LIGHTS, CAME

SOUND TRACKS

MARTIN C. STRONG has been researching and compiling discographies for around 25 years, among them *The Great Metal Discography*, *The Great Alternative Discography*, *The Great Indie Discography*, *The Great Psychedelic Discography* and, of course, *The Great Rock Discography* and *The Essential Rock Discography*. He lives in Falkirk, Scotland.

BRENDON GRIFFIN has worked sporadically on the *Great Rock* series since the late 90s. His work has also appeared in *Record Collector*, and he's a regular contributor to *HMV Choice* and www.popmatters.com. When not writing about music, he's often wandering abroad for Rough Guides, contributing to various Latin American and European titles, writing *Spain: 25 Ultimate Experiences* and editing guides to Cancún and New York. He lives in Fife, Scotland.

First published in Great Britain in 2008
by Canongate Books Ltd,
14 High Street, Edinburgh EH1 1TE

British Library Cataloguing-in-Publication Data
A catalogue record for this book is available upon request from the British Library.

All plate section images supplied by Redferns.

ISBN 978 184767 003 8
US ISBN 978 184767 021 2

Typeset by TexturAL, Dundee

Printed and bound in Germany by Bercker, Kevelaer

www.meetatthegate.com

LIGHTS, CAMERA, SOUNDTRACKS

MARTIN C. STRONG
with
BRENDON GRIFFIN

CANONGATE
Edinburgh · London · New York · Melbourne

This book is dedicated to …

my mother JEAN FOTHERINGHAM
(born: 6th of January 1929,
died of cancer: 31st of August 1985)

Still missing you
and thanks for still
guiding me through all
the hard times.

my dad GERRY/GEOFF STRONG
(born: 28th of July 1930,
died of a heart attack: 20th October 1998)

Will miss you always.
You were also a great friend, inspiration
and someone who could make me laugh.

Hope you're both getting on up there.
If only …

* * * * *

Contents

Acknowledgments

Firstly I'd like to thank the plethora of contributors to *LIGHTS, CAMERA, SOUNDTRACKS*:

Mark Robertson *(MR)*
James Zdzieblo *(JZ)*
Dan Franklin *(DF)*
Ninian Dunnett *(ND)*
Christopher McLean *(CM)*
Sean Welsh *(SW)*
Lloyd Fay *(LF)*
Stewart Smith *(SS)*
Keith Munro *(KM)*
David Graham *(DG)*
Adam Stafford *(AS)*
Sharon McHendry *(SM)*
Stef Lewandowski *(SL)*

not forgetting…

Martin C. Strong *(MCS)* and
Brendon Griffin *(BG)*

To the aforementioned Sean, Lloyd, Stewart and Sharon, I hope to eventually meet all of you at the book launch – who knows? I'd like to thank the people at Canongate from (Sir) Jamie Byng to Sheila McAinsh, plus Dan F (of course), phenomenal proofreader Helen Bleck (& Lynda Carey), Amanda and Kathleen. And how can one forget typesetter Alan Lawson?

Thanks also to my great long-time friends Allan & Elaine Brewster who supplied the goods and some interest-free finances to support the cause. Special love to my long-suffering fiancée Dawn and our wee four-year-old Samantha, who kept the ambition alive when I was trailing well behind. Love to my older daughters Shirley and Suzanne (and my grandchildren Ivor, Jade and Lyla), I would have liked to have seen more of you, but I suppose we'll save that time for another day – thanks from a distance anyway. Also thanks to Suzy's long-time partner, Damian, for his computer wizardry. Because of my hectic schedule I've also missed my Auntie Joyce, cousins Paul, Stephen, Brian, Maureen (who sadly died) and Kevin McElroy from Portobello. And just around the corner, see you soon Auntie Isobel and Uncle Danny. A tip of my hat also goes to my brother Graeme Strong, who I sadly fell out with prior to his death a few years ago. After all that happened I hope you're OK, wherever you are.

And now my pub friends (and I'll keep this as brief as I can – if I forget you, please forgive me). To everyone past and present at (Alex) Smith's in Falkirk, the drinks are on y'all (Fantasy Island, indeed), so come on down: Allan Brewster (again!), Andrew Risk, Stan Lyon, Tony Hughes, Vic Zdzieblo, Dougie Niven (now deceased), James Zdzieblo (again!), Wattie Morrison, Ian 'Harry' Harrison, Adam Stafford (again!), Paul Hughes, Peter McGuckin, Stef Lewandowski (& Marie), Danny Dickson, Brian (& Margaret) Hunter, Derek Grant, Davie Blair, Laurie Doolan, Archie & Caroline (both now sadly passed away), Gordon Murray, uncle John McArdle (deceased), Ian 'Dark Eyes', Davie Galloway, Martin McDermot, Tony Weir, Barry Devlin, Mikey Kinnaird, Michael Fletcher, Paul Klemm (now deceased), Barry & Katriona Moore, Martin McFarlane, Jock Hill (deceased), Iain McLean, Billy & Ann Ross, Rab Bell, Scott McKean, Cliff Pattenden, Brian Kerragher, Johnny Parker, Bobby Callaghan, Jock McLeish, Grahame Winters & Doreen McLeish, Paul Cox, George Dickson, Bill Fisher (deceased), Chris Reid (deceased), Martin No.7, Scotty Honeyman, Tam Morrison, Jimmy & wee Greg, Allan Mann (still in Oz), Jock & Wendy, Alison Wyles, Sean Harris, Janice, Eleanor, et al; plus from The Wheatsheaf: George Main, Sherida, Davie Seath, Martin L; and last but not least, all the way from America, Edward 'Kip' Hannon.

The following sources were very helpful during the writing of this book: imdb.com, amazon.com, ebay.com, allmovie.com, allmusic.com, blaxploitation.com, soundtrackcollector.com, *REDMuze* and *Halliwell's Film Guide.*

MCS

Introduction

A long six years ago in 2002, in between updating/compiling the *GREAT ROCK DISCOGRAPHY* series, I came up with an idea to tackle a book of soundtracks: little did I know where this would lead and how hard a task it would become.

By 2004, it had evolved into a fully-fledged post-Rock'n'Roll Soundtrack tome, omitting – for now! – the numerous classically-edged OSTs that hog the market (by Ennio Morricone, etc). Anything that connected the Rock & Pop world with film I would include. When that became a little too much – finding that ex-Oingo Boingo mainman Danny Elfman (he of 'Beetlejuice' & 'Simpsons' fame) had supplied over 40 CDs to this genre – I would have needed two volumes to include all these, and other, scores.

In its embryonic stage, I phoned and wrote to a number of publishers and, while most were enthusiastic about the idea, the nature of the beast was somewhat daunting to them – it seemed I was alone with my vision. But Canongate Books (publishers of the *GRD* series) came along as usual and snapped it up. One thing it was important to establish with them was that this would be a Rock book, not a Scores book (that would come at a later date). I was better known for my Rock writing, rather than writing about film, or indeed film soundtracks. So where better place to start then writing about movies such as 'PURPLE RAIN', 'WOODSTOCK' and 'PARIS, TEXAS' – films with real Rock credentials.

Initially I called the book *POP IN THE MOVIES*, and although everyone I knew loved it, Canongate and my second-in-command at the time, Brendon Griffin, thought it too corny. I came up with another, *LIGHTS, CAMERA, SOUNDTRACKS*, which (nearly) everyone agreed was a much stronger title.

The arrangement between myself and co-reviewer BG was that I would research every film released (even ones not associated with this particular volume), maintain the database of around 2000 flicks, do half the storylines, half the reviews and all 1750 of the Off The Record (OTR) sections, while BG would tackle the other half of the reviews and storylines and as many artist biographies as needed. There are hundreds of rock movies included that don't even have an accompanying OST release.

My work would entail around 70 hours a week (a nasty bout of blood clots in November 2005 was supposed to have reduced my workload to zero!). Everything was going hunky dory when the book just grew and grew. I found a plethora of entries as I went along and what was meant to be around 1000 film entries expanded to 1700. Under the increasing pressure, relations between the two authors became strained, but that's a story to be told elsewhere. The result was I needed to find a new crew of reviewers, and about a dozen (picked from over 50 CVs) were supplied by Mark Robertson at *The List*. Incidentally, thanks to Mark for giving me album review work at the mag.

Time was running out on my deadline(s), and with my workload going up to 100 hours a week, something had to give. And with various problems mounting up, the decision was taken to delay the book, moving the publication date from summer 2007 to September 2008. One thing that annoyed me profusely was when my old Windows 98 computer broke down (and my internet access was curtailed due to lack of funds), and someone who was in a position to help just said 'it should work!' – no fairy godmother was forthcoming and I had to buy and adapt to a new £500 laptop, leaving stacks of data in cyberspace. Thanks to Dan The Man at Canongate London (also the reviewer DF), who helped me pick up the pieces and finally get back to work.

With this encouragement I brought back some reviewers (BG was now out of the scene completely) and slowly but surely we filled in the gaps, while I took the time to find more stuff and incorporate the numerous proofreading inclusions. I was exhausted. But I was committed to the project; I never give up at anything I do. Ten years spent trying to get the *GRD* published and 26 years (and counting) working on the series tell you everything you need to know about MY dedication.

Anyway, I am pleased with most of everyone's contributions. Although the book has evolved through many incarnations, I've set it out in three sections:

1. Rock Movies/Musicals and Pop Fiction;
2. Rockumentaries and Performance Movies; and
3. Pop/Rock Scores and Blaxploitation.

I hope readers and participants out there have a great time ploughing through these facts. Whatever the cost, it was worth every bit of my time, effort and stress.

Martin C. Strong
Falkirk, May 2008

A Brief History of Popular Music in the Movies

The Birth of the Rock 'n' Roll Movie

There are many different types of Rock movies (musicals, biopics, Rockumentaries, etc.); original soundtracks (or OSTs) come in a multitude of line-ups and musical styles.

Dating way back to 1956's 'LOVE ME TENDER' (a Western credited to subsequent soundtrack veteran and star ELVIS PRESLEY) and Various Artists ensemble 'THE GIRL CAN'T HELP IT' (1956), the rock'n'roll movie was born. The previous year's 'BLACKBOARD JUNGLE' featured a certain BILL HALEY & HIS COMETS over the end credits, a riotous outro that resulted in some cinema seats going skywards. 'DON'T KNOCK THE ROCK' (1951), 'ROCK, PRETTY BABY' (1951), and anything with the word 'Rock' in it hit the cinemas during a peak period in the late 50s. Across the pond in Blighty, barrow-boy TOMMY STEELE had hits with two pop-orientated films, the questionably titled 'THE TOMMY STEELE STORY' (1957) and 'THE DUKE WORE JEANS' (1958); his 'Half A Sixpence' was thankfully one step too far to be described as Rock. Elvis clone CLIFF RICHARD launched his rock'n'roll musical film career in the early 60s (see 'SUMMER HOLIDAY', 'THE YOUNG ONES', etc). Back in the USA, probably to match the cuteness of one-time lady of rock'n'roll, CONNIE FRANCIS (and her series of starring-role movie OSTs), the 'Beach Movie' was created by way of several sand-in-your-face flicks featuring ANNETTE FUNICELLO and FRANKIE AVALON. Subsequent movies such as 'AMERICAN GRAFFITI' (1973), 'GREASE' (1978), two versions of 'HAIRSPRAY' (1988 & 2007), plus biopics 'LA BAMBA' (1987) and 'GREAT BALLS OF FIRE!' (1989) recreated the time of bobbysocks and tight jeans.

With the British Invasion underway and ELVIS on his umpteenth OST in the States, the BEATLES gave us 'A HARD DAY'S NIGHT' in 1964 and 'HELP!' a year later. And who could hold back GERRY & THE PACEMAKERS, the DAVE CLARK FIVE and HERMAN'S HERMITS, who aped their mop-topped counterparts on various levels and to different degrees?

Scores of Rockumentaries

As far as Rock-Pop scores were concerned, the late 60s produced 'THE GRADUATE' (1967) by SIMON & GARFUNKEL (co-credited alongside jazzplayer Dave Grusin), while PINK FLOYD opened their OST account with 'MORE' (1969). The ROLLING STONES were the subject of Jean-Luc Godard's documentary, 'SYMPATHY FOR THE DEVIL' (1968), plus concert movies 'GIMME SHELTER' (1970) and the canned 'ROCK AND ROLL CIRCUS' (from 1968, released 1996). MICK JAGGER was also the star of two cult movies at the time, 'NED KELLY' (1969) and 'PERFORMANCE' (1970). Brian Jones' mysterious death was finally unveiled (or was it?) with biopic 'STONED' (2005).

The 70s was the time of the excessive Rock Performance movie, none more so than 'WOODSTOCK' (1970), the definitive document of the concert from 1969 featuring soon-to-be-deceased JIMI HENDRIX and JANIS JOPLIN, among others. The tragedy of the former's death was reinforced with two posthumous documentaries, 'RAINBOW BRIDGE' (1971) and 'JIMI HENDRIX' (1973), while the story of the latter was told in 'JANIS' (1975). The genre went into self-indulgence overload with NEIL YOUNG's 'JOURNEY THROUGH THE PAST' (1974), LED ZEPPELIN's 'THE SONG REMAINS THE SAME' (1976) and the marathon 'THE GRATEFUL DEAD MOVIE' (1977), the latter displaying signs of weariness – amongst the audience at least. Martin Scorsese's 'THE LAST WALTZ' (1978) (featuring THE BAND and various friends in concert) rectified this mediocrity somewhat in 1978. Subsequent movies (and soundtracks) such as U2's 'RATTLE AND HUM' (1988), Depeche Mode's '101' (1989) and a plethora of Blues films split public opinion: many were bemused as to why it was necessary to release them in the cinema, when video (and later DVD) would deliver them to the buying masses anyway. By way of a slight apology, the Rockumentaries and Performance Movies section has only a worthy *selection* of films rather than every one issued (it got beyond a joke when I tried to include video/DVD releases).

The prog-rock soundtrack flourished in the 70s, and while PINK FLOYD were underway with their sophomore score, 'OBSCURED BY CLOUDS' (aka 'La VALLEE') (1972), Krautrock counterparts (no, not TANGERINE DREAM!) POPOL VUH hit the buttons of doom on 'AGUIRRE, WRATH OF GOD' (1972); TD kicked off their soundtrack career with 'SORCERER' in 1977. While rarely heard in the UK, Italian film scorers GOBLIN emerged between the releases of their contemporaries with 'SUSPIRIA' (1975). 'PROFONDO ROSSO' (1977) was the first of many OSTs to follow. Former Yes man, keyboard wizard and ex-Sex Pistols foe RICK WAKEMAN found his way into the movies via Ken Russell's 'LISZTOMANIA' (1975), 'WHITE ROCK' (1976) and 'G'OLE' (1977), the last two both sport documentaries. Former Genesis chameleon PETER GABRIEL finally shifted from prog singer to composer via 1985's 'BIRDY'. To balance out these psychedelic sounds and mind-blowing flicks, and on the cusp of a religious wave, born-again devotees of the gospel found their niche courtesy of stage-to-screen epics 'GODSPELL' (1973), Andrew Lloyd Webber's 'JESUS CHRIST SUPERSTAR' (1973) and 'HAIR' (1979). The first of many TV pop series also came about around this time. 'ROCK FOLLIES' (1977) showed that the rock movie could be a hit in a small screen format, and 30 years on we have 'Rock Rivals'.

MCS

The Blaxploitation Era

In the words of Jimmy Castor, let's go back, way back, back into time, to an era when black representation in Hollywood, if not in its troglodyte stage, was limited to the sophisticated yet ultimately compliant characters played by Sidney Poitier. While films such as 'Guess Who's Coming to Dinner' (1967) and 'In the Heat of the Night' (also 1967) addressed race issues, they ultimately reinforced the prevailing societal structures and middle class mores governing black/white relations… relations all too easily sent up by MELVIN VAN PEEBLES in his 1970 breakthrough, 'WATERMELON MAN', wherein a white racist quite literally wakes up to the reality of being black. It might have been a comedy but its subtext was serious. Van Peebles followed up with 1971's 'SWEET SWEETBACK'S BAADASSSSS SONG', a gritty minor masterpiece, cathartic in its violent reaction to racism and radical in its unflinching portrayal of sex and the reality of ghetto life. Unsurprisingly, the major studios would not touch it, so the director funded it himself, pitching it to a handful of black cinemas where word of mouth turned it into a major underground success. As both a bulletin from the heart of ghetto darkness and a catalyst for cinematic change, its shock waves are still being felt today.

Back then, its most immediate effect was the birth of Blaxploitation – with an x, if you please – and an avalanche of big money melodramas focusing on black gangsters, pimps, hookers and sexually rampant police detectives. While these films made token comments on social/race issues, their presentation of sexy, charismatic and, above all, powerful black characters, regardless of their moral ambivalence, was the irresistible pull behind their popularity. And if they were attempts to replicate – and inevitably dilute – the primitive force of 'SWEETBACK' on a bigger budget, they were also attempts to match the million dollar success and unrivalled marriage of sound and vision which was 'SHAFT' (1971). MGM had been working on the movie as 'SWEETBACK' had begun its limited run, casting muscular model Richard Roundtree as virile black detective John Shaft. More glamourous and conventionally plotted than 'SWEETBACK', and minus that film's claustrophobic realism, the true genius of 'SHAFT' lay in its seminal, Oscar-winning, ISAAC HAYES-scored soundtrack. The hi-hat hissed suggestively, wicka-wacka-wicka went the guitar, with a regal fanfare the strings announced HAYES' indomitably cool entrance: Blaxploitation funk was born.

While 'SWEETBACK's soundtrack – also scored by VAN PEEBLES with a helping hand from a fledgling EARTH, WIND & FIRE – was a classic groovefest, 'Theme From Shaft' rubber-stamped the kind of wah-wah funk which would be imitated, expanded upon and eventually done to death over the course of the Blaxploitation genre's early to mid-70s golden era. Given Shaft's success, the inevitable sequels came thick and fast: 'SHAFT'S BIG SCORE' (1972) featured a soundtrack written by the film's director, GORDON PARKS. It didn't quite measure up to HAYES' effort but it did feature a side-long chase theme with a brilliant line in alliteration. 'SHAFT IN AFRICA' appeared in 1973, the final chapter in the Shaft saga with a fine score by experienced jazz player/Impressions arranger JOHNNY PATE. Bigger than any of these sequels was 'SUPERFLY' (1972), another Gordon Parks film, and one which arguably more than any other helped formulate the violent, drug-dealing gangster chic still so prevalent in certain strands of black music and culture. CURTIS MAYFIELD was the man who gave voice to the emptiness and nihilism at the heart of that narco dream in what has come to be regarded as the all-time great Blaxploitation score. At once mellow, chilling and sympathetic, MAYFIELD's silky croon and running lowlife commentary made for hypnotic and slyly funky listening.

MARVIN GAYE also got in on the soundtrack action in 1972 with 'TROUBLE MAN' – for this writer's money the most alluring and timeless of all Blaxploitation scores. GAYE might not have needed a career boost coming off the back of 'What's Going On', but the record allowed him to stretch out into even more experimental territory, a hitherto unavailable opportunity to explore the full emotional range of the black experience. It was this artistic scope, as well as the possibility of career advancement, which made the Blaxploitation soundtrack a magnet for both established and more obscure artists: MAYFIELD and HAYES both had their careers turbo-charged with 'SUPERFLY' and 'SHAFT', while both albums' multi-faceted dramatisation of black urban life reinvented the soundtrack as an entity in its own right; EARTH, WIND & FIRE got their first break with 'SWEETBACK'; ROY AYERS facilitated his gradual move towards funk, disco and fusion with 'COFFY' (1973); while BOBBY WOMACK was inspired to create one of the most deliciously bittersweet moments in soul history with 'ACROSS 110th STREET' (1972). Of course, JAMES BROWN's conscious funk was also tailor-made for the genre and while 'BLACK CAESAR' (1973) and 'SLAUGHTER'S BIG RIP-OFF' (1974) appeared too late to exert any great influence, they remain essential additions to the Godfather's catalogue.

Aside from the soul giants, lesser figures and more specialist artists and composers also pitched in with great albums. GENE PAGE composed the fiendishly funky 'BLACULA' (1972) as Blaxploitation plundered horror; jazz guitarist GRANT GREEN successfully sparred with funk rhythms on 'THE FINAL COMEDOWN' (1972); Motown veterans such as EDWIN STARR and WILLIE HUTCH were lent new leases of life with soundtracks to 'FOXY BROWN' (1974) and 'HELL UP IN HARLEM' (1973); the aforementioned JOHNNY PATE scored the memorable 'BROTHERS ON THE RUN' (1973); cult soul-jazz dude CHARLES EARLAND scored 'THE DYNAMITE BROTHERS' (1974), itself a precursor to the late 70s explosion of underground kung-fu movies; even commercially ailing soul legend SOLOMON BURKE got in on the act with 'COOL BREEZE' (1972).

In most cases, these soundtracks outshone and outlived their intended function as auditory aids to the onscreen action, even when the movies inevitably degenerated into ever more ludicrous parody and cartoon-like caricature as Hollywood sucked the genre dry. By the mid-70s it had more or less exhausted itself. ISAAC HAYES bookended his Blaxploitation years with 'THREE TOUGH GUYS' (1974) and 'TRUCK TURNER' (1974), although CURTIS MAYFIELD scored 1975's 'LET'S DO IT AGAIN' for the STAPLE SINGERS, and cut a last gasp Blaxploitation score with 'SHORT EYES' in 1977. While the wildcard fashions, street slang and misogyny left more of a visible mark, the films and even the soundtracks were subsequently submerged by tides of cultural change, partially re-emerging through 80s hip-hop samples and finally getting their due come the 90s' obsession with the 70s.

While hip-hop films such as 'Juice' and 'Boyz N The Hood' were perhaps a more enlightened, intelligent mirror-image of Blaxploitation, Quentin Tarantino homed in on the ultraviolence and kitsch of the originals for films like 'PULP FICTION' (1994) and 'JACKIE BROWN' (1997), the latter featuring BOBBY WOMACK's 'ACROSS 110th STREET'. It's fair to say these originals remain period touchstones, artefacts with seismic aftershocks. Their soundtracks, however, stand apart, as dynamic and as fresh as the day they were scored. *BG*

Bass Culture and Country Folk

Along the same lines as Blaxploitation, but coming from the third world of Jamaica, 1972's reggae-fied 'THE HARDER THEY COME' (featuring JIMMY CLIFF), identified with the black community settling in England at the time. Subsequent movies such as 'ROCKERS' (1980), 'COUNTRYMAN' (1982) and a handful of BOB MARLEY documentaries took the reggae genre to a new global fanbase.

Country music had been on the fringes of rock'n'roll music since the days of Hank Williams. A biopic of Williams' drink-fuelled life was released in 1964 as 'YOUR CHEATIN' HEART' (starring his son, HANK WILLIAMS JR.), while other Country & Western movies include 'COAL MINER'S DAUGHTER' (1980) and 'SWEET DREAMS' (1985) – starring C&W starlets Loretta Lynn and Patsy Cline respectively. Combining acting and songwriting skills, there's no one better than the effervescent DOLLY PARTON ('9 To 5' to 'STRAIGHT TALK'), WILLIE NELSON ('THE ELECTRIC HORSEMAN' to 'The Dukes Of Hazzard') and KRIS KRISTOFFERSON ('PAT GARRETT & BILLY THE KID' to 'Blade'); the latter hard-grafting twosome also collaborated for the film 'SONGWRITER' in 1984. *MCS*

The Rock Star as Movie Icon

Rock star icons taking on the mantle of the movie star (figures such as ELVIS, CLIFF, DAVID ESSEX and numerous glam bands) was best exemplified when Starman DAVID BOWIE took the role of an alien in 'The Man Who Fell To Earth' (1976). The music was provided by an ex-Mamas & Papas man, JOHN PHILLIPS. The jury was out when BOWIE returned alongside Catherine Deneuve in 1982's 'The Hunger' (featuring Bauhaus with 'Bela Lugosi's Dead') and alongside Ryuichi Sakamoto (ex-Yellow Magic Orchestra) in 1983's 'Merry Christmas Mr. Lawrence'. Among others, 70s stars MEAT LOAF, BLONDIE's Deborah Harry, IGGY POP and STING would subsequently follow in his thespian footsteps. The 1975 Ken Russell stab at OTT rock'n'roll, 'TOMMY', featured a host of contemporary rock stars including The WHO (all four of them!), plus TINA TURNER, ELTON JOHN and ERIC CLAPTON, while you had to admire the bollocks of 'Wild Thing' luvvy Oliver Reed. 'Your senses will never be the same' the film's poster declared, although The WHO's next Rock Opera 'QUADROPHENIA' (1979) settled easier on the mind and soul of the post-punk aficionado.

John Travolta would find his feet – quite literally – when he funked till dawn under the disco ball spotlight of 'SATURDAY NIGHT FEVER' (1977), a multi-million selling soundtrack to die for by messrs Gibb under the BEE GEES and various artists banner. Travolta and dance partner OLIVIA NEWTON-JOHN smooched and shimmied their way through some 'Summer Nights' in the following year's hit musical, 'GREASE' (1978). Dance movies were in abundance with 1982's 'FAME', 1983's 'FLASHDANCE' and 1984's AOR hit 'FOOTLOOSE'. A word of warning to the uninitiated: the late 70s & early 80s also gave us disco duds such as 'THE WIZ' (1978) (starring Diana Ross and Michael Jackson), 'THANK GOD IT'S FRIDAY' (1978), 'THE APPLE' (1980), 'CAN'T STOP THE MUSIC' (1980) (starring the Village People) and ONJ's 'XANADU' (1980). Who's bad?

The 80s also proved to be a mega-decade for the rock movie, kicking off as it did with the fun-packed 'BLUES BROTHERS' (1980), the everything-goes punk movie 'THE GREAT ROCK'N'ROLL SWINDLE' (1980) and even 'BREAKING GLASS' (1986). Surpassing all before it and taking excess to new levels, hard rock mockumentary 'THIS IS SPINAL TAP' (1984) left others trailing, even if one did happen upon a Marshall amplifier that could turn up to 11. That same year, PRINCE (and THE REVOLUTION) found fame and fortune when he wrote, starred and performed the soundtrack to 'PURPLE RAIN' (1984). Subsequent movies such as 'UNDER THE CHERRY MOON' (1986) and 'GRAFFITI BRIDGE' (1990) suffered by comparison – to put it mildly – but PRINCE did deliver two non-starring OSTs, 'BATMAN' (1989) and 'GIRL 6' (1996). MADONNA grabbed her chance with both hands when she starred in girly flicks such as 'Desperately Seeking Susan' (1985) and 'WHO'S THAT GIRL?' (1987). The debate raged as to whether she could actually act, as her performances ranged from the awful 'Bloodhounds Of Broadway' (1989) and 'DICK TRACY' (1990) to her award-winning portrayal of 'EVITA' in 1996.

Taking the title of showbusiness 'Funny Girl', Barbra Streisand and stand-up comedienne BETTE MIDLER fought off the critics with grand roles in movies such as 'THE ROSE' (1979) and 'BEACHES' (1988). Although who could surpass the Oscar-winning DIANA ROSS in her portrayal of jazz legend Billie Holiday in 1972's 'THE LADY SINGS THE BLUES'? Jazz music is represented by Rock fusion giants such as MILES DAVIS ('DINGO', etc.) and HERBIE HANCOCK ('DEATH WISH', etc.), although regrettably the likes of Quincy Jones (a musician/producer turned composer) are left for another edition.

While Randy Newman's career was virtually taken over by the world of soundtracks (that's why he's not included in this edition), the likes of RY COODER and MARK KNOPFLER combined a prolific solo career with numerous scores, nearly all released. COODER's best work was in his sparse dust bowl scores such as 'THE LONG RIDERS' (1980) and 'PARIS, TEXAS' (1983), while KNOPFLER's best pieces came by way of 'LOCAL HERO' (1983) and 'WAG THE DOG' (1997). Of course, the likes of Sir ELTON, DYLAN, NEIL DIAMOND and NILSSON had already achieved a modicum of success via soundtrack work, while CLAPTON finally cut his OST teeth writing the music to cult TV series, 'Edge Of Darkness' (1985). Although differing in styles somewhat and harking back to the continental side of things, former Aphrodite's Child star VANGELIS found fame and fortune with 'CHARIOTS OF FIRE' (1981) and the long-awaited 'BLADE RUNNER' (1982). He would eventually go epic film-style with '1492: Conquest of Paradise' (1992) and 'Alexander' (2004). Meanwhile back at alt-versus-weirdo ranch, messrs NICK CAVE, DAVID BYRNE, TOM WAITS and JOHN LURIE all provided the world of film with some exquisite scores, none more so than the former's recently released 'THE PROPOSITION' (2005) and 'THE ASSASSINATION OF JESSE JAMES BY THE COWARD ROBERT FORD' (2007) – both collaborations with ex-Dirty Three and Bad Seed musician WARREN ELLIS.

MCS

Don't Look Back

With over 100 films and counting (from 'HOUSE PARTY' to 'GET RICH OR DIE TRYIN'') under the production wing and guidance of indulgent rappers and hip-hop stars, the genre of music-based movies has shifted in the last two decades. If the films were slightly less than below par, the accompanying CD soundtracks were above reprehension – arguments and drive-by shootings excepted. And then came EMINEM, a star and piston-packing white rapper (post-Vanilla Ice of the disastrous 'COOL AS ICE') and his semi-biopic '8 MILE' (2002) – a masterpiece for a new generation, an overblown anti-rock movie for others.

However, the Rock movie continued unabated via Cameron Crowe's 'ALMOST FAMOUS' (2000), the post-'ROCKY HORROR PICTURE SHOW' (1975) shocker, 'HEDWIG AND THE ANGRY INCH' (2001) and the Jack Black (of Tenacious D) vehicle 'SCHOOL OF ROCK' (2003). Where BJORK's Palme d'Or-winning 'DANCER IN THE DARK' (2000) fits doesn't matter really – just file it under awesome. While the mid 00s found a new line in Rock biopics hitting the big screen, 'RAY' (2004), 'WALK THE LINE' (2005) and 'CONTROL' (2007) – about RAY CHARLES, JOHNNY CASH and Ian Curtis respectively – the mockumentary saw new light, courtesy of the post-'SPINAL TAP' comedies 'A MIGHTY WIND' (2003), 'BROTHERS OF THE HEAD' (2006) and the John C. Reilly-vehicle 'WALK HARD: THE DEWEY COX STORY' (2007).

MCS

MARTIN C. STRONG's SELECTIONS

Top Rock Movies/Musicals (non-Pop Fiction) of all time, combination of both film & soundtrack:–

1. DANCER IN THE DARK (Bjork), 2000
2. THE GREAT ROCK'N'ROLL SWINDLE (The Sex Pistols), 1980
3. CONTROL (Various Artists), 2007
4. HEDWIG AND THE ANGRY INCH (Various Cast), 2001
5. 24 HOUR PARTY PEOPLE (Various Artists), 2002
6. THIS IS SPINAL TAP (Spinal Tap), 1974
7. TOMMY (The Who & Cast), 1975
8. SCHOOL OF ROCK (Various Artists), 2003
9. MOULIN ROUGE (Various Cast), 2001
10. WALK THE LINE (Various Cast), 2005

Top Pop Fiction (non-Rock Movie), combination of both film & soundtrack:–

1. TRAINSPOTTING (Various Artists), 1996
2. REPO MAN (Various Artists), 1984
3. EASY RIDER (Various Artists), 1969
4. PULP FICTION (Various Artists), 1994
5. QUADROPHENIA (The Who & Various Artists), 1979

Top Rockumentaries/Performance Movies, combination of both film & soundtrack:–

1. THE DEVIL & DANIEL JOHNSTON (Daniel Johnston), 2004
2. DIG! (Brian Jonestown Massacre & The Dandy Warhols), 2004
3. WOODSTOCK (Various Artists), 1970
4. LET IT BE (The Beatles), 1970
5. STOP MAKING SENSE (Talking Heads), 1984
6. THE LAST WALTZ (The Band & Various Artists), 1978
7. RUST NEVER SLEEPS (Neil Young & Crazy Horse), 1979
8. ZIGGY STARDUST: THE MOTION PICTURE (David Bowie), 1983
9. THE SONG REMAINS THE SAME (Led Zeppelin), 1976
10. LIVE AT POMPEII (Pink Floyd), 1974

Top Rock/Pop Scores, combination of both film & soundtrack:–

1. AGUIRRE, WRATH OF GOD (Popol Vuh), 1972
2. PASSION: MUSIC FOR THE LAST TEMPTATION OF CHRIST (Peter Gabriel), 1989
3. PARIS, TEXAS (Ry Cooder), 1984
4. THE WICKER MAN (Paul Giovanni & Magnet), 1973
5. HAROLD AND MAUDE (Cat Stevens), 1971
6. SON DE MAR (Piano Magic), 2001
7. OBSCURED BY CLOUDS: LA VALLEE (Pink Floyd), 1972
8. FIRST LOVE, LAST RITES (Shudder To Think & Various Artists), 1997
9. SORCERER (Tangerine Dream), 1977
10. SUPERFLY (Curtis Mayfield), 1972

How to Read the Book

Here is some guidance as to the style of layout used in the book, as well as the different sub-sections of information provided within each main entry.

<u>Titles</u> that are displayed inverse (white on black) are Biographical entries, not films; where these are biogs of Blaxploitation artists, the type is italic.

In Section 1, grey-boxed titles (about 50+) are Pop Fiction movies. In Section 3, grey-boxed titles are Blaxploitation movies.

---

the MOVIE TITLE

alternative title (if any)

year (US/UK/other time) Moviemakers (certificate)

Film genre: Rock Music drama, thriller, comedy, etc.

Top guns: dir: = director / s-w: = screenwriter (au: = author)

Stars: Actor *(character in italics)* ← PAST MOVIES, **Pop Actor/Performer** *(character/performer)* → POST MOVIES, **Pop ACTOR with MOVIE history in caps & bold** *(character)*, etc.

Storyline: Brief synopsis of movie. *writer's initials*

Movie rating: *0 – *10 (*.5 inclusive)

Visual: video +/or dvd availability (no audio OST mention)

Off the record: exclusive **Pop Actor** film to music info or potted history. Also a feature of tracks on the unreleased soundtrack. *MCS* = Martin C Strong

—

POP/ROCK ARTIST(S)/PERFORMER(S) (composer name/s*)

iss-date. (format) *Label; <US cat.no.> (UK cat.no) chart =* [US] alt. [UK]
– Track (ARTIST/GROUP) / Track (ARTIST * associated with composer) / etc. *(re-iss. cd date; catalogue number)* – extra tracks, etc.

S/track review: The album under the spotlight – the tracks, the PEOPLE behind the music and the associated ARTISTS (note that only LCS MOVIES, the PEOPLE & the ARTISTS relevant to the tracks are in CAPS, and not biog/filmography entries). *writer's initials*

Album rating: *0 – *10

– spinoff hits/releases, etc. –

POP/ROCK ARTISTS(S): Single 'A' side / 'B' side

iss- date. (format) *Label; <US cat.no.> (UK cat.no.) charts =* [US] diff. [UK]

—— note: chart boxes can be swapped – UK then US – if UK cat.no. first

—— other countries (Australia, Italy, etc.) are in boxes () not <>

MOVIE TITLE (sub-category)

ARTIST/GROUP (biography)

note: Italics are used for Blaxploitation artists

- **filmography** (composer or acting)

Chronological Movie List *(year; {* = star})* / **Film in bold type** *(year; {a = acting part} OST => Original Sound Soundtrack in this book)* / **Other relevant Movies** *(year; {b = bit-actor} {c = cameo} (v = voice of} {p = performance} OST by V/A = Various Artists)*

Formats & Abbreviations

VINYL (black-coloured unless stated): *lp* = long player record... circular 12" plays at $33^{1/3}$ r.p.m., and has photo or artwork sleeve. *d-1p* = double-long player. *t-1p* = triple-long player. *4-1p-box* = boxed-long player. *m-lp* = mini-long player. *pic-1p* = picture disc-long player. *col-lp* = coloured-long player, eg *red-lp.*

Singles: 7" (also 10" and 12" for most formats): *7"* = 7-inch single. *7" m* = 7-inch maxi. *7" ep* = 7-inch extended play. *d7"* = double 7-inch. *7" pic-d* = 7-inch picture-disc. *7" sha-pic-d* = 7-inch shaped-picture-disc. *7" col* = 7-inch coloured. *7" flexi* = 7-inch flexible.

CASSETTES : *c* = cassette album... in case $4^{1/2}$ inches high. *d-c* = double-cassette album. *c-s* = cassette-single. *c-ep* = cassette-extended play single.

COMPACT DISCS (and others) *cd* = compact disc album, all 5" circular and mostly silver on its playing side. *d-cd* = double-compact disc album. *cd-s* = compact disc-single. *pic-cd-s* = picture-compact disc-single, also *pic-cd-ep*. *vid-pic-s* = video-compact-disc-single, video cd. *dvd-s* = digital-video-disk-single. *dl-s* = download-single – internet single. *dat* = digital audio tape album.

Other abbreviations: *repl.* = replaced; *comp.* = compilation; *re-iss.* = re-issued; *re-dist.* = re-distributed.

Section 1

Rock Musicals/Movies and Pop Fiction

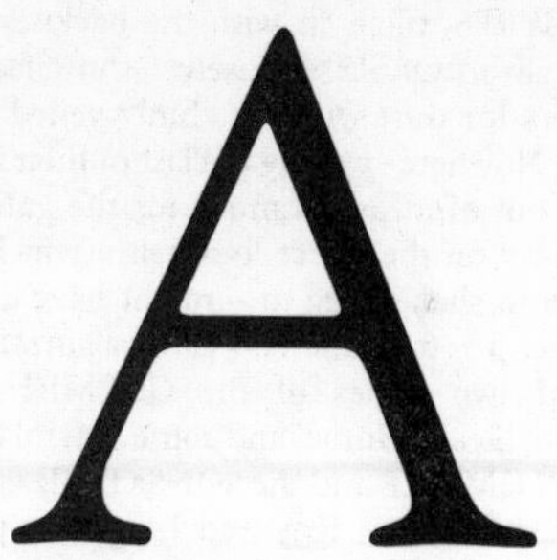

☐ AALIYAH segment
(⇒ QUEEN OF THE DAMNED)

☐ ABBA: THE MOVIE
(⇒ Rockumentaries/Performance movies)

☐ Paula ABDUL segment
(⇒ MR. ROCK'N'ROLL: THE ALAN FREED STORY)

ABSOLUTE BEGINNERS

1986 (UK 107m) Goldcrest Films / Palace Pictures (15)

Film genre: coming-of-age/teen Pop-Rock Musical drama

Top guns: dir: Julien Temple ← the GREAT ROCK'N'ROLL SWINDLE / → RUNNING OUT OF LUCK → EARTH GIRLS ARE EASY → AT THE MAX → the FILTH AND THE FURY → GLASTONBURY → the FUTURE IS UNWRITTEN / s-w: Richard Burridge, Christopher Wicking, Don MacPherson (nov: Colin MacInnes)

Stars: Eddie O'Connell *(Colin / narrator)*, Patsy Kensit *(Crepe Suzette)* → GRACE OF MY HEART → THINGS BEHIND THE SUN, **David BOWIE** *(Vendice Partners)*, James Fox *(Henley of Mayfair)* ← PERFORMANCE, **Ray DAVIES** *(Arthur, Colin's dad)*, Eve Ferret *(Big Jill)*, Lionel Blair *(Harry Charms)* ← a HARD DAY'S NIGHT ← PLAY IT COOL, Mandy Rice-Davies *(Flora)*, **Sade Adu** *(Athene Duncannon)*, Steven Berkoff *(the fanatic)* ← McVICAR / → UNDER THE CHERRY MOON, Graham Fletcher-Cook *(wizard)* → SID & NANCY → STRAIGHT TO HELL → SIESTA, Anita Morris *(Dido Lament)* → BLUE CITY, **Tenpole Tudor** *(Ed the Ted)* ← the GREAT ROCK'N'ROLL SWINDLE / → SID & NANCY → STRAIGHT TO HELL → WALKER, Bruce Payne *(Flikker)*, **Smiley Culture** *(DJ entertainer)*, **Jess Conrad** *(Cappuccino man)* ← the GREAT ROCK'N'ROLL SWINDLE, Sylvia Syms *(Cynthia Eve)*, Alan Freeman *(call-me-cobber)* ← JUST FOR FUN ← IT'S TRAD, DAD!, Robbie Coltrane *(Mario)* ← GHOST DANCE ← SUBWAY RIDERS ← FLASH GORDON / → EAT THE RICH → TUTTI FRUTTI, **Slim Gaillard** *(party singer)*, **G.B. Zoot Money** *(Chez)* ← BREAKING GLASS, Peter-Hugo Daly *(Vern; aka Jaws)*, Pat Hartley *(Ms. Cool Snr.)* ← JIMI HENDRIX ← RAINBOW BRIDGE, Irene Handl *(Mrs. Larkin)* ← the GREAT ROCK'N'ROLL SWINDLE ← WONDERWALL ← SMASHING TIME ← JUST FOR FUN, Johnny Shannon *(Saltzman)* ← FLAME ← THAT'LL BE THE DAY ← PERFORMANCE, **Sandie Shaw** *(Baby Boom's mum)* → EAT THE RICH

Storyline: In late 50s, London, England, the birth of the cool, the hip and the emerging British trad-jazz scene are witnessed through the eyes of wannabe fashion photographer, Colin. When he is spurned by love-of-his-life, Crepe Suzette, he turns to well-groomed ad exec, Vendice Partners. *BG*

Movie rating: *5

Visual: video

Off the record: Apart from the usual suspects (see own entries for BOWIE and Ray DAVIES), there was an eclectic array of pop stars on film here: **Sade** (responsible for cool-jazz hits, 'Your Love Is King', 'Smooth Operator', etc.), **Slim Gaillard** (pioneering jazz pianist and singer who penned 'Tutti Frutti'), **Zoot Money** (former bluesy 'Big Time Operator' in 1966), **Smiley Culture** (reggae star – real name David Emanuel; one hit wonder via 'Police Officer'), **Tenpole Tudor** (former part-time SEX PISTOLS singer, Eddie, who'd had hits such as 'Swords Of A Thousand Men'), **Sandie Shaw** (recently darling of the Smiths indie sect and a Eurovision Song Contest in 1967 with 'Puppet On A String') and early 60s pop star, **Jess Conrad** (biggest hit in 1961, 'Mystery Girl'). *MCS*

Various Artists (score: GIL EVANS *)

Mar 86. (d-lp/c)<lp/c> *Virgin; (VD/TCVD 2514) EMI; <SV5 17182>* [19] [62]
– Absolute beginners (DAVID BOWIE) / Killer blow (SADE) / Have you ever had it blue (STYLE COUNCIL) / Quiet life (RAY DAVIES) / Va va voom (*) / That's motivation (DAVID BOWIE) / Having it all (EIGHTH WONDER feat. PATSY KENSIT) / Rodrigo Bay (WORKING WEEK) / Selling out (SLIM GAILLARD) / Riot city (JERRY DAMMERS) // Boogie stop shuffle (rough and the smooth) (*) / Ted ain't dead (TENPOLE TUDOR) / Volare (DAVID BOWIE) / Napoli (CLIVE LANGER) / Little cat (you've never had it so good) (JONAS) / Better get hit in yo' soul (*) / So what? (SMILEY CULTURE) / Absolute beginners (refrain) (*). *(cd-iss. Jun87; CDV 2386) (re-iss. Apr86 1-lp/c; OVED/+C 225) (re-iss. May91 on 'Virgin-VIP' cd/c; VVIP D/C 112)*

S/track review: Not many soundtrack compilers would merge an array of cool/hip stars such as smooth operator SADE ('Killer Blow'), Paul Weller's post-Jam hit collective, the STYLE COUNCIL ('Have You Ever Had It Blue') and Patsy Kensit's own backers EIGHTH WONDER ('Having It All') with jazz musos such as GIL EVANS; the latter two giants contributed 'Va Va Voom' (among other film compositions) and 'Selling Out' respectively. However, it would be movie star, DAVID BOWIE, who kicked off proceedings via the crooning smash-hit title track; he was featured on two further cuts, 'That's Motivation' and his interpretation of 'Volare'. In every respect, the remainder of the LP disc 1 – which some film soundtrack fans ended up with instead of the double-set! – consisted of 'Riot City', a sort of modernized 'Ghost Town' by ex-Specials songsmith JERRY DAMMERS, a rendition of 'Rodrigo Bay' via London's WORKING WEEK and the groovily-arranged 'Quiet Life' by the Kinks' RAY DAVIES. Like the rest, not exactly absolute beginners, more absolute becrooners. Sorry, couldn't resist it. *BG*

Album rating: *7

– spinoff hits, etc. –

DAVID BOWIE: Absolute Beginners / dub version
Mar 86. (7"/7"sha-pic-d)(ext.12") *(VS/+S 838)(VS 838-12) <8308>* [2] [53]
(re-iss. 3"cd-s Nov88; CDT 20)

the STYLE COUNCIL: Have You Ever Had It Blue / Mr. Cool's Dream
Mar 86. (7"/12") *Polydor; (CINEX 1/+12)* [14] [–]

RAY DAVIES: Quiet Life / Voices In The Dark *[from 'Return To Waterloo' OST]*
May 86. (7"/12") *(VS 865/+12)* [ ] [–]

the ACID HOUSE

1998 (UK 118m) Channel 4 / Zeitgest Films (18)

Film genre: coming-of-age/seXual urban black comedy(s)

Top guns: dir: Paul McGuigan / s-w: Irvine Welsh (+ au) ← TRAINSPOTTING

Stars: Maurice Roeves *(1. God / 2. the drunk / 3. the priest)* ← TUTTI FRUTTI / → HALLAM FOE, 1. "The Granton Star Cause":- Stephen

McCole *(Boab)* → the YOUNG PERSON'S GUIDE TO BECOMING A ROCK STAR, Garry Sweeney *(Kev)*, Jenny McCrindle *(Evelyn)*, Simon Weir *(Tambo)*, Irvine Welsh *(Parkie)* ← TRAINSPOTTING, Alex 'Happy' Howden *(Boab Sr.)*, Pat Stanton *(barman)*, **Garry McCormack** *(workmate; + "Larry" in . . .)* / 2. "A Soft Touch":- Kevin McKidd *(Johnny)* ← TRAINSPOTTING, Michelle Gomez *(Catriona)*, Tam Dean Burn *(Alec)*, Cas Harkins *(Skanko)* / 3. "The Acid House":- Ewen Bremner *(Colin 'Coco' Bryce)* ← MOJO ← TRAINSPOTTING / → HALLAM FOE, Martin Clunes *(Rory)*, Jemma Redgrave *(Jenny)*, Jane Stabler *(Emma)*, Barbara Rafferty *(Dr. Callaghan)* ← TUTTI FRUTTI ← the WICKER MAN / → the YOUNG PERSON'S GUIDE TO BECOMING A ROCK STAR, Kirsty Mitchell *(Julie)* → a SHOT AT GLORY

Storyline: De-selection from his local pub team is just the start of a terminally bad day for the hapless Boab in the first part of this typically blacker than black trilogy, 'Granton Star Cause'. Like 'TRAINSPOTTING' without the window dressing, the Irvine Welsh follow-up finds Boab, in short order, chucked by his girlfriend, politely asked to move out of his mum and dad's and roughed up by the police, finally forced to drown his sorrows down his local where he literally falls into conversation with a pint-swilling God. After a philosophical chinwag in which the Big Man points out his multiple inadequacies, God decides to turn him into a fly. Buzzing around Granton, Edinburgh, Boab catches his pal getting it on with his girlfriend and proceeds to take revenge by leaving a little gift in his takeaway. Being a fly on the wall, though, leaves him privy to even more wretched revelations, and an insight into exactly why his mum and dad wanted him out of the house in the first place. In 'A Soft Touch', the easygoing Johnny finds himself at the mercy of an abusive, parasitic neighbour without so much as an ASBO to help him, while the title short has an acid-tripping druggie morph into the infant body of a yuppie couple's baby. *BG*

Movie rating: *7.5

Visual: video + dvd

Off the record: Garry McCormack was formerly of punk/oi band the Exploited, while in stark contrast, Pat Stanton was former Hibernian, Celtic and Scotland right-half/midfielder. *MCS*

—

Various Artists (score: Dan Mudford)

Nov 98. (cd/c) *Capitol; (<4 98207-2/-4>)* ☐ Aug99 ☐
– Insect royalty (PRIMAL SCREAM) / Break (the GYRES) / Nothing to be done (the PASTELS) / Sweetest embrace (BARRY ADAMSON & NICK CAVE) / This is carbootechnodiscotechnobooto (BENTLEY RHYTHM ACE) / You'll never know (the SOUL RENEGADES with TEXAS) / Precious maybe (BETH ORTON) / Hot love (T. REX) / Slow graffiti (BELLE & SEBASTIAN) / I still miss you (ARAB STRAP) / Going nowhere (OASIS) / Leave home (the CHEMICAL BROTHERS) / Bobby dazzler (the SONS OF SILENCE) / Claiming Marilyn (DEATH IN VEGAS) / Toujours l'amore (DIMITRI FROM PARIS) / On your own (VERVE) / Leave home – Underworld mix 1 (the CHEMICAL BROTHERS).

S/track review: Equalling the caustic rush of 'Trainspotting' was always going to be nigh on impossible. Irvine Welsh just about managed it with his episodically hilarious book, 'THE ACID HOUSE', and while Paul McGuigan's screen version was a fine attempt, critics baulked at its unrelenting misanthropy. The accompanying soundtrack found itself in a similar position, attempting to follow what is generally regarded as the definitive score of the 90s. Incredibly, it almost succeeds, following roughly the same blueprint of indie suss, clubland hedonism and ageless oldie, albeit with the kind of Scottish bent which the original 'Trainspotting' soundtrack should, by rights, have followed in the first place. PRIMAL SCREAM make another appearance, kicking things off with 'Insect Royalty', the kind of churning, dissonant instrumental which announced their late 90s return to darker musical territory. Their veteran Glasgow brethren the PASTELS make an unlikely appearance with 'Nothing To Be Done', while BELLE & SEBASTIAN's inevitable, and inevitably winsome, contribution, 'Slow Graffiti', is less in keeping with the spirit of the film than ARAB STRAP's reliably lugubrious dissection, 'I Still Miss You'. The slightest of the native talent, much touted Oasis wannabes the GYRES, pitch in with the hackneyed, if enjoyable enough 'Break'. Even OASIS themselves show face, leaving their young pretenders for dust with the thinly veiled Burt Bacharach homage, 'Going Nowhere', among the last of their truly great songs before they ran out of ideas. So much for the guitar music. If the film's title – a play on the dancefloor genre which Welsh himself has been known to shake a leg to – might have led less informed punters to expect a retrograde 808 extravaganza, the soundtrack presents instead two mixes of the CHEMICAL BROTHERS' technoid anthem, 'Leave Home' and some playful beat frolics from BENTLEY RHYTHM ACE and the SONS OF SILENCE. 'Hot Love' by T. REX almost matches Iggy and Lou for retrospective cool, although tellingly enough, one of the best things here, a philosophic chamber meditation by BARRY ADAMSON & NICK CAVE, doesn't fit into any formula. Nevertheless, outside of 'Trainspotting' itself, you'll struggle to find a more compelling or diverse showcase of mid-to-late 90s music. *BG*

Album rating: *7.5

ACROSS THE UNIVERSE

2007 (US 129m) Sony Pictures (PG-13)

Film genre: romantic Rock Musical drama

Top guns: dir: Julie Taymor (+ story w/ . . .) / s-w: Dick Clement ← STILL CRAZY, Ian La Frenais ← STILL CRAZY ← the TOUCHABLES

Stars: Evan Rachel Wood *(Lucy)*, Jim Sturgess *(Jude)*, Joe Anderson *(Max Carrigan)* ← CONTROL, Dana Fuchs *(Sadie)*, Martin Luther McCoy *(JoJo)* ← BLOCK PARTY, T.V. Carpio *(Prudence)*, Spencer Liff *(Daniel)* ← HAIRSPRAY, **Joe COCKER** *(bum/pimp/mad hippie)*, **Bono** *(Dr. Robert)* <= U2 =>, Eddie Izzard *(Mr. Kite)* ← ROMANCE & CIGARETTES ← REVENGERS TRAGEDY ← VELVET GOLDMINE, Salma Hayek *(singing nurse)* ← 54 ← FROM DUSK TILL DAWN ← FOUR ROOMS

Storyline: Jude and Lucy find transatlantic love in the midst of the sixties psychedelic, rock'n'roll and anti-war movements. Lucy's brother Max has just been drafted and, guided by gurus Dr Robert and Mr Kite, they begin a voyage of self-discovery amidst the peace movements and protest marches which made the headlines on an almost daily basis in those troubled times. The songs of the Beatles come to life. *JZ*

Movie rating: *7

Visual: dvd

Off the record: (see below)

—

Various (songwriters: the BEATLES) (score: Elliot Goldenthal)

Sep 07. (cd) *Interscope; <(0009801 02)>* ☐ ☐
– All my loving (JIM STURGESS) / I want to hold your hand (T.V. CARPIO) / It won't be long (EVAN RACHEL WOOD) / I've just seen a face (JIM STURGESS) / Let it be (CAROL WOODS & TIMOTHY T. MITCHUM) / Come together (JOE COCKER) / I am the walrus (BONO and SECRET MACHINES) / Something (JIM STURGESS) / Oh! darling (DANA FUCHS BAND and MARTIN LUTHER McCOY) / Strawberry fields forever (JIM STURGESS and JOE ANDERSON) / Across the universe (JIM STURGESS) / Helter skelter (DANA FUCHS) / Happiness is a warm gun (JOE ANDERSON feat. SALMA HAYEK) / Blackbird (EVAN RACHEL WOOD) / Hey Jude (JOE ANDERSON) / Lucy in the sky with diamonds (BONO feat. THE EDGE).

S/track review: BEATLES covers are a bit like cheese on toast, get it right and nothing tastes better, but get it wrong and you're close to throwing up. This album follows both examples to the letter with some hit and miss renditions of the Fab Four hits. Actor JIM STURGESS is excellent via the rockabilly 'I've Just Seen A Face', but awful in opener 'All My Loving', where he sounds like he belongs in McFly. T.V. CARPIO's a cappella beginning to 'I Want To Hold Your Hand' and CAROL WOODS and TIMOTHY T. MITCHUM's gospel 'Let It Be' are excellent; however 'It Won't Be Long' by EVAN RACHEL WOOD and 'Oh Darling' by DANA FUCHS and MARTIN LUTHER McCOY sound like rejects from a Ben Elton musical. It's not only the actors trying to be singers that let the album down, the ubiquitous BONO somehow manages to murder both 'I Am The Walrus' and 'Lucy In The Sky With Diamonds', with the EDGE as an accessory to the latter. The best tracks on the album, though, come from both an actor and a singer. JOE ANDERSON, along with SALMA HAYEK, offer a very credible 'Happiness Is A Warm Gun', although the show is stolen by JOE COCKER (once famous for his classic interpretation of 'With A Little Help From My Friends') delivering a rasping and downright funky take of 'Come Together', one of the consistently well-covered BEATLES songs it has to be said. There are better BEATLES cover albums out there, although it may be advisable to stick to the originals as a rule of thumb. *CM*

Album rating: *5.5

the ADVENTURES OF FORD FAIRLANE

1990 (US 103m) 20th Century Fox (12)

Film genre: cop/detective mystery & Rock-music parody

Top guns: dir: Renny Harlin / s-w: James Cappe (+ story), David Arnott (+ story), Daniel Waters

Stars: Andrew Dice Clay *(Ford Fairlane)* ← PRETTY IN PINK, **Wayne Newton** *(Julian Grendel)*, Priscilla Presley *(Colleen Sutton)*, Lauren Holly *(Jazz)*, **Morris Day** *(Don Cleveland)* ← PURPLE RAIN / → GRAFFITI BRIDGE, Maddie Corman *(Zuzu Petals)*, Gilbert Gottfried *(Johnny Crunch)*, David Patrick Kelly *(Sam)* → WILD AT HEART → the CROW → CROOKLYN → HEAVY → LAST MAN STANDING, Robert Englund *(Smiley)* ← a STAR IS BORN, Ed O'Neill *(Lt. Amos)* → WAYNE'S WORLD → WAYNE'S WORLD 2, **Vince Neil** *(Bobby Black)*, **Sheila E.** *(club singer)* ← SIGN 'O' THE TIMES ← KRUSH GROOVE, Kurt Loder *(MTV VJ)* → WHO'S THE MAN? → FEAR OF A BLACK HAT → AIRHEADS → TUPAC: RESURRECTION → RAMONES: RAW → LAST DAYS, **Black Plague:- Randy Castillo, Phil Soussan & Carlos Cavazo** *(performers)*, **Tone Loc** *(Slam the rapper)*, **Rick Marotta** *(studio musician)*, **James Zavala** *(sax man)*

Storyline: Ford Fairlane, is to his clients the great rock'n'roll detective, to everyone else he's just a dick. Our hero gets involved when some hot shots in the music world start getting bumped off. Along for the ride is persistent assistant Jazz and the fascinatingly-named Zuzu Petals. Can Ford solve the case in time before his obnoxious personality sees him next on the hit list? *JZ*

Movie rating: *5

Visual: video + dvd

Off the record: Alongside comedian, Andrew Dice Clay, star an eclectic crew of pop people: **Wayne Newton** (a Las Vegas legend who'd first hit the charts in 1963 with 'Danke Schoen'), **Morris Day** (a Prince sidekick, who had summer 1990 hit with the Times, 'Jerk-Out'), **Sheila E.** (another Prince associate), **Vince Neil** (was of Motley Crue), **Randy Castillo** (ex-drummer of Ozzy Osbourne band (w/ **Phil Soussan**), **Carlos Cavazo** (was of Quiet Riot), **Kurt Loder** was former editor of Rolling Stone mag & co-author of 'I, Tina' (What's Love Got To Do With It), **Tone Loc** (was the man behind 'Funky Cold Medina' & 'Wild Thing'), **Rick Marotta** (had sessioned with Steely Dan, Carly Simon and Stevie Nicks) and **James Zavala** (was saxophonist with Etta James). *MCS*

—

Various Artists (score: BORIS BLANK *)

Jun 90. (cd)(lp/c) *Elektra; <(7559 60952-2)>(EK 74/+C* [66] [ ]
– Cradle of love (BILLY IDOL) / Sea cruise (DION) / Funky attitude (SHEILA E.) / Glad to be alive (TEDDY PENDERGRASS and LISA FISHER) / Can't get enough (TONE LOC) / Rock 'n roll junkie (MOTLEY CRUE) / I ain't got you (ANDREW DICE CLAY) / Last time in Paris (QUEENSRYCHE) / Unbelievable (theme from "Ford Fairlane") (YELLO) * / The wind cries Mary (RICHIE SAMBORA).

S/track review: 1990 was a rather desperate time for music, which this album demonstrates in abundance. After listening to this it is understandable why Nirvana came along about a year later and kicked everybody's arse with 'Nevermind'. Apart from the swaggering, sneering brilliance of BILLY IDOL's 'Cradle Of Love' and 'Last Time In Paris' from nu-prog rockers QUEENSRYCHE, listening to "..FORD FAIRLANE' is like having to wear an itchy Christmas sweater your gran knitted; you grin and bear it for the day but know it will be stuffed down the back of a cupboard come Boxing Day. TONE LOC's 'Can't Get Enough' gives rap a bad name, sounding like the slaverings of some pre-pubescent Casanova wannabe. It is difficult to work out whether or not 'Unbelievable (Theme From Ford Fairlane)' by YELLO is trying to be funny or cool when in fact it's not even close to either, while MOTLEY CRUE's 'Rock'n'Roll Junkie' is cock-rock at its absolute worst. 'Glad To Be Alive' from TEDDY PENDERGRASS and LISA FISHER is condescending nonsense that'll have you sticking two fingers down your throat before it even reaches the chorus and DION should not have bothered turning up to sing 'Sea Cruise'. And finally, Bon Jovi guitarist RICHIE SAMBORA should have all his guitars taken away from him and his fingers cut off before being locked in a box never to be seen or, even more importantly, heard ever again after what is quite frankly a sacrilegious destruction of the Jimi Hendrix classic 'The Wind Cries Mary'. The next time you come across this soundtrack in a bargain bin I urge you to throw it to the ground and stamp on it until it is impossible for any other poor, unfortunate soul to suffer such torture before thanking whoever you normally thank for the existence of 'Nevermind'. *CM*

Album rating: *2

– spinoff hits, etc. –

BILLY IDOL: Cradle Of Love / (non-OST songs)

Apr 90. (7"/c-s/12"/cd-s) *Chrysalis <23509> (IDOL/+C/X/CD 14)* [2] [34]

☐ the ADVENTURES OF RAT PFINK AND BOO BOO alt. (⇒ RAT PFINK A BOO-BOO)

AGONIA

1969 (Greece 100m b&w) unknown

Film genre: romantic showbiz/pop-music drama

Top guns: dir: Odysseas Kosteletos / s-w: Nikos Antonakos

Stars: Tolis Voskopoulos *(Alexis)*, Eleni Anousaki *(Anna)*, Despina Nikolaidou *(Katy Andreou)*, Lavrentis Dianellos, Theodoros Exarchos, Yiorgos Mazis, **Giorgos Zambetas** *(singer)*

Storyline: Alexis and Anna are next door neighbours who have been lovers as long as they can remember. Marriage seems just around the corner but when Alexis impresses a record company with his singing Anna suddenly becomes surplus to requirements. Fame and fortune drag Alexis away from his beloved into the clutches of singer Katy but can she keep him from seeing the error of his ways? *JZ*

Movie rating: *3

Visual: none

Off the record: Giorgos Zambetas was a singer (and bouzouki-strummer) in real life with a plethora of romantic-styled dramas and scores behind him – too numerous to mention at this stage. *MCS*

AIRHEADS

1994 (US 92m) 20th Century Fox (PG-13)

Film genre: showbiz/music teen comedy

Top guns: dir: Michael Lehmann / s-w: Rich Wilkes

Stars: Brendan Fraser *(Chazz/Chester Darby)*, Steve Buscemi *(Rex)* ← PULP FICTION ← RESERVOIR DOGS ← MYSTERY TRAIN ← the WAY IT IS / → the WEDDING SINGER → COFFEE AND CIGARETTES → ROMANCE & CIGARETTES → the FUTURE IS UNWRITTEN, Adam Sandler *(Pip)* → the WEDDING SINGER, Chris Farley *(officer Wilson)* ← WAYNE'S WORLD 2 ← WAYNE'S WORLD, Joe Mantegna *(Ian)* ← ELVIS: THE MOVIE / → ALBINO ALLIGATOR, Michael McKean *(Milo)* ← EARTH GIRLS ARE EASY ← LIGHT OF DAY ← THIS IS SPINAL TAP / → GIGANTIC (A TALE OF TWO JOHNS) → a MIGHTY WIND, Judd Nelson *(Jimmie Wing)* ← EVERYBREATH ← BLUE CITY / → MR. ROCK'N'ROLL: THE ALAN FREED STORY, Ernie Hudson *(Sergeant O'Malley)* ← the CROW ← ROAD HOUSE ← the JAZZ SINGER ← LEADBELLY / → the BASKETBALL DIARIES → a STRANGER IN THE KINGDOM, Amy Locane *(Kayla)* ← CRY-BABY, Nina Siemaszko *(Suzzi)* ← TUCKER: THE MAN AND HIS DREAM, Marshall Bell *(Carl Mace)* ← DICK TRACY ← TUCKER: THE MAN AND HIS DREAM ← BIRDY / → a SLIPPING-DOWN LIFE, David Arquette *(Carter)* → RAVENOUS, Mike Judge *(voice; Beavis/Butt-Head)* → BEAVIS AND BUTT-HEAD DO AMERICA → SOUTH PARK: BIGGER, LONGER & UNCUT, Allen Covert *(cop)* → the WEDDING SINGER → the LONEST YARD, Kurt Loder *(himself)* ← FEAR OF A BLACK HAT ← WHO'S THE MAN? ← the ADVENTURES OF FORD FAIRLANE / → TUPAC: RESURRECTION → RAMONES: RAW → LAST DAYS, Harold Ramis *(Chris Moore)* ← HEAVY METAL / → KNOCKED UP → WALK HARD: THE DEWEY COX STORY, Reg E. Cathey *(Marcus)* → POOTIE TANG, **LEMMY** *(school newspaper rocker)*, **White Zombie:- Robert/Rob Cummings/Zombie** *(himself)* → MAYOR OF THE SUNSET STRIP, **Sean Yseult** *(herself)*, ***Jay Yuenger*** *(himself)*, **Philo Buerstatte** *(himself)*

Storyline: A typical US comedy about an unsigned rock band called the Lone Rangers, who, frustrated by their unsuccessful attempts to get a record deal, decide to take drastic action, holding up their local radio station with water pistols loaded with hot pepper sauce in an attempt to force them to play their demo. When the tape reel is accidentally incinerated in a fire, the group try to escape but find themselves surrounded by police. The publicity finds them with a record contract offer, followed by a platinum album and a prison sentence. *KM*

Movie rating: *5.5

Visual: video + dvd

Off the record: White Zombie (featuring ROB ZOMBIE, Yseult, Yuenger & Buerstatte) cameo alongside Motorhead's **LEMMY**.

Various Artists (score: Carter Burwell)

Aug 94. (cd/c) *Fox-Arista; <(07822 11014-2/-4)>* [ ] Oct94 [ ]
– Born to raise hell (MOTORHEAD w/ ICE-T & WHITFIELD CRANE) / I'm the one (4 NON BLONDES) / Feed the gods (WHITE ZOMBIE) / No way out (DGENERATION) / Bastardizing jellikit (PRIMUS) / London (ANTHRAX) / Can't give in (CANDLEBOX) / Curious George blues (DIG) / Inheritance (PRONG) / Degenerated (the LONE RANGERS) / I'll talk my way out of it (STUTTERING JOHN) / Fuel (STICK) / We want the airwaves (RAMONES).

S/track review: Although heavy metal was distinctly out of vogue in 1994, this film bravely harks back to the latter half of the 80s and even resurrects a couple of fallen heroes along the way. First up for a career revival were MOTORHEAD with 'Born To Raise Hell'; although pointlessly joined by ICE-T half way through, it's not enough to spoil what makes for a decent start. Things go rapidly downhill, however, when 4 NON BLONDES – sounding like Republica at their direst – make an unwelcome appearance on 'I'm The One'. WHITE ZOMBIE bring some contemporary respite with their acquired-taste bayou thrash, rendering DGENERATION's 'No Way Out' tame in comparison. PRIMUS proceed to trawl through the never ending 'Bastardizing Jellikit' (nice title though.., and where can we buy one?), while ANTHRAX's entry, 'London', is but a pale shadow of their mighty 1987 classic, 'Among The Living'. Even worse is DIG's bamboozling 'Curious George Blues', marred by an instrumental middle 8 which sounds like it's been edited in from another album. Coming on like a lumberjack-shirted cross between Pearl Jam and the Black Crowes, only CANDLEBOX's 'Can't Give In' lights the way, with an incendiary vocal from KEVIN MARTIN. Let's just be thankful the LONE RANGERS didn't inspire a tribute band called Tonto (Spanish for dumb, incidentally). *KM*

Album rating: *3.5

– spinoff hits, etc. –

MOTORHEAD with ICE-T & WHITFIELD CRANE: Born To Raise Hell
Nov 94. (7"/c-s/12"/cd-s) *(74321 23915-7/-4/-1/-2)* [–] [47]

□ ALICE COOPER: THE NIGHTMARE alt. (⇒ the NIGHTMARE)

ALICE'S RESTAURANT

1969 (US 111m) United Artists (R)

Film genre: coming-of-age comedy drama

Top guns: s-w: Arthur Penn (+ dir) → LITTLE BIG MAN, Venabel Herndon

Stars: Arlo Guthrie *(Arlo)* → WOODSTOCK → RENALDO AND CLARA → ROADSIDE PROPHETS → the BALLAD OF RAMBLIN' JACK, Pat Quinn *(Alice Brock)* → ZACHARIAH, James Broderick *(Ray Brock)*, Michael McClanathan *(Shelly)*, Geoff Outlaw *(Roger)*, Tina Chen *(Mari-chan)*, **Pete SEEGER** *(himself)*, Lee Hays *(himself)*, Kathleen Dabney *(Karin)*, Monroe Arnold *(Blueglass)* ← GOODBYE, COLUMBUS, M. Emmet Walsh *(group sergeant)* ← MIDNIGHT COWBOY / → LITTLE BIG MAN → BOUND FOR GLORY → BLADE RUNNER → CATCH ME IF YOU CAN → ALBINO ALLIGATOR, Seth Allen *(evangelist)*

Storyline: Guitar-wielding hippy Arlo meanders around the countryside until he meets his friends Alice and Ray in Stockbridge. There he becomes a member of their commune which holds court in a disused church. Alice at least tries to keep in touch with society when she and Ray open a restaurant, but she's in the minority as most of the others prefer lazing around getting stoned. Meanwhile, Arlo has a couple of brushes with the establishment due to his disastrous attempts at litter-dumping and his eligibility for the US army (no connection). *JZ*

Movie rating: *7

Visual: video + dvd (on 'MGM')

Off the record: ARLO GUTHRIE (see below)

ARLO GUTHRIE (w/ Various / composer: Garry Sherman)

Oct 69. (lp) *United Artists; <5195> (UAS 29061)* [63] Mar70 [44]
– Travelin' music / Alice's restaurant massacree – 1 / The let down / Songs to aging children (TIGGER OUTLAW) / Amazing Grace (GARRY SHERMAN CHORUS) / Trip to the city / Alice's restaurant massacree – 2 / Crash pad improvs / You're a fink (AL SHACKMAN) / Harps and marriage. *<(cd-iss. Oct98 on 'Rykodisc'+=; RCD 10737)>* – Opening credits (Amazing Grace) / Travelin' guitars / Cafe Harris rag / Revival meeting (Amazing Grace) / Alice's Restaurant radio jingle / Pastures of plenty (PETE SEEGER) / Car song (with PETE SEEGER) / Big city garbage / Wedding festivities / Farewell (Alice's Restaurant) / End title (Amazing Grace).

S/track review: Films aren't often inspired by the title song of their soundtracks but Arthur Penn's droll, Oscar-nominated meditation on ARLO GUTHRIE's even droller draft saga is a slap-happy exception. Originally recorded for GUTHRIE's 1967 debut (also titled 'Alice's Restaurant' and often erroneously – and confusingly – listed as a soundtrack), 'Alice's Restaurant Massacree' has aged well; offering humorous implements-of-destruction relief in an eve-of-destruction era, its tale of garbage-dumping, inadvertent draft dodging and rock'n'roll in-church living (itself recalling bittersweet Iain Banks' classic, 'Espedair Street'), is recounted with impeccable comic timing in a style midway between his dad Woody, Bob Dylan's own take on Woody, and the contained, cadenced hysteria of a Deep South preacher. Here the 20-minute original is split in half, divided into two more easily digestible – and arguably funnier – parts, putting the meat into a soundtrack otherwise fleshed out with typically arcane tidbits. Just who is TIGGER OUTLAW? Some claim she's a pseudonymous Joni Mitchell; those of a more cautious disposition claim she's just a Joni Mitchell wannabe; great name though, and a definitively earnest reading of one of Mitchell's definitively earnest creations, 'Songs To Aging Children'. "Music Supervisor" Garry Sherman, the man behind some of 'MIDNIGHT COWBOY's heavier arrangements, contributes the excellent breakbeat blues, 'Harps And Marriage', and – together with GUTHRIE – pens a wry piece of pedal steel heartbreak for a rare AL SHACKMAN vocal. GUTHRIE himself rounds it off with a couple of preliminary folk-bluegrass instrumentals, collectivising a rather fine soundtrack too often written off as GUTHRIE marginalia. The 'Ryko' CD chucks in a full ten tracks of extra/related material, but – despite a lavish sleevenote – offers no comment on them at all. Aside from PETE SEEGER's assiduously annunciated cover of Woody's 'Pastures Of Plenty', and the raspberry-blowing joyride of 'Car Song', most are spirited, inconsequential stringed-instrumental sketches clocking in at well under two minutes. As a belated dessert on top of the main dish, they're just about worth the thirty year wait. The rootsy account of 'Amazing Grace' dreamed up for the film's opening and closing credits is the least of what should have made it to the vinyl. To that you might add the short but ineffably sweet snatch of dulcimer chime and kazoo called 'Café Harris Rag', and the ratchet-ribbing, freakbeat-folk of 'Wedding Festivities', but – in this ragtag diner – tipping is at the listener's discretion. *BG*

Album rating: *6.5

– spinoff hits, etc. –

ARLO GUTHRIE: Alice's Rock'n'Roll Restaurant / (non-OST-song)

Nov 69. (7") *Reprise; <0877> (RS 20877)* 97 Jan70 ☐

ALIEN SEX PARTY

aka MOBY PRESENTS: ALIEN SEX PARTY

2003 (US 87m) Next in Line Productions Inc. (R)

Film genre: seXual Pop-Rock musical comedy

Top guns: s-w: (+ dir) Paul Yates, Jonee Eisen

Stars: Moby *(Dildo Head)* ← MY GENERATION ← BETTER LIVING THROUGH CIRCUITRY ← MODULATIONS ← JOE'S APARTMENT / → AMERICAN HARDCORE, Joe Smith *(Joe)*, Tina Carlucci *(Tina)*, Dyanna Lauren *(herself)*, Adam Sarner *(Adam)*, **Christian Urich** *(Christian)*, Dean Haspiel *(Dean)*, Brian O'Halloran *(clerk)*

Storyline: It's Christmas Eve, and in an adult video store, owner Joe whiles away the hours talking to his employees, the highly promiscuous Tina and self-opinionated Adam. Also in the store are two gay security guards, who have to deal with the weird and wonderful customers who come in. Tonight's bunch, a fairly typical lot, include a porn star, freaks, nerds and a mad bomber, so an interesting evening is guaranteed. *JZ*

Movie rating: *2

Visual: dvd (no audio OST by MOBY, etc.)

Off the record: MOBY was born Richard Melville Hall, 11 Sep'65, New York City, USA. After being raised by his middle-class mother in Darien, Connecticut, he joined hardcore outfit the Vatican Commandos, which led to him having a brief stint in the similar, Flipper. MOBY, however, didn't record anything with the band and moved back to New York to become a DJ, making hardcore techno/dance records under the guise of Brainstorm and UHF3, etc. He subsequently became a mixer for the Pet Shop Boys, Erasure and even Michael Jackson, before and during his return into solo work in the early 90s. His UK debut, 'Go', hit the Top 10 in October '91, having just breached the charts three months earlier. Sampling the 'Twin Peaks' theme, the song was a compelling piece of techno-pop that remains a dancefloor favourite. Little was then heard of him barring a few US imports, although this led to UK semi-indie, 'Mute', taking him on board in mid '93. First up was his near Top 20 single, 'I Feel It', beginning a series of hits, albeit sporadic. Early in 1995, his album 'Everything Is Wrong' had critics lavishing praise on the man for his combination of acid-dance and ambience. 'Animal Rights', the 1996 follow-up added a new dimension; heavy industrial punk-metal which gave him a new found Kerrang! audience. Towards the tail-end of '97, the shaven-headed Christian vegan released the James Bond Theme to 'Tomorrow Never Dies', and although it rocketed into the UK Top 10, the accompanying soundtracks album, 'I Like To Score', failed to gain the same chart momentum. Eager to once more turn up his amps to number 11, MOBY this time took elements of Southern Blues (courtesy of Bessie Jones' 'Sometimes') and threw it into his punk/dance melting pot for next single, 'Honey'. Although it deserved a better chart placing than No.33, it did pave the way for a series of diverse releases kicking off with Canned Heat-esque 'Run On' (aka 'Run On For A Long Time' by Bill Landford), a taster from his fourth 'Mute' album, 'Play' (1999). '18' (2002) was as warm and self-assured as its predecessor while pointedly not attempting to repeat that record's singular fusion. **Christian Urich** (b. John Christian Urich) was a solo musician who also featured in Cooly's Hot Box. *AS & MCS*

☐ ALL YOU NEED IS CASH alt.
(⇒ the RUTLES)

☐ Davie ALLAN AND THE ARROWS segment
(⇒ the WILD ANGELS)

ALMOST FAMOUS

2000 (US 122m) Columbia Pictures (R)

Film genre: coming-of-age showbiz/music comedy drama

Top guns: s-w + dir: Cameron Crowe ← SINGLES ← FAST TIMES AT RIDGEMONT HIGH

Stars: Patrick Fugit *(William Miller)*, Frances McDormand *(Elaine Miller)* → LAUREL CANYON, Billy Crudup *(Russell Hammond)*, Kate Hudson *(Penny Lane)* → DR. T & THE WOMEN, Jason Lee *(Jeff Bebe)*, Philip Seymour Hoffman *(Lester Bangs)* ← MAGNOLIA ← BOOGIE NIGHTS / → COLD MOUNTAIN, Zooey Deschanel *(Anita Miller)*, Anna Paquin *(Polexia Aphrodisia)*, **Mark Kozelek** *(Larry Fellows)*, **Peter Frampton** *(Reg)* ← SGT. PEPPER'S LONELY HEARTS CLUB BAND ← SON OF DRACULA, Fairuza Balk *(Sapphire)* ← GAS FOOD LODGING, Rainn Wilson *(David Felton)* → HOUSE OF 1000 CORPSES, **Bijou Phillips** *(Estrella Starr)* ← BLACK AND WHITE ← SUGAR TOWN / → OCTANE, Charles Walker *(principal)* ← GOIN' COCONUTS ← a PIECE OF THE ACTION, Eion Bailey *(Jann Wenner)* ← FIGHT CLUB, Noah Taylor *(Dick Roswell)* ← DOGS IN SPACE / → the PROPOSITION, Jay Baruchel *(Vic Munoz)* → KNOCKED UP, **Pauley Perrette** *(Alice Wisdom)* → BADSVILLE → BROTHER BEAR, Jesse Caron *(Darryl)* ← the BEACH BOYS: AN AMERICAN FAMILY, **Pete Droge** *(Hyatt singer)*, Emmy Collins *(hotel loadie)* ← TO HELL AND BACK / → ROCK STAR

Storyline: Assigned to a Rolling Stone cover scoop when most of his peers are still on their paper rounds, 15 year-old William Miller charts his own rites of passage in the company of up and coming blues-rockers Stillwater. His mentor is none other than legendary journo Lester Bangs, who memorably dismisses Stillwater as "swill merchants" but cautiously encourages him all the same, warning him off free drugs, friendships and compromise. On the road across America, shepherded by kindly groupies, he encounters all of these, as well as a minefield of ego battles, musical politics and marital strain. *BG*

Movie rating: *7.5

Visual: dvd

Off the record: NANCY WILSON (b.16 Mar'54, San Francisco, California). As one half of femme rockers Heart, NANCY WILSON enjoyed two distinct periods of fame: during the FM million-selling era of the late 70s, and during the band's MTV-era, pop-rock reinvention of the mid-80s, during which time she married music journalist turned director Cameron Crowe. Having already appeared in both Amy Heckerling's adaptation of Crowe's novel, 'FAST TIMES AT RIDGEMONT HIGH' (1982) and the Crowe-scripted 'The Wild Life' (1984), she went on to swap acting in the man's films to scoring them. While her most high profile screen appearance had been the Fred Williamson effort, 'The Big Score' (1983), she first made the move from acting to composing with Crowe's directorial debut, 'Say Anything . . .' (1989), providing additional score to the OST by with Richard Gibbs and Art Of Noise alumni Anne Dudley, and having her power ballad theme song, 'All For Love', featured on the soundtrack, itself the first of Crowe's Nick Hornby-esque trawls through the back pages of his record collection. To his 1992 slacker classic, 'SINGLES', NANCY and her sister contributed a cover of LED ZEPPELIN's 'The Battle Of Evermore', credited to their occasional side project Lovemongers, while Crowe's Oscar-winning 'Jerry Maguire' (1996) served as NANCY's first solo scoring project, with her mellow main theme, 'We Meet Again' and the elegiac 'Sandy' making it to the rock-centric soundtrack. The partnership was still going strong come the new millennium with WILSON scoring two of Crowe's most talked about films to date: the bittersweet remembrances of his rock journalist apprenticeship, 'ALMOST FAMOUS' (2000) and his mind-bending psych-thriller, 'Vanilla Sky' (2001). Sidling up to the former's roll call of 70s soundtrack nuggets was her acoustic sketch 'Lucky Trumble', with the similarly pastoral 'Elevator Heat' and the Sheryl Crowe-esque 'I Fall Apart' (in tandem with her hubby and actress Cameron Diaz) representing her score on the more eclectic soundtrack to the Alejandro Amenábar remake. *BG*
Note that, **Mark Kozelek** (is of Red House Painters and a solo artist), **Bijou Phillips** (daughter of JOHN PHILLIPS, ex-MAMAS & THE PAPAS – a pro singer since she was 17, her album 'I'd Rather Eat Glass' was produced by Jerry Harrison, ex-Talking Heads), **Peter Frampton** (was ex-Humble Pie and the man behind multi-platinum double-LP, 'Frampton Comes Alive'), **Pete Droge** (was of the Droges). *MCS*

—

Various Artists (score: NANCY WILSON *)

Sep 00. (cd) *DreamWorks; <(4 50279-2)>* [43] Feb01 [ ]
– America (SIMON & GARFUNKEL) / Sparks (the WHO) / It wouldn't have made any difference (TODD RUNDGREN) / I've seen all good people – Your move (YES) / Feel flows (the BEACH BOYS) / Fever dog (STILLWATER) / Every picture tells a story (ROD STEWART) / Mr. Farmer (the SEEDS) / One way out (the ALLMAN BROTHERS) / Simple man (LYNYRD SKYNYRD) / That's the way (LED ZEPPELIN) / Tiny dancer (ELTON JOHN) / Lucky trumble (*) / I'm waiting for the man (DAVID BOWIE) / The wind (CAT STEVENS) / Slip away (CLARENCE CARTER) / Something in the air (THUNDERCLAP NEWMAN).

S/track review: The cocaine-stuffed caviar to 'HIGH FIDELITY's humble pie, 'ALMOST FAMOUS' inhabits an era when music, if no longer likely to save the world, was at least decadent enough to let you forget it for a while. Unsurprisingly given Crowe's real life cachet as a former rock journo, he cherry-picks that music with the same fondness – if not the same ear for hip obscurity – as Quentin Tarantino or VINCENT GALLO. And even if this is much more of a straight rock job than 'HIGH FIDELITY', and more or less restricted to a single decade (the 70s), it pretty much manages to avoid the easy options which marred that soundtrack. Crowe sticks to the big names but generously digs into the mustier corners of their respective catalogues (and pulls off a historical coup by successfully licensing a LED ZEPPELIN track). Like SPINAL TAP with a humour bypass, Peter Frampton-schooled hard rockers STILLWATER want to be Led Zep so much it hurts, and – along with played-to-pulp offerings from SIMON & GARFUNKEL and THUNDERCLAP NEWMAN – is the only wrong turn on what is otherwise a discerning, occasionally surprising evocation of a less cynical, more soulful time. ROD STEWART's 'Every Picture Tells A Story' also falls into the overexposed bracket, but as one of his ageless paeons to global philandering, it's hard to resist. Those enjoying only a passing acquaintance with the 70s will scarcely believe that the skittering psychedelia of 'Feel Flows' is credited to the BEACH BOYS, may well start checking out the unsung works of TODD RUNDGREN, perhaps never regard ELTON JOHN in quite the same way again, and realise that LYNYRD SKYNYRD were capable of writing a ballad without a headbanging finale. The tracklist is admittedly whiter than white (no Jimi Hendrix?), but – with the inclusion of CLARENCE CARTER's revelatory 'Slip Away' – Crowe at least concedes there's more to the Deep South than rebel flags and sideburns. Figure in wife NANCY WILSON's score excerpt, 'Lucky Trumble', and 'ALMOST FAMOUS' is almost a classic album. *BG*

Album rating: *8

AMERICAN GRAFFITI

1973 (US 109m) Universal Pictures (PG)

Film genre: coming-of-age/teen comedy drama (w/ Rock'n'roll)

Top guns: s-w: George Lucas (+ dir), Gloria Katz & Willard Huyck → HOWARD THE DUCK

Stars: Richard Dreyfuss *(Curt Henderson)* ← HELLO DOWN THERE / → DOWN AND OUT IN BEVERLY HILLS, Ronny Howard *(Steve Bolander)* → MORE AMERICAN GRAFFITI, Paul Le Mat *(John Milner)* → MORE AMERICAN GRAFFITI → ROCK & RULE, Charlie Martin Smith *(Terry 'The Toad' Fields)* ← PAT GARRETT & BILLY THE KID / → the BUDDY HOLLY STORY → COTTON CANDY → MORE AMERICAN GRAFFITI → TRICK OR TREAT, Cindy Williams *(Laurie Henderson)* ← GAS-S-S-S! / → MORE AMERICAN GRAFFITI, **Mackenzie Phillips** *(Carol)* → MORE AMERICAN GRAFFITI → MAYOR OF THE SUNSET STRIP, Candy Clark *(Debbie Dunham)* → MORE AMERICAN GRAFFITI → COOL AS ICE, Joe Spano *(Vic)* → ROADIE, Bo Hopkins *(Joe Young)* → MORE AMERICAN GRAFFITI → SOUTH OF HEAVEN, WEST OF HELL → DON'T LET GO, Harrison Ford *(Bob Falfa)* ← ZABRISKIE POINT / → MORE AMERICAN GRAFFITI → BLADE RUNNER → WORKING GIRL, Kathy Quinlan *(Peg)* → the DOORS → EVENT HORIZON, Manuel Padilla Jr. *(Carlos)* → COTTON CANDY → MORE AMERICAN GRAFFITI, Wolfman Jack *(XERB DJ)* → DEADMAN'S CURVE → SGT. PEPPER'S LONELY HEARTS CLUB BAND → MORE AMERICAN GRAFFITI, **Flash Cadillac & The Continental Kids:- Sam "Flash Cadillac" McFadden, Lin "Spike" Phillips, Dwight "Spider" Bement, Chris "Angelo" Moe, Warren "Butch" Knight, Jeff "Wally" Stuart** *(prom band)*, Jim Bohan *(Officer Holstein)* → BUCKTOWN, Kay Ann Kemper *(Jane; girl at the dance)* → FALLING FROM GRACE

Storyline: Modesto, California, one end of summer night in 1962, four teenage boys desperately cruise for girls while listening to DJ, Wolfman Jack, playing all the hits on the radio. Their lives will change – and they know it – when they'll be whisked off to various colleges the following day. *MCS*

Movie rating: *8

Visual: video + dvd

Off the record: Colorado's fifties-styled rockers, **Flash Cadillac** went on to have a few Top 50 hits, namely 'Good Times, Rock & Roll' and 'Did You Boogie (With Your Baby)', the latter featuring another "AMERICAN GRAFFITI"-ite, Wolfman Jack. *MCS*

—

Various Artists

Aug 73. (d-lp/d-c) *M.C.A.; <2-/4-8001> (MCSP/+C 253)* [10] Apr74 [37]
– (We're gonna) Rock around the clock (BILL HALEY & HIS COMETS) * / Sixteen candles (the CRESTS) / Runaway (DEL

SHANNON) * / Why do fools fall in love? (FRANKIE LYMON & THE TEENAGERS) * / That'll be the day (BUDDY HOLLY) * / Fannie Brown (BUSTER BROWN) / At the hop (FLASH CADILLAC & THE CONTINENTAL KIDS) / She's so fine (FLASH CADILLAC & THE CONTINENTAL KIDS) / The stroll (the DIAMONDS) / See you in September (the TEMPOS) / Surfin' safari (the BEACH BOYS) / (He's the) Great imposter (the FLEETWOODS) / Almost grown (CHUCK BERRY) / Smoke gets in your eyes (the PLATTERS) * / Little darlin' (the DIAMONDS) * / Peppermint twist (JOEY DEE & THE STARLITERS) / Barbara Ann (the REGENTS) * / Book of love (the MONOTONES) / Maybe baby (BUDDY HOLLY) * / Ya ya (LEE DORSEY) / The great pretender (the PLATTERS) // Ain't that a shame (FATS DOMINO) * / Johnny B. Goode (CHUCK BERRY) * / I only have eyes for you (the FLAMINGOS) * / Get a job (the SILHOUETTES) / To the aisle (the FIVE SATINS) * / Do you wanna dance (BOBBY FREEMAN) / Party doll (BUDDY KNOX) / Come go with me (the DEL-VIKINGS) * / You're sixteen (JOHNNY BURNETTE) * / Love potion No.9 (the CLOVERS) * / Since I don't have you (the SKYLINERS) * / Chantilly lace (BIG BOPPER) / Teen angel (MARK DINNING) / Crying in the chapel (SONNY TIL & THE ORIOLES) / A thousand miles away (the HEARTBEATS) / Heart and soul (the CLEFTONES) / Green onions (BOOKER T. & THE MG'S) / Only you (and you alone) (the PLATTERS) * / Goodnight, sweetheart, goodnight (the SPANIELS) * / All summer long (the BEACH BOYS) *. *<re-iss. Sep85 as * 'Highlights From . . .' lp/c/cd; MCLD/MCLDC/DMCLD 617> (d-cd/d-c iss.Oct92; MCLDD/MCLC 19150) <re-iss. d-cd Mar03 on 'Universal'; AAMCAD 28001>*

S/track review: '41 Original Hits From The Soundtrack Of AMERICAN GRAFFITI' to give you its full title, just about sums up what this cult teenage rock'n'roll compilation was all about. How else would you start this historical timepiece than with BILL HALEY & HIS COMETS' cinema seat-smashing '(We're Gonna) Rock Around The Clock'. Every one a gem, although revamped versions of 'At The Hop' & 'She's So Fine' by R&R revivalists, FLASH CADILLAC & THE CONTINENTAL KIDS, were a little too squeaky for my polished tastes; and just where was the King, ELVIS? Everything else seems to be on show here, from the mid-50s to the movie's early 60s setting, most ear-bashing R&R jukebox classics from the likes of iconic legends BUDDY HOLLY, CHUCK BERRY, FATS DOMINO, the PLATTERS, FRANKIE LYON & THE TEENAGERS and the BEACH BOYS representing a time when bobby socks and leather jackets were in fashion. An album (or two!) that can whisk you back in time, it also featured numbers from one-hit wonders such as the MONOTONES ('Book Of Love'), BUSTER BROWN ('Fannie Mae'), MARK DINNING ('Teen Angel') and the TEMPOS ('See You In September'), though to my knowledge, doo-wop vocalists the SPANIELS got nowhere with 'Goodnight, Sweetheart, Goodnight'. Personal faves (from the crest of the pack) include, DEL SHANNON's 'Runaway', BUDDY KNOX's 'Party Doll', the BIG BOPPER's Jerry Lee Lewis-sounding 'Chantilly Lace' and BOOKER T.'s mod classic, 'Green Onions'. If the 41 tracks – and the sound of rasping disc jockey WOLFMAN JACK contributing several abridged intros – were too much for one sitting, single-CD versions are also available. There was also a second double LP released a few years later, and this comprised 25 more jukebox faves from DION, LITTLE RICHARD and the KINGSMEN. *MCS*

Album rating: *9 (1-cd *7.5) / More . . . *8

– spinoff releases, etc. –

Various Artists: More American Graffiti

1975. (d-lp) *M.C.A.; <2-8007>* [ ] [–]
– See you later, alligator (BILL HALEY & HIS COMETS) / Maybe (the CHANTELS) / Bony Maronie (LARRY WILLIAMS) / Shoop shoop song (it's in his kiss) (BETTY EVERETT) / Teenager in love (DION & THE BELMONTS) / Ready Teddy (LITTLE RICHARD) / Poison Ivy (the COASTERS) / I'm sorry (BRENDA LEE) / Speedo (the CADILLACS) / Duke of Earl (GENE CHANDLER) / Peggy Sue (BUDDY HOLLY) / One summer night (the DANLEERS) / / Locomotion (LITTLE EVA) / He will break your heart (JERRY BUTLER) / Twilight time (the PLATTERS) / Tutti frutti (LITTLE RICHARD) / Will you still love me tomorrow (the SHIRELLES) / Could this be magic (the DUBS) / Stagger Lee (LLOYD PRICE) / Gee (the CROWS) / My heart is an open book (CARL DOBKINS JR.) / Oh, boy! (BUDDY HOLLY & THE CRICKETS) / Happy happy birthday baby (the TUNE WAVERS) / Louie, Louie (the KINGSMEN) / It might as well rain until September (CAROLE KING).

AMERICAN HOT WAX

1978 (US 95m) Paramount Pictures (PG)

Film genre: Rock'n'roll Musical bio-pic/drama

Top guns: dir: Floyd Mutrux / s-w: John Kaye (+ story) → WHERE THE BUFFALO ROAM (story: Art Linson) → WHERE THE BUFFALO ROAM

Stars: Tim McIntire *(Alan Freed)*, Laraine Newman *(teenage Louise)*, John Lehne *(D.A. Coleman)*, ← BROTHERS ← BOUND FOR GLORY / → CARNY → LADIES AND GENTLEMEN, THE FABULOUS STAINS, Jay Leno *(Mookie/Michael)* → WAG THE DOG, **Chuck BERRY** *(himself)*, **Jerry Lee LEWIS** *(himself)*, Fran Drescher *(Sheryl)* ← SATURDAY NIGHT FEVER / → THIS IS SPINAL TAP → ROCK'N'ROLL MOM → UHF, Hamilton Camp *(Louie Morgan)* → ROADIE → DICK TRACY, Moosie Drier *(Artie Moress)*, **the Chesterfields:- Carl Weaver** *(performer)*, **Al Chalk** *(performer)*, **Sam Harkness** *(performer)*, **Arnold McCuller** *(performer)*, → CROSSROADS → BEACHES / → DUETS, **Frankie Ford** *(himself)*, **Screamin' Jay Hawkins** *(himself)* ← MISTER ROCK AND ROLL / → JOEY → MYSTERY TRAIN → I PUT A SPELL ON ME, **Kenny Vance** *(Prof. LaPlano)* → EDDIE AND THE CRUISERS → LOOKING FOR AN ECHO, Olivia Barash *(Susie)* → REPO MAN, Keene Curtis *(Mr. Leonard)* → LAMBADA, Arnold Johnson *(Arnold; musician in bar)* ← PIPE DREAMS ← SHAFT / → the FIVE HEARTBEATS, Cameron Crowe *(delivery boy)* → SINGLES, Pat McNamara *(Gordie)* → CRIMES OF PASSION → FIGHT CLUB, Garry Goodrow *(Louise's dad)* ← STEELYARD BLUES / → HARD TO HOLD → DIRTY DANCING, Elmer Valentine *(union man)* ← CHASTITY, Larry Hankin *(Diamond's manager)* ← STEELYARD BLUES ← the PHYNX

Storyline: Musical bio-pic following the career of pioneering DJ Alan Freed and his role in popularising 50s pop music, particularly his efforts to stage America's inaugural rock'n'roll gig in New York. *BG*

Movie rating: *5

Visual: video

Off the record: Alan Freed was born in Johnstown, Pennsylvania on 15th December, 1921. As a DJ in the mid-50s, he brought rock'n'roll (a coin he is said to have phrased) to millions of teenagers that listened to his radio shows. However, a subsequent payola scandal in the early 60s, led to humiliation in the broadcasting industry. Freed (or Moondog as he was affectionately known) sadly died on 20th January, 1965. *MCS*

Various Artists

Mar 78. (d-lp) *A&M; <SP 6500> (AMLM 66500)* [31] [ ]
– (Live recordings):- introduction of Alan Freed / Hot Wax theme (BIG BEAT BAND) / Rock and roll is here to stay (PROF. LaPLANO & THE PLANOTONES) / Mister Lee (DELIGHTS) / Maybe (DELIGHTS) / Hey little girl (CLARK OTIS) / Reelin' and rockin' (CHUCK BERRY) / Roll over Beethoven (CHUCK BERRY) / Why do fools fall in love (the CHESTERFIELDS) / That is rock & roll (the CHESTERFIELDS) / I put a spell on you (SCREAMIN' JAY HAWKINS) / Mister Blue (TIMMY & THE TULIPS) / Whole lotta shakin' goin' on (JERRY LEE LEWIS) / Great balls of fire (JERRY LEE LEWIS) // (Mono recordings):- Sweet little sixteen (CHUCK BERRY) / That's why (I love you so) (JACKIE WILSON) / Sincerely (the MOONGLOWS) / There goes my baby (the DRIFTERS) / Hushabye (the MYSTICS) / Rave on (BUDDY HOLLY) / Stay (MAURICE WILLIAMS AND THE ZODIACS) / Tutti frutti

(LITTLE RICHARD) / Zoom (the CADILLACS) / Little star (the ELEGANTS) / When you dance (the TURBANS) / Splish splash (BOBBY DARIN) / Sea cruise (FRANKIE FORD) / Goodnight, it's time to go (the SPANIELS).

S/track review: As a tribute to the "Father of Rock & Roll" – the man who started it all – Alan Freed, 'AMERICAN HOT WAX' pays tribute to the man and the groups whom he championed way back in the 50s and early 60s. Alongside decent cuts from the fictional acts created for the movie, classic cuts from the likes of JERRY LEE LEWIS, the maniacal SCREAMIN' JAY HAWKINS, the CHESTERFIELDS and CHUCK BERRY (all of whom appeared in the film) make this worth searching out, the latter contributing a reassuringly lascivious and suggestive version of 'Reelin' And Rockin'". Fictitious as they were, PROF. LaPLANO & THE PLANOTONES (i.e. music supervisor/producer KENNY VANCE, Joe Esposito, Bruce Sudano and Ed Hokenson), the DELIGHTS (featuring Brenda Russell, Stephanie Spruill, Joyce King & Yolanda Howard), TIMMY & THE TULIPS (a one-guy/two-gal outfit – the Human League of their day!) all contributed their retro doo-wops as if lifted from the 50s. Split into two discs, Record One deals with stereo "live" recordings, while Record Two (sides 3 & 4) highlights standards from the likes of LITTLE RICHARD ('Tutti Frutti'), BOBBY DARIN ('Splish Splash'), BUDDY HOLLY ('Rave On'), FRANKIE FORD ('Sea Cruise') and the aforementioned CHUCK BERRY ('Sweet Little Sixteen'). All'n'all, a glorious introduction to rock and roll, and a worthy musical addition next to the likes of 'AMERICAN GRAFFITI' and 'THAT'LL BE THE DAY'. *MCS*

Album rating: *7

AMERICAN POP

1981 (US 96m w/anim.) Columbia Pictures (R)

Film genre: animated Pop-Rock Musical drama

Top guns: dir: Ralph Bakshi ← HEAVY TRAFFIC ← FRITZ THE CAT / s-w: Ronni Kern

Voices: Ron Thompson *(Tony / Pete)*, Jeffrey Lippa *(Zalmie)*, Jerry Holland *(Louie)*, Marya Small *(Frankie)* ← THANK GOD IT'S FRIDAY / → MAN ON THE MOON, Lisa Jane Persky *(Bella)* ← KISS MEETS THE PHANTOM OF THE PARK / → GREAT BALLS OF FIRE! → TO HELL AND BACK, Roz Kelly *(Eva Tanguay)* ← NEW YEAR'S EVIL ← YOU'VE GOT TO WALK IT LIKE YOU TALK IT . . . ← the OWL AND THE PUSSYCAT, Richard Singer *(Benny)*, Eric Taslitz *(little Pete)*, Frank DeKova *(Crisco)* ← HEAVY TRAFFIC, Amy Levitt *(Nancy)* ← WHO IS HARRY KELLERMAN . . ., Vincent Schiavelli → FAST TIMES AT RIDGEMONT HIGH

Storyline: Spanning four generations of an immigrant family of musicians, the story begins in 1890s Russia when a rabbi's wife and son flee to America to avoid a pogrom. Over the course of the 20th century they and their descendants find themelves having to cope with wars, gangsters and drugs but each generation is determined to continue their musical tradition. *JZ*

Movie rating: *7

Visual: video + dvd on Columbia TriStar

Off the record: nothing yet!

Various Artists (score/m.a.: Lee Holdridge)

Feb 81. (lp/c) *M.C.A.; <MCA/+C 5201>* □ □
– Hell is for children (PAT BENATAR) / Summertime (BIG BROTHER & THE HOLDING COMPANY) / California dreamin' (the MAMAS AND THE PAPAS) / This train (PETER, PAUL AND MARY) / Somebody to love (MARCY LEVY) / Purple haze (the JIMI HENDRIX EXPERIENCE) / Take five (the DAVE BRUBECK QUARTET) / You send me (SAM COOKE) / Turn me loose (FABIAN) / People are strange (the DOORS).

S/track review: With a plethora of classic 20th-century pop tunes from the 'AMERICAN POP' animation movie to choose from (eg 'A Hard Rain's A-Gonna Fall', 'Free Bird', 'Night Moves' and 'Pretty Vacant'), how in hell's children did the OST supervisors come up with such dull-oids from girl rocker PAT BENATAR, folkie trio PETER, PAUL AND MARY, teen idol FABIAN and future Shakespear Sister, MARCY LEVY? (the latter doing a copycat "Stars-In-Yer-Eyes" rendition of Jefferson Airplane's psych-out number, 'Somebody To Love'). One awaits some kind of response . . . and then nothing. Here we get only just over half an hour on record and one can feel slightly cheated in the fact that this was to represent the ultimate collection of er . . . "AMERICAN POP". What was wrong with the elementary double-LP? – so fashionable around the early 80s with similarly-themed movies, 'ROADIE', 'NO NUKES', etc. Having said all the negative, side 2 does contain "real" classics, including contender for the greatest 60s track, 'Purple Haze' by the JIMI HENDRIX EXPERIENCE. The DOORS' 'People Are Strange' keeps the MORRISON memories alive, while side 1's George Gershwin standard ('Summertime') is ground out by another dead pop star, JANIS JOPLIN, through her psychedelic blues unit, BIG BROTHER AND THE HOLDING COMPANY. The jazz element is down to one song, the cooler than cool 'Take Five' by the DAVE BRUBECK QUARTET, while soul is catered for via SAM COOKE's 1957 smooching chart-topper, 'You Send Me'. All'n'all, according to this LP, the 20th-century was half great, half mediocre; the ratings then exemplify this. *MCS*

Album rating: *5

AMERICAN REEL

2003 (US 100m) KiMina Entertainment

Film genre: Country-music/showbiz comedy drama

Top guns: dir: Mark Archer / s-w: Junior Burke, Scott Fivelson

Stars: David Carradine *(James Lee Springer)* ← ROADSIDE PROPHETS ← the LONG RIDERS ← BOUND FOR GLORY / → KILL BILL VOL.1 → KILL BILL VOL.2, Michael Maloney *(Jason Fields)*, Mariel Hemingway *(Disney Rifkin)* ← FALLING FROM GRACE, Kevin Ferguson *(Tony Marty)*, Matt Socia *(Blair Whiteman)*

Storyline: Jamie Lee Springer is a singer-songwriter who has been struggling for twenty years to hit the big time. At last he is beginning to make a breakthrough but his manager and best friend Jason tells him the only way to reach stardom is to sacrifice his principles and kowtow to the smart-suit record executives, who would prefer to see him do commercials and music videos rather than just write songs. *JZ*

Movie rating: *6.5

Visual: dvd (no audio OST; score: Thom Bishop)

Off the record: David Carradine had also tried his hand at singing via, 'BOUND FOR GLORY'.

AMOR A RITMO DE GO-GO

1966 (Mex 95m) Peliculas Mexicanas S.A. / TV Producciones S.A.

Film genre: Pop-Rock Musical teen comedy

Top guns: dir: Miguel M. Delgado / s-w: Adolfo Torres Portillo

Stars: Javier Solis *(Javier)*, Rosa Maria Vazquez *(Lupe)*, Leonorilda Ochoa *(Leonor)*, Eleazar Garcia 'Chelelo' *(Lucio)*, Raul Astor *(Don Guillermo)*, Arturo Cobo 'Cobitos' *(Hector)*, Yolanda Montes 'Tongolele' *(Tongolele)*, **Los Hooligans** *(performers)*, **Los Rockin Devil's:- Francisco Estrada, Alejandro Robles, Elias Amabilis Palmam Jaime Gonzalez, Miguel Angel Osuna,**

Victor Mariano Rojas & Blanca Estrada *(performers)* ← JUVENTUD SIN LEY, **La Orquestra de Leo Acosta** *(performers)*

Storyline: Set in a Mexican discotheque, there's dance action a-plenty in this Spanish-language "Rocanrolero Phenomenon" movie. *MCS*

Movie rating: *6

Visual: video / + dvd (with audio CD-R)

Off the record: Los Hooligans (not to be confused with 90s third-wave ska outfit) released a plethora of Mexican 45s and LPs in the 60s, mainly of the rock'n'roll covers variety; example 2005 compilation 'El Rock De Los 60s', the group consisted of Ortega, Novarro, Becerra & Ramos. **Los Rockin Devils** * (six guys and a girl!) were of the same ilk, contributions from the three groups included 'Hey Lupe'*, 'Bule Bule'*, 'Si Soy Graciosa', 'Watussi Go-Go', 'Que Flojera', 'Go Go Tropical' and the title track. *MCS*

AMY

1998 (Aus 103m) Cascade Films / Film Victoria (PG-13)

Film genre: coming-of-age family comedy/drama

Top guns: dir: Nadia Tass ← RIKKY AND PETE / s-w: David Parker ← RIKKY AND PETE

Stars: Alana De Roma *(Amy Enker)*, Rachel Griffiths *(Tanya Rammus)* ← TO HAVE AND TO HOLD / → STEP UP, Ben Mendelsohn *(Robert Buchanan)*, **Nick Barker** *(Will Enker)*, Kerry Armstrong *(Sarah Trendle)* → LANTANA → ONE PERFECT DAY, William Zappa *(Bill Trendle)*, Jeremy Trigatti *(Zac Trendle)*, Torquil Neilson *(Luke Lassister)*, Sullivan Stapleton *(Wayne Lassiter)*, Frank Gallacher *(Dr. Urquhart)* ← HAMMERS OVER THE ANVIL ← PROOF / – ONE PERFECT DAY, Susie Porter *(Anny Buchanan)*, Mary Ward *(Mrs. Mullins)*, Dino Marnika *(Mike Cialano)* → QUEEN OF THE DAMNED

Storyline: Traumatised by witnessing her father's death live on stage, eight year old Amy no longer hears or speaks. Her mother Tanya tries her best to cope, but when the government threatens to take Amy away from her, they run off from their farm into the big city. They end up in a bad neighbourhood, but just when things are at their worst they meet musician Robert, who finds he alone can communicate with Amy in a special way – music. *JZ*

Movie rating: *7

Visual: dvd

Off the record: PHIL JUDD was a founding member of New Zealand art-rock act, Split Enz; while other members evolved into Crowded House, he subsequently formed Swingers who had a No.1 with 'Counting The Beat'; he went solo in the early 80s and contributed several songs to Australian rock musical, 'STARSTRUCK' (1982). The following decade, Judd was commissioned for a string of film OST's, 'The Big Steal' (1990), 'Death In Brunswick' (1991), 'Hercules Returns' (1993), 'Mr. Reliable' (1996) and 'AMY' (1998); the expanded 2nd edition will look into his film work more closely. *MCS*

—

Various Cast/Artists (composer: PHIL JUDD *)

Aug 98. (cd) *Best Boy – Festival; (D 31876)* [–] Austra [–]
– Shamrock (NICK BARKER) / Somedays (NENEH CHERRY) / By your side (Mr Popular) (NICK BARKER) / Ain't no sunshine (ALANA) / Amy suite: [I] Secret angel [II] Dilemma [III] Two little doves (*) / Real wild life (ED KUEPPER) / Paper cut (NICK BARKER) / Colours (DONOVAN) / Goreki (LAMB) / You & me (NICK BARKER and ALANA). *<Japanese iss.Sep99; QTCY 73013>* – (last track first).

S/track review: Scanning the track list to the soundtrack of Australian film, 'AMY', does generate a bit of expectancy due to the presence of some respected artists such as NENEH CHERRY, LAMB and DONOVAN; however, one shouldn't get carried away. The album is led by Aussie singer/songwriter NICK BARKER, who also stars in the movie, and is the former frontman of punksters the Reptiles and Wreckery. He contributes a few soft-rock numbers that are probably better off remaining anonymous as they do little to even raise an eyebrow, never mind pulses. Dance singer ALANA offers a truly awful version of the Bill Withers classic 'Ain't No Sunshine' that is devoid of any trace of intensity or passion. 'Real Wild Life' from former Saints/Laughing Clowns frontman, ED KUEPPER, is good in a kind of Cure-meets-Cocteau Twins way, while former Split Enz man PHIL JUDD provides the orchestral 'Amy Suite'. The best tracks on the album are delivered by the aforementioned artists. 'Somedays' by NENEH CHERRY is a wonderfully atmospheric and tense ballad, while DONOVAN's 'Colours' offers a welcome infusion of blues-tinged folk and the widely used 'Goreki' by Mancunian electro-pioneers LAMB is also excellent. The soundtrack to 'AMY' is okay without being spectacular and the best tracks can be found elsewhere. *CM*

Album rating: *5

AND THE BEAT GOES ON: THE SONNY & CHER STORY

1999 (US 87m TV) Larry Thompson Organization / ABC (PG)

Film genre: Pop-music/showbiz bio-pic/comedy/drama

Top guns: dir: David Burton Morris → COME ON, GET HAPPY: THE PARTRIDGE FAMILY STORY / s-w: Ellen Weston (book: **Sonny Bono**)

Stars: Jay Underwood *(Sonny Bono)*, Renee Faia *(Cher)*, Christian Leffler *(Phil Spector)*, Jim Pirri *(Buddy Black)*, Bruce Nozick *(Art Rupe)*, Carl Gilliard *(Bumps Blackwell)*, Walter Franks *(Little Richard)* → MR. ROCK'N'ROLL: THE ALAN FREED STORY, Thomas Tofel *(Charlie Green)*, Mahryah Shain *(David Geffen)*

Storyline: Charting the rise to fame of Sonny & Cher, the story begins with Sonny Bono trying to sell his music to anyone in the business who is interested. At last he gets a break thanks to producer Phil Spector, but things really start to happen when he meets and falls in love with struggling singer Cher. Soon they get married and begin their singing career together, but dark clouds are already gathering on the horizon. *JZ*

Movie rating: *5.5

Visual: video + dvd (no audio OST by Bob Mann & Steve Tyrell)

Off the record: Jess Harnell and Kelly van Hoose Smith took on the singing voices of Sonny & Cher respectively.

ANGEL, ANGEL, DOWN WE GO

aka 'CULT OF THE DAMNED'

1970 (US 93m) American International Pictures (R)

Film genre: Rock'n'roll crime drama

Top guns: s-w: (+ dir) Robert Thom ← WILD IN THE STREETS

Stars: Jennifer Jones *(Astrid Steele)*, Jordan Christopher *(Bogart Peter Stuyvesant)*, Roddy McDowall *(Santoro)* ← HELLO DOWN THERE ← the COOL ONES / → MEAN JOHNNY BARROWS → CLASS OF 1984, Holly Near *(Tara Nicole Steele)*, **Lou Rawls** *(Joe)* → BLUES BROTHERS 2000, Charles Aidman *(Willy Steele)*, Davey Davison *(Anna Livia)*

Storyline: The Steele family have sunk into a wealthy decadence and it shows – when daughter Tara brings home new boyfriend Bogart, he soon susses out how rotten they all are and begins a campaign of mindgames with psychedelic drugs to seduce them for his own ends. He and his motley entourage think up "entertainment" using everything from diving boards to parachutes – but the fun 'n' games soon turn deadly serious. *JZ*

Movie rating: *4

Visual: none (no audio OST; composer/score: Barry Mann)

Off the record: Lou Rawls (b. 1 Dec'33, Chicago, Illinois) raised by his grandmother and a subsequent classmate of Sam Cooke (for whom he subsequently sung backing vocals), he joined gospel troupe the Pilgrim Travelers. In the mid-60s, Rawls had a number of US chart hits including 'Love Is A Hurtin' Thing', while he also charted with the theme, 'Down On Here On The Ground', from 'Cool Hand Luke' (1968). He went on to became a serious actor, the voice of many a Budweiser ad and a near chart-topper in 1976 with the smoochy R&B gem, 'You'll Never Find Another Love Like Mine'. In 'ANGEL, ANGEL,..' he's a member of fictitious band, the Rabbit Habit (alongside Roddy McDowall, Jordan Christopher and Davey Davison), who contribute several songs: 'Mother Lover', 'Hey Hey Hey And Hi Ho', 'Angel, Angel, Down We Go', 'The Fat Song', 'Revelation' & 'Lady Lady'. On a sad footnote, Rawls died of cancer on the 6th of January, 2006. *MCS*

ANIMAL HOUSE

aka NATIONAL LAMPOON'S ANIMAL HOUSE

1978 (US 109m) Universal Pictures (R)

Film genre: anarchic coming-of-age comedy

Top guns: dir: John Landis → the BLUES BROTHERS → BLUES BROTHERS 2000 / s-w: Harold Ramis → CADDYSHACK → CLUB PARADISE, Douglas Kenney → CADDYSHACK, Chris Miller → CLUB PARADISE story

Stars: John Belushi *(John "Bluto" Blutarsky)* ← the RUTLES / → the BLUES BROTHERS, Tim Matheson *(Eric "Otter" Stratton)* → ALMOST SUMMER → the STORY OF US, Peter Riegert *(Donald "Boon" Schoenstein)* → LOCAL HERO, John Vernon *(Dean Vernon Wormer)*, Verna Bloom *(Marion Wormer)* ← the HIRED HAND / → HONKYTONK MAN → the LAST TEMPTATION OF CHRIST, Thomas Hulce *(Larry "Pinto" Kroger)*, Donald Sutherland *(Prof. Dave Jennings)* ← STEELYARD BLUES / → RED HOT → COLD MOUNTAIN, Stephen Furst *(Kent "Flounder" Dorfman)* → SHAKE, RATTLE & ROCK!, Cesare Danova *(Mayor Carmime DePasto)*, Mary Louise Weller *(Mandy Pepperidge)*, Kevin Bacon *(Chip Diller)* → FOOTLOOSE, Sarah Holcomb *(Clorette DePasto)* → CADDYSHACK, James Daughton *(Greg Marmalard)*, Bruce McGill *(Daniel "D-Day" Simpson)* → CLUB PARADISE → the INSIDER, Mark Metcalf *(Doug Neidermeyer)* → WHERE THE BUFFALO ROAM, **Stephen Bishop** *(charming guy with guitar)* → the BLUES BROTHERS, DeWayne Jessie *(Otis Day)* ← THANK GOD IT'S FRIDAY ← CAR WASH ← SPARKLE / → WHERE THE BUFFALO ROAM, Karen Allen *(Katy)* → SWEET TALKER, **Robert Cray** *(guitarist with Otis Day & The Knights)* → HAIL! HAIL! ROCK'N'ROLL, Sunny Johnson *(Otter's co-ed)* → WHERE THE BUFFALO ROAM → FLASHDANCE

Storyline: The students of Faber College, Pennsylvania, are split into two houses, Delta and Omega. The Deltas' sole reason for existence is to flunk exams and cause as much mayhem as possible. Meanwhile the Omegas, along with dean Wormer, would rather obliterate the Deltas from the face of the earth and keep the college to themselves. When the dean introduces "double secret probation" things look grim for the doughball Deltas. *JZ*

Movie rating: *9.5

Visual: video + dvd

Off the record: STEPHEN BISHOP (see below). Bluesman **Robert Cray** was still trying to break through (his first LP, 'Who's Been Talkin', was released in 1980). *MCS*

Various Artists (conductor: Elmer Bernstein *)

Aug 78. (lp/c) *M.C.A.; <3046> (MCF/TC-MCF 2868)* [71] Mar79 [ ]
– Faber College theme (*) / Louie, Louie (JOHN BELUSHI) / Twistin' the night away (SAM COOKE) / Tossin' and turnin' (BOBBY LEWIS) / Shama lama ding dong (LLOYD WILLIAMS) / Hey Paula (PAUL & PAULA) / Animal house (STEPHEN BISHOP) / Intro / Money (that's what I want) (JOHN BELUSHI) / Let's dance (CHRIS MONTEZ) / Dream girl (STEPHEN BISHOP) / (What a) Wonderful world (SAM COOKE) / Shout (LLOYD WILLIAMS) / Faber College theme (*). *(re-iss. Nov87 lp/c/cd; MCL/MCLF/DMCL 1867) (re-iss. Jun92 cd/c; MCL D/C 19086) <cd re-iss. 1995; MCAD 31023> <cd re-iss. Sep98; MCADE 11808>*

S/track review: In the words of JOHN BELUSHI: "Let's Toga!". Yes, "Welcome to Delta House", and who better to kick off his muddy boots and get this rock'n'roll party started (song-wise, at least!), than the film's star gonzo and spiritual Blues Brother, Mr JOHN BELUSHI. 'Louie, Louie' (that Kingsmen staple written by Richard Berry) showcases the man's maniacal aura, while a second bite at the proverbial cherry sees him tackle Barrett Strong's 'Money (That's What I Want)'. Sheer unadulterated class, and you just have to admire anyone who could break wind then break an acoustic guitar over a certain bit-part thespian STEPHEN BISHOP's nut, albeit in an acting role – aye right. The aforementioned BISHOP supplies two tongue-in-cheek songs, the falsetto, Frankie Valli-esque 'Animal House' and 'Dream Girl', augmented by virtually the same session band as BELUSHI: Bob Bobbitt (bass), Gary Mure (drums), Bob Rose & Jeff Layton (guitars) and Rob Mounsey (keys). Reminiscent of coming-of-age movies like 'AMERICAN GRAFFITI' and 'AMERICAN HOT WAX', one is spared an exhaustive double-LP account of rock'n'roll history, instead getting a single-LP with R&B tidbits alongside some whimsical dialogue. The golden nuggets loved on campus are as follows:- BOBBY LEWIS' 'Tossin' And Turnin'' (made famous in Britain by the Searchers), CHRIS MONTEZ' 'Let's Dance', PAUL & PAULA's 'Hey Paula' and SAM COOKE's twosome, 'Twistin' The Night Away' & '(What A) Wonderful World'. From the movie itself, Otis Day (alias DeWayne Jessie) mimes to the voice of LLOYD WILLIAMS for a pair of rehashed oldies, 'Shama Lama Ding Dong' & 'Shout'. Much like the short intro at the soundtrack's beginning, all is quietened down somewhat by conductor ELMER BERNSTEIN's 'Faber College Theme'. *MCS*

Album rating: *6.5

– spinoff hits, etc. –

JOHN BELUSHI: Louie, Louie / Money (That's What I Want)

Sep 78. (7") *<40950>* [89] [–]

STEPHEN BISHOP: Animal House / Dream Girl

Dec 78. (7") *A.B.C.; <12435> (ABC 4254)* [73] Feb79 [ ]

the ANIMALS

Formed: 1960 in Newcastle-Upon-Tyne, England, as the Alan Price Combo. After supporting the likes of legendary bluesmen, Sonny Boy Williamson and John Lee Hooker, the line-up of ALAN PRICE, singer ERIC BURDON, John Steel, Chas Chandler and Hilton Valentine moved to London early in '64, where they were promptly signed to EMI's 'Columbia' roster by then virtually unknown producer Mickie Most. Re-christened the ANIMALS by their fans, the quintet hit paydirt in summer '64 with their rendition of blues standard, 'The House Of The Rising Sun'. A massive hit on both sides of the Atlantic, with BURDON's ominous vocal phrasing and PRICE's wailing organ, the record remains the band's defining moment. Rarely, if ever, has the United Kingdom produced a white guy who could sing the blues like ERIC BURDON. The whisky-soaked menace of his voice sounded at times like Old Nick incarnate and was a key component in the ANIMALS' feisty challenge to the ROLLING STONES' throne at the height of the 60s R&B Boom. It was around this time that the band first appeared on film, 'GET YOURSELF A COLLEGE GIRL' (1964) and 'POP GEAR' (1965), highlighting a time just prior to the untimely departure of PRICE. With Dave Rowberry as PRICE's replacement, the band cut a few more albums including the semi-classic 'Animalization'; however, it all fell apart towards the end of '66; Chandler went on to manage and work with JIMI HENDRIX and SLADE. BURDON moved to San Francisco, where he immersed himself in the nascent psychedelic scene, consuming liberal quantities of LSD. Under the new and improved moniker ERIC BURDON & THE ANIMALS, he released in 1967 his paeon to the emerging hippy culture, 'Winds Of Change'. Other highlights of this period include BURDON's tribute to the narcotic delights of the Swiss pharmaceutical industry, 'A Girl Named Sandoz' and 'Monterey', his reverential recollection of the legendary Pop Festival. BURDON tasted major success for the last time with soul/funk band, WAR, their debut single 'Spill The Wine' climbing into the Top 3 in the States mid 1970. The original ANIMALS line-up (minus PRICE, of course, who subsequently scored 'O LUCKY MAN') re-formed in 1977 and again in '83, although the new material was met with a lukewarm response. While BURDON had busied himself with numerous solo albums over the 70s and 80s (including the 1982 soundtrack, 'COMEBACK', from a neo-autobiographical effort which he also starred in), he continued to earn favourable reviews into the 90s on the likes of 'Lost Within The Halls Of Fame' (1995); he also appeared in 'The DOORS' movie. Following on from his published autobiography, Don't Let Me Be Misunderstood: A Memoir, the former ANIMALS frontman set some of his personal reminiscences and experience to song in quasi-concept set, 'My Secret Life' (2004), a tribute to the soul, blues and jazz that first inspired him.

MCS & BG

- **filmography** – {starring} (composer) –

Get Yourself A College Girl *(1964 {p} OST by V/A =>)* / **Pop Gear** *(1965 {p})* / **It's A Bikini World** *(1967 {p})* / **Tonite Let's All Make Love In London** *(1967 {c} OST by V/A =>)* / **Monterey Pop** *(1968 {p as ERIC BURDON & the ANIMALS} OST by V/A =>)* / Gibbi – Westgermany *(1979 {* ERIC})* / 11th Victim *(1979 TV {a ERIC})* / **Comeback** *(1982 {* ERIC} OST by BURDON =>)* / **the Doors** *(1991 {c} OST by the DOORS =>)* / the Big Pink *(1994 {p ERIC})* / O Adelfos Mou Ki Ego *(1998 {* ERIC})* / Schnee In Der Neujahrsnacht *(1999 {a ERIC})* / Plaster Caster *(2001 {c ERIC})* / **I Put A Spell On Me** *(2001 {c ERIC} =>)* / Fabulous Shiska In Distress *(2003 {a ERIC})*

ANNA

1967 (Fra 87m TV) Office de Radiodiffusion Télévision Française

Film genre: romantic Pop Musical

Top guns: dir: Pierre Koralnik → CANNABIS / s-w: Jean-Loup Dabadie → the WOMAN IN RED

Stars: Anna Karina *(Anna)*, J.C. Briarly *(Serge)*, **Marianne Faithfull** *(une jeune femme dans la soirée dansante)* → DON'T LOOK BACK → LUCIFER RISING → the WALL: LIVE IN BERLIN → ROCK AND ROLL CIRCUS, **Serge GAINSBOURG** *(l'ami de Serge)*, Barbara Sommers + Isabelle Felder *(une tante de Serge)*, Henri Virlojeux *(L'homme du banc)*, Hubert Deschamps *(le TV présentateur)*

Storyline: In wintry but still gay Paris, gravel-voiced Serge – in echoes of Antonioni's 'BLOW UP' – becomes obsessed with a photograph. Rather than glimpsing the anatomy of a murder, however, he falls head over heels for the girl in the photo, whom he then determines to hunt down all over the city; little does he know she's actually right there in the ad agency where he works.

BG

Movie rating: *6

Visual: video

Off the record: According to the biography, the song 'Hier Ou Demain' was heard in the film (performed by **Marianne Faithfull**) but didn't appear on the OST/album, and was subsequently recorded and put on an EP by Faithfull, herself apparently director Pierre Koralnik's original choice for the part of Anna.

BG

—

ANNA KARINA (*) / JEAN-CLAUDE BRIARLY (**) / SERGE GAINSBOURG (***) (+ composer)

1967. (lp) *Philips; (P70.391L)* [–] French [–]
– Sous le soleil exactement (w/ orchestre) / Sous le soleil exactement (*) / C'est la cristallisation comme dit Stendhal (** & ***) / Pas mal, pas mal du tout (** & ***) / J'étais fait pour les sympathies (**) / Photographes et religieuses (w/ orchestre) / Rien, rien, j'disais ça comme ça (*** & *) / Boomerang (**) / Un poison violent c'est l'amour (** & ***) / De plus en plus, de moins en moins (** & *) / Roller girl (*) / Ne dis rien (** & *) / Pistolet Jo (*) / G.I. Jo (*) / Je n'avais qu'un seul mot à lui dire (** & *). *(UK cd-iss. Oct98 on 'Mercury'; 558837-2)*

S/track review: 'ANNA' was SERGE GAINSBOURG's second TV project of 1966, trailed by the tense, finger-picked folk timbre he'd sounded for gumshoe hero, 'Vidocq'. Michel Colombier is the common denominator, GAINSBOURG's musical director and arranger through the most commercially successful, pop-orientated period of his career, a man whose talents were shown to be alive and swooning as recently as Air's 'Talkie Walkie' (2004). If you've ever wondered at the way Saint Etienne seemingly plucked their out-of-time, space-clipper echo from nowhere, 'Sous Le Soleil Exactement' offers up an irresistible precedent. The bassline is a revelation but the voice – and the film's title and iconic promo shot – is ANNA KARINA, French screen goddess and then wife and muse of Jean-Luc Goddard, who added pop star to her CV after the song made the French charts. Her petulant magnetism makes this soundtrack tick, whether balladeering with tack-throated co-star JEAN-CLAUDE BRIARLY on 'Ne Dis Rien', jauntily tipping her cowboy hat on SERGE's mandatory Americana piss-take, 'Pistolet Jo', or grinding her vowels like a boho satyr on 'Roller Girl', the last word in Gallic bubblegum-fuzz. It's BRIARLY, though, who gets to play the trump card as the GAINSBOURG-Colombier dynamic shifts ever subtly on its future-pop axis, growling away in phlegmatic outrage as 'Boomerang' traces a deceptive arc of piano, bass and strings before spinning back on a relentless, coppery gut-ache of treated guitar. GAINSBOURG, in fact, walks his favourite tightrope between provocative populism and the sublime right to the end, almost tripping himself on cheerleading stars'n'stripes satire, 'G.I. Jo', but, in 'Je N'Avais Qu'un Seul Mot A Lui Dire', finishing up with a baroque reverberation of his masterpiece to come, 'Histoire De Melody Nelson' (1971).

BG

Album rating: *7.5

– spinoff releases, etc. –

SERGE GAINSBOURG: EP

1967. (7"ep) *(437.279 BE)* [–] French [–]
– Sous le soleil exactement (*) / Roller girl (*) / Ne dis rien (* & SERGE) / Un poison violent, c'est ca l'amour (w/ JEAN CLAUDE BRIARLY).

ANNETTE

Born: Annette Funicello, 22 Oct'42, Utica, New York, USA. Performing since the age of 10, ANNETTE became the darling of TV's Mickey Mouse Club, which led to an opportunity to star in her own show. With a string of hit 45's behind her (including 'Tall Pall' & 'O Dio Mio') – Walt Disney always at the helm – ANNETTE was part of late 50s/early 60s productions such as 'The Shaggy Dog' and 'Babes In Toyland', although it was not until the "BEACH PARTY" movies she made her name in celluloid. Co-starring alongside pop star FRANKIE AVALON, ANNETTE (who never paraded in a bikini herself!) featured in around six films between 1963-66: the aforementioned 'BEACH PARTY', 'MUSCLE BEACH PARTY', 'BIKINI BEACH', 'PAJAMA PARTY', 'BEACH

BLANKET BINGO' and 'HOW TO STUFF A WILD BIKINI'. When this genre was put to bed, ANNETTE went on to star in other youth movies such as: 'Fireball 500' (1966), 'THUNDER ALLEY' (1967), and the MONKEES' vehicle, 'HEAD' (1968). Subsequently settling down to family life, ANNETTE returned to her "BEACH PARTY" roots via the co-financed 1987 reunion, 'BACK TO THE BEACH' (alongside AVALON). However, that same year, she was diagnosed with multiple sclerosis, a degenerative disease which she has bravely fought with over the last two decades. ANNETTE's autobiography was published and made into a movie in the mid 90s; it also featured her son Jason Gilardi, drummer with rock act, Caroline's Spine. *MCS*

- filmography {actress} –

the Shaggy Dog *(1959 {*})* / Babes In Toyland *(1961 {*})* / Escapade In Florence *(1962 {*})* / **Beach Party** *(1963 {*} OST to ANNETTE =>)* / **Muscle Beach Party** *(1964 {*} OST by ANNETTE + FRANKIE AVALON =>)* / **Bikini Beach** *(1964 {*} OST by ANNETTE + CANDY JOHNSON =>)* / **Pajama Party** *(1964 {*} OST by ANNETTE =>)* / **Beach Blanket Bingo** *(1965 {*} OST by DONNA LOREN =>)* / **How To Stuff A Wild Bikini** *(1966 {*} OST by the KINGSMEN =>)* / Fireball 500 *(1966 {*})* / **Thunder Alley** *(1967 {*} OST by V/A =>)* / **Head** *(1968 {*} OST by MONKEES =>)* / Lots Of Luck *(1985 TV {*})* / **Back To The Beach** *(1987 {*} OST by V/A =>)* / Troop Beverly Hills *(1989 {c})* / **a Dream Is A Wish Your Heart Makes: The Annette Funicello Story** *(1995 TV {c})*

the APPLE

1980 (W.Ger/US 90m) Cannon Films / NF Geria III-Produktion (PG-13)

Film genre: Disco/Pop Musical sci-fi fantasy

Top guns: s-w: Menahem Golan (+ dir), Coby Recht, Iris Recht

Stars: Catherine Mary Stewart *(Bibi)* → SCENES FROM THE GOLDMINE → DUDES, George Gilmour *(Alphie)*, Joss Ackland *(Mr. Topps; hippie leader)* → IT COULDN'T HAPPEN HERE → BILL & TED'S BOGUS JOURNEY, Vladek Sheybal *(Mr. Boogalow)*, Grace Kennedy *(Pandi)*, Allan Love *(Dandi)*, Ray Shell *(Shake)* → VELVET GOLDMINE, Iris Recht *(Domini)*, Coby Recht *(Jean-Louis)*, **George S. Clinton** *(Joe Pittman; reporter)*, Derek Deadman *(Bulldog)*, Miriam Margoyles *(Alphie's landlady)* → ELECTRIC DREAMS → MAGNOLIA, Finola Hughes *(dancer)* → STAYING ALIVE

Storyline: A cult favourite among fans of superannuated kitsch, this ridiculous music biz satire (set in 1994) focuses on the ambitions of folk singer Bibi, who is lured into the machinations of the music industry by the shady Mr Boogalow. Her erstwhile partner Alphie – who righteously refrains from any such Faustian pact – is predictably proved right as Bibi comes to regret her life of dubious glamour. *BG*

Movie rating: *3

Visual: video

Off the record: George S. Clinton (see below)

—

Various Cast (composers: Coby & Iris Recht, George S. Clinton)

Nov 80. (lp) *Cannon; <1001>* ☐ ☐
– BIM / Universal melody / Coming / I found me / The apple / Cry for me / Speed / Creation / Where has love gone / Showbizness / Made for me / How to be a master / Child of love.

S/track review: As kitsch as can be expected, this soundtrack was masterminded by one George S. Clinton, although a cursory listen to the record's campy pop-disco will reveal that it's a decidedly different Clinton from the one who made such a colourfully defiant, late 70s stand against the genre. Dancing on rollerskates might not help the out-of-tune singing, but it was all done in the best possible taste – not. The truly goddamn awful Worldvision Song Festival of a film (something akin to our Eurovision equivalent, but miraculously worse!) opens with outlandish "pseudo hit song" 'BIM'. Sung by Dandi & Pandi (couldn't find Andy Pandy one supposes), the track takes on a Barbarella-meets-glam persona with odious results. The Carpenters-styled 'Universal Melody' (by Bibi & Alphie) is straight-laced but cringeworthy, 'The APPLE' falling from grace rather than rapidly falling from a tree. George Gilmour (as Alphie) gets his fair share of the spotlight, while even the evil Mr. Boogalow gets to exercise his tonsils on the self-explanatory 'Showbizness' and 'How To Be A Master'. The equally risqué 'Coming', the er . . . patriotic 'Speed' ("reds, whites & blues, are in our blood") and the "bible-camp" title track are tasteless and indeed rotten to the core. But one expects some brave person to release the CD soon. *BG & MCS*

Album rating: *2

APRIL LOVE

1957 (US 98m) 20th Century Fox (PG)

Film genre: romantic Pop Musical drama

Top guns: dir: Henry Levin ← BERNARDINE / → WHERE THE BOYS ARE / s-w: Winston Miller → HOUND-DOG MAN (au: George Agnew Chamberlain)

Stars: Pat Boone *(Nick Conover)* ← BERNARDINE ← the PIED PIPER OF CLEVELAND, Shirley Jones *(Liz Templeton)*, Dolores Michaels *(Fran Templeton)*, Arthur O'Connell *(Jed Bruce)* → HOUND-DOG MAN → FOLLOW THAT DREAM → KISSIN' COUSINS → YOUR CHEATIN' HEART, Jeanette Nolan *(Henrietta)*, Matt Crowley *(Dan Templeton)*, Brad Jackson *(Al Turner)*

Storyline: Nick Conover leaves the Windy City for the fields of Kentucky after a run-in with the cops. His uncle isn't exactly overjoyed to see him as he has just lost his son Jed, so Nick has a wander to the neighbour's farmstead. There he meets mother and daughter Fran and Liz Templeton, whose trotting horse won't let anyone handle him since Jed died. Nick begins the conquest of both the horse and Liz and begins to enjoy his new way of life. *JZ*

Movie rating: *5

Visual: none

Off the record: PAT BOONE (see below)

—

Various Cast (songs: Paul Francis Webster and Sammy Fain)

Dec 57. (lp) *Dot; <DPL 9000> London; (HA-D 2078)* 12 Jan58 —
– Main title / Clover in the meadow (PAT BOONE) / Tugfire / Give me a gentle girl (PAT BOONE) / First meeting / Give me a gentle girl (SHIRLEY JONES) / April love (PAT BOONE) / Tugfire's escape / April love (PAT BOONE and SHIRLEY JONES) / The sulky race / Do it yourself (PAT BOONE, SHIRLEY JONES & ensemble) / Lovers' quarrel / Tugfire's illness / The Bentonville fair (PAT BOONE, SHIRLEY JONES & ensemble) / Finale (PAT BOONE, SHIRLEY JONES & ensemble).

S/track review: Featuring his fifth US chart-topper ('April Love') – his first four were 'Ain't That A Shame', 'I Almost My Mind', 'Don't Forbid Me' & 'Love Letters In The Sand', PAT BOONE was given full billing on parent soundtrack to 'APRIL LOVE'. However, most of the set, was down to composer, Lionel Newman and a host of songwriters, Sammy Fain, Paul Francis Webster, etc. Breaking slightly away from the usual run-of-the-sawmill song and dance musicals such as 'Oklahoma' and getting down to brass tacks pop, BOONE and co-star SHIRLEY JONES (a future Partridge Family mum!), tried in vain for something to get them on to the rock'n'roll bandwagon. 'APRIL LOVE' is part orchestral, part BOONE, the man from Jacksonville, Florida afforded three solo cues, 'Clover

In The Meadow', 'Give Me A Gentle Girl' (also sung by SHIRLEY JONES) and the chart-topping title track. Side two, sees PAT (a direct descendent of Daniel Boone!) combine with SHIRLEY JONES on four duets, the title track (again!), 'Do It Yourself', 'The Bentonville Fair' and the 'Finale'. A mixture of the day's pop style (un-rock'n'roll one might add!) and old-style romanticism or pre-50s sentimentalism. BOONE's vox is deep, smooth and velvety, JONES' is dreamy and pre-Julie Andrews, while the orchestral numbers are dramatic without being convuluting. All'n'all, this is one you can file under easy-listening and strictly one for the grannies and grandads. *MCS*

Album rating: *4

– spinoff hits, etc. –

PAT BOONE: April Love

Oct 57. (7") *<15660> (HLD 8512)* [1] Nov57 [7]

ASPHALTNACHT

aka ASPHALT NIGHT

1980 (W.Ger 90m) Tura-Film / Zweites Deutsches Fernsehen

Film genre: Rock-music buddy film/drama

Top guns: s-w + dir: Peter Fratzscher ← PANISCHE ZEITEN

Stars: Thomas Davis *(Johnny)*, Gerd Udo Heinemann *(angel)*, Ralf Hermann *(Frank)* ← PANISCHE ZEITEN, Petra Jokisch *(Debbie Noone)* → KAMIKAZE 1989, Christina Plate *(girl)*, Michael Zens *(Kamikaze)*, Charly Wierczejewski *(L.A. Peters)*, Herbert Rimbach *(the critic)*

Storyline: Punk meets rock'n'roll in the unlikely setting of Berlin's concrete jungle of back streets and tenement blocks. Searching for inspiration, Angel drives round the streets day after day. Eventually he meets Johnny, a man with a talent for upsetting almost everyone he comes across. But when Johnny plays a chord or two on his guitar (his only companion) it seems to be exactly the tune Angel is looking for. *JZ*

Movie rating: *4

Visual: video (no audio OST; score: LOTHAR MEID)

Off the record: LOTHAR MEID was a member of both Amon Duul II and Passport; he subsequently took on more score work in the 80s including 'Neonstadt' (1982) and 'die Heartbreakers' (1983). *MCS*

AT ANY COST

2000 (US 90m TV) Charter Films Inc. / Wilshire Court / VH-1

Film genre: Rock'n'roll showbiz drama

Top guns: dir: Charles Winkler / s-w: **Roderick Taylor**, Bruce A. Taylor

Stars: Eddie Mills *(Lance)*, James Franco *(Mike)*, Glenn Quinn *(Ben)*, Maureen Flannigan *(Chelsea)*, Cyia Batten *(Rebecca)*, J.D. Evermore *(cop #1)*, **Gene Simmons** *(Dennis Berg)* <= KISS =>, Jesse Adams *(apartment manager)* → TOO LEGIT: THE MC HAMMER STORY

Storyline: Singer-songwriter Lance is frontman for rock band Beyond Gravity. He's promised his wife Chelsea there'll be no more screw-ups when they get a good contract with Rage records. But his young brother Mike throws a spanner in the works with his increasing addiction to drugs and long stays in rehab. His subsequent arrest and death are too much for Chelsea and soon Beyond Gravity are beyond recall. *JZ*

Movie rating: *5

Visual: video

Off the record: Roderick Taylor (as Rod Falconer) released a couple of guitar-orientated albums in the 70s, including 'New Nation' and 'Victory In Rock City' (both on 'U.A.'). Cyia Batten was an original member of the Pussycat Dolls between 2000-2002. *MCS*

—

Various Artists incl. BEYOND GRAVITY * (score: Joel Goldsmith)

Aug 00. (cd) *Reprise; <9362 47830-2>* [ ] [–]

– Pinch me (BARENAKED LADIES) / Been here once before (EAGLE-EYE CHERRY) / Beat from underground (*) / Meant for you (*) / Don't look back (*) / Happens every day (*) / Glorious (ANDREAS JOHNSON) / What reason (DECKARD) / Thoughtless innuendos (KEVIN MARTIN) / Talking with your eyes (*) / It's over now (*).

S/track review: Coffee shop rock and one hit wonders make up the soundtrack for 'AT ANY COST'. Most of the tracks are written by bit-part actor/musician RODERICK TAYLOR and performed by the film's fictional band BEYOND GRAVITY. SPINAL TAP or even The COMMITMENTS they are most definitely not. Limp, acoustic-led soft-rock is the order of the day that would be better served as background music in an episode of Friends. Not one single song is worthy of mention. So, as for the one hit wonders. BARENAKED LADIES, EAGLE-EYE CHERRY or ANDREAS JOHNSON anyone? Unfortunately, it's only ANDREAS JOHNSON who sings the song that won him his five minutes of fame, 'Glorious', a pop rock number that makes good use of the dramatic accompanying strings. 'Pinch Me' by BARENAKED LADIES does not have the catchiness of their infectious hit 'One Week' but EAGLE-EYE CHERRY does stand out with the well-written 'Been Here Once Before', a folk-rock tune in a similar vein to his hit 'Save Tonight'. Probably the most successful artist on the album is KEVIN MARTIN, frontman of post-grunge rockers Candlebox, who chips in with the heartfelt ballad 'Thoughtless Innuendos', the only other track on the album worthy of mention. The band from a TV film about the music industry were never going to be exactly chart-toppers but this is a woeful effort which isn't even saved by the real artists that feature alongside them. Avoid at any cost. *CM*

Album rating: *3.5

□ ATTACK OF THE DEMONS alt.
(⇒ KISS MEETS THE PHANTOM OF THE PARK)

Frankie AVALON

Born: Francis Thomas Avallone, 18 Sep'39, Philadelphia, Pennsylvania, USA. The definitive teen idol, preceding Frankie going to Hollywood, the AVALON Frankie had a plethora of hits including 1959 chart-toppers, 'Venus' & 'Why'. Combining a busy singing career with serious roles in top movies (notably 'Guns Of The Timberland' & 'The Alamo'), the clean-cut young man couldn't buy a Top 20 hit during the early 60s. Just in the nick of time, AVALON's career was given a boost when he was paired with another former star, ANNETTE (Funicello), in the start of the 'BEACH PARTY' (1963-66) film series. However, "proper" film roles kept him busy throughout the 60s & 70s, and he was even invited to play a part in the teen flick, 'GREASE' (1978). In 1987, he reunited for a one-off role in 'BACK TO THE BEACH', alongside ANNETTE, a film which they both co-produced. *MCS*

- **filmography** {acting} –

Jamboree *(1957 {p} OST by V/A =>)* / Alakazam The Great *(1960 {v})* / Guns Of The Timberland *(1960 {*})* / the Alamo *(1960 {*})* / Voyage To The Bottom Of The Sea *(1961 {a})* / Sail A Crooked Ship *(1961 {*})* / Panic In The Year Zero! *(1962 {*})* / Operation Bikini *(1963 {*})* / Come Fly With

Me *(1963 title theme)* / el Valle De Las Espadas *(1963 {a})* / Drums Of Africa *(1963 {*})* / **Beach Party** *(1963 on OST by ANNETTE =>)* / **Muscle Beach Party** *(1964 {*} on OST =>)* / **Bikini Beach** *(1964 {*} on OST =>)* / **Pajama Party** *(1964 {a} on OST =>)* / **Beach Blanket Bingo** *(1965 {*} on OST =>)* / I'll Take Sweden *(1965 {*})* / **Ski Party** *(1965 {*} =>)* / Sergeant Dead Head *(1965 (*})* / Dr. Goldfoot & The Bikini Machine *(1965 {*})* / **How To Stuff A Wild Bikini** *(1966 {b} OST by V/A & the KINGSMEN =>)* / Fireball 500 *(1966 {*})* / the Million Eyes Of Sumuru *(1966 {*})* / **Thunder Alley** *(1967 {b} OST by V/A =>)* / **Skidoo** *(1968 {a} OST by NILSSON =>)* / the Haunted House Of Horror *(1969 {a})* / Saga Of Sonora *(1973 TV {a})* / the Take *(1974 {a})* / **Grease** *(1978 {a} OST by V/Cast =>)* / Blood Song *(1982 {a})* / **Back To The Beach** *(1987 {*} on OST by V/A =>)* / Troop Beverly Hills *(1989 {a})* / the Stoned Age *(1994 {b})* / Casino *(1995 {c}; see future edition)* / **a Dream Is A Wish Your Heart Makes: The Annette Funicello Story** *(1995 {*c} =>)*

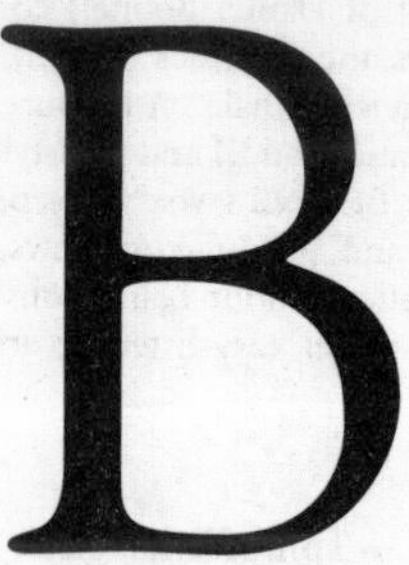

□ B2K segment
(⇒ YOU GOT SERVED)

BABYLON

1980 (UK/Ita 95m TV) Pan-Canadian (18)

Film genre: crime thriller/drama

Top guns: s-w: (+ dir) Franco Rosso, Martin Stellman ← QUADROPHENIA

Stars: Brinsley Forde *(Blue)*, Karl Howman *(Ronnie)* ← STARDUST ← THAT'LL BE THE DAY, Trevor Laird *(Beefy)* ← QUADROPHENIA, Brian Bovell *(Spark)*, Victor Romero Evans *(Lover)*, Archie Pool *(Dreadhead)*, David N. Haynes *(Errol)*, T-Bone Wilson *(Wesley)*, Mel Smith *(Alan)* → the PRINCESS BRIDE, Mark Monero *(Carlton)* → SID & NANCY, Maggie Steed *(woman at lockup)* → LIPSTICK ON YOUR COLLAR

Storyline: Blue is front man for a reggae sound system crew in 1980s London. His problems are not just about winning the forthcoming competition – just at the wrong time he gets fired from his day job, beaten up by the police and has his equipment smashed by the neighbours. If it wasn't for his love of reggae none of these things would have happened, but it's that same love that keeps him going come what may. *JZ*

Movie rating: *6

Visual: none

Off the record: Brinsley Forde (b. Guyana, 1952) was a child actor (early 70s 'Here Come The Double Deckers!' TV series & 'Please Sir!') before becoming an integral member of London reggae outfit, ASWAD. Signed by 'Island' records in 1976, the band struggled to break through into the mainstream until they had a UK chart-topper in '88 with a Tina Turner B-side, 'Don't Turn Around'. *MCS*

Various Artists (score: DENNIS BOVELL *)

Oct 80. (lp/c) *Chrysalis; (CHR/ZCHR 1294)* □ [-]
– Deliver me from my enemies (YABBY U) / Turn me loose (MICHAEL PROPHET) / Free Africa (YABBY U) / Whap'n bap'n (I-ROY) / Thank you for the many things you've done (CASSANDRA) / Hey jah children (ASWAD) / Warrior charge (ASWAD) / Beefy's tune (*) / Manhunter (*) / Jazterpiece (*). *(cd-iss. Feb05 on 'E.M.I.'+=; 584321-2)* – School skanking (*'s DUB BAND) / Living in Babylon (*) / Runnin' away (*) / Chief inspector (*'s DUB BAND) / B flat reggae concerto (*'s DUB BAND) / Jazterpiece – reggae version (*) / Beefy's tune – long version (*).

S/track review: While Jamaica will always be automatically associated with reggae, it's easy to forget or even dismiss the relevance of British reggae. 'BABYLON', the first black British film, goes some way to amending this discrepancy with a soundtrack overseen by London born and former Matumbi front man, DENNIS BOVELL. The sound is a marriage of heavy Jamaican dub and Beatles-esque harmonics that create a very melodic alternative to native reggae. In the late 70s the burgeoning British reggae scene had a vibrancy that spoke to a disenfranchised youth in much the same way as punk did and was centred on the sound systems peppered around London. BOVELL uses this sound to create the instrumentals to accompany the film, such as 'Beefy's Tune' with its catchy grooves accompanied by an excellent brass-led melody. On 'Jazzterpiece' and 'Manhunter' he combines the dub reggae feel with jazz style improvisation and saxophones to create a fascinating fusion. ASWAD, another British reggae outfit, also appear on the soundtrack with the powerful 'Warrior Charge' and the atmospheric 'Hey Jah Children' while CASSANDRA offers a dose of sublime pop reggae via 'Thank You For The Many Things You've Done'. There is also a considerable Jamaican presence in the shape of YABBY U who weighs in with the trumpet-led dub groove of 'Deliver Me From My Enemies' and the rousing 'Free Africa'. Anyone who thinks that reggae begins and ends with Bob Marley will be treated to an eye opening experience with 'BABYLON', a recording that catches the spirit and energy of a scene that is often unjustly overlooked. *CM*

Album rating: *7.5

– spinoff releases, etc. –

ASWAD: Warrior Charge / (version)

Sep 80. (7") *Island; (WIP 6646)* ☐ [-]

BACK TO THE BEACH

1987 (US 92m) Paramount Pictures (PG)

Film genre: Pop/Rock Musical comedy

Top guns: dir: Lyndall Hobbs / s-w: Peter Krikes, Christopher Thompson, Steve Meerson (story: James Komack, B.W.L. Norton, Bruce Kirschbaum)

Stars: Frankie AVALON *(Frankie, the Big Kahuna)*, **ANNETTE Funicello** *(Annette)*, Connie Stevens *(Connie)* ← GREASE 2 / → TAPEHEADS, Lori Loughlin *(Sandi)*, Tommy Hinkley *(Michael)*, Demian Slade *(Bobby)*, John Calvin *(Troy)* / **Fishbone:- Angelo Moore** → TAPEHEADS → IDLEWILD, **Kendall Jones, Norwood Fisher, Walter Kibby II, Christopher Dowd, Phillip Fisher** *(performers)* / Pee-Wee Herman *(himself)* ← the BLUES BROTHERS / → MOONWALKER → SOUTH OF HEAVEN, WEST OF HELL → OVERNIGHT → MAYOR OF THE SUNSET STRIP, Edd Byrnes *(valet)* ← GREASE ← STARDUST ← BEACH BALL, **Dick Dale** *(himself)* ← MUSCLE BEACH PARTY ← BEACH PARTY, **Stevie Ray Vaughan** *(himself)*, Alan Hale *(bartender's buddy)* ← ADVANCE TO THE REAR, Rodney Bingenheimer *(himself)* ← UNCLE MEAT ← X: THE UNHEARD MUSIC ← REPO MAN ← UP IN SMOKE / → ROCKULA → RAGE: 20 YEARS OF PUNK ROCK WEST COAST STYLE → END OF THE CENTURY → MAYOR OF THE SUNSET STRIP → PUNK'S NOT DEAD

Storyline: Twenty years on and Frankie and Annette have finally tied the knot and settled down in Ohio. They decide to take a trip to Malibu to visit their daughter Sandi and meet up with some of their old chums. It's not long before Frankie has to flex his creaking muscles when he learns a gang of punks are threatening to take over the beach. Things come to a head with Frankie throwing away his zimmer and launching his surf board one last time in a competition with the bad guys. *JZ*

Movie rating: *5

Visual: video

Off the record: Funk-rockers, **Fishbone**, seemed to be always on the threshold of making it big, although albums such as 'Truth And Soul' (1988), 'The Reality Of My Surroundings' (1991) and 'Give A Monkey A Brain And He'll Swear He's The Center Of The Universe' (1993), sold relatively well. When Living Color and Red Hot Chili Peppers found fame, FISHBONE's took a dive, not even a naked saxophone player could save them. *MCS*

—

Various Artists

Aug 87. (lp/c/cd) *Columbia; <CL/SCT/CK 40892>* ☐ [-]
– Catch a ride (EDDIE MONEY) / Pipeline (STEVIE RAY VAUGHAN & DICK DALE) / Sign of love (AIMEE MANN) / Absolute perfection (PRIVATE DOMAIN) / Surfin' bird (PEE-WEE HERMAN) / Sun, sun, sun, sun, sun (MARTI JONES) / Jamaica ska (ANNETTE FUNICELLO & FISHBONE) / Wipe out (HERBIE HANCOCK) / California sun (FRANKIE AVALON) / Wooly bully (DAVE EDMUNDS).

S/track review: From 1963 to 1966, there were half a dozen "BEACH PARTY" movies, the last of which, 'HOW TO STUFF A WILD BIKINI', failed miserably. So what's new? Nothing really. "BEACH PARTY" stars on parade, Frankie Avalon and Annette Funicello had waited a long time for another sequel and were no spring chickens in 1987 having just reached their mid-40s. 'BACK TO THE BEACH' identified with the fun side of life by the ocean, a hark back to the early half of the 60s when beaches were about surf, sea and sand – oh, and parties. New kid on the block, PEE-WEE HERMAN (aka comic entertainer, Paul Reubens), unearths another "big adventure" and plenty of corny laughs courtesy of his rendition of the Trashmen's classic 'Surfin' Bird'. Exclusive songs come by way of 'Til Tuesday singer, AIMEE MANN, who goes Bananarama via 'Sign Of Love', while the similar, ex-Color Me Gone pop star, MARTI JONES, gets upbeat with 'Sun, Sun, Sun, Sun, Sun'. Blue-collar rocker EDDIE MONEY sticks out a hand to 'Catch A Ride', while he's tracked by dual-axemen STEVIE RAY VAUGHAN & DICK DALE covering the Chantays' 'Pipeline'. On a similar instrumental surf theme, surprise package HERBIE HANCOCK apes Prince on the Surfaris' 'Wipe Out' (vinyl cameos come courtesy of Dweezil Zappa & Terry Bozzio); usual soundtrack suspect, DAVE EDMUNDS, takes on Sam The Sham's 'Wooly Bully'. The aforementioned FRANKIE AVALON comes up trumps here via "BEACH PARTY" nugget 'California Sun' (a song better known by Ramones fans), while ANNETTE FUNICELLO & FISHBONE take on her old Mouseketeer number, 'Jamaica Ska'. Coming up for air and on a similar reggae beat, 'Absolute Perfection' by the chameleon-ish PRIVATE DOMAIN, with special appearance by Pato Banton, brought up the rear. *MCS*

Album rating: *6

BACKBEAT

1994 (UK 100m w/b&w) Channel Four Films / PolyGram (15)

Film genre: Pop/Rock-music bio-pic drama

Top guns: s-w: Iain Softley (+ dir), Michael Thomas ← COUNTRYMAN, Stephen Ward

Stars: Stephen Dorff *(Stuart Sutcliffe)* ← JUDGMENT NIGHT ← an AMBUSH OF GHOSTS / → S.F.W. → I SHOT ANDY WARHOL, Ian Hart *(John Lennon)* ← the HOURS AND TIMES / → MOJO, Sheryl Lee *(Astrid Kirchherr)*, Gary Bakewell *(Paul McCartney)* → the LINDA McCARTNEY STORY, Kai Wiesinger *(Klaus Voormann)*, Scot Williams *(Pete Best)* → SWING → IN HIS LIFE: THE JOHN LENNON STORY, Chris O'Neill *(George Harrison)* → JULIE AND THE CADILLACS, Wolf Kahler *(Bert Kaempfert)*, James Doherty *(Tony Sheridan)*, Paul Duckworth *(Ringo Starr)*, Gertan Klauber *(pimp)* ← PIED PIPER ← DATELINE DIAMONDS

Storyline: The early days of Liverpool's finest in less than glamourous Hamburg, with Stuart Sutcliffe as the precocious art student come reluctant fifth Beatle. While McCartney rails against Sutcliffe's lack of professionalism, an obnoxious Lennon defends him till his last pilsner. In the end, Sutcliffe opts out under his own steam, devoting himself to his art and the enigmatic Astrid, a photographer and socialite with whom he spends his final days. *BG*

Movie rating: *7.5

Visual: video + dvd

Off the record: None of the film's music was penned by Lennon or McCartney, all of it stemming from their rock'n'roll idols. *MCS*

---

the BACKBEAT BAND (composers: Various)

Apr 94. (cd/c/lp) *Virgin; (CD/TC/+V 2729) <V2/V4 39386>* [39] [ ]
– Money / Long tall Sally / Bad boy / Twist and shout / Please Mr. Postman / C'mon everybody / Rock'n'roll music / Slow down / Roadrunner / Carol / Good golly Miss Molly / 20 flight rock.

S/track review: Let's face it, whatever early Beatles influence there was on the American post-punk/grunge class of the early to mid-90s, it wasn't readily apparent. The idea of someone like Sonic Youth's THURSTON MOORE shimmying his way through standards more often seen making weight on the likes of a Dire Straits' greatest hits set, was, to say the least, unappealing. Some of the tracks – 'Money', 'C'mon Everybody', 'Roadrunner' – had already been made over by punk twenty years earlier, but the project still looked like a non-starter. Somehow, the collective efforts of MOORE, GREG DULLI (Afghan Whigs), DAVE GROHL (then Nirvana, now Foo Fighters), DAVE PIRNER (Soul Asylum), MIKE MILLS (R.E.M.) and grunge guru DON FLEMING (Gumball) were naturalistic enough to make it halfway convincing. These largely ageing alt-rockers couldn't have hoped – and presumably didn't try – to replicate the hormonal brinkmanship of the original performances, but they did reclaim a lot of these songs from dinosaur rock redundancy. And at their best – on a flailing 'Rock'n'Roll Music' and a terse, sneering 'Bad Boy' – the BACKBEAT BAND do the memory of Stuart Sutcliffe as proud as a sucker punch. *BG*

Album rating: *6 / Don Was score *5

– spinoff hits, etc. –

the BACKBEAT BAND: Money / He's Wearing My Bathrobe

Mar 94. (7"/c-s) *(VS/+C 1489)* [48] [–]
(12"+=/cd-s+=) *(VSA/VSCDX 1489)* – Dizzy Miss Lizzy

the BACKBEAT BAND: Please Mr. Postman / C'mon Everybody

May 94. (7"/c-s) *(VS/+C 1502)* [69] [–]
(cd-s+=) *(VSCDX 1502)* – the BACKBEAT BAND: Long Tall Sally

DON WAS

Apr 94. (cd) *(CDV 2740) <V2 39413>* [ ] [ ]
– You asked, I came / Darkroom / What do they call this drink? / He's wearing my bathrobe / Just read the poems / You asked, I came (early version) / He's wearing my bathrobe (end title).

BAD CHANNELS

1992 (US 88m) Full Moon Entertainment (R)

Film genre: sci-fi Rock-music comedy

Top guns: dir: Ted Nicolaou / s-w: Jackson Barr (story: Charles Band ← NETHERWORLD)

Stars: Paul Hipp *(Dan O'Dare)*, Martha Quinn *(Lisa Cummings)* ← EDDIE AND THE CRUISERS II: EDDIE LIVES! ← TAPEHEADS, Aaron Lustig *(Vernon Locknut)* → ROADSIDE PROPHETS, Robert Factor *(Willis)*, Charlie Spradling *(Cookie)* ← the DOORS ← WILD AT HEART, Ian Patrick Williams *(Dr. Payne)*, Sonny Carl Davis *(Peanut)* ← ROADIE ← WHERE THE BUFFALO ROAM, Michael Huddleston *(Corky)* ← the WOMAN IN RED, Tim Thomerson *(dollman)* ← EDDIE PRESLEY ← NEAR DARK ← RHINESTONE ← HONKYTONK MAN ← CARNY ← RECORD CITY ← CAR WASH

Storyline: "Dangerous" Dan O' Hare is famous for his publicity stunts and pranks over the airwaves. Just his bad luck that when a real alien turns up and takes over the studio no-one believes his running commentary broadcast. Soon our little green man is using a shrinking device to transport female listeners to the studio where they're bunged up in foot high bottles. It's up to DJ Dan to stop the alien and save the day. *JZ*

Movie rating: *3.5

Visual: dvd on 'Cold Fusion'

Off the record: To many diserning pop/rock music fans, BLUE OYSTER CULT might be only famous for one song, '(Don't Fear) The Reaper', but there was more . . . Formed in Long Island, New York in 1970 as Soft White Underbelly, BUCK DHARMA, ALLEN LANIER and AL BOUCHARD subsequently became Stalk-Forrest Group and signed a deal with 'Elektra' (one 45 exists, 'What Is Quicksand'). In late 1971, they renamed themselves the BLUE OYSTER CULT, their manager/guru Sandy Pearlman securing them a recording contract with 'Columbia'. The group's first two albums 'Blue Oyster Cult'(1972) and 'Tyranny And Meditation' (1973) – containing lyrics by producer Richard Meltzer – were sophisticated proto-metal classics, infusing the crunching guitar and rhythm with a keen sense of melody and keeping a tight enough a rein on proceedings to avoid the hoary bombast that characterised other bands of their ilk. Lyrically the band peddled fairly clichéd, if more intelligent than average, dark musings and with 1974's 'Secret Treaties', the music began to sound similarly predictable. Throughout the remainder of the 70s, the band gravitated to a cleaner cut, hard rock sound, although the darkly shimmering ' . . . Reaper' was a one-off return to their 60s psychedelic roots. The song gave the band a surprise Top 20 UK hit, and while they continued to enjoy minor chart successes with their subsequent releases, the quality of their output struggled to rise above stale cliché. 'BAD CHANNELS' did little to rectify any past glories. *BG & MCS*

BLUE OYSTER CULT (& Various Artists)

1992. (cd) *Moonstone; <12936-2>* [ ] [–]
– Demon kiss / The horsemen arrive / That's how it is (JOKER) / Jane Jane (the hurricane) (JOKER) / Somewhere in the night (FAIR GAME) / Blind faith (FAIR GAME) / Manic depresso (SYKOTIK SINFONEY) / Mr. Cool (SYKOTIK SINFONEY) / Myth of freedom (DMT) / Touching myself again (DMT) / Little old lady polka (the UKELALIENS) / Bad channels overture / Power station / Shadow / V.U. / Cosmos rules, but lump controls / Battering ram / This dude is fucked / Pick up her feed / Spray that scumbag / Out of station / Tree full of owls / Cookie in bottle / Corky gets it / Eulogy for Corky / Spore bomb / Remodeling / Ginger snaps / The Moon gets it. *<(re-iss. Nov99 & Jun01 on 'Angel Air'; SJPCD 046)>*

S/track review: Rock veterans BLUE OYSTER CULT scored this film from the early 90s and provide two of its stand-out featured tracks. 'Demon's Kiss' is a throbbing uptempo rocker, its lyrical themes of sowing wild oats are tempered by its insouciant musical fluidity, though a shout it out loud chorus taints the track with 80s metallurgy. But its effortless, effects-drenched guitars, revelling in legato runs and Slayer-like dive bombs are tempered by its tasteful bluesy lead breaks. 'The Horsemen Arrive' takes things down a few gears, as power chords ring out its strident mid-tempo middle section rails against the government, greed and corruption (though it all feels quite harmless). JOKER arrive with some bad MOR synth-driven pop-rock in the form of 'That's How It Is': their currency is gently stabbing diminished chords, before opening out to a bombastic chorus and mandatory lead guitar squealing. FAIR GAME's two contributions are similarly unremarkable, although vocalist Ron Keel's Joe Cocker-ish tone redeems things somewhat. The album is single-handedly raised a level by SYKOTIK SINFONEY's 'Manic Depresso', a very rare recorded outing for the group. Its melding of circus freakery and Pantera-esque post-thrash attack, with the bleak and grim incantations that presage black metal, is a heady concoction. A great shredding solo blows away the questions about whether these guys or fellow Mike Patton-led misfits Mr Bungle got to this hybrid sound first. 'Mr. Cool' echoes Bungle again in tones and effects, and throws a pinch of Zappa into the mix for extra seasoning, it boasts an excellent off-kilter mid-section and triple-picking thrash tastiness. DMT's harsher, more metallic atonal stylings, allied with Pumpkins-esque clean sections render the cut and paste riffage of 'Myth Of Freedom' and 'Touching Myself' a refreshing change in direction. The UKELALIENS (a re-constituted SYKOTIK SINFONEY) keep things strictly silly on 'Little Old Lady Polka'. The rest of the album is made up of the original score, largely a synthetic industrial soundscape, awash with synths and heavily reverberating blues guitar licks. They aspire to Vangelis on 'Power Station', whereas 'Battering Ram' recalls New Wave and Kraftwerk, 'Ginger Snaps' is so up front it's almost Faithless. *DF*

Album rating: *5

BADDING

2000 (Fin 104m) Fennada Film / YLE (K-12)

Film genre: Pop/Rock-music comedy/drama bio-pic

Top guns: s-w: (+ dir) Markku Polonen, Heikki Metsamaki

Stars: Janne Reinikainen *(Rauli "Badding" Somerjoki)*, Karoliina Blackburn *(Mari)*, Peter Franzen *(Ossi)*, Puntti Valtonen *(Arde)*, Pertti Koivula *(Frans Hilton)*, Ilkka Koivula *(Albert Hilton)*, Vappu Jurkka *(Aiti)*, Hannu Virolainen *(Yki-Laakio)*

Storyline: Rauli "Badding" Somerjoki was a pop superstar in Finland in the 1970s, but now ten years later he's retired into oblivion after developing severe stage fright and chronic alcoholism. However, he reluctantly agrees to perform a sell-out comeback concert and his reporter friend Ossi offers to drive him there, hoping for a scoop or two along the way. Can Rauli conquer his nerves or is he really all Finnished up? *JZ*

Movie rating: *6

Visual: video

Off the record: RAULI "BADDING" SOMERJOKI performed several tracks including:- 'Sydamessain', 'Ja Rokki Soi', 'Valot', 'Arpiset Haavat', 'Rakkauden Myrkky Surut Tappaa', 'Mielitauti-rock', 'Omista Minut', 'Tahdet, Tahdet', 'Paratiisi', 'Ma Jain Kii', 'Kuihtuu Kesainen Maa' & 'Fiilaten Ja Hoylaten' – we'll do a profile of the man in a later edition. *MCS*

BAJA OKLAHOMA

1988 (US 105m TV) HBO

Film genre: Country-music drama

Top guns: s-w: (+ dir) Bobby Roth ← HEARTBREAKERS / → DEAD SOLID PERFECT → the MAN INSIDE → BRAVE NEW GIRL, Dan Jenkins (+ au) → DEAD SOLID PERFECT

Stars: Lesley Ann Warren *(Juanita Hutchins)* ← SONGWRITER / → PURE COUNTRY, Peter Coyote *(Slick Henderson)* ← HEARTBREAKERS ← TIMERIDER: THE ADVENTURE OF LYLE SWANN / → the MAN INSIDE → a LITTLE TRIP TO HEAVEN → COMMUNE, Swoosie Kurtz *(Doris Steadman)* ← TRUE STORIES / → REALITY BITES, **Billy Vera** *(Lonnie Slocum)* → SUMMER DREAMS: THE STORY OF THE BEACH BOYS → the DOORS, Anthony Zerbe *(Ol' Jeemy Williams)* ← KISS MEETS THE PHANTOM OF THE PARK / → TOUCH, William Forsythe *(Tommy Earl Browner)* → DICK TRACY → the DEVIL'S REJECTS, John M. Jackson *(Lee Steadman)* ← SID & NANCY ← LOCAL HERO / → DEAD SOLID PERFECT → GINGER ALE AFTERNOON, Bruce Abbott *(Dove Christian)*, Julia Roberts *(Candy Hutchins)* ← SATISFACTION, Carmen Argenziano *(Roy Simmons)* ← HEARTBREAKERS, Paul Bartel *(minister)* ← GET CRAZY ← ROCK'N'ROLL HIGH SCHOOL / → JOE'S APARTMENT, Linda Dona *(Martha Healy)* → DEAD SOLID PERFECT → SUMMER DREAMS: THE STORY OF THE BEACH BOYS, Alice Krige *(Patsy Cline)* ← CHARIOTS OF FIRE, **Willie NELSON** *(performer)*, **Emmylou HARRIS** *(performer)*, **John Mayall** *(performer)* ← SGT. PEPPER'S LONELY HEARTS CLUB BAND ← DON'T LOOK BACK / → RED, WHITE & BLUES → the SOUL OF A MAN

Storyline: Juanita is fed up with her dead-end waitressing job and dreams of becoming a C&W songwriter. However it seems most of her life is taken up with a string of bad relationships and it's not until her old high school flame Slick returns to town that things start to improve. He is the one person who believes in her talent and, together with local DJ Ole' Jeemy who becomes her manager they set off on the road to stardom. *JZ*

Movie rating: *5

Visual: video (no audio OST; score: Stanley Myers)

Off the record: **Willie NELSON + Emmylou HARRIS** were of course C&W icons, while others such as **Billy Vera** (& the Beaters) from L.A. were a little low key, that is until an earlier live hit, 'At This Moment', found its way to US No.1 in 1986, due to its play on TV's 'Family Ties'. *MCS*

BALLAD IN BLUE

US title 'BLUES FOR LOVERS' (1966)

1964 (UK 89m b&w) 20th Century Fox / Alsa Productions

Film genre: R&B/Pop-music-based drama

Top guns: dir: (+ story) Paul Henreid / s-w: Burton Wohl

Stars: **Ray CHARLES** *(himself)*, Mary Peach *(Peggy Harrison)*, Tom Bell *(Steve Collins)* → ALL THE RIGHT NOISES, Dawn Addams *(Gina Graham)*, Piers Bishop *(David)*, Betty McDowall *(Mrs. Babbidge)*, Lucy Appleby *(Margaret)*

Storyline: Set in London, a blind pianist (Ray Charles as himself!), befriends a recently blinded English boy, helping him to arrange to visit an eye-specialist in Paris and reconcile his parents. *MCS*

Movie rating: *2.5

Visual: video + dvd as US title (no audio OST)

Off the record: **RAY CHARLES** (score by Stanley Black) contributed a dozen or so tracks including, 'Let The Good Times Roll', 'Careless Love', 'Hit The Road Jack', 'That Lucky Old Sun', 'Unchain My Heart', 'Hallelujah, I Love Her So', 'Don't Tell Me Your Troubles', 'I Got A Woman', 'Busted', 'Talkin' 'Bout You', 'Light Of Darkness' and 'What'd I Say'. The giant of R&B/Gospel & Soul was the subject of a feature film bio-pic, 'RAY' (2004). *MCS*

BALLER BLOCKIN

2000 (US 60m str8-to-video) Universal Pictures (R)

Film genre: urban Musical drama

Top guns: s-w + dir: Steven Esteb

Stars: **B.G.** *(Chopper)*, **Juvenile** *(Tanuk)*, **Lil' Wayne** *(Iceberg Shorty)*, Jerry Kato *(Curlyhead)*, Jeanette Branch *(Nettie)*, Mykel Shannon *(Garr)*, **Turk** *(Teke)*, **Bryan 'Baby' Williams** *(Beatrice)*, **Mannie Fresh** *(himself)*, **Ronald 'Suga Slim'** *(himself)*, A.J. Johnson *(himself)*, T.K. Kirkland *(himself)*

Storyline: Cash Money record's rap stars Juvenile, B.G. and Lil' Wayne are among the non-actors taking to the silverscreen in this ultra low budget, and extremely brief, hour-long look at life on the streets of New Orleans; a life of doing what you have to survive, legal, criminal or otherwise. A slice of life filled with dodgy deals, corrupt policemen, brutal rivalries and hard struggles. *MR*

Movie rating: *4

Visual: dvd

Off the record: Solo southern rap stars, **B.G.** (alias Christopher Dorsey), **Juvenile** (alias Terius Gray), **Turk** (aka Young Turk, alias Tab Virgil, Jr.) and **Brian 'Baby' Williams** (aka The Birdman) are all CASH MONEY MILLIONAIRES. Turk is now in a state penitentiary (as of April 2006) after being sentenced to 12 years for the murder of a police deputy in January 2004. *MCS*

CASH MONEY MILLIONAIRES

Sep 00. (cd) *Uptown-Universal; <(AA121 153291-2)>*
– Intro (feat. LOVELY & ATRICE) / Baller blockin (BABY, TURK, JUVENILE & E-40) / Family affair (UGK) / Rover truck (JUVENILE) / skit (BIG CHIEF – ZIGGY) / Project b!#$h (BIG TYMERS, LIL WAYNE & JUVENILE) / Ballin' Gs (EIGHTBALL & MJG) / Thugged out (BG) / Don't cry (UNPLUGGED) / What you gonna do (NAS & the BRAVEHARTS) / Calling me killer (LIL WAYNE) / I got to go (TQ) / Whatever (BABY, LAC AND STONE) / Let us stunt (BIG TYMERS) / skit (ZIGGY) / Milk & honey (w/ MAC 10 feat. the COMRADES) / Uptown (TURK) / I don't know (UNPLUGGED feat. LIL WAYNE) / Win or lose (RAPPIN' 4 TAY).

S/track review: From a cottage industry to multi-million dollar operation, 'Cash Money' was for a period, the biggest underground record label in the world. But while 50 Cent deals in bottle water and signature shoes, the lucrative DVD market in the US is where Cash Money flourish with low rent gangster tales like this. Their veritable production line was selling serious amounts of albums all over America with having a video on MTV once. And while their entrepreneurial skills must be lauded, lyrically, they should be shamed. The only thing liberal here is the dousing of lyrics with hateful, mysoginistic, homophobic, greedy, antisocial, thuggish nihilism. They may believe they are keeping it real with such talk, but as true to the cold real world as this may be, it makes for hard listening. This wouldn't be a problem of course if innovation was a part of the mix too but dial-a-cliché must have been ringing off the hook when EIGHTBALL & MJG called up for the lyrics for 'Ballin' Gs', Similarly, 'Project Bitch' is as bluntly feminist as the title might suggest and the B.G.'s 'Thugged Out' is even more unpleasant in that it nails sloppy lyrical flows to a peculiarly camp ballad backbeat. The squeaking, creaking, rumbling Southern take of hip hop is truly mind-blowing when executed correctly but too much of this is a cheap bastardisation of the original gangsta rap template commercially pioneered by Dr Dre in the early 90s. The big ballers, shot callers and general bad asses at 'Cash Money' go for a quick, route one fix, but for the most part, that's a fairly unoriginal, cynical and clichéd ride. The arrival of a real class A star in the shape of NAS signals hope perhaps, but his contribution is a mere token appearance. Only JUVENILE gives as good as he gets on the bouncing, trouncing 'Rover Truck', a track that harnesses the energy, swing and dark intentions of the music as well as the misanthropic lyrical ideas. Unsurprising really that he was one of the first to fly the 'Cash Money' coup for bigger and better things. *MR*

Album rating: *3

BANDITS

1997 (Ger 111m) Olga-Film / Buena Vista International (R)

Film genre: Rock/Pop-music road movie/comedy/drama

Top guns: s-w: Katja von Garnier (+ dir), Uwe Wilhelm

Stars: Katja Riemann *(Emma)*, Jasmin Tabatabai *(Luna)*, Nicolette Krebitz *(Angel)*, Jutta Hoffmann *(Marie)*, Hannes Jaenicke *(Inspector Schwarz)*, Werner Schreyer *(West)*, Oliver Hasenfratz *(Schneider)*, Andrea Sawatzki *(Ludwig)*, Peter Sattmann *(Gold)*, August Schmolzer *(Gunther)*

Storyline: Four female convicts escape their bleak environs by forming a rock band. Not surprisingly, during a policeman's convention, a real escape provides them with a chance to find some long-lost stash and play spontaneous concerts along the way. *MCS*

Movie rating: *6

Visual: dvd

Off the record: Don't get mixed up with other 2001 film/OST of the same name.

Various Cast

1997. (cd) *Druck – Polydor; (357 863-2)* German
– Puppet / If I were God / It's alright / Crystal cowboy / Catch me (short) (*) / Another sad song / Blinded / Like it / All along the watchtower (*) / Shadows / Time is now / Photograph / Ain't nobody's buziness if I do / Wenn ich ein voglein war / Puppet (Luna & Angel) / Catch me (film) (*) / Puppet chase. *<US-iss.Oct99 on 'Sire'; 31051-2>*

S/track review: Full of overdriven guitars, snapping snares and screaming Hammond organs, topped off with carefree melodies, 'BANDITS' presents plenty of upbeat numbers (musically, if not lyrically) such as 'Puppet' and 'It's Alright' alongside the naive lo-fi charm of the rattling 'If I Were God'. 'Blinded' is decent skewed guitar pop whilst there are changes in mood and tempo with the smoky stripped bare sensual funk of 'Like It' and a surprisingly atmospheric high-tempo cover of Dylan's 'All Along The Watchtower' which is forcefully driven by the drums and bass. Meanwhile, 'Catch Me' is genuinely moving, with its ambitious big chorus, U2-esque drumming and 80s sounding anthemics, and 'Time Is Now' is a pleasingly original goth/new-wave hybrid that bizarrely sounds like the dark cousin of Red Hot Chili Peppers' 'Give It Away'. There are some failed offerings that miss the mark here, like 'Another Sad Song', 'Shadows' and the cumbersome 'Crystal Cowboy'. Things end, however, with some rousing tracks, none more so than 'Ain't Nobody's Business If I Do' which sounds like a bleary bad-mouthed take on Randy Newman (and a little like the theme from the long running TV show 'Minder'), before racing into a punky thrasharound. *LF*

Album rating: *6.5

BANDWAGON

1996 (US 103m) Lakeshore Entertainment / Pamlico Pictures (M)

Film genre: Rock-music/showbiz drama

Top guns: s-w + dir: **John Schultz**

Stars: Kevin Corrigan *(Wynn Knapp)* → WALKING AND TALKING → BUFFALO '66 → DETROIT ROCK CITY → CHELSEA WALLS, Lee Holmes *(Tony Ridge)*, Steve Parlavecchio *(Eric Ellwood)*, **Doug MacMillan** *(Linus Tate)*, Matthew Hennessey *(Charlie Flagg)*, Doug McCallie *(Chester Mealy)*, Steph Robinson *(Dizz)*, **David Palmer** *(manifestation of death)*

Storyline: Neurotic Tony Ridge is persuaded to join rock band Circus Monkey after he loses his old job. However, Tony is too shy to play in front of anybody at first and the other band members all have problems of their own too. When they recruit worldly-wise manager Linus they begin to get a few gigs and after much coaching and soul-searching they start their climb to the top with hope and encouragement. *JZ*

Movie rating: *6.5

Visual: video

Off the record: Doug MacMillan is lead singer of North Carolina favourites, the Connells (remember ''74-'75'); filmmaker **John Schultz** was their original drummer way back in the mid 80s, while **David Palmer** was in ABC! (new romantics from the latter period). *MCS*

Various Artists (composer/score: GREG KENDALL *)

Aug 97. (cd) *Milan; <35824-2>*
– So long (Ann) (CIRCUS MONKEY) * / It couldn't be Ann (CIRCUS MONKEY) * / 'Til the end of time (INCINERATOR) / Kick the can (POUNDCAKE) / Wynn & Linus go fishing (* & BOB KENDALL) / Get the net (*, BOB KENDALL & MARK RIVERS) / Wheat penny (TACKLE BOX) * / Rest of the world (CIRCUS MONKEY) * / Nashville diner (*, BOB KENDALL & MARK RIVERS) / Mudda mudda faddah (SPITTLE) * / What you hide

(JUDY JUDY JUDY) / Living in France (under an assumed name) (the FLIPTONES) / Lampshade (INCINERATOR) / Open the door (MANCHILD) / Don't put her down (TACKLE BOX) * / Spin U round (INCINERATOR) / Ann it goes (CIRCUS MONKEY) * / A suitable ending (*).

S/track review: America's underground movement (represented this time by North Carolina and further afield) had been written and re-written so many times: was it ready for another rock'n'roll supplement? The jury's out on that one. There seems to be one guy instrumental – so to speak – in holding this 'BANDWAGON' project together: GREG "SKEG" KENDALL. He is leader of relatively unknown alt-rockers, TACKLE BOX, exampled here via two tracks, 'Wheat Penny' (from their 1993 album, 'Grand Hotel') and new song, 'Don't Put Her Down'. Songwriter/guitarist, GREG, his brother BOB on vocals, MICHAEL LEAHY (guitar), BRIAN DUNTON or KEVIN SWEENEY (bass) and PAUL HARDING or STACEY JONES (drums), are indeed the main musicians behind the fictitious movie band, CIRCUS MONKEY, who, in turn, deliver four exclusive and catchy tracks, 'So Long (Ann)', 'It Couldn't Be Ann', 'Rest Of The World' & 'Ann It Goes' – you just wonder who he fell out with. Not content with two featured bands, GREG also supplies the score guitar music and a solitary grindcore effort, 'Mudda Mudda Faddah' by SPITTLE, virtually CIRCUS MONKEY (minus his brother) but with lead shouter, Ed Silvia (aka Eddie Wad). Without discarding power-poppers MANCHILD ('Open The Door'), Dick Dale-esque the FLIPTONES ('Living In France (Under An Assumed Name)', and L.A.-based post-grungers JUDY JUDY JUDY ('What You Like'), the best songs stem from two other outfits. Boston's Nirvana-cloned POUNDCAKE fit like a glove via 'Kick The Can', while the female-led INCINERATOR (featuring Lilia Mercedes-Halpern) supply three Primitives-ish tracks, ''Til The End Of Time', 'Lampshade' & 'Spin U Round'. All'n'all an okay sort of album and with reasonably funny film dialogue interspersing several of the cues, the soundtrack works hard to get the listener on board. Question is – where are they now? *MCS*

Album rating: *6

the BANGER SISTERS

2002 (US 98m) Fox Searchlight Pictures (R)

Film genre: buddy movie/comedy

Top guns: s-w + dir: Bob Dolman

Stars: Goldie Hawn *(Suzette)*, Susan Sarandon *(Lavinia)* ← DEAD MAN WALKING ← the ROCKY HORROR PICTURE SHOW ← JOE / → ALFIE re-make → ROMANCE & CIGARETTES, Geoffrey Rush *(Harry Plumber)* ← LANTANA ← STARSTRUCK, Erika Christensen *(Hannah)*, Eva Amurri *(Ginger)* ← DEAD MAN WALKING, Matthew Carey *(Jules)*, Robin Thomas *(Raymond Kingsley)*, Andre Ware *(Jake)*, Adam Tomei *(club owner)* → MY DINNER WITH JIMI, Sal Lopez *(pump attendant)* ← SELENA, **Buckcherry:- Josh Todd, Yugomir Lonich, Devon Glenn, Keith Nelson, Jonathan Brightman** *(themselves)* ← WOODSTOCK 99

Storyline: When raunchy barmaid Suzette is fired she decides to go in search of her old groupie pal Vinnie. On the drive down to Phoenix she picks up stressed out writer Harry and tells him about the old times when they were known as the Banger Sisters. Suzette gets a shock when she discovers that Vinnie has turned into respectable housewife Lavinia, but the glam gals decide to have a last fling at the high school graduation, ensuring it will be a day to remember. *JZ*

Movie rating: *6

Visual: video + dvd

Off the record: L.A. rock group, **Buckcherry** had already released a couple of Top 75 albums prior to this film, 'Buckcherry' (1999) & 'Time Bomb' (2001). *MCS*

—

Various Artists (score: TREVOR RABIN *)

Sep 02. (cd) *Sanctuary; <84565> (SANCD 152)* ☐ Jan03 ☐
– The red road (CHRIS ROBINSON) / Fame 02 (TOMMY LEE) / Home (DISHWALLA) / Burning down the house (TALKING HEADS) / One last goodbye (RICHIE SAMBORA) / Don't let me be misunderstood (*) / Doctor my eyes (BEN FOLDS) / Hour of need (PETER FRAMPTON) / Trippin' (JP) / Child of mine (ROGER DALTREY feat. G TOM MAC) / Crushed (BUCKCHERRY) / Burn out (SLACK) / Rock me (STEPPENWOLF).

S/track review: 'The BANGER SISTERS' offers little in the way of inspiration, despite the inclusion of several rock "legends" and some "hapnin'" young bucks (circa 2002 anyway). Black Crowes frontman CHRIS ROBINSON leads us in with his solo effort, 'The Red Road', a soft-rock ballad that, without being a total disaster, does nothing to quicken any heartbeats. Next up is Motley Crue drummer TOMMY LEE with a quite frankly woeful attempt at trying to sound like Nine Inch Nails in his cover of Bowie's 'Fame'. On ballad 'One Last Goodbye', Bon Jovi guitarist RICHIE SAMBORA leaves us in no doubt as to why he is the guitarist and Jon is the singer. TREVOR RABIN sticks closely to the Nina Simone version of 'Don't Let Me Be Misunderstood', as opposed to the Animals', but fails to get near the brilliance of either, while those "young bucks" alluded to earlier, DISHWALLA, BUCKCHERRY, JP and SLACK, are merely filling in space. ROGER DALTREY and STEPPENWOLF should be given a mention out of respect more than their actual contributions of 'Child Of Mine' and 'Rock Me' respectively. The album is not a total washout, however; TALKING HEADS' classic 'Burning Down The House' would brighten up anyone's day, while BEN FOLDS' excellent version of the Jackson Browne hit 'Doctor My Eyes' and the quite frankly brilliant 'Hour Of Need' from PETER FRAMPTON at least make listening to this soundtrack a bit more worthwhile. *CM*

Album rating: *5.5

☐ Toni BASIL segment
(⇒ ROCKULA)

the BASKETBALL DIARIES

1995 (US 102m) Island Pictures (R)

Film genre: coming-of-age showbiz/Rock-music bio-pic drama

Top guns: dir: Scott Kalvert / s-w: Bryan Goluboff (au: **Jim Carroll**)

Stars: Leonardo DiCaprio *(Jim Carroll)*, Lorraine Bracco *(Jim's mother)* ← EVEN COWGIRLS GET THE BLUES ← SING / → DEATH OF A DYNASTY, Bruno Kirby *(Swifty)* ← GOOD MORNING, VIETNAM ← BIRDY ← THIS IS SPINAL TAP ← WHERE THE BUFFALO ROAM ← ALMOST SUMMER / → a SLIPPING-DOWN LIFE, **Mark Wahlberg** *(Mickey)* → BOOGIE NIGHTS → ROCK STAR → OVERNIGHT, Ernie Hudson *(Reggie Porter)* ← AIRHEADS ← the CROW ← ROAD HOUSE ← the JAZZ SINGER ← LEADBELLY / → a STRANGER IN THE KINGDOM, Jimmy Papiris *(Iggy)*, Patrick McGaw *(Neutron)*, Nick Gaetani *(referee)*, Alexander Gaberman *(Bobo)*, Ben Jorgensen *(Tommy)*, Josh Mostel *(counterman)* ← JESUS CHRIST SUPERSTAR, Juliette Lewis *(Diane Moody)* ← NATURAL BORN KILLERS → the RUNNIN' KIND / → STRANGE DAYS → FROM DUSK TILL DAWN → the FEARLESS FREAKS → CATCH AND RELEASE, Michael Imperioli *(Bobby)* ← JUNGLE FEVER / → I SHOT ANDY WARHOL → GIRL 6 → LAST MAN STANDING → DISAPPEARING ACTS, Brittany Daniel *(Blinkie)*, Toby Huss *(Kenny)* → CLUBLAND → the COUNTRY BEARS, Michael Rapaport *(bald punk)* → PAPER SOLDIERS → DEATH OF A DYNASTY, Barton Heyman *(confessional priest)* ← ROADSIDE PROPHETS ← LIVING PROOF: THE HANK WILLIAMS JR. STORY / → DEAD MAN WALKING, Vinnie Pastore *(construction worker)* ← WHO'S THE MAN? ← BLACK ROSES / → WALKING AND TALKING → JOE'S APARTMENT

Storyline: The real life story of an adolescent Jim Carroll's collapse into heroin addiction and crime marketed under the tag line, "the death of innocence and the birth of an artist" begins with Jim as a future basketball star tempted into drug experimentation. He soon finds himself out on the seedy streets of New York stealing, dealing drugs and even prostituting himself as his habit tightens its grip. Finding solace in Reggie, an old neighbourhood friend and ex user himself, Jim begins his long, painful road to recovery. *KM*

Movie rating: *6.5

Visual: video + dvd

Off the record: JIM CARROLL (b. 1950, New York) released three LP's in the early early 80s period, 'Catholic Boy' (1980), 'Dry Dreams' (1982) and 'I Write Your Name' (1983), while 90s sets included the spoken-word 'Praying Mantis' (1991) and vocal comeback, 'Pools Of Memory' (1998). *MCS*

Various Artists (score: GRAEME REVELL *)

May 95. (cd) *Island; <(524093-2)>*
– Catholic boy (JIM CARROLL w/ PEARL JAM) / Devil's toe (* & JIM CARROLL) / Down by the water (PJ HARVEY) / What a life (ROCKERS HI-FI) / I am alone (* & JIM CARROLL) / People who died (JIM CARROLL) / Riders on the storm (the DOORS) / Dizzy (GREEN APPLE QUICK STEP) / It's been hard (* & JIM CARROLL) / Coming right along (the POSIES) / Strawberry wine (MASSIVE INTERNAL COMPLICATIONS) / Star (the CULT) / Dream massacre (*) / I've been down (FLEA) / Blind dogs (SOUNDGARDEN).

S/track review: While 'The BASKETBALL DIARIES' the film, modernises JIM CARROLL's early 70s experiences, the soundtrack attempts to bring up to date his 1980 cult new wave recording, 'Catholic Boy' by pairing him with stadium grungers PEARL JAM on the compilation's opener. Eddie Vedder's suffocating roar replaced with a stripped down semi-spoken CARROLL vocal, PEARL JAM sound refreshingly different, almost timeless if you can ignore the unnecessary solos. Continuing the contemporary punk sound PJ HARVEY steps in with 'Down By The Water', a disturbing ode to infanticide with its knurled bass and hissing refrains, it gives the compilation an intimidating feel that's quickly lost to less controversial label mates ROCKERS HI-FI, following on with an unchallenging song about growing up. JIM CARROLL confronts more sombre experiences with his pogo paced 'People Who Died' which, despite its late 70s vintage, feels relevant enough to warrant inclusion on this soundtrack. That's more than can be said for the DOORS classic, 'Riders On The Storm' which is one decade too far even if they were enjoying an unexpected renaissance in the mid 90s. The glitch is temporary as the POSIES pace themselves with 'Coming Right Along', a beautifully restrained mix of distortion and ballad while SOUNDGARDEN fail to power their way through the lethargic 'Blind Dogs' (it might sound better played at 45rpm) and FLEA strips off his Chili Peppers to contribute the pleasant, unplugged 'I've Been Down'. Their inclusion makes this soundtrack read like a who's who of 90s alternative rock even if the recordings within are not always the best examples of their work. *KM*

Album rating: *7

la BATTAGLIA DEI MODS

aka 'CRAZY BABY' / German 'SIEBZEHN JAHR, BLONDES HAAR'

1966 (Ita/W.Ger 97m) Ultra Film / Roxy Film GmbH

Film genre: Pop-Rock Musical comedy/drama

Top guns: dir: Franco Montemurro / s-w: Adriano Bolzoni, Ennio De Concini → AMO NON AMO / Michael A. Chreiber

Stars: Ricky Shayne *(Ricky Fuller)*, Joachim Fuchsberger *(Robert Fuller)*, Elga Andersen *(Sonia)*, Eleonora Brown *(Martine)*, Rudolf Lenz *(Landers)*, Solvi Stubing *(Diana)*, Hans Elwenspoek *(Jeremy)*, Jurgen Draeger *(Steve)*, **Udo Jurgens** *(cameo)*, **DONOVAN** *(himself)*

Storyline: A continental slant on the gangs of mods and rockers from Liverpool, a city better known for Merseybeat rather than its violence between two of that generation's musical fractions. The main protagonist is rich kid turned mod guitarist, Rickym, who, after one of his gang fights results in the death of his girlfriend, jets off to Rome, where he has an affair with his businessman dad's mistress. Not so much "The Battle Of The Mods", more the battle of the bods. *MCS*

Movie rating: *5

Visual: none (no audio OST)

Off the record: Ricky Shayne (b. George Albert Tabett, 4 Jun'44, Cairo, Egypt) was raised in Beirut, ironically out of wealthy stock; father was a Lebanese oilman, mother was an Egyptian painter. He subsequently found a little pop music fame after he relocated from France to Italy, where a few singles under his new moniker were released. After his starring role in 'CRAZY BABY', he further ventured into acting and singing and won many awards including Luxembourg's Golden Lion; look out for his 1997 compilation, 'Mamy Blue' on 'B.M.G.' records. Austrian-born **Udo Jurgens** was a lot more successful having written songs for Shirley Bassey ('Reach For The Stars') in 1960 and subsequently winning the 1966 Eurovision Song Contest for Austria with 'Merci, Cherie' (in previous years he'd come 4th & 6th!); in 1978, Udo and the full West German World Cup Squad had a big hit with the country's official theme, 'Buenos Dias, Argentina'. *MCS*

BE COOL

2005 sequel (US 119m) Metro-Goldwyn-Mayer Pictures (PG-13)

Film genre: Pop-music/showbiz/crime caper

Top guns: dir: F. Gary Gray / s-w: Peter Steinfeld (nov: Elmore Leonard ← JACKIE BROWN ← TOUCH)

Stars: John Travolta *(Chili Palmer)* ← SWORDFISH ← PRIMARY COLORS ← PULP FICTION ← SHOUT ← STAYING ALIVE ← URBAN COWBOY ← GREASE ← SATURDAY NIGHT FEVER / → HAIRSPRAY re-make, Uma Thurman *(Edie Athens)* ← CHELSEA WALLS ← PULP FICTION ← EVEN COWGIRLS GET THE BLUES, Vince Vaughn *(Raji)* ← THUMBSUCKER ← SOUTH OF HEAVEN, WEST OF HELL / → INTO THE WILD, Cedric The Entertainer *(Sin LaSalle)* ← RIDE, **Andre Benjamin** *(Dabu)* → IDLEWILD, **Steven Tyler + AEROSMITH** *(himself/themselves)*, Robert Pastorelli *(Joe Loop)*, **Christina Milian** *(Linda Moon)*, Debi Mazar *(Marla)* ← the INSIDER ← GIRL 6 ← EMPIRE RECORDS ← SINGLES ← JUNGLE FEVER ← the DOORS ← DOWNTOWN 81, The Rock *(Elliot Wilhelm)* ← LONGSHOT, Harvey Keitel *(Nick Carr)* ← FINDING GRACELAND ← FROM DUSK TILL DAWN ← PULP FICTION ← RESERVOIR DOGS ← the LAST TEMPTATION OF CHRIST ← the BORDER ← THAT'S THE WAY OF THE WORLD, Danny DeVito *(Martin Weir)* ← MAN ON THE MOON ← the VIRGIN SUICIDES ← CAR WASH, James Woods *(Tommy Athens)* ← STRAIGHT TALK, **Wyclef Jean** *(himself)* ← the COUNTRY BEARS ← CARMEN: A HIP HOPERA ← RHYME & REASON / → BLOCK PARTY, **RZA** *(himself)* ← COFFEE AND CIGARETTES ← GHOST DOG: THE WAY OF THE SAMURAI ← RHYME & REASON, **Fred Durst** *(himself)* ← WOODSTOCK '99, **Gene Simmons** *(himself)* <= KISS =>, **Sergio Mendes** *(himself)*, **the Black Eyed Peas:- Will i Am, Fergie, Apl.de.Ap & Taboo** *(performers)* / **the Pussycat Dolls:- Nicole Scherzinger, Kimberly Wyatt, Ashley Roberts, Kasey Campbell & Melody Thornton** *(themselves)*, Seth Green *(music video director)* ← JOSIE AND THE PUSSYCATS ← PUMP UP THE VOLUME / → ELECTRIC APRICOT: QUEST FOR FESTEROO

Storyline: The sequel to 'Get Shorty'. Bored with the movie making business, reformed gangster Chili Palmer decides to branch out in to the music industry, helping out his friends wife, Edie, after her husband is bumped off by the Russian mafia. Fame and fortune on discovery of singing sensation seem a dead cert on discovery of Linda Moon except that the Russians are after Chili as he was a witness to their hit and Linda is in legal wrangles with a previous deal that Chili needs to get her out of. *MR*

Movie rating: *5.5

Visual: dvd

Off the record: **Steven Tyler** (Aerosmith), **Andre Benjamin** (Outkast), **Fred Durst** (Limp Bizkit), **the RZA** (Wu-Tang Clan), **Gene Simmons** (Kiss), all have cameos along with **the Black Eyed Peas, the Pussycat Dolls** and even **Sergio Mendes** (remember Brasil '66?).

—

Various Artists (score: JOHN POWELL *)

Mar 05. (cd) *TVT Soundtrax; <TV-6720-2>*
– Fantasy (EARTH, WIND & FIRE) / Hollywood swinging (KOOL & THE GANG) / Be thankful for what you got (WILLIAM DeVAUGHN) / Roda (ELIS REGINA) / Sexy (BLACK EYED PEAS) / Suga suga – reggae mix (BABY BASH) / The boss (JAMES BROWN) / Ain't no reason (CHRISTINA MILIAN) / Believer (CHRISTINA MILIAN) / Brand new old skool (777) / G's & soldiers (PLANET ASIA feat. KURUPT) / Cool Chili (*) / A cowboy's work is never done (SONNY & CHER) / You ain't woman enough (THE ROCK).

S/track review: There's always a preoccupation retaining a degree of authenticity when making sequels. If a follow up is deserved, it is all important to ensure it captures the essence of what made the first film so compelling. 'BE COOL' didn't quite manage this, and instead of expanding on the charm of 'Get Shorty' it sabotages it in a well-intentioned but untidy shambles. 'BE COOL', from its truly ironic title, right down to its cameo-ridden, pop star-heavy cast smelt funny from the start but while the film comes up short, the soundtrack has a few pleasant surprises. Taking obvious inspiration from the eclectic 'PULP FICTION' soundtrack, there's some damn fine songs on here: EARTH, WIND & FIRE's massive 'Fantasy', KOOL & THE GANG's 'Hollywood Swinging' and WILLIAM DeVAUGHN's take on 'Be Thankful For What You Got' are as strong an opening triumvirate as you could hope to find. Their nerve goes after such a joyously unselfconscious start however, and when contemporary artists rub shoulders with old hands we find the young 'uns lacking. That's not to say BLACK EYED PEAS' 'Sexy', or PLANET ASIA & KURUPT's 'G's And Soldiers' aren't great tunes in their own right it's just that the mix feels forced. 'BE COOL' is trying hard and there are some great moments here, but the overall effect is oddly self-conscious and less than the sum of its parts. Quite fitting perhaps then, given that the reuniting of Travolta and Thurman on screen turned out to be such a damp squib in the end. A wasted opportunity. *MR*

Album rating: *5.5

BE MY GUEST

1965 sequel (UK 82M b&w) Three Kings / Columbia Pictures USA

Film genre: Pop-Rock Musical comedy drama

Top guns: dir: Lance Comfort / s-w (+ story): Lyn Fairhurst ← LIVE IT UP

Stars: David Hemmings *(Dave Martin)* ← LIVE IT UP ← SOME PEOPLE ← PLAY IT COOL / → BLOW-UP → PROFONDO ROSSO → la VIA DELLA DROGA, **Steven Marriott** *(Ricky)* ← DATELINE DIAMONDS ← LIVE IT UP / → TONITE LET'S ALL MAKE LOVE IN LONDON, John Pike *(Phil)* ← LIVE IT UP, Andrea Monet *(Erica)*, Ivor Salter *(Herbert Martin)*, Diana King *(Margaret Martin)*, Avril Angers *(Mrs. Pucil)* → the FAMILY WAY → TWO A PENNY, Douglas Ives *(Stewars)* ← JUST FOR FUN ← LIVE IT UP, **the Nashville Teens:- John Hawkens, Ray Phillips, Pete Shannon, Arthur Sharp** *(performers)* → BEACH BALL → POP GEAR, **Jerry Lee LEWIS** *(performer)*, **the Plebs:- Danny McCulloch *, Terry Crowe, Mick Dunford** *(performers)* → MONTEREY POP *, **the Zephyrs** *(aka Slash Wildly & The Cut-Throats)*:- **John Peeby, John Carpenter, Mike Lease *, John Hinde** *(performers)* → * NEROSUBIANCO, **Kenny & the Wranglers:- Kenny Bernard** *(performer/s)*, **the Niteshades** *(performers)*

Storyline: Dave's mum and dad inherit a seaside hotel in Brighton but have bother getting it off the ground until the singer turns up with a few ideas – and his American girlfriend. Together with his re-formed R&B outfit, the Smart Alecs, he sets up a battle of the bands competition, which hits a dead end when suggestions of unscrupulous rigging and the likes are uncovered. *MCS*

Movie rating: *5.5

Visual: video (no audio OST)

Off the record: Child-actor, **Steve Marriott**, was of course frontman for the Small Faces (later of Humble Pie). British R&B band **the Zephyrs** (managed by Shel Talmy) appeared in the film as Slash Wildly & The Cut-Throats and had a minor UK hit with 'She's Lost You'. Other R&B acts were **Kenny & The Wranglers** who had just had two flop 45s, **the Plebs** (one flop) and the unknown Niteshades. *MCS*

BEACH BALL

1965 (US 83m) La Honda Services / Paramount Pictures

Film genre: teen Pop-Rock Musical comedy

Top guns: dir: Lennie Weinrib → WILD, WILD WINTER → OUT OF SIGHT / s-w: Sam Locke i.e. David Malcolm ← the GIRLS ON THE BEACH / → WILD, WILD WINTER

Stars: Edd Byrnes *(Dick Martin)* → STARDUST → GREASE → BACK TO THE BEACH, Chris Noel *(Susan Collins)* ← GIRL HAPPY ← GET YOURSELF A COLLEGE GIRL / → WILD, WILD WINTER, Robert Logan *(Bango)*, Aron Kincaid *(Jack Williams)* ← SKI PARTY ← the GIRLS ON THE BEACH → the GHOST IN THE INVISIBLE BIKINI, Mikki Jamison *(Augusta)* ← SKI PARTY, Don Edmonds *(Bob)* → WILD, WILD WINTER, Brenda Benet *(Samantha)* ← the GIRLS ON THE BEACH ← GIRL HAPPY / → HARUM SCARUM, James Wellman *(Bernard Wolf)* → WILD, WILD WINTER, Dick Miller *(cop #1)* ← SKI PARTY ← the GIRLS ON THE BEACH ← ROCK ALL NIGHT ← CARNIVAL ROCK / → WILD, WILD WINTER → the WILD ANGELS → the TRIP → TRUCK TURNER → I WANNA HOLD YOUR HAND → ROCK'N'ROLL HIGH SCHOOL → GET CRAZY → SHAKE, RATTLE & ROCK! tv, Gail Gilmore *(Deborah)* ← the GIRLS ON THE BEACH ← GIRL HAPPY / → HARUM SCARUM, Jack Bernardi *(Mr. Wilk)* → the WILD ANGELS → IT'S A BIKINI WORLD → WILLIE DYNAMITE → FOXY BROWN, **the Supremes:- Diana ROSS, Mary Wilson *, Florence Ballard** *(performers)* ← the T.A.M.I. SHOW * / → STANDING IN THE SHADOWS OF MOTOWN → * JACKIE'S BACK, **the Four Seasons:- Frankie Valli *, Tommy DeVito, Nick Massi, Bob Gaudio** *(performers)* → SGT. PEPPER'S LONELY HEARTS CLUB BAND, **the Righteous Brothers:- Bobby Hatfield, Bill Medley** *(performers)* ← a SWINGIN' SUMMER, Sid Haig *(their drummer)* → IT'S A BIKINI WORLD → BLACK MAMA, WHITE MAMA → COFFY → FOXY BROWN → the FORBIDDEN DANCE → JACKIE BROWN → HOUSE OF 1000 CORPSES → KILL BILL: VOL.2 → the DEVIL'S REJECTS, **the Walker Brothers:- Scott WALKER *, Gary Leeds, John Maus** *(performers)* ← SURF PARTY * → 30 CENTURY MAN *, **the Hondells:- Homer Hondells, Jethro Hondells** *(performers)*, **the Nashville Teens:- Barry Jenkins *, Ray Phillips, John Allen , John Hawkens, Ken Osborn** *(performers)* ← BE MY GUEST ← POP GEAR / → MONTEREY POP *

Storyline: Three (or four) teen rockers in drag try to impress the surf fraternity with disastrous results, well.. film-wise anyway. *MCS*

Movie rating: *2.5

Visual: video (no audio OST)

Off the record: The SUPREMES entered the fray with two numbers, 'Come To The Beach Ball With Me' and 'Surfer Boy', while the WIGGLERS (can't remember them in the film!) completed four songs, 'I Feel So Good', 'Surfin' Shindig', 'We've Got Money' and 'Wigglin' Like You Tickled'. The FOUR SEASONS contributed one song, 'Dawn (Go Away)' and the WALKER BROTHERS (Scott Walker was in the Routers & later composed OST for 'POLA X') contributed 'Doin' The Jerk'. The RIGHTEOUS BROTHERS performed 'Baby, What You Want Me To Do, while the HONDELLS stuck with 'My Buddy Seat'. *MCS*

BEACH BLANKET BINGO

1965 sequel-4 (US 96m) American International Pictures (PG)

Film genre: teen Pop/Rock Musical comedy

Top guns: s-w: William Asner (+ dir) ← BIKINI BEACH ← MUSCLE BEACH PARTY ← BEACH PARTY / → HOW TO STUFF A WILD BIKINI, Leo Townsend ← BIKINI BEACH / → HOW TO STUFF A WILD BIKINI

Stars: Frankie AVALON *(Frankie)*, **ANNETTE Funicello** *(Dee Dee)*, Deborah Walley *(Bonnie Graham)* → SKI PARTY → the GHOST IN THE INVISIBLE BIKINI → SPINOUT → IT'S A BIKINI WORLD, Harvey Lembeck *(Eric Von Zipper)* ← PAJAMA PARTY ← BIKINI BEACH ← BEACH PARTY / → HOW TO STUFF A WILD BIKINI → the GHOST IN THE INVISIBLE BIKINI → HELLO DOWN THERE, John Ashley *(Steve Gordon)* ← BIKINI BEACH ← MUSCLE BEACH PARTY ← BEACH PARTY ← HOT ROD GANG / → HOW TO STUFF A WILD BIKINI, **Donna Loren** *(Donna)* ← PAJAMA PARTY ← BIKINI BEACH ← MUSCLE BEACH PARTY, Jody McCrea *(Bonehead)* ← PAJAMA PARTY ← BIKINI BEACH ← MUSCLE BEACH PARTY ← BEACH PARTY / → HOW TO STUFF A WILD BIKINI, Marta Kristen *(Lorelei)*, Linda Evans *(Sugar Kane)*, Don Rickles *(Big Drop)* ← PAJAMA PARTY ← BIKINI BEACH ← MUSCLE BEACH PARTY, Timothy Carey *(South Dakota Slim)*, Paul Lynde *(Bullets)* ← BYE BYE BIRDIE, Buster Keaton *(himself)* ← PAJAMA PARTY / → HOW TO STUFF A WILD BIKINI, Bobbi Shaw *(Bobbi)* ← PAJAMA PARTY / → SKI PARTY → HOW TO STUFF A WILD BIKINI → the GHOST IN THE INVISIBLE BIKINI → PIPE DREAMS, Luree Holmes *(beach girl)* ← PAJAMA PARTY ← BIKINI BEACH ← MUSCLE BEACH PARTY ← BEACH PARTY / → SKI PARTY → HOW TO STUFF A WILD BIKINI → the GHOST IN THE INVISIBLE BIKINI → THUNDER ALLEY → the TRIP, **Brian Wilson** *(a beach boy)* ← BEACH PARTY / → SKI PARTY → HOW TO STUFF A WILD BIKINI → MAYOR OF THE SUNSET STRIP, Patti Chandler *(Patti)* ← PAJAMA PARTY ← BIKINI BEACH / → SKI PARTY → HOW TO STUFF A WILD BIKINI, Salli Sasche *(beach girl)* ← PAJAMA PARTY ← BIKINI BEACH ← MUSCLE BEACH PARTY / → SKI PARTY → HOW TO STUFF A WILD BIKINI → the GHOST IN THE INVISIBLE BIKINI → THUNDER ALLEY → the TRIP → WILD IN THE STREETS, Mike Nader *(Butch)* ← PAJAMA PARTY ← BIKINI BEACH ← MUSCLE BEACH PARTY ← BEACH PARTY / → SKI PARTY → HOW TO STUFF A WILD BIKINI → the TRIP, Mickey Dora *(beach boy)* ← BIKINI BEACH ← MUSCLE BEACH PARTY ← SURF PARTY ← BEACH PARTY / → SKI PARTY → HOW TO STUFF A WILD BIKINI, Mary Hughes *(beach girl)* ← PAJAMA PARTY ← BIKINI BEACH ← MUSCLE BEACH PARTY / → SKI PARTY → HOW TO STUFF A WILD BIKINI → THUNDER ALLEY → DOUBLE TROUBLE

Storyline: Yet again Dee Dee finds herself out of favour with frolicking Frankie, this time because of singing starlet Sugar Kane. She arrives on the scene with her sleazy manager Bullets, who soon gets the gang sky-diving for his latest promotional stunt. Regular knucklehead Eric Von Zipper is up to his usual no good but the real villain of the piece is South Dakota Slim, who introduces Sugar Kane to his favourite buzz-saw. *JZ*

Movie rating: *4.5

Visual: video + dvd

Off the record: DONNA LOREN (b. Donna Zukor, 1947, Boston, Massachusetts) was similar in many respects to her musical counterpart, ANNETTE, in the fact she cut her teeth as a member of the Mickey Mouse Club. LOREN subsequently became the face for soft-drink TV ad, Dr. Pepper, before she branched out in to the "Beach Party" flicks. *MCS*

DONNA LOREN (composer: Les Baxter)

Oct 65. (lp) *Capitol; <ST 2323>* ☐ ☐
– Cycle set / I think, you think / It only hurts when I cry / These are the good times / I'll never change him / Fly boy / New love / I am my ideal / Beach blanket bingo / Freeway. *<cd-iss. Jan01 as 'The Very Best Of Donna Loren – Beach Blanket Bingo' on 'Collectables'+=; COL-CD 2793>* – (nine extra non-OST songs).

S/track review: Another in the "BEACH PARTY" series of movie soundtracks, although this time previous girl-next-door ANNETTE is supplanted by the gorgeous Ann-Margret soundalike, DONNA LOREN. With an arsenal of Hemric & Styner songs (bar Hondells' cover 'Cycle Set' and MIKE CURB's instrumental 'Freeway'), LOREN is said to have recorded 'BEACH BLANKET BINGO' in a single 14-hour-long session. The effect and production work (arranged and conducted by H.B. Barnum) is somewhat hurried-along and in a way, not far removed from the Phil Spector or Brill Building sound. Adding up to a mere 20 minutes in total, the LP's highlights – or passable fluff – come by way of the aforementioned 'Cycle Set', 'I Think, You Think', the speeded-up take of 'It Only Hurts When I Cry', the Beach Boys-esque 'Fly Boy', 'New Love' and 'I Am My Ideal' – all reminiscent and derivative of the manufactured-pop times. The re-issue CD added another dimension to LOREN, but none of the songs were ' . . .BINGO' tracks. *MCS*

Album rating: *3.5

the BEACH BOYS: AN AMERICAN FAMILY

2000 (US 100m x 2 TV-mini) ABC / Columbia TriStar

Film genre: Rock/Pop-music bio-pic/drama

Top guns: dir: Jeff Bleckner / s-w: Kirk Ellis

Stars: Frederick Weller *(Brian Wilson)*, Nick Stabile *(Dennis Wilson)*, Ryan Northcott *(Carl Wilson)*, Matt Letscher *(Mike Love)*, Ned Vaughn *(Al Jardine)*, Kevin Dunn *(Murry Wilson)*, Alley Mills *(Audree Wilson)*, Erik Passoja *(Charles Manson)* → THANK YOU, GOOD NIGHT, Jesse Caron *(Bruce Johnston)* → ALMOST FAMOUS, Emmanuelle Vaugier *(Pamela)*, Anthony Rapp *(Van Dyke Parks)*, David Polcyn *(Phil Spector)*, Clay Wilcox *(Tommy Schaeffer)* ← COME ON, GET HAPPY: THE PARTRIDGE FAMILY STORY ← ROCK'N'ROLL MOM

Storyline: Featuring the ups and downs of the 60s supergroup, the film focuses on the often abusive relationship between dictatorial father Murry Wilson and his sons. The low points of the film include Carl's tragic death, Dennis' flirtation with the Charles Manson set and Brian's increasing dependence on drugs, although their triumphant musical successes offset the trials and tribulations they encounter. *JZ*

Movie rating: *6.5

Visual: video (no audio OST)

Off the record: The **BEACH BOYS** contributed over a dozen songs to the movie:- 'Surfin'', 'Wouldn't It Be Nice', 'Surfin' Safari', 'Surfin' USA', 'Surf City', 'In My Room', 'Surfer Girl', 'Be True To Your School', 'Little Deuce Coupe', 'I Get Around', 'Don't Worry, Baby', 'I Live For The Sun' (the SUNRAYS), 'God Only Knows', 'Good Vibrations' & 'Add Some Music To Your Day'. *MCS*

BEACH PARTY

1963 (US 101m) American International Pictures (PG)

Film genre: teen Pop/Rock Musical comedy

Top guns: dir: William Asher → MUSCLE BEACH PARTY → BIKINI BEACH → BEACH BLANKET BINGO → HOW TO STUFF A WILD BIKINI / s-w: Lou Rusoff ← HOT ROD GANG ← SHAKE, RATTLE & ROCK!

Stars: Bob Cummings *(Prof. Robert O. Sutwell)*, Dorothy Malone *(Marianne)*, **Frankie AVALON** *(Frankie)*, **ANNETTE Funicello** *(Dolores de Rio)*, Harvey Lembeck *(Eric Von Zipper)* → BIKINI BEACH → PAJAMA PARTY → BEACH BLANKET BINGO → HOW TO STUFF A WILD BIKINI → the GHOST IN THE INVISIBLE BIKINI → HELLO DOWN THERE, Jody McCrea *(Deadhead)* → MUSCLE BEACH PARTY → BIKINI BEACH → PAJAMA PARTY → BEACH BLANKET BIKINI → HOW TO STUFF A WILD BIKINI, John Ashley *(Ken)* ← HOT ROD GANG / → MUSCLE

BEACH PARTY → BIKINI BEACH → BEACH BLANKET BINGO → HOW TO STUFF A WILD BIKINI, Morey Amsterdam *(Cappy)*, Eva Six *(Ava)*, **Dick Dale** *(himself)* → MUSCLE BEACH PARTY → BACK TO THE BEACH, Meredith MacRae *(beach girl)* → BIKINI BEACH → NORWOOD → the CENSUS TAKER, **Brian Wilson** *(surfer)* <= the BEACH BOYS =>, Vincent Price *(Big Daddy)* → the TROUBLE WITH GIRLS → CUCUMBER CASTLE → the NIGHTMARE → WELCOME TO MY NIGHTMARE → the MONSTER CLUB, Andy Romano *(J.D.)* → PUMP UP THE VOLUME, **Candy Johnson** *(perpetual motion dancer)* → MUSCLE BEACH PARTY → BIKINI BEACH → PAJAMA PARTY, Luree Nicholson *(girl)* → MUSCLE BEACH PARTY → BIKINI BEACH → BEACH BLANKET BINGO → SKI PARTY → HOW TO STUFF A WILD BIKINI → THUNDER ALLEY → the TRIP, Linda Rogers *(Rat Pack member)* → BIKINI BEACH → PAJAMA PARTY → TICKLE ME → WINTER A-GO-GO → WILD, WILD WINTER, Mike Nader *(beach boy)* → MUSCLE BEACH PARTY → BIKINI BEACH → PAJAMA PARTY → BEACH BLANKET BINGO → SKI PARTY → HOW TO STUFF A WILD BIKINI → the TRIP, Mickey Dora *(beach boy)* → SURF PARTY → MUSCLE BEACH PARTY → BIKINI BEACH → BEACH BLANKET BINGO → HOW TO STUFF A WILD BIKINI

Storyline: Anthropologist Professor Sutwell is conducting a study of mating habits, not of gorillas or chimps but of teenage Americans. Assistant Marianne notes he's spending too much time with the female of the species, but it's all for a worthy cause. His subjects on the beach include the quarrelsome Frankie and Dolores, the vivacious Ava and dumb biker Eric Von Zipper. What conclusions will the professor draw, or will he just bury his head in the sand? *JZ*

Movie rating: *5

Visual: video + dvd

Off the record: Glimpse and you might miss the original Beach Boy himself, **Brian Wilson.**

—

ANNETTE: Annette's Beach Party (composer: Les Baxter)

Aug 63. (lp) *Buena Vista; <BB/STER 3316> H.M.V.; (CLP 1782)* **39** 1964 ☐
– Beach party (FRANKIE AVALON & ANNETTE FUNICELLO) / Treat him nicely / Don't stop now (FRANKIE AVALON) / Promise me anything (give me love) / Secret surfin' spot (with DICK DALE AND THE DEL TONES) / Song of the islands / California sun / Battle of San Onofre / Swingin' and a-surfin' (with DICK DALE AND THE DEL TONES) / Date night in Hawaii / Surfin' Luau / Pineapple princess. *<re-iss. 1984 on 'Rhino'; RNDF 204> <cd-iss. 1992 on 'Pony Canyon' Japan; PCCD 00069>*

S/track review: The first of six "BEACH PARTY" movies starts right here. Former Mouseketeer, ANNETTE (FUNICELLO), who hadn't had a major US chart hit since she was a teenager in 1960, takes top billing. That certain hit, 'Pineapple Princess', was restored here on 'BEACH PARTY', a quirky, Hawaiian-infused dirge that recalled both Connie Francis, Brenda Lee or Ann-Margret. Hawaii is indeed the theme for a handful of other attempts ('Song Of The Islands' and 'Date Night In Hawaii'), while the opening title track – with the lyrics "Vacation is here/Beach party tonight" – surfs on the sands of time like there's no tomorrow. Two Hemric-Styner ballads, 'Treat Him Nicely' & 'Promise Me Anything (Give Me Love)', slow the album's pace a little, both songs deserving of a comeback hit for ANNETTE – even now. On the original recording, DICK DALE & THE DEL TONES feature on a couple of tracks, 'Secret Surfin' Spot' & 'Swingin' And A-Surfin'', although it's ANNETTE's cutesy-pie vocal chords that steal the show. Her 'BEACH PARTY' boyfriend, FRANKIE AVALON – once a teen idol himself with two late 50s chart-toppers under his belt ('Venus' & 'Why') – also gets to grips with a couple of cues including 'Don't Stop Now'. ANNETTE shows her versatilty via the narrative versus choral (or is that coral!), 'The Ballad Of San Onofre', while the hotter than hot 'California Sun' (a minor hit for Joe Jones) is first class; punks the Ramones would subsequently give it a new lease of life in 1977. It's no surprise that 'BEACH PARTY' – the album – would reach Top 40 status, and that's without an accompanying hit single! *MCS*

Album rating: *7.5

– spinoff hits, etc. –

ANNETTE: Treat Him Nicely / Promise Me Anything

Sep 63. (7") *<F 427>* ☐ [–]

LU ANN SIMMS: Treat Him Nicely / Promise Me Anything

Sep 63. (7") *Vee-Jay; <63-3404>* ☐ [–]

FRANKIE AVALON: Beach Party / Don't Stop Now

Dec 63. (7") *Chancellor; <1139>* ☐ [–]

DICK DALE: Secret Surfin' Spot / Swingin' And A-Surfin'

Dec 63. (7") *Capitol; <4967>* ☐ [–]

BEACHES

1988 (US 123m) Buena Vista / Touchstone Pictures (PG-13)

Film genre: buddy Pop-music melodrama/comedy

Top guns: dir: Garry Marshall / s-w: Mary Agnes Donoghue (au: Iris Rainer Dart)

Stars: Bette MIDLER *(Cecilia Carol "CC" Bloom)*, Barbara Hershey *(Hillary Whitney Essex)* ← the LAST TEMPTATION OF CHRIST ← SHY PEOPLE / → LANTANA, John Heard *(John Pierce)* ← BEST REVENGE, Spalding Gray *(Dr. Richard Milstein)* ← TRUE STORIES ← the KILLING FIELDS / → STRAIGHT TALK → HOW HIGH, Lainie Kazan *(Leona Bloom)* ← ONE FROM THE HEART, James Read *(Michael Essex)*, Grace Johnston *(Victoria Cecilia Essex)*, Mayim Bialik *("CC", age 11)*, Marcie Leeds *(Hillary, age 11)*, **Arnold McCuller** *(Hollywood Bowl backup singer)* ← CROSSROADS ← AMERICAN HOT WAX / → DUETS, Jenifer Lewis *(diva)* → WHAT'S LOVE GOT TO DO WITH IT → SHAKE, RATTLE & ROCK! tv → GIRL 6 → the PREACHER'S WIFE → the TEMPTATIONS → JACKIE'S BACK! → LITTLE RICHARD, Jane Dulo *(Hillary's neighbor)* ← ROUSTABOUT, Hector Elizondo *(judge)* ← the LANDLORD / → HOW HIGH, Judith Baldwin *(screaming woman)* ← MADE IN USA

Storyline: The lifelong on-off-on friendship of earthy, ambitious Bronx gal CC Bloom and her strait-laced opposite Hillary Essex, charting their relationship from childhood penpals to unlikely adult flatmates. Trifles like romantic rivalry and incompatability of their other halves separate them for long periods, and although they finally wind up free, single – if not exactly young – and splitting the rent once more, fate has the final, tragic say. *BG*

Movie rating: *6

Visual: video + dvd

Off the record: Arnold McCuller went on to release a string of light-weight albums, including 'Exception To The Rule'.

—

BETTE MIDLER (composer: Marc Shaiman / score: Georges Delerue)

Jan 89. (lp/c/cd) *Atlantic; <(7567 81933-1/-4/-2)>* **2** Jun89 **21**
– Under the boardwalk / Wind beneath my wings / I've still got my health / I think it's going to rain today / Otto Titsling / I know you by heart / The glory of love / Baby mine / Oh industry / The friendship theme.

S/track review: "A classic piece of self-serving showbiz tripe" is how Rolling Stone summed up 'Wind Beneath My Wings', the Grammy-winning single which rejuvenated BETTE MIDLER's career. You can find it here in all its late 80s defining, keyboard-orchestrated, "did you ever know that you're my heeeeroooo.." melodrama; if you've never seen the film, you'll almost certainly have heard the song at your mum's golden anniversary, or maybe your big sister's 40th. If you've managed to somehow avoid it, congratulations. Still, it's not quite the loudest cluck on this overproduced turkey; Nina Simone fans can look forward to wincing at MIDLER's assault on

Randy Newman's 'I Think It's Going To Rain Today'. Soul was never one of MIDLER's strengths and it's likewise hard to believe Drifters' fans will get much mileage from a cod-salsa-intro'd 'Under The Boardwalk'. In fact, it's saying something when the tired, taste-free cabaret of 'Otto Titsling' is actually preferable to the cover versions, generic, written-to-order pop floss, appalling, sub-Depeche Mode arrangements and goth-Wagnerian straining of 'Oh Industry'. Only her spicy kick on Cole Porter's 'I've Still Got My Health', and the brief piano solo of Georges Delerue's 'Friendship Theme', really escape the slush. As beaches go, this one's the musical equivalent of the Costa del Sol: overdeveloped, overfamiliar and just plain tacky. *BG*

Album rating: *3.5

– spinoff hits, etc. –

BETTE MIDLER: Wind Beneath My Wings / Oh Industry

Feb 89. (7"/c-s/cd-s) *<88972> (A 8972/+C/CD)* [1] Jun89 [5]

the BEAT

2003 (US 85m) Symbolic / Tripped-Out Productions LLC (M)

Film genre: urban/coming-of-age (part)Rap-music drama/fantasy

Top guns: s-w + dir: Brandon Sonnier

Stars: Rahman Jamaal *(Flip)*, Kazz Wingate IV *(Cassius 'Cash' Bernard)*, Michael Colyar *(Chi-Barnes)*, **Jazsmin Lewis** *(Tawanna)*, Keith Ewell *(Tony)*, **Coolio** *(MC)* ← GET OVER IT!, **Chino XL** *(Crazy 8)*, John Cothran Jr. *(Bumma)* → BLACK SNAKE MOAN, **Brian McKnight** *(record executive)*, **4-Zone** *(himself)*

Storyline: Flip and Cash are two brothers who want to become big names in the rap business. Their dream is cruelly shattered when Cash is murdered in a back alley, leaving Flip to decide whether he wants to go solo or follow his father's wishes and become a cop. We see two different futures as Flip is portrayed as living in the ghetto learning about life on the streets, and as a young cop patrolling the ghetto learning about life on the streets. Which side of the coin will Flip choose? *JZ*

Movie rating: *4

Visual: dvd (no audio OST; score JAMAAL, etc.)

Off the record: Brian McKnight was part of R&B/gospel/vocal outfit, Take 6, who had a string of Top 100 album entries between 1989 and 1994; as a solo artist he chalked up several hits including Top 3 smash, 'Back At One'. Hardcore rapper, **Chino XL**, from East Orange, New Jersey, debuted in 1996 with the much-touted album, 'Here To Save You All'. Pre-acting work, **Jazsmin Lewis**, played bass and sang for the likes of George Clinton and Zapp. *MCS*

BEAT STREET

1984 (US 106m) Orion Pictures (PG)

Film genre: R&B/Dance/teen musical drama

Top guns: dir: Stan Lathan ← SAVE THE CHILDREN/ s-w: Andy Davis, David Gilbert, Paul Golding (au: Steven Hager)

Stars: Rae Dawn Chong *(Tracy Carlson)* → RUNNING OUT OF LUCK, **Guy Davis** *(Kenny 'Double K' Kirkland)* → HELLHOUNDS ON MY TRAIL, Jon Chardiet *(Ramon)*, Leon W. Grant *(Chollie)* → PLAYING FOR KEEPS, Robert Taylor *(Lee)*, Saundra Santiago *(Carmen Cararro)*, Lee Chamberlin *(Alicia)* ← LET'S DO IT AGAIN, Mary Alice Smith *(Cora)* ← SPARKLE ← the EDUCATION OF SONNY CARSON, Hope Clarke *(dancing instructor)* ← a PIECE OF THE ACTION ← BOOK OF NUMBERS, **Shawn Elliott** *(Domingo)* ← SHORT EYES, **Grandmaster Melle Mel & The Furious Five** *(themselves)*, **Afrika Bambaataa & the Soul Sonic Force** *(themselves)* → the SHOW → MODULATIONS → SCRATCH, **Andy B. Bad** *(himself)*, **Tina B.** *(herself)*, **the System** *(themselves)*, **Dougie/Doug E. Fresh** *(himself)* → TAPEHEADS → WHITEBOYS → BROWN SUGAR → AWESOME: I FUCKIN' SHOT THAT!, **Rock Steady Crew:- Frosty Freeze, Mr. Freeze, Crazy Legs & Prince Ken Swift** *(themselves)* ← WILD STYLE, **Us Girls:- Lisa Lee** *(themselves)* ← WILD STYLE, **the Treacherous Three/Kool Moe Dee** *(themselves)* ← WILD STYLE / → BEEF, **Brenda K. Starr** *(herself)*, **DJ Jazzy Jay** *(performer)* → SCRATCH

Storyline: The heady first days of hip hop get the Hollywood treatment in the form of a musical interlinking the dreams and ambitions of its interracial New York protagonists: Lee the breakdancer, big brother Kenny the budding DJ and Ramon the graffiti artist. Cameos from seminal figures Kool Herc, Afrika Bambaataa, Melle Mel, Kool Moe Dee, Jazzy Jay and Doug E Fresh (and a teenaged RZA!), as well as a semi-legendary face-off between the Rock Steady Crew and New York City Breakers ensure cult status. *BG*

Movie rating: *5

Visual: video + dvd

Off the record: Son of filmmakers/activists, Ossie Davis and Ruby Dee, self-taught guitarist **Guy Davis** (b.12 May'52, New York City) released his first traditional blues LP in 1978, 'Dreams About Life'. After his starring role in 'BEAT STREET', GUY scored a couple of TV/Broadway movies before releasing a string of contemporary soul-blues albums in the 90s & 00s, 'Stomp Down The Rider' (1995) to 'Give In Kind' (2002). *MCS*

Various Artists (score: Arthur Baker, Harry Belafonte & Webster Lewis)

May 84. (lp/c/cd) *Atlantic; <80154> (780154-1/-4/-2)* [14] Jun84 [30]
– Beat Street breakdown (GRANDMASTER MELLE MEL & THE FURIOUS FIVE) / Baptize the beat (the SYSTEM) / Strangers in a strange world (JENNY BURTON & PATRICK JUDE) / Frantic situation (AFRIKA BAMBAATAA & THE SOUL SONIC FORCE) / Beat Street strut (JUICY) / Us girls (SHARON GREEN, LISA COUNTS & DEBBIE D.) / This could be the night (CINDY MIZELLE) / Breaker's revenge (ARTHUR BAKER) / Tu carino – Carmen's theme (RUBEN BLADES).

S/track review: This Harry Belafonte-produced movie – while relatively gritty for its genre – was one of the first to document a scene that was already way ahead of the big screen, and would pretty much stay that way. It was also the very first film to be blessed with more than one spin-off album, and although the two volumes could've been edited down to a definitive single disc, there's some classic stuff here only otherwise available on hard-to-track-down CD's and pricey vinyl. Crucially, as a sound that held all the fantastical shock of the new and promise of the future in its 808 ricochet, whoosing effects and turntablist trickery, vintage electro still fascinates; the promise was never fully realised, either by techno or hip hop, but back then there really was nothing like it. Fronted by the zealous owner of a bark as apocalyptic as MELLE MEL, 'Beatstreet Breakdown' – like 'The Message' before it – was (is) truly an epochal epistle, a bulletin from the soul of the Bronx: as its six-plus minutes of soapbox sample'n'scratch serves to remind, once upon a time mainstream hip hop really did hold the power of social comment in its grasp. When MEL holds court with lines like "water tastes funny, it's forever too sunny" and "peoples in terror, the leaders made an error", the ferocious timbre of that voice assures you that not only is it all horribly true, but it's way ahead of its time, both in the sense of laying the stylistic blueprint for the likes of Public Enemy but also in raising issues that'd still be relevant more than twenty years later. It's a lasting irony that the breakdancing craze and movie cash-ins which accompanied it at least partially muffled Flash and Co's unexpected and unflinching brand of realism. But AFRIKA BAMBAATAA – between slippery brass samples – was also setting his phasers to stun, rapping about global knowledge and empowerment over the funkiest effects money could buy in the early 80s, cheekily incorporating the old 'Do It

Any Way You Wanna' melody and manipulating studio technology to create something meaningful rather than embarrassing. Save for ARTHUR BAKER collage, 'Breaker's Revenge', the rest of the original album wasn't up to much but at least the Latino love theme was binned when Vol.1 hooked up with Vol.2 on a CD two-fer. JAZZY JAY steps up with the lesser theme, 'Son Of Beat St.', and the great ROCKERS REVENGE supply the 'White Lines'-like thrum of 'Battle Cry'. But the prize cultural artefact is TREACHEROUS THREE's 'Santa's Rap', where triviality and threadbare humour battle with retrospectively quaint bleeps; hard to believe that hip hop not only had a self-censoring sense of irony, but MC's actually joked about how hard up they were, or – in the case of a novelty cut like 'Phony Four MC's' – how crap they were. *BG*

Album rating: *6.5

– spinoff hits, etc. –

GRANDMASTER MELLE & THE FURIOUS FIVE: Beat Street Breakdown – Part I / Part II

May 84. (7"/12") *<89659> (A/TA 9659)* [86] Jun84 [42]

JENNY BURTON & PATRICK JUDE: Strangers In A Strange World / (instrumental)

May 84. (7") *<89660> (A 9660)* [54] Jun84 [ ]

Various Artists: Beat Street, Volume 2

Sep 84. (lp/c) *<80158> (780158-1/-4)* [ ] Oct84 [ ]
– Son of Beat Street (JAZZY JAY) / Give me all (JUICY) / Nothin's gonna come easy (TINA B.) / Santa's rap (TREACHEROUS THREE) / It's alright by me (JENNY BURTON) / Battle cry (ROCKERS REVENGE) / Phony four MC's-wappin' (RALPH ROLLE) / Into the night (LA LA).

BEATLEMANIA: THE MOVIE

1981 (US 86m) American Cinema Releasing (PG)

Film genre: pop/rock Musical drama

Top guns: dir: Joseph Manduke ← CORNBREAD, EARL AND ME

Stars: David Leon *(John Lennon)*, Mitch Weissman *(Paul McCartney)*, Tom Teely *(George Harrison)*, Ralph Castelli *(Ringo Starr)*, Christina Applegate

Storyline: From the popular stage production, 'Beatlemania!', this feature film was actually tagged: "Not The Beatles, But An Incredible Simulation" (a running joke in pop circles). It charts the development of the Fab Four from their early Cavern days to their break-up in the late 60s. *MCS*

Movie rating: *3

Visual: none (no audio OST)

Off the record: Songs tackled by the actors included 'I Wanna Hold Your Hand', 'Eleanor Rigby' and a cover of 'Let's Twist Again'. Mitch Weissman subsequently formed Beatlefest in the early 90s, mimicking McCartney of course. *MCS*

the BEATLES

Formed: Liverpool, England . . . by JOHN LENNON and PAUL McCARTNEY as schoolboy band the Quarrymen in 1957. Despite recent, unprecedented advances in gobal communication and increasing homogenization of entertainment, the BEATLES remain as universal a pop cultural phenomenon as the world has yet witnessed. In many ways, the fact that America's roots music was transformed into as complex and readily, wondrously accessible a format by a group of working class lads from Liverpool can perhaps still be considered slightly surreal. To the four distinctive personalities – including the late GEORGE HARRISON, who'd joined in 1958, and RINGO STARR, who'd replaced original drummer Pete Best – caught up in the initial rush of "Beatlemania" it must've seemed even more surreal, a sense at least partly conveyed by the quartet's Richard Lester-directed screen debut, 'a HARD DAY'S NIGHT' (1964). Famously dubbed "the Citizen Kane of juke box movies" by American critic Andrew Sarris, the film's visually and technically striking, whirlwind snaphot of a fantastical day and a half in the life, boasted an equally pioneering, all-original soundtrack which served as a surrogate third album. It proved so successful, in fact, that the same director was held over for a follow-up, 'HELP!' (1965). Shot in colour rather than black and white, and adding a convoluted plot to the established formula of Liverpudlian wit, slapstic gags and musical performance, the movie didn't make quite as much of a splash as its predecessor although the soundtrack showcased some of the most fully realised songwriting LENNON and McCARTNEY had produced up to that point. Two years on and in the wake of the group's narcotic experimentation and definitive, all conquering contribution to psychedelia, 'Sgt. Pepper's Lonely Hearts Club Band' (1967), they attempted to apply their expanded consciousness to the art of filmaking. The result was 'MAGICAL MYSTERY TOUR' (1967), an amateurish mini road movie inspired by Ken Kesey's crusading vagabaonds, the Merry Pranksters. While the film remains a muddled relic of its era, again the accompanying soundtrack has weathered the vagaries of time as an occasionally brilliant comapanion piece to 'Sgt. Pepper's . . .' It was also the last BEATLES album to display any sense of a unified entity as personal friction began to undo their collective spirit. In a tentative indication of his initial emergence as the most compelling post-BEATLES solo artist, GEORGE HARRISON subsequently composed the experimental score for voyeuristic fantasy, 'WONDERWALL' (1968). HARRISON also furnished the best songs for 'YELLOW SUBMARINE' (1968), a garish, contract-filling exercise in animated surealism to which the band contributed little save for the soundtrack and a brief live-action scene. The BEATLES' final, drawn out demise was captured in unforgiving detail by Michael Lindsay-Hogg in 'LET IT BE' (1970), an Oscar winning document of the sessions for the band's last album. In film scoring terms, it was PAUL McCARTNEY who went on to make the biggest impression after the BEATLES had imploded. While he'd previously lent his composing talents to Roy Boulting's romantic comedy, 'The FAMILY WAY' (1966), he excelled himself with one of the most memorable 007 theme tunes in the James Bond series' long running history. As performed by his post-BEATLES aggregation, Wings, the epic 'Live And Let Die' almost topped the US chart (UK Top 10) and was later covered by sleaze rockers Guns 'N Roses amongst others. And while JOHN LENNON had previously starred in Richard Lester's military satire, 'How I Won The War' (1967), and went on to appear in cult pseudo-documentary, 'Dynamite Chicken' (1972) and the Jonas Mekas film, 'Diaries, Notes And Sketches' (1970), it was RINGO STARR who most visibly built on the droll comedic talent he'd flourished in those early BEATLES movies. Having already appeared as a Mexican gardener (what else?!) in Christian Marquand's 'CANDY' (1968) and starred opposite Peter Sellers in 'The MAGIC CHRISTIAN' (in which LENNON also appeared), he subsequently popped up in FRANK ZAPPA's '200 MOTELS' (1971), starred in spaghetti western 'Il Cieco' (1972), directed his own Marc Bolan/T.Rex documentary, 'BORN TO BOOGIE' (1972) and did a voiceover on HARRY NILSSON animation, 'The POINT!' (1971). NILSSON was in fact, such good pals with STARR that he took a leading role opposite him in Freddie Francis' 'SON OF DRACULA' (1974) even though he regarded the script as second rate. STARR also landed a major part in rock'n'roll musical 'THAT'LL BE THE DAY' (1973) opposite David Essex, and even made a cameo as the

Pope in Ken Russell's demented 'LISZTOMANIA' (1975). Along with NILSSON, WHO drummer KEITH MOON was another of STARR's drinking buddies and they were reunited on screen in both Mae West's final stab at reliving her youth, 'Sextette' (1978) and WHO documentary, 'The KIDS ARE ALRIGHT' (1979). Towards the end of the decade, it was HARRISON who began making waves in the film world. Having already produced the all-star benefit show, 'The CONCERT FOR BANGLA DESH' (1972), and British political satire, 'Little Malcolm And His Struggle Against The Eunuchs' (1974), HARRISON rather serendipitously became more closely involved in cinema after the filming of Monty Python's 1979 classic, 'The Life Of Brian' (in which he also made a cameo) ran into financial difficulties. Being a huge fans of John Cleese and Co, HARRISON allegedly even mortgaged his own home to save the movie from oblivion. The resulting production company, 'Handmade Films', became a prolific UK player during the 80s, handling such acclaimed features as 'The Long Good Friday' (1980), 'The Missionary' (1982), the BAFTA award winning 'Mona Lisa' (1986), 'Withnail & I' (1987), 'Five Corners' (1987) and Terry Gilliam's 'Time Bandits' (1981), in which HARRISON co-composed the score with MIKE MORAN. While JOHN LENNON's career was brought to a brutal end with his murder on 8th December 1980, and HARRISON was also savagely attacked in his later years, the latter finally passed away on 29th November 2001 after fighting a losing battle with cancer. Of the remaining BEATLES, STARR's big screen career tapered off in the 80s although he did star as a neolithic misfit in 'Caveman' (1981), narrated children's TV animation series, 'Thomas The Tank Engine', and made an inevitable appearance in McCARTNEY's vanity project, 'GIVE MY REGARDS TO BROAD STREET' (1984). With its paper thin, self-penned screenplay and BEATLES reworkings, the movie received a critical hammering. Sir PAUL nevertheless continued to make the occasional screen dalliance, turning up as a dinner guest in Comic Strip satire, 'EAT THE RICH' (1987), penning the title track for Cameron Crowe's 'Vanilla Sky' (2001) and composing the music for kids animation, 'Tropic Island Hum' (2003). *BG*

- **filmography** (composers) {acting} –

a Hard Day's Night *(1964 {* all} OST =>)* / **Pop Gear** *(1965 {* all} V/A =>)* / **Help!** *(1965 {* all} OST =>)* / **the Family Way** *(1966 OST by McCARTNEY =>)* / **Magical Mystery Tour** *(1967 {* all} OST + V/A =>)* / How I Won The War *(1967 {* JOHN})* / **Rock And Roll Circus** *(1968 {* JOHN} OST by the ROLLING STONES & V/A =>)* / **Candy** *(1968 {* RINGO} OST by V/A & DAVE GRUSIN =>)* / **Wonderwall** *(1968 OST by HARRISON =>)* / **Yellow Submarine** *(1968 OST w/ George Martin =>)* / **the Magic Christian** *(1969 {* RINGO} {b JOHN} hit theme by BADFINGER =>)* / John Lennon And Yoko Ono: The Bed-In *(1969 {* JOHN})* / **Let It Be** *(1970 {*p all} OST =>)* / Diaries, Notes And Sketches *(1970 {c JOHN})* / **200 Motels** *(1971 {a RINGO} OST by FRANK ZAPPA =>)* / Dynamite Chicken *(1972 {c JOHN})* / il Cieco *(1972 {* RINGO} no s/t)* / **the Concert For Bangla Desh** *(1972 {*p GEORGE} {p RINGO} OST by HARRISON & V/A =>)* / **Imagine** *(1972 {*p JOHN} =>)* / **Born To Boogie** *(1972 {* RINGO} OST by MARC BOLAN & T. REX =>)* / **That'll Be The Day** *(1973 {* RINGO} OST by V/A =>)* / Live And Let Die *(1973 hit/theme by McCARTNEY & WINGS on OST by George Martin)* / **Son Of Dracula** *(1974 {* RINGO} OST by NILSSON =>)* / **Lisztomania** *(1975 {a RINGO} OST by RICK WAKEMAN =>)* / **All This And World War II** *(1976 OST by V/A =>)* / **the Last Waltz** *(1978 {p RINGO} OST by the BAND =>)* / Fire In The Water *(1977 {c JOHN})* / **I Wanna Hold Your Hand** *(1978 score by LENNON)* / **the Rutles** *(1978 {c GEORGE} OST by the RUTLES =>)* / **Sgt. Pepper's Lonely Hearts Club Band** *(1978 OST by V/A =>)* / Sextette *(1978 {* RINGO})* / **the Kids Are Alright** *(1979 {c RINGO} OST by the WHO =>)* / **Rockshow** *(1980 {*p PAUL & WINGS} =>)* / **Concert For Kampuchea** *(1980 {p PAUL, WINGS & ROCKESTRA} on OST by V/A =>)* / Caveman *(1981 {* RINGO})* / Les Jocondes *(1982 no OST by LENNON & Jacques Dutronc)* / **the Compleat Beatles** *(1982 {* all} =>)* / Princess Daisy *(1983 TV {a RINGO})* / **Give My Regards To Broad Street** *(1984 {* PAUL} {* RINGO] OST by McCARTNEY =>)* / Alice In Wonderland *(1985 TV {a RINGO})* / Water *(1985 {b GEORGE} {b RINGO} OST by MIKE MORAN see; future editions =>)* / Shanghai Surprise *(1986 {b GEORGE} score by HARRISON & V/A)* / Walking After Midnight *(1988 {p RINGO})* / **Imagine: John Lennon** *(1988 {*p JOHN} {p GEORGE} OST by LENNON =>)* / **Get Back** *(1991 {*p PAUL} =>)* / the Beatles Anthology *(1995 {p all} compilation OST; see future edition =>)* / Wingspan: An Intimate History *(2001 TV {*p PAUL / WINGS})* / Tropic Island Hum *(2003 score by McCARTNEY)* / **Concert For George** *(2003 {*p PAUL} {*p RINGO} by V/A =>)*

– compilations, etc. –

the BEATLES: Reel Music

Mar 82. (lp/c) *Capitol; <SV/4XV 12199>* [–] [19]
– A hard day's night / I should have known better / Can't buy me love / And I love her / Help! / You've got to hide your love away / Ticket to ride / Magical mystery tour / I am the walrus / Yellow submarine / All you need is love / Let it be / Get back / The long and winding road.

the BEATLES: Beatles Movie Medley / (non-OST B-side)

May 82. (7") *Parlophone; (R 6055) Capitol; <5107>* [10] Mar82 [12]
– (medley):- Magical Mystery Tour – All You Need Is Love – You've Got To Hide Your Love Away – I Should Have Known Better – A Hard Day's Night – Ticket To Ride – Get Back.

the BEATNICKS

2000 (US 98m) Exile Pictures (PG-13)

Film genre: buddy film/comedy

Top guns: s-w: (+ dir) Nicholson Williams, Nina Jo Baker

Stars: Norman Reedus *(Nick Nero)* ← REACH THE ROCK / → OCTANE → OVERNIGHT, Mark Boone Jr. *(Nick Beat)* ← LAST EXIT TO BROOKLYN ← the WAY IT IS, Elodie Bouchez *(Nica)*, Eric Roberts *(Mack Drake)*, Patrick Bauchau *(Hank)* ← EVERYBREATH ← PHENOMENA / → RAY

Storyline: Started out as a film short in 1996; also scripted and directed by Nicholson Williams. The BeatNicks – semi-professional musician Nick Nero and poet Nick Beat – are a pair of care-free, truth-seekers who will find themselves homeless if they don't find a gig. Their luck changes when they discover a box of infinite beats on the beach, a mystical treasure that ensures them their ultimate goal: a billing at their local Monkey Club. When love complications for Nero come to light courtesy of club owner's captive bride, Nica (and other hard knocks), they set to return the box to its rightful owner – the sea. *MCS*

Movie rating: *4

Visual: dvd (no audio OST; score: ZANDER SCHLOSS)

Off the record: ZANDER SCHLOSS (ex-Circle Jerks) contributed three tracks to the movie soundtrack, 'Nero's Theme', 'To The Beatnicks' & 'Do The Thing'. *MCS*

the BEATNIKS

1960 (US 78m b&w) Barjul International Pictures Inc.

Film genre: showbiz/crime drama

Top guns: s-w: (+ dir) Paul H. Frees, Arthur Julian

Stars: Tony Travis *(Eddy Crane)* ← JAMBOREE, Joyce Terry *(Helen Tracy)*, Karen Kadler *(Iris)*, Peter Breck *(Bob "Moon" Mooney)* → HOOTENANNY HOOT → TERMINAL CITY RICOCHET → HIGHWAY 61, Bob Wells *(Chuck)*, Sam Edwards *(Red)*, Charles Delaney *(Harry Bayliss)*, Martha Wentworth *(Nadine)*, Stanley Farrar *(Ray Morrissey)*

Storyline: Eddie Crane and his tough-guy pals like nothing better than pulling on rubber masks and terrorizing local shopkeepers. After a successful stick-up, Eddie mimics a love song to some background music and is spotted by agent Harry Bayliss, who puts two and two together and makes five. Eddie is invited to star in Harry's TV show the next day, but can young Mr Crane hoist himself away from his beatnik pals before he's pulled up for murder? *JZ*

Movie rating: *1

Visual: video + dvd (no audio OST)

Off the record: Tony Travis sings 'Leather Coats', etc.

BEAVIS AND BUTT-HEAD DO AMERICA

1996 (US 81m) Geffen Pictures / Paramount Pictures (PG-13)

Film genre: animated road/buddy movie/comedy

Top guns: dir: Mike Judge (+ s-w), Yvette Kaplan / s-w: Joe Stillman

Voices: Mike Judge *(Beavis / Butt-Head / Mr. Van Driessen / Tom Anderson / Principal McVicar)* ← AIRHEADS / → SOUTH PARK, BIGGER, LONGER & UNCUT, Cloris Leachman *(old woman)*, Robert Stack *(ATF Agent Fleming)*, Eric Bogosian *(ranger at Old Faithful / White House press secretary)*, Pamela Blair *(flight attendant / White House tour guide)*, Kristofor Brown *(man on plane / old guy/Jim / man in confession #2)*, David Letterman/Earl Hofart *(a Motley Crue roadie)* → PRIVATE PARTS → MEETING PEOPLE IS EASY → MAN ON THE MOON → GRIZZLY MAN, Demi Moore *(Dallas Grimes)*, Bruce Willis *(Muddy Grimes)* ← LAST MAN STANDING ← FOUR ROOMS ← PULP FICTION / → the STORY OF US → OVER THE HEDGE, Greg Kinnear *(ATF agent Bork)*, Richard Linklater *(voice; tour bus driver)* ← JANIS JOPLIN SLEPT HERE / → CHELSEA WALLS

Storyline: The dysfunctional duo endure a catastrophe of cataclysmic proportions when, shock! horror! their TV is stolen. Spurred into action, the pair of potato heads set off across America in search of the culprit (and sex). On their travels they come into possession of a top secret weapon and are pursued by the FBI and other weirdos. Will B & B manage to save the world and, more importantly, recover their TV? *JZ*

Movie rating: *6

Visual: video + dvd

Off the record: The TV series for 'Beavis and Butt-Head' started off its life in 1993, the nasty animation characters slagging off every non-metal video until 1997. *MCS*

Various Artists (score: John Frizzell)

Nov 96. (cd/c) *Geffen; <GED/GEC 25002>* 20 –

– Two cool guys (ISAAC HAYES) / Love rollercoaster (RED HOT CHILI PEPPERS) / Ain't nobody (LL COOL J) / Ratfinks, suicide tanks and cannibal girls (WHITE ZOMBIE) / I wanna riot (RANCID & STUBBORN ALL-STARS) / Walk on water (OZZY OSBOURNE) / Snakes (NO DOUBT) / Pimp'n ain't Ez (MADD HEAD) / Lord is a monkey (the BUTTHOLE SURFERS) / White trash (SOUTHERN CULTURE ON THE SKIDS) / Gone shootin' (AC/DC) / Lesbian seagull (ENGELBERT HUMPERDINCK).

S/track review: As a South Park regular it seems appropriate that ISAAC HAYES should feature here with his self-parodying rendition of 'Two Cool Guys', setting our eponymous heroes as the exact opposite of what they are, underpinned by a catchy wah-wah riff. 'Love Rollercoaster' features a joyous RED HOT CHILI PEPPERS in retro funk mode. As for LL COOL J, he once again proves that nobody does it better on 'Ain't Nobody'. After a deceptive start it's not long before Beavis & Butt-Head's beloved metal genre raises its head; WHITE ZOMBIE's 'Ratfinks, Suicide Tanks & Cannibal Girls' relies heavily on electronics in a Marilyn Manson/NIN neo-industrial style, more so than the raw riffage of their Astro Creep days. RANCID & STUBBORN ALL-STARS rage in a pastiche Brit punk manner through 'I Wanna Riot', OZZY OSBOURNE stalks into the room with the run of the mill 'Walk On Water'. Some time before 'Don't Speak' and Gwen Stefani's reinvention as a bling bling RnB songstress, is the NO DOUBT b-side 'Snakes' in which the bass and drums' duel riffing coils around the melody in an entrancing manner. MADD HEAD's West Coast Hip hop is so G that it's almost H. Gibby Haynes gibbers manically over 'Lord Is A Monkey', an intoxicating super-funky, distorted grind. An injection of straight-up AC/DC retro riffage, 'Gone Shootin'' will always add a touch of thoroughbred class to proceedings. And ENGELBERT HUMPERDINCK's credibility is single-handedly raised a thousandfold with the lounge-ish, 'Lesbian Seagull'. *DF*

Album rating: *6.5

– spinoff hits, etc. –

LL COOL J: Ain't Nobody / MADD HEAD: Pimp'n Ain't Ez

Dec 96. (c-s/12"/cd-s) *<19410> (GFS C/T/TD 22195)* 46 Jan97 1

RED HOT CHILI PEPPERS: Love Rollercoaster / ENGELBERT HUMPERDINCK: Lesbian Seagull

Jun 97. (7"/c-s/cd-s) *(GFS/+C/TD 22188)* – 7

the BEE GEES

Formed: By the brothers Gibb: Maurice, Robin and Barry, in Brisbane, Australia (although they originally hailed from the Isle of Man via Manchester, England) in 1958. Given the mercilessly short shelf life of most rock and pop bands, who could've predicted that these siblings would not only still be together twenty years on from their inception but would be responsible in large part for the biggest selling soundtrack of all time? Yet that's exactly what happened. The BEE GEES (temporarily minus Robin) kicked off the 70s with their soundtrack to TV Rock Musical comedy, 'CUCUMBER CASTLE' (1970), featuring Blind Faith, LULU and even Spike Milligan. Although the three contributed a bevvy of tried and tested songs to the – all but forgotten – British teen romance, 'MELODY' (1971), during their initial burst of late 60s/early 70s success as a heavily Beatles-influenced pop act, the BEE GEES finally came good with 'SATURDAY NIGHT FEVER' (1977). In the wake of their Arif Mardin-abetted re-invention as mid-70s white boy funk pretenders, the BEE GEES really got on the good foot with this phenomenally popular disco exploitation movie, stealing the show on the soundtrack with some of the most enduring dancefloor numbers ever recorded. All the more unfortunate, then, that they had to go and contribute to the disaster that was 'SGT. PEPPER'S LONELY HEARTS CLUB BAND', the failed late 70s BEATLES tribute. Supplying half of the songs for similarly pilloried '. . .Fever' follow-up, 'STAYING ALIVE' (1983), was also a wrong move and one which effectively closed this phase of their career. Maurice and Barry continued on solo work and film soundtracks, 'A Breed Apart' (1984) and 'HAWKS' (1987) respectively. Although the BEE GEES as a group subsequently stayed away from soundtracks, they remain the most vivid example of a pop act marrying their songs to a movie. Few have done it with such style, and it's hard to imagine anyone doing it with such huge cultural and global impact in the future. *BG*

- **filmography** {acting}, etc.-

Cucumber Castle *(1970 OST =>)* / **Melody** *(1971 OST =>)* / **All This And World War II** *(1976 {*p BARRY} {*p ROBIN} {*p MAURICE} OST by V/A =>)* / **Saturday Night Fever** *(1977 OST by BEE GEES w/ V/A =>)* / **Sgt. Pepper's Lonely Hearts Club Band** *(1978 {*p BARRY} {*p ROBIN} {*p MAURICE} OST by V/A =>)* / **Staying Alive** *(1983 OST by BEE GEES w/ V/A =>)* / a Breed Apart *(1984 score by MAURICE GIBB =>)* / **Hawks** *(1987 OST by BARRY GIBB w/ John Cameron =>)*

BERNARDINE

1957 (US 94m) 20th Century Fox (PG)

Film genre: teen-Pop Musical comedy

Top guns: dir: Henry Levin → APRIL LOVE → WHERE THE BOYS ARE / s-w: Theodore Reeves (play: Mary Chase)

Stars: Pat Boone *(Arthur "Beau" Beaumont)* ← the PIED PIPER OF CLEVELAND / → APRIL LOVE, Terry Moore *(Jean Cantrick)*, Janet Gaynor *(Mrs. Ruth Wilson)*, Dean Jagger *(J. Fullerton Weldy)* → KING CREOLE → VANISHING POINT, Richard Sergent *(Sanford Wilson)* → LIVE A LITTLE, LOVE A LITTLE, James Drury *(Lt. Langley Beaumont)* ← LOVE ME TENDER, Ronnie Burns *(Griner)*, Jack Costanzo *(orchestra leader)*

Storyline: Arthur "Beau" Beaumont and his classmates sit at their desks and contemplate Bernardine, their "perfect girl", who they know is out there somewhere. Surprise surprise, when Arthur's mate Sanford meets telephone operator Jean he realizes she's the girl they've all been dreaming about and starts dating her. But gosh, it's nearly exam time and best friend Langley is told to keep Jean away from the other guys while Sanford does his swotting. But Jean is Langley's idea of the perfect girl too. *JZ*

Movie rating: *5.5

Visual: none (no audio OST)

Off the record: From this movie, **Pat Boone** scored his 4th US chart-topper with 'Love Letters In The Sand'.

– spinoff hits, etc. –

PAT BOONE: Love Letters In The Sand / Bernardine

Apr 57. (7"/78) *Dot; <15570> London; (HLD 8445)* [1] [14] Jun57 [2]

☐ Alan BERNHOFT segment
(⇒ the DR. JEKYLL & MR. HYDE ROCK 'N ROLL MUSICAL)

☐ Adele BERTEI segment
(⇒ the OFFENDERS)

the BEST LITTLE WHOREHOUSE IN TEXAS

1982 (US 114m) Universal Pictures (R)

Film genre: romantic Country/Pop Musical comedy

Top guns: s-w: Colin Higgins (+ dir) ← HAROLD AND MAUDE, Larry L. King & Peter Masterton (musical)

Stars: Burt Reynolds *(Sheriff Ed Earl Dodd)* ← DELIVERANCE / → BOOGIE NIGHTS → BROKEN BRIDGES, **Dolly PARTON** *(Mona Stangely)*, Dom DeLuise *(Melvin P. Thorpe)* ← WHO IS HARRY KELLERMAN AND WHY IS HE SAYING THOSE TERRIBLE THINGS ABOUT ME? ← NORWOOD, Charles Durning *(governor)* ← I WALK THE LINE / → FAR NORTH → DICK TRACY → O BROTHER, WHERE ART THOU?, **Jim Nabors** *(Deputy Fred)*, Robert Mandan *(Senator Charles Wingwood)*, Barry Corbin *(C.J.)* ← URBAN COWBOY / → HONKYTONK MAN → PERMANENT RECORD, **Mickey Jones** *(Henry)* → LIVING PROOF: THE HANK WILLIAMS JR. STORY / → SLING BLADE

Storyline: Gentlemen's club the Chicken Ranch moves from the New York stage to the Hollywood screen, but even then it's not safe from Christian right preachers and moral majority Texas authorities, as local sheriff – and enthusiastic patron – Ed Earl Dodd battles TV evangelist Melvin P. Thorpe's campaign for closure. *BG*

Movie rating: *5

Visuals: video + dvd

Off the record: Jim Nabors was an easy-listening actor-cum-balladeer whose LPs in the mid-60s sold quite well; most older people will remember him as Gomer Pyle in the popular Andy Griffith Show. *MCS*

—

Various Artists (composer: Carol Hall)

Jul 82. (lp/c) *M.C.A.; <MCA/+C 1499>* [63] [–]
– 20 fans (narration by JIM NABORS) / A lil' ole bitty pissant country place (DOLLY PARTON, TERESA MERRITT, THE WHOREHOUSE GIRLS & CUSTOMERS) / Sneakin' around (DOLLY PARTON AND BURT REYNOLDS) / Watching report – Texas has a whorehouse in it (DOM DeLUISE AND THE DOGETTES) / Courtyard shag / The Aggie song / The sidestep (CHARLES DURNING) / Hard candy Christmas (DOLLY PARTON AND THE WHOREHOUSE GIRLS) / I will always love you (DOLLY PARTON). *(UK-iss.Jan89 lp/c; MCA/+C 37218) (UK cd-iss. Jan89; MCAD 31007) <(cd re-iss. Mar03 on 'Universal'; AAMCAD 31007)>*

S/track review: Time Out's critical punchline – "stale air on a G-string" – is hard to trump, summing up the corn-shucking, Benny Hill-goes-Hair set pieces that also make up the clap-ridden meat and two veg of the soundtrack. DOLLY PARTON's cheek-chewing, buttermilk twang is better churned on less self-consciously-slapstick and more self-consciously-suffering material, but this was the early 80s and – with two catalogue classics – she's about all this album's got going for it. At just over half an hour, it's actually a mercifully short haul, and – if you programme out rubbish like 'The Aggie Song' – flounces by in no time. The jazz patina of Burt Reynolds duet, 'Sneakin' Around', gets under your skin like a bad case of scabies, 'Courtyard Shag' chafes satisfyingly against expectations for what turns out to be an almost Harry Nilsson/Van Dyke Parks-esque saloon bonanza, and then there's Oscar-winner Charles Durning's star turn, albeit weakened offscreen. As for madame DOLLY, she warbles a climactic ballad which, ironically, was to be afforded massive exposure way out of context, even more ironically by way of another soundtrack. We are, of course, talking 'I Will Always Love You'; if you've never heard the original, you're in for a wee country treat, a homespun ode to everlasting lurve which bears little trace of Whitney's all-conquering, subtlety-strangling bombast. And then there's 'Hard Candy Christmas', a Carol Hall composition from the original stage show, transfigured by DOLLY into one of the most poignant entries in what wasn't exactly a golden era in her recording career. *BG*

Album rating: *6

– spinoff hits, etc. –

DOLLY PARTON: I Will Always Love You / (non-OST song)

Jul 82. (7") *R.C.A.; <13260> (RCA 270)* [53] Sep82 [ ]

☐ BEYOND THE DOORS alt.
(⇒ DOWN ON US)

BEYOND THE SEA

2004 (US/Ger/UK 121m) Lions Gate Films (PG-13)

Film genre: Pop-music/showbiz bio-pic drama

Top guns: s-w: Kevin Spacey (+ dir) ← ALBINO ALLIGATOR, Lewis Colick

Stars: Kevin Spacey *(Bobby Darin)* ← ORDINARY DECENT CRIMINAL ← WORKING GIRL, Kate Bosworth *(Sandra Dee)*, John Goodman *(Steve Blauner)* ← OVERNIGHT ← MASKED AND ANONYMOUS ← STORYTELLING ← the EMPEROR'S NEW GROOVE ← COYOTE UGLY ← O BROTHER, WHERE ART THOU? ← BLUES BROTHERS 2000 ← TRUE STORIES ← SWEET DREAMS, Bob Hoskins *(Charlie Cassotto Maffia)* ← SPICEWORLD ← the WALL / → DANNY THE DOG, Brenda Blethyn *(Polly Cassotto)*, Greta Scacchi *(Mary Duvan)*, Caroline Aaron *(Nina Cassotto Maffia)* ← PRIMARY COLORS ← THIS IS MY LIFE ← WORKING GIRL

Storyline: Playing as fast and loose with time and ageing as the contemporaneous Cole Porter bio-pic, 'De-Lovely', the movie at least broaches the thorny subject of being too old in the opening scenes, cutting back to Darin's boyhood sickbed and his introduction to music. All grown up, disconcertingly high-kicking in red trousers and armed with "a public relations man who had never related to the public", he makes it to toupee teen idol status through sheer force of will. Nightclub crooning is his real vocation, though, and he's soon bewitching diamond-studded crowds with the itchy mannerisms of 'Mack The Knife'. His tenacious character nets him the waif-ish Sandra Dee as his stratospheric career culminates in an Oscar nomination. The 60s are less kind and it's not long before his reinvention as an anti-war folk singer has him as the butt of sneering audiences. The identity crisis deepens when it emerges that his sister is actually his mother, but his heart is stout enough for one final Vegas fling. *BG*

Movie rating: *6.5

Visual: dvd

Off the record: BOBBY DARIN (see above)

—

KEVIN SPACEY & the John Wilson Orchestra

Nov 04. (cd) *Atco; <(8122 78444-2)>* ☐ ☐
– Hello young lovers / Once upon a time / Fabulous places / Simple song of freedom / Mack the knife / Beyond the sea / By myself – When your lover has gone / Some of these days / Change / If I were a carpenter / Artificial flowers / That's all / Dream lover / Splish splash / Lazy river / Charade / As long as I'm singing / The curtain falls.

S/track review: KEVIN SPACEY, the high priest of sardonica, assuming the trip and tux of Bobby Darin? It's an improbable fit, made all the more improbable by SPACEY's careworn countenance. But then you won't see his coupon on the soundtrack, only a voice that exhumes Darin with real ardour and phantom accuracy. As contemporaneous Cole Porter biopic, 'De-Lovely', proved, faithfully arranged big-band/supper-club material is still Hollywood's best friend; SPACEY throws himself into it body and soul, but it's the Darin/Tim Hardin dynamic that supplies some of the real story's most fascinating marginalia, and inspires some of Spacey's most poignant performances. Sharing more than a death before their time, Darin and Hardin supplied each other with their respective final hits (no pun intended in Hardin's case): Darin's protest anthem, 'Simple Song Of Freedom' was, in fact, Hardin's only hit, and Darin made the Top 10 in 1966 with Hardin signature, 'If I Were A Carpenter'. While it's perhaps difficult to reconcile the actor's trademark ambiguity with Brill Building fluff like 'Splish Splash', archetypal SPACEY is more easily disseminated in the wandering, what-if rumination of '..Carpenter', or Darin's perversely buoyant murder-ballad-turned-big-band blast, 'Mack The Knife'. Other highlights include a billowing 'Dream Lover' and victorious title track, proof that Spacey's devotion to his subject matter is above and beyond the call of duty. *BG*

Album rating: *7

BEYOND THE VALLEY OF THE DOLLS

1970 (US 110m) 20th Century Fox (18)

Film genre: Pop/Rock-music showbiz/seXploitation satire/comedy

Top guns: s-w: Russ Meyer (+ dir), Roger Ebert

Stars: Dolly Read *(Kelly MacNamara)* ← TONITE LET'S ALL MAKE LOVE IN LONDON, Cynthia Myers *(Casey Anderson)*, Marcia McBroom *(Petronella Danforth)* → COME BACK, CHARLESTON BLUE → JESUS CHRIST SUPERSTAR → WILLIE DYNAMITE, John LaZar *(Ronnie "Z-Man" Barzell)*, Michael Blodgett *(Lance Rocke)* ← BEYOND THE VALLEY OF THE DOLLS ← the TRIP / → DISCO FEVER, David Gurian *(Harris Allsworth)*, Edy Williams *(Ashley St. Ives)* ← GOOD TIMES ← PARADISE, HAWAIIAN STYLE, Erica Gavin *(Roxanne)*, Harrison Page *(Emerson Thorne)* → TROUBLE MAN, Jim Iglehart *(Randy Black)* → SAVAGE!, Charles Napier *(Baxter Wolfe)* → the BLUES BROTHERS → SPIRIT: STALLION OF THE CIMARRON, Pamela Grier *(partygoer)* → BLACK MAMA, WHITE MAMA → COOL BREEZE → COFFY → FOXY BROWN → FRIDAY FOSTER → SHEBA, BABY → BUCKTOWN → BILL & TED'S BOGUS JOURNEY → JACKIE BROWN → BONES, **the Carrie Nations** *(themselves)*, **Strawberry Alarm Clock** *(themselves)* ← PSYCH-OUT

Storyline: "You're a groovy boy, I'd like to strap you on sometime"; Hollywood Babylon never looked – or sounded – so peerlessly trashy, or so blackly comic. Meyer's major studio one-off follows the rise, fall and redemption of three rock chicks and their naïve manager, with Kelly McNamara as chief rock chick, buxom, doe-eyed and the proud owner of one of the best transatlantic-mangling accents in B-movie history. Together with bassist Casey, Afro-funky drummer Petronella, and lover cum manager Harris, she heads for the industry sleazepit of L.A. where her fashionista aunt reveals she has a claim on an inheritance. Poor old David is out of the game almost as soon as he arrives, usurped by transexual svengali Rodney 'Z-Man' Barzell, a dude fond of throwing decadent soirees and spouting brilliant Shakespearian verbiage. Throw into the mix insatiable porn star Ashley St. Ives, a bronzed gigolo named Lance Rocke and the motliest bunch of freaks this side of the Manson Family, and the girlzzz – renamed the Carrie Nations – are soon up to their crotches in sex and substance abuse, lost in "the oft times nightmare world of show business". Kelly even gives it up for the balding lawyer holding up her money and only comes to her senses when David – looking up from a near fatal bottom – tries to end it all on live TV. While matters reach a bloody climax as Barzell gets his hooters out and goes on a murderous rampage, it all comes good in the end with the kind of priceless, moose-voiced faux-moralising that Scooby Doo could only have dreamt of. Look out for the Pam Grier cameo. *BG*

Movie rating: *7.5

Off the record: Strawberry Alarm Clock from Santa Barbara, California, consisted of Ed King (future Lynyrd Skynyrd guitarist), Lee Freeman (guitar), Mark Weitz (keyboards), Gary Lovetro + George Bunnel (bass) and Randy Seol (drums). With the Shapes 16-year-old singer, Greg Munford, the band topped the charts in 1967 with 'Incense And Peppermints' – a classic psychedelic song from the flower-power era. *MCS*

—

Various Artists (score: STU PHILLIPS *)

Nov 70. (lp) *Stateside; <(SSL 10311)>* ☐ Jan71 ☐
– Main title sequence (*) / Find it (the CARRIE NATIONS) / Come with the gentle people (the CARRIE NATIONS) / Dinner party (*) / Girl from the city (STRAWBERRY ALARM CLOCK) / I'm comin' home (STRAWBERRY ALARM CLOCK) / Ampersand (*) / Sweet talking candy man (the CARRIE NATIONS) / In the long run (the CARRIE NATIONS) / Back stage (*) / Hang cool teddybear! (*) / Late night visit (*) / Look on up at the bottom (*). *<(cd-iss. Jun97 on 'Screen Gold'+=; SGLDCD 0010)>* – Groupie Girl *(cd re-iss. Mar03 on 'Harkit'+=; HRKCD 8032)* – Find it – movie version (the CARRIE NATIONS) / Randy throws in the towel / I need you so very much – Checkmate / Let the games begin! / Methinks you remind me of certain things . . . / I am Superwoman! / Murder on the beach / Gun stroke / Beyond The Valley Of The Dolls theme (the SANDPIPERS) / Sweet talkin' candy man (movie version) (the CARRIE NATIONS) / Come with the gentle people (movie version) (the CARRIE NATIONS) / Look on up at the bottom (movie version) (the CARRIE NATIONS). *<cd re-iss. Aug04 on 'Sound Track Classics';*

S/track review: One of the juiciest sleevenote snippets in the superb, patience-of-Job-awaited re-issue is screenwriter Roger Ebert's anecdote on Johnny Rotten, recounting how he and Russ Meyer were "non-plussed" when the Sex Pistols' frontman admitted "that he liked Beyond The Valley Of The Dolls because it was so true to life". Perhaps Rotten was really talking about the soundtrack, dominated as it is by one of the meanest girl groups ever to stalk Hollywood. Rock bands have long taken to naming themselves after Meyer movies (Faster Pussycat and Mudhoney to name two), but the CARRIE NATIONS were a 100% Meyer creation, a technicolour wet dream gone stereo. And the great-but-daft 'Come

With The Gentle People' aside, they were no Spinal Tap, or at least they didn't get caught stuffing cotton wool down their bras. LYNNE CAREY (whose vocals were substituted on the original over contractual wrangles with her management) admittedly treads a bollock-rupturing fine line, challenging old Percy Page himself with a Valhalla-terrorising intro to the raucous 'Find It'. The lady's Grace Slick-meets-Nico wail likewise scours its own potential on the garage-funk-anthemic 'Look On Up At The Bottom' and the peerless 'Sweet Talkin' Candy Man' ("he's talkin' good-ahhh!!!"), workin' the kind of proto-riot grrrrrl mojo that real life psyche-popsters the STRAWBERRY ALARM CLOCK – good as 'I'm Comin' Home' and the Beatles-y 'City Girl' are – can't touch. Just as Meyer liked his films to straddle various genres simultaneously, he perversely preferred his soundtracks "to have as little continuity as possible", or so claims composer STU PHILLIPS in his notes. What you end up with then, is a Wagnerian opening that cheekily snatches a few bars of 'Ride Of The Valkyries' before segueing into the deliciously fey, SANDPIPERS-do-Ferrero Rocher main theme. Faithful to Meyers' brief, PHILLIPS punctuates the psych numbers with beautifully worked cocktail-symphonies, soul jazz and some demonically swinging big band material (check the shamelessly Mancini-esque 'Murder On The Beach'). He even manages to dissociate Paul Dukas' galumphing 'Let The Games Begin' from its Walt Disney context, and somehow it all hangs together, like a late 60s concept album that actually works. And as a concept album, you don't need to be able to grasp the concept – nor even see the film, though it's mandatory before-you-die viewing – to appreciate this soundtrack for the priceless cultural artefact it is. *BG*

Album rating: *8

the BIG BEAT

1958 (US 81m b&w) Universal Pictures

Film genre: Rock'n'roll Musical comedy

Top guns: dir: William J. Cowen / s-w: David P. Harmon

Stars: William Reynolds *(John Randall)*, Andra Martin *(Nikki Collins)*, **Gogi Grant** *(Cindy Adams)*, Bill Goodwin *(Joseph Randall)*, Jeffrey Stone *(Danny Phillips)*, Rose Marie *(May Gordon)*, Hans Conried *(Vladimir Skilsky)*, Howard Miller *(himself)* ← JAMBOREE, Steve Drexel *(piano player)* → HOT ROD GANG, **Fats DOMINO** *(performer)*, **the Diamonds:- Dave Somerville, Ted Kowalski, Phil Leavitt, Bill Reed** *(performers)*, **the Mills Brothers** *(performers)*, **Carl Tjader** *(performer)*, **Harry James** *(performer)*, **George Shearing** *(performer)*, **Buddy Bregman** *(performer)*

Storyline: John Randall is a young record executive who works for his father Joseph. John is determined to prove to his stuffy dad that the future is in rock'n'roll, and with the help of his secretary and admirer Nikki he books the top acts of the 1950s to put on a show to remember. Will the great Fats Domino and the Mills Bros be enough to show daddy-o that he's a square by the day's standards. *JZ*

Movie rating: *5

Visual: video (no audio LP; score: Henry Mancini)

Off the record: Jazz singer, **Gogi Grant** (b. Myrtle Audrey Arinsberg, 20th September, 1924, Philadelphia, Pennsylvania) had a flirtation with pop music when she topped the charts in 1956 with 'The Wayward Wind'. The **Diamonds** were Canada's biggest R'n'R exports at the time (next to the Crew-Cuts and also from Toronto), although covering popular doo wop numbers was their forte. Frankie Lymon's 'Why Do Fools Fall In Love', the Gladiolas' 'Little Darlin' and Buddy Holly's 'Words Of Love', were all hits just prior to this film, although they had a dance original, 'The Stroll', which hit US Top 5; in 1961, the group's Dave Somerville went solo. Old style acts such as the **Mills Brothers, Buddy Bregman, George Shearing, Carl Tjader & Harry James** were also featured in the movie. *MCS*

– spinoff releases, etc. –

FATS DOMINO: The Big Beat

Dec 57. (7",78) *Imperial; <5477> London; (HLP 8575)* [26] Mar58 [20]

GOGI GRANT: The Big Beat EP

1958. (7"ep) *R.C.A.; <EPA 4185>* [ ] [–]

□ BIG COMMOTION!
(⇒ the SPIDERS filmography)

BIG DREAMS & BROKEN HEARTS: THE DOTTIE WEST STORY

1995 (US 90m* TV) CBS Entertainment

Film genre: Country-music bio-pic/drama

Top guns: dir: Bill D'Elia / s-w: Theresa Rodgerton

Stars: Michele Lee *(Dottie West)*, **Kenny Rogers** *(himself)*, Rhoda Griffis *(Diane March)* → BROKEN BRIDGES, David James Elliott *(Byron Metcalf)*, **Larry Gatlin** *(performer)*, **Chet Atkins** *(himself)* → IN DREAMS, **Kris KRISTOFFERSON** *(himself)*, **Larry Gatlin** *(himself)*, **Loretta Lynn** *(herself)* ← NASHVILLE REBEL, **Dolly PARTON** *(herself)*, **Willie NELSON** *(himself)*, William Russ *(Bill West)* ← the BORDER / → COME ON, GET HAPPY: THE PARTRIDGE FAMILY STORY, Lisa Akey *(Shelly West)*, Tere Myers *(Patsy Cline)*, Norm Woodel *(Jim Reeves)*, Stuart Greer *(Owen)* ← CROCODILE SHOES / → ELVIS

Storyline: Just what it says on the tin, the sad story of Nashville C&W star, Dottie West. Backed by a plethora of "real" country stars, acting as themselves, it's a sort of warts'n'all depiction of life as a rags to riches C&W/ pop star. *MCS*

Movie rating: *6

Visual: video (no audio OST; score: Edgar Struble)

Off the record: If one told you the tragic life of **Dottie West**, it would certainly spoil the thread of the film.

– helpful release –

DOTTIE WEST: The Essential Dottie West

Jan 96. (cd/c) *R.C.A.; <66782>* [ ] [ ]
– Love is no excuse / Here comes my baby back again / Would you hold it against me / What's come over my baby / Me today and her tomorrow / Mommy, can I still call him daddy / Paper mansions / His eye is on the sparrow / Like a fool / Childhood places / Country girl / Reno / Rings of gold / There's a story (goin' round) / Forever yours / Slowly / Six weeks every summer (Christmas every other year) / Country sunshine / House of love / Last time I saw him.

BIG MONEY HUTLA

INSANE CLOWN POSSE: BIG MONEY HUTLA

2000 (US 97m) Non-Homogenized / Island Def Jam Music Group (15)

Film genre: gangster/crime caper

Top guns: dir: John Cafiero → RAMONES: RAW / s-w: **Violent J** as Joseph Bruce

Stars: Insane Clown Posse:- Violent J *(Big Baby Sweets / Ape Boy)*, **Shaggy 2 Dope** *(Sugar Bear)* / Johnny Brennan *(Chief of Police)*, Rudy Ray Moore *(Dolemite)* ← JACKIE'S BACK! ← DISCO GODFATHER ← PETEY WHEATSTRAW ← the MONKEY HUSTLE ← DOLEMITE, Mick Foley *(Cactus Sac)*, Fred Berry *(Bootleg Greg)*, Kamal Ahmed *(Kissel)*, Jump Steady *(Hack Benjamin / etc.)*, Harland Williams *(Officer Harry Cox)* ← WAG THE DOG, Alex Abbiss *(Hazad)*, **Twiztid:- Monoxide Child** *(Lil' Poot)*, **Jamie**

Madrox *(Big Stank)* / **Myzery** *(Green Willie)*, Floyd Vivino *(Uncle Floyd)* ← GOOD MORNING, VIETNAM / → RAMONES: RAW, **Mike E. Clark** *(himself)*, **the Misfits:- Jerry Only, Michale Graves, Doyle Wolfgang von Frankenstein, Dr. Chud** *(themselves)*

Storyline: Poetic cop Sugar Bear is summoned from the streets of San Francisco to rid New York of crime boss Big Baby Sweets. His task is not helped by the fact that his two sidekicks appear to be uniformly hopeless, but never mind – the ghost of Dolemite is on hand to spook out the villains and stop them from clowning around (even though Dolemite ain't quite dead yet). *JZ*

Movie rating: *5

Visual: video + dvd (no audio OST; score: Mike E. Clark)

Off the record: Insane Clown Posse were formed in Detroit, Michigan, USA . . . 1989 as the Inner City Posse, by Shaggy 2 Dope and Violent J, two face-painted rappers with er . . . a wicked sense of fun. They changed their moniker in 1992, releasing their debut album 'Carnival Of Carnage' the same year. Championed by the metal press, INSANE CLOWN POSSE are basically nevertheless a dyed-in-the-wool rap duo, albeit an extremely offensive one with a bizarre line in twisted circus trappings. Following a little contretemps with the Walt Disney corporation (and a short-lived spell with 'Jive' records), the gruesome jokers delivered their breakthrough release, 'The Great Milenko' in 1997, although this initially ran into difficulties with the all-powerful moral majority (their old record company recalling all copies due to its offensive content). Predictably, sales of the album (released by 'Island') soared, culminating in a US Top 75 placing. 1998 saw a further couple of minor UK hit singles while 'The Amazing Jeckel Brothers' (1999) amazingly made the US Top 5. Yet the posse's most ambitious moment was still to come: in the year 2000, the jokers released 'Bizzar' – accompanied by the US-only 'Bizaar'. Confused? You might well be, especially by the former's choice of cover material, a reading of the 80s Sly Fox hit, 'Let's Go All The Way'. If Beavis And Butt-Head were still running their TV show, the INSANE ones would be up there for all to see. Others in their first and only venture into celluloid were, Alex Abbiss, head of their record label, 'Psychopath', which included in the ranks similar rap-rock acts, **Twiztid** and **Myzery** (only one EP in 1998, 'Para La Isla'); label songwriter/producer, **Mike E. Clark**, was also on board. Johnny Brennan & Kamal Ahmed are noneother than comic/ phone-prank duo the Jerky Boys. *MCS*

BIGGER THAN TINA

1999 (Aus 91m) Backyard Productions / Palace Films

Film genre: showbiz/Pop-music mockumentary/satire

Top guns: s-w + dir: Neil Foley

Stars: Michael Dalley *(Dan Vardy-Cobb)*, Sally Lightfoot *(Chrystal Furnon)*, Anni Finsterer *(Jacinta Fellows)* ← TO HAVE AND TO HOLD / → QUEEN OF THE DAMNED, Fraser Gray *(Wes Grieves)*, Barry Friedlander *(John Vardy-Cobb)*, Philippa Chapple *(Bridget Vardy-Cobb)*, John Murphy *(Arthur Furnon)* ← DOGS IN SPACE ← GIVE MY REGARDS TO BROAD STREET, Steve Adams *(Mick Jewell)*, Pam Murphy *(Vi Furnon)*

Storyline: Aussie new age warrior Dan Vardy-Cobb is "discovered" by a record company talent spotter at a local show. Deciding that a showbiz career has more to offer than working at his dad's lawnmower shop, he ploughs all his money into producing his first album. However it soon becomes apparent that Dan's talent only stretches to one song, and his album is a disaster. Things get even worse when a shopping mall gig becomes a heckler's paradise. *JZ*

Movie rating: *5

Visual: video

Off the record: (see below)

—

Various Artists/Cast inc. DAN VARDY-COBB (*)

1999. (cd) *Festival; (D 32148)* [–] Austra [–]
– Bigger than Tina II (the FAUVES) / We can get together (CUSTARD with *) / Better the devil you know (the MEANIES feat. *) / State of the heart (POLLYANNA feat. *) / Bigger than Tina I (the FAUVES) / Am I ever gonna see your face again (MACH PELICAN feat. *) / We can't be beaten (28 DAYS feat. *) / Science fiction (MOLER feat. *) / Love is blindness – radio edit (the DUMPMASTERS feat. DVC) / Sound of your heart (REBECCA'S EMPIRE feat. *) / Chrystalized (by your touch) (* AND THE DEEVEECEES) / Goodbye (* AND THE DEEVEECEES) / Ways of love (* AND THE DEEVEECEES) / Prisoner of love (* AND THE DEEVEECEES) / Send me an angel (HONEYSMACK feat. DVC). *(bonus +=)* – Love is blindness – extended (the DUMPMASTERS feat. DVC).

S/track review: 'BIGGER THAN TINA' is pretty much filled with anonymous Australian bands that for all intents and purposes, at least based on this album, should remain anonymous. The FAUVES, CUSTARD, the MEANIES, POLLYANNA and MACH PELICAN anyone? All of them seem to be attempting to sound like British/American indie bands from the 80s, like the Pixies, early R.E.M. or Teenage Fanclub, although they fail to grasp any of the qualities that make those bands great. None of the songs here stand out at all, preferring to merge into one another creating a dull, lifeless monotone. There is little in the way of energy, intensity or anything for that matter. Most of the bands are accompanied by the fictional "star" of the film, which is barely noticeable, either on the sleeve notes or in the songs themselves, and the appearance of the main star, who goes by the name of DAN VARDY-COBB, and his band will only have you reaching for the razorblades, or at very least the skip button. Whatever you do, do not buy this album, it's certified bargain bin material. *CM*

Album rating: *1

– spinoff singles, etc. –

LES FAUVES: Bigger Than Tina I / Bigger Than Tina II

1999. (cd-s) [–] Austra [–]

BIKINI BEACH

1964 sequel-2 (US 100m) American International Pictures (PG)

Film genre: romantic teen Pop Musical comedy

Top guns: s-w: William Asner (+ dir) ← MUSCLE BEACH PARTY ← BEACH PARTY / → BEACH BLANKET BINGO → HOW TO STUFF A WILD BIKINI, Robert Dillon ← MUSCLE BEACH PARTY, Leo Townsend → BEACH BLANKET BINGO → HOW TO STUFF A WILD BIKINI

Stars: Frankie AVALON *(Frankie / Potato bug)*, **ANNETTE Funicello** *(Dee Dee)*, Martha Hyer *(Vivien Clements)*, Keenan Wynn *(Harvey Huntington Honeywagon III)* → NASHVILLE → the LAST UNICORN, Harvey Lembeck *(Eric Von Zipper)* ← BEACH PARTY / → PAJAMA PARTY → BEACH BLANKET BINGO → HOW TO STUFF A WILD BIKINI → the GHOST IN THE INVISIBLE BIKINI → HELLO DOWN THERE, Don Rickles *(Big Drag)* ← MUSCLE BEACH PARTY / → PAJAMA PARTY → BEACH BLANKET BINGO, John Ashley *(Johnny)* ← MUSCLE BEACH PARTY ← BEACH PARTY ← HOT ROD GANG / → BEACH BLANKET BINGO → HOW TO STUFF A WILD BIKINI, **Candy Johnson** *(Candy)* ← MUSCLE BEACH PARTY ← BEACH PARTY / → PAJAMA PARTY, Jody McCrea *(Deadhead)* ← MUSCLE BEACH PARTY ← BEACH PARTY / → PAJAMA PARTY → BEACH BLANKET BINGO → HOW TO STUFF A WILD BIKINI, Meredith MacRae *(animal)* ← BEACH PARTY / → NORWOOD → the CENSUS TAKER, Boris Karloff *(art dealer)* → the GHOST IN THE INVISIBLE BIKINI, **Donna Loren** *(Donna)* ← MUSCLE BEACH PARTY / → PAJAMA PARTY → BEACH BLANKET BINGO, Luree Holmes *(beach girl)* ← MUSCLE BEACH PARTY ← BEACH PARTY / → PAJAMA PARTY → BEACH BLANKET BINGO → SKI PARTY → HOW TO STUFF A WILD BIKINI → the GHOST IN THE INVISIBLE BIKINI → THUNDER ALLEY → the TRIP, Salli Sachse *(beach girl)* ← MUSCLE BEACH PARTY / → PAJAMA PARTY → BEACH BLANKET BINGO → SKI PARTY → HOW TO STUFF A WILD BIKINI → the GHOST IN THE INVISIBLE BIKINI → THUNDER

ALLEY → the TRIP → WILD IN THE STREETS, Linda Rogers *(Rat Pack member)* ← BEACH PARTY / → PAJAMA PARTY → TICKLE ME → WINTER A-GO-GO → WILD, WILD WINTER, Patti Chandler *(beach girl)* → PAJAMA PARTY → BEACH BLANKET BINGO → SKI PARTY → HOW TO STUFF A WILD BIKINI, Michael Nader *(beach boy)* ← MUSCLE BEACH PARTY ← BEACH PARTY / → PAJAMA PARTY → BEACH BLANKET BINGO → SKI PARTY → HOW TO STUFF A WILD BIKINI → the TRIP, **Little Stevie WONDER** *(himself)*, **the Pyramids** *(themselves)*, Mary Hughes *(beach girl)* ← MUSCLE BEACH PARTY / → PAJAMA PARTY → BEACH BLANKET BINGO → SKI PARTY → HOW TO STUFF A WILD BIKINI → THUNDER ALLEY → DOUBLE TROUBLE

Storyline: Feckless Frankie finds himself yet another love rival, this time in the form of English rock star the Potato Bug. He wins Dee Dee over after singing to her but that's just the start of Frankie's problems. A millionaire developer wants to clear the beach for his own purposes, and uses his pet monkey Clyde to show that American teenagers behave worse than apes. Finally a win-or-bust drag race is the only way to settle the feud between Frankie and the Bug. *JZ*

Movie rating: *4.5

Visual: video + dvd

Off the record: Songs from the movie, not the soundtrack: 'Love's A Secret Weapon' (DONNA LOREN), 'Gimmie Your Love' (FRANKIE AVALON & ANNETTE FUNICELLO), 'How About That?' (the PYRAMIDS), 'Happy Feeling (Dance And Shout)' (LITTLE STEVIE WONDER), 'Bikini Drag' (FRANKIE AVALON), 'Record Run' (FRANKIE AVALON), 'Got You Where I Want You' (the EXCITERS BAND) and 'Because You're You' (FRANKIE AVALON & ANNETTE FUNICELLO). Go-go dancer, **Candy Johnson** (favorite color pink) released a few singles including a version of Elvis' 'Hound Dog'. *MCS*

—

ANNETTE: At Bikini Beach (composer: Les Baxter)

Sep 64. (lp) *Buena Vista; <BV/STER 3324>*
– Bikini beach / Because you're you / Secret weapon / This time it's love / How about that / Happy feeling / The Clyde / Let's twist again / The Wah Watusi / Blame it on the bossa nova / The Jamaica ska / The monkey's uncle.

S/track review: One thing that strikes you when you see the cover shot of 'BIKINI BEACH' (another in the long-line of "BEACH PARTY" movies), is that Disney "it"-girl ANNETTE (Funicello) is not in bikini pose, rather a flowery-patterned, parent-approved one-piece, suggesting – as they say in Bonnie Scotland – that she "dis-nae" (sorry – ed!). As usual (like in many of the "BEACH PARTY" genre), it's a mixture of songs from the movie itself and other outsider tracks, the latter ilk stemming via generic early 60s dance routines, "the twist", "the bossa-nova", "the Jamaica ska" and one cue that particularily appeals to my Caledonian side, "The Clyde". Concentrating strictly on Side One's OST numbers, composers Styner-Hemric are behind ANNETTE's finest on show, 'Because You're You', a love-ly mezzo soprano ballad that somewhat overshadowed her other pieces, 'Secret Weapon', 'This Time It's Love' and the title track. While you can expect to pay over $100 for the privilege – if that's the right term – to own a copy of the album, hold your breath for the price of the private pressing of CANDY JOHNSON's version: $649.99 and that's not mint. If you've seen the four "BEACH PARTY" flicks she's appeared in (as a blonde bimbette in skimpy two-piece), there just might be a reason behind this madness, the other is that 'Can-Jo' her label only saw fit to release a limited number of records. *MCS*

Album rating: *3 / Candy Johnson *2

– spinoff releases, etc. –

ANNETTE: Bikini Beach Party / The Clyde

Sep 64. (7") *<F 436>*

ANNETTE: The Wah Watusi / The Clyde

Oct 64. (7") *<F 437>*

CANDY JOHNSON & HER EXCITERS: The Candy Johnson Show At Bikini Beach

Sep 64. (lp) *CanJo; <LRLP 1002>*
– Bikini beach / Two-timin' angel / Secret weapon / Gimme your love / Looney gooney bird / Dreams that never come true / Gotcha where I want you / Happy feeling / This time it's love / How about that / Because you're you / Little heartbreaker.

CANDY JOHNSON & HER EXCITERS: Because You're You / Gotcha Where I Want You

Oct 64. (7") *CanJo; <C 105>*

BILL & TED'S BOGUS JOURNEY

1991 (US 93m) Orion Pictures Corporation (PG)

Film genre: teen comedy/sci-fi fantasy

Top guns: dir: Peter Hewitt / s-w: Chris Matheson & Ed Solomon ← BILL & TED'S EXCELLENT ADVENTURE

Stars: Keanu Reeves *(Ted "Theodore" Logan)* ← BILL & TED'S EXCELLENT ADVENTURE ← PERMANENT RECORD / → EVEN COWGIRLS GET THE BLUES → THUMBSUCKER, Alex Winter *(Bill S. Preston, Esq. / Evil Bill / Granny Preston)* ← BILL & TED'S EXCELLENT ADVENTURE, William Sadler *(Grim Reaper)* → RUSH → TRESPASS → REACH THE ROCK, George Carlin *(Rufus)* ← BILL & TED'S EXCELLENT ADVENTURE ← CAR WASH, Joss Ackland *(Chuck DeNomolos)* ← IT COULDN'T HAPPEN HERE ← the APPLE, Pam Grier *(Ms. Wardroe)* ← SHEBA, BABY ← BUCKTOWN ← FRIDAY FOSTER ← FOXY BROWN ← COFFY ← COOL BREEZE ← BLACK MAMA, WHITE MAMA ← BEYOND THE VALLEY OF THE DOLLS / → JACKIE BROWN → BONES, David Carrera *(Ted's Double)*, Jeff Miller *(Bill's Double)*, Amy Stock-Poynton *(Missy Logan)* ← BILL & TED'S EXCELLENT ADVENTURE, William Shatner *(James T. Kirk)*, Ed Cambridge *(George Washington Carver)* ← FRIDAY FOSTER ← TROUBLE MAN ← MELINDA ← the FINAL COMEDOWN ← COOL BREEZE, **Taj MAHAL** *(gatekeeper)*, Michael 'Shrimp' Chambers *(good robot Bill)* ← BREAKIN' 2: ELECTRIC BOOGALOO ← BREAKIN', Ed Gale *(station #1)* ← HOWARD THE DUCK / → O BROTHER, WHERE ART THOU?, **Primus:- Les Claypool** *(performer)* → WOODSTOCK 94 → PINK AS THE DAY SHE WAS BORN → WE SOLD OUR SOULS FOR ROCK 'N ROLL → RISING LOW → ELECTRIC APRICOT: QUEST FOR FESTEROO, **Tim "Herb" Alexander & Larry Lalonde** *(performers)*

Storyline: In the 27th century evil mastermind De Nomolos is fed up with everyone being nice to each other, thanks to the legendary Bill and Ted. He builds two time-travelling clones to terminate them and take their place, ensuring chaos in his own world. Bill and Ted are immediately bumped off and find themselves having to escape from Hell and plead their case to God. Can they stop the "evil" Bill and Ted from winning the Battle of the Bands and incidentally save the Universe along the way? *JZ*

Movie rating: *5.5

Visual: video + dvd

Off the record: **Primus** went on to have two US Top 10 albums, 'Pork Soda' (1993) and 'Tales From The Punchbowl' (1995).

—

Various Artists (score: David Newman)

Jul 91. (cd/c/lp) *Interscope; <(7567 91725-2/-4/-1)>* **28** Jan92 **3**
– Shout it out (SLAUGHTER) / Battle stations (WINGER) / God gave rock and roll to you II (KISS) / Drinking again (NEVERLAND) / Dream of a new day (RICHIE KOTZEN) / The reaper (STEVE VAI) / The perfect crime (FAITH NO MORE) / Go to hell (MEGADETH) / Tommy the cat (PRIMUS) / Junior's gone wild (KING'S X) / Showdown (LOVE ON ICE) / The reaper rap (STEVE VAI).

S/track review: You love hard rock, right? You have a backcombed hairstyle? Then this is the soundtrack for you, as self-consciously reverential and ridiculous in its love of hard rock as the film's eponymous heroes. A snaking bass line and defiant stomp announce

SLAUGHTER's 'Shout It Out' with brash confidence, a slice of unashamed preening hard rock, indulging its squealing guitars and overt cheesiness, even breaking into a swinging, good times outro. WINGER bring more virtuosity to the table in 'Battle Stations', and somehow manage to make the genre's trademark multi-layered choruses shine more brightly in the process. Well, what can you say about KISS and 'God Gave Rock And Roll To You II'? True titans of the genre, this is either the greatest anthem ever penned in the name of Rock, or the nadir of an execrable movement. Either way its hooks are positively deadly, the chorus a true killer. Whereas NEVERLAND have been 'Drinking Again' and are drunk on stadium rock excess, RICHIE KOTZEN brings a whiskey-soaked rawness to 'Dream Of A New Day' that in its slinking blues rock licks recalls vintage Robin Trower, sadly besmirched by the mandatory synth accompaniment. STEVE VAI brings some true class and maverick musicianship to the party, 'The Reaper' showcases his always fluid, astonishingly deft guitar playing. Not just for the geeks, he brings colour and personality to his variation of shred soloing, his glissandos are perfectly histrionic and he extracts fire from the overdriven squeals. From one maverick to another, Mike Patton's peerless voice and melodic instinct make FAITH NO MORE's 'The Perfect Crime' an urgent and necessary heavy funk-rock hybrid, built upon a churning, percussive bass line, overlaid with razorwire guitars and tastefully (hear that WINGER?) embellished with keys. Metal rears its moody head with MEGADETH's 'Go To Hell', opening with a series of neo-classical fretboard ascents and descents, as Dave Mustaine sneers in customarily petulant fashion, the rhythm section keeping everything locked down into a rock solid mid tempo groove, all the better for the solos to spiral over. Les Claypool's wet, funky basslines single 'Tommy The Cat' out as the real oddity of the collection, its rhythmic contortions, searing guitar work and melodic unorthodoxy setting PRIMUS a class apart from the hairspray pack. KING'S X deliver a punchy, heavy going cut with 'Junior's Gone Wild', whereas LOVE ON ICE's 'Showdown' is overlong and fights a losing battle. VAI returns, and although 'The Reaper Rap' re-hashes his earlier contribution with excerpts of dialogue from the film, the musicianship is still exemplary. *DF*

Album rating: *6.5

– spinoff hits, etc. –

KISS: God Gave Rock And Roll To You II / KING'S X: Junior's Gone Wild

Jan 92. (7") *(A 8696)* [–] [4]
(12"+=/cd-s+=) *(A 8696 T/CD)* – SLAUGHTER: Shout It Out.

BILL & TED'S EXCELLENT ADVENTURE

1989 (US 90m) Orion Pictures Corporation (PG)

Film genre: teen comedy/sci-fi fantasy

Top guns: dir: Stephen Herek → ROCK STAR / s-w: Chris Matheson & Ed Solomon → BILL & TED'S BOGUS JOURNEY

Stars: Keanu Reeves *(Ted "Theodore" Logan)* ← PERMANENT RECORD / → BILL & TED'S BOGUS JOURNEY → EVEN COWGIRLS GET THE BLUES → THUMBSUCKER, Alex Winter *(Bill S. Preston, Esq.)* → BILL & TED'S BOGUS JOURNEY, George Carlin *(Rufus)* ← CAR WASH / → BILL & TED'S BOGUS JOURNEY, Bernie Casey *(Mr. Ryan)* ← BROTHERS ← CORNBREAD, EARL AND ME ← CLEOPATRA JONES, Terry Camilleri *(Napoleon)*, Dan Shor *(Billy The Kid)* ← MIKE'S MURDER / → ELVIS AND THE COLONEL: THE UNTOLD STORY, Robert V. Barron *(Abraham Lincoln)* ← HONKYTONK MAN ← COTTONPICKIN' CHICKENPICKERS ← LAS VEGAS HILLBILLYS, **Jane Wiedlin** *(Joan Of Arc)* ← URGH! A MUSIC WAR, Rod Loomis *(Dr. Sigmund Freud)*, Clifford David *(Ludwig van Beethoven)*, Amy Stock-Poynton *(Missy Preston)* → BILL & TED'S BOGUS JOURNEY, Hal Landon Jr. *(Captain Logan)* → TRESPASS, Al Leong *(Genghis Khan)*, Tony Steedman *(Socrates)*, Kimberley LaBelle *(Princess Elizabeth)* → BLUE VALLEY SONGBIRD, **Fee Waybill** *(one of "the three most important people in the world")* ← LADIES AND GENTLEMEN, THE FABULOUS STAINS ← XANADU, **Martha Davis** *(one of . . .)*, **Clarence Clemons** *(one of . . .)* → BLUES BROTHERS 2000 → SWING

Storyline: An emissary from the future visits the suburbs of L.A. (in a phone box) to save his timeline from extinction. In Rufus' future, society depends on the music and philosophy of Bill and Ted, the two dopiest high school students ever. They'll be split apart if they fail their Oral History, they'll never make music, and the future will cease to be. It's up to Rufus to take Bill and Ted through history to meet the Greats so that his dodgy future is a thing of the past. *JZ*

Movie rating: *7

Visual: video + dvd

Off the record: Jane Wiedlin (was ex-Go-Go's), **Fee Waybill** (the Tubes), **Martha Davis** (ex-Motels) and **Clarence Clemons** (played sax with the E-Street Shuffle; Bruce Springsteen's backing band).

—

Various Artists (score: David Newman)

Mar 89. (lp/c/cd) *A&M; <(AMA/AMC/CDA 3915)>* [ ] Apr90 [ ]
– Play with me (EXTREME) / The boys and girls are doing it (VITAL SIGNS) / Not so far away (GLEN BURTNIK) / Dancing with a gypsy (TORA TORA) / Father Time (SHARK ISLAND) / Breakaway (BIG PIG) / Dangerous (SHARK ISLAND) / Walk away (BRICKLIN) / In time (ROBBIE ROBB) / Two heads are better than one (POWER TOOL). *(re-iss. Feb92 cd/c; 393915-2/-4)*

S/track review: Constituted by a smattering of bands purveying 80s stadium rock, as rendered in the seedy clubs of the Sunset Strip, this is a smooth blend of cocky, histrionic good times metal. EXTREME's Van Halen-esque 'Play With Me' is a hi-energy, rowdy call to excess, opening with an electric rendition of Schubert, revelling in squealing harmonics and pitch bends. VITAL SIGNS put the "cock" into "cock rock" with the swaggering 'The Boys And Girls Are Doing It', but GLEN BURTNICK only succeeds in demonstrating that he still hasn't found what he's looking for in the U2-worshipping 'Not So Far Away'. TORA TORA fare better with Zeppelin-y Eastern melodic riffing and helium vocals before launching into full-on arpeggiated soloing that revels in its excesses. The two contributions from SHARK ISLAND betray a fascination with perennial Strip Kings Motley Crüe, whereas BIG PIG bring a bass-heavy tribal vibe that veers to the left of the largely MOR rock proceedings. In fact nothing is more firmly centred in the middle of the FM dial than the balladry of ROBBIE ROBB's 'In Time', and it's the perfect gumby accompaniment for our eponymous heroes to get together with their girlfriends. The aptly named POWER TOOL could do with some self-administered DIY, but as an example of post "Back In Black" hard rock it is adequate enough. Like much of this album, derivative of the greats as it is, it's no wonder these bands struggled to escape L.A. on an excellent adventure. *DF*

Album rating: *5

BIRTH OF THE BEATLES

1979 (UK/US 100m TV) Dick Clark Productions / ABC

Film genre: Pop/Rock Musical bio-pic/drama

Top guns: dir: Richard Marquand → HEARTS OF FIRE / s-w: Jacob Eskendar, John Kurland (+ story)

Stars: Stephen MacKenna *(John Lennon)*, Rod Culbertson *(Paul McCartney)*, John Altman *(George Harrison)* ← QUADROPHENIA, Ray Ashcroft *(Ringo Starr)*, Ryan Michael *(Pete Best)*, David Wilkinson *(Stu Sutcliffe)*, Brian

Jameson *(Brian Epstein)*, Wendy Morgan *(Cynthia Lennon)*, Gary Olsen *(Rory Storm)* → BREAKING GLASS → the WALL, Nigel Havers *(George Martin)* → CHARIOTS OF FIRE, Linal Haft *(agent)* → PSYCHODERELICT, Harry Ditson *(reporter)* → TOP SECRET!, Perry Benson *(page boy)* → SID & NANCY → THIS IS ENGLAND

Storyline: "The excitement of being there when it all first happened" was the poster billing. Yes, the Beatles story from the beginning in Liverpool and Hamburg – when there was five of them including Stu Sutcliffe, who sadly died of a brain haemorrhage – until their major US breakthrough early in 1964. *MCS*

Movie rating: *7

Visual: none (no audio OST; score – Carl Davis)

Off the record: Some astute casting here, most noteably 'Chariots Of Fire' actor, Nigel Havers, as Beatles producer, George Martin. *MCS*

BJORK

Born: Bjork Gudmundsdottir, 21 Nov'65, Reykjavik, Iceland. While Iceland has traditionally been more readily identifiable for its thermal baths and outrageous beer prices than its music, the emergence of the country's first bonafide pop star has put the northern nation firmly on the global map. A child star, BJORK may have been familiar to Icelandic fans since the late 70s yet it took a further decade before she graduated to cult international acclaim with the Sugarcubes. The collective's freewheeling avant-pop briefly charmed the European indie scene (and spun off a few minor hits, among them the inimitable 'Birthday') before its diminutive, hyperkinetic singer went solo in the early 90s. If her 1993 'Debut' album didn't exactly set the heather alight upon its initial release, the subsequent tacking on of her Top 20 David Arnold collaboration, 'Play Dead', gave it sufficient commercial push to take it Top 5. Framed by Arnold's nu-orchestration, the track – the theme to British crime drama, 'The Young Americans' (1993) – expanded upon the electronic experimentation of her debut, and while it wasn't the first time the singer had dabbled in cinema (the Sugarcubes had previously collaborated with composer Hilmar Orn Hilmarsson on the score to late 80s Icelandic feature, 'Skytturmar'), nor was she a stranger to the big screen, having appeared (with her scatalogically titled first band, Tappi Tikarrass) in musical document, 'ROKK I REYKJAVIK' (1982) and starred in the Icelandic Brothers Grimm update, 'The Juniper Tree' (1990). Save for a cameo in Robert Altman's 'Prêt-À-Porter' (1994), BJORK's next film project was the feted 'DANCER IN THE DARK' (2000), controversial Danish director Lars Von Trier's Palme d'Or winning musical. As the star of the film and the composer of its reliably experimental routines (released on soundtrack as 'Selmasongs'), the Icelandic songstress bagged a plethora of nominations and awards, including a Best Song Oscar nomination (for the track 'I've Seen It All') and a European Film Academy award for Best European Actress. *BG*

- **filmography** {acting} (composer) –

Rokk I Reykjavik *(1982 {p w/ TAPPI TIKARRASS} OST by V/A =>)* / Skytturmar *(1987 OST w/ SUGARCUBES + HILMAR ORN HILMARSSON)* / the Juniper Tree *(1990 {*})* / the Young Americans *(1993 hit theme on OST w/ David Arnold see; future editions)* / Prêt A Porter *(1994 {b})* / Anton *(1996 w/ HILMAR ORN HILMARSSON)* / **Popp I Reykjavik** *(1998 {p} on OST by V/A =>)* / **Dancer In The Dark** *(2000 {*} OST 'SelmaSongs' by BJORK =>)* / **Drawing Restraint 9** *(2005 {*} + OST =>)* / **Screaming Masterpiece** *(2005 {p} on OST by V/A =>)*

BLACK AND WHITE

1999 (US 98m) Palm Pictures (R)

Film genre: urban music film & psychological crime drama

Top guns: s-w + dir: James Toback

Stars: Robert Downey Jr. *(Terry Donager)* ← NATURAL BORN KILLERS / → the SINGING DETECTIVE, Jared Leto *(Casey)* → FIGHT CLUB, Brooke Shields *(Sam Donager)* → MAYOR OF THE SUNSET STRIP, **Raekwon** *(Cigar)* ← RHYME & REASON ← the SHOW, Ben Stiller *(Mark Clear)* ← REALITY BITES / → the PICK OF DESTINY → AWESOME: I FUCKIN' SHOT THAT!, Power *(Rich Bower)*, Elijah Wood *(Wren)*, Allan Houston *(Dean Carter)*, Gaby Hoffman *(Raven)* ← THIS IS MY LIFE, Scott Caan *(Scotty)*, Joe Pantoliani *(Bill King)* ← the IN CROWD ← ROCK'N'ROLL MOM ← LA BAMBA ← SCENES FROM THE GOLDMINE ← EDDIE AND THE CRUISERS ← RISKY BUSINESS ← the IDOLMAKER, Kidada Jones *(Jesse)* ← THICKER THAN WATER, Hassan Johnson *(Iniko)* → PRISON SONG, **Bijou Phillips** *(Charlie)* ← SUGAR TOWN / → ALMOST FAMOUS → OCTANE, William Lee Scott *(Will King)* → KILLER DILLER, Claudia Schiffer *(Greta)*, **Ghostface** *(himself)* → FADE TO BLACK → WALK HARD: THE DEWEY COX STORY, **Inspectah Deck** *(himself)*, **Fredro Starr** *(himself)* ← RIDE / → SAVE THE LAST DANCE, **Sticky Fingaz** *(himself)* ← RIDE, Mike Tyson *(himself)*, **Daz Dillinger** ← MURDER WAS THE CASE

Storyline: Voyeuristic, young white filmmaker Sam is making a documentary exploring the inner sanctums of the New York hip hop scene. But this sprawling tale unfolds to be more than just about the rap game as main player Rich Bower has his fingers in altogether more dubious pies. When his basketball star best friend Dean takes a hunk of cash to throw some matches, it divides the two men and Rich nominates one of his coterie of gullible white hangers-on to be the assassin of his friend. Obviously of course, a murder plot like this was never going to be so straight-forward. *MR*

Movie rating: *5

Visual: dvd

Off the record: Jared Leto was also in a band called 30 Seconds To Mars; Oli 'Power' Grant is a rap producer; others such as **Bijou Phillips** (solo artist), **Fredro Starr & Sticky Fingaz** (both Onyx), **Raekwon, Ghostface Killah, Inspectah Deck** turn up elsewhere in the book.

Various Artists

Mar 00. (cd/c/lp) *Loud-Sony;* <62200-2/-4/-1> [ ] [–]
– It's not a game (AMERICAN CREAM TEAM feat. RAEKWON) / Year 2000 – remix (XZIBIT feat. JONATHAN DAVIS) / Don't be a follower (PRODIGY of MOBB DEEP) / Dramacide (X-ECUTIONERS feat. BIG PUN & KOOL G RAP) / Life's a bitch (EVERLAST) / Wake up (RAEKWON) / Dem crazy (DEAD PREZ feat. STEPHEN MARLEY & GHETTO YOUTHS CREW) / Stand for something (CHIP BANKS feat. Tha OUTLAWZ) / Middle finger attitude (AMERICAN CREAM TEAM) / You'll never be better than me – I'm that s*** (QUEEN PEN feat. JOE HOOKER) / You – feel good remix (SAMUEL CHRISTIAN feat. MOS DEF) / You're a big girl now (LV) / Free (MICHAEL FREDO).

S/track review: A welcome antidote to the relentless gangsterisms of the 90s, this eclectic mix draws from all corners of the hip hop world to prove that the genre is a many splintered thing, but when the tunes are good no one minds. Okay, so there are the inevitable moments of bravado – AMERICAN CREAM TEAM's spooked up Scarface tributes on 'Middle Finger Attitude' for one – but it's a great tune where in they employ some spooky strings to great effect. DEAD PREZ couldn't be more contrasting, dropping scholarly, positive verses over a mellow soul beat on 'Dem Crazy'. A song rendered oddly melancholy, thanks to some droopy-lidded vocal hook from STEPHEN MARLEY. SAMUEL CHRISTIAN and MOS DEF's 'You' follows a similar reggae-fied vibe on their clarion call to those who reckon themselves streetwise. The sweetest beats and more complex rhymes however, come from the RAEKWON (who also has a cameo in the film). The excellent 'Wake Up' has him counting through his reasoning to the trill of a harpsichord. The X-ECUTIONER's 'Dramacide' even gives the turntables centre stage momentarily, a deft barrage of scratches trading punches with a few verses from BIG PUN, whose contribution is some seriously good double-time rhymes. Only the token drippy R&B songs by MICHAEL FREDO and LV are definitely worth skipping. Some may decry an album like this as an indication of the state of flux hip hop was in around 2000, but conversely, it is more interesting for its lack of a single dominating theme. No one name is shouting for centre stage and no one track stands out. The strength of this album is very much about it being the sum of its parts. *MR*

Album rating: *6.5

BLACK ROSES

1988 (US 90m) Rayvan Productions / Shapiro Entertainment (R)

Film genre: Heavy-Rock Musical supernatural horror

Top guns: dir: John Fasano ← ROCK'N'ROLL NIGHTMARE / s-w: Cindy Sorrell

Stars: John Martin *(Matthew Moorhouse)*, Ken Swofford *(Mayor Farnsworth)*, Sal Viviano *(Damien)*, Frank Dietz *(Johnny Pratt)* ← ROCK'N'ROLL NIGHTMARE, Vincent Pastore *(Mr. Ames; Tony's dad)* → WHO'S THE MAN? → the BASKETBALL DIARIES → WALKING AND TALKING → JOE'S APARTMENT, Julie Adams *(Mrs. Miller)* ← TICKLE ME, Carla Ferringno *(Miss Priscilla Farnsworth)*, **Carmine Appice** *(Vinny Apache)* → CHASING DESTINY, Paul Kelman *(Julie's stepdad)*, Karen Planden *(Julie Windham)*, Anthony C. Bua *(Tony Ames)*, Ron Mazza *(Black Roses; guitarist)*, Paul Phenomenon *(Black Roses; keyboardist)*, Glenn Deveau *(Demon bassist)*, Chester Nakelski *(Demon drummer)*

Storyline: The Black Roses are a devil-worshipping heavy metal band whose lead singer just happens to be called Damien (hmm, there's a clue). They are about to play a gig at the sleepy town of Mills Basin, to the consternation of the locals who know of their reputation. However, the concert goes ahead and the sneaky supergroup behave themselves until the adults go away – only then do they switch to their Satanic silliness. It's up to English teacher Mr Moorhouse to do battle with demonic Damien and save his students. *JZ*

Movie rating: *3.5

Visual: video

Off the record: **Carmine Appice** was an original member of Vanilla Fudge, and went on to work with JEFF BECK and Rod Stewart.

BLACK ROSES (*) (& Various) (score: Elliot Solomon, etc.)

Oct 90. (cd) *Metal Blade-Enigma; <7 73353-2>* [ ] [-]
– Dance on fire (*) / Soldiers of the night (*) / I'm no stranger (BANG TANGO) / Rock invasion (*) / Paradise (we're on our way) (*) / Me against the world (LIZZY BORDEN) / Take it off (KING KOBRA) / King of kool (DAVID MICHAEL-PHILLIPS) / Streetlife warrior (TEMPEST) / D.I.E. (HALLOW'S EVE).

S/track review: Hard-rock or Heavy-metal, you decide, but this OST is a mixture of lower-league Kerrang! acts along with movie band, BLACK ROSES, led by drummer CARMINE APPICE. It would be hard to criticise something so spontaneous as this makeshift get-together of anthemic-rock, but I'm going to, by way of stating the tracks are bog-standard, cod-piece, hair-metal: 'Dance On Fire' (sounds like "pants on fire", or am I being a little childish), 'Soldiers Of The Night' (is post-Rainbow), 'Rock Invasion' (ditto) and 'Paradise (We're On Our Way)' (is the customary metal ballad). Track six, 'Me Against The World', confuses the bleary-eyed among us, because the song belongs to LIZZY BORDEN (at least here on record), while BLACK ROSES mime their way through it in the movie itself. Although there are the usual guitar histrionics, one would have to be a metal fan airhead to appreciate this derivative stab at glorified metal. Example the Ac/Dc-like KING KOBRA ('Take It Off') and DAVID MICHAEL-PHILLIPS ('King Of Kool'). Hook-line'n'stinker BANG TANGO ('I'm No Stranger') fizzes out like a damp squib, while commercial flop – never mind critical – outfits TEMPEST and HALLOW'S EVE (the latter with Sabbath-esque 'D.I.E.') bring the curtain down with post-Spinal Tap aplomb. Expect to empty your pockets out for 'BLACK ROSES' – it must be for the splendid cover artwork. *MCS*

Album rating: *3

BLACK SNAKE MOAN

2007 (US 116m) New Deal Productions / Paramount Vantage (R)

Film genre: psychological romantic Blues-music drama

Top guns: s-w + dir: Craig Brewer ← HUSTLE & FLOW

Stars: Samuel L. Jackson *(Lazarus)* ← KILL BILL: VOL.2 ← KILL BILL: VOL.1 ← JACKIE BROWN ← PULP FICTION ← JUICE ← JOHNNY SUEDE ← JUNGLE FEVER ← SCHOOL DAZE ← MAGIC STICKS, Christina Ricci *(Rae)* ← the FEARLESS FREAKS ← MONSTER ← FEAR AND LOATHING IN LAS VEGAS ← BUFFALO 66, **Justin Timberlake** *(Ronnie)* ← LONGSHOT, S. Epatha Merkerson *(Angela)*, John Cothran, Jr. *(Reverend R.L.)* ← the BEAT, David Banner *(Tehronne)* ← BEEF 3, Michael Raymond-James *(Gill)*, Amy Laverne *(Jesse)* ← WALK THE LINE

Storyline: Taking the title from a 1927 Blind Lemon Jefferson song, the movie is a modern romanticised tale of the blues. When boyfriend Ronnie leaves for his tour of duty, nymphomaniac Rae immediately begins searching for a replacement man. There is no shortage of takers but needless to say she ends up used and abused by a roadside. Enter Lazarus, who takes her home and, discovering her addiction to men, promptly chains her to the radiator and tries to save her soul. So begins a battle of the spiritual against the physical and Lazarus finds he can still be arisen by a woman's charms. *JZ*

Movie rating: *7

Visual: dvd

Off the record: **Justin Timberlake** got to grips with acting here. SCOTT BOMAR (was ex-Jack O. & The Tearjerkers).

Various Artists/Original Cast (score: SCOTT BOMAR *)

Jan 07. (cd) *New West; <NW 3021> (NW 6105-2)* [ ] Feb07 [ ]
– Opening theme (*) / Ain't but one kind of blues (SON HOUSE) / Just like a bird without a feather (SAMUEL L. JACKSON and KENNY BROWN) / When the lights go out (the BLACK KEYS) / Standing in my doorway crying (JESSIE MAE HEMPHILL) / Chicken heads (BOBBY RUSH) / Black snake moan (SAMUEL L. JACKSON and JASON FREEMAN) / Morning train (PRECIOUS BRYANT) / The losing kind (JOHN DOE) / Lord have mercy on me (OUTRAGEOUS CHERRY) / Ronnie and Rae's theme (*) / The chain (*) / Alice Mae (SAMUEL L. JACKSON, KENNY BROWN and CEDRIC BURNSIDE) / Stackolee (SAMUEL L. JACKSON, KENNY BROWN, LUTHER DICKINSON and CEDRIC BURNSIDE) / Old black Mattie (R.L. BURNSIDE) / That's where the blues started (SON HOUSE) / Mean ol' wind died down (NORTH MISSISSIPPI ALLSTARS).

S/track review: Is there anything SAMUEL L. JACKSON can't do? Apart from being a bible-quoting manic gangster, Jedi knight, and appearing in almost every film ever made since the mid-80s, he also plays golf and even manages to make a kilt look like a new fashion accessory. Now it seems he thinks himself a down at heel, Delta bluesman and, in what may be his own words, he ain't half bad, motherf***er. JACKSON takes on two R.L. BURNSIDE numbers, 'Just Like A Bird Without A Feather' and 'Alice Mae', accompanied on guitar by BURNSIDE's adopted son

KENNY BROWN for the former and his backing band for the latter. Both are heartfelt interpretations with JACKSON's deep and dry voice good enough to make you believe he's a bonafide pro singer. 'Stackolee', along with 'Alice Mae', are live, raucous stamp-alongs while 'Black Snake Moan' is a slow, tense dirge. 'Old Black Mattie', an original R.L. BURNSIDE tune, chugs along, as does 'PRECIOUS BRYANT's 'Morning Train', an acoustic ballad in the southwest Georgia tradition. Punk legend JOHN DOE contributes the uncharacteristically subtle and rootsy song 'The Losing Kind' and SCOTT BOMAR experiments with some Hill Country Blues to create a sinister, atmospheric piece. The soundtrack to 'BLACK SNAKE MOAN' is an entertaining journey through various forms of blues and SAMUEL L. JACKSON carries off the role of bluesman with enough aplomb to suggest that he's been doing it all his life. *CM*

Album rating: *6.5

BLACKBOARD JUNGLE

1955 (US 101m b&w) M.G.M.

Film genre: urban teen drama

Top guns: s-w + dir: Richard Brooks (au: Evan Hunter)

Stars: Glenn Ford *(Richard Dadier)* → ADVANCE TO THE REAR, Sidney Poitier *(Gregory W. Miller)* → TO SIR, WITH LOVE → LET'S DO IT AGAIN → a PIECE OF THE ACTION, Anne Francis *(Anne Dadier)*, Louis Calhern *(Jim Murdock)*, Vic Morrow *(Artie West)* → KING CREOLE, Margaret Hayes *(Lois Judby Hammond)*, John Hoyt *(Mr. Warneke)*, Richard Kiley *(Joshua J. Edwards)*, Warner Anderson *(Dr. Bradley)*, Basil Ruysdael *(Prof. A.R. Kraal)*, Rafael Campos *(Pete V. Morales)*, Paul Mazursky *(Emmanuel Stoker)* → a STAR IS BORN → DOWN AND OUT IN BEVERLY HILLS → HEY HEY WE'RE THE MONKEES → TOUCH → WHY DO FOOLS FALL IN LOVE, Jameel Farah / Jamie Farr *(Santini)*, **Bill HALEY & His Comets** *(soundtrack performers)*

Storyline: War veteran Richard Dadier finds himself in his toughest battle so far when he goes to teach at a tough New York high school. Here it's the kids who run the classrooms while the teachers timidly put up with violence and abuse, especially from gang ringleader Artie West. Appalled, Dadier starts to fight back and accuses Artie of sending malicious letters to his wife – but that's just the excuse Artie's been waiting for to declare a new "class war". *JZ*

Movie rating: *7.5

Visual: video + dvd (no audio OST; score: Charles Wolcott)

Off the record: We included this film in here because of its historical significance although its not actually a Rock'n'roll movie per se, just a film that resulted in cinema seats being ripped up after they heard the sound of BILL HALEY's 'Rock Around The Clock'. *MCS*

– spinoff hits, etc. –

BILL HALEY & HIS COMETS: Rock Around The Clock

May 55. (7",78) *Decca; <29124> Brunswick; (05317)* 1 Oct55 1
(above actually iss.May54 US & Sep54 UK – only a hit after movie)

BLAME IT ON THE NIGHT

1984 (US 85m) Columbia Tri-Star Pictures (PG-13)

Film genre: rock-Music showbiz melodrama

Top guns: dir: Gene Taft (+ story w/ **Michael Philip Jagger** <= the ROLLING STONES =>) / s-w: Len Jenkin

Stars: Nick Mancuso *(Chris Dalton)* ← HEARTBREAKERS / → PAROLES ET MUSIQUE → NIGHT MAGIC → BRAVE NEW GIRL → IN THE MIX, Byron Thames *(Job Dalton)*, Leslie Ackerman *(Shelly)*, Richard Bakalyan *(Manzini)*, Rex Ludwick *(Animal)* ← HONEYSUCKLE ROSE, Leeyan Granger *(Melanie)*, Michael Wilding, Jr. *(Terry)*, **Dennis Tufano** *(Leland)*, **Billy PRESTON** *(performer)*, **Merry Clayton** *(performer)*, **Ollie E. Brown** *(performer)*, Richard Caruso *(sax player)*

Storyline: Rock star Chris finds he has an unexpected companion on tour when his illegitimate son Job appears after his mother's death. Job is used to the strict life of a military academy and has to cope with the culture shock of the slightly less disciplinarian routine of a rock musician. For Chris too, getting to know his son in between being famous is not as easy as it seems – let's hope he makes a good Job of it. *MCS*

Movie rating: *3.5

Visual: video (no audio OST; score: Ted Neeley & Tom Scott)

Off the record: **Dennis Tufano** was the frontman for 60s rock act, the Buckinghams (who had a No.1 hit in 1966 with 'Kind Of A Drag') – alongside guitarist Carl Giammarese they formed a duo in 1973; **Merry Clayton** sang backing vocals for the 'Stones and had a handful of minor hits from 'Gimme Shelter' to 'Yes' (the latter from 'DIRTY DANCING'); **Ollie E. Brown** was one-half of Ollie & Jerry, hitmakers in '84 with 'Breakin' . . . There's No Stopping Us' (from the movie, 'BREAKIN''); **Michael Philip Jagger** is noneother than a certain Rolling Stone. *MCS*

BLANK GENERATION

1980 (US 85m) International Harmony

Film genre: Punk-rock-music drama

Top guns: s-w: Ulli Lommel (+ dir), **Richard HELL**, Bob Madero, Roger Deutsch

Stars: Carole Bouquet *(Nada)*, **Richard HELL** *(Billy)*, Ulli Lommel *(Hoffritz)*, Suzanna Love *(Lizzy)* ← HAIR, Ben Weiner *(Kellerman)*, Howard Grant *(Jack)*, Andy Warhol *(himself)* ← IMAGINE ← COCKSUCKER BLUES ← the VELVET UNDERGROUND AND NICO / → NICO ICON → ROCK AND ROLL HEART → DETROIT ROCK CITY → END OF THE CENTURY, Bob Madero *(Harry)*, **the Void-Oids:- Ivan Julian, Robert Quine + Mark Bell** *(performers)* <= RAMONES =>

Storyline: A rising punk rock poet, Billy, falls for gorgeous French journalist, Nada. Their fickle relationship, set to the backdrop of the New York underground punk scene, is the main crux of the story as she tries to set up a meeting with the estranged Andy Warhol. *MCS*

Movie rating: *4.5

Visual: video + dvd

Off the record: Incidentally, only three – live at CBGB's – **RICHARD HELL** & The Void-Oids songs appear in the film. **Mark Bell** went on to join the RAMONES. *MCS*

☐ the BLASTERS / Dave ALVIN segment
(⇒ STREETS OF FIRE)

BLAST-OFF GIRLS

1967 (US 83m) Creative Film Enterprises Inc. / Dominant (R)

Film genre: Rock Musical comedy drama

Top guns: dir + s-w: Herschell Gordon Lewis

Stars: Dan Conway *(Boojie Baker)*, Ray Sager *(Gordie)*, Tom Tyrell, Ron Liace, Dennis Hickey, Chris Wolski, Ralph Mullin *(Big Blast musicians)*, Lawrence J. Aberwood *(Marty Dunn)*, Steve White, Bob Compton, Ray Barry, Tom Eppolito, Tony Sorci *(Charlie band members)*, Colonel Sanders *(himself)* → the PHYNX

Storyline: Unscrupulous music promoter come rock manager, Boojie Baker, finds some naive and female-hungry garage band members and moulds them into the Big Blast. Offering them go-go girls but little of the proceeds, the group get into fights and trouble with the police. *MCS*

Movie rating: *3

Visual: video + dvd (no audio OST)

Off the record: The two groups, the Big Blast and Charlie, are of course fictitious.

BLONDIE

Formed: New York, USA ... 1974 as Angel And The Snake by DEBORAH HARRY, CHRIS STEIN, Clem Burke, Gary Valentine and Jimmy Destri. Fronted by platinum siren HARRY and plying the most seductive, addictive hit of the original CBGB's scene, BLONDIE were first filmed in seminal Amos Poe/Ivan Kral documentary, 'BLANK GENERATION' (1976), alongside peers such as RAMONES and Patti Smith Group. HARRY made her feature debut with a singing cameo in obscure Don Murray crime thriller, 'Deadly Hero' (1976), and a part in Poe's Jean Luc Godard tribute, 'Unmade Beds' (1976). After going on to appear in Poe's 'The FOREIGNER' (1978), she graduated to more accomplished character-acting in 'Union City' (1979), a New Wave noir for which STEIN composed the score. By 1980, BLONDIE had stylised the modernist throb of disco so seamlessly and commercially successfully, they'd supply the No.1 theme for slick, Giorgio Moroder-scored Richard Gere vehicle, 'American Gigolo'. Also in 1980, the band were sighted in Alan Rudolph's 'ROADIE', performing – after a quick fix from MEAT LOAF – Johnny Cash's 'Ring Of Fire', and also gracing the double-disc soundtrack. With John Waters' scratch'n'sniff comedy, 'Polyester' (1981), Stein furthered his film scoring career in tandem with HARRY and Michael Kamen, while Divine took the starring role. While both HARRY and STEIN were inevitable sightings in cult NY classic, 'DOWNTOWN '81' (shot in '81 but unreleased until 2000), BLONDIE's hip hop hybrid, 'Rapture', set the context for 'WILD STYLE' (1983), the landmark hip hop film/soundtrack which STEIN would score (along with Fab Five Freddy) and perform following the band's split in 1982. The same year, HARRY netted her most high profile role up to that point, starring in cult David Cronenberg effort, 'Videodrome', and setting the pattern for a career which alternated acting with post-BLONDIE solo work. In 1983, she re-teamed with Moroder for the 'Scarface' soundtrack excerpt, 'Rush Rush', and contributed to the score of cult animation, 'ROCK & RULE', alongside the likes of LOU REED and Cheap Trick. While much of her time during this period was devoted to STEIN, who'd been diagnosed with a rare genetic disease (from which he later made a full recovery), she returned to recording in the mid-80s with a Jellybean Benitez-produced contribution to the 'KRUSH GROOVE' soundtrack, 'Feel The Spin'. Her screen career likewise stuttered into life again with a starring role alongside Alex Baldwin in comedy, 'Forever, Lulu' (1987) and a part in Waters' riotous classic, 'HAIRSPRAY' (1988), as well as a cameo in Scorsese/Coppola/Allen trilogy, 'New York Stories' (1989) and an appearance in teen rock drama, 'SATISFACTION' (1988). Soundtrack wise, she recorded a cover of the Castaways' 'Liar, Liar' for Jonathan Demme's 'Married To The Mob' (1988). Following multiple TV projects and a reunion with STEIN, the blonde one starred in serial killer drama, 'Dead Beat' (1994), and put in a memorable performance as a jaded waitress (a job she held down in pre-BLONDIE days) alongside Liv Tyler and Evan Dando in James Mangold's engagingly offbeat debut, 'HEAVY' (1995). As the 'TRAINSPOTTING' soundtrack gifted BLONDIE a back catalogue coup and new remix opportunities, HARRY appeared in metal satire, 'DROP DEAD ROCK' (1996), Mangold sophomore, 'Cop Land' (1997) and – with another waitressing role – in black comedy, 'Zoo' (1999), as well as crime comedy, 'Six Ways To Sunday' (1997). In one of her unlikeliest soundtrack cameos, she even performed an electro cover of 'Ghost Riders In The Sky' for Alex Cox's Prey For Rain-scored 'Three Businessmen' (1998). While BLONDIE themselves returned with a vengeance in the late 90s (and Deborah became the oldest women to have a No.1 UK hit, 'Maria') and on into the new millennium, she continued to maintain a prolific sideline in acting with supporting roles in gay porn drama, 'The Fluffer' (2001), Jonas Akerlund's Billy Corgan-scored drug piece, 'Spun' (2002) and Scott 'The Basketball Diaries' Kalvert's gang drama, 'Deuces Wild' (2002), as well as a lead part in Elijah Wood coming-of-age comedy, 'All I Want' (2001) alongside Mandy Moore. A familiarly motherly role in Spanish director Isabel Coixet's 'My Life Without Me', followed in 2003, as did a cameo in Martha Graham drama, 'Ghostlight', a part in indie crime thriller, 'A Good Night To Die' (2003) and contributions to Harold Arlen tribute, 'Stormy Weather', RAMONES documentary, 'END OF THE CENTURY', and docu-tribute to legendary L.A. mover and shaker, Rodney Bingenheimer, 'MAYOR OF THE SUNSET STRIP'. A series of shorts from Christopher Romero ('Patch'), veteran music video director Bob Giraldi ('Honey Trap') and Henry S Miller ('I Remember You Now') followed in 2005, with HARRY also set to appear in Miller's 2007-scheduled 'Anamorph'. *BG*

- **filmography** DEBBIE {acting} / CHRIS (composer) –

Deadly Hero *(1976 {s})* / **Blank Generation** *(1976 {c})* / **the Foreigner** *(1978 {*})* / Mr. Mike's Mondo Video *(1979 {c})* / Unmade Beds *(1980 {a})* / **Roadie** *(1980 {c BLONDIE} OST by V/A =>)* / Union City *(1980 {*} on OST by STEIN)* / American Gigolo *(1980 hit theme by BLONDIE on OST by Giorgio Moroder see future edition)* / **Downtown 81** *(1981 {a} {p CHRIS} OST by V/A =>)* / **Wild Style** *(1982 OST by STEIN & FAB FIVE FREDDY =>)* / **Rock & Rule** *(1983 {sv} =>)* / Videodrome *(1983 {*} OST by Howard Shore; see future edition)* / Forever, Lulu *(1987 {*})* / **Satisfaction** *(1988 {a} OST by Justine Bateman =>)* / **Hairspray** *(1988 {*} OST by V/A =>)* / New York Stories *(1989 {b} OST by V/A; see future edition)* / Tales From The Darkside: The Movie *(1990 {*})* / Mother Goose Rock'n'Rhyme *(1990 {a} OST by V/A)* / Intimate Stranger *(1992 TV {*})* / Body Bags *(1993 TV {*})* / Dead Beat *(1994 {*})* / Texas Chainsaw Massacre: The Next Generation *(1994 single by DEBORAH HARRY & Robert Jacks on OST)* / **Drop Dead Rock** *(1995 {a} OST by V/A =>)* / Wigstock: The Movie *(1995 {c})* / **Heavy** *(1995 {*} OST by THURSTON MOORE & V/A =>)* / L.A. Johns *(1997 TV {a})* / Cop Land *(1997 {a} OST by Howard Shore; see future edition =>)* / Six Ways To Sunday *(1997 {*})* / Joe's Day *(1998 {*})* / Zoo *(1999 {a})* / Red Lipstick *(2000 {a})* / In Bad Taste *(2000 {c})* / Pie In The Sky: The Brigid Berlin Story *(2000 OST by STEIN)* / the Fluffer *(2001 {a})* / Deuces Wild *(2002 {a})* / Spun *(2002 {a})* / Try Seventeen *(2002 {*})* / **End Of The Century** *(2003 {c})* / My Life Without Me *(2003 {*})* / a Good Night To Die *(2003 {a})* / **Mayor Of The Sunset Strip** *(2003 {c} =>)* / the Tulse Luper Suitcases, Part 1: The Moab Story *(2003 {b})* / **Ramones: Raw** *(2004 {c})* / Bettie Page: Dark Angel *(2004 STEIN on OST by Danny B. Harvey; see future edition)* / **New York Doll** *(2005 {c; FRANK & CLEM} =>)* / Full Grown Men *(2006 {*})* / **Too Tough To Die: A Tribute To Johnny Ramone** *(2006 {p})*

□ BLOODSTONE segment
(⇒ TRAIN RIDE TO HOLLYWOOD)

BLUE HAWAII

1961 (US 101m) Paramount Pictures

Film genre: romantic Rock'n'roll Musical comedy

Top guns: dir: Norman Taurog ← G.I. BLUES / → GIRLS! GIRLS! GIRLS! → IT HAPPENED AT THE WORLD'S FAIR → TICKLE ME → SPINOUT → DOUBLE TROUBLE → SPEEDWAY → LIVE A LITTLE, LOVE A LITTLE / s-w: Hal Kanter ← LOVING YOU / (story: Allan Weiss → GIRLS! GIRLS! GIRLS! → ROUSTABOUT)

Stars: Elvis PRESLEY *(Chad Gates)*, Joan Blackman *(Maile Duval)* → KID GALAHAD → RETURN TO WATERLOO, Nancy Walters *(Abigail Prentice)*, Roland Winters *(Fred Gates)*, John Archer *(Jack Kelman)*, Angela Lansbury *(Sarah Lee Gates)* → the LAST UNICORN, Pamela Kirk *(Selena/ Sandy Emerson)* → HOOTENANNY HOOT → KISSIN' COUSINS, Howard McNear *(Mr. Chapman)* → FUN IN ACAPULCO, Darlene Tompkins *(Patsy Simon)* → FUN IN ACAPULCO, Steve Brodie *(Tucker Garvey)* → ROUSTABOUT, Iris Adrian *(Enid Garvey)* ← CARNIVAL ROCK

Storyline: Returning home to Honolulu, G.I. Chad Gates is loathed to take on his family's lucrative pineapple business. Instead, he spends as much time as he can at the beach with predictably glamourous female acquaintances. *BG*

Movie rating: *5.5

Visual: video + dvd

Off the record: Angela Lansbury starred in the film – yes, she of 'Bedknobs & Broomsticks' and 'Murder She Wrote'. *MCS*

—

ELVIS PRESLEY (composers: Joseph Lilley, etc.)

Oct 61. (lp) *R.C.A.; <LSP 2426> (RD 27238)(SF 5115)* [1] Dec61 [1]
– Blue Hawaii / Almost always true / Aloha oe / No more / Can't help falling in love / Rock-a-hula baby / Moonlight swim / Ku-u-i-po (Hawaiian sweetheart) / Ito eats / Slicin' sand / Hawaiian sunset / Beach boy blues / Island of love / Hawaiian wedding song. *(re-iss. Sep77; SF 8145)* – (hit UK No.26) *(re-iss. Aug84 lp/c; NL/NK 83683) (cd-iss. Oct87; ND 83683) <(cd re-iss. Feb98 +=; 07863 66959-2)>* – (bonus film tracks). *(lp re-mast.Sep01 on 'Castle'++=; ELVIS 107)* – (bonus 7" tracks).

S/track review: Sun, sea, sand and songs – as many and as genial as possible – was the order of the day on 'BLUE HAWAII', ELVIS PRESLEY's most commercially successful film and, as a result, one which pretty much set the pattern for the rest of the decade. Chock full of all the contrived, pseudo-native exotica and elastic-band-twanging Hawaiian guitars even the most S.A.D.-scarred ELVIS fan could handle, the soundtrack nevertheless finds the King in as incredible vocal form as ever and features some classic moments, not least the gorgeous 'Can't Help Falling In Love', inspired by Giovanni Martini's 'Plaisir d'Amour'. The ethnic baubles are kept to a minimum here, although the same can't be said for the film's other huge hit, 'Rock-A-Hula Baby', a slice of mindless grass-skirt fun which probably best sums up the soundtrack as a whole. The first single to be lifted from it was actually the title track, a song first crooned by Bing Crosby in the 1937 movie, 'Waikiki Wedding'. Of the three tracks cut from the final print, Wise/Weisman/Fuller's 'Steppin' Out Of Line' was resurrected for the 1997 CD re-issue. A red-blooded rocker bolstered by Boots Randolph's fiery sax, it's not difficult to see why it didn't fit with the film's mood. That it nevertheless plays as one of the most convincing numbers on the re-issue speaks volumes, although fans of prime ELVIS kitsch certainly won't be disappointed. *BG*

Album rating: *5.5

– spinoff hits, etc. –

ELVIS PRESLEY: Rock-A-Hula Baby / Can't Help Falling In Love

Nov 61. (7") *<47-7968> (RCA 1270)* [23]
[2] Jan62 [1]
(re-iss. May77; PB 2703)

ELVIS PRESLEY: Rock-A-Hula Baby / Can't Help Falling In Love

Feb 05. (cd-s) *Sony-BMG; (82876 66673-2)* [–] [3]
(10"+=) *(82876 66673-1)* – Can't Help Falling In Love (alt.)

BLUE VALLEY SONGBIRD

1999 (US 91m TV) Southern Light Productions (PG)

Film genre: Country/Pop Musical drama

Top guns: dir: Richard A. Colla / s-w: Ken Carter, Annette Haywood-Carter

Stars: Dolly PARTON *(Leanna Taylor)*, John Terry *(Hank)*, Billy Dean *(Bobby)*, Beth Grant *(Ruby)* → DANCE WITH ME → ROCK STAR, Kimberley Kates *(Thelma Russell)* ← BILL & TED'S EXCELLENT ADVENTURE, **Sam Bush** *(fiddler #1)*, Randall Franks *(fiddler #2)*

Storyline: Leanne Taylor is a country and western singer with the Blue Valley Ramblers. For the last 15 years, she has toured the same old places with nothing to show, and her relationship with domineering boyfriend and manager Hank is becoming stale. When new band member Bobby comes on the scene, he convinces Leanne that she can do much better with her genuine talent if she is willing to forget the past and look to a better future. *JZ*

Movie rating: *4.5

Visual: video + dvd (no audio OST; score: Velton Ray Bunch)

Off the record: Sam Bush was in fact the accomplished bluegrass fiddle and mandolin player who sessioned for others as well as releasing a handful of albums, mainly for 'Sugar Hill' – check out the live 'Ice Caps: Peaks Of Telluride' (2000). **DOLLY PARTON** performed several tracks (old & new) including:- 'Blue Valley Songbird', 'I Hope You're Never Happy' (with BILLY DEAN), 'Wildflowers', 'We Might Be In Love' (with BILLY DEAN), 'My Blue Tears', 'Runaway Feeling' (with BILLY DEAN), 'Amazing Grace' & 'Angel Band'. *MCS*

the BLUES BROTHERS

1980 (US 135m) Universal Pictures (R)

Film genre: anarchic R&B/Rock Musical buddy comedy

Top guns: s-w: John Landis (+ dir) ← ANIMAL HOUSE / → BLUES BROTHERS 2000, Dan Aykroyd → BLUES BROTHERS 2000

Stars: John Belushi *("Joliet" Jake Blues)* ← ANIMAL HOUSE ← the RUTLES, Dan Aykroyd *(Elwood Blues)* ← the RUTLES / → THIS IS MY LIFE → BLUES BROTHERS 2000, **James BROWN** *(Rev. Cleophus James)*, **Cab Calloway** *(Curtis)*, **Ray CHARLES** *(Ray)*, John Candy *(Burton Mercer)* → HEAVY METAL → LITTLE SHOP OF HORRORS, Carrie Fisher *(mystery woman)* → THIS IS MY LIFE, Kathleen Freeman *(Sister Mary Stigmata; aka The Penguin)* → BLUES BROTHERS 2000, **Aretha Franklin** *(Mrs. Murphy; soulfood cafe owner)* → BLUES BROTHERS 2000, Henry Gibson *(head Nazi)* ← NASHVILLE / → a STRANGER IN THE KINGDOM → MAGNOLIA, **John Lee Hooker** *(Street Slim)* → SURVIVORS: THE BLUES TODAY → FEEL LIKE GOING HOME, Murphy Dunne *(Murph)* → BLUES BROTHERS 2000, **Steve Cropper** *(Steve "The Colonel" Cropper)* → SATISFACTION → BLUES BROTHERS 2000, **Donald Dunn** *(Donald "Duck" Dunn)*, **Matt "Guitar" Murphy** *(himself)* → BLUES BROTHERS 2000, **Willie "Too Big" Hall** *(himself)* → BLUES BROTHERS 2000, **Tom Malone** *(himself)* → BLUES BROTHERS 2000, **"Blue Lou" Marini** *(himself)* → BLUES BROTHERS 2000, **Alan Rubin** *(Mr. Fabulous)* → BLUES BROTHERS 2000, **Steve Lawrence** *(Maury Sline)* → BLUES BROTHERS 2000, **Stephen Bishop** *(charming trooper)* ← ANIMAL HOUSE, **Chaka Khan** *(choir soloist)* → STANDING IN THE SHADOWS OF MOTOWN, Frank Oz *(corrections officer)* → BLUES BROTHERS 2000, Jeff Morris *(Bob)* ← PAYDAY ← KID GALAHAD / → the BORDER → BLUES BROTHERS 2000, Paul Reubens *(waiter)* → BACK TO THE BEACH → MOONWALKER → SOUTH OF HEAVEN, WEST OF HELL → OVERNIGHT → MAYOR OF THE SUNSET STRIP, Steven Spielberg *(cook county clerk)*, **Joe Walsh** *(prisoner)* ← ZACHARIAH, Frank Oz *(corrections officer)*, Steve Lawrence *(Maury Sline)*, Twiggy *(chic lady)* ← POPCORN / → CLUB PARADISE → EDGE OF SEVENTEEN, **'Pinetop' Perkins** *(Luther Jackson)* ← the LAST WALTZ / → PIANO BLUES, Charles Napier *(Tucker McElroy)* ← BEYOND THE VALLEY OF THE DOLLS / → SPIRIT: STALLION OF THE CIMARRON, Steve Williams *(trooper Mount)*, Devoreaux White *(young guitar thief)* → TRESPASS

Storyline: Fresh out of prison, sharp suited Jake Blues joins his portly sibling Elwood in a chaotic bid to raise money for the ailing Catholic home they were raised in. Blessed by the formidable Sister Mary Stigmata aka The Penguin, they round up their old band, which just happens to include legendary Stax players Steve Cropper and Donald 'Duck' Dunn, yet can only scrape a gig at a shit-kicking redneck joint in the middle of nowhere. Despite making a game attempt at playing country, they escape in a hail of broken bottles, only to run afoul of neo-Nazis in the middle of a training exercise. The whole mess ends in one of the biggest car pile-ups in screen history, which, of course, the boys escape without a crease in their shirts. *BG*

Movie rating: *8

Visual: video + dvd

Off the record: BLUES BROTHERS (see above/below)

——

the BLUES BROTHERS (& Various Artists)

Jun 80. (lp/c) *Atlantic; <SD/CS 16017> (K/K4 50715)* [13] Oct80 [ ]
– She caught the Katy / Peter Gunn theme / Gimme some lovin' / Shake a tail feather (w/ RAY CHARLES) / Everybody needs somebody to love / The old landmark (JAMES BROWN) / Think (ARETHA FRANKLIN) / Theme from Rawhide / Minnie the moocher (CAB CALLOWAY) / Sweet home Chicago / Jailhouse rock. *<(cd-iss. Feb87; K2 50715)> <(cd re-iss. Nov95; 7567 82787-2)>*

S/track review: Met with critical derision on its original release – 'Time Out' dubbed it a "27 million dollar whoopee cushion" – John Landis' suited-and-booted R&B romp has since become one of the most celebrated rock movies of all time. Titular soul brothers JOHN BELUSHI and DAN AYKROYD are comedians by trade, singers by default, elevated from 'Saturday Night Live' to big screen immortality with a sharp line in synchronised fashion and a dog-eared, wholly predictable songbook. If you haven't seen the film, you'd be forgiven for failing to grasp the point of this soundtrack. There's not an original song in sight, only one which qualifies as blues and assorted soul-royalty performing songs they've performed better elsewhere. But there's no arguing with the 'BROTHERS' enthusiasm; it seeps and sweats from every note. And it's especially pungent on Solomon Burke's 'Everybody Needs Somebody To Love', the one track which really gives a flavour of the film's deadpan momentum. BELUSHI isn't blessed with a voice to match his dress sense but black music clearly runs in his blood, and it helps that STEVE CROPPER and DONALD 'DUCK' DUNN – the 'Stax'/ M.G.'s engine room – are backing him up. It also helps that RAY CHARLES partners him on 'Shake A Tail Feather', but even on solo turns like 'She Caught The Katy' and 'Sweet Home Chicago', he sings with the shining-eyed glee of a honky kid in a black candy store. CAB CALLOWAY and ARETHA FRANKLIN both make decent cameos but if for nothing else, this record is worth hearing for JAMES BROWN sermonising in the spirit of his righteous Georgian forebear, the Rev. J.M. Gates. Say it loud, they're Blues and they're proud. *BG*

Album rating: *6

– spinoff releases, etc. –

the BLUES BROTHERS: Gimme Some Lovin' / She Caught The Katy

May 80. (7") *<3666> (K 11499)* [18] Jun80 [ ]

the BLUES BROTHERS: Everybody Needs Somebody To Love / Jailhouse Rock

Oct 80. (7") *(K 11625)* [ ] [ ]

the BLUES BROTHERS: Everybody Needs Somebody To Love / ARETHA FRANKLIN: Think

Mar 90. (7"/c-s) *East West; (A 7951/+C)* [–] [12]
(12"+=/cd-s+=) *(A 7951 T/CD)* – (other non-OST song).

the BLUES BROTHERS: Complete

Sep 99. (d-cd) *(7567 80840-2)* [–] [ ]
– (Briefcase Full Of Blues / **the Blues Brothers** / Made In America / The Best Of The Blues Brothers)

BLUES BROTHERS 2000

1998 (US 123m) Universal Pictures (PG-13)

Film genre: R&B/Rock Musical road comedy

Top guns: s-w: John Landis (+ dir) ← the BLUES BROTHERS ← ANIMAL HOUSE, Dan Aykroyd ← the BLUES BROTHERS

Stars: Dan Aykroyd *(Elwood Blues)* ← THIS IS MY LIFE ← the BLUES BROTHERS ← the RUTLES, John Goodman *(Mighty Mack McTeer)* ← TRUE STORIES ← SWEET DREAMS / → O BROTHER, WHERE ART THOU? → COYOTE UGLY → the EMPEROR'S NEW GROOVE → STORYTELLING → MASKED AND ANONYMOUS → OVERNIGHT → BEYOND THE SEA, Joe Morton *(Cab Chamberlain)* ← CROSSROADS / → STEALTH, J. Evan Bonifant *(Buster Blues)*, Nia Peeples *(Lt. Elizondo)*, Kathleen Freeman *(Mother Mary Stigmata)* ← the BLUES BROTHERS, Frank Oz *(warden)* ← the BLUES BROTHERS, **Steve Lawrence** *(Maury Sline)* ← the BLUES BROTHERS, Darrell Hammond *(Robertson)*, **Erykah Badu** *(Queen Mousette)*, **Aretha Franklin** *(Mrs. Murphy)* ← the BLUES BROTHERS, **James BROWN** *(Rev. Cleophus James)*, **B.B. KING** *(Malvern Gasperon)*, **Junior Wells** *(himself)* ← CHICAGO BLUES, **Lonnie Brooks** *(himself)* ← PRIDE AND JOY / → GODFATHERS AND SONS, **Steve Cropper** *(himself)* ← SATISFACTION ← the BLUES BROTHERS, **Donald Dunn** *(himself)* ← the BLUES BROTHERS, Murphy Dunne *(Murph)* ← the BLUES BROTHERS, **Jonny Lang** *(custodian)*, **Matt "Guitar" Murphy** *(himself)* ← the BLUES BROTHERS, **Willie "Too Big" Hall** *(himself)* ← the BLUES BROTHERS, **Tom Malone** *(himself)* → the BLUES BROTHERS, **"Blue Lou" Marini** *(himself)* ← the BLUES BROTHERS, **Alan Rubin** *(Mr. Fabulous)* ← the BLUES BROTHERS, Jeff Morris *(Bob)* ← the BORDER ← the BLUES BROTHERS ← PAYDAY ← KID GALAHAD, **Sam Moore** *(Reverend Morris)* ← TAPEHEADS ← ONE-TRICK PONY, **Eddie Floyd** *(Ed)*, **Wilson Pickett** *(Mr. Pickett)* ← SGT. PEPPER'S LONELY HEARTS CLUB BAND ← SAVE THE CHILDREN ← SOUL TO SOUL / → BLUES ODYSSEY → ONLY THE STRONG SURVIVE, **Blues Traveler:- John Popper** ← *PRIVATE PARTS* ← *WOODSTOCK '94* / → *MY GENERATION*, **Bobby Sheehan, Chan Kinchla, Brendan Hill** *(themselves)* / **Louisiana Gator Boys:- Eric Clapton** ← **TOMMY**, **Gary U.S. Bonds** *(performer)*, **Bo DIDDLEY** *(performer)*, **Isaac HAYES** *(performer)*, **KoKo Taylor** *(performer)* ← PRIDE AND JOY ← WILD AT HEART ← CHICAGO BLUES / → GODFATHERS AND SONS, **DR. JOHN** *(performer)*, **Lou Rawls** *(performer)* ← ANGEL, ANGEL, DOWN WE GO, **Billy PRESTON** *(performer)*, **Travis Tritt** *(performer)* → DILL SCALLION, **Joshua Redman** *(performer)*, **Charlie Musselwhite** *(performer)*, **Jack de Johnette** *(performer)*, **Jeff Baxter** *(performer)* → OVERNIGHT, **Jimmie Vaughan** *(performer)* ← GREAT BALLS OF FIRE! ← LIGHT OF DAY, **Steve Winwood** *(performer)* ← WOODSTOCK 94 ← GLASTONBURY FAYRE ← CUCUMBER CASTLE ← the GHOST GOES GEAR / → RED, WHITE & BLUES, **Clarence Clemons** *(performer)* ← BILL & TED'S EXCELLENT ADVENTURE / → SWING, **Grover Washington Jr., Jon Faddis, Tommy McDonnell, Wylie Weeks, Prakash John** *(Tent revival bassist)* ← WELCOME TO MY NIGHTMARE

Storyline: Finally out of the slammer, Blues Brother (singular, now that his bro is dead) Elwood wastes little time in seeking out the fearsome Mother Mary, who reveals he has a long lost step brother, Cabel, and unwisely charges him with the mentorship of an orphaned child. Although he fails miserably with his step sibling (who just happens to be a police chief), he promotes the kid to honorary little Blues Brother, rounds up the rest of the band (Duck Dunne and Steve Cropper have been reduced to counselling criminals on a radio phone-in), and succeeds in provoking the ire of the local Russian mafia who solemnly promise to "drink vodka from their skulls". Much car chasing (the biggest, most brainless car pile-up in screen history), capering and choreography ensue (including a performance of Eddie Floyd's '634-5789' in a sexline call centre) as Elwood strives to save music from "digitally sampled techno grooves, quasi-synth rhythms, pseudo songs of violence laden gangster rap, acid pop and simpering, saccharine, soul-less slush". Right on bro. *BG*

Movie rating: *5.5

Visual: dvd

Off the record: (see above/below)

——

Various Artists (BLUES BROTHERS BAND *) (score: Paul Shaffer)

Feb 98. (cd/c) *Universal;* <*(UND 53116)*> [12] [ ]
– Born in Chicago (PAUL BUTTERFIELD BLUES BAND) / Blues don't bother me (MATT "GUITAR" MURPHY) / Harmonica musings (JOHN POPPER) / Cheaper to keep her (DAN AYKROYD, LONNIE BROOKS, JUNIOR WELLS & *) / Perry Mason theme (*) / Looking for a fox (JOHN GOODMAN, DAN AYKROYD & *) / I can't turn you loose (*) / R-E-S-P-E-C-T (ARETHA FRANKLIN & *) / 634-5789 (Soulsville, U.S.A.) (EDDIE FLOYD, WILSON PICKETT, JONNY LANG & *) / Maybe I'm wrong (BLUES TRAVELER) / Riders in the sky (a cowboy legend) (DAN AYKROYD, JOHN GOODMAN & *) / John the revelator (TAJ MAHAL, SAM MOORE, JOE MORTON, SHARON RILEY & FAITH CHORALE) / Let there be drums (CARL LaFONG TRIO) / Season of the witch (DR. JOHN & *) / Funky Nassau (JOE MORTON, DAN AYKROYD, JOHN GOODMAN, PAUL SHAFFER, ERYKAH BADU & *) / How blue can you get? (LOUISIANA GATOR BOYS) / Turn on your love light (JOE MORTON, DAN AYKROYD, JOHN GOODMAN, J. EVAN BONIFANT & *) / New Orleans (LOUISIANA GATOR BOYS & *).

S/track review: With John Belushi and Cab Calloway long dead, this pre-millennial nostalgia project was never going to inspire much beyond disparaging reviews, many of which excused the film by way of its soundtrack. The music isn't bad, especially considering that all-star get-togethers often have a surprisingly consistent staleness-to-superstar ratio, and that this one's literally buckling under big names. The LOUISIANA GATOR BOYS has to be one of the most comprehensive supergroups ever assembled: BB KING, onetime Steely Dan guitarist JEFF "Skunk" BAXTER, ERIC CLAPTON, CLARENCE CLEMMONS, former Miles Davis drummer JACK DeJOHNETTE, BO DIDDLEY, DR JOHN, session trumpet legend JON FADDIS, ISAAC HAYES, LOU RAWLS, BILLY PRESTON, GROVER WASHINGTON JR., STEVE WINWOOD, CHARLIE MUSSELWHITE and TRAVIS TRITT amongst others; do they exceed the sum of their legendary parts? Is it reasonable to expect them to? Nope, and not really. The question of whether any soundtrack really needs yet another run through ARETHA's 'R-E-S-P-E-C-T' (great as its car showroom choreography is in the movie), seems so rhetorical as to be irrelevant, and attempts at humour/parody (see 'Cheaper To Keep Her', 'Riders In The Sky') are simply tired. Far worthier of all those travel expenses – and about the only time the record really taps the black music motherlode – is the Son House blues, 'John The Revelator', performed by SAM MOORE and the late, great JAMES BROWN, whose beseeching screen coda has taken on a certain poignancy now that he's gone for ever; even better would've been the TAJ MAHAL a cappella sung over the movie's main title, but let's be thankful for small mercies. In a different bag but nearly as soulful is a sweaty, swampy incarnation of Donovan's 'Season Of The Witch', growled by DR JOHN over the slimiest grooves the regrouped Blues Brothers Band lays down all programme. Among the younger generation, ERYKAH BADU shines, scats and squeals on a surprisingly spry 'Funky Nassau', oiled by RALPH McDONALD's percussion, while the PAUL BUTTERFIELD BAND's 'Born In Chicago' is as hard-driving a slab of vintage white-boy blues as you're going to get. *BG*

Album rating: *6

□ BLUES FOR LOVERS alt.
(⇒ BALLAD IN BLUE)

BODY ROCK

1984 (US 93m) New World Pictures (PG-13)

Film genre: Pop/Dance Musical drama

Top guns: dir: Marcelo Epstein / s-w: Desmond Nakano → LAST EXIT TO BROOKLYN (+ story w/ Kimberley Lynn White)

Stars: Lorenzo Lamas *(Chilly D)* ← GREASE / → the MUSE, Vicki Frederick *(Claire)*, Cameron Dye *(E-Z)* → SCENES FROM THE GOLDMINE, Michelle Nicastro *(Darlene)*, Ray Sharkey *(Terrence)* ← DU-BEAT-E-O ← the IDOLMAKER, Seth Kaufman *(Jama)*, La Ron A. Smith *(Magick)*, Rene Elizondo *(Snake)*, Russell Clark *(Jay)*, Joseph Whipp *(Donald)*, Oz Rock *(Ricky Riccardo)*, Robin Menken *(Jodie)* ← THIS IS SPINAL TAP ← THANK GOD IT'S FRIDAY ← the STRAWBERRY STATEMENT ← FOOLS, Carol White *(unemployed lady)* ← MADE

Storyline: With breakdance all the rage – well it certainly angered me – the movie was supposed to cash-in on similar celluloid features such as 'WILD STYLE', 'BREAKIN'' and 'BEAT STREET', all delivered to the big screen just prior to this box office flop. King of the breakdancers, Chilly D, fine-tunes his talents to find fame and fortune in the Big Apple, while all around him including his steady girlfriend get the heave-ho. *MCS*

Movie rating: *3

Visual: video

Off the record: Lorenzo Lamas' performance – although a little OTT – was the highlight of the film, while his singing was definitely well above par. *MCS*

Various Artists (score/composer: Sylvester Levay)

Sep 84. (lp) *EMI America;* <*SO 17140*> [ ] [–]
– Body rock (MARIA VIDAL) / Teamwork (DAVID LASLEY) / Why you wanna break my heart? (DWIGHT TWILLEY) / One thing leads to another (ROBERTA FLACK) / Let your body rock (don't stop) (RALPH McDONALD) / Vanishing point (BAXTER ROBERTSON) / Sharpshooter (LAURA BRANIGAN) / The jungle (ASHFORD & SIMPSON) / Deliver (MARTIN BRILEY) / The closest to love (ASHFORD & SIMPSON).

S/track review: At first glance, the album features only a few hitmakers of their day, 'Solid As A Rock'-crew ASHFORD & SIMPSON, 'Killing Me Softly'-diva ROBERTA FLACK and 'Gloria' hitmaker, LAURA BRANIGAN – it's a pity these tracks couldn't have entered the fray here. On closer inspection, you'll find Tulsa-born rocker, DWIGHT TWILLEY, who'd recently cracked the US Top 20 with 'Girls'; his song, featured in the movie, 'Why Do You Wanna Break My Heart?', was typical of the day, safe FM for MOR buffs into anything soft-rock. English session man, MARTIN BRILEY (who'd scored in the US charts with 'The Salt In My Tears') was present and correct here courtesy of mild AOR number, 'Deliver'. LORENZO LAMAS' contribution, 'Smooth Talker' (a subsequent minor hit B-side and penned by Danny Sembello) was not included here among the guff that was unknowns DAVID LASLEY, RALPH McDONALD and BAXTER ROBERTSON; a session man's paradise. The most recognizable track was indeed the title track, a blistering dancefloor-filler that reached the Top 50 and even the UK Top 20, albeit a year later. *MCS*

Album rating: *3.5

– spinoff hits, etc. –

MARIA VIDAL: Body Rock / ASHFORD & SIMPSON: Do You Know Who I Am

Aug 84. (7"/12") *EMI America;* <*8233*> *(EA/12EA 189)* [48] Aug85 [11]

the BODYGUARD

1992 (US 130m) Kasdan Pictures / Warner Bros. (R)

Film genre: romantic showbiz/R&B/Pop-music drama

Top guns: dir: Mick Jackson / s-w: Lawrence Kasdan

Stars: Kevin Costner *(Frank Farmer)*, **Whitney HOUSTON** *(Rachel Marron)*, **Gary Kemp** *(Sy Spector)*, Bill Cobbs *(Bill Devaney)* ← ROADSIDE PROPHETS ← a HERO AIN'T NOTHIN' BUT A SANDWICH / → THAT

THING YOU DO! → a MIGHTY WIND, Ralph Waite *(Herb Farmer)* ← TROUBLE MAN, Tomas Arana *(Greg Portman)* ← the LAST TEMPTATION OF CHRIST, Michelle Lamar Richards *(Nikki Marron)*, Mike Starr *(Tony Scipelli)* ← WHO'S THAT GIRL ← MAGIC STICKS, Robert Wuhl *(Oscar host)* ← BATMAN ← GOOD MORNING, VIETNAM ← FLASHDANCE, Richard Schiff *(Skip Thomas; Oscar show director)* ← YOUNG GUNS II / → GRACE OF MY HEART → TOUCH → I AM SAM → RAY, Joe Unger *(journalist)* ← ROAD HOUSE / → SOUTH OF HEAVEN, WEST OF HELL, Susan Traylor *(dress designer)* → FINDING GRACELAND → MASKED AND ANONYMOUS

Storyline: Our Whitney mirrors her real-life role as a megastar in this Lawrence Kasdan scripted blockbuster which belatedly handed the role of bodyguard and romantic foil to Kevin Costner rather than Kasdan's original choice of Steve McQueen. As Rachel Marron, Houston inevitably falls in love with her overly assiduous protector, whom she's been forced to hire after receiving a series of death threats. *BG*

Movie rating: *5

Visual: video + dvd

Off the record: Gary Kemp (older brother of 'Eastenders' actor, Martin; also lead roles as the twins in the film, 'The Krays') was the guitarist with new romantics, Spandau Ballet. *MCS*

—

WHITNEY HOUSTON (*) & Various (score: ALAN SILVESTRI **)

Nov 92. (cd/c/lp) *Arista; <(07822 18699-2/-4/-1)>* [1] [1]
– I will always love you (*) / I have nothing (*) / I'm every woman (*) / Run to you (*) / Queen of the night (*) / Jesus loves me (*) / Even if my heart would break (KENNY G & AARON NEVILLE) / Someday (I'm coming back) (LISA STANSFIELD) / It's gonna be a lovely day (the S.O.U.L. S.Y.S.T.E.M.) / (What's so funny 'bout) Peace, love and understanding (CURTIS STIGERS) / Waiting for you (KENNY G) *[UK-only]* / Trust in me (JOE COCKER & SASS GORDON) / Theme from The Bodyguard (**).

S/track review: A multi-million selling, Grammy-winning phenomenon which outsold WHITNEY HOUSTON's regular studio albums, 'THE BODYGUARD' drew most of its momentum from the success of its Dolly Parton-penned lead single, 'I Will Always Love You'. Parton had already performed the song in the 1982 Burt Reynolds vehicle, 'The BEST LITTLE WHOREHOUSE IN TEXAS', but HOUSTON commercialised it with typically polished, neo-gospel power, holding the US No.1 spot for almost three months and rendering it the second-biggest selling single performed by a female artist in UK chart history. The rest of the soundtrack is split pretty much equally between HOUSTON songs and airbrushed add-ons from the likes of KENNY G and CURTIS STIGERS. The WHITNEY tracks are actually among the most accomplished of her career, lending the soundtrack much of its enduring appeal. Ballads aside, Ashford & Simpson's 'I'm Every Woman' is the epitome of early 90s R&B-oriented dance-pop, not exactly on a par with Aretha's 'A Deeper Love', but on the same wavelength, while her version of 'Jesus Loves Me', tame as it is, illuminates HOUSTON's gospel roots more overtly than anything else in her catalogue. Among the best of the rest, the hallowed tonsils of AARON NEVILLE were a welcome bonus on G's 'Even If My Heart Would Break', rendering it – ironically – the most soulful cut on the album. The then-ubiquitous Clivilles & Cole/the S.O.U.L. S.Y.S.T.E.M.'s dancefloor-friendly take on Bill Withers' 'It's Gonna Be A Lovely Day' remains amusing nostalgia fare, dated beyond its years, while the calibre of Nick Lowe's writing saves the great '(What's So Funny 'Bout) Peace, Love And Understanding' from too ignominious a fate at the hands of STIGERS. Hidden away at the end of the album, meanwhile, Alan Silvestri's 'Theme From The Bodyguard' sounds like an afterthought. *BG*

Album rating: *5.5

– spinoff hits, etc. –

WHITNEY HOUSTON: I Will Always Love You / Jesus Loves Me
Nov 92. (7"/c-s/12"/cd-s) *<12490> (74321 12065-7/-4/-1/-2)* [1] [1]

the S.O.U.L. S.Y.S.T.E.M. introducing Michelle Visage: It's Gonna Be A Lovely Day / (version)
Nov 92. (c-s/cd-s) *<12486> (74321 12569-4/-2)* [34] Jan93 [17]

LISA STANSFIELD: Someday (I'm Coming Back) / (mixes)
Dec 92. (7"/c-s/12"/cd-s) *(74321 12356-7/-4/-1/-2)* [–] [10]

WHITNEY HOUSTON: I'm Every Woman / (mixes)
Dec 92. (7"/c-s/12"/cd-s) *<12519> (74321 13150-7/-4/-1/-2)* [4] Feb93 [4]

WHITNEY HOUSTON: I Have Nothing
Feb 93. (7"/c-s/12"/cd-s) *<12527> (74321 14614-7/-4/-1/-2)* [4] Apr93 [3]

WHITNEY HOUSTON: Run To You
Jun 93. (7"/c-s/cd-s) *<12570> (74321 15333-7/-4/-2)* [31] Jul93 [15]

WHITNEY HOUSTON: Queen Of The Night
Oct 93. (7"/c-s/12"/cd-s) *(74321 16930-7/-4/-1/-2)* [–] [14]

□ Sonny BONO
(⇒ SONNY & CHER)

BOOGIE NIGHTS

1997 (US 155m) New Line Cinema (R)

Film genre: showbiz comedy drama

Top guns: s-w + dir: Paul Thomas Anderson → MAGNOLIA

Stars: Mark Wahlberg *(Eddie Adams / Dirk Diggler)* ← the BASKETBALL DIARIES / → ROCK STAR → OVERNIGHT, Burt Reynolds *(Jack Horner)* ← the BEST LITTLE WHOREHOUSE IN TEXAS ← DELIVERANCE / → BROKEN BRIDGES, Julianne Moore *(Maggie / Amber Waves)* → MAGNOLIA → I'M NOT THERE, John C. Reilly *(Reed Rothchild)* ← GEORGIA / → MAGNOLIA → the PICK OF DESTINY → WALK HARD: THE DEWEY COX STORY, Heather Graham *(Brandy; rollergirl)* ← EVEN COWGIRLS GET THE BLUES ← SHOUT / → COMMITTED, Don Cheadle *(Buck Swope)* ← ROADSIDE PROPHETS / → THINGS BEHIND THE SUN → SWORDFISH, Philip Seymour Hoffman *(Scotty)* → MAGNOLIA → ALMOST FAMOUS → COLD MOUNTAIN, William H. Macy *(Little Bill)* ← COLIN FITZ LIVES! ← the LAST DRAGON / → WAG THE DOG → MAGNOLIA, Luis Guzman *(Maurice TT Rodriguez)* ← SHORT EYES / → MAGNOLIA, Thomas Jane *(Todd Parker)* → MAGNOLIA, Philip Baker Hall *(Floyd Gondolli)* ← THREE O'CLOCK HIGH / → MAGNOLIA → the INSIDER, Ricky Jay *(Kurt Longjohn)* → MAGNOLIA → LAST DAYS, Alfred Molina *(Rahad Jackson)* ← DEAD MAN / → MAGNOLIA → COFFEE AND CIGARETTES, Nicole Ari Parker *(Becky Barnett)* ← the END OF VIOLENCE / → BROWN SUGAR, Melora Walters *(Jessie St. Vincent)* → MAGNOLIA → COLD MOUNTAIN, Robert Downey Sr. *(Burt; studio manager)* ← TO LIVE AND DIE IN L.A. ← YOU'VE GOT TO WALK IT LIKE YOU TALK IT . . . / → MAGNOLIA, Robert Ridgely *(the Colonel James)* ← THAT THING YOU DO!, **John DOE** *(Andrew's father)*, **Jon Brion** *(awards ceremony band member)*

Storyline: The L.A. porn industry comes under scrutiny, albeit aside the burgeoning 70s disco scene. Greenhorn Eddie becomes hardcore's "big-boy" centre spread (with a new moniker Dirk Diggler in place), while life under the proverbial spotlight drags him into the world of drugs. The sort-of mirrorball effect also shows his newfound dysfunctional porn family at its most gruesome and brazen. *MCS*

Movie rating: *8

Visual: video + dvd

Off the record: Jon Brion, now a film composer in his own right, was a one-time member of indie supergroup, the Grays, alongside ex-Jellyfish guitarist Jason Faulkner. *MCS*

—

Various Artists (score: MICHAEL PENN *)

Oct 97. (cd/c) *Capitol; <(8 55631-2/-4)>* 84 Jan98
– Intro (Feel the heat) (JOHN C. REILLY & MARK WAHLBERG) / Best of my love (the EMOTIONS) / Jungle fever (CHAKACHAS) / Brand new key (MELANIE) / Spill the wine (ERIC BURDON & WAR) / Got to give it up – part 1 (MARVIN GAYE) / Machine gun (the COMMODORES) / Magnet and steel (WALTER EGAN) / Ain't no stoppin; us now (McFADDEN & WHITEHEAD) / Sister Christian (NIGHT RANGER) / Livin' thing (ELECTRIC LIGHT ORCHESTRA) / God only knows (the BEACH BOYS) / The big top – theme from 'Boogie Nights' (* & PATRICK WARREN).

S/track review: Under the backdrop of the booming 70s porn industry comes 'BOOGIE NIGHTS', the disco mirrorball of the day, although shockingly without the presence of Heatwave's hit song of the same name. Dancefloor fillers of the era stem from the EMOTIONS ('Best Of My Love'), McFADDEN & WHITEHEAD ('Ain't No Stoppin' Us Now'), MARVIN GAYE ('Got To Give It Up – Part 1'), CHAKACHAS ('Jungle Fever') and a COMMODORES' funky instrumental ('Machine Gun'), while there are extreme oddities aboard. One such oddity is the inclusion of MELANIE's kooky folk song, 'Brand New Key', while soft-rock & power ballad are represented by WALTER EGAN ('Magnet And Steel') and NIGHT RANGER ('Sister Christian') respectively. The oldest cue on the soundtrack comes via 'God Only Knows' by the BEACH BOYS, while two other songs, 'Spill The Wine' (by ERIC BURDON & WAR) and 'Livin' Thing' (by ELECTRIC LIGHT ORCHESTRA) fit into the scheme of things quite well. Opening cut, 'Feel The Heat' matches up actors JOHN C. REILLY and MARK WAHLBERG (Marky Mark to his fans), but it's the 10-minute finale score cue by MICHAEL PENN and PATRICK WARREN that produces the film's gripping emotion. 'Volume 2' combines another interesting collage of recycled pop disco and light rock – a better idea would've been to stick them into the one double-CD package.

Album rating: *7.5 / Vol.2 *6.5

– spinoff releases, etc. –

Various Artists: Boogie Nights 2

Jan 98. (cd/c) *<93076-2>* –
– Mama told me not to come (THREE DOG NIGHT) / Fooled around and fell in love (ELVIN BISHOP) / You sexy thing (HOT CHOCOLATE) / Boogie shoes (KC & THE SUNSHINE BAND) / Do your thing (CHARLES WRIGHT & THE WATTS 103RD STREET RHYTHM BAND) / Driver's seat (SNIFF N' THE TEARS) / Feel too good (the MOVE) / Jessie's girl (RICK SPRINGFIELD) / J.P. walk (SOUND EXPERIENCE) / I want to be free (the OHIO PLAYERS) / Joy (APOLLO 100).

☐ Pat BOONE segment
(⇒ APRIL LOVE)

BOP GIRL

aka BOP GIRL GOES CALYPSO

1957 (US 80m b&w) United Artists

Film genre: showbiz/Pop Musical comedy

Top guns: dir: Howard W. Koch ← UNTAMED YOUTH / s-w: Arnold Belgard (story: Hendrik Vollaerts)

Stars: Judy Tyler *(Jo Thomas)* → JAILHOUSE ROCK, **Bobby Troup** *(Robert Hilton)*, Margo Woode *(Marion Hendricks)*, Lucien Littlefield *(Prof. Winthrop)*, George O'Hanlon *(Barney; the club owner)*, Jerry Barclay *(Jerry; backup band leader)* ← UNTAMED YOUTH, **Lord Flea** *(performer)* ← CALYPSO JOE, Judy Harriet *(YMCA rehearsal vocalist)*, **Mary Kaye** *(performer)*, **Nino Tempo** *(speciality act)* ← the GIRL CAN'T HELP IT, **the Titans:- Larry Green, Charles Wright, Sam Barnett, Alvin Branom, Curtis McNair** *(performers)*, **the Goofers** *(performers)*, **the Cubanos** *(performers)*

Storyline: Bob Hilton is a music student doing a graduate thesis on rock n' roll. Using his invention the "applausemeter", he becomes convinced that calypso will be the next musical craze, and to prove his theory he recruits bop singer Jo Thomas and gets her to sing her songs calypso style. Could this be the end of bop music in Jamaica? Probably. *JZ*

Movie rating: *3.5

Visual: none (no audio OST; score: Les Baxter)

Off the record: Bobby Troup (b.18 Oct'1918, Harrisburg, Pennsylvania) was famous for at one classic song, 'Route 66', covered by the likes of Nat 'King' Cole (in 1946), Chuck Berry, Nelson Riddle, the Rolling Stones, Depeche Mode, etc. Bobby was married to cool jazz singer, Julie London, until his heart attack/death on the 7th of February, 1999, at his home in Sherman Oaks, California. Nicknamed "the First Lady of Rock and Roll", **Mary Kaye** (b. 9 Jan'24, Detroit, Michigan) sang and played Hawaiian guitar – Fender Stratocaster named after her – along with her own jazz trio; one minor hit in 1959, 'You Can't Be True Dear'. The Hawaiian descendent of the last reigning monarch, Mary recently died on 17th February, 2007, of heart and respiratory failure. *MCS*

BORDER RADIO

1987 (US 87m b&w) Coyote Productions (R)

Film genre: urban showbiz road movie

Top guns: s-w + dir: Allison Anders → GAS, FOOD LODGING → FOUR ROOMS → GRACE OF MY HEART → SUGAR TOWN → THINGS BEHIND THE SUN, Dean Lent, Kurt Voss → DELUSION → SUGAR TOWN → THINGS BEHIND THE SUN → DOWN AND OUT WITH THE DOLLS

Stars: Chris D. *(Jeff Bailey)*, Chris Shearer *(Chris)* → GRACE OF MY HEART, Luanna Anders *(Lu)*, **Dave Alvin** *(Dave)* ← STREETS OF FIRE, Iris Berry *(scenester)*, **John DOE** *(Dean)*, Devon Anders *(Devon)*, **Eddie Flowers** *(thug)*, **Texacala Jones** *(babysitter)* ← DU-BEAT-E-O, **Green On Red:- * Dan Stuart, Chris Cacavas, Chuck Prophet, Daren Hess, Jack Waterson** *(themselves)* * → HIGH AND DRY, **Julie Christensen** *(door girl)*

Storyline: Jeff Bailey is the leader of a punk band who are rather cheesed off with life as a club owner hasn't paid them for a gig. Undeterred, Jeff turns into an amateur safecracker and makes off with the club's loot to Mexico. His wife and band-mates cover for him as the list of his pursuers grows longer, and soon Jeff will have to decide whether to stay in Tequila-land or come back to face the music. *JZ*

Movie rating: *4

Visual: video

Off the record: Eddie Flowers (b. 8 Aug'57, Jackson, Mississippi, USA; aka Crawlin' Ed) was leader of two seminal punk/hardcore outfits, the Gizmos (in '76-'77) and Crawlspace. *MCS*

—

Various Artists (score: DAVE ALVIN composer *)

Nov 87. (lp/c) *Enigma; <SJ/4XSJ 73221>* –
– Border radio (the TONYS) * / La frontera I (* and STEVE BERLIN) / Drugs (the LAZY COWGIRLS) / Burning guitar (* and STEVE BERLIN) / Mi vida loca – acoustic (*) / Little honey (JOHN DOE and *) / Mother's worry (DIVINE HORSEMEN) / Sixteen ways (GREEN ON RED) / La frontera II (* and STEVE BERLIN) / Lilly white hands (CHRIS D.) / Driving to Mexico (* and STEVE BERLIN) / Mi vida loca – Border Radio theme (*).

S/track review: Los Angeles has probably the most vibrant and diverse music scene in America, if not the world, and this 'BORDER RADIO' OST (from vintage year, 1987) features the cream of the "cowpunk" crop. Kicking off with the title track by the movie's supergroup of sorts, the TONYS (i.e. Rank & File brothers, Tony &

Chip Kinman, Blasters bassist John Bazz, plus Long Ryders posse Steve McCarthy and Greg Sowders), the alt-country-rock song combines elements of Duane Allman's 'Happily Married Man' and Gordon Lightfoot's 'Sundown'. The Blasters' connection was focal to 'BORDER RADIO' via guitarist DAVE ALVIN, who actually wrote the said track, as he did most of the instrumental score cues, some with another Blasters player, STEVE BERLIN (sax, keyboards). Desert-bowl dirges such as 'La Frontera I & II' and 'Burning Guitar', conjure up a sort of "meeting by the river-plate" performed by Cooder and Eno – what a soundtrack that would make. ALVIN also contributes the 'Paris, Texas'-like 'Mi Vida Loca' film theme, while X-man, JOHN DOE, provides the vocals for the collaborative, 'Little Honey'; X's DJ Bonebrake, Los Lobos' David Hidalgo and the Blasters' pairing of Bazz (again!) and Bill Bateman were additional musicians. Highlights from 'BORDER . . .' stem conclusively from the LAZY COWGIRLS (not a female in sight!) on the buzzsaw, garage-rock number 'Drugs', while picked from the same recording year (1985) is the classic GREEN ON RED staple, 'Sixteen Ways'. Just when you think it can't get any better, up pops CHRIS D (Desjardins) for two Gun Club-ish cuts, the solo 'Lilly White Hands' (from '84) and his DIVINE HORSEMEN's 'Mother's Worry'. Never been released on CD as of 2007 – shame on you 'Enigma' records. *MCS*

Album rating: *8.5

BORN TO LOSE

1999 (US 90m; str8-to-vid) Vanguard Cinema (R)

Film genre: Rock/Pop Musical comedy drama

Top guns: s-w: Doug Cawker (+ dir), Howard Roth

Stars: Joseph Rye *(Stevie Monroe)*, **Francis Fallon** *(Johnny)*, Elyse Ashton *(Lisa)*, David Goldman *(Bob)*, Alex Lange *(Walter)*, Wendy Latta *(Janie)*

Storyline: The Spoilers are a struggling punk band in downtown L.A. Lead singer Stevie is a bit of a headbanger, but that's as much due to his doped-up bandmates as his own drug problem. Just as it seems they're destined for oblivion they get "noticed" by PR girl Lisa, who convinces a recording company to give them a chance. However Lisa turns out to be as big a junkie as Stevie and the Spoilers look like spoiling their chance of the big time. *JZ*

Movie rating: *4

Visual: dvd

Off the record: Francis Fallon (was of the band, Nero) and **Greg Kuehn** (was ex-keyboards w/ T.S.O.L.).

—

Various Artists (score: Greg Kuehn / film *)

Jun 99. (cd) *Bomp; <(LAFF 6997)>*
– Tight pants (IGGY & THE STOOGES) / Loose is good (*) / A little sex & death (the LAZY COWGIRLS) / Baby's gotta have her way (the ZEROS) / Don't give it away (WHITE FLAG) / I can't feel it (*) / Little Tokyo (the STREETWALKIN' CHEETAHS) / Ultra fuck (the DARLINGS) / Pill box (JONESES) / The Social Distortions (*) / Beat girl (LOVEMASTERS) / (Ride on) Silver surfer (TRASH CAN SCHOOL) / Danceteria (BLACK ANGEL'S DEATH SONG) / It sucks (*) / Goin' down (the BEES) / Black & white (the ZEROS) / Criminal (the JONESES) / This ain't our last goodbye (SACRED HEARTS) / I have no idea (*) / Pain killer (BED OF EYES) / Frustration (FANCY LADS) / Situation (TEXAS TERRI & THE STIFF NOTES) / Liquor store (the SPOILERS) / I'm straight (the MODERN LOVERS).

S/track review: Flying the flag for Greg Shaw's legendary independent imprint, 'Bomp', this OST stretches the listener's punk-rock brain to new extremes. Featuring nearly twenty songs from L.A.'s rife underground punk scene, completed further by some splendid dialogue. How else would you kick off a punk album, than with the "Godfather" himself, IGGY POP (here as 1973 incarnation, IGGY & THE STOOGES). His er . . . 'Tight Pants' comes across as another "Godfather", soul brother James Brown, well, at least in blood, sweat and enthusiasm. Second on the proverbial bill, the LAZY COWGIRLS (with 'A Little Sex & Death') produce a garage-like sound once right at home with Dr Feelgood, while the Zeros chalk up two gritty, Jam-tastic numbers, 'Baby's Gotta Have Her Way' and 'Black'n'White'. Another band with two songs, the JONESES ('Pill Box' and 'Criminal'), although little known from Boston, are one of the best punk revivalists of the 90s, example their 'Criminal History' comp for 'Sympathy For The Record Industry' label. From Sunnymead, California, WHITE FLAG (featuring Kim Shattuck & Ronnie Barnett of the Muffs) fire in the Go-Go's-esque, 'Don't Give It Away', while grrrl-outfit, the DARLINGS smash it up with 'Ultra Fuck'. With a few listens, this album brings it all back, whether in true '77 style or in retro-fied motion, the other highlights being the Vibrators-ish STREETWALKIN' CHEETAHS ('Little Tokyo'). Taking their moniker from a Velvet Underground track, BLACK ANGEL'S DEATH SONG contribute 'Danceteria', next to the Link Wray-esque TRASH CAN SCHOOL growl with '(Ride On) Silver Surfer' (Jim Miller was a member of the mid-90s outfit). If IGGY was an inspired choice for the opener, then there could be no one better than Jonathan Richman and his MODERN LOVERS to close it, 'I'm Straight' (out of the Kim Fowley sessions) very convincingly indeed. *MCS*

Album rating: *7

BOUND FOR GLORY

1976 (US 148m) United Artists Pictures (PG)

Film genre: trad-Folk-music road movie/bio-pic

Top guns: dir: Hal Ashby ← HAROLD AND MAUDE ← the LANDLORD / → LET'S SPEND THE NIGHT TOGETHER / s-w: Robert Gretchell → SWEET DREAMS (book: **Woody Guthrie**)

Stars: David Carradine *(Woody Guthrie)* → the LONG RIDERS → ROADSIDE PROPHETS → AMERICAN REEL → KILL BILL: VOL.1 → KILL BILL: VOL.2, Ronny Cox *(Ozark Bule)* ← DELIVERANCE, Melinda Dillon *(Mary Guthrie)* → SONGWRITER → MAGNOLIA, Gail Strickland *(Pauline)* → ONE ON ONE, John Lehne *(Locke)* → BROTHERS → AMERICAN HOT WAX → CARNY → LADIES AND GENTLEMEN, THE FABULOUS STAINS, Ji-Tu Cumbuka *(Slim Snedeger)* ← BLACULA ← UP TIGHT, Randy Quaid *(Luther Johnson)* → the LONG RIDERS → DEAD SOLID PERFECT → ELVIS, James Hong *(chili joint owner)* ← DYNAMITE BROTHERS / → BLADE RUNNER → the KAREN CARPENTER STORY → WAYNE'S WORLD 2 → EXPERIENCE, M. Emmet Walsh *(husband in trailer automobile)* ← LITTLE BIG MAN ← ALICE'S RESTAURANT ← MIDNIGHT COWBOY / → BLADE RUNNER → CATCH ME IF YOU CAN → ALBINO ALLIGATOR, Brion James *(pick-up trucker at border)* → BLADE RUNNER, Harry Holcombe *(minister)* ← FOXY BROWN, David Clennon *(Carl; man in gas station)* → LADIES AND GENTLEMEN, THE FABULOUS STAINS → SWEET DREAMS → GRACE OF MY HEART, Susan Barnes *(singer at migrant camp)* → REPO MAN, **Mary Kay Place** *(Sue Ann)* → MORE AMERICAN GRAFFITI → JUST MY IMAGINATION → MANNY & LO → COMMITTED → KILLER DILLER

Storyline: The story of dust bowl protest singer/balladeer Woody Guthrie, tracing the legendary troubadour's journey to California and his subsequent involvement in union agitation amid the grinding poverty and brutality of the 1930s Depression. *BG*

Movie rating: *8

Visual: video

Off the record: WOODY GUTHRIE was born Woodrow Wilson Guthrie, 14th July 1912, Okemah, Oklahoma, USA. The son of a professional boxer,

GUTHRIE first began performing in public in his teens before landing a job as a DJ in Los Angeles. By the time musicologist Alan Lomax made his first field recordings of GUTHRIE in 1940, the self-confessed ramblin' man had amassed a staggering catalogue of songs, many based on his experiences as a traveling hobo living on his wits, talent and staunch political beliefs. While he was refused membership of the US communist party after refusing to give up his religious beliefs, socialist ideals permeated much of his work nevertheless; with the now famous message 'This machine kills fascists' (imitated countless times since) emblazoned across his battered acoustic guitar, few were left in doubt as to where his heart lay. 'This Land Is Your Land', perhaps his best known track, remains a populist anthem and an unofficial alternative to 'The Star Spangled Banner' although this message of equality somehow rings hollow in the corporate miasma of modern day America. GUTHRIE's views had been shaped by years of struggling on the breadline and huddling in boxcars, watching his people leaving their homes to escape the "dustbowl" of Oklahoma, only to arrive in sunny California and be turned back, beaten up or worse. Songs like 'I Ain't Got No Home', 'Talkin' Dust Bowl Blues' and 'Hard Travelin', sung by GUTHRIE in his weatherbeaten, heavily accented husk of a voice evoke the trials of the migrants just as vividly as Steinbeck's 'Grapes Of Wrath'. Lomax's Library Of Congress recordings were subsequently issued commercially by 'R.C.A.' although GUTHRIE's work wasn't afforded any significant recognition in his own lifetime. Suffering from alcohol problems, he was consigned to a mental institution before being diagnosed with the genetic degenerative disease, Huntington's Chorea. Confined to a hospital bed for the latter stages of his life, the illness finally claimed him on October 3rd, 1967. By this time, a young BOB DYLAN had already been crowned America's king of cool, his inspiration (particularly his earlier work and indeed the whole Greenwich Village folk revival) taken largely from GUTHRIE; during the ailing troubadour's final years, DYLAN had been a regular visitor at his bedside, including tribute 'Song To Woody' on his 1962 debut set. Aside from the obvious influence of his work on artists like DYLAN, Pete Seeger and his own son ARLO, everyone from U2 to BRUCE SPRINGSTEEN paid tribute to the man on 1988's 'Folkways: A Vision Shared'. Round about the same time, 'Folkways' the label released a split album of GUTHRIE and LEADBELLY material. More recently, GUTHRIE's wife unearthed and submitted some of his unfinished "work in progress" to the combined talents of US roots rockers WILCO & English protest bard, BILLY BRAGG. The results were issued in 1998 in the shape of the critically acclaimed 'Mermaid Avenue', a highly entertaining and often moving collection of songs interpreted with surprising sensitivity and intuition. It also sounded utterly relevant, some thirty years after the man's death. A veritable cornerstone of popular music, both GUTHRIE's fame and the continuing influence of his music grow with each passing year. *BG*

WOODY GUTHRIE music (vocal: DAVID CARRADINE *) (score: LEONARD ROSENMAN **)

1976. (lp) *EMI America; <LA 695-H> United Artists; (UAG 30035)* ☐ ☐

– Hard travelin' (*) / This train is bound for glory – The drifters (**) – I ain't got no home / So long: it's been good to know yuh (dusty old dust) / Hobo's lullaby (*) / Dust storm (**) – Pastures of plenty / Do re mi (*) / Running for the train (**) – So long: it's been good to know yuh (dusty old dust) – This train is bound for glory – Arrival in Los Angeles (**) / Oklahoma hills (*) / So long: it's been good to know yuh (dusty old dust) (*) – Howdido (*) / So long: it's been good to know yuh (dusty old dust) – Pastures of plenty – Hitchhiking (**) – Ramshackle (**) / Pastures of plenty (*) / Curly headed baby – Talking dust bowl blues – This land is your land / Deportee (*) / Hobo's lullaby – On the road again (**) – Going down the road: I ain't going to be treated this way / This land is your land (*).

S/track review: The unlikely combination of folk music's populist genius and one of Hollywood's great composers turns up a diverting (and Oscar-winning) triumph. LEONARD ROSENMAN was at the height of his fame, an exploratory maverick who had scored 'Rebel Without A Cause' (he was a room-mate and close friend of James Dean), 'Fantastic Voyage' and the movie that had just given him his first Oscar, 'Barry Lyndon'. Working with the life story of a musician whose central virtue was directness, ROSENMAN allows WOODY GUTHRIE's songs plenty of room to breathe, seamlessly weaving the songwriter's melodies and traditional instruments into orchestral interludes that are craftily atmospheric and sophisticated. Songs like 'Deportee' and 'Bound For Glory' stand unadorned, and if DAVID CARRADINE's voice is a shade too smooth to recapture GUTHRIE's unvarnished zest, these are admirably straight readings of what are effectively anthems of North America's heartland. Only once, on 'This Land Is Your Land', does the composer submit to conventional musical motifs with a chorus and orchestra, at a climactic final moment where it is wholly forgivable. And if the combination of adventurous orchestration and GUTHRIE-by-CARRADINE makes this more of a soundtrack recording than a record for WOODY fans, it nevertheless does its job to a degree of excellence. *ND*

Album rating: *8

☐ BRATZ segment
(⇒ ROCK ANGELZ)

BRAVE NEW GIRL

2004 (US 120m TV) LionsGate / Park Lane Productions (PG)

Film genre: coming-of-age/teen Rock Musical drama

Top guns: dir: Bobby Roth ← the MAN INSIDE ← DEAD SOLID PERFECT ← BAJA OKLAHOMA ← HEARTBREAKERS / s-w: Amy Talkington (+ story) (nov: 'A Mother's Gift' by **Britney Spears** + Lynne Spears)

Stars: Lindsey Haun *(Holly Lovell)*, Virginia Madsen *(Wanda Lovell)* ← DUNE, Barbara Mamabolo *(Angela)*, Nick Roth *(Grant)*, Joanne Boland *(Zoe Moscatel)*, Jackie Rosenbaum *(Ditz; aka Portia)*, Nick Mancuso *(Ditz's father)* ← NIGHT MAGIC ← PAROLES ET MUSIQUE ← BLAME IT ON THE NIGHT ← HEARTBREAKERS → IN THE MIX

Storyline: Holly dreams desperately to be a pop star, but although she has all the qualities, she's stuck in a humdrum suburban life with her enthusiastic single mother. Fortunately, with the financial and spiritual help of said mom, Holly gets a few breaks, but its not all plain sailing – much like mother/daughter co-writers Lynne and Britney Spears, we suppose. *MCS*

Movie rating: *4

Visual: dvd (no audio OST)

Off the record: Britney Spears is of course better known as the chart-topping pop singer with a plethora of hits behind her including debut, '. . .Baby One More Time' and 2004's 'Toxic'. *MCS*

BREAKIN'

aka BREAKDANCE

1984 (US 87m) Cannon Pictures / MGM-UA (PG)

Film genre: R&B/Dance Musical teen drama

Top guns: dir: Joel Silberg → RAPPIN' → LAMBADA / s-w: Allen DeBevoise (+ story), Charles Parker (+ story), Gerald Scaife

Stars: Lucinda Dickey *(Kelly)* ← GREASE 2 / → BREAKIN' 2: ELECTRIC BOOGALOO, Adolfo "Shabba Doo" Quinones *(Ozone)* ← XANADU / → BREAKIN' 2: ELECTRIC BOOGALOO → LAMBADA, Michael Chambers *(Turbo)* → BREAKIN' 2: ELECTRIC BOOGALOO → BILL & TED'S BOGUS JOURNEY, Ben Lokey *(Franco)*, Chris McDonald *(James)* ← GREASE 2 / → SLC PUNK, Phineas Newborn III *(Adam)*, **ICE-T** *(hip hop MC)*, Lela Rochon *(extra)* → BREAKIN' 2" ELECTRIC BOOGALOO → WHY DO FOOLS FALL IN LOVE

Storyline: New dance sensation Kelly throws away her tutu and the prospect of a glittering career after her coach Franco tries it on with her once too often. Instead she changes her style (and costume) and joins up with street dancers Ozone and Turbo. After perfecting their new routine, they enter a ballet competition where they're determined to show up the prima donnas and prove how good they are by breakin' new ground. *JZ*

Movie rating: *4.5

Visual: video + dvd

Off the record: **ICE-T** kicked off his celluloid career here.

—

Various Artists: Breakdance

May 84. (lp/c) *Polydor; <821919-1/-4> (POLD/+C 5147)* [8] Jun84 [6]
– Breakin' . . . there's no stopping us (OLLIE & JERRY) / Freakshow on the dance floor (the BAR-KAYS) / Body work (HOT STREAK) / 99 1/2 (CAROL LYNN TOWNES) / Showdown (OLLIE & JERRY) / Heart of the beat (3-V) / Street people (FIRE FOX) / Cut it (RE-FLEX) / Ain't nobody (RUFUS with CHAKA KHAN) / Reckless (CHRIS "THE GLOVE" TAYLOR & DAVID STORRS; rap by ICE-T). *<(cd-iss. Jun87; 821919-2)>*

S/track review: While breakdancing's roots lie in hip hop culture, much of the music here has less to do with that and more to do with the fusion pop, than with the burgeoning electro sound emanating from America's inner cities in the early 80s. These ideas were being run with by upstarts like John 'Jellybean' Benitez, who produced Madonna's debut album and handles the mix on a couple of tracks here, drawing the music further into the pop realm through his understanding of both camps. That said, much of it sounds dated, and lacking in dynamics by contemporary standards, but there's still some fizzing tracks that harness the energy of the time. 'Freakshow' by the BAR-KAYS alludes to that same high-powered funk that Cameo broke the charts with, while HOT STREAK's 'Body Work' throws in all the tricks of the era: vocoders, electronic percussion, fat keyboard riffs and over-the-top soul vocal hooks. The caterwauling of CAROL LYNN TOWNES is generously doused with some of the most gratuitous guitar soloing since Eddie Van Halen donned his axe. Weep with joy though at the inclusion of CHAKA KHAN's sublime 'Ain't Nobody', which shows colossal pop could come from such roots. Cash-ins like this album give up relatively few gems retrospectively – there's maybe four out of the ten here worth playing for more than nostalgic indulgence – but in an age when two big hits and ten tracks of your pals vomiting-up filler can be a bestseller – thanks Mariah! Thanks 50 Cent! – this album is of historical interest for those who understood the value of linoleum outside the kitchen. *MR*

Album rating: *6

– spinoff hits, etc. –

the BAR-KAYS: Freakshow On The Dancefloor / (non-OST song)

May 84. (7") *Mercury; <818631>* [73] [–]

OLLIE & JERRY: Breakin' . . . There's No Stopping Us / Showdown

May 84. (7"/12") *<821708> (POSP/+X 690)* [9] Jun84 [5]

CAROL LYNN TOWNES: 99 1/2 / CHRIS "THE GLOVE" TAYLOR & DAVID STORRS feat. ICE-T: Reckless

Jun 84. (7") *<881008> (POSP 693)* [77] Jul84 [47]
(12"+=) *(POSPX 693)* – HOT STREAK: Body work.

BREAKIN' 2: ELECTRIC BOOGALOO

1984 (US 94m) Cannon Group / TriStar (R)

Film genre: Pop/Rock teen Musical drama

Top guns: s-w: Sam Firstenberg (+ dir), Julia Reichert, Jan Ventura

Stars: Lucinda Dickey *(Kelly)* ← BREAKIN' ← GREASE 2, Adolfo "Shabba Doo" Quinones *(Ozone)* ← BREAKIN' ← XANADU / → LAMBADA, Michael Chambers *(Turbo)* ← BREAKIN' / → BILL & TED'S BOGUS JOURNEY, Susie Coelho Bono *(Rhonda)*, Harry Caesar *(Byron)* ← LADY SINGS THE BLUES / → ROADSIDE PROPHETS, **Paulette McWilliams** *(Fire Fox)*, Jo De Winter *(Mrs. Dickey)*, **ICE-T** *(Radiotron rapper)*, **Martika aka Marta Marrero** *(kid)*, Frankie Crocker *(Emcee)* ← THAT'S THE WAY OF THE WORLD ← FIVE ON THE BLACK HAND SIDE ← JIMI HENDRIX ← CLEOPATRA JONES, Donovan Leitch *(featured dancer)* → the IN CROWD → GAS FOOD LODGING → I SHOT ANDY WARHOL, Lela Rochon Quinones *(dancer)* ← BREAKIN' / → WHY DO FOOLS FALL IN LOVE

Storyline: Breakdancing dons Turbo and Ozone return, legs and arms akimbo, to save their community centre from the clutches of corrupt local authorities and a ruthless developer with plans for a shopping centre. *BG*

Movie rating: *3.5

Visual: video + dvd

Off the record: Paulette Williams was the original Rufus vocalist before Chaka Khan. Cuban-American singer/dancer, **Martika** (b.18 May'69) went on to bigger and better things when she had a US No.1 with 'Toy Soldiers', a song later utilized by EMINEM for his hit, 'Like Toy Soldiers'. *MCS*

—

Various Artists (score: Michael Linn)

Dec 84. (lp/c/cd) *Polydor; <(823696-2)> (POLD/C 5168)* [52] [ ]
– Electric boogaloo (OLLIE & JERRY) / Radiotron (FIREFOX) / Trommeltanz (din daa daa) (GEORGE KRANZ) / When I.C.U. (OLLIE & JERRY) / Gotta have the money (STEVE DONN) / Believe in the beat (CAROL LYNN TOWNES) / Set it out (MIDWAY) / I don't wanna come down (MARK SCOTT) / Stylin', profilin' (FIREFOX) / Oye mamacita (RAGS & RICHES).

S/track review: Everyone should see this sleeve at least once: a baseball boot glowing like the holy grail, worshipped by superimposed breakers in disco jodhpurs. Listening to the damn thing is another matter. While most self-respecting B-Boys were appalled at the original film and its multi-platinum soundtrack, it at least had early 80s BAR-KAYS, CHAKA KHAN and a novice ICE-T. 'BREAKIN' 2' carries over the weakest artists and adds a few more, reducing the alien thrill of electro to inconsequential pop music, and laughably trying to pass it off as hip hop. Most of the tracks sport sub-Prince R&B bolted to an 808, or in OLLIE & JERRY's case, come on like 'Ghostbusters' without the humour. MARK SCOTT does a remarkable Michael Jackson impression and CAROL LYNNE TOWNE's 'Believe In The Beat' at least makes its bubblegum ambitions clear, but the record's sole redeeming features are the tangents which, given the watered-down premise, almost appear avant-garde: it's saying something when a German producer – GEORGE KRANZ – can beat the New Yorkers at their own game with the much sampled scat attack, 'Din Daa Daa', while minor dancefloor staple, RAGS & RICHES' 'Oye Mamacito', still sounds like a weirdly out-of-time update of Chakachas' 'Jungle Fever'. What you can say is that 'BREAKIN' 2' flaunts the real spirit of the 80s: it's gaudy, overproduced and monotonous (with proto-bling bling lyrics about city-break shopping..), desirable only in as far as the songs recall the movie's kitschy choreography, or as far as nostalgia distorts reality. *BG*

Album rating: *4

– spinoff hits, etc. –

CAROL LYNN TOWNES: Believe In The Beat / (instrumental)

Jan 85. (7"/12") *(POSP/+X 720)* [–] [56]

OLLIE & JERRY: Electric Boogaloo / (non-OST song)

Jan 85. (7"/12") *(POSP/+X 730)* [–] [57]

BREAKING GLASS

1980 (UK 104m) GTO Films / Paramount Pictures (R)

Film genre: Rock Musical/showbiz drama

Top guns: dir (+ s-w): Brian Gibson → WHAT'S LOVE GOT TO DO WITH IT → STILL CRAZY

Stars: Hazel O'Connor *(Kate)*, Phil Daniels *(Danny)* ← QUADROPHENIA / → STILL CRAZY → SEX, CHIPS AND ROCK N' ROLL, Jon Finch *(Woods)* ← MACBETH, Jonathan Pryce *(Ken)* → EVITA → STIGMATA → BROTHERS OF THE HEAD, Peter-Hugo Daly *(Mick)* → ABSOLUTE BEGINNERS, Mark Wingett *(Tony)* ← QUADROPHENIA, **Gary Tibbs** *(Dave)*, Hugh Thomas *(Davis)* ← O LUCKY MAN!, **Derek Thompson** *(Andy)* ← GONKS GO BEAT, **Zoot Money** *(promotion man)* → ABSOLUTE BEGINNERS, Richard Griffiths *(studio engineer)*, **Gary Holton** *(punk guitarist)* ← QUADROPHENIA, Jim Broadbent *(station porter)* → RUNNING OUT OF LUCK → MOULIN ROUGE!, Gary Olsen *(guy at bar)* ← BIRTH OF THE BEATLES / → the WALL

Storyline: Set against Britain's Winter of Discontent in 1979, punk singer Kate does the rounds in backstreet London nightclubs. Her anti-government music draws her to the attention of band manager Danny who reckons her songs will strike a chord with the long-suffering British youth. Sure enough the seedy nightclubs become a thing of the past and when record promoter Woods gives her a chance to work for him it seems like Kate is set for the top – but there's a price to be paid for success. *JZ*

Movie rating: *5.5

Visual: video + dvd

Off the record: HAZEL O'CONNOR (see below). **Gary Tibbs** was the guitarist with Adam & The Ants.

HAZEL O'CONNOR

Jul 80. (lp/c) *A&M; (AMLH/CAM 64820) <4820>* [5] [ ]
– Writing on the wall / Monsters in disguise / Come into the air / Big brother / Who needs it / Will you? / Eighth day / Top of the wheel / Calls the tune / Blackman / Give me an inch / If only. *(re-iss. Mar91 cd/c; CD/C MID 124) (cd re-iss. Sep95 on 'Spectrum'; 551356-2)*

S/track review: Relatively unknown singer/actress (and former exotic dancer and English teacher abroad) HAZEL O'CONNOR was virtually thrust into the limelight with post-punk Brit-movie, 'BREAKING GLASS'. It was now the 80s and the race was on between Hazel and her fellow actress, Toyah, to become the new punk-pop princess. Coventry-born Hazel had just returned to London (she'd previously had small roles in films, 'Girls Come First' 1975 'Double Exposure' 1976), where she signed on the dotted line with 'Albion' records; both her singles failed to sell. With the help of musical director, Tony Visconti (once the man behind Bowie) and newbie filmmaker Brian Gibson, Hazel wrote and sang all the songs herself, her dreams and aspirations were literally rolled into this one project. With a dozen tracks on the album, Hazel's anti-government/system lyrics took on an anti-Thatcher zeitgeist and the doom of the impending 1984/Big Brother cloud (not just the dismal EURYTHMICS film soundtrack!); in fact there's a song called 'Big Brother' on 'BREAKING GLASS'. 'Writing On The Wall' gets the whole show underway, an anthemic post-punk dirge (with sax appeal) warning of the shape of things to come. For most of the album, we can hear influences such as X-Ray Spex, Penetration, Toyah, and voice-wise at least, Lene Lovich and Marianne Faithfull. Many older fans of the film will remember Hazel's robotic attire and stage performance, others might just recall one or two hit songs, 'Will You?' and the Utopian classic 'Eighth Day'. The latter anthem is very 'Metropolis' (the futuristic silent flick) with a hint of Toyah-to-come, while the former song is a post-New Wave ballad featuring a sax-to-die-for (who is the man?). Of the other tracks, 'Calls The Tune', 'Give Me An Inch' and the CND-infected 'Who Needs It' (about the rising nuclear energy), all switched the power on to the people and for a short while – an hour and a half – one forgot rising unemployment and the 'Monsters In Disguise'. Still contracted to 'Albion' ('BREAKING GLASS' was on 'A&M'), Hazel released a follow-up LP, 'Sons And Lovers' (1981), although her only other major hit was 'D-Days'. Much like in this movie, Hazel's career was like one big rollercoater ride, one minute she was enjoying star parts in 'Jangles' (1982) TV series and the film 'Car Trouble' (1985), other times she was struggling to break back into the UK Top 50. At the turn of the millennium, she released the acoustic 'Beyond The Breaking Glass', and she's regularly performed at the Edinburgh Festival. *MCS*

Album rating: *6

– spinoff hits, etc. –

HAZEL O'CONNOR: Writing On The Wall / Big Brother
Jun 80. (7") *(AMS 7530)* [ ] [–]

HAZEL O'CONNOR: Eighth Day / Monsters In Disguise
Aug 80. (7") *(AMS 7553)* [5] [–]

HAZEL O'CONNOR: Give Me An Inch / If Only
Oct 80. (7") *(AMS 7569)* [41] [–]

HAZEL O'CONNOR: Will You? / Big Brother
Nov 80. (7") [–] [ ]

HAZEL O'CONNOR: Eighth Day / Big Brother
Jan 81. (7") [–] [ ]

HAZEL O'CONNOR: Will You?
May 81. (7") *(AMS 8131)* [8] [–]

HAZEL O'CONNOR: Calls The Tune / Eighth Day / Give Me An Inch
Jan 82. (7"m) *(AMS 8203)* [60] [–]

BRING ME THE HEAD OF MAVIS DAVIS

1997 (UK 99m) BBC Films / Goldcrest Films International (15)

Film genre: crime caper/comedy

Top guns: dir: John Henderson / s-w: Craig Strachan (idea: Joanne Reay)

Stars: Rik Mayall *(Marty Starr)* ← EAT THE RICH ← SHOCK TREATMENT, Jane Horrocks *(Marla Dorland / Mavis Davis)* → BROTHERS OF THE HEAD, Danny Aiello *(Mr. Rathbone)*, Ronald Pickup *(Percy Stone)*, Jaclyn Mendoza *(Cynthia)*, Philip Martin-Brown *(Insp. Clint Furse)*, Mark Heap *(Duncan)* → ABOUT A BOY, Paul Keating *(Paul; Rathbone's son)*, Daniel Albineri *(Bruce)*

Storyline: Record producer Marty Starr has decided that his one-time starlet Mavis Davis is well past her sell-by date, while the financial side of the business is just as bad. Scheming Starr produces his master-stroke:- have Mavis assassinated and turn her into a legend, thus bringing money and fame to his company (and himself). However, hitman Clint does not have an easy time of things when Mavis proves tougher to bump off than he first expected. *JZ*

Movie rating: *4

Visual: dvd (no audio OST; score: Christopher Tyng)

Off the record: While 'Absolutely Fabulous' actress JANE HORROCKS went on to screen-test her 'Little Voice' in a subsequent movie, Rik Mayall had already been to the top of the charts in the early 80s via the spin-off to 'The Young Ones' TV series. JANE HORROCKS actually sings on the soundtrack: 'Shine On Me' & 'Untouchables'; the latter a duet with PAUL KEATING. Apart from a few score cues by MARC ELDRIDGE and NICK BATTLE, various artists included ELVIS PRESLEY ('The Wonder Of You'), KENNY LOGGINS ('I'm Alright'), CHRIS REA ('Let's Dance') and KIPPER & SIMON HUMPHREY ('The Love Song (I L.O.V.E. U)'). *MCS*

BROKEN BRIDGES

2006 (US 104m) MTV Films / Paramount Pictures (PG-13)

Film genre: Country-music rural drama

Top guns: dir: Steven Goldmann / s-w: Cherie Bennett, Jeff Gottesfeld

Stars: Toby Keith *(Bo Price)* ← NASHVILLE SOUNDS, Kelly Preston *(Angela Dalton)*, Lindsey Haun *(Dixie Leigh Delton)*, Tess Harper *(Dixie Rose Delton)* ← FAR NORTH ← FLASHPOINT ← TENDER MERCIES, Burt Reynolds *(Jake Delton)* ← BOOGIE NIGHTS ← the BEST LITTLE WHOREHOUSE IN TEXAS ← DELIVERANCE, **Willie NELSON** *(himself)*, Josh Henderson *(Wyatt)* ← STEP UP, Katie Finneran *(Patsi)*, **BeBe Winans** *(himself)*, Anna Maria Horsford *(Loretta)* ← HOW HIGH ← TIMES SQUARE, Rhoda Griffis *(Ida Mae Chalmers)* ← BIG DREAMS & BROKEN HEARTS: THE DOTTIE WEST STORY, Leland L. Jones *(club manager)* ← the GOSPEL

Storyline: Back in his hometown after the death of his brother, jaded country idol Bo Price doesn't bargain for an emotional re-acquaintance with both his first love and the teenaged daughter he bore her. *BG*

Movie rating: *4.5

Visual: dvd

Off the record: Toby Keith (see below). **BeBe Winans** (b. Benjamin Winans, 17 Sep'62, Detroit, Michigan) is a renowned gospel singer who peaked in 2000 with his Top 30 album, 'Love And Freedom'. *MCS*

Various Artists/Cast incl. TOBY KEITH *

Aug 06. (cd) *Show Dog Nashville; <001>* ☐ ☐–
– Broken bridges (LINDSEY HAUN & *) / Thinkin' 'bout you (FRED EAGLESMITH) / Crash here tonight (*) / Broken (LINDSEY HAUN) / Along for the ride (MATRACA BERG) / Uncloudy day (*, WILLIE NELSON & BeBe WINANS) / What's up with that (SCOTTY EMERICK) / High on the mountain (FLYNNVILLE TRAIN) / Battlefield (SONYA ISAACS) / Can't go back (*) / The waiting game – instrumental (POOR RICHARD'S HOUND) / Bug bull rider (*) / Zig zag stop (*) / Jacky Don Tucker (play by the rules miss all the sun) (*).

S/track review: Forever linked with his controversial 9-11 missive, 'Courtesy Of The Red, White And Blue (The Angry American)', country reactionary TOBY KEITH might sit on the other side of the political fence from the likes of Steve Earle but he's almost as much of a maverick. His post-millennial rise to prominence inevitably ended in Hollywood (Hollyweird?), where his starring role as a country star on the skids came with a soundtrack commission and poster that cast him in classic thinking-man's-outlaw-with-guitar-in-hand-walking-down-the-highway mode. Yet disappointingly given KEITH's redneck reputation, it really doesn't do enough to dispel the notion of contemporary country as written-to-order pop fodder in a cowboy hat: SCOTTY EMERICK's 'What's Up With That' takes top prize for glibness, MATRACA BERG's amiable 'Along For The Ride' is more coffee table roots than country and LINDSEY HAUN's power balladry lies way outside even the most charitable definition of the form. It may have a strong Celtic folk streak, but SONYA ISAAC's 'The Battlefield' is much more like it. And thank God for WILLIE NELSON, a man who supplies sweet succour in the unlikeliest of places. 'Uncloudy Day' just about makes the opening sequence worth sitting through, and raises the curtain on a more assertive, genuinely countrified second half. Lynyrd Skynyrd, the Allman Brothers; .38 Special; all of them glint through the lockjawed grind of both FLYNVILLE TRAIN and KEITH's own contributions, unfairly shuffled to the end of the pack. 'Big Bull Rider' is great, even if it does sound like Spinal Tap's Southern rock encore, and 'Zig Zag Stop' toys with the white-boy boogie of Joe Satriani and ZZ Top. But in the layered steel of 'The Waiting Game' it's POOR RICHARD'S HOUND who successfully carry off genuine Southern soundtrack music; the whole album should have been given over to them, whoever they are. *BG*

Album rating: *5.5

BROOKLYN BABYLON

2001 (US 89m) Bac Films / Off Line / Artisan Entertainment (R)

Film genre: romantic urban/Hip-Hop drama

Top guns: s-w: (+ dir) Marc Levin ← WHITEBOYS / → GODFATHERS AND SONS, Bonz Malone, Pam Widener

Stars: Tariq Trotter *(Sol/Solomon; member of the Lions)* ← FREESTYLE: THE ART OF RHYME ← WOODSTOCK '99 / → BROWN SUGAR → BLOCK PARTY, Karen Goberman *(Sara)*, Bonz Malone *(Scratch)* ← WHITEBOYS, David Vadim *(Judah)* ← LOOKING FOR AN ECHO, **Rahzel** *(narrator)* → 5 SIDES OF A COIN, Earl Contasti *(Ras Don)*, Carol Woods *(Cislyn)* ← JOE'S APARTMENT, **Slick Rick** *(Buddah)* ← TRUE VINYL ← WHITEBOYS ← the SHOW ← TOUGHER THAN LEATHER / → BROWN SUGAR → FADE TO BLACK, **Mad Cobra** *(key bouncer)* ← KLA$H, **Ahmir-Khalib Thompson** *(member of the Lions)* ← FREESTYLE: THE ART OF RHYME ← WOODSTOCK '99 / → BROWN SUGAR → FADE TO BLACK → BLOCK PARTY, **James 'Kamal' Gray** *(member of the Lions)* → BLOCK PARTY, **Leonard 'Hub' Hubbard** *(member of the Lions)* ← WOODSTOCK '99 / → BROWN SUGAR → BLOCK PARTY, **Kyle 'Scratch' Jones** *(member of the Lions)*, Joanne Baron *(Aunt Rose)*

Storyline: In the Crown Heights district of Brooklyn, the black and Jewish communities live uneasily side by side. Sol and Scratch are two friends trying to start a career in the music business, while Sara and her fiancé Judah are preparing for their marriage. These four people find their lives suddenly linked by a car accident, and while Scratch and Judah get ready for fisticuffs Sol and Sara fall in love. But their romance causes tensions in both communities and some people are determined to stop it at all costs. *JZ*

Movie rating: *5

Visual: dvd (no audio OST by the ROOTS)

Off the record: The Roots are in fact, **Tariq** (Black Thought), **Rahzel, Ahmir, Kamal, Hub** & **Scratch.**

the BROS.

2006 (US 91m) Reachfar Films Inc. / Lionsgate (R)

Film genre: Hip-Hop-music crime caper

Top guns: s-w + dir: Jonathan Figg

Stars: John Tindall *(Lanny)*, Joachim Wiese *(Pete)*, **Joey Fatone** *(Anthony Sabatino)* ← LONGSHOT, Dennis Scott *(Daddy)*, Jimmy Hart *(Randy)*, Sean O'Toole *(Eric)*, Shaquille O'Neal *(himself)*, **Ludacris** *(himself)* ← HUSTLE & FLOW, **Vanilla Ice** *(himself)* ← BETTY BLOWTORCH AND HER AMAZING TRUE LIFE ADVENTURES ← COOL AS ICE, Jon Freda *(Les McCorkle)*, Scott 'Carrot Top' Thompson *(himself)*

Storyline: Pete and Lanny have been failures at everything they've tried, but they're convinced they're headed for stardom in the hip-hop business. However, the $10,000 they need to launch their album is way beyond their means, so they go on a wild crime spree one night to raise the readies (and establish some street cred as well). The bungling burglars lurch from one disaster to another but fate lends a hand to stop them taking the rap for their misdemeanours. *JZ*

Movie rating: *4

Visual: dvd (no audio OST; score: Kays Al-Atrakchi)

Off the record: Joey Fatone is ex-N'Sync.

BROTHERS OF THE HEAD

2006 (UK 88m) IFC and Film Four with EMI Media (18)

Film genre: Punk-rock-music mockumentary comedy/drama

Top guns: dir: Keith Fulton, Louis Pepe / s-w: Tony Grisoni ← FEAR AND LOATHING IN LAS VEGAS (nov: Brian Aldiss)

Stars: Harry Treadaway *(Tom Howe; guitarist/vocalist)* → CONTROL, Luke Treadaway *(Barry Howe; vocalist)*, Bryan Dick *(Paul Day; live bassist in the 70s)*, Sean Harris *(Nick Sydney)* ← 24 HOUR PARTY PEOPLE, Jonathan Pryce *(Henry Couling)* ← STIGMATA ← EVITA ← BREAKING GLASS, Howard Attfield *(Zak Bedderwick)*, John Simm *(Boatman)* ← 24 HOUR PARTY PEOPLE ← HUMAN TRAFFIC, Ken Russell *(himself)*, Tania Emery *(Laura Ashworth in the 70s)*, Steven Eagles *(Steve Spitz; guitarist)*, **Nicholas Millard** *(Tubs Puller; drummer)*, Jack Dunkley *(technician/studio bassist)*, Jane Horrocks *(Roberta Howe)* ← BRING ME THE HEAD OF MAVIS DAVIS, Ed Hogg *(Chris Dervish)*, Tania Emery *(Laura Ashworth; in the 70s)*, **Ray Cooper** *(himself)* ← CONCERT FOR GEORGE ← POPEYE

Storyline: Tom and Harry are Siamese twins conjoined at the waist. Their father realizes that the teenagers must somehow earn a living and when unscrupulous showbiz agent Zak offers him a contract, the boys' fate is sealed. At first the twins are regarded as freaks, but in 1970s punk Britain they soon blend into the scene. Drugs, sex and alcohol become part of their daily lives but the twins are living on borrowed time. *JZ*

Movie rating: *6.5

Visual: dvd

Off the record: **Nicholas Millard** was drummer with Crackout (two albums for 'Hut' records, 'This Is Really Neat' 2002 and 'Oh No!' 2004); he's now with Blackholes. **Ray Cooper** is/was the percussionist with Elton John. *MCS*

the BANG-BANG (songs: CLIVE LANGER)

Jul 06. (cd) *Milan; (399 045-2)*
– 2-way Romeo / Sitting in a car / I am a sock / Nelson's blood / Doola and Dawla / My friend (u c***) / Sink or swim / D-rive / Hey hey / Bonus Tracks:- My friend (acoustic) / No money (CLIVE'S HIGH FIVE) / I am a sock (the NOIZE) / Sink or swim (acoustic) / Every little moment (live) / Sink or swim (live) / Two way Romeo (live) / Doola & Dawla (acoustic) / Two way Romeo (alternate version).

S/track review: Who better to employ as songwriter/producer than veteran of the UK punk and new wave scene of the mid-70s, CLIVE LANGER. His credentials stretched to having been part of Merseyside outfit, Deaf School (and a solo artist with the Boxes), to being a renowned producer (alongside Alan Winstanley) for the likes of Elvis Costello, Madness and Lloyd Cole & The Commotions. Among his film songwriting credits are another mock-rock movie, 'STILL CRAZY' (1998), plus a call-up as one of the many on the earlier 'ABSOLUTE BEGINNERS' (1986). Unauthentically co-billed as 'the BANG-BANG: The Original Unreleased Album – Remastered', this CD was not recorded way back in 1975 as some of the sleevenotes suggest, but by the "band" of actors themselves (see above). The trick does work at times, as the music is as raw and tinny as anything that dated back to these embryonic punk days. Opener, '2-Way Romeo' . . . "Giving Me a bone-io", certainly captured the essence of the times – lyrically speaking at least – while its anthemic punk potion was a kind of Sex Pistols, Damned and Buzzcocks hybrid and reminiscent of the Adverts' 'One Chord Wonder'. The excellent 'Sitting In A Car' could well be Alternative TV or even the Leyton Buzzards ('Saturday Night Beneath The Plastic Palm Trees'), while 'I Am A Sock' is ATV ditto with a hint of "new kids on the block", the Libertines. 'I Am A Sock' is retro personified and takes us back to psychedelic times (1968) when mock bassist Paul Day was in a band called the Noize; mock lead singer and journalist Chris Dervish (aka Ed Hogg) sounds a little like Robert Wyatt. 'Nelson's Blood' is one for the pogo brigade, all fast'n'furious, but never fast'n'bulbous. For 'Doola And Dawla', LANGER and Buzzcocks supremo PETE SHELLEY find use for a 'Shot By Both Sides' guitar riff, the sleevenotes suggest it was Shelley who was in Magazine rather than another former Buzzcock, Howard Devoto. An intentional mix-up or what. 'My Friend (U C***)' uses the C word with a blitzkrieg spitting edge, while the grungy 'Sink Or Swim' gets in a few F's to boot. The edgy 'D-Rive' and 'Hey Hey' are basically fill-ins for the first half of the CD, or even the fictitious BANG-BANG LP of old. The er . . . bonus tracks therefore give out the impression LANGER and Co had run out of ideas. Rather the reverse. The acoustic 'My Friend' is a sedated but effective lovelorn lament, while others of the acoustic ilk ('Sink Or Swim' & 'Doola & Dawla') are definitely of the demo variety. LANGER gets his own shot as CLIVE'S HIGH FIVE on 'No Money', a Booker T-type of cool retro. The BANG-BANG close the show – so to speak – with live August/October 1975 renditions of er . . . crowd-pleasers, the Buzzcocks-esque 'Every Little Moment', 'Sink Or Swim' and 'Two Way Romeo'; the latter gets in a third "alternate version" to finish up. *MCS*

Album rating: *6.5

BROWN SUGAR

2002 (US 109m) Twentieth Century Fox (PG-13)

Film genre: romantic R&B-music/showbiz comedy

Top guns: s-w: Rick Famuyiwa (+ dir), Michael Elliot ← CARMEN: A HIP HOPERA

Stars: Taye Diggs *(Dre)* → MALIBU'S MOST WANTED → RENT, Sanaa Lathan *(Sidney)* ← DISAPPEARING ACTS, **Mos Def** *(Chris Shawn)* ← CARMEN: A HIP HOPERA / → BLOCK PARTY, Nicole Ari Parker *(Reese Marie Wiggam Ellis)* ← BOOGIE NIGHTS ← the END OF VIOLENCE, Boris Kodjoe *(Kelby Dawson)*, **Queen Latifah** *(Francine)* ← the COUNTRY BEARS ← WHO'S THE MAN? ← JUICE ← HOUSE PARTY 2 ← JUNGLE FEVER / → HAIRSPRAY re-make, Erik Weiner *(Ren)*, Reggi Wyns *(Ten)*, Wendell Pierce *(Simon)* → the FIGHTING TEMPTATIONS → RAY, **Kool G. Rap** *(himself)* ← WHO'S THE MAN? / → BLOCK PARTY, **Pete Rock** *(himself)* ← WHO'S THE MAN?, **Talib Kweli** *(performer)* ← FREESTYLE: THE ART OF RHYME / → BLOCK PARTY, **the Roots:- Ahmir-Khalib Thompson** *(performer)* ← BROOKLYN BABYLON ← FREESTYLE: THE ART OF RHYME ← WOODSTOCK '99 / → FADE TO BLACK, **Black Thought** *(performer)* ← BROOKLYN BABYLON ← FREESTYLE: THE ART OF RHYME ← WOODSTOCK '99 / → BLOCK PARTY, **Leonard 'Hub' Hubbard** *(performer)* ← BROOKLYN BABYLON ← WOODSTOCK '99 / → BLOCK PARTY / **Jermaine Dupri** *(himself)* ← CARMEN: A HIP HOPERA, Angie Martinez *(herself)* ← PAPER SOLDIERS ← RIDE, **Common** *(himself)* → GODFATHERS AND SONS → BEEF → FADE TO BLACK → BLOCK PARTY, **Method Man** *(himself)* ← HOW HIGH ← BLACK AND WHITE ← BACKSTAGE ← RHYME & REASON ← the SHOW, **Russell Simmons** *(himself)* <= RUN-D.M.C. =>, **Big Daddy Kane** *(himself)* → BLOCK PARTY, **Doug E. Fresh** *(himself)* ← WHITEBOYS ← TAPEHEADS ← BEAT STREET / → AWESOME: I FUCKIN' SHOT THAT!, Nicole Ari Parker *(Reese Marie Wiggam Ellis)* ← 200 CIGARETTES ← the END OF VIOLENCE, **Slick Rick** *(himself)* ← BROOKLYN BABYLON ← TRUE VINYL ← WHITEBOYS ← the SHOW ← TOUGHER THAN LEATHER / → FADE TO BLACK, **Beanie SIGEL** *(himself)*, **De La Soul:- Trugoy The Dove, Plugwon Posdnuos + Vincent L. Mason** *(themselves)* ← FREE TIBET, Marc John Jeffries *(young Dre)* → GET RICH OR DIE TRYIN', **Ralph E. Tresvant** *(Royale)* ← PAPER SOLDIERS ← HOUSE PARTY 2 ← KRUSH GROOVE

Storyline: Calling this an African-American 'When Harry Met Sally' isn't so far off the mark as it centres around a game of cat and mouse between a couple of friends. Dre and Sidney have known each other since childhood and, when after some years apart the two reconvene in New York, they find themselves feeling drawn into being more than just friends, despite the fact that Dre is engaged and Sidney is being wooed by a basketball player. One common thread for the pair is their love of hip hop, but is there potentially more? *MR*

Movie rating: *6

Visual: dvd

Off the record: Kool G. Rap (b. Nathaniel Wilson, 20 Jul'68, Elmhurst, Queens, New York) had a one-off hit, 'Fast Life', taken from his Top 30 set, '4,5,6' (1995); the G stand for "Genius" by the way. **Talin Kwele + Ahmir + Black Thought** were all Roots. *MCS*

Various Artists (score: Robert Hurst)

Sep 02. (cd) *M.C.A.; <(113028-2)>* [16] [ ]
– Brown sugar – extra sweet (MOS DEF feat. FAITH EVANS) / Love of my life (an ode to hip hop) (ERYKAH BADU feat. COMMON) / Bring your heart (ANGIE STONE) / Brown sugar – raw (BLACK STAR) / Easy conversation (JILL SCOTT) / It's going down (BLACKALICIOUS feat. LATEEF THE TRUTH SPEAKER & KEKE WYATT) / Breakdown (MOS DEF) / You make life so good (RAHSAAN PATTERSON) / Time after time (CASSANDRA WILSON) / Paid in full – 7 minutes of madness – the Coldcut remix (ERIC B. and RAKIM) / No one knows her name (HI-TEK feat. BIG D and PIAKHAN) / Act too (love of my life) – remix (the ROOTS) / Never been (MARY J. BLIGE) / Brown sugar – fine (MOS DEF). *(bonus track+=)* – You changed (introducing JULLY BLACK).

S/track review: MOS DEF numbers among the rap game's strongest and most magnetic personalities and it is used to good effect on this soundtrack. His fingerprints are all over this, he contributes a trio of tracks, plus his various acolytes fill up the rest of the disc and he even has a role in the film. Lucky then that he is a man of exquisite taste and this is a thoughtfully compiled, compelling collection of future rap and sparkling nu soul. Incidentally, MOS DEF's tracks are produced by Kanye West. At the time of release, West hadn't yet stepped out from behind the mixing desk at this point but was still producer du jour and these cuts are illustrative of exactly why. Given the subject matter, there's no shortage of slow jams here as supplied by JILL SCOTT, ERYKAH BADU and CASSANDRA WILSON while MARY J BLIGE employs MISSY ELLIOTT to inject a bit of va-va-voom into 'Never Been' The hidden gem here however is almost 15 years older than any track here. Coldcut's seven minutes of madness remix of ERIC B AND RAKIM's 'Paid In Full'. A song which remains not only one of the finest re-workings in all hip hop history – it was also the first remix of this ilk done entirely with turntables, without the aid of studio trickery – but inexplicably manages to take a platinum track and make it double platinum quality and is worth the admission price alone. Genius pure and simple. Everything here is passable, even asentimental cover of Cyndi Lauper's 'Time After Time' by the aforementioned CASSANDRA WILSON and a syrupy slice of hip hop soul from the normally sparkling BLACKALICIOUS. In general however, this collection is good, if not amazing, filled with unpretentious hip hop with unashamed pop sensibilities, hardly the stuff of political revolution perhaps but fitting with the feelgood visual focus. *MR*

Album rating: *6.5

– spinoff hits, etc.

ERYKAH BADU feat. COMMON: Love Of My Life (An Ode To Hip Hop)
Aug 02. (12") *<113987>* [9] [–]

BUBBA HO-TEP

2002 (US 92m) Vitagraph Films (R)

Film genre: horror mystery/comedy

Top guns: s-w + dir: Don Coscarelli (au: Joe R. Lansdale)

Stars: Bruce Campbell *(Elvis Presley / Sebastian)* ← EDDIE PRESLEY, Ossie Davis *(John Fitzgerald Kennedy / Jack)* ← JUNGLE FEVER ← SCHOOL DAZE ← COUNTDOWN AT KUSINI ← LET'S DO IT AGAIN, Ella Joyce *(the nurse)*, Bob Ivy *(Bubba Ho-Tep)*, Heidi Marnhout *(Callie)*, Larry Pennell *(Kemosabe)* ← ELVIS

Storyline: Elvis and JFK are both alive and well – allegedly – in a Texas nursing home. However, the two reclusive geriatrics' quiet existence is shattered when they discover the resident cockroaches are in fact scarab beetles, and the home is under attack from an ancient Egyptian soul-sucker. It's up to our super-oldies to save the day but can Elvis see it through? After all, we all know how much he loved his Mummy. *JZ*

Movie rating: *7

Visual: dvd (audio OST on La-La Land by Brian Tyler cancelled)

Off the record: A limited edition of the score was released by 'Silver Sphere' (SS 002)

the BUDDY HOLLY STORY

1978 (US 113m) Columbia Pictures (PG)

Film genre: Rock'n'roll-music bio-pic drama

Top guns: dir: Steve Rash / s-w: Robert Gittler (based/book: John Goldrosen)

Stars: Gary Busey *(Buddy Holly)* ← a STAR IS BORN / → CARNY → FEAR AND LOATHING IN LAS VEGAS, Don Stroud *(Jesse)* ← SLAUGHTER'S BIG RIP-OFF, Charles Martin Smith *(Ray Bob)* ← AMERICAN GRAFFITI ← PAT GARRETT & BILLY THE KID / → COTTON CANDY → MORE AMERICAN GRAFFITI → TRICK OR TREAT, William Jordan *(Riley Randolph)*, Maria Richwine *(Maria Elena Holly)*, Conrad Janis *(Ross Turner)* ← LET'S ROCK, Albert Popwell *(Eddie Foster)* ← CLEOPATRA JONES / → WHO'S THAT GIRL, Amy Johnston *(Cindy Lou)*, John F. Goff *(T.J.)*, Gailard Sartain *(The Big Bopper)* ← NASHVILLE / → ROADIE → HARD COUNTRY → SONGWRITER, Paul Mooney *(Sam Cooke)*, Arch Johnson *(Lawrence O. Holly)* ← G.I. BLUES, M.G. Kelly *(Lenny Lawrence)* ← a STAR IS BORN / → ROLLER BOOGIE → VOYAGE OF THE ROCK ALIENS → UHF, Will Jordan *(Ed Sullivan)* ← I WANNA HOLD YOUR HAND / → ELVIS: THE MOVIE → the DOORS, **Buddy Miles** *(tour musician)* ← JIMI HENDRIX ← SUPERSHOW

Storyline: Acclaimed bio-pic following the inspired but devastatingly short-lived career of rock'n'roll pioneer Buddy Holly, as he battles against small-town prejudice and ignorance to realise his vision. *BG*

Movie rating: *7.5

Off the record: Ex-Electric Flag musician, **Buddy Miles**, found fame in the late 60s/early 70s as drummer with Jimi Hendrix's Band Of Gypsys. *MCS*

Various Cast (md: Joe Renzetti)

Jul 78. (lp/c) *Epic; <35412> Warwick; (WW/+4 5064)* [86] Jul79 [ ]
– Rave on / It's so easy / True love ways / Clear Lake medley: That'll be the day – Oh boy! – Peggy Sue – Maybe baby – Not fade away / I'm gonna love you too / Whole lotta shakin' goin' on / Well all right / Listen to me / Maybe baby / Everyday / Roller Rink medley: Rock around with Ollie Vee – That'll be the day. *<cd-iss. Mar88; EK 35412>*

S/track review: This Oscar-winning soundtrack features the surprisingly authentic vocals and guitar of actor GARY BUSEY, who convincingly carried off the part of Holly. He works his way through the cream of the Buddy Holly & The Crickets' repertoire, augmented by actor/players CHARLES MARTIN SMITH on bass and DON STROUD on drums. GARY BUSEY, hats off to the guy, is Buddy Holly reincarnated. Instead of trying to nail the perfect vocals and risk sounding flat, he has taken a rough sketch of what Buddy Holly sounds like and, more importantly, grabbed the energy and intensity of the original to create a soundtrack that is as close as you'll get to the real thing. You'd be forgiven for thinking it was the birth of rock'n'roll over again. The favourites, 'That'll Be The Day', 'Rave On', 'Peggy Sue', 'Oh Boy', 'Maybe Baby' and 'Everyday', are all brought to life with an electric edge and the fact that most of the tracks are recorded live just adds to authenticity. Lesser known ballads 'It's So Easy' and 'True Love Ways' are handled with care, showing that BUSEY has a tenderness to match the throaty growl that accompanies the rock'n'roll numbers, which is reinforced by a rapturous a cappella version of 'I'm Gonna Love You Too'. The soundtrack to 'The BUDDY HOLLY STORY' captures not only the sound but also the spirit of one of rock'n'roll's greatest founding icons with a vibrancy and panache befitting the legend himself. *BG/CM*

Album rating: *8

BUDDY'S SONG

1991 (UK 106m) Castle Premier (R)

Film genre: coming-of-age showbiz/Pop-music drama

Top guns: dir: Claude Whatham ← THAT'LL BE THE DAY / s-w: Nigel Hinton (+ nov)

Stars: Roger Daltrey *(Terry Clark)* <= the WHO =>, Sharon Duce *(Carol Clark)*, **Chesney Hawkes** *(Buddy)*, Michael Elphick *(Des King)* ← QUADROPHENIA ← STARDUST ← O LUCKY MAN!, Douglas Hodge *(Brian Rosen)*, Paul McKenzie *(Julius)*, Lee Ross *(Jason)*, Nick Moran *(Mike)* → CHRISTIE MALRY'S OWN DOUBLE-ENTRY, Julia Sawalha *(Kelly)*

Storyline: Londoner Buddy Clark is an up and coming musician who finds himself under parental pressure to do better than his dad Terry, himself a teddy boy rocker. Buddy does indeed go on to better things, unlike Terry who ends up doing porridge for his dodgy pal Des. Meanwhile, mum Carol has problems of her own, and when Terry is released she finds herself piggy in the middle between father and son and arguments abound. *JZ*

Movie rating: *4.5

Visual: video

Off the record: CHESNEY HAWKES was born on the 22nd September, 1971, Windsor, Berkshire, England, son of TREMELOES singer Len "Chip" Hawkes and 'Golden Shot' TV hostess and actress, Carol Dilworth. At the age of 19, he landed the main role in 'BUDDY'S SONG', and for a time in 1991 he was adorned by a horde of teenage girls. His star faded as quickly as it arrived and the young man concentrated on songwriting, working with the likes of Howard Jones, Nik Kershaw and Stewart Copeland. Now married with a couple of children, he launched his second comeback in May 2005 via a single, 'Another Fine Mess', which scraped into the Top 50. *MCS*

—

CHESNEY HAWKES (score: Alan Shacklock)

Mar 91. (cd/c/lp) *Chrysalis; (CCD/ZCHR/CHR 1812)* [18] [–]
– The one and only / Nothing serious / Feel so alive / I'm a man not a boy / It's gonna be tough / Torn in half / I'm young / Secrets of the heart / This is me / Ordinary girl / A crazy world like this / Say mama.

S/track review: Love it or loathe it, 'BUDDY'S SONG' captured the outgoing zeitgeist of 80s pop-rock (despite being released in 1991 – the same year Nirvana's 'Nevermind' blew away this type of music once and for all) with its over-reliance on synthesizers, horrible chiming keyboards and, strangely enough, the virtual absence of guitars (until the "big solo"). Built around the perennial student favourite and Nik Kershaw-penned mega-hit, 'The One And Only' made a brief and unlikely teen heart-throb of CHESNEY HAWKES and hit No.1 in the UK, staying there for five weeks. Whilst admittedly catchy, the rest of the soundtrack is unoriginal and uninspired soft-rock replete with formulaic and boisterous big choruses, dramatic key changes and strained faux emoting. 'I'm A Man Not A Boy' is the only other memorable moment here, a driving "coming of age" number that HAWKES and Co try and fail to replicate elsewhere on the likes of the unconvincing 'I'm Young' and 'This Is Me'. Elsewhere we have the flat balladeering of 'Torn In Half' and the world weary 'Secret Of The Heart' which take their cue from the stadium rock successfully peddled by Def Leppard and Bon Jovi, and at the same time reminiscent of some offerings from Bryan Adams' 'Waking Up The Neighbours' (also 1991). Still worse is HAWKES sounding like Cher on 'A Crazy World Like This', the patronising Roy Orbison-lite 'Ordinary Girl' and the embarrassing attempt at 50s rock'n'roll that is 'Say Mama'. Avoid. *LF*

Album rating: *3

– spinoff hits, etc. –

CHESNEY HAWKES: The One And Only / It's Gonna Be Tough

Feb 91. (7") *(CHSLH 3627)* [1] [ ]
(cd-s+=) *(CDCHS 3627)* – It's gonna be tough – film version / Say mama.

CHESNEY HAWKES: I'm A Man Not A Boy / Torn In Half – orchestral

Jun 91. (7") *(CHSP 3708)* [27] [–]
(cd-s+=) *(CDCHS 3708)* – Ordinary girl / ('A'-film version).

CHESNEY HAWKES: Secrets Of The Heart

Sep 91. (7") *(CHSP 3681)* [57] [–]
(cd-s+=) *(CDCHS 3681)* – ('A'-live).

BUMMER!

1973 (US 90m) Entertainment Ventures Inc. (R)

Film genre: psychological/horror Rock Musical drama

Top guns: dir: William Allen Castleman / s-w: Alvin L. Fast → BLACK SHAMPOO

Stars: Kipp Whitman *(Duke)*, Dennis Burkley *(Butts)* → WHO'S THAT GIRL → LAMBADA → the DOORS → RUSH → TOUCH, Connie Strickland *(Barbara)*, Carol Speed *(Janyce)* → the MACK → SAVAGE! → DYNAMITE BROTHERS → DISCO GODFATHER, David Buchanan *(Gary)*, David Ankrum *(Mike)*, Diane Lee Hart *(Dolly)*, Leslie McRae *(Morrie)* → COFFY → WILLIE DYNAMITE

Storyline: The antics of a psycho rock band get out of control, resulting in the manager giving the bassman the boot. He in turn, goes a rape and murder spree – "A far out trip thru a hard rock tunnel". *MCS*

Movie rating: *3

Visual: double dvd on Magnum (no OST by William Loose)

Off the record: Carol Speed provided the theme to the movie, 'Abby' (1974).

□ Eric BURDON
(⇒ the ANIMALS entry)

□ T-Bone BURNETT segment
(⇒ O BROTHER, WHERE ART THOU?)

BYE BYE BIRDIE

1963 (US 112m) Columbia Pictures (PG)

Film genre: showbiz/teenPop-Rock Musical comedy

Top guns: dir: George Sidney → VIVA LAS VEGAS / s-w: Irving Brecher (play: Michael Stewart → BYE BYE BIRDIE remake)

Stars: Janet Leigh *(Rosie DeLeon)*, Dick Van Dyke *(Albert F. Peterson)* → DICK TRACY → CURIOUS GEORGE, **Ann-Margret** *(Kim McAfee)* → VIVA LAS VEGAS → TOMMY, Maureen Stapleton *(Mama Mae Peterson)*, **Bobby Rydell** *(Hugo Peabody)* → MR. ROCK'N'ROLL: THE ALAN FREED STORY, Jesse Pearson *(Conrad Birdie)*, Ed Sullivan *(himself)* → the PHYNX → the COMPLEAT BEATLES → ELVIS BY THE PRESLEYS, Paul Lynde *(Harry McAfee)* → BEACH BLANKET BINGO, Mary LaRoche *(Doris McAfee)*

Storyline: Rock'n'roll sensation Conrad Birdie is about to be drafted into the army, which is bad news for up and coming songwriter Albert Peterson. He needs the Birdman to go on the Ed Sullivan show and sing his only worthwhile song, so that his sweetheart Rosie will finally marry him. Things go wrong when Conrad almost starts a riot in Sweet Apple and Albert finds himself up against Rosie's terrifying mother. Maybe his chemistry set will help him get his girl. *JZ*

Movie rating: *6

Visual: video + dvd

Off the record: (see below)

—

Various Cast (music: Charles Strouse / lyrics: Lee Adams)

Apr 63. (lp) *RCA Victor; <1081> (RD/SF 7580)* [2] [ ]
– Bye bye Birdie (ANN-MARGRET) / Opening credits (the COLUMBIA STUDIO ORCHESTRA CONDUCTED BY JOHNNY GREEN) / The telephone hour (the SWEET APPLE TEENAGERS) / How lovely to be a woman (ANN-MARGRET) / We love you Conrad *[film version]* * / Honestly sincere (JESSE PEARSON) / Hymn for a Sunday evening (PAUL LYNDE, MARY LA ROCHE, BRYAN RUSSELL, BRYAN RUSSELL) / One boy (ANN-MARGRET, BOBBY RYDELL, JANET LEIGH) / Put on a happy face (DICK VAN DYKE, JANET LEIGH) / Kids (PAUL LYNDE, MAUREEN STAPLETON, DICK VAN DYKE, BRYAN RUSSELL) / One last kiss *[gym rehearsal outtake]* (JESSE PEARSON) * / A lot of livin' to do (JESSE PEARSON, ANN-MARGRET, BOBBY RYDELL) / The sultans' ballet *[film version]* (the COLUMBIA STUDIO ORCHESTRA CONDUCTED BY JOHNNY GREEN) * / One last kiss (JESSE PEARSON) / Rosie (DICK VAN DYKE, JANET LEIGH, ANN-MARGRET, BOBBY RYDELL) / Bye bye Birdie (reprise) (ANN-MARGRET, JANET LEIGH, DICK VAN DYKE, BOBBY RYDELL). *<cd-iss. 1988; 1081-2R> <(cd-iss. 2003 on 'RCA-BMG'+= *; 82876 54217-2)>*

S/track review: As it proudly boasts on the sleevenotes: "The first of the great rock musicals, 'BYE BYE BIRDIE' is a rollicking uptempo joyride through a candy-colored early 1960s landscape which takes good-natured swipes at popular culture, rock'n'roll, and American family life" – mmmm . . . in a word, no. One thinks only "Rock Musical" by the proverbial skin of its whiter than white teeth. Its Broadway origins overpower any pretence of becoming credited as a bonafide ROCK'n'roll outing, although some cues give the impression (and I mean impression: ELVIS-like) of being pop songs rather than song and dance numbers. The "songs" in question are undoubtedly, 'Honestly Sincere' and 'One Last Kiss', actor JESSE PEARSON (Conrad Birdie himself) taking the Elvis mantle like Bobby Pickett chewing on a bit of his own "Monster Mash". The star of the show singing-wise is ANN-MARGRET, a 22-year-old redhead at the time, and ironically a future rock starlet of sorts when she starred opposite "the real" ELVIS PRESLEY in his movie, 'VIVA LAS VEGAS' (and who can forget her part(s) in the subsequent WHO rock opera, 'TOMMY'). Although born in Sweden (she moved to the US when she was six), her "Nu Yoik" accent and kittenesque innocence/sex appeal are all over the show on numbers such as 'Bye Bye Birdie' and 'How Lovely To Be A Woman'. Alongside other cast members such as BOBBY RYDELL (whose hits C.V. included 'Swingin' School', 'Volare' & 'The Cha-Cha-Cha'), JANET LEIGH (don't mention 'Psycho') and DICK VAN DYKE (don't mention 'Mary Poppins', 'Chitty Chitty Bang Bang' or anything with an English accent!), ANN-MARGRET was also involved on 'Rosie', 'Bye Bye Birdie (Reprise)', 'One Boy' (without VAN-DYKE) and 'A Lot Of Livin' To Do' (without VAN-DYKE and LEIGH). The latter two superstars of the movie world got on their dancing shoes for 'Put On A Happy Face', while ANN-MARGRET was credited again on 'Hymn For A Sunday Evening', this time with PAUL LYNDE, MARY LA ROCHE and BRYAN RUSSELL. Pre-'GREASE' by a good decade and a half, the SWEET APPLE TEENAGERS congregated for 'The Telephone Hour', while these goddamn 'Kids' (shucks!) were more or less the subject for a kitschy, Charleston-type, song-and-dance number. Re-released for a 40th anniversary, the CD contained three extra cues, including the film version of 'We Love You Conrad' (complete with male equivalent chorus "we hate you Conrad") by the aforementioned SWEET APPLE TEENAGERS. *MCS*

Album rating: *5.5

– spinoff releases, etc. –

BILL POTTS: Bye Bye Birdie

May 63. (lp) *Colpix; <CP 451>* [ ] [-]
– Bye bye Birdie / Rosie / How lovely to be a woman / Put on a happy face / One last kiss / A lot of livin' to do / Baby, talk to me / Kids / One boy (one girl) / The closer.

JAMES DARREN: Bye Bye Birdie

May 63. (lp) *Colpix; <CP 454>* [ ] [-]

BYE BYE BIRDIE

1995 re-make (US 133m TV) RHI Entertainment / Columbia TriStar (PG)

Film genre: romantic Pop-Rock Musical comedy/drama

Top guns: dir: Gene Saks (play: Michael Stewart ← BYE BYE BIRDIE)

Stars: Jason Alexander *(Albert Peterson)* ← the BURNING, **Vanessa Williams** *(Rose Alvarez)* ← the JACKSONS: AN AMERICAN DREAM / → DANCE WITH ME, Marc Kudisch *(Conrad Birdie)*, Chynna Phillips *(Kim MacAfee)*, Tyne Daly *(Mae Peterson)*, George Wendt *(Harry MacAfee)* → SPICEWORLD → GARAGE: A ROCK SAGA → MY DINNER WITH JIMI, Sally Mayes *(Doris MacAfee)*, Jason Gaffney *(Hugo Peabody)*, Blair Slater *(Randolph MacAfee)*, Murray Weinstock *(Talk To Me quartet)* → LOOKING FOR AN ECHO

Storyline: Pop star Conrad Birdie gets his National Service call up and his manager Albert decides to give him a memorable send off. He sets up a concert in a small town called Sweet Apple and plans to get Conrad to sing his latest song 'One Last Kiss'. Confident that the song will be an instant hit, poor Albert hasn't reckoned with his overbearing mother or his girl's possessive boyfriend. *JZ*

Movie rating: *5

Visual: video + dvd

Off the record: Vanessa Williams was concurrently in the US singles chart (peaking at No.4) with the theme tune ('Colors Of The Wind') to the Disney animation, 'Pocahontas'. *MCS*

—

Various Cast (music: Charles Strouse / lyrics: Lee Adams)

Jul 95. (cd) *RCA Victor; <9026 68356-2>* [ ] [-]
– Main title (Bye Bye Birdie) (the SWEET APPLE TEENS) / An English teacher (VANESSA WILLIAMS) / The telephone hour (the SWEET APPLE TEENS) / How lovely to be a woman (CHYNNA PHILLIPS) / Put on a happy face (JASON ALEXANDER) / A healthy, normal American boy (JASON ALEXANDER, VANESSA WILLIAMS & ENSEMBLE) / One boy (CHYNNA PHILLIPS with SHELLEY HUNT and MARLOWE WINDSOR-MENARD) / Let's settle down (VANESSA WILLIAMS) / Honestly sincere (MARC KUDISCH) / Hymn for a Sunday evening (Ed Sullivan) (GEORGE WENDT, SALLY MAYES, CHYNNA PHILLIPS, BLAIR SLATER & ENSEMBLE) / One last kiss (MARC KUDISCH with the SWEET APPLE TEENS) / What did I ever see in him (VANESSA WILLIAMS & CHYNNA PHILLIPS) / A lot of livin' to do (MARC KUDISCH, CHYNNA PHILLIPS & the SWEET APPLE TEENS) / Kids (GEORGE WENDT & SALLY MAYES) / Spanish rose (VANESSA WILLIAMS) / Talk to me (JASON ALEXANDER with PETER DAVIS, DARYL TOOKES, AL DANA & MURRAY WEINSTOCK) / A mother doesn't matter anymore (TYNE DALY) / A giant step (JASON ALEXANDER) / Rosie (JASON ALEXANDER & VANESSA WILLIAMS) / End credits (ORCHESTRA).

S/track review: It'd been 33 years since the original film & soundtrack was released, and as usual short of new ideas, Hollywood delivered the customary remake. The 1963 version was a mixture of "pleasant valley Sunday" music (see above), and this was no different while adding some new numbers to the fold. There's déjà vu memories of Ann-Margret through the solo singing voice of CHYNNA PHILLIPS ('How Lovely To Be A Woman'), while the earthy vocal chords come via VANESSA WILLIAMS (on fresh cues 'An English Teacher', 'Let's Settle Down' & 'Spanish Rose'); the pair also manage a duet, 'What Did I Ever See In Him'. The Elvis-cloned rock'n'roll numbers belong to MARC KUDISCH, who attempts the impersonation on the likes of 'Honestly Sincere', 'One Last Kiss' and 'A Lot Of Livin' To Do' (with PHILLIPS). The latter two tracks also feature the SWEET APPLE TEENS, an ensemble of squeaky-clean kids who are best on the 'Main Title', 'The Telephone Hour', etc. For the golden oldies among you, Seinfeld's JASON ALEXANDER sings (among other cuts) the Dick Van Dyke number 'Put On A Happy Face', while Cheers-staple GEORGE WENDT and SALLY MAYES croak out 'Kids' & 'Hymn For A Sunday Evening (Ed Sullivan)'; Cagney & Lacey star TYNE DALY puts the miserabilist tone back into this musical soup courtesy of 'A Mother Doesn't Matter Anymore'. Does anything matter anymore? *MCS*

Album rating: *4

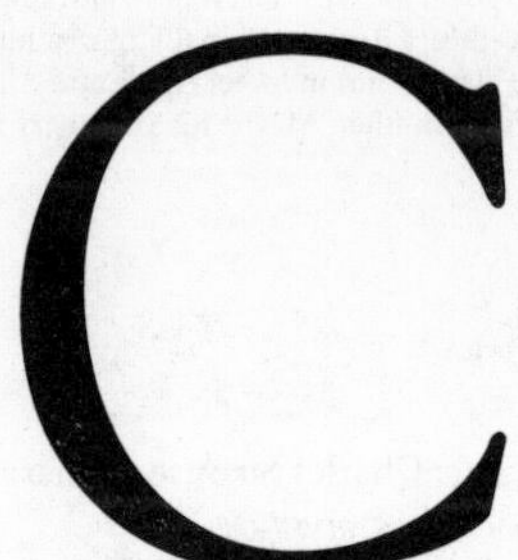

CB4: THE MOVIE

1993 (US 89m) Universal Pictures (R)

Film genre: Hip Hop-music/showbiz satire/comedy

Top guns: dir: Tamra Davis / s-w: Chris Rock (+ story), Nelson George (+ story), Robert LoCash

Stars: Chris Rock *(Albert)* → POOTIE TANG, Allen Payne *(Euripides)*, **Deezer D** *(Otis)* ← COOL AS ICE / → FEAR OF A BLACK HAT → BONES → IN THE MIX, Chris Elliott *(A. White)* ← MEDUSA: DARE TO BE TRUTHFUL, Phil Hartman *(Virgil Robinson)*, Khandi Alexander *(Sissy)* → WHAT'S LOVE GOT TO DO WITH IT → HOUSE PARTY 3, Charles Q. Murphy *(Gusto)* ← JUNGLE FEVER / → MURDER WAS THE CASE → PAPER SOLDIERS → DEATH OF A DYNASTY → ROLL BOUNCE, Art Evans *(Albert Sr.)* ← TRESPASS ← SCHOOL DAZE ← YOUNGBLOOD ← BIG TIME ← LEADBELLY ← CLAUDINE / → the STORY OF US, Theresa Randle *(Eve)* ← JUNGLE FEVER ← the FIVE HEARTBEATS / → GIRL 6, Richard Gant *(Baa Baa Ack)* ← KRUSH GROOVE, **Isaac HAYES** *(owner)*, Halle Berry *(herself)* ← JUNGLE FEVER / → GIRL 6 → WHY DO FOOLS FALL IN LOVE → SWORDFISH, **Eazy E** *(himself)*, **ICE-T** *(himself)*, **Flavor Flav** *(himself)* → WHO'S THE MAN? → PRIVATE PARTS → DEATH OF A DYNASTY, **ICE CUBE** *(himself)*, Allen Payne *(Euripedes/Dead Mike)* → DOUBLE PLATINUM, Tommy Davidson *(Weird Warren)*, Willard E. Pugh *(Trustus)* ← EDDIE PRESLEY ← BLUE CITY, Shaquille O'Neal *(himself)*, **the Butthole Surfers** *(themselves)*, Lance Crouther *(well dressed man)* → FEAR OF A BLACK HAT → POOTIE TANG, Stoney Jackson *(Wacky Dee)* ← TRESPASS ← KNIGHTS OF THE CITY ← SWEET DREAMS ← STREETS OF FIRE ← ROLLER BOOGIE

Storyline: This spoof rapumentary does for hip hop what 'THIS IS SPINAL TAP' did for rock music: lays it all open for all to see its ridiculous shortcomings. We follow the rise and fall of a group of would be gangsta rappers who are in fact not quite as street wise or hardcore as they have first suggested. This is illustrated when it is revealed one band member borrowed his moniker (MC Gusto) from a local incarcerated hood who, on hearing of their scam, now wants a piece of their action. *MR*

Movie rating: *5

Visual: video + dvd

Off the record: Also in 1993, director Tamra Davis married MIKE D of the Beastie Boys.

Various Artists (score: John Barnes)

Mar 93. (lp/c/cd) *M.C.A.; <(MCA/+C/D 10758)>* **41** Apr93 ☐
– The 13th message / Livin' in a zoo (PUBLIC ENEMY) / Black cop (BOOGIE DOWN PRODUCTIONS) / May day on the front line (MC REN) / Stick 'em up (HURRICANE feat. the BEASTIE BOYS) / Sneaking up on ya (FU-SCHNICKENS) / Lifeline (PARENTAL ADVISORY) / The noctural is in the house (P.M. DAWN) / Baby be mine (BLACKSTREET feat. TEDDY RILEY) / It's alright (TRACIE

SPENCER) / Sweat of my balls (CB4) / Straight out of Locash (CB4) / Rapper's delight (CB4). *<clean version; 10803>*

S/track review: CB4 may play mostly for laughs but it still tries to convey some pertinent points about the hypocrisy of the music industry. Following suit, the music on the soundtrack is a blend of hardline politicos, gangster fantasists and jokers. First, dispense with the three spoof tracks tucked at the end of this disc, recorded for the film by CHRIS ROCK and his cohorts. The three are take offs of tracks by NWA, Kool G Rap and the Sugarhill Gang that are fun in context but pointless otherwise. It kicks off with a meaty, vitriolic spoken word diatribe from PUBLIC ENEMY's Chuck D on the subjugation of hardcore hip hop. From then on its down to BOOGIE DOWN PRODUCTIONS to provide some tough love and grimy beats on the brutal 'Black Cop' while one-time NWA man MC REN does a passable turn on 'May Day On The Front Line'. Erstwhile Beastie Boys collaborator HURRICANE commends himself with the cut'n'paste bounce of 'Stick 'Em Up' while FU-SCHNICKENS change the pace and provide the other real highlight with a manic tumbling double speed rhyme on 'Sneaking Up On Ya'. Even the R&B cut, the hip hop soundtrack equivalent of that lone bottle of Babycham at a 70s house party (that is: something for the ladies) is worth a mention. There's a funksome chunk of vocoder new jack pop from über-producer Teddy Riley and BLACKSTREET to round things off nicely. *MR*

Album rating: *6.5

– spinoff releases, etc. –

BLACKSTREET feat. TEDDY RILEY: Baby Be Mine / (mixes)

Mar 93. (c-s)(12"/cd-s) *<54561><54634> (MCST/+D 1772)* [ ] May93 [37]

John CAFFERTY

Born: c.1950, Narragansett, Rhode Island, USA. From New England barroom covers act in the early 70s, singer/guitarist JOHN CAFFERTY and his Brown Beaver Band (Gary Gramolini – guitar, Robert Cotoia – keyboards, Michael Antunes – sax, Pat Lupo – bass & Jo Silva – drums) shot to fame in 1983 when he/they composed the music for the "heartland" rock-themed movie, 'EDDIE & THE CRUISERS'. Sounding like a cross between Bruce Springsteen, John Cougar Mellencamp and Bob Dylan, the band also reached the Top 10 with 'On The Dark Side', a previously released CAFFERTY solo 45. After another hit ('Tender Years') from the movie, the sextet subsequently made the Top 30 a further twice: 'Tough All Over' and 'C-I-T-Y'. Back at the movies – sort of – JOHN CAFFERTY AND THE BROWN BEAVER BAND found more chart success in 1985 via a couple of Sylvester Stallone flicks, 'Rocky IV' (featuring 'Heart's On Fire') and 'Cobra' ('Voice Of America's Sons'). With the band at a loss towards the end of the 80s, they provided a second instalment of 'EDDIE & THE CRUISERS II: EDDIE LIVES!' (1989; and also released on 'Scotti Brothers'), not the most revered film by any manner of means. *MCS*

- **filmography** (composer) –

Eddie And The Cruisers *(1983 OST =>)* / Rocky IV *(1985 hit single on OST by V/A)* / Cobra *(1986 hit single on OST by V/A)* / **Eddie And The Cruisers II: Eddie Lives!** *(1989 OST =>)*

CAKE BOY

2005 (US 90m; straight-to-dvd) Kung Fu Films (15)

Film genre: Rock-music comedy

Top guns: dir: **Joe Escalante** / s-w: **Warren Fitzgerald**

Stars: Warren Fitzgerald *(Selwyn Hills)* ← THAT DARN PUNK ← GODMONEY ← DUDES / → PUNK'S NOT DEAD, Pam Gidley *(Becky)* ← S.F.W. ← PERMANENT RECORD ← DUDES, Mia Crowe *(Catherine)* ← THAT DARN PUNK, Scott Aukerman *(Mickey)* ← THAT DARN PUNK, Kyle Gass *(Nathan)* ← THAT DARN PUNK / → the PICK OF DESTINY, Bob Odenkirk *(Darnell Hawk, P.I.)*, Patton Oswalt *(cake pervert)* ← MAN ON THE MOON ← MAGNOLIA, Brian Posehn *(Darrel)* ← the DEVIL'S REJECTS, **No Use For A Name** *(themselves/performers)*, Paul Goebel *(Maurice)* ← GRAND THEFT PARSONS, **Fat Mike** *(sheriff)* ← PUNK ROCK HOLOCAUST, Akemi Royer *(conselling group)* ← THAT DARN PUNK

Storyline: Misunderstood Selwyn is so fed up with the abuse he gets from the locals (he's a naughty cake-maker) he decides to quit town and become a roadie with a punk band. His half-baked scheme soon brings him romance and he learns a few lessons in the school of life on his travels. The icing on the cake comes when he does battle on TV against ze greatest French cake baker in ze world – let's hope Selwyn doesn't get whipped. *JZ*

Movie rating: *4.5

Visual: dvd on Image Entertainment

Off the record: Warren Fitzgerald + Joe Escalante (are in the Vandals, **Fat Mike** is leader of NOFX and Me First & The Gimme Gimmes. **No Use For A Name** were formed in Sunnydale, California, USA ... 1987 by leader/songwriter, Tony Sly (guitar), along with Chris Dodge (guitar), Steve Papoutsis (bass) and Rory Koff (drums). Like many acts of their ilk, NUFaN received early coverage through US hardcore fanzine 'Maximum Rock'n'Roll', releasing their first recorded track, 'Turn It Around' via a special maxi-7" produced by the publication. After a further single, 'Let Them Out', their long-awaited debut album, 'Incognito', was finally issued at the turn of the decade. Sophomore effort 'Don't Miss The Train' (1991) preceded a deal with 'Fat Wreck Chords' and a third album, 'The Daily Grind' (1993). By the release of 'Leche Con Carne' (1994), the group had undergone numerous personnel changes with only a couple of survivors from the original line-up. Sly and Koff welcomed Matt Riddle (on bass) and Chris Shiflett into the fold for 'Making Friends' (1997), the latter jumping ship to the Foo Fighters after the recording of 'More Betterness!' (1999). Erstwhile Suicidal Tendencies guitarist, Dave Nassie, was subsequently recruited for the millennium. Two further studio sets, 'Hard Rock Bottom' (2002) and 'Keep Them Confidential' (2005), saw them finally pick up some deserved airplay. *MCS*

Various Artists (score: Warren Fitzgerald)

May 05. (dvd+cd) *Kung Fu; <78795-9>* [ ] [–]

– No way to live (NO USE FOR A NAME) / Selwyn's got a problem (NO USE FOR A NAME) / Fatal flu (NO USE FOR A NAME) / 1945 (NO USE FOR A NAME) / Coming too close (NO USE FOR A NAME) / Long nights (PIEBALD) / Here comes hollow (JACKSON) / Weird rock (USELESS ID) / Stop the bleeding (the BRONX) / Jason (AUDIO KARATE) / It's kinda like a body bag (UNDERMINDED) / My special moment (the VANDALS) / Rock star land (YELLOWCARD) / Game over (OZMA) / 24 hour party zone (HUNTER REVENGE).

S/track review: Available only with the DVD (much in the same way as 'OUR BURDEN IS LIGHT'), the 'CAKE BOY' soundtrack is down to NO USE FOR A NAME and various other lower-league punk bands. Of the five exclusive NUFaN numbers, the opener 'No Way To Live' and '1945' seem the most effective but they're so derivative – think Green Day pre-'Dookie'. Of the other ten bands on show – and there's not too much difference on most! – the award for best track goes to 'It's Kinda Like A Body Bag' by UNDERMINDED. The award for punk group with the most staying power goes to the VANDALS (who disappoint with 'My Special Moment'), while best newcomers to the BRONX, who subsequently inked a deal with 'Island' records. Closing track, '24 Hour Party Zone', presses all the right funky buttons – if you're a Prince fan. *MCS*

Album rating: *3.5

□ CALIFORNIA HOLIDAY alt.
(⇒ SPINOUT)

CALYPSO HEAT WAVE

1957 (US 86m b&w) Clover Productions / Columbia Pictures

Film genre: Pop-Rock Musical comedy

Top guns: dir: Fred F. Sears ← DON'T KNOCK THE ROCK ← ROCK AROUND THE CLOCK / s-w: David Chandler (story: Orville H. Hampton → RIOT ON SUNSET STRIP → a TIME TO SING → FRIDAY FOSTER)

Stars: Paul Langton *(Mack Adams)*, Merry Anders *(Marti Collins)* → TICKLE ME, Michael Granger *(Barney Pearl)*, **Johnny Desmond** *(Johnny Conroy)*, Meg Myles *(Mona DeLuce)*, Joel Grey *(Alex Nash)* → DANCER IN THE DARK, George E. Stone *('Books')*, **Maya Angelou** *(singer from Trinidad)*, **Darla Hood** *(Johnny's duet partner)*, **Alan Arkin** *(Tarriers lead singer)* → the LAST UNICORN, **Mac Niles** *(performer)*, **the Treniers** *(performers)*, **the Hi-Los** *(performers)*

Storyline: A jukebox magnate forces his way into control of a record company and begins changing things round the way he wants them. However the company's biggest star refuses to go with the flow and the intransigent new owner forces him to quit. However profits soon begin to drop with the demise of our hero, and unless a solution is found there will be no way back from disaster. *JZ*

Movie rating: *4

Visual: video (no audio OST)

Off the record: Big band singer, **Johnny Desmond** performed a song ('Oh, My Darlin'') with **Darla Hood**, while poetess **Maya Angelou** recited 'Run, Joe'. Folk-pop act, the **Tarriers** (aka **Alan Arkin**, Bob Carey & Erik Darling) performed their recent Top 5 smash, 'The Banana Boat Song'; Arkin went on to star in films such as 'Catch-22' and 'M*A*S*H'. **Mac Niles** (aka King Charles MacNiles) contributed 'Stewed Pig Knuckles', while **the Treniers** were responsible for two tracks, 'Rock Joe' and 'Day Old Bread And Canned Beans'. *MCS*

CALYPSO JOE

1957 (US 75m b&w) Allied Artists Pictures Corporation

Film genre: romantic Pop Musical drama

Top guns: s-w: (+ dir) Edward Dein, Mildred Dein

Stars: Herb Jeffries *(Calypso Joe)*, Angie Dickinson *(Julie; stewardess)* → EVEN COWGIRLS GET THE BLUES → DUETS, Ed Kemmer *(Lee Darling)*, Stephen Bekassy *(Rico Vargas)*, Claudia Drake *(Astra)*, Laurie Mitchell *(Leah)*, **Lord Flea and his Calypsonians** *(performers)* → BOP GIRL, **the Easy Riders** *(performers)*, the Lester Horton Dancers *(performers)*

Storyline: Flight stewardess Julie has had a lovers' tiff with TV celebrity Lee Darling, but not content with slamming down the phone on him she jumps on the first plane to South America to prove a point. Distraught Darling sees the error of his ways and races off after her, and the pair try to reconcile their differences with the sun, sea and calypso music to help them along. *JZ*

Movie rating: *3

Visual: none + audio; score: Richard Hazard & Herb Jeffries)

Off the record: Lord Flea (b. Norman Thomas, 1932, Kingston, Jamaica) was at the height of his calypso/"mento" (precursor to reggae and ska) when he died on May 18th 1959, of Hodgkin's Disease. As a resident of Miami, Florida since the early 50s, the multi-talented and multi-instrumentalist was a force on songs such as 'Where Did The Naughty Little Flea Go?'; look out for his rare LP, 'Swingin' Calypsos' (1957). *MCS*

CAMP

2003 (US 115m) IFC Films (PG-13)

Film genre: teen Pop-musical comedy drama

Top guns: s-w + dir: Todd Graff

Stars: Daniel Letterle *(Vlad Baumann)*, Joanna Chilcoat *(Ellen Lucas)*, Robin De Jesus *(Michael Flores)*, Tiffany Taylor *(Jenna Malloran)*, Sasha Allen *(Dee)*, Alana Allen *(Jill Simmons)*, Anna Kendrick *(Fritzi Wagner)*, Kahiry Bess *(Petie)*, Steven Cutts *(Shaun)*, Vince Rimoldi *(Spitzer)*, **Don Dixon** *(Bert)*, Dequina Moore *(Dequina)*, Tracee Beazer *(Tracee)*

Storyline: Bert Hayley is trying to make a new show at the summer camp, but he has to contend with the usual suspects – bitchy teenage girls, an alcoholic teacher and an obese child whose jaws are wired shut to help her lose weight (watch her reciting Shakespeare). Meanwhile, newcomer Vlad's good looks attract the attention of all the male luvvies, especially Michael. Can Bert bring this bunch of misfits together in time? *JZ*

Movie rating: *6

Visual: dvd

Off the record: Don Dixon (b. North Carolina) was the producer of Let's Active, Marshall Crenshaw, Guadalcanal Diary, R.E.M., the Smithereens and a solo artist in his own right ('Most Of The Girls Like To Dance But Only Some Of The Boys Do' 1985 to 'The Invisible Man' 2000); he's also married to singer Marti Jones. *MCS*

Various Cast // Various Artists (score: Stephen Trask)

Jul 03. (cd) *Decca; <B 0000667-12> (038280-2)* ☐ Sep03 ☐
– How shall I see you through my tears (SASHA ALLEN, STEVEN CUTTS and the COMPANY) / Century plant (the COMPANY) / Here's where I stand (TIFFANY TAYLOR and the COMPANY) / I sing for you (DANIEL LETTERLE) / The want of a nail (the COMPANY) / Wild horses (DANIEL LETTERLE) / The ladies who lunch (ALANA ALLEN and ANNA KENDRICK) / Turkey lurkey time (ALANA ALLEN, DEQUINA MOORE, TRACEE BEAZER and the COMPANY *) // Skyway (the REPLACEMENTS) / The size of a cow (the WONDER STUFF) / On/off (SNOW PATROL) / Right on be free (the VOICES OF EAST HARLEM) / I believe in us (WARREN WIEBE) / Round our way (OASIS).

S/track review: Featuring an array of original songs offered by seasoned Broadway composers Michael Gore and Lynn Ahrens, 'CAMP' kicks off with the rambunctious old-school gospel-tinged soul of 'How Shall I See You Through My Tears', which has strong lead vocals from SASHA ALLEN, backed by the glorious choir of the COMPANY and rounded out by a full band replete with tinkling piano and smooth guitar. TIFFANY TAYLOR joins forces with the COMPANY on 'Here's Where I Stand', a jaunty piano ballad the likes of which Whitney Houston built much of her career on. Meanwhile 'Century Plant' is early 70s hippie rock'n'roll stuck somewhere between Neil Young and Donovan which, despite some interesting tempo changes, suffers from having too many vocalists, whilst 'The Want Of A Nail' adds even more upbeat gospel to proceedings. 'I Sing For You' features some nice acoustic fingerstyle akin to Extreme's 1991 hit 'More Than Words' but the sickeningly clichéd lovelorn lyrics delivered by DANIEL LETTERLE are devoid of passion, much like his wafer-thin emotionless performance on an otherwise pleasant cover of the Rolling Stones classic 'Wild Horses'. The REPLACEMENTS show how it should be done on 'Skyway' with its strummed acoustic guitars à la Ryan Adams before the Stephen Sondheim-penned 'The Ladies Who Lunch' brings to mind Randy Newman and Broadway on a jazzy venture dripping with cynicism despite the obvious youth of vocalists ALANA ALLEN and ANNA KENDRICK. Things then go off on a tangent as the WONDER STUFF bustle into the action with the hyperactively upbeat 'Size Of A Cow' which surprisingly isn't so sonically dissimilar to OASIS's 'Round Our Way' which features an unlikely boisterous brass section. Between those offerings we also have the dreamy lo-fi of SNOW PATROL's 'On/Off' as well as a slice of 70s funk with 'Right On Be Free' by the VOICES OF EAST HARLEM and the slick mushy piano ballad of WARREN WIEBE's 'I Believe In Us' which both feel rather tacked on at the end. *LF*

Album rating: *6

Glen CAMPBELL

Born: 22 Apr'36, Delight, Arkansas, USA. A studio stalwart who juggled high profile session work before his sporadic solo career finally bore fruit, GLEN CAMPBELL straddled the often opposing spheres of pop, easy listening and country with an unrivalled finesse and homey Southern charm. Definitive interpretations from writers like JIMMY WEBB, turned CAMPBELL into a late 60s/early 70s superstar with the obligatory TV chat show to match. After initially appearing in music biz satire, 'The COOL ONES', an inevitable shot at real acting came with a starring role opposite John Wayne in Henry Hathaway's western masterpiece, 'True Grit' (1969). This was followed with a lead role as a Vietnam vet with wanderlust in 'NORWOOD' (1970); he even provided most of the soundtrack. Although his star had faded by the time he popped up in Clint Eastwood sequel, 'Any Which Way You Can' (1980), CAMPBELL continued to make occasional screen appearances in dramas such as 'Family Prayers' (1992) and 'I Love Your Work' (2004). *BG*

- **filmography** {acting} (composer) –

the T.A.M.I. Show *(1964 {p} =>)* / Baby, The Rain Must Fall *(1965 {a})* / Star Route USA *(1966 {*})* / **the Cool Ones** *(1967 {p} =>)* / **the Man, His World, His Music** *(1969 {c} OST by JOHNNY CASH =>)* / True Grit *(1969 {*} hit theme on OST by Elmer Bernstein)* / **Norwood** *(1970 {*} OST =>)* / Strange Homecoming *(1974 TV {a})* / Any Which Way You Can *(1980 {c} on OST by V/A)* / Uphill All The Way *(1985 TV {*})* / Family Prayers *(1992 {c})* / **Rock-A-Doodle** *(1992 {v} on OST by V/A =>)* / **Endless Harmony: The Beach Boys Story** *(1998 TV {c} =>)* / I Love Your Work *(2004 {p})*

CANDY MOUNTAIN

1988 (Swi/Can/Fra 91m) Antenne 2 / Films Plain Chant (R)

Film genre: Road movie comedy/drama

Top guns: dir: Rudy Wurlitzer (+ s-w) ← WALKER ← PAT GARRETT & BILLY THE KID, Robert Frank ← COCKSUCKER BLUES

Stars: Kevin J. O'Connor *(Julius)*, Harris Yulin *(Elmore Silk)* ← GOOD TO GO / → the MILLION DOLLAR HOTEL → CHELSEA WALLS, **Tom WAITS** *(Al Silk)*, Bulle Ogier *(Cornelia)* ← la VALLEE ← les IDOLES, **David Johansen** *(Keith Burns)* <= NEW YORK DOLLS =>, **Leon Redbone** *(Huey)*, **Joe STRUMMER** *(Mario)*, **DR. JOHN** *(himself)*, Roberts Blossom *(Archie)* ← FLASHPOINT, **Rita MacNeil** *(Winnie)*, Laurie Metcalf *(Alice)*, Tantoo Cardinal *(Annie)* → WHERE THE RIVERS FLOW NORTH → a STRANGER IN THE KINGDOM, **Arto Lindsay** *(Eric Mitchell (Gunther) ← the FOREIGNER*, **Mary Margaret O'Hara** *(Darlene)* → APARTMENT HUNTING, David Margulies *(lawyer)* ← MAGIC STICKS ← TIMES SQUARE / → LOOKING FOR AN ECHO, Nancy Fish *(maid)* ← HOWARD THE DUCK ← BIRDY ← MORE AMERICAN GRAFFITI ← STEELYARD BLUES, Wayne Robson *(Buddy Burke)* ← POPEYE / → AFFLICTION, Rockets Redglare *(van driver)* ← DOWN BY LAW / → MYSTERY TRAIN → WHAT ABOUT ME, Jim Jarmusch *(cameo)* ← STRAIGHT TO HELL / → LENINGRAD COWBOYS GO AMERICA → SLING BLADE → YEAR OF THE HORSE → I PUT A SPELL ON ME → the FUTURE IS UNWRITTEN

Storyline: Promising rock star, Julius, goes on a long quest to locate an elusive and legendary guitar-maker, Elmore Silk, a meeting he hopes will bring him the rewards of fame and wealth. *MCS*

Movie rating: *5

Visual: video (no audio OST)

Off the record: Leon Redbone (b.29 Oct'29, New York City, NY) was a bit of a mystery, his past hidden under his persona of a neo-vaudeville (ragtime jazz and blues) act; the Groucho Marx moustache, dark glasses and omnipresent fedora, were hand in glove with his deep baritone crooning. It is believed Leon moved to Toronto, Canada in the 70s and while performing on the 'Saturday Night Live' TV shows, he made his first 'Warner Bros.' record, 'On The Track' (1976), a US Top 100 entry; his second, 'Double Time' (1977), reached the Top 40, although 'Champagne Charlie' (1978) only peaked at No.163. Leon subsequently co-wrote the score for 'CANDY MOUNTAIN' (1988) – alongside DR. JOHN, DAVID JOHANSEN and RITA MacNEIL (all of whom starred in the film) – and composed additional material for the 1990 movie, 'Everybody Wins'. **Rita MacNeil** (b.28 May'44, Big Pond, Cape Breton, Nova Scotia) has been a folk singer from the age of 17, her debut album, 'Born A Woman', being issued in '75. In 1987, having released a few independent sets, she signed a major deal with 'Virgin', who issued 'Flying On Your Own'. The larger than life lady was given the Order Of Canada in 1992 and is still going strong in 2006 having just delivered her umpteenth album, 'Songs My Mother Loved'. *MCS*

CAN'T STOP THE MUSIC

1980 (US 120m) EMI Films (PG)

Film genre: Disco-Pop musical comedy

Top guns: dir: Nancy Walker / s-w: Allan Carr, Bronte Woodard ← GREASE

Stars: Valerie Perrine *(Samantha Simpson)* → the BORDER → 54, Steve Guttenberg *(Jack Morrell)*, Bruce Jenner *(Ron White)*, Jack Weston *(Benny Murray)* → DIRTY DANCING, **Randy Jones** *(Randy the cowboy)*, **Ray Simpson** *(Ray the police officer)*, **David Hodo** *(David the construction worker)*, **Felipe Rose** *(Felipe the Indian chief)*, **Alex Briley** *(Alex the G.I.)*, **Glenn Hughes** *(Glenn the leather man)*, June Havoc *(Helen Morell)*, Barbara Rush *(Norma White)*, Altovise Davis *(Alicia Edwards)* ← PIPE DREAMS, Leigh Taylor-Young *(Claudia Walters)*, Paul Sand *(Steve Waits)*, Tammy Grimes *(Sydney Channing)* → HIGH ART, Dick Patterson *(Mr. Schultz; record store manager)* ← GREASE / → GREASE 2, **Blackie Lawless** *(metal man with leash)*, Bobo Lewis *(bread woman)* ← HOOTENANNY HOOT, Gene Montoya *(dancer)* ← WELCOME TO MY NIGHTMARE ← the NIGHTMARE

Storyline: Struggling songwriter Jack Morrell has the talent, has the songs, but doesn't have the right group to sing them. Who should he have as his best friend but ex-supermodel Samantha (lucky so-and-so) who with her huge list of contacts in the music business soon finds Jack the required band. Despite the fact they dress very strangely Samantha persuades her lawyer friend Ron to give them a chance, and a gay old time is had by all. *JZ*

Movie rating: *3.5

Visual: video

Off the record: Blackie Lawless was of metal act, W.A.S.P.

—

the VILLAGE PEOPLE (& Various) (score: Jacques Morali)

Jun 80. (lp/c) *Casablanca; <NBLP 7220> Mercury; (6399/7199 051)* [47] Aug80 [9]
– Can't stop the music / Samantha (DAVID LONDON) / Give me a break (the RITCHIE FAMILY) / Liberation / Magic night / The sound of the city (DAVID LONDON) / Milkshake / Y.M.C.A. / I love you to death / Sophistication (the RITCHIE FAMILY). *<re-iss. Sep96 on 'Mercury' cd/c; 314 532932-2/-4>*

S/track review: The VILLAGE PEOPLE were big in 1978 when the disco dancefloor scene was all the rage, and everybody else and their grannies knew what else they were "into". The brainchild of French-born, New York-based songwriter Jacques Morali (aka Ritchie Rome), the group of singers (ALEX BRILEY – the sailor, DAVID "SCAR" HODO – the construction worker, GLENN HUGHES – the leatherman, RANDY JONES – the cowboy, FELIPE ROSE – the Indian chief and RAY SIMPSON – the police officer) had a handful of hits including 'Y.M.C.A.', 'Macho Man', 'In The Navy' & 'Go West'. 'CAN'T STOP THE MUSIC' saw the VP at their OTT best, but most of their numbers on show here were not up to scratch except, for many, the UK hit title track, the rock-ish 'Liberation', plus the aforementioned oldie, 'Y.M.C.A.'. The instructional 'Milkshake' is indeed one of the most embarrassingly bad songs of all time, while 'Magic Night' is over-produced and over-orchestrated; 'I Love You To Death' is just basically out of place. There was also room for Morali's other protégés, the RITCHIE FAMILY (Cheryl Jacks, Cassandra Wooten & Gwen Oliver), plus newbie on the block, DAVID LONDON. While not much is known about the latter pop singer (who actually shines on his two contributions, the Toto-like 'Samantha' & the NYC-anthem of 'The Sound Of The City'), the RITCHIE FAMILY had a couple of high chart entries by way of 'Brazil' & 'The Best Disco In Town'. The trio of robotic disco divas from Philadelphia were no Sister Sledge or LaBelle – although they tried hard to be – and if there was any proof needed one could just check out 'Give Me A Break' and 'Sophistication'. One sad footnote to the movie was the AIDS-related death of Jacques Morali on the 15th of November, 1991. *MCS*

Album rating: *4.5

– spinoff hits, etc. –

the VILLAGE PEOPLE: Can't Stop The Music / I Love You To Death

Jul 80. (7") *(MER 16)* ☐ 11

the RITCHIE FAMILY: Give Me A Break

Jul 80. (7") *(MER 17)* ☐ ☐

the VILLAGE PEOPLE: Magic Night / Liberation

Sep 80. (7") *(MER 39)* ☐ ☐

☐ Mariah CAREY segment
(⇒ GLITTER)

CARMEN: A HIP HOPERA

2001 (US 88m TV) New Line Television / MTV (PG-13)

Film genre: Hip-Hop musical/drama

Top guns: dir: Robert Townsend ← LIVIN' FOR LOVE: THE NATALIE COLE STORY ← LITTLE RICHARD ← JACKIE'S BACK! ← the FIVE HEARTBEATS / s-w: Michael Elliot → BROWN SUGAR

Stars: Beyonce Knowles *(Carmen)* → the FIGHTING TEMPTATIONS → FADE TO BLACK → DREAMGIRLS, Mekhi Phifer *(Sgt. Derek Hill)* ← GIRL 6 / → 8 MILE → HONEY, **Mos Def** *(Frank Miller)* → BROWN SUGAR → BLOCK PARTY, **Rah Digga** *(Rasheeda)*, Joy Bryant *(Nikki)* → HONEY → GET RICH OR DIE TRYIN', **Da Brat** *(voice; narrator)* ← RHYME & REASON / → GLITTER, Sam Sarpong *(Nathaniel)* ← MASKED AND ANONYMOUS ← CARMEN: A HIP HOPERA, **Wyclef Jean** *(fortune teller)* ← RHYME & REASON / → the COUNTRY BEARS → BE COOL → BLOCK PARTY, **Jermaine Dupri** *(Pockets)* → BROWN SUGAR, Casey Lee *(Blaze)*, **Bow Wow** *(Jalil)* ← MURDER WAS THE CASE / → ROLL BOUNCE, Fred Williamson ← RIDE ← FROM DUSK TILL DAWN ← MR. MEAN ← THREE TOUGH GUYS ← THREE THE HARD WAY ← ADIOS AMIGO ← MEAN JOHNNY BARROWS ← BUCKTOWN ← HELL UP IN HARLEM ← BLACK CAESAR

Storyline: Set in modern-day Philadelphia, Carmen still manages to cause trouble wherever she goes. The aspiring actress even skips jail when her arresting officer Derek "Don José" Hill falls so much in love with her he almost floats away up into the sky. However, our haughty heroine has her eye on rapster Blaze, and the fact that the lovestruck cop gives up everything for her cuts no ice. The scene is set for a tragic ending as Carmen's chaos catches up with her – fatal consequences ensue. *JZ*

Movie rating: *4

Visual: dvd

Off the record: Rah Digga (b. Rashia Fisher, 18 Dec'72, Newark, New Jersey, USA) was part of rap outfits, Flipmode Squad and the Outsidaz, the latter along with boyfriend Young Zee; her solo album, 'Dirty Harriet' (2000), hit the Top 20. *MCS*

—

Various Artists: MTV's Hip Hopera: Carmen (score: Kip Collins & Sekani Williams)

Jun 01. (cd) *Columbia; <CK 85846> (503324-2)* ☐ ☐
– The introduction (DA BRAT) / Survivor remix (DESTINY'S CHILD feat. DA BRAT) / Boom (ROYCE DA 5'9") / What we gonna do (RAH DIGGA) / If looks could kill (you would be dead) (BEYONCE KNOWLES, MOS DEF, SAM SARPONG) / Cards never lie (BEYONCE KNOWLES, WYCLEF JEAN, RAH DIGGA) / The last great seduction (BEYONCE KNOWLES, MEKHI PHIFER) / B.L.A.Z.E. (CASEY LEE, RAH DIGGA, JOY BRYANT) / Black & blue (MOS DEF, MEKHI PHIFER) / Stop that! (BEYONCE KNOWLES, MEKHI PHIFER) / B.L.A.Z.E. finale (CASEY LEE) / Immortal beloved – outro (DA BRAT) / Bootylicious – Rockwilder remix (DESTINY'S CHILD feat MISSY "MISDEMEANOR" ELLIOTT).

S/track review: Remaking and updating is common practice in Hollywood but lifting from the classical canon and bringing to bear on a contemporary audience is a real challenge. 'CARMEN: A HIP HOPERA' is bold in that it brought out the biggest guns in hip hop and R&B around for a post-Baz Luhrmann's Romeo And Juliet-style over the top shindig. BEYONCE KNOWLES as our eponymous heroine means we get a pair of prime DESTINY'S CHILD cuts, 'Survivor' and sticky reworking of 'Bootylicious' plus BEYONCE throwing her weight about on pretty much all the other tracks on this specially recorded collection. She may be a fine warbler and balladeer but her rap skills are sadly lacking. She sounds like she's trying that little bit too hard and that breathiness is supposed to sound sexy, but comes off faintly asthmatic. Conversely, RAH DIGGA's wide-mouth vowels on 'What We Gonna Do' and DA BRAT's grimy intro and outro show what a fine line it is for women to play the men in hip hop at their own game however; both manage to sound tough but credible. This whole album is surprising palatable, although for the most part it's just too clean. It feels contrived rather than inspired. Even a few verses thrown in by co-star MOS DEF on 'If Looks Could Kill' and 'Black & Blue' add a little bit of random tension but then there are way too many flaccid planks. The prime turkey is 'Cards Never Lie', which features that musical kiss of death, a contribution from WYCLEF JEAN. *MR*

Album rating: *4.5

CARNIVAL ROCK

1957 (US 75m b&w) Roger Corman Productions

Film genre: Romantic melodrama

Top guns: dir: Roger Corman → ROCK ALL NIGHT → the WILD ANGELS → the TRIP → GAS-S-S-S / s-w: Leo Lieberman

Stars: Susan Cabot *(Natalie Cook)*, Brian Hutton *(Stanley)* → KING CREOLE, David J. Stewart *(Christy Cristakos)*, Dick Miller *(Benny)* → ROCK ALL NIGHT → BEACH BALL → SKI PARTY → the GIRLS ON THE BEACH → WILD, WILD WINTER → the WILD ANGELS → the TRIP → TRUCK TURNER → I WANNA HOLD YOUR HAND → ROCK'N'ROLL HIGH SCHOOL → GET CRAZY → SHAKE, RATTLE & ROCK! tv, Iris Adrian *(Celia)* → BLUE HAWAII, Jonathan Haze *(Max)* → ROCK ALL NIGHT, Ed Nelson *(Cannon; lawyer)* → ROCK ALL NIGHT → THAT'S THE WAY OF THE WORLD, Chris Alcaide *(Slug)* → ROCK ALL NIGHT, Dorothy Neumann *(Clara; matron)* → HOT ROD GANG → LOOKING FOR LOVE → GET YOURSELF A COLLEGE GIRL, Horace Logan *(MoC)*, Bruno VeSota *(Mr. Kirsch; editor)* → ROCK ALL NIGHT → DADDY-O → YOUR CHEATIN' HEART → the GIRLS ON THE BEACH, **Bob Luman & the Shadows** *(performers)*, **the Platters:- David Lynch, Herb Reed, Zola Taylor, Paul Robi + Tony Williams** *(performers)* ← the GIRL CAN'T HELP IT ← ROCK AROUND THE CLOCK / → ROCK ALL NIGHT, **David Houston** *(performer)*, **the Blockbusters** *(performers)* → ROCK ALL NIGHT

Storyline: Director/producer gets his teeth into his first rock'n'roll movie about a carnival night-club singer and two men in her life, Christy and Stanley. The former (the club owner down on his luck) is besotted by the girl, but she only has eyes for the latter, a gambler who wants to buy out his business. *MCS*

Movie rating: *3

Visual: video + dvd

Off the record: David Houston (b. 9 Dec'33, Newark, New Jersey – a descendant of Robert E. Lee and Sam Houston) became a country pop singer in the 60s, and went on to have a string of US hits, the greatest of them being 'Almost Persuaded', which reached the Top 30 in 1966. He died of a ruptured brain aneurysm on 25th November, 1993. Rockabilly singer, **Bob Luman** (b.15 Apr'37, Nacoqdoches, Texas), meanwhile, switched his musical allegiences to country and had a Top 10 novelty hit in 1960 with 'Let's Think About Living'. Sadly, although he survived a serious heart attack a few years previously, Luman died (at his home in Nashville) of pneumonia on the 27 December, 1978. *MCS*

Various Artists

Oct 03. (cd) *And More Bears; <25003>* ☐ ☐
– The creep (SHADOWS) / This is the night (BOB LUMAN) / All night long (BOB LUMAN) / One and only (DAVID HOUSTON) / Teen age Frankie and Johnny (DAVID HOUSTON) / O-shoo-bla-d (teen age bop) (SUSAN CABOT & the BLOCKBUSTERS) / There's no place to go (SUSAN CABOT) / Carnival rock (BLOCKBUSTERS) / Remember when (PLATTERS) / Teen age kisses (DAVID HOUSTON) *[not in film]*.

S/track review: Not issued at the time (LPs weren't really kicking until 1958), the recordings saw light on CD some 46 years later. Switching from rockabilly and C&W in the shape of BOB LUMAN (& the SHADOWS; featuring guitarist JAMES BURTON) and DAVID HOUSTON respectively, the songs were prime cuts in their heyday. The doo-wop of the PLATTERS, who'd already had several hits prior to 1957 (including chart-toppers, 'The Great Pretender' and 'My Prayer') were undoubtedly on a high with 'Remember When'. All 'n all, an average piece of nostalgia that deserved better recognition at the time. *MCS*

Album rating: *5

☐ David CASSIDY segment
(⇒ the DAVID CASSIDY STORY)

CATALINA CAPER

aka 'NEVER STEAL ANYTHING WET'

1967 (US 84m) Crown International Pictures

Film genre: Pop-Rock Musical crime caper/mystery

Top guns: dir: Lee Sholem / s-w: Clyde Ware (ss au: Sam Pierce)

Stars: Tommy Kirk *(Don Pringle)* ← IT'S A BIKINI WORLD ← the GHOST IN THE INVISIBLE BIKINI ← PAJAMA PARTY, Del Moore *(Arthur Duval)*, Peter Duryea *(Tad Duval)*, Robert Donner *(Fingers O'Toole)* → SKIDOO → VANISHING POINT, Ulla Stromstedt *(Katrina Corelli)*, Jim Begg *(Larry)* ← IT'S A BIKINI WORLD ← the COOL ONES / → DEATH WISH II, Michael Blodgett *(Bob Draper)* ← the TRIP / → BEYOND THE VALLEY OF THE DOLLS → DISCO FEVER, **LITTLE RICHARD** *(performer)*, **the Cascades:- John Gummoe, Eddie Snyder, David Stevens, David Wilson, David Zabo** *(performers)*, **Carol Connors Shaw** *(performer)*

Storyline: The beach (Catalina Island) is the setting for this youthful crime malarky mystery, which revolves around the thieves of a stolen antique scroll from an art gallery and the attempts to steal it back. *MCS*

Movie rating: *2.5

Visual: video (no audio OST)

Off the record: The **Cascades** were a vocal pop group from San Diego led by singer/guitarist, John Gummoe. In 1963, they had a Top 3 smash with 'Rhythm Of The Rain'; further minor hits included 'The Last Leaf'. The quintet contributed one Ray Davies-penned number, 'There's A New World Opening For Me', while **LITTLE RICHARD** contributed 'Scuba Party', co-written with Jerry Long, who also scored the opening and closing version of 'Never Steal Anything Wet' by MARY WELLS; actress/singer CAROL CONNORS SHAW sang 'Book Of Love'. *MCS*

CATCH MY SOUL

1973 (US 95m) Metromedia Productions / Cinerama (PG-13)

Film genre: Pop/Rock musical drama

Top guns: dir: Patrick McGoohan / s-w: Jack Good (based on William Shakespeare's 'Othello')

Stars: Richie Havens *(Othello)* ← WOODSTOCK / → HEARTS OF FIRE → GLASTONBURY → I'M NOT THERE, Lance LeGault *(Iago)*, Season Hubley *(Desdemona)* → ELVIS: THE MOVIE, **Tony Joe White** *(Cassio)*, Susan Tyrell *(Emilia)* → FORBIDDEN ZONE → SUBWAY RIDERS → TAPEHEADS → ROCKULA → CRY-BABY → PINK AS THE DAY SHE WAS BORN → MASKED AND ANONYMOUS, **Delaney & Bonnie Bramlett** * *(performers)* ← VANISHING POINT ← MEDICINE BALL CARAVAN / → the DOORS * → FESTIVAL EXPRESS, **Billy Joe Royal** ← WEEKEND REBELLION

Storyline: New Mexico, the early 70s; rather than a Venenian general in the eastern Med, Othello is an itinerant Afro-American preacher who holds sway over a hippy commune, while convert Michael Cassino is "a wino from Baton Rouge". Encouraging Cassino and co to restore a ruined chapel, and cosummating his love for Desdemona, he doesn't suspect the ulterior motives of devil-in-disguise, Iago, a man with a black tour bus of demonic musos – "a supergroup of hell". *BG*

Movie rating: *3.5

Visual: video (very rare!)

Off the record: Richie Havens + TONY JOE WHITE (see below)

JACK GOOD (*) / TONY JOE WHITE (**) / Various Cast (composer: Paul Glass)

Nov 73. (lp) *Metromedia; <BML 1-0176> Polydor; (2383 035)* ☐ ☐
– Othello 1 (**) / Wash us clean (* & **) / Catch my soul 1 (* & **) / Working on a building (**) / Othello 2 (**) / Catch my soul 2 (*, ** & LANCE DeLAULT) / Open our eyes (LEON LUMKINS) / Backwoods preacher man (**) / Looking back (DELANEY BRAMLETT & TONY JOE WHITE) / Eat the bread – drink the wine (* & **) / That's what God said (DELANEY BRAMLETT) / Chug-a-lug (the drinking song) (DELANEY BRAMLETT) / I found Jesus (DELANEY BRAMLETT) / Rin, shaker life / Catch my soul 3 (* & **) / Book of prophecy (* & RICHIE HAVENS) / Othello 3 (**) / Lust of the blood (* & RAY POHLMAN) / Tickle his fancy (ALLENE LUBIN) / Why (* & EMILE DEAN ZOGHBY) / Othello 4 (**) / Catch my soul 4 (* & **) / Put out the light (* & RAY POHLMAN) / Othello 5 (**).

S/track review: Filmed at the height of rock-opera fever in the early 70s, Jack Good's stage-to-screen version of Shakespeare's 'Othello' isn't well remembered, if it's remembered at all. Yet the likes of Time Out's verdict of "grade-school Shakespeare and grade-school religion" glosses over another excellent Americana-brings-it-all-back-home-to-the-desert soundtrack performed by the likes of RICHIE HAVENS, DELANEY & BONNIE BRAMLETT and the great TONY JOE WHITE. Naturally, gospel is the common denominator, with all parties working out their own peace: HAVENS with his mocha-rich proclamations, delivering oracularly phrased sermons over the burning-bush, bluegrass-breakbeat funk of 'Working On A Building' and the relentless 'Run Shaker Life'; WHITE with his Southern "swamp fox" persona and country-got-so-much-soul-it-hurts timbre; the ubiquitous DELANEY & BONNIE (in one of her funkiest ever performances over the second line groove of 'Chug A Lug') with the husband-and-wife belief, and soul-saturated country-rock which had so taken Clapton. Each of them takes turns on lead or rafter-charging backup, each contributes more or less equally to the songwriting and WHITE together with actor Lance LeGault – a man with bit parts in several late period Elvis movies (as well as a lengthy run in the 'A-Team'..) and no slouch as a multi-range, soul-stealing Southern growler himself, born to sing lines like "we're gonna have a black mass on Othello's black ass" – are afforded their own themes in multiple parts. More importantly, the bombast more commonly associated with the term "rock opera" is all but absent, replaced with the loose bonhomie, easy ardour and unfettered acoustics of an ad hoc Southern ensemble. The themes – sin, temptation, adultery, murder, damnation, etc. – may be heavy but the music is almost wholly redemptive, a seamless roots-rock classic unjustly lost in its own vinyl limbo. *BG*

Album rating: *7.5

– spinoff releases, etc. –

TONY JOE WHITE: Backwoods Preacher Man

Nov 73. (7") *Warners; (K 16294)* [ ] [ ]

DELANEY BRAMLETT: That's What God Said / I Found Jesus

Nov 73. (7") *Columbia; C.B.S.; (1914)* [ ] [ ]

CATCH US IF YOU CAN

US title 'HAVING A WILD WEEKEND'

1965 (UK 91m) Columbia Pictures

Film genre: Pop-Rock Musical comedy

Top guns: dir: John Boorman → DELIVERANCE / s-w: Peter Nichols

Stars: the Dave Clark Five:- Dave Clark *(Steve/performer)* ← GET YOURSELF A COLLEGE GIRL, + **Lenny Davidson, Rick Huxley, Mike Smith, Denis Payton** *(themselves/performers)* ← GET YOURSELF A COLLEGE GIRL, Robin Bailey *(Guy)*, Barbara Ferris *(Dinah)*, Robert Lake *(columnist)* → HAWKS, David Lodge *(Louis)* ← IDLE ON PARADE, Yootha Joyce *(Nan)* → ALL THE RIGHT NOISES, Julian Holloway *(asst. director)* ← a HARD DAY'S NIGHT / → the GREAT ROCK'N'ROLL SWINDLE, Alan Lake *(cameraman)* → FLAME, Peter Eyre *(art director)* → PIED PIPER

Storyline: Sulky Steve and depressed Dinah meet on a cold winter's day while filming a meat commercial – romantic stuff. The pair cheer each other up with their tales of woe and head for an island off the coast of Devon to escape the rat race, without telling anyone about their mini-elopement. Villain of the piece Lenny follows Dinah's tracks in the snow and makes sure their flight to Utopia will not be an easy one. *JZ*

Movie rating: *4

Visual: video + in 2007 dvd

Off the record: The **DAVE CLARK FIVE** (see below)

—

the DAVE CLARK FIVE: Catch Us If You Can

Aug 65. (lp) *Columbia; (SX 1756)* [8] [–]
– Catch us if you can / On the move / If you come back / Long ago / Any time you want love / I can't stand it / Your turn to cry / Hurtin' inside / Don't be taken in / Don't you realize / I cried over you / Sweet memories.

—

the DAVE CLARK FIVE: Having A Wild Weekend

Aug 65. (lp) *Epic; <BN 26162>* [–] [15]
– Having a wild weekend / New kind of love / Dum-dee-dee-dum / I said I was sorry / No stopping / Don't be taken in / Catch us if you can / When I'm alone / If you come back / Sweet memories / Don't you realize / On the move.

S/track review: Tottenham lads the DAVE CLARK FIVE were London's answer to the BEATLES, in fact, the quintet followed the Fab Four in 1964 on a successful jaunt to America (and on to the Ed Sullivan show!) as the "British Invasion" took hold. Leader and former movie stuntman DAVE (on drums!), MIKE SMITH (vocals/keys), LENNY DAVIDSON (lead guitar), RICK HUXLEY (bass) and DENIS PAYTON (rhythm guitar/sax/harmonica) were on the crest of a wave up to now, hitting both the UK and US charts with the thumpin'/stompin' beats of 'Glad All Over' and 'Bits And Pieces', and this film was indeed the icing on the cake. Helped by the Top 5 title track, the soundtrack did well commercially, although critics failed to see the wisdom of another Beatles-type movie (the DC5 had also turned up for 'GET YOURSELF A COLLEGE GIRL'). Flipside to the title track 45, 'On The Move', showed the quintet weren't just Beatles clones, rawcous instrumentalists Duane Eddy and Link Wray were also presumably idols. But this was a one-off. With mainman CLARK and DAVIDSON writing the bulk of the songs (including pop ballads/R&B screamers 'If You Come Back', 'Long Ago', 'Any Time You Want Love' and 'I Can't Stand It'), you wonder what all the fuss was about. And there was more on side two ('Don't Be Taken In', etc). Whether the American version was better – it did vary greatly from its UK counterpart – is conjecture, although one title 'Dum-Dee-Dee-Dum' suggests otherwise. *MCS*

Album rating: *4

– spinoff hits, etc. –

the DAVE CLARK FIVE: Catch Us If You Can / On The Move

Jul 65. (7") *(DB 7625) <9833>* [5] Aug65 [4]

CENTER STAGE

2000 (US 115m) Columbia Pictures (PG-13)

Film genre: teen/Dance-musical drama

Top guns: dir: Nicholas Hytner / s-w: Carol Heikkinen ← EMPIRE RECORDS ← the THING CALLED LOVE

Stars: Amanda Schull *(Jody Sawyer)*, Zoe Saldana *(Eva Rodriguez)* → GET OVER IT → TEMPTATION, Susan May Pratt *(Maureen Cummings)*, Peter Gallagher *(Jonathan Reeves)* ← the IDOLMAKER, Donna Murphy *(Juliette Simone)*, Debra Monk *(Nancy Cummings)*, Ethan Stiefel *(Cooper Nielson)*

Storyline: Twelve teen hopefuls enrol at New York's American Ballet Academy, all hoping to learn how to fly (high) and live forever, or at least get the nod to join the American Ballet Company. *BG*

Movie rating: *5.5

Visual: video + dvd

Off the record: nothing of interest

—

Various Artists (score: George Fenton)

May 00. (cd/c) *Sony; <63969-2/-4> (498227-2)* [ ] Oct00 [ ]
– I wanna be with you (MANDY MOORE) / First kiss (INTERNATIONAL FIVE) / Don't get lost in the crowd (ASHLEY BALLARD) / We're dancing (P.Y.T.) / Friends forever (THUNDERBUGS) / Get used to this (CYRENA) / A girl can dream (P.Y.T.) / Cosmic girl (JAMIROQUAI) / Higher ground (RED HOT CHILI PEPPERS) / Come baby come (ELVIS CRESPO & GIZELLE D'COLE) / The way you make me feel (MICHAEL JACKSON) / If I was the one (RUFF ENDZ) / Canned heat (JAMIROQUAI) / I wanna be with you – Soul Solution remix (MANDY MOORE). *(re-iss. May04; same)*

S/track review: Salve Miooooooooo!! Giving your subjective tuppenceworth on other folks' art can be a drag sometimes. But having to write, produce and market the sonic cornflakes on this travesty of a soundtrack? It doesn't bear thinking about. Unless you've just started high school, you'll probably struggle to figure out where one lachrymose, cynically produced arrangement ends and another begins. About the only distinguishing features your poor reviewer could discern was a harpsichord and some pseudo-acid effects. Still, JAMIROQUAI must be kicking his 'Canned Heat' heels. His cat-in-the-hat funk and bloke-must-be-black vocals have always been a chipper combination; slumming it with the so-called "pop" dredged up here, he sounds like the second coming of Stevie Wonder. Talking of which, the RED HOT CHILI PEPPERS profit from the same equation with their wonderful, crusty old cover of one of Stevie's best songs. So desperately seeking some boardroom formula of prefabricated-pap-meets-stadium-weightiness is this album, you almost half expect Metallica to supply a grand finale. But no, only a terminally predictable Diane Warren ballad and an even more terminally predictable dance remix of MANDY MOORE. Come back Kids From Fame, all is forgiven. *BG*

Album rating: *3.5

– spinoff hits, etc. –

MANDY MOORE: I Wanna Be With You

May 00. (cd-s) *Epic; <radio> (669592-2)* [24] Aug00 [21]

CHA CHA

1979 (Neth 99m; US 90m) Black Tulip / Concorde (R)

Film genre: Punk Rock Musical drama

Top guns: s-w: (+ dir) Herbert Curiel, **Herman Brood, Nina Hagen, Lene Lovich**

Stars: Nina Hagen *(punk)* → ROCK'N'ROLL JUNKIE → NINA HAGEN = PUNK + GLORY, **Lene Lovich** *(punk)*, **Herman Brood** *(punk)* → ROCK'N'ROLL JUNKIE → NINA HAGEN = PUNK + GLORY, **Les Chappell** *(himself)*, Nelly Frijda

Storyline: "There she was a bank robber" sang the Clash in 1980; the movie's plot centered around "real" German New Wave star, Nina Hagen, trying to give up this jailbound occupation for a better life as a rock star in and around Amsterdam's thriving punk scene. What would she and her cohorts get up to next? *MCS*

Movie rating: *5

Visual: video + dvd

Off the record: HERMAN BROOD's career was documented in the 1994 film, 'ROCK'N'ROLL JUNKIE'. **NINA HAGEN**'s story was revealed later in the movie, 'NINA HAGEN = PUNK + GLORY' (1999). No such celluloid journal has been afforded **LENE LOVICH** (b. Lili-Marlene Premilovich, 30 Mar'49, Detroit, Michigan), who by all accounts was as much to the New Wave scene as the aforementioned Hagen. Raised by her Yugoslavian father and English mother, Lovich found it hard going when her family moved to Hull, England – she subsequently took off to London and found jobs as a go-go dancer and street busker playing saxophone. Having worked as a songwriter to French disco star, Cerrone, Lene signed a deal with 'Stiff' records, who immediately packaged her as a wacky, post-Punk singer. *MCS*

—

HERMAN BROOD, NINA HAGEN and LENE LOVICH
(& Various back-up)

Jan 80. (lp) *Ariola; (200.649)* [–] Dutch [–]
– I love you like I love myself (HERMAN BROOD, NINA, LENE, LESS & THE WILD ROMANCE) / Home (LENE LOVICH & LESS CHAPELL) / Pick up (PHONEY & THE HARDCORE) / Sweet memories (FLOOR VAN ZUTPHEN) / Take it all in ((HUGO SINSZHEIMER &) THE METEORS) / (You don't) Fit (INSIDE NIPPLES) / Herman's door (NINA HAGEN & THE WILD ROMANCE) / Two together (MONIKA TJEN A KWOEI & THE HOUSEBAND) / Blues (SONNY & THE DULFERGANG) / Doin' it (HERMAN BROOD & HIS WILD ROMANCE) / It's you (Smersz) ((HUGO &) THE METEORS) / Beat (HERMAN BROOD & HIS WILD ROMANCE) / (No more) Conversation (STREETBEATS) / Bop (DULFERGANG) / Herman ist high (NINA & THE WILD ROMANCE) / Jilted (HERMAN BROOD & THE DULFERGANG) / Don't wanna loose (HANNEKE &) WHITE HONEY) / (Can't stop) Foolin' myself (PHONEY & THE HARDCORE) / Never be clever (HERMAN BROOD & HIS WILD ROMANCE) / Blues (SONNY & THE DULFERGANG). *(UK-iss.Feb80 on 'Ariola'; ARL 5039) (cd-iss. Dec96; 436282)*

S/track review: No doubt inspired by an earlier HERMAN BROOD & HIS WILD ROMANCE set from 1978: 'Cha-Cha', this subsequent (and rare) Dutch various-artists LP could be filed under: eclectic. Recorded for the most part in '79, 'CHA CHA' the soundtrack credited HERMAN BROOD, but this time alongside lucky ladies, NINA HAGEN (from Berlin, Germany) and LENE LOVICH (from Detroit, USA), plus several Dutch-based outfits. The album kicks off with all three (and BROOD's band the WILD ROMANCE) on one of his better-known songs, 'I Love You Like I Love Myself', a self-deprecating bit of Springsteen-esque hokum. The English-speaking, eccentric post-New Wave threesome were a hit all over Northern Europe, the squealing LOVICH more so in Great Britain where she had chalked up three Top 40 entries including chart debut, 'Lucky Number'; 'CHA CHA' credits Lene's 'Home' (from Top 20 LP, 'Stateless') with her musical collaborator Les Chappell – here as LESS CHAPELL. HERMAN BROOD & HIS WILD ROMANCE spread themselves evenly around the set, their fusion of funky disco-rock apparent on at least three cuts, 'Doin' It', 'Beat' and the rock'n'roller, part (for Elvis)-tribute, 'Never Be Clever'. Talking of tributes, NINA took turns with HIS WILD ROMANCE – although not literally one hopes – on two tracks, the high-pitched 'Herman Ist High' (complete with spit & grog) and 'Herman's Door', the latter a deconstruction of Dylan's 'Knocking On . . .' that was more centered on Sid Vicious! The rest of the BROOD-ing bunch of post-New Wave affiliates were indeed clones of one or other Westernised pop & rock acts. For instance, if you liked Stretch ('Why Did You Do It'), the Dutch equivalent might be FLOOR VAN ZUTPHEN and their 'Sweet Memories', while Penetration might come to mind via INSIDE NIPPLES' '(You Don't) Fit'. Ditto Graham Parker & sub-Bowie for (HUGO &) the METEORS on their two contributions 'Take It All In' & 'It's You (Smersz)'. Double ditto ('Pick Up' & '(Can't Stop) Foolin' Myself') by way of the Springsteen-meets-Clash-types PHONEY & THE HARDCORE, while STREETBEATS juxtapose Joe Jackson on '(No More) Conversation'. The ultimate is (HANNEKE &) WHITE HONEY's take of the Electric Chairs & Rush on 'Don't Wanna Loose' (the Dutch spelling of 'Lose' apparently!). The less said about funky-tonk dirge, 'Two Together' by MONIKA TJEN & KWOEI, the better, and where the hell did BROOD dig up SONNY & THE DULFERGANG ('Blues' twice!?); the latter jazzateers deliver 'Bop' and back BROOD on his 'Jilted' cut. If twenty songs equate to value for money, then okay – it's just one might like a bit quality now . . . and then. *MCS*

Album rating: *4.5

– spinoff singles, etc. –

HERMAN BROOD & HIS WILD ROMANCE: I Love You Like I Love Myself

Nov 79. (7") *(101.085)* [–] Dutch [–]

– associated release –

HERMAN BROOD & HIS WILD ROMANCE: Cha-Cha

1978. (lp/c) *Ariola; (200/400 230)* [–] Dutch [–]
– Hit / Too slow / Street / Still believe / True fine mama / Rock 'n roll

junkie / One more dose / Speedo / Dope suds / City / Blue / Can't stand up / Phony / Pop.

CHANGE OF HABIT

1969 (US 94m) N.B.C. / Universal Pictures (PG)

Film genre: Rock'n'roll Musical/medical drama

Top guns: dir: William A. Graham → ELVIS AND THE COLONEL: THE UNTOLD STORY / s-w: James Lee, John Joseph (+ story), Richard Morris (+ story), S.S. Paddy Schweitzer

Stars: Elvis PRESLEY *(Dr. John Carpenter)*, Mary Tyler Moore *(Sister Michelle Gallagher)*, Barbara McNair *(Sister Irene Hawkins)*, Edward Asner *(Lt. Moretti)* ← KID GALAHAD, Jane Elliot *(Sister Barbara Bennett)*, Leora Dana *(Mother Joseph)*, Robert Emhardt *(the banker)*

Storyline: A singing, philanthropic doctor helps the inner city poor with the aid of some defrocked nuns. The local priest is none too impressed with the sisters' secular experiments and eventually forces them back into their habits. *BG*

Movie rating: *2.5

Visual: video + dvd

Off the record: Mary Tyler Moore had been in the song and dance musical, 'Thoroughly Modern Millie'.

—

ELVIS PRESLEY: Live A Little, Love A Little / Charro! / The Trouble With Girls / Change Of Habit

Mar 95. (cd) *R.C.A.; <(07863 66559-2)>* ☐ ☐
– (LIVE A LITTLE, LOVE A LITTLE tracks) / (CHARRO! tracks) / (THE TROUBLE WITH GIRLS tracks) / Have a happy / Let's be friends / Change of habit / Let us pray / Rubberneckin'.

S/track review: The final chapter of ELVIS' sorry Hollywood sojourn, 'CHANGE OF HABIT' didn't exactly send him off with a bang, although it has to be said it towers over most of his other late 60s efforts. The rootsy title track was his best since 'VIVA LAS VEGAS' five years previous, complete with fuzz-fired guitar, a funky drummer, and a swaggering, soulful vocal; it doesn't quite match 'A Little Less Conversation' but it comes close. 'Let Us Pray' is almost as funky, a holy-rolling diversion into gospel/country-rock, while 'Let's Be Friends' – not used in the original film – boasts a piano line which could've easily graced an early 70s Faces number. Semi-legendary southern soul don Chips Moman co-produced 'Rubberneckin', a decidedly secular little ditty wherein Dr. PRESLEY has to stifle his laughter amid all manner of dirty mac girly panting. All of which adds to the bargain factor of the 4-on-1 CD re-issue (mentioned previously), with enough decent tracks spread over the whole to make it worthwhile, many of which are unavailable on any of the myriad ELVIS comps. *BG*

– spinoff hits, etc. –

ELVIS PRESLEY: Rubberneckin'

Nov 69. (7") *R.C.A.; <47-9768> (RCA 1916)* 6 Feb70 8

ELVIS PRESLEY: Rubberneckin' remix with Paul Oakenfold / (extended)

Sep 03. (12") *<(82876 54218-1)>* 94 5
(cd-s+=) *(82876 54341-2)* – (original).

Ray CHARLES

Born: Ray Charles Robinson, 23 Sep'30, Albany, Georgia, USA. The late RAY CHARLES is often credited with making one of the most important evolutionary leaps in rhythm and blues, a man blind from the age of six whose disability meant he played with even more gut feeling than he doubtless would've anyway. CHARLES' influence was especially acute in Britain, where his hammering piano grooves set many a future icon to dreams of blues-ness, (VAN MORRISON, in a recent interview in Word magazine, talked about instinctively knowing 'What'd I Say' was a RAY CHARLES record the first time he heard it, even though he'd never previously heard any of his stuff. MORRISON finally got to duet with him – on 'Crazy Love' – upon the Belfast bard's induction into the Songwriters Hall Of Fame in 2003. While many of his most innovative recordings were already behind him by the time he made his big screen debut – in comedy don Charles Barton's 'SWINGIN' ALONG' (1962), appearing as himself alongside the likes of crooner Bobby Vee – his landmark 'Modern Sounds In Country And Western Music' (1962) crossed the tracks in a way no other black artist had done before, bringing country to an urban Afro-American audience and making Southern Soul more possible than it already was. He also played his benevolent self (and served as musical director) in his first starring role, doing his performance bit in a school for the blind in veteran actor-turned-director Paul Henreid's final feature, 'BALLAD IN BLUE' (1966). CHARLES' most notable cinematic contribution of the 60s, though, was his performance of the title theme to one of his protégé QUINCY JONES' most widely heard scores, 'In The Heat Of The Night' (1967). While JONES went on to record some of the most significant soundtracks of the blaxploitation era, CHARLES spent much of his 70s screen time as a tireless variety show guest, also appearing on several country music tributes. An impromptu performance in a music shop (as more or less himself) endeared the man to a whole new audience with John Landis landmark, 'The BLUES BROTHERS' (1980), while a more unlikely role as a heavy in Roger Moore's final James Bond film, 'Octopussy' (1983), was at least lent a bit of authenticity via the trademark dark glasses. As well as a concert performance with WILLIE NELSON and an appearance on 'We Are The World' (1985), CHARLES also contributed to 80s documentaries on Aretha Franklin, Fats Domino and Percy Mayfield. Come the 90s, CHARLES was a natural invite to NELSON's birthday bash, 'Willie Nelson: The Big Six-0' (1993), and made a further couple of feature cameos, as himself in Warren Beatty/Katharine Hepburn romance, 'Love Affair' (1994), and as a bus driver in Leslie Nielsen spoof, 'Spy Hard' (1996). He also paid tribute to his indefatigable onetime student QUINCY JONES in Jeff Margolis' documentary tribute, 'Quincy Jones, The First Fifty Years' (1998). In 2000, he was the voice of G-Clef The Keyboard in US animated feature, 'Blue's Big Musical Movie', and in 2003, he was the keyboard in Clint Eastwood's contribution to the Martin Scorsese blues series, 'PIANO BLUES', side by side at the piano in one of his most engaging latter day appearances. He also appeared in Mike Figgis' Scorsese entry, 'RED, WHITE & BLUES' (2003) and put in his tuppence worth on 'Tom Dowd And The Language Of Music' (2003), a documentary tribute to one of the greatest producers in popular music history. CHARLES himself was to be honoured with 'RAY' (2004), a lavish Hollywood biopic directed by Taylor Hackford. As well as putting Jamie Foxx through his piano paces prior to shooting, CHARLES personally selected the songs Foxx was to lip-synch. Cruelly, he didn't live to see the film's release (or its critical acclaim), passing away from liver disease on 10th June 2004. *BG*

- **filmography** (composer) {acting/performance} –

Swingin' Along *(1961 {*c} =>)* / **Ballad In Blue** *(1964 {*} OST =>)* / **the Big T.N.T. Show** *(1966 {p} =>)* / **the Blues Brothers** *(1980 {*/p} on OST by V/Cast =>)* / Limit Up *(1989 {a/*p})* / Listen Up: The Lives Of Quincy Jones *(1990 {p} =>)* / Love Affair *(1994 {c})* / Spy Hard *(1996 {b})*

CHARRO!

1969 (US 98m) National General Pictures (PG)

Film genre: revisionist western drama

Top guns: s-w + dir: Charles Marquis Warren (au: Frederic Louis Fox)

Stars: Elvis PRESLEY *(Jess Wade)*, Ina Balin *(Tracey Winters)*, Barbara Werle *(Sara Ramsey)* ← HARUM SCARUM ← TICKLE ME, Victor French *(Vince Hackett)*, Lynn Kellogg *(Marcie)*, Solomon Sturges *(Billy Roy)*

Storyline: Former outlaw Jess Wade comes a cropper at the hands of his old gang, themselves the scourge of decent citizens whom they threaten with a stolen cannon, and the theft of which Wade finds himself framed for. *BG*

Movie rating: *4

Visual: video + dvd

Off the record: PRESLEY only sings a couple of songs in the film, but because he's ELVIS, this entry goes into the Rock Movies section. *MCS*

—

ELVIS PRESLEY: Live A Little, Love A Little / Charro! / The Trouble With Girls / Change Of Habit

Mar 95. (cd) *R.C.A.; <(07863 66559-2)>* ☐ ☐
– (LIVE A LITTLE, LOVE A LITTLE tracks) / Charro / Let's not forget about the stars / (THE TROUBLE WITH GIRLS tracks) / (CHANGE OF HABIT tracks).

S/track review: Also featured on the 4-in-1 package alongside 'LIVE A LITTLE, LOVE A LITTLE', 'The TROUBLE WITH GIRLS' and 'CHANGE OF HABIT'. With the boisterous wine-women-and-song formula long having long lost its box office draw, ELVIS was hopefully cast as a Clint Eastwood-style gunfighter, match-striking stubble and all. With the singing kept to a minimum in line with the movie's pseudo-Spaghetti pretensions, his vocals were only showcased on the opening credits, backed by the portentous brass and maracas of the Hugo Montenegro Orchestra. Aiming for a kind of 'Gun for Ringo'-era Morricone feel, 'CHARRO!'s title song certainly isn't the worst of ELVIS' soundtrack efforts and stands up well alongside the Western-themed material on 'STAY AWAY, JOE' (which, conceivably, it might've been more sympathetically paired with). The song was originally released as the B-side to the 1968 TV-comeback-vintage 'Memories' single. The 1995 CD re-issue adds the more conventional ballad, 'Let's Forget About The Stars', which was cut from the film's final print. *BG*

CHASING DESTINY

2001 (US 91m TV) Pretty Brunette Films / Prosperity Pictures

Film genre: romantic pop-music comedy/drama

Top guns: dir: Tim Boxell / s-w: Guy Thomas

Stars: Christopher Lloyd *(Jet James)*, Lauren Graham *(Jessy James)* ← DILL SCALLION, Casper Van Dien *(Bobby Moritz)*, **Roger Daltrey** *(Nehemiah Peoples)* <= the WHO =>, Deborah Van Valkenburgh *(Suzy Aquado)* ← STREETS OF FIRE ← the WARRIORS / → the DEVIL'S REJECTS, Stuart Pankin *(Mike Ditlow)*, Justin Henry *(Eddie McDermot)* → MY DINNER WITH JIMI, **Spencer Davis** *(himself)*, **Carmine Appice** *(rock legend)* ← BLACK ROSES, **Denny Laine** *(band member #2)* ← CONCERTS FOR THE PEOPLE OF KAMPUCHEA ← ROCKSHOW

Storyline: Old rock star Jet James is fading fast, and his mountain of debts is reaching Everest proportions. Luckily his daughter Jesse is there to keep the repo men at bay, especially as Jet's beloved Ford Mustang is hidden nearby. Bobby is an ex-writer turned collector who uses his silver tongue to cajole his clients into paying up, but Jesse doesn't fall for his charms when he phones her up. In fact it's Bobby who ends up falling in love with Jesse, the best adversary he's ever come across. *JZ*

Movie rating: *5

Visual: none (no audio OST; score Michael Whalen)

Off the record: The 60s were on show in full force here via: the Who's **Roger Daltrey**, **Spencer Davis**, **Carmine Appice** was the drummer with Vanilla Fudge and **Denny Laine** was with the Moody Blues; he later became part of Paul McCartney & Wings. *MCS*

☐ Chubby CHECKER segment
(⇒ DON'T KNOCK THE TWIST)

CHEECH & CHONG

Formed: Vancouver, Canada ... late 60s by Richard – aka CHEECH – Marin and Tommy CHONG. The two stooges of grass-addled 70s slackerdom, CHEECH & CHONG were an ethnic hippy comedy duo who somehow made it onto Grammy-winning record and, inevitably, the big screen. Directed by music biz guru Lou Adler, 'UP IN SMOKE' (1978) packed them in at American cinemas, following the lads on a cannabis-centric sojourn through California. The accompanying soundtrack combined typically slack-jawed skits and dialogue with stoned acoustic odes (including their previous hit, 'Earache My Eye'), contributions from L.A. Chicanos, WAR, and even a reggae pastiche, all in the pair's long established, pot-smoke shrouded tradition. As the stoned 70s turned into the sharply focused 80s, follow-ups 'Cheech & Chong's Next Movie' (1980), 'Cheech & Chong's Nice Dreams' (1981), 'Things Are Tough All Over' (1982) and 'Still Smokin' (1983) generated diminishing returns in terms of both laughs and box office revenues, nor were any soundtracks forthcoming. Following last gasp efforts, 'The Corsican Brothers' (1984) and 'Get Out Of My Room' (1985), the pair finally called it a day, although they subsequently both appeared in Martin Scorsese's black comedy, 'After Hours' (1985). Of the two, it was to be Marin who established himself as a viable character actor, starring in his own directorial debut, 'Born In East L.A.' (1987) and hippie time capsule spoof, 'Rude Awakening' (1989). Ironically, he also made a cameo in Tom Holland's anti-drugs drama, 'Fatal Beauty' (1987), as well as cameos in 'Troop Beverly Hills' (1989), 'Ghostbusters 2' (1989) and CHONG's directorial debut, 'Far Out Man' (1989). As well as starring in the latter, CHONG made occasional screen appearances in such negligible fare as 'Tripwire' (1989), 'The SPIRIT OF '76' (1990) and 'McHale's Navy' (1997) as well as a more memorable cameo alongside the likes of WILLIE NELSON and SNOOP DOGG in 70s nostalgia effort, 'Half Baked' (1998), and a major – if predictably pot addled – part in high school franchise, 'National Lampoon's Senior Trip' (1995). Come the 90s, MARIN's career took off in earnest, with a voiceover on high grossing Disney animation, 'The LION KING' (1994), and starring roles in such high profile Robert Rodriguez features as 'Desperado' (1995), 'FROM DUSK TILL DAWN' (1996) and 'Once Upon A Time In Mexico' (2003) as well as Ron Shelton sports comedy, 'Tin Cup' (1996), John Roberts' Parrot-themed caper, 'Paulie' (1998) and Woody Allen black comedy, 'Picking Up The Pieces' (2000). Additionally, he secured supporting roles and smaller parts in the likes of boxing satire, 'The Great White Hype' (1996), Rodriguez's 'Spy Kids' (2001), BOB DYLAN vehicle, 'MASKED AND ANONYMOUS' (2003) and John Sayles' 'Silver City' (2004) amongst others. *BG*

- filmography [s-w + dir] (composers) {acting} –

Up In Smoke *(1978 [s-w x2] {* x2} OST by CHEECH & CHONG =>)* / Cheech & Chong's Next Movie *(1980 [s-w x2] {* x2})* / Cheech & Chong's Nice Dreams *(1981 [s-w x2] {* x2})* / Things Are Tough All Over *(1982 [s-w x2] {* x2})* / It Came From Hollywood *(1982 {* x2})* / Still Smokin' *(1983 [s-w x2] {* x2})* / Yellowbeard *(1983 {a x2})* / the Corsican Brothers *(1984*

TV; *[s-w x2] {* x2}*) / Get Out Of My Room *(1985 [s-w + dir: CHEECH] {* x2})* / After Hours *(1985 {a x2})* / Echo Park *(1985 {a CHEECH})* / Born In East L.A. *(1987 [s-w + dir: CHEECH] {* CHEECH})* / Fatal Beauty *(1987 {a CHEECH})* / Oliver And Company *(1988 {v CHEECH})* / Troup Beverly Hills *(1989 {c CHEECH})* / Ghostbusters II *(1989 {a CHEECH})* / Rude Awakening *(1989 {* CHEECH})* / Tripwire *(1990 {a CHONG})* / Far Out Man *(1990 [s-w + dir: CHONG] {* CHONG} {c CHEECH})* / the Shrimp On The Barbie *(1990 {* CHEECH})* / **the Spirit Of '76** *(1990 {a CHONG})* / Mother Goose Rock'n'Rhyme *(1990 {b CHEECH})* / la Pastorela *(1992 {v CHEECH})* / Ferngully: The Last Rainforest *(1992 {v x2})* / the Cisco Kid *(1994 TV {* CHEECH})* / a Million To One *(1994 {a CHEECH})* / **the Lion King** *(1994 {v CHEECH})* / the Magic Of The Golden Bear: Goldy III *(1994 {* CHEECH})* / the Ring Of The Musketeers *(1994 {* CHEECH})* / Charlie's Ghost *(1994 {* CHEECH})* / Desperado *(1995 {* CHEECH})* / the Courtyard *(1995 {a CHEECH})* / National Lampoon's Senior Trip *(1995 {* CHONG})* / Tin Cup *(1996 {a CHEECH})* / the Great White Hype *(1996 {a CHEECH})* / **From Dusk Till Dawn** *(1996 {* CHEECH})* / McHale's Navy *(1997 {a CHONG})* / Paulie *(1998 {* CHEECH})* / Half Baked *(1998 {a CHONG})* / the Venice Project *(1999 {c CHEECH})* / the Nuttiest Nutcracker *(1999 TV {v CHEECH})* / Luminarias *(2000 {a CHEECH})* / Picking Up The Pieces *(2000 {* CHEECH})* / Spy Kids *(2001 {a CHEECH})* / the Wash *(2001 {b CHONG})* / Spy Kids 2: The Island Of Lost Dreams *(2002 {a CHEECH})* / Pinocchio *(2002 {v CHEECH})* / **Masked And Anonymous** *(2003 {b CHEECH})* / Once Upon A Time In Mexico *(2003 {a CHEECH})* / Good Boy! *(2003 {a CHEECH})* / Spy Kids 3-D: Game Over *(2003 {b CHEECH})* / High Times' Potluck *(2003 {b CHONG})* / Silver City *(2004 {b CHEECH})* / the Lion King 1 1/2 *(2004 {v CHEECH})* / Christmas With The Kranks *(2004 {a CHEECH})* / the Underclassman *(2005 {* CHEECH})*

the CHEETAH GIRLS

2003 (US 95m TV) Disney Channel

Film genre: coming-of-age/teen-Pop Musical drama

Top guns: dir: Oz Scott ← BUSTIN' LOOSE / s-w: Alison Taylor → the CHEETAH GIRLS 2 (books: Deborah Gregory)

Stars: the Cheetah Girls:- Raven-Symone *(Galleria Garibaldi)*, **Adrienne Bailon** *(Chanel Simmons)*, **Kiely Williams** *(Aqua; Aquanette Walker)*, **Sabrina Bryan** *(Dorinda Thomas)* all → the CHEETAH GIRLS 2, Lynn Whitfield *(Dorothea Garibaldi)* → the CHEETAH GIRLS 2, Kyle Schmid *(Derrick)*, Sandra Caldwell *(Drinka Champagne)*, Vincent Corazza *(Jackal Johnson)*, Lori Alter *(Juanita)* ← SING / → the CHEETAH GIRLS 2

Storyline: Four high school students form an all-girl band as an alternative to the highly intellectual world of fashion design. The Cheetah Girls are soon spotted (ahem!) by drama teacher Drinka Champagne, who gives them the inspiration (and bottle) to succeed in the cut throat world of pop. Record producer Jackal Johnson, who invented the word "exploit", is also interested. Can the girls make it big before he sinks his claws into them? *JZ*

Movie rating: *3

Visual: video + dvd

Off the record: (see below)

—

the CHEETAH GIRLS & Various (score: John Van Tongeren)

Aug 03. (m-cd) *Walt Disney; <60126-7>* [33] [–]
– Cheetah sisters / Cinderella / Girl power / Together we can / C'mon (SONIC CHAOS) / Girlfriend (CHAR) / Breakthrough (HOPE 7) / End of the line (HOPE 7). *(re-iss. Jun04 +=; 61104-7)* – Cinderella (remix) / Girl power (remix) / (8 karaoke tracks).

S/track review: "Girl Power" takes another step backwards with the 00s fashion-accessorised answer to the Spice Girls, the CHEETAH GIRLS. Spawned from a series of tween-girl books, these adopted Disney (or is that dizzy) females were another in a long line of manufactured dance-pop acts to ruin a good night in watching telly. The effervescent CHEETAH GIRLS (featuring 'That's So Raven!' actress RAVEN-SYMONE as Galleria) predated another prepubescent Disney channel product 'HIGH SCHOOL MUSICAL' by a couple of years, but there was really no difference separating the two choreographed collectives; 'Lizzie McGuire' & 'Hannah Montana' were even more reasons to feel old. 'The CHEETAH GIRLS' mini-soundtrack is split between CG songs and various artists, aided and abetted by writer/producer, Ray Cham. Opener, 'Cheetah Sisters' and predictable track 3 'Girl Power', are so Britney (with a smidgen of Sugababes), while 'Cinderella' is virtually All Saints reincarnated. 'Together We Can' has all of the above and more, derivative of any pop-pap on the scene. The cod-hip hop of SONIC CHAOS on the short-n-sweet 'C'mon' is purile to the max, although CHAR's "Stars-In-Your-Eyes" impersonation of Beyonce or Janet on 'Girlfriend' would certainly please the Paula Abdul fans among you. Two numbers, 'Breakthrough' (a flop single) and 'End Of The Line' by power-popsters HOPE 7 (aka singer KRISTI McKLAVE and band), are nice enough to close the show; incidentally, a few CHEETAH GIRLS remixes are added onto the 2004 re-issue. *MCS*

Album rating: *4

the CHEETAH GIRLS 2

2006 (US 96m TV) Disney Channel

Film genre: family/teen comedy/drama

Top guns: dir: Kenny Ortega ← HIGH SCHOOL MUSICAL / → HIGH SCHOOL MUSICAL 2 / s-w: Alison Taylor ← the CHEETAH GIRLS, Bethesda Brown (books: Deborah Gregory)

Stars: the Cheetah Girls:- Raven, Adrienne Bailon, Sabrina Bryan, Kiely Williams (Galleria, Chanel, Dorinda, Aqua) ← the CHEETAH GIRLS, Belinda Peregrin *(Marisol)*, Lori Alter *(Juanita)* ← the CHEETAH GIRLS ← SING, Lynn Whitfield *(Dorothea)* ← the CHEETAH GIRLS, Golan Yosef *(Joaquin)*, Peter Vives *(Angel)*

Storyline: Galleria, Chanel, Aqua and Dorinda change their spots for sombreros as they head for a big music festival in Barcelona. Various sexy Spaniards begin to lead the girls astray but the trouble really starts when local vocal Marisol plans a sneaky duet with Chanel without letting on to the other felines. Will the girls throw Chanel into the sea or will they paws for thought and stick together? *JZ*

Movie rating: *4

Visual: dvd

Off the record: Mexican actress Belinda Peregrin released her first album, 'Belinda' in mid 00s, featuring hits such as 'Lo Siento', 'Angel' & 'Vivir'. *MCS*

—

the CHEETAH GIRLS (& Various Cast)

Aug 06. (cd) *Walt Disney; <61592-7>* [5] [ ]
– The party's just begun / Strut / Dance with me (DREW SEELEY feat. BELINDA) / Why wait (BELINDA) / A la nanita nana (ADRIENNE BAILON & BELINDA) / Do your own thing (RAVEN-SYMONE) / It's over / Step up / Amigas Cheetahs / Cherish the moment / Cheetah sisters (Barcelona mix) / Everyone's a star (RAVEN-SYMONE) / It's gonna be alright (RAVEN-SYMONE). *(bonus video track +=)* – (studio session). *(d-cd re-iss. Nov06 w/ dvd+=; 61630-7)* – Route 66 / Strut (Ming mix) / (DVD in concert in Disneyland).

S/track review: "Girls just wanna have fun" was a term coined by Cheetah-styled girls way back in the 80s, Galleria, Dorinda, Aquanette and Chanel subsequently giving the kids what they want two decades on. Nothing changes. Everything evolves – or does it? When the clean-cut Bananarama were top of their class, it was hard to imagine anything getting sweeter, especially when the naughty Spice Girls were princesses of sleazy, girl-power pop in the 90s; and stop press, the Pussycat Dolls are showing that lap-dancing pop is now in vogue. Anyway, the innocent CHEETAH GIRLS have a second chance to redeem themselves after the first mini-CD debacle. With more than a hint of exotic, flamenco-styled pop on board (the film was sub-titled 'When In Spain'), the girls spin into action via 'The Party's Just Begun', 'Everyone's A Star' and 'Strut', three of the better numbers in this made-for-teens flick. The sophistication comes via 'It's Over' and Symone's number, 'Do Your Own Thing', but one's heard it all before a thousand times. Now where's the remote to record X Factor? Aye right! *MCS*

Album rating: *4

– spinoff hits, etc. –

the CHEETAH GIRLS: The Party's Just Begun

Sep 06. (-) *<radio>* [85] [–]

the CHEETAH GIRLS: Strut

Nov 06. (-) *<radio>* [53] [–]

□ CHER (⇒ SONNY & CHER)

CHOICES – THE MOVIE

2001 (US 90m str8-to-video) Three 6 Mafia & Hypnotize Minds

Film genre: psychological crime drama

Top guns: dir: Gil Green

Stars: Rodney Wickfall *(Pancho Villa)*, Isley Nicole Melton *(Lexxus)* → the WASH, Project Pat *(Big Pat)*, **D.J. Paul** *(DJ)* → HUSTLE & FLOW, Reginald Boyland *(Alonzo)*, Daniel Iorio *(Ray Wilkes)*, **Jordan Houston** *(Juice)*, **La' Chat** *(Chat)*, Dennis Larkin *(fast food manager)*, Cassie Betts *(Keisha)*

Storyline: An ex-con returns home determined to change his life for the better. However his home town of Memphis appears to be only slightly less corrupt than Sodom and Gomorrah, and temptation lurks around every corner. Money, drugs and loose women are all available at a price, but that price could prove to be too high for our reformed rapper. *JZ*

Movie rating: *5

Visual: dvd

Off the record: **THREE 6 MAFIA** were formed in Memphis, Tennessee, initially a horror hardcore rap outfit. With a revolving door personnel in place (including Crunchy Black, Gangsta Boo, Koopsta Knicca, Lord Infamous, etc), there were only really two core members, **Juicy J (Jordan Houston)** and **DJ Paul (Paul Beauregard)**. Steady growth in popularity ensued until they finally hit paydirt with Top 40 set, 'Chpt.2: "World Domination"' (1997); 'When The Smoke Clears Sixty 6, Sixty 1' hit the Top 10 on the wisp of the new millennium. Released in conjunction with the movie was 'Choices – The Album', misleading in that there were only bits and pieces lifted from the celluloid, the majority was unassociated. Of late, THREE 6 MAFIA, have hit the Top 30 singles chart with both 'Stay Fly' & 'Poppin' My Collar'. *MCS*

– associated release –

THREE 6 MAFIA (*) & featuring Various Artists [& skits]

Aug 01. (cd) *Relativity; <1972>* [ ] [–]
– 2-way freak (LA' CHAT & *) / [The restaurant scene] / Mafia (HYPNOTIZE CAMP POSSE & *) / Gangsta niggaz (*) / Wona get some, I got some (T-ROCK, TEAR DA CLUB UP THUGS & *) / [1st crime scene] / O.V. (LORD INFAMOUS & *) / U got da game wrong (LA' CHAT & *) / We shootin' 1st (GANGSTA BOO, CRUNCHY BLACK & LORD INFAMOUS) / Dis bitch, dat hoe (PROJECT PAT, LUDACRIS & CRUNCHY BLACK) / Pass me (CRUNCHY BLACK & LA' CHAT) / [Big Pat's warehouse] / They don't fuck wit U (*) / Slang & serve (T-ROCK & *) / War wit us (LA' CHAT & *) / Mean mug (LA' CHAT & *) / [How it went down] / I ain't goin' (a hustler's theme) (*) / Ridin' on chrome (PROJECT PAT) / Talkin' (DJ PAUL, JUICY J & *).

□ Tommy CHONG
(⇒ CHEECH & CHONG)

CHRISTIANE F.

aka WIR KINDER VOM BAHNHOF ZOO; trans 'We Children From..'

1981 (W.Ger 120m) Maran Film / Solaris Film Productions

Film genre: urban/coming-of-age drama

Top guns: dir: Uli Edel / s-w: Herman Weigel (au: Kai Hermann, Horst Rieck)

Stars: Natja Brunckhorst *(Christiane)*, Thomas Haustein *(Detlef)*, Jens Kuphal *(Axel)*, Christiane Reichelt *(Babsi)*, Daniela Jaeger *(Kessi)*, **David BOWIE** (archive performer)

Storyline: Christiane is a 14-year-old on a mission to do nothing. It's no surprise when she falls for a Bowie-loving drug-pusher, Detlef, who procures her into prostition. *MCS*

Movie rating: *7

Visual: video in 1984 (track listing different)

Off the record: BOWIE and band were filmed late in 1978, although the music was overdubbed into the movie. Incidentally, the additional film-only score was provided by Jurgen Kneiper. *MCS*

—

DAVID BOWIE: Christiane F. – Wir Kinder Vom Bahnhof Zoo

May 81. (lp/c) *R.C.A.; (RCA LP/K 3074) <AFl1/AFK1 4239>* [ ] Mar82 [ ]
– V-2 Schneider / TVC 15 / Heroes (Helden) / Boys keep swinging / Sense of doubt / Station to station / Look back in anger / Stay / Warszawa. *(<cd-iss. Aug01 on 'E.M.I.'; 5 33093-2>)*

S/track review: The return of the Thin White Duke was best sampled on other products as this is really a "Best Of Bowie" (mostly not live!) compilation from his '76 to '78 period. Okay, then, this is strictly for BOWIE completists, all of them already owning LPs, 'Station To Station', 'Low', 'Heroes', 'Stage' and even 'Lodger', the latter set actually released in '79. Having said all that, the songs themselves (half co-written with BRIAN ENO) are still quality, with not only BOWIE fans giving an arm and a leg for the 'Heroes (Helden)' English-to-German segue'd mix, emotionally presented here; cuts from the same 1977 album – his second of that year – were 'V-2 Schneider' and the eerie instrumental, 'Sense Of Doubt'. The show-stealer – so to speak – was the "real" live, 8-minute+ rendering of 'Station To Station', complete with that aforementioned, immortal opening line, "The return of the . . ." – BOWIE has never sounded more at ease on record. Stemming from the same class recording of 1976, were 'Stay' and 'TVC-15', soulful and funky respectively, while the 1977 'Low' set, only donated 'Warszawa', a cinematic mood-piece with a "World Music" feel pre-dating Peter Gabriel in his solo soundtrack mission. 'Look Back In Anger' – again augmented by a great band including guitarist EARL SLICK – and 'Boys Keep Swinging' (both from 'Lodger') were probably a little out of place on record, but not in the cult movie. *MCS*

Album rating: *6.5

□ CINCO AMIGAS alt.
(⇒ VIVIR INTENTANDO)

CLAMBAKE

1967 (US 98m) United Artists

Film genre: Rock'n'roll Musical drama

Top guns: dir: Arthur H. Nadel / s-w: Arthur Browne Jr.

Stars: Elvis PRESLEY *(Scott Hayward)*, Shelley Fabares *(Dianne Carter)* ← SPINOUT ← HOLD ON! ← GIRL HAPPY ← RIDE THE WILD SURF ← SUMMER LOVE ← ROCK, PRETTY BABY / → a TIME TO SING, Bill Bixby *(James J. Jamison III)* → SPEEDWAY, Will Hutchins *(Tom Wilson)* ← SPINOUT, James Gregory *(Duster Hayward)* ← HEY BOY! HEY GIRL!, Gary Merrill *(Sam Burton)*, **Jack Good** *(Mr. Hathaway)*, Suzie Kaye *(Bee Bee Vendemeer)* ← IT'S A BIKINI WORLD ← C'MON, LET'S LIVE A LITTLE ← WILD, WILD WINTER, Teri Garr *(dancer)* ← the COOL ONES ← ROUSTABOUT ← VIVA LAS VEGAS ← PAJAMA PARTY ← the T.A.M.I. SHOW ← KISSIN' COUSINS ← FUN IN ACAPULCO / → HEAD → ONE FROM THE HEART, Angelique Pettyjohn *(Gloria)* → REPO MAN → the CENSUS TAKER

Storyline: Worried that the ladies want his money rather than him, singing Texas oil scion Scott Heyward changes places with skint water-skiing instructor Tom Wilson. *BG*

Movie rating: *2.5

Visual: video + dvd

Off the record: Middlesex-born Englishman, **Jack Good**, went on to write and produce the 1973 movie, 'CATCH MY SOUL'.

ELVIS PRESLEY (composers: Jeff Alexander, etc.)

Feb 68. (lp; mono/stereo) *R.C.A.; <LSP 3893> (RD/SF 7917)* [40] Apr68 [19]
– Clambake / Who needs money / A house that has everything / Confidence / Hey, hey, hey / You don't know me / The girl I never loved / How can you lose what you never had / Big boss man / Singing tree / Just call me lonesome / Guitar man. *(re-iss. Aug80 on 'RCA Int.'; INTS 5040) (re-iss. Jan84 lp/c; NL/NK 82565)*

S/track review: While this was actually among the handful of truly worthwhile soundtracks ELVIS recorded, part of its draw was the quality of the last-minute, non-film additions like 'Guitar Man' and 'Big Boss Man', both of which were released as singles at the time and which, unfortunately, the compilers of the CD re-issue (a three-on-one with 'KISSIN' COUSINS' and 'STAY AWAY, JOE') chose to jettison. If space really was an issue, it remains a mystery why they didn't dispense with barely listenable tat like 'Who Needs Money' and the Sesame Street-style 'Confidence' instead. In any case, the bulk of the tracks in the film were different versions from the ones which appeared on the original soundtrack. Only 'Hey Hey Hey', a groovy, soul/jazz-influenced number with a killer breakbeat (and perhaps a primitive blueprint for 'A Little Less Conversation'), was the same version. On the CD, however, the film version of 'You Don't Know Me', a dignified ballad previously covered by RAY CHARLES, was reinstated. Among the other highlights, the King puts in first class performances on the slow-burning 'The Girl I Never Loved' and the loose-limbed, bluesy shuffle, 'How Can You Lose What You Never Had'. *BG*

Album rating: *4.5

– spinoff hits, etc. –

ELVIS PRESLEY: Big Boss Man / You Don't Know Me

Oct 67. (7") *<47-9341> (RCA 1642)* [38] Nov67 [ ]

ELVIS PRESLEY: Guitar Man

Jan 68. (7") *<47-9425> (RCA 1663)* [43] Feb68 [19]

☐ the Dave CLARK FIVE segment
(⇒ CATCH US IF YOU CAN)

CLASS OF 1984

1982 (Can 98m) Guerilla High Productions / Citadel Films (R)

Film genre: juvenile crime drama

Top guns: s-w: (+ dir) Mark Lester ← ROLLER BOOGIE / → FIRESTARTER, Tom Holland → SCREAM FOR HELP, John Saxton

Stars: Perry King *(Andrew Norris)*, Merrie Lynn Ross *(Diane Norris)*, Timothy Van Patton *(Peter Stegman)*, Roddy McDowall *(Terry Corrigan)* ← MEAN JOHNNY BARROWS ← the COOL ONES / → HELLO DOWN THERE → ANGEL, ANGEL, DOWN WE GO, **Stefan Arngrim** *(Drugstore)*, Michael Fox *(Arthur)* → LIGHT OF DAY → WHERE THE RIVERS FLOW NORTH, Al Waxman *(Detective Stewiski)* ← HEAVY METAL, **Teenage Head** *(performers)*

Storyline: Andrew Norris is the new music teacher at Abraham Lincoln High School. He soon finds that there is a reign of terror in the classroom caused by a gang of punks led by the vicious Stegman. When his students are threatened Norris has a showdown with Stegman, but he and his wife Diane soon find themselves the targets of the gang as the classroom violence begins to escalate out of control. *JZ*

Movie rating: *4

Visual: dvd (no audio OST; score: Lalo Schifrin *)

Off the record: Tracks featured in the film:- 'I Am The Future' * (ALICE COOPER), 'Fresh Flesh' (the FEAR), 'Let's Have A War' (the FEAR), 'Ain't Got No Sense' (TEENAGE HEAD), 'Stegman's Concerto' (TIMOTHY VAN PATTON), 'Suburbanite' * (JEFFREY BAXTER), 'You Better Not Step Out Of Line' * (RANDALL BRAMLETT) & 'Alimony' (TEENAGE HEAD). **Stefan Arngrim** subsequently formed L.A. band, the Knights Of The Living Dead, an outfit who signed to Capitol records but were unfortunate enough to find themselves on the scrapheap; he co-wrote songs with Warren Zevon on his 'Transverse City'. *MCS*

CLEAN

2004 (Can/Fra/UK 111m) TVA Films / ARP Selection (R)

Film genre: domestic drama

Top guns: s-w: Olivier Assayas (+ dir) ← DEMONLOVER / → NOISE, Malachy Martin, Sarah Perry

Stars: Maggie Cheung *(Emily Wang)*, Nick Nolte *(Albrecht Hauser)* ← AFFLICTION ← DOWN AND OUT IN BEVERLY HILLS / → OVER THE HEDGE, Beatrice Dalle *(Elena)* ← TROUBLE EVERY DAY ← NIGHT ON EARTH, Jeanne Balibar *(Irene Paolini)*, Don McKellar *(Vernon)* ← HIGHWAY 61, Martha Henry *(Rosemary Hauser)*, James Johnston *(Lee Hauser)*, James Dennis *(Jay)*, **David Roback** *(himself)*, **Metric:- Emily Haines & James Shaw** *(performers)*, **Tricky & Liz Densmore** *(performers)*

Storyline: Emily Wang's past is filled with regrets – she has been in prison for drug possession; she is blamed by her mother-in-law for the premature death of her husband, and she has lost her son Jay to his grandparents through the courts. Now once and for all Emily decides to stay clean. She moves to France and gets a job, but finds it much more difficult to kick the habit than she had hoped. Only her father-in- law Albrecht can help save the family and reunite Emily with her son, provided her courage and faith is strong enough. *JZ*

Movie rating: *7

Visual: dvd

Off the record: Emily Haines (Metric & Broken Social Scene), **Tricky** (is the Bristol-born trip-hoppers), **David Roback** (of Opal & ex-Rain Parade).

Various Artists (incl. MAGGIE CHEUNG *)

Aug 04. (cd) *Naive; (NV 802111)* [–] French [–]
– An ending (ascent) (BRIAN ENO) / Strawberry stain (*) / Taking tiger mountain (BRIAN ENO) / Breakaway (TRICKY & LIZ DENSMORE) / Down in the light (*) / Dead disco (METRIC) / Spider and I (BRIAN ENO) / Neon golden (the NOTWIST) / Wait for me (*) / Knives from Bavaria (BRITTA PHILLIPS & DEAN WAREHAM) / She can't tell you (*). *(bonus +=)* – Dead disco – "clean" live film version (METRIC). *(<UK/US-iss.Sep05 on 'Silva Screen'; SILVA 1180>)*

S/track review: A Cannes Film Festival Best Actress Award for MAGGIE CHEUNG owed as much to the oriental lady's newfound singing ability, as to her thespian role-playing. London-raised since she was eight, MAGGIE was no newcomer to the world of showbiz, having already been just pipped to win Miss Hong Kong in 1983. Her fortieth birthday approaching, the former model was asked to perform a handful of songs by writer/director (and former husband) Olivier Assayas. For the soundtrack, CHEUNG featured on four cuts, two penned by former Galaxie 500 man, DEAN WAREHAM (who also incidentally gets in a track of his own with partner, BRITTA PHILLIPS: 'Knives From Bavaria'), and two by founding Rain Parade giant, DAVID ROBACK. Squeezed in between a few BRIAN ENO gems from his heyday ('An Ending (ascent)' and 'Taking Tiger Mountain'), WAREHAM's 'Strawberry Stain' was very Margo Timmins/Cowboy Junkies, sultry, smooth and dreamy; the similarly-composed track 9 was ditto. ROBACK's two CHEUNG donations, 'Down In The Light' & 'She Can't Tell You', were alt-country flavoured, both with Cooder-esque, dustbowl sliding frets and lo-fi acoustics. If you've watched the movie you'll also have heard several ENO cuts, only three of which made it to album, the aforementioned openers and 'Spider And I'; the four discarded tracks numbered, 'The Lost Day', 'Third Uncle', 'The Jezebel Spirit' (with David Byrne) and 'Stars' (with Daniel Lanois & Roger Eno). A pity indeed. 'City Slang' outfit, the NOTWIST, were certainly the surprise act, their 'Neon Golden' harking back to the early 70s Eagles, Quicksilver and another of ROBACK's outfits, Opal. On a slightly critical note, cinematic performances by LIZ DENSMORE (backed by Brit-trip-hop artist, TRICKY) on 'Breakaway' and METRIC's Republica-like meanderings on 'Dead Disco', were a little out of their depth here and just didn't quite push the right buttons for me. *MCS*

Album rating: *7

Jimmy CLIFF

Born: James Chambers, 1 Apr'48, St. Catherine, Jamaica. A leading light of the Jamaican Ska movement and a reggae singer who successfully crossed over to the British pop charts, it's nevertheless difficult to believe that JIMMY CLIFF only had two major British hit singles in his long career. Or that he remains best remembered for his leading role in Perry Henzell's cult classic, 'The HARDER THEY COME' (1972). While the film's grainy tale of country boy turned bad was a compelling portrait of Jamaican society and its cut throat music industry, the soundtrack – to which CLIFF contributed three of his best loved songs – was an instant classic, and one which accelerated the appreciation of reggae in both Britain and the USA, despite not even charting in Britain and not being released in the States until 1975. It remains a mystery, however, as to why the movie's success didn't boost CLIFF's career at a time when he was signed to 'Island' in the UK and when his albums were still garnering critical acclaim. Disillusioned, he moved on to various major record labels over the couple of decades without ever regaining commercial success. He did, however, have further brushes with film, being the subject of a West German documentary, 'Bongo Man' (1981) and co-starring as a revolutionary in Caribbean-set tourism farce, 'CLUB PARADISE' (1986), to which he also contributed some tracks. More successful was his US Top 20 cover of Johnny Nash's 'I Can See Clearly Now', featured on the soundtrack for Jon Turteltaub's sports comedy, 'Cool Runnings' (1993). *BG*

- **filmography** (composer) {acting/performance} –

the Harder They Come *(1972 {*} OST by CLIFF & V/A =>)* / Bongo Man *(1981 {*p})* / **Club Paradise** *(1986 {*} OST by CLIFF & V/A =>)* / Marked For Death *(1990 {c} on OST by V/A see; future editions =>)* / Cool Runnings *(1993 hit on OST by V/A see; future editions =>)*

□ Patsy CLINE segment
(⇒ SWEET DREAMS)

CLUBLAND

1999 (US 93m) Interpid Entertainment / Shoreline (R)

Film genre: Pop/Rock-music comedy/drama

Top guns: dir: Mary Lambert ← SIESTA / s-w: **Glen Ballard**, Todd Robinson

Stars: Jimmy Tuckett *(Kennedy)*, Brad Hunt *(King)* → MAGNOLIA, Rodney Eastman *(Mondo)*, Buddy Quaid *(Vernon)* → PSYCHO BEACH PARTY, Sky James *(Harpo)*, Phil Buckman *(Paul)*, Heather Stephens *(Sophie)*, Lisa Robin Kelly *(Carla)*, Lori Petty *(India)* → PREY FOR ROCK & ROLL, Jon Sklaroff *(Eddie)* → MASKED AND ANONYMOUS, Toby Huss *(Rastus)* ← the BASKETBALL DIARIES / → the COUNTRY BEARS, **Terence Trent D'Arby** *(Toby)* → SHAKE, RATTLE & ROLL: AN AMERICAN LOVE STORY, **Steven Tyler** *(David Foster)* <= AEROSMITH =>, Grant Heslov *(Matt)* ← CATCH ME IF YOU CAN, Alexis Arquette *(Steven)* ← the WEDDING SINGER ← LAST EXIT TO BROOKLYN, Mark Pellegrino *(Lipton T)*

Storyline: Front man Kennedy tours the nightspots of L.A. with his band, who by the sound of their playing would be better off sticking to their day jobs. At last manager King gets Radar Records to take an interest in them, but the band's short-lived joy turns to anger when it turns out they're only interested in Kennedy. Now he has to make the choice between staying with his not-so-hot friends or going solo towards fame and fortune. *JZ*

Movie rating: *4.5

Visual: video + dvd

Off the record: Terence Trent D'Arby had been conspicuous by his absence of late, his star fading fast since his heyday as moody prince of pop on late 80s hits such as 'If You Let Me Stay', 'Wishing Well' and 'Sign Your Name'. *MCS*

Various Artists (composer/score: Glen Ballard)

Mar 99. (cd/c) *Capitol; <93051-2/-4>* □ ⊟

– Away from me (JIMMY TUCKETT) / Bi-sexual chick (JOHN OSZAJCA) / Games you play (SPLASHDOWN) / Check (ZEBRAHEAD) / Stayin' alive (SUPPLE) / Why are you so mean to me? (VITREOUS HUMOR) / Not me (JIMMY TUCKETT) / Purple (CRUSTATION) / Closer to myself (RADFORD) / 200,000 (in counterfeit fifty dollar bills) (CITIZEN COPE) / Here we go (FRISBIE) / Watch her walk out (FLOOD) / Burning down the house (STAR 69) / Far out (BRENDAN LYNCH) / Good advice (LUCIE GAMELON) / Gemini (JIMMY TUCKETT) / I used to manage PM Dawn (BLOCK). *(hidden track +=)* – Living the oblivion (JIMMY TUCKETT).

S/track review: Yet another soundtrack to yet another film about trying to make it big in the music industry. Hold me back! 'CLUBLAND' may, however, have got something right in its approach. Whereas other films surround the fictional performer's songs with good "proper" songs in an attempt to disguise the fact that the fictional songs are, well, rubbish, this actually surrounds itself with songs that are just as mediocre or indeed worse than those of the fictional artist. Although, instead of making the fictional artist's songs sound better as a result, 'CLUBLAND' slowly grinds away your will to live. The only track out of seventeen that can hold its head up without being pummelled by rotten tomatoes is SUPPLE's cover of the Bee Gees' disco classic 'Stayin' Alive'. Transforming it into a laid back acoustic affair complete with oboe and muted hand claps was a stroke of genius that provides a new perspective on a song that, let's face it, can get on your nerves at times, despite its excellence. The fictional artist referred to above is the amusingly named JIMMY TUCKETT, who isn't exactly terrible, he's just not very good either. In saying that, 'Not Me', a song about the lack of fresh rock'n'roll heroes, has the potential to be good, if only a bit more imagination was put into it or it was given to someone like Bruce Springsteen. Sadly it wasn't and we are left with wishy-washy nonsense. Even legendary producer, FLOOD, cannot lift this album from its stupor with the woeful 'Watch Her

Walk Out', while JOHN OSZAJCA's 'Bi-Sexual Chick' is derogatory nonsense with about as much taste as a soggy hula hoop. The rest is not worth mentioning and if you are brave, or daft, enough to listen to this album, then just remember that good music does exist and all hope is not lost. *CM*

Album rating: *2.5

C'MON, LET'S LIVE A LITTLE

1967 (US 84m) All-Star Productions / Paramount Pictures

Film genre: Rock'n'roll Musical comedy drama

Top guns: dir: David Butler / s-w: June Starr

Stars: Bobby Vee *(Jesse Crawford)* ← JUST FOR FUN ← PLAY IT COOL ← SWINGIN' ALONG, **Jackie DeShannon** *(Judy Grant)* ← SURF PARTY, **Eddie Hodges** *(Eddie Stewart)* → LIVE A LITTLE, LOVE A LITTLE, Suzie Kaye *(Bee Bee Vendemeer)* ← WILD, WILD WINTER / → IT'S A BIKINI WORLD → CLAMBAKE, Patsy Kelly *(Mrs. Fitts)*, Russ Conway *(John W. Grant)*, John Ireland Jr. *(Rego)*, Mark Evans *(Tim Grant)*, Jill Banner *(Wendy)*, Ken Osmond *(the Beard)*, **Kim Carnes** *(Melinda)*, Don Crawford *(Jeb Crawford)*, **Ethel Smith** *(Aunt Ethel)*

Storyline: A folk-rock singer becomes a hero to a small college when he rescues the dean's daughter from a car crash. This enables his free speech and radical teachings to virtually become part of the curiculum, while attempts to woo the daughter. *BG*

Movie rating: *4

Visual: none (cable/satellite channel AMC)

Off the record: By the time **Bobby Vee** starred in this movie, he had amassed several Top 10 hits, including 'Rubber Ball', 'Take Good Care Of My Baby', 'Run To Him' and 'The Night Has A Thousand Eyes'. **Jackie DeShannon** , meanwhile, hit Top 10 in 1965 with 'What The World Needs Now Is Love'; **Kim Carnes** went on to have a chart-topper courtesy of the rasping, 'Bette Davis Eyes', incidentally co-written with DeShannon. **Eddie Hodges** kicked off his US chart career back in 1961 when 'I'm Gonna Knock On Your Door' hit No.12. **Ethel Smith** was also a organist in her own right, known to many golden oldies for her novelty smash, 'Tico Tico'. *MCS*

Various Artists (score: DON RALKE *)

1966. (lp; mono/stereo) *Liberty; <LRP 3430/LST 7430>* [ ] [–]
– C'mon, let's live a little – opening main title (*) / Instant girl (BOBBY VEE) / Baker man (JACKIE DeSHANNON) / C'mon, let's live a little (SUZIE KAYE) / What fool this mortal be (BOBBY VEE) / Tonight's the night (the PAIR) / For granted (JACKIE DeSHANNON) / Back-talk (BOBBY VEE & JACKIE DeSHANNON) / Over and over (BOBBY VEE) / Let's go go (EDDIE HODGES) / Way back home (ETHEL SMITH & DON CRAWFORD) / C'mon, let's live a little – end title (*).

S/track review: Brill Building pop with a host of top stars on show here, featuring main stars BOBBY VEE and JACKIE DeSHANNON on several numbers including romantic duet, 'Back-Talk'. Sadly, nothing was deemed good enough for a spinoff hit single, although VEE's solo recording, 'Instant Girl' and DeSHANNON's 'For Granted', just might've been awarded that accolade. EDDIE HODGES, a duo called the PAIR, ETHEL SMITH and DON CRAWFORD brought up the rear, so to speak, although only the first's 'Let's Go Go' came out with any credibility. *BG*

Album rating: *4.5

COAL MINER'S DAUGHTER

1980 (US 125m) Universal Pictures (PG)

Film genre: Country-music bio-pic/drama

Top guns: dir: Michael Apted ← STARDUST / → BRING ON THE NIGHT / s-w: Tom Rickman (au: Loretta Lynn & George Vescey)

Stars: Sissy Spacek *(Loretta Lynn)* → AFFLICTION, Tommy Lee Jones *(Doolittle "Mooney" Lynn)* → the PARK IS MINE → NATURAL BORN KILLERS, Beverly D'Angelo *(Patsy Cline)* ← HAIR / → SUGAR TOWN, **Levon Helm** *(Ted Webb)* <= the BAND =>, Phyllis Boyens *(Clara Webb)*, Ernest Tubb *(himself)*, Robert Elkins *(Bobby Day)*, Bob Hannah *(Charlie Dick)*, William Sanderson *(Lee Dollarhide)* → BLADE RUNNER → LAST MAN STANDING, **Jim Webb** *(bus driver)*, **Billy Strange** *(Speedy West)*, **Merle Kilgore** *(cowboy at Tootsie's)* ← NASHVILLE / → ROADIE → LIVING PROOF: THE HANK WILLIAMS JR. STORY

Storyline: Loretta Lynn's life of extreme poverty lasts until the ripe old age of 13, when she marries and rattles off four kids by the time she's 20. So much for motherhood. When her horny hubby buys her a guitar for her birthday, her unfulfilled musical talent comes to fruition and her Country & Western career takes off in earnest. How will she cope with the transition from a coal mine to a gold mine? *JZ*

Movie rating: *7.5

Visual: video + dvd

Off the record: Loretta Lynn (see storyline)

Various Cast incl. SISSY SPACEK * & BEVERLY D'ANGELO **

Mar 80. (lp/c) *M.C.A.; <5107> (MCF/+C 3068)* [40] Apr80 [ ]
– The Titanic (*) / Blue moon of Kentucky (LEVON HELM) / There he goes (*) / I'm a honky tonk girl (*) / Amazing Grace (FUNERAL GUESTS) / Walking after midnight (**) / Crazy (**) / I fall to pieces (*) / Sweet dreams (**) / Back in baby's arms (* & **) / One's on the way (*) / You ain't woman enough to take my man (*) / You're lookin' at country (*) / Coal miner's daughter (*). *(re-iss. Mar87 lp/c; MCL/+C 1847) <(cd-iss. Jun00; 088 170 122-2)>*

S/track review: SISSY SPACEK mopped up every major film award and was Grammy-nominated for the title song – and, produced by veteran Owen Bradley, the album is crafted with a care and integrity that seems to get the best from everybody. The range includes BEVERLY D'ANGELO's creditably polished impersonation of Patsy Cline on 'Walking After Midnight' and 'Crazy', and a fabulously rough-edged a cappella 'Amazing Grace' from a chorus of funeral guests. LEVON HELM makes the most of limited vocal resources on a rootsy 'Blue Moon Of Kentucky' (the BAND drummer would go on to extend the session at the legendary Bradley's Barn studios into what became his acclaimed 'American Son' album). But above all, it's SISSY SPACEK's show. A capable singer (she had recorded a novelty single in 1969 under the name "Rainbo"), SPACEK spent weeks shadowing Loretta Lynn on the road, and from her rough-hewn Kentucky-accented debut on the Carter family's 'Titanic' to the practised swagger of hits like 'You Ain't Woman Enough To Take My Man' she is utterly persuasive and appealing, even if you are not a devotee of Lynn's fairly humdrum songwriting. SPACEK would go on to record an album with Rodney Crowell and Vince Gill ('Hangin' Up My Heart', 1983, on which she co-wrote a song with Lynn) without ever coming close to emerging from the shadow of this huge-selling success. *ND*

Album rating: *7.5

COFFEE AND CIGARETTES

2003 (US 96m b&w; comp. of shorts 1986/89/93) United Artists (R)

Film genre: urban comedy

Top guns: s-w + dir: Jim Jarmusch ← GHOST DOG: THE WAY OF THE SAMURAI ← YEAR OF THE HORSE ← DEAD MAN ← NIGHT ON EARTH ← MYSTERY TRAIN ← DOWN BY LAW

Stars: Steven Wright *(Steven)* ← RESERVOIR DOGS, Roberto Benigni *(Roberto)* ← NIGHT ON EARTH ← DOWN BY LAW, Joie Lee *(good twin)* ← GIRL 6 ← CROOKLYN ← SCHOOL DAZE, Cinque Lee *(evil twin / kitchen guy)* ← MYSTERY TRAIN ← SCHOOL DAZE, Steve Buscemi *(waiter)* ← the WEDDING SINGER ← DESPERADO ← AIRHEADS ← PULP FICTION ← RESERVOIR DOGS ← MYSTERY TRAIN ← the WAY IT IS / → ROMANCE & CIGARETTES → the FUTURE IS UNWRITTEN, **Iggy POP** *(Iggy)*, **Tom WAITS** *(Tom)*, Joe Rigano *(Joe)* ← GHOST DOG: THE WAY OF THE SAMURAI ← HEY, LET'S TWIST, Vinny Vella *(Vinny Jr.)* ← GHOST DOG: THE WAY OF THE SAMURAI, Renee French *(Renee)*, **E.J. Rodriguez** *(waiter)*, Alex Descas *(Alex)* ← TROUBLE EVERY DAY ← NENETTE ET BONI, Isaach De Bankole *(Isaach)* ← GHOST DOG: THE WAY OF THE SAMURAI ← NIGHT ON EARTH, Cate Blanchett *(Cate/Shelly)* → the LIFE AQUATIC WITH STEVE ZISSOU → I'M NOT THERE, **Mike Hogan** *(waiter)*, **Jack White** *(Jack)* → COLD MOUNTAIN → the FEARLESS FREAKS → TWO HEADED COW → WALK HARD: THE DEWEY COX STORY, **Meg White** *(Meg)* → the FEARLESS FREAKS, Alfred Molina *(Alfred)* ← MAGNOLIA ← BOOGIE NIGHTS ← DEAD MAN, Steve Coogan *(Steve)* ← 24 HOUR PARTY PEOPLE, Katy Hansz *(Katy)*, Bill Rice *(Bill)* ← SUBWAY RIDERS ← the OFFENDERS, **GZA** *(GZA)*, **the RZA** *(RZA)* ← GHOST DOG: THE WAY OF THE SAMURAI ← RHYME & REASON / → BE COOL, Bill Murray *(Bill Murray)* ← LOST IN TRANSLATION ← LITTLE SHOP OF HORRORS ← CADDYSHACK ← WHERE THE BUFFALO ROAM ← the RUTLES / → the LIFE AQUATIC WITH STEVE ZISSOU, Taylor Mead *(Taylor)*

Storyline: A compendium of deadpan café cultural shorts make this perhaps the most Jarmusch-esque of all the man's films. Against a monochrome backdrop of tattered formica and milk jugs, Iggy Pop and Tom Waits get uncharacteristically tongue tied, Steve Coogan gets a lesson in humanity and Bill Murray gets a lecture in holistic medicine. Jack and Meg White, and even Cate Blanchett also chew the fat in a movie which comically deflates fame to the level of the humdrum without losing the fascination. *BG*

Movie rating: *7.5

Visual: dvd

Off the record: Mike Hogan (was bassist with the Cranberries), **E.J. Rodriguez** (percussionist with John Lurie), **Jack & Meg White** (the White Stripes, of course!), **GZA & RZA** (of Wu-Tang Clan).

—

Various Artists

May 04. (cd) *Milan; <M2 36077> (5046 73712-2)* ☐ ☐
– Louie, Louie (RICHARD BERRY & THE PHAROAHS) / Nappy dugout (FUNKADELIC) / Crimson and clover (TOMMY JAMES & THE SHONDELLS) / Down on the street (the STOOGES) / Nimblefoot ska (the SKATALITES) / Baden Baden (MODERN JAZZ QUARTET) / Hanalei moon (JERRY BYRD) / Fantazia 3 in G minor (FRETWORK) / Enna bella (ERIC "MONTY" MORRIS) / Saw sage (C-SIDE & TOM WAITS) / A joyfull process (FUNKADELIC) / Louie, Louie (IGGY POP) / Ich bin der weit abhanden gekommen (JANET BAKER).

S/track review: A Jim Jarmusch soundtrack almost counts as a brand name in its own right; unlike Tarantino, he doesn't usually go for the straight compilation, but this is a masterclass in how it should be done, skanking, educating and agitating its way into your CD player/I-pod and refusing to budge. White Stripes and Wu Tang types appear in the movie, but Jarmusch is clearly keener on the recorded past than the present, and he uses this album to show us why. As funk sage Keb Darge once commented (in his sleevenotes to 'The Kings Of Funk' comp): "enough good music has already been made to last anyone born tomorrow until their grave without boredom setting in". Hear, hear. Not being tied to any particular era, Mr Jim rifles through the decades and gives more than a few starting points for further adventures in stereo, most obscurely ska pioneer ERIC 'MONTY' MORRIS' sweet 'Enna Bella' and steel guitarist JERRY BYRD's 'Hanalei Moon'. And he doesn't think twice about throwing together Henry Purcell, Mahler and the STOOGES on the same album. It works of course, but then all the compositions are definitions of their respective art forms, and the electrifying throb of 'Down On The Street' (has a cooler rock song ever been sweated out?) would work anywhere. A couple of lesser heard FUNKADELIC nuggets, a clanking TOM WAITS/C-SIDE incantation and IGGY POP's own 'Louie, Louie' (a big, dumb, politically slanted update of the original, also included) are pure Jarmusch, but his most revealing choice is 'Crimson And Clover'. TOMMY JAMES & THE SHONDELLS sold more singles than the Beatles in the late 60s, but receive a fraction of the retrospective coverage. 'Crimson And Clover' is bubblegum-psych symphony reclaimed, praise the Lord. And that's without even mentioning the SKATALITES or the MODERN JAZZ QUARTET; you won't get a buzz this addictive – or eclectic – from coffee or fags. *BG*

Album rating: *8

COLIN FITZ LIVES!

1997 (US 91m) River One Films (R)

Film genre: screwball rock-music comedy

Top guns: dir: Robert Bella / s-w: Tom Morrissey

Stars: Matt McGrath *(Paul)* ← PUMP UP THE VOLUME, Andy Fowle *(Grady)*, Mary McCormack *(Moira)* → PRIVATE PARTS, Martha Plimpton *(Ann)* ← I SHOT ANDY WARHOL ← SHY PEOPLE, William H. Macy *(Mr. O'Day)* ← the LAST DRAGON / → BOOGIE NIGHTS → WAG THE DOG → MAGNOLIA, John C. McGinley *(groundskeeper)*, Julianne Phillips *(Justice Fitz)*, Will McCormack *(Todd)*, Erik Jensen *(Dean)*, Chris Bauer *(Tony Baby Shark)*, Robert Bella *(Pepe)*

Storyline: It's been exactly a year since the tragic death of rock star, Colin Fitz, and to mark the anniversary, his widow decides to employ two contrasting security guards to protect his grave from the anticipated hordes of suicidal fans. In a night of beer drinking and bizarre stories (plus the weird characters/fans that come and go), the pair find an alliance of sorts while finding the mystique behind the life and death of the legend that was Colin Fitz. *MCS*

Movie rating: *4

Visual: none (no audio OST)

Off the record: The film opens with ASTROPUPPEES' 'Dead Around Here'. Julianne Phillips was married to Bruce Springsteen between May 1985 and 1990. *MCS*

COME ON, GET HAPPY: THE PARTRIDGE FAMILY STORY

1999 (US 100m TV) Columbia TriStar Television Inc. / ABC

Film genre: Pop-music bio-pic comedy/drama

Top guns: dir: David Burton Morris ← AND THE BEAT GOES ON: THE SONNY AND CHER STORY / s-w: Jacqueline Feather, Jon S. Denny, David Seidler ← TUCKER: THE MAN AND HIS DREAM

Stars: Eve Gordon *(Shirley Jones/Partridge)*, Rodney Scott *(David Cassidy / Keith Partridge)*, Kathy Wagner *(Susan Dey / Laurie Partridge)* → HOW HIGH, Shawn Pyfrom *(Danny Bonaduce/Partridge)*, Michael Chieffo *(Dave Madden / Reuben Kincaid)*, William Russ *(Joseph Bonaduce)* ← BIG DREAMS

& BROKEN HEARTS: THE DOTTIE WEST STORY ← the BORDER, Roxanne Hart *(Betty Bonaduce)*, Richard Fancy *(Harold)* ← TOUCH / → PSYCHO BEACH PARTY, **Debby Boone** *(Beth)*, Clay Wilcox *(Wes)* ← ROCK'N'ROLL MOM / → the BEACH BOYS: AN AMERICAN FAMILY, Danny Bonaduce *(narrator)*

Storyline: Just what it says on the tin, the rise to stardom of TV's popular music-loving, sit-com family from the early 70s starring "genuine" singers David Cassidy and Shirley Jones; Danny Bonaduce of the Partridge Family narrated the TV movie, having already received a bit of noteriety on his own talk show in the 90s. *MCS*

Movie rating: *5

Visual: video (no audio OST; score: Guy Moon & Steve Tyrell)

Off the record: The **Partridge Family** had a sackful of hits in the early 70s, their biggest being 'I think I Love You', 'Doesn't Somebody Want To Be Wanted', 'I'll Meet You Halfway' and 'I Woke Up In Love This Morning'. **Debby Boone** (was the daughter of Pat Boone): see 'YOU LIGHT UP MY LIFE'. *MCS*

COMEBACK

1982 (W.Ger 105m) Rocco-Film / Pro-ject Filmproduktion (R)

Film genre: Blues/Rock-music showbiz drama

Top guns: s-w + dir: Christel Buschmann

Stars: Eric Burdon *(Rocco)* <= the ANIMALS =>, John Aprea *(lawyer)*, Michael Cavanaugh *(manager)*, Julie Carmen *(Tina)*, Rosa King *(Rosa)*, Bob Lockwood *(Marilyn)*, **Louisiana Red** *(Louisiana)*

Storyline: Jaded by corruption and excess, rock star Rocco retreats from the music business to the relative anonymity of the then West Germany where he plans his comeback of the title. *BG*

Movie rating: *6.5

Visual: video on MGM/UA 1996

Off the record: ERIC BURDON (see the ANIMALS biography); bluesman **Louisiana Red** had a minor hit in 1964 with 'I'm Too Poor To Die'. *MCS*

ERIC BURDON

1983. (lp) *Blackline; (BL 712)* – W.Ger –
– No more Elmore / The road / Crawling King Snake / Take it easy / Dey won't / Wall of silence / Streetwalker / It hurts me too / Lights out / Bird on the beach. *(UK-iss.Jun84 as 'THE ROAD' on 'Thunderbolt'; THBL 1017) (cd-iss. Sep94 on 'Line'; LICD 900058) <(d-cd iss.Apr01 on 'Burning Airlines'+=; PILOT 081)>* – (extra tracks).

S/track review: Now this really is an obscurity: a good old rags-to-riches-to-rags music biz movie which just happened to feature ERIC BURDON in a starring role and an ostensibly fictional script "close to biography". Printed in an annoying, retina-challenging script, the 'Burning Airlines' sleevenotes go on to quote the film's director, Christel Buschmann, on the soundtrack's dubious, German-only beginnings, but this latest, expanded version is hardly without its flaws: grainy stills, no songwriting credits, sloppy mistakes like paragraphs printed twice and songs listed in the wrong order. But what about the music? Even taking into account the early 80s recording date, it's suprisingly close to the bone. BURDON's voice is still a British Northern-cum-American Southern force of nature, and it's put to especially effective use on the straight blues covers and end-of-tether originals. He leers though a version of John Lee Hooker's 'Crawling King Snake' with the kind of degenerate hysteria once the preserve of Mick Jagger and Lux Interior. The spirit of Jagger – albeit the late 70s model – also flutters around 'Bird On A Beach', with BURDON mincing to some Blockhead-ed funk. For the most part, though, he sounds in no mood to mince, making some not so veiled threats on the the coruscating 'Kill My Body' and a menacing cover of Louisiana Red's 'Sweet Blood Call', and pledging lyrical – if not literal – allegiance with Lou Reed, another 60s/70s refugee wracking his soul in an attempt to come to some kind of accommodation with the 80s. "I feel like I'm good for nothing.. I hope you've enjoyed my suffering", he roars on 'Who Gives A Fuck', over what sounds like a greasy variation on 'Mannish Boy'. Easy listening it's not, but it's often car-crash compelling and even if he runs the gamut of classic rock, he's still his own man. Inevitably, he also trawls through a contemporary, sax-doctored update of 'House Of The Rising Sun'. The 'Burning Airlines' CD comes with a bonus disc of blooze-sodden live cuts recorded largely in Berlin prior to filming, including an epically ravaged, reggae-tinged 'Don't Let Me Be Misunderstood'. *BG*

Album rating: *5 / re-CD *5.5

the COMMITMENTS

1991 (Ire/UK/US 116m) First Film / Beacon / Dirty Hands (15)

Film genre: Pop/R&B-music urban drama

Top guns: dir: Alan Parker ← BIRDY ← the WALL ← FAME / → EVITA / s-w: Dick Clement → STILL CRAZY, Ian La Frenais → STILL CRAZY (au: Roddy Doyle)

Stars: Robert Arkins *(Jimmy Rabbitte)*, Michael Aherne *(Steven Clifford)*, Angeline Ball *(Imelda Quirke)*, Maria Doyle *(Natalie Murphy)*, Bronagh Gallagher *(Bernie McGloughlin)* → PULP FICTION, Johnny Murphy *(Joey 'Fat Lips' Fagan)*, Dave Finnegan *(Mickah Wallace)*, Andrew Strong *(Deco Cuffe)*, **Glen Hansard** *(Outspan Foster)* → ONCE, Kenneth McCluskey *(Derek Scully)*, Dick Massey *(Billy Mooney)*, Colm Meaney *(Mr. Rabbitte)* ← DICK TRACY, Felim Gormley *(Dean Fay)*, **Andrea Corr** *(Sharon Rabbitte)* → EVITA, **Jim Corr** *(avante-garde-a-clue band)*, **Sharon Corr** *(fiddle player)*, Caroline Corr *(extra)*, Sean Hughes *(Dave from Eejit Records)*, John Cronin *(kid with horse)* → the LAST BUS HOME

Storyline: In pre-Celtic Tiger Dublin, self-styled hustler Jimmy Rabbitte assembles an unlikely raggle taggle army of soul boys and girls from the urban wastes of the city's Northside district. With expletives flying thicker and faster than a hail of gobsh**e, the group inch their way to citywide acclaim and the promise of the big time even as internal personality clashes threaten to become calamities. *BG*

Movie rating: *7.5

Visual: video + dvd

Off the record: The **Corrs** subsequently charted numerous times with singles, 'Runaway', 'Dreams', 'What Can I Do', 'So Young' & 'Breathless'; the latter their first UK No.1. *MCS*

---

the COMMITMENTS (composers: Various)

Aug 91. (lp/c/cd) *M.C.A.; (<MCA/+C/D 10286>)* 4 8
– Mustang Sally / Take me to the river / Chain of fools / The dark end of the street / Destination anywhere / I can't stand the rain / Try a little tenderness / Treat her right / Do right woman do right man / Mr. Pitiful / I never loved a man / In the midnight hour / Bye bye baby / Slip away.

S/track review: What else but the charm of the film can explain the outrageous success of this soundtrack? After hearing it – in all likelihood – more times than either the director and band themselves, anyone unlucky enough to be working in a record store in the early 90s probably still knows and silently curses every last lyric and the "craic" that spawned them. Only 'Bat Out Of Hell II' inspired more shop floor discontent. Barbed humour aside (though there's plenty of that here as well), and for the benefit of those unfamiliar with it, 'The COMMITMENTS' is the sound of Irish tenacity projected onto the broken heart and gospel conscience of black music, recorded and released at a serendipitously receptive moment in time. It's also gratifyingly, organically arranged and produced, green-eyed soul with a hefty dose of the black stuff, performed with a lot of heart and an audibly deep affinity with the tradition. The title implies hard graft rather than prodigious talent (although at only 16 years old, ponytailed lead vocalist STRONG – no relation.. – sounds ancient before his time) and that's what you get, Embassy Regal-singed odysseys in search of Deep South totems, in the days before Dublin was a smoke-free zone. STRONG is equally intimate with the shouters as he is the ballads, backed up by a cast of Celtic soul divas who occasionally double on lead, and who hit banshee point on 'Treat Her Right'. By dint of both the familiarity of the material, and the earthy affability of the performers, it's a record which wins your confidence pretty much instantaneously but, like the Guinness on a bender, gets a little too stodgy after one spin too many. *BG*

Album rating: *6 / Vol.2 *5

– spinoff releases, etc. –

the COMMITMENTS: Try A Little Tenderness / Mr. Pitiful

Oct 91. (c-s) *<54128>* [–] [67]
(cd-s+=) *<54128>* – I can't stand the rain.

the COMMITMENTS: Mustang Sally / Take Me To The River

Nov 91. (7") *(MCS 1598)* [63] [–]
(cd-s) *(MCSCD 1598)* – ('A') / Chain of fool / Do right woman do right man.

the COMMITMENTS: Vol.2

Apr 02. (lp/c/cd) *(<MCA/+C/D 10506>)* [13] Mar92 [ ]
– Hard to handle / Grits ain't groceries / I thank you / That's the way love is / Show me / Saved / Too many fish in the sea / Fa-fa-fa-fa (sad song) / Land of a thousand dances / Nowhere to run / Bring it home to me. *(<cd re-iss. Oct95; MCLD 19312>)*

the COMMITMENTS: The Best Of The Commitments featuring Andrew Strong

Mar 04. (cd) *(80050)* [ ] [ ]
– Mustang Sally / Chain of fools / Treat her right / Same old me / The dark end of the street / Do right woman, do right man / Take me to the river / Mr. Pitiful / Try a little tenderness / I never loved a man / Hard to handle / (She's) Some kind of wonderful / Fa-fa-fa-fa (sad song) / Bring it on home to me / I can't stand the rain / Ain't nothing you can do / Half a man / In the midnight hour.

CONCRETE ANGELS

1987 (Can 97m) Shapiro Entertainment (R)

Film genre: Pop/Rock-music drama

Top guns: dir: Carlo Liconti / s-w: Jim Purdy

Stars: Joseph di Mambro *(Bello Vecchio)*, Luke McKeehan *(Sean)*, Omie Craden *(Ira)*, Dean Bosacki *(Josse)*, Tom Maccarone *(Mr. Vecchio)*, Anna Migliarisi *(Mrs. Vecchio)*, Simon Craig *(Mick)*, Derrick Jones *(Bullet)*

Storyline: When the Beatles come to Toronto, the competition to be chosen as a warm up band reaches fever pitch. Enter the Concrete Angels, who must out-perform the opposition to play alongside John, Paul, George and Ringo. Can they cope with the pressure-cooker atmosphere or will they mess up and lose the chance of a lifetime? *JZ*

Movie rating: *4

Visual: video on Academy Home Entertainment (no audio OST)

Off the record: The fictitious QUASI HANDS (*) or 1964 (**) bands performed covers of (mainly Beatles songs):- 'She Loves You' (*), 'Love Me Do' (**), 'From Me To You' (*), 'Misery' (*), 'P.S. I Love You' (*), 'Johnny B. Goode' (CHUCK BERRY), 'A Hard Day's Night' (**), 'Johnny B. Goode' (*), 'I Saw Her Standing There' (**), 'Not Fade Away' (BLUSHING BRIDES), 'Money (That's What I Want)' (**), '(The) Loco-Motion' (LITTLE EVA), 'Will You Still Love Me Tomorrow (the SHIRELLES), 'One Fine Day' (the CHIFFONS), 'Runaround Sue' (DION), 'Mr. Bass Man' (*), 'Twist And Shout' (**) & 'Big Town Boy' (SHIRLES MATTHEWS).

CONFESSIONS OF A POP PERFORMER

aka TIMOTHY LEA'S CONFESSION OF A POP PERFORMER

1975 (UK 91m) Columbia Pictures (X)

Film genre: Rock/Pop-music seXual comedy

Top guns: dir: Norman Cohen / s-w: Christopher Wood (+ au)

Stars: Robin Askwith *(Timothy Lea)*, Anthony Booth *(Sidney Noggett)* → REVENGERS TRAGEDY, Bill Maynard *(Mr. Lea)*, Doris Hare *(Mrs. Lea)*, Sheila White *(Rosie Noggett)* ← MRS. BROWN, YOU'VE GOT A LOVELY DAUGHTER ← HERE WE GO ROUND THE MULBERRY BUSH ← the GHOST GOES GEAR / → SILVER DREAM RACER, Lin Harris *(Jason Noggett)*, Bob Todd *(Mr. Barnwell)*, Jill Gascoine *(Mrs. Barnwell)* → RED HOT, Peter Jones *(Maxy Naus)* ← SMASHING TIME, Carol Hawkins *(Jill Brown)*, Kipper:- Peter Cleall *(Nutter Normington)*, David Auker *(Zombie)*, Maynard Williams *(Eric)*, Richard Warwick *(Petal)*, Mike King *(Blow)* / Diane Langton *(Ruby Climax)*, Linda Regan *(Brenda Climax)*, Ian Lavender *(Rodney)*, Rita Webb *(Fanny's mother)* ← PERCY ← the MAGIC CHRISTIAN ← MRS. BROWN, YOU'VE GOT A LOVELY DAUGHTER ← TO SIR, WITH LOVE, Rula Lenska *(receptionist)* → ROCK FOLLIES → ROCK FOLLIES OF '77

Storyline: The second in the "Confessions Of A . . ." series of gaudy adult entertainment, the first being the equally titilating 'Confessions Of A Window Cleaner'. Timothy Lea gets into the world of pop music (and naked females) courtesy of glam-rock band, Kipper. On tour, they team up with the Climax Sisters and have a couple of er . . . hits. *MCS*

Movie rating: *2

Visual: video

Off the record: Benny Hill sidekick, Bob Todd, was forever immortalized by Merseyside Scouse indie funsters Half Man Half Biscuit in the track, '99% Of Gargoyles Look Like Bob Todd', from their album, 'Back In The DHSS'. Talking of Scousers, Anthony Booth ('Till Death Us Do Part' layabout) is the father of Cherie, the wife of our former Prime Minister, Tony Blair. *MCS*

Various Cast/Artists (songwriters: Dominic Bugatti & Frank Musker)

Sep 75. (lp) *Polydor Super; (2383 350)* [ ] [–]
– This is your life Timmy Lea (THREE'S A CROWD) / The Clapham / Oh sha la la / I need you (like a hole in the head) / Kipper / Accidents will happen / (other tracks from 'Confessions Of A Window Cleaner').

S/track review: An interesting artefact from the days of glam and unusual in that it features instrumental tracks such as the funky 'Charlie Snowgarden' (by SAM SKLAIR) from Robin Askwith's previous "Confessions . . ." film, ' . . .Window Cleaner'. Of the ' . . .POP PERFORMER' tracks, only the opening title track is worthy of note, 'This Is Your Life Timmy Lea', written by former Blue Mink composers, Roger Cook & Roger Greenaway. The bulk of the other songs are written by Dominic Bugatti and Frank Musker (both later responsible for 'FAME'), with actor Robin Askwith getting in with some awful dialogue; be ready to pay over £60 for the privilege. *MCS*

Album rating: *2.5

CONFESSIONS OF A TEENAGE DRAMA QUEEN

2004 (US 89m) Buena Vista / Disney / Touchstone Pictures (PG)

Film genre: Pop-music teen comedy

Top guns: dir: Sara Sugarman / s-w: Gail Parent (au: Dyan Sheldon)

Stars: Lindsay Lohan *(Mary Elizabeth Cep / Lola)*, Megan Fox *(Carla Santini)*, Adam Garcia *(Stu Wolff)*, Glenne Headly *(Karen)*, Alison Pill *(Ella Gerard)*, Eli Marienthal *(Sam Creek)*, Carol Kane *(Miss Baggoli)*, Adam MacDonald *(Steve)*, Gerry Quigley *(slimy guy)*

Storyline: It's the Battle of the Bitches as new girl Lola takes on Most Popular Girl At School, Carla Santini. Handbags are first raised when the lead role in Pygmalion comes up for grabs and the war intensifies when Carla buys up all the spare tickets for the Stu Wolff farewell concert, denying Lola a last chance to see her heart-throb. Can Lola rise to the challenge or will Carla remain Queen of the Classroom? *JZ*

Movie rating: *4

Visual: dvd

Off the record: (see below)

—

Various Artists (score: Mark Mothersbaugh)

Feb 04. (cd) *Hollywood; <2061 62442-2> (5046 73940-2)* [51] Jun04 [ ]
– Drama queen (that girl) (LINDSAY LOHAN) / Ready (CHERIE) / Ladies night (ATOMIC KITTEN feat. KOOL & THE GANG) / Perfect – acoustic version (SIMPLE PLAN) / Tomorrow (LILLIX) / What are you waiting for (LINDSAY LOHAN) / Na na (SUPERCHIC[K]) / 1,2,3 (NIKKI CLEARY) / Don't move on – Living for the city – Changes: medley (LINDSAY LOHAN) / Boom (FAN_3) / A day in the life (LINDSAY LOHAN) / The real me (ALEXIS) / Un-sweet sixteen (WAKEFIELD) / Only in the movies (DIFFUSER).

S/track review: Star of the film LINDSAY LOHAN kicks things off with the toe-tapping slick American pop of 'Drama Queen (That Girl)' although CHERIE's 'Ready' is more like the bland filler you would expect from a teen movie soundtrack. ATOMIC KITTEN's 'Ladies Night' may feature KOOL AND THE GANG but is just pointless and devoid of any passion, however it is still nowhere near as embarrassing as the whiny wuss-rock offered by SIMPLE PLAN on the mawkish and self-pitying 'Perfect'. LILLIX's 'Tomorrow' is familiar self-affirming rock-pop reminiscent of a less angry Pink which LOHAN's 'What Are You Waiting For' and SUPERCHIC(K)'s 'Na Na' do less convincingly. Meanwhile, '1,2,3' by NIKKI CLEARY is terrible pop that belongs in the 80s – a feat matched by the annoyingly weak 'Boom' by FAN_3. We also have a medley featuring Stevie Wonder's 'Living For The City' and David Bowie's 'Changes' which is just plain insulting before LOHAN returns to the routine guitar-pop of 'A Day In The Life Of', which is at least better than the horribly oversung 'The Real Me' by ALEXIS. Indeed, the likes of Green Day and Blink 182 have a lot to answer for as WAKEFIELD ape their sound on the excruciating 'Un-Sweet Sixteen' much like DIFFUSER who also try to play the lovable-loser card on 'Only In The Movies' but fail miserably. *LF*

Album rating: *3.5

– spinoff hits, etc. –

ATOMIC KITTEN featuring KOOL & THE GANG: Ladies Night

Jan 04. (c-s,cd-s) *E.M.I.; <547773> Innocent; (SIN C/CD 53)* [ ] Dec03 [8]

the CONTINENTAL TWIST

aka 'TWIST ALL NIGHT' / UK title 'the YOUNG AND THE COOL'

1961 (US 76m b&w) Keelou / American International Pictures

Film genre: Dance/Rock'n'roll Musical comedy

Top guns: dir: Allan David, William J. Hole Jr. / s-w: Berni Gould

Stars: **Louis Prima** *(Louis Evans)* ← HEY BOY! HEY GIRL!, June Wilkinson *(Jenny Watson)*, **Sam Butera** *(himself)* ← HEY BOY! HEY GIRL!, **& the Witnesses** *(performers)*, Gertrude Michael *(Letitia Clunker)*, David M. Whorf *(Riffy)*, Tom Mathews & The All-Stars *(performers)*, Parisian Twisters *(performers)*, Manhattan Twisters *(performers)*, Joe Cavalier *(himself)*, Dick Winslow *(M. Dubois)* ← KING CREOLE / → RIOT ON SUNSET STRIP

Storyline: A new dance craze is all the rage in America and its called The Twist, unfortunately – as in early rock'n'roll movies – old timers are getting in on the act. Oh! and there's a plot centering around a small nightclub and its owner, Louis Evans, who is trying to keep it from falling into the unscrupulous hands of some nasty neighbours. *MCS*

Movie rating: *2.5

Visual: video (no audio OST w/drawn on 'Capitol')

Off the record: Old-time (pre-rock'n'roll) jazz & blues bandleaders are all featured here including the legendary **Louis Prima** and one-time cohort **Sam Butera** – but they do twist. *MCS*

CONTROL

2007 (UK/US 90m* b&w) Monumentum Pictures (18)

Film genre: indie-Rock-music biopic/drama

Top guns: dir: Anton Corbijn / s-w: Matt Greenhalgh (book: 'Touching From A Distance' by Deborah Curtis)

Stars: **Sam Riley** *(Ian Curtis)* ← 24 HOUR PARTY PEOPLE, Samantha Morton *(Deborah Curtis)*, Alexandra Maria Lara *(Annik Honore)*, Craig Parkinson *(Tony Wilson)*, James Anthony Pearson *(Bernard Sumner)*, Joe Anderson *(Hooky)* → ACROSS THE UNIVERSE, Harry Treadaway *(Stephen Morris)* ← BROTHERS OF THE HEAD, Ben Naylor *(Martin Hannett)*, Toby Kebbell *(Rob Gretton)*, Tim Plester *(Earnest Richards)* ← IT'S ALL GONE PETE TONG, Nicola Harrison *(Corrine Lewis)*

Storyline: A biopic of Ian Curtis, the legendary and iconic figurehead of post-punk, alt-rock outfit, Joy Division. The story goes way back to when Curtis won a scholarship at Kings School, Macclesfield. It's only when he sees the Sex Pistols live on stage in Manchester that he is convinced he can make it too. Sadly, it's only when his aforementioned band hit the headlines that Ian's problems begin. *JZ & MCS*

Movie rating: *9

Visual: dvd

Off the record: *IAN CURTIS* (b.15 Jul'56, Stretford, Gr. Manchester, England) and his post-punk rock outfit, Joy Division, were to many the greatest band to emerge from Britain's bleak, Thatcher-ite, late 70s time zone. From their embryonic period as the Stiff Kittens and Warsaw, CURTIS emerged as Rock's saviour to the pop-fuelled new wave. CURTIS's despondent lyrics and matching morose vox worked together alongside his emotive and implosive, "dance, dance, dance, to the radio" body movements – he actually suffered from epileptic fits both on and off stage. Joy Division albums such as 'Unknown Pleasures' (1979) and 'Closer' (1980), have become regarded as classics, while 'Transmission' (see "lyrics" above!), 'Atmosphere' and 'She's Lost Control', should be on everybody's i-pods. As the classic single, 'Love Will Tear Us Apart', was just about to make JOY DIVISION a household name by filtering into the radio airwaves and the Top 20, CURTIS, sadly, hung himself in his wife Deborah's kitchen on the 18th of May, 1980. His widow subsequently wrote her book (published in the mid-90s) and Joy Division became New Order, fronted by JD guitarist, Bernard Sumner; the appropriately-titled 'Movement' (1981) was their debut LP. The man who played the role of CURTIS, **Sam Riley** was once frontman for Leeds indie outfit, 10,000 Things, who released an eponymous set in April 2005 featuring the singles 'Food Chain' and 'Titanium'. *MCS*

—

Various Artists incl. JOY DIVISION ** (score: NEW ORDER *)

Oct 07. (cd) *Warners; (5051442 4478 2 8) Rhino; <333372>* ☐ ☐
– Exit (*) / What goes on (the VELVET UNDERGROUND) / Shadowplay (the KILLERS) / Boredom (live at the Roxy) (the BUZZCOCKS) / Dead souls (**) / She was naked (SUPERSISTER) / Sister midnight (IGGY POP) / Love will tear us apart (**) / Problems (live) (SEX PISTOLS) / Hypnosis (*) / Drive in Saturday (DAVID BOWIE) / Evidently chickentown (live) (JOHN COOPER CLARKE) / 2HB (ROXY MUSIC) / Transmission (cast version) (**) / Autobahn (KRAFTWERK) / Atmosphere (**) / Warszawa (DAVID BOWIE) / Get out (*).

S/track review: The story of Joy Division's fractious frontman comes to life via this inspired set of eclectic alt rock'n'roll. JOY DIVISION are here of course, five numbers in fact: 'Dead Souls' (from 'Unknown Pleasures'), the hit single 'Love Will Tear Us Apart', the cast/movie version of 'Transmission', the funereal 'Atmosphere' and the KILLERS' worthy take of 'Shadowplay'. Offshoot outfit, the recently disbanded NEW ORDER (featuring original JD members Bernard Sumner, Peter Hook & Stephen Morris), produce the score, actually only three exclusive short-ish cues, 'Exit', 'Hypnosis' and 'Get Out'. The rest of the album sees some Curtis favourites, first up two sides of the BOWIE coin, heads: the glam 'Drive In Saturday' and tails: the Eno experimental collaboration 'Warszawa'; the mainman's old punk mucker IGGY POP finds solace in 'Sister Midnight' (incidentally co-written with The Great White Duke himself!). Another Bowie cohort, Lou Reed, pops up with the VELVET UNDERGROUND on 'What Goes On', while the aforementioned Brian Eno adjusts the dials for early ROXY MUSIC via '2HB'. Seminal punk rock rears its ugly head courtesy of two live cuts, the SEX PISTOLS' 'Problems' and post-Devoto BUZZCOCKS on 'Boredom' – "bdm bdm". The humour – and you ask yourself why? – comes by way of Mancunian punk poet JOHN COOPER CLARKE (former beau of VU chanteuse Nico) and his all-too-brief "fucking" live recital of 'Evidently Chickentown'. On another tangent of sorts is 'Autobahn' by German men machines KRAFTWERK; we're spared the full version but it still clocks in at double figures. Surprise package is undoubtably 'She Was Naked' by early 70s psych-progsters SUPERSISTER (fronted by Dutchman, Robert Jan Stips), a fave of Stephen Morris no less. One thinks IC might be quite pleased with 'CONTROL' the soundtrack, while the album is dedicated to the recently deceased guru/manager Tony Wilson, one of the original 24 Hour Party People – R.I.P. 1980 & 2007. *MCS*

Album rating: *7.5

COOL AS ICE

1991 (US 100m) Universal Pictures (PG)

Film genre: romantic biker drama

Top guns: dir: David Kellogg / s-w: David Stenn

Stars: Vanilla Ice *(Johnny Van Owen)* → BETTY BLOWTORCH AND HER AMAZING TRUE LIFE ADVENTURES → the BROS., Kristin Minter *(Kathy Winslow)*, John Haymes Newton *(Nick)*, Candy Clark *(Grace Winslow)*, Michael Gross *(Gordon Winslow)*, Sidney Lassick *(Roscoe McCallister)*, **Deezer D** *(Jazz)* → CB4: THE MOVIE → FEAR OF A BLACK HAT → BONES → IN THE MIX, Naomi Campbell *(singer)* → GIRL 6, Dody Goodman *(Mae McCallister)* ← GREASE 2 ← GREASE, Candy Clark *(Grace Winslow)* ← MORE AMERICAN GRAFFITI ← AMERICAN GRAFFITI

Storyline: So awful it's good, this teen rebel flick sees VANILLA ICE starring as Johnny, a bike gang leader, in a "Rebel Without A Cause"-with-rappers remake. While out riding with his gang, Johnny spies a beautiful young woman on a horse and unintentionally causes her to take a tumble when he jumps a fence to meet her. She later forgives him at the local barn dance when he pulls the plug on the band and does his rap thang. Their burgeoning romance is forbidden by the girl's father who thinks Johnny is part of a gang trying to recover money he owes them. When the gang kidnap the girl's brother, Johnny and his bike go to the rescue. *KM*

Movie rating: *2

Visual: video

Off the record: White rapper, **Vanilla Ice** (b. Robert Van Winkle, 31 Oct'68, Miami Lakes, Florida) first splashed on to the scene via his 'Under Pressure'-sampled chart-topper, 'Ice Ice Baby'. **Deezer D** (was a Christian rapper). *MCS*

—

Various Artists (incl. VANILLA ICE *) (score: STANLEY CLARKE **)

Oct 91. (cd/c/lp) *S.B.K.; <K2/K4 97722> (SBK CD/MC/LP 16)* 89 Jan92 ☐
– Cool as ice (everybody get loose) (* feat. NAOMI CAMPBELL) / Gonna catch you (LONNIE GORDON) / You've got to look up (DEREK B) / Love 2 love U (PARTNERS IN KRYME feat. DEBBE COLE) / The people's choice (*) / Never wanna be without you (*) / Forever (D'NEW feat. TEMPLE) / Faith (ROZALLA) / Drop that zero (**) / Get wit' it (*).

S/track review: NAOMI CAMPBELL will be thankful she didn't give up the day job following her bewildering cameo as the unconvincing soul diva on 'Cool As Ice (Everybody Get Loose)'. Her solitary four lines unwisely looped and pasted throughout the duet with regrettable frequency while the on par VANILLA ICE holds things together with a solid rap performance on what could otherwise have been a big hit back in 1991. ICE then turns slush puppy, unwittingly exposing his limitations as he tunelessly whispers his way through the banal love song 'Never Wanna Be Without You'. Returning to what he's good at, ICE pulls off another funky recital about how amazing he is in 'The Peoples Choice' before closing the album with the inspired 'Get Wit' It' which, save the appalling backing vocals (again!), had many of the merits of ICE's contemporaries, like NWA's classy samples and pounding bass. Sadly, despite what he might have claimed, ICE lacked the genuine anger or real life experience to make music or lyrics as good as the aforementioned group and his rap credentials were exposed and discredited shortly before this film's release causing it and the soundtrack to be a commercial flop. However, with a mixture of good pop and soul hits like, ROZALLA's 'Faith' and LONNIE GORDON's 'Gonna Catch You' filling the large space left by ICE's miserly four contributions, this album sounds more like an antiquated cassette sampler you might have found free on the cover of Smash Hits 20 years or so ago rather than a bona fide VANILLA ICE album. *KM*

Album rating: *3

– spinoff hits, etc. –

VANILLA ICE feat. NAOMI CAMPBELL: Cool As Ice (Everybody Get Loose) / (version)

Oct 91. (c-s) *<07369>* 81 –

the COOL ONES

1967 (US 98m) Warner Bros. Pictures

Film genre: Pop-Rock Musical comedy

Top guns: s-w: Gene Nelson (+ dir) ← HARUM SCARUM ← YOUR CHEATIN' HEART ← KISSIN' COUSINS ← HOOTENANNY HOOT, Robert Kaufman ← SKI PARTY, Joyce Geller

Stars: Roddy McDowall *(Tony Krum)* ← the SUBTERRANNEANS / → HELLO DOWN THERE → ANGEL, ANGEL, DOWN WE GO → MEAN JOHNNY BARROWS → CLASS OF 1984, Debbie Watson *(Hallie Rogers)*, Gil Peterson *(Cliff Donner)*, Phil Harris *(MacElwaine)* → ROCK-A-DOODLE, Robert Coote *(Stan)*, Nita Talbot *(Dee Dee)* ← GIRL HAPPY, **Mrs. Miller** *(performer)*, Jim Begg *(Charlie)* → IT'S A BIKINI WORLD → CATALINA CAPER → DEATH WISH II, James Millhollin *(manager)* ← GET YOURSELF A COLLEGE GIRL, **Glen CAMPBELL** *(Patrick)*, **the Bantams** *(performers)*, **the Four Forte:- Ernie Earnshaw, Dan Anthony, Guy Watson, John Case Schaeffer II** *(performers)*, **the Leaves** *(performers)*, Teri Garr *(Hallie's friend)* ← ROUSTABOUT ← PAJAMA PARTY ← the T.A.M.I. SHOW ← VIVA LAS VEGAS ← KISSIN' COUSINS ← FUN IN ACAPULCO / → CLAMBAKE → HEAD → ONE FROM THE HEART

Storyline: Rich entrepreneur/manager, Tony Krum, finds pop music promotion an ordeal until he finds a romantic boy/girl duo in Cliff and Hallie, the latter a go-go dancer. *MCS*

Movie rating: *3

Visual: video (no audio OST)

Off the record: **Mrs. Miller** (b. Elva Ruby Connes, 5 Oct 1907, Joplin, Missouri – d. 28 Jun'97, Claremont, California) was an unusual choice for inclusion; she was a classically-trained tone-deaf singer whose operatic singing found a novelty niche in 1966 with US Top 20 LP, 'Mrs. Miller's Greatest Hits'; she sings 'It's Magic' in the film. Not much is known about **the Four Forte + the Bantams**, while **the Leaves** were the folk-rock group from L.A. famous for having a massive US hit with 'Hey Joe' (also covered by Jimi Hendrix). **Glen CAMPBELL** was better known for his country singing and his major role & soundtrack work on 'NORWOOD' (1970); he sings 'Just One Of Those Things', while 'Secret Love' is by Gil Peterson. Other songs in the film – mainly by Gil and Debbie – include, 'The Cool Ones', 'A Bad Woman's Love', 'High', 'The Tantrum', 'Whiz Bam Opener', 'This Town', 'Up Your Totem Pole With Love' and 'Where Did I Go Wrong?'; Ernie Freeman was the composer. *MCS*

COTTON CANDY

aka Ron Howard's COTTON CANDY

1978 (US TV 97m) Ron Howard & Major H Productions / NBC-TV

Film genre: Pop-Rock Musical comedy/drama

Top guns: s-w: (+ dir) Ron Howard, Clint Howard

Stars: Kevin Lee Miller *(Barry Bates)*, Leslie E. King *(Brenda Matthews)*, Charles Martin Smith *(George Smalley)* ← the BUDDY HOLLY STORY ← AMERICAN GRAFFITI ← PAT GARRETT & BILLY THE KID / → MORE AMERICAN GRAFFITI → TRICK OR TREAT, Manuel Padilla Jr. *(Julio Sanchez)* ← AMERICAN GRAFFITI / → MORE AMERICAN GRAFFITI, Clint Howard *(Corky MacPherson)* → ROCK'N'ROLL HIGH SCHOOL → GET CRAZY → THAT THING YOU DO! → CURIOUS GEORGE

Storyline: A group of geeky high school students decide to form a band which they name Cotton Candy. However, they soon find themselves in competition with their classmates' much more hip rock band, Rapid Fire. Lessons take a back seat as the groups vie for supremacy and at the annual Battle of the Bands competition (held in the local shopping mall of all places) the rivalry between the groups reaches its peak. *JZ*

Movie rating: *5

Visual: video (no audio OST)

Off the record: Clint Howard, is the older brother of former 'Happy Days' actor turned director, Ron Howard. *MCS*

the COUNTRY BEARS

2002 (US 88m) Gunn Films / Walt Disney

Film genre: children's/family musical comedy

Top guns: dir: Peter Hastings / s-w: Mark Perez

Stars: Haley Joel Osment *(voice; Beary Barrington)*, Diedrich Bader *(voice; Ted Bedderhead / officer Cheets)*, Candy Ford *(voice; Trixie St. Clair)*, James Gammon *(voice; Big Al)* ← URBAN COWBOY / → COLD MOUNTAIN, Brad Garrett *(voice; Fred Bedderhead)* → MUSIC AND LYRICS, Toby Huss *(voice; Tennessee O'Neal)* ← CLUBLAND ← the BASKETBALL DIARIES, Kevin Michael Richardson *(voice; Henry Dixon Taylor)*, Stephen Root *(voice; Zeb Zoober)* ← O BROTHER, WHERE ART THOU?, Christopher Walken *(Reed Thimple)* ← TOUCH ← LAST MAN STANDING ← PULP FICTION ← WAYNE'S WORLD 2 ← HOMEBOY / → ROMANCE & CIGARETTES → HAIRSPRAY re-make, Stephen Tobolowsky *(Norbert Barrington)* ← ROADSIDE PROPHETS ← GREAT BALLS OF FIRE! / → the INSIDER, **Daryl "Chill" Mitchell** *(officer Hamm)* ← FLY BY NIGHT ← HOUSE PARTY 2 ← HOUSE PARTY, M.C. Gainey *(roadie)*, Eli Marienthal *(Dex Barrington)* ← FIRST LOVE, LAST RITES, **Queen Latifah** *(Cha-Cha)* ← WHO'S THE MAN? ← JUICE ← HOUSE PARTY 2 ← JUNGLE FEVER / → BROWN SUGAR → HAIRSPRAY re-make, **Jennifer Paige** *(waitress)*, **Krystal Marie Harris** *(herself)*, **Don Henley** *(himself / singing voice; Tennessee)*, **Bonnie RAITT** *(herself / singing voice; Trixie)*, **E.G. Daily** *(herself / singing voice; Beary)* ← STREETS OF FIRE ← LADIES AND GENTLEMEN, THE FABULOUS STAINS / → the DEVIL'S REJECTS, **John Hiatt** *(himself / singing voice; Ted Bedderhead)*, **Wyclef Jean** *(himself)* ← CARMEN: A HIP HOPERA ← RHYME & REASON / → BE COOL → BLOCK PARTY, **Xzibit** *(himself)* ← 8 MILE ← the WASH, **Brian Setzer** *(himself)* ← WOODSTOCK '99 ← LA BAMBA, **Elton JOHN** *(himself)*, **Don Was** *(himself)* ← STANDING IN THE SHADOWS OF MOTOWN, **Willie NELSON** *(himself)*, **Colin Hay** *(singing voice)*, **Brian Dresel** *(drummer)*

Storyline: Beary Barrington is an adolescent orphan brought up by humans after being abandoned in the forest. He decides to head to Tennessee to trace his real parents and at the same time resurrect his favourite, long defunct band the Country Bears. He finds one of the band members who tells him that the Country Bear Hall will be demolished unless the money can be found to save it from greedy banker Reed Thimple. With the cops hot on his tail, Beary must organise a Country Bears reunion concert to save the day. *JZ*

Movie rating: *3.5

Visual: dvd

Off the record: A star's paradise here – too numerous to mention any or all.

Various Artists/Cast (score: CHRIS YOUNG *)

Jul 02. (cd) *Disney; <86774>* 100 –
– Let it ride (JOHN HIATT) / Where nobody knows my name (JOHN HIATT) / Can love stand the test (DON HENLEY & BONNIE RAITT) / The kid in you (KRYSTAL MARIE HARRIS) / I'm only in it for the honey (BRIAN SETZER '68 COMEBACK SPECIAL w/ STEPHEN ROOT) / Kick it into gear (JENNIFER PAIGE) / Straight to the heart of love – live (JOHN HIATT w/ E.G. DAILY, COLIN HAY, DON HENLEY, BONNIE RAITT) / Bear mountain hop (BELA FLECK) / Just the goin' (JOHN HIATT) / Where nobody knows my name – reprise (E.G. DAILY) / So you want to be a rock'n'roll star (the BYRDS) / Friends (ELTON JOHN) / Bearly home (*) / Nylon hymn (*).

S/track review: An array of hidden talent (in furry bear-suits it seems) feature on this star-studded, Disney musical spectacular. Daddy Bear is country-roots-rocker, JOHN HIATT, who contributes several songs to the soundtrack, three of them solo: 'Let It Ride', 'Just The Goin' and the boogie-ing, Canned Heat-esque 'Where Nobody Knows My Name'; the last of these gets kid-friendly by actress/singer E.G. DAILY. If you like your honky tonk stripped "bear", this album might just shake your tree, although not with the same bite of southern boys, 'Skynyrd or ZZ. The pace slows somewhat for the BONNIE RAITT/DON HENLEY love ballad/

duet, 'Can Love Stand The Test', while both singers combine with HIATT, DAILY and COLIN HAY (of Men At Work fame) for a live all-star rendition of 'Straight To The Heart Of Love'. Follow-on BELA FLECK twang-fest instrumental, the Grammy-nominated 'Bear Mountain Hop', is a meeting of Pure Prairie League vs. Barefoot Jerry, while ex-Stray Cat BRIAN SETZER and Co showcase neo-rockabilly via the corny, 'I'm Only In It For The Honey'. To show you didn't have to be a southern COUNTRY BEAR to feature, the soundtrack also gets down, deep and funky with diva KRYSTAL MARIE HARRIS' 'The Kid In You'; it gets worse when the country-pop diva doesn't quite 'Kick It Into Gear' as the song title suggested. And just why the inclusion of the BYRDS' timeless classic 'So You Want To Be A Rock'n'Roll Star' and ELTON's 'Friends', surely both incidental to the kids under ten. Score composer, CHRIS YOUNG, finally gets his respective two-pennorth in via a couple of uptempo and sombre instrumentals. OK, I've certainly heard worse. *MCS*

Album rating: *5

COUNTRY MUSIC HOLIDAY

1958 (US 81m b&w) Aurora / Paramount Pictures

Film genre: er.. Country-music drama

Top guns: dir: Alvin Ganzer → WHEN THE BOYS MEET THE GIRLS / s-w: H.B. Cross

Stars: **Ferlin Husky** *(Pvt. Verne Brand)* ← MISTER ROCK AND ROLL / → LAS VEGAS HILLBILLYS → HILLBILLYS IN A HAUNTED HOUSE → THAT'S COUNTRY, **June Carter Cash** *(Marietta)* → ROAD TO NASHVILLE → the MAN, HIS WORLD, HIS MUSIC → JOHNNY CASH AT SAN QUENTIN → GOSPEL ROAD → THAT'S COUNTRY, Jesse White *(Sonny Moon)* → LOOKING FOR LOVE → PAJAMA PARTY → the GHOST IN THE INVISIBLE BIKINI → NASHVILLE GIRL, Al Fisher *(himself)* ← MISTER ROCK AND ROLL ← DON'T KNOCK THE ROCK, Lou Marks *(Sgt. Lou Marks)* ← MISTER ROCK AND ROLL, Rocky Graziano *(Rocky)* ← MISTER ROCK AND ROLL / → TEENAGE MILLIONAIRE, Zsa Zsa Gabor *(Zsa Zsa)*, Rod Brasfield *(Pappy Brand)*, **Faron Young** *(Clyde Woods)* → NASHVILLE REBEL → SECOND FIDDLE TO A STEEL GUITAR → WHAT AM I BID? → ROAD TO NASHVILLE, Patty Duke *(Sis Brand)*, Cliff Norton *(Morty Chapman)* → FRANKIE AND JOHNNY, **the Jordanaires** *(performers)* → G.I. BLUES → KID GALAHAD, **La Dell Sisters** *(performers)*, **Drifting Johnny Miller** *(performer)*, **Lonzo & Oscar** *(performers)*

Storyline: Verne Brand is a hillbilly singer whose talents go a lot further than homespun hoedowns. He's spotted by agent Sonny Moon who launches his professional career, but Verne needn't say bye y'all to Pappy, Ma and Sis just yet because Hungarian Zsa Zsa owns half his contract and she's out to cause trouble. Can Verne fight his way to the top of the haybale or is he just a straw man? *JZ*

Movie rating: *2.5

Visual: none (no audio OST)

Off the record: Songs featured in the film, number 'Wang Dang Doo', 'Albuquerque', 'Terrific Together', 'Goodbye My Darlin'', 'Ninety Nine Percent', 'Don't Walk Away From Me', 'Little Miss Ruby' & 'My Home Town'.

COUNTRYMAN

1982 (Jama 102m) Island Pictures (R)

Film genre: jungle adventure/drama

Top guns: s-w: Dickie Jobson (+ dir), Michael Thomas → BACKBEAT

Stars: Hiram Keller *(Bobby Lloyd / Countryman)* ← LIFESPAN, Carl Bradshaw *(Capt. Benchley)* ← the HARDER THEY COME / → CLUB PARADISE → KLA$H → DANCEHALL QUEEN → ONE LOVE, Basil Keane *(Colonel Sinclair)* ← the HARDER THEY COME, Freshey Richardson *(Mosman)*, Kristina St. Clair *(Beau Porter)*, Jahman *(himself)*, Ronnie McKay *(Wax)*

Storyline: The dreadlocked dude known only as Countryman lives a solitary, righteous life until the rude arrival of an American couple. After crashlanding in a jungle swamp, Countryman has them partake of the weed as he hides them from Jamaican authorities duped into believing that the plane was commandeered by the opposition party in cahoots with the CIA. *BG*

Movie rating: *7

Visual: video

Off the record: nothing really

—

Various Artists (incl. BOB MARLEY & THE WAILERS *) (score: WALLY BADAROU **)

May 82. (d-lp/c) *Island: (ISTDA/ZISTDA 1)* ☐ [-]

– Natural mystic (*) / Rastaman chant (*) / Theme from Countryman (**) / Rat race (*) / Jah live (*) / Ramble (RICO) / Rebel music (3 o'clock roadblock) (*) / Sound system (STEEL PULSE) / Mosman skank (ASWAD) / Small axe (*) / Sitting and watching (DENNIS BROWN) / Bam bam (TOOTS AND THE MAYTALS) / Ooh! aah! (FABULOUS 5) / Wisdom (JAH LION) / Carry us beyond (HUMAN CARGO) / Dreadlocks in moonlight (LEE "SCRATCH" PERRY) / Time will tell (*) / Theme from Countryman ** (REBOP KWAKU BAAH) / Pass it on (*) / Guidance (**) / Obeah man dub (**) / Theme from Countryman (**). *<US cd-iss. 1992 on 'Mango'; 16253 9001-2> (UK cd-iss. May94 on 'Refreshers'; RRCD 44)*

S/track review: 'COUNTRYMAN' couldn't hope to loot'n'shoot its way into the Jamaican zeitgeist as stylishly as 'The HARDER THEY COME' (1972), but it's still a great soundtrack, part alternative WAILERS anthology, part early 80s 'Island' sampler. Most of MARLEY's 70s albums get a look-in, with the pressure on the rootsier tracks rather than the hits which made up 'Legend' (1984). Conscious totems like 'Natural Mystic', 'Jah Live', 'Small Axe' and the hymnal 'Rastaman Chant' are coconut bread and butter to most reggae fans, and it's great to hear the folky 'Time Will Tell' (later covered by the Black Crowes of all people). But it's the ubiquitous LEE PERRY who's really in the jungle groove. His mesmeric production on JAH LION's 'Wisdom' out-mysticises anything here, a gooseflesh scroll spoken in tongues. He also sneaks into the credits of the aforementioned 'Jah Live', and makes the tracklist with his own 'Dreadlocks In Moonlight'. The mighty RICO's 'Ramble' acknowledges the debt to ska, but some of the (excellent) cuts from the less famous artists – ASWAD, HUMAN CARGO – as well as WALLY BADAROU's title theme, are the sound of reggae at the nexus of 80s technology and 70s roots/dub legacy. BADAROU's electro-nyahbingi-meets-Jan Hammer theme stretches the definition of the genre, and compromises itself with annoying film dialogue, but it's an interesting experiment. *BG*

Album rating: *8

COYOTE UGLY

2000 (US 100m) Touchstone Pictures (PG-13)

Film genre: urban/coming-of-age comedy drama

Top guns: dir: David McNally / s-w: Gina Wendkos ← GINGER ALE AFTERNOON

Stars: Piper Perabo *(Violet Sanford)* ← WHITEBOYS, Adam Garcia *(Kevin McDonnell)*, Maria Bello *(Lil)* → DUETS, John Goodman *(Bill)* ← O BROTHER, WHERE ART THOU? ← BLUES BROTHERS 2000 ← TRUE STORIES ← SWEET DREAMS / → the EMPEROR'S NEW GROOVE → STORYTELLING → MASKED AND ANONYMOUS → OVERNIGHT →

BEYOND THE SEA, Melanie Lynskey *(Gloria)* ← DETROIT ROCK CITY, Izabella Miko *(Cammie)* → BYE BYE BLACKBIRD → SAVE THE LAST DANCE 2, Bridget Moynahan *(Rachel)*, Tyra Banks *(Zoe)*, Del Pentacost *(Lou the bouncer)* ← O BROTHER, WHERE ART THOU?, Michael Weston *(Danny)*, **LeAnn Rimes** *(performer)* ← DILL SCALLION, Victor Argo *(Pete)* ← GHOST DOG: THE WAY OF THE SAMURAI ← the LAST TEMPTATION OF CHRIST ← the ROSE, Bud Cort *(Romero)* ← the MILLION DOLLAR HOTEL ← SOUTH OF HEAVEN, WEST OF HELL ← ELECTRIC DREAMS ← HAROLD AND MAUDE ← GAS-S-S-S ← BREWSTER McCLOUD ← the STRAWBERRY STATEMENT / → the LIFE AQUATIC WITH STEVE ZISSOU, Freeze Luv *(Fiji Mermaid bouncer)* ← JACKIE'S BACK! ← MURDER WAS THE CASE ← HOUSE PARTY 3, Johnny Knoxville *(college guy)* → GRAND THEFT PARSONS

Storyline: Rags to no stitches drama as would-be singer-songwriter Violet Sanford gets her kit off for the bar in downtown New York. If Coyote Ugly was the name of a boozer in real life, it would probably be the worst named boozer in the world, but that's where Sanford gets in training for the life of a pop star, setting the bar on fire along with her tough chick colleagues on a nightly basis. *BG*

Movie rating: *5

Visual: dvd

Off the record: LeAnn Rimes was born 28th August, 1982, Jackson, Mississippi; raised in Garland, Texas. As a 14-year-old she signed a contract with 'Curb' records and immediately became a star overnight with such hits as 'Blue', 'How Do I Live' and a version of 'You Light Up My Life'. *MCS*

Various Artists (score: Trevor Horn)

Aug 00. (cd) *Curb; <78703> Curb-London; (8573 85254-2)* 10 Aug00 16
– Can't fight the moonlight (LeANN RIMES) / Please remember (LeANN RIMES) / The right kind of wrong (LeANN RIMES) / But I do love you (LeANN RIMES) / All she wants to do is dance (DON HENLEY) / Unbelievable (EMF) / The power (SNAP) / Need you tonight (INXS) / The Devil went down to Georgia (CHARLIE DANIELS BAND) / Boom boom boom (RARE BLEND) / Didn't we love (TAMARA WALKER) / We can get there (MARY GRIFFIN).

S/track review: She didn't earn a Grammy for it (she'd already scooped a Best New Artist award) but LeANN RIMES' UK No.1, 'Can't Fight The Moonlight' (Theme From 'Coyote Ugly') is so obviously the millennial equivalent of Bette Midler's 'Wind Beneath My Wings'. In its ultra-slick choreography and mini-me-diva phrasing, it suggests that the difference between contemporary country and Diane Warren-penned AOR-in-teen-clothing really doesn't amount to much. The soft rock ballad, 'Please Remember', is actually closer in substance to MIDLER's calling card, but it's that theme which updates the chick flick kleenex factor. Both 'But I Do Love You' and 'The Right Kind Of Wrong' pedal more of the same, shoring up her country chameleon careerism. Inevitably, the album also opportunistically pushes another couple of girly-friendly, 'Curb'-signed artistes: RIMES clone, TAMARA WALKER, and R&B diva, MARY GRIFFIN, but if you've made it that far you're probably due a Grammy yourself. After RIMES' front-loaded contributions, the album boldly plunges into the kind of vacuum-sucking synth territory DON HENLEY – and most Eagles fans – have doubtless long ago offered up to voluntary amnesia. Where 80s/90s oldies from SNAP, EMF and INXS – never mind CHARLIE DANIELS nugget, 'The Devil Went Down To Georgia' – fit into all this is ultimately a question only those behind the 'Flashdance'-meets-'Cocktail' farrago of a movie can answer. *BG*

Album rating: *4.5

– spinoff hits, etc. –

LeANN RIMES: Can't Fight The Moonlight

Aug 00. (c-s/cd-s) *<73116> (CUB C/CD 58)* 11 Nov00 1

Various Artists: More Music From . . .

Jan 03. (cd) *<78765> (5046 63931-2)* ☐ ☐
– One way or another (BLONDIE) / Rebel yell (BILLY IDOL) / Rock this town (the STRAY CATS) / Keep your hands to yourself (the GEORGIA SATELLITES) / Out of my head (FASTBALL) / Battle flag (PIGEONHED) / It takes two (ROB BASE & DJ EZ ROCK) / Love machine (the MIRACLES) / We can get there (MARY GRIFFIN) / Can't fight the moonlight (LeANN RIMES) / But I do love you (LeANN RIMES).

CRAZY

2006 (US 90m*) Favored Nations Crazy Film LLC

Film genre: Country-music bio-pic/drama

Top guns: s-w: (+ dir) Rick Bieber, Jason Ehlers, Brent Boyd

Stars: Waylon Payne *(Hank Garland)* ← WALK THE LINE, Ali Larter *(Evelyn Garland)*, Lane Garrison *(Billy Garland)*, Scott Michael Campbell *(Billy Byrd)*, David Conrad *(Ryan Bradford)*, John Fleck *(Lloyd "Cowboy" Copas)*, Tim Omundson *(Paul Howard)* ← SWORDFISH, Brent Briscoe *(Doug)* ← MAN ON THE MOON ← SLING BLADE, Mandy Barnett *(Patsy Cline)*, **Shawn Colvin** *(Kitty Wells)* ← GRACE OF MY HEART, Danny Bergen *(Ernest Tubb)*, Evans Forde *(Chet Atkins)*, Brad Hawkins *(Bobby Helms)* ← DON'T LET GO ← SHAKE, RATTLE AND ROLL: AN AMERICAN LOVE STORY, Brian Jones *(Roy Orbison)*, Jason Alan Smith *(Elvis Presley)*, **Steve Vai** *(Hank Williams)* ← CROSSROADS, Gerald Emerick *(Red Foley)*, **Larry Klein** ← SUGAR TOWN ← GRACE OF MY HEART

Storyline: Hank Garland joins the Grand Ol' Opry aged 15 and begins a glittering career as a songwriter/guitarist in Nashville. He soon finds that success brings its own problems and his wife Evelyn finds herself competing against his passion for his music. Artists like Roy Orbison, Elvis and Patsy Cline are all after Hank's recordings but his career is about to be tragically cut short at the height of his success. *JZ*

Movie rating: *7.5

Visual: dvd (no audio OST)

Off the record: Former Suzanne Vega backing singer, **Shawn Colvin** (b.10 Jan'58, Vermillion, South Dakota) was a one-hit wonder in 1996 with 'Sunny Came Home', a track taken from her only US Top 40 album, 'A Few Small Repairs'. Hard-rock axeman, **Steve Vai** (b. 6 Jun'60, Long Island, New York) was a journeyman of sorts who sidelined with FRANK ZAPPA (1979-84) and Whitesnake (in 1989), prior to releasing his only Top 20 album, 'Passion And Warfare' (1990). *MCS*

☐ CRAZY BABY alt.
(⇒ la BATTAGLIA DEI MODS)

CROCODILE SHOES

1994 (UK 55m x 7 epi TV-mini) BBC

Film genre: Roots/C&W-music drama

Top guns: dir: Robert Knights, Malcolm Mowbray, David Richards / s-w: **Jimmy NAIL**

Stars: Jimmy NAIL *(Jed Sheppard)*, Sammy Johnson *(Archie)* → CROCODILE SHOES II, Melanie Hill *(Emma Sheppard)* → CROCODILE SHOES II, Amy Madigan *(Carmel Cantrell)* ← ALAMO BAY ← PLACES IN THE HEART ← STREETS OF FIRE, James Wilby *(Ade Lynn)*, Burt Young *(Lou Benedetti)* ← LAST EXIT TO BROOKLYN ← ACROSS 110th STREET, Alex Kingston *(Caroline Carrison)*, Brian Capron *(Rex Hall)* → STILL CRAZY, Christopher Fairbank *(Alan Clark)* ← BATMAN / → CROCODILE SHOES II, Stuart Greer *(Pete)* → BIG DREAMS & BROKEN HEARTS: THE DOTTIE WEST STORY → ELVIS, John Bowler *(Pep)* -< CROCODILE SHOES II, **Nadeshda Brennicke** *(Roxanne)* → CROCODILE SHOES II, Robert Morgan *(Warren Bowles)* → CROCODILE SHOES II, Elizabeth Carling *(Wendy)* → CROCODILE SHOES II, Kenneth MacDonald *(McCluskey)* → CROCODILE SHOES II, Sara Stewart *(Lucy)*

Storyline: Jed Sheppard is a factory worker who dreams of becoming a famous singer-songwriter. On his rollercoaster road to success the country and western crooner has to contend with shady record producers from down south who reckon anyone with an accent like his must be soft in the head. Adventure and romance are never far away as Jed sings his way to stardom while avoiding the perils and pitfalls along the way. *JZ*

Movie rating: *6

Visual: video

Off the record: Nadeshda Brennicke played keyboards for German popsters, Munchner Freiheit.

JIMMY NAIL

Nov 94. (cd/c) *East West; (<4509 98556-2/-4>)* [2] Mar95 [ ]
– Crocodile shoes / Calling out your name / Cowboy dreams / Once upon a time / Only one heart / Bitter and twisted / Love will find someone for you / Angel / Between a woman and a man / Don't wanna go home / Dragons.

S/track review: 'Crocodile Shoes' (the track) is an amiable enough beginning with its plodding minor-key Nashville country. A UK No.2, the single successfully launched the TV series and accompanying album, but is ultimately let down by JIMMY NAIL's straining and uncomfortably high vocals. Meanwhile, 'Calling Out Your Name' and 'Angel' are inoffensive and uncomplicated strum-a-longs that recall a time when Mike & The Mechanics ruled the airwaves. 'Cowboy Dreams' takes the easy going Eagles sound as a template and drifts by without notable impact, like much here, whilst 'Once Upon A Time' sees NAIL ditch his slightly embarrassing and inauthentic country crooning for a more Celtic traditional sound. Unfortunately, 'Only One Heart' is an out of place sub-Disney big ballad, so slick it will make you sick and similarly, 'Love Will Find Someone For You' is so poor you might consider giving it your spare change. 'Between A Woman And A Man' is a better stab at a love song due largely to a well used string section, before 'Angel' returns the album to its rightful MOR place and things are rounded off with a surprising twist with the pleasant pop of 'Dragons' which could easily have been lifted from Sting's ultra-successful 'Ten Summoners' Tales'. It's hard to hate this soundtrack as it was clearly not as cynically constructed as most TV tie-ins, and it's delivered in a harmlessly heartfelt manner by the affable big Geordie. That said, however, it doesn't disguise the fact that this is a patchy, unimaginative and peculiarly sentimental collection that doesn't linger long in the memory and suffers from being tiresomely hung up on painting NAIL as some kind of downtrodden cowboy. *LF*

Album rating: *5

– spinoff hits & releases, etc. –

JIMMY NAIL: Crocodile Shoes / Calling Out Your Name (Jed's demo)

Nov 94. (c-s) *(YZ 867C)* [4] [–]
(cd-s+=) *(YZ 867CD)* – Once Upon A Time (Jed's demo).

JIMMY NAIL: Cowboy Dreams / Bitter And Twisted (Jed's demo).

Feb 95. (7"/c-s) *(YZ 878/+C)* [13] [–]
(cd-s+=) *(YZ 878CD)* – Don't Wanna Go Home (Jed's demo).

JIMMY NAIL: Calling Out Your Name / Fear No Evil

Apr 95. (7"/c-s) *(YZ 935/+C)* [65] [–]
(cd-s+=) *(YZ 935CD)* – ('A'-radio remix).

JIMMY NAIL: Only One Heart / Angel

Jun 95. (7"/c-s) *(YZ 949/+C)* [ ] [–]
(cd-s+=) *(YZ 949CD)* – Between A Woman And A Man.

CROCODILE SHOES II

1996 (UK 50m x 7 epi TV-mini) BBC

Film genre: Roots/C&W-music comedy drama

Top guns: dir: Roger Bamford, Baz Taylor / s-w: Nick Mead → SWING, **Jimmy NAIL**

Stars: Jimmy NAIL *(Jed Sheppard)*, Melanie Hill *(Emma Sheppard)* ← CROCODILE SHOES, Sammy Johnson *(Archie)* ← CROCODILE SHOES, Christopher Fairbank *(Alan Clark)* ← CROCODILE SHOES, John Bowler *(Pep)* ← CROCODILE SHOES, Nadeshda Brennicke *(Roxanne)* ← CROCODILE SHOES, Robert Morgan *(Warren Bowles)* ← CROCODILE SHOES, Elizabeth Carling *(Wendy)* ← CROCODILE SHOES, Kenneth MacDonald *(Detective Inspector McCluskey)* ← CROCODILE SHOES, Marcus Hutton *(Alan Morton)*

Storyline: Unlikely working-class hero, Jed Sheppard, returns with a few more tales of woe and fascination, as the man tries his damnedest to succeed in the bigger, wider world outside Geordieland. *MCS*

Movie rating: *6

Visual: video

Off the record: Sadly, Gateshead-born Sammy Johnson – one-time musician with Pigmeat, among others – subsequently died of a heart attack while out jogging in Malaga, Spain, 1998. *MCS*

JIMMY NAIL

Nov 96. (cd/c) *East West; (<0630 16935-2/-4>)* [10] Jan97 [ ]
– Country boy / Blue roses / Running man / Fear no evil / I'm a troubled man / My buddy / Gentle's lament / Still I dream of it / Just can't win / Until the day I die / I refuse to lie down.

S/track review: With JIMMY NAIL buoyed by two years of constant chart success, 'CROCODILE SHOES II' tries to take off from where its predecessor left, whilst at the same time trying to embellish the formula with a bit of anthemics on the cringingly rubbish 'Country Boy'. But this largely forgettable follow-up is basically a rushed cash-in with its tried-and-tested, watered down imitation of the first soundtrack. 'Blue Roses' is so insipid a ballad that it could be mistaken for Chris De Burgh's 'Lady In Red', whilst the plaintive and earnest 'I'm A Troubled Man' falls way short of its emotive ambition and will have you banging your head against the wall, or simply skipping forward to the equally unpleasant 'Gentle's Lament' which is shrill and calamitous, like a shit-kicking version of Black Lace's 'Agadoo'. 'Still I Dream Of It' is an American style big ballad, delivered in a horrible trans-Atlantic voice, saved in part by its cynical lyrics, and whilst 'Just Can't Win' shares similar lyrical themes it actually manages to stir up a decent pub-rock-meets-Van Morrison jam. 'Running Man' is about the only track that successfully captures the breezy and inoffensive feel of its passable parent album, before 'Until The Day I Die' returns us to horrible ballad territory all too soon on an album that can't be over quick enough. *LF*

Album rating: *3

– spinoff hits, etc. –

JIMMY NAIL: Country Boy / Until The Day I Die / Just Can't Win

Nov 96. (c-s/cd-s) *(EW 070 C/CD)* [25] [–]

CROOKLYN

1994 (US 112m) 40 Acres & A Mule / Universal Pictures (PG-13)

Film genre: urban comedy drama

Top guns: s-w: Spike Lee (+ dir) as below + → HE GOT GAME, Joie Lee, Cinque Lee

Stars: Alfre Woodard *(Carolyn Carmichael)* → the SINGING DETECTIVE → TAKE THE LEAD, Delroy Lindo *(Woody Carmichael)* ← MORE AMERICAN GRAFFITI, David Patrick Kelly *(Jim)* ← the CROW ← WILD AT HEART ← the ADVENTURES OF FORD FAIRLANE / → HEAVY → LAST MAN STANDING, Zelda Harris *(Troy)* → HE GOT GAME, Carlton Williams *(Clinton)*, Sharif Rashed *(Wendell)*, Spike Lee *(Snuffy)* ← JUNGLE FEVER ← SCHOOL DAZE / → GIRL 6, Joie Lee *(Aunt Maxine)* ← SCHOOL DAZE / → GIRL 6 → COFFEE AND CIGARETTES, Isaiah Washington *(Vic)*, **RuPaul** *(Bodega woman)*, Arthur French *(West Indian store manager)*, Vondie Curtis-Hall *(Uncle Brown)* ← the MAMBO KINGS ← MYSTERY TRAIN / → TURN IT UP, Frances Foster *(Aunt Song)*, Bokeem Woodbine *(Richard)* → RAY

Storyline: Laughter and sadness in equal measure as the Carmichaels struggle to cope with life in a Brooklyn brownstone. Dad Woody is a musician who gave up the money for serious stuff (income = 0). Mum Carolyn therefore is the breadwinner which she just about manages, apart from the odd nervous breakdown. Meanwhile their several dozen children are rogues and rascals and the neighbours weird and wonderful. Ring any bells? *JZ*

Movie rating: *6.5

Visual: video + dvd

Off the record: **RuPaul** (b. RuPaul Andre Charles, 17 Nov'60, San Diego, California) was a black male transvestite who had a minor hit with 'Supermodel'.

—

Various Artists (score: Terence Blanchard)

May 94. (cd) *M.C.A.; <(MCD 11036)>* [59] Jun94 [ ]
– Crooklyn (CROOKLYN DODGERS) / Respect yourself (the STAPLE SINGERS) / Everyday people (SLY & THE FAMILY STONE) / Pusher man (CURTIS MAYFIELD) / Thin line between love and hate (the PERSUADERS) / El pito (I'll never go back to Georgia) (JOE CUBA) / ABC (the JACKSON 5) / Oh girl (CHI-LITES) / Mighty love (SPINNERS) / Mr. Big stuff (JEAN KNIGHT) / O-o-h child (the FIVE STAIRSTEPS) / Pass the peas (JB's) / Time has come today (the CHAMBERS BROTHERS) / People make the world go round (MARC DORSEY).

S/track review: Spike Lee took inspiration from one of the other great New York storytellers Martin Scorsese in realising the power of pop music in movie making. 'CROOKLYN' was a fairly insignificant film in the Spike Lee canon but the soundtrack is right up there, mixing old school classics to bring out a vivid picture of 70s black America in this most celebrated of New York Boroughs. 'Crooklyn' by CROOKLYN DODGERS is an incongruous start though, a snappy slice of mid-90s East Coast rap that enjoys some nice production but lacks a lyrical spark. From there on in we head back to the past as the STAPLE SINGERS' 'Respect Yourself' heralds half a dozen absolute diamond tunes. 'Everyday People' by SLY AND THE FAMILY STONE . . . 'Pusherman' by CURTIS MAYFIELD . . . 'Thin Line Between Love And Hate' by the PERSUADERS . . . 'ABC' by the JACKSON 5 – come on people, it doesn't get much better than this. You can almost hear the burr of tight corduroy, the rustle of a polyester shirt the music is so evocative of its era. We can pop out to grab a cold one while the oldies head to the floor for the CHI-LITES and the SPINNERS but be back in time for the crucial magic of JEAN KNIGHT's mighty 'Mr Big Stuff'. The bottom line is we could go home sated but there's still the righteous 'Time Has Come Today' by the CHAMBERS BROTHERS. If you forget the sloppy contemporary closer tacked on for the credits you've got the perfect summer mixtape. And then there's ' . . . Volume II'. Wow! *MR*

Album rating: *8.5 / Volume II *7

– spinoff releases, etc. –

the CROOKLYN DODGERS: Crooklyn / (instrumental)
May 94. (c-s/cd-s) *<54837>* [60] [–]

Various Artists: Crooklyn – Volume II
Oct 94. (cd) *<MCD 11065>* [ ] [–]
– People make the world go round (the STYLISTICS) / Signed, sealed, delivered I'm yours (STEVIE WONDER) / Bra (CYMANDE) / I'm stone in love with you (the STYLISTICS) / Everybody is a star (SLY & THE FAMILY STONE) / Never can say goodbye (the JACKSON 5) / Soul power (JAMES BROWN) / Soul makossa (MANU DIBANGO) / La la (means I love you) (the DELFONICS) / I'll take you there (the STAPLE SINGERS) / Puerto Rico (EDDIE PALMIERI) / Theme from Shaft (ISAAC HAYES) / The tears of a clown (SMOKEY ROBINSON & THE MIRACLES) / I can see clearly now (JOHNNY NASH).

CROSSROADS

1986 (US 100m) Columbia Pictures (R)

Film genre: coming-of-age/road movie/drama

Top guns: dir: Walter Hill ← the LONG RIDERS ← STREETS OF FIRE / → JOHNNY HANDSOME → TRESPASS → GERONIMO: AN AMERICAN LEGEND → LAST MAN STANDING / s-w: John Fusco → YOUNG GUNS II → SPIRIT: STALLION OF THE CIMARRON

Stars: Ralph Macchio *(Eugene Martone)*, Joe Seneca *(Willie Brown)* → SCHOOL DAZE, Jami Gertz *(Frances)*, Joe Morton *(Scratch's assistant)* → BLUES BROTHERS 2000 → STEALTH, Robert Judd *(Scratch)*, **Steve Vai** *(Jack Butler)* → CRAZY, Dennis Lipscomb *(Lloyd)*, Allan Arbus *(Dr. Santis)* ← COFFY ← HEY, LET'S TWIST, Tim Russ *(Robert Johnson)*, Wally Taylor *(O.Z.)* ← LORD SHANGO ← SHAFT'S BIG SCORE! ← COOL BREEZE ← COTTON COMES TO HARLEM, Harry Carey Jr. *(bartender)* ← the LONG RIDERS, **Arnold McCuller** *(guitar duel sequence singer #3)* ← AMERICAN HOT WAX / → BEACHES → DUETS, Royce Wallace *(hotel proprietress)* ← WILLIE DYNAMITE ← COOL BREEZE ← GOODBYE, COLUMBUS, Gretchen Palmer *(beautiful dancer)* ← FAST FORWARD

Storyline: Celebrated re-imagining of the evergreen Robert Johnson legend with young guitar whizz Eugene Martone eager to uncover a mythical blues song long lost to history. He duly enlists the help of grizzled blues legend Willie Brown, a contemporary of the song's original author and a man with his own diabolical interests in the pair's subsequent road trip. *BG*

Movie rating: *6

Visual: video + dvd

Off the record: "Real" guitar virtuoso (and ex-ZAPPA axeman and hit soloist with 'Passion And Warfare'), **Steve Vai**, subsequently scored the music to the 1994 feature, 'PCU'. *MCS*

—

RY COODER

May 86. (lp/c) *Reprise; <(9 25399-1/-4)>* [85] Jul86 [ ]
– Crossroads / Down in Mississippi / Cotton needs pickin' / Viola Lee blues / See you in Hell, blind boy / Nitty gritty Mississippi / He made a woman out of me / Feel it (bad blues) / Somebody's callin' my name / Willie Brown blues / Walkin' away blues. *<(cd-iss. Oct91; 9 25399-2)>*

S/track review: The most popular of COODER's soundtracks in his pre-'BUENA VISTA' days (alongside 'PARIS, TEXAS'), 'CROSSROADS' is not necessarily his best. Occasionally substituting 80s studio slickness for gritty blues authenticity, this is a product of its era, albeit an eminently listenable one. Despite the creative arrangement of Robert Johnson's own 'Crossroads', COODER's rollicking version of this most covered of all blues songs teeters on the verge of the kind of crowded, rock-centric treatment which too often makes modern blues a chore to listen to (and which, ironically, this song has too often been subjected to). In contrast, 'Cotton Needs Pickin', grinds and lurches to its own eccentric rhythms, while Frank Frost provides grizzled, soul-food vocals on a track which effectively harnesses the studio and individual players rather than using them as padding. The great J.B. Lenoir's 'Down In Mississippi' is convincingly brooding and Noah Lewis' 'Viola Lee Blues' could've featured – production aside –

on COODER's 1970 debut album, with some beguiling brass and mandolin interplay and a rare, ravaged vocal from the man himself. While the record's holy rolling backing vocals lend some fervent, if occasionally overwrought religiosity to proceedings, the most enduring tracks are the stripped down instrumentals like 'Walkin' Away Blues', with Sonny Terry contributing some mean harmonica, and 'Feelin' Bad Blues', a skeletal slide meditation with more than a ghostly hint of Johnson's 'Love In Vain'. 'Somebody's Callin' My Name', meanwhile, is a faithful acappella rendition of the old spiritual, although it doesn't hold a candle to the haunting Hugh Masakela version (on his 1971 'Union of South Africa' album). *BG*

Album rating: *7

– spinoff releases, etc. –

RY COODER: Crossroads / Feel It (Bad Blues)

Jul 86. (7") <28723> ☐ [-]

the CROW

1994 (US 102m) Miramax Films (R)

Film genre: comic-strip fantasy

Top guns: dir: Alex Proyas → GARAGE DAYS / s-w: David J. Schow, John Shirley (comic strip: James O'Barr)

Stars: Brandon Lee *(Eric Draven)*, Ernie Hudson *(Sgt. Albrecht)* ← ROAD HOUSE ← the JAZZ SINGER ← LEADBELLY / → AIRHEADS → the BASKETBALL DIARIES → a STRANGER IN THE KINGDOM, Michael Wincott *(Top Dollar)* ← the DOORS / → DEAD MAN → STRANGE DAYS, Rochelle Davis *(Sarah)*, David Patrick Kelly *(T-Bird)* ← WILD AT HEART ← the ADVENTURES OF FORD FAIRLANE / → CROOKLYN → HEAVY → LAST MAN STANDING, Angel David *(Skank)*, Bai Ling *(Myca)*, Sofia Shinas *(Shelly Webster)*, Anna Thomson *(Darla)* → I SHOT ANDY WARHOL, Laurence Mason *(Tin Tin)* → FRONTERZ, Tony Todd *(Grange)*, Tierre Turner *(Jugger)* ← BUCKTOWN ← CORNBREAD, EARL AND ME ← FRIDAY FOSTER, Jon Polito *(Gideon; pawn shop owner)* ← HOMEBOY / → the SINGING DETECTIVE

Storyline: Killed along with his fiancée by a ruthless gang who had broken into his apartment, rock guitarist Eric Draven – daubed in Gothic make-up and dressed in leather – is resurrected a year later by a crow to seek revenge on his murderers, one by one. *DF*

Movie rating: *8

Visual: video + dvd

Off the record: The film won the BMI Film Music Award and won the 1995 MTV Movie award for Best Movie Song ('Big Empty' by Stone Temple Pilots). *DF*

—

Various Artists (score: Graeme Revell)

Apr 94. (cd/c) *Atlantic; <(7567 82519-2/-4)>* [1] Jun94 [13] – Burn (the CURE) / Golotha tenement blues (MACHINES OF LOVING GRACE) / Big empty (STONE TEMPLE PILOTS) / Dead souls (NINE INCH NAILS) / Darkness (RAGE AGAINST THE MACHINE) / Color me once (VIOLENT FEMMES) / Ghost rider (ROLLINS BAND) / Milquetoast (HELMET) / The badge (PANTERA) / Slip slide melting (FOR LOVE NOT LISA) / After the flesh (MY LIFE WITH THE THRILL KILL KULT) / Snakedriver (JESUS & MARY CHAIN) / Time baby III (MEDICINE) / It can't rain all the time (JANE SIBERRY). *<(cd re-iss. Jun02 on 'WEA'; 0927 45479-2)>*

S/track review: Released into the alternative cultural landscape of 1994, 'The CROW's OST is an MTV-friendly hybrid of the best alternative, industrial, goth-rock and heavy metal of the period. The album opens with the propulsive bass line of the CURE's 'Burn', all resounding piano chords and tribal drum patterns, a solipsistic and moody track that forms the dark heart of the film's alterno-Goth aesthetic. It is Eric Draven's anthem as he steps out menacingly into the night: "Every night I burn / Waiting for the world to end". MACHINES OF LOVING GRACE do a fantastic impression of Nine Inch Nails with one of the most memorable guitar lines from the film, which maybe explains why Trent Reznor (and NINE INCH NAILS) plump for a cover of Joy Division's 'Dead Souls', re-working it with insistent drum machine and serrated riffing. The alternative rock flag is waved by STONE TEMPLE PILOTS with a cut also available on their album 'Purple'. 'Big Empty' finds them in lounge act mode, their cigarette end eroticism to the fore, before breaking into an anthemic stadium rock chorus that demonstrates how the Sunset Strip outfit sold 30 million albums, and provides a template for the film's commodified sleek and shiny grunge posturing. RAGE AGAINST THE MACHINE, HELMET and the ROLLINS BAND all pitch in with enjoyable taut, funky bursts of aggression. RATM's contribution 'Darkness' seems a jarringly political choice, with de la Rocha's condemnation of Western government inaction over confronting the AIDS crisis in Africa a rare moment of looking outward in an otherwise sulky and self-centred film soundscape; it also features an excellent, reverb-drenched Tom Morello solo spot. PANTERA sledgehammer their way into the proceedings with 'The Badge', carried off with their customary braggadocio, Phil Anselmo barking out a measured critique of what truly motivates cops ("the badge means you suck"), that builds to a riotous double bass drum run-in and crashes to a close with a sample of the frenzied conclusion of.. say 'Taxi Driver'. Following that heavy metal injection, MY LIFE WITH THE THRILL KILL KULT unleash a gnashing piece of techno-rock, and JESUS & MARY CHAIN contribute a cool piece of slacker alterno-rock, 'Snakedriver'. The album closes with two examples of the dark side of the 90s, MEDICINE's washed-out, pseudo-psychedelia has a very memorable hook but little else. JANE SIBERRY's cheesy synthscape 'It Can't Rain All the Time' forms a central sentiment in the film but that doesn't redeem it. *DF*

Album rating: *7

CRY-BABY

1990 (US 85m) Universal Pictures (PG-13)

Film genre: teen musical comedy/satire

Top guns: s-w + dir: John Waters ← HAIRSPRAY

Stars: Johnny Depp *(Wade "Cry-Baby" Walker)* → DEAD MAN → FEAR AND LOATHING IN LAS VEGAS → the FUTURE IS UNWRITTEN, Amy Locane *(Allison Vernon-Williams)* → AIRHEADS, Susan Tyrrell *(Ramona Rickettes)* ← ROCKULA ← TAPEHEADS ← SUBWAY RIDERS ← FORBIDDEN ZONE ← CATCH MY SOUL / → PINK AS THE DAYS SHE WAS BORN → MASKED AND ANONYMOUS, Polly Bergen *(Mrs. Vernon-Williams)*, **Iggy POP** *(Uncle Belvedere Rickettes)*, Ricki Lake *(Pepper Walker)* ← LAST EXIT TO BROOKLYN ← WORKING GIRL ← HAIRSPRAY / → JACKIE'S BACK! → HAIRSPRAY re-make, Traci Lords *(Wanda Woodward)* → SHOCK 'EM DEAD, Kim McGuire *(Hatchet-Face)*, David Nelson *(Wanda's father)* ← UP IN SMOKE, Darren E. Burrows *(Milton Hackett)*, Patricia Hearst *(Wanda's mother)*, Mink Stole *(Hatchet's mother)* ← HAIRSPRAY / → MONSTER MASH: THE MOVIE → PINK AS THE DAY SHE WAS BORN → SPLENDOR, Stephen Mailer *(Baldwin; Allison's boyfriend)*, Troy Donahue *(Hatchet's father)* ← HARD ROCK NIGHTMARE ← SUMMER LOVE / → SHOCK 'EM DEAD → SHAKE, RATTLE & ROLL: AN AMERICAN LOVE STORY, Joe Dallesandro *(Milton's father)* ← JE T'AIME MOI NON PLUS / → ROCK & ROLL HEART, Willem Dafoe *(hateful guard)* ← the LAST TEMPTATION OF CHRIST ← TO LIVE AND DIE IN L.A. ← STREETS OF FIRE / → WILD AT HEART → AFFLICTION → OVERNIGHT → the LIFE AQUATIC WITH STEVE ZISSOU, **James Intveld** *(singing voice; Johnny Depp)* → SHAKE, RATTLE & ROCK! tv

Storyline: Bad boy, Wade "Cry-Baby" Walker, is the leader of the 'Drapes' in 1950s Baltimore. They are the official juvenile delinquents while their rivals the Squares are the boring college-type kids. Enter Allison, a Square, who falls for the permanently tear-stained Cry-Baby and wants to cross sides and be bad (have fun). However the good guy Baldwin (boring) has other ideas and he'll do anything to keep Allison on the side of the saints. *JZ*

Movie rating: *6

Off the record: Traci Lords is the infamous porn star turned actress and singer!; David Nelson is the brother of singer/actor, Ricky Nelson; Patricia "Patty" Hearst was the "kidnapped" granddaughter of tycoon William Randolph Hearst. *MCS*

—

Various Artists (score: Patrick Williams)

Mar 90. (lp/c/cd) *M.C.A.; <MCA/+C/D 8038> (MCG/MCGC/ DMCG 6089)* ☐ Jul90 ☐
– King Cry-Baby (JAMES INTVELD) / Sh boom (BALDWIN AND THE WHIFFLES) / Doin' time for bein' young (JAMES INTVELD) / A teenage prayer (RACHEL SWEET) / Please, Mr. Jailer (RACHEL SWEET) / Cry baby (the HONEY SISTERS) / Teardrops are falling (JAMES INTVELD) / Nosey Joe (BULL MOOSE JACKSON) / Mister Sandman (BALDWIN AND THE WHIFFLES) / High school hellcats (JAMES INTVELD) / Bad boy (the JIVE BOMBERS) / The flirt (SHIRLEY & LEE) / I'm so young (the STUDENTS) / (My heart goes) Piddily patter, patter (NAPPY BROWN) / I'm a bad, bad girl (LITTLE ESTHER) / Jungle drums (EARL BOSTIC) / Cherry (the JIVE BOMBERS) / Rubber biscuit (the CHIPS). *(cd re-iss. Jun94; MCLD 19260) <(cd re-iss. Mar03 on 'Universal'; AAMCAD 8038)>*

S/track review: Initially disappointing in that there's no Iggy Pop songs on parade, filmmaker John Waters (the oldest juvenile delinquent on the Hollywood block) steering clear of possibly Iggy's only out'n'out, retro rock'n'roll number, 'Real Wild Child'. Anyway, there's no shortage of tracks here (18 in all!) and with a running-time of over 50 minutes, many would think they're getting value for money. Similar in style and composition to Waters' original 'HAIRSPRAY' movie soundtrack, 'CRY-BABY', he moves the musical goal-posts slightly to ensure more outsider production work was in order. Lead actor Johnny Depp was no lead vocalist, so his singing voice was handed to Elvis-soundalike JAMES INTVELD, who rumbled his way through 50s-esque numbers, 'King Cry-Baby' (penned by songwriting legend, Doc Pomus and the album's producer, DAVE ALVIN – ex-Blasters), 'Doin' Time For Bein' Young' (penned by JD Souther & Waddy Wachtel), 'High School Hellcats' (written by Alvin, again) and the falsetto 'Teardrops Are Falling'. The latter track was produced by yet another giant of rock music, AL KOOPER, who was also the man at the controls for RACHEL SWEET's 'A Teenage Prayer' and the Wynona Carr-penned 'Please, Mr. Jailer', records that give you a sort of "Back To The Future" feeling. Under the guise of BALDWIN AND THE WHIFFLES, messrs GERRY BECKLEY (of America), ANDREW GOLD (of Wax) and TIMOTHY B. SCHMIT (of Eagles), delivered two nuggets from the past, 'Sh Boom' and 'Mister Sandman', although the latter featured RACHEL SWEET not former "Lonely Boy", GOLD. Doo-wop was also in vogue on the title track by the HONEY SISTERS (BETH ANDERSEN, SUZIE BENSON, ROSEMARY BUTLER and TERRY WOOD) under the guidance of Jai Winding, a case of saccharine and bubblegum rather than honey. We all know early blues music had more metaphors and double-entendres than you could shake a tail-feather at, BULL MOOSE JACKSON's Leiber-Stoller-penned 'Nosey Joe' was the genuine article – or was it just me with a dirty mind. The JIVE BOMBERS, meanwhile, were indeed the b's and e's, the distinctive and characteristic vibrato vox of Clarence Palmer, here the highlight of two 50s hits, 'Bad Boy' (written by Lillian Armstrong, wife of Louis) and 'Cherry'. Glossing over SHIRLEY & LEE, LITTLE ESTHER, EARL BOSTIK and the STUDENTS, one can't warn you enough about '(My Heart Goes) Piddily Patter, Patter' by the unfortunately monikered NAPPY BROWN. Saving the best for last, Waters unearths something of a hidden treasure by way of the CHIPS' 'Rubber Biscuit', a Coasters-ish, novelty track that is now featured in a TV ad for Muller Vitality. Now check that out you hep-cats. *MCS*

Album rating: *6.5

CUCKOO PATROL

1967 (UK 76m b&w) Grand National Pictures / Eternal Films

Film genre: Pop-Rock Musical comedy/farce

Top guns: dir: Duncan Wood / s-w: Lew Schwartz

Stars: Freddie & The Dreamers:- Freddie Garrity, Derek Quinn, Roy Crewsdon, Peter Birrell, Bernie Dwyer *(themselves/performers)* ← DISK-O-TEK HOLIDAY ← OUT OF SIGHT ← EVERY DAY'S A HOLIDAY ← JUST FOR YOU ← WHAT A CRAZY WORLD, Kenneth Connor *(Wick)* ← GONKS GO BEAT / → the MAGIC CHRISTIAN, Victor Maddern *(Dicko)* ← BUNNY LAKE IS MISSING → the MAGIC CHRISTIAN, John Le Mesurier *(Gibbs)* ← FINDERS KEEPERS / → the MAGIC CHRISTIAN, Arthur Mullard *(Yossle)* ← IT'S TRAD, DAD! / → SMASHING TIME, Ernest Clark *(Marshall)* ← FINDERS KEEPERS

Storyline: Freddie & The Dreamers (without a hit to their name since 1965) dress as boy scouts in a "cuckoo patrol" to get out of a sticky situation. Boys will be boys and men will be downright idiots. *MCS*

Movie rating: *2.5

Visual: video (no audio OST)

Off the record: Freddie Garrity died nearly forty years later at his Bangor, Wales home on 19th May 2006.

CUCUMBER CASTLE

1970 (UK 56m TV) Robert Stigwood Organization

Film genre: Pop/Rock musical fantasy

Top guns: dir: Hugh Gladwish ← the GHOST GOES GEAR / devised by: **Barry Gibb, Maurice Gibb**

Stars: the BEE GEES:- Barry Gibb *(Prince Frederick, King of Cucumber)*, **Maurice Gibb** *(Prince Marmaduke, King of Jelly)*, Eleanor Bron *(Lady Margerie Pee)* ← HELP!, Vincent Price *(Wicked Count Voxville)* ← the TROUBLE WITH GIRLS ← BEACH PARTY / → WELCOME TO MY NIGHTMARE → the NIGHTMARE, Julian Orchard *(Julian the Lord Chamberlaine)*, Pat Coombs *(nurse Sarah Charles Bottom)*, Frankie Howerd *(dying king)* → SGT. PEPPER'S LONELY HEARTS CLUB BAND, Spike Milligan *(the court jester)* ← the MAGIC CHRISTIAN, **LULU** *(Lulu the cook)*, **Blind Faith:- Eric CLAPTON** *(performer)*, **Steve Winwood** *(performer)* ← the GHOST GOES GEAR / → GLASTONBURY FAYRE → WOODSTOCK 94 → BLUES BROTHERS 2000 → RED, WHITE & BLUES, **Ric Grech** *(performer)*, **Ginger Baker** *(performer)* ← GONKS GO BEAT / **Mick Jagger** *(himself)* <= the ROLLING STONES =>, **Marianne Faithfull** *(herself)* ← LUCIFER RISING ← DON'T LOOK BACK ← ANNA / → the WALL: LIVE IN BERLIN → ROCK AND ROLL CIRCUS

Storyline: Medieval and bizarre, the BBC showed this as a Xmas Special on a Saturday afternoon, 26th December, 1970 – how did I miss it! *MCS*

Movie rating: *5

Visual: none (there should be a dvd soon!)

Off the record: Quite an array of stars to join two of the **BEE GEES** (Robin Gibb had left)

—

the BEE GEES

Apr 70. (lp) *Polydor; (2383 010) Atco; <327>* [57] [94]
– If only I had my mind on something else / I.O.I.O. / Then you left me / The Lord / I was the child / I lay down and die / Sweetheart / Bury me down by the river / My thing / The chance of love / Turning tide / Don't forget to remember. *(cd-iss. Nov89; 833783-2)*

S/track review: "Bowzey wow wowzey!", it's 'CUCUMBER CASTLE', fifth official BEE GEES album and vague tie-in to a TV film of the same name, confusingly titled after a track on the band's debut and usually remembered as the record-without-ROBIN (the tremulous GIBB sibling having abdicated in favour of a solo album). Left to their own devices, love-knights-in-shining-armour (the sleeve is a kitsch novelty in itself) BARRY and MAURICE lay on the sentiment and strings with the proverbial trowel. 'If Only I Had My Mind On Something Else' is the catchy title of the opening track, setting in Arthurian stone the lachrymose, heavily arranged, sub-Beatles/neo-Bacharach mood that permeates much of the rest of the album. About the only exceptions are 'i.o.i.o', dropping an enjoyably tokenistic, tropical-percussive hint of the dancefloor conquering to come, and the dippy pop-psych rhyming of 'My Thing' (see above). This being 1970, the brothers even made their own attempt at country-rock, without much of the rock. They work themselves into some half-convincing holy rolling – as well as some daft redneck accents – on 'The Lord', but Nashville Sound-alike 'Don't Forget To Remember' was the big hit (a near UK No.1), their last of the 60s. 'Sweetheart' is more Brotherhood Of Man, but some of the ballads are worth persevering with: 'Then You Left Me' is ambitious enough to border quasi-film-score territory, with echoes of both Ennio Morricone and 'PAT GARRETT & BILLY THE KID', and 'I Lay Down And Die' aspires to the level of pop symphony. Not the band's greatest moment, but undeserving of its bad rap. *BG*

Album rating: *5

– spinoff hits, etc. –

the BEE GEES: Don't Forget To Remember / The Lord

Aug 69. (7") *(56343) <6702>* [2] Sep69 [73]

the BEE GEES: If Only I Had My Mind On Something Else / Sweetheart

Mar 70. (7") *<6741>* [–] [91]

the BEE GEES: I.O.I.O. / Sweetheart

Mar 70. (7") *(56377)* [49] [–]

the BEE GEES: I.O.I.O. / Then You Left Me

Jun 70. (7") *<6752>* [–] [94]

☐ CULT OF THE DAMNED alt.
(⇒ ANGEL, ANGEL, DOWN WE GO)

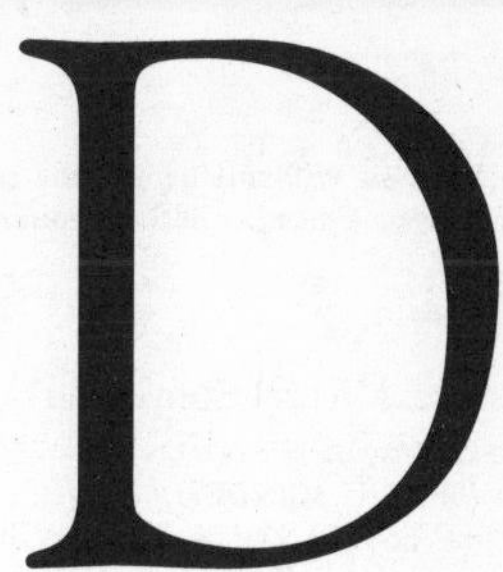

DADDY-O

1958 (US 74m b&w) American International Pictures

Film genre: rock'n'roll Music crime mystery

Top guns: dir: Lou Place / s-w: David Moessinger

Stars: Dick Contino *(Phil Sandifer)*, Sandra Giles *(Jana Ryan)* → IT HAPPENED AT THE WORLD'S FAIR, Bruno VeSota *(Sidney Chillas)* ← ROCK ALL NIGHT ← CARNIVAL ROCK / → YOUR CHEATIN' HEART → the GIRLS ON THE BEACH, Ron McNeil *(Duke)*, Gloria Victor *(Marcia Hayes)*, Jack McClure *(Bruce Green)*, Sonia Torgeson *(Peg Lawrence)*

Storyline: Singer and truck driver Daddy-O (Phil to his pals) decides to skip challenge races for a while when his friend is murdered and he's beaten by a woman. Instead he goes driving undercover for the local crime boss who he suspects is behind the killing. His job is to deliver mysterious packages up from Mexico (just chili beans, honest) and soon finds his life in danger when he exposes the baddies to the cops. *JZ*

Movie rating: *2.5

Visual: video (no audio OST; debut score: John Williams)

Off the record: Songs include 'Angel Eyes' & 'Rock Candy Baby', etc. (Contino was a professional accordionist). *MCS*

☐ Jimmy DALEY & THE DING-A-LINGS
(⇒ ROCK, PRETTY BABY)

DANCE WITH ME

1998 (US 126m) Mandalay / Columbia Pictures (PG)

Film genre: romantic Dance/Pop musical drama

Top guns: dir: Randa Haines/ s-w: Daryl Matthews

Stars: Vanessa L. Williams *(Ruby Sinclair)* ← BYE BYE BIRDIE re-make ← the JACKSONS: AN AMERICAN DREAM, **Chayanne** *(Rafael Infante)*, **Kris Kristofferson** *(John Burnett)* ← FLASHPOINT ← SONGWRITER ← a STAR IS BORN ← PAT GARRETT & BILLY THE KID / → the BALLAD OF RAMBLIN' JACK → CHELSEA WALLS, Joan Plowright *(Bea Johnson)* ← BRIMSTONE & TREACLE / → CURIOUS GEORGE, Jane Krakowski *(Patricia)* → ALFIE re-make → OPEN SEASON, Beth Grant *(Lovejoy)* → BLUE VALLEY SONGBIRD → ROCK STAR, Rick Valenzuela *(Julian Marshall)*, **Albita Rodriguez** *(performer)*, **DLG:- Eustace Dunbar IV, James De Jesus & Wilfredo A. Crispin** *(performers)*

Storyline: After his mother dies, young Cuban Rafael heads to the States to meet his father John. John runs a dance school and as everyone there gets ready for the World Open Dance Contest Rafael gets a handyman job as he wonders how to tell John that he is his son. When it becomes obvious that

Rafael is a better dancer than a joiner he gets to partner John's star pupil Ruby as competition day draws nearer. *JZ*

Movie rating: *5.5

Visual: video + dvd

Off the record: The **Vanessa Williams** here is the model/Miss America turned actress. **Chayanne** was a member of the Menudo group, Los Chicos, before he went solo.

—

Various Artists (score: Michael Convertino)

Aug 98. (cd/c) *Sony; <EK/ET 68905> Epic; (491125-2/-4)* [ ] Sep98 [ ]
– Magalenha (SERGIO MENDES) / Heaven's what I feel – dance remix (GLORIA ESTEFAN) / You are my home (VANESSA L. WILLIAMS & CHAYANNE) / Jibaro – Dance With Me '98 mix (ELECTRA) / Fiesta pa'los rumberos (ALBITA) / Want you, miss you, love you (JON SECADA) / Jazz machine (BLACK MACHINE) / Echa pa'lante – Spanglish cha-cha mix (THALIA) / Atrevete (no puedes conmigo) (DLG: DARK LATIN GROOVE) / Eres todo en mi (You're my everything) (ANA GABRIEL) / Refugio de amor (You are my home) – salsa (VANESSA L. WILLIAMS & CHAYANNE) / Tres deseos (Three wishes) – 12" remix (GLORIA ESTEFAN) / Patria (RUBEN BLADES) / Pantera en libertad – Apollo 440 remix – radio edit (MONICA NARANJO) / Suavemente – tropical Spanglish mix (ELVIS CRESPO).

S/track review: 'DIRTY DANCING' has a lot to answer for. Dance-based movies that don't take themselves too seriously tend to work best and 'DANCE WITH ME', plays to its strengths and has a soundtrack delivering high-octane rhythms to propel the spectacular dance sequence. The mix is fairly balanced, a blend of old world classics and contemporary takes, many of which sound tacky in comparison on disc, even if they work well on screen. In an unsubtle attempt to gain some cultural overlap, Latin music's biggest ever crossover name GLORIA ESTEFAN appears twice, with the upbeat electropop of 'Heaven's What I Feel' and the furiously paced 'Tres Desos (Three Wishes)'. The other smart tactic is to concede some modern takes on Latin classics. In particular, the updating of 'Jibaro' by ELECTRA is perhaps the most accomplished. It keeps the breadth and colour of the original while infusing it with some contemporary energy. ALBITA create something tremendous from a more traditional musical palette with the excellent 'Fiesta Pa' Los Rumberos' – fit to challenge the most skilled of feet. On the downside, JON SECADA trades in some unnerving Michael Bolton-esque balladry and the horns'n'beats'n'chants of BLACK MACHINE's 'Jazz Machine' sound woefully dated. There are several moments where it strays into cliché territory but this is about filling dancefloors, not blowing minds with new musical equations. For the most part this is party music and it fits the bill handsomely. *MR*

Album rating: *6.5

– spinoff hits, etc. –

GLORIA ESTEFAN: Heaven's What I Feel (mixes)

May 98. (c-s/12"/cd-s) *<78875/78926/78908> (666004--4/-6/-2)* [27] [17]

DANCEHALL QUEEN

1997 (Jama 98m) Hawk's Nest Productions / Island Group (R)

Film genre: domestic melodrama

Top guns: dir: (+ s-w) **Don Letts** ← the PUNK ROCK MOVIE / → WESTWAY TO THE WORLD → ONE LOVE → PUNK: ATTITUDE, Rick Elgood → ONE LOVE (other s-w: Ed Wallace & Suzanne Fenn)

Stars: Audrey Reid *(Marcia)*, Paul Campbell *(Priest)* ← KLA$H, Carl Davis *(Lany)*, Pauline Stone-Myrie *(Mrs. Gordon)*, Mark Denvers *(Junior)*, Cherine Anderson *(Tanya)* → ONE LOVE, Carl Bradshaw *(police officer #1)* ← KLA$H ← CLUB PARADISE ← COUNTRYMAN ← the HARDER THEY COME / → ONE LOVE, **Beenie Man** *(himself)*, **Lady Saw** *(herself)*

Storyline: Jamaican street vendor Marcia has two big problems – moneylender 'Uncle' Larry who's got the hots for her daughter, and notorious thug Priest who's got his eye on her stall. Marcia takes things into her own hands and dresses herself up incognito so that she can take part in the $100,000 Dancehall Queen contest. With a bit of luck she might set Larry and Priest against each other and win first prize as well. *JZ*

Movie rating: *7

Visual: video + dvd

Off the record: Beenie Man (b. Anthony Davis, 22 Aug'73, Kingston, Jamaica) was one of the first to fuse rap with reggae – well certainly in the mainstream pop world. Just around the corner of '97, the man had his first US Top 40 hit, 'Who Am I'. *MCS*

—

Various Artists (score: Wally Badarou)

Aug 97. (cd) *Mercury; <(524396-2)>* [ ] Sep97 [ ]
– Dancehall queen – Bonzai mix (BEENIE MAN & CHEVELLE FRANKLYN) / Badman sonata (BUCCANEER) / What's the move (CHAKA DEMUS & PLIERS) / Unbelievable (MARLEY GIRLS) / My Jamaican guy (GRACE JONES & BOUNTY KILLER) / Dancehall queen – Delano renaissance mix (BEENIE MAN & CHEVELLE FRANKLYN) / Tune in (BOUNTY KILLER & SUGAR MINOTT) / Little and cute (FRISCO KID) / Boof n' baff n' biff (BLACK UHURU) / Nuff gal (BEENIE MAN) / Joyride (WAYNE WONDER & BABY CHAM) / Dancehall queen – Maurice Joshua club hall mix (BEENIE MAN & CHEVELLE FRANKLYN). *<(re-iss. Mar03 on 'Universal'; AA314 524396-2)>*

S/track review: A new breed of reggae stars feature here. Kicking off with relative newcomer to the scene, BEENIE MAN, he delivered the rap-stylee title track with the aid of CHEVELLE FRANKLYN. Most of you will recognise the song, 'My Jamaican Guy', an old GRACE JONES nugget that here sees her combine with BOUNTY KILLER, the latter hardcore ragga man also getting into the groove alongside ("Good Thing Going" hitmaker from '81) SUGAR MINOTT on 'Tune In'. CHAKA DEMUS & PLIERS put the spanner in the works – so to speak – with a soulful reggae-pop take of 'What's The Move', while the MARLEY GIRLS chime in with 'Unbelievable'. BEENIE MAN serves up another slice of Shaggy-style ragga in the shape of 'Nuff Gal', only to be bettered by top guns WAYNE WONDER & BABY CHAM on the smoochy, 'Joy Ride'. Putting them in the shade is by far the best track ('Badman Sonata') by surprise package, BUCCANEER, a song at least relating to the thug-life in the movie. *MCS*

Album rating: *6.5

– spinoff hits, etc. –

BEENIE MAN & CHEVELLE FRANKLYN: Dancehall Queen (mixes)

Jun 97. (12"/cd-s) *<572036> (IJCD 2018)* [90] Sep97 [70]

DANCER IN THE DARK

2000 (Den/Swe/Fra 137m) Film i Vast / Trust Film Svenska (18)

Film genre: Dance/Rock Musical melodrama (remake)

Top guns: s-w + dir: Lars von Trier

Stars: BJORK *(Selma Jezkova)*, Catherine Deneuve *(Kathy)* ← POLA X ← PAROLES ET MUSIQUE ← JE VOUS AIME, David Morse *(Bill Houston)* → the SLAUGHTER RULE, Joel Grey *(Oldrich Novy)* ← CALYPSO HEAT WAVE, Peter Stormare *(Jeff)* ← the MILLION DOLLAR HOTEL, Vincent Paterson *(Samuel)*, Cara Seymour *(Linda Houston)*, Jean-Marc Barr *(Norman)*, Udo Kier *(Dr. Porkorny)* ← NINA HAGEN = PUNK + GLORY

← the END OF VIOLENCE ← EVEN COWGIRLS GET THE BLUES ← SUSPIRIA / → PIGS WILL FLY → 30 DAYS UNTIL I'M FAMOUS, Vladica Kostic *(Gene Jezkova)*, Zeljko Ivanek *(D.A.)*, Siobhan Fallon *(Brenda)*, Luke Reilly *(new defense counsel)* ← PRIVATE PARTS ← NIGHTHAWKS, Stellan Skarsgard *(doctor)* ← GOOD WILL HUNTING, Paprika Steen *(woman on night shift)*

Storyline: Set in a town in Washington state in 1964, Czech factory worker Selma faces a dilemma, she is going blind and, due to a genetic disorder, so will her 10-year-old boy if he doesn't have an operation. To forget her day-to-day woes, she and her helpful friend, Cvalda, take trips to the cinema, watching (or indeed trying to watch) Hollywood musicals. Unselfishly, Selma secretly puts away money in a kitchen cupboard tin each week until it amasses to a couple of thousand dollars. When the cash suddenly vanishes, she confronts the culprit (her landlord Bill), but things go awry in the process. This was the third in von Trier's 'Golden Heart Trilogy', the previous couple were 'Breaking The Waves' (1996) and 'The Idiots' (1998). *MCS*

Movie rating: *9.5

Visual: video + dvd

Off the record: From the time he witnessed BJORK prancing about in the Spike Jonze-directed video for her song and dance-styled musical hit, 'It's Oh So Quiet', screenwriter/director Lars Von Trier wanted her in a movie. *MCS*

—

BJORK: Selmasongs

Sep 00. (lp/cd) *One Little Indian; (TPLP 151/+CD) Elektra; <62533>* [34] [41]
– Overture / Cvalda / I've seen it all (w/ THOM YORKE) / Scatterheart / In the musicals / 107 steps / New world.

S/track review: Before this venture, BJORK had only ever contributed the odd exclusive song/track to various feature films ('Play Dead' to 1993's 'The Young Americans', 'Nu Flyver Anton' to 'Anton' in 1996 and 'Amphibian' to 'Being John Malkovich' 1999 – all I might add alongside bona fide film composers). The Icelandic pixie (this description must irritate her sometimes!) certainly didn't do things by half though, having starred in the movie while composing, arranging and producing the music (the lyrics were down to von Trier and Sjon Sigurosson). The album opened its account with an orchestral theme, 'Overture' (augmented by Vincent Mendoza who features throughout), a sad but melodious lament with a brass section for effect. 'Cvalda', starts off as part industrial, in fitting with the machination of the movie, while BJORK (along with trusty sidekicks, MARK BELL and MARK "SPIKE" STENT) finally marks her noisy entrance with that clatter, crash and bang, that was oh so prevalent in her 40s-styled, Big Band hit, 'It's Oh So Quiet'. Not the greatest of singers, Catherine Deneuve (Selma's best friend in the movie), nevertheless gives 'Cvalda' that je ne sais quoi appeal. The voice of Radiohead's THOM YORKE combines effectively with BJORK for the romanticised, Oscar-nominated, 'I've Seen It All', a hark back to post-war musicals with a hint of what was to come with Baz Luhrmann's 'MOULIN ROUGE' (2001). 'Scatterheart' was a beat-box lullaby in which BJORK acclaims and repeats "You're gonna have to find out for yourself", a song better addressed in the film than in the grooves. BJORK's technicolour vision so-to-speak, is in full flow on track five, 'In The Musicals' (with a mind-blowing chorus of "You will always be there to ca-a-a-tch me"), an uptempo BJORK record that displayed her full emotional "voca-a-a-a-argh-l" range. The serious side of the film is intensified on '107 Steps', BJORK counting as she walks to the gallows, memories of the scene come flooding back. Closing track, 'New World', is another to get you reaching for the handkerchiefs (especially if you've seen the movie), reprised from the opening orchestral score and theatrically performed with heart and soul by BJORK. She could hit as many high notes as Japanese journalists in my book. If there's one criticism, it's a tad short at just over 32 minutes! *MCS*

Album rating: *7.5

□ Bobby DARIN segment
(⇒ BEYOND THE SEA)

□ August DARNELL
(⇒ KID CREOLE & THE COCONUTS)

DATELINE DIAMONDS

1965 (UK 73m b&w) Viscount Films / J. Arthur Rank Productions

Film genre: Pop-Rock Musical crime caper/mystery

Top guns: dir: Jeremy Summers → FERRY 'CROSS THE MERSEY / s-w: Tudor Gates (idea: Harold Shampan ← LIVE IT UP

Stars: William Lucas *(Maj. Fairclough)*, Kenneth Cope *(Lester Benson; aka Arthur Gittins)*, George Mikell *(Paul Verlekt)*, Conrad Phillips *(Tom Jenkins)*, Patsy Rowlands *(Mrs. Edgecomb)*, Burnell Tucker *(Dale Meredith)* → FINDERS KEEPERS → FLASH GORDON → SCREAM FOR HELP, Gertan Klauber *(Meverhof)* → PIED PIPER → BACKBEAT, **the Small Faces:- Steven Marriott */**, Ronnie Lane *, Kenney Jones *, Jimmy Langwith** *(performers)* ← BE MY GUEST * ← LIVE IT UP * / → TONITE LET'S ALL MAKE LOVE IN LONDON ** → THIRTY YEARS OF MAXIMUM R&B LIVE **, **the Chantelles:- Riss Chantelle, Jay Adams, Sandra Orr** *(performers)*, **Kiki Dee** *(performer)*, **Mark Richardson** *(performer)*, **Rey Anton & Pro Formula** *(performers)*, Kenny Everett *(himself)*

Storyline: An ex-con turned rock band manager (of the Small Faces, no less!) wants to get back into the business of crime. With the help of like-minded crooks and said band, Lester Benson plans to ship a case of diamonds to Amsterdam. "The hottest rocks in Britain being smuggled by the hottest rockers in Britain" was the appropriate tagline. *MCS*

Movie rating: *3.5

Visual: video (no audio OST)

Off the record: Quite an array of pop stars/singers of the mid-60s, including **the Small Faces** (responsible for the UK hit, 'Whatcha Gonna Do About It?'). They contributed four songs to the movie, 'I've Got Mine', 'It's Too Late', 'Come On Children' and 'Don't Stop What You're Doing', while others stemmed from no-hopers – at the time – MARK RICHARDSON ('What 'Ma Gonna Do?'), the CHANTELLES ('I Think Of You' & 'Please Don't Kiss Me'), REY ANTON & PRO FORMULA ('First Taste Of Love'), plus KIKI DEE ('Small Town'); of course, KIKI went on to be a star in the 70s with hits such as 'Amoureuse', 'I've Got The Music In Me' and No.1 duet with Elton John, 'Don't Go Breaking My Heart'. Kenny Everett became a Radio One DJ and TV presenter/comedian; he also had a couple of hits, 'Captain Kremmen (Retribution)' and 'Snot Rap'. *MCS*

the DAVID CASSIDY STORY

2000 (US 88m TV) Dennis Hammer Productions / NBC Productions (PG-13)

Film genre: Pop-music bio-pic/drama

Top guns: dir: Jack Bender / s-w: Duane Poole

Stars: Andrew Kavovit *(David Cassidy)*, Malcolm McDowell *(Jack Cassidy)* ← GET CRAZY ← the COMPLEAT BEATLES ← O LUCKY MAN!, Dey Young *(Shirley Jones)* ← SHAKE, RATTLE AND ROCK! tv ← ROCK'N'ROLL HIGH SCHOOL, Roma Maffia *(Ruth Aarons)* ← SMITHEREENS, Chandra West *(Sue Shifrin)*, Matthew John Armstrong *(Nick Hiller)*, Katie Wright *(Susan Dey)*, Paul Ben-Victor *(Wes Farrell)*, Sibel Ergener *(Kay Lenz)*

Storyline: Tells the story of how David got into the music business thanks to his father, film star Jack, who gets him his first break with his showbiz contacts. David lands the part in a TV series about a family of singers (The Partridge Family) and never looks back, much to the jealous annoyance of his dad. The twist in the tale comes when the public finally have had enough of David's music, which David was never a great fan of himself. *JZ*

Movie rating: *5

Visual: video (no audio OST; score: Michael Melvoin)

Off the record: David Cassidy was born in New York City on the 12th of April, 1950. A hitmaker with the Partridge Family in the early 70s, David subsequently rose to be the ultimate boy-next-door, teen pin-up (alongside Donny Osmond) when most of his 45s such as 'Could It Be Forever', 'How Can I Be Sure', 'I'm A Clown' and 'Daydreamer', hit UK No.1 or the Top 3 (his only US Top 10 hit was 'Cherish'). *MCS*

– associated compilation –

DAVID CASSIDY & the PARTRIDGE FAMILY: The Definitive Collection

Jan 00. (cd) *Arista; <14640>* ☐ ☐
– I think I love you / I woke up in love this morning / I'll meet you halfway / Doesn't somebody want to be wanted / Cherish / It's one of those nights (yes love) / Am I losing you / I am a clown / Could it be forever / How can I be sure / Breaking up is hard to do / Rock me baby / Point me in the direction of Albuquerque / Looking through the eyes of love / Friend and lover / Daydreamer / If I didn't care / Walking in the rain / Some kind of summer / Please please me. *<re-iss. Aug01 on 'BMG International' +=; 78560>* – Puppy song / Darlin' / Get it up for love / I write the songs.

Ray DAVIES

Born: 21 Jun'44, Muswell Hill, London, England. Together with his younger brother Dave, RAY DAVIES formed the KINKS, recruiting Peter Quaife from the Ravens and drummer Mick Avory. With help from managers Robert Wace and Grenville Collins, the band met up with Larry Page who arranged the recording of a few demos, which were soon heard by American A&R boss, Shel Talmy. After two flop 45s for 'Pye' records, their third, 'You Really Got Me', stormed to the top of the UK charts and US Top 10. With its scuzzy, propulsive guitar riff, the song is oft cited as one of the first real "heavy rock" records, although it's debatable whether RAY DAVIES would admit to inspiring a multitude of poodle-maned Van Halen soundalikes. A top-selling eponymous LP followed, as did a series of Top 10 sixties singles, including two more UK No.1's, 'Tired Of Waiting For You' and 'Sunny Afternoon'. As Ray's songwriting developed, the band moved to a quieter, more reflective sound, his semi-camp, semi-detached vocals complementing the wry observations and quintessential Englishness of the lyrical themes. Come 1967, when every band worth their weight in spiked sugarcubes were looking towards the "East", DAVIES looked no further than his proverbial back garden. 'Something Else', with its heartfelt eulogies to a mythical England past, still stands as the KINKS' greatest moment, the aching melancholy of 'Waterloo Sunset' its crowning glory. DAVIES' nostalgic bent continued on 1968's '. . .The Village Green Preservation Society', an enchanting concept album that reached ever further into a faded history of rural simplicity. The bard's lyrical obsessions were given centre stage once more on 'Arthur (Or The Decline Of The Roman Empire)' (1969), wherein the rosy hue of the past was contrasted with the grey decline of modern day Britain. The mood lightened somewhat with 1970s surprise No.2 hit single, 'Lola', a tongue in cheek tribute to a male cross-dresser and the standout track from the subsequent album, 'Lola Versus Powerman . . .'. 1971's 'Muswell Hillbillies' echoed 'Village Green's collection of storybook vignettes, although the band were beginning to lose their focus and the hits were about to dry up. Unfair but poor reviews for the KINKS' first trip into soundtracks, 'PERCY' (1971), didn't do them many favours, although the band did return with a Top 20 single, 'Supersonic Rocketship', in '72. The remainder of the 70s saw the KINKS become bogged down in ill-advised concept albums and self-parody, although while the band were virtually ignored in the UK, they still had a sizeable following in America; the patchy 'Sleepwalker' album nearly went Top 20 in 1977. With the release of the harder rocking 'Low Budget' a couple of years later, the band were embraced fully by the US rock fraternity and hitched a lucrative ride on the stadium rock circuit as well as gaining a sizeable piece of chart action. While the early 80s albums 'Give The People What They Want' and 'State Of Confusion' were competent albeit largely uninspired, the Americans lapped them up and the band even found themselves back in the UK Top 20 with the classy 'Come Dancing' single. Throughout the 80s the band once again descended into inconsistency and commercial wilderness, their live shows being the sole factor in keeping the KINKS' spirit intact. Ray's 1998 'The Storyteller', meanwhile, was his first solo effort since 1985's low-key 'RETURN TO WATERLOO' soundtrack, which incidentally led to a role in the movie, 'ABSOLUTE BEGINNERS' (1986). *BG & MCS*

- **filmography** (composer) {acting} [s-w + dir] –

Percy *(1971 OST by the KINKS =>)* / **Punk And Its Aftershocks** *(1980 {p w/ the KINKS} =>)* / **Return To Waterloo** *(1985 [s-w + dir] {a} OST =>)* / **Absolute Beginners** *(1986 {a} on OST by V/A =>)* / Weird Nightmare *(1993 [dir])*

☐ Spencer DAVIS GROUP segment
(⇒ HERE WE GO 'ROUND THE MULBERRY BUSH)

DAYDREAM BELIEVERS: THE MONKEES STORY

2000 (Can/US 100m* TV) Pebblenut Productions / Rhino Films (PG-13)

Film genre: Pop-Rock music biopic/drama

Top guns: dir: Neill Fearnley → INSIDE THE OSMONDS / s-w: Ron McGee → TO HELL AND BACK (au: Harold Bronson)

Stars: George Stanchev *(Davy Jones)* → MY DINNER WITH JIMI, Aaron Lohr *(Mickey Dolenz)*, Jeff Geddis *(Mike Nesmith)*, L.B. Fisher *(Peter Tork)*, Wallace Langham *(Don Kirschner)*, Stephen Bogaert *(Harris Green)*, Polly Shannon *(Phyllis Nesmith)*, Tony Springer *(Jimi Hendrix)*, **Peter Tork** *(cameo)* <= MONKEES =>), Colin Ferguson *(van foreman)* → INSIDE THE OSMONDS, Jason Knight *(Paul)* → INSIDE THE OSMONDS

Storyline: From 1966, America's answer to the Beatles, the Monkees, branched out of their little worlds via an eponymous TV show (produced by Rob Rafaelson & Bert Schneider) that sparked an overnight pop phenomenon. This is how four young men (actors Davy Jones and Mickey Dolenz, plus musicians Mike Nesmith and Peter Tork) took on the might of the record industry moguls to subsequently play their own music, not the classy but manufactured pop they had to mime. *MCS*

Movie rating: *5

Visual: video + dvd (no audio OST)

Off the record: Non-Monkees tracks include 'Left-Handed Strat' (STAN MEISSNER) and '(All In The) All In All' (the KNACK). *MCS*

– associated release –

the MONKEES: Greatest Hits

May 99. (cd) *Rhino; <(8122 75785-2)>* ☐ ☐
– (Theme from) The Monkees / Last train to Clarksville / I wanna be free / I'm a believer / (I'm not your) Steppin' stone / Mary, Mary / A little bit me, a little bit you / The girl I knew somewhere / Randy Scouse git / Pleasant valley Sunday / Words / Daydream believer / Goin' down / Valleri / D.W. Washburn / It's nice to be with you / Porpoise song (theme from 'Head') / Listen to the band / That was then, this is now / Heart and soul.

☐ Stephanie DE SYKES segment
(⇒ SIDE BY SIDE)

DEADMAN'S CURVE

1978 (US 100m TV) Roger Gimbel Productions / EMI TV; 3rd Feb'78

Film genre: Pop-Rock Music biopic/drama

Top guns: dir: Richard Compton / s-w: Dalene Young (story: Paul Morantz)

Stars: Richard Hatch *(Jan Berry)* → LIVING LEGEND: THE KING OF ROCK'N'ROLL, Bruce Davison *(Dean Torrence)* ← SHORT EYES ← the STRAWBERRY STATEMENT / → CRIMES OF PASSION → an AMBUSH OF GHOSTS → GRACE OF MY HEART, Wolfman Jack *(the Jackal)* ← AMERICAN GRAFFITI / → SGT. PEPPER'S LONELY HEARTS CLUB BAND / → MORE AMERICAN GRAFFITI, Susan Sullivan *(Rainbow)*, Pamela Bellwood *(Annie)*, June Dayton *(Mrs. Berry)*, George D. Wallace *(Mr. Berry)*, Leonard Stone *(Herb Alpert)* → AMERICAN POP, Dick Clark *(himself)* ← the PHYNX ← WILD IN THE STREETS ← JAMBOREE, **Bruce Johnston & Mike Love** *(themselves)* <= the BEACH BOYS =>, **Jan Berry** *(himself)* ← the T.A.M.I. SHOW, Papa Doo Run Run:- Jimmy Armstrong, Mark Ward, Don Zirilli, Jim Rush, Jim Shippey

Storyline: The biopic of Californian surf-pop vocal duo, Jan & Dean, all their highs and lows – especially their lows when Jan was critically injured in a car crash in 1966. *MCS*

Movie rating: *7

Visual: video (no audio OST)

Off the record: JAN & DEAN were of course, Los Angeles surf boys Jan Berry (b. 3 Apr'41) and Dean Torrence (b.10 Mar'40), a fact that surprises many is that they pre-dated fellow surf-ites the Beach Boys by a good few years. From 1958 to 1966 (when JAN had a near-fatal car accident), Jan & Dean notched up numerous Top 20 hits, including debut 'Jennie Lee' (actually credited to Jan & Arnie because DEAN was drafted into the army!), 'Baby Talk' (which nearly hit the same fate – Arnie was called up for the navy!), 1963 chart-topper 'Surf City', 'Dead Man's Curve' (of course!), 'The Little Old Lady (From Pasadena)' and 'Popsicle' (their last hit). In between all the good times was their work on 1964 soundtrack, 'RIDE THE WILD SURF' and a rare television spot on 'THE T.A.M.I. SHOW' around the same time. However, 1966 became a year to forget (the Beach Boys would hit No.1 with 'Good Vibrations'), especially when JAN just barely survived after his Corvette Stingray crashed on April 19th. After a healthy response to the 'DEADMAN..' TV movie, Jan & Dean made a comeback of sorts; sadly, Jan finally suffered a heart attack on March 26th, 2004. For the said TV movie (not to be confused with their 1964 LP, 'Dead Man's Curve / The New Girl In School' (& others of that ilk on combination CDs), JAN & DEAN's music was the source of numerous soundbites. The **BEACH BOYS** were heard on 'Surfin', while a song from the BB repertoire, 'Barbara Ann', was tackled by BRUCE DAVISON; DEAN TORRENCE was vocalist on 'Like A Summer Rain'. *MCS*

– associated UK release –

JAN & DEAN: The Jan & Dean Story

Jun 80. (lp/c) *K-Tel; (NE1/CE2 084)* [–] [67]
– Surf city / Dead man's curve / Ride the wild surf / Help me Rhonda / Little deuce coupe / Fun fun fun / I get around / Sidewalk surfin' / Drag city / The little old lady (from Pasadena) / Baby talk / Gee / We go together / There's a girl / Cindy / My heart sings / Judy / You're on my mind / Clementine / Heart and soul.

DEATH OF A DYNASTY

2003 (US 92m) Roc-a-fella Films / TLA Releasing (R)

Film genre: Hip-Hop Musical mockumentary/comedy

Top guns: dir: Damon Dash ← PAPER SOLDIERS / s-w: Adam Moreno

Stars: Ebon Moss-Bachrach *(Dave Katz)*, Kevin Hart *(P-Diddy / etc.)* ← PAPER SOLDIERS / → IN THE MIX, Rob Stapleton *(Jay-Z / etc.)*, Rashida Jones *(Layna Hudson)* ← TUPAC SHAKUR: THUG ANGEL, Devon Aoki *(Picasso)*, Charlie Murphy *(Dick James / etc.)* ← PAPER SOLDIERS ← MURDER WAS THE CASE ← CB4: THE MOVIE ← JUNGLE FEVER / → ROLL BOUNCE, Damon Dash *(Harlem)* ← PAPER SOLDIERS ← BACKSTAGE / → FADE TO BLACK, **JAY-Z** *(himself)*, Note *(bouncer at Lotus)*, **Capone** *(Damon Dash)* ← PAPER SOLDIERS, Loon *(Turk)*, Carson Daly *(himself)*, Ed Lover *(himself)* ← DOUBLE PLATINUM ← RIDE ← WHO'S THE MAN? ← JUICE / → TUPAC: RESURRECTION, **Flavor Flav** *(reporter #1)* ← PRIVATE PARTS ← WHO'S THE MAN? ← CB4: THE MOVIE, **Mariah Carey** *(herself)* ← GLITTER, Jamie-Lynn Sigler *(sexy woman No.3)*, **Beanie SIGEL** *(Charles 'Sandman' Patterson / himself)*, Chloe Sevigny *(sexy woman No.1)* ← DEMONLOVER ← KIDS / → the BROWN BUNNY, Lorraine Bracco *(Enchante R&B singer No.2)* ← the BASKETBALL DIARIES ← EVEN COWGIRLS GET THE BLUES ← SING, **RUN-D.M.C.** *(rappers/themselves)*, **Kid Capri** *(party DJ)* ← the SHOW ← FLY BY NIGHT ← WHO'S THE MAN?, **Duncan Sheik** *(well-dressed man)*, **Sean 'P. Diddy' Combs** *(cameo)* ← TUPAC: RESURRECTION ← BIGGIE AND TUPAC ← RHYME & REASON ← the SHOW / → FADE TO BLACK, Doctor Dre *(himself)* ← RIDE ← WHO'S THE MAN? ← JUICE, **Rell** *(himself)* ← STREETS IS WATCHING, Michael Rapaport *(cameo)* ← PAPER SOLDIERS ← the BASKETBALL DIARIES, **Q-TIP** *(cameo)*, **Cam'ron** *(himself)* ← PAPER SOLDIERS, **Memphis Bleek** *(cameo)* ← PAPER SOLDIERS ← BACKSTAGE / → FADE TO BLACK, **M.O.P.** *(themselves)*, **Busta Rhymes** *(cameo)* ← RHYME & REASON ← WHO'S THE MAN?, **Russell Simmons** *(himself)* ← BEEF ← BROWN SUGAR ← the SHOW ← TOUGHER THAN LEATHER ← KRUSH GROOVE

Storyline: Journalist David Katz thinks he's getting an insider's view of the hip hop industry from businessman Dash and rapper Jay-Z (no relation). Over the course of three weeks, the naive scribbler is strung along by the partners who set up a scam and have a good laugh at the gossip columns at the same time. However, as David dreams of getting his own column some of his articles start to cause friction between the two schemers. *JZ*

Movie rating: *4

Visual: dvd (no audio OST)

Off the record: In 1997, singer-songwriter and guitarist, **Duncan Sheik** (b.18 Nov'69, Hilton Head, North Carolina), was at No.16 in the US charts with 'Barely Breathing'. *MCS*

☐ Joey DEE segment
(⇒ HEY, LET'S TWIST)

☐ the DEL-AIRES segment
(⇒ the HORROR OF PARTY BEACH)

☐ Terry DENE segment
(⇒ the GOLDEN DISC)

☐ John DENVER segment
(⇒ TAKE ME HOME: THE JOHN DENVER STORY)

DESPERATE TEENAGE LOVEDOLLS

1984 (US 60m) We Got Power Films (18)

Film genre: Punk Rock Musical comedy drama

Top guns: s-w: (+ dir) **Dave MARKEY**, Jennifer Schwartz, Jordan Schwartz

Stars: Jennifer Schwartz *(Kitty Carryall)* → LOVEDOLLS SUPERSTAR, Hilary Rubens *(Bunny Tremelo)*, Janet Housden *(Patch Kelly)* → LOVEDOLLS SUPERSTAR, Kim Pilkington *(Alexandria)*, Tracy Lea *(Patricia Ann Cloverfield)* → LOVEDOLLS SUPERSTAR, Michael F. Glass *(Matt)*, **Jeffrey McDonald** *(Tears Brunell)* <= REDD KROSS =>, **Dez Cadena** *(Flaco)* ← the SLOG MOVIE / → BETTY BLOWTORCH AND HER AMAZING TRUE LIFE ADVENTURES → AMERICAN HARDCORE, **Steven McDonald** *(Johnny Tremaine)* <= REDD KROSS =>, **Victoria Peterson** *(hippie mob killer)* → LOVEDOLLS SUPERSTAR, the She Devils:- **Annette Zilinskas**, Stephanie Shaw, Cathy Sample, Pam Douglas, **Sky Saxon** → LOVEDOLLS SUPERSTAR, Tracy Marshak-Nask *(Tanya Hearst)* → LOVEDOLLS SUPERSTAR, Jordan Schwartz *(doctor/mom)* ← the SLOG MOVIE / → REALITY 86'D → AMERICAN HARDCORE

Storyline: "Thanks for killing my mom, man" may sound a trifle nonchalant, but all-girl group the Love Dolls are used to death and violence. Lead singer Kitty bashes a tramp to death with a guitar and helps her band-mates Bunny and Patch do in their arch-rivals the She Devils. Meanwhile their agent Johnny propels them onwards and upwards but makes the slight mistake of raping one of the girls. You've guessed it, Johnny's next on the list and that glass of wine he's drinking looks suspiciously fizzy. *JZ*

Movie rating: *4

Visual: dvd

Off the record: **Dez Cadena** (was of Black Flag), **Annette Zilinskas** + **Victoria Peterson** (were in the Bangles) and **Sky Saxon** (the Seeds).

Various Artists incl. REDD KROSS (*)

1984. (lp) *Gasatanka;* [ ] [-]
– Ballad of a lovedoll (*) / Legend (come on up to me) (*) / Fox on the run (NIP DRIVERS) / Out of focus (*) / Life of pain (BLACK FLAG) / Self respect (*) / Running fast (GREG GRAFFIN & GREG HETSON) / Johnny Tremaine's theme (WHITE FLAG) / 12 hour trip (SIN 34) / Survive (the BAGS) / Charlie (*) / Stairway to Heaven – instrumental (*) / Purple haze – instrumental (*) / Right's right (DARKSIDE) / You got me (WHITE FLAG) / Hot bitch (with an electric guitar) (WHITE FLAG) / Ballad of a lovedoll – instrumental (*). *<re-iss. 1990 on 'S.S.T.'; SST 072> <(cd-iss. Aug97 on 'Sympathy For The Record Industry'+=; SFTRI 497)>* – Desperate Teenage Lovedolls radio spot (DAVID MARKEY) / interview with Jeff & Steve McDonald (with Edith Massey & Stella).

S/track review: Featuring a plethora of bratty 80s punks, 'DESPERATE TEENAGE LOVEDOLLS' opens with main protagonists, REDD KROSS, and their thrashy but tuneful 'Ballad Of A Lovedoll' before 'Legend' kicks in with its hooky guitars and glorious harmonies, like the Stooges meeting the West Coast pop of the Beach Boys in a sweet and sweaty frenzied battle. Next up, NIP DRIVERS bridge the gap between fuzzy Ramones-esque punk and glam rock on 'Fox On The Run', whilst in contrast the influential battering-ram that is BLACK FLAG offer the pugnacious 'Life Of Pain'. Breaking the mould, Bad Religion's GREG GRAFFIN and GREG HETSON provide the excellent lo-fi rolling acoustic strum-a-long, 'Running Fast'. Normal service is soon resumed, however, with '12 Hour Trip' by SIN 34 which is a phenomenal blissful blast of early Sonic Youth before REDD KROSS reappear with the sinister 'Charlie' and two unnecessary, yet joyful, covers of Led Zeppelin's 'Stairway To Heaven' and Hendrix's 'Purple Haze'. DARKSIDE provide a huge slab of distorted and direct aggressive punk with 'Right's Right', let down by out of tune vocals, and WHITE FLAG get their teenage kicks with two trashy numbers before REDD KROSS bookend this splendid, thrilling album with an instrumental version of 'Ballad Of A Lovedoll'. *LF*

Album rating: *7

DETROIT ROCK CITY

1999 (US 95m) New Line Cinema (R)

Film genre: Rock-music teen movie

Top guns: dir: Adam Rifkin / s-w: Carl V. DuPre

Stars: Edward Furlong *(Hawk)*, Giuseppe Andrews *(Lex)*, James DeBello *(Trip Hurudie)*, Sam Huntington *(Jeremiah 'Jam' Bruce)*, Lin Shaye *(Mrs. Bruce)* ← LAST MAN STANDING ← EVEN COWGIRLS GET THE BLUES ← ROADSIDE PROPHETS ← PUMP UP THE VOLUME ← the LONG RIDERS, Melanie Lynskey *(Beth Bumsteen)* → COYOTE UGLY, Natasha Lyonne *(Christine)*, Emmanuelle Chriqui *(Barbara)* → IN THE MIX, Shannon Tweed *(Amanda Finch)*, **KISS:- Gene Simmons, Paul Stanley, Ace Frehley, Peter Criss** *(themselves)* / Kevin Corrigan *(mechanic 1)* ← WALKING AND TALKING ← BANDWAGON / → BUFFALO '66 → CHELSEA WALLS, Ron Jeremy *(MC)* ← 54 / → OVERNIGHT, Julian Richings *(ticket taker)* ← HARD CORE LOGO ← the TOP OF HIS HEAD, Andy Warhol *(cameo at Studio 54)* ← ROCK AND ROLL HEART ← NICO-ICON ← BLANK GENERATION ← IMAGINE ← COCKSUCKER BLUES ← the VELVET UNDERGROUND AND NICO / → END OF THE CENTURY

Storyline: Four loyal Kiss fans desperately want to see their favourite hard rock band performing in Detroit. True to christian fundamentalist type, however, one of their mothers, believing the band are Devil worshippers, burns the tickets and sends her son to religious school. The remaining three manage to win more tickets, break their friend out of school and head out on the road Detroit bound. Co-produced by Mr Rock School himself, Gene Simmons. *KM*

Movie rating: *5.5

Visual: dvd

Off the record: Ron Jeremy is/was an iconic porn star with er . . . the biggest credentials in Hollywood – one hears.

Various Artists (score: J. Peter Robinson)

Aug 99. (cd) *Mercury: <546389-2)>* [68] Oct99 [ ]
– The boys are back in town (EVERCLEAR) / Shout it out loud (KISS) / Runnin' with the Devil (VAN HALEN) / Cat scratch fever (PANTERA) / Iron man (BLACK SABBATH) / Highway to Hell (MARILYN MANSON) / 20th Century boy (DRAIN STH) / Detroit Rock City (KISS) / Jailbreak (THIN LIZZY) / Surrender – live (CHEAP TRICK) / Rebel rebel (DAVID BOWIE) / Strutter (the DONNAS) / School days (the RUNAWAYS) / Little Willy (SWEET) / Nothing can keep me from you (KISS).

S/track review: Hardly as rockin' as its title suggests (if anyone made Detroit a rock city it was the Stooges and MC5), 'DETROIT ROCK CITY' hosts a passable mix of classic rawk tunes and bizarro covers, the first of which finds EVERCLEAR gamely attempting a grungey update of 'The Boys Are Back In Town' (THIN LIZZY's own 'Jailbreak' is used to satisfyingly cheesy effect in the film when the Kiss fan breaks out of boarding school..). Keeping up the pace, KISS (who also – inevitably – have the honour of the title track) follow with their 1976 party-hard anthem, 'Shout It Out Loud', a cunning production conveniently disguising their vocal failings under a wall of bass and guitar. And let's hear it for the DONNAS punky revision of sidewalk classic, 'Strutter', as shamelessly upfront as David Lee Roth caterwauling his way through 'Runnin' With The Devil', arguably one of VAN HALEN's lesser recordings yet infinitely more promising than PANTERA's mauling of the Ted Nugent classic, 'Cat Scratch Fever'. Things gets back on track with BLACK SABBATH's 'Iron Man' as the album takes a walk on the dark side, MARILYN MANSON losing his stilettos-down-a-blackboard vocals on a barely recognisable 'Highway To Hell' and Marc Bolan's '20th Century Boy' undergoing a traumatic assault by Swedish femme-grungesters DRAIN STH. Easier on the earhole but still an endurance test is CHEAP TRICK's overproduced 'Surrender', the uniquely tuneless RUNAWAYS likewise. The cheese turns mouldy for KISS' rock ballad finale but doesn't spoil an otherwise enjoyable platter. *KM*

Album rating: *6.5

the DEVIL'S REJECTS

2005 sequel (US 109m) Lions Gate Films / UMe (R)

Film genre: slasher/horror movie

Top guns: s-w + dir: **Rob Zombie** ← HOUSE OF 1000 CORPSES

Stars: Sid Haig *(Captain Spaulding)* ← KILL BILL: VOL.2 ← HOUSE OF 1000 CORPSES ← JACKIE BROWN ← the FORBIDDEN DANCE ← FOXY BROWN ← COFFY ← BLACK MAMA, WHITE MAMA ← IT'S A BIKINI WORLD ← BEACH BALL, Bill Moseley *(Otis)* ← HOUSE OF

1000 CORPSES, Sheri Moon Zombie *(Baby)* ← HOUSE OF 1000 CORPSES, Ken Foree *(Charlie Altamont)*, Matthew McGrory *(Tiny)* ← HOUSE OF 1000 CORPSES, William Forsythe *(Sheriff John Wydell)* ← DICK TRACY ← BAJA OKLAHOMA, Leslie Easterbrook *(Mother Firefly)*, Geoffrey Lewis *(Roy Sullivan)* ← CATCH ME IF YOU CAN, Danny Trejo *(Rondo)*, **E.G. Daily** *(Candy)* ← the COUNTRY BEARS ← STREETS OF FIRE ← LADIES AND GENTLEMEN, THE FABULOUS STAINS, P.J. Soles *(Susan)* ← SHAKE, RATTLE & ROCK! tv ← SWEET DREAMS ← ROCK'N'ROLL HIGH SCHOOL, Dave Sheridan *(Officer Ray Dobson)* ← the FIGHTING TEMPTATIONS, Steve Railsback *(Sheriff Ken Dwyer)* ← SCENES FROM THE GOLDMINE, Deborah Van Valkenburgh *(Casey)* ← CHASING DESTINY ← STREETS OF FIRE ← the WARRIORS, Daniel Roebuck *(Morris Green)* ← EDDIE PRESLEY ← DUDES, Brian Posehn *(Jimmy)* → CAKE BOY, Michael Berryman *(Clevon)* ← VOYAGE OF THE ROCK ALIENS, Duane Whitaker *(Dr. Bankhead)* ← PULP FICTION ← SATURDAY NIGHT SPECIAL ← EDDIE PRESLEY

Storyline: The game appears to be up for the murderous Firefly family as an armed-to-the-teeth SWAT team surrounds their house. However, all but Ma Firefly manage to escape the siege and immediately go on the rampage, pursued by Sheriff Wydell, half the State Police, and a couple of deranged bounty hunters. After a massacre at a motel the net closes in on Tiny, Baby, Otis and Captain Spaulding but the pursuers seem to be losing their sanity just as much as the Fireflys. *JZ*

Movie rating: *6

Visual: dvd

Off the record: Sheri Moon is the wife of Rob Zombie. Matthew McGrory is/was the tallest man in the world; he died of natural causes aged 32 (9th August 2005) after making this movie. **E.G. Elizabeth Daily** was actually a Rugrats Movies voiceover. *MCS*

Various Artists incl. "dialogue" (score: Tyler Bates)

Jun 05. (cd) *Hip-O; <04846-2>* □ [-]

– "You ain't getting me" / Midnight rider (the ALLMAN BROTHERS BAND) / "I call 'em like I see 'em" / Shambala (THREE DOG NIGHT) / "Find a new angle" / Brave awakening (TERRY REID) / "It's just so depressing" / It wasn't God who made honky tonk angels (KITTY WELLS) / "Would you say that again" / Satan's got to get along without me (BUCK OWENS & HIS BUCKAROOS) / "This is insane" / Fooled around and fell in love (ELVIN BISHOP) / "Chinese, Japanese" / I can't quit you baby (OTIS RUSH) / "Top secret clown business" / Funk #49 (the JAMES GANG) / "Have fun scrapping them brains" / Rock on (DAVID ESSEX) / "Tootie fruitie" / Rocky mountain way (JOE WALSH) / "What'd you call me?" / To be treated (TERRY REID) / "You have got it made" / Free bird (LYNYRD SKYNYRD) / "We've always been Devil slayers" / Seed of memory (TERRY REID) / "Banjo & Sullivan radio spot #1" / I'm at home getting hammered (while she's out getting nailed) (BANJO & SULLIVAN) / "Banjo & Sullivan radio spot #2".

S/track review: A music enthusiast's compilation – as you would expect from the man behind White Zombie – this is perfect fare for the inner teenager. The meat is classic 70s guitar rock from the likes of the ALLMAN BROTHERS, JOE WALSH and LYNYRD SKYNYRD, interspersed on the DualDisc edition with potty-mouthed vignettes from the film ("Boy, the next word that comes out of your mouth better be some brilliant f***ing Mark Twain shit, because it's definitely getting chiselled on your tombstone."). There's plenty of room for more exotic morsels, too, including DAVID ESSEX's throbbing 'Rock On', a slice of mighty blues from OTIS RUSH and some perky country in KITTY WELLS' 1952 'It Wasn't God Who Made Honky Tonk Angels' (a big-selling answer-song to 'Wild Side Of Life') and BUCK OWENS' less-known 'Satan's Gotta Get Along Without Me' from 1966. A dose of solemnity comes, rather more obscurely, from TERRY REID – the English singer who had turned down the lead role with both Deep Purple and the early Led Zeppelin, but never quite made the breakthrough on his own. Three tracks from his Graham Nash-produced 1976 album 'Seed of Memory' make a gentle introduction to REID's country and folk-flavoured rock: passionate and pleasant if not groundbreaking. Things pick up splendidly for us shallow teen spirits with Zombie's closing country spoof 'I'm At Home Getting Hammered (While She's Out Getting Nailed)'. *ND*

Album rating: *7.5

□ Barry DEVLIN segment
(⇒ SOUL SURVIVOR)

DEVO

Formed: Akron, Ohio, USA ... 1972 by two sets of brothers, Mark and Bob Mothersbaugh together with Gerald and Bob Casale (drummer Alan Myers completed the line-up). From the early 70s, they had been known as the De-Volution Band, before sensibly abbreviating the name to DEVO. This bunch of lab-coated weirdos (taking up the RESIDENTS' terminally skewed vision) issued two obscure 45s on their own indie label, 'Booji Boy'. These were heavily imported into Britain through leading indie outlet, 'Stiff,' late in 1977, and early the following year, both the double A-sided, 'Mongoloid'/'Jocko Homo', and a hilarious electro-fied rendition of the Rolling Stones' '(I Can't Get No) Satisfaction', were re-pressed due to popular demand. A debut album, inspiringly titled 'Q: Are We Not Men? A: We Are Devo!' (produced by BRIAN ENO, who else!?), was released a month later to a confused but appreciative audience who helped propel the record into the Top 20 (Top 100 US). However, their follow-up set, 'Duty Now For The Future' (1979), suffered a slight backlash, the novelty wearing thin without the impact of a hit single. 1980s 'Freedom Of Choice' would have suffered a similar fate, but for a freak US Top 20 single, 'Whip It'. The rest of their 80s output lacked their early wit, although the cinema was graced with their potato-faced glamour in the shape of alt-rockumentary, 'URGH! A MUSIC WAR' (1981), the hit single, 'Working In A Coalmine' from 'HEAVY METAL' (1981) and another hit theme from 'Doctor Detroit' (1983). Having disbanded in the middle of the decade, DEVO (with new drummer, David Kendrick) re-formed in 1988, signing to 'Enigma', but with one non-event album after another (and parts for all in 'SPIRIT OF 76' – 1990 – alongside David Cassidy!), they folded. It's just recently, 2007, that DEVO (with serious film composer Mark Mothersbaugh in their ranks) were back. Incidentally, the solo film score work of Mothersbaugh and the rest of the crew will be in a second edition. *MCS*

- **DEVO filmography** {performance/acting} –

Pray TV *(1980 {p})* / **Urgh! A Music War** *(1981 {p} on OST by V/A =>)* / **Heavy Metal** *(1981 hit single on OST by V/A =>)* / **Human Highway** *(1982 {p/a} =>)* / Doctor Detroit *(1983 hit theme on OST by V/A; see future edition)* / **the Spirit Of '76** *(1990 {a} on OST by V/A =>)* / Shakespeare's Plan 12 From Outer Space *(1991 {p MARK})* / Mystery Men *(1999 {b MARK} on OST by V/A; see future edition)* / **Derailroaded** *(2005 {c} =>)*

DICK TRACY

1990 (US 105m) Buena Vista Pictures (PG)

Film genre: comic-strip gangster/crime comedy

Top guns: dir: Warren Beatty / s-w: Jim Cash, Jack Epps Jr. (comic strip: Chester Gould)

Stars: Warren Beatty *(Dick Tracy)* → TRUTH OR DARE, Charlie Korsmo *('Kid' / Dick Tracy Jr.)*, Glenne Headly *(Tess Trueheart)*, **MADONNA** *(Breathless Mahoney)*, Al Pacino *(Big Boy Caprice)* → the INSIDER, Dustin

Hoffman *(Mumbles)* ← WHO IS HARRY KELLERMAN AND WHY IS HE SAYING THOSE TERRIBLE THINGS ABOUT ME? ← the POINT! ← LITTLE BIG MAN ← MIDNIGHT COWBOY ← the GRADUATE / → WAG THE DOG, William Forsythe *(Flattop)* ← BAJA OKLAHOMA / → the DEVIL'S REJECTS, Charles Durning *(Chief Brandon)* ← FAR NORTH ← the BEST LITTLE WHOREHOUSE IN TEXAS ← I WALK THE LINE / → O BROTHER, WHERE ART THOU?, Mandy Patinkin *(88 Keys)* ← the PRINCESS BRIDE, Paul Sorvino *(Lips Manlis)* → LONGSHOT, R.G. Armstrong *(Pruneface)* ← WHERE THE BUFFALO ROAM ← MEAN JOHNNY BARROWS ← PAT GARRETT & BILLY THE KID ← the FINAL COMEDOWN, Dick Van Dyke *(D.A. Fletcher)* ← BYE BYE BIRDIE / → CURIOUS GEORGE, Kathy Bates *(Mrs. Green)* → PRIMARY COLORS, James Caan *(Spaldoni)* ← THIEF, Estelle Parsons *(Mrs. Trueheart)* ← I WALK THE LINE ← WATERMELON MAN, Henry Silva *(Influence)* ← MAN AND BOY / → the END OF VIOLENCE → GHOST DOG: THE WAY OF THE SAMURAI, Colm Meaney *(cop at Tess')* → the COMMITMENTS, Michael J. Pollard *(Bug Bailey)* ← LITTLE FAUSS AND BIG HALSY ← the WILD ANGELS, Catherine O'Hara *(Texie Garcia)* ← ROCK & RULE / → a MIGHTY WIND → OVER THE HEDGE, Marshall Bell *(Lips' cop)* ← TUCKER: THE MAN AND HIS DREAM ← BIRDY / → AIRHEADS → a SLIPPING-DOWN LIFE, Mary Woronov *(welfare person)* ← ROCK'N'ROLL HIGH SCHOOL FOREVER ← GET CRAZY ← ROCK'N'ROLL HIGH SCHOOL ← the VELVET UNDERGROUND AND NICO / → SHAKE, RATTLE & ROCK! tv, Allen Garfield *(reporter)* ← GET CRAZY ← ONE FROM THE HEART ← ONE-TRICK PONY ← NASHVILLE ← YOU'VE GOT TO WALK IT LIKE YOU TALK IT . . . ← the OWL AND THE PUSSYCAT, Tom Signorelli *(Mike)* ← THIEF ← SORCERER ← the TRIP, Bert Remsen *(bartender)* ← FAST BREAK ← NASHVILLE ← the STRAWBERRY STATEMENT, Charles Fleischer *(reporter)* → STRAIGHT TALK, Hamilton Camp *(store clerk)* ← ROADIE ← AMERICAN HOT WAX, Henry Jones *(night clerk)* ← the GIRL CAN'T HELP IT, James Keane *(Pat Patton)* ← the ROSE / → DON'T LET GO, Bing Russell *(Club Ritz patron)* ← ELVIS: THE MOVIE, Jack Kehoe *(customer at raid)* ← CAR WASH / → YOUNG GUNS II

Storyline: Hey youse guys! Big Boy Caprice ain't messin' around no more as he launches a gang war for control of the underworld, and Lips Manlis is the sucker feeling the heat as Caprice steals his girl and his nightclub. But the forces of law and order (our Dick) are out to get Caprice but his moll, the ridiculously sexy Breathless Mahoney (phew!) is sent on a sabotage mission to tempt Tracy from his stay-at-home sweetheart and divert him from Caprice's crooked capers. *JZ*

Movie rating: *5.5

Visual: video + dvd

Off the record: (see below)

—

MADONNA: I'm Breathless *[* in film]*

May 90. (cd)(lp/c) *Sire; <(7599 26209-2)>(WX 351/+C)* [2] [2]
– He's a man / Sooner or later [*] / Hanky panky / I'm going bananas / Cry baby / Something to remember / Back in business / More [*] / What can you lose [*] / Now I'm following you (part I) / Now I'm following you (part II) / Vogue.

—

Various Artists (score: Danny Elfman)

Jun 90. (cd/c/lp) *Sire; <(7599 26236-2/-4/-1)>* [ ] [ ]
– Ridin' the rails (k.d. LANG and TAKE 6) / Pep, vim and verve (JEFF VINCENT and ANDY PALEY) / It was the whiskey talkin' (not me) (JERRY LEE LEWIS) / You're in the doghouse now (BRENDA LEE) / Some lucky day (ANDY PALEY) / Blue nights (TOMMY PAGE) / Wicked woman, foolish man (AUGUST DARNELL) / The confidence man (PATTI AUSTIN) / Looking glass sea (ERASURE) / Dick Tracy (ICE-T) / Slow rollin' mama (LaVERN BAKER) / Rompin' & stompin' (AL JARREAU) / Mr. Fix-It (1930s version) (DARLENE LOVE) / Mr. Fix-It (DARLENE LOVE) / It was the whiskey talkin' (not me) (rock & roll version) (JERRY LEE LEWIS) / Dick Tracy (90s mix) (ICE-T).

S/track review: As MADONNA strove to break out of her role as the Princess of 80s pop – a title she won and steadily defended for over half a decade – she branched out into cinema. 'Desperately Seeking Susan' worked because, the story goes, she was playing herself. As soundtrack recordings go, the three associated 'DICK TRACY' movie albums take the proverbial biscuit. Bypassing Danny Elfman's underscore (see classical & orchestral scores soundtrack book), there are two that fit into the Pop category. The first is MADONNA's 'I'm Breathless', not really an OST as it's "music from and inspired by the film DICK TRACY" and only three Stephen Sondheim, 40s-era-penned cues ('Sooner Or Later', 'More' & 'What Can You Lose') from the movie feature. The second is an ANDY PALEY-produced/written Various Artists set with nearly all the numbers appearing at some stage in the movie. The source and inspiration are relatively the same, although we are taken a further decade back into the swing-era 30s. Opening with 'Ridin' The Rails' (by country diva k.d. LANG and nostalgia a cappella group TAKE 6) one knows where one's going right from the start, and PALEY even affords himself a few cues. From golden rock'n'roll oldies JERRY LEE LEWIS (who turns in two versions of 'It Was The Whiskey Talkin' (Not Me)'), LaVERN BAKER (with the overtly-suggestive 'Slow Rollin' Mama') and BRENDA LEE ('You're In The Doghouse Now') to new kids on the block, AUGUST DARNELL (aka Kid Creole, on 'Wicked Woman, Foolish Man'), ERASURE ('Looking Glass Sea') and rapper ICE-T (on two versions of the title track). All'n'all, okay if you're that way inclined. Meanwhile, the aforementioned MADONNA 'I'm Breathless' album features non-soundtrack hits such as the risqué, but truly irritating 'Hanky Panky' and global hit 'Vogue'. While the latter MADONNA gem was co-penned with Shep Pettibone, others such as 'He's A Man', 'Cry Baby', 'Something To Remember', 'Back In Business' and 'Now I'm Following You' (in 2 parts) were co-scribed alongside Patrick Leonard. The aforementioned academy award winner: the smoky ballad 'Sooner Or Later' (and Best Song at the Oscars goes to . . . Stephen Sondheim!), does make up for the fact that the rest of MADONNA's 'I'm Breathless' is unashamedly atrocious. Cheeky rhumbas ('I'm Going Bananas'), sickly-sweet show tunes ('Cry Baby'), laborious retro-pop, 'Back In Business' are part of a barrage of cloying tack, while 'Vogue' it must be stated is a genuine pop diamond. So, all'n'all, two albums for the price of er . . . two! *MCS & MR*

Album rating: *2.5 / Various Artists *5.5

– associated hits, etc. –

MADONNA: Vogue

Mar 90. (7"/7"pic-d/c-s) *(W 9851/+P/C)* [–] [1]
(12"+=/cd-s+=) *(W 9851 TX/CD)* – (Strike-a-pose dub mix).
(12"pic-d+=) *(W 9851TW)* – (Bette Davis dub).

MADONNA: Vogue / (Bette Davis dub)

Apr 90. (7"/c-s) *<19863>* [1] [–]
(12"+=/c-s+=/cd-s+=) *<21513-0/-4/-2>* – (Strike-a-pose dub).

MADONNA: Hanky Panky / More

Jun 90. (7"/c-s) *<19789> (W 9789/+C)* [10] Jul90 [2]
('A'-Bare Bottom mix;12"+=/12"pic-d+=/cd-s+=) *<21577> (W 9789 T/TP/CD)* – ('A'-Bare Bones mix).

ICE-T: Dick Tracy (mixes)

Jul 90. (12"/cd-s) *<0-/7599-21704>* [ ] [–]

DILL SCALLION

1999 (US 91m) Brady Oil Entertainment / Pedestrian Films (PG-13)

Film genre: Pop/Rock Musical mockumentary/comedy

Top guns: s-w + dir: Jordan Brady

Stars: Billy Burke *(Dill Scallion)*, Lauren Graham *(Kristie Sue)* → CHASING DESTINY, David Koechner *(Bubba Pearl)* ← WAG THE DOG / → MAN ON

THE MOON, Jason Priestey *(Jo Joe Hicks)*, Kathy Griffin *(Tina)* ← FOUR ROOMS ← PULP FICTION ← MEDUSA: DARE TO BE TRUTHFUL, Henry Winkler *(Larry Steinberg)*, Peter Berg *(Nate Clumson)* ← GIRL 6, Robert Wagner *(Tony Llama)* → HOOT, **Willie NELSON** *(himself)*, **Travis Tritt** *(himself)* ← BLUES BROTHERS 2000, **LeAnn Rimes** *(herself)* → COYOTE UGLY, Drake Bell *(Eugene Bob)* → HIGH FIDELITY, Kevin Fry *(Doug Bob)* ← WHY DO FOOLS FALL IN LOVE

Storyline: Almost by accident, a "singing" school bus driver from central Texas going by the name of Dill Scallion, lands his big chance to be a country music star on Nashville radio. Helped along the way by his hick promoter, Dick also invents a new dance craze courtesy of a wounded foot. *MCS*

Movie rating: *6

Visual: video (no audio OST; score by SHERYL CROW)

Off the record: Along with the more conventional country music stars, **Willie NELSON, LeAnn Rimes & Travis Tritt**, child actor/musician **Drake Bell** subsequently emerged from the indie music scene via well-received debut album, 'Telegraph' (2005); he's since signed to 'Universal' records for sophomore effort, 'It's Only Time' (2006). *MCS*

DIRTY DANCING

1987 (US 100m) Vestron Films (PG-13)

Film genre: romantic/coming-of-age Dance-Musical drama

Top guns: dir: Emile Ardolino / s-w: Eleanor Bergstein

Stars: Jennifer Grey *(Frances "Baby" Houseman)*, Patrick Swayze *(Johnny Castle)* → ROAD HOUSE → OVERNIGHT → DIRTY DANCING: HAVANA NIGHTS, Jerry Orbach *(Dr. Jake Houseman)* → STRAIGHT TALK, **Cynthia Rhodes** *(Penny Johnson)* ← STAYING ALIVE ← FLASHDANCE, Jack Weston *(Max Kellerman)* ← CAN'T STOP THE MUSIC, Jane Brucker *(Lisa Houseman)*, Kelly Bishop *(Marjorie Houseman)* → PRIVATE PARTS, Lonny Price *(Neil Kellerman)*, Max Cantor *(Robbie Gould)*, Miranda Garrison *(Vivian Pressman)* ← XANADU / → SALSA → the FORBIDDEN DANCE, Garry Goodrow *(Moe Pressman)* ← HARD TO HOLD ← AMERICAN HOT WAX ← STEELYARD BLUES

Storyline: Set in 1963, a naive 17 year-old (Baby Houseman) spends the summer season with her family in the Catskills where she falls head-over-heels with hunky dancing instructor, Johnny Castle. She gets her big opportunity to get close to him when his dancefloor partner, Penny (played by Animotion's Cynthia Rhodes), falls pregnant. Step by step we're taken through her sensual but rocky path in the search for love and romance. A coming-of-age film that hits all the right buttons. *MCS*

Movie rating: *8

Visual: video + dvd

Off the record: Cynthia Rhodes was in the techno-pop outfit, Animotion (hits, 'Obsession', etc) and married well-maned singer Richard Marx. *MCS*

Various Artists (score: John Morris)

Sep 87. (lp/c/cd) *R.C.A.; <6408-1/-4/-2 R> (BL/BK/BD 86408)* 1 Oct87 4
– (I've had) The time of my life (BILL MEDLEY & JENNIFER WARNES) / Be my baby (the RONETTES) / She's like the wind (PATRICK SWAYZE) / Hungry eyes (ERIC CARMEN) / Stay (MAURICE WILLIAMS & THE ZODIACS) / Yes (MERRY CLAYTON) / You don't own me (BLOW MONKEYS) / Hey baby (BRUCE CHANNEL) / Overload (ZAPPACOSTA) / Love is strange (MICKEY & SYLVIA) / Where are you tonight? (TOM JOHNSTON) / In the still of the night (the FIVE SATINS). *<2xcd re-iss. Jul99 +=; 07863 67786-2>* – More Dirty Dancing

S/track review: Smooth, silky and elegant in all the right places, this AOR-friendly soundtrack found success initially via three major US hits. The first of which, '(I've Had) The Time Of My Life' waltzed to the top of the charts and won a Best Song Oscar for BILL MEDLEY & JENNIFER WARNES. The former had of course found fame as part of the Righteous Brothers, while the latter had won her first Academy Award five years previously singing 'Up Where We Belong' (from 'An Officer And A Gentleman') alongside Joe Cocker. 'Hungry Eyes' by ERIC CARMEN (he of 'All By Myself' fame) nearly followed the same chart route and surprisingly didn't register at all in the UK, while the incredible hunk himself, PATRICK SWAYZE secured a surprise one-hit-wonder with 'She's Like The Wind'. Apart from modern-pop tracks by MERRY CLAYTON (who hit with the track 'Yes'), the BLOW MONKEYS, TOM JOHNSTON and ZAPPACOSTA, the remainder of the album was mainly taken up by classic golden oldies such as 'Hey! Baby', 'Stay', 'In The Still Of The Night', 'Be My Baby' and the effervescent, 'Love Is Strange'. A second batch in spring '88, 'More Dirty Dancing', kept the commercial fires burning with a plethora of timeless pop pieces, 'Big Girls Don't Cry', 'Do You Love Me', 'Will You Love Me Tomorrow' and 'Wipe Out', segued between a few numbers by scoreman JOHN MORRIS and musical director MICHAEL LLOYD. *MCS*

S/track review: There's nothing particularly dirty about this album, more's the pity. It's about as risqué as 'FOOTLOOSE' and just as evocative of its era. It also sold by the skipful (one of the biggest selling soundtracks of all time) to a female demographic lusting over lead hunk PATRICK SWAYZE. His name's in capitals because even he got a look-in on the soundtrack with the dry ice, wet knickers atmospherics of 'She's Like The Wind'. There's similar, overproduced slush from ex-Raspberries man ERIC CARMEN and Doobie Brother TOM JOHNSTON. ZAPPACOSTA sounds like a stodgy prophecy of Tom Jones' late 90s comeback, but perhaps the most disheartening thing here is the spectacle of MERRY CLAYTON's still impressive voice subjected to an 80s studio on the sub-Prince schtick that is 'YES', her talent for jangling nerves ('PERFORMANCE'), and invoking disaster ('Gimme Shelter') a distant memory. BILL MEDLEY and JENNIFER WARNES' Oscar-winning main theme, '(I've Had) The Time Of My Life', is about the only song with enough real class to rise above the synthetic mire, and remains a totem of written-to-measure 80s pop. Still, sequencing it next to the RONETTES only magnifies how bloodless 80s pop really was. The 50s/60s nuggets (a ploy which many a soundtrack fell back on in those dark days) surely deserve better company. *BG*

Album rating: *6 / More Dirty Dancing *5.5

– spinoff hits, etc. –

BILL MEDLEY & JENNIFER WARNES: (I've had) The Time Of My Life / MICKEY & SYLVIA: Love Is Strange

Sep 87. (7") *<5224> (PB 49625)* 1 Oct87 6

ERIC CARMEN: Hungry Eyes / TOM JOHNSTON: Where Are You Tonight?

Oct 87. (7") *<5315> (PB 49593)* 4 Jan88
(12"+=/cd-s+=) *(PT/PD 49594)* – (I've had) The time of my life.

PATRICK SWAYZE (featuring WENDY FRASER): She's Like The Wind / MAURICE WILLIAMS & THE ZODIACS: Stay

Dec 87. (7"/12") *<5363> (PB/PT 49565)* 3 Mar88 17

MERRY CLAYTON: Yes / the FIVE SATINS: In The Still Of The Night

Feb 88. (7") *<6989> (PB 49563)* 45 May88 70

Various Artists: More Dirty Dancing

Mar 88. (lp/c/cd) *<6965-1/-4/-2 R> (BL/BK/BD 86965)* 3 Apr88 3
– (I've had) The time of my life (JOHN MORRIS ORCHESTRA) / Big girls don't cry (the 4 SEASONS) / Merengue (MICHAEL LLOYD & LE DISC) / Some kind of wonderful (the DRIFTERS) / Johnny's mambo (MICHAEL LLOYD & LE DISC) / Do you love me (the CONTOURS) / Love man (OTIS REDDING) / Wipeout (SURFARIS) / These arms of mine (OTIS REDDING) / De todo un poco (MICHAEL LLOYD & LE DISC) / Cry to me (SOLOMON BURKE) / Trot the fox (MICHAEL LLOYD & LE DISC) / Will you love me tomorrow (the SHIRELLES) / Kellerman's anthem (EMILE

BERGSTEIN CHORALE) / (I've had) The time of my life (JOHN MORRIS ORCHESTRA).

Various Artists: Dirty Dancing Live In Concert

Apr 89. (lp/c/cd) *<9660-1/-4/-2> (PL/PK/PD 90336)* [ ] May89 [19]
– (tracks by MERRY CLAYTON, ERIC CARMEN, the CONTOURS, BILL MEDLEY and the DIRTY DANCING CAST).

DIRTY DANCING: HAVANA NIGHTS

2004 (US 86m) Lions Gate Films / Miramax Films (PG-13)

Film genre: romantic teen drama

Top guns: dir: Guy Ferland / s-w: Boaz Yakin, Victoria Arch (story: Kate Gunzinger, Peter Sagal)

Stars: Diego Luna *(Xavier Suarez)*, Romola Garai *(Katey Miller)*, Sela Ward *(Jeannie Miller)* ← 54, John Slattery *(Bert Miller)*, Jonathan Jackson *(James Phelps)*, January Jones *(Eve)*, Mike Boorem *(Susie Vendetto)*, Rene Lavan *(Carlos Suarez)*, **Mya Harrison** *(Lola Martinez)* → HOW SHE MOVE, **Heather Headley** *(Rosa Negra singer)*, **Shawn Kane** *(country club singer)*, Patrick Swayze *(dance class instructor)* ← OVERNIGHT ← ROAD HOUSE ← DIRTY DANCING

Storyline: Katey and her parents move to Havana just before Castro's revolution. Her parents think she will soon meet a rich socialite, but she secretly begins dating waiter Javier who introduces her to Cuban dance music. As the revolution looms, Katie's parents decide to return to America in fear of their lives. Should Katey go with them, or will her love for Javier tempt her to stay behind? JZ

Movie rating: *5

Visual: dvd

Off the record: **Mya** Harrison (was part of the 'Moulin Rouge' – 'Lady Marmalade' No.1 collaboration with Christina Aguilera, etc.

—

Various Artists (score: Heitor Pereira)

Feb 04. (cd) *J-Records; <57758> B.M.G.; (82876 59838-2)* [46] Mar04 [ ]
– Dance like this (WYCLEF JEAN feat. CLAUDETTE ORTIZ) / Dirty dancing (BLACK EYED PEAS) / Guajira (I love U 2 much) (YERBA BUENA) / Can I walk by (JAZZE PHA feat. MONICA) / Satellite (SANTANA feat. JORGE MORENO) / El beso del final (CHRISTINA AGUILERA) / Represent, Cuba (ORISHAS feat. HEATHER HEADLEY) / Do you only wanna dance (MYA) / You send me (SHAWN KANE) / El estuche (ATERCIOPELADOS) / Do you only wanna dance (JULIO DAVIEL BIG BAND conducted by CUCCO PENA) / Satellite – nave espacial (SANTANA feat. JORGE MORENO).

S/track review: The original 'DIRTY DANCING' stands alongside the likes of 'GREASE' and 'SATURDAY NIGHT FEVER' among the biggest film soundtracks of all time, so it stands to reason then, that this "re-imaging" of the 'DIRTY DANCING' legend – that is, it's not quite a remake but not exactly a sequel either – means we get a hamfisted attempt at musical crossover (R&B pop meets Latin) that ultimately leaves both genres wanting. Let's be honest, if you are looking for a genuine introduction to Latin music you'd be silly to look here, this is an unsubtle Spanglish hybrid, hence why artists like WYCLEF JEAN, MYA and the BLACK EYED PEAS are on hand to water down any fire. The original might have seemed random on paper but the songs shared an aesthetic that worked for the film and the disc. This is a jumble of contemporary styles, bastardised trad Latin flavours and too few decent ideas. You can't fault the energy of some of this, the rap meets acoustic guitar blend on YERBA BUENA's 'Guajira' is the most passable attempt at a credible synergy. Then there's the likes of SHAWN KANE, he should expect some kind of jail term for his reedy take on Sam Cooke's 'You Send Me'. Only JULIO DAVIEL BIG BAND's 'Do You Only Wanna Dance' suggests what kind of expansive brass-driven live sound should dominate an album like this motley collection of flaccid grooves. They're just plain dirty. MR

Album rating: *2.5

DISAPPEARING ACTS

2000 (US 116m TV) Amen Ra Films / HBO

Film genre: romantic urban comedy drama

Top guns: dir: Gina Prince-Bythewood / s-w: Lisa Jones (story: Terry McMillan

Stars: Sanaa Lathan *(Zora Banks)* → BROWN SUGAR, Wesley Snipes *(Franklin Swift)* ← JUNGLE FEVER, Regina Hall *(Portia)* → MALIBU'S MOST WANTED, Lisa Arrindell Anderson *(Claudette)*, **Kamaal Fareed** *(Reg Baptiste)* <= Q-TIP =>, Clark Johnson *(Jimmy)*, John Amos *(Mr. Swift)* ← LET'S DO IT AGAIN ← SWEET SWEETBACK'S BAADASSSSS SONG ← VANISHING POINT, CCH Pounder *(Mrs. Swift)*, Aunjanue Ellis *(Pam)* → RAY, Michael Imperioli *(Vinney)* ← LAST MAN STANDING ← GIRL 6 ← I SHOT ANDY WARHOL ← the BASKETBALL DIARIES ← JUNGLE FEVER

Storyline: When schoolteacher Zora and construction worker Franklin meet it's lust at first sight. Zora has ambitions to be a singer, while Franklin has just lost his job through the demon drink. When they discover there's a baby on the way, the couple find out that living together is not easy, as their conflicting personalities force them apart. Can they find true love through their unborn child or will they simply drift away from one another as time goes on? JZ

Movie rating: *6.5

Visual: dvd

Off the record: **Kamaal Fareed** is actually Q-TIP.

—

Various Artists (score: Allen Cato)

Dec 00. (cd) *Artemis; <622014-2>* [ ] [–]
– Got to know you better (ANGIE STONE) / Remember (MESHELL NDEGEOCELLO) / Sweet revenge (SPOOKS) / Love language (TALIB KWELI feat. LES NUBIANS) / Brooklyn (MELKY SEDECK) / Do I love you enough (TONY KURTIS) / A song for you (DONNY HATHAWAY) / Call on me (TERRY ELLIS) / Have a little faith in me (CHAKA KHAN) / Just for my baby (MELKY SEDECK) / Unconditional (KURUPT feat. SKY) / Flesh not bone (SPOOKS) / Head over heels (SHAWN STOCKMAN) / Super people (CURTIS MAYFIELD & THE NOTATIONS) / Y.O.Y. (BOREALIS).

S/track review: You'd think after 50 odd years of singing "I Love You" songs we'd get bored of it. But hell, no, there's still plenty of mileage in those three little words. Or at least the build up to them or the aftermath of them. And this showing would indicate there's still plenty of life left in the subject yet. Starting off quietly and rising to a roar, 'DISAPPEARING ACTS' means tracks by ANGIE STONE, SPOOKS and MESHELL NDEGEOCELLO are so slow burn they could be overlooked when in fact they are the strongest here, managing to be both fresh and understated. TALIB KWELI might not seem like such a romantic but he spins some glorious syncopated verses round an innovative beat while French vocal outfit LES NUBIANS counter with some gossamer harmonies. Things take a turn for the worst mid-way where there's a pile up of syrupy, by-the-numbers ballads. You can actually hear the chicken-in-a-basket being served in the background. Only the great DONNY HATHAWAY can break the torpor with the wistful, affecting beauty of 'A Song For You'. Skip on then to CURTIS MAYFIELD's excellent bumping, thumping 'Super People' while BOREALIS close with a righteous funk-rock blaster that lies somewhere between Lenny Kravitz's retro rumble and Rage Against The Machine's eloquent aggression. An odd finish perhaps given what has come before but proof that love is a many splintered thing. *MR*

Album rating: *7

□ DISC JOCKEY JAMBOREE alt. (⇒ JAMBOREE!)

DISCO FEVER

1978 (US 91m) Group 1 International (R)

Film genre: Pop/Disco-music drama/thriller

Top guns: dir: Lamar Card / s-w: John Arnoldy

Stars: FABIAN *(Desmond)*, Casey Kasem *(manager)*, Michael Blodgett *(disco singer)* ← BEYOND THE VALLEY OF THE DOLLS ← CATALINA CAPER ← the TRIP, Phoebe Dorin *(Cybill)*, George Barris, Susette Carroll, Tanya George, Joel Kramer, Kate Netter, Stephanie Black, Eduardo Nieto

Storyline: Signed up by a dodgy club owner, former 50s acapulco teen idol, Desmond (and his horny manager), becomes the opening act to a newbie disco singer – and end up performing in an aeroplane. *MCS*

Movie rating: *3

Visual: none (no audio OST)

Off the record: FABIAN was the star here singing three non-disco songs (including 'Movin' On'). Actor, Casey Kasem, was author of all these American chart books. *MCS*

DISK-O-TEK HOLIDAY

1966 (US 80m) Allied Artists (w/ Canterbury / Delmore)

Film genre: Pop-Rock musical

Top guns: dir: Douglas Hickox ← JUST FOR YOU ← IT'S ALL OVER TOWN, Vincent Scarza

Stars: Casey Paxton *(himself/performer)*, Katherine Quint *(herself/performer)*, Hy Lit *(himself)* → the IN CROWD, **a Band Of Angels** *(performers)*, **the Bachelors** *(performers)* ← I'VE GOTTA HORSE ← JUST FOR YOU ← IT'S ALL OVER TOWN, **the Vagrants** *(performers)*, **Peter & Gordon** *(performers)* ← POP GEAR ← JUST FOR YOU, **the Chiffons** *(performers)*, **Freddie & The Dreamers:- Freddie Garrity, Derek Quinn, Roy Crewsdon, Pete Birrell, Bernie Dwyer** *(performers)* ← EVERY DAY'S A HOLIDAY ← JUST FOR YOU ← WHAT A CRAZY WORLD / → OUT OF SIGHT → CUCKOO PATROL, **Johnny B. Great** *(performer)* ← JUST FOR YOU, **Louise Cordet** *(performer)*, **the Applejacks** *(performers)* ← JUST FOR YOU, **Jackie & The Raindrops** *(performers)*, **the Merseybeats** *(performers)* ← JUST FOR YOU, **the Rockin' Ramrods** *(performers)*, **the Orchids** *(performers)* ← JUST FOR YOU, **Millie Small** *(performer)*, **Freddy Cannon & the Ramrods** *(performer)* ← JUST FOR FUN

Storyline: Understandibly disjointed, in the fact they pieced two films together for this, 'DISCOTHEQUE HOLIDAY' and 1964's 'JUST FOR YOU'. However, you do get a basic plot. Casey Paxton, is an up and coming pop star who attempts to kickstart his musical career by convincing A&R people, through many trips to the studio with his girlfriend, that he's the one. *MCS*

Movie rating: *3.5

Visual: (no audio) dvd adds 30 min doc on Screaming Lord Sutch

Off the record: The track order listing is as follows:- 'Hide & Seek' (a BAND OF ANGELS), 'Teenage Valentino' (the BACHELORS), 'The Fox' (the BACHELORS), 'Oh Those Eyes' (the VAGRANTS), 'Leave Me Alone (PETER & GORDON), 'Nobody Knows' (the CHIFFONS), 'You Were Made For Me' (FREDDIE & THE DREAMERS), 'If I Had A Hammer' (JOHNNY B. GREAT), 'It's So Hard To Be Good' (LOUISE CORDET), 'Tell Me When' (the APPLEJACKS), 'Locomotion' (JACKIE & THE RAINDROPS), 'Milkman' (the MERSEYBEATS), 'Play It' (ROCKIN' RAMRODS), 'Low In The Valley' (the BACHELORS), 'Mr. Scrooge' (the ORCHIDS), 'Sugar Dandy' (MILLIE SMALL), 'Soft As The Dawn' (PETER & GORDON), 'Tallahassee' + 'Abigail Beecher' + 'Buzz, Buzz A-Diddle It' + 'Beachwood City' (all live) (FREDDY CANNON with the RAMRODS), 'Just For You' (FREDDIE & THE DREAMERS). *MCS*

the DR. JEKYLL & MR. HYDE ROCK 'N ROLL MUSICAL

2003 (US 91m) Andre Champagne Productions / Omega Entertainment

Film genre: Pop/Rock Musical horror

Top guns: dir: Andre Champagne / s-w: **Alan Bernhoft**, Robert Ricucci (nov: Robert Louis Stevenson)

Stars: Alan Bernhoft *(Henry Jekyll & Edward Hyde)*, Lisa Peterson *(Anne)*, Terence Marinan *(Lanyon)*, Susannah Devereux *(Amanda Lennox)*, John Heffron *(Utterson)*, Robert Ricucci *(Poole)*, William Knight *(Inspector McCree)*, Maria Kress *(Ellie; the hooker)*, **Hal Blaine** *(the wino)* ← MAN ON THE MOON ← GIRLS! GIRLS! GIRLS! / → BEAUTIFUL DREAMER: BRIAN WILSON AND STORY OF 'SMiLE'

Storyline: The classic RLS story is updated to modern day L.A. where Dr Jekyll is busy creating a potion which will bring out the inner demon in men (so the Nobel Peace Prize is off the cards anyway). Meanwhile, fiancée Anne and her friend Henry try to stop Jekyll from interfering with the unknown, but sure enough Mr Hyde soon emerges onto the streets of L.A. causing mayhem with his heavy wooden cane. Can Henry and Anne stop Jekyll in time or will he continue playing Hyde and seek with them? *JZ*

Movie rating: *4

Visual: dvd

Off the record: Alan Bernhoft was born in Jackson, Mississippi, USA. After becoming a "serious" drummer at the age of eight, his music tastes developed from the blues to the Beatles. His first band was an arty punk act, the Wedgeheads, who subsequently evolved into the Mice! A debut single, 'I Like Her', was promptly followed by 'I Can Fly', a rare 45 issued for Greg Shaw's L.A.-based 'Voxx' records. The main songwriter with groups such as Mary Kelly (four-song EP, 'Living In A Pay Toilet'), Alan found time to score his own rock opera, 'The Strange Case Of Jekyll & Hyde', a musical on which he "produced, played all the instruments and created all the vocal characterizations". The film version (which received many awards) showed he was a man of many talents; his tributes to the Beatles (especially Lennon) are apparently worth checking out. Watch out for a new horror musical, 'Frankenstein Rock Musical' (re-scheduled – one thinks – for 2008). *MCS*

– associated release –

Original Cast (composer: ALAN BERNHOFT)

Sep 03. (cd) *Jaxalon; <none>* [–] net [–]
– Jekyll's theme / Overture / Jekyll's theme – Hyde's theme / Listen, Jekyll / Some things / Henry / Anne / The London fog / All that really matters / Another bottle of beer / Little girls / Midnight tonight / Where is Henry? / Time for a kill – medley / I'm comin' for you / King of the night.

John DOE

Born: John Nommensen, 25 Feb'54, Decatur, Illinois, USA. A leading figure in the L.A. underground punk scene, having been a part (i.e. bass player) of the rootsy, cowpunk band, X, alongside his then wife and vocalist, Exene Cervenka. X released a string of studio LPs from 1980s debut 'Los Angeles' to 1987's disappointing 'See How We Are', their most influential being all the ones inbetween: 'Wild Gift' (1981), 'Under The Big Black Sun' (1982), 'More Fun In The New World' (1983) and 'Ain't Love Grand' (1985). The split was inevitable with the divorce in 1985 of JOHN and Exene (he remarried in '87 to Gigi Blair). A celluloid testament to their seminal work lies in some live footage in performance flicks such as 'URGH! A MUSIC WAR' (1981), Penelope Spheeris' 'The DECLINE OF WESTERN CIVILIZATION' (1981) and 'The UNHEARD MUSIC' (1986). While DOE ventured into a low-key solo sojourn (debut album, 'Meet John Doe' in 1990), the man with the rugged looks also carved out a lucrative acting career. From humble beginnings in 1986's 'Salvador' to 'BOOGIE NIGHTS' (1997) to 'The Sandpiper' in 2007, DOE has combined serious roles with a plethora of countrified, rock-orientated movies such as 'BORDER RADIO' (1987), 'GREAT BALLS OF FIRE!' (1989), 'ROADSIDE PROPHETS' (1992), 'PURE COUNTRY' (1992) and 'GEORGIA' (1995). JOHN DOE is still going strong music-wise in 2007, having released his umpteenth set, 'A Year In The Wilderness' for 'Yep Roc' records. *MCS*

- **filmography** {acting} –

Urgh! A Music War *(1981 {p w/ X} on OST by V/A =>)* / **the Decline Of Western Civilization** *(1981 {p w/ X} on OST by V/A =>)* / **the Unheard Music** *(1986 {*p w/ X} =>)* / Salvador *(1986 {a})* / 3:15 – The Moment Of Truth *(1986 {b})* / Slam Dance *(1987 {a} OST by Mitchell Froom)* / **Border Radio** *(1987 {*})* / Road House *(1989 {a} OST by V/A; see future edition)* / **Great Balls Of Fire!** *(1989 {*} OST by JERRY LEE LEWIS =>)* / a Matter Of Degrees *(1990 {a})* / Liquid Dreams *(1991 {a})* / **Roadside Prophets** *(1992 {*} on OST by V/A =>)* / **Pure Country** *(1992 {*} OST by GEORGE STRAIT =>)* / **Shake, Rattle And Rock!** *(1994 TV {a})* / Wyatt Earp *(1994 {a})* / **Georgia** *(1995 {*})* / Scorpion Spring *(1996 {a})* / *Black Circle Boys (1997 {*})* / Vanishing Point *(1997 TV {*})* / **Touch** *(1997 {a} OST by DAVE GROHL =>)* / the Piece Of Kissing *(1997 {a})* / **Boogie Nights** *(1997 {b} OST by V/A =>)* / Get To The Heart: The Barbara Mandrell Story *(1997 TV {a})* / Lone Greasers *(1998 {a})* / the Pass *(1998 {b})* / Black Cat Run *(1998 TV {a})* / Odd Man *(1998 {b})* / *Drowning On Dry Land (1999 {b})* / **Sugar Town** *(1999 {a})* / Knocking On Death's Door *(1999 {a})* / Forces Of Nature *(1999 {a})* / the Rage: Carrie 2 *(1999 {a})* / Wildflowers *(1999 {b})* / Brokedown Palace *(1999 {a})* / the Specials *(2000 {a})* / Lucky 13 *(2001 {a})* / **Gypsy 83** *(2001 {a})* / Jon Good's Wife *(2001 {a})* / the Employee Of The Month *(2002 {a})* / the Good Girl *(2002 {a})* / Bug *(2002 {b})* / Wuthering Heights *(2003 TV {*})* / **the Mayor Of Sunset Strip** *(2003 {p} on OST by V/A =>)* / Torque *(2004 {a})* / Tom 51 *(2005 {a})* / Pledge Of Allegiance *(2005 {a})* / the Darwin Awards *(2006 {a})* / the Sandpiper *(2007 {*})*

DOGS IN SPACE

1987 (Aus 103m) Burrowes Film Group / Skouras Pictures (R)

Film genre: urban Rock-music drama

Top guns: dir: (+ s-w) Richard Lowenstein ← AUSTRALIAN MADE: THE MOVIE ← WHITE CITY

Stars: Michael Hutchence *(Sam)* → AUSTRALIAN MADE: THE MOVIE, Saskia Post *(Anna)* → PROOF, Nique Needles *(Tim)* ← SHOUT! THE STORY OF JOHNNY O'KEEFE, Deanna Bond *(the girl)*, Tony Helou *(Luchio)*, Chris Haywood *(chainsaw man)* → SWEET TALKER, Peter Walsh *(Anthony)*, Laura Swanson *(Clare)*, Adam Briscomb *(Grant)*, **Ollie Olsen** *(Bowie fan)*, **Hugo Race** *(Pierre)* → QUEEN OF THE DAMNED, Marie Hoy *(herself)*, Noah Taylor *(Bowie fan)* → ALMOST FAMOUS → the PROPOSITION, **Edward Clayton-Jones** *(Nick)*, **Glenys Osborne** *(Cathy McQuade)*, **John Murphy** *(Leanne's brother)* ← GIVE MY REGARDS TO BROAD STREET / → BIGGER THAN TINA, **Chuck Meo** *(Charles)*, **Tim Millikan**

Storyline: It's 1978 and punk rock is sweeping Australia. In a run-down suburb of Melbourne new wave/punk group, Dogs In Space, sit in their flat waiting for the Skylab satellite to crash to earth (there's a reward if you recover a piece). Their apartment block is a magnet for every misfit and outcast of the day, and alcohol, drugs and rock music are the mainstay of their existence. *JZ*

Movie rating: *6

Visual: video

Off the record: Ollie Olsen (b. Ian Olsen, Norway; raised Melbourne) collaborated with **Michael Hutchence** in the band, Max Q; he also scored the film 'Head On' in 1998. Ollie was also the leader of electronic outfit, Whirlywirld, who released a couple of EPs in 1979/80 for 'Missing Link' records. **Hugo Race** was bass player with Nick CAVE & the Bad Seeds. **Chuck Meo** was drummer with the Ears, **Edward Clayton-Jones** played guitar for Wreckery and **Glenys Osborne** played bass with Deckchair Overboard. *MCS*

—

Various Artists incl. MICHAEL HUTCHENCE (*)

Sep 87. (lp/c) *Chase; <CLPX 14>* [–] Austra [–]
– Dog food (IGGY POP) / Dogs in space (*) / Win/lose (OLLIE OLSEN) / Anthrax (GANG OF FOUR) / Skysaw (BRIAN ENO) / True love (the MARCHING GIRLS) / Shivers (BOYS NEXT DOOR) / Diseases – instrumental (THRUSH & THE C**TS) / Pumping ugly muscle – instrumental (PRIMITIVE CALCULATORS) / Golf course (*) / The green dragon (*) / Shivers (MARIE HOY & FRIENDS) / Endless sea (IGGY POP) / Rooms for the memory (*). *<US-iss.Dec87 on 'Atlantic' lp/c/cd; 81789-1/-4/-2> (UK-iss.May88 on 'Mercury' lp/c (cd); MERH/+C 122 (832748-2)*

S/track review: A timepiece that encapsulates the late 70s, post-punk era in and around Melbourne, Australia, 'DOGS IN SPACE' is definitely the only soundtrack of its kind. To attain a certain sense of where with all, filmmaker Richard Lowenstein hired the semi-legendary OLLIE OLSEN to be musical director/producer. OLSEN's experience with Suicide-esque, electro outfit, Whirlywirld, and others such as PRIMITIVE CALCULATORS (here with 'Pumping Ugly Muscle') was just the ticket to inspire the latter band plus THRUSH & THE C**TS (who kick off side two with 'Diseases') to re-form. Both partly instrumental except for the odd "ooh" and "aah", etc, these tracks were re-recorded (from 1979 tapes) exclusively for the film, Ollie even contributing piano on 'Diseases'. The delightfully-named THRUSH & THE . . . er . . . C**TS (didn't know Celts was a sweary word!) were led by bassist Denise Grant and vocalist Jules Taylor (David Light played drums), while the CALCULATORS featured frontman Stuart Grant and Denise, again, this time keyboards, with Light on bass. But OLSEN is everywhere. Solo, he re-records an old Whirlywirld number from early 1980, 'Win/Lose' (very Fad Gadget), produces three songs for INXS frontman, MICHAEL HUTCHENCE: 'Dogs In Space' and 'Golf Course' (both incidentally penned by former Ears members, Sam Sejavka and Mick Lewis), plus 'Rooms For The Memory' (OLSEN as writer, producer, programmer); a 4th cue by the Australian hunk is a storytelling segment from the movie entitled 'The Green Dragon'. Last but not least, OLSEN works with actress MARIE HOY (& FRIENDS) on her celluloid version of Rowland Howard's indie-rock ballad 'Shivers', the original by BOYS NEXT DOOR (featuring Ollie's old pre-Birthday Party buddie, Nick Cave) also finding a place on the soundtrack. Another nugget from Down Under comes by way of the MARCHING GIRLS, a trio of ex-pat Kiwis whose film song, 'True Love', was licensed to Bob Last's Edinburgh-based independent 'Fast Product' offshoot, 'Pop Aural', way back in 1980. The British connection also saw classics from GANG OF FOUR ('Anthrax') and BRIAN ENO ('Skysaw'), the latter from the man's 1975 set, 'Another Green World'. Leaving the best till last, there are two tracks by the Godfather Of Punk himself, IGGY POP: soundtrack opener 'Dog Food' and unlucky for some track 13, 'Endless Sea', both featuring one-time Sex Pistol, Glen Matlock. If energy and sweat equalled brilliance, this album would've warranted a ten out of ten; the fact that it isn't even near that elusive number shows some sort of failure to communicate on both levels – film and soundtrack. *MCS*

Album rating: *5.5

– spinoff releases, etc. –

MICHAEL HUTCHENCE: Rooms For The Memory / Golf Course

Sep 87. (7") *WEA; (7-258441)* [–] Austra [–]

DOING TIME FOR PATSY CLINE

1997 (Austra 95m) Oilrag Productions (PG)

Film genre: C&W Musical/showbiz comedy/drama/road movie

Top guns: s-w + dir: Chris Kennedy

Stars: Richard Roxburgh *(Boyd)* → MOULIN ROUGE! → STEALTH, Miranda Otto *(Patsy)*, Matt Day *(Ralph)*, Tony Barry *(Dwayne)*, Roy Billing *(dad)*, Kiri Paramore *(Ken)*, Jeff Truman *(Warren)*

Storyline: Farmer's son Ralph wants to swap the Outback for Nashville, Tennessee, but first he must make his way across New South Wales to get to the airport. He hitches a lift with a con-man called Boyd and his girlfriend Patsy, who sings just like the famous Ms. Cline. However, Ralph soon finds himself on the wrong side of the law when Boyd's shenanigans land them in jail – where Ralph learns that deep down Boyd is a good man at heart. *JZ*

Movie rating: *6

Visual: video

Off the record: Not to be confused with the French film, 'C.R.A.Z.Y.'.

—

Various Artists/Cast (score: Peter Best *)

1997. (cd) *Wild Sound; (OST 005)* [–] Austra [–]
– The road to Nashville (*) / Sweet old world (EMMYLOU HARRIS) / Life's railway to Heaven (PATSY CLINE) / Midnight special (MATT DAY) / Roses for Patsy (*) / Crazy (MIRANDA OTTO) / She's not for us (*) / Gaol train (*) / Girl's night out (GINA JEFFREYS) / Steppin' on love ('KEN', 'ALFIE' and 'DWAYNE') / Mexicali punch-up (*) / My mother's silver hair ('KEN', 'ALFIE' and 'DWAYNE') / The Grand Ol' Opry (*) / If only I could stay asleep (PATSY CLINE) / Boyd's jazz (*) / Boulder to Birmingham (EMMYLOU HARRIS) / Every little thing (CARLENE CARTER) / Crash (*) / Goodbye Patsy (*) / Dead red roses (MIRANDA OTTO, MATT DAY & CHRISTINE MOY).

S/track review: Ah! Patsy Cline, the greatest female C&W singer of all time, she simply blew away the opposition with her crystal-clear, but lived-in vocal style. CLINE finds herself among some other modern-day Nashville singers such as EMMYLOU HARRIS and CARLENE CARTER, but it's the former who shines through via 'Life's Railway To Heaven' (altogether now "choo-choo-puh-puh") and 'If Only I Could Stay Asleep'. However, it's a score piece ('The Road To Nashville') that opens up the record, Australian Peter Best getting to grips with combining a moody rootsy feel (as with 8 other cues) to sit next to some fine, if not outstanding country nostalgia. If there was one comparison for his short'n'sweet dirges, it's probably the "infinite" guitar sound of U2's The Edge – 'Roses For Patsy' and 'She's Not For Us', other prime examples. Already a staple of the Grand Ol' Opry, the aforementioned EMMYLOU HARRIS switches the mood into mournful but uplifting courtesy of Lucinda Williams' 'Sweet Old World' and golden nugget 'Boulder To Birmingham' – simply delightful. Ditto 'Every Little Thing' by CARLENE CARTER. Cast members too get a share of the country musical spoils – if that's the correct terminology. However, MATT DAY comes across as quite amateur with his version of 'Midnight Special', although he would probably admit to being in a no-win situation next to the aforementioned country legends. MIRANDA OTTO, meanwhile, tries her damnedest to shine through on a Patsy gem, 'Crazy' (incidentally penned by another giant, Willie Nelson), while both latter thespians get together with CHRISTINE MOY for finale 'Dead Red Roses'. The novelty value comes by way of two numbers by 'KEN', 'ALFIE' AND 'DWAYNE', while GINA JEFFREYS gets all Timbuk 3 on 'Girl's Night Out'. Now these were spoilers. *MCS*

Album rating: *6

Fats DOMINO

Born: Antoine Domino, 26 Feb'28, New Orleans, Louisiana, USA. Growing up in a musical family, Fats began playing local honky tonk clubs before he even reached his teens. Nicknamed "Fats" – due to his 16-stone stature – by his bass player, Billy Diamond, he was soon tinkling the ivories alongside Crescent City masters like Professor Longhair and Champion Jack Dupree, while "digging" the records of Fats Waller and Louis Jordan. DOMINO was only sixteen when he joined the band of trumpeter/producer/composer extrordinaire, Dave Bartholomew, although the pair would subsequently strike up a long and fruitful partnership. Also working as an A&R man for 'Imperial', Bartholomew helped the youngster sign to the label in 1949, the same year the pair co-penned what would become DOMINO's debut single, 'The Fat Man'. A rollicking piano groove oft cited as the first rock'n'roll record (alongside a host of others), the track was release by 'Imperial' in the spring of 1950 and went on to sell a million copies over the ensuing three years. More importantly, it created a sizeable market for Fats' laid-back, free-rolling take on classic New Orleans R&B. It was only a matter of time before he crossed over to the mainstream pop charts and in summer 1955 Fats took his propulsive boogie-woogie to the masses with 'Ain't That A Shame', a US Top 10 smash. Along with his appearance in teen movies, 'SHAKE, RATTLE & ROCK!', 'The GIRL CAN'T HELP IT' and 'JAMBOREE', his success grew to almost a decade of regular chart action, his best-loved and most well known song, 'Blueberry Hill', making the Top 10 on both sides of the pond; another classic 'It Keeps Rainin'', has been cited as a precursor to Jamaican ska/reggae after import copies caused a musical storm – Bitty McLean took it to UK No.2 in 1993. All this and more consolidated Fats as one of the most popular and respected performers of the rock'n'roll era, his unique encapsulation of his native city's multicultural musical heritage seeing him rack up more sales than any other American artist save ELVIS PRESLEY. Among the best and biggest of his 45s were 'Blue Monday' (sadly not an early version of New Order's electro classic), 'I'm Walkin'', 'Whole Lotta Loving' and 'Walking To New Orleans', all million-selling US Top 10 hits. By the time of Fats' move to 'ABC Paramount' in 1963, the hits were becoming thinner on the ground as the British Invasion heated up. Ironically, the BEATLES were big DOMINO fans and were no doubt both thrilled and amused when the Big Man covered 'Lady Madonna' in 1968, one of his first singles for 'Reprise' and his last chart entry. Nevertheless, he continued to tour and record right up until the early 80s, when he finally retired from the music business. DOMINO was back in the news in August 2005, when it was thought the New Orleans giant might be one of the casualties of Hurricane Katrina. However, after a day or two he was lifted to safety, and was even planning to get back on the road. 'MAKE IT FUNKY' the movie – a benefit for the lost people of the tragedy – marked the man's return. *BG & MCS*

- **filmography** {performance} –

Shake, Rattle & Rock! *(1956 {p} =>)* / **the Girl Can't Help It** *(1956 {p} on OST by V/A =>)* / **Jamboree** *(1957 {p} =>)* / **the Big Beat** *(1958 {p} =>)* / **Let The Good Times Roll** *(1973 {p} on OST by V/A =>)* / Any Which Way You Can *(1980 {p})* / **the Compleat Beatles** *(1984 {p} =>)* / Twist *(1992 {p} =>)* / **Make It Funky!** *(2005 {a/p} =>)*

DON'T KNOCK THE ROCK

1956 (US 84m b&w) Clover Productions / Columbia Pictures

Film genre: Rock'n'roll Musical drama

Top guns: dir: Fred F. Sears ← ROCK AROUND THE CLOCK / → CALYPSO HEAT WAVE / s-w: Robert Kent ← ROCK AROUND THE CLOCK / → TWIST AROUND THE CLOCK → HOOTENANNY HOOT → GET YOURSELF A COLLEGE GIRL → WHEN THE BOYS MEET THE GIRLS → the FASTEST GUITAR ALIVE → a TIME TO SING

Stars: Alan Dale *(Arnie Haines)*, Alan Freed *(himself)* ← ROCK AROUND THE CLOCK / → ROCK, ROCK, ROCK! → MISTER ROCK AND ROLL → GO, JOHNNY, GO!, Patricia Hardy *(Francine MacLaine)*, Fay Baker *(Arlene MacLaine)*, Jana Lund *(Sunny Everett)*, **Bill HALEY & the Comets** *(performer/s)*, **LITTLE RICHARD** *(performer)*, **the Treniers** *(performers)*, **Dave Appell & His Applejacks** *(performer/s)*, Al Fisher *(Al)* → MISTER ROCK AND ROLL → COUNTRY MUSIC HOLIDAY

Storyline: Singer Arnie Haines decides he needs a rest after two years on the circuit. He and his group return home to Mellonville, but any thoughts of peace and quiet are shattered when catty columnist Arlene MacLaine and the mayor publicly denounce rock'n'roll as a bad influence on teenagers. Arnie puts on an all-star rock show to prove them wrong, but the unwelcome attentions of a jealous teenage girl throw things into turmoil. *JZ*

Movie rating: *4.5

Visual: video (no audio OST)

Off the record: Tracks featured in the film are as follows:- 'Don't Knock The Rock', 'Calling All Comets', 'Rip It Up' & 'Goofin' Around' (by BILL HALEY AND HIS COMETS), 'Long Tall Sally' (by LITTLE RICHARD), 'Rockin' On Saturday Night' (by the TRENIERS), 'Applejack' & 'Country Dance' (by DAVE APPELL & THE APPLEJACKS) and 'I Cry More' & 'Don't Knock The Rock' (by ALAN DALE). *MCS*

– spinoff hits, etc. –

BILL HALEY & HIS COMETS: Don't Knock The Rock

Dec 56. (7",78) *Decca; <30148> Brunswick; (05640)* Jan57 7

DON'T KNOCK THE TWIST

1962 (US 87m b&w) Four-Leaf Productions / Columbia Pictures

Film genre: Rock'n'roll Musical drama

Top guns: dir: Oscar Rudolph ← TWIST AROUND THE CLOCK / s-w: Robert E. Kent as James B. Gordon ← TWIST AROUND THE CLOCK ← ROCK AROUND THE CLOCK / → HOOTENANNY HOOT → GET YOURSELF A COLLEGE GIRL → WHEN THE BOYS MEETS THE GIRLS → the FASTEST GUITAR ALIVE → a TIME TO SING

Stars: Gene Chandler *(the Duke of Earl)*, Lang Jeffries *(Ted Haver)*, Mari Blanchard *(Dulcie Corbin)*, Georgine Darcy *(Madge Albright)*, Stephen Preston *(Billy Albright)*, Barbara Morrison *(Mrs. Morrison)*, James Chandler *(Joe Albright)*, Hortense Petra *(Mrs. Kay)* → KISSIN' COUSINS → GET YOURSELF A COLLEGE GIRL → YOUR CHEATIN' HEART → WHEN THE BOYS MEET THE GIRLS → HOLD ON! → RIOT ON SUNSET STRIP, **Chubby Checker** *(himself)* ← IT'S TRAD, DAD! ← TWIST AROUND THE CLOCK ← TEENAGE MILLIONAIRE / → LET THE GOOD TIMES ROLL → PURPLE PEOPLE EATER → TWIST, **Linda Scott** *(herself)*, **Vic Dana** *(himself)*, **the Dovells:- Len Barry, Arnie Silver, Mike Dennis, Jerry Summers** *(performers)* → a SWINGIN' SUMMER

Storyline: TV executive Ted Haver is given a month to prepare a "Twist Special" before the rival TV station does theirs. After recruiting Chubby Checker to help with the show, Ted obviously feels he's done enough as he goes on vacation. As the whole universe is twisting away he soon discovers siblings Billy and Madge and ropes them into proceedings, even giving Madge star billing. This leads to jealous girlfriend Dulcie seeking revenge, and more twists in the plot follow. *JZ*

Movie rating: *4

Visual: video + dvd

Off the record: (see below)

—

CHUBBY CHECKER & Various Artists (composers: Various)

May 62. (lp) *Parkway; <P-7011> Columbia; (33SX 1446)* 29 Jul62

– Twistin' / Bristol stomp (the DOVELLS) / La Paloma twist / Mashed potato time (DEE DEE SHARP) / Bo Diddely (the CARROLL BROTHERS) / I love to twist / Don't knock the twist / Do the New Continental (the DOVELLS) / Salome twist (the CARROLL BROTHERS) / The fly / Smashed potatoes (the CARROLL BROTHERS) / Slow twistin'.

S/track review: With a fistful of hits, CHUBBY CHECKER and his twisting compadres danced the bobby socks off most post-rock'n'roll competitors. His second "Twist" musical (the first was 'TWIST AROUND THE CLOCK'), CHUBBY contributed six numbers to the film OST, a mixture of fresh cuts, 'Twistin'', 'I Love To Twist', 'La Paloma Twist' and of course, 'Don't Knock The Twist', plus recent hits, 'Slow Twistin'' and 'The Fly'; presumably the latter "electric shaver" couldn't do the twist, although one thinks it'd do a better job than a certain inanimate vegetable. The veggie in question, DEE DEE SHARP's 'Mashed Potato Time' (a rip-off of 'Please Mr. Postman'), had already just zoomed up to No.2, while she was also credited on CHUBBY's 'Slow Twistin'' at the same time. Born Dione LaRue in Philadelphia, 1945, the teen sensation went on to have further Top 10 hits, 'Gravy (For My Mashed Potatoes)', 'Ride!' & 'Do The Bird' (plus a collaborative LP with CHECKER, 'Down To Earth'), all really quite derivative of Little "Loco-motion" Eva and the Twist movement. The snappy and tuneful DOVELLS (aka the pseudonymous Len Barry, Arnie Silver, Jerry Summers, Mike Dennis & Danny Brooks) provided the film with two of their hits, the near-chart-topper 'Bristol Stomp' (a town near Philadelphia) and 'Do The New Continental'. Incidentally, Len Barry (real name Leonard Borisoff) had a No.2 solo hit with '1-2-3' in 1965. That leaves us the CARROLL BROTHERS, a quintet (Pete Carroll, Jimmy Chick, Dick Noble, Billy McGraw and Kenneth Dom) who were afforded three numbers, a cover of 'Bo Diddely' (yes, it was spelt incorrectly!), 'Salome Twist' (complete with great tinny guitar) and their take on the dancin' tattie theme, 'Smashed Potatoes'. *MCS*

Album rating: *4.5

DON'T LET GO

2002 (US 87m) Hemisphere Entertainment / Jimmy Ray Productions (R)

Film genre: Rock'n'roll musical drama

Top guns: s-w + dir: Max Myers

Stars: Scott Wilson *(Jimmy Ray Stevens)* ← SOUTH OF HEAVEN, WEST OF HELL ← DEAD MAN WALKING ← SOUL SURVIVOR ← GERONIMO: AN AMERICAN LEGEND ← ELVIS AND THE COLONEL: THE UNTOLD STORY ← YOUNG GUNS II ← JOHNNY HANDSOME ← BLUE CITY / → MONSTER, Katharine Ross *(Charlene Stevens)* ← FOOLS ← the GRADUATE, Brad Hawkins *(Johnny Blue Stevens)* ← SHAKE, RATTLE AND ROLL: AN AMERICAN LOVE STORY / → CRAZY, Levi Kreis *(Billy Joe Stevens)*, James Keane *(Wes)* ← DICK TRACY ← the ROSE, Justin Shilton *(young Billy Joe)*, MIchael Davison *(young Jimmy Ray)*, Christine Carlo *(Christina)*, Irma P. Hall *(Hazel)* ← a SLIPPING-DOWN LIFE ← STRAIGHT TALK ← BOOK OF NUMBERS, Tanya Garrett *(Sueanne)*, Bo Hopkins *("The Boss")* ← SOUTH OF HEAVEN, WEST OF HELL ← MORE AMERICAN GRAFFITI ← AMERICAN GRAFFITI

Storyline: Jimmy Ray Stevens was king of rockabilly in the 1950s. After his brother was murdered, Jimmy hit the booze and never played again. 40 years later, Jimmy Ray's sons have followed in his footsteps and are doing the business with their own group, the Texas Two-Tones. As their special commemoration concert (in tribute to their uncle) approaches, Jimmy Ray must decide whether to turn back the clock and play again or drown his sorrows in another bottle. *JZ*

Movie rating: *7

Visual: video (no audio OST; score: KEITH ALLISON)

Off the record: Lead guitarist, KEITH ALLISON, was a member of Paul Revere & the Raiders between 1968 and 1975 before touring with ex-Monkees formation Dolenz, Jones, Boyce & Hart; he became an actor and movie composer from the 70s onwards, noteably 'Where Does It Hurt?' (1972) and 'The Night The Lights Went Out In Georgia' (1981). *MCS*

the DOORS

1991 (US 135m) Tri-Star Pictures (R)

Film genre: Rock-music bio-pic/drama

Top guns: s-w: Oliver Stone (+ dir) → NATURAL BORN KILLERS → EVITA, J. Randall Johnson ← DUDES (book: 'Riders On The Storm' John Densmore)

Stars: Val Kilmer *(Jim Morrison)* ← TOP SECRET! / → MASKED AND ANONYMOUS, Meg Ryan *(Pamela Courson)*, Kyle MacLachlan *(Ray Manzarek)* ← DUNE, Kevin Dillon *(John Densmore)*, Frank Whaley *(Robby Kreiger)* → PULP FICTION → WENT TO CONEY ISLAND ON A MISSION FROM GOD ... BE BACK BY FIVE → SHAKE, RATTLE & ROLL: AN AMERICAN LOVE STORY → CHELSEA WALLS → the HOTTEST STATE, **Billy IDOL** *(Cat)*, Michael Madsen *(Tom Baker)* → RESERVOIR DOGS / → STRAIGHT TALK, Dennis Burkley *(Dog)* ← LAMBADA ← WHO'S THAT GIRL ← BUMMER! / → RUSH → TOUCH, Kathleen Quinlan *(Patricia Kennealy)* ← AMERICAN GRAFFITI / → EVENT HORIZON, Crispin Glover *(Andy Warhol)* ← WILD AT HEART / → EVEN COWGIRLS GET THE BLUES → DEAD MAN, Josh Evans *(Bill Siddons)*, Michael Wincott *(Paul Rothchild)* ← the CROW / → DEAD MAN → STRANGE DAYS, Kristina Fulton *(Nico)*, **Eric Burdon** *(backstage manager)* <= the ANIMALS =>, Hawthorne James *(Chuck Vincent)* → the FIVE HEARTBEATS, Will Jordan *(Ed Sullivan)* ← ELVIS: THE MOVIE ← the BUDDY HOLLY STORY ← I WANNA HOLD YOUR HAND, **Floyd Red Crow Westerman** *(shaman)*, **Billy Vera** *(Miami promoter)* ← SUMMER DREAMS: THE STORY OF THE BEACH BOYS ← BAJA OKLAHOMA, **Bonnie Bramlett** *(bartender)*, ← CATCH MY SOUL ← MEDICINE BALL CARAVAN ← VANISHING POINT / → FESTIVAL EXPRESS, Debi Mazar *(whiskey girl)* ← DOWNTOWN 81 / → JUNGLE FEVER → SINGLES → EMPIRE RECORDS → GIRL 6 → the INSIDER → BE COOL, Tudor Sherrard *(office publicist)* ← HEARTBREAK HOTEL, **Harmonica Fats** *(blues singer on Venice boardwalk)*, Alan Manson *(judge)* ← LEADBELLY, Kelly Hu *(Dorothy)* → STRANGE DAYS, Wes Studi *(Indian in desert)* → GERONIMO: AN AMERICAN LEGEND, Steve Reevis *(Indian in desert)* → GERONIMO: AN AMERICAN LEGEND, **Fiona** *(Fog groupie)* ← HEARTS OF FIRE, **Paul Williams** *(Warhol PR)* ← PHANTOM OF THE PARADISE ← WATERMELON MAN, Rodney Grant *(patron at Barney's)* → GERONIMO: AN AMERICAN LEGEND, Annie McEnroe *(secretary)* ← TRUE STORIES / → S.F.W., Karina Lombard *(Warhol actress)* → LAST MAN STANDING, **Eagle Eye Cherry** *(roadie)* → the SOUL OF A MAN, **John Densmore** *(engineer; last session)* ← DUDES ← GET CRAZY ← the DOORS ARE OPEN / → MESSAGE TO LOVE: THE ISLE OF WIGHT FESTIVAL, Jennifer Rubin *(Edie)* ← PERMANENT RECORD / → DELUSION, David Allen Brooks *(roadie)* ← SCREAM FOR HELP, Bill Graham *(New Haven promoter)* ← the RETURN OF BRUNO ← a STAR IS BORN ← FILLMORE ← MUSCLE BEACH PARTY, Charlie Spradling *(CBS girl backstage)* ← WILD AT HEART / → BAD CHANNELS

Storyline: Oliver Stone pays overblown tribute to his overblown hero, Jim Morrison, charting the singer's troubled, messianic life from a childhood memory of a dying Indian to his bohemian days in L.A. and his rise and untimely fall with the Doors. *BG*

Movie rating: *7.5

Visual: video + dvd

Off the record: The **DOORS** were formed in Los Angeles, California, USA ... mid 1965, by RAY MANZAREK and JIM MORRISON; a year later after some initial personnel changes, JOHN DENSMORE and ROBBY KRIEGER finalised the line-up, taking their name from Aldous Huxley's work 'The Doors Of Perception'. When they were released from an ill-advised 'Columbia' recording contract, Arthur Lee (of Love), recommended them to his 'Elektra' label boss Jac Holzman. Early in '67, a the peak of the "flower-power" era, their eponymous debut album was issued. It soon climbed to No.2 after an edited version of 'Light My Fire' topped the charts. Both the single and the album showcased MORRISON's overtly sexual vocal theatrics against a backdrop of organ-dominated, avant-garde blues. The classic debut also contained two cover versions ('Back Door Man' & 'Alabama Song'), along with the extremely disturbing 11-minute epic, 'The End' (a record which was later used on the soundtrack for the 1979 Francis Ford Coppola film, 'Apocalypse Now'). While other bands of the era were into peace and love, the DOORS found their salvation in a much darker vision, again in evidence on the follow-up (also in '67), 'Strange Days'. As MORRISON's drink and drug antics became increasingly problematic, he was arrested many times (on stage and off), mostly for lewd simulation of sexual acts and indecent exposure. Nevertheless, in the late summer of '68, the DOORS found themselves at the top of the US charts again with 'Hello I Love You' and the album, 'Waiting For The Sun'. A disappointing 4th album, 'The Soft Parade', was overshadowed later in 1969 when MORRISON was accused of interfering with an airline stewardess while a flight was in progress. He was later acquitted, but was later sentenced to eight months hard labour after being found guilty of a separate charge of indecent exposure and profanity at a Miami gig. He was freed on appeal and began work on 1970s, 'Morrison Hotel / Hard Rock Cafe', a return to rawer, more basic rock'n'roll. After the recording of 'L.A. Woman', JIM relocated to Paris in the spring of '71 with his girlfriend Pamela, amid rumours of an imminent split from the group. The aforementioned album was delivered in June, a masterpiece that carried on the re-evaluation of their blues roots. His over-indulgence in drugs and booze, had given his vocal chords a deeper resonance, showcased on such classics as, 'Riders On The Storm' (a Top 30 hit), 'Love Her Madly' and the freewheeling title track. Ironically, just as the band seemed to have found their feet again, JIM MORRISON was found dead in his bathtub on the 3rd of July 1971. Speculation was rife at the time, but it later became apparent he had died from a drugs/drink induced heart attack. He was also buried in Paris, his grave becoming a shrine to all but his parents, who disowned him in 1967. The others continued as a trio for the next two years, but sadly the public refused to acknowledge them as the real DOORS. **JOHN DENSMORE** appears in 'The DOORS' movie, while there's also room for rockers **Eric Burdon, Billy Idol, Fiona** and future pop star and brother of Neneh, **Eagle Eye Cherry**. *BG & MCS*

---

the DOORS (*) (& Various others)

Mar 91. (lp/c)(cd) *Elektra; (EKT 85/+C)<(7559 61047)>* 8 11
– The movie (JIM MORRISON *) / Riders on the storm (*) / Love street (*) / Break on through (*) / The end (*) / Light my fire (*) / Ghost song (JIM MORRISON *) / Roadhouse blues (*) / Heroin (the VELVET UNDERGROUND & NICO) / Carmina burana: introduction (ATLANTA SYMPHONY ORCHESTRA AND CHORUS) / Stoned immaculate (JIM MORRISON *) / When the music's over (*) / The severed garden (adagio) (JIM MORRISON *) / L.A. woman (*).

S/track review: As vivid and visceral as Oliver Stone's bio-pic was, the decision to use a straightforward greatest hits (and a poor man's greatest hits at that; pretty much any of the anthologies released since the early 70s offer an equally comprehensive – and often better – summary) was disappointing. There's nothing here save for maybe 'Carmina Burana', or, even more unlikely, VELVET UNDERGROUND touchstone 'Heroin', that hardcore DOORS fans haven't heard before, or even that hardcore Stone fans haven't heard before. In reality, there's little that even casual fans will be unfamiliar with; the fairground rhyme of 'Love Street', maybe, or the solipsistic fragments culled from posthumously released poetry anthology, 'An American Prayer'; hearing MORRISON rap – in a manner of speaking.. – over the 70s slap bass funk of 'Ghost Song' is a novelty that never fades. From the vantage point of almost two decades, though, the whole early 90s DOORS revival appears more random than ever, an out-of-time irony that MORRISON would doubtless have relished. *BG*

Album rating: *6

– spinoff hits, etc. –

the DOORS: Break On Through / Love Street

Apr 91. (7") *(EKR 121)* [–] [64]
(12"+=/cd-s+=) *(EKR 125 TW/CD)* – Hello I love you / Touch me.

the DOORS: Light My Fire / People Are Strange

May 91. (7") *(EKR 125)* [ ] [7]
(ext; 12"+=/cd-s+=) *(EKR 125 TW/CD)* – Soul kitchen.

D'OU VIENS-TU, JOHNNY?

trans: Where Are You From, Johnny?

1964 (Fra 100m) Hoche Productions / SNC / Imperia

Film genre: Pop-Rock Musical crime drama

Top guns: s-w: (+ dir) Noel Howard, Christian Plume, Yvan Audouard

Stars: Johnny Halliday *(Johnny)* → a TOUT CASSER, Sylvie Vartan *(Gigi)* ← JUST FOR FUN, Evelyne Dandry *(Magali Thibault)*, Pierre Barouh *(Django)*, Fernand Sardou *(Gustave; dit "Le sherif")*, Mick Besson *(Fred)*

Storyline: Struggling musician Johnny sings in the bars and nightclubs of Paris to keep his happy-go-lucky lifestyle going. When the money gets tight he sometimes runs errands for some rather sinister men involving shady packages which are surely nothing to do with drugs (!). When the police try to inspect his latest package, Johnny finally puts two and two together and dumps the lot in the Seine, to the annoyance of his dodgy friends. Johnny hot-foots it to his uncle's ranch in the Camargue with the mafia close behind. *JZ*

Movie rating: *4.5

Visual: video (no audio OST by Eddie Vartan)

Off the record: JOHNNY HALLIDAY spun out a handful of songs including 'Pour Moi La Vie Va Commencer' & 'Rien N'a Change'.

DOUBLE PLATINUM

1999 (US 92m TV) Columbia TriStar (PG)

Film genre: Pop/R&B Musical + domestic drama

Top guns: dir: Robert Allan Ackerman / s-w: Nina Shengold

Stars: Diana ROSS *(Olivia King)*, **Brandy** *(Kayla Harris)*, Christine Ebersole *(Peggy)*, Allen Payne *(Ric Ortega)* ← CB4: THE MOVIE, Brian Stokes Mitchell *(Adam Harris)*, Roger Rees *(Marc Reckler)*, Samantha Brown *(Royana)*, Ed Lover *(Party Ardie)* ← RIDE ← WHO'S THE MAN? ← JUICE / → DEATH OF A DYNASTY → TUPAC: RESURRECTION, Peter Francis James *(Martin Holly)*, Harvey Fierstein *(Gary Millstein)*

Storyline: When Olivia finally gets the chance to go to New York to pursue her singing career, she is faced with the toughest decision of her life – to leave behind her baby daughter Kayla or pass up her chance of fame. In the end the lure of the Big Apple proves too strong and Kayla is left motherless in St Louis. Eighteen years on and Olivia, now a success, is about to meet the winner of a local singing contest – and the winner just happens to be Kayla. *JZ*

Movie rating: *5

Visual: video + dvd (no ost; score: David Shire)

Off the record: Brandy (Norwood) is now a judge on X-Factor-type TV show, 'America's Got Talent'. *MCS*

□ DOUBLE TROUBLE alt.
(⇒ SWINGIN' ALONG)

DOUBLE TROUBLE

1967 (US 92m) Metro-Goldwyn-Mayer

Film genre: Rock'n'roll Musical drama

Top guns: dir: Norman Taurog ← SPINOUT ← TICKLE ME ← IT HAPPENED AT THE WORLD'S FAIR ← GIRLS! GIRLS! GIRLS! ← BLUE HAWAII ← G.I. BLUES / → SPEEDWAY → LIVE A LITTLE, LOVE A LITTLE / s-w: Jo Heims (au: Marc Brandel)

Stars: Elvis PRESLEY *(Guy Lambert)*, Annette Day *(Jill Conway)*, John Williams *(Gerald Waverly)*, Yvonne Romain *(Claire Dunham)*, Chips Rafferty *(Archie Brown)*, Norman Rossington *(Arthur Babcock)* ← a HARD DAY'S NIGHT, Monte Landis *(Georgie)* ← WHAT A CRAZY WORLD ← PLAY IT COOL, Michael Murphy *(Morley)* → NASHVILLE → PRIVATE PARTS → MAGNOLIA, Mary Hughes *(Watusi dancer)* ← THUNDER ALLEY ← HOW TO STUFF A WILD BIKINI ← SKI PARTY ← BEACH BLANKET BINGO ← PAJAMA PARTY ← BIKINI BEACH ← MUSCLE BEACH PARTY

Storyline: Despite the fact that Elvis famously got no further than Prestwick Airport in real life, here he tours the UK in the fictional guise of hearthrob singer Guy Lambert. The threadbare plot involves a star struck fan's neurotic ardour, which catches up with Guy in Belgium of all places. *BG*

Movie rating: *4

Visual: video + dvd

Off the record: nothing I'm afraid

ELVIS PRESLEY (composers: Jeff Alexander, etc.)

Jun 67. (lp; mono/stereo) *R.C.A.; <LSP 3787> (RD/SF 7892)* [47] Aug67 [34]
– Double trouble / Baby, if you'll give me all your love / Could I fall in love / Long legged girl (with the short dress on) / City by night / Old MacDonald / I love only one girl / There is so much world to see / It won't be long / Never ending / Blue river / What now, what next, where to. *(re-iss. Aug80 on 'RCA Int.'; INTS 5039) (cd-iss. Oct04 on 'Follow That Dream'+=; FTD 1010)* – (extra takes).

S/track review: On the evidence of 'Old Macdonald' (yes, that one.. bolstered with an unfortunate, retrospectively tasteless "hamburger medium rare" line) and the dire 'I Love Only One Girl', it's clear PRESLEY was fulfilling contractual obligations, going through the motions but needlessly scraping the barrel anyhow. Like all his soundtracks, there are a few saving graces: PRESLEY is in fine vocal form on the opening double whammy of the Doc Pomus/Mort Shuman title track and the brassy 'Baby, If You'll Give Me All Of Your Love'. He's accompanied by some fine, moanin' trombone on the refreshingly jazzy 'City By Night', while 'Long Legged Girl (With The Short Dress On)' stands as the King's heaviest, hardest rocking film track of the 60s, offering a tantalising glimpse of that sneering genius of old. If you can handle the low points (and be assured, they really are low), this is worth picking up in its two-on-one re-packaging with 'SPINOUT'. *BG*

Album rating: *4

– spinoff hits, etc. –

ELVIS PRESLEY: Long Legged Girl (With The Short Dress On)

May 67. (7") *<47-9115> (RCA 1616)* [63] Aug67 [49]

DOWN & OUT WITH THE DOLLS

2001 (US 88m) Whyte House Productions / Indican (R)

Film genre: Rock-music comedy drama

Top guns: s-w + dir: Kurt Voss ← THINGS BEHIND THE SUN ← SUGAR TOWN ← DELUSION ← BORDER RADIO (+ co-story w/ Nalini Cheriel)

Stars: Zoe Poledouris *(Fauna)*, **Kinnie Starr** *(Reggie)*, Nicole Barrett *(Kali)*, Melody Moore *(Lavender)*, **Coyote Shivers** *(Levi)* ← EMPIRE RECORDS, Sierra Feldner-Shaw *(Heather)*, **Inger Lorre** *(Shade)*, **LEMMY Kilmister** *(Joe)*, **Janis Tanaka** *(Trudie)*

Storyline: "The harder they rock, the harder they fall" seems to be the motto for all-girl band the Paper Dolls. New lead singer Fauna could pick an argument in an empty room but she's got the talent and motivation to get to the top. Kali, Lavender and Reggie all have their fair share of problems and when the foursome end up sharing a flat things start to boil over. However a new contract with a major Indie label could just about keep the quarrelsome quartet together. *JZ*

Movie rating: *5.5

Visual: dvd

Off the record: **Janis Tanaka** was a brief member of all-girl L.A. sleeze-rockers, L7, before joining up in 1999 with hard-rockers, Fireball Ministry (check out 'The Second Great Awakening' in 2003); the bassist also performed with Hammers Of Misfortune. *MCS*

Various Artists (score: ZOE POLEDOURIS *)

Feb 03. (cd) *Lakeshore; <33746>*
– Rock star (LO-BALL) / He's a groupie (the BANGS) / Sick dance (the ANGORAS) / One night stand (the PAPER DOLLS) / Got balls (the PAPER DOLLS) / Hot as fuck (BOMBER) / Warm (KINNIE STARR) / Be a volunteer (FONDA) / She's not your friend (INGER LORRE) / Dig (the PAPER DOLLS) / Round & square (FONDA) / Taking it on (*).

S/track review: For a film about a fictional all-girl rock group it is perhaps fitting that the soundtrack be filled with all-girl groups, or at least bands with female lead singers. Almost all the artists on 'DOWN AND OUT WITH THE DOLLS', including the film's fictional group the PAPER DOLLS, fall somewhere in a Bermuda Triangle between Blondie, Hole and the Donnas featuring gritty, pop punk tunes laced with venomous vocals. Hell hath no fury and all that. LO-BALL's 'Rock Star', the BANGS' 'He's A Groupie' and 'Sick Dance' from the ANGORAS are all infectious little numbers with some almost sinister undertones. The PAPER DOLLS themselves are surprisingly good for a fictional band and there is definitely a healthy dose of tongue in bubble-gummed cheek that has a certain charm to it. INGER LORRE (formerly of the Nymphs) pops up with the epic 'She's Not Your Friend', while KINNIE STAR contributes the tender 'Warm'. This breaks up the album nicely before FONDA hits us with another pop punk left and right in the shape of 'Be A Volunteer' and 'Round & Square'. Unfortunately it's not all great, 'Hot As Fuck' by BOMBER is just three minutes of pointless screeching and ZOE POLEDOURIS's score track, 'Taking It On', is incidental. Nothing's perfect but this soundtrack is a decent album with some good tunes. *CM*

Album rating: *6.5

DOWN ON US

1984 (US 117m) Omni Leisure International (R)

Film genre: political Rock Musical drama/bio-pic(s)

Top guns: s-w + dir: Larry Buchanan

Stars: Sandy Kenyon *(Alex Stanley)* ← EASY COME, EASY GO, Joe Camp *(Hunter)*, Toni Sawyer *(Mrs. Stanley)* → SWEET DREAMS, Steven Tice *(Frank Stanley)*, Jennifer Wilde *(Ellen)*, Gregory Allen Chatman *(Jimi Hendrix)*, David DeShay *(Al Long)*, Mark Madison *(stage manager)*, Riba Meryl *(Janis Joplin)*, Brian Wolf *(Jim Morrison)*

Storyline: Conspiracy theorist, Larry Buchanan, takes a self-absorbed and unbelievable tale of what could've happened to legendary rock icons, Jim Morrison, Jimi Hendrix and Janis Joplin, who all died prematurely due to drugs. Did the US government assign assassins to kill the trio due to their anti-Vietnam stance? Tosh! *MCS*

Movie rating: *2

Visual: video in 1989 on 'Unicorn' as 'BEYOND THE DOORS'

Off the record: (no audio OST)

□ DOWNHILL CITY
(⇒ Rock/Pop Scores)

DOWNTOWN 81

aka NEW YORK BEAT MOVIE

2000 (US 71m) Kinetique / Sagittaire Films (15)

Film genre: urban comedy docu-drama

Top guns: dir: Edo Bertoglio / s-w: Glenn O'Brien

Stars: **Jean Michel Basquiat** (himself), Anna Schroeder *(Beatrice)*, Danny Rosen *(Danny)*, Marshall Chess *(the thief)* ← COCKSUCKER BLUES / → GODFATHERS AND SONS, Lisa Rosen *(the maid)*, 'Lee' George Quinones *(graffiti artist)* → WILD STYLE, **Vincent GALLO** *(himself)*, **John LURIE** *(himself)*, **BLONDIE:- Deborah Harry** *(fairy godmother)*, **Clem Burke** *(Felons band member)*, **Chris Stein** *(Felons band member)*, **Jimmy Destri** *(taxi driver)* / **James Chance** *(James White)*, Giorgio Gomelsky *(the landlord)*, **Tav Falco** *(conversationalist at Mudd Club)*, **Fab Five Freddy** *(himself)* → WILD STYLE → JUICE → WHO'S THE MAN?, **August Darnell + Coati Mundi** *(himself)* <= KID CREOLE & THE COCONUTS =>, **Lori Eastside** *(herself)* → GET CRAZY, Glenn O'Brien *(Neil Barlowe)* → WILD STYLE, **Saul Williams** *(voice of Basquiat)*, **Bradley Field** *(studio manager)* ← the OFFENDERS, **Kristian Hoffman** *(A&R person)* ← the OFFENDERS / → the NOMI SONG, Amos Poe *(conversationist at Mudd Club)* ← the FOREIGNER / → SUBWAY RIDERS → SMITHEREENS, David McDermott *(himself)* → the NOMI SONG, **Blaine Reininger** *(himself)* → BLACK MILK, Michael Holman *(Michael)* ← FILLMORE, Debi Mazar *(Peppermint Lounge dancer)* → the DOORS → JUNGLE FEVER → SINGLES → EMPIRE RECORDS → GIRL 6 → the INSIDER → BE COOL

Storyline: An urban fairytale of sorts (shot in Manhattan district in the very early 80s) featuring real life pop/rock stars (Blondie = the Felons) as street actors, hipsters and colorful people – but really this is a showcase for the all-round talents of artist, Jean Michel Basquiat. He's seen coming out of hospital and wandering around the Big Apple, reality becoming fantasy in the – at times – surreal streets of the city. Subsequently re-dubbed due to the damage done in the losing process of the original master reels/tapes. *MCS*

Movie rating: *6.5

Visual: dvd 2001 as 'DOWNTOWN 81' on 'Zeitgeist'

Off the record: **Basquiat** featured with his band, Gray.

Various Artists (score: JOHN LURIE)

Sep 01. (cd) *E.M.I.; <810163>*
– So far so real (GRAY) / K pasa – Pop I (KID CREOLE & THE COCONUTS) / Desire (TUXEDOMOON) / Cavern (LIQUID LIQUID) / Blonde redhead (DNA) / Sax maniac (JAMES CHANCE) / I'm a doggy (LOUNGE LIZARDS) / Contort yourself (JAMES CHANCE) / Drum mode (GRAY) / The closet (LYDIA LUNCH) / Palabras con ritmo (COATI MUNDI) / Bob the bob (LOUNGE LIZARDS) / Tangita (PABLO CALOGERO) / Mr. Softee (KID CREOLE & THE COCONUTS) / 15 minutes (CHRIS STEIN) / Detached (DNA) / Cheree (SUICIDE) / Copy (the PLASTICS) / New day (WALTER STEDING & THE DRAGON PEOPLE) / Beat bop (ROB K. RAMMELLZEE).

S/track review: To complement the DVD re-issue and premiere (as 'DOWNTOWN 81') at Cannes 2000 of the long lost master tapes, we at last have a record of these No Wave times. Understandably, the album kicks off with a short tune ('So Far So Real') from main man Basquiat under the guise of GRAY – a fairytale beginning indeed; GRAY would also contribute a second track 'Drum Mode'. KID CREOLE & THE COCONUTS (featuring COATI MUNDI) were, without a doubt, the surprise package of the 20-long song CD, their 7-minute, calypso-rap meets avant-disco fusion of 'K Pasa' and debut hit (Me No) 'Pop I', truly a gift from the gods. Now if this version had been released as a single way back in 1981? . . . Anyway, back to reality and the narrative that was TUXEDOMOON, BLAINE REININGER and Co dispatching 'Desire', a favourite of the experimental bourgeoise and sadly their only outing here. Ditto 'Cavern' by LIQUID LIQUID, a record exploding out of its funk grooves courtesy of its angular, bass-heavy beats; it would become the hip hop rhythm behind Grandmaster Flash's 'White Lines'. DNA were No Wave's answer to Gang Of Four (or even NY comedian/actor, Bobcat Goldthwait) their maniacal freakout messages relayed on two workouts, 'Blonde Redhead' and 'Detached'. Sandwiched between a couple of JAMES CHANCE classics ('Sax Maniac' & 'Contort Yourself') once heard on the excellent early 80s comp 'No New York', was one of the two John Lurie/LOUNGE LIZARDS contributions, 'I'm A Doggy'; not this time under the guise of his gravel-voiced alter-ego, Marvin Pontiac. Talking of alter-egos, the sultry LYDIA LUNCH had her fair share of them, Teenage Jesus & The Jerks, Beirut Slump, 8 Eyed Spy, but here she was solo, singing – did I say singing! – her heart out on 'The Closet', er sadly . . . not out of a closet. Thankfully, the beats were uptempo again when COATI MUNDI donned his Gil Scott-Heron & the Last Poets overcoat – so to speak – for the existential rap delivery, 'Palabras Con Ritmo'. PABLO CALOGERO's 'Tangita' was a nice uptempo addition to the proceedings, the actor of sorts more at home in the movie, 'The MAMBO KINGS' (1992), than he was squatting here. After another "Noo Yoik" gem from KID CREOLE ('Mr. Softee'), a sharp intake of breath was needed for one of SUICIDE's best known tracks, 'Cheree'. In complete contrast, the PLASTICS (and their 'Copy' ditty) were of the Devo imprint, while violinist WALTER STEDING & THE DRAGON PEOPLE ('New Day') was the modern-day hybrid of Johnny Preston's 'Running Bear'. Last, but not least, the Basquiat-produced, Cypress Hill-referenced 'Beat Bop' (by ROB K. RAMMELLZEE), was Grandmaster/hip hop-like to the max, "like the break-a-dawn". *MCS*

Album rating: *8.5

a DREAM IS A WISH YOUR HEART MAKES: THE ANNETTE FUNICELLO STORY

1995 (US 95m TV) Savoy Pictures / CBS Television

Film genre: Pop-music/showbiz bio-pic/drama

Top guns: dir: Bill Corcoran / s-w: John McGreevey ← HELLO DOWN THERE, Peter Torokvei (same titled book by **ANNETTE Funicello** & Patricia Romanowski)

Stars: Eva La Rue *(Annette Funicello)*, Len Cariou *(Walt Disney)*, Frank Crudele *(Joe Funicello)*, Jack Gilardi *(himself)*, David Lipper *(Paul Anka)*, Don S. Davis *(Glen Holt)*, **Frankie AVALON** *(himself)*, **ANNETTE Funicello** *(herself)*, Justin Lewis *(young Frankie Avalon)*, Andrea Nemeth *(Annette Funicello; aged 12-15)*, Lorraine Landy *(young Shelley Fabares)*, Austin Basile *(Jack Gilardi, Jr.)*, Rob Stewart *(Jack Gilardi)*, Shelley Fabares *(herself)*

Storyline: Annette's story begins as a shy 1950s youngster who reluctantly joins TV's Mouseketeers. So begins her acting and singing career, during which her friendly relationship with Frankie Avalon and romance with Paul Anka are shown. By the time of her second marriage, after her big comeback, she realises she has MS but bravely comes to terms with the disease. Indeed the whole film is less concerned with Annette the actress than Annette the person, as seen through the eyes of friends and family. *JZ*

Movie rating: *6

Visual: none (no audio OST)

Off the record: Only a very rare cassette version of the soundtrack by ANNETTE was issued around April '95 (see ← ANNETTE for full story)

□ the DREAM MAKER alt.
(⇒ IT'S ALL HAPPENING)

DREAMGIRLS

2006 (US 130m) DreamWorks / Paramount Pictures (PG-13)

Film genre: R&B/Soul-musical drama

Top guns: s-w + dir: Bill Condon (au: Tom Eyen)

Stars: Jamie Foxx *(Curtis Taylor, Jr.)* ← STEALTH ← RAY, **Beyonce Knowles** *(Deena Jones)* ← FADE TO BLACK ← the FIGHTING TEMPTATIONS ← CARMEN: A HIP HOPERA, Eddie Murphy *(James "Thunder" Alley)*, Danny Glover *(Marty Madison)* ← PLACES IN THE HEART, Jennifer Hudson *(Effie White)*, Anika Noni Rose *(Lorrell Robinson)* ← the TEMPTATIONS ← FROM JUSTIN TO KELLY, Keith Robinson *(C.C. White)*, Sharon Leal *(Michelle Morris)*, Hinton Battle *(Wayne)*, Loretta Devine *(jazz singer)* ← I AM SAM ← the PREACHER'S WIFE, John Lithgow *(Jerry Harris)* ← FOOTLOOSE, Robert Curtis Brown *(technical director)* → HIGH SCHOOL MUSICAL 2

Storyline: Desperate for stardom in a pre-Pop Idol era, Dreamettes Effie White, Deena Jones and Lorrell Robinson are taken under the wing of smooth talking manager, Curtis Taylor Jr, who hooks them up with legendary soul man, James "Thunder" Early. He's their passport to the big time but also their undoing, promoting Deena at the expense of Effie as fame spells the end of personal friendships. *BG*

Movie rating: *7

Visual: dvd

Off the record: Jennifer Hudson was the American Idol 2004; 7th place.

—

Original Cast (composer: Henry Krieger)

Dec 06. (cd) *Sony-Urban; <82876 88953-2>* [1] Jan07 [ ]
– I'm lookin' for something (*) / Goin' downtown (*) / Take the long way home (*) / Move / Fake your way to the top / Big (*) / Cadillac car / Steppin' to the bad side / Love you I do / I want you baby / Family / Dreamgirls / Heavy (*) / It's all over / And I am telling you I'm not going // I'm somebody (*) / When I first saw you / Patience / I am changing / Perfect world (*) / I meant you no harm – Jimmy's rap / Lorrell loves Jimmy (*) / Step on over (*) / I miss you old friend (*) / Effie, sing my song (*) / One night only / One night only (disco) / Listen / Hard to say goodbye / Dreamgirls (finale) / Curtain call (*) / Family (end title) (*) / When I first saw you (duet). *<(deluxe edition d-cd+= *; 88697 02012-2)>* – One night only (dance mix) (*) / I am telling you I'm not going (dance mix) (*) / Patience (composer demo) (*).

S/track review: A "Motown-inspired musical that's indebted to the melisma-addicted exhibitionism of modern R&B" is how Time Out called it, "without a single hummable song". That might be going a bit far, but the soundtrack too often gives in to its Broadway baggage and blusters itself blind to any actual soul, summed up in the pointless diaphragm-bionics of American Idol protégé JENNIFER HUDSON's 'And I Am Telling You I'm Not Going' ('And I Am Changing' – another catchy title – isn't far behind). If the Supremes had indulged in such anonymous posturing they'd never have made it out of Studio A. 'Move' launches the whole thing with hustling percussion and passably authentic call and response, and then goes and rhymes "satanic" and "titanic". 'Fake Your Way To The Top' has the boys take over, with 'Steppin' To The Bad Side' fixing some Stevie-style clavinet and supporting harmonies, but it doesn't last. Period disco arrangements on 'One Night Only' at least rein in HUDSON's showboating, and provide a bit of respite from the not-so-quiet storm plod, the ensemble harmonies of 'Hard To Say Goodbye' just about get into the headspace of a classic girl group, and BEYONCE's self-penned 'Listen' strives for elder soul stateswomanliness, but isn't exactly the stuff dreams are made of. BG

Album rating: *5.5 / d-cd *6

– spinoff hits, etc. –

BEYONCE: Listen
Jan 07. (cd-s) *<05886> (88697 05960-2)* 61 Feb07 16

DROP DEAD ROCK

1996 (US 93m; straight-to-video) Spazz-O Productions

Film genre: showbiz/Rock-music mockumentary/comedy

Top guns: s-w: (+ dir) Adam Dubin, Ric Menello ← TOUGHER THAN LEATHER

Stars: Shoshana Ami *(Bonnie)*, Shelly Mars *(Andie)*, Ian Maynard *(Spazz-O)*, Robert Occhipinti *(Chick)*, **Adam Ant** *(Dave Donovan)* ← JUBILEE / → SWEETWATER: A TRUE ROCK STORY, **Deborah Harry** *(Thor)* <= BLONDIE =>, Eddie Brill *(Lieutenant Cole)*, Apollo Smile *(Alana Payne)*

Storyline: The plot follows a bizarre heavy-metal outfit, Hindenburg, who are just about as disastrous as the German zeppelin namesake (that crashed from the skies in 1937). Going nowhere fast, they hatch a plan to kidnap producer, Spazz-O, and in turn, blackmail his unyielding ex-pornstar wife. Apparently "The comedy that will ROCK your world" . . . you decide! MCS

Movie rating: *5

Visual: video + dvd (no audio OST; score John Hill)

Off the record: Adam Ant (aka Stuart Goddard, ex-Adam & The Ants; hits 'Ant Music', 'Prince Charming' and 'Goody Two Shoes') acted and starred in several movies after appearing in Derek Jarman's 'JUBILEE' (1977), noteably 'Slam Dance' (1987) and 'Sunset Heat' (1991). MCS

DU-BEAT-E-O

1984 (US 84m) H-Z-H / duBeat-e-o (R)

Film genre: showbiz comedy drama

Top guns: s-w: (+ dir) Alan Sacks, **El Duce**, Marc Sheffler

Stars: Ray Sharkey *(duBEAT-e-o)* ← the IDOLMAKER / → BODY ROCK, **Joan Jett** *(herself)* <= the RUNAWAYS =>, **Derf Scratch** *(Benny)* ← GET CRAZY ← the SLOG MOVIE ← the DECLINE OF WESTERN CIVILIZATION, Nora Gaye *(Sharon)*, Len Lesser *(Hendricks)* ← HOW TO STUFF A WILD BIKINI, Johanna Went *(Benny's nightmare)*, Texacala Jones *(herself)* → BORDER RADIO, **El Duce** *(himself)* → POPULATION: ONE → KURT & COURTNEY, **Chuck E. Weiss** *(Hendricks' sidekick)*, Zachary *(performer)*, **Cheryl Smith** *(herself; Runaways member!)*

Storyline: Film producer DuBEAT-e-o has just 31 hours (for some reason) to finish his latest project about the career of ex-Runaways starlet, Joan Jett. So says the shady financier of the film who threatens nasty things unless the work is completed on time. Dubeat knuckles down to it in his ramshackle studio with the help of long-suffering editor Benny and a woman called Sharon. As the clock whirrs round the stress becomes more and more palpable and DuBEAT goes more and more doolally. JZ

Movie rating: *3

Visual: video (no audio OST)

Off the record: Derf Scratch (aka Frederick Charles Miller III) was the bassman for punk outfit, the Fear. Musician and friend of Tom Waits, **Chuck E. Weiss** was momentarily famous when singer-songwriter, Rickie Lee Jones, attributed the man in her debut 1979 hit single, 'Chuck E.'s In Love'. He subsequently released his own debut LP, 'The Other Side Of Town', a few years later which was actually early demo tapes. After an 18-year gap, Weiss produced his follow-up album, 'Extremely Cool' (1999) – at the time of writing he had just released another, '23rd & Stout' (2006). Actress, Cheryl Smith (who sadly died of hepatitis in October 2002), was in fact a mock member of **the RUNAWAYS** when only **Joan Jett** remained. The music in the film was mainly supplied by JOAN JETT ('You Don't Know What You've Got', 'I Want You', 'Tell Me', 'You Can't Get Me' and 'We're All Crazy Now', SOCIAL DISTORTION ('Hour Of Darkness', 'Creeps' & 'It's Not A Pretty Picture'), the MODIFIERS w/ DERF SCRATCH ('You're My Next Victim'), RAY SHARKEY ('Stickball'), TEX AND THE HORSEHEADS ('Lock Me Up'), CHUCK E. WEISS ('Sidekick'), ZACHARY ('A Little Lesson In The Movie Biz'), JOHANNA WENT ('Theme To Benny's Nightmare'), the MENTORS w/ EL DUCE ('Get Up And Die'), DR. KNOW ('Up Your Ass'), EVEN WORSE ('We Suck'), RAINBOW SMITH ('Sure Sure'), LOUNGE LIZARDS ('No Bikers, Just Punkers') and RENE INOUYE ('I Was Dancing With You Under An Amethyst Sky'. MCS

DUDES

1987 (US 90m / UK 86m) New Century Vista Film Company (R)

Film genre: Punk-rock western/road movie/comedy

Top guns: dir: Penelope Spheeris ← SUBURBIA ← the DECLINE OF WESTERN CIVILIZATION / → the DECLINE OF WESTERN CIVILIZATION 2: THE METAL YEARS → WAYNE'S WORLD → the DECLINE OF WESTERN CIVILIZATION PART III → WE SOLD OUR SOULS FOR ROCK'N'ROLL / s-w: Randall Johnson → the DOORS

Stars: Jon Cryer *(Grant)* ← PRETTY IN PINK / → WENT TO CONEY ISLAND ON A MISSION FROM GOD . . . BE BACK BY FIVE, Daniel Roebuck *(Biscuit)* → EDDIE PRESLEY → the DEVIL'S REJECTS, **Flea** *(Milo)* <= the RED HOT CHILI PEPPERS =>, **Lee VING** *(Missoula)*, Billy Ray Sharkey *(Blix)*, Catherine Mary Stewart *(Jessie)* ← SCENES FROM THE GOLDMINE ← the APPLE, Glenn Withrow *(Wes)*, Michael Melvin *(Logan)*, Pamela Gidley *(Elyse)* → PERMANENT RECORD → S.F.W. → CAKE BOY, Tiny Wells *(McGrorty)* ← MADE IN USA, **John Densmore** *(Beeson)* ← GET CRAZY ← the DOORS ARE OPEN / → the DOORS → MESSAGE TO LOVE: THE ISLE OF WIGHT FESTIVAL, **the Vandals:- Joe Escalante** *(performer)* ← SUBURBIA, **Jan Ackerman** *(performer)* ← SUBURBIA, **Warren Fitzgerald** *(performer)* → GODMONEY → THAT DARN PUNK → CAKE BOY → PUNK'S NOT DEAD, **Dave Quackenbush** *(performer)* → THAT DARN PUNK → PUNK'S NOT DEAD

Storyline: Grant, Biscuit and Milo are three punks who give up the big city to follow the wagon trail out west. On the way Milo is brutally murdered by some rednecks, and the punks' appeal to the local sheriff for justice falls on deaf ears. The pair decide to take things into their own hands and seek retribution with the rednecks in their own way – the old laws of the west where it's an eye for an eye and a tooth for a tooth. JZ

Movie rating: *4

Visual: video

Off the record: the Vandals were a punk band formed in Huntington Beach, California in 1980 (check out their video/dvd, 'Sweatin' To The Oldies').

—

Various Artists (composer: CHARLES BERNSTEIN *)

1987. (lp) *M.C.A.; <MCA 6212>* ☐ –
– Rock 'n' roll outlaw (KEEL) / Urban struggle (the VANDALS) / Show no mercy (W.A.S.P.) / Vengeance is mine (SIMON STEELE & THE CLAW) / These boots are made for walkin' (MEGADETH) / Time forgot you (LEGAL WEAPON) / Jesus came driving along (the LEATHER NUN) / Mountain song (JANE'S ADDICTION) / Lost highway (the LITTLE KINGS) / Dudes showdown (* & Co.) / Amazing Grace (STEVE VAI).

S/track review: An excellent primer in late 80s American alternative rock. There's a percentage of ballast – things begin unpromisingly with the airbrushed metal of KEEL, while LEGAL WEAPON had long since let their punk roots wither in the mud of commercial pap – but on the whole this collection musters the freshness, energy and sheer eccentricity to match the movie. MEGADETH's carefully-crafted assault on Lee Hazlewood's 'These Boots Are Made for Walkin'' had aroused Hazlewood's ire when it appeared on the band's debut album in 1985 (and has been bleeped or omitted from all pressings since 1995), but it's here in its foul-mouthed glory. The early JANE'S ADDICTION sound raw and fresh on 'Mountain Song', several years before they became alternative rock icons and founded the Lollapalooza festival. Californian punks the VANDALS deliver a welcome serving of spaghetti western riffs and cornball rapping, while W.A.S.P. (of the famous exploding cod-piece) contribute 1984's happily over-the-top 'Show No Mercy': "I hear the mighty engines roar/And I unleash the savage dogs of war". There's also a taste of under-appreciated Swedes, the LEATHER NUN, and a moody piece from the LITTLE KINGS (whose sometime guitarist was future 'Pirates of the Caribbean' director Gore Verbinski). Guitar hero STEVE VAI provides a soothing conclusion to the tongue-in-cheek mayhem with a fingerpicked 'Amazing Grace' that is slight but atmospheric. *ND*

Album rating: *7.5

DUETS

2000 (US 112m) Buena Vista Pictures (R)

Film genre: Pop/Rock-music road movie/comedy

Top guns: dir: Bruce Paltrow / s-w: John Byrum

Stars: Maria Bello *(Suzi Loomis)* → COYOTE UGLY, Andre Braugher *(Reggie Kane)* → STANDING IN THE SHADOWS OF MOTOWN, Paul Giamatti *(Todd Woods)* ← MAN ON THE MOON ← PRIVATE PARTS ← SINGLES / → STORYTELLING, Gwyneth Paltrow *(Liv)* ← SHOUT, **Huey Lewis** *(Ricky Dean)*, Scott Speedman *(Billy Hannan)*, Angie Dickinson *(Blair)* ← EVEN COWGIRLS GET THE BLUES ← CALYPSO JOE, Marian Seldes *(Harriet Gahagan)* ← AFFLICTION, Arnold McCuller *(Reggie Kane; singing voice)* ← BEACHES ← CROSSROADS ← AMERICAN HOT WAX, Angie Phillips *(Arlene)* ← MANNY & LO, Kiersten Warren *(Candy Woods)* → HOOT, **Michael Buble** *(finale singer)*, **John Pinette** *(finale singer)*, Erin Wright *(Finale singer)* ← SWEETWATER: A TRUE ROCK STORY / → BONES

Storyline: The lives of six karaoke singers become intertwined as the national karaoke competition in Omaha draws near. Father and daughter Ricky and Liv meet for the first time at a funeral and discover they both sing karaoke. Todd and Reggie meet by chance in a bar and discover they're a perfect match too. Meanwhile, waitress Suzi serves out the songs with her friend Billy and there's a battle to see who'll be the most dynamic duet in town. *JZ*

Movie rating: *5

Visual: dvd

Off the record: **Huey Lewis** had a string of hits in the 80s including 'Do You Believe In Love', 'Heart And Soul', 'I Want A New Drug', plus chart-toppers, 'The Power Of Love', 'Stuck With You' & 'Jacob's Ladder'.

—

Various Cast/Artists (score: DAVID NEWMAN *)

Sep 00. (cd/c) *Hollywood; <1 62241> (0122412HWR)* [ ] Nov00 [ ]
– Feeling alright (HUEY LEWIS) / Bette Davis eyes (GWYNETH PALTROW) / Cruisin' (GWYNETH PALTROW and HUEY LEWIS) / Just my imagination (running away with me) (BABYFACE and GWYNETH PALTROW) / Try a little tenderness (PAUL GIAMATTI and ARNOLD McCULLER) / Hello, it's me (PAUL GIAMATTI) / I can't make you love me (MARIA BELLO) / Sweet dreams (are made of this) (MARIA BELLO) / Lonely teardrops (HUEY LEWIS) / Copacabana (JOHN PINETTE) / Free bird (ARNOLD McCULLER) / Beginnings – Endings (*).

S/track review: What would you expect from a film about karaoke? – and I don't mean a documentary about the X-Factor. Had it been a British film it would've featured a collection of drunks slavering 'I Will Survive' or 'My Way' over some keyboard tune that bears little resemblance to the actual song. Might have been a good laugh but this is American and even something as trivial as karaoke has to be taken seriously and done properly. Therefore we have a series of polished songs sung by a mixture of actors and proper singers, complete with full musical accompaniment and backing vocals. The whole album is a haven of sobriety and therefore lacks the fun that karaoke is supposed to be about. The best track by a mile is 'Try A Little Tenderness', sung in the Otis Redding style by actor PAUL GIAMATTI and singer ARNOLD McCULLER. Indeed, GIAMATTI is the only actor who sounds like he's having fun and not trying to be note perfect. GWYNETH PALTROW lacks any strength in her voice when she duets with HUEY LEWIS on the Smokey Robinson hit 'Crusin'' but he does perform a passable, throaty version of 'Bette Davis Eyes'. LEWIS himself opens the set with 'Feeling Alright', a one-time hit for Joe Cocker, then adds 'Lonely Teardrops', both of which are distinctly average. JOHN PINETTE sounds like the only one to make it to the bar before singing the Barry Manilow staple 'Copacabana' while ARNOLD McCULLER sings a soulful version of Lynyrd Skynyrd's 'Free Bird'. The whole album just tries to be too perfect with a couple of old hits but mostly misses. You can't imagine any of them being allowed to hog the mic down your local Dog & Bone. *CM*

Album rating: *4.5

the DUKE WORE JEANS

1958 (UK 90m b&w) Insignia / Anglo-Amalgamated Films

Film genre: Rock'n'roll Musical comedy

Top guns: dir: Gerald Thomas / s-w: Norman Hudis ← the TOMMY STEELE STORY / → the 6.5 SPECIAL (story: Lionel Bart, Michael Pratt)

Stars: **Tommy Steele** *(Tony Whitecliffe / Tommy Hudson)* ← the TOMMY STEELE STORY / → IT'S ALL HAPPENING, June Laverick *(Princess Maria)*, Michael Medwin *(Cooper)* → IT'S ALL HAPPENING → I'VE GOTTA HORSE → O LUCKY MAN!, Eric Pohlmann *(Bastini)* → FOLLOW THE BOYS, Alan Wheatley *(King of Ritallia)*, Noel Hood *(Lady Marguerite)*, Mary Kerridge *(Queen)*, Cyril Chamberlain ← the TOMMY STEELE STORY

Storyline: The Hon. Tony Whitecliffe cares more about his beloved cattle than finding a wife, so when his parents arrange a marriage for him with the Princess of Rittalia he desperately tries to find a way out. Luckily for him, who should appear but his exact lookalike Tommy, and with a little prompting and cajoling Tommy is sent off to Europe to stand in for our country gentleman. At first the princess is not amused by the lower-class Lothario, but after a while his cockney charm begins to win her over. *JZ*

Movie rating: *3.5

Visual: nothing official

Off the record: **TOMMY STEELE** (see own biog)

—

TOMMY STEELE (composers: Bart; Pratt; Bennett)

Mar 58. (10"m-lp) *Decca; (LF 1308)* [1] [–]
– It's all happening / What do you do / Family tree / Happy guitar / Hair-down hoe-down / Princess / Photograph (duet with JUNE LAVERICK) / Thanks a lot.

S/track review: TOMMY STEELE had come a long way (but not in a long time) since his rock'n'roll heydays and his chart-topping

'Singing The Blues', although with 'The DUKE WORE JEANS' the rock was now indeed rolling down the proverbial hill – fast! The cheeky cockney had a cheek alright, calling this rock'n'roll, when this mini-LP by all accounts was old-fashioned West End music hall variety stuff-and-nonsense. It's hardly surprising when you see who's behind the songs: Lionel Bart, etc., a person who would subsequently take fame from choreographed musicals such as 'Oliver!'. Only 'Happy Guitar' (a Top 20 hit) and 'Hair-Down Hoe-Down' are plucky enough to reach anything barely resembling rock'n'roll, but with none of his Steelmen aboard the good ship Tommy, this might've suited the likes of Anthony Newley better (Bart just might've seen the latter Artful Dodger in 1948's 'Oliver Twist'). Listening to 'Photograph' (STEELE's duet with co-star JUNE LAVERICK) is never "easy-listening" but one can definitely file under that particular category. As Tommy's "Knees-Up-Mother-Brown" finale rings out, one can only say 'Thanks A Lot' – not.

MCS

Album rating: *2.5

– spinoff hits, etc. –

TOMMY STEELE: Happy Guitar / Princess

Apr 58. (7") *Decca; (F 10976)* 20 –

Bob DYLAN

Born: Robert Allan Zimmerman, 24 May'41, Duluth, Minnesota, USA. One of the human foundation stones of modern popular music, BOB DYLAN is quite probably the most talented, most misunderstood, most covered and certainly the most written about songwriter and performer of recent history. His early work inspired the BEATLES and furnished countless songs for US counterparts the Byrds, while his politicised folk and flights of poetic genious gave voice to the fledgling counter culture. Famously booed by outraged luddites when he swapped an acoustic guitar for an electric one, DYLAN courted controversy as casually as he wooed the gypsy women in his songs. His mid-60s albums set the bar before he went into seclusion up in Woodstock, eventually emerging in the 70s with the best work of his career. But what of the great man's dalliances with the big screen? Aside from 'DON'T LOOK BACK' (1967), D.A. Pennebaker's account of Bob's 1965 British tour, it'd be 1973 before DYLAN was given a bonafide opportunity to appear in a major Hollywood film. That film was Sam Peckinpah's outlaw tale, 'PAT GARRETT & BILLY THE KID', a movie whose on-set anecdotes were almost as legendary as its subjects. While DYLAN was given a fairly minor role as Alias, the Kid's laconic sidekick, he excelled himself with the soundtrack, his first, and one that stands among the cream of Western scores. The experience had him all fired up about making his own film, one conceived as a kind of arthouse concert movie documenting his famous Rolling Thunder Revue of the mid-70s, and one which made liberal use of improvisation. Finally released in 1978 (as was his large contribution the Band's 'The LAST WALTZ'), the four hour 'RENALDO AND CLARA' was an unmitigated failure, pulled from screens before it had even finished its limited run. The movie had also been a serious drain on DYLAN's finances and dampened his enthusiasm for further celluloid experiments. In fact, it'd be the mid-80s before he dabbled in film again, agreeing to take on the part of a jaded rock star in the forgettable 'HEARTS OF FIRE'. It was to be an underwhelming epitaph for director Richard Marquand, who passed away soon after the movie was completed. By the time of DYLAN's next major film involvement, he'd enjoyed his biggest critical and commercial comeback since the 70s with great albums either side of the millennium. He'd also picked up an unexpected Best Music (Song) Oscar for the gritty 'Things Have Changed', featured in the acclaimed Michael Douglas vehicle, 'Wonder Boys' (2000). That he proceeded to compromise all these achievements with a starring role (as . . . an aged rock star..) in a failed movie could be viewed as either mystifying, or reverting to type. 'MASKED AND ANONYMOUS' (2003) received short thrift from critics, and DYLAN's performance can only be described as inscrutable. Even more so when his barely noticeable acting is contrasted with his considerably more compelling stage presence, especially with such a cracking band behind him. Yet again the soundtrack was his saving grace, with great live performances and a sprinkling of inspired covers from around the globe. It seems fair to conclude that BOB's relationship with film – at least beyond the realms of the soundtrack – has been an uneasy one, although it's hard to hold this against the man when the music does such a consistently eloquent job of speaking for itself.

BG

- **filmography** (composer) {acting} –

Don't Look Back *(1967 {*p})* / **Festival** *(1967 {*p})* / Scruggs *(1970 {p})* / **the Concert For Bangla Desh** *(1972 {p} OST by GEORGE HARRISON & V/A =>)* / **Eat The Document** *(1972 {p})* / **Pat Garrett & Billy The Kid** *(1973 {*} OST =>)* / **Renaldo And Clara** *(1978 {p/*})* / **the Last Waltz** *(1978 {p} on OST by the BAND =>)* / Parole *(1982 TV score by DYLAN & STING)* / Band Of The Hand *(1986 theme-only by DYLAN)* / **Hearts Of Fire** *(1987 {*} OST by DYLAN & V/A =>)* / High Stakes *(1989 score by DYLAN & Mira J. Spektor)* / Backtrack *(1991 TV)* / Paradise Cove *(1999 {b})* / Wonder Boys *(2000 on V/A OST see; future editions =>)* / **Godfathers And Sons** *(2003 {p} on OST by V/A =>)* / **Masked And Anonymous** *(2003 {*} OST by DYLAN & V/A =>)* / **No Direction Home** *(2006 {p} OST =>)*

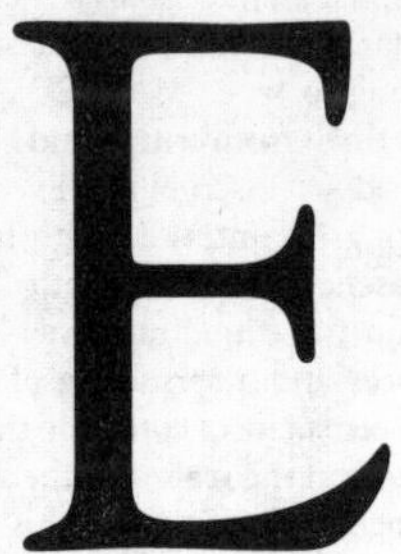

EARTH GIRLS ARE EASY

1989 (US/UK 100m) Kestral Films Production / Vestron Pictures (PG)

Film genre: romantic sci-fi Rock Musical comedy

Top guns: dir: Julien Temple ← RUNNING OUT OF LUCK ← ABSOLUTE BEGINNERS ← the GREAT ROCK'N'ROLL SWINDLE / → AT THE MAX → the FILTH AND THE FURY → GLASTONBURY → the FUTURE IS UNWRITTEN / s-w: Julie Brown ← MEDUSA: DARE TO BE TRUTHFUL, Charlie Coffey ← MEDUSA: DARE TO BE TRUTHFUL, Terrence E. McNally

Stars: Geena Davis *(Valerie Dale)*, Jeff Goldblum *(Mac)* ← THANK GOD IT'S FRIDAY ← NASHVILLE ← DEATH WISH / → BARENAKED IN AMERICA, Jim Carrey *(Wiploc)* ← MAN ON THE MOON, Julie Brown *(Candy Pink)* → the SPIRIT OF 76 → MEDUSA: DARE TO BE TRUTHFUL, Damon Wayans *(Zeebo)* → MARCI X, Michael McKean *(Woody; pool boy)* ← LIGHT OF DAY ← THIS IS SPINAL TAP / → AIRHEADS → GIGANTIC (A TALE OF TWO JOHNS) → a MIGHTY WIND, Charles Rocket *(Dr. Ted Gallagher)*, Larry Linville *(Dr. Bob)* → ROCK'N'ROLL HIGH SCHOOL FOREVER, Rick Overton *(Dr. Rick)* → POPSTAR, Stacey Travis *(Tammy)* → the MUSE

Storyline: What would you do if a spaceship crash landed in your swimming pool? When exactly that happens to manicurist Valerie she knows just what's required – a total makeover for the aliens at the Curl Up and Dye beauty salon. Poor Valerie's just dumped two-timing fiancé Ted and wants some fun. What better way than to take Mac, Whiploc and Zeebo out dancing and introduce them to earth culture – once they've had their fur shaved off. *JZ*

Movie rating: *5

Visual: video + dvd

Off the record: Rick Overton's mother Nancy Overton was a member of the Chordettes at a time when they recorded 'Lollipop'.

—

Various Artists (producer: NILE RODGERS: composer *)

May 89. (lp/c/cd) *Sire-WEA; <(9 25835-1/-4/-2)>* ☐ Nov89 ☐
– Love train (DARYL HALL & JOHN OATES) / Baby gonna shake (ROYALTY) / Hit me (INFORMATION SOCIETY) / The ground you walk on (JILL JONES) / Earth girls are easy * (the N) / Shake that cosmic thing (the B-52's) / Route 66 (the Nile Rodgers mix) (DEPECHE MODE) / Who do you love? (the JESUS AND MARY CHAIN) / Throb (STEWART COPELAND) / Brand new girl (JULIE BROWN) / 'Cause I'm a blonde (JULIE BROWN).

S/track review: NILE RODGERS looms large, producing and/or playing on seven of the eleven tracks, and the Chic maestro's funky take on 80s synth pop sets the pace for a quirkily likeable collection that is wholly of its time. The template encompasses both the B-52's' cheerfully bouncy retro 'Cosmic Thing' and DARYL HALL & JOHN OATES redrafting Philly soul with an electronic 'Love Train'. RODGERS remixes Depeche Mode's bubbling cover of 'Route 66' to infectious effect with a pleasingly wayward instrumental break, and the JESUS AND MARY CHAIN's trademark chainsaw guitars are orchestrated to throbbing, programmed drums on a dark 'Who Do You Love?' The spirit of Madonna also lurks unattractively, though; having established impeccable credentials the best part of a decade before with the likes of 'Good Times', RODGERS was the man who had produced 'Like A Virgin', and the multi-talented screenwriter JULIE BROWN (a perennial on US television) was the most famous and incisive mimic of the Material Girl's po-faced posturing. Still, RODGERS and BROWN fail to rise above the level of cabaret on their two collaborations. And even worse, the contribution of Madonna's ex-boyfriend and long-serving hit-writer Stephen Bray with his band ROYALTY, 'Baby Gonna Shake', is identikit 80s Madonna – and still no better sung. *ND*

Album rating: *5.5

☐ EARTH, WIND & FIRE segment
(⇒ THAT'S THE WAY OF THE WORLD)

EASY COME, EASY GO

1966 (US 96m) Paramount Pictures (PG)

Film genre: Rock'n'roll Musical adventure

Top guns: dir: John Rich ← ROUSTABOUT / s-w: Allan Weiss ← PARADISE, HAWAIIAN STYLE ← ROUSTABOUT ← FUN IN ACAPULCO ← GIRLS! GIRLS! GIRLS! ← BLUE HAWAII, Anthony Lawrence ← PARADISE, HAWAIIAN STYLE ← ROUSTABOUT / → ELVIS: THE MOVIE

Stars: Elvis PRESLEY *(Ted Jackson)*, Dodie Marshall *(Jo Symington)* ← SPINOUT, Pat Priest *(Dina Bishop)* ← LOOKING FOR LOVE, Pat Harrington *(Judd Whitman)*, Skip Ward *(Gil Carey)*, Frank McHugh *(Capt. Jack)*, Elsa Lancaster *(Mme. Neherina)* ← PAJAMA PARTY, Sandy Kenyon *(Lt. Marty Schwartz)* → DOWN ON US

Storyline: Singing skindiver (we kid you not..) Ted Jackson attempts to salvage a haul of treasure from a sunken wreck with the help of sassy yoga practitioner Jo Symington. *BG*

Movie rating: *3.5

Visual: video + dvd

Off the record: nothing really

—

ELVIS PRESLEY: Easy Come, Easy Go / Speedway

Mar 95. (cd) *<(07863 66558-2)>* ☐ ☐
– Easy come, easy go / The love machine / Yoga is as yoga does / You gotta stop / Sing you children / I'll take love / She's a machine / The love machine (take 11) / Sing you children (take 1) / She's a machine (take 13) / Suppose (alt.) / (SPEEDWAY tracks).

S/track review: While many ELVIS soundtracks suffered from weak sound and production, 'EASY COME, EASY GO' was one of the worst, possibly because, as the CD sleevenote suggests, it was recorded on-site, on the Paramount scoring stage. Worse, 'Yoga Is As Yoga Does' comes perilously close to 'Old MacDonald' in the cringe stakes, a plodding, preposterous attempt at a hip 60s reference during a time when PRESLEY was so far out of fashion he was almost off the cultural map. Gripes aside, there are some half decent-songs here, or at least ELVIS' delivery makes them seem half decent. The spirited contributions of a larger-than-usual brass section are also a plus point, spicing up the likes of 'You Gotta Stop' and the celebratory, biblically-themed 'Sing You Children', and lending 'The Love Machine' a rootsy Southern Soul feel. The

Latin brass and percussion – courtesy of Cal Tjader's brother, Curry (seriously) – on 'I'll Take Love' also works fairly well. Originally released as an EP (the last of ELVIS' career), these songs were collected along with alternate takes ('The Love Machine' is a particularly welcome addition with some jamming organ, bolshier brass and meaner guitar) on a CD with the full-length soundtrack from 'SPEEDWAY'. *BG*

Album/EP rating: *3 / CD with 'Speedway' *5

– spinoff releases, etc. –

ELVIS PRESLEY: You Gotta Stop / The Love Machine

May 67. (7") *(RCA 1593)* [–] [38]

ELVIS PRESLEY

May 67. (7"ep) *R.C.A.; <EPA 4387> (RCX 7187)* [ ] Jun67 [ ]
– Easy come, easy go / The love machine *[US-only]* / Yoga is as yoga does / You gotta stop *[US-only]* / Sing you children / I'll take love.

EASY RIDER

1969 (US 94m) Columbia Pictures (R)

Top guns: Americana biker/road movie

Top guns: s-w: Peter Fonda, Dennis Hopper (+ dir), Terry Southern ← CANDY / → the MAGIC CHRISTIAN

Stars: Peter Fonda *(Wyatt, aka Captain America)* ← the TRIP ← the WILD ANGELS / → the HIRED HAND → GRACE OF MY HEART → SOUTH OF HEAVEN, WEST OF HELL, Dennis Hopper *(Billy)* ← HEAD ← the TRIP / → HUMAN HIGHWAY → WHITE STAR → RUNNING OUT OF LUCK ← STRAIGHT TO HELL, Jack Nicholson *(George Hanson)* ← HEAD ← PSYCHO-OUT / → TOMMY → the BORDER → BATMAN, Karen Black *(Karen)* ← YOU'RE A BIG BOY NOW / → NASHVILLE → HOUSE OF 1000 CORPSES, Robert Walker *(Jack)* ← the SAVAGE SEVEN, Luana Anders *(Lisa)* ← the TRIP, **Phil Spector** *(drug connection)* ← the BIG T.N.T. SHOW ← the T.A.M.I. SHOW / → the CONCERT FOR BANGLADESH → IMAGINE → IMAGINE: JOHN LENNON → MAYOR OF THE SUNSET STRIP, Antonio Mendoza *(Jesus)*, **Toni Basil** *(Mary)* ← HEAD ← PAJAMA PARTY ← the T.A.M.I. SHOW / → ROCKULA, Luke Askew *(stranger on highway)* → PAT GARRETT & BILLY THE KID → MACKINTOSH & T.J. → SOUTH OF HEAVEN, WEST OF HELL

Storyline: Released a matter of months before the hippie dream was slain at Altamont, 'Easy Rider' was both a low-budget, loose limbed celebration of America's oldest freedom of all: the open road; and an anticipation of the fragility and contradictions of the US counter-culture. The movie follows two footloose, chopper riding dreamers as they cruise eastwards towards New Orleans on the proceeds of a cocaine deal. Along the way they pick up a sympathetic lawyer who gets them out of a tight spot, before indulging in a drugs 'n' sex blow-out at the Mardi Gras. The dream finally turns sour as good old American values bite back in the form of trigger happy rednecks. *BG*

Movie rating: *9.5

Visual: video + dvd

Off the record: Toni Basil (she of 'Mickey' fame!) actually got a bit hippy-chic here and er . . . naked.

—

Various Artists

Aug 69. (lp) *Dunhill; <DSX 50063> Stateside; (SSL 5018)* [6] Nov69 [2]
– The pusher (STEPPENWOLF) / Born to be wild (STEPPENWOLF) / The weight (SMITH) / Wasn't born to follow (the BYRDS) / If you want to be a bird (the HOLY MODAL ROUNDERS) / Don't bogart me (the FRATERNITY OF MAN) / If 6 was 9 (the JIMI HENDRIX EXPERIENCE) / Kyrie Eleison – Mardi gras (when the saints) (the ELECTRIC PRUNES) / It's alright, ma (I'm only bleeding) (ROGER McGUINN) / The ballad of Easy Rider (ROGER McGUINN). *(re-iss. Feb82 on 'M.C.A.' lp/c; MCL/+C 1647) (re-iss. 1987 on 'Castle' lp/c; CLA LP/MC 139) <(cd-iss. Nov90 on 'M.C.A.'; DMCL 1647) (c/cd re-iss. Sep94 on 'Quality'; NTLC/+D 027) <US cd re-iss. 2000 on 'M.C.A.'; 088 119 153-2> <d-cd-iss. Mar04 "inspired by . . ." on 'Hip-O'+=; B0002115-02>* – Pushin' too hard (the SEEDS) / I had too much to dream (last night) (the ELECTRIC PRUNES) / (We ain't got) Nothing yet (BLUES MAGOOS) / San Franciscan nights (ERIC BURDON & THE ANIMALS) / White rabbit (JEFFERSON AIRPLANE) / I can see for miles (the WHO) / A whiter shade of pale (PROCOL HARUM) / Groovin' (the YOUNG RASCALS) / High flyin' bird (RICHIE HAVENS) / The weight (the BAND) / You ain't going nowhere (the BYRDS) / Time has come today (the CHAMBERS BROTHERS) / With a little help from my friends (JOE COCKER) / Summertime blues (BLUE CHEER) / Nights in white satin (the MOODY BLUES) / Mendocino (SIR DOUGLAS QUINTET) / Get together (the YOUNGBLOODS) / My uncle (the FLYING BURRITO BROTHERS) / Something in the air (THUNDERCLAP NEWMAN).

S/track review: Despite being one of the first films to assemble a rundown of the most popular, hip contemporary tracks of the day rather than commission them especially, 'EASY RIDER' easily and thrillingly matched the music on vinyl with the action on screen. The combination of a distant horizon and the BYRDS' psych-country classic, 'Wasn't Born To Follow' is still enough to make anyone want to give up their 9 to 5, while STEPPENWOLF's 'Born To Be Wild' (a hit a year earlier!) was defined as the ultimate biker anthem. The latter act's second best-loved track, 'The Pusher' (penned by Hoyt Axton), fits in well with a mind-blowing version of 'If 6 Was 9' by the JIMI HENDRIX EXPERIENCE, for many the "high" points of this tripped-out rock extravaganza. Whimsical relief came courtesy of the HOLY MODAL ROUNDERS ('If You Want To Be A Bird') and the FRATERNITY OF MAN ('Don't Bogart Me'), while ROGER McGUINN's 'The Ballad Of Easy Rider' (co-written with Bob Dylan) over the movie's denouement remains as poignant as ever. *BG & MCS*

Album rating: *9

EDDIE AND THE CRUISERS

1983 (US 93m) Embassy Pictures Corporation (PG)

Film genre: Rock/Pop-music showbiz drama

Top guns: s-w: Martin Davidson (+ dir) ← ALMOST SUMMER / → LOOKING FOR AN ECHO, Arlene Davidson (au: P.F. Kluge)

Stars: Michael Pare *(Eddie Wilson)* → STREETS OF FIRE → EDDIE AND THE CRUISERS II: EDDIE LIVES! → the VIRGIN SUICIDES, Tom Berenger *(Frank Ridgeway)*, Joe Pantoliano *(Doc Robbins)* ← RISKY BUSINESS → the IDOLMAKER / → SCENES FROM THE GOLDMINE → LA BAMBA → ROCK'N'ROLL MOM → the IN CROWD → BLACK AND WHITE, Helen Schneider *(Joann Carlino)*, Matthew Laurance *(Sal Amato)* → STREETS OF FIRE → EDDIE AND THE CRUISERS II: EDDIE LIVES!, David Wilson *(Kenny Hopkins)*, **Michael "Tunes" Antunes** *(Wendell Newton)*, Ellen Barkin *(Maggie Foley)* ← TENDER MERCIES ← UP IN SMOKE / → DOWN BY LAW → SIESTA → JOHNNY HANDSOME → FEAR AND LOATHING IN LAS VEGAS, **Kenny Vance** *(Lew Elson)* ← AMERICAN HOT WAX / → LOOKING FOR AN ECHO, John Stockwell *(Keith Livingston)*, Joey Balin *(Eddie's replacement)*

Storyline: After his badly damaged car is discovered on a bridge, the lead singer (Eddie Wilson) of fictional 60s band the Cruisers mysteriously disappears, as do the tapes for the group's second album. Twenty years later, with Eddie presumed dead, the group's re-vamped debut starts climbing the charts again sparking renewed interest in their story and a successful quest to seek out the missing tapes. The mystery intensifies when, just before the titles, an unnoticed middle aged figure cuts a striking resemblance to Eddie at the rediscovered album's launch. *KM*

Movie rating: *6

Visual: video

Off the record: Michael "Tunes" Antunes was actually the sax player with the BROWN BEAVER BAND.

—

JOHN CAFFERTY AND THE BEAVER BROWN BAND
(score: KENNY VANCE *)

Sep 83. (lp/c) *Scotti Bros.; <ZK/ZC 38929> (SCT/40 25702)* 9 Apr85
– On the dark side / Mockingbird / Runaround Sue / Down on my knees / Hang up my rock & roll shoes / Runaway / Boardwalk angel / Betty Lou's got a new pair of shoes (*) / Those oldies but goodies (remind me of you) (*) / Season in Hell (fire suite). *<cd-iss. Dec90 on 'Volcano-Zomba'; 32001-2> <cd re-iss. May04 as 'Extended Versions'>*

S/track review: Thrust out of playing in bars and into the limelight overnight, JOHN CAFFERTY AND THE BEAVER BROWN BAND received plaudits and multi-platinum success for this derivative, three-chords-are-plenty soundtrack. Modelling their songs on the Bruce Springsteen/E-Street Shuffle sound, CAFFERTY and Co penned the majority of this album with the brazen confidence that helped them go Top 10 with 'On The Dark Side'. Its fist-pounding bass and scratchy 80s sax sound punctuates the album regularly in tracks like 'Down On My Knees' and the blithe 'Wild Summer Nights'. Equally at home playing rock'n'roll numbers, they enlist the talents of KENNY VANCE, a little-known doo wop enthusiast turned soundtrack writer, to compose a couple of R'n'R standards like 'Those Oldies But Goodies (Remind Me Of You)' (obviously modelled on the Crewcuts's drippy last dance, 'Earth Angel'). They needn't have bothered though; their joyous self-penned doo wopper 'Runaround Sue' temporarily shook off the Springsteen mould that the group would carry to their grave . . . or at least to the bars from whence they emerged. *KM*

Album rating: *5.5

– spinoff hits, etc. –

EDDIE AND THE CRUISERS: On The Dark Side / Wild Summer Nights

Sep 83. (7") *<04107>* 64 –

JOHN CAFFERTY AND THE BEAVER BROWN BAND: Tender Years / Down On My Knees

Jan 84. (7") *<04327>* 78 –

JOHN CAFFERTY AND THE BEAVER BROWN BAND: On The Dark Side / Wild Summer Nights

Aug 84. (7"/12") *<04594> (A/SCT 4867)* 7 Apr85

JOHN CAFFERTY AND THE BEAVER BROWN BAND: Tender Years / Down On My Knees

Nov 84. (7") *<04682>* 31 –

EDDIE AND THE CRUISERS II: EDDIE LIVES!

1989 (US/Can 104m) Scotti Brothers Pictures (PG-13)

Film genre: Rock/Pop-music/showbiz drama

Top guns: dir: Jean-Claude Lord / s-w: Charles Zev Cohen, Rick Doehring

Stars: Michael Pare *(Eddie Wilson / Joe West)* ← STREETS OF FIRE ← EDDIE AND THE CRUISERS / → the VIRGIN SUICIDES, Marini Orsini *(Diane Armani)*, Bernie Coulson *(Rick Diesel)* → HARD CORE LOGO, Matthew Laurance *(Sal Amato)* ← STREETS OF FIRE ← EDDIE AND THE CRUISERS, Michael Rhoades *(Dave Pagent)*, Anthony Sherwood *(Hilton)* → HONEY, Mark Holmes *(Quinn Quinley)*, David Matheson *(Stewart Fairbanks)*, **Bo DIDDLEY** *(legendary guitarist)*, Martha Quinn *(music video hostess)* ← TAPEHEADS / → BAD CHANNELS, Vlasta Vrana *(Frank)* ← HEAVY METAL, Orville Thompson *(sax player)*, Warren Williams *(bassist)*

Storyline: Joe West is a construction worker living quietly in Montreal, but when he takes off his false moustache he amazingly becomes – Eddie Wilson! Yes, the iconic lead singer of the Cruisers survived the plunge all those years ago and is living reclusively, longing for the good old days. When "Eddiemania" breaks out after the release of his old album, Eddie decides to form a new band and settle some scores from the past. *JZ*

Movie rating: *4

Visual: video

Off the record: BO DIDDLEY (see own biog)

JOHN CAFFERTY AND THE BEAVER BROWN BAND
(score: Marty Simon, Kenny Vance & Leon Aronson)

Aug 89. (lp/c/cd) *Scotti Bros; <ZK/ZC/ZD 45297> (842046-1/-4/-2)* Jul90
– Runnin' thru the fire / Just a matter of time / Open road / Maryia / Emotional storm / Pride & passion / Garden of Eden / N.Y.C. song / Some like it hot / (Keep my love) Alive. *<cd re-iss. Dec90 on 'Volcano-Zomba'; 32002-2>*

S/track review: Six years since the last "EDDIE" episode and one might think there'd be some progression by JOHN CAFFERTY and Co as the 90s get closer. No chance, in fact it's rather the opposite, all retro with a Springsteen vocal sheen that even "The Boss" himself would be proud of, the sax meanwhile, is pure Clarence Clemons. Tracks such as 'Open Road', 'Runnin' Thru The Fire', 'Just A Matter Of Time', 'NYC Song', etc. were very derivative of the three-chord-wonder, all-American boy and not a patch on his greatest success, 'The Dark Side'. Another prime example if you needed one more, comes by way of the bombastic 'Pride & Passion' single, which only managed a minor chart placing, while the album itself reached a lowly No.121; not their worst so far as CAFFERTY's previous long-player ('Roadhouse') didn't manage to reach the Top 200 at all. The 'Garden Of Eden' and 'Some Like It Hot' tracks do try a different approach, but JC only swops a Springsteen signature for that of Jerry Lee Lewis or Elvis. One supposes there might be listeners that might love this type of dull-oid rock'n'roll, but this LP suggests that "Eddie Dies!" rather than "EDDIE LIVES!". Fact. *MCS*

Album rating: *3.5

– spinoff hits, etc. –

JOHN CAFFERTY AND THE BEAVER BROWN BAND: Pride & Passion / Heat Of The Night

Jul 89. (7") *<68999>* 66

JOHN CAFFERTY AND THE BEAVER BROWN BAND: Runnin' Thru The Fire /

May 90. (7") *(PO 86)* –

EDDIE PRESLEY

1992 (US 106m) Raven Pictures International

Film genre: psychological comedy drama

Top guns: dir: Jeff Burr / s-w: Duane Whitaker

Stars: Duane Whitaker *(Eddie Presley)* → SATURDAY NIGHT SPECIAL → PULP FICTION → the DEVIL'S REJECTS, Clu Gulager *(Sid)* ← TAPEHEADS ← the RETURN OF THE LIVING DEAD ← LIVING PROOF: THE HANK WILLIAMS JR. STORY, Roscoe Lee Browne *(Doc)* ← SUPERFLY T.N.T. ← UP TIGHT!, Ted Raimi *(Scooter)*, Daniel Roebuck *(Keystone the magnificent)* ← DUDES / → the DEVIL'S REJECTS, Willard Pugh *(Nick)* ← BLUE CITY / → CB4: THE MOVIE, Stacie Bourgeois *(Tyranny)*, Ian Ogilvy *(Starch)*, Lawrence Tierney *(West)* → RESERVOIR DOGS, Tim Thomerson *(shock comic)* ← NEAR DARK ← RHINESTONE ← HONKYTONK MAN ← CARNY ← RECORD CITY ← CAR WASH / → BAD CHANNELS, Quentin Tarantino *(asylum attendant)* → RESERVOIR DOGS → PULP FICTION → FOUR ROOMS → FROM DUSK TILL DAWN → GIRL 6, Bruce Campbell *(asylum attendant)* → BUBBA HO-TEP

Storyline: Eddie Presley is an ex-Elvis impersonator who now works as a security guard. He is divorced, overweight and has depression. One day he is offered the chance to recapture the old days when a club hires him to do an

Elvis show, but Eddie's luck is out when the club's music system flops. Instead of going home, however, he stays on stage and tells the audience all about the trials and tribulations of his life. *JZ*

Movie rating: *5.5

Visual: d-DVD on 'Tempe' 2004 (no audio OST; score: Jim Manzie)

Off the record: Ian Ogilvy took on the role of TV's 'The Saint' after the James Bond departure of Roger Moore. *MCS*

□ the EDGE OF HELL alt. (⇒ ROCK'N'ROLL NIGHTMARE)

EDGE OF SEVENTEEN

1998 (US 99m) Blue Streak Films / Luna Pictures (R)

Film genre: romantic coming-of-age/teen comedy drama

Top guns: dir: David Moreton / s-w: Todd Stephens → GYPSY 83

Stars: Chris Stafford *(Eric Hunter)*, Tina Holmes *(Maggie)* → STORYTELLING, Anderson Gabrych *(Rod)* → GYPSY 83, Stephanie McVay *(Bonnie Hunter; mom)* → GYPSY 83, John Eby *(dad)*, **Lea DeLaria** *(Angie)*, Antonio Carriero *(Andy)*, Twiggy *(Marlene Dicktrick)* ← CLUB PARADISE ← the BLUES BROTHERS ← POPCORN

Storyline: It's 1984 and small-town Eurythmics fan, Eric, is coming out, and going out to gay bars for the first time. Ohio lad, Eric, subsequently meets Rod, while his girlfriend of sorts, Maggie, waits patiently for some affection from her sartorially-dressed, bleached-hair pop lover. *MCS*

Movie rating: *7

Visual: video + dvd

Off the record: Twiggy (Lawson) (b. Lesley Hornby) was the 60s model/icon turned actress and singer; she starred in song and dance musical, 'The Boyfriend' (1971) and later became a one-hit wonder in 1976 with 'Here I Go Again'. *MCS*

Various Artists (score: Tom Bailey *)

May 99. (cd) *Razor & Tie; <(RE 82847-2)>* □ Jul99 □

– Right by your side (EURYTHMICS) / Smalltown boy (BRONSKI BEAT) / Wishing (I had a photograph of you) (A FLOCK OF SEAGULLS) / Obsession (ANIMOTION) / The politics of dancing (RE-FLEX) / Love plus one (HAIRCUT 100) / Destination unknown (MISSING PERSONS) / So many men, so little time (MIQUEL BROWN) / High energy (EVELYN THOMAS) / Mickey (TONI BASIL) / Why? (BRONSKI BEAT) / Modern love is automatic (A FLOCK OF SEAGULLS) / In the name of love (THOMPSON TWINS) * / You're my world (CILLA BLACK) / Blue skies (LEA DeLARIA).

S/track review: Ah! the 80s! A decade, it seems, derided by many critics and music observers. A time when gay pride came of age and music slipped out of its Studio 54 dress & drag (a la 70s) and into a post-new romantic suited'n'booted weird-o hairstyle. This soundtrack encompasses all of that and more, the more being closing tracks from 60s Scouser and gay icon, CILLA BLACK ('You're My World') and lesbian comic, turned jazz/lounge singer, LEA DeLARIA ('Blue Skies'). Back to the futuristic 80s (self-acclaimed, no doubt) and how could you not open proceedings with the theme of the movie, by the EURYTHMICS. Surprisingly though, the duo's only inclusion here, 'Right By Your Side' (a big hit in '84 on both sides of the Atlantic), a pity as the film itself carries more ANNIE and DAVE interest. Two tracks each respectively go to gay Anglo-Scots BRONSKI BEAT and Merseyside quiff-quartet A FLOCK OF SEAGULLS, Jimmy Somerville's vox lifting the listener higher and higher on 'Smalltown Boy' & 'Why?', while AFOS' Mike Score delivered UK hits, 'Wishing (I Had A Photograph Of You)' & 'Modern Love Is Automatic'. Talking of haircuts, HAIRCUT 100 (featuring the boyish Nick Heyward), delivered probably their best three-minute pop tune in 'Love Plus One', while on the er . . . fringe of transatlantic new wave-dom was ANIMOTION (featuring Astrid Plane) and their Top 5 smash, 'Obsession'. Understated at the time (only Top 30 in 1984), but deserving of a mention is RE-FLEX, 'The Politics Of Dancing', a song that could transport the listener back to a time when 'The Tube' was the only decent pop programme on the telly. US acts such as choreographer/actress TONI BASIL (and the excruciatingly catchy chart-topper, 'Mickey'), Frank Zappa pop-offshoots MISSING PERSONS ('Destination Unknown'), the topical MIQUEL BROWN ('So Many Men, So Little Time') and Chicago dancing diva EVELYN THOMAS ('High Energy'), were all on show on this electro-pop testament to a near forgotten era. It's just a pity too, that OST arranger, TOM BAILEY, couldn't get more of his 80s "trio" THOMPSON TWINS (with 'In The Name Of Love') into the mix. *MCS*

Album rating: *6.5

EEGAH

aka EEGAH: THE NAME WRITTEN IN BLOOD

1962 (US 90m) Fairway International Pictures (PG)

Film genre: Rock horror musical!

Top guns: dir: (+ story) Arch Hall Sr. → WILD GUITAR / s-w: Bob Wehling → WILD GUITAR

Stars: **Arch Hall, Jr.** *(Tom Nelson)* → WILD GUITAR, Marilyn Manning *(Roxy Miller)*, Richard Kiel *(Eegah)* → ROUSTABOUT → SKIDOO, William Watters as Arch Hall, Sr. *(Robert Miller)* → WILD GUITAR, Bob Davis *(George)*, Addalyn Pollitt *(George's wife)*, Clay Stearns + Deke Lussier *(band members)*, William Lloyd *(Kruger)* → WILD GUITAR, Ray Steckler *(Mr. Fishman)* → WILD GUITAR, Carolyn Brandt *(Fishman's girl)* → WILD GUITAR → RAT PFINK A BOO-BOO

Storyline: Teenagers driving through Mojave Desert stumble upon a neanderthal 7-foot caveman, Eegah! He fancies pulling a bit of bikini- clad Roxy, so he kidnaps the damsel and her father, but when she escapes the big man goes on a teenage rampage all over Palm Springs; the only obstacle it seems is some pitiful rock'n'roll played by her paramour, Tom Nelson and his god awful band. *MCS*

Movie rating: *2 (regarded as the worst movie of all time!)

Visual: Rhino Home Video / dvd: Platinum Disc (no audio OST; score by Henri Price, aka Andre Brummer – died pneumonia May 2006)

Off the record: **Arch Hall, Jr.** (and the Archers) performed three gloriously bad tracks, 'Nobody Lives On Brownsville Road', 'Valerie' and 'Vickie', all available on their 2005 compilation, 'Wild Guitar!'; Arch Jr's mother was Addalyn Pollitt, wife of Arch Sr – keeping it in the family. Viewers might recognise the character Eegah as "Jaws" in the subsequent Bond movies, 'The Spy Who Loved Me' and 'Moonraker'. *MCS*

8 MILE

2002 (US 110m) Universal Pictures (R)

Film genre: Hip Hop/Rap-music urban drama

Top guns: dir: Curtis Hanson / s-w: Scott Silver

Stars: **Eminem** *(Jimmy "B-Rabbit" Smith Jr.)*, Kim Basinger *(Stephanie Smith)* ← WAYNE'S WORLD 2 ← BATMAN ← HARD COUNTRY, Brittany Murphy *(Alex)*, Mekhi Phifer *(David 'Future' Porter)* ← CARMEN: A HIP HOPERA ← GIRL 6 / → HONEY, Evan Jones *(Cheddar Bob)*, Omar Benson Miller *(Sol George)* → GET RICH OR DIE TRYIN', Eugene Byrd *(Wink)* ←

WENT TO CONEY ISLAND ON A MISSION FROM GOD . . . BE BACK BY FIVE ← WHITEBOYS ← DEAD MAN, De'Angelo Wilson *(DJ Iz)*, Taryn Manning *(Janeane)* → COLD MOUNTAIN → HUSTLE & FLOW, Anthony Mackie *(Papa Doc)*, **Obie Trice** *(second parking lot rapper)*, **Proof** *(Lil' Tic)*, **Xzibit** *(male lunch truck rapper)* → the COUNTRY BEARS

Storyline: In the grim environs of inner city Detroit, Jimmy Smith aka Rabbit is the token white boy among the black hip hop majority, slaving in the factory by day and pitting his lyrical wits against the other freestyle hopefuls by night. The fact that his mom is an alcoholic mess is only one more negative factor in a blighted existence which – in time honoured Hollywood fashion – he can only escape if he makes the grade on the mic. *BG*

Movie rating: *7

Visual: dvd

Off the record: EMINEM was born Marshall Bruce Mathers III, 17 Oct'72, St Joseph, Missouri, USA. Spending his childhood roaming from one State to the next, the gifted rapper and one time Soul Intent member began freestyling in his friend's basement at the age of fifteen. Five years (and, apparently, a lot of mushrooms and NWA albums) later, the white MC decided to try his luck in the increasing world of hip hop. He debuted with the poorly distributed album 'Infinite' (1996) and failed blindly at attracting attention from any major labels. Legend Dr Dre apparently discovered EMINEM (a word play on his initials) when he found a demo tape on Interscope's Jimmy Iovines' garage floor. To be fully convinced by the rapper, Dre travelled to watch him perform in the 1997 Rap Olympics, before rushing over and signing him on the spot. His major label debut, 'The Slim Shady LP', appeared in the spring of '99, sales boosted after the rather offensive massive hit single, 'My Name Is'. The aforementioned platter rocketed to the top spot in America and sent parents into a fit of rage over the filth and obscenities our white chump was slobbering about on tape. The American media, senseless rock stars and a few bad words about his dear old momma were all mentioned in the single, that had such an infectious chorus it made listeners fall under the spell of EMINEM's crazy, high-speed, nasal-pinching slur. The sophomore album did not do so bad either, selling nearly a million copies in its first week and a further million in the months after its release. The crown king of confrontation returned in 2001 with 'The Marshall Mathers LP', an even darker journey through his tortured psych-scape, shot through with as much humour as ever but pinned back with (un)healthy doses of stark realism. The pairing of Mathers and cooing pop songbird Dido on 'Stan' was a true stroke of genius, one that resulted in a huge UK No.1 single. This was preceded by 'The Real Slim Shady', a shuffling, propulsive groove taking it to the top; he was now taking the alter-ego of the Texas Chainsaw Massacre on stage – a tough life indeed! 2001 saw the emergence of D-12, a project from the preceding decade initiated by Bizarre and **Proof** (aka Rufus Johnson and DeShaun Holton respectively). Joined by Kon Artis, Kuniva plus Bugz (although the latter was shot dead in 1998 and replaced by Swifty McVay), the alter-ego outfit that was the Dirty Dozen soon got together with childhood buddy EMINEM. The enfant terrible of the rap scene returned in May 2002 with his ego firmly in place, delivering 'The Eminem Show'. The album consisted of the usual disgruntled outbursts at his critics and enemies, personal and international; if 'The Marshall Mathers LP' was a concept album about his emotional strife, then this was centered upon the ever-looming media circle that surrounded him. And then there was a starring role in the movie, '8 MILE', proof if need be he could actually act outside his circle of videos. *AS & MCS*

—

Various Artists (incl. EMINEM *)

Oct 02. (cd/lp) *Interscope; <493508-2/-1> (493530-2)* [1] [1]
– Lose yourself (*) / Love me (*, OBIE TRICE & 50 CENT) / 8 mile (*) / Adrenaline rush (OBIE TRICE) / Places to go (50 CENT) / Rap game (D-12 & 50 CENT) / 8 miles and runnin' (JAY-Z & FREEWAY) / Spit shine (XZIBIT) / Time of my life (MACY GRAY) / U wanna be me (NAS) / Wanksta (50 CENT) / Wasting my time (BOOMKAT feat. TARYN MANNING) / R.A.K.I.M. (RAKIM) / That's my nigga fo' real (YOUNG ZEE) / Battle (GANG STARR) / Rabbit run (*).

S/track review: Having already reinvented the concept of Caucasian rap, EMINEM proceeded to drag both the hip hop movie and the hip hop soundtrack cursing and swearing into the 21st century. Searing, underdog-made-good opener, 'Lose Yourself', was a massive UK No.1, but the best thing here by a mile – or even eight miles – remains the title track, its neo-autobiographical baggage and revelations of self-doubt more hardcore than any of the standard lyrical posturing, driven on by a piston-packing production and queasy jazz piano loop. Taken together, they're rightly recognised as the most brutally satisfying documents in his rapidly expanding file. As sharp at sniffing out new talent as cutting a honky swathe through the competition, EMINEM also used this soundtrack to showcase his then-new protégé, 50 CENT: on both 'Places To Go' and 'Wanksta', the man's insinuating, narcoleptic energy predicted an infamous career. The two of them (together with Obie Trice) got together on 'Love Me', veering from the gloriously ridiculous – EM comparing his talent to the nascent rapping skills of George Bush – to the predictably misogynous (L'il Kim and Lauryn Hill coming in for flak). The fact that the other half of the record is generously given over to big names like JAY-Z, NAS, RAKIM and, erm, MACY GRAY, only underlined the inevitability of EMINEM's ascendence: witness the man's outclassing of D-12 on 'Rap Game'. GANG STARR's sampledelic, Afro-brassy 'Battle' leads the charge for the old skool but ultimately, this is Marshall Mathers' baby and he goes out with all syllables blazing on closer Rabbit Run, the sheer bloody-minded momentum and petulant, adenoidal outrage of his delivery serving notice that the noughties belonged to him. *BG*

Album rating: *7.5

– spinoff releases, etc. –

Various Artists: More Music From 8 Mile

Nov 02. (cd/d-lp) *<(450979-2/-1)>* [ ] Jan03 [ ]
– Shook ones (part 2) (MOBB DEEP) / Juicy (NOTORIOUS B.I.G.) / Gotta get mine (MC BREED & 2 PAC) / Feel me flow (NAUGHTY BY NATURE) / Player's ball (OUTKAST) / Get money (JUNIOR M.A.F.I.A.) / You're all I need to get by (Puff Daddy mix) (METHOD MAN & MARY J. BLIGE) / Shimmy shimmy ya (OL' DIRTY BASTARD) / Bring da pain (METHOD MAN) / C.R.E.A.M. (WU TANG CLAN) / Runnin' (PHARCYDE) / Survival of the fittest (MOBB DEEP).

EMINEM: Lose Yourself / (instrumental)

Dec 02. (c-s/cd-s) *<497815> (497828-4/-2)* [ ] [1]
(12") *(497828-1) <INTR 7815>* – ('A' & mixes).

ELECTRIC APRICOT: QUEST FOR FESTEROO

2007 (US 80m*) National Lampoon (R)

Film genre: Rock-music mockumentary/comedy

Top guns: s-w + dir: **Les Claypool**

Stars: Electric Apricot:- Adam Gates *(Steve Hampton Trouzdale, aka "Aiwass"; bass guitar)*, **Bryan Kehoe** *(Steven Allan Gordon, aka "Gordo; vocals, lead guitar)*, **Les Claypool** *(Lapland Miclovich, aka Lapdog; drums, vocals)* ← RISING LOW ← WE SOLD OUR SOULS FOR ROCK 'N ROLL ← PINK AS THE DAY SHE WAS BORN ← WOODSTOCK 94 ← BILL & TED'S BOGUS JOURNEY, **Jonathan Korty** *(Herschel Tambor Brilstein; keyboards, vocals)*, Jason McHugh *(Smilin' Don Kleinfeld)*, Kyle McCulloch *(Drew Shackleford)*, Dian Bachar *(Stacey "Skip" Holmes)*, Brian Kite *(Dr. Brian "Bucky" Lefkowitz)*, **Mike Gordon** *(himself)* ← RISING LOW ← OUTSIDE OUT ← BITTERSWEET MOTEL, **Warren Haynes** *(himself)* ← RISING LOW, **Matt Abts** *(himself)* ← RISING LOW, **Bob Weir** *(himself)* <= GRATEFUL DEAD =>, Arj Barker *(the Cube)*, Seth Green *(Jonah "the taper")* ← BE COOL ← JOSIE AND THE PUSSYCATS ← PUMP UP THE VOLUME, Matt Stone *(Tom "the taper")*, **Gabby La La** *(performer)*

Storyline: A young filmmaker decides to do a documentary about the music business and picks the unlikely sounding Electric Apricot as his study band. As he gets more and more into their psychedelic style of music he discovers whole new vistas of musical enlightenment and comes to know more about man's spiritual place in the cosmos (as he tours pubs and clubs with them). Not bad for a first effort, then. *JZ*

Movie rating: *8

Visual: dvd (the CD will be released by CLAYPOOL in 2008)

Off the record: Electric Apricot were made up of ex-Primus man **Les Claypool**, **Mike Gordon** (from Phish), **Warren Haynes & Matt Abts** (from Gov't Mule & the Allman Brothers Band). Indie newcomer **Gabby La La** (aka Gabby Lang, is ex-DJ J-Boogie, Dakah Hip Hop Orchestra) had just released her Claypool-produced debut set, 'Be Careful What You Wish For' (2005); described as Tiny Tim on helium. *MCS*

ELECTRIC DREAMS

1984 (UK/US 112m) Metro-Goldwyn-Mayer / United Artists (PG)

Film genre: romantic fantasy comedy/drama

Top guns: dir: Steve Barron / s-w: Rusty Lemorande

Stars: Lenny von Dohlen *(Miles Harding)*, Virginia Madsen *(Madeline Robistat)* → DUNE, Maxwell Caulfield *(Bill)* ← GREASE 2 / → EMPIRE RECORDS, Bud Cort *(voice; Edgar)* ← HAROLD AND MAUDE ← GAS-S-S-S ← the STRAWBERRY STATEMENT / → SOUTH OF HEAVEN, WEST OF HELL → the MILLION DOLLAR HOTEL → COYOTE UGLY → the LIFE AQUATIC WITH STEVE ZISSOU, Don Fellows *(Mr. Ryley)*, Alan Polonsky *(Frank)*, **Giorgio Moroder** *(radio producer)*, Koo Stark *(girl in soap opera)* ← the ROCKY HORROR PICTURE SHOW, Miriam Margoyles *(ticket girl)* ← the APPLE → MAGNOLIA

Storyline: With a God-like superhuman computer apparently not too far off, this daft comedy seems less daft than it once did. Back in the 80s, though, all you had to fear from artificial intelligence was an interest in your love life. Miles Harding is the architect who goes head to head with his hardware over the girl upstairs, a sexy cellist named Madeline. The computer – which calls itself Edgar – initially helps Harding in his efforts to woo her before deciding it fancies some of the action for itself. *BG*

Movie rating: *6

Visual: video + dvd

Off the record: Giorgio Moroder appears in the movie – his many post-pop scores will appear in a further edition.

Various Artists (score: GIORGIO MORODER *)

Aug 84. (lp/c/cd) *Virgin; (V/TCV/CDV 2318) <39600>* [46] [94]
– Electric dreams (P.P. ARNOLD) / Video! (JEFF LYNNE) / The dream (CULTURE CLUB) / The duel (*) / Now you're mine (HELEN TERRY) / Love is love (CULTURE CLUB) / Chase runner (HEAVEN 17) / Let it run (JEFF LYNNE) / Madeline's theme (*) / Together in electric dreams (* & PHILIP OAKEY). *(cd re-iss. Oct94; CDVIP 127)*

S/track review: Having worked his Midas touch on divas Donna Summer and DEBBIE HARRY, electro wunderkind GIORGIO MORODER paired off with a bloke – Human League's PHIL OAKEY – for what became the biggest solo hit of his career, 'Together In Electric Dreams'. A sentimental guilty pleasure to top all guilty pleasures (can any pop record evoke the sta-pressed awkwardness of an 80s school disco as poignantly as this, PETER FRAMPTON's masturbatory, oh-my-giddy-aunt guitar freakout and all?), its Top 3 success spawned an album in its own right. MORODER, alas, didn't have quite the same effect on either HELEN TERRY or 60s soul swinger P.P. ARNOLD, whose title track – released a month before the OAKEY effort – failed to chart. With ELO on the brink of redundancy, JEFF LYNNE wasn't exactly at the top of his game in the mid-80s; neither 'Video!' nor the bizarre rock'n'roll-reggae pastiche, 'Let It Run' hold a candle to his work on 'XANADU'. Which is part of this soundtrack's problem: by late '84, HEAVEN 17's best work was behind them and even CULTURE CLUB had lost their lipgloss (OK, 'Love Is Love' is admittedly one of the album's better tracks, but is it just me, or does it sound like the Style Council?). As for MORODER, left to his own devices he's doomed to his own cod-classical pretensions – 'The Duel' sounds like something Mike Oldfield might have cobbled together for his music O-grade. If executive producer Richard Branson had rounded up these artists just a couple of years earlier, he might have had a half-decent album on his hands. *BG*

Album rating: *5.5

– spinoff releases, etc. –

JEFF LYNNE: Video!
Jul 84. (7"/12") *(VS 695/+12) Epic; <04570>* [ ] [85]

P.P. ARNOLD: Electric Dreams / GIORGIO MORODER: instrumental
Aug 84. (7"/12") *10-Virgin; (TEN 29/+12)* [ ] [–]

GIORGIO MORODER & PHILIP OAKEY: Together In Electric Dreams / GIORGIO MORODER: instrumental
Sep 84. (7"/7"pic-d/ext.12") *(VS/+Y 713/+12)* [–] [3]

HELEN TERRY: Now You're Mine / GIORGIO MORODER: instrumental
Nov 84. (7"/12") *(VS 710/+12)* [ ] [–]

GIORGIO MORODER: The Duel / Madeline's Theme
Dec 84. (7") *(VS 732)* [ ] [–]

□ ELECTRIC LIGHT ORCHESTRA segment
(⇒ XANADU)

ELEKI NO WAKADAISHO

aka The Young General's Electric Guitar / US 'CAMPUS A-GO-GO'

1965 (Jap 94m) Toho Company

Film genre: Rock'n'roll Musical

Top guns: dir: Katsumi Iwauchi / dir: Yasuo Tanami

Stars: Yuzo Kayama *(Yuichi Tanuma)*, Takeshi Terauchi, Yukiro Hoshi, Tatsuyoshi Ehara, Machiki Naka, Kunie Tanaka

Storyline: The Young Beats are an instrumental "Eleki" outfit from Japan (think the Ventures, the Astronauts & Dick Dale). They enter a battle of the bands contest and even perform Beatles/"Help!"-like in front of groups of mini-skirted females. *MCS*

Movie rating: *5

Visual: dvd in Japan (no audio OST)

Off the record: A plethora of guitar instrumentals by the YOUNG BEATS include:- Black Sand Beach', 'Blonde Jennie', 'Yozora To Itsumademo', 'Yozora No Hoshi', 'Blues Of Wakadaisho', etc. Director, Katsumi Iwauchi, subsequently despatched further "Eleki" pop musicals, namely 'Retsu Go! Wakadaisho' (1967), 'Go! Go! Wakadaisho' (1967), 'Rio No Wakadaisho' (1968) & 'Hi! London' (1969). *MCS*

□ ELVIS biog
(⇒ PRESLEY, Elvis)

ELVIS

aka ELVIS: THE MOVIE

1979 (US 117m TV) Dick Clark Productions / ABC (G)

Film genre: Rock'n'roll-music biopic/drama

Top guns: dir: John Carpenter / s-w: Anthony Lawrence ← EASY COME, EASY GO ← PARADISE, HAWAIIAN STYLE ← ROUSTABOUT

Stars: Kurt Russell *(Elvis Presley)* ← IT HAPPENED AT THE WORLD'S FAIR, Shelley Winters *(Gladys Presley)* ← CLEOPATRA JONES ← WILD IN THE STREETS / → PURPLE PEOPLE EATER → HEAVY, Bing Russell *(Vernon Presley)* → DICK TRACY, Season Hubley *(Priscilla Presley)* ← CATCH MY SOUL, Pat Hingle *(Colonel Tom Parker)* ← NORWOOD / → MAXIMUM OVERDRIVE → BATMAN, Elliott Street *(Bill Black)* ← RECORD CITY, James Canning *(Scotty)*, Ed Begley, Jr. *(D.C. Fontana)* ← RECORD CITY / → GET CRAZY → THIS IS SPINAL TAP → STREETS OF FIRE → EVEN COWGIRLS GET THE BLUES → a MIGHTY WIND, Charles Cyphers *(Sam Phillips)* ← TRUCK TURNER ← COOL BREEZE / → DEATH WISH II → HONKYTONK MAN, Galen Thompson *(Hank Snow)*, Joe Mantegna *(Joe Esposito)* → AIRHEADS → ALBINO ALLIGATOR, Will Jordan *(Ed Sullivan)* ← the BUDDY HOLLY STORY ← I WANNA HOLD YOUR HAND / → the DOORS, Melody Anderson *(Bonnie)* → FLASH GORDON, Larry Pennell → BUBBA HO-TEP, **Ronnie McDowell** *(singing voice; Elvis)*

Storyline: This summary of the life of Elvis Presley begins with his sensitive relationship with his mother when he was still a boy. As he grows older and his career takes off meteorically, he finally comes to terms with his mother's death and marries Priscilla. However the pressure of making records and films, and his superstar status begin to take their toll on his health and his marriage. *JZ*

Movie rating: *7

Visual: video

Off the record: (see below)

—

RONNIE McDOWELL: Elvis – The Soundtrack Of The Movie

Feb 79. (lp) *Arcade; ADE P 40)* ☐ ☐
– Mystery train / The wonder of you / That's alright mama / Blue moon of Kentucky / My happiness / Old Shep / Concert medley: Mystery train (instrumental); Lawdy Miss Clawdy; Mystery train (instrumental); Shake, rattle & roll; Mystery train (instrumental); Long tall Sally; Mystery train (instrumental); A fool such as I; Mystery train (instrumental) / Heartbreak hotel / Rip it up / Love me tender / Are you lonesome tonight / Crying in the chapel / Until it's time for you to go / Pledging my love / Separate ways / Suspicious minds / Burning love / Blue suede shoes / Final: Dixie – battle hymn of the Republic.

S/track review: For a time listening to 'ELVIS' (the soundtrack of the movie) one could be forgiven if one thought it was actually the king of rock'n'roll himself behind the vocals of main actor Kurt Russell, who, incidentally played the part magnificently. In fact, the vox was all down to Elvis impersonator, RONNIE McDOWELL. Born in Fountain Head, Portland, Tennessee (26th March '50), the one-time country singer had already coined it in via his posthumous Elvis tribute 45, 'The King Is Gone', which hit the Top 20 almost immediately after Presley's untimely death on the 16th August, 1977. With former Elvis in Nashville session man on board, Charlie McCoy (who'd also played for Bob Dylan and Area Code 615) on harmonica, plus guitarists Chip Young & Dale Sellers, bassist Mike Leech, keyboard-players David Briggs & Bobby Ogden, drummer Bobby Harmon and not forgetting one-time Elvis back-up singers, the Jordanaires on tow, it certainly had some credentials of being the genuine article. Wrong. Once you know it's not the Elvis on 'ELVIS', it somehow puts it all into a pale significance, although McDOWELL's performances are indeed commendable by any standards. All the classic early Elvis hits are on board, 'That's Alright Mama', 'Heartbreak Hotel', 'Love Me Tender' and even 'Old Shep', while post-army crooners 'Are You Lonesome Tonight', 'Crying In The Chapel' and 'The Wonder Of You', take their historical place setting, but you get the feeling you're on one big 'Mystery Train' ride going as far away from Graceland as one could possibly go. 'Mystery Train' the track, is at center of one of the biggest botch-up "concert" medleys of all time (having already been the album's opening salvo), saddling up five times on either side of some hollow, un-Elvis, rock'n'roll nuggets. The "As seen on T.V." (as depicted on the UK-only album sleeve) didn't represent a television promo ad, more the TV movie itself. It'd be another two years – for another biopic 'THIS IS ELVIS' – before the "authentic" King truly shined through. *MCS*

Album rating: *4

ELVIS

aka ELVIS: THE EARLY YEARS

2005 (US 200m* TV-mini) Greenblatt / Jaffe Bernstein / CBS TV (12)

Film genre: Rock'n'roll Musical bio-pic/drama

Top guns: dir: James Steven Sadwith / s-w: Patrick Sheane Duncan

Stars: Jonathan Rhys Meyers *(Elvis Presley)* ← OCTANE ← VELVET GOLDMINE, Randy Quaid *('Colonel' Tom Parker)* ← DEAD SOLID PERFECT ← the LONG RIDERS ← BOUND FOR GLORY, Rose McGowan *(Ann-Margret)*, Tim Guinee *(Sam Phillips)*, Antonia Bernath *(Priscilla Presley)*, Jack Noseworthy *(Steve Binder)* ← EVENT HORIZON ← S.F.W., Robert Patrick *(Vernon Presley)* ← ALL THE PRETTY HORSES ← WAYNE'S WORLD / → WALK THE LINE, Camryn Manheim *(Gladys Presley)*, Clay Steakley *(Bill Black)* → WALK THE LINE, Mark Adam *(Scotty Moore)*, Doug M. Griffin *(Chet Atkins)*, John Boyd West *(Red West)*, Jennifer Rae Westley *(Dixie Locke)*, Eric William Pierson *(D.J. Fontana)*, Stuart Greer *(Captain Beaulieu)* ← BIG DREAMS & BROKEN HEARETS: THE DOTTIE WEST STORY ← CROCODILE SHOES

Storyline: As well as Elvis the pop legend, the story of Elvis the man is told through the three main relationships of his life:- his stormy marriage to Priscilla; his loyalty to wheeler-dealer manager 'Colonel' Tom Parker, and perhaps most importantly of all to his beloved mother Gladys, who guides him to success in the early days of his career. *JZ*

Movie rating: *6.5

Visual: dvd (no audio OST; score: Steve Dorff)

Off the record: The archive of ELVIS PRESLEY was responsible for several songs in the film:- 'Don't Be Cruel', 'Love Me Tender', 'Too Much', 'One Night', 'All Shook Up', 'Are You Lonesome Tonight?', 'Surrender' & 'Return To Sender'. *MCS*

ELVIS AND THE BEAUTY QUEEN

1981 (US 96m TV) Columbia Pictures Television / NBC

Film genre: romantic Pop-music docu-drama

Top guns: dir: Gus Trikonis ← NASHVILLE GIRL / s-w: Julia Cameron

Stars: Stephanie Zimbalist *(Linda Thompson)*, Don Johnson *(Elvis Presley)* ← ZACHARIAH / → the HOT SPOT, Ann Dusenberry *(Jeannie)*, Richard Lenz *(David Briggs)*, Ann Wedgeworth *(Aunt Betty)* → SWEET DREAMS → FAR NORTH, Richard Herd *(Thompson)*, Jay W. MacIntosh *(Mrs. Thompson)* ← SGT. PEPPER'S LONELY HEARTS CLUB BAND, Ruta Lee *(Su-Su)* ← HOOTENANNY HOOT

Storyline: Once upon a time there was a legend called Elvis who was married to a girl called Priscilla. When Elvis and Priscilla had an irreversible parting of the ways in 1972, a beauty queen called Linda magically appeared in Priscilla's place. Linda looked after Elvis' every need and Elvis loved her so much he even gave her some of his special pills to take away the stress of fame and stardom, and they didn't live happily ever after. Sadly, some fairy tales don't have good endings. *JZ*

Movie rating: *4

Visual: video (no audio OST; score: Allyn Ferguson)

Off the record: Don Johnson had a few post-'Miami Vice' hits, including his highest placing (No.5), 'Heartbeat'. *MCS*

ELVIS AND THE COLONEL: THE UNTOLD STORY

1993 (US 100m TV) NBC

Film genre: Pop/Rock-music bio-pic/drama

Top guns: dir: William A. Graham ← CHANGE OF HABIT / s-w: Phil Penningroth (+ story w/ Frank V. Furino)

Stars: Beau Bridges *(Col. Tom Parker)* ← SILVER DREAM RACER ← the LANDLORD, Rob Youngblood *(Elvis Presley)*, Dan Shor *(Jass)* ← BILL & TED'S EXCELLENT ADVENTURE ← MIKE'S MURDER, Scott Wilson *(Vernon Presley)* ← YOUNG GUNS II ← JOHNNY HANDSOME ← BLUE CITY / → GERONIMO: AN AMERICAN LEGEND → SOUL SURVIVOR → DEAD MAN WALKING → SOUTH OF HEAVEN, WEST OF HELL → DON'T LET GO → MONSTER, Micole Mercurio *(Gladys Presley)* ← FLASHDANCE / → the THING CALLED LOVE, Kehli O'Byrne *(Priscilla)*, Ben Slack *(Oscar Davis)*, Don Stark *(Dutch)*, Lois De Banzie *(Marie)*

Storyline: The relationship between No.1 king of rock'n'roll, Elvis Presley, and his tougher than tough manager, Colonel Tom Parker, comes under the spotlight in this one-sided – Elvis-beyond-the-grave – view. *MCS*

Movie rating: *4

Visual: none (no audio OST; score: Chris Boardman)

Off the record: nothing really

□ EMINEM segment
(⇒ 8 MILE)

EMPIRE RECORDS

1995 (US 91m) New Regency / Warner Bros. (PG-13)

Film genre: teen/buddy comedy drama

Top guns: dir: Allan Moyle ← PUMP UP THE VOLUME ← TIMES SQUARE / → MAN IN THE MIRROR: THE MICHAEL JACKSON STORY / s-w: Carol Heikkinen ← the THING CALLED LOVE / → CENTER STAGE

Stars: Anthony LaPaglia *(Joe Reaves)*, Liv Tyler *(Corey Mason)* ← HEAVY / → THAT THING YOU DO! → DR. T & THE WOMEN, Johnny Whitworth *(A.J.)*, Rory Cochrane *(Lucas)* → SOUTHLANDER, Renee Zellweger *(Gina)* ← SHAKE, RATTLE & ROCK! tv ← REALITY BITES / → COLD MOUNTAIN, Maxwell Caulfield *(Rex Manning)* ← ELECTRIC DREAMS ← GREASE 2, Debi Mazar *(Jane)* ← SINGLES ← JUNGLE FEVER ← the DOORS ← DOWNTOWN 81 / → GIRL 6 → the INSIDER → BE COOL, Robin Tunney *(Debra)*, Ethan Randall *(Mark)* → THAT THING YOU DO!, Ben Bode *(Mitchell Beck)* → MY DINNER WITH JIMI, **Coyote Shivers** *(Berko)* → DOWN & OUT WITH THE DOLLS → BADSVILLE, **Gwar w/ Oderus Urungus** *(themselves)*

Storyline: Centering on one day of an independent record shop and the people working there, who try at all costs to raise money for their boss and avoid a large megachain turning it into Music Town. *MCS*

Movie rating: *4

Visual: video + dvd

Off the record: **GWAR** (God What an Awful Racket) were a pseudonymous hard-rock outfit from Richmond, Virginia. 'America Must Be Destroyed' (1992) was the most successful album, peaking as it did at No.177. Their God damn awful videos will be the subject of an up and coming future edition. *MCS*

Various Artists (score: Mitchell Leib)

Aug 95. (cd/c) *A&M; <540384-2/-4> (540437-2)* [63] Feb98 [ ]
– Til I hear it from you (GIN BLOSSOMS) / Liar (the CRANBERRIES) / A girl like you (EDWYN COLLINS) / Free (the MARTINIS) / Crazy life (TOAD THE WET SPROCKET) / Bright as yellow (the INNOCENCE MISSION) / Circle of friends (BETTER THAN EZRA) / I don't want to live today (APE HANGERS) / Whole lotta trouble (CRACKER) / Ready, steady, go (the MEICES) / What you are (DRILL) / Nice overalls (LUSTRE) / Here it comes again (PLEASE) / The ballad of El Goodo (EVAN DANDO) / Sugarhigh (COYOTE SHIVERS) / The honeymoon is over (the CRUEL SEA).

S/track review: If you like your alt-rock music a little lighter and a little folkier, this collection is for you. From hit single opener, 'Til I Hear It From You' by GIN BLOSSOMS (for me, the poor man's Tom Petty & The Heartbreakers) to Australia's new rock'n'roll find, the CRUEL SEA and their title track from a 1993 ARIA (an Aussie Grammy!) set, 'The Honeymoon Is Over', little wavered from the safe. Needless to say, all the music accompanying film of Liv Tyler (daughter of Steven), has added benefits. The big alt-rock names of the day from other parts of the globe take a bow here, Ireland's CRANBERRIES ('Liar'), Scotland's EDWYN COLLINS (with mid-90s classic 'A Girl Like You') and New Orleans newcomers BETTER THAN EZRA ('Circle Of Friends'). The MARTINIS were a short-lived splinter of the Pixies, featuring Joey Santiago – his wife Linda Mallari on vocals – and Dave Lovering, although their 'Free' was a little too twee; connections all round, the latter drummer was to later join the ranks of Cracker (on tour), who featured here courtesy of the country-tinged, 'Whole Lotta Trouble'. For an album of this nature, only two covers surfaced from the pack, Generation X's 'Ready, Steady, Go' by the MEICES and Big Star's 'The Ballad Of El Goodo' by Lemonhead balladeer EVAN DANDO – nice'n'easy does it. Liveliest track award goes to COYOYE SHIVERS (also a star in the film!) who rocked the joint with his retro-fied 'Sugarhigh', while others like DRILL, APE HANGERS, PLEASE and the 10,000 Maniacs-inspired INNOCENCE MISSION were just along for the ride. And who could forget TOAD THE WET SPROCKET? Er . . . me. *MCS*

Album rating: *6.5

– spinoff hits, etc. –

EDWYN COLLINS: A Girl Like You / (non-OST song)

Oct 95. (c-s/cd-s) *Bar None; <58-1234>* [32] [–]
(above was already a major UK hit – twice!)

GIN BLOSSOMS: Til I Hear It From You / (non-OST song)

Jan 96. (c-s/cd-s) *<1380>* [11] [–]

GIN BLOSSOMS: Til I Hear It From You / (diff. non-OST songs)

Jan 96. (c-ep/cd-ep) *(581227-4/-2)* [39] [–]

EVERY DAY'S A HOLIDAY

aka SEASIDE SWINGERS

1965 (UK/US 94m) Embassy Pictures (PG)

Film genre: Pop/Rock Musical comedy

Top guns: s-w: James Hill (+ dir), Anthony Marriott (+ story), Jeri Matos

Stars: **John Leyton** *(Gerry)* ← IT'S TRAD, DAD!, Ron Moody *(the professor)* ← SUMMER HOLIDAY, **Mike Sarne** *(Tim)*, **Grazina Frame** *(Christina)* ← WHAT A CRAZY WORLD, Liz Fraser *(Miss Slightly)* → the FAMILY WAY → UP THE JUNCTION → the GREAT ROCK'N'ROLL SWINDLE, Susan Baker *(Susan)* → TOMMY, Nicholas Parsons *(Julian Goddard)* → the GHOST GOES GEAR, Jennifer Baker *(Jennifer)* → TOMMY, Michael Ripper *(Mr. Pulman)* ← WHAT A CRAZY WORLD, Hazel Hughes *(Mrs. Barrington de Witt)*, Richard O'Sullivan *(Jimmy)* ← WONDERFUL LIFE ← the YOUNG ONES, Charles Lloyd Pack *(Mr. Close)* → TWO A PENNY, Peter Gilmore *(Kenneth)* ← I'VE GOTTA HORSE, **Freddie & The Dreamers:- Freddie Garrity, Roy Crewsdon, Bernie Dwyer, Peter Birrell, Derek Quinn** *(chefs)* ← JUST FOR YOU ← WHAT A CRAZY WORLD / → DISK-O-TEK HOLIDAY → OUT OF SIGHT → CUCKOO PATROL, **the Mojos:- Stuart**

Slater, Nicholas Crouch, John Conrad, Keith Alcock & Terence O'Toole *(performers)*

Storyline: Back we go to the nostalgic days of the British holiday camp – leaky chalets, lousy food and dreadful weather. So the teenagers imprisoned in this camp get together to form a band for the big televised talent show. However, there's competition aplenty from rival groups (and chefs) and a curmudgeonly old aunt who wants to take home her charge Christina before she becomes corrupted by our seaside swingers. *JZ*

Movie rating: *4

Visual: none

Off the record: the MOJOS's 'Everything's Alright' was featured in the film, but not on the LP.

—

Various Artists: Seaside Swingers (composer: Tony Osborne)

Aug 65. (lp) *Capitol; <ST 6132>* [-] [ ]
– What's cooking (FREDDIE & THE DREAMERS) / Every day's a holiday (JOHN LEYTON – MIKE SARNE – GRAZINA FRAME) / All I want is you (JOHN LEYTON) / Love me please (MIKE SARNE) / A boy needs a girl (JOHN LEYTON – GRAZINA FRAME) / Don't do that to me (FREDDIE & THE DREAMERS) / Say you do (JOHN LEYTON – MIKE SARNE – GRAZINA FRAME) / Indubitably me (MIKE SARNE) / Second time shy (GRAZINA FRAME) / Crazy horse saloon (JOHN LEYTON).

S/track review: 'SEASIDE SWINGERS' as it was billed in the States, sets out its stall by describing itself thus: "10 swingin' song hits" . . . "Freddie and the Dreamers meet the screamers and it's the swingin'est!" – no, really. Yes, Manchester's zany London Palladium faves, FREDDIE & THE DREAMERS, kick off the set by way of a culinary and conceptual novelty in the shape of 'What's Cooking', a fun five and a half minute medley of sorts to whet one's appetite; their side 2 opener, 'Don't Do That To Me' (written by FREDDIE GARRITY himself), is more strictly to the point. With only three other major UK pop stars on parade, it's hardly various artists:- war-movie screen idol JOHN LEYTON (famous for chart-topper, 'Johnny Remember Me', way back in '61), MIKE SARNE (a former Venice DJ who'd also topped the charts – in 1962 with 'Come Outside' – alongside future 'Are You Being Served/ Eastenders' actress, Wendy Richards) and GRAZINA FRAME (a bubbly newbie who'd featured in 'WHAT A CRAZY WORLD'). All lumped together in one melting-pot of musical mayhem, they delivered 'Say You Do', (UK) title track, 'Every Day's A Holiday' and the SARNE-less croon ballad, 'A Boy Needs A Girl'. Of their solo spots, GRAZINA (on 'Second Time Shy') comes across as a girl groomed for success as the next Shapiro or Lulu, while both LEYTON (on 'All I Want Is You' and the embarrassing 6-minute western showstopping finale, 'Crazy Horse Saloon') plus SARNE (with the Beatles-esque 'Love Me Please' & 'Indubitably Me') looked to have had their day a long, long time ago. *MCS*

Album rating: *3.5

☐ EVERYBODY'S FAMOUS! alt.
(⇒ IEDEREEN BEROEMD!)

EVITA

1996 (US 134m) Buena Vista Pictures / Hollywood Pictures (PG)

Film genre: Pop/Rock Musical bio-pic/drama

Top guns: s-w: Alan Parker (+ dir) ← the COMMITMENTS ← BIRDY ← the WALL ← FAME ← MELODY, Oliver Stone ← NATURAL BORN KILLERS ← the DOORS (play: Tim Rice ← JESUS CHRIST SUPERSTAR)

Stars: MADONNA *(Eva Peron)*, Antonio Banderas *(Che)* ← FOUR ROOMS ← TRUTH OR DARE / → TAKE THE LEAD, Jonathan Pryce *(Juan Peron)* ← BREAKING GLASS / → STIGMATA → BROTHERS OF THE HEAD, Jimmy NAIL *(Agustin Magaldi)*, Victoria Sus *(Dona Juana)*, Julian Littman *(Brother Juan)*, Olga Merediz *(Blanca)*, **Andrea Corr** *(Peron's mistress)* ← the COMMITMENTS, Peter Polycarpou *(Domingo Mercante)* → JULIE AND THE CADILLACS, **Gary Brooker** *(Juan Bramuglia)* → BRITISH ROCK SYMPHONY → BLUES ODYSSEY → CONCERT FOR GEORGE

Storyline: Alan Parker begins with a tale of two funerals: the national mourning of Eva 'Evita' Peron's own send-off and a flashback to a very brown and Hispanic looking Eva 'Evita' Duarte and her gatecrashing of her own middle class father's funeral, a man to whom she was born illegitimately. Older, conspicuously whiter and very un-Hispanic looking, she takes up with a tango singer and gravitates to the bright lights of Buenos Aires. Collecting progressively more influential lovers as easily as she generates Porteño gossip, Evita claws her way up from poverty to the highest echelons of Argentine society, where she's snubbed by the great and the good but where her champagne socialism makes its iconic mark. *BG*

Movie rating: *6.5

Visual: video + dvd

ON the record: MADONNA needs no introduction (she knew she'd land the part), ANTONIO BANDERAS (**) sings!, **JIMMY NAIL** (***) removes his 'Crocodile Shoes', JONATHAN PRYCE (****) forgets 'Breaking Glass', JULIAN LITTMAN (*****), **ANDREA CORR** (******) edges away from the Corrs and **GARY BROOKER** (ex-Procol Harum) sings alongside Peter Polycarpou & John Gower (*******).

—

MADONNA & Cast (composer: Andrew Lloyd Webber *)

Nov 96. (d-cd/d-c) *Warners; <(9362 46346-2/-4)>* [2] [1]
– A cinema in Buenos Aires, 26 July 1952 (*) / Requiem for Evita (*) / Oh what a circus (w/ **) / On this night of a thousand stars (***) / Eva and Magaldi – Eva beware of the city (w/ ***, ** & *****) / Buenos Aires / Another suitcase in another hall / Goodnight and thank you (w/ **) / The lady's got potential (**) / Charity concert – The art of the possible (w/ ***, ***** & **) / I'd be surprisingly good for you (w/ ****) / Hello and goodbye (w/ ****** & ****) / Peron's latest flame (w/ **) / A new Argentina (w/ **** & **) // On the balcony of the Casa Rosada 1 (****) / Don't cry for me Argentina / On the balcony of the Casa Rosada 2 / High flying, adored (w/ **) / Rainbow high / Rainbow tour (w/ **, ******* & ****) / The actress hasn't learned the lines (you'd like to hear) (w/ **) / And the money kept rolling in (and out) (**) / Partido feminista / She is a diamond (****) / Santa Evita (*) / Waltz for Eva and Che (w/ **) / Your little body's slowly breaking down (w/ ****) / You must love me / Eva's final broadcast / Latin chant (*) / Lament (w/ **).

S/track review: After desperately seeking some decent reviews for most of her screen career, MADONNA finally found her métier in the Hollywood musical. 'EVITA' was tinsel town's first gamble on the genre since the early 80s, one which paid off fairly handsomely for its ambitious lead, and for whom its subject matter presumably ticked all the right boxes (female identity and power, the iconography of sainthood etc.). Vocally, she doesn't have the range of stage predecessors Elaine Page or Patti LuPone, but she so obviously identifies with the material that technical limitations are easily overlooked. Her pop sensibilities don't always serve her well – 'Buenos Aires' is brash and fresh if ultimately slightly stilted – but when they do, as on 'Another Suitcase In Another Hall' and 'I'd Be Suprisingly Good For You', they trade on the Venusian passion and mystique of her best 80s ballads and remakes these standards in her own image. She also gets a new ballad – the Oscar winning 'You Must Love Me' – specifically written for her, one which became perhaps the most unlikely hit of her career. Antonio Banderas, for his part, is a compelling variation on David Essex, moving smoulderingly, shadily through the film like an Argentine Nick Cotton (villain of 'Eastenders' soap fame). He's the owner of a surprisingly expressive tenor, even if he struggles with the more bombastic parts of his opening showcase, 'What A Circus'. With the movie itself being a non-stop barrage of musical performance, the DVD is actually better value than the soundtrack, with the added bonus of seeing Jimmy Nail as one of the unlikliest Latin lotharios in screen history. *BG*

Album rating: *6

– spinoff hits, etc. –

MADONNA: You Must Love Me / Rainbow High

Oct 96. (c-s/cd-s) *<17495> (W 0378 C/CD)* [18] [10]

MADONNA: Don't Cry For Me Argentina / Santa Evita

Dec 96. (c-s/cd-s) *(W 0384 C/CD)* [–] [3]
(cd-s+=) *(W 0384CDX)* – Latin chant.

MADONNA: Don't Cry For Me Argentina / ('A'-mixes; Spanglish / Miami dub & instrumental / etc).

Feb 97. (c-s/cd-s) *<43809-4/-2>* [8] [–]

MADONNA: Another Suitcase In Another Hall / Don't Cry For Me Argentina

Mar 97. (c-s) *(W 0388C)* [–] [7]
(cd-s+=) *(W 0388CDX)* – Waltz for Eva and Che.
(cd-s) *(W 0388CD)* – ('A'-dance mix) / Hello and goodbye / You must love me.

MADONNA : selections from Evita

Aug 97. (cd) *<9362 46692-2>* [ ] [–]

EXPRESSO BONGO

1959 (UK 111m) Britannia Films / British Lion Films

Film genre: Rock'n'Roll Musical drama

Top guns: dir: Val Guest / s-w: Wolf Mankowitz (+ play)

Stars: Lawrence Harvey *(Johnny Jackson)*, Sylvia Syms *(Maisie King)*, Yolande Donlan *(Dixie Collins)*, **Cliff RICHARD** *(Bongo Herbert)*, Meier Tzelniker *(Mayer)*, Gilbert Harding *(himself)*, Ambrosine Phillpotts *(Lady Rosemary)*, Eric Pohlmann *(Leon)*, Wilfred Lawson *(Mr. Rudge)*, Hermoine Baddeley *(Penelope)*, Reginald Beckwith *(Rev. Tobias Craven)*, Martin Miller *(Kakky)*

Storyline: Impresario Johnny Jackson roams the seedy night clubs and strip joints looking for new talent. One day he spots a youngster, Bert Rudge, singing rock'n'roll in a coffee house and realises the kid has got what it takes. He signs him up, renames him Bongo Herbert and begins dreaming of the lucrative contracts with radio and TV. Little does he realise that Bongo is a minor, underage thus making the deal null and void. *JZ*

Movie rating: *5

Visual: video + dvd

Off the record: Released the same year as 'Serious Charge', 'EXPRESSO BONGO' found CLIFF RICHARD still in thrall to King Elvis and once again attempting to match his hip-swivelling, hormonal appeal on 'Love', the soundtrack EP's frantic, bongo-assisted lead track. Yet the presence of two ballads reflected the prior success of 'Living Doll', and predicted the future direction of Cliff's career: 'A Voice In The Wilderness' pitched Cliff's honey-wouldn't-melt vocals against Hank Marvin's swaying, slow-motion glissandos and almost topped the chart (even if the version on the EP was different from the single release) while 'The Shrine On The Second Floor' remains the most lugubriously unnerving of all the man's ballads, all the more so considering his subsequent religious conversion. *BG*

– spinoff hits, etc. –

CLIFF RICHARD AND THE DRIFTERS

Jan 60. (7"ep) *Columbia; (SEG 7971/ESG 7783)* [ ] [–]
– Love / A voice in the wilderness / The shrine on the second floor / (1 by DRIFTERS, "Shadows").

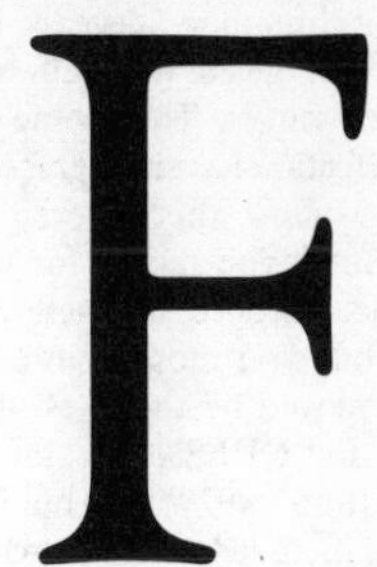

FM

1978 (US 104m) Universal Pictures (PG)

Film genre: workplace/showbiz comedy

Top guns: dir: John A. Alonzo / s-w: Ezra Sacks

Stars: Michael Brandon *(Jeff Dugan)* → ROCK'N'ROLL MOM, Eileen Brennan *(the mother)*, Alex Karras *(Doc Holiday)* → BUFFALO 66, Cleavon Little *(Prince)* ← VANISHING POINT ← COTTON COMES TO HARLEM, Martin Mull *(Eric Swan)*, Cassie Yates *(Laura Coe)*, Jay Fenichel *(Bobby Douglas)*, Joe Smith *(Albert Driscoll)* → ONE-TRICK PONY, James Keach *(Lt. Reach)* → the LONG RIDERS → WALK THE LINE, Norman Lloyd *(Carl Billings)*, Tom Tarpey *(Regis Lamar)*, Janet Brandt *(Alice)* → the JAZZ SINGER, **Linda Ronstadt** *(herself)* → UNCLE MEAT → HAIL! HAIL! ROCK'N'ROLL → MAYOR OF THE SUNSET STRIP, **Tom Petty** *(himself)* → CONCERT FOR GEORGE, **Jimmy BUFFETT** *(himself)*, **REO Speedwagon** *(themselves)*

Storyline: The staff of an American radio station stage a coup after the boss announces a commercially minded playlist shake-up. The hijacker's rock-centric selection underpins this film's short sighted, rather boorish plotline, one which no doubt fuelled the misguided anti-disco movement of the late 70s. *BG*

Movie rating: *4.5

Visual: video + dvd

Off the record: LINDA RONSTADT was filmed at the The Summit in Houston, Texas, although a lot of the concert footage has remained in the can, waiting for use in possibly another movie. *MCS*

Various Artists

Apr 78. (d-lp/d-c) *M.C.A.; <12000> (MCLD/+C 621)* [5] May78 [37]
– FM (STEELY DAN) / Night moves (BOB SEGER) / Fly like an eagle (STEVE MILLER) / Cold as ice (FOREIGNER) / Breakdown (TOM PETTY & THE HEARTBREAKERS) / Bad man (RANDY MEISNER) / Life in the fast lane (EAGLES) / Do it again (STEELY DAN) / Lido shuffle (BOZ SCAGGS) / More than a feeling (BOSTON) // Tumbling dice (LINDA RONSTADT) / Poor poor pitiful me (LINDA RONSTADT) / Livingston Saturday night (JIMMY BUFFETT) / There's a place in the world for a gambler (DAN FOGELBERG) / Just the way you are (BILLY JOEL) / It keeps you runnin' (DOOBIE BROTHERS) / Your smiling face (JAMES TAYLOR) / Life's been good (JOE WALSH) / We will rock you (QUEEN) / FM – reprise (STEELY DAN). *<d-cd-iss. Jun00; 112313> (UK cd-iss. Mar03; same)*

S/track review: 'FM' is often touted as rock's answer to 'SATURDAY NIGHT FEVER', but there's a crucial difference (besides the awful, sub-Ac/Dc or 'FLASH GORDON' sleeve): this is little more than a carefully selected 'Now That's What I

Call Decadence Vol.1', a late 70s greatest hits package before its marketing departmental time. STEELY DAN were commissioned to write a title theme, but they allegedly knew little about the film, maybe just as well given the gulf between the plot and the complexity of their music. The theme's furtive bassline and 'Gaucho'-tentative perfection has since graced several of the band's own hits packages, so now there's even less reason for this soundtrack to exist. But if you take it for what it is, or if you're too young to have been wooed by these shag-pile classics first time round, it'll still buy you more than a few thrills. Given the massive 80s success enjoyed by the likes of FOREIGNER, TOM PETTY, BILLY JOEL and QUEEN, it's not quite the end-of-the-line wake that 'NO NUKES' (1979) was, but it's the end-of-the-line artists – STEELY DAN included – who provide the peak moments, BOB SEGER with his Van Morrison-esque phrasing and heartland parallel to Morrison's own nostalgic Americana interpretations (no-one phrases "Summertime" with quite as much devotion), the EAGLES with their ode to frozen-nosed meltdown, LINDA RONSTADT with steaming live versions of a 'Stones classic that had set the tone for the decade in the first place, and a – gamely gender-reversed – slice of Warren Zevon sarcasm that later summed it up. The hurtling electronics of 'Fly Like An Eagle' predict his eccentric one-off, 'Abracadabra', but even STEVE MILLER faded in the 80s, and while it took a lager ad to put the wind back in BOSTON's air guitar, only the most determinedly masochistic music snob could still turn their nose up at 'More Than A Feeling'. *BG*

Album rating: *7.5

– spinoff hits, etc. –

STEELY DAN: FM (No Static At All) / FM (reprise)

May 78. (7") *<40894> (MCA 374)* [22] Jul78 [49]

JOE WALSH: Life's Been Good

Jun 78. (7") *Asylum; <45493> (K 13129)* [12] [14]

JIMMY BUFFETT: Livingston Saturday Night

Jul 78. (7") *A.B.C.; <12391>* [52] [–]

□ Shelley FABARES segment
(⇒ GIRL HAPPY)

FABIAN

Born: Fabiano Forte, 6 Feb'43, Philadelphia, Pennsylvania. FABIAN made his acting debut in 'HOUND-DOG MAN' (1959); he was already a clean-cut teenage idol at fifteen, plucked from obscurity – and virtually his back porch! – by 'Chancellor' records owner, Bob Marcucci. In 1959, the boy had four major hits, 'I'm A Man', 'Turn Me Loose', 'Tiger' (a Top 3) and 'Come On And Get Me'. The next year, FABIAN crossed-over into crooning land via a co-starring role in songbook-style musical, 'High Time', alongside Bing Crosby – but soon the hits dried up. The Fab one continued to increase his film profile with top roles in subsequent movies such as 'North To Alaska' (1960), college comedy 'Love In A Goldfish Bowl' (1961) – with TOMMY SANDS – plus 'The Longest Day' (1962). *MCS*

- filmography {acting} –

Hound-Dog Man *(1959 {*} =>)* / High Time *(1960 {*})* / North To Alaska *(1960 {*})* / **Love In A Goldfish Bowl** *(1961 {*} =>)* / Mr. Hobbs Takes A Vacation *(1962 {*})* / Five Weeks In A Balloon *(1962 {*})* / the Longest Day *(1962 {a})* / **Ride The Wild Surf** *(1962 {*} OST by JAN & DEAN =>)* / Dear Brigitte *(1965 {*})* / Ten Little Indians *(1965 {*})* / Fireball 500 *(1966 {*})* / Dr. Goldfoot And The Girl Bombs *(1966 {*})* / **Thunder Alley** *(1967 {*} OST by V/A =>)* / Maryjane *(1968 {*})* / the Wild Racers *(1968 {*})* / the Devil's 8 *(1969 {*})* / a Bullet For Pretty Boy *(1970 {a})* / Little Laura And Big John *(1973 {a})* / the Day The Lord Got Busted *(1976 {a})* / Getting Married *(1978 TV {*})* / Katie: Portrait Of A Centerfold *(1978 TV {a})* / **Disco Fever** *(1978 {*} =>)* / Crisis In Mid-Air *(1979 TV {a})* / Kiss Daddy Goodbye *(1981 {a})* / **Get Crazy** *(1983 {b} =>)* / Lo Negro Del Negro *(1986 {a})* / Runaway Daughters *(1994 TV {b})* / Up Close & Personal *(1996 {a})* / **Mr. Rock'n'Roll: The Alan Freed Story** *(1999 TV {p} =>)*

□ Adam FAITH segment
(⇒ McVICAR)

FALL AND SPRING

1996 (US 100m w/b&w) Anytown Anywhere Productions

Film genre: showbiz/Rock-music drama

Top guns: s-w + dir: Steven Sobel

Stars: Jason Cottle *(Cadix)* → WAG THE DOG → the WEDDING SINGER, Michael Healey *(Chet)*, Nicole Von Riesen *(Tanya)*, Mark Theodorf *(Dexter)*, Michael Sulprizio *(Bucky)*, Brandon Beckner *(Mark Anthony)*

Storyline: Cadix is a rising rock star intent on self destruction, Chet is his childhood friend whose parents have just died. Will the pair hit it off again or will they both drown in their own sorrows. *MCS*

Movie rating: *4

Visual: none (no audio OST; score: Brandon Beckner)

Off the record: Brandon Beckner is not Buckner, he of Wookieback.

FALLING FROM GRACE

1992 (US 100m) Little B / Columbia Pictures (PG-13)

Film genre: romantic family drama

Top guns: dir: **John Mellencamp** / s-w: Larry McMurtry

Stars: John Mellencamp *(Bud Parks)*, Mariel Hemingway *(Alice Parks)* → AMERICAN REEL, Claude Akins *(Speck Parks)* ← HOUND-DOG MAN, Dub Taylor *(Grandpa Parks)* ← MAN AND BOY ← HOT ROD GANG, Kay Lenz *(P.J. Parks)* ← AMERICAN GRAFFITI, Larry Crane *(Ramey Parks)*, Kate Noonan *(Linda)*, Deirdre O'Connell *(Sally Cutler)* → STRAIGHT TALK, **John Prine** *(Mitch Cutler)*, Brent Huff *(Parker Parks)*, Joanne Jacobson *(Marian Parks)*, the Pure Jam Band:- Glenn Dalton, Eric Austin, Bentley Austin, Craig Austin *(performers)*

Storyline: Rock star Bud Parks heads to Indiana for his father's birthday after spending years away from home on the road. With him are his wife Alice and his daughter Terri Jo, but any hopes of a happy reunion are soon dashed when Bud discovers that his family are still as pernicious and backbiting as ever. His wife Alice has to defend herself from the advances of his father Speck, and it's not long before he begins an affair with his brother's wife PJ, an uncomfortable reminder that he is not so different from his father. *JZ*

Movie rating: *4.5

Visual: video + dvd (no audio OST by JOHN MELLENCAMP)

Off the record: John Mellencamp to keep it brief had his best times in the 80s when he had a plethora of US hits, including Top 3 smashes 'Hurts So Good', 'Jack & Diane' & 'R.O.C.K. In The U.S.A.'. Note that Larry McMurtry is the father of rock star, James McMurtry. **John Prine** contributes 'All The Best (acoustic version)' to the soundtrack. *MCS*

FAME

1980 (US 134m) MGM – United Artists (PG)

Film genre: showbiz/Pop-Dance Musical drama

Top guns: dir: Alan Parker → the WALL → BIRDY → the COMMITMENTS → EVITA / s-w: Christopher Gore

Stars: Irene Cara *(Coco Hernandez)* ← SPARKLE ← AARON LOVES ANGELA, Lee Curreri *(Bruno Martelli)*, Laura Dean *(Lisa Monroe)*, Paul McCrane *(Montgomery MacNeil)*, Gene Anthony Ray *(Leroy Johnson)*, Barry Miller *(Raul/Ralph Garcia/Garcey)* ← SATURDAY NIGHT FEVER / → the LAST TEMPTATION OF CHRIST, Antonia Franceschi *(Hilary van Doren)*, Albert Hague *(Benjamin Shorofsky)*, Anne Meara *(Mrs. Elizabeth Sherwood)* → REALITY BITES, Maureen Teefy *(Doris Finsecker)* → GREASE 2, Debbie Allen *(Lydia Grant)*, Steve Inwood *(Francois Lafete)* → STAYING ALIVE, Eddie Barth *(Angelo)* ← SHAFT, Jim Moody *(Mr. Farrell)* → the LAST DRAGON → WHO'S THE MAN?, Michael DeLorenzo *(dancer)* → FAST FORWARD → SATISFACTION

Storyline: Prefiguring 'Fame Academy' by a good few decades, this is the original star spangled soap opera, following a posse of bright, underprivileged young things as they attempt to make New York's High School Of Performing Arts a springboard to the big time, and their life one long dance routine. *BG*

Movie rating: *6.5

Visual:

Off the record:

—

Various Cast (composers: Michael Gore * w/ Lesley Gore)

May 80. (lp/c) *R.S.O.; <3080> (2479 253)* 7 Aug80 1
– Fame (IRENE CARA) / Out here on my own (IRENE CARA) / Hot lunch jam (IRENE CARA) / Dogs in the yard (PAUL McCRANE) / Red light (LINDA CLIFFORD) / Is it okay if I call you mine? (PAUL McCRANE) / Never alone (CONTEMPORARY GOSPEL CHORUS) / Ralph and Monty (dressing room piano) (*) / I sing the body electric (LAURA DEAN, IRENE CARA & PAUL McCRANE). *(re-iss. Nov84 lp/c; SPE LP/MC 82) <(cd-iss. Nov84; 800034-2)> <(cd re-iss. Apr03/Jul03 on 'Rhino'+=; 8122 73862-2)>* – Miles from here / Out here on my own – piano and vocal / Fame – instrumental.

S/track review: Legwarmers, Britney Spears, "R&B". If you're going to blame anything, you have to blame the screen cheese factory that is 'FAME', culpable for every dodgy dance routine and X-Factor folly vacuum-packed in its wake. The film's choreographed legacy really has lived for what seems like forever, as has the title track, pure, unadulterated nostalgia even as it blazed a trail: there's nothing that heralds the 80s as cheap-thrillingly as that designer guitar, post-disco rhythm and IRENE CARA warbling. Unlike its MTV-surfing successor, 'FOOTLOOSE' (lyricist Dean Pitchford is the missing link), 'FAME' still has one lycra'd toe in the 70s, and the music of Michael Gore (sister of LESLEY "It's My Party" GORE) is surprisingly untainted by the hi-tech dross of the decade it sings to life; the polyphonic, prog rock-symphonic bombast of 'I Sing The Body Electric' might've been written for 'JESUS CHRIST SUPERSTAR'. And though you really have to hear it to believe it, the CARA-arranged 'Hot Lunch Jam' flirts – however mildly – with cacophonous free jazz. Ironically, jazz heavyweights like RON CARTER and MARCUS MILLER show up on cheesier synth-rock tracks like 'Dogs In The Yard'. Slap bass funk jam, 'Red Light', also lists the likes of RANDY BRECKER and JON FADDIS, with onetime 'Curtom' artiste, LINDA CLIFFORD – along with the Gospel Chorus on 'Never Alone' – paying the most soulful dues on the whole soundtrack. Ultimately – and paradoxically – 'FAME' transcends what it purports to be, and it probably still deserves at least 15 minutes of anyone's time. *BG*

Album rating: *6.5

– spinoff hits, etc. –

IRENE CARA: Fame / CONTEMPORARY GOSPEL CHORUS: Never Alone

Jun 80. (7") *<1034> (2090 450)* 4
(re-iss. Mar86 on 'Old Gold'; OG 9595)

LINDA CLIFFORD: Red Light / MICHAEL GORE: Ralph And Monty

Jul 80. (7") *<1041> (RSO 64)* 41 Sep80

IRENE CARA: Out Here On My Own / (piano and vocal)

Aug 80. (7") *<1048>* 19 –

IRENE CARA: Out Here On My Own / PAUL McCRANE: Is It Okay If I Call You Mine?

Nov 80. (7") *(RSO 66)* –
(re-dist.Aug82; same) – hit No.58

IRENE CARA: Fame / Never Alone / Hot Lunch Jam

Jun 82. (7"m) *(RSO 90)* – 1

FANTASTICA

1980 (Can/Fra 110m) El Productions / Gaumont Films (X)

Film genre: psychological drama

Top guns: s-w + dir: Gilles Carle

Stars: Carole Laure *(Lorca)* → HEARTBREAKERS → NIGHT MAGIC, **Lewis Furey** *(Paul)* → NIGHT MAGIC, Serge Reggiani *(Euclide)*, John Vernon *(Jim McPherson)*, Claudine Auger *(Johanne McPherson)*, Claude Blanchard *(Hector)*, Denise Filiatrault *(Emma)*, Michel Labelle *(Louis)*

Storyline: In the wilds of Canada, local fishermen discover that salmon are no longer swimming upriver to spawn. Putting two and two together, they realize that there must be pollution from the new factory. A fight begins between the factory owner and the people, who are led by an ageing ecologist and a travelling actress. The two find romance when they're taking time off from battlng the businessmen but like the salmon their love looks doomed to fail. *JZ*

Movie rating: *5

Visual: video

Off the record: **LEWIS FUREY** (see 'NIGHT MAGIC')

—

CAROLE LAURE – LEWIS FUREY

Oct 80. (lp) *Acapella; (AC 108)* – Canada –
– Fantastica (title theme) / Funny funny / Be my baby tonight / This could have been the song / Fantastica / Goodbye love / What's wrong with me / Happy's in town / Lorca in three movements / This could have been the song (reprise). *(cd-iss. 1990s on 'Saravah Mantra' France; 020)*

S/track review: As well as their domestic relationship at home in Montreal, common-law husband-and-wife team LEWIS FUREY and CAROLE LAURE's singing partnership started to blossom right here. 'FANTASTICA' is not so complex as their other work together – LAURE released 3 solo sets – songwriter (and pianist) FUREY finding a sort of mainstream pop niche in a line somewhere between Cohen and Abba. With an orchestra conducted by JOHN LISSAUER (who also plays electric piano & sax), the accordion-rife opening title theme is jaunty enough, but it's the lyrical Englishness, yes Englishness of songs such as 'Funny Funny', 'Be My Baby Tonight', 'This Could Have Been The Song', 'Fantastica' and 'Goodbye Love' that give it a certain savoir faire. Less band (i.e. BARRY LAZAROWITZ on drums, JAY LEONHART on bass and JEFF LAYTON on banjo & guitar), side two is a lot deeper and melodramatic, 'Happy's In Town' and the lengthy 'Lorca In Three Movements', both complex and very OTT theatrical. Was this FUREY's 'Phantom Of The Opera'? If so, it worked on a lesser scale but with no real gusto. *MCS*

Album rating: *5

FAREWELL PERFORMANCE

1963 (UK 73m) Sevenay

Film genre: crime drama/Rock Musical

Top guns: dir: Robert Tronson / s-w: Aileen Burke, Leone Stuart, Jim O'Connolly

Stars: David Kernan *(Ray Baron)* → the EDUCATION OF SONNY CARSON, Delphi Lawrence *(Janice Marlon)* → BUNNY LAKE IS MISSING, Frederick Jaeger *(Paul Warner)*, Derek Francis *(Supt. Raven)* → the WICKED LADY, Alfred Burke *(Marlon)*, John Kelland *(Mitch)*, James Copeland *(Andrews)*, Toni Gilpin *(Carol)*, Ron Perry *(Dennis)*, **Heinz / the Tornados:- Alan Caddy, George Bellamy, Clem Cattini, Roger LaVern** *(performer/s)* ← LIVE IT UP! ← JUST FOR FUN / → the LONDON ROCK AND ROLL SHOW

Storyline: Marlon is used to taming wild lions and tigers, but his wife Janice is a different matter. He knows she has been having an affair with a pop star and, guess what, the aforementioned star is mysteriously murdered. Who on earth could possibly do such a thing? Janice decides to rack her two braincells when the police give up this difficult case, but will she suspect her cuckolded husband? This could be one for Sherlock Holmes. *JZ*

Movie rating: *2.5

Visual: none

Off the record: Heinz (Burt) performed one track in the film, the Joe Meek-penned 'Dreams Do Come True'. *MCS*

FAST FORWARD

1985 (US 110m) Columbia Pictures (PG)

Film genre: coming-of-age Pop/Dance Musical drama

Top guns: dir: Sidney Poitier ← a PIECE OF THE ACTION ← LET'S DO IT AGAIN / s-w: Richard Wesley ← LET'S DO IT AGAIN (au: Timothy March ← a PIECE OF THE ACTION ← LET'S DO IT AGAIN)

Stars: John Scott Clough *(Matt Sherman)*, Don Franklin *(Michael Stafford)*, Tamara Mark *(June Wolsky)*, Tracy Silver *(Meryl Stanton)*, Cindy McGee *(Francine Hackett)*, Gretchen F. Palmer *(Valerie Thompson)* → CROSSROADS, Monique Cintron *(Rita Diaz)*, Irene Worth *(Ida Sabol)*, Robert DoQui *(Mr. Hughes)* ← NASHVILLE ← COFFY ← UP TIGHT! / → GOOD TO GO, Michael DeLorenzo *(Caesar Lopez)* ← FAME / → SATISFACTION

Storyline: Eight high school kids from the sticks travel to the Big Apple for the Big Showdown dance competition. They find that in the city you actually need money to buy food and things, and so they begin touring the dance clubs to earn a crust. They soon learn that all their dance routines went out with the Ark, and the only way they'll win the Showdown is to learn some new stuff – fast. *JZ*

Movie rating: *3

Visual: video in 1998

Off the record: Not on the OST are the tracks, 'That's Just The Way It Is' by NARADA MICHAEL WALDEN, 'Lolli Poppin' by TOM SCOTT, 'How Do You Do by DECO, 'Mystery' by the LIVING DAYLIGHTS and 'Pretty Girl' by JEF SCOTT; HERBIE HANCOCK also had music featured in the film. *MCS*

—

Various incl. DECO (*) (score: Tom Scott & Jack Hayes)

Jun 85. (lp/c) *Island; <90193-1/-4> Warners; (9 25263-1)* ☐ ☐
– Breakin' out (*) / Do you want it right now (SIEDAH GARRETT) / Long as we believe (SIEDAH GARRETT and DAVID SWANSON) / Curves (*) / Taste (*) / Showdown (PULSE feat. ADELE BERTEI) / Survive (*) / Fast forward (*).

S/track review: With QUINCY JONES as executive music producer (it was also released on his label, 'Qwest'), and Sidney Poitier as director, 'FAST FORWARD' should've been the next 'FLASHDANCE' or 'FOOTLOOSE'. Instead, the film and soundtrack moved to its own beat, ultimately choosing to stick to one or two disco guns rather than a proper various artists selection (the tracks were available). DECO were main transgressors here, a session group of sorts to back singer SIEDAH GARRETT featuring NARADA MICHAEL WALDEN (drums & percussion), RANDY "THE KING" JACKSON (bass), PRESTON GLASS and WALTER "BABY LOVE" AFANASIEFF (keyboards), CORRADO RUSTICI (guitars), etc. Confusingly, these players were only used for two DECO cuts, 'Curves' and 'Taste', the latter Prince-meets-Pointer Sisters number also seeing Michael Jackson-esque DAVID SWANSON move up from backing singer to co-lead. DECO (Mk.II) saw SIEDAH relegated to backing singer, while KIP LENNON took the mic for tracks, 'Survive', 'Fast Forward' and 'Breakin' Out'; main musicians on the first two tracks were JOHN VAN TONGEREN and TOMMY FARAGHER (keyboards & synths), ROBBIE NEVIL (guitar) and CARLOS VEGA (drums), while the latter opening cue retained TONGEREN and NEVIL alongside MARK VIEHA and JAY KENNEDY and JOHN ROBINSON. It beats me why both sections were billed as DECO, but one thing was clear, all five songs were ridiculously similar. The aforementioned GARRETT (a protégé of QUINCY JONES and hitmaker courtesy of Dennis Edwards' duet, 'Don't Look Any Further'), bounced off the dancefloor walls for 'Do You Want It Right Now', balanced with the smooth ballad 'Long As We Believe', the latter credited SWANSON and featuring the DECO line-up Mk.I. The former song showcased STEPHEN BRAY (on programming) who subsequently brought the LP's connection full circle by performing with PULSE (on 'Showdown'), another JOHN "JELLYBEAN" BENITEZ production – one will know his other protégé, MADONNA. *MCS*

Album rating: *4

FAST TIMES AT RIDGEMONT HIGH

1982 (US 91m) Universal Pictures (R)

Film genre: coming-of-age/teen seX comedy

Top guns: dir: Amy Heckerling / s-w: Cameron Crowe (+ au) → ALMOST FAMOUS

Stars: Sean Penn *(Jeff Spicoli)* → DEAD MAN WALKING → I AM SAM, Jennifer Jason Leigh *(Stacy Hamilton)* → LAST EXIT TO BROOKLYN → RUSH → GEORGIA, Judge Reinhold *(Brad Hamilton)*, Robert Romanus *(Mike Damone)*, Brian Backer *(Mark 'Rat' Ratner)* ← the BURNING, Phoebe Cates *(Linda Barrett)* → SHAG: THE MOVIE, Ray Walston *(Mr. Hand)* ← POPEYE, Scott Thomson *(Arnold)*, Forest Whitaker *(Charles Jefferson)*, Eric Stoltz *(stoner bud)*, Nicolas Cage/Coppola *(Brad's bud)* → BIRDY → WILD AT HEART, Tom Nolan *(Dennis Taylor)* ← CHASTITY / → VOYAGE OF THE ROCK ALIENS → the THING CALLED LOVE, Vincent Schiavelli *(Mr. Vargas)* ← AMERICAN POP, Eric Stoltz *(stoner bud)* → SINGLES → PULP FICTION → GRACE OF MY HEART → THINGS BEHIND THE SUN, **Nancy Wilson** *(girl in car)*

Storyline: The students of Ridgemont High seem to be obsessed with dating each other as often as possible. Stacy and Linda are the sexy 6th formers who have an eye for the boys, especially Mike and Mark who end up as rivals over the "spoils of war". Meanwhile, permanently stoned Jeff (aloha!) has a running battle with history teacher Mr Hand, who is convinced all the kids are sex mad and high on dope. He may not be wrong. *JZ*

Movie rating: *8

Visual: video + dvd

Off the record: Nancy Wilson was of the rock group Heart.

—

Various Artists

Aug 82. (d-lp/c) *Full Moon; <60158-1/-4>* 54 –
– Somebody's baby (JACKSON BROWNE) / Waffle stomp (JOE WALSH) / Love rules (DON HENLEY) / Uptown boys (LOUISE GOFFIN) / So much in love (TIMOTHY B. SCHMIT) / Raised on the

radio (RAVYNS) / The look in your eyes (GERARD McMAHON) / Speeding (the GO-GO'S) / Don't be lonely (QUARTERFLASH) / Never surrender (DON FELDER) / Fast times (the best years of our lives) (BILLY SQUIER) / Fast times at Ridgemont High (SAMMY HAGAR) / I don't know (Spicoli's theme) (JIMMY BUFFET) / Love is the reason (GRAHAM NASH) / I'll leave it up to you (POCO) / Highway runner (DONNA SUMMER) / Sleeping angel (STEVIE NICKS) / She's my baby (and she's outta control) (PALMER/JOST) / Goodbye, goodbye (OINGO BOINGO). *<cd-iss. Mar95 on 'Elektra'; 60158-2>*

S/track review: With a cursory glance at the names on show here, one thing that sticks out is the array of solo Eagles: JOE WALSH ('Waffle Stomp'), DON HENLEY ('Love Rules'), TIMOTHY B. SCHMIT ('So Much In Love') and DON FELDER ('Never Surrender'), while other West Coast soft-rock associates also get the nod, namely JACKSON BROWNE ('Somebody's Baby'), GRAHAM NASH ('Love Is The Reason'), POCO ('I'll Leave It Up To You') and STEVIE NICKS ('Sleeping Angel'). While a handful of the tracks come up trumps (WALSH, BROWNE and NICKS shine out), the majority of these tracks fit into the corporate mainstream early 80s. With a smidgen of new wave (aka OINGO BOINGO, RAVYNS, the GO-GO's and DAVE PALMER & PHIL JOST) alongside some AOR hair-metal (SAMMY HAGAR, QUARTERFLASH and BILLY SQUIER), why the choice of flash-in-the-pan GERARD McMAHON ('The Look In Your Eyes'), retro Brill-Building offspring LOUISE GOFFIN ('Uptown Boys') or ex-disco queen-turned-rock-chick DONNA SUMMER ('Highway Runner'). Note, in some European countries a single LP was initially released. *MCS*

Album rating: *6

– spinoff hits, etc. –

JACKSON BROWNE: Somebody's Baby / (non-OST song)

Jul 82. (7") *Asylum; <69982> (K 13185)* [7] Aug82 [ ]

TIMOTHY B. SCHMIT: So Much In Love / DAVE PALMER & PHIL JOST: She's My Baby (And She's Outta Control)

Sep 82. (7") *<69939>* [59] [–]

the FASTEST GUITAR ALIVE

1968 (US 88m) Metro-Goldwyn-Mayer (PG)

Film genre: Country & Western Musical comedy

Top guns: dir: Michael Moore ← PARADISE, HAWAIIAN STYLE / s-w: Robert E. Kent ← WHEN THE BOYS MEET THE GIRLS ← GET YOURSELF A COLLEGE GIRL ← HOOTENANNY HOOT ← DON'T KNOCK THE TWIST ← DON'T KNOCK THE ROCK ← ROCK AROUND THE CLOCK / → a TIME TO SING

Stars: Roy Orbison *(Johnny Banner)* → ROADIE → HAIL! HAIL! ROCK'N'ROLL → a BLACK & WHITE NIGHT, Sammy Jackson *(Steve Menlo)*, Maggie Pierce *(Flo)*, Joan Freeman *(Sue)* ← ROUSTABOUT, Lyle Bettger *(Charlie)*, Patricia Donahue *(Stella)*, John Doucette *(Sheriff Max Cooper)* ← PARADISE, HAWAIIAN STYLE, Ben Lessy *(Indian chief)* ← PAJAMA PARTY, **Sam The Sham** *(first expressman)*

Storyline: It looks like the end of the Civil War as the money begins to run out for the Southern army. Enter superspy Johnny Banner and his sidekick Steve, who are sent to San Francisco to "liberate" a shipment of Yankee gold. It seems an impossible task but with our hero's secret weapon – a rifle hidden inside a guitar – they try to pull it off, bringing a new concept to the phrase "duelling banjos". *JZ*

Movie rating: *5

Visual: video + dvd

Off the record: Sam The Sham (aka Domingo "Sam" Samudio) was born in Dallas, Texas, 1940. With his backing group the Pharaohs, Sam The Sham knocked out several US hits, including his biggest, 'Wooly Bully' and 'Lil' Red Riding Hood', which both reached No.2 in 1965 and '66 respectively. *MCS*

—

ROY ORBISON (composer; w/ Bill Dees)

Jan 68. (lp) *M.G.M.; <E/SE 4475> London; (HA-U/SH-U 8358)* [ ] Feb68 [ ]
– Whirlwind / Medicine man / River / The fastest guitar alive / Rollin' on / Pistolero / Good time party / Heading south / Best friend / There won't be many coming home. *(re-iss. Jan89 on 'M.C.A.' lp/c; MCA/+C 1437) <cd-iss. 1985 on 'Columbia'; AK 45405> (cd-iss. Apr90 on 'M.G.M.'+=; CDMGM 18)* – HANK WILLIAMS JR.: Your Cheatin' Heart.

S/track review: 'The FASTEST GUITAR ALIVE' sees the screen debut of ROY ORBISON, a multi-million-selling singer-songwriter on a mission to become Nashville's answer to Elvis – well, somebody might've told him that. One thinks WAYLON JENNINGS' 'NASHVILLE REBEL' (1966) tried this already. Anyway, Roy 'O' supplies the OST with seven fresh songs (augmented by Bill Dees), while the other three cues on the 27-minute set are versions of older tracks. At a time when the "Spaghetti Western" was the in-thing, ORBISON goes old-style Western revisionism and tries to become the new John Wayne or Alan Ladd rather than Clint Eastwood or Lee Van Cleef. Musically, his "Big Country" sound is awash with echoing cowboy tunes, although one song in particular, the opening number 'Whirlwind', stands out from the rest. The swirling strings and atmospheric backing shoot straight from the hip and combine with Roy's falsetto vox – a minor classic indeed. Rather than gallop into town to save us all from the world of late 60s bubblegum-pop music, Roy very rarely hits the proverbial heights of his once-great singing career. Track 2, 'Medicine Man', typically rumbles along like something akin ("bom, bom, bom"-like) to Johnny Preston's 'Running Bear', Red Indian chants et al. If you've heard it all before, it's because it's just so derivative of everything that B-movie cowboy films of the previous two decades, uptempo balladry and romantic; example 'River'. The title track is reasonably up-to-date, but it's no 'Ring Of Fire', which it suggests throughout. Just when you think the LP should lie buried in a dust-bowl desert, ORBISON comes up trumps (well, nearly) courtesy of 'Rollin' On', a splendid exercise at last for his warbling, crescendo-loving vox. 'Pistolero', meanwhile, sees him getting in a Flamenco-cum-Mexicali mood, and dare one say it – Morricone-influenced, while 'Good Time Party' attempts a sing-a-long. If there was one "golden-oldie" track – from Roy's bulging back catalogue – befitting an inclusion, surely it must've been 'Running Scared'. But no, the listener has to settle for three add-on fillers in the shape of 'Heading South', the lilting-lullaby of 'Best Friend' and the heart-rending, glory-hallelujah ballad, 'There Won't Be Many Coming Home'. Shed a tear, one just might. *MCS*

Album rating: *5

FEAR AND LOATHING IN LAS VEGAS

1998 (US 119m) Rhino Films / Universal Pictures (R)

Film genre: experimental road movie/comedy

Top guns: s-w: Terry Gilliam (+ dir), Tod Davies, Tony Grisoni → BROTHERS OF THE HEAD, Alex Cox ← STRAIGHT TO HELL ← SID & NANCY ← REPO MAN (au: Hunter S. Thompson ← WHERE THE BUFFALO ROAM)

Stars: Johnny Depp *(Raoul Duke)* ← DEAD MAN ← CRY-BABY / → the FUTURE IS UNWRITTEN, Benicio Del Toro *(Dr. Gonzo / Oscar Z. Acosta)*, Tobey Maguire *(hitchhiker)* ← S.F.W., Ellen Barkin *(North Star Cafe waitress)* ← JOHNNY HANDSOME ← SIESTA ← DOWN BY LAW ← EDDIE AND THE CRUISERS ← TENDER MERCIES ← UP IN SMOKE, Gary Busey *(highway patrolman)* ← CARNY ← the BUDDY HOLLY STORY ← a STAR IS BORN, Christina Ricci *(Lucy)* ← BUFFALO '66 / → MONSTER → the FEARLESS FREAKS → BLACK SNAKE MOAN, Mark Harmon *(Mint 400 magazine reporter)*, Cameron Diaz *(TV reporter)* ← SHE'S THE ONE / → the INVISIBLE CIRCUS, Michael Jeter *(L. Ron Bumquist)* ← HAIR / → SOUTH OF HEAVEN, WEST OF HELL, Penn Jillette *(carnie talker)* ← ROCK & ROLL HEART ← the BAND THAT WOULD BE KING, **Lyle Lovett** *(road guy)* → DR. T & THE WOMEN, **Flea** *(musician)* <= the RED HOT CHILI PEPPERS =>, Harry Dean Stanton *(judge)* ← WILD AT HEART ← the LAST TEMPTATION OF CHRIST ← PRETTY IN PINK ← PARIS, TEXAS ← REPO MAN ← ONE FROM THE HEART ← the ROSE ← RENALDO AND CLARA ← RANCHO DELUXE ← PAT GARRETT & BILLY THE KID, Richard Portnow *(wine colored tuxedo)* ← PRIVATE PARTS ← S.F.W. ← GOOD MORNING, VIETNAM ← ROADIE / → GHOST DOG: THE WAY OF THE SAMURAI

Storyline: Sports journalist, Raoul Duke, heads to Las Vegas in search of the "American Dream", though he's not quite sure exactly what that is. Accompanied by attorney Dr Gonzo he drives through the Mojave Desert sustained mainly by a bootload of drugs and liquor. As the dope takes effect the twosome have splendid fun trashing various hotel rooms and working out reality from hallucination, as well as covering (of all things) a Narcotics Convention for the paper. *JZ*

Movie rating: *7

Visual: video + dvd

Off the record: New film composer, RAY COOPER (b. 9 Aug'42, Watford, England) was the percussionist with many acts including ELTON JOHN, PINK FLOYD, STING, ERIC CLAPTON, GEORGE HARRISON, etc. For the latter, COOPER performed on the tribute film/soundtrack, 'CONCERT FOR GEORGE' (2003). *MCS*

Various (score: RAY COOPER & TOMOYASU HOTEI *)

May 98. (cd/c) *Geffen; <(GED/GEC 25218)>*
– Combination of the two (BIG BROTHER & THE HOLDING COMPANY) / One toke over the line (BREWER & SHIPLEY) / She's a lady (TOM JONES) / For your love (the YARDBIRDS) / White rabbit (JEFFERSON AIRPLANE) / A drug score – part 1: Acid spill (*) / Get together (the YOUNGBLOODS) / Mama told me not to come (THREE DOG NIGHT) / Stuck inside of Mobile with the Memphis blues again (BOB DYLAN) / Time is tight (BOOKER T. & THE MGs) / Magic moments (PERRY COMO) / A drug score – part 2: Adrenochrome, the Devil's dance (*) / Tammy (DEBBIE REYNOLDS) / A drug score – part 3: Flashbacks (*) / Expecting to fly (BUFFALO SPRINGFIELD) / Viva Las Vegas (DEAD KENNEDYS).

S/track review: This musical excursion into the savage heart of the American dream leans heavily towards the psych rock and pop of the late 60s and early 70s (unsurprisingly), interspersed with choice doses of dialogue. Three of the most entertaining form a 'Drug Score' trilogy by TOMOYASU HOTEI and RAY COOPER, woozily swinging from uncomfortable vibes to the full-blown terror of being informed "You took too much, man . . .". Things begin in bright and breezy fashion as we begin our dabbling, 'Combination Of The Two' by BIG BROTHER AND THE HOLDING COMPANY is fuzzed up 60s psychedelia, and 'One Toke Over The Line' by BREWER AND SHIPLEY, a jaunty countrified excursion. The YARDBIRDS contribute 'For Your Love', its neo-baroque shuffle shifting gears into a more rampant, chugging mid-section, before settling back again. The glittering Las Vegas nightmare is invoked by its long serving bare-chested, medallion-sporting crooner TOM JONES: 'She's A Lady' is a stone-cold classic, and his latter day incarnation – bloated boyo from the Valleys – hangs in the background of 'Mama Told Me Not To Come' performed by THREE DOG NIGHT, written by Randy Newman, and latterly butchered by JONES with the Stereophonics. If that song is a warning of the darkness to come, 'White Rabbit' is the palpitating heartbeat of the album; the counterculture anthem par excellence for the compulsive, acid tripping bather in all of us, a stark admonition to those who believed that their "energy would simply prevail" in the battle against the forces of old and evil. The frazzled, Timothy Leary-worshipping hordes were always fighting a losing battle, enacted by the strung-out drawling of BOB DYLAN on 'Stuck Inside Of Mobile With the Memphis Blues Again', and the walls-closing-in vibes of 'Time Is Tight' by BOOKER T & THE MG'S. PERRY COMO's 'Magic Moments' is an affront to the drug-addled proceedings of madness encroaching, and DEBBIE REYNOLDS' wholesome-is-as-wholesome-does rendition of 'Tammy' is simply disconcerting. The Floyd-ish stylings of BUFFALO SPRINGFIELD's 'Expecting To Fly' act as summation of the failure of the countercultural dream, as an overambitious, naive happening which imploded upon itself due to its own excesses and egotistical self-regard. All the more fitting that it is left to the DEAD KENNEDYS and Jello Biafra's crazed re-invigoration of that other bloated denizen of Vegas to blow it all away with a manic, frenetic blast through 'Viva Las Vegas', the city it is great to leave. *DF*

Album rating: *7.5

FEAR OF A BLACK HAT

1994 (US/UK 87m) Samuel Goldwyn Company / ITC (R)

Film genre: Hip Hop/Rap Musical mockumentary

Top guns: s-w (+ dir): Rusty Cundieff ← HOUSE PARTY 2

Stars: Rusty Cundieff *(Ice Cold)* ← SCHOOL DAZE, Mark Christopher Lawrence *(Tone Def)* → SHAKE, RATTLE & ROLL: AN AMERICAN LOVE STORY, Larry B. Scott *(Tasty Taste)* ← a HERO AIN'T NOTHIN' BUT A SANDWICH, Kasi Lemmons *(Nina Blackburn)* ← the FIVE HEARTBEATS ← SCHOOL DAZE, Howie Gold *(Guy Friesch)*, Faizon Love *(jam boy)* → the FIGHTING TEMPTATIONS → IDLEWILD, **Deezer D** *(jam boy)* ← CB4: THE MOVIE ← COOL AS ICE / → BONES → IN THE MIX, Lamont Johnson *(MC Slammer)* ← the FIVE HEARTBEATS, Kurt Loder *(himself)* ← WHO'S THE MAN? ← the ADVENTURES OF FORD FAIRLANE / → AIRHEADS → TUPAC: RESURRECTION → RAMONES: RAW → LAST DAYS, **Bobby Mardis** *(promoter #1)* ← HOUSE PARTY 3 ← the FIVE HEARTBEATS, Lance Crouther *(street vendor)* ← CB4: THE MOVIE / → POOTIE TANG, Eric Laneuville *(Jike Spingleton)* ← BLACK BELT JONES ← DEATH WISH

Storyline: "Don't shoot till you see the whites of their eyes? No, don't shoot till you see the whites". Following gangsta rappers Niggaz With Hats over the course of a year, we find they only employ white managers as they keep getting killed: their security guards take body searches to extremes (especially women fans) and shootings occur almost on an hourly basis. Somehow Ice Cold, Tasty Taste and Tone Def manage to keep on rappin' throughout the mayhem. *JZ*

Movie rating: *6

Visual: video + dvd

Off the record: NWH (NIGGAZ WITH HATS) see below. **Bobby Mardis** was an R&B singer who had a minor hit in 1986 with 'Keep On' (for 'Profile' records).

N.W.H. (N*GGAZ WITH HATS)

Sep 00. (cd) *Avatar; <10006-2>*
– Ice froggy frog / Come pet the P.U.S.S.Y. / Guerrillas in the midst / I'm just a human / Booty juice / Fuck the security guards / Granny says kick yo black ass / Wear yo hat (buried and bald) / Grab yo stuff / White cops on dope / My peanuts.

S/track review: As the gangsta rap answer to 'THIS IS SPINAL TAP', 'FEAR OF A BLACK HAT' sports a similarly supremely dumb, novelty soundtrack. The whole gamut of hip hop disciplines are sent-up by N*GGAZ WITH HATS – aka RUSTY CUNDIEFF, MARK CHRISTOPHER LAWRENCE & LARRY B SCOTT – of the film in derivative, low-brow rip-offs of late 80s and early 90s US hits. So Snoop Dogg's 'Who Am I (What's My Name?)' becomes 'Ice Froggy Frog', 'Fuck The Police' by NWA is readdressed as 'Fuck The Security Guards' and LL Cool J's 'Mama Said Knock You Out' is chewed up and spat out as 'Granny Says Kick Yo Black Ass'. Yes, it is on this level at which the NWH humour operates, often lower. 'I'm Just A Human', based musically on PM Dawn's 'Set Adrift On Memory Bliss', proves especially base in its opening verse assertion that everyone's fecal matter exhibits largely the same properties. That said, the contents of this album are intended as a satire on the dubious ideals and general crassness of mainstream hip hop of the period and one or two tracks almost capture the sound and feel of the originals. Appreciation of 'FEAR OF A BLACK HAT's appropriated covers really depends on the sophistication of an individual listener's own sense of humour, and their patience for novelty recordings, but for most the dubious laughs don't translate so successfully from film to soundtrack, and as an album the joke soon wears thin. *MR*

Album rating: *4.5

FEEL THE NOISE

2007 (US 88m) TriStar Pictures (PG-13)

Film genre: urban hip-hop Musical drama

Top guns: dir: Alejandro Chomski / s-w: Albert Leon

Stars: Omarion Grandberry *(Rob Vega)* ← YOU GOT SERVED, Rosa Arredondo *(Marivi)*, Zulay Henao *(Carol "CC" Reyes)*, James McCaffrey *(Jeffrey Skylar)*, Melonie Diaz *(Mimi)*, Kellita Smith *(Tanya)* ← ROLL BOUNCE, Malik Yoba *(the mayor)* ← RIDE, Giancarlo Esposito *(Roberto Vega)* ← KLA$H ← NIGHT ON EARTH ← SCHOOL DAZE ← MAXIMUM OVERDRIVE, Victor Rasuk *(Javi Vega)*, **Pras Michel** *(Electric)* ← BLOCK PARTY ← TURN IT UP, **Julio 'Volito' Ramos** *(Volito)*, **Jerome I. Jones** *(young Rome)* ← YOU GOT SERVED ← HOUSE PARTY 3, Luis Lozada *(Vico C.)*, Raul Ortiz *(Alexis)*, Joel "Fido" Martinez *(Fido)*, Norman Darnell Howell *(Notch)*

Storyline: New York rapper Rob feels the heat from the local bully boys and decides to head off to even hotter Puerto Rico for safety. There he gets to know his long-lost father and his half-brother Javi, who introduces him to Reggaeton, a mix of hip-hop, Latin and (surprise! surprise!) reggae. Along with dancer CC, the brothers head back to New York for the big Puerto Rico day Parade and a possible record contract, bully boys notwithstanding. *JZ*

Movie rating: *2

Visual: dvd

Off the record: Omarion (b. Omari Ishmael Grandberry, 12 Nov'84, Inglewood, California, USA) was the main singer behind B2K, a group who split in 2004, leaving the man to release a solo album, 'O' (2005). **Jerome I. Jones** was in the rap group Immature. *MCS*

—

Various Artists (composer: Andres Levin)

Sep 07. (cd) *Norte-Columbia; <715283-2>* ☐ ☐
– Cut off time (OMARION feat. KAT DeLUNA) / Pa la calle (VICO C. feat. CUCU DIAMANTES & PRAS) / Coqui (OMARION feat. WYCLEF JEAN) / Chulin, culin, chunfly (VOLITO feat. RESIDENTE CALLE 13) / Eso ehh ...!!! (ALEXIS & FIDO) / Atrevete te te (CALLE 13) / No quiere novio (NEJO feat. TEGO CALDERON) / Chevere (VOLITO feat. NOTCH) / Espaldota (DOMBI) / Get down (W7).

S/track review: Main actor and Latin-rapper, OMARION, steals the show here with a handful of songs including the smooth opening "Reggaeton" number, 'Cut Off Time', featuring KAT DeLUNA. His slick, bling-worthy presence also affords him another song, 'Coqui', alongside former Fugees star, WYCLEF JEAN; another from the old Refugees Camp, PRAS, gets in on the act via a guest spot with CUCU DIAMANTES on VICO C.'s 'Pa La Calle'. If one is looking for a highlight in amongst the chaff, one could do no better than VOLITO's groovy, 'Chulin, Culin, Chunfly', although what it all means is a mystery to the pop layman; a second from VOLITO, 'Chevere' (featuring NOTCH), is also worth checking out. TEGO CALDERON is also in attendance on NEJO's 'No Quiere Novio', but with 'FEEL THE NOISE' you can virtually taste the sweat on the dancefloor, but whether that's a good thing or a bad thing, that's for you to decide. *MCS*

Album rating: *4.5

☐ the FEELIES segment
(⇒ SMITHEREENS)

FEELIN' GOOD

1966 (US 85m) Pike Productions Inc.

Film genre: Rock'n'roll Musical comedy/drama

Top guns: s-w: (+ dir) James A. Pike, Mildred Maffei

Stars: Travis E. Pike *(Ted)*, Patricia Ewing *(Karen)*, Judi Reeve *(Judi)*, Leslie Burnham *(Elaine)*, Ronald Stafford *(Danny)*, Frank Dolan *(landlord)* → CHARLY, **Brenda Nichols** *(performer)*, the **Brattle Street East** *(performers)*, **the Montclairs** *(performers)*

Storyline: G.I. Ted comes back from the wars to find his old girlfriend has discovered rock'n'roll in a big way. She now performs in a band called the Brattle Street East but not to worry, Karen hasn't forgotten Ted and the two make up for his enforced absence in the time-honoured fashion. However, when Ted disappears for a suspiciously long time with Karen's ravishing room-mate (the car broke down, honest darling) she goes into a jealous rage and the future of Brattle Street East looks to be going West. *JZ*

Movie rating: *2

Visual: none (no audio OST; score: Arthur Korb)

Off the record: Travis E. Pike (b. 1944, Boston, Massachusetts; son of director James A.) was a prolific songwriter and led many bands in the early 60s: the Jesters, Teen Beats and the New Jesters, before forming bizarre rock act, Travis Pike's Tea Party. Other than the title song and 'Summertime' by the MONTCLAIRS (a Cleveland R&B outfit band led by Don Gregory?), the 'FEELIN' GOOD' soundtrack featured several songs by the **Brattle Street East**: 'Don't Hurt Me Again', 'The Way That I Need You', 'Wicked Woman', 'Watch Out Woman', 'Isn't It Right', 'Ute Ute', 'I Beg Your Pardon' & 'Foolin' Around'; another track 'Ride The Rainbow' was by English folk singer, **Brenda Nichols**. In 1973, Pike scored the music for the documentary film, 'The Second Gun', and subsequently wrote, directed, composed and acted in TV production, 'Grumpuss' (1998). *MCS*

FERRY 'CROSS THE MERSEY

1964 (UK 88m w/ b&w) United Artists Pictures (U)

Film genre: Pop/Rock Musical drama

Top guns: dir: Jeremy Summers ← DATELINE DIAMONDS / s-w: David Franden (story: Tony Warren)

Stars: Gerry & The Pacemakers:- Gerry Marsden *(Gerry)* **Freddie Marsden** *(Fred)*, **Leslie Maguire** *(Les)*, **Les Chadwick** *(Chad)* ← the T.A.M.I. SHOW / → the COMPLEAT BEATLES / Eric Barker *(Col. Dawson)*, George A. Cooper *(Mr. Lumsden)*, Patricia Lawrence *(Miss Kneave)* → O LUCKY MAN!, T.P. McKenna *(Hanson)* → PERCY → SILVER DREAM RACER, Mona Washbourne *(Aunt Lil)* → TWO A PENNY → MRS. BROWN, YOU'VE GOT A LOVELY DAUGHTER → O LUCKY MAN!, Mischa De La Motte *(Dawson's butler)*, Andy Ho *(Chinese restaurant manager)*, Deryck Guyler *(Trasler)* ← a HARD DAY'S NIGHT ← IT'S TRAD, DAD!, Margaret Nolan

(Norah) ← a HARD DAY'S NIGHT / → TOOMORROW, Keith Smith *(Dawson's chauffeur)*, with cameos from **Cilla Black** *(herself)*, Jimmy Saville ← JUST FOR FUN / → POP GEAR, Donald Gee

Storyline: Gerry and his pals are art students in 1960s Liverpool. To make ends meet they form a band and play gigs at the local clubs, especially The Cavern. After a diet of bread and water for months they finally get noticed and hire a manager. From then on their success is assured, but wait – the big concert is tonight and their instruments are mistakenly en route for the airport. Stop that ferry! *JZ*

Movie rating: *4

Visual: video + dvd

Off the record: GERRY & THE PACEMAKERS (see below)

—

GERRY & THE PACEMAKERS (& Various Artists)

Jan 65. (lp) *Columbia; (33SX 1693)* [19] [–]
– It's gonna be alright / Why oh why / Fall in love / Think about love / I love you too (the FOURMOST) / All quiet on the Mersey front (the GEORGE MARTIN ORCHESTRA) / This thing called love / Baby you're so good to me / I'll wait for you / She's the only girl for me / Is it love (CILLA BLACK) / Ferry cross the Mersey. *(re-iss. Mar88 on 'Beat Goes On'; BGOLP 10) (cd-iss. Aug94 on 'Repertoire'+=; REP 4423)* – (14 tracks).

—

GERRY & THE PACEMAKERS (& Various Artists)

Feb 65. (lp) *United Artists; <UAL 3387>* [–] [13]
– Ferry cross the Mersey / It's gonna be alright / Why oh why / I gotta woman (the BLACK KNIGHTS) / Fall in love / Think about love / This thing called love / Baby you're so good to me / I'll wait for you / Shake a tail feather (EARL ROYCE & THE OLYMPICS) / She's the only girl for me / Why don't you love me (the BLACKWELLS).

S/track review: Much like the BEATLES (on 'a HARD DAY'S NIGHT'), two differing versions of 'FERRY CROSS THE MERSEY' were released over both sides of the Atlantic. Liverpool's GERRY & THE PACEMAKERS up to now had been record breakers in the fact that they were the only outfit to have their first three 45s ('How Do You Do It?', 'I Like It' & 'You'll Never Walk Alone') to consecutively top the UK charts. But this was way back in 1963, although it must be said they were still up there with the best having subsequently produced two hits from the movie, 'It's Gonna Be Alright' and the classic 'Ferry Cross The Mersey'. The band's jovial leader of the pack, GERRY MARSDEN, penned all the group's nine quirky tunes aboard this rocking Mersey-boat of foot-tapping pop. Many songs don't come up to the surface (or even up to the 2-minute mark!), easy-going dirges such as 'This Thing Called Love', 'Think About Love', 'I'll Wait For You' and 'Fall In Love', too twee and romance-riddled for the more discerning rock'n'roll fan. The other BEATLES connection comes courtesy of musical director, GEORGE MARTIN, whose orchestra features with 'All Quiet On The Mersey Front' on the UK version. While the same LP highlights other Liverpudlian top acts such as the FOURMOST ('I Love You Too') and "Surprise, Surprise" CILLA BLACK ('Is It Love'), the US equivalent marks the introduction of three unsung Merseybeat bands, the BLACK KNIGHTS ('I Gotta Woman') featuring Ken Griffiths, the BLACKWELLS ('Why Don't You Love Me') with messrs McDermott, Trimnell, Little & Gormall, and EARL ROYCE & THE OLYMPICS ('Shake A Tail Feather') fronted by Billy Kelly. The six outsider tracks spread over both UK & US counterparts competed equally with the Gerry's contributions, and it was easy to predict the group's days were indeed numbered. *MCS*

Album rating: *5

– spinoff hits, etc. –

GERRY & THE PACEMAKERS: It's Gonna Be Alright
Aug 64. (7") *(DB 7353)* [24] [–]

GERRY & THE PACEMAKERS: Ferry Cross The Mersey
Dec 64. (7") *(DB 7437)* [8] [–]

the BLACKWELLS: Why Don't You Love Me
Dec 64. (7") *(DB 7442)* [ ] [–]

the BLACK KNIGHTS: I Gotta Woman
Dec 64. (7") *(DB 7443)* [ ] [–]

GERRY & THE PACEMAKERS: Ferry Cross The Mersey
Jan 65. (7") *Laurie; <3284>* [–] [6]

GERRY & THE PACEMAKERS: It's Gonna Be Alright
Mar 65. (7") *Laurie; <3293>* [23] [–]

□ 50 CENT segment
(⇒ GET RICH OR DIE TRYIN')

54

1998 (US 92m) Miramax Films (R)

Film genre: Disco-music urban drama

Top guns: s-w + dir: Mark Christopher

Stars: Ryan Phillippe *(Shane O'Shea)*, Salma Hayek *(Anita Randazzo)* ← FROM DUSK TILL DAWN ← FOUR ROOMS / → ACROSS THE UNIVERSE, Mike Myers *(Steve Rubell)* ← WAYNE'S WORLD 2 ← WAYNE'S WORLD, Sela Ward *(Billie Auster)* → DIRTY DANCING: HAVANA NIGHTS, Neve Campbell *(Julie Black)*, Breckin Meyer *(Greg Randazzo)* ← TOUCH, Sherry Stringfield *(Viv)*, **Coati Mundi** *(DJ)* <= KID CREOLE & THE COCONUTS =>, **Art Garfunkel** *(Elaine's patron)* <= SIMON & GARFUNKEL =>, Valerie Perrine *(Elaine's patron)* ← the BORDER ← CAN'T STOP THE MUSIC, Lorna Luft *(Elaine's patron)* ← GREASE 2, Lauren Hutton *(Liz Vangelder)* ← LITTLE FAUSS AND BIG HALSY, Ellen Albertini Dow *(Disco Dottie)* ← the WEDDING SINGER → LONGSHOT, Mark Ruffalo *(Ricko)* → COMMITTED, **Sheryl Crow** *(VIP patron)* ← WOODSTOCK 94 / → DILL SCALLION → WOODSTOCK '99, **Thelma Houston** *(herself)* → BRITISH ROCK SYMPHONY, Sean Sullivan *(Andy Warhol)* ← WAYNE'S WORLD ← the IN CROWD ← WHO'S THAT GIRL?, Michael York *(ambassador)* ← the GURU ← SMASHING TIME, Ron Jeremy *(Ron)* → DETROIT ROCK CITY → OVERNIGHT

Storyline: The story of the famous Studio 54 nightclub as seen through the eyes of new barman Shane. It's the summer of '79 and disco music is still all the rage. But things are about to go disastrously wrong for owner Steve Rubell – an old dancer dies on the floor, cash goes missing and the IRS get involved, and Rubell himself is arrested and jailed. Amidst all these goings on, shirtless Shane meets the rich and famous but comes to realize the club's future is far from secure. *JZ*

Movie rating: *4

Visual: video + dvd

Off the record: Thelma Houston (see below OST)

—

Various Artists: 54 – Volume 1 (score: Marco Beltrami)

Aug 98. (cd) *Tommy Boy; <TBCD 1293>* [77] [–]
– Studio 54 (the 54 ALL-STARS) / Keep on dancin' (GARY'S GANG) / The boss (DIANA ROSS) / Dance dance dance (yowsah yowsah yowsah) (CHIC) / Vertigo – Relight my fire (DAN HARTMAN) / You make me feel (mighty real) (SYLVESTER) / Move on up (DESTINATION) / Love machine (part 1) (the MIRACLES) / Contact (EDWIN STARR) / Knock on wood (MARY GRIFFIN) / Let's start the dance (BOHANNON) / I got my mind made up (INSTANT FUNK) / Young hearts run free (CANDI STATON) / Native New Yorker (ODYSSEY) / Que sera mi vida (the GIBSON BROTHERS) / Wishing on a star (ROSE ROYCE).

—

Various Artists: 54 – Volume 2 (score: Marco Beltrami)

Aug 98. (cd) *Tommy Boy; <TBCD 1294>* [74] [–]
– If you could read my mind (STARS ON 45: ULTRA NATE, AMBER & JOCELYN ENRIQUEZ) / Haven't stopped dancing yet (GONZALEZ) / Heaven must have sent you (BONNIE POINTER) / Loving is really my game (BRAINSTORM) / Disco nights (rock-freak) (GQ) / Found a cure (ASHFORD & SIMPSON) / Don't leave me this way (THELMA HOUSTON) / Come to me (FRANCE JOLI) / Take your time (do it right) (S.O.S. BAND) / Please don't let me be misunderstood (SANTA ESMERALDA) / Spank (JIMMY "BO" HORNE) / Galaxy (WAR) / I need a man (GRACE JONES) / Heart of glass (BLONDIE) / Cherchez la femme – Se si bon (DR. BUZZARD'S ORIGINAL SAVANNAH BAND) / Fly Robin fly (SILVER CONVENTION).

S/track review: Disco had never been so skilfully encapsulated than with the biggest selling soundtrack album of all time: 'SATURDAY NIGHT FEVER', but relative latecomer '54' makes up for its late arrival at the party with a mammoth two-volume, 32-track set which cherry picks many of the populist dancefloor fillers, and crowd-pleasing is the modus operandi here over a historically exact representation of the era. Disco is such a pure musical form and the endless swathes of strings, the brass stabs, the chukka-chukka-wah-wah guitar and vocal gymnastics all work as ingredients to make the biggest, fluffiest funk soufflé you've ever heard. This is pure, unadulterated dance music, but akin to that other pure dance form, northern soul, there is often incredible songcraft contained within. Among the solid gold here is the MIRACLES's 'Love Machine', CHIC's 'Dance, Dance, Dance (Yowsah, Yowsah, Yowsah)', EDWIN STARR with 'Contact' and 'You Make Me Feel (Mighty Real)' by SYLVESTER. There's more anthems here than at the United Nations, lest we forget 'Young Hearts Run Free', 'Native New Yorker' and 'Wishing On A Star'. And that's only volume/disc one. The second follows in similar style with less crossover hits and a more varied palette of gossamer delights. There's the odd ringer – a truly pointless contemporary house rehash of 'If You Could Read My Mind' ruins the flow of classics – but for the most part this is big, bold and beautiful stuff. *MR*

Album(s) rating: Volume 1 *7.5 / Volume 2 *7

the FIGHTING TEMPTATIONS

2003 (US 123m) MTV Films / Paramount Pictures (PG-13)

Film genre: showbiz/R&B-music comedy

Top guns: dir: Jonathan Lynn / s-w: Elizabeth Hunter (+ au), Saladin K. Patterson

Stars: Cuba Gooding Jr. *(Darrin Hill)* ← JUDGMENT NIGHT ← SING, **Beyonce Knowles** *(Lilly)* ← CARMEN: A HIP HOPERA / → FADE TO BLACK → DREAMGIRLS, **Melba Moore** *(Bessie Cooley)* ← HAIR ← COTTON COMES TO HARLEM, Mike Epps *(Lucius)* ← MALIBU'S MOST WANTED ← HOW HIGH / → ROLL BOUNCE, Reverend Shirley Caesar *(herself)*, **Faith Evans** *(Maryann Hill)* ← TURN IT UP / → TUPAC: RESURRECTION, LaTanya Richardson *(Paulina Pritchett)*, Wendell Pierce *(Reverend Lewis)* ← BROWN SUGAR / → RAY, **Montell Jordan** *(Eric Johnson)* ← STANDING IN THE SHADOWS OF MOTOWN, **Angie Stone** *(Alma)*, **T-Bone** *(Bee-Z Briggs)*, Dave Sheridan *(Bill)* → the DEVIL'S REJECTS, **Bilal** *(nightclub singer)* ← MOONWALKER / → BLOCK PARTY, **the O'Jays:- Eddie Levert Sr.** *(Joseph)*, **Walter Williams Sr.** *(Frank)*, James E. Gaines *(Lilly's grandfather)* ← FIVE ON THE BLACK HAND SIDE, **Eric Nolan Grant** *(Samuel)*, **Ann Nesby** *(Aunt Sally Walker)*, **Zane Copeland Jr.** *(Derek)*, **Yolanda Adams** *(herself)*, **Donnie McClurkin** *(himself)*, Faizon Love *(prison warden)* ← FEAR OF A BLACK HAT / → IDLEWILD, Daphnee Duplaix *(Tiffany)*, Steve Harvey *(Miles Smoke)* → YOU GOT SERVED, **Mary Mary:- Erica & Tina Atkins** *(performers)*, **the Mighty Falcons:- Bob Mardis** *(performer)* → HOUSE PARTY 3 → FEAR OF A BLACK HAT, **Jimmy Woodard** *(performer)* → HOUSE PARTY 3 / **the Blind Boys Of Alabama** *(performers)*, **Ramiyah** *(performers)*

Storyline: Decades after his mother was thrown out of the local gospel choir for singing the devil's music, blasé but ambitious ad man Darrin winds up heading back to the deep south to attend his dead aunt's funeral. The revelation that one of her dying wishes was for him to lead the choir in the Gospel Explosion competition doesn't much enthrall him, until he finds out the incentive is thousands of dollars' worth of telecom stock. While his city slicker charms fail to impress single mum cum nightclub siren Lilly, she eventually agrees to join his motley bunch of singers for a crack at the annual Gospel Explosion competition. Worth seeing if only for Melba Moore's demented dancing. *BG*

Movie rating: *5.5

Visual: dvd

Off the record: Beyonce (see below)

Various Artists (md: Jimmy Jam & Terry Lewis)

Sep 03. (cd/c) *Sony; <90286> Columbia; (513514-2)* [19] [ ]
– Fighting temptation (BEYONCE & MISSY ELLIOTT feat. MC LYTE & FREE) / I know (DESTINY'S CHILD) / Rain down (ANGIE STONE & EDDIE LEVERT SR.) / To da river (T-BONE, ZANE & MONTELL JORDAN) / I'm getting ready (ANN NESBY) / The stone (SHIRLEY CAESAR & ANN NESBY) / Heaven knows (FAITH EVANS) / Fever (BEYONCE) / Everything I do (BEYONCE & BILAL) / Love me like a rock (O'JAYS) / Swing low, sweet chariot (BEYONCE) / He still loves me (BEYONCE & WALTER WILLIAMS SR.) / Time to come home (BEYONCE, ANGIE STONE & MELBA MOORE) / Don't fight the feeling (SIKANGE feat. PAPA REU) / Summertime (BEYONCE feat. P. DIDDY).

S/track review: Swapping her bootymama persona for the church pew, BEYONCE's single-mum-goes-gospel makes for some interesting moments. The Missy Elliott-produced title track, though, isn't quite one of them, an annoyingly enjoyable Dubya-style abstinence anthem masquerading as femme-hop. As every R&B siren knows, though, "chicks were born to give you fever" and it's only when she bins the beats and the bluster, and gets down with the legacy of Peggy Lee that the temptation is actually worth fighting. As a window on what the singer might be capable of in another musical life, it's tantalising. While DESTINY'S CHILD get a look-in with the Lauryn Hill-esque 'I Know', KNOWLES follows fellow CHILD, Michelle Williams, into the bosom of the Lord with the ensemble a cappella, 'Swing Low Sweet Chariot'. Spiritual healing-wise, it's more convincing than the farcical freestyle-seeks-salvation patter of 'To Da River' as barked by T-BONE, ZANE and MONTELL JORDAN (funny in the film, though) and less formulaic than the ANGIE STONE-meets-EDDIE LEVERT number, 'Rain Down'. BEYONCE gets her own duet with an O'JAY on the 'Lean On Me'-esque Jam & Lewis production, 'He Still Loves Me', as well as a threesome with STONE and MELBA MOORE on 'Time To Come Home'. It's the venerable SHIRLEY CAESAR, though, who really takes it to the believers with 'The Stone', as well as supplying ANNE NESBY's testifying soul-hymn, 'I'm Getting Ready'. The atmosphere of happy-clappy abandon even moves the O'JAYS to cover Paul Simon and Jam & Lewis to randomly reprise vintage Giorgio Moroder/Donna Summer. And it's easy to be seduced by the mellow P-DIDDY pairing, 'Summertime', even if it is a shameless tack-on. A real reverend's egg of a soundtrack, then, but worth a spin if only for the sound of BEYONCE raising a temperature. *BG*

Album rating: *5.5

FINDERS KEEPERS

1966 (UK 89m) United Artists (U)

Film genre: Pop/Rock Musical comedy

Top guns: dir: Sidney Hayers / s-w: Michael Pertwee

Stars: Cliff RICHARD *(Cliff)*, **Hank B. Marvin** *(Hank)* ← WONDERFUL LIFE ← SUMMER HOLIDAY ← the YOUNG ONES, **Bruce Welch** *(Bruce)* ← WONDERFUL LIFE ← SUMMER HOLIDAY ← the YOUNG ONES, **Brian Bennett** *(Brian)* ← WONDERFUL LIFE ← SUMMER HOLIDAY, **John Rostill** *(John)* ← WONDERFUL LIFE, Robert Morley *(Colonel Roberts)* ← the YOUNG ONES, John Le Mesurier *(Mr. X)* → CUCKOO PATROL → the MAGIC CHRISTIAN, Graham Stark *(Burke)* → the MAGIC CHRISTIAN, Peggy Mount *(Mrs. Bragg)*, Vivienne Ventura *(Emilia)*, Ernest Clark *(air marshall)* → CUCKOO PATROL, Burnell Tucker *(pilot)* ← DATELINE DIAMONDS / → FLASH GORDON → SCREAM FOR HELP

Storyline: When the US Air Force accidentally drop a bomb on a small Spanish town (were they aiming for Iraq?) the people are evacuated until the bomb disposal squad get there. Meanwhile Cliff and Co arrive for a gig and find the place empty, so with a cavalier disregard for a health and safety policy they go in search of the UXB. Also in the hunt is the sinister Mr X who wants the bomb for his own purposes. He keeps himself well hidden in the er . . . Shadows. *JZ*

Movie rating: *4.5

Visual: video + dvd

Off the record: nothing really

CLIFF RICHARD AND THE SHADOWS (composers: Norrie Paramor/the SHADOWS)

Dec 66. (lp; mono/stereo) *Columbia; (SX/SCX 6079)* [6] [–]
– Finders keepers / Time drags by / Washerwoman / La la la song / My way (SHADOWS) / Oh señorita / Spanish music fiesta (SHADOWS) / This day / Paella medley (SHADOWS) / Run to the door / Where did the summer go / Into each life some rain must fall.

S/track review: On this, CLIFF RICHARD's last musical with longtime backing band the SHADOWS, the production glitz was mercifully stripped away in favour of a rootsy sound designed to soundtrack the film's Spanish setting but actually more Americana character. It was also the first of his soundtracks which, released from Musicians Union restrictions, featured the actual versions heard in the movie. While the influence of CLIFF's new competitors, the Beatles, is more pronounced than ever, it's perhaps the folk-pop smarts of John Sebastian and his Lovin' Spoonful which the SHADOWS – writers of all the material here – lean most heavily on, at least if the likes of the groovy 'Time Drags By' and 'Oh Señorita' are anything to go on. Much like Elvis' late 60s soundtracks, there are some great, unsung tracks here and it all hangs together much better than its bad press would have you believe; it's certainly more consistently listenable than the inispid 'WONDERFUL LIFE'. Perhaps just to prove how much all that Iberian sun had gone to his head, CLIFF even addresses a love song ('Paella') to some traditional Spanish cuisine. Tasty but past its sell-by date. *BG*

Album rating: *4.5

– spinoff hits, etc. –

CLIFF RICHARD & THE SHADOWS: Time Drags By / La La La Song

Oct 66. (7") *(DB 8017)* [10] [–]

CLIFF RICHARD & THE SHADOWS: In The Country / Finders Keepers

Dec 66. (7") *(DB 8094)* [6] [–]

FINDING GRACELAND

1998 (US 106m) Largo Entertainment / TCB Productions (PG-13)

Film genre: road movie comedy/drama

Top guns: dir: David Winkler (+ story +) / s-w: Jason Horwitch

Stars: Harvey Keitel *(Elvis)* ← FROM DUSK TILL DAWN ← PULP FICTION ← RESERVOIR DOGS ← the LAST TEMPTATION OF CHRIST ← the BORDER ← THAT'S THE WAY OF THE WORLD / → BE COOL, Johnathon Schaech *(Byron Gruman)* ← THAT THING YOU DO! / → SPLENDOR, Bridget Fonda *(Ashley)* ← JACKIE BROWN ← TOUCH ← GRACE OF MY HEART ← SINGLES ← SHAG: THE MOVIE / → SOUTH OF HEAVEN, WEST OF HELL, Gretchen Mol *(Beatrice Gruman)* ← GIRL 6, John Aylward *(Sheriff Haynes)*, Susan Traylor *(Maggie)* ← the BODYGUARD / → MASKED AND ANONYMOUS, Peggy Gormley *(Fran)* ← the LAST TEMPTATION OF CHRIST

Storyline: Byron Gruman decides to go on a pilgrimage to Memphis after the death of his wife. Not long into the journey (in a car far from roadworthy) he picks up a hitchhiker who casually informs him he is Elvis Presley and could he kindly be taken back home to Graceland? Of course Byron thinks the guy is two strings short of a guitar but as Memphis draws nearer "Elvis" begins getting through to him, especially when they stop to pick up a second passenger – who happens to be the double of Marilyn Monroe. *JZ*

Movie rating: *6

Visual: dvd (no audio OST; score: Stephen Endelman)

Off the record: Songs featured in the film include:- 'Rip It Up' (ELVIS PRESLEY), 'Wayward Soul' (JOE COCKER), 'Restless' (CARL PERKINS & TOM PETTY & THE HEARTBREAKERS), 'Baby, For Your Love' (MAC CURTIS), 'Playing With A Memory' (JESSE DAYTON), 'Come To Me' (CATIE CURTIS), 'How Can You Be So Mean' (JOHNNY ACE), 'It's Raining' (IRMA THOMAS), 'Kiddio' (JOHN LEE HOOKER), 'One Night' (ELVIS PRESLEY), 'Anytime, Anyplace, Anywhere' (HADDA BROOKS), 'Suspicious Minds' (MARK CAMPBELL), 'You'd Be Surprised' (BRIDGET FONDA), 'Long Black Limousine' (ELVIS PRESLEY), 'Walking In Memphis' (MARC COHN), 'If I Can Dream' (ELVIS PRESLEY) and old-style orchestrations by Larry Hochman. *MCS*

□ FIONA segment
(⇒ HEARTS OF FIRE)

the FIVE HEARTBEATS

1991 (US 122m) Twentieth Century-Fox Film Corporation (R)

Film genre: showbiz/R&B/Pop Musical drama

Top guns: s-w: Robert Townsend (+ dir) → JACKIE'S BACK! → LITTLE RICHARD → LIVIN' FOR LOVE: THE NATALIE COLE STORY → CARMEN: A HIP HOPERA, Keenan Ivory Wayans

Stars: Robert Townsend *(Donald 'Duck' Matthews)* ← STREETS OF FIRE, Michael Wright *(Eddie King, Jr.)*, Leon *(James Thomas 'J.T.' Matthews)* → the TEMPTATIONS → MR. ROCK'N'ROLL: THE ALAN FREED STORY → LITTLE RICHARD → GET RICH OR DIE TRYIN', Harry J. Lennix *(Terrance 'Dresser' Williams)* → RAY → STOMP THE YARD, Tico Wells *(Anthony 'Choirboy' Stone)* → TRESPASS, Diahann Carroll *(Eleanor Potter)* ← CLAUDINE / → JACKIE'S BACK!, Chuck Patterson *(Jimmy Potter)* ← HAIR, Hawthorne James *(Big Red Davis)* ← the DOORS, Theresa Randle *(Brenda)* → JUNGLE FEVER → CB4: THE MOVIE → GIRL 6, Paul Benjamin *(Eddie King Sr.)* ← LEADBELLY ← FRIDAY FOSTER ← the EDUCATION OF SONNY CARSON ← ACROSS 110th STREET ← MIDNIGHT COWBOY, John Witherspoon *(Wild Rudy)* ← HOUSE PARTY ← the JAZZ SINGER / → RIDE, Norma Donaldson *(Mrs. Sawyer)* ← HOUSE PARTY ← STAYING ALIVE ← WILLIE DYNAMITE ← ACROSS 110th STREET, Kasi Lemmons *(Cookie)* ← SCHOOL DAZE / → FEAR OF A BLACK HAT, Arnold Johnson *(Mr. Matthews)* ← AMERICAN HOT WAX ← PIPE DREAMS ← SHAFT, Lamont Johnson *(Bobby Casanova)* → FEAR OF A BLACK HAT, Harold Nicholas *(Ernest 'Sarge' Johnson)* ← DISCO 9000, Eddie Griffin *(ventriloquist)* → HOUSE PARTY 3, Barry Diamond *(the five horsemen)* ← HOUSE PARTY ← GET CRAZY / → HOUSE PARTY 2, Tommy Redmond Hicks *(Pastor Blake)* → DELUSION → WARMING BY THE DEVIL'S FIRE

Storyline: The good old Hollywood rise and fall from an Afro-American perspective, alighting on fantasy soul league quintet the Five Heartbeats. Starting out in the early 60s as harmony amateurs on the chitlin circuit, it's not long before Duck, Eddie, JT and co taste the rewards, double standards and terminal pitfalls of fame, brought into even sharper relief by endemic racism. *BG*

Movie rating: *7

Visual: video & dvd

Off the record: The DELLS were responsible for a few songs on the films to 'Come Together' (1971) and 'NO WAY BACK' (1976). *MCS*

Various Artists/Cast (score: Stanley Clarke)

Apr 91. (cd/c/lp) *Virgin; <91609> (CD/TC+/VMM 4)* [58] Sep92 ☐
– A heart is not a house for love (the DELLS) / We haven't finished yet (PATTI LaBELLE with TRESSA THOMAS & BILLY VALENTINE) / Nights like this (AFTER 7) / Bring back the days (U.S. MALE) / Baby stop running around (BIRD AND THE MIDNIGHT FALCONS) / In the middle (FLASH AND THE FIVE HEARTBEATS) / Nothing but love (the FIVE HEARTBEATS) / Are you ready for me (FLASH AND THE EBONY SPARKS) / Stay in my corner (the DELLS) / I feel like going on (EDDIE, BABY DOLL AND THE L.A. MASS CHOIR).

S/track review: With the film's plot a jigsaw-like aggregation of biz lore and soul apocrypha, and the group themselves a mongrel hybrid of the Temptations, Sam Cooke, Smokey Robinson and the DELLS amongst others, there's nothing that isn't familiar here, even if much of the music was written to order, and some of it re-recorded for the soundtrack. It's rather an affectionate tribute to soul's troubled youth, too often compromised by vapid production and arrangements but capturing just enough old skool spirit to make it listenable. As consultants and performers, 50s vintage troopers the DELLS have the luxury of a direct input, yet thanks to an 80s sheen with the consistency of powdered custard, opener 'A Heart Is A House For Love' doesn't come close to either their classic 45's or their one-off blaxploitation soundtrack; MARVIN "The Magnum" JUNIOR still sounds great though, almost as good as he does on orchestrated 'Cadet' oldie, 'Stay In My Corner' (a US Top 10 in 1968). Even if you can get over the appalling pun, U.S. MALE's 'Bring Back The Days' is lifeless, and, despite singing her lungs out, PATTI LaBELLE is likewise let down by dishwater arrangements, doubly disappointing given that her contribution replaced the Tressa Thomas film version. BIRD AND THE MIDNIGHT FALCONS, FLASH AND THE EBONY SPARKS: now there's a couple of soul names to bear proudly; together with Indiana soulsters AFTER-7, they do a reasonable job of recreating the space, urgency and anticipation of vintage 'Motown', FLASH and co recalling one of Berry Gordy's first hits in the Contours' 'Do You Love Me'. But what of the 'FIVE HEARTBEATS' themselves? Ironically, they put most of the professionals to shame with the slick retro stylings of the VALENTINE-led 'Nothing But Love'. Held at arm's length from the film, 'The FIVE HEARTBEATS' isn't going to set many pulses racing, but – like its Celtic counterpart 'The COMMITMENTS' – its workaday soul will keep it in print for a good few years to come. *BG*

Album rating: *5.5

– spinoff hits, etc. –

AFTER 7: Nights Like This / BIRD AND THE MIDNIGHT FALCONS: Baby Stop Running Around

May 91. (c-s/cd-s) *<98798>* [24] ☐

☐ the 5.6.7.8's segment
(⇒ KILL BILL: VOL.1)

FLAME

aka SLADE IN FLAME

1975 (UK 91m) Goodtimes Enterprises (PG)

Film genre: Glam-Rock Musical drama

Top guns: dir: Richard Loncraine → BRIMSTONE & TREACLE / s-w: Andrew Birkin ← PIED PIPER, Dave Humphries → QUADROPHENIA

Stars: Slade:- Noddy Holder *(Stoker)*, **Dave Hill** *(Barry)*, **Don Powell** *(Charlie)*, **Jim Lea** *(Paul)* / Tom Conti *(Robert Seymour)*, Johnny Shannon *(Ron Harding)* ← THAT'LL BE THE DAY ← PERFORMANCE / → ABSOLUTE BEGINNERS, Alan Lake *(Jack Daniels)* ← CATCH US IF YOU CAN, Kenneth Colley *(Tony Devlin)* ← PERFORMANCE / → LISTZOMANIA → RETURN TO WATERLOO, Sara Clee *(Angie)* ← THAT'LL BE THE DAY, John Dicks *(Lenny)* → QUEEN OF THE DAMNED, Jimmy Gardner *(Charlie's dad)* ← TAKE ME HIGH ← the COMMITTEE, Sheila Raynor *(Charlie's mum)*, Tommy Vance *(Ricky Storm)*, Emperor Rosko *(himself)* ← YOU ARE WHAT YOU EAT

Storyline: After getting locked in a coffin on stage and spending the night in the clink, mutton-chopped Stoker leaves his sub-goth no-hoper of a band and becomes lead singer of rival band Flame. Outside of a decent songbook, Stoker's livewire personality and Basil Brush bark are about the only things they've got going for them; they're manipulated by their repulsive agent, patronised by plum-throated executive Robert Seymour and shot at while doing an interview (with the late Tommy Vance no less!) at a pirate radio station housed in a grim, wartime sea fort in the Thames Estuary. Forget the soundtrack's Bee Gees-gone-cosmic cover art, this is more shithouse than arthouse, and in this case that's a compliment. It's also one of the most sobering portraits of the music industry committed to celluloid, written by Andrew 'Cement Garden' Birkin (brother of Jane). *BG*

Movie rating: *7

Visual: video + dvd

Off the record: SLADE were formed in 1964 as the Vendors by **Dave Hill** and **Don Powell**, while their first moniker change came shortly afterwards when they metamorphosed into the In-Be-Tweens. Their official debut 45, 'You Better Run', introduced **Noddy Holder** and **Jim Lea**, although it flopped when it was released in late '66. Returning in 1969 as Ambrose Slade – at the suggestion of 'Fontana' label's Jack Baverstock – a belated debut album, 'Beginnings', sold poorly although ex-ANIMALS bass player, Chas Chandler (who'd helped to bring JIMI HENDRIX into Britain); he subsequently became their manager/producer. Kitted out in bovver boots, jeans, shirt and braces, SLADE topped their newly adopted 'ard look with skinheads all round, Chandler moulding the band's image and sound in an attempt to distance them from the fading hippy scene. Although they attracted a sizeable grassroots following, SLADE's appropriately titled first album, 'Play It Loud' failed to translate into sales. However, they finally cracked the UK Top 20 in May 1971 via a rousing cover of Bobby Marchan's 'Get Down And Get With It', the track bringing SLADE into the living rooms of the nation through a Top Of The Pops appearance. By this point, HOLDER and co had grown some hair, painted their boots sci-fi silver and initiated the roots of "Slademania" (foot-stomping now all the rage). The noisy, gravel-throated Holder (complete with tartan trousers, top hat and mutton-chop sideburns), the bare-chested, glitter-flecked Hill and the not so flamboyant Lea and Powell, became part of the glam-metal brigade later in the year, 'Coz I Luv You' hitting the top of the charts for 4 weeks. Competing with the likes of GARY GLITTER, T.REX and Sweet, the lads amassed a string of anthemic UK chart toppers over the ensuing two years, namely 'Take Me Back 'ome', 'Mama Weer All Crazee Now', 'Cum On Feel The Noize', 'Skweeze Me Pleeze Me' and the perennial festive fave 'Merry Xmas Everybody'. The noize level was markedly lower on the pop-ballad, 'Everyday' (1974), a song that only hit No.3, glam-rock/pop shuddering to a halt around the same time. Their chart-topping albums, 'Slayed?' (1972), 'Sladest' (1973) and 'Old New Borrowed And Blue' (1974) were now shoved to the back of people's record collections, PINK FLOYD, Mike Oldfield and Genesis now vying for the attention of the more discerning rock fan. *BG & MCS*

SLADE : Slade In Flame

Nov 74. (lp) *Polydor; (2442 126) Warners; <2865>* [6] Jun75 [93]
– How does it feel? / Them kinda monkeys can't swing / So far so good / Summer song (wishing you were here) / O.K. yesterday was yesterday / Far far away / This girl / Lay it down / Heaven knows / Standin' on the corner. *(re-iss. Nov82 on 'Action Replay'; REPLAY 1000) (cd-iss. May91; 849 182-2)*

S/track review: Wolverhampton's finest were in their foot-stomping pomp when they recorded 'FLAME', before the movie's grainy anti-glamour prefigured punk and ushered in a late-decade trough. The music isn't nearly as as gratifyingly jaded as the film, but it's more of a piece than the No.1 albums which it followed and it's weathered the years with most of its hard-knock soul intact. The tartan-scarf-waving 'Far Far Away' was their last big hit until 'Merry Xmas Everybody' got its second wind almost a decade later, but it's the Beatles-esque ennui of 'How Does It Feel?' which really carries the tired spirit of the movie. By sequencing the song back to back with the furious, quasi-punk thrash of 'Them Kinda Monkeys Can't Swing', SLADE (i.e. NODDY HOLDER, DAVE HILL, JIM LEA and DON POWELL) come off as more than just the terrace-friendly Oasis template they're often bracketed as. They can't quite maintain that pace over the course and they're not averse to tipping a mirror-plated top hat to past glories – the see-saw melody of 'Summer Son (Wishing You Were Here)' is far too similar to '..Xmas..' to ever make it sound like a t-shirts'n'beer anthem – but there are enough highlights (the Faces-esque slide-groove of 'O.K. Yesterday Was Yesterday' and the anthemic 'So Far So Good' included) to make it a serious competitor to 'Slayed' (1973) as HOLDER and co's finest non-anthology long player, one which easily stands apart from the film but equally makes it mandatory viewing. *BG*

Album rating: *7.5

– spinoff hits, etc. –

SLADE: Far Far Away / O.K. Yesterday Was Yesterday

Oct 74. (7") *(2058 522)* [2] [–]

SLADE: How Does It Feel? / So Far So Good

Feb 75. (7") *(2058 547)* [15] [–]

SLADE: How Does It Feel? / O.K. Yesterday Was Yesterday

Apr 75. (7") *<8134>* [–] [ ]

FLAMING STAR

1960 (US 93m) 20th Century Fox (PG)

Film genre: Western drama (w/ bit of Rock'n'roll)

Top guns: dir: Don Siegel ← HOUND-DOG MAN / s-w: Clair Huffaker (+ au), Nunnally Johnson

Stars: Elvis PRESLEY *(Pacer Burton)*, Steve Forrest *(Clint Burton)*, Dolores Del Rio *(Neddy Burton)*, Barbara Eden *(Roslyn Pierce)*, John McIntire *(Sam Burton)* ← SING BOY SING / → HONKYTONK MAN, Rudolph "Rudy" Acosta *(Buffalo Horn)*, Richard Jaeckel *(Angus Pierce)* → PAT GARRETT & BILLY THE KID

Storyline: Pacer Burton is the mixed race young buck in the Old West, whose family is caught up in the animosity between white settlers and native indians. *BG*

Movie rating: *4.5

Visual: video

Off the record: Barbara Eden was the star of US TV series, 'I Dream Of Jeannie'.

ELVIS PRESLEY: Flaming Star / Wild In The Country / Follow That Dream

Mar 95. (cd) *R.C.A.; <66557> (74321 90612-2)* [ ] [ ]
– Flaming star / Summer kisses, winter tears *[not in film]* / Britches / A cane and a high starched collar / Black star *[not in film]* / Summer kisses, winter tears (movie version) *[not in film]* / Flaming star (alt.) / (WILD IN THE COUNTRY tracks) / (FOLLOW THAT DREAM tracks).

S/track review: Banned in South Africa due to its racial plot line, this has got to be PRESLEY's most controversial and challenging film. Then again, given the overall blandness of his Hollywood vehicles, that's not saying much. The music certainly doesn't have the rebellious kick of his 50s material, although 'Black Star' (the original title of the film) has a faintly ominous air to it, ELVIS sounding marginally more haunted than on the re-recorded, re-titled version which featured in the film. 'Summer Kisses, Winter Tears', another song recorded for the film but deleted from the final print, was from the same drawing board as 'Earth Boy' right down to the wafting vocals of the JORDANAIRES. It was also re-recorded, appearing with the film's title song on 1961's 'Elvis By Request' EP. 'Girl In Britches' is cowpoke ELVIS kitsch with lyrics to match; wisely, the film's producers decided to cut it. 'A Cane And A High Starched Collar', a barn-dance-style trifle which could've also done with cutting, was the only other ELVIS performance to make it onto the commercial print. The various versions of all these tracks – including the brief, atmospheric end title of 'Flaming Star' – were finally gathered together on a CD along with retrospective "soundtracks" from 'WILD IN THE COUNTRY' and 'FOLLOW THAT DREAM'. *BG*

Album (CD compilation) rating: *4.5

– spinoff releases, etc. –

ELVIS PRESLEY: Elvis By Request

Apr 61. (7"ep) *R.C.A.; <LPC 128>* [14] [–]
– Flaming star / (+ 3 others not in film).

ELVIS PRESLEY: Flaming Star And Summer Kisses

Sep 65. (mono-lp) *R.C.A.; (RD 7723)* [–] [11]
– (compilation of 'Elvis By Request' EP & others)

ELVIS PRESLEY: Elvis Sings Flaming Star

Apr 69. (lp) *<CAS 2304> (INTS 1012)* [96] Jun69 [2]
– (only 1 track from the movie) *(re-iss. Apr79 on 'RCA Camden' lp/c; CDS/CAM 1185) (cd-iss. Apr06;)*

FLASHDANCE

1983 (US 95m) Paramount Pictures (R)

Film genre: romantic Pop/Dance Musical drama

Top guns: dir: Adrian Lyne / s-w: Joe Eszterhas → HEARTS OF FIRE, Thomas Hedley Jr. (+ au) → HARD TO HOLD

Stars: Jennifer Beals *(Alex Owens)* → FOUR ROOMS, Michael Nouri *(Nick Hurley)* ← GOODBYE, COLUMBUS, Lilia Skala *(Hanna Long)* ← CHARLY, Sunny Johnson *(Jeanie Szabo)* ← WHERE THE BUFFALO ROAM ← ANIMAL HOUSE, Kyle T. Heffner *(Richie)* → the WOMAN IN RED, Belinda Bauer *(Katie Hurley)* ← TIMERIDER: THE ADVENTURE OF LYLE SWANN / → UHF, **Cynthia Rhodes** *(Tina Tech)* → STAYING ALIVE → DIRTY DANCING, Liz Sagal *(Sunnt)* ← GREASE 2 / → HOWARD THE DUCK, **Lee VING** *(Johnny C.)*, **Rocksteady Crew:- Wayne Frost/Frosty Freeze, Marc Lemberger/Mr. Freeze *, Kenneth Gabbert/Prince Ken Swift, Richard Colon/Crazy Legs** *(themselves)* ← WILD STYLE / → KNIGHTS OF THE CITY *, Robert Wuhl *(one of Mawby's regulars)* → GOOD MORNING, VIETNAM → BATMAN → the BODYGUARD, Micole Mercurio *(Rosemary Szabo)* → ELVIS AND THE COLONEL: THE UNTOLD STORY → the THING CALLED LOVE

Storyline: Muscling her way through a Pittsburgh steel mill by day, working up a sweat in a blue collar club by night, Alex Owens is a lady with proverbial naked ambition. Tired of slumming it, she dreams of turning her talents to ballet dancing, eventually getting a shot at an audition where she turns humid choreography into 80s iconography, and Giorgio Moroder turns her theme tune into high melodrama. *BG*

Movie rating: *6

Visual: video + dvd

Off the record: The **Rocksteady Crew** (from South Bronx, New York) were UK one-hit-wonders in October 1983 via '(Hey You) The Rocksteady Crew'. Their claim to fame was an association with Afrika Bambaataa (through his Zulu Nation), while newcomers to the fold have to fight and win a battle with an existing member! *MCS*

Various Artists (score/composer: Giorgio Moroder)

Apr 83. (lp/c) *Casablanca; <811492-1/-4> (CANH/+C 5)* [1] Jun83 [9]
– Flashdance ... what a feeling (IRENE CARA) / He's a dream (SHANDI) / Love theme from "Flashdance" (HELEN ST. JOHN) / Manhunt (KAREN KAMON) / Lady, lady, lady (JOE "BEAN" ESPOSITO) / Imagination (LAURA BRANIGAN) / Romeo (DONNA SUMMER) / Seduce me tonight (CYCLE V) / I'll be here where the heart is (KIM CARNES) / Maniac (MICHAEL SEMBELLO). *<(cd-iss. Dec83; 811492-2)> (re-iss. Jun87 on 'Mercury'; PRICE 111) <(cd re-iss. Aug98 on 'Polydor'; 558682-2)>*

S/track review: Ooops.. she did it again; after her indelible, star-crossed turn on 'FAME', IRENE CARA was back with the Oscar-winning theme for bazillion-grossing Jerry Bruckheimer megabuster, 'FLASHDANCE'. This time it was 80s for keeps, drum machines, spondylitic synth, lipgloss emotion and all; somehow, though, the aerobic workout of Giorgio Moroder music and CARA mantra bore that same burden of nostalgia even as it busted its sweatshirt moves, or at least until the Harold Faltermeyer-style breakdown. Moroder's best stuff was well behind him by 1983; his love theme is archetypal banks-of-the-Seine (in Pennsylvania) cinetronica but 'Seduce Me Tonight' by CYCLE V (sounding for all the world like the Sweet making an 80s comeback) has to represent a nadir of sorts. DONNA SUMMER comes on like a congested cross between Toni Basil and Hazel O'Connor; despite barking about her 'Romeo', she clearly wasn't feeling much love. And, save for maybe JOE BEAN ESPOSITO and the SHANDI oddity, 'He's A Dancer' (check the almost Kurt Cobain-esque guitar part), that goes for the album as a whole – soul-leached pop in all its lurid glory, MICHAEL SEMBELLO's 'Maniac' (inspired by the notorious slasher flick of the same name) included. The album even commits the cardinal sin of leaving out LAURA BRANIGAN's 'Gloria' at the expense of the dire 'Imagination', and criminally omits breakin' classic, 'It's Just Begun'; then again, putting Jimmy Castor on this album would have been like inviting Ghandi for a rare steak. *BG*

Album rating: *5.5

– spinoff hits, etc. –

IRENE CARA: Flashdance ... What A Feeling / HELEN ST. JOHN: Love Theme From "Flashdance"

Mar 83. (7") *<811440> (CAN 1016)* [1] May83 [2]

MICHAEL SEMBELLO: Maniac / GIORGIO MORODER – instrumental

May 83. (7") *<812516> (CAN 1017)* [1] Aug83 [43]

JOE "BEAN" ESPOSITO: Lady, Lady, Lady

Oct 83. (7") *<811430>* [86] [–]

FLY BY NIGHT

1993 (US 100m) Lumiere Productions (R)

Film genre: urban Hip Hop-music buddy drama

Top guns: dir: Steve Gomer / s-w: Todd Graff

Stars: Jeffrey D. Sams *(Rich)*, Ron Brice *(I Tick)*, **MC Lyte** *(Akusa)*, **Daryl Mitchell** *(Kayam)* ← HOUSE PARTY 2 ← HOUSE PARTY / → the COUNTRY BEARS, Leo Burmester *(Rickey Tick)* ← the LAST TEMPTATION OF CHRIST / → SHAKE, RATTLE & ROLL: AN AMERICAN LOVE STORY, Maura Tierney *(Denise)* → PRIMARY COLORS, Yul Vazquez *(Sam)* ← the MAMBO KINGS, Larry Gillard *(Jed-Lite)*, Todd Graff *(Naji)*, Ebony Jo-Ann *(Charlotte)* → POOTIE TANG

Storyline: Struggling MC, Rich, leaves his wife and son to become a hip hop rapper and meets up with hardcore gangsta, I Tick, along the way. Now billed as the King And I, they combine forces in an attempt to break into the big time – "how MUCH will you go for the DREAM . . . how MUCH will you risk for the MUSIC..". *MCS*

Movie rating: *3

Visual: dvd (no audio OST: score: Sidney Mills)

Off the record: **MC Lyte** (b. Lana Moorer, 11 Oct'71, Queens, New York) female rapper who broke through in 1989 with album, 'Eyes On This'; subsequent Top 10 hits included 'Keep On, Keepin' On' (from the 1996 movie, 'Sunset Park') and 'Cold Rock A Party'. *MCS*

FOLLOW THAT DREAM

1962 (US 110m) United Artists / Mirisch Corporation (PG)

Film genre: Rock'n'roll Musical comedy/drama

Top guns: dir: Gordon Douglas → SLAUGHTER'S BIG RIP-OFF / s-w: Charles Lederer (novel: 'Pioneer Go Home' by Richard Powell)

Stars: **Elvis PRESLEY** *(Toby Kwimper)*, Arthur O'Connell *(Pop Kwimper)* ← HOUND-DOG MAN ← APRIL LOVE / → KISSIN' COUSINS → YOUR CHEATIN' HEART, Joanna Moore *(Alicia Claypoole)*, Anne Helm *(Holly Jones)*, Jack Kruschen *(Carmine)*, Simon Oakland *(Nick)*

Storyline: The Kwimpers are a clan of itinerant hillbillies who occupy a Florida beach, coming into conflict with the local populace and ending up in court. Toby, the family's most likeable member, is the prime target of the locals' misdirected ire. *BG*

Movie rating: *4.5

Visual: video + dvd

Off the record: nothing

ELVIS PRESLEY: Flaming Star / Wild In The Country / Follow That Dream

Mar 95. (cd) *R.C.A.; <66557> (74321 90612-2)* [ ] [ ]
– (FLAMING STAR tracks) / (WILD IN THE COUNTRY tracks) / Follow that dream / Angel / What a wonderful life / I'm not the marrying kind / A whistling tune / Sound advise.

S/track review: More archetypically Hollywood ELVIS than the relatively oblique, downbeat material which accompanies them on the three-on-one CD re-issue (alongside 'FLAMING STAR' & 'WILD IN THE COUNTRY'), the songs from 'FOLLOW THAT DREAM' reflect the lightweight drama of the film's plot. The likes of 'Sound Advice' and 'I'm Not The Marrying Kind' are the epitome of the kind of instantly forgettable fare which compromised PRESLEY's earlier achievements and offered glaringly inadequate exercise for his stymied talent. Again, one of the most memorable songs – the title song – is a spirited Wise/Weisman number, driven on by Floyd Cramer's flamboyant piano. 'Angel' is a passable ballad, and the rollicking 'What A Wonderful Life' at least gives ELVIS something to get his teeth into. 'A Whistling Tune' wasn't included in the film but was subsequently re-recorded for 'KID GALAHAD', complete with corny whistling. *BG*

Album (CD compilation) rating: *4.5

– spinoff hits, etc. –

ELVIS PRESLEY: Follow That Dream EP

May 62. (7"ep) *R.C.A.; <EPA 4368> (RCX 211)* [15] Jun62 [34]
– Follow that dream / Angel / What a wonderful life / I'm not the marrying kind.

FOLLOW THE BOYS

1963 (US 95m) Metro-Goldwyn-Mayer (PG)

Film genre: romantic Pop Musical comedy

Top guns: dir: Richard Thorpe ← JAILHOUSE ROCK / → FUN IN ACAPULCO / s-w: David T. Chantler, David Osborn (story: Lawrence P. Bachmann)

Stars: Connie FRANCIS *(Bonnie Pulaski)*, Paula Prentiss *(Toni Denham)* → LOOKING FOR LOVE, Dany Robin *(Michele)*, Russ Tamblyn *(Lt. Wadsworth "Smitty" Smith)* ← HIGH SCHOOL CONFIDENTIAL! / → HUMAN HIGHWAY, Janis Paige *(Liz Bradville)*, Richard Long *(Lt. Peter Langley)*, Ron Randell *(Cmdr. Ben Bradville)*, Robert Nichols *(Hulldown)*, Eric Pohlmann *(Italian farmer)* ← the DUKE WORE JEANS, Roger Perry *(radarman Billy Pulaski)* → ROLLER BOOGIE

Storyline: The boys have relocated to the French Riviera from Florida, but that won't stop Bonnie and Toni from their traditional man-hunt. Along with French amie Michele, they meet up with their sailor boyfriends who are on shore leave. There's also some ooh-la-la from Commander Ben which doesn't impress wife Liz, and as usual girls and boys swap dates at the drop of a hornpipe. *JZ*

Movie rating: *4.5

Visual: none

Off the record: One of the CONNIE FRANCIS outtakes not used in the movie was 'Sleepyland'. *MCS*

CONNIE FRANCIS (composers: Benny Davis & Ted Murry)

Mar 63. (lp;mono/stereo) *M.G.M.; <E/ES 4123> (MGM-C/-CS 931)* [66] [ ]
– Follow the boys / Tonight's my night / Intrigue (version with voices) / Waiting for Billy / Italian lullaby / Intrigue (Dixieland instrumental) / *[Side Two – not in film]*: For every young heart / On a little street in Venice / In your arms / Somewhere near someplace / My dearest possession / I can't reach your heart.

S/track review: CONNIE FRANCIS gets her second chance to shine on film and soundtrack (her first was 'WHERE THE BOYS ARE' in 1960), only this time the 34-year-old pop balladeer is awarded only Side One of the LP. Penned by Davis-Murry and arranged/conducted by LeRoy Holmes, four out of six numbers belong to CONNIE, the heartbreaking Top 20 title track, 'Follow The Boys', 'Tonight's The Night', 'Waiting For Billy' and her own song 'Italian Lullaby'. While the film raised Italian-American CONNIE's profile a little, the nondescript part-soundtrack did nothing but put it in reverse, critically at least. Soft, pastel, Brill-Building nostalgia superseded her brief R&R of old, and without her, side 1 just plummets further into despair with a Dixieland instrumental of 'Intrigue'. One can't review non-film CONNIE songs on side 2, but if one could, maybe the up tempo 'In Your Arms' would get top marks. All the aforementioned 'FOLLOW THE BOYS' movie songs feature on her "In Hollywood" compilation CD, 'Where The Boys Are', for 'Rhino' records. *MCS*

Album rating: *2

– spinoff hits, etc. –

CONNIE FRANCIS: Follow The Boys / Waiting For Billy

Feb 63. (7") *<13127>* [17] [–]

CONNIE FRANCIS: Follow The Boys / Tonight's My Night

Feb 63. (7") *(1193)* [–] [ ]

FOOTLOOSE

1984 (US 107m) Paramount Pictures (R)

Film genre: Dance/Rock Musical drama

Top guns: dir: Herbert Ross ← the OWL AND THE PUSSYCAT / s-w: Dean Pitchford → SING

Stars: Kevin Bacon *(Ren McCormack)* ← ANIMAL HOUSE, Lori Singer *(Ariel Moore)* → MADE IN USA, John Lithgow *(Reverend Shaw Moore)* → DREAMGIRLS, Dianne Wiest *(Vi Moore)* → I AM SAM, Christopher Penn *(Willard Hewitt)* → MADE IN USA → RESERVOIR DOGS → MASKED AND ANONYMOUS, Sarah Jessica Parker *(Rusty)*, John Laughlin *(Woody)* → CRIMES OF PASSION, Jim Youngs *(Chuck Cranston)*, Timothy Scott *(Andy Beamis)* ← VANISHING POINT, Russ McGinn *(Herb)* ← SLAUGHTER'S BIG RIP-OFF, Oscar Rowland *(Mr. Walsh)* ← SIDE BY SIDE: THE TRUE STORY OF A MAGICAL FAMILY, H.E.D. Redford *(Widdoes)* ← SIDE BY SIDE: THE TRUE STORY OF A MAGICAL FAMILY

Storyline: Brush-haired Ren is the new kid in town, one where the minister has banned dancing lest it lead his flock into lewdness. If the prospect of a dance free zone in the mid-1980s wasn't preposterous enough, the locals work themselves into the kind of book burning frenzy last seen in the middle ages. As a snake-hipped kinda dude, Ren does his utmost to remedy this state of affairs, quoting from the bible, breaking into embarrassing dance routines at the first sign of an AOR power chord and eventually organising a tuxedo'd shindig in the local flour mill. Aaarrrgghhh. *BG*

Movie rating: *5

Visual: video + dvd

Off the record: Like many of the songs featured on the soundtrack, **Kenny LOGGINS** co-wrote them with Dean Pitchford, a man also involved in another pop musical, 'SING' (1989). *MCS*

Various Artists (songs: KENNY LOGGINS *)

Feb 84. (lp/c) *Columbia; <39242> C.B.S.; (CBS/40 70246)* [1] Apr84 [7]
– Footloose (*) / Let's hear it for the boy (DENIECE WILLIAMS) / Almost Paradise . . . love theme from Footloose (MIKE RENO & ANN WILSON) / Holding out for a hero (BONNIE TYLER) / Dancing (SHALAMAR) / I'm free (Heaven helps the man) (*) / Somebody's eyes (KARLA BONOFF) / The girl gets around (SAMMY HAGAR) / Never (MOVING PICTURES). *(cd-iss. Aug84; CD 70246) (re-iss. Nov88 lp/c/cd; 463000-1/-4/-2) <cd re-iss. Oct98 on 'Columbia/Legacy'+=; CK 65781>* – Bang your head (metal health) (QUIET RIOT) / Hurts so good (JOHN COUGAR MELLENCAMP) / Waiting for a girl like you (FOREIGNER) / Dancing in the sheets – 12" mix (SHALAMAR). *(cd re-iss. May99 on 'Sony'+=; 493000-2)*

S/track review: Ah, those heady days of 1984, when young folks were too busy fighting for their right to go to the hop and racing tractors to concern themselves with curfews, Buckfast and anti-social behaviour orders. They don't make rock stars like KENNY LOGGINS anymore, and they certainly don't make Welsh divas as stout-throated as BONNIE TYLER. Both were 70s renegades who'd somehow found their footing in the new decade, unreconstructed roots rockers who somehow managed to shoehorn (OK, no more foot puns) their style into an 80s aesthetic. Dean Pitchford was the key to it all, LOGGINS' co-writer and the man behind the film's dubious screenplay. He also co-wrote every song on the soundtrack and, crucially, conceived the MTV-esque incorporation of those songs into the film. Divorced from their glibly choreographed screen routines, the best of these songs still have enough nostalgia value to make the soundtrack viable. Rock never did sit well with those pesky 80s production values, at least not as well as soul and pop, and it's DENIECE WILLIAMS who's weathered the years better than anyone. Bouncing along on the mini-moog squelch of ex-Zappa associate George Duke, 'Let's Hear It For The Boy' conjures the disposable hedonism of those years more evocatively than any amount of "power-balladeering", even if TYLER's 'Holding Out For A Hero' still commands attention, plugging in Meat Loaf mastermind Jim Steinman's bombastic hallmark to the hollow pulse of a Linn drum machine. Likewise, the title track still comes on like a guiltily pleasurable cross between the Stray Cats and Shakin' Stevens, even if LOGGINS' other contribution, 'I'M FREE', sounds like a dry run sortie for 'Top Gun' (1987). The rest of the original soundtrack – and most of the CD bonus cuts – are for incurable 80s cases only, taking the tepid temperature of mid-80s mainstream America via chronically dated cock rock and AOR. Pass the hairspray. *BG*

Album rating: *5.5

– spinoff hits, etc. –

KENNY LOGGINS: Footloose

Jan 84. (7"/12") *<04310> (A/TA 4101)* [1] Mar84 [6]

BONNIE TYLER: Holding Out For A Hero

Feb 84. (7"/12") *<04370> (A/TA 4251)* [34] Aug85 [2]

SHALAMAR: Dancing In The Sheets

Feb 84. (7"/12") *<04372> (A/TA 4171)* [17] Mar84 [41]

DENIECE WILLIAMS: Let's Hear It For The Boy

Mar 84. (7"/12") *<04417> (A/TA 4319)* [1] Apr84 [2]

MIKE RENO & ANN WILSON: Almost Paradise . . . Love Theme From Footloose

Apr 84. (7"/12") *<04418> (A/TA 4480)* [7] Jun84 [ ]

KENNY LOGGINS: I'm Free (Heaven Helps The Man)

May 84. (7"/12") *<04452> (A/TA 4495)* [22] Jun84 [ ]

the FORBIDDEN DANCE

1990 (US 96m) Columbia Pictures (PG-13)

Film genre: romantic Dance-music drama

Top guns: dir: Greydon Clark ← BLACK SHAMPOO / s-w: Roy Langsdon, John Platt

Stars: Laura Herring *(Princess Nisa)*, Jeff James *(Jason Anderson)*, Barbra Brighton *(Ashley)*, Miranda Garrison *(Mickey)* ← SALSA ← DIRTY DANCING ← XANADU, Sid Haig *(Joa)* ← FOXY BROWN ← COFFY ← BLACK MAMA, WHITE MAMA ← IT'S A BIKINI WORLD ← BEACH BALL / → JACKIE BROWN → HOUSE OF 1000 CORPSES → KILL BILL: VOL.2 → the DEVIL'S REJECTS, Angela Moya *(Carmen)*, Richard Lynch *(Benjamin Maxwell)*, **KID CREOLE & THE COCONUTS** *(performers)*

Storyline: First there was 'LAMBADA' (1988), and if that wasn't enough for fans of the Latin-dance scene, 'The FORBIDDEN DANCE' was forged. Nisa is a young princess happy and content in the Amazon rainforests, until, that is, she and her people are threatened by the corporate businessmen of America. She decides to fly to Los Angeles with a witch doctor, but when (w.d.) Joa is thrown in jail, she has to come up with another plan. A chance meeting with dancer Jason finds her in a televised competition that might be just the ticket to save her good-cause mission. *MCS*

Movie rating: *2.5

Visual: video + dvd (no audio OST)

Off the record: Songs from the film include: three from KID CREOLE & THE COCONUTS ('Lambada A La Creole (Llorando Se Fue – Chorando Se Foi)', 'It's A Horror' & 'Automatic'), MENDY LEE ('You And Me Alone'), JOSE FELICIANO ('Lambada The Forbidden Dance'), KAOMA ('Lambada'), JOYCE KENNEDY ('Always You'), the DREAM MACHINE ('Capoiera'), REGINALDO PI ('Limba Limba Lambada'), VICTOR MERINO ('Good Girls Like Bad Boys'), MARA GETZ ('Hand To Hold You Over'), JEFF HARPER ('It's Never Too Late'), EXPOSE ('Stop, Look, Listen And Think'), BOB MIDOFF ('BH Disco') and two by GENE EVARO ('Reaction To Passion' & 'Last Lover'). *MCS*

FORBIDDEN ZONE

1980 (US 76m b&w) Hercules Films (R)

Film genre: Alt/New Wave Musical fantasy comedy/spoof

Top guns: s-w: (+ dir) **Richard Elfman, Matthew Bright, Nick James, Nick L. Martinson**

Stars: Herve Villechaize *(King Fausto)*, Susan Tyrell *(Queen Doris / Ruth Henderson)* ← SUBWAY RIDERS ← CATCH MY SOUL / → TAPEHEADS → ROCKULA → CRY-BABY → PINK AS THE DAY SHE WAS BORN → MASKED AND ANONYMOUS, Marie-Pascale Elfman *(Susan B. "Frenchy" Hercules)*, **Matthew Bright as Toshiro Boloney** *(Squeezit & Renee Henderson)*, **Gene Cunningham as Ugh-Fudge Bwana** *(Huckleberry B. Jones / Pa Hercules)*, Virginia Rose *(Ma Hercules)*, Hyman Diamond *(Gramps Hercules)*, Phil Gordon *(Flash Hercules)*, Viva *(ex-queen)* → FLASH GORDON → PARIS, TEXAS → NICO ICON, **Richard Elfman** *(masseuse/ prisoner)*, **Danny Elfman** *(Satan)*, Dennis Olivieri *(stuttering student)* ← PHANTOM OF THE PARADISE ← the NAKED APE, Joe Spinell *(Squeezit's father)* ← SORCERER ← RANCHO DELUXE

Storyline: Lambasted initially for its truly mad display of OTT, this midnight movie of sorts tells the tale of the Hercules family and their daughter Frenchy who discovers a door in the basement leading to the Sixth Dimension. This other fantasy world comes complete with a King and Queen plus a whole bunch of "wicked" beings including red hot attraction, Satan. *MCS*

Movie rating: *6.5

Visual: video + dvd in 2004

Off the record: OINGO BOINGO (see below)

—

the MYSTIC KNIGHTS OF THE OINGO BOINGO
(composer: Danny Elfman)

1983. (lp) *Varese Sarabande; <(STV 81170)>* [ ] [ ]
– Forbidden Zone / "Hercules" family theme / Some of these days (CAB CALLOWAY) / Journey through the intestines / Squeezit's vision of his "sister" / Queen's revenge / Factory / Love theme – Squeezit and the chickens / Flash and Gramps / Squeezit the moocher (Minnie the moocher) / Alphabet song / Cell 63 / Witch's egg / Yiddishe Charleston (R. YOSSELE ELFMAN) / Bim bam boom (MIGUELITO VALDES) / Chamber music / Pleure (with MARIE PASCALE) / Battle of the queens / Love theme – King and queen / Finale. *<(cd/c-iss.Oct90; VSD/VSC 5268)>*

S/track review: Love them or loathe them, Oingo Boingo – here billed under their original MYSTIC KNIGHTS OF THE OINGO BOINGO – were certainly different, like a cross between Devo and Split Enz. The fact that the L.A. ensemble were instigated in 1979 to provide music for this actual movie, was even more bizarre; the co-writer and director, RICHARD ELFMAN recruiting talented younger brother DANNY ELFMAN to compose the score (the young "Elf" is now a top film composer in his own right with over 50 movies to his name, 'Beetlejuice', 'BATMAN', 'DICK TRACY' & 'Charlie And The Chocolate Factory'). RICHARD and DANNY (alongside other Boingo members) even gave themselves roles in the film, the latter landing the part of Satan. 'FORBIDDEN ZONE', has been a slow-burner of sorts for DANNY, RICHARD and Co, while they concentrated on the rise of Oingo Boingo; early synth-pop LPs included 'Only A Lad' (1981), 'Nothing To Fear' (1982), 'Good For Your Soul' (1983) and US Top 100 breakthrough 'Dead Man's Party' (1985). Essential embryonic history aside (well, nearly!), the off-the-wall antics of both the movie and its accompanying OST, should be inspirational to many a newbie band, the 'FORBIDDEN . . .' album (first released in 1983 we think) certainly is. From the opening Devo-meets-Xtc title track, the listener could be forgiven for thinking this was just another run-of-the-mill, 80s electro set. Wrong. Track 2, 'Hercules Family Theme' – a reference to the character played by diminutive Fantasy Island actor, Herve Villechaize – bounces away like a Hawaiian surfer (on the crest of another New Wave, quite possibly) and reminiscent of Spirit the band rather than any spirit from a faraway land or time zone. That time span was filled by follow-on track, 'Some Of These Days' by Big Band/Swing veteran, CAB CALLOWAY, a track that might've instead graced a Marx Brothers film, although its inclusion here is both refreshing and inspirational. Now watch those happy feet. The pre-war 40s theme was constantly trialed throughout the set, 'Squeezit The Moocher' (aka Minnie The Moocher, c. CALLOWAY), the Groucho Marx-ish 'Yiddishe Charleston' and 'Bim Bam Boom' OTT but excellent. Little tunes or short-stoppers (rather than show-stoppers) were DANNY's forte, 'Journey Through The Intestines', the bouncy 'Factory', 'Cell 63' and 'Chamber Music' being the pick of that particular batch. Stand-out was the busy, 'Queen's Revenge', its military dirge like something out of a foreign-dubbed 'Wizard Of Oz'. Truly space-dust, man, and without the presence of ZAPPA or Judy Garland. A must-have album for all the family, quite possibly (although beware the film is rated R for adult viewing), the fun aspect of tracks such as 'Flash And Gramps' and the Eartha Kitt-esque, 'Witch's Egg' would amuse everyone from 6 to 66. On a low negative note (and God knows there's a few here!), the album's 'Finale' was a little weak, but this was a minor tweak on an album that delivered more than its share of shocks and surprises. Maybe now I'll search through the Oingo Boingo catalogue, although I'm unlikely to find something as weird and truly wonderful. *MCS*

Album rating: *7.5

the FOREIGNER

1978 (US 77m b&w) Amos Poe Visions (15)

Film genre: spy adventure/drama

Top guns dir (+ s-w): Amos Poe ← the BLANK GENERATION / → SUBWAY RIDERS → JUST AN AMERICAN BOY

Stars: Eric Mitchell *(Max Menace)* → CANDY MOUNTAIN, Anya Phillips *(Doll)*, Patti Astor *(Fili Harlow)* → WILD STYLE, **Debbie Harry** *(Dee Trik)* <= BLONDIE =>, **(Terens) Severine** *(Zazu Weather)*, Amos Poe *(Amos Nitrate)* → DOWNTOWN 81 → SUBWAY RIDERS → SMITHEREENS, **the Cramps:- Lux Interior, Poison Ivy Rorschach, Bryan Gregory + Miriam Linna** *(punk thugs)* → URGH! A MUSIC WAR. **the Erasers:- Susan Springfield, Jody Beach + Jane Fire**

Storyline: Secret agent Max Menace is assigned to pursue some weirdos and punks in the seedy world that is New York City. Why? *MCS*

Movie rating: *4.5

Visual: video + dvd (Electric DVD Distribution)

Off the record: Debbie Harry was the main pop feature here, although **Severine** (b. Josiane Grizeau) had also pop credentials; the French diva was the 1971 Eurovision Song Contest winner with subsequent UK Top 10 song, 'Un Blanc, Un Arbre, Une Rue'. Two punk-rock acts were also present, **the Cramps + the Erasers. Ivan Kral** (guitarist of the Patti Smith Group) composed the unreleased soundtrack. *MCS*

Connie FRANCIS

Born: Concetta Rosemarie Franconero, 12 Dec'38, Newark, New Jersey, USA. Little "Queenie" (as she was affectionately nicknamed) cut her shiny white teeth at the age of 11 when she featured as a singer and accordionist with the Arthur Godfrey Show. While still a teenager, Connie provided the singing voice for Tuesday Weld in the 1956 movie, 'ROCK, ROCK, ROCK!' and for Freda Holloway in the following year's 'JAMBOREE'. Signed to 'M.G.M.', the 5'1" starlet had her first of many Top 20 hits via the ballad, 'Who's Sorry Now', a song that dated way back to 1923 and which she was reputed to have disliked. Connie's subsequent late 50s hits ranged from classy rock'n'roll ('Stupid Cupid' – written by Neil Sedaka – & 'Lipstick On Your Collar') to old-time ballads ('My Happiness' & 'Among My Souvenirs'), while in the early 60s she had three chart-toppers, 'Everybody's Somebody's Fool', 'My Heart Has A Mind Of Its Own' & 'Don't Break The Heart That Loves You'. In the meantime, Connie had already found her way into the world of film acting and singing. 'WHERE THE BOYS ARE' (1960) – also the title of her umpteenth hit single – was the first of many movie roles including 'FOLLOW THE BOYS' (1963), 'LOOKING FOR LOVE' (1964) and 'WHEN THE BOYS MEET THE GIRLS' (1965). Hit themes – however minor – also came in the shape of 'Al Di La' (from 1962's 'Rome Adventure') and 'Forget Domani' (from 1965's 'The Yellow Rolls Royce'), although by the mid-60s her star was fading fast. Following her return to stage work, an ordeal of horrendous proportions came about, when on November 8th, 1974 (after a concert at the Westbury Music Fair), Connie was raped at knifepoint while staying at New York's Howard Johnson Motel. She subsequently won a lawsuit of a reputed $3m, and later found out she had been, and still was a manic depressive (bipolar disorder). Gradually, she ventured back into the spotlight, but only worked on a very limited basis. *MCS*

- **filmography** {actress} -

Where The Boys Are *(1960 {a} theme-song =>)* / **Follow The Boys** *(1963 {*} OST =>)* / **Looking For Love** *(1964 {*} OST =>)* / **When The Boys Meet The Girls** *(1965 {*} on OST w/ V/A =>)*

– her movie music compilations, etc. –

CONNIE FRANCIS: Where The Boys Are: Connie Francis In Hollywood

Apr 97. (cd) *Rhino; <RCD 72774>*
– Main title – Where the boys are / Turn on the sunshine / Follow the boys / Tonight's my night / Waiting for Billy / Italian lullabye / Looking for love (rock'n'roll version) / When the clock strikes midnight / Whoever you are, I love you / Let's have a party / Be my love / I can't believe that you're in love with me / This is my happiest moment / Looking for love (jazz version) / When the boys meet the girls / Mail call / Embraceable you / I got rhythm / But not for me / Finale: Where the boys are – Do you love me (orchestral) – Where the boys are (vocal) / Looking for you (jazz version demo) / When the clock strikes midnight (jazz version) / Let's have a party / Looking for love (rock'n'roll version).

FRANKIE AND JOHNNY

1966 (US 87m) United Artists

Film genre: romantic Rock'n'roll Musical comedy

Top guns: dir: Frederick de Cordova / s-w: Alex Gottlieb (story: Nat Perrin)

Stars: Elvis PRESLEY *(Johnny)*, Donna Douglas *(Frankie)*, Sue Ann Langdon *(Mitzi)* ← WHEN THE BOYS MEET THE GIRLS ← ROUSTABOUT / → HOLD ON!, Harry Morgan *(Cully)*, Nancy Kovack *(Nelly Bly)*, Audrey Christie *(Peg)*, Robert Strauss *(Blackie)* ← GIRLS! GIRLS! GIRLS!, Cliff Norton *(Eddie)* ← COUNTRY MUSIC HOLIDAY

Storyline: Johnny, a singing gambler on a Mississippi riverboat, plays true to the traditional ballad by fraternising with Nelly Bly and incurring the wrath of his woman, Frankie. *BG*

Movie rating: *5.5

Visual: video + dvd

Off the record: nothing

ELVIS PRESLEY (composers: Freddy Karger, etc.)

Apr 66. (lp; mono/stereo) *R.C.A.; <LSP 3553> (RD/SF 7793)* [20] [11]
– Frankie and Johnny / Come along / Petunia, the gardener's daughter / Chesay / What every woman lives for / Look out Broadway / Beginner's luck / Down by the riverside / When the saints go marching in / Shout it out / Hard luck / Please don't stop loving me / Everybody come aboard. *(re-iss. Aug80 on 'RCA Int.'; INTS 5036) (re-iss. Apr84 lp/c; NL/NK 82559) (cd-iss. Jul04 on 'Follow That Dream'+=; FTD 1005)* – (extra takes).

S/track review: A welcome diversion from the patchwork pastiche normally passing for an ELVIS soundtrack, this goes squarely for a bold, brassy New Orleans feel in keeping with the film's plot, much more overtly – if much less effectively – than 'KING CREOLE'. Which isn't to say the songs are any better ("I'm as daffy as a daffodil"?!! please..) although it does have its moments. The title track finds PRESLEY bringing his sterling vocal chops to bear on the old cheatin' ballad and there's also a campy romp through 'Down By The Riverside – When The Saints Go Marching In'. Of the original material, 'Hard Luck' is a surprisingly gritty, downbeat blues with some mean harmonica from Charlie McCoy, while 'Come Along' is probably the best of the Dixie-flavoured songs, although all are equally enjoyable if ultimately disposable, and 'Petulia, The Gardener's Daughter' wins hands-down the prize for cheesy innuendo. In terms of unadulterated kitsch, meanwhile, 'Chesay' approaches Cher's 'Gypsies, Tramps and Thieves' albeit minus that song's pop hooks. Overall, this record is worth hearing, if only for the novelty of listening to ELVIS in a context so far removed from almost everything else he recorded. *BG*

Album rating: *4

– spinoff hits, etc. –

ELVIS PRESLEY: Frankie And Johnny / Please Don't Stop Loving Me

Mar 66. (7") *<47-8780> (RCA 1509)* [25] [21]

ELVIS PRESLEY: Frankie And Johnny / Paradise, Hawaiian Style

Jun 94. (cd) *<(07863 66360-2)>* [ ] [ ]

□ Aretha FRANKLIN segment
(⇒ SPARKLE)

□ Alan FREED segment
(⇒ AMERICAN HOT WAX)

FROM DUSK TILL DAWN

1996 (US 107m) Dimension Films / Miramax Films (R)

Film genre: black comedy vampire horror/thriller

Top guns: dir: Robert Rodriguez ← FOUR ROOMS / s-w: Quentin Tarantino ← FOUR ROOMS ← NATURAL BORN KILLERS ← PULP FICTION ← RESERVOIR DOGS / → JACKIE BROWN → KILL BILL: VOL.1 → KILL BILL: VOL.2 (story: Robert Kurtzman)

Stars: Harvey Keitel *(Jacob Fuller)* ← PULP FICTION ← RESERVOIR DOGS ← the LAST TEMPTATION OF CHRIST ← the BORDER ← THAT'S THE WAY OF THE WORLD / → FINDING GRACELAND → BE COOL, George Clooney *(Seth Gecko)* → SOUTH PARK: BIGGER, LONGER AND UNCUT → O BROTHER, WHERE ART THOU?, Quentin Tarantino *(Richard Gecko)* ← FOUR ROOMS ← PULP FICTION ← RESERVOIR DOGS ← EDDIE PRESLEY / → GIRL 6, Juliette Lewis *(Kate Fuller)* ← STRANGE DAYS ← the BASKETBALL DIARIES ← NATURAL BORN KILLERS ← the RUNNIN' KIND / → the FEARLESS FREAKS → CATCH AND RELEASE, Ernest Liu *(Scott Fuller)*, **Cheech Marin** *(border guard / Chet pussy / Carlos)* <= CHEECH & CHONG =>, Fred Williamson *(Frost)* ← MR. MEAN ← NO WAY BACK ← ADIOS AMIGO ← MEAN JOHNNY BARROWS ← BUCKTOWN ← THREE THE HARD WAY ← TOUGH GUYS ← HELL UP IN HARLEM ← the SOUL OF NIGGER CHARLEY ← BLACK CAESAR / → RIDE → CARMEN: A HIP HOPERA, Salma Hayek *(Santanico Pandemonium)* ← FOUR ROOMS / → 54 → ACROSS THE UNIVERSE, Danny Trejo *(Razor Charlie)*, Tom Savini *(Sex Machine)* ← DAWN OF THE DEAD, John Saxon *(FBI agent Stanley Chase)* ← SUMMER LOVE ← ROCK PRETTY BABY, **Tito Larriva** *(Titty Twister; guitarist & vocalist)* ← ROAD HOUSE ← TRUE STORIES / → the MILLION DOLLAR HOTEL, Kelly Preston *(newscaster; Kelly Houge)*

Storyline: The Gecko brothers are on the run after a string of robberies and shootings makes them most wanted north of the border. Salvation is seemingly at hand in a Mexican bar where they are due to meet the local Mr Big who, for a price, will provide them with Mexican citizenship and safety. Taking along a minister and his children as hostages, the Geckos arrive in the bar towards nightfall. However, after dark in this vampire-ridden joint a Bloody Mary is more likely to be a customer than a drink. *JZ*

Movie rating: *6.5

Visual: video + dvd

Off the record: Tito Larriva was a member of Latin-punk band, the Plugz (see REPO MAN)

Various Artists (score: GRAEME REVELL *)

Jan 96. (cd/c) *Epic Soundtrax; <EK 67523> (483617-2/-4)* [ ] Mar96 [ ]
– Everybody be cool (dialogue; George Clooney) / Dark night (the BLASTERS) / Mexican blackbird (ZZ TOP) / Texas funeral (JON WAYNE) / Foolish heart (the MAVERICKS) / Would you do me a favor? (dialogue; Juliette Lewis & Quentin Tarantino) / Dengue woman blues (JIMMIE VAUGHAN) / Torquay (the LEFTOVERS) / She's just killing me (ZZ TOP) / Chet's speech (dialogue; Cheech Marin) / Angry cockroaches (cucarachas enojadas) (TITO & TARANTULA) / Mary had a little lamb (STEVIE RAY VAUGHAN AND DOUBLE TROUBLE) / After dark (TITO & TARANTULA) / Willie the wimp (and his cadillac coffin) (STEVIE RAY VAUGHAN AND DOUBLE TROUBLE) / Kill the band (dialogue; Tom Savini) / Mexican standoff (*) / Sex machine attacks (*).

S/track review: Put together by bloodthirsty gore merchants, Robert Rodriguez, Lawrence Bender and of course, Quentin Tarantino, it's inevitably the record kicks off with some typically smart dialogue, this time in the shape of George Clooney instructing: "Everybody Be Cool". Similar in many aspects to 'RESERVOIR DOGS' and 'PULP FICTION', the snippets of movie soundbites are systematic to all Tarantino flicks, and there are a number of crackers here. Music-wise, it's equally cool, the seminal 'Dark Night' by cowpunks the BLASTERS (a band led by Dave Alvin) can be tracked all the way back to 1985. Not one of ZZ TOP's better-known numbers, 'Mexican Blackbird' (from 1975's 'Fandango!' set) is good-ol'-boy Southern-fried country with that derivative drawl and solo guitar-licking twang that only Gibbons and Co could get away with. The boogie-ing trio bring the soundtrack and themselves up-to-date via exclusive number, 'She's Just Killing Me' (later picked for their Top 30 album, 'Rhythmeen'), not their greatest but effective and appropriate for inclusion on this road movie-meets-vampire film. Tarantino's remarkable skill at finding the very obscure and novelty-value numbers is now legendary, the 1983 track, 'Texas Funeral' (by the un-cool JON WAYNE, aka David Vaught) was no exception, lyrically out-there (carpet urination, etc) and a precursor to the Handsome Family – perhaps. Who else but QT could sit the aforementioned cue back to back with retro-country act, the MAVERICKS, who soften the joint up via 'Foolish Heart' – think Hank Williams or Chris Isaak. If you preferred your music, or indeed your blues back to basics and traditional, then JIMMIE VAUGHAN (on 'Dengue Woman Blues') was your man. His late brother and band, STEVIE RAY VAUGHAN AND DOUBLE TROUBLE, supplied two finger-pickingly good tracks, 'Mary Had A Little Lamb' (yes, the old nursery rhyme!) and 'Willie The Wimp (And His Cadillac Coffin)'. Bypassing the LEFTOVERS' 'Torquay', which was basically the Champs' 'Tequila', the Latino-flavour continues with the film's bar-band, TITO (Larriva) & TARANTULA, who take Los Lobos one step further on two cuts, 'Angry Cockroaches (Cucarachas Enojadas)' and 'After Dark'. Add-on orchestral score tracks by GRAEME REVELL (ex-SPK) end the show and seem way out of place, but then this was indeed all-eclectic if not all-electric. Incidentally, hidden track (#18) carries on from 'Chet's Speech', which sees CHEECH Marin (doorman) peddling a variety of cats or indeed "pusseeeee!". *MCS*

Album rating: *7

FROM JUSTIN TO KELLY

2003 (US 81m +9m dvd) 19 Entertainment / Twentieth Century Fox (PG)

Film genre: romantic Pop Musical comedy

Top guns: dir: Robert Iscove / s-w: Kim Fuller ← SEEING DOUBLE ← SPICEWORLD

Stars: Kelly Clarkson *(Kelly)*, **Justin Guarini** *(Justin)*, Katherine Bailess *(Alexa)*, Anika Noni-Rose *(Kaya)* → TEMPTATION → DREAMGIRLS, Greg Siff *(Brandon)*, Brian Dietzen *(Eddie)*, Jason Yribar *(Carlos)*

Storyline: Kelly, Kaya and Alexa head for the beaches of Miami for some fun in the sun. Also on their way are Justin, Brandon and Eddie, and amidst the millions of sunbathers, Justin and Kelly manage to fall in love with each other at first sight. A hastily scribbled phone number is soon lost and while Kelly frantically tries to find her Romeo, her friend Alexa does a little Justin-hunting herself. May the best girl win! *JZ*

Movie rating: *2.5

Visual: video + dvd (no audio OST; score: Michael Wandmacher)

Off the record: Justin Guarini (b.28 Oct'78, Columbus, Georgia, USA) was the runner-up to Kelly Clarkson in the very first 'American Idol' TV show/ contest in 2002; his subsequent eponymous album reached the Top 20. Meanwhile, the aforementioned winner **Kelly Clarkson** (b.24 Apr'82, Fort Worth, Texas) has since had three Top 3 sets, 'Thankful' (2003), 'Breakaway' (2004) and 'My December' (2007). In this movie KELLY sings several songs:- 'I Won't Stand In Line', the Go-Go's 'Vacation', 'The Luv (The Bounce' (with above cast), 'Forever Part Of Me' (w/ JUSTIN), 'Timeless' (w/ JUSTIN), 'Madness' (w/ ANIKA), 'Anytime' (w/ JUSTIN) and a version of KC & The Sunshine Band's 'That's The Way I Like It' (w/ cast). Other tracks include 'Brandon's Rap' (GREG SIFF), 'Boom Boom Boom' (LEWIS MARTINEE), 'You're So Beautiful' (LOUIS CASTLE), 'Pull It Out' (NATARAJ feat. NOLITA), 'The Game' (GERARD McMAHON & JOHN VAN EPS), 'It's Meant To Be' (ANIKA NONI ROSE), 'Ghetto Blaster' (CULTURE CLASH DANCE PARTY), 'Party Up' (KEELY HAWKES), 'Wish Upon A Star' (KATHERINE BAILESS), 'Workin' (ALEX STIFF), 'Get Up' (HEATHER BRADLEY), etc. *MCS*

FRONTERZ

2004 (US 95m) Babe Wilson Entertainment

Film genre: showbiz comedy

Top guns: dir: Courtney Jones / s-w: Garth Belcon ← WHITEBOYS

Stars: Reno Wilson *(Tracy Baker / Lil' Problem)* ← WHITEBOYS, Dennis Pressey *(Ron Lewis / Big Spoon)*, Garth Belcon *(Malikai Cameron / Pimp Mississippi Messiah)* ← WHITEBOYS, Ted Danson *(executive)*, Henry Winkler *(executive)*, Tamara Lynch, Blair Underwood ← MALIBU'S MOST WANTED ← KRUSH GROOVE, Laurence Mason ← the CROW, Chastity Bono

Storyline: Three black actors decide to form rap group Large Money Mercenaries as it seems they only make gangsta films at Hollywood these days. Ron, Tracey and Malikai become Big Spoon, L'il Problem and Pimp Mississippi Messiah, so that's most of America represented, and sure enough the movie moguls soon launch the trio to stardom. However it's not easy for the boys to live a double life and their fake personas are beginning to take them over. *JZ*

Movie rating: *3

Visual: dvd (no audio OST; score: Kathryn Bostic & David Shaw)

Off the record: Chastity Bono is the daughter of Sonny & Cher.

FUBAR

2002 (Can 76m) Xenon Pictures (R)

Film genre: buddy film mockumentary/comedy

Top guns: s-w: (+ dir) Michael Dowse → IT'S ALL GONE PETE TONG, Paul Spence, David Lawrence

Stars: Paul Spence *(Dean Murdoch)* → IT'S ALL GONE PETE TONG, David Lawrence *(Terry Cahill)* → IT'S ALL GONE PETE TONG, Gordon Skilling *(Farrel Mitchener)* → IT'S ALL GONE PETE TONG, Tracey Lawrence *(Trixie Anderson)*, Sage Lawrence *(Chastity Anderson)*, Rose Martin *(Rose Murdoch)*

Storyline: Filmmaker Farrel Mitchener follows the adventures of Canadian headbangers Dean and Terry as they pontificate on the science of beer drinking, wrecking bus shelters and of course playing heavy metal music. When Dean is diagnosed with testicular cancer, the pair go up country for a final fling with the locals before his treatment begins. Beer and fights galore, and Dean in particular is going to have a ball. *JZ*

Movie rating: *6

Visual: dvd

Off the record: Paul Spence (b.29 Jan'76, Calgary, Alberta, Canada) fronts punk revival band CPC Gangbangs; one CD release in 2007, 'Mutilation Nation'. *MCS*

Various Artists (composer: PAUL SPENCE) (& "dialogue")

Nov 03. (cd) *Phantom; <00605>* [–] Canada [–]
– "Turn up the good, turn down the suck" / Rock you (PAIN FOR PLEASURE / SUM 41) / "Guidance counsellor" / Heavy metal shuffle (GOB) / Your daddy don't know (the NEW PORNOGRAPHERS) / "Where's Tron?" / Blockbuster (the SWEET) / "It wasn't so much the thing . . ." / Roller (TREBLE CHARGER) / "Shotgun a few beers" / In the mood (SLOAN) / "A band called Creeper" / Handsome hose (CREEPER) / "You can't just back it up!" / C'mon let's go (GIRLSCHOOL) / "Giver: Plan B" / Raise a little hell (GRIM SKUNK) / Four wheel drive (the ENGLISH TEETH) / Garden gate of evil (CREEPER) / Garden of evil (CREEPER) / "Fingerbang" / The kid is hot tonight (CHIXDIGGIT) / "I got attacked by a hawk" / FUBAR is a super rocker (THOR) / Eyes of a stranger (BREACH OF TRUST) / Hey hey my my (NOMEANSNO) / Rock and roll is my guitar (CREEPER).

S/track review: Featuring some exclusive tracks from Canada's youthful alt-indie-punk revival acts such as SUM 41, the NEW PORNOGRAPHERS, CHIXDIGGIT, SLOAN, TREBLE CHARGER, etc., alongside the ageing Canadian bodybuilding rocker THOR, 80s indie punks NOMEANSNO, and all-girl-Brit-group, GIRLSCHOOL, was indeed a masterstroke. What wasn't clever was the time between paying lots for the elusive CD and the months it took to arrive from the certain internet music retailer – an angry . . . *MCS*

Album rating: *7

FUN IN ACAPULCO

1963 (US 97m) Paramount Pictures (PG)

Film genre: Rock'n'roll Musical drama

Top guns: dir: Richard Thorpe ← FOLLOW THE BOYS ← JAILHOUSE ROCK / s-w: Allan Weiss ← GIRLS! GIRLS! GIRLS! ← BLUE HAWAII / → ROUSTABOUT → PARADISE, HAWAIIAN STYLE → EASY COME, EASY GO

Stars: Elvis PRESLEY *(Mike Windgren)*, Ursula Andress *(Marguerita Dauphin)*, Paul Lukas *(Maximillian Dauphin)*, Elsa Cardenas *(Dolores Gomez)*, Alejandro Rey *(Moreno)*, Larry Domasin *(Raoul Almeido)*, Robert Carricart *(Jose Garcia)*, Howard McNear *(Dr. John Stevens)* ← BLUE HAWAII, Darlene Tompkins *(Miss Stevens)* ← BLUE HAWAII, Teri Hope/Garr *(Janie Harkins)* → KISSIN' COUSINS → PAJAMA PARTY → the T.A.M.I. SHOW → VIVA LAS VEGAS → ROUSTABOUT → the COOL ONES → CLAMBAKE → HEAD → ONE FROM THE HEART, Mary Treen *(Mrs. Stevens)* ← GIRLS! GIRLS! GIRLS! / → PARADISE, HAWAIIAN STYLE

Storyline: Having given up his career due to vertigo, trapeze artist Mike Windgren is forced to take a job as a lifeguard at a Mexican holiday resort, where his romatic intrigues include the attentions of a female bullfighter. *BG*

Movie rating: *4.5

Visual: video + dvd

Off the record: nothing

—

ELVIS PRESLEY (composers: Joseph Lilley, etc.)

Dec 63. (lp; mono/stereo) *R.C.A.; <LSP 2756> (RD/SF 7609)* 3 Mar64 9
– Fun in Acapulco / Vino, dinero y amor / Mexico / El toro / Marguerita / The bullfighter was a lady / (There's) No room to rhumba in a sports car / I think I'm gonna like it here / Bossa nova baby / You can't say no in Acapulco / Guadalajara / Love me tonight * / Slowly but surely *. *(re-iss. Oct79 lp/c; PL/PK 42357) (re-iss. Aug81 on 'RCA Int.'; INTS 5106) <(cd/c-iss.Mar93 [* not on cd] +=; 74321 13431-2/-4)>* – IT HAPPENED AT THE WORLD'S FAIR (tracks). *(cd re-iss. Apr03 on 'Follow That Dream'+=; FTD 24)* – (bonus takes).

S/track review: Now this really is escapist fare, swapping the tropical hula-hooping of Hawaii for the tropical maraca-shaking of Mexico. If you approach it in this knowledge, you won't be disapppointed; if you approach it seriously, you're missing the point. Most of the songs are interchangeable as ELVIS limbers up on his Spanish pronunciation amid parping mariachi horns, rattling marimbas and mucho Latin high spirits. 'El Toro' is worth a special mention for its melodramatic, castanet kitsch, ditto 'Guadalajara', where ELVIS really lets loose on his language skills. 'The Bullfighter Was A Lady', meanwhile, will have you crying – or laughing – into your nachos. Ironically given its title, the Hispanic high jinks only let up on 'Bossa Nova Baby' (a US Top 10 hit), although even here there's a horn breakdown, as well as a completely incongruous Manfred Mann-style organ part. Save this soundtrack for your next Mexican-themed fancy dress party; it sounds great after a bottle of tequila, honest . . . *BG*

Album rating: *4

– spinoff hits, etc. –

ELVIS PRESLEY: Bossa Nova Baby / Witchcraft

Oct 63. (7") *(RCA 1374) <47-8243>*

8 / 32 13

GARAGE: A ROCK SAGA

2001 (US 86m str8-to-dvd) Planet Ant

Film genre: Rock Musical comedy/mockumentary

Top guns: dir: Mikey Brown / s-w: **Joshua Funk**, Nancy Hayden

Stars: Joshua Funk *(Frank Pluczinski)*, George Wendt *(the pitching coach)* ← SPICEWORLD ← BYE BYE BIRDIE / → MY DINNER WITH JIMI, Nancy Hayden *(Harriet Pluczinski)*, Tim Hayden *(Louie)*, Hal Soper *(Frank's dad)*, Ron West *(Rock god)*, Samantha Bennett *(Mrs. Rock god)*, Chad Krueger *(Gilbert Schultz)*, **Chuck Bartels** *(Dwayne Dubois)*, Jamie Taunten *(Swamp Bucket; bassist)*, Joe Lapham *(Swamp Bucket; drummer)*, Mikey Brown *(Betty Jablonski)*

Storyline: Actually started out as a pre-millennium stage play. 25 years (in 5-year excursions) in the life of rock star, Frank Pluczinski (whose father has just passed away), recalls his band, his relationships and er, Satanism. *MCS*

Movie rating: *4

Visual: dvd (no audio OST; see below)

Off the record: Guitarist/vocalist, **Joshua Funk** (and co-founder of the Planet Ant Theater in Hamtramck, Chicago), has self-financed two solo CD's, 'A Jukebox Envy' and 'Grits'. The movie's resident outfit, PARK: A ROCK BAND (aka Joshua Funk, Chad Krueger (not Kroeger!), Stunning Amazon's **Chuck Bartels**, etc.), contributed nearly a dozen songs, 'Funky Train To Hamtramck', 'Lady', 'Digital Reaction', 'Slim Slam', 'The DJ Plays The Songs He Wants To Play', 'Hey Where You Goin'', 'Leap Of Love', 'Rosa's Song', 'Rock And Roll Is Gonna Kick Your Ass' & 'It's The End Of The Movie'. *MCS*

GARAGE DAYS

2002 (Austra 105m) AFFC / Mystery Clock Cinema (MA) (R) (15)

Film genre: Rock Musical comedy/drama

Top guns: s-w: (+ dir + story) Alex Proyas ← the CROW, Dave Warner (+ story), Michael Udesky

Stars: Kick Gurry *(Freddy)*, Maya Stange *(Kate)*, Pia Miranda *(Tanya)* ← QUEEN OF THE DAMNED, Russell Dykstra *(Bruno)*, Brett Stiller *(Joe)*, Chris Sadrinna *(Lucy)*, Andy Anderson *(Kevin)*, Marton Csokas *(Shad Kern)* ← RAIN, Yvette Duncan *(Angie)* ← PRAISE, Tiriel Mora *(Thommo)* ← QUEEN OF THE DAMNED, Holly Brisley *(Scarlet)*, Matthew Le Nevez *(Toby)*, **Johnathan Devoy** *(punky lead singer)* ← QUEEN OF THE DAMNED, **David McCormack** + Andrew Lancaster *(York pub band)*

Storyline: Freddy is lead singer in a garage band trying to make a mark on the Sydney music scene. As he dreams of fame and fortune the rest of the band seem more concerned with their love lives, and at their first public gig the punters are overcome – with apathy. However, a chance meeting with top music executive Shad Kern gives Freddy the chance to tout his band, but first he must find $1200 for a venue, which leads to him resorting to skulduggery. "Live the dream . . . Love the trip" – or try your best, at least. *JZ*

Movie rating: *5

Visual: video + dvd

Off the record: Johnathan Devoy was the frontman with hard rock band Jerk until 2004.

—

Various Artists (* score: DAVID McCORMACK & ANDREW LANCASTER)

Sep 02. (cd) *20th Century Fox; <33585>* [–] Aus [–]
– High voltage (the D4) / Alright (SUPERGRASS) / Kooks (MOTOR ACE) / Buy me a pony (SPIDERBAIT) / Rockin' it (*) / Garage days (* feat. KATIE NOONAN) / Love is the drug (ROXY MUSIC) / Add it up (SONICANIMATION) / Walk up (*) / Ghost town (RHOMBUS) / Smash it up (INTERNATIONAL NOISE CONSPIRACY) / Say what? (28 DAYS) / That's entertainment (the JAM) / Master plan (*; McCORMACK-only) / Stop thinking about it (JOEY RAMONE) / Mad man (the HIVES) / Get the trap (* & ANTHONY PARTOS) / Lucky number nine (the MOLDY PEACHES) / Help yourself (TOM JONES).

S/track review: The OST to Aussie film 'GARAGE DAYS' is an eclectic mix of old and new, of stadium-fillers and those who would struggle to sell out their own garage. 'Alright' from SUPERGRASS is enough to get your head bopping and your feet tapping but SPIDERBAIT's 'Buy Me A Pony' will soon have you reaching for the skip button. ROXY MUSIC are the epitome of cool with 'Love Is The Drug' and a perfect contrast to the brash punk rockers of INTERNATIONAL NOISE CONSPIRACY's Damned cover, 'Smash It Up' or 'Mad Man' from the HIVES. The JAM's suburban opus 'That's Entertainment' makes a welcome appearance along with the poignant 'Stop Thinking About It' from the late, great JOEY RAMONE, while indie upstarts MOLDY PEACHES contribute 'Lucky Number Nine', a song that gives a nod to the likes of Weezer and Pavement. To close the album we are given 'Help Yourself' by the one and only TOM JONES, which will at least bring a smile to your face if nothing else. Of the others, D4's cover of Ac/Dc's 'High Voltage', MOTOR ACE's Bowie rendition, 'Kooks' and RHOMBUS' unusual take of the Specials' 'Ghost Town', are also worthy of a return visit. Score composers DAVID McCORMACK (from Brisbane band, Custard) and ANDREW LANCASTER contributed a few cues including the title track with singer KATIE NOONAN. There is no need to send this soundtrack back to the garage, with or without the motor running, as it is a good and varied selection of songs. *CM*

Album rating: *6

GAROTA DOURADA

aka 'Golden Girl'

1984 (Braz 105m) Embrafilme / Luiz Carlos Barreto Producoes..

Film genre: Disco/Pop Musical comedy teen drama

Top guns: s-w: (+ dir) Antonio Calmon, Flavio R. Tambellini

Stars: Andrea Beltrao *(Gloria)*, Geraldo Del Rey *(Aguia)*, Roberto Bataglin *(Betinho)*, Sergio Mallandro *(Zeca)*, Bianca Byington *(Diana)*, Andre de Biase *(Valente)*, Claudio Magno *(Patricia)*, **Marina Lima** *(herself)*, **Ritchie** *(himself)* → RUNNING OUT OF LUCK, **Guilherme Arantes** *(himself)*

Storyline: A young Brazilian man heads for sun, sea and sand after his wife walks out on him. Luckily enough his best pal is a famous rock star so it shouldn't be too difficult to find a replacement señorita. However, the way to win the girls' hearts and minds these days is to be the sexiest surfer in town, and our hero finds plenty of competition from the locals in his quest for a Brazilian beach babe. *JZ*

Movie rating: *4

Visual: video (no audio OST; score: Guilherme Arantes)

Off the record: From a very young age **Ritchie** (b. Richard David Court, 6 Mar'52, Beckenham, Kent, England) had lived a cosmopolitan lifestyle, moving from numerous places in Europe and Asia before settling back in London where he was part of folk-protest congregation/group, Everyone Involved. A friendship with guitarist Mike Klein and Rio outfit, Os Mutantes, led to his emigration to Brazil. His subsequent work with A Barca Do Sol (as flautist) and Vimana (as vocalist) led to a production role on Jim Capaldi's 'Let The Thunder Cry' (1980) album. For the rest of the 80s, Ritchie became a solo star with many credits and Latin-pop albums to his name. **Marina Lima** and **Guilherme Arantes** were also of Brazilian jazz-pop fame. *MCS*

GAS-S-S!

1970 (US 79m) American International Pictures (GP)

Film genre: sci-fi road movie/comedy

Top guns: dir: Roger Corman ← the TRIP ← the WILD ANGELS ← ROCK ALL NIGHT ← CARNIVAL ROCK / s-w: George Armitage

Stars: Robert Corff *(Coel)*, Elaine Giftos *(Cilla)*, Alex Wilson *(Jason)*, Lou Procopio *(Marshall McLuhan)* ← the WILD ANGELS, Ben Vereen *(Carlos)* → WHY DO FOOLS FALL IN LOVE → IDLEWILD, Tally Coppola, aka Talia Shire *(Coralee)*, Cindy Williams *(Marissa)* → AMERICAN GRAFFITI → MORE AMERICAN GRAFFITI, Bud Cort *(Hooper)* ← BREWSTER McCLOUD ← the STRAWBERRY STATEMENT / → HAROLD AND MAUDE → ELECTRIC DREAMS → SOUTH OF HEAVEN, WEST OF HELL → the MILLION DOLLAR HOTEL → COYOTE UGLY → the LIFE AQUATIC WITH STEVE ZISSOU, George Armitage *(Billy the kid)*, **Country Joe McDONALD** *(AM radio)*

Storyline: A poisonous gas is mistakenly released into the atmosphere and everyone in the world over 25 years of age is killed. Oh dear. Coel and Cilla survive and decide to head for a hippie utopia in darkest New Mexico. On their travels they encounter various post-apocalyptic oddballs and eccentrics and find their lives at risk from a fearsome football team out for women and plunder. *JZ*

Movie rating: *3.5

Visual: dvd

Off the record: Robert Corff (see below)

—

Various Artists (composer: BARRY MELTON) *(vocals by ROBERT CORFF *)*

Dec 70. (lp; stereo/mono) *A.I.R.; <ST-A 1038>* [ ] [–]
– I'm looking for a world (*) / First time, last time (the GOURMET'S DELIGHT) / Please don't bury my soul (*) / Cry a little (JOHNNY & THE TORNADOS) / Maybe it really wasn't love (*) / Juke box serenade (JOHNNY & THE TORNADOS) / Castles (JOHNNY & THE TORNADOS) / World that we all dreamed of (*) / Today is where (the GOURMET'S DELIGHT) / Don't chase me around (*) / The Pueblo pool (JOHNNY & THE TORNADOS) / Gas man (JOHNNY & THE TORNADOS) / Got to get movin' (*) / Bubble gum girl (JOHNNY & THE TORNADOS) / This is the beginning (*).

S/track review: The one thing that probably holds this curio together is BARRY MELTON, songwriter extraordinaire and second in command of the legendary Country Joe & The Fish. MELTON is behind most of the songs here, several for star of the show, ROBERT CORFF (ex-Purple Gang) and roughly the same amount for Country Joe/Fish splinter outfit, JOHNNY & THE TORNADOS (featuring MELTON himself, GREG DEWEY,

MARK KAPNER and DOUG METZLER). The aforementioned CORFF had just been released from 'Hair' duties on Broadway (and by all accounts his 'GAS-S-S!' mop-top was looking rather fetching), when he was chosen by cult director Roger Corman to become youthful hippie leader, Coel. Sounding rather Jagger-esque on the opening, 'I'm Looking For A World', CORFF also plied a sort of soulful rock to several other MELTON-penned numbers, 'Please Don't Bury My Soul', 'Maybe It Really Wasn't Love', 'Don't Chase Me Around', 'Got To Get Movin'' and the LP's highlight 'This Is The Beginning'; also of note is his rendition of Country Joe McDonald's 'World That We All Dreamed Of'. The eclectic JOHNNY & THE TORNADOS instrumental trips consist of the funky 'Cry A Little', the comedic 'Juke Box Serenade', the laid-back 'Castles', the MELTON-only-penned, Zeppelin/'Bron-Y-Aur'-like 'The Pueblo Pool', the hard-rockin' 'Gas Man' and the organic 'Bubble Gum Girl' – phew!. Most of the tracks featured (many of them under the 2-minute mark!) don't quite get underway for this reviewer and therefore become quite a novelty. Of the CORFF cuts, lyrically, they were too contrived, and one cannot leave without mentioning obscure female act, the GOURMET'S DELIGHT (led by T. BROWN), who supplied two short'n'sweet harmony-versus-piano songs, 'First Time, Last Time' & 'Today Is Where'. *MCS*

Album rating: *3.5

□ Crystal GAYLE segment
(⇒ ONE FROM THE HEART)

GEORGIA

1995 (US 117m) CiBy 2000 / Miramax Films (R)

Film genre: Pop music-based domestic drama

Top guns: dir: Ulu Grosbard ← WHO IS HARRY KELLERMAN AND WHY IS HE SAYING THOSE TERRIBLE THINGS ABOUT ME? / s-w: Barbara Turner

Stars: Jennifer Jason Leigh *(Sadie Flood)* ← RUSH ← LAST EXIT TO BROOKLYN ← FAST TIMES AT RIDGEMONT HIGH, **Mare Winningham** *(Georgia)* ← MIRACLE MILE ← SHY PEOPLE ← ONE-TRICK PONY, Ted Levine *(Jake)*, *Max Perlich (Axel)* ← SHAKE, RATTLE & ROCK! tv ← RUSH, **John DOE** *(Bobby)*, John C. Reilly *(Herman)* → BOOGIE NIGHTS → MAGNOLIA → TENACIOUS D: THE PICK OF DESTINY → WALK HARD: THE DEWEY COX STORY, **Jimmy Witherspoon** *(trucker)*, Jason Carter *(Chasman)*, Tom Bower *(Erwin Flood)*, **Smokey Hormel** *(Leland)*, Bill Johns *(promoter)* → *SLAVES TO THE UNDERGROUND*

Storyline: Sadie dreams of being a music star like her elder, C&W singer, Georgia. Unfortunately, envy and ambition don't always lead to success and Sadie is left turning to other rock'n'roll problems such as booze and drugs. "The toughest act to follow was their dreams" *MCS*

Movie rating: *6

Visual: dvd on Miramax Classics

Off the record: Jimmy Witherspoon (b.18 Aug'21, Gurdon, Arkansas) was the legendary post-war blues singer (he had roles in 'The Black Godfather' 1974 and 'To Sleep With Anger' 1990). He recorded for numerous labels in the 40s culminating with his best loved hit, 'Ain't Nobody's Business (parts 1 & 2)' in 1949. With blues out of the limelight for a period in the 50s, Witherspoon found his way back the following decade, the ANIMALS' Eric Burdon (whom he subsequently recorded an album, 'Guilty' in 1973), giving him the respect he deserved. Sadly, Jimmy died on the 18th September, 1997, in L.A. **Smokey Hormel** is better known for his multi-instrumentalist session work (Beck, Tom Waits, Johnny Cash, etc.) – see future edition.. *MCS*

—

JENNIFER JASON LEIGH * & MARE WINNINGHAM **
& Various others (score: J. STEVEN SOLES ***)

Jun 96. (cd) *Discovery-WEA; <0603 10881-2>* □ □
– Hard times (**) / Ain't nobody's business (JIMMY WITHERSPOON) / There she goes again (JOHN DOE) / Almost blue (*) / Sally can't dance (JOHN DOE & *) / Optimistic voices (JOHN DOE & *) / Yosel yosel (*) / I'll be your mirror (*, JOHN DOE & SMOKEY HORMEL) / Arizona moon (RANCH ROMANCE) / If I wanted (** & *) / Mercy (**, *** & KEN STRINGFELLOW) / Take me back (*) / Midnight train to Georgia (*) / Hard times (*).

S/track review: This is no Georgia peach by any stretch of the imagination. 'GEORGIA' is the good, the bad and the ugly of soundtracks and Morricone is nowhere to be found. The good comes courtesy of actress-turned-singer, MARE WINNINGHAM (does anyone recall 'The Gong Show' in '76), who opens the album with the excellently-executed, Stephen Foster-penned country song, 'Hard Times'. The bad comes by way of mostly anything JENNIFER JASON LEIGH attempts, and if proof be needed sample her part (alongside JOHN DOE) on Lou Reed's 'Sally Can't Dance' & 'I'll Be Your Mirror', Steinberg's 'Yosel Yosel', Van Morrison's lengthy 'Take Me Back', James D Weatherly's 'Midnight Train To Georgia' and her own rendition of 'Hard Times'; she just about gets away with it on her whispering version of Elvis Costello's 'Almost Blue'. Yes, the screen sisters were doing it for themselves (especially on dual cut, 'If I Wanted'), but all live and uncut, maybe it was a bit too much of a gamble by producer, J Steven Soles. There's one good thing, JJL makes Velvet Underground chanteuse, Nico, quite excellent. Of the other tracks, JIMMY WITHERSPOON croaks a bit on 'Ain't Nobody's Business', RANCH ROMANCE breathe a bit fresh air into Jo Miller's 'Arizona Moon', while 'Mercy' is down to WINNINGHAM, SOLES and a Big Star Posie, KEN STRINGFELLOW. Oh, and by the way, there's no ugly unless you count JOHN DOE on his punk version of Lou Reed's 'There She Goes Again' – stagedoor left presumably as there was no sign of LEIGH. *MCS*

Album rating: *3.5

GERACAO BENDITA

trans: 'Blessed Generation' – 1973 title 'E ISSO AI BICHO'

1971 (Braz 90m*) Meldy Filmes Ltda.

Film genre: romantic comedy drama

Top guns: dir: Carlos Bini / s-w: Carl Kohler

Stars: Rita de Cassia *(Sonia)*, Carlos Bini *(Carlos)*, Charlote Garcia *(Sonia's mother)*, Sebastiao Goncalves *(Paolo)*, Carl Kohler, Carlos Doady, Jao Carlos Teixeira

Storyline: Carlos is a moustachio'd lawyer who rebels against the boredom and humdrum of everyday living, and joins a hippie commune. He falls for the sultry Sonia, although he has to share her with her dim-witted fiancé, Paolo – a love and peace triangle of sorts! This was indeed "the first Brazilian hippie movie" – don't ask me what was the second or the last. *MCS*

Movie rating: *4

Visual: none

Off the record: SPECTRUM were initiated by Fernando Gomes Correa Jr and his brother Ramon, under the wing of a hippie commune around 1967 in Nova Friburgo, a city in the state of Rio De Janeiro. While still at school, they found two other musicians (Jose Luiz Caetano Da Silva and Nando) with similar interests in rock music and they began practicing and rehearsing, at first at home, then in their school. During rehearsals, Ramon (who wore a dental brace) was given an electric shock after touching the microphone; the name 2000 Volts was quickly adapted. The addition of Caetano's brother Tiao (to replace ill Ramon), and a little later, Serginho (there was no Nando at this point) saw the band adopting the name of SPECTRUM – Brazilian psychedelia was finally born. It was at this stage that Toby (alias Jose Carlos

Correa Da Rocha) was drafted in for the departing Tiao, while additional member David John Giecco was invited into the fold to participate in the writing process of their new project, the movie 'GERACAO BENDITA'. *MCS*

——

SPECTRUM

1971. (lp) *TodoAmerica; <80005>* [–] Brazil [–]
– Quiabo's / Mother Nature / Trilha Antiga / Mary you are / Maria imaculada / Concerto do pantano / Pingo e letra / 15 years old / Tema de amor / Thank you my God / On my mind / A paz, o amor, voce. *<(cd-iss. Sep02 on 'Shadoks'; SHADOKS MUSIC 027)>*

S/track review: The history of this movie & soundtrack has been a lot clearer since its German CD issue over three decades on from the LP's original homeland release date of 1971. Filmed and recorded in parts of Rio, youngsters vocalist TOBY, lead guitarist CAETANO, bassist SERGINHO, drummer FERNANDO and DAVID (aka SPECTRUM) pieced together their post-'WOODSTOCK' attempt at living the South American dream of "peace, love and the age of Aquarius". Progressive rock had taken Europe by storm in the early 70s, however, across the pond, and more so south of the Mexican border, psychedelic rock was still in vogue. Opening salvo, 'Quiabo's', was a primeval example, a fuzz guitar frenzy and fusion of Steppenwolf or Hendrix jamming with the Mamas & The Papas. 'Mother Nature' (one of a handful of cues sung in English not Portuguese) showed their folky roots by way of Crosby, Stills & Nash, the Incredible String Band . . . one could go on forever. Acid rock was at the forefront during 'Trilha Antiga' (one of the many TOBY-FERNANDO compositions), the Beatles-esque harmonies here overshadowed by the squeaky vox of SPECTRUM's frontman. The missing link between the Beatles and Gorky's Zygotic Mynci or the Beta Band (also think Can, Aphrodite's Child, Brainticket), several of the songs such as 'Many You Are', 'Maria Imaculada', 'Thank You My God', 'Pingo E Letra' & 'On My Mind' (the latter virtually Lennon-McCartney's 'In My Life') are derivative of the early 70s era. On track 8, '15 Years Old', the wake-up call is complete courtesy of the loudest, f***ed up intro of all time, a song that could make Prog/Krautrock aficionados break out in a cold sweat. Slowing it all down, 'Tema De Amor', was tranquility personified, all peace and love and harmony without the hairspray. Closing track, 'A Paz, O Amor, Voce', is a celebratory sing-a-long of sorts (if you're Portuguese-Brazilian), and a nice and horizontal way to end proceedings. The downside to the album is that at only just under half an hour, it's a little short on running time. *MCS*

Album rating: *7

☐ GERRY & THE PACEMAKERS segment
(⇒ FERRY 'CROSS THE MERSEY)

GET CRAZY

1983 (US 92m) Rosebud Films (R)

Film genre: Pop-Rock Musical comedy/spoof

Top guns: dir: Allan Arkush ← ROCK'N'ROLL HIGH SCHOOL / → SHAKE, RATTLE & ROCK! tv → the TEMPTATIONS / s-w: Danny Opatoshu, Henry Rosenbaum, David Taylor

Stars: Malcolm McDowell *(Reggie Wanker)* ← the COMPLEAT BEATLES ← O LUCKY MAN! / → the DAVID CASSIDY STORY, Allen Garfield *(Max Wolfe)* ← ONE FROM THE HEART ← ONE-TRICK PONY ← NASHVILLE ← YOU'VE GOT TO WALK IT LIKE YOU TALK IT . . . ← the OWL AND THE PUSSYCAT / → DICK TRACY, Daniel Stern *(Neil Allen)* ← ONE-TRICK PONY, Gail Edwards *(Willy Loman)*, Miles Chapin *(Sammy Fox)* ← HAIR / → MAN ON THE MOON, Ed Begley Jr. *(Colin Beverly)* ← ELVIS: THE MOVIE ← RECORD CITY / → THIS IS SPINAL TAP → STREETS OF FIRE → EVEN COWGIRLS GET THE BLUES → a MIGHTY WIND, Stacy Nelkin *(Susie)*, **Bill Henderson** *(King Blues)* ← CORNBREAD, EARL AND ME ← TROUBLE MAN ← COOL BREEZE, **Lou REED** *(Auden)*, **Howard Kaylan** *(Capt. Cloud)* ← 200 MOTELS, **Lori Eastside** *(Nada)* ← DOWNTOWN 81, **Lee VING** *(Piggy)*, **John Densmore** *(Toad)* ← the DOORS ARE OPEN → DUDES → the DOORS → MESSAGE TO LOVE: THE ISLE OF WIGHT FESTIVAL, Anna Bjorn *(Chantamina)* ← MORE AMERICAN GRAFFITI, **Bobby Sherman** *(Mark)*, **FABIAN Forte** *(Marv)*, Franklyn Ajaye *(Cool)* ← the JAZZ SINGER ← CAR WASH / → QUEEN OF THE DAMNED, Mary Woronov *(Violetta)* ← ROCK'N'ROLL HIGH SCHOOL ← the VELVET UNDERGROUND AND NICO / → ROCK'N'ROLL HIGH SCHOOL FOREVER → DICK TRACY → SHAKE, RATTLE & ROCK! tv, Robert Picardo *(O'Connell)* → LEGEND, Paul Bartel *(Dr. Carver)* ← ROCK'N'ROLL HIGH SCHOOL / → BAJA OKLAHOMA → JOE'S APARTMENT, Barry Diamond *(stagehand)* → HOUSE PARTY → the FIVE HEARTBEARTS → HOUSE PARTY 2, Sam Laws *(minister)* ← TRUCK TURNER ← COOL BREEZE, Dick Miller *(Susie's dad)* ← ROCK'N'ROLL HIGH SCHOOL ← I WANNA HOLD YOUR HAND ← TRUCK TURNER ← the TRIP ← the WILD ANGELS ← WILD, WILD WINTER ← BEACH BALL ← SKI PARTY ← the GIRLS ON THE BEACH ← ROCK ALL NIGHT ← CARNIVAL ROCK / → SHAKE, RATTLE & ROCK! tv, Clint Howard *(usher)* ← ROCK'N'ROLL HIGH SCHOOL ← COTTON CANDY / → THAT THING YOU DO! → CURIOUS GEORGE, **Philo Cramer** *(Jews band)* ← the DECLINE OF WESTERN CIVILIZATION, Daniel Davies *(Jews band)* ← ROCK'N'ROLL HIGH SCHOOL, **Coati Mundi** *(Reggie's band)* <= KID CREOLE & THE COCONUTS =>, **Jonathan Melvoin** *(Reggie's band)*, **Derf Scratch** *(Reggie's band)* ← the SLOG MOVIE ← the DECLINE OF WESTERN CIVILIZATION / → DU-BEAT-E-O

Storyline: It's New Year's Eve 1982 and all is in readiness in the Saturn Theatre for the big concert – almost. In fact most of the musicians haven't arrived yet and the only people backstage are a dodgy drug dealer and a safety inspector who's threatening to close the place. Meanwhile, record producer Colin Beverley is determined to stop the show by fair means or foul, and by the looks of this shambles it shouldn't be too much of a problem for him. *JZ*

Movie rating: *6.5

Visual: video

Off the record: The **Bill Henderson** here is the Chicago jazz singer (b. 1926) not the better-know Chicago bluesman (b. 1930); **Howard Kaylan** (ex-Mothers Of Invention/Frank Zappa & ex-Turtles); **Lori Eastside & Coati Mundi** (both ex-Kid Creole & The Coconuts stalwarts); **Lee VING, Philo Cramer & Derf Scratch** (were of the Fear); **John Densmore** (ex-Doors); Santa Monica singer **Bobby Sherman** had a string of hits in the late 60s/early 70s including four Top 10s: 'Little Woman', 'La La La (If I Had You)', 'Easy Come, Easy Go' & 'Julie, Do Ya Love Me'. **Jonathan Melvoin** is the keyboard player with the Smashing Pumpkins & brother of Wendy (Wendy & Lisa). *MCS*

——

Various Cast/Artists (score: MICHAEL BODDICKER *)

1983. (lp) *Morocco – Motown; <6065CL>* [ ] [–]
– Get crazy (SPARKS) / You can't make me (LORI EASTSIDE & NADA) / Chop Suey (RAMONES) / It's only a movie (a.k.a. "but, but") (MARSHALL CRENSHAW) / Baby sister (LOU REED) / I'm not gonna take it (LORI EASTSIDE & NADA) / Hot shot (MALCOLM McDOWELL) / The blues had a baby and they named it rock & roll (BILL HENDERSON) / Hoochie coochie man (FEAR) / Starscape (*) / Auld lang syne (HOWARD KAYLAN & Cast).

S/track review: The old football cliché, "a game of two halves", is the perfect metaphor to describe the soundtrack to 'GET CRAZY'. SPARKS kick us off with the title track which is followed by 'You Can't Make Me' by LORI EASTSIDE & NADA, both are energetic synth-led pop songs that are surprisingly good. The pace is kept up by 'Chop Suey' from the RAMONES, a track that combines their abrasive punk sound with pop backing vocals to great effect, before MARSHALL CRENSHAW offers 'It's Only A Movie (a.k.a. "But, But")', which could easily be Roy Orbison playing at the Grand Ol' Opry. Side one is closed by arguably the best track on the album, which comes in the shape of LOU REED's 'Baby Sister', an acoustic-led semi-folk tune with the former Velvet Underground frontman's trademark monotone vocals. Unfortunately, it's now time to change sides with side two taking the form of a kind of live show. LORI EASTSIDE & NADA kick off with 'I'm Not Gonna Take It', a kind of Blondie-meets-Ronettes affair that picks up where the first side left off. It really goes downhill from there, with actor MALCOLM McDOWELL trying, and failing miserably, to sound like Alice Cooper on 'Hot Shot', while 'The Blues Had A Baby And They Named It Rock'n'Roll' by BILL HENDERSON (a faux blues track) is even worse than it sounds and manages to take every famous bluesman's name in vain. Punk band FEAR appear with a frankly awful version of 'Hoochie Coochie Man' before the album is finished off with a cringeworthy attempt (especially for a listening Scotsman) at 'Auld Lang Syne' sung by HOWARD KAYLAN & CAST (he of ex-Turtles fame). If you ever deign to buy this album then I would recommend you only pay half price because it only has one side worth listening to. *CM*

Album rating: *5

GET OVER IT!

2001 (US 87m) Miramax Films (PG-13)

Film genre: romantic Pop Musical teen comedy

Top guns: dir: Tommy O'Haver / s-w: R. Lee Fleming Jr.

Stars: Kirsten Dunst *(Kelly Woods / Helena)*, Ben Foster *(Berke Landers / Lysander)*, Melissa Sagemiller *(Allison McAllister / Hermia)*, **Sisqo** *(Dennis Wallace)*, Shane West *(Bentley "Striker" Scrumfield / Demetrius)*, Colin Hanks *(Felix Woods)*, Zoe Saldana *(Maggie)* ← CENTER STAGE / → TEMPTATION, Swoosie Kurtz *(Beverly Landers)*, Ed Begley Jr. *(Frank Landers)*, Martin Short *(Dr. Desmond Forrest Oates)*, **Carmen Electra** *(Mistress Moira)*, **Coolio** *(himself)* → the BEAT, **Colleen Fitzpatrick as Vitamin C** *(herself)*, **Shawn Fernandez** *(attendant/fairie)* → HONEY → HOW SHE MOVE

Storyline: Berke Landers suddenly becomes the centre of attention when he gets a date with the hottest chick in class, the alluring Allison. However she soon dumps Berke, but our lovestruck hero means to win her back. He hatches a cunning plan which sees him taking acting lessons from his friend's sister Kelly so that he can worm his way into the school play in which Allison is (of course) the leading lady. But when Berke finds himself "proclaiming true love" to Kelly in his lessons, he wonders if he might actually mean it. *JZ*

Movie rating: *6

Visual: dvd

Off the record: **Sisqo** (b. Mark Andrews, 9 Nov'78, Baltimore, Maryland, USA) was the leading light in R&B quartet, Dru Hill, who had several hits in the late 90s including 'In My Bed', 'Never Make A Promise', 'Tell Me', 'How Deep Is Your Love' & 'These Are The Times'. As a silver-haired solo star, he furthered his music credentials with 'The Thong Song'. **Carmen Electra** was actually a recording artist in 1992! while **Colleen Fitzpatrick** (aka singer Vitamin C) was in alt-rock act, Eve's Plum. *MCS*

—

Various Artists (score: Steve Bartek)

Mar 01. (cd) *Uptown – Universal; <(AA314 548693-2)>* [ ] May01 [ ]
– Get with me (SHORTY 101) / Sho' nuff (FATBOY SLIM) / Bingo bango (BASEMENT JAXX) / Another perfect day (AMERICAN HI-FI) / Perfect world (MIKAILA) / Alison (ELVIS COSTELLO & THE ATTRACTIONS) / The shining (BADLY DRAWN BOY) / Goldmine (CAVIAR) / Love will keep us together (CAPTAIN & TENNILLE) / Dream of me (KIRSTEN DUNST) / Arnoldo said (WONDERMINTS) / I'll never fall in love again (SPLITSVILLE) / Get on it (RESIDENT FILTERS) / Would you . . .? (TOUCH & GO) / That green Jesus (MR. NATURAL).

S/track review: There's no shortage of dance cues on show here, although there's the odd rock-pop dirge littered about. 'GET OVER IT' opens with a fairly successful stab at the big production pop of Britney Spears in the form of the horrendously named SHORTY 101's 'Get With Me', an achievement not replicated by 'Perfect World' which has MIKAILA overdoing the Britney-isms and ending up like Shakira; actress KIRSTEN DUNST surprisingly comes off better on the Disney-esque piano-ballad 'Dream Of Me'. The classic "bumpin' & thumpin'-Jeans On" dance beat of FATBOY SLIM's 'Sho' Nuff' and near-Pigbag retrogression of BASEMENT JAXX's 'Bingo Bango' shake it up somewhat, generating needed excitement all round. The listener has to wait to the very end for a trio of song-by-numbers dance by way of RESIDENT FILTER's 'Get On It', TOUCH AND GO's Big Beat/Euro hit 'Would You . . .?' (from 1998's 'I Find You Very Attractive'), and MR. NATURAL's dull 'That Green Jesus'. We take a sharp left turn with ELVIS COSTELLO & THE ATTRACTIONS' 'Alison' and the subtle lo-fi acoustic strum of BADLY DRAWN BOY on 'The Shining'. CAPTAIN & TENNILLE's jaunty 70s hit 'Love Will Keep Us Together' is then followed by the absolutely appalling Weezer-aping geek-rock of CAVIAR's 'Goldmine'. Sliding with ease into cool rock territory are Boston's "Flavor Of The Week" AMERICAN HI-FI and 'Another Perfect Day', whilst the WONDERMINTS' 'Arnoldo Said' is just plain bubblegum-pop and a bit smug. SPLITSVILLE offer up another unnecessary part-croon/part-power-pop take on Burt Bacharach and Hal David's classic 'I'll Never Fall In Love Again'. Ultimately, this is a collection of largely low quality and irksome offerings which due to its constant changing of genres lacks any identity. *LF*

Album rating: *5

GET RICH OR DIE TRYIN'

2005 (US 118m) MTV Films / Paramount Pictures (R)

Film genre: urban showbiz/music drama

Top guns: dir: Jim Sheridan / s-w: Terence Winter

Stars: Curtis '50 Cent' Jackson *(Marcus)* ← BEEF, Adewale Akinnuoye-Agbaje *(Majestic)*, Joy Bryant *(Charlene)* ← HONEY, Omar Benson Miller *(Keryl)* ← 8 MILE, Terrence Howard *(Bama)* ← HUSTLE & FLOW ← RAY ← GLITTER ← WHO'S THE MAN? ← the JACKSONS: AN AMERICAN DREAM / → IDLEWILD, Tory Kittles *(Justice)*, **Ashley Walters** *(Antwan)* → LIFE & LYRICS, Marc John Jeffries *(young Marcus)* ← BROWN SUGAR, Viola Davis *(grandma)*, Sullivan Walker *(grandpa)*, Bill Duke *(Levar)* ← CAR WASH, Leon *(Slim)* ← LITTLE RICHARD ← MR. ROCK'N'ROLL: THE ALAN FREED STORY ← the TEMPTATIONS ← the FIVE HEARTBEATS

Storyline: An autobiographical 'Cinderella with an Uzi' story of one young man Marcus (Curtis '50 Cent' Jackson) and his battle to turn his back on a life of pimping, hustling and drug dealing on the streets to take a shot of the million dollar rap game. He may fancy a change of career but his gangsta fraternity aren't so keen on letting him move on. *MR*

Movie rating: *5

Visual: dvd

Off the record: **Ashley Walters** is Asher D of London rappers So Solid Crew, and a child actor in Grange Hill (as Andy Phillips) way back in 1997. **50 CENT** (see below) *MCS*

—

Various Artists incl. 50 CENT (*) (score: Quincy Jones, Gavin Friday & Maurice Seezer)

Nov 05. (cd/lp) *Interscope; <56060-2/-2> (988799-2)* [2] [18]
– Hustlers ambition (*) / What if (*) / Things change (SPIDER LOC & * feat. LLOYD BANKS) / You already know (LLOYD BANKS & * feat. YOUNG BUCK) / When death becomes you (* & MOP) / Have a party (MOBB DEEP & * feat. NATE DOGG) / We both think alike (* & OLIVIA) / Don't need no help (YOUNG BUCK) / Get

low (LLOYD BANKS) / Fake love (TONY YAYO) / Window shopper (*) / Born alone, die alone (LLOYD BANKS) / You a shooter (MOBB DEEP & *) / I don't know officer (*, LLOYD BANKS, PRODIGY, SPIDER LOC & MA$E) / Talk about me (*) / When it rains it pours (*) / Cloud 9 (OLIVIA) / Best friend (*) / I'll whip ya head boy (* & YOUNG BUCK).

S/track review: It all seemed so straightforward on paper. The rags to riches rap fairytale had been done with considerable success and credibility by 50 CENT's mentor Eminem with '8 MILE' and in Craig Brewer's excellent 'HUSTLE & FLOW'. It seemed natural than that the protégé should be able to replicate the success with his own hard knock life story. What the movie and the subsequent soundtrack was missing one vital thing, humility. Where '8 MILE' was grimy and angry, but shot through with a ray of hope, 'GET RICH OR DIE TRYIN'' is just downright bleak. You can almost smell the brutal nihilism oozing from the CD. The frustration however, is that for the greater part of this album (not to be confused with 50 CENT's solo set of the same name in 2003) the bleaker the lyrics get, the better the music does. Swaying unsteadily between thunderous death marches ('I'll Whip Ya Head Boy', 'I Don't Know Officer') and lightweight, 70s-soul sampling G-funk grooves like 'Hustler's Ambition' and 'Window Shopper', the album is most successful when it is attempting to spark something truly itchy and funky from the bones of 70s mainstream soul of Barry White et al. 50 CENT's nine tracks showcase his trademark growl and addictive, high-sheen beats while cohorts LLOYD BANKS and YOUNG BUCK prove why they deserve to remain in the shadows with their ham-fisted metaphors. It is left to MOBB DEEP and SPIDER LOC to provide some real tension with three tracks of memorable, seedy swing Isaac Hayes would have been proud of. When Malcolm X declared he'd get things done "by any means necessary" you can be sure he didn't think his sentiment would be hijacked and applied to the gangsta rap movie world. 'GET RICH OR DIE TRYIN'' has some addictive grooves that go for the jugular but the overlying sentiment is that movies and their soundtracks sit among the commodities in any aspirant rap star's portfolio, between the signature sneakers ranges and energy drinks. *MR*

Album rating: *5

– spinoff hits, etc. –

50 CENT: Window Shopper / I'll Whip Ya Head Boy / Window Shopper – versions

Dec 05. (cd-s) *<(9888358)>* [20] Nov05 [11]

GET YOURSELF A COLLEGE GIRL

UK title 'The SWINGIN' SET'

1964 (US 86m) M.G.M. (PG)

Film genre: Pop/Rock Musical comedy

Top guns: dir: Sidney Miller / s-w: Robert E. Kent ← HOOTENANNY HOOT ← DON'T KNOCK THE TWIST ← TWIST AROUND THE CLOCK ← DON'T KNOCK THE ROCK ← ROCK AROUND THE CLOCK / → WHEN THE BOYS MEET THE GIRLS → the FASTEST GUITAR ALIVE → a TIME TO SING

Stars: Mary Ann Mobley *(Teresa 'Terry' Taylor)* → GIRL HAPPY → HARUM SCARUM, Chad Everett *(Gary Underwood)*, Joan O'Brien *(Marge Endicott)* ← IT HAPPENED AT THE WORLD'S FAIR, **Nancy Sinatra** *(Lynne)* → the GHOST IN THE INVISIBLE BIKINI → the WILD ANGELS → SPEEDWAY → MAYOR OF THE SUNSET STRIP, Chris Noel *(Sue Ann Mobley)* → GIRL HAPPY → BEACH BALL → WILD, WILD WINTER, Willard Waterman *(Senator Hubert Morrison)*, Hortense Petra *(Donna; the photographer)* ← KISSIN' COUSINS ← DON'T KNOCK THE TWIST / → YOUR CHEATIN' HEART → WHEN THE BOYS MEET THE GIRLS → HOLD ON! → RIOT ON SUNSET STRIP, **Freddie Bell & The Bellboys** *(themselves)*, **the ANIMALS:- Eric Burdon, Alan Price, Chas Chandler, John Steele, Hilton Valentine** *(performers)* / **the Standells:- Dick Dodd, John Fleck, Tony Valentino, Gary Lane, Larry Tamblyn** *(performers)* → RIOT ON SUNSET STRIP, **Stan Getz** *(performer)*, **Astrud Gilberto** *(performer)*, **Jimmy Smith Trio** *(performers)*, **Dave Clark Five:- Dave Clark, Mike Smith, etc.** *(performers)* → CATCH US IF YOU CAN, Roberta Linn *(herself)*, Dorothy Neumann *(Miss Martha Stone)* ← LOOKING FOR LOVE ← HOT ROD GANG ← CARNIVAL ROCK, **Donnie Brooks** *(Donnie)* → a SWINGIN' SUMMER, James Millhollin *(Gordon)* → the COOL ONES, Percy Helton *(senator's chauffeur)* ← WHERE THE BOYS ARE ← JAILHOUSE ROCK ← SHAKE, RATTLE AND ROCK! / → HEAD

Storyline: Poor Terry finds herself expelled from college when she is exposed as the culprit behind some saucy songs which she writes in her spare time. She promptly heads off to a ski resort where she meets sleazy senator, Hubert Morrison, who wants to meet the ski set and attract the "youth" vote. Can Terry and the senator use each other to achieve their aims or will they just head off on the piste? *JZ*

Movie rating: *3.5

Visual: video + dvd

Off the record: (see below)

Various Artists (composer: Freddy Karger)

Dec 64. (lp) *M.G.M.; <E/SE 4273> (MGM-C 8012)* [ ] 1966 [ ]
– Whenever you're around (the DAVE CLARK FIVE) / Girl from Ipanema (STAN GETZ & ASTRUD GILBERTO) / Around and around (the ANIMALS) / The sermon (JIMMY SMITH TRIO) / Get yourself a college girl (MARY ANN MOBLEY) / Bony Moronie (the STANDELLS) / Thinking of you baby (the DAVE CLARK FIVE) / Sweet rain (STAN GETZ) / Blue feeling (the ANIMALS) / Comin' home Johnny (JIMMY SMITH TRIO) / Talkin' about love (FREDDIE BELL with ROBERTA LINN & THE BELL BOYS) / The swim (the STANDELLS).

S/track review: The mid-60s spawned a handful of Rock musicals featuring various pop acts: 'GONKS GO BEAT', 'EVERY DAY'S A HOLIDAY' & 'WHERE THE BOYS ARE' – to name but a few. None of them outstanding by any stretch of the imagination. 'GET YOURSELF A COLLEGE GIRL' (a poorly received movie!) was another in a lengthy conveyor belt of youth-infused films that spread the word of popular music. Split into two camps (maybe three), this soundtrack is part R&B-pop, part lounge-jazz. The DAVE CLARK FIVE (having already picked up "Bits And Pieces" of awards) kicked off the record with a Beatles-ish love ballad, 'Whenever You're Around', although they get back into top gear via another original, 'Thinking Of You Baby'. Chalk and cheese-like, track 2 on the LP, 'The Girl From Ipanema' by saxophonist STAN GETZ & singer ASTRUD GILBERTO, exudes class from the very first note to the last – a sort of "GETZ Yourself Astrud GILBERTO" (if only). If cool, laid back and sophisticated was your bag, more of the GETZ man himself was on show via perfect cinematic track, 'Sweet Rain', a precursor to Tortoise and Trans Am – one thinks. While GETZ was behind one of the great jazz soundtracks that year, 'MICKEY ONE', another jazz dude, Hammond-playing JIMMY SMITH was responsible for 'la METAMORPHOSE DES CLOPORTES' around the same time. The JIMMY SMITH TRIO delivered two scorching, Booker T-ish instrumentals, 'The Sermon' & 'Comin' Home Johnny', the latter an arrangement of the traditional tune 'When Johnny Comes Marching Home'. The Rock party was underway again with the ANIMALS' rendition of Chuck Berry's 'Around And Around' (although the song was overturned by the 'Stones first!). You just couldn't fault BURDON and the boys as they upstaged all and sundry on a second R&B gem, Jimmy Henshaw's 'Blue Feeling'. US garage act and soon to be hitmakers with 'Dirty Water', the STANDELLS donated their interpretation of Larry Williams' 'Bony Moronie' (sounding more DC5 than the DC5!) & lead guitarist Larry Tamblyn's 'The Swim' (very 'Twist And Shout'). MARY ANN MOBLEY (Miss America 1959) displayed her vocal charms on the Fred Karger/S. Miller title song, although why she had to tell us that "S.E.X. spells sex" is anyone's guess. Penultimate ' . . .COLLEGE GIRL' number, 'Talkin' About Love', saw Stateside golden oldie FREDDIE BELL – who'd charted in the UK 1956 with 'Giddy-Up-A Ding Dong' – team up with ROBERTA LINN & THE BELL BOYS to put the bop back into rock. All'n'all, most of the tracks here have stood the test of time – 40-odd years and counting . . . *MCS*

Album rating: *7

the GHOST GOES GEAR

1967 (UK 79m) Associated British-Pathe Limited

Film genre: Pop/Rock Musical comedy

Top guns: s-w: (+ dir) Hugh Gladwish → CUCUMBER CASTLE (+ story), Roger Dunton (+ story)

Stars: the Spencer Davis Group:- Spencer Davis + Muff Winwood *(performer)* ← POP GEAR / → HERE WE GO ROUND THE MULBERRY BUSH, **Steve Winwood** *(performer)* → CUCUMBER CASTLE → GLASTONBURY FAYRE → WOODSTOCK 94 → BLUES BROTHERS 2000 → RED, WHITE & BLUES, **Pete York** *(performer)* → HERE WE GO ROUND THE MULBERRY BUSH, Nicholas Parsons *(Algernon Rowthorpe Plumley)* ← EVERY DAY'S A HOLIDAY, Sheila White *(Polly)* → HERE WE GO ROUND THE MULBERRY BUSH → MRS. BROWN, YOU'VE GOT A LOVELY DAUGHTER → CONFESSIONS OF A POP PERFORMER → SILVER DREAM RACER, Jack Haig *(old Edwards)*, **Lorne Gibson** *(ghost/performer)*, Arthur Howard *(vicar)*, Joan Ingram *(Lady Rowthorpe)*, Tony Sympson *(Lord Plumley)*, **Acker Bilk** *(performer)* ← IT'S ALL OVER TOWN ← IT'S TRAD, DAD!, **Dave Berry** *(performer)*, **Sue Bell/the Three Bells** *(performers)*, **M6** *(performers)*

Storyline: Fictitious manager of the Spencer Davis Group, Algernon, inherits a haunted house, although renovating the run down property will require a lot of money – money they haven't got. After seeing that the abode has several uninvited ghosts, the group come up with an idea to charge admission; the ghouls have different ideas. *MCS*

Movie rating: *4.5

Visual: dvd (no audio OST)

Off the record: the Spencer Davis Group subsequently performed and composed some of the tracks for the film, 'HERE WE GO ROUND THE MULBERRY BUSH' (1967). **Lorne Gibson** (b. 1940, Edinburgh, Scotland) had a string of UK singles; he died on 12th May 2003. **Acker Bilk** was the man behind clarinet classic, 'Stranger On The Shore', while **Dave Berry** was responsible for three UK Top 5 hits, 'The Crying Game' (later used for the film of the same name in 1992), 'Little Things' and 'Mama'; he was last seen on the revival circuit. Other acts included **the Three Bells + M6 + St. Louis Union** *MCS*

the GHOST IN THE INVISIBLE BIKINI

1966 sequel-6 (US 82m) American International Pictures

Film genre: beach movie fantasy/comedy

Top guns: dir: Don Weis ← PAJAMA PARTY ← LOOKING FOR LOVE / s-w: Louis M. Heyward ← PAJAMA PARTY, Elwood Ullman ← TICKLE ME

Stars: Tommy Kirk *(Chuck Phillips)* ← PAJAMA PARTY / → IT'S A BIKINI WORLD → CATALINA CAPER, Deborah Walley *(Lili Morton)* ← SKI PARTY ← BEACH BLANKET BINGO / → SPINOUT → IT'S A BIKINI WORLD, Aron Kincaid *(Bobby)* ← BEACH BALL ← SKI PARTY ← the GIRLS ON THE BEACH, Quinn O'Hara *(Sinistra)* ← a SWINGIN' SUMMER, Jesse White *(J. Sinister Hulk)* ← PAJAMA PARTY ← LOOKING FOR LOVE ← COUNTRY MUSIC HOLIDAY / → NASHVILLE GIRL, Harvey Lembeck *(Eric Von Zipper)* ← HOW TO STUFF A WILD BIKINI ← BEACH BLANKET BINGO ← PAJAMA PARTY ← BIKINI BEACH ← BEACH PARTY / → HELLO DOWN THERE, **Nancy Sinatra** *(Vicki)* ← GET YOURSELF A COLLEGE GIRL / → the WILD ANGELS → SPEEDWAY → MAYOR OF THE SUNSET STRIP, Basil Rathbone *(Reginald Ripper)*, Boris Karloff *(the corpse; Hiram Stokely)* ← BIKINI BEACH, Piccola Pupa *(Piccola)*, Bobbi Shaw *(Princess Yolanda)* ← HOW TO STUFF A WILD BIKINI ← SKI PARTY ← BEACH BLANKET BINGO ← PAJAMA PARTY / → PIPE DREAMS, Claudia Martin *(Lulu)*, Luree Holmes *(Luree)* ← HOW TO STUFF A WILD BIKINI ← SKI PARTY ← BEACH BLANKET BINGO ← PAJAMA PARTY ← MUSCLE BEACH PARTY ← BEACH PARTY / → THUNDER ALLEY → the TRIP, Susan Hart *(Cecily; the ghost)* ← PAJAMA PARTY ← RIDE THE WILD SURF, Salli Sachse *(Salli)* ← HOW TO STUFF A WILD BIKINI ← SKI PARTY ← BEACH BLANKET BINGO ← PAJAMA PARTY ← BIKINI BEACH ← MUSCLE BEACH PARTY / → THUNDER ALLEY → the TRIP → WILD IN THE STREETS, other "Beach Party" trippers:- Mary Hughes, Ed Garner, Alberta Nelson, Andy Romano, Patti Chandler, Frank Alesia, Sue Hamilton, **the Bobby Fuller Four:- Bobby Fuller, Randy Fuller, DeWayne Quirico, Jim Reese** *(performers)*

Storyline: The ghost in question being Cecily, who must help the newly-dead Hiram get into Heaven within 24 hours (oh hell!). Hiram decides to help his heirs and their beach pals from being swindled by lawyer Reginald Ripper and his henchman. Meanwhile, bozo biker Eric von Zipper drags his knuckles into the sand for a piece of the action, and the scene is set for a big showdown at the pool party, with plenty of wine and spirits. *JZ*

Movie rating: *2

Visual: dvd dbl feature (no audio OST; score Les Baxter)

Off the record: All songs stemmed from the pens of Guy Hemric & Jerry Styner: 'Geronimo' (NANCY SINATRA), 'Stand Up And Fight' (PICCOLA PUPA), 'Don't Try To Fight It Baby' (QUINN O'HARA), 'Make The Music Pretty' & 'Swing A-Ma Thing' (the BOBBY FULLER FOUR). **Bobby Fuller** himself was murdered on the 18th June, 1966, found in his car stabbed to death and doused in petrol – the police initially thought it suicide! ('I Fought The Law', indeed). Claudia Martin was the daughter of actor/crooner Dean Martin. *MCS*

G.I. BLUES

1960 (US 104m) Paramount Pictures (PG)

Film genre: pop/rock musical drama

Top guns: dir: Norman Taurog → BLUE HAWAII → GIRLS! GIRLS! GIRLS! → IT HAPPENED AT THE WORLD'S FAIR → TICKLE ME → SPINOUT → DOUBLE TROUBLE → SPEEDWAY → LIVE A LITTLE, LOVE A LITTLE / s-w: Edmund Beloin, Henry Garson

Stars: Elvis PRESLEY *(Tulsa McLean)*, Juliet Prowse *(Lili)*, Robert Ivers *(Cookey)*, Leticia Roman *(Tina)*, Sigrid Maier *(Maria)*, James Douglas *(Rick)*, Arch Johnson *(Sgt. McGraw)* ← the BUDDY HOLLY STORY, Jeremy Slate *(Turk)* → GIRLS! GIRLS! GIRLS!, Kenneth Becker *(Mack)* ← LOVING YOU / → GIRLS! GIRLS! GIRLS! → ROUSTABOUT, Beach Dickerson *(Warren)* ← LOVING YOU ← ROCK ALL NIGHT / → the TRIP → the SAVAGE SEVEN, **the Jordanaires** *(performers)* ← COUNTRY MUSIC HOLIDAY / → KID GALAHAD

Storyline: Tulsa Mclean is a guitar-toting American soldier stationed in the then West Germany. He persuades one of his superiors to put some money into a nightclub, and wagers that he can ensnare cabaret singer Lili, whom he subsequently ends up falling in love with. *BG*

Movie rating: *5

Visual: video + dvd

Off the record: The **Jordanaires** were of course backing musicians of Elvis.

ELVIS PRESLEY (composers: Joseph Lilley, etc.)

Oct 60. (lp) *R.C.A.; <LSP 2256> (RD 27192)(SF 5078)* 1 Dec60 1
– Tonight is so right for love / What's she really like / Frankfurt special / Wooden heart / G.I. blues / Pocketful of rainbows / Shoppin' around / Big boots / Didja' ever / Blue suede shoes / Doin' the best I can. *(re-iss. Sep77; same)* – (hit UK No.14) *(re-iss. Aug81 on 'RCA Int.'; INTS 5104) (re-iss. Jan84 lp/c; NL/NK 83735) (cd-iss. Oct87; ND 83735) <(cd-iss. Feb98 +=; 07863 66960-2)>* – (alternate bonus tracks). *(lp re-mast.Sep01 on 'Castle'++=; ELVIS 106)* – (bonus 7"ep).

S/track review: Dissing German food and raving about "frantic frauleins", the ELVIS of 'G.I. BLUES' is the archetypal American soldier in Europe, singing equally clichéd, featherweight material. While an underwhelming sign of things to come, this was PRESLEY's first post-war flick and it's to his credit that he manages to rescue – with his ever impressive voice and gutsy delivery – much of the soundtrack from easy-listening oblivion. Having had its definitive version recorded three years earlier, 'Blue Suede Shoes' doesn't really count although it's still the best thing here by a country mile. The Bert Kaempfert- inspired 'Wooden Heart' maintains a certain mawkish charm, and remains essential listening if only for the surreal sound of the King singing in German. ELVIS also brings a dreamy charm to 'Pocketful Of Rainbows' and a genuine tenderness to Doc Pomus/Mort Shuman's 'Doin' The Best I Can', where JIMMIE HASKELL's accordion affords a vaguely Tex-Mex feel. *BG*

Album rating: *5.5

– spinoff releases, etc. –

ELVIS PRESLEY: Wooden Heart / Tonight Is So Right For Love

Mar 61. (7") *(RCA 1226)* – 1
(re-iss. May77; PB 2700) – (hit UK No.49 Aug77)

ELVIS PRESLEY: G.I. Blues – The Alternate Takes

Feb 82. (7"ep) *(RCX 1)* –
– Shoppin' around / Big boots / Frankfurt special / Tonight's all right for love.

ELVIS PRESLEY: G.I. Blues – The Alternate Takes Vol.2

Oct 82. (7"ep) *(RCX 2)* –

ELVIS PRESLEY: Wooden Heart / Puppet On A String

Feb 05. (cd-s) *Sony-BMG; (82876 66661-2)* – 2
(10"+=) *(82876 66661-1)* – Tonight Is So Right For Love.

☐ Alex GIBSON segment
(⇒ SUBURBIA)

GIRL

1998 (US 99m) HSX Films / Kushner-Locke Company (18)

Film genre: romantic coming-of-age/teen drama

Top guns: dir: Jonathan Kahn / s-w: David E. Tolchinsky)nov: Blake Nelson)

Stars: Dominique Swain *(Andrea Marr)*, Sean Patrick Flanery *(Todd Sparrow)* → OVERNIGHT → 30 DAYS UNTIL I'M FAMOUS, Summer Phoenix *(Rebecca Fernhurst)* → SLC PUNK! → COMMITTED, Tara Reid *(Cybil)* → DR. T & THE WOMEN → JOSIE AND THE PUSSYCATS, Selma Blair *(Darcy)* → STORYTELLING; Channon Roe *(Kevin)* → PSYCHO BEACH PARTY, Portia di Rossi *(Carla Sparrow)*, David Moscow *(Greg)* → HONEY, Bodhi Elfman *(Derek)*, Jay R. Ferguson *(Parker Blackman)* ← PINK AS THE DAY SHE WAS BORN, John Philbin *(Mr. Jones)* ← SHY PEOPLE ← the RETURN OF THE LIVING DEAD, Adam Scott *(Scott)* → WHO LOVES THE SUN, Clea Duvall *(Gillian)* → A SLIPPING-DOWN LIFE → COMMITTED → the SLAUGHTER RULE, James Karen *(dad)* ← the RETURN OF THE LIVING DEAD ← the JAZZ SINGER

Storyline: Bright teenager Andrea discovers there's more to life than schoolbooks and study periods, and plunges headlong into the Washington club scene. Here she finds life very different from classes as she encounters weird and wonderful people, some of whom even dye their hair! She begins a flighty affair with rock singer Todd Sparrow to speed up her coming of age, but relationships count for little if you're a new groupie in the big bad world of the music industry. *JZ*

Movie rating: *5.5

Visual: dvd (no audio OST; score: Michael Tavera)

Off the record: Bodhi Elfman is the son of Richard Elfman and the nephew of Danny Elfman, both formerly of 80s New Wave act, Oingo Bongo, the latter also one of the top modern day film composers. Tracks on the soundtrack are as follows:- 'I Will Arrive' (MELISSA FERRICK), 'Ever So So' (OPERATOR), 'Declan (Man Of Mystery)' (the MITCHENERS), 'Into The Cloud Forest' (BRAIN GARDEN), 'Which Way' (MAGNET), 'Forget The World' (the HIPPOS), 'She's So Cool' (JEFFRIES FAN CLUB), 'I Can't Catch You' (SIXPENCE NONE THE RICHER), 'Never (aka Cybil's Song)' (CROOKED TOM), 'Stealing Away' (FOAMILAYE), "The Way That I Feel' (FLO 13), 'L.I.N.U.S.' (JFT), 'I Walk The Mole' (the MOLES), 'One More Time' (JEFFRIES FAN CLUB), 'Farewell' (the SMOOTHS), 'Who's Got The Yea-yo' (the BEERNUTS), 'Solid' (POWERMAN 5000), 'We Have Forgotten' (SIXPENCE NONE THE RICHER), 'Blood Brothers' (MIKE PARNELL), 'One Step Forward' (the JON KAHN BAND), 'Girl' (the JON KAHN BAND), 'Beast In The Joungle' (the JON KAHN BAND), 'Refuge' (the JON KAHN BAND), 'Look My Way' (JON KAHN BAND), 'Strange' (CROOKED TOM), 'Rations' (CROOKED TOM), 'Evil Ways' (CROOKED TOM), 'Stand In Line' (CROOKED TOM) & 'History's Burning' (the SMOOTHS). *MCS*

the GIRL CAN'T HELP IT

1956 (US 97m) 20th Century Fox (U)

Film genre: Rock'n'roll Musical comedy

Top guns: s-w: Frank Tashlin (+ dir), Herbert Baker → LOVING YOU → KING CREOLE → the JAZZ SINGER (story 'Do Re Mi' by Garson Kanin)

Stars: Jayne Mansfield *(Jerri Jordan)* → LAS VEGAS HILLBILLYS, Tom Ewell *(Tom Miller)*, Edmond O'Brien *(Marty Murdock)* → SING BOY SING, Henry Jones *(Mousie)* → DICK TRACY, John Emery *(Wheeler)*, Juanita Moore *(Hilda)* → UP TIGHT! → the MACK, plus **Julie London** *(performer)*, **Ray Anthony** *(performer)*, **Barry Gordon** *(performer)*, **LITTLE RICHARD** *(performer)*, **Fats DOMINO** *(performer)*, **Eddie Cochran** *(performer)* → UNTAMED YOUTH → HOT ROD GANG → GO, JOHNNY, GO! → BLUE SUEDE SHOES → the COMPLEAT BEATLES, **Eddie Fontaine** *(performer)*, **Nino Tempo** *(performer)* → BOP GIRL, **Abbey Lincoln** *(performer)*, **Johnny Olenn** *(performer)*, **Gene Vincent & The Blue Caps** *(performers)* → HOT ROD GANG → IT'S TRAD, DAD! → LIVE IT UP → BLUE SUEDE SHOES → NO DIRECTION HOME, **the Platters** *(performers)* ← ROCK AROUND THE CLOCK / → CARNIVAL ROCK → ROCK ALL NIGHT, **the Treniers** *(performers)*, **the Chuckles** *(performers)*, **Teddy Randazzo** *(performer)* → ROCK, ROCK, ROCK! → MISTER ROCK AND ROLL → HEY, LET'S TWIST

Storyline: Theatrical agent Tom is hired by mob boss Murdock to promote his voluptuous girlfriend Jerri. A slight complication arises when Jerri turns out to be completely useless on stage and instead wants to be a housewife. Tom informs Murdock who threatens to shoot him unless he somehow gets Jerri to sing his prison hit 'Rock Around The Rockpile' at his club. And things get worse when Tom and Jerri stop playing cat and mouse with each other and fall in love. *JZ*

Movie rating: *6

Visual: video + dvd

Off the record: (see below)

—

Various (composers: Lionel Newman / BOBBY TROUP)

Nov 56. (lp) *Capitol; <EAP1 823>* –
– The girl can't help it (LITTLE RICHARD) / Rock around the rockpile (BOBBY TROUP) / Cry me a river (JULIE LONDON) / Be-bop-a-lula (GENE VINCENT & THE BLUE CAPS) / You'll never never know (the PLATTERS) / She's got it (LITTLE RICHARD) / You

got it made (BOBBY TROUP) / Cool it baby (EDDIE FONTAINE) / Tempo's tempo (NINO TEMPO) / Rockin' is our business (the TRENIERS) / Blue Monday (FATS DOMINO). *(cd-iss. May92 on 'E.M.I.'+=; CDGO 2037)* – Big band boogie (RAY ANTHONY) / I wish I could shimmy like my sister Kate (ARMAND PIRON) / Spread the word (ABBEY LINCOLN) / Twenty flight rock (EDDIE COCHRAN).

S/track review: If you had to mention only one rock'n'roll movie of the 50s, 'The GIRL CAN'T HELP IT' would have to be your choice. Featuring no less than eleven cameos from the world of 50s pop music, it's definitely the business. Where better to start than with LITTLE RICHARD and the title track. Written by BOBBY TROUP, a one-time husband of JULIE LONDON (who also features in the movie with the sultry jazz ballad, 'Cry Me A River'), the song was a Top 50 hit. 'The GIRL CAN'T HELP IT' conjured up the appropriate lurid suggestion for the pink-gowned singer, who also delivers two other rollickin' tracks to the film, 'Reddy Teddy' and 'She's Got It' (although not for the LP). NINO TEMPO (future hitmaker with 'Deep Purple') provides the only instrumental in the film, with his rather simple but very exotic 'Tempo's Tempo'. Heavily influenced by Louis Prima's famous backing band of the time, Sam Butera's Witnesses, the track has cool. EDDIE FONTAINE gives us 'Cool It Baby', a fine example of the more "socially acceptable" white rock'n'roll of the time and penned in the mould of another rock'n'roller, Bill Haley. Rockabilly was also in vogue around this time, and GENE VINCENT & THE BLUE CAPS were without doubt thee band to 'Be-Bop A Lula' to. His old mucker EDDIE COCHRAN also provided one song to the soundtrack, but his minor hit 'Twenty Flight Rock' would go on to be one of the most important songs in the history of modern music. The TRENIERS tell us that 'Rockin' Is Our Business', and although the song has some nice honkin' sax solos, it seems somewhat contrived at times. FATS DOMINO was already a major recording star when he had a hit with his superb 'Blue Monday', a rolling blues track, a record which is a perfect example of the New Orleans sound that FATS still performs to this day. The PLATTERS, meanwhile, were one of the most commercially successful of all doo-wop vocal groups, and their 'You'll Never Never Know' highlights Buck Ram's entrancing vocal. In addition to all the aforementioned tracks, there are several performances, which were included in the film, but omitted on the "songs from the film" CD released in the early 90s by 'E.M.I.'. The CHUCKLES accordion-driven pop track, 'Cinnamon Sinner' is one, ABBEY LINCOLN'S monumental 'Spread The Word, Spread The Gospel' is another. Three performances of 'Rock Around The Rockpile' (featuring Jayne Mansfield, Ray Anthony and Edmond O'Brien on vocals respectively) also show up. *MCS*

Album rating: *7.5

– spinoff hits, etc. –

FATS DOMINO: Blue Monday

Dec 56. (7",78) *Imperial; <5417> London; (HLP 8377)* 5 Mar57 23

LITTLE RICHARD: The Girl Can't Help It

Jan 57. (7",78) *Speciality; <591>* 49 –

the PLATTERS: You'll Never Never Know

Jan 57. (7",78) *Mercury; (MT 130)* – 23

LITTLE RICHARD: She's Got It / The Girl Can't Help It

Feb 57. (7",78) *London; (HLO 8382)* – 15 9

JULIE LONDON: Cry Me A River

Mar 57. (7",78) *London; (HLU 8240)* – 22
(above single was released in 1956 but re-actified for the movie)

GIRL HAPPY

1965 (US 96m) Metro-Goldwyn-Mayer (PG)

Film genre: romantic Rock'n'roll Musical comedy

Top guns: dir: Boris Sagal / s-w: Harvey Bullock, R.S. Allen

Stars: Elvis PRESLEY *(Rusty Wells)*, Shelley Fabares *(Valerie Frank)* ← RIDE THE WILD SURF ← SUMMER LOVE ← ROCK, PRETTY BABY / → HOLD ON! → SPINOUT → CLAMBAKE → a TIME TO SING, Harold J. Stone *(Big Frank)*, Gary Crosby *(Andy)* ← TWO TICKETS TO PARIS, Joby Baker *(Wilbur)* ← LOOKING FOR LOVE ← HOOTENANNY HOOT / → WHEN THE BOYS MEET THE GIRLS, Nita Talbot *(Sunny Daze)* → the COOL ONES, Mary Ann Mobley *(Deena Shepherd)* ← GET YOURSELF A COLLEGE GIRL, Jackie Coogan *(Sgt. Benson)* ← HIGH SCHOOL CONFIDENTIAL!, Chris Noel *(Betsy)* ← GET YOURSELF A COLLEGE GIRL / → BEACH BALL → WILD, WILD WINTER, Tommy Farrell *(Louie)* ← KISSIN' COUSINS ← SWINGIN' ALONG, Norman Grabowski *('Wolf Call' O'Brien)* ← ROUSTABOUT / → OUT OF SIGHT → the NAKED APE, Gary Crosby *(Andy)*, Peter Brooks *(Brentwood von Durgenfeld)* → the GIRLS ON THE BEACH, Gail Gilmore *(Nancy)* → the GIRLS ON THE BEACH → BEACH BALL → HARUM SCARUM, Nancy Czar *(blonde on beach)* ← WILD GUITAR / → WINTER A-GO-GO → SPINOUT, Beverly Adams *(girl #2)* ← ROUSTABOUT / → HOW TO STUFF A WILD BIKINI → WINTER A-GO-GO

Storyline: Rock'n'roll singer Rusty Wells is charged with guarding the chastity of college girl Valerie Frank, the daughter of a Chicago kingpin. Accompanying the girl and her friends down to Florida, Rusty survives her inevitable crush on him, only to see her getting fresh with an Italian. *BG*

Movie rating: *4

Visual: video + dvd

Off the record: Shelley Fabares (b. Michele Fabares, 19 Jan'44, Santa Monica, California, USA) – niece of actress/comedienne Nanette Fabray – got her first real break at the age of 12 starring opposite Rock Hudson as his daughter in the film, 'Never Say Goodbye' (1956). Her "kid sister" roles carried on in the subsequent rock'n'roll-themed movies such as 'ROCK, PRETTY BABY' (1956) and its 1958 sequel, 'SUMMER LOVE'. Her teen-idol status was assured when she also starred – as Mary Stone – alongside Donna Reed in the latter's 1958 long-running TV series. With every girl in the neighbourhood taking up the art of singing, Fabares, too, joined this illustrious club, astonishingly topping the charts early in 1962 with the sensual, 'Johnny Angel'. However, her chart run of three further hits (including No.21 'Johnny Loves Me') fizzled out by summer '63. Things picked up again when she married record producer Lou Adler in 1964, her "luck" changing dramatically when her bikini-clad figure appeared in "Beach Movie" 'RIDE THE WILD SURF' and Elvis movies such as 'GIRL HAPPY', 'SPINOUT' (1966) and 'CLAMBAKE' (1967). With even a Brit-flick behind her, 'HOLD ON!' (1966) – starring HERMAN'S HERMITS – her appeal was indeed getting ever more so global. She continued to co-star in various movies and has been married to second husband, Mike Farrell (remember 'M*A*S*H') since 1984 having divorced Adler in 1980. *MCS*

ELVIS PRESLEY (composers: George Stoll, etc.)

Apr 65. (lp; mono/stereo) *R.C.A.; (RD/SF 7714) <LSP 3338>* 8 8
– Girl happy / Spring fever / Fort Lauderdale chamber of commerce / Startin' tonight / Wolf call / Do not disturb / Cross my heart and hope to die / The meanest girl in town / Do the clam / Puppet on a string / I've got to find my baby. *(re-iss. Aug81 on 'RCA Int.'; INTS 5034) (re-iss. Nov84 lp/c; NL/NK 83338) (cd-iss. Apr03 on 'Follow That Dream'; FTD 25)*

S/track review: Sure, it opens with the kind of exuberantly dumb, feel-good energy rush that'll soften even the most hardened Hollywood ELVIS cynic, but 'GIRL HAPPY', Doc Pomus' brilliant title track aside, doesn't leave much of a lasting impression. 'Do Not Disturb' is well measured, semi-acoustic pop, 'Wolf Call' the token concession to 60s musical fashion, while both 'Startin' Tonite' and 'The Meanest Girl In Town' work up a decent sweat, the latter complete with hysterical backing singers. 'Puppet On A String' is a professionally rendered ballad (released in the UK as the b-side to the 'Tell Me Why' single), although its most memorable element is Floyd Cramer's tears-in-the-beer, country-tinged piano. Granted, most of 'GIRL HAPPY's lyrics deal with females in some form or other but what is it about ELVIS movies, girls and clams?! No sniggering at the back please.. whatever, 'Do The Clam' (a dance invented for the film, apparently..), Benny Hill-style sax and all, like most of this flimsy soundtrack, is instantly forgettable. *BG*

Album rating: *5

– spinoff releases, etc. –

ELVIS PRESLEY: Do The Clam

Feb 65. (7") *<47-8500> (RCA 1443)* [21] Mar65 [19]

ELVIS PRESLEY: Puppet On A String

Nov 65. (7") *<447-0650>* [14] [–]

ELVIS PRESLEY: Puppet On A String

Nov 65. (7"; B-side) *(RCA 1489)* [–] [15]

GIRLS! GIRLS! GIRLS!

1962 (US 106m) Paramount Pictures (PG)

Film genre: romantic Rock'n'roll Musical comedy

Top guns: dir: Norman Taurog ← BLUE HAWAII ← G.I. BLUES / → IT HAPPENED AT THE WORLD'S FAIR → TICKLE ME → SPINOUT → DOUBLE TROUBLE → SPEEDWAY → LIVE A LITTLE, LOVE A LITTLE / s-w: Edward Anhalt, Allan Weiss ← BLUE HAWAII / → FUN IN ACAPULCO → ROUSTABOUT → PARADISE, HAWAIIAN STYLE → EASY COME, EASY GO

Stars: Elvis PRESLEY *(Ross Carpenter)*, Stella Stevens *(Robin Gantner)* → ADVANCE TO THE REAR → POPSTAR, Laurel Goodwin *(Laurel Dodge)*, Jeremy Slate *(Wesley Johnson)* ← G.I. BLUES, Benson Fong *(Kin Yung)*, Robert Strauss *(Sam; owner of Pirate's Den)* → FRANKIE AND JOHNNY, **Jack Nitzsche** *(piano player in lounge band)* → JOURNEY THROUGH THE PAST, Kenneth Becker *(Mack)* ← G.I. BLUES ← LOVING YOU / → ROUSTABOUT, Mary Treen *(Mrs. Figgot)* → FUN IN ACAPULCO → PARADISE, HAWAIIAN STYLE, **Hal Blaine** *(lounge drummer)* → MAN ON THE MOON → the DR. JEKYLL & MR. HYDE ROCK 'N ROLL MUSICAL → BEAUTIFUL DREAMER: BRIAN WILSON AND THE STORY OF 'SMiLE'

Storyline: Hawaii is once again the setting as tuna-fishing club singer Ross Carpenter juggles his many female admirers but fails to find true love, at least not until we've already endured too much of the wafer-thin/bordering-on-non-existent plot. *BG*

Movie rating: *5

Visual: video + dvd

Off the record: Hal Blaine was the legendary session drummer behind Phil Spector's "Wall Of Sound", featuring as he did on records by the Crystals, the Ronettes, etc. In 1964, alongside GLEN CAMPBELL and other West Coast session men at the time, Hal had a Top 10 hit ('Little Honda') with the Hondells. *MCS*

ELVIS PRESLEY (composers: Joseph Lilley, etc.)

Nov 62. (lp; mono/stereo) *R.C.A.; <LSP 2621> (RD/SF 7534)* [3] Jan63 [2]
– Girls! girls! girls! / I don't wanna be tied / Where do you come from / I don't want to / We'll be together / A boy like me, a girl like you / Earth boy / Return to sender / Because of love / Thanks to the rolling stone / Song of the shrimp / The walls have ears / We're coming in loaded. *(re-iss. Oct79; lp/c; PL/PK 42354) (re-iss. Aug81 on 'RCA International'; INTS 5107) (re-iss. Jun84 lp/c; NL/NK 89048) (re-iss. Sep86 on 'RCA-Camden' lp/c; CDS/CAM 1221)*

S/track review: Chiefly famous for the hip-swinging 'Return To Sender', which deservedly topped the US chart at the close of 1962, this uneven soundtrack has more than its fair share of listenable if inconsequential filler. But oh for the un-PC days of yore when a "red-blooded boy" could sing about "peaches" and "tight sweaters" without fear of a moral furore; it's hard to believe that even clean-cut soul boys like the Drifters had already cut the licentious Leiber/Stoller title track. ELVIS-approved testosterone aside, there are some truly surreal, maritime-themed moments here: 'Thanks To The Rolling Sea' boasts a lyric straight out of a "Captain Birdseye" ad and a vocal as melodramatically ridiculous as it is fascinating. 'Song Of The Shrimp', meanwhile, is 'Banana Boat Song' meets Marty Robbins, sheer kitsch genius complete with exotic, grass-skirt arrangements. Among the best of the rest are 'Plantation Rock' (not included on the original LP release), 'I Don't Wanna Be Tied', the Mexican-style 'We'll Be Together' and the pseudo-oriental 'Earth Boy'. Overall, there are enough gems and oddities on here to make it a worthwhile acquisition, even for non-diehards, and especially in its two-on-one CD coupling with 'KID GALAHAD'. *BG*

Album rating: *4.5

– spinoff hits, etc. –

ELVIS PRESLEY: Return To Sender / Where Do You Come From

Oct 62. (7") *<47-8100> (RCA 1320)* [2]
[99] Nov62 [1]
(re-iss. May77; PB 2706) (hit UK No.42 in Aug'77)

ELVIS PRESLEY: Kid Galahad / Girls! Girls! Girls!

Mar 05. (cd) *<(74321 13430-2)>* [ ] [ ]
– (+=) extra Girls! Girls! Girls! takes

ELVIS PRESLEY: Return To Sender / Where Do You Come From

Mar 05. (cd-s) *Sony-BMG; (82876 66677-2)* [–] [5]
(10"+=) *(82876 66677-1)* – Girls! Girls! Girls!

the GIRLS ON THE BEACH

1965 (US 83m) Lebin Brothers / Paramount Pictures (PG-13)

Film genre: Pop-Rock Musical comedy

Top guns: dir: William N. Witney / s-w: David Malcolm → BEACH BALL → WILD, WILD WINTER

Stars: Martin West *(Duke)* ← a SWINGIN' SUMMER / →, Noreen Corcoran *(Selma)*, Peter Brooks *(Stu)*, Linda Marshall *(Cynthia)*, Steven Rogers *(Brian)* → SKI PARTY → WILD, WILD WINTER, Anna Capri *(Arlene)* → PAYDAY, Aron Kincaid *(Wayne)* → SKI PARTY → BEACH BALL → the GHOST IN THE INVISIBLE BIKINI, Nancy Spry *(Betty)*, Mary Mitchell *(Emily)* ← a SWINGIN' SUMMER ← TWIST AROUND THE CLOCK, Gail Gerber *(Georgia)* ← GIRL HAPPY / → BEACH BALL → HARUM SCARUM, Peter Brooks *(Stu Rankin)* ← GIRL HAPPY, Bruno VeSota *(Pops)* ← YOUR CHEATIN' HEART ← DADDY-O ← ROCK ALL NIGHT ← CARNIVAL ROCK, **the BEACH BOYS:- Brian Wilson, Carl Wilson, Dennis Wilson, Mike Love, Al Jardine** *(performers)*, **the Crickets:- Jerry Allison, Sonny Curtis *, Jerry Naylor *** *(performer/s)* ← JUST FOR FUN, **Lesley Gore** *(performer)* ← the T.A.M.I. SHOW / → SKI PARTY, Dick Miller *(first waiter)* ← ROCK ALL NIGHT ← CARNIVAL ROCK / → SKI PARTY → BEACH BALL → WILD, WILD WINTER → The WILD ANGELS → the TRIP → TRUCK TURNER → I WANNA HOLD YOUR HAND → ROCK'N'ROLL HIGH SCHOOL → GET CRAZY → SHAKE, RATTLE & ROCK! tv

Storyline: Sorority girls from the Alpha Beta fraternity have to raise $10,000 the save their house, and when three boys boast of knowing the Beatles, they plan a concert with the Liverpool Fab Four at the helm. Will they be there? *MCS*

Movie rating: *3.5

Visual: video (no audio OST)

Off the record: The CRICKETS (contributing 'La Bamba' here) were once the backing band of the late, great Buddy Holly, while LESLEY GORE ('Leave Me Alone' & 'It's Gotta Be You') went on to contribute songs to the movie, 'SKI PARTY'. The **BEACH BOYS** also delivered two tracks, 'The Girls On The Beach' & 'Little Honda'. *MCS*

GIVE MY REGARDS TO BROAD STREET

1984 (UK 109m) 20th Century Fox (PG)

Film genre: Pop-Rock Musical drama

Top guns: dir: Peter Webb / s-w: **Paul McCartney**

Stars: Paul McCartney *(Paul)* <= the BEATLES =>, Bryan Brown *(Steve)* → SWEET TALKER, **Ringo Starr** *(Ringo)* <= the BEATLES =>, Barbara Bach *(journalist)*, **Linda McCartney** *(Linda)* ← CONCERTS FOR THE PEOPLE OF KAMPUCHEA ← ROCKSHOW – < SGT. PEPPER'S LONELY HEARTS CLUB BAND ← ONE HAND CLAPPING ← LET IT BE / → GET BACK, **Tracey Ullman** *(Sandra)*, Ralph Richardson *(Jim)* ← O LUCKY MAN!, Ian Hastings *(Harry)*, Jeremy Child *(record company executive)* ← QUADROPHENIA ← PRIVILEGE, **George Martin** *(producer)* ← the COMPLEAT BEATLES ← LET IT BE / → IMAGINE: JOHN LENNON → BEAUTIFUL DREAMER: BRIAN WILSON AND THE STORY OF 'SMiLE', Philip Jackson *(Alan)* → a LITTLE TRIP TO HEAVEN, **Jody Linscott** *(performer)* → THIRTY YEARS OF MAXIMUM R&B LIVE → LIFEHOUSE, David Easter *(Apache dancer)* ← the MUSIC MACHINE, Gary Shail *(Apache dancer)* ← SHOCK TREATMENT ← QUADROPHENIA ← the MUSIC MACHINE, John Murphy *(Windo)* → DOGS IN SPACE → BIGGER THAN TINA, **Eric Stewart** *(himself)* ← TO SIR, WITH LOVE

Storyline: When the master tapes of Paul McCartney's new album mysteriously disappear (wishful thinking?), the loveable scouser – between the inevitable whirlwind creative and business appointments and nostalgic gags of an ex-Beatle – has a mere 24 hours to sniff them out before his label falls into the clutches of The Man. The cameo roll call includes 80s wrestling don, Giant Haystacks. *BG*

Movie rating: *4

Visual: video

Off the record: Tracey Ullman (b.30 Dec'59, Slough, Berkshire, England) acted in this film as a reciprocal favour to Paul McCartney who appeared in her video for the Top 10 hit single, 'They Don't Know' (penned by Kirsty MacColl). Once a star of a UK hit TV comedy series alongside Lenny Henry and David Copperfield (no, not the magic man), her subsequent US TV work began with The Tracey Ullman Show, which, incidentally, kicked off the embryonic 'Simpsons' animation. In 2003, she became an American citizen, having flitted between her London and L.A. homes from the late 80s. *MCS*

PAUL McCARTNEY

Oct 84. (d-lp/c)(cd) *Parlophone; (PCTC/TCPCTC 2)(CDP 746043-2) Columbia; <39613>* [1] [21]
– No more lonely nights (ballad) / Good day sunshine – Corridor music / Yesterday / Here, there and everywhere / Wanderlust / Ballroom dancing / Silly love songs / Not such a bad boy / No values – No more lonely nights (reprise) / For no one / Eleanor Rigby – Eleanor's dream / The long and winding road / No more lonely nights (play out version). *(re-iss. Mar91 lp/c; ATAK/TC-ATAK 165) (cd re-iss. Mar91; CZ 395) (re-iss. Aug93 cd+=/c+=; CD/TC PMCOL 14)* – Good night princess.

S/track review: PAUL McCARTNEY's mid-80s vanity project is one of those records upon which critics routinely converge like a school of starving piranhas. Is it really as bad as all that? Well, yes and no. At the very least it can claim his best song of the decade, one of the best of his solo career: 'No More Lonely Nights'; as long as you give the alternate versions ('2' is particularly appalling) a wide berth, you'll find a song which, incredibly, manages to replicate the swelling poignancy of his Beatles ballads from dubious 80s raw materials/production. And talking of the BEATLES, there's the small fact that McCARTNEY went and included a bevy of their songs here for no readily apparent reason (although he was famously unhappy with Phil Spector's production on 'The Long And Winding Road'). Re-records of such sacred cows as 'Yesterday', 'For No One' and 'Eleanor Rigby', modified with McCARTNEY's filmic/classical/brass leanings, were guaranteed to run afoul of rock critics; the reality is they could have been a lot worse, and the production could have been worse still. A jazz fusion-esque 'The Long And Winding Road' pushes sympathy to the limit but for the most part they're palatable enough in their own right; after all, they're among the best pop songs ever written and it'd take more than a quasi-contemporary makeover to mess with their DNA. The case for the defence gets a bit shakier with the rest of the 80s material, most of which should've been left to moulder on the album(s) they hailed from. The most notable exception is 'So Bad', a dulcet ballad reprised from 'Pipes Of Peace', while 'Wanderlust' sounds like a cross between a 'No More Lonely Nights' clone and a passably updated excerpt from 'The FAMILY WAY'. With the Frog Chorus still to croak its way into being, let's just be thankful he couldn't re-do 'We All Stand Together'. *BG*

Album rating: *4.5

– spinoff hits, etc. –

PAUL McCARTNEY: No More Lonely Nights / extended

Sep 84. (7") *(R 6080) <04581>* [2] [6]
(12"+=/12"pic-d+=) *(12R/+P 6080)* – Silly love songs.

GLITTER

2001 (US 104m) Columbia Pictures (PG-13)

Film genre: romantic showbiz/music drama

Top guns: dir: Vondie Curtis-Hall / s-w: Kate Lanier ← WHAT'S LOVE GOT TO DO WITH IT (story: Cheryl L. West)

Stars: Mariah Carey *(Billie Frank)* → DEATH OF A DYNASTY → STATE PROPERTY 2, Max Beesley *(Julian Dice)*, **Da Brat** *(Louise)* ← CARMEN: A HIP HOPERA ← RHYME & REASON, Tia Texada *(Roxanne)*, Valarie Pettiford *(Lillian Frank)* → STOMP THE YARD, **Ann Magnuson** *(Kelly)* → the NOMI SONG, Terrence Howard *(Timothy Walker)* ← WHO'S THE MAN? ← the JACKSONS: AN AMERICAN DREAM / → RAY → HUSTLE & FLOW → GET RICH OR DIE TRYIN' → IDLEWILD, Dorian Harewood *(Guy Richardson)* ← HENDRIX ← SPARKLE, Bill Sage *(Billie's father)* ← HIGH ART ← I SHOT ANDY WARHOL / → MYSTERIOUS SKIN

Storyline: Little more than a vanity project for Mariah Carey, where she plays Billie, a mixed race child who is abandoned by her mother and grows up in a foster home. She has eyes on a career as a singer, meets a DJ and conveniently becomes a superstar overnight. She then decides to go seek out her birthmother to reconcile. *MR*

Movie rating: *2

Visual: dvd

Off the record: MARIAH CAREY was born on 27th March 1969 in Long Island, New York, USA – of Irish-American and African-American/Venezuelan parentage. A true pop/R&B phenomenom in the 90s, Mariah hit the US No.1 spot no less than 15 times in that decade, from her breakthrough in 1990, 'Vision Of Love' to 'Thank God I Found You', in 1999. Studio albums such as 'Mariah Carey' (1990), 'Emotions' (1991), 'Music Box' (1993), 'Daydream' (1995), 'Butterfly' (1997) and 'Rainbow' (1999) nearly all followed suit, America had found its new Whitney Houston. And then she signed to 'Virgin' records for an estimated $80m . . . *MCS*

MARIAH CAREY (score: Terence Blanchard)

Sep 01. (cd/c/d-lp) *Virgin; <10797> (CDVUS/VUSMC/VUSLP 201)* [7] [10]
– Loverboy remix (feat. DA BRAT, LUDACRIS, TWENTY II, SHAWNNA) / Lead the way / If we (feat. NATE DOGG and JA

RULE) / Didn't mean to turn you on / Don't stop (funkin' 4 Jamaica) (feat. MYSTIKAL) / All my life / Reflections (care enough) / Last night a DJ saved my life (feat. BUSTA RYMES, FABULOUS, DJ CLUE) / Want you (feat. ERIC BENET) / Never too far / Twister / Loverboy (feat. CAMEO).

S/track review: MARIAH CAREY may command more octaves than the conductor at the Proms but she's no polymath. Singer? Sure! In a terrifying showboating, raspy, warbling kind of way, yes. But actor? Hell no! She is the queen of chicken in a basket soul, all echoey rim shots, honking organ parts and syrup-drenched strings, and this torturous collection is divided between a handful of such ballads and a clutch of CAREY's other signature: frothy, over-familiar R&B pop. The resulting album has virtually no redeeming qualities whatsoever. With more guests than a mafia wedding, 'GLITTER' the soundtrack is as ill-conceived and overblown as the original movie. It boasts a veritable production line of rappers with hands out, ready for their cheque, tossing in a verse: BUSTA RHYMES, JA RULE, MYSTIKAL, DA BRAT, LUDACRIS, and FABOLOUS more or less all sound like they're phoning it in, particularly the normally lucid and avuncular LUDACRIS and BUSTA who resort to throwing out glib catchphrases. Tracks like 'If We' genuinely sound like they were knocked up in half an hour, a cheap drum loop, a few vocal lines, CAREY topping it with an obligatory warble fest to 'til fade. Vain attempts to capture the spirit of the 80s through the kidnapping of CAMEO on 'Loverboy' and the hijacking of Robert Palmer's 'I Didn't Mean To Turn You On' and 'All My Life' are remarkable in their vacuity. What takes the cake however is the reworking of 'Last Night A DJ Saved My Life', possibly the most pointless piece of work in living memory; a rambling example of hip hop disco karaoke. 'GLITTER' is as subtle as a brick and the contrived, shallow nature of this supposed soul music reflects how low expectations are for populist tastes. There is some justice however, the film and soundtrack both bombed. Maybe there is a God after all. *MR*

Album rating: *1

– spinoff hits, etc. –

MARIAH CAREY featuring CAMEO: Loverboy / (MJ Cole remix) / (Club of love remix)

Jul 01. (c-s/cd-s) *<38791> (VUS C/CD 211)* [2] [12]
(12"+=) *(VUST 211)* – ('A'remix).
(12") *(VUSTX 211)* – ('A'-Drums of love remix) / ('A'-dub love remix) / ('A'-MJ Cole London dub mix).

MARIAH CAREY: Never Too Far

Dec 01. (cd-s) *<38813>* [81] [–]

MARIAH CAREY: Never Too Far / Loverboy (MJ Cole London dub mix)

Dec 01. (c-s) *(VUSC 228)* [–] [32]
(cd-s+=) *(VUSCD 228)* – Don't stop (funkin' 4 Jamaica) (w/ MYSTIKAL) / Loverboy (drums of love).
(12") *(VEST 228)* – ('A') / Never too far / Don't stop (funkin' 4 Jamaica) (instrumental).

☐ Gary GLITTER segment
(⇒ REMEMBER ME THIS WAY)

☐ GO FORWARD!!
(⇒ the SPIDERS filmog...)

GO, JOHNNY, GO!

1959 (US 75m b&w) Valiant Films (G)

Film genre: Rock'n'roll Musical drama

Top guns: dir: Paul Landres / s-w: Gary Alexander

Stars: Alan Freed *(himself)* ← MISTER ROCK AND ROLL ← ROCK, ROCK, ROCK! ← DON'T KNOCK THE ROCK ← ROCK AROUND THE CLOCK, **Jimmy Clanton** *(Johnny Melody)* → TEENAGE MILLIONAIRE, Sandy Stewart *(Julie Arnold)*, Herb Vigran *(Bill Barnett)*, **Chuck BERRY** *(performer)*, **Eddie Cochran** *(performer)* ← HOT ROD GANG ← UNTAMED YOUTH ← the GIRL CAN'T HELP IT / → BLUE SUEDE SHOES → the COMPLEAT BEATLES → the BEATLES ANTHOLOGY, **Ritchie Valens** *(performer)*, **Jackie Wilson** *(performer)*, **Jo-Ann Campbell** *(performer)* → HEY, LET'S TWIST, **Harvey (Fuqua)** *(performer; the Moonglows)* ← MISTER ROCK AND ROLL ← ROCK, ROCK, ROCK!, **the Cadillacs** *(performers)*, **the Flamingos** *(performers)* ← ROCK, ROCK, ROCK!, Frank Wilcox *(Mr. Arnold)*, Barbara Woodell *(Mrs. Arnold)*, Milton Frome *(Mr. Martin)*, Phil Arnold *(call boy)* → YOUR CHEATIN' HEART → HOLD ON! → GOOD TIMES → SKIDOO

Storyline: Young orphan Johnny Melody is kicked out of the church choir for the heinous crime of liking rock'n'roll. He lurches from one job to the next and scrapes together enough cash to make a demo tape for promoter Alan Freed. When Freed hears the anonymous tape he broadcasts an appeal on his show for the "mystery voice" to come forward, but Johnny is more interested in girlfriend Julie and has the radio switched off. Fate, however, is about to lend a hand to help Johnny fulfil his destiny. *JZ*

Movie rating: *5

Visual: dvd

Off the record: Jimmy Clanton (see below)

Various Artists

1985. (lp) *Swift; (JN 5705)* [–] [ ]
– My love is strong (JIMMY CLANTON) / It takes a long time (JIMMY CLANTON) / Ship on a stormy sea (JIMMY CLANTON) / Angel face (JIMMY CLANTON) / Johnny B. Goode (CHUCK BERRY) / Little Queenie (CHUCK BERRY) / Memphis (CHUCK BERRY) / Playmates (SANDY STEWART) / Heavenly father (SANDY STEWART) / Ooh! my head (RITCHIE VALENS) / You'd better know it (JACKIE WILSON) / Teenage heaven (EDDIE COCHRAN) / Jay walker (the CADILLACS) / Please Mr. Johnson (the CADILLACS) / Jump children (the FLAMINGOS) / Momma, can I go out (JO ANN CAMPBELL) / Don't be afraid to love me (HARVEY FUQUA).

S/track review: While only a rare promo LP of 'GO, JOHNNY, GO!' was released at the time (and another in 1985), the soundtrack is a must-have for any rock'n'roll fan – just make sure you have plenty cash to spare. "See! 10 Great Rock'n'Roll Stars! – Hear! 17 Great New Rock'n'Roll Hits!" was the billing, and who could say they were wrong. CHUCK BERRY kicks off the film (although not the record) with the title track of sorts, 'Johnny B. Goode', and before he can shout 'Little Queenie' and 'Memphis', he and Alan Freed are introducing new talent, JIMMY CLANTON. This film was certainly a vehicle for the cherub-faced CLANTON, who's afforded four numbers, the best of which is 'It Takes A Long Time'. The FLAMINGOS ('Jump Children'), JACKIE WILSON ('You'd Better Know It'), HARVEY FUQUA ('Don't Be Afraid To Love Me') and the CADILLACS ('Jay Walker' & 'Please Mr. Johnson') see the R&B side shine through, while rockers EDDIE COCHRAN ('Teenage Heaven'), RITCHIE VALENS ('Ooh! My Head') and even a double by SANDY STEWART provide the pop balance. *MCS*

Album rating: *6.5

– spinoff releases, etc. –

CHUCK BERRY: Little Queenie

Mar 59. (7",78) *<1722> (HLM 8853)* [80] Apr59 [ ]
(above was flip side to BERRY's 'Almost Grown')

JIMMY CLANTON: Jimmy Clanton In . . . Go, Johnny Go!

1959. (7"ep) *Ace; <EP 101>* [ ] [–]

GODSPELL

or 'GODSPELL: A MUSICAL BASED ON THE GOSPEL ACCORDING TO ST MATTHEW'

1973 (US 103m) Columbia Pictures (G)

Film genre: religious Rock Musical drama

Top guns: s-w: David Greene (+ dir) → HARD COUNTRY, John-Michael Tebelak (+ play)

Stars: Victor Garber *(Jesus Christ)*, David Haskell *(Judas/John)*, Robin Lamont *(Robin)*, Lynne Thigpen *(Lynne)* → STREETS OF FIRE → the INSIDER, Jerry Sroka *(Jerry)*, Katie Hanley *(Katie)* → XANADU, Merrell Jackson *(Merrell)*, Gilmer McCormick *(Gilmer)*, Joanne Jonas *(Joanne)*, Jeffrey Mylett *(Jeffrey)*, Jerry Sroka *(Jerry)*

Storyline: In a God bothering presentiment of Milos Forman's 'Hair', a Broadway musical finds itself relocated to New York for real, playing out Matthew's Gospel as a contemporary post-hippy analogy. Taking the guise of a clown, Jesus heads up a bunch of long hairs baptised in Central Park, with the not so mean looking streets forming a backdrop for modern day miracles to happen. *BG*

Movie rating: *6

Visual: video + dvd

Off the record: nothing

—

Various Cast & Company . . . (composer: Stephen Schwartz)

Apr 73. (lp/c) *Bell; <1118>* [50] [–]

– Prepare ye (the way of the Lord) (DAVID HASKELL & . . .) / Save the people (VICTOR GARBER & . . .) / Day by day (ROBIN LAMONT & . . .) / Turn back, O man (JOANNE JONAS, VICTOR GARBER & . . .) / Bless the Lord (LYNNE THIGPEN & . . .) / All for the best (VICTOR GARBER, DAVID HASKELL & . . .) / All good gifts (MERRELL JACKSON & . . .) / Light of the world (JERRY SROKA, GILMER McCORMICK, JEFFREY MYLETT, ROBIN LAMONT & . . .) / Alas for you (VICTOR GARBER) / By my side (KATIE HANLEY & . . .) / Beautiful city (. . .) / On the willows (STEPHEN REINHARDT, RICHARD LaBONTE & VICTOR GARBER) / Finale (VICTOR GARBER & . . .). *(UK-iss.Jan89 on 'Silva Screen' lp/c; ALB 6/AC86 8337) <cd-iss. 1990 on 'Arista'; ARCD 8337>*

S/track review: Rock operas as a rule tend to degenerate in quality the further they stray from the counter-culture that spawned them. Bearing a 1973 birth date, 'GODSPELL' is more or less an original, a worthy companion piece to both 'JESUS CHRIST SUPERSTAR' and the underrated 'CATCH MY SOUL', with respectable credentials in the likes of session guitarist HUGH McCRACKEN and session keyboard ace/talk show luminary/'BLUES BROTHERS' musical director PAUL SHAFFER (who'd already directed the stage version of 'Godspell' in his native Canada). Maximising the creative and budgetary opportunities presented by the big screen transfer, stage composer Stephen Schwartz subjected the arrangements to the equivalent of a religious conversion, enriching the instrumental and stylistic communion and rarifying the ensemble harmonies. After all, if George Harrison could work such melodic wonders with Hare Krishna, why not Christianity? Schwartz occasionally attempts to squeeze too many elocutionary exclamations into too tight a space but the less gratuitously theatrical numbers glow with spiritual health: whipped into a fervour by McCRACKEN's fat, Mike Oldfield-esque treble, opener 'Prepare Ye (The Way Of The Lord) builds from lone supplication to zealous mantra, 'Day By Day' from Burt Bacharach-esque waltz to ecstatic Harrison homage. Katie Hanley, meanwhile, is just bewitching on 'By My Side', close harmony folk that'd now be commanding vast sums had it been released on obscure 70s vinyl. Schwartz also dallies with ragtime, music hall and – on the bass-heavy 'Light Of The World' – soul and funk, while the one song written especially for the soundtrack, 'Beautiful City', bears all the hallowed, buttoned-down guilelessness of the Carpenters. So hear ye this, heathens, 'GODSPELL' is worthy of your sheckels even if the smell of greasepaint normally has you running for a darkened crypt. *BG*

Album rating: *7

GOIN' COCONUTS

1978 (US 93m) a Kolob production (PG)

Film genre: Pop Musical comedy/adventure

Top guns: dir: Howard Morris / s-w: Raymond Harvey

Stars: Donny Osmond *(Donny)* → INSIDE THE OSMONDS, **Marie Osmond** *(Marie)* → SIDE BY SIDE: THE TRUE STORY OF A MAGICAL FAMILY → INSIDE THE OSMONDS, Herb Edelman *(Sid)*, Kenneth Mars *(Kruse)*, Chrystin Sinclaire *(Tricia)*, Ted Cassidy *(Mickey)*, Marc Lawrence *(Webster)* ← a PIECE OF THE ACTION / → FOUR ROOMS, Jack Collins *(Charlie)* ← ROCK, ROCK, ROCK!, Danny Wells *(Al)* → the WOMAN IN RED → MAGNOLIA, Charles Walker *(Jake)* ← a PIECE OF THE ACTION / → ALMOST FAMOUS, Harold Sakata *(Ito)* ← RECORD CITY

Storyline: Donny and Marie get out the grass skirts and garlands as they head off to sunny Hawaii. Hot on their heels are a bunch of do-baddies who're after Marie's shiny new necklace, and Donny's eyes are straying towards temptress Tricia instead of looking after her. Luckily the villains are particularly incompetent and the sibling songsters should have no problems sorting them out. *JZ*

Movie rating: *2

Visual: video

Off the record: DONNY & MARIE (see below)

—

DONNY & MARIE (part of soundtrack *)

Oct 78. (lp) *Polydor; <6169> (2391 371)* [98] Jan79 [ ]

– On the shelf (*) / Don't play with the one who loves you / You don't have to say you love me / Baby, now that I've found you / Gimme some time / Let's fall in love / You bring me sunshine (*) / Fallin' in love again (*) / Doctor dancin' (*) / You never can tell / May tomorrow be a perfect day.

S/track review: Arriving towards the end of their glittering time at the top, DONNY & MARIE's 'GOIN' COCONUTS' musical extravaganza showcased the singing and dancing talents of the brother and sister duo (it has to said one could indeed "go coconuts" after enduring this LP). Of course, both had cut their perfect, whiter than white teeth as part of the multi-talented Osmond family (young DONNY was the shining star of the Mormon boy-band) and both had platinum-selling solo singles, while also pairing up as a duo. While MARIE's time at the top was brief ('Paper Roses' hit Top 5), DONNY's stretched out a little longer via No.1s 'Puppy Love', 'The Twelfth Of Never' & 'Young Love'; DONNY & MARIE's 'I'm Leaving It All Up To You' also reached Top 5 in 1974. Having been stars on their own TV series between 1976 and 1978, 'GOIN' COCONUTS', one supposes was their attempt to cash in on movie fame. It didn't work. Their star was fading fast – DONNY was nearly key-of-the-door 21, fantasy-girl MARIE had just turned 19 – and this manufactured package was definitely one for their loyal fanbase, who only managed to scrape it into the US Top 100. Produced as always by Mike Curb (and part-songwriter Michael Lloyd), the LP played safe, not taking too many risks in the process. And to make things worse and confusing, the record isn't even a bona fide soundtrack, having only four songs featured in the movie itself ('On The Shelf' a Top 40 hit, 'You Bring Me Sunshine', 'Fallin' In Love Again' & 'Doctor Dancin''). Covers/standards such as 'You Don't Have To Say You Love Me', 'Baby, Now That I've Found You', 'Let's

Fall In Love' and Chuck Berry's 'You Never Can Tell', were wishy-washy cuts not allowed to fester on celluloid, doomed only to make a good punk suffer. The aforementioned 'On The Shelf' (never more poignantly put!) takes cheesy disco one step (and indeed four feet) into cringeland, DONNY obviously fixated by John Travolta and the previous year's 'SATURDAY NIGHT FEVER'. The other soundtrack-associated songs (all written by brothers, Alan, Wayne & Merrill Osmond) were run-of-the-mill, easy-listening pop-pap. One good thing about the "Crazy Horses" Osmonds, was that at least you knew what to buy your granny every birthday. Ten years on, we had to endure it all again courtesy of clone-like duo, Kylie & Jason (although not in a sibling-loving way) – was it just a coincidence that both DONNY and Jason Donovan have worn Joseph's coat of many colours? *MCS*

Album rating: *2

– spinoff hits, etc. –

DONNY & MARIE: On The Shelf

Sep 78. (7") *<14510> (2066 981)* [38] Nov78 [ ]

the GOLDEN DISC

US title 'the INBETWEEN AGE' (1959)

1958 (UK 78m b&w) Butcher's Film Service / Allied Artists Pictures

Film genre: Rock'n'roll Musical drama

Top guns: s-w: Don Sharp (+ dir) → IT'S ALL HAPPENING, Don Nicholl (story: Gee Nicholl)

Stars: Lee Patterson *(Harry Blair)*, Mary Steele *(Joan Farmer)*, **Terry Dene** *(himself/performer)*, Linda Gray *(Aunt Sarah)*, Ronald Adam *(Mr. Dryden)*, Peter Dyneley *(Mr. Washington)*, David Jacobs *(himself)* → IT'S TRAD, DAD! → JUST FOR FUN → STARDUST, **Sonny Stewart's Skiffle Kings** *(performers)*, **the Terry Kennedy Group** *(performers)*, **Don Rendell's Six** *(performers)*, **Nancy Whiskey** *(performer)* ← the TOMMY STEELE STORY

Storyline: A teenage couple, Lee and Mary – with the help of their auntie – extend their coffee bar to include a record store/recording outlet. With rock'n'roll all the rage, they look to handyman turned singing sensation, Terry Dene, to bring them some luck. *MCS*

Movie rating: *4.5

Visual: video + dvd (no audio OST)

Off the record: Terry Dene (b. Terrence Williams, 20 Dec'38, Elephant and Castle, London) didn't really set the world alight as predicted, even after three Top 20 hits including 'A White Sport Coat'. This was due to a drunken incident caught by the press and an all to brief call-up for National Service. He would suffer a nervous breakdown due to all the stress, although he did return in the 70s producing gospel music; the cabaret circuit would be his subsequent destiny. **Nancy Whiskey** (b. Nancy Wilson, 4 Mar'35, Glasgow, Scotland) sang and played guitar with the Charles McDevitt Skiffle Group on 'Freight Train' and recorded with C&W artist, Hank Garland; she died on 1st Feb'03. *MCS*

– spinoff releases, etc. –

TERRY DENE: The Golden Age / (non OST-song)

Feb 58. (7"/78) *Decca; (F 10977)* [ ] [-]

TERRY DENE: The Golden Disc EP

Feb 58. (7"ep) *Decca; (DFE 6427)* [ ] [-]
– I'm gonna wrap you up / Dynamo / The in-between age / The golden age.

□ GONE segment (⇒ LOVEDOLLS SUPERSTAR)

GONKS GO BEAT

1965 (UK 90m) Titan Films

Film genre: Pop/Rock Musical comedy

Top guns: dir: Robert Hartford-Davis (+ story w/ Peter Newbrook) / s-w: Jimmy Watson

Stars: Kenneth Connor *(Wilco Roger)* → CUCKOO PATROL → the MAGIC CHRISTIAN, Pamela Brown *(Helen)*, Jerry Desmonde *(Great Galaxian)*, Iain Gregory *(Steve)*, Frank Thornton *(Mr. A&R)* ← IT'S TRAD, DAD! / → the MAGIC CHRISTIAN → SIDE BY SIDE, Reginald Beckwith *(Professor)* ← JUST FOR FUN, Terry Scott *(P.M.)*, **LULU** *(performer)*, & **the Luvers** *(themselves)*, **Graham Bond Organisation:- Graham Bond** *(vocalist, guitarist)* → THAT'LL BE THE DAY, **John McLaughlin** *(guitarist)* → 'ROUND MIDNIGHT, **Dick Heckstall-Smith** *(saxophonist)*, **Jack Bruce** *(bassist)* → KLODEN ROKKER → RISING LOW → RED, WHITE & BLUES, **Ginger Baker** *(drummer)* → CUCUMBER CASTLE, **Alan David** *(performer)*, **Barbara Brown & Perry Ford** *(performers)*, Elaine & **Derek (Thompson)** → BREAKING GLASS

Storyline: The two nations of Ballad Isle and Beat Land are irreconcilable foes. Inept alien Wilco Rogers (no relation to Buck) is sent to Earth to mediate between the two sides but finds it impossible to negotiate a solution. He cunningly brings together a boy and girl from each nation in the hope that love will conquer all, including presumably the small furry gonks (cushion-like soft toys with arms and legs) which appear all over the place. *JZ*

Movie rating: *2.5

Visual: dvd

Off the record: (see below)

Various Artists

Apr 65. (lp) *Decca; (LK 4673)* [ ] [-]
– Choc ice (LULU & THE LUVERS) / Harmonica (the GRAHAM BOND ORGANISATION) / Broken pieces (ELAINE & DEREK) / Bum up (the TITAN STUDIO ORCHESTRA) / Love is a dream (ALAN DAVID) / Take this train (the LONG AND THE SHORT) / As young as we are (DOUGIE ROBINSON with the TITAN STUDIO ORCHESTRA) / Drum battle (ALAN GRINDLEY, RONNIE VERRELL, ANDY WHITE, RONNIE STEPHENSON) / In love with you today (PERRY FORD) / Penny for your thoughts (BARBARA BROWN) / Loving you (BARBARA BROWN and PERRY FORD) / Gonks go beat (the TITAN STUDIO ORCHESTRA) / The only one (LULU & THE LUVERS) / Poor boy (the NASHVILLE TEENS) / Take two to make love (BARBARA BROWN and PERRY FORD) / Finale (the TITAN STUDIO ORCHESTRA). *<cd-iss. Apr04 on 'Bridge' Japan; BRIDGE-016>*

S/track review: 'GONKS GO BEAT' is as schizoid a record as one's likely to hear, then, now, or in the future as depicted in the movie itself. The "GONKS" here either "rock'd" their tiny little butts off (LULU, the GRAHAM BOND ORGANISATION, the NASHVILLE TEENS, the LONG AND THE SHORT, the TITAN STUDIO ORCHESTRA . . .) or they "roll'd" right off the musical map. For acts such as ELAINE AND DEREK (Derek Thompson now in 'Casualty' – the TV series that is!), ALAN DAVID (a cross between Adam Faith and himself!), BARBARA BROWN & PERRY FORD (who were actually afforded four love ballads!), bubblegum pap is too sticky a term to use. That leaves the aforementioned "rock" movers, also booked, one might add, because of their signing to 'Decca' records. Up first was wee Scots lass LULU with a rasping Mike Leander, R&B arrangement of 'Choc Ice', surely a candidate for one-that-got-away, had it been released by the label in the first place. Sheer class. A second LULU & THE LUVERS song, 'The Only One' (Luvvers again spelt wrong here!) calmed it down dramatically, no doubt someone in the studio not a fan of her Top 10 hit, 'Shout!'. That man of 'PRIVILEGE' – one could say (see 1967 film) – MIKE LEANDER was also behind another Brit-blues band, the NASHVILLE TEENS, who came up trumps via the 'Not Fade Away'-esque 'Poor Boy'. If your bag was the Bluesbreakers, the Yardbirds or the Animals, then 'Harmonica' by the GRAHAM BOND ORGANISATION (a supergroup of sorts featuring enigmatic frontman BOND, sax-man DICK HECKSTALL-SMITH, bassist JACK BRUCE and drummer GINGER BAKER) just might've been right up your street – the blues had a baby . . . as they say. If a weird future was the movie's cinematic theme, then a handful of acts here were well ahead of their proverbial time, none more so than "house band" and surprise package all-round, the TITAN STUDIO ORCHESTRA, who struck up more than one chord on 'Burn Up'. Penned by bandleader Robert Richards, the track fuelled memories of early 60s sci-fi outfits, the Sputniks, the Tornados, etc., although one can also think Dick Dale, Link Wray, Johnny & The Hurricanes . . . all in one room with Joe Meek!; it's just a pity their subsequent back-to-basics dirges didn't stand up to the first. Off-kilter to the point of obscurity, the LONG AND THE SHORT (who'd originally had a minor Top 50 hit with Leander's 'Choc Ice' in 1964/5), produced a hybrid of futuristic R&B via 'Take This Train'; probably sought after by fans of Beefheart. Last, but not least (in terms of a cracking first half), 'Drum Battle' showcased a plethora of sticksmen (definitely a precursor to solo Prog-solos by ELP: Palmer or Powell – you decide), but did it have to take eight of them, and why only credit four? *MCS*

Album rating: *6.5

☐ Jack GOOD segment
(⇒ CATCH MY SOUL)

GOOD MORNING, VIETNAM

1987 (US 120m) Touchstone Pictures (R)

Film genre: military/war comedy drama

Top guns: dir: Barry Levinson → WAG THE DOG / s-w: Mitch Markowitz

Stars: Robin Williams *(Adrian Cronauer)* ← CLUB PARADISE / → GOOD WILL HUNTING, Forest Whitaker *(Edward Garlick)* → JOHNNY HANDSOME → GHOST DOG: THE WAY OF THE SAMURAI → a LITTLE TRIP TO HEAVEN, Tung Thanh Tran *(Tuan)*, Chintara Sukapatana *(Trinh)*, Bruno Kirby *(2nd Lt. Steven Hauk)* ← BIRDY ← THIS IS SPINAL TAP ← WHERE THE BUFFALO ROAM ← ALMOST SUMMER / → the BASKETBALL DIARIES → a SLIPPING-DOWN LIFE, J.T. Walsh *(Sgt. Major Phillip 'Dick' Dickerson)*, Robert Wuhl *(SSgt. Marty Lee Dreiwitz)* ← FLASHDANCE / → BATMAN → the BODYGUARD, Noble Willingham *(Brig. Gen. Taylor)* ← LA BAMBA ← LIVING PROOF: THE HANK WILLIAMS JR. STORY / → SOUTH OF HEAVEN, WEST OF HELL, **Richard Edson** *(Pvt. Abersold)* ← WALKER ← HOWARD THE DUCK / → TOUGHER THAN LEATHER → WHAT ABOUT ME → STRANGE DAYS → the MILLION DOLLAR HOTEL → SOUTHLANDER, Juney Smith *(Sgt. Phil McPherson)*, Richard Portnow *(Dan 'the man' Levitan)* ← ROADIE / → S.F.W. → PRIVATE PARTS → FEAR AND LOATHING IN LAS VEGAS → GHOST DOG: THE WAY OF THE SAMURAI, Floyd Vivino *(Eddie Kirk)* → BIG MONEY HUTLA → RAMONES: RAW

Storyline: Robin Williams gives a manically brilliant performance as Adrian Cronauer, an army DJ plying his trade in Vietnam. Stinging satire, wildly inspired improvisation and a rebelliously eclectic playlist conspire to make Cronauer the troops' unequivocal favourite. He pushes his superiors one step too far, however, when he blows the whistle on the realities of the war. *BG*

Movie rating: *7

Visual: video + dvd

Off the record: **Richard Edson** was drummer with SONIC YOUTH.

—

Various Artists (& Robin Williams dialogue *)

Jan 88. (lp/c/cd) *A&M; <(AMA/AMC/CDA 3913)>* [10] Feb88 [50]
– (*) / Nowhere to run (MARTHA & THE VANDELLAS) / I get around (the BEACH BOYS) / Game of love (WAYNE FONTANA & THE MINDBENDERS) / (*) / Sugar and spice (the SEARCHERS) / (*) / Liar, liar (the CASTAWAYS) / The warmth of the sun (the BEACH BOYS) / (*) / I got you (I feel good) (JAMES BROWN) / (*) / Baby please don't go (THEM) / (*) / Danger heartbreak dead ahead (the MARVELETTES) / Five o'clock world (the VOGUES) / California sun (the RIVIERAS) / (*) / What a wonderful world (LOUIS ARMSTRONG). *(hit UK No.7 in compilation charts Jul'89)*

S/track review: 'GOOD MORNING, VIETNAM' – or "Goo-ood Morrnninng, Vietnaaam!!!" as real comic DJ Adrian Cronauer would've put it – is essentially a sound selection of classic, mid-60s pop, soul and R&B. Setting the scene, after unhinged lead actor ROBIN WILLIAMS gets his two-penneth monologue(s) in, is MARTHA & THE VANDELLAS' 'Nowhere To Run'. Balance this track with the sheer godlike genius of the BEACH BOYS' 'I Get Around' and follow-on cue 'Game Of Love' from Manchester's chart-topping MINDBENDERS, and you get a sort of cross-Atlantic pop challenge. Not only once does this happen, but three times as the CASTAWAYS' 'Liar, Liar' lies in wait for the SEARCHERS' 'Sugar And Spice', while THEM (featuring VAN MORRISON's lead vox on 'Baby Please Don't Go') takes on 'California Sun' by the RIVIERAS and! . . . 'Five O'Clock World' by the VOGUES. The Brits seem outnumbered three to one here. But like in all good American war movies, the Yanks always win the day, in this instance sheer numbers take the medals. Stateside heroes firing all of their guns at once stem from JAMES BROWN ('I Got You (I Feel Good)') and LOUIS ARMSTRONG's 'What A Wonderful World'. Only the BEACH BOYS' second contribution, 'The Warmth Of The Sun', lets the side down – now give us 50 press-ups, boys. *MCS*

Album rating: *7.5

– spinoff hits, etc. –

LOUIS ARMSTRONG: What A Wonderful World / WAYNE FONTANA & THE MINDBENDERS: Game Of Love

Feb 88. (7") *<3010> (AM 435)* [32] Mar88 [53]

MARTHA & THE VANDELLAS: Nowhere To Run / JAMES BROWN: I Got You (I Feel Good)

Jul 88. (7") *(AM 444)* [–] [52]

Various Artists: More Songs From The Good Morning Vietnam Era

Oct 92. (cd) *Universal; <515766-2>* [ ] [–]

GOOD TIMES

1967 (US 91m) Columbia Pictures (PG)

Film genre: Pop/Rock Musical comedy/fantasy

Top guns: dir: William Friedkin → SORCERER → TO LIVE AND DIE IN L.A. / s-w: Tony Barrett (au: Nicholas Hyams)

Stars: **Sonny Bono** *(himself)* → HAIRSPRAY, **CHER** *(herself)*, George Sanders *(Mr. Mordicus)*, Norman Alden *(Warren)* ← the WILD ANGELS, Larry Duran *(Smith)*, Kelly Thordsen *(tough hombre)*, Lennie Weinrib *(Garth)* → the POINT!, Peter Robbins *(Brandon)*, Edy Williams *(Mordicus' girl)* ← PARADISE, HAWAIIAN STYLE / → BEYOND THE VALLEY OF THE DOLLS, Phil Arnold *(Solly)* ← HOLD ON! ← YOUR CHEATIN' HEART ← GO, JOHNNY, GO! / → SKIDOO, Morris Buchanan *(proprietor)* → COFFY, **Mickey Dolenz** *(Jungle Gino)* → HEAD

Storyline: Sonny and Cher take an irreverent look at the movie world. When Sonny is offered a part in a new film, he reckons the script is so bad he could do a better job himself. The producer gives him 10 days to come up with something and, with Cher's able assistance, he spends most of this time daydreaming about various scenarios, with himself as the hero in everything from Tarzan to the Maltese Falcon. *JZ*

Movie rating: *4

Visual: video + dvd

Off the record: Sonny BONO (see Sonny & CHER →)

—

SONNY & CHER (composer: SONNY BONO)

May 67. (lp) *Atco; <S33 214>* [73] [–]
– I got you babe (instrumental) / It's the little things / Good times / Trust me / Don't talk to strangers / I'm gonna love you / Just a name / I got you babe. *<cd-iss. 1999 on 'One Way'; OW 35140>*

S/track review: SONNY & CHER go to the movies. Husband and wife team (married since 1963) star and perform all the songs in the movie soundtrack, SONNY also on songwriting credits. Image-conscious SONNY had learned a lot since the duo first stormed to the top of the charts with the pop-tastic 'I Got You Babe' two years previously. Here, the song makes an appearance twice (both very different to the original): first as a kooky, Bacharach-esque instrumental opener with strings, child-like verses and harmonies substituting SONNY & CHER's vocalising, second as a melancholy bookend, love ballad complete with flamenco. Influenced by producer-kings Brian Wilson and more so, Phil Spector, SONNY brings in his own "wall of sound" on 'It's The Little Things', a belated Top 50 hit. Track 3, 'Good Times', starts with some sexy CHER and SONNY on dialogue, intentionally hamming up the song to great effect. Ditto pop ballad, 'Trust Me', albeit with added jazz waltz to complement William Friedkin's fun movie. If there's one mediocre song on the LP it must be 'Don't Talk To Strangers', relegated to the B-side of '. . .Little Things'. Traditional blues takes over for 'I'm Gonna Love You', its 6/8 time procession march uncharacteristic of anything the pair had experimentated with in the past. The longest song by far (at 6 and 1/2 minutes), 'Just A Name', once again begins with some turkey-acting dialogue, although when it opens into a carousel, bitter-sweet love song, it has all the hallmarks of a great S&C song; remarkably it predates the similar "Butch Cassidy" themes by a couple of years. Maybe Burt Bacharach was returning the compliment. It was a fun time for the fashion-conscious SONNY & CHER, however nothing lasts forever – the pair divorced in 1974 (see CHER biog for more details). *MCS*

Album rating: *6.5

– spinoff hits, etc. –

SONNY & CHER: It's The Little Things / Don't Talk To Strangers
Aug 67. (7") *<6507>* [50] [–]

GOOD TO GO

aka SHORT FUSE

1986 (US 87m) Island Alive (R)

Film genre: Hip Hop Musical drama

Top guns: s-w + dir: Blaine Novak

Stars: Art Garfunkel *(S.D. Blass)* <= SIMON & GARFUNKEL =>, Robert DoQui *(Max)* ← FAST FORWARD ← NASHVILLE ← COFFY ← UP TIGHT!, Harris Yulin *(Harrigan)* → CANDY MOUNTAIN → the MILLION DOLLAR HOTEL → CHELSEA WALLS, Reginald Daughtry *(Little Beats)*, Richard Brooks *(Chemist)*, Paula Davis *(Evette)*, Michael White *(Gil Colton)*, Hattie Winston *(mother)*, Anjelica Huston ← THIS IS SPINAL TAP / → BUFFALO 66

Storyline: Washington DC reporter S.D. Blass finds himself caught in a web of intrigue and deceit when he is wrongly told that a nurse's murder took place in a Go-Go dance bar. When Blass finds similar cases of misinformation spread by racist police chief Harrigan, he threatens to go public in his newspaper column. However, Harrigan has too much to lose and, after another murder, Blass realizes that he's next on the list. *JZ*

Movie rating: *3

Visual: video on Vidmark Entertainment

Off the record: nothing

—

Various Artists (score: Billy Goldenberg)

Aug 86. (lp) *Island; <90509-1>* [ ] [–]
– Good to go (TROUBLE FUNK) / Meet me at the go-go (HOT, COLD SWEAT) / Still smokin' (TROUBLE FUNK) / Make 'em move" "The Wrecking Crew's Theme" (SLY DUNBAR & ROBBIE SHAKESPEARE) / E.U. freeze (E.U.) / Keys: "The chemist's theme" (WALLY BADAROU) / We need money (CHUCK BROWN & THE SOUL SEARCHERS) / Status quo: "Little Beat's theme" (DONALD BANKS) / Drop the bomb (TROUBLE FUNK) / Riot zone (call the police) (INI KAMOZE) / I like it (TROUBLE FUNK) / Movin' and groovin' (REDDS AND THE BOYS) / Good to go: "reprise" (TROUBLE FUNK).

S/track review: Rarely do the movie-making entrepreneurs who jump on a musical fad manage to get their bearings fast enough to avoid serving up a turkey – but they avoid the pitfalls here, at least on the soundtrack. It's partly a matter of time and place; Go Go had been exalting its movers and shakers since the late 70s in the vibrant nightlife of Washington DC, and 'Island' records boss Chris Blackwell (who had been inspired by hearing Chuck Brown on the radio in New York) had the experience and clout to sign them up at their peak. The result is a creditable sampler of Go Go's top stars getting the best out of the genre: funk with a nimbler, swinging beat and a good dose of early hip-hop. TROUBLE FUNK, the music's biggest successes, contribute four songs including 'Drop The Bomb', and CHUCK BROWN & THE SOUL SEARCHERS (whose breakthrough 1978 hit 'Bustin' Loose' is a big miss) provide the staple 'We Need Money'. Other stalwarts include HOT, COLD SWEAT, E.U. and REDDS AND THE BOYS; and if history has made Go Go something of a musical side alley this collection nevertheless captures the excitement of a riotous party in full flight. *ND*

Album rating: *7.5

GRACE OF MY HEART

1996 (US 116m) Gramercy Pictures / Universal Pictures (R)

Film genre: showbiz/Pop-music drama

Top guns: s-w + dir: Allison Anders ← FOUR ROOMS ← GAS, FOOD LODGING ← BORDER RADIO / → SUGAR TOWN → THINGS BEHIND THE SUN

Stars: Illeana Douglas *(Denise Waverly / Edna Buxton)*, John Turturro *(Joel Milner)* ← GIRL 6 ← JUNGLE FEVER ← TO LIVE AND DIE IN L.A. / → HE GOT GAME → O BROTHER, WHERE ART THOU?, Eric Stoltz *(Howard Caszatt)* ← PULP FICTION ← SINGLES ← FAST TIMES AT RIDGEMONT HIGH / → THINGS BEHIND THE SUN, Bruce Davison *(John Murray)* ← an AMBUSH OF GHOSTS ← CRIMES OF PASSION ← DEADMAN'S CURVE ← SHORT EYES ← the STRAWBERRY STATEMENT, Patsy Kensit *(Cheryl Steed)* ← ABSOLUTE BEGINNERS / → THINGS BEHIND THE SUN, Matt Dillon *(Jay Phillips)* ← SINGLES / → ALBINO ALLIGATOR → the FUTURE IS UNWRITTEN, Jennifer Leigh Warren *(Doris Shelley)*, Lucinda Jenney *(Marion)* → SUGAR TOWN → the MOTHMAN PROPHECIES, Bridget Fonda *(Kelly Porter)* ← SINGLES ← SHAG: THE MOVIE / → TOUCH → JACKIE BROWN → FINDING GRACELAND → SOUTH OF HEAVEN, WEST OF HELL, Christina Pickles *(Mrs. Buxton)* → the WEDDING SINGER, **Jill Sobule** *(talent show contestant)*, **Larry Klein** *(record producer)* → SUGAR TOWN → CRAZY, **Chris Isaak** *(Matthew Lewis)* → THAT THING YOU DO!, **Shawn Colvin** *(commune guitarist)* → CRAZY, **REDD KROSS:- Steve McDonald, Jeff McDonald, Brian Reitzell**

(the Riptides), David Clennon *(Dr. 'Jonesy' Jones)* ← SWEET DREAMS ← LADIES AND GENTLEMEN, THE FABULOUS STAINS ← BOUND FOR GLORY, **J. Mascis** *(the Riptides' engineer)* ← GAS, FOOD LODGING ← 1991: THE YEAR PUNK BROKE / → THINGS BEHIND THE SUN, Peter Fonda *(Guru Dave)* ← the HIRED HAND ← EASY RIDER ← the TRIP ← the WILD ANGELS / → SOUTH OF HEAVEN, WEST OF HELL, Amanda De Cadenet *(receptionist #2)* ← FOUR ROOMS, Richard Schiff *(record producer auditioner)* ← the BODYGUARD ← YOUNG GUNS II / → TOUCH → I AM SAM → RAY, **For Real** *(Brill Building hallway singers)*, **David Williams** *(click brother #1)*, **Andrew Williams** *(click brother #2)*, Chris Shearer *(security expert)* ← BORDER RADIO, **Kristen Vigard** *(singing voice for Illeana)* → THINGS BEHIND THE SUN, Latanyia Baldwin *(Brill Building hallway singer)* ← SHAKE, RATTLE & ROCK! tv, Jade Gordon *(coffee shop girl)* → SUGAR TOWN → THINGS BEHIND THE SUN

Storyline: Set in the 60s and remarkably similar to the real life story of Carole King, Denise Waverly is the daughter of an important steel tycoon whose dreams to become a musician take a positive turn after winning a talent contest. The ensuing record contract brings her to New York where she quickly realises she's not the only girl in town looking for a break. When her first single sinks without trace she turns her hand to songwriting and begins to work with in-house composer, Howard Cazsatt. Co-writing songs for other aspiring new acts, their pairing is a massive success as they score successive hits while their relationship becomes more intimate. A tumultuous and brief marriage follows before Waverly packs her bags for California where she starts a turbulent relationship with a surfer. *KM*

Movie rating: *6

Visual: video + dvd

Off the record: Kristen Vigard was a relatively unknown alt/folk-rock singer-songwriter from Manhattan, New York, whose eponymous debut in 1988 received some rave reviews. *MCS*

—

Various Artists (composers: Various)

Sep 96. (cd) *M.C.A.; <(MCD 11554)>* [ ] Feb97 [ ]
– God gave me strength (BURT BACHARACH & ELVIS COSTELLO) / Love doesn't ever fail us (WILLIAMS BROTHERS) / Take a run at the sun (J. MASCIS) / I do (FOR REAL) / Between two worlds (SHAWN COLVIN) / My secret love (MISS LILY BANQUETTE) / Man from Mars (KRISTEN VIGARD) / Born to love that boy (FOR REAL) / Truth is you lied (JILL SOBULE) / Unwanted number (FOR REAL) / Groovin' on you (JUNED) / In another world (PORTRAIT) / Don't you think it's time (J. MASCIS) / Absence makes the heart grow fonder (TIFFANY ANDERS & BOYD RICE) / A boat on the sea (KRISTEN VIGARD).

S/track review: Love 'em or loathe 'em, ELVIS COSTELLO's BURT BACHARACH collaboration, 'God Give Me Strength' opens this album with the unrivalled confidence that might be expected of such a pedigree face-off. With its touchingly understated horns, strings and piano contrasting nicely with COSTELLO's wavering and sometimes overbearingly brittle voice, this song's success led to a full album's worth from the pair. Other luminaries of similar magnitude weren't exactly in short supply for this OST, and a good thing too since without the use of cover versions it would require a near miracle to pen a whole album's worth of convincing 60s vintage classics. So it is then, that Gerry Goffin graces the writing credits of three of the album's originals including the tender Temptations-esque 'In Another World' (co-written with Los Lobos) performed by PORTRAIT, and the classicist 'Between Two Worlds', with SHAWN COLVIN delivering a weedy vocal over lush production. Alas, Brian Wilson couldn't be hired to write the album's surf song, 'Love Doesn't Ever Fail Us', in which the WILLIAMS BROTHERS bravely engage every trick in the West Coast book including the Dick Dale-esque tremolo, un-spooky electro-theremin and the inevitable hand-stitched harmonies. More convincing is KRISTEN VIGARD's second contribution to the album, the beautiful Joni Mitchell sound-a-like, 'A Boat On The Sea', ironically more enjoyable than her other effort, 'Man From Mars', an actual JONI composition, and an irony summing up a soundtrack trying – and to some extent succeeding – to match the music of the 60s using the same instruments, production techniques and lyrics. *KM*

Album rating: *7

GRAFFITI BRIDGE

1990 (US 95m) Paisley Park Films / Warner Bros. Pictures (PG-13)

Film genre: R&B/Rock Musical drama

Top guns: s-w + dir: **PRINCE**

Stars: PRINCE *(The Kid)*, **Ingrid Chavez** *(Aura)*, **Morris Day** *(Morris)* ← the ADVENTURES OF FORD FAIRLANE ← PURPLE RAIN, **Jerome Benton** *(Jerome)* ← UNDER THE CHERRY MOON ← PURPLE RAIN, **Mavis Staples** *(Melody Cool)* <= the STAPLE SINGERS =>, **George Clinton** *(himself)* ← HOUSE PARTY → MACEO → NINA HAGEN = PUNK + GLORY, **Tevin Campbell** *(Tevin)*, **T.C. Ellis** *(T.C.)*, **Robin Power** *(Robin)*, **Jill Jones** *(Jill)* ← PURPLE RAIN, **the Revolution:- Mico Weaver, Michael Bland, Rosie Gaines, Damon Dickson, Levi Seacer Jr., Tony Mosley, Kirk Johnson**, *(Kid's band)*, **the Time:- Garry Johnson** *(performer)* ← PURPLE RAIN, **Jesse Johnson** *(performer)* ← PURPLE RAIN, **Jimmy Jam, Terry Lewis, Monte Moir**, *(themselves)*, **Funkestra:- George Clinton** *(performer)*, **Atlanta Bliss** *(performer)* ← SIGN 'O' THE TIMES

Storyline: Another Prince turkey has the diminutive, Adam Ant-striped Kid locked in a battle of wits with the Time's pimp-strutting Morris Day. Trouble is that he spends so much time moping around in his future-shock subterranean den that he neglects to write any decent songs. Day doesn't get the girl but he proves that the bad guys have the best tunes. *BG*

Movie rating: *3

Visual: video + dvd

Off the record: Ingrid Chavez co-penned (with Lenny Kravitz) 'Justify My Love' for MADONNA. Discovered by **QUINCY JONES**, **Tevin Campbell** (straight outta TV show, 'Wally & The Valentines) went on to have a plethora of post-'GRAFFITI BRIDGE' hits including 'Tell Me What You Want Me To Do', 'Can We Talk' & 'I'm Ready'. *MCS*

—

PRINCE (& Various Artists)

Aug 90. (cd)(d-lp/c) *Paisley Park; <(927493-2)>(WX 361/+C)* [6] [1]
– Can't stop this feeling I got / New power generation / Release it (TIME) / The question of U / Elephants and flowers / Round and round (TEVIN CAMPBELL) / We can funk (GEORGE CLINTON & PRINCE) / Joy in repetition / Love machine (TIME) / Tick, tick, bang / Shake! (TIME) / Thieves in the temple / The latest fashion (the TIME & PRINCE) / Melody Cool (MAVIS STAPLES) / Still would stand all time / Graffiti bridge (MAVIS STAPLES & TEVIN CAMPBELL) / New power generation (pt.II) (MAVIS STAPLES, TEVIN CAMPBELL, T.C. ELLIS & ROBIN POWER).

S/track review: Dated is the adjective of choice most often bandied about by critics in re-appraising PRINCE's last-gasp soundtrack. If anything, 'GRAFFITI BRIDGE' hasn't even aged as well as its superhero predecessor. The opening 'Can't Stop This Feeling I Got' is PRINCE doing his best Kenny Loggins-cum-Bruce Springsteen routine, and while what worked in the early 80s doesn't necessarily cut the purple mustard a decade later, its author is clearly more inspired looking backwards than he is forwards. With its lumpen R&B and tired 'Times-they-are-a-changin' theme, 'New Power Generation' was his poorest-performing single since the mid-80s. Given that the NPG were actually his new backing band, things looked grim. 'Release It' picks up the tempo with a slap bass and breakbeat groove as raw as could feasibly be expected for 1990. But it's not PRINCE; the fact is, this album only really breaks sweat when he rather charitably makes way for his old pals the TIME: 'Love Machine' offers a peep-show preview of the new model, x-rated funk which the NPG would – at least initially – carry off on the underrated 'Diamonds And Pearls' (1991). Among the other guests, Amp Fiddler's 'Knee Deep'-like keyboards animate the otherwise disappointing GEORGE CLINTON collaboration, 'We Can Funk', and MAVIS STAPLES at least brings a bit of old skool sass to 'Melody Cool'. 'Thieves In The Temple' was the big single, and while it's not one of PRINCE's most memorable, at least it's got a hook, something which – for all their neo-psychedelic promise and impressive guitar work – the likes of 'Joy In Repitition' and 'The Question Of U' lack. Even more ominous than the cloying production and half-written songs was the sleeve artwork: a pallid-looking PRINCE sporting a "symbol" earring. In terms of the identity crises and creative freefall to come, the graffiti wasn't so much on the bridge as already on the wall. *BG*

Album rating: *5.5

– spinoff hits, etc. –

PRINCE: Thieves In The Temple / (Part 2)

Jul 90. (7"/c-s) *<19751> (W 9751/+C)* [6] [7]
(12"+=/cd-s+=/12"pic-d+=) *(W 9751 T/CD/TP)* – ('A'-dub).

PRINCE: New Power Generation / (Part 2)

Oct 90. (7"/c-s) *<19525> (W 9525/+C)* [64] [26]
(12"+=/cd-s+=/12"pic-d+=) *(W 9525 T/CD/TP)* – Melody Cool (extended remix).

TEVIN CAMPBELL: Round And Round / (soul dub)

Dec 90. (7"/c-s) *<21740> (W 0115/+C)* [12] [ ]
(12"+=/cd-s+=) *<921740-0/-2> (W 0115 T/CD)* – (versions).

GRAND THEFT PARSONS

2003 (UK/US 87m) Redbus Pictures / Swipe Films (PG-13)

Film genre: road movie/comedy

Top guns: dir: David Caffrey / s-w: Jeremy Drysdale

Stars: Johnny Knoxville *(Phil Kaufman)* ← COYOTE UGLY, Gabriel Macht *(Gram Parsons)*, Christina Applegate *(Barbara Mansfield)* ← VIBRATIONS ← BEATLEMANIA, Marley Shelton *(Susie)*, Robert Forster *(Stanley Parsons)* ← JACKIE BROWN, Michael Shannon *(Larry Oster-Berg)*, Mike Shawyer *(Barney)*, Phil Kaufman *(handcuffed felon)* ← BABY SNAKES / → FALLEN ANGEL → the LIFE AND HARD TIMES OF GUY TERRIFICO, Kay E. Kuter *(undertaker)* ← WATERMELON MAN, Paul Goebel *(petrol station attendant)* → CAKE BOY

Storyline: Road manager/"Executive Nanny" Phil Kaufman stays true to his word and respects his recently deceased ward Gram Parsons' wishes to be cremated in the Joshua Tree desert. Easier said than done, of course, especially as Parsons happened to be a country rock prodigy on the cusp of solo stardom, with a host of interested parties converging on the scene after his death. Nor do Kaufman's attempts to transport Gram's body in a flower powered hearse make either him or his grisly task any less conspicuous. *BG*

Movie rating: *6

Visual: dvd

Off the record: Gram Parsons' story is better told in the documentary bio-pic, 'FALLEN ANGEL'.

Various Artists (score: RICHARD G MITCHELL *)

Mar 04. (cd) *Fly-Cube; (FLYCUB 20106)* [ ] [–]
– Hot burrito #2 (STARSAILOR) / Sister surround (SOUNDTRACK OF OUR LIVES) / Movin' on up (PRIMAL SCREAM) / Big bird (EDDIE FLOYD) / Parsons' boy (*) / Wild horses (FLYING BURRITO BROTHERS) / A song for you (GRAM PARSONS) / Hickory wind (GILLIAN WELCH) / Hot burrito #1 – instrumental (LEE RUSSELL) / Brass buttons (LEMONHEADS) / Love hurts (GRAM PARSONS) / Joshua Tree Inn (*) / Dark end of the street (FLYING BURRITO BROTHERS) / How much I've lied – live (EVAN DANDO) / Older guys – live (COALPORTERS) / One hundred years from now (WILCO) / Christine's tune (aka Devil in disguise) (OLIVER BROTHERS) / Gram's ghost (*) / Bad penny (RORY GALLAGHER) / Flying high (COUNTRY JOE & THE FISH) / Rhinestones in the ashes (ROGER ALAN WADE) / Cosmic American spirit (*).

S/track review: Given the intense interest in GRAM PARSONS over the last decade or so it was only a matter of time before someone attempted to transfer his story – or at least the story of his demise – to the big screen. While the movie approached the aftermath of his death as meandering farce, at least the accompanying soundtrack – an impressive effort of will over a tiny budget and licensing restrictions – imparts some of the passion of PARSONS' music. The decision to include more than half a dozen cover versions not featured in the film means that the only thing which differentiates this disc from the various tribute sets on the market is Ivor Novello winner Richard G Mitchell's score and a handful of unrelated rock tracks. Of these, only Knoxville's cousin ROGER ALAN WADE's gratifyingly threadbare, blackly bittersweet 'Rhinestones In The Ashes' and, at a push, PRIMAL SCREAM's 'Movin' On Up', sound spiritually at home among the PARSONS' memorabilia, yet the whole thing still hangs together surprisingly well. EDDIE FLOYD's 'Big Bird' would sound great on any soundtrack although brawny inclusions from artists as diverse as RORY GALLAGHER (the searing 'Bad Penny') and the SOUNDTRACK OF OUR LIVES are harder to justify; they might have worked well in the film but here they sound jarringly out of sync. Which leaves Mitchell's rather oblique score. Ranging from jazzy electronica to orchestral ambience, it at least partly succeeds in projecting PARSONS' vision into the 21st century on the likes of 'Gram's Ghost' and 'Cosmic American Spirit', with veteran Al Perkins' pedal steel dissolving into the desert ether. Among the covers, LEE RUSSELL's instrumental, Beatles-influenced take on 'Hot Burrito #1' is the most imaginative and revealing, in part because – wisely – he doesn't even attempt to interpret PARSONS' singularly wracked singing. STARSAILOR's overbearing vocals, on the other hand, remain an acquired taste, marring an otherwise decent cover of 'Hot Burrito #2' (played over the movie's end titles), while WILCO display impeccable taste but precious little subtlety in resurrecting one of GRAM's lesser known but most affecting efforts from his Byrds tenure. As for the actual GP tracks, there are better introductions, sure, but the there's no arguing with the selections that are here, especially 'Love Hurts'; the chemistry between PARSONS and EMMYLOU HARRIS remains one of the most sublime in the history of popular music. Still, putting originals next to covers – as fond and accomplished as many of them are – only accentuates a chasm of truly Cosmic American proportions between the man and his admirers. And for that we should probably all be thankful. *BG*

Album rating: *7

GREASE

1978 (US 110m) Paramount Pictures (PG)

Film genre: romantic teen-Pop/Rock'n'roll Musical

Top guns: dir: Randal Kleiser / s-w: Bronte Woodard → CAN'T STOP THE MUSIC (stage musical: Jim Jacobs & Warren Casey)

Stars: John Travolta *(Danny Zuko)* ← SATURDAY NIGHT FEVER / → URBAN COWBOY → STAYING ALIVE → SHOUT → PULP FICTION → PRIMARY COLORS → SWORDFISH → BE COOL → HAIRSPRAY re-make, **Olivia Newton-John** *(Sandy Olsson)* ← TOOMORROW / → XANADU, Stockard Channing *(Rizzo)*, Jeff Conaway *(Kenickie)*, Didi Conn *(Frenchy)* ← YOU LIGHT UP MY LIFE / → ALMOST SUMMER → GREASE

2, Eve Arden *(Principal McGee)* → GREASE 2, Joan Blondell *(Vi)* ← the PHYNX ← STAY AWAY, JOE ← ADVANCE TO THE REAR, Barry Pearl *(Doody)*, Michael Tucci *(Sonny)*, Kelly Ward *(Putzie)*, Susan Buckner *(Patty Simcox)*, Eddie Deezen *(Eugene Felnic)* ← I WANNA HOLD YOUR HAND / → GREASE 2 → ROCK-A-DOODLE, Lorenzo Lamas *(Tom Chisum)* → BODY ROCK → the MUSE, Dennis C. Stewart *(Leo)*, Annette Charles *(Cha Cha DiGregorio)*, Dick Patterson *(Mr. Rudie)* → CAN'T STOP THE MUSIC → GREASE 2, Sid Caesar *(Coach Calhoun)* → GREASE 2, Dody Goodman *(Blanche; school secretary)* → GREASE 2 → COOL AS ICE, Edd Byrnes *(Vince Fontaine)* ← STARDUST ← BEACH BALL / → BACK TO THE BEACH → SHAKE, RATTLE & ROLL: AN AMERICAN LOVE STORY, Alice Ghostley *(Mrs. Murdock)* ← RECORD CITY ← the GRADUATE, **Frankie AVALON** *(teen angel)*, **Sha Na Na:- Jon 'Bowzer' Bauman *, Donald 'Donny' York, Jocko Marcellino, Johnny Cartado, 'Screamin' Scott Simon, Frederick 'Dennis' Greene, Lennie Barker** *(Johnny Casino and the Gamblers)* ← DYNAMITE CHICKEN * ← WOODSTOCK * / → FESTIVAL EXPRESS *

Storyline: Adapted from the Broadway hit, the movie found a slicked back Danny caught between a chick – Sandy – and a hard place as his leather-clad, T-Bird pals pooh-pooh his whiter than white choice of girlfriend. So white, in fact, that she's shunned by girly in-crowd, the Pink Ladies. Amid much swooning, snogging and shimmying, the pair attempt to overcome the social boundaries standing between their undying, impressively choreographed love. *BG*

Movie rating: *10

Visual: video + dvd

Off the record: Sha-Na-Na were also featured in the rockumentary/concert movie, 'WOODSTOCK' (1970).

—

Various Cast (composers: Jim Jacobs & Warren Casey)

May 78. (d-lp) *R.S.O.; <4002> (RSD 2001)* [1] Jun78 [1]
– Grease (FRANKIE VALLI) / Summer nights (JOHN TRAVOLTA & OLIVIA NEWTON-JOHN) / Hopelessly devoted to you (OLIVIA NEWTON-JOHN) / You're the one that I want (JOHN TRAVOLTA & OLIVIA NEWTON-JOHN) / Sandy (JOHN TRAVOLTA) / Beauty school drop-out (FRANKIE AVALON) / Look at me, I'm Sandra Dee (STOCKARD CHANNING) / Greased lightnin' (JOHN TRAVOLTA) / It's raining on prom night (CINDY BULLENS) / Alone at the drive-in movie (instrumental) / Blue moon (SHA NA NA) / Rock'n'roll is here to stay (SHA NA NA) / Those magic changes (SHA NA NA) / Hound dog (SHA NA NA) / Born to hand jive (SHA NA NA) / Tears on my pillow (SHA NA NA) / Mooning (LOUIS ST. LOUIS & CINDY BULLENS) / Freddy my love (CINDY BULLENS) / Rock'n'roll party queen (LOUIS ST. LOUIS) / There are worse things I could do (STOCKARD CHANNING) / Look at me, I'm Sandra Dee (reprise) (OLIVIA NEWTON-JOHN) / We go together (JOHN TRAVOLTA & OLIVIA NEWTON-JOHN) / Love is a many splendored thing (instrumental) / Grease (reprise) (FRANKIE VALLI). *(re-iss. Jan84 on 'Polydor'; SPDLP 4) <(cd-iss. Apr91; 817998-2)> <cd re-iss. Oct03 on 'Universal'; 3755-2>*

S/track review: The teen movie to end all teen movies, 'GREASE' captured the 50s cum late 70s zeitgeist and set it forever in stone, or possibly Brylcreem. While JOHN TRAVOLTA and OLIVIA NEWTON-JOHN's pristine pop chemistry dragged 50s musical finesse into the disco era with the ageless 'You're The One That I Want', Barry Gibb's FRANKIE VALLI-sung title track was a notable highlight among the dusted-down golden oldies and Jim Jacobs/ Warren Casey-penned numbers. While other highlights included 'Hopelessly Devoted To You', 'Sandy' and 'Greased Lightnin'', it was the ultimate of boy/girl duos, 'Summer Nights', that stole the show. The rock'n'roll element comes in the shapes'n'drapes of SHA NA NA, who fire in no less than six consecutive golden oldie nuggets including 'Blue Moon', 'Rock'n'Roll Is Here To Stay' and 'Hound Dog'. The Western-styled song and dance cue, 'Look At Me, I'm Sandra Dee', finds actress STOCKARD CHANNING in fine fettle, while a reprised version comes via OLIVIA NEWTON-JOHN. There are some well-chewed bits of bubblegum on 'GREASE', but in the end it's good clean fun. *BG & MCS*

Album rating: *7.5

– spinoff hits, etc. –

JOHN TRAVOLTA & OLIVIA NEWTON-JOHN: You're The One That I Want / Alone At The Drive-In Movie – instrumental

Mar 78. (7") *<891> (RSO 6)* [1] May78 [1]

FRANKIE VALLI: Grease / instrumental

May 78. (7") *<897> (RSO 12)* [1] Aug78 [3]

OLIVIA NEWTON-JOHN: Hopelessly Devoted To You / Love Is A Many Splendored Thing – instrumental

Jun 78. (7") *<903> (RSO 17)* [3] Oct78 [2]

JOHN TRAVOLTA & OLIVIA NEWTON-JOHN: Summer Nights / LOUIS ST. LOUIS: Rock'n'roll Party Queen

Jul 78. (7") *<906> (RSO 18)* [5] Sep78 [1]

JOHN TRAVOLTA: Greased Lightnin' / SHA NA NA: Rock'n'roll is here to stay

Sep 78. (7") *<909>* [47] [–]

JOHN TRAVOLTA: Sandy

Sep 78. (7") *Polydor; (POSP 6)* [2] [–]

JOHN TRAVOLTA: Greased Lightnin'

Nov 78. (7") *Polydor; (POSP 14)* [11] [–]

JOHN TRAVOLTA & OLIVIA NEWTON-JOHN: You're The One That I Want

Jul 98. (cd-s) *Polydor; (044133-2)* [4] [–]

GREASE 2

1982 (US 114m) Paramount Pictures (PG)

Film genre: romantic teen-Pop/Rock Musical

Top guns: dir: Patricia Birch / s-w: Ken Finkleman → WHO'S THAT GIRL

Stars: Maxwell Caulfield *(Michael Carrington)* → ELECTRIC DREAMS → EMPIRE RECORDS, Michelle Pfeiffer *(Stephanie Zimone)* → the STORY OF US → I AM SAM → HAIRSPRAY re-make, Adrian Zmed *(Johnny Nogerelli)*, Lorna Luft *(Paulette Rebchuck)* → 54, Maureen Teefy *(Sharon Cooper)* ← FAME, Alison Price *(Rhonda Ritter)*, Eve Arden *(Ms. McGee)* ← GREASE, Sid Caesar *(Coach Calhoun)* ← GREASE, Tab Hunter *(Mr. Stuart)* ← RIDE THE WILD SURF, Connie Stevens *(Ms. Mason)* → BACK TO THE BEACH → TAPEHEADS, Dick Patterson *(Mr. Spears)* ← CAN'T STOP THE MUSIC ← GREASE, Didi Conn *(Frenchy)* ← ALMOST SUMMER ← GREASE ← YOU LIGHT UP MY LIFE, Peter Frechette *(Louis DiMucci)*, Dody Goodman *(Blanche Hodel)* ← GREASE / → COOL AS ICE, Liz Sagal *(sorority girl)* → FLASHDANCE → HOWARD THE DUCK, Christopher McDonald *(Goose McKenzie)*, Eddie Deezen *(Eugene Felnic)* ← GREASE ← I WANNA HOLD YOUR HAND / → ROCK-A-DOODLE, Matt Lattanzi *(Brad)* ← XANADU / → CATCH ME IF YOU CAN, Lucinda Dickey *(girl greaser)* → BREAKIN' → BREAKIN' 2: ELECTRIC BOOGALOO

Storyline: English exchange student Michael Carrington arrives at Rydell High and a few seconds later falls in love with Stephanie, head of the Pink Ladies. However, the Ladies have solemnly sworn only to date members of the T-Birds gang, so Michael drops the top hat and tails, buys a bike and a mask, and promptly rescues Steph from some ruffians. Does Michael keep up the mystery man guise or will he reveal all to his admiring angel? *JZ*

Movie rating: *3

Visual: video + dvd

Off the record: Already a star in the making after appearing in the movies, 'Young And Dangerous', 'Dragstrip Riot' and 'Rock-A-Bye Baby', Brooklyn-born Connie Stevens set her sights a little higher when she had two Top 5 hits in 1959/60: 'Kookie, Kookie (Lend Me Your Comb)' (with Edward Byrnes) and 'Sixteen Reasons'. *MCS*

—

Various Cast/Artists (composer: Louis St. Louis)

Jun 82. (lp/c) *R.S.O.; <RS-1/-4 3803> (RSD/TRSD 5020)* 71

– Back to school again (FOUR TOPS) / Cool rider (MICHELLE PFEIFFER) / Score tonight (the T-BIRDS & the PINK LADIES) / Girl for all seasons (MAUREEN TEEFY, LORNA LUFT, ALISON PRICE & MICHELLE PFEIFFER) / Do it for our country (PETER FRECHETTE) / Who's that guy? (Cast) / Prowlin' (the T-BIRDS) / Reproduction (TAB HUNTER) / Charades (MAXWELL CAULFIELD) / (Love will) Turn back the hands of time (MAXWELL CAULFIELD & MICHELLE PFEIFFER) / Rock-a-hula-luau (summer is coming) (Cast) / We'll be together (MAXWELL CAULFIELD & Cast). *(cd-iss. Apr94 on 'Polydor'; 825096-2)*

S/track review: While Travolta and his 'GREASE' screen partner Newton-John were furthering their respective acting and singing careers, someone in Hollywood brought about this celluloid "Son Of Grease" cash-in. And are rising thespian substitutes MAXWELL CAULFIELD and MICHELLE PFEIFFER worthy of any merit? Definitely, maybe. For all that, it's not this pair that kick off the LP, but soulful R&B stalwarts, the FOUR TOPS, who had the only hit from the movie, 'Back To School Again'. The cast get to work on the remainder of the cues, PFEIFFER in particular sets the pulses racing with 'Cool Rider', although one doesn't think spelling lessons for the title were necessary. MAXWELL CAULFIELD appears on subsequent numbers, 'Charades' (very Manilow!), '(Love Will) Turn Back The Hands Of Time' (a Rundgren-esque duet with PFEIFFER) and 'We'll Be Together' (with the rest of the cast). Like in the original 'GREASE', there are the odd suggestive songs, the bubblegum 'Score Tonight' (by T-BIRDS & the PINK LADIES), 'Reproduction' (by TAB HUNTER) and to a lesser effect, 'Prowlin'' (by the T-BIRDS). Songs to get one pressing the next track button on your remote control are:- the schmaltzy 'Girl For All Seasons', the jingo-istic 'Do It For Our Country' and the sing-a-long-a-doo-wop-a-sap of 'Rock-A-Hula-Luau (Summer Is Coming)'. Throw in the Eagles-esque, 'Who's That Guy?' and you have one hell of a soundtrack – with the emphasis on the word Hell. *MCS*

Album rating: *3

– spinoff hits, etc. –

FOUR TOPS: Back To School Again / Cast: Rock-A-Hula-Luau (Summer Is Coming)

May 82. (7") *R.S.O.; <1069> (RSO 89)* 71 62

GREAT BALLS OF FIRE!

1989 (US 107m) Orion Pictures (R)

Film genre: Rock'n'roll-music bio-pic/drama

Top guns: s-w: Jim McBride (+ dir) → TO HELL AND BACK, Jack Baran (book: Myra Lewis, Murray Silver)

Stars: Dennis Quaid *(Jerry Lee Lewis)* ← the LONG RIDERS, Winona Ryder *(Myra Gale Lewis)* → NIGHT ON EARTH → REALITY BITES, Alec Baldwin *(Jimmy Lee Swaggart)* ← WORKING GIRL, **John DOE** *(J.W. Brown)*, John Bloom as Joe Bob Briggs *(Dewey "Daddy-O" Phillips)*, Trey Wilson *(Sam Phillips)*, Stephen Tobolowsky *(Jud Phillips)* → ROADSIDE PROPHETS → the INSIDER → the COUNTRY BEARS, Steve Allen *(himself)*, Lisa Blount *(Lois Brown)*, **Mojo Nixon** *(James Van Eaton)* → ROCK'N'ROLL HIGH SCHOOL FOREVER → TWO HEADED COW, **Jimmie Vaughan** *(Roland Janes)* ← LIGHT OF DAY / → BLUES BROTHERS 2000, Booker T. Laury *(Piano Slim)* → DEEP BLUES, Michael St. Gerard *(Elvis Presley)* ← HAIRSPRAY, **Rufus Thomas** *(Haney's big house dancer)* ← WATTSTAX / → MYSTERY TRAIN → ONLY THE STRONG SURVIVE → the ROAD TO MEMPHIS, **Tav Falco** *(new bass player)*, Peter Cook *(English reporter)* ← the PRINCESS BRIDE, Lisa Jane Persky *(Babe)* ← AMERICAN POP ← KISS MEETS THE PHANTOM OF THE PARK / → TO HELL AND BACK

Storyline: The colourful – and colourfully portrayed – life story of rock'n'roll pioneer/wayward genius Jerry Lee Lewis, as he rides roughshod over the charts, only to earn his due opprobrium after marrying his 13 year-old cousin. *BG*

Movie rating: *5.5

Visual: video + dvd

Off the record: Modern-day rock'n'rollers are here in force, **John DOE** (ex-X), **Tav Falco** (ex-Panther Burns), **Mojo Nixon** (Jello Biafra associate) and **Jimmie Vaughan** (Double Trouble musician and brother of the late, great Stevie Ray). *MCS*

—

JERRY LEE LEWIS (& Various Artists)

Nov 89. (lp/c/cd) *Polydor; <(839 516-1/-4/-2)>* Jul89 62

– Great balls of fire / High school confidential / Big legged woman (BOOKER T. LAURY) / I'm on fire / Rocket 88 (JACKIE BRENSTON & THE DELTA CATS) / Whole lotta shakin' goin' on / Whole lotta shakin' goin' on (VALERIE WELLINGTON) / Breathless / Crazy arms / Wild one / That lucky old sun / Great balls of fire (original).

S/track review: While the film's lead, Dennis Quaid, was originally pencilled in to handle LEWIS' songbook, "the Killer" himself stepped into the breach at the last minute, giving a valedictory lesson in who was actually best qualified to sing his own, ever electrifying songs. Yes, JERRY LEE (bar, a few from other R'n'R nuggets!) on eight newly-recorded golden oldies plus an original take of the title track. With a backing band that included guitarist GERALD McGEE, bassist JERRY SCHEFF, drummer DAVID KEMPER (under the watchful eye of arranger/orchestrator David Miner), 50-something, living legend LEWIS assumed the mantle of full responsiblity; actor DENNIS QUAID gets in with a croaking shout – so to speak – when he duets on 'Crazy Arms'. 'GREAT BALLS OF FIRE!' (and its opening title track) showcases an extrovert still in control of his faculties, with subsequent songs such as 'High School Confidential', 'I'm On Fire', 'Breathless', 'Wild One' and 'Whole Lotta Shakin' Goin' On', all perilously risky even by today's un-PC standards. Rock'n'roll was indeed here to stay – if "The Killer" had his way – and if LEWIS wanted "great balls of fire", he got 'GREAT BALLS OF FIRE!'. Only his version of Johnny O'Keefe's 'Wild One' (where was Iggy Pop when you needed him) and 'That Lucky Old Sun', fall short of the task. Of the three "outsider" tracks, the best comes via 'Rocket 88' by JACKIE BRENSTON & THE DELTA CATS (which claims to be the first rock & roll recording from 1951), while not far behind are 'Big Legged Woman' by barrelhouse bluesman BOOKER T. LAURY, and VALERIE WELLINGTON's take of 'Whole Lotta Shakin' . . .'. Sadly, the latter Chicago blues newcomer was to die of a brain aneurysm on 2nd of January, 1993 (aged only 33), while the aforementioned LAURY also popped his clogs a few years later in Memphis (aged 81). JERRY LEE LEWIS is still going strong (as of July 2007) and it'll take a "whole lotta shakin'" before he gets, er . . . "breathless". *BG & MCS*

Album rating: *7

– spinoff releases, etc. –

JERRY LEE LEWIS: Great Balls Of Fire / Breathless

Sep 89. (7"/12") *(PO/PZ 57)*

the GREAT ROCK'N'ROLL SWINDLE

1980 (UK 103m) Kendon Films Ltd. / Virgin Films (18)

Film genre: Punk Rock Musical & documentary bio-pic

Top guns: dir (+ s-w): Julien Temple → ABSOLUTE BEGINNERS → RUNNING OUT OF LUCK → EARTH GIRLS ARE EASY → AT THE MAX → the FILTH AND THE FURY → the GLASTONBURY → the FUTURE IS UNWRITTEN

Stars: Malcolm McLaren *("the Embezzler")* → the FILTH AND THE FURY, **Johnny Rotten/John Lydon** *("the Collaborator")* → the FILTH AND THE FURY, **Sid Vicious** *("the Gimmick")*, **Paul Cook** *("the Tea-maker")* → the FILTH AND THE FURY, **Steve Jones** *("the Crook")* → the FILTH AND THE FURY, Ronald Biggs *("the Exile")*, **Jess Conrad** *(Jess)* → ABSOLUTE BEGINNERS, **Eddie Tenpole Tudor** *(kiosk attendant)* → ABSOLUTE BEGINNERS → SID & NANCY → STRAIGHT TO HELL → WALKER, Irene Handl *(usherette)* ← WONDERWALL ← SMASHING TIME ← JUST FOR FUN / → ABSOLUTE BEGINNERS, Mary Millington *(Mary, the Crook's partner)*, Liz Fraser *(woman in cinema)* ← UP THE JUNCTION ← the FAMILY WAY ← EVERY DAY'S A HOLIDAY, Julian Holloway *(man)* ← CATCH US IF YOU CAN ← a HARD DAY'S NIGHT, Helen Of Troy *(Helen)* ← JUBILEE / → the FILTH AND THE FURY, Jordan *(t-shirt girl)* ← JUBILEE / → WESTWAY TO THE WORLD → the FILTH & THE FURY, Nancy Spungen *(herself)* → D.O.A. → the FILTH & THE FURY

Storyline: Part performance documentary, part bio-pic, part everything under the sun, Malcolm McLaren tells you a story of the rise and fall of number one punk group, the Sex Pistols. Manager McLaren tells HIS account of the "Swindle", all the advances, the swearing, the arguments and there's even a piece directed by Russ Meyer. *MCS*

Movie rating: *7

Visual: video + dvd

Off the record: Malcolm McLaren subsequently found more worldly backing (the World's Famous Supreme Team) on a couple of massive UK dance hits, namely 'Buffalo Gals' and 'Double Dutch'. *MCS*

---

the SEX PISTOLS (& Various Artists)

Mar 79. (d-lp/d-c) *Virgin; (VD/TCV 2510) Warners; <45083>* [7] [ ]
– God save the Queen (symphony) / Rock around the clock / Johnny B Goode / Road runner / Black arabs / Anarchy in the UK / Watcha gonna do about it / Who killed Bambi? / Silly thing / Substitute / Don't give me no lip child / I'm not your stepping stone / Lonely boy / Something else / Anarchie pour le UK / Einmal war Belsen bortrefflich / Einmal war Belsen wirflich bortrefflich / No one is innocent / My way / C'mon everybody / Emi (orch) / The great rock'n'roll swindle / You need hands / Friggin' in the riggin'. *(re-iss. 1-lp Jan80; V 2168)* – hit No.11 *(re-iss. Apr89 lp/c; OVED/+C 234) (d-cd iss.Jul86; CDVD 2510) (cd re-iss. May93; CDVDX 2510)*

S/track review: Never mind the bollocks, here's the swindle, 'The GREAT ROCK'N'ROLL SWINDLE', an album of unadulterated fun and crap in equal measures. Long gone was their sensational "Bollocks" debut LP of '77, this was the muck'n'brassic-necked divulgence that 'Pistols fans were subjected to. Released on record a month after the controversial o.d. death of bassist SID VICIOUS (2nd of February 1979), manager/guru MALCOLM McLAREN – not JOHNNY ROTTEN, well almost! – and his remaining motley crue of STEVE JONES, PAUL COOK, and other honorary PISTOLS helped put together this hit or miss double-set. The project being manager MALCOLM McLAREN's brainchild, the man himself opens the album's account via a hoarse and coarse narrative of the 'Pistols story over a "symphony" version of 'God Save The Queen'. Honorary Pistol No.1, TEN POLE TUDOR hits the extremely high notes for a rollickin', bollockin' rendition of Bill Haley's 'Rock Around The Clock', in fact EDDIE (TPT) puts in the best performance by far courtesy of his (and fashion guru, Vivienne Westwood's) 'Who Killed Bambi?'. Has it really been twenty-five-odd years since this one had me rolling in the aisles with laughter at the local cinema, and how many ways can you say "Bamboiii / Bambaaeee / Bambarrgh!". The funniest film song of all time – no question. Compare this to JOHNNY ROTTEN and his shambolic rehearsal covers of 'Johnny B Goode' and 'Road Runner'; punk at its most embryonic and with the ginger one forgetting the words, a total embarrassment. The Swindle goes from scrag-end to scrag-end with the 'Black Arabs" run-through disco, Stars On 45-like medley of all the 'PISTOLS best-loved numbers, until now that is. Would the real SEX PISTOLS stand up? – thankfully 'Anarchy In The UK' (the 45 in all its glory) gave the album the kick up the proverbial arse it needed. That old 60s, Small Faces nugget, 'Watcha Gonna Do About It', sees ROTTEN and Co get back to their old boyish antics what the great Steve Marriott and Ronnie Lane would think of this is anyone's guess; we can't ask them now. Post-ROTTEN (he'd now become John Lydon), Messrs COOK and JONES (with the former on vocals) carried on regardless courtesy of rousing Top 10 hit song, 'Silly Thing', while JONES got his turn through 'Lonely Boy'. Squeezed somewhat precariously between the two aforementioned dirges, three ROTTEN/rotten (delete as appropriate) covers, the Who's 'Substitute', 'Don't Give Me No Lip Child' (Dave Berry originally recorded this!) and Boyce & Hart's 'I'm Not Your Stepping Stone' (written for the Monkees). Another anomaly and oddity stems from JERZIMY's Frenchy accordion take of 'Anarchie Pour Le UK'; Jacques Brel or Plastic Bertrand anyone? Where did McLAREN dig them up from? Shocking even by today's standards – although life has become a bit predictable since the demise of Punk and the Pistols – the extremely un-PC "Belsen Was A Gas" (aka 'Einmal Belsen War – Wirflich – Bortrefflich') and you can vote for your fave rendition by either ROTTEN or another "swindler" the Great Train Robber, RONNIE BIGGS (intro by real Nazi, Martin Borman). The latter wins it in spades. Brazilian exile, BIGGS (with JONES as co-writer) gets into the "thick of it" again with Top 10 hit, 'No One Is Innocent', surely he was the oldest punk rocker in town (well, Rio, to be exact!), although there was a UK Sub who could contest that. Ahh! The vicious Sidney, his epitaph is written all over this film and soundtrack. SID gets his three-pennorth in, courtesy of a trio of accompanying Top 10 smashes, all going back two decades and a bit, Eddie Cochran's 'Something Else' and 'C'mon Everybody', plus Sinatra's 'My Way' (penned by Paul Anka). It was SID's classic reading (the B-side of the aforementioned BIGGS hit) that got fans and pundits raving. How could a man with seemingly no vocal talent whatsoever (although this was accentuated and acted out in its full cinematic glory) achieve so much? Maybe raw talent and bravado had more power over manufactured pop shite after all. Anyway, VICIOUS never got to sing/shout much else after that, as his drugged-up lifestyle saw only one outcome – death. The latter quarter of the double-set also featured an orchestral "posh among the dosh" version of 'EMI', never mind the dog's bollocks here's STEVE JONES as we've never heard him before – and never likely to hear him again either. The abysmal McLAREN is but a joke on 'You Need Hands' and er.. I'll tell you a story – no, a fact! . . . you're no friggin' Max Bygraves! (stick to Buffalo Gals, Malky). Talking about friggin', the whole Jolly Roger cast gets plastered and with er . . . all hands on deck (or indeed, dick!) the fun explodes on 'Friggin' In The Riggin'', a naughty schoolboy sing-a-long that complemented the preceding JONES/TEMPLE/COOK title track. Chaos? In abundance – "Cause there was fuck all else to do". *MCS*

Album rating: *7.5

– spinoff hits, etc. –

the SEX PISTOLS: No One Is Innocent (A Punk Prayer By Ronnie Biggs / My Way

Jun 78. (7") *(VS 220)* [7] [–]
(12") *(VS 220-12 A1/2)* – The Biggest Blow (a punk prayer by Ronnie Biggs) / My Way.
(12"+=) *(VS 220-12 A3)* – (interview).

the SEX PISTOLS: Something Else / Friggin' In The Riggin'

Feb 79. (7") *(VS 240)* [3] [–]

the SEX PISTOLS: Silly Thing / Who Killed Bambi?

Apr 79. (7") *(VS 256)* [6] [–]

the SEX PISTOLS: C'mon Everybody / God Save The Queen (symphony) / Watcha Gonna Do About It?

Jun 79. (7") *(VS 272)* [3] [–]

the SEX PISTOLS: The Great Rock'n'Roll Swindle / Rock Around The Clock
Oct 79. (7") *(VS 290)* 21 –

the SEX PISTOLS: I'm Not Your Stepping Stone
Jun 80. (7") *(VS 339)* 21 –

GREENDALE

2003 (US 83m) Shakey Pictures

Film genre: experimental/political Rock Musical drama

Top guns: s-w + dir: Bernard Shakey (aka **Neil YOUNG**

Stars: Sarah White *(Sun Green)*, **Eric Johnson** *(Jed Green/Devil)*, **Ben Keith** *(Arius J. "Grandpa" Green)* → HEART OF GOLD, Erik Markegard *(Earth Brown)*, James Mazzeo *(Earl Green)*, Elizabeth Keith *(Grandma Green)*, Paul Supplee *(Officer Carmichael)*, **Pegi Young** *(Edith Green)* → HEART OF GOLD, Sydney Stephan *(widow)*, **Echobrain:- Adam Donkin** *(imitator)*, **Dylan Donkin** *(imitator)* SOME KIND OF MONSTER, **Brian Sagrafena** *(imitator)* → SOME KIND OF MONSTER / **Neil YOUNG as Bernard Shakey** *(Wayne Newton)*

Storyline: 'Six Feet Under' goes country, right down to the radical, misunderstood daughter, but without much of the black humour or eclectic music. Jed Green kills a cop and moves in with the Devil in the local jailhouse, while his uncle Earl finally manages to sell some paintings with Beelzebub's help. It's all too much for Grandpa, who keels over from a heart attack during the ensuing media feeding frenzy. His death serves as a catalyst for his young grandaughter Sun, who chains herself to a statue, gets harassed by the FBI and ultimately heads to Alaska to stave off impending environmental disaster. *BG*

Movie rating: *5.5

Visual: dvd

Off the record: **Echobrain** were a Bay Area, San Francisco heavy metal outfit and friends of Jason Newstead (then of Metallica). So far, they've released two full-length albums, 'Echobrain' (2002) and 'Glean' (2004). *MCS*

NEIL YOUNG & CRAZY HORSE

Aug 03. (cd) *Reprise; <(9362 48543-2)>* 24 22
– Falling from above / Double E / Devil's sidewalk / Leave the driving / Carmichael / Bandit / Grandpa's interview / Bringin' down dinner / Sun Green / Be the rain.

S/track review: The awkward equation of NEIL YOUNG (Bernard Shakey) + film-making has generally succeeded only in a straightforward live performance context. As an extended and often self-conscious series of grainy, lip-synching music videos knitted into a vague narrative, 'GREENDALE' didn't do much to alter that impression, even if its social protest was laudable and its ambition a kick up the backside for YOUNG's floundering career. The "musical novel" of a soundtrack works a little better, but if it's possible to roughly categorise the man's albums into bluesy plodder, rocker and acoustic, this one leans a bit too heavily on the plod. YOUNG's latter-day CRAZY HORSE outings haven't been his best, but it's RALPH MOLINA and bassist BILLY TALBOT who yet again set the meandering pace here. Their grizzled sponsor nods and noodles along like the sage Grandpa Green, recounting his backwater vignettes in a tone halfway between barroom anecdote and kitchen table confessional. It's a tone he nails handsomely on 'Bandit', a whispered elegy for rootless, penniless artists everywhere, one with a ghost of YOUNG's great 70s meditation on human desperation, 'Tired Eyes'. And it's hardly a coincidence that 'Bandit' is a slack-stringed acoustic ballad rather than a bluesy chugger. With the rambling sleevenotes shedding as much light on YOUNG's creative process as they do the characters or plot, the convoluted story itself is interesting primarily as a vehicle for its well-aimed socio-political barbs; after the plangent 'Falling From Above', the only other time the music really rises above the concept is when YOUNG varies the texture with some pump organ on 'Bringin' Down Dinner', and especially when CRAZY HORSE accelerate into a semi-gallop on closing Earth Mother anthem, 'Be The Rain': the harmonies fly, YOUNG's guitar heaves and writhes, and suddenly the years fall away like so much small-town gossip. To be fair, 'GREENDALE' is a song cycle, designed to be listened to in a single sitting, and while it isn't such a bad place to be, like every small town it only really comes alive in fits and starts. *BG*

Album rating: *6.5

GROOVE

2000 (US 83m) Sony Pictures (R)

Film genre: Rave/Dance-music drama

Top guns: s-w + dir: Greg Harrison

Stars: Lola Glaudini *(Leyla Heydel)*, Mackenzie Firgens *(Harmony Stitts)*, Denny Kirkwood *(Colin Turner)*, Hamish Linklater *(David Turner)*, Rachel True *(Beth Anderson)* ← CB4, Steve Van Wormer *(Ernie Townsend)*, **Vincent Riverside** *(Anthony Mitchell)*

Storyline: Invited to a word-of-mouth San Francisco rave by his brother Colin, bookish would-be writer David Turner finds the key to his inner groove-man unlocked by drugs, music and an opposites-attract bond with hardened party girl Leyla Heydel. The blissed-out mood bottoms out, though, when Colin's fiancée discovers his secret. *BG*

Movie rating: *6

Visual: dvd

Off the record: **Vincent Riverside** released four albums (1996-2002) as frontman with Gasoline.

Various Artists

Jun 00. (cd) *Kinetic; <47765>* –
– "No obstacles, only challenges" / Girls like us (B-15 PROJECT feat. CRISSY D & LADY G) / Champagne beat boogie (BOOZY & SWAN) / You're the lucky one (BABY D LOVE) / Duke's up – Joshua's dubwise mix (WADE HAMPTON) / 20 minutes of disco glory – Simon's come-unity mix (DJ GARTH & E.T.I.) / Perpetual (CHRISTIAN SMITH & E.B.E. PRESENT TIMELINE) / Halcyon and on and on (ORBITAL) / Anomaly (calling your name) – Ferry Corsten remix (LIBRA PRESENTS TAYLOR) / Heaven scent (BEDROCK) / Beachcoma (HYBRID) / Protocol (SYMBIOSIS) / "Wanna go to the Endup?" / Infinitely gentle blows – Scott Hardkiss aural hallucination mix (ALTER]RING).

S/track review: Much more a mellow, West Coast connoisseur's choice than the chav anthems which filled out this movie's satirical, turn-of-the-millennium cousin, 'KEVIN & PERRY GO LARGE', the soundtrack actually shares a producer in HYBRID, here supplying the trance-goes-turntablist 'Beachcoma'. And in ORBITAL's 'Halcyon + On + On', there's at least one cut guaranteed to get middle-aged rave veterans babbling about muddy fields off the M25. As well as putting the whole thing together, soundtrack designer WISHFM/WADE RANDOLPH HAMPTON is credited with the most soulful, evocative and addictive groove of the programme in 'Duke's Up', layering Afro-Eastern brass parts over a funky loop and asteroids effects. BOOZY & SWAN's 'Champagne Beat Boogie' solicits a disco pulse and a classicist, Loose Joints-esque vibe. Other highlights include the trembling, 'White Lines'-like bassline and percussive thrust of DJ GARTH & E.T.I.'s '20 Minutes Of Disco Glory', but 'GROOVE' is merely a good DJ mix rather than a great one, and the relative anonymity of the music means that unlike cult youth culture B-soundtracks of the past, it isn't likely to be remembered in ten years never mind thirty. *BG*

Album rating: *5.5

GROUPIE GIRL

US title 'I AM A GROUPIE'

1970 (UK 86m) Salon Production for Eagle Films (X)

Film genre: showbiz/Pop/Rock-music drama

Top guns: s-w: Derek Ford (+ dir), Suzanne Mercer

Stars: Esme Johns *(Sally)*, Billy Boyle *(Wes)* → SIDE BY SIDE, Donald Sumpter *(Steve)*, Richard Shaw *(Morrie)*, Neil Hallett *(detective)* → MELODY, Charles Finch *(dog handler)*, Eliza Terry *(mooncake girl)*, Jimmy Edwards *(Bob)*, Madeleine + Mary Collinson *(twin groupies)* ← PERMISSIVE, **Opal Butterfly:- Tom Doherty, Trevor Adams, Ken Hutchison, Simon King** *(the Sweaty Betty group)*

Storyline: "Sex-hungry Superfan of the Pop Stars ... they don't collect autographs any more!". Bored teenager Sally is desperate to meet her rock star heroes the Sweaty Betty Group, so one night she sneaks on board their van and becomes their groupie. When she gets to London she finds a new world of sex and drugs and discovers a groupie's life is not an easy one. Following a murder the police raid her flat, and Sal does the only thing she can to hide the hash – she swallows it. Stoned out of her mind, now her troubles really begin. *JZ*

Movie rating: *3

Visual: video

Off the record: Opal Butterfly's drummer **Simon King** chose the path of former member, LEMMY, and eventually found employment with Hawkwind.

—

Various Artists (score: John Fiddy & Alan Hawkshaw *)

Dec 70. (lp) *Polydor; (2384 031)* ☐ ☐
– You're a groupie girl (OPAL BUTTERFLY) / To Jackie (ENGLISH ROSE) / Four wheel drive (SALON BAND) * / Got a lot of life (VIRGIN STIGMA) * / I wonder did you (BILLY BOYLE) / Gigging song (OPAL BUTTERFLY) / Disco 2 (SALON BAND) * / Now you're gone (I'm a man) (VIRGIN STIGMA) * / Yesterday's hero (ENGLISH ROSE) / Love me (give a little) (VIRGIN STIGMA) * / Looking for love (BILLY BOYLE) / Sweet motion (SALON BAND) * / Love's a word away (ENGLISH ROSE) / True blue (SALON BAND) * / Groupie girl (it doesn't matter what you do) (VIRGIN STIGMA) *.

S/track review: This is a 1970 soundtrack that sounds as if it's from around 1965, albeit with heavier undertones. Two "proper" rock groups were on board for 'GROUPIE GIRL': OPAL BUTTERFLY (subsequent stamping ground for Hawkwind/Motorhead-bound LEMMY and Mott The Hoople's Ray Major) and ENGLISH ROSE, the latter including former Love Affair organist, Lynton Guest and frontman/songwriter Edwards. OPAL BUTTERFLY (cameo band, the Sweaty Betty group – with another future Hawkwind member – see line-up above) seduced us with two Hollies-like numbers, 'You're A Groupie Girl' & 'Gigging Song', both also available as an A&B-sided single. ENGLISH ROSE (presumably named after a recent Fleetwood Mac LP), also spun out A&B sides, 'To Jackie' & 'Yesterday's Hero', the first very reminiscent of the Moody Blues although juxtaposing mellotron with strings/brass, the second scribed by John Sebastian. For the wailing instrumental pop score, composers Alan Hawkshaw and John Fiddy take on the guise of SALON BAND, completing four tracks, 'Four Wheel Drive', 'Disco 2', 'Sweet Motion' and 'True Blue'. The same pairing was also behind follow-on act, VIRGIN STIGMA (fronted by funky vocalist Peter Lee Stirling), on a further four cuts, 'Got A Lot Of Life', 'Now You're Gone (I'm A Man)', 'Love Me (Give A Little)' and closer 'Groupie Girl (It Doesn't Matter What You Do)', best described as the Spencer Davis Group fused with Steam. Dublin-born star-turn, BILLY BOYLE, strummed and sang his way through two film tracks, 'I Wonder Did You' & 'Looking For Love'. *MCS*

Album rating: *5.5

– spinoff releases, etc. –

ENGLISH ROSE: Yesterday's Hero / To Jackie
Dec 70. (7") *(2058 040)* ☐ ☐

OPAL BUTTERFLY: You're A Groupie Girl / Gigging Song
Dec 70. (7") *(2058 041)* ☐ ☐

☐ the GURU
(⇒ Pop/Rock Scores)

☐ Arlo GUTHRIE segment
(⇒ ALICE'S RESTAURANT)

☐ Woody GUTHRIE segment
(⇒ BOUND FOR GLORY)

GYPSY 83

2001 (US 94m) Luna Pictures / Staccato Films / Velvet Films (R)

Film genre: coming-of-age comedy & road movie

Top guns: s-w: (+ dir) Todd Stephens ← EDGE OF SEVENTEEN (+ story w/ Tim Kaltenecker)

Stars: Sara Rue *(Gypsy Vale)* ← a SLIPPING-DOWN LIFE, Kett Turton *(Clive Webb)*, Karen Black *(Bambi LeBleau)* ← NASHVILLE ← EASY RIDER ← YOU'RE A BIG BOY NOW / → HOUSE OF 1000 CORPSES, **John DOE** *(Ray Vale)*, Anson Scoville *(Zachariah Peachey)*, Paulo Costanzo *(Troy)* ← JOSIE AND THE PUSSYCATS, Stephanie McVay *(Polly Pearl)* ← EDGE OF SEVENTEEN, Carolyn Baeumler *(Lois)*, Andersen Gabrych *(Banning)* ← EDGE OF SEVENTEEN

Storyline: Overweight goth Gypsy is fed up with her boring life in Sandusky, Ohio. Her only escape is listening to her idol Stevie Nicks along with her strange friend Clive, whose main pastime is recording Gypsy singing in the cemetery. When they learn of the "Night of 1000 Stevies" competition in New York, they hop on the Trans-Am and go for first prize. Gypsy might also meet her long-lost mother so it should be a night to remember for a thousand and one reasons. *JZ*

Movie rating: *6

Visual: video + dvd

Off the record: Tracks not featured on the album are as follows:- 'Surround You With Love' (PJ LAQUERICA), 'Crystal Sea' (SARA RUE & JOHN DOE), 'Talk To Me' (SARA RUE), 'Crystal Sea' (CHE ZERO), 'Turn Up The Radio' (AUTOGRAPH), 'When Sunny Gets Blue' (KAREN BLACK), 'I'm Too Sexy' (the FRAT BOYS), 'Country Road Show' (JOHN REED KEKAR), 'Just Like Heaven' (the CURE). *MCS*

—

Various Cast/Artists (score: Marty Beller)

Oct 03. (cd) *Metropolis; <297>* ☐ ☐
– Pieces (CLAIRE VOYANT) / Talk to me (DIVA DESTRUCTION) / Doing the unstuck (the CURE) / Walking in the jungle (KAREN BLACK & the SMARTMEN) / Eccentricity (MAGENTA) / Nothing special (MECHANICAL CABARET) / Twenty-four years (CLAIRE VOYANT) / I want a lip (KAREN BLACK & the SMARTMEN) / Severance (BAUHAUS) / Dilaudid (postponed) (VELVET ACID CHRIST) / Suffer in silence (APOPTYGMA BERZERK) / Iolite – Francis A. Preve remix (CLAIRE VOYANT) / Voice so sweet (SARA RUE).

S/track review: Often there is more in what you don't say than what you do. In the case of 'GYPSY 83', it seems to be more about what is not included rather than what is. The film is about two goth-types on a road trip to New York for a Stevie Nicks convention, however the soundtrack is not a goth heavy album. Is the soundtrack trying to be more accessible to the uninitiated or just showing the unseen side of their culture to an ignorant audience? It's difficult to say. There are no, what might be considered, major goth acts such as Marilyn Manson or Cradle Of Filth to name but two. Nor, indeed, is there any Stevie Nicks songs. Instead the soundtrack is a smattering of heavy, dark and atmospheric songs such as 'Eccentricity' by MAGENTA, 'Nothing Special' from MECHANICAL CABARET, CLARE VOYANT's 'Twenty-Four Years' and APOPTYGMA BEZERK's 'Dilaudid (Postponed)' that would be considered goth. There is a strong melodic electro feel running through many of these and other tracks that isn't always acknowledged in goth music. There are also a couple of dark jazz numbers from KAREN BLACK, while BAUHAUS weigh in with an epic cover of 'Severance'. Arguably the best track comes from the CURE with 'Doing The Unstuck', a swirling acoustic-led pop song reminiscent of 'Inbetween Days' or 'Just Like Heaven'. It comes as no surprise to see the CURE feature on a goth album, Robert Smith and co., while not exactly an outright goth band, do have a large following in the community, which might have something to do with the music or just the liberal application of mascara. Who knows? 'GYPSY 83' is a decent soundtrack that is accessible to anyone interested in goth music while remaining true to what is often a very misunderstood culture. *CM*

Album rating: *6

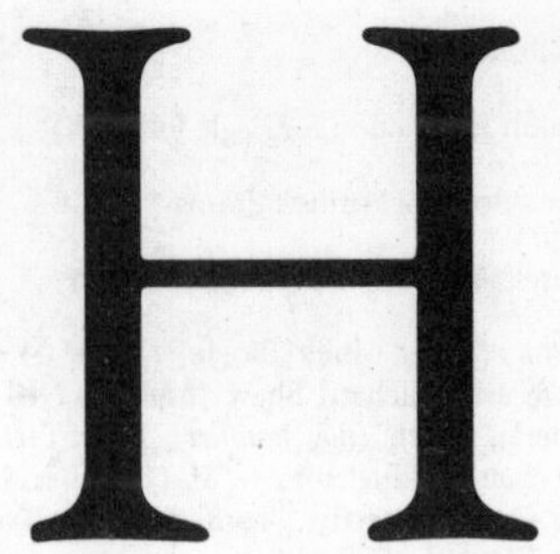

HAIR

1979 (US/W.Ger 121m) CIP Filmproduktion / United Artists (PG)

Film genre: Pop/Rock Musical comedy/drama

Top guns: dir: Milos Forman → MAN ON THE MOON / s-w: Michael Weller

Stars: John Savage *(Claude)* ← STEELYARD BLUES, Treat Williams *(Berger)* → FLASHPOINT → WHERE THE RIVERS FLOW NORTH, Beverly D'Angelo *(Sheila)* → COAL MINER'S DAUGHTER → SUGAR TOWN, **Annie Golden** *(Jeannie)* → THIS IS MY LIFE → TEMPTATION, Dorsey Wright *(Hud)*, Don Dacus *(Woof)*, Nicholas Ray *(the General)*, **Cheryl Barnes** *(Hud's fiancée)*, Richard Bright *(Fenton)* ← RANCHO DELUXE ← PAT GARRETT & BILLY THE KID / → the IDOLMAKER → WHO'S THE MAN?, **Melba Moore** *("3-5-0-0" soloist)* ← COTTON COMES TO HARLEM / → the FIGHTING TEMPTATIONS, **Ronnie Dyson** *("3-5-0-0" soloist)*, **Ellen Foley** *("Black Boys")*, Nell Carter *("Ain't Go No" / "White Boys")*, Kurt Yahjian *("Ain't No Go")* ← JESUS CHRIST SUPERSTAR, Charlaine Woodward *("White Boys")* → the MILLION DOLLAR HOTEL, Chuck Patterson *("White Boys")* → the FIVE HEARTBEATS, Ren Woods *('Aquarius' soloist)* ← YOUNGBLOOD ← CAR WASH ← SPARKLE / → XANADU, Michael Jeter *(Sheldon)* → FEAR AND LOATHING IN LAS VEGAS → SOUTH OF HEAVEN, WEST OF HELL, Miles Chapin *(Steve)* → GET CRAZY → MAN ON THE MOON, Leata Galloway *(Electric Blues)* → PANISCHE ZEITEN, Charlotte Rae *(lady in pink)* ← HELLO DOWN THERE, Suki Love *(debutante #2)* → BLANK GENERATION

Storyline: Naive hick Claude arrives in New York with a few days to kill before signing up for the Vietnam war. As well as turning the head of posh chick Sheila, he attracts the less welcome attentions of the local hippies, led by the bushy eyebrowed Berger. In a moment of unrestrained surrealism, Berger tails Sheila and her snooty pals around Central Park on horseback to the controversial strains of 'Sodomy', before leading the gang in gatecrashing Sheila's party, all in the name of uniting her with the object of her affections. Inane, episodic events cling vainly to the concept of a plot as Claude goes off to the army, leaving his friends and lover to the bitter blast of a Big Apple winter. *BG*

Movie rating: *6

Visual: video + dvd

Off the record: Brooklyn-raised **Ronnie Dyson** had been in the original Broadway version of 'Hair'. He even reached the US Top 10 in 1970 with 'Why Can't I Touch You', coming not long after an appearance in the movie, 'Putney Swope' (1969). Many will remember his high-pitched vox in 1971's minor US/UK hit, 'When You Get Right Down To It' (with lyrics "Gonna make you an offer you can't refuse..". Sadly, he died of a heart failure on the 10th November, 1990, having just turned 40. **Ellen Foley**'s claim to fame was her dual role squeezed beside MEAT LOAF in the 'Bat Out Of Hell' number, 'Paradise By The Dashboard Lights'. She was the girlfriend of the CLASH's Mick Jones around the time of her moderately successful LPs, 'Night Out' (1979), 'Spirit Of St. Louis' (1981) and 'Another Breath' (1983). She subsequently worked with JOE JACKSON, while maintaining her career as an actress ('Fatal Attraction' & 'Married To The Mob'). *MCS*

Various Cast/Company (*) (score/composer: GALT MacDERMOT / lyrics: James Rado & Gerome Ragni)

Mar 79. (d-lp/c) *RCA Victor; <(BL/BK 03274>* 65 May79
– Aquarius (RONNIE DYSON) / Sodomy (*) / Donna – Hashish (TREAT WILLIAMS) / Colored spade (DORSEY WRIGHT) / Manchester (JOHN SAVAGE) / Abie baby – Fourscore (DORSEY WRIGHT, NELL CARTER, CHARLAINE WOODARD & DON DACUS) / I'm black – Ain't got no (DON DACUS & DORSEY WRIGHT) / Air (ANNIE GOLDEN) / Party music *[not on cd]* / My conviction *[not on cd]* / I got life (JOHN SAVAGE) / Frank Mills (BEVERLY D'ANGELO) / Hair (JOHN SAVAGE & TREAT WILLIAMS) / L.B.J. (*) / Electric blues – Old fashioned melody (RICHARD BRIGHT) / Hare Krishna (*) / Where do I go? (JOHN SAVAGE) / Black boys / White boys (TRUDY PERKINS, NELL CARTER & CHARLAINE WOODARD) / Walking in space (*) / Easy to be hard (CHERYL BARNES) / 3-5-0-0 (MELBA MOORE) / Good morning starshine (BEVERLY D'ANGELO, NELL CARTER, JOHN SAVAGE & TREAT WILLIAMS) / What a piece of work is man / Somebody to love / Don't put it down (*) / The flesh failures – Let the sunshine in (JOHN SAVAGE & TREAT WILLIAMS). *<(cd-iss. Sep99 on 'R.C.A.'; 07863 67812-2)>*

S/track review: Like 'GREASE', this was a late 70s nostalgia job before that decade became nostalgia fodder in its own right. Released amid the aftershocks of a punk coup d'état, it was never going to make much of an impression beyond ageing baby boomers. A band like the Tubes might easily have come up with the neo-doo-wop subversion of 'Sodomy', but the frazzled, free love radicalism indulged in most of the score must have appeared glaringly out of step in 1979. In 'Donna', our hero lays his mutated head at the feet of a 16 year-old virgin ("psychedelic urchin") who's been "busted for her beauty", before the cast recite a list of unfashionable drugs. Time Out trashed the film as a "National Lampoon parody", and while there's enough soundbite-campy vocalising to back that up (as well as the presence of BEVERLY D'ANGELO, who, strangely enough, almost became one of Ronnie Hawkins' Hawks in another life, and who puts in a charming enough turn on the calypso-lite of 'Good Morning Starshine'), the soundtrack has just enough of a 70s funk-rock sheen to keep it viable, and is worth picking up for the heraldic, almost Deodato-dramatic update of 'Aquarius' alone. Annoyingly, even the anniversary reissue offers no credits for the singers, never mind any musicians. There's no mistaking MELBA MOORE, though, a lone survivor from the original production performing the heavy duty slap bass vamp-cum-ensemble dixie-gospel of '3-5-0-0'. And CHERYL BARNES (a non-professional pulled from her job as a hotel maid in New England) surely deserves a credit for her coruscating soul ballad 'Easy To Be Hard', a minor US hit. The late NELL CARTER flaunts a larynx like no other, the anonymous rhythm section hold down some great funk breaks (see 'Electric Blues', 'Abie Baby', 'Hare Krishna', 'White Boys', etc.) if you can get past the warbling, and at times – 'Walking In Space', the climactic 'Let The Sunshine In' – even the ensemble pieces get over their own theatricality. *BG*

Album rating: *6

– spinoff hits, etc. –

CHERYL BARNES: Easy To Be Hard / Good Morning Starshine

Apr 79. (7") *<11548> (PB 1548)* 64 Jul79

HAIRSPRAY

1988 (US 94m) New Line Cinema (PG)

Film genre: Pop/Rock Musical comedy

Top guns: s-w + dir: John Waters (+ story) → CRY-BABY

Stars: **Sonny Bono** *(Franklin von Tussle)* ← GOOD TIMES, **Ruth Brown** *(Motormouth Maybelle)* ← ROCK'N'ROLL REVUE ← RHYTHM AND BLUES REVUE / → SHAKE, RATTLE & ROCK! tv → LIGHTNING IN A BOTTLE, Divine *(Edna Turnblad / Arvin Hodgepile)*, **Deborah Harry** *(Velma von Tussle)* <= BLONDIE =>, Ricki Lake *(Tracy Turnblad)* → WORKING GIRL → LAST EXIT TO BROOKLYN → CRY-BABY → JACKIE'S BACK! → HAIRSPRAY re-make, Michael St. Gerard *(Link Larkin)* → GREAT BALLS OF FIRE!, Jerry Stiller *(Wilbur Turnblad)* → HAIRSPRAY re-make, **Colleen Fitzpatrick** *(Amber von Tussle)* → ROCK STAR, Leslie Ann Powers *(Penny Pingleton)*, Mink Stole *(Tammy)* → CRY-BABY → MONSTER MASH: THE MOVIE → PINK AS THE DAY SHE WAS BORN → SPLENDOR, **Ric Ocasek** *(beatnik cat)*, Pia Zadora *(beatnik chick)* ← VOYAGE OF THE ROCK ALIENS, **Toussaint McCall** *(himself)*, Josh Charles *(Iggy)*, John Waters *(psychiatrist)* → HAIRSPRAY re-make

Storyline: Every teenage girl in 60s Baltimore dreams of appearing on the Corny Collins Show, and when Tracy Turnblad is the unlikely winner of a featured spot she sets her mind on ridding the show of its discrimination against blacks, who are only allowed to appear once a week. On her adventures she steals her arch rival's boyfriend and gets arrested demonstrating at a theme park, but it's all part of the coming of age process for Tracy and her friends. *JZ*

Movie rating: *7

Visual: video + dvd

Off the record: **Ric Ocasek** was a member of the Cars.

Various Artists (score: Kenny Vance)

Mar 88. (lp/c/cd) *M.C.A.; <(MCA/+C/D 6228)>* Jul88
– Hairspray (RACHEL SWEET) / The Madison time – part 1 (RAY BRYANT COMBO) / I'm blue (the gong-gong song) (the IKETTES) / Mama didn't lie (JAN BRADLEY) / Town without pity (GENE PITNEY) / The roach (dance) (GENE & WENDELL) / Foot stomping – part 1 (the FLARES) / Shake a tail feather (the FIVE DU-TONES) / The bug (JERRY DALLMAN & THE KNIGHTCAPS) / You'll lose a good thing (BARBARA LYNN) / I wish I were a princess (LITTLE PEGGY MARCH) / Nothing takes the place of you (TOUSSAINT McCALL).

S/track review: Nostalgia and art of the dance craze in the early 60s gets full-on treatment by filmmaker John Waters. Former "jailbait" darling of the 'Stiff' label, 24-year-old RACHEL SWEET exclusively came out of retirement for the fresh-faced opening title track. In stark comparison, 'The Madison Time – Part I', a Top 30 hit from 1960 by bandleader/group RAY BRYANT COMBO, was instructionally narrative ("hit it and away we go") to the point of tedium. The dance craze theme finally got rockin' courtesy of the . . . er "squish, squash" of 'The Roach' and the similarly-themed Cliff-meets-Mizell treasure, 'The Bug'; in those days they hit the dancefloors rather than call pest-control. If the vermin weren't altogether dead after a bit of 'Foot Stomping' by the FLARES (another Top 30 smash), then the deep baritone of the FIVE DU-TONES on 'Shake A Tail Feather' would certainly "Twist" them all about. Other highlights were the Ike-less IKETTES, backing singer TINA TURNER on top form with Top 20 R&B track, 'I'm Blue (The Gong-Gong Song)', the similarly-charting, CURTIS MAYFIELD-penned 'Mama Didn't Lie' by JAN BRADLEY and the sad lament that was GENE PITNEY's cinematic title theme to a 'Town Without Pity'. The set culminated with a trio of "rainy day" soul ballads in the shape of 'You'll Lose A Good Thing' (a Top 10'er by BARBARA LYNN in 1962), 'I Wish I Were A Princess' (Top 40, 1963) and the rather late-in-the-day (1967!) hit, 'Nothing Takes The Place Of You' by Louisiana R&B exponent, TOUSSAINT McCALL. On reflection, to be part of America in the early 60s, pre-BEATLES era, mightn't've been all that bad after all. *MCS*

Album rating: *7

HAIRSPRAY

2007 re-make (US 107m) New Line Cinema (PG)

Film genre: teen Dance-pop Musical comedy

Top guns: dir: Adam Shankman / s-w: Leslie Dixon (musical play: Mark O'Donnell) (1988 s-w: John Waters)

Stars: John Travolta *(Edna Turnblad)* ← BE COOL ← SWORDFISH ← PRIMARY COLORS ← PULP FICTION ← SHOUT ← STAYING ALIVE ← URBAN COWBOY ← GREASE ← SATURDAY NIGHT FEVER, Michelle Pfeiffer *(Velma Von Tussle)* ← I AM SAM ← the STORY OF US ← GREASE 2, Christopher Walken *(Wilbur Turnblad)* ← ROMANCE & CIGARETTES ← the COUNTRY BEARS ← TOUCH ← LAST MAN STANDING ← PULP FICTION ← WAYNE'S WORLD 2 ← HOMEBOY, Amanda Bynes *(Penny Pingleton)* James Marsden *(Corny Collins)*, **Queen Latifah** *(Motormouth Maybelle)* ← BROWN SUGAR ← the COUNTRY BEARS ← WHO'S THE MAN? ← JUICE ← HOUSE PARTY 2 ← JUNGLE FEVER, Brittany Snow *(Amber Von Tussle)*, Zac Efron *(Link Larkin)* ← HIGH SCHOOL MUSICAL / → HIGH SCHOOL MUSICAL 2, Allison Janney *(Prudy Pingleton)* ← OVER THE HEDGE ← PRIMARY COLORS ← PRIVATE PARTS ← WALKING AND TALKING, Elijah Kelley *(Seaweed)* ← TAKE THE LEAD, Nikki Blonsky *(Tracy Turnblad)*, Taylor Parks *(Little Inez)*, Paul Dooley *(Mr. Spritzer)* ← a MIGHTY WIND ← POPEYE, Jerry Stiller *(Mr. Pinky)*, John Waters *(flasher)* ← HAIRSPRAY, Ricki Lake *(talent agent)* ← JACKIE'S BACK! ← CRY-BABY ← LAST EXIT TO BROOKLYN ← WORKING GIRL ← HAIRSPRAY, Spencer Liff *(Mikey)* → ACROSS THE UNIVERSE, Marc Shaiman *(talent agent #2)*

Storyline: Tracy Turnblad has one ambition – to dance on the Corny Collins show. When she impresses Corny with her moves at an audition her dream comes true and she is selected to appear. However, when she finds out that black dancers are only allowed on the show once a month, she begins an equal-rights campaign to get this changed. Meanwhile, she has a score to settle with arch-rival Amber von Tussle at the Miss Teenage Hairspray competition – if she can avoid being arrested first. *JZ*

Movie rating: *7

Visual: dvd

Off the record: Queen Latifah was born Dana Elaine Owens on the 18th March 1970 in Newark, New Jersey. The first lady of hip-hop (or was that Roxanne Shante?), she has been on the fringes of major success since her debut album, 'All Hail The Queen', was released by 'Tommy Boy' in '89. Her acting work (see above) has included films 'Barbershop 2: Back In Business' and 'Chicago'. *MCS*

—

Various Artists (music: Marc Shaiman)

Jul 07. (cd) *New Line; <39089-2>* ☐ ☐
– Good morning Baltimore (NIKKI BLONSKY) / The nicest kids in town (JAMES MARSDEN) / It takes two (ZAC EFRON) / (The legend of) Miss Baltimore Crabs (MICHELLE PFEIFFER) / I can hear the bells (NIKKI BLONSKY) / Ladies' choice (ZAC EFRON) / The new girl in town (BRITTANY SNOW) / Welcome to the 60s (NIKKI BLONSKY and JOHN TRAVOLTA) / Run and tell that (ELIJAH KELLEY) / Big, blonde and beautiful (QUEEN LATIFAH) / Big, blonde and beautiful – reprise (JOHN TRAVOLTA and MICHELLE PFEIFFER) / (You're) Timeless to me (JOHN TRAVOLTA and CHRISTOPHER WALKEN) / I know where I've been (QUEEN LATIFAH) / Without love (ZAC EFRON, NIKKI BLONSKY, ELIJAH KELLEY and AMANDA BYNES) / (It's) Hairspray (JAMES MARSDEN) / You can't stop the beat (NIKKI BLONSKY, ZAC EFRON, ELIJAH KELLEY, AMANDA BYNES, JOHN TRAVOLTA and QUEEN LATIFAH) / Come so far (got so far to go) (QUEEN LATIFAH, NIKKI BLONSKY, ZAC EFRON and ELIJAH KELLEY) / Cooties (AIMEE ALLEN) / Mama, I'm a big girl now (RICKI LAKE, MARISSA JARET WINOKUR and NIKKI BLONSKY).

S/track review: Okay, so, in order to be fair and impartial in reviewing the soundtrack to the remake of 'HAIRSPRAY', it is imperative to (try and) strip away the rock-snob-pretensions and review it for what it is, which is a musical. Yep, a musical, lots of sing-a-long tunes, dance routines, greased-lightning and such like. Therefore, 'HAIRSPRAY' is as you would expect, I suppose, with over-produced, big band numbers that you know will get stuck in your head and are more irritating than an itch in an awkward area. Sorry, didn't think remaining objective would be so difficult. Try again. The music probably works better in the film than on its own, though, because in listening to the album you only get part of the story and the songs aren't suited to standing out on their own. The choruses are big and bold with plenty of gospel-type backing vocals and I suppose stand-out track 'Welcome To The 60s' could easily have been sung by the Supremes in another life. Oh, sod it. It's terrible. The songs couldn't get anymore patronising and cloying if they tried, the music is predictable to put it politely and there is something extremely disconcerting about JOHN TRAVOLTA and CHRISTOPHER WALKEN dueting on cheesy love song '(You're) Timeless To Me'. Let's just say I wouldn't want to see the DVD. There, I said it, I've had enough. Unless you like your musicals cheap, cheerful and smothered in cheese, stay well away, or go rent 'GREASE' instead. *CM*

Album rating: *3.5

Bill HALEY

Born: William Haley, 6 Jul'25, Highland Park, Detroit, USA. After leaving school in Pennsylvania, Bill became a travelling musician and yodeller for country bands such as the Down Homers and the Range Drifters. In 1948, at a time when HANK WILLIAMS was king of C&W, HALEY was hired as a DJ for the local WPWA station in Chester, taking up the opportunity to air recordings of his new outfit, the Four Aces. He subsequently abandoned them in the early 50s, recruiting new backers, the Saddlemen, whose reputation was beginning to spread around the hillbilly community. In 1952, HALEY signed to 'Essex' records and issued the double-playlisted 78, 'Icy Heart' / 'Rock The Joint', although this was only a minor seller. Renaming the outfit BILL HALEY & HIS COMETS, they hit upon a winning combination of rockabilly fused with their own interpretation of black R&B, scoring their first Top 20 hit with 'Crazy Man Crazy'. In 1954, the group shifted stables to 'Decca', where they cut 'Thirteen Women' as a single; however, this was to initially flop. The record's flip side, 'Rock Around The Clock', began to garner airplay from some of the more non-conformist radio stations and their follow-up single, 'Shake, Rattle & Roll', became a Top 20 hit (on both! sides of the Atlantic). Due to unprecedented public demand, the aforementioned 'Rock Around The Clock' was re-issued, this landmark track eventually becoming a transatlantic chart-topper. It was undeniably the birth of popular rock'n'roll, the youth culture transforming virtually overnight (parents hated its rebellious overtones, their offspring bopping uninhibitedly around the nation's dancehalls and indeed, cinemas, where it was played on the closing credits to the movie 'The BLACKBOARD JUNGLE'). HALEY was now giving legendary performances up and down the States, although his clean-cut and well-dressed appearance disappointed his newfound British following who were looking for a thinner, unmarried figurehead to portray this hip new sound. The formula was repeated on subsequent platters throughout the mid to late 50s, various rock'n'roll permutations dominating the charts, while modern-day musicals such as 'ROCK AROUND THE CLOCK' (1956) and 'DON'T KNOCK THE ROCK' (1956) lifted the man's profile even higher. The 60s were virtually a non-starter for HALEY, although his revival concerts of the following decade (featured in flicks, 'LET THE GOOD TIMES ROLL' & 'The LONDON ROCK AND ROLL SHOW' – both 1973) saw the obligatory re-issue of 'Rock Around The Clock' hit the UK Top 20. Sadly, after a year spent in and out of hospital with a brain tumor, Bill died of a heart attack (9th of February, 1981) at his home in Harlingen, Texas. *MCS*

- filmography {performance} (composer) –

the Pied Piper Of Cleveland *(1955 {p} =>)* / **Blackboard Jungle** *(1955 hit single =>)* / **Rock Around The Clock** *(1956 {p} =>)* / **Don't Knock The Rock** *(1956 {p} =>)* / Besito A Papa *(1961 {p})* / Juventud Rebelde *(1961 {p})* / a Ritmo De Twist *(1962 {p})* / Adios Cunado! *(1967 score w/ Raul Lavista)* / **Let The Good Times Roll** *(1973 {p} on OST by V/A =>)* / **the London Rock And Roll Show** *(1973 {p} OST =>)* / **Blue Suede Shoes** *(1980 {p} =>)*

HALF-COCKED

1995 (US 90m) Matador Records

Film genre: alt/indie-Rock mockumentary road movie

Top guns: s-w: Suki Hawley (+ dir), Michael Galinsky

Stars: Tara Jane O'Neil *(Rhoda)*, **the Make-Up:- Ian Svenonious** *(Otis)*, **James Canty** *(James)*, **Steve Gamboa** *(Steve)* / **the Grifters:- Dave Shouse** *(Dave)*, **Scott Taylor** *(Scott)*, **Tripp Lamkins** *(Tripp)*, **Stan Gallimore** *(Stan)* / **Sean Meadows** *(Jackson)*, **Jason Noble** *(Jason)*, **Jeff Mueller** *(Jeff)*, **Cynthia Lynn Nelson** *(Cynthia)*, **Jon Cook** *(Elliott)*

Storyline: Rhoda and her friends are bored hanging out at the same old place in Louisville, Kentucky. One night they steal her brother's van which is full of musical instruments and equipment and head off in search of adventure. Soon without money or food, they resort to desperate measures and pretend to be rock band Truckstop to try and make some money. They soon bluff their way onto the bill of a show, and, though none of them can play a note, they somehow pull it off and start to learn to play properly. They decide to continue as Truckstop and drive off for more adventures. *JZ*

Movie rating: *5

Visual: video + 10th anniversary dvd

Off the record: Tara Jane O'Neil (ex-Rodan) & **Cynthia Nelson** (ex-Ruby Falls) had just formed Retsin in 1993 and were about to release their debut indie-country album, 'Salt Lick' (1995), for 'Simple Machines' records. **Jon Cook** (ex-Rodan). Other ex-Rodan affiliates, **Jason Noble** was now in post-rock trio Rachel's, while **Jeff Mueller** moved to NY and formed June Of 44 with ex-Lungfish guy **Sean Meadows** (the latter also subsequently half of Sonora Pine with Tara). *MCS*

—

Various Artists (score: Michael Galinsky)

Jul 95. (cd/d-lp) *Matador; <(OLE 152-2/-1)>* ☐ Aug95 ☐
– Snoopy (SNOOPY) / Dragnalus (UNWOUND) / Time expired (SLANT 6) / No space (TRUCKSTOP) / Tron (RODAN) / CB (SLEEPYHEAD) / Dusty (RUBY FALLS) / Drunk friend (FREAKWATER) / excerpt (SALMON SKIN) / B-9 (VERSUS) / Can I ride (POLVO) / excerpt (RETSIN) / Flowers in our hair (BIG HEIFER) / Invertabrate (BOONDOGGLE) / All-nighter (TRUCKSTOP) / Hey cops (CRAIN) / Magic box (HELIUM) / The man went out (DUNGBEETLE) / Truckstop theme (TRUCKSTOP) / The want (the GRIFTERS). *(d-lp+=)* – 37 push-ups (SMOG) / Star 60 (TWO $ GUITAR) / Satellite (KICKING GIANT) / Crazy man (FREAKWATER).

S/track review: An assortment of post-grunge, nu-indie-rock acts (all in the movie I might add), and worth the asking price alone for the embryonic POLVO song, 'Can I Ride', a quirky collision between Husker Du and Dinosaur Jr. Of the others on this 'Matador' records showcase, only UNWOUND's 'Dragnalus', the folkie FREAKWATER's 'Drunk Friend' and BIG HEIFER's 'Flowers In Our Hair', come close. The grunge came via the monstertruck sound of BOONDOGGLE on 'Invertabrate', while Mudhoney aficionados RODAN ('Tron') and the rarely heard DUNGBEETLE ('The Man Went Out') were just grinding to the core. If one was looking for complete copyists, one would have to point the finger at Lydia Lunch-sounding RUBY FALLS ('Dusty'), who could well have just been better screeching in front of a Sonic Youth backing tape. Another with the feedback more on a high than themselves, the GRIFTERS (and 'The Want'), were to lo-fi what thieving is to a store detective. A taster for many acts from the 'Matador' roster, I went to buy material by POLVO and DUNGBEETLE and couldn't find anything associated with the latter. Who were they? Anybody? *MCS*

Album rating: *5.5 / d-lp *5.5

HALLAM FOE

2007 (UK 95m) FilmFour / Buena Vista International (15)

Film genre: psychological domestic drama

Top guns: s-w: (+ dir) David Mackenzie ← YOUNG ADAM ← the LAST GREAT WILDERNESS, Ed Whitmore (au: Peter Jinks)

Stars: Jamie Bell *(Hallam Foe)*, Sophia Myles *(Kate Breck)*, Ciaran Hinds *(Julius Foe)*, Jamie Sives *(Alasdair)*, Maurice Roeves *(Raymond)* ← the ACID HOUSE ← TUTTI FRUTTI, Ewen Bremner *(Andy)* ← the ACID HOUSE ← MOJO ← TRAINSPOTTING, Claire Forlani *(Verity Foe)*, Ruth Milne *(Jenny)*

Storyline: Hallam Foe is a troubled teen. Mourning the loss of his dead mother, he is edged out of the family home by his stepmother and moves to Edinburgh where he surreptitiously spies on, and subsequently falls for the charms of Kate, who looks remarkably like his dead mother. They develop a complex relationship as Hallam tries to come to terms with the blossoming love for Kate while coming to terms with his mother's passing. *MR*

Movie rating: *8

Visual: dvd

Off the record: nothing

—

Various Artists

Aug 07. (cd) *Domino; (WIGCD 091)* ☐ ☐
– Blue boy (ORANGE JUICE) / Here on my own (U.N.P.O.C.) / The someone else (KING CREOSOTE) / Broken bones (SONS AND DAUGHTERS) / Double shadow (JUNIOR BOYS) / If you could read your mind (CLINIC) / Battle at the gates of dub (FUTURE PILOT AKA) / Lines low to frozen ground (the HOOD) / Hallam Foe dandelion blow (FRANZ FERDINAND) / Tricycle (PSAPP) / Surf song (JAMES YORKSTON) / Also in white (BILL WELLS) / Salvese quien pueda (JUANA MOLINA) / They nicknamed me Evil (CINEMA) / I hope you get what you want (WOODBINE) / Ocean song (MOVIETONE).

S/track review: 'Domino' Records is a rare beast, an independent record label that has stuck to its guns through thick and thin, championing music they loved only for them to hit paydirt with a massive act. Or in this case two: FRANZ FERDINAND and Arctic Monkeys. Only the former appear here, they supply the woozy ballad 'Hallam Foe Dandelion Blow' which was written for the film, while the other 15 tracks here plunder the label's capacious back catalogue for other treats. Fife's lauded Fence Collective supply three of the highlights here: U.N.P.O.C.'s winsome 'Here On My Own', JAMES YORKSTON's magical 'Surf Song', while KING CREOSOTE beguiles on the tremendous 'The Someone

Else', a familiar acoustic paean rendered even more plaintive thanks to some affecting banjo and accordion backing. In stark contrast, Glaswegian quartet SONS AND DAUGHTERS bring some PJ Harvey/Nick Cave-esque tension to bear on the terse and brooding 'Broken Bones', while the artful clamour of ORANGE JUICE's 'Blue Boy' sounds as fresh now as when Edwyn Collins first rattled through it in the early 80s. Turning at right angles from that are CLINIC's nervy 'If You Could Read Your Mind', FUTURE PILOT AKA's dreamy 'Battle At The Gates Of Dub' and the HOOD's barely-there 'Lines Low To Frozen Ground'. Only the suburban electropop of JUNIOR BOYS' 'Double Shadow' fails to be completely convincing, in this context it feels flimsy in the company of so many weighty musos. It is leftfield, Falkirk-born jazzer BILL WELLS, however, who provides the finest moment here. 'Also In White' is a wistful harmonica-led instrumental that could be a homage to John Barry's theme from 'MIDNIGHT COWBOY'. A heady dose of melancholic magic. *MR*

Album rating: *8

HARD CORE LOGO

1996 (Can 96m) Rolling Thunder Pictures (R)

Film genre: mockumentary road movie/comedy

Top guns: dir: Bruce McDonald ← HIGHWAY 61 ← ROADKILL / s-w: Noel S. Baker (au: Michael Turner)

Stars: Hugh Dillon *(Joe Dick)*, Callum Keith Rennie *(Billy Tallent)*, John Pyper-Ferguson *(John Oxenberger)* ← EVERYBREATH, Bernie Coulson *(Pipefitter)* ← EDDIE AND THE CRUISERS II: EDDIE LIVES!, Julian Richings *(Bucky Haight)* ← the TOP OF HIS HEAD / → DETROIT ROCK CITY, **Joey Ramone** *(himself)* <= RAMONES =>, **Art Bergmann** *(himself)* ← HIGHWAY 61, **Joe Keithley** *(performer)*, Trevor Roberts *(skinhead)* → SWEETWATER: A TRUE ROCK STORY, Molly Parker *(Jenifur band member)* → LOOKING FOR LEONARD → WHO LOVES THE SUN

Storyline: Legendary punk band Hard Core Logo re-unite after five years when they hear that their old mentor Bucky has had his legs amputated. Their benefit concert is such a hit that lead singer Joe persuades the others to go on tour and recapture the good old days. But not for nothing did the band split up and soon personality clashes between Joe and lead guitarist Billy threaten to turn the tour into a shambles. *JZ*

Movie rating: *6

Visual: video + dvd

Off the record: Vancouver-born **Art Bergmann** had been around the Canadian underground scene since 1977 performing with the Schmorgs and the K-Tels (i.e. the Young Canadians). After two EP's with the latter, he finally completed his debut solo set, 'Crawl With Me' (1988); further recordings included 'Sexual Roulette' (1990). **Joey 'Shithead' Keithley** was of the same origin and a founding member of hardcore punks, D.O.A., Canada's answer to JELLO BIAFRA and Dead Kennedys. **Hugh Dillon** (see below). *MCS*

—

HUGH DILLON AND SWAMP BABY // Various Artists

Nov 98. (cd) *Velvel; <63467-79762-2>* ☐ ☐
– Who the hell do you think you are? / Rock 'n' roll is fat and ugly / Something's gonna die tonight / Blue tattoo / Sonic reducer / Edmonton block heater / China white (ten buck f**k) / One foot in the gutter / Hawaii (SWAMP BABY) / Bonerack (TEENAGE HEAD) / Touring (RAMONES) / Wild wild women (CHRIS SPEDDING).

S/track review: The third in filmmaker Bruce McDonald's music-biased trilogy, 'HARD CORE LOGO', is virtually down to one eponymous punk band, aka/or SWAMP BABY, headed by frontman and star of the show HUGH DILLON (or Michael Turner of "real band" the Headstones). With RANDALL BERGS and MARK BOSA (on guitars), RICK SENTENCE (on bass), JIM MATTACHIONE (on drums) and STEVE COWAL (on backing vox), Toronto comes up trumps here as the band produce something lying between deceased punk icons Johnny Thunders and Stiv Bators. Like a bare-knuckle fight (witness the movie for an example), this soundtrack is out'n'out, no holds barred hardcore punk, never more so than with the opener 'Who The Hell Do You Think You Are'. Easily the best track on the album, it stands spit-over-shoulders above the likes of 'Rock'n'Roll Is Fat And Ugly' and 'Something's Gonna Die Tonight' – all trash'n'thrash and headbangingly sing-a-long. 'Blue Tattoo' pushes the sentimental ballad button and slows it all down a pace where the Gin Blossoms meets Poison. Ditto 'China White (Ten Buck F**k)'. HUGH DILLON AND SWAMP BABY pay tribute to the aforementioned Stiv Bators by way of a Dead Boys cover, 'Sonic Reducer', while 'Edmonton Block Heater' and 'One Foot In The Gutter' clone the New York Dolls and the Rolling Stones. Track 9, 'Hawaii' (penned by Art Bergmann), saw COWAL taking on lead vox, a song possibly inspired by Dead Kennedys or Ramones. Talking of the latter (the film featured Joey in cameo), they contributed 'Touring' (very 'Rock'n'Roll High School'), one of three various artists tracks that complemented the film. 'Bonerack' (by TEENAGE HEAD) is riff-tastically "Somethin' Else" (Eddie Cochran's that is), while surprise-package CHRIS "Motor Biking" SPEDDING gets into 'Wild Wild Women' – think Lemmy or Mark Knopfler. Toronto's never looked healthier music-wise. *MCS*

Album rating: *6

HARD COUNTRY

1981 (US 104m) ITC / Associated Film Distribution (PG-13)

Film genre: romantic Country (& Western)-music drama

Top guns: dir: David Greene ← GODSPELL / s-w: Michael Kane (+ story w/ **Michael Martin Murphey**)

Stars: Jan-Michael Vincent *(Kyle Richardson)*, Kim Basinger *(Jodie)* → BATMAN → WAYNE'S WORLD 2 → 8 MILE, Michael Parks *(Royce)* → KILL BILL: VOL.1 → KILL BILL: VOL.2, Gailard Sartain *(Johnny Bob)* ← ROADIE ← the BUDDY HOLLY STORY ← NASHVILLE / → SONGWRITER, Sierra Pecheur *(Mama)*, John Chappell *(Daddy)* ← FAST BREAK ← KISS MEETS THE PHANTOM OF THE PARK, **Tanya Tucker** *(Caroline)*, Daryl Hannah *(Loretta)* → BLADE RUNNER → KILL BILL: VOL.1 → KILL BILL: VOL.2, Ted Neeley *(Wesley)* ← JESUS CHRIST SUPERSTAR, Curtis Credel *(Dale)* → FIRESTARTER, Richard Lineback *(Larry)* → NATURAL BORN KILLERS, **Michael Martin Murphey** *(Michael)*, **Katy Moffatt** *(special guest)* → the THING CALLED LOVE

Storyline: Kyle Richardson is a typical Texas dude – by day he works in the factory, at night he drinks with his buddies in the local saloon. However his ambitious girlfriend Jodie has her own plans for the good ol' boy – a quick trip down the aisle and then straight off to the city lights to seek fame and fortune. It's decision time for Kyle:- to keep his woman or keep his batchelor-boy lifestyle. *JZ*

Movie rating: *5

Visual: video

Off the record: Tanya Tucker was no stranger to acting having appeared in the 1972 movie, 'Jeremiah Johnson'. Raised in Wilcox, Arizona, the country singer had several hits throughout the 70s including two Top 50 entries, 'Would You Lay Down With Me (In A Field Of Stone)' & 'Lizzie And The Rainman'. **Michael Martin Murphey** (aka Travis Lewis) was a member of the Lewis & Clarke Expedition (band), who released an eponymous LP for 'Colgems' way back in 1967. *MCS*

—

MICHAEL MURPHEY, TANYA TUCKER, JERRY LEE LEWIS and JOE ELY (score: Jimmie Haskell)

Apr 81. (lp) *Epic; <SE 37367>* [ ] [–]
– Hard country (MICHAEL MURPHEY with KATY MOFFATT) / Hard partyin' country darlin' (MICHAEL MURPHEY) / Texas (when I die) (TANYA TUCKER) / Cowboy cadillac (MICHAEL MURPHEY) / Break my mind (MICHAEL MURPHEY) / Take it as it comes (MICHAEL MURPHEY with KATY MOFFATT) / Somebody must have loved you right last night (TANYA TUCKER) / Gonna love you anyway (TANYA TUCKER) / I love you so much it hurts (JERRY LEE LEWIS) / West Texas waltz (JOE ELY).

S/track review: Now known as the showboating "singing cowboy poet" who tours 40 American cities every winter with his 'Cowboy Christmas' show, MICHAEL MARTIN MURPHEY was once a lauded songwriter who worked with the likes of Willie Nelson, Lyle Lovett and Mike Nesmith. In between these two extremes he veered influentially into the sort of easy-listening country that proved fertile for later musical horrors like Lonestar and Alabama, and this movie – derived from a song by the Texan – finds him sounding wholly routine on five self-penned songs of formulaic fodder. Fellow Texan TANYA TUCKER shows off her superior raunchy voice on three numbers from her 1970s heyday, including the likeable pop country hit 'Texas (When I Die)'. And JERRY LEE LEWIS and JOE ELY each contribute a waltz; the former's take on Floyd Tillman's doleful 'I Love You So Much It Hurts' was one of his earliest country recordings, and the latter delivers a spry tune by another Texan, Butch Hancock. Apart from these bright spots, the soundtrack serves the film's barroom hokum and the coffers of Texas songwriters without coming close to explaining why its title should since have developed into a label for independent-minded, gritty roots music. *ND*

Album rating: *4.5

a HARD DAY'S NIGHT

1964 (UK 85m b&w) United Artists (U)

Film genre: anarchic Pop/Rock Musical comedy

Top guns: dir: Richard Lester ← IT'S TRAD, DAD! / → HELP! → GET BACK / s-w: Alun Owen

Stars: **the BEATLES:- John Lennon** *(John)*, **Paul McCartney** *(Paul)*, **George Harrison** *(George)*, **Ringo Starr** *(Ringo)*, Wilfrid Brambell *(Paul's grandfather)*, Norman Rossington *(Norm)*, Victor Spinetti *(television director)* → HELP! → MAGICAL MYSTERY TOUR → UNDER THE CHERRY MOON → JULIE AND THE CADILLACS, John Junkin *(Shake)*, Anna Quayle *(Millie)*, Deryck Guyler *(police inspector)* ← IT'S TRAD, DAD! / → FERRY 'CROSS THE MERSEY, Richard Vernon *(man on train)*, Lionel Blair *(TV choreographer)* ← PLAY IT COOL / → ABSOLUTE BEGINNERS, Julian Holloway *(Adrian; Simon's assistant)* → CATCH US IF YOU CAN → the GREAT ROCK'N'ROLL SWINDLE, John Bluthall *(man stealing car)* → HELP!, Derek Nimmo *(Leslie Jackson; magician)* ← IT'S TRAD, DAD!, Anna Quayle *(Millie)* → SMASHING TIME, Kenneth Haigh *(Simon Marshall)*, Margaret Nolan *(grandfather's girl at casino)* → FERRY CROSS THE MERSEY → TOOMORROW, **Phil Collins** *(seated necktie fan)*

Storyline: Director Richard Lester's pioneering 1964 film captures the fantasy whirlwind of a supposedly average 36 hours in the life of the Beatles, at that time the hottest item on the planet. Jump-cuts, madcap antics and wry wit – not to mention some great performances – abound as the band attempt to make the deadline for a crucial TV engagement. *BG*

Movie rating: *9

Visual: video + dvd

Off the record: Yes, a young 13-year-old **Phil Collins** appeared in the film – blink and you'll miss it.

—

the BEATLES

Jul 64. (lp) *Parlophone; (PMC 1230)(PCS 3058)* [1] [–]
– A hard day's night / I should have known better / If I fell / I'm happy just to dance with you / And I love her / Tell me why / Can't buy me love / Anytime at all / I'll cry instead / Things we said today / When I get home / You can't do that / I'll be back. *(re-iss. Jan71; same); hit 39) (cd-iss. Feb87; CDP 746437-2); hit No.30) (re-iss. Nov88 lp/c; PMC/TC-PMC 1230)*

—

the BEATLES (composer: GEORGE MARTIN *)

Jul 64. (lp) *Capitol; <6366>* [–] [1]
– A hard day's night / Tell me why / I'll cry instead / I should have known better (*) / I'm happy just to dance with you / And I love her (*) / I should have known better / If I fell / And I love her / This boy (*) / Can't buy me love / A hard day's night (*).

S/track review: Even taking into the account the turkey-clucking competition (Elvis' 'KISSIN' COUSINS' and 'ROUSTABOUT'; Cliff's 'WONDERFUL LIFE'), 'A HARD DAY'S NIGHT' was a watershed in the world of rock soundtracks, as it was in rock albums. As the sleevenotes understatedly made clear, it was "interesting to remember" that all the songs were LENNON-McCARTNEY originals. Their author can't have known just how revolutionary the pair's rapidly developing writing skills would become, even as they began taking separate paths. "I've got a chip on my shoulder that's bigger than my feet", warned LENNON, but twenty-something angst had never sounded so candy-sweet. The toothy harmonies, the infatuated melodies, the breathless Rickenbacker jangle; pop music had never had it so good, or seemingly so easy. 'Can't Buy Me Love', 'I'll Be Back', 'I Should Have Known Better', the title track, all tripped off the vinyl like they'd been written in a lunch-break. Their energy and superficial simplicity endeared them to half the planet, and eventually forced the band to give up touring for the respite of the recording studio where, happily, they came up with more ballads in the haunted spirit of 'And I Love Her'. The transition from mop-top to meditation moved a step closer only a month after this album's release, when they had their first fateful encounter with Bob Dylan and dope. Granted, only one side of the British album featured songs from the film (the American release was closer to the movie, featuring score material by GEORGE MARTIN), but this is where the BEATLES first predicted their own legend. *BG*

Album rating: *8.5 (UK) / *6 (US)

– spinoff hits, etc. –

the BEATLES: A Hard Day's Night / Things We Said Today

Jul 64. (7") *(R 5160)* [1] [–]
(re-iss. Jul84; same); hit No.52) (re-iss. cd-s.1989)

the BEATLES: A Hard Day's Night / I Should Have Known Better

Jul 64. (7") *<5222>* [–] [1] [53]

the BEATLES: I'll Cry Instead / I'm Happy Just To Dance With You

Aug 64. (7") *<5234>* [–] [25] [95]

the BEATLES: And I Love Her / If I Fell

Aug 64. (7") *<5235>* [–] [12] [53]

– other bits & pieces, etc. –

PETER SELLERS: A Hard Day's Night / Help!

Dec 65. (7") *Parlophone; (R 5393)* [14] [–]
(re-iss. Nov93 cd-s; CDEMS 293) – hit UK No.52

HARD ROCK NIGHTMARE

1988 (US 87m) Manley Productions (R)

Film genre: Rock'n'roll horror drama

Top guns: s-w + dir: Dominick Brascia

Stars: Greg Joujon-Roche *(Charlie)*, Annie Mikan *(Tina)*, Lisa Guggenheim *(Sally)*, Robert D. Peverley *(Sammy)*, Bryan Kovacs *(John)*, Tom Shell *(Paul)*, Troy Donahue *(Uncle Gary)* ← SUMMER LOVE / → CRY-BABY → SHOCK 'EM DEAD → SHAKE, RATTLE & ROLL: AN AMERICAN LOVE STORY, Nikki McQueen *(Connie)*, Gary Hays *(Tim)*

Storyline: A rock band are fed up being harrassed by the police for practising in a quiet neighbourhood. They decide to go to an abandoned cabin in the forest where no one can hear them, but when one of the band has nightmares about a werewolf which begin to come true, blood begins to flow and the band and their groupies start disappearing one by one. *JZ*

Movie rating: *6

Visual: video (no audio OST; score: Johnny Marchello)

Off the record: nothing of pop culture interest

HARD ROCK ZOMBIES

1984 (US 98m) Cannon Film Distributors (R)

Film genre: Hard-Rock horror musical comedy/spoof

Top guns: s-w: (+ dir) Krishna Shah, David Allen Ball

Stars: E.J. Curcio *(Jesse)*, Sam Mann *(Chuck)*, Geno Andrews *(Tommy)*, Mick Manz *(Robby)*, Lisa Toothman *(Elsa)*, Jennifer Coe *(Cassy)*, Gary Friedkin *(Buckey)*, Crystal Shaw *(Mrs. Buff)*, Ted Wells *(Ron)*, Jack Bliesener *(Hitler)*, John Fleck *(Arnold)* → HOWARD THE DUCK → TAPEHEADS → CRAZY

Storyline: A heavy metal band (Holly Moses) stops off at the little-known town of Grand Guignol to play a gig, despite mysterious warnings from a girl called Cassy. Sure enough the residents of the town include mad dwarfs, perverts, werewolves and of course Adolf Hitler. The band end up as sacrificial victims (they weren't that bad, surely) and with Hitler plotting to take over the world it's up to Cassy to raise the band from the dead and save the guys and ghouls from the zombie legions. "Their farewell concert is to die for". *JZ*

Movie rating: *3

Visual: video

Off the record: Crystal Shaw Martell released an album, 'Thank Ya Baby', on 'Mercury', a collection of 40s-styled ballads and er, hip hop. *MCS*

—

"HOLLY MOSES": Rock Zombies (composer: PAUL SABU)

1984. (lp) *Trema-Ariola; (310.175)* [–] German [–]
– Angel's first victim / Shake it out / Cassy's warning / Cassy / Death montage / It don't come easy / Zombies revenge / Cassy's theme / Angel's trophy room / Street angel (mark of the Devil) / Midjet gets the beef / Bucky dines in / Arnold's picnic / Matson's last deal / Zombies lure ghouls / Hitler's gas chamber / Zombies reprise.

S/track review: PAUL SABU was a singer/guitarist who loved both hard rock and disco, as both 'Sabu' LPs (released in 1980 on 'M.C.A.' & 'Ocean' records respectively) will testify. After a long sabbatical, Paul returned to the fold in '84, first with session outfit, Kidd Glove (for one eponymous LP), then with the soundtrack to 'HARD ROCK ZOMBIES'. If one liked his/her metal served up with hookline and melody, then 'Rock Zombies' (as it was re-titled), could be one's cup of char. The instrumental guitar-friendly dirge, 'Angel's First Victim', kicked off the album in melodic style, like all of the tracks, performed by HOLLY MOSES (and not, it seems . . . PAUL SABU himself). The set drifted between subsequent score cues such as 'Death Montage' (a mess of a track!) and the 80s pop-rock machinations of 'Shake It Out', the nice-but-dim 'Cassy' and 'It Don't Come Easy'. Side two shapes up with 'Miami Vice'-meets-Rick Wakeman-styled cues such as 'Zombies Revenge', 'Cassy's Theme' and the minute-long 'Angel's Trophy Room'. The hard rock factor comes by way of the Dio-esque 'Street Angel (Mark Of The Devil)', while the remainder of this weird album is taken up by short amusement arcade numbers or eerie cuts. The only redeeming factor on show is arguably the 'Zombies Lure Ghouls' track, the vocals quite possibly a precursor to grindcore with heavy grunting et al. Schizoid to the max. SABU (the son of Indian 'Elephant Boy' actor, Selar Shaik Sabu) went on to issue non-soundtrack set 'Heartbreak' in 1985 and formed Only Child, a band who delivered only one self-titled album before they too disbanded. Where is he now? *MCS*

Album rating: *4

HARD TO HOLD

1984 (US 93m) Universal Pictures (PG)

Film genre: romantic Pop/Rock-music comedy drama

Top guns: dir: Larry Peerce ← GOODBYE, COLUMBUS ← the BIG T.N.T. SHOW / s-w: Thomas Hedley Jr. (+ story) → FLASHDANCE, Richard Rothstein

Stars: Rick Springfield *(James Roberts)*, Janet Eilber *(Diana Lawson)*, Patti Hansen *(Nicky Nides)*, Albert Salmi *(Johnny Lawson)*, Gregory Itzin *(Owen)*, Peter Van Norden *(Casserole)*, Tracy Brooks Swope *(Toby)*, Cindy Perlman *(Ethel)* ← RHINESTONE ← STAYING ALIVE, Garry Goodrow *(maitre d')* ← AMERICAN HOT WAX ← STEELYARD BLUES / → DIRTY DANCING, Bill Mumy *(keyboard player)* ← WILD IN THE STREETS / → DERAILROADED

Storyline: James Roberts has reached the top of the tree in the music business. Adored by his fans, wealthy beyond measure, James is still not happy. His latest album just isn't coming together and the sulking superstar is so distraught he runs his car into the back of child psychologist Diana. When James fails to impress Diana he massages his bruised ego by wooing her, to the annoyance of ex-girlfriend Nicky. Can James find true love at last or will the psychologist shrink away from him? *JZ*

Movie rating: *3.5

Visual: video + dvd

Off the record: RICK SPRINGFIELD was born Richard Springthorpe, 23rd August '49, Sydney, Australia. As an aspiring singer-songwriter in the late 60s, Rick formed teeny-bop hitmakers Zoot; his high school band Rock House actually entertained the troops in Vietnam. In 1972, he embarked on a solo career for 'Capitol' records and moved to the States when his debut 45, 'Speak To The Sky', hit their Top 20. SPRINGFIELD found it difficult to emulate earlier triumph and took up acting to help pay the bills. In 1976, while still working as a solo artist for 'Chelsea' records, he appeared in a handful of hit TV series including 'The Rockford Files', 'The Six Million Dollar Man', 'Wonder Woman' & 'The Incredible Hulk'. In 1977, he starred in his first soap opera 'The Young And The Restless', and went on to play Dr. Drake in 'General Hospital'. Now a TV star, he signed to 'R.C.A.' records in 1981 and immediately achieved a US No.1 via 'Jessie's Girl'. Although pitched as a teen pop idol, he subsequently tried to tread on the same path as SPRINGSTEEN and Mellencamp, while having hit after hit courtesy of 'I've Done Everything For You' (penned by Sammy Hagar), 'Love Is Alright Tonite', 'Don't Talk To Strangers', 'What Kind Of Fool Am I', 'I Get Excited', 'Affair Of The Heart' and 'Souls'. After starring in the movie 'HARD TO HOLD', SPRINGFIELD had something of a novelty hit by way of 'Bruce', an autobiographical track of mistaken identity. *MCS*

—

RICK SPRINGFIELD (w/ Various) (score: Tom Scott)

Mar 84. (lp/c/cd) *R.C.A.; <4935> (BL/BK/BD 84935)* [16] Aug84 [ ]
– Love somebody / Don't walk away / Bop 'til you drop / Taxi dancing

(w/ RANDY CRAWFORD) / S.F.O. / Stand up – live / When the lights go down (GRAHAM PARKER) / The great lost art of conversation / Heart of a woman (NONA HENDRYX) / I go swimming – live (PETER GABRIEL).

S/track review: With no less than three major hits on show here, RICK SPRINGFIELD (a man now in his mid-30s), still found it hard to shrug off his Springsteen comparisons – for many reasons, he couldn't sing 'Born In The U.S.A.'. One of said hits, opening track 'Love Somebody' is mainstream power-pop at its best, while – with added sax-appeal – the Loverboy-esque 'Don't Walk Away' is lightweight by comparison. Fuse Daryl Hall, Phil Collins and Lou Gramm, and you'd probably come up with 'Bop 'Til You Drop', while his only collaboration on 'HARD TO HOLD' is the silly love-ballad 'Taxi Dancing' with one-time Crusaders cohort, RANDY CRAWFORD. Bypassing the oddness of Rick's instrumental, 'S.F.O.', and the awful ballad, 'The Great Lost Art Of Conversation', the man in the spotlight goes for the J.Geils-meets-Huey Lewis approach on live number, 'Stand Up'. The remainder of the 10-track set is filled up by other artists, one by former pub-rocker GRAHAM PARKER ('When The Lights Go Down'), the other by ex-LaBelle R&B singer NONA HENDRYX ('Heart Of A Woman'), and the funky finale of 'I Go Swimming' sung live by PETER GABRIEL. *MCS*

Album rating: *4.5

– spinoff hits, etc. –

RICK SPRINGFIELD: Love Somebody / The Great Lost Art Of Conversation

Feb 84. (7"/12") *<13738> (RICK/+T 3)* [5] May84 [ ]

RICK SPRINGFIELD: Don't Walk Away / S.F.O.

May 84. (7") *<13813>* [26] [–]

RICK SPRINGFIELD: Bop 'Til You Drop / RICK SPRINGFIELD with RANDY CRAWFORD: Taxi Dancing

Aug 84. (7") *<13861>* [20] [59] [–]

the HARDER THEY COME

1972 (Jama 110m) International Films (R)

Film genre: urban showbiz/Reggae-music drama

Top guns: s-w: Perry Henzell (+ dir), Trevor D. Rhone → ONE LOVE

Stars: Jimmy CLIFF *(Ivan Martin)*, Janet Barkley *(Elsa)*, Carl Bradshaw *(Jose)* → COUNTRYMAN → CLUB PARADISE → KLA$H → DANCEHALL QUEEN → ONE LOVE, Ras Daniel Hartman *(Pedro)*, Basil Keane *(preacher)* → COUNTRYMAN, Robert Charlton *(Hilton)*, Winston Stona *(Detective Ray Jones)* → ONE LOVE, **Prince Buster** *(DJ at dance)*

Storyline: Ivanhoe Martin arrives in Kingston Town with high hopes of releasing a record. However, he soon finds business is conducted on lines which are far from straight and narrow, and ends up becoming involved in the marijuana trade. After a shootout with some policemen he becomes Jamaica's most wanted man just as his record finds success. Will this help the police weed him out? *JZ*

Movie rating: *7

Visual: video + dvd

Off the record: Prince Buster (aka Buster Campbell) had a UK Top 20 hit in 1967 with 'Al Capone'.

JIMMY CLIFF (& Various Artists)

Nov 72. (lp) *Island; (<ILPS 9202>)* [ ] Mar75 [ ]

– You can get it if you really want / Draw your breaks (SCOTTY) / Rivers of Babylon (the MELODIANS) / Many rivers to cross / Sweet and dandy (the MAYTALS) / The harder they come / Johnny too bad (the SLICKERS) / Shanty town (DESMOND DEKKER) / Pressure drop (the MAYTALS) / Sitting in limbo. *(re-iss. Sep86 lp/c/cd; ILPM/ICM/CCD 9202) (re-iss. Oct90 on 'Reggae Refreshers' cd/c; RRCD/RRCT 11) (cd re-iss. Jul01; RRCD 61) (d-cd-iss. Aug03 on 'Island'+=; 6949529)* – You can get it if you really want / The harder they come.

S/track review: "Shanty Town – Jamaica – where the best grass in the world sells for two dollars an ounce, where shooting a film can be held up when an actor is shot (2 alone have died since it was completed), where people sing in church till they have an orgasm (thank you Lord)" . . .so begin the sleevenotes to a record which introduced a whole generation to the musical delights of the Caribbean. Although JIMMY CLIFF's name and flamboyantly clad character dominates the sleeve, pistols, leopardskin shirt, shades and all, this is actually a various-artists soundtrack, and possibly one of the finest ever released. Alongside the iconic title track, the buoyant CLIFF talisman, 'You Can Get It If You Really Want', and a couple of the man's late 60s/early 70s classics, 'Many Rivers To Cross' and the gorgeous 'Sitting In Limbo', the album's handful of peerlessly sequenced reggae classics is as thrilling an introduction to the genre as you'll find anywhere. Every track is a highlight: the MELODIANS' revelatory original version of 'Rivers Of Babylon', the SLICKERS' deceivingly laid-back rude-boy fable, 'Johnny Too Bad' and DESMOND DEKKER's brilliant '007 (Shanty Town)', transplanting Hollywood imagery to the Kingston ghettos. And that's without even mentioning the two MAYTALS numbers. If you've ever had the slightest interest in reggae, you probably own this already; if not, you need it. *BG*

Album rating: *9

– spinoff releases, etc. –

JIMMY CLIFF: The Harder They Come / Many Rivers To Cross

Oct 72. (7") *(WIP 6139)* [ ] [–]

□ HAREM HOLIDAY alt.
(⇒ HARUM SCARUM)

□ Jesse HARRIS segment
(⇒ the HOTTEST STATE)

□ Deborah HARRY
(⇒ BLONDIE)

HARUM SCARUM

aka HAREM HOLIDAY

1965 (US 95m) Metro-Goldwyn-Mayer (PG)

Film genre: romantic Rock'n'roll Musical drama

Top guns: dir: Gene Nelson ← YOUR CHEATIN' HEART ← KISSIN' COUSINS ← HOOTENANNY HOOT / → the COOL ONES / s-w: Gerald Drayson Adams ← KISSIN' COUSINS

Stars: Elvis PRESLEY *(Johnny Tyrone)*, Mary Ann Mobley *(Princess Shalimar)* ← GIRL HAPPY ← GET YOURSELF A COLLEGE GIRL, Fran Jeffries *(Aishah)*, Michael Ansara *(Prince Dragna)* → the PHYNX, Theodore Marcuse *(Sinan)*, Billy Barty *(Baba)* ← ROUSTABOUT / → LEGEND → UHF, Jay Novello *(Zacha)*, Dick Harvey *(Makar)*, Barbara Werle *(Leilah)* ← TICKLE ME / → CHARRO!, Brenda Benet *(Emerald)* ← BEACH BALL, Gail Gilmore *(Sapphire)* ← BEACH BALL ← the GIRLS ON THE BEACH ← GIRL HAPPY

Storyline: Hollywood bigshot Johnny Tyrone finds himself at the mercy of Middle Eastern kidnappers after being abducted on a foreign promotional tour. Help comes in the form of the avaricious Zacha who offers his assistance for a hefty price. *BG*

Movie rating: *4

Visual: video + dvd

Off the record: nothing

—

ELVIS PRESLEY (composers: Freddy Karger, etc.)

Nov 65. (lp; mono/stereo) *R.C.A.; <LSP 3468> (RD/SF 7767)* [8] Jan66 [11]
– Harem holiday / My desert serenade / Go east young man / Mirage / Kismet / Shake that tambourine / Hey little girl / Golden coins / So close, yet so far (from paradise) / Animal instinct / Wisdom of the ages. *(re-iss. Aug80 on 'RCA Int.'; INTS 5035) (re-iss. Apr84 lp/c; NL/NK 82558) (cd-iss. Nov03 on 'Follow That Dream'+=; FTD 1006)* – (extra takes).

S/track review: 'Go East Young Man', councils the King – not particularly convincingly it must be said – on this pedestrian Hollywood vehicle. ELVIS dazzles with his vocal depth and power, but the material just isn't there: most of these attempts at hackneyed exoticism fall fairly flat. Only 'Mirage', with its bossa rhythms, the campy 'Shake That Tambourine' and the bluesy, breathless 'Hey Little Girl' are in the least bit memorable, while PRESLEY only really sounds like he means it on the ballad, 'So Close, Yet So Far (From Paradise)'. Ironically, the two tracks cut from the final print but reinstated for the CD re-issue, 'Animal Instinct' and 'Wisdom Of The Ages', are marginally more successful at conjuring up a convincing marriage of ELVIS and the East, the former with some surprisingly funky flute arrangements and the latter conflating a mildly trippy guitar part with an epic, Righteous Brothers-style pop/soul structure. *BG*

Album rating: *3.5

– spinoff releases, etc. –

ELVIS PRESLEY: Harum Scarum / Girl Happy

Mar 93. (cd) *<(74321 13433-2)>* [ ] [ ]

□ HAVING A WILD WEEKEND alt.
(⇒ CATCH US IF YOU CAN)

□ Chesney HAWKES segment
(⇒ BUDDY'S SONG)

□ Ron HAYDOCK segment
(⇒ RAT PFINK A BOO-BOO)

HEAD

1968 (US 85m) Columbia Pictures (G)

Film genre: anarchic Pop/Rock Musical satire/comedy

Top guns: s-w: Bob Rafelson (+ dir), Jack Nicholson ← the TRIP

Stars: the MONKEES:- David Jones *(Davy)*, **Mickey Dolenz** *(Mickey)*, **Mike Nesmith** *(Mike)*, **Peter Tork** *(Peter)* / **ANNETTE Funicello** *(Minnie)*, Victor Mature *(Big Victor)*, Abraham Sofaer *(Swami)*, Timothy Carey *(Lord High'n'Low)*, **Frank ZAPPA** *(the critic)*, Vito Scotti *(I. Vitteloni)*, Teri Garr *(Testy True)* ← CLAMBAKE ← the COOL ONES ← ROUSTABOUT ← VIVA LAS VEGAS ← PAJAMA PARTY ← the T.A.M.I. SHOW ← KISSIN' COUSINS ← FUN IN ACAPULCO / → ONE FROM THE HEART, Percy Helton *(heraldic messenger)* ← GET YOURSELF A COLLEGE GIRL ← WHERE THE BOYS ARE ← JAILHOUSE ROCK ← SHAKE, RATTLE AND ROCK!, Carol Doda *(Sally Silicone)*, T.C. Jones *(Mr. & Mrs. Ace)*, Logan Ramsey *(Officer Faye Lapid)*, Charles Macauley *(Inspector Shrink)* → BLACULA, Jack Nicholson *(himself)* ← PSYCH-OUT / → EASY RIDER → TOMMY → the BORDER → BATMAN, Dennis Hopper *(himself)* ← the TRIP / → EASY RIDER → HUMAN HIGHWAY → WHITE STAR → RUNNING OUT OF LUCK → STRAIGHT TO HELL, Toni Basil *(dancer)* ← PAJAMA PARTY ← the T.A.M.I. SHOW / → EASY RIDER → ROCKULA

Storyline: Actually, there's no storyline to speak of. In trashing the acceptable face of the Monkees, Bob Rafelson contrived an anarchic cut-up untethered to any conventional notions of cinematic form. Parodic skits, reportage, vintage film clips, cryptic jokes and ad hoc snatches of music are all thrown into the blender, with the resulting psychedelic soup best served in small doses. *BG*

Movie rating: *5.5

Visual: video + dvd

Off the record: The **MONKEES** (see own entry)

—

the MONKEES (composers: Various)

Dec 68. (lp; mono/stereo) *R.C.A.; <5008> (RD/SF 8051)* [45] Sep69 [ ]
– (Opening ceremony) / The porpoise song (theme from 'Head') / Ditty Diego – War chant / Circle sky / (Supplicio) / Can you dig it / (Gravy) / (Superstitious) / As we go along / (Dandruff?) / Daddy's song / (Poll) / Long title: Do I have to do this all over again / Swami – Plus strings. *<re-iss. Oct86 on 'Rhino'; 70146> (cd-iss. Dec94 on 'Warners'+=; 4509 97659-2)* – Ditty Diego – War chant / Circle sky / Happy birthday to you / Can you dig it / Daddy's song / Head radio spot.

S/track review: There aren't many soundtracks co-ordinated by Jack Nicholson (you can actually hear his wily drawl on the CD's bonus version of 'Ditty Diego-War Chant') and the freewheeling spirit of the Nicholson/Rafelson partnership is stamped all over this. While that partnership would go on to concoct the brilliant 'Five Easy Pieces' (1970), their oft-quoted aim for 'HEAD' was to subvert the MONKEES' teen dream image. As Peter Tork puts it in the re-issue's copious sleevenotes, "Basically, the movie Head is not the story of the Monkees' release, it is Rafelson's idea of who the Monkees are". The movie might indeed have scuppered both their image and career, but, from a purely musical perspective, they'd already proved – with the previous year's 'Headquarters' (1967) – that they weren't just pretty, marketable faces. 'HEAD' nevertheless relies for the most part on session heavyweights as well as the likes of RY COODER, Jack Nitzsche and Russ Titelman, a triumvirate more famous – at least cinematically – for their work on Nic Roeg's 'PERFORMANCE' (1970). Composition-wise, the record features two songs by PETER TORK, a previously recorded MIKE NESMITH tune and a couple of tracks by the group's regular writers, Gerry Goffin and Carole King. The normally indomitable Goffin/King axis supply the lead track – and lead single – 'Porpoise Song (Theme From Head)' a meandering, self-conscious stab at 'Magical Mystery Tour'-esque psychedelia which promises a lot but winds up sounding half-finished. They fare better with the rootsy, if slight, 'As We Go Along', featuring NEIL YOUNG no less. With its quasi-Eastern motifs and shadowy bongos, TORK's own 'Can You Dig It' is a more engaging psychedelic confection, while NESMITH's sole contribution, 'Circle Sky', is a caterwauling rocker prefiguring his underrated 70s material. If, on this evidence, it's surprising that TORK's solo career never got off the starting blocks, NESMITH's position as a recording artist outwith the MONKEES seems guaranteed. HARRY NILSSON also makes an appearance, supplying the brassy and very Beatles-y 'Daddy's Song'. In some ways – the most annoying ones – 'HEAD' occasionally resembles Nilsson's own 60s soundtrack, 'SKIDOO' (1968); the inter-song skits aren't as facile – they're a lot more subversive, creative and some are actually pretty funny – but they're just as wearing after the fourth or fifth listen. If you really can't get enough of them, the 'Rhino' CD adds a few more for good measure, as well as the superior live version of 'Circle Sky' featured in the film. *BG*

Album rating: *6

– spinoff hits, etc. –

the MONKEES: Daddy's Song / The Porpoise Song

Aug 69. (7") *(RCA 1862)* [–] [ ]

□ Jeff HEALEY segment (⇒ ROAD HOUSE)

HEARTBREAK HOTEL

1988 (US 97m) Touchstone Pictures (PG-13)

Film genre: showbiz/Rock'n'roll music teen comedy

Top guns: dir: (+ s-w) Chris Columbus → RENT

Stars: David Keith *(Elvis Presley)* ← FIRESTARTER ← the ROSE / → RAISE YOUR VOICE, Tuesday Weld *(Marie Wolfe)* ← THIEF ← I WALK THE LINE ← WILD IN THE COUNTRY ← ROCK, ROCK, ROCK! / → CHELSEA WALLS, Charlie Schlatter *(Johnny Wolfe)*, Angela Goethals *(Pam Wolfe)* → STORYTELLING, Chris Mulkey *(Steve Ayres)* ← TIMERIDER: THE ADVENTURE OF LYLE SWANN ← the LONG RIDERS / → GAS FOOD LODGING → SUGAR TOWN → MYSTERIOUS SKIN, Jacque Lynn Colton *(Rosie Pantangellio)*, Karen Landry *(Irene)*, Tudor Sherrard *(Paul Quinine)* → the DOORS, Paul Harkins *(Brian Gasternick)* ← LIGHT OF DAY, John Hawkes *(M.C.)* → a SLIPPING-DOWN LIFE

Storyline: It's been a bad day for Johnny Wolfe. His rock band has just been kicked out of the school competition and his mum is laid up after a road accident. Not to worry, Elvis is playing up the road on Saturday night, and what better way to cheer everyone up than to kidnap him for a few hours and show him round. And so it proves, Elvis being lured away with diabolical cunning (a false wig) and beginning a new chapter in his life at the Wolfe's lair. *JZ*

Movie rating: *4

Visual: video + dvd

Off the record: Actress Tuesday Weld had appeared in an original Elvis movie, 'WILD IN THE COUNTRY' (1961).

—

Various Artists (score: Georges Delerue)

Oct 88. (lp/c/cd) *R.C.A.; <8533-1/-4/-2 R>* [ ] [–]
– Heartbreak hotel (ELVIS PRESLEY) / One night (ELVIS PRESLEY) / Drift away (DOBIE GRAY) / Can't help falling in love (DAVID KEITH with The T. GRAHAM BROWN BAND) / Burning love (ELVIS PRESLEY) / Love me (DAVID KEITH) / Ready Teddy (ELVIS PRESLEY) / I'm eighteen (ALICE COOPER) / Soul on fire (CHARLIE SCHLATTER with ZULU TIME) / If I can dream (ELVIS PRESLEY) / Heartbreak hotel (DAVID KEITH & CHARLIE SCHLATTER with ZULU TIME).

S/track review: The moviemakers' fixation with everything rock'n'roll and nostalgic (i.e. 'HAIRSPRAY', 'SHAG', 'PURPLE PEOPLE EATER', etc.) was beginning to grate on the discerning buying public of the late 80s. Covered head to foot-tappin' toe by ELVIS numbers, either sung by the man himself or indeed interpreted by the film's star attraction, DAVID KEITH, 'HEARTBREAK HOTEL' was no exception. The King ghosted on no less than five of the eleven tracks, 'Heartbreak Hotel', 'One Night', 'Burning Love', 'Ready Teddy' and 'If I Can Dream', while the aforementioned KEITH notched up three: 'Can't Help Falling In Love' (augmented by the T. GRAHAM BROWN BAND), 'Love Me' and 'Heartbreak Hotel' – again. On the latter track, the man is joined by co-star CHARLIE SCHLATTER (who'd contributed 'Soul On Fire') and the ZULU TIME BAND, which consisted of DAVE DAVIES (guitars, vocals), MICHAEL MOYER (bass, vocals), COLE HANSON (guitar, vocals) and KEVIN PEARSON (drums). Incidentally, it wouldn't therefore be fair to leave out the line-up of his T. GRAHAM BROWN BAND, which featured MICHAEL THOMAS (guitar), JOE McGLOHON (saxophone & guitar), GARLAND (keyboards), GREG WATZEL (keyboards), LARRY MARS (bass) and GARY KUBAL (drums), but not a guy called T. Graham Brown. It must also be said that the impersonation of Elvis by DAVID KEITH is commendable of any white-suited, Las Vegas crooner, and at least he tackles his subject full-on, unlike Kurt Russell in 1979's 'ELVIS: The Movie'. Two non-Elvis classics make up the rest of the 30-minute album, 'Drift Away' by DOBIE GRAY and 'I'm Eighteen' by ALICE COOPER. Schizoid, or what!? *MCS*

Album rating: *6

the HEARTBREAKERS

1983 (W.Ger 113m) Pro-ject Filmproduktion / Tura-Film (15)

Film genre: coming-of-age/teen Rock-music comedy/drama

Top guns: dir: Peter F. Bringmann / s-w: Matthias Seelig

Stars: Mary Ketikidou *(Lisa)*, Sascha Disselkamp *(Fretag)*, Michael Klein *(Pico)*, Uwe Enkelmann *(Schmittchen)*, Mark Eichenseher *(Hornchen)*, Esther Christinat *(Sieglinde)*, Harmut Isselhorst *(Guido Fischer)*, Rolf Zacher *(Lisa's father)*

Storyline: Police arrest a group of teenagers after a riot at a Rolling Stones concert in West Germany. The kids get to know each other at the police station and decide to form a band, the Heartbreakers. They scrape together enough to buy instruments, find themselves a lead singer, and get ready to launch themselves on the rock circuit – personal problems and conflicts notwithstanding. *JZ*

Movie rating: *6

Visual: video (no audio OST; score: LOTHAR MEID)

Off the record: LOTHAR MEID was formerly of German progsters, Amon Duul II. *MCS*

HEARTS OF FIRE

1987 (US/UK 95m) Phoenix Entertainment / Lorimar Productions (R)

Film genre: Rock Musical drama

Top guns: dir: Richard Marquand ← BIRTH OF THE BEATLES / s-w: Joe Eszterhas ← FLASHDANCE, Scott Richardson

Stars: **Fiona Flanagan** *(Molly McGuire)* → the DOORS, **Bob DYLAN** *(Billy Parker)*, Rupert Everett *(James Colt)*, Julian Glover *(Alfred)*, **Ian DURY** *(Bones)*, **Richie Havens** *(Pepper Ward)* ← CATCH MY SOUL ← WOODSTOCK / → GLASTONBURY → I'M NOT THERE, Maury Chaykin *(Charlie Kelso)*, Larry Lamb *(Jack Rosner)*, Suzanne Bertish *(Anne Ashton)*, **Ron Wood** *(himself)* ← the RUTLES ← the LAST WALTZ, **Steve Bolton** *(Spyder)* → THIRTY YEARS OF MAXIMUM R&B LIVE

Storyline: Reclusive rocker Billy Parker meets Molly, a young waitress who wants to try her hand in the music business. He takes Molly to England for the beginning of his tour, which he hopes will give her the experience she needs. However, she gets a completely different experience when she meets promoter James Colt and falls for him, leading to an old fashioned tug of love between the two men. Molly must choose where her affections really lie, and her choice could be a surprise for both her suitors. *JZ*

Movie rating: *3

Visual: video + dvd

Off the record: Starring alongside the likes of rock legends, **BOB DYLAN, Ian Dury & Richie Havens**, there was the petite figure of **FIONA** (b. Fiona Flanagan, 13 Sep'61, New York City, New York, USA). After playing in a number of local bands, FIONA finally got a break when 'Atlantic' signed her to a solo deal in 1985. Alongside Starz guitarist Bobby Messano and a few session players, she cut an eponymous debut set, an eventual Top 75 entry later that summer. Moving away somewhat from the lightweight pop-metal sound of the debut, a Beau Hill-produced second set, 'Beyond The Pale' (1986), failed to break the Top 100 despite its more considered approach and guest appearances by glam/hair crew, Winger. Despite being given a lucrative co-starring role in the Rock Musical, 'HEARTS OF FIRE', further chart success continued to elude the singer. After a final effort for 'Atlantic', 'Heart Like A Gun', and a one-off set for 'Geffen', 'Squeeze' (1992), she retired from the rock scene. *MCS*

Various Artists (incl. FIONA * & BOB DYLAN **)

Aug 87. (lp/c/cd) *Columbia; <SC 40870> C.B.S.; (460000-1/-4/-2)* ☐ Oct87 ☐
– Hearts of fire (*) / The usual (**) / I'm in it for love (*) / Tainted love (RUPERT EVERETT) / Hair of the dog (that bit you) (*) / Night after night (**) / In my heart (RUPERT EVERETT) / The night we spent on Earth (*) / Had a dream about you, baby (**) / Let the good times roll (*).

S/track review: Like in the movie itself, what we have here is an unusual combination of "rock" stars: one-time folk legend BOB DYLAN playing hard AOR, leather-clad rocker FIONA and English "toff" boy RUPER EVERETT. Coming across like an AOR-fusion of Pat Benatar, Joan Jett, Heart and Bonnie Tyler, FIONA performs half of the songs on the set, while DYLAN contributes three and EVERETT two. FIONA opens her musical account via a typical 80s title track rock ballad, while the rest ('I'm In It For Love', 'Hair Of The Dog (That Bit You)', 'The Night We Spent On Earth' & 'Let The Good Times Roll') are of the same hollerin' "hair-rock" persuasion. Meanwhile, DYLAN – a man in his mid-40s – finds he wants to get down and rock with the rest of them, taking on John Hiatt's 'The Usual', the Los Lobos-esque 'Night After Night' and the boogie-fuelled 'Had A Dream About You, Baby'. The RUPERT EVERETT fillers (Soft Cell's 'Tainted Love' and the Howard Jones-ish 'In My Heart') are worth mentioned for the fact that not every actor should try singing. The now rare album was recorded in London in two days – 26th & 27th of August, 1986! – and is a collector's dream (and especially the CD!) selling on eBay for top dollar; John Barry's score has never seen the light of day. *MCS*

Album rating: *4.5

– spinoff releases, etc. –

FIONA: Hearts Of Fire / (non-OSTrack)

Nov 87. (7") *<07596>* ☐ ☐

HEAVEN TONIGHT

1990 (Austra 96m) Boulevard Films / Century Park Pictures (R)

Film genre: Rock-music comedy/drama

Top guns: dir: Pino Amenta / s-w: Frank Howson, Alister Webb

Stars: John Waters *(Johnny Dysart)*, Rebecca Gilling *(Annie Dysart)*, Kym Gyngell *(Baz Schultz)*, Sean Scully *(Tim Robbins)*, Guy Pearce *(Paul Dysart)* → a SLIPPING-DOWN LIFE → RAVENOUS → the PROPOSITION, Matthew Quartermaine *(Stevo)*

Storyline: Failed rock star Johnny Dysart still dreams of that one last comeback, but his level-headed wife would rather he concentrated on the day job. Meanwhile, son Paul is getting rave reviews from those in the know and he and his band look set for the big time. Is dad jealous? Of course he is! Johnny has to decide whether to put the past behind him once and for all, or try, try, try again to be like his more successful son. *JZ*

Movie rating: *4.5

Visual: video (no audio OST; score John Capek)

Off the record: John Waters was in an R&B band called the Riots.

HEAVY METAL

1981 (US/Can 95m) Columbia Pictures (R)

Film genre: animated sci-fi fantasy

Top guns: dir: Gerald Potterton, Jimmy T. Murakami → WHEN THE WIND BLOWS / s-w: Len Blum → PRIVATE PARTS → OVER THE HEDGE, Daniel Goldberg (story: Dan O'Bannon → the RETURN OF THE LIVING DEAD, Corny Cole, Berni Wrightson)

Voices: Rodger Bumpass *(Hanover Fiste / Dr. Anrak)*, John Candy *(desk sergeant / Dan / Den / robot)* ← the BLUES BROTHERS / → LITTLE SHOP OF HORRORS, Eugene Levy *(Sternn / male reporter / Edsel)* → CLUB PARADISE → a MIGHTY WIND → CURIOUS GEORGE → OVER THE HEDGE, Harold Ramis *(Zeke)* → AIRHEADS → KNOCKED UP → WALK HARD: THE DEWEY COX STORY, Richard Romanus *(Harry Canyon)*, Joe Flaherty *(lawyer / general)* → CLUB PARADISE, Jackie Burroughs *(Katherine)*, Martin Lavut *(Ard)*, Marilyn Lightstone *(whore / queen)*, Alice Playten *(Gloria)* → LEGEND, John Vernon *(prosecutor)* ← ANIMAL HOUSE, Don Francks *(Grimaldi/co-pilot/barbarian)* → ROCK & RULE → MADONNA: INNOCENCE LOST → MR. MUSIC → I'M NOT THERE, **Zal Yanovsky** *(navigator / barbarian)* ← ONE-TRICK PONY ← WHAT'S UP, TIGER LILY?, Al Waxman *(Rudnick)* → CLASS OF 1984, Vlasta Vrana *(barbarian leader)* → EDDIE AND THE CRUISERS II: EDDIE LIVES!, Douglas Kenney *(Regolian)* ← CADDYSHACK ← ANIMAL HOUSE, Susan Roman *(girl/Satellite)* → ROCK & RULE

Storyline: A mysterious green orb is brought back to Earth, where it reveals its identity to a frightened young girl. Calling itself Loc-Nar, it claims to be the embodiment of all evil in the universe and proves it by showing all the terrible things it has done to mankind since its arrival. Various humans are resurrected as zombies, transported to alien worlds, and turned into murderous barbarians just so Loc-Nar can have his bit of fun. Boo! Hiss! *JZ*

Movie rating: *5

Visual: dvd

Off the record: Zal Yanovsky was of the **LOVIN' SPOONFUL**

Various Artists (score: Elmer Bernstein)

Jul 81. (d-lp) *Asylum; <90004> Epic; (EPC 88558)* 12 Nov81 ☐
– Heavy metal (SAMMY HAGAR) / Heartbeat (RIGGS) / Working in the coal mine (DEVO) / Veteran of the psychic wars (BLUE OSTER CULT) / Reach out (CHEAP TRICK) / Heavy metal (takin' a ride) (DON FELDER) / True companion (DONALD FAGEN) / Crazy (a suitable case for treatment) (NAZARETH) / Radar radar (RIGGS) / Open arms (JOURNEY) / Queen bee (GRAND FUNK RAILROAD) / I must be dreamin' (CHEAP TRICK) / Mob rules (BLACK SABBATH) / All of you (DON FELDER) / Prefabricated (TRUST) / Blue lamp (STEVIE NICKS). *<cd-iss. Mar95 on 'Elektra'; 60691> (cd-iss. Apr97 on 'Columbia'; 486749-2)*

S/track review: Caught somewhere between the raw earthiness of the early 70s, and the streamlined aggression of the thrash movement, this album represents a nadir in the long life of the metal genre. Back when Heavy Metal was a by-word for poodle hairstyles, Sunset Strip excesses and utter shallowness, this is a barren hinterland where the old dinosaurs have come to die and middle of the road was the path best taken. It's not without its moments, witness SAMMY HAGAR's call to arms 'Heavy Metal', a strident and chunkier version of Van Halen, which presages the stripped back riffage of AC/DC's 'Back In Black' a year before that album's release, and BLACK SABBATH's 'Mob Rules', a Dio-era belter, before they slid into inexorable decline then surprised everyone with a millennial resurgence (and recent reunion with Dio himself). The Eagles' DON FELDER re-emerges from the shadows to torture us with two neon-lit bluesy excursions, 'Heavy Metal (Takin' A Ride)' (always beware an album that includes two tracks with that moniker) and the smooth grooves and parping bass lines of 'All Of You'. The mediocrity on show makes the leftfield inclusion of new wave art punks DEVO all the more incongruous, but 'Working

In The Coal Mine' is an interesting inclusion, with a synthesized electro sound, off-beat and off-kilter; its intriguing vocal interplay singlehandedly proves that the era was not beyond redemption. Other stalwarts include BLUE OYSTER CULT with 'Veteran Of The Psychic Wars', with lyrics penned by British author Michael Moorcock, and its evocation of the Eternal Champion battling the forces of chaos as "the winds of limbo roar", its overblown, silly themes elide well with the concerns of the lurid animated subject matter of the film. GRAND FUNK RAILROAD weigh in with 'Queen Bee', taken from their "comeback" album, 'Grand Funk Lives', its Zeppelin-like propulsion is marred by the 80s sheen but it still holds its head above water. Unlike the contributions from RIGGS, JOURNEY and STEVIE NICKS, which are uniformly execrable. *DF*

Album rating: *4.5

– spinoff hits, etc. –

DON FELDER: Heavy Metal (Takin' A Ride) / All Of You

Jul 81. (7") *Full Moon; <WBS 47175>* 43 –

DEVO: Working In The Coal Mine

Aug 81. (7") *Full Moon; <WBS 47204>* 43 –

DEVO: Working In The Coal Mine

Oct 81. (7") *Virgin; (VS 457)* –

JOURNEY: Open Arms

Jan 82. (7") *Columbia; <02687> Epic; (A 2057)* 2 Apr82

HEDWIG AND THE ANGRY INCH

2001 (US 95m) New Line Cinema (R)

Film genre: glam-Rock Musical comedy/drama

Top guns: s-w + dir: John Cameron Mitchell (+ play w/ **Stephen Trask**)

Stars: John Cameron Mitchell *(Hedwig/Hansel Robinson)* ← GIRL 6, Andrea Martin *(Phyllis Stein)* ← WAG THE DOG ← CLUB PARADISE, Miriam Shor *(Yitzhak)*, **Stephen Trask** *(Skszp)*, Michael Pitt *(Tommy Gnosis)* → LAST DAYS, Theodore Liscinski *(Jacek)*, Rob Campbell *(Krzysztof)*, Alberta Watson *(Hedwig Schmitt, Hansel's mom)* ← BEST REVENGE, Michael Aronov *(Schlatko)*, Taylor Abrahamse *(singing boy)* → INSIDE THE OSMONDS

Storyline: In 1999 there was the Broadway box-office smash (accompanied by a stage musical OST), a few years later came the movie, a cult classic by all accounts. It tells of an Iron Curtain rock performer, Hansel (from East Berlin) whose dreams are to become a hit in the USA. Raised by his trailer-trash mother, the lad subsequently falls for an American G.I., who pressurises Hedwig into having the ultimate snip so they can officially marry. When the operation goes wrong, Hedwig is left with an inch of manhood, satisfying no-one, especially his flighty boyfriend. Now virtually ignored by the fickle music business, he meets up with rising star, Tommy Gnosis, who in turn steals his image and more so, his songs. His inch, indeed gets angrier. *MCS*

Movie rating: *8.5

Visual: dvd

Off the record: Brooklyn metal act, Type O Negative, subsequently covered the song 'Angry Inch' on their 2003 set, 'Life Is Killing Me'. *MCS*

Various Cast (composer: STEPHEN TRASK *)

Jul 01. (cd) *Hybrid (Red); <HY 20024-2>* –
– Tear me down / Origin of love / Angry Inch / Wicked little town (Tommy Gnosis version) / Wig in a box / The long grift / Hedwig's lament / Exquisite corpse / Midnight radio / Nailed / Sugar daddy / Freaks (w/ GIRLS AGAINST BOYS) / In your arms tonight / Wicked little town (Hedwig version). *<re-iss. Oct03 on 'Off'; OFF 994>*

S/track review: First there was 'The ROCKY HORROR PICTURE SHOW' (1975), then its low-key sequel, 'SHOCK TREATMENT' (1981), now two decades on, comes another camp glam rock musical straight from Broadway. 'HEDWIG AND THE ANGRY INCH' – and that inch makes all the difference! – is something of a cult classic in both cinematic and audio terms, its meteoric rise from the depths of composer STEPHEN TRASK's "time warped" mind, a welcome shock in every respect. The noble appointment of JOHN CAMERON MITCHELL as Hedwig (also on Broadway) and therefore leading "man"/lead singer was another considered ploy, it's a shame his subsequent career didn't take off in the same way. His David Johansen-meets-Ziggy/Bowie persona is what makes the film (and soundtrack) so special, all glitter and glam with a capital G. Conceptual from opening track, 'Tear Me Down' (a "semi"-political rock'n'roll dirge of a song about the erection . . . of the Berlin Wall), 'HEDWIG . . .' the soundtrack gets to grips quite literally with the emotion of the schlock plot. In slight contrast, the rawk-ballad-ish 'Origin Of Love', could've been straight out of the Lou Reed songbook, while 'Angry Inch' ("six inches forward and five inches back") is pure cabaret Stooges, or even Albertos Y Lost Trios Paranoias. Explicit to the point of untrollable laughter, the lyrics take some getting used to, but if you're liberally-minded you'll enjoy all the puns. 'Wicked Little Town' (featuring STEPHEN TRASK taking on the vocals – although not his role in the film – of Tommy Gnosis) was pure Terry Jacks/'Seasons In The Sun' er . . . "soft"-rock, although its not a criticism. Arguably the best track on the OST is 'Wig In A Box', a self-analytic, Meat Loaf/Jim Steinman-type of old-style musical tune and the catchiest sing-a-long ("I put on some make-up, turn on the 8-track, I'm pulling the wig down from the shelf . . .") you'll hear since Chuck Berry's er.. 'My Ding-A-Ling'. Echoes of punk rock, and indeed Wayne County & The Electric Chairs, are rife, never more so than in 'Exquisite Corpse' & the Iggy-esque, 'Freaks' (complete with a Billy Preston 'That's The Way God Planned It' chorus!), a hark back to the heady days of '77 with a smidgen of Nirvana grunge thrown in for good measure. 'Midnight Radio' was HEDWIG's 'Rock'n'roll Suicide' or 'Ziggy Stardust', the track as climactic and uplifting as anything I've heard from "real" bands in recent times; TRASK is the 21st Century Paul Williams ('PHANTOM OF THE PARADISE'). Of the rest, 'Nailed', was a little sugar-coated, 'Sugar Daddy' was C&W w/ saccharine, and the sensitised 'In Your Arms Tonight' was Sugar-orientated featuring the legendary SUGAR frontman BOB MOULD on guitar (the Angry Inch rhythm section consisted of TED LISCINSKI on bass and PERRY JAMES on drums). A Hedwig/JCM version of 'Wicked Little Town' closes the show on a lighter note, but overall the 'HEDWIG' soundtrack has plenty of balls and unlike its namesake, is outstanding in all departments. *MCS*

Album rating: *8

HELLO DOWN THERE

1969 (US 88m) Paramount Pictures (G)

Film genre: family sci-fi adventure/comedy

Top guns: dir: Jack Arnold, Ricou Browning / s-w: John McGreevey → a DREAM IS A WISH YOUR HEART MAKES: THE ANNETTE FUNICELLO STORY, Frank Telford (story: Art Arthur, Ivan Tors)

Stars: Tony Randall *(Fred Miller)*, Janet Leigh *(Vivian Miller)*, Jim Backus *(T.R. Hollister)* ← ADVANCE TO THE REAR / → FRIDAY FOSTER, Ken Berry *(Mel Cheever)*, Roddy McDowall *(Nate Ashbury)* ← the COOL ONES / → ANGEL, ANGEL, DOWN WE GO → MEAN JOHNNY BARROWS → CLASS OF 1984, Charlotte Rae *(Myrtle Ruth)* → HAIR, Richard Dreyfuss *(Harold Webster)* → AMERICAN GRAFFITI → DOWN AND OUT IN BEVERLY HILLS, Gary Tigerman *(Tommie Miller)*, Kay Cole *(Lorrie Miller)*, Lou Wagner *(Marvin Webster)*, Merv Griffin *(himself)* → ONE-TRICK PONY, Harvey Lembeck *(Sonarman)* ← the GHOST IN THE INVISIBLE

BIKINI ← HOW TO STUFF A WILD BIKINI ← BEACH BLANKET BINGO ← PAJAMA PARTY ← BIKINI BEACH ← BEACH PARTY, Arnold Stang *(Jonah)* ← SKIDOO

Storyline: Fred Miller designs an underwater house. His boss, however, is not convinced it is feasible and would rather put his money into an underwater gold detecting machine. However Fred persuades him to let him have a 30 day trial and soon the Miller household find themselves up against sharks, hurricanes and even the US navy, who are convinced the rock and roll music coming from the depths is actually secret Russian activity. *JZ*

Movie rating: *4.5

Visual: dvd (no audio OST; score: JEFF BARRY)

Off the record: Film tracks include JEFF BARRY's 'Hello Down There', HAROLD AND THE HANG-UPS' 'Hey, Little Goldfish', 'I Can Love You', 'Glub' & 'Just One More Chance'; songwriters Arthur Johnston (music) & Sam Coslow (lyrics). *MCS*

HELP!

1965 (UK 92m) United Artists (U)

Film genre: anarchic Pop/Rock Musical comedy/satire

Top guns: dir: Richard Lester ← a HARD DAY'S NIGHT ← IT'S TRAD, DAD! / → GET BACK/ s-w: Charles Wood (story: Marc Behm)

Stars: the BEATLES:- John Lennon *(John)*, **Paul McCartney** *(Paul)*, **George Harrison** *(George)*, **Ringo Starr** *(Ringo)* / Leo McKern *(Clang)*, Eleanor Bron *(Ahme)* → CUCUMBER CASTLE, Victor Spinetti *(Prof. Foot)* ← a HARD DAY'S NIGHT / → MAGICAL MYSTERY TOUR → UNDER THE CHERRY MOON → JULIE AND THE CADILLACS, Patrick Cargill *(superintendent)* → the MAGIC CHRISTIAN, Roy Kinnear *(Algernon)* → MELODY → PIED PIPER, John Bluthal *(Bhuta)* ← a HARD DAY'S NIGHT, Alfie Bass *(doorman)* → UP THE JUNCTION, Peter Copley *(jeweller)*, Warren Mitchell *(Abdul)*, Dandy Nichols *(the neighbour)* → O LUCKY MAN!, Bruce Lacey *(lawnmower)* ← IT'S TRAD, DAD!

Storyline: Richard Lester's follow-up Beatles feature, extending the formula of 'A Hard Day's Night' with the patented blend of slapstick, irreverent humour and classic pop music, as the group flee a religious cult with designs on Ringo's ring. The wafer thin plot takes the Fab Four halfway across the world, in as much of a tail-flapping frenzy as ever. *BG*

Movie rating: *7

Visual: video + dvd

Off the record: nothing

—

the BEATLES

Jul 65. (lp) *Parlophone; (PMC 1255)(PCS PCS 3071)* [1] [-]
– Help! / The night before / You've got to hide your love away / I need you / Another girl / You're going to lose that girl / Ticket to ride / Act naturally / It's only love / You like me too much / Tell me what you see / I've just seen a face / Yesterday / Dizzy Miss Lizzy. *(re-iss. Jul71 lp/c; same); hit No.33) (cd-iss. Apr87; CDP 746439-2); hit No.61) (re-iss. Nov88 lp/c; PMC/TC-PMC 1255)*

—

the BEATLES (composer: KEN THORNE *)

Aug 65. (lp) *Capitol; <2386>* [-] [1]
– Help! / The night before / From me to you fantasy (*) / You've got to hide your love away / I need you / In the tyrol (*) / Another girl / Another hard day's night (*) / Ticket to ride / The bitter end (*) / You're gonna lose that girl / The chase (*).

S/track review: The final chapter in the first phase of the BEATLES' career, 'HELP!' presaged the band's inevitable move into more experimental territory, with both McCARTNEY and LENNON contributing the best songs of their career to date: LENNON's title track was possessed of a hitherto unwitnessed emotional urgency, while McCARTNEY raised the creative bar with his plaintive 'Yesterday'. Elsewhere 'Ticket To Ride', 'You've Got To Hide Your Love Away' and 'You're Going To Lose That Girl' were all enduring additions to the mushrooming BEATLES songbook. Again, only the US version of the album counted as a comprehensive soundtrack, featuring only the songs actually heard in the film plus instrumental pieces composed by KEN THORNE. *BG*

Album rating: *8 (UK) *6 (US)

– spinoff hits, etc. –

the BEATLES: Help! / I'm Down

Jul 65. (7") *(R 5305) <5476>* [1] [1]
(re-iss. Apr76; same); hit No.37) (re-iss. Jul85; same) (re-iss. cd-s.1989)

the BEATLES: Yesterday / Act Naturally

Sep 65. (7") *<5498>* [-] [1]

– other bits & pieces, etc. –

MATT MONRO: Yesterday

Oct 65. (7") *(R 5348)* [8] [-]

MARIANNE FAITHFUL: Yesterday

Oct 65. (7") *Decca; (F 12268)* [36] [-]

RAY CHARLES: Yesterday

Dec 67. (7") *Stateside; (SS 2071) A.B.C.; <11009>* [44] Oct67 [25]

TINA TURNER: Help

Feb 84. (7") *Capitol; (CL 325)* [40] [-]

BANANARAMA & LA NA NEE NEE NOO NOO: Help

Feb 89. (7") *London; (LON 222)* [3] [-]

WET WET WET: Yesterday

Aug 97. (cd-s) *Precious; (JWLCD 31)* [4] [-]

HENDRIX

2000 (US 101m TV) Showtime Networks / MGM Television (R)

Film genre: Rock-music bio-pic/drama

Top guns: dir: Leon Ichaso / s-w: Hal Roberts, Art Washington, Butch Stein (+ story)

Stars: Wood Harris *(Jimi Hendrix)*, Billy Zane *(Michael Jeffrey)* → OVERNIGHT, Dorian Harewood *(Al Hendrix)* ← SPARKLE, Vivica A. Fox *(Faye Pridgeon)* ← WHO DO FOOLS FALL IN LOVE / → KILL BILL: VOL.1, Christian Potenza *(Chas Chandler)*, Michie Mee *(Devon Wilson)*, Kristen J. Holdenried *(Noel Redding)*, Christopher Ralph *(Mitch Mitchell)*, Kevin Hanchard *(Little Richard)* → TAKE THE LEAD, Mark Holmes *(Pete Townshend)*, Jim Corbett *(Eric Clapton)*, Nigel Graham *(Roger Daltrey)*, Derek Aasland *(Ginger Baker)* ← TWO OF US, Michael Dunston *(Buddy Miles)* ← MR. ROCK'N'ROLL: THE ALAN FREED STORY, Cle Bennett *(Billy Cox)* ← MR. MUSIC / → LIVIN' FOR LOVE: THE NATALIE COLE STORY → HOW SHE MOVE, Louis Mercier *(Little Richard)*, Kevin Duhaney *(young Jimi)* → HONEY → HOW SHE MOVE, Joe Bostick *(reporter)* ← TWO OF US, Jeremy Tracz *(hippy at concert)* ← TWO OF US + loads of archive stars

Storyline: The film begins in his London flat in 1970, Jimi giving an interview, with his life so far shown in a series of flashbacks. After a brief glimpse of his pre-stardom days, we see him in New York with Chas Chandler, making the deal which results in him going to London and ending with the infamous Monkees gig. From then Hendrix's slide into drugs and sex parties is (rather graphically) shown, as well as his time at Woodstock and Monterey, before his sad ending not long afterwards. *JZ*

Movie rating: *4

Visual: video + dvd (no audio OST; score Daniel Licht, Andrew Rollins & Spencer Proffer)

Off the record: A who's who of stars appear in the movie, a pity they're only played by actors! *MCS*

HERE WE GO 'ROUND THE MULBERRY BUSH

1967 (UK 96m) Lopert Films / United Artists (18)

Film genre: coming-of-age/teen comedy/drama

Top guns: dir: Clive Donner ← SOME PEOPLE / s-w: Hunter Davis (+ au)

Stars: Barry Evans *(Jamie McGregor)*, Judy Geeson *(Mary Gloucester)*, Angela Scoular *(Caroline Beauchamp)*, Adrienne Posta *(Linda)* → UP THE JUNCTION → PERCY, Sheila White *(Paula)* ← the GHOST GOES GEAR / → MRS. BROWN, YOU'VE GOT A LOVELY DAUGHTER → CONFESSIONS OF A POP PERFORMER → SILVER DREAM RACER, Vanessa Howard *(Audrey)*, Diane Keen *(Claire)* → SILVER DREAM RACER, Denholm Elliott *(Mr. Beauchamp)* → PERCY → BRIMSTONE & TREACLE → the WICKED LADY, Christopher Timothy *(Spike)*, Moyra Fraser *(Mrs. McGregor)* → TAKE ME HIGH, Michael Bates *(Mr. McGregor)*, **the Spencer Davis Group:- Spencer Davis, Muff Winwood, Pete York** *(band at the church)* ← the GHOST GOES GEAR ← POP GEAR

Storyline: The suburbs of southeast England and the burgeoning mod culture provide the background and context for this colourfully attired tale of one adolescent's amusing, fumbling attempts to pop his cherry. Even a few days in the company of his school's most sought after chick brings final year pupil Jamie McGregor more regret than relief. *BG*

Movie rating: *6

Visual: video + dvd

Off the record: (see below)

---

the SPENCER DAVIS GROUP (*) / TRAFFIC (**)

Dec 67. (lp; stereo/mono) *United Artists; (S+/ULP 1186) <UAS 5175>* ☐ Apr68 ☐

– Here we go 'round the mulberry bush (**) / Healthy young lad (***) / Taking out time (*) / Every little thing (*) / Dear unknown teacher (***) / Virginals dream (*) / Utterly simple (**) / It's been a long time (ANDY ELLISON) / Looking back (*) / Picture of her (*) / Just like me (*) / Waltz for Caroline (*) / Upside down (***) / Possession (*) / Am I what I was or am I what I am (**). *(cd-iss. Jun97 on 'R.P.M.'+=; RPM 179)* – Taking out time (alt.) / Picture of her (alt.) / Just like me (alt.) / Possession (alt.). *<US cd-iss. 1998 on 'Rykodisc'+= *** dialogue; RCD 10717> (lp re-iss. Apr02 on 'Simply Vinyl'; SVLP 356)*

S/track review: Given the film's forgettably lightweight subject matter, it's the soundtrack which continues to generate interest in this movie. The majority of the tracks were commissioned from the SPENCER DAVIS GROUP, the chart-topping Midlands R&B act who had nurtured a young STEVE WINWOOD and who, to their inevitable detriment, had just lost him to psychedelic popsters TRAFFIC. Happily for Winwood fans, there were also a handful of TRAFFIC songs here, including the obligatory sitar wig-out, 'Utterly Simple', and the soulful, mildly psychedelic title theme, a UK Top 10 hit and the soundtrack's strident pièce de résistance. The aforementioned SPENCER DAVIS GROUP (without Winwood and brother Muff) contribute several cues, 'Taking Out Time', 'Every Little Thing', 'Looking Back' and 'Picture Of Her', the best of the vocal bunch and featuring recent frontman PHIL SAWYER combining well with DAVIS, drummer PETE YORK and the screeching organ of EDDIE HARDIN; the latter excels on instrumentals 'Virginals Dream' and 'Waltz For Caroline'. ANDY ELLISON, a former John's Children member (a band who included Marc Bolan), pleas for something – or the other – via 'It's Been A Long Time', the trumpet snippets being the highlight. Interspersed with witty dialogue snippets from the film's "virgin" star, Barry Evans, this soundtrack can safely be filed under the 60s. *BG & MCS*

Album rating: *6

– spinoff hits, etc. –

TRAFFIC: Here We Go 'Round The Mulberry Bush

Nov 67. (7") *Island; (WIP 6025) United Artists; <50232>* 8 –

– other bits & pieces, etc. –

the SPENCER DAVIS GROUP: The Mulberry Bush

Sep 99. (cd) *R.P.M.; (RPM 188)* ☐ –

– (film tracks). *(lp-iss.Dec99 on 'Get Back'; GET 548)*

HERMAN'S HERMITS

Formed: Manchester, England ... 1964 out of the Heartbeats by singer Peter Noone (b. 5 Nov'47), guitarist Keith Hopwood (b.26 Oct'46), lead guitarist Derek "Lek" Leckenby (b.14 May'45), bassist Karl Green (b.31 Jul'47) and drummer Barry Whitwam (b.21 Jul'46). With fellow Mancunians the Hollies, Freddie & The Dreamers and Wayne Fontana & The Mindbenders already high in the charts (and with the British Invasion about to explode across the Atlantic), HERMAN'S HERMITS were the archetypal clean-cut, English pop band. The good looks of Noone certainly drew in the girl power, while singles such as 'I'm Into Something Good' (their chart-topping debut), 'Silhouettes', 'Wonderful World' and 'A Must To Avoid' all cracked the Top 10. Inevitably, they couldn't resist the draw of the movies, having seen the success of the BEATLES' 'a HARD DAY'S NIGHT' & 'HELP!'; 'POP GEAR' (1965) and 'WHEN THE BOYS MEET THE GIRLS' (also '65) saw their initial foray into celluloid. 'HOLD ON!' (1966) and 'MRS. BROWN, YOU'VE GOT A LOVELY DAUGHTER' (1968) saw the lads star attractions, while they also provided both the soundtracks. Meanwhile, the hits just kept rolling on (although not now in the US); 'Sunshine Girl', 'Something's Happening' & 'My Sentimental Friend' were all Top 10, although when Noone left in 1970, the band tailed off. Sadly, Derek has since died (4th June, 1994) of non-Hodgkins lymphoma. *MCS*

- **filmography** {acting} (composers) –

Pop Gear *(1965 {* all} =>)* / **When The Boys Meet The Girls** *(1965 {* all} on OST by V/A =>)* / **Hold On!** *(1966 {* all} OST =>)* / **Mrs. Brown, You've Got A Lovely Daughter** *(1968 {* all} OST =>)* / **Never Too Young To Rock** *(1975 {a PETER} =>)* / **Sgt. Pepper's Lonely Hearts Club Band** *(1978 {c PETER} OST by V/A =>)* / **Hey Hey We're The Monkees** *(1997 {c PETER} =>)*

☐ Greg HETSON
(⇒ the CIRCLE JERKS)

HEY BOY! HEY GIRL!

1959 (US 83m b&w) Columbia Pictures

Film genre: romantic trad-Jazz/Rock'n'roll Musical drama

Top guns: dir: David Lowell Rich / s-w: James West, Raphael Hayes

Stars: Louis Prima *(himself)* → the CONTINENTAL TWIST, **Keely Smith** *(Dorothy Spencer)*, James Gregory *(Father Burton)* → CLAMBAKE, Kim Charney *(Buzz)*, Henry Slate *(Marty Moran)* → LOOKING FOR LOVE, Asa Maynor *(Shirley)*, Barbara Heller *(Grace Dawson)*, **Sam Butera** *(performer)* → the CONTINENTAL TWIST

Storyline: Dorothy Spencer is devoted to her local parish. As well as constantly raising funds for that leaky church roof, she finds time to bring up her young brother and be a wonderful singer. When kindly band-leader Louis Prima meets Dorothy, he falls for her housewifely charms and agrees to do a concert for her, all proceeds to go towards a new scout camp. Romance and happy ending guaranteed. *JZ*

Movie rating: *5.5

Visual: dvd

Off the record: Louis Prima was born in New Orleans (from Sicilian stock) in 1910. A master of many instruments (including his favourite, the trumpet) as well as being a big bandleader, composer, showman, etc., the man with the gravel-pit scat vocal chords worked his way up to become "King Of The Swingers". In the 30s, Hollywood invited him to perform/act in numerous movies (including 'Rhythm On The Range' with Bing Crosby), while he was also recognised as writing jazz/swing staple, 'Sing Sing Sing'. Arranger/saxophonist **Sam Butera** and the Witnesses were to provide backing for Louis and his new wife in the 50s. **Keely Smith** was born Dorothy Keely (9 Mar'32) of Cherokee/Irish descent in Norfolk, Virginia. A gifted teenager, she began her professional career in 1948/9 alongside Louis, whom she married four years later (his fourth wife incidentally). The Sonny & Cher of their day, their musical partnership subsequently blossomed, and in 1958 they had their first Top 20 hit ('That Old Black Magic') via the movie, 'Senior Prom'; solo, she sang 'Whippoorwill' in the film, 'Thunder Road'. After their Las Vegas lounge act faded after 'HEY BOY! HEY GIRL!', they divorced in 1961, Keely citing Louis' away from home activities and the physical abuse. Keely continued to work with composer Nelson Riddle and signed a contract with 'Reprise' records in 1964, where she had a UK Top 20 hit ('You're Breaking My Heart') straight from her 'Lennon-McCartney Songbook' LP. Meanwhile, **Prima** was gearing up to play his biggest role yet, as the rumbustious orangutan King Louie in the Disney animation, 'The Jungle Book'. He married his fifth wife along the way, but tragedy struck when, in 1975, he was diagnosed with brain cancer – three years later and never out of the resulting coma, Louis died on the 24th of August, 1978. Although a swinger (in more ways than one!), he was to influence the likes of rockers, Bill Haley & His Comets, Alex Harvey, Brian Setzer, David Lee Roth and Big Bad Voodoo Daddy, while his songs appear on many soundtracks. *MCS*

—

LOUIS PRIMA & KEELY SMITH (composer: Nelson Riddle)

May 59. (lp) *Capitol; <(T 1160)>* [37] [ ]
– Hey boy! hey girl! / Banana split for my baby / You are my love / Fever / Oh Marie / Lazy river / Nitey nite / When the saints go marching in / Autumn leaves / Hey boy! hey girl!.

S/track review: Not necessarily rock'n'roll per se, but trad-jazz with gusto and spirit, 'HEY BOY! HEY GIRL!' (and don't hum the Chemical Brothers tune when you think out loud!) was a showcase for man and wife double act at the time, LOUIS PRIMA and KEELY SMITH. With only ten tracks on this wee LP, the pair split the songs into solo and duets, with arranger Nelson Riddle always in tow (sax man, SAM BUTERA, and the Witnesses also augmented). PRIMA's rasping, Louis Armstrong-style scat-cattin' (and his trumpet!) on numbers such as 'Oh Marie' and 'When The Saints Go Marching In' were highlights, while KEELY gets her chance to shine on 'Nitey Nite' and 'You Are My Love'. Squeezed somewhere in the middle of two great title track versions, is SAM BUTERA rendition of 'Lazy River'. Fans of all parties concerned await that elusive CD release. *MCS*

Album rating: *5.5

– spinoff releases, etc. –

LOUIS PRIMA & KEELY SMITH: Hey Boy! Hey Girl!

May 59. (7"ep) *<T 1160>* [ ] [–]

HEY, LET'S TWIST!

1961 (US 80m b&w) Paramount Pictures

Film genre: Rock'n'roll Musical drama

Top guns: dir: Greg Garrison ← TWO TICKETS TO PARIS / s-w: Hal Hackady ← LET'S ROCK / → TWO TICKETS TO PARIS

Stars: Joey Dee *(Joey Dee)* → TWO TICKETS TO PARIS, **Teddy Randazzo** *(Rickey Dee)* ← MISTER ROCK AND ROLL ← ROCK, ROCK, ROCK! ← the GIRL CAN'T HELP IT, **Kay Armen** *(Angie)*, **Jo-Ann Campbell** *(Piper)* ← GO, JOHNNY GO!, Zohra Lampert *(Sharon)*, Dino DiLuca *(Papa)*, Allan Arbus *(the doctor)* → COFFY → CROSSROADS, **Joe Pesci** *(dancer at the Peppermint Club)* → MOONWALKER, Sally Kirkland *(dancer)* → PIPE DREAMS → a STAR IS BORN → HUMAN HIGHWAY → THANK YOU, GOOD NIGHT, Richard Dickens *(Rore)* ← TWO TICKETS TO PARIS, Joseph Rigano *(Vinnie)* → GHOST DOG: THE WAY OF THE SAMURAI → COFFEE AND CIGARETTES

Storyline: Joey and Rickey Dee are two brothers who want to get involved in the music scene, now dominated by the Twist craze. When they tell this to their stressed-out dad he promptly collapses, as he had hoped his boys would be doctors or lawyers. Entrusted with poorly dad's restaurant, the boys swiftly turn it into a dance club while the old boy convalesces, and the Peppermint Twist can soon be heard all over town. *JZ*

Movie rating: *4

Visual: video

Off the record: **JOEY DEE** (see below).

—

JOEY DEE & THE STARLITERS (*) / JO-ANN CAMPBELL (**) / TEDDY RANDAZZO (***) / KAY ARMEN (****)

Feb 62. (lp;stereo/mono) *Roulette; <S+/R 25168> Columbia; (33SX 1421)* [18] [ ]
– Hey, let's twist (*) / Roly poly (*) / I wanna twist (****) / Peppermint twist – part 1 (*) / Keelee's twist (instrumental) / It's a pity to say goodnight (***) / Mother Goose twist (***) / Joey's blues (DAVE & The STARLITERS) / Let me do my twist (**) / Blue twister (alto sax solo by BILL RAMMEL) / Shout (*) / 'Na voce, 'na chitarra E'o poco 'E luna (****).

S/track review: The Peppermint Lounge in Manhattan's west side, New York, takes centre stage for the latest teenage dance craze (nay, epidemic!): "the twist". Hank Ballard had instigated this dancefloor sensation, while Chubby Checker subsequently coined it in big time during a chart spree in the early 60s. JOEY DEE & THE STARLITERS (a group who used to have actor Joe Pesci as a guitarist!) became the dance's latest recruits, heading the bill on 'HEY, LET'S TWIST!', with a handful of hit singles. A surprise chart-topper, 'Peppermint Lounge – part 1', caught the nation's attention, while the equally rambunctious Top 20 title track, the un-PC 'Roly Poly' and an excellent cover of the Isley's 'Shout!' (also Top 10), conjured up a time when the teenager ruled the globe. Anthemic and frenetic, the bubblegum-chewing youth fashioned out their own goody-two-shoes kind of rock'n'roll. Veteran of pop musicals of the late 50s, TEDDY RANDAZZO, gets to grips with two varying cuts, the "reelin' & rockin'" of 'Mother Goose Twist' and the crooning ballad that was 'It's A Pity To Say Goodnight'. Former 40s radio starlet, KAY ARMEN (who'd starred in 1955's song-and-dance movie, 'Hit The Deck'), was also up for a bit of crooning via ''Na Voce, 'Na Chitarra E'o Poco 'E Luna' along with the Brenda Lee-esque 'I Wanna Twist'. Florida-born JO ANN CAMPBELL (with a previous cameo in 'GO, JOHNNY GO!' behind her), was afforded only one cue, 'Let Me Do My Twist', while the best instrumental on show was 'Blue Twister', featuring a sexy alto sax performed by BILL RAMMEL. *MCS*

Album rating: *4.5

– spinoff hits, etc. –

JOEY DEE & THE STARLITERS: Peppermint Twist – part 1 / Peppermint Twist – part 2

Nov 61. (7") *<4401> (DB 4758)* [1] Jan62 [33]

JOEY DEE & THE STARLITERS: Hey, Let's Twist / Roly Poly

Feb 62. (7") *<4408> (DB 4803)* [20]
[74] Mar62 [ ]

JOEY DEE & THE STARLITERS: Shout – part 1 / Shout – part 2

Mar 62. (7") *<4416> (DB 4842)* 6 Apr62

– other bits & pieces, etc. –

JOEY DEE & THE STARLITERS: Hey, Let's Twist!

Aug 90. (cd/c) *<(CD/TC ROU 5010)>*
– (compilation featuring 6 film tracks).

□ HEY YOU, GO!
(⇒ the JAGUARS)

HIGH FIDELITY

2000 (US 113m) Buena Visa Pictures (R)

Film genre: romantic workplace comedy/drama

Top guns: dir: Stephen Frears / s-w: D.V. De Vincentis, Steve Pink, Scott Rosenberg, John Cusack (au: Nick Hornby)

Stars: John Cusack *(Rob Gordon)* ← ROADSIDE PROPHETS ← TAPEHEADS / → the FUTURE IS UNWRITTEN, Iben Hjejle *(Laura)*, Jack Black *(Barry)* ← DEAD MAN WALKING / → SCHOOL OF ROCK → the PICK OF DESTINY → WALK HARD: THE DEWEY COX STORY, Lisa Bonet *(Marie DeSalle)*, Todd Louiso *(Dick)*, Joan Cusack *(Liz)* ← WORKING GIRL / → SCHOOL OF ROCK, Catherine Zeta Jones *(Charlie Nicholson)*, Tim Robbins *(Ian)* ← JUNGLE FEVER ← TAPEHEADS ← HOWARD THE DUCK / → the PICK OF DESTINY, Sara Gilbert *(Annaugh Moss)*, Joelle Carter *(Penny)*, Chris Rehmann *(Vince)*, Lili Taylor *(Sarah)* ← a SLIPPING-DOWN LIFE ← I SHOT ANDY WARHOL ← FOUR ROOMS, Ben Carr *(Justin)*, Natasha Gregson Wagner *(Caroline)* ← FIRST LOVE, LAST RITES ← S.F.W., **Bruce SPRINGSTEEN** *(himself)*

Storyline: Stupefied with inertia and secure in his motto that it's not what someone's like but what they like that counts, Rob Gordon navigates the choppy waters of thirty-something crisis in tandem with running a backstreet record shop. His girlfriend's finally left him, apparently for good, and when he's not splitting discographical hairs with his employees, he's wondering just where it all started to go wrong. To find out, he roots out his former lovers one by one, encounter by squirmingly uncomfortable encounter. *BG*

Movie rating: *8

Visual: dvd

Off the record: Welsh lass Catherine Zeta Jones (from being "A Darling Bud Of May" to marrying Hollywood actor Michael Douglas after this film was released) has hit the UK Top 40 charts twice in her life, in 1992 with 'For All Time' and in 1994 with 'True Love Ways', the latter a duet with DAVID ESSEX. *MCS*

—

Various Artists

Apr 00. (cd/d-lp) *Hollywood; <62188> (011218-2/-1 HWR)* Jul00
– A town called Malice (the JAM) *[track 1 UK-only]* / You're gonna miss me (the 13TH FLOOR ELEVATORS) *[track 2 UK]* / Everybody's gonna be happy (the KINKS) *[track 13 UK]* / I'm wrong about everything (JOHN WESLEY HARDING) *[track 3 US-only]* / I'm gonna love you a little more babe (BARRY WHITE) *[track 4 UK-only]* / Oh! sweet nuthin' (the VELVET UNDERGROUND) *[track 10 UK]* / Always see your face (LOVE) *[track 5 US-only]* / Rock steady (ARETHA FRANKLIN) *[track 6 UK-only]* / Most of the time (BOB DYLAN) *[track 11 UK]* / Fallen for you (SHEILA NICHOLLS) *[track 9 UK]* / Dry the rain (the BETA BAND) *[track 7 UK]* / Shipbuilding (ELVIS COSTELLO & THE ATTRACTIONS) *[track 8 UK]* / Cold blooded old times (SMOG) *[track 3 UK]* / Let's get it on (JACK BLACK) *[track 14 UK]* / Lo boob oscillator (STEREOLAB) *[track 14 UK]* / Inside game (ROYAL TRUX) *[track 13 US-only]* / Who loves the sun (the VELVET UNDERGROUND) *[track 5 UK]* / I believe (when I fall in love it will be forever) (STEVIE WONDER).

S/track review: Relocating Nick Hornby's shambling vinyl junkie from London to Chicago should surely have been a cue for indulging the poor sod's love of rare black music; if there was ever an excuse to get some dusty grooves on a Hollywood (as in L.A., not the label) soundtrack this was it. It's a good collection, but it could've been great – and a lot more soulful. There's not nearly enough arcane or imaginatively selected stuff to satisfy the kind of trainspotter the movie sends up, if doubtless more than enough to get less crusty, less obsessive music fans and cinema-goers digging deeper. Even taking into account licensing considerations, there are some glaring omissions from the music actually heard and/or namedropped in the film. In place of some rare 45's we get some done-to-death BARRY WHITE and STEVIE WONDER, and surely Rob Fleming would have preferred the funkier Marvels' version of 'Rock Steady' to the ARETHA FRANKLIN original? Still, even that's an improvement on the US release, which indefensibly includes only STEVIE's 'I Believe (When I Fall In Love It Will Be Forever)' alongside the 60s/indie perennials. A heavy VELVET UNDERGROUND vibe – two Lou Reed-less tracks from 'Loaded' (1971), and a proxy VELVETS number in the form of STEREOLAB's wonderful, Nico-goes-Gallic 'Lo Boob Oscillator' – and an even heavier, slacker vibe supply a theme of sorts: the late, lamented BETA BAND stand slouched but proud among the superstars, and SMOG (aka Bill Callahan) is in unmissably pungent form on 'Cold Blooded Old Times', a drawling, Gen X inversion of Willie Nelson's 'Good Times'. But would even the most self-conscious, crisis-addled music geek really have a copy of SHEILA NICHOLLS' 'Fallen For You'? *BG*

Album rating: *7.5

HIGH SCHOOL CONFIDENTIAL!

1958 (US 85m b&w) Albert Zugsmith Productions / M.G.M.

Film genre: crime/detective mystery teen drama

Top guns: dir: Jack Arnold / s-w: Robert Blees (+ story), Lewis Meltzer

Stars: Russ Tamblyn *(Tony Baker)* → FOLLOW THE BOYS → HUMAN HIGHWAY, Jan Sterling *(Arlene Williams)*, John Drew Barrymore *(J.I. Coleridge)*, Mamie van Doren *(Gwen Dulaine)* ← UNTAMED YOUTH / → LAS VEGAS HILLBILLYS, Diane Jergens *(Joan Staples)* ← SING BOY SING / → TEENAGE MILLIONAIRE, **Jerry Lee LEWIS** *(performer)*, Ray Anthony *(Bix)*, Jackie Coogan *(Mr. A)* → GIRL HAPPY, Charles Chaplin Jr. *(Quinn)*, Michael Landon *(Steve Bentley)*, William Wellman Jr. *(wheeler-dealer)* → a SWINGIN' SUMMER → WINTER A-GO-GO → BLACK CAESAR, Jody Fair *(Doris)* → HOT ROD GANG

Storyline: Tough guy Tony Baker is the new kid on the block at high school and soon he's involved in all the usual ex-curricular activities of the 50s that we know and love – drag racing, sleazy night clubs and of course pot-smoking (as well as fending off his sex-starved aunt). At last Tony draws himself to the attention of drug baron Mr A, and as he hustles for a piece of the action we find out which side Tony is really on. *JZ*

Movie rating: *5

Visual: video + dvd (no audio OST)

Off the record: Ray Anthony was a big band leader/trumpeter from Bentleyville, Pennsylvania, who worked with Glenn Miller, Jimmy Dorsey and Frank Sinatra. *MCS*

– spinoff hits, etc. –

JERRY LEE LEWIS: High School Confidential

May 58. (7",78) *Sun; <296> London; (HLS 8780)* 21 Jan59 12

HIGH SCHOOL MUSICAL

2006 (US 98m TV) First Street Films / Walt Disney Pictures (PG)

Film genre: romantic teen Pop Musical comedy/drama

Top guns: dir: Kenny Ortega → the CHEETAH GIRLS 2 → HIGH SCHOOL MUSICAL 2 / s-w: Peter Barsocchini → HIGH SCHOOL MUSICAL 2

Stars: Zac Efron *(Troy Bolton)* → HAIRSPRAY re-make → HIGH SCHOOL MUSICAL 2, Vanessa Anne Hudgens *(Gabriella Montez)* → HIGH SCHOOL MUSICAL 2, Ashley Tisdale *(Sharpay Evans)* → HIGH SCHOOL MUSICAL 2, Monique Coleman *(Taylor McKessie)* → HIGH SCHOOL MUSICAL 2, Lucas Grabeel *(Ryan Evans)* → HIGH SCHOOL MUSICAL 2, Corbin Bleu *(Chad Danforth)* → HIGH SCHOOL MUSICAL 2, Bart Johnson *(coach Jack Bolton)* → HIGH SCHOOL MUSICAL 2, Alyson Reed *(Ms. Darbus)* → HIGH SCHOOL MUSICAL 2

Storyline: Troy (captain of the East High basketball team) and Gabriella (a member of the school's academic team) are two very different students who discover a mutual love for music and theatre. When the other students realise they are spending too much time together, they decide to join forces and split them up. However they haven't reckoned with the couple's desire and ambition to succeed and things come to a head with the big musical audition and the make or break basketball decider. *JZ*

Movie rating: *6.5

Visual: dvd (+ 2-disc)

Off the record: nothing

—

Various Cast/Composers (score: DAVID LAWRENCE *)

Jan 06. (cd) *Walt Disney; <861426>* [1] Sep06 [ ]
– Start of something new (GABRIELLA & TROY) / Get'cha head in the game (TROY & WILDCATS) / What I've been looking for (SHARPAY & RYAN) / What I've been looking for – reprise (GABRIELLA & TROY) / Stick to the status quo (SHARPAY) / When there was me and you (SHARPAY) / Bop to the top (SHARPAY & RYAN) / Breaking free (GABRIELLA & TROY) / We're all in this together (the Cast) / I can't take my eyes off of you (GABRIELLA, TROY, SHARPAY & RYAN) / Get'cha head in the game (B5) / Start of something new (karaoke) / Breaking free (karaoke). *(also iss.May06 d-cd+=)* – (other karaoke versions).

S/track review: A made-for-TV film loosely based around a modern day Romeo and Juliet plotline, 'HIGH SCHOOL MUSICAL' is the latest wholesome Disney pop product. Overly sweet, the soundtrack features sugary piano laden ballads, bright and cheery urban pop rapping and chirpy latin numbers. For the older listeners, it leaves a bit of a sick feeling in the stomach but then that's the way it should be. In fairness, many of the songs on the album are positive, it's a more palatable musical for the teen market and you can hear the influence of popular artists from Akon to Puff Daddy and Mariah Carey. It's the type of musical that, as a budding young entertainer, you would die to be involved with and as a parent you are completely dumbfounded as to why your 10-year-old loves it so much. The opening ballad 'Start Of Something New', a sappy duet by leads ZAC EFRON and VANESSA ANNE HUDGENS, is the type of song that Disney does best (think 'Beauty And The Beast'). Much more listenable though is the urban rapping of 'Get'cha Head In The Game' performed by ANDREW SEELEY, which is reminiscent of artists such as Missy Elliott and Justin Timberlake. 'Bop to the Top', a fun and danceable latin infused number, performed by LUCAS GRABEEL and ASHLEY TISDALE, continues the eclecticism. The dance tracks continue with 'We're All In This Together' sung by the HIGH SCHOOL MUSICAL CAST (another US Hot 100 hit!), which sounds like a school band backed up by a cheerleading team. All very S Club 7 and not very interesting. 'I Can't Take My Eyes Off of You' performed by ANDREW SEELEY, ZAC EFRON, VANESSA ANNE HUDGENS, LUCAS GRABEEL and ASHLEY TISDALE, is slightly better with a tropical feel. It sounds like the younger siblings of Justin Timberlake harmonising together. Parents may guffaw and cringe at this rather average effort but give the kids a break, before long they'll graduate onto more mature sounds. *SM*

Album rating: *6

– spinoff hits, etc. –

High School Musical: Breaking Free / Start Of Something New
Jun 06. (cd-s) *<(373085-2)>* [4] [28] Sep06 [9]

High School Musical: Bop To The Top
Jul 06. (-) *<radio>* [61] [–]

High School Musical: Get'cha Head In The Game
Jul 06. (-) *<radio>* [23] [–]

High School Musical: Stick To The Status Quo
Aug06. (-) *<radio>* [43] [–]

High School Musical: What I've Been Looking For – Reprise
Sep 06. (-) *<radio>* [66] [–]

High School Musical: What I've Been Looking For
Sep 06. (-) *<radio>* [35] [–]

High School Musical: We're All In This Together
Oct 06. (cd-s) *<377159-2>* [34] [–]

High School Musical: When There Was Me And You
Nov 06. (-) *<radio>* [71] [–]

HIGH SCHOOL MUSICAL 2

2007 (US 90m TV) First Street Films / Disney Channel

Film genre: teen-pop Musical comedy

Top guns: dir: Kenny Ortega ← the CHEETAH GIRLS 2 ← HIGH SCHOOL MUSICAL / s-w: Peter Barsocchini ← HIGH SCHOOL MUSICAL

Stars: Zac Efron *(Troy Bolton)* ← HAIRSPRAY ← HIGH SCHOOL MUSICAL, Vanessa Anne Hudgens *(Gabriella Montez)* ← HIGH SCHOOL MUSICAL, Ashley Tisdale *(Sharpay Evans)* ← HIGH SCHOOL MUSICAL, Lucas Grabeel *(Ryan Evans)* ← HIGH SCHOOL MUSICAL, Corbin Bleu *(Chad Danforth)* ← HIGH SCHOOL MUSICAL, Monique Coleman *(Taylor McKessie)* ← HIGH SCHOOL MUSICAL, Mark L. Taylor *(Mr. Fulton)*, Bart Johnson *(Jack Bolton)* ← HIGH SCHOOL MUSICAL, Alyson Reed *(Ms. Darbus)* ← HIGH SCHOOL MUSICAL, Robert Curtis Brown *(Vance Evans)* ← DREAMGIRLS

Storyline: Things are hotting up at the Lava Springs Country Club when Troy, Gabriella and their friends all land summer jobs there. This isn't a coincidence – Sharpay's family own the club and she's sneakily got Troy a job to lure him away from his true love. With the big talent show looming, will he succumb to Sharpay's scholarship bait or will glamorous Gabby win the siege of Troy? *JZ*

Movie rating: *5

Visual: dvd

Off the record: nothing

—

Various Cast (score: David Lawrence)

Aug 07. (cd) *Walt Disney; <D 00065102> (505420-0)* [1] [ ]
– What time is it? (HIGH SCHOOL MUSICAL 2 CAST) / Fabulous (RYAN and SHARPAY) / Work this out (HIGH SCHOOL MUSICAL 2 CAST) / You are the music in me (GABRIELLA and TROY) / I don't dance (CHAD and RYAN) / You are the music in me – Sharpay version (SHARPAY) / Gotta go my own way (GABRIELLA and TROY) / Bet on it (TROY) /

Everyday (HIGH SCHOOL MUSICAL 2 CAST) / All for one (HIGH SCHOOL MUSICAL 2 CAST). *(bonus track +=)* – Humuhumunukunukuapua'a (SHARPAY).

S/track review: So soon – or indeed too soon – after the original Disney cable smash, this is a blatant rip-off to cash in on the kids just before they start junior school (or indeed, primary). The music here is unadulterated supermarket fodder, likely to find a home with any child who would've loved the Spice Girls or East 17 – had they been around at the time. Opener, 'What Time Is It?', represents all that's rich, safe and cutesy in a selfish world of sports-loving, fashion-daft, designer-label Bratz. In one word, schmaltz. It harks back to a time (in the mid-90s) when girl and boy bands were all the rage, while you could even take it one dance-step further back to the 80s and the 'FAME' and 'FLASHDANCE' era; and what about the Osmonds? The likelihood of such goody-two-shoes running about the halls of American schools, while armed security walk among them, is downright hokum. But one has diverted too long. The boy and girl next door, in this case TROY and GABRIELLA, have their best moment on love ballad, 'You Are The Music In Me'; there's also a SHARPAY version if you want more. All'n'all, one thinks there might be a case for "AOR-rock" balladeers such as Nickelback or Journey for example, (lawyers-are-us.com) to check out some of the sappy-fied, new-look tunes on display here. You heard it here first, unfortunately I was the first "grown-up" to hear it for myself. *MCS*

Album rating: *1

– spinoff hits, etc. –

High School Musical 2: What Time Is It?

Jul 07. (cd-s) *<501647-0>* 6 20

High School Musical 2: All For One

Aug 07. (-) *<radio>* 92 –

High School Musical 2: Bet On It

Aug 07. (-) *<radio>* 46 –

High School Musical 2: Everyday

Aug 07. (-) *<radio>* 90 –

High School Musical 2: Gotta Go My Own Way

Aug 07. (-) *<radio>* 34 –

High School Musical 2: I Don't Dance

Aug 07. (-) *<radio>* 74 –

High School Musical 2: You Are The Music In Me

Aug 07. (-) *<radio>* 31 –

HIGHWAY 61

1991 (Can/US/UK 110m) Skouras Pictures (R)

Film genre: road movie/comedy

Top guns: s-w: Bruce McDonald (+ dir) ← ROADKILL / → HARD CORE LOGO, Don McKellar ← ROADKILL, Allan Magee (story: Colin Brunton)

Stars: Valerie Buhagiar *(Jackie Bangs)* ← ROADKILL, Don McKellar *(Pokey Jones)* ← ROADKILL / → CLEAN, Earl Pastko *(Mr. Skin / Satan)* ← ROADKILL, Peter Breck *(Mr. Watson)* ← TERMINAL CITY RICOCHET ← HOOTENANNY HOOT ← the BEATNIKS, **Art Bergmann** *(Otto)* → HARD CORE LOGO, **Jello BIAFRA** *(customs agent #1)*, Hadley Obodiac *(customs agent #2)*, **Tav Falco** *(motorcycle gang leader)*, Elizabeth Pritchard *(Louise Watson)*, Larry Hudson *(Nathan; manservant)* ← ROADKILL

Storyline: Barber Pokey Jones finds a corpse in his garden (well, it is Canada after all). Soon a woman turns up claiming to be the dead man's sister, and asks Pokey to drive both her and the body down Highway 61 to New Orleans. But all is not as it seems – there's a stash of drugs hidden in the body, and a certain gentleman usually seen with pitchfork, horns and tail is after them to fulfil a binding contract. It looks like our bemused barber is about to experience a close shave of his own. *JZ*

Movie rating: *6

Visual: video + dvd

Off the record: NASH THE SLASH (see below)

—

Various Artists (score: NASH THE SLASH *)

Dec 91. (cd) *Intrepid; <N21S 0009>* □ –

– Into the land of the fire (*) / Highway 61 revisited (RITA CHIARELLI feat. COLIN LINDEN) / Put your head on (BOURBON TABERNACLE CHOIR) / Dance (ACID TEST) / Momma's waitin' (JANE HAWLEY) / Sally on (SAM LARKIN) / My way or the highway (the RAZORBACKS) / It's not unusual (TOM JONES) / Torture (TAV FALCO) / Mr. Skin (ACID TEST) / The erlking (JELLYFISHBABIES) / Can't nobody do me like Jesus (ANNE MARIE STERN, CARLTON RANCE, VANESSA YOUNGER and ROSIE WESTNEY) / Zydeco heehaw (BOOZOO CHAVIS).

S/track review: The first thing one notices when looking at 'HIGHWAY 61's line-up of eclectic outfits is its lack of big-name acts – TOM JONES' 1965 smash 'It's Not Unusual' is the notable exception. Where Quentin Tarantino opted for the obscure in subsequent movies such as 'RESERVOIR DOGS' and 'PULP FICTION', Canadian filmmaker Bruce McDonald (and complier Peter J. Moore) find a lower-league all-sorts of indie rockabilly, hard-rock, folk, zydeco and nu-dance. NASH THE SLASH – who gets in his own full soundtrack below – kicks off with a hard-rock anthem of sorts, 'Into The Land Of Fire', while segued from film dialogue arrives a Dylan cover of 'Highway 61 Revisited' by RITA CHIARELLI featuring COLIN LINDEN. Very Eagles-versus-Pat Benatar. Getting all funky and retro are BOURBON TABERNACLE CHOIR with alt-rock Canadian hit, 'Put Your Head On', while two A Certain Ratio-meets-Paul Hardcastle numbers, 'Dance' and 'Mr. Skin' stem from ACID TEST (aka Lucy DiSanto & Steve Fall). Roots-rock and country-folk comes by way of singer-songwriters, JANE HAWLEY ('Momma's Waitin'') and SAM LARKIN ('Sally On'), who compete with rockabilly rockers the RAZORBACKS ('My Way Or The Highway') and the Sid Vicious-sounding TAV FALCO ('Torture'). With no RAMONES' 'Rock'n'Roll Radio' on the OST, a shoegazing track 'The Erlking' (courtesy of JELLYFISHBABIES) and a gospel cue are overshadowed by superb finale cue, 'Zydeco Heehaw' by BOOZOO CHAVIS. *MCS*

Album rating: *4.5

—

NASH THE SLASH with DOC SATAN'S ORCHESTRA

Dec 91. (cd) *Cut-Throat; <CUTCD 1>* □ –

– Pokey remembers / Pickeral falls sunrise / Pokey finds a body / Afternoon in the barbershop / Pokey meets the Devil / Jackie prepares the body / Jackie hitches out of nowhere / Country driving / Into the land of the fire / Pokey remembers / Nightime drive / The clothesline / The getaway / Ice blues / 'War' (Margo's song) / Bikers get a shave / Pokey's blues / Jackie bin baptized / The Devil's playground / Fires of Hell / Doc Satan / The getaway (reprise).

S/track review: If there were a few snippets of dialogue in the Various Artists equivalent, there were several more tasty segments on the NASH THE SLASH score version. The mysterious Canadian (Jeff Plewman, anyone?) was of the eccentric and weird variety, the ex-FM musician guarding his identity by swathing his face in surgical bandages. Performing to packed audiences since his solo inception in the late 70s, NASH and his audio-visuals have supported the likes of Gary Numan and Iggy Pop. Several LPs have surfaced up to 'HIGHWAY 61': 'Bedside Companion' (1978), 'Dreams And Nightmares' (1979), 'Children Of The Night' (1980), 'Decomposing' (1981; and plays at any speed!),

his greatest achievement 'And You Thought You Were Normal' (1982) and 'American BandAges' (1984). After returning to FM, NASH also made a cameo appearance and wrote the music for Bruce McDonald's debut feature, 'ROADKILL' (1989) – and then there was 'HIGHWAY '61'. Described as laying somewhere between a David Lynch soundtrack or a Velvets/Reed experiment (gone wrong!), the electronic score finds itself in a dark and brooding place, uneasy, unnerving and unsettling. Okay, there are a fair share of rock numbers on board ('Into The Land Of The Fire' – for one!), but this album is strictly for the primitive and primeval among you.
MCS

Album rating: *5

HOLD ON!

1966 (US 85m) Metro-Goldwyn-Mayer (PG)

Film genre: Pop/Rock Musical comedy

Top guns: dir: Arthur Lubin / s-w: James B. Gordon

Stars: HERMAN'S HERMITS:- Peter Noone, Karl Green, Barry Whitwam, Keith Hopwood + Derek Leckenby *(as themselves)* ← WHEN THE BOYS MEET THE GIRLS / → MRS. BROWN, YOU'VE GOT A LOVELY DAUGHTER, Shelley Fabares *(Louisa)* ← GIRL HAPPY ← RIDE THE WILD SURF ← SUMMER LOVE ← ROCK, PRETTY BABY / → SPINOUT → CLAMBAKE → a TIME TO SING, Sue Ane Langdon *(Cecilie)* ← FRANKIE AND JOHNNY ← WHEN THE BOYS MEET THE GIRLS ← ROUSTABOUT, Herbert Anderson *(lindquist)*, Bernard Fox *(Dudley)*, Mickey Deems *(publicist)*, Hortense Petra *(Mrs. Page)* ← WHEN THE BOYS MEET THE GIRLS ← YOUR CHEATIN' HEART ← GET YOURSELF A COLLEGE GIRL ← KISSIN' COUSINS ← DON'T KNOCK THE TWIST / → RIOT ON SUNSET STRIP, Phil Arnold *(photographer)* ← YOUR CHEATIN' HEART ← GO, JOHNNY, GO! / → GOOD TIMES → SKIDOO

Storyline: The Hermits arrive in Los Angeles for their big concert at the Rose Bowl, although they act more like a tourist group than a pop group. They pay the price for fame when they find themselves pursued by an odd bunch of people who want to annoy them as much as possible. Amongst others, there's a wannabe actress who desperately needs publicity, and a NASA scientist who wants to use their name on a new spaceship to boldly go where no pop group has gone before.
JZ

Movie rating: *4

Visual: video + dvd

Off the record: (see below)

—

HERMAN'S HERMITS

Mar 66. (lp;mono/stereo) *M.G.M.; <E/SE-4342ST>* [14] [–]
– Hold on! / The George and Dragon / Got a feelin' / Wild love / Leaning on a lamp post / Where were you when I needed you / All the things I do for you baby / Gotta get away / Make me happy (w/ SHELLEY FABARES) / A must to avoid.

S/track review: On first reflection: did pop pickers really love this? – or was it just overhyped pop? Anyway, stars of the show, Manchester's HERMAN'S HERMITS (characterised by their debut No.1, 'I'm Into Something Good') were an integral part of the British pop invasion that started a few years previously with the Fab Four. Produced by Mickie Most, the toothy PETER NOONE (Colgate's best ambassador!) and Co sing and perform with all the cheeky Englishness that made them so appealing Stateside. That very Englishness was evident on at least two of the tracks, 'The George And Dragon' (a ye olde fantasy about their local pub/inn, complete with harpsichord and showing shades of their medieval US chart-topper, 'I'm Henry VIII, I Am') and the George Formby ukelele timepiece, 'Leaning On The Lamp Post'; even Freddie And The Dreamers would've passed up this cringeworthy effort. Many will find it difficult to comprehend that the latter actually hit the US Top 10. Novelty records aside, HERMAN'S HERMITS were at their best on post-Beatles/Hollies-like numbers such as 'Got A Feeling', which displayed great lead guitar work. Ditto 'Wild Love' and 'Gotta Get Away', also from the pens of Karger-Weisman-Wayne. Highlighting fellow star, actress SHELLY FABARES (see numerous Elvis movies), the quintet smoothed out their hard edges on pop ballad 'Make Me Happy', while songwriter P.F. Sloan (some alongside Barri) supplied the 'Hermits with a handful of songs, the title track, 'Where Were You When I Needed You' (a subsequent hit for the Grass Roots!), 'The Things I Do For You Baby' and another US Top 10 smash, 'A Must To Avoid' (think Freddie And The Dreamers – again!). Now, what was that song, "I'm Into Something . . . [not very] Good".
MCS

Album rating: *4.5

– spinoff hits, etc. –

HERMAN'S HERMITS: A Must To Avoid / (non-OST song)
Dec 65. (7") *<13437> Columbia; (DB 7791)* [8] [6]

HERMAN'S HERMITS: Leaning On The Lamp Post / Hold On!
Mar 66. (7") *<13500>* [9] [–]

– others, etc.

the GRASS ROOTS: Where Were You When I Needed You
Jun 66. (7") *Dunhill; <4029> R.C.A.; (1532)* [28] [ ]

HOMER

1970 (US 91m) Palomar Pictures Inc. / National General (PG)

Film genre: showbiz/Rock-music teen drama

Top guns: dir: John Trent → BEST REVENGE / s-w: Claude Harz (au: Matt Clark)

Stars: Chelo/Don Scardino *(Homer Edwards)*, Alex Nicol *(Mr. Harry Edwards)*, Tisa Farrow *(Laurie Grainger)*, Lenka Peterson *(Mrs. Edwards)*, Ralph Endersby *(Hector)*, Tim Henry *(Eddie Cochran)*, Tom Harvey *(Mr. Tibbet)*

Storyline: Wisconsin teenager Homer Edwards is an angry young man. His parents don't understand him, his pal is fighting deep in the jungles of Vietnam, and he gets his kicks through rock music and dope. The only way to make himself heard is to form a rock band, and he does this when Eddie returns from the wars and his other mate Hector helps out. Now everyone will have to sit up and listen!
JZ

Movie rating: *5.5

Visual: none

Off the record: Don Scardino (nowadays a TV series/film director) had already featured in the movie, 'The People Next Door' (1970), while he furthered his CV career by acting in 'Rip-Off' (1971) and 'Cruising' (1980).
MCS

—

Various Artists

Dec 70. (lp) *Cotillion; <SD 9037> Polydor; (2400 137)* [ ] Aug71 [ ]
– Turn! turn! turn! (to everything there is a season) (the BYRDS) / Bluebird (BUFFALO SPRINGFIELD) / Nashville cats (LOVIN' SPOONFUL) / Rock n' roll woman (BUFFALO SPRINGFIELD) / How many more times (LED ZEPPELIN) / Brave new world (STEVE MILLER BAND) / Man of music (DON SCARDINO) / Rock n roll gypsies (HEARTS AND FLOWERS) / Spoonful (CREAM) / For what it's worth (BUFFALO SPRINGFIELD).

S/track review: Although 'HOMER' was released towards the end of 1970, it was firmly embedded in the 60s, BUFFALO SPRINGFIELD (featuring main songsmith, Stephen Stills) taking top billing here with three seminal cues, 'Bluebird', 'Rock n' Roll Woman' & 'For What It's Worth'. 'Atlantic' subsidiary 'Cotillion' had an enviable habit of getting it right soundtrack-wise having just produced the voluminous, triple-set, 'WOODSTOCK'; coincidentally, Yasgur Farm star John Sebastian also got his two-pennorth in here by way of his LOVIN' SPOONFUL "gone country" gem, 'Nashville Cats'. From the BYRDS', Pete Seeger-penned classic, 'Turn! Turn! Turn!', CREAM's Willie Dixon cover, 'Spoonful' and LED ZEPPELIN's 'How Many More Times' (Plant, Page & Co at eight and a half minutes!), the listener is in for a God almighty treat. If there's a low point, well there's three of them, the easy-on-the-ear 'Man Of Music' by the film's star-turn, DON SCARDINO, 'Rock n Roll Gypsies' by country-folkers HEARTS AND FLOWERS (featuring future Eagles guitarist, Bernie Leadon) and 'Brave New World' by the STEVE MILLER BAND (the title track from their 3rd LP). *MCS*

Album rating: *7.5

HONEY

2003 (US 94m) Universal Pictures (PG-13)

Film genre: urban R&B/Dance Musical drama

Top guns: dir: Bille Woodruff / s-w: Alonzo Brown, Kim Watson

Stars: Jessica Alba *(Honey Daniels)*, **Lil' Romeo** *(Benny)*, Mekhi Phifer *(Chaz)* ← 8 MILE ← CARMEN: A HIP HOPERA ← GIRL 6, Joy Bryant *(Gina)* → GET RICH OR DIE TRYIN', David Moscow *(Michael Ellis)* ← GIRL, Zachary Isaiah Williams *(Raymond)*, **Lonette McKee** *(Mrs. Daniel)* ← HE GOT GAME ← JUNGLE FEVER ← SPARKLE, **Missy Elliott** *(herself)* ← POOTIE TANG / → FADE TO BLACK, Anthony Sherwood *(Mr. Daniels)* ← EDDIE AND THE CRUISERS II: EDDIE LIVES!, Kevin Duhaney *(Otis)* ← HENDRIX / → HOW SHE MOVE, **Ginuwine** *(himself)*, **Silkk Tha Shocker** *(himself)*, **Jay-Z** *(himself)*, **Sheek** *(himself)*, **Tweet** *(herself)*, **Jadakiss** *(himself)*, **Blaque:- Brandi Williams, Natina Reed, Shamari Fears** *(themselves)*, **3rd Storee** *(themselves)*, Lyriq Bent *(barber)* → the LIFE AND HARD TIMES OF GUY TERRIFICO → TAKE THE LEAD, **Shawn Desman** *(himself)* ← GET OVER IT! / → HOW SHE MOVE, Tracey Armstrong *(dancer)* → SAVE THE LAST DANCE 2 → HOW SHE MOVE

Storyline: Honey is good clean living kid from a relatively poor background who, in between shifts at the local record store teaches dance classes at the local community centre. At night she can be found at the downtown clubs, busting out her newly perfected moves. When she catches the eye of a music video producer, he offers her a chance to become a choreographer. What she has to sacrifice in return however is more than she first thinks. *MR*

Movie rating: *4

Visual: dvd

Off the record: A plethora of hip hop acts feature here (mostly cameos): **Lil' Romeo** (b. Romeo Miller, 19 Aug'89, New Orleans, Louisiana) is the son of rapper Master P and has hit No.3 with 'My Baby' in 2001. His uncle is **Silkk Tha Shocker** (b. Vyshonn King Miller), the younger brother of Master P and Murder-C whose had a No.1 album, 'Made Mann' (1999). Others on parade: Ex-The Lox, **Jadakiss** (b. Jason Phillips) – Top 5 album 'Kiss Tha Game Goodbye' (2001), **Tweet** (b. Charlene Keys) – Top 3 album, 'Southern Hummingbird' (2002), **Ginuwine** (b. Elgin Baylor Lumpkin) – Top 3 album 'The Life' (2001), **Sheek** Louch (aka Shawn Jacobs) – Top 10 album, 'Walk Witt Me' (2003) and girl group **Blaque** and newcomers **3rd Storee**. *MCS*

Various Artists (score: Mervyn Warren)

Nov 03. (cd) *Elektra; <(7559 62925-2)>* ☐ Dec03 ☐
– Hurt sumthin (MISSY ELLIOTT) / I'm good (BLAQUE IVORY) / Gimme the light (SEAN PAUL) / React (ERICK SERMON feat. REDMAN) / Leave her alone (NATE DOGG feat. MEMPHIS BLEEK, FREEWAY and YOUNG CHRIS) / Ooh wee (MARK RONSON feat. GHOSTFACE KILLAH, NATE DOGG, TRIFE & SAIGON) / It's a party (TAMIA) / Thugman (TWEET feat. MISSY ELLIOTT) / Now ride (FABOLOUS) / J-A-D-A (JADAKISS and SHEEK) / Think of you (AMERIE) / Closer (GOAPELE) / I believe (YOLANDA ADAMS).

S/track review: Certain soundtracks capture a very particular moment in pop culture. 'PULP FICTION', 'TRAINSPOTTING' and 'The GREAT ROCK'N'ROLL SWINDLE' all represent pivotal moments in the zeitgeist – the death of US indie cinema, the maturity of Britpop and the death of punk respectively – odd to think you could add 'HONEY' to that influential list but it captured the urban pop zeitgeist of 2003 perfectly. It might not have seemed like such a pivotal time as it was when crosspollination in urban music finally made it out of the underground and into the charts. It was also the time when SEAN PAUL's made dancehall a genuine mainstream concern with his nuclear hit 'Gimme The Light' which is included here. Similarly, MISSY ELLIOTT's transformation from futuristic R&B queen to old school party hip hop cheerleader was made complete on 'Hurt Sumthin', one of a wheen of retroistic funk tracks she unveiled that year. ERICK SERMON teaming up with hip hop's original nutter REDMAN on the inspired, Bollywood sampling 'React' which is also blindingly good. MARK RONSON's Studio 54 inspired bump 'Ooh Wee' gives hip hop a glittery disco wig and somehow gets away with it. MISSY ELLIOTT pops up yet again on TWEET's lolloping 'Thugman', a tremendous, stumbling, tumbling tribute to baaaaad men. Thundering tunes from FABOLOUS and JADAKISS continue the fun and it's only AMERIE's Mary J Blige by numbers on 'Think Of You' and GOAPELE's 'Closer' that fail to keep up the pace. 'HONEY' the movie was compared to Mariah Carey's 'GLITTER'. Be sure however, the two soundtracks couldn't be more different. *MR*

Album rating: *7

– spinoff hits, etc. –

BLAQUE IVORY: I'm Good

Sep 03. (12") *<67479-1>* ☐ ☐-

HONEYSUCKLE ROSE

1980 (US 120m) Warner Bros. Pictures (PG)

Film genre: romantic showbiz/music drama

Top guns: dir: Jerry Schatzberg / s-w: John Binder, William D. Wittliff, Carol Sobieski (story: Gosta Stevens, Gustaf Molander)

Stars: Willie NELSON *(Buck Bonham)*, Dyan Cannon *(Viv Bonham)*, Amy Irving *(Lily Ramsey)*, Slim Pickens *(Garland Ramsey)* ← RANCHO DELUXE ← PAT GARRETT & BILLY THE KID ← SKIDOO, Joey Floyd *(Jamie Bonham)*, Charles Levin *(Sid)* → THIS IS SPINAL TAP, Lane Smith *(Brag, Cotton's manager)* → PLACES IN THE HEART → WHY DO FOOLS FALL IN LOVE, Pepe Serna *(Rooster)*, Priscilla Pointer *(Rosella Ramsey)*, Diana Scarwid *(Jeanne)*, Mickey Raphael *(Kelly)* → SONGWRITER → TEATRO, **Emmylou HARRIS** *(herself)*, **Johnny Gimble** *(fiddler)* → HONKYTONK MAN → SONGWRITER → ALAMO BAY, **Hank Cochran** *(Hank)*, **Grady Martin** *(Grady)* → SONGWRITER, **Jody Payne** *(Jonas)* → SONGWRITER, **Paul English** *(Paul)* → SONGWRITER, **Bee Spears** *(Bo)* → SONGWRITER, **Bobbie Nelson** *(Bobbie)* → SONGWRITER, **Chris Ethridge** *(Easter)* ← CELEBRATION AT BIG SUR, Rex Ludwick *(Tex)* → BLAME IT ON THE NIGHT, Bobby Aster *(bartender)* ← PELVIS

Storyline: The quiet man of country is transformed into a babe magnet, "living out his own love songs" and agonising between the women in his life. In a simplified, C&W take on 1939 weepie, 'Intermezzo', the hard drinking, road loving Buck Bonham (no relation to John, presumably) must choose between domestic bliss and a shot a stardom, life with his wife and family or freewheeling love on the run with his new guitarist. *BG*

Visual: video + dvd
Movie rating: *5.5
Off the record: Chris Etheridge was a member of the International Submarine Band and the Flying Burrito Brothers.

—

WILLIE NELSON & FAMILY (score: Richard Baskin)

Aug 80. (d-lp) *Columbia; <S2 36752> C.B.S.; (CBS 22080)* 11 Nov80 ☐
– On the road again / Pick up the tempo / Heaven or Hell / Fiddlin' around (JOHNNY GIMBLE) / Blue eyes crying in the rain / Working man blues / Jumpin' cotton eyed Joe (JOHNNY GIMBLE) / Whiskey river / Bloody Mary morning / Loving her was easier (than anything I'll ever do again) (w/ DYAN CANNON) / I don't do windows (HANK COCHRAN) / Coming back to Texas (KENNETH THREADGILL) / It's not supposed to be that way / You show me yours (and I'll show you mine) (w/ AMY IRVING) / If you could touch her at all / Angel flying too close to the ground / I guess I've come to live here in your eyes / Angel eyes (w/ EMMYLOU HARRIS) / So you think you're a cowboy (EMMYLOU HARRIS) / Make the world go away (HANK COCHRAN & JEANNIE SEELY) / Two sides to every story (DYAN CANNON) / A song for you / Uncloudy day (w/ DYAN CANNON). *<US d-cd iss.Apr03 +=; CK 89259>* – Yesterday's wine / If you want me to love you I will (AMY IRVING) / Good hearted woman.

S/track review: Hundreds have sung his songs but only WILLIE NELSON could play Willie Nelson. Sporting the sweatiest, hardest touring bandana in country music, chewing over his words like a particularly flavoursome T-Bone, the man remains the icon's icon in a genre where they've long dried up. By end of the 70s he'd earned enough kudos to warrant a neo-autobiographical film in his own right, and was long enough in the songwriting tooth to reel off signature tunes on demand. According to the man himself (as recounted in Jonny Whiteside's reissue sleevenotes), the Oscar-nominated 'On The Road Again' was penned ad hoc in mid-air, written to order for Sydney Pollack and Jerry Schatzberg. A Top 20 (US) hit in 1980, it's the enduring legacy of a soundtrack which is basically an extended live set with NELSON indulging his fine love and playing music with his friends. And with the reissue bumped up to 26 tracks, there's no question that you get a lot of love and a lot of music for your dollar. All roses need pruned, though, and dispensing with some of the bit players in NELSON's family might have made it easier to plough through. Erstwhile Texas Playboy JOHNNY GIMBLE's 'Jumpin' Cotton Eyed Joe' (the original B-side of 'On The Road Again') swings with abandon but is difficult not to associate with its novelty pop doppelganger, and KENNETH THREADGILL yodelling through 'Coming Back To Texas' is probably one for the specialists. 'Pick Up The Tempo' is still one of NELSON's most emblematic titles: an ironically mellow plea for bottom and balls (musically speaking) from a dude who treats tempo as just another technical quirk to be toyed with. But still the crowd go nuts when he belts out the unlikely couplet, "I'm wild and I'm mean, I'm creating the scene, goin' crazy"; and only Willie can get away with rhyming "gravy" and "navy", while 'Blue Eyes Crying In The Rain' gets the most tantalising of Tex-Mex glosses and the fans whoop it up on redneck existentialist classic, 'Yesterday's Wine'. Guitarist JODY PAYNE stays faithful to the Outlaw ethic even as it'd already run its course, shredding the near 'Skynyrd-strength 'Whisky River' and bruising through Merle Haggard's 'Working Man Blues', while WILLIE himself showboats with dazzling, Latin-influenced flair on divorce-concept classic, 'It's Not Supposed To Be That Way'. There's no Waylon at all, but HANK COCHRAN almost makes up for his absence, if only in spirit. NELSON's duets with his female leads are pleasant diversions from the main event (and 'Uncloudy Day' makes for a barnstorming closer), but it's when the real angel, EMMYLOU HARRIS, flies too close to the bone that a high voltage charge rips through the crowd, her quartz-pure soprano ringing off NELSON's mahogany and invoking memories of those otherworldly duets with Gram Parsons; "Emmylou I love you", drools a besotted fan before HARRIS launches solo into NELSON's 'So You Think You're A Cowboy'. Ultimately, 'HONEYSUCKLE ROSE' is a reminder of a time when loving country music was easier than it'll ever be again. *BG*

Album rating: *7.5

– spinoff hits, etc. –

WILLIE NELSON: On The Road Again / JOHNNY GIMBLE: Jumpin' Cotton Eyed Joe
Aug 80. (7") *<11351> (CBS 1632)* 20 Sep80 ☐

HONKYTONK MAN

1982 (US 122m) The Malpaso Company / Warner Bros. Pictures (PG-13)

Film genre: Road movie – Country-music drama/comedy

Top guns: dir: Clint Eastwood → PIANO BLUES / s-w: Clancy Carlile (+ nov)

Stars: Clint Eastwood *(Red Stovall)* → PIANO BLUES, Kyle Eastwood *(Whit)*, John McIntire *(Grandpa)* ← FLAMING STAR ← SING BOY SING, Alexa Kenin *(Marlene)* → PRETTY IN PINK, Verna Bloom *(Emmy)* ← ANIMAL HOUSE ← the HIRED HAND / → the LAST TEMPTATION OF CHRIST, Matt Clark *(Virgil)* ← OUTLAW BLUES ← PAT GARRETT & BILLY THE KID / → SOUTH OF HEAVEN, WEST OF HELL, Barry Corbin *(Arnspringer)* ← the BEST LITTLE WHOREHOUSE IN TEXAS ← URBAN COWBOY / → PERMANENT RECORD, Jerry Hardin *(Snuffy)* → HEARTBREAKERS, **Johnny Gimble** *(Bob Wills)* ← HONEYSUCKLE ROSE / → SONGWRITER → ALAMO BAY, **Marty Robbins** *(Smoky)* ← THAT'S COUNTRY ← FROM NASHVILLE WITH MUSIC ← ROAD TO NASHVILLE, **Linda Hopkins** *(blues singer)* ← the EDUCATION OF SONNY CARSON ← ROCKIN' THE BLUES, **Ray Price** *(Bob Wills singer)*, **David Frizzell** *(Opry singer)*, Charles Cyphers *(Stubbs)* ← DEATH WISH II ← ELVIS: THE MOVIE ← TRUCK TURNER ← COOL BREEZE, **Shelly West** *(Opry singer)*, Roy Jenson *(Dub)* → BUSTIN' LOOSE → HONKYTONK MAN, Tim Thomerson *(highway patrolman)* ← CARNY ← RECORD CITY ← CAR WASH / → RHINESTONE → NEAR DARK → EDDIE PRESLEY → BAD CHANNELS, **Porter Wagoner** *(Dusty)* ← the NASHVILLE SOUND ← ROAD TO NASHVILLE ← NASHVILLE REBEL, John Russell *(Jack Wade)* ← UNTAMED YOUTH, Tracey Walter *(Pooch)* ← TIMERIDER: THE ADVENTURE OF LYLE SWANN / → REPO MAN → BATMAN → YOUNG GUNS II → DELUSION → MAN ON THE MOON → HOW HIGH → MASKED AND ANONYMOUS, Robert V. Barron *(undertaker)* ← COTTONPICKIN' CHICKENPICKERS ← LAS VEGAS HILLBILLYS / → BILL & TED'S EXCELLENT ADVENTURE, **Texas Playboys:- Merle Travis, Tommy Alsopp, Gordon Terry**

Storyline: Deep in the days of the depression, alcoholic country singer Red Stovall visits his sister and family and quickly bonds with nephew, Whit. With Red's health deteriorating through some heavy drinking bouts, he, Whit, grandpa and protégé Marlene, go on a last chance but problematic journey to the Grand Ole Opry, Nashville. *MCS*

Movie rating: *6

Visual: video + dvd

Off the record: Johnny Gimble (frontman for the Texas Playboys), **Ray Price** (C&W singer and songwriter of a plethora of hits including 'Please Release Me' and 'Crazy Arms'), **Linda Hopkins** (blues singer), **Marty Robbins** (Rockabilly C&W singer-songwriter responsible for 'El Paso', 'That's All Right', 'Singing The Blues', etc. – died December 1982), **Shelly West** (daughter of country legend Dottie West; had a few hits in the early 80s), other country singers **David Frizzell, Porter Wagoner** (latter producer/songwriter and singing partner of Dolly Parton in the late 60s/early 70s). Clint Eastwood's son, Kyle (also in film), has subsequently scored several jazz albums. *MCS*

—

Various Artists (md: Snuff Garrett)

Dec 82. (lp) *Warners; <1-23739>* ☐ [–]
– San Antonio rose (RAY PRICE with Johnny Gimble & The Texas

Swing Band) / Turn the pencil over (PORTER WAGONER) / Please surrender (FRIZZELL & WEST) / When I sing about you (CLINT EASTWOOD) / Ricochet rag (JOHNNY GIMBLE & THE TEXAS SWING BAND) / Honkytonk man (MARTY ROBBINS) / One fiddle, two fiddle (RAY PRICE with Johnny Gimble & The Texas Swing Band) / In the jailhouse now (MARTY ROBBINS, JOHN ANDERSON, DAVID FRIZZELL, CLINT EASTWOOD) / No sweeter cheater than you (CLINT EASTWOOD) / These cotton patch blues (JOHN ANDERSON) / Texas moonbeam waltz (JOHNNY GIMBLE & THE TEXAS SWING BAND) / When the blues come around this evening (LINDA HOPKINS).

S/track review: Even if you've never come across 'Clint Eastwood Sings Cowboy Favourites' (from his 1960s TV days) you might suspect that singing is not Eastwood's forte, but there's no question the man knows his music – and like the movie, this is a soundtrack of considerable eccentric charm. Overseen by veteran producer Snuff Garrett, the album leans on some exemplary Western Swing by JOHNNY GIMBLE AND THE TEXAS SWING BAND, sometimes with RAY PRICE on vocals. There are several songs penned by Dewayne Blackwell in rather more maudlin vein than his memorable 'I'm Gonna Hire A Wino To Decorate Our Home' (Eastwood the director is unafraid of lachrymose anthems); Blackwell's nuts-and-bolts title song was to be one of Marty Robbins' last recordings, and a posthumous hit single. JOHN ANDERSON and blues singer LINDA HOPKINS deliver a couple of excellent pick-me-ups, and if Eastwood's two workaday vocal outings find the familiar leathery rasp modulated by an endearing waver, it would take a hard heart to resist the overall mix of craft and warmth. The director went on to demonstrate his musical gifts beyond question with a series of highly accomplished orchestral scores in his later career. *ND*

Album rating: *6.5

HOOTENANNY HOOT

1963 (US 91m b&w) Metro-Goldwyn-Mayer

Film genre: Country/Folk Musical comedy

Top guns: dir: Gene Nelson → KISSIN' COUSINS → YOUR CHEATIN' HEART → HARUM SCARUM → the COOL ONES / s-w: James B. Gordon ← DON'T KNOCK THE TWIST ← TWIST AROUND THE CLOCK ← ROCK AROUND THE CLOCK / → GET YOURSELF A COLLEGE GIRL → WHEN THE BOYS MEET THE GIRLS → the FASTEST GUITAR ALIVE → a TIME TO SING

Stars: Peter Breck *(Ted Grover)* ← the BEATNIKS / → TERMINAL CITY RICOCHET → HIGHWAY 61, Ruta Lee *(A.G. Bannister)* → ELVIS AND THE BEAUTY QUEEN, Joby Baker *(Steve Laughlin)* → LOOKING FOR LOVE → GIRL HAPPY → WHEN THE BOYS MEET THE GIRLS, Pam Austin *(Billy-Jo Henley)* ← BLUE HAWAII / → KISSIN' COUSINS, Bobo Lewis *(Claudia Hoffer)* → CAN'T STOP THE MUSIC, **Sheb Wooley** *(performer)*, **the Brothers Four** *(performers)*, **Johnny CASH** *(performer)*, **the Gateway Trio** *(performers)*, **Judy Henske** *(performer)*, **George Hamilton IV** *(performer)* / **Joe & Eddie** *(performers)*, **Cathie Martin** *(performer)*, **Chris Crosby** *(performer)*

Storyline: And lo! After the twist craze came the folk music craze, and producer Ted Grover has about ten minutes to discover a completely new music concept to fill the gap. He cobbles together a collection of up and coming stars to hootenanny away, and becomes the unofficial agony aunt of the group as he sorts out the love lives of the various performers in between organizing the show. *JZ*

Movie rating: *5

Visual: none

Off the record: (see below)

—

Various: Soundtrack Recordings and Other Hootenanny Favorites

Aug 63. (lp) *M.G.M.; <E/SE 4172>* □ [-]
– Hootenanny hoot (SHEB WOOLEY) / Country boy (MARK DINNING) / Puttin' on the style (the GATEWAY TRIO) / Sweet, sweet love (CHRIS CROSBY) / Frozen logger (CATHIE TAYLOR) / There's a meetin' here tonight (JOE AND EDDIE) / Foolish questions (the GATEWAY TRIO) / Black is the color of my true love's hair (MARK DINNING) / Buildin' a railroad (SHEB WOOLEY) / Lost highway (MARK DINNING) / Papa's ole fiddle (SHEB WOOLEY) / That's my pa (SHEB WOOLEY).

S/track review: Hootenanny apparently means an impromptu folk party/concert, and this I suppose applies to some of the tracks here, the others are just Hootenanny favourites as it says on the package. As Joan Baez once put it: "a hootenanny is to folk singing what a jam session is to jazz". Moving quickly along, and with the accent on variety (much like its TV show before it), this 'HOOTENANNY' takes the slant of country rather than traditional folk, although there are exceptions. The fusion is certainly there for all to hear. Forgetting the goddamn awful MARK DINNING (who'd actually had a US No.1 in 1960 with 'Teen Angel') and his crooning renditions of 'Country Boy', 'Black Is The Color Of My True Love's Hair' & 'Lost Highway', this 1963 LP might just've got over its point – whatever that was. Ditto for nephew of Bing Crosby, CHRIS CROSBY, who tells us of his 'Sweet, Sweet Love'. With the folk music revival set to emerge alongside every hand-painted lyric of the "Master Of Anti-War" himself, Bob Dylan, this 'HOOTENANNY' was downright embarrassing. Forget the troops abroad, just stay home have a folk'n'country party and dance till you drop! – or have to drop. This is the only message one gets here. Down from the soapbox mountain so to speak, if there is a good point to this "shindig" (there's another appropriate word!) it's the "Purple People Eater" himself, SHEB WOOLEY; the man just oozes fun. Take the opening title track (complete with Benny Hill-meets-Beverly Hillbillies-styled intersections!), along with three other novelty records on side 2 (including the glorious US No.51 hit, 'That's My Pa') and you'll probably appreciate why they made this record/film in the first place. Of the remainder, one can't swear too much with Bible-punchers JOE & EDDIE in the room (well, at least on record), and as for the very unfunny CATHIE TAYLOR – only 18 at the time – comedy was probably not her strong point. *MCS*

Album rating: *2.5 (all for the WOOLEY track!)

□ Linda HOPKINS segment
(⇒ ROCKIN' THE BLUES)

the HORROR OF PARTY BEACH

1964 (US 78m b&w) Twentieth Century-Fox Corporation

Film genre: teen sci-fi horror rock-Musical

Top guns: dir: Del Tenney / s-w: Richard Hilliard (added dialogue: Lou Binder + Ronald Gianettino)

Stars: John Scott *(Hank Green)*, Alice Lynn *(Elaine)*, Allan Laurel *(Dr. Gavin)*, Eulabelle Moore *(Eulabelle)*, Marilyn Clarke *(Tina)*, Augustin Mayer *(Mike)*, Damon Kebroyd *(Lt. Wells)*, **the Del-Aires:- Ronnie Linares, Gary Robert Jones, Wilfred Holcombe, Edward Earle** *(performers)*

Storyline: A glop of sludge on the sea bed suddenly comes to life after being hit by a barrel of radioactive waste. Unsuspecting beach party-goers on the California coast are soon gobbled up by the mess which has now turned into several blood-sucking monsters. Despite coming from the ocean, it appears the monsters are allergic to salt (?), but can Dr Gavin, the world's dopiest scientist, work this out before all the beach teenies are devoured? Take your time, Doc. *JZ*

Movie rating: *2.5

Visual: video + dvd (no audio OST)

Off the record: The **Del-Aires** (ex-Treble Tones & Ronnie And The Del-Aires; from Patterson, New Jersey) contributed half a dozen rock tracks to the movie:- 'Elaine', 'Just Wigglin' And Wobblin'' (an A&B sided 45 in 1963), 'Drag', 'Joy Ride', 'The Zombie Stomp' & 'You Are Not A Summer Love', the latter three penned by Wilfred Holcombe and Edward Earl. The latter two had replaced Bobby Osborne on sax and drummer John Becker prior to the movie. *MCS*

HOT ROD GANG

1958 (US 71m b&w) American International Pictures

Film genre: Rock'n'roll Musical drama

Top guns: dir: Lew Landers / s-w: Lou Rusoff ← SHAKE, RATTLE & ROCK! / → BEACH PARTY

Stars: John Ashley *(John Abernathy III)* → BEACH PARTY → MUSCLE BEACH PARTY → BIKINI BEACH → BEACH BLANKET BINGO → HOW TO STUFF A WILD BIKINI, Jody Fair *(Lois Cavendish)* ← HIGH SCHOOL CONFIDENTIAL!, Steve Drexel *(Mark)* ← the BIG BEAT, Scott Peters *(Jack)*, Dub Taylor *(Al Berrywhiff)* → MAN AND BOY → FALLING FROM GRACE, Helen Spring *(Abigail Abernathy)*, Dorothy Neumann *(Anastasia Abernathy)* ← CARNIVAL ROCK / → LOOKING FOR LOVE → GET YOURSELF A COLLEGE GIRL, Doodles Weaver *(Wesley Cavendish)* → ROAD TO NASHVILLE, Russ Bender *(motorcycle cop)* → WILD ON THE BEACH, **Gene Vincent & His Blue Caps** *(performers)* ← the GIRL CAN'T HELP IT / → IT'S TRAD, DAD! → LIVE IT UP → BLUE SUEDE SHOES → NO DIRECTION HOME, **Eddie Cochran** *(cameo)* ← UNTAMED YOUTH ← the GIRL CAN'T HELP IT / → GO, JOHNNY, GO! → BLUE SUEDE SHOES → the COMPLEAT BEATLES → the BEATLES ANTHOLOGY

Storyline: Teenager Jack Abernathy III has a problem – he's going to inherit his aunts' fortune but only if he behaves like a gentleman – and he's already in trouble with the law. The only way he can afford to enter his hot rod in drag races (apart from stealing hub caps) is to earn money singing in Gene Vincent's rock'n'roll band. Can he keep it all a secret from aunts Anastasia and Abigail or will his fortune end up cooked? Inspiration and cult icon, James Dean, had a lot to answer for. *JZ*

Movie rating: *4.5

Visual: video + dvd (no audio LP)

Off the record: Gene Vincent was already a major hitmaker; 'Be-Bop-A-Lula' has since become one of the all-time rock'n'roll greats. Main actor, John Ashley, also sang two songs in the film, 'Hit And Run Lover' & 'Annie Laurie'. *MCS*

– spinoff releases, etc. –

GENE VINCENT & HIS BLUE CAPS

Sep 58. (7"ep) *Capitol; <(EAP 1-985)>* ☐ ☐
– Hot rod gang / Dance in the street / Baby blue / Lovely Loretta / Dance to the bop.

the HOTTEST STATE

2007 (US 117m) Baracuda Films / ThinkFilm (PG-13)

Film genre: romantic drama

Top guns: s-w + dir: Ethan Hawke (+ au)

Stars: Mark Webber *(William Harding)* ← CHELSEA WALLS ← STORYTELLING ← WHITEBOYS, Catalina Sandino Moreno *(Sarah Garcia)*, Ethan Hawke *(Vince)*, Laura Linney *(Jesse)* ← the MOTHMAN PROPHECIES, Michelle Williams *(Samantha)*, Sonia Braga *(Mrs. Garcia)*, **Jesse Harris** *(Dave Afton)*, Frank Whaley *(Harris)* ← CHELSEA WALLS ← SHAKE, RATTLE AND ROLL: AN AMERICAN LOVE STORY ← WENT TO CONEY ISLAND ON A MISSION FROM GOD . . . BE BACK BY FIVE ← PULP FICTION ← the DOORS

Storyline: Actor William moves from Texas to New York in search of the big time. Instead, he meets songwriter Sarah in a bar and they begin an affair. However, it soon becomes apparent that wishy-washy William is not the man of Sarah's dreams, and when she gives him the heave-ho he resorts to writing love letters on his windows for her to read. Looks like Sarah did the right thing. *JZ*

Movie rating: *6.5

Visual: dvd

Off the record: New York-born singer-songwriter **JESSE HARRIS** was the guitarist with Once Blue (alongside Rebecca Martin), a one-off album unit who released only one eponymous set in 1995. The rootsier Fernandos were subsequently formed, releasing a handful of self-financed CDs before he augmented Norah Jones on her Grammy-winning debut, 'Come Away With Me'. Since this partnership, HARRIS has delivered four solo albums, 'Secret Sun' (2003), 'While The Music Lasts' (2004), 'Mineral' (2006) and 'Feel' (2007). *MCS*

Various Artists (songwriter: JESSE HARRIS)

Aug 07. (cd) *Hickory; <90057>* ☐ ⊟
– Ya no te veria mas (Never see you) (ROCHA) / Always seem to get things wrong (WILLIE NELSON) / Somewhere down the road (FEIST) / Big old house (BRIGHT EYES) / The speed of sound (EMMYLOU HARRIS) / It will stay with us (JESSE HARRIS) / If you ever slip (the BLACK KEYS) / Crooked lines (M. WARD) / World of trouble (NORAH JONES) / Never see you (BRAD MEHLDAU) / It's alright to fail (CAT POWER) / One day the dam will break (JESSE HARRIS) / You, the queen (TONY SCHERR) / Morning in a strange city / No more (ROCHA) / Dear Dorothy (JESSE HARRIS) / Never see you (ROCHA) / There are no second chances.

S/track review: Prolific songwriter, JESSE HARRIS, has his stamp on all of the 18 exclusive numbers on 'The HOTTEST STATE' OST, a feat in itself, although getting another 11 top-notch stars to perform his songs in the studio was downright incredible. Old hats at the country store, WILLIE NELSON and EMMYLOU HARRIS, take their respective places via the melancholic, 'Always Seem To Get Things Wrong' and 'The Speed Of Sound'. Relative newbies on the block (in respect to the aforementioned country icons, at least), BRIGHT EYES, CAT POWER and NORAH JONES are also present and correct. Many will know young Conor Oberst's BRIGHT EYES since their inception in the mid-90s (when he was just 14!), here he takes on the uplifting 'Big Old House'. The equally-fashioned, one person/one group CAT POWER (alias Chan Marshall) brings down the tempo somewhat with 'It's Alright To Fail', while Jesse's boss (of sorts) NORAH JONES does her usual bluesy best courtesy of 'World Of Trouble'; the latter also tinkles the ivories and provides backing vox for M. WARD on 'Crooked Lines'. The little-known ROCHA (who is the singing voice of Sarah in the movie) turns in three beautiful cues, 'Ya No Te Veria Mas (Never See You)', 'No More' and 'Never See You' (again!), but if you've been searching for the next Eva Cassidy, listen to FEIST's 'Somewhere Down The Road'. JESSE HARRIS himself performs four songs, three rootsy vocal tracks 'It Will Stay With Us', 'One Day The Dam Will Break' and 'Dear Dorothy', plus two acoustic instrumentals 'Morning In A Strange City' and 'There Are No Second Chances'. On session for Jesse and Co on either guitar or bass, TONY SCHERR comes into the spotlight on 'You, The Queen', although this and the piano piece by BRAD MEHLDAU seem a little too subdued. The rockiest track by far stems from the White Stripes-meets-Cream-like BLACK KEYS, who carry it off via 'If You Ever Slip'. All'n'all, HARRIS, Hawke and Co should be proud of this unique collection. *MCS*

Album rating: *7

HOUND-DOG MAN

1959 (US 87m) 20th Century Fox (U)

Film genre: romantic Rock'n'roll Musical comedy/drama

Top guns: dir: Don Siegel → FLAMING STAR / s-w: Winston Miller ← APRIL LOVE (au: Fred Gipson)

Stars: FABIAN *(Clint)*, Stuart Whitman *(Blackie Scantling)* → MEAN JOHNNY BARROWS → the MONSTER CLUB, Carol Lynley *(Dony Wallace)* → BUNNY LAKE IS MISSING → NORWOOD, Arthur O'Connell *(Aaron McKinley)* ← APRIL LOVE / → FOLLOW THAT DREAM → KISSIN' COUSINS → YOUR CHEATIN' HEART, **Dodie Stevens** *(Nita Stringer)*, Betty Field *(Cora McKinney)*, Royal Dano *(Fiddling Tom Walker)*, Edgar Buchanan *(Doc Cole)*, Claude Akins *(Hog Peyson)* → FALLING FROM GRACE, Jane Darwell *(Grandma Wilson)*, Dennis Holmes *(Spud Kinney)*

Storyline: Set on a rural farm – Oklahoma!-style – in the early 20th Century, Clint and his buddy Blackie take a farmboy hunting in the backwoods. They find that the prey comes in all shapes and sizes, especially a couple of hillbilly females, although Clint seems more interested in singing several pop songs. *MCS*

Movie rating: *5

Visual: none (no audio OST; score: Cyril Mockridge)

Off the record: Dodie Stevens (b. Geraldine Ann Pasquale, 17 Feb'46, Chicago) was an even younger teen sensation having aleady had a Top 3 smash, 'Pink Shoe Laces', after just turning thirteen; by 1961 Dodie was all but forgotten. *MCS*

– spinoff hits, etc. –

FABIAN: Hound Dog Man / This Friendly World

Nov 59. (7"/78) *Chancellor; <1044> / H.M.V.; (POP 695)* 9 — 12 Feb60 46

the HOURS AND TIMES

1992 (US 60m b&w) Antarctic Pictures / Good Machine (R)

Film genre: showbiz drama

Top guns: s-w + dir: Christopher Munch

Stars: David Angus *(Brian Epstein)*, Ian Hart *(John Lennon)* → BACKBEAT → MOJO, Stephanie Pack *(Marianne)*, Robin McDonald *(Quinones)*, Sergio Moreno *(Miguel)*, Unity Grimwood *(mother)*

Storyline: "What might have happened between John Lennon and Brian Epstein on a weekend the two spent in Barcelona in 1963", just about describes the hour-long movie about the relationship on holiday between Beatles icon, John Lennon, and his/their manager, Brian Epstein. *MCS*

Movie rating: *7

Visual: video + dvd

Off the record: Only two songs are featured in the film, 'I'm In Love Again' by LITTLE RICHARD and 'The Goldberg Variations' by Johann Sebastian Bach. Brian Epstein was a renowned loner and homosexual who died of a drug overdose at 32 years of age, 27th August, 1967. *MCS*

HOUSE PARTY

1990 (US 100m) New Line Cinema (R)

Film genre: teen/buddy film/comedy

Top guns: s-w + dir: Reginald Hudlin

Stars: Christopher Reid *(Kid/Christopher)* → HOUSE PARTY II → HOUSE PARTY 3 → the TEMPTATIONS, **Christopher Martin** *(Play/Peter Martin)* → HOUSE PARTY II → HOUSE PARTY 3, Robin Harris *(Pop)*, Martin Lawrence *(Bilal)* → HOUSE PARTY II → OPEN SEASON, Tisha Campbell *(Sydney)* ← SCHOOL DAZE ← LITTLE SHOP OF HORRORS / → HOUSE PARTY II → HOUSE PARTY 3, A.J. Johnson *(Sharane)* ← SCHOOL DAZE, **Paul Anthony** *(Stab)* ← KRUSH GROOVE / → HOUSE PARTY II → WHO'S THE MAN? → LONGSHOT, **B-Fine** *(Zilla)* ← KRUSH GROOVE / → HOUSE PARTY II → WHO'S THE MAN? → LONGSHOT, **Bow-Legged Lou** *(Pee Wee)* → HOUSE PARTY 2 → WHO'S THE MAN? → LONGSHOT, Clifton Powell *(Sharane's brother)* → WHY DO FOOLS FALL IN LOVE → BONES → RAY, Ronn Riser *(guy)*, **George Clinton** *(himself)* → GRAFFITI BRIDGE → NINA HAGEN = PUNK + GLORY, Norma Donaldson *(Mildred)* ← STAYING ALIVE ← WILLIE DYNAMITE ← ACROSS 110th STREET / → the FIVE HEARTBEATS, J. Jay Saunders *(Sidney's dad)* ← THIEF ← CORNBREAD, EARL AND ME ← SLAUGHTER'S BIG RIP-OFF, **Eugene Allen** *(Groove)* → HOUSE PARTY II → WHAT'S LOVE GOT TO DO WITH IT, **Daryl Mitchell** *(Chill)* → HOUSE PARTY II → FLY BY NIGHT → the COUNTRY BEARS, **Anthony Johnson** *(E.Z.E.)* → HOUSE PARTY 3, Barry Diamond *(cop #1 / Wynarski)* ← GET CRAZY → the FIVE HEARTBEATS → HOUSE PARTY II, Joe Torry *(student in cafe)* → HOUSE PARTY 3, Reginald Hudlin *(burglar #1)* → JOE'S APARTMENT

Storyline: Kid 'n Play decide to throw a huge party when Play's parents crazily leave their house unguarded. Kid's high school horseplay gets him in trouble and his dad grounds him on the day of the party. However Kid is determined to show off his rapping skills to the chicks and manages to sneak away, but just when he thinks he's free for the night, who should turn up at the party but his angry dad, his high school enemies and the cops – can Kid outsmart them all? *JZ*

Movie rating: *6

Visual: video + dvd

Off the record: KID 'N PLAY (see below)

Various Artists (score: Marcus Miller & Lenny White)

Mar 90. (cd/c/lp) *Motown; <3746362962> (ZD/ZK/ZL 72699)* — Apr90
– Why you get funky on me (TODAY) / What a feeling (ARTS & CRAFTS) / Jive time sucker (FORCE M.D.'s) / House party (FULL FORCE FAMILY feat. LISA LISA & CULT JAM, U.T.F.O., CHERYL "PEPSII" RILEY, DOCTOR ICE, EX-GIRLFRIEND and E-CROF) / This is love (KENNY VAUGHAN and the ART OF LOVE) / I can't do nothing for you, man! (FLAVOR FLAV) / Fun house (KID 'N PLAY) / To da break of dawn (L.L. COOL J. and MARLEY MARL) / Kid vs. Play (the battle) (KID 'N PLAY) / I ain't going out like that (ZAN) / Surely (ARTS & CRAFTS). *<cd re-iss. Jul01 on 'Universal'; AA4400 14593-2>*

S/track review: The late 80s and early 90s were an odd time for hip hop. The genre, heading into its early teens, was going through the first stages of puberty and all awkward, unable to fully comprehend its own powers. Technology was racing and it was a time where to contemporary ears, the music sounds most dated. The mood was jocular, saucy and fun but the songs were often suffocated under the burgeoning technology. The original 'HOUSE PARTY' movie was written with DJ Jazzy Jeff & Fresh Prince in mind and it shows, you could imagine Will Smith's tongue-in-cheek banter fitting in right at home in this caper. KID 'N PLAY were the C-list substitutes who took up the baton and supply a couple of their own nuggets of gentle rap tomfoolery amidst a disc of gawky, pre-house music electronic funk, synthetic soul balladeering and a random Public Enemy spin-off, a solo track by FLAVOR FLAV of all things! This kind of sums up the aspirations of this collection. The strongest cut here is the James Brown pilfering 'Fun House', sadly not a hip house re-interpretation of the Stooges' classic but a hunk of goofy, clumsy pop. A by-the-numbers LL COOL J cue is the only track that stands up to any scrutiny. 'HOUSE PARTY' is very much a product of his time. *MR*

Album rating: *4

– spinoff releases, etc. –

KID 'N PLAY: Funhouse

Mar 90. (12"/cd-s) [ ] [-]

HOUSE PARTY 2

1991 sequel (US 94m) New Line Cinema (R)

Film genre: teen movie/comedy

Top guns: dir: Doug McHenry, George Jackson / s-w: Rusty Cundieff → FEAR OF A BLACK HAT, Daryl G. Nickens

Stars: Christopher Reid *(Kid)* ← HOUSE PARTY / → HOUSE PARTY 3 → the TEMPTATIONS, **Christopher Martin** *(Play)* ← HOUSE PARTY / → HOUSE PARTY 3, Martin Lawrence *(Bilal)* ← HOUSE PARTY / → OPEN SEASON, Tisha Campbell *(Sydney)* ← HOUSE PARTY ← SCHOOL DAZE ← LITTLE SHOP OF HORRORS / → HOUSE PARTY 3, **Bow-Legged Lou** *(Pee-Wee)* ← HOUSE PARTY / → WHO'S THE MAN? → LONGSHOT, **Paul Anthony** *(Stab)* ← HOUSE PARTY ← KRUSH GROOVE / → WHO'S THE MAN? → LONGSHOT, **B-Fine/Brian George** *(Zilla)* ← HOUSE PARTY ← KRUSH GROOVE / → WHO'S THE MAN? → LONGSHOT, **Kamron** *(Jamal)*, Iman *(Sheila Landreaux)*, **Queen Latifah** *(Zora)* ← JUNGLE FEVER / → JUICE → WHO'S THE MAN? → the COUNTRY BEARS → BROWN SUGAR → HAIRSPRAY re-make, Helen Martin *(Mrs. Deevers)* ← REPO MAN ← a HERO AIN'T NOTHIN' BUT A SANDWICH ← DEATH WISH ← COTTON COMES TO HARLEM, **Eugene Allen** *(Groove)* ← HOUSE PARTY / → WHAT'S LOVE GOT TO DO WITH IT, **Daryl Mitchell** *(Chill)* ← HOUSE PARTY / → FLY BY NIGHT → the COUNTRY BEARS, **Ralph E. Tresvant** *(performer)* ← KRUSH GROOVE / → PAPER SOLDIERS → BROWN SUGAR, **Tony! Toni! Tone!:- Raphael Saadiq, Dwayne Wiggins & Tim Riley** *(performers)* → PANTHER, Barry Diamond *(cop #2)* ← the FIVE HEARTBEATS ← HOUSE PARTY ← GET CRAZY, **Ralph Tresvant** *(himself)* → RAY

Storyline: Kid graduates from high school and is all set for the dizzy heights of Harris Uni. His buddy Play throws a spanner in the works when he loses Kid's scholarship money to a con artist posing as a music producer. Undeterred, Kid tries to earn a crust by helping out in the college cafe, but the dastardly Dean will have none of it – pay up or get out! The only solution, of course, is to throw another party – $10 a time (but women wearing only their underwear get in free). *JZ*

Movie rating: *4.5

Visual: video

Off the record: The usual gatecrashers appear on this sequel + 'Feels Good' R&B/funk hitmakers from Oakland, California: **Tony! Toni! Tone!**

Various Artists (score: Vassal Benford)

Oct 91. (cd/c) *M.C.A.; <10397>* [55] [-]

– (announcement of Pajama Jammi Jam) / House party (I don't know what you come to do) (TONY! TONI! TONE!) / (The Christopher Robinson scholarship fund) / Ready or not (House Party II New Jack theme) (WRECKS N-EFFECT) / (Kid 'N Play wreck shop!) / Ain't gonna hurt nobody (House Party II theme) (KID 'N PLAY) / I like your style (House Party II swing theme) (BUBBA) / (Kid & Sydney break up) / Candlelight & you (House Party II love theme) (feat. KEITH WASHINGTON and introducing CHANTE' MOORE) / I lust 4 U (House Party II passion theme) (LONDON JONES) / (Bilal gets off) / Let me know something?! (House Party II mental theme) (BELL BIV DeVOE) / Yo, baby, yo! (House Party II Harris U theme) (RALPH TRESVANT) / (The F.F.F. rap) / What's on your mind (House Party II rap theme) (ERIC B & RAKIM) / Big ol' jazz (House Party II memorial) (M.C. TROUBLE) / (You gotta pay what you owe) / It's so hard to say goodbye to yesterday (House Party II film theme) (the FLEX) / (Confidence to Marcus Garvey) / It's so hard to say goodbye to yesterday (acappela reprise) (the FLEX) / (Kid's goodbye "thanks to Pops").

S/track review: Some people just can't seem to get enough of a mediocre thing and lo, it was decreed that we deserved a sequel to KID 'N PLAY's residential comedy of errors 'HOUSE PARTY'. This album was compiled at the time when the latest hot idea was new jack swing, a brief flash in the pan hybrid of swing rhythms and beats with R&B pop sensibilities. WRECKS N-EFFECT show how its done on 'Ready Or Not', one of the few tunes that would justify a second listen here. The multi-layered harmonies add some smoothness to an addictive sub-Prince backing. The only other presentable tracks here are from more soul funk horn-fest from BELL BIV DeVOE called 'Let Me Know Something' and a bumping pop rap blend entitled 'Big Ol' Jazz' from squeaky teen rhymer MC TROUBLE. Other than that, there's a hugely disappointing shuffle flop from the normally excellent ERIC B & RAKIM. The rest may come in handy for clearing your front room should your own house party guests overstay their welcome. *MR*

Album rating: *3.5

– spinoff hits, etc. –

TONY! TONI! TONE!: House Party (I Don't Know What You Come To Do)

Aug 91. (c-s/cd-s) *<54170>* [ ] [-]

KID 'N PLAY: Ain't Gonna Hurt Nobody (mixes)

Oct 91. (c-s/cd-s) *Select; <64847>* [51] [-]

HOUSE PARTY 3

1994 sequel-2 (US 99m) New Line Cinema (R)

Film genre: teen movie/comedy

Top guns: dir: Eric Meza / s-w: Takashi Bufford (+ story w/ David Toney)

Stars: Christopher Reid *(Kid)* ← HOUSE PARTY 2 ← HOUSE PARTY / → the TEMPTATIONS, **Christopher Martin** *(Play)* ← HOUSE PARTY 2 ← HOUSE PARTY, Angela Means *(Veda)*, Khandi Alexander *(Janelle)* ← WHAT'S LOVE GOT TO DO WITH IT ← CB4: THE MOVIE, Bernie Mac *(Uncle Vester)* ← WHO'S THE MAN?, David Edwards *(Stinky)*, Michael Colyar *(Showboat)* ← WHAT'S LOVE GOT TO DO WITH IT, **Ketty Lester** *(Aunt Lucy)* ← BLACULA ← UP TIGHT!, **Marques Houston** *(himself)* → YOU GOT SERVED, **Jerome Jones** *(himself)* → YOU GOT SERVED → FEEL THE NOISE, Tisha Campbell *(Sydney)* ← HOUSE PARTY 2 ← HOUSE PARTY ← SCHOOL DAZE ← LITTLE SHOP OF HORRORS, **Sex As A Weapon:- Tionne 'T-Boz' Watkins** *(performer)*, **Lisa 'Left Eye' Lopes** *(performer)*, **Rozonda 'Chilli' Thomas** *(performer)* / Freez Luv *(ex con caterer)* → MURDER WAS THE CASE → JACKIE'S BACK! → COYOTE UGLY, Joe Torry *(D-Trick)*, Anthony Johnson *(butcher)*, **Chuckii Booker** *(musician)*, Chris Tucker *(Johnny Booze)* → JACKIE BROWN, Eddie Griffin *(guest at Kid's bachelor party)* ← the FIVE HEARTBEATS, **Bobby Mardis** *(Master Cataract(* ←the FIVE HEARTBEATS / → FEAR OF A BLACK HAT, Jimmy Woodard *(M.C. Cane)* ← the FIVE HEARTBEATS, **R.A.S. Posse:- Bigga Don & Soul Gee**

Storyline: While Play tries to break into the music business, the only sound Kid can hear is wedding bells, as he has finally decided to tie the knot with sweetheart Veda. Play sets up the biggest ever bachelor party for his pal, but the red-hot rappers haven't reckoned on some unexpected gatecrashers – Kid's ex girlfriend Sydney and his crazy young cousins are on the way to spoil the wedding – and maybe even the party! *JZ*

Movie rating: *3

Visual: video

Off the record: Breakthrough R&B/hip hop artists include **Immature** (all male trio from L.A.), **TLC as Sex As A Weapon and R.A.S. Posse** – most appearing on the soundtrack album. *MCS*

Various Artists (score: David Allen Jones)

Mar 94. (cd/c/lp) *Select Street; <2-/4-/1-21647> M.C.A.; (MCL D/C 19246)* [ ] Apr94 [ ]

– Bounce (KID 'N PLAY) / Wakes you up – house party

(IMMATURE) / Two fingers (KID 'N PLAY) / How about some hardcore (M.O.P.) / Drop down (SYLK SMOOV) / Rock the house (R.A.S. POSSE) / The illest (RED HOT LOVER TONE) / Butt booty naked (AMG) / Make noize (KID 'N PLAY) / How'm I doin' (KID 'N PLAY) / Void (KID 'N PLAY) / We got it goin' on (TO DA CORE) / Here and now (KID 'N PLAY) / I just love the man (Veda's theme) (EVERYDAY EMOTIONS) / The cure (NERISSA). *<cd re-iss. Sep99; same>*

S/track review: For their third and final instalment KID 'N PLAY are getting all grown up. The stupid hairdos are concealed under skip caps and there's an injection of bullish heavy hip hop tracks in contrast to the hip house pop which dominated this movie's two predecessors. That's not to say things are getting any better. God no, the ratio of turkey to stuffing here is still 2 to 1 in favour of the undercooked padding. Our aforementioned heroes dominate the tracklisting, with half a dozen tunes, including some woeful, sub-LL Cool J, hands in the air, cliché-ridden chanting. Only the mid-tempo trudge of 'Here And Now' is worthy of singling out for having any redeeming features. There's barely any groove, no swing, no funk, no weight, no power, barely any lyrical twists and no more than a scraping of passable humour. It's no shock to note that America was in the thrall of gangsta rap and grunge at the time, and there is little to recommend KID 'N PLAY's damp lyrical ballistics. The party was well and truly over. Time to go to bed methinks. *MR*

Album rating: *2.5

☐ David HOUSTON segment (⇒ CARNIVAL ROCK)

Whitney HOUSTON

Born: 9 Aug'63, East Orange, New Jersey, USA. As the daughter of singer Cissy Houston and the cousin of Dionne Warwick, WHITNEY HOUSTON actually bucked the trend of America's underachieving pop progeny. While critics mourned the squandering of her formidable vocal talent on forgettable material, the record buying public saw things differently. Like all soul singers worth their salt, Whitney cut her teeth in a Baptist church before scoring sitcom acting roles. In one of popular music's more unlikely and in fact barely believable recording debuts, her first appearance on vinyl was as a vocalist in Bill Laswell's avant-garde ensemble, Material. Any affinity with pop's wayward fringe was soon ironed out amid the corporate confines of 'Arista', and HOUSTON went on to sell singles and albums by the skipload. In the early 90s, just as her commercial clout was beginning to ebb slightly, she resumed her acting career and rejuvenated her recording career into the bargain. In Mick Jackson's high grossing romantic thriller, 'The BODYGUARD' (1992), HOUSTON pretty much played herself, starring alongside Kevin Costner and breaking all manner of records with her quavering cover of DOLLY PARTON's 'I Will Always Love You'. The multi-million selling, Grammy-winning soundtrack also featured another five Whitney songs, two of which also reached the US Top 5. 1995's girly bonding effort, 'Waiting To Exhale' (1995) was another respectable addition to her CV, and while the R&B-weighted soundtrack only sold half as many records as 'The BODYGUARD', that was still a serious amount of product. Of her three songs, the film's theme, 'Exhale (Shoop Shoop)' again topped the American singles charts. In 1996, the tenacious superstar appeared in her third starring role, alongside Denzel Washington in the religious themed romantic comedy, 'The PREACHER'S WIFE' (1996). Neither the film nor the heavily gospel-oriented soundtrack – featuring a clutch of HOUSTON songs alongside spirituals from her mother Cissy as well as the likes of Shirley Caesar and the Georgia Mass Choir – received a particularly warm critical reception and the singer belatedly resumed her pop career. While Whitney subsequently collaborated with MARIAH CAREY on a song ('When You Believe') for the Dreamworks animation, 'Prince Of Egypt' (1998), more recently she's turned her hand to producing, with two instalments of Gary Marshall's teen comedy, 'The Princess Diaries'. *BG*

- **filmography** {acting} –

the Bodyguard *(1992 {*} OST w/ V/A =>)* / Waiting To Exhale *(1995 {*} on OST by V/A see; future edition =>)* / **the Preacher's Wife** *(1996 {*} OST =>)* / Scratch The Surface *(1997 {c})*

HOW HIGH

2001 (US 93m) Universal Pictures (R)

Film genre: buddy film/comedy

Top guns: dir: Jesse Dylan / s-w: Dustin Lee Abraham

Stars: Method Man *(Silas P. Silas)* ← BLACK AND WHITE ← BACKSTAGE ← RHYME & REASON ← the SHOW / → BROWN SUGAR, **Redman** *(Jamal King)* ← BACKSTAGE ← RIDE ← RHYME & REASON, Obba Babatunde *(Dean Cain)* ← the TEMPTATIONS, Mike Epps *(Baby Powder)* → MALIBU'S MOST WANTED → the FIGHTING TEMPTATIONS → ROLL BOUNCE, Anna Maria Horsford *(Mrs. King)* ← TIMES SQUARE / → MY BIG PHAT HIP HOP FAMILY → BROKEN BRIDGES, Fred Willard *(Chancellor Huntley)* ← THIS IS SPINAL TAP ← MODEL SHOP / → a MIGHTY WIND → KILLER DILLER, Lark Voorhies *(Lauren)* ← LONGSHOT, Tracey Walter *(Prof. Wood)* ← MAN ON THE MOON ← YOUNG GUNS II ← BATMAN ← REPO MAN / → MASKED AND ANONYMOUS, Jeffrey Jones *(vice president)* ← RAVENOUS ← HOWARD THE DUCK, Spalding Gray *(Prof. Jackson)* ← STRAIGHT TALK ← BEACHES ← TRUE STORIES ← the KILLING FIELDS, Amber Smith *(Prof. Garr)* ← PRIVATE PARTS, **Cypress Hill:- B-Real/Louis Freese** *(himself)* ← THICKER THAN WATER ← RHYME & REASON ← WHO'S THE MAN?, **Sen Dog/Senen Reyes** *(himself)* ← (as above), **Bobo/Eric Correa** *(himself)* ← (as above) / Hector Elizondo *(Bill the crew coach)* ← BEACHES ← the LANDLORD, Tyrin Turner *(Shirley Locks)* ← PANTHER, Chris Elwood *(Bart)* → MY DINNER WITH JIMI, Garrett Morris *(PCC agent)* ← LITTLE RICHARD ← the CENSUS TAKER ← CAR WASH, Kathy Wagner *(intellect)* ← COME ON, GET HAPPY: THE PARTRIDGE FAMILY STORY

Storyline: A permanently stoned amateur botanist who deals in herbal remedies through a hatch in his door, Silas isn't your average Harvard undergrad, nor is fellow stoner, Jamal, harangued into studying by his battleaxe of a mother. After Silas' best friend accidentally burns himself to death with a stray reefer, his ghost returns to reveal the mind-expanding secrets of supernatural weed smoking. The pair pass their entrance exam with flying colors, ending up at Harvard where they shake up the ivory towers to the point of anarchy, baking pot-laced brownies for the dean and enlisting a couple of prostitutes to show their roommates a good time. When their brainpower finally deserts them, they decide to exhume and smoke the corpse of 19th century US President, John Quincy Adams . . . *BG*

Movie rating: *5.5

Visual: dvd

Off the record: METHOD MAN & REDMAN (see below)

—

Various Artists incl. METHOD MAN ** & REDMAN ***
*(both *)*

Dec 01. (cd/c) *Def Jam; <(586628-2/-4)>* **38** ☐
– (intro) / Part II (*) / Round & round – remix (JONELL & **) / Cisco kid (* feat. WAR & CYPRESS HILL) / America's most wanted (*) / Let's do it (*) / We don't know how 2 act (***) / N2gether (LIMP BIZKIT feat. **) / Party up (DMX) / What's your fantasy (LUDACRIS feat. SHAWNNA) / Da Rockwilder (*) / Bring da pain (**) / How to roll a blunt (***) / All I need (** feat. MARY J. BLIGE) / Big dogs (*) / How high (*).

S/track review: Pausing for breath between collaborations, the Cheech & Chong of freestyle recorded at least half a new album as a quasi-follow-up to 1999's 'Blackout!', rounding it out with previously released material and calling it a soundtrack. With a punchline as clichéd and generally inhaled-to-death as "smoke cheeba cheeba smoke cheeba cheeba", the reworked title doesn't hold out much promise for the rest of the album. The ganja-addled worldview of men RED and METHOD probably sounds funnier after a few draws of California's finest, but their sibilant excess is mildly entertaining in coughing fits and starts. Blue of both face and air, RED's Pete Rock-produced 'How To Roll A Blunt' instructs lesser mortals in how to consume manly quantities of weed; despite the fact it's been around the block once already it's still a highlight, built around the Keni Burke rare groover, 'Keep Rising To The Top'. The funkiest production by a mile is War's 'Cisco Kid', which the duo – with help from CYPRESS HILL – rip pretty much wholesale, alternating rapid-fire profanity over Lee Oskar's rattling harmonica. Elsewhere the pickings are slim: the Mantronixed electro of 'Da Rockwilder'; the Wu-gothica of both 'Bring Da Pain' and 'N2Gether Now' (though you'll have to put up with LIMP BIZKIT); and the memorable METHOD revelation, "it ain't easy bein' greasy". And of course, there's more macho boasting and misogyny than you can shake a designer puffa jacket at: among the most objectionable is REDMAN's 'We Don't Know How To Act', referencing Public Enemy on a stream of bile. But the Ashford & Simpson-sampling MARY J. BLIGE love-in, 'All I Need', suggests there's some serious madonna-whore (or should that be "ho"?) shit going on muthafu**ahhhh . . . Next to RZA's peerless 'GHOST DOG' score, 'HOW HIGH' isn't even at the races. *BG*

Album rating: *5.5

– spinoff hits, etc. –

METHOD MAN & REDMAN: Part II

Dec 01. (cd-s) *<588891>* 72 –

HOW SHE MOVE

2007 (Can 98m) Paramount Vantage (rel. UK March '08)

Film genre: urban coming-of-age/dance drama

Top guns: dir: Ian Iqbal Rashid / s-w: Annmarie Morais

Stars: Rutina Wesley *(Raya)*, Tracey Armstrong *(Michelle)*, Brennan Gademans *(Quake)* ← MAN IN THE MIRROR: THE MICHAEL JACKSON STORY, Cle Bennett *(Garvey)* ← LIVIN' FOR LOVE: THE NATALIE COLE STORY ← HENDRIX ← MR. MUSIC, Nina Dobrev *(tall Britney)*, Kevin Duhaney *(E.C.)* ← HONEY ← HENDRIX, **Shawn Fernandez** *(Trey)* ← HONEY ← GET OVER IT!, **Jason Harrow** *(himself)*, **Mya** *(herself)* ← DIRTY DANCING: HAVANA NIGHTS, Jai Jai Jones *(Lester Johnson)* ← LIVIN' FOR LOVE: THE NATALIE COLE STORY

Storyline: The passionate world of step dancing comes under the proverbial spotlight, as a young career girl gets to grip with her new ghetto surroundings following the untimely o.d. death of her sister. *MCS*

Movie rating: *5

Visual: none as yet (no audio OST; score: Andrew Lockington)

Off the record: Jason Harrow is Kardinal Offishall, while **Shawn Fernandez** is Shawn Desman. **Mya** will be best known for her part in 'MOULIN ROUGE!'/'Lady Marmalade' chart-topper. *MCS*

HOW TO STUFF A WILD BIKINI

1966 sequel-5 (US 93m) American International Pictures (PG)

Film genre: teen/beach Pop/Rock Musical comedy

Top guns: s-w: William Asner (+ dir) ← BEACH BLANKET BINGO ← BIKINI BEACH ← MUSCLE BEACH PARTY ← BEACH PARTY, Leo Townsend ← BEACH BLANKET BINGO ← BIKINI BEACH

Stars: ANNETTE Funicello *(Dee Dee)*, Dwayne Hickman *(Ricky)* ← SKI PARTY, Brian Donlevy *(B.D.; Big Daddy)*, Harvey Lembeck *(Eric Von Zipper)* ← BEACH BLANKET BINGO ← PAJAMA PARTY ← BIKINI BEACH ← BEACH PARTY / → the GHOST IN THE INVISIBLE BIKINI → HELLO DOWN THERE, Buster Keaton *(Bwana)* ← PAJAMA PARTY ← BEACH BLANKET BINGO, Beverly Adams *(Cassandra)* ← GIRL HAPPY ← ROUSTABOUT / → WINTER A-GO-GO, Mickey Rooney *(Peachy Keane)* → SKIDOO, Jody McCrea *(Bonehead)* ← BEACH BLANKET BINGO ← PAJAMA PARTY ← BIKINI BEACH ← MUSCLE BEACH PARTY ← BEACH PARTY, Bobbi Shaw *(Khola Koku)* ← SKI PARTY ← BEACH BLANKET BINGO ← PAJAMA PARTY / → the GHOST IN THE INVISIBLE BIKINI → PIPE DREAMS, Luree Holmes *(beach girl)* ← BEACH BLANKET BINGO ← PAJAMA PARTY ← BIKINI BEACH ← MUSCLE BEACH PARTY ← BEACH PARTY / → the GHOST IN THE INVISIBLE BIKINI → THUNDER ALLEY → the TRIP, John Ashley *(Johnny)* ← BEACH BLANKET BINGO ← BIKINI BEACH ← MUSCLE BEACH PARTY ← BEACH PARTY ← HOT ROD GANG, **Frankie AVALON** *(Frankie)*, **the Kingsmen** *(themselves)*, Salli Sasche *(bookend #2)* ← SKI PARTY ← BEACH BLANKET BINGO ← PAJAMA PARTY ← BIKINI BEACH ← MUSCLE BEACH PARTY / → thye GHOST IN THE INVISIBLE BIKINI → THUNDER ALLEY → the TRIP → WILD IN THE STREETS, Patti Chandler *(Patti)* ← SKI PARTY ← BEACH BLANKET BINGO ← PAJAMA PARTY ← BIKINI BEACH, Len Lesser *(North Dakota Pete)* → DU-BEAT-E-O, **Brian Wilson** *(a beach boy)* <= the BEACH BOYS =>, Rick Jones *(a beach boy)*, Michael Nader *(Mike)* ← SKI PARTY ← BEACH BLANKET BINGO ← PAJAMA PARTY ← BIKINI BEACH ← MUSCLE BEACH PARTY ← BEACH PARTY / → the TRIP, Mickey Dora *(beach boy)* ← SKI PARTY ← BEACH BLANKET BINGO ← BIKINI BEACH ← MUSCLE BEACH PARTY ← SURF PARTY ← BEACH PARTY, Mary Hughes *(beach girl)* ← SKI PARTY ← BEACH BLANKET BINGO ← PAJAMA PARTY ← BIKINI BEACH ← MUSCLE BEACH PARTY / → THUNDER ALLEY → DOUBLE TROUBLE

Storyline: Navy boy Frankie is a worried man – while he's off patrolling the South Pacific his girlfriend Dee Dee is at the mercy of all the hunks back on the beach. So he finds the local witch-doctor Bwana and gets him to send a pelican back home to spy on her – as you do. Then, his worst fears confirmed, he gets Bwana to magic up Cassandra, a femme fatale irresistible to all men, and sends her beachwards with disastrous consequences. *JZ*

Movie rating: *4

Visual: new DVD

Off the record: The **Kingsmen** (see below)

Various Artists (incl. the KINGSMEN *) (composer: Les Baxter)

May 66. (lp) *Wand; <WD 671>* – –

– How to stuff a wild bikini (JOHN ASHLEY & cast *) / That's what I call a healthy girl (JOHN ASHLEY & cast) / If it's gonna happen (LU ANN SIMMS, FRANKIE AVALON, ANNETTE FUNICELLO and DWAYNE HICKMAN) / How about us (MICKEY ROONEY and the BEACH GIRLS) / The boy next door (HARVEY LEMBECK and the RAT PACK) / After the party (the Cast) / Better be ready (ANNETTE FUNICELLO) / Follow your leader (HARVEY LEMBECK and the RAT PACK) / The perfect boy (ANNETTE FUNICELLO and the BEACH GIRLS) / Madison avenue (MICKEY ROONEY, BRIAN DONLEVY and the AD MEN) / Give her lovin' (*) / How to stuff a wild bikini (the Cast *).

S/track review: If one was a KINGSMEN fan (ye of 'Louie Louie' fame) way back in the mid 60s, one'd certainly be cheesed off with this beach exploitation OST that has the group's moniker emblazoned on the front sleeve. Alright, they (most certainly drummer-turned-singer LYNN EASTON and guitarist MIKE MITCHELL, along with three sessioners) do make several appearances in the movie itself, but to give full billing to the garage band from Portland, Oregon, when they only knocked out one old B-side ('Give Her Lovin'') was downright shameful and very misleading – the trades description act might well've been informed. It must be said though, that the KINGSMEN did feature with the rest of the cast on various numbers, including the closing title track. Anyway, back to the beach balls-up and the kitschy frolics of 'HOW TO STUFF A . . .'. It seemed the whole cast and crew were asked to appear on camera and sound, even the wee man MICKEY ROONEY himself, although you can take it from me, his grating attempts were strictly of the Hollywood/Broadway variety. Where were the rock and the roll you might ask. With crooner FRANKIE AVALON reduced to a bit-part/collaboration with Rochester-born LU-ANN SIMMS, ANNETTE FUNICELLO (star of the five previous "Beach Party" movies), was the soundtrack's only saving grace. 'If It's Gonna Happen' & 'The Perfect Boy', were indeed her two biggest assets from the pop movie since she was covered up, sarong-like, for the most part. Oh yes, that fun one was talking about, that comes courtesy of a couple of novelty songs by HARVEY LEMBECK and his RAT PACK. Aye, right! *MCS*

Album rating: *4

– spinoff releases, etc. –

LU ANN SIMMS: If It's Gonna Happen / After The Party

Jun 66. (7") *Wand; <196>* ☐ ☐-

HUMAN HIGHWAY

aka NEIL YOUNG: HUMAN HIGHWAY

1982 (US 88m) Shakey Pictures

Film genre: sci-fi Rock Musical comedy

Top guns: dir: (+ s-w) Dean Stockwell, **Neil YOUNG** as Bernard Shakey

Stars: Neil YOUNG *(Lionel Switch)*, Russ Tamblyn *(Fred Kelly)* ← FOLLOW THE BOYS ← HIGH SCHOOL CONFIDENTIAL!, Dean Stockwell *(Otto Quartz)* ← PSYCH-OUT / → PARIS, TEXAS → DUNE → TO LIVE AND DIE IN L.A. → TUCKER: THE MAN AND HIS DREAM → MADONNA: INNOCENCE LOST, Dennis Hopper *(Cracker)* ← EASY RIDER ← HEAD ← the TRIP / → WHITE STAR → RUNNING OUT OF LUCK → STRAIGHT TO HELL, **DEVO:- Mark Mothersbaugh, Bob Mothersbaugh, Bob Casale, Jerry Casale, Alan Myers** *(themselves/performers)*, Sally Kirkland *(Katherine)* ← a STAR IS BORN ← PIPE DREAMS ← HEY, LET'S TWIST / → THANK YOU, GOOD NIGHT, Charlotte Stewart *(Charlotte Goodnight)*

Storyline: Lionel Switch is a none-too bright mechanic who has an obsession with crooner Frankie Fontaine. When Fontaine turns up at the garage one day Lionel can barely contain himself when he gets the honour of fixing his car. Meanwhile Otto Quartz, boss of the diner next door, has devised a scheme to burn down his establishment and claim the insurance, bad news for Lionel's sweetheart Charlotte who works there. And the ancient nuclear power station nearby is slowly but surely turning everything radioactive. *JZ*

Movie rating: *4.5

Visual: video on Warner Bros.

Off the record: DEVO complete several scenes from the film featured in their video compilations, 'We're All Devo' and 'The Complete Truth About De-Evolution'; edited for one complete track, 'Worried Man'. *MCS*

HUMAN TRAFFIC

1999 (UK/Ire 95m) Renaissance Films / Fruit Salad Films (R)

Film genre: urban/buddy movie/comedy

Top guns: s-w + dir: Justin Kerrigan

Stars: John Simm *(Jip)* → 24 HOUR PARTY PEOPLE → BROTHERS OF THE HEAD, Lorraine Pilkington *(Lulu)*, Shaun Parkes *(Koop)*, Danny Dyer *(Moff)*, Dean Davies *(Lee)*, Nicola Reynolds *(Nina)*, Justin Kerrigan *(Ziggy Marlon)*, Peter Albert *(Lulu's Uncle Eric)*, Jan Anderson *(Karen Benson)*, Jo Brand *(Reality)*, Giles Thomas *(Martin)* ← LIPSTICK ON YOUR COLLAR, **Carl Cox** *(Pablo Hassan)* ← BETTER LIVING THROUGH CIRCUITRY ← MODULATIONS / → IT'S ALL GONE PETE TONG, Howard Marks *(himself)*

Storyline: A typical weekend in the life of nineties youth sees Jip, Koop, Nina and Moff forget about the problems of the past week as they begin a two-day drink and drugs binge around the Cardiff club scene. Each of the five has their own personal troubles but they rarely let that interfere with their determination to have a blow-out come what may. After all, Monday morning is still a long, long way away. *JZ*

Movie rating: *6

Visual: dvd

Off the record: DJ **Carl Cox** had a string of minor-esque UK hits from the early 90s including 'I Want You (Forever)' & 'Does It Feel Good To You'. In 1996, he had a Top 30 album, 'At The End Of The Cliché'. *MCS*

Various Artists (md: Pete Tong)

Jun 99. (d-cd/d-c) *London; (556109-2/-4) <27950>* 14 ☐
– (The weekend has landed) / It ain't gonna be (CJ BOLLARD) / Build it up, tear it down (FATBOY SLIM) / (Moff's lyrical madness) / Cookies (JACKNIFE LEE) / Scared (LUCID) / (Spliff politics) / Bucket wipe (POSITION NORMAL) / (Hip hop – intro) / My last request (GRIM) / (Hip hop – outro) / You're gonna get yours (PUBLIC ENEMY) / Dirt (DEATH IN VEGAS) / (Jungle – intro) / Never believe (DILLINJA) / The mood club (FIRST BORN) / (What was I talking about?) / Ogive (WILLIAM ORBIT) / All day (INTERFEARENCE) / King Titos gloves (DEADLY AVENGER) / (Comedown sermon) / Belfast (ORBITAL) / Human traffic theme (MATTHEW HERBERT & ROBERT MELLO) / (Star Wars theory) / Flowerz (ARMAND VAN HELDEN & ROLAND CLARK) / Under the water (BROTHER BROWN & FRANKEE) / Atlanta (PETE HELLER) / Push it (QUAKE) / 5:55 (DURANGO) / My fellow boppers (THEE MADKATT COURTSHIP III) / The age of love (AGE OF LOVE) / Cafe Del Mar '98 (ENERGY 52) / Diving faces (LIQUID CHILD) / Out of the blue (SYSTEM F) / The Latin theme (Dave Angel mix) (CARL COX) / Kittens (UNDERWORLD) / Dark air (QUAKE) / The tingler (CJ BOLLARD) / (We're all in this together) / Come together (PRIMAL SCREAM).

S/track review: If the double CD soundtrack to Brit flick 'HUMAN TRAFFIC' was a weekend then it would be a pretty rubbish Friday night followed by a great Saturday night. Disc one is just too disjointed to work at all and features rave favourites spliced with sound clips from the film and a dash of rap. Some heavy hitters from the 90s club scene are present, including FATBOY SLIM, JACKNIFE LEE, ORBITAL and WILLIAM ORBIT, who all offer pretty standard fare. However, the standout tracks come from PUBLIC ENEMY and DEATH IN VEGAS with 'You're Gonna Get Yours' and 'Dirt' respectively. The former is classic old skool CHUCK D et al while the latter features a monster riff over grimy synths and sinister beats. 'Belfast' (by ORBITAL) is also worth a mention as a great come down track, complete with falsetto vocals – but the real action arrives on the second disc. Made up like a mix tape, it is what the whole soundtrack for a film about the club scene should've sounded like. The few sound clips there are, are mixed in wonderfully with the music, unlike the stop start of disc one. After the insightful 'Star Wars Theory', ARMAND VAN HELDEN kicks us off with 'Flowerz', a breezy dance number that is soon followed by some hardcore club tunes. 'Push It' by QUAKE and SYSTEM F's 'Out Of The Blue' are happy hardcore at its finest while THEE MADKATT COURTSHIP III sound like an updated and spaced-out Kraftwerk on 'My Fellow Boppers'. Some classic UNDERWORLD and a touch of CARL COX are thrown into the mix before the grand finale, 'Come Together' by PRIMAL SCREAM. Although completely different from what had gone before it, and following the best quote from the film (courtesy of Bill Hicks, "It's an insane world but I'm proud to be part of it"), the song just seems like the perfect way to lead us into Sunday. *CM*

Album rating: *6.5

HUSTLE & FLOW

2005 (US 115m) Homegrown Pictures / MTV Films / Paramount (R)

Film genre: urban/Rap-music drama

Top guns: s-w + dir: Craig Brewer → BLACK SNAKE MOAN

Stars: Terrence Howard *(DJay)* ← RAY ← GLITTER ← WHO'S THE MAN? ← the JACKSONS: AN AMERICAN DREAM / → GET RICH OR DIE TRYIN' → IDLEWILD, Anthony Anderson *(Key)* ← MALIBU'S MOST WANTED, Taryn Manning *(Nola)* ← COLD MOUNTAIN ← 8 MILE, Taraji P. Henson *(Shug)*, D.J. Qualls *(Shelby)*, Paula Jai Parker *(Lexus)* ← WHY DO FOOLS FALL IN LOVE / → IDLEWILD, Elise Neal *(Yevette)*, **Isaac HAYES** *(Arnel)*, **Ludacris** *(Skinny Black)* → the BROS., **Jordan Houston as Juicy J** *(Tigga)* ← CHOICES – THE MOVIE, **DJ Paul** *(R.L.)* ← CHOICES: THE MOVIE, **Al Kapone** *(himself)*, **Bobby 'I-20' Sandimanie** *(Yellow Jacket)*, **Haystak** *(Mickey)*, **Josey Scott** *(Elroy)*

Storyline: Under-achieving Djay up till now has been a pimp and dealer in Memphis. Now turning 40, he decides to change his philosophy and transform himself into a rap artist, something he actually enjoys and is good at. He has many an obstacle to overcome, but he sees his big chance when his childhood friend Skinny Black, now a millionaire rapper, is due back in town. Will Skinny pick out Djay's demo among the hundreds of others he gets every day? *JZ*

Movie rating: *7.5

Visual: dvd

Off the record: Taryn Manning auditioned for PopStars US in February 2001 and formed own group, BoomKat, with her brother Kellin. **Juicy J** is Jordan Houston; **Paul Beauregard** is DJ Paul; **Al Kapone** wrote some of the cues from 'HUSTLE..'; **Bobby Sandimanie** is in 'Self-Explanatory' Southern rappers, I-20; **Haystak** is Nashville-born, Southern hardcore rapper Jason Winfree; **Josey Scott** is frontman for Saliva, a heavy-metal band! *MCS*

—

Various Artists (score: Scott Bomar)

Jul 05. (cd) *Atlantic; <83822>* ☐ ☐
– I'm a king – remix (P$C feat. T.I. & LIL SCRAPPY) / Swerve (LIL' BOOSIE & WEBBIE) / (Microphone skit feat. DJAY & pawn shop owner) / It's hard out here for a pimp (DJAY feat. SHUG) / Tell me why (8BALL & MJG) / P***y n***az (E-40 feat. BOHAGON & LIL SCRAPPY) / Whoop that trick (DJAY) / (Bum guy skit feat. DJAY & Arnel's drunk) / Man up (TRILLVILLE) / Carbon 15's, A.K.'s & Mac 11's (BOYZ N DA HOOD) / Lil' daddy (YOUNG CITY a.k.a. CHOPPER) / Let's get a room (NASTY NARDO) / Booty language (JUVENILE feat. SKIP & WACKO) / Bad b**ch – remix (WEBBIE feat. TRINA) / (We in charge skit feat. DJAY & NOLA) / Hustle and flow (it ain't over) (DJAY) / Still tippin' – It's a man's world remix (MIKE JONES feat. NICOLE WRAY) / Murder game (P$C) / Get crunk, get buck (AL KAPONE) / (Man ain't like a dog skit feat. DJAY).

S/track review: Craig Brewer's intense, claustrophobic take on one man trying to make it in the rap game was way more gritty than anything Eminem or 50 Cent could conjure up in their own celluloid dalliances, and this is one of the few times where an actor convinces as a rapper. Terence Howard is DJAY and his three tracks are among the best here. His style is throaty and aggressive, trading on power and weight rather than fluidity of his rhymes. The title track, and the song which is the catalyst for Howard's character in the movie, 'It's Hard Out Here For A Pimp', are ominous, rumbling beasts. The latter won an Oscar for the Three 6 Mafia, who penned the track. After 16 tracks of hard-necked pimping, the gunshots are ringing in your ears and you become a little numb to it all. You wonder if there's anyone at all in gainful employment outside the pimping business, such are the frequency of those claiming it to be their occupation. The monotony of subject matter does not completely diminish what is a fine collection of southern fried beats, slow, deliberate, unctuous backing for some deftly laid down rhymes. The bad-tempered nature of the whole album is exhausting but nuggets here from JUVENILE, P$C and MIKE JONES give us a taste of the dirty south undiluted. *MR*

Album rating: *6.5

HUSTLETOWN MOBBIN'

2003 (US 94m str8-to-dvd) Reptile Films / Nexus Entertainment (R)

Film genre: urban showbiz/Rap-music drama

Top guns: dir: John Darbonne / s-w: Billy Daniels, Kevin Squyres, Marq DeChambres

Stars: **Lil' Troy** *(Rodney / 24/7)*, **Lil' Flip** *(D)* → BEEF 3, **Jacob "Word" Richardson** *(Word)*, **C-Note** *(himself)*, **the Botany Boyz** *(themselves)*, **South Park Mexican/SPM** *(performer)*, Song *(Rodney's girlfriend)*, Cliff Alexander *(rapper in studio)*

Storyline: Young rap star 24/7 (Rodney to his friends) is determined to make it to the top of the tree. But in the cut-throat world of the rap industry it doesn't pay to tread on too many toes, and Rodney is soon at odds with two rival record labels which are run by the street gang bosses. Helped along by girlfriend Song, Rodney must risk life and limb to make sure his promising career isn't over prematurely at the hands of the mobsters. *JZ*

Movie rating: *2.5

Visual: dvd on Maverick

Off the record: Putting other rappers to one side, **SPM** (aka Carlos Coy) spent five years as a jailbird after dealing drugs. **C-Note** (not the male vocal group from Orlando, Florida) is another foul-mouthed southern rapper. *MCS*

—

Various Artists

Dec 06. (cd) *Paid In Full; <PIF 0067 2>* ☐ ☐
– West Coast, Gulf Coast, East Coast (SPM) / South side fook (RP COLA) / Leanin' hard down south (BIG SNAP) / Money in my life (C-NOTE) / Everybody wanna be somebody (SOUTHERN KLICK) / Who dat (LIL KEKE) / Choppers, swangers, discs and vogues (EMC) / Thug life (LIL FLIP) / Respect (MEANMUG) / Rich (HSE) / Mr. Headbanger (NUKRUK) / Million dollar stars (LIFESTYL) / Cafe love (BILLY COOK).

S/track review: In many people's heads, the notion of "straight to DVD" is an admission of failure, a realisation that a movie isn't good enough to deserve even the shortest of theatrical releases. In the vast markets of the US, the DVD market is a legitimate place for film sub genres to thrive. There is a whole subculture of hip hop movies, making flesh the lyrical conceits discussed in the raps. 'HUSTLE TOWN MOBBIN'' is a prime example of the low budget gangsta-centric films being made. And unsurprisingly, they have a soundtrack to match. This one features 13 cuts from a variety of rappers from the south: Houston, Texas and beyond.

Despite the popularity of DJ SCREW's chopped and screwed style of production popularised in the south, only LIL FLIP's 'Thug Life' and the peculiar heavy metal sampling 'Mr Headbanger' adopt the detuned production trademarks. The majority here plough a furrow fairly faithful to the familiar gangsta rap template. LIL KEKE proves perhaps why he's the most recognisable name here, a star in his home of the Lone Star state but his 'Who Dat' is one of the few tracks here that engages. Some sound like glorified karaoke they're so bad, like EMC's 'Choppers, Swangers, Discs And Vogues'. The fact that the artists are fiercely territorial and loyal to the sound, language and styles of southern hip hop means it all sounds a bit samey and the relentless gangsta posturing gets wearing after a while. *MR*

Album rating: *3.5

HYSTERIA: THE DEF LEPPARD STORY

2001 (US 90m TV) LS Productions / Viacom Productions Inc. (R)

Film genre: Rock-music/showbiz bio-pic/drama

Top guns: dir: Robert Mandel / s-w: Christopher Ames, Carolyn Shelby

Stars: Nick Bagnall *(Pete Willis)*, Karl Geary *(Steve Clark)*, Orlando Seale *(Joe Elliott)*, Adam MacDonald *(Rick Savage)*, Esteban Powell *(Phil Collen)*, Tat Whalley *(Rick Allen)*, Dean McDermott *(Peter Mensch)*, Amber Valletta *(Lorelei Shellist)*, Anthony Michael Hall *(Mutt Lange)*, Brett Watson *(Tony Kenning)*

Storyline: The film opens with Rick Allen's car accident when he loses an arm while subsequently wondering if he'll ever play drums again. A sense of tragedy runs through the film as it deals with the various group members' brushes with alcohol and drugs, and the determination of Joe Elliot to make his band the best in the world. From the back streets of Sheffield to the lights of London and beyond it's the band's comradeship which pulls them through adversity and stops Def Leppard changing their spots. *JZ*

Movie rating: *5

Visual: video + dvd (no audio OST)

Off the record: Def Leppard (see above)

□ I AM A GROUPIE alt.
(⇒ GROUPIE GIRL)

I AM SAM

2001 (US 132m) New Line Cinema (PG-13)

Film genre: part courtroom melodrama

Top guns: s-w: Jessie Nelson (+ dir) ← the STORY OF US, Kristine Johnson

Stars: Sean Penn *(Sam Dawson)* ← DEAD MAN WALKING ← FAST TIMES AT RIDGEMONT HIGH, Michelle Pfeiffer *(Rita Harrison)* ← the STORY OF US ← GREASE 2 / → HAIRSPRAY remake, Dakota Fanning *(Lucy Diamond Dawson)*, Dianne Wiest *(Annie Cassell)* ← FOOTLOOSE, Loretta Devine *(Margaret Calgrove)* ← the PREACHER'S WIFE / → DREAMGIRLS, Richard Schiff *(Mr. Turner)* ← TOUCH ← GRACE OF MY HEART ← the BODYGUARD ← YOUNG GUNS II / → RAY, Laura Dern *(Randy Carpenter)* ← DR.T & THE WOMEN ← WILD AT HEART ← LADIES AND GENTLEMAN, THE FABULOUS STAINS, Mary Steenburgen *(Dr. Blake)*, Rosalind Chao *(Lily)*, Scott Paulin *(Duncan Rhodes)* ← PUMP UP THE VOLUME, Kathleen Robertson *(Big Boy waitress)* ← PSYCHO BEACH PARTY ← SPLENDOR

Storyline: Autistic Sam Dawson (at a mental age of 7) raises his child Lucy until she turns eight, only to have the authorities insist on him giving up parental rights. With a reluctant female lawyer on his case, he goes to court to fight for custody. Sam has more than a penchant for everything Beatles, citing the Fab Four's recorded history on a plethora of occasions. *MCS*

Movie rating: *7

Visual: dvd

Off the record: nothing.

—

Various (songwriters: LENNON & McCARTNEY) (score: John Powell)

Jan 02. (cd/c) *V2; <63881 27119-2> (VVR 101941-2)* □ May02 □
– Two of us (AIMEE MANN & MICHAEL PENN) / Blackbird (SARAH McLACHLAN) / Across the universe (RUFUS WAINWRIGHT) / I'm looking through you (the WALLFLOWERS) / You've got to hide your love away (EDDIE VEDDER) / Strawberry fields forever (BEN HARPER) / Mother Nature's son (SHERYL CROW) / Golden slumbers (BEN FOLDS) / I'm only sleeping (the VINES) / Don't let me down (STEREOPHONICS) / Lucy in the sky with diamonds (BLACK CROWES) / Julia (CHOCOLATE GENIUS) / We can work it out (HEATHER NOVA) / Help! (HOWIE DAY) / Nowhere man (PAUL WESTERBERG) / Revolution (GRANDADDY) / Let it be (NICK CAVE). *(UK+=)* – Lucy in the sky with diamonds (AIMEE MANN) / Two of us (NEIL FINN & LIAM) / Here comes the sun (NICK CAVE).

S/track review: A clutch of Americans (with a smattering of Canadians, Aussies and some token Welshmen) tackling the songbook of the Beatles for an underachieving indie "Rain Man" take-off? Alarm bells should be ringing. Far from being surprising – if you want that, seek out the mighty Laibach's industrial cover of the 'Let It Be' album or Danger Mouse's Beatles/Jay-Z mash-up 'The Grey Album' – it's safe to say nothing is reinvented here, everything is faithful, some to a fault; just ask the VINES and their plastic Scouse accents to boot on their pointless take of 'I'm Only Sleeping'. At the opposite end of the spectrum, GRANDADDY manage to make 'Revolution' exactly like a GRANDADDY song, and not a very good one at that. The BLACK CROWES try to sound tripped out on 'Lucy In The Sky With Diamonds' but are so consciously digging the detail they forget to inject the song with any of the trademark swagger and passion. There are a few whose strong performances shine through. PAUL WESTERBERG excels on a skeletal 'Nowhere Man', SARAH McLACHLAN's creamy tones are suited to the simplicity of 'Blackbird' and HEATHER NOVA's sleepy delivery adds a feminine touch to her languid rendition of 'We Can Work It Out'. STEREOPHONICS promise much, taking on 'Don't Let Me Down' and while Kelly Jones puts in a creditable vocal performance, they don't deliver the money shot with some of their trademark bombast, opting for an anti-climactic, acoustic take instead. NICK CAVE stays on the right side of a smirk and applies the right amount of gravitas for 'Let It Be', while father and son NEIL and LIAM FINN close proceedings with a rousing and harmonious 'Two Of Us'. A decidedly patchy collection of renditions focussing predominantly on the sentimental side of LENNON and McCARTNEY's musical cache which fails to capture much of the joyful oddness and tender humour in their music. Maybe that's what made the Beatles really quite good then, huh? *MR*

Album rating: *5.5

I SHOT ANDY WARHOL

1996 (UK/US 103m) Samuel Goldwyn Company (R)

Film genre: showbiz/music bio-pic drama

Top guns: s-w: Mary Harron (+ dir), Daniel Minahan → SERIES 7: THE CONTENDERS

Stars: Lili Taylor *(Valerie Jean Solanas)* ← FOUR ROOMS / → a SLIPPING-DOWN LIFE → HIGH FIDELITY, Jared Harris *(Andy Warhol)* ← DEAD MAN ← NATURAL BORN KILLERS / → TWO OF US, Lothaire Bluteau *(Maurice Girodias)*, Martha Plimpton *(Stevie)* ← SHY PEOPLE / → COLIN FITZ LIVES!, Anna Thompson *(Iris)* ← the CROW, Stephen Dorff *(Candy Darling)* ← S.F.W. ← BACKBEAT ← JUDGMENT NIGHT ← an AMBUSH OF GHOSTS, Reg Rogers *(Paul Morrisey)*, Donovan Leitch *(Gerard Malanga)* ← GAS, FOOD LODGING ← the IN CROWD ← BREAKIN' 2: ELECTRIC BOOGALOO, Michael Imperioli *(Ondine)* ← the BASKETBALL DIARIES ← JUNGLE FEVER / → GIRL 6 → LAST MAN STANDING → DISAPPEARING ACTS, Bill Sage *(Tom Baker)* → HIGH ART → GLITTER → MYSTERIOUS SKIN, Jill Hennessy *(Laura)*, Marian Quinn *(Jean)* ← HEAVY, Gabriel Mick/Mann *(clean cut boy)* → HIGH ART → THINGS BEHIND THE SUN → JOSIE AND THE PUSSYCATS, Anh Doung *(Contesse de Courcy)* ← the MAMBO KINGS / → HIGH ART, Miriam Cyr *(Ultra Violet)* ← GOTHIC, Eric Mabius *(revolutionary #2)* → SPLENDOR, Mark Margolis *(Louis Solanas)* ← WHERE THE RIVERS FLOW NORTH ← SHORT EYES, **Yo La Tengo:- Ira Kaplan, Georgia Hubley, James McNew** plus **Tara Key** (as the Velvet Underground), Edoardo Ballerini *(school paper editor)* → LOOKING FOR AN ECHO

Storyline: The true story of troubled feminist Valerie Solanas, who forms her infamous SCUM manifesto (Society for Cutting Up Men) after suffering terrible abuse as a prostitute in New York. Finally escaping from that life, she writes a screenplay and finds herself in Andy Warhol's circle of friends. When Warhol ignores her efforts at writing and distances himself from her, she begins to plot a frightening revenge. *JZ*

Movie rating: *6

Visual: video + dvd

Off the record: Yo La Tengo were formed in Hoboken, New Jersey, USA in 1984 by husband/wife team Ira Kaplan (vocals, guitar) and Georgia Hubley (vocals, drums). Finally, through much time and varied personnel, the pair stabilised their line-up with Dave Schramm and Mike Lewis. This configuration recorded the 1986 debut album, 'Ride The Tiger', introducing the band's countrified acoustic-rock which drew on the likes of the Velvet Underground, Love and the Rain Parade. Following the departure of Schramm and Lewis, Kaplan assumed writing duties for 'New Wave Hot Dogs' (1987), providing the band with their first of many credible and critically acclaimed albums. 1989's 'President Yo La Tengo' was more experimental, while 'Fakebook' (1990) was a beguiling album of rootsy covers. Throughout the 90s, the band (with James McNew on bass) have released a string of albums for 'Matador', taking an increasingly left-field direction; check out 'May I Sing With Me' (1992), 'Painful' (1993), 'Electr-O-Pura' (1995) and 'I Can Hear The Heart Beating As One' (1997). Filmmaker fan of the group, Hal Hartley, often invites YO LA TENGO to supply some songs for his movies ('Simple Men' 1992 was one), while Georgia's sister, Emily (a short filmmaker), does likewise. Post-millennium, YO LA TENGO, completed a number of sets ('And Then Nothing Turned Itself Inside-Out' – 2000, 'Summer Sun' – 2003 and 'I Am Not Afraid Of You And I Will Beat Your Ass' – 2006), but their most cinema-orientated being the 2002 ambient workout for French underwater documentarian, Jean Painleve: 'The Sounds Of The Sounds Of Science'. Of late and working to a tight schedule, YO LA TENGO have scored the music for no less than four films, 'Junebug' (2005), 'Game 6' (2005), 'Old Joy' (2006) and 'Shortbus' (2006), the latter actually released but credited to Various Artists. *MCS*

—

Various Artists (score: JOHN CALE *)

Mar 96. (cd/c) *Warners; (<7567 92690-2/-4>)* ☐ Apr96 ☐
– Season of the witch (LUNA) / Do you believe in magic? (the LOVIN' SPOONFUL) / Love is all around (R.E.M.) / Burned (WILCO) / Itchycoo park (BEN LEE) / Sunshine Superman (JEWEL) / Mais que nada (SERGIO MENDES AND BRASIL '66) / Gimi a little break (LOVE) / Sensitive Euro man (PAVEMENT) / Kick out the jams (MC5) / I'll keep it with mine (BETTIE SERVEERT) / Demons (YO LA TENGO) / I Shot Andy Warhol suite (*).

S/track review: There are thirteen tracks on 'I SHOT ANDY WARHOL', one is a beautiful orchestral suite from JOHN CALE of the Velvet Underground, the closest link to Andy Warhol on the album, and the remaining twelve are halved into tracks which are covers and those which are originals. None of the covers are wildly different from the originals but that shouldn't detract the listener from what are basically excellent versions. Donovan's 'Season Of The Witch' and 'Sunshine Superman' are covered brilliantly by LUNA and JEWEL respectively, both retaining a psychedelic edge to what are rocked up version of the originals. R.E.M. drummer BILL BERRY takes up vocal duties on a stripped down, laid back rendering of the Troggs' 'Love Is All Around' while BEN LEE sticks close to the original on the Small Faces' 'Itchycoo Park'. WILCO take on Neil Young's 'Burned' and BETTIE SERVEERT do Bob Dylan's 'I'll Keep It With Mine', again both do justice to their originals. Add to those the raucous 'Kick Out The Jams' from the MC5, 'Do You Believe In Magic' by the LOVIN' SPOONFUL and LOVE's 'Gimi A Little Break', as well as PAVEMENT's 'Sensitive Euro Man', 'Mais Que Nada' by SERGIO MENDES AND BRASIL '66 and the atmospheric 'Demons' from YO LA TENGO and TARA KEY and you have a great set. 'I SHOT ANDY WARHOL' is indeed an excellent collection of songs that mixes some classics with a nice dose of one-off cover versions to make it worth buying. *CM*

Album rating: *7.5

I WANNA HOLD YOUR HAND

1978 (US 104m) Universal Pictures (PG)

Film genre: Pop/Rock-music-based screwball/teen comedy

Top guns: s-w (+ dir): Robert Zemeckis + Bob Gale → TRESPASS

Stars: Nancy Allen *(Pam Mitchell)*, Bobby Di Cicco *(Tony Smerko)* → WAVELENGTH, Marc McClure *(Larry Dubois)* → THAT THING YOU DO!, Susan Kendall Newman *(Janis Goldman)*, Theresa Saldana *(Grace Corrigan)*, Wendie Jo Sperber *(Rosie Petrofsky)*, Eddie Deezen *(Richard "Ringo" Klaus)* → GREASE → GREASE 2 → ROCK-A-DOODLE, Will Jordan *(Ed Sullivan)* → the BUDDY HOLLY STORY → ELVIS: THE MOVIE → the DOORS, Read Morgan *(Pete's father)*, James Houghton *(Eddie)* ← ONE ON ONE / → MORE AMERICAN GRAFFITI → PURPLE PEOPLE EATER, Dick Miller *(Sgt. Brenner)* ← TRUCK TURNER ← the TRIP ← the WILD ANGELS ← WILD, WILD WINTER ← BEACH BALL ← SKI PARTY ← the GIRLS ON THE BEACH ← ROCK ALL NIGHT ← CARNIVAL ROCK / → ROCK'N'ROLL HIGH SCHOOL → GET CRAZY → SHAKE, RATTLE & ROCK! tv, **the BEATLES** *(archive performance)*, Brian Epstein *(archive)* → the COMPLEAT BEATLES → IMAGINE: JOHN LENNON, Victor Brandt *(theatre cop Foley)* ← THREE THE HARD WAY / → NEON MANIACS

Storyline: Three goofy New Jersey teenagers have been struck with the "Beatlemania" bug and aspire to meeting their idols on the upcoming Ed Sullivan Show. Each has a particular want from the Fab Four, although what they really want is tickets. *MCS*

Movie rating: *6.5

Visual: video + dvd (no audio OST)

Off the record: Will Jordan has portrayed Ed Sullivan several times in the movies.

ICE CUBE

Born: O'Shea Jackson, 15 Jun'69, Los Angeles, California, USA. A founding member of inflammatory, highly influential hip hop crew NWA, and a man whose big screen multi-tasking has long since taken over from his MC'ing, ICE CUBE couldn't have hoped for a more auspicious debut than 'Boyz N The Hood' (1991). Although drawing generous notices for his magnetic portrayal of an ex-con, as well as contributing to the soundtrack (with 'How To Survive In South Central'), CUBE was just getting started, using the John Singleton landmark as proof of his ability to face down his near namesake ICE-T in Walter Hill's 'TRESPASS' (1992). While RY COODER came good on the score, CUBE teamed up with ICE-T for the heavy duty title track. Both went on to play themselves in hip hop send-up, 'CB4' (1993), before the former NWA man finally teamed up with old mucker Dr Dre for a contribution ('Natural Born Killaz') to SNOOP DOGG vehicle, 'MURDER WAS THE CASE' (1994). Continuing to work with credible Afro-American directors, he appeared in Isaac Julien's more sober look at hip hop, 'Darker Side Of Black' (1994) and, continuing to excel in roles on the wrong side of the law, he also starred in Charles Burnett's 'The Glass Shield' (1994), before taking on a subtler, more ambiguous role as an eternal student in Singleton's 'Higher Learning' (1995), as well as contributing a couple of songs to the stylistically educational soundtrack. CUBE's penchant for comedy asserted itself on the spliff-fragranced 'Friday' (1995), his first, highly successful shot at scriptwriting, sketching another wry role for himself and honing his increasingly impressive acting chops into the bargain. His production debut was just as impressive: Darrell James Roodt's 'Dangerous Ground' (1997); the movie furnished an even more politically slanted part than the Burnett film, witnessing ICE CUBE – alongside Elizabeth Hurley – imagining himself into the role of a longtime exile returning to post-apartheid South Africa. He also graced the (strictly hip hop) soundtrack's cover art and penned its lead cut, 'The World Is Mine'. Less promising was jungle farce, 'Anaconda' (1997), playing a serpent-baiting cameraman for a pre-J.Lo Jennifer Lopez. In what was by this point becoming an established pattern, CUBE swung back to grittier material for his directorial debut (which he also wrote and produced), dabbling in Spike Lee-patented sexual politics with 'The Players Club' (1997), to the soundtrack of which he contributed his usual handful of thematic rhymes alongside the likes of Master P. P returned the favour with his own production/writing vehicle, 'I Got The Hook-Up' (1998), giving him a cameo and gracing the soundtrack with 'Ghetto Vet', one of the best tracks from CUBE's acclaimed comeback album, 'War & Peace, Vol.1' (1998). David O. Russell's acclaimed 'Three Kings' (1999) cast him in a real-life (Gulf) war role alongside George Clooney, while the hip hop themed 'THICKER THAN WATER' (1999) focused on war closer to the streets he grew up on. The new millennium saw the release of belated follow-up, 'Next Friday' (2000), CUBE writing the script and taking a starring role but relinquishing the director's chair. For the soundtrack, he lifted a cut, 'You Can Do It', from his second volume of 'War & Peace' (2000), one which went on to have an unlikely remixed wind as a near UK No.1 in 2004. Having mastered earthbound gangstas, CUBE went on to star as a criminal in outer space in John Carpenter's 'Ghosts Of Mars' (2001), a role which presaged the more action-orientated bent of some of his roles in the decade to come. While 'Friday After Next' (2002) milked a third film from his comedy sideline, with the rapper again credited as writer and producer while leaving the direction to music video maestro Marcus Raboy, a braided CUBE put a bit more Hollywood largesse into his next writing/acting/producing project, 'All About The Benjamins' (2002), also directed by a music video expert in Kevin Bray. ICE CUBE's talent for homespun comedy was again underlined with a gregarious starring role in neighbourhood ensemble piece, 'Barbershop' (2002), while a Paul Oakenfold link-up for the same year's 'BLADE II' soundtrack predicted the aforementioned club makeover of 'You Can Do It'. Yet another music video player, Joseph Khan, was CUBE's director on unapologetically high-octane actioner, 'Torque' (2004), while 'XXX: State Of The Union' (2005) finally saw him line up (once again as a dangerous con) with Samuel L Jackson, taking up where Vin Diesel left off and contributing his mandatory lyric ("Anybody Seen The PoPo's?") to the soundtrack. Punctuating the rough stuff was a second volume of 'Barbershop', an executive production credit on the concept's Queen Latifah spin-off, 'Beauty Shop' (2005), and a role as a de facto father in family comedy, 'Are We There Yet' (2005). 2006 saw a link-up with award-winning documentarian R.J. Cutler, a reality TV project putting an experimental, sociological spin on the time-honoured concept of a white person (in this case a whole family) living – with the help of modern make-up techniques – in the guise of a black person, and vice versa. And as a dude who likes a good sequel, he took up the domestic baton once more on 2007 follow-up, 'Are We Done Yet', perhaps signalling a mellowing of one of hip hop's original – and most successful – gangstas, long since a father in real life. *BG*

- filmography {acting} [s-w + dir] –

Boyz N The Hood *(1991 {*} on OST by V/A; future edition)* / **Trespass** *(1992 {*} on OST by V/A & RY COODER =>)* / **CB4: The Movie** *(1993 {c} OST by V/A =>)* / the Glass Shield *(1994 {a})* / **Murder Was The Case** *(1994 {c} OST by V/A =>)* / Higher Learning *(1995 {*} on OST; future edition)* / Friday *(1995 [s-w] {*} on OST by V/A; see future edition)* / Dangerous Ground *(1997 {*} on OST by V/A; future edition)* / Anaconda *(1997 {*} OST; see future editions =>)* / the Players Club *(1998 [s-w + dir] {*} on OST by V/A; future edition)* / I Got The Hook-Up *(1998 {b} on OST by V/A; future edition)* / **Thicker Than Water** *(1999 {*} OST by V/A =>)* / Three Kings *(1999 {*})* / Next Friday *(2000 [ch s-w] {*} hit single on OST by V/A; see future edition)* / Ghosts Of Mars *(2001 {*})* / All About The Benjamins *(2002 [s-w] {*} on OST by V/A; future* *edition)* / BarberShop *(2002 {*} on OST by V/A; see future edition)* / Friday After Next *(2002 [ch s-w] {*} OST by V/A; see future edition)* / **Beef** *(2003 {p} on OST by V/A =>)* / BarberShop 2: Back In Business *(2004 {*} OST by V/A; future edition)* / the N Word *(2004 {c})* / **Beef 2** *(2004 {p})* / Torque *(2004 {*})* / Are We There Yet? *(2005 {*})* / xXx: State Of The Union *(2005 {*} on OST by V/A; future edition)*

ICE-T

Born: Tracy Morrow, 16 Feb'58, Newark, New Jersey, USA. A generation older than his namesake ICE CUBE (and inspired by the same legendary pimp, Iceberg Slim), Original Gangsta ICE-T entered the rap game in its formative years, although he's never quite managed the same level of screen success. He got out on something approaching the good foot, though, making his acting/soundtrack debut with an MC cameo ('Reckless') in Hollywood B-Boy cash-in, 'BREAKIN' (1983), following it up in sequel, 'BREAKIN' 2: ELECTRIC BOOGALOO' (1984), and making an appearance in early Mario Van Peebles vehicle, 'RAPPIN'' (1985). Less well known are his backroom contributions to bizarre motivational b-movie turned cult favourite, 'Mr. T's Be Somebody . . . Or Be Somebody's Fool' (1984), wherein the A-Team bruiser dispensed all-American advice in proto-rap stylee. With T's (ICE, not Mr.) pioneering, major label music career beginning in earnest in the mid-late 80s, he also moved up the movie big league, writing title tracks for both Dennis Hopper's acclaimed L.A. gang drama 'Colors' (1988) and Warren Beatty's 'DICK TRACY' (1990). He also netted his first starring roles in Denzel Washington actioner, 'Ricochet' (1991) and Van Peebles' seminal nu-blaxploitation feature 'New Jack City' (1991), for which he also supplied the thematic 'New Jack Hustler (Nino's Theme)'. While the irony of his playing a police officer can't have been lost on afficionados of the politicised hardcore rap style he'd incubated and which NWA put their own brutal spin on (the 'New Jack City' soundtrack also featured the era's bass-quaking anthem, 'Straight Outta Compton'), and certainly not on those expressing outrage over his infamous 'Cop Killer' track from the same year, ICE-T used the role in his defence. As debate raged over music censorship and 'Warners' fielded death threats, T defended his right to write in character and got on with his acting/soundtrack career, starring opposite ICE CUBE in Walter Hill's 'TRESPASS' (1992), with whom he also composed the title theme (as well as contributing the track 'Depths Of Hell'). In addition to a link-up with Slayer on the 'JUDGMENT NIGHT' soundtrack, and a bit part in Perry Farrell's directorial debut, 'Gift', 1993 brought a bit of light relief in rap satire, 'CB4: THE MOVIE', and alongside Dr Dre in Ted Demme-directed hip hop comedy, 'WHO'S THE MAN?'. Come the mid-90s, T was being hunted by Rutger Hauer in 'Surviving The Game' (1994), locking horns with LEMMY for the 'AIRHEADS' soundtrack and starring in crusty comic book adaptation, 'Tank Girl' (1995), to which he contributed the track, 'Big Gun'. He even branched into sci-fi, starring in William Gibson adaptation, 'Johnny Mnemonic' (1995), and, with 'Mean Guns' (1997), began an association with cult b-director Albert Pyun. Between comedy ('The Deli') and kids' stuff ('Jacob Two Two Meets The Hooded Fang'), the flyest man in rap starred in Pyun's 'Crazy Six' (1998) and appeared in the SNOOP DOGG-starring 'Urban Menace' (1999) as well as both producing and starring in 'Corrupt' (1999) and 'The Wrecking Crew' (1999). In what was a busy end of the millennium for him, he also appeared in various other low budget efforts including 'Sonic Impact', 'The Heist' and 'Frezno Smooth', as well as straight-to-video Mario Van Peebles meteor drama, 'Judgement Day'. While the year 2000 brought perhaps the most surreal hip hop feature of all time, 'Leprechaun In The Hood', and roles in the by now mandatory slew of sci-fi/action straight-to-video material, he at least got a credit alongside Hopper and Michael Madsen in Luca Bercovici's 'Luck Of The Draw', teamed up with SNOOP DOGG and Ja Rule in Donald Goines' adaptation, 'Crime Partners' (2001), and landed a role in the Kurt Russell/Kevin Costner head-to-head, '3000 Miles To Graceland' (2001). 2001 also saw him putting on that police badge once again alongside Coolio in futuristic thriller, 'Gangland', and in erotic low budget job, 'Kept', returning to cinemas and the wrong side of the tracks with a rare, typically gritty feature ('R Xmas') from a (relatively) big name director in Abel Ferrara. 'Out Kold' saw yet another hip hop pairing, this time with old skool legend Kool Moe Dee, while the Fred Williamson-directed 'On The Edge' (2002) had T mixing it with original blaxploitation icon Ron O'Neal. While he continued working with Pyun – notably with a cameo in terrorism drama, 'Ticker' (2001) – ICE-T's feature appearances became even more marginal as the decade wore on, comprising another Fred Williamson film, 'Lexie' (2004), and prison drama, 'Tracks' (2005). More interesting were his many TV/documentary appearances, where his well-earned reputation as an intelligent, provocative and humorous commentator on subjects dear to his heart (hip hop, pimps, politics, etc.) has yet to fail him. Like his namesake and old sparring partner ICE CUBE, he even moved into reality TV with 'Ice-T's Rap School', working a similar premise of white culture encountering black. *BG*

- **filmography** {acting} (composer) –

Breakin' *(1984 {p} on OST by V/A =>)* / **Breakin' 2: Electric Boogaloo** *(1984 {p} OST by V/A =>)* / Colors *(1988 hit single on OST by V/A; see future editions)* / the Return Of Superfly *(1990 hit single w/ CURTIS MAYFIELD on OST by V/A; future edition)* / New Jack City *(1991 {*} hit single on OST by V/A; see future edition)* / Ricochet *(1991 {*} on OST by Alan Silvestri)* / **CB4: The Movie** *(1993 {c} OST by V/A =>)* / **Who's The Man?** *(1993 {*} OST by V/A =>)* / Surviving The Game *(1994 {*})* / Tank Girl *(1995 {*} on OST by V/A; see future edition)* / Johnny Mnemonic *(1995 {*})* / Frankenpenis *(1996 {b})* / **Rhyme & Reason** *(1997 {p} on OST by V/A =>)* / Mean Guns *(1997 {*})* / the Deli *(1997 {*})* / Below Utopia *(1997 {*})* / Crazy Six *(1998 {*})* / Exiled *(1998 TV {a})* / the Wrecking Crew *(1999 {*} + score w/ Tony Riparetti)* / Sonic Impact *(1999 {*})* / Judgment Day *(1999 {*})* / the Heist *(1999 {*})* / Frezno Smooth *(1999 {*})* / Urban Menace *(1999 {*n})* / Stealth Fighter *(1999 {a})* / Final Voyage *(1999 {*})* / Jacob Two Two Meets The Hooded Fang *(1999 {a})* / Corrupt *(1999 + score w/ Anthony Riparetti)* / Guardian *(2000 {*})* / Gangland *(2000 {a})* / Leprechaun In The Hood *(2000 {*})* / Luck Of The Draw *(2000 {*})* / the Alternate *(2000 {*})* / Lost Angeles *(2000 {*c})* / the Disciples *(2000 TV {*})* / Tara *(2001 {*})* / Stranded *(2001 {*})* / Kept *(2001 {*})* / Crime Partners *(2001 {*})* / 3000 Miles To Graceland *(2001 {a})* / Point Doom *(2001 {a})* / Deadly Rhapsody *(2001 {*})* / 'R Xmas *(2001 {*})* / Ticker *(2001 {a})* / Out Kold *(2001 {*})* / Ablaze *(2001 {*})* / Air Rage *(2001 {*})* / Pimpin' 101 *(2002 {*})* / On The Edge *(2002 {*})* / Tracks *(2002 {*})* / Lexie *(2004 {*})* / There's A God On The Mic *(2005 {*p/c})* / F*ck *(2005 {c})* / the Magic 7 *(2006 {*v} + co-OST)*

IDLE ON PARADE

1959 (UK 88m b&w) Warwick Film Productions / Columbia Pictures

Film genre: Pop-music military comedy

Top guns: dir: John Gilling / s-w: John Antrobus (au: William Camp)

Stars: William Bendix *(Sgt. Lush)*, Anthony Newley *(Jeep Jackson)*, Anne Aubrey *(Caroline)*, Lionel Jeffries *(Bertie)*, Sid James *(Herbie)*, David Lodge *(Shorty)* → CATCH US IF YOU CAN, Dilys Laye *(Renee)*, Victor Kendall *(commanding officer)*, Bernie Winters *(Joseph Jackson)* → PLAY IT COOL, Harry Fowler *(Ron)* → JUST FOR FUN

Storyline: Pop idol Jeep Jackson gets his call-up papers and changes from stage-bashing to square-bashing. The usual chaos ensues when the army tries to transform unwilling civilians into soldiers, despite the best efforts of despairing Sergeant Lush. However Jeep happily sings his way through his National Service and even manages to woo the Colonel's daughter. What would G.I. Elvis have made of it all? *JZ*

Movie rating: *6

Visual: none (no audio OST; score: Johnny Gregory)

Off the record: Child actor/star, Anthony Newley (b.24 Sep'31, Hackney, East London) – famous for playing the role of the Artful Dodger in 1948 film version of 'Oliver Twist' – kicked off his pop singing career on the cusp of this particular movie (see below singles). Further monster hits included, 'Personality', chart-toppers 'Why' & 'Do You Mind', plus 'If She Should Come To You', a David Jones/BOWIE fave 'Strawberry Fair', 'And The Heavens Cried' & the excrutiating 'Pop Goes The Weasel'. He was subsequently married to actress Joan Collins for several years (1963-1970). Tony finally went back to the Bow Bells of his Cockney upbringing by acting as a dodgy car salesman in Eastenders (c.1998); sadly he died of renal cancer on the 14th April, 1999. *MCS*

– spinoff hits, etc. –

ANTHONY NEWLEY: I've Waited So Long / Saturday Night Rock-a-boogie

Apr 59. (7") *Decca; (F 11127)* [3] [–]

ANTHONY NEWLEY: Idle On Parade / Idle Rock-a-boogie

May 59. (7") *Decca; (F 11137)* [ ] [–]

ANTHONY NEWLEY: Idle On Parade (EP)

May 59. (7"ep) *Decca; (DFE 6566)* [13] [–]
– I've waited so long / Idle rock-a-boogie / Idle on parade / Saturday night rock-a-boogie.

IDLEWILD

2006 (US 121m) Universal Pictures (R)

Film genre: gangster/crime Hip Hop Musical

Top guns: s-w + dir: Bryan Barber

Stars: Andre Benjamin *(Percival)* ← BE COOL, **Antwan A. Patton** *(Rooster)*, Paula Patton *(Angel)*, Terrence Howard *(Trumpy)* ← GET RICH OR DIE TRYIN' ← FOUR BROTHERS ← HUSTLE & FLOW ← RAY ← GLITTER ← WHO'S THE MAN? ← the JACKSONS: AN AMERICAN DREAM, Faizon Love *(Sunshine Ace)* ← the FIGHTING TEMPTATIONS ← FEAR OF A BLACK HAT, Malinda Williams *(Zora)*, **Macy Gray** *(Taffy)*, Cicely Tyson *(Mother Hopkins)* ← BUSTIN' LOOSE ← a HERO AIN'T NOTHIN' BUT A SANDWICH ← SOUNDER, Ben Vereen *(Percy Sr.)* ← WHY DO FOOLS FALL IN LOVE ← GAS-S-S-S!, Paula Jai Parker *(Rose)* ← HUSTLE & FLOW ← WHY DO FOOLS FALL IN LOVE, **Patti LaBelle** *(Angel Davenport)* ← SING, Ving Rhames *(Spats)* ← BEEF ← PULP FICTION, Bill Nunn *(GW)* ← HE GOT GAME ← SCHOOL DAZE, **Angelo Moore** *(band director)* ← TAPEHEADS ← BACK TO THE BEACH

Storyline: In the Deep South of the 30s, Idlewild is the speakeasy of choice, Rooster the singing host with the most and Percival his right hand piano man. Things are peachy until the local mob decide they want a piece of the action and a time-served conflict ensues. *BG*

Movie rating: *6

Visual: dvd

Off the record: OUTKAST (see below)

OUTKAST (feat. Various guests)

Aug 06. (cd/d-lp *LaFace-Zomba; <(82876 75792-2/75266-1)>* [2] Sep06 [16]
– Intro / Mighty "O" / Peaches (feat. SLEEPY BROWN & SCAR) / Idlewild blue (don'tchu worry 'bout me) / Infatuation – interlude / N2U (feat. KHUJO GOODIE) / Morris Brown (feat. SCAR & SLEEPY BROWN) / Chronomentrophobia / The train (feat. SLEEPY BROWN & SCAR) / Life is like a musical / No bootleg DVDs / Hollywood divorce (feat. LIL' WAYNE & SNOOP DOGG) / Zora – interlude / Call the law (feat. JANELLE MONAE) / Bamboo & cross – interlude / BuggFace / Makes no sense at all / In your dreams (feat. KILLER MIKE & JANELLE MONAE) / PJ & Rooster / Mutron angel (feat. WHILD PEACH) / Greatest show on Earth (feat. MACY GRAY) / You're beautiful – interlude / When I look in your eyes / Dyin' to live / A bad note.

S/track review: Like most vanity projects this one didn't quite live up to the hype but, as one of the few hip hop acts who audibly cherish an eclectic record collection rather than just manipulating an inferior one, OUTKAST weren't going to turn out anything less than a bespoke soundtrack. As sprawling as 'Speakerboxxx/ The Love Below', if minus the poplife highs, 'IDLEWILD' plays as a postmodern update of a tradition that runs back through 'BOOK OF NUMBERS', 'COTTON COMES TO HARLEM' and 'COME BACK, CHARLESTON BLUE', telescoping the paranoia and closed-doors pizazz of the Prohibition era through a 'Paisley Park' lens and the disillusion of encroaching middle age. DRE and BIG BOI maintain an almost late-period Lennon/McCartney-esque distance in their respective writing corners, and there's not so much full-on hip hop per se ('Mighty "O"' being a bristling exception), but those who've followed the group through their own whistle-stop trainride to 'Hollywood Divorce' (itself a show-stealing, sing-rapping indictment listing LIL' WAYNE and SNOOP DOGG) will find plenty to pore over. The period jazz isn't as prevalent as it might have been but gets memorably channelled through the marching band swing of 'Morris Brown' and the click track ragtime of 'Call The Law', JANELLE MONAE's vocals dripping like Deep South candlewax. DRE's 'Chronomentrophobia' draws in the mood of spatz and loathing, with 'The Train' as its brassy-bittersweet counterpart, and the Terry Callier-meets-Shuggie Otis vibe of 'Life Is Like A Musical' as its bright-eyed twin. MONAE gets ambitious on the Prince-ly jazz/soul of 'Make No Sense At All' and 'Mutron Angel', makes for a sultry foil to BOI's swordsman on 'In Your Dreams' and gilds DRE's séance with the ghosts of Nina Simone and Donny Hathaway on 'Dyin' To Live', but the furthest limb OUTKAST have ever gone out on swims into double vision on closer 'A Bad Note', a shuddering, Funkadelicised miasma recalling the hearing-voices experimentation of Sonny Terry and Brownie McGhee on the aforementioned 'BOOK OF NUMBERS'. Make no mistake, with few obvious hits and no concession to expectations, 'IDLEWILD' isn't a pop record, or even a hip hop/R&B record, more the 'White Album' and 'Black Album' boiled down with bootleg liquor, best sampled in moderation. *BG*

Album rating: *6.5

– spinoff hits, etc. –

OUTKAST: Mighty "O"

Jun 06. (12") *<87269>* [77] [–]

OUTKAST: Morris Brown

Aug 06. (cd-s) *<82876 80842-2>* [95] [–]

OUTKAST: Morris Brown / Mighty "O"

Sep 06. (cd-s) *(82876 80842-2)* [–] [43]

OUTKAST: Idlewild Blue (Don'tchu Worry 'Bout Me)

Oct 06. (-) *<radio>* [100] [–]

les IDOLES

UK title 'the IDOLS'

1968 (Fra 95m) International Thanos Films (18)

Film genre: Pop/Rock Musical comedy/satire

Top guns: dir + s-w: Marc'o *(adapted from stage play)*

Stars: Pierre Clementi *(Charlie le Rurineur)*, Bulle Ogier *(Gigi la folle)* → la VALLEE → CANDY MOUNTAIN, Jean-Pierre Kalfon *(Simon le magicien)* → la VALLEE, Valerie Lagrange *(Rosine)* → la VALLEE, Michele Moretti *(Mme.*

Canasson), Joel Barbouth *(M. Canasson)*, Bernadette Lafont *(la Nyasse)*, Daniel Pommereule, **the Rollsticks:- Didier Malherbe** *(performers)*

Storyline: Centres around three French avant-pop singers, the wild and rebellious Charlie, the sweet and innocent Gigi and the mystical but frantic Simon, all inspired by "real" pop idols, Johnny Hallyday, France Gall and Andy Warhol/the Velvets respectively. *MCS*

Movie rating: *5

Visual: none

Off the record: Session man, Michel Portal, performed on the LP, while sax/wind man **Didier Malherbe** (future GONG) also appeared. *MCS*

—

Various Cast (composers: Patrick Greussay & Stephane Vilar)

Jun 68. (lp) *C.B.S.; (62812)* [–] France [–]
– (unavailable)

S/track review: What's the saying? "hen's teeth" – wanted!

Album rating: *?

the IDOLMAKER

1980 (US 119m) United Artists Pictures (PG)

Film genre: showbiz/Pop-music drama

Top guns: dir: Taylor Hackford → HAIL! HAIL! ROCK'N'ROLL → RAY / s-w: Edward Di Lorenzo

Stars: Ray Sharkey *(Vincent Vacarri)* → DU-BEAT-E-O → BODY ROCK, Tovah Feldshuh *(Brenda Roberts)*, Paul Land *(Tommy Dee)*, Peter Gallagher *(Caesare)* → CENTER STAGE, Olympia Dukakis *(Mrs. Vacarri)* → WORKING GIRL, Joe Pantoliano *(Gino Pilato)* → RISKY BUSINESS → EDDIE AND THE CRUISERS → SCENES FROM THE GOLDMINE → LA BAMBA → ROCK'N'ROLL MOM → the IN CROWD → BLACK AND WHITE, Richard Bright *(Uncle Tony)* ← HAIR ← RANCHO DELUXE ← PAT GARRETT & BILLY THE KID / → WHO'S THE MAN?

Storyline: Vincent Vacarri is The Idolmaker, the man who can turn raw talent (and sometimes no talent at all) into stars. Tommy Dee and Caesare are two typical young artists in Vacarri's stable, and their rags to riches stories are told here. But of course Vacarri is not averse to milking his teen superstars for all they're worth and enjoying the financial rewards of success. *JZ*

Movie rating: *6

Visual: video

Off the record: JEFF BARRY was a renowned songwriter (Sam Cooke used his 'Teenage Sonata', the Archies hit the top with 'Sugar, Sugar') and released solo singles in the late 50s; he appeared in the TV movie, 'HEY HEY WE'RE THE MONKEES' (1997). *MCS*

—

Various Artists/Cast (composer/score: Jeff Barry)

Dec 80. (lp) *<SP 4840>* [ ] [–]
– Here is my love (JESSE FREDERICK) / Ooo-wee baby (DARLENE LOVE) / Come and get it (NINO TEMPO) / Sweet little lover (JESSE FREDERICK) / I can't tell (COLLEEN FITZPATRICK) / However dark the night (PETER GALLAGHER) / Baby (PETER GALLAGHER) / I know where you're goin' (NINO TEMPO) / A boy and a girl (the SWEET INSPIRATIONS & the LONDON FOG) / I believe it can be done (RAY SHARKEY) / I believe it can be done – instrumental (NINO TEMPO).

S/track review: A rock and roll past master, JEFF BARRY co-wrote a host of all-time classics like 'River Deep, Mountain High', 'Iko Iko', 'Leader Of The Pack', and 'Baby I Love You'; but he fails to recapture the magic of his heyday in this leadenly-produced potboiler. Barry's history gave him access to legends like DARLENE LOVE, who is in terrific voice re-creating the sound of the famous girl-group songs she recorded with Phil Spector. There are esteemed session musicians like saxman NINO TEMPO (who can be heard on John Lennon's 1975 album 'Rock And Roll'), and the James Cleveland gospel choir make an admirable contribution. But aside from the fact that BARRY doesn't come up with a song to touch his best, the music is cruelly hobbled by turn-of-the-80s production fads. It's at its most infuriating on 'A Boy And A Girl', which begins with an entirely pleasing a cappella duel between 60s groups the SWEET INSPIRATIONS and the LONDON FOG – and then succumbs to clattering drums, its harmonies collapsing into a unison chorus, strings and handclaps. DARLENE LOVE's Spector-pastiche 'Ooo-wee Baby' is similarly clobbered, with the thudding rhythm section mixed way up, and the chorus way down. As consolation, the prodigiously-browed PETER GALLAGHER in his first movie role proves to have a serviceable baritone and a deal of stagey dramatics on two songs where he sounds like nothing so much as late 70s spangle-shirted Neil Diamond. The similarity is no coincidence, of course: it was JEFF BARRY who discovered Diamond, and produced his breakthrough hits. *ND*

Album rating: *4

□ the IDOLS alt.
(⇒ les IDOLES)

IEDEREEN BEROEMD!

US title 'EVERYBODY'S FAMOUS!'

2000 (Belg/Neth/Fra 97m subt.) Canal+ / Eurimages / Miramax (R)

Film genre: Music-based comedy/drama

Top guns: dir (+ s-w): Dominique Deruddere

Stars: Josse De Pauw *(Jean Vereecken)*, Eva van der Gucht *(Marva Vereecken)*, Werner de Smedt *(Willy Van Outreve)*, Thekla Reuten *(Debbie)*, Victor Low *(Michael Jensen)*, Gert Portael *(Chantal Vereecken)*, Alice Reys *(Lizzy)*, Ianka Fleerackers *(Gaby)*

Storyline: A hard working-class father (and part-time songwriter) tries to live his rock'n'roll dreams by pinning his long lost ambitions on his overweight daughter, Marva. After losing his job at the local bottle factory, Jean has a chance meeting with well-known pop star, Debbie, and proceeds to kidnap her, with the intension of getting his daughter a chance to sing on TV. *MCS*

Movie rating: *7

Visual: video + dvd

Off the record: Orchestral composer, Raymond Van Het Groenewoud, wrote the score – a hard to find Various Artists CD was released on Belgium's 'Double T Music'; *DTM 228101-2)*

□ Frank IFIELD segment
(⇒ UP JUMPED A SWAGMAN)

I'M NOT THERE

2007 (US 135m) The Weinstein Co. / Paramount Pictures (R)

Film genre: rock-Music biopic/drama

Top guns: s-w: (+ dir) Todd Haynes ← VELVET GOLDMINE, Oren Moverman

Stars: Cate Blanchett *(Jude Quinn)* ← the LIFE AQUATIC WITH STEVE ZISSOU ← COFFEE AND CIGARETTES, Ben Whishaw *(Arthur Rimbaud)* ← STONED, Christian Bale *(Jack Rollins / Pastor John)* ← LAUREL CANYON ← VELVET GOLDMINE ← METROLAND, Richard Gere *(Billy the Kid)* ← the MOTHMAN PROPHECIES ← DR. T & THE WOMEN,

Marcus Carl Franklin *(Woody Guthrie)*, Heath Ledger *(Robbie Clark)*, **Kris KRISTOFFERSON** *(narrator)*, Don Francks *(Hobo Joe)* ← MR. MUSIC ← MADONNA: INNOCENCE LOST ← ROCK & RULE ← HEAVY METAL, Roc LaFortune *(Hobo Moe)*, **Richie Havens** *(old man Alvin)* ← GLASTONBURY ← HEARTS OF FIRE ← CATCH MY SOUL ← WOODSTOCK, Julianne Moore *(Alice Fabian)* ← MAGNOLIA ← BOOGIE NIGHTS, **Kim Gordon** *(Carla Hendricks)* <= SONIC YOUTH =>

Storyline: The remarkable career of folk-rock legend, Bob Dylan, with the focus on the six characters who play him. Awaiting one's ticket to the UK premiere as we speak (aye, right!). *MCS*

Movie rating: *8.5

Visual: dvd

Off the record: Cate Blanchett was subsequently nominated for an Oscar as best actress in a supporting role.

—

Various Artists (songwriter: BOB DYLAN)

Oct 07. (d-cd/d-lp) *Columbia; <88697 12038-2/-1>* [95] [–]
– All along the watchtower (EDDIE VEDDER & THE MILLION DOLLAR BASHERS) / I'm not there (SONIC YOUTH) / Goin' to Acapulco (JIM JAMES & CALEXICO) / Tombstone blues (RICHIE HAVENS) / Ballad of a thin man (STEPHEN MALKMUS & THE MILLION DOLLAR BASHERS) / Stuck inside of Mobile with the Memphis blues again (CAT POWER) / Pressing on (JOHN DOE) / Fourth time around (YO LA TENGO) / Dark eyes (IRON & WINE & CALEXICO) / Highway 61 revisited (KAREN O & THE MILLION DOLLAR BASHERS) / One more cup of coffee (ROGER McGUINN & CALEXICO) / The lonesome death of Hattie Carroll (MASON JENNINGS) / Billy 1 (LOS LOBOS) / Simple twist of fate (JEFF TWEEDY) / Man in the long black coat (MARK LANEGAN) / Señor (tales of yankee power) (WILLIE NELSON & CALEXICO) / / As I went out one morning (MIRA BILLOTTE) / Can't leave her behind (STEPHEN MALKMUS & LEE RANALDO) / Ring them bells (SUFJAN STEVENS) / Just like a woman (CHARLOTTE GAINSBOURG & CALEXICO) / Mama, you've been on my mind – A fraction of last thoughts on Woody Guthrie (JACK JOHNSON) / I wanna be your lover (YO LA TENGO) / You ain't goin' nowhere (GLEN HANSARD & MARKETA IRGLOVA) / Can you please crawl out your window? (the HOLD STEADY) / Just like Tom Thumb's blues (RAMBLIN' JACK ELLIOTT) / The wicked messenger (the BLACK KEYS) / Cold irons bound (TOM VERLAINE & THE MILLION DOLLAR BASHERS) / The times they are a-changin' (MASON JENNINGS) / Maggie's farm (STEPHEN MALKMUS & THE MILLION DOLLAR BASHERS) / When the ship comes in (MARCUS CARL FRANKLIN) / Moonshiner (BOB FORREST) / I dreamed I saw St. Augustine (JOHN DOE) / Knockin' on Heaven's door (ANTONY & THE JOHNSONS) / I'm not there (BOB DYLAN with THE BAND).

S/track review: This OST, like the film it scores, is epic in scale, with 29 different singers covering 34 different tracks from DYLAN's monolithic back catalogue. Some are faithful (a few to a fault), while others choose to go down a path less travelled with varying degrees of success. This feels more like a feat of organisation rather than one of creative brilliance. There's still plenty to intrigue here though, Yeah Yeah Yeah's KAREN O doing a high school marching band thing on 'Highway 61 Revisited' for starters and CAT POWER who successfully adds her own guile and humour to 'Stuck Inside Of Mobile With The Memphis Blues Again'. MARK LANEGAN plays up the drama and lust on 'Man In The Long Black Coat'. SONIC YOUTH, meanwhile, just sound sheepish on the title track. JEFF TWEEDY, JACK JOHNSON and the HOLD STEADY dish out the earnest tributes while MASON JENNINGS, STEPHEN MALKMUS and SUFJAN STEVENS resort to peculiar Bob karaoke. That singular, acquired taste, ANTONY AND THE JOHNSONS put a ghostly sheen via 'Knockin' On Heaven's Door' which, depending on where you stand on tremulous wailing, is a pleasure or a pain. CALEXICO are utilized as house band for a clutch of tracks and few could invoke their own dusty atmosphere as John Convertino's mariachi rock outfit courtesy of their collaboration with WILLIE NELSON on 'Señor (Tales Of Yankee Power)' and their languid backing of JIM JAMES for a sublime 'Goin' To Acapulco'. Similar plaudits go to CALEXICO for their work with a downright frail sounding ROGER McGUINN on a brilliant 'One More Cup Of Coffee'. The whole shebang is rounded off with DYLAN himself performing the title track (with the BAND recorded in 1967), a take from the legendary 'Basement Tapes' era. It sounds quiet and slightly hollow, DYLAN feeling like someone who's turned up late for a surprise party, everyone being left to get on without him. A curio to end a curious collection that doesn't do anyone any real favours but leaves the man's legacy untarnished. *MR*

Album rating: *7

IMMORTAL

1995 (US 105m) Spectrum Films / Sprocketz (R)

Film genre: Swing/Pop-music psychological horror

Top guns: s-w + dir: Walt Bost, Steven D. White

Stars: Andrew Taylor *(Dex Drags)*, Meredith Leigh Sause *(Linda)*, Steve Willard *(Steve)*, Randy Jones *(Randy)*, George Taylor *(George)*, **Tom Maxwell** *(Jared)*, Trent McDevitt *(Evan)*, Frank Aard *(Wiley)*, Matt Brookshire *(Pete Gonnabedead)*, **Greg Humphreys** *(movie star)*, Walt Bost *(consessionaire)*, K.K./Ken Kupstis *(Candyman)*, Phillip O'Brian Metcalf *(Ox)*, Phil Ford *(museum curator)*, Mike Shaw *(Mike)*

Storyline: Dex Drags has an almost superhuman ability on electric guitar, but that's not surprising as he's not quite the same as most other humans. Dex has a craving for human blood which he has somehow managed to keep a secret from his band and his girlfriend, but as he tries to find a cure for his vampiric tendencies he knows the trail of blood is growing ever longer and the "stakes" are getting higher. *JZ*

Movie rating: *4

Visual: video + dvd

Off the record: **Tom Maxwell** is a member of Chapel Hill retro-swing outfit, Squirrel Nut Zippers (current album, 'The Inevitable'). **Greg Humphreys** had just disbanded Dillon Fence and moved on to Hobex. Meredith Leigh Sause subsequently formed her own band, My Little Phony (no recordings!). *MCS*

—

Various Artists/Cast (score: Donny Black)

Jan 96. (cd) *Permanent; <3>* [ ] [–]
– Danny Diamond – live (SQUIRREL NUT ZIPPERS) / Tours in progress (PHIL FORD, ANDREW TAYLOR and MEREDITH LEIGH SAUSE) / Don't ask (REVERB-A-RAY) / Weeble (PSYCHO SONIC CINDI) / Linda's theme (ANDREW TAYLOR and MIKE SHAW) / Column shifter (CAPSIZE 7) / The '72 Strat (ANDREW TAYLOR and MIKE BROOKSHIRE) / You and me girl – live (VERTIGO JOYRIDE) / Valentine (REVERB-A-RAY) / Candy counter (WALT BOST and K.K.) / Show me (GREG HUMPHREYS) / Bees in a jar (JUNE) / Ear to ear (SEX POLICE) / Cheesy B movie (GREG HUMPHREYS; actor) / Coffee cup – live (DILLON FENCE) / Don't take me for the fool (the TROUT BAND) / Myths and legends (FRANK AARD and ANDREW TAYLOR) / Ballad in a blue (DEXTER ROMWEBER).

S/track review: 'IMMORTAL' is filled with largely unknown acts but it's none the worse for it. While many of the tracks here aren't exactly earth shattering, there are a few notables that make it worth a listen. Possibly the most well known are the SQUIRREL NUT ZIPPERS who achieved a couple of minor hits in the US during the 90s with their own particular brand of tongue-in-cheek swing and feature here with the quasi-funeral live dirge 'Danny Diamond'. REVERB-A-RAY contribute two tracks to the proceedings, the punky 'Don't Ask', which could be mistaken for

'Color And The Shape'-era Foo Fighters, and the ballad 'Valentine', both of which are o.k. songs. Then we have 'Weeble' by the wonderfully named PSYCHO SONIC CINDI that is reminiscent of the Smashing Pumpkins and a dose of post-grunge rock with CAPSIZE 7's 'Column Shifter'. There are a couple of lovely instrumental pieces with the delicate 'Linda's Theme' by ANDREW TAYLOR & MIKE SHAW and the equally tender 'Show Me' from GREG HUMPHREYS, front man of DILLON FENCE, who also appear with a live rendition of 'Coffee Cup'. The album closes with the atmospheric warbling of DEXTER ROMWEBER's 'Ballad In A Blue' which seems like a fitting way to end what is an interesting album without being something that would make you rush to write home about. *CM*

Album rating: *5.5

the IN CROWD

1988 (US 95m) Force 10 Productions / Orion Pictures (PG)

Film genre: romantic Rock Musical teen drama

Top guns: s-w: (+ dir) Mark Rosenthal, Lawrence Konner

Stars: Donovan Leitch *(Del Green)* ← BREAKIN' 2: ELECTRIC BOOGALOO / → GAS, FOOD LODGING → I SHOT ANDY WARHOL, Joe Pantoliano *(Perry Parker)* ← ROCK'N'ROLL MOM ← LA BAMBA ← SCENES FROM THE GOLDMINE ← EDDIE AND THE CRUISERS ← RISKY BUSINESS ← the IDOLMAKER / → BLACK AND WHITE, Jennifer Runyon *(Vicky)*, Wendy Gazelle *(Gail)*, Sean Gregory Sullivan *(Popeye)* ← WHO'S THAT GIRL? / → WAYNE'S WORLD → 54, Charlotte d'Amboise *(Ina)* → the PREACHER'S WIFE, Bruce Kirby *(Morris)* ← SWEET DREAMS, Page Hannah *(Lydia)* → SHAG: THE MOVIE, Peter Boyle *(Uncle Pete)* ← WALKER ← WHERE THE BUFFALO ROAM ← STEELYARD BLUES ← JOE, **the Contours** *(performers)*

Storyline: A popular Ivy League-bound college student lands a spot on a TV dance show and instantly becomes a hit. Now he has a dilemma, will he continue to be a rock'n'roll teen idol and leave his past behind him, or will he find notice his biggest fan . . . his dance partner. "Clean-cut Dirty Dancing meets Flashdance". *MCS*

Movie rating: *4.5

Visual: video (no audio OST; score: Mark Snow)

Off the record: Calvin Klein male model, Donovan Leith, is the son of 60s pop icon, Donovan, and had a brief spell in the mid-90s as frontman with alt-rock outfit, Nancy Boy (one set, 'Promosexual' 1995); Camp Freddy is his most recent band project (2006). The **Contours** vocal R&B group in the movie were not the original 60s outfit. Music from the movie comes via VINCE GUARALDI TRIO ('Cast Your Fate To The Wind') and a version of 'Land Of 1000 Dances'. *MCS*

IN HIS LIFE: THE JOHN LENNON STORY

2000 (US 88m TV) Michael O'Hara Productions / NBC Studios (PG-13)

Film genre: Pop/Rock-music bio-pic/drama

Top guns: dir: David Carson / s-w: Michael O'Hara

Stars: Philip McQuillan *(John Lennon)*, Blair Brown *(Mimi Smith)* ← ONE-TRICK PONY, Daniel McGowan *(Paul McCartney)*, Mark Rice-Oxley *(George Harrison)*, Lee Williams *(Stuart Sutcliffe)* ← STILL CRAZY, Christine Kavanagh *(Julia Lennon)*, Gillian Kearney *(Cynthia Lennon)* ← SEX, CHIPS AND ROCK N' ROLL, Jamie Glover *(Brian Epstein)*, Christian Ealey *(Ringo Starr)*, Scot Williams *(Pete Best)* ← SWING ← BACKBEAT, Paul Usher *(Freddie Lennon)* ← SWING, Alex Cox *(Bruno)* → REVENGERS TRAGEDY, Dean Anthony *(Rory Storm)*

Storyline: "From a boy with a dream . . . to the Beatle who rocked the world!" – as it says on the cover – just about says it all. The early years of singer/musician John Lennon and his development into being the integral part of 60s icons, the Beatles. *MCS*

Movie rating: *6.5

Visual: video + dvd (no audio OST by Dennis McCarthy)

Off the record: Philip McQuillan is also part of the Sundogs (although this was not the San Fran-based swamp rockers who released albums in the 90s. Scot Williams had already played ex-Beatle, Pete Best, in another early Fab Four bio-pic, 'BACKBEAT'. *MCS*

IN THE MIX

2005 (US 95m) Lions Gate Films / Twentieth Century Fox (R)

Film genre: romantic crime comedy

Top guns: dir: Ron Underwood / s-w: Jacqueline Zambrano (story: Chanel Capra, Brian Rubenstein & Cara Dellaverson)

Stars: Usher *(Darrell)* ← FADE TO BLACK, Chazz Palminteri *(Frank Pacelli)* ← the LAST DRAGON, Emmanuelle Chriqui *(Dolly)* ← DETROIT ROCK CITY, Robert Davi *(Fish)*, Matt Gerald *(Jackie)* ← MAGNOLIA, **Deezer D** *(JoJo)* ← BONES ← FEAR OF A BLACK HAT ← CB4: THE MOVIE ← COOL AS ICE, Kevin Hart *(Busta)* ← DEATH OF A DYNASTY ← PAPER SOLDIERS, Nick Mancuso *(Salvatore)* ← BRAVE NEW GIRL ← NIGHT MAGIC ← PAROLES ET MUSIQUE ← BLAME IT ON THE NIGHT ← HEARTBREAKERS

Storyline: Successful DJ Darrell plays Sir Galahad to a mobster by taking a bullet in the shoulder for him, and is rewarded with a job as his daughter's bodyguard. As Dolly and Darrell become more attracted to each other, jealousy and rivalry abound as a gang war breaks out and Dolly becomes the centre of attention. It's time for DJ Darrell to face the music or go back to the day job. *JZ*

Movie rating: *2.5

Visual: dvd

Off the record: Usher first came to light when he acted in 1998's 'The Faculty' movie.

Various Artists: USHER Presents . . . In The Mix

Nov 05. (cd) *J-Records; <(82876 72019-2)>* ☐ ☐
– Settle down (RICO LOVE) / That's my word (ONE CHANCE) / Be what it's gonna be (CHRISTINA MILIAN) / Which one (CHRIS BROWN feat. NOAH) / Hands & feet (KERI HILSON) / Sweat (RICO LOVE feat. USHER) / Get acquainted (RYON LOVETT) / Could this be love (ONE CHANCE) / Some kind of wonderful (ANTHONY HAMILTON) / Against the world (ROBIN THICKE) / Murda (YOUNGBLOODZ feat. CUTTY & FAT DOG) / On the grind (RICO LOVE feat. JUELZ SANTANA & PAUL WALL).

S/track review: Appearances can be deceptive. For a minute you might be fooled into believing you've picked up the soundtrack to a mobster movie given gangsta imagery and presence of dial-a-hood Chaz Palminteri. But this is a vanity project for USHER, the crown prince of US R&B. 'Usher Presents . . .' is emblazoned across the front and it draws tightly from his coterie of protégés and collaborators while the man himself guests on selected tracks. The music is incredibly slick, stylised R&B, soul and hip hop that is synthetic, studio-bound and over-produced. The performances are by the numbers, the arrangements pedestrian, the lyrics are often little more than strung together clichés. It lacks that essential thing for good soul music: soul. USHER's finest moment yet was his globe-straddling single 'Yeah!' and this album lacks the thing that made that song so good: an edge. LIL' JON's feverish production is a distant memory to this stilted, underplayed fluff. Even the rougher hip hop tracks lack bite. Sure, there's some scholarly, sub-Donny Hathaway soul work from ANTHONY HAMILTON, some sweet pop from CHRISTINA MILIAN and some passable come hither suggestiveness on RICO LOVE's slippery hip hop pop 'Settle Down', but for the most part this is just tripe. The genius of the best machine funk music is that it swings. This doesn't swing, it flops. *MR*

Album rating: *2.5

□ the INBETWEEN AGE alt.
(⇒ the GOLDEN DISC)

□ INSANE CLOWN POSSE segment
(⇒ BIG MONEY HUTLA)

INSIDE THE OSMONDS

2001 (US 2x50m TV-mini) Merv Griffin Entertainment / ABC

Film genre: Pop-music bio-pic/drama

Top guns: dir: Neill Fearnley ← DAYDREAM BELIEVERS: THE MONKEES STORY / s-w: Matt Dorff ← MR. ROCK'N'ROLL: THE ALAN FREED STORY

Stars: Bruce McGill *(George Osmond)*, Veronica Cartwright *(Olive Osmond)*, Joel Berti *(Alan Osmond)*, Pat Kirkpatrick *(Merrill Osmond)*, Jason Knight *(Wayne Osmond)* ← DAYDREAM BELIEVERS: THE MONKEES STORY, Miklos Perlus *(Jay Osmond)*, Patrick Levis *(Donny Osmond)*, Janaya Stephens *(Marie Osmond)*, Trevor Blumas *(Jimmy Osmond)*, Thomas Dekker *(young Donny)*, Taylin Wilson *(young Marie)*, Taylor Abrahamse *(young Jimmy)* ← HEDWIG AND THE ANGRY INCH, Colin Ferguson *(Mike Curb)* ← DAYDREAM BELIEVERS: THE MONKEES STORY, George & Olive Osmond *(themselves)* ← SIDE BY SIDE: THE TRUE STORY OF A MAGICAL FAMILY, **Donny Osmond** *(himself)* ← GOIN' COCONUTS, **Marie Osmond** *(herself)* ← SIDE BY SIDE: THE TRUE STORY OF A MAGICAL FAMILY ← GOIN' COCONUTS, **Alan Osmond** *(himself)*, **Jay Osmond** *(himself)*, **Merrill Osmond** *(himself)*, **Wayne Osmond** *(himself)*, **Jimmy Osmond** *(himself)*, **Andy Williams** *(himself)*

Storyline: "They couldn't live without the spotlight: they couldn't share it either". Starting with their first concert flop in California, the band change their image (and manager) and straight away hit the big time. Untainted by alcohol, sex or drugs, the family go from strength to strength under the stern gaze of father George. The end comes with bankruptcy on a massive scale, but the family still manages to keep on smiling, at least to the public. *JZ*

Album rating: *5

Visual: video (no audio OST; score: Patrick Williams)

Off the record: Songs by the **Osmonds** ('One Bad Apple (Don't Spoil The Whole Bunch)', 'Hold Her Tight', 'Yo-Yo', 'Goin' Home', 'He Ain't Heavy (He's My Brother)', 'Are You Up There?', 'Crazy Horses' & 'Down By The Lazy River') are featured on boxed-set below, as are 'Sweet And Innocent' & 'Puppy Love' by (DONNY OSMOND), 'Long Haired Lover From Liverpool' (LITTLE JIMMY OSMOND), 'Paper Roses' & 'I'm Leaving It All Up To You' (DONNY & MARIE OSMOND) plus 'Utah' by the whole OSMOND family. *MCS*

– helpful compilation –

the OSMOND FAMILY: The All-Time Greatest Hits Of . . .

Feb 00. (3xcd-box) *Curb; <77955-2>* □ [–]

INTERSTELLA 5555: THE 5TORY OF THE 5ECRET 5TAR 5YSTEM

2003 (Japan/Fra 68m) Daft Life Ltd. Co. / Soda Pictures (PG)

Film genre: animated sci-fi Techno Pop-music fantasy

Top guns: dir: Kazuhisa Takenochi / s-w: **Thomas Bangalter, Guy-Manuel De Homem-Christo**, Cedric Hervet

Voices: Romanthony *(Octave)*, **DJ Sneak, Todd Edwards, Daft Punk**, etc.

Storyline: Galactic super-villain (and record producer) Earl de Darkwood kidnaps an alien techno band from their home planet and transports them to Earth. There they are brainwashed and given new human identities, but not before space pilot Shep receives their distress call and flies Earthwards in pursuit. The evil Earl plans to conquer the world when he gets 5,555 Gold Records and it's up to Shep and the aliens to thwart him. *JZ*

Movie rating: *7.5

Visual: dvd Nov'03 on 'Virgin' (score: DAFT PUNK)

Off the record: DAFT PUNK . . . tracks order (see below for associated mix):- 'One More Time', 'Aerodynamic', 'Digital Love', 'Harder, Better, Faster, Stronger', Crescendolls', 'Nightvision', 'Superheroes', 'High Life', 'Something About Us', 'Voyager', 'Veridis Quo', 'Short Circuit', 'Face To Face', 'Too Long' & 'Aerodynamic'.

– associated releases –

DAFT PUNK: Daft Club *(remixes)*

Dec 03. (cd) *Virgin; (CDV 2982) <596389>* □ □
– Ouverture / Aerodynamic *[Daft Punk remix]* / Harder, better, faster, stronger *[the Neptunes remix]* / Face to face *[Cosmo Vitelli remix]* / Phoenix *[Basement Jaxx remix]* / Digital love *[Boris Dlugosch remix]* / Harder, better, faster, stronger *[Jesse & Crabbe remix]* / Face to face *[Demon mix]* / Crescendolls *[Laidback Luke remix]* / Aerodynamic *[Slum Village remix]* / Too long *[Gonzales version]* / Aerodynamite / One more time *[Romanthony's unplugged]* / Something about us (love theme from Interstella 5555).

DAFT PUNK: Something About Us (Love Theme from Interstella 5555) / Veridis Quo / Voyager / ('A'-video mix)

Dec 03. (cd-s) *Virgin; <547645>* [–] □

IT COULDN'T HAPPEN HERE

1987 (UK 87m) EMI Films / PMI (15)

Film genre: Pop/Rock Musical comedy/drama

Top guns: s-w: (+ dir) Jack Bond, James Dillon

Stars: Pet Shop Boys:- Neil Tennant & Chris Lowe *(themselves)*, Joss Ackland *(priest/murderer)* ← the APPLE / → BILL & TED'S BOGUS JOURNEY, Neil Dickson *(pilot/car salesman)* ← EAT THE RICH, Gareth Hunt *(Uncle Dredge/ventriloquist/postcard seller)*, Barbara Windsor *(seaside landlady/Neil's mother)*

Storyline: Neil and Chris go on a self-discovery tour round their version of modern-day England. On their travels they hark back to their childhood days and how things have changed, not necessarily for the better. Beaches, boarding houses and a blind preacher all play their part, along with biker gangs and SS nuns, in this symbolic pastiche of Pet Shop Britain. *JZ*

Movie rating: *5.5

Visual: video (no audio OST; see below)

Off the record: The 80s belonged to the camp and the **PET SHOP BOYS** (formed in London, England in 1981 by assistant editor of Smash Hits Neil Tennant and architecture student Chris Lowe), were no exception. 'West End Girls', a flop at first, was re-worked by producer Stephen Hague in 1985, hitting No.1 in many countries including both sides of the "big pond". Their debut album, 'Please' (1986) was a classy collection of intelligent synth-pop, infectious melodies and wryly observant lyrics becoming the campy duo's trademark. 'Opportunities' (another recent miss) was hastily re-released in clanking, mechanically remixed form and almost reached the Top 10, while a further single ('Suburbia') from the album made No.8. Visually, the band were akin to a more stylish Sparks or Erasure, sharing the latter's sizeable gay following, while ironically also being idolised by thugish football "casuals" for their immaculate taste in designer wear. 'It's A Sin' gave the act their second No.1 in 1987, while they also teamed up with 60s songstress Dusty Springfield for the hit 'What Have I Done To Deserve This' near chart-topper. The fact that the Americans had taken so keenly to PET SHOP BOYS was odd, given that nation's notorious inability to appreciate irony; it's arguably a testament to the group's finely honed melodic mastery and perfectionist production that they broke the US market where other quintessentially English pop bands have consistently failed. 'Actually' (1987) was another successful slice of sophisticated pop nous, containing the aforementioned two singles as well as the poignant 'Rent' and two further No.1 singles in 'Heart' and a flamboyant synth/strings remake of Elvis' 'Always On My Mind'; all incidentally featured in the duo's first and only movie, 'IT COULDN'T HAPPEN HERE'.

MCS & BG

– associated releases, etc. –

PET SHOP BOYS: It's A Sin / (non-OST songs/versions)

Jun 87. (7"/12"/c-s/cd-s) *Parlophone; (R/12R/TCR/CDR 6158)* *EMI America; <43027>* [1] Aug87 [9]

PET SHOP BOYS & DUSTY SPRINGFIELD: What Have I Done To Deserve This? / (non-OST songs/versions)

Aug 87. (7"/12"/c-s/cd-s) *Parlophone; (R/12R/TCR/CDR 6163)* *EMI America; <50107>* [2] Dec87 [2]

PET SHOP BOYS: Actually

Sep 87. (cd/c/lp) *Parlophone; (CD/TC+/PCSD 104) EMI America; <46972>* [2] [25]
– One more chance / What have I done to deserve this? / Shopping / Rent / Hit music / It couldn't happen here / It's a sin / I want to wake up / Heart / King's Cross. *(re-iss. May88; PCSDX 104) (w/free US 12" or cd-s)* – Always on my mind.

PET SHOP BOYS: Rent / (non-OST songs/versions)

Oct 87. (7"/12"/c-s/cd-s) *Parlophone; (R/12R/TCR/CDR 6168)* [8] [–]

PET SHOP BOYS: Always On My Mind / (non-OST songs/versions)

Nov 87. (7"/12"/c-s/cd-s) *Parlophone; (R/12R/TCR/CDR 6171)* *EMI America; <50123>* [1] Mar88 [4]

IT HAPPENED AT THE WORLD'S FAIR

1963 (US 104m) Metro-Goldwyn-Mayer (PG)

Film genre: Rock'n'roll Musical drama

Top guns: dir: Norman Taurog ← GIRLS! GIRLS! GIRLS! ← BLUE HAWAII ← G.I. BLUES / → TICKLE ME → SPINOUT → DOUBLE TROUBLE → SPEEDWAY → LIVE A LITTLE, LOVE A LITTLE / s-w: Si Rose, Seaman Jacobs

Stars: Elvis PRESLEY *(Mike Edwards)*, Joan O'Brien *(Diane Warren)* → GET YOURSELF A COLLEGE GIRL, Gary Lockwood *(Danny Burke)* ← WILD IN THE COUNTRY / → MODEL SHOP, Vicky Tiu *(Sue-Lin)*, Yvonne Craig *(Dorothy Johnson)* → KISSIN' COUSINS → ADVANCE TO THE REAR → SKI PARTY, H.M. Wynant *(Vince Bradley)*, Edith Atwater *(Miss Steuben)*, Sandra Giles *(Lily)* ← DADDY-O, Kurt Russell *(boy who kicks Mike)* → ELVIS: THE MOVIE

Storyline: The World's Fair in Seattle is the backdrop for the trifling adventures of Mike Edwards and his right hand man, Danny Burke, a pair of crop-dusting pilots who find love at the expo. *BG*

Movie rating: *4

Visual: video + dvd

Off the record: nothing

ELVIS PRESLEY (composers: Leith Stevens, etc.)

Apr 63. (lp; mono/stereo) *R.C.A.; <LSP 2697> (RD/SF 7565)* [4] May63 [4]
– Beyond the bend / Relax / Take me to the fair / They remind me too much of you / One broken heart for sale / I'm falling in love tonight / Cotton candy land / A world of our own / How would you like to be? / Happy ending. *(re-iss. Aug81 on 'RCA Int.'; INTS 5033) (re-iss. Jan84 lp/c; NL/NK 82568) <(cd/c-iss.Mar93 +=; 74321 13431-2/-4)>* – Fun In Acapulco (tracks). *(cd re-iss. Apr03 on 'Follow That Dream'+=; FTD 23)* – (bonus takes).

S/track review: While this record lacks the breadth of its predecessor, it still ranks as one of the best of ELVIS' early soundtracks, selling by the bucketload and attracting rave reviews for its lead single, 'One Broken Heart For Sale'. An exuberant, doo-wop-influenced shuffle in the same vein as 'Return To Sender', the song nevertheless inexplicably broke with a long line of No.1's upon its UK release; perhaps it was just too similar to 'Return..' Whatever, the Don Robertson-penned ballads 'I'm Falling In Love Tonight' and 'They Remind Me Too Much Of You', as well as 'A World Of Our Own', are as impressive a showcase as you'll find for PRESLEY's vocals at this stage in his career, sounding just fine alongside mandatory escapist fare like 'Take Me To The Fair' and 'Happy Ending'. *BG*

Album rating: *4.5

– spinoff hits, etc. –

ELVIS PRESLEY: One Broken Heart For Sale / They Remind Me Too Much Of You

Feb 63. (7") *<47-8134> (RCA 1337)* [11] [53] [12]

IT'S A BIKINI WORLD

1967 (US 86m) Trans America (PG-13)

Film genre: Pop/Rock Musical comedy

Top guns: s-w: (+ dir) Stephanie Rothman, Charles S. Swartz

Stars: Deborah Walley *(Delilah Dawes)* ← SPINOUT ← the GHOST IN THE INVISIBLE BIKINI ← SKI PARTY ← BEACH BLANKET BINGO, Tommy Kirk *(Mike/Herbert Samson)* ← the GHOST IN THE INVISIBLE BIKINI ← PAJAMA PARTY / → CATALINA CAPER, **Bob Pickett** *(Woody)* → MONSTER MASH: THE MOVIE, Suzie Kaye *(Pebbles)* ← C'MON, LET'S LIVE A LITTLE ← WILD, WILD WINTER / → CLAMBAKE, Jack Bernardi *(Harvey Pulp)* ← the WILD ANGELS ← BEACH BALL / → WILLIE DYNAMITE → FOXY BROWN, William O'Connell *(McSnigg)*, Sid Haig *(Daddy)* ← BEACH BALL / → BLACK MAMA, WHITE MAMA → COFFY → FOXY BROWN → the FORBIDDEN DANCE → JACKIE BROWN → HOUSE OF 1000 CORPSES → KILL BILL: VOL.2 → the DEVIL'S REJECTS, Pat McGee *(Cindy)*, Jim Begg *(boy)* ← the COOL ONES / → CATALINA CAPER → DEATH WISH II, Lori Williams *(girl)*, **the ANIMALS: Eric Burdon, Hilton Valentine, Barry Jenkins, Dave Rowberry, Chas Chandler** *(performers)*, **the Gentrys:- Larry Raspberry, Jimmy Hart, Bruce Bowles, Bobby Fisher, Neal, Jimmy Johnson, Larry Wall** *(performers)*, **the Toys:- Barbara Harris, June Montiero, Barbara Parritt** *(performers)*, **the Castaways:- Richard Robey, Roy Hensley, Robert Folschow, James Donna, Dennis Craswell** *(performers)*, **Lolly & Pat Vegas** *(performers)*

Storyline: Another beach romp with a plot thinner than the bikini-clad babes who literally bust out all over the movie. Mike is a hunky chauvinist surfer who is surprisingly shunned by feminist Delilah. As a ploy to win her affections, he decides to pose as his imaginary bespectacled brother, Herbert, but he becomes smitten by her intelligence rather than her beauty. *MCS*

Movie rating: *3.5

Visual: none (no audio OST; score: MIKE CURB & BOB SUMMERS)

Off the record: The **Gentrys** were US hitmakers from Memphis, their biggest being Top 5 smash, 'Keep On Dancing'; here they sing 'Spread It On Thick'. The **Toys** (from Woodrow Wilson High School, Jamaica, New York) nearly topped the charts with 'A Lover's Concerto', a song adapted from Bach's 'Minuet From The Anna Magdalena Notebook'; their follow-up Top 20 gem, 'Attack' features here. The **Castaways** (from St. Paul, Minnesota) scored a #12 hit via, 'Liar, Liar'; all performed in the film. All the aforementioned tracks charted in 1965. Brothers **Lolly & Pat Vegas** sang non-hit 'Walk On (Right Out Of My Life)' in the film; as Redbone they had three subsequent Top 50 hits in the 70s, 'Maggie', 'The Witch Queen Of New Orleans' & 'Come And Get Your Love'. The **ANIMALS** have their own entry but contribute their 1965 classic, 'We Gotta Get Out Of This Place', to the movie. *MCS*

IT'S ALL GONE PETE TONG

2005 (UK/Can 90m) Vertigo Films (15)

Film genre: mockumentary; Rave-music satire

Top guns: s-w + dir: Michael Dowse ← FUBAR

Stars: Paul Kaye *(Frankie Wilde)*, Mike Wilmot *(Max Haggar)*, Beatriz Batarda *(Penelope)*, Kate Magowan *(Sonja)* ← 24 HOUR PARTY PEOPLE, David Lawrence *(Horst)* ← FUBAR, **Paul Spence** *(Alfonse)* ← FUBAR, Tim Plester *(Brent Tufford)* ← CONTROL, **Pete Tong** *(himself)*, **Carl Cox** *(himself)* ← HUMAN TRAFFIC ← BETTER LIVING THROUGH CIRCUITRY ← MODULATIONS, **Fatboy Slim/Norman Cook** *(Lol Hammond)*, **Tiesto** *(himself)*, Gordon Skilling *(Coke Badger)* ← FUBAR

Storyline: Paul Kaye, (who up until this film had been famous only for accosting stars on the red carpet and asking them rude questions as Dennis Pennis) dons the headphones as a celebrated Ibiza superstar DJ Frankie Wilde who finds himself going deaf while at the peak of his powers. How does a man who relies on his hearing survive? The tragic/ridiculous premise sets this one up meaning you know you're not going to get Battleship Potemkin. *MR*

Movie rating: *6.5

Visual: dvd

Off the record: **Pete Tong** (b.30 Jul'60, Dartford, Kent, England) was indeed a proper DJ/producer and the most inspirational guy ever to sit at the mixing desk or feature at dance/rave nights. His numerous 'Essential Section' volumes and 'Dance Nation' sets of the 90s are an indie music man's nightmare. *MCS*

—

Various Artists (score: GRAHAM MASSEY *)

May 05. (d-cd) *Positiva; (311213-2)* ☐ ☐
– Pacific state – Massey's conga mix (808 STATE) * / Cloud watch (LOL HAMMOND) / Dry pool suicide (*) / Moonlight sonata (*) / Baby piano (LOL HAMMOND) / Ku da ta (PETE TONG & CHRIS COX) / Mirage (MOROCCAN BLONDE) / Troubles (the BETA BAND) / Parlez moi d'amour (LUCIENNE BOYER) / Need to feel loved – horizontal mix (REFLEKT feat. DELLINE BASS) / It's over (the BETA BAND) / Halo – Goldfrapp remix (DEPECHE MODE) / How does it feel? (AFTERLIFE) / Holding on – album version (FERRY CORSTEN feat. SHELLEY HARLAND) / Four-four-four (FRAGILE STATE) / Music for a found harmonium (PENGUIN CAFE ORCHESTRA) / Learning to lip-read (*) / Good vibrations (the BEACH BOYS) / interlude / White lines (BAREFOOT) // intro / DJs in a row (SCHWAB) / Flashdance – Raul Rincon remix (DEEP DISH) / Good to go – mix with Christophe Monier & DJ Pascal Representent (JUGGERNAUT) / Blue water – original mix (BLACK ROCK feat. DEBRA ANDREW) / Back to basics – main vocal mix (SHAPESHIFTERS) / Up & down – superclub (SCENT) / Serendipity (PETE TONG & STEVE MAC presents LINGUA FRANCA) / Plastic dreams – Tayo & Acid Rockers remix (JAYDEE) / Rock your body rock – Rennie Pilgrem'a hum remix (FERRY CORSTEN) / Can you hear me now? – club mix (DOUBLEFUNK feat. FRANKIE WILDE) / Musak – Steve Lawler remix (TRISCO) / Yimanya (FILTERHEADZ) / Need to feel loved – Seb Fontaine's & Jay P's Type remix (REFLEKT feat. DELLINE BASS) / More intensity (PETE TONG & CHRIS COX) / Frenetic – short mix (ORBITAL).

S/track review: This isn't the Ibiza of Union Jack-blazoned beer monsters and vomiting ladettes, this is an island where dancing, partying and general good vibes prevail. What chemicals inspire such spirited behaviour remain up for debate but the modus operandi is downright positive and this expansive 2-disc collection captures a rhythmical 24 hours with flair without relying on obvious big hitters of the day. Like 'HUMAN TRAFFIC' before it, 'IT'S ALL GONE PETE TONG' effortlessly captures the euphoria and escapism of clubbing, something that's partly down to cunning sound editing but also, as is illustrated here, the choice of music. GRAHAM MASSEY of Manchester electronica dons 808 State throws in a few cunning atmospheric nuggets to warm things up including a mix of the timeless 'Pacific State', a genius tune that, like much of this, is a product of its time but is still incredibly evocative. Meanwhile, the inclusion of crackers from the BETA BAND ('Troubles' & 'It's Over'), PENGUIN CAFE ORCHESTRA ('Music For A Found Harmonium'), 'Good Vibrations' by the BEACH BOYS and a piano bar jazz reworking of 'White Lines' suggest the notion of chill out is entirely in the ear of the beholder. Disc two kicks off as the sun goes down and ups the tempo but never gets too manic, the throbbing house enjoying a lick of disco joy to ensure things don't get too banging. ORBITAL bring things full circle, 'Frenetic' being the ideal song to watch the sun rise to. Despite its length, this is a fairly consistent, considered blend of warm up, freak out and come down tunes. The occasional clanger is acceptable, as no mixtape is ever perfect, but this is a soundtrack that captures a moment as sweetly (if not succinctly) as that of 'a HARD DAY'S NIGHT'. The film may not be a smash but much of the music is spot on. *MR*

Album rating: *7

IT'S ALL HAPPENING

US title 'the DREAM MAKER'

1963 (UK 74m) British Lion Films / Columbia Pictures

Film genre: children's Rock'n'roll Musical comedy

Top guns: dir: Don Sharp ← the GOLDEN DISC / s-w: Leigh Vance

Stars: **Tommy STEELE** *(Billy Bowles)*, Angela Douglas *(Julie Singleton)* ← SOME PEOPLE, Michael Medwin *(Max Catlin)* ← the DUKE WORE JEANS / → I'VE GOTTA HORSE → O LUCKY MAN!, Walter Hudd *(J.B. Madgeburg)*, Bernard Bresslaw *(Parsons)*, Jean Harvey *(Delia)*, Richard Goolden *(Lord Sweatstone)*, **Russ Conway** *(himself)*, **Danny Williams** *(performer)* ← PLAY IT COOL

Storyline: A&R talent scout, Billy Bowles is a good sort. A one-time orphan, he goes back to his stamping ground every Saturday to play with the children. Inspired by his uneviable background and the kids, he sets up a benefit gig to provide neccessary monies. With numerous song and dance people on parade, it is surprisingly crooning Billy that gains most of the attention. *MCS*

Movie rating: *4

Visual: dvd

Off the record: (see below)

—

Various Artists (composer: Philip Green)

1963. (lp) *Columbia; (33SX 1533/SCX 3486)* ☐ ☐
– tracks by: – What do you want (TOMMY STEELE) / The dream maker (TOMMY STEELE) / Eggs and chips (TOMMY STEELE) / You are (MARION RYAN) / Lover man (MARION RYAN) / On a day without you (DANNY WILLIAMS) / Whittling time away (TONY MERCER) / Somebody else not me (SHANE FENTON & THE FENTONES) / (JOHN BARRY) / (CLYDE VALLEY STOMPERS) / It's summer (GEORGE MITCHELL SINGERS) / Once upon a time in Venice (GEORGE MITCHELL SINGERS)

S/track review: An array of British talent fits the musical bill here on 'IT'S ALL HAPPENING'. Whether it was or not, people at the time had their own opinions whether it was indeed "happening". Of course, many will already know of the cherub-faced TOMMY STEELE, a singer with several musicals under his belt ('The TOMMY STEELE STORY' & 'The DUKE WORE JEANS') and who'd charted numerous times since 1956/7's 'Rockin' With The Caveman' and chart-topper 'Singing The Blues'. Here, he only got three chances to shine, 'What Do You Want', 'The Dream Maker' (a failed 45) and the not so delicious 'Eggs And Chips'; when the er ... novelty wore off, he struck a better chord as Arthur Kipps in 1963's 'Half A Sixpence'. South African-born/English-based, velvet-voxed crooner, DANNY WILLIAMS (who'd also had a UK No.1 – 'Moon River' in '61), found it hard to be here 'On A Day Without You', while MARION RYAN (one-hit-wonder-maker in 1958 with 'Love Me Forever') popped out with her 'Lover Man'. The Scots were on full parade also, Falkirk-born GEORGE MITCHELL (and his Singers, rather than his "un-PC" Black & White Minstrels!) plus the CLYDE VALLEY STOMPERS both found time to supply a few showpieces each. Multi-talented film composer-to-be, JOHN BARRY (here as arranger on 4 numbers and who'd been working on 'Zulu' around the same time), was indeed man of the moment, while SHANE "I'm A Moody Guy" FENTON (& HIS FENTONES) would find his moment(s) a decade later when as Alvin Stardust he charted with 'My Coo-Ca-Choo'. *MCS*

Album rating: *3.5

– spinoff releases, etc. –

TOMMY STEELE: The Dream Maker / Eggs And Chips

May 63. (7") *(DB 7070)* ☐ ⊟

IT'S ALL OVER TOWN

1963 (UK 55m) British Lion Films

Film genre: Rock'n'roll Musical comedy

Top guns: dir: Douglas Hickox → JUST FOR YOU / s-w: Stewart Farrar, Lance Percival

Stars: Lance Percival *(Richard Abel)* → MRS. BROWN, YOU'VE GOT A LOVELY DAUGHTER → YELLOW SUBMARINE, William Rushton *(fat friend)*, **Frankie Vaughan** *(performer)*, **Wayne Gibson** *(performer)*, **Alan Davison** *(performer)*, **Clodagh Rodgers** *(performer)*, **the Bachelors:- Declan Cluskey, Con Clusky, John Stokes** *(performers)* → JUST FOR YOU → DISK-O-TEK HOLIDAY → I'VE GOTTA HORSE, **the Springfields: Dusty Springfield, Tom Springfield, Mike Hurst** *(performers)*, **the Hollies:- Allan Clarke** *(performer)*, **Tony Hicks** *(performer)*, **Graham Nash** *(performer)* <= CROSBY, STILLS & NASH =>, **Eric Haycock** *(performer)*, **Bobby Elliott** *(performer)* / **Acker Bilk** *(performer)* ← IT'S TRAD, DAD! / → the GHOST GOES GEAR, **Ivor Cutler** *(himself)* → MAGICAL MYSTERY TOUR

Storyline: Some people want to visit every football ground in the country, others to climb every mountain. Stagehand Richard Abel and his fat friend decide to take in every show in town no matter what the cost or the strain on the London Underground. On their travels they get to see the best of British pop bands on stage and go behind the scenes, proving that the West End has not met its Waterloo just yet. *JZ*

Movie rating: *4.5

Visual: video

Off the record: (see below)

—

Various Artists

Dec 63. (lp) *Philips; (BL 7609)* ☐ ⊟
– Down and out (the SPRINGFIELDS) / Moraca mamba (the SPRINGFIELDS) / The stars will remember (the BACHELORS) / Please let it happen (ALAN DAVISON) / Come on let's go (WAYNE GIBSON) / Give me the moonlight (FRANKIE VAUGHAN) / Wouldn't you like it (FRANKIE VAUGHAN) / Alley alley O (FRANKIE VAUGHAN) / Gonna be a good boy now (FRANKIE VAUGHAN) / It's all over town (FRANKIE VAUGHAN) / Now's the time (the HOLLIES) / My love will still be there (CLODAGH RODGERS).

S/track review: Quite an array of Brit talent on show here, including opening act the SPRINGFIELDS (featuring Dusty!), who'd already had five hits, their biggest being Top 10'ers 'Island Of Dreams' and 'Say I Won't Be There'. For 'IT'S ALL OVER TOWN', the folk trio contributed the similarly-themed 'Down And Out' and 'Moraca Mamba', while future minor hitmaker WAYNE GIBSON (with 1964's 'Kelly') rocked a bit via 'Come On Let's Go'. Dublin-based vocal trio the BACHELORS (1963 being their breakthrough year via 'Charmaine', 'Faraway Places' & 'Whispering') supplied easy-listening ballad, 'The Stars Will Remember'; another Irish singer (and future Eurovision hitmaker), CLODAGH RODGERS, appeared here with 'My Love Will Still Be There'. Manchester's newest chartbusters, the HOLLIES (in the hit parade at the time with 'Stay'), were the closest thing to rock here courtesy of 'Now's The Time'. Star of the show, before he indeed went to Hollywood, FRANKIE VAUGHAN (best known for UK version of 'The Green Door'), sang five cues, the best of which was flop 45, 'Alley Alley O'. Sequel movie ('JUST FOR YOU') by Hickox was a vehicle for new protégés Peter (Asher) And Gordon (Waller). *MCS*

Album rating: *3

– spinoff releases, etc. –

FRANKIE VAUGHAN: Alley Alleh O / Gonna Be A Good Boy Now

Jan 64. (7") *(BF 1310)* ☐ ⊟

IT'S TRAD, DAD!

1962 (UK 73m b&w) British Lion Films / Columbia Pictures

Film genre: Rock'n'jazz Musical comedy

Top guns: dir: Dick Lester → a HARD DAY'S NIGHT → HELP! → GET BACK / s-w: Milton Subotsky ← JAMBOREE ← ROCK, ROCK, ROCK! / → JUST FOR FUN

Stars: Helen Shapiro *(heroine)* → PLAY IT COOL, **Craig Douglas** *(hero)*, Timothy Bateson *(coffeeshop owner)*, Frank Thornton *(TV director)* → GONKS GO BEAT → the MAGIC CHRISTIAN → SIDE BY SIDE, Felix Felton *(mayor)*, Derek Nimmo *(head waiter)* ← a HARD DAY'S NIGHT, Arthur Mullard *(police chief)* → CUCKOO PATROL → SMASHING TIME, Deryck Guyler *(narrator)* → a HARD DAY'S NIGHT → FERRY 'CROSS THE MERSEY, **Gene Vincent** *(himself)* ← HOT ROD GANG ← the GIRL CAN'T HELP IT / → LIVE IT UP → BLUE SUEDE SHOES → NO DIRECTION HOME, **John Leyton** *(himself)* → EVERY DAY'S A HOLIDAY, **Gene McDaniels** *(performer)* → the YOUNG SWINGERS, **Chubby Checker** *(performer)* ← TWIST AROUND THE CLOCK ← TEENAGE MILLIONAIRE / → DON'T KNOCK THE TWIST → LET THE GOOD TIMES ROLL → PURPLE PEOPLE EATER → TWIST, Bruce Lacey *(gardener)* → HELP!, Hugh Lloyd *(usher)* → JUST FOR FUN / → QUADROPHENIA, **Acker Bilk** *& His Paramount Jazz Band (performers)* → IT'S ALL OVER TOWN → the GHOST GOES GEAR, **Temperance Seven** *(performers)*, **the Paris Sisters** *(performers)*, **Kenny Ball & His Jazzmen** *(performers)* → LIVE IT UP, **Del Shannon** *(performer)*, **the Brook Brothers** *(performers)*, **Gary "U.S." Bonds** *(performer)*, **Chris Barber** *(performer)* → RED, WHITE & BLUES, **Bob Wallis & His Storyville Jazzmen** *(performer/s)*, **Terry Lightfoot & His New Orleans Jazzband** *(performer/s)*, **Sounds Incorporated** *(performers)* → LIVE IT UP → JUST FOR FUN / → POP GEAR, **Ottilie Patterson**, Alan Freeman *(disc jockey)* → JUST FOR FUN → ABSOLUTE BEGINNERS, David Jacobs *(disc jockey)* ← the GOLDEN DISC / → JUST FOR FUN → STARDUST, Pete Murray *(disc jockey)* ← the 6.5 SPECIAL

Storyline: In a typical English town at the start of the 60s, the mayor and council try to banish the trad jazz music craze. Fear not! Helen and Craig are on hand to prove to the old fuddy-duddies that their music is not in fact one step away from anarchy. This they do by organizing a concert featuring all the big names of the jazz scene, who turn up to save the day. *JZ*

Movie rating: *5.5

Visual: none

Off the record: Tracks that didn't make it on to the OST are:- 'You

Never Talk About Me' (DEL SHANNON), 'Seven Day Weekend' (GARY "U.S." BONDS), 'Dream Away Romance' (the TEMPERANCE SEVEN), 'Aunt Flo' (BOB WALLIS AND HIS STORYVILLE JAZZMEN), 'Bellissima' (BOB WALLIS AND HIS STORYVILLE JAZZMEN), 'Maryland' (TERRY LIGHTFOOT'S NEW ORLEANS JAZZMEN) and 'Now That We Are Through With Love' (the PARIS SISTERS). *MCS*

—

Various Artists (composer: Ken Thorne)

Apr 62. (lp) *Columbia; (33SX 1412)* [3] [–]
– Tavern in the town (TERRY LIGHTFOOT'S NEW ORLEANS JAZZMEN) / Lonely city (JOHN LEYTON) / Another tear falls (GENE McDANIELS) / In a Persian market (MR. ACKER BILK AND HIS PARAMOUNT JAZZ BAND) / Let's talk about love (HELEN SHAPIRO) / Down by the riverside (CHRIS BARBER'S JAZZ BAND with OTTILIE PATTERSON) / Ring-a-ding (CRAIG DOUGLAS) / Space-ship to Mars (GENE VINCENT) / Everybody loves my baby (the TEMPERANCE SEVEN) / Rainbows (CRAIG DOUGLAS) / Frankie and Johnny (MR. ACKER BILK AND HIS PARAMOUNT JAZZ BAND) / The lose-your-inhibitions twist (CHUBBY CHECKER) / Sometime yesterday (HELEN SHAPIRO) / When the saints go marching in (CHRIS BARBER'S JAZZ BAND with OTTILIE PATTERSON).

S/track review: Overseen by musical supervisor/producer, Norrie Paramor (who also co-wrote a handful of songs!), 'IT'S TRAD, DAD!' is all about Brit-based jazz-pop. Artists such as TERRY LIGHTFOOT, Mr ACKER BILK and CHRIS BARBER (with female accompaniment OTTILIE PATTERSON) all fitted the bill, although traditional songs, 'Tavern In The Town' (LIGHTFOOT), 'Frankie And Johnny' & 'In A Persian Market' (both BILK) plus 'Down By The Riverside' & 'When The Saints Go Marching In' (both BARBER), were miles away from rock'n'roll, R&B or the dancefloor crazes of the time. Ditto the weird and wonderful, Vaudevillian TEMPERANCE SEVEN, whose 'Everybody Loves My Baby' is a precursor to the Bonzos. Yes, this is definitely something your grandad would love. On some sort of mission to retain its teenage audience, there were Brit-pop stars a-plenty, "Johnny Remember Me" chart-topper, JOHN LEYTON with 'Lonely City', "Only Sixteen" chart-topper CRAIG DOUGLAS with two up-tempo cues, 'Ring-A-Ding' & 'Rainbows', plus "Walkin' Back To Happiness" chart-topper, HELEN SHAPIRO also on two numbers, 'Let's Talk About Love' & 'Sometime Yesterday' – mostly written by PARAMOR-Lewis. However, the stars of the show came courtesy of America. "Be-Bop-A-Lula" cool-cat, GENE VINCENT and his 'Space-Ship To Mars' (definitely "Somethin' Else"), dance-floor icon CHUBBY CHECKER with 'The Lose-Your-Inhibitions Twist' and "Tower Of Strength" himself GENE McDANIELS on the David-Bacharach smoocher, 'Another Tear Falls'. 'IT'S TRAD, DAD!' is decidedly split between two camps (maybe three), so take two (maybe three!) of something before you taste this heady cocktail of musical mirth. *MCS*

Album rating: *3.5

– spinoff hits, etc. –

BOB WALLIS / KENNY BALL & HIS JAZZMEN: It's Trad, Dad

1962. (7"ep) *Pye Jazz; (NJE 1083)* [ ] [–]

TERRY LIGHTFOOT & HIS NEW ORLEANS JAZZMEN: Tavern In The Town / Maryland

Apr 62. (7") *(DB 4822)* [49] [–]

HELEN SHAPIRO: Let's Talk About Love / Sometime Yesterday

Apr 62. (7") *(DB 4824)* [23] [–]

JOHN LEYTON: Lonely City

May 62. (7") *H.M.V.; (POP 1014)* [14] [–]

I'VE GOTTA HORSE

1965 (UK 92m) Pathe Films / Warner Bros. Pictures

Film genre: Pop Musical comedy

Top guns: s-w: Kenneth Hume (+ dir), Ronald Wolfe, Ronald Chesney, Larry Parnes

Stars: Billy Fury *(Billy)* ← PLAY IT COOL / → THAT'LL BE THE DAY, Michael Medwin *(Hymie Campbell)* ← IT'S ALL HAPPENING ← the DUKE WORE JEANS / → O LUCKY MAN!, Amanda Barrie *(Jo)*, Bill Fraser *(Mr. Bartholemew)* ← WHAT A CRAZY WORLD, Marjorie Rhodes *(Mrs. Bartholemew)* → the FAMILY WAY → MRS. BROWN, YOU'VE GOT A LOVELY DAUGHTER, John Pertwee *(costumer's assistant)*, Fred Emney *(Lord Bentley)* → BUNNY LAKE IS MISSING → the MAGIC CHRISTIAN, Peter Gilmore *(Jock)* → EVERY DAY'S A HOLIDAY, Leslie Dwyer *(Berl)* → the MAGIC CHRISTIAN, Michael Cashman *(Peter)* → MADE, **the Bachelors** *(performers)* ← DISK-O-TEK HOLIDAY ← JUST FOR YOU ← IT'S ALL OVER TOWN

Storyline: In this nags-to-riches story, pop star Billy is so mad about animals he'd rather play with his pet dogs than turn up for the big summer show rehearsal. Things get worse when he buys a racehorse and trains it up for the Derby, which happens to be on the same day as the concert. As Billy's manager worriedly looks at his watch, will the forgetful singer get to the show on time from the racetrack – will he even remember the show's on at all? *JZ*

Movie rating: *4

Visual:

Off the record: BILLY FURY (see below); Michael Cashman gave up acting in 1997 and went into politics (he's now an MEP). *MCS*

—

BILLY FURY / Various (composers: David Heneker & John Taylor)

Apr 65. (lp) *Decca; (LK 4677)* [ ] [–]
– I've gotta horse (BILLY FURY) / Stand by me (BILLY FURY & THE GAMBLERS) / Do the old soft shoe (BILLY FURY & SHEILA O'NEILL) / I cried all night (the GAMBLERS) / Far far away (the BACHELORS) / I like animals (BILLY FURY) / Find your dream (BILLY FURY) / Dressed up for a man (SHEILA O'NEILL & AMANDA BARRIE) / He's got the whole world in his hands (the BACHELORS) / Won't somebody tell me why (BILLY FURY) / Problems (AMANDA BARRIE & MICHAEL MEDWIN) / You've got to look right for the part (AMANDA BARRIE & JON PERTWEE) / Finale medley (BILLY FURY).

S/track review: 'I'VE GOTTA HORSE' was the er ... vehicle for one-time prince of British pop, BILLY FURY (born Ronald Wycherley, 1940, Liverpool), who'd had numerous hits in the early 60s including Top 3 entries:- 'Halfway To Paradise', 'Jealousy', 'Like I've Never Been Gone' and 'When Will You Say I Love You'. With his heyday behind him then, why oh why did he attempt to venture into the fickle world of movie soundtracks – maybe the celluloid success of a certain Liverpudlian Fab Four might've swayed him. Anyway, FURY virtually put the last nail in his musical coffin, by agreeing to do this. Picturing him on the sleeve with "Carry On" actress/singer (and future Coronation Street soap star) AMANDA BARRIE, and his own racehorse, the LP also features some outsider tracks from the likes of Dublin pop-ballad trio, the BACHELORS ('Far Far Away' and the traditional 'He's Got The Whole World In His Hands'). While the aforementioned work of AMANDA BARRIE is only collaborative and not alongside BILLY FURY, the album cover is therefore slightly misleading. FURY, meanwhile (backed at times by the GAMBLERS: Jim Crawford – lead guitar, Alan George – keyboards, Tony Damond – guitar, trumpet, Ken Brady – sax, Alan Sanderson – bass, and Andy Mac – drums), sings the majority of the songs, although only the title track, the duet 'Do The Old Soft Shoe' (with SHEILA O'NEILL) and 'Find Your Dream' resemble a decent track. If this was indeed a horse, it would've been pulled up after a few furlongs; instead the blame probably lies on colours of main songwriters, David Heneker and John Taylor, while a certain Mike Leander (later the pen of GARY GLITTER) was the musical director. Neigh good, as they say in horsey circles. *MCS*

Album rating: *2

JACKIE BROWN

1997 (US 155m) Miramax Films (R)

Film genre: crime thriller

Top guns: s-w + dir: Quentin Tarantino ← FROM DUSK TILL DAWN ← FOUR ROOMS ← NATURAL BORN KILLERS ← PULP FICTION ← RESERVOIR DOGS / → KILL BILL: VOL.1 → KILL BILL: VOL.2 (nov: 'Rum Punch' by Elmore Leonard ← TOUCH / → BE COOL)

Stars: Pam Grier *(Jackie Brown)* ← BILL & TED'S BOGUS JOURNEY ← SHEBA, BABY ← BUCKTOWN ← FRIDAY FOSTER ← FOXY BROWN ← COFFY ← COOL BREEZE ← BLACK MAMA, WHITE MAMA ← BEYOND THE VALLEY OF THE DOLLS / → BONES, Samuel L. Jackson *(Ordell Robbie)* ← PULP FICTION ← JUICE ← JOHNNY SUEDE ← JUNGLE FEVER ← SCHOOL DAZE ← MAGIC STICKS / → KILL BILL: VOL.1 → KILL BILL: VOL.2 → BLACK SNAKE MOAN, Robert Forster *(Max Cherry)* → GRAND THEFT PARSONS, Bridget Fonda *(Melanie)* ← TOUCH ← GRACE OF MY HEART ← SINGLES ← SHAG: THE MOVIE / → FINDING GRACELAND → SOUTH OF HEAVEN, WEST OF HELL, Robert De Niro *(Louis Gara)* ← WAG THE DOG, Michael Keaton *(Ray Nicolette)* ← BATMAN / → a SHOT AT GLORY, Michael Bowen *(Mark Dargus)* → MAGNOLIA, Chris Tucker *(Beaumont Livingston)* ← HOUSE PARTY 3, Tommy 'Tiny' Lister Jr. *(Winston)* ← TRESPASS ← BLUE CITY, Lisa Gay Hamilton *(Sheronda)* ← KRUSH GROOVE, Sid Haig *(judge)* ← the FORBIDDEN DANCE ← FOXY BROWN ← COFFY ← BLACK MAMA, WHITE MAMA ← IT'S A BIKINI WORLD ← BEACH BALL / → HOUSE OF 1000 CORPSES → KILL BILL: VOL.2 → the DEVIL'S REJECTS

Storyline: Centres around sexy air stewardess Jackie Brown, who's been caught smuggling cash into the country (by ATF agents/cops, Ray Nicolette and Mark Dargus), cash owned by merciless gun-runner Ordell Robbie. He frees Jackie with the aid of lonely bail bondsman Max Cherry, who in turn takes a shine to the feisty lady and helps her hatch a plan to steal $500,000. Meanwhile, Ordell's bikini-clad house-bunny (Melanie) and newfound partner-in-crime (Louis Gara) are also planing to double-cross their pony-tailed benefactor. Tarantino's third movie proper. *MCS*

Movie rating: *9

Visual: video + dvd

Off the record: nothing

Various Artists

Jan 98. (cd/c) *Maverick; <(9362 46841-2/-4)>* **73** Mar98 ☐
– Across 110th Street (BOBBY WOMACK) / (Beaumont's lament – dialogue; Samuel L. Jackson & Robert De Niro) / Strawberry letter 23 (the BROTHERS JOHNSON) / (Melanie, Simone and Sheronda – dialogue; Samuel L. Jackson & Robert De Niro) / Who is he (and what is he to you)? (BILL WITHERS) / Tennessee stud (JOHNNY CASH) / Natural high (BLOODSTONE) / Long time

woman (PAM GRIER) / (Detroit 9000 – dialogue; Council Cargle) / (Holy matrimony) Letter from the firm (FOXY BROWN) / Street life (RANDY CRAWFORD) / Didn't I (blow your mind this time) (the DELFONICS) / Midnight confessions (the GRASS ROOTS) / Inside my love (MINNIE RIPERTON) / (Just ask Melanie – dialogue; Samuel L. Jackson & Robert De Niro) / The lions and the cucumber (VAMPIRE'S SOUND INCORPORATION) / Monte Carlo nights (ELLIOT EASTON TIKI GODS).

S/track review: Ever since the infamous scene in 'RESERVOIR DOGS' where a psychotic Mr Blonde cuts off the cop's ear to the sounds of Stealers Wheel's 'Stuck In The Middle With You', Quentin Tarantino has been hailed for the choice of songs to accompany his films and 'JACKIE BROWN' is no exception. 'Across 110th Street', BOBBY WOMACK's gritty description of growing up in the ghetto sets a precedent which rarely falters throughout. Interspersed with clips from the film, are several soul and funk classics including the excellent 'Who Is He (And What Is He To You)?' from BILL WITHERS, 'Strawberry Letter 23' by BROTHERS JOHNSON and the DELFONICS' 'Didn't I (Blow Your Mind This Time)'. Then there is 'Street Life' by RANDY CRAWFORD, the GRASS ROOTS' 'Midnight Confessions' and 'The Lions And The Cucumber' from VAMPIRE'S SOUND INC.. These tracks are perfectly chosen to reinforce the Blaxploitation themes from the film but it just wouldn't be Tarantino if there wasn't a curveball in their somewhere. Here it comes in the shape of 'Tennessee Stud' by JOHNNY CASH, the tale of one man and his horse is a bit surreal in the context but somehow manages to blend in with its surroundings. Then there is closing track 'Monte Carlo Nights' by (ex-Cars) ELLIOT EASTON, an instrumental track which sounds a bit like a spaced out Chris Isaak taking on the Shadows 'Apache'. 'JACKIE BROWN' is an excellent compilation that shows that a soundtrack can work as an album on its own if the director knows how to pick them. *CM*

Album rating: *8

JACKIE'S BACK!

1999 (US 100m TV) Hearst Entertainment

Film genre: mockumentary/showbiz/R&B-music comedy

Top guns: dir: Robert Townsend ← the FIVE HEARTBEATS / → LITTLE RICHARD → LIVIN' FOR LOVE: THE NATALIE COLE STORY → CARMEN: A HIP HOPERA / s-w: Dee LaDuke, Mark Alton Brown

Stars: Jenifer Lewis *(Jackie Washington)* ← the TEMPTATIONS ← the PREACHER'S WIFE ← GIRL 6 ← SHAKE, RATTLE & ROCK! tv ← WHAT'S LOVE GOT TO DO WITH IT ← BEACHES, Tim Curry *(Edward Whatsett St. John)* ← the WALL: LIVE IN BERLIN ← LEGEND ← TIMES SQUARE ← ROCK FOLLIES OF '77 ← the ROCKY HORROR PICTURE SHOW, T.V. Blake *(Antandra Washington)*, Tangie Ambrose *(Shaniqua Summers Wells)*, Whoopi Goldberg *(nurse Ethyl Washington Rue Owens)* ← the LION KING, David Hyde Pierce *(Perry)*, Tom Arnold *(Marv Pritz)* ← TOUCH, Julie Hagerty *(Pammy Dunbar)* → the STORY OF US → STORYTELLING, JoBeth Williams *(Jo Face)*, Kyla Pratt *(little Jackie)*, Jackie Collins *(herself)* ← ROCK YOU SINNERS, Diahann Carroll *(herself)* ← the FIVE HEARTBEATS ← CLAUDINE, **Patti Austin** *(herself)* ← TUCKER: THE MAN AND HIS DREAM ← ONE-TRICK PONY ← the WIZ ← IT'S YOUR THING, **Dolly PARTON** *(herself)*, **Bette MIDLER** *(herself)*, **Melissa Etheridge** *(herself)* ← WOODSTOCK '94 / → MY GENERATION, Liza Minnelli *(herself)*, Rudy Ray Moore *(bad guy)* ← DISCO GODFATHER ← PETEY WHEATSTRAW ← the MONKEY HUSTLE ← DOLEMITE / → BIG MONEY HUTLA, Ricki Lake *(herself)* ← CRY-BABY ← LAST EXIT TO BROOKLYN ← WORKING GIRL ← HAIRSPRAY / → HAIRSPRAY re-make, Rosie O'Donnell *(herself)*, → TARZAN, Penny Marshall *(herself)* ← the SAVAGE SEVEN, **Taylor Dayne** *(herself)*, Don Cornelius *(himself)* ← TAPEHEADS ← ROADIE ← NO WAY BACK ← CLEOPATRA JONES, Robert Bailey Jr. *(Wilson Wells)* → TOO LEGIT: THE MC HAMMER STORY, **Grace Slick** *(herself)* ← FILLMORE ← GIMME SHELTER ← a NIGHT AT THE FAMILY DOG ← MONTEREY POP, **Mary Wilson** *(Vesta Crotchley)* ← BEACH BALL ← the T.A.M.I. SHOW, **Freez Luv** *(Larry; die-hard fan)* ← MURDER WAS THE CASE ← HOUSE PARTY 3 / → COYOTE UGLY

Storyline: R&B-soul singer from the 60s and 70s, Jackie Washington, has been on a slippery slope to downsville of late, but with the organisation of a comeback gig, she thinks the late 90s will see her star re-born. Things don't quite go to plan, however. The movie was first aired on the 14th June, 1999 for Lifetime. *MCS*

Movie rating: *5

Visual: video + dvd (no audio OST; score: Marc Shaiman)

Off the record: A plethora of famous singers feature here, Jefferson Airplane's **Grace Slick**, the Supremes' **Mary Wilson, Patti Austin, Taylor Dayne, Melissa Etheridge, PARTON + MIDLER**. Jackie's songs include 'Yield' & 'Look At Me (My Love For You Has Only Made Me Love Me More)'. *MCS*

the JACKSONS: AN AMERICAN DREAM

1992 (US 4 epi x 55m mini-TV) Motown / De Passe / ABC

Film genre: Pop/Rock-music/showbiz bio-pic/drama

Top guns: dir: Karen Arthur / s-w: Joyce Eliaison ← ELVIS AND ME

Stars: Lawrence Hilton-Jacobs *(Joseph Jackson)* ← YOUNGBLOOD ← CLAUDINE ← DEATH WISH / → SOUTHLANDER, Angela Bassett *(Katherine Jackson)* → WHAT'S LOVE GOT TO DO WITH IT → STRANGE DAYS → MASKED AND ANONYMOUS, Holly Robinson *(Diana Ross)* ← HOWARD THE DUCK, Margaret Avery *(Martha)* ← HELL UP IN HARLEM ← COOL BREEZE, Alex Burrall *(Michael Jackson; aged 6-8)*, Jason Weaver *(Michael Jackson; aged 9-14)*, Jermaine Jackson II *(Jermaine Jackson; aged 13-17)*, Bumper Robinson *(Jackie; aged 12-16)*, Floyd Roger Myers Jr. *(Marlon; aged 7-9)*, Monica Calhoun *(Rebbie)*, Angel Vargas *(Tito)*, Terrence Dashon Howard *(Jackie)* → WHO'S THE MAN? → GLITTER → RAY → HUSTLE & FLOW → GET RICH OR DIE TRYIN' → IDLEWILD, Billy Dee Williams *(Berry Gordy)* ← BATMAN ← NIGHTHAWKS ← LADY SINGS THE BLUES ← the FINAL COMEDOWN, **Vanessa Williams** *(Suzanne de Passe)* → DANCE WITH ME, Grady Harrell *(Jackie Wilson)*, **Jimmy Castor** *(Royal)*, Lamman Rucker *(Rebbie's husband)* → the TEMPTATIONS

Storyline: The Jacksons were a working class family brought up as Jehovahs Witnesses and taught strict discipline. The children turned to music as a release and when father Joe realised they had talent he began to plan a musical career for them. At first performing in their neighbourhood, they soon began touring Indiana and made their first full recording in 1967. As we all know, success and fame were soon at hand. *JZ*

Movie rating: *6

Visual: dvd (no audio OST)

Off the record: **Jimmy Castor** had a solo hit ('Hey, Leroy, Your Mama's Callin' You') in early 1967, and as the Jimmy Castor Bunch, he had three more funk/R&B smashes, including 1972's Top 10 'Troglodyte'. *MCS*

JACQUES BREL IS ALIVE AND WELL AND LIVING IN PARIS

1974 (Fra/Can 97m) The Ely Landau Prganization and Cinevision

Film genre: theatrical Pop-Rock Musical drama

Top guns: dir: Denis Heroux / s-w: Eric Blau (+ play w/ **Mort Shuman, Jacques Brel**

Stars: Elly Stone *(lady with shopping bag/performer)*, **Mort Shuman** *(taxi driver/performer)*, Joe Masiell *(marine/performer)*, **Jacques Brel** *(himself/performer)*

Storyline: Three strangers take shelter from a rainstorm in an old theatre alongside a group of cranks and weirdos. Jacques Brel himself sits in the balcony and watches a puppet show which portrays the three strangers as marionettes. From there they undergo a Dali-esque series of events which take them directly from backstage to the beach wondering when they get to go home to the real world. *JZ*

Movie rating: *6

Visual: video (no audio OST; composer: JACQUES BREL)

Off the record: Watch out for a plethora of off-Broadway/London Cast album releases which are not connected to the actual movie. *MCS*

ELLY STONE / MORT SHUMAN / JOE MASIELL
with JACQUES BREL (himself)

Dec 74. (d-lp) *Atlantic; <SD2-1000>*
– Madeleine / Marathon (les Flamandes) / My childhood (Mon enfance) / The statue (la Statue) / Brussels (Bruxelles) / Jackie (la chanson de Jacky) / Timid Frieda (les Timides) / The taxicab (le Gaz) / Old folks (les Vieux) / Alone (Seul) / I loved (J'aimais) / Funeral tango (tango Funebre) / Bachelor's dance (la Bouree du celibataire) // Amsterdam / Ne me quitte pas / The desperate ones (les Deseperes) / Sons of . . . (Fils de . . .) / The bulls (les Toros) / Marieke / The last supper (le Dernier repas) / Mathilde / Middle class (les Bourgeois) / Song for old lovers (la Chanson des vieux amants) / Next (au Suivant) / Carousel (la Valse a mille temps) / If we only had love (Quand on n'a que l'amour).

S/track review: It's a pity the title of the movie doesn't bear true in today's post-millennium, naughty noughties, although in 1974, JACQUES BREL was indeed alive and well and living in Paris. Here, we celebrate the classic Belgian-born singer-songwriter (and you can't say that too often!) and all his remarkable songs. In the 60s, "BREL was to Europe what Dylan was/is to America" as sleevenotes by playwright Eric Blau suggested; it was the latter's idea in 1967 to get BREL's work onto stage and screen. 'JACQUES BREL IS ALIVE . . .' is not a "rock" soundtrack, more like 'Cabaret' meets 'The Producers', but it is important to the "rock" world due to the many artists who were inspired enough to cover his songs. With music conducted and arranged by Francois Rauber, this double-LP totally differs from its original stage-production cousin, while crediting the film's stars, ELLY STONE (funny lady and long-standing BREL fan), MORT SHUMAN (the same man who wrote for Elvis, Ray Charles, etc in the 50s/60s) and the underrated JOE MASIELL. The latter of the said troupe sounded a little like Gene Pitney in his heyday, while ELLY took on a Nana Mouskouri-meets-Mary Hopkin pitch. For most of the songs on record, with all their tragi-comedy and World War I themes, one can almost feel the pain of BREL via one's lonely bedsit where the reverbs of Leonard Cohen once played. Marc Almond was once (and still is) a major fan, and here we see why, courtesy of 'The Bulls'. Ditto SCOTT WALKER, who also completed a BREL covers album with most of the film's highlights, including the bitter-sweet 'Mathilde'. Speeding up to a climactic crescendo and spinning to a new degree in musical dizziness, 'Carousel' and its spiralling accomplice ELLY STONE take you a place called Vertigo. 'Amsterdam', meanwhile, finds solace in the easy canyons of your mind and soul, the song soon-to-be the flipside of Bowie's re-issued 'Space Oddity' chart-topper. Lyrically excellent throughout, BREL's mission is to save souls through his wayward transfigurations, prime examples being 'The Taxicab', drunken barroom drawl, 'The Middle Class' and by far his greatest three minutes, the MASIELL-sung, brothel-creeper 'Next'. The latter had already become "rock" folklore and the loot of the (Sensational) Alex Harvey (Band), the Scotsman even naming his/their second LP after the track. With lyrics like "One day I'll cut my legs off/I'll burn myself alive", how could you not be a cult icon. Just when think you've had enough, up pops 'Alone', 'If We Only Had Love' and 'Ne Me Quitte Pas', all classics in their own right, with the latter featuring a cameo from BREL himself. Sadly, BREL had virtually retired from the limelight when he died in 1978. *MCS*

Album rating: *8.5

the JAGUARS

Formed: Tokyo, Japan . . . mid-60s by Yukio Miya, Shin Okamoto, Hisayuki Okitsu, Yasuji Sato, Mikio Morida, Kiochi Miyazaki and Takeshi Hameno, a Japanese Group Sounds (GS) outfit, who were in the shadow of their country's finest, the SPIDERS. The Japanese fixation with the Beatles movie, 'HELP!', was all too obvious in the JAGUARS' one and only entry into celluloid history, 'HEY YOU, GO' (1968). Psychedelic prism effects, Buddhist monks going through customs, fuzz guitars and without a word in English (until they sing!), the band's time in the music scene was all too brief and they disbanded in 1971. *MCS*

JAILBIRD ROCK

aka 'PRISIONEROS DE LA DANZA'

1988 (Arg/Pan/US 92m) Continental Motion Pictures (R)

Film genre: Rock Musical drama

Top guns: dir: Phillip Schuman / s-w: Edward Kovach, Carole Stanley (story: Eduard Sarlui)

Stars: Robin Antin *(Jessie Harris)*, Valerie Gene Richards *(Peggy)*, Robin Cleaver *(Echo)*, Rhonda Aldrich *(Max)*, Jacquelyn Houston *(Samantha)*, Debra Laws *(Lisa)*, Erica Jordan *(Judy)*, Perry Lang *(Denny)*, Ron Lacey *(Warden Bauman)*, Maria Noel *(Mary)*, **Arthur Brown** *(guard)* ← CLUB PARADISE ← TOMMY ← the COMMITTEE / → I PUT A SPELL ON ME, **George Black, Howard Huntsberry & Lucy Sustar** *(singing voices)*

Storyline: Tagged "Prison took away her freedom, but not her dreams" (her = Jessie Harris), this is basically an adult women-in-prison movie inspired by the likes of 'Flashdance' and 'Scrubbers'. The usual cliché'd things happen: knife fights, butch lesbians, and er . . . choreographed dancing, as the movie (and its badly dubbed acting!) never lets you forget that its a musical. *MCS*

Movie rating: *3.5

Visual: video 1988 (no audio OST)

Off the record: Songs featured in the movie are performed by WORLD WITHOUT END (and sung by . . .):- 'Can't Shake The Beat' (GEORGE BLACK), 'Over And Out' (HOWARD HUNTSBERRY), 'Wind On My Wings' (GEORGE BLACK), 'Heart Of Me' (DEBRA LAWS), 'Just Luck' (LUCY SUSTAR) & 'Gotta Move' (DEBRA LAWS). *MCS*

JAILHOUSE ROCK

1957 (US 96m b&w) Avon Productions / M.G.M. (PG)

Film genre: Rock'n'roll Musical comedy

Top guns: dir: Richard Thorpe → FOLLOW THE BOYS → FUN IN ACAPULCO / s-w: Guy Trosper (story: Nedrick Young)

Stars: Elvis PRESLEY *(Vince Everett)*, Judy Tyler *(Peggy Van Alden)* ← BOP GIRL, Mickey Shaughnessy *(Hunk Houghton)*, Vaughn Taylor *(Mr. Shores)*, Dean Jones *(Teddy Talbot)*, Jennifer Holden *(Sherry Wilson)*, Anne Neyland *(Laury Jackson)*, Percy Helton *(Sam Brewster)* ← SHAKE, RATTLE AND ROCK! / → WHERE THE BOYS ARE → GET YOURSELF A COLLEGE GIRL → HEAD, Don Burnett *(Mickey Alba)* ← UNTAMED YOUTH

Storyline: The story of Vince Everett, a talented con who wows his fellow inmates with hip-swivelling charisma and a stunning voice, scoring a surprise hit single while still in stir. Upon his release, Vince sets up his own record label although he soon discovers the seedier side of the music business. *BG*

Movie rating: *7.5

Visual: video + dvd

Off the record: On a tragic note, 23-year-old Judy Tyler (with her new husband Gregory LaFayette) was killed in a road accident on the 3rd of July, 1957. *MCS*

—

ELVIS PRESLEY (composers: Various)

1983. (lp) *R.C.A.; (PL 42792)* [–] German [–]
– Jailhouse rock / Treat me nice / I want to be free / Don't leave me now / Young and beautiful / (You're so square) Baby I don't care / (movie versions on B-side). *(UK-iss.May92 on 'Ariola Express' cd+=/ c+=; 2/4 95051) <(cd re-iss. Feb98 +=; 07863 67453-2)>* – (bonus tracks; some not from the movie). *(lp re-mast.Jan02 on 'Castle'++=; ELVIS 111)* – (bonus 7" singles).

S/track review: One of only a handful of films which captured the full-force swagger of a pre-army PRESLEY, 'JAILHOUSE ROCK' is the one movie, the one song, and probably the one dance routine (even the one guitar part, courtesy of Scotty Moore) which everyone knows, ELVIS buff or otherwise. The title song remains one of the most inspired to emanate from the golden pens of Jerry Leiber and Mike Stoller, and PRESLEY grabs it by the proverbial balls, possessing it with an almost supernatural self-belief, sexuality and subversive authority. The same writers came up trumps yet again with the fluid, rolling groove of 'Treat Me Nice', wherein ELVIS gets to show off some of his finest syllable-swallowing vocals. Released as a single, these two tracks (different versions – in the case of 'Jailhouse . . .' minus the backing vocal parts – from the ones which appeared in the movie) topped the US chart for just under two months in late 1957, going on to scale the British Top 40 early the following year. The soundtrack EP – with 'Jailhouse Rock' as its lead track – also went to No.1, featuring 'Treat Me Nice', and Leiber/ Stoller's hat trick, '(You're So Square) Baby I Don't Care' amongst others. The CD re-issue collects together both the EP/single and all the original movie versions, as well as the usual alternate takes. *BG*

Album rating: *6

– spinoff hits, etc. –

ELVIS PRESLEY: Jailhouse Rock / Treat Me Nice

Oct 57. (7",78) *R.C.A.; <47-7035> (RCA 1028)* [1]
[18] Jan58 [1]
(re-iss. May77; PB 2695) – (hit UK No.44 in Aug'77) *(re-iss. Jan83, hit No.27, also on 7"pic-d diff B-side THE ELVIS MEDLEY)*

ELVIS PRESLEY: Jailhouse Rock EP

Nov 57. (7"ep) *<EPA 4114> (RCX 106)* [ ] Jan58 [18]
– Jailhouse rock / Young and beautiful / I want to be free / Don't leave me now / (You're so square) Baby I don't care. *(re-iss. Mar60 + Feb82)*

ELVIS PRESLEY: Jailhouse Rock / Treat Me Nice

Jan 05. (cd-s) *Sony-BMG; (82876 66715-2)* [–] [1]
(10"+=) *(82876 66715-1)* – Treat Me Nice (alt.)

JAMBOREE!

UK title 'DISC JOCKEY JAMBOREE'

1957 (US 71m b&w) Warner Bros. (PG)

Film genre: romantic Rock'n'roll Musical comedy

Top guns: dir: Roy Lockwood / s-w: Milton Subotsky ← ROCK, ROCK, ROCK! / → IT'S TRAD, DAD! → JUST FOR FUN, Leonard Kantor → HONEYBABY, HONEYBABY

Stars: Kay Medford *(Grace Show)* → TWO TICKETS TO PARIS, Paul Carr *(Pete Porter)*, Bob Pastine *(Lew Arthur)*, David King-Wood *(Warren Sykes)*, Freda Holloway *(Honey Wynn)*, Jean Martin *(Cindy Styles)*, Tony Travis *(stage manager)* → the BEATNIKS, **Aaron Schroder** *(songwriter)*, **Connie FRANCIS** *(singing voice; Honey Wynn)*, **Fats DOMINO** *(performer)*, **Jerry Lee LEWIS** *(performer)*, Howard Miller *(himself)* → the BIG BEAT, **Carl Perkins** *(performer)* → the MAN, HIS WORLD, HIS MUSIC → JOHNNY CASH AT SAN QUENTIN → LITTLE FAUSS AND BIG HALSY, **Jodie Sands** *(performer)*, **Frankie AVALON** *(performer)*, **Buddy Knox** *(performer)* → SWEET COUNTRY ROAD, **the Four Coins** *(performer)*, **Jimmy Bowen** *(performer)*, **Slim Whitman** *(performer)*, **Louis Lymon & the Teenchords** *(performer/s)*, **Joe Williams** *(performer)* → SING SING THANKSGIVING → PETEY WHEATSTRAW, **Charlie Gracie** *(performer)*, Dick Clark *(himself)* → WILD IN THE STREETS → the PHYNX → DEADMAN'S CURVE, **Count Basie** *(performer)*

Storyline: Pete Porter and Honey Wynn are a singing duo whose romantic numbers on stage lead to romantic encounters back stage. However, our lovebirds are at the mercy of scheming showbiz agent Grace Shaw, who splits them up for her own purposes. Of course, this is only in a background to numerous rock'n'roll stars of the day who literally steal the show. *JZ*

Movie rating: *6

Visual: video on Warners (ext. to 86m)

Off the record: (see below)

—

Various Artists

1957. (lp) *Warners; <promo>* [–] promo [–]
– Jamboree! (COUNT BASIE & HIS ORCHESTRA) / Record hop tonight (ANDY MARTIN) / For children of all ages (CONNIE FRANCIS) / Glad all over (CARL PERKINS) / Who are we to say (CONNIE FRANCIS & PAUL CARR) / Teacher's pet (FRANKIE AVALON) / Sampre (CONNIE FRANCIS) / Cool baby (CHARLIE GRACIE) / Sayonara (JODIE SANDS) / Great balls of fire (JERRY LEE LEWIS) / Toreador (RON COLEY) / Your last chance (LOUIS LYMON & THE TEENCHORDS) / If not for you (PAUL CARR) / Unchain my heart (SLIM WHITMAN) / A broken promise (the FOUR COINS) / One o'clock jump (COUNT BASIE & HIS ORCHESTRA) / I don't like you no more (JOE WILLIAMS) / Crazy to care (MARTHA LOU MARY) / Cross over (JIMMY BOWEN) / Hula love (BUDDY KNOX) / Wait and see (FATS DOMINO) / Twenty four hours a day (CONNIE FRANCIS & PAUL CARR).

S/track review: Only a promo LP/EP was released; the score was by Otis Blackwell & Neal Hefti. Billed as "18 Great Stars 22 Wonderful songs". Apart from FATS DOMINO's 'Wait And See' hit, the movie also features JERRY LEE LEWIS ('Great Balls Of Fire'), CARL PERKINS ('Glad All Over'), COUNT BASIE & HIS ORCHESTRA ('One O'Clock Jump') & BUDDY KNOX ('Hula Love'). Teddy Randazzo & Cirino Colacrai penned two songs for CONNIE (Freda Holloway in the movie):- 'Toreador' & 'I Don't Like You No More'. Songwriter/producer/publisher, Aaron Schroder, co-penned numerous hits for Elvis, Bobby Vee, etc. Expect to pay up to $500 on ebay. *MCS*

Album rating: *4

– spinoff hits, etc. –

BUDDY KNOX: Hula Love / Devil Woman

Aug 57. (7"/78) *Roulette; <4018> Columbia; (DB 4014)* [9] Sep57 [ ]

FATS DOMINO: Wait And See

Oct 57. (7",78) *Imperial; <5467> London; (HLP 8519)* [23] Nov57 [ ]

□ JAN & DEAN segment
(⇒ DEADMAN'S CURVE)

JANIS ET JOHN

2003 (Fra 104m) Fidelite / Mars Films (15)

Film genre: workplace crime caper/comedy

Top guns: s-w: (+ dir) Samuel Benchetrit, Gabor Ressov

Stars: Sergi Lopez *(Pablo Sterni)*, Marie Trintignant *(Brigitte Sterni)*, Francois Cluzet *(Walter Kingkate)*, Christopher Lambert *(Leon)* ← PAROLES ET MUSIQUE, Jean-Louis Trintignant *(Mr. Cannon)*, Amparo Soler Leal *(la mere de Pablo)*

Storyline: Insurance salesman Pablo Sterni finds himself in a tight spot when it looks like his "creative accountancy" will be uncovered, to the tune of half a million francs. However salvation is at hand in the unlikely figure of his cousin Leon, who has just inherited a million francs and whose sole purpose in life is to await the Second Coming of Janis Joplin and John Lennon. Can Pablo pull off the impossible and make Leon's dream come true – and con him out of his inheritance at the same time? *JZ*

Movie rating: *6

Visual: dvd

Off the record: On the verge of completion, the film was marred by the death of lead actrees, Marie Trintignant, who murdered on 1st of August, 2003, by her boyfriend and lead singer of Noir Desir, Bertrand Cantat; at the time of her death she was still married to the film's first-time director, Samuel Benchetrit. *MCS*

Various Artists (+ dialogue)

Nov 03. (cd) *Fidelite – Virgin; (94355-2)* [–] French [–]
– (dialogue Pablo) / Janie Jones (the CLASH) / (dialogue Pablo + Leon) / Tonight (IGGY POP) / (dialogue Pablo + Walter) / I woke up this morning (TEN YEARS AFTER) / (dialogue Brigitte) / Down on me – live (JANIS JOPLIN) / (dialogue Pablo + Brigitte + Walter) / 50,000 miles beneath my brain (TEN YEARS AFTER) / (dialogue Walter) / I sing (the KEATLES) / Taking some time on (BARCLAY JAMES HARVEST) / (dialogue Brigitte + Pablo) / If you should love me (TEN YEARS AFTER) / (dialogue Brigitte) / Workin' together (IKE & TINA TURNER) / (dialogue Mr. Cannon) / Cosmic dancer (T REX) / Kozmic blues (JANIS JOPLIN) / Isolation (JOHN LENNON) / Where is my mind (the PIXIES). *(w/ bonus video bande annonce teaser, etc.).*

S/track review: You have to hand it to whoever had the job of selecting the music for French flick, 'JANIS ET JOHN', because here is a collection of some fantastic songs that will send shivers down your spine. Indeed, it could easily be someone's tape for their car masquerading as a soundtrack. The only annoying thing is the dialogue clips between almost every song, which I am sure are either hilarious or insightful but, alas, are in French, so I wouldn't know. The soundtrack explodes into life with the thumping drums of 'Janie Jones' from the CLASH, arguably still the best opening track of all time, and is closely followed by IGGY POP's lavishly epic 'Tonight'. TEN YEARS AFTER appear with a handful of classic English blues-rock tracks, 'I Woke Up This Morning', '50,000 Miles Beneath My Brain' and 'If You Should Love Me', all of which are full of bass-heavy licks, killer guitar solos and wailing vocals. IKE & TINA TURNER's 'Workin' Together' is beautifully gritty soul at its best, 'Cosmic Dancer' from T REX just oozes class and the PIXIES' wonderfully disorientating 'Where Is My Mind' just seems like the perfect way to finish before reaching for the play button again. Finally, it wouldn't be a film about people thinking they are JANIS JOPLIN and JOHN LENNON without some input from the actual artists. The former is represented with the intense 'Kozmic Blues' and a live version of stomper 'Down On Me', while the latter appears with 'Isolation', a tender piano-led ballad close to the man's heart at the time. It's a great feeling when you listen to a bunch of songs that someone else has put together and find that you love every single one, especially if you haven't heard them for a long time or not at all. The soundtrack to 'JANIS ET JOHN' is one of those albums. *CM*

Album rating: *8

the JAZZ SINGER

1980 (US 115m) E.M.I. Films (PG)

Film genre: showbiz/Pop-Rock Musical drama

Top guns: dir: Richard Fleischer / s-w: Herbert Baker ← KING CREOLE ← LOVING YOU ← the GIRL CAN'T HELP IT, Arthur Laurents, Stephen H. Foreman (au: Samson Raphaelson)

Stars: Neil DIAMOND *(Yussel Rabinovitch)*, Laurence Olivier *(Cantor Rabinovitch)* ← BUNNY LAKE IS MISSING, Lucie Arnaz *(Molly Bell)*, Catlin Adams *(Rivka Rabinovitch)*, Franklyn Ajaye *(Bubba)* ← CAR WASH / → GET CRAZY → QUEEN OF THE DAMNED, **Paul NICHOLAS** *(Keith Lennox)*, Sully Boyar *(Eddie Gibbs)* ← CAR WASH, Mike Kellin *(Leo)* ← the PHYNX, James Booth *(Paul Rossini)* ← THAT'LL BE THE DAY, Janet Brandt *(Aunt Tillie)* ← FM, Hank Garrett *(police sergeant)* ← DEATH WISH, James Karen *(Barney Callahan)* → the RETURN OF THE LIVING DEAD → GIRL, Ernie Hudson *(heckler)* ← LEADBELLY / → ROAD HOUSE → the CROW → AIRHEADS → the BASKETBALL DIARIES → a STRANGER IN THE KINGDOM, John Witherspoon *(MC at Cinderella club)* → HOUSE PARTY → the FIVE HEARTBEATS → RIDE

Storyline: Hackneyed remake of the Al Jolson classic with Diamond as Yussel Rabinovitch, a likeably bland Jewish cantor/ageing wannabe who doesn't fancy singing in the local synygogue for the rest of his life. He gets his big break after a snotty new wave band cover one of his songs, but soon cracks under the twin pressures of L.A. and marital breakdown. What's a man to do when his orthodox father disowns him? Grow a beard, of course, and hit the road with furrowed brow. Oh, and become a cowboy troubadour. *BG*

Movie rating: *3.5

Visual: video

Off the record: (see own entries)

NEIL DIAMOND

Nov 80. (lp/c) *Capitol; <(EAST/TCEAST 12120)>* [3] [14]
– America / Adon olom / You baby / Love on the rocks / Amazed and confused / On the Robert E. Lee / Summerlove / Hello again / Acapulco / Hey Louise / Songs of life / Jerusalem / Kol nidre – My name is Yussel / America (reprise). *(cd-iss. Jul84; CDEAST 12120) <cd-iss. 1992; 46026> <US cd-iss. 1996 on 'Columbia'; 67569> (re-iss. Jul98 on 'Columbia' cd/c; 483927-2/-4)*

S/track review: "What is jazz to Neil Diamond and what is Neil Diamond to jazz?" asked 'Variety' back in the day, and they had a point. The Jewish Elvis had about as much of a handle on jazz as glam rockers Slade, whose mid-70s biopic 'FLAME' (1974) was as brutally realistic a portrait of the music business as DIAMOND's effort was an embarrassing, PG-certificate gloss on it. And despite the pointless title, and the fact that it was sandwiched between two of the poorest albums of his career, the soundtrack sold by the skipful. Such is showbusiness, and that's what 'The JAZZ SINGER' deals in – flag-waving bombast like 'America', where tinny 80s synth and hollow platitudes ("freedom's light burning warm") schlep together like hot dogs and mustard. 'You Baby' ends with a scrum of movie dialogue: "That ain't no brother, it's a white boy!", lifted from one of the movie's dodgiest scenes; no matter how much boot polish DIAMOND puts on his face he's just not going to sound black. He's blessed with one of rock's great voices, but it's the voice of a "blue-eyed" balladeer; one that Rick Rubin admired enough to engineer a Johnny Cash-style resurgence with '12 Songs' (2005). That album was acclaimed as his best in decades, exploding the Vegas clichés and stripping back the schlock to recover the singer-songwriter of yore.

This soundtrack is where the schlock gets out of hand, overpowering decent songs like 'Love On The Rocks' and 'Hello Again', and even kitsch belters like 'Hey Louise'. While 'The JAZZ SINGER' will likely attract more attention and even more apologists as DIAMOND's star rises again, the fact is it raised the curtain on an era he'll probably want to forget, as will most of his discerning fans. *BG*

Album rating: *5.5

– spinoff hits, etc. –

NEIL DIAMOND: Love On The Rocks / Acapulco

Oct 80. (7") *<4939> (CL 16173)* 2 17

NEIL DIAMOND: Hello Again / Amazed And Confused

Jan 81. (7") *<4960> (CL 16176)* 6 51

NEIL DIAMOND: America / Songs Of Life

Apr 81. (7") *<4994> (CL 16197)* 8

JESUS CHRIST SUPERSTAR

1973 (US 108m) Universal Pictures (G)

Film genre: religious Pop/Rock Musical drama

Top guns: s-w: Norman Jewison (+ dir), Mervyn Bragg (book: Tim Rice → EVITA)

Stars: Ted Neeley *(Jesus Christ)* → HARD COUNTRY, Carl Anderson *(Judas Iscariot)*, **Yvonne Elliman** *(Mary Magdalene)* → SGT. PEPPER'S LONELY HEARTS CLUB BAND, Barry Deenen *(Pontius Pilate)* → SHOCK TREATMENT, Bob Bingham *(Caiaphas; High Priest)*, Kurt Yaghjian *(Annas)*, Larry T. Marshall *(Simon Zealotes)* → ROADIE, Joshua Mostel *(King Herod)* → the BASKETBALL DIARIES, Kurt Yaghjian *(Annas)* → HAIR, Philip Toubus *(Peter)*, Marcia McBroom *(woman)* ← COME BACK, CHARLESTON BLUE ← BEYOND THE VALLEY OF THE DOLLS / → WILLIE DYNAMITE

Storyline: Concentrates on the last few weeks of the life of Jesus as seen through the eyes of Judas Iscariot. Judas becomes more and more concerned at his master's behaviour after his rampage at the moneylenders' temple and his growing affinity with Mary Magdalene. In despair, he visits the High Priest and begins to conspire against Jesus. Don't worry, I won't give away the ending. *JZ*

Movie rating: *6.5

Visual: video + dvd

Off the record: Honolulu-born **Yvonne Elliman** (who'd already had a hit with the stage version of 'I Don't Know How To Love Him') remained part of the Robert Stigwood Organisation (R.S.O.) and had four subsequent UK Top 30 hits between 1976-78: 'Love Me', 'Hello Stranger', 'I Can't Get You Out Of My Mind' & 'If I Can't Have You' (the latter from 'SATURDAY NIGHT FEVER'). *MCS*

—

Various Cast (music: Andrew Lloyd Webber / lyrics: Tim Rice)

Jun 73. (d-lp/c) *M.C.A.; <11000> (MCX/+C 502)* 21 Sep73 23
– Overture / Heaven on their minds / What's the buzz / Strange thing mystifying / Then we are decided / Everything's alright / This Jesus must die / Hosanna / Simon Zealotes / Poor Jerusalem / Pilate's dream / The temple / I don't know how to love him / Damned for all time – Blood money // The last supper / Gethsemane (I only want to say) / The arrest / Peter's denial / Pilate and Christ / King Herod's song / Could we start again, please? / Judas' death / Trial before Pilate / Superstar / The crucifixion / John nineteen forty one. *<(d-cd iss.Mar98/Dec99 on 'Universal'; MCA 11757)> (1-cd-iss. Oct00 on 'Sony'; 501092-2)*

S/track review: 'JESUS CHRIST SUPERSTAR' is a difficult one to assess as it relies on the listener/audience to forego years of Sunday worship doctrine and take on a revisionist OTT hippy-glam. The Rock Opera (double-album) soundtrack also integrates overbearing symphonics with conventional "rock" musicians and, of course, the all-singing, all-dancing cast. Conducted by classical composer, André Previn, with music and orchestration by Andrew Lloyd Webber and lyrics by Tim Rice (all three very established in the high faluting bow-tie world), one knows exactly what's in store. 'Overture' opens the story, a guitar-vs-orchestra piece that segues into (Judas) CARL ANDERSON's first vocal cue, 'Heaven On Their Minds'. Funky beats and gospel singing (provided by Jesus – TED NEELEY, Mary Magdalene – YVONNE ELLIMAN and the cast of Apostles) emerge and register via 'What's The Buzz', one of several songs that have lasted the pace of time. The other highlight from side one is Mary Magdalene, Jesus, Judas & the Apostles' uplifting sing-a-long, 'Everything's Alright'. Without using too many spiritual, divine and celestial clichés, "JESUS CHRIST SUPERSTAR transcends the boundaries of both set and stage to become a statement of historical and contemporary significance", as it says on the back cover/sleeve. Side two, however, is just too dramatical for it to work musically, although there is one timeless number, YVONNE ELLIMAN's 'I Don't Know How To Love Him', rated one of Lloyd Webber/Rice's best tunes ever. Side three kicks off and continues relentlessly with shards of melancholy, possibly the subject matter too solemn to just "jolly-it-up" for the sake of it, that's until the uptempo, pastiche and vaudevillean 'King Herod's Song'. ELLIMAN is unquestionably the superSTAR here, her crystal-clear vox opening side four by way of 'Could We Start Again, Please?'. To fit a Batman theme into the intro of follow-on track 'Judas' Death' is plain sacrilegious, although there was definitely no intention. 'Superstar' is another song to "retro-fry" the brain into submission, but there's no denying its appeal – TED NEELEY simply shines out. *MCS*

Album rating: *6.5

JOE'S APARTMENT

1996 (US 80m) Geffen Pictures / Warner Bros. Pictures (PG-13)

Film genre: Pop-Rock Musical fantasy comedy

Top guns: s-w + dir: John Payson

Stars: Jerry O'Connell *(Joe)*, Megan Ward *(Lily Dougherty)*, Jim Sterling *(Jesus Bianco / voice; cockroach)*, Jim Turner *(Walter Shit / voice; cockroach)*, Shiek Mahmud-Bey *(Vladimir Bianco)*, Don Ho *(Alberto Bianco)*, **Sandra Denton** *(Blank)*, Billy West *(voice; Ralph Roach)*, Reginald Hudlin *(voice; Rodney Roach)* ← HOUSE PARTY, Robert Vaughn *(Sen. Dougherty)* → POOTIE TANG, David Huddleston *(P.I. Smith)* ← NORWOOD, Paul Bartel *(NEA scout)* ← GET CRAZY ← ROCK'N'ROLL HIGH SCHOOL, **Richard 'MOBY' Hall** *(performer)* → MODULATIONS → BETTER LIVING THROUGH CIRCUITRY → MY GENERATION → ALIEN SEX PARTY → AMERICAN HARDCORE, **Boss Hog:- Jon Spencer *, Cristina Martinez, Jens Jurgensen, Hollis Yungblut** *(performers)* → YOU SEE ME LAUGHIN' * → the SOUL OF A MAN * → MONKS: THE TRANSATLANTIC FEEDBACK *, Carol Woods *(pt. the Roach Chorus)* → BROOKLYN BABYLON, Nick Zedd *(pizza couple guy)* ← WHAT ABOUT ME, Vincent Pastore *(apartment broker #2)* ← WALKING AND TALKING ← the BASKETBALL DIARIES ← WHO'S THE MAN? ← BLACK ROSES

Storyline: Based on a short film made for MTV in 1992, this is a somewhat gross-out version of a nice couple (Joe and Lily) living in a run-down apartment in New York. They take on the mite (sic!) of 50,000+ all-singing, all-dancing cockroaches and of course a landlord whose interests are to get rid of his hapless tenants. "Sex, Bugs, Rock'n'Roll" – indeed! *MCS*

Movie rating: *4

Visual: video + dvd (no audio OST; score: Carter Burwell)

Off the record: Songs written by KEVIN WEIST & JOHN PAYSON and performed by the ROACH CHORUS (*) are as follows:- 'Joe's

Apartment Theme' (MEL TORME & *), 'Rotten Apple' (OPERATION RATIFICATION), 'Garbage In The Moonlight' (*), 'Cat Rodeo' (*), 'Funky Towel' (*), 'Sewer Surfin'' (*), 'Hold My Feeler' (*); other tracks of the alt-rock & rave/dance variety include 'Discharge' (LAST EXIT), 'New York City' (MADBALL), 'Shoo Bee Do Bee Do' (LA BOUCHE), 'Impossible Mission' (DIAMOND D), 'Nod Off' (SKELETON KEY), 'Winn Coma' (BOSS HOG), 'The Incumbent' (SOUL COUGHING), 'The Tallest Building In The World' (MOBY), 'Loi Sai Da' (MOBY), 'Love Theme' (MOBY), 'Waiting' (the RENTALS), 'On The Sand' (GROOVE THING), 'Involved' (VELDT), 'Apiary' (YUM-YUM), 'Prayin' (For A Jeapbeat)' (NIGHTMARES ON WAX), 'De La F.U.N.K.Y. Towel' (DE LA SOUL) and '86' (GREEN DAY). **Sandra Denton** is the Pepa from Salt-N-Pepa. *MCS*

JOEY

1986 (US 97m) Rock & Roll Productions / Satori Entertainment (PG)

Film genre: Rock'n'roll Musical teen drama

Top guns: dir + s-w: Joseph Ellison (story: Ellen Hammill)

Stars: Neill Barry *(Joey/Joseph King Jr.)*, Frank R. Lanziano *(Frankie Lanz)*, James Quinn *(Joseph King Snr.)*, Ellen Hammill *(Bobbie)*, Linda Thorson *(Principal O'Neill)*, Elisa Heinsohn *(Janie)*, Dan Grimaldi *(Ted)*, **the Limeliters** *(performers)*, **the Silhouettes** *(performers)*, **the Elegants** *(performers)*, **the Teenagers** *(performers)*, **the Ad-Libs** *(performers)*, **Vito Balsamo Group** *(performers)*, **Screamin' Jay Hawkins** *(performer)* ← AMERICAN HOT WAX ← MISTER ROCK AND ROLL / → MYSTERY TRAIN → I PUT A SPELL ON ME

Storyline: Joey is a 17-year old guitarist who gets a chance to perform with a 50s-style vocal outfit, much to the envious dismay of his one-time Doo Wop singer dad, Joe Sr. *MCS*

Movie rating: *5.5

Visual: video + dvd (no audio OST)

Off the record: Besides the late, great **Screamin' Jay Hawkins** other pop groups included **the Limeliters** (i.e. Alex Hassilev, Lou Gottlieb and Ernie Sheldon), **the Silhouettes** who had a No.1 hit in 1958 with 'Get A Job', and **the Elegants** who followed them to the top that year via Doo-Wop classic 'Little Star'. In 1965, **the Ad-Libs** gatecrashed the US Top 10 with 'The Boy From New York City', while **the Teenagers** were once the backing singers for Frankie Lymon, 'Why Do Fools Fall In Love', etc. *MCS*

JOHNNY SUEDE

1991 (US/Fra/Swi 93m) Vega / Balthazar / Arena / Starr Films (R)

Film genre: romantic Rock-Music/Showbiz comedy

Top guns: dir (+ s-w): Tom DiCillo

Stars: Brad Pitt *(Johnny Suede)* → FIGHT CLUB → the ASSASSINATION OF JESSE JAMES . . ., Catherine Keener *(Yvonne)* → WALKING AND TALKING → INTO THE WILD, Calvin Levels *(Deke)*, Alison Moir *(Darlette)*, **Nick CAVE** *(Freak Storm)*, Peter McRobbie *(Flip Doubt)*, Dennis Palato *(Dalton)*, Ron Vawter *(Winston)*, Ashley Gardner *(Ellen)*, Tina Louise *(Mrs. Fontaine)*, Samuel L. Jackson *(B-Bop)* ← JUNGLE FEVER ← SCHOOL DAZE ← MAGIC STICKS / → JUICE → PULP FICTION → JACKIE BROWN → KILL BILL: VOL.1 → KILL BILL: VOL.2 → BLACK SNAKE MOAN

Storyline: Johnny Suede dreams of becoming a rock star as he sits in his flat listening to vintage rock'n'roll records. One day a pair of black suede shoes literally falls out of the sky at his feet, and he thinks this is the sign he's been waiting for. However things don't change right away and Johnny ends up selling his guitar to pay the rent. He meets Darlette, who soon tells him she doesn't love him, and it's not until he meets the worldly-wise Yvonne that things finally begin to fall into place. *JZ*

Movie rating: *6

Visual: video + dvd (no audio OST)

Off the record: **Nick CAVE** (see own entry)

JOSIE AND THE PUSSYCATS

2001 (US 98m) Universal Pictures (PG-13)

Film genre: showbiz/Pop-music teen comedy

Top guns: s-w + dir: Harry Elfont, Deborah Kaplan

Stars: Rachael Leigh Cook *(Josie McCoy)*, Tara Reid *(Melody Valentine)* ← DR. T & THE WOMEN ← GIRL, Rosario Dawson *(Valerie Brown)* ← HE GOT GAME ← KIDS / → CHELSEA WALLS → RENT, Alan Cumming *(Wyatt Frame)* ← SPICEWORLD, Parker Posey *(Fiona)* ← SUBURBI@ / → a MIGHTY WIND, Gabriel Mann *(Alan M.)* ← THINGS BEHIND THE SUN ← HIGH ART ← I SHOT ANDY WARHOL, Paulo Costanzo *(Alexander Cabot)* → GYPSY 83, Missi Pyle *(Alexandra Cabot)*, Alex Martin *(Les; Du Jour musician)*, Zak Alam *(megastore DJ)* ← LATE NIGHT SESSIONS ← SWEETWATER: A TRUE ROCK STORY, Kurt Max Runte *(German delegate)* ← SWEETWATER: A TRUE ROCK STORY, Seth Green *(Travis; Du Jour band member)* ← PUMP UP THE VOLUME / → BE COOL → ELECTRIC APRICOT: QUEST FOR FESTEROO, Katharine Isabelle *(laughing girl)* → BONES

Storyline: Warning: tHere may bE a subliminaL message hidden in this pLot synOpsis. Manager Wyatt Frame and his boss Fiona have sneakily been inserting subliminal messages into boy supergroup Du Jour's music, and when the band finds out their plane mysteriously crashes. Enter replacements Josie And The Pussycats, but will Wyatt and Fiona pull the wool over their eyes too or will they get the message and reveal the truth? *JZ*

Movie rating: *6

Visual: dvd

Off the record: Josie And The Pussycats stemmed from the Hanna-Barbera cartoon series of the early 70s!

JOSIE AND THE PUSSYCATS (score: John Frizzell)

Mar 01. (cd) *Play-Tone; <85683> Epic; (503179-2)* **16** Aug01
– 3 small words / Pretend to be nice / Spin around / You don't see me / You're a star / Shapeshifter / I wish you well / Real wild child / Come on / Money (that's what I want) / Du Jour around the world (DU JOUR) / Backdoor lover (DU JOUR) / Josie And The Pussycats theme.

S/track review: Surprisingly for a teen movie soundtrack 'JOSIE AND THE PUSSYCATS' features a healthy dose of short blasts of fierce yet melodic heavy rock, akin to the Go-Go's but closer to the grunge of Veruca Salt, particularly on 'Shapeshifter' and the 'Josie And The Pussycats Theme'. '3 Small Words' has pleasing slabs of crushing guitars and the likes of 'Spin Around' are reminiscent of the not-quite-punk polished sound of Jimmy Eat World and Weezer, thanks largely to the presence of Fountains Of Wayne's Adam Schlesinger. 'You're A Star', replete with chugging guitars, has an altogether more alternative life-affirming message than your average girl-band offering, whilst 'I Wish You Well' successfully marries sweet vocals with towering Marshall stacks, and 'Come On' similarly showcases the vocal talents of KAY HANLEY (from Letters To Cleo). Although it is hardly going to change rock history this is a decent little album that races by and is edgier than most posturing teen rockers clogging up the charts, despite it having its fair share of dumb moments, with the covers of 'Money (That's What I Want)' and 'Real Wild Child' particularly weak. It is then left to the pastiche of fictional boyband DU JOUR to close things with their slick parodies featuring some mischievous lyrics. *LF*

Album rating: *6.5

JUBILEE

1978 (UK 104m) Cinegate / Libra Films International (cert X)

Film genre: surreal satire/fantasy

Top guns: s-w: Derek Jarman (+ dir) → IN THE SHADOW OF THE SUN → GLITTERBUG, Christopher Hobbs

Stars: Jenny Runacre *(Queen Elizabeth I / Bod)* ← SON OF DRACULA, Little Nell Campbell *(Crabs)* ← ROCK FOLLIES OF '77 ← LISTZOMANIA ← the ROCKY HORROR PICTURE SHOW / → SHOCK TREATMENT → the WALL → the KILLING FIELDS, **TOYAH Willcox** *(Mad)*, Jordan *(Amyl Nitrate)* → the PUNK ROCK MOVIE → WESTWAY TO THE WORLD → the FILTH AND THE FURY, Hermine Demoriane *(Chaos)*, Linda Spurrier *(Viv)*, Ian Charleson *(Angel)* → ROCK FOLLIES OF '77 → CHARIOTS OF FIRE, Richard O'Brien *(John Dee)* ← the ROCKY HORROR PICTURE SHOW / → FLASH GORDON → SHOCK TREATMENT → SPICEWORLD, **Adam Ant** *(Kid)* → DROP DEAD ROCK → SWEETWATER: A TRUE ROCK STORY, Karl Johnson *(Sphinx)* ← ROCK FOLLIES OF '77, Neil Kennedy *(Max)*, Orlando/Jane Birkett *(Borgia Ginz)*, David Haughton/ Brandon *(Ariel)*, **Wayne County** *(Lounge Lizard)* ← PUNK IN LONDON ← the BLANK GENERATION / → the PUNK ROCK MOVIE → STADT DER VERLORENEN SEELEN → END OF THE CENTURY, Helen Wellington-Lloyd *(lady in waiting)* → the GREAT ROCK'N'ROLL SWINDLE → the FILTH AND THE FURY, **Gene October** *(Happy Days/performer Chelsea)* ← PUNK IN LONDON / → D.O.A. → URGH! A MUSIC WAR, Lindsay Kemp *(cabaret performer)* ← the WICKER MAN / → VELVET GOLDMINE, **Siouxsie** *(performer)* → the PUNK ROCK MOVIE → WESTWAY TO THE WORLD → the FILTH & THE FURY → 24 HOUR PARTY PEOPLE → PUNK: ATTITUDE

Storyline: Queen Elizabeth I is transported 400 years into the future to see what has become of her kingdom. Instead of the glorious splendour she imagined, she finds a London which has become a desolate wasteland where teenage punk girls roam around looking for trouble to relieve the monotony of their lives. Just as bad are the fascist State Police and control freak Borgia Ginz who owns most of the Establishment. Elizabeth finds an unexpected rapport with a group of female rebels who, rather like her, hate convention. *JZ*

Movie rating: *6.5

Visual: video + dvd

Off the record: (see below)

Various Artists (score: BRIAN ENO *)

Apr 78. (lp) *Polydor; (2302 079)* [ ] [-]
– Deutscher girls (ADAM AND THE ANTS) / Paranoia paradise (WAYNE COUNTY AND THE ELECTRIC CHAIRS) / Right to work (CHELSEA) / Nine to five (MANEATERS) / Plastic surgery (ADAM AND THE ANTS) / Rule Britannia (SUZI PINNS) / Jerusalem (SUZI PINNS) / Wargasm in Pornotopia (AMILCAR) / Slow water (*) / Dover beach (*). *(cd-iss. Jan87 on 'E.G.'; EGLP 34) (<cd re-iss. Sep97 on 'Caroline'; 1112>)*

S/track review: The inaugural British punk movie soundtrack, this paved the way for the likes of 'The GREAT ROCK'N'ROLL SWINDLE', etc. Boasting several of the cast of 'The ROCKY HORROR PICTURE SHOW' (1975), including Richard O'Brien and Jordan/Amyl Nitrate, the latter was as SUZI PINNS on two OST numbers, the un-jingo-istic, avant-punk versions of traditional national anthems, 'Rule Britannia' & 'Jerusalem'. Old guard Cockney punks, ADAM AND THE ANTS also featured on a few tracks, the opener 'Deutscher Girls' and 'Plastic Surgery', very simplistic but effective nevertheless, and an exploitative twin-sided Top 20 hit in 1982 when ADAM ruled the pop kingdom. Billed as MANEATERS, the ANT man even combined efforts with JUBILEE actress, TOYAH (Willcox), to kickstart her singing career on the screaming 'Nine To Five'. Embarrassing, to say the least. The Birmingham-born-lass would find her own new wave pop niche via a subsequent solo career and marry a King Crimson. Pick of the punk pack was definitely/defiantly (delete as appropriate), Gene October and his CHELSEA crew, their anthemic 'Right To Work' poignant in an era of spiky-topped dole kids and a futuristic look to an even bigger crisis when Thatcher and the Tories came to power in '79. The inspiration (quite possibly!) for 'HEDWIG AND THE ANGRY INCH' came in the shape of the outrageous Max's Kansas City stalwarts, WAYNE COUNTY AND THE ELECTRIC CHAIRS, and their glam-punk cut, 'Paranoia Paradise'; little did one know back in '77, that he would subsequently become a she and take a walk on the proverbial wild side as Jayne County. The closing three tracks on this hit or "Miss" LP, were of the chalk and cheese variety. Unknowns AMILCAR (and still so!) on funky, mirrorball number, 'Wargasm In Pornotopia' and BRIAN ENO bowing out on two exclusive score soundscapes, 'Slow Water' and 'Dover Beach'. A weird ending indeed. And a number of questions arise: why ENO's inclusion was thought necessary . . . and why AMILCAR, when the film's best piece, 'Love In A Void' by SIOUXSIE & THE BANSHEES was shunted . . . and where were the Slits? *MCS*

Album rating: *6

– spinoff releases, etc. –

ADAM AND THE ANTS: Deutscher Girls / Plastic Surgery

Feb 82. (7") *E.G.; (Ego 5)* [13] [-]

MANEATERS: Nine To Five / SUZI PINNS: Jerusalem

Jul 82. (7") *E.G.; (Ego 8)* [ ] [-]

JUDGMENT NIGHT

1993 (US 109m) Universal Pictures (R)

Film genre: crime thriller

Top guns: dir: Stephen Hopkins / s-w: Lewis Colick → BEYOND THE SEA (+ story w/ Jere Cunningham)

Stars: Emilio Estevez *(Frank Wyatt)* ← YOUNG GUNS II ← MAXIMUM OVERDRIVE ← REPO MAN, Cuba Gooding Jr. *(Mike Peterson)* ← SING / → the FIGHTING TEMPTATIONS, Denis Leary *(Fallon)* ← WHO'S THE MAN? / → WAG THE DOG, Stephen Dorff *(John Wyatt)* ← an AMBUSH OF GHOSTS / → BACKBEAT → S.F.W. → I SHOT ANDY WARHOL, Jeremy Piven *(Ray Cochran)* ← SINGLES, Peter Greene *(Sykes)* → PULP FICTION, **Erik Schrody/Everlast** *(Rhodes)* ← WHO'S THE MAN? / → WOODSTOCK '99, Michael Wiseman *(Travis)*

Storyline: Four young men drive through Chicago on their way to a boxing match. A quick short cut to avoid a traffic jam seems a good idea at the time, but soon the guys are lost in gangland territory and no-one's going to stop and help them. When they witness a cold-blooded shooting they realize they're next as the killers want no traces of the crime. Then comes a life or death chase around the city blocks as the mobsters close in on their prey. *JZ*

Movie rating: *5.5

Visual: video + dvd

Off the record: Erik Schrody.. is Everlast of House Of Pain (opened with Helmet on OST)

Various Artists (score: Alan Silvestri)

Sep 93. (cd/c/lp) *Immortal-Epic; <EK/ET/E 57144> (474183-2/ -4/-1)* [17] Oct93 [16]
– Just another victim (HELMET & HOUSE OF PAIN) / Fallin' (TEENAGE FANCLUB & DE LA SOUL) / Me, myself & my microphone (LIVING COLOUR & RUN D.M.C.) / Judgment night (BIOHAZARD & ONYX) / Disorder (SLAYER & ICE-T) / Another body murdered (FAITH NO MORE & BOO-YAA T.R.I.B.E.) / I love you Mary Jane (SONIC YOUTH & CYPRESS HILL) / Freak momma (MUDHONEY & SIR MIX-A-LOT) / Missing link (DINOSAUR JR. & DEL THE FUNKY HOMOSAPIEN) / Come and die (THERAPY? & FATAL) / Real thing (PEARL JAM & CYPRESS HILL).

S/track review: This unique collision of the worlds of rap and heavy rock presaged the rap metal explosion of the mid to late 90s, and its cult status has only increased over time. The jump-up riff of 'Just Another Victim' kicks things into gear, Page Hamilton's cut glass vocals sear through the sledgehammer riffing. HELMET and HOUSE OF PAIN literally divide the tune between them, starting with the taut, white hot rage of the NYC mob, before the riff is slowed down, the mix made murkier and the effortless flow of Everlast allowed to exude malevolent nonchalance all over the track. The contrast couldn't be more stark as TEENAGE FANCLUB and DE LA SOUL's wonderfully laidback 'Fallin'' breezes along on a funky bass line, its minimalist clean guitar shimmering. LIVING COLOR and RUN DMC's thick, Cream-y heavy blues riffage are set off against RUN's confident proclamations, the bassline pops along, layered guitars widdle, but it's a focused ultra-groovy contribution, bookended by a devastating Sabbath-inspired, doomy breakdown. You wouldn't be surprised to bump into BIOHAZARD and ONYX in a neon-lit dive, and if you did you'd high tail it out fast. With the titular 'Judgment Night' it's a collision of tough guy braggadocio, BIOHAZARD lend themselves very easily to this musical template, their backstreet hardcore aimed squarely at the same streetwise audience as the ONYX crew. Its complete lack of subtlety and grace is compensated by sheer meathead charm. The early 90s were tough for SLAYER, unsure of their direction after their seminal output during the 80s, and embracing a more overtly punk outlook, their pairing with firebrand and political outcast ICE-T is well made. The latter's sole contribution seems to be to shout along with singer Tom Araya, adding little in the way of rap flavouring to the track, but after a cautious mid-tempo start, an upstart riff announces its intent and the track storms off in an Agnostic Front-style direction for its commentary on police brutality in L.A. Jeff Hanneman and Kerry King indulge the anti-soloing that is their trademark, before the whole thing goes off in a blitzkrieg of thrash ferocity. It's breathtaking, though far from groundbreaking. Mike Patton's superb vocal refrain marks 'Another Body Murdered's collaboration with BOO-YA T.R.I.B.E. as the album's highlight, melding uncharacteristically weighty riffola, decorative piano and Patton's gibbering vocal weirdisms, all of which is offset against the T.R.I.B.E's overt Gangsta credentials and exhortations to bang the head. B-Real has made a career out of extolling the virtues of his beloved herb and 'I Love You Mary Jane' is no different from much of CYPRESS HILL's woozy output, SONIC YOUTH's backing vocals and guitar minimalism instill a sleek alterno vibe which only just raises itself above decoration. You have to smile at big-butt-loving SIR MIX-A-LOT's self-referential raps over MUDHONEY's fuzzed-up proto-grunge, and it's a well-worked tune, allowing both sides to shine, executed with humour and slacker cool. It leads into the extremely funky DINOSAUR JR track, with a distinctly psychedelic vibe and effortlessly tripped-out soloing; DEL THE FUNKY HOMOSAPIEN's rich intonation, animated articulation and wordplay give the grainy guitars a refined sheen. FATAL is a very angry man if 'Come And Die' is anything to judge by, and his strained screams verge on silliness, under him THERAPY's energetic combination of ragged punk and solid chunk compensate for a dull programmed drum sound. Back for their second (bonus) contribution, CYPRESS HILL bring out a lo-fi PEARL JAM to get in the mixer with them, but lacking any stand-out contribution from vocalist Eddie Vedder, the effect is to make an intriguing proposition actually pretty bland, groovy as it is. *DF*

Album rating: *8.5

– spinoff releases, etc. –

FAITH NO MORE & BOO-YAA T.R.I.B.E.: Another Body Murdered / HELMET & HOUSE OF PAIN: Just Another Victim

Oct 93. (12"/c-s/cd-s) *(659794-6/-4/-2)* [–] [26]

TEENAGE FANCLUB & DE LA SOUL: Fallin' / Fallin' – final mix / BIOHAZARD & ONYX: Judgment Night – Jam Master Jay mix

Mar 94. (c-s/cd-s) *(660262-2)* [–] [59]

JUICE

1992 (US 95m) Paramount Pictures (R)

Film genre: urban crime drama

Top guns: s-w: Ernest R. Dickerson (+ dir), Gerard Brown

Stars: Omar Epps *(Quincy "Q")* → ALFIE re-make, **Tupac SHAKUR** *(Bishop)*, Jermaine Hopkins *(Steel)*, Khalil Kain *(Raheem)*, **Cindy Herron** *(Yolanda)*, Vincent Laresca *(Radames)*, Samuel L. Jackson *(Trip)* ← JOHNNY SUEDE ← JUNGLE FEVER ← SCHOOL DAZE ← MAGIC STICKS / → PULP FICTION → JACKIE BROWN → KILL BILL: VOL.1 → KILL BILL: VOL.2 → BLACK SNAKE MOAN, Rony Clanton *(Det. Markham)* ← RAPPIN' ← the EDUCATION OF SONNY CARSON, **Queen Latifah** *(Ruffhouse M.C.)* ← HOUSE PARTY 2 ← JUNGLE FEVER / → WHO'S THE MAN? → the COUNTRY BEARS → BROWN SUGAR → HAIRSPRAY re-make, **Oran "Juice" Jones** *(Snappy Nappy Dugout)*, Doctor Dre *(contest judge)* → WHO'S THE MAN? → RIDE → DEATH OF A DYNASTY, Ed Lover *(contest judge)* → WHO'S THE MAN? → RIDE → DOUBLE PLATINUM → DEATH OF A DYNASTY → TUPAC: RESURRECTION, **EPMD:- Erick Sermon** *(bar patron)* → RHYME & REASON → RIDE + **Parrish Smith** *(bar patron)* / **Fab 5 Freddy** *(himself)* ← WILD STYLE ← DOWNTOWN 81 / → WHO'S THE MAN? → TUPAC: RESURRECTION, Flex Alexander *(contest announcer)* → MAN IN THE MIRROR: THE MICHAEL JACKSON STORY

Storyline: Four young black men from Harlem at that first crossroads in life, on the way to becoming men. Initially depicting four kids skipping school, playing at the arcades and indulging in some innocent fun, the tone turns dark as the boys try to deal with growing up and wanting respect. Dealing with life, loves, families, run-ins the with police, the four begin to fragment as each chooses his own path and we witness the often bitter consequences of their reckless or reticent actions. *MR*

Movie rating: *6

Visual: video + dvd

Off the record: Doctor Dre is not thee Dr. Dre, while **Cindy Herron** was singer in En Vogue and **Oran "Juice" Jones** had a 'Def Jam' Top 10 smash in 1986 with 'The Rain'. *MCS*

—

Various Artists (score: GARY G-WIZ)

Jan 92. (cd/c) *M.C.A.; <(MCA D/C 10462)>* [17] Sep92 [ ]
– Uptown anthem (NAUGHTY BY NATURE) / Juice (know the ledge) (ERIC B. & RAKIM) / Is it good to you (TEDDY RILEY feat. TAMMY LUCAS) / Sex, money & murder (M.C. POOH) / Nuff' respect (BIG DADDY KANE) / So you want to be a gangster (TOO $HORT) / It's going down (EPMD) / Don't be afraid (AARON HALL) / He's gamin' on ya (SALT N' PEPA) / Shoot 'em up (CYPRESS HILL CREW) / Flipside (JUVENILE COMMITTEE) / What could be better bitch (SON OF BAZERK) / Does your man know about me (RAHIEM) / People get ready – remix (the BRAND NEW HEAVIES feat. N'DEA DAVENPORT). *(cd re-iss. Oct95; MCLD 19306)*

S/track review: 'JUICE' was intended to be realistic depiction of the urban experience for young black America and it needed a soundtrack to truly reflect this. It was ingrained with hip hop from day one; with Tupac Shakur cast in one of the lead roles and Public Enemy's lauded production team the BOMB SQUAD providing a creditable score. The soundtrack also brought together many of the real credible heavyweights of the scene at this time. Producer of the moment TEDDY RILEY, threw in the album's best non-hip hop moment, a futuristic G-funk swinger called 'Is It Good To You' with TAMMY RILEY on vocals. This is and contributions from SALT

N' PEPA and the BRAND NEW HEAVIES are brief glimmers of light among some seriously dark cuts. MC POOH's slouchy but sinister 'Sex, Money And Murder' and the tremendous 'So You Wanna Be A Gangster' performed by TOO $HORT share a lethargic pace and some sobering guns+glitz=death lyrical subject matter. BIG DADDY KANE teams up with the BOMB SQUAD for the incendiary 'Nuff' Respect' but it takes the mighty EPMD to really blow the bloody doors off. Their rugged rhymes remain among the finest in the rap game and this shows his talents at their very best managing to be insanely catchy but still hard as nails. CYPRESS HILL – who were relative newcomers at this point, it wasn't long before they exploded globally. Their contribution, 'Shoot 'Em Up' only hints at what they were capable of. Only the super smooth R&B vibe of RAHIEM sounds incongruous in the mix here but makes sense within the context of the film. 1992 was still the era of air raid siren samples and big jacking drum machine beats – as pioneered by the aforementioned BOMB SQUAD – and their influence looms large here but this film surfaced on the cusp of when West Coast rap begun to truly become the dominant force (commercially at least) with one rapper as its spiritual figurehead: Tupac Shakur. *MR*

Album rating: *7.5

– spinoff hits, etc. –

ERIC B. & RAKIM: Juice (Know The Ledge)

Feb 92. (c-s/cd-s) <54333> [96] [–]

AARON HALL: Don't Be Afraid

Mar 92. (c-s/cd-s) *<54330> (MCS 1632)* [44] May92 [56]

JULIE AND THE CADILLACS

1999 (UK 102m) Capricorn / Parker Mead Limited

Film genre: showbiz/Pop/Rock Musical drama

Top guns: dir: Bryan Izzard / s-w: John Dean

Stars: Tina Russell *(Julie Carr)*, Ben Richards *(Mike Williams)*, Peter Polycarpou *(Phil Green)* ← EVITA, Victor Spinetti *(Cyril Wise)* ← UNDER THE CHERRY MOON ← MAGICAL MYSTERY TOUR ← HELP! ← a HARD DAY'S NIGHT, **TOYAH Willcox** *(Barbara "Babs" Gifford)*, Thora Hird *(Julie's grandmother)*, James Grout *(Mr. Watkins)*, **Mike Berry** *(Mac MacDonald)*, the Cadillacs:- Billy Boyd *(Jimmy Campbell)* + David Habbin *(John Wood)* + Chris O'Neill *(Tony Henderson)* ← BACKBEAT + Matt Rayner *(Roy Holgate)*, Cameron Blakely *(the Big Rocker)*, Moya Ruskin *(Mandi Spring)*, Linzi Hateley *(Polly Winter)*, Lucy Williamson *(Cindy)*, Jacqueline Kennedy *(Sue)*

Storyline: Julie Carr is lead singer of the Cadillacs, a struggling rock band from Liverpool. She finally gets a break when two London PR men "discover" her band and promise them fame and fortune down south. Like Dick Whittington, the band dream of streets paved with gold, but when their first release is a non-event all hopes of stardom vanish. Julie, thwarted in love as well as her music, becomes a waitress waiting on her luck to turn. *JZ*

Movie rating: *2.5

Visual: none

Off the record: **Mike Berry** had three hits in the early 60s (augmented by the Outlaws): 'Tribute To Buddy Holly', 'Don't You Think It's Time' (a Top 10) & 'My Little Baby'. In 1980, he crooned his way back into the UK Top 10 via, 'The Sunshine Of Your Smile'. In February '93, Brighton-born Peter Polycarpou had a UK Top 30 hit with the theme tune to the BBC drama, 'Love Hurts'. *MCS*

—

Various / JULIE AND THE CADILLACS (*) (composer: John Dean)

Oct 99. (cd) *Red Ball; (BALL CD 114)* [ ] [–]

– Sweat (*) / Best damn party (*) / Everybody needs PR (ADAM, PHIL, BABS AND POLLY) / I want only you (BOBBY JAMES AND THE BELLTONES) / That's the music biz (MIKE AND THE COFFEE BAR CROWD) / First words of love (MIKE AND JULIE) / Rockin' blood (the BIG ROCKER) / Saw a boy (*) / No one plays the 'B' side (PHIL AND ADAM) / Hey Mr Sun (MANDI) / Down (BIG ROCKER AND THE COFFEE BAR CROWD) / Love you more (JULIE) / Out of money (the CADILLACS) / Bubbles (JULIE, CINDY AND SUE) / Maybe I thought you didn't love me (MIKE) / Saw a boy – finale concert (JULIE, MIKE AND THE CADILLACS) / Mr Teaser – finale concert (*).

S/track review: Why this "feel-good" movie was ever released is anybody's guess. It's nothing better than a British stage show (filmed!), while the OST cast production is the audio equivalent of a rock'n'roll pantomime. Derivative sounding – and "where have I heard that song before?" – 'JULIE AND THE CADILLACS' comes under scrutiny right from the opening lines of 'Sweat' and 'Best Damn Party'. Granted, they can all sing in tune, and on track 3 you can even hear former punkette Toyah Willcox (as BABS) on 'Everybody Needs PR' – a song by numbers. Retro-fied to the point of ridicule, 'JULIE . . .' (and its writer, JOHN DEAN), try in vain to whisk us back to a time when doo-wop was the in-thing, although groups like that never ventured across the pond to Blighty. If Chas & Dave (or indeed, Eric Idle) were indeed younger, they might've charmed their way around some of these 50s/60s-styled pop songs. If music be your food of love, stay clear of 'Rockin' Blood' (by the BIG ROCKER), a vampire-themed dirge of banal proportions. 'No One Plays The 'B' Side' is somewhat of a poignant reminder of what happens to crap songs – the bin. I recently bought this for 1p (p+p was £1.24) – tells "shoo-be-doo" everything really. *MCS*

Album rating: *2

JUST FOR FUN

1963 (UK/US 84m b&w) Columbia Pictures

Film genre: Rock'n'roll Musical comedy

Top guns: dir: Gordon Flemyng / s-w: Milton Subotsky ← IT'S TRAD, DAD! ← JAMBOREE ← ROCK, ROCK, ROCK!

Stars: **Mark Wynter** *(Mark)*, Cherry Roland *(Cherry)*, Richard Vernon *(Prime Minister)* → a HARD DAY'S NIGHT, Reginald Beckwith *(opposition leader)* → GONKS GO BEAT, Jeremy Lloyd *(Prime Minister's son)* → SMASHING TIME → the MAGIC CHRISTIAN, Hugh Lloyd *(plumber)* ← IT'S TRAD, DAD! / → QUADROPHENIA, Dick Emery *(juror)* → YELLOW SUBMARINE → LOOT, Irene Handl *(housewife)* → SMASHING TIME → WONDERWALL → the GREAT ROCK'N'ROLL SWINDLE → ABSOLUTE BEGINNERS, Harry Fowler *(interviewer)* ← IDLE ON PARADE, David Jacobs *(disc jockey)* ← IT'S TRAD, DAD! ← the GOLDEN DISC / → STARDUST, Alan Freeman *(disc jockey)* ← IT'S TRAD, DAD! / → ABSOLUTE BEGINNERS, Jimmy Saville *(disc jockey)* → FERRY 'CROSS THE MERSEY → POP GEAR, **Sounds Incorporated w/ Tony Newman** *(performers)* ← LIVE IT UP ← IT'S TRAD, DAD! / → POP GEAR, **the Spotnicks** *(performers)*, **the Springfields** *(performers)*, **Johnny Tillotson** *(performer)*, **the Vernon Girls** *(performers)*, **Joe Brown** *(performer)* → WHAT A CRAZY WORLD → CONCERT FOR GEORGE, **Bobby Vee** *(performer)* ← PLAY IT COOL ← SWINGIN' ALONG / → C'MON, LET'S LIVE A LITTLE, **the Crickets:- Sonny Curtis *, Glen D. Hardin & Jerry Naylor *** *(performers)* → the GIRLS ON THE BEACH, **the Tornados w/ Heinz *** *(performers)* ← * FAREWELL PERFORMANCE ← LIVE IT UP! / → the LONDON ROCK AND ROLL SHOW, **Clodagh Rodgers** *(performer)*, **Louise Cordet** *(performer)* → DISK-O-TEK HOLIDAY, **Kenny Lynch** *(performer)*, **Freddy Cannon** *(performer)* → DISK-O-TEK HOLIDAY, **Ketty Lester** *(performer)*, **Karl Denver** *(performer)*, **Jet Harris & Tony Meehan** *(performers)* ← the YOUNG ONES, **the Tremeloes w/ Brian Poole** *(performers)*, **Jimmy Powell** *(performer)*, Sylvie Vartan *(performer)* → D'OU VIENS-TU, JOHNNY?, Douglas Ives ← LIVE IT UP / → BE MY GUEST

Storyline: Teenage popsters take on the politicians in swinging 60s England.

The old geriatrics in the House of Commons certainly don't want to give these juvenile delinquents the vote (as there's no way the kids would vote for them) so the teeny-boppers decide to form their own political party. They enlist the help of various pop stars and DJ's to publicize their cause and soon the politicians are getting worried. *JZ*

Movie rating: *4

Visual: dvd (new)

Off the record: (see below)

Various Artists (composer: Franklyn Boyd)

Jun 63. (lp) *Decca; (LK 4524)* [ ] [–]
– Go (SOUNDS INCORPORATED) / My Bonnie lies over the ocean (the SPOTNIKS) / Little boat (the SPRINGFIELDS) / Ups and downs of love (FREDDY CANNON) / Judy, Judy (JOHNNY TILLOTSON) / All the stars in the sky (the TORNADOS) / Just for fun (MARK WYNTER & CHERRY ROLAND) / Vote for me (MARK WYNTER) / Happy with you (MARK WYNTER) / Just another girl (the VERNON GIRLS) / The night has a thousand eyes (BOBBY VEE) / (All I gotta do is) Touch me (BOBBY VEE) / Let her go (JOE BROWN) / What's the name of the game? (JOE BROWN) / Which way the wind blows (LOUISE CORDET) / Kisses can lie (LYNN CORNELL) / My little girl (the CRICKETS) / Teardrops fell like rain (the CRICKETS) / Crazy crazes (KENNY LYNCH) / Monument (KENNY LYNCH) / The man from nowhere (JET HARRIS) / Hully gully (JET HARRIS) / Warm summer day (KETTY LESTER) / Keep on dancing (BRIAN POOLE) / Everyone but you (JIMMY POWELL) / Sweet boy (CLODAGH RODGERS).

S/track review: If you're a little older than a certain reviewer, names like BOBBY VEE, JOE BROWN, BRIAN POOLE, JET HARRIS and the CRICKETS should just roll off the tongue. The same can't be said for LYNN CORNELL, LOUISE CORDET, JIMMY POWELL, the VERNON GIRLS and at the time a fresh-faced CLODAGH RODGERS, although the latter name cropped up several years later (with 'Jack In The Box') as United Kingdom's entry into the cheesy Eurovision Song Contest. Another girl-next-door one might recognise is a certain Dusty, who fronts orchestral-folkies the SPRINGFIELDS on 'Little Boat'. KENNY LYNCH was at the time having his second UK Top 10 entry ('You Can Never Stop Me Loving You') when he was afforded two numbers here, 'Crazy Crazes' & 'Monument'; he went into stand-up comedy soon afterwards. Former Shadow, JET HARRIS, supplied 'The Man From Nowhere' and 'Hully Gully', while JOE BROWN does his best to shake and twist to 'Let Her Go' & 'What's The Name Of The Game?'. Clean-cut crooner MARK WYNTER (a Buddy Holly-clone if ever there was one!) smooches his way through 'Happy With You' and 'Vote For Me', but it's BOBBY VEE who steals the limelight here via 'The Night Has A Thousand Eyes'. The Holly connection fits in nicely when fellow Stateside stars the CRICKETS sing 'My Little Girl', while FREDDY CANNON and JOHNNY TILLOTSON keep the American flag flying with two further cuts. Sweden's the SPOTNIKS find nostalgia and tradition and come up with 'My Bonnie Lies Over The Ocean', although 'Go' by SOUNDS INCORPORATED had suggested they had already kicked off their minor music chart careers, when it was indeed the opposite. *MCS*

Album rating: *4

JUST FOR YOU

1964 (UK 63m) Delmore / British Lion Film Corporation

Film genre: Pop-Rock-music concert drama

Top guns: dir: Douglas Hickox ← IT'S ALL OVER TOWN / → DISK-O-TEK HOLIDAY / s-w: David Edwards

Stars: the Applejacks:- Al Jackson, Phil Cash, Martin Baggott, Don Gould, Megan Davies, Gerry Freeman *(performers)*, **Peter & Gordon:- Peter Asher, Gordon Waller** *(performers)* → POP GEAR → DISK-O-TEK HOLIDAY, **Freddie & The Dreamers:- Freddie Garrity, Roy Crewsdon, Derek Quinn, Peter Birrell, Bernie Dwyer** *(performers)* ← WHAT A CRAZY WORLD / → EVERY DAY'S A HOLIDAY → DISK-O-TEK HOLIDAY → OUT OF SIGHT → CUCKOO PATROL, **Johnny B. Great** *(performer)* → DISK-O-TEK HOLIDAY, **the Bachelors** *(performers)* ← IT'S ALL OVER TOWN / → DISK-O-TEK HOLIDAY → I'VE GOTTA HORSE, **the Merseybeats:- Tony Crane, Bolly Kinsley, Aaron Williams, John Banks** *(performers)* → DISK-O-TEK HOLIDAY, **the Orchids** *(performers)* → DISK-O-TEK HOLIDAY, **a Band Of Angels:- Mike D'Abo, John Baker, Christian Gaydon, Dave Wilkinson, James Rugge-Price** *(performers)* → DISK-O-TEK HOLIDAY

Storyline: Basically a rock'n'roll movie without much plot. Some of the film was utilised for another movie in 1966, 'Disk-O-Tek Holiday'(!). *MCS*

Movie rating: *3

Visual: none (see 'DISK-O-TEK HOLIDAY')

Off the record: (see below)

Various Artists

Jun 64. (lp) *Decca; (LK 4620)* [ ] [–]
– Hide & seek (a BAND OF ANGELS) / Tell me when (the APPLEJACKS) / Milkman (the MERSEYBEATS) / You were made for me + Just for you (FREDDIE & THE DREAMERS) / Leave me alone + Soft as the dawn (PETER & GORDON) / Teenage Valentino + The fox + Low in the valley (the BACHELORS) / If I had a hammer (JOHNNY B. GREAT) / Mr. Scrooge (the ORCHIDS).

S/track review: With the previous year's 'JUST FOR FUN' there's loads of pop-tastic talent on show here (most of it turning up in the 1966 US movie, 'DISK-O-TEK HOLIDAY'). England's own, the APPLEJACKS, contributed their recent UK Top 10 hit, 'Tell Me When', while recent No.1 hitmakers (with 'A World Without Love') PETER AND GORDON, who were unfairly described by the press as the ugliest act in pop, supply two, 'Leave Me Alone' and 'Soft As The Dawn'. The all-singing, all-dancing FREDDIE AND THE DREAMERS were definitely the stars of the show, their 1963 smash, 'You Were Made For Me', and the film's minor-hit title track putting the fun back into popular music. Liverpool's the MERSEYBEATS hadn't quite established themselves yet (although 'I Think Of You' got into the Top 5); here, they turn in one track, 'Milkman'. The ORCHIDS ('Mr. Scrooge') were Liverpool's answer to the Crystals, having already had three misses produced by Shel Talmy. Other flops came courtesy of Harrow-educated, Fab Four clones, A BAND OF ANGELS (featuring 'Handbags & Gladrags' writer/vocalist Mike D'Abo), on 'Hide & Seek'. With three croon-fuelled cues, 'Teenage Valentino', 'Low In The Valley' and skiffle-tribute 'The Fox', Irish singing trio the BACHELORS toned the whole script down somewhat. The Juke Box Jury panel were out to lunch on this one, but I say "miss". *MCS*

Album rating: *3.5

– spinoff releases, etc. –

the APPLEJACKS: Tell Me When / (non-OST song)

Feb 64. (7") *Decca; (F 11833)* [7] [–]

FREDDIE & THE DREAMERS: Just For You / (non OST-song)

Jul 64. (7") *Columbia; (DB 7322)* [41] [–]

Various Artists

1964. (7"ep) *Columbia; (SEG 8337)* [ ] [–]
– Leave me alone + Soft as the dawn (PETER & GORDON) / You were made for me + Just for you (FREDDIE & THE DREAMERS)

JUST MY IMAGINATION

1992 (US 100m TV) unknown

Film genre: Pop/Rock-music comedy

Top guns: dir: Jonathan Sanger / s-w: Lynn Roth (book: Marianne Gingher)

Stars: Tom Wopat *(Bobby Rex)*, Jean Smart *(Pally Thompson)* ← FLASHPOINT, **Mary Kay Place** *(Shilda Hawk)* ← MORE AMERICAN GRAFFITI ← BOUND FOR GLORY / → MANNY & LO → COMMITTED → KILLER DILLER, Yvette Freeman *(Mrs. DeWitt)*, Cristine Rose *(Brenda Sands)*

Storyline: When a smalltown woman hears a hit song citing her as the romance, she opts to confront her old college beau turned pop star. *MCS*

Movie rating: *5

Visual: video (no audio OST)

Off the record: Tom Wopat took the role of Luke Duke in the long-running TV series, 'The Dukes Of Hazzard'. *MCS*

JUVENTUD SIN LEY: REBELDES A GO-GO

aka Lawless Youth

1965 (Mex 90m b&w) Producciones Sotomayor

Film genre: Spanish-language Rock/Pop Musical drama

Top guns: dir: Gilberto Martinez Solares / s-w: Rafael Garcia Travesi

Stars: Marga Lopez *(Elisa Duran)*, Arturo de Cordova *(Licenciado Luis Ordorica)*, Jose Elias Moreno, Kitty de Hoyos *(Ordorico's wife)*, Roberto Jordan *(Ricardo Silva)*, Fanny Cano *(Ofelia)*, Fernando Lujan *(Jorge Ordorico)*, Columba Dominguez *(Sra. Silva)*, Manolo Munoz *(Flaco)*, **Los Rockin Devil's** *(musicians)* → AMOR A RITMO DE GO-GO

Storyline: Rock'n'roll Mexican style and the old subject of wild youths protesting against parents and society. *MCS*

Movie rating: *6

Visual: video + dvd (no audio OST)

Off the record: **Los Rockin Devil's** (yes, correct spelling!) and some of their music from the movie can be heard on a compilation CD, 'Musica De Las Peliculas'. *MCS*

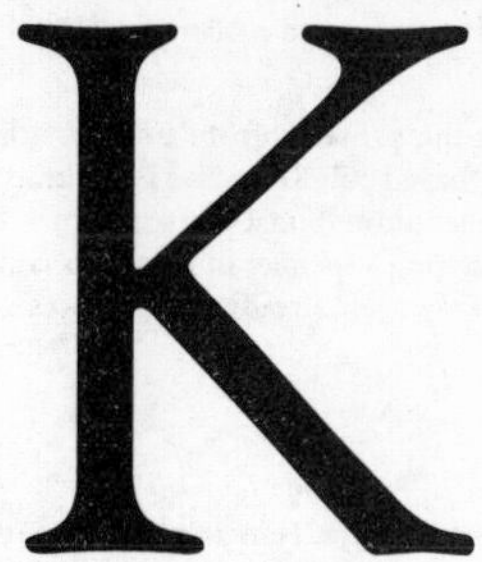

the KAREN CARPENTER STORY

1989 (US 97m TV) Weintraub Entertainment Group

Film genre: Pop-music biopic/drama

Top guns: dir: Joseph Sargent, **Richard Carpenter** / s-w: Barry Morrow

Stars: Cynthia Gibb *(Karen Carpenter)*, Mitchell Anderson *(Richard Carpenter)*, Peter Michael Goetz *(Harold Carpenter)*, Lise Hilboldt *(Lucy)*, Michael McGuire *(Sherwin Bash)*, Louise Fletcher *(Agnes Carpenter)* ← FIRESTARTER, Josh Cruze *(Herb Alpert)*, James Hong *(Dr. Dentworth)* ← BLADE RUNNER ← BOUND FOR GLORY ← the DYNAMITE BROTHERS / WAYNE'S WORLD 2 → EXPERIENCE

Storyline: The biopic of Karen Carpenter who first showed musical talent at High School when she played glockenspiel in the band. Soon she bought herself a proper drum kit and by the time she was fifteen the first Carpenter trio was formed. It was a year later when Karen performed her first singing audition, and after winning the "Battle of the Bands" contest at Hollywood Bowl the same year there was no doubt that a star had been born. *JZ*

Movie rating: *6

Visual: video (no audio OST; see below)

Off the record: The CARPENTERS were behind most of the songs featured in the film (except where note *):- 'Rainy Days And Mondays', 'The End Of The World' (CYNTHIA GIBB), 'All Of My Life', 'I'll be Yours', 'Don't Be Afraid', 'Eve', '(They Long To Be) Close To You', 'We've Only Just Begun', 'Love Is Surrender', 'Superstar', 'A Song For You', 'You're The One', 'Top Of The World', 'For All We Know', 'This Masquerade', 'Where Do I Go From Here?', 'Now', 'A Song For You Reprise', 'Karen's Theme' (RICHARD CARPENTER). There are numerous CARPENTERS compilations out there with most (or some) of these tracks; I suggest UK No.1 from March 1990, 'Only Yesterday'. *MCS*

□ KEEP IT COOL alt.
(⇒ LET'S ROCK)

□ Toby KEITH segment
(⇒ BROKEN BRIDGES)

KEVIN & PERRY GO LARGE

2000 (UK 82m) Tiger Aspect / Icon Films / Fragile Films (15)

Film genre: anarchic teen comedy

Top guns: dir: Ed Bye / s-w: Harry Enfield, **Dave Cummings**

Stars: Harry Enfield *(Kevin)*, Kathy Burke *(Perry)* ← WALKER ← STRAIGHT TO HELL ← EAT THE RICH ← SID & NANCY, **Rhys Ifans**

(Eyeball Ball), Laura Fraser *(Candice)*, James Fleet *(dad)*, Louisa Rix *(mum)*, Tabitha Wady *(Gemma)* → CHRISTIE MALRY'S OWN DOUBLE-ENTRY, Natasha Little *(Anne Boleyn)*, Kenneth Cranham *(vicar)*, Paul Whitehouse *(bouncer 1)*, Frank Harper *(armed robber)* ← TWENTYFOURSEVEN / → THIS IS ENGLAND

Storyline: Agog with the proceeds from unexpectedly heading off a bank robbery, adenoidal teenaged pals Kevin and Perry head to the hedonist mecca that is turn-of-the-millennium Ibiza. Only problem is, they've got Kev's mum and dad in tow. Also setting a spanner in the works is sleazy A-list DJ, Eyeball Paul, putting in jeopardy their already slim chances with geekettes Gemma and Candice. *BG*

Movie rating: *4.5

Visual: dvd

Off the record: Comedian/actor, Harry Enfield, was responsible for UK Top 5 novelty hit, 'Loadsamoney (Doin' Up The House), way back in 1988. **Dave Cummings** was the guitarist of Glasgow-based 90s hitmakers, Del Amitri, ('Nothing Ever Happens', etc.); he'd already written screenplay for 'The Last Seduction II' (1999). **Rhys Ifans** (acting resume:- 'Twin Town', 'Notting Hill' and 'Once Upon A Time In THe Midlands') was briefly lead singer of Welsh indie faves, Super Furry Animals (he subsequently featured in the promo for their 1996 Top 40 hit, 'God Show Me Magic' and, more recently showed up alongside Oasis on their 2005 chart-topper, 'The Importance Of Being Idle'. *MCS*

Various Artists (score: Cecily Fay & Philip Pope)

Apr 00. (d-cd) *Virgin-E.M.I.; (VTDCDX 298)* [4] [–]
– Big girl (PRECOCIOUS BRATS feat. KEVIN & PERRY) / Kid 2000 (HYBRID feat. CHRISSIE HYNDE) / I'm in the mood for love (JOOLS HOLLAND AND HIS RHYTHM & BLUES ORCHESTRA feat. JAMIROQUAI) / Ooh la la (the WISEGUYS) / Love island – 4-4 mix (FATBOY SLIM) / Straight to hell (the CLASH) / King of Snake – Straight Mate mix (UNDERWORLD) / Another day – Perfecto dub (SKIP RAIDERS feat. JADA) / Mystery land – Sickboy Courtyard remix (Y TRAXX) / Ayla – DJ Taucher mix (AYLA) / Crazy Ivan (VER VLADS) / Chicago (GROOVE ARMADA) / The look of love (GLADYS KNIGHT) / Ethnic majority (NIGHTMARES ON WAX) / F**k dub (TOSCA) / Emotion – Sweet Harry (NIGHTMARES ON WAX) / Mi amor (PHIL POPE & LOS LIDOS) / The partee (ROGER SANCHEZ) / Follow me (LANGE feat. the MORRIGHAN) / Eyeball (SUNBURST) / Luvstruck (SOUTHSIDE SPINNERS) // Don't give up (CHICANE feat. BRYAN ADAMS) / Must be the music (JOEY NEGRO feat. TAKA BOOM) / Get get down (PAUL JOHNSON) / Needin' U – original mistake (DAVID MORALES presents the FACE) / Horny (MOUSSE T. Vs. HOT 'N' JUICY) / Get wicked (PERFECT PHASE presents THOSE 2) / Dreaming (RUFF DRIVERZ presents ARROLA) / Sound of bamboo (FLICKMAN) / I feel love – R.A.F. zone mix (CRW) / Sunshine (YOMANDA) / Lizard – Claxxix mix (MAURO PICOTTO) / Coming on strong – Bobellow Vs. Euphoria (SIGNUM feat. SCOTT MAC) / A9 (ARIEL) / Toca's miracle (FRAGMA) / Toca me – In Petto mix (FRAGMA) / 9pm (till I come) – Signum remix (ATB) / After love – Signum remix (BLANK & JONES) / Everyday (AGNELLI & NELSON) / Sparkles – Airscape mix (DJ TIESTO) / Pumpin' – Eniac 99 mix (NOVY Vs. ENIAC) / Everybody (2000 BC) / Big girl – Yomanda mix (PRECOCIOUS BRATS feat. KEVIN & PERRY).

S/track review: In lieu of the chemical assistance enhancing your average Ibiza mix, 'KEVIN & PERRY GO LARGE' leavens trance's prog-in-hotpants fantasies (or prog-in-hotpants fantasies plus BRYAN ADAMS) with the satirical humour of Harry Enfield. Mercifully so, given the likes of 'Crazy Ivan', 'Don't Give Up' (a UK No.1) and PRETENDERS cover, 'Kid 2000'. But credit where it's due; with the rattling synth-dub atmospherics of CLASH sleeper, 'Straight To Hell' and a GLADYS KNIGHT cover from deep in the crates, there's at least some lip service to the Balearic spirit of yore. The mod jazz and grunting of 'Big Girl' (Top 20) were made for each other, while veteran beatheads NIGHTMARES ON WAX, the rolling devilment of the WISEGUYS and a Top 30 JOOLS 'n' JK duet (pity it wasn't 'Sunny') offer contemporary respite from the not-so-super star DJ'ing. ROGER SANCHEZ, to be fair, comes good with some rousing Latin-jazz-house, GROOVE ARMADA loop some ingratiatingly funky guitar and UNDERWORLD go large on the spirit of Giorgio Moroder. The cheesemonger really gets raided on disc 2 though, going straight for the jugular with every head-clobbering, neo hi-NRG beat, x-ray/hoover synth and tabloid refrain you thought you'd heard for the last time. *BG*

Album rating: *5.5

– spinoff hits, etc. –

JOEY NEGRO feat. TAKA BOOM: Must Be The Music

Feb 00. (cd-s) *Incentive; (CENT 4CDS)* [8] [–]

CHICANE feat. BRYAN ADAMS: Don't Give Up

Mar 00. (cd-s) *Xtravaganza; (XTRAV 9CDS)* [1] [–]

PRECOCIOUS BRATS featuring KEVIN & PERRY: Big Girl (mixes)

Apr 00. (cd-s) *(VTSCD 1)* [16] [–]

HYBRID featuring CHRISSIE HYNDE: Kid 2000 (mixes)

May 00. (cd-s) *(VTSCD 2)* [32] [–]

JOOLS HOLLAND AND HIS RHYTHM & BLUES ORCHESTRA featuring JAMIROQUAI: I'm In The Mood For Love

Feb 01. (cd-s) *Warner.esp; (WSMS 001CD)* [29] [–]

KID CREOLE & THE COCONUTS

Formed: New York City, New York, USA . . . 1980 by AUGUST DARNELL (b. Thomas August Darnell Browder, 12 Aug'50, Montreal, Canada) – the son of Dominican father and French-Canadian mother – and COATI MUNDI (b. Andy Hernandez, 3 Jan'63, NY), both having been part of swing/disco outfit, Dr Buzzard's Original "Savannah" Band. Led by August's brother, Stony Browder, the group had a Top 30 hit in 1976 with an old Paul Whiteman/Eartha Kitt number, 'Whispering – Cherchez La Femme – Se Si Bon' (a track lifted from their Top 30 eponymous LP). Four years on and split from Dr Buzzard, August, now working at 'Ze' records, assumed the new moniker of KID CREOLE (inspired by a certain Elvis flick) and pieced together his er . . . Coconuts. This ensemble included three female singers (fronted by his wife, Adriana "Addy" Kaegi) and his old mucker/wee retainer, vibraphone-player COATI MUNDI. Taking a leaf from the sound of Dr Buzzard but with an added Latin-esque twist of Cab Calloway for style (zoot suit, broad-rimmed hat and pencil-line moustache), KID CREOLE & the Coconuts were a fresh and exciting nuance to the dead end "No Wave" scene. Two relatively low-key LPs were released in the early 80s: 'Off The Coast Of Me' (1980) and 'Fresh Fruit In Foreign Places' (1981), the former highlighted by the excellent 'Mister Softee', while the latter should've featured their UK breakthrough hit, 'Me No Pop I' (check out their live versions on the movie soundtrack to 'DOWNTOWN '81'). It was indeed Britain (not America) that took KID CREOLE . . . to their hearts and minds, 1982 seeing a Top 3 album, 'Tropical Gangsters' and three Top 10 singles, 'I'm A Wonderful Thing, Baby', 'Stool Pigeon' and 'Annie, I'm Not Your Daddy'. Although their follow-up, 'Doppelganger' (1983), also produced hits (as did a COCONUTS solo outing and also a COATI MUNDI offering), it fared less well than its predecessor, it being only a matter of time before the KC's star faded. Turning to the movies, the group displayed their talents performing in 'GET CRAZY' (1983) and 'Against All Odds' (1984), while COATI himself branched out in a bit of acting: 'KRUSH GROOVE' (1985), 'SID & NANCY' (1986), 'WHO'S THAT GIRL?' (1987), 'TAPEHEADS' (1988), 'Mo' Better Blues' (1990), 'Car 54, Where Are You?' (1994), 'GIRL 6' (1996), etc; his score to 'Spike

Of Bensonhurst' was never issued. When the group split in 1985, so did August and Addy, although the man did resurrect his persona of KID CREOLE many times, none more so than in 1990 when he and the band re-united with former Dr Buzzard singer Cory Daye on comeback, PRINCE-penned Top 40 single, 'The Sex Of It' (taken from 7th album, 'Private Waters In The Great Divide'). The rest of the 90s saw KID CREOLE . . . in full swing once again, releasing the odd album here and there (one in Germany, 'The Conquest Of You' 1997), while the main man himself starred in London's West End revival musical show, 'Oh! What A Night', in 1999. *MCS*

- **filmography** {acting} (composers) –

Downtown 81 *(1981 {c} on OST by V/A =>)* / **Get Crazy** *(1983 {p COATI} OST by V/A =>)* / Against All Odds *(1984 {p})* / Mixed Blood *(1985 score by MUNDI)* / **Krush Groove** *(1985 {b COATI} OST by V/A =>)* / **Sid & Nancy** *(1986 {b COATI} OST by the POGUES, etc. =>)* / **Who's That Girl?** *(1987 {a COATI} OST by MADONNA & V/A =>)* / **Tapeheads** *(1988 {b COATI} OST by SWANKY MODES =>)* / Pathos – Segreta Inquietudine *(1988 {a AUGUST])* / Spike Of Bensonhurst *(1988 score by MUNDI)* / Identity Crisis *(1989 {b COATI})* / New York Stories *(1989 OST by DARNELL & V/A; see future edition)* / **the Forbidden Dance** *(1990 {p})* / Mo' Better Blues *(1990 {a COATI} OST by Branford Marsalis; see future edition)* / Cattive Ragazze *(1992 {c AUGUST})* / Only You *(1992 {p AUGUST})* / Carlito's Way *(1993 {p COATI})* / Car 54, Where Are You? *(1994 {p COATI})* / Species *(1995 {p COATI})* / **Girl 6** *(1996 {a COATI} OST by PRINCE =>)* / a Further Gesture *(1997 {a COATI})* / **He Got Game** *(1998 {b COATI} OST by PUBLIC ENEMY =>)* / **54** *(1998 {b COATI} OST by V/A =>)* / Bamboozled *(2000 {b COATI})* / Serving Sara *(2002 {b COATI})* / 25th Hour *(2002 {a COATI})* / Jon E. Edwards Is In Love *(2003 {c COATI})* / God Has A Rap Sheet *(2003 {a COATI})* / Undefeated *(2003 TV {a COATI})* / Red Doors *(2005 {a COATI})* / All The Invisible Children *(2005 {a})* / One Last Thing *(2005 {b})* / I Believe In America *(2006 {*})*

KID GALAHAD

1962 re-make (US 96m) United Artists / Mirisch Corporation (PG)

Film genre: Rock'n'roll Musical/sports drama

Top guns: dir: Phil Karlson / s-w: William Fay (au: Francis Wallace)

Stars: Elvis PRESLEY *(Walter Gulick / Kid Galahad)*, Lola Albright *(Dolly Fletcher)*, Gig Young *(Willy Grogan)*, Joan Blackman *(Rose Grogan)* ← BLUE HAWAII / → RETURN TO WATERLOO, Charles Bronson *(Lew Nyack)* → DEATH WISH → DEATH WISH II, Ned Glass *(Max Lieberman)*, Robert Emhardt *(Mr. Maynard)*, David Lewis *(Otto Danzig)*, Ed Asner *(Asst. Dist. Atty. Frank Gerson)* → CHANGE OF HABIT, Michael Dante *(Joie Shakes)* → THAT'S THE WAY OF THE WORLD, Jeffrey Morris *(Ralphie)* → PAYDAY → the BLUES BROTHERS → the BORDER → BLUES BROTHERS 2000, **the Jordanaires** *(performers)* ← G.I. BLUES ← COUNTRY MUSIC HOLIDAY

Storyline: All singing remake of the 1937 boxing flick, following the fortunes of Walter, a discharged soldier who earns the respect of gym owner Willie Grogan in a run-in with the local hoods. Christened Kid Galahad, he subsequently channels his talents into the ring although he's up against more than just a worthy opponent. *BG*

Movie rating: *5.5

Visual: video + dvd

Off the record: The **Jordanaires** were of course, Elvis' backing singers.

ELVIS PRESLEY: Kid Galahad / Girls! Girls! Girls!

Mar 93. (cd) *R.C.A.; <(74321 13430-2)>* ☐ ☐
– (see EP tracks) / (GIRLS! GIRLS! GIRLS!) + (extras).

S/track review: An EP rather than an album, with a running time of just over ten minutes, this is a short and occasionally sweet snatch of Hollywood ELVIS conveniently re-issued on CD as two-for-one with the meatier 'GIRLS! GIRLS! GIRLS!'. Aside from its intro bearing a surreal similarity with Abba's 'Waterloo', lead track 'King Of The Whole Wide World' is a hugely enjoyable, R&B-ish romp with some nifty sax from Boots Randolph, although it's Fuller/ Weisman/Wise's 'I Got Lucky' which leaves the deepest impression, ELVIS sounding pained even when he sings about good fortune in the lady stakes. *BG*

Album/EP rating: *3.5 / CD *4

– spinoff releases, etc. –

ELVIS PRESLEY

Sep 62. (7"ep) *R.C.A.; <EPA 4371> (RCX 7106)* 30 Jan63 16
– King of the whole wide world / This is living / Riding the rainbow / Home is where the heart is / I got lucky / A whistling tune.

KILL BILL: VOL.1

2003 (US 107m w/ anim.) Miramax Films (R)

Film genre: martial arts thriller/drama

Top guns: s-w + dir: Quentin Tarantino ← JACKIE BROWN ← FROM DUSK TILL DAWN ← FOUR ROOMS ← NATURAL BORN KILLERS ← PULP FICTION ← RESERVOIR DOGS / → KILL BILL: VOL.2

Stars: Uma Thurman *(the bride)*, Lucy Liu *(O-Ren Ishii)*, Vivica A. Fox *(Vernita Green)* ← HENDRIX ← WHY DO FOOLS FALL IN LOVE, Daryl Hannah *(Elle Driver)* ← BLADE RUNNER ← HARD COUNTRY / → KILL BILL: VOL.2, Julie Dreyfus *(Sophie Fatale)*, Michael Madsen *(Budd)*, David Carradine *(Bill)* ← AMERICAN REEL ← ROADSIDE PROPHETS ← the LONG RIDERS ← BOUND FOR GLORY / → KILL BILL: VOL.2, Samuel L. Jackson *(Rufus)* ← JACKIE BROWN ← PULP FICTION ← JUICE ← JOHNNY SUEDE ← JUNGLE FEVER ← SCHOOL DAZE ← MAGIC STICKS / → KILL BILL: VOL.2 → BLACK SNAKE MOAN, Liu Chia-hui *(Pai Mei)*, Bo Svenson *(Reverend Harmony)*, Michael Jai White *(Alburt)*, Chiaki Kuriyama *(Go Go Yubari)*, Caitlin Keats *(Janeen)*, Michael Parks *(Earl McGraw)* ← HARD COUNTRY / → KILL BILL: VOL.2, **the 5.6.7.8's:- Sachiko Fujii, Yoshiko "Ronnie" Fujiyama, Yoshiko Yamaguchi** *(performers)*

Storyline: A badly beaten-up bride takes a bullet in the head at her own wedding. Four and half years later she emerges from a coma. Her brutal, death-list revenge quite literally "kicks-off" when she appears at the door of one of her attackers, a co-member of the Deadly Viper Assassination Squad. "Revenge is a dish best served cold." [Proverb] *MCS*

Movie rating: *9.5

Visual: dvd (w/ special 5.6.7.8's tracks)

Off the record: Tokyo-based all-girl trio, the **5.6.7.8's** (sisters Sachiko Fujii – drums, and Yoshiko "Ronnie" Fujiyama – vocals, guitar, plus new bassist Yoshiko Yamaguchi) had already disbanded before 'KILL BILL: VOL.1' was premiered. Their garage surf-rock and kitschy style (think the Cramps meets the Pandoras), evident of a handful of sets such as 'The 5.6.7.8's Can't Help It' (1993), 'The 5.6.7.8's' (1994), 'Bomb The Twist' mini-set (1996) and 'Pin Heel Stomp' (1997). After Quentin Tarantino discovered their sounds in a Tokyo clothing store, they were urged to re-form for the movie; 'Teenage Mojo Workout' (2002) saw them return to vinyl. 1996's 'Woo-Hoo', one of their songs from the movie – others were 'I Walk Like Jayne Mansfield', 'I'm Blue' & 'The House Of Blue Leaves' – subsequently featured in a Carling lager TV commercial and the UK Top 30 in 2004. *MCS*

Various Artists (score: RZA *)

Sep 03. (cd) *Maverick; <48570> WEA; (9362 48588-2)* 45 ☐
– Bang bang (my baby shot me down) (NANCY SINATRA) / That certain female (CHARLIE FEATHERS) / The grand dual (parte prima) (LUIS BACALOV) / Twisted nerve (BERNARD HERRMANN) / (Queen of the crime council – dialogue; Lucy Liu & Julie Dreyfus) / Ode to Oren Ishii (*) / Run Fay run (ISAAC HAYES) / Green hornet theme (AL HIRT) / Battle without honor or humanity (TOMOYASU HOTEI) / Don't let me be misunderstood

(SANTA ESMERALDA) / Woo hoo (the 5.6.7.8's) / Crane – White lightning (* – CHARLES BERNSTEIN) / The flower of carnage (MEIKO KAJI) / The lonely shepherd (ZAMFIR) / (You're my wicked life – dialogue; David Carradine, Julie Dreyfus & Uma Thurman) / Ironside – excerpt (QUINCY JONES) / Super 16 (excerpt) (NEU!) / Yakuza Oren 1 (*) / Banister fight (*) / (Flip sting) – (Sword swings) – (Axe throws).

S/track review: Unlike some other directors and even more soundtrack compilers, Quentin Tarantino is a man who knows his music; there are few, if any people in the film industry who can draw on such an obvious depth of pop cultural knowledge and ability to marry it with stylized visuals. Selected with the obscurantist eye of a true trainspotter and ordered with the skill of a great DJ, you know that a Tarantino record is guaranteed, at worst, to educate you, and, at best, to leave you goggle-eared and gasping at the man's audacity. Who else could follow QUINCY JONES with NEU! and make it sound like the most natural link in the world? One of the man's shrewder moves has been to incorporate the work of bonafide movie composers into his soundtracks, and again, he's done it with the meticulous craft of an incurable film buff. Spaghetti don, Luis Bacalov, the mighty Bernard Herrmann and even Charles Bernstein all have their work spliced into the Tarantino masterplan. While NANCY SINATRA's rarely heard cover of the Sonny & Cher chestnut, 'Bang Bang (My Baby Shot Me Down)', kicks things off in an unnaturally low gear before CHARLIE FEATHERS' 'That Certain Feeling' – a typical Tarantino track, if such a thing exists – noises it up rockabilly style, chief among the pop excavations is SANTA ESMERALDA's majestically sexy 'Don't Let Me Be Misunderstood', from the same school of vaguely cheesy yet peerless mid-70s ethno-disco as the likes of Kongas and Black Blood. Throw in an early 70s Japanese ballad in the vein of Francoise Hardy, a killer RZA rhyme and some reliably profane Uma Thurman dialogue and you have the best non-original soundtrack of 2003, hands down. *BG*

Album rating: *8

– spinoff hits, etc. –

the 5.6.7.8's: Woo Hoo / (non-OST song)

Jul 04. (cd-s) *Sweet Nothing; (CSSN 028)* [–] [28]

– others, etc. –

AUDIO BULLYS featuring NANCY SINATRA: Shot You Down

May 05. (12"/cd-s) *Source; (SOUR T/CDX 11)* [–] [3]

KILL BILL: VOL.2

2004 (US 137m w/ b&w) Miramax Films (R)

Film genre: Martial arts thriller/drama

Top guns: s-w + dir: Quentin Tarantino ← KILL BILL: VOL.1 ← JACKIE BROWN ← FROM DUSK TILL DAWN ← FOUR ROOMS ← NATURAL BORN KILLERS ← PULP FICTION ← RESERVOIR DOGS

Stars: Uma Thurman *(the bride)*, David Carradine *(Bill)* ← KILL BILL: VOL.1 ← AMERICAN REEL ← ROADSIDE PROPHETS ← the LONG RIDERS ← BOUND FOR GLORY, Michael Madsen *(Budd)*, Daryl Hannah *(Elle Driver)* ← KILL BILL: VOL.1 ← BLADE RUNNER ← HARD COUNTRY, Gordon Liu *(Pai Mei)*, Michael Parks *(Esteban Vihaio)* ← KILL BILL: VOL.1 ← HARD COUNTRY, Bo Svenson *(Reverend Harmony)*, Jeannie Epper *(Mrs. Harmony)*, Samuel L. Jackson *(Rufus)* ← KILL BILL: VOL.1 ← JACKIE BROWN ← PULP FICTION ← JUICE ← JOHNNY SUEDE ← JUNGLE FEVER ← SCHOOL DAZE ← MAGIC STICKS / → BLACK SNAKE MOAN, Sid Haig *(Jay)* ← HOUSE OF 1000 CORPSES ← JACKIE BROWN ← the FORBIDDEN DANCE ← FOXY BROWN ← COFFY ← BLACK MAMA, WHITE MAMA ← IT'S A BIKINI WORLD ← BEACH BALL / → the DEVIL'S REJECTS

Storyline: Battered bride Beatrix Kiddo takes her one-woman revenge quest against the Deadly Viper Assassination Squad to its bitter and invariably bloody conclusion. Along the way she gets buried alive, although that's a minor inconvenience compared to the venomous demise of her sleazy tormenter Budd. Meatier flashbacks and less martial arts shenanigans deliver a more psychologically compelling experience than Volume 1. Just don't try the Five Point Palm Exploding Heart Technique at home kids. *BG*

Movie rating: *7.5

Visual: dvd

Off the record: nothing

Various Artists (score: Robert Rodriguez & RZA)

Apr 04. (cd) *Maverick; <(9362 48676-2)>* [58] [ ]

– A few words from the bride (dialogue: Uma Thurman) / Goodnight moon (SHIVAREE) / Il tramonto (ENNIO MORRICONE) / Can't hardly stand it (CHARLIE FEATHERS) / Tu mira (LOLE Y MANUEL) / Summertime killer (LUIS BACALOV) / The chase (ALAN REEVES, PHIL STEELE & PHILIP BRIGMAN) / The legend of Pai Mei (dialogue: David Carradine & Uma Thurman) / L'arena (ENNIO MORRICONE) / A satisfied mind (JOHNNY CASH) / A silhouette of doom (ENNIO MORRICONE) / About her (MALCOLM McLAREN) / Truly and utterly Bill (dialogue: David Carradine & Uma Thurman) / Malaguena saleroso (CHINGON) / Urami bushi (MEIKO KAJI).

S/track review: Tarantino's latest double-barrelled triumph might've achieved a violently fantastical conflation of East and Western, but the second 'KILL BILL' soundtrack – like the film it accompanies – serves up more Spaghetti than Saki. This time around, the wily director just couldn't resist slipping in a bit of prime ENNIO MORRICONE, and who can blame him. The Italian composer's vast body of work generates more interest with each passing year (a tongue-in-cheek MORRICONE tribute was one of the highlights of the 2005 Edinburgh Festival) and the inclusion of brooding cues like 'L'Arena' and 'A Silhouette Of Doom' will doubtless generate more. To his credit, Tarantino at least manages to dig out a great Spaghetti-style nugget (veteran actress/singer URAMI BUSHI's 'Meiko Kaji') from Japan, achieving a more accurate synergy with his cinematic cross-hatching, but it's that naggingly fatalistic Latin spirit which looms largest. In part, this is down to Tarantino's relationship with fellow film director Robert Rodriguez, the man behind the likes of 'El Mariachi' (1992) and 'Once Upon A Time In Mexico' (2003). His band CHINGON – who played at the 'Kill Bill: Volume 2' premiere – supply the haunting cross-border bombast of 'Malaguena Salerosa', a traditional Mariachi which Rodriguez originally earmarked for his own 'Desperado' (1995). An instalment of vintage, neo-psychedelic flamenco from legendary practitioners LOLE Y MANUEL deepens the Hispanic theme while the obligatory 70s chase music comes courtesy of LUIS BACALOV (the brilliant, bongo-funk fury of 'Summertime Killer') and the combined music library-style efforts of ALAN REEVES, PHIL STEELE and PHILIP BRIGHAM. Even modern stuff like SHIVAREE's 'Goodnight Moon' quivers with moody vibrato, as does the mandatory CHARLIE FEATHERS track. Tarantino also makes his own tribute to the departed JOHNNY CASH with the redemptive 'Satisfied Mind'. After almost two decades in the movie business, and more than a decade compiling movie music, the maverick director has gradually forged a sonic trademark which – at least in spirit and attitude – has remained surprisingly constant, regardless of the artists/composers who make his final cut. And, in an age of homogenous soundtrack cash-ins, that's surely a talent worth having around. When today's blockbuster scores have long been deleted and forgotten, this – like all Tarantino's soundtracks – will still be around, aiming a flying, gravity-defying karate kick into your ear-hole. *BG*

Album rating: *8

KILLER DILLER

2004 (US 95m) Bulwark . . . & Sprocketdyne Entertainment (PG-13)

Film genre: Rock Musical comedy drama

Top guns: dir + s-w: Tricia Brock (au: Clyde Edgerton)

Stars: Lucas Black *(Vernon Jackson)* ← COLD MOUNTAIN ← ALL THE PRETTY HORSES ← SLING BLADE / → FRIDAY NIGHT LIGHTS, William Lee Scott *(Wesley Benfield)* ← BLACK AND WHITE, Fred Willard *(Ned Sears)* ← a MIGHTY WIND ← HOW HIGH ← THIS IS SPINAL TAP ← MODEL SHOP, John Michael Higgins *(Deermont Sears)* ← a MIGHTY WIND ← WAG THE DOG, W. Earl Brown *(Holister Jackson)* ← TO HELL AND BACK, Ashley Johnson *(Angie Gold)*, **Mary Kay Place** *(Dr. Gwen Bradley)* ← COMMITTED ← MANNY & LO ← JUST MY IMAGINATION ← MORE AMERICAN GRAFFITI ← BOUND FOR GLORY, **Taj MAHAL** *(J.R. Cox)*, Robert Wisdom *(Charlie Moker)* ← MASKED AND ANONYMOUS ← STORYTELLING ← THAT THING YOU DO! / → RAY, RonReaco Lee *(Ben Ashley)*, Niki J. Crawford *(Shanita Scott) (Lonnie Ledford)*, Lawrence Lowe *(Raymond Cole)*

Storyline: Blues guitarist Wesley has an unfortunate passion for other people's motor cars. When he is summoned before the judge for his misdemeanours, he is sent to a Baptist "halfway house" as part of his rehab. There he meets Vernon, an autistic pianist (who drives an invisible car), and together they try to introduce some Blues into the gospel music they're made to play. Let's hope they don't undergo a baptism of fire. *JZ*

Movie rating: *6

Visual: dvd

Off the record: The movie featured a number of tracks, one in particular ('Judge Boushay's Blues'), was arranged by Tree Adams. *MCS*

KING CREOLE

1958 (US 116m b&w) Paramount Pictures (PG)

Film genre: Rock'n'roll Musical drama

Top guns: dir: Michael Curtiz / s-w: Herbert Baker ← LOVING YOU ← the GIRL CAN'T HELP IT / → the JAZZ SINGER, Michael Vincent Gazzo (novel: 'A Stone For Danny Fisher' by Harold Robbins)

Stars: Elvis PRESLEY *(Danny Fisher)*, Carolyn Jones *(Ronnie)*, Walter Matthau *(Maxie Fields)* → CANDY, Dean Jagger *(Mr. Fisher)* ← BERNARDINE / → VANISHING POINT, Dolores Hart *(Nellie)* ← LOVING YOU, Paul Stewart *(Charlie LeGrand)*, Liliane Montevecchi *("Forty" Nina)*, Vic Morrow *(Shark)* ← BLACKBOARD JUNGLE, Val Avery *(Ralph)* → BLACK CAESAR → LET'S DO IT AGAIN, Jan Shepard *(Mimi Fisher)* → PARADISE, HAWAIIAN STYLE, Brian Hutton *(Sal)* ← CARNIVAL ROCK, Dick Winslow *(Eddie Burton)* → the CONTINENTAL TWIST → RIOT ON SUNSET STRIP

Storyline: An adpatation of a best selling Harold Robbins novel, with Danny Fisher as the stymied student obliged to pack in his studies to support his father. A singing gig in a New Orleans nightclub only leads to more grief as he becomes mixed up with the local gangsters and their molls, eventually facing the prospect of robbing his own father's store. *BG*

Movie rating: *6.5

Visual: video + dvd

Off the record: nothing

ELVIS PRESLEY (composers: Walter Scharf, etc.)

Sep 58. (lp) *R.C.A.; <LPM 1884> (RD 27088)* [2] Oct58 [4]
– King Creole / As long as I have you / Hard headed woman / Trouble / Dixieland rock / Don't ask me why / Lover doll / Crawfish / Young dreams / Steadfast, loyal and true / New Orleans. *(re-iss. 1963 & Feb69; same) (re-iss. Aug81 on 'RCA Int.'; INTS 5013) (re-iss. Jan84 lp/c; NL/NK 83733) (cd-iss. Oct87; ND 83733)*
<(cd re-iss. Feb98 +=; 07863 67454-2)> – King Creole (alt. take 18) / As long as I have you (movie version take 4) / Danny / Lover doll (undubbed) / Steadfast, loyal and true (alt.) / As long as I have you (movie version take 8) / King Creole (alt. take 3). *(lp re-mast.Jan02 on 'Castle'++=; ELVIS 112)* – (bonus 7" singles).

S/track review: With 'KING CREOLE' widely regarded as one of PRESLEY's few accomplished acting roles and the last before his army call-up (he had to apply for a two-month deferment from his local draft board in order to get the picture finished), it's unsurprising that the soundtrack also rises well above much of the inferior material he churned out during his 60s Hollywood heyday. The curled-lip urgency of the famous Leiber/Stoller title track aside, 'Crawfish' is rivetting, a creeping voodoo mambo and a prime reference point for trash fiends such as the Cramps and the B-52's. Kitty White is the damsel in sultry distress, suggesting that ELVIS might've benefitted from a more regular female foil. Leiber and Stoller also supplied the Muddy Waters-style 'Trouble', a swaggering, straight talkin' ode to sheer badness and the only time ELVIS proudly declared "I'm evil as can be"; a pity the songwriting dream team then had to go and spoil it with the downright nauseating 'Steadfast, Loyal And True'. Other highlights include the hard swinging 'Hard Headed Woman', drunk on boisterous New Orleans brass and attitude. The ballads aren't quite so compelling although Wise/Weisman's 'As Long As I Have You' at least showcase PRESLEY's incredibly rich timbre. *BG*

Album rating: *6

– spinoff hits, etc. –

ELVIS PRESLEY: Hard Headed Woman / Don't Ask Me Why

Jun 58. (7",78) *<47-7280> (RCA 1070)* [1] [25] Jul58 [2]

ELVIS PRESLEY: King Creole / Dixieland Rock

Sep 58. (7",78) *(RCA 1081)* [–] [2]

ELVIS PRESLEY: King Creole Volume 1

Sep 58. (7"ep) *<EPA 4319> (RCX 117)* [ ] [ ]
– King Creole / New Orleans / As long as I have you / Lover doll. *(re-iss. Mar60 + Feb82) <US re-iss. Apr61 on 'RCA Gold'>*

ELVIS PRESLEY: King Creole Volume 2

Sep 58. (7"ep) *<EPA 4321> (RCX 118)* [ ] [ ]
– Trouble / Young dreams / Crawfish / Dixieland rock. *(re-iss. Mar60 + Feb82; 7201) <US re-iss. Apr61 on 'RCA Gold'>*

KISS

Formed: New York City, New York, USA . . . late 1971 by ex-Wicked Lester members GENE SIMMONS (guitar & vocals) and Paul Stanley (bass); guitarist Ace Frehley and drummer Peter Criss were added not long afterwards. Albums 'Kiss' (1974), 'Hotter Than Hell' (1974) and 'Dressed To Kill' (1975) set the grease-painted scene for what was to follow; low-rent glitter-metal so tacky it almost stuck to the speakers. Though these early albums sound like they were recorded on a cheap Walkman in a sawmill, they contained some of KISS's finest groin-straining moments; 'Strutter', 'Deuce' and 'Rock And Roll All Nite' were anthemic shout-alongs for white college kids who could pretend to be rebellious for three minutes. But KISS undoubtedly built their reputation on a garish image and the sensory overkill of their live show, Alice Cooper-style make-up and onstage schlock the order of the day. Accordingly, it was the double live album, 'Alive' (1975), that finally powered the band into the US Top 10 and the stadium major league. With 'Destroyer' (produced by ALICE COOPER mentor, Bob Ezrin), KISS refined their sound slightly, even recording a ballad, the Peter Criss-penned/crooned teen heartbreaker, 'Beth', which furnished the band with their biggest ever hit single. This mid-70s career peak also saw a further three releases achieve platinum status, 'Rock And Roll Over' (1976), 'Love Gun' (1977) and 'Alive II'. KISS had struck a resounding chord in some back alley of the American consciousness and now boasted a merchandise line almost as long as SIMMONS' grotesque tongue, a perverted, proto-SPICE GIRLS marketing job from the dark side. And you couldn't get a much better marketing coup than releasing four solo albums on the same day, which is exactly what KISS did (one by each member), probably because they knew they could get away with it. Unsurprisingly, most of the material was self-indulgent rubbish and, with the threat of punk never far away, the band began to falter; a film project 'KISS MEETS THE PHANTOM OF THE PARK' (1978) also bombed. Although the 'Dynasty' (1979) album went Top 10 and provided a massive hit with 'I Was Made For Lovin' You', Criss soon bowed out, the drum stool filled by session man Anton Fig for the 'Unmasked' (1980) album. A permanent replacement was found in Eric Carr, who made his debut on the ill-advised concept nonsense of 'The Elder' (1981), though the new musical direction was just too much for Frehley to take and he wisely departed the following year. His place was filled by Vinnie Vincent, who played on the back to basics 'Creatures Of The Night' (1982). When this album failed to revive their commercial fortunes, the band did the unthinkable, removing their make-up for the 'Lick It Up' (1983) album. Perhaps as a result of the public discovering they weren't blood-sucking ghouls after all but (relatively) normal-looking people, the album went Top 30. Ironically, KISS had just started to re-establish themselves in Britain, where the latter set reached the Top 10, no doubt giving them heart in their struggle back to world domination. KISS then went through more line-up changes, with Vincent being replaced first by Mark St John, then Bob Kulick. With the unashamedly commercial 'Crazy Crazy Nights' single in '87 and a similarly-titled set, the band enjoyed their biggest success since their 70s heyday, both releases reaching No.4 in the UK. By this point, SIMMONS had expanded his horizons by appearing in a few movies ('Runaway', 'Never Die Too Young' & 'TRICK OR TREAT'), while the band themselves featured in a second instalment of Penelope Spheeris' 'The DECLINE OF WESTERN CIVILIZATION: THE METAL YEARS' (1988). After another reasonably successful album, 'Hot In The Shade' (1989), tragedy struck the band in the early 90s when Carr died following heart problems and cancer. Shaken but unbowed, the band carried on with Eric Singer on drums, going back to the hoary sound of old with the 'Revenge' (1992) opus, an album that saw them showing the young bucks who had patented the moves. It had to happen, of course; 1996 marked a money-spinning, full-blown reunion tour with the original line-up and re-applied warpaint, the perfect KISS-off to those who had written them off for dead. Of course, this now meant that Kulick and Singer were surplus to requirement. With 'Psycho Circus' (1998) making the US Top 3, despite the fact it offered little or nothing new, people – moviemakers in particular – were obsessed by their fantasy rock world, and the 1999 film 'DETROIT ROCK CITY' (about teenagers trying to gatecrash their concert) cameoed the group yet again. SIMMONS radioactivated his solo career in 2004 with a couple of very different albums, the first of which, '***HOLE', was a bizarre mish-mash of covers ('Firestarter' anyone?), writing collaborations and out of character ballads. The other record was a stand-up (as in "comedy") effort, 'Speaking In Tongues', performed before an appreciative Australian audience. From 2005, British fans could tune in to his weekly patter on Reality TV show, 'Rock School', shaking up a staid, private school music department in much the same way as the 2003 movie, 'SCHOOL OF ROCK'.

BG & MCS

- **filmography** {acting} –

KISS Meets The Phantom Of The Park *(1978 TV {*} =>)* / Runaway *(1984 {* GENE})* / Never Die Too Young *(1986 {* GENE})* / **Trick Or Treat** *(1986 {a GENE} OST by FASTWAY =>)* / Wanted Dead Or Alive *(1987 {* GENE})* / **the Decline Of Western Civilization Part II: The Metal Years** *(1988 {p*} on OST =>)* / Red Surf *(1990 {* GENE})* / **Detroit Rock City** *(1999 {*p} on OST by V/A =>)* / **At Any Cost** *(2000 TV {c GENE})* / the New Guy *(2002 {c GENE})* / Wish You Were Dead *(2002 {a})* / **Tupac: Resurrection** *(2003 {c} OST by TUPAC SHAKUR =>)* / Remedy *(2005 {c ACE})* / **Be Cool** *(2005 {c GENE} =>)*

KISS MEETS THE PHANTOM OF THE PARK

aka 'ATTACK OF THE DEMONS'

1978 (US 96m TV) NBC / Hanna-Barbera Productions

Film genre: sci-fi Rock Musical mystery

Top guns: dir: Gordon Hessler / s-w: Jan Michael Sherman, Don Buday

Stars: KISS:- Peter Criss *(Cat Man)*, **Ace Frehley** *(Space Man)*, **Gene Simmons** *(the Demon)*, **Paul Stanley** *(Star Child)* / Anthony Zerbe *(Abner Devereaux)* → BAJA OKLAHOMA → TOUCH, Deborah Ryan *(Melissa)*, Carmine Caridi *(Calvin Richards)* ← CAR WASH, Lisa Jane Persky *(Dirty Dee)* → AMERICAN POP → GREAT BALLS OF FIRE! → TO HELL AND BACK, Terry Lester *(Sam)*, John Dennis Johnston *(Chopper)* → the ROSE → STREETS OF FIRE, Brion James *(guard)* ← BOUND FOR GLORY

Storyline: With children's animation icons, Hanna-Barbera at the helm, it was no surprise this came across as an episode of 'Scooby-Doo' – only with rock group, Kiss, supplanting Scooby, Shaggy, et al. Filmed in California's Six Flags Magic Mountain amusement park, the theme is basically centered on "demented genius inventor" Abner Devereaux's efforts to sabotage a forthcoming Kiss concert and turn everybody – including the hard-rock group – into cyborgs/androids. *MCS*

Movie rating: *4

Visual: video + dvd (no audio OST by Hoyt S. Curtin)

Off the record: KISS do perform versions of smash hits, 'Shout It Out Loud' and the acoustic 'Beth', as well as opening the film with 'Rock & Roll All Nite'. *MCS*

KISSIN' COUSINS

1964 (US 96m) Metro-Goldwyn-Mayer (PG)

Film genre: romantic Rock'n'roll Musical drama

Top guns: s-w (+ dir): Gene Nelson ← HOOTENANNY HOOT / → YOUR CHEATIN' HEART → HARUM SCARUM → the COOL ONES, Gerald Drayson Adams → HARUM SCARUM

Stars: Elvis PRESLEY *(Jodie Tatum / Josh Morgan)*, Arthur O'Connell *(Pappy Tatum)* ← FOLLOW THAT DREAM ← HOUND-DOG MAN ← APRIL LOVE / → YOUR CHEATIN' HEART, Glenda Farrell *(Ma Tatum)*, Jack Albertson *(Capt. Robert Salbo)* → ROUSTABOUT, Pamela Austin *(Selena Tatum)* ← HOOTENANNY HOOT ← BLUE HAWAII, Cynthia Pepper *(Cpl. Midge Riley)*, Yvonne Craig *(Azalea Tatum)* ← IT HAPPENED AT THE WORLD'S FAIR / → ADVANCE TO THE REAR → SKI PARTY, Tommy Farrell *(MSgt. William George Bailey)* ← SWINGIN' ALONG / → GIRL HAPPY, Donald Woods *(Gen. Alvin Donford)* → a TIME TO SING, Beverly Hills *(Trudy)* → SPEEDWAY, Hortense Petra *(Dixie Cate)* ← DON'T KNOCK THE TWIST / → GET YOURSELF A COLLEGE GIRL → YOUR CHEATIN' HEART → WHEN THE BOYS MEET THE GIRLS → HOLD ON! → RIOT ON SUNSET STRIP, Joan Staley *(Jonesy)* → ROUSTABOUT, Terri Garr *(extra)* ← FUN IN ACAPULCO / → VIVA LAS VEGAS → PAJAMA PARTY → ROUSTABOUT → the COOL ONES → CLAMBAKE → HEAD → ONE FROM THE HEART

Storyline: Elvis famously gets two roles here, playing both Air Force Lieutenant Josh Morgan and blonde haired Jody Tatum ("Elvis Has a Blonde-Hair Twin The Gals Swoon Over!", ran the ads), a member of a backwoods bumpkin family whose land the government has designs on. *BG*

Movie rating: *4

Visual: video + dvd

Off the record: nothing

ELVIS PRESLEY (composers: Fred Karger, etc.)

Apr 64. (lp; mono/stereo) *R.C.A.; <LSP 2894> (RD/SF 7645)* 6 Jun64 5
– Catchin' on fast / Tender feeling / Anyone (could fall in love with you) / Barefoot ballad / Once is enough / Kissin' cousins / Echoes of love / (It's a) Long, lonely highway / Smokey mountain way / There's gold in the mountains / One boy, two little girls / Kissin' cousins (reprise). *(re-iss. Oct79 lp/c; PL/PK 42355) (re-iss. Aug81 on 'RCA Int.'; INTS 5108) (re-iss. Nov84 lp/c; NL/NK 84115) (re-iss. Sep86 on 'RCA Camden' lp/c; CDS/CAM 1222)*

S/track review: The sleevenote on the CD re-issue says it all: "the producers . . . wanted the soundtrack to be recorded in Nashville to recreate the authentic "country" sound. However, the songs were pure Hollywood and could have been recorded anywhere". It's not unfair to add that the low budget nature of this movie extended to the music. As usual, ELVIS made the most of the largely throwaway material he's saddled with: he certainly raises the title track above its pedestrian potential, at least on its rockier version, while the approaching influence of the swinging sixties is evident on 'Catchin' On Fast', with Floyd Cramer showing his fleet-fingered talent at the piano. 'There's Gold In The Mountains' is a campy, catchy, guilty pleasure, 'Once Is Enough' an enjoyably forgettable slice of R&B, while ELVIS is in fine voice on 'Tender Feeling' and 'Anyone (Could Fall In Love With You)' rendering middling ballad material a little more memorable, even if the latter was cut from the final print. 'Barefoot Ballad', a cringeworthy collision between cod-Appalachian country, Hollywood gimmickry and what sounds like a cuckoo clock, deserves special mention for a down-home, gravel-throated vocal that has to be heard to be believed. *BG*

Album rating: *4

– spinoff hits, etc. –

ELVIS PRESLEY: Kissin' Cousins

Feb 64. (7") *<47-8307> (RCA 1404)* 12
29 Jun64 10

KLA$H

1995 (Can/US 95m) Xenon Entertainment / Hollywood Independents (R)

Film genre: romantic Reggae-music mystery/thriller

Top guns: s-w: (+ dir) Bill Parker, Peter Allen

Stars: Jasmine Guy *(Blossom)* ← SCHOOL DAZE / → TUPAC: RESURRECTION, Giancarlo Esposito *(Stoney)* ← NIGHT ON EARTH ← SCHOOL DAZE ← MAXIMUM OVERDRIVE / → FEEL THE NOISE, **Cedella Marley** *(Inspector Lovelace)*, Lucien Chen *(Mr. Lee)*, Stafford Ashani *(Ragga)*, Carl Bradshaw *(Walker)*, Paul Campbell *(Ultimate)* → DANCEHALL QUEEN, **Mad Cobra** *(performer)* → BROOKLYN BABYLON, **Snow** *(performer)* → PRISON SONG, **Shaggy** *(performer)*, **Steel Pulse** *(performers)*, **Bounti Killa** *(performer)*, **Shabba Ranks** *(performer)*, **Ninja Man** *(performer)*, **Capleton** *(performer)*, **Patra** *(performer)*, **Prince Midas** *(performer)*, **Beanie Man** *(performer)*, **Born Jamericans** *(performers)*

Storyline: Set in Jamaica to a backdrop of a reggae music, a photojournalist assigned to cover the Kla$h concert (a Battle Of The Bands contest) falls for a dancehall girl, employed by a local crime boss. Things become a little uneasy for Stoney when Blossom convinces him to steal some money from a neigbouring island paradise. *MCS*

Movie rating: *4

Visual: video + dvd

Off the record: Lead actress Jasmine Guy starred in the Cosby Show TV spin-off, 'A Different World' (as Whitley Gilbert from 1987-1993), while also becoming a top R&B singer. She had two US hits in 1991: 'Another Like My Lover' & 'Just Want To Hold You', both lifted from her eponymous set. Canadian reggae rapper, **Snow**, had a No.1 a few years earlier with 'Informer', while the similarly-styled Kingston-born **Mad Cobra** had a Top 20 smash courtesy of 'Flex' around the same period. **Cedella Marley** is the daughter of reggae icon, Bob Marley, and is a member of offspring, sibling outfit, Ziggy Marley & the Melody Makers; 'Tomorrow People' was a US Top 40 hit in 1988. *MCS*

—

Various Artists: Kla$h – The Soundtrak: Kaught Up In Da Mix

May 97. (cd) *Thug; <30072>* –
– Watch your speech (SHAGGY) / I spy (STEEL PULSE) / Down in de ghetto – live (BOUNTI KILLA) / Sex therapist (COBRA) / Gun stupid (TERROR FABULOUS) / First blood (PRINCE MIDAS & BRIAN & TONY GOLD) / Luv 2 luv U (JASMINE GUY) / Sweetie (CHAKA DEMUS & PLIERS) / Nastee (BORN JAMERICANS & K.O. BOYS) / Breakfast in bed (LORNA BENNETT) / Monday morning blues (LOOSE CABOOSE) / Complaint (GARNETT SILK) / Rivertown – medley – live (SNOW) / Free style (NINJA MAN).

S/track review: Despite claiming to be a representation of Jamaica's underground dancehall scene circa 1995, 'KLA$H: KAUGHT UP IN DA MIX' – to give the album its full title – leans towards an earlier, more slickly produced reggae sound but is all the more accessible as a result. As such, you have the bouncing proto-basement of STEEL PULSE and cross-over success SHAGGY rubbing up against COBRA's lovers rock and an oddly doo-wop inflected 'Sweetie' by fellow exports CHAKA DEMUS & PLIERS. LORNA BENNETT makes a sultry, stripped-down return to 1974 hit 'Breakfast In Bed' and PRINCE MIDAS & BRIAN & TONY GOLD offer a deeply atmospheric consciousness on 'First Blood'. Dancehall's symbiotic relationship with US hip hop is present and correct on tracks by TERROR FABULOUS, BORN JAMERICANS & K.O. BOYS and SNOW, all espousing a subtle updating of the classic reggae sound with crisper, machine-driven drums, while the film's female lead, 'A Different World's JASMINE GUY, contributes by means of the straight US soul sizzler 'Luv 2 Luv U'. It is the sparse, synthesized sound on GARNETT SILK's 'Complaint' and the live performances from the feature courtesy of BOUNTI KILLA and NINJA MAN that represent the emergent dancehall scene proper, the atmosphere of 'KLA$H' further conveyed through snippets of dialogue interspersed amongst the tracks. The overall impact of the album thus proves a surprisingly approachable and perfectly pleasant, sun-kissed, head-nodding synopsis of early-90s reggae in all its forms. *MR*

Album rating: *6

KNIGHTS OF THE CITY

1986 (US 87m) Grace / New World Pictures (R)

Film genre: crime/Rap-music adventure

Top guns: dir: Dominic Orlando / s-w: Leon Isaac Kennedy

Stars: Leon Isaac Kennedy *(Troy)*, Nicholas Campbell *(Joey)* → GUITARMAN, John Mengatti *(Mookie)*, Stoney Jackson *(Eddie)* ← SWEET DREAMS ← STREETS OF FIRE ← ROLLER BOOGIE / → TRESPASS → CB4: THE MOVIE, Dino Henderson *(Dino)*, Curtis Lema *(Ramrod)*, Marc Lemberger *(Mr. Freeze)* ← FLASHDANCE ← WILD STYLE, Jeff Moldovan *(Carlos)*, **the Fat Boys:- Darren Robinson, Damon Wimbley, Mark Morales** *(themselves)* ← KRUSH GROOVE, **Kurtis Blow** *(himself)* ← KRUSH GROOVE / → the SHOW → RHYME & REASON, **Smokey Robinson** *(himself)* ← the T.A.M.I. SHOW / → the TEMPTATIONS

Storyline: Troy, Joey and Mookie find themselves in the middle of a gang war when they would rather be rapping away in the record business. Arch rivals the Mechanix (maybe they're more into garage) are preparing for the big showdown with our heroes, and if they win the rapsters' next audience will be the other patients in hospital. Will the three Sir Dancealots chicken out of the fight and continue their music, or will this be a knight to remember for all the wrong reasons? *JZ*

Movie rating: *3.5

Visual: video (no audio OST; score: Misha Segal)

Off the record: The **Fat Boys** went on to have a few US cover hits, namely 'Wipeout' and 'The Twist (Yo, Twist!)', while they also starred in the movie, 'Disorderlies' (1987). *MCS*

□ George KRANZ segment
(⇒ MAGIC STICKS)

Kris KRISTOFFERSON

Born: 22 Jun'36, Brownsville, Texas, USA. In common with many singers who've successfully graduated to Hollywood, KRIS KRISTOFFERSON is something of a multi-dimensional talent, a one-time Oxford scholar and teacher as well as an army veteran. He intially drew recognition as a Nashville-based songwriter, simultaneously shaking up the country establishment and charming the rock world with classic, pioneeringly pared-down material for the likes of JOHNNY CASH and JANIS JOPLIN. In 1971, at the behest of his pal Dennis Hopper, KRISTOFFERSON travelled to Peru where the 'EASY RIDER' star was shooting an experimental western, 'The Last Movie' (1971). While the film's notorious critical and commercial failure put paid to Hopper's budding directorial career, it furnished the bearded, raggedly photogenic singer with his first film part (as himself) as well as his first attempt at film scoring, and it wasn't long before he'd snagged his first leading role, in cult drama 'Cisco Pike' (1971). Playing a faded, drug-haunted rock star blackmailed by Gene Hackman's crooked cop, KRISTOFFERSON also got a chance to saturate the soundtrack with songs from his contemporary album, 'The Silver-Tongued Devil And I' (1971), a handful of which appeared on a specially issued EP. Another appearance as a singer in Paul Mazursky's marital comedy, 'Blume In Love' followed in 1973 before the country outlaw got a chance to play a real outlaw alongside James Coburn and BOB DYLAN in Sam Peckinpah's revisionist/outlaw western, 'PAT GARRETT & BILLY THE KID' (1973). He also appeared in Peckinpah's 'Bring Me The Head Of Alfredo Garcia' (1973) before a breakthrough role opposite Oscar winner Ellen Burstyn in Martin Scorsese's Hollywood debut, 'Alice Doesn't Live Here Anymore' (1974). Despite the film's success, KRISTOFFERSON chose to concentrate on his flagging music career for a couple of years before returning to the big screen as a Vietnam vet in 'Vigilante Force' (1976) and alongside Sarah Miles in steamy drama, 'The Sailor Who Fell From Grace With The Sea' (1976). Yet it would be his role alongside Barbra Streisand as a frozen-nosed rock star on the skids, which would define the man's movie career; 'a STAR IS BORN' (1976), bare chested publicity shot and all, was a massive box office success while the soundtrack – to which Kris contributed a clutch of solo tracks alongside the duets with Streisand – sold by the millions. Unfortunately, KRISTOFFERSON's role was too close for comfort and his struggles with drink and drugs reached a late 70s trough. He nevertheless contined to act, draw some laughs even, alongside Burt Reynolds in American Football satire, 'Semi-Tough' (1977) and as everyone's favourite trucker, Rubber Duck, in Sam Peckinpah's CB radio drama, 'Convoy' (1978). His screen career began to go the way of his personal struggles, however, with an appearance in Michael Cimino's infamous, studio-breaking failure, 'Heaven's Gate' (1981), a fate compounded later that year by his starring role in failed Jane Fonda vehicle, 'Rollover', whose tagline – "the most erotic thing in their world was money" hardly inspired confidence. 1984 saw him back on form, if not in forgotten drama 'FLASHPOINT' (1984), then alongside WILLIE NELSON in Alan Rudolph's music biz drama, 'SONGWRITER' (1984), returning to the tattered troubadour persona of his early movies and bringing his career full circle. A starring role in Rudolph's 'Trouble In Mind' (1986) was also well received and while he spent most of the remainder of the decade working on TV westerns, he did make an unlikely appearance in the Pee Wee Herman comedy, 'Big Top Pee-Wee' (1988) and sci-fi dud, 'Millennium' (1989). Having already spoken out about America's involvement in Nicaragua, KRISTOFFERSON began the 90s with a starring role in a Spanish biopic of Nicaraguan guerilla hero, Augusto C. Sandino. Less inspiring were a series of forgettable roles in the likes of 'Night Of The Cyclone' (1990), 'Original Intent' (1991), 'Knights' (1993), 'Cheatin' Hearts' (1993) and 'Sodbusters' (1994) although things finally began looking up again with his role as a preacher in American civil war drama, 'Pharaoh's Army' (1995) and especially with his memorably nasty turn in John Sayles' highly acclaimed 'Lone Star' (1996), which rejuvenated his film career and led to a number of high profile parts. While he continued to take on sub-par fare like 'Fire Down Below' (1997), 'DANCE WITH ME' (1998), 'Girls' Night' (1998) and 'Payback' (1999), these were balanced with more credible roles in superhero fantasy, 'Blade' (1998), James Ivory's 'A Soldier's Daughter Never Cries' (1998) and Sayles' Alaskan-cum-desert island drama, 'Limbo' (1999). Into the new millennium, KRISTOFFERSON has proved he's one of the most versatile singers-turned-actors in the business, continuing to appear in hip indies such as Ethan Hawke's directorial debut, 'CHELSEA WALLS' (2001) and Sayles' political satire, 'Silver City' (2004), as well as major studio efforts like the updated 'Planet Of The Apes' (2001) and two further assignments as Wesley Snipe's imperturbable sidekick in the hugely successful 'Blade' series. *BG*

- **filmography** {acting} (composer) –

the Last Movie *(1971 {a})* / Cisco Pike *(1971 {*} OST EP see; future editions)* / Fat City *(1972 score by KRIS)* / Blume In Love *(1973 {*})* / **Pat Garrett & Billy The Kid** *(1973 {*} OST by BOB DYLAN =>)* / **the Gospel Road** *(1973 {p} score w/ JOHNNY CASH)* / Alice Doesn't Live Here Anymore *(1974 {*})* / Bring Me The Head Of Alfredo Garcia *(1974 {a})* / Vigilante Force *(1975 {*})* / the Sailor Who Fell From Grace With The Sea *(1976 {*})* / **a Star Is Born** *(1976 {*} shared OST w/ BARBRA STREISAND =>)* / Semi-Tough *(1977 {*})* / Convoy *(1978 {*})* / Freedom Road *(1979 TV {*})* / Heaven's Gate *(1981 {*})* / Rollover *(1981 {*})* / Hawk *(1982 docu {*})* / the Lost Honor Of Kathryn Beck *(1984 TV {*})* / **Flashpoint** *(1984 {*} =>)* / **Songwriter** *(1984 {*} OST shared w/ WILLIE NELSON =>)* / Trouble In Mind *(1985 {*})* / Stagecoach *(1986 TV {*})* / the Last Days Of Frank & Jesse James *(1986 TV {*})* / Blood And Orchids *(1986 TV {*})* / Big Top Pee-Wee *(1988 {*})* / the Tracker *(1988 TV {*})* / Millennium *(1989 {*})* / Welcome Home *(1989 TV {*})* / a Pair Of Aces *(1990 TV {*})* / Night Of The Cyclone *(1990 {*})* / Sandino *(1990 {*})* / Original Intent *(1991 {*})* / Another Pair Of Aces: Three Of A Kind *(1991 TV {*})* / Miracle Of The Wilderness *(1991 TV {*})* / Christmas In Connecticut *(1992 TV {*})* / Cheatin' Hearts *(1993 {*})* / Knights *(1993 {*})* / No Place To Hide *(1993 {*})* / Sodbusters *(1994 {*})* / Tad *(1995 TV {*})* / **Big Dreams & Broken Hearts: The Dottie West Story** *(1995 TV {a} =>)* / Pharaoh's Army *(1995 {*})* / Lone Star *(1996 {*})* / Long Road Home *(1996 {*})* / **Message To Love: The Isle Of Wight Festival** *(1997 {p} on OST by V/A =>)* / Two For Tea *(1997 TV {*})* / Fire Down Below *(1997 {*})* / Outlaw Justice *(1998 TV {*})* / **Dance With Me** *(1998 {*} =>)* / Blade *(1998 {*})* / a Soldier's Daughter Never Cries *(1998 {*})* / Girls' Night *(1998 {*})* / **Payback** *(1999 {a} =>)* / Limbo *(1999 {*})* / the Joy Riders *(1999 {*})* / Father Damien *(1999 {*})* / Netforce *(1999 TV {*})* / D-Tox *(2000 {a})* / Perfect Murder, Perfect Town *(2000 {*})* / **the Ballad Of Ramblin' Jack** *(2000 {p} =>)* / Planet Of The Apes (re-make) *(2001 {*} =>)* / **Chelsea Walls** *(2002 {*} OST by JEFF TWEEDY =>)* / Blade II *(2002 {*})* / Where The Red Fern Grows *(2003 {*})* / Silver City *(2004 {*})* / Blade: Trinity *(2004 {*})* / the Jacket *(2005 {*})* / **the Life And Hard Times Of Guy Terrifico** *(2005 {*} on OST by MATT MURPHY =>)* / the Wendell Baker Story *(2005 {*})* / 14 Hours *(2005 TV {*})* / Dreamer: Inspired By A True Story *(2007 {*})* / Disappearances *(2006 {*})* / Fast Food Nation *(2006 {a})* / **I'm Not There** *(2007 {n} OST by V/A =>)*

KRUSH GROOVE

1985 (US 100m) Warner Bros. Pictures (R)

Film genre: showbiz/Hip Hop-music drama

Top guns: dir: Michael Schultz ← the LAST DRAGON ← SGT. PEPPER'S LONELY HEARTS CLUB BAND ← CAR WASH / → ROCK'N'ROLL MOM / s-w: Ralph Farquhar

Stars: Blair Underwood *(Russell Walker)* → MALIBU'S MOST WANTED → FRONTERZ, **Sheila E.** *(herself)* → SIGN 'O' THE TIMES → the ADVENTURES OF FORD FAIRLANE, **RUN-D.M.C.:- Joseph Simmons, Daryll McDaniels, Jason Mizell** *(themselves)* / **the Fat Boys:- Mark "Prince Markie Dee" Morales, Damon "Kool Rock Ski" Wimbley, Darren "the Human Beat Box" Robinson** *(themselves)* → KNIGHTS OF THE CITY / **Kurtis Blow** *(himself)* → KNIGHTS OF THE CITY → the SHOW → RHYME & REASON, **Rick Rubin** *(Rick)* → TOUGHER THAN LEATHER → END OF THE CENTURY → FADE TO BLACK → SHUT UP & SING, Daniel Simmons *(Rev. Walker)* → TOUGHER THAN LEATHER, **Russell Simmons** *(Crocket)* → TOUGHER THAN LEATHER → the SHOW → BROWN SUGAR → BEEF → DEATH OF A DYNASTY, Richard E. Gant *(Jay B.)* → CB4: THE MOVIE, **BEASTIE BOYS:- Adam Horovitz, Adam Yauch, Mike D** *(performers)* / **LL Cool J** *(himself)* → TOUCH, Lisa Gay Hamilton *(Aisha)* → JACKIE BROWN, **New Edition:- Bobby Brown, Ralph Tresvant → HOUSE PARTY → PAPER SOLDIERS → BROWN SUGAR, Ricky Bell, Michael Lamone Bivins, Ronald De Voe** *(themselves)* / **Coati Mundi** *(record shop owner)* <= KID CREOLE & THE COCONUTS =>, **Dr. Jekyll/Andre Harrell** *(performer)* → the SHOW, **Mr. Hyde** *(performer)*, **Full Force:- B-Fine** *(enforcer #1)* → HOUSE PARTY 2 → HOUSE PARTY 2 → WHO'S THE MAN? → LONGSHOT, **Paul Anthony** *(enforcer #2)* → HOUSE PARTY → HOUSE PARTY 2 → WHO'S THE MAN? → LONGSHOT, Raymond White *(Hollis crew)* → TOUGHER THAN LEATHER

Storyline: On the back of Run-D.M.C.'s debut hit, aspiring hip hop mogul Russell Walker (read Simmons) needs dosh to further his label 'Krush Groove' (read 'Def Jam'), home to the likes of Kurtis Blow amongst others. Forced to borrow from a loan shark only to see his protégés step up to the big time, Walker – who's also competing with his brother Run for the charms of Sheila E – has a music biz baptism of fire amid some classic old skool performances. *BG*

Movie rating: *5

Visual: video + dvd

Off the record: **Sheila E.** (future PRINCE associate) hit the Top 10 in 1984 with 'The Glamorous Life'.

—

Various Artists

Oct 85. (lp/c) *Warners; <(9 25295-1/-4)>* [79] Mar86 [ ]
– (Krush groove) Can't stop the street (CHAKA KHAN) / I can't live without my radio (LL COOL J) / If I ruled the world (KURTIS BLOW) / All you can eat (the FAT BOYS) / Feel the spin (DEBBIE HARRY) / Holly rock (SHEILA E.) / She's on it (BEASTIE BOYS) / Love triangle (the GAP BAND) / Tender love (FORCE M.D.'S) / Krush groovin' (the FAT BOYS, RUN-D.M.C., SHEILA E. & KURTIS BLOW).

S/track review: Fetishized to the point that the Japanese CD (the only existing reissue, and that was back in the mid-80s) fetches upwards of £200, the 'KRUSH GROOVE' soundtrack is routinely filed alongside the likes of 'WILD STYLE' (1983) and 'BEAT STREET' (1984). In reality, it's not quite up to such elevated company, dragged down by turgid, hopelessly dated tracks from the likes of CHAKA KHAN, SHEILA E and DEBBIE HARRY. For a document of the rise and rise of 'Def Jam'/RUN-D.M.C./Russell Simmons, the DVD is a far wiser investment, and at least you'll get to hear D.M.C. signatures, 'King Of Rock', 'Can You Rock It Like This' and 'It's Like That'. In its favour – though hardly exclusive – are a couple of pioneering 'Def Jam' classics: 'I Can't Live Without My Radio', four fiercely minimalistic minutes introducing a Kangol-coiffed LL COOL J, and the magnificently dumb 'She's On It' from a pre-Buddhist BEASTIE BOYS. KURTIS BLOW's moment had already passed by 1985; 'If I Ruled The World' is too self-consciously old – as in really old – skool to compete with the new boys; some fine scratching though. HARRY's tinny 'Feel The Spin' ham-fistedly parrots the "Uno, dos, tres, cuatro" intro from Gil Scott-Heron's 'The Bottle', while SHEILA E's seemingly James Brown-inspired rhyming skills – allegedly booed in Big Apple cinemas – are probably best left in the bedroom. *BG*

Album rating: *6

– spinoff hits, etc. –

SHEILA E.: A Love Bizarre / (part II)
Nov 85. (7") *Paisley Park; <28890>* [11] [ ]

FORCE M.D.'S: Tender Love / (instrumental)
Jan 86. (7") *<28818>* [10] [–]

FORCE M.D.'S: Tender Love / (non-S/track)
Mar 86. (7"/12") *Tommy Boy; (IS/12IS 269)* [–] [23]

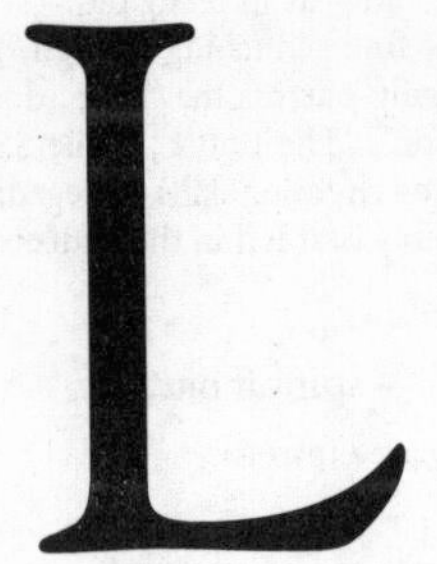

LA BAMBA

1987 (US 99m) New Vision / Columbia Pictures (PG-13)

Film genre: Rock'n'roll Musical drama/bio-pic

Top guns: s-w + dir: Luis Valdez

Stars: Lou Diamond Phillips *(Ritchie Valens)* → YOUNG GUNS II, Esai Morales *(Bob Morales)*, Rosanna DeSoto *(Connie Valenzuela)*, Elizabeth Pena *(Rosie Morales)* ← DOWN AND OUT IN BEVERLY HILLS ← TIMES SQUARE / → STRANGELAND → THINGS BEHIND THE SUN, Danielle von Zerneck *(Donna Ludwig)*, Joe Pantoliano *(Bob Keene)* ← SCENES FROM THE GOLDMINE ← EDDIE AND THE CRUISERS ← RISKY BUSINESS ← the IDOLMAKER / → ROCK'N'ROLL MOM → the IN CROWD → BLACK AND WHITE, **Marshall Crenshaw** *(Buddy Holly)*, **Rick Dees** *(Ted Quillin)* ← RECORD CITY, **Brian Setzer** *(Eddie Cochran)* → WOODSTOCK '99 → the COUNTRY BEARS, Howard Huntsberry *(Jackie Wilson)*, Stephen Lee *(Big Bopper)* ← CRIMES OF PASSION, Daniel Valsez *(Lelo)*, Noble Willingham *(Howard)* ← LIVING PROOF: THE HANK WILLIAMS JR. STORY / → GOOD MORNING, VIETNAM → SOUTH OF HEAVEN, WEST OF HELL

Storyline: The story of celebrated rock'n'roll prodigy Ritchie Valens, narrating the Hispanic singer's rags to riches life as he leaves behind his fellow migrant workers for the bright lights of the music business. Tragedy strikes, however, in the form of the infamous plane crash which claimed not only the life of Valens, but those of Buddy Holly and the Big Bopper. *BG*

Movie rating: *6

Visual: video + dvd

Off the record: *Ritchie Valens* (b. Richard Valenzuela, 13 May'41, Pacoima, California) managed to have a few chart hits before his untimely death on 3rd February, 1959: 'Come On, Let's Go' and the double-A-sided 'Donna' / 'La Bamba'. **LOS LOBOS** meanwhile, were formed in Los Angeles, California, 1974 by David Hidalgo, Luis Perez, Cesar Rosas and Conrad Lozano. Covers band stalwarts, who defiantly yet seamlessly incorporated a Latin heritage into their sweaty roots-rock agenda, LOS LOBOS were merely another cult alternative act prior to their unexpected Hollywood entree. Yet the soundtrack to high grossing 'LA BAMBA' (1987) made for an opportunity to record the kind of period covers LOS LOBOS could reel off in their sleep. While the handful of Mexican numbers featured in the film failed to make it to the accompanying soundtrack, the band's buoyant take on the title tune earned them a transatlantic No.1, followed up with the near transatlantic Top 20 success of 'Come On, Let's Go'. While their more opaque studio albums couldn't hope to match this success, who else but LOS LOBOS could've scored the Antonio Banderas vehicle, 'Desperado' (1995), Robert Rodriguez's follow-up to his low-budget favourite, 'El Mariachi' (1992). While further commissions included the Keanu Reeves/Cameron Diaz comedy, 'Feeling Minnesota' (1996) and – along with a raft of other modern ex-Rock composers including Danny Elfman – Rodriguez's family espionage yarn, 'Spy Kids' (2001), both of which were released as Various Artists soundtracks. *MCS & BG*

LOS LOBOS (& Various Artists)

Aug 87. (lp/c)(cd) *Slash; <25605> (LON LP/C 36)(828058-2)* [1] [24]
– La Bamba / Come on, let's go / Ooh! my head / We belong together / Framed / Donna / Lonely teardrops (HOWARD HUNTSBERRY) / Crying, waiting, hoping (MARSHALL CRENSHAW) / Summertime blues (BRIAN SETZER) / Who do you love (BO DIDDLEY) / Charlena / Goodnight my love.

S/track review: Latin rockers LOS LOBOS were an obvious choice for this soundtrack, having previously cut a blistering version of Valens' 'Come On, Let's Go' for their 1984 album, 'And A Time To Dance'. Handed the opportunity of a more extensive foray into the man's songbook, they anchored the piledriving 'Ooh! My Head' with a grungy, chugging riff and faithfully rendered the Valens ballad, 'Donna'. Where their empathy with the Hispanic legend really hits home is on the irresistible, all-conquering 'La Bamba', a Mexican mariachi which the doomed singer originally adapted as the B-side of 'Donna'. Ironically, Valens didn't actually speak a word of Spanish, giving LOS LOBOS' version the edge over the 1959 original. Its trebly, signature riff was all over the place during the summer of '87, a ubiquitous transatlantic No.1 which might've been a millstone round the band's neck ever since but – regardless of its commercial appeal – remains one of the most vibrant and enduring splicings of traditional Latin music and American rock ever recorded. Eddie Cochran gets a bristling version of his own signature, 'Summertime Blues', aired courtesy of Stray Cats singer, BRIAN SETZER, while Buddy Holly is honoured with MARSHALL CRENSHAW's cover of 'Crying, Waiting, Hoping', more notable for its Southern-fried guitar than CRENSHAW's vocal. None of the covers can match BO DIDDLEY's swaggering R&B nugget, 'Who Do You Love', but its inclusion isn't as incongruous as it might've been, highlighting 'LA BAMBA's most gratifying revelation: the fact that it remains relatively unscathed by the dead hand of 80s production values. *BG*

Album rating: *6

– spinoff hits, etc. –

LOS LOBOS: La Bamba / Charlena

Jul 87. (7"/c-s) *<28336> (LASH/LASCS 13)* [1] [1]
(12"+=) *(LASHX 13)* – Rip it up.

LOS LOBOS: Come On, Let's Go / Ooh! My Head

Sep 87. (7") *<28186> (LASH 14)* [21] [18]
(10"+=/12"+=) *(LASH T/X 14)* – MARSHALL CRENSHAW: Crying, waiting, hoping.

LOS LOBOS: Donna / Framed

Nov 87. (7") *(LASH 16)* [–] [ ]
(12"+=)(10"+=) *(LASHX 16)(HL 8803)* – Goodnight my love.

LADIES AND GENTLEMEN, THE FABULOUS STAINS

1982 (Can/US 87m) Barclays Mercantile / Paramount Pictures (R)

Film genre: Punk Rock Musical drama

Top guns: dir: Lou Adler ← UP IN SMOKE / s-w: Jonathan Demme ← BLACK MAMA, WHITE MAMA / → STOP MAKING SENSE, Nancy Dowd

Stars: Diane Lane *(Corinne Burns)* → STREETS OF FIRE, Peter Donat *(Harley Dennis)*, David Clennon *(Dave Robell – the agent)* ← BOUND FOR GLORY / → SWEET DREAMS → GRACE OF MY HEART, John Lehne *(Stu McGrath)* ← CARNY ← AMERICAN HOT WAX ← BROTHERS ← BOUND FOR GLORY, Laura Dern *(Jessica McNeil)* → WILD AT HEART → DR. T & THE WOMEN → I AM SAM, Cynthia Sikes *(Alicia Meeker)*, Marin Kanter *(Tracy Burns)*, **Steve Jones** *(Steve)* <= the SEX PISTOLS =>, **Paul Cook** *(Danny)* <= the SEX PISTOLS =>, **Paul Simonon** *(Johnny)* <= the

CLASH/Joe STRUMMER =>, Ray Winstone *(Billy)* ← QUADROPHENIA / → SEXY BEAST → COLD MOUNTAIN → the PROPOSITION → BREAKING AND ENTERING, **Fee Waybill** *(Lou Corpse)* ← XANADU / → BILL & TED'S EXCELLENT ADVENTURE, **Vince Welnick** *(Jerry Jervy of Metal Corpses)* ← XANADU, **Elizabeth Daily** *(motel maid)* → STREETS OF FIRE → the COUNTRY BEARS → the DEVIL'S REJECTS

Storyline: Orphaned teenager Diane Lane goes on the road with her all-girl punk band, the Stains. They soon team up with another band, the Looters, and through a series of clever promotional stunts they gain media recognition even though they haven't yet released a single. They become celebrities almost overnight, but fate can be fickle, and it's not long before fame is replaced by notoriety – can the advent of the rock video save them from disaster? *JZ*

Movie rating: *6

Visual: video (no audio OST)

Off the record: Fee Waybill + Vince Welnick were both members of the Tubes (the latter subsequently joined the GRATEFUL DEAD).

LADY SINGS THE BLUES

1972 (US 144m) Motown Productions / Paramount Pictures (R)

Film genre: showbiz/Jazz-music bio-pic drama

Top guns: dir: Sidney J. Furie ← LITTLE FAUSS AND BIG HALSY ← WONDERFUL LIFE ← the YOUNG ONES / s-w: Terence McCloy, Chris Clark, Suzanne de Passe (book: Billie Holiday & William Dufty)

Stars: Diana ROSS *(Billie Holiday)*, Billy Dee Williams *(Louis McKay)* ← the FINAL COMEDOWN / → NIGHTHAWKS → BATMAN → the JACKSONS: AN AMERICAN DREAM, Richard Pryor *(piano man)* ← YOU'VE GOT TO WALK IT LIKE YOU TALK IT . . . ← the PHYNX ← WILD IN THE STREETS / → WATTSTAX → the MACK → ADIOS AMIGO → CAR WASH → the WIZ → BUSTIN' LOOSE, James T. Callahan *(Reg)*, Sid Melton *(Jerry)*, Paul Hampton *(Harry)*, Tracee Lyles *(whore)* ← COOL BREEZE, Scatman Crothers *(Big Ben)* → SLAUGHTER'S BIG RIP-OFF → BLACK BELT JONES → TRUCK TURNER → FRIDAY FOSTER, **Yvonne Fair** *(Yvonne)*, Milton Selzer *(the doctor)* → SID & NANCY → WALKER → TAPEHEADS, Harry Caesar *(rapist)* → BREAKIN' 2: ELECTRIC BOOGALOO → ROADSIDE PROPHETS, Charles Woolf *(reporter #3)* → NO WAY BACK, Virginia Capers *(Mama Holiday)* ← NORWOOD / → TROUBLE MAN → FIVE ON THE BLACK HAND SIDE → HOWARD THE DUCK → WHAT'S LOVE GOT TO DO WITH IT, Jayne Kennedy *(Louis's date)* → LET'S DO IT AGAIN → BIG TIME

Storyline: Billie Holiday's story is a complex one, familiarly told: a Dickensian upbringing and apprenticeship in a brothel before a rise to fame and a drawn out fall amid ill starred relationships and heroin addiction, with some admittedly fine performances from the Hollywood Holiday en-route. Diana Ross was nominated for an Oscar. *BG*

Movie rating: *6.5

Visual: video + dvd

Off the record: Yvonne Fair (b. 1942, Virginia, USA) had been a part of the JAMES BROWN Revue and the Chantels in the 60s. After augmenting the likes of soul man Chuck Jackson, she signed to a contract with 'Motown' records; she was also married to Sammy Strain, ex-Little Anthony & The Imperials and the O'Jays. After a Norman Whitfield-produced album, 'The Bitch Is Black' (1975) – featuring 'Funky Music Sho 'Nuff Turns Me On' and the UK Top 5 hit, 'It Should Have Been Me' (incidentally written by Kim Weston & Gladys Knight) – she retired from the music biz. Sadly, Yvonne died in Las Vegas on the 6th March, 1994. *MCS*

DIANA ROSS (composer: Michel LeGrand *)

Nov 72. (d-lp/d-c) *Motown; <758> (TMSP/CTMSP 1131)* 1 Mar73 50

– (the arrest) / Lady sings the blues / (Baltimore brothel) / (Billie sneaks into Dean and Dean's – Swinging uptown) / T'ain't nobody's bizness if I do (BLINKY WILLIAMS) / (Big Ben – C.C. rider blues) / All of me / The man I love / Them there eyes / Gardenias from Louis / Cafe Manhattan – Had you been around (MICHELE ALLER) – Love theme (*) / (Any happy home) / (I cried for you) / (Billie and Harry – Don't explain) / Mean to me / (Fine and mellow) / What a little moonlight can do / Louis visits Bilie on tour – Love theme (*) / Cafe Manhattan party / Persuasion – T'ain't nobody's bizness if I do / (Agent's office) / Love is here to stay / Fine and mellow / Lover man (oh where can you be?) / You've changed / Gimme a pigfoot and a bottle of beer / Good morning heartache / All of me / Love theme (*) / My man / Don't explain / I cried for you / Strange fruit / God bless the child / Closing theme (*). *(re-iss. Oct81; same) (cd-iss. Jul86; WD 72610) (cd-iss. Apr93; 530135-2)*

S/track review: While Billie Holiday herself had to make do with playing a singing house servant (in Jules Levy's 1947 jazz quickie, 'New Orleans'), by the 70s Hollywood had at least moved on to the extent that a contemporary black female singer could take a leading role in a biopic about a legendary black female singer, even if it was – in the end – backed by a black record mogul ('Motown' don Berry Gordy). Even then, DIANA ROSS had to negotiate a blizzard of critical flack, much of it from within the black community. Jazz writers and fans were up in arms about the prospect of a youthful soul/pop star taking on the mantle of such a singular, iconic talent. Newly divorced from the Supremes and determined to justify Motown's hefty investment in her solo career, ROSS also had something to prove to her own supporters. Ironically, the film's soap-operatic treatment of a troubled, ambiguous life actually rendered ROSS' performances one of its few saving graces. She doesn't sound like Holiday, but then no-one realistically expected her to. Instead she gets round what would have been a technically impossible feat by simply extending the limitations of her own style to fit the asymmetric conventions of jazz, and at least approximate Holiday's phrasing. And while she couldn't have hoped to communicate the full extent of Lady Day's emotional turmoil, she gives it her all in trying. Minus the dialogue and Michel LeGrand's overbearing and largely superfluous score, this could've been a pretty accomplished soundtrack. As it is, ROSS' interpretations are too often cut short, even on the a cappella title track, where she comes closest – along with 'My Man (Mon Homme)' and inevitably, 'Strange Fruit' – to Holiday's signature combination of finesse and trouble. The presence of many of the original musicians nevertheless adds authenticity, while Edwin Starr associate BLINKY WILLIAMS offers a very un-Holiday-esque and refreshingly raw counterpoint with her own reading of 'T'Ain't Nobody's Bizness If I Do'. This is the album (a double!) that ended her tenure with Motown greats the Supremes. Together with composer Michel LeGrand, she soared the US charts with her rendition of Holiday classics including 'God Bless The Child'. *BG*

Album rating: *6

– spinoff hits, etc. –

DIANA ROSS: Good Morning Heartache / God Bless The Child

Feb 73. (7") *<1211> (TMG 849)* Mar73 34

LAMBADA

1990 (US 104m) Cannon Films / Warner Bros. Pictures (PG-13)

Film genre: R&B/Dance Musical drama

Top guns: s-w: (+ dir) Joel Silberg (+ story) ← RAPPIN' ← BREAKIN', Sheldon Renan

Stars: J. Eddie Peck *(Kevin 'Blade' Laird)*, Melora Hardin *(Sandy Thomas)*, Ricky Paull Goldin *(Dean)*, Shabba-Doo *(Ramone)* ← BREAKIN' 2: ELECTRIC BOOGALOO ← BREAKIN' ← XANADU, Basil Hoffman *(Supt. Leland)*, Dennis Burkley *(Uncle Big)* ← WHO'S THAT GIRL ← BUMMER! / → the DOORS → RUSH → TOUCH, Keene Curtis *(Principal Singleton)*

← AMERICAN HOT WAX, Thalmus Rasalala *(Wesley Wilson)* ← ADIOS AMIGO ← BUCKTOWN ← FRIDAY FOSTER ← CORNBREAD, EARL AND ME ← WILLIE DYNAMITE ← BLACULA ← COOL BREEZE, Eddie Garcia *(Chili)*

Storyline: By day Kevin Laird teaches maths at a posh Beverly Hills school, but every night he becomes Blade, king of the lambada down at the Barrio. His double life remains a secret until one of his students spots Kevin in the night club instead of marking maths papers. When Principal Singleton is told the truth it's Kevin who's put in detention and finds his job on the line. *JZ*

Movie rating: *2

Visual: video + dvd

Off the record: Can't understand why the producers left out other tracks:- 'I Can't Live Without My Rock'n'roll' (MICKI FREE), 'When We Make Love' (BELVA HANEY), 'Computer Dance' (GREG DE BELLES) & 'Heat Of The Night (SOUL II SOUL).

Various Artists: Lambada: Set The Night On Fire

Mar 90. (cd/c) *Epic; <EK/ET 46129>* ☐ ☐
– Set the night on fire (SWEET OBSESSION) / This moment in time (ABSOLUTE) / Perfect (DINA D!) / Tease me, please me (TONY TERRY) / Lambada dancin' (KATHY SLEDGE) / Gotta lambada (ABSOLUTE) / I like the rhythm (CARRIE LUCAS) / Rock lambada (JOHNNY THOMAS, JR.) / Wes' groove (BILL WOLFER) / Sata (BRENDA K. STARR) / Give it up (JUDETTE WARREN).

S/track review: Do you remember the lambada? That dance sensation that swept through 80s pop culture quicker than the Rubik's Cube. And for a brief moment looked like it could be more than just a flash in the pan. It was not to be as it went the way of 'Buffalo Gals' and 'Vogue' into the shadowy vaults of dancefloor history. What we have left to remember such a phenomenon is the eponymous movie and this accompanying soundtrack. The eleven tracks here share one thing in common: they are all terrible. There is nothing to redeem this set in any way, plain and simple, it's just bloody awful. If we had to say something nice, the pseudo hip hop break used on DINA D!'s 'Perfect' is quite catchy, but even that is second or third hand. 'LAMBADA: SET THE NIGHT ON FIRE' manages to encapsulate everything that is dated, shoddy and corny about bad music from the late 80s, filling up as it does, on thin-sounding electronic instrumentation, second-hand riffs and trite lyrical insights. It is astounding in its vacuity, the sub-Prince-ian hooks on 'Gotta Lambada' by ABSOLUTE are atrocious, the fake brass on 'Wes' Groove' equally poor. At one point CARRIE LUCAS runs out of words in the chorus of 'I Like The Rhythm' and absentmindedly dashes off some "la-la-la-la-la-la"s to fill the gap. There might be ways to make this album worse, but it's not exactly clear how. Maybe if it was longer? *MR*

Album rating: *1

– inspirational single –

KAOMA: Lambada / (instrumental)

Feb 90. (7"/cd-s) *Epic; <73090> CBS; (655011-7/-2)* 46 Oct89 4

LAS VEGAS HILLBILLYS

1966 (US 85m) Woolner Brothers Pictures Inc.

Film genre: Country Musical comedy

Top guns: dir: Arthur C. Pierce / s-w: Larry Jackson → COTTONPICKIN' CHICKENPICKERS

Stars: Ferlin Husky *(Woody)* ← COUNTRY MUSIC HOLIDAY ← MISTER ROCK AND ROLL / → HILLBILLYS IN A HAUNTED HOUSE → THAT'S COUNTRY, Jayne Mansfield *(Tawny)* ← the GIRL CAN'T HELP IT, Mamie Van Doren *(Boots Malone)* ← HIGH SCHOOL CONFIDENTIAL! ← UNTAMED YOUTH, Robert V. Barron *(Donald)* → COTTONPICKIN' CHICKENPICKERS → HONKYTONK MAN → BILL & TED'S EXCELLENT ADVENTURE, Billie Bird *(Aunt Clementine)*, Don Bowman *(Jeepers)* → HILLBILLYS IN A HAUNTED HOUSE, **Wilma Burgess** *(performer)*, **Roy Drusky** *(performer)* ← the GOLD GUITAR, **Sonny James** *(performer)* ← NASHVILLE REBEL / → SECOND FIDDLE TO A STEEL GUITAR → HILLBILLYS IN A HAUNTED HOUSE, **Del Reeves** *(performer)* → the GOLD GUITAR → SECOND FIDDLE TO A STEEL GUITAR → COTTONPICKIN' CHICKENPICKERS, **Connie Smith** *(performer)* → ROAD TO NASHVILLE → SECOND FIDDLE TO A STEEL GUITAR, **Bill Anderson** *(performer)* → ROAD TO NASHVILLE → the GOLD GUITAR → FROM NASHVILLE WITH SOUND → the NASHVILLE SOUND

Storyline: Jeepers Maw! Woody has inherited a saloon in Las Vegas, and after dusting down the Arkansas Chug-A-Bug he drives off to his new life in the big city. However, it looks like he's only struck fool's gold when singer Boots tells him how much debt his uncle left him. In a burst of inspiration he decides to turn the sleepy saloon into a sort of hillbilly tourist centre, to the bemusement of the regular biker boys. Ten cents a hoedown and $38,000 to raise. *JZ*

Movie rating: *3.5

Visual: video + dvd (no audio OST by Dean Elliott)

Off the record: FERLIN HUSKY delivered a handful of songs for the film, 'White Lightning Eyes', 'I Feel Better All Over' & 'Money Greases The Wheel', while others included 'Bright Lights And Country Music' (BILL ANDERSON, the PO BOYS & the JUNIOR CAROLINA CLOGGERS), 'Nobody But A Fool' (CONNIE SMITH), 'Baby, Sweet Sweet Baby' (WILMA BURGESS), 'What Makes A Man Wonder', 'I'll Keep Holding On To You' & 'True Love's A Medicine' (SONNY JAMES), 'That Makes It' (JAYNE MANSFIELD), 'I Don't Believe You Love Me Anymore' (ROY DRUSKY), 'Watching The Bell Of Southern Bell Go By' & 'Women Do Funny Things To Me' (DEL REEVES). *MCS*

the LAST BUS HOME

1997 (Ire 93m) Goutte d'Or

Film genre: road movie melodrama

Top guns: s-w + dir: Johnny Gogan

Stars: Annie Ryan *(Reena)*, Brian F. O'Byrne *(Jessop)*, Barry Comerford *(Joe)*, John Cronin *(Petie)* ← the COMMITMENTS, Gemma Craven *(Reena's mother)*, Anthony Brophy *(Billy)*, Brendon Coyle *(Steve Burkett)*, Donal O'Kelly *(Richie)*, Eileen Walsh *(Carole)*

Storyline: Set in Dublin at the end of '79, Reena and Jessop get it together and then form an energetic punk quartet, the Deep Patriots. Three years down the line and based in London, they are not so enthusiastic about the music business or each other, although they have just signed a major record deal. *MCS*

Movie rating: *4.5

Visual: none (no audio OST; score: CATHAL COUGHLAN)

Off the record: CATHAL COUGHLAN (formerly of Microdisney, Fatima Mansions) had recently released his first solo album, 'Grand Necropolitan' (1996) for the revamped 'Kitchenware' imprint. The Cork-born Scott Walker fan, subsequently delived a sophomore set, 'Black River Falls' (2000), before he turned to film once again with the unreleased score to 'The Mapmaker' (2001). *MCS*

LAST DAYS

2005 (US 93m) HBO Films / Meno Film Company (15)

Film genre: Psychological Rock-music drama

Top guns: dir (+ s-w): **Gus Van Sant** ← GOOD WILL HUNTING ← EVEN COWGIRLS GET THE BLUES

Stars: Michael Pitt *(Blake)* ← HEDWIG AND THE ANGRY INCH, Lukas Haas *(Luke)* → WHO LOVES THE SUN, Asia Argento *(Asia)* ← la CHIESA, Scott Green *(Scott)* ← EVEN COWGIRLS GET THE BLUES, Nicole Vicius *(Nicole)*, Ricky Jay *(detective)* ← MAGNOLIA ← BOOGIE NIGHTS, Ryan Orion *(Donovan)*, Harmony Korine *(guy in club)* ← GOOD WILL HUNTING ← KIDS, **Kim Gordon** *(record executive)* <= SONIC YOUTH =>, **Rodrigo Lopresti** *(band in club)*, Kurt Loder *(TV voiceover)* ← RAMONES: RAW ← TUPAC: RESURRECTION ← AIRHEADS ← FEAR OF A BLACK HAT ← WHO'S THE MAN? ← the ADVENTURES OF FORD FAIRLANE, Michael Azerrad *(TV voiceover)* ← GIGANTIC (A TALE OF TWO JOHNS) ← the SHIELD AROUND THE K

Storyline: Inspired by the final hours of grunge-rock spokesman, Kurt Cobain, this is a truly fictional account of the troubled Nirvana singer's lifestyle. Blake is a depressed musician who lives in an old shabby mansion but chooses to frequent the woods and the peaceful tranquility of the garden house. His friends and hangers-on use his mansion as their own property, and maybe that's the message of this overrated and pedestrian film. Paint dries quicker. *MCS*

Movie rating: *4

Visual: dvd

Off the record: Filmmaker, **Gus Van Sant**'s (b.24 Jul'52, Louisville, Kentucky), artistic liaisons began way back in the mid-70s when he attended the same design college in Rhode Island as Talking Heads. In the early 80s, he worked on some home recordings and also formed the band, Destroy All Blondes; his feature film work was instigated after the release of 'Mala Noche' in 1985. Having made his name with films such as 'Drugstore Cowboy' (1989), 'My Own Private Idaho' (1991) and 'GOOD WILL HUNTING' (1997), an independent record company ('Pop Secret') unearthed some earlier tapes, '18 Songs About Golf' (1998) and 'Gus Van Sant' (1999); a collaboration with poet, William S. Burroughs, 'The Elvis Of Letters' was the debut for the 'Tim/Kerr' imprint way back in '85. **Rodrigo Lopresti** (aka the Hermitt), played in the style of Nirvana and scored and performed the music in the film; he's delivered one album to date, 'The Hermitt & The Story Of The Insects' (2003). There was no audio release for the movie, although the VELVET UNDERGROUND's 'Venus In Furs', is spun a few times. *MCS*

the LAST DRAGON

aka BERRY GORDY'S THE LAST DRAGON

1985 (US 109m) Motown Productions / TriStar Pictures (PG-13)

Film genre: urban/martial arts comedy

Top guns: dir: Michael Schultz ← SGT. PEPPER'S LONELY HEARTS CLUB BAND ← CAR WASH / → KRUSH GROOVE → ROCK'N'ROLL MOM / s-w: Louis Venosta

Stars: Taimak *(Leroy Green)*, Vanity *(Laura Charles)*, Christopher Murney *(Eddie Arcadian)* → MAXIMUM OVERDRIVE → LAST EXIT TO BROOKLYN, Julius J. Carry III *(Sho'nuff; the Shogun of Harlem)* ← DISCO GODFATHER, Leo O'Brien *(Richie)* → RAPPIN', Faith Prince *(Angela)*, Ernie Reyes Jr. *(Tai)*, W.H. Macy *(J.J.)* → COLIN FITZ LIVES! → BOOGIE NIGHTS → WAG THE DOG → MAGNOLIA, Chazz Palminteri *(hood #2)* → IN THE MIX

Storyline: Leroy Green is a martial arts expert searching for "the glow" (known well to fans of Ready Brek). While inner contemplation leads him closer to that warm-all-over feeling, he must also rescue singer Laura from a nasty promoter and do battle with an evil martial arts genius. Can our born-again Bruce Lee light up the night or will he finally get the chop? *JZ*

Movie rating: *5

Visual: video + dvd

Off the record: Vanity (b. Denise Katrina Matthews, 4 Jan'59, Niagara Falls, Ontario, Canada) was a former model from African-American & German parentage before she took up acting in 1980: 'Klondike Fever', 'Terror Train' and 'Tanya's Island' (the latter two as D.D. Winters) were all from that year. Establishing herself as frontgirl for Vanity 6, she was to have played opposite PRINCE in his 1984 movie, 'PURPLE RAIN', however one thinks 'Motown' got there first when they released minor hit 45, 'Pretty Mess', the same year. After 'Motown' vehicle, 'The LAST DRAGON' and another minor hit single ('Under The Influence' in '86), Vanity starred in 'Never Too Young To Die' (1986), '52 Pick-Up' (1986), 'Deadly Illusion' (1987), 'Action Jackson' (1988), 'Memories Of Murder' (1990 for TV), 'Neon City' (1992), 'South Beach' (1992) and 'DaVinci's War' (1993) – all them virtual box-office flops. A brief marriage to ex-pro footballer, Anthony Smith, and her newfound Christian faith saw her retire from Hollywood. *MCS*

—

Various Artists (score: Bruce Miller & Misha Segal)

Mar 85. (lp/c/cd) *Motown; <6128> (ZL/ZK/ZD 72363)* [58] May85 [ ]
– The last dragon (title song from "Berry Gordy's The Last Dragon") (DWIGHT DAVID) / 7th Heaven (VANITY) / Star (ALFIE) / Fire (CHARLENE) / The glow (WILLIE HUTCH) / Rhythm of the night (DeBARGE) / Upset stomach (STEVIE WONDER) / First time on a ferris wheel (love theme from "Berry Gordy's The Last Dragon") (SMOKEY ROBINSON and SYREETA) / Peeping tom (ROCKWELL) / Inside you (WILLIE HUTCH with the TEMPTATIONS). *<(cd re-iss. Aug01; 530386-2)>*

S/track review: 'Motown' records and Berry Gordy's 'The LAST DRAGON' is a feast for the soulful R&B fan, with artists such as STEVIE WONDER, his former wife SYREETA (Wright) together with SMOKEY ROBINSON, WILLIE HUTCH combined with the TEMPTATIONS, DeBARGE and youngster ROCKWELL. All of the aforementioned performers feature on side two, the "Western side", with HUTCH contributing a solo, part-rapping song, 'The Glow', to side one. The "Eastern side" – as it was billed – also featured misfiring solo wannabes, DWIGHT DAVID (with the opening title track), one-hit-wonder CHARLENE (with 'Fire'), high-octave female ALFIE (by way of 'Let's Hear It For The Boy'-cloned 'Star') and the film's pouting co-star, VANITY (with the forgettable, '7th Heaven') – all poor by anybody's standards. Back to basics and the all-improved side two, we kick off with DeBARGE and their classic, Diane Warren-penned Caribbean cut, 'Rhythm Of The Night' – at last, a hit. ROCKWELL (aka Berry's son Kenneth Gordy), meanwhile, once again gets a little risqué via another pervy/voyeuristic, 'Peeping Tom', as the theme of 'Somebody's Watching Me' & 'Obscene Phone Caller' continued unabound. The three numbers from the aforementioned STEVIE WONDER ('Upset Stomach' – eh!), SMOKEY ROBINSON & SYREETA ('First Time On A Ferris Wheel') and WILLIE HUTCH with the TEMPTATIONS ('Inside You') were certainly exclusive, although they gave the impression of being outtakes from another project or indeed planet. *MCS*

Album rating: *4

– spinoff hits, etc. –

DeBARGE: Rhythm Of The Night / (non-OST song)

Feb 85. (7"/12") *Gordy; <1770> (TML/+T 1376)* [3] Mar85 [4]

LATE NIGHT SESSIONS

1999 (Can 82m) Arc2 Entertainment / Minna Street Flick Inc. (R)

Film genre: psychological urban drama

Top guns: s-w: (+ dir) Joshua B. Hamlin, Stephanie Seifert

Stars: Ryan Robbins *(Ben)*, Christine Chatelain *(Zoie)*, Michael Nyuis *(Shaggy)*, Caterpillar MacLaggan *(Nina)*, Kimani Ray Smith *(Manni)*, Terry Chen *(Dax)*, Zak Alam *(Danny)* ← SWEETWATER: A TRUE ROCK STORY / → JOSIE AND THE PUSSYCATS, Alisen Down *(Candy)*

Storyline: Ben and Zoie are working 24/7 to organize the United Get Down, the biggest rave party in Vancouver. The fact they haven't found anywhere to stage it yet poses a slight problem, but their troubles really begin when they find out that local bad guys Danny and Dax are planning to open their new club on the same night. As their ticket sales can be counted on the fingers of one hand, the Double Ds decide to ruin Ben and Zoie's "get down" by all means possible as they are quite depraved. *JZ*

Movie rating: *5

Visual: dvd (no audio OST)

Off the record: nothing

LAUREL CANYON

2002 (US 103m) Sony Pictures Classics (R)

Film genre: psychological/erotic drama

Top guns: s-w + dir: Lisa Cholodenko ← HIGH ART

Stars: Frances McDormand *(Jane)* ← ALMOST FAMOUS, Christian Bale *(Sam)* ← VELVET GOLDMINE ← METROLAND / → I'M NOT THERE, Kate Beckinsale *(Alex)*, Natascha McElhone *(Sara)*, Alessandro Nivola *(Ian McKnight)* ← REACH THE ROCK, Melissa De Sousa *(Claudia)* ← RIDE, **Louis Knox Barlow** *(Fripp)*, **Russell Pollard** *(Rowan)*, **Imaad Wasif** *(Dean)*, **Mark Linkous** *(himself)*, **Daniel Lanois** *(himself)* ← ALL THE PRETTY HORSES, **Justin Meldal-Johnsen** *(soft rocker)*

Storyline: When Harvard graduate Sam and his fiancée Alex relocate to Los Angeles, they decide to live with Sam's estranged mother Jane while looking for a new home. Sam is a record producer and her latest project involves her new toy-boy Ian, though drink and drugs seem more important to them than doing the actual work. Alex soon becomes drawn to the wild party lifestyle in the house while Sam begins paying much more attention to Alex's work colleague Sara. *JZ*

Movie rating: *6

Visual: dvd

Off the record: Louis Knox Barlow is noneother than Lou Barlow, ex-Dinosaur Jr. player and the man behind Sebadoh and FOLK IMPLOSION (see 'KIDS'); the former band included **Russell Pollard** who was also a member of offshoot San Franciscan-based outfit Alaska! alongside another Barlow-associate and ex-Lowercase singer/guitarist **Imaad Wasif** and **Mark Linkous** (of Sparklehorse). Eugene, Oregon-based **Justin Meldal-Johnsen** was bassist for L.A.-based alt-rock band, Ima Robot. *MCS*

Various Artists (score: Craig Wedren)

Mar 03. (cd) *Hollywood; <1 62392-2>* ☐ ☐
– In a funny way (MERCURY REV) / Do it again (STEELY DAN) / Shade and honey (ALESSANDRO NIVOLA) / Do you know what I mean (LEE MICHAELS) / Someday I will treat you good (ALESSANDRO NIVOLA) / Planet Queen (T. REX) / The shame of life (the BUTTHOLE SURFERS) / Good time (LEROY) / Harmony (CLINIC) / Crawling (SCAPEGOAT WAX) / Oscar Brown (BAXTER DURY) / Ma rencontre (BERTRAND BURGALAT) / C'est si bon (EARTHA KITT) / It's a wonderful life (SPARKLEHORSE).

S/track review: With ex-Shudder To Think man, Craig Wedren, taking a back seat on this one, it was left to a diverse Various Artists selection to shine through. 'In A Funny Way' by the mercurial MERCURY REV opened the album's account, not their best song ever and one of their more recent efforts, it's bright and psychedelic enough to stand out here. In fact, it's not too far removed from the album's other golden nuggets such as T.REX's 'Planet Queen' and STEELY DAN's 'Do It Again'. Another stemming from the early 70s, 'Do You Know What I Mean', was a white-funk, blue-eyed soul gem from the Top 10 of 1971, while we had to further back in time for EARTHA KITT's 'C'est Si Bon'. Having already featured on the soundtrack to '10 Things I Hate About You' (2001), the Beck-like LEROY was also present and correct here for 'Good Time', although the impression is he's the second coming of Lenny Kravitz; ditto SCAPEGOAT WAX and 'Crawling'. The little curio in the pack was Gallic newbie BERTRAND BURGALAT ('Ma Rencontre'), his interpretations not from the swinging 60s but more inspired from the likes of Stereolab. Modern-day Mersey-beaters, CLINIC, deliver 'Harmony', a song that was 60s Velvets meeting Can. Son of Ian, BAXTER DURY pulls off the album's surprise psychedelic cut, 'Oscar Brown', a song to make one-time weirdos, the BUTTHOLE SURFERS and their entry 'The Shame Of Life' weep into their Alabama 3-esque pint jugs. The film's fictional act(or), ALESSANDRO NIVOLA (augmented by alt-rockers LOU BARLOW and RUSS POLLARD), go dream-pop for two songs, 'Shade And Honey' and 'Someday I Will Treat You Good', both written by Mark Linkous, whose band SPARKLEHORSE also closes the OST with the dour, but excellent, 'It's A Wonderful Life'. *MCS*

Album rating: *7.5

LEADBELLY

1976 (US 126m) Paramount Pictures (PG)

Film genre: Blues-music bio-pic/drama

Top guns: dir: Gordon Parks ← SHAFT'S BIG SCORE! ← SHAFT / s-w: Ernest Kinoy

Stars: Roger E. Mosley *(Huddie Ledbetter)* ← the MACK / → BIG TIME, Paul Benjamin *(Wes Ledbetter)* ← FRIDAY FOSTER ← the EDUCATION OF SONNY CARSON ← ACROSS 110th STREET ← MIDNIGHT COWBOY / → the FIVE HEARTBEATS, Madge Sinclair *(Miss Eula)* ← CORNBREAD, EARL AND ME / → the LION KING, Alan Manson *(prison chief/guard)* → the DOORS, Albert P. Hall *(Dicklicker)* ← WILLIE DYNAMITE ← COTTON COMES TO HARLEM, Art Evans *(Blind Lemon Jefferson)* ← CLAUDINE / → BIG TIME → YOUNGBLOOD → SCHOOL DAZE → TRESPASS → CB4: THE MOVIE → the STORY OF US, James Brodhead *(John Lomax)*, John Henry Faulk *(Governor Neff)*, **Pete SEEGER** *(himself)* → NO DIRECTION HOME, Loretta Greene *(Lethe)* ← BLACK GIRL, Ernie Hudson *(cameo)* → the JAZZ SINGER → ROAD HOUSE → the CROW → AIRHEADS → the BASKETBALL DIARIES → a STRANGER IN THE KINGDOM

Storyline: The rise of Huddie Ledbetter, who spent his teen years wandering around the deep south taking jobs in the fields to stay alive. There he learned his huge repertoire of blues, folk ballads and spirituals which would help him to fame in later years. A strong man with a fiery temper, "Leadbelly" spent time inside on charges of murder, but his amazing musical ability earned him pardons from the prison governors and started his showbiz career. *JZ*

Movie rating: *6.5

Visual: none

Off the record: LEADBELLY was born Hudson William Ledbetter on the 29th of January, 1889, Mooringsport, Los Angeles, USA. A blues legend in his own right, "Huddie" displayed a unique musical talent at an early age and had ambition beyond range or scope. When he was thirteen, he had managed to learn to read and write (a very difficult thing to achieve for a black man at the start of the century) and had a substantial grasp on the ethics of guitar playing and performing. The teenager spent most of his nights wandering aimlessly through the red light districts and town squares on his home turf, attracting an audience with his own take-on of popular blues and spiritual music. After his marriage soured in the first decade of the 20th century, LEADBELLY changed his guitar format from 6-string to 12-string, a choice that bettered his career and enabled him to broaden his musical style. He re-worked a traditional song called 'Irene', which became one of his most treasured songs, and impressed Blind Lemon Jefferson so much that he decided to teach LEADBELLY slide guitar. However, success was not forthcoming, and due to his violent outbursts LEADBELLY constantly found himself on the wrong side of the law. In 1917, he was given a life sentence for murder and was sent to Texas State prison, where, ironically, he wrote his best material. His songs became increasingly popular with the prison inmates and governers, and in 1925, the man performed for one particular Texas governer who subsequently pardoned the enigmatic guitarist. When he was released from prison, LEADBELLY tried his best to keep on a straight path by doing odd and regular jobs. He was arrested again in 1930 and sentenced to life imprisonment for attempted murder. In Louisiana prison he met John Lomax (a travelling researcher for the Library of Congress) who was gathering Americana and blues related music with his son, Alan. Lomax was more than impressed with LEADBELLY's talents and managed to record material on his small portable studio in prison. In 1934, Lomax persuaded the Congress to free the bluesman, and with the aid of father and son, he became a minor hero in the white community. Lomax subsequently booked LEADBELLY for sessions at the "American record company", which brought coherence to his creations with smooth, clean and professionally recorded songs. However, LEADBELLY's relationship with Lomax was on the rocks due to manipulative and manufactured concerts where he was forced to dress up in a striped prison uniform; ultimately a gimmick to spread LEADBELLY's notoriety. Their partnership expired with LEADBELLY subsequently flitting to New York City in search of a more respectful audience – and that he found. Members of the Bohemian intelligentsia and folk/roots fans created a huge and almost cult following which attracted the attention of Moe Asch, manager of 'Folkway' records. It was here that perhaps the man's finest works were drawn: songs depicting the horrors of World War II were particularly ahead of their time. He continued to record for 'Asch' and 'Capitol' records throughout the 40s although inevitably he fell ill and died on the 6th of December 1949. Like many blues legends, fame came to LEADBELLY in death: the Weavers (featuring PETE SEEGER who cropped up in the movie itself) had a hit single with a folkie rendition of 'Goodnight Irene' in 1951, while skiffle-king Lonnie Donegan had a handful of UK smashes including 'Rock Island Line' and 'Bring A Little Water, Sylvie'; in 1970, the BEACH BOYS went to No.5 with 'Cotton Fields'. *AS & MCS*

—

Various (songs: LEADBELLY) (arranged: FRED KARLIN *)

1976. (lp) *A.B.C.; <ABDP 939>* ☐ [–]
– Go down, ol' Hannah / Fannin' street / Good morning blues / See that my grave is kept clean / The midnight special / Cotton fields (the cotton song) / The challenge (*) / Silver city bound / Rock island line / Goodnight Irene / Black girl / Green corn / Bring me a li'l water, Silvy / Old Riley (in dem long hot summer days).

S/track review: Do the blues work on a level backed by a full orchestra? Here's part of your answer, 'LEADBELLY', the movie soundtrack featuring a plethora of Blaxploitation actors transcending the music full-circle from the blues-meets-jazz song and dance musical 'Porgy And Bess' (1959). From opener, 'Go Down, Ol' Hannah', we get a-hollerin' – like most of LP sung by LEADBELLY voice stand-in, HI TIDE HARRIS – while the aforesaid orchestra, conducted by FRED KARLIN, set the ethereal mood. The latter also provided score track, 'The Challenge', while there was also a Blind Lemon Jefferson-penned gem (voice by ART EVANS), 'See That My Grave Is Kept Clean'. Blues soundtrack albums were thin on the ground, although the Blaxploitation movement had seen a few by TAJ MAHAL and one by BROWNIE McGHEE and SONNY TERRY ('BOOK OF NUMBERS'), who incidentally provided 6-string and harmonica respectively to 'LEADBELLY' movie tracks, 'Good Mornin' Blues' & the uptempo 'Green Corn'. The importance of folklorists John Lomax (and his son Alan) cannot be ignored, classics such as 'The Midnight Special', 'Rock Island', 'Bring Me A Li'l' Water, Silvy', might never've been heard but for their righteous attempts to document ALL the blues. What the late LEADBELLY might've thought of these blues-by-numbers film recordings is anyone's guess, but they certainly brought to the table an ageless appeal; example the character duet by Leadbelly and Blind Lemon on 'Silver City Bound'. If you're looking for melancholia through bluesy nostalgia you'll do no wrong in searching out two tracks at least, 'Black Girl' and closer 'Old Riley (In Dem Long Hot Summer Days)', the eerie, train-chuggin' strings on the latter are hair-raisin' – orchestral blues at its most effective. *MCS*

Album rating: *6.5

LENINGRAD COWBOYS GO AMERICA

1989 (Fin/Swe 78m) Finnkino Oy / Svenska Filminstitutet (PG-13)

Film genre: Road movie mockumentary (music comedy)

Top guns: s-w: (+ dir) Aki Kaurismaki (+ story w/ **Sakke Jarvenpaa** * + **Mato Valtonen**) * → ZOMBIE JA KUMMITUSJUNA → TOTAL BALALAIKA SHOW → LENINGRAD COWBOYS MEET MOSES

Stars: Matti Pellonpaa *(Vladimir; the manager)* + Kari Vaananen *(Igor; the village idiot)* → NIGHT ON EARTH ** → ZOMBIE JA KUMMITUSJUNA → LENINGRAD COWBOYS MEET MOSES, **the Leningrad Cowboys:- Mauri Sumen *, Mato Valtonen *, Sakke Jarvenpaa *, Silu Seppala *, Sakari Kuosmanen **, Pimme Korhonen, Puka Oinonen, Heikki Keskinen + Pekka Virtanen** *(themselves/performers)* * → ZOMBIE JA KUMMITUSJUNA → TOTAL BALALAIKA SHOW → LENINGRAD COWBOYS MEET MOSES, **Nicky Tesco** *(lost cousin)* ← URGH! A MUSIC WAR / → LENINGRAD COWBOYS MEET MOSES, Jim Jarmusch *(New York car dealer)* ← CANDY MOUNTAIN ← STRAIGHT TO HELL / → SLING BLADE → YEAR OF THE HORSE → I PUT A SPELL ON ME → the FUTURE IS UNWRITTEN

Storyline: A Soviet rock band – played by a Finnish band – attempt to find fame and fortune on the American small venue scene, albeit with varied degrees of success/failure (delete as appropriate). The goal is a Mexican wedding, the trouble is a village idiot wants to join their troupe. Spinal Tap for Trotsky-ites or students, it's actually based on the Marx Brothers movie, 'Go West'. *MCS*

Movie rating: *7

Visual: Essete Video / Artificial Eye

Off the record: **Nicky Tesco** was the frontman for punk band, the Members, who had a few hits in the late 70s including 'The Sound Of The Suburbs' (he also had bit parts in indie films, 'Thru The Wire' (1987), 'I Hired A Contract Killer' (1990) and 'Iron Horsemen' (1995). *MCS*

—

LENINGRAD COWBOYS

Oct 90. (cd) *Chlowig; (611539)* [–] Finn [–]
– L.A. woman / Marching / Flight AY 105 / Thru the wire / Sunday morning / Highway / Rocky VI / Blue swing / On the road / That's alright / Glamour cowboy / No man's land / Born to be wild / Ten lost gringos / Mambo from Sakkijarvi / Desconsolado / Ballad of the Leningrad Cowboys / Tequila / Chasing the light.

S/track review: Whether you're a Richard Marx-ist or a John "Lennongrad"-ist, you'll enjoy the basic toilet humour music of these Russian invaders (er, actually double-figured Finnish ensemble the SLEEPY SLEEPERS!); there was a "Cold War" front now indeed hitting parts of the United States via 'LENINGRAD COWBOYS GO AMERICA'. If ZZ Top & Van Morrison ever get together to cover the Doors' classic, 'L.A. Woman', the opening song would be what it sounds like. An excellent rock and rollicking start by my book. The full Soviet Red Army seems to have been invited into the studio for the appropriately-titled 'Marching', although I got a little "brassed-off" by the end. The jazzy, 'Flight AY 105', is upbeat, cool and funky in places and segues between 'The Star-Spangled Banner' and a saxxy "stripper" instrumental. Another saxxy one, 'Thru The Wire' – probably the "saddest" song I've ever heard! – conjures up Springsteen and Tom Waits sharing a microphone, although it's 'Sounds Of The Suburbs' man NICKY TESCO who actually does the er ... damage. The 'COWBOYS (featuring MAURI SUMEN) were nostalgic in an old cinematic way during the melancholic, 'Sunday Morning', while 'Highway' sounds like what Glenn Miller would have sounded like post-rock'n'roll, had he not previously kicked the "big band" bucket. We go foreign-film-intro-turns-disco for track 7, 'Rocky VI', just imagine Sylvester Stallone doing 'SATURDAY NIGHT FEVER', not

John Travolta, er . . . mouth-shattering. Passing by some tin pan alley lounge instrumentals, the Finnish congregation get all Elvis on us by taking on 'That's Alright', while 'Glamour Cowboy' is pure 'Moondance'-meets-Mancini. Track 12, 'No Man's Land', calls out "Godfather-like" to their fictional homeland for forgiveness, but I think these comics had crossed the line, even before their Martin C Strong/karaoke version of Steppenwolf's classic 'Born To Be Wild'. If you were to guess what 'Ten Lost Gringos' sounded like, most folks out there might be forgiven for thinking of Ennio Morricone, you'd be wrong as this has Ry Cooder's stamp (with a hint of Jim Reeves' 'You'll Have To Go') emblazoned on its picturesque acoustics and piano. Did I mention the 'Cowboys liked to polka? Polka they did on accordion-biased 'Mambo From Sakkijarvi' and the Mexicano 'Desconsolado'. Ditto the latter for the alcoholic-inspired 'Tequila', an old chestnut from the Champs, while 'Chasing The Light' is indeed NICKY TESCO's country song, country in a way that Finland/Russia meets England/America. *MCS*

Album rating: *6

LENINGRAD COWBOYS MEET MOSES

1994 sequel (Fin/Ger/Fra 91m) La Sept Cinema / Sputnik Oy

Film genre: Rock Musical road movie/comedy

Top guns: s-w + dir: Aki Kaurismaki ← TOTAL BALALAIKA SHOW ← ZOMBIE JA KUMMITUSJUNA ← LENINGRAD COWBOYS GO AMERICA (+ story w/ **Sakke Jarvenpaa + Mato Valtonen**; see above)

Stars: Leningrad Cowboys:- Mauri Sumen *, Sakke Jarvenpaa *, Mato Valtonen *, Silu Seppala *, Pemo Ojala, Lyle Narvanen, Ekke Niiva, Twist-Twist Erkinharju, Ben Granfelt, Jore Marjaranta *(themselves/performers)* * ← TOTAL BALALAIKA SHOW ← ZOMBIE JA KUMMITUSJUNA ← LENINGRAD COWBOYS GO AMERICA, Matti Pellonpaa *(Vladimir / Moses)* + Kari Vaananen *(the mute)* ← ZOMBIE JA KUMMITUSJUNA ← NIGHT ON EARTH ← LENINGRAD COWBOYS GO AMERICA, Andre Wilms *(Lazarus / Johnson)*, **Nicky Tesco** *(American cousin)* ← LENINGRAD COWBOYS GO AMERICA ← URGH! A MUSIC WAR

Storyline: Dubbed "the worst rock'n'roll band in the world" – by themselves! – the Leningrad Cowboys have settled in Mexico (the land of tequila) having had a Top 10 hit. Their mysterious manager, Vladimir (now thinking he's Moses!), surfaces from out of the blue, and it's his mission to return them back to Russia, via "the promised land" – Siberia. *MCS*

Movie rating: *4

Visual: video + dvd (no audio OST)

Off the record: The LENINGRAD COWBOYS (i.e. songwriter/arranger **Mauri Sumen**, and Co), let loose some of their usual novelty canon, 'Rosita', 'Nolo Tengo Dinares', 'Kili Watch', 'Kasatchok', 'Lonely Moon', 'Wedding March', 'I Woke Up This Morning Last Night', 'Matuschka', 'Uralin Pihlaja', 'The Sunbeam And The Goblin', 'U.S. Border' & 'Rivers Of Babylon'. *MCS*

□ John LENNON
(⇒ the BEATLES)

□ LET IT ROCK alt.
(⇒ WHITE STAR)

LET'S ROCK

UK title 'KEEP IT COOL'

1958 (US 79m b&w) Columbia Pictures

Film genre: Rock musical drama

Top guns: dir: Harry Foster / s-w: Hal Hackady → HEY, LET'S TWIST → TWO TICKETS TO PARIS

Stars: Julius LaRosa *(Tommy Adane)*, Phyllis Newman *(Kathy Abbott)*, Conrad Janis *(Charlie)* → the BUDDY HOLLY STORY, Harold Gary *(Shep Harris)*, Ned Wertimer *(studio manager)*, **Paul Anka** *(performer)* → SHAKE, RATTLE & ROCK! tv, **Danny & The Juniors** *(performers)*, **Della Reese** *(performer)*, **Wink Martindale** *(performer)* → MEDUSA: DARE TO BE TRUTHFUL, **Roy Hamilton** *(performer)* ← the PIED PIPER OF CLEVELAND, **the Tyrones:- Tyrone DeNittis, George Lesser, Al DeNittis** *(performers)*, **the Royal Teens w/ Bob Gaudio** *(performer)* → BEACH BALL, Joy Harmon *(pick-up girl)* → ROUSTABOUT

Storyline: Flagging pop swingers and balladeers (such as Tommy Adane) are trying to get in on the game of rock'n'roll, but are they just too old to shake their hips daddy-o. *MCS*

Movie rating: *2.5

Visual: video (no audio OST)

Off the record: Famous for being sacked by radio and TV personality Arthur Godfrey, Brooklyn-born **Julius LaRosa** (he was 38 when this movie was made) was an old-style crooner in the wake of Frank Sinatra; he sang four songs here, 'Crazy, Crazy Party', 'Two Perfect Strangers', 'These Are Times' and 'Casual' (the latter with Phyllis Newman). Actor/musician, Conrad Janis, was (and still is, to a certain degree) a Dixieland/jazz trombonist who released a string of albums in the early 50s. **Paul Anka** is of course, the crooner behind classic song 'My Way', covered en mass by Sinatra, etc. **Roy Hamilton** ('Here Comes Loves' in the movie) was in the same mould although he was primarily a singer, not a songwriter ('You'll Never Walk Alone' and 'Unchained Melody'); he died in 1969, having earlier suffered a stroke. Childhood chum of Elvis, **Wink Martindale**, was a DJ in the 50s and had a narrative country hit, 'Deck Of Cards' around the same time; one song here, 'All Love Broke Loose'. **Della Reese** (contributing 'Lonelyville' here), starting singing at an early age and progressed to being a top gospel/R&B singer; subsequently responsible for the 1959 No.2 hit, 'Don't You Know'. **the Tyrones** (from Philadelphia) were discovered and sponsored by Bill Haley and had a string of local hits including 'Blast Off' (featured in the movie); the 1999 movie, 'The Iron Giant' featured a few Tyrones numbers. **Bob Gaudio** of the Royal Teens ('Short Shorts' a Top 3 just prior to the film) was soon a member of the Four Seasons. Another highlight of the film, saw the inclusion of **Danny & The Juniors** recent chart-topping smash, 'At The Hop'. *MCS*

□ LEVIATAN alt.
(⇒ MONSTER DOG)

Jerry Lee LEWIS

Born: 29 Sep'35, Ferriday, Louisiana, USA. In 1949, Jerry Lee's parents mortgaged their house to buy him a piano which he mastered in two weeks! A few years later, after being expelled from a religious school that taught music, he married a preacher's daughter; he soon deserted her however, bigamously marrying another girl in true shotgun style. In 1956, LEWIS went to Memphis, Tennessee with his father and through perseverance, set up recording time in Sam Phillips' 'Sun' studios. The following year, after his debut, 'Crazy Arms', was banned from airplay, LEWIS secured a couple of appearances on the Steve Allen TV Show, the exposure leading to massive sales of his second single, 'Whole Lotta Shakin' Goin' On'. Although LEWIS didn't actually write any of his material, his demented rock'n'roll performances (he even pummelled the piano with his feet!) earned him the rather unfortunate nickname, "The Killer". Later in '57, Jerry Lee bigamously married again!, this time secretly to his 13 year-old second cousin, Myra Gale Brown. Perhaps inspired by his recent activities, LEWIS scored two enormous worldwide classics in the appropriately titled 'Great Balls Of Fire' (used in the 1957 movie, 'JAMBOREE') and 'Breathless'. Meanwhile, he divorced his second wife and brought the wrath of the religious establishment and moral majority when his questionable lifestyle was disclosed; LEWIS' UK arrival (in May '58) caused uproar and near tour cancellation after newspapers had a field day over his "minor" misdemeanours. His second celluloid appearance came via his performance in 'HIGH SCHOOL CONFIDENTIAL' (1958); a single was released to coincide with the movie. Although Jerry Lee made a few more sporadic returns to the charts, his career had been severely dented by this late 50s hysteria. While Myra gave birth to his second son in February '59, LEWIS's intake of alcohol and pills was increasing every month. Tragedy struck in April '62, when his aforementioned son drowned in a swimming pool accident. Around a year and a half later, coinciding with LEWIS' signature for new imprint 'Smash', Myra produced another child, this time a daughter. Two further movie appearances came about with 'BE MY GUEST' (1965) and 'KEEP ON ROCKIN'' (1969), while in the early 70s, Myra finally divorced him, claiming neglect, etc. It didn't stop him marrying a fourth time, although this time he did it legally in late '71. Enjoying something of a resurrection in 1973 – see 'The LONDON ROCK AND ROLL SHOW' (and by which time he'd traded in his blue suede shoes for Stetson-styled country-pop), tragedy struck again when his son (his drummer on tour) Jerry Lee, Jr. was killed in a motoring accident. In 1976, LEWIS was involved in two gun incidents, one when he accidently shot his bassman, Norman Owens, the other occurring outside Gracelands (Elvis Presley's home) hours after being charged with drunk driving. LEWIS signed to 'Elektra' in 1978, although a few albums and a serious stomach ulcer operation later, he sued the label. In 1982, his estranged fourth wife, Jaren Gunn Lewis (ne Pate), drowned in a mysterious swimming pool incident just prior to their divorce settlement. The following year, coming up for his 50th birthday, the irrepressible LEWIS tied the knot yet again, this time to a 25 year-old, Shawn Michelle Stevens; just over two months later, she was to be found dead in their home. Although suspected of foul play, no case was brought and LEWIS, proving that he was a family man at heart, went on to marry his sixth wife, the 22 year-old, Kerrie McCarver, who, in early '87, gave birth to a son, Jerry Lee Lewis III. A few years later, after a guest spot in Chuck Berry's 'HAIL! HAIL! ROCK'N'ROLL' in '87, his biopic film story, 'GREAT BALLS OF FIRE!' (1989) was premiered, featuring new re-recordings of his golden oldies; actor Dennis Quaid played LEWIS. *BG & MCS*

- **filmography** {performance/acting} [s-w] –

Jamboree *(1957 {p} =>)* / **High School Confidential** *(1958 {p} =>)* / **Be My Guest** *(1965 {p} =>)* / **Keep On Rockin'** *(1969 {p} =>)* / **the London Rock And Roll Show** *(1973 {p} on OST by V/A =>)* / **American Hot Wax** *(1978 {c} on OST by V/A =>)* / Middle Age Crazy *(1980 [s-w])* / **the Compleat Beatles** *(1984 {a/p} =>)* / I Am What I Am *(1987 TV {p} =>)* / **Hail! Hail! Rock'n'Roll** *(1987 {p} on OST by CHUCK BERRY =>)* / **Great Balls Of Fire!** *(1989 {m} OST by LEWIS =>)* / In Dreams: The Roy Orbison Story *(1999 TV)* / **Mayor Of The Sunset Strip** *(2003 {c} OST by V/A =>)*

LIALEH

1973 (US 80m) Arrow Releasing (X)

Film genre: erotic/soft-porn Musical drama

Top guns: s-w + dir: Barron Borcovichy

Stars: Jennifer Leigh *(Lialeh)*, Larry Perillar *(Arlo)*, **Bernard Purdie** *(pimp)*, Darryl Speer *(Chasin)*, Amy/Any Mathiew *(French girl)*, Inger Kissen aka **Andrea True** *(cameo)*, Terrance Brady

Storyline: Oft cited as the first Afro-erotic film (described as "the black Deep Throat"), this threadbare-plotted tale centres on a pimp's efforts to stage a sex musical and a black girl's desperation to make it as a soul singer. *BG*

Movie rating: *5

Visual: video

Off the record: Nashville-born **Andrea True** Connection had subsequent disco hits in the 70s, 'More, More, More (How Do You Like It)', was her biggest asset – musically speaking. **Bernard Purdie** (see below) *MCS*

—

BERNARD "PRETTY" PURDIE

Jan 04. (cd/lp) *Light In The Attic; <LITA 003 CD/LP>* □ [-]
– Lialeh / Touch me again / Conscious / Easy / All pink on the inside / Pass me not / Hap'nin.

S/track review: Even if you're unfamiliar with the name BERNARD 'PRETTY' PURDIE, chances are he's credited on one of your favourite albums. Since the 60s, he's been one of the most in-demand and most sampled drummers in the business, with more than 3000 sessions to his name including gigs with the likes of Aretha Franklin, James Brown and the Rolling Stones. With 'LIALEH' (1974), an irredeemably obscure low-budget effort infamous for being the first black porn flick, PURDIE jumped at the chance of taking full writing/composing credits on his first – and to date only – film soundtrack. He even appeared in the movie itself, as the CD reissue's sleevenotes humorously recount. Bass player Wilbur 'Bad' Bascomb fills in the picture: "And they started shooting a nude scene with some girl and some guy! I said "Hey, man, what kind of stuff is – " and he {Purdie} said "Never mind, man, just keep playing!". Gifted full creative control, PURDIE took that same insouciance into the studio, creating something far classier than bog-standard porn-funk fare. Sure, there's kitschy innuendo galore, not least on 'Touch Me Again' and, ahem, 'All Pink On The Inside', but that's hardly the reason this record has traditionally fetched such astronomical prices on the collectors' market. While 'Hap'nin' offers a locomotive, highly sought-after masterclass in polyrhythm, the man rarely showboats and isn't exactly a slouch on the songwriting front either- 'Easy' sounds like the kind of soulfood ballad Ronnie Lane might have written for the Faces had he been born black. The CD booklet even throws in stills of PURDIE nonchalantly pounding the skins despite the nubile distractions of Jennifer Leigh. Now that must've taken willpower. *BG*

Album rating: *7

the LIFE AND HARD TIMES OF GUY TERRIFICO

2005 (Can 86m) Darius Films / Alliance Atlantis (R)

Film genre: Country-music mockumentary comedy

Top guns: s-w + dir: Michael Mabbott

Stars: **Matt Murphy** *(Guy Terrifico)*, **Kris KRISTOFFERSON** *(himself)*, **Donnie Fritts** *(himself)* ← SONGWRITER ← a STAR IS BORN ← PAT GARRETT & BILLY THE KID, Phil Kaufman *(himself)* ← FALLEN ANGEL ← GRAND THEFT PARSONS ← BABY SNAKES, **Merle Haggard** *(himself)* ← WAG THE DOG ← FROM NASHVILLE WITH MUSIC ← HILLBILLYS IN A HAUNTED HOUSE, **Levon Helm** *(himself)* <= the BAND =>, **Ronnie Hawkins** *(himself)* ← RENALDO AND CLARA ← the LAST WALTZ, Lyriq Bent *(Mr. Stuff)* ← HONEY / → TAKE THE LEAD, Natalie Radford *(Mary Lou)*, Rob Bowman *(himself)* ← FESTIVAL EXPRESS, Jane Sowerby ← the LINDA McCARTNEY STORY

Storyline: The unusual life of semi-legend in his lunchtime, Guy Terrifico, who alongside his talent and good looks had a unique ability to trip over his own feet. It all went wrong for the (fairly) great man when a lottery win led to the wobbly warbler opening a bar and recording his own music (with accompanying dwarf). Things go from bad to worse and he's reduced to appearing on a religious musical programme, whose host makes a bit of a fist of things. *JZ*

Movie rating: *5

Visual: dvd

Off the record: **MATT MURPHY** (see below)

—

GUY TERRIFICO: Bring It Back Home *(aka MATT MURPHY – songwriter & Michael Mabbott)*

Jan 06. (cd) *Outside; <9012>* [–] Can [–]
– Saturday night / Just a show – rehearsal / Just a show / Worth a song / Friend of the Devil / Rambler / Walking back to Houston / Let's make love again / Si señor / Whiskey, you can save me – live in Toronto / Midnight rider / I'm only make believe / Alberta son / New Mr. Me (duet w/ KRIS KRISTOFFERSON). *(bonus +=)* – Perogie moon / The gospel song / Going to the country / The pilgrim: Chapter 33 (live at the Opera House, Toronto w/ KRIS KRISTOFFERSON) / (My life would make) A damn good country song.

S/track review: The brainchild of filmmaker/songsmith, Michael Mabbott, who, with his writing partner MATT MURPHY, worked to recreate something their "imaginary" hillbilly friend, Guy Terrifico, could only have dreamt of. Putting country legends aside, in reality "Bring It Back Home" was a vehicle – or just an excuse – to highlight the country-roots alter-ego MURPHY, a singer/guitarist who once trod the indie-rock boards with Super Friendz and offshoots, the Flashing Lights. With a backing band that boasted BOB EGAN on pedal steel guitar, JOHN BORRA or TRACY STEVENS on bass, CHRIS MURPHY or DAVE MARSH on drums, and JAMES GREY or BILL STEVENSON on piano, MATT MURPHY metamorphosed into "Guy Terrifico", albeit for a brief moment in time. 'Saturday Night' opens up the country charade, while 'Just A Show' (another one of many from Terrifico's faux set, 'Retribution Honky Tonkus') gives a good impression of say . . . Tom Petty fronting the Grateful Dead. The fact that Terrifico/MURPHY re-"hash" Garcia & Co's 'Friend Of The Devil' is no coincidence, while other covers come by way of the Allman Brothers' 'Midnight Rider' and Bruce Cockburn's 'Goin' To The Country' (the latter one of the bonus tracks not featured in the film). 'Worth A Song', 'Rambler', 'Walking Back To Houston', 'I'm Only Make Believe', the all-too-brief 'Alberta Son' and 'Let's Make Love Again' (with guest vox by RUTH MINNIKIN) kept the country-rock flag flying, while 'Si Señor' took a leaf out from the Area Code 615 book of instrumentals. The Dylan/Petty-like "live in Toronto" track, 'Whiskey, You Can Save Me', is probably the most derivative (and best) of country tunes, the crowd noises giving it an extra oomph. A namecheck to hero DONNIE FRITTS tagged at the end of the song leads to the latter's own pastiche bonus contribution from 1975, '(My Life Would Make) A Damn Good Country Song'. Another country/songwriting idol arrives courtesy of KRIS KRISTOFFERSON, who duets with MURPHY on 'New Mr. Me' and goes solo for bonus cut, 'The Pilgrim'. Country fans with a sense of irony (or humour) will enjoy this set without getting into too much hysterics. *MCS*

Album rating: *6

LIFE & LYRICS

2006 (UK 99m) Fiesta Productions / UIP (15)

Film genre: romantic urban/Rap-music drama

Top guns: dir: Richard Laxton / s-w: Ken Williams

Stars: **Ashley Walters** *(DJ Danny 'D-Biz' Lewis)* ← GET RICH OR DIE TRYIN', **Louise Rose** *(Carmen)*, Christopher Steward *(Fable)*, Alexis Rodney *(Cashflow)*, Patrick Regis *(Money Man)*, Cat Simmons *(Sista Twista)*, Jade Williams *(Lady Gees)*, Jason Maza *(Ant)*

Storyline: South London is the setting for Britain's answer to '8 Mile' (throw into the mix, 'Hustle & Flow', 'Boyz N The Hood' and even 'Romeo & Juliet', and you have most of the ingredients to make this movie work – emphasise on most). 20-something Danny Lewis is the man getting all loved up in between some DJ rap battles for the coveted Mic Masters competition. "Live Life At Full Volume" . . . if you like that sort of thing. *MCS*

Movie rating: *5

Visual: dvd

Off the record: **Ashley Walters** is noneother than Asher D, bad-boy of Brit Hip-Hop aggregate, So Solid Crew, who had a string of Top 10 hits including No.1 debut, '21 Seconds'. **Louise Rose** had her own degree of success, when as Precious, she was United Kingdom's entry (with 'Say It Again') into the 1999 Eurovision Song Contest; it came 12th, the record hit No.6, and Precious had a few other chart entries in 2000. *MCS*

—

Various Artists

Sep 06. (cd) *Cinetracks; (CINECD 001)* [ ] [–]
– Brown eyes (KANO) / Coast 2 coast (LIL KEKE) / Yeek! (SKY HY) / Whut it do (MARZ) / Party hard (the PERCEPTIONISTS ft GURU & CAMUTAO) / That sound (OHMEGA WATTS) / (Keeps on) Burning (GUM DROP) / Dance with me (ESTELLE) / Cupid (SHERRISA STEWART) / The Royalpriesthood (the ROYAL PRIESTHOOD) / Catch me if U can (C-MONE) / Perfect world (CAGE) / No pills, no frills (STYLY CEE ft MIDNYTE) / Broke ballers anthem (SKY HY ft C'BEYOHN) / Video tape it (MARZ) / Treading water (DEEP VARACOUZO) / Epiphany (HKB FINN) / Month in the summer (SWAY ft TEDDY).

S/track review: However poorly received the film 'LIFE & LYRICS' was, the soundtrack was a stellar compilation of British urban sounds. How representative it is of the capital's cutting edge music scene is anyone's guess outside the street-level culture, but with cockney rhyming over hard-hitting bass and beats, this is at very least a thorough workout for your stereo. London's bigger grime exports such as Dizzee Rascal, Skinnyman and Roll Deep might be conspicuous by their absence, but a sugary closer from emerging talent SWAY (here featuring TEDDY) is typical of the high standard in cut selection. Opening proceedings with an early reference to 'Eastenders' is the other celebrated name in the line-up and KANO's 'Brown Eyes' makes for a winning mid-tempo introduction. From there the net is cast wide to encapsulate a myriad metropolitan soul flavours. Attitude abounds in the garage, grime and hip hop of LIL KEKE, SKY HY and C-MONE, supplemented by the occasional left-of-centre US artist such as OHMEGA WATTS. The pace is changeable, UK street bangers enjoying the majority rule but interspersed with silky, nu-soul grooves like ESTELLE's 'Dance With Me' and the down-tempo, off-kilter '(Keeps On) Burning' by GUM DROP. It isn't all stone-cold London 'tude, however; some might find the throwback soul-pop of SHERRISA STEWART's 'Cupid' a turn-off and the lush orchestration of 'Epiphany' can't save HKB FINN from an out of place earnestness. *MR*

Album rating: *7

LIGHT OF DAY

1987 (US 107m) Taft Entertainment / Tri-Star Pictures (PG-13)

Film genre: domestic showbiz/Rock-music drama

Top guns: s-w (+ dir): Paul Schrader → the LAST TEMPTATION OF CHRIST → TOUCH → AFFLICTION

Stars: Michael J. Fox *(Joe Rasnick)* ← CLASS OF 1984 / → WHERE THE RIVERS FLOW NORTH, Gena Rowlands *(Jeanette Rasnick)* → NIGHT ON EARTH, **Joan Jett** *(Patti Rasnick)* <= the RUNAWAYS =>, Michael McKean *(Bu Montgomery)* ← THIS IS SPINAL TAP / → EARTH GIRLS ARE EASY

→ AIRHEADS → GIGANTIC (A TALE OF TWO JOHNS) → a MIGHTY WIND, Thomas G. Waites *(Smittie)*, Jason Miller *(Benjamin Rasnick)*, Cherry Jones *(Cindy Montgomery)*, Michael Dolan *(Gene Bodine)*, Paul J. Harkins *(Billy Tatton)* → HEARTBREAK HOTEL, Michael Rooker *(Oogie)*, **the Fabulous Thunderbirds:- Jimmie Vaughan** *(guitarist)* → GREAT BALLS OF FIRE! → BLUES BROTHERS 2000, **Kim Wilson, Fran Christina, Preston Hubbard** *(themselves)* / **Trent Reznor** *(member of the Problems)* → WOODSTOCK 94, the Hunzz:- Mark Diamond, Jimi Bell, Joe Aparo, Mark Franco / John Rubano *(arguing man)* → SPIRIT: STALLION OF THE CIMARRON

Storyline: Joe and Patti play in Cleveland rock band the Barbusters. The brother and sister have different priorities – Patti wants to put her life and soul into her music while Joe is more concerned with patching up the differences between Patti and her mother Jeanette, and looking after Patti's young son Benji. Things reach meltdown with mum when the band quit their day jobs and go on tour, taking Benji with them. *JZ*

Movie rating: *4.5

Visual: video

Off the record: Trent Reznor was of course future brainchild of industrial rockers, Nine Inch Nails.

—

Various Artists/Cast (score: THOMAS NEWMAN *)

Mar 87. (lp/c/cd) *Blackheart; <ZK/ZT/ZD 40654> (450501-1/-4/-2)* [82] May87 [ ]
– Light of day (the BARBUSTERS) / This means war (the BARBUSTERS) / Twist it off (the FABULOUS THUNDERBIRDS) / Cleveland rocks (IAN HUNTER) / Stay with me tonight (DAVE EDMUNDS) / It's all coming down tonight (the BARBUSTERS) / Rude mood (the BARBUSTERS) / Only lonely (BON JOVI) / RABBIT'S GOT THE GUN (the HUNZZ) / You got no place to go (MICHAEL J. FOX) / Elegy – instrumental (RICK COX, CHAS SMITH, JON C. CLARKE & MICHAEL BODDICKER) *.

S/track review: A record that has no trouble at all living down to the phenomenal mullet hairstyles on its cover, this is curiously difficult to dislike – but then, who hasn't got a soft spot for a good mullet? Things start encouragingly with a gung-ho performance that makes the most of the workaday Springsteen-penned title track (the New Jersey star was friends with writer/director Paul Schrader). Led by JOAN JETT and MICHAEL J FOX, the screen band, the BARBUSTERS had apparently earned their stripes playing in real bars before production began, and on their other four songs they deliver catchy 80s mainstream guitar rock with a practised efficiency that equals (and frankly exposes) the bland genre's "genuine" celebrities. It must be said, too, that there isn't much threat from the competition: the FABULOUS THUNDERBIRDS – a mighty steamroller of a band at their best – trundle by inoffensively; DAVE EDMUNDS brings a typically endearing slice of rockabilly-lite; and IAN HUNTER and Mick Ronson upchuck a wobbling, wayward and frankly falling-over live version of HUNTER's 'Cleveland Rocks' long before it was the theme tune to the Drew Carey Show. BON JOVI's risible 1984 single 'Only Lonely' also makes an appearance. It's undeniably disappointing, too, to find Spinal Tap's David St Hubbins (actor Michael McKean, who plays bass for the BARBUSTERS) in such blithely humdrum fare. *ND*

Album rating: *5.5

– spinoff hits, etc. –

the BARBUSTERS: Light Of Day / (non-OST song)

Feb 87. (7") *<06692>* [33] [–]

the LINDA McCARTNEY STORY

2000 (Can/US 90m TV) Lions Gate / Mandalay / Columbia TriStar

Film genre: Pop/Rock-music bio-pic/drama

Top guns: dir: Armand Mastroianni / s-w: Christine Berardo

Stars: Elizabeth Mitchell *(Linda McCartney)*, Gary Bakewell *(Paul McCartney)* ← BACKBEAT, David Lewis *(Danny Field)*, Matthew Harrison *(Mick Jagger)*, George Segal *(Lee Eastman)* ← the OWL AND THE PUSSYCAT, Tim Piper *(John Lennon)*, Aaron Grain *(Jim Morrison)*, Moya O'Connell *(Heather McCartney)*, Alexander Ruurs *(James McCartney)*, Chris Cound *(George Harrison)*, Michael McMurtry *(Ringo Starr)*, Jane Sowerby *(Chrissie Hynde)* → the LIFE AND HARD TIMES OF GUY TERRIFICO, Linda Ko *(Yoko Ono)*, Claude Duhamel *(Keith Richards)*, Rafe McDonald *(Brian Jones)*, Mitchell Parsons *(Bill Wyman)*

Storyline: Concentrating on the relationship between Linda and Paul, the film begins with her photographs of the rich and famous, reminding us that she was a successful snapper before her more fruitful musical career. However, it's pretty much love at first sight for Paul and Linda and soon they marry. Her long battle against breast cancer is portrayed and her determination to have an active life is shown in her last years by her well-publicised involvement with vegetarianism. Throughout it all Paul remained loyal and steadfast until the end. *JZ*

Movie rating: *5

Visual: video (no audio OST; score: J. Peter Robinson)

Off the record: *Linda McCartney* (see above)

the LION KING

1994 (US 89m) Walt Disney Pictures (G)

Film genre: animated family/children's fantasy/Musical

Top guns: dir: Roger Allers → OPEN SEASON / s-w: Irene Mecchi, Jonathan Roberts, Linda Woolverton

Voices: Matthew Broderick *(Simba)*, Jeremy Irons *(Scar)*, Rowan Atkinson *(Zazu the hornbill)*, Niketa Calame *(young Nala)*, Whoopi Goldberg *(Shenzi the hyena)* → JACKIE'S BACK!, Moira Kelly *(Nala)*, Ernie Sabella *(Pumbaa the warthog)*, Jim Cummings *(Ed)*, Robert Guillaume *(Rafiki)* ← SUPERFLY T.N.T., **Cheech Marin** *(Banzai the hyena)* <= CHEECH & CHONG =>, James Earl Jones *(King Mufasa)* ← a PIECE OF THE ACTION ← CLAUDINE / → PRIMARY COLORS, Madge Sinclair *(Queen Sarabi)* ← LEADBELLY ← CORNBREAD, EARL AND ME, Jonathan Taylor Thomas *(young Simba)*, Nathan Lane *(Timon the meerkat)*, Jason Weaver *(young Simba; singing)*, **Joseph Williams** *(adult Simba; singing)*

Storyline: The Lion King tells the story of Simba, a lion cub who is the son of old lion King Mufasa. When the evil Scar murders Mufasa, Simba is forced to flee into the jungle to save himself. There he befriends Pumbaa the warthog and Timon the meerkat. But when his father's ghost visits Simba and tells him he must reclaim the throne which is rightfully his, Simba begins a coming-of-age quest which must inevitably culminate in a life-or-death battle with Scar to see who will be the Lion King. *JZ*

Movie rating: *7.5

Visual: video + dvd

Off the record: Joseph Williams (son of composer John Williams) was the singer in the rock band, Toto, from 1986. *MCS*

—

ELTON JOHN & TIM RICE (score: HANS ZIMMER *)

Jun 94. (cd) *Walt Disney; <60858> Mercury; (522690-2)* [1] Oct94 [4]
– The circle of life (CARMEN TWILLIE) / I just can't wait to be king (JASON WEAVER) / Be prepared (JEREMY IRONS) / Hakuna matata (NATHAN LANE & ERNIE SABALLA) / Can you feel the love tonight? (JOSEPH WILLIAMS & SALLY DWORSKY) / This

land (*) / To die for (*) / Under the stars (*) / King of pride rock (*) / The circle of life (ELTON JOHN) / I just can't wait to be king (ELTON JOHN) / Can you feel the love tonight? (ELTON JOHN).

S/track review: Initially the Disney conglomerate was unsure about the commission of contemporary pop icon, ELTON JOHN, after they heard the early drafts of one of the pieces, 'The Circle Of Life'; thoughts were, why change the winning Alan Menken-penned formula that had given them 'The Little Mermaid', 'Beauty And The Beast' and 'Aladdin'. However, when the Disney team signed up Academy Award-winning lyricist TIM RICE ('JESUS CHRIST SUPERSTAR', etc.) and the multi-faceted HANS ZIMMER for the score, things looked a bit more promising, especially when Elton chose an overall South African/Paul Simon-Graceland theme. The aforementioned Top 20 single 'Circle . . .' opened the album, albeit with CARMEN TWILLIE hitting the high notes instead of JOHN himself. His opportunity came towards the end and preceded two other solo gems, 'I Just Can't Wait To Be King' and the Top 5, 'Can You Feel The Love Tonight?'; a shortened version of the latter was also performed by JOSEPH WILLIAMS & SALLY DWORSKY. The Jungle Book-esque, 'Be Prepared' and 'Hakuna Mata' (er . . . "sung" by actors JEREMY IRONS and NATHAN LANE respectively) were of the unadultered comical variety and were best accompanied in the cinema by your not-too-discerning offspring. The sad part is what little kids (and big kids for that matter!) would make of the four ZIMMER instrumental pieces, serious stuff for today's pop-centric teenyboppers. *MCS*

Album rating: *4.5

– spinoff hits, etc. –

ELTON JOHN: Can You Feel The Love Tonight? / JOSEPH WILLIAMS & SALLY DWORSKY: Can You Feel The Love Tonight?

May 94. (7"/c-s) *<64543> (EJS/+MC 34)* [4] Jun94 [14]
(cd-s+=) *(EJCD 34)* – NATHAN LANE & ERNIE SABELLA: Hakuna Matata / HANS ZIMMER: Under the stars.

ELTON JOHN: The Circle Of Life / CARMEN TWILLIE: The Circle Of Life

Aug 94. (c-s) *<64516> (EJSMC 35)* [18] Sep94 [11]
(cd-s+=/pic-cd-s+=) *(EJS CD/CX 35)* – ELTON JOHN: I just can't wait to be king / HANS ZIMMER: Under the stars.

LIPSTICK ON YOUR COLLAR

1993 (UK 50 x 6 epi; TV mini) Whistling Gypsy / Channel 4

Film genre: surreal romantic Rock'n'roll Musical comedy drama

Top guns: dir: Renny Rye / s-w: Dennis Potter (+ story) ← BRIMSTONE & TREACLE / → the SINGING DETECTIVE

Stars: Giles Thomas *(Pvt. Francis Francis)* → HUMAN TRAFFIC, Louise Germaine *(Sylvia Berry)*, Ewan McGregor *(Pvt. Mick Hopper)* → TRAINSPOTTING → VELVET GOLDMINE → MOULIN ROUGE → YOUNG ADAM, Peter Jeffrey *(Col. Bernwood)* ← O LUCKY MAN!, Douglas Henshall *(Cpl. Pete Berry)*, Clive Francis *(Maj. Hedges)*, Roy Hudd *(Harold Atterbow)*, Shane Rimmer *(Lt. Col. Trekker)*, Nicholas Farrell *(Maj. Church)* ← CHARIOTS OF FIRE, Nicholas Jones *(Maj. Carter)*, Kim Huffman *(Lisa Trekker)* → LOOKING FOR LEONARD, Bernard Hill *(Uncle Fred)*, Maggie Steed *(Aunt Vickie)* ← BABYLON, Jim Carter *(the inspector)* ← TOP SECRET! ← FLASH GORDON / → HEARTLANDS

Storyline: It's 1956 and Old Blighty is in the middle of the Suez Canal crisis. Foreign Office employees at Whitehall, noteably Russian translators Francis Francis and Mick Hopper, have daydreams outwith their humdrum work environs and of course pulling a couple of birds – so to speak. All do the Dennis Potter thing: lipsync to the music. *MCS*

Movie rating: *7.5

Visual: video

Off the record: One of the birds in question was Louise Germaine, famous for being a Page 3 girl and other centrefold exploits – so I've been informed. *MCS*

Various Artists

Apr 93. (cd/c/d-lp) *Universal TV; (516086-2/-4/-1)* [ ] [–]
– Lipstick on your collar (CONNIE FRANCIS) / Don't be cruel (to a heart that's true) (ELVIS PRESLEY) / The great pretender (the PLATTERS) / Earth angel (will you be mine) (the CREW CUTS) / Little bitty pretty one (THURSTON HARRIS) / The green door (FRANKIE VAUGHAN) / Only you (the PLATTERS) / The story of my life (BILLIE HOLIDAY) / Blueberry hill (FATS DOMINO) / It's almost tomorrow (the DREAM WEAVERS) / Your cheatin' heart (HANK WILLIAMS) / The garden of Eden (FRANKIE VAUGHAN) / My prayer (the PLATTERS) / Blue suede shoes (CARL PERKINS) / Raining in my heart (BUDDY HOLLY & THE CRICKETS) / Unchained melody (LES BAXTER) / I see the Moon (the STARGAZERS) / Be-bop-a-lula (GENE VINCENT) / I'm in love again (FATS DOMINO) / Young love (SONNY JAMES) / The fool (SANFORD CLARK) / It'll be me (JERRY LEE LEWIS) / Love is strange (MICKEY & SYLVIA) / Sh-boom (life could be a dream) (the CREW CUTS) / Lotta lovin' (GENE VINCENT) / Lay down your arms (ANNE SHELTON) / Makin' love (FLOYD ROBINSON) / The man with the golden arm (BILLY MAY & HIS ORCHESTRA).

S/track review: "Rock'n'roll is here to stay" you could say as we source back three decades or so to the 50s and in particular 1956/7, a time when doo wop, the balladeer and of course, rock'n'roll, was king. In fact, "the King" ELVIS PRESLEY gets into gear early on in the set, via his classic, 'Don't Be Cruel', while other rockers of the day, CARL PERKINS, FATS DOMINO, JERRY LEE LEWIS, GENE VINCENT and a posthumous 1959 track ('Raining In My Heart') from BUDDY HOLLY stole the show. Nostalgia rears its not so ugly head time after time, the pick of the bunch being the rhetorical duet, 'Love Is Strange' by MICKEY & SYLVIA. Doo-wop gets in a fair share of timeless beauties, notably three PLATTERS gems, 'The Great Pretender', 'Only You' and 'My Prayer', plus the much-revived and commercialised 'Sh-Boom (Life Could Be A Dream)' and 'Earth Angel (Will You Be Mine)' by Toronto sons, the CREW-CUTS. The surprise package comes courtesy of Liverpool lad, FRANKIE VAUGHAN, who excelled himself on UK chart-toppers, 'The Green Door' (actually only reached No.2) and 'The Garden Of Eden' – FRANKIE indeed went to Hollywood, but not for long. Of the non-hits, were blues diva BILLIE HOLIDAY on 'The Story Of My Life' and pre-RnR, C&W champion HANK WILLIAMS on 'Your Cheatin' Heart'. The theme from 'The Man With The Golden Arm' movie by BILLY MAY & HIS ORCHESTRA ends a well-crafted, hand-picked album that cracks open the champagne right from the opening bars of the film's title track by CONNIE FRANCIS. It ticks all the right boxes. *MCS*

Album rating: *7

LISZTOMANIA

1975 (UK 104m) Warner Bros. / Goodtimes (18)

Film genre: (classical) Rock Musical bio-pic comedy/drama

Top guns: dir (+ s-w): Ken Russell ← TOMMY / → CRIMES OF PASSION → GOTHIC

Stars: **Roger Daltrey** *(Franz Liszt)* <= the WHO =>, Sara Kestelman *(Princess Carolyn)*, **Paul NICHOLAS** *(Richard Wagner)*, **Ringo Starr** *(the Pope)* <= the BEATLES =>, Fiona Lewis *(Countess Marie d'Agoult)*, John Justin *(Count d'Agoult)*, Veronica Quilligan *(Cosima)*, Nell Campbell *(Thor)* ← the ROCKY HORROR PICTURE SHOW / → ROCK FOLLIES OF '77 → JUBILEE → SHOCK TREATMENT → the WALL → the KILLING FIELDS, **Rick WAKEMAN** *(Thor)*, Andrew Reilly *(Hans Von Buelow)*, Imogen Claire

(George Sand) ← the ROCKY HORROR PICTURE SHOW ← TOMMY / → FLASH GORDON → SHOCK TREATMENT → HAWKS, Kenneth Colley *(Frederic Chopin)* ← FLAME ← PERFORMANCE / → RETURN TO WATERLOO, Oliver Reed *(Princess Carolyn's servant)* ← TOMMY / → CAPTIVE

Storyline: Ken Russell's modern pop take on the controversial life and times (the mistresses and groupies!) of 19th Century composer/performer, Franz Liszt. A tortured genius it seemed (much like Amadeus Mozart), it tells of his rivalry – not a fact! – with operatic composer and son-in-law-to-be, Richard Wagner, although by all accounts the director took artistic licence on much of the facts. A bit Brahms and Liszt for everybody's palette. *MCS*

Movie rating: *4.5

Visual: video

Off the record: **Paul NICHOLAS**'s part as Wagner is a little OTT to say the least, although it did fit nicely into Russell's vulgar and outlandish world. *MCS*

RICK WAKEMAN (w/ ROGER DALTREY)

Nov 75. (lp) *A&M; (AMLH 64546) <SP 4546>* [ ] [ ]
– Rienzi – Chopsticks – Fantasia / Love's dream / Dante period / Orpheus song / Hell / Hibernation / Excelsior song / Master race / Rape, pillage and clap / Funerailles / Free song / Peace at last.

S/track review: Prog-meister RICK WAKEMAN (who also starred as Viking, Thor, in the movie!) provided the classically-slanted score for the film. However, although it does feature ROGER DALTREY (Liszt) – on some vocals – as a project on its own, it doesn't get anywhere near to WAKEMAN's previous grandoise compositional albums, '. . .Henry VIII', '. . .Centre Of The Earth' and '. . .King Arthur'. On a commercial front it failed dismally, as did the ROGER DALTREY-credited single, 'Orpheus Song' (complete with diabolical lyrics), and many other tracks such as the goddam awful 'Rape, Pillage And Clap' and the Nazi-fixated 'Master Race'; 'Peace At Last' is just that. *MCS*

Album rating: *3.5

– spinoff singles, etc. –

ROGER DALTREY: Orpheus Song / Love's Dream

Nov 75. (7") *(AMS 7206)* [ ] [–]

RICK WAKEMAN & ROGER DALTREY: Wagner's Dream / Love's Dream / Count Your Blessings

1976. (7"flexi) *Lyntone-A&M; (LYN 3176/7)* [–] [–]

LITTLE RICHARD

2000 (US 120m TV) Davis Entertainment / 20th Century Fox Television

Film genre: Rock'n'roll-music/showbiz drama/biopic

Top guns: dir: Robert Townsend ← JACKIE'S BACK! ← the FIVE HEARTBEATS / → LIVIN' FOR LOVE: THE NATALIE COLE STORY → CARMEN: A HIP HOPERA / s-w: Bill Kerby ← SHAKE, RATTLE & ROLL: AN AMERICAN LOVE STORY ← the ROSE, Daniel Taplitz

Stars: Leon *(Little Richard)* ← MR. ROCK'N'ROLL: THE ALAN FREED STORY ← the TEMPTATIONS ← the FIVE HEARTBEATS / → GET RICH OR DIE TRYIN', Jenifer Lewis *(Muh Penniman)* ← JACKIE'S BACK! ← the TEMPTATIONS ← the PREACHER'S WIFE ← GIRL 6 ← SHAKE, RATTLE & ROCK! tv ← WHAT'S LOVE GOT TO DO WITH IT ← BEACHES, Carl Lumbly *(Bud Penniman)*, Tamala Jones *(Lucille)* ← TURN IT UP, Mel Jackson *(Bump Blackwell)* ← the TEMPTATIONS, Garrett Morris *(Carl Rainey)* ← the CENSUS TAKER ← CAR WASH / → HOW HIGH, **Warren G.** *(studio musician)* ← the SHOW

Storyline: This biopic examines the career of Little Richard Penniman, from the early days when he ran away from home to start his rock'n'roll career. Religion plays a part throughout his life but the film is all about his music, and the brutal murder of his father; hints of homosexuality are merely touched upon. Finally we see the moment when religion wins out over music and he retires to his faith. *JZ*

Movie rating: *5.5

Visual: video + dvd (no audio OST; score: Velton Ray Bunch)

Off the record: Ex-basketball player, Leon (Robinson), has portrayed other R&B/soul singers, Jackie Wilson and David Ruffin. *MCS*

LITTLE SHOP OF HORRORS

1986 remake (US 94m) the Geffen Company / Warner Bros. (PG-13)

Film genre: Pop-Rock sci-fi Musical comedy

Top guns: dir: Frank Oz / s-w (1960): Charles B. Griffith ← the WILD ANGELS ← ROCK ALL NIGHT (play: Howard Ashman)

Stars: Rick Moranis *(Seymour Krelborn)* ← CLUB PARADISE ← STREETS OF FIRE / → BROTHER BEAR, Ellen Greene *(Audrey)*, Vincent Gardenia *(Mr. Mushnik)* ← DEATH WISH II ← DEATH WISH, Steve Martin *(Orin Scrivello, DDS)* ← SGT. PEPPER'S LONELY HEARTS CLUB BAND, Tichina Arnold *(Crystal)*, Michele Weeks *(Ronette)*, Tisha Campbell *(Chiffon)* → SCHOOL DAZE → HOUSE PARTY → HOUSE PARTY 2 → HOUSE PARTY 3, **Levi Stubbs** *(voice; Audrey II)*, James Belushi *(Patrick Martin)* ← THIEF / → WAG THE DOG, John Candy *(Wink Wilkinson)* ← HEAVY METAL ← the BLUES BROTHERS, Bill Murray *(Arthur Denton)* ← CADDYSHACK ← WHERE THE BUFFALO ROAM ← the RUTLES / → LOST IN TRANSLATION → COFFEE AND CIGARETTES → the LIFE AQUATIC WITH STEVE ZISSOU, Christopher Guest *(customer #1)* ← THIS IS SPINAL TAP ← the LONG RIDERS ← DEATH WISH / → the PRINCESS BRIDE → a MIGHTY WIND, Michael J. Shannon *(TV reporter)* ← ROCK FOLLIES

Storyline: The big screen version of Alan Menken and Howard Ashman's tongue-in-cheek and darkly comic musical adaptation of the 1960 film of the same name. A nerdy, down on his luck orphan in 50s America dreams of a better life where he can provide for the girl of his dreams. When a strange and mysterious (talking!) plant finds its way into his hands he suddenly gains notoriety and is on the road to fulfilling his dreams, but it is a case of "be careful what you wish for" as the sinister and manipulative plant turns out to be an alien invader with a serious appetite for human blood! *LF*

Movie rating: *6.5

Visual: video + dvd

Off the record: **Levi Stubbs** (b. Levi Stubbles, 6 Jun'36, Detroit, Michigan, USA) was a member of 'Motown' singing group, the Four Tops, until ill health (cancer and diabetes) put paid to his career in 2000; his baritone vox features on classic hits such as 'Baby I Need Your Loving', 'I Can't Help Myself', 'It's The Same Old Song', 'Reach Out I'll Be There', 'Standing In The Shadows Of Love' and 'Bernadette'. *MCS*

Various Cast (composers: Howard Ashman & Alan Menken)

Jan 87. (lp/c) *Geffen; <(K9 24125-1/-4)>* [47] Mar87 [ ]
– Prologue (Little Shop Of Horrors) / Skid row (downtown) / Da-doo / Grow for me / Somewhere that's green / Some fun now / Dentist! / Feed me (git it) / Suddenly, Seymour / Suppertime / The meek shall inherit / Mean green mother from outerspace / Finale (don't feed the plants). *<(cd-iss. Oct87; K9 24125)>*

S/track review: Held together by the strong voices of the narrative chorus, TICHINA ARNOLD, MICHELLE WEEKS and TISHA CAMPBELL reprising the sound of the Motown girl trio, 'LITTLE SHOP OF HORRORS' showcases a range of expected stage musical standards suffused with a soulful backbone and complemented by occasional doo-wop leanings and calypso rhythms. The could-have-only-been-written-for-Broadway big number 'Skid Row (Downtown)' is a powerful and bombastic opening, earnestly detailing the hardship, poverty and helplessness of life at the very bottom of the pile (honestly!). This serious tone does not last long as the weedy voice of geeky florist Seymour Krelborn (RICK MORANIS) takes on the light hearted 'Da-Doo' and 'Grow For Me'. In contrast, ELLEN GREENE, playing the love interest Audrey, shows off her powerful vocal gymnastics on the unlikely ballad 'Suddenly Seymour' and the Disney-esque, American Dream satirising 'Somewhere That's Green' (perhaps it's not surprising that both Menken and Ashman would go on to write for Disney). STEVE MARTIN does his best to steal the show with the hilarious high-camp of 'Dentist', a comedy jewel celebrating his character's sadistic tendencies. But it is the Four Tops' LEVI STUBBS, as the voice of the evil man-eating bloodthirsty plant Audrey II, who really cuts loose on the glorious OTT rock romps that are 'Feed Me (Get It)' and 'Mean Green Mother From Outerspace'. The comedy takes a backseat again as the eerie piano, subtle melodies and an entrancing bassline on 'Suppertime' offer a darker moment before the raucous and righteous 'The Meek Shall Inherit' explodes with its tonsil shattering climax. The 80s obsession of overusing synthesizers means the music often lacks the expansiveness of the impressive vocal tracks, however, 'LITTLE SHOP OF HORRORS' remains a delightfully entertaining collection of unlikely and unique high quality show tunes. *LF*

Album rating: *7

LIVE A LITTLE, LOVE A LITTLE

1968 (US 90m) Metro-Goldwyn-Mayer (PG)

Film genre: romantic drama

Top guns: dir: Norman Taurog ← SPEEDWAY ← DOUBLE TROUBLE ← SPINOUT ← TICKLE ME ← IT HAPPENED AT THE WORLD'S FAIR ← GIRLS! GIRLS! GIRLS! ← BLUE HAWAII ← G.I. BLUES / s-w: Michael A. Hoey (au: Dan Greenburg)

Stars: Elvis PRESLEY *(Greg Nolan)*, Michele Carey *(Bernice/Betty/Alice/Suzie)*, Don Porter *(Mike Lansdown)*, **Rudy Vallee** *(Louis Penlow)*, Dick Sargent *(Harry Baby)* ← BERNARDINE, Sterling Holloway *(milkman)* ← SHAKE, RATTLE & ROCK, **Eddie Hodges** *(Woodrow; the delivery boy)* ← C'MON, LET'S LIVE A LITTLE, Joan Shawlee *(Robbie's mother)* ← the WILD ANGELS, Ann Doran *(landlady)* → the HIRED HAND

Storyline: A photographer, Greg, attempts to earn a crust moonlighting for a soft porn mag without his morally upstanding newspaper boss, Penlow, finding out.

Movie rating: *2.5

Visual: video

Off the record: Rudy Vallee was a former big band leader very popular on Broadway. *MCS*

—

ELVIS PRESLEY: Live A Little, Love A Little / Charro! / The Trouble With Girls / Change Of Habit

Mar 95. (cd) *R.C.A.; <(07863 66559-2)>* [ ] [ ]
– Almost in love / A little less conversation / Wonderful world / Edge of reality / A little less conversation (album version) / (CHARRO! tracks) / (THE TROUBLE WITH GIRLS tracks) / (CHANGE OF HABIT tracks).

S/track review: Never released as a soundtrack in its own right until the mid-90s CD reissue (a 4-on-1 with the soundtracks to 'CHARRO', 'THE TROUBLE WITH GIRLS' and 'CHANGE OF HABIT'), 'LIVE A LITTLE, LOVE A LITTLE's music originally trickled out on singles and b-sides. First up was 'A Little Less Conversation', a brassy slice of honky funk whose lowly chart position belied its testifiying, pelvis-swivelling genius. Unfortunately, the heady combination of PRESLEY's towering vocal presence, funk breakbeats and chicken-scratch guitar was pretty much a one-off; we can but dream of what other dancefloor nuggets The King might've turned up had he chosen to pursue this avenue. It's also incredible to think that this classic lay pretty much forgotten until JXL's club-friendly reinvention became the soundtrack to the 2002 Fifa World Cup. Was ELVIS turning in his grave? More likely he was cracking open a beer for that crucial/controversial USA v Iran clash. The pleasant, bossa-tinged ballad, 'Almost In Love', appeared as the B-side to the original single, while the inferior, vaguely psychedelic 'Edge Of Reality' ironically enjoyed a higher chart position as the B-side to the 1969 single, 'If I Can Dream'. 'Wonderful World', meanwhile, was originally included on 'Singer Presents . . . Flaming Star And Others' (1968), a promotional tool for Singer sewing machines . . . *BG*

Album rating: *6

– spinoff hits, etc. –

ELVIS PRESLEY: A Little Less Conversation / Almost In Love

Sep 68. (7") *<47-9610> (RCA 1768)* [69]
[95] Dec68 [ ]

ELVIS VS. JXL: A Little Less Conversation / ELVIS (original)

Jun 02. (c-s) *<060575> (74321 94357-4)* [50] [1]
(12"+=/cd-s+=) *(74321 94357-1/-2)* – ('A'-version).

LIVE IT UP

US title 'SING AND SWING'

1963 (UK 75m b&w) Three Kings / Rank Film Distributors

Film genre: Pop-Rock Musical comedy

Top guns: dir: Lance Comfort → BE MY GUEST / Lyn Fairhurst → BE MY GUEST (idea: Harold Shampan → DATELINE DIAMONDS)

Stars: David Hemmings *(Dave Martin)* ← SOME PEOPLE ← PLAY IT COOL / → BE MY GUEST → BLOW-UP → PROFONDO ROSSO → la VIA DELLA DROGA, Jennifer Moss *(Jill)*, John Pike *(Phil)* → BE MY GUEST, **Heinz Burt** *(Ron)* → FAREWELL PERFORMANCE → JUST FOR FUN → the LONDON ROCK AND ROLL SHOW, **Steven Marriott** *(Ricky)* → BE MY GUEST → DATELINE DIAMONDS → TONITE LET'S ALL MAKE LOVE IN LONDON, Peter Glaze *(Mike Moss)*, **Dave CLARK** *(recording man)*, **John Mitchell** *(Andrews)* <= Jimi HENDRIX =>, **Patsy Ann Noble** *(performer)*, Douglas Ives *(Bingo)* → JUST FOR FUN → BE MY GUEST, **Kenny Ball** *(performer)* ← IT'S TRAD, DAD!, **the Outlaws:- Ritchie Blackmore, Ken Lundgren, Chas Hodges, Mick Underwood** *(performers)*, **the Saints:- Andy Cavell, Roy Phillips** *(performers)*, **Sounds Incorporated:- Tony Newman** *(performer)* ← IT'S TRAD, DAD! / → JUST FOR FUN → POP GEAR, **Gene Vincent** *(performer)* ← IT'S TRAD, DAD! ← HOT ROD GANG ← the GIRL CAN'T HELP IT / → BLUE SUEDE SHOES → NO DIRECTION HOME, **Kim Roberts** *(performer)*

Storyline: With Beatlemania probably an inspiration, a quartet of delivery boys decide to give pop stardom a go. The Smart Alecs – Dave, Ron, Phil and Ricky – think their destiny is just a stones throw away, but can they hit it big. *MCS*

Movie rating: *5.5

Visual: video (no audio OST)

Off the record: Heinz was of the Tornados and had a solo hit with 'Just Like Eddie' – a tribute to Eddie Cochran; his old mucker **Gene Vincent** also turned up here. **Steve Marriott** subsequently fronted the Small Faces and later Humble Pie before going solo. **John Mitchell** became drummer Mitch Mitchell, later of the Jimi Hendrix Experience. Instrumental act, **the Outlaws**, were made up of future rock and pop stars.. **Ritchie Blackmore** would surface as lead guitarist with Deep Purple and Rainbow, while **Mick Underwood** joined Episode Six which contained Deep Purple members. **Chas Hodges** joined Heads, Hands & Feet before becoming one-half of cockney pop duo,

Chas & Dave. **Patsy Ann Noble** (b. 3 Feb'44, Sydney, Australia) was from a showbiz family and she made her recording debut in 1960 with the single, 'I Love You So Much It Hurts'. After a one-off 45 – 'Good Looking Boy' – for 'H.M.V.' records, she signed a deal with 'Columbia', but had no luck in the UK charts with several further attempts; her subsequent acting work was mainly for British, then American TV. **Sounds Incorporated** and **Kenny Ball** (and his Jazzmen) had a number of UK hits repectively. In the movie, **Kim Roberts**, performed 'For Loving Me This Way', later a B-side. Peter Glaze, was the original Crackerjack! children's TV presenter. Producer **Joe Meek** wrote several of the songs, except spinoff 45 for Patsy Ann Noble (see below) *MCS*

– spinoff releases, etc. –

the OUTLAWS: Law And Order / (non-OST song)

1963. (7") *H.M.V.; (POP 1241)* ☐ ⊟

PATSY ANN NOBLE: Accidents Will Happen / (non OST-song)

1963. (7") *Columbia; (DB 7088)* ☐ ⊟

GENE VINCENT: Temptation Baby / (non-OST song)

1963. (7") *Columbia; (DB 7174)* ☐ ⊟

LIVING LEGEND: THE KING OF ROCK AND ROLL

1980 (US 93m) Maverick Pictures International (PG)

Film genre: Country-music/showbiz drama

Top guns: dir: Worth Keeter / s-w: Thom McIntyre

Stars: Earl Owensby *(Eli Canfield)*, William T. Hicks *(Jim Cannon)*, Ginger Alden *(Jeannie Loring)*, Jerry Rushing *(Chad)* ← CARNY, Greg Carswell *(Teddy)*, Toby Wallace *(Dean)*, Kristina Reynolds *(Susan)*

Storyline: Eli Canfield is the "King Of Rock'n'Roll" (but is not pretending to be Elvis, honestly) and a hit wherever he goes. Offstage his personal life lurches from one trauma to another (nothing like you-know-who) with broken relationships and a barrowload of happy pills to help his deteriorating health (it's all a coincidence). Let's hope his manager isn't a nosey Parker. *JZ*

Movie rating: *5

Visual: video (no audio OST)

Off the record: ROY ORBISON performs several songs in the movie.

LIVING PROOF: THE HANK WILLIAMS JR. STORY

1983 (US 89m TV) Melpimene Productions / NBC

Film genre: Country-music bio-pic/drama

Top guns: dir: Dick Lowry / s-w: Stephen Kandel, I.C. Rapoport (book: 'Living Proof' by **Hank WILLIAMS Jr.** & Michael Bane)

Stars: Richard Thomas *(Hank Williams, Jr.)*, Lenora May *(Lisa)*, Liane Langland *(June Bradshaw)*, Ann Gillespie *(Becky)*, **Merle Kilgore** *(himself)* ← ROADIE ← COAL MINER'S DAUGHTER ← NASHVILLE, Allyn Ann McLerie *(Audrey Williams)*, Clu Gulager *(J.R. Smith)* → the RETURN OF THE LIVING DEAD → TAPEHEADS → EDDIE PRESLEY, Barton Heyman *(Bobby Deane)* → ROADSIDE PROPHETS → the BASKETBALL DIARIES → DEAD MAN WALKING, Noble Willingham *(Dr. Graham)* → LA BAMBA → GOOD MORNING, VIETNAM → SOUTH OF HEAVEN, WEST OF HELL, Jay O. Sanders *(Dick Willey)* → TUCKER: THE MAN AND HIS DREAM, Christian Slater *(Walt Willey)* → TUCKER: THE MAN AND HIS DREAM → YOUNG GUNS II → PUMP UP THE VOLUME → MASKED AND ANONYMOUS, **Mickey Jones** *(Mickey)* ← the BEST LITTLE WHOREHOUSE IN TEXAS / → SLING BLADE, **Naomi Judd** *(redhead)* ← MORE AMERICAN GRAFFITI

Storyline: Hank Williams, Jr. from an early age has to live in the shadow of his famous father; indeed his mother uses him as a novelty act on stage dressed up as his dearly-departed daddy. Unsurprisingly, given his dad's success, his attempts to break away and create his own musical style lead to depression and alcoholism, but his terrible fall down snowy Mt Ajax shows a deep-down will to live and succeed through adversity. *JZ*

Movie rating: *5

Visual: video (no audio OST; see below)

Off the record: Merle Kilgore was the manager of Hank (he sadly died 6th February, 2005). **Mickey Jones** was ex-drummer with the New Christy Minstrels, Kenny Rogers' First Edition and Bob Dylan. **Naomi Judd** went on to be part of massive country duo, the Judds (with Wynonna Judd), who hit the US Top 75 with album, 'Why Not Me' (1984); she subsequently starred in low-key movies, 'A Holiday Romance' (1999) and 'Family Tree' (2000). *MCS*

– associated release –

HANK WILLIAMS, Jr.: Hank Williams, Jr.'s Greatest Hits

Nov 82. (lp/c) *Curb-Elektra; <1-/4-60193>* ☐ ⊟
– FAmily tradition / Whiskey bent and hell bound / Women I've never had / Old habits / Kaw-liga / Dixie on my mind / Texas women / The American dream / A country boy can survive / All my rowdy friends (have settled down). *<cd-iss. 1984; 2-60193>*

the LIZZIE McGUIRE MOVIE

2003 (US 93m) Buena Vista / Walt Disney Pictures (PG)

Film genre: romantic teen comedy

Top guns: dir: Jim Fall / s-w: Susan Estelle Jansen, John J. Strauss, Ed Decter

Stars: Hilary Duff *(Lizzie McGuire / Isabella Parichi)* → RAISE YOUR VOICE, Adam Lamberg *(David "Gordo" Gordon)*, Hallie Todd *(Mrs. Jo McGuire)*, Yani Gellman *(Paolo Valisari)*, **Robert Carradine** *(Mr. Sam McGuire)* ← WAVELENGTH ← the LONG RIDERS ← JOYRIDE, Jake Thomas *(Matt McGuire)*, Ashley Brillaut *(Kate Sanders)*, Clayton Snyder *(Ethan Craft)*, Alex Borstein *(Miss Ungermeyer)*

Storyline: Lizzie and her classmates celebrate their graduation with a trip to Rome. They say everyone has a doppelganger, and Lizzie finds out hers is pop starlet Isabella, whose duets with pin-up boy Paolo are the talk of the town. When Isabella's hot Latin temperament gets the better of her, Paolo talks Lizzie into standing in for her on stage and off, but can she cope with her new-found stardom especially with her family on their way for a share of the spoils. *JZ*

Movie rating: *5

Visual: dvd

Off the record: Hilary Duff (b.28 Dec'87, Houston, Texas) has since had four Top 3 albums, 'Hilary Duff' (2004), 'Metamorphosis' (2005), 'Most Wanted' (2005) and 'Dignity' (2007), all containing the odd teen-pop Top 50 hit (including 'So Yesterday' & 'Come Clean'). *MCS*

Various Artists (score: CLIFF EIDELMAN *)

Apr 03. (cd) *Disney; <860080> (50466 6312-2)* 6 Aug03 ☐
– Why not (HILARY DUFF) / The tide is high (get the feeling) (ATOMIC KITTEN) / All around the world (COOLER KIDS) / What dreams are made of – ballad version (PAOLO & ISABELLA) / Shining star (JUMP5) / Volare (VITAMIN C) / Open your eyes (to love) (LMNT) / You make me feel like a star – Lizzie mix (the BEU SISTERS) / Supermodel (TAYLOR DAYNE) / What dreams are made of (LIZZIE McGUIRE / HILARY DUFF) / On an evening in Roma (DEAN MARTIN) / Girl in the band (HAYLIE DUFF) / Orchestral suite from The Lizzie McGuire Movie (*) / Why not – McMix (HILARY DUFF).

S/track review: Lizzie McGuire herself (HILARY DUFF) opens things with the reasonable upbeat offering 'Why Not' which is a predictable but well executed slice of Avril Lavigne-esque guitar-pop that manages to race through all the cornerstones and clichés of that sound in just three minutes. Whilst it probably contains some life affirming moments for seven-year-old girls the world over, it also suffers from a glut of embarrassing lyrics, as you would expect when grown men are writing for teenage girls. It is all downhill from this relatively pleasant beginning though, followed as it is by ATOMIC KITTEN's insipid karaoke readthrough of Blondie's 'The Tide Is High' and COOLER KIDS' 'All Around The World' which sounds like a creepy mix of the Spice Girls and Daft Punk. Similarly, listening to TAYLOR DAYNE's cringingly camp, yet humourlessly drivel 'Supermodel' is possibly the worst way you could spend four minutes of your life. Then again, there is the frankly horrible 'Open Your Eyes (To Life)' by the Backstreet Boys-shaped LMNT. The mood is temporarily lifted by VITAMIN C's energetic rendition of 'Volare' and Hilary's little sister HAYLIE DUFF getting in on the act too with more of the expected girlie-guitar-pop on 'Girl In The Band' before CLIFF EIDELMAN's 'Orchestral Suite' ends things on a genuinely pleasant note, bearing that Disney mark of quality. Ultimately, though, this is just another throwaway piece of merchandise, patched up with mainly middle-of-the-road inoffensive dance music that went on to sell millions in America regardless. *LF*

Album rating: *4.5

Kenny LOGGINS

Born: 7 Jan'48, Everett, Washington, USA. An aw-shucks singer-songwriter who – initially in tandem with former Poco man Jim Messina – very successfully traded on the inoffensive middle ground between country rock and easy going pop, KENNY LOGGINS made his entry into the film world in 1980 with a theme tune contribution – the US Top 10 'I'm Alright' – to Harold Ramis' comedy classic, 'CADDYSHACK'. This was followed by his hugely successful theme (US No.1/UK Top 10) for the inexplicably popular 80s teen movie, 'FOOTLOOSE' (1984), the crunching 80s rawk of 'Danger Zone' (US No.2) for Tom Cruise vehicle, 'Top Gun' (1986) and hit contributions (US Top 20) to both Sly Stallone hokum, 'Over The Top' (1986) and 'Caddyshack II' (1988). *BG*

- filmography (composer) –

Caddyshack *(1980 OST w/ JOHNNY MANDEL & V/A =>)* / **Footloose** *(1984 OST w/ V/A =>)* / Top Gun *(1986 hit on OST by V/A see future editions =>)* / Over The Top *(1987 hit on OST by V/A see future editions =>)* / Caddyshack II *(1988 hit on OST by V/A see future editions =>)*

LONGSHOT

2000 (US 93m) Trans Continental Pictures (PG-13)

Film genre: crime drama

Top guns: dir: Lionel C. Martin / s-w: Tony DeCamillis, Louis J. Pearlman

Stars: Tony DeCamillis *(Jack Taylor)*, Hunter Tylo *(Rachel)*, Joey Sculthorpe *(Alex Taylor)*, Paul Sorvino *(Laszlo Pryce)* ← DICK TRACY, Danielle Fishel *(Gloria)*, Antonio Sabato Jr. *(Tommy Sutton)*, Lewis J. Pearlman *(Captain Lewis)*, **Innosense: Jenny Morris, Veronica Finn, Nikki DeLoach, Mandy Ashford, Danay Ferrer** *(performers)*, **'N Sync:- Justin Timberlake** *(valet)* → BLACK SNAKE MOAN, **Joey Fatone** *(pizza chef)* → the BROS., **Lance Bass** *(flight engineer)*, **Britney Spears** *(flight attendant)*, Ellen Albertini Dow *(Mrs. Fleischer)* ← 54 ← the WEDDING SINGER, Dwayne Johnson *(mugger)* → BE COOL, **Take 5:- Stevie Sculthorpe, Tilky Jones, Timothy 'T.J.' Christofore, Ryan Goodell, Jeffrey 'Clay' Goodell** *(performers)* / **O-Town:- Ashley Parker Angel, Erik-Michael Estrada, Dan Miller, Trevor Penick, Jacob Underwood** *(performers)* / **C-Note:- David Perez & Raul Molina** *(performers)*, **LFO:- Rich Cronin** *(NYC police officer)*, **Devin Lima** *(Chippendales dancer)*, **Brad Fischetti** *(himself)* / Dustin Diamond *(waiter)*, Lark Voorhies *(woman at the bar)* → HOW HIGH / **Full Force:- Lou George, Paul A. George, Brian George** ← WHO'S THE MAN? ← HOUSE PARTY 2 ← HOUSE PARTY, **Curtis Bedeau, Gerald Charles & Hugh Clarke** *(themselves)* / **Brian 'Brizz' Gillis** *(himself)*, Traci Bingham *(herself)*, **Jermaine Jackson** *(himself)* ← VOYAGE OF THE ROCK ALIENS ← SAVE THE CHILDREN, **Robert Kool Bell** *(announcer)*, **Jerod Mixon** *(himself)*, **Jamal Mixon** *(himself)*, **Yolanda Whitaker** *(herself)* ← WHO'S THE MAN? / → PAPER SOLDIERS, **Kenny Rogers** *(pilot)*, **Art Garfunkel** *(himself)* <= SIMON & GARFUNKEL =>, Darrin Henson → STOMP THE YARD

Storyline: Beverly Hills gigolo, Jack, falls in with the wrong crowd and finds himself blackmailed by shady businessman Pryce. Meanwhile his young brother Alex is down in the dumps after messing up in the big basketball game. Even worse, his life might be in danger if Jack doesn't do what Pryce wants. It's only when Rachel and Gloria meet the unhappy brothers that things start to look up. *JZ*

Movie rating: *3

Visual: dvd

Off the record: A plethora of hot pop stars appear in the film, most of them featured in the soundtrack below.

Various Artists (score: LALO SCHIFRIN *)

Mar 02. (cd) *Transcontinental; <4066>*
– Feel the love (*NSYNC) / Me (boom shalak) (LFO) / See you again (O-TOWN) / Put your arms around me (NATURAL) / Let's get this party started (TAKE 5) / Wishing on every star (INNOSENSE) / So often (C-NOTE) / It don't bother me (BRIZZ) / She's a mystery to me (BECKER) / In & out (ALI DEE) / I just wanna be (with you) (BON VOYAGE) / Happy (KELI MICHAELS) / Fall in love (NICHOLE CARTER) / A reason to love me (JOEY SCULTHORPE) / Longshot theme (*) / Longshot theme – remix (*).

S/track review: It seems every single Identikit slick American boyband on the production line is present and correct on 'LONGSHOT', beginning with the prototype, mega-selling NSYNC on the OTT 'Feel The Love', which shows up O-TOWN's contrasting 'See You Again' for its copycat feel, lesser production and simple lyrics that nearly entirely consist of singing the song title over and over again. This is followed by the self-aggrandising frat-boy RnB of LFO which is unsurprisingly similar to former member BRIZZ's 'It Don't Bother Me'. 'Put Your Arms Around Me' is an inoffensive, pleasant enough radio-friendly mid-tempo ballad let down by NATURAL's wet and wimpy delivery whilst TAKE 5's 'Let's Get This Party Started' is sickeningly slick teen-pop, slightly disturbing in its inappropriate sleazy lyrics, like the creepy 'In And Out' by ALI DEE which seems to be deliberately aurally offensive and, it hardly needs mentioning, is absolute shite. 'Wishing On Every Star' sounds familiar and would not be out of place in any quirky 80s romantic comedy, whilst C-NOTE's 'So Often' is simply filler, ploughing a similar furrow to everything else here. Then from nowhere the glacial guitar-chiming pop of BON VOYAGE's 'I Just Wanna Be (With You)' will catch you off guard with its Blondie-meets-the Sundays charm. KELI MICHAELS' 'Happy' returns us to familiar ground, although it does retain a certain 90s feeling, akin to the chart-friendly RnB of Lisa Stansfield, and is at least better than NICHOLE CARTER's embarrassing Britney Spears impression on 'Fall In Love'. The boys get back in on the act with JOEY SCULTHORPE's 'A Reason To Love Me', which adds nothing new to the mix before the intriguing silky score track of LALO SCHIFRIN's 'Longshot Theme' signals the end of this trying affair. *LF*

Album rating: *3

Released in 1984, *Purple Rain* was one of the first mega-albums of the 80s that capitalised on the CD/MTV revolution. Lacking a decent plot, the film functioned better as a series of video promos for the multi-million-selling soundtrack, which showcased Prince as 'an amalgam of Marc Bolan, Nijinsky and the Scarlet Pimpernel' (*Time Out*).

For the soundtrack to Cameron Crowe's 2000 coming-of-age movie/fictional rock biopic, the music journo-turned-film director cherry-picked big names from the early 70s, including Lynyrd Skynyrd and Rod Stewart, and even pulled off the historical coup of licensing a Led Zeppelin track. Elton John's 'Tiny Dancer' will never sound the same again.

John Landis' suited and booted R&B romp is one of the most celebrated musical movies of all time. The titular brothers, played by John Belushi and Dan Aykroyd – singers by default – blaze through the soundtrack, fuelled by pure enthusiasm. Star cameos come in the form of Ray Charles (duetting on 'Shake A Tail Feather'), Cab Calloway, Aretha Franklin and a sermonising James Brown.

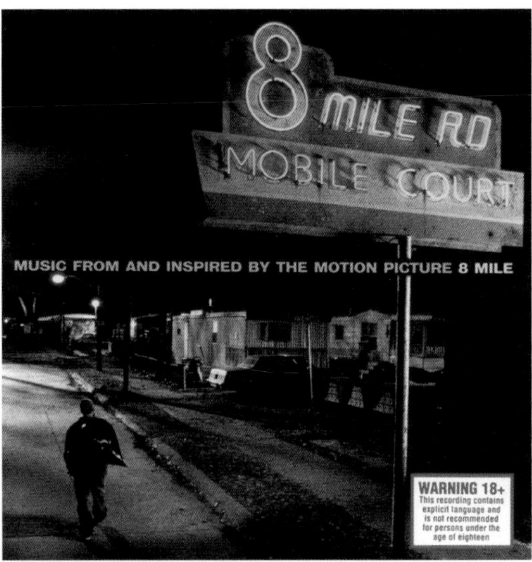

As a white rapper who broke the Vanilla Ice mould, Eminem's heavily autobiographical biopic boasts a hip-hop soundtrack brought into the 21st century. Featuring tracks by luminaries such as Jay-Z, 50 Cent, Nas and Rakim, this is still Eminem's album. He stamps his authority all over the searing, massive No.1 'Lose Yourself', the piston-packing album highlight '8 Mile' and he goes out all syllables blazing on 'Rabbit Run'.

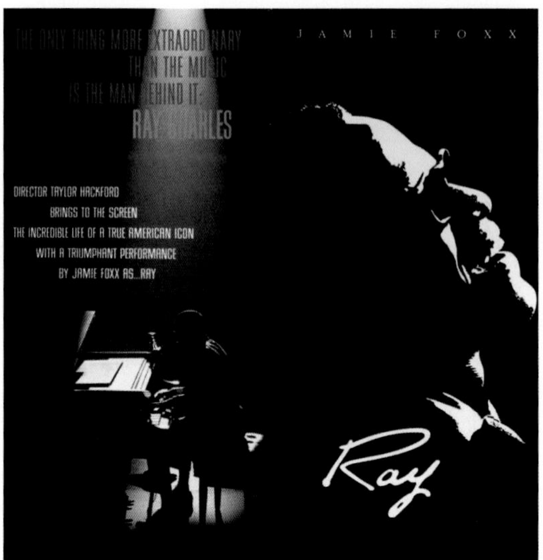

Released just a few months after Ray Charles passed away, the soundtrack to Taylor Hackford's inspiring 2004 biopic is far from a casually thrown-together hits package. From the rarely heard, self-penned cuts like 'Mary Ann', through difficult-to-find 'Born To Lose', to the freshened-up 'Mess Around' and 'I've Got A Woman', it delineates a pioneering career and a cultural fault line.

Jailhouse Rock is one of only a handful of films which captured the full-force swagger of a pre-army Presley. The soundtrack EP went to No.1 following the film's release in 1957. The title song is one of the most inspired to come from the pens of Jerry Leiber and Mike Stoller, and witnesses Elvis possessed with an almost supernatural self-belief, sexuality and subversive authority.

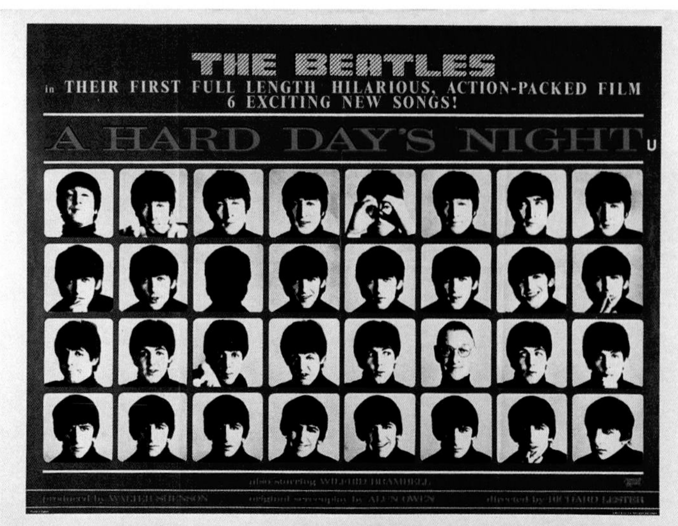

Richard Lester's 1964 film captures the fantasy whirlwind of a supposedly average 36 hours in the life of The Beatles, at that time the hottest band on the planet. It was a watershed in the world of rock soundtracks: 'Can't Buy Me Love', 'I'll Be Back', 'I Should Have Known Better' and the title track demonstrated that pop music had never had it so good, or seemingly so easy.

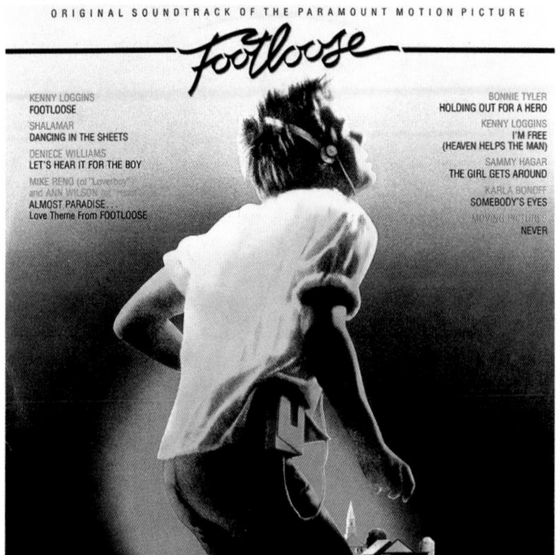

The film that saw Kevin Bacon break into embarrassing dance routines at the first sign of an AOR power chord has a soundtrack that belongs to incurable 80s headcases only. It showcases unreconstructed 70s roots rockers Kenny Loggins and Bonnie Tyler, who found their footing in the new decade. Screenwriter Dean Pitchford co-wrote every song and conceived the MTV-esque incorporation of those songs into the film.

The source of no doubt much record shop discontent on its release in 1991, when it was ubiquitous, this is the sound of Irish tenacity melded with the broken heart and gospel conscience of black music. Ponytailed lead vocalist Andrew Strong sounds ancient before his time, equally at home with the shouters as he is the ballads, backed up by a cast of Celtic soul divas who hit banshee point on 'Treat Her Right'.

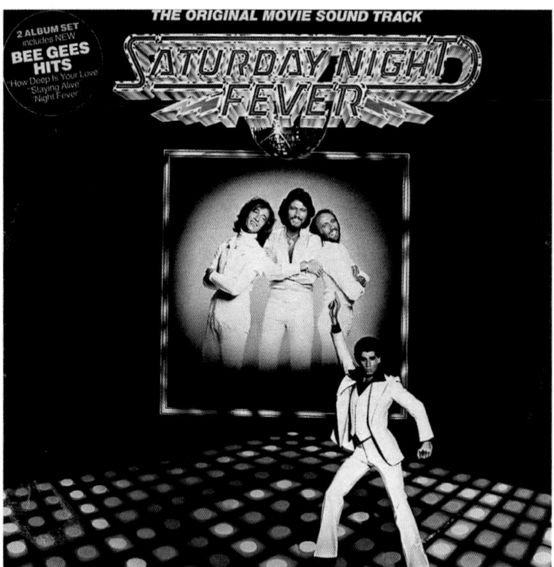

The biggest-selling soundtrack of all time, and one of the defining albums of the disco era. With 'Stayin' Alive', 'More Than A Woman' and 'Night Fever', blessed with an irresistible dancefloor pulse and a charming naivety, the Bee Gees popularised and commercialised the disco genre. Also boasting a range of funky hits, from Yvonne Elliman's 'If I Can't Have You' to The Trammps' 'Disco Inferno', this double-set still sounds fresh thirty years on.

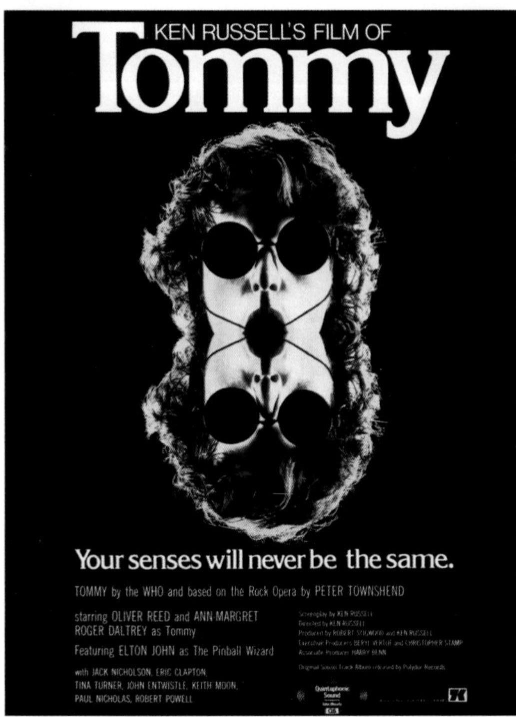

The Who's landmark 'Rock Opera' was given its definitive visual realisation in Ken Russell's arresting film adaptation, made in 1975. The Who themselves dominate the soundtrack in the guise of Townshend and Daltrey, but the star performances come in the form of Tina Turner's 'The Acid Queen' and Elton John's rendition of 'Pinball Wizard'.

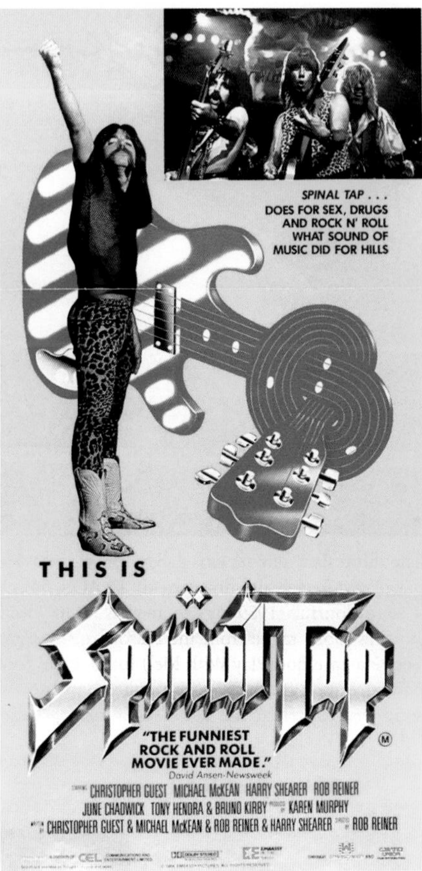

Released in 1984, Rob Reiner's pitch-perfect satire of all things heavy endures to this day thanks to stand-out performances and a superb soundtrack that charts the Tap's regression from 60s beat-sound roots to Puppet Show-straddling Rock behemoths. All the songs were co-written by the main players with Reiner: 'Hell Hole' sends up Deep Purple, 'Tonight I'm Gonna Rock You Tonight' is clearly a Kiss parody, but 'Sex Farm', 'Big Bottom' and the legendary 'Stonehenge' have impacted on popular consciousness to such an extent that they have since gained a cultural currency of their own.

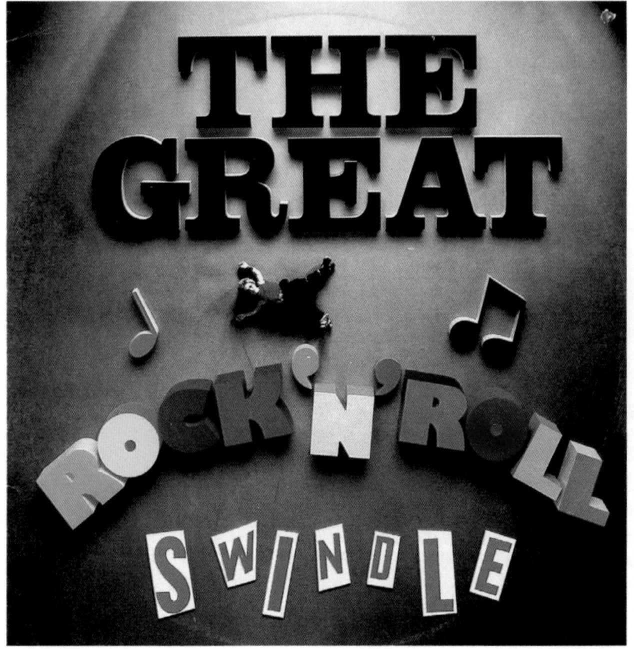

Part-performance documentary, part-biopic, part-everything under the sun, Julien Temple's film of the rise and fall of the Sex Pistols features a soundtrack as chaotic, inspired and hit-and-miss as you might expect. Highlights include one of the funniest film songs of all time, 'Who Killed Bambi?', a French accordion re-working of 'Anarchy In The UK', Sid Vicious' legendary 'My Way' and a host of butchered rock 'n' roll standards.

Alongside Wayne and Garth, Bill and Ted are the archetypal brainless Metal-worshipping dudes, as immortalised in this colourful 1989 sci-fi fantasy comedy. Soundtrack contributions range from the reasonably credible (Extreme's Van Halen-esque 'Play With Me') to the downright ridiculous (Shark Island, anyone?), but air guitar action is guaranteed.

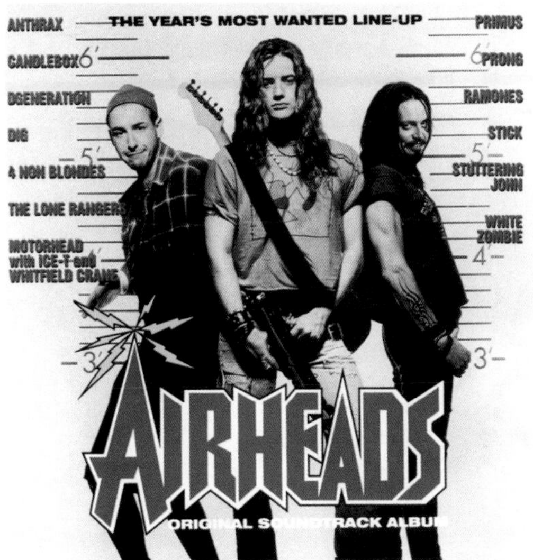

US comedy about an unsigned rock band called The Lone Rangers (yes, they pluralised it) who hold up the local radio station with water pistols to force them to play their demo. Although Heavy Metal was distinctly out of vogue in 1994, the old guard – in the form of Motörhead and Anthrax – stand alongside newer blood like White Zombie, Primus and Prong on the patchy soundtrack.

Inspired by the line-up changes of Judas Priest in the late 90s, 2001's *Rock Star* features ('Marky') Mark Wahlberg as Chris Cole, who is lifted from Steel Dragon tribute band Blood Pollution to front Steel Dragon itself. Their six contributions to the soundtrack feature Jason Bonham on drums and Zakk Wylde on guitar, ably supported by scene stalwarts Mötley Crüe, Bon Jovi, Ted Nugent and, er, INXS.

This 1978 comedy saw the staff of an American radio station stage a coup after their boss announces a commercially minded playlist shake-up. Steely Dan were commissioned to write a title theme. Touted at the time as Rock's answer to *Saturday Night Fever*, there are contributions from Bob Seger, Foreigner, Tom Petty, Billy Joel and Queen.

Nostalgia and the art-of-the-dance craze in the early 60s got the full-on treatment by filmmaker John Waters in the original 1988 screen version of *Hairspray*. The Flares and the deep baritone of the Five Dutones get the dance craze theme rockin', and other highlights include the Ike-less Ikettes (with backing singer Tina Turner) and Curtis Mayfield-penned 'Mama Didn't Lie', performed by Ian Bradley. Pre-Beatles era America might not have been that bad after all.

Boasting the talents of Jamie Foxx and Beyoncé Knowles, the cast of *Dreamgirls* provide the soundtrack to the 2006 biopic based on the story of The Supremes. But too often it gives in to its Broadway baggage and replaces soul with bluster, summed up in the pointless diaphragm bionics of American Idol *protégée* Jennifer Hudson's 'And I Am Telling You I'm Not Going'.

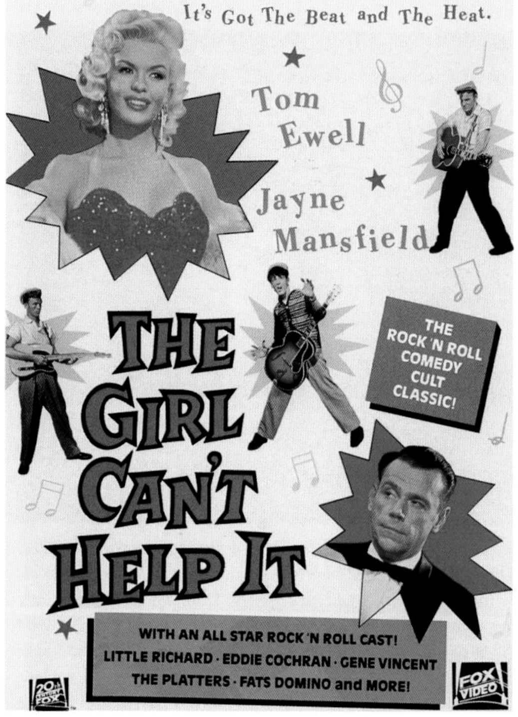

If you had to mention only one rock 'n' roll movie of the 50s, *The Girl Can't Help It!* would be the one. More than a Jayne Mansfield vehicle, it features no less than eleven cameos from the world of 50s pop music, none better than the title track featuring Little Richard.

Manfred Mann's former frontman, Paul Jones, took his newly found solo career one step further by starring/performing in 1967 cult movie *Privilege*. Under the guidance of composer/arranger/conductor Mike Leander, soundtrack highlights include 'Free Me', reconstructed a decade later by punk rock poetess Patti Smith.

Ivanhoe Martin's aspirations to release a record are complicated by his involvement in the Jamaican marijuana trade in this 1972 Reggae classic. Its star Jimmy Cliff dominates the soundtrack, which introduced a whole generation to the musical delights of the Caribbean. Possibly one of the finest various-artists soundtracks ever released, it also features the Melodians, Desmond Dekker and the Maytals.

David Essex starred as Jim Maclaine, lead singer of rock group the Stray Cats, who starts on a rollercoaster of drink, drugs and sex when the band hits the big time and he finds things too hard to handle. Essex delivers the priceless title track, which hit the UK Top Ten, and there is a breadth of 60s sounds on offer, including an easy flow into the flower-power movement via the Mamas & the Papas, The Lovin' Spoonful and Jefferson Airplane.

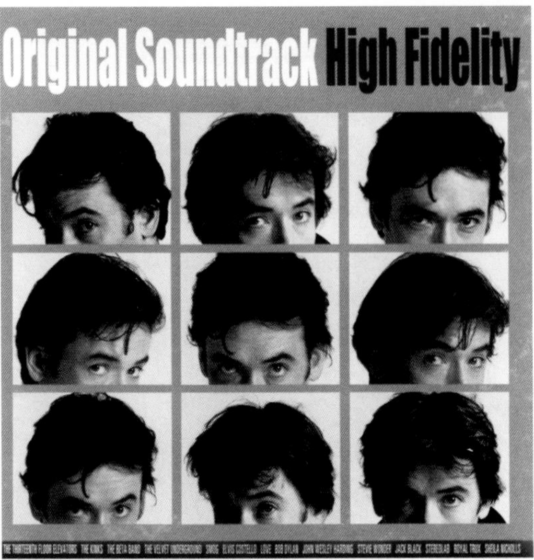

John Cusack starred as Rob Gordon, struggling with a thirty-something crisis in tandem with running a backstreet record shop in Stephen Frears' adaptation of Nick Hornby's novel. The soundtrack does not deliver enough arcane or imaginatively selected stuff to satisfy the trainspotter it sends up. In place of some rare 45s we have done-to-death Barry White and Stevie Wonder, but Smog, the Velvet Underground and The Beta Band instil a heavier, slacker vibe.

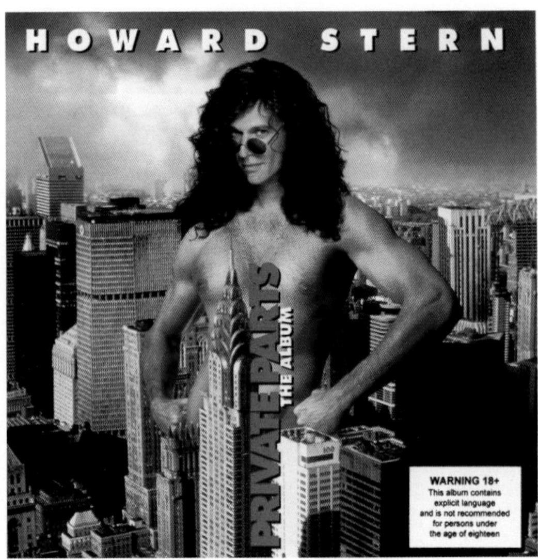

The 1997 story about, and starring, shock jock Howard Stern, a nerdy college kid who wanted above all else to be a famous disc jockey, and succeeds with tasteless toilet humour and various studio sexploits. The soundtrack is composed of classic rock and heavier stuff: Deep Purple, Van Halen and AC/DC as well as Green Day covering The Kinks, and Ozzy Osbourne covering Status Quo.

Julien Temple's 1986 portrait of London in the late 50s, as the birth of the cool, the hip and British trad-jazz scene is witnessed through the eyes of wannabe fashion photographer Colin. David Bowie (who stars as well-groomed ad exec Vendice Partners) features on the soundtrack, which puts 80s stars Sade and the Style Council alongside jazz muso Gil Evans.

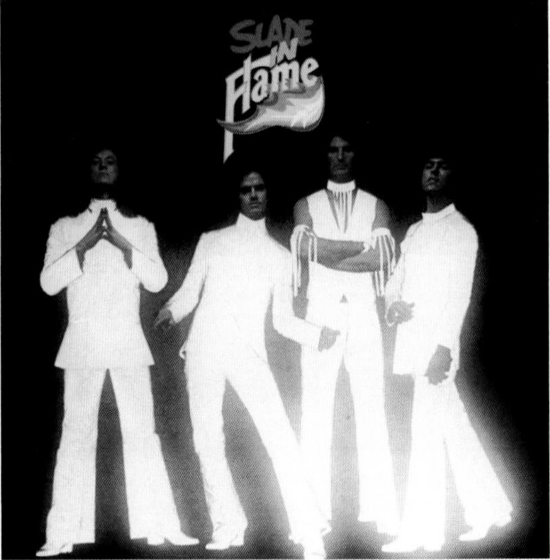

Slade starred as the band Flame in this 1975 film, one of the most sobering portraits of the music industry ever made. They provided the soundtrack when they were still in their foot-stomping pomp, but its gratifyingly jaded soul prefigures the anti-glamour of punk. It stands apart from the film but equally makes it mandatory viewing.

LOOKING FOR AN ECHO

1999 (US 97m) Steve Tisch Company / Regent Releasing (R)

Film genre: psychological romantic melodrama (w/ doo-wop)

Top guns: s-w: (+ dir) Martin Davidson ← EDDIE AND THE CRUISERS ← ALMOST SUMMER, Jeffrey Goldenberg, Robert Held

Stars: Armand Assante *(Vince 'Vinnie' Pirelli)* ← the ROAD TO EL DORADO, Diane Venora *(Joanne)* ← the INSIDER, Tom Mason *(Augustus 'Augie' MacAnnally III)*, Tony Denison *(Ray 'Nappy' Napolitano)*, Johnny Williams *(Phil 'Pooch' Puccirelli)* ← the SPOOK WHO SAT BY THE DOOR, Edoardo Ballerini *(Anthony Pirelli)* ← I SHOT ANDY WARHOL, Christy Carlson Romano *(Tina Pirelli)*, David Vadim *(Tommie Pirelli)* → BROOKLYN BABYLON, David Margulies *(Dr. Ludwig)* ← CANDY MOUNTAIN ← MAGIC STICKS ← TIMES SQUARE, Murray Weinstock *(Orchid Blue vocalist)* ← BYE BYE BIRDIE re-make ← the LEMON SISTERS, **Kenny Vance** *(vocals; Vince)* ← EDDIE AND THE CRUISERS ← AMERICAN HOT WAX

Storyline: Widower Vince works as a barman in the Bay Ridge Bistro, determined to forget his past life with his doo-wop band the Dreamers. Now his life centres around his children, especially 14 year-old Tina who is battling leukemia. Romance may be in the air when he becomes friendly with Tina's nurse Joanne, but all of that is put on hold when he and his old bandmates from the Dreamers get together one last time to re-release their smash hit. Can Vince put his old regrets behind him and begin anew? *JZ*

Movie rating: *6

Visual: video + dvd

Off the record: Master of retro 50s doo-wop, **Kenny Vance** (b. Kenneth Rosenberg), has been treading the boards for some time since his early 60s heyday with US hitmakers, Jay & The Americans. His subsequent work in numerous films (mainly as Musical Director) saw him supply sounds to 'YOU'VE GOT TO WALK IT . . .' (1971), 'AMERICAN HOT WAX' (1978), 'EDDIE AND THE CRUISERS' (1983), 'HAIRSPRAY' (1988), 'The Heart Of Dixie' (1989), 'EDDIE AND THE CRUISERS II: EDDIE LIVES!' (1989), etc., while he also carved out a solo career. *MCS*

KENNY VANCE & THE PLANOTONES (*)

Nov 00. (cd) *Sindrome; <8952>* –
– Bridge prelude / This I swear (*) / I'm so happy (*) / Your way (*) / I want to (do everything for you) (*) / Life is but a dream / Doo wop medley / This magic moment (*) / Hushabye / Sh-boom / Please say you want me / It's alright / Wisdom of a fool / Looking for an echo (*) / It's so hard to say goodbye to yesterday.

S/track review: The music here is based on a recent KENNY VANCE AND THE PLANOTONES album of the same name released for the '32 Jazz' imprint in 1996 – so watch out! VANCE and his barbershop-like PLANOTONES go back in time to re-create something out of the doo-wop field of dreams, echoing times when nearly every boy was clean-cut and every gal was of the next-door variety, while each romanticised tune is stretched to its vocal limit, 'This I Swear', 'I'm So Happy' and 'Your Way' prime examples. Whether one can appreciate something from the 50s moving into the new millennium, well that's for the listener to decide. Golden nuggets like 'Sh-boom', the softer rendition 'Life Is But A Dream' and the old Jay & The Americans number, 'This Magic Moment', make their easy-listening entrances, and if one was a fan of laid-back blues, 'I Want To (Do Everything For You)' was indeed "for you". *MCS*

Album rating: *6

– associated release –

KENNY VANCE and THE PLANOTONES: Looking For An Echo

May 96. (cd) *32 Jazz; <32001>* –
– (some tracks above * corresponded with later sound tracks).

LOOKING FOR LOVE

1964 (US 83m) Metro-Goldwyn-Mayer (PG)

Film genre: romantic Pop Musical drama

Top guns: dir: Don Weis → PAJAMA PARTY → the GHOST IN THE INVISIBLE BIKINI / s-w: Ruth Brooks Flippen

Stars: Connie FRANCIS *(Libby Caruso)*, Jim Hutton *(Paul Davis)* ← WHERE THE BOYS ARE, Susan Oliver *(Jan McNair)* → YOUR CHEATIN' HEART, Joby Baker *(Cuz Rickover)* ← HOOTENANNY HOOT / → GIRL HAPPY → WHEN THE BOYS MEET THE GIRLS, Barbara Nichols *(Gaye Swinger)*, Jay C. Flippen *(Mr. Ralph Front)*, Jesse White *(Tiger Shay)* ← COUNTRY MUSIC HOLIDAY / → PAJAMA PARTY → the GHOST IN THE INVISIBLE BIKINI → NASHVILLE GIRL, Charles Lane *(screen test director)*, Joan Marshall *(Miss Devine)*, Johnny Carson *(himself)*, George Hamilton *(himself)* ← WHERE THE BOYS ARE / → YOUR CHEATIN' HEART, Paula Prentiss *(herself)* ← FOLLOW THE BOYS, Yvette Mimieux *(herself)*, Henry Slate *(bar owner)* ← HEY BOY! HEY GIRL!, Dorothy Neumann *(Rose)* ← HOT ROD GANG ← CARNIVAL ROCK / → GET YOURSELF A COLLEGE GIRL, Pat Priest *(waitress)* → EASY COME, EASY GO

Storyline: Libby Caruso has the hots for dashing Paul Davis, but he takes about as much notice of her as a fly on the wall. However Libby's new clothes creation does attract his attention and she gets a spot on his Tonight Show. Her idea turns out to be a flop but her singing is a success and after a stuttering start her musical career and love life finally get better. *JZ*

Movie rating: *6

Visual: video

Off the record: nothing

CONNIE FRANCIS (composers: Mark Hunter, Stan Vincent)

Jul 64. (lp) *M.G.M.; <E/ES 4229> (MGM-C/-CS 6079)* Jan65
– Looking for love (rock 'n roll version) / Whoever you are I love you (vocal) / When the clock strikes midnight / Rock dem bells / This is my happiest moment / Be my love / Looking for love (jazz version) / Let's have a party / I can't believe that you're in love with me / Connie Francis – Lady Valet theme / Whoever you are I love you (inst.) / Looking for love (reprise).

S/track review: CONNIE FRANCIS returns briefly to her rock'n'roll roots via her third starring motion picture, 'LOOKING FOR LOVE'. Three times the hit title track pops up, the best versions by far bookending the MGM soundtrack, while a big band/jazz version spoils the start of Side Two. Written by Mark Hunter and Stan Vincent (who also supplied 'When The Clock Strikes Midnight' and the Brenda Lee-esque, Papa Oom Mow Mow-chiming 'Let's Have A Party'), the LP also fulfils its R&R obligation on the Claus Ogerman instrumental 'Rock Dem Bells' (his 'Connie Francis – Lady Valet Theme' was poor by comparison). With Connie's hits all but drying up – and I say that very carefully – the girl of Italian descent decided old-time nostalgic crooning was her field. While she was definitely the "material girl" twenty years before Madonna got in tune, most of her songs here are sub-standard. Check out 'This Is My Happiest Moment' and I can assure you it was quite the reverse. Ditto 'Be My Love' and 'Whoever You Are I Love You'; it was as if the Beatles and the 'Stones had never happened. At 30 minutes of play, you wonder if a couple of EPs should've sufficed. Anyway, if you can't purchase the rare LP, you'll find all the best bits on a CONNIE FRANCIS In Hollywood collection, 'Where The Boys Are', released on 'Rhino' records in 1997. *MCS*

Album rating: *3.5

– spinoff hits, etc. –

CONNIE FRANCIS: Looking For Love / This Is My Happiest Moment

Jul 64. (7") *<13256>* 45 –

☐ Donna LOREN segment
(⇒ BEACH BLANKET BINGO)

☐ LOS LOBOS segment
(⇒ LA BAMBA)

☐ LOVE IN LAS VEGAS alt.
(⇒ VIVA LAS VEGAS)

LOVE ME TENDER

1956 (US 89m b&w) 20th Century Fox (PG)

Film genre: romantic Rock'n'roll Musical western

Top guns: dir: Robert D. Webb / s-w: Robert Buckner (au: Maurice Geraghty)

Stars: Richard Egan *(Vance Reno)*, Debra Paget *(Cathy Reno)*, **Elvis PRESLEY** *(Clint Reno)*, Robert Middleton *(Mr. Siringo)*, William Campbell *(Brett Reno)*, Neville Brand *(Mike Gavin)*, Mildred Dunnock *(Marlha Reno)*, Bruce Bennett *(Maj. Kincaid)*, James Drury *(Ray Reno)* → BERNARDINE, Ken Clark *(Mr. Kelso)*, Barry Coe *(Mr. Davis)*, Russ Conway *(Ed Galt)*

Storyline: Three brothers rob a Union payroll just as the American Civil War comes to a close. Faced with the realisation that they're squarely on the losing side, they divide up the loot although sibling relations become strained once they head home. *BG*

Movie rating: *5.5

Visual: video

Off the record: Given that this wasn't an ELVIS film per se, the King's screen debut featured a mere four songs, released as an EP and dominated by the treacle-rich, tearjerking croon of its classic title track, alongside the lesser known likes of 'Poor Boy', a farmyard hoedown with a vaguely cajun vibe which comes perilously close to fulfilling the hillbilly jibes trundled out by ELVIS' detractors. 'We're Gonna Move', meanwhile, may well have paved the way for Shakin' Stevens' 'This Ol' House'. They're all worth hearing, if only for novelty value; you can find them – along with alternate stereo versions – tacked onto the 'JAILHOUSE ROCK' CD re-issue. *BG*

– spinoff hits, etc. –

ELVIS PRESLEY: Love Me Tender

Oct 56. (7",78) *R.C.A.; <47-6643> H.M.V.; (POP 253)* [1] Sep56 [11]

ELVIS PRESLEY: Love Me Tender

Nov 56. (7"ep) *R.C.A.; <EPA 4006> H.M.V.; (7EG 8199)* [22] Dec56 [ ]
– Love me tender / Let me / Poor boy / We're gonna move.
(UK re-iss. Oct77; RCX 7191)

—— <the 3rd track from the EP actually hit US No.24 on its own>

– other bits & pieces, etc. –

RICHARD CHAMBERLAIN: Love Me Tender

Sep 62. (7") *M.G.M.; <13097> (1173)* [21] Sep62 [15]

ROLAND RAT SUPERSTAR: Love Me Tender

Apr 84. (7") *Rodent; (RAT 2)* [–] [32]

LOVEDOLLS SUPERSTAR

1986 sequel (US 80m) We Got Power (R)

Film genre: Punk Rock Musical & religious satire

Top guns: s-w + dir: **Dave MARKEY**

Stars: Jennifer Schwartz *(Kitty Carryall)* ← DESPERATE TEENAGE LOVEDOLLS, **Steven McDonald** *(Rainbow Tremaine)* ← REDD KROSS =>, Janet Housden *(Patch Christ)* ← DESPERATE TEENAGE LOVEDOLLS, Kim Pilkington *(Alexandria "Cheetah" Azethrasher)* ← DESPERATE TEENAGE LOVEDOLLS, **Jeff McDonald** *(Carl Celery)* <= REDD KROSS =>, Tracy Lea *(Patricia Ann Cloverfield)* ← DESPERATE TEENAGE LOVEDOLLS, Michael F. Glass, **Vicki Peterson** *(Jeannie)*← DESPERATE TEENAGE LOVEDOLLS, **Sky Saxon** ← DESPERATE TEENAGE LOVEDOLLS, **Jello BIAFRA**, Tracy Marshak-Nash *(Patricia Hearst)* ← DESPERATE TEENAGE LOVEDOLLS

Storyline: The Lovedolls are back where they came from – in the brothels, communes and gutters of L.A. However, the fed-up girls decide to re-form the band and rampage their way back to the top by the usual methods – violence, depravity and a plot to do away with Bruce Springsteen (well, why not?). Meanwhile, the past comes back to haunt them as a she-devil's mum is out for revenge and their ex-manager's brother Rainbow shows his true colours. *JZ*

Movie rating: *6

Visual: dvd

Off the record: **Sky Saxon** (was of 60s garage outfit, the Seeds), **Vicky Peterson** (was of the Bangles). **Gone** were the outfit of former Black Flag guitarist, Greg Ginn, who disgarded hardcore for a fusion of instrumental jazz-rock and heavy metal a la Black Sabbath style. In between solo albums on his newly-formed 'Cruz' imprint, Ginn and Gone unleashed several albums (on 'S.S.T.') namely 'Let's Get Real, Real Gone For A Change' (1986), 'Gone II – But Never Too Gone' (1987), 'Criminal Mind' (1994), 'All The Dirt THat's Fit To Print' (1994), 'Best Left Unsaid' (1996) and 'Country Dumb' (1998). *MCS*

——

Various Artists incl. LOVEDOLLS (*) & GONE (**)

1986. (d-lp/c) *S.S.T.; <SST 062/+C>* [ ] [–]
– Lovedoll superstar (REDD KROSS) / Beer and ludes (*) / Rex Smith 9 (I wanna be a Cholo Chuck) (*) / Now that I've tasted blood (*) / Sunshine day (*) / Kickin' & stickin' (BLACK FLAG) / Purple haze (REDD KROSS) / Baby don't go (ANNETTE) / Slick's thang (**) / Love machine (*) / Hallowed be thy name (SONIC YOUTH) / Darling Shelah (PAINTED WILLIE) / Wingtips (LAWNDALE) / Lord of the wasteland (**) / Slam, spit, cut your hair, kill your mom! (ANARCHY 6) / Goodbye forever (**) / No values (MEAT PUPPETS) / Atomic jam (**) / One-way ticket to Pluto (DEAD KENNEDYS) / I won't stick any of you unless and until I can stick all of you! (**) / March (**) / Material jam (**) / Day in India (on acid) (**). *<cd-iss. 1990; SST/+CD 062>*

S/track review: People will tell you that if you have nothing nice to say then don't say anything at all. Unfortunately, one has a couple of hundred words to fill and therefore don't have that luxury. The title track by REDD KROSS is some kind of faux metal anthem that has enough cheese to satisfy an army of starving mice while their instrumental version of 'Purple Haze' leaves a lot to be desired. LOVEDOLLS, the film's fictional band that sound like a cheap Siouxsie & The Banshees rip-off, throw in five songs that make you wish they hadn't, including a comical version of Brady Bunch anthem 'Sunshine Day'. Even the presence of SONIC YOUTH, BLACK FLAG or DEAD KENNEDYS do little to lift the soundtrack above what can only be described as bog standard, their contributions sounding forced and laboured as opposed to their usual intensity. Friends of Kurt Cobain, MEAT PUPPETS are quite frankly awful with 'No Values' while not one of GONE's eight fiddly instrumentals are worth a mention. There is too much dumb punk rock here that lacks any sort of charm or charisma to make 'LOVEDOLLS SUPERSTAR' worth a listen. It also lacks any kind of energy or vibrancy which, coupled with bad songs, makes this a terrible record and one that should be consigned to a locked drawer in order to protect the population at large. *CM*

Album rating: *3

☐ Lene LOVICH segment
(⇒ CHA CHA)

LOVING YOU

1957 (US 101m) Paramount Pictures (A)

Film genre: Rock'n'roll Musical drama

Top guns: s-w: Hal Kanter (+ dir) → BLUE HAWAII , Herbert Baker ← the GIRL CAN'T HELP IT / → KING CREOLE → the JAZZ SINGER (au: Mary Agnes Thompson)

Stars: Elvis PRESLEY *(Jimmy Tompkins / Deke Rivers)*, Lizabeth Scott *(Glenda Markle)*, Wendell Corey *(Walter "Tex" Warner)*, Dolores Hart *(Susan Jessup)* → KING CREOLE, James Gleason *(Carl Meade)*, Kenneth Baker *(Wayne)* → G.I. BLUES → GIRLS! GIRLS! GIRLS! → ROUSTABOUT, Beach Dickerson *(Glenn)* ← ROCK ALL NIGHT / → G.I. BLUES → the TRIP → the SAVAGE SEVEN, Yvonne Lime *(Sally)* ← UNTAMED YOUTH

Storyline: Deke Rivers, a hillbilly truck driver with a sideline in singing and a winning way with women, is recruited by hard-nosed publicity agent Glenda Markle to shore up her erstwhile lovers' fading C&W outfit. Predictably, Rivers' causes a nationwide sensation amid claims of moral degeneracy. *BG*

Movie rating: *4.5

Visual: video + dvd

Off the record: nothing

ELVIS PRESLEY (composers: Walter Scharf, etc.)

Jul 57. (10"lp) *RCA Victor; <LPM 1515> R.C.A.; (RC 24001)* [1] Aug57 [*]
– Mean woman blues / (Let me be your) Teddy bear / Loving you / Got a lot o' livin' to do / Lonesome cowboy / Hot dog / Party / Blueberry hill / True love / Don't leave me now / Have I told you lately that I love you / I need you so. *(re-iss. Sep77 lp/c +=; PK/PL 42358)* – (hit UK No.24) *(re-iss. Aug81 on 'R.C.A. Int.' INTS 5109) (re-iss. Jan84 lp/c; NL/NK 81515) (cd-iss. Oct87; ND 81515) <(cd-iss. Feb98 +=; 07863 67452-2)>* – (bonus tracks; some not from movie). *(lp re-iss. Jan02 on 'Castle'++=; ELVIS 110)* – (bonus 7" singles).

S/track review: As a pseudo-autobiographical tale of ELVIS' rise to fame (director Hal Kanter actually did some on-the-road research with PRESLEY and his band), this movie coaxed some of his best musical performances before Hollywood ironed out the grit and dumbed down the material. Reunited with Scotty Moore, Tiny Timbrell, the Jordanaires et al after 20th Century Fox had spurned them (for their supposedly primitive Nashville pedigree) on 'LOVE ME TENDER', PRESLEY sounded more relaxed here than he would at almost any other time in his celluloid career. The high standard of the songs certainly helped, with ELVIS rising to first-rate material from Claude Demetrius ('Mean Woman Blues'), Lowe/Mann ('Teddy Bear'), Leiber/Stoller ('Loving You' and 'Hot Dog') and Schroder/Wiseman ('Got A Lot O' Livin' To Do!') amongst others. Hardcore fans will revel in the prime "C'mon baby" hollers liberally sprinkled throughout the latter (its finale perhaps a source of inspiration for Vic Reeves' inimitable "club singing"..?) while 'Lonesone Cowboy' mines the spirit of the Old West more convincingly than many country troubadours. Yet this wasn't a conventional soundtrack as such, featuring a whole side of slower songs not included in the film, among them Ivory Joe Hunter's excellent 'I Need You So' and a decent version of 'Blueberry Hill'. The CD re-issue bumps up the package even further with a slew of bonus tracks and alternate takes, chief among them the magnificent 'One Night Of Sin', a raw, emotionally bruising ballad with a 'Blueberry..'-esque groove, and a crackly reprise of the rocking 'Got A Lot O' Lovin' To Do'. *BG*

Album rating: *6

– spinoff hits, etc. –

ELVIS PRESLEY: Loving You

Jun 57. (7"ep) *<EPA1 1515>* [ ] [–]
– Loving you / Let's have a party / Teddy bear / Got a lot of lovin' to do. *(UK-iss.Oct77; RCX 7192)*

ELVIS PRESLEY: Loving You, Volume 2

Jun 57. (7"ep) *<EPA2 1515>* [–] lp-cht [18]

ELVIS PRESLEY: (Let Me Be Your) Teddy Bear / Loving You

Jun 57. (7",78) *<47-7000> (1013)* [1] [20] Jul57 [3]

ELVIS PRESLEY: Party / Got A Lot Of Lovin' To Do

Oct 57. (7",78) *(1020)* [–] [2]

□ Bob LUMAN segment
(⇒ CARNIVAL ROCK)

□ Frankie LYMON segment
(⇒ WHY DO FOOLS FALL IN LOVE)

□ Liam LYNCH segment
(⇒ the PICK OF DESTINY)

□ Loretta LYNN segment
(⇒ COAL MINER'S DAUGHTER)

□ Rita MacNEIL segment
(⇒ CANDY MOUNTAIN)

MADE

1972 (UK 104m) Anglo / EMI Films (18)

Film genre: domestic drama

Top guns: dir: John MacKenzie / s-w: Howard Barker (+ au: 'No One Was Saved')

Stars: Carol White *(Valerie)* → BODY ROCK, **Roy Harper** *(Mike Preston)* → the SONG REMAINS THE SAME, John Castle *(Father Dyson)* ← BLOW-UP, Margery Mason *(Mrs. Marshall)*, Richard Vanstone *(Ray)* ← TWO A PENNY, Sam Dastor *(Mahdav)*, Michael Cashman *(Joe)* ← I'VE GOTTA HORSE, Brian Croucher *(Arthur)*, Bob Harris *(interviewer)*

Storyline: Valerie is a young woman struggling to cope with a lot of frustration and stress as a one-parent mother while also dealing with her terminally-ill mother. When an insecure rock star and a young priest vie for her attentions, she secretly enjoys the attention at first but soon sees where her superfluous priorities lie. *MCS*

Movie rating: *5

Visual: none as yet (score: John Cameron)

Off the record: Roy Harper also composed the songs for the movie, some excerpts of which ('The Lord's Prayer', 'Highway Blues' – live, 'Little Lady' – live session, 'Bank Of The Dead' – aka 'Social Casualty' & 'Valerie's Song') appeared on the 1973 set, 'Lifemask'. *MCS*

– associated releases, etc. –

ROY HARPER: Bank Of The Dead (Valerie's Song) / Little Lady

Oct 72. (7") *Harvest; (HAR 5059)* □ [-]

ROY HARPER: Lifemask

Feb 73. (lp) *Harvest; (SHVL 808)* □ [-]
– Highway blues / All Ireland / Little lady / Bank of the dead (Valerie's song) / South Africa / The Lord's prayer: a) Poem, b) Modal song parts 1-4, c) Front song, d) Middle song, e) End song (Front song (reprise). *<US-iss.1978 on 'Chrysalis'; 1162> (re-iss. Apr87 on 'Awareness' lp/c; AWL/AWT 1007) (cd-iss. Sep94 & Oct96 & Sep02 on 'Science Friction'+=; HUCD 005)* – (other tracks).

MADONNA

Born: Madonna Louise Veronica Ciccone, 16 Aug'59, Rochester, Michigan, USA. Where she's so often been the exception to the rule in musical, stylistic and cultural terms, pop icon MADONNA has pretty much reinforced the old adage that the world of popular music and the world of the Hollywood motion picture are mutually exclusive. Given her background in dance and love of choreography, it was perhaps inevitable that she'd seek to take her interest in the visual side of music to its ultimate conclusion and strive for acceptance as a major league actress. In fact, she'd already dabbled in film before she'd even had her first club hit, starring in grimy seXploitation flick, 'A Certain Sacrifice' (1980). She later wished she hadn't of course, attempting unsuccessfully to prevent the film's release on video. Not that she was averse to flirting with sexual controversy although in future, crucially, she would be in control. Her first major film role, alongside Rosanna Arquette in Susan Seidelman's boisterous femme comedy, 'Desperately Seeking Susan' (1985), came amid her first flush of chart success as she toyed with her 'Like A Virgin' and 'Material Girl' personas, and successfully translated her New York nous to the big screen. It was a decent start, and one which earned her a surpise No.1 (her fourth) with spin-off single 'Into The Groove'. Harold Becker's coming-of-age drama, 'Vision Quest' (1985), also earned her a huge hit with 'Crazy For You' that same summer (she also made a cameo appearance in the film). Much less promising was the unverisally panned ("astonishingly abysmal" even, as one critic ventured), 'Shanghai Surprise' (1986), a George Harrison-scored romantic comedy in which MADONNA starred alongside her then husband Sean Penn. Her critical stock continued to plummet with the poorly received 'WHO'S THAT GIRL?' (1987), a makeweight comedy in which the singer played a feisty ex-con. If the soundtrack's four new MADONNA tracks – including the title song – weren't her best, the remainder of the album was largely forgettable filler. More interesting was the brassy period nostalgia of 'I'm Breathless' (1990), a set "inspired by the film DICK TRACY" but also standing as her fifth studio album. In actual fact, only four of the record's songs were featured in the Warren Beatty-directed movie, excluding the two singles, 'Vogue' and the wonderful 'Hanky Panky'. While she couldn't hope to match the movie idols she reels off so casually in 'Vogue' (itself the cue for a much hyped but short lived dance craze), her role as a nightclub singer was actually one of her better performances, enhaced by the film's visual flair. While Alek Keshishian's intimate documentary, 'TRUTH OR DARE' (aka 'In Bed With Madonna' – 1991), revealed a more accurate picture of its media savvy subject than even she probably intended, her role as a female baseball player in Penny Marshall's 'A League Of Their Own' (1992) found her acting ambitions finally taking off both critically and commercially. Contrary (and as controversial) as ever, MADONNA undid these plaudits with her slated soft-porn book, 'Sex' (1992) and disappointingly one-dimensional role in Udi Edel's erotic thriller, 'Body Of Evidence' (1993). Despite a disarmingly convincing performance in Abel Ferrara's 'Dangerous Game' (1993), the film was a commercial disaster and, with only cameos in Wayne Wang/Paul Auster's celeb spangled, engagingly off-beat 'Blue In The Face' (1995) and multi-directed black comedy, 'FOUR ROOMS' (1995) to go on over the next few years, Maddie's movie profile remained low. Until 'EVITA' (1996) that is, when the singer's well documented pleas to director Alan Parker finally paid off and he successfully cast her as Argentine icon Eva Peron. The lavish, long-time-coming big screen adaptation of the Andrew Lloyd Webber & Tim Rice musical was widely regarded as a triumph, or at least a stylistic one, and MADONNA's performace of the movie's sole new song, 'You Must Love Me', won an Oscar for its aforementioned composers. A cameo in Spike Lee's phone-sex spoof, 'GIRL 6' (1996) seemed to put the lid on her acting career, and for the remainder of the decade she concentrated on her rejuvenated pop career. Save a sassy contribution ('Beautiful Stranger') to spy spoof sequel, 'Austin Powers: The Spy Who Shagged Me' (1999), MADONNA was absent from the big screen until her uninspiring role in the John Schlesinger melodrama,

'The Next Best Thing' (2000). She nevertheless contributed an impressively updated version of Don McLean's 'American Pie' to the various artists soundtrack, released on her own 'Maverick' label. More high profile than any of this was her wedding to English film director Guy Ritchie, its Scottish Highlands location a cue for maximum media fawning. The pair's inevitable celluloid collaboration, 'Swept Away' (2002), a remake of an obscure mid-70s Italian movie, turned out to be one of MADONNA's most ill-advised projects to date, with critics damning her unconvincing portrayal of an aloof and emotionally barren heiress. A star turn on the David Arnold-masterminded Bond soundtrack, 'Die Another Day' (2002) was more suited to her talents, talents which, as her screen career hits an all-time low, it looks likely she'll stick to in future. *BG*

- **filmography** {acting} -

a Certain Sacrifice *(1980 {*})* / Vision Quest *(1985 {c} hit single on OST by V/A see; future editions =>)* / Desperately Seeking Susan *(1985 {*} hit single but not on OST by THOMAS NEWMAN see; future editions =>)* / Shanghai Surprise *(1986 {*})* / **Who's That Girl?** *(1987 {*} OST =>)* / Bloodhounds Of Broadway *(1989 {*})* / **Dick Tracy** *(1990 {*} OST =>)* / **Truth Or Dare** *(1991 {*})* / Shadows And Fog *(1992 {*})* / a League Of Their Own *(1992 {*} OST by V/A see; future edition =>)* / Body Of Evidence *(1993 {*})* / Dangerous Game *(1993 {*})* / Blue In The Face *(1995 {a} OST by V/A =>)* / **Four Rooms** *(1995 {*} OST by COMBUSTIBLE EDISON =>)* / **Girl 6** *(1996 {a} OST by PRINCE =>)* / **Evita** *(1996 {*} OST w/ Cast =>)* / Austin Powers: The Spy Who Shagged Me *(1999 hit theme on V/A; see future edition)* / the Next Best Thing *(2000 {*} hit single on OST by V/A see; future edition =>)* / Swept Away *(2002 {*})* / Die Another Day *(2002 {b} hit single on OST)*

MADONNA: INNOCENCE LOST

1994 (US 76m TV) Fox Network

Film genre: Pop/Rock-music biopic/drama

Top guns: dir: Bradford May / s-w: Michael J. Murray (book: 'Madonna: Unauthorized' by Christopher Andersen)

Stars: Terumi Matthews *(Madonna)*, Wendie Malick *(Camille Barbone)* → the EMPEROR'S NEW GROOVE, Jeff Yagher *(Paul)* ← SHAG: THE MOVIE, Diana Leblanc *(Ruth Novak)*, Dean Stockwell *(Tony Ciccone)* ← TUCKER: THE MAN AND HIS DREAM ← TO LIVE AND DIE IN L.A. ← DUNE ← PARIS, TEXAS ← HUMAN HIGHWAY ← PSYCH-OUT, Nigel Bennett *(Bennett)*, Don Francks *(Jerome Kirkland)* ← ROCK & RULE ← HEAVY METAL / → MR. MUSIC → I'M NOT THERE, Maia Filar *(Madonna at 10)*, Cyndy Preston *(Jude O'Mally)* ← WHALE MUSIC, Matthew Godfrey *(Peter Barbone)*, Rod Wilson *(Mitch Roth)*

Storyline: The early life and rise to fame of talented dancer-turned-pop-singer, Madonna. Determined and obsessed to become a star, the "material girl" loses faith in her religion after her mother's death, but this only gives her more drive to succeed. *MCS*

Movie rating: *4

Visual: none (no audio OST; score: Tony Shimkin)

Off the record: nothing

MAGIC STICKS

1987 (W.Ger/US 97m) Tale Films / Wolfgang Odenthal Filmproduktion

Film genre: Pop/Dance-music comedy

Top guns: s-w: (+ dir) Peter Keglevic, **George Kranz**, Christopher Ragazzo

Stars: George Kranz *(Felix)*, Kelly Curtis *(Shirley)*, **Chico Hamilton** *(Mr. Jazz)*, Joe Silver *(pawnbroker)* ← YOU LIGHT UP MY LIFE, David Margulies *(Goldfarb)* ← TIMES SQUARE / → CANDY MOUNTAIN → LOOKING FOR AN ECHO, James Lally *(Chris)* → WORKING GIRL, Sam Jackson *(bum)* → SCHOOL DAZE → JUNGLE FEVER → JOHNNY SUEDE → JUICE → PULP FICTION → JACKIE BROWN → KILL BILL: VOL.1 → KILL BILL: VOL.2 → BLACK SNAKE MOAN, Mike Starr *(debt collector #2)* → WHO'S THAT GIRL → the BODYGUARD

Storyline: Would-be drummer Felix thinks he'll never hit the big time, until one day as he wanders New York he buys a pair of drumsticks from a street vendor. But these aren't just ordinary drumsticks – Felix soon discovers they have the magical ability to make New Yorkers dance till they drop. Can Felix use the sticks to win the heart of music student Shirley and avoid another visit to the pawnbroker? *JZ*

Movie rating: *4

Visual: video

Off the record: GEORGE KRANZ (AND ZOOM) . . . see below

—

GEORGE KRANZ

1987. (lp) *Virgin; (208 479)* [–] German [–]
– Wipe / Zoom / Magic drums – Ken leaves / You and me (duo GEORGE KRANZ & ELSE NABU) / Wipe / Magic drums – Central Park / Magic drums – Tiffany / Magic sticks – Gangster theme / Happy good byes / Wipe / Wild vocals with CHICO HAMILTON / You and me (theme) / Laws of dancing part II / Magic drums – Guard dances / Zoom – And gangster theme / Magic sticks – I've got the beat.

S/track review: German dance/house producer/percussionist, GEORGE KRANZ, was the brainchild behind the film and the music for 'MAGIC STICKS'. Having spread his Euro-electro message around the globe via one-off hit in '84, 'Din Daa Daa', KRANZ formed ZOOM, who were MICHAEL CRETU (on keys), MICHAEL BRANDT (guitar) and AXEL KOTTMANN (bass). The track, 'I've Got The Beat (Magic Sticks)' – a subsequent German 12" on 'Virgin' in 1990 – was co-written with Enigma brainchild, Michael Cretu. Meanwhile, sticksman extraordinaire, KRANZ, seemed to be having a whale of a time on film and record, although the total running time for the soundtrack only comes to around 25 minutes. If one was a fan of post-New Wave New Romantics such as Re-Flex (remember 'The Politics Of Dancing'), Howard Jones or, dare I say it, the Art Of Noise, 'MAGIC STICKS' might be up your street. 'Zoom' – the track – was very derivative of all three aforementioned stars and many other English acts, while the best song goes to 'You And Me' (his duet with ELSE NABU). Rhythmically-speaking, the three-parter at the end of side one is two-parts effective, one-part annoying, themes such as 'Central Park', 'Tiffany' and 'Gangster Theme', very Euro-fied. The scatty "Wild Vocals" on er . . . 'Wild Vocals' belong to JOCHEN SCHWARZAT, while also sitting in on the brief New York session is the legendary CHICO HAMILTON. *MCS*

Album rating: *4.5

MAGICAL MYSTERY TOUR

1967 (UK/US 55m; TV) Apple Corps (1973: New Line Cinema)

Film genre: Pop/Rock Musical road movie

Top guns: dir: Bernard Knowles + **the BEATLES** *(below)*

Stars: the BEATLES:- John Lennon *(John / ticket salesman / magician with coffee / narrator)*, **Paul McCartney** *(Paul / Major McCartney / brown-nosed magician)*, **George Harrison** *(George / magician looking through telescope)*, **Ringo Starr** *(Ringo / talkative magician)* / Victor Spinetti *(army sergeant)* ← HELP! ← a HARD DAY'S NIGHT / → UNDER THE CHERRY MOON → JULIE AND THE CADILLACS, Derek Royle *(Jolly Jimmy Johnson the courier)*, **Vivian Stanshall** *(singer: Bonzo Dog Band)* → THAT'LL BE THE DAY,

Neil Innes *(member: Bonzo Dog Band)* → the RUTLES → CONCERT FOR GEORGE, Maggie Wright *(the lovely starlet)*, **Ivor Cutler** *(Buster Bloodvessel)* ← IT'S ALL OVER TOWN, Jessie Robins *(Ringo's auntie)* ← WHAT A CRAZY WORLD / → UP THE JUNCTION, George Claydon *(Little George the photographer)* → BORN TO BOOGIE

Storyline: One of the more indulgent oddities from 1967's "summer of love", the Beatles' psychedelic-inpsired, self-directed foray into the English countryside was virtually plotless, leaving the – admittedly rather fine – music to do the talking. Features a host of famous actors/musicians from the era. *BG*

Movie rating: *4.5

Visual: video + dvd

Off the record: The film is full of eccentric musicians/singers, **Ivor Cutler** (a Glasgow-born comic-poet who will be remembered for LPs such as 'Life In A Scotch Sitting Room Volume 2', 'Jammy Smears' & 'Gruts'); plus ex-Bonzos **Neil Innes** ('Erik The Viking') and **Vivian Stanshall** ('Sir Henry At Rawlinson End'). *MCS*

---

the BEATLES

Dec 67. (d7"ep; stereo/mono) *Parlophone; (S+/MMT 1)* [2] [–]
– Magical mystery tour / Your mother should know / Flying / Fool on the hill / Blue Jay way / I am the walrus.

---

the BEATLES

Dec 67. (lp) *Capitol; (import) <SMAL 2835>* [31] [1]
– Magical mystery tour / The fool on the hill / Flying / Blue Jay way / Your mother should know / I am the walrus / Hello goodbye / Strawberry fields forever / Penny lane / Baby you're a rich man / All you need is love. *(UK-iss.Oct76 lp/c; same as US cd-iss. Sep87; CDP 748 062-2); hit UK 52)*

S/track review: In its original incarnation as a 6-track double EP, the soundtrack functioned as a kind of hazy coda to 'Sgt. Pepper's . . .', notable primarily for McCARTNEY's much loved ballad, 'The Fool On The Hill', and LENNON's surrealistic minor masterpiece, 'I Am The Walrus'. In its US – and eventual British – format, adding as it did the complete run of 1967's groundbreaking singles (including the chart-topping 'All You Need Is Love') and their B-sides, the album became an essential part of the BEATLES' legacy. *BG*

Album/d-EP review: *9 / EP *6

– spinoff hits, etc. –

the BEATLES: All You Need Is Love / Baby You're A Rich Man

Jul 67. (7") *(R 5620) <5964>* [1] [1] [34]

(re-iss. 7"pic-d/c-s/12" Nov87; RP/TCR/12R 5620); hit No.47) (3"cd-s iss.Jun89; CD3R 5620)

the BEATLES: Hello Goodbye / I Am The Walrus

Nov 67. (7") *(R 5655) <2056>* [1] [1] [56]

(re-iss. 7"pic-d Jul87; RP 5655); hit No.63) (3"cd-s iss.Jul89; CD3R 5655)

MALIBU'S MOST WANTED

2003 (US 86m) Karz Entertainment / Warner Bros. Pictures (PG-13)

Film genre: teen/crime comedy

Top guns: dir: John Whitesell / s-w: Fax Bahr, Adam Small ← ANOTHER STATE OF MIND, Jamie Kennedy, Nick Swardson

Stars: Jamie Kennedy *(Brad 'B-Rad' Gluckman)*, Taye Diggs *(Sean)* ← BROWN SUGAR / → RENT, Anthony Anderson *(PJ)* → HUSTLE & FLOW, Regina Hall *(Shondra)*, Blair Underwood *(Tom Gibbons)* ← KRUSH GROOVE / → FRONTERZ, Damien Dante Wayans *(Tec)*, Ryan O'Neal *(Bill Gluckman)* ← GREEN ICE, Bo Derek *(Bess Gluckman)*, Jeffrey Tambor *(Dr. Feldman)* ← THREE O'CLOCK HIGH, Kal Penn *(Hadji)*, Terry Crews *(8 Ball)*, **SNOOP DOGG** *(voice; Ronnie Rizzat)*, **Young Dre** *(himself)*, **Hi-C** *(himself)*, **Drop Da Bomb** *(himself)*, **Felli Fel** *(himself)*, Big Boy *(himself)*, Mike Epps *(rap-battle compere)* ← HOW HIGH / → the FIGHTING TEMPTATIONS → ROLL BOUNCE

Storyline: Brad Gluckman might be white on the outside but as far as on the inside he's a thug life living, hard knock givin', black dude from the ghettos of America. When his father, a wealthy Jewish politician wishes to run for Governor of California, he stages his own son's kidnap with the hopes that exposure to the real life terrors of life in the black inner cities will scare him "white" again. A plan that is guaranteed to go wrong. *MR*

Movie rating: *5

Visual: dvd

Off the record: Young Dre released the album, 'Hated By Many' (1997) for 'Kryptic'; Louisiana rapper **Hi-C** issued three albums:- 'Skanless' (1991) on 'Warners', 'Swing'n' (1993) for 'Skanless' and 'The Hi-Life Hustle' (2003) for 'D.M.G.'; **Felli Fel** issued two sets in 2002; **Drop (Da Bomb)** featured on this OST.

Various Artists (score: John Van Tongeren & themes John Debney)

Apr 03. (cd) *Universal; <(AAB 00003110-2)>* [ ] [ ]
– Girls, girls (SNOOP DOGG feat. E-WHITE, DELANO & JAMIE KENNEDY aka B-RAD) / I told ya (GRANDADDY SOUF) / Most wanted in Malibu (BABY JAYMES & JAMIE KENNEDY aka B-RAD) / Chug-a-lug (PASTOR TROY) / Really don't wanna go (DAVID BANNER feat. MR. MARCUS & B FLAT) / Crush on you (MR. CHEEKS feat. MARIO WINANS) / Blah, blah, blah, blah (702) / In here ta nite (RATED R) / That's dirty (DIRTY feat. MANNIE FRESH) / Play that funky music (white boy) (HI-C, BIG STEELE, DROP, YOUNG DRE & MR. KANE) / I want you girl (BUTCH CASSIDY) / California (AKIA feat. KAREEM OSBOURNE) / Choppa style (CHOPPA F / MASTER P) / Get back (504 BOYZ).

S/track review: Given the frankly silly nature of the film it might have been expected to get a disc of throwaway filler and an obligatory inclusion of Offspring's 'Pretty Fly (For A White Guy)'. Instead, we get a mix of straight commercial hip hop tracks plus a sprinkling recorded with Jamie Kennedy rapping in character as B-RAD. And the fusion is surprisingly credible. SNOOP DOGG's laconic drawl has been used to better effect than on opener 'Girls, Girls', a song which makes you crave the Jay-Z track of the same name but there's notable highlights include the doomy mechanical stutter of PASTOR TROY's 'Chug-a-Lug', a sloping roller powered by incessant brass stabs. Similarly DAVID BANNER mixes smooth vocal hooks and vicious guitar spikes on 'Really Don't Wanna Go' and CHOPPA F and MASTER P wind things up in brutal, compelling style on 'Choppa Style'. The grimy rhymes are broken up with some patchy pop, the lone star being an itchy groove from 702 where they diss inconsiderate paramours on 'Blah, Blah, Blah, Blah'. They may be Destiny's Child lite but this is a welcome spark. In contrast, RATED R needs a greased pole and a dictionary as 'In Here Ta Nite' amounts to more than poorly spelled filth. There's no dominant force here, more an amalgam of style sounds and weights. A real mixed bag where grizzly dirty southern beats are as welcome as frothy R&B. They couldn't resist the temptation completely and therefore their cover of 'Play That Funky Music (White Boy)' is fluff, although it reminds us that this kind of film just can't take itself too seriously, a good thing in a musical genre that allows too little space for humour. *MR*

Album rating: *6

the MAMBO KINGS

1992 (US/Fra 104m) Canal+ Alcor Films / Warner Bros. (R)

Film genre: showbiz/nostalgia Musical drama

Top guns: dir: Arnold Glimcher / s-w: Cynthia Cidre (au: Oscar Hijuelos)

Stars: Armand Assante *(Cesar Castillo)*, Antonio Banderas *(Nestor Castillo)*, Cathy Moriarty *(Lanna Lake)*, Maruschka Detmers *(Delores Fuentes)*, Desi Arnaz Jr. *(Desi Arnaz Sr.)*, **the Mambo Kings Band**:- Pablo Calogero *(Ramon)*, Scott Cohen *(Bernadito)* → VIBRATIONS → PRIVATE PARTS, Mario Grillo *(Mario)*, Pete Macnamara *(Johnny Bing)*, Ralph Irizarry *(Pito)*, James Medina *(Manny)*, J.T. Taylor *(Frankie Suarez)*, Marcos Quintanilla *(Willie)*, William Thomas Jr. *(Xavier)*, **Yul Vazquez** *(Flaco)* → FLY BY NIGHT / **Tito Puente** *(himself)*, **Celia Cruz** *(Evalina Montoya)*, Anh Duong *(Ismelda Perez)* → I SHOT ANDY WARHOL → HIGH ART, Vondie Curtis-Hall *(Miguel Montoya)* ← MYSTERY TRAIN / → CROOKLYN → TURN IT UP

Storyline: Hermanos in music and exile, Cesar and Nestor Castillo swap revolutionary Cuba for New York where they try their luck on a music scene afire with the energy of ex-pat Latinos. Gigging as the Mambo Kings, their different characters ultimately shape their destinies as nostalgic and lovelorn Nestor pines for Cuba while Cesar exults in the proto-rock'n'roll lifestyle. *BG*

Movie rating: *6

Visual: video + dvd

Off the record: Tito Puente + Celia Cruz (see below)

—

Various Artists (score: Robert Kraft & Carlos Franzetti)

Mar 92. (cd/c) *Elektra; <(7559 61240-2/-4)>* [50] May92 [ ]
– La dicha mia (CELIA CRUZ) / Ran kan kan (TITO PUENTE) / Cuban Pete (TITO PUENTE) / Mambo caliente (ARTURO SANDOVAL) / Quiereme mucho (LINDA RONSTADT) / Sunny Ray (MAMBO ALL-STARS) / Melao de cana (moo la lah) (CELIA CRUZ) / Beautiful Maria of my soul (Bella Maria de mi alma) (MAMBO ALL-STARS w/ ANTONIO BANDERAS) / Para los rumberos (TITO PUENTE) / Perfidia (LINDA RONSTADT) / Guantanamera (CELIA CRUZ) / Tea for two (MAMBO ALL-STARS) / Accidental mambo (MAMBO ALL-STARS) / Como fue (BENY MORE) / Tanga, rumba-Afro-Cubana (MAMBO ALL-STARS) / Beautiful Maria of my soul (LOS LOBOS).

S/track review: The undying popularity of mambo manifested itself in the 90s mainstream more forcefully than it had done for decades, thanks variously to a Perez Prado-excavating Guinness ad, a global megahit in Lou Bega's 'Mambo No.5' and, most memorably, the screen adaptation of Oscar Hijuelos' Pulitzer Prize-winning novel. Released a good few years before Latin music really came back into vogue (with the attendant avalanche of identikit compilations), 'The MAMBO KINGS' soundtrack was a fine sampler of its then-untapped riches. There's no Prado but there is plenty of TITO PUENTE and CELIA CRUZ, both still alive and active at the time. CRUZ is simply electric, the first and last word in Latin sass and the embodiment of female power in a culture not exactly known for its sympathy to women. Her laugh alone is lusty enough to make a harridan blush, and even singing in English – on 'Melao De Caña' and the drolly autobiographical 'La Dicha Mia' – her phrasing and delivery are mesmerising. It's difficult to see the logic, then, in sequencing LINDA RONSTADT next to her. With no disrespect to the lady – her contributions to 70s roots rock still sound great and her Mexican folk albums fine in their own right – it's questionable whether she should really be here at all. RONSTADT may have Latin ancestry but her polished, string-saturated ballads all but extinguish the album's momentum, especially when she's singing in English. It's not a charge which could be levelled against PUENTE, who's best represented by his frantic late 50s signature, 'Ran Kan Kan', and the even faster 'Para Los Rumberos'. The MAMBO ALL-STARS fire up the big band business and Cuban trumpet veteran ARTURO SANDOVAL proves why he moves in elite jazz circles. The only real bum note is the remixed 'Ran Kan Kan' which opens the millennial reissue, choking PUENTE's groove with horrible synth, four-square bludgeon and the random shrieks of OLGA TANON. *BG*

Album rating: *6.5

MAN IN THE MIRROR: THE MICHAEL JACKSON STORY

2004 (US 87m TV) Blueprint / Nomadic / VH-1 (PG-13)

Film genre: R&B/Pop-music biopic/drama

Top guns: dir: Allan Moyle ← EMPIRE RECORDS ← PUMP UP THE VOLUME ← TIMES SQUARE / s-w: Claudia Salter

Stars: Flex Alexander *(Michael Jackson)* ← JUICE, Eugene Clark *(Bobby)* ← TURN IT UP, Peter Onorati *(Ziggy)*, Lynne Cormack *(Liz Taylor)*, Frederic Tucker *(Joe Jackson)*, Samantha Banton *(Diana Ross)*, Amy Sloan *(Holly)*, Jason Griffith *(Jermaine Jackson)*, Barbara Mamabolo *(Janet Jackson)*, Krista Rae *(Lisa Marie Presley)*, Gerrick Winston *(Tito Jackson)*, Brennan Gademans *(young Michael)* → HOW SHE MOVE, April Telek *(Debbie Rowe)*, Cedric De Souza *(Martin Bashir)*, Carrie Schiffler *(surgeon)* ← ROCK'N'ROLL NIGHTMARE

Storyline: The somewhat controversial rise and fall of iconic pop star, Michael Jackson, from his early days with the Jackson 5, the multi-selling 'Thriller' album in '82 and up to the child molestation charges and court proceedings that took place in 2004. The film was aired on August 6th, 2004. *MCS*

Movie rating: *3

Visual: dvd (no audio OST)

Off the record: Michael Jackson was aquitted of all ten charges on June 13th, 2005, although a few jurors believed he was guilty of previously committing child sex crimes stating there was not enough evidence; Jackson subsequently relocated to Bahrain where he was planning his musical return for 2008. *MCS*

□ CHEECH Marin
(⇒ CHEECH & CHONG)

MASKED AND ANONYMOUS

2003 (US/UK 112m) Sony Pictures Classics / BBC Films (PG-13)

Film genre: political Rock Musical satire/comedy

Top guns: s-w (+ dir): Larry Charles aka Rene Fontaine, Sergei Petrov aka **Bob DYLAN** (au: Enrique Morales)

Stars: Bob DYLAN *(Jack Fate)*, Jeff Bridges *(Tom Friend)* ← TUCKER: THE MAN AND HIS DREAM ← the LAST UNICORN ← RANCHO DELUXE, Penelope Cruz *(Pagan Lace)* ← ALL THE PRETTY HORSES, John Goodman *(Uncle Sweetheart)* ← STORYTELLING ← the EMPEROR'S NEW GROOVE ← COYOTE UGLY ← O BROTHER, WHERE ART THOU? ← BLUES BROTHERS 2000 ← TRUE STORIES ← SWEET DREAMS / → OVERNIGHT → BEYOND THE SEA, Jessica Lange *(Nina Veronica)* ← FAR NORTH ← SWEET DREAMS, Luke Wilson *(Bobby Cupid)* ← COMMITTED / → HOOT, Angela Bassett *(mistress)* ← STRANGE DAYS ← WHAT'S LOVE GOT TO DO WITH IT ← the JACKSONS: AN AMERICAN DREAM, Steven Bauer *(Edgar)*, Bruce Dern *(editor)* ← ALL THE PRETTY HORSES ← LAST MAN STANDING ← PSYCH-OUT ← the TRIP ← the WILD ANGELS, Val Kilmer *(animal wrangler)* ← the DOORS ← TOP SECRET!, **Cheech Marin** *(Prospero)* <= CHEECH & CHONG =>, Ed Harris *(Oscar Vogel)* ← WALKER ← SWEET DREAMS ← ALAMO BAY ← PLACES IN THE HEART, Giovanni Ribisi *(soldier)* ← the VIRGIN SUICIDES ← FIRST LOVE, LAST RITES ← SUBURBI@ ← THAT THING YOU DO! / → LOST IN TRANSLATION → COLD MOUNTAIN, Chris Penn *(crew guy #2)* ← RESERVOIR DOGS ← MADE

IN USA ← FOOTLOOSE, Mickey Rourke *(Edmund)* ← BUFFALO 66 ← JOHNNY HANDSOME ← HOMEBOY, Christian Slater *(crew guy #1)* ← PUMP UP THE VOLUME ← YOUNG GUNS II ← TUCKER: THE MAN AND HIS DREAM ← LIVING PROOF: THE HANK WILLIAMS JR. STORY, Robert Wisdom *(Lucius)* ← STORYTELLING ← THAT THING YOU DO! / → KILLER DILLER → RAY, Sam Sarpong *(Blunt)* ← CARMEN: A HIP HOPERA, Fred Ward *(drunk)* ← TIMERIDER: THE ADVENTURE Oñ LYLE SWANN ← CARNY, **Simple Twist Of Fate:- Charlie Sexton** *(guitarist)*, **Tony Garnier** *(bassist)*, **Larry Campbell** *(guitarist)* / Susan Tyrell *(Ella the fortune teller)* ← PINK AS THE DAY SHE WAS BORN ← CRY-BABY ← ROCKULA ← TAPEHEADS ← SUBWAY RIDERS ← FORBIDDEN ZONE ← CATCH MY SOUL, Jon Sklaroff *(young Jack)* ← CLUBLAND, Tracey Walter *(desk clerk)* ← HOW HIGH ← MAN ON THE MOON ← DELUSION ← YOUNG GUNS II ← BATMAN ← REPO MAN ← HONKYTONK MAN ← TIMERIDER: THE ADVENTURE OF LYLE SWANN, Susan Traylor *(Mrs. Brown)* ← FINDING GRACELAND ← the BODYGUARD, Richard C. Sarafian *(President)* ← SONGWRITER

Storyline: Having failed to secure Paul McCartney, Eric Clapton or any of the usual suspects for his benefit concert, sleazy promoter Uncle Sweetheart has been forced to turn to jailed and all but forgotten rock star Jack Fate. Upon his release, the almost catatonic Fate braves a rebel hold-up, a muck-raking journalist, and various random characters spouting inane profundities, hollow clichés and pop cultural references, against an improbable backdrop of ethnic minority dictatorship and endemic civil war. Confused? You will be. *BG*

Movie rating: *4

Visual: dvd

Off the record: Larry Campbell, Tony Garnier & Charlie Sexton are all part of DYLAN's backing band, Simple Twist Of Fate. The latter gifted guitarist was born (11 August 1968) in San Antonio, Texas, and was signed by 'M.C.A.' records while he was only 16. Towards the end of 1985, a single ('Beat's So Lonely') and an album ('Pictures For Pleasure') both hit the Top 20, although a long-awaited eponymous follow-up in 1989 narrowly failed to break into the Top 100. In between sets, Charlie worked with DYLAN, BOWIE and his brother Will's debut album, 'Will & The Kill'. The early 90s saw Charlie branch out a little, appearing and contributing music to 'Thelma & Louise' (1991), while forming rock band Arc Angels (for one eponymous album) with ex-backing members of Stevie Ray Vaughan. Charlie periodically worked with DYLAN and had a bit part in the movie, 'F.T.W.' (1994); further work saw him as leader of Charlie Sexton & The Sextet for the Celtic-meets-blues album, 'Under The Wishing Tree' (1995), more film work in 'Natural Selection' and as producer/player for Edie Brickell's 'Volcano' set in 2003. *MCS*

BOB DYLAN (performer *) (w/ Various Artists)

Jul 03. (cd) *Columbia; <90336> (512556-2)* [94] [ ]
– My back pages (MAGOKORO BROTHERS) / Gotta serve somebody (SHIRLEY CAESAR) / Down in the flood (new version *) / It's all over now, baby blue (GRATEFUL DEAD) / Most of the time (SOPHIE ZELMANI) / On a night like this (LOS LOBOS) / Diamond Joe (*) / Come una pietra scalciata (Like a rolling stone) (ARTICOLO 31) / One more cup of coffee (SERTAB) / Non dirle che non e' cosi' (If you see her, say hello) (FRANCESCO DE GREGORI) / Dixie (*) / Señor (tales of Yankee power) (JERRY GARCIA) / Cold irons bound (new version *) / City of gold (DIXIE HUMMINGBIRDS).

S/track review: Given that the film has all the surface enigma and a little of the wit of a typical DYLAN song, but none of the underlying emotion, it's surprising that the soundtrack works so well. In fact, it's about the only thing that does work in the movie and inevitably becomes its sole focus, and not just because we're treated to DYLAN cranking his way through old classics and folk adaptations. The idea of filling up the rest of the film with cover versions would be tired if it wasn't for refreshingly cosmopolitan reworkings such as ARTICOLO 31's 'Come Una Pietra Scalciata' (that's 'Like A Rolling Stone' to you and me!), where the Italians chop up those famous organ chords into bite sized hip hop chunks and weld a sassy female chorus onto BOB's grizzled chorus. From Japan, the MAGOKORO BROTHERS bring us glad, folksy tidings in the shape of 'My Back Pages', while Turkish diva SERTEB ERENER luxuriates in the Eastern promise of 'One More Cup Of Coffee' and SOPHIE ZELMANI brilliantly invests 'Most Of The Time' with the icy sensuality of prime Velvet Underground. Ok, JERRY GARCIA wasn't very foreign but his haunting cover of 'Señor (Tales Of Yankee Power)' comes closest to evoking the atmosphere of societal apocalypse the film so resolutely fails to achieve. Apart from a Mozambican R&B version of, erm, 'Mozambique', what more could we ask for? Well, the poignant, all-too-short rendering of pint-sized TINASHE KACHINGWE's 'The Times They Are A-Changin' for one, an a cappella delight mystifyingly left off the album. Instead we get SHIRLEY CAESAR doing 'Gotta Serve Somebody' and the DIXIE HUMMINGBIRDS' version of 'City Of Gold', neither of which are featured in the film. Of the actual DYLAN numbers, 'Dixie' is mined from the seam of primal American myth which has always worked so well for him, and benefits from the rootsy, Band-like depth of his current backing group, as does the loose, sinuous version of 'Cold Irons Bound'. The biggest criticism of this record has to be the performances left out; no 'Blind Willie McTell' or 'Dirt Road Blues' amongst others. Apart from that, it's a compelling collection, and pretty much an essential purchase for DYLAN diehards. *BG*

Album rating: *5.5

- ☐ Linda McCARTNEY segment
(⇒ the LINDA McCARTNEY STORY)
- ☐ Paul McCARTNEY
(⇒ the BEATLES)
- ☐ Clyde McPHATTER segment
(⇒ MISTER ROCK AND ROLL)

MEAT LOAF

Born: Marvin Lee Aday, 27 Sep'47, Dallas, Texas, USA. A man with a musical landmark/millstone as hefty as his own bulky frame, MEAT LOAF will forever be identified with his Jim Steinman collaboration, 'Bat Out Of Hell' (1977), one of the highest-grossing albums in the history of this thing called popular music. By the time of its release, MEAT was already an old screen hand (and a Broadway veteran who got his break in 'Hair'), having made his adolescent acting debut with a cameo in Rodgers and Hammerstein musical-turned-Pat Boone vehicle, 'State Fair' (1962), and graduated to the part of Eddie in cult classic, 'The ROCKY HORROR PICTURE SHOW' (1975). Comedic cameos in Michael Schultz's 'Scavenger Hunt' (1979) and Neal Israel's farsighted satire, 'Americathon' (1979), were followed by a memorably buffoonish starring role in Alan Rudolph's minor groupie classic, 'ROADIE' (1980). Despite the year-round presence of 'Bat Out Of Hell' on the album charts, though, the 80s weren't particularly kind to MEAT. He played himself (twice) in comedy musical, 'Dead Ringer' (1982), but subsequently fell off the radar with bit parts in forgotten 80s fare like 'Out Of Bounds' (1987), 'Feel The Motion' (1987) and 'The Squeeze' (1987). Road movie, 'Motorama' (1991), offered him his biggest role in a decade – as a biker – but it wasn't until the likes of 'WAYNE'S WORLD' and Steve Martin vehicle, 'Leap Of Faith' (1992), that both his profile and his dramatic stock began to rise, compounded by the massive success of a follow-up which finally resurrected his rock career, 'Bat Out Of Hell II: Back To Hell' (1993). After a relatively successful follow-up in 'Welcome To The Neighbourhood' (1995), he returned to the big screen with a vengeance in 1998, co-starring in Kevin Hooks actioner, 'Black

Dog', alongside Patrick Swayze and country singer Randy Travis, playing the part of a radio boss to Taj Mahal's DJ in 'Outside Ozona', and both scoring a bit part in Peter Chelsom drama, 'The Mighty' and joining the endless list of star cameos in Spice Girls showcase, 'SPICE WORLD'. MEAT's screen star continued to rise the following year with a supporting role in Antonio Banderas' directorial debut, 'Crazy In Alabama' (1999), and a starring role – the most credible of his career – in David Fincher's satirical classic, 'FIGHT CLUB' (1999). Into the millennium, MEAT starred as a truck driver in Canadian thriller, 'Blacktop' (2000), and as an anti-Semitic bigot in Arthur Miller adaptation, 'Focus' (2001), while biopic, 'TO HELL AND BACK' (2000), loosely based on the man's autobiography of the same name, documented his early success, late 70s/early 80s trough and recovery. Minor parts in indie comedy 'Face To Face' (2001), gritty drug thriller 'The Salton Sea' (2002) and supernatural fantasy, 'Wishcraft' (2002), as well as starring roles as a coach in American Football player-turned-director Rick Johnson's screen debut, 'Rustin' (2001), and Samuel Jackson-goes-to-Liverpool drama, 'The 51st State' (2001), puffed up his CV further, as did a turn in 'Ugly Betty'/'The L Word' director Tricia Brock's offbeat short, 'The Car Kid' (2003). A great performance in Richard Leddes' 'A Hole In One' (2004) marked his most credible character part since 'FIGHT CLUB' five years earlier, while more credible roles followed in Tarantino cinematographer Andrzej Sekula's ensemble piece, 'The Pleasure Drivers' (2005), and alongside another Tarantino veteran, Michael Madsen, in serial killer noir, 'Chasing Ghosts' (2005). A part (alongside Ronnie James Dio and DAVE GROHL) in Jack Black/Tenacious D comedy, 'The PICK OF DESTINY' (2006), was a reminder of his sporadic music career, one which – as the 'Bat Out Of Hell' suite of a concert film, 'Meat Loaf: Live With The Melbourne Symphony Orchestra' (2004) and the 2006 release of 'Bat Out Of Hell III: The Monster Is Loose' illustrated – is still at least partly based on his indestructible operatic wonder from the late 70s. *BG*

- **filmography** {acting} [story] –

State Fair *(1962 {b})* / **the Rocky Horror Picture Show** *(1975 {a} OST by the Cast =>)* / **Americathon** *(1979 {a})* / Scavenger *(1979 {a})* / **Roadie** *(1980 {*} OST by V/A =>)* / Dead Ringer *(1981 [story] {*c/p})* / Out Of Bounds *(1986 {a})* / the Squeeze *(1987 {a})* / Motorama *(1991 {a})* / **Wayne's World** *(1992 {a} OST by V/A =>)* / the Gun In Betty Lou's Handbag *(1992 {a})* / Leap Of Faith *(1992 {a})* / To Catch A Yeti *(1995 TV {*})* / **Spice World** *(1997 {a} OST by the SPICE GIRLS =>)* / Gunshy *(1998 {a})* / Black Dog *(1998 {*})* / the Mighty *(1998 {a})* / Everything That Rises *(1998 TV {*})* / Outside Ozona *(1998 {a})* / A Tekerolantos Naploja *(1999 {*})* / Crazy In Alabama *(1999 {*})* / **Fight Club** *(1999 {*} OST by the DUST BROTHERS =>)* / Blacktop *(2000 {*})* / Trapped *(2001 {*})* / Polish Spaghetti *(2001 {*})* / the Ballad Of Lucy Whipple *(2001 {*})* / Face To Face *(2001 {a})* / Rustin *(2001 {*})* / Focus *(2001 {*})* / the 51st State *(2001 {*})* / the Salton Sea *(2002 {a} OST by Thomas Newman; see future edition)* / Wishcraft *(2002 {a})* / the Car Kid *(2003 {*})* / Leaving Curves *(2003 {a})* / Extreme Dating *(2004 {a})* / a Hole In One *(2004 {*})* / Chasing Ghosts *(2005 {*})* / Crazylove *(2005 {a})* / Bloodrayne *(2005 {a})* / **the Pick Of Destiny** *(2006 {b} OST by TENACIOUS D =>)*

MEDUSA: DARE TO BE TRUTHFUL

1992 (US 51m TV w/b&w) Columbia Showtime Television (15)

Film genre: Pop-music mockumentary/comedy

Top guns: s-w: Julie Brown ← EARTH GIRLS ARE EASY (+ dir w/ John Fortenberry), Charlie Coffey ← EARTH GIRLS ARE EASY

Stars: Julie Brown *(Medusa)* ← the SPIRIT OF '76 ← see above, Chris Elliott *(Andy)* → CB4: THE MOVIE, Bobcat Goldthwait *(himself)* ← TAPEHEADS, Wink Martindale *(himself)* ← LET'S ROCK, Carol Leifer *(angry mom)*, Charlie Coffey *(Jeff)*, Donal Logue *(Shane Pencil)* → FIRST LOVE, LAST RITES → the MILLION DOLLAR HOTEL, Kathy Griffin *(Taffy)* → PULP FICTION → FOUR ROOMS → DILL SCALLION

Storyline: Comedienne Julie Brown takes off Madonna's 'Truth Or Dare' flick, and with more than a whiff of tongue-in-cheek she duplicates the "material girl" to a tee. It's all here on "The Blonde Leading The Blonde" tour: the ego, the self-obsession, the costumes and the er, hyper-sex . . . giving fellatio to a watermelon. *MCS*

Movie rating: *7

Visual: video + dvd (no audio OST by Brown & Coffey)

Off the record: Songs (sung by JULIE BROWN) include 'Expose Yourself', 'Vague', 'Everybody, Be Excited', 'Party In My Pants', 'Dare To Be Truthful', 'Special Friend', 'Like A Video', etc. *MCS*

Bette MIDLER

Born: 1 Dec'45, Paterson, New Jersey, USA. After spending her childhood years in Hawaii, MIDLER moved to the bright lights of New York, where her early interest in acting and singing paid dividends with a role in Broadway's 'Fiddler On The Roof' which lasted for three years. Indeed it was here that she would learn the acting skills which would serve her so well in her future film career. By the early 70s she had perfected a nightclub routine (alongside accompanist Barry Manilow) which parodied some of the top performers of that era in a mixture of comedy and song. Her increasing fame led to a contract with 'Atlantic' records which saw 'The Divine Miss M' (1972) go gold, including a release of the single, 'Boogie Woogie Bugle Boy' (1972), a record which made it into the Top 10. For the next few years, MIDLER concentrated on the tour circuit as her album sales began to dwindle, although her wheel of fortune had spun around by the end of the decade when she was nominated for an Oscar in 'The ROSE' (1979), a would-be biopic of Janis Joplin which led to another Top 10 hit via the title track. Next year she followed this up with 'DIVINE MADNESS' (1980); however, her next attempt at the silver screen was indeed 'Jinxed' (1982), so much so that it took MIDLER four years to reappear in 'DOWN AND OUT IN BEVERLY HILLS' (1986), complete with a new, comedy-style persona which re-established her film career. 'BEACHES' (1988) and 'Stella' (1989) saw MIDLER successfully broaden her acting horizons and yet again a pop spin-off from her movies, 'Wind Beneath My Wings', made it to No.1. This in turn spurred her on to further musical success with 'From A Distance' and her album soundtrack to 'For The Boys' (1991). After a brief diversion into the world of animated movie voice-overs, she triumphed in a TV production of the Broadway hit 'Gypsy', a sign perhaps of things to come. For the moment, however, her star was in the ascendant and yet another gold album 'Bette Of Roses' (1995), was followed by a role in 'Get Shorty' (1995), although co-starring alongside Goldie Hawn in the highly successful 'The First Wives Club' (1996) would prove to be her last really major film role for some time. MIDLER celebrated her change to 'Warner Bros.' records with her new album 'Bathhouse Betty' (1998) and followed this up with the imaginatively-named 'Bette' (2000). However, she increasingly turned her attention to TV around this time and starred as herself in 'JACKIE'S BACK!' (1999) and a half-hour comedy series called, surprise surprise, 'Bette' (2000). By now middle-aged, MIDLER was perhaps slowing down just a tad, although starring roles ('Isn't She Great', 'Drowning Mona' & 'The Stepford Wives') were still coming in thick and fast. MIDLER continues to perform to sell-out concerts and her legions of admirers no doubt await her next film/TV/album venture with baited breath. *JZ*

- **filmography** {actress & performer} [s-w] –

Hawaii *(1966 {b})* / the Divine Mr. J *(1974 {*})* / **the Rose** *(1979 {*} OST to MIDLER =>)* / **Divine Madness** *(1980 {*p} [s-w] OST to MIDLER =>)* / Jinxed! *(1982 {*})* / **Down And Out In Beverly Hills** *(1986 {*} =>)* / Ruthless People *(1986 {*}; see future edition)* / Outrageous Fortune *(1987 {*})* / Big

Business *(1988 {*})* / Oliver & Company *(1988 {v} on OST by V/A & J.A.C. Redford; see future edition)* / **Beaches** *(1988 {*} OST to MIDLER =>)* / Stella *(1990 {*})* / Scenes From A Mall *(1991 {*})* / For The Boys *(1991 {*} OST to MIDLER; see future edition)* / Hocus Pocus *(1993 {*})* / Gypsy *(1993 TV {*} OST to MIDLER & Cast; see future edition)* / Get Shorty *(1995 {a} see future edition)* / the First Wives Club *(1996 {*} on OST by V/A; see future editions =>)* / That Old Feeling *(1997 {*})* / **Jackie's Back** *(1999 TV {c} =>)* / Get Bruce! *(1999 TV {*c})* / Fantasia 2000 *(2000 {n})* / Isn't She Great *(2000 {*} see future edition)* / Drowning Mona *(2000 {*})* / What Women Want *(2000 {b} =>)* / the Stepford Wives *(2004 {*})* / Then She Found Me *(2007 {*})*

a MIGHTY WIND

2003 (US 91m) Warner Brothers (PG-13)

Film genre: mockumentary Folk-rock Musical comedy

Top guns: s-w: Christopher Guest (+ dir) ← THIS IS SPINAL TAP, Eugene Levy

Stars: Bob Balaban *(Jonathan Steinbloom)* ← the STRAWBERRY STATEMENT ← MIDNIGHT COWBOY, the Folksmen:- Harry Shearer *(Mark Shubb)* ← GIGANTIC (A TALE OF TWO JOHNS) ← GHOST DOG: THE WAY OF THE SAMURAI ← WAYNE'S WORLD 2 ← THIS IS SPINAL TAP ← ONE-TRICK PONY ← ANIMALYMPICS, Christopher Guest *(Alan Barrows)* as above + ← the PRINCESS BRIDE ← LITTLE SHOP OF HORRORS ← THIS IS SPINAL TAP ← the LONG RIDERS ← DEATH WISH, Michael McKean *(Jerry Palter)* ← GIGANTIC (A TALE OF TWO JOHNS) ← AIRHEADS ← EARTH GIRLS ARE EASY ← LIGHT OF DAY ← THIS IS SPINAL TAP / Mitch & Mickey:- Eugene Levy *(Mitch Cohen)* ← CLUB PARADISE ← HEAVY METAL / → CURIOUS GEORGE → OVER THE HEDGE, Catherine O'Hara *(Mickey Devlin Crabbe)* ← DICK TRACY ← ROCK & RULE / → OVER THE HEDGE with Joe Godfrey *(acoustic bassist)* & Bruce Gaitsch *(guitarist)* / the New Main Street Singers:- Jane Lynch *(Laurie Bohner)* ← STRAIGHT TALK, John Michael Higgins *(Terry Bohner)* ← WAG THE DOG / → KILLER DILLER, Parker Posey *(Sissy Knox)* ← JOSIE AND THE PUSSYCATS ← SUBURBI@, Paul Dooley *(George Menschell)* ← POPEYE / → HAIRSPRAY re-make, Patrick Sauber *(Jerald Smithers)*, Christopher Moynihan *(Sean Halloran)*, David Alan Blasucci *(Tony Pollono)*, Steve Pandis *(Johnny Athenakis)* / Fred Willard *(Mike LaFontaine)* ← HOW HIGH ← THIS IS SPINAL TAP ← MODEL SHOP / → KILLER DILLER, Ed Begley Jr. *(Lars Olfen)* ← EVEN COWGIRLS GET THE BLUES ← STREETS OF FIRE ← THIS IS SPINAL TAP ← GET CRAZY ← ELVIS: THE MOVIE ← RECORD CITY, Bill Cobbs *(bluesman)* ← THAT THING YOU DO! ← the BODYGUARD ← ROADSIDE PROPHETS ← a HERO AIN'T NOTHIN' BUT A SANDWICH, Michael Hitchcock *(Lawrence Turpin)*, Jennifer Coolidge *(Amber Cole)* ← POOTIE TANG, Larry Miller *(Wally Fenton)*

Storyline: How better to commemorate the death of a living legend than to bring together some of his protégés. When Irving Steinbloom goes to the Great Folk Music Hall In The Sky his son Jonathan does exactly that, and some of the nearly-greatest talents in Folk gather in New York for the big event. Watch out for the Folksmen, who never quite got the hang of electric guitars, and colour-coded "neuftet" the New Main Street Singers along with Mitch & Mickey. *JZ*

Movie rating: *7

Visual: dvd

Off the record: Comedy actress Catherine O'Hara is the sister of singer-songwriter Mary Margaret O'Hara.

—

Various Cast: the FOLKSMEN (*) / MITCH & MICKEY (**) / the NEW MAIN STREET SINGERS (***)

Apr 03. (cd) *Columbia; <89222> (512656-2)* ☐ Jan04 ☐
– Old Joe's place (*) / Just that kinda day (***) / When you're next to me (**) / Never did no wanderin' (*) / Fare away (***) / One more time (**) / Loco man (*) / The good book song (***) / Skeletons of Quinto (*) / Never did no wanderin' (***) / The ballad of Bobby and June (**) / Blood on the coal (*) / Main Street rag (***) / Start me up (*) / Potato's in the paddy wagon (***) / A kiss at the end of the rainbow (**) / A mighty wind (*, ** & ***).

S/track review: The boys from 'THIS IS SPINAL TAP' are back, only this time they're soft-rock folkers, not heavy hard-rockers. 'SPINAL TAP' trio CHRISTOPHER GUEST, MICHAEL McKEAN and HARRY SHEARER become the FOLKSMEN (a mocku-take of the Kingston Trio), while "non-TAPpers" MITCH & MICKEY (like Ian & Sylvia or Richard & Mimi Farina in their heyday) and the NEW MAIN STREET SINGERS (the equivalent of another early 60s folk act, the New Christy Minstrels) were equally nostalgic. Treading a thin line between deadpan tribute and cut-throat parody, the three outfits (and what outfits!) took easy-listening to new extremes without grasping the more serious side of protest-folk, aka Dylan & Ochs. The aforementioned FOLKSMEN kick-off the album with 'Old Joe's Place', a breathless, tongue-twisting ditty that only messers GUEST, McKEAN and SHEARER (playing their own instruments) could achieve without it all going belly-up. The fun-poking trio achieve virtual cult status here by way of other dirges such as the cowboy-esque 'Never Did No Wanderin', the calypso-cloned 'Loco Man' and a song about Spanish-American hostilities, 'Skeletons Of Quinto', the latter very Gene Pitney, was he a folk artist. Two bonus, non-film numbers by the FOLKSMEN also feature on the album, 'Blood On The Coal' (eat your heart out, the Levellers!) and 'Start Me Up' (yes, the Rolling Stones hit!), just too hilarious to omit: repeat after me "You make a dead man kum/ You make a dead man kum . . . baya". The more serious MITCH & MICKEY (EUGENE LEVY & CATHERINE O'HARA) get snuggled-up and romantic on flowery nuggets such as 'When You're Next To Me', 'One More Time', 'The Ballad Of Bobby And June' (very 'Billy Don't Be A Hero') and 'A Kiss At The End Of The Rainbow'. Last, but not least, vocal group the NEW MAIN STREET SINGERS, aka JOHN MICHAEL HIGGINS, DAVID ALAN BLASUCCI (also guitars), JANE LYNCH, CHRISTOPHER MOYNIHAN, STEVE PANDIS (also acoustic bass), PARKER POSEY, PATRICK SAUBER (banjo, mandolin), CJ VANSTON (multi) and DON SHELTON, find that Partridge Family-meets-Brady Bunch feel on 'Just That Kinda Day', the seafaring 'Fare Away', the bible-punching 'The Good Book Song', their choral, C&W-tinged version of 'Never Did No Wanderin', the short-n-sweet 'Main Street Rag' and the downright hilarious 'Potato's In The Paddy Wagon' (co-written w/ Annette O'Toole). All "acts" get together for one last blow-out finale of 'A Mighty Wind', sadly the last we'll probably hear from GUEST, McKEAN and SHEARER . . . or can one hear SPINAL TAP turning amps up to 11 for a "Live Earth" Wembley Stadium gig (7th July, 2007). *MCS*

Album rating: *7.5

MR MUSIC

1999 (Can 92m TV) DLP Productions

Film genre: Pop-music/showbiz comedy

Top guns: s-w + dir: Fred Gerber

Stars: Jonathan Tucker *(Rob Tennant)* → the VIRGIN SUICIDES, **Mick Fleetwood** *(Simon Eckstal)* → BLUES ODYSSEY → RED, WHITE & BLUES, Cle Bennett *(Larry McGuire)* → HENDRIX → LIVIN' FOR LOVE: THE NATALIE COLE STORY → HOW SHE MOVE, Dan Gallagher *(Louie Liberti)*, Sarah Mitchell *(Helen Sage)*, Jackie Richardson *(Rhonda Grace)*, Don Francks *(Zal Adamchyk)* ← MADONNA: INNOCENCE LOST ← ROCK & RULE ← HEAVY METAL / → I'M NOT THERE, Peter Keleghan *(Harley Yates)*, Stephanie Mills *(Olivia)*

Storyline: Simon Eckstal is the boss of strugging company 'Tone' records. In a burst of inspiration he hires a completely unknown 15 year-old kid, Rob

Tennant, and in a blaze of publicity makes him vice president of the firm. Suddenly everyone wants to know about the record company and why they're making juniors into seniors. Can young Rob save the company or will the scheming bosses send him back to the school playground? *JZ*

Movie rating: *4.5

Visual: dvd

Off the record: **Mick Fleetwood** was the leader and drummer of Fleetwood Mac, although the bearded one will now be best remembered for his embarrassing Brit-awards host attempts (alongside page 3 model-turned singer, Sam Fox) in 1989. The Stephanie Mills here is Canadian, not the American R&B singer who had hits from the late 70s. *MCS*

—

Various Artists (score: SPENCER PROFFER & LARRY BROWN *)

Mar 99. (cd) *Sonic Images; (SID 8903)* [–] [ ]
– At the top of the world (CARAMEL) / Friend of mine (TREBLE CHARGER) / River of love (PAT BENATAR) / Songbird (EVA CASSIDY) / Our house (GRAHAM NASH) / Crossing the bridge (*) / My new home (*) / Out of habit (BLUE FLANNEL) / Only you (PAT BENATAR) / Feels like a Sunday (CARAMEL) / Circles (KEITH CHAGALL) / Teach your children (GRAHAM NASH) / Understandin' (*) / Street strut (ANDREW ROLLINS) / Snoop dog, baby (REEL BIG FISH) / Puppy Munchies (the MORLETTES) / Strawberry wine (PAT BENATAR) / Road to nowhere (CARAMEL).

S/track review: Easily the most disappointing thing about the soundtrack to 'MR MUSIC' (and this is saying something) is the fact that, although he plays a major part in the film, Mick Fleetwood doesn't actually contribute any songs of his own. And, believe me, this soundtrack needed it. There are a few highlights here, like the delicate 'Songbird' by EVA CASSIDY and REEL BIG FISH's brass-led ska-pop number 'Snoop Dog, Baby', while Grammy winner PAT BENATAR's soulful rock on 'River Of Love', 'Only You' and 'Strawberry Wine' is also worth a listen. Unfortunately, there are more cringeworthy moments than watching 'The Full Monty' being performed by a troupe of drunken uncles at a wedding reception. GRAHAM NASH better not let Crosby, Stills or Young hear 'Our House' or 'Teach Your Children' in case he isn't allowed back into the team. CARAMEL, made up from former members of metal band Soho 69, sound limp and boring on 'At The Top Of The World', 'Feels Like A Sunday' and 'Road To Nowhere', which, thankfully, is not an attempt at the Talking Heads hit, while the instrumentals provided by SPENCER PROFFER and friends are uninspiring at best. It is quite fitting that 'MR MUSIC' was a Canadian TV film because the soundtrack is the musical equivalent. *CM*

Album rating: *3.5

MISTER ROCK AND ROLL

1957 (US 86m) Aurora Productions LLC / Paramount Pictures

Film genre: Rock'n'roll Musical bio-pic/drama

Top guns: dir: Charles S. Dubin / s-w: James Blumgarten

Stars: Alan Freed *(himself)* ← ROCK, ROCK, ROCK! ← DON'T KNOCK THE ROCK ← ROCK AROUND THE CLOCK / → GO, JOHNNY, GO!, **Teddy Randazzo** *(himself)* ← ROCK, ROCK, ROCK! ← the GIRL CAN'T HELP IT / → HEY, LET'S TWIST, Lois O'Brien *(Carole Hendricks)*, Jay Barney *(Joe Prentiss)* → the KILLING FIELDS, Al Fisher *(Al)* ← DON'T KNOCK THE ROCK / → COUNTRY MUSIC HOLIDAY, Lou Marks *(Lou)* → COUNTRY MUSIC HOLIDAY, **Clyde McPhatter** *(performer)*, **Chuck BERRY** *(performer)*, **Screamin' Jay Hawkins** *(performer)* → AMERICAN HOT WAX → JOEY → MYSTERY TRAIN → I PUT A SPELL ON ME, **Brook Benton** *(performer)*, **LITTLE RICHARD** *(performer)*, **LaVern Baker** *(performer)* ← ROCK, ROCK, ROCK! ← the PIED PIPER OF CLEVELAND, **Frankie Lymon & the Teenagers:- Frankie Lymon, Herman Santiago, Joe Negroni, Sherman Garnes, Jimmy Merchant** *(performers)* ← ROCK, ROCK, ROCK!, **the Moonglows** ← ROCK, ROCK, ROCK! / → GO, JOHNNY, GO!, **Lionel Hampton & His Band** *(performers)*, **Ferlin Husky** *(performer)* → COUNTRY MUSIC HOLIDAY → LAS VEGAS HILLBILLYS → HILLBILLYS IN A HAUNTED HOUSE → THAT'S COUNTRY, Rocky Graziano *(himself)* → COUNTRY MUSIC HOLIDAY → the TEENAGE MILLIONAIRE

Storyline: After his editor criticises the rock music disc jockey, Alan Freed makes an impassioned appeal on air to his audience asking them to raise money for a heart fund. A special concert is arranged and performers include Freed himself, Teddy Randazzo and LaVerne Baker, as well as the cream of 1950s rock talent. *JZ*

Movie rating: *4

Visual: video (no audio OST)

Off the record: **LITTLE RICHARD** sang 'Keep A Knockin'' and 'Lucille' hits, while **CHUCK BERRY** delivered 'Oh Baby Doll'. **CLYDE McPHATTER** (b.15 Nov'32, Durham, North Carolina, USA) marked a rare performance here with 'Rock And Cry'. A one-time member of Billy Ward & The Dominoes, they had crossover R&B pop hits in the early 50s ('Have Mercy Baby' & 'I'd Be Satisfied') before Clyde departed in 1953. The lead vocalist subsequently joined the Drifters who turned in a handful of hits, before the man went solo. During the mid-50s to the early 60s, Clyde chalked up several US Top 30 entries, including 'Treasure Of Love', 'Without Love (There Is Nothing')', 'Just To Hold My Hand', 'A Lover's Question', 'Ta Ta', the Billy Swan-penned 'Lover Please' and 'Little Bitty Pretty One'. In the early 60s, Clyde moved to Britain, where he carved out a career as a club singer, although along the way he picked up a heavy drinking habit. Returning to America in the early 70s, Clyde inked a deal with 'Decca' records, who issued his comeback LP, 'Welcome Home'. Sadly, due to years of alcohol abuse, McPHATTER died of a heart attack on the 13th of June, 1972. *MCS*

– spinoff hits, etc. –

LaVERN BAKER: Humpty Dumpty Heart / Love Me Right

Sep 57. (7"78) *Atlantic; <1150> / London: HLE 8254)* [71] Dec57 [ ]

LITTLE RICHARD: Keep A Knockin' / (non OST-song)

Sep 57. (7"/78) *Speciality; <611> / London; (HLO 8509)* [8] Nov57 [21]

CLYDE McPHATTER: Rock And Cry / (non-OST-song)

Nov 57. (7"/78) *Atlantic; <1158> London; (HLE 8525)* [93] Dec57 [ ]

MR. ROCK'N'ROLL: THE ALAN FREED STORY

1999 (US 95m TV) Von Serneck Sertner Films / NBC

Film genre: Rock'n'roll-music bio-pic/drama

Top guns: dir: Andy Wolk / s-w: Matt Dorff (au: John A. Jackson)

Stars: Judd Nelson *(Alan Freed)* ← AIRHEADS ← EVERYBREATH ← BLUE CITY, Madchen Amick *(Jackie McCoy)*, **Leon** *(Jackie Wilson)* ← the TEMPTATIONS ← the FIVE HEARTBEATS / → LITTLE RICHARD → GET RICH OR DIE TRYIN', **Paul Abdul** *(Denise Walton)*, David Gianopoulos *(Morris Levy)*, Daniel Kash *(Hooke)*, James C. Victor *(Jerry Lee Lewis)*, Walter Franks *(Little Richard)* ← AND THE BEAT GOES ON: THE SONNY AND CHER STORY, Michael Dunston *(Bo Diddley)* → HENDRIX, Michael Daingerfield *(Bill Haley)*, Joe Warren Davis *(Buddy Holly)*, LeRoy D. Brazile *(Frankie Lymon)*, Mark Wilson *(Leo Mintz)*, Ross Petty *(J. Elroy McCaw)*, Fulvio Cecere *(Pete Bell)*, **FABIAN** *(interviewee)*, **Bobby Rydell** *(himself)* ← BYE BYE BIRDIE

Storyline: The life story of Alan Freed, 50s Cleveland radio DJ extraordinaire and the man who virtually single-handedly broadcast rock'n'roll and R&B music to the American people. Freed bravely played the risqué platters every day on air despite howls of protest from the racists and conservatives. Undaunted, he married and moved to New York, becoming the top DJ overnight. After film and record success came the payola scandal, the $20,000 loan, the meetings with DA Levy, the cancellations and finally the sack. Freed died a broken man aged just 43. The 1978 movie, 'AMERICAN HOT WAX', painted its own picture of the man known as Moondog. *JZ*

Movie rating: *5

Visual: video (no audio OST)

Off the record: The film does include music by BUDDY HOLLY, JERRY LEE LEWIS, LITTLE RICHARD, BILL HALEY AND HIS COMETS, BO DIDDLEY, etc. **Paula Abdul** (b.19 Jun'62, San Fernando Valley, California) was from Brazilian and French-Canadian parentage and cut her teeth as a cheerleader before becoming a video choreographer for the likes of Janet Jackson, Deborah Gibson and George Michael. In the late 80s and early 90s, Paula had no less than six US chart-topping singles, 'Straight Up', 'Forever Your Girl' (also the title of her No.1 album), 'Cold Hearted', 'Opposites Attract', 'Rush, Rush' and 'The Promise Of A New Day' (the latter two from her No.1 follow-up set, 'Spellbound'). Her connection to the world of movies subsequently came about when she married Emilio Estevez in April 1992 (they divorced two years later), while she starred in another TV film, 'The Waiting Game' (1998). In 2002, she became a panel judge on American Idol, alongside adversory, Simon Cowell – Opposites don't Attract. *MCS*

MRS. BROWN, YOU'VE GOT A LOVELY DAUGHTER

1968 (UK 95m) Metro-Goldwyn-Mayer (PG)

Film genre: Pop/Rock Musical comedy

Top guns: dir: Saul Swimmer → the CONCERT FOR BANGLADESH / s-w: Thaddeus Vane

Stars: HERMAN'S HERMITS:- Peter Noone *(Herman)*, **Keith Hopwood, Derek Leckenby, Karl Green, Barry Whitwam** *(themselves)* / Stanley Holloway *(George G. Brown)*, Mona Washbourne *(Mrs. Brown)* ← TWO A PENNY ← FERRY 'CROSS THE MERSEY / → O LUCKY MAN!, Lance Percival *(Percy Sutton)* ← IT'S ALL OVER TOWN / → YELLOW SUBMARINE, Marjorie Rhodes *(Grandma)* ← the FAMILY WAY ← I'VE GOTTA HORSE, Sheila White *(Tulip)* ← HERE WE GO ROUND THE MULBERRY BUSH ← the GHOST GOES GEAR / → CONFESSIONS OF A POP PERFORMER → SILVER DREAM RACER, Joan Hickson *(landlady)* → FRIENDS, Avis Bunnage *(Tulip's mother)* ← WHAT A CRAZY WORLD, Tom Kempinski *(Vince Hobart)* ← the COMMITTEE, Hugh Futcher *(Swothard)*, James Myers *(page boy)* → SHAFT IN AFRICA, Rita Webb *(woman in pub)* ← TO SIR, WITH LOVE / → the MAGIC CHRISTIAN → PERCY → CONFESSIONS OF A POP PERFORMER

Storyline: Mrs Brown has four legs, a tail, a wet nose and enjoys chasing hares. Yes, she is a greyhound owned by diehard Mancunian Herman. When the dog starts winning, Herman and his mates form a band and do some gigs to raise the cash to enter Mrs Brown in the big races down south. After a few trials and tribulations the guys make it to swinging London and begin to show their stripes in the music business. *JZ*

Movie rating: *4.5

Visual: video

Off the record: nothing

HERMAN'S HERMITS

Sep 68. (lp) *Columbia; (SCX 6303) M.G.M.; <4548>* ☐ ☐
– It's nice to be out in the morning / Holiday Inn / Ooh, she's done it again / There's a kind of hush (all over the world) / Lemon and lime / The most beautiful thing in my life / Daisy chain part I / Daisy chain part II / The world is for the young / Mrs. Brown, you've got a lovely daughter. *(cd-iss. Mar00 & Apr03 on 'Repertoire'+=; REP 4857)* – (10 subsequent bonus songs not from the film).

S/track review: Now into their second full film soundtrack ('HOLD ON' being their first in '66), HERMAN'S HERMITS based 'MRS. BROWN, YOU'VE GOT A LOVELY DAUGHTER' around one of their earlier hits of the same name; it's also the cheeky closing song on the LP, while fans will recognise 'There's A Kind Of Hush (All Over The World)'. With a plethora of "usual suspect" songwriters (including Graham Gouldman (later of 10cc), Geoff Stephens, Kenny Young and Trevor Peacock, PETER NOONE and his HERMITS (see film stars above) tried in vain to attract a more mature fanbase. Of the four Gouldman-penned numbers, 'It's Nice To Be Out In The Morning' (with a reference to Manchester United F.C.) and 'Ooh, She's Done It Again', is typical HH, while the Small Faces-esque 'Lemon And Lime' and 'The World Is For The Young' (both featuring veteran thespian, Stanley Holloway and other cast!) are pure novelty. With records such as 'Holiday Inn' and 'The Most Beautiful Thing In My Life' (both very derivative of the Hollies), it was no wonder the British Invasion was all but washed up. The only group composition(s), 'Daisy Chain Part I', saw HERMAN'S HERMITS wig-out in an instrumental frenzy of sorts, while 'Part II' saw the quintet chill-out, but just ever so slightly. The Arctic Monkeys of their day, maybe so . . . but 'I'm Into Something Good' – and this was certainly not it. *MCS*

Album rating: *5

– spinoff releases, etc. –

HERMAN'S HERMITS: The Most Beautiful Thing In My Life / Ooh, She's Done It Again

Nov 68. (7") *<13994>* ☐ ☐

☐ MOBY segment
(⇒ ALIEN SEX PARTY)

MOJO

1997 (UK 91m) Portobello Pictures / Mojo Films

Film genre: showbiz/Pop/Rock-music drama

Top guns: s-w + dir: Jez Butterworth (+ play)

Stars: Ian Hart *(Mickey)* ← BACKBEAT ← the HOURS AND TIMES, Ewen Bremner *(Skinny)* ← TRAINSPOTTING / → the ACID HOUSE → HALLAM FOE, Hans Matheson *(Silver Johnny)* → STILL CRAZY, Aidan Gillen *(Baby)* ← the COURIER, Martin Gwynn Jones *(Sweets)*, Andy Serkis *(Potts)* → 24 HOUR PARTY PEOPLE, Ricky Tomlinson *(Ezra)*, Harold Pinter *(Sam Ross)*

Storyline: Silver Johnny is the star of the Atlantic Club, a dive in the heart of Soho. The young rockster is the protégé of club manager Ezra, and soon the two of them are invited to a meeting with local boss man Sam Ross. Sam is impressed with Johnny and wants to discuss a contract, but things take a sinister turn when Ezra is found sawn in half and Ross suddenly wants to be the new club owner. *JZ*

Movie rating: *4.5

Visual: dvd

Off the record: You might slightly recognise actor Andy Serkis, he played the Golam in Lord Of The Rings!

Various Artists (score: Murray Gold)

Jul 98. (cd) *Premier-EMI; (821718-2)* ☐ ☐
– Christo redentor (DONALD BYRD) / Crazy crazy momma (LITTLE LEWIS) / Ooh ma Liddi (JJ JACKSON & THE JACKAELS) / Please (ST. ETIENNE) / The big hurt (NICK CAVE & GALLON DRUNK) / Chained to loving you (HANS MATHESON) / Stone cold stroll (the STONE COLD STROLLERS) / Sequins and stars (MARC ALMOND) / Write my name (WARM JETS) / Constantly (ST. ETIENNE) / Ooh my soul (the STONE COLD STROLLERS) / Since I don't have you (the SKYLINERS) / I put a spell on you (DAVID McALMONT) / Don't make me wait (LITTLE LEWIS) / I

love how you love me (BETH ORTON) / One night of sin (MARC ALMOND) / Mojo (NICK CAVE).

S/track review: When Jez Butterworth's play, MOJO, hit the stage the Tarantino comparisons piled up due to its sharp dialogue and witty observations. The soundtrack to the film adaptation shows a similar ear for a tune that characterised films like 'RESERVOIR DOGS' and 'PULP FICTION'. Opener 'Christo Redentor' is classic Blue Note, with DONALD BYRD's hauntingly smooth trumpet playing over staccato piano. There are several early rock'n'roll numbers from the likes of LITTLE LEWIS, JJ JACKSON & THE JACKAELS and movie band the STONE COLD STROLLERS that instantly conjure up images of the swinging Soho jazz club featured in the film. However, it is the other songs featured here that lend it credibility and prevent it sounding like 'GREASE'. ST ETIENNE's fragile vocals and xylophonic melodies on 'Please' and 'Constantly' are the perfect antithesis to the abrasive caterwaul of NICK CAVE, who combines with GALLON DRUNK on Wayne Shanklin's 1958 hit, 'The Big Hurt'. CAVE also appears on his own with the devilishly malicious title track, 'Mojo'. Imagine Isaac Hayes's 'Shaft' pumped full of amphetamines before being dragged through a black hole and chewed over by Hannibal Lector. DAVID McALMONT chips in with a unique and slightly psychedelic update of the Jay Hawkins standard 'I Put A Spell On You' while BETH ORTON's version of 'I Love How You Love Me' is a beautifully tender ballad. 'MOJO' is a royal rumble of styles and artists, with NICK CAVE being the likely king of the ring, however the Aussie doom merchant is almost thrown over the top by MARC ALMOND. The former Soft Cell frontman uses two opportunities to show off his range of vocal talents. His own composition, 'Sequins And Stars' is a delicate, Righteous Brothers-style warble, while 'One Night Of Sin' is as downright sleazy as the title suggests, complete with erogenous saxophone and wailing vocals. 'MOJO' does not fall into the trap that many films set around the birth of rock'n'roll do, which is to jam pack it with Chuck Berry or Elvis standards. Instead, 'MOJO' mixes its rock'n'roll with a healthy helping of other styles to remind you that it is a soundtrack to a dark and melancholic film, not a Best Rock'n'Roll Hits Ever-type album. *CM*

Album rating: *6.5

the MONKEES

Formed: Los Angeles, California, USA . . . 1965 as a made-for-NBC boy band featuring Mike Nesmith, Micky Dolenz, Davy Jones and Peter Tork. Given that they were actually founded as a weekly dose of Beatles-esque slapstick with added songs and old Three Stooges stage sets, the MONKEES, of all 60s bands (which, with the huge success of the series, is what they became), cultivated the most obvious relationship with moving pictures, primarily on the small screen but ultimately on the large, the artificiality of their position generating an ambiguous relationship with the mainstream and progressively more hostile reaction to it. The narrative-busting musical segments in their series are often credited as blueprints for music video, a format Nesmith would further pioneer in the late 70s with his 'Popclips' series. As the 60s counterculture gathered strength the band got in on the action with cult film/soundtrack, 'HEAD' (1968), MONKEES producer (and future 'Five Easy Pieces' director) Bob Rafelson roping in Jack Nicholson as co-writer and conceiving its guerrilla montage as a parody of the band's corporate gloss. A commercial non-event, the movie put the lid on the TV series and, at least in Nesmith's case, precipitated a relatively high profile solo career. His aforementioned 'Popclips' series anticipated MTV, a fertile market for the many videos his own 'Pacific Arts' company produced throughout the 80s, with his own 'Elephant Parts' (1981) harking, at least in spirit, back to 'HEAD'. He would serve as writer/producer/composer on sci-fi western, 'TIMERIDER: THE ADVENTURE OF LYLE SWANN' (1983), and as executive producer on both Alex Cox's cult debut 'REPO MAN' (1984) and video production parody 'TAPEHEADS' (1988), coming from behind the scenes to make a rare cameo as a taxi driver in Whoopi Goldberg comedy, 'Burglar' (1987). A post-MONKEES Dolenz, meanwhile, appeared in B-movies 'Night Of The Strangler' (1973) and 'Linda Lovelace For President' (1975) before moving to the UK (initially to star in Nilsson's stage version of 'The POINT', no less), where he established himself as a successful director and producer, working for the BBC, London Weekend Television (co-masterminding award-winning children's show, 'Metal Mickey') and Channel 4. Beginning with a mid-80s revival, all four MONKEES sporadically re-formed (albeit with Nesmith only briefly in the frame) for both live and studio work, with attendant video 'Heart and Soul' (1987), re-formation spoof 'HEY, HEY WE'RE THE MONKEES' (1997) and video collection 'Justus' (1997), the latter a spin-off from the sole album of newly recorded material to feature all four members. Upon his return to the USA, Dolenz appeared alongside the likes of Nicolas Cage and Peter Fonda in crime thriller 'Deadfall' (1993), and with Jones (who'd appeared in the original 70s series) and TORK in warped nostalgia piece, 'The Brady Bunch Movie' (1995). A made-for-TV biopic (not featuring any of the MONKEES themselves), 'DAYDREAM BELIEVERS: THE MONKEES STORY', appeared in 2000. *BG*

- **filmography** {acting/performance} –

Wild In The Streets *(1968 {b PETER} OST by V/A =>)* / **Head** *(1968 {*} OST =>)* / Lollipops And Roses *(1971 {a DAVY})* / Treasure Island *(1972 {v DAVY})* / Oliver Twist *(1973 {v DAVY})* / Night Of The Strangler *(1973 {a MICKY})* / Linda Lovelace For President *(1975 {a MICKY})* / Northfield Cemetery Massacre *(1976 score NESMITH)* / **Timerider: The Adventure Of Lyle Swann** *(1982 [s-w] {b MICHAEL} NESMITH OST =>)* / Burglar *(1987 {a MICHAEL})* / **Tapeheads** *(1988 {a MICHAEL} OST by V/A =>)* / Deadfall *(1993 {a MICKY})* / the Brady Bunch Movie *(1995 {c DAVY + PETER})* / **Hey, Hey We're The Monkees** *(1997 TV {*})* / the Love Bug *(1997 TV {a MICKY})* / Invisible Mom 2 *(1998 {a MICKY})* / Mom, Can I Keep Her? *(1999 {a MICKY})* / **Daydream Believers: The Monkees Story** *(2000 TV {c PETER} =>)* / Mixed Signals *(2001 {b PETER})* / Easy Riders, Raging Bulls *(2003 {c MICKY})* / **Mayor Of The Sunset Strip** *(2003 {c DAVY})* / Cathedral Pines *(2006 {a})* / **Bound To Lose** *(2006 {c} =>)* / **Who Is Harry Kellerman (And Why Is Everybody Talkin' About Him)?** *(2006 {c MICKY})*

the MONSTER CLUB

1981 (UK 104m) Pathfinder Home Entertainment

Film genre: monster movie

Top guns: dir: Roy Ward Baker / s-w: Edward Abraham, Valerie Abraham (au: R. Chetwynd-Hayes)

Stars: Vincent Price *(Erasmus)* ← WELCOME TO MY NIGHTMARE ← the NIGHTMARE ← CUCUMBER CASTLE ← the TROUBLE WITH GIRLS ← BEACH PARTY, John Carradine *(R. Chetwynd-Hayes)* ← the TROUBLE WITH GIRLS, Donald Pleasence *(Pickering)* ← SGT. PEPPER'S LONELY HEARTS CLUB BAND ← PIED PIPER / → PHENOMENA, Britt Ekland *(Lintom's mother)* ← the WICKER MAN ← PERCY, Anthony Steel *(Lintom Busotsky; film producer)*, Richard Johnson *(Lintom's father)*, Stuart Whitman *(Sam)* ← MEAN JOHNNY BARROWS ← HOUND-DOG MAN, Barbara Kellerman *(Angela)*, James Laurenson *(Raven)* → the WALL → HEARTBREAKERS → the MAN INSIDE, Simon Ward *(George)*, Anthony Valentine *(Mooney)* ← PERFORMANCE, Geoffrey Bayldon *(psychiatrist)* ← BORN TO BOOGIE ← TO SIR, WITH LOVE ← TWO A PENNY, Patrick Magee *(innkeeper)* → CHARIOTS OF FIRE, **B.A. Robertson** (performer), **the Night** *(performers)*, **Chris Thompson** *(performer)*, **the Pretty Things:- Phil May, Dick Taylor** *(performers)*

Storyline: Horror writer R. Chetwynd-Jones bumps into his greatest fan, Erasmus, who naturally enough turns out to be a vampire. Erasmus invites his hero to an exclusive club where they see a striptease which really does go all the way (right to the bones), and entertains the author with three stories of his own concerning vampires, ghouls and a creature which can kill by whistling, which must pose problems if it ever becomes a referee. Tagged: "a tongue-in-cheek trilogy of horror". *JZ*

Movie rating: *4.5

Visual: video (no audio OST; score: Douglas Gamley)

Off the record: Tracks in the film include 'Monsters Rule O.K.' (the VIEWERS), 'Sucker For Your Love' (B.A. ROBERTSON), 'The Stripper' (the NIGHT), '25 Per Cent' (UB40), 'Monster Club' (the PRETTY THINGS), 'Valentino's Had Enough' (EXPRESSOS), 'Ghouls Galore' (JOHN HACKSHAW), 'Pavane' (JOHN WILLIAMS), 'Vienna Blood' & 'Transylvanian Terrors' (JOHN GEORGIADIS). **Chris Thompson** was the singer with a plethora of outfits including Manfred Mann's Earth Band ('Blinded By The Light', etc.). *MCS*

MONSTER DOG

aka LEVIATAN

1985 (Spa/US 81m) Continental Motion Pictures / Trans World

Film genre: monster/horror movie

Top guns: s-w + dir: Claudio Fragasso

Stars: **Alice COOPER** *(Vincent Raven)*, Victoria Vera *(Sandra)*, Carlos Sanurio *(Frank)*, Pepita James *(Angela)*, Emilio Linder *(Jordan)*, Maria Jose Sarsa *(Marilou)*, Luis Maluenda *(deputy)*, Ricardo Palacios *(sheriff Morrison)*, B. Barta Barri *(old man)*, Charlie Bravo *(townie)*

Storyline: Rock star Vincent needs some inspiration, so he heads back home to shoot a new video on familiar ground. However, he and girlfriend Sandra find themselves in the middle of a police manhunt (or rather doghunt) after a series of gruesome murders. Vincent knows his dad had "canine tendencies" and fears that he's on the prowl again. More worryingly, has Vincent any werewolf tendencies of his own or is it all just a shaggy dog story? *JZ*

Movie rating: *3

Visual: video + dvd (no audio OST; score: GRUPO DICHOTOMY)

Off the record: **ALICE COOPER** provided two songs, 'Identity Crisis' & 'See Me In The Mirror', the ALAN PARSONS PROJECT also two, 'A Dream Within A Dream' & 'The Raven'. *MCS*

MONSTER MASH: THE MOVIE

1995 (US 82m) Prism Pictures (PG)

Film genre: Rock'n'roll comedy/horror Musical

Top guns: dir: Joel Cohen, Alec Sokolow / s-w: Sheldon Allman + **Bobby Pickett**

Stars: Ian Bohen *(Scott/Romeo)*, Candace Cameron Bure *(Mary/Juliet)*, Sarah Douglas *(Countess Natasha 'Nasty' Dracula)*, **Bobby Pickett** *(Dr. Victor Frankenstein)* ← IT'S A BIKINI WORLD, **John Kassir** *(Igor)*, Adam Shankman *(Wolfie)* ← ROCKULA, Mink Stole *(Wolfie's mother)* CRY-BABY ← HAIRSPRAY / → PINK AS THE DAY SHE WAS BORN → SPLENDOR, Jimmy Walker *(Hathaway)* ← LET'S DO IT AGAIN ← SING SING THANKSGIVING, Anthony Crivella *(Dracula)*, E. Aaron Price *(Elvis/ Mummy)*

Storyline: Based on the 1967 play, 'I'm Sorry The Bridge Is Out, You'll Have To Spend The Night' (but incorporating the song, 'Monster Mash'), Scott and Mary go off to a Halloween party dressed as Romeo and Juliet. However, when their vehicle comes to a halt just outside an eerie mansion, things take a sinister turn when they discover inside another party, a party of monsters! Fright-nightingly unfunny! *MCS*

Movie rating: *3

Visual: video (no audio OST)

Off the record: **Bobby Pickett** (b.11 Feb'40, Somerville, Massachusetts) was the man behind the original song, 'Monster Mash', which became a huge novelty No.1 in 1962 for Bobby "Boris" Pickett And The Crypt-Kickers. Having had limited success with a few other "Monster"-themed 45s and a TV/film acting career, the Boris Karloff-inspired '..Mash' hit the Top 10 again (and in the UK) in 1973. *MCS*

MOONWALKER

aka MICHAEL JACKSON: MOONWALKER

1988 (US 93m; video 84m) Ultimate Productions / Warner Bros.

Film genre: episodic Pop-R&B Musical fantasy + performance

Top guns: dir: Jerry Kramer (+ segments: Jim Blashfield + Colin Chilvers) / s-w: David Newman + **Michael Jackson** (+ story)

Stars: **Michael Jackson** *(performer/Michael)* ← the WIZ ← SAVE THE CHILDREN, **Joe Pesci** *(Mr. Big)* ← HEY, LET'S TWIST, **Sean Lennon** *(Sean)* → IMAGINE: JOHN LENNON → ENDLESS HARMONY: THE BEACH BOYS STORY → FREE TIBET, Kellie Parker *(Katie)*, Brandon Quinton Adams *(Zeke)*, **the Boys:- Khiry + Hakeem + Tajh + Bilal Abdul-Samad** * *(performers)* → the FIGHTING TEMPTATIONS * → BLOCK PARTY *, **Mick Jagger** *(himself)* <= the ROLLING STONES =>, Paul Reubens *(voice)* ← the BLUES BROTHERS / → OVERNIGHT → MAYOR OF THE SUNSET STRIP, Garland Spencer *(dancer)* → YOU GOT SERVED, Jermaine Jackson II *(dancer)*, Dante Basco → TAKE THE LEAD

Storyline: Apart from exhaustive concert footage and a retrospective look at his life, there are a couple of story segments, a claymation sequence courtesy of Disney and one where he plays the role of hero when he saves children from a drug-touting gang leader. *MCS*

Movie rating: *4.5

Visual: video + dvd (no audio OST: score: Bruce Broughton)

Off the record: The **Boys** (actually brothers aged around 9-14 at this time) were from Northridge, California, a vocal quartet who had just hit the US Top 20 with 'Dial My Heart'. **Joe Pesci** ('Goodfellas' & 'Casino') was actually a member of early 60s outfit, Joey Dee & the Starliters, before he was an actor. **Sean Lennon** is the son of the late great John Lennon and also released an album, 'Into The Sun' (1996), in his own right; having dated Yuka Honda – of Cibo Matto – he's just recently followed it up with 'Friendly Fire' (2006). Jermaine Jackson II is the son of one-time Jackson 5 singer Jermaine and nephew of Rockwell. **Michael Jackson** sang live versions of recent hits, etc.:- 'Man In The Mirror', 'A Retrospective Of 24 Years Of Hits', 'Badder', 'Speed Demon', 'Leave Me Alone', 'Smooth Criminal', 'Come Together' and 'The Moon Is Walking'. *MCS*

MORE AMERICAN GRAFFITI

1979 (US 111m) Lucasfilm / Universal Pictures (PG)

Film genre: coming-of-age comedy drama

Top guns: s-w + dir: Bill L. Norton

Stars: Candy Clark *(Debbie Dunham)* ← AMERICAN GRAFFITI / → COOL AS ICE, Bo Hopkins *(Little Joe)* ← AMERICAN GRAFFITI / → SOUTH OF HEAVEN, WEST OF HELL, Ron Howard *(Steve Bolander)* ← AMERICAN GRAFFITI, Paul Le Mat *(John Milner)* ← AMERICAN GRAFFITI / → ROCK & RULE, Mackenzie Phillips *(Carol/Rainbow)* ← AMERICAN GRAFFITI / → MAYOR OF THE SUNSET STRIP, Cindy Williams *(Laurie Bolander)* ← AMERICAN GRAFFITI ← GAS-S-S-S!, Anna Bjorn *(Eva)* → GET CRAZY, Scott Glenn *(Newt)* ← NASHVILLE / → URBAN COWBOY → the VIRGIN SUICIDES, Richard Bradford *(Major Creech)*, Charles Martin Smith *(Terry 'The Toad' Fields)* ← COTTON CANDY ← the BUDDY HOLLY STORY ← AMERICAN GRAFFITI ← PAT GARRETT & BILLY THE KID / → TRICK

OR TREAT, Harrison Ford *(motorcycle cop)* ← AMERICAN GRAFFITI ← ZABRISKIE POINT / → BLADE RUNNER → WORKING GIRL, Manuel Padilla *(Carlos)* ← AMERICAN GRAFFITI ← COTTON CANDY, **Doug Sahm** *(Bobbie)*, **Country Joe (McDONALD) & The Fish** *(themselves)*, Rosanna Arquette *(girl in commune)* → PULP FICTION → BUFFALO '66 → SUGAR TOWN → THINGS BEHIND THE SUN, Delroy Lindo *(army sergeant)* → CROOKLYN, Wolfman Jack *(himself)* ← SGT. PEPPER'S LONELY HEARTS CLUB BAND ← DEADMAN'S CURVE ← AMERICAN GRAFFITI, James Houghton *(Sinclair)* ← I WANNA HOLD YOUR HAND ← ONE ON ONE / → PURPLE PEOPLE EATER, Nancy G. Fish *(police matron)* ← STEELYARD BLUES / → BIRDY → HOWARD THE DUCK → CANDY MOUNTAIN, **Mary Kay Place** *(Teensa)* ← BOUND FOR GLORY / → JUST MY IMAGINATION → MANNY & LO → COMMITTED → KILLER DILLER, Morgan Upton *(Mr. Hunt)* ← BUCKTOWN ← SPACE IS THE PLACE ← STEELYARD BLUES / → TUCKER: THE MAN AND HIS DREAM → the SPIRIT OF 76, **Naomi Judd** *(girl in bus)* → LIVING PROOF: THE HANK WILLIAMS JR. STORY

Storyline: Life moves on for the original characters as we enter the era of flower power, Vietnam and Ban The Bomb. Debbie has become involved with a bunch of pot-smoking hippies and works as a stripper to help bail out her boyfriend. Meanwhile, Steve and Laurie have settled down as a steady couple but find themselves at each other's throats every few seconds, and John continues his quest for speed with a career in drag racing which draws towards its tragic conclusion. *JZ*

Movie rating: *4.5

Visual: video + dvd

Off the record: Doug Sahm was the man behind Sir Douglas Quintet, a Tex-Mex rock outfit who had three Top 30 hits in the mid to late 60s, 'She's About A Mover', 'The Rains Came' & 'Mendocino'. Sadly, he died on a heart attack in Taos, New Mexico, 18th November '99, aged 58. *MCS*

Various Artists

Jul 79. (d-lp) *<(2-11006)>* [84] [ ]
– Heat wave (MARTHA & THE VANDELLAS) / Moon river (ANDY WILLIAMS) / Mr. Tambourine man (the BYRDS) / My boyfriend's back (the ANGELS) / The sound of silence (SIMON & GARFUNKEL) / Season of the witch (DONOVAN) / Stop! in the name of love (the SUPREMES) / Strange brew (CREAM) / Just like a woman (BOB DYLAN) / Respect (ARETHA FRANKLIN) / She's not there (the ZOMBIES) / 96 tears (? & THE MYSTERIANS) / Pipeline (the CHANTAYS) / Since I fell for you (LENNY WELCH) / Beechwood 4-5789 (the MARVELETTES) / Mr. Lonely (BOBBY VINTON) / Cool jerk (the CAPITOLS) / I feel like I'm fixin' to die rag (COUNTRY JOE & THE FISH) / Ballad of the Green Berets (BARRY SADLER) / My guy (MARY WELLS) / I'm a man (DOUG SAHM) / Hang on Sloopy (the McCOYS) / When a man loves a woman (PERCY SLEDGE) / Like a rolling stone (BOB DYLAN).

S/track review: Like in the movie sequel itself, the double-LP soundtrack switches from the late-50s/early 60s of 'AMERICAN GRAFFITI', to early to mid-60s. There are several classics a-poppin' out here, PERCY SLEDGE's 'When A Man Loves A Woman' (from 1966) and the McCOYS' 1965 chart-topper, 'Hang On Sloopy', among them. Girl groups and female singers broke through from 1962 onwards, the 'Tamla/Motown/Gordy' roster producing the MARVELETTES' 'Beechwood 4-5789', MARTHA & THE VANDELLAS' 'Heat Wave', MARY WELLS' 'My Guy' and the SUPREMES' 'Stop! In The Name Of Love', while other gems included the 1963 No.1 'My Boyfriend's Back' (by the ANGELS), plus ARETHA FRANKLIN's Otis-tribute 'Respect'. Forgetting nostalgic alumni ANDY WILLIAMS, BOBBY VINTON and LENNY WELCH, 'MORE AMERICAN GRAFFITI' takes us on a journey to when BOB DYLAN was King of Folk. Represented here by three of his greatest songs, 'Just Like A Woman', 'Like A Rolling Stone' and the BYRDS' interpretation of 'Mr. Tambourine Man', you kinda get the message the music supervisor is in with the "in-crowd". Not as iconic perhaps, but just as important in these anthemic, revolutionary times is 'I Feel Like I'm Fixin' To Die Rag' (by COUNTRY JOE & THE FISH), 'Seasons Of The Witch' (DONOVAN) and 'The Sound Of Silence' (SIMON & GARFUNKEL). Throw into the mix, the heavier 'Strange Brew' (CREAM), the psychedelic '96 Tears' (by ? & THE MYSTERIANS) and the pop-rock of 'She's Not There' (the ZOMBIES), and you have quite an eclectic cocktail soundtrack of our lives and times. *MCS*

Album rating: *7.5

MOULIN ROUGE!

2001 (Aus/US 128m) Twentieth Century Fox (PG-13)

Film genre: romantic Pop/Rock Musical drama

Top guns: s-w: Baz Luhrmann (+ dir), Craig Pearce

Stars: Nicole Kidman *(Satine)*, Ewan McGregor *(Christian)* ← VELVET GOLDMINE ← TRAINSPOTTING ← LIPSTICK ON YOUR COLLAR / → YOUNG ADAM, Jim Broadbent *(Zidler)* ← RUNNING OUT OF LUCK ← BREAKING GLASS, John Leguizamo *(Toulouse-Lautrec)*, Richard Roxburgh *(Duke of Worcester)* ← DOING TIME FOR PATSY CLINE / → STEALTH, Garry McDonald *(the doctor)* ← the PIRATE MOVIE / → RABBIT-PROOF FENCE, Matthew Whittet *(Satie)*, Jacek Koman *(the unconscious Argentinian)*, Kerry Walker *(Marie)*, **Kylie Minogue** *(the green fairy)*, David Wenham *(Audrey)* → the PROPOSITION, **Ozzy OSBOURNE** *(voice; the green fairy)*, Don Reid *(Character Rake)* ← RIKKI AND PETE

Storyline: Another love-it-or-hate-it Luhrmann extravaganza, updating the 1952 original with a stage set from kitsch Valhalla. Fin-de-siècle Monmartre is the location of his queasy neon wonderland, where naive young writer Christian gets mixed up with Toulouse-Lautrec's Bohemian crowd, freefalling into the position of house writer in the 18th arrondissement's premier fleshpot, the Moulin Rouge. While his wit and charm win over the club's in-demand but consumptive courtesan, Satine, their illicit romance can only last as long as the Duke – to whom she's promised – has patience and her illness allows. *BG*

Movie rating: *9

Visual: dvd

Off the record: Former "Neighbours" girl, **Kylie Minogue**, had a series of Top 3 singles & albums from the late 80s onwards, including 'I Should Be So Lucky', 'Got To Be Certain', 'The Loco-Motion', 'Je Ne Sais Pas Pourquoi', 'Especially For You' (with "Neighbours" boyfriend Jason Donovan), 'Hand On My Heart', 'Wouldn't Change A Thing', 'Tears On My Pillow', 'Better The Devil You Know', etc. Her film acting career kicked off with a starring role in 'The Delinquents' (1989), and subsequent work included 'Street Fighter' (1994), 'Hayride To Hell' (1995), 'Bio-Dome' (1996), 'Cut' (2000) and 'Sample People' (2000). *MCS*

Various Cast & Artists (score: Craig Armstrong *)

May 01. (cd) *Interscope; <(493035-2)>* [3] Sep01 [2]
– Lady Marmalade (CHRISTINA AGUILERA, LIL' KIM, MYA & PINK) / Diamond dogs (BECK with TIMBALAND) / Children of the revolution (BONO, GAVIN FRIDAY & MAURICE SEEZER) / Nature boy (DAVID BOWIE & MASSIVE ATTACK) / Le tango de Roxanne (EWAN McGREGOR with JOSE FELICIANO) / Because we can (FATBOY SLIM) / Sparkling diamonds (NICOLE KIDMAN, JIM BROADBENT with LARA MULCAHY) / One day I'll fly away (NICOLE KIDMAN) / Rhythm of the night (VALERIA) / Hindi sad diamonds (NICOLE KIDMAN with JOE LEGUABE) / Your song (EWAN McGREGOR with ALESSANDRO SAFINA) / Elephant love medley (EWAN McGREGOR & NICOLE KIDMAN) / Come what may (NICOLE KIDMAN & EWAN McGREGOR) / Compliante de la butte (RUFUS WAINWRIGHT). *[UK tracks vary in order & appearance] (d-cd-iss. Mar02 +=; 493259-2)* – (extra CD of original versions & remixes).

S/track review: Back in the mid-90s, Baz Luhrmann's pop deconstructionism lit up the film/soundtrack world like an Olympic-strength sparkler; 'When Doves Cry' is still up there as a beacon of choral-kitsch. When the curtain finally came up on 'MOULIN ROUGE', it revealed nothing quite as revelatory. "Truth; Beauty; Freedom; Love" boasted the sleeve, but the music could only aspire to such Bohemian ideals. The regulation 70s disco cover (CHRISTINA AGUILERA et al.'s cynical trawl through LaBelle's 'Lady Marmalade') and GAVIN FRIDAY cameo (a workaday cover of T.Rex's 'Children Of The Revolution', with BONO and MAURICE SEEZER in tow..) don't make the grade. Ditto the thin Ewan McGregor/Nicole Kidman medleys, alternate versions from those used in the film. Even the indomitable FATBOY SLIM tosses off a one-dimensional headbanger of a track, and did we really need a fromage-pungent excavation of a Diane Warren-penned DeBarge hit?! Mon Dieu!! Whirled into the frothy cocktail of the film, these songs buzz with lurid synergy. Isolated on the soundtrack, they just grate. In contrast, BECK's deadpan version of Bowie's own 'Diamond Dogs' sounds as out of place as a nun in the Pigalle, and all the better for it. RUFUS WAINWRIGHT's 'Complainte De La Butte'- sung half in French, half English – is the other highlight, lavished with the kind of Gallic sophistication which Luhrmann steamrollers elsewhere. This album's a good idea in theory, but its simplistic set pieces don't really survive the morning after. If you're a fan of the film, save your francs for the second volume, featuring CRAIG ARMSTRONG's score alongside the original version of the Kidman-performed 'Sparkling Diamonds' and Zidler's demented 'Like A Virgin'. *BG*

Album rating: *6 / Moulin Rouge 2 *6

– spinoff hits, etc. –

CHRISTINA AGUILERA, LIL' KIM, MYA & PINK: Lady Marmalade / (Thunderpuss club mix)

Jun 01. (c-s) *(497561-4)* [1] [1]
(12"+=/cd-s+=) *<497066> (497561-1/-2)* – (Thunderpuss mix).

NICOLE KIDMAN & EWAN McGREGOR: Come What May

Sep 01. (cd-s) *(497630-2)* [–] [27]

Various Artists: Moulin Rouge 2

Feb 02. (cd) *<(493228-2)>* [90] Mar02 [ ]
– Your song – instrumental from the score cue "rehearsal montage" (*) / Sparkling diamonds (NICOLE KIDMAN, JIM BROADBENT & LARA MULCAHY) / One day I'll fly away – Tony Phillips remix (NICOLE KIDMAN) / The pitch (spectacular spectacular) (NICOLE KIDMAN, EWAN McGREGOR & JIM BROADBENT) / Come what may (NICOLE KIDMAN & EWAN McGREGOR) / Like a virgin (JIM BROADBENT, RICHARD ROXBURGH & ANTHONY WEIGH) / Meet me in the red room (AMIEL) / Your song – instrumental from the score cue "After the storm" (*) / The show must go on (NICOLE KIDMAN, JIM BROADBENT & ANTHONY WEIGH) / Ascension – Nature boy (EWAN McGREGOR) / Bolero – closing credits (SIMON STANDAGE).

NICOLE KIDMAN: One Day I'll Fly Away / (Tony Phillips remix)

Mar 02. (c-s) *(497703-4)* [–] [ ]
(cd-s+=) *(497703-2)* – Your song (instrumental rehearsal).

□ Coati MUNDI
(⇒ KID CREOLE & THE COCONUTS)

MURDER WAS THE CASE

1994/5 (US 18m short/ 50m video) Ventura (R)

Film genre: crime drama + rapumentary

Top guns: s-w: Dr. Dre (+ dir), Phillip G. Atwell (story: **SNOOP Doggy DOGG**)

Stars: SNOOP Doggy DOGG *(performer)*, Charles Q. Murphy *(JC)* ← CB4: THE MOVIE ← JUNGLE FEVER / → PAPER SOLDIERS → DEATH OF A DYNASTY → ROLL BOUNCE, Gregory Scott Cummings *(Devil)*, Freez Luv *(himself)* ← HOUSE PARTY 3 / → JACKIE'S BACK! → COYOTE UGLY, **ICE CUBE** *(performer)*, **Dr. Dre** *(himself)* → the SHOW → RHYME & REASON → WHITEBOYS → TUPAC: RESURRECTION, **Kurupt** *(himself)* → TUPAC: RESURRECTION, **Dat Nigga Daz** *(performer)* → BLACK AND WHITE, **Sam Sneed** *(himself)*, **Bow Wow** *(kid jumping on couch)* → CARMEN: A HIP HOPERA → ROLL BOUNCE

Storyline: To call this a film per se is stretching it a little; this is in the tradition of Michael Jackson's 'Thriller', an extended music video. Snoop Doggy Dogg lives the treacherous gangster life and when he gets shot he has to make a deal with the Devil to survive. *MR*

Movie rating: *4

Visual: video + dvd

Off the record: SNOOP DOGG (see own entry)

Various Artists (incl. SNOOP DOGGY DOGG *)

Oct 94. (cd/c/d-lp) *Death Row; <(6544 92484-2/-4/-1)>* [1] [ ]
– Murder was the case – remix (*) / Natural born killaz (DR. DRE & ICE CUBE) / What would U do? (Tha DOGG POUND) / 21 Jump Street (* & TRAY DEEE) / One more day (NATE DOGG) / Harvest for the world (JEWELL) / Who got some gangsta shit? (* feat. Tha DOGG POUND, LIL' STYLE 7 YOUNG) / Come when I call (DANNY BOY) / U better recognize (SAM SNEED feat. DR. DRE) / Come up to my room (JODECI feat. Tha DOGG POUND) / Woman to woman (JEWELL) / Dollars and sense (D.J. QUIK) / The eulogy (SLIP CAPONE & CPO) / Horny (B-REZELL) / East side – west side (YOUNG SOLDIERZ). *(cd re-iss. Feb97 on 'Interscope'; IND 92484)* *<(cd re-iss. Dec02; DROW 106)>*

S/track review: Something of a legend in gangster rap terms, 'MURDER WAS THE CASE' was a showcase of the cream of the (sub) genre's most strident prime movers of the time. In the early 90s, Suge Knight and Death Row Records could do no wrong. With SNOOP DOGGY DOGG (he has since dropped the "Doggy" feeling it was childish and he'd grown up), DR DRE and Tha DOGG POUND they were conquering the US charts and this was before 2PAC, the real cash cow arrived. This, however, is less of a soundtrack and more a compilation built around that tremendous lead track. 'Murder was the case' sums up all that was so compelling about gangster rap: the bass, the classic 70s funk samples, the tireless grooves and the bleak lyrical insight into a criminal mind. The title track encapsulates all of this with considerable style and is one of the definitive gangsta rap tracks. 'Natural Born Killaz' is also significant in that it was the first time former NWA cohorts ICE CUBE and DR DRE would appear on record together since their original band split acrimoniously four years earlier, and showed them back to their bad-tempered selves again. SNOOP and Dre's canine sidekicks Tha DOGG POUND also aquit themselves well with the excellent 'What Would U Do?' where DRE's signature parping bass and trippy analogue keys are a delight. The smut fest that is JODECI's 'Come Up To My Room' indicates why they were the go-to guys when a soundtrack needed some near-the-knuckle R&B gloss: big on lyrical hooks delivered with virtuosic twists. There's little surprise, however, why JEWELL, a Millie Jackson style soul singer showcased here, made her first and last appearance on this soundtrack; she is the weakest link, sounding flimsy amid the battery of beats and wanton displays of testosterone. From here SNOOP the pup grew up and would become one of the planet's biggest rap stars and would make it back on the silver screen for cult horror movies 'BONES' less than a decade later. *MR*

Album rating: *7

– spinoff releases, etc. –

JEWELL: Woman To Woman / DR. DRE & ICE CUBE: Natural Born Killaz

Jan 95. (c-s/cd-s) *<98185>* [72] [–]

DR. DRE & ICE CUBE: Natural Born Killaz / THA DOGG POUND: What Would U Do?

Mar 95. (7"/c-s/cd-s) *(A 8197/+C/CD)* [–] [45]

SAM SNEED feat. DR. DRE: U Better Recognize

Mar 95. (c-s/12"/cd-s) *<98168>* [ ] [–]

MUSCLE BEACH PARTY

1964 sequel-2 (US 94m) American International Pictures (PG)

Film genre: teen-Pop/Rock Musical comedy

Top guns: dir: William Asher ← BEACH PARTY / → BIKINI BEACH → BEACH BLANKET BINGO → HOW TO STUFF A WILD BIKINI / s-w: Robert Dillon → BIKINI BEACH

Stars: Frankie AVALON *(Frankie)*, **ANNETTE Funicello** *(Dee Dee)*, Luciana Paluzzi *(Julie)*, John Ashley *(Johnny)* ← BEACH PARTY ← HOT ROD GANG / → BIKINI BEACH → BEACH BLANKET BINGO → HOW TO STUFF A WILD BIKINI, Don Rickles *(Jack Fanny)* → BIKINI BEACH → PAJAMA PARTY → BEACH BLANKET BINGO, Jody McCrea *(Deadhead)* ← BEACH PARTY / → BIKINI BEACH → PAJAMA PARTY → BEACH BLANKET BINGO → HOW TO STUFF A WILD BIKINI, Peter Lupus as Rock Stevens *(Flex Martian)*, **Candy Johnson** *(Candy)* ← BEACH PARTY / → BIKINI BEACH → PAJAMA PARTY, **Donna Loren** *(Donna)* → BIKINI BEACH → PAJAMA PARTY → BEACH BLANKET BINGO, Morey Amsterdam *(Cappy)* ← BEACH PARTY, Buddy Hackett *(S.Z. Matts)*, Peter Turgeon *(Theodore)*, Luree Holmes *(beach girl)* ← BEACH PARTY / → BIKINI BEACH → PAJAMA PARTY → BEACH BLANKET BINGO → SKI PARTY → HOW TO STUFF A WILD BIKINI → the GHOST IN THE INVISIBLE BIKINI → THUNDER ALLEY → the TRIP, Salli Sachse *(surfer girl)* → BIKINI BEACH → PAJAMA PARTY → BEACH BLANKET BINGO → SKI PARTY → HOW TO STUFF A WILD BIKINI → the GHOST IN THE INVISIBLE BIKINI → THUNDER ALLEY → the TRIP → WILD IN THE STREETS, Mike Nader *(surfer boy)* ← BEACH PARTY / → BIKINI BEACH → PAJAMA PARTY → BEACH BLANKET BINGO → SKI PARTY → HOW TO STUFF A WILD BIKINI → the TRIP, **Dick Dale** *(himself)* ← BEACH PARTY / → BACK TO THE BEACH, **Little Stevie WONDER** *(himself)*, Peter Lorre *(Mr. Strangdour)*, Mary Hughes *(surfer girl)* → BIKINI BEACH → PAJAMA PARTY → BEACH BLANKET BINGO → SKI PARTY → HOW TO STUFF A WILD BIKINI → THUNDER ALLEY → DOUBLE TROUBLE, Mickey Dora *(surfer boy)* ← SURF PARTY ← BEACH PARTY / → BIKINI BEACH → BEACH BLANKET BINGO → SKI PARTY → HOW TO STUFF A WILD BIKINI, Bill Graham *(surfer boy)* → FILLMORE → a STAR IS BORN → the RETURN OF BRUNO → the DOORS

Storyline: A group of macho muscle men encamp next door to our bunch of beach beauties and soon the guys and gals find themselves in trouble. Pick of the pecs Flex Martian (he's green with envy) is supposed to be the latest lover for wealthy Contessa Julie, but she sets her sights on Frankie instead. Old girlfriend Dee Dee is not best pleased with this and more surfing squabbles are guaranteed. *JZ*

Movie rating: *5

Visual: dvd double feature w/ 'SKI PARTY'

Off the record: (see below)

ANNETTE (score: Les Baxter)

Apr 64. (lp) *Buena Vista; <BV/STER 3314>* [ ] [–]
– Muscle beach party / A girl needs a boy / Surfer's holiday / I dream about Frankie / Muscle hustle / *(other tracks not in the movie:-)* Merlin Jones / Custom city / Draggin' U.S.A. / Rebel rider / Waikiki / Shut down again / The scrambled egghead. *<re-iss. 1984 on 'Rhino'; RNDF 205> <cd-iss. 1992 on 'Pony Canyon' Japan; PCCD 00068>*

FRANKIE AVALON: Muscle Beach Party And Other Movie Songs

Apr 64. (lp; m/s) *United Artists; <ual 3371/uas 6371> (ULP 1078)* [ ] [ ]
– Muscle beach party / Surfer's holiday / A boy needs a girl / Beach party / Don't stop now / Runnin' wild // *(. . .and other movie songs)* Nevertheless / More / Days Of Wine And Roses / Moon river / The stolen hours / Again.

S/track review: To confuse matters here, there's two actual soundtracks, one by ANNETTE (Funicello) and the other by FRANKIE AVALON, both similar in the fact that their respective first sides have anything to do with the movie itself. Displaying her apparent affection for beach hunks (as depicted on the sleeve!), ANNETTE gets to grips with a handful of cues, including 'The Loco-Motion'-cloned, muscle-fixated opening title track; she seemingly condoned sand-kicking in the faces of geeks. But 'A Girl Needs A Boy' shows she had a soft spot for anything in tight trunks. Dick Dale's 'Surfer's Holiday' comes in for the Little Eva-meets-Brenda Lee treatment, and one has just learned that "a woody" means a surfboard – I hope! 'I Dream About Frankie' is a nightmare and 'Muscle Hustle' gets back to everybody kicking up the sand – in a new dance craze. Where was "the Shag" when you needed it. Tracks 'Merlin Jones' and 'The Scrambled Egghead' were from an earlier Disney film, while the best pieces come via non-movie numbers, 'Custom City' and 'Rebel Rider'. FRANKIE AVALON, meanwhile, tries his hand at six cues (Annette only had five film numbers!), three of them crooning takes of ANNETTE's opening OST songs. 'Beach Party', 'Don't Stop Now' and 'Runnin' Wild' state they're from 'MUSCLE BEACH . . .', although one thinks they were actually from ANNETTE's previous "BEACH PARTY" ventures. Side Two, for the once-talented AVALON, sees him tackle songs from other movies such as 'Three Little Words', 'Mondo Cane', 'Days Of Wine & Roses', 'Breakfast At Tiffany's', 'The Stolen Hours' & 'Road House' – he never appeared in any of them. *MCS*

Album rating: Annette *3.5 / Frankie Avalon *2.5

– spinoff releases, etc. –

ANNETTE: Muscle Beach Party / I Dream About Frankie

Jul 64. (7") *<F 433>* [ ] [–]

MUSIC AND LYRICS

2007 (US 96m) Castle Rock / Village Roadshow / Warner Bros. (PG-13)

Film genre: romantic Pop Musical comedy

Top guns: s-w + dir: Marc Lawrence

Stars: Hugh Grant *(Alex Fletcher)* ← ABOUT A BOY, Drew Barrymore *(Sophie Fisher)* ← CURIOUS GEORGE ← the WEDDING SINGER ←WAYNE'S WORLD 2 ← FIRESTARTER, Brad Garrett *(Chris Riley)* ← the COUNTRY BEARS, Kristen Johnston *(Rhonda Fisher)*, Haley Bennett *(Cora Corman)*, Campbell Scott *(Sloan Cates)* ← SINGLES, Toni Trucks *(Tricia)*, **Andrew Wyatt Blakemore** *(guitarist)*, **Nick Bacon** *(bassist)*, **Seth Matthew Faulk** *(Cora's drummer)*, **Zak Soulam** *(Cora's guitarist)*, **Conrad Korsch** *(Cora's upright bassist)*, **Ben Butler** *(Cora's guitarist)*, **Rachel Golub** *(Cora's sitarist)*

Storyline: 1980s pop star Alex Fletcher gets a last-chance-saloon offer from new starlet Cora Corman – write a song and record it with her in a week, and she'll give him a spot on her show. Alex promptly agrees but then remembers he's completely useless at writing lyrics – his old partner did that for him. It's just as well he's got Sophie Fisher helping out around the house, as her poetic talents can be put to better use than just talking to the plants. *JZ*

Movie rating: *6

Visual: dvd

Off the record: Andrew Wyatt is the guitarist of the A.M. (one eponymous set 2003), **Nick Bacon** played guitar (not bass) with Lost City Angels (two albums, 'Lost City Angels' 2002 & 'Broken World' 2005). **Seth Matthew Faulk** drums with the Fire Flies; **Zak Soulam** plays guitar with reggae artist, Fefe Dobson, **Conrad Korsch** performs with Rod Stewart, while **Rachel Golub**

plays chamber jazz with the Sutton Ensemble; **Ben Butler** was a one-time member of jazz-rock outfit, Edison With The Weather. *MCS*

—

Various Cast/Artists (composer: ADAM SCHLESINGER *)

Feb 07. (cd) *Atlantic; <(7567 89995-3)>* [63] [ ]
– Pop! goes my heart (HUGH GRANT) / Buddha's delight (HALEY BENNETT) / Meaningless kiss (HUGH GRANT) / Entering bootytown (HALEY BENNETT) / Way back into love (demo) (HUGH GRANT & DREW BARRYMORE) / Tony the beat (*) / Dance with me tonight (HUGH GRANT) / Slam (HALEY BENNETT) / Don't write me off (HUGH GRANT) / Way back into love (HUGH GRANT & HALEY BENNETT) / Different sound (TEDDYBEARS) / Love autopsy (HUGH GRANT).

S/track review: 'MUSIC AND LYRICS' is commendable in that the film's creators didn't just mix'n'match a soundtrack of various artists, instead they whisked the main actors off to a "real" studio with bona fide music producers and songwriters. But can just about anybody have that hidden X Factor. It seems so, if one has the necessary backing. HUGH GRANT, HALEY BENNETT and crew, must've spent a lot of overtime at rehearsals and in the studio, the end results having a nice MOR sheen. We await the show going on the road – mmm. For many pop critics and music lovers, the thought of former Oxford grad HUGH GRANT singing was beyond comprehension, for others with more liberal tastes, the man (now 46 years old) was at least adventurous. Combining vocal sounds from a fusion of New Romantic acts such as ABC and the Human League, GRANT comes up trumps in many respects, example being opening salvo, 'Pop! Goes My Heart'. Written – like many of the songs – by ex-Fountains Of Wayne guy, ADAM SCHLESINGER (who'd worked on the movie 'THAT THING YOU DO!' with Tom Hanks), it has a lot of mainstream qualities and trites. Of the other GRANT efforts, 'Meaningless Kiss' (a tongue-in-cheek send-up of George Michael's 'Careless Whisper') is the most interesting, while 'Dance With Me Tonight' (Spandau Ballet on a bad night out), 'Don't Write Me Off' and 'Love Autopsy', are indeed rhyming slang for trite. It must be said though that HUGH's duet(s) of 'Way Back Into Love' (the demo version alongside DREW BARRYMORE is better!), are head and shoulders above anything on the soundtrack. As for HALEY BENNETT, is she the new Britney Spears? Well, songs like 'Buddha's Delight' (very 'Toxic'), 'Entering Bootytown' (very 'Overprotected') and 'Slam' (very 'I'm A Slave 4 U'), seem to point in that direction. Outsider cues, the Salt-N-Pepa-esque 'Tony The Beat' (by the SOUNDS) and the Duran Duran-ish 'Different Sound' (by TEDDYBEARS), complement the 40-minute one-off pop project. *MCS*

Album rating: *5

the MUSIC MACHINE

1979 (UK 93m) Target Int. / Norfolk International Pictures (A)

Film genre: Disco/Pop Musical drama

Top guns: dir: Ian Sharp / s-w: James Kenelm Clarke

Stars: Gerry Sundquist *(Gerry)*, **Patti Boulaye** *(Claire)*, David Easter *(Howard)* → GIVE MY REGARDS TO BROAD STREET, Michael Feast *(Nick Dryden)*, Ferdy Mayne *(Basil Silverman)*, Mandy Perryment *(Candy)*, Clarke Peters *(Laurie)* → SILVER DREAM RACER, Gary Shail *(Aldo)* → QUADROPHENIA → SHOCK TREATMENT → GIVE MY REGARDS TO BROAD STREET, Thomas Baptiste *(Claire's father)* ← COUNTDOWN AT KUSINI ← SHAFT IN AFRICA, Brenda Fricker *(Mrs. Pearson)*, **John Gorman** *(newsagent)* ← MELODY, Esther Rantzen *(herself)*

Storyline: Working class Gerry's life revolves around the disco at the weekend. At the moment his dancing skills are slightly worse than a bear at the circus, so his chances of winning the heart of his amour are approximately zero. However, by some miracle he gets to practise with the best disco babe in town just in time for the big North vs. South London contest. Gerry at last has a chance to impress the apple of his eye, but will she be impressed by him? *JZ*

Movie rating: *2

Visual: video

Off the record: **John Gorman** was a member of comic novelty outfit the Scaffold.

—

MUSIC MACHINE Cast (guest: PATTI BOULAYE *)

May 79. (lp/c) *Pye; (NH/ZCNH 106)* [ ] [-]
– Let me feel your heartbeat / Disco dancer (*) / The Dilly / Get the feel right (*) / Jumping the gun / Music machine / Move with the beat / Music's my thing / Ready for love (*) / Music machine.

S/track review: The sleeve boasts it "at last.." has "..the definitive Disco Band – Music Machine", adding that they're "all world class musicians who regularly fly from Munich to L.A. and back to London to record with the biggest names in Disco – Artists like Donna Summer, Olivia Newton-John and Elton John. They are the Band the box-office smash motion picture MUSIC MACHINE demanded". The beautiful people had taken one step into the disco arena, and numerous steps back out as they quickly stumble and fall head over heels and mind over matter. "This is not just another soundtrack album. For Disco Dancers this is a MUST – the first monster album by a band who are just too talented to stay behind the scenes one minute longer!". Who are they? Answer: session people and songwriters such as TREVOR BASTOW (keyboards), PAUL KOOGH (guitar), LES HURDLE (bass), HAROLD FISHER (drums), FRANK RICOTTI (percussion), plus singers TONY JACKSON, JEANNIE KYTE and GLORIA MACARI, all subsequent household names – weren't they!? The celluloid introduction of New Faces singing sensation, PATTI BOULAYE, was the only "name" – well at least in the UK or her birthplace, Nigeria – to pull the punters into the low-budget cinematic ballroom of their, indeed, very small minds. While the aforementioned BOULAYE gets her larynx around three cues, 'Disco Dancer', 'Get The Feel Right' and 'Ready For Love' – none of them startling – there are other dancefloor dirges including the title track twice! The 'MUSIC MACHINE's only redeeming factor comes via the underrated 'Move With The Beat', surely a song better aimed at queen of disco divas, Donna Summer, or even Tina Charles. *MCS*

Album rating: *2.5

– spinoff releases, etc. –

the MUSIC MACHINE: Music Machine / Let Me Feel Your Heartbeat
Jun 79. (7"/12") *(7N/+L 46199)* [ ] [-]

PATTI BOULAYE: Disco Dancer / Ready For Love
Jun 79. (7") *Polydor; (PB 61)* [ ] [-]

MUSICAL MUTINY

1970 (US 74m) Cineworld

Film genre: Rock-music concert/fantasy/drama

Top guns: dir: Barry Mahon

Stars: **Iron Butterfly:- Doug Ingle, Erik Braunn, Mike Pinera** *(themselves/ performers)*, **the Fantasy** *(performers)*, **Grit** *(performers)*, **the New Society Band** *(performers)*, Terri De Sario, Brad Grinter

Storyline: The ghost of a Caribbean pirate appears out of the sea and visits Pirate World Amusement Park. Annoyed that the park has been built over one of his old haunts, he gets a biker to go round and start a "mutiny". All the local Flower Children who gather at the park are delighted to find the gates open and entry is free. Not so delighted is the park boss, whose takings plummet. At last star attraction Iron Butterfly take to the stage and save the day. *JZ*

Movie rating: *3

Visual: Something Weird Video (VHS)

Off the record: Iron Butterfly perform heavy metal opus, 'In-A-Gadda-Da-Vida', 'In The Times Of Our Lives' & 'Soul Experience', before the plug gets pulled. **The Fantasy** here are not the obscure Californian psychedelic quartet who released one much-sought after eponymous LP in 1970. *MCS*

MY DINNER WITH JIMI

2003 (US 90m) Fallout Entertainment / Rhino Entertainment

Film genre: Pop/Rock-music bio-pic/drama

Top guns: dir: Bill Fishman ← TAPEHEADS / s-w: **Howard Kaylan** ← 200 MOTELS

Stars: Justin Henry *(Howard Kaylan)* ← CHASING DESTINY, Royale Watkins *(Jimi Hendrix)*, Jason Boggs *(Mark Volman)*, George Wendt *(Bill Uttley)* ← GARAGE: A ROCK SAGA – ← SPICEWORLD ← BYE BYE BIRDIE re-make, Brett Gilbert *(John Barbata)*, Sea Maysonet *(Jim 'Tucko' Tucker)*, Kevin Cotteleer *(Jim Pons)*, George Stanchev *(Al Nichol)* ← DAYDREAM BELIEVERS: THE MONKEES STORY, Brian Groh *(John Lennon)*, Quinton Flynn *(Paul McCartney)*, Ben Bode *(Ringo Starr)* ← EMPIRE RECORDS, Nate Dushku *(George Harrison)*, Jay Michael Ferguson *(Brian Jones)*, Lisa Brounstein *(Mama Cass)*, John Corbett *(Henry Diltz)* → RAISE YOUR VOICE, Bret Roberts *(Jim Morrison)*, Chris Soldevilla *(Graham Nash)*, Adam Tomei *(Frank Zappa)* ← the BANGER SISTERS, Curtis Armstrong *(Herb Cohen)* ← RISKY BUSINESS / → RAY, Robert Patrick Benedict *(Donovan)*, Chris Elwood *(Justin Hayward)* ← HOW HIGH, Todd Lowe *(John Lodge)*, Jill Marie Simon *(Jane Asher)*

Storyline: The memories of the early career of Turtles lead singer, Howard Kaylan, beginning with the bad old days playing in smoky nightclubs for next to nothing. Then comes fame and fortune as they knock the Beatles from the top of the charts and follow this up with a tour of England, including a meeting with the Fab Four themselves. However, the film's highlight is the famous "dinner" with the legend (and personal hero, Jimi Hendrix) and their long conversation together. *JZ*

Movie rating: *6

Visual: dvd (no audio OST; score: Andrew Gross)

Off the record: The TURTLES were formed by **Howard Kaylan** and Mark Volman in Westchester, Los Angeles, California, USA, 1961, initially as the Nightriders. With additional members, Al Nichol, Chuck Portz and Don Murray, they subsequently became the Crossfires and released two flop singles. In 1965, Ted Feigen, co-owner of the 'White Whale' label, signed them up, while manager Reb Foster re-christening the band the Tyrtles, in line with local folk-rock big cheeses, the Byrds. Although this was speedily altered to the TURTLES, it was obvious the band were infatuated with their L.A. rivals on the evidence of their debut single, an inspired cover of Dylan's 'It Ain't Me Babe'. Despite two more hits penned by "protest" writer P.F. Sloan, 'Let Me Be' and 'You Baby', the band's albums stiffed. The quintet then decided that earnest folk-protest wasn't their bag anyway. They found their true calling with the arrival of flower power in 1967, taking the classic hippy-pop of 'Happy Together' to No.1 in America; the equally effervescent 'She'd Rather Be With Me', was also a big hit later that summer. Branching out from the patented TURTLES sound, the group released an eccentric concept album, 'The Turtles Present The Battle Of The Bands' (1969), an entertaining collection of easy going parody that spawned the single 'Elenore'. With the band line-up in continual flux, the TURTLES recorded one more album, the RAY DAVIES-produced 'Turtle Soup' (1969), before finally bowing out with a belated cover of Sloan's 'Eve Of Destruction' in 1970. Kaylan and Volman metamorphosed into Flo & Eddie, lending their satirical expertise to FRANK ZAPPA (on his '200 MOTELS' film project) before venturing out on their own. In 1974, both Kaylan and Volman composed the music for the movie, 'Down And Dirty Duck', an X-rated animation in the mould of 'FRITZ THE CAT'. *MCS & BG*

– helpful compilation –

the TURTLES: Happy Together – The Very Best Of..

Sep 04. (cd) *Shout! Factory; <37488-2> Sony; (519134-2)* ☐ Jun05 ☐
– Happy together / She'd rather be with me / Let me be / You know what I mean / You baby / Elenore / It ain't me babe / She's my girl / Eve of destruction / You showed me / Outside chance / Can I get to know you better / You don't have to walk in the rain / Grim reaper of love.

MY LIFE WITH MORRISSEY

2003 (US 80m) Overt Pictures / Twelve Angry Films (15)

Film genre: romantic dark comedy

Top guns: dir: (+ s-w) Andrew Overtoom

Stars: Jackie Buscarno *(Jackie)*, Eduardo Acosta *(Ed)*, Carla Jimenez *(Virginia)*, Ben Watson *(Routly)*, Alan Smart *(Stan)*, John O. Nelson *(Bob)*, Jose Maldonado *(Morrissey)*

Storyline: Studio worker Jackie is a Morrissey fan, but not in the normal sense of the word. Her bedroom is a shrine to her idol and includes a blow-up doll with a cut-out of his face stuck to it. When she actually meets the man himself the experience sends her completely loopy – she appears at work the next day wearing a wedding dress and insists she and Moz are getting married. However, to everyone else it looks like the only bells Jackie will be hearing are the ones on top of the yellow ambulance. *JZ*

Movie rating: *4.5

Visual: dvd (no audio OST; score: Andrew Overtoom)

Off the record: The music is provided by HI-FIVES, BROOKLYN BRIDGE, ABERDEEN, NERF HERDER, MOPES and QUASI.

MYSTERY TRAIN

1989 (US 115m) JVC / Orion Pictures (R)

Film genre: pop-music-inspired urban comedy

Top guns: s-w + dir: Jim Jarmusch ← DOWN BY LAW / → NIGHT ON EARTH → DEAD MAN → YEAR OF THE HORSE → GHOST DOG: THE WAY OF THE SAMURAI → COFFEE AND CIGARETTES

Stars: Masatoshi Nagase *(Jun)*, Youki Kudoh *(Mitsuko)*, **Screamin' Jay Hawkins** *(night clerk)* ← JOEY ← AMERICAN HOT WAX ← MISTER ROCK AND ROLL / → I PUT A SPELL ON ME, Nicoletta Braschi *(Luisa)* ← DOWN BY LAW, Cinque Lee *(bellboy)* ← SCHOOL DAZE / → COFFEE AND CIGARETTES, **Rufus Thomas** *(man in station)* ← GREAT BALLS OF FIRE! ← WATTSTAX / → ONLY THE STRONG SURVIVE → the ROAD TO MEMPHIS, Elizabeth Bracco *(Dee Dee)*, **Joe STRUMMER** *(Johnny aka Elvis)*, **Sy Richardson** *(News vendor)* ← TAPEHEADS ← WALKER ← STRAIGHT TO HELL ← SID & NANCY ← REPO MAN ← PETEY WHEATSTRAW, Rick Aviles *(Will Robinson)*, Steve Buscemi *(Charlie the barber)* ← the WAY IT IS / → RESERVOIR DOGS → PULP FICTION → AIRHEADS → the WEDDING SINGER → COFFEE AND CIGARETTES → ROMANCE & CIGARETTES → the FUTURE IS UNWRITTEN, Vondie Curtis-Hall *(Ed)* → the MAMBO KINGS → CROOKLYN → TURN IT UP, **Tom WAITS** *(voice of radio DJ)*, Rockets Redglare *(liquor store clerk)* ← CANDY MOUNTAIN ← DOWN BY LAW / → WHAT ABOUT ME

Storyline: Three stories of people who all stay at the same downtrodden hotel in Memphis and, one way or another, are influenced by the "spirit of Elvis". A Japanese couple come on holiday to see the sights, convinced that Elvis is God and Memphis is the Holy Land. Italian Luisa stops over on her way home with her dead husband's body in a casket, and Brit Johnny is on the run after shooting a shopkeeper. Elvis' ghost would appear to have its work cut out. *JZ*

Movie rating: *7.5

Visual: video + dvd

Off the record: If you were to ask anyone who **Rufus Thomas** was, you'd probably get a reply: "didn't he do, Walking The Dog"? Born 26th March 1917, Cayce, Mississippi, USA, Rufus initially cut his teeth as a comedian before becoming a radio DJ in the 40s. Having recorded for the iconic 'Sun' label in the 50s, he subsequently signed for 'Stax' records, the aforementioned 'Walking The Dog' hitting the Top 10 towards the close of 1963. Many subsequent hits (some crediting his daughter Carla Thomas) were only minor, although in the early 70s the R&B-cum-dance legend reeled off four Top 50 breakers, 'Do The Funky Chicken', '(Do The) Push And Pull', 'The Breakdown' and 'Do The Funky Penguin'. Sadly, at the age of 84 on the 15th December, 2001, Rufus died of heart failure. *MCS*

Various Artists // JOHN LURIE

Nov 89. (lp/c/cd) *Milan; <(A/C/CD 509)>* ☐ ☐
– Mystery train (ELVIS PRESLEY) / Mystery train (JUNIOR PARKER) / Blue moon (ELVIS PRESLEY) / Pain in my heart (OTIS REDDING) / Domino (ROY ORBISON) / The Memphis train (RUFUS THOMAS) / Get your money where you spend your time (BOBBY "BLUE" BLAND) / Soul finger (the BAR-KAYS) // Mystery Train suite: Long spell of cold day – Banjo blues – Chaucer Street / Tuesday night in Memphis suite:- Tuesday night in Memphis – To be alive and in a truck / Girls suite: Girls – Random Screamin' Jay / Italian walk / A lawyer can't take you to another planet suite: Groove truck – Drunk blues / Big harmonica escape / Dream sun king / Chaucer Street / Tuesday night in Memphis. *<US cd re-iss. Oct01; 73138 35967-2>*

S/track review: Inspired by the song 'Mystery Train', the album is as about as schizoid as the Jim Jarmusch movie itself. Split into two sections, the first part of eight Memphis-soaked tracks, the second is the score from ex-Lounge Lizard, JOHN LURIE, a man responsible for several avant-jazz soundtracks including 'Down By Law' and 'Stranger Than Paradise'. The listener is left in no doubt that filmmaker Jarmusch knows his R&B, his RnR and his R in rockabilly. Opening with back-to-back versions of the title track by ELVIS and the original by JUNIOR PARKER, there was a slight risk of the King being upstaged. No way, and to make sure PRESLEY is awarded another 'Sun'-recorded gem, 'Blue Moon'. Another track from that mid-50s era, and worth the admission price alone, is ROY ORBISON's version of 'Domino', better known to punk-rockabilly fans of the Cramps. The soul and the rhythm comes via four numbers, 'Pain In My Heart' (by the late, great OTIS REDDING), 'The Memphis Train' (by RUFUS THOMAS), 'Get Your Money Where You Spend Your Time' (by BOBBY "BLUE" BLAND) and 'Soul Finger' (partly a re-working of 'Lucille' by retro-mod princes the BAR-KAYS). Section two is all LURIE, a cooler than cool score that was definitely his most rock-orientated ever. 'Mystery Train Suite' harks back to one of his better known compositions, 'Little Doggy', although this is instrumental, all guitar and banjo. Mostly short'n'sweet but effective (example 'Tuesday Night Suite' & 'Italian Walk'), LURIE and his reverberating, Cooder-like guitar-plucking give us the mystery hotel on a plate. The Lounge Lizard takes us on another journey courtesy of the samba-riddled 'Groove Truck' from 'A Lawyer Can't Take You To Another Planet Suite', while 'Drunk Blues' swaggers like the title suggests. A few reprise tracks close the show, 'Tuesday Night In Memphis', the one that carries the soul of LURIE into the wee small hours. *MCS*

Album rating: *7

Jimmy NAIL

Born: James Michael Aloysius Bradford, 16 Mar'54, Newcastle-Upon-Tyne, England. Not the most likely pop star, or actor for that matter, NAIL – who received his nickname due to him standing on a 15cm spike – did in fact take to music quite early on. After a delinquency-tinged youth, followed by a brief spell in prison, NAIL toured the northern toilet circuit with late 70s pub rock band, the King Crabs; there's even pictures somewhere of him wearing a dress on stage! Without success, Jimmy turned to acting, landing a major role in the 1983 British comedy-drama series, 'Auf Wiedersehen Pet'. This role and subsequent others gave him the platform he needed to get into the music market. In 1985, NAIL had a UK Top 3 cover of the melancholy love-lost Rose Royce song, 'Love Don't Live Here Anymore'. Unfortunately, a subsequent single and the album, 'Take It Or Leave It' (1986), released the following year, failed to make much impression on the charts. NAIL then returned to television, in which he thrived, especially in the title role of the detective series, 'Spender'. After a long-run in this part, Jimmy decided to flex his musical muscles again, and in 1992 he rocketed to No.1 with, 'Ain't No Doubt', from his near chart-topping sophomore album, 'Growing Up In Public'. Another hugely successful television series ('CROCODILE SHOES') followed in '94, with NAIL writing the screenplay, the songs – including the Top 5 hit title track – and taking on the major role of Country & Western crooner, Jed Sheppard. The following few years saw more musical fortune come to Jimmy, via another long-player, 'Big River' (1995), a second TV series/album of 'CROCODILE SHOES II' (1996) and a notable part alongside MADONNA in the musical, 'EVITA' (1996). The rock-band concept movie, 'STILL CRAZY' (1998), was rocking Jimmy's next port of call, the soundtrack as the fictitious band, Strange Fruit, managed a whole OST – featuring NAIL, Billy Connolly, etc. – and a minor UK hit, 'The Flame Still Burns'. The man with "that nose" continued to work on films such as 'SWING' (1999) – a vehicle for another Northerner, Lisa Stansfield – and fantasy TV series, 'The 10th Kingdom' (2000); the following year saw the release of his seventh, rather modestly titled, covers album, '10 Great Songs And An Ok Voice'. This summed up NAIL's appeal as a bit of a coarse, but hard-working and honest labourer of the rock and entertainment world. *MCS*

- **filmography** {actor / composer}

Morons From Outer Space *(1985 {*})* / Wallenberg: A Hero's Story *(1985 TV {a})* / Howling II: Stirba – Werewolf Bitch *(1985 {a})* / Shoot For The Sun *(1986 TV {*})* / Diamond's Edge *(1988 {a})* / Dream Demon *(1988 {*})* / Crusoe *(1989 {a})* / Danny, The Champion Of The World *(1989 TV {a})* / **Crocodile Shoes** *(1994 TV-mini {*} + OST by NAIL =>)* / **Crocodile Shoes**

II *(1996 TV-mini {*} + OST by NAIL =>)* / **Evita** *(1996 {*} on OST by MADONNA/Cast =>)* / **Still Crazy** *(1998 {*} on OST by V/Cast =>)* / **Swing** *(1999 {a} OST by LISA STANSFIELD =>)* / the 10th Kingdom *(2000 TV-mini {a})*

□ NASH THE SLASH segment (⇒ HIGHWAY 61)

NASHVILLE

1975 (US 159m) Paramount Pictures (R)

Film genre: Americana showbiz/music drama

Top guns: dir: Robert Altman → POPEYE → DR. T & THE WOMEN / s-w: Joan Tewkesbury

Stars: Henry Gibson *(Haven Hamilton)* → the BLUES BROTHERS → a STRANGER IN THE KINGDOM → MAGNOLIA, Lily Tomlin *(Linnea Reese)*, Keith Carradine *(Tom Frank)* → the LONG RIDERS, David Arkin *(Norman; chauffeur)*, Barbara Baxley *(Lady Pearl)*, Geraldine Chaplin *(Opal)*, Shelley Duvall *(Marthe aka "L.A. Joan")*, Allen Garfield *(Barnett)* ← YOU'VE GOT TO WALK IT LIKE YOU TALK IT . . . ← the OWL AND THE PUSSYCAT / → ONE-TRICK PONY → ONE FROM THE HEART → GET CRAZY → DICK TRACY, Ned Beatty *(Delbert Reese)* ← DELIVERANCE / → PURPLE PEOPLE EATER → HE GOT GAME, Karen Black *(Connie White)* ← EASY RIDER ← YOU'RE A BIG BOY NOW / → HOUSE OF 1000 CORPSES, **Ronee Blakley** *(Barbara Jean)* → RENALDO AND CLARA → I PLAYED IT FOR YOU, Keenan Wynn *(Mr. Green)* ← BIKINI BEACH → the LAST UNICORN, Timothy Brown *(Tommy Brown)* ← DYNAMITE BROTHERS, Scott Glenn *(Pfc. Glenn Kelly)* → MORE AMERICAN GRAFFITI → URBAN COWBOY → the VIRGIN SUICIDES, Richard Baskin *(Frog)*, Jeff Goldblum *(tricycle man)* ← DEATH WISH / → THANK GOD IT'S FRIDAY → EARTH GIRLS ARE EASY → BARENAKED IN AMERICA, Robert DoQui *(Wade Cooley)* ← COFFY ← UP TIGHT! / → FAST FORWARD → GOOD TO GO, Michael Murphy *(John Triplette)* ← DOUBLE TROUBLE / → PRIVATE PARTS → MAGNOLIA, Merle Kilgore *(Trout)* → COAL MINER'S DAUGHTER → ROADIE → LIVING PROOF: THE HANK WILLIAMS JR., Julie Christie *(herself)* ← TONITE LET'S ALL MAKE LOVE IN LONDON / → the ANIMALS FILM, Bert Remsen *(star)* ← the STRAWBERRY STATEMENT / → FAST BREAK → DICK TRACY, Cristina Raines *(Mary)* → SILVER DREAM RACER, Barbara Harris *(Albuquerque)* ← WHO IS HARRY KELLERMAN AND WHY IS HE SAYING THOSE TERRIBLE THINGS ABOUT ME?, Gailard Sartain *(man at lunch counter)* → the BUDDY HOLLY STORY → ROADIE → HARD COUNTRY → SONGWRITER

Storyline: Following the life and times of a group of individuals pulled together by two events at Nashville:- a music festival and a political conference. The Replacement Party are out to foist their agenda on an unsuspecting public and try to persuade the festival singers to perform for them, but British commentator Opal finds herself reporting on a fruity assassination story instead of music and politics. *JZ*

Movie rating: *9

Visual: video + dvd

Off the record: (see below)

Various Cast (composers: see Cast & Richard Baskin)

Jul 75. (lp/c) *A.B.C.; <ABCD 893>* **80** –
– It don't worry me (KEITH CARRADINE) / Bluebird (TIMOTHY BROWN) / For the sake of the children (HENRY GIBSON) / Keep a-goin' (HENRY GIBSON) / Memphis (KAREN BLACK) / Rolling stone (KAREN BLACK) / 200 years (HENRY GIBSON) / Tapedeck in his tractor (RONEE BLAKLEY) / Dues (RONEE BLAKLEY) / I'm easy (KEITH CARRADINE) / One, I love you (HENRY GIBSON) / My Idaho home (RONEE BLAKLEY) / It don't worry me (BARBARA HARRIS & KEITH CARRADINE). *<cd-iss. May00 on 'M.C.A.'; 170133>*

S/track review: Here's an idea: forget professional composers and source music; get your actors to write the songs instead. C&W's always been an easy target but Altman's cast hold up a mirror to both the genius and the farce, leavening the film's subtextual venality with country's life-affirming whine. KEITH CARRADINE picked up an Oscar for his efforts, even though the winning song (if not the scene it hails from), 'I'm Easy', was outgunned by his totemic opener, 'It Don't Worry Me'. Rattling along on the kind of anthemic, saddlepack chorus that harks back to the Dylan-via-Byrds chestnut, 'You Ain't Goin' Nowhere', satire never sounded so gloriously self-helpful. The tragically toupeed HENRY GIBSON ups the ante with 'Keep A-Goin' and raids country's stock-in-trade sentiment 'For The Sake Of The Children', but it's his acutely observed gobbets of patter that raise the biggest smiles ("now let's take another one and do it with a little more religious fervour"..). There's no joking about the calibre of the musicians: WELDON MYRICK contributes some dazzling pedal steel and KAREN BLACK gets to introduce legendary fiddler VASSAR CLEMENT on ensemble tearjerker, 'Rolling Stone'. The sorely put-upon RONEE BLAKLEY goes for the jugular with the frantic 'Tapedeck In His Tractor' ("There's nothing like the muscles of a hard drivin' cowboy man"..), and while she's no Dolly Parton, she lays her soul bare in both 'Dues' and 'My Idaho Home'. Maybe this amateurs-come-good album's most telling legacy is its verdict on modern-day Nashville; it sounds like a Hall of Fame classic next to much of the overproduced slurry coming out of a 21st Century Music Row. *BG*

Album rating: *7.5

– spinoff hits, etc. –

KEITH CARRADINE: I'm Easy / HENRY GIBSON: 200 Years

Aug 75. (7") *<12117> (ABC 4086)* **17** Oct75 □
<above actually didn't hit chart until Apr'76>

NASHVILLE GIRL

aka NEW GIRL IN TOWN

1976 (US 90m) New World Pictures (R)

Film genre: Country-music drama

Top guns: dir: Gus Trikonis → ELVIS AND THE BEAUTY QUEEN / s-w: Peer J. Oppenheimer

Stars: Monica Gayle *(Jamie)*, Glenn Corbett *(Jeb)*, Roger Davis *(Kelly)* ← RIDE THE WILD SURF, **Johnny Rodriguez** *(himself)*, Jesse White *(C.Y. Ordell)* ← the GHOST IN THE INVISIBLE BIKINI ← PAJAMA PARTY ← LOOKING FOR LOVE ← COUNTRY MUSIC HOLIDAY, Judith Anna Roberts *(Fran)*, Leo Gordon *(Burt)*, Marcie Barkin *(Alice)*, Shirley Jo Finney *(Frisky)*

Storyline: Kentucky teenager Jamie Barker straps on her guitar and ups sticks for Nashville to become a Country & Western star. She quickly realizes her best asset is her body and in the corrupt music business the way ahead is to sleep with as many producers as possible and hope for a lucky break. She is of course used and abused and ends up in prison for her sins, but once she's let out her final chance seems to lie with superstar Jeb Hubbard, who ominously has a particular liking for cute 16-year-olds. *JZ*

Movie rating: *4.5

Visual: video (title 'COUNTRY MUSIC DAUGHTER')

Off the record: Johnny Rodriguez (b. Juan Rodriguez, 10 Dec'51, Sabinal, Texas, USA) was a C&W singer who had three minor hits between 1973-74: 'You Always Come Back (To Hurting Me)', 'Ridin' My Thumb To Mexico' and the Beatles' 'Something'. *MCS*

NASHVILLE REBEL

1966 (US 95m) American International Pictures

Film genre: showbiz/Country-music drama

Top guns: s-w: Jay Sheridan (+ dir), Ira Kerns

Stars: Waylon JENNINGS *(Arlin Grove)*, Mary Frann *(Molly Morgan)*, Cece Whitney *(Margo Powell)*, Gordon Oas-Heim *(Wesley Lang)*, **Sonny James** *(himself)* → LAS VEGAS HILLBILLYS → SECOND FIDDLE TO A STEEL GUITAR → HILLBILLYS IN A HAUNTED HOUSE, **Faron Young** *(himself)* ← COUNTRY MUSIC HOLIDAY / → SECOND FIDDLE TO A STEEL GUITAR → WHAT AM I BID? → ROAD TO NASHVILLE, **Loretta Lynn** *(herself)* → BIG DREAMS & BROKEN HEARTS: THE DOTTIE WEST STORY, **Tex Ritter** *(himself)* → WHAT AM I BID? → the NASHVILLE SOUND, **Porter Wagoner** *(himself)* → ROAD TO NASHVILLE → the NASHVILLE SOUND → HONKYTONK MAN, Henry Youngman *(himself)*, Archie Campbell *(himself)*

Storyline: Arlin Grove is demobbed from the army and decides to give C&W music a go. He's good, and soon builds up a reputation at the local clubs. He meets gorgeous Molly Morgan who soon becomes Mrs Grove, but all good things must come to an end, and Arlin discovers he's been duped by his manager and begins hitting the bottle big time. "Jailhouse Rock for country lovers". *JZ*

Movie rating: *4.5

Visual: video

Off the record: (see below)

—

WAYLON JENNINGS (composer: S. Jagmohan)

Dec 66. (lp) *RCA Victor; <LSP-3736e>*
– Silver ribbons / Nashville bum / Green river / Nashville rebel / I'm a long way from home / Tennessee / Norwegian wood / Hoodlum (instrumental) / Spanish penthouse (instr.) / Lang's theme (instr.) / Rush Street blues (instr.) / Lang's mansion (instr.).

S/track review: WAYLON JENNINGS had already lived a life (he gave up his seat to the Big Bopper on the plane in which Buddy Holly and Richie Valens died in 1959), and would soon be caught up in the amphetamine addiction which had shackled his room-mate and fellow hellraiser JOHNNY CASH. In the meantime, he was just beginning to score his first country hits, and this low-budget potboiler opened another door – though he was displeased with his performance, and it would turn out to be his only starring role. Disappointingly, the Chet Atkins-produced soundtrack fails to find space for any of the shedload of country stars who appear with JENNINGS on screen, instead packing in some formulaic instrumentals by writer-director JAY SHERIDAN. JENNINGS' seven songs include an ambitious but ill-advised stab at 'Norwegian Wood' (not featured in the movie) and a slew of easy-to-like, impeccably-crafted mid-sixties "Hear that lonesome whistle blow" country fodder by top writers like Harlan Howard. JENNINGS' baritone is lighter than the world-weary growl which would become familiar in his 70s heyday, but still rings with the authority of experience. And six or seven years on, rebellion would become a career coup rather than a genre-movie affectation when JENNINGS and Willie Nelson declared their independence from music biz control, gave their considerable talents free rein and ushered in a triumphant backlash against the Nashville Sound. *ND*

Album rating: *5

NATURAL BORN KILLERS

1994 (US 117m w/b&w) New Regency / Warner Bros. Pictures (R)

Film genre: romantic crime thriller

Top guns: s-w: Oliver Stone (+ dir) ← the DOORS / → EVITA, David Veloz, Richard Rutowski (story: Quentin Tarantino ← PULP FICTION ← RESERVOIR DOGS / → FOUR ROOMS → FROM DUSK TILL DAWN → JACKIE BROWN → KILL BILL: VOL.1 → KILL BILL: VOL.2)

Stars: Woody Harrelson *(Mickey Knox)* → WAG THE DOG, Juliette Lewis *(Mallory Knox)* ← the RUNNIN' KIND / → the BASKETBALL DIARIES → STRANGE DAYS → FROM DUSK TILL DAWN → the FEARLESS FREAKS → CATCH AND RELEASE, Robert Downey, Jr. *(Wayne Gale)* → BLACK AND WHITE → the SINGING DETECTIVE, Tommy Lee Jones *(Dwight McClusky)* ← the PARK IS MINE ← COAL MINER'S DAUGHTER, Tom Sizemore *(Det. Jack Scagnetti)* → STRANGE DAYS, Rodney Dangerfield *(Mallory's dad)* ← CADDYSHACK, Edie McClurg *(Mallory's mom)*, Pruitt Taylor Vince *(deputy warden Kavanaugh)* ← WILD AT HEART ← SHY PEOPLE / → HEAVY → the END OF VIOLENCE → MONSTER, O-Lan Jones *(Mabel)* → TOUCH → the END OF VIOLENCE, Jared Harris *(London boy)* → DEAD MAN → I SHOT ANDY WARHOL → TWO OF US, Richard Lineback *(Sonny)* ← HARD COUNTRY, Jeremiah Bitsui *(young Indian boy)*

Storyline: The story of Mickey and Mallory, who both share a passion for murder. After Mickey helps his lover dispose of her parents, the two begin the devil of a journey down route 666 spreading mayhem and violence wherever they go, always leaving one survivor to tell the tale. Reporter Wayne Gale is soon on the story of a lifetime and his column glorifies the pair even when they're in prison, leading to a nationwide debate on the values and morals of modern America. *JZ*

Movie rating: *6.5

Visual: video + dvd

Off the record: Jared Harris is the son of 'MacArthur Park' hitmaker, Richard Harris.

—

Various Artists (md: TRENT REZNOR)

Aug 94. (cd/c) *Nothing; <(6554 92460-2/-4)>* 19 Sep94 10
– Waiting for the miracle (LEONARD COHEN) / Shitlist (L7) / Moon over Greene County (DAN ZANES) / Rock'n'roll nigger (PATTI SMITH) / Sweet Jane (the COWBOY JUNKIES) / You belong to me (BOB DYLAN) / The trembler (DUANE EDDY) / Burn (NINE INCH NAILS) / Route 666 ("BB TONE" BRIAN BERDAN) / Totally hot (REMMY ONGALA & ORCHESTRA) / Back in baby's arms (PATSY CLINE) / Taboo (PETER GABRIEL & NUSRAT FATEH ALI KHAN) / Sex is violent (JANE'S ADDICTION & DIAMANDA GALAS) / History repeats itself (A.O.S.) / Something I can never have (NINE INCH NAILS) / I will take you home (RUSSELL MEANS) / Drums a go-go (the HOLLYWOOD PERSUADERS) / Hungry ants (BARRY ADAMSON) / The day the niggaz took over (DR. DRE) / Born bad (JULIETTE LEWIS) / Fall of the rebel angels (SERGIO SERVETTI) / Forkboy (LARD) / Batonga in Batongaville (the BUDAPEST PHILHARMONIC ORCHESTRA) / A warm place (NINE INCH NAILS) / Allah, Mohammed, Char, Yaar (NUSRAT FATEH ALI KHAN); incl. Judgement day (DIAMANDA GALAS) / The future (LEONARD COHEN) / What would U do? (THA DOGG POUND). *(d-lp iss.Sep99 on 'Simply Vinyl'; SVLP 118)*

S/track review: If it was 'RESERVOIR DOGS' that set the trend and 'PULP FICTION' that did it most successfully, then the soundtrack to 'NATURAL BORN KILLERS' was the compilation tape-as film-soundtrack in extremis. With curmudgeonly NINE INCH NAILS' master of the intense TRENT REZNOR as album producer it sure wasn't going to be an easy ride. We are treated to 70 minutes of sensory overload, less a mixtape, more an extended aural collage. REZNOR took the principle of reusing dialogue snippets from the film something that worked so well in Quentin Tarantino's flicks and blended them into the music as a DJ would in a club. Mickey and Mallory's bloodthirsty antics act as brutal punctuation between hunks of the music. As well as shamefacedly throwing in a clutch of his own tracks, REZNOR wildly blends campfire country of the COWBOY JUNKIES with the L.A. gangsta rap throb of DR DRE and the acerbic punk poetry of PATTI SMITH with the ethereal vocal gymnastics of NUSRAT FATEH ALI KHAN. The result is a furiously eclectic mix which is as reckless, dark, brutal and lacking in morals as Oliver Stone's original film. Before she was in her own band, the Licks, JULIETTE LEWIS also performed on this set via 'Born Bad'; a good stab at early stardom you could say. It is rare for soundtracks to enjoy a life on their own entirely independent of the film but 'NATURAL BORN KILLERS' is an entity in itself. It has a life all its own. *MR*

Album rating: *8.5

□ Ricky NELSON segment
(⇒ ORIGINAL TEEN IDOL)

Willie NELSON

Born: 30 Apr'33, Fort Worth, Texas, USA. One of the few remaining living legends of country, WILLIE NELSON is still going strong even as his contemporaries pass away with what feels like increasing regularity. Universally respected for his songwriting talent, independent mindset and refusal to be pigeonholed, NELSON initially rose to fame as the driving force – alongside drinking buddy WAYLON JENNINGS – of the mid-70s Outlaw movement, taking country away from the Nashville tastemakers and back to its roots. Prior to this, he'd been one of Music Row's most in-demand writers, famously penning 'Crazy' for Patsy Cline and furnishing scores of other artists with classic material. Yet it wasn't until the massive success of his 1978 pop standards album, 'Stardust' (1978), that he truly achieved superstar status. He made his acting debut not long afterwards, appearing alongside Jane Fonda and Robert Redford in Sydney Pollack's 'The ELECTRIC HORSEMAN', for which he also recorded the soundtrack. His performance was sufficiently well received to furnish him with a starring role in 'HONEYSUCKLE ROSE' (1980), a vaguely autobiographical tale of a Texan country singer struggling to hit the big time. Again, WILLIE handled the soundtrack, for which he penned one of his most enduring and talismanic songs, 'On The Road Again'. Further screen appearances in such high calibre movies as Michael Mann's 'Thief' (1981) and Fred Schepisi's 'Barbarosa' (1982) confirmed NELSON as an actor of some merit, while Alan Rudolph's 'SONGWRITER' (1984) again cast him in the familiar mould of time-served country troubadour, this time alongside KRIS KRISTOFFERSON with whom he also co-composed the soundtrack. If an unlikely appearance in lurid fantasy flick, 'Amazons' (1986), a starring role as a vengeful preacher in 'The Red Headed Stranger' (1987), a bit part in rural Texas rape drama, 'Trespasses' (1987) and ruminations on reincarnated cowboys in quirky Canadian film, 'Walking After Midnight' (1988) weren't quite so high profile, his 1990 run-in with the IRS was. By the mid-90s, he'd paid off his tax bill and began to get his career back on track. While roles in celluloid duds such as 'Starlight' (1996) and 'Gone Fishin'' (1997) didn't help his cause, he scored his best part in years as a songwriter in Barry Levinson's acclaimed political satire, 'WAG THE DOG' (1997). NELSON's position as one of the few trad country singers it's OK to admit to liking was underlined with his appearance as interview subject alongside the likes of John Waters, Chuck D and the late Hunter S Thompson in road-trip docu, 'Anthem' (1997), an appearance alongside SNOOP DOGG and Tommy CHONG in stoner comedy, 'Half Baked' (1998), his 'TEATRO' documentary and a cameo as himself in 'Austin Powers: The Spy Who Shagged Me' (1999). He was even the unlikely subject of a documentary on notoriously highbrow UK TV arts institution, 'The South Bank Show', although he continued with parts in films as varied as 'Journeyman' (2001), 'The COUNTRY BEARS' (2002), 'The Big Bounce' (2003) and – as his hip self once more – in cannabis comedy, 'High Times' Potluck' (2003). Of late, NELSON's also worked with Jessica Simpson on 'The Dukes Of Hazzard' (2005) movie. *BG*

- **filmography** (composer) {acting} –

the Electric Horseman *(1979 {*} OST =>)* / **Honeysuckle Rose** *(1980 {*} OST =>)* / **Thief** *(1981 {*} OST by TANGERINE DREAM =>)* / Coming Out Of The Ice *(1982 TV {a})* / Barbarosa *(1982 {*})* / Hell's Angels Forever *(1983 docu {*})* / **Songwriter** *(1984 {*} OST w/ KRIS KRISTOFFERSON =>)* / Amazons *(1986 {a})* / the Last Days Of Frank & Jesse James *(1986 TV {*})* / Stagecoach *(1986 TV {*})* / Trespasses *(1987 {a})* / the Red Headed Stranger *(1987 {*})* / **Baja Oklahoma** *(1987 TV {a})* / Once Upon A Texas Train *(1988 TV {*})* / Walking After Midnight *(1988 {p})* / Dynamite And Gold *(1988 TV {*})* / a Pair Of Aces *(1990 TV {*})* / Another Pair Of Aces: Three Of A Kind *(1991 TV {*} no OST by JAY GRUSKA)* / Wild Texas Wind *(1991 TV {*})* / Dust To Dust *(1994 {*} no OST)* / Starlight *(1996 {*})* / **Nashville Sounds** *(1996 {p} on OST by the BEACH BOYS =>)* / Gone Fishin' *(1997 {*})* / **Wag The Dog** *(1997 {a} OST by MARK KNOPFLER =>)* / Outlaw Justice *(1998 TV {*})* / Half Baked *(1998 {c})* / **Teatro** *(1998 OST →)* / Austin Powers: The Spy Who Shagged Me *(1999 {c} OST by V/A)* / **Dill Scallion** *(1999 {c} =>)* / the Journeyman *(2001 {*} + score)* / **the Country Bears** *(2002 {v} OST by V/A =>)* / High Times' Potluck *(2003 {c})* / the Big Bounce *(2003 {*})* / **Be Here To Love Me: A Film About Townes Van Zandt** *(2004 {c} OST by TOWNES VAN ZANDT =>)* / the Dukes Of Hazzard *(2005 {*} on OST by V/A; future edition =>)* / **Broken Bridges** *(2006 {c} on OST by TOBY KEITH =>)*

NEON MANIACS

1986 (US 90m) Bedford Entertainment (R)

Film genre: horror/monster movie/comedy

Top guns: dir: Joseph Mangine / s-w: Mark Patrick Carducci

Stars: Allan Hayes *(Steven)*, Leilani Sarelle *(Natalie)* → SHAG: THE MOVIE, Donna Locke *(Paula)*, Victor Brandt *(Devin)* ← I WANNA HOLD YOUR HAND ← THREE THE HARD WAY, David Muir *(Wylie)*, Marta Kober *(Lorraine)*, P.R. Paul *(Eugene)*, Jeff Tyler *(Wally)*, Amber Denyse Austin *(Lisa)*

Storyline: Something even scarier than Karl Malden walks the streets of San Francisco at night, slaughtering innocent teenagers and making off with various body parts (but how to get a brain)? Rock singer Steven and pretty Paula witness one such bloodfest and with the help of the police set out to destroy the creatures, who appear to be vulnerable to water, holy or normal. Let's hope the usual hosepipe ban is relaxed for the duration. *JZ*

Movie rating: *2.5

Visual: video + dvd (no audio OST; score: Kendall Schmidt)

Off the record: Tracks on the film include:- 'Baby Lied' & 'The Choice You Made' & 'Let Me Ruin Your Evening' (RICK BOWLES), 'We Had Enough' (SPLIT SYDNEY), 'Treat Me' (PAUL SIMPSON CONNECTION), 'I Don't Want To Be Alone Tonight' & 'Rock Me All Night' (SNEAUX).

□ NEVER STEAL ANYTHING WET alt.
(⇒ CATALINA CAPER)

NEVER TOO YOUNG TO ROCK

1975 (UK 99m) G.T.O. / Libert Films International (1976)

Film genre: Glam-Rock Musical comedy

Top guns: s-w: (+ dir) Dennis Abey, Ron Inkpen ← NEVER TOO YOUNG TO ROCK ← REMEMBER ME THIS WAY

Stars: Peter Denyer *(hero)*, Freddie Jones *(Mr. Rockbottom)* ← SON OF DRACULA / → DUNE → WILD AT HEART, Sheila Steafel *(cafe proprietress)*

← MELODY ← PERCY, John Clive *(bandsmen)* ← YELLOW SUBMARINE ← SMASHING TIME, Joe Lynch *(Russian soldier)*, **Peter Noone** *(army captain)* <= HERMAN'S HERMITS =>, **Mud** *(performers)* → SIDE BY SIDE, **the Rubettes** *(performers)* → SIDE BY SIDE, **the Glitter Band** *(performers)* ← REMEMBER ME THIS WAY, **Scott Fitzgerald** *(performer)*, **Slik:- Midge Ure** *(performers)*, **Bob Kerr's Whoopee Band** *(performers)*, Sally James

Storyline: A hero tries to save us from TV companies banning rock'n'roll from our screens, and with a reluctant Mr. Winterbottom and some futuristic glam rock groups on parade, they set about on their mission. Quite ironic in a way as Glam-"pop" was pushed aside for Punk-"rock" a few years later. *MCS*

Movie rating: *3

Visual: none (no audio OST)

Off the record: the Rubettes and **Mud** take top pop-billing here, the former had been responsible for a string of teeny-bop chartbusters, including No.1, 'Sugar Baby Love', 'Tonight' and Juke Box Jive' (all in the film!); the soundtrack also featured their title track. Mud, meanwhile, carved their career out a little earlier and scored a number of UK smashes, 'Dyna-Mite', 'Tiger Feet', 'The Cat Crept In' and 'Rocket'. **the Glitter Band** showcased three of their hits, 'Angel Face', 'Just For You' and 'Let's Get Together Again'. Glasgow band, **Slik**, were at the time, on a threshold of a No.1, 'Forever And Ever', although the film only highlighted their flop, 'The Boogiest Band In Town'. Relative unknowns, **Bob Kerr's Whoopee Band** were showcased in the movie's finale song, 'Bless My Soul, It's Rock'n'Roll'. **Scott Fitzgerald** (b. William McPhail) finally had a hit in 1978, when his soppy duet with Yvonne Keeley, 'If I Had Words', reached the Top 3. Sally James subsequently became one of the presenters on Saturday morning TV show, 'Tiswas', alongside Who Wants To Be A Millionaire presenter, Chris Tarrant. *MCS*

□ NEW GIRL IN TOWN alt.
(⇒ NASHVILLE GIRL)

NEW YEAR'S EVIL

1980 (US 90m) Cannon Group (R)

Film genre: slasher/horror thriller/comedy

Top guns: s-w: (+ dir) Emmett Alston, Leonard Neubauer

Stars: Roz Kelly *(Diane Sullivan)* ← YOU'VE GOT TO WALK IT LIKE YOU TALK IT . . . ← the OWL AND THE PUSSYCAT / → AMERICAN POP, Kip Niven *(Richard Sullivan)*, Chris Wallace *(Lt. Clayton)*, Grant Creamer *(Derek Sullivan)*, Louisa Moritz *(Sally)* ← UP IN SMOKE, Jed Mills *(Ernie)*, Taaffe O'Connell *(Jane)*

Storyline: As the last hours of the old year tick away, punk icon Diane Sullivan hosts a mega-party live on TV. Celebrations are rudely interrupted by a phone call from a mystery voice who announces that a girl will be killed each hour before midnight, one per time zone (Hawaii doesn't count). Ominously, Diane herself will be the last victim as the clock strikes twelve. The first murder duly occurs but the show goes on with extra security and with the clock running down . . . *JZ*

Movie rating: *4

Visual: video + dvd (no audio OST; score: W. Michael Lewis & Laurin Rinder)

Off the record: Eddie del Barrio & Roxanne Seeman composed the title track, the groups are MADE IN JAPAN and SHADOW, the rock'n'roll/punk songs 'When I Wake Up', 'Suicide Ways', 'The Cooler', 'Cold Hearted Lover', 'Temper Tantrum', 'Headwind', 'Dumb Blondes', 'Simon Bar Sinister' & 'Auld Lang Syne'. *MCS*

□ NEW YORK BEAT MOVIE alt.
(⇒ DOWNTOWN 81)

□ Olivia NEWTON-JOHN segment
(⇒ XANADU)

Paul NICHOLAS

Born: Paul Oscar Beuselinck, 3 Dec'45, Peterborough, England. Paul cut his teeth playing piano in 1964 for the Savages, backing band for the infamous raving loony, Screaming Lord Sutch. A solo career seemed the way to go for NICHOLAS, however songs donated by DAVID BOWIE ('Over The Wall We Go') and PETE TOWNSHEND ('Join My Gang') couldn't keep that particular dream alive. With acting now his main game, NICHOLAS found a top role as Claude in the rock musical, 'Hair', and through its producer, Robert Stigwood (who brought 'Jesus Christ Superstar' to the theatre), he featured in subsequent movie productions such as 'TOMMY' (1975), 'LISZTOMANIA' (1975) and 'SGT. PEPPER'S LONELY HEARTS CLUB BAND' (1978); Paul had already starred in films, 'CANNABIS' (1970) and 'STARDUST' (1974). With high profile roles in such mid-70s cult-ish Brit flicks, Paul turned again to singing and surprised many by having three UK Top 20 disco-pop hits: 'Reggae Like It Used To Be', 'Dancing With The Captain' and 'Grandma's Party'. At the turn of the decade, he starred in three films, the rather inconsequential 'The World Is Full Of Married Men' (1979), 'Yesterday's Hero' (1979) and 'The JAZZ SINGER' (1980), the latter a Hollywood re-make opposite NEIL DIAMOND and Sir Laurence Olivier. Aside from three subsequent roles in 'Nutcracker' (1982), 'Alicja' (1982) and 'Invitation To The Wedding' (1985), NICHOLAS found his niche in TV sitcom-land, 'Just Good Friends', for which he sang the theme tune. Acting work has been somewhat sporadic post-millennium, although you might've spotted him in TV series such as 'Sunburn', 'Burnside', 'Holby City' and most recently (2006), 'Heartbeat'. *MCS*

- **filmography** {acting}

Cannabis *(1970 {*} OST by SERGE GAINSBOURG =>)* / die Weibchen *(1970 {b})* / Blind Terror *(1971 {a})* / What Became Of Jack And Jill? *(1972 {a})* / **Stardust** *(1974 {a} =>)* / **Tommy** *(1975 {a} on OST by the WHO & V/A =>)* / Three For All *(1975 {a})* / **Lisztomania** *(1975 {*} on OST by RICK WAKEMAN & ROGER DALTREY =>)* / **Sgt. Pepper's Lonely Hearts Club Band** *(1978 {a} on OST by V/A =>)* / the World Is Full Of Married Men *(1979 {*})* / Yesterday's Hero *(1979 {*})* / **the Jazz Singer** *(1980 {*} OST by NEIL DIAMOND =>)* / Nutcracker *(1982 {*/p})* / Alicja *(1982 {a/p})* / Invitation To The Wedding *(1985 {a})*

NIGHT MAGIC

1985 (Can/Fra 92m) Fildebroc Productions / RSL Films (X)

Film genre: Rock Opera/Musical drama

Top guns: s-w: **Lewis Furey** (+ dir), **Leonard Cohen**

Stars: Nick Mancuso *(Michael)* ← PAROLES ET MUSIQUE ← BLAME IT ON THE NIGHT ← HEARTBREAKERS / → BRAVE NEW GIRL → IN THE MIX, Carole Laure *(Judy)* ← HEARTBREAKERS ← FANTASTICA, Stephane Audran *(Janice)*, Jean Carmet *(Sam)* ← les YEUX FERMES, Lyne Tremblay *(Stardust)*, Frank Augustyn *(Frank)*, Barbara Eve Harris *(Doubt)*, Danielle Godin *(Moonbeam)*

Storyline: Michael is a singer who is trying to put together a show to save a theatre from closing down, so far with little success. One night, however, he is visited by three angels who give him help and inspiration to make the show a world beater. One of the angels, Judy, falls in love with Michael and gives up her immortality to become Michael's wife. *JZ*

Movie rating: *4.5

Visual: video

Off the record: (see below)

—

LEWIS FUREY (lyrics: LEONARD COHEN)

Dec 85. (d-lp) *RCA Sararvah;* [–] French [–]
– Ouverture / I've counted what I have / Wishing window / Throne of desire part 1 / Throne of desire variations / Angel eyes / The law / The promise – The marriage march / Third invention / Clap, clap! / Hunter's lullaby / We told you so / Fire / Song of destruction / Walls / Coming back – Song to my assassin / The bells. *(cd-iss. Mar04 on 'Disques CineMusique' Canadian; DCM 112)*

S/track review: The French Connection, albeit through the collaborative pens of French-Canadians, LEWIS FUREY and LEONARD COHEN (both born in Quebec), this 78-minute musical double-LP is by comparison a little Andrew Lloyd Webber, a little 'Sound Of Music'. With the help of singer/real-life wife, CAROLE LAURE (the angel Judy in the movie), FUREY takes on a rock opera of sorts, a project that could well have landed the composer better results in the West End or even Broadway. 'NIGHT MAGIC' scrapes into this book by the skin of its ceremonial teeth and the fact Mr. LEONARD COHEN is lending his not too inconsiderable hand. From its orchestral conception, 'NIGHT MAGIC' tries to spellbind the listener into submission with its lullaby-esque trimmings. Sadly, it's too theatrical and initially twee for my liking, although it did get more brooding and darker after a time. With Abba out of the way, it could be that FUREY and Co were merely trying to fill the void the "Super Trooper" left in 1982 after their acrimonious split. 'The Throne Of Desire' (and more so its follow-on variations) does have its overblown moments, but like most of the set it fails to take off in any one direction, the session players virtually at odds with a backing orchestra who'd be advised not to listen to ELP albums before they hit the studio. I'd probably have to hear the album a hundred times before I could see its appeal, although one track stood wings and shoulders above the rest, the smoochy, Genie award-winning – for Best Song in a Canadian Movie – 'Angel Eyes'; it must've been a hard decision for the judges as there was a plethora of great Canadian movie tunes that year . . . it's just that I can't remember any of them. Put your hands together for 'Clap, Clap!' (pardon my Anglo-sized slang!), a 6-minute ditty that could sit well in 'Les Miserables', or better still background to FUREY and LAURE's full-on fantasy porn roles in the likes of the similarly-themed 'L'Ange Et La Femme' (1977). *MCS*

Album rating: *4

the NIGHTMARE

aka ALICE COOPER: THE NIGHTMARE

1975 (US 66m TV) Alive Enterprises Inc.

Film genre: Hard Rock Musical horror drama

Top guns: dir: Jorn Winther / s-w: Alan Rudolph → WELCOME TO MY NIGHTMARE → ROADIE, Tony Hudz

Stars: Alice COOPER *(Steven)*, Vincent Price *(the Spirit of the Nightmare)* ← CUCUMBER CASTLE ← the TROUBLE WITH GIRLS ← BEACH PARTY / → WELCOME TO MY NIGHTMARE → the MONSTER CLUB, Linda Googh *(Cold Ethyl)*, Robyn Blythe *(dancer)* → WELCOME TO MY NIGHTMARE, Sheryl Goddard *(dancer)* → WELCOME TO MY NIGHTMARE → SGT. PEPPER'S LONELY HEARTS CLUB BAND → ROADIE, Eugene Montoya *(dancer)* → WELCOME TO MY NIGHTMARE → CAN'T STOP THE MUSIC, Uchi Sugiyama *(dancer)* → WELCOME TO MY NIGHTMARE

Storyline: A late-night weekend TV surprise for ABC's "Wide World Of Entertainment", after the success of Alice Cooper's conceptual LP, 'Welcome To My Nightmare'. Steven is a young boy whose imagination dreams up "the Spirit Of The Nightmare" (aka horror legend/icon, Vincent Price; who also appears on the album) and between them they conjure up all sorts of ghoulish and spooky themes. *MCS*

Movie rating: *6.5

Visual: video (the music stems from below set)

Off the record: The films adds a few extra tracks to the 'Welcome To My Nightmare' album:- 'Years Ago (reprise)', 'Ballad Of Dwight Fry' & 'The Awakening (reprise)'. *MCS*

– associated release –

ALICE COOPER: Welcome To My Nightmare

Mar 75. (lp/c) *Atlantic; <18130> Anchor; (ANC L/K 2011)* [5] [19]
– Welcome to my nightmare / Devil's food / The black widow / Some folks / Only women bleed / Department of youth / Cold Ethyl / Years ago / Steven / The awakening / Escape. *<cd-iss. Sep87 on 'Atlantic'; SD 19157> <(cd re-iss. Mar02 on 'Rhino'+=; RCD 74383)>* – Devil's food (alt.) / Cold Ethyl (alt.) / The awakening (alt.).

9 SONGS

2004 (UK 66m) Revolution Films (18)

Film genre: seXual(hardcore)/romantic/Rock-music drama

Top guns: dir (+ s-w): Michael Winterbottom ← 24 HOUR PARTY PEOPLE

Stars: Keiran O'Brian *(Matt)* ← 24 HOUR PARTY PEOPLE, Margo Stilley *(Lisa)*, **Black Rebel Motorcycle Club:- Peter Hayes** *(performer)* ← DIG!, **Nick Jago** *(performer)*, **Robert Turner** *(performer)* / **the Von Bondies:- Jason Stollsteimer, Marcie Bolen, Carrie Smith, Don Blum** *(performers)* / **Elbow:- Gus Garvey, Pete Turner, Mark Potter, Craig Potter, Richard Jupp** *(performers)* / **Primal Scream:- Bobby Gillespie** *(performer)* → LOVE STORY, **Mani** *(performer)* ← 24 HOUR PARTY PEOPLE, **Robert Young** *(performer)* / **the Dandy Warhols:- Courtney Taylor-Taylor, Zia McCabe** *(performers)* ← DIG!, **Super Furry Animals:- Gruff Rhys, Huw Bunford, Cian Ciaran, Dafydd Ieuan + Guto Pryce** *(performers)*, **Franz Ferdinand:- Alex Kapranos, Nick McCarthy, Bob Hardy + Paul Thomson** *(performers)*, **Michael Nyman** *(performer)*

Storyline: A young glaciologist (Matt) takes off in a bi-plane to work in the South Pole. He recalls the last year spent with girlfriend, Lisa, whom he met at a rock concert at Brixton Academy. They had a deep, intense relationship interspersed with going to live concerts and a nudie show. Warning – this is the most sexually explicit film to be awarded an 18 certificate by the BBFC, as it says on the sleeve. *MCS*

Movie rating: *6

Visual: dvd on 'Optimum' with a music-only opt-out

Off the record: The "9 SONGS" featured are 'Whatever Happened To My Rock And Roll' (BLACK REBEL MOTORCYCLE CLUB), 'C'mon C'mon' (the VON BONDIES), 'Fallen Angel' (ELBOW), 'Movin' On Up' (PRIMAL SCREAM), 'The Last High' (the DANDY WARHOLS), 'Slow Life' (SUPER FURRY ANIMALS), 'Jacqueline' (FRANZ FERDINAND), 'Nadia' (MICHAEL NYMAN) and 'Love Burns' (BLACK REBEL MOTORCYCLE CLUB). *MCS*

NORWOOD

1970 (US 95m) Paramount Pictures (G)

Film genre: romantic comedy/drama

Top guns: dir: Jack Haley Jr. / s-w: Marguerite Roberts (au: Charles Portis)

Stars: Glen CAMPBELL *(Norwood Pratt)*, Kim Darby *(Rita Lee Chipman)* ← the STRAWBERRY STATEMENT, Joe Namath *(Joe William Reese)* → the LAST REBEL, Carol Lynley *(Yvonne Phillips)* ← BUNNY LAKE IS MISSING ← HOUND-DOG MAN, Pat Hingle *(Grady Fring)* → ELVIS: THE MOVIE → MAXIMUM OVERDRIVE → BATMAN, Tisha Sterling *(Marie)*, Dom DeLuise *(Bill Bird)* → WHO IS HARRY KELLERMAN AND WHY IS HE SAYING THOSE TERRIBLE THINGS ABOUT ME? → the BEST LITTLE WHOREHOUSE IN TEXAS, Leigh French *(Vernell Bird)*, Meredith MacRae *(Kay)* ← BIKINI BEACH ← BEACH PARTY / → the CENSUS TAKER,

Billy Curtis *(Edmund B. Ratner)* ← OUT OF SIGHT, Jimmy Boyd *(Jeeter)* → THAT'S THE WAY OF THE WORLD, Virginia Capers *(Ernestine)* → LADY SINGS THE BLUES → TROUBLE MAN → FIVE ON THE BLACK HAND SIDE → HOWARD THE DUCK → WHAT'S LOVE GOT TO DO WITH IT, David Huddleston *(Uncle Lonnie)* → JOE'S APARTMENT

Storyline: Musician Norwood journeys from Texas to New York in the hope of a reunion with fellow 'Nam vet Reese. After much adventure he discovers Reese now lives in Arkansas and, his talents unappreciated by the people of the Village, he sets off in pursuit with new friend Rita, plus a performing chicken and a midget (welcome to America). At last Norwood gets the chance of a big audition, but when Rita reveals she's pregnant he has much more to worry about than talented farmyard animals. *JZ*

Movie rating: *5

Visual: none

Off the record: (see below)

GLEN CAMPBELL (score: AL DE LORY *)

Jun 70. (lp) *Capitol; <E-SW 475>* 90 Sep70
– Ol' Norwood's comin' home / Country girl (*) / Marie / The brass ensemble of Ralph, Texas (*) / The repo man / Hot wheels (*) / I'll paint you a song / Norwood (me and my guitar) / The fring thing / Down home / Chicken out (Joann's theme) (*) / I'll paint you a song – reprise / A different kind of rock (*) / Everything a man could ever need.

S/track review: As country superstars go, GLEN CAMPBELL didn't have the animal magnetism of Elvis, the musical gravity of Johnny Cash, nor the lyricism of Dolly Parton, but despite being Mr Nice Guy, he did, however, have huge hits in his expansive career. He was hand-picked by John Wayne for his role in 'True Grit' – a gig which earned him a Golden Globe nomination as well as an Academy Award for his theme song. 'NORWOOD' seems slight in comparison and while it taps into CAMPBELL's country pop sensibility he never really pushes it anywhere particularly interesting. To be fair, he's up against it from the start, having to contribute anything with an ounce of gravitas to the soundtrack of a romantic comedy that was never really going to be that rewarding a job. Of the 14 songs here, 6 were written in collaboration with Texan MAC DAVIS (the writer of 'In The Ghetto' for Elvis), who had an ear for a pop crossover, something that 'Norwood (Me And My Guitar)' and 'I'll Paint You A Song' illustrate in timely fashion. The problem is, however, nothing here fully grabs the attention in a way a truly great CAMPBELL (or Davis) composition could. The funky 'Chicken Out (Joann's Theme)', one of the half dozen instrumentals scored by AL DE LORY for the film, is twitchy and fun, but that's it. This album of sweet country pop lacks a killer touch to lift it out of the realms of the mediocre. *MR*

Album rating: *4.5

– spinoff hits, etc. –

GLEN CAMPBELL: Everything A Man Could Ever Need / Norwood (Me And My Guitar)

Jun 70. (7") *<2843> (CL 15653)* 52 Aug70 32

O BROTHER, WHERE ART THOU?

2000 (US 106m) Buena Vista Pictures (PG-13)

Film genre: Americana crime caper & road/buddy movie

Top guns: s-w: Joel Coen (+ dir), Ethan Coen

Stars: George Clooney *(Ulysses Everett McGill)* ← SOUTH PARK: BIGGER, LONGER AND UNCUT ← FROM DUSK TILL DAWN, John Turturro *(Pete)* ← HE GOT GAME ← GRACE OF MY HEART ← GIRL 6 ← JUNGLE FEVER ← TO LIVE AND DIE IN L.A., Tim Blake Nelson *(Delmar)* ← THIS IS MY LIFE / → HOOT, John Goodman *(Big Dan Teague)* ← BLUES BROTHERS 2000 ← TRUE STORIES ← SWEET DREAMS / ← COYOTE UGLY → the EMPEROR'S NEW GROOVE → STORYTELLING → MASKED AND ANONYMOUS → OVERNIGHT → BEYOND THE SEA, Charles Durning *(Pappy O'Daniel)* ← DICK TRACY ← FAR NORTH ← the BEST LITTLE WHOREHOUSE IN TEXAS ← I WALK THE LINE, Holly Hunter *(Penny)*, Michael Badalucco *(George "Babyface" Nelson)* ← JUNGLE FEVER, **Chris Thomas King** *(Tommy Johnson)* → DOWN FROM THE MOUNTAIN → LAST OF THE MISSISSIPPI JUKES → the SOUL OF A MAN → LIGHTNING IN A BOTTLE → RAY, Del Pentecost *(Junior O'Daniel)* → COYOTE UGLY, Wayne Duvall *(Homer Stokes)*, Ed Gale *(the little man)* ← BILL & TED'S BOGUS JOURNEY ← HOWARD THE DUCK, **Gillian Welch** *(Soggy Bottom customer)* → DOWN FROM THE MOUNTAIN, **the Cox Family:- Willard Cox, Suzanne Cox, Sidney Cox, Evelyn Cox** *(performers)* → DOWN FROM THE MOUNTAIN, **the Whites: Buck White, Cheryl White, Sharon White** *(performers)* → DOWN FROM THE MOUNTAIN, **Jerry Douglas** *(dobro player)* → DOWN FROM THE MOUNTAIN, Stephen Root *(radio station man)* → the COUNTRY BEARS

Storyline: In this parody of the Odyssey, erstwhile jail-breakers and small-time crooks, Ulysses Everett McGill, Delmar O'Donnell and Pete Hogswallop cast off their chains and prison garb in false pursuit of Everett's fabulous lost treasure. In reality, all he wants to do is to contact his wife who is about to marry someone else. Surprises and fun abound in this eventful romp through 1930s small-town Mississippi. Supported (and jinxed) by McGill's homespun philosophy, the trio are chased by the law, befriended by blues legend Tommy Johnson, signed to a recording contract, beaten up by a bible salesman, duped by sirens, chased by the Ku Klux Klan, hit on by corrupt politicians, etc., etc. and all to the authentic down-home music of the time. Needless to say, Everett comes off with the treasure – but not as the others envision it. If yo likes yo philo-suphie homespun, then this movie dee-livers it in spades! Yee-haw! *SL*

Movie rating: *9

Visual: dvd

Off the record: T-BONE BURNETT was born Joseph Henry Burnett, 18 Jan'48, St. Louis, Missouri, USA. A highly regarded producer and a cult, critically acclaimed artist in his own right, T-Bone is the archetypal Texas maverick. Having grown up in the lone star state and used its rawhide musical heritage to inform much of his work, BURNETT was on familiar ground with his debut film score for forgotten cross-border comedy, 'In 'n Out' (1986). Yet in tandem with his pioneering productions for country roots artists such as Gillian Welch, it was his sterling work on Joel Coen's Deep South epic, 'O BROTHER, WHERE ART THOU?' (2000) which really got his film career in gear. By gathering the likes of of Welch, Alison Krauss, EMMYLOU HARRIS, Ralph Stanley and John Hartford to perform a collection of defiantly traditional and unadorned American roots music, BURNETT not only addressed his own oft cited spiritual concerns but created one of the starkest, most cohesive soundtracks in years, an achievement which was subsequently recognised with a Grammy. In his role as musical director, the man once again demonstrated his unimpeachable taste on the soundtracks to both Callie Khouri's 'Divine Secrets Of The Ya-Ya Sisterhood' (2002), assembling an impressive cast of largely Afro-American past masters, contemporary talent and even the odd Cajun wild card, and Anthony Minghella's 'COLD MOUNTAIN' (2003), which successfully combined Gabriel Yared's score with sparse blues courtesy of White Stripes don, Jack White, more bluegrass from Alison Krauss and luminous gospel from Sacred Harp Singers At Liberty Church. For the latter he contributed three songs under the name Henry Burnett. *BG*

Various Artists (score/md: T-BONE BURNETT)

Dec 00. (cd) *Polydor;* <(170069-2)> [11] Apr01 [ ]
– Po Lazarus (JAMES CARTER & THE PRISONERS) / Big rock candy mountain (HARRY McCLINTOCK) / You are my sunshine (NORMAN BLAKE) / Down to the river to pray (ALISON KRAUSE) / I am a man of constant sorrow (the SOGGY BOTTOM BOYS feat. DAN TYMINSKI) / Hard time killing floor blues (CHRIS THOMAS KING) / I am a man of constant sorrow – instrumental (NORMAN BLAKE) / Keep on the sunny side (the WHITES) / I'll fly away (GILLIAN WELCH & ALISON KRAUSS) / Didn't leave nobody but the baby (GILLIAN WELCH, ALISON KRAUSS & EMMYLOU HARRIS) / In the highways (SARAH, HANNAH & LEAH PEARSALL) / I am weary (let me rest) (the COX FAMILY) / I am a man of constant sorrow – instrumental (JOHN HARTFORD) / O death (RALPH STANLEY) / In the jailhouse now (the SOGGY BOTTOM BOYS feat. TIM BLAKE NELSON) / I am a man of constant sorrow – with band (the SOGGY BOTTOM BOYS feat. DAN TYMINSKI) / Indian war whoop (JOHN HARTFORD) / Lonesome valley (the FAIRFIELD FOUR) / Angel band (the STATLER BROTHERS).

S/track review: The Coen Brothers certainly struck pay dirt big-time in 2000 with their down-home 30s depression adaptation of Homer's Odyssey. A blend of classical mythology and gallows humour, served up with a fricassee of old time, gospel, blues and country music, this movie's soundtrack went on to sell in excess of seven million copies worldwide and collect numerous film and music awards. Despite a rather tenuous storyline, the film is nevertheless a showcase for American traditional music – coloured and white – and it certainly satisfied millennium America's desire to re-establish contact with their country roots. The opening track, 'Po Lazarus', a 1957 field recording by collector Alan Lomax, of black inmate JAMES CARTER and fellow prisoners, was taped in Mississippi State Penitentiary and sets the mood perfectly for the ensuing escape scene. 'Big Rock Candy Mountain', sung by HARRY McCLINTOCK started life as a bawdy turn-of the century hobo ballad. Aka "Haywire Mac", he recorded this original (cleaned-up!) version in 1928, although some readers may be more familiar with the Burl Ives 1948 version; it resurfaced in 1960 as a a Billboard hit for Dorsey Burneyye. Throughout the soundtrack, NORMAN BLAKE's stylish guitar and dobro interweave with the captivating special effects and the fiddle of one-time steamboat pilot JOHN HARTFORD. 'Man Of Constant Sorrow', a STANLEY BROTHERS classic, is featured by them both as incidental music throughout the picture and also vocally in the hilarious recording shack scene by the unlikely-named SOGGY BOTTOM BOYS (aka Nashville stalwarts DAN TYKINSKI from UNION STATION, Nashville Bluegrass Band's PAT ENRIGHT and songwriter HARLEY ALLEN. Newgrass alumni, ALISON KRAUSS and GILLIAN WELCH pay further homage to the Stanleys with 'I'll Fly Away', while country queen EMMYLOU HARRIS leads them in a close harmony trio in the hypnotic "siren scene" via 'Didn't Leave Nobody But The Baby', a kinda a blues-cum-lullaby effort. Cleverly complementing the aforementioned all-star cast are a trio of genuine back porch bluegrass: the COX FAMILY, the WHITES and the sickeningly-cute child act the PEASALS. In direct contrast is the wonderful acting and blues singing of CHRIS THOMAS KING who turns in a great performance as Tommy Johnson; his version of Skip James' 'Hard Time Killing Floor' is a spine-tingler. Long-time black gospel quartet, the FAIRFIELD FOUR, manage to shake the foundations with their deep southern harmony singing of 'Lonesome Valley'. Doctor RALPH STANLEY (possibly the greatest living exponent of this mountain music genre) gives the score his stamp of approval with a spooky version of the Stanley Brothers' classic, 'O Death' in the KKK ceremony scene. This film and soundtrack is a must see for anyone seriously interested in American old-timey music and its portrayal on the big screen. If this whets your appetite then give a listen to the Nitty Gritty Dirt Bands' 'Will The Circle Be Unbroken' triple album from the early 70s. This featured all of the major players of this genre, many of whom have since gone on to that Grand Ol' Opry in the sky. *SL*

Album rating: *8

☐ Hazel O'CONNOR segment
(⇒ BREAKING GLASS)

☐ Johnny O'KEEFE segment
(⇒ SHOUT!: THE STORY OF JOHNNY O'KEEFE)

the OFFENDERS

1980 (US 100m) B Movies (R)

Film genre: urban melodrama

Top guns: dir: Beth B., Scott B. (Billingsly) → SALVATION!

Stars: William Rice *(Dr. Moore)* → SUBWAY RIDERS → COFFEE AND CIGARETTES, **Adele Bertei** *(Laura)*, **John LURIE** *(The Lizard)*, **Evan Lurie, Lydia Lunch** → KILL YOUR IDOLS, Robin Winters, Scott B., **Judy Nylon, Bradley Field** ← DOWNTOWN 81, **Kristian Hoffman** → DOWNTOWN 81 → the NOMI SONG, **Walter Lure** → END OF THE CENTURY, **Robert Smith, Diego Cortez**

Storyline: Centered around the kidnapping of punkette Laura and her father by Young Turks. The 8mm feature film was initially serialised in vignettes at the legendary punk club, Max's Kansas City. *MCS*

Movie rating: *5

Visual: video (no audio OST; composers above)

Off the record: ADELE BERTEI was born in Germany before moving to New York in the late 70s. Part of the city's underground scene (that included **Lydia Lunch** and **John & Evan Lurie**), ADELE became an intergral piece of No Wave/jazz outfit, James Chance & The Contortions, her organ-playing and singing featurured on the LP, 'Buy The Contortions' (1979). BERTEI broke into film work at this point, contributing music to two punk melodramas, 'The OFFENDERS' and 'Vortex' (1981). In '83, she had a disco hit with 'Build Me A Bridge' (produced by THOMAS DOLBY), although after acting in two further movies, 'Born In Flames' (1983) and the MADONNA-launching 'Desperately Seeking Susan' (1985), BERTEI's career took a slight dip until her collaboration with Jellybean on his 1988 UK Top 20 hit, 'Just A Mirage'. A solo debut album, 'Little Lives', was pushed out by 'Chrysalis' shortly afterwards and she just might've had her first hit with 'Little Lives, Big Love'. Where is she now? **Judy Nylon** was leader of punk/New Wave act, Snatch, while **Bradley Field** (+ Lydia Lunch) were Teenage Jesus & The Jerks; **Walter Lure** (Johnny Thunders/the Heartbreakers); **Robert Smith** (the Cure); **Kristian Hoffman** (the Mumps), **Diego Cortez** was a singer-songwriter (b. 1946), although the author, lecturer/professor and video director, was more into art than music production. *MCS*

□ OINGO BOINGO segment
(⇒ FORBIDDEN ZONE)

ONCE

2007 (Ire 85m) Samson Films / Summit Entertainment (15)

Film genre: Folk-rock Musical drama

Top guns: s-w + dir: **John Carney**

Stars: Glen Hansard *(the busker guy)* ← the COMMITMENTS, **Marketa Irglova** *(the girl)*, Bill Hodnett *(busker guy's dad)*, Danuse Ktreatova *(the girl's mother)*, Hugh Walsh *(Timmy; drummer)*, Alastair Foley *(bassist dude)*, Geoff Minogue *(Eamon)*, Gerard Hendrick *(lead guitarist)*, Marcella Plunkett *(ex-girlfriend)*, Mal Whyte *(Bill)*, Catherine Hansard *(singer at party)*

Storyline: A busker sings the same old songs on the Dublin streets to earn a crust. When a foreign girl asks him why he doesn't sing what the crowds want, he tells her it's all about what the songs do for him. The pair meet again and soon find a rapport when the girl, herself a piano player, helps him express his emotions through her playing and as love blossoms they decide to record an album together. Real life couldn't be like that – could it? *JZ*

Movie rating: *6

Visual: dvd

Off the record: John Carney was also ex-Frames. The film's music was subsequently nominated for an Oscar.

—

GLEN HANSARD (*) & MARKETA IRGLOVA (**)

May 07. (cd) *Canvasback-Columbia; <88697 10586-2>* □ □
– Falling slowly (* & **) / If you want me (** & *) / Broken hearted hoover fixer sucker guy (*) / When your mind's made up (* & **) / Lies (*) / Gold (INTERFERENCE) / The hill (**) / Fallen from the sky (*) / Leave (*) / Trying to pull myself away (*) / All the way down (*) / Once (* & **) / Say it to me now (*).

S/track review: This is the perfect kind of album as background music for a candlelit dinner with your significant other. This is down to the abundance of acoustic-led fireside folk ballads about love and longing. Unfortunately, as a soundtrack it doesn't quite work due to the lack of variety in the songs themselves. Therefore you don't really get any kind of feel for what the film is about or how the music fits in, unless it happened to be about a perpetual dinner date. All bar one of the tracks is performed by former Frames member GLEN HANSARD and Czech singer-songwriter MARKETA IRGLOVA, either separately or together. Vocally, the pair complement each other well; HANSARD's pained wailing is the perfect foil for IRGLOVA's soft yet resonant warble. This is evident on the likes of 'If You Want Me', 'Say It To Me Now' and 'Lies', where their voices merge almost as one. The only song that really breaks the album up is HANSARD's humorous busking on 'Broken Hearted Hoover Fixer Sucker Guy', while INTERFERENCE are the only other artists present, chipping in with the folky 'Gold'. There is nothing bad about this album, it's just that it isn't that exciting either, especially as a soundtrack, but there are some beautiful vocals and lovely, delicate songs here that do make it a decent enough listen. *CM*

Album rating: *6.5

ONE FROM THE HEART

1982 (US 101m) Columbia Pictures (R)

Film genre: romantic Pop-Rock Musical comedy drama

Top guns: s-w (+ dir): Francis Ford Coppola → YOU'RE A BIG BOY NOW / → TUCKER: THE MAN AND HIS DREAM, Armyan Bernstein (+ story) ← THANK GOD IT'S FRIDAY

Stars: Frederic Forrest *(Hank)* ← the ROSE / → TUCKER: THE MAN AND HIS DREAM / → the END OF VIOLENCE → SWEETWATER: A TRUE ROCK STORY, Teri Garr *(Frannie)* ← HEAD ← CLAMBAKE ← the COOL ONES ← ROUSTABOUT ← VIVA LAS VEGAS ← PAJAMA PARTY ← the T.A.M.I. SHOW ← KISSIN' COUSINS ← FUN IN ACAPULCO, Raul Julia *(Ray)*, Nastassja Kinski *(Leila)* → PARIS, TEXAS, Lainie Kazan *(Maggie)* → BEACHES, Harry Dean Stanton *(Moe)* ← the ROSE ← RENALDO AND CLARA ← RANCHO DELUXE ← PAT GARRETT & BILLY THE KID / → REPO MAN → PARIS, TEXAS → PRETTY IN PINK → the LAST TEMPTATION OF CHRIST → WILD AT HEART → FEAR AND LOATHING IN LAS VEGAS, Allen Garfield as Allen Goorwitz *(restaurant owner)* ← ONE-TRICK PONY ← NASHVILLE ← YOU'VE GOT TO WALK IT LIKE YOU TALK IT . . . ← the OWL AND THE PUSSYCAT / → GET CRAZY → DICK TRACY, **Tom WAITS** *(trumpet player)*, Rebecca De Mornay *(understudy)* → RISKY BUSINESS → RAISE YOUR VOICE

Storyline: Francis Ford Coppola's visually and technically dazzling labour of love pivots around the paper-thin, Indpendence Day exploits of bored lovers Hank and Franny. Letting loose in Las Vegas after a domestic, the pair each indulge in their own one-night stand fantasies before realising that they love each other after all, ahhh . . . *BG*

Movie rating: *6

Visual: video + dvd

Off the record: CRYSTAL GAYLE was responsible for at least one hit classic, 'Don't It Make Your Brown Eyes Blues'.

—

TOM WAITS & CRYSTAL GAYLE (*); WAITS solo (**) / GAYLE solo (***)

Feb 83. (lp/c) *Columbia; <37703> C.B.S.; (CBS/40 70215)* □ □
– Opening montage: Tom's piano intro – Once upon a town – The wages of love (*) / Is there any way out of this dream? (***) / Picking up after you (*) / Old boyfriends (***) / Broken bicycles (**) / I beg your pardon (**) / Little boy blue (**) / Instrumental montage: The tango – Circus girl (*) / You can't unring a bell (**) / This one's from the heart (*) / Take me home (***) / Presents (*). *(re-iss. Jan91 cd/c/lp; 467609-2/-4/-1) <cd re-mast.Jan04 on 'Legacy-Columbia'+=; CK 85813> –* Candy apple red (**) / Once upon a town – Empty rockets (**).

S/track review: Originally released in 1982 just before he reincarnated himself with 'Swordfishtrombones', 'ONE FROM THE HEART' finds TOM WAITS bidding sour-throated adieu to the bloodshot, tattered-tux sermonising of his 70s albums. That he's assisted in this endeavour by CRYSTAL GAYLE, her of chaste-voiced country fame, is, for the most part, fairly incongruous. Which is perhaps why sumptuously orchestrated duets (originally intended to feature the earthier BETTE MIDLER, whose previous collaboration with WAITS on his 'Foreign Affairs' set was reportedly the inspiration for Coppola's movie in the first place) such as 'Once Upon A Town' ebb and flow with cultured ease yet never really pack the emotional punch they were presumably intended to. WAITS, for his part, is in his upmarket boho element, yet GAYLE's formal, note-perfect vocals fail to smoulder against the jazzy arrangements (although they come close on the downbeat 'Old Boyfriends'), never mind igniting any kind of sexual tension with WAITS' scuzzy croon. More telling than any amount of Broadway torch-singing on either participant's part is the fact that WAITS' sloppy, cracked carnival piano and vaguely ominous accordion and brass arrangements on 'Instrumental Montage' are the most striking things here, frowning petulantly at the tasteful fare around them and – along with the wire-taut 'Little Boy Blue' and spiteful tympani dirge, 'You Can't Unring A Bell' – pointing the way towards the man's future experiments. *BG*

Album rating: *8

ONE LOVE

2003 (Jama/Nor/UK 100m) One Love Films / Blue Dolphin Ltd. (12)

Film genre: romantic Reggae-music drama

Top guns: dir: Rick Elgood ← DANCEHALL QUEEN, **Don Letts** ← WESTWAY TO THE WORLD ← DANCEHALL QUEEN ← the PUNK ROCK MOVIE / → PUNK: ATTITUDE / s-w: Trevor D. Rhone ← the HARDER THEY COME

Stars: Ky-Mani Marley *(Kassa)*, Cherine Anderson *(Serena)* ← DANCEHALL QUEEN, Vas Blackwood *(Scarface)*, Carl Bradshaw *(Obeah man)* ← DANCEHALL QUEEN ← KLA$H ← CLUB PARADISE ← COUNTRYMAN ← the HARDER THEY COME, Idris Elba *(Aaron)*, Winston Stona *(Pastor Johnson)* ← the HARDER THEY COME, Alex Rosen *(music manager)*

Storyline: Much jealousy in Jamaica when reggae musician Kassa teams up with churchy singer, Serena, to combine in a double act which crosses the cultural boundaries. Serena's father, a devout preacher, would rather she kept with her own kind, as would her fiancé. Meanwhile, Kassa's band has become entangled with a dodgy music producer and his romance with Serena will have to be rock solid to survive. JZ

Movie rating: *5.5

Visual: dvd (no audio OST; score: Simon Bass)

Off the record: Son of legendary reggae singer, Bob Marley, **Ky-Mani Marley** (b.26 Feb'76) had already released a couple of albums, 'The Journey' (1999) and 'Many More Roads' (2001) before he starred in the movies, 'Shottas' (2002) and this Elgood-Letts movie. MCS

ONE NIGHT THE MOON

2001 (Aus 57m) Dendy Films

Film genre: psychological drama (+ Rock Musical)

Top guns: s-w: Rachel Perkins (+ dir), John Romeril

Stars: Paul Kelly *(father)*, Kaarin Fairfax *(mother)* ← STARSTRUCK, Memphis Kelly *(child)*, Kelton Pell *(Albert)* → AUSTRALIAN RULES, **Ruby Hunter** *(Albert's wife)*, Chris Haywood *(sergeant)*, David Field *(Allman)* ← CHOPPER ← TO HAVE AND TO HOLD ← GHOSTS . . . OF THE CIVIL DEAD / → SILENT PARTNER

Storyline: After listening to dad's bedtime story, a young girl wanders into the night entranced by the Moon. But it's not long before she's lost in the Outback and the police call in aboriginal tracker Albert to help find her. However, the bigoted father wants nothing to do with the black tracker and forms a posse of farmers to begin his own search. Needless to say the white men get nowhere, and it's up to the girl's mother and Albert to find her. JZ

Movie rating: *7

Visual: dvd

Off the record: (see below)

—

PAUL KELLY (*) / KEV CARMODY (**) & MAIREAD HANNAN (***)

Sep 01. (cd) *E.M.I.; (7243 535987-2)* [–] Austra [–]
– I don't know anything anymore (*) / Flinders theme (***) / One night the moon (KAARIN FAIRFAX and MEMPHIS KELLY) / Moon child (*** & DEIRDRE HANNAN) / The gathering (***) / Now listen here – intro (***) / This land is mine (* & KELTON PELL) / The march goes on – The gathering 2 (***) / Spirit of the ancients (**) / What do you know (KAARIN FAIRFAX and KELTON PELL) *** & ** & * / Carcass – The gathering 3 (***) / Night shadows (* & ***) / Black and white (**) / Moment of death (***) / Hunger (***) / Unfinished business (KELTON PELL and KAARIN FAIRFAX) ** & * / Spirit of the ancients (**) / Moody broody (***) / Little bones (KAARIN FAIRFAX) *** & * / Oh breathe on me (RUBY HUNTER) / Moonstruck (**).

S/track review: When he sings, PAUL KELLY (also one of the stars of the film) is Australia's modern-day Leonard Cohen or Bob Dylan; testament to this is the soundtrack's moody opening song, 'I Don't Know Anything Any More'. But 'ONE NIGHT THE MOON' was not just down to KELLY, it also belongs to violinist MAIREAD HANNAN and Aboriginal musician KEV CARMODY. With her uplifting folk fiddle, the former gets into the heritage side of things via 'Flinders Theme' and 'The Gathering' (think Scots act Ossian, or Irish traditionalists, the Chieftains), while the lilting title track is sung by cast KAARIN FAIRFAX and PAUL's young daughter MEMPHIS KELLY. Augmented by her sister DEIRDRE HANNAN (on lute, bodhran, mandolin, etc.), MAIREAD also exerts her Clannad-like vocal chords via 'Moon Child'. Sounding more like Men At Work or Midnight Oil, PAUL KELLY and KELTON PELL duet on 'This Land Is Mine', while other Kelly-Carmody compositions include 'What Do You Know' and 'Unfinished Business' (both sung by FAIRFAX and PELL – the Joni Mitchell and Warren Zevon of down under). The acoustic CARMODY and didgeridoo turn up again on 'Spirits Of The Ancients' (twice!); he also sang solo on 'Black And White' and 'Moonstruck'. FAIRFAX is back once more on the M.Hannan/P.Kelly dirge, 'Little Bones', while Aborigini RUBY HUNTER takes on ancient Irish melody, 'Oh Breathe On Me'. There's a lot of creepiness in the atmospheric music, none more so than 'Night Shadows', while MAIREAD's folk tracks 'Moment Of Death' & 'Hunger' seem to play out on a lonely outback, summoning some kind of spirit for help. MCS

Album rating: *6.5

ONE PERFECT DAY

2004 (Aus 106m) Lightstream Films

Film genre: Pop/Dance/classical-music drama

Top guns: s-w: Paul Currie (+ dir), Chip Richards

Stars: Dan Spielman *(Tommy Matisse)*, Leeanna Walsman *(Alysee Green)*, Nathan Phillips *(Trig)* ← AUSTRALIAN RULES, Kerry Armstrong *(Carolyn Matisse)* ← LANTANA ← AMY, Leigh Whannell *(Chris)*, Frank Gallacher *(Malcolm)* ← AMY ← HAMMERS OVER THE ANVIL ← PROOF, Abbie Cornish *(Emma Matisse)* → SOMERSAULT, Malcolm Robertson *(Beck)*, Syd Brisbane *(Hamish)* ← SILENT PARTNER ← HAMMERS OVER THE ANVIL

Storyline: Brilliant musician Tommy Matisse is well on his way to composing his operatic masterpiece, but his devotion to his work causes him to ignore his sister Emma's increasing slide into drug addiction. His girlfriend Alysse takes Emma clubbing one night, with tragic consequences, and Tommy wakes up to find his sister dead and Alysse heartbroken with grief. Tommy only then recognises his loss and begins a voyage of discovery in the Melbourne club scene. JZ

Movie rating: *5

Visual: dvd

Off the record: Kerry Armstrong was married to Australian Crawl guitarist, Brad Robinson, who died in 1996. MCS

—

Various Artists (score: JOSH G. ABRAHAMS * / DAVID HOBSON **)

Feb 04. (d-cd) *Universal; (9809589)* [–] Austra [–]
– Blow wind blow (the RAIRBIRDS) / Break it (down James Brown) – * remix (the OFFCUTS) / Krazy krush (MS DYNAMITE) / What is the problem? (GRAFITI) / Don't let the man get you down (FATBOY SLIM) / Are you ready for love – Radio Slave remix

(ELTON JOHN) / One perfect day (LYDIA DENKER) / No one knows – UNKLE remix (QUEENS OF THE STONE AGE) / Two months off (UNDERWORLD) / Late at night (FUTURESHOCK) / All of me (GROOVE ARMADA) / Schoolgirl (SANDRINE) / Feathers and down (the CARDIGANS) / Hector's demise (the DUST BROTHERS) / Ordinary world – * remix (MANDY KANE) / Pictures of you – Paulmac remix (ROBERT SMITH) / One and the same – OPD remix (ROB DOUGAN) // Design music (SVEN VATH) / The man with the red face (LAURENT GARNIER) / Horsepower (C.J. BOLLAND) / Graffiti part 2 (STEREO MCs) / No transmission (LHB) / To know (NuBREED) / Gorecki (LAMB) / Just show me (GRANDADBOB) / Sleepwalking (EUROBOY) / Sly-ed (MAN WITH NO NAME) / Drop some drums ([LOVE] TATTOO) / One perfect sunrise (ORBITAL feat. LISA GERRARD) / One perfect day epic dance mix – Paul Van Dyk remix (ALI McGREGOR) / TV screen memories (** and LISA GERRARD) / Final moments (**) / Orchestral finale (**) / Ride (HELMUT).

S/track review: As sprawling epics go, this two-disc, 34-track collection should really be accompanying a four-hour odyssey rather than an Australian clubbing movie, but the cliché is that: size isn't everything after all. This expansive collection may cover a variety of bases but it doesn't hold together terribly well. Spectral techno is thrown up against plaintive chill-out tracks against torpid big beat in an unholy mash up, which is as much an indication of the unfocussed state of dance music at the turn of the century as anything. There are some truly great tunes here though, a few surprises and a smattering of unsung classics. Among the highlights are LAMB's heartbreaking 'Gorecki', which captured that moment when trip hop met quality songwriting, while GRAFITI's excellent 'What Is The Problem?' is a perfect synergy of chunky house and Mike Skinner-esque vocal stylings. Lest we forget the throbbing genius of UNDERWORLD who delight here with 'Two Months Off' and LAURENT GARNIER, whose absolute classic 'Man With The Red Face' is a soundclash of free saxophone over a throbbing techno underscore. Then there's the odd crossover favourite: UNKLE's moody drum and bass reworking of 'No One Knows' stands up well, as does a sweet CURE remix as 'Pictures Of You' gets rendered even more dreamy. The almost magpie-like selection, it was always going to be a bit hit and miss. For the most part though, the set has passable tunes with a smattering of brilliance amidst an undertow of below par bedroom boffinry. *MR*

Album rating: *6.5

ONE-TRICK PONY

1980 (US 98m) Warner Bros. Pictures (R)

Film genre: Pop/Rock Musical drama

Top guns: dir: Robert M. Young ← SHORT EYES / s-w: **Paul Simon**

Stars: Paul Simon *(Jonah)* <= SIMON & GARFUNKEL =>, Blair Brown *(Marion)* → IN HIS LIFE: THE JOHN LENNON STORY, Rip Torn *(Walter Fox)* ← PAYDAY ← YOU'RE A BIG BOY NOW / → SONGWRITER → FLASHPOINT → WHERE THE RIVERS FLOW NORTH → the INSIDER, Joan Hackett *(Lonnie Fox)*, Allen Garfield as Allan Goorvitz *(Cal van Damp)* ← NASHVILLE ← YOU'VE GOT TO WALK IT LIKE YOU TALK IT . . . ← the OWL AND THE PUSSYCAT / → ONE FROM THE HEART → GET CRAZY → DICK TRACY, Mare Winningham *(Modeena Dandridge)* → SHY PEOPLE → MIRACLE MILE → GEORGIA, Michael Pearlman *(Matty Levin)*, **Lou REED** *(Steve Kunelian)*, **Steve Gadd** *(Danny Duggin)*, **Eric Gale** *(Lee-Andrew Parker)*, **Tony Levin** *(John DiBatista)*, **Richard Tee** *(Clarence Franklin)*, Harry Shearer *(Bernie Wepner)* ← ANIMALYMPICS / → THIS IS SPINAL TAP → WAYNE'S WORLD 2 → GHOST DOG: THE WAY OF THE SAMURAI → GIGANTIC (A TALE OF TWO JOHNS) → a MIGHTY WIND, **Samuel D. Moore** *(himself)* → TAPEHEADS → BLUES BROTHERS 2000 / → ONLY THE STRONG SURVIVE, **Dave Prater** *(himself)*, Joe Smith *(narrator at convention)* ← FM, **the B-52's: Kate Pierson, Fred Schneider, Keith Strickland, Ricky Wilson, Cindy Wilson** *(themselves)* → ATHENS, GA. – INSIDE / OUT, **Tiny Tim** *(himself)* ← YOU ARE WHAT YOU EAT / → MESSAGE TO LOVE: THE ISLE OF WIGHT FESTIVAL → PRIVATE PARTS, **David Sanborn** *(himself)*, **the LOVIN' SPOONFUL, Zal Yanovsky, Joe Butler, Steve Boone** *(performers)* / **Patti Austin** *(backing singer)* ← the WIZ ← IT'S YOUR THING / → TUCKER: THE MAN AND HIS DREAM → JACKIE'S BACK!, Merv Griffin *(acappella singer)* ← HELLO DOWN THERE, Daniel Stern *(hare krishna)* → GET CRAZY

Storyline: Jonah, a walking hangover from the 60s folk-protest movement, attempts to the get his music biz career back on track in the brave, unforgiving new wave world of the late 70s. Steering his way through industry sharks and hucksters, not to mention the detritus of his marriage, he's forced to choose between artistic integrity and commercial survival. *BG*

Movie rating: *5.5

Visual: video

Off the record: Sam Moore & Dave Prater were actually soul hitmaker, Sam & Dave.

PAUL SIMON

Aug 80. (lp/c) *Warners; <3472> (K/K4 56846)* [12] [17]
– Late in the evening / That's why God made the movies / One-trick pony / How the heart approaches what it yearns / Oh, Marion / Ace in the hole / Nobody / Jonah / God bless the absentee / Long, long day. *<(cd-iss. 1987; K2 56846)> <(cd re-iss. Jul04 +=; 8122 78902-2)>* – (bonus non-OST tracks).

S/track review: Poor old PAUL SIMON hasn't exactly had an easy time of it with his dramatic side projects. Long before his Broadway debut, 'The Capeman' left tumbleweed blowing in the aisles, 'ONE-TRICK PONY' bombed at the box office, a failure which, he admitted to Playboy in the mid-80s, left him with a "severe loss of faith". By the time 'Graceland' (1986) had restored his critical stock to mid-70s levels, this soundtrack had long been consigned to history, shape-shifting from a pony into a dark horse as the least debated and least heard of all his solo albums. Save for the brassy, syncopated rattle of 'Late In The Evening' – a song firmly in the Latin-pop tradition of 'Me And Julio . . .' on down – it's also one of his most introspective. It's no coincidence that the sophisti-fusion-session calibre of his backing band resembles the one which accompanied him on his pensive masterpiece, 'Still Crazy After All These Years' (1975), and at least four of that number are present here: late 'Motown' pianist RICHARD TEE, percussionist RALPH McDONALD, drummer STEVE GADD and singer PATTI AUSTIN. Add to that the likes of Dave Grusin and legendary guitarist ERIC GALE and the muso credentials of 'ONE-TRICK PONY' tell their own story. It's not quite Steely Dan but in its tastefulness and barbed disillusion, it's getting there. And if SIMON only really sounds alive on the relatively straightforward arrangement and gilded memories of 'Late In . . .', the rest of the songs chug by so innocuously it's difficult to tell them apart. The Dire Straits-meets-Bob James canter of the title track comes closest to a definable hook, and GALE at least gets into something resembling a groove on 'Ace In The Hole', TEE likewise on 'God Bless The Absentee'. Yet while the lyrics sketch the protagonist's struggle using insight and humanist wit, SIMON assumes Jonah's mantle of emotionally frazzled world weariness all too convincingly; for all its musical slickness, much of this record feels like an ad hoc, after-hours session, great for setting a mood but seriously lacking in songs. *BG*

Album rating: *5.5

– spinoff releases, etc. –

PAUL SIMON: Late In The Evening / How The Heart Approaches What It Yearns

Aug 80. (7") *<49511> (K 17666)*  [58]

PAUL SIMON: One-Trick Pony / Long, Long Day

Oct 80. (7") *<49601>* *(K 17715)* [40] Nov80 [ ]

PAUL SIMON: Oh, Marion / God Bless The Absentee

Jan 81. (7") *<49675>* *(K 17745)* [ ] [ ]

ORIGINAL TEEN IDOL

aka 'RICKY NELSON: ORIGINAL TEEN IDOL'

1999 (Can/US 100m TV) Pebblehut Nelson Inc. / VH1 Television

Film genre: Rock'n'roll-music biopic/drama

Top guns: dir: Sturla Gunnarsson / s-w: Arlene Sarner

Stars: Gregory Calpakis *(Ricky Nelson)*, Jamey Sheridan *(Ozzie Nelson)*, Sara Botsford *(Harriet Nelson)*, Anthony Lemke *(David Nelson)*, Vincent Corazza *(Freddie)*, Larissa Laskin *(Helen Blair)*, Nicky Guadagni *(Donna Fontana)*, David Keeley *(Bobby Neal)*, Melody Johnson *(Lorrie Collins)* ← the VIRGIN SUICIDES, Peter Oldring *(Terry)*, Tara Rosling *(Suzanne Fontana)*, Rob Fenton *(Elvis)*, Christopher Dignan *(Johnny Burnette)*, Sean Dignan *(Dorsey Burnette)*, Chris Loane *(James Burton)*, Kelly Harms *(Randy Meisner)*

Storyline: Ricky Nelson sits in the airport lounge awaiting his last, fatal flight and tells his life story to a fan. He first appears in 'Here Come The Nelsons' alongside his mother and overbearing father. However his stardom begins in 1957 with the launch of his first album, and its not long before he starts a film career spanning over 25 years. He marries Kris, becomes a songwriter, and fights a personal battle against drug addiction. Still in demand in the 1980s, he doesn't realise his career will tragically soon be over. *JZ*

Movie rating: *5

Visual: video (no audio OST; score: Jonathan Goldsmith)

Off the record: RICKY NELSON was indeed the original teen idol, having had a plethora of hits including 'A Teenager's Romance', 'I'm Walking', 'Be-Bop Baby', 'Poor Little Fool' & 'Travelin' Man', before he shortened his moniker to Rick Nelson. *MCS*

□ Donny & Marie OSMOND segment (⇒ GOIN' COCONUTS)

OUR BURDEN IS LIGHT

2005 (US 88m) Lightburden Productions / BCI Eclipse LLC (R)

Film genre: romantic/psychological drama (w/ Rock-music)

Top guns: s-w + dir: Denise Coates

Stars: Denise Coates *(Karen Moone)*, Nathan Webb *(Kyle)*, **Jessica Ballard** *(Marnie Lowell)*, **Jack Rooney** *(Sam Heartman)*, **Nate Mendel** *(Devin)* ← FREE TIBET, Nato Morris *(Douglas Moone)*, **Abe Brennan** *(Tim Hunter)*, **Jason Livermore** *(Drunken Pete)*, William Stobo *(guitar prophet)*

Storyline: Set in Colorado, Karen, is a lonely and depressed artist in search of meaning to her art and life. When Karen's mother fatally slashes her wrists in the bathtub, well-meaning rock star friends rally round, but most are just as desperate and insecure as her. When Karen retreates to an introverted world of drink, drugs – with the contemplation of suicide – she and a brief liaison get mugged and beaten at a bus stop. Losing their memories, they are both nursed back to health by a good samaritan and subsequently fall in love, only too aware they might have unwanted pasts. When they eventually find their old haunts, will they embrace a new beginning or just return sadly to their mundane lives. *MCS*

Movie rating: *4

Visual: dvd on Revelation (w/ CD below)

Off the record: WILLIAM STOBO sang 'Rose Garden' & 'You Can', while **Abe Brennan + Jason Livermore** were of local Fort Collins punk-pop quartet Wretch Like Me, who've released three albums to date, 'Calling All Cars' (2000), 'New Ways To Fall' (2000) and 'I Am Become Death' (2002). **Jack Rooney** released 'The Eternal Upgrade' in 2002 on his own imprint. *MCS*

—

Various Artists (score: NATE MENDEL *)

May 05. (dvd w/cd) *Brentwood; <46053>* [–] dvd [–]
– Alone (WRETCH LIKE ME) / Carry you (ALL) / Crash (into me) (the DAVE MATTHEWS BAND) / Falling free (DAVID GRAY) / February stars (FOO FIGHTERS) * / Left of center (BLEEDER) * / Little trip to Heaven (TOM WAITS) / Negativity (BLEEDER) * / River rise (MARK LANEGAN) / Running from mercy (RICKIE LEE JONES & LEO KOTTKE) / Tearjerker (WRETCH LIKE ME) / Say hello, wave goodbye (DAVID GRAY).

S/track review: A good idea in the making: exclusively package the CD soundtrack with the DVD, especially when they combine the acting skills of a musician (NATE MENDEL of Foo Fighters) and his film music composition abilities. The movie is also a bit dull. With the aforementioned MENDEL at the helm, why would they need another Foo Fighters-esque outfit, WRETCH LIKE US (on 'Alone'), to steal the opening limelight; ditto their 'Tearjerker'. Maybe the answer is something to do with WLU cohorts Abe Brennan and Jason Livermore also having integral acting parts in the indie film. Music-wise, the same can be said for ex-Descendents, ALL, who, I suppose, were the hardcore-pop precursors to the Foo's. The pace drops somewhat when big-in-America star(s) the DAVE MATTHEWS BAND find a way in via 'Crash (Into Me)', almost like a meeting of an old Peter Gabriel and a young John Martyn. Yuk! England's DAVID GRAY keeps the folky fires burning via, 'Falling Free' and he even gets another chance when he closes the CD with a cover of Soft Cell's 'Say Hello, Wave Goodbye'. Will the real FOO FIGHTERS stand up, please stand up, was certainly my call to arms. Their only contribution saw 'February Stars' waste a good three minutes before they broke a sweat and Rock-crescendo'd their way out of a soft-rock wilderness. MENDEL just might've persuaded someone upstairs to release some 'OUR BURDEN . . .' score tracks such as 'Danger', 'Depths', 'The Bottom', 'The Dream', 'Your Past', 'Redemption' & the title song, although his band BLEEDER (with Jessica Ballard and Taylor Hawkins) contributed two Hole-like songs, 'Left Of Center' & 'Negativity', displayed either side of an old TOM WAITS nugget, 'Little Trip To Heaven'. Incidentally, Icelandic film scorist Mugison also gives his rendition a go in the subsequent 'a LITTLE TRIP To Heaven' (2006) movie/ OST. Two songs remain, the anthemic, acoustic-based 'River Rise' from ex-Screaming Trees man, MARK LANEGAN, and the one-off collaboration ('Running From Mercy') by RICKIE LEE JONES and LEO KOTTKE. Maybe one day all soundtrack CD/DVDs will be packaged thus, I just hope they are of better quality. *MCS*

Album rating: *5.5

OUT OF SIGHT

1966 (US 87m) Universal Pictures (PG)

Film genre: teen-Pop/Rock Musical spy comedy

Top guns: dir: Lennie Weinrib ← WILD, WILD WINTER ← BEACH BALL / s-w: Larry Hovis (au: Davis Asher)

Stars: Jonathan Daly *(Homer)*, Karen Jensen *(Sandra Carter)*, Carole Shelyne *(Marvin)*, Robert Pine *(Greg)*, Wende Wagner *(Scuba)*, Maggie Thrett *(Wipeout)*, Deanna Lund *(Tuff Bod)* → SPINOUT, Rena Horten *(Girl from F.L.U.S.H.)*, Billy Curtis *(Man from F.L.U.S.H.)* → NORWOOD, Norman Grabowski *(Huh!)* ← GIRL HAPPY ← ROUSTABOUT / → the NAKED APE, Coby Denton *(Tom)* → the WILD ANGELS, **Freddie & The Dreamers:- Freddie Garrity, Derek Quinn, Roy Crewsdon, Peter Birrell, Bernie Dwyer** *(performers)* ← DISK-O-TEK HOLIDAY ← EVERY DAY'S

A HOLIDAY ← JUST FOR YOU ← WHAT A CRAZY WORLD / → CUCKOO PATROL, **Dobie Gray** *(performer)*, **Gary Lewis & The Playboys:- Gary Lewis, Nick Rather, Mike Arturi, Tom Tripplehorn** *(performers)* ← a SWINGIN' SUMMER, **the Knickerbockers:- Jimmy Walker, Buddy Randell, Beau Charles, Johnny Charles** *(performers)*, **the Astronauts:- Bob Demmon, Dennis Lindsey, Rick Fifield, Storm Patterson, Jim Gallagher** *(performers)* ← WILD, WILD WINTER ← SURF PARTY

Storyline: Oh No! Nefarious organization FLUSH plans to do away with rock'n'roll! When hare-brained Homer gets a tip off meant for his secret agent brother, he decides to live the dream and be an agent himself. His villainous adversary Big Daddy plans a dastardly deed at a music fair, but along with girlfriend Sandra Homer is sure to save the day and FLUSH out the baddies. *JZ*

Movie rating: *4.5

Visual: video

Off the record: For the numerous pop outfits, see below review.

—

Various Artists (incl. the NICK VENET ORCHESTRA *)

May 66. (lp; mono/stereo) *Decca; <DL/+7 4751>* ☐ [–]
– Malibu run (GARY LEWIS AND THE PLAYBOYS) / It's not unusual (the KNICKERBOCKERS) / Hip city (*) / Funny over you (FREDDIE AND THE DREAMERS) / Main theme from "Out Of Sight" (*) / Baby, please don't go (the ASTRONAUTS) / She'll come back (the TURTLES) / Tailgate strings (*) / (Out of sight) Out on the floor (DOBIE GRAY) / Camp sight (*) / Z.Z.R. theme (*) / A love like you (FREDDIE AND THE DREAMERS).

S/track review: Back in 1966 you might've thought, wowee! Ring-a-ding-g-g! What a line-up. Four decades and the relative and subsequent underachievements of some of the movie's pop star acts, were in fact not "OUT OF SIGHT". Served up first on the musical menu L.A. hitmakers, GARY LEWIS AND THE PLAYBOYS, who'd incidentally turned in no less than five US Top 5 hits (including chart-topper debut, 'This Diamond Ring') in 1965. Born Cary Levitch and the son of comedian Jerry Lewis, GARY plus his team of PLAYBOYS (session men Jim Keltner and Carl Radle on board) delivered the surfin', Leon Russell-co-penned 'Malibu Run', not in any shape their greatest song ever. Second on the soundtrack and all the way from Bergenfield, New Jersey, the KNICKERBOCKERS' glory arrived via Welsh boyo, Tom Jones and their rock-ish rendition of his UK No.1, 'It's Not Unusual'. From another state entirely, Colorado to be exact, surfers the ASTRONAUTS (famous for a minor hit in 1963, 'Baja' and hitmakers in Japan!), got to grips with Big Joe Williams' blues staple, 'Baby, Please Don't Go'. Accompanied by an orchestra rather than instruments, the TURTLES (aka Howard Kaylan & Mark Volman) excelled themselves beyond that of Dylan folk-clone-ites, via psychedelic, Byrds-esque number, 'She'll Come Back' – the LP's mind-blowing highlight and a precursor to the LA's if ever there was one. Next on the musical conveyor belt was the mod-ish, soulful gem by Mr. Smooth and silky himself, DOBIE GRAY, a man (think Otis Redding fronting the Drifters!) in with "The In-Crowd" and indeed '(Out Of Sight) Out On The Floor'. All the way from Manchester, England, FREDDIE AND THE DREAMERS (like a singing Shadows) were the spoilers here, 'A Love Like You' and 'Funny Over You', derivative of everything they'd done in the last year – not really representative of the "OUT OF SIGHT" British Invasion. The various artists sections aside, I suppose you can't ignore the five eclectic score ditties by The NICK VENET ORCHESTRA (all written by Fred Darian & Al V. de Lory), including the swinging 'Louie Louie'-esque main theme and the clownish, 'Camp Sight'. But you can try! *MCS*

Album rating: *5

OUTLAW BLUES

1977 (US 100m) Warner Bros. (PG)

Film genre: road/romantic comedy drama

Top guns: dir: Richard T. Heffron ← FILLMORE / s-w: Bill L. Norton

Stars: Peter Fonda *(Bobby Ogden)*, Susan Saint James *(Tina Waters)*, John Crawford *(Buzz Cavenaugh)*, James T. Callahan *(Garland Dupree)*, Michael Lerner *(Hatch)*, Matt Clark *(Billy Bob)* ← PAT GARRETT & BILLY THE KID ← IN THE HEAT OF THE NIGHT / → HONKYTONK MAN → SOUTH OF HEAVEN, WEST OF HELL, **Steve Fromholz** *(Elroy)* → SONGWRITER, Richard Rockmiller *(associate Warden)*

Storyline: Bobby Ogden is an aspiring C&W singer who writes a sad, weepy ballad while he is in prison. When sneaky superstar Garland Dupree hears the song he promptly puts his name to it and releases it, so when skint Bobby emerges from the can he goes after Garland seeking royalties and compensation. Needless to say, none is forthcoming, but things go from bad to worse when Dupree is shot and Bobby is the prime suspect. *JZ*

Movie rating: *5

Visual: video

Off the record: Steve Fromholz (see below)

—

Various Artists (score: CHARLES BERNSTEIN *)

Nov 77. (lp) *Capitol; <(E-ST 11691)>* ☐ ☐
– Everybody's goin' on the road (STEVE FROMHOLZ) / Jailbirds don't fly (PETER FONDA) / I dream of highways (PETER FONDA & SUSAN SAINT JAMES) / Outlaw on the run (*) / Beyond these walls (STEVE FROMHOLZ) / Outlaw blues (PETER FONDA) / Love theme from Outlaw Blues (*) / Water for my horses (PETER FONDA) / Whisper in a velvet night (HOYT AXTON) / Little more holy (STEVE FROMHOLZ).

S/track review: Why is country music the genre above all others that persuades filmmakers they can get away with singers who can't sing (see 'HONKYTONK MAN', 'TENDER MERCIES', etc). Shaped by time-served songwriters HOYT AXTON and STEVE FROMHOLZ, and featuring considerable musical talent, this is a soundtrack that never gets off the ground. Part of the problem is Axton's production; by the late 70s mainstream country had succumbed to TV and Vegas, and though the session band includes top-flight players like JIM KELTNER, JEFF BAXTER and DOUG DILLARD, virtually every song is horribly hobbled by intrusive electric bass. Interspersed with capable instrumental atmospherics from Charles Bernstein (a movie score stalwart who most recently worked on 'KILL BILL'), the songs are mainly unexceptional middle-of-the-road stuff – except, that is, for the four sung by PETER FONDA. The actor has many talents, but carrying a tune isn't one of them. The film's most important musical contribution may be in its celebration of Austin, Texas, where the 'OUTLAW BLUES' crew's arrival remains a well-remembered early milestone in that town's evolution into "the live music capital of the world". *ND*

Album rating: *5

OUTSIDE OUT

2000 (US 83m) Cactus Unlimited

Film genre: experimental Rock-music movie

Top guns: dir: **Mike Gordon** → RISING LOW

Stars: Jimi Stout *(Rick Bault)*, **Col. Bruce Hampton, Ret.** *(himself)* ← SLING BLADE, Ashley Scott Shamp *(Bill Bault)*, Ree Hartwell *(Mrs. Bault)*, Elizabeth Combs Beglin *(Ms. Foster)*, Elena McSherry *(Missy)*, Richard Valyou Jr. *(Ben)*,

Mike Gordon *(Matt Gizzard)* ← BITTERSWEET MOTEL / → RISING LOW → ELECTRIC APRICOT: QUEST FOR FESTEROO

Storyline: Rick is a young musician who's been trying to master the guitar, and he must do so to avoid his disapproving father sending him off to military school. With the help of do-it-yourself "the Outstructional Video" and accomplished guitar maestro Colonel Bruce Hampton, he seeks outs his inner being through the "unlearning" of his skills. *MCS*

Movie rating: *4

Visual: dvd March 2003 (no audio OST by MIKE GORDON)

Off the record: Mike Gordon is the bass player with nu-psychedelic jam outfit, Phish. In the film soundtrack, MIKE is assisted by James Harvey, Russ Lawton and Gordon Stone with also Buddy Cage, Vassar Clements, Jon Fishman, Bela Fleck, Adam Frehm, Gabe Jarrett, Craig Johnson, Stuart Paton, Mark Van Allen & Heloise Williams. Other tracks included are mostly oldies from COL. BRUCE HAMPTON:- 'Fixin' To Die', 'J. Thaddeus Toad' (the AQUARIUM RESCUE UNIT), 'Jack The Rabbit', 'One Of Us Is Truly Blessed' (ASHLEY SCOTT SHAMP) & 'Rehearsals For Fainting (Been False Accused)' (the LATE BRONZE AGE). Like Phish, Grateful Dead, Commander Cody and even Captain Beefheart, COL. BRUCE HAMPTON and his associate outfits had been around since his first incarnation the Hampton Grease Band issued, 'Music To Eat', for 'Columbia' in 1969; his LATE BRONZE AGE were responsible for inspirational LP, 'Outside Looking Out' (1980). *MCS*

□ OZ alt.
(⇒ 20th CENTURY OZ)

PAJAMA PARTY

1964 sequel-3 (US 82m) American International Pictures (PG)

Film genre: romantic sci-fi/teen comedy

Top guns: dir: Don Weis ← LOOKING FOR LOVE / → the GHOST IN THE INVISIBLE BIKINI / s-w: Louis M. Heyward → the GHOST IN THE INVISIBLE BIKINI

Stars: Tommy Kirk *(Go-Go)* → the GHOST IN THE INVISIBLE BIKINI → IT'S A BIKINI WORLD → CATALINA CAPER, **ANNETTE Funicello** *(Connie)*, Elsa Lanchester *(Aunt Wendy)* → EASY COME, EASY GO, Jody McCrea *(Big Lunk)* ← BIKINI BEACH ← MUSCLE BEACH PARTY ← BEACH PARTY / → BEACH BLANKET BINGO → HOW TO STUFF A WILD BIKINI, Harvey Lembeck *(Eric Von Zipper)* ← BIKINI BEACH ← BEACH PARTY / → BEACH BLANKET BINGO → HOW TO STUFF A WILD BIKINI → the GHOST IN THE INVISIBLE BIKINI → HELLO DOWN THERE, Buster Keaton *(chief Rotten Eagle)* → HOW TO STUFF A WILD BIKINI ← BEACH BLANKET BINGO, Jesse White *(J. Sinister Hulk)* ← LOOKING FOR LOVE ← COUNTRY MUSIC HOLIDAY / → the GHOST IN THE INVISIBLE BIKINI → NASHVILLE GIRL, **Donna Loren** *(Vikki)* ← BIKINI BEACH ← MUSCLE BEACH PARTY / → BEACH BLANKET BINGO, Ben Lessy *(Fleegle)* → the FASTEST GUITAR ALIVE, Susan Hart *(Jilda)* ← RIDE THE WILD SURF / → the GHOST IN THE INVISIBLE BIKINI, Bobbi Shaw *(Helga)* → BEACH BLANKET BINGO → SKI PARTY → HOW TO STUFF A WILD BIKINI → the GHOST IN THE INVISIBLE BIKINI → PIPE DREAMS, **Candy Johnson** *(Candy)* ← BIKINI BEACH ← MUSCLE BEACH PARTY ← BEACH PARTY, Luree Holmes *(perfume girl)* ← BIKINI BEACH ← MUSCLE BEACH PARTY ← BEACH PARTY / → BEACH BLANKET BINGO → SKI PARTY → HOW TO STUFF A WILD BIKINI → the GHOST IN THE INVISIBLE BIKINI → THUNDER ALLEY → the TRIP, Dorothy Lamour *(head saleslady)*, Teri Hope *(pajama girl)* ← VIVA LAS VEGAS ← the T.A.M.I. SHOW ← KISSIN' COUSINS ← FUN IN ACAPULCO / → ROUSTABOUT → the COOL ONES → CLAMBAKE → HEAD → ONE FROM THE HEART, Salli Sachse *(pajama girl in sand on beach)* ← BIKINI BEACH ← MUSCLE BEACH PARTY / → BEACH BLANKET BINGO → SKI PARTY → HOW TO STUFF A WILD BIKINI → the GHOST IN THE INVISIBLE BIKINI → THUNDER ALLEY → the TRIP → WILD IN THE STREETS, Don Rickles *(Big Bang the Martian)* ← BIKINI BEACH ← MUSCLE BEACH PARTY / → BEACH BLANKET BINGO, **Frankie AVALON** *(Socum)*, Mike Nader *(pajama boy)* ← BIKINI BEACH ← MUSCLE BEACH PARTY ← BEACH PARTY / → BEACH BLANKET BINGO → SKI PARTY → HOW TO STUFF A WILD BIKINI → the TRIP, **Toni Basil** *(pajama girl)* ← the T.A.M.I. SHOW / → HEAD → EASY RIDER → ROCKULA, Patti Chandler *(pajama girl)* ← BIKINI BEACH / → BEACH BLANKET BINGO → SKI PARTY → HOW TO STUFF A WILD BIKINI, Linda Rogers *(Rat Pack member)* ← BIKINI BEACH ← BEACH PARTY / → TICKLE ME → WINTER A-GO-GO → WILD, WILD WINTER, Mary Hughes *(pajama girl)* ← BIKINI BEACH ← MUSCLE BEACH PARTY / → BEACH BLANKET BINGO → SKI PARTY → HOW TO STUFF A WILD BIKINI → THUNDER ALLEY → DOUBLE TROUBLE

Storyline: Teenage Martian Go-Go is sent beachwards to study Earth teenagers (and prepare for an invasion as an afterthought). Meanwhile the action centres around Aunt Wendy's dress shop where Chief Rotten Eagle and J Sinister Hulk are trying to swizzle Aunt's inheritance money. Eric Von Zipper and his beastly bikers are also on the scene, and it's up to the by-now bewildered Go-Go to save the day and win the heart of Connie at the pajama party. *JZ*

Movie rating: *4.5

Visual: video

Off the record: nothing

—

ANNETTE: Annette's Pajama Party (composer: Les Baxter)

Nov 64. (lp) *Buena Vista; <BV/STER 3325>* □ [-]

– Pajama party / There has to be a reason / Beach ball (instrumental) / It's that kind of day / Among the young / The maid and the Martian / Pajama party (instrumental) / Stuffed animal / Among the young (instrumental) / Where did I go wrong (DOROTHY LAMOUR) / It's that kind of day (instrumental).

S/track review: Another in the long line of "BEACH PARTY" movie soundtracks, the conveyor-belt churning along nicely (albeit, too nicely!) with ANNETTE'S 'PAJAMA PARTY'. Disney gets a bit risqué for the sleeve courtesy of a teasing FUNICELLO posing in a baby-doll nightie, actually showing more than a bit of leg, thigh and er . . . furry slippers. As for the songs, one could just about stop right here, but anyway . . . Kicking off with the highlights – and there ain't many aboard here – ANNETTE sings solo on the uptempo title track plus a couple of Styner-Hemric cues, including 'There Has To Be A Reason' (sung with co-star Tommy Kirk in the movie) and 'Stuffed Animal'. The downside is three dance-orientated instrumentals and a cover of 'Beach Ball', which sort of say: "Why credit ANNETTE?". The latter question is also apparent when the musical directors let ageing 30s/40s Hollywood starlet DOROTHY LAMOUR (screen partner of many a Bob Hope/Bing Crosby "Road To . . ." movie) loose on the appropriately-titled 'Where Did I Go Wrong'. That's all folks! *MCS*

Album rating: *3

PANISCHE ZEITEN

aka PANIC TIMES

1980 (W.Ger 101m) Amazonas / Regina Ziegler / Roba Music

Film genre: Pop/Rock Musical comedy

Top guns: dir: Peter Fratzscher → ASPHALTNACHT + **Udo Lindenberg** (+ s-w w/ Karlheinz Freynik)

Stars: Udo Lindenberg *(himself / Kuhlmann)* → NINA HAGEN = PUNK + GLORY, Leata Galloway *(Vera)* ← HAIR, Walter Kohut *(Minister Dr. Kling)*, Vera Tschechowa *(frau doktor)*, Hark Bohm *(Peitschenperverser Kuhn)*, Werner Boehm *(Entfuhrer)*, Karl Dall *(Vogelwart)*, Beate Jensen *(Wiebke Stinksterff von Lololand)*, Eddie Constantine *(Lemmy Caution)*, Ralf Hermann → ASPHALTNACHT

Storyline: If you're crazy enough to hire a midget as one of your bodyguards then you pretty well deserve all you get, and that's what happens to Udo when he gets kidnapped after a show. Detective Kuhlmann is assigned to the case but at first he takes it all with a pinch of salt as it seems to be another of Udo's publicity stunts. However, it transpires that the kidnapper is actually a government agent who thinks Udo's music is corrupting the nation – is he playing 1950s rock'n'roll? *JZ*

Movie rating: *3.5

Visual: dvd 2005 on 'Turbine Medien' (audio OST by UDO LINDENBERG & David A. King; rare LP on 'Telefunken' 624311)

Off the record: Stetson-wearing **Udo Lindenberg** (b.17 May'46, Gronau, Westphalia, Germany) was a member of mid-70s jazz-fusion outfit, Passport (led by fellow subsequent film composer, Klaus Doldinger), who had a surprise following in the US where LPs such as 'Cross-Collateral' (1975), 'Iguacu' (1977), 'Sky Blue' (1978), 'Oceanliner' (1980) & 'Blue Tattoo' (1981), all reached the lower regions of the US Top 200. *MCS*

PAPER SOLDIERS

2002 (US 88m) Universal Studios (R)

Film genre: Hip-Hop crime caper

Top guns: dir: David Daniel, **Damon Dash** → DEATH OF A DYNASTY / s-w: Brian Ash, Charles Q. Murphy

Stars: Kevin Hart *(Shawn)* → DEATH OF A DYNASTY → IN THE MIX, **Beanie SIGEL** *(Stu)*, **Damon Dash** *(himself)* ← BACKSTAGE / → DEATH OF A DYNASTY → FADE TO BLACK, **Memphis Bleek** *(himself)* ← BACKSTAGE / → DEATH OF A DYNASTY → FADE TO BLACK, Jason Cerbone *(Mike O)*, Kevin Carroll *(Larry)*, Paul Sado *(Johnnie)*, Michael Rapaport *(Mike E)* ← the BASKETBALL DIARIES / → DEATH OF A DYNASTY, Charles Q. Murphy *(Johnson)* ← MURDER WAS THE CASE ← CB4: THE MOVIE ← JUNGLE FEVER / → DEATH OF A DYNASTY → ROLL BOUNCE, Kamal Ahmed *(store owner)*, Stacey Dash *(Tamika)*, Angie Martinez *(parole officer)* ← BROWN SUGAR ← RIDE, **Ralph E. Tresvant** *(cameo)* ← HOUSE PARTY 2 ← KRUSH GROOVE / → BROWN SUGAR, **Cam'ron** *(masked gunman)*, **Capone** *(himself)* → DEATH OF A DYNASTY, **Victor Santiago** *(himself)* ← PRISON SONG / → STILL NOT A PLAYER, **JAY-Z** *(himself)*, **Jimmy Jones** *(himself)* → BEEF 3, **Yo-Yo** *(herself)* ← WHO'S THE MAN?, **Lil' Cease** *(himself)*

Storyline: Originally written as a drama, the comedy plot revolves around rookie crook Shawn, a ghetto guy trying very hard to be a burglar and succeed in the world of crime – all this just to feed and clothe his child and girlfriend. The Hip-Hop world around him also has center stage. *MCS*

Movie rating: *5

Visual: straight-to-video + dvd (no audio OST)

Off the record: Cam'ron (Giles) was a New York rapper with two Top 20 sets behind him, 'Confessions Of Fire' (1998) and 'S.D.E.' (2000). Kiam **Capone** Holley (ex-QB Finest) and Victor **Noreaga** Santiago were part of rap duo, Capone-n-Noreaga, who had two US Top 40 albums, 'The War Report' (1997) and 'The Reunion' (2000). NY rapper, **Jim Jones**, subsequently broke into the US Top 20 with albums, 'On My Way To Church' (2004), 'Harlem: Diary Of A Summer' (2005) and 'Hustler's P.O.M.E. (Product Of My Environment)' (2006), the latter containing massive hit single, 'We Fly High'. **Yo-Yo** is hip-hop star Yolanda Whitaker. Kamal was one-half of phone-in comedy duo, the Jerky Boys. *MCS*

PARADISE, HAWAIIAN STYLE

1966 (US 91m) Paramount Pictures (G)

Film genre: romantic Rock'n'roll Musical

Top guns: dir: Michael Moore → the FASTEST GUITAR ALIVE / s-w: Allan Weiss ← ROUSTABOUT ← FUN IN ACAPULCO ← GIRLS! GIRLS! GIRLS! ← BLUE HAWAII / → EASY COME, EASY GO, Anthony Lawrence ← ROUSTABOUT / → EASY COME, EASY GO → ELVIS: THE MOVIE

Stars: Elvis PRESLEY *(Greg "Rick" Richards)*, Suzanna Leigh *(Judy Hudson / Friday)* → SON OF DRACULA, James Shigeta *(Danny Kohana)*, Irene Tsu *(Pua)* → THREE THE HARD WAY, Donna Butterworth *(Jan Kohana)*, Marianna Hill *(Lani Kaimana)* ← ROUSTABOUT, Linda Wong *(Lehua Kawena)*, Jan Shepard *(Betty Kohana)* ← KING CREOLE, Edy Williams *(brunette girl)* → GOOD TIMES → BEYOND THE VALLEY OF THE DOLLS, John Doucette *(Donald Belden)* → the FASTEST GUITAR ALIVE, Mary Treen *(Mrs. Belden)* ← FUN IN ACAPULCO ← GIRLS! GIRLS! GIRLS!, Julie Parrish *(Joanna)* ← WINTER A-GO-GO, Philip Ahn *(Moki Kaimana)* → JONATHAN LIVINGSTON SEAGULL

Storyline: Womanising pilot Rick returns to Hawaii to set up a tourist helicopter service after being suspended from commercial flying. Of course, he's not averse to a bit of singing on the side, although this doesn't help his ailing business. *BG*

Movie rating: *3.5

Visual: video + dvd

Off the record: nothing

—

ELVIS PRESLEY (composers: Joseph Lilley, etc.)

Jul 66. (lp; mono/stereo) *R.C.A.; <LSP 3643> (RD/SF 7810)* 15 7
– Paradise, Hawaiian style / Queenie Wahine's papaya / Scratch my back (then I'll scratch yours) / Drums of the islands / Datin' / A dog's life / House of sand / Stop where you are / This is my heaven / Sand castles. *(re-iss. Aug80 on 'RCA Int.'; INTS 5037) (re-iss. Apr84 lp/c; NL/NK 89010) (cd-iss. Jul04 on 'Follow That Dream'+=; FTD 1009) – (extra takes).*

S/track review: While the slack-key guitar and Polynesian atmospherics aren't laid on quite so thickly, it's difficult to regard this soundtrack as anything other than a poor cousin to 'BLUE HAWAII'. There really isn't much on the songwriting front to commend this record (there wasn't even a single release), and it falls down on both the music and the words, not to mention the poor sound quality; granted, the songs on ELVIS' Hollywood efforts have never exactly been known for their lyrical wit, but this album plumbs new depths, particularly with nudge-nudge wink-wink nonsense like 'Queen Wahine's Papaya'. In fact, the best thing about this record is probably the snatches of tropical percussion, as heard in the title track and 'Drums Of The Island'. This was the third ELVIS film in only six months and it showed; the level of creative jetlag suggested its authors had bypassed Hawaii and gone all the way to Easter Island. *BG*

Album rating: *4

PAROLES ET MUSIQUE

aka 'Words And Music'; US-title 'LOVE SONGS' in 1986

1984 (Fra/Can 107m) 7 Films Cinema / Spectrafilm

Film genre: romantic melodrama

Top guns: s-w + dir: Elie Chouraqui

Stars: Catherine Deneuve *(Margaux)* → JE VOUS AIME → POLA X → DANCER IN THE DARK, Christophe Lambert *(Jeremy)* → JANIS ET JOHN, Richard Anconina *(Michel)*, Jacques Perrin *(Yves)*, Dayle Haddon *(Corinne)* ← MADAME CLAUDE, Nick Mancuso *(Peter)* ← BLAME IT ON THE NIGHT ← HEARTBREAKERS / → NIGHT MAGIC → BRAVE NEW GIRL → IN THE MIX, Charlotte Gainsbourg *(Charlotte Marker)*, Dominique Lavanant *(Florence)*

Storyline: Music promoter Margaux's unhappy marriage looks like finally ending when hubby stomps off to New York to write a book and singer Jeremy steps into his shoes. She hides her affair from her children who nevertheless leave her too and go after dad. Meanwhile, Jeremy's musical partner Michel gets a chance of stardom after a successful audition, and things come to a head for Jeremy when he must choose between moping Margaux or his curtailed career. *JZ*

Movie rating: *4.5

Visual: video

Off the record: Gene McDaniels writes some songs for Guy Thomas (voice of Jeremy) or Terry Lauber (voice of Michel) to sing. Charlotte is the London-born daughter of SERGE GAINSBOURG and Jane Birkin. *MCS*

—

MICHEL LeGRAND

Jun 84. (lp) *WEA; (240578-1)* – French –
– From the heart / We can dance / One more moment (ouverture) / Human race / Theme (3) / One more moment / Leave it to me / Theme (12) / I'm with you now / Psychic flash. *<US-iss.Nov86 on 'Silva Screen'; STV 81258>*

S/track review: (see future orchestral edition)

Album rating: unknown

Dolly PARTON

Born: 19 Jan'46, Sevierville, Tennessee, USA. A grand dame of country, DOLLY PARTON remains the genre's most visible female figurehead, a seemingly shining example of the American Dream's rags to riches promise. It's a story compellingly told in some of her more autobiographical songs, songs which have also marked her out as one of country's most talented female writers, as well as performers. After battling through the early years and developing an impressive solo career alongside an apprenticeship with Porter Wagoner, Dolly went her own way in the mid-70s, veering ever more into pop crossover territory as the decade drew to a close. By 1980, she'd become a Las Vegas mainstay, diversifying still further into acting and film composing. Her wisecracking part opposite Jane Fonda and Lily Tomlin, in feminist comedy '9 To 5' (1980) was sufficiently well received to secure her a starring role in the screen version of Broadway musical, 'The BEST LITTLE WHOREHOUSE IN TEXAS' (1982). Dolly composed the themes for both movies, with the classic '9 To 5' single topping both the US pop and country charts. Another starring role, this time opposite Sylvester Stallone in 'RHINESTONE' (1984), wasn't quite so successful, nor was the soundtrack, her first attempt at scoring a full movie. Although it'd be another five years before she returned to the big screen, she again put in a noteable performance in the film version of stage play 'Steel Magnolias' (1989), another comedy vehicle where she essentially played herself and made creative capital out of her own downhome personality. DOLLY's acting career continued into the early 90s with starring roles in 'STRAIGHT TALK' (1992), for which she also composed the score, and Penelope Spheeris' film version of US TV series 'The Beverly Hillbillies' (1993), in which she really did play herself. Since then she's worked solely in TV, although who needs Hollywood when you have Dollywood(?!), a perennially popular Smoky Mountain theme park which the shrewd singer added to her bulging business portfolio in the mid-80s. *BG*

- **filmography** (composer) {acting} –

9 To 5 *(1980 {*} hit theme on OST)* / **the Best Little Whorehouse In Texas** *(1982 {*} OST w/ V/A =>)* / **Rhinestone** *(1984 {*} OST =>)* / Captain Kangaroo And His Friends *(1985 TV {a})* / a Smoky Mountain Christmas *(1986 TV {*})* / Steel Magnolias *(1989 {*})* / Wild Texas Wind *(1991 TV {*})* / **Straight Talk** *(1992 {*} OST =>)* / the Beverly Hillbillies *(1993 {a})* / Love Can Build A Bridge *(1995 TV {a})* / Unlikely Angel *(1996 TV {*})* / **Jackie's Back** *(1999 {a} =>)* / **Blue Valley Songbird** *(1999 TV {*} =>)* / Frank McKlusky, C.I. *(2002 {a})*

□ the PARTRIDGE FAMILY segment
(⇒ COME ON, GET HAPPY . . .

PAYDAY

1973 (US 102m) Fantasy Films / Cinerama Releasing Corporation (R)

Film genre: Country-music melodrama

Top guns: dir: Daryl Duke / s-w: Don Carpenter

Stars: Rip Torn *(Maury Dann)* ← YOU'RE A BIG BOY NOW / →

ONE-TRICK PONY → SONGWRITER → FLASHPOINT → WHERE THE RIVERS FLOW NORTH → the INSIDER, Ahna Capri *(Mayleen Travis)* ← the GIRLS ON THE BEACH, Elayne Heilveil *(Rosamond McClintock)*, Michael C. Gwynne *(Clarence McGinty)* → PRIVATE PARTS, Jeff Morris *(Bob Tally)* ← KID GALAHAD / → the BLUES BROTHERS → the BORDER → BLUES BROTHERS 2000, Cliff 'Fatty' Emmich *(Chicago)*, Henry O. Arnold *(Ted)*

Storyline: Maury Dann is finding it hard to keep his career as a C&W singer on the straight and narrow. While on stage he may be "a good ol' boy" his true character only comes to light once the show is over. He hires and fires colleagues at will, changes girlfriends at the drop of a hat and is not averse to throwing a punch or two. Drink and drugs are also on the agenda and it's not long before things begin to get out of control. *JZ*

Movie rating: *6.5

Visual: video (no audio OST; add. score: ED BOGAS)

Off the record: Songs featured in the movie were mainly by SHEL SILVERSTEIN ('She's Only A Country Girl', 'Slowly Fadin' Circle', 'Lovin' You More' & 'Baby Here's A Dime'), TOMMY McKINNEY ('Road To Nashville' & 'Flatland') plus IAN & SYLVIA ('Payday'). *MCS*

PELVIS

1977 (US 84m) Funky Films / William Mishkin Motion Pictures (R)

Film genre: seXual showbiz/Pop-music spoof/comedy

Top guns: dir: Robert T. Megginson / s-w: Straw Weisman

Stars: Luther Bud Whaney *(Pelvis)*, Mary Mitchell *(Betty Lu)*, Bobby Astyr *(Snake Gianetti)* → HONEYSUCKLE ROSE, Chris Thomas *(Candy)*, Cindy Tree *(Susie)*, Billy Padgett *(Rev.)*, Carol Baxter *(Skate)*

Storyline: Pelvis (a sort of youthful country version of Elvis) relocates to New York and is "mis"-guided into the world of glam-rock. Peeved off by the music industry as a whole, his world becomes one big roller-coaster ride as his life becomes a joke. Tagged "Where what goes on usually comes off" describes what the movie becomes. *MCS*

Movie rating: *4

Visual: video as 'TOGA PARTY'

Off the record: Bobby Astyr was known as "the Clown Prince Of Porno".

PERFORMANCE

1970 (UK 105m w/b&w) Warner Bros. Pictures (X)

Film genre: psychological/experimental drama

Top guns: dir: Nicolas Roeg, Donald Cammell (+ s-w)

Stars: James Fox *(Chas Devlin)* → ABSOLUTE BEGINNERS, **Mick Jagger** *(Turner)* <= the ROLLING STONES =>, Anita Pallenberg *(Pherber)* ← CANDY ← WONDERWALL / → le BERCEAU DE CRISTAL, Michele Breton *(Lucy)*, Ann Sidney *(Dana)*, Josh Binden *(Moody)* → QUADROPHENIA, Stanley Meadows *(Rosebloom)*, Allan Cuthbertson *(the lawyer)*, Johnny Shannon *(Harry Flowers)* → THAT'LL BE THE DAY → FLAME → ABSOLUTE BEGINNERS, Anthony Valentine *(Joey Maddocks)* → the MONSTER CLUB, John Sterland *(chauffeur)*, Ken Colley *(Tony Farrell)* → FLAME → LISZTOMANIA → RETURN TO WATERLOO, Billy Murray *(thug 1)* ← UP THE JUNCTION ← WHAT A CRAZY WORLD / → ROCK FOLLIES → McVICAR

Storyline: Donald Cammell and Nicolas Roeg's masterpiece takes a still Swinging London as the backdrop to its unsettling, claustrophobic study of sexual identity. Mick Jagger revels in the role of Turner, a rock star turned reclusive junkie who takes in Chas, a hard man on the run. Far from enjoying the decadent pleasures of Turner's mansion, Chas finds himself at the mercy of his host's penetrating mind games. *BG*

Movie rating: *6.5

Visual: video + dvd

Off the record: Anita Pallenberg (who had simulated sex on screen with **Mick Jagger**) was actually the girlfriend of another 'Stone, Keith Richards.

Various Artists (score: JACK NITZSCHE *)

Sep 70. (lp) *Warners; (WS 2554) <BS 1846>*
– Gone dead train (*) / Performance (MERRY CLAYTON) / Get away (RY COODER) / Powis Square (RY COODER) / Rolls Royce and acid (*) / Dyed, dead, red (BUFFY SAINTE-MARIE) / Harry Flowers (*) / Memo from Turner (MICK JAGGER) / The hashishin (BUFFY SAINTE-MARIE & RY COODER) / Wake up, niggers (the LAST POETS) / Poor white hound dog (MERRY CLAYTON) / Natural magic (*) / Turner's murder (the MERRY CLAYTON SINGERS). *(<cd-iss. Oct93; 7599 26400-2>)*

S/track review: Even the most casual glance at JAGGER's elegantly wasted cover shot tells you that the Mick/Keef contribution, 'Memo From Turner', is going to be of the vintage variety. A bluesy, low-slung, semi-spoken monologue with reliably sordid lyrics, it plays like an excerpt from 'Beggars Banquet' minus the Deep South affectations. Listen closely and you'll hear Mick trying to stifle laughter. It must've been contagious: RANDY NEWMAN is also at it on 'Gone Dead Train', perhaps amused at himself and his uncharacteristic – and actually pretty impressive – rock freak-out. If this suggests boisterous studio shenanigans, don't be fooled; composer JACK NITZSCHE's material is often as unsettling as the movie itself, employing trippy studio effects, ethnic percussion and unusual arrangements like mouth bow and dulcimer for some seriously spaced-out ear candy. RY COODER contributes typically prodigious bottleneck slide, MERRY CLAYTON and BUFFY SAINTE-MARIE supply disturbingly disembodied vocals, while the LAST POETS' proto-rap sermon, 'Wake Up Niggers', is about as far ahead of its time as it was possible to be in 1970. *BG*

Album rating: *7.5

– spinoff hits, etc. –

MICK JAGGER: Memo From Turner / JACK NITZSCHE: Natural Magic

Nov 70. (7") *Decca; (F 13067)* 32 –

PERMISSIVE

1970 (UK 86m) Tigon Film Distributors Ltd. (18)

Film genre: Faux documentary-style drama

Top guns: dir: Lindsay Shonteff / s-w: Jeremy Craig Dryden

Stars: Maggie Stride *(Suzy)*, Gilbert Wynne *(Jimi)*, Gay Singleton *(Fiona)*, Robert Daubigny *(Pogo)*, Madeleine Collinson *(groupie)* → GROUPIE GIRL, Mary Collinson *(groupie)* → GROUPIE GIRL, **Forever More:- Stuart Francis** *(Kip)*, **Alan Gorrie** *(Lee)*, **Mick Travis** *(Mick)*, **Onnie Mair** *(Onnie)*, Nicola Austine *(groupie)*, Maria Frost *(groupie)*, Samantha Bond *(groupie)*, **Titus Groan:- Stuart Cowell** *(Rick/performer)*, **Tony Priestland** *(performer)*, **Jim Toomey** *(performer)*, **John Lee** *(performer)*

Storyline: London's groupie scene and the swinging sixties is at the crux (or crutch!) of this morality tale about two young girls and a new generation of free love and music. *MCS*

Movie rating: *3.5

Visual: video on Jezebel Films Ltd. (no audio score by COMUS)

Off the record: Forver More were a folk-styled blues quartet from Dundee, Scotland; they contributed several tracks, 'Beautiful Afternoon', 'Good To Me', 'Home Country Blues', 'Sylvester's Last Voyage' and 'We Sing', all available on their debut LP, 'Yours Forever More' (on 'R.C.A.'); Onnie Mair and Alan Gorrie eventually formed Average White Band. Mervyn Peake-inspired Prog-rockers, **Titus Groan**, performed a live version of 'Can't Find

The Words To Say', a lengthy track NOT available on their eponymous LP (for 'Dawn' records). *MCS*

□ PET SHOP BOYS segment (⇒ IT COULDN'T HAPPEN HERE)

PHANTOM OF THE PARADISE

1974 (US 92m) Twentieth Century-Fox Film Corporation (PG)

Film genre: Pop/Rock Musical horror/satire

Top guns: s-w + dir: Brian De Palma

Stars: Paul Williams *(Swan)* ← WATERMELON MAN / → the DOORS, William Finley *(Winslow Leach / The Phantom)*, Jessica Harper *(Phoenix)* → SUSPIRIA → SHOCK TREATMENT, George Memmoli *(Philbin)*, Gerrit Graham *(Beef)* → WALKER → SHAKE, RATTLE & ROCK! tv, **Ray Kennedy** *(Beef's singing voice)*, Dennis Olivieri *(reporter)* ← the NAKED APE / → FORBIDDEN ZONE, Adam Wade *(reporter)* ← CLAUDINE ← GORDON'S WAR ← ACROSS 110th STREET ← COME BACK, CHARLESTON BLUE ← SHAFT, the Undead:- Harold Oblong *(vocals)* / the Juicy Fruits:- Archie Hahn *(vocals)* / the Beach Bums:- Jeffrey Comanor *(vocals)*, **Keith Allison** *(country & western singer)*

Storyline: It was only a matter of time before the idea of silent classics, 'The Phantom Of The Opera' and 'Faust', would fuse together to become this fully-fledged "Rock Opera". "He Sold His Soul For Rock And Roll" was its Black Sabbath-esque tagline, but this was director Brian De Palma's vision. Updating the plot somewhat, we have loner composer, Winslow Leach, writing his masterwork, only to be thwarted by plagiarist Swan, who steals his music for a production at his palace, Paradise. Just as the rightful composer meets the beautiful Phoenix, he's unlawfully imprisoned due to the scheming Swan. When Winslow escapes, he sets up trying to destroy Swan's recording plant, but things go awry when he's disfigured in the process. *MCS*

Movie rating: *6.5

Visual: video + dvd

Off the record: Keith Allison (cousin of Crickets drummer, Jerry Allison) was a member of Paul Revere & The Raiders and went on to be a session man for Monkees offshoot, 'Dolenz, Jones, Boyce & Hart. *MCS*

Various Cast & (composer/score: PAUL WILLIAMS)

Dec 74. (lp/c) *A&M; <SP/CS 3176>* □ □
– Goodbye Eddie, goodbye (the JUICY FRUITS) / Faust (BILL FINLEY) / Upholstery (the BEACH BUMS) / Special to me (Phoenix audition song) (JESSICA HARPER) / Phantom's theme (beauty and the beast) (PAUL WILLIAMS) / Somebody super like you (beef construction song) (UNDEAD) / Life at last (RAY KENNEDY) / Old souls (JESSICA HARPER) / Faust (PAUL WILLIAMS) / The hell of it (PAUL WILLIAMS). *(UK-iss.Jan89; same) <cd-iss. Jun98; CD 69831>*

S/track review: PAUL WILLIAMS – a guy more at home writing for the likes of the Carpenters and Three Dog Night – was commissioned to score this pastiche rock'n'roll score. Sources mainly stemmed from 50s doo-wop & 70s glam-pop – think Zappa, the Rubettes and Flo & Eddie – while others were typical WILLIAMS-styled love ballads. Opener, 'Goodbye, Eddie, Goodbye' (featuring ARCHIE HAHN on vocals), was of the former "Bop Showaddy" ilk, while 'Old Souls' (sung by 'Rhoda' actress, JESSICA HARPER) is of the latter style, very Carpenters 'Rainy Days And Mondays' and 'We've Only Just Begun'. HARPER also lent her vocal chords to 'Special To Me (Phoenix Audition Song)', a song remarkable in that it sounds like a 1975 Fleetwood Mac (w/ Buckingham-Nicks!); maybe they all shared a studio or something, who knows. The sinister and indeed "Faustian" 'Faust', was delivered in two parts, the shorter, quirkier version by BILL FINLEY, and the laid back country-funk 5-minutes by WILLIAMS himself. 'Upholstery' (by the BEACH BUMS) was very – as you can predict – all surf on the crest of a Brian Wilson wave, the fun, fun, fun coming via its whimsical, lispy vox; "Upholstery . . . when my baby sits up close to me" is in its own lyrical wonderland. We get all sentimental for The Phantom Of The Opera-ish, 'Phantom's Theme (Beauty And The Beast)' – and why not! – singer-songwriter WILLIAMS at ease performing at the piano, only Elton and Nilsson could do better. The UNDEAD (featuring actor HAROLD OBLONG) were up next, 'Somebody Super Like You (Beef Construction Song)' very Alice Cooper circa late 60s, while 'Life At Last' (vocals courtesy of future KGB supergrouper, RAY KENNEDY) was Little Shop Of Horrors before its time. 'The Hell Of It' closed the show, a nostalgic, campy resolution, better all – like most of the LP – witnessed in front of the DVD/TV. It was no surprise that the similarly-themed 'ROCKY HORROR PICTURE SHOW' (1975) movie was next in line, music not too distanced from this effective slice of operatic shenanighans. *MCS*

Album rating: *6.5

– spinoff singles, etc. –

JESSICA HARPER: Old Souls / PAUL WILLIAMS: The Hell Of It

May 75. (7") *(AMS 7166)* □ □

the PHYNX

1970 (US 81m) Cinema Organization / Warner Bros. Pictures (PG)

Film genre: Pop-Rock Musical spy spoof

Top guns: dir: Lee H. Katzin / s-w: Stan Cornyn (story: Bob Booker & George Foster)

Stars: the Phynx:- Michael A. Miller, Lonnie Stevens *, Dennis Larden, Ray Chippeway *(themselves/performers)* * ← UP TIGHT!, Lou Antonio *(Corrigan)*, Mike Kellin *(Bogey)* → the JAZZ SINGER, Michael Ansara *(Col. Rostinov)* ← HARUM SCARUM, George Tobias *(Markevitch)*, Joan Blondell *(Ruby)* ← STAY AWAY, JOE ← ADVANCE TO THE REAR / → GREASE, Martha Raye *(Foxy)*, Larry Hankin *(Philbaby)* → STEELYARD BLUES → AMERICAN HOT WAX, Ruby Keeler *(herself)*, Maureen O'Sullivan *(herself)*, Ed Sullivan *(himself)* ← BYE BYE BIRDIE / → the COMPLEAT BEATLES → ELVIS BY THE PRESLEYS, **James BROWN** *(performer)*, Joe Louis *(himself)*, Guy Lombardo *(himself)*, Richard Pryor *(himself)* ← WILD IN THE STREETS / → YOU'VE GOT TO WALK IT . . . → LADY SINGS THE BLUES → WATTSTAX → the MACK → ADIOS AMIGO → CAR WASH → the WIZ → BUSTIN" LOOSE, Rudy Vallee *(himself)*, Johnny Weissmuller *(himself)*, Dorothy Lamour *(herself)*, **Trini Lopez** *(performer)*, Dick Clark *(himself)* ← WILD IN THE STREETS ← JAMBOREE / → DEADMAN'S CURVE, Busby Berkeley *(himself)*, Butterfly McQueen *(herself)*, Xavier Cugat *(himself)*, Pat O'Brien *(himself)*, Patty Andrews *(herself)*

Storyline: A mix'n'match of runaway ideas and people take center stage in this rock'n'roll spy movie featuring a fictitious quartet, the Phynx. On a secret mission from the U.S. Intelligence (S.S.A.), they tour beyond the Iron Curtain (Albania), where a madman of a general is kidnapping celebrities. Mental indeed and a Golden Turkey. *MCS*

Movie rating: *3

Visual: video (no audio OST)

Off the record: In between a plethora of vintage celebrity actors, sportsmen and old-time performers (Xavier Cugat, Rudy Vallee, Patty Andrews, etc.), there were a few post-rock'n'roll acts such as **JAMES BROWN** and **Trini Lopez**. The latter folk-pop singer/guitarist was born Trinidad Lopez III in Dallas, Texas (15 May'37) and was discovered by Frank Sinatra, who signed him to 'Reprise' records. Trini had several US Top 50 hits, including the Pete Seeger-penned, 'If I Had A Hammer' and 'Kansas City', both in 1963. Songs in the film were provided by Mike Stoller (he of Leiber-Stoller/Elvis fame):- 'What Is Your Sign?', etc. *MCS*

the PICK OF DESTINY

aka TENACIOUS D in: THE PICK OF DESTINY

2006 (US 93m) New Line Cinema (R)

Film genre: Rock Musical comedy/road movie

Top guns: s-w: (+ dir) **Liam Lynch**, Jack Black, Kyle Gass

Stars: Jack Black *(JB)* ← SCHOOL OF ROCK ← HIGH FIDELITY ← DEAD MAN WALKING / → WALK HARD: THE DEWEY COX STORY, Kyle Gass *(KG)* ← CAKE BOY ← THAT DARN PUNK, Jason Reed *(Lee)*, **Ronnie James Dio** *(himself)* ← METAL: A HEADBANGER'S JOURNEY, Troy Gentile *(lil' JB)*, Paul F. Tompkins *(open mic host)*, Ned Bellamy *(security guard #1)*, **Fred Armisen** *(security guard #2)* ← I AM TRYING TO BREAK YOUR HEART, Tim Robbins *(the stranger)* ← HIGH FIDELITY ← JUNGLE FEVER ← TAPEHEADS ← HOWARD THE DUCK, **Dave Grohl** *(Satan)* ← FREE TIBET ← 1991: THE YEAR PUNK BROKE, Ben Stiller *(guitar store guy)* ← AWESOME: I FUCKIN' SHOT THAT! ← BLACK AND WHITE ← REALITY BITES, **MEAT LOAF** *(Bud Black)*, John C. Reilly *(Sasquatch)* ← MAGNOLIA ← BOOGIE NIGHTS ← GEORGIA / → WALK HARD: THE DEWEY COX STORY

Storyline: A simple story about two simple rock wannabes (JB and KG), who go on an epic quest to find a magical guitar plectrum, er.. the Pick. They (Tenacious D) aspire to attain musical immortality and take their destiny as the greatest rock band of all time. JB's breakaway from his mid-western, christian roots to Venice Beach, California (where he meets slacker, KG), seems a distance from the "heavy-metal" fire-and-brimstone he garners along the way. *MCS*

Movie rating: *6.5

Visual: dvd

Off the record: **TENACIOUS D** (see below). **Liam Lynch** had a novelty Top 10 hit late in 2002 with 'United States Of Whatever' (a track from the album 'Fake Songs' 2003). **Ronnie James Dio** was ex-singer of Dio, etc. **Dave Grohl** Foo Fighters (see 'TOUCH' entry).

TENACIOUS D (score: Andrew Gross & John King)

Nov 06. (cd) *Sony; <94891> Columbia; (88697 00737-2)* [8] [10]
– Kickapoo / Classico / Baby / Destiny / History / The government totally sucks / Master exploder / The divide / Papagenu (he's my sassafrass) / Dude (I totally miss you) / Break in city (storm the gate!) / Car chase city / Beelzeboss (the final showdown) / POD / The metal.

S/track review: JACK BLACK has had a chequered career of late ('Nacho Libre' & 'King Kong') since his rise to fame via two Rock-music-orientated movies, 'HIGH FIDELITY' (2000) & 'SCHOOL OF ROCK' (2003). The resurrection of TENACIOUS D – with sterling sidekick KYLE GASS – through 'The PICK OF DESTINY' was as much anticipated as the TV episodes that spanned American TV into the latter years of the 90s; and who could forget their self-acclaimed "Greatest Song On Earth", 'Tribute'. The latter Satan-baiting, hard-rock gem, should've, could've, would've, been a worthy addition to this set (or the movie for that matter), although their er ... "one-joke" MTV-playlisted-to-death video had weathered the storm reasonably well. If your humour stretches from 'THIS IS SPINAL TAP' – an inspiration to JB since its release to the public in 1984 – and Monty Python, then from track one, 'Kickapoo' (featuring MEAT LOAF and RONNIE JAMES DIO), you're going to be slapping your thighs while trying to play acoustic air-guitar – heads down, no nonsense boogie as the Albertos Y Lost Trios Paranoia once chorused. In a complete contrast, the one-minute 'Classico' was indeed another to "f-ing rock your f-ing roll", albeit with a touch of Beethoven ('Fleur De Lys') and Mozart. TENACIOUS D get into their singer-songwriter mood with the Neil Young-esque, 'Baby', but just as it gets into gear – like most of the tracks – it stops short at 1 1/2 minutes; the half-minute 'Destiny' is virtually a Metallica soundbite. The self-explanatory, 'History', truly rides the rock'n'roll horse as the Two Horsemen Of The Apocalypse, more 1-2-3 than an A-Z. The rest of the album is standard AC/DC-ish rock ('Break-In City (Storm The Gate!)' & 'Car Chase City') with at times a capital R, although JACK BLACK surpasses himself as one of music's affective vocalists – just listen to 'Master Exploder' for the evidence. His influences are all over the shop by 'Papagenu (He's My Sassafrass)', a sort of Cheech & Chong-meets-Zappa, while 'Dude (I Totally Miss You)' gets melancholic to the Nth degree. The monster-truck of the bunch comes courtesy of "rude-imentary" epic, 'Beelzeboss (The Final Showdown)', probably the best song Iron Maiden and Alice Cooper never recorded – and just listen to each rock-tastic crescendo! It's just a pity it didn't end there as 'POD' and 'The Metal' were poor cousins to Sabbath and Priest. Nevertheless, JB and KG are without doubt the new comic kings of 21st Century Rock. *MCS*

Album rating: *7

– spinoff hits, etc. –

TENACIOUS D: POD / (non-OST song; Kong)

Nov 06. (7"pic-d) *(88697 03027-2)* [ ] [24]
(cd-s) *(88697 02961-2)* – ('A') / Master exploder / Training medley / ('A'-video).

□ Bobby PICKETT segment
(⇒ MONSTER MASH: THE MOVIE)

PINK AS THE DAY SHE WAS BORN

1997 (US 90m*) Global Entertainment Network Inc. (18)

Film genre: seXual Rock'n'roll-music comedy

Top guns: dir: Steve Hall / s-w: **Linda Perry**, Cathee Wilkins

Stars: Alanna Ubach *(Cherry)* → 30 DAYS UNTIL I'M FAMOUS, Nicole Eggert *(Tiffany)* → THANK YOU, GOOD NIGHT, Christine Harnos *(Rhonda)*, Bojesse Christopher *(Nick)*, Margaret Cho *(Donna)*, Jay R. Ferguson *(Brad)* → GIRL, Susan Tyrrell *(Lana)* ← CRY-BABY ← ROCKULA ← TAPEHEADS ← SUBWAY RIDERS ← FORBIDDEN ZONE ← CATCH MY SOUL / → MASKED AND ANONYMOUS, Andrew Shaifer *(Mark)*, Ogie Zuletta *(Tim)*, Saul Stein *(Bad Baby)* → HE GOT GAME, Mink Stole *(Vera)* ← MONSTER MASH: THE MOVIE ← CRY-BABY ← HAIRSPRAY / → SPLENDOR, **Stuart D. Johnson** *(J.D.)*, **Les Claypool** *(Stevie)* ← WOODSTOCK 94 ← BILL & TED'S BOGUS JOURNEY / → WE SOLD OUR SOULS FOR ROCK 'N ROLL → RISING LOW → ELECTRIC APRICOT: QUEST FOR FESTEROO

Storyline: Young rock singer Cherry leaves dusty Arizona for the bright lights and stardom of L.A. However, no band is interested in taking her on and so to support herself she is forced to take on a job in a sex parlour, where she must pander to the quirky whims of the customers. It remains to be seen if she can dominate the music business as well as she dominates in her other job. *JZ*

Movie rating: *2.5

Visual: none (no audio OST)

Off the record: **Linda Perry** is one of the top songwriters in the business and was formerly the leader of 4 Non Blondes. Drummer **Stuart D. Johnson** sessioned for JOHN DOE and Matthew Sweet and subsequently joined alt-rockers, Simon Dawes. **Les Claypool** was leader of Primus.

the PIRATE MOVIE

1982 (Aus 105m; cut to 98m US) Joseph Hamilton International (PG)

Film genre: romantic Rock-"opera" Musical comedy/adventure

Top guns: dir: Ken Annakin / s-w: Trevor Farrant (operetta: William S. Gilbert)

Stars: Kristy McNichol *(Mabel)*, Christopher Atkins *(Frederic)*, Ted Hamilton *(the pirate king)*, Bill Kerr *(Major-General)* → SWEET TALKER, Maggie Kirkpatrick *(Ruth)*, Garry McDonald *(sergeant/inspector)* → MOULIN ROUGE → RABBIT-PROOF FENCE, Chuck McKinney *(Samuel)* → SHOUT! THE STORY OF JOHNNY O'KEEFE

Storyline: Disaster strikes for poor Mabel when she literally misses the boat at a pirate festival on the beach. Undeterred, she commandeers a small boat and sets off after her friends – only to be shipwrecked in a storm. Lying unconscious, she imagines herself in a real pirate adventure as she tries to recover her father's treasure from the Pirate King with the help of Pirate of Penzance, Frederick. She and Frederick fall in love (inevitably) but Frederick must choose between a life on the high seas or his beloved. *JZ*

Movie rating: *3.5

Visual: video on CBS-Fox

Off the record: nothing

—

Various Cast (score: Peter Sullivan & orchestra *)

Aug 82. (d-lp) *Polydor; (POLD 5074) <PD 2-9503>* ☐ ☐
– Victory (the PIRATES feat. MIKE BRADY) / First love (KRISTY McNICHOL & CHRISTOPHER ATKINS) / How can I live without her? (CHRISTOPHER ATKINS) / Hold on (KRISTY McNICHOL) / We are the pirates (IAN MASON) / Pumpin' and blowin' (KRISTY McNICHOL) / Stand up and sing (KOOL AND THE GANG) / Happy ending (the PETER CUPPLES BAND) / The chase (*) / (The Pirate Movie) I am a pirate king (TED HAMILTON & the PIRATES) // Happy ending (the cast) / The Chinese battle (*) / (The Pirate Movie) The modern Major General's song (BILL KERR & the cast) / We are the pirates (the PIRATES feat. TED HAMILTON) / Medley (*) / (The Pirate Movie) Tarantara (GARRY McDONALD & the policemen) / The duel (*) / The sisters' song (the SISTERS) / Pirates, police and pizza (*) / Come friends, who plough the sea (TED HAMILTON & THE PIRATES).

S/track review: For the first half of this OTT double-LP, there is little to take you into the world of (bar 'I Am The Pirate King') Gilbert & Sullivan and their 'The Pirates Of Penzance'. The second disc is rather different, when the ghost-like opera bards get into the full orchestral swing of things, courtesy of update takes on 'The Modern Major General's Song', 'Medley', 'Tarantara', 'The Sister's Song' and 'Come Friends, Who Plough The Sea', albeit with the aid of conductor/arranger, Peter Sullivan (any relation?) and "The Pirate King" himself, actor TED HAMILTON. Yes, a ship of two halves, and enough to "shiver me timbers". On the other hand (on sides 1 & 2), they steer a long way away from the olde shores of Penzance – but not so as to drift out to sea completely – the whole thing was mostly recorded in Melbourne, Australia. Side one, track one, 'Victory' sees the PIRATES/the cast shout it all out, while there's a guitar riff very reminiscent of something else I just can't put my finger on – for now. 'First Love', is the er . . . the first of many Donny & Marie-like love ballad duets by CHRISTOPHER ATKINS and KRISTY McNICHOL, while there's plenty of solo heartstring-pullers from the young actors/singers. The man behind the songs is TERRY BRITTEN, one-time compadre of Glenn Shorrock (Little River Band) while both members of 60s outfit, the Twilights; other writers featured are:- Kit Hain, Sue Shifrin and B.A. "Bang Bang" Robertson. With all these songsmiths on board the good ship, how could it fail? But it did. Possibly it was all a bit déjà vu, with disco one plundering the styles of Chicago, Foreigner, Styx, etc. 'The PIRATE MOVIE's saving grace is undoubtedly KOOL & THE GANG track, 'Stand Up And Sing', plus side 1 anthem, 'We Are The Pirates', the latter having three potions Alice Cooper, one dose Adam Ant. Embarrassingly good – now walk the plank you landlubbers! *MCS*

Album rating: *5

PLAY IT COOL

1962 (UK 82m b&w) Allied Artists

Film genre: Pop-Rock Musical drama

Top guns: dir: Michael Winner → DEATH WISH II → the WICKED LADY → SCREAM FOR HELP / s-w: Jack Henry

Stars: Billy Fury *(Billy Universe)* → I'VE GOTTA HORSE → THAT'LL BE THE DAY, Michael Anderson Jr. *(Alvin)*, Dennis Price *(Sir Charles Bryant)* → the MAGIC CHRISTIAN, Richard Wattis *(nervous man)* → UP JUMPED A SWAGMAN → BUNNY LAKE IS MISSING → WONDERWALL → TAKE ME HIGH, Anna Palk *(Ann)*, Ray Brooks *(Freddy)* → SOME PEOPLE, Jeremy Bullock *(Joey)* → SUMMER HOLIDAY → O LUCKY MAN!, Peter Barkworth *(Skinner)* → TWO A PENNY, Max Bacon *(Lotus proprietor)* → PRIVILEGE, Keith Hamshere *(Ring-a-Ding)*, Monte Landis *(beatnik man)* → WHAT A CRAZY WORLD → DOUBLE TROUBLE, **Helen Shapiro** *(performer)* ← IT'S TRAD, DAD!, **Bobby Vee** *(performer)* ← SWINGIN' ALONG / → JUST FOR FUN → C'MON, LET'S LIVE A LITTLE, **Shane Fenton** *(performer)* → IT'S ALL HAPPENING, **& the Fentones:- Bill Bonney, Tony Hinchcliffe, Jerry Wilcock** *(performers)*, **Danny Williams** *(performer)* → IT'S ALL HAPPENING, Bernie Winters *(Sydney Norman)* ← IDLE ON PARADE, Lionel Blair *(himself)* → a HARD DAY'S NIGHT → ABSOLUTE BEGINNERS, David Hemmings → SOME PEOPLE → LIVE IT UP → BE MY GUEST → BLOW-UP → PROFONDO ROSSO → la VIA DELLA DROGA

Storyline: Billy Universe & the Satellites head off to Brussels (to participate in a contest) after a series of successful gigs in London. En route, they meet up with Ann Bryant, whose relationship with another pop star, Larry Grainger, has been curtailed by her millionaire father. Director, Michael Winner's debut. *MCS*

Movie rating: *3.5

Visual: video (no audio OST)

Off the record: Billy Fury sings the bulk of the tracks, while **Helen Shapiro** performs 'I Don't Care' + 'To Cry My Heart Out For You'; **Bobby Vee** sings 'At A Time Like This'. **Shane Fenton** (& the Fentones) – with three UK Top 30 hits under their belt, 'I'm A Moody Guy', 'It's All Over Now' and 'Cindy's Birthday', contributed 'Like Magic' to the film; in 1973, he became Alvin Stardust and had several UK hits including 'My Coo-Ca-Choo' and the No.1 'Jealous Mind'. South African crooner **Danny Williams** whose biggest hit was a version of 'Moon River', supplied 'Who Can Say?'. *MCS*

– spinoff releases, etc. –

BILLY FURY: Once Upon A Dream / (non OST-song)

Jul 62. (7") *Decca; (F 11485)* 7 –

BILLY FURY: Play It Cool EP

Aug 62. (7"ep) *Decca; (DFE 6708)* ☐ –
– Play it cool / I think you're swell / Once upon a dream / Let's paint the town.

PLAYING FOR KEEPS

1986 (US 103m) Miramax Films (PG-13)

Film genre: coming-of-age comedy drama

Top guns: s-w + dir: Bob Weinstein, Harvey Weinstein ← the BURNING

Stars: Daniel Jordano *(Danny D'Angelo)*, Matthew Penn *(Spikes)*, Leon W. Grant *(Silk)* ← BEAT STREET, Mary B. Ward *(Chloe)*, Marisa Tomei *(Tracy)*

→ FOUR ROOMS → ALFIE re-make, Harold Gould *(Rockerfeller)*, Kim Hauser *(Marie)*, Bruce Kluger *(Gene Epstein)* ← the BURNING, Hildy Brooks *(Danny's mom)* ← the ROSE

Storyline: Danny, Spikes and Silk are three high school grads who find to their surprise they have inherited a hotel deep in the Catskills. They decide to turn the rickety resort into a rock'n'roll hotel (complete with Mick Jagger suite) but it's going to take all their time and money to put things right. Meanwhile, the property developer and head of the council have their greedy eyes on the site and the locals don't want no interferin' outsiders neither! It looks as if the boys' establishment is more likely to become a last chance saloon. *JZ*

Movie rating: *2.5

Visual: video on 'MCA-Universal'

Off the record: Silk's band was made of bit-part actors.

—

Various (score: George Acogny, Daniel Bechet, etc. *)

Oct 86. (lp/c) *Atlantic; <81678-1/-4> Parlophone; (PCS/TCPCS 7306)* ☐ ☐
– Life to life ("Playing For Keeps" title song) (PETE TOWNSHEND) / It's not over ("Playing For Keeps" anthem) (CHRIS THOMPSON) / Distant drums (PETER FRAMPTON) / It's gettin' hot (EUGENE WILDE) * / Think we're gonna make it (HINTON BATTLE) / We said hello, goodbye (don't look back) (PHIL COLLINS) / Here to stay (SISTER SLEDGE) * / Say the word (theme from "Playing For Keeps") (ARCADIA) / Make a wish (JOE CRUZ) / Stand by me (JULIAN LENNON).

S/track review: 'PLAYING FOR KEEPS' features a stellar line-up of big-name artists such as PETE TOWNSHEND, PETER FRAMPTON, PHIL COLLINS, SISTER SLEDGE, ARCADIA and, erm, JULIAN LENNON. Unfortunately, despite this, it's a rather lacklustre album that has a very mid-eighties pop feel about it. TOWNSHEND's rousing 'Life To Life' is one of the few highlights, even if it is a long way from his best work, and PETER FRAMPTON's 'Distant Drums' is a fine addition to the album. ARCADIA (Simon Le Bon and Nick Rhodes' Duran Duran offshoot) appear with 'Say The Word', a synth and guitar-led track full of edgy verses and bold choruses, while JULIAN LENNON provides a live cover of the Ben E. King classic 'Stand By Me' which, while not being a patch on his father's version, is still a decent effort. That's about as good as it gets though. Noel Gallagher once described PHIL COLLINS as "the anti-Christ" and, while that may have been a bit strong, the Oasis man's judgement isn't far off if 'We Said Hello, Goodbye' – a dull and over-sentimental piano ballad – is anything to go by. The bold-as-brass cheesiness is continued by SISTER SLEDGE with the disco-orientated 'Here To Stay' and 'Think We're Gonna Make It' by HINTON BATTLE. 'It's Not Over' and 'Make A Wish' by CHRIS THOMPSON and JOE CRUZ respectively also follow in the same vein. While there are a few decent songs on 'PLAYING FOR KEEPS', there is just too much mawkish nonsense to make it worth listening to without reaching for the reject button, or a sick bowl. *CM*

Album rating: *3.5

POOTIE TANG

2001 (US 81m) Alphaville Films / MTV / 3 Arts / Paramount (PG-13)

Film genre: Pop-Rock Musical adventure comedy

Top guns: s-w + dir: Louis C.K.

Stars: Lance Crouther *(Pootie Tang)* ← FEAR OF A BLACK HAT ← CB4: THE MOVIE, Wanda Sykes *(Biggie Shorty)* → OVER THE HEDGE, Chris Rock *(JB/radio DJ/Pootie's father)* ← CB4: THE MOVIE, Jennifer Coolidge *(Ireenie)* → a MIGHTY WIND, Robert Vaughn *(Dick Lecter)* ← JOE'S APARTMENT, Dave Attell *(Frank)*, Reg E. Cathey *(Dirty Dee)* ← AIRHEADS, J.B. Smoove *(Trucky)*, Tara Jeffers, Qiana Drew & Lorria Richards *(singers)*, **Missy Elliott** *(diva)* → HONEY → FADE TO BLACK, Ebony Jo-Ann *(Pootie's mother)* ← FLY BY NIGHT, Andy Richter *(record executive)* ← DR. T & THE WOMEN

Storyline: Superhero Pootie Tang relentlessly does battle with the forces of evil in America, personified by the villainous Dick Lecter. He's out to corrupt American children with burgers, booze and cigarettes (looks like he's done a good job so far), so Pootie, with the help of his special belt, must try to stop him. However, when our unintelligible Ulysses manages to lose said belt, it's up to the oxymoronic Biggie Shorty to nurse him back to health and help him save America. *JZ*

Movie rating: *4

Visual: video + dvd

Off the record: **Missy Elliott** (aka Melissa Arnette Elliott from Portsmouth, Virginia) has been R&B/hip hop's diva queen for over a decade now having broke through in 1997 with her groundbreaking, 'Supa Dupa Fly'. *MCS*

—

Various Artists (score: QD3 aka Quincy Jones III)

Jun 01. (cd) *Hollywood; <HR 62329-2>* ☐ ☐
– Pootie tangin' (702) / Dirty Dee (MAJIC feat. MASTER P) / Comin' up on somp'n (E-40 and SUGA T.) / Poison (BELL BIV DeVOE) / Make em say ugh (MASTER P) / Southern girl (ERYKAH BADU feat. RAHZEL) / I should've told you (IDEAL) / I want to be your man (ZAPP & ROGER) / A woman needs to be loved (K.K.) / You know how we do (SHAQUILLE O'NEAL) / You know what? (LIL J) / Yesterday (ROSCOE and NATE DOGG) / Why Pootie why? (KARL CLANTON) / Ode to Pootie (TARA JEFFERS, QIANA DREW and LORRIA RICHARDS).

S/track review: After 55 minutes of this album, one's unlikely to understand much more about 'Pootie Tangin'' or the eponymous hero, despite what femme R&B outfit 702 might breathily intone on their sub-Destiny's Child title track. Similarly, given the film's premise of satirising the Blaxploitation genre, odd then that there's only one song – K.K's 'A Woman Needs To Be Loved' – makes any attempt to hark back to that era. Instead we get a rather uninspired hotch-potch of tepid southern-fried hip hop and powdery, inconsequential soul. There's not much to redeem this throwaway slection, other than the rather quaint 'Poison' by BELL BIV DeVOE, it's instrumentation sounding incredibly dated to contemporary ears, but it's one of only a pair of tracks that feel like proper songs and not just a loose collection of half ideas committed to tape. The other is RAHZEL & ERYKAH BADU's understated 'Southern Girl', a song uncomplicated and beautiful, a paean to BADU's southern roots that is conspicuous by its presence. 'No Limit' records impresario MASTER P pops up twice here and fails to impress, while the rest are a motley collection of rap nearly men and almost interesting starlets. *MR*

Album rating: *3.5

Iggy POP

Born: James Osterberg, 21 Apr'47, Ann Arbor, Michigan, USA. The son of an English father and American mother, Osterberg joined the Iguanas as a drummer in 1964. A few years later in 1967, Iggy (as he was now billed) returned to Michigan and formed the (Psychedelic) Stooges with Ron (a fellow Prime Movers member) and his drummer brother Scott Asheton; Dave Alexander was to join soon afterwards. In 1968, the Stooges gigged constantly. On one occasion Iggy was charged with indecent exposure. The following year, A&R man Danny Fields, while looking to sign rivals MC5, instead signed the Stooges to 'Elektra' records, furnishing them with a $25,000 advance. Their eponymous debut (produced by John Cale – another Velvet Underground connection) later proved to be way ahead of its time. Tracks such as 'No Fun', '1969' and 'I Wanna Be Your Dog', were howling proto-punk, garage classics, later covered by the SEX PISTOLS, Sisters Of Mercy and Sid Vicious respectively. The album just failed to secure a Top 100 placing, the second album faring even worse commercially, although it was hailed by the more discerning critics of the day as a seminal work. From the primal nihilism of 'Dirt', to the psychedelic kiss-off, 'I Feel Alright (1970)', it seemed, to the Stooges at least, as if flower-power had never happened. They were duly dropped by their label, following drug-related problems and dissension in the ranks; Iggy had already marked his celluloid debut in the avant-garde, François De Menil short, 'Evening Of Light' (1969) with girlfriend at the time, NICO. He subsequently moved to Florida, becoming a greenkeeper while taking up golf more seriously, a healthier pastime than his penchant for self-mutilation. In 1972, he had a chance meeting with DAVID BOWIE and his manager Tony DeFries, who persuaded Iggy to re-form the Stooges and sign a MainMan management deal; this in turn led to a 'C.B.S.' contract. After his/their flawed classic, 'Raw Power' (not one of BOWIE's best productions), they folded again, citing drugs as the cause. It was, in retrospect, even more of an embryonic punk record, the amphetamine rush of 'Search And Destroy' highly influential on the "blank generation" that would trade in their Steely Dan albums for anything with two chords and a sneering vocal. In 1975, Iggy checked into a psychiatric institute, weaning himself off heroin. His only true friend, BOWIE, who regularly visited him in hospital, invited him to appear on his 'Low' album. Iggy signed to 'R.C.A.' in '77, issuing his BOWIE-produced debut solo album, 'The Idiot', which, due to the recent "new wave" explosion, broke him into the UK Top 30 and US Top 75. It featured the first fruitful BOWIE/POP collaboration, 'China Girl', later a smash hit for BOWIE himself. Iggy's second solo release, 'Lust For Life' (also produced by BOWIE in '77), was another gem, again deservedly reaching the UK Top 30 (the title track was later resurrected in 1996 after appearing on the soundtrack to the cult Scottish movie, 'TRAINSPOTTING'). In 1979, Iggy moved along the corridor to 'Arista' records, while the first half of the 80s saw the man desperately trying to carve out a successful solo career while combating his continuing drug problems, with albums such as 'Soldier' (1980), 'Party' (1981) and 'Zombie Birdhouse' (1982) marking the nadir of POP's chequered career. Finally teaming up again with BOWIE for 1986's 'Blah Blah Blah', the proclaimed "Godfather Of Punk" at last gained some belated recognition, his revival of a 1957 Johnny O'Keefe hit, 'Real Wild Child', giving Iggy his first Top 10 hit (UK). Still with 'A&M' records, he consolidated his recovery with 'Instinct' (1988), while he also raised his profile somewhat by appearing in films 'ROCK & RULE' (well, at least his voice!), 'SID & NANCY' (1986) and 'The Color Of Money' (1986). This new lease of life prompted 'Virgin America' to give Iggy a new contract, the 1990 set 'Brick By Brick' featuring the GN'R talents of Slash and Duff McKagan. More film work came about via 'Hardware' (1990), 'CRY-BABY' (1990) and an instalment of 'COFFEE AND CIGARETTES' (1993/2003), and musically he was back once again in 1993 with 'American Caesar'. Subsequently busying himself with more film work ('Atolladero', 'Tank Girl', 'DEAD MAN', 'The Crow: City Of Angels' and 'PRIVATE PARTS'), the Ig eventually broke his recording silence with 'Naughty Little Doggie' (1996); the album 'Avenue B' followed it in 1999. Diverse as ever, Iggy lent his voice of a newborn baby in the children's animation, 'The Rugrats Movie' (1998) and was higher up in the acting pecking order courtesy of a worthy performance in the family comedy 'Snow Day' (2000). Apart from anything else, 'Beat 'Em Up' (2001) should surely have scooped the most gratuitously tasteless sleeve of the year award, while his film appearances were strictly of the Rockumentary sort: 'YOU SEE ME LAUGHIN'' (2002), the RAMONES' 'END OF THE CENTURY' (2003), 'MAYOR OF THE SUNSET STRIP' (2003) and 'NEW YORK DOLL'. In 2003, Iggy brought out yet another dose of high-octane retro-punk via 'Skull Ring', but it was the man's subsequent decision to re-IGnite the Stooges that got the world of music spinning. 'Telluric Chaos' (2005) was a veritable Stooge-fest recorded in Japan; for those unlucky enough not to get one of the hottest tickets of the last few years, this live set wiped the floor with most of the bootlegs which had been doing the rounds since the band's heyday. *BG & MCS*

- **filmography** {acting} (composer) –

Rock & Rule *(1983 {v} =>)* / **Repo Man** *(1984 theme on OST by V/A =>)* / **Sid & Nancy** *(1986 {b} OST by the POGUES, PRAY FOR RAIN & V/A =>)* / the Color Of Money *(1986 {b} OST by V/A; see future edition)* / Hardware *(1990 {*} OST by Simon Boswell; see future edition)* / **Cry-Baby** *(1990 {*} OST by V/A =>)* / Atolledero *(1995 {*})* / Tank Girl *(1995 {a} OST by V/A; see future edition)* / **Dead Man** *(1995 {a} OST by NEIL YOUNG =>)* / Va Mourire *(1995 score w/ Tino Rossi, Josephine Baker & Georges Blaness)* / the Crow: City Of Angels *(1996 {*} OST by Graeme Revell & OST; see future edition)* / the Brave *(1997 {b} + score)* / **Private Parts** *(1997 {c} OST by V/A =>)* / the Rugrats Movie *(1998 {v} OST by V/A; see future edition)* / Snow Day *(2000 {*} OST by V/A; see future edition)* / **You See Me Laughin'** *(2002 {c})* / **Coffee And Cigarettes** *(2003 {*c} OST by V/A =>)* / **End Of The Century** *(2003 {p} =>)* / **Mayor Of The Sunset Strip** *(2003 {c} OST by V/A =>)* / **New York Doll** *(2005 {c} =>)*

POPEYE

1980 (US 114m) Paramount Pictures (PG)

Film genre: comic-book superhero Pop Musical comedy

Top guns: dir: Robert Altman ← NASHVILLE / → DR. T & THE WOMEN / s-w: Jules Feiffer (comic strip: E.C. Segar)

Stars: Robin Williams *(Popeye)*, Shelley Duvall *(Olive Oyl)*, Ray Walston *(Poopdeck Poppy)* → FAST TIMES AT RIDGEMONT HIGH, Paul Dooley *(Wimpy)* → a MIGHTY WIND → HAIRSPRAY re-make, Paul L. Smith *(Bluto)* ← the GOSPEL ROAD / → DUNE, Richard Libertini *(Geezil)*, **Van Dyke Parks** *(Hoagy)* → the BEACH BOYS: AN AMERICAN BAND → BEAUTIFUL DREAMER: BRIAN WILSON AND THE STORY OF 'SMiLE', **Klaus Voormann** *(Von Schnitzel)* ← SON OF DRACULA ← the CONCERT FOR BANGLADESH / → WHITE STAR → CONCERT FOR GEORGE, **Doug Dillard** *(Clem)*, **Ray Cooper** *(the preacher)* → CONCERT FOR GEORGE → BROTHERS OF THE HEAD, Roberta Maxwell *(Nana Oyl)* → DEAD MAN WALKING, Linda Hunt *(Mrs. Oxheart)* → DUNE, Geoff Hoyle *(Scoop)* → the SPIRIT OF '76, Wayne Robson *(Chizzleflint; the pawnbroker)* → CANDY MOUNTAIN → AFFLICTION

Storyline: The animated seaman comes to life in Altman's satirically barbed, brilliantly designed port of Sweethaven (actually Malta), where God-fearin', hamburger-eatin' folks are "safe from democracy" under the despotic rule of Captain Bluto. After putting up with miserly merchants, a marauding taxman and a you-ain't-from-round-these-parts silent treatment, he cracks over taunts in the local tavern and shows the locals exactly why his forearms are so disturbingly overdeveloped. While his affections for a torn-faced Olive Oyl are initially snubbed, his unexpected custodianship of a clairvoyant baby soon wins her over. The townsfolk waste little time in getting the baby to predict a narrow victory for Cat's Pygamas over Warped Values in the local betting shop; Popeye is "disgustipated", showing his distaste by breaking into song in the nearby "house of ill repukes". Bluto, meanwhile, bribes Uncle Wimp to kidnap the baby and foretell the location of the Commodore's treasure. As it turns out, the misanthropic mariner is actually Popeye's long lost pappy, and his "treasure" a stash of tinned veg. *BG*

Movie rating: *7

Visual: video

Off the record: Doug Dillard (b. 6 Mar'37, East St. Louis, Illinois, USA) and his brother Rodney, were part of bluegrass/country-rock outfit, the Dillards, although Doug left the band in 1967 to form Dillard & Clark (alongside ex-Byrds man, Gene Clark). *MCS*

—

Various Cast (composer: HARRY NILSSON / md: VAN DYKE PARKS)

Dec 80. (lp/c) *Boardwalk; <SW 36880> Epic; (EPC/40 70203)* ☐ Apr81 ☐
– I yam what I yam (ROBIN WILLIAMS) / He needs me (SHELLEY DUVALL) / Swee'Pea's lullaby (ROBIN WILLIAMS) / Din' we / Sweethaven / Blow me down / Sailin' (ROBIN WILLIAMS & SHELLEY DUVALL) / It's not easy being me (RAY WALSTON) / He's large (SHELLEY DUVALL) / I'm mean (PAUL L. SMITH) / Kids (RAY WALSTONE) / I'm Popeye the sailor man (ROBIN WILLIAMS & CHORUS).

S/track review: The bow-legged, muscle-bound mariner as conceived by Robert Altman and arch-tin-pan-alley cats HARRY NILSSON and Van Dyke Parks. "Kurt Weill meeting Lionel Newman" according to Robert Christgau. It's difficult to think of two sonic auteurs less suited to this bizarro project; together they mould gloriously eccentric orchestral pop to the convulsive mutterings of Robin Williams, the absent-minded warblings of Shelley Duvall and the drunken baritone of Robert Fortier. If this sounds like your idea of music-hall hell, plough on dear reader; NILSSON and Parks' subversive waltzes have you in their sights: 'Sweethaven' is as classic, clanging Parks – an ensemble saloon singalong with grand Yankee strings – as 'Blow Me Down' is vintage NILSSON, a grown-up nursery rhyme crooned by HARRY himself over a wheezing sea shanty. Duval sets a screen moment in stone with her 'Nina Simone and Piano!'-spirited lament, 'He Needs me', wails a wonderful, off-key ode to Bluto and renders 'Sailin' as an errant highlight, a salt-and-pepper face-off with Williams, absolutely nothing to do with Rod Stewart although that might have been interesting . . . Jon Brion recently paid tribute to 'POPEYE' on his Parks-ish score for Paul Thomas Anderson's 'Punch-Drunk Love' (2002), but is there a composer alive – Parks aside – who can condense so many decades of cinema and music into one soundtrack, and still make it funny and relevant? And is HARRY NILSSON one of the most underappreciated, heroically flawed geniuses in modern history? Maybe the masses just haven't been eating enough spinach to realise it. *BG*

Album rating: *6.5

POPSTAR

2005 (US 94m) Tag Entertainment / Downtown the Movie LLC (PG)

Film genre: romantic teen/family comedy

Top guns: dir: Richard Gabai / s-w: Timothy Barton

Stars: Aaron Carter *(JD McQueen)*, Alana Austin *(Jane Brighton)*, **David Cassidy** *(Grant)* ← the SPIRIT OF '76, Kimberly Kevon Williams *(Abby Banks)*, Adrianne Palicki *(Whitney Addison)*, Mary Elise *(Bobette)*, Deena Dill *(Faith Brighton)*, Andrew Stevens *(Professor Stevens)*, **Leif Garrett** *(janitor)* ← the SPIRIT OF '76 ← SGT. PEPPER'S LONELY HEARTS CLUB BAND, Rick Overton *(Mr. Thomas)* ← EARTH GIRLS ARE EASY, Stella Stevens *(Henrietta)* ← ADVANCE TO THE REAR ← GIRLS! GIRLS! GIRLS!, Tom Bosley *(Harvey)*, **Nicki Fox** *(London; JD's ex)*

Storyline: Teen superstar JD McQueen may be a singing sensation, but his brain grinds to a halt with anything more complex than a songline. Which is bad news as his parents have threatened to cancel his big summer tour unless he passes his maths test. Enter brainy Jane Brighton, the hottest kid on the block when it comes to equations. Soon JD and Jane are doing more than revision together as the tour looms closer. *JZ*

Movie rating: *3.5

Visual: dvd

Off the record: The music of **Aaron Carter** can be heard on the soundtrack to 'Pokemon: The First Movie', while albums such as 'Aaron's Party (Come Get It)' (2000), 'Oh Aaron' (2001) and 'Another Earthquake!' (2002), have reached the US Top 20. Way before the birth of Aaron, 70s pop idols **David Cassidy & Leif Garrett** were cutting their musical teeth via massive hits all over the world. *MCS*

—

Various Cast/Artists incl. AARON CARTER (*)

Oct 05. (cd) *Madacy; <MLG2 51683>* ☐ ☐
– Saturday night (*) / Enuff of me (*) / Your vibe (JORDAN KNIGHT) / Say yes (JASPER & KELLI) / Boom ba boom (SEAN VAN DER WILT) / Maria (US 5) / Tell me (SMILEZ AND SOUTHSTAR) / Forgive me (C NOTE) / I want candy – live (*) / Saturday night – live (*) / One better – live (*) / Do you remember – live (*) / Tear up this town (LEIF GARRETT).

S/track review: This vehicle for star AARON CARTER opens with the arrogant and obnoxious frat-boy pop of 'Saturday Night' with its massive production and horrible nasal vocals. 'Enuff Of Me' makes a decent fist of trying to copy N.E.R.D.'s 'Rockstar' in building itself around an admittedly kick-ass Tom Morello-esque funky rock riff, however CARTER's spoilt-kid teen-star posturing angst is extremely grating to say the least. Meanwhile, JORDAN KNIGHT's 'Your Vibe' is more of the expected über-produced slick RnB and 'Say Yes' by JASPER & KELLI is exactly the same acoustic guitar-led soul peddled by Britain's Craig David. SEAN VAN DER WILT provides the obligatory and predictable onomatopoeic 'Boom Ba Boom' whilst US 5's smooth breathy Latino vibes on 'Maria' just sound uncomfortably sleazy. 'Tell Me' by SMILEZ AND SOUTHSTAR is a third rate attempt at a bombastic boy-girl duet lacking in edge and C NOTE's emasculated wet and weak ballad 'Forgive Me' is custom-made for the last dance at the school disco. There then follows a clutch of live songs from CARTER, delivered in his customary nasal whine, which are really just formulaic filler and only serve to irritate further. *LF*

Album rating: *3

POPULATION: ONE

1986 (US 70m) American Scenes (18)

Film genre: Music-based psychological drama

Top guns: s-w + dir: Rene Daalder

Stars: Screamers:- **Tomata Du Plenty, K.K. Barrett, Tommy Gear** *(himself/ performers)* → RAGE: 20 YEARS OF PUNK ROCK WEST COAST STYLE, the Fabulous **Sheela Edwards** *(herself)*, **Paul Ambrose** *(performer)*, **Gorilla Rose aka Michael Farris** *(performer)*, Jane Gaskill *(herself)*, Mike Doud *(himself)*, **El Duce** *(performer)* ← DU-BEAT-E-O / → KURT & COURTNEY, **Beck Campbell aka Hansen** *(performer)*, Shari Penquin *(herself)*, Vampira *(herself)*

Storyline: A post-apocalyptic affair, where the supposedly sole-survivor of a nuclear holocaust (a civil defense worker into avant-garde punk-rock) hordes up in a high tech bunker and creates his own multimedia musical déjà vu to depict the decline of the human race. *MCS*

Movie rating: *2.5

Visual: video (no audio score by Daniel Schwartz)

Off the record: Screamers consisted of **Tomata Du Plenty** (b. David Xavier Harrigan, 28 May'48, Coney Island, NY) – songs included 'Vertigo', 'Beat Goes On', Punish Or Be Damned', 'Another World', 'Last 4 Digits', '122 Hours Of Fear' and 'Magazine Love', all on the video, 'Live In San Francisco Sept 2nd 1978' (available 2004 on 'Target' DVD. Look out too for **Beck** (Hansen) and **el Duce** in the film. *MCS*

Elvis PRESLEY

Born: Elvis Aaron Presley, 8th January 1935, Tupelo, Mississippi, USA; one of twin sons (the other Jesse was stillborn), he was raised in Memphis, Tennessee. Between the summer of '53 and '54, Elvis spent time in Sam Phillips' 'Sun' studios, cutting demos. With the arrival of back-up session players, Scotty Moore and Bill Black, his first single, a rousing cover of Arthur Crudup's 'That's All Right Mama', gained local airplay even before its release on the 'Sun' label. After a brief flirtation with country music, he opted for R&B after his young audiences lapped up his unique pelvic action. Although Sam Phillips initially thought PRESLEY was a black blues singer, he still chose to feature Elvis' country recordings on the flip sides. Colonel Tom Parker became his manager in 1955, subsequently securing a large 5-figure deal with 'R.C.A.', who also bought out his contract with 'Sun' records; the attention attracted by PRESLEY's riotous stage shows had prompted an intense bidding war. His major debut 45, 'Heartbreak Hotel', sparked off a new phenomenon at the start of 1956 which soon gave him a massive-selling No.1. His story now concentrates on his film work only. Everyone and his hound dog knows that ELVIS PRESLEY's film career was a dud, yet how many people have actually listened to the soundtracks or, God forbid, even sat through the films themselves? The idea that ELVIS' Hollywood years were less Honolulu than horror show has become one of popular music's self-perpetuating myths, up there with subliminal messages and Jim Morrison still roaming the earth. While it's true that the bulk of these films were little more than disposable star vehicles, they did actually have some good songs tucked away in the furthest recesses of their soundtracks, some of which stand alongside the cream of PRESLEY's career and which casual observers probably wouldn't have imagined emanating from one of the King's much lampooned movies. It all began with 'LOVE ME TENDER', Elvis' 1956 screen debut and one which turned up one of his most emotionally fraught songs. He wasn't even given a starring role, although he acquitted himself reasonably well. In fact, his lead roles in the semi-autobiographical 'LOVING YOU', the B-movie grit of 'JAILHOUSE ROCK' and the superior 'KING CREOLE' suggested that, if not exactly pushing the envelope, PRESLEY was serious about his acting career and committed to developing it. His performances were as promising as the music was galvanising, showcasing bona fide classic title tracks, heavy-duty Leiber/Stoller material and one-off pearls like 'Crawfish'. Then came the army, with Elvis' enforced layoff and its artistic consequences as good an argument as any for scrapping military service. Buttoned-up in his army threads, there was really no way the King could convincingly continue to portray a dangerous, anti-establishment, angry young man. Instead, he scored the biggest box office success of his career to date with 'G.I. BLUES', a good-time army base romp which foisted 'Wooden Heart' upon his growing legions of fans. Yet even at this point, all was not lost. Both 'FLAMING STAR' and 'WILD IN THE COUNTRY' were brave, if ultimately failed attempts to cast ELVIS in challenging roles, with the musical content kept to a minimum. Come 1961's 'BLUE HAWAII', however, the die was cast: a combination of exotic setting, transparent plot, Elvis' stunningly photogenic looks and easygoing persona, and copious quantities of scantily clad ladies set the tills ringing. They didn't stop until the recipe had been cooked to mush. But it's the music we're concerned about here, music which was no longer cutting edge and all too often cutting floor, but which still showcased one of the most resonant voices of that or any time. In amidst 'BLUE HAWAII's slack-keyed guitars and traditional adaptations was 'Can't Help Falling In Love', one of Elvis' most poignant performances and reason alone to watch the film. The movie's huge success was replicated with the likes of 'KID GALAHAD' and 'GIRLS! GIRLS! GIRLS!', vehicles whose soundtracks showcased great songs – 'King Of The Whole Wide World' and 'Return To Sender' – as well as great vocal presence. 1964's 'VIVA LAS VEGAS' was probably the most successful of Elvis' all-singing, all-dancing extravaganzas, if only because its sense of showmanship was equalled in the screen partnership between PRESLEY and Ann-Margret, while its brilliant title song was a campy celebration and encapsulation of Elvis' Hollywood years. It couldn't last, though. Dire, plotless disasters like 'ROUSTABOUT' and 'HARUM SCARUM', a last gasp Polynesian sequel to the sequel, 'PARADISE, HAWAIIAN STYLE', and other equally forgettable films challenged even the most committed Elvis fans and really began to drive the nails into his rapidly fading reputation. The received wisdom is that PRESLEY's manager, Colonel Tom Parker, was the man who allegedly tied Elvis to these dismal movies and novelty songs, loath to allow his protégé weightier dramatic roles. Elvis expert Alanna Nash has even suggested that Parker's strategy – inadvertently or otherwise – saved PRESLEY from having to compete with the British Invasion. Regardless, the King was in serious danger of finally losing his crown in the mid to late 60s as he churned out movies like 'SPEEDWAY' and 'STAY AWAY, JOE' in order to fulfil contractual obligations. It didn't help that the songwriting material he was being supplied with had gone, in general, from bad to terminal, although there were still memorable moments in all but the worst soundtracks: 'Goin' Home', for instance, a country-rock classic sequestered on 'STAY AWAY, JOE', or 'CLAMBAKE's 'Guitar Man'. Finally, in 1968, Elvis' live televised comeback opened up a new, and to many, definitive, chapter in his career. Most of the songs which peppered his Hollywood soundtracks were promptly abandoned to history, at least until the CD re-issue bonanza. For rock purists, granted, there can be no amnesty; ELVIS' transformation from taboo-busting, sexually-charged rock'n'roll rebel to malleable, clean-cut film staple is a waste of his talent and a betrayal of his establishment-baiting roots. It's only too easy, though, to swallow the line that the King's 60s film output was one big, indelible black mark on his considerable overall achievements. No-one's under the illusion that these movies constitute anything more than a proven formula, yet dig a little deeper and who knows, you might just find yourself humming 'GIRL HAPPY' while flicking furtively through a Hawaiian short-breaks brochure. His work in the 70s showed him moving away from celluloid and into the money-spinning cabaret circuit as his live appearances were mainly in Las Vegas and Hawaii. While "The King" was still a top performer, as loyal fans old and new flocked to see his larger frame (squeezing out of a white glitzy suit) churn out another exhaustive show, he was barely a shadow of the rock'n'roll hero he once was. A combination of a special diet, prescribed drugs, junk food (binges) and alcohol eventually proved too much for his ailing heart and, tragically, on the 16th of August, 1977, he was found dead in his Graceland home by girlfriend at the time, Ginger Alden. His funeral saw over 75,000 fans/mourners flocking to the gates of his home in Gracelands. The King Of Rock was dead. Following the death of ELVIS, many tabloids reported sightings of a living ELVIS and speculation about his doomed life has been catapulted into the ridiculous. The King should've been laid to rest in peace, his music the only thing to live on. The fact is, PRESLEY went on to have numerous hit compilations and the odd hit single, none more so than when Junkie XL sent his updated remixed version of 'A Little Less Conversation' (taken from the movie remake of 'Ocean's Eleven') to the top of the UK charts in summer 2002. The Paul Oakenfold twist on ELVIS' 'Rubberneckin'' nearly followed suit in 2003, both giving the King crossover dance hits a quarter of a century after his death! After 'That's All Right' hit the UK Top 3 in October 2004, his label kept the ELVIS gravy train rolling early the following year with a weekly series of cannily-marketed re-issues, primed to break PRESLEY's record of No.1

singles but just falling short as the schedule progressed. A wider look at the non-Soundtrack work of ELVIS between 1956 and 1970 is included in the Essential Rock Discography. *BG & MCS*

- filmography {acting} –

the Pied Piper Of Cleveland *(1955 {*p} =>)* / **Love Me Tender** *(1956 {*} OST =>)* / **Loving You** *(1957 {*} OST =>)* / **Jailhouse Rock** *(1957 {*} OST =>)* / **King Creole** *(1958 {*} OST =>)* / **G.I. Blues** *(1960 {*} OST =>)* / **Flaming Star** *(1960 {*} OST =>)* / **Wild In The Country** *(1961 {*} =>)* / **Follow That Dream** *(1961 {*} =>)* / **Blue Hawaii** *(1961 {*} OST =>)* / **Kid Galahad** *(1962 {*} =>)* / **Girls! Girls! Girls!** *(1962 {*} OST =>)* / **It Happened At The World's Fair** *(1963 {*} OST =>)* / **Fun In Acapulco** *(1963 {*} OST =>)* / **Kissin' Cousins** *(1964 {*} OST =>)* / **Viva Las Vegas** *(1964 {*} =>)* / **Roustabout** *(1964 {*} OST =>)* / **Girl Happy** *(1965 {*} OST =>)* / **Tickle Me** *(1965 {*} =>)* / **Harum Scarum** *(1965 * OST =>)* / **Frankie And Johnny** *(1965 {*} OST =>)* / **Paradise, Hawaiian Style** *(1966 {*} OST =>)* / **Spinout** *(1966 {*} OST =>)* / **Easy Come, Easy Go** *(1967 {*} =>)* / **Double Trouble** *(1967 {*} OST =>)* / **Clambake** *(1967 {*} OST =>)* / **Stay Away, Joe** *(1968 {*} =>)* / **Speedway** *(1968 {*} OST =>)* / **Live A Little, Love A Little** *(1968 {*} =>)* / **Charro!** *(1969 {*} =>)* / **the Trouble With Girls** *(1969 {*} =>)* / **Change Of Habit** *(1969 {*} =>)* / **Elvis: That's The Way It Is** *(1970 {*p} OST =>)* / **Elvis On Tour** *(1972 {*p} =>)* / **This Is Elvis** *(1981 OST =>)*

– movietrack compilations, etc. –

ELVIS PRESLEY: Elvis Sings Hits From His Movies, Vol.1

Jun 72. (lp/c) *RCA Camden; <2567> (CDS 1110/CAM 423)* [87] Jul72 [ ]
– Down by the riverside / When the saints go marching in / They remind me too much of you / Confidence / Frankie and Johnny / Guitar man / Long legged girl (with the short dress on) / You don't know me / How would you like to be / Big boss man / Old MacDonald.

ELVIS PRESLEY: Burning Love And Hits From The Movies, Vol.2

Nov 72. (lp/c) *RCA Camden; <2595>* [22] [–]
– Burning love / Tender feeling / Am I ready / Tonight is so right for love / Guadalajara / It's a matter of time / La paloma / Santa Lucia / We'll be together / I love only one girl.

ELVIS PRESLEY: Pictures Of Elvis

Sep 77. (lp) *R.C.A.; (HY 1023)* [–] [ ]
– Return to sender / Roustabout / Little Egypt / Paradise, Hawaiian style / Girls! girls! girls! / Double trouble / Do the clam / Fun in Acapulco / Bossa nova baby / Clambake / Girl happy / Rock-a-hula baby. *(re-iss. Mar80 on 'RCA Int.'lp/c; INT S/K 5001)*

ELVIS PRESLEY: Elvis Aron Presley

Aug 80. (8xlp-box) *R.C.A.; <(CPL8 3699)>* [27] [21]
– (disc 3):- They remind me too much of you / Tonight is so right for love / Follow that dream / Wild in the country / Datin' / Shoppin' around / Can't help falling in love / A dog's life / I'm falling in love tonight / Thanks to the rolling sea / Jailhouse rock.

ELVIS PRESLEY: Elvis In Hollywood

Jul 82. (lp/c) *Everest; (CBR 1014/KCBR/1014)* [–] [ ]
– Jailhouse rock / Rock-a-hula baby / G.I. blues / Kissin' cousins / Wild in the country / King Creole / Blue Hawaii / Fun in Acapulco / Follow that dream / Girls! girls! girls! / Viva Las Vegas / Bossa nova baby / Flaming star / Girl happy / Frankie and Johnny / Roustabout / Spinout / Double trouble / Charro / They remind me too much of you.

ELVIS PRESLEY: Pictures Of Elvis II

Feb 83. (pic-lp) *R.C.A.; (AR30 002)* [–] [ ]

ELVIS PRESLEY: Jailhouse Rock / Love In Las Vegas

Apr 83. (pic-lp) *R.C.A.; (RCALP 9020)* [–] [40]

ELVIS PRESLEY: 32 Film Hits

Aug 84. (d-lp/d-c/cd) *R.C.A.; (NL/NK/PD 89388)* [–] [ ]
– Fun in Acapulco / Mexico / Marguerita / Bossa nova baby / Blue Hawaii / Can't help falling in love / Rock-a-hula baby / Ky-u-i-po / King Creole / Hard headed woman / Trouble / Dixieland rock / Frankie and Johnny / Please don't stop loving me / Easy come, easy go / Sing you children / Tonight is so right for love / Frankfurt special / Wooden heart / G.I. blues / Blue suede shoes / Doin' the best I can / A dog's life / Charro / Roustabout / Little Egypt / Poison Ivy league / Girls! girls! girls! / Where do you come from / Return to sender / Follow that dream / Angel.

ELVIS PRESLEY: 32 Film Hits Vol.2

Jul 85. (d-lp/d-c/cd) *R.C.A.; (NL/NK/PD 89550)* [–] [ ]
– Jailhouse rock / Young and beautiful / (You're so square) Baby I don't care / They remind me too much of you / Beyond the bend / Relax / One broken heart for sale / I'm falling in love tonight / No more (la paloma) / Island of love / Moonlight swim / Hawaiian sunset / Beach boy blues / Hawaiian wedding song / The love machine / I'll take love / Rubberneckin' / Change of habit / Let us pray / El toro / Vino, dinero y amor / Hard knocks / One track heart / Wheels on my heels / Lover doll / Crawfish / New Orleans / Shoppin' around / What's she really like / Pocketful of rainbows / I'm not the marrying kind / What a wonderful life.

ELVIS PRESLEY: Essential Elvis: The First Movies *(* alt. & unreleased takes)*

Dec 86. (lp/c/cd) *R.C.A.; (PL/PK/PD 89979)* [–] [ ]
– Love me tender / Let me / Poor boy / We're gonna move / Loving you (*) / Party (*) / Hot dog / (Let me be your) Teddy bear / Loving you (*) / Mean woman blues (*) / Got a lot of livin' to do (*) / Loving you (*) / Party / Lonesome cowboy / Jailhouse rock (*) / Treat me nice (*) / Young and beautiful (*) / Don't leave me now (*) / I want to be free (*) / (You're so square) Baby I don't care (*) / Jailhouse rock (*) / Got a lot of livin' to do / Love me tender (*).

ELVIS PRESLEY: Elvis Movies

Jul 00. (cd) *R.C.A.; <(74321 68241-2)>* [ ] [ ]
– Got a lot of livin' to do / Love me tender / (You're so square) Baby I don't care / Crawfish / I slipped, I stumbled, I fell / Doin' the best I can / Flaming star / Return to sender / Loving you / G.I. blues / Girls! girls! girls! / I needed somebody to lean on / A little less conversation / Follow that dream / Viva Las Vegas / Trouble / Swing down sweet chariot / Bossa nova baby / Rubberneckin' / They remind me too much of you.

PRETTY IN PINK

1986 (US 96m) Paramount Pictures (PG-13)

Film genre: coming-of-age/teen comedy drama

Top guns: dir: Howard Deutch / s-w: John Hughes → REACH THE ROCK

Stars: Molly Ringwald *(Andie Walsh)*, Jon Cryer *(Philip "Duckie" Dale)* → DUDES → WENT TO CONEY ISLAND ON A MISSION FROM GOD . . . BE BACK BY FIVE, Andrew McCarthy *(Blane McDonnagh)*, Harry Dean Stanton *(Jack Walsh)* ← PARIS, TEXAS ← REPO MAN ← ONE FROM THE HEART ← the ROSE ← RENALDO AND CLARA ← RANCHO DELUXE ← PAT GARRETT & BILLY THE KID / → the LAST TEMPTATION OF CHRIST → WILD AT HEART → FEAR AND LOATHING IN LAS VEGAS, Annie Potts *(Iona)* ← CRIMES OF PASSION, James Spader *(Steff McKee)*, **Dweezil Zappa** *(Simon)*, Gina Gershon *(Trombley)* → TOUCH → the INSIDER → DEMONLOVER → PREY FOR ROCK & ROLL, Kate Vernon *(Benny Hanson)*, Andrew 'Dice' Clay *(bouncer at CATS)* → the ADVENTURES OF FORD FAIRLANE, Alexa Kenin *(Jena Hoeman)* ← HONKYTONK MAN, **the Rave-Ups:- Jimmer Podrasky, Tom Blatnik, Terry Wilson, Timothy Jimenez** (themselves) / **Orchestral Manoeuvres In The Dark** *(prom band)* ← URGH! A MUSIC WAR

Storyline: Student outcast Andie Walsh is out with the in crowd until she manages to attract the eye of the high school hunk Blane McDonnagh. Unfortunately, her longtime new waver friend Philip "Duckie" Dale also secretly worships her and does not respond well to the blossoming relationship. Andie and Blane, from vastly removed social backgrounds (she works in a record store), also fend off criticism from their respective social circles when they try to take things further. Could this be the undoing of the relationship before it has even started and how should Andie respond to Duckie's adoration? *SM*

Movie rating: *7

Visual: video + dvd

Off the record: L.A.'s the **Rave-Ups** were formed in 1984 by frontman **Jimmer Podrasky** (a native of Pittsburgh), who, after a time inbetween jobs found other likeminded musicians, **Timothy Jiminez** (drums), **Terry Wilson** (guitar) and **Tommy Blatnik** (bass). An album 'Town + Country' (1985) was released on 'Demon' records (home to nu-roots contemporaries Green On Red, Giant Sand, etc), a record which resulted in star actress Molly Ringwald getting the quartet a spot in the film, 'PRETTY IN PINK' (her sister Beth was to subsequently give birth to Jimmer's child). Now signed to 'Epic' records, the Rave-Ups delivered two further albums, 'The Book Of Your Regrets' (1988) and 'Chance' (1990), the latter featuring their best-known track, 'Respectfully King Of Pain'. *MCS*

—

Various Artists (score: Michael Gore)

Feb 86. (lp/c/cd) *A&M; <39 5113-1/-4/-2> (AMA/AMC/CDA 5113)* [5] Jul86 [ ]

– If you leave (ORCHESTRAL MANOEUVRES IN THE DARK) / Left of center (SUZANNE VEGA feat. JOE JACKSON on piano) / Get to know ya (JESSE JOHNSON) / Do wot you do (INXS) / Pretty in pink (the PSYCHEDELIC FURS) / Shell-shock (NEW ORDER) / Round, round (BELOUIS SOME) / Wouldn't it be good (DANNY HUTTON HITTERS) / Bring on the dancing horses (ECHO & THE BUNNYMEN) / Please please please let me get what I want (the SMITHS).

S/track review: For many, the 80s was a vacuous, turgid decade with distinct lack of cultural substance. An era they would much rather bury the dayglo, shoulder pad remnants from in a time capsule 100ft underground. Thankfully, some gems were salvaged from the murky waters. This album came shining through, a combination of the success of the Bratpack movie it supported, a careful smattering of leftfield post punk, and various popular musicians who dominated the scene at the time. Specially selected by director Howard Deutch and writer John Hughes, the insert insists the ten tracks were not an afterthought and it is clear care and consideration were employed. With forethought, they would surely have relegated the odd track on here to the cringeworthy bin. This is most definitely true of 'Get To Know Ya' by JESSE JOHNSON which sounds rather dated and pseudo Prince-like, unfortunately with a type of Rick Wakeman's synth equivalent flexing his fingers a little too enthusiastically on the keys. The guitarist too, if we imagine him, definitely has to be sporting a poodle perm judging merely by his cheesy, queasy rock solos. Arguably one of the album's standout tracks is 'Left Of Center' by SUZANNE VEGA featuring JOE JACKSON on piano. The singer's trademark whispery, soothing vocals, almost spoken, are teamed with straightforward lyrics for this infectious composition. Famously, the PSYCHEDELIC FURS had already recorded 'Pretty In Pink' in 1981 for their album 'Talk Talk Talk'. Used at the start of the movie in its original format and re-recorded for the end credits, it also re-hit the UK Top 20 and reached the US chart. ORCHESTRAL MANOEUVRES IN THE DARK (aka OMD) scored a massive Stateside smash via 'If You Leave', their pop-centric electro surprisingly the toast of a discerning US audience at the time. The SMITHS' 'Please Please Please Let Me Get What I Want' is a gentle ballad of tempestuous proportions and yet another example of Morrissey's brilliance as a songwriter. The 80s soundtrack band of choice, ECHO AND THE BUNNYMEN (they also feature on 'The Lost Boys' soundtrack amongst others), display their fondness for the equestrian pursuit with 'Bring On The Dancing Horses', which, despite being a perfectly pleasing indie track, is more insipid and weaker than earlier releases such as 'The Cutter'. 'Shell-Shock' is classic NEW ORDER; a flowing bank of synths, drum machines and Bernard Sumner's anthemic vocals. The beauty is that it was an upbeat breath of fresh air at the time and it still is today. INXS 'Do What You Do' doesn't have the immediacy of their numerous hits but it's an understated, likeable pop song. 'Wouldn't it Be Good by the DANNY HUTTON HITTERS, written by Nik Kershaw, is pop pap through and through but manages to be one of those nostalgic guilty pleasures that you do find yourself reminiscing to (when no-one is around). Generally, 'PRETTY IN PINK' is an 80s soundtrack which, thanks to the cult status of many of the artists, will only gain credibility over time. *SM*

Album rating: *6.5

– spinoff hits, etc. –

ORCHESTRAL MANOEUVRES IN THE DARK: If You Leave / (non-OST song)

Feb 86. (7") *<2811>* [4] [–]

the PSYCHEDELIC FURS: Pretty In Pink / (dub version)

Apr 86. (7") *<2826>* [41] [–]

ORCHESTRAL MANOEUVRES IN THE DARK: If You Leave / (non-OST song)

Apr 86. (7"/12") *Virgin; (VS 843/+12)* [–] [48]

the PSYCHEDELIC FURS: Pretty In Pink / (non-OST songs)

Aug 86. (7"/7"pic-d/12"/d7") *Epic; (A/WA/TA/DA 7242)* [–] [18]

PREY FOR ROCK & ROLL

2003 (US 104m) Samy Boy Entertainment / Mac

Film genre: showbiz/Punk-music drama

Top guns: dir: Alex Steyermark / s-w (+ play): **Cheri Lovedog** , Robin Whitehouse

Stars: Gina Gershon *(Jacki; vocalist/guitarist)* ← DEMONLOVER ← the INSIDER ← TOUCH ← PRETTY IN PINK, Drea de Matteo *(Tracy; bassist)* ← SWORDFISH, Lori Petty *(Faith; lead guitarist)* ← CLUBLAND, Shelly Cole *(Sally; drummer)*, Marc Blucas *(Animal)*, Ivan Martin *(Nick)*, Eddie Driscoll *(Chuck)*

Storyline: Life's supposed to begin at 40, but for Clamdandy lead singer Jacki that's when it's due to end, unless she finally leads the band to success. For years they've struggled with nothing to show, and if this last producer gives them the thumbs down, it's back to the hubby, kids and ironing board for our Jacki. Will the band manage to pull together just this once or is Jacki living on a wing and a prayer? *JZ*

Movie rating: *6

Visual: dvd

Off the record: Cheri Lovedog was indeed singer/guitarist in an 80s L.A. punk band named Lovedog, while she was a columnist for local rock fanzines such as 'Hollywood Trash & Tinsel' in the mid-80s. *MCS*

—

Various Cast (songs: CHERI LOVEDOG / score: Stephen Trask)

Oct 03. (cd) *Hybrid (Red); <HY 20030-2>* [ ] [–]

– Ms. Tweak / Give me / Stupidstar (GINA GERSHON, LINDA PERRY and PATTY SCHEMEL) / Prey for rock & roll / 4 into 3 / The ugly / Pretty pretty / Every six minutes / My favorite sin / Sam / That was me / Bitter pill / Punk rock girl / Post nuclear celebration party song.

S/track review: 'PREY FOR ROCK & ROLL' is another in the 'JOSIE AND THE PUSSYCATS' and 'DOWN & OUT WITH THE DOLLS' mould, full of post-grrrl rock. Now let us "prey" this is better. The Marshall stack crunch and bratty, sneering vocals of opener 'Ms. Tweak' is close to the glam-punk hybrid of the New York Dolls and (very) early Guns N' Roses, whilst the euphoric 'Stupidstar' is rollicking Stooges or Generation X for the 2000s. However, 'PREY FOR ROCK & ROLL' runs out of legs very quickly. By the time the title track and 'Sam' come around things are quite pedestrian with '4 into 3' sounding particularly tired. GINA GERSHON overdoes the bitchiness on 'The Ugly' and ups the brattiness to pantomime level on 'That Was Me' as things get very one-dimensional. 'Every 6 Minutes' fares much better with its dark bass-led textured atmospherics, though 'Bitter Pill' is a throwaway angst-ridden piano ballad which is, like so much here, lacking lyrically. 'My Favorite Sin' and 'Pretty Pretty' are returns to the better sound of the earlier tracks and closer 'Post Nuclear Celebration Party Song' is overblown cartoon Green Day, but will leave you wondering just who this music is for. Incidentally, CLAM DANDY are the band behind the music:- the aforementioned GINA GERSHON (vocals), GINA VOLPE (guitar, piano, vocals; ex-Lunachicks), CHERI LOVEDOG (lead guitar; ex-Lovedog), SARA LEE (bass; ex-Gang Of Four, ex-Indigo Girls), SAMANTHA MOLONEY (drums; ex-Hole, ex-Motley Crue). "Prey-ers", players or prayers answered then? *LF*

Album rating: *6

□ Louis PRIMA segment
(⇒ HEY BOY! HEY GIRL!)

PRINCE

Born: Prince Rogers Nelson, 7 Jun'58, Minneapolis, Minnesota, USA. The archetypal mystery wrapped inside an enigma, PRINCE has delighted and confounded the world of popular music for nigh on three decades. He's done much the same thing with film, albeit not to the same extent, and if his acting has never never been much cop, his soundtracks stand, at best, as career highlights, and at worst, glorious failures. The big news in the early days was his 'Warners' solo deal, in which he negotiated comprehensive creative control over his entire recording process. If this was something pretty much unheard of for a young black artist, the company's faith was rewarded in the early 80s when, together with multi-racial backing band the Revolution, this voraciously talented musical polymath opened up both the white and black markets with his patented blend of risqué pop, synth-heavy new wave, post-funk R&B and Hendrix-influenced rock. Having already capitalised on the emergence of MTV, PRINCE duly went the whole hog and essentially made one long, extended music video in the form of neo-autobiographical movie, 'PURPLE RAIN' (1984). If the film's plot and premise were fairly dubious, the soundtrack was world beating, scaling the US chart itself and spawning two US No.1 singles in 'Let's Go Crazy' and 'When Doves Cry'. The album became one of the biggest selling of the decade, and, if it rendered PRINCE a genuine global phenomenon, it also presented a hell of a challenge in following it up. In the event, and as contradictory as ever, the diminutive genius didn't even try; instead he went to ground in his Paisley Park studios and furthered his mystical musings with 'Around The World In A Day' (1985). 'Parade' (1986) was even less of a follow-up, continuing with a similar philosophical tack but nevertheless featuring the killer (US) No.1 funk of 'Kiss' and belatedly achieving semi-forgotten, semi-classic status. Sub-titled 'UNDER THE CHERRY MOON', the album actually contained only a handful of songs featured in the film, itself PRINCE's unfairly slated directorial debut and not one which improved his acting chops. It wasn't surprising when the wee man offered up a feature concert video to accompany his next album project, 'SIGN 'O' THE TIMES' (1987), a film that featured ex-pat Scots lass, Sheena Easton. The critics were much kinder to his next cinematic project, the soundtrack to Tim Burton's 'BATMAN' (1989), in which he clipped back his more esoteric tendencies and turned in the kind of tight, funky set such a commission demanded. Again, there was a spin-off US No.1, 'Batdance', and an unlikely one at that. Unfortunately, such box office magic didn't rub off on PRINCE's sophomore vanity project, 'GRAFFITI BRIDGE' (1990), a critical and commercial disaster touted as a follow-up to 'PURPLE RAIN'. If the accompanying soundtrack mitigated some of the pain, it certainly wasn't his best. By the time he came to score Spike Lee comedy, 'GIRL 6' (1996), he'd taken to billing himself with a symbol instead of a name (although he was usually referred to – not without some mockery – as The Artist Formerly Known As Prince), releasing self-indulgent contract-fillers in an attempt to free himself from his recording contract. True to form, he duly changed his name back to PRINCE in 1999. If his ever more unfathomable behaviour and record company problems haven't exactly boosted his career, he remains an important Afro-American icon and a hugely influential musician and songwriter, and while it doesn't seem likely he'll return to the film world any time soon, in 'PURPLE RAIN' he remains the author of one of the best selling and most accomplished soundtracks of all time. *BG*

- **filmography** (composer) {acting} –

Purple Rain *(1984 {*} OST =>)* / **Under The Cherry Moon** *(1986 {*} OST as 'Parade' =>)* / **Sign 'O' The Times** *(1987 {*p} OST =>)* / **Batman** *(1989 OST =>)* / **Graffiti Bridge** *(1990 {*} OST =>)* / Billboards *(1994)* / **Girl 6** *(1996 OST =>)*

□ PRISIONEROS DE LA DANZA alt.
(⇒ JAILBIRD ROCK)

PRISON SONG

2001 (US 99m) New Line Cinema (R)

Film genre: coming-of-age prison drama/pt.musical

Top guns: s-w: (+ dir) Darnell Martin, **Q-TIP**

Stars: **Q-TIP** *(Elijah Butler)*, **Mary J. Blige** *(Mrs. Butler)* → FADE TO BLACK, Harold Perrineau *(uncle Cee)*, **Fat Joe** *(Big Pete)* ← WHITEBOYS ← THICKER THAN WATER, Danny Hoch *(cameo)* ← WHITEBOYS, **Snow** *(officer McIntyre)* ← KLA$H, Hassan Johnson *(Jay)* ← BLACK AND WHITE, **Victor 'Noreaga' Santeago** *(rapper)* → PAPER SOLDIERS, **Clay Da Raider** *(KT)*, **Elvis COSTELLO** *(public defender/teacher)*

Storyline: Elijah has been shunted around children's homes since he was ten years old. Several years on, the adolescent Elijah is living with his hard-working mother who also lives with her boyfriend, until, that is, he is unjustly incarcerated for life on the three strikes law. The lad subsequently rebels against the system that put his "uncle" there (plus the mental breakdown and the institutionalization of his poor mum) and also ends up behind bars. Note that this was to be a fully-fledged musical until a lot of the numbers were removed after an unsuccessful premiere. *MCS*

Movie rating: *6

Visual: video + dvd (no audio OST)

Off the record: ELVIS COSTELLO contributed a few songs ('A Teacher's Tale (Oh Well)' and 'Soul For Hire') to the completed soundtrack (a lot of Hip-Hop was disgarded); MARY J. BLIGE's 'Mom's Song' was the highlight. **Noreaga** was of duo, 'Capone-n-Noreaga. **Snow** (b. Darrin O'Brien, 30 Oct'68, Toronto, Ontario, Canada) was a white reggae/rapper who scored a US No.1 (UK No.2) with the single, 'Informer' in 1993; **Clay Da Raider** was also a rapper. *MCS*

PRIVATE PARTS

1997 (US 109m) Rysher Entertainment / Paramount Pictures (R)

Film genre: media bio-pic/comedy

Top guns: dir: Betty Thomas / s-w: Len Blum ← HEAVY METAL / → OVER THE HEDGE, Michael Kalesniko (book: Howard Stern)

Stars: Howard Stern *(Howard Stern)*, Robin Quivers *(Robin Quivers)*, Mary

McCormack *(Alison Stern)* ← COLIN FITZ LIVES!, Fred Norris *(Fred Norris)*, Paul Giamatti *(Kenny 'Pig Vomit' Rushton)* ← SINGLES / → MAN ON THE MOON → DUETS → STORYTELLING, Jackie Martling *(himself)*, Gary Dell'Abate *(himself)*, Richard Portnow *(Ben Stern)* ← S.F.W. ← GOOD MORNING, VIETNAM ← ROADIE / → FEAR AND LOATHING IN LAS VEGAS → GHOST DOG: THE WAY OF THE SAMURAI, Kelly Bishop *(Ray Stern)* ← DIRTY DANCING, Henry Moti *(Moti)*, Michael Murphy *(Roger Erlick)* ← NASHVILLE ← DOUBLE TROUBLE / → MAGNOLIA, Allison Janney *(Dee Dee)* ← WALKING AND TALKING / → PRIMARY COLORS → OVER THE HEDGE → HAIRSPRAY re-make, Amber Smith *(Julie)* → HOW HIGH, Jenna Jameson *(Mandy)*, **Chris Barron** *(himself)*, **Flavor Flav** *(himself)* ← WHO'S THE MAN? ← CB4: THE MOVIE / → DEATH OF A DYNASTY, **MC Hammer** *(himself)*, **Ted Nugent** *(himself)* ← TAPEHEADS, **Ozzy Osbourne** *(himself)* ← the DECLINE OF WESTERN CIVILIZATION 2: THE METAL YEARS ← TRICK OR TREAT / → MOULIN ROUGE → WE SOLD OUR SOULS FOR ROCK'N'ROLL, **Slash** *(himself)*, **Dee Snider** *(himself)* → STRANGELAND → METAL: A HEADBANGER'S JOURNEY, **Ac/Dc:- Brian Johnson, Angus Young *, Malcolm Young *, Cliff Williams *, Phil Rudd *** *(themselves)* ← LET THERE BE ROCK, **Tiny Tim** *(himself)* ← MESSAGE TO LOVE: THE ISLE OF WIGHT FESTIVAL ← ONE-TRICK PONY ← YOU ARE WHAT YOU EAT, **John Popper** *(himself)* ← WOODSTOCK '94 / → BLUES BROTHERS 2000 → MY GENERATION, Mia Farrow *(herself)* ← the LAST UNICORN ← the COMPLEAT BEATLES, **Iggy POP** *(himself)*, Michael Gwynne *(Duke of Rock)* ← PAYDAY, Scott Cohen *(friend)* ← VIBRATIONS ← the MAMBO KINGS, Luke Reilly *(Don Imus)* ← NIGHTHAWKS / → DANCER IN THE DARK

Storyline: The story of Howard Stern, a nerdy college kid who wants above all else to be a disc jockey. After some early setbacks, he finally gets his chance when he meets newscaster Robin Quivers in Washington. Determined to succeed this time, Stern goes all out to shock his audience with tasteless toilet humour and various studio sexploits. The radio executives try to muzzle him but the ratings keep going up, leading to a fantastic climax at a Central Park rally. *JZ*

Movie rating: *6

Visual: video + dvd

Off the record: A long list of Rock stars are present here:- **Chris Barron** (Spin Doctors), **John Popper** (Blues Traveler, **Flavor Flav** (Public Enemy), **MC Hammer**, **Ted Nugent**, **Slash** (Guns N' Roses), **Dee Snider** (Twisted Sister), **Ac/Dc** , **Ozzy**, **Iggy**, etc.

HOWARD STERN * (w/ Various Artists)

Feb 97. (cd/c) *Warner Bros.; <(9 46477-2/-4)>* [1] Mar97 [ ]
– Pig virus (*) / The great American nightmare (ROB ZOMBIE with *) / Mama look – – a boo boo (*) / I make my own rules (LL COOL J with FLEA, DAVE NAVARRO and CHAD SMITH) / The match game (*) / Hard charger (PORNO FOR PYROS) / Moti (*) / The suck for your solution (MARILYN MANSON) / Lance eluction (*) / Pictures of matchstick men (OZZY OSBOURNE with TYPE O NEGATIVE) / The contest (*) / Tired of waiting for you (GREEN DAY) / WRNW (*) / Pinhead (RAMONES) / Oh Howard (*) / The Ben Stern megamix / The Howard Stern experience (*) / Smoke on the water (DEEP PURPLE) / WCCC (*) / I want you to want me (CHEAP TRICK) / The antichrist (*) / Cat scratch fever (TED NUGENT) / WNBC (*) / Jamie's Cryin' (VAN HALEN) / Crackhead Bob (*) / You shook me all night long – live (AC/DC) / Howard you stink (*) / Ladies & gentlemen (*) / Tortured man (* and the DUST BROTHERS).

S/track review: It would be fair to say that Howard Stern is probably more famous for the controversy he created as opposed to the music he played, which is reflected in the soundtrack to his biopic, 'PRIVATE PARTS'. Featuring more sound clips from the film than actual songs reflects this fact, as does the actual music chosen, which doesn't exactly leave you drooling in anticipation. The format is mostly classic rock with some heavier stuff thrown in. DEEP PURPLE's 'Smoke On The Water', CHEAP TRICK's 'I Want You To Want Me', 'Cat Scratch Fever' by TED NUGENT, 'Jamie's Cryin'' from VAN HALEN, and a live 'You Shook Me All Night Long' from AC/DC throw up little in the way of surprises. As for the rest, 'Hard Charger' by PORNO FOR PYROS is easily one of the better tracks released by Perry Farrell's post-Jane's Addiction indiscretion. Anything by the RAMONES is always welcome and 'Pinhead' is no exception, while MARILYN MANSON's 'Suck For Your Solution' is okay if not the best one can expect from the dark one. Easily the best track on the album though is GREEN DAY's cover of the Kinks' 'Tired of Waiting For You' because, although it doesn't stray far from the original, it's good to hear an American band retain the subtle understatement of a great British band. Unfortunately, the antithesis of this previous statement is produced by OZZY OSBOURNE & TYPE O NEGATIVE's version of 'Pictures Of Matchstick Men', originally a hit in 1968 for Status Quo – truly awful. Also languishing in the atrocious category are Stern's own attempts at creating music rather than playing it, even with the help of the likes of ROB ZOMBIE and the DUST BROTHERS. 'PRIVATE PARTS' would suit the Hard-Rock crowd who don't mind a little trip down memory lane, and some of the clips are quite funny, but apart from that, the album has a tendency to recall rather than recreate. *CM*

Album rating: *6

PRIVILEGE

1967 (UK 102m) Universal Pictures (X)

Film genre: political Pop-music satire/mockumentary

Top guns: s-w: Peter Watkins (+ dir), Norman Bogner (story: Johnny Speight)

Stars: **Paul Jones** *(Steven Shorter)* → the COMMITTEE, Jean Shrimpton *(Vanessa Ritchie)*, **Mark London** *(Alvin Kirsch)*, Max Bacon *(Julie Jordan)* ← PLAY IT COOL, William Job *(Andrew Butler)*, Jeremy Child *(Martin Crossley)* → QUADROPHENIA → GIVE MY REGARDS TO BROAD STREET, James Cossins *(Professor Tatham)* → MELODY, Victor Henry *(Freddie K.)*, Frederick Danner *(Marcus Hooper)*, **the George Bean Group** *(the Runner Beans)*

Storyline: Tagged as "a film so bizarre, so controversial, it shall crucify your mind to the tree of conscious." In a future Great Britain it's the government who control what we do and what we think. But "youth will out" and in this case the outlet is pop star Steven Shorter, whose concerts are stage managed to perfection by the apparatchiks. Although the kids identify with Steven, he knows his life is just a facade, and when the establishment tell him to change his image to a squeaky-clean nice guy he decides it's time to take on the system for real. *JZ*

Movie rating: *5.5

Visual: video

Off the record: (see below)

---

the MIKE LEANDER ORCHESTRA (songs w/ Mark London)

Sep 67. (lp) *H.M.V.; (CLP/CSD 3623) Uni; <7 3005>* [ ] [ ]
– Privilege (vocal: PAUL JONES) / Stephen / Vanessa / Free me (vocal: PAUL JONES) / It's overotherness time / Free me (reprise) (vocal: PAUL JONES) / I've been a bad, bad boy (vocal: PAUL JONES) / Onward christian soldiers (vocal: GEORGE BEAN and THE RUNNER BEANS) / I'm alright jackboot / Alvin / Jerusalem (vocal: GEORGE BEAN and THE RUNNER BEANS) / Birmingham, oh Birmingham.

S/track review: God almighty! Manfred Mann's former frontman, PAUL JONES, takes his newly-found solo career one step further by starring/performing ("rock star" mode) in cult movie, 'PRIVILEGE'. Once a man who could put the pop into R&B via a plethora of Manfred Mann mid-60s hits (including '5-4-3-2-1', 'Do Wah Diddy Diddy', 'Come Tomorrow' & 'Pretty Flamingo'), here, it's all rather different. Under the guidance of composer/arranger/conductor, MIKE LEANDER, JONES gets to surge musically with songs such as 'Privilege' (the opener), recent hit 'I've Been A Bad, Bad Boy' (very repentive) and easily the LP's best tune, 'Free Me' (organ-ically mind-bending); the latter was reconstructed a decade later by punk-rock poetess, Patti Smith, for her 'Easter' set. The aforementioned LEANDER (who subsequently co-wrote numerous hits for Gary Glitter, etc.) was only 25 at the time, his classically-orchestrated numbers very effective at re-producing the "holier than thou" aspect. However, the music goes into OTT religious overdrive, when two hymnal songs, 'Onward Christian Soldiers' & 'Jerusalem' (by the GEORGE BEAN GROUP), take embarrassment to a new level – the worst I've ever heard! What would wannabe rock'n'roll star and political preacher, Tony Blair, have made of this? Answer: If he's not seen or heard it already, one thinks he'd probably love it. *MCS*

Album rating: *6

– spinoff releases, etc. –

PAUL JONES: I've Been A Bad, Bad Boy / (non-OST song)

Jan 67. (7") *(POP 1576)* 5

PAUL JONES: Privilege EP

Sep 67. (7"ep) *(7EG 8975)* –
– Privilege / Free me / Breaking / I've been a bad, bad boy.

PSYCH-OUT

1968 (US 101m) American International Pictures (R)

Film genre: psychedelic crime thriller

Top guns: dir: Richard Rush → the SAVAGE SEVEN / s-w: E. Hunter Willett (+ au), Betty Tusher, Betty Ulius

Stars: Susan Strasberg *(Jenny Davis)* ← the TRIP / → the RUNNIN' KIND, Dean Stockwell *(Dave)* → HUMAN HIGHWAY → PARIS, TEXAS → DUNE → TO LIVE AND DIE IN L.A. → TUCKER: THE MAN AND HIS DREAM → MADONNA: INNOCENCE LOST, Jack Nicholson *(Stoney)* → HEAD → EASY RIDER → TOMMY → the BORDER → BATMAN, Bruce Dern *(Steve Davis)* ← the TRIP ← the WILD ANGELS / → LAST MAN STANDING → ALL THE PRETTY HORSES → MASKED AND ANONYMOUS, Adam Roarke *(Ben)* ← PSYCH-OUT, Max Julien *(Elwood)* → the SAVAGE SEVEN → UP TIGHT! → the MACK, Tommy Flanders *(Wesley)*, Robert Kelljan *(Arthur)*, Henry Jaglom *(Warren)*, Linda G. Scott *(Lynn)* → LITTLE FAUSS AND BIG HALSY, **the Seeds w/ Sky Saxon** *(themselves)*, **the Strawberry Alarm Clock:- Ed KIng, Mark Weitz, Lee Freeman, Gary Lovetro, George Bunnel, Randy Seol** *(themselves)* → BEYOND THE VALLEY OF THE DOLLS, **the Storybook** *(themselves)*, **the Boenzee Cryque:- Rusty Young, George Grantham, Malcolm Mitchell, Joe E. Neddo, Sam Bush** *(themselves)*, Barbara London *(Sadie)* → CHASTITY, William Bonner *(thug)* → CLEOPATRA JONES → BLACK SHAMPOO

Storyline: Worth catching purely for Jack Nicholson's scrawny pony tail and Fillmore-stage guitar preening, 'Psych-Out' is less compelling in terms of narrative. The plot retches and gurns as queasily as Jenny's STP trip, mooning around after the teenage runaway and her doomed attempts to locate her brother Steve (who, like woaaah man, is nicknamed The Seeker) before he arsons his life up completely. *BG*

Movie rating: *5

Visual: video + dvd

Off the record: (see below)

—

Various Artists (score: Ronald Stein *)

Mar 68. (lp) *Sidewalk; <ST 5913>* –
– The pretty song from Psych-Out (the STORYBOOK) / Rainy day mushroom pillow (the STRAWBERRY ALARM CLOCK) / Two fingers pointing on you (the SEEDS) / Ashbury Wednesday (BOENZEE CRYQUE) / The world's on fire (the STRAWBERRY ALARM CLOCK) / Psych-out sanctorum (the STORYBOOK) * / Beads of innocence (the STORYBOOK) * / The love children (the STORYBOOK) * / Psych-out (the STORYBOOK) * / The world's on fire – long version (the STRAWBERRY ALARM CLOCK).

S/track review: In 1968, flower-power had blossomed into experimental psychedelia, but there was little to shout about the genre by way of a soundtrack. 'PSYCH-OUT' proved to be the catalyst. The album kicks off with 'The Pretty Song From Psych-Out', a harmony-fuelled Byrds-meets-Strawberry Alarm Clock-like number by the STORYBOOK (the latter was in fact written by S.A. Clock – clue, anyone?); the aforementioned STRAWBERRY ALARM CLOCK had a version of said song on a B-side to an 'Incense And Peppermints' follow-up, 'Sit With The Guru'. On track 2, the 'ALARM CLOCK rise to the occasion by way of 'Rainy Day Mushroom Pillow', a track slipping easily into top gear Pink Floyd, the harpsichord interlude proving very cinematic. An edited version of 'The World's On Fire' fits neatly on to the end of side one, its Doors-'Light My Fire'-like organ very intense if not a little twee by today's standards. One-off oddities by the SEEDS (featuring Sky Saxon) with 'Two Fingers Pointing On You' and country-rockers BOENZEE CRYQUE (comprising future Poco musicians, Rusty Young & George Grantham) on 'Ashbury Wednesday' nearly spoil the show, the latter track a clone of Jimi Hendrix's 'Purple Haze'. On side two, Ronald Stein (their writer and head honcho, it seemed) and the STORYBOOK are afforded a further four Pink Floyd-ish numbers, 'Psych-Out Sanctorum', 'Beads Of Innocence', 'The Love Children' and the title track, all suspiciously similar to a certain act with the initials SAC. The climax comes courtesy of an 8-minute-plus long version of 'The World's On Fire', so just set the controls for the heart of the sun and explode into space. *MCS*

Album rating: *7

PULP FICTION

1994 (US 153m) Miramax Films (R)

Film genre: crime/gangster comedy

Top guns: s-w: Quentin Tarantino (+ dir) ← RESERVOIR DOGS / → NATURAL BORN KILLERS → FOUR ROOMS → FROM DUSK TILL DAWN → JACKIE BROWN → KILL BILL: VOL.1 → KILL BILL: VOL.2, Roger Avary

Stars: John Travolta *(Vincent Vega)* ← SHOUT ← STAYING ALIVE ← URBAN COWBOY ← GREASE ← SATURDAY NIGHT FEVER / → PRIMARY COLORS → SWORDFISH → BE COOL → HAIRSPRAY re-make, Samuel L. Jackson *(Jules Winnfield)* ← JUICE ← JOHNNY SUEDE ← JUNGLE FEVER ← SCHOOL DAZE ← MAGIC STICKS / → JACKIE BROWN → KILL BILL: VOL.1 → KILL BILL: VOL.2 → BLACK SNAKE MOAN, Uma Thurman *(Mia Wallace)* ← EVEN COWGIRLS GET THE BLUES / → CHELSEA WALLS → BE COOL, Bruce Willis *(Butch Coolidge)* → FOUR ROOMS → LAST MAN STANDING → BEAVIS AND BUTT-HEAD DO AMERICA → the STORY OF US → OVER THE HEDGE, Harvey Keitel *(the Wolf)* ← RESERVOIR DOGS ← the LAST TEMPTATION OF CHRIST ← the BORDER ← THAT'S THE WAY OF THE WORLD / → FROM DUSK TILL DAWN → FINDING GRACELAND → BE COOL, Tim Roth *(Pumpkin)* ← RESERVOIR DOGS ← RETURN TO WATERLOO / → FOUR ROOMS → the MILLION DOLLAR HOTEL, Amanda Plummer *(Honey Bunny)* → the MILLION DOLLAR HOTEL, Ving Rhames *(Marsellus Wallace)* → BEEF → IDLEWILD, Maria De Medeiros *(Fabienne)*, Peter Greene *(Zed)* ← JUDGMENT NIGHT, Eric Stoltz *(Lance)* ← SINGLES ← FAST TIMES AT RIDGEMONT HIGH / → GRACE OF MY HEART → THINGS BEHIND THE SUN, Christopher Walken *(Capt. Koons)* ← WAYNE'S WORLD 2 ← HOMEBOY / → LAST MAN STANDING → TOUCH → the COUNTRY BEARS → ROMANCE & CIGARETTES →

HAIRSPRAY re-make, Bronagh Gallagher *(Trudi)* ← the COMMITMENTS, Rosanna Arquette *(Jody)* ← MORE AMERICAN GRAFFITI / → BUFFALO '66 → SUGAR TOWN → THINGS BEHIND THE SUN, Duane Whitaker *(Maynard)* ← SATURDAY NIGHT SPECIAL ← EDDIE PRESLEY / → the DEVIL'S REJECTS, Frank Whaley *(Brett)* ← the DOORS / → WENT TO CONEY ISLAND ON A MISSION FROM GOD . . . BE BACK BY FIVE → SHAKE, RATTLE & ROLL: AN AMERICAN LOVE STORY → CHELSEA WALLS → the HOTTEST STATE, Quentin Tarantino *(Jimmie Dimmick)* ← RESERVOIR DOGS ← EDDIE PRESLEY / → FOUR ROOMS → FROM DUSK TILL DAWN → GIRL 6, Steve Buscemi *(Buddy Holly look-alike)* ← RESERVOIR DOGS ← MYSTERY TRAIN ← the WAY IT IS / → AIRHEADS → the WEDDING SINGER → COFFEE AND CIGARETTES → ROMANCE & CIGARETTES → the FUTURE IS UNWRITTEN, Don Blakely *(Wilson's trainer)* ← the SPOOK WHO SAT BY THE DOOR ← SHORT EYES ← SHAFT'S BIG SCORE!, Kathy Griffin *(Kathy Griffin)* ← MEDUSA: DARE TO BE TRUTHFUL / → FOUR ROOMS → DILL SCALLION

Storyline: Interlocking four offbeat tales; a couple (Pumpkin and Honey Bunny) robbing a restaurant, two fast-talking hitmen (Vincent and the righteous Jules), a boxer on the take (Butch) from gangland boss (Marcellis Wallace), his coke-snorting missus (Mia), etc. – "Royale with cheese" best describes this MF of a film. *MCS*

Movie rating: *10

Visual: video + dvd

Off the record: (see below)

Various Artists (w/ "dialogue")

Oct 94. (cd/c) *M.C.A.; <(MCD/MCC 11103)>* [21] [5]
– "Pumpkin and Honey Bunny" – Misirlou (DICK DALE & HIS DEL-TONES) / "Royale with cheese" / Jungle boogie (KOOL & THE GANG) / Let's stay together (AL GREEN) / Bustin' surfboards (the TORNADOES) / Lonesome town (RICKY NELSON) / Son of a preacher man (DUSTY SPRINGFIELD) / "Zed's dead, baby" – Bullwinkle part II (the CENTURIANS) / "Jack Rabbit Slims twist contest" – You never can tell (CHUCK BERRY) / Girl, you'll be a woman soon (URGE OVERKILL) / If love is a red dress (hang me in rags) (MARIA McKEE) / "Bring out the gimp" – Comanche (the REVELS) / Flowers on the wall (the STATLER BROTHERS) / "Personality goes a long way" / Surf rider (the LIVELY ONES) / "Ezekiel 25:17". *<(re-iss. Oct02 +=; 113043-2)>* – Since I first met you (the ROBINS) / Rumble (LINK WRAY & HIS RAY MEN) / Strawberry letter #23 (BROTHERS JOHNSON) / Out of limits (the MARKETTS) / (interview with Quentin Tarantino).

S/track review: Having already resurrected the soundtrack genre with 'RESERVOIR DOGS' in '92, Quentin Tarantino made good on his early promise with as rip-snorting a follow-up as any in the history of film music. Until 'Trainspotting' surfaced a couple of years later, the 'PULP FICTION' soundtrack was the whitest-knuckle ride in town. A decade on it's still a blast. Film buffs routinely bemoan the surfeit of dialogue on movie soundtracks but – casting a backwards glance to the innovations of Melvin Van Peebles – Tarantino applies it with the same style, humour, timing and crafted anarchy which make his scripts so compelling in the first place. And while '. . .DOGS' raided the 70s for its little green bag of oldies, here Tarantino digs in the crates for an infinitely evocative stash of 60s surf tunes. The opening, expletive-happy gambit of 'Pumpkin And Honey Bunny', chased by the roiling, spidery runs of DICK DALE's 'Miserlou' sets the breakneck surf 'n' violence pace. It's a pace which lesser compilers would struggle to maintain over the course, but Tarantino just about carries it off. Nuggets from the likes of the TORNADOES, the CENTURIANS and the REVELS make up his impressive arsenal of treble mongering, strategically positioned like sonic landmines. DUSTY SPRINGFIELD's luscious 'Son Of A Preacher Man', URGE OVERKILL's peerless reading of NEIL DIAMOND's 'Girl, You'll Be A Woman Soon' (a US Top 10 in 1967) and MARIA McKEE's 'If Love Is A Red Dress (Hang Me In Rags)' supply emotional balance to an unhinged, peripatetic plot while the biblical fury of Samuel L. Jackson's closing dialogue, 'Ezekiel 25:17', literally provides a smoking gun in support of Tarantino's nomination as mad genius. *BG*

Album rating: *9

– spinoff hits, etc. –

URGE OVERKILL: Girl, You'll Be A Woman Soon / the TORNADOES: Bustin' Surfboards

Nov 94. (c-s) *<54935> (MCSC 2024)* [59] [37]
(cd-s+=) *(MCSTD 2024)* – the CENTURIANS: Bullwinkle part II.

PUMP UP THE VOLUME

1990 (Can/US 105m) New Line Cinema (R)

Film genre: coming-of-age/teen drama

Top guns: dir (+ s-w): Allan Moyle ← TIMES SQUARE / → EMPIRE RECORDS → MAN IN THE MIRROR: THE MICHAEL JACKSON STORY

Stars: Christian Slater *(Mark Hunter)* ← YOUNG GUNS II ← TUCKER: THE MAN AND HIS DREAM ← LIVING PROOF: THE HANK WILLIAMS JR. STORY / → MASKED AND ANONYMOUS, Ellen Greene *(Jan Emerson)* → ROCK-A-DOODLE, Scott Paulin *(Brian Hunter)* → I AM SAM, Samantha Mathis *(Nora Diniro)* → THIS IS MY LIFE → the THING CALLED LOVE, Cheryl Pollak *(Paige)*, **Annie Ross** *(Mrs. Loretta Creswood)*, Andy Romano *(Murdock)* ← BEACH PARTY, Ahmet Zappa *(Jamie)*, Mimi Kennedy *(Marla Hunter)*, Lin Shaye *(PTA parent #3)* ← the LONG RIDERS / → ROADSIDE PROPHETS → EVEN COWGIRLS GET THE BLUES ← LAST MAN STANDING → DETROIT ROCK CITY, James Hampton *(Arthur Watts)* ← MACKINTOSH & T.J., Seth Green *(Joey)* → JOSIE AND THE PUSSYCATS → BE COOL → ELECTRIC APRICOT: QUEST FOR FESTEROO, Billy Morrissette *(Mazz Mazzilli)* ← CATCH ME IF YOU CAN, Matt McGrath *(Chris)* → COLIN FITZ LIVES!

Storyline: Mark is a student at an Arizona high school. His parents give him a short wave radio so he can talk to his pals back East, but Mark has other ideas. He sets up a pirate radio station down in his cellar and broadcasts to the community by night as Hard Harry. Soon his show becomes cult listening as he encourages anarchy at the high school and incurs the wrath of the authorities. *JZ*

Movie rating: *6.5

Visual: video + dvd

Off the record: **Annie Ross** was actually an easy-listening jazz singer who went on to star and perform in the movie, 'Short Cuts' (1993). *MCS*

Various Artists (score: Cliff Martinez)

Aug 90. (lp/c/cd) *M.C.A.; <MCA/+C/D 8039> (MCG/MCGC/ DMCG 6121)* [50] Nov90 [ ]
– Everybody knows (CONCRETE BLONDE) / Why can't I fall in love (IVAN NEVILLE) / Stand! (LIQUID JESUS) / Wave of mutilation (UK surf) (PIXIES) / I've got a miniature secret camera (PETER MURPHY) / Kick out the jams (BAD BRAINS & HENRY ROLLINS) / Freedom of speech (ABOVE THE LAW) / Heretic (SOUNDGARDEN) / Titanium exposé (SONIC YOUTH) / Me and the Devil blues (COWBOY JUNKIES) / Tale o' the twister (CHAGALL GUEVARA).

S/track review: Playing like Christian Slater's character's volatile mixtape, it opens with CONCRETE BLONDE's cover of Leonard Cohen's 'Everybody Knows', a reverb-heavy and sexy rumination on the slight betrayals that make up our lives, which reaches a soaring climax. IVAN NEVILLE then longingly pleads 'Why Can't I Fall In Love', replete with session guitar solo. LIQUID JESUS cover Sly and the Family Stone's 'Stand!' in a rather conventional way, but PIXIES' 'Wave of Mutilation (U.K. Surf)'s use of thudding bass and intriguing surfy chords makes amends in a strangely soothing manner. PETER MURPHY's sly electronica gives way to the unholy union of BAD BRAINS & HENRY ROLLINS reigniting MC5's firebrand classic 'Kick Out The Jams' (which does prompt the question, just how many times has this song been covered?!), although it sets itself out from the crowd with some wonderfully twisted soloing to deliver its Metallic K.O. ABOVE THE LAW's effortless hip-hop is offset by SOUNDGARDEN's grinding 'Heretic', with several arresting tempo changes and Chris Cornell imperious as ever, raw as the recording is. Supporting the heavy alternative rock charge are SONIC YOUTH with 'Titanium Exposé', a quirky and frenetic piece of music which eases into a more ethereal mid-paced jam. Some screwed-up soloing presages its pounding, doomy outro. Surprisingly, COWBOY JUNKIES' version of Robert Johnson's 'Me And The Devil Blues' slinks into view and out again without making much of an impression. *DF*

Album rating: *6

PUNK ROCK HOLOCAUST

2004 (US 95m; straight-to-dvd) Backseat / Springman Records (R)

Film genre: Rock-music slasher-horror comedy

Top guns: s-w: Doug Sakmann (+ dir), Nick Esposito, Christopher Stella

Stars: Kevin Lyman *(Warped tour founder)* → PUNK'S NOT DEAD, Heather Vantress *(Warped tour reporter)*, Lloyd Kaufman *(Belial/Satan)* ← FRIENDS FOREVER, Steven Smith *(Fuse Action news reporter)*, Jeff Rosenstock *(Brutal Enigma guitarist)*, J.T. Turret *(Brutal Enigma keyboards player)*, **Andrew W.K.** *(performer)*, **Atmosphere:- Slug, Mr. Dibbs, Murs** *(performers)*, **Beret!:- Jacques Merde, Henri En Coute, Ramone Sanchez, Albert Fausse Couche** *(performers)*, **Big D and the Kids Table:- Tom Bishop, Sean Murphy, Sean Rogan, Daniel Stoppelman, Stephen Foote, Chris Bush, David McWane, David Lagveaux** *(performers)*, **Bowling For Soup:- Jaret Reddick, Gary Wiseman, Erik Chandler, Chris Burney** *(performers)*, **Destruction Made Simple:- Raul Landers, Andy Rodrigues, Adrian Montes, Isiah Hernandez** *(performers)*, **Dropkick Murphys:- Scruffy Wallace, James Lynch, Texas Bob, Stephanie** *(performers)*, **Face To Face:- Scott Shiflett, Pete Parada, Trever Keizt** *(performers)*, **Glassjaw:- Daryl Palumbo, Larry Gorman** *(performers)*, **Horrorpops:- Patricia Day, Kim Nekroman, Karsten, Kamilla, Millie** *(performers)*, **the Kids Of Widney High:- Tanesa Tarvin, Cain Fonseca, Elisa De La Torre, Fabian Castillo, Shelly Goodhope** *(performers)*, **Less Than Jake:- Chris Hagar, Roger Thig, Louis 'Buddy' Schaub** *(performers)*, **Me First and the Gimme Gimmes w/ Fat Mike *, R. Joseph Cape, Sean Slawson, Dave Raun, Chris Shiflett** *(performers)* → CAKE BOY *, **M.E.S.T.:- Tony Lovato, Matt Lovato, Nick Gigler** *(performers)*, **Never Heard Of It:- Greg Lynch, Rick Avery, Seth Noack, Janoshka Creager, David J. Dellosa** *(performers)*, **Pennywise:- Jim Lindberg, Fletcher Dragge, Byron McMackin, Randy Bradbury** *(performers)*, **the Phenomenauts:- Commander Angel Nova, Corp. Joe Bot, Prof. Greg Arius, Colonel Re Hotch, Captain Chree-hos** *(performers)*, **Rancid:- Tim Armstrong *, Lars Fredricksen **, Matt Freeman, Brett Reed** *(performers)* ← END OF THE CENTURY / ** → PUNK'S NOT DEAD, **Simple Plan:- Pierre Bouvier, Sebastien Lefebure, Chuck Corneau, David Desrosiers, Jeff Stinco** *(performers)*, **Suicide Machines:- Jay Navarro, Ryan Vandeberghe, Rich Tschirhart, Dan Lukacinsky** *(performers)*, **Treephort:- Lee Satterfield, Joe Klein, Kyle Knight, London May, Sonny Harding, Oscar Velez** *(performers)*, **Tsunami Bomb:- Agent M., Dominic Davi, Gabriel Linderman, Mike Griffen** *(performers)*, **the Used:- Bert McCracken, Jeph Howard, Quinn Allman, Branden Steinedart** *(performers)*, **Vendetta Red:- Joseph Childres** *(themselves)*

Storyline: "Punk's not dead, but it's about to be". In this gorefest, various punk bands in the Vans Warped Tour are reduced one by one by a manic killer, who has a penchant for smashed skulls and trailing intestines. Meanwhile, sinister record producer Belial is keeping a close eye on what's left of the tour and as the body count rises by the minute it's up to the plucky tour reporter to solve this Brutal Enigma before she becomes the next victim. *JZ*

Movie rating: *4

Visual: dvd on 'Springman' (no audio OST; clips on dvd)

Off the record: A plethora of new – and old! – punk kids on the block are present including:- ANDREW WK ('Party Hard' & 'Get Ready To Die'), RANCID ('Dead Bodies'), HORRORPOPS ('Where They Wander'), BERET! ('Tete d'Hamburger'), the KIDS OF WIDNEY HIGH ('Doctor, Doctor'), SUICIDE MACHINES ('Feeling Of Dread'), the PHENOMENAUTS ('Y2K' & 'Space Flight'), DESTRUCTION MADE SIMPLE ('Trouble And Chaos'), TREEPHORT ('(Why Do) Fat Kids Like Metallica'), etc. – there was a sequel, 'PUNK ROCK HOLOCAUST 2' (2005). *MCS*

PURE COUNTRY

1992 (US 113m) Warner Bros. Pictures (PG)

Film genre: romantic showbiz/Country-music drama

Top guns: dir: Christopher Cain / s-w: Rex McGee

Stars: George Strait *(Dusty Wyatt Chandler)*, Lesley Ann Warren *(Lula Rogers)* ← BAJA OKLAHOMA ← SONGWRITER, Isabel Glasser *(Harley Tucker)*, Kyle Chandler *(Buddy Jackson)*, **John DOE** *(Earl Blackstock)*, Rory Calhoun *(Ernest Tucker)*, Jeff Prettyman *(Bobby Louis)* ← SUBURBIA

Storyline: Country star Dusty Chandler realizes he has forgotten his roots when he misreads his lines at a concert and no-one even notices. He gets away from hi-tech special effects and escapes to dear old granny and the Tucker ranch away in the back country. Wise words and a haircut do wonders and Dusty ends up with his new girlfriend Harley getting ready for the big rodeo competition. But when he learns he's been replaced on stage by the manager's girlfriend, the Stetson comes off for the big showdown. *JZ*

Movie rating: *6

Visual: video

Off the record: GEORGE STRAIT (b.18 May'52, Poteet, Texas, USA) has been around the Nashville C&W scene since around 1973, however it would take another decade before he broke into the mainstream pop charts. 80s sets, including 'Right Or Wrong' (1983), 'Does Fort Worth Ever Cross Your Mind' (1984), '#7' (1986), 'Ocean Front Property' (1987), 'If You Ain't Lovin' You Ain't Livin'' (1988) and 'Beyond The Blue Neon' (1989), all found the man on the brink of major success, but it wasn't until the 90s that STRAIT's career took off. 'Livin' It Up' in 1990 to 'Always Never The Same' in 1999, the country hunk (who was once chosen by People magazine as one of the 50 Most Beautiful) had album hit after album hit; 'Easy Come, Easy Go' (1993) cracked the Top 5 for the first time, while 'Carrying Your Love With Me' (1997) topped the charts. The man could no wrong. *MCS*

GEORGE STRAIT (songwriters: various) (md: Steve Dorff)

Sep 92. (cd/c) *M.C.A.; <(MCD/MCC 10651)>* 6 Apr93
– Heartland / Baby your baby / I cross my heart / When did you stop loving me / She lays it all on the line / Overnight male / Last in love / Thoughts of a fool / The king of broken hearts / Where the sidewalk ends / Heartland (main title sequence).

S/track review: GEORGE STRAIT's loyalty to the honky-tonk and Western Swing styles of his Texas roots has fostered twenty-five years of hit records (seeing off Garth Brooks and a wagonful of briefly vogueish "hat acts" along the way), so it's no surprise to find his one starring role pursuing issues of musical integrity. Still, you'd think a story about stardom's corrupting influence would give the singer a good excuse to flirt with some different styles, but not this cowboy: there are none of the rock-addled wanderings which sabotaged Brooks' later career. Instead, it's another opportunity for STRAIT to position himself as the voice of middle America ("When you hear twin fiddles and a steel guitar/You're listening to the sound of the American heart.") The result is a straight-up country album, faultlessly arranged, paced and played by top-notch sidemen like RANDY SCRUGGS and BUDDY EMMONS. From the clunking double entendres of 'Overnight Male' to the bleeding heart of 'When Did You Stop Loving Me?' there are few surprises, and the childish contribution of GEORGE STRAIT JR will be too cute for many. But whether this polished and heartfelt collection sounds like cliché or classic will hang on your view of mainstream country and its sentiments. *ND*

Album rating: *6.5

PURPLE PEOPLE EATER

1988 (US 91m) MPCA / Concorde Pictures (PG)

Film genre: Pop/Rock-music sci-fi comedy

Top guns: s-w + dir: Linda Shayne

Stars: Neil Patrick Harris *(Billy Johnson)*, Ned Beatty *(grandpa)* ← NASHVILLE ← DELIVERANCE / → HE GOT GAME, Shelley Winters *(Rita)* ← ELVIS: THE MOVIE ← CLEOPATRA JONES ← WILD IN THE STREETS / → HEAVY, Peggy Lipton *(mom)*, James Houghton *(dad)* ← MORE AMERICAN GRAFFITI ← I WANNA HOLD YOUR HAND ← ONE ON ONE, **Sheb Wooley** *(Harry Skinner)*, **Chubby Checker** *(himself)* ← LET THE GOOD TIMES ROLL ← DON'T KNOCK THE TWIST ← IT'S TRAD, DAD! ← TWIST AROUND THE CLOCK ← TEENAGE MILLIONAIRE / → TWIST, **LITTLE RICHARD** *(mayor)*, Linda Shayne *(nurse)*

Storyline: Young Billy Johnson is being looked after by Grandpa while his parents are abroad. When he plays an old record of 'Purple People Eater', a spaceship lands outside and a one-eyed, furry, purple thingy appears from within. It has not come to conquer Earth or meet world leaders, but, much worse, to play in a rock'n'roll band. However, PPE's musical career is put on hold when he and Billy must save Gramps' old folk's village from the greedy landlord. *JZ*

Movie rating: *3.5

Visual: video

Off the record: Sheb Wooley (see below)

Various Artists/Cast (score: Dennis Dreith)

1988. (lp/c/cd) *AJK Music; <A 227-1/-4/-2>* [ ] [–]
– The purple people eater (D.K. AND THE FLAMZ) / Twist it up (CHUBBY CHECKER) / See you in September (the HAPPENINGS) / Good golly Miss Molly (LITTLE RICHARD) / Georgie Porgie (JEWEL AKENS) / When you dance (D.K. AND THE FLAMZ) / Fun, fun, fun (JAN & DEAN) / The birds and the bees (SHA-NA-NA) / Rockin' robin (BOBBY DAY) / Dance with me (the BLENDELLS) / Anyone but you (MIKE HARRIS with PENNY & SONDRA and the BOB SUMMERS ORCHESTRA) / Do the Purple (LONGFELLOW).

S/track review: Taking rock'n'roll nostalgia to new depths, 'PURPLE PEOPLE EATER' is definitely one for the kids and the grandmas – well it does star Ned Beatty and Shelley Winters. SHEB WOOLEY's novelty chart-topper from 1958 made into celluloid fun, although most would disagree. Where else would you start than with a version of "a rock'n'roll, one-eyed, one-horned, flying . . . Purple People Eater", done here (and I emphasize, done) by D.K. AND THE FLAMZ; the latter get another chance to redeem themselves via 'When You Dance'. And did they? In a word, NO. However, there are a few old RnR/R&B nuggets here: CHUBBY CHECKER's 'Twist It Up', LITTLE RICHARD's 'Good Golly Miss Molly', JAN & DEAN's Beach Boys take 'Fun, Fun, Fun' and BOBBY DAY's 'Rockin' Robin'. Whether it's because they stand out next to the likes of mid-60s, bubblegum hits by the HAPPENINGS ('See You In September'), JEWEL AKENS ('Georgie Porgie') and Latino flops from L.A. the BLENDELLS ('Dance With Me'), we'll never know. *MCS*

Album rating: *3

PURPLE RAIN

1984 (US 113m) Purple Films / Warner Bros. Pictures (R)

Film genre: romantic Pop/Rock Musical drama

Top guns: s-w: Albert Magnoli (+ dir), William Blinn

Stars: PRINCE *(the kid)*, **Apollonia Kotero** *(Apollonia)*, **Morris Day** *(Morris)* → the ADVENTURES OF FORD FAIRLANE → GRAFFITI BRIDGE, Olga Karlatos *(mother)*, Clarence Williams III *(father)*, Billy Sparks *(Billy)*, **Wendy Melvoin** *(Wendy)*, **Lisa Coleman** *(Lisa)*, **Jerome Benton** *(Jerome)* → UNDER THE CHERRY MOON → GRAFFITI BRIDGE, **Eric Leeds** *(stage hand)*, **Jill Jones** *(Jill)* → GRAFFITI BRIDGE, **Bobby Z.** *(performer)*, **Brown Mark** *(performer)*, **Matt Fink** *(performer)*, **Dez Dickerson** *(performer)*, **Susan Moonsie** *(Susan)*, **Garry Johnson** *(Jellybean)* → GRAFFITI BRIDGE, **Jesse Johnson** *(Jesse)* → GRAFFITI BRIDGE

Storyline: An Afro-American dandy with more self-belief than Muhammad Ali, The Kid is convinced that his strange new music is the way forward but folks just don't understand, especially the owner of the club where he's resident. To make matters worse, his parents are constantly at each other's throats and his nemesis Morris Day (frontman with The Time) plots to steal his thunder as well as his woman. On a good night though, he has the audience wide eyed under their new wave haircuts, making like an "amalgam of Marc Bolan, Nijinsky and the Scarlet Pimpernel" – as colourfully described by Time Out. *BG*

Movie rating: *7.5

Visual: video + dvd

Off the record: PRINCE (see own entry)

PRINCE & THE REVOLUTION

Jul 84. (lp,purple-lp/c/cd) *Warners; <(9 25110-1/-4/-2)>* [1] [7]
– Let's go crazy / Take me with U / The beautiful ones / Computer blue / Darling Nikki / When doves cry / I would die 4 U / Baby I'm a star / Purple rain. *(re-iss. cd/c Feb95; 925110-2/-4) (lp re-iss. Jun99; same)*

S/track review: For the likes of Michael Jackson and PRINCE, the CD/MTV revolution couldn't have been more convenient. Both pretty much made their careers on the back of early 80s mega-albums which themselves milked the novelty value of a new format and a video revolution. Lacking a decent plot, 'Purple Rain' functioned better as a series of video promos for the multi-million selling soundtrack. And if the metronomic pop-funk of '1999' (1983) had set the parameters of the so-called Minneapolis sound, that soundtrack made its architect a superstar, while the film furthered the careers of the Time, Apollonia 6 and Sheila E amongst others. It helped that an advance single, 'When Doves Cry' – a singularly haunting piece of kitchen-sink electro-pop – became his first UK No.1, proving that if anyone could make synth material soulful, it was PRINCE. 'Let's Go Crazy' had brand new-retro funk-rock in the bag, a No.1 chaser a couple of months later. Balladry bombastic enough to sink a battleship; proto-spiritual enough to count as post-modern gospel? The title track almost made it a hat trick, concluding with a guitar solo which "stakes his claim as Hendrix's musical heir", according to writer Craig Werner. The continuing wonder of PRINCE is not just the stylistic breadth which prompted Miles Davis to hail to him as a successor to Duke Ellington, but how his material – at the time as contemporary as legwarmers but now dredged from the decade with the shortest shelf life – has aged as well as it has. Even at his most synthetically effete ('I Would Die 4 U'), naughtily baroque (the Tipper Gore-baiting 'Darling Nikki') or doggedly 80s-sounding ('Computer Blue'), the man has a sureness of touch – no pun intended – convinced of its own longevity. This isn't his best album, or his funkiest, but it's by far the most cohesive. And for as overarchingly ambitious an artist as PRINCE, that's no mean praise. *BG*

Album rating: *8

– spinoff hits, etc. –

PRINCE & THE REVOLUTION: When Doves Cry

May 84. (7"/12"/c-s) *<29286> (W 9296/+T/C)* [1] Jun84 [4]

PRINCE & THE REVOLUTION: Let's Go Crazy

Jul 84. (7") *<29216>* [1] [–]

PRINCE & THE REVOLUTION: Purple Rain

Sep 84. (7"/7"sha-pic-d/12") *<29174> (W 9174/+P/T)* [2] [8]

PRINCE & THE REVOLUTION: I Would Die 4 U

Nov 84. (7"/12"/12") *<29121> (W 9121/+T/TE)* [8] [58]

PRINCE & THE REVOLUTION: Let's Go Crazy / Take Me With U

Feb 85. (7"/12") *(K 2000/+T)* [7] [–]

PRINCE & THE REVOLUTION: Take Me With U / Baby I'm A Star

Feb 85. (7") *<29079>* [–] [25]

QUADROPHENIA

1979 (UK 115m) The Who Films / Brent Walker Films (18)

Film genre: coming-of-age/teen drama

Top guns: s-w: Franc Roddam (+ dir), Dave Humphries ← FLAME, Martin Stellman → BABYLON, **Pete Townshend** <= the WHO =>

Stars: Phil Daniels *(Jimmy Michael Cooper)* → BREAKING GLASS → STILL CRAZY → SEX, CHIPS AND ROCK N' ROLL, Mark Wingett *(Dave)* → BREAKING GLASS, Philip Davis *(Chalky)* → the WALL → STILL CRAZY, Leslie Ash *(Steph)*, Garry Cooper *(Peter)* → 1984 → BEAUTIFUL THING, **TOYAH Willcox** *(Monkey)*, **STING** *(Ace Face)*, Trevor Laird *(Ferdy)*, Michael Elphick *(Mr. Cooper; Jimmy's father)* ← STARDUST ← O LUCKY MAN! / → BUDDY'S SONG, Kate Williams *(Jimmy's mother)* ← MELODY, Raymond Winstone *(Kevin)* → LADIES AND GENTLEMEN, THE FABULOUS STAINS → SEXY BEAST → COLD MOUNTAIN → the PROPOSITION → BREAKING AND ENTERING, Gary Shail *(Spider)* ← the MUSIC MACHINE / → SHOCK TREATMENT → GIVE MY REGARDS TO BROAD STREET, Kim Neve *(Yvonne)*, Benjamin Whitrow *(Mr. Fulford)* → BRIMSTONE & TREACLE, Jeremy Child *(Aganey man)* ← PRIVILEGE / → GIVE MY REGARDS TO BROAD STREET, Timothy Spall *(projectionist)* → GOTHIC → STILL CRAZY → ROCK STAR, John Binden *(Harry)* ← PERFORMANCE, Trevor Laird *(Ferdy)* → BABYLON, Hugh Lloyd *(Mr. Cale)* ← JUST FOR FUN ← IT'S TRAD, DAD!, **Gary Holton** *(aggressive rocker)* ← BREAKING GLASS, John Altman *(John)* → BIRTH OF THE BEATLES

Storyline: Frank Roddam's unsentimental film adaptation of the WHO's rock opera centres on the growing pains and misadventures of Jimmy, a rebellious working class youth with an identity crisis. Enamoured with Mod culture, the pill-popping, scooter-riding teenager ends up in Brighton battling his sworn enemies, the Rockers, and getting sweaty up an alley with Mod babe Stephanie. *BG*

Movie rating: *7.5

Visual: video + dvd

Off the record: Before **Gary Holton** literally said "Auf Wiedersehen, Pet" on 25th October, 1985 (morphine and alcohol poisoning), the Londoner was actually in a mid-70s band, the Heavy Metal Kids. After a brief outing as lead singer with the Damned, he just might've become frontman for AC/DC after the tragic death of Bon Scott. *MCS*

the WHO (& Various Artists)

Sep 79. (d-lp)(d-c) *Polydor; (2625 037)(3577 352) <6235>* [23] [46]
– I am the sea / The real me / I'm one / 5:15 / Love reign o'er me / Bell boy / I've had enough / Helpless dancer / Doctor Jimmy / Zoot suit (the HIGH NUMBERS) / Hi heel sneakers (the CROSS SECTION) / Get out and stay out / Four faces / Joker James / The punk and the godfather / Night train (JAMES BROWN) / Louie Louie (the KINGSMEN) / Green onions (BOOKER T. & THE MG'S) / Rhythm

of the rain (the CASCADES) / He's so fine (the CHIFFONS) / BE MY BABY (the RONETTES) / Da doo ron ron (the CRYSTALS) / I'm the face (the HIGH NUMBERS). *(d-cd iss.1988; 831074-2) (cd re-iss. Jun96; 531971-2)*

S/track review: You get the feeling that in the 70s, the WHO – like Led Zep and the 'Stones – could have done practically anything and people would have lapped it up. Few bands however, would have had the nerve to try a third rock opera. 'TOMMY' was a huge success and PETE TOWNSHEND nearly killed himself with the aborted 'LIFEHOUSE' project. 'QUADROPHENIA' was another overblown, epic musical folly that worked best when honed to become the soundtrack to Franc Roddam's simultaneously boisterous and ponderous teen tribe fable. The film plays out in hunks as an extended rock video, such is the dominating power of the music. The first two sides of the original double soundtrack album find the WHO at their persuasive, bombastic best. The feral stomp of 'The Real Me' or '5.15' leave no doubt who was the ace face in the crowd is here and, while the film itself is riddled with holes, it hardly mattered, this is a trip and the WHO are in the driving seat, revving up their Vespa, raring to go. They get, fast and furious ('I've Had Enough'), grand and tragic ('Love Reign O'er Me') even just plain silly ('Bell Boy'). Only moments of lyrical cheese tarnish an otherwise compelling WHO collection. Additionally, the inclusion of tracks by JAMES BROWN, MARVIN GAYE, BOOKER T & THE MGs, the CHIFFONS and other notables of the late 60s give a distinct, if cursory overview of the original Mod era at its peak. Throwing in 'Hi Heel Sneakers' by a second generation Mod outfit the CROSS SECTION – which they perform in a scene in the movie itself – makes this an untidy mix which may jump around chronologically but wears fairly well, the familiar moody cool that the Mods aspired to is the tie that binds the music together. A recent remastered edition throws in a few more tracks for good measure but in truth, they add little to the original product. The original double vinyl was just enough. Bar the clutch of new tracks, etc., it's probably worth referring back to the earlier record for a more comprehensive sense of what TOWNSHEND was trying to achieve. *MR*

Album rating: *7

– spinoff hits, etc. –

the WHO: 5:15 / I'm One

Sep 79. (7") *(WHO 3) <2022>* [ ] [45]

– associated release –

the WHO: Quadrophenia

Nov 73. (d-lp) *Track; (2657 002) M.C.A.; <10004>* [2] [2]
– I am the sea / The real me / Quadrophenia / Cut my hair / The punk and the godfather / I'm one / Dirty jobs / Helpless dancer / Is it in my head? / I've had enough / 5:15 / Sea and sand / Drowned / Bell boy / Doctor Jimmy / The rock / Love, reign o'er me. *(re-iss. Sep79 on 'Polydor' d-lp)(d-c; 2657013)(3526001) (d-cd-iss. Jan87 on 'Polydor'; 831074-2)*

QUEEN OF THE DAMNED

2002 (US/Aus 101m) Warner Bros. Pictures (R)

Film genre: occult horror

Top guns: dir: Michael Rymer / s-w: Scott Abbott, Michael Petroni (nov: 'The Vampire Chronicles' Anne Rice)

Stars: Aaliyah *(Queen Akasha)*, Stuart Townsend *(Lestat de Lioncourt / the vampire Lestat)*, Marguerite Moreau *(Jesse Reeves)*, Vincent Perez *(Marius de Romanus)*, Paul McGann *(David Talbot)*, Lena Olin *(Maharet)*, Christian Manon *(Mael)*, Claudia Black *(Pandora)*, Bruce Spence *(Khayman)* ← SWEET TALKER ← RIKKY AND PETE ← 20th CENTURY OZ, Pia Miranda *(Jesse's roommate)* → GARAGE DAYS, Tiriel Mora *(Roger)* → GARAGE DAYS, **Rowland S. Howard** *(vampire guitarist)*, **Hugo Race** *(vampire bassman)* ← DOGS IN SPACE, **Aimee Nash** *(vampire singer)*, **Robin Casinader** *(vampire pianist)*, **Jonathan Davis** *(scalper)*, Franklyn Ajaye *(French dealer)* ← GET CRAZY ← the JAZZ SINGER ← CAR WASH, John Dicks *(talamascan)* ← FLAME, Johnathan Devoy *(James)* → GARAGE DAYS, Anni Finsterer *(Euro Trash vampire)* ← BIGGER THAN TINA ← TO HAVE AND TO HOLD, Dino Marnika *(music journalist)* ← AMY

Storyline: Loosely based on the 2nd and 3rd novels of Anne Rice's vampire trilogy that began with 'Interview With A Vampire', the movie's central character is the vampire, Lestat, who is awakened from decades of sleep by a heavy rock band. He proceeds to join the group as lead singer and becomes a huge international sensation while upsetting Marius – the vampire who created him – for drawing too much attention. Undeterred, Lestat's powerful music awakens Akasha, the vampire queen who takes Lestat to be her king leading to the inevitable confrontation with the old vampire order. *KM*

Movie rating: *4.5

Visual: dvd

Off the record: AALIYAH was born Aaliyah Dani Houghton, 16th January '79, Brooklyn, New York, USA; pronounced Ah-lee-yah. Tragedy was to befall one of R&B's most talented and gifted young artists in August 2001, when AALIYAH, a revered and respected figure in the music industry was killed in a plane crash after a video shoot in the Bahamas. She was only 22, but left an amazing legacy behind her with everyone from Sean Combs (P. Diddy), R. Kelly and Usher expressing their deep regrets that such a blossoming talent had to die so young. AALIYAH was raised in Detroit by her musical mother, who was also a soul singer. She had other musical connections in her family; her uncle, an entertainment lawyer, was married to GLADYS KNIGHT, whom AALIYAH appeared on stage with aged only eleven. Her debut album 'Age Ain't Nothing But A Number' (1994), made it into the Top 10 but she also courted controversy, quite literally, when she married her producer R Kelly at the tender age of fifteen. However, the relationship was not to last, with AALIYAH departing from the R&B millionaire in 1996. She collaborated with rising stars Timbaland and Missy Elliott on her sophomore set 'One In A Million' (1996), a collection of sassy R&B tracks, mixed with hip-hop and a fruity dance, funk/soul style. Eventually, AALIYAH made her way into the world of movies, starring in the Jet Li-vehicle 'Romeo Must Die' and signing up to star in the two sequels in 'The Matrix' series. AALIYAH issued her self-titled album in 2001, after a long recording hiatus and began work on her second feature film 'QUEEN OF THE DAMNED', in which she played a sexy, femme fatale, who just so happened to be a vampire. The young actress/artist's career was finally reaching boiling point when the tragedy struck. But with such a detailed and enigmatic legacy, she was becoming the most respected and dearly missed artist of her generation. 2002's posthumous 'I Care 4 U' paid tribute to that legacy with a measured selection of past glories from early hits like 'Back And Fourth', right through to cuts from 2001's eponymous 'Aaliyah' album. *BG & MCS*

Various (composers: JONATHAN DAVIS & RICHARD GIBBS *)

Feb 02. (cd) *Warners; <(9362 48288-2)>* [28] Mar02 [ ]
– Not meant for me (WAYNE STATIC) * / Forsaken (DAVID DRAIMAN) * / System (CHESTER BENNINGTON) * / Change (in the house of flies) (DEFTONES) / Redeemer (MARILYN MANSON) * / Dead cell (PAPA ROACH) / Penetrate (GODHEAD) / Slept so long (JAY GORDON) * / Down with the sickness (DISTURBED) / Cold (STATIC-X) / Headstrong (EARSHOT) / Body crumbles (DRY CELL) / Excess (TRICKY) / Before I'm dead (KIDNEYTHIEVES).

S/track review: With music befitting of a vampire flick, this nu-metal compilation showcases the best and worst of a genre obsessed with all things black. Five tracks here were written by Korn's JONATHAN DAVIS together with soundtrack composer, RICHARD GIBBS, but contractual reasons mean that the DAVIS vocals which appear on the actual film score have been re-recorded here by other artists. Not necessarily a bad thing when you look at the list of veritable nu-metallers taking the mantle like MARILYN MANSON and Linkin Park's CHESTER BENNINGTON, whose version of 'System' ably displays the glaring contrast between gentle yet sinister verses and bellowing, cod-evil choruses that underlie most nu-metal music. No exception is WAYNE STATIC with his two contributions, the inspired funk metaller, 'Cold' and the lyrically inferior DAVIS/GIBBS penned 'Not Meant For Me'. MARILYN MANSON's cover ('Redeemer') may have had better lines but his typical overdependence on multiple vocal layers leaves the background music sounding half-finished. Slicker production follows on DEFTONES' 'Change (In The House Of Flies)', which, although not specifically written for the film, fits in well and brings a certain level of sophistication and originality to the album. That's more than can be said for RAGE AGAINST THE MACHINE copycats, PAPA ROACH, whose laudably convulsive rap-metal display renders the soundtrack more inclusive if a little past its sell by date. *KM*

Album rating: *6

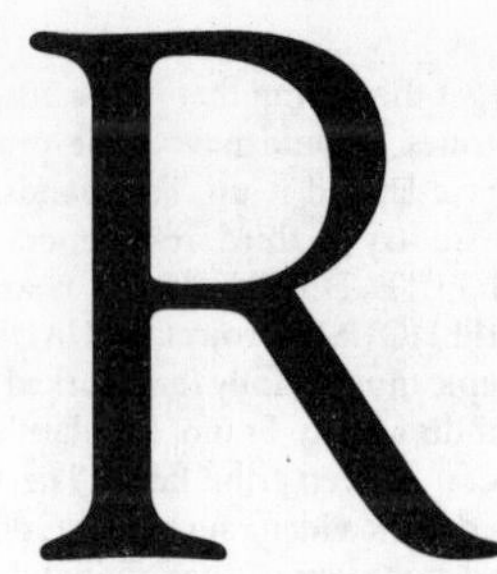

RADIO ON

1980 (UK/W.Ger 104m b&w) NFFC / Road Movies Filmproduktion (18)

Film genre: Road movie/mystery

Top guns: s-w: Christopher Petit (+ dir), Heidi Adolph

Stars: David Beames *(Robert)* → McVICAR, Lisa Kreuzer *(Ingrid)*, Sandy Ratcliff *(Kathy)*, Andrew Byatt *(deserter)*, **Sue Jones-Davies** *(girl)* ← ROCK FOLLIES OF '77, **STING** *(Just Like Eddie)*, Sabina Michael *(aunt)* → STILL CRAZY

Storyline: Robert is a DJ for an obscure radio station in London. His life is dull and commonplace, until one day he is told that his brother has died in Bristol. He sets off to get more information from those who knew him, but as time goes on Robert seems to take less and less interest in his brother's death and loses himself in long journeys through the cold winter landscape. Produced by German director Wim Wenders, the film was revisited, shortened and remixed in 1988 – unusual! *JZ*

Movie rating: *5.5

Visual: video + dvd (no audio OST)

Off the record: Sue Jones-Davies performed for Welsh-speaking recording artists (2 LPs), Cusan Tan. Sandy Ratcliff actually played bass for pop-rock outfits, Tropical Appetite and Escalator (nothing recorded) / the songs stem from BOWIE ('Heroes/Helden'), KRAFTWERK, ROBERT FRIPP, DEVO, LENE LOVICH, IAN DURY, WRECKLESS ERIC ('Whole Wide World') and even **STING** performing himself (he was at the time a member of the Police). *MCS*

RAISE YOUR VOICE

2004 (US 103m) New Line Cinema (PG)

Film genre: romantic teen Pop/family Musical drama

Top guns: dir: Sean McNamara / s-w: Sam Schreiber (story: Mitch Rotter)

Stars: Hilary Duff *(Terri Fletcher)* ← the LIZZIE McGUIRE MOVIE, Oliver James *(Jay Corgan)*, David Keith *(Simon Fletcher)* ← HEARTBREAK HOTEL ← FIRESTARTER ← the ROSE, Rita Wilson *(Francis Fletcher)* ← the STORY OF US ← THAT THING YOU DO!, Rebecca De Mornay *(Aunt Nina)* ← RISKY BUSINESS ← ONE FROM THE HEART, Jason Ritter *(Paul Fletcher)*, John Corbett *(Mr. Torvald)* ← MY DINNER WITH JIMI, Dana Davis *(Denise Gilmore)*, **Three Days Grace:- Adam Gontier, Barry Stock, Brad Walst, Neil Sanderson** *(performers)*, John Gipson *(sax player)*, **Steven "T7" Palmer** *(street drummer)*, Sean McNamara *(Doctor Mark Farley)*, **Seis Cuerdas** *(Flamenco guitarists)*, **Mitch Rotter** *(folk singer)*

Storyline: After her brother's death in a car crash, teen singer Terri enrols at a summer music academy in L.A. against the wishes of her father. Terri has bags of talent but no proper training, and when she gets an attack of nerves, new boyfriend Jay helps her conquer her stage fright. Just as she is geared up for the big scholarship competition her father appears, determined to march her straight back home, and Terri suddenly finds she's not the only one raising her voice. *JZ*

Movie rating: *4.5

Visual: dvd (no audio OST; score: Aaron Zigman)

Off the record: HILARY DUFF sang a handful of songs including 'Someone's Watching Over Me', 'Jericho' & 'Fly'. Also check out the appearance of Ontario alt-rockers, **Three Days grace**, who are now (2006/7) massive in the States courtesy of sophomore album, 'One-X'. Formed in 1997 as (a trio) Groundswell, they built up a steady following which eventually led to a signing with 'Jive' records. An eponymous US Top 75 set in 2003 featuring hit single, '(I Hate) Everything About You', marked the band's entry into the big time. The following year they were now a 4-piece and contributing 'Home & 'Are You Ready' to the 'Raise Your Voice' soundtrack. Never released, it also featured various tracks from MxPx ('Play It Loud'), SUSAN J. PAUL ('Poor Poor Mary'), KATRINA AND THE WAVES ('Walking On Sunshine'), SEIS CUERDAS ('Recuerdos'), TINA SUGANDH ('Lift Off'), FT ('Just Do It'), SALOME ('Because Of You'), KEEGAN ('Change In My Condition'), KEANE ('We Might As Well Be Strangers') and MITCH ROTTER ('Take It Back Now'); his compadre ADAM SCHIFF and metal act MACHINE HEAD were also on the playlist alongside a couple of standards, 'Joy To The World' (written by Hoyt Axton) & 'The Way You Do The Things You Do' (Smokey Robinson & The Miracles). *MCS*

RAPPIN'

1985 (US 92m) Cannon Pictures (PG)

Film genre: urban Rap/Hip Hop Musical drama

Top guns: dir: Joel Silberg ← BREAKIN' / → LAMBADA / s-w: Adam Friedman, Robert Jay Litz

Stars: Mario Van Peebles *(John Hood)* ← SWEET SWEETBACK'S BAADASSSSS SONG, Rony Clanton *(Cedric)* ← the EDUCATION OF SONNY CARSON / → JUICE, Charles Flohe *(Duane)*, Eriq La Salle *(Ice)*, Leo O'Brien *(Allan)* ← the LAST DRAGON, Tasia Valenza *(Dixie)*, Melvin Plowden *(Fats)*, Rutanya Alda *(Cecilia)* ← PAT GARRETT & BILLY THE KID, Kadeem Hardison *(Moon)* → SCHOOL DAZE, **Force M.D.'s:- Jesse Daniels, Trisco Pearson, Charles Nelson, Stevie Lundy, Antoine Lundy** *(performers)*, **Eugene Wilde** *(performer)*, **ICE-T** *(himself)* + **David Storrs** *(Ice-T's group)*

Storyline: John "Rappin'" Hood is an ex-con turned good guy who stops all aggression and violence by the unique method of breaking into a dance routine. His equally dance-happy neighbourhood is glad to have him back as they are getting evicted one by one by a dodgy real estate developer and his gang of ruffians. At the big council meeting to decide the neighbourhood's future, Rappin' must dance like never before if he wants to rap the rich and jive to the poor. *JZ*

Movie rating: *2.5

Visual: video (no audio OST; score: Michael Linn)

Off the record: Force M.D.'S were responsible for one major hit, 'Tender Love', from the film 'KRUSH GROOVE'. R&B specialist, **Eugene Wilde**, had two minor hits in 1985, 'Gotta Get You Home Tonight' & 'Don't Say No Tonight'. **David Storrs** was a drummer turned producer who founded the 'Louie' imprint. *MCS*

RAT PFINK A BOO-BOO

aka 'The ADVENTURES OF RAT PFINK AND BOO BOO'

1966 (US 72m b&w) Craddock Films (15)

Film genre: Rock-music comic-book caper/comedy

Top guns: dir: Ray Dennis Steckler (+ story) ← WILD GUITAR / s-w: **Ronald Haydock**

Stars: Carolyn Brandt *(Cee Bee Beaumont)* ← WILD GUITAR ← EEGAH, **Vin Saxon** *(Lonnie Lord / Rat Pfink)*, Titus Moede *(Titus Twimbly / Boo Boo)*, George Caldwell *(Linc)*, Mike Kannon *(Hammer)*, James Bowie *(Benjie)*, Keith Wester/Dean Danger *(Cowboy)*

Storyline: When the beautiful girlfriend of rock'n'roll superstar Lonnie Lord is kidnapped by an evil chain gang, he transends to superhero and dons the disguise of Rat Pfink. With his trusty sidekick and gardener, Titus Twimbly (aka Boo Boo), the masked marvels unleash the American right to justice, truth and er, everything else, albeit with a few sing-songs and go-go parties along the way. *MCS*

Movie rating: *2

Visual: video + dvd (no audio OST; score: Henri Price)

Off the record: Ronald Haydock (b.17 Apr'40, Chicago, Illinois) had originally fronted his own late 50s combo, Ron Haydock & The Boppers, singing and playing guitar. Towards the end of that decade, the Gene Vincent clone with band issued a couple of rockabilly 45s, '99 Chicks' – listen for the f-word! (flipped with 'Be Bop A Jean') and a rendition of Chuck Berry's 'Maybellene' (flipped w/ 'Baby Say Bye Bye'). When Haydock disbanded the Boppers, he turned his hand to writing for a number of monster movie mags as well as porn novels under the moniker of **Vin Saxon**; among them 'Animal Lust' & 'Pagan Lesbians'. After several years in the minor celebrity wilderness in and around L.A., Ron succumbed to an untimely death (13 August 1977) when he was struck by an 18-wheeler truck while trying to hitch a ride near Victorville, California. *MCS*

– associated release –

RON HAYDOCK & THE BOPPERS: 99 Chicks

Jun 96. (cd) *Norton; (247)* [-] [ ]
– (other than the aforementioned singles, the excellent 29-track album includes 'Rat Pfink', 'You're Running Wild', 'Big Boss A-Go-Go Party', 'Eaffin' And Surfin' (theme from 'Rat Pfink') and movie dialogue).

□ the RAVE-UPS segment
(⇒ PRETTY IN PINK)

□ Lou RAWLS segment
(⇒ ANGEL, ANGEL, DOWN WE GO)

RAY

2004 (US 152m) Universal Pictures (PG-13)

Film genre: R&B/Pop bio-pic drama

Top guns: s-w: Taylor Hackford (+ dir + story) ← HAIL! HAIL! ROCK'N'ROLL ← the IDOLMAKER, James L. White (+ story)

Stars: Jamie Foxx *(Ray Charles)* → STEALTH → DREAMGIRLS, Kerry Washington *(Della Bea Robinson)* ← SAVE THE LAST DANCE, Regina King *(Margie Hendricks)*, Clifton Powell *(Jeff Brown)* ← BONES ← WHY DO FOOLS FALL IN LOVE ← HOUSE PARTY, Aunjanue Ellis *(Mary Ann Fisher)* ← DISAPPEARING ACTS, Harry Lennix *(Joe Adams)* ← the FIVE HEARTBEATS / → STOMP THE YARD, Bokeem Woodbine *(Fathead Newman)* ← CROOKLYN, Sharon Warren *(Aretha Robinson)*, Larenz Tate *(Quincy Jones)* ← WHY DO FOOLS FALL IN LOVE, Curtis Armstrong *(Ahmet Ertegun)* ← MY DINNER WITH JIMI ← RISKY BUSINESS, Terrence Howard *(Gossie McKee)* ← GLITTER ← WHO'S THE MAN? ← the JACKSONS: AN AMERICAN DREAM / → HUSTLE & FLOW → GET RICH OR DIE TRYIN' → IDLEWILD, Richard Schiff *(Jerry Wexler)* ← I AM SAM ← TOUCH ← GRACE OF MY HEART ← the BODYGUARD ← YOUNG GUNS II, **Chris Thomas King** *(Lowell Fulsom)* ← LIGHTNING IN A BOTTLE ← the SOUL OF A MAN ← LAST OF THE MISSISSIPPI JUKES ← DOWN FROM THE MOUNTAIN ← O BROTHER, WHERE ART THOU?, C.J. Sanders *(young Ray)*, David Krumholtz *(Milt Shaw)*, Wendell Pierce *(Wilbur Brassfield)* ← the FIGHTING TEMPTATIONS ← BROWN SUGAR, Thomas Jefferson Byrd *(Jimmy)* ← HE GOT GAME ← GIRL 6, Robert Wisdom *(Jack Lauderdale)* ← KILLER DILLER ← MASKED AND

ANONYMOUS ← STORYTELLING ← THAT THING YOU DO!, Rick Gomez *(Tom Dowd)*, Tom Clark *(Alan Freed)*, **Ralph Tresvant** *(Sam Cooke)* ← HOUSE PARTY 2, Vernel Bagneris *(Dancin' Al)* ← DOWN BY LAW, Patrick Bauchau *(Dr. Hacker)* ← the BEATNICKS ← EVERYBREATH ← PHENOMENA

Storyline: Ray Charles wasn't the first musician to be both black and blind, but in triumphing over both his own sensory disability and the Deep South's endemic racism, his story is an endlessly inspiring one. A celebration of his life even in death, this colourful, fast-paced biopic concentrates on the turbulent early years, from rural poverty and the glaucoma which brought on his blindness to his taboo-busting marriage of jump-blues and gospel, and equally transgressive embrace of country. *BG*

Movie rating: *7.5

Visual: dvd

Off the record: Protégé of sorts, **Ralph Tresvant** was a former member of New Edition and a solo artist (highest charting single, 'Sensitivity', No.4 in 1990). *MCS*

—

RAY CHARLES

Oct 04. (cd) *Rhino; <(8122 76540-2)>* 9 Jan05 36
– Mess around / I've got a woman / Hallelujah I love her so (live) / Drown in my own tears / (Night time is) The right time / Mary Ann / Hard times (no one knows better than I) / What'd I say (live) / Georgia on my mind / Hit the road Jack / Unchain my heart / I can't stop loving you (live) / Born to lose / Bye bye, love / You don't know me (live) / Let the good times roll (live) / Georgia on my mind (live). *<(re-iss. Feb05; 8122 79597-2)>*

S/track review: Released just a few months after he passed away, the 'RAY' soundtrack might have come across like the obligatory posthumous compilation, even if its compilers never intended it as such. But it's far from a casually thrown-together hits package; rarely heard, self-penned cuts like the slinky 'Mary Ann' from his – only very recently reissued – sophomore album, 'Ray Charles / Hallelujah I Love Her So' (1957), betray the hand of a discerning compiler. Incredibly, the man's country-soul masterpiece, 'Modern Sounds In Country And Western Music' (1962), is still awaiting re-issue and – outside of the original vinyl or the pricey 'Rhino' box set – 'RAY' is about the only place you're going to hear the likes of 'Born To Lose' and his startling big band take on Boudleaux Bryant's 'Bye, Bye, Love'. A handful of live cuts – including a great version of his No.1 Don Gibson cover, 'I Can't Stop Loving You' – from the long deleted 'Ray Charles In Japan' (1976) sweeten the package further. With Taylor Hackford admitting to the sprucing up of some of the horn parts, even the more familiar classics sound fresher, and the likes of 'Mess Around' and 'I've Got A Woman' delineate not only the launch of a pioneering career but a cultural fault line; by the time he'd released 1965's 'Live In Concert' (from which Hackford pulls a raucous 'What'd I Say'), British beat bands had already begun interpreting his innovations and selling them back to America. This soundtrack – like the film it accompanies – necessarily concentrates its energies on a particular phase of CHARLES' career, and even then only scratches the surface. But it's obviously produced with a great deal of love, and, as a primer for his vast archives, you could do far worse. There was of course, 'More Music From Ray' and a Craig Armstrong-released score. *BG*

Album rating: *8 / More Music From Ray *7

– spinoff releases, etc. –

RAY CHARLES: More Music From Ray

Jan 05. (cd) *Rhino; <(8122 78703-2)>* May05
– Leave my woman alone / Lonely avenue / Rockhouse (pts.1 & 2) / I believe to my soul / Losing hand / I'm movin' on / But on the other hand baby / Baby, it's cold outside / The danger zone / Busted / Makin' whoopee / Let's go get stoned / Drifting blues / Baby let me hold your hand / Drown in my own tears – You don't know me / Everyday I have the blues / America the beautiful / *(+ dvd +=)* – Don't set me free / Carry me back to Old Virginny / (O-Genio trailer).

REALITY BITES

1994 (US 99m) Universal Pictures (PG-13)

Film genre: coming-of-age/romantic comedy

Top guns: dir: Ben Stiller / s-w: Helen Childress

Stars: Winona Ryder *(Lelaina Pierce)* ← NIGHT ON EARTH ← GREAT BALLS OF FIRE!, Ethan Hawke *(Troy Dyer)* → the HOTTEST STATE, Ben Stiller *(Michael Grates)* → BLACK AND WHITE → the PICK OF DESTINY → AWESOME: I FUCKIN' SHOT THAT!, Janeane Garofalo *(Vickie Miner)* → TOUCH → GIGANTIC (A TALE OF TWO JOHNS), Steve Zahn *(Sammy Gray)* → THAT THING YOU DO! → SUBURBI@ → CHELSEA WALLS, Swoosie Kurtz *(Charlane McGregor)* ← BAJA OKLAHOMA ← TRUE STORIES, Joe Don Baker *(Tom Pierce)*, John Mahoney *(Grant Gubler)* → SHE'S THE ONE, Harry O'Reilly *(Wes McGregor)*, Barry Sherman *(Grant's producer)*, Renee Zellweger *(Tami)* → SHAKE, RATTLE & ROCK! tv → EMPIRE RECORDS → COLD MOUNTAIN, Keith David (Roger) ← ROAD HOUSE ← DISCO GODFATHER, Anne Meara *(Louise)* ← FAME, David Spade *(hot dog vendor Mgr.)* → the EMPEROR'S NEW GROOVE, **Evan Dando** *(actor "Roy")* <= the LEMONHEADS =>

Storyline: The story of four Generation X college grads starts with Lelaina, who lands a job as a TV presenter. Her best friend and wannabe-rock-star Troy would rather idle away the days than find a job. When Lelaina meets TV executive Michael, she is torn between his practical views on life and Troy's philosophical musings. Their friends/ flatmates are sex-mad sales assistant Vickie and her gay friend Sammy. *JZ*

Movie rating: *7.5

Visual: video + dvd

Off the record: (see below)

—

Various Artists (score: KARL WALLINGER *)

Feb 94. (cd/c) *R.C.A.; <(07863 66364-2/-4)>* 13 Aug96
– My Sharona (the KNACK) / Spin the bottle (JULIANA HATFIELD THREE) / Bed of roses (the INDIANS) / When you come back to me (WORLD PARTY) * / Going, going, gone (the POSIES) / Stay (I missed you) (LISA LOEB & NINE STORIES) / All I want is you (U2) / Locked out (CROWDED HOUSE) / Spinning around over you (LENNY KRAVITZ) / I'm nuthin' (ETHAN HAWKE) / Turnip farm (DINOSAUR JR.) / Revival (ME PHI ME) / Tempted '94 (SQUEEZE) / Baby, I love your way (BIG MOUNTAIN). *<(cd re-iss. Jun04 – 10th Anniversary Edition – +=; same)>* – Stay (I missed you) – living room mix (LISA LOEB) / Add it up (ETHAN HAWKE) / Confusion (NEW ORDER) / Disco inferno (the TRAMMPS) / Give a man a fish (ARRESTED DEVELOPMENT) / Fools like me (LISA LOEB).

S/track review: You'd have to be a spoilsport not to nod along with the KNACK's knockabout classic 'My Sharona' as a way of kicking things into gear, but the momentum is stalled by JULIANA HATFIELD THREE's mawkish alterno folky rock. The funk is re-installed by 'When You Come Back To Me' by WORLD PARTY, and 'Going, Going Gone' by the POSIES is perfectly affable as it makes its way in a lilting fashion. 'Stay' by LISA LOEB & NINE STORIES is something of an alt-pop classic and still holds up as a sophisticated and bittersweet tune from the era when alterno-songstresses like Alanis Morissette and Fiona Apple ruled the roost. U2's 'All I Want Is You' is a fine example of their particular variety of anthemic and stirring love songs, and LENNY KRAVITZ's 'Spinning Around Over You' also bears all the hallmarks of his heavy rock with Funkadelic overtones. It all rolls along on a lazy, assured groove, with a spiralling refrain and a tasteful, dry, bluesy solo to boot. ETHAN HAWKE is another actor who can't resist getting into the fray, putting on his best whiskey-soaked drawl over his acoustic troubadeering. It's all blown away by the proto-grunge, psychedelic fuzz of J Mascis and DINOSAUR JR's 'Turnip Farm'; the distended riffs roll into each other, and its overarching guitar soloing outshines all around it, a masterpiece of trippy, educated garage rock. Hip-hop manages to stick its head above the parapet of this alternative rock landscape, with the woozy, crackling ME PHI ME, harmonica and all. Things come to a close with the rather ridiculous good-time quasi dub reggae of BIG MOUNTAIN and 'Baby I Love Your Way'. *DF*

Album rating: *8 / re-CD *8.5

– spinoff hits, etc. –

BIG MOUNTAIN: Baby, I Love Your Way / Baby, Te Quiero Ati

Feb 94. (7"/c-s/cd-s) *<62780> (74321 19806-7/-4/-2)* [6] May94 [2]

LENNY KRAVITZ: Spinning Around Over You

Mar 94. (c-s/cd-s) *Virgin; <38412>* [80] b-side [–]

LISA LOEB & NINE STORIES: Stay (I Missed You) / (remixes)

Apr 94. (7"/c-s/cd-s) *<62870> (74321 21252-7/-4/-2)* [1] Aug94 [6]

JULIANA HATFIELD THREE: Spin The Bottle

Aug 94. (c-s/10"/cd-s) *East West; (YZ 819 C/TE/CD)* [–] [ ]

JULIANA HATFIELD THREE: Spin The Bottle / ETHAN HAWKE: I'm Nuthin'

Oct 94. (c-s/cd-s) *<64207>* [97] [–]

RECORD CITY

1978 (US 90m) American International Pictures (PG)

Film genre: workplace Pop Musical comedy

Top guns: dir: Dennis Steinmetz / s-w: Ron Friedman

Stars: Ruth Buzzi *(Olga)*, Michael Callan *(Eddie)*, Jack Carter *(Manny)*, **Rick Dees** *(Gordon)* → LA BAMBA, **Kinky Friedman** *(himself)*, Alice Ghostley *(worried wife)* ← the GRADUATE / → GREASE, Frank Gorshin *(Chameleon)* ← SKIDOO ← WHERE THE BOYS ARE, Joe Higgins *(Doyle)*, Ted Lange *(the Wiz)* ← FRIDAY FOSTER ← BLACK BELT JONES ← WATTSTAX, Larry Storch *(deaf man)*, Elliott Street *(Hitch)* → ELVIS: THE MOVIE, Ed Begley Jr. *(Pokey)* → ELVIS: THE MOVIE → GET CRAZY → THIS IS SPINAL TAP → STREETS OF FIRE → EVEN COWGIRLS GET THE BLUES → a MIGHTY WIND, Tim Thomerson *(Marty)* ← CAR WASH / → CARNY → HONKYTONK MAN → RHINESTONE → NEAR DARK → EDDIE PRESLEY → BAD CHANNELS, Harold Sakata *(Gucci)* → GOIN' COCONUTS, Sorrell Brooke *(Coznowski)* → ROCK-A-DOODLE

Storyline: Forget the post-indie irony of 'EMPIRE RECORDS' and 'HIGH FIDELITY', this is the original slice-of-vinyl-life, spinning at 33 gags per minute on 'Car Wash'-patented 70s pizazz, as the employees and clientele of an L.A. record shop negotiate cross dressing, leopard print shirts and, erm, Gorilla Man. *BG*

Movie rating: *3.5

Visual: none

Off the record: **Kinky Friedman** was a country music singer/satirist/author from Texas, famous for un-PC songs such as 'They Ain't Makin' Jews Like Jesus Anymore', 'Somethin's Wrong With The Beaver' & 'Get Your Biscuits In The Oven And Your Buns In The Bed'. **Rick Dees** was responsible for 'Disco Duck' – one of the contenders for Worst Song Of The Century . . . Ever! *MCS*

Various Artists/Cast (score: FREDDIE PERREN *)

Feb 78. (lp) *M.V.P.; <PD-1-8002>* [–] promo [–]
– Record city (vocal: KENI ST. LEWIS) / Mr Feel Good (vocal: KENI ST. LEWIS) / Make way for the lover (vocal: JAMES GADSON) / Mucho macho (vocal: FRITZ DIEGO) / Night music (* & the TEAM PLAYERS) / X-sight-me (* & the TEAM PLAYERS) / Gorilla man (vocal: RICK DEES) / Ecstasy (* & the TEAM PLAYERS) / Shine on (* & the TEAM PLAYERS) / Hold me baby (* & the TEAM PLAYERS) / Steppin' out (vocal: 'RIC & ROBYN' WYATT) / You're my reason (vocal: GARY STARBUCK).

S/track review: If only for the fact that it doesn't rely on the usual rock jukebox-jury of a soundtrack, the original record store film also has the best music. Your man FREDDIE PERREN is writer, arranger and producer, fresh from being voted both "Disco Producer Of The Year" and "Top Pop Producer Of The Year" in the 1976 Billboard Awards, and doubtless champing at the bit to have a whole two sides of soundtrack to himself after collaborating with Fonce Mizell on the excellent 'HELL UP IN HARLEM' (1974), and sharing space with a raft of 'Motown' hits on 'Cooley High' (1975), as well as masterminding two of the biggest songs on 'SATURDAY NIGHT FEVER' (1977). 'RECORD CITY' is actually one of the most obscure neo-blaxploitation albums out there, sinking without trace along with the no-budget film soon after release. Not that the personnel are bargain basement: legendary funk drummer JAMES GADSON (the man behind such sampled-to-death breaks as Charles Wright and the Watts 103rd Street Rhythm Band's 'Express Yourself'), Brazilian percussion maestro Paulinho Da Costa on bongos and conga, and the sublime vocals of Minnie Riperton, herself to tragically pass away less than two years later. GADSON even sings lead on one of the more conventional soul-disco tracks ('Make Way For The Lover'), but the polyester core of this record is in its instrumentals. While it never quite clicks into the 9-to-5 rhythm of 'CAR WASH', the prevailing tone is unashamedly feel-good/tongue-in-cheek – PERREN assembles a template for the Village People on 'Mucho Macho' (growled by one Fritz Diego – a pseudonym?), and pens the pre-PC nonsense-kitsch of 'Gorilla Man' (where else can you hear Riperton cooing "Go-Go-Go-Gorilla, Get Down, Get Down"?), and there are some engrossing tangents. Chief among them is 'Shine On', a great if slightly generic example of how to blend Gibson Brothers-style horn charts and haughty, Moroder-esque electro-disco; PERREN even spools it out with a roaming solo and still comes up smelling of synthesized roses. Both 'Ecstasy' and 'Hold Me Baby' are sweet, idling incidental pieces of the mellowest order, full of weird little synth/counter melodies and sub-Abba harmonies. Figure in the Southern Soul title and grinding disco-funk-rock of 'X-Sight-Me', and it's difficult to see how – with almost everything PERREN touched literally turning to gold at the time – this album has such a low profile. It boasts some of the strangest fruit PERREN put his name to, and it deserves at least a footnote in his discography. *BG*

Album rating: *7

☐ RED ELVISES segment
(⇒ SIX-STRING SAMURAI)

RED HOT

1993 (Can 95m) SC Entertainment International (PG)

Film genre: Rock'n'roll-music drama

Top guns: s-w: (+ dir) Paul Haggis, Michael Maurer

Stars: Balthazar Getty *(Alexi)* ← YOUNG GUNS II, Hugh O'Conor *(Yuri)*, Jason Kristofer *(Sasha)*, Colin Buchanan *(Vladimir)*, Carla Gugino *(Valentina)*, Jan Niklas *(Yorgi)*, Tusse Silberg *(Klara)*, Diane Fletcher *(Mrs. Kirov)*, Donald Sutherland *(Kirov)* ← ANIMAL HOUSE ← STEELYARD BLUES / → COLD MOUNTAIN, Armin Mueller-Stahl *(Dimitri)* ← NIGHT ON EARTH, Jill Gascoine *(waitress)* ← CONFESSIONS OF A POP PERFORMER

Storyline: Young Alexi thinks he'll soon be a Red Star after listening to rock'n'roll records smuggled from the West by his uncle Dimitri. He decides to form the first garage band in the Soviet Union with some help from his friends Sasha, Yuri, Vlad and Valentina. But when their record comes to the attention of Valentina's frosty father and the KGB, it looks like the Iron Curtain will be pulled down on their act. *JZ*

Movie rating: *4

Visual: video (no audio OST; score: Peter Breiner)

Off the record: nothing

□ Leon REDBONE segment (⇒ CANDY MOUNTAIN)

REDD KROSS

Formed: Hawthorne, California, USA . . . late 1978 by schoolboy brothers Jeffrey (b.10 Aug'63) and Steve McDonald (b. 1967). Completing the line-up with Greg Hetson and Ron Reyes, Red Cross (as they were known then) played their first gig in 1979, opening for pioneers of hardcore punk, Black Flag. Spotted by DJ and entrepreneur, Rodney Bingenheimer, they subsequently recorded an EP for 'Posh Boy' which led to the "real" International Red Cross threatening to sue them if they didn't change the group name! Now as REDD KROSS, they lost Hetson and Reyes, both moving on to similar respective hardcore acts, CIRCLE JERKS and the aforementioned Black Flag. Over the course of the early to mid-80s, personnel changed like the weather and output was sparse. However, a few albums had emerged during this lean period, namely 'Born Innocent' (1982) and covers mini-set, 'Teen Babes From Monsanto' (1984). REDD KROSS were not exactly in any hurry to find fame with their take on trashy psychedelic punk/glam; their embryonic grunge sound was definitely ahead of its time. Meanwhile, both brothers had contributed performance and acting skills in underground punk movies such as 'The SLOG MOVIE' (1982), 'DESPERATE TEENAGE LOVEDOLLS' (1984) and its sequel 'LOVEDOLLS SUPERSTAR' (1986). Just when recognition seemed to be forthcoming with 1987's 'Neurotica', luck ran out as their label 'Big Time' came a cropper. The McDonald brothers re-appeared in 1990 with their one-off covers side project, Tater Totz, before the pair resurfaced with a new REDD KROSS line-up and a major deal courtesy of 'Atlantic' records. A comeback album, 'Third Eye', appeared in 1991, while Jeffrey featured in cult movies, 'The SPIRIT OF '76' (1990 with Steve) and 'GAS FOOD LODGING' (1992). With another new line-up in place (namely, Eddie Kurdziel, Gere Fennelly and Brian Reitzel), 1993's 'Phaseshifter' spawned three classy singles, 'Switchblade Sister', 'Lady In The Front Row' and 'Visionary'. Later that summer, the band indulged their love of classic 70s pop with a kitschy cover of the Carpenters' 'Yesterday Once More', a shock UK Top 50 hit which featured SONIC YOUTH paying tribute to Karen & Richard on the B-side. A long hiatus ensued before REDD KROSS entered the fray once more in early '97 with another set of multi-coloured sonic-pop, 'Show World', a collection that featured another minor hit single, 'Get Out Of Myself'. With film credits expanding to 'GRACE OF MY HEART' (1996), 'SUGAR TOWN' (1999) and a performance in 'THINGS BEHIND THE SUN' (2001), the brothers REDD KROSS had ceased to be. With a long lay-off, Jeff was back in 2002 with new husband/wife album project, Ze Malibu Kids (on 'Sound It Out'), alongside Anna Waronker. *MCS*

- filmography {actors/performance} –

the Slog Movie *(1982 {p} =>)* / **Desperate Teenage Lovedolls** *(1984 {*/p} OST by REDD KROSS & V/A =>)* / **Lovedolls Superstar** *(1986 {*} on OST by V/A =>)* / **the Spirit Of '76** *(1990 {a} on OST by V/A =>)* / **Gas Food Lodging** *(1992 {b JEFFREY} OST by BARRY ADAMSON, J MASCIS & V/A =>)* / **Grace Of My Heart** *(1996 {a} OST by V/A =>)* / the Heist *(1999 {a JEFFREY})* / **Sugar Town** *(1999 {a JEFF} =>)* / **Things Behind The Sun** *(2001 {p} =>)*

Lou REED

Born: Louis Firbank, 2 Mar'42, Freeport, Long Island, New York, USA. A member of a plethora of bands from the late 50s (the Jades and the Primitives, among them), Lou first established himself as leader of the seminal Velvet Underground. An integral part of the group's songwriting prowess, he and co-Primitives conspirator, John Cale, formed the band in New York City early in 1965. Meeting up with Svengali pop artist, Andy Warhol, he/they invited German chanteuse NICO to join the set-up alongside Sterling Morrison and Mo/Maureen Tucker. Early in 1966, the Velvets signed to 'MGM-Verve', and soon began work on what was to be their debut album, 'The Velvet Underground & Nico'. The album (accompanied by a Warhol-directed film of the same name) was a revelation, strikingly different from the love and peace psychedelia of the day; the band's vision was decidedly darker and more disturbing. Combining sublime melodies and nihilistic noise, it featured eleven superb ahead-of-their-time classics, notably the brutally frank and frenetic 'Heroin', 'Venus In Furs' and the garage raunch of 'Waiting For The Man'. The record only managed a brief stay in the US Top 200, as did the 1967 follow-up, 'White Light, White Heat', which included the 17-minute white noise freak-out of 'Sister Ray'. With Cale now out of the picture, the focus fell on REED's songwriting for the self-titled third album. An altogether mellower set of more traditionally structured songs, the highlight was undoubtedly REED's beautiful lullaby, 'Pale Blue Eyes'. The band's last studio album, 'Loaded', was the closest they ever came to mainstream rock and an indicator of the direction REED would take in his solo career. 'Sweet Jane' and 'Rock'n'Roll' marked his creative peak, a final glorious burst of guitar noise before the group disbanded and the myth started to crystallise. REED subsequently signed a contract with 'R.C.A.', although a badly-timed eponymous 1972 debut (with Richard Robinson on production) only just scraped into the US Top 200, gaining nothing in renewed respect. Later that year, helped by stablemates DAVID BOWIE and his Spiders From Mars sidekick, Mick Ronson, Lou unleashed 'Transformer', a Top 30 triumph and critical success on both sides of the Atlantic. It was boosted by 'Walk On The Wild Side' (a classic Top 20 single), the piano-led melancholy of 'Perfect Day', the raw glam of 'Vicious' and one-that-got-away 'Satellite Of Love'. His next album, 'Berlin' (1973), although unfairly panned by US critics, still managed a Top 10 placing in Britain. On reflection, its subject matter of suicide and child neglect ('The Bed' and 'The Kids') didn't help win any new friends but it still stands as one of the most unrelentingly bleak listens in the history of rock. After the claustrophobic confessions of his last LP, the live 'Rock'n'Roll Animal' (1974) must have come as something of a relief to his record company. A technically faultless back-up band roared through a selection of old Velvets numbers with REED hollering over the top, and while the set represented something of a concession to commercial credibility (by REED's standards anyway) it captured little of the Velvet Underground's subtlety. It also saw REED sinking further into self-parody, hamming up his studied image of sleazy decadence to the max. 'Sally Can't Dance', released later the same year, was REED in full emotionless flight, an icy collection of biting cynicism. But laughing Lou hadn't played his ace card yet, that musical two-fingered salute fell to 1975's 'Metal Machine Music', the one everyone talks about but has never had the will or mental endurance to listen to the whole way through. A double album of impenetrable feedback noise interspersed with inhuman screams, hums etc., the record successfully alienated most of REED's long-suffering fans amid critical meltdown. In true contrary style, he sashayed sweetly back with the mellow 'Coney Island Baby' (1976), although the lyrics remained as brutally frank as ever. His first record for 'Arista', 'Rock'n'Roll Heart' (1976), was indeed as vacantly awful as the title suggests, though the punk-inspired follow-up, 'Street Hassle' (1978), showcased a re-energised REED, most impressively on the malicious guitar workout of 'Dirt' and the swaggering title track. After a tedious live album, REED started to show uncharacteristic signs of maturity in both his music and lyrics with 'The Bells' (1979) and 'Growing Up In Public' (1980). At the turn of the 80s, having just appeared in Paul Simon's 'ONE-TRICK PONY' movie, Lou hooked up with former Void-Oid/RICHARD HELL sidekick, Robert Quine, a partnership that resulted in two of the most consistent and accomplished sets in REED's solo career, 'The Blue Mask' and the similarly focused 'Legendary Hearts'. Celluloid work surfaced as Lou featured in three 1983 films, the animation 'ROCK & RULE' (1983), the feature 'GET CRAZY' (1983) and the concert video 'A Night With . . .'. 1984's 'New Sensations' was fairly low-key, while 'Mistrial' (1986) saw REED introduce a few drum machine tracks in typical 80s style. These were competent albums but hardly essential and only the most devout REED believer could've predicted the creative, commercial and critical renaissance that would ensue with 1989's 'New York' album. A skeletal strum-athon, this was LOU REED in the raw with the sparsest of musical accompaniment. Back on familiar territory, his sardonic tales of the Big Apple's seedier side made for compelling listening. 'Songs For Drella' (1990) – a reunification with John Cale – was a heartfelt tribute to his mentor Warhol, while 'Magic And Loss' (1992) was a sincere series of stark meditations on life and death. Despite an ill-advised Velvet Underground reunion, REED retained critical favour, going on to release another well-received album in 1996, 'Set The Twilight Reeling'. Squeezed somewhere in between film work ('Blue In The Face' 1995 and 'Lulu On The Bridge' 1998), Various Artists "Children In Need" charity single 'Perfect Day' was a belated chart-topper in November '97. The aptly titled 'Ecstasy' (2000) found the cantankerous ex-Velvet fearlessly analysing the more uncomfortable dimensions of man's primal urges. 'The Raven' (2003), meanwhile, has to rank as one of the more unconventional projects REED has undertaken in recent years. In setting the works of Edgar Allan Poe to music at the request of theatre director Robert Wilson, REED exorcised some of his own demons in line with Poe's dark imaginings. The resulting album – the double-set version which came complete with the production's spoken word performances from the likes of actors Willem Dafoe and Steve Buscemi – ran the gamut of REED's stylistic arsenal, while musical guests included everyone from his old mucker BOWIE and Ornette Coleman to the Five Blind Boys Of Alabama. Neither this nor his subsequent live album, 'Animal Serenade' (2004), did much chart-wise, although some commercial consolation came the old trooper's way later that year when he finally had a hit with another old 'Transformer' perennial, 'Satellite Of Love', after it was remixed into the UK Top 10. *BG & MCS*

- **filmography** {acting} –

the Velvet Underground And Nico *(1966 {p} =>)* / **Jimi Hendrix** *(1973 {p} OST by JIMI HENDRIX =>)* / **One-Trick Pony** *(1980 {a} OST by PAUL SIMON =>)* / **Rock & Rule** *(1983 {v} =>)* / **Get Crazy** *(1983 {a} on OST by V/A =>)* / a Night With Lou Reed *(1983 {p})* / the Secret Policeman's Third Ball *(1987 {p} OST by V/A =>)* / **Permanent Record** *(1988 {c} on OST by JOE STRUMMER & V/A =>)* / Superstar: The Life And Times Of Andy Warhol *(1990 docu {c})* / **Nico Icon** *(1995 {c} =>)* / Blue In The Face *(1995 {*} on OST by V/A =>)* / Lulu On The Bridge *(1998 {b})* / **Rock & Roll Heart** *(1998 {p} =>)* / Prozac Nation *(2001 {c})* / **the Soul Of A Man** *(2003 {p} OST by V/A =>)*

RENT

2005 (US 135m) 1492 Pictures / Columbia Pictures (PG-13)

Film genre: romantic Pop-Rock Musical drama

Top guns: dir: Chris Columbus ← HEARTBREAK HOTEL / s-w: Stephen Chbosky (musical play: Jonathan Larson)

Stars: Anthony Rapp *(Mark Cohen)* ← the BEACH BOYS: AN AMERICAN FAMILY, Adam Pascal *(Roger Davis)* ← TEMPTATION ← SCHOOL OF ROCK ← SLC PUNK!, Rosario Dawson *(Mimi Marquez)* ← CHELSEA WALLS ← JOSIE AND THE PUSSYCATS ← HE GOT GAME ← KIDS, Jesse L. Martin *(Tom Collins)*, Wilson Jermaine Heredia *(Angel Dumott Schunard)* ← WENT TO CONEY ISLAND ON A MISSION FROM GOD . . . BE BACK BY FIVE, Idina Menzel *(Maureen Johnson)*, Tracie Thoms *(Joanne Jefferson)*, Taye Diggs *(Benjamin Coffin III)* ← MALIBU'S MOST WANTED ← BROWN SUGAR, Sarah Silverman *(Alexi Darling)* ← the SCHOOL OF ROCK

Storyline: The late Jonathan Larson's rock operatic, Tony and Pullitzer-winning reimagining of Puccini's 'La Bohème' transplanted to the screen, following the year-in-the-life trials of a close-knit group of Bohemians living in New York's East Village, with lack of money, the reality of AIDS and the agonies of infidelity/sexual identity all shaping their strained interrelationships. *BG*

Movie rating: *6.5

Visual: dvd

Off the record: Jonathan Rapp fronts the group, Albino Kid (no records as yet)

—

Original Cast (composer: Jonathan Larson)

Sep 05. (d-cd) *Warners; <49455-2>* [40] [–]
– Seasons of love (*) / Rent (*) / You'll see / One song glory (*) / Light my candle (*) / Today 4 U (*) / Tango: Maureen (*) / Life support / Out tonight (*) / Another day / Will I / Santa Fe (*) / I'll cover you (*) / Over the moon // La vie boheme (*) / I should tell you (*) / La vie boheme B (*) / Seasons of love B / Take me or leave me (*) / Without you (*) / I'll cover you (reprise) (*) / Halloween / Goodbye love / What you own (*) / Finale A / Your eyes / Finale B (*) / Love heals (*).

S/track review: If you're familiar with the Broadway album, 'RENT', the movie soundtrack is akin to an old pal after an unexpected nip and tuck. Save for Rosario Dawson and Tracie Thomas, the cast is more or less unchanged. The performances have been tightened up and much of the dramatic gristle sheared off, but they're still theatre; if you're not familiar with the show at all, or you've got a problem with the unholy alliance of musicals and period arrangements, you might find it hard going. 'Today 4 U' employs an arsenal of 80s dancefloor devices, the title track comes on like a cross between Billy Idol and Green Day, and 'Tonight' bears all the hallmarks of a Pat Benatar-style MTV extravaganza. It's an alliance shored up by the tonal and stylistic echoes of 'Let's Dance'-era David Bowie in Adam Pascal showcase, 'One Song Glory', a reedy whine reprised in Queen-scale closer, 'Your Eyes'. The tango number sounds tokenistic and even the dalliances with jazz, soul and gospel are often overpolished, exemplified by the otherwise talismanic 'Seasons Of Love'. While one of the few vocal segments held over from the Cast album is 'Over The Moon', with its surreal, intermittently a cappella imagery and ad hoc moo-ing actually coming as light relief from the ensemble bombast, the generally more reflective Disc 2 is an immediate improvement; 'La Vie Boheme' offers a raucous, mildly humorous gospel countdown of alternative touchstones including "Sontag", "fruits", "the Village Voice", "Langston Hughes", "tofu", "Buddha", "lezzies", "Bertolucci", "dildos" and "mucho masturbation" (though not necessarily in that order..). Less brazen but no less of a highlight is

Dawson's acoustic ballad, 'Without You'; like every performance on the album, though, its emotional context is inevitably compromised outwith the movie. If this kind of stuff lights your stage, better spend your rent money on the DVD. *BG*

Album rating: *6 / selections from . . . *5.5

– spinoff releases, etc. –

Original Cast: Rent – selections from . . . *(* above)*

Nov 05. (cd) *<49468-2>* [43] [–]

Original Cast: Seasons Of Love *remixes*

Jan 06. (cd-s) *<42866-2>* [ ] [–]

Original Cast: Take Me Or Leave Me *remixes*

Apr 06. (cd-s) *<42922-2>* [ ] [–]

REPO MAN

1984 (US 94m) Edge City / Universal Pictures (R)

Film genre: sci-fi/crime comedy

Top guns: dir (+ s-w): Alex Cox → SID & NANCY → STRAIGHT TO HELL → WALKER → FEAR AND LOATHING IN LAS VEGAS → REVENGERS TRAGEDY

Stars: Harry Dean Stanton *(Bud)* ← ONE FROM THE HEART ← the ROSE ← RENALDO AND CLARA ← RANCHO DELUXE ← PAT GARRETT & BILLY THE KID / → PARIS, TEXAS → PRETTY IN PINK → the LAST TEMPTATION OF CHRIST → WILD AT HEART → FEAR AND LOATHING IN LAS VEGAS, Emilio Estevez *(Otto Maddox)* → MAXIMUM OVERDRIVE → YOUNG GUNS II → JUDGMENT NIGHT, Tracey Walter *(Miller)* ← HONKYTONK MAN ← TIMERIDER: THE ADVENTURE OF LYLE SWANN / → BATMAN → YOUNG GUNS II → DELUSION → MAN ON THE MOON → HOW HIGH → MASKED AND ANONYMOUS, Olivia Barash *(Leila)* ← AMERICAN HOT WAX, **Sy Richardson** *(Lite)* ← PETEY WHEATSTRAW / → SID & NANCY → STRAIGHT TO HELL → WALKER → TAPEHEADS → MYSTERY TRAIN, Susan Barnes *(agent Rogersz)* ← BOUND FOR GLORY, Vonetta McGee *(Marlene, secretary)* ← BROTHERS ← SHAFT IN AFRICA ← BLACULA ← MELINDA, Helen Martin *(Mrs. Parks)* ← a HERO AIN'T NOTHIN' BUT A SANDWICH ← DEATH WISH ← COTTON COMES TO HARLEM / → HOUSE PARTY 2, **the CIRCLE JERKS:- Keith Morris *, Greg Hetson, Chuck Biscuits, Earl Liberty** *(nightclub band)* / **Zander Schloss** *(Kevin the nerd)* <= the CIRCLE JERKS =>, **Dick Rude** *(Duke the punk)* → SID & NANCY → STRAIGHT TO HELL → WALKER → ROADSIDE PROPHETS → LET'S ROCK AGAIN!, Jennifer Balgobin *(Debbi the punk)* → STRAIGHT TO HELL → TAPEHEADS → ROADSIDE PROPHETS, Biff Yeager *(Agent B)* ← DYNAMITE BROTHERS / → SID & NANCY → STRAIGHT TO HELL → WALKER → ROADSIDE PROPHETS, Michael Sandoval *(Archie the punk)* → HOWARD THE DUCK → SID & NANCY → STRAIGHT TO HELL → WALKER → JUNGLE FEVER, **Jimmy Buffet** *(additional blond agent)* ← FM, **the Untouchables:- Clyde Grimes, Jerry Miller, Chuck Askerneese, Herman Askerneese, Rob Lampron, Kevin Long, Josh Harris** *(scooter guys)*, Rodney Bingenheimer *(himself)* ← UP IN SMOKE / → X: THE UNHEARD MUSIC → UNCLE MEAT → BACK TO THE BEACH → ROCKULA → RAGE: 20 YEARS OF PUNK ROCK WEST COAST STYLE → END OF THE CENTURY → MAYOR OF THE SUNSET STRIP → PUNK'S NOT DEAD, Angelique Pettyjohn *(Repo man #2)* ← CLAMBAKE / → the CENSUS TAKER

Storyline: Punk rocker Otto has lost his boring supermarket job and is dumped by his girlfriend. Wandering the streets, he meets repossession agency man Bud and becomes his apprentice. So begins a series of adventures involving UFO cultists, the police and government agents, who take an interest in a missing 1964 Chevy Malibu with a deadly package in the boot and a $20,000 dollars repossession prize. *JZ*

Movie rating: *8

Visual: video + dvd

Off the record: The **Untouchables** were actually formed just prior to the making of 'REPO MAN'. Consisting of **Chuck Askerneese** (vocals), **Clyde Grimes** (guitar and vocals) plus **Jerry Miller, Josh Harris, Herman Askerneese, Rob Lampron & Kevin Long**, they subsequently added two guys named Carruthers and Symmons, signing to UK label, 'Stiff', in the process. 'Wild Child' (1985) – like a meeting of the Specials and the Jam – nearly cracked the Top 50 in Britain, while 'Free Yourself' & 'I Spy (For The F.B.I.)' hit Nos.26 and 59 respectively. They continued to be a hit around the US ska revival scene and released further sets including sophomore, 'Agent Double O Soul' (1989). *MCS*

Various Artists

May 84. (lp/c) *M.C.A.; <MCA/+C 39019> (MCF/+C 3223)* [ ] Jun84 [ ]

– Repo man (IGGY POP) / TV party (BLACK FLAG) / Institutionalized (SUICIDAL TENDENCIES) / Coup d'etat (the CIRCLE JERKS) / El clavo y la Cruz (the PLUGZ) / Pablo Picasso (BURNING SENSATIONS) / Let's have a war (FEAR) / When the shit hits the fan (the CIRCLE JERKS) / Hombre secreto (secret agent man) (the PLUGZ) / Bad man (JUICY BANANAS) / Reel ten (the PLUGZ). *<(cd-iss. Jan93; MCAD 39019)> (cd re-iss. Oct95; MCLD 19311)*

S/track review: The ultimate Various Artists US hardcore/punk OST . . . ever! 'REPO MAN' is indeed the ultimate cult package, made by cult director, Alex Cox, a man with a revered musical knowledge and sharp wit besides. Who better to kick out the jams and kick off the show, than "Godfather of Punk" IGGY POP, who puts a capital A into the adrenalin-fuelled exclusive title theme; augmented incidentally by former Sex Pistol Steve Jones and Blondie guys, Clem Burke and Nigel Harrison. The Los Angeles hardcore scene at the turn of the 80s are well represented here, none more so than BLACK FLAG (featuring the classic line-up of HENRY ROLLINS, Greg Ginn, Dez Cadena, Charles Dubowski and Robo) and their boisterous "Friggin' In The Riggin'"-ish 'TV Party'. Future actor, LEE VING, gets his two-pennorth in via his band, FEAR, although 'Let's Have A Party' is slightly overshadowed by a couple of CIRCLE JERKS gems, 'Coup d'Etat' and the slo-acoustic 'When The Shit Hits The Fan', the latter featuring different 'Jerks (see stars above). Skater-punks, SUICIDAL TENDENCIES (with 'Institutionalized') – featuring Mike Muir on angst-ridden vox – were also present and correct, while fun lovin' Hispanics, the PLUGZ (highlighting singer/guitarist Tito Larriva) get in three numbers, 'El Clavo Y La Cruz', the cinematic 'Reel Ten' and a rendition of P.F. Sloan's 'Hombre Secreto (Secret Agent Man)'. Talking of covers, BURNING SENSATIONS pull off a clever, 'Peter Gunn'-like version of Jonathan's Richman's arty 'Pablo Picasso'. Man of the moment, Alex Cox, became part-time lyricist for mock blaxploitation outfit, JUICY BANANAS, vocalist SY RICHARDSON getting all super-'Bad Man' (Isaac'n'Barry-wise) on a cool cut featuring Zander Schloss (guitar), Billy Ferrick (keys/synths), Ron White (bass) and Eric Thompson (drums). Now go and buy. *MCS*

Album rating: *8.5

RESERVOIR DOGS

1992 (US 99m) Miramax Films (R)

Film genre: crime/gangster thriller

Top guns: s-w + dir: Quentin Tarantino → PULP FICTION → NATURAL BORN KILLERS → FOUR ROOMS → FROM DUSK TILL DAWN → JACKIE BROWN → KILL BILL: VOL.1 → KILL BILL: VOL.2

Stars: Harvey Keitel *(Mr. White/Larry Dimmick)* ← the LAST TEMPTATION OF CHRIST ← the BORDER ← THAT'S THE WAY OF THE WORLD / → PULP FICTION → FROM DUSK TILL DAWN → FINDING GRACELAND → BE COOL, Tim Roth *(Mr. Orange/Freddy Newandyke)* ← RETURN TO WATERLOO / → PULP FICTION → FOUR ROOMS → the MILLION

DOLLAR HOTEL, Chris Penn *(Nice Guy Eddie Cabot)* ← MADE IN USA ← FOOTLOOSE / → MASKED AND ANONYMOUS, Steve Buscemi *(Mr. Pink)* ← MYSTERY TRAIN ← the WAY IT IS / → PULP FICTION → AIRHEADS → the WEDDING SINGER → COFFEE AND CIGARETTES → ROMANCE & CIGARETTES → the FUTURE IS UNWRITTEN, Michael Madsen *(Mr. Blonde/Vic Vega)* ← the DOORS / → STRAIGHT TALK, Randy Brooks *(Holdaway)*, Lawrence Tierney *(Joe Cabot)* ← EDDIE PRESLEY, Kirk Baltz *(Marvin Nash)*, Eddie Bunker *(Mr. Blue)*, Quentin Tarantino *(Mr. Brown)* ← EDDIE PRESLEY / → PULP FICTION → FOUR ROOMS → FROM DUSK TILL DAWN → GIRL 6, Steven Wright *(K-Billy DJ)* → COFFEE AND CIGARETTES

Storyline: Quentin Tarantino reinvents the gangster genre and cements his career for the coming decade via a slew of hip cultural references, razor sharp dialogue, twisted humour, a great soundtrack and lashings of gratuitous violence. The action seesaws between the planning and the gory aftermath – although not the execution – of a botched jewellery heist, as the colour coded characters start cracking under the strain of sniffing out the traitor in their midst. *BG*

Movie rating: *9.5

Visual: video + dvd

Off the record: nothing

—

Various Artists (& intros by Steven Wright *)

Nov 92. (cd/c) *M.C.A.; <MCA D/C 10541> (MCDMCC 10793)* ☐ Feb93 16
– And now Little Green Bag (*) / Little green bag (GEORGE BAKER SELECTION) / Rock flock of five (*) / Hooked on a feeling (BLUE SWEDE) / Bohemiath (*) / I gotcha (JOE TEX) / Magic carpet ride (BEDLAM) / (Madonna speech – dialogue; Quentin Tarantino & Harvey Keitel) / Fool for love (SANDY ROGERS) / Super sounds (*) / Stuck in the middle with you (STEALERS WHEEL) / Harvest moon (BEDLAM) / Let's get a taco (Harvey Keitel & Tim Roth; dialogue) / Keep on truckin' (*) / Coconut (HARRY NILSSON) / Home of rock (*). *<US re-dist.Feb95>* – hit No.24

S/track review: Not only did Tarantino resurrect the gangster genre but he gave the increasingly tired soundtrack format its biggest dressing-down since the Blaxploitation era. The blueprint was simple: a combination of classic R&B, obscure 70s pop and select snippets of dialogue, in this instance all strung together by the brilliantly slack-jawed introductions of comedian Steven Wright. Highlights include the opening 'Little Green Bag' by the GEORGE BAKER SELECTION, BLUE SWEDE's swinging 'Hooked On A Feeling', and who could forget the unhinged Mr. Blonde indulging in a notorious spot of ear-slicing to the strains of STEALERS WHEELS' 'Stuck In The Middle With You'. Further smash hits from NILSSON ('Coconut') and JOE TEX ('I Gotcha') sat side by side with a few obscurities by unknown quantities, BEDLAM ('Harvest Moon' & Steppenwolf's 'Magic Carpet Ride'), but all'n'all it's over far too quickly. *BG & MCS*

Album rating: *8

the RETURN OF THE LIVING DEAD

1985 (US 91m) Hemdale / Fox Films Ltd. / Orion Pictures (R)

Film genre: sci-fi horror comedy/drama

Top guns: s-w (+ dir): Dan O'Bannon ← HEAVY METAL (story: Rudy Ricci, Russell Steiner / book: John A. Russo)

Stars: Clu Gulager *(Burt Wilson)* ← LIVING PROOF: THE HANK WILLIAMS JR STORY / → TAPEHEADS → EDDIE PRESLEY, James Karen *(Frank)* ← the JAZZ SINGER / → GIRL, Don Calfa *(Ernie Kaltenbrunner)* ← the ROSE, Thom Matthews *(Freddy)* ← the WOMAN IN RED, Brian Peck *(Scuz)* → MAN ON THE MOON, Miguel A. Nunez Jr. *(Spider)* → WHY DO FOOLS FALL IN LOVE, Linnea Quigley *(Trash)*, Beverly Randolph *(Tina)*, John Philbin *(Chuck)* → SHY PEOPLE → GIRL, Jewel Shepard *(Casey)* → SCENES FROM THE GOLDMINE, Mark Venturini *(Suicide)*

Storyline: Frank and Freddy are two employees at a warehouse which supplies corpses and skeletons to medical people. When they inadvertently release a canister of a top secret chemical into the atmosphere, the corpses suddenly spring to life and look for something to eat – human brains are a particular favourite. Is it the end of civilization as we know it, or will it be a real no-brainer for the good guys? *JZ*

Movie rating: *7

Visual: video + dvd

Off the record: (see below)

—

Various Artists (score: Matt Clifford)

Jun 85. (lp/c) *Restless; <72085-1/-4> Big Beat; (WIK/+C 38)* ☐ ☐
– Surfin' dead (the CRAMPS) / Partytime (zombie version) (45 GRAVE) / Nothing for you (TSOL) / Eyes without a face (the FLESHEATERS) / Burn the flames (ROKY ERICKSON) / Dead beat dance (the DAMNED) / Take a walk (TALL BOYS) / Love under will (the JET BLACK BERRIES) / Tonight (we'll make love until we die) (SSQ) / Trash's theme (SSQ). *(pic-lp iss.Jul85 on 'New Rose'; ROSE 66P) (cd-iss. Jun88; CDWIK 38) <cd-iss. Jul93; 7 72004-2>*

S/track review: For a film about spiky-topped ghouls (with names like Scuz, Trash and Suicide on display), it was little wonder the album's producer chose to serve the celluloid with an array of varying 70s punk rock bands. The CRAMPS come out to play on the psychobilly opener, 'Surfin' Dead', an exclusive cut that shakes 'n' shimmies its way through a musical graveyard and into the proverbial crematorium (as in the film itself) – not their best ever. The minor Orange County band, 45 GRAVE (think Suzi Quatro & the Runaways), surface next with a zombie version of their best song, 'Partytime', also a lyrically-cloned "fight-for-your-right-to-party" precursor to the Beastie Boys – without the wit. TSOL (another act to promote the movie's US indie imprint, 'Restless') were the epitomy of anthemic hardcore angst, and 'Nothing For You' was no exception. 'Eyes Without A Face' (no relation to the subsequent Billy Idol song), from the bleeding hearts of the inconquerable FLESHEATERS and their unique screamer/singer Chris Desjardins (think Ramones or the Gun Club), is a definite highlight. Another surprise gem from the soundtrack is the exquisitely ghoulish 'Burn The Flames', from the legendary 13th Floor Elevators leader, ROKY ERICKSON, a 6-minute dirge delivering maniacal vox and a solo guitar spot to boot. The only major Brit-punks on display are the DAMNED, who don't really "smash it up" for the exclusive, but slightly disappointing, 'Dead Beat Dance', while on a similar theme, the little-known TALL BOYS (also from London) are out of their depth on 'Take A Walk'. Newcomers on the block, the JET BLACK BERRIES, were just as obscure at the time, although the track here, 'Love Under Will', is just too nice. The female-led SSQ conclude the 10-track soundtrack with two electro-beat squeaks, 'Tonight (We'll Make Love Until We Die)' and the instrumental 'Trash's Theme' – hardly riveting. With great reviews elsewhere for 'The RETURN OF THE LIVING DEAD', one was more than underwhelmed by the set, although most of these coffin-dodgers on display certainly come from a gothic-punk underground somewhere. Dust to dust – as they say. *MCS*

Album rating: *6

RETURN TO WATERLOO

1985 (UK 95m TV) Channel 4 Television (PG-13)

Film genre: Pop-Rock Musical drama

Top guns: s-w + dir: **Ray DAVIES**

Stars: Kenneth Colley *(the traveller)* ← LISZTOMANIA ← FLAME ← PERFORMANCE, Valerie Holliman *(traveller's wife)*, Dominique Barnes *(traveller's daughter)*, Hywel Williams Ellis *(young businessman)*, Aaron Probyn *(small boy traveller)*, Joan Blackman *(mother)* ← KID GALAHAD ← BLUE HAWAII, **Ray DAVIES** *(subway singer)*, Tim Roth *(boy punk)* → RESERVOIR DOGS → PULP FICTION → FOUR ROOMS → the MILLION DOLLAR HOTEL, Michael Fish *(himself)*, Sheila Collings *(middle-aged lady)* ← SIDE BY SIDE, Claire Rayner *(herself)*

Storyline: Conceptual musical layering the bittersweet early years, tainted adulthood, disturbing present and bleak future of a balding estate agent, telescoped into the recurring metaphor of a journey on good old British Rail. He might be the rapist pictured by the tabloids, he's not averse to a tryst with a woman half his age or even the full blown affair his miserable wife suspects, at least in his mind. Suited and booted, Dennis Potter-esque singalongs are choreographed on depressing station platforms, a gang of obnoxious teenagers terrorise a carriage of stiff upper-lipped pensioners in classic punk-iconographic style and the dead-eyed hero hallucinates all the while, oblivious to the accusing stares and whispered insults of his fellow passengers. *BG*

Movie rating: *6

Visual: video on RCA

Off the record: (see below)

—

RAY DAVIES

Jul 85. (lp) *Arista; <8380>* ☐ ☐
– Intro / Return to Waterloo / Going solo / Missing persons / Sold me out / Lonely hearts / Not far away / Expectations / Voices in the dark – end title. *<cd-iss. Feb05 on 'Velvel'; VELV 79820>*

S/track review: Re-issued in 2005 to coincide with the release of RAY DAVIES' first ever solo studio set, 'RETURN TO WATERLOO' is a KINKS catalogue oddity, a band album (with seasoned musicians IAN GIBBONS – keyboards, JIM RODFORD – bass and drummers BOB HENRITT and MICK AVORY) in all but name and the presence of brother DAVE. If you're familiar with the band's 80s work you'll pretty much know what to expect here. There's nothing of the calibre of the underrated 'PERCY', especially in the ballad department but – as with 'Come Dancing' – DAVIES occasionally manages to square his urban nostalgia with synth-padded studio ethics, most successfully on 'Going Solo' (previously heard – along with 'Missing Persons' and 'Sold Me Out' – on 1984's 'Word Of Mouth' album). Even then, though, what stands out is the message rather than the music, chafing against the tawdry reality of Thatcher's Britain on the likes of 'Expectations' and the cockney-punk 'Sold Me Out'. The soundtrack's most perversely enjoyable moment (and definitely its most memorable) is actually the end title, 'Voices In The Dark', buttery 80s pop which – unwittingly or otherwise – congeals ELO and OMD; it's outrageously dated but it fits his reedy voice like a fingerless glove. Cautiously recommended for DAVIES diehards then, but those curious about the KINKS' screen career should probably start with 'PERCY'. *BG*

Album rating: *5.5

☐ RHEOSTATICS segment
(⇒ WHALE MUSIC)

RHINESTONE

1984 (US 120m) Twentieth Century-Fox Films (PG)

Film genre: showbiz/Country-music comedy

Top guns: dir: Bob Clark / s-w: Phil Alden Robinson (+ story), Sylvester Stallone ← STAYING ALIVE

Stars: Sylvester Stallone *(Nick Martinelli)* ← BEST REVENGE, **Dolly PARTON** *(Jake Ferris)*, Richard Farnsworth *(Noah Ferris)* ← the SOUL OF NIGGER CHARLEY, Ron Leibman *(Freddie Ugo)*, Tim Thomerson *(Barnett Cale)* ← HONKYTONK MAN ← CARNY ← RECORD CITY ← CAR WASH / → NEAR DARK → EDDIE PRESLEY → BAD CHANNELS, Penny Santon *(Mother Martinelli)*, Phil Rubenstein *(Maurie)* ← the ROSE, Cindy Perlman *(Esther Jean)* ← STAYING ALIVE / → HARD TO HOLD, Russell Buchanan *(Elgart)*, **Floyd & Randy Parton** *(members of the Cut N' Slice Band)*

Storyline: Frustrated country singer, Jake Ferris, is held back by a New York bar owner who wants to keep her performing there instead of letting her go onwards and upwards. In order to escape, Jake strikes a bet with her boss claiming that she can teach anyone to be a country singer in two weeks. The "anyone" happens to be loudmouth taxi driver Nick Martinelli, who gets his kicks from terrifying his passengers. As he's a useless singer, Jake's bet is looking a bit rocky. *JZ*

Movie rating: *3

Visual: video + dvd

Off the record: (see below)

—

DOLLY PARTON (* w/ + ** by SYLVESTER STALLONE)

Jul 84. (lp/c) *R.C.A.; <5032> (BL/BK 85032)* ☐ Aug84 ☐
– Tennessee homesick blues (*) / Too much water (RANDY PARTON) / The day my baby died (RUSTY BUCHANAN) / One emotion after another (*) / Goin' back to Heaven (STELLA PARTON & KIN VASSY) / What a heartache (*) / Stay out of my bedroom (** & *) / Woke up in love (** & *) / God won't get you (*) / Drinkin'stein (**) / Sweet lovin' friends (** & *) / Waltz me to Heaven (FLOYD PARTON) / Butterflies (*) / Be there (** & *).

S/track review: Having been redirected from 'The BEST LITTLE WHOREHOUSE IN TEXAS' – so to speak – leading C&W star DOLLY PARTON and sidekick "Rocky Bilbao" himself, SYLVESTER STALLONE, work up a sweat while striving to put a few songs together. 5-foot DOLLY is head and shoulders above her other singing contenders, which incidentally include wee sister STELLA and younger brothers RANDY and FLOYD. Not one of DOLLY's best moves in the fickle world of Hollywood showbusiness, record-wise she still manages to air that high-octave singing larynx to everywhere in the room; she also wrote "every" song. But Glen Campbell (writer of the film's inspirational song, 'Rhinestone Cowboy') might well've been handy to have around. On lonesome ground, DOLLY tracks such as 'Tennessee Homesick Blues' (competing with annoying canned clap-ter), 'One Emotion After Another' & 'What A Heartache' were basically bread-and-butter dirges, like some leftovers from previous sets. Her best solo cues stem from the spiritual 'God Won't Get You' (with enough country song clichés to sink any boat) and her ever-present theme of 'Butterflies'. However, when "The Backwoods Barbie" meets "The Italian Stallion", things go from quite bad to warbling worse as the big two (no pun intended) get to grips with some duelling duets. 'Stay Out Of My Bedroom' strikes me as the most embarrassing song of all time; the monotone STALLONE obviously listened to Springsteen's 'Born In The USA' before he went into the studio. The clapping was ever-present, of course, and thankfully the sheep-ish DOLLY comes in for a chorus or two just at the right time. If you get past "the bedroom song", there's 'Woke Up In Love', 'Sweet Lovin' Friends' (here Sly becomes Neil Diamond) and 'Be There', and as for the two STALLONE solo cuts, just don't go there. Meanwhile, back at the Dolly ranch, aforementioned kinsfolk RANDY PARTON (with 'Too Much Water'), FLOYD PARTON (with 'Waltz Me To Heaven') and STELLA PARTON ('Goin' Back To Heaven', alongside Charles KINdred VASSY) spread the country gospel – but not to me. Whether it's my sense of humour, I laughed at the country pastiche of RUSTY BUCHANAN's 'The Day My Baby Died', which just about says it all. Boo! *MCS*

Album rating: *3.5

– spinoff releases, etc. –

DOLLY PARTON & SYLVESTER STALLONE: Sweet Lovin' Friends / DOLLY PARTON: God Won't Get You

Oct 84. (7") *<13883>* ☐ -

Cliff RICHARD

Born: Harry Roger Webb, 14 Oct'40, Lucknow, India. An ELVIS wannabe who shook up a staid, pre-BEATLES British pop scene in the late 50s before mellowing into a celibate, MOR elder statesman, CLIFF RICHARD – like his idol PRESLEY – made more than his fair share of all-singing, all-dancing films. That said, his debut screen appearance was in 'Serious Charge' (1959), a movie which boasted fairly explosive subject matter for its day. Although his part was pretty minor, among the soundtrack's trio of RICHARD songs was one of the most enduring, 'Living Doll', featured in its rawer original version rather than the ballad which topped the charts and announced a toning down of his pelvis-pushing image. The satirical, pseudo-autobiograpical music business drama, 'EXPRESSO BONGO' (1959), cast Cliff as Bongo Herbert, a young wannabe transformed into a huge star by a wily Soho suit. While an EP of songs from 'Serious Charge' failed to chart, 'EXPRESSO BONGO's soundtrack EP hit the top 20 as his film career really began to kick in. Yet along with the toning down of his image came a switch from gritty cinematic realism to inoffensive musicals. Inspired by a Rodgers & Hart production, 'The YOUNG ONES' (1962) landed Cliff his biggest role to date as the son of a millionaire determined to foil his father's designs on the local youth centre. Chief in the lad's armoury was, of course, songs, largely of the shiny happy variety and which pushed the attendant soundtrack to No.1 in the UK (where it spent almost a year on the chart). In line with the movie's MGM-esque pretensions, the soundtrack featured a full studio orchestra on top of Cliff's regular backing band, the SHADOWS, while the film itself remains one the man's best loved vehicles, infamously lending its name to the anarchic 80s comedy of Rik Mayall et al. 1963's 'SUMMER HOLIDAY' proved even more successful, breaking box office records and mimicking the proven formula of the ELVIS movies with its heady brew of glamourous location, beautiful women and escapist song. The fact that Cliff was actually playing a London Transport mechanic who travels by bus rather than private jet merely added a bit of stolid British modesty to proceedings. Again the soundtrack topped the chart and even generated a couple of spin-off EP's as well as a No.1 title track. Just as it seemed there was no stopping RICHARD's inexorable rise to cinematic fame, the emergence of the BEATLES served to put something of a brake on the success of his next film, 'WONDERFUL LIFE' (1964). While its tale of romance and movie-making in the Canary Islands seemed to have all the right ingredients, the picture failed to repeat the financial success of its predecessor and, tellingly, the soundtrack was kept off the No.1 spot by its BEATLES counterpart, 'a HARD DAY'S NIGHT'. But if Cliff couldn't hope to compete with the either the BEATLES' songwriting or their skewed Scouse humour, at least he still had an appeciative and commercially viable audience. Neither its rather convoluted, espionage-style plot nor the pared down music in 'FINDERS KEEPERS' (1966) were regarded as matching previous standards although both the film and soundtrack (Cliff's last with the SHADOWS) performed well financially. 1966 also found Cliff famously providing the singing voice for his puppet likeness in Gerry Anderson's 'Thunderbirds Are Go', although the song in question, 'Shooting Star', failed to chart. His next film proper, 'TWO A PENNY' (1968) was a bizarre vehicle for American evangelist Billy Graham (Cliff had recently converted to Christianity), substituting the youthful dance routines for overly simplistic religious moralising. Only one of the soundtrack's four RICHARD songs was performed in the film, while the soundtrack itself – bolstered by extra material – was his first not to chart. By the time he recorded his next – and to date, final – movie, 'TAKE ME HIGH' (1973), RICHARD was getting on a bit, and while much of his audience had probably aged with him, his movie-musical formula – like PRESLEY's before him – had long since passed its sell by date. While he continued to record and tour right through the 80s, 90s and noughties, Sir Cliff (he was knighted in 1995) has yet to resume his acting career and given that he's apparently so unfashionable his Xmas '99 No.1, 'The Millennium Prayer', was pretty much ignored by the media, it looks increasingly unlikely that's ever going to happen. *BG*

- **filmography** {acting} –

Serious Charge *(1959 {a} EP but no OST)* / **Expresso Bongo** *(1959 {*} OST w/ DRIFTERS/SHADOWS =>)* / **the Young Ones** *(1961 {*} OST w/ SHADOWS =>)* / **Summer Holiday** *(1963 {*} OST w/ SHADOWS =>)* / **Wonderful Life** *(1964 {*} OST w/ SHADOWS =>)* / **Finders Keepers** *(1966 {*} OST w/ SHADOWS =>)* / **Two A Penny** *(1968 {*} OST =>)* / His Land *(1970 {*} OST w/ Cliff Barrows)* / **Take Me High** *(1973 {*} OST =>)*

– compilations, etc. –

CLIFF RICHARD: At The Movies 1959-1974

Jul 96. (4xcd-box/d-c) *E.M.I.; (CD/TC EMD 1096) <52790>* ☐ -

– No turning back / Living doll / Mad about you / Love / A voice in the wilderness / The shrine on the second floor / Friday night / Got a funny feeling (alt. take) / Nothing's impossible / The young ones / Lessons in love / When the girl in your arms / We say yeah! / (It's) Wonderful to be young (alt. take) / Outsider / Seven days to a holiday / Summer holiday / Let us take you for a ride / A stranger in town / Bachelor boy / A swingin' affair / Dancing shoes / The next time / Big news / Wonderful life / A girl in ever port / A little imagination (edited) / On the beach / Do you remember / Look don't touch / In the stars / What've I got to do / A matter of moments / Wonderful life (alt. take) / Shooting star / Finders keepers / Time drags by / Washerwoman / La la la song / Oh señorita (extended) / This day / Paella / Two a penny / Twist and shout / I'll love you forever today / Questions / It's only money / Midnight blue / The game / Brumberger duet / Take me high / The anti-brotherhood of man / Winning / The young ones (film version) / Lessons in love (edited film version) / Bachelor boy (film version) / Summer holiday.

RIDE

1998 (US 84m) Dimension Films (R)

Film genre: showbiz road comedy

Top guns: s-w + dir: Millicent Shelton

Stars: Malik Yoba *(Poppa)* → FEEL THE NOISE, Melissa De Sousa *(Leta)* → LAUREL CANYON, John Witherspoon *(Roscoe)* ← the FIVE HEARTBEATS ← HOUSE PARTY, **Fredro Starr** *(Geronimo)* → BLACK AND WHITE → SAVE THE LAST DANCE, Cedric The Entertainer *(Bo)* → BE COOL, **Sticky Fingaz** *(Brotha X)* → BLACK AND WHITE, Kellie Williams *(Tuesday)*, **the Lady Of Rage** *(Peaches)*, Dartanyan Edmonds *(Byrd)*, **Luther 'Luke' Campbell** *(Freddy B.)*, Doctor Dre *(Eight)* ← WHO'S THE MAN? ← JUICE / → DEATH OF A DYNASTY, Ed Lover *(Six)* ← WHO'S THE MAN? ← JUICE / → DOUBLE PLATINUM → DEATH OF A DYNASTY → TUPAC: RESURRECTION, **SNOOP Doggy DOGG** *(Mente)*, Fred Williamson *(Caspar's dream dad)* ← FROM DUSK TILL DAWN ← MR. MEAN ← NO WAY BACK ← ADIOS AMIGO ← MEAN JOHNNY BARROWS ← THREE THE HARD WAY ← THREE TOUGH GUYS ← the SOUL OF NIGGER CHARLEY ← BLACK CAESAR ← HELL UP IN HARLEM / → CARMEN: A HIP HOPERA, **Dave Hollister** *(himself)*, Guy Torry *(Indigo)*, **Erick Sermon** *(himself)* ← RHYME & REASON ← JUICE, **Redman** *(himself)* ← RHYME & REASON / → BACKSTAGE → HOW HIGH, **Keith Murray** *(himself)* ← RHYME & REASON, Angie Martinez *(herself)* → BROWN SUGAR → PAPER SOLDIERS → STATE PROPERTY 2

Storyline: New York graduate Leta takes her first job escorting a group of aspiring actors, dancers and singers to Florida for a promotional video. Leta's learning curve rises sharply when the drawbacks occur – their tour bus was built in biblical times, the personalities of the troupe clash like Scylla and Charybdis, and the final straw is when the bus is held up by two gangsters who're after one of the rappers. Can Leta save the day? *JZ*

Movie rating: *4

Visual: dvd

Off the record: **Fredro Starr** (is of Onyx); **Luther 'Luke' Campbell** (2 Live Crew); **Dave Hollister** (ex-BlackStreet); **Erick Sermon** (of EPMD – also solo star with two Top 40 albums: 1993's 'No Pressure' & 1995's 'Double Or Nothing'); **Redman** (numerous albums in the 90s, 'Whut? Thee Album', 'Dare Iz A Darkside', 'Muddy Waters', 'Doc's Da Name 2000', etc.), R&B **Keith Murray** (has had three Top 40 sets between 1994 & '9;: 'The Most Beautifullest Thing In This World', 'Enigma' & 'It's A Beautiful Thing'); Angie Martinez was hip hop's lady of radio (station Hot 97, to be precise). *MCS*

Various Artists (score: Dunn Pearson Jr.)

Feb 98. (d-lp/cd) *Tommy Boy; <TB/+CD 1227>* [54] [–]
– The weekend (DAVE HOLLISTER feat. REDMAN + ERICK SERMON) / The worst (WU-TANG CLAN + ONYX) / Blood money – part 2 (NOREAGA feat. NAS + NATURE) / Outta sight (RUFUS BLAQ) / Soldier funk (MIA X feat. FIEND + MAC) / The game (MACK 10, BIG MIKE + D.J. U-NEEK feat. EWF) / The symptoms (BLACK CAESAR) / Feels so good (EASTSIDERS feat. SNOOP DOGGY DOGG) / Mourn you til I join you (NAUGHTY BY NATURE) / Jam on it (CARDAN feat. JERMAINE DUPRI) / Higher (SEXIONS) / Callin' (AMARI) / Why (ERIC BENET + the ROOTS) / No one (SOMETHIN' FOR THE PEOPLE feat. TRINA + TAMARA) / Can't get enough (RAPHAEL SAADIQ introducing WILLIE MAX) / Never say goodbye (ADRIANA EVANS feat. PHIFE of A TRIBE CALLED QUEST).

S/track review: There often appears to be little correlation between the quality of a movie and its soundtrack, as the excellent cache of beats racked up to soundtrack 'RIDE' attests. A vibrant disc of two halves: one downpour of chunky hip hop bangers, followed by a rainbow of earthy, soulful, considered R&B. The collection reflects a time post-Biggie and 2Pac when the focus in black American music shifted away from the beefs and bling and momentarily back to the music. It is the collaborations here that bring forth the most fruitful results. One-time Blackstreet crooner DAVID HOLLISTER gets in the vocal booth with REDMAN and ERICK SERMON to show how the sharp contrasts between smooth R&B and roughneck rap can make comfortable bedfellows. The collaboration between Queens heavies ONYX and Staten Island's wayward sons, WU-TANG CLAN, 'The Worst', was both a critical and commercial success at the time. A sparse, demonic drum-loop driving a dozen verses of dextrous hip hop doom. NAUGHTY BY NATURE get serious and sincere on their tribute to 2Pac, 'Mourn You Til I Join You', which injects a degree of melancholy into the heart of a boisterous tribute. CARDAN and JERMAINE DUPRI team up to deliver a bit of stripped down, back to '84 electro beats for their gem of a cut 'Jam On It'. Similarly effective is the ROOTS and ERIC BENET's 'Why', BENET's Prince-like tones sliding over the ROOTS' fluid live funk. SOMETHIN' FOR THE PEOPLE follow the post-Prince, D'Angelo route for R&B jams with 'No One' and TRINA + TAMARA are on hand to slather it with luscious harmonics. The set is brought to a close with ADRIANA EVANS and PHIFE from A TRIBE CALLED QUEST combining for some sweet supper club jazz and EVANS' emphatic, chocolatey tones. From start to finish, there's not a weak cut here. *MR*

Album rating: *8.5

– spinoff hits, etc. –

NAUGHTY BY NATURE: Mourn You Til I Join You / (non-OST song)

Oct 97. (c-s/12"/cd-s) *<427>* [51] [–]

RIKKY AND PETE

1988 (Aus 102m) Cascade Films / MGM / United Artists (R)

Film genre: road movie comedy/drama

Top guns: dir: Nadia Tass → AMY / s-w: David Parker → AMY

Stars: Stephen Kearney *(Pete Menzies)*, Nina Landis *(Rikky Menzies)*, Tetchie Agbayani *(Flossie)*, Bill Hunter *(Whitstead)* ← NED KELLY / → BAD EGGS, Bruno Lawrence *(Sonny)*, Bruce Spence *(Ben)* ← 20th CENTURY OZ / → SWEET TALKER → QUEEN OF THE DAMNED, Lewis Fitz-Gerald *(Adam)*, Don Reid *(Mr. Menzies)* → MOULIN ROUGE, Ralph Cotterill *(George Pottinger)* → SONS OF STEEL → the PROPOSITION

Storyline: Rikky and her brother Pete head for a mining community in the Australian outback after deciding city life is not for them. Pete has a talent for inventing gadgets which can do the impossible (to the annoyance of the local police) while Rikky dreams of becoming a country and western singer. How will the oddball siblings cope with the change from modern suburbia to the slow pace of life in the outback, and will they strike gold when they join with a group of miners out to make their fortune? *JZ*

Movie rating: *6

Visual: video on Warner Bros.

Off the record: EDDIE RAYNER and BRIAN BAKER subsequently produced The Makers on their 1990 debut set.

Various Artists (score: EDDIE RAYNER and BRIAN BAKER *)

Jun 88. (lp) *E.M.I.; (EMX 790678)* [–] Austra [–]
– Pete's theme (*) / Recurring dream (CROWDED HOUSE) / Rikky's sample (*) / (NOEL'S COWARD'S):- Finger's crossed / Cold shoulder / In the dark / Tears of joy / Just like you / Hard to believe // Pete's ride (*) / As good as it gets (*) / Run a mile (SCHNELL FENSTER) / Return to Melbourne (*) / Perfect world (BLUE HEALERS) / Couldn't happen to a nicer guy (*) / Last call for love (KEITH GLASS AND THE HONKY TONKS) / How many more moves (KEITH GLASS and the HONKY TONKS) / Hell of a job (KEITH GLASS and the HONKY TONKS) / Whitstead (*). *(<UK/US-iss.Feb90 on 'D.R.G.' cd/lp; CD+/SBL 12593>)*

S/track review: Australian OST, 'RIKKY AND PETE', is a bit of a misnomer, suggesting as it does it will be "featuring CROWDED HOUSE", when in reality only the jangle-pop of track #2, 'Recurring Dream', is by the multi-platinum-to-be antipodean band. However, there are connections a-plenty. Most of you pop-pickers out there will have heard of CROWDED HOUSE's fledgling outfit, Split Enz, who featured numerous personnel throughout the 70s and 80s including future Schnell Fenster musicians PHILIP JUDD (main songwriter, co-producer & guitarist), NOEL CROMBIE (drummer) and NIGEL GRIGGS (bassist). With other members, WENDY MATTHEWS (vocalist), MICHAEL den ELZEN (guitarist & co-producer), MICHAEL HARRIS (on fiddle), LOUIS McMANUS (on mandolin), etc., and for the sake of the movie, SF became NOEL'S COWARD'S – the grammatical error very mysterious. Anyway, this indie-folk outfit contributed several consecutive tunes, namely 'Finger's Crossed', 'Cold Shoulder', 'In The Dark', 'Tears Of Joy', 'Just Like You' and 'Hard To Believe', all highlighting the raspy vox of MATTHEWS – think Pat Benatar or Pussycat (remember 'Mississippi'). Incidentally, the aforementioned SCHNELL FENSTER supply one Fad Gadget/The The-esque dirge, 'Run A Mile'. Bar the sing-a-long sole contribution by BLUE HEALERS ('Perfect World'), the remainder of 'RIKKY AND PETE' is down to two further acts, EDDIE RAYNER (another

Split Enz affiliate) and BRIAN BAKER providing the short, acoustic score cues, while the self-evident KEITH GLASS AND THE HONKY TONKS are afforded three country cues. *MCS*

Album rating: *5

– spinoff releases, etc. –

NOEL'S COWARD'S: Fingers Crossed / Tears Of Joy
Jul 88. (7") *(2101)* [–] Austra [–]

RIOT ON SUNSET STRIP

1967 (US 87m) American International Pictures (18)

Film genre: cop/detective drama

Top guns: dir: Arthur Dreifuss → a TIME TO SING / s-w: Orville H. Hampton ← CALYPSO HEAT WAVE / → a TIME TO SING → FRIDAY FOSTER

Stars: Aldo Ray *(Lt. Walt Lorimer)* → the DYNAMITE BROTHERS → SHOCK 'EM DEAD, Mimsy Farmer *(Andy)* → MORE → CODENAME: WILDGEESE, Michael Evans *(Sgt. Tweedy)*, Laurie Mock *(Liz-Ann)*, Tim Rooney *(Grady)*, Gene Kirkwood *(Flip)*, Hortense Petra *(Marge)* ← HOLD ON! ← WHEN THE BOYS MEET THE GIRLS ← YOUR CHEATIN' HEART ← GET YOURSELF A COLLEGE GIRL ← KISSIN' COUSINS ← DON'T KNOCK THE TWIST, **the Chocolate Watchband:- David Aguilar, Tim Abbott, Mark Loomis, Gary Andrijasevich, Bill Flores, Mark Whitaker, Sean Tolby, Danny Phay** *(themselves)*, **the Standells:- Dick Dodd, Gary Lane, John Fleck, Larry Tamblyn, Tony Valentino** *(themselves)* ← GET YOURSELF A COLLEGE GIRL, **Debra Travis** *(herself)*, **the Enemies** *(themselves)*, **the Longhairs** *(themselves)*, Dick Winslow *(Curtis)* ← the CONTINENTAL TWIST ← KING CREOLE

Storyline: Churned out on the back of real life anti-curfew riots, this B-quickie ("The Most Shocking Film Of Our Generation!") is remembered – when remembered at all- for vintage footage of garage perennials the Standells and the Chocolate Watchband (as well as the Enemies), with a plot revolving around clichéd cop Walt Lorimer and his handling of intergenerational tensions. Initially sympathetic to letting the kids have their fun, he changes his tune when his naïve, estranged daughter takes up with a gang of hippies, who, of course, turn out to be good old fashioned degenerates.. funny that. *BG*

Movie rating: *4

Visual: none

Off the record: (see below)

—

Various Artists (score: Freddy Karger)

Mar 67. (lp; mono/stereo) *Tower; <T/DT 5065>* [–] [–]
– Riot on Sunset Strip (the STANDELLS) / Sunset Sally (the MUGWUMPS) / The Sunset theme (the SIDEWALK SOUNDS) / Old country (DEBRA TRAVIS) / Don't need your lovin' (the CHOCOLATE WATCHBAND) / Children of the night (the MOM'S BOYS) / Make the music pretty (the SIDEWALK SOUNDS) / Get away from here (the STANDELLS) / Like my baby (DREW) / Sitting there standing (the CHOCOLATE WATCHBAND). *(UK cd-iss. Jun93 on 'Big Beat'+=; CDWIKD 113)* – the STANDELLS – Rarities (tracks).

S/track review: A vintage Mike Curb/'Tower' records exploitation job, reissued in the early 90s with full sleevenotes shedding at least some light on its motley conception. Disdainfully dispensing the kind of lyrics which might've been written on a matchbook five minutes before showtime, the STANDELLS' title theme sticks up three chords to the cops; "it's causin' a riot!" yelps drummer Dick Dodd, channelling the kind of whey-faced fervour inherited by Bobby Gillespie. It's a belief that makes their on-screen club performance easier to digest, even if 'Get Away From Here' is dreary in comparison. Fellow-Ed Cobb protégés the CHOCOLATE WATCHBAND go a fair distance to matching the STANDELLS' fury on their own mime-thrash, 'Don't Need Your Lovin'". Mainman DAVE AGUILAR agonises over a hopeless Mick Jagger fixation, shouting himself hoarse under a bassline so thick it could be a trombone. So far, so nuggets; it's worth investing in the soundtrack for these two cuts alone but there's also the CHOCOLATE WATCHBAND blues, 'Sitting There Standing', the MOM'S BOYS frazzled mystic-funk (think 'White Bird' meets 'Bring Down The Birds'; tragically, the sleevenotes fail to shed any further light on it) and a pretty folk number from little-known DEBRA TRAVIS, snipped from successive prints. Curb's 'Sunset Theme' – billed to the SIDEWALK SOUNDS – is likewise unrelated to the movie, a surf-style instrumental every bit as clichéd as the cheesy 'Make The Music Pretty'. Curb also gets half the blame for DREW's shameless regurgitation of the Byrds' 'Spanish Harlem Incident', while the MUGWUMPS credited on the gummy 'Sunset Sally' are NOT, according to the notes, the same band that hosted Mama Cass, John Sebastian et al. So now you know. *BG*

Album rating: *5.5 / re-CD *6

ROAD HOUSE

1989 (US 115m) Silver Pictures / United Artists (R)

Film genre: music-backed crime thriller/drama

Top guns: dir: Rowdy Herrington / s-w: Hilary Henkin → WAG THE DOG, David Lee Henry

Stars: Patrick Swayze *(James Dalton)* ← DIRTY DANCING / → OVERNIGHT → DIRTY DANCING: HAVANA NIGHTS, Kelly Lynch *(Dr. Elizabeth Clay)* → the SLAUGHTER RULE, Sam Elliott *(Wade Garrett)* → RUSH, Ben Gazzara *(Brad Wesley)* → BUFFALO 66, Marshall Teague *(Jimmy; Wesley's No.1 thug)*, Julie Michaels *(Denise)*, Red West *(Red Webster)* ← bit parts in all ELVIS films, Sunshine Parker *(Emmet)*, **Jeff Healey** *(Cody)*, **Joseph Rockman** *(bassist w/ Cody's band)*, **Thomas Stephen** *(drummer w/ Cody's band)*, **John DOE** *(Pat McGurn)*, **Tito/Humberto Larriva** *(Crusades' singer/leader)* ← TRUE STORIES / → FROM DUSK TILL DAWN → the MILLION DOLLAR HOTEL, Ernie Hudson *(bartender)* ← the JAZZ SINGER ← LEADBELLY / → the CROW → AIRHEADS → the BASKETBALL DIARIES, Joe Unger *(Karpis)* → the BODYGUARD → SOUTH OF HEAVEN, WEST OF HELL, Keith David *(Ernie Bass, Double Deuce bartender)* ← DISCO GODFATHER / → REALITY BITES, Kevin Tighe *(Frank Tilghman; owner of Double Deuce)* → GERONIMO: AN AMERICAN LEGEND, Marshall Rohner *(Crusades)* ← VOYAGE OF THE ROCK ALIENS

Storyline: Dalton is a man with a mullet and a mission, not to mention a Phd. Preferring the sound of broken glass to the silence of a library, he's established himself as the most unassuming, sought after 'cooler' in the business, a chief bouncer who can sort out bad eggs with a chop suey flick of the wrist. Lured to the back of beyond to sort out the white trash clientele of a blues-music bar-cum-warzone called the Double Deuce, he's sucked into a confrontation with local kingpin Brad Wesley. Things turn nasty as one of Wesley's top stooges sets fire to his landlord's cottage; Dalton proceeds to literally rip his throat out and, after his buddy is fatally stabbed, goes after Wesley himself. *BG*

Movie rating: *6

Visual: video + dvd

Off the record: Blind since developing eye cancer (retinoblastoma) at the age of one, **Jeff Healey** (b.25 Mar'66, Toronto, Ontario, Canada) subsequently overcame his disability to become a talented blues/rock guitarist with a distinctive guitar-in-lap playing style. Having received his first guitar at the age of three, he later formed his first band, Blue Direction, whilst at high school, gigging frequently in the Toronto area. Adopting a style that conjured up images of BB King, Robin Trower and even more so, Hendrix, Healey's talent was sufficiently impressive to catch the eye of blues giant, Albert Collins, who, in turn, introduced him to Stevie Ray Vaughan; the Jeff Healey Band (bassist **Joe Rockman** and drummer **Thomas Stephen**), was formed the same year and began performing all over Canada. The group released singles on their own 'Forte' label before signing to 'Arista' in 1987 and setting out on their rapid rise to blues stardom. A much anticipated debut album, 'See The Light' (1988), featured the blues/rock of John Hiatt's 'Confidence Man' alongside Healey's own, 'My Little Girl', the bluesy title track and covers of ZZ Top's, 'Blue Jean Blues' and Freddie King's, 'Hideaway', the record selling nearly two million copies on its way to the US Top 30 (UK Top 60), while a single, 'Angel Eyes', made the American Top 5. The same year, the Canadian appeared in the feature film, 'ROAD HOUSE', in which he played a familiar role as a blind blues guitarist performing versions of the Doors' 'Roadhouse Blues', etc. (but where was his rendition of Canned Heat's 'On The Road Again' on the soundtrack)? *MCS*

—

Various Artists (score: Michael Kamen)

May 89. (lp/c/cd) *Arista; <+/AC/ARCD 8576> (209/409/259 948)* 67 Jul89
– Roadhouse blues (JEFF HEALEY BAND) / Blue Monday (BOB SEGER) / I'm torn down (JEFF HEALEY BAND) / These arms of mine (OTIS REDDING) / When the night comes falling from the sky (JEFF HEALEY BAND) / Rad gumbo (LITTLE FEAT) / Raising heaven (in Hell tonight) (PATRICK SWAYZE) / A good heart (KRIS McKAY) / (I'm your) Hoochie coochie man (JEFF HEALEY BAND) / Cliff's edge (PATRICK SWAYZE).

S/track review: Combining a blind blues wunderkind and a kung-fu-fighting Patrick Swayze, there's no question that 'ROAD HOUSE' fed into some kind of zeitgeist, although its genesis remains nebulous; a last-gasp, noised-up 'Dirty Bouncing' that saw out the 80s with behemoths from a decade earlier. Alongside JEFF HEALEY's lap prowess, BOB SEGER and a Lowell George-less LITTLE FEAT reminded the world they were still standing, SEGER with a New Orleans-buffed 'Blue Monday' and the recently reformed LITTLE FEAT with 'Rad Gumbo', a so-so Cajun number recorded for 1990s 'Representing The Mambo'. OTIS REDDING, by contrast, reminds us that he exited all too soon; the inclusion of 'These Arms Of Mine' underlines just how close un-neutered soul was to extinction by 1989. HEALEY himself convincingly rewrites Dylan's 'All Along The Watchtower' as 'When The Night Comes Falling From The Sky' (on-the-verge-of-stardom MARIA McKEE on backing vocals), generally dazzles with his casual technique, and finishes up with a gurning trawl through 'Hoochie Coochie Man'. If you actually lived through the 80s you'll be surprised how easily you can bear hearing – the McKEE-penned, Feargal Sharkey-famed – 'A Good Heart' one more time, Kim Carnes-style; and if only for a pungent, mind's ear flashback of how wretched an 80s production could be, it's worth copping an earful of Swayze's 'Raising Heaven (In Hell Tonight)' . . .ahh, the smell of dry ice in the morning. *BG*

Album rating: *5.5

ROAD TO NASHVILLE

1967 (US 88m) Crown International Pictures

Film genre: showbiz/Country Musical comedy

Top guns: dir: (+ s-w) Will Zens

Stars: Marty Robbins *(himself/performer)* → FROM NASHVILLE WITH MUSIC → THAT'S COUNTRY → HONKYTONK MAN, **Johnny CASH** *(himself/performer)*, **Waylon JENNINGS** *(himself/performer)*, **June Carter Cash** *(performer)* ← COUNTRY MUSIC HOLIDAY / → the MAN, HIS WORLD, HIS MUSIC → GOSPEL ROAD → THAT'S COUNTRY, **Helen Carter + Mother Maybelle Carter + Anita Carter** *(performers)* → the MAN, HIS WORLD, HIS MUSIC, Doodles Weaver *(Colonel Feitlebaum)* ← HOT ROD GANG, Richard Arlen *(studio boss)*, **Connie Smith** *(herself)* ← the LAS VEGAS HILLBILLYS ← SECOND FIDDLE TO A STEEL GUITAR, **Hank Snow** *(performer)* → the NASHVILLE SOUND, **Porter Wagoner** *(performer)* ← NASHVILLE REBEL / → the NASHVILLE SOUND → HONKYTONK MAN, **the Stoneman Family:- Roni Stoneman Hemrick + Donna Stoneman** *(performers)*, **Dottie West** *(performer)* ← SECOND FIDDLE TO A STEEL GUITAR, **Lefty Frizzell** *(performer)* ← SECOND FIDDLE TO A STEEL GUITAR, **Faron Young** *(performer)* ← WHAT AM I BID? ← SECOND FIDDLE TO A STEEL GUITAR ← NASHVILLE REBEL ← COUNTRY MUSIC HOLIDAY, **the Osborne Brothers:- Sonny + Bobby** *(performers)*, **Kitty Wells** *(performer)* ← SECOND FIDDLE TO A STEEL GUITAR, **Margie Singleton** *(performer)*, **Bill Anderson** *(performer)* ← the GOLD GUITAR ← LAS VEGAS HILLBILLYS / → the NASHVILLE SOUND, **Webb Pierce** *(performer)* ← SECOND FIDDLE TO A STEEL GUITAR, **Quinine Gumstump & Buck** *(performers)*, **Bobby Sykes** *(performer)*, **Don Winters** *(performer)*, **Bill Phillips** *(performer)* ← SECOND FIDDLE TO A STEEL GUITAR, **Johnny Wright** *(performer)* ← SECOND FIDDLE TO A STEEL GUITAR, **Ruby Wright** *(performer)*

Storyline: Big boss JB sends hopelessly incompetent Colonel Beedlebaum to Nashville to recruit fresh talent for his new country and western film. Unfortunately the chaotic colonel has such a good time meeting the stars and watching them rehearse that he completely forgets to sign them up, much to the annoyance of his boss. *JZ*

Movie rating: *4

Visual: video on Rhino / DVD on Umbrella Australia (no OST)

Off the record: A plethora of country stars & songs feature in the film:- MARTY ROBBINS: 'Devil Woman', 'Begging To You', 'El Paso', 'Count Me Out' & 'Working My Way Through A Heartache'; WEBB PIERCE: 'You Ain't No Better Than Me' & 'Love's Something I Can't Understand'; WAYLON JENNINGS: 'Anita'; DON WINTERS: 'Annie Lou'; BOBBY SYKES: 'Back To Me'; QUININE GUMSTUMP & BUCK: 'Cutting Room Floor'; KITTY WELLS: 'Is Love Worth All The Heartache' & 'A Woman Half My Age'; FARON YOUNG: 'I Miss You Already' & 'Dreams'; BILL PHILLIPS: 'Put It Off Until Tomorrow'; LEFTY FRIZZELL: 'I Love You A Thousand Ways'; DOTTIE WEST: 'Here Comes My Baby' & 'Would You Hold It Against Me'; BILL ANDERSON: 'I Love You Drops' & 'Poor Folks'; CONNIE SMITH: 'Never Get Over Loving You' & 'Nobody But A Fool'; MARGIE SINGLETON: 'For Just A Moment'; the STONEMAN FAMILY: 'Cripple Creek' & 'Send Me A Letter'; HANK SNOW: 'I've Been Everywhere' & 'Just A Fades Petal From A Beautiful Bouquet'; the OSBORNE BROTHERS: 'Be Alright Tomorrow' & 'Up This Hill'; PORTER WAGONER: 'Skid Row Joe' & 'Howdy Neighbor'; JOHNNY CASH: 'The One On The Right Is On The Left', 'Were You There' (with CARTER FAMILY): + 'I Walk The Line'. *MCS*

ROADIE

1980 (US 106m) Alive Enterprises / United Artists (PG)

Film genre: Country & Rock-music comedy/drama

Top guns: s-w: Alan Rudolph ← WELCOME TO MY NIGHTMARE ← the NIGHTMARE (+ dir → SONGWRITER), Bruce Robinson, Michael Ventura, James Big Boy Medlin

Stars: MEAT LOAF *(Travis W. Redfish)*, Kaki Hunter *(Lola Bouilliabase)* → PORKY'S REVENGE, Art Carney *(Corpus C. Redfish)*, Gailard Sartain *(B.B. Muldoon)* ← the BUDDY HOLLY STORY ← NASHVILLE / → HARD COUNTRY → SONGWRITER, Rhonda Bates *(Alice Poo Redfish)*, Don Cornelius *(Mohammed Johnson)* ← NO WAY BACK ← CLEOPATRA JONES / → TAPEHEADS → JACKIE'S BACK!, Joe Spano *(Ace)* ← AMERICAN GRAFFITI, Hamilton Camp *(Grady)* ← AMERICAN HOT WAX / → DICK TRACY, **Alice COOPER** *(himself)*, & band:- **Davey Johnstone, Roger Powell, Kasim Sulton, Fred Mandel, John Wilcox** *(themselves)*, Sheryl Cooper *(herself)* ← SGT. PEPPER'S LONELY HEARTS CLUB BAND ← WELCOME TO MY NIGHTMARE ← the NIGHTMARE, **BLONDIE:- Deborah Harry, Chris Stein, Clem Burke, Jimmy Destri, Nigel Harrison, Frank Infante** *(themselves)* / Sonny Davis *(Bird)* ← WHERE THE BUFFALO ROAM / → BAD CHANNELS, **Roy ORBISON** *(himself)*, **Hank WILLIAMS Jr.** *(himself)*, **Ramblin' Jack Elliott** *(himself)* ← RENALDO AND CLARA ← BANJOMAN / → the BALLAD OF RAMBLIN' JACK, Richard Portnow *(first New York wino)* → GOOD MORNING, VIETNAM → S.F.W. → PRIVATE PARTS → FEAR AND LOATHING IN LAS VEGAS → GHOST DOG: THE WAY OF THE SAMURAI, Kurtwood Smith *(security guard)* → STAYING ALIVE → FLASHPOINT, Larry Marshall *(2nd roadie)* ← JESUS CHRIST SUPERSTAR, **Asleep At The Wheel:- Ray Benson** *(himself)* → ALAMO BAY, **Chris O'Connell, Bobby Black, Dan Levin, Francis**

Christina, Pat Ryan, John Nicholas, Dean DeMerritt *(themselves)* / **the Pleasant Valley Boys** *(themselves)*

Storyline: Galumphing Texan hick Travis Redfish hasn't heard of rock'n'roll but rapidly develops a taste for it after meeting virgin groupie Lola Bouilliabase. His talent for electrical improvisation comes in handy, his periodic pathological fits less so. While he pines for Lola like a corpulent puppy, all she can think about is meeting her hero, Alice Cooper. Travis trails her all the way to New York, stopping off to help out a power-cut Blondie en-route. *BG*

Movie rating: *5.5

Visual: video + dvd

Off the record: **Asleep At The Wheel** (see line-up above) were a country group established in the early 70s; LP's 'Comin' Right At Ya' (1973), 'Asleep At The Wheel' (1974), 'Texas Gold' (1975), 'Wheelin' And Dealin'' (1976), 'The Wheel' (1977), 'Framed' (1980), etc. *MCS*

Various Artists

Jun 80. (d-lp/c) *Warners; <3441> (K/K4 66093)* ☐ ☐
– Everything works if you let it (CHEAP TRICK) / You better run (PAT BENATAR) / Brainlock (JOE ELY BAND) / Road rats (ALICE COOPER) / Can't we try (TEDDY PENDERGRASS) / Drivin' my life away (EDDIE RABBIT) / Your precious love (STEPHEN BISHOP and YVONNE ELLIMAN) / A man needs a woman (JAY FERGUSON) // Crystal ball (STYX) / Double yellow line (SUE SAAD AND THE NEXT) / Ring of fire (BLONDIE) / Pain (ALICE COOPER) / That lovin' you feelin' again (ROY ORBISON and EMMYLOU HARRIS) / (Hot damn) I'm a one woman man (JERRY LEE LEWIS) / The American way (HANK WILLIAMS, JR.) / Texas, me and you (ASLEEP AT THE WHEEL).

S/track review: A double album stuffed with pop Hall of Famers, overseen by inspirational producers like Todd Rundgren, Steve Cropper and George Martin: what more could you want? The whole rich tapestry of musical life is here, from pomp rock to country when it still hung around with Western – but sadly, this is a badly-made knockoff, boasting bargain length and breadth and absolutely no quality at all. ALICE COOPER, CHEAP TRICK, STYX and BLONDIE were all past their best, bypassing the opportunity to serve up a reliable favourite in favour of fresh-minted mediocrities from the downslope. (Strike all the above, if you think the idea of Debbie Harry delivering a whimsical take on 'Ring of Fire' sounds appealing). A side from TEDDY PENDERGRASS, EDDIE RABBIT, STEPHEN BISHOP and JAY FERGUSON tells more than anybody should need to know about the Habitat sofa of nice-but-dim 1970s easy listening, while even diehard fans of ROY ORBISON & EMMYLOU HARRIS (with 'That Lovin' You Feelin' Again'), JERRY LEE LEWIS and ASLEEP AT THE WHEEL must regret the talent-draining magic 'ROADIE' works on a string of tunes whose sloppiness goes beyond the merely careless. There is, all the same, a redeeming feature: Meat Loaf doesn't sing. *ND*

Album rating: *4

– spinoff hits, etc. –

CHEAP TRICK: Everything Works If You Let It

May 80. (7") *Epic; <50887> (EPC 8755)* [44] Jul80 ☐

EDDIE RABBIT: Drivin' My Life Away

Jun 80. (7") *Elektra; <46656> <K 12460>* [5] Jul80 ☐

ROY ORBISON & EMMYLOU HARRIS: That Lovin' You Feelin' Again

Jun 80. (7") *<49262>* [55] [–]

PAT BENATAR: You Better Run

Jul 80. (7") *Chrysalis; <2450>* [42] [–]

TEDDY PENDERGRASS: Can't We Try

Aug 80. (7") *Philadelphia; <3107>* [52] [–]

ROADKILL

1989 (Can 85m b&w) Cinephile (R)

Film genre: historical rock'n'road movie

Top guns: dir: Bruce McDonald (+ story) → HIGHWAY 61 → HARD CORE LOGO / s-w: Don McKellar → HIGHWAY 61

Stars: Valerie Buhagiar *(Ramona)* → HIGHWAY 61, Gerry Quigley *(Roy Seth; the promoter)*, Larry Hudson *(Buddy; the cab driver)* → HIGHWAY 61, Bruce McDonald *(Bruce Shack)* → HARD CORE LOGO, Don McKellar *(Russel; the serial killer)* → HIGHWAY 61 → CLEAN, Shawn Bowring *(Mathew)*, **Joey Ramone** *(himself)* <= RAMONES =>, **Nash The Slash** *(live performer)*

Storyline: "A rock'n'road movie about a girl who learns to drive". Ramona works for a concert promoter who sends her to the wilds of Canada to track down a rock band who have gone AWOL. She hires a taxi as she can't yet drive, but the continually-ticking meter is the least of her worries as she encounters a variety of weird and wonderful people. Oddballs like an unemployed serial killer, a camera crew who want blood, and a strangely silent man can't have any connection – can they? *JZ*

Movie rating: *7

Visual: video + dvd

Off the record: Pop composer, **Nash The Slash** was subsequently commissioned to score Bruce's next film project, 'HIGHWAY 61'.

Various Artists w/ "dialogue" (*)

1990. (cd) *Denon; <CAN 9006>* ☐ [–]
– "Hinterland" (*) / Instant death (RAZOR) / "Mr. Shack explains" (*) / The sound (LESLIE SPIT TREE-O) / "Ramona on the road" (*) / Street people (GRAEME KIRKLAND & THE WOLVES with JULIE MASSI) / "Spiritual quest" (*) / Nostradamus (SUFFER MACHINE) / She ain't no use to me (the UGLY DUCKLINGS) / "Russell the serial killer" (*) / Put the blame on me (HANDSOME NED & THE SIDEWINDERS) / The weenie boy song (STEVE "THE BUTCHER" MUNRO) / Burning rain (TEN SECONDS OVER TOKYO) / "Thangst for the angst" – "Buddy & Biff" / Magic people (the PAUPERS) / "Luke" / Dancing cadavars (TEKNAKULLAR RAINCOATS) / "The driving lesson" / Have you seen my shoes? (RITA CHIARELLI) / It's Saturday night (the RAZORBACKS) / "Joey say hey" / Howlin' at the Moon (RAMONES) / "Ramona gets ready" / Roadkill (NASH THE SLASH) / "Weenie boy reprise".

S/track review: Stemming from award-winning Canadian film-maker, Bruce McDonald (in his first feature), this rare set features a Lemmy-type title track by weirdo muso, NASH THE SLASH, an electro-punk 'Howlin' At The Moon' by RAMONES and a plethora of wannabe Canadian garage-punk acts. Alongside interspersed movie dialogue, the pick of the bunch are the RAZORBACKS ('It's Saturday Night'), SUFFER MACHINE ('Nostradamus') and TEN SECONDS OVER TOKYO ('Burning Rain'). For the non-punks among you, the best-of batch comes via the countrified 'Put The Blame On Me' by HANDSOME NED & THE SIDEWINDERS, 'Street People' – a jazzy torch song of sorts – by GRAEME KIRKLAND & THE WOLVES (featuring JULIE MASSI), and the folk-pop ditty 'The Sound' by the Peter, Paul & Mary of alternative pop, LESLIE SPIT TREE-O. Kickstarting her blues-rock career right here on 'ROADKILL', Hamilton-born RITA CHIARELLI (fuse Melissa Etheridge, Bonnie Raitt and Timbuk 3), performed 'Have You Seen My Shoes?' – she won Canada's Maple Leaf Awards in 2000. On a different note entirely and alongside the speed-metal attack of 'Instant Death' by RAZOR, this album certainly exemplifies everything on the wild side of rock, fashioned by an eclectic composite of McDonald's warped psyche. It was reported that when he picked up a $25,000 prize at the Toronto Film Festival in 1990, he told an audience he was going to "buy a big chunk of hash". Cheech & Chong were said to be almost immediately on the blower to Bruce and Co. *MCS*

Album rating: *6.5

ROADSIDE PROPHETS

1992 (US 96m) New Line Cinema (R)

Film genre: road movie/comedy

Top guns: s-w (+ dir): Abbe Wool ← SID & NANCY

Stars: **John DOE** *(Joe Mosely)*, **Adam Horowitz** *(Sam)* <= BEASTIE BOYS =>, David Carradine *(Othello Jones)* ← the LONG RIDERS ← BOUND FOR GLORY / → AMERICAN REEL → KILL BILL: VOL.1 → KILL BILL: VOL.2, Timothy Leary *(Salvadore)*, **Arlo Guthrie** *(Harvey)* ← RENALDO AND CLARA ← WOODSTOCK ← ALICE'S RESTAURANT / → the BALLAD OF RAMBLIN' JACK, John Cusack *(Caspar)* ← TAPEHEADS / → HIGH FIDELITY → the FUTURE IS UNWRITTEN, Jennifer Balgobin *(Ms. Labia Mirage)* ← TAPEHEADS ← STRAIGHT TO HELL ← REPO MAN, Barton Heyman *(Sheriff Quentin Durango)* ← LIVING PROOF: THE HANK WILLIAMS JR. STORY / → the BASKETBALL DIARIES → DEAD MAN WALKING, Lin Shaye *(Celeste)* ← PUMP UP THE VOLUME ← the LONG RIDERS / → EVEN COWGIRLS GET THE BLUES → LAST MAN STANDING → DETROIT ROCK CITY, Bill Cobbs *(Oscar)* ← a HERO AIN'T NOTHIN' BUT A SANDWICH / → the BODYGUARD → THAT THING YOU DO! → a MIGHTY WIND, John Snyder *(Hank)* ← SID & NANCY, Biff Yeager *(bartender)* ← WALKER ← STRAIGHT TO HELL ← SID & NANCY ← REPO MAN ← DYNAMITE BROTHERS, Stephen Tobolowsky *(ranger Bob)* ← GREAT BALLS OF FIRE! / → the INSIDER → the COUNTRY BEARS, Don Cheadle *(Happy Days manager)* → BOOGIE NIGHTS → THINGS BEHIND THE SUN → SWORDFISH, Harry Caesar *(Jesse)* ← BREAKIN' 2: ELECTRIC BOOGALOO ← LADY SINGS THE BLUES, **Too Free Stooges:- Dick Rude** *(performer)* ← WALKER ← STRAIGHT TO HELL ← SID & NANCY ← REPO MAN / → LET'S ROCK AGAIN!, Aaron Lustig *(morning desk clerk)* ← BAD CHANNELS, Nancy Lenehan *(Vegas motel 9 desk clerk)* ← ROCK'N'ROLL MOM, **Billy Ferrick** ← TAPEHEADS, **Flea** *(cameo)* <= RED HOT CHILI PEPPERS =>, **Manny Chevrolet, Tony Ruglio, Pete Weiss**

Storyline: Factory worker Joe sets off for the town of El Dorado to scatter his late friend Dave's ashes there (cause of death – electrocuted by video game). On the way he is persistently dogged by a lad called Sam who insists on staying in Motel 9s. They encounter several strange characters on their journey who educate them about gladiators, anarchism and prehistoric fish amongst other things. No wonder they go gambling mad when they hit Las Vegas. *JZ*

Movie rating: *6

Visual: video + dvd

Off the record: (see below)

—

Various Artists (score: PRAY FOR RAIN *)

Oct 92. (cd/c) *Vanguard; <VHD/VHC 79463>* ☐ ☐
– Beer, gas, ride forever (JOHN DOE) / Helmets are bullshit (*) / Make yourself at home in my heart (HARRY DEAN STANTON) / Vegas (*) / Springtime (TOO FREE STOOGES) / Gridlock (the POGUES) / Out of Barstow (*) / Clean like tomorrow (EXENE CERVENKA) / Down by the roadside (the BROKEN HOMES) / Valley of zoom (*) / Hot white sun (*) / The mist (ERIN KENNEY & ETHAN JAMES) / The loneliest road in America (*) / Dinosaur tracks (DIFFERENT WORLD) / Horses (*) / El Dorado (BUG LAMP).

S/track review: As filmmaker Abbe Wool expressed in the sleevenotes: "ROADSIDE PROPHETS is about discovering freedom and friendship". And that is what defines this collection of songs. They're eclectic, but they're not random." With a host of friends from her days as screen-writer on 'SID & NANCY' (1986), including her brother Dan's band PRAY FOR RAIN, the POGUES plus ex-Circle Jerks, Zander Schloss & Keith Morris (now with TOO FREE STOOGES and BUG LAMP respectively), Abbe's Californian underground collection was just about in place. Interspersed between the TOO FREE STOOGES (on the excellent lounge-punk 'Springtime') and BUG LAMP ('El Dorado'), Alex Cox staples PRAY FOR RAIN get to grips with several short cuts and a proper vocal song, 'Hot White Sun'. Where the latter band ventured, the POGUES would be right behind them, 'Gridlock', being a slight diversion from the usual poetical folk-punk. The X-factor was also on parade as former X cohorts, JOHN DOE (with Tony Gilkyson & D.J. Bonebrake on board) plus EXENE CERVENKA saddled up to the studio for two differing cues, the latter with the hard-country 'Beer, Gas, Ride Forever', the former courtesy of avant-lo-fi-banjo cut, 'Clean Like Tomorrow' (can I hear Courtney Love, anyone!). With no Beastie Boy Adam Horowitz to speak of, co-star HARRY DEAN STANTON crooned his way through Billy Swann's 'Make Yourself At Home In My Heart', while other competent "country-rockers" the BROKEN HOMES ('Down By The Roadside'), DIFFERENT WORLD ('Dinosaur Tracks') and ERIN KENNEY & ETHAN JAMES ('The Mist'), were too 70s or 80s to live in the 90s. *MCS*

Album rating: *7

ROCK ALL NIGHT

1957 (US 65m b&w) Sunset / American International Pictures

Film genre: Rock'n'roll Musical drama

Top guns: dir: Roger Corman ← CARNIVAL ROCK / → the WILD ANGELS → the TRIP → GAS-S-S-S / s-w: Charles B. Griffith → the WILD ANGELS → LITTLE SHOP OF HORRORS (story: David P. Harmon)

Stars: Abby Dalton *(Julie)*, Robin Morse *(Al)*, Dick Miller *(Shorty)* ← CARNIVAL ROCK / → BEACH BALL → SKI PARTY → the GIRLS ON THE BEACH → WILD, WILD WINTER → the WILD ANGELS → the TRIP → TRUCK TURNER → I WANNA HOLD YOUR HAND → ROCK'N'ROLL HIGH SCHOOL → GET CRAZY → SHAKE, RATTLE & ROCK! tv, Russell Johnson *(Jigger)*, Mel Welles *(Sir Bop)*, Bruno VeSota *(Charlie)* ← CARNIVAL ROCK / → DADDY-O → YOUR CHEATIN' HEART → the GIRLS ON THE BEACH, Chris Alcaide *(Angie)* ← CARNIVAL ROCK, Richard H. Cutting *(Steve)*, Barboura Morris *(Syl)* → the WILD ANGELS → the TRIP, Ed Nelson *(Pete)*, Clegg Hoyt *(Marty)*, Jonathan Haze *(Joey)* ← CARNIVAL ROCK, Ed Nelson *(Pete)* ← CARNIVAL ROCK / → THAT'S THE WAY OF THE WORLD, Beach Dickerson *(the kid)* → LOVING YOU → G.I. BLUES → the TRIP → the SAVAGE SEVEN, **the Platters:- Tony Williams, Herb Reed, Zola Taylor, David Lynch, Paul Robi** *(performers)* ← CARNIVAL ROCK ← the GIRL CAN'T HELP IT ← ROCK AROUND THE CLOCK, **the Blockbusters** *(performers)* ← CARNIVAL ROCK

Storyline: Every bar has its hangers on, and Cloud Nine is no exception. Shorty is the guy with a grudge in this case, but for once he gets to play the hero when a couple of gangsters storm the club and take hostages to keep the cops at bay. The regulars turn out to be particularly useless at coping with the baddies, but super-cool Shorty is just the man for a crisis. *JZ*

Movie rating: *4.5

Visual: video

Off the record: (see below)

—

Various Artists (composer: Buck Ram) (score: Ronald Stein)

Apr 57. (lp) *Mercury; <MG 20293> (MPT 7527)* ☐ ☐
– Rock all night (the BLOCKBUSTERS) * / Pussy foot (EDDIE BEAL COMBO) / Rock 'n roll guitar – pt.1 (the BLOCKBUSTERS) * / Rock 'n roll guitar – pt.2 (the BLOCKBUSTERS) * / The great pretender (NORA HAYES) * / He's mine (the PLATTERS) / I guess I won't hang around anymore (NORA HAYES) * / Honey buggin' (EDDIE BEAL COMBO) * / I'm sorry (the PLATTERS) / Breezin' (EDDIE BEAL

COMBO) * / I wanna rock now (the BLOCKBUSTERS) * / Leadfoot (EDDIE BEAL COMBO). *(cd-iss. Jul00 on 'Ace'*tracks +=; <(CDCHD 763)>* – (20 non-sound tracks by the BLOCKBUSTERS, etc.)

S/track review: 'ROCK AROUND THE CLOCK' (1956) instigated a plethora of similarly-themed rock'n'roll movies in the 50s, and 'ROCK ALL NIGHT' was one of the first in the subsequent production line. The fact that the title track (the first of many written by music director Buck Ram) was delivered Bill Haley-style by the BLOCKBUSTERS, a group that seem to have four tracks here. Wrong. There were indeed several BLOCKBUSTERS incarnations in the mid-50s, all thought up by label boss/manager, BUCK RAM, although only two outfits are featured in the film. The aforementioned 'Rock All Night' and its musical counterpart 'I Wanna Rock Now', were by the Philadelphian BLOCKBUSTERS (featuring Gene Labadi, Dennis Clark and Al Pommetto), a group who nearly had a hit with George Jones' 'Why Baby Why'. The second BLOCKBUSTERS to appear on record were fronted by Italian-American singer Bill Peck (real name William Pecchi), formerly a big band drummer in the 40s who turned to rockabilly in the 50s. 'Rock n' Roll Guitar – pts.1 & 2' (written by Peck and his hunchbacked session guitarist, Jimmy Rollins) clones Chuck Berry to a tee; a double-A single by the New Blockbusters was previously issued by 'Antler' records and it's these versions that appear on the re-issued "inspired" compilation CD issued in 2000. Omitted from the latter but sitting right there on the rare LP, were two hits ('I'm Sorry' & 'He's Mine') by the PLATTERS, a group very much under the guidance of manager/songwriter, Buck Ram. America's leading vocal group, they'd already had two chart-toppers ('My Prayer' & 'The Great Pretender') in 1956. A version of the latter song found its way on to the OST, courtesy of relatively unknown crooner, NORA HAYES (alias Patti Anne Mesner), whose voice substitutes Abby Dalton's character, Julie, on this and another Buck Ram-penned cut, 'I Guess I Won't Hang Around Here Anymore' – intentionally out-of-key to fail the role-playing audition. That just leaves EDDIE BEAL (and COMBO), a 46-year-old pianist/arranger/composer who puts the big band jazz sound into pseudo rock'n'roll instrumentals, 'Honey' Buggin'', 'Breezin'', 'Pussy Foot' & 'Leadfoot', the last two not included on the aforementioned CD. *MCS*

Album rating: *4

– spinoff hits, etc. –

the PLATTERS: I'm Sorry / He's Mine

Mar 57. (7") *<71032> (MT 145)* [11] [16] May57 [18]

ROCK & RULE

1983 (Can 85m) Canada Trust / MGM/UA Entertainment (PG)

Film genre: animated sci-fi Rock Musical fantasy

Top guns: dir: Clive A. Smith / s-w: John Halfpenny (story: Patrick Loubert & Peter Sauder)

Voices: Don Francks *(Mok)* ← HEAVY METAL / → MADONNA: INNOCENCE LOST → MR. MUSIC → I'M NOT THERE, Susan Roman *(Angel)* ← HEAVY METAL, Paul Le Mat *(Omar)* ← MORE AMERICAN GRAFFITI ← AMERICAN GRAFFITI, Dan Hennessey *(Dizzy)*, Chris Wiggins *(Toad)*, Samantha Langevin *(Mok's computer)*, Catherine Gallant *(Cindy)*, **Lou REED** *(Mok; singing)*, **Debbie Harry** *(Angel; singing)* <= BLONDIE =>, **Iggy POP** *(monster from another dimension)*, **Robin Zander** *(Omar; singing)*, Melleny Brown *(Carnegie Hall groupie)*, Catherine O'Hara *(Aunt Edith)* → DICK TRACY → a MIGHTY WIND → OVER THE HEDGE, John Halfpenny *(Uncle Mikey)*

Storyline: In a post-apocalyptic future, megalomaniac rock star Mok plans to summon a demon from another dimension. He can only do this by kidnapping new rock singer Angel and use her voice to open a portal. It's up to Angel's band to save her from the clutches of villainous Mok and send the demon back where it came from. *JZ*

Movie rating: *6

Visual: video + d-DVD (no audio OST; score: Patricia Cullen)

Off the record: Tracks featured in the movie are as follows:- 'Angel's Song' (DEBBIE HARRY), 'Invocation Song' (DEBBIE HARRY), 'Send Love Through' (DEBBIE HARRY), 'Pain And Suffering' (IGGY POP), 'My Name Is Mok' (LOU REED), 'Triumph' (LOU REED), 'Born To Raise Hell' (CHEAP TRICK) with ROBIN ZANDER, 'I'm The Man' (CHEAP TRICK), 'Ohm Sweet Ohm' (CHEAP TRICK), 'Dance, Dance, Dance' (EARTH, WIND & FIRE) & 'Hot Dogs And Sushi' (MELLENY BROWN). *MCS*

ROCK ANGELZ

aka BRATZ: ROCK ANGELZ

2005 (US 73m) VoiceWorks Productions Inc.

Film genre: children's animated Pop Musical

Top guns: dir: Mucci Fassett / s-w: Peggy Nicoll

Voices: Lacey Chabert *(Kaycee)*, Tia Mowry *(Sasha)*, Olivia Hack *(Chloe)*, Soleil Moon Frye *(Jade)*, Dionne Quan, Wendie Malick, Kaley Cuoco

Storyline: Turning their hand to the fashion magazine world, the popular animated quartet, Bratz, embark on a new adventure in "girl power" when they dash off to London to get the scoop on a cool new rock group's concert. Things take a turn for the worse when the dastardly rivals from fashion mag, 'Your Thing', pinch the girls' tickets leaving them unable to get in . . . unless . . . they quickly get some guitars and pretend to be a rock group. Imagination runs wild as the Bratz steal the show and go on to have a number one hit. *KM*

Movie rating: *3

Visual: dvd

Off the record: **BRATZ** (see below)

—

BRATZ

Jul 05. (cd) *Hip-O; <00049020-2> Universal TV; (988425-9)* [79] Oct05 [42]
– So good / Change the world / I don't care / All about you / Who I am / So what / You think / It could be yours / Lookin' good / Rock the world / Stand out / Nobody's girl / Se siente.

S/track review: Replicating the anthemic mélange of 80s hair rock and teeny pop associated with the likes of Hilary Duff and Avril Lavigne, the uncredited performers for BRATZ sing their over optimistic hearts out to empower their blatantly obvious demographic (girls under 10) to be who they want to be, as long as they're in bed on time. To many parents, this brazen commercialism from MGA Entertainment's BRATZ brand especially with the CD's accompanying booklet chock full of adverts would be reason enough to hold back the pocket money. However, the life affirmingly positive lyrics on topics like self belief and discovery, together with the synthy guitars and sing-a-long choruses make this largely harmless record seem a whole lot more fun than Barbie. Certainly Barbie never donned a Flying V and exclaimed "So What, If I'm Talking Too Loud"! Fear not, such dissent is a rare feature of an album which is more interested in building up pre-adolescent confidence and personality illustrated on songs like the album's excitable standout track 'So Good' and the Def Leppard-esque 'All About You' with its big sister advice: "You Don't Need To Be Who You're Not, Believe In Yourself". However, big sister would probably also advise buying an overall less monotonous pop record like one of the aforementioned Avril Lavigne's. *KM*

Album rating: *3.5

– spinoff hits, etc. –

BRATZ: So Good / Sparkle & Shine / Who I Am

Oct 05. (cd-s) *(988528-0)* [–] [23]

ROCK AROUND THE CLOCK

1956 (US 77m b&w) Columbia Pictures

Film genre: Rock'n'roll Musical drama

Top guns: dir: Fred F. Sears → DON'T KNOCK THE ROCK → CALYPSO HEAT WAVE / s-w: Robert Kent → DON'T KNOCK THE ROCK → TWIST AROUND THE CLOCK → DON'T KNOCK THE TWIST → HOOTENANNY HOOT → GET YOURSELF A COLLEGE GIRL → WHEN THE BOYS MEET THE GIRLS → the FASTEST GUITAR ALIVE → a TIME TO SING

Stars: Bill HALEY & His Comets *(performers)*, **the Platters** *(performers)* → the GIRL CAN'T HELP IT → CARNIVAL ROCK → ROCK ALL NIGHT, **Tony Martinez** *(performer)*, **Freddie Bell & The Bellboys** *(performers)*, **LITTLE RICHARD** *(performer)*, Johnny Johnston *(Steve Hollis)*, Alan Freed *(himself)* → DON'T KNOCK THE ROCK → ROCK, ROCK, ROCK! → MISTER ROCK AND ROLL → GO, JOHNNY, GO!, Lisa Gaye *(Lisa Johns)* → SHAKE, RATTLE AND ROCK!, Alix Talton *(Corrine Ralbot)*, Henry Slate *(Corny LaSalle)*, Earl Barton *(Jimmy Johns)*, John Archer *(Mike Dennis)*

Storyline: Small-time promoter Steve Hollis thinks his career is going nowhere until he bumps into rock'n'roll band Bill Haley & His Comets. Impressed by their new style of music, Hollis becomes their manager and with the help of DJ Alan Freed books them a spot in New York. There they get to perform alongside the Platters and Freddie Bell & His Bell Boys, but a shady booking agent has his own agenda for the band. *JZ*

Movie rating: *7

Visual: video + dvd (no audio OST released)

Off the record: Tracks from the film are as follows (BILL HALEY & HIS COMETS *): 'Rock Around The Clock' (*), 'See You Later Alligator' (*), 'Rock-A-Beatin' Boogie' (*), 'A.B.C. Boogie' (* excerpt), 'Cuero (Skins)', 'Mambo Capri', 'Solo Y Triste (Sad And Lonely) & 'Bacaloa Con Papa (Codfish And Potatoes)' (all by TONY MARTINEZ AND HIS BAND), 'Razzle-Dazzle' (*), 'Teach You To Rock' (FREDDIE BELL AND THE BELLBOYS), 'Only You (And You Alone)' (the PLATTERS), 'R-O-C-K' (*), 'Happy Baby' (* excerpt), 'Mambo Rock' (* excerpt), 'Giddy Up A Ding Dong' (FREDDIE BELL AND THE BELLBOYS), 'The Great Pretender' (the PLATTERS) and 'Rudy's Rock' (*). *MCS*

– spinoff hits, etc. –

BILL HALEY & HIS COMETS: R-O-C-K

Mar 56. (7",78) *Decca; <29870> Brunswick; (05565)* [16] May56 [5]
(above was on flip side to HALEY's 'The Saints Rock 'n Roll')

the PLATTERS: The Great Pretender / Only You (And You Alone)

Aug 56. (7",78) *Mercury; (MT 117)* [–] [5]
(re-iss. Mar57; same) – hit No.18

FREDDIE BELL AND THE BELLBOYS: Giddy Up A Ding Dong

Aug 56. (7",78) *Mercury; (MT 122)* [ ] [4]

BILL HALEY & HIS COMETS: Rock Around The Clock

Sep 56. (7",78) *Brunswick; (05317)* [–] [5]
(above single was re-actified after film; had already hit No.1)

□ ROCK AROUND THE WORLD alt.
(⇒ the TOMMY STEELE STORY)

ROCK BABY ROCK IT

1957 (US 84m b&w) Freebar

Film genre: Rock'n'roll Musical crime drama

Top guns: dir: Murray Douglas Sporup / s-w: Herbert H. Margolis ← ROCK, PRETTY BABY / → SUMMER LOVE, William Raynor

Stars: Kay Wheeler *(herself)*, **Don Coates & The Bon-Aires** *(performers)*, **Johnny Carroll & The Hot Rocks** *(performers)*, Joan Arnold *(herself)*, **Lee Young** *(performer)*, **Rosco Gordon & the Red Tops** *(performer/s)* → the ROAD TO MEMPHIS, **the 5 Stars** *(performers)*, **the Belew Twins: Benny & Bobby** *(performers)*, **the Cell Block 7** *(performers)*, **Preacher Smith & the Deacons** *(performers)*

Storyline: A group of Texas teenagers find their "nightclub" (room for three tables and a piano) under threat from a bunch of mobsters who presumably want to use their place as a kitchen cupboard. The only way to save the premises is, of course, to have a concert to raise enough money to buy out the baddies. If they squeeze in any more bodies to watch the show they'll have to rename the club the Black Hole Of Calcutta. *JZ*

Movie rating: *4.5

Visual: video

Off the record: (see below)

Various Artists

1980s. (lp) *Rhino; <RNSP 309> Magnum Force; (MFLP 040)* [ ] 1989 [ ]
– Hot rock (the CELL BLOCK 7) / Stop the world (DON COATES & THE BON-AIRES) / Molly Molly (the 5 STARS) / Your love is all I need (the 5 STARS) / Eat your heart out (PREACHER SMITH & THE DEACONS) / Chicken in the rough (ROSCO GORDON & THE RED TOPS) / Bop it (ROSCO GORDON & THE DEACONS) / Crazy crazy lovin' (JOHNNY CARROLL & THE HOT ROCKS) / Wild wild woman (JOHNNY CARROLL & THE HOT ROCKS) / Lonesome (the BELEW TWINS) / Love me baby (the BELEW TWINS) / The saint song (the CELL BLOCK 7) / Roogie doogie (PREACHER SMITH & THE DEACONS) / Love never forgets (DON COATES & THE BON-AIRES) / Rockin' Maybelle (JOHNNY CARROLL & THE HOT ROCKS) / Hey Juanita (the 5 STARS) / Sugar baby (JOHNNY CARROLL & THE HOT ROCKS) / Hot rock (the CELL BLOCK 7). *<(cd-iss. Nov01 on 'Goofin'; GRCD 6111)>*

S/track review: Fifty years ago everybody was rock'n'roll crazy and since the groundbreaking 'ROCK AROUND THE CLOCK' (1956), it seemed anybody who was anybody and could sing or play an instrument was on the rock musical bandwagon. Yes, it was a time to swing and dance, get down and boogie and of course, tear up the theatre seats. One guy who would probably not condone the latter actions of youth, was one JOHNNY CARROLL, a new singing sensation signed to 'Decca' records. The songwriter turns up everywhere on this record, firstly as leader of the CELL BLOCK 7, who deliver a couple of cues, namely 'The Hot Rock' (a Bill Haley-type number) and 'The Saint Song' (aka 'When The Saints Go Marching In'). With the 5 STARS, J.C. takes the mantle of the day's stars during recitals of 'Molly Molly', 'Your Love Is All I Need' and the Coasters-esque 'Hey Juanita'. No matter how much you like the songs, everything's spoiled by the super-imposed dialogue, which results in songs being turned down to the minimum. Annoying. His best pseudonym – if that's what it was – JOHNNY CARROLL & THE HOT ROCKS scored big time with 'Crazy Crazy Lovin'' (very 'That's Alright Mama'), 'Wild Wild Women' (very Chuck Berry), 'Rockin' Maybelle' (very Be-Bop-A-Lula) & 'Sugar Baby' (very Elvis). Other highlights, but at the same time derivative, stemmed from ROSCOE GORDON & THE RED TOPS: 'Chicken In The Rough' & 'Bop It', giving it all their 88 keys so to speak. The BELEW TWINS (Carl was one) were the new Everly Brothers ("Everlish" as it says in the sleevenotes!), the duo bopping on 'Love Me Baby' & 'Lonesome' (the latter covered by the Horton Brothers 40 years later). Add a sax to PREACHER SMITH & THE DEACONS on 'Roogie Doogie' (a dance!) and 'Eat Your Heart Out' (not a dance – I hope!) and you get one rocking record. And who can forget DON COATES & THE BON-AIRES? . . . – er me, that's who! *MCS*

Album rating: *4

□ ROCK 'EM DEAD alt.
(⇒ SHOCK 'EM DEAD)

ROCK FOLLIES

1976 (UK 6 epi x 50m mini-TV) Thames Television / ITV

Film genre: Pop-Rock Musical drama

Top guns: dir: Brian Farnham → ROCK FOLLIES OF '77, Jon Scoffield / s-w: Howard Schuman → ROCK FOLLIES OF '77

Stars: Julie Covington *(Devonia "Dee" Rhoades)* → ROCK FOLLIES OF '77, Rula Lenska *(Nancy "Q" Cunard de Longchamps)* ← CONFESSIONS OF A POP PERFORMER / → ROCK FOLLIES OF '77, Charlotte Cornwell *(Anna Ward)* ← STARDUST / → ROCK FOLLIES OF '77, Emlyn Price *(Derek Huggins)*, Angela Bruce *(Gloria)*, Beth Porter *(Kitty Schreiber)*, Billy Murray *(Spike)* ← PERFORMANCE ← UP THE JUNCTION ← WHAT A CRAZY WORLD / → McVICAR → BUDDY'S SONG, Stephen Moore *(Jack)*, Simon Jones *(Juan)* → CLUB PARADISE, Michael J. Shannon *(Carl 'Tubes' Benson)* → LITTLE SHOP OF HORRORS, Bill Stewart *(Bob)*, Ellis Dale *(Schubert Birnbaum)*, Michael Angelis *(David)*, the Group:- Peter John Van Hooke, Tony Stevens, Ray Russell, Brian Chatton

Storyline: Three struggling actresses are encouraged to try their luck in the music business after yet another stage flop. The girls do the rounds as a rock band, receiving mixed receptions in the pubs and clubs. Just as the last coin is being rattled in the piggy bank Greek entrepreneur Stavros takes them under his wing and gives "The Little Ladies" a new image. However, when they play at his new restaurant's opening night (the well-named Blitz), they fail to realize that the loud ticking noise is not coming from the clock on the wall. *JZ*

Movie rating: *7.5

Visual: video (+ d-dvd)

Off the record: (see below)

—

Original Cast (composer: ANDY MACKAY / lyrics: Howard Schuman)

Apr 76. (lp) *Island; (ILPS 9362)* [1] [–]
– Sugar mountain / Good behaviour / Stairway / Daddy / Lamplight / The road / Glenn Miller is missing / Biba nova / Talking pictures / Hot neon / Roller coaster / Rock follies. *(re-iss. 1980 on 'E.G.'; EGLP 23) (cd-iss. 2001 on 'E.M.I.'+=; 849231)* – War brides.

S/track review: Way back in '77, with Bryan Ferry now into a fully-fledged solo sabbatical from Roxy Music (or so it seemed at the time), co-songwriter and saxophonist ANDY MACKAY found himself with time on his hands. His solo LP in 1974 ('In Search Of Eddie Riff') had been poorly received, and MACKAY gladly picked up the challenge to write for TV's "Little Ladies" (aka, actresses JULIE COVINGTON, RULA LENSKA and CHARLOTTE CORNWELL). With Howard Schuman behind the clever lyrics, it was down to MACKAY and regular session players, BRIAN CHATTON (keyboards), TONY STEVENS (bass), RAY RUSSELL (guitar) and PETE VAN HOOKE (percussion), to augment the girls on a six-track. Never intended for commercial release, the mono recordings were turned into proper stereo cues after the mighty success of the 'ROCK FOLLIES' TV series. The Little Ladies were a powerhouse of vocal talent, headed by Evita/'Don't Cry For Me Argentina' chart-topper, JULIE COVINGTON, RULA LENSKA (future wife of singing actor Dennis Waterman) and CHARLOTTE CORNWELL (sister of best-selling author John Le Carre). A three-way cocktail of Suzi Quatro's, one might say. 'Sugar Mountain' and 'Good Behavoiur' kicked off proceedings, two up-tempo dirges that rocked with a much needed raw edge to sit in with the new punk movement. Slowing the pace down somewhat, 'Stairway' harks back to girl groups of the early 60s, fusing Spector over a kitschy Roxy Music/Eno tune. There are a few Racey-like bummers on board the 'Follies: 'Daddy', a prime example of how ROCK can go POP without realising it and 'Lamplight', a song Buffy Sainte-Marie would've been proud of. 'The Road' (with MACKAY on sax and a Mike Oldfield-styled guitar) is probably the most spiritual song on the album, while 'Glenn Miller Is Missing' (like a cool Steely Dan tune) has had the most staying power. MACKAY did not discard his Roxy, glam-rock days entirely, as 'Biba Nova' would testify, while 'Hot Neon' wasn't too far removed from a bit of Fanny (the 70s all-girl group, that is). With soft-core in mind, 'Talking Pictures', takes the listener through the sleazy porn industry, while – squeezed after the 'Batman'-themed 'Rollercoaster' – the title track finale is Phil Spector-esque fused with old prog/keyboard trips. The CD has a bonus B-side, 'War Brides', a boogie-woogie-woodpecker of a song, that would've fitted neatly into the Bette Midler 'For The Boys' movie. *MCS*

Album rating: *6

– spinoff singles, etc. –

ROCK FOLLIES: Glenn Miller Is Missing / Talking Pictures
Mar 76. (7") *(WIP 6293)* [ ] [–]

ROCK FOLLIES: Sugar Mountain / War Brides
Jun 76. (7") *(WIP 6310)* [ ] [–]

ROCK FOLLIES OF '77

1977 sequel (UK 6 epi x 50m mini-TV) Thames Television / ITV

Film genre: Pop-Rock Musical drama

Top guns: dir: Brian Farnham ← ROCK FOLLIES / s-w: Howard Schuman ← ROCK FOLLIES

Stars: Julie Covington *(Dee)* ← ROCK FOLLIES, Rula Lenska *(Q)* ← ROCK FOLLIES ← CONFESSIONS OF A POP PERFORMER, Charlotte Cornwell *(Anna)* ← ROCK FOLLIES ← STARDUST, Tim Curry *(Stevie Streeter)* ← the ROCKY HORROR PICTURE SHOW / → TIMES SQUARE → LEGEND → the WALL: LIVE IN BERLIN → JACKIE'S BACK!, Little Nell Campbell *(Sandra)* ← LISZTOMANIA ← the ROCKY HORROR PICTURE SHOW / → JUBILEE → SHOCK TREATMENT → the WALL → the KILLING FIELDS, Karl Johnson *(Charlie Chime)* ← JUBILEE, Sam Dale *(Rawls)*, Denis Lawson *(Ken Church)*, **Sue Jones-Davis** *(Rox)* → RADIO ON, Trevor Ward *(the angel)* → FLASH GORDON, Ian Charleson *(Jimmy Smiles)* ← JUBILEE / → CHARIOTS OF FIRE

Storyline: The Little Ladies are back on the club circuit all by themselves, after they literally brought the house down at The Blitz. New manager Kitty soon takes things over, and under her domineering gaze the trio are pushed to the big time, not without several embarrassments along the way ("cans means headphones, dear"). However, as the band's musical direction changes, tensions between old and new members reach breaking point and battle lines are drawn between Kitty and the girls. *JZ*

Movie rating: *4

Visual: video (+ d-DVD)

Off the record: (see below)

—

Original Cast (composer: ANDY MACKAY / lyrics: HOWARD SCHUMAN)

Jun 77. (lp)(c) *Polydor; (2302 072)(3100 387)* ☐ ☐
– Follies of '77 / Struttin' ground / Round 1 / The hype / Dee's hype / The things you have to do / The band that wouldn't die / Wolf at the door / Loose change / Jubilee / OK? / Real life. *(re-iss. 1980 on 'E.G.'; EGLP 29)*

S/track review: Nothing much between this and its predecessor, except, that is – quality songs. Only a matter of months since 'ROCK FOLLIES' was on our TV screens and was leading the way for Girl Power, but 'ROCK FOLLIES OF '77' failed to emulate anything the original established. Roxy Music sax-player ANDY MACKAY was still on board, as was lyricist HOWARD SCHUMAN, but with punk-rock all the rage by summer '77, the Little Ladies were in for a rough ride. The poignant opening lyrics on 'Follies Of '77' ("Old year, old show, about to fold/the single was truly a dismal flop . . . New year, new show, new fantasy") bring us up-to-date on the story so far; one can even hear the piano-piece to Queen's 'Seven Seas Of Rhye'. COVINGTON, LENSKA and CORNWALL faced somewhat of a dilemma here having to sing lines such as "nothing really changes in the Follies". Track 2, 'Struttin' Ground', hooks in the funk and fuses a sound not too dissimilar to the Climax Blues Band's 1976 smash hit 'Couldn't Get It Right' with anything from the disco bargain bin basket – luckily it's saved by MACKAY's sax solo. The girls get back in the ring (no pun intended!) for their hard-life-knock-musical equivalent of a boxing match, 'Round 1'; this is certainly where the listener could be prone to getting punch-drunk. The self-explanatory 'The Hype' is a knock-out track, a sucker-punch indeed, but just why track 11, 'OK?', hit the UK Top 10 beats me. Slower version, 'Dee's Hype', sounds like Barbara Dickson walked into the session arm-in-arm with MACKAY's old Roxy chum, Brian Eno, but of course that was all fantasy. The upbeat, 'The Things You Have To Do', is full of climactic chord changes, something akin to the Moody Blues orchestrating 'Evita' – you just can't shrug off the COVINGTON connection. With the said little belter in the forefront vocally, some of the other "Little Ladies" get caught in the crossfire, example 'Wolf At The Door' if not the rest of the numbers. For track 10, 'Jubilee', the album politically challenges the Royal Family and the government of the day courtesy of a cod-reggae dirge. A challenge to the SEX PISTOLS' 'God Save The Queen' it was not, while 'Real Life' was as effective a finale as I've ever heard. And then God created 'BREAKING GLASS', although we'd have to wait until a new decade dawned for that one. *MCS*

Album rating: *4.5

– spinoff singles, etc. –

JULIE COVINGTON, RULA LENSKA, CHARLOTTE CORNWELL & SUE JONES-DAVIES: OK? / B Side

May 77. (7") *(2001 714)* 10 –

ROCK N' ROLL COWBOYS

1987 (Aus 83m TV) Somerset Film Productions / Nine Network (R)

Film genre: sci-fi Musical comedy

Top guns: dir: Rob Stewart / s-w: David Young

Stars: Peter Phelps *(Mickey LaGrange)*, John Doyle *(Damien Shard)*, David Franklin *(Eddie)*, Ben Franklin *(Harvey Glutzman)* ← STARSTRUCK, Nikki Coghill *(Teena Tungsten)*, Greg Parke *(Stevie Van Blitz)*, Dee Krainz *(Karla)*, Ron Blanchard *(Uncle Sam)*, Robin Copp *(James)*

Storyline: Mickey is a busy roadie/soundman for a futuristic heavy metal band, although he dreams daily of his own groupies and becoming the next Bon Scott. His visions just might come true via Damien Shard and the fictitious Psychotronic Alpha Sampler, but is Mickey ready for the long rock'n'roll trip? *MCS*

Movie rating: *2.5

Visual: none (no audio OST)

Off the record: Peter Phelps (Phelpsy) was to become part of the 'Baywatch' team playing the role of Trevor Cole. *MCS*

ROCK'N'ROLL HIGH SCHOOL

1979 (US 93m) Warner Bros.

Film genre: anarchic Punk Rock Musical comedy

Top guns: dir: Allan Arkush → GET CRAZY → SHAKE, RATTLE & ROCK! tv → the TEMPTATIONS (+ story w/ Joe Dante) / s-w: Richard Whitley, Russ Dvonch, Joseph McBride

Stars: P.J. Soles *(Riff Randell)* → SWEET DREAMS → SHAKE, RATTLE & ROCK! tv → the DEVIL'S REJECTS, Vincent Van Patten *(Tom Roberts)*, Clint Howard *(Eaglebauer)* ← COTTON CANDY / → GET CRAZY → THAT THING YOU DO! → CURIOUS GEORGE, Dey Young *(Kate Rambeau)* → SHAKE, RATTLE & ROCK! tv → the DAVID CASSIDY STORY, Mary Woronov *(Miss Evelyn Togar)* ← the VELVET UNDERGROUND AND NICO / → GET CRAZY → ROCK'N'ROLL HIGH SCHOOL FOREVER → DICK TRACY → SHAKE, RATTLE & ROCK! tv, Paul Bartel *(Mr. McGree)* → GET CRAZY → JOE'S APARTMENT, Dick Miller *(police chief)* ← I WANNA HOLD YOUR HAND ← TRUCK TURNER ← the TRIP ← the WILD ANGELS ← WILD, WILD WINTER ← the GIRLS ON THE BEACH ← SKI PARTY ← BEACH BALL ← ROCK ALL NIGHT ← CARNIVAL ROCK/ → GET CRAZY → SHAKE, RATTLE & ROCK! tv, Don Steele *(Screamin' Steve Stevens)*, Alix Elias *(coach Steroid)* → TRUE STORIES, Daniel Davies *(Fritz Gretel)* → GET CRAZY, Lynn Farrell *(Angel Dust)*, **RAMONES:- Joey, Johnny, Dee Dee + Marky** *(themselves/performers)*

Storyline: Riff Randell is a high school student into the Ramones, and she wants to meet them, big time. However, new principal, Miss Evelyn Togar is out to stiffle her ambitious intentions. Enough is enough when the teacher and like-minded, rock'n'roll-hating parents decide to burn some records, and understandably the pupils rebel. *MCS*

Movie rating: *7

Visual: video + dvd

Off the record: The video/dvd represents even further value, adding a plethora of RAMONES songs:- 'Sheena Is A Punk Rocker', 'I Wanna Be Sedated', 'I Just Want To Have Something To Do', 'I Wanna Be Your Boyfriend', 'Do You Wanna Dance' & 'Questioningly'. ENO gets in a couple more, 'Spirits Drifting' & 'Alternative 3', while the VELVET UNDERGROUND fit in 'Rock & Roll', MC5 contribute 'High School' and FLEETWOOD MAC – the early version – contribute 'Albatross' & 'Jigsaw Puzzle Blues', etc. *MCS*

RAMONES // Various Artists

May 79. (lp/c) *Sire; <(SRK/SRC 6070)>* ☐ Oct79 ☐
– Rock'n'roll high school / I want you around / Come on let's go (w/ PALEY BROTHERS) / Blitzkrieg bop – Teenage lobotomy – California sun – Pinhead – She's the one // So it goes (NICK LOWE) / Energy fools the magician (BRIAN ENO) / Rock'n'roll high school (P.J. SOLES) / Come back Jonee (DEVO) / Teenage depression (EDDIE & THE HOT RODS) / Smokin' in the boys' room (BROWNSVILLE STATION) / School days (CHUCK BERRY) / A dream goes on forever (TODD RUNDGREN) / School's out (ALICE COOPER). *<cd-iss. May90; 2-6070> <re-iss. May02; same>*

S/track review: New York's iconic punks, the RAMONES were 1-2-3-4! LPs into their career when they dusted off their landmark diversion into the cult movie business. Teenagers loved them, so with high school rebellion the theme to the film, and New Wave the catalyst, the quartet introduced us to their "unabashed lunacy" via this partly nostalgic, 50s-styled vehicle. The RAMONES take up virtually half of the album, while side 2 was "principally" classroom classics from various acts such as the unadulterated 'Smokin' In The Boys' Room' (by BROWNSVILLE STATION), 50s R&R gem 'School Days' (CHUCK BERRY) and prototype punk giant, 'School's Out' (by ALICE COOPER). Back to the future and back to the RAMONES. They indeed opened proceedings with the title track, a sort of 50s pastiche record harking back to a time (er, 'At The Hop') when the cartoon-esque punks were only just ripping up their diapers – not their jeans; actress P.J. SOLES' version on the flip side is better left unsaid. If you liked your RAMONES downbeat and gooey, then the romantically-inclined, 'I Want You Around', was up your proverbial street; for me though, it 'Don't Come Close'. A collaboration with power-pop, 'Sire' labelmates, the PALEY BROTHERS, for an update of Ritchie Valens' 'Come On, Let's Go', took another step back, quite literally. The RAMONES really got into top gear with a 1-2-3-4 . . . 5! song "best of" live medley, featuring pogo-tastic numbers, 'Blitzkrieg Bop', 'Teenage Lobotomy', 'California Sun', the "Gabba Gabba Hey" 'Pinhead' and 'She's The One'; 11 minutes that was pure head-on headbanging. Of the other various new-wave ditties, DEVO's rollicking 'Come Back Jonee' was the pick of the bunch, while England's NW pub rock culture (via NICK LOWE's 'So It Goes' and EDDIE & THE HOT RODS' 'Teenage Depression') was a welcome inclusion. Of the more sombre pieces, ENO's bass-tastic instrumental 'Energy Fools The Magician' (from his 'Before And After Science' set), shone out, while FM-styled avant-rock could not be better represented than by TODD RUNDGREN and the appropriately-titled 'The Dream Goes On Forever'. *MCS*

Album rating: *7.5

– spinoff releases, etc. –

RAMONES: Rock'n'Roll High School / Do You Wanna Dance?
May 79. (7") *<1051>* [ ] [–]

RAMONES: Rock'n'Roll High School / Sheena Is A Punk Rocker
Sep 79. (7") *(SIR 4021)* [–] [67]

ROCK'N'ROLL HIGH SCHOOL FOREVER

1991 sequel (US 94m) Live Entertainment (PG-13)

Film genre: Rock Musical teen comedy

Top guns: s-w + dir: Deborah Brock ← SLUMBER PARTY MASSACRE II

Stars: Corey Feldman *(Jessie Davis)*, Mary Woronov *(Doctor Vadar)* ← GET CRAZY ← ROCK'N'ROLL HIGH SCHOOL ← the VELVET UNDERGROUND AND NICO / → DICK TRACY → SHAKE, RATTLE & ROCK! tv, Larry Linville *(Principal McGree)* ← EARTH GIRLS ARE EASY, Liane Alexandra Curtis *(Stella)*, **Mojo Nixon** *(Spirit of Rock'n'Roll)* ← GREAT BALLS OF FIRE! / → TWO HEADED COW, Evan Richards *(Mag)*, Jason Lively *(Donovan)*, Brynn Horrocks *(Tabatha)*, **Michael Cerveris** *(Eaglebauer)* → TEMPTATION

Storyline: The worst-behaved students in the world are back at the new Ronald Reagan High School (they blew up the old one). Prankster-in-chief Jessie Davis comes up against a worthy adversary in the form of Doctor Vadar, the new head teacher (the Force is surely with her). She wants to cancel the school riot – sorry, er dance, and run the place like a boot camp, but will the kids let her? Let battle commence! *JZ*

Movie rating: *3

Visual: dvd Australia-only (no audio OST)

Off the record: COREY FELDMAN AND THE ERADICATORS performed five cues, 'I'm Walkin'', 'Tutti Frutti', 'Riot In The Playground', 'Rock Us Danny' & 'Dare Dreamer'. While **Mojo Nixon** released several albums in the 80s & 90s, **Michael Cerveris** (who's worked on theatre projects with Pete Townshend) released only one solo, and that was 'Dog Eared' in 2004; his band Retriever released 'Hinterlands' in 2001. *MCS*

ROCK'N'ROLL MOBSTER GIRLS

1988 (US 110m str-8-to-vid) Donna Michelle Productions

Film genre: Rock-music mockumentary/horror

Top guns: s-w + dir: Rick Werner Fahr

Stars: the Doll Squad:- **Hell'n** *(vocals, acoustic guitar)*, **Cathy Watson** *(guitar)*, **Mara** *(vocals)*, **Annette Billesbach** *(bass)*, **Patty Schemel** *(drums)* / Fred Hopkins *(Bruno Multrock)*, Robert Gus Blue *(Jack)*, **Scott McCaughey** → **HYPE!, the Backtrackers:- Jeff Simmons** (performer/s)

Storyline: It's Seattle and "grunge rock" is all the rage. Wannabes, the Doll Squad, an all-girl outfit, are part of the scene, but they have hit on bad times resorting to eating from diner dumpsters. Thinking they'll never get the breaks, the band take on manager Bruno Multrock, but this psycho serial killer has other things on his mind, mainly the decapitated head of his brother he still talks to! *MCS*

Movie rating: *3

Visual: video-only 1992 (no audio OST)

Off the record: Although they did play some local gigs and guested on the Spud Goodman Show, the fabricated Doll Squad (featuring **Patty Schemel** of Hole), delivered several tracks to the movie, including 'You're Gone', 'Love Van', 'Seduce & Destroy', 'Black Leather Rocker', 'Psycho Girls', 'Fox On The Run', 'American Woman', 'I Got You Babe' & 'Get Off The Road'; the latter four being covers. In the 1989 follow-up, 'Attack Of The Hideopoid' (1989), the Young Fresh Fellows (with **Scott McCaughey**) play the local band. Seattle grunge/heavy outfits, CAT BUTT (a supergroup of sorts!), the BACKTRACKERS (fronted by **Jeff Simmons**, ex-ZAPPA/Mothers Of Invention), SPY DELLE and CRISIS PARTY were involved on the soundtrack. **Simmons** was also the man behind the obscure "acid-fuzz" instrumental soundtrack to 'NAKED ANGELS' (1969), described as the worst biker movie of all-time. *MCS*

ROCK'N'ROLL MOM

1988 (US 95m TV) Buena Vista / Walt Disney Television

Film genre: family Pop-music/showbiz comedy

Top guns: dir: Michael Schultz ← KRUSH GROOVE ← the LAST DRAGON ← SGT. PEPPER'S LONELY HEARTS CLUB BAND ← CAR WASH / s-w: Gen LeRoy

Stars: Dyan Cannon *(Annie Hackett)*, Michael Brandon *(Jeff Robins)* ← FM, **Telma Hopkins** *(Edda)*, Heather Locklear *(Darcy X)* ← FIRESTARTER / → WAYNE'S WORLD 2, Nancy Lenehan *(Connie)* → ROADSIDE PROPHETS, Fran Drescher *(Jody Levin)* ← THIS IS SPINAL TAP ← AMERICAN HOT WAX ← SATURDAY NIGHT FEVER / → UHF, Joe Pantoliano *(Ronnie)* ← LA BAMBA ← SCENES FROM THE GOLDMINE ← EDDIE AND THE CRUISERS ← RICKY BUSINESS ← the IDOLMAKER / → the IN CROWD → BLACK AND WHITE, Nina Blackwood *(video DJ)*, Josh Blake *(Nicky)*, Amy Lynne *(Emma)*, David Paymer *(Boris)* ← HOWARD THE DUCK / → GANG RELATED, Clay Wilcox *(Eric)* → COME ON, GET HAPPY: THE PARTRIDGE FAMILY STORY → the BEACH BOYS: AN AMERICAN FAMILY, **Waddy Watchel** *(himself)*

Storyline: Annie Hackett is a single mother with two teenage girls. Much to the girls' embarrassment, Annie sings and dances to music while she does the housework and takes part in local talent contests. Producer Jeff Robins hears a tape of her singing and is impressed – soon she is making her first single under her new stage name – Mystere. *JZ*

Movie rating: *5

Visual: video (no audio OST; score: Lee Ritenour)

Off the record: Workhorse session guitarist **Waddy Watchel** (real name,

Robert) augmented the late, great Warren Zevon, DYLAN, Randy Newman, Linda Ronstadt, etc.; he also scored several movies from 'UP IN SMOKE' (1978) to 'The Last Request' (2006). **Telma Hopkins** (b.28 Oc'48, Louisville, Kentucky) was one-half of Dawn, the singing group behind Tony Orlando ('Knock Three Times' & 'Tie A Yellow Ribbon..'). She was also the mysterious woman who yells "shut your mouth" on ISAAC HAYES' 'Shaft' theme, and a backing singer for Johnnie Taylor's biggest hit, 'Disco Lady'; check out her acting in the film/s, 'Trancers' and mid-80s TV series 'Gimme A Break!' *MCS*

ROCK'N'ROLL NEVER DIES

2006 (Fin 131m) Filmtotal Oy

Film genre: Rock-music comedy drama

Top guns: s-w + dir: Juha Koiranen

Stars: Samuli Edelmann *(Tiger)*, Laura Birn, Marjukka Halttunen *(mother)*, Seppo Halttunen *(teacher)*, Risto Tuorila *(father)*, Ilkka Koivula *(Jack Nevada)* ← BADDING, Hennariikka Laaksola *(Kiti)*, Kari-Pekka Toivonen *(Pumppu)*

Storyline: A modern parable about Tiger, a backward, near-forty-something man, who lives with his parents and sleeps most of the time with his beloved, homemade guitar. His only goal it seems is to write and perform songs, while bittersweet flashbacks of his surrounding family and old friend, Jack Nevada, give us an idea of his eventful past. *MCS*

Movie rating: *7

Visual: none yet! (no audio OST)

Off the record: Actor/singer, SAMULI EDELMANN, performed a couple of songs (Brian May-like), namely 'I Wanna Be Somebody' & 'Smoke On The Water'; ILKKA KOIVULA contributed 'Sininen Ja Valkoinen'. *MCS*

ROCK'N'ROLL NIGHTMARE

aka the EDGE OF HELL

1987 (Can 83m) Synapse Films (R)

Film genre: Heavy Metal-music horror thriller

Top guns: dir: John Fasano → BLACK ROSES / s-w: **Jon Mikl Thor**

Stars: **Jon Mikl Thor** *(John Triton)*, Jillian Peri *(Lou Anne)*, Frank Dietz *(Roger Eburt)* → BLACK ROSES, David Lane *(Max)*, Teresa Simpson *(Randy)*, Liane Abel Dietz *(Mary Eburt)*, Denise Dicandia *(Dee Dee)*, Jim Cirile *(Stig)*, Gene Kroth *(Karl)*, Carrie Schiffler *(Cindy Connelly)* → MAN IN THE MIRROR: THE MICHAEL JACKSON STORY, Chris Finkel *(father)*, Clara Pater *(mother)*, Jesse D'Angelo *(little boy)* → BLACK ROSES

Storyline: Heavy metal band the Tritons need to find somewhere quiet to record their latest album. When lead singer John finds an old country house which has been converted into a recording studio, all seems well. But the old spooky house just happens to be inhabited by demons and various band members start acting strangely and disappearing. Soon it's only John that's left to do battle with Big S himself but our hero has an angel or two up his sleeve. "When the band starts to rock . . . heads start to roll!" *JZ*

Movie rating: *2.5

Visual: video + dvd (latter 2006)

Off the record: Canadian-born THOR (aka **Jon Mikl Thor**) was a one-time Mr North America and body-builder, the man mountain taking his name from the Norse God of thunder. Initiating his own-named band comprising of John Shand (on guitar), Terry McKeown (on bass) and Bill Wade (on drums), THOR signed a recording contract. In 1978, us mere mortals were promised a musclebound extravaganza in the form of the band's Alice Cooper-meets-Kiss-like debut set, 'Keep The Dogs Away', many critics panning its lack of originality. In the event, its rather lame metal posturing and poor production probably didn't even keep the odd stray chihuahua at bay. Early in '84, he relaunched a new band (Steve Price on guitar, Keith Zazzi on bass, Mike Favata on drums and wife Pantera on backing vox) and once more he was unleashed on the unsuspecting British public through a set of Marquee gigs and a mini-set, appropriately titled 'Unchained'. THOR and his muscular frame subsequently returned to his homeland (North America, not Valhalla!) and with a stage show that SPINAL TAP would've been proud of, the caged THOR proceeded to display his immortal powers by blowing up hot water bottles (as normal earthlings would do with balloons!). On the vinyl front, the rampant THOR released 'Only The Strong' (1985), while the following year saw JON MIKL THOR (as he was now known) enter the film industry with a role in the movie, 'Recruits', a project that inspired his next album, 'Recruits: Wild In The Streets' (1986). Self-financed movies, 'Zombie Nightmare' (1986) and 'ROCK'N'ROLL NIGHTMARE' (1987), followed in quick succession, the latter featuring new sidekicks The TRITONS:- FRANK SODA (guitar), ROB BEGG (keys), UMBERTO SODA (bass), ADAM RIDDLE (rhythm guitar) and BEN FRITH (drums). THOR – the man and yet another line-up – are still going strong in 2005, having released 'Thor Against The World'. *MCS*

THOR AND THE TRITONZ (composer: JON MIKL THOR)

Jul 06. (cd) *La-La Land; <(LLLCD 1048)>* ☐ ☐
– RNRN intro / Spiralling terror / Wild life / The magic voice / Winds of evil / Live it up / Heads will turn / Calm before the fear / We live to rock (let's tune our weapons) / Damage control (let's rock one) / Energy / Nocturnal invader (Phil's demise) / Mad as hell / Ghost walker / Steal your thunder / I heard Luanne scream / March of the purple star fish / Somewhere when rises the Moon / Attack of the minions / Face off (the final confrontation) / I knew I pissed you off / We accept the challenge / See you again Old Scratch / Unknown stranger / Rock n'roll nightmare / Tritonz theme / Lend me your ears.

S/track review: It'd be a cheap shot to say 'ROCK'N'ROLL NIGHTMARE' best describes itself, because this heavy-metal-thunder OST – released nearly two decades after the movie! – is not at all bad, in fact, it's one of his better albums. Had it really been ten or so years since ALICE COOPER's 'Welcome To My Nightmare', well the bridge was gapped here by way of spine-tingling opening score tracks 'RNRN Intro' and 'Spiralling Terror', JON MIKL THOR proving he was no one-trick stallion. Back-to-basics hard-rock rears its ugly head on more than one occasion through vocal tracks, 'Wild Life', 'Live It Up', 'We Live To Rock', 'Mad As Hell', 'Steal Your Thunder', 'Somewhere When Rises The Moon' and 'We Accept The Challenge', conjure up images of Twisted Sister, Judas Priest and Iron Maiden, while the Toto-esque 'Heads Will Turn' (written by their agent, Alan Solomon) is hairy-head-and-shoulders above the rest of the pack. The uplifting and narrative 'The Magic Voice' exudes atmosphere, although some of the good work is marred by a squeaky cover of 'Energy'. The all-too-brief dialogue skits are hardly necessary, while the short bursts of score dirges become either incidental or effectively eerie. Tagged on at the end of the CD are a couple of interesting non-soundtrack numbers – 25 and 27, to be exact – 'Rock N' Roll Nightmare' and the lengthy, Hawkwind-esque 'Lend Me Your Ears', freshly recorded for the value-for-money album. *MCS*

Album rating: *5.5

ROCK, PRETTY BABY

1956 (US 89m b&w) Universal Pictures

Film genre: teen Rock'n'roll Musical drama

Top guns: dir: Richard Bartlett / s-w: William Raynor → ROCK BABY: ROCK IT / → SUMMER LOVE, Herbert H. Margolis ← ROCK BABY: ROCK IT / → SUMMER LOVE

Stars: Sal Mineo *(Nino Barrato)*, John Saxon *(Jimmy Daley)* → SUMMER LOVE → FROM DUSK TILL DAWN, Luana Patten *(Joan Wright)*, Edward Platt *(Dr. Thomas Daley)* → SUMMER LOVE, Fay Wray *(Beth Daley)* →

SUMMER LOVE, **Rod McKuen** *("Ox" Bentley)* → SUMMER LOVE, Alan Reed, Jr. *("Sax" Lewis)*, John Wilder *("Fingers" Porter)* → SUMMER LOVE, Douglas Fowley *("Pop" Wright)*, Bob Courtney *("Half-Note" Harris)* → SUMMER LOVE, Shelley Fabares *(Twinkey Daley)* → SUMMER LOVE → RIDE THE WILD SURF → GIRL HAPPY → HOLD ON! → SPINOUT → CLAMBAKE → a TIME TO SING, George Winslow *(Tommy)* → SUMMER LOVE, Johnny Grant *(DJ, himself)*

Storyline: "The story of today's rock'n'roll generation, told the way they want it told". Jimmy Daley is the typical rebellious teenager who's into the new rock'n'roll craze. His dad Thomas believes rock music is a one way ticket to crime and delinquency, and puts his foot down when Jimmy organizes a student band. When the band ends up on TV in a talent competition, the battle between the generations is on. *JZ*

Movie rating: *3

Visual: video

Off the record: Subsequent film composer and former beat-poet, **Rod McKuen**, will have own entry in a further edition.

—

JIMMY DALEY AND THE DING-A-LINGS (composer: Henry Mancini *)

Feb 57. (lp) *Decca; <DL 8429> Brunswick; (LAT 8162)* [16] [ ]
– Rock, pretty baby / Dark blue (*) / Free and easy (*) / What's it gonna be (*) / Rockin' the boogie (*) / Rockabye lullaby blues / Teen age bop (*) / The most (*) / Can I steal a little love / Juke box rock (*) / The saints rock 'n roll / Picnic by the sea / Young love (*) / Happy is a boy named me / Hot rod (*) / Big band rock and roll (*). *<(re-iss. 1983 on 'Jasmine'; JASM 1028)>*

S/track review: JIMMY DALEY AND THE DING-A-LINGS were indeed the first mock-up outfit, featuring as they did top young actors at the time, John Saxon (aka JIMMY DALEY) on guitar frets and Sal Mineo on wee drumkit! And just who was the sax man pop pickers? The one thing that seems to hold it all together is the sounds of "real" music man, Henry Mancini, a Universal staff composer from 1952-58 and a one-time member of Mel Torme's Mel-Tones. He wrote 10 of the 16 cuts on 'ROCK, PRETTY BABY', a far cry from his subsequent and numerous movie Oscars and Grammys ('Breakfast At Tiffany's', etc.). Taking rock'n'roll as its cue, Mancini (and the film's stars) pull off a fast one here, Mancini playing the cool daddy-o on instrumentals such as 'Dark Blue', 'Teen Age Bop', 'The Most', 'Juke Box Rock' and 'Hot Rod' – not bad for a jazz composer/lover in his un-cool thirties (he was born in Cleveland in 1924). The non-Mancini songs are of the Haley-meets-Presley variety. Check out Sonny Burke's ALAN COPELAND-sung title track, the Bobby Troup-scribed 'Rockabye Lullaby Blues', plus the ROD McKUEN-performed & penned 'Happy Is A Boy Named Me' & 'Picnic By The Sea'. If you're looking for a minor highlight (lyrically, at least), and to seriously avoid the lounge-jazz chaff, go no further than side 2 opener, 'Can I Steal A Little Love' (from the pen of Phil Tuminello), featuring vox by the DING-A-LINGS. One to avoid is the film interpretation of Bill Haley & Milt Gobler's 'The Saints Rock 'n Roll', aka "The Saints Go Marching In". *MCS*

Album rating: *4

– spinoff releases, etc. –

JIMMY DALEY AND THE DING-A-LINGS: Jimmy Daley and the Ding-A-Lings

Feb 57. (7"ep) *Decca; <ED 2480>* [ ] [–]

JIMMY DALEY AND THE DING-A-LINGS: Rock, Pretty Baby / Can I Steal A Little Love

Mar 57. (7",78) *Brunswick; (05648)* [–] [ ]

– other bits & pieces, etc. –

JIMMY DALEY: Rock, Pretty Baby

2004. (cd) *(TLR 97445)* [–] German [–]
– Rock, pretty baby / Ding a ling (*) / Sox hop (*) / Night walk (*) / The hole in the wall (w/ ROD McKUEN) (*) / Boppin' at the bash (*) / Beatin' on the bongos (w/ MOLLY BEE) (*) / The most / Love is something (w/ MOLLY BEE) (*) / Juke box rock / Calypso rock (w/ ROD McKUEN) (*) / The rock talks / Red lips and green eyes (w/ ROD McKUEN) (*) / Soft touch (*) / How's about a little kiss (*) / Summer love (w/ KIP TYLER) / Rockin' the boogie / Can I steal a little love (w/ ROD McKUEN) / The saints rock'n'roll / Big band rock and roll / Rockabye lullabye blues.

ROCK, ROCK, ROCK!

1956 (US 85m b&w) Vanguard Productions

Film genre: Rock'n'roll teen Musical

Top guns: dir: Will Price / s-w: Milton Subotsky → JAMBOREE → IT'S TRAD, DAD! → JUST FOR FUN (au: Phyllis Coe)

Stars: Tuesday Weld *(Dori)* → WILD IN THE COUNTRY → I WALK THE LINE → THIEF → HEARTBREAK HOTEL → CHELSEA WALLS, **Teddy Randazzo** *(Tommy)* ← the GIRL CAN'T HELP IT / → MISTER ROCK AND ROLL → HEY, LET'S TWIST, Jacqueline Kerr *(Gloria)*, Alan Freed *(recording artist)* ← DON'T KNOCK THE ROCK ← ROCK AROUND THE CLOCK / → MISTER ROCK AND ROLL → GO, JOHNNY, GO!, Fran Manfred *(Arabella)*, Carol Moss *(mother)*, Jack Collins *(father)* → GOIN' COCONUTS, Eleanor Swayne *(Miss Silky)*, Bert Conway *(Mr. Barker)* → LITTLE BIG MAN → RANCHO DELUXE, **Frankie Lymon & the Teenagers:- Frankie Lymon, Sherman Garnes, Herman Santiago, Joe Negroni, Jimmy Merchant** *(performers)* → MISTER ROCK AND ROLL, **Chuck BERRY** *(performer)*, **the Johnny Burnette Trio** *(performers)*, **Fats DOMINO** *(performer)*, **the Flamingos:- Johnny Carter, Jake Carey, Zeke Carey** *(performers)* → GO, JOHNNY, GO!, **the Moonglows:- Harvey Fuqua** *(performer)* → MISTER ROCK AND ROLL → GO, JOHNNY, GO!, **LaVern Baker** *(performer)* ← the PIED PIPER OF CLEVELAND / → MISTER ROCK AND ROLL, **Jimmy Cavallo & The House Rockers** *(themselves)*, **Connie FRANCIS** *(voice; Dori)*

Storyline: It's time for the annual school prom, and teenager Dori simply HAS to be there. But grumpy old dad won't give her the 30 dollars she needs for that special blue dress in the shop window. After much head-scratching Dori comes up with a way of raising the money herself, with one eye on arch-rival Gloria who's got her sights set on boyfriend Tommy. Can Dori do a Cinderella and get to the ball with her Prince Charming? *JZ*

Movie rating: *6

Visual: video + dvd

Off the record: (see below)

—

Various Artists

Dec 56. (lp) *Chess; <LP 1425>* [ ] [–]
– I knew from the start (the MOONGLOWS) / Would I be crying (if I were lying to you) (the FLAMINGOS) / Maybellene (CHUCK BERRY) / Sincerely (the MOONGLOWS) / Thirty days (CHUCK BERRY) / The vow (the FLAMINGOS) / You can't catch me (CHUCK BERRY) / Over and over again (the MOONGLOWS) / Roll over Beethoven (CHUCK BERRY) / I'll be home (the MOONGLOWS) / See saw (the MOONGLOWS) / A kiss from your lips (the FLAMINGOS). *(UK cd-iss. Jun88 on 'Charly-MCA'; CHD 31270)* *<(cd re-iss. Mar04 on 'Universal'+=; AAB 00017510-2)>* – I'm not a juvenile delinquent (FRANKIE LYMON & THE DELINQUENTS) / Rock & roll boogie (ALAN FREED & HIS ROCK'N'ROLL ORCHESTRA) / Lonesome train (on a lonesome track) (JOHNNY BURNETTE'S ROCKABILLY TRIO).

S/track review: Not exactly a various-artists soundtrack per se, as only three major acts are featured – at least on the original LP version. The MOONGLOWS (highlighting singer Harvey Fuqua) were first up their blend of cool R&B doo-wop had already witnessed them having two major hits, 'Sincerely' & 'See Saw' (both featured here), while the film produced three other numbers, 'I

Knew From The Start', 'I'll Be Home' and 'Over And Over Again'. The similar – in respect of their doo-wop sound – the FLAMINGOS were still in search of that elusive chart entry when a trio of cuts, 'The Vow' and double-A side flop, 'Would I Be Crying (If I Were Lying To You)' / 'A Kiss From Your Lips', also flopped. The "Rock" (and, of course, the R&B) part comes by way of the legendary CHUCK BERRY, who's afforded four excellent cuts, 'Maybellene', 'Thirty Days', 'Roll Over Beethoven' and 'You Can't Catch Me'. For CD buffs, there was finally the soundtrack's re-issue in 2004, containing extra tracks from the likes of FRANKIE LYMON & THE TEENAGERS, JOHNNY BURNETTE and even disc-jockey, ALAN FREED. *MCS*

Album rating: *6.5 (cd *7)

– spinoff hits, etc. –

LaVERN BAKER: Jim Dandy *(not in movie)* / Tra La La

Dec 56. (7") *Atlantic; <1116>* [17] [94] [–]

the FLAMINGOS: Would I Be Crying (If I Were Lying To You) / A Kiss From Your Lips

Jan 57. (7") *Chess; <?> London; (HLN 8373)* [ ] Feb57 [ ]

FRANKIE LYMON & THE TEENAGERS: I'm Not A Juvenile Delinquent

Mar 57. (7") *Columbia; (DB 3879)* [ ] [12]

ROCK STAR

2001 (US 105m) Warner Bros. Pictures (R)

Film genre: Hard Rock-music drama/comedy

Top guns: dir: Stephen Herek ← BILL & TED'S EXCELLENT ADVENTURE / s-w: John Stockwell

Stars: Mark Wahlberg *(Chris 'Izzy' Cole)* ← BOOGIE NIGHTS ← the BASKETBALL DIARIES / → OVERNIGHT, Jennifer Aniston *(Emily Poule)* ← SHE'S THE ONE, Steel Dragon:- Jason Flemyng *(Bobby Beers; lead singer)* ← SPICEWORLD, Dominic West *(Kirk Cuddy; guitarist)* ← SPICEWORLD, **Zakk Wylde** *(Ghode; guitarist)*, **Jeff Pilson** *(Jorgen; bassist)*, **Jason Bonham** *(A.C.; drummer)* ← the SONG REMAINS THE SAME, Timothy Spall *(Mats; road manager)* ← STILL CRAZY ← GOTHIC ← QUADROPHENIA, Blood Pollution:- Timothy Olyphant *(Rob Malcolm; guitarist)* → CATCH AND RELEASE, **Nick Catanese** *(Xander Cummins; guitarist)*, **Brian Vander Ark** *(Ricki Bell; bassist)*, **Blas Elias** *(Donny Johnson; drummer)*, Matthew Glave *(Joe Cole)* ← the WEDDING SINGER, Dagmara Dominczyk *(Tania Asher; PR for Steel Dragon)*, **Stephan Jenkins** *(Bradley; lead singer of Black Babylon)*, Michael Shamus Wiles *(Mr. Cole)* ← MAGNOLIA ← FIGHT CLUB, Beth Grant *(Mrs. Cole)* ← BLUE VALLEY SONGBIRD ← DANCE WITH ME, Rachel Hunter *(A.C.'s wife)*, **Colleen Fitzpatrick** *(guitarist in crowd outside mansion)* ← HAIRSPRAY, Valerie Landsburg ← THANK GOD IT'S FRIDAY, Emmy Collins *(roadie)* ← ALMOST FAMOUS ← TO HELL AND BACK

Storyline: With more than just a nod to the real life story of Judas Priest, Chris Cole is a photocopy machine repairman during the day and frontman for Steel Dragon tribute band, Blood Pollution by night. His dreams of rock stardom receive an unexpected boost when he is offered the chance to front the hugely successful Steel Dragon after his ignominious sacking from the band he founded. Catapulted into stardom, Chris soon discovers his new found success isn't all he had hoped for. *KM*

Movie rating: *5.5

Visual: dvd

Off the record: Mark Wahlberg is better known as dance-pop performer Marky Mark; **Jason Bonham** is the drummer son of Led Zeppelin's John Bonham and featured in own late 80s hard-rock band, Bonham; **Jeff Pilson** is the bassist with hard-rockers, Dokken; guitarist **Zakk Wylde** was mainstay of Ozzy Osbourne and subsequently his own outfit, Black Label Society, a metal outfit who also featured **Nick Catanese**; **Blas Elias** was the drummer with hard-rock band, Slaughter; **Brian Vander Ark** fronted rock group, the Verve Pipe; **Stephan Jenkins** led the rock band Third Eye Blind. *MCS*

—

Various Artists (score: TREVOR RABIN *)

Aug 01. (cd) *Priority; <50238> (CDPTY 222)* [ ] Nov01 [ ]
– Rock star (EVERCLEAR) / Livin' the life (STEEL DRAGON) / Wild side (MOTLEY CRUE) / We all die young (STEEL DRAGON) / Blood pollution (STEEL DRAGON) / Livin' on a prayer (BON JOVI) / Stand up (STEEL DRAGON) / Stranglehold (TED NUGENT) / Wasted generation (STEEL DRAGON) / Lick it up (KISS) / Long live rock'n'roll (STEEL DRAGON) / Devil inside (INXS) / Colorful (VERVE PIPE) / Gotta have it – music from Rock Star (*).

S/track review: Dredging the barrel of forgotten late 80s metal cast-offs like Steelheart vocalist, MIKE MATIJEVIC and Dokken's JEFF PILSON, the producers of 'ROCK STAR' somehow managed to cobble together a surprisingly authentic sounding motley crew of musicians to form the film's core. Although STEEL DRAGON's six contributions to this soundtrack deserve little more than album filler status, they feature competent performances like the Bon Scott-style rasp delivered on 'Stand Up And Shout' (sadly without the Young brothers' backbeat) and the lively if a little widdly interpretation of Rainbow's 'Long Live Rock'n'Roll'. However gallant their efforts, the soundtrack relies heavily on well known artists like KISS and BON JOVI to entice its audience to keep listening as well as Oregon grunge punks, EVERCLEAR, to provide 'ROCK STAR' the film's main titles. Notably absent from the list are leather clad Brummys, Judas Priest, whose own story provided the majority of the film's plot albeit a decade prior to 'ROCK STAR's own setting. Instead, most tracks here come from a time when metal took itself less seriously, cuts like L.A. revellers MOTLEY CRUE's nostalgic party anthem 'Wild Side' and KISS' 'Lick It Up' which sounds contemporary by comparison. Party poopers, VERVE PIPE, provide an unexpected but welcome element of sentimentality to proceedings with 'Colorful', their ode to a certain, special groupie while TED NUGENT stretches the patience with a reliably proficient but predictable eight-minute long 'Stranglehold'. Save the last two, this record provides an enjoyable if partial insight into a time when heavy metal lost its way but found its sense of humour. *KM*

Album rating: *6

ROCK YOU SINNERS

1957 (UK 59m b&w) Small Films

Film genre: Rock'n'roll Musical

Top guns: dir: Dennis Kavanagh / s-w: Beatrice Scott

Stars: Philip Gilbert *(Johnny)*, Adrienne Scott *(Carol)*, Beckett Bould *(McIver)*, Colin Croft *(Pete)*, Michael Duffield *(Selway)*, Jackie Collins *(Jackie)* → JACKIE'S BACK!, Diana Chesney, **Tony Crombie & His Rockets** *(performers)*, **Joan Small** *(performer)*, **Rory Blackwell & The Blackjacks** *(performers)*, **Art Baxter & His Rockin' Sinners** *(performers)*, **Don Sollash & His Rockin' Horses** *(performers)*, **Dickie Bennett** *(performer)*, **George 'Calypso' Browne** *(performer)*, **Curly Pat Berry** *(performer)*, **Tony Hall** *(performer)*

Storyline: This was the first British-produced Rock'n'Roll movie. A hip-to-be-square disc jockey, Johnny (now a TV presenter), becomes over-indulgent in his vision to turn anybody and everybody into rock'n'rollers. And we mean anybody. *MCS*

Movie rating: *2

Visual: video in 1996 (no audio OST)

Off the record: Pick of the bunch of music hall rockers were **Tony Crombie & His Rockets** who'd recently hit the UK Top 30 with double-header, 'Teach You To Rock' / 'Short'nin Bread'; they subsequently moved into soundtrack/ score work in the early 60s – he died on 27th August, 1999. **Dickie Bennett** with three flop singles behind him, contributed three songs to the film, 'Heartbreak Hotel', 'How Many Times' and 'Cry Upon My Shoulder'; various others – **George Browne** delivered 'Calypso Rock'n'Roll', **Don Sollash & His Rockin' Horses** 'Rockin' The Blues', **Rory Blackwell** 'Rockin' With Rory' & 'Intro To The Rock' (see spinoffs for more). Non-singer, Jackie Collins, on the other hand (sister of Joan Collins), shakes her booty here before becoming one of the best-selling authors of the 80s. *MCS*

– spinoff releases, etc. –

TONY CROMBIE & HIS ROCKETS: London Rock / Brighton Rock

1957. (7"/78) *Columbia; (DB 3921)* ☐ ☐ -

JOAN SMALL: Gonna Get Along Without You Now / You Can't Say I Love You To A Rock & Roll Tune

1957. (7"/78) *Parlophone; (R 4269)* ☐ ☐ -

ART BAXTER & HIS ROCKIN' SINNERS: Rock You Sinners

1957. (10"lp) *Philips; (BBR 8107)* ☐ ☐ -
– Rock you sinners / Art's theme / Dixieland rock / etc.

TONY CROMBIE & HIS ROCKETS: Let's You And I Rock

1957. (7"ep) *Columbia; (SEG 7686)* ☐ ☐ -

TONY CROMBIE & HIS ROCKETS: Rockin' With . . .

1957. (10"lp) *Columbia; (33S 1108)* ☐ ☐ -

Various Artists: Rock You Sinners – The Dawn Of British Rock & Roll

Jan 07. (cd) *Rev-Ola; (CRBAND 10)* ☐ ☐ -
– (contains material from the film)

ROCK-A-DOODLE

1992 (US/Ire 77m) Goldcrest Films / Samuel Goldwyn Company (G)

Film genre: animated children's fantasy Musical

Top guns: dir: Don Bluth, Dan Kuenster / s-w: David N. Weiss

Stars: Glen CAMPBELL *(Chanticleer)*, Ellen Greene *(Goldie)* ← PUMP UP THE VOLUME, Christopher Plummer *(Grand Duke)* → the INSIDER, Charles Nelson Reilly *(Hunch)* ← TWO TICKETS TO PARIS, Eddie Deezen *(Snipes)* ← GREASE 2 ← GREASE ← I WANNA HOLD YOUR HAND, Sorrell Brooke *(Pinky)* ← RECORD CITY, Phil Harris *(Patou)*, Sandy Duncan *(Peepers)*, Will Ryan *(Stuey)*

Storyline: Chanticleer the rooster leaves the farm in disgrace when he fails to crow one morning and the sun consequently doesn't rise. As stormclouds, darkness and the Grand Duke Owl all gather ominously the rock'n'roll rooster finds fame in the city as "The King". Meanwhile, his farmyard friends launch an expedition to persuade Chanticleer to come home and save them from a torrential flood, thus giving the tale a happy ending. *JZ*

Movie rating: *4

Visual: video + dvd

Off the record: (see below)

—

Various Cast (songs: T.J. Kuenster) (score: Robert Folk)

Apr 92. (m-cd) *Liberty; <(CDP-7 98911-2)>* ☐ ☐
– Sun do shine (GLEN CAMPBELL) / We hate the sun (CHRISTOPHER PLUMMER) / Come back to you (GLEN CAMPBELL) / Rock-a-doodle (GLEN CAMPBELL) / The bouncer's song (the DON BLUTH PLAYERS) / Tweedle-le-dee (CHRISTOPHER PLUMMER) / Treasure huntin' fever (GLEN CAMPBELL) / Sink or swim (ELLEN GREENE) / Kiss 'n coo (GLEN CAMPBELL & ELLEN GREENE) / Back to the country (GLEN CAMPBELL) / The owls' picnic (CHRISTOPHER PLUMMER) / Tyin' your shoes (PHIL HARRIS).

S/track review: One for the kiddies here, although the recording's down to grandpappies in the shape of GLEN CAMPBELL and thespian elder statesman CHRISTOPHER PLUMMER, the former turning in several pseudo-Elvis-in-Vegas-meets-C&W performances. You'd have to go way back in time to discover Mr. CAMPBELL starring in a musical-orientated film ('NORWOOD'; 1970), even further if you wanted to find 60-something Mr. PLUMMER ('The Sound Of Music'; 1965). Once a country star and a short-term member of the Beach Boys, GLEN CAMPBELL disguises himself (and his vocal chords, it seems) as a big ol' gospel-singing, Elvis-styled, rockin' rooster on ditties such as 'Sun Do Shine', 'Come Back To You', 'Rock-A-Doodle', 'Treasure Huntin' Fever', 'Kiss 'N Coo' (with co-star ELLEN GREENE) and the Billy Ray Cyrus-esque 'Back To The Country'. The whispering ELLEN GREENE gets all cutesy-pie, Marilyn Monroe-ish, on her one and only short solo cue, 'Sink Or Swim', like nearly every other track here (including PHIL HARRIS' 'Tyin' Your Shoes') backed by one-time Elvis cohorts and backing group, the JORDANAIRES. All writing credits go to T.J. KUENSTER, a pianist who led the DON BLUTH PLAYERS (here with 'The Bouncer's Song') and backing band the NASHVILLE RHYTHM SECTION who included CAMPBELL (again!) and Billy Joe Walker, Jr. on guitars. It's just left to say the aforementioned PLUMMER produces his OTT theatrical monotone on three narrative numbers, 'We Hate The Sun', 'Tweedle-Le-Dee' and 'The Owls' Picnic', the latter two short'n'sweet much like the album itself, which runs in at just over 21 minutes. *MCS*

Album rating: *3

ROCKERS

1978 (Jama 100m) Rockers Film Corporation

Film genre: crime/gangster drama

Top guns: s-w + dir: Ted Bafaloukos

Stars: Leroy Wallace *(Horsemouth)*, Richard Hall *(Dirty Harry)*, Marjorie Norman *(Sunshine)*, **Gregory Isaacs** *(Jah Tooth)* → LAND OF LOOK BEHIND → COOL RUNNINGS: THE REGGAE MOVIE → MADE IN JAMAICA, **Jacob Miller** *(Jakes)* → HEARTLAND REGGAE, **Frank Dowding** *(Kiddus I)*, **Winston Rodney** *(Burning Spear)* → REGGAE SUNSPLASH → the REGGAE MOVIE, **Leroy Smart** *(himself)*, Monica Craig *(Madgie)*, **Errol Brown** *(Natty Garfield)*, **Robbie Shakespeare** *(Robbie)* → MADE IN JAMAICA, **Theophilus Beckford** *(Easy Snapping)*, **Manley Buchanan** *(Big Youth)*, **Peter Tosh** *(himself)* → REGGAE SUNSPLASH → HEARTLAND REGGAE → the BOB MARLEY STORY; CARIBBEAN NIGHTS → STEPPING RAZOR RED X, **Bunny Wailer** *(himself)* → the BOB MARLEY STORY; CARIBBEAN NIGHTS, **Lester Bullocks** *(Dillinger)*, **Herman Davis** *(Bongo Herman)*

Storyline: The great, the bad and the good of 70s reggae pepper this comic romp of a movie like hot rocks, making random cameos in the misadventures of drummer/hustler Leroy 'Horsemouth' Wallace and his beloved red motorbike. Bought with the hard sweat of his long suffering wife, the bike aids his efforts as a record distributor, until it's stolen during a party. With the help of his pals, he eventually gets it back along with a cache of luxury goods which he and his homies proceed to deliver, Robin Hood style, to Kingston's downpressed masses. *BG*

Movie rating: *8

Visual: video + dvd

Off the record: Leroy Wallace (as Horsemouth) released 'Original Armageddon Dub' – Recorded 1978 – his "First Release" as it states on the cover. Two decades on, **Robbie Shakespeare** wrote the score for Various "reggae" Artists film soundtrack, 'Third World Cop' (1999). *MCS*

—

Various Artists

Sep 79. (lp/c) *Island; (ILPS/ZCI 9587)* ☐ ☐

– We 'A' rockers (INNER CIRCLE) / Money worries (the MAYTONES) / Police and thieves (JUNIOR MURVIN) / Book of rules (the HEPTONES) / Stepping razor (PETER TOSH) / Tenement yard (JACOB MILLER) / Fade away (JUNIOR BYLES) / Rockers (BUNNY WAILER) / Slave master (GREGORY ISAACS) / Dread lion (the UPSETTERS) / Graduation in Zion (KIDDUS I) / Jah no dead (BURNING SPEAR) / Satta massagana (JUSTIN HINDS & the DOMINOES) / Natty take over (JUSTIN HINDS & the DOMINOES). *(cd-iss. Jul90; CCD 9587) (cd re-iss. May94 on 'Reggae Refreshers'; RRCD 45)*

S/track review: Just as 'The HARDER THEY COME' (1972) had spread the reggae gospel further and wider than ever before, 'ROCKERS' drew a line under what had been the most successful decade in the history of Jamaican music, just before the 80s ushered in a brash new era. As a movie, it's a funnier, more colourful and sympathetic window onto Kingston life and rasta culture than its predecessor. Musically, it was more of a contemporary overview. Its greatest song, 'Tenement Yard', remains a dyed-in-the-dreadlocks classic with a tragic resonance; larger than life singer JACOB MILLER died in a car crash some six months after the soundtrack's release. INNER CIRCLE also lost their frontman. He'd been one of Jamaica's biggest stars, newly returned from a trip to Brazil with Bob Marley at the time of the accident. Marley's former partner PETER TOSH was also to die, albeit in murkier circumstances; 'Stepping Razor' is testament to his hard-nosed philosophy, shredded – like BUNNY WAILER's title track – by American funk. Famous for its Clash cover, JUNIOR MURVIN's 'Police And Thieves' supplies unflinching social commentary in creamy falsetto, BURNING SPEAR's 'Jah No Dead' is a haunting, a cappella mantra with tidal effects, and while LEE PERRY would infamously torch his 'Black Ark' studios not long after the movie's release, 'Dread Lion' – from the excellent 'Super Ape' (1976) – is a mesmerising example of the kind of tropico-mystical sounds he conjured there. Older harmony cuts from the MAYTONES, JUSTIN HINES and the HEPTONES round out what is still one of the best samplers of 70s reggae on the market, with an iconoclastic, end-of-an-era feel. *BG*

Album rating: *9

ROCKIN' THE BLUES

1955 (US 68m b&w) Fritz Pollard Associates / Austin Productions

Film genre: Rock'n'roll Musical comedy

Top guns: dir: Arthur Rosenblum / s-w: Irvin C. Miller

Stars: Hal Jackson *(MC)*, Mantan Moreland *(himself)*, F.F. Miller *(himself)*, **Connie Carroll** *(performer)*, **the Wanderers** *(performers)*, **the Hurricanes** *(performers)*, **Linda Hopkins** *(performer)*, **Reese La Rue** *(performer)*, **Pearl Woods** *(performer)*, **the Harptones** *(performers)*, **the Five Miller Sisters** *(performers)*

Storyline: Energetic at least, it centres on a music and comedy revue for black GI's – a sort of MOBO awards for the 50s, except there's no presentations. "Rock'n'Roll at its tingling, exciting best" was the misinformed tagline. *MCS*

Movie rating: *3

Visual: Norton Video / R&B Video DVD

Off the record: Linda Hopkins (b.14 Dec'24, New Orleans, Louisiana) is a larger-than-life figure in the world of jazz, gospel and the blues. Besides recording a plethora of singles in the 50s, she was best known for her subsequent hit collaboration ('Shake A Hand') with the late, great, Jackie Wilson. Her vocal dexterity also landed her major roles in the theatre, none more satisfying than when she portrayed her idol, Bessie Smith, in the stage production, 'Jazz Train'. Her film work included bit parts in the movies such as 'Roots: The Next Generation' (1979) and she is still on the circuit performing in the "Wild Women Blues" revue around Europe and L.A. *MCS*

ROCKTOBER BLOOD

1985 (US 93m) Panarecord (R)

Film genre: Heavy Rock-music horror drama

Top guns: s-w: (+ dir) Beverly Sebastian, Ferd Sebastian

Stars: Tray Loren *(Billy "Eye" Harper)*, Donna Scoggins *(Lynn Starling)*, Cana Cockrell *(Honey Bear)*, Renee Hubbard *(Donna Lewis)*, Ben Sebastian *(head security)*, Nigel Benjamin *(Chris Keane)*, Tony Rista *(Tony Leland)*, Headmistress:- **Richard Taylor** *(guitarist)* ← STUNT ROCK, **Rich King** *(bassist)* ← STUNT ROCK, **Perry Morris** *(drummer)* ← STUNT ROCK

Storyline: Rock star Billy "Eye" Harper suddenly goes insane and begins a gory killing spree at his recording studio. His girlfriend Donna manages to escape and testifies against him, and he is duly found guilty and executed. Two years later on Donna is now a singer with Rocktober Blood and thinks she has put the past behind her – until someone looking and sounding very much like Billy reappears and begins terrorising the band once more. *JZ*

Movie rating: *3.5

Visual: dvd extended (no audio OST by RICHARD SMOKEY TAYLOR)

Off the record: Richard Taylor (aka Smokey Huff) also scored the music for 1978's 'STUNT ROCK'. *MCS*

ROCKULA

1990 (US 87m) Cannon Film Distributors (PG-13)

Film genre: Rock Musical comedy-horror

Top guns: s-w: Luca Bercovici (+ dir), Jefery Levy → S.F.W., Christopher Verwiel

Stars: Dean Cameron *(Ralph LaVie)*, **Toni Basil** *(Phoebe LaVie)* ← EASY RIDER ← HEAD ← PAJAMA PARTY ← the T.A.M.I. SHOW, **Thomas DOLBY** *(Stanley)*, Tawny Fere *(Mona)*, Susan Tyrell *(Chuck the bartender)* ← TAPEHEADS ← SUBWAY RIDERS ← FORBIDDEN ZONE ← CATCH MY SOUL / → CRY-BABY → PINK AS THE DAY SHE WAS BORN → MASKED AND ANONYMOUS, **Bo DIDDLEY** *(Axman/performer)*, Rodney Bingenheimer *(himself)* ← BACK TO THE BEACH ← UNCLE MEAT ← X: THE UNHEARD MUSIC ← REPO MAN ← UP IN SMOKE / → RAGE: 20 YEARS OF PUNK ROCK WEST COAST STYLE → END OF THE CENTURY → MAYOR OF THE SUNSET STRIP → PUNK'S NOT DEAD, Adam Shankman *(driver)* → MONSTER MASH: THE MOVIE

Storyline: Four centuries ago, a virgin vampire did nothing to prevent his damsel from dying at the hands of a pirate with a stone peg leg. He's been cursed ever since, which has prevented him from getting his end away, although he stands a better chance as a Rock star – or does he? *MCS*

Movie rating: *4

Visual: video

Off the record: Dean Cameron subsequently played bass with Hollywood rock quartet, the Thornbirds (formerly, the Ducks); look out for the album, 'All The Same' (2004). **Toni Basil** (b. Antonia Christina Basilotta, 22 Sep'43, Philadelphia, Pennsylvania) was raised and schooled in Las Vegas, where incidentally she was a cheerleader, a fact that probably led to the cheesy choreography (by Toni, herself) for her video on the 1982 debut hit single, 'Mickey' – a US No.1. However, this was not an overnight success, as she had worked on TV shows such as 'Shindig', 'The T.A.M.I. Show', 'Hullabaloo', etc. while also appearing in several movies (mainly bit parts). Choreography was her main vocation and it was while working on films such as 'AMERICAN GRAFFITI' and 'THE ROSE' plus stage and video shoots for DAVID BOWIE and TALKING HEADS, that she gained notariety. Although her album, 'Word Of Mouth', hit the Top 30, her name would be synonymous with the phrase one-hit-wonder. She still works as an actress and dance choreographer, mainly for television (the Gap ad) and film. **Thomas DOLBY**'s career (see own entry). Luca's brother, Hilary, completed the score, although it was never released. *MCS*

the ROCKY HORROR PICTURE SHOW

1975 (UK 100m) Twentieth Century-Fox Films (R)

Film genre: Pop/Rock Musical comedy/horror

Top guns: s-w: Jim Sharman (+ dir) ← SHIRLEY THOMPSON VERSUS THE ALIENS / → SHOCK TREATMENT, Richard O'Brien → SHOCK TREATMENT

Stars: Tim Curry *(Dr. Frank-n-furter)* → ROCK FOLLIES OF '77 → TIMES SQUARE → LEGEND → the WALL: LIVE IN BERLIN → JACKIE'S BACK!, Susan Sarandon *(Janet Weiss)* ← JOE / → DEAD MAN WALKING → the BANGER SISTERS → ALFIE re-make → ROMANCE & CIGARETTES, Barry Bostwick *(Brad Majors)*, Richard O'Brien *(Riff Raff)* → JUBILEE → FLASH GORDON → SHOCK TREATMENT → SPICEWORLD, Jonathan Adams *(Dr. Everett V. Scott)*, Patricia Quinn *(Magenta)* → SHOCK TREATMENT, Little Nell Campbell *(Columbia)* → LISZTOMANIA → ROCK FOLLIES OF '77 → JUBILEE → SHOCK TREATMENT → the WALL → the KILLING FIELDS, **MEAT LOAF** *(Eddie)*, Peter Hinwood *(Rocky Horror)*, Koo Stark *(bridesmaid)* → ELECTRIC DREAMS, Jeremy Newson *(Ralph Hapschatt)* → SHOCK TREATMENT, Charles Gray *(criminologist)* → SHOCK TREATMENT, Sadie Corre *(the Transylvanians)* ← the BODY, Imogen Claire *(the Transylvanians)* ← TOMMY / → LISZTOMANIA → FLASH GORDON → SHOCK TREATMENT → HAWKS

Storyline: Straight-laced couple Janet Weiss and Brad Majors get a salutory lesson in decadence after getting stranded in the sticks. Making the mistake of seeking help at an isolated mansion, they're ushered into a world of high class gender-bending populated by transvestite aliens. Frank-N-Furter is their host, a mascara'd mad scientist with a penchant for sussies and spike heels, who proceeds to regale them with his latest creation: an artificially engineered blonde bombshell named Rocky Horror. As butler Riff-Raff explains in his typed sleevenote: "all have missed the blindingly obvious ingredient, simply, that it is an astonishing, yet true story." You have been warned. *BG*

Movie rating: *9

Visual: video + dvd

Off the record: Tim Curry (b.19 Apr'46, Grappenhall, Cheshire, England) subsequently released three LPs for 'A&M': 'Ready My Lips' (1978), a near US Top 50 entry 'Fearless' (1979) – featuring minor hit 'I Do The Rock' – and 'Simplicity' (1981); he also supplied backing vox on friend CARLY SIMON's 1979 album, 'Spy'. *MCS*

—

Various Cast (composer/score: Richard O'Brien)

Oct 75. (lp) *Ode; (ODE 78332) <21653>* [ ] Apr78 [49]

– Science fiction double feature / Dammit Janet / Over at the Frankenstein place / Time warp / Sweet transvestite / I can make you a man / Hot patootie – Bless my soul / I can make you a man (reprise) / Touch-a, touch-a, touch me / Eddie / Rose tint my world / I'm going home / Super heroes / Science fiction double feature (reprise). *(re-iss. Jan86 lp/pic-lp/c/cd; OSV+/P/C/CD 21653) <re-iss. 1989 on 'Rhino' lp/c/cd+=; R1/R4/R2 70712>* – Time warp (1989 extended remix) / Time warp (U-mix). *(re-iss. Aug93 on 'Griffin' c/cd; MC+/GRF 231) (cd re-iss. Jul01 on 'Castle'; CMRCD 296)*

S/track review: It's regarded as one of the greatest cult films of all time, still has them dancing in the aisles three decades after its box office debut and has probably done more for the humble fishnet stocking than all the dodgy 80s videos ever filmed. Prior to 'ROCKY HORROR . . .', though, rock operas were a serious business, high-minded concepts attempting to push the boundaries of popular music. Richard O'Brien's B-movie tribute took a different tack, pushing at the boundaries of popular taste instead. Unlike Rocky Horror himself, the songs – brazen couplings of bubblegum rock'n'roll and early 70s glam-pop/rock (think the Bonzo Dog Band and Alice Cooper auditioning for 'Grease') – are nigh on indestructible, even without the screen theatrics or communal cross-dressing. The hooks are sharper than Nosferatu's fangs, the lyrics ("Satanic mechanic" anyone?); the vocal interplay kitschier than Lady Marmalade; and the monocled, ask-Jeeves asides and cod-Transylvanian accents guaranteed to get a smile out of the pastiest goth. Readers of a certain age will recognise 'The Time Warp' (a huge hit for Damian – yes, just Damian – back in the late 80s) on sight; some may even have endured the 'Agadoo'-like trauma of dancing to it. With 'Hot Patootie', MEAT LOAF previewed the kind of fist-pumping rock with which he'd conquer the world at the turn of the decade, and who can resist Susan Sarandon writhing her way through the technicolour smut of 'Touch-a, Touch-a, Touch Me'? Like the man says, "swim the warm waters of sins of the flesh", you know you want to. *BG*

Album rating: *8

– spinoff hits, etc. –

Original Cast: 15th Anniversary Boxed Set

Nov 87. (4xlp-box) *(RHBXLP 1)* [ ] [–]
(re-iss. Jan89 as 4xcd-box; RHBXCD 1)

Original Cast: 25th Anniversary Anthology

Jul 00. (d-cd) *Essential; (<ESDCD 908>)* [ ] [ ]

— there are of course at plethora of Cast recordings, etc.

– other bits & pieces, etc. –

DAMIAN: The Time Warp 2

Dec 87. (7") *Jive; (JIVE 160)* [51] [–]

DAMIAN: The Time Warp 2

Aug 88. (7") *Jive; (JIVE 182)* [64] [–]

DAMIAN: The Time Warp (re-mix)

Aug 89. (7") *Jive; (JIVE 209)* [7] [–]

ROLL BOUNCE

2005 (US 107m) Fox Searchlight Pictures (PG-13)

Film genre: coming-of-age comedy drama

Top guns: dir: Malcolm D. Lee / s-w: Norman Vance Jr.

Stars: Bow Wow *(Xavier "X" Smith)* ← CARMEN: A HIP HOPERA ← MURDER WAS THE CASE, Chi McBride *(Curtis)* ← WHAT'S LOVE GOT TO DO WITH IT, Marcus T. Paulk *(Boo)* → TAKE THE LEAD, Meagan Good *(Naomi Phillips)* ← YOU GOT SERVED / → STOMP THE YARD, **Nick Cannon** *(Bernard)*, Wesley Jonathan *(Sweetness)*, Kellita Smith *(Vivian)* → FEEL THE NOISE, Mike Epps *(Byron)* ← the FIGHTING TEMPTATIONS ← MALIBU'S MOST WANTED ← HOW HIGH, Charlie Murphy *(Victor)* ← DEATH OF A DYNASTY ← PAPER SOLDIERS ← MURDER WAS THE CASE ← CB4: THE MOVIE ← JUNGLE FEVER, **Darryl 'DMC' McDaniels** *(garden DJ; Smooth Dee)* <= RUN-D.M.C. =>

Storyline: You can almost imagine the pitch at the meeting in some Hollywood execs office "this is The Karate Kid . . . on rollerskates!" And that's what it is, 1978 and Xavier's mother has died and his local roller rink has shut down so he and his crew have to bust their moves at the swanky Sweetwater rink uptown. A rivalry springs up between the local champs and Xavier and his boys, but Xavier has as many troubles with his home life as he does on the rink. *MR*

Movie rating: *5

Visual: dvd

Off the record: Kid rapper, **Bow Wow** (b. Shad Gregory Moss, 9th March '87, Columbus, Ohio), has grown a lot since his youthful post-millennium Top 10 breakthrough as Lil Bow Wow. Since his debut album, 'Beware Of Dog' (2000), he's subsequently hit high with further sets: 'Doggy Bag' (2002), 'Unleashed' (2003) and 'Wanted' (2005). Fellow rapper, **Nick Cannon** (ex-Da Bomb Squad), issued his eponymous debut album late in 2003. *MCS*

—

Various Artists (score: Stanley Clarke)

Sep 05. (cd) *Sanctuary; <87539>*
– Boogie oogie oogie (BROOKE VALENTINE with FABOLOUS & YO-YO) / Bounce, rock, skate, roll (VAUGHAN MASON AND CREW) / Pure gold (EARTH, WIND & FIRE) / Wishing on a star (BEYONCE) / Quit actin' (RAY J feat. R KELLY & SHORTY MACK) / Superman lover (JOHNNY "GUITAR" WATSON) / Hollywood swingin' (KOOL & THE GANG feat. JAMIROQUAI) / Let's stay together (MICHELLE WILLIAMS) / Lovely day (BILL WITHERS) / I wanna know your name (KEITH SWEAT) / Get off (FOXY) / Le freak (CHIC).

S/track review: This is an unsubtle co-joining of mid-70s disco, funk and pop (plus contemporary R&B schmaltz), a familiar tactic when trying to capture the credibility of the past but the commercial pull of the present. While many might be tempted to head down the Austin Powers pastiche route 'ROLL BOUNCE' is all the better for playing it relatively straight, drawing on old hands like EARTH WIND & FIRE, CHIC, BILL WITHERS and KOOL & THE GANG to give this trunk some funk. The latter's much sampled 'Hollywood Swingin'' has a JAMIROQUAI vocal refit which leaves you craving the original but the rest are untouched and sound fresh as the creases on their polyester pant suits. The most enjoyable oddity here however (and all good soundtracks should have one ringer on it) is JOHNNY 'GUITAR' WATSON's 'Superman Lover' where the original funk eccentric brews up bubbling tale of his superhuman prowess between the sheets. Meanwhile, in the 2000s, BEYONCE and MICHELLE WILLIAMS of DESTINY'S CHILD shimmy through a couple of soul standards: 'Wishing On A Star' and 'Let's Stay Together' respectively. Only WILLIAMS adds anything new: a little bounce to the arrangement and a little feminine wile to the vocal, but its just different rather than an improvement. More commendable is RAY J, who drafts in R KELLY and SHORTY MACK to give some poke to his already excellent bump'n'grind party tune 'Quit Actin''. Its clichéd as hell but ultimately good fun. A line that pretty much sums up the whole record. 'ROLL BOUNCE' keeps things lightweight and is all the better for it. *MR*

Album rating: *6.5

ROLLER BOOGIE

1979 (US 104m) Compass International Pictures / United Artists (PG)

Film genre: romantic disco-Musical drama

Top guns: dir: Mark L. Lester → CLASS OF 1984 → FIRESTARTER / s-w: Barry Schneider (story: Irwin Yablans)

Stars: Linda Blair *(Theresa "Terry" Barkley)*, Jim Bray *(Bobby James)*, Beverly Garland *(Lillian Barkley)*, Roger Perry *(Roger Barkley)* ← FOLLOW THE BOYS, Jimmy Van Patten *(Hoppy)*, Kimberly Beck *(Lana)*, Sean McClory *(Jammer Delaney)*, Mark Goddard *(Mr. Thatcher)*, Albert Insinnia *(Gordo)*, Stoney Jackson *(Phones)* → STREETS OF FIRE → SWEET DREAMS → KNIGHTS OF THE CITY → TRESPASS → CB4: THE MOVIE, M.G. Kelly *(DJ)* ← the BUDDY HOLLY STORY ← a STAR IS BORN / → VOYAGE OF THE ROCK ALIENS → UHF, Chris Nelson *(Franklin Potter)*, Nina Axelrod *(Bobby's friend)*

Storyline: Back in the late 70s, the kids of Venice, California didn't have a care in the world. With ears glued to transistor radios, they'd skate happily up and down all day, and have let's-get-tipsy alcoholic parties before bedtime at nine o'clock. Now, horror of horrors, all this may be coming to an end as their skating rink is to be pulled down and replaced by a shopping mall! Can the kids beat the baddies and keep the rink open, or are they just skating on thin ice? *JZ*

Movie rating: *3

Visual: video + dvd

Off the record: Kimberly Beck was a brief recording starlet, having sang 'Let's Take A Walk', a song penned with her stepfather Tommy Leonetti and Bob Russell. *MCS*

—

Various Artists (score/composer: BOB ESTY *)

Jun 80. (d-lp) *Casablanca; <NBLP-2 7194>*
– Hell on wheels (CHER) / Good girls (JOHNNIE COOLROCK) / All for one, one for all (MAVIS VEGAS DAVIS) / Boogie wonderland (EARTH, WIND & FIRE with the EMOTIONS) / We got the power (RON GREEN) / Top jammer (CHEEKS) / Summer love (*) / Takin' life in my own hands (RON GREEN) // Elektronix (roller dancin') (* & CHEEKS) / Cunga (*) / Evil man (MAVIS VEGAS DAVIS) / Lord is it mine (*) / Rollin' up a storm (the eye of the hurricane) (*) / The roller boogie (*) / Love fire (* & MICHELE ALLER).

S/track review: Propagating the double-LP somewhat with a blue sticker to announce the inclusion of two of last year's summer disco hits from CHER ('Hell On Wheels') and EARTH, WIND & FIRE with the EMOTIONS ('Boogie Wonderland'), 'ROLLER BOOGIE' stings the listener into believing this is the cat's whiskers. The fact is, apart from the two aforementioned floor-fillers (and that's pushing it a bit for pop-rocker CHER), the remainder of the songs skate on thin ice rather than any rollerskate. The likes of the cheesily-monikered unknowns JOHNNIE COOLROCK (on 'Good Girls'), MAVIS VEGAS DAVIS (on 'All For One, One For All' & 'Evil Man'), CHEEKS ('Top Jammer' & 'Elektronix (Roller Dancin')) and er . . . RON GREEN ('We Got The Power' & 'Takin' Life In My Own Hands'), one tries seriously to avoid any other blades that might be lying around. The aforementioned producer, arranger, conductor and songwriter, BOB ESTY, pens, or co-pens with MICHELE ALLER, most of the dance numbers here, while he tackles 'Summer Love', 'Elektronix' (as mentioned with CHEEKS), 'Cunga' and Supertramp's 'Lord Is It Mine'; he literally takes over side four with three further forgettable solo cuts, 'Rollin' Up A Storm (The Eye Of The Hurricane)', 'The Roller Boogie' and the MICHELE ALLER duet, 'Love Fire' (listen out for Toto guitarist, Steve Lukather). ESTY would subsequently work on the music for the dance movie, 'SALSA', taking with him MAVIS, while he also scored 'You Can't Hurry Love' (1988), 'Galactic Gigolo' (1988) and 'The Secret Of The Ice Cave' (1989) – you have been warned. *MCS*

Album rating: *2.5

ROMANCE & CIGARETTES

2006 (US 115m) GreeneStreet Films / United Artists (R)

Film genre: romantic Pop-Musical comedy drama

Top guns: s-w: (+ dir) John Turturro

Stars: James Gandolfini *(Nick Murder)*, Susan Sarandon *(Kitty Kane Murder)* ← ALFIE re-make ← the BANGER SISTERS ← DEAD MAN WALKING ← the ROCKY HORROR PICTURE SHOW ← JOE, Kate Winslet *(Tula)*, Steve Buscemi *(Angelo)* ← COFFEE AND CIGARETTES ← the WEDDING SINGER ← AIRHEADS ← PULP FICTION ← RESERVOIR DOGS ← MYSTERY TRAIN ← the WAY IT IS / → the FUTURE IS UNWRITTEN, Bobby Cannavale *(Fryburg)*, **Mandy Moore** *(Baby Murder)*, Mary-Louise Parker *(Constance Murder)* → the ASSASSINATION OF JESSE JAMES . . ., Aida Turturro *(Rosebud / 'Rara')*, Christopher Walken *(cousin Bo)* ← the COUNTRY BEARS ← TOUCH ← LAST MAN STANDING ← PULP FICTION ← WAYNE'S WORLD 2 ← HOMEBOY / → HAIRSPRAY re-make, Barbara Sukowa *(Gracie)*, Elaine Stritch *(Nick's mother)*, Eddie Izzard *(Father Gene Vincent)* ← REVENGERS TRAGEDY ← VELVET GOLDMINE / → ACROSS THE UNIVERSE

Storyline: Construction worker Nick Murder is a builder of bridges, and he'll need to produce his best ever day's work if he's to rebuild the bridge with his partner Kitty. She's just found out he's been having a torrid affair with shopgirl Tula and "sends him to Coventry" as punishment. Problems with their teenage daughter and the trauma of cancer leave Nick no choice but to seek reconciliation however hard it may be. *JZ*

Movie rating: *6

Visual: dvd (no audio; score: Paul Chihara & Marilyn D'Amato)

Off the record: Songs featured in the film included:- 'Delilah' (TOM JONES), 'A Man Without Love' (ENGELBERT HUMPERDINCK), 'Piece Of My Heart' (DUSTY SPRINGFIELD), 'Answer Me, My Love' (GENE AMMONS), 'Red Headed Woman' (BRUCE SPRINGSTEEN), 'Scapricciatiello (Do You Love Me Like You Kiss Me)' (CONNIE FRANCIS), 'Hot Pants' (BOBBY CANNAVALE), 'Quando M'innamoro' (ANNA IDENTICI), 'Little Water Song' (UTE LEMPER), 'El Cuarto De Tula' (BUENA VISTA SOCIAL CLUB), 'Prisoner Of Love' (CYNDI LAUPER), 'Trouble' (ELVIS PRESLEY), 'Piece Of My Heart' (JANIS JOPLIN), 'I Want Candy' (MANDY MOORE, AIDA TURTURRO & MARY-LOUISE PARKER), 'It's A Man's Man's World' (JAMES BROWN), 'It Must Be Him' (VICKI CARR), 'The Girl That I Marry' (JAMES GANDOLFINI & SUSAN SARANDON), 'Ten Commandments Of Love' (the MOONGLOWS), 'I Wonder Who's Kissing Her Now' (AIDA TURTURRO), 'Piece Of My Heart' (ERMA FRANKLIN), 'Banks of The Ohio' (DAVID PATRICK KELLY & KATHERINE BOROWITZ), & 'When The Saviour Reached Down For Me' (the R&C CHOIR). *MCS*

the ROSE

1979 (US 125m) Twentieth Century-Fox Films (R)

Film genre: Pop/Rock Musical/showbiz drama

Top guns: dir: Mark Rydell / s-w: Michael Cimino, Bo Goldman, (story: Bill Kerby → SHAKE, RATTLE & ROLL: AN AMERICAN LOVE STORY → LITTLE RICHARD)

Stars: Bette MIDLER *(Mary Rose Foster)*, Alan Bates *(Rudge Campbell)* → the WICKED LADY → the MOTHMAN PROPHECIES, Frederic Forrest *(Huston Dyer)* → ONE FROM THE HEART → TUCKER: THE MAN AND HIS DREAM → the END OF VIOLENCE → SWEETWATER: A TRUE ROCK STORY, Harry Dean Stanton *(Billy Ray)* ← RENALDO AND CLARA ← RANCHO DELUXE ← PAT GARRETT & BILLY THE KID / → ONE FROM THE HEART → REPO MAN → PARIS, TEXAS → PRETTY IN PINK → the LAST TEMPTATION OF CHRIST → WILD AT HEART → FEAR AND LOATHING IN LAS VEGAS, Barry Primus *(Dennis)*, David Keith *(Pfc. Mal)* → FIRESTARTER → HEARTBREAK HOTEL → RAISE YOUR VOICE, Sandra McCabe *(Sarah Willingham)*, Ted Harris *(reporter)* ← BLACULA, Victor Argo *(lockerman)* → the LAST TEMPTATION OF CHRIST → GHOST DOG: THE WAY OF THE SAMURAI → COYOTE UGLY, Phil Rubenstein *(Pot Belly)* → RHINESTONE, Jack Starrett *(Dee)*, James Keane *(Sam)* → DICK TRACY → DON'T LET GO, Don Calfa *(Don Frank)* → the RETURN OF THE LIVING DEAD, **John Dennis Johnston** *(Milledge)* ← KISS MEETS THE PHANTOM OF THE PARK / → STREETS OF FIRE, **Sylvester** *(Supremes drag queen)*, **Danny Weis** *(leader/guitarist of Rose Band)*, **Doug Dillard, Byron Berline, Rodney Dillard** *(country band members)*, Hildy Brooks *(Arlene)* → PLAYING FOR KEEPS, Jonathan Banks *(television promoter)*, **Whitey Glan + Steve Hunter** *(Rose band members)* ← WELCOME TO MY NIGHTMARE

Storyline: Unofficially based on the life of Janis Joplin, this fictional biopic plots the gin-stoked rise and blearily predictable fall of American blues dame Mary Rose Foster, a woman caterwauling in a man's, man's man's world, an arena controlled by familiarly Mephistophelian characters like English manager Rudge. *BG*

Movie rating: *7

Visual: video + dvd

Off the record: Pioneering fiddler **Byron Berline** (b. 6 Jul'44, Caldwell, Kansas) remains one of the most respected and adventurous bluegrass practitioners in an often traditionalist minded field. Initially cutting his teeth with Bill Monroe, he was also a pivotal figure in the insurgent late 60s/early 70s country rock movement, a member of the Dillard And Clark Expedition and familiar face on records by the likes of the Flying Burrito Brothers and Gram Parsons himself. He was also the author of the sawing, heaving fiddle lines behind Mick Jagger on the ROLLING STONES' 'Country Honk', a countrified update of 'Honky Tonk Women'. Having already worked in TV scoring, Berline (in collaboration with cult sessioneer BRUCE LANGHORNE) scored his one and only feature, Bob Rafelson's 'Stay Hungry' (1976), featuring a fiddle-playing Arnie Schwarzeneggar (we kid you not!). Byron subsequently made an unlikely cameo in blockbusting Sharon Stone flick, 'Basic Instinct' (1992). *BG*

BETTE MIDLER (composer: Paul A. Rothchild)

Dec 79. (lp/c) *Atlantic; <SD/CS 16010> (K/K4 50681)* [12] Jan80 [68]
– Whose side are you on / Midnight in Memphis / Concert monologue / When a man loves a woman / Sold my soul to rock'n'roll / Keep on rockin' / Love me with a feeling / Camelia / Homecoming monologue / Stay with me / Let me call you sweetheart / The Rose. *(cd-iss. Jan84; K2 50681) <(cd-iss. Nov95 on 'East West'; 7567 82778-2)>*

S/track review: As spiritual heir to 'a STAR IS BORN', this Janis Joplin-inspired biopic saw BETTE MIDLER – like Streisand before her – assuming the kind of thesp-rooted rock divadom attuned to the excess of the late 70s but lumberingly out of step with its music. MIDLER struts the walk and authentically bawls the talk but even in 1979, 'The ROSE' was a massively successful, Oscar-nominated anachronism. It drops all the right names – legendary producer (and Joplin veteran) Paul Rothchild, ex-Mitch Ryder/Lou Reed/ Alice Cooper guitarist Steve Hunter – but ends up coming off like an honorary 'Blooze Sister', replacing the 'BLUES BROTHERS' self-mocking humour with self-conscious banter. Reading like some manifesto for a keep-it-vinyl campaign, irony and imagination-free titles (and lyrics) like 'Keep On Rockin' and 'Sold My Soul To Rock'n'Roll' make it difficult to take seriously. To her credit, and regardless of the jaded predictability of much of the material and arrangements, MIDLER consistently goes the extra length for maximum emotional heft, fulfilling the role's neo-Joplin theatrics with a truly frazzled ferocity on the likes of 'Stay With Me', if inevitably leaching most of the tenderness and subtlety from Percy Sledge's 'When A Man Loves A Woman'. 'Midnight In Memphis' alone is a lock-tight revelation, the best soul performance of her career, but the double entendres of the blues, and the bluster of its rock-revivalist reincarnation are much more up MIDLER's street. The US Top 10 success of the title ballad sent the album platinum but behind the hype, 'The ROSE' is still a musical, Hollywood's same old rise, fame and fall game as played out by a Broadway Tina Turner. *BG*

Album rating: *5.5

– spinoff releases, etc. –

BETTE MIDLER: When A Man Loves A Woman / Love Me With A Feeling

Jan 80. (7") *<3643> (K 11433)* [35] [ ]

BETTE MIDLER: The Rose / Stay With Me

Mar 80. (7") *<3656> (K 11459)* [3] Apr80 [ ]

Diana ROSS

Born: 26th March '44, Detroit, Michigan, USA. Many will know the iconic DIANA ROSS as she rose to fame as lead singer with the Supremes. From 1962 onwards, she helped define the sound of 'Motown' with No.1 hits such as 'Where Did Our Love Go', 'Baby Love', 'Come See About Me', 'Stop! In The Name Of Love', 'Back In My Arms Again', 'I Hear A Symphony', 'You Can't Hurry Love', 'You Keep Me Hangin' On', 'The Happening', 'Love Child' & 'Someday We'll Be Together'. She was subsequently groomed for solo superstardom by Berry Gordy as the 70s loomed. With the Supremes continuing (quite successfully) without her, Diana unveiled her new sophisticated soul sound with the Top 20 hit, 'Reach Out And Touch (Somebody's Hand)'. 1970 also saw her first solo chart-topper with 'Ain't No Mountain High Enough', while she repeated the feat in the UK via 'I'm Still Waiting' (although surprisingly the ballad was a relative flop in the USA, only reaching No.63). A 1972 Motown-produced biopic of legendary jazz singer Billie Holiday, 'The LADY SINGS THE BLUES', found ROSS taking the starring role and being nominated for an Oscar in the process. If the chart-topping 'Touch Me In The Morning' – from the 1973 album of the same name – saw the quality control begin to slip, her album of duets with Marvin Gaye ('Diana & Marvin') later that year proved she was still value for money, the record spawning a trio of hits including 'You Are Everything'. ROSS once again turned her hand to acting with 1975's 'Mahogany', the accompanying soundtrack (scored by Michael Masser) furnishing her with another No.1 in the shape of the heart-wrenching theme 'Do You Know Where You're Going To'. Nothing if not versatile, ROSS flagged down the disco bandwagon for her 1976 boogie classic (and US No.1), 'Love Hangover'. Following a further venture into singing/acting with the disastrous musical, 'The WIZ' (1978) – alongside Richard Pryor and Michael Jackson – ROSS again aimed for the dancefloor with the Ashford & Simpson-written 'The Boss' (1979) and 'Diana' (1980), Chic's Nile Rodgers and Bernard Edwards whipping up a mean groove on the latter. It was back to movie theme slush in 1981 with title themes to 'It's My Turn' & 'Endless Love', the latter a duet with Lionel Richie that was both the biggest single of her career and indeed her last for 'Motown'. Signing for 'R.C.A.' records, Diana hit the US Top 10 almost immediately with a cover of Frankie Lymon And The Teenagers' 'Why Do Fools Fall In Love', her album of the same name spawning a second Top 10 hit in 'Mirror, Mirror'. Playing safer than safe, ROSS chugged along with another couple of big-selling albums, 'Silk Electric' (1982) – which featured the Michael Jackson-penned US Top 10 hit, 'Muscles' – and 'Swept Away', the latter utilising the guitar talents of one JEFF BECK. The latter half of the decade proved more difficult for the ageing but still youthful-looking superstar, her only chart success of any note being a rare UK No.1 with 'Chain Reaction' – a cutesy BEE GEES-penned update of the classic Supremes sound – in 1986. Finally, after 1987's flop album, 'Red Hot Rhythm And Blues' (1987), she returned to 'Motown' and despite a flurry of hype, neither her comeback effort, 'Workin' Overtime' (1989), nor its successor, 'The Force Behind The Power' (1991), made any commercial headway. Her 1994 autobiography, 'Secrets Of A Sparrow', didn't do much better and although she's still a hot ticket live, the "First Lady Of Motown" – as she's affectionately known by her doting fans – struggled to make her return. In 1994 and 1999, ROSS returned to acting, starring in TV movies, 'Out Of Darkness' and 'DOUBLE PLATINUM', respectively; the latter coincided with the release of umpteenth comeback set, 'Every Day Is A New Day'. In 2007, many critics who regarded her as a spent force were made to eat their words when her album, 'I Love You', nearly reached the Top 30. *BG & MCS*

- filmography {acting} –

Lady Sings The Blues *(1972 {*} OST to DIANA ROSS, score by Michel LeGrand =>)* / Mahogany *(1975 {*} theme on OST by Lee Holdridge; see future edition)* / **the Wiz** *(1978 {*} OST by QUINCY JONES =>)* / It's My Turn *(1980 theme on OST by Patrick Williams; see future edition)* / Endless Love *(1981 theme with Lionel Richie on OST by Jonathan Tunick; see future edition)* / Out Of Darkness *(1994 TV {*})* / **Double Platinum** *(1999 TV {*})*

ROUSTABOUT

1964 (US 101m) Paramount Pictures (PG)

Film genre: romantic Rock'n'roll Musical drama

Top guns: dir: John Rich → EASY COME, EASY GO / s-w: Anthony Lawrence → PARADISE, HAWAIIAN STYLE → EASY COME, EASY GO → ELVIS: THE MOVIE, Paul Nathan (story: Allan Weiss ← GIRLS! GIRLS! GIRLS! ← BLUE HAWAII / → PARADISE, HAWAIIAN STYLE)

Stars: Elvis PRESLEY *(Charlie Rogers)*, Barbara Stanwyck *(Maggie Morgan)*, Joan Freeman *(Cathy Lean)* → the FASTEST GUITAR ALIVE, Sue Ann Langdon *(Mme. Mijanou)* → WHEN THE BOYS MEET THE GIRLS → FRANKIE AND JOHNNY → HOLD ON!, Leif Erikson *(Joe Lean)* → MAN AND BOY, Pat Buttram *(Harry Carver)*, Joan Staley *(Marge)* ← KISSIN' COUSINS, Steve Brodie *(Fred the pitcher)* ← BLUE HAWAII, Billy Barty *(Billy the midget)* → HARUM SCARUM → LEGEND → UHF, Teri Hope *(college student)* ← FUN IN ACAPULCO, Teri Garr *(carny dancer)* ← VIVA LAS VEGAS ← PAJAMA PARTY ← the T.A.M.I. SHOW ← KISSIN' COUSINS ← FUN IN ACAPULCO / → the COOL ONES → CLAMBAKE → HEAD → ONE FROM THE HEART, Jack Albertson *(Lou; tea house manager)* ← KISSIN' COUSINS, Norman Grabowski *(Sam)* → GIRL HAPPY → OUT OF SIGHT → the NAKED APE, Kenneth Becker *(Gregg)* ← GIRLS! GIRLS! GIRLS! ← G.I. BLUES ← LOVING YOU, Jane Dulo *(Hazel)* → BEACHES, Marianna Hill *(Viola)* ← PARADISE, HAWAIIAN STYLE, Joy Harmon *(college girl)* ← LET'S ROCK, Beverly Adams *(Cora)* → GIRL HAPPY → HOW TO STUFF A WILD BIKINI → WINTER A-GO-GO, Richard Kiel *(strongman)* ← EEGAH / → SKIDOO, Raquel Welch *(blue-bowed college girl)* → a SWINGIN' SUMMER → the MAGIC CHRISTIAN

Storyline: Charlie Rogers, a hard-nosed, leather-clad singer joins a travelling carnival, where he makes advances to sexie carnie Cathy Lean and earns the wrath of her father in return. *BG*

Movie rating: *4.5

Visual: video + dvd

Off the record: nothing

ELVIS PRESLEY (composers: Joseph Lilley, etc.)

Nov 64. (lp; mono/stereo) *R.C.A.; <LSP 2999> (RD/SF 7678)* [1] Jan65 [12]
– Roustabout / Little Egypt / Poison Ivy league / Hard knocks / It's a wonderful world / Big love big heartache / One track heart / It's carnival time / Carny town / There's a brand new day on the horizon / Wheels on my heels. *(re-iss. Oct79 lp/c; PL/PK 42356) (re-iss. Aug81 on 'RCA Int.'; INTS 5110) (re-iss. Nov84 lp/c; NL/NK 89049)*

S/track review: Not the best of ELVIS soundtracks, it has to be said, especially on the back of the vivacious 'Viva Las Vegas'. It's nevertheless hard to disgree with the sentiments of 'Poison Ivy League' even if the song itself is a stinker. The rocking 'Hard Knocks', one of the few tracks which merit a second listen, offers a similar don't-mess-with-this-poor-boy message, rather ironic given ELVIS' increasing real-life riches. 'One Track Heart' offers enjoyably cheap pop thrills, while some credibility is at least salvaged with Leiber/Stoller's 'Little Egypt', an R&B shuffle with more than a hint of the carnival's racy undercurrent. 'It's Carnival Time', by contrast, is downright awful, enough to persuade anybody that 9-to-5 bank-telling is a more exciting occupation. *BG*

Album rating: *3.5

RUDE BOY

aka RUDE BOY: THE CLASH

1980 (UK 133m) Atlantic / Buzzy (15)

Film genre: semi-documentary/concert drama

Top guns: dir: Jack Hazan, David Mingay (+ s-w w/ Ray Gange)

Stars: Ray Gange *(Ray; Rude Boy)*, **the Clash:- Joe STRUMMER** *(himself/performer)*, **Mick Jones** *(himself/performer)* ← PUNK IN LONDON / → D.O.A. → WESTWAY TO THE WORLD → NEW YORK DOLL, **Paul Simonon** *(himself/performer)* → LADIES AND GENTLEMEN, THE FABULOUS STAINS → WESTWAY TO THE WORLD, **Nick "Topper" Headon** *(himself/performer)* → WESTWAY TO THE WORLD, Johnny Green *(road manager)* → TERROR ON TOUR, **Jimmy Pursey** *(performer)*

Storyline: Part rockumentary, part drama, Rude Boy is a fictionalized account of one man's social and political environs – Margaret Thatcher was Prime Minister – involving punk-rock quartet the Clash. *MCS*

Movie rating: *6

Visual: video + dvd (no audio OST)

Off the record: Jimmy Pursey (was Sham 69 frontman).

the RUNNIN' KIND

1989 (US 101m) M.G.M. / United Artists (R)

Film genre: coming-of-age road drama/comedy

Top guns: s-w: Max Tash (+ dir), **Pleasant Gehman**

Stars: David Packer *(Joey Curtis)* → STRANGE DAYS, **Pleasant Gehman** *(Linda)*, **Brie Howard** *(Thunder)* ← TAPEHEADS, **Rosie Flores** *(Carla)*, Marilyn Reins *(Marsky)*, John Carter *(Richard Curtis)*, James Cromwell *(uncle Phil)* → SPIRIT: STALLION OF THE CIMARRON → the LONGEST YARD, Juliette Lewis *(Amy Curtis)* → NATURAL BORN KILLERS → the BASKETBALL DIARIES → STRANGE DAYS → FROM DUSK TILL DAWN → the FEARLESS FREAKS → CATCH AND RELEASE, Susan Strasberg *(Carol Curtis)* ← PSYCH-OUT ← the TRIP

Storyline: Shunning the world of law his father expected him to follow, Joey Curtis uses his summer off to befriend a drummer and her all-girl rock band. *MCS*

Movie rating: *4

Visual: video (89m) (no audio OST; score: Guy Moon)

Off the record: Pleasant Gehman + Rosie Flores were part of all-female country-punkettes, Screamin' Sirens – one 1984 LP 'Fiesta'; they appeared together in the 1986 movie, 'Vendetta'. The talented Gehman is an actress, singer, poet, writer, screenwriter, promoter, belly dancer, etc. She was the first girlfriend of Pat Smear (of the Germs, now Foo Fighters) and once shared a room with Go-Go's singer, Belinda Carlisle. Rosie is now a thriving solo artist on the country circuit, while actress, Juliette Lewis has formed her own band Juliette Lewis & the Licks. **Brie Howard** (mother of ex-Playboy playmate, Brandi Brandt, who married/divorced Nikki Sixx of Motley Crue) was part of Boxing Gandhis; also dated Nikki! *MCS*

RUNNING OUT OF LUCK

aka 'MICK JAGGER: RUNNING OUT OF LUCK'

1986 (US 81m) CBS Records (R)

Film genre: Rock-music fantasy comedy/drama adventure

Top guns: s-w: (+ dir) Julien Temple ← ABSOLUTE BEGINNERS ← the GREAT ROCK'N'ROLL SWINDLE / → EARTH GIRLS ARE EASY → AT THE MAX → the FILTH AND THE FURY → GLASTONBURY → the FUTURE IS UNWRITTEN, **Mick Jagger**

Stars: Mick Jagger *(Mick)* <= the ROLLING STONES =>, Jerry Hall *(herself)* ← LET'S SPEND THE NIGHT TOGETHER ← URBAN COWBOY / → BATMAN → 25x5: THE CONTINUING ADVENTURES OF THE ROLLING STONES → the WALL: LIVE IN BERLIN, Dennis Hopper *(video director)* ← WHITE STAR ← HUMAN HIGHWAY ← EASY RIDER ← HEAD ← the TRIP / → STRAIGHT TO HELL, Rae Dawn Chong *(slave girl)* ← BEAT STREET, Jim Broadbent ← BREAKING GLASS / → MOULIN ROUGE!, Nicholas Ball, **Tony Tornado** *(bunkhouse card player)*, **Ritchie** *(himself)* ← GAROTA DOURADA

Storyline: Mick Jagger is in Rio to shoot his latest music video. After a row with Jerry Hall, he storms off with three women who turn out to be transvestites (well, anyone can make a mistake) who rob him and dump him in the jungle. Quite believably, poor Mick is then kidnapped and forced to work on a banana plantation (for peanuts) and he begins a desperate escape attempt with some prostitutes to win his freedom. *JZ*

Movie rating: *3

Visual: video – of course! (no "official" audio OST; see below)

Off the record: The aforementioned video added JAGGER's versions of 'Jumpin' Jack Flash' & 'Brown Sugar'. *MCS*

– associated releases, etc. –

MICK JAGGER: Just Another Night / Turn The Girl Loose

Feb 85. (7") *Columbia; <04743> C.B.S.; (A 4722)* [12] [32]
(ext-12"+=) *(TA 4722)* – ('A'-dub version).

MICK JAGGER: She's The Boss

Mar 85. (lp/c/cd) *Columbia; <39940> C.B.S.; (CBS/40/CD 86310)* [13] [6]
– Lonely at the top / Half a loaf / Hard woman / Lucky in love / Secrets / Just another night / She's the boss / Running out of luck / Turn the girl loose. *(<cd re-iss. Aug95 on 'East West'; 7567 82553-2>)*

MICK JAGGER: Lucky In Love / Running Out Of Luck

Apr 85. (7"/12") *Columbia; <04893> C.B.S.; (A/TA 6213)* [38] [ ]

the RUTLES

aka 'THE RUTLES: ALL YOU NEED IS CASH'

1978 (UK/US 70m TV) Warner Bros. Pictures (12)(PG-13)

Film genre: Pop/Rock-music mockumentary/comedy

Top guns: dir: Eric Idle (+ s-w), Gary Weis ← JIMI HENDRIX

Stars: Eric Idle *(Dirk McQuickley / narrator, Stanley J. Krammerhead III, Jr.)* ← SIDE BY SIDE / → SOUTH PARK: BIGGER, LONGER & UNCUT, **Neil Innes** *(Ron Nasty)* ← MAGICAL MYSTERY TOUR / → CONCERT FOR GEORGE, Rikki Fataar *(Stig O'Hara)*, John Halsey *(Barry Womble)*, Michael Palin *(Eric Manchester)* → CONCERT FOR GEORGE, Bianca Jagger *(Martini McQuickly)* ← COCKSUCKER BLUES / → 25X5: THE CONTINUING ADVENTURES OF THE ROLLING STONES, John Belushi *(Ron Decline)* → ANIMAL HOUSE → the BLUES BROTHERS, Dan Aykroyd *(Brian Thigh)* → the BLUES BROTHERS → BLUES BROTHERS 2000, Bill Murray *(Bill Murray the K.)* → WHERE THE BUFFALO ROAM → CADDYSHACK → LITTLE SHOP OF HORRORS → LOST IN TRANSLATION → COFFEE AND CIGARETTES → the LIFE AQUATIC WITH STEVE ZISSOU, Terence Bayler *(Leggy Mountbatten)* ← MACBETH, Henry Woolf *(Arthur Sultan)*, Gilda Radner *(Mrs. Emily Pules)* ← ANIMALYMPICS / → the WOMAN IN RED, **Ron Wood** *(Hells Angel)* ← the LAST WALTZ / → HEARTS OF FIRE, **George Harrison** *(the interviewer)* ← the BEATLES =>, **Ollie Halsall** *(Leppo, 5th Rutle)*, **Mick Jagger** *(himself)* <= the ROLLING STONES =>, **Paul Simon** *(interviewee)* <= SIMON & GARFUNKEL =>, **Roger McGough** *(himself)*

Storyline: "A living legend after all the other living legends have died", the "pre-fab four" of Nasty, Barry, Stig and Dirk appear on Rutland TV for a documentary. From their basement beginnings at the Rat Kellar in Hamburg, we see their triumphs and tragedies as their meteoric career takes off. Finally we find out "what are they doing now" after their last record 'Let It Rot' signalled the end of the megagroup. *JZ*

Movie rating: *8

Visual: video + dvd

Off the record: In 2002, the "fun-fab four" returned to celluloid via the reunion movie, 'THE RUTLES 2: CAN'T BUY ME LUNCH'; featured **Jewel, Bowie, Billy Connolly**, Robin Williams, Carrie Fisher, Tom Hanks, Steve Martin, etc. *MCS*

---

the RUTLES

Mar 78. (lp/c) *Warners; (K/K4 56459) <HS 3151>* [12] [63]
– Hold my hand / Number one / With a girl like you / I must be in

love / Ouch! / Living in hope / Love life / Nevertheless / Good times roll / Doubleback alley / Cheese and onions / Another day / Piggy in the middle / Let's be natural. *<cd; see spinoff releases)*

S/track review: It is a certifiable fact that ERIC IDLE is a comic genius. He can also write a tune or two, just think of 'Always Look On The Bright Side Of Life' from 'The Life Of Brian' or the TV theme tune to 'One Foot In The Grave'. Eric has all the qualities of those great British comedians of old; subtlety, timing, an acute eye for detail and an ability to produce hilarity from even the most mundane sources. All of this is clearly evident on 'The RUTLES' soundtrack. It takes a brave man to attempt to parody the Beatles, such is the reverence in which the Fab Four are held, indeed it may even be a hanging offence in some parts of the globe. Eric is joined by ex-Bonzo Dog Band muso NEIL INNES, JOHN HALSEY and RIKKI FATAAR to complete the line-up. As for the songs, there are some straight alternative-lyrics-over-the-original-tunes, for example 'Twist & Shout' becomes 'Number One', 'All You Need Is Love' is transformed into 'Love Life', 'Help!' is 'Ouch!' and 'I Am The Walrus' morphs into 'Piggy In The Middle'. There are also more intricate parodies with the likes of 'Hold My Hand' which has a title reference to 'I Wanna Hold Your Hand' but musically it's more like 'All My Lovin''. Lyrically, the album has its tongue planted firmly in its cheek with some neat word play, double entendres, innuendo and an effective use of nursery rhymes and working class self-deprecation. Some are just downright side-splitting on first listen while others require a second hearing to catch the joke and, if that's not enough, the sleeve notes must be the funniest ever penned. It is a shame that this kind of intelligent comedy is hard to find nowadays but at least we can sit back and listen to the RUTLES with a kind of warm and fuzzy nostalgic glow, while we piss ourselves laughing. *CM*

Album rating: *7 / re-CD *7.5

– spinoff releases, etc. –

the RUTLES: I Must Be In Love / Cheese And Onions

Mar 78. (7") *(K 17125)* 39 –

the RUTLES: Let's Be Natural / Piggy In The Middle

Jun 78. (7") *(K 17180)* – –

the RUTLES – The Rutles *(w/ added tracks *)*

Jul 90. (cd) *Rhino; <R2 75760>* –
– Goose-step mama (*) / Number one / Baby let me be (*) / Hold my hand / Blue suede Schubert (*) / I must be in love / With a girl like you / Between us (*) / Living in hope / Ouch! / It's looking good (*) / Doubleback alley / Good times roll / Nevertheless / Love life / Piggy in the middle / Another day / Cheese and onions / Get up and go (*) / Let's be natural.

□ S CLUB segment (⇒ SEEING DOUBLE)

S.F.W.

1994 (US 92m) A&M Films / Gramercy Pictures (R)

Film genre: showbiz/media satire/comedy

Top guns: s-w: Jefery Levy (+ dir) ← ROCKULA, Danny Rubin (au: Andrew Wellman)

Stars: Stephen Dorff *(Cliff Spab)* ← BACKBEAT ← JUDGMENT NIGHT ← an AMBUSH OF GHOSTS / → I SHOT ANDY WARHOL, Reese Witherspoon *(Wendy Pfister)* → WALK THE LINE, Jake Busey *(Morrow Streeter)* → OVERNIGHT, Joey Lauren Adams *(Monica Adams)*, Pamela Gidley *(Janet Streeter)* ← PERMANENT RECORD ← DUDES / → CAKE BOY, David Barry Gray *(Scott Spab)* → WHY DO FOOLS FALL IN LOVE, Jack Noseworthy *(Joe Dice)* → EVENT HORIZON → ELVIS, Richard Portnow *(Gerald Parsley)* ← GOOD MORNING, VIETNAM ← ROADIE / → PRIVATE PARTS → FEAR AND LOATHING IN LAS VEGAS → GHOST DOG: THE WAY OF THE SAMURAI, Edward Wiley *(Mr. Spab)*, Lela Ivey *(Mrs. Spab)*, Natasha Gregson Wagner *(Kristen)* → FIRST LOVE, LAST RITES → HIGH FIDELITY, Annie McEnroe *(Dolly)* ← the DOORS ← TRUE STORIES, Tobey Maguire *(Al)* → FEAR AND LOATHING IN LAS VEGAS, Jim True *(David Bailey)* → AFFLICTION, **Babes In Toyland:- Kat Bjelland *, Lori Barbero *, Maureen Herman** *(themselves)* ← 1991: THE YEAR PUNK BROKE * / → NOT BAD FOR A GIRL *

Storyline: Alienated and unshaven, archetypal slacker Cliff Spab can't find the energy to get terrified, or even mildly scared, when he finds himself at the centre of a convenience store hold up. As the crisis is beamed live into America's homes at the request of his captors, Cliff's sardonic disinterest taps a deep vein of unlikely (and unwanted) sympathy. *BG*

Movie rating: *5

Visual: video + dvd

Off the record: Babes In Toyland created quite a stir around the early 90s, the Minneapolis-based all-girl grunge act carving out a UK fanbase resulting in third set, 'Fontanelle' (1992) hitting Top 30 status. *MCS*

Various Artists (score: GRAEME REVELL *)

Sep 94. (cd/c) *A&M; <(540246-2/-4)>*
– Jesus Christ pose (SOUNDGARDEN) / Get your Gunn (MARILYN MANSON) / Can I stay? (PRETTY MARY SUNSHINE) / Teenage whore (HOLE) / Negasonic teenage warhead (MONSTER MAGNET) / Like suicide (acoustic) (CHRIS CORNELL) / No fuck'n problem (SUICIDAL TENDENCIES) / Surrender (PAW) / Creep (RADIOHEAD) / Two at a time (COP SHOOT COP) / Say what you want (BABES IN TOYLAND) / S.F.W. (GWAR) / Spab 'n' Janet evening – Green room (*).

S/track review: As a low-rent spin on the same Gen X/media mirror theme as 'Natural Born Killers', 'S.F.W.' has weathered the years better as an identi-grunge soundtrack than a film, a convenient opportunity for 'A&M' to sell some of the bands they'd inked during the grunge goldrush. Compiling the likes of BABES IN TOYLAND, PRETTY MARY SUNSHINE and HOLE, it's less of a boys' club than the more famous 'SINGLES' from two years earlier, although MONSTER MAGNET, SOUNDGARDEN and the dependably ludicrous GWAR beat their collective chests in time. The hoary behemoth that is MONSTER MAGNET are at their most accessible on 'Negasonic Teenage Warhead', the best title the Ramones never dreamt up. CHRIS CORNELL and COURTNEY LOVE make rival claims to Seattle supremacy with, respectively, 'Jesus Christ Pose' and 'Teenage Whore'; both define their disquiet, with LOVE's heavily accented squall, more than any other voice on this album, burning through the years like crystallised bleach. CORNELL also croons the obligatory grunge-acoustic track, 'Like Suicide', a rare decent example of one of the most mercilessly flogged genres ever invented. Even SUICIDAL TENDENCIES had gone grunge by the mid-90s but the forced attitude of 'No F**k'n Problem' is a long way from genially surreal missives like 'Institutionalised'. GWAR aren't in such deliberately bad taste parted from their messy visuals but the deadpan vocals offer some light relief on the title theme, as does GRAEME REVELL's bravely pleasant (almost Chris Rea-esque) score excerpt. MARILYN MANSON spits the anti-social revenge of grunge but RADIOHEAD – along with funky prog-industrialists COP SHOOT COP – are the exception to the lurid rule here; more than a decade late they're about the only featured band still on the media A-list. *BG*

Album rating: *7

SLC PUNK

1999 (US 97m) Beyond Films / Blue Tulip (R)

Film genre: coming-of-age/buddy comedy drama

Top guns: s-w + dir: James Merendino

Stars: Matthew Lillard *(Stevo)*, Michael A. Goorjian *(Heroin Bob)*, Annabeth Gish *(Trish)*, Jennifer Lien *(Sandy)*, Christopher McDonald *(father)* ← BREAKIN' ← GREASE 2, Devon Sawa *(Sean)*, Summer Phoenix *(Brandy)* ← GIRL / → COMMITTED, Adam Pascal *(Eddie)* → SCHOOL OF ROCK → TEMPTATION → RENT, Til Schweiger *(Mark)*, Jason Segel *(Mike)* → KNOCKED UP, Jimmy Duval *(John the mod)* ← an AMBUSH OF GHOSTS

Storyline: Stevo and Heroin Bob are two anarchic punks who get bored with ordinary life and decide to go on the rampage in Salt Lake City, home of the Mormons. Cue chaos – punks, rednecks, beer, women and violence all explode in the cleanest-living community in the States. But Stevo gets a wake up call when things go bad for Bob and the chance of law school and respectability beckons. *JZ*

Movie rating: *7

Visual: dvd

Off the record: Summer Phoenix is the younger sister of actors River, Joaquin, Rain and Liberty. With her sister Rain on lead vox, she is part of NY alt-rock act, the Paper Cranes, playing keyboards and guitar on a one-off EP. *MCS*

Various Artists (score: Melanie Miller)

Mar 99. (cd) *Hollywood; <1 62178>* ☐ ⊟
– I never promised you a rose garden (the SUICIDE MACHINES) / Sex and violence (the EXPLOITED) / I love livin' in the city (FEAR) / 1969 (the STOOGES) / Too hot (the SPECIALS) / Cretin hop (RAMONES) / Dreaming (BLONDIE) / Kiss me deadly (GENERATION X) / Rock and roll (the VELVET UNDERGROUND) / Gasoline rain (MOONDOGG) / Mirror in the bathroom (FIFI) / Amoeba (ADOLESCENTS) / Kill the poor (DEAD KENNEDYS).

S/track review: Salt Lake City, Utah, doesn't readily spring to mind when thinking of global punk hotspots and it is therefore understandible that none of the artists on the soundtrack call it home, preferring the likes of New York, Los Angeles, Detroit, London, Edinburgh and even Coventry. Beginning with the SUICIDE MACHINES sublime, ska infused punk cover of the Lynn Anderson country hit, 'I Never Promised You A Rose Garden', 'SLC PUNK' rarely lets up, as you might expect. FEAR provide a dose of dumb, 100mph punk that lacks the charm of the RAMONES, who appear with 'Cretin Hop', a proper pogo-ing tune. The STOOGES' '1969' is of course, class, as is 'Rock'n'Roll' by the VELVET UNDERGROUND, while 'Kiss Me Deadly' is almost a ballad and about as poignant as GENERATION X ever got. The DEAD KENNEDYS brand of speed punk and the SPECIALS rootsy, Two-Tone reggae continue the credibility drive with 'Kill The Poor' and 'Too Hot' respectively. However the EXPLOITED's refrain of 'Sex And Violence' is just downright irritating and 'Dreaming' is far from BLONDIE's best. The inclusion of MOONDOGG's 'Gasoline Rain' is a strange one. The drum and base-led piece of atmospheric electro is reminiscent of 'Mezzanine'-era Massive Attack or Everything But The Girl, just nowhere near as good, and is out of place in this particular line-up. Apart from the opening track, 'SLC PUNK' doesn't throw up any surprises and the best tracks can be bought elsewhere, where they are in better company. *CM*

Album rating: *6

☐ Paul SABU segment
(⇒ HARD ROCK ZOMBIES)

SALSA

1988 (US 100m) Golan-Globus / Cannon Films (PG)

Film genre: urban Pop/Dance Musical drama

Top guns: s-w: Boaz Davidson (+ dir + story), Tomas Benitez, Shepard Goldman

Stars: **Robi Rosa** *(Rico)*, Rodney Harvey *(Ken)*, Magali Alvarado *(Rita)*, Miranda Garrison *(Luna)* ← DIRTY DANCING ← XANADU / → the FORBIDDEN DANCE, Moon Orona *(Lola)*, **Tito Puente** *(himself)*, Angela Alvarado *(Vicki)*, **Chain Reaction** *(themselves)*, **Grupo Niche** *(themselves)*, **Celia Cruz** *(herself)*, **Willie Colon** *(himself)*, **Michael Sembello** *(himself)*, **Ramon "Mongo" Santamaria** *(himself)*, **H. Wilkins** *(himself)*, **Mavis Vegas Davis** *(herself)*, **Kenny Ortega** *(himself)*, **Marisela Esqueda** *(herself)*, Leroy Anderson *(himself)*, **Bobby Caldwell** *(himself)*, **Edwin Hawkins Singers** *(themselves)*, **Dimencion** *(themselves)*

Storyline: Rico is determined to be the King of Salsa at the forthcoming contest at La Luna. Not really understanding the concept of modesty, he struts around the dance floor surrounded by a bevy of bimbos, alienating his family and friends by the minute with his arrogant attitude. Soon the only person he'll dance with is club owner Luna, who has the misfortune of being old and nasty. When the unstoppable dance force meets the immovable dance object, what unique thing will occur? *JZ*

Movie rating: *3.5

Visual: video

Off the record: (see below)

Various Artists (composers: Various)

Jun 88. (lp/c/cd) *M.C.A.; <(IMCA/+C/D 6232)>* ☐ Aug88 ☐
– Margarita (WILKINS) / Chicos y chicas (MAVIS VEGAS DAVIS) / Cali pachanguero (GRUPO NICHE) / Your love (LAURA

BRANIGAN) / Good lovin' (KENNY ORTEGA) / Under my skin (ROBI ROSA) / Oye como va (give it all you got) (TITO PUENTE) / I know (MARISELA) / Spanish Harlem (BEN E. KING) / Puerto Rico (BOBBY CALDWELL).

S/track review: If your bag is 'SALSA' then this dance soundtrack will blow your mind. While most non "salsa" afficionados will have discovered R&B/pop artists such as BEN E. KING ('Stand By Me', etc.) and LAURA BRANIGAN (remember 'Gloria'), the likes of KENNY ORTEGA, ROBI ROSA and TITO PUENTE might've eluded you somewhat. The legendary BEN E is in great form with his standard classic, 'Spanish Harlem', while the sadly-missed BRANIGAN (she died of a brain aneurysm on 26th of August 2004) has her moments via 'Your Love'. The aforementioned ORTEGA (here with 'Good Lovin'') had a number of film choreography credits to his name, including 'XANADU', 'ONE FROM THE HEART', 'PRETTY IN PINK' and 'DIRTY DANCING', before he turned his hand to screenwriting and directing. TITO PUENTE was a Latin jazz legend who was responsible for one of the salsa genre's greatest hits (featured here), 'Oye Como Va', a track covered by Santana; sadly, he too died aged 77 on 31st May 2000. Colombian ensemble GRUPO NICHE had been brewing up a tropical storm from their inception in the early 80s, one of their best-known numbers 'Cali Pachanguero' is another 'SALSA' highlight. Latin music's answer to Madonna, MARISELA, was another to shine out via 'I Know', while the soundtrack's best cue is undoubtably 'Under My Skin' by NY-born, Puerto Rican-raised ROBI ROSA. *MCS*

Album rating: *7

□ Tommy SANDS segment
(⇒ SING BOY SING)

SATISFACTION

1988 (US 92m) 20th Century Fox / NBC (PG-13)

Film genre: romantic Pop-Rock Musical comedy/drama

Top guns: dir: Joan Freeman / s-w: Charles Purpura

Stars: Justine Bateman *(Jennie Lee)*, Liam Neeson *(Martin Falcon)*, Julia Roberts *(Daryle Shane)* → BAJA OKLAHOMA, Trini Alvarado *(May "Mooch" Stark)* ← TIMES SQUARE, Scott Coffey *(Nickie Longo)* → SHAG: THE MOVIE → SHOUT → WAYNE'S WORLD 2, **Britta Phillips** *(Billy Swan)*, **Deborah Harry** *(Tina)* <= BLONDIE =>, Michael DeLorenzo *(Bunny Slotz)* ← FAST FORWARD ← FAME, **Steve Cropper** *(Sal)* ← the BLUES BROTHERS / → BLUES BROTHERS 2000

Storyline: The Mystery are an up and coming rock band consisting of three young women and a guy, all keen about performing at a resort in the summer. However, slight complications beset the quartet when they have to share a room together, while lead girl, Jennie, falls head over heels with the bar owner. Debutant actress, Julia Roberts, subsequently found fame and fortune away from rock'n'role-playing. *MCS*

Movie rating: *3.5

Visual: video + dvd (no audio OST by Michel Colombier)

Off the record: **Britta Phillips** had been a singing voice of Jem in the mid-80s cartoon series of the same name. She subsequently took her own group, shoegazers the Belltower from New York to London, releasing a solitary album, 'Popdropper' (1992), before partnering ex-Galaxie 500 man, Dean Wareham in indie supergroup, Luna. Now retired from mid-00s, the pair have scored two major movies, 'The Squid And The Whale' (2005) and 'Just Like The Son' (2006). **Steve Cropper** was one of the men behind Booker T & the MG's, while Beau Charles (ex-Knickerbockers) wrote the song, 'Lies', for covers act JUSTINE BATEMAN & THE MYSTERY; other songs 'Mystery Dance', 'C'mon Everybody', 'Satisfaction', 'Talk To Me', 'Knock On Wood', 'Mr. Big Stuff' and 'Iko, Iko' – JOHN KAY & STEPPENWOLF contributed 'Rock And Roll Rebels'. *MCS*

SATURDAY NIGHT FEVER

1977 (US 119m) RSO / Paramount Pictures (R)

Film genre: urban Pop/Dance-music drama

Top guns: dir: John Badham / s-w: Norman Wexler ← JOE / → STAYING ALIVE (story: Nik Cohn → STAYING ALIVE)

Stars: John Travolta *(Tony Manero)* → GREASE → URBAN COWBOY → STAYING ALIVE → SHOUT → PULP FICTION → PRIMARY COLORS → SWORDFISH → BE COOL → HAIRSPRAY re-make, Karen Lynn Gorney *(Stephanie)*, Barry Miller *(Bobby C.)* → FAME → the LAST TEMPTATION OF CHRIST, Paul Pape *(Double J.)*, Joseph Cali *(Joey)*, Donna Pescow *(Annette)*, Bruce Ornstein *(Gus)*, Julie Bovasso *(Flo Manero)* → STAYING ALIVE, Denny Dillon *(Doreen)*, Fran Drescher *(Connie)* → AMERICAN HOT WAX → THIS IS SPINAL TAP → ROCK'N'ROLL MOM → UHF, Sam J. Coppola *(Fusco)*, Val Bisoglio *(Frank Manero Sr.)*, William Andrews *(detective)*, Murray Moston *(haberdashery salesman)* ← THAT'S THE WAY OF THE WORLD

Storyline: Saturday nights would never be quite the same again after John Travolta donned that white suit and cut some wildly impressive rug. By day, Tony Manero is the paint shop sales peasant with no prospects; by night, he's the lord of the disco dancefloor, busting those famous moves with his lady Stephanie. There's more to it than that of course, but it was Travolta's dance routines – together with the Bee Gees' soundtrack – which inspired a generation and raked in multi- millions at the box office. *BG*

Movie rating: *9.5

Visual: video + dvd

Off the record: Prior to his 'SNF' success, John Travolta had a few flop singles including 'Let Her In', 'Whenever I'm Away From You', 'All Strung Out' & 'Slow Dancing (Feels So Good)'. *MCS*

—

the BEE GEES (composers) (& Various Artists)

Nov 77. (d-lp)(d-c) *R.S.O.; <4001> (2658 123)(3517 014) <4001>* [1] Mar78 [1]
– Stayin' alive / How deep is your love / Night fever / More than a woman / If I can't have you (YVONNE ELLIMAN) / A fifth of Beethoven (WALTER MURPHY) / More than a woman (the TAVARES) / Manhattan skyline (DAVID SHIRE) / Calypso breakdown (RALPH MacDONALD) / If I can't have you (YVONNE ELLIMAN) / Night on disco mountain (DAVID SHIRE) / Open sesame (KOOL & THE GANG) / Jive talkin' / You should be dancing / Boogie shoes (K.C. & THE SUNSHINE BAND) / Salsation (DAVID SHIRE) / K-Jee (M.F.S.B.) / Disco inferno (the TRAMMPS). *(d-cd-iss. Nov83; 800068-2) (d-lp re-iss. Jan84; SPDLP 5) (d-cd re-iss. Oct95; 825389-2)*

S/track review: The biggest-selling soundtrack of all time and one which nominated the BEE GEES and Robert Stigwood (their manager, the financial muscle behind the film and the one who originally persuaded them to contribute) as having come closest to capturing that oft cited and much abused cultural phenomenon known as the Zeitgeist. They certainly captured something: having already laid the bass-popping, falsetto harmonising foundations with albums such as 'Main Course' (1975) and 'Children of the World' (1976), the BEE GEES tapped into a latent mania for something which, at the time, was the exclusive preserve of inner-city black, Hispanic and gay communities. That something was disco, and through ageless songs like 'Stayin' Alive', 'More Than A Woman' and 'Night Fever', the BEE GEES popularised and commercialised it, taking it overground and into the suburbs. Blessed with both an irresistible dancefloor pulse and a charming naivety, these songs – together with the previously released 'Jive Talkin'' and ballads like 'How Deep Is Your Love' and the

YVONNE ELLIMAN-sung 'If I Can't Have You' – defined an era and catapulted the band into the superstar bracket. Throw in the TRAMMPS' 'Disco Inferno' and funky classics by the likes of KOOL & THE GANG and MFSB, and you have a double-set which still sounds fresh almost thirty years on. *BG*

Album rating: *9

– spinoff hits, etc. –

the BEE GEES: How Deep Is Your Love
Sep 77. (7") *<882> (2090 259)* 1 Oct77 3

the TAVARES: More Than A Woman
Nov 77. (7") *Capitol; <4500> (CL 15977)* 32 Apr78 7

the BEE GEES: Stayin' Alive / YVONNE ELLIMAN: If I Can't Have You
Dec 77. (7") *<885> (2090 267)* 1 Jan78 4

K.C. & THE SUNSHINE BAND: Boogie Shoes
Jan 78. (7") *T.K.; <1025> (TKR 6025)* 35 Apr78 34

the BEE GEES: Night Fever
Jan 78. (7") *<889> (2090 272)* 1 Apr78 1

the TRAMMPS: Disco Inferno
Feb 78. (7") *Atlantic; <3389> (K 11135)* 11 Jun78 47

SATURDAY NIGHT SPECIAL

1994 (US 86m) Concorde – New Horizons (R)

Film genre: Country-music erotica – eh!

Top guns: s-w + dir: Dan Golden

Stars: Billy Burnette *(Travis)*, Maria Ford *(Darlene)*, Rick Dean *(T.J.)*, Duane Whitaker *(Reno)* ← EDDIE PRESLEY / → PULP FICTION → the DEVIL'S REJECTS, William Edwards *(Tommy)* ← EDDIE PRESLEY, band members:- **Dwight Twilley, Rocky Burnette, Carla Olsen**, Billy Woo & Peter Smith

Storyline: Wandering C&W minstrel Travis finds his luck doubly in when redneck proprietor TJ offers him a job in his bar and then introduces his voluptuous wife Darlene. Soon it's apparent to all and sundry (except TJ) that Travis and Darlene have the hots for each other but boring old TJ stands in the way. The sheriff too begins taking an interest when an ex-con friend of Travis' turns up at the diner and it looks as if one way or another TJ's days are numbered. *JZ*

Movie rating: *3.5

Visual: video + dvd (no audio OST; score: Nicolas Rivera)

Off the record: Billy Burnette joined the ranks of Fleetwood Mac for 'Tango In The Night' in 1987; he's in other films, 'Not Like Us' (1995) and 'Carnosaur 3: Primal Species' (1996). Billy's cousin, **Rocky Burnette**, was among a handful of new country stars present here including **Dwight Twilley** & **Carla Olsen.** *MCS*

the SAVAGE SEVEN

1968 (US 96m) American International Pictures (R)

Film genre: biker movie/drama

Top guns: dir: Richard Rush ← PSYCH-OUT / s-w: Michael Fisher (au: Rosalind Ross)

Stars: Robert Walker *(Johnnie)* → EASY RIDER, Larry Bishop *(Joint)* ← WILD IN THE STREETS, Joanna Frank *(Marcia)*, John Garwood *(Stud)* → CLEOPATRA JONES, Adam Roarke *(Kisum)* ← PSYCH-OUT, Max Julien *(Grey Wolf)* ← PSYCH-OUT / → UP TIGHT! → the MACK, Richard Anders *(Bull)*, Mel Berger *(Fillmore)*, Billy Green Bush *(Seely)* → ELECTRA GLIDE IN BLUE → MACKINTOSH & T.J., **Duane Eddy** *(Eddie)*, Fabian Gregory *(Tommy)*, Beach Dickerson *(Bruno)* ← the TRIP ← G.I. BLUES ← LOVING YOU ← ROCK ALL NIGHT, Penny Marshall *(Tina)* → JACKIE'S BACK!

Storyline: Knuckle-scraping, proto-'Easy Rider' fare as rival biker gangs fight a turf war on an Indian reservation with twangmeister Duane Eddy taking a starring role. *BG*

Movie rating: *5

Visual: video

Off the record: Duane Eddy (b.26 Apr'38, Corning, New York) was just a little bit out of place here, his heyday way back in the late 50s/early 60s via a plethora of classic "twangy" instrumental hits including 'Rebel-Rouser', 'Cannonball', 'Forty Miles Of Bad Road', 'Because They're Young', 'Peter Gunn' & '"Pepe"'. *MCS*

Various Artists (composer/arranger: Jerry Styner *)

May 68. (lp) *Atco; <SD33-245>* –
– Anyone for tennis (theme from The Savage Seven) (CREAM) / Desert ride (*) / Maria's theme (vocal) (BARBARA KELLY & THE MORNING GOOD) / Shacktown revenge (*) / The medal (*) / Here comes the fuzz (*) / Iron Butterfly theme (IRON BUTTERFLY) / Unconscious power (IRON BUTTERFLY) / Everyone should own a dream (*) / The deal (*) / Desert love (*) / Ballad of The Savage Seven (BARBARA KELLY & THE MORNING GOOD) / Maria's theme (instrumental) (*) / The savage struggle (*).

S/track review: No Blue Cheer but plenty of greasy, surprisingly heavy psychedelic rock from IRON BUTTERFLY, notably their eponymous 'Iron Butterfly Theme' (a B-side to their shortened version of 'In-A-Gadda-Da-Vida'). Just about to blast onto the scene via the magnum opus of the aforementioned 17-minute title track, Doug Ingle and Co fire all of their guns via further number, 'Unconscious Power' (from their debut 'Heavy' album). Brit blues-rock giants CREAM (CLAPTON, Bruce & Baker) make a rare soundtrack appearance with their laid-back UK Top 40 hit, 'Anyone For Tennis' (the theme from the movie). BARBARA KELLY & THE MORNING GOOD (one thinks this was the BARBARA that featured on the OST to 'The WILD ANGELS') also fitted in two cues, 'Maria's Theme' (the vocal version) and the Brill-Building-esque 'Ballad Of The Savage Seven'. Composer, JERRY STYNER, fills out the remainder of the album with orchestral/band arrangements of 'Desert Ride', 'Shacktown Revenge' (a sprightly instrumental), 'The Medal' & 'Here Comes The Fuzz' (both the latter short'n'sweet). Ditto for side two efforts from 'Everyone Should Own A Dream' to 'The Savage Struggle'. Mike Curb would further his career by forming Congregation (had a hit with 'Softly Whispering I Love You') and becoming a fully-fledged Conservative. *MCS*

Album rating: *4

SAVE THE LAST DANCE

2001 (US 112m) Paramount Pictures (PG-13)

Film genre: romantic teen/Dance Musical drama

Top guns: dir: Thomas Carter / s-w: Duane Adler (+ story) → the WAY SHE MOVES → STEP UP, Cheryl Edwards

Stars: Julia Stiles *(Sara Johnson)* → a LITTLE TRIP TO HEAVEN, Sean Patrick Thomas *(Derek Reynolds)*, Kerry Washington *(Chenille Reynolds)* → RAY, **Fredro Starr** *(Malakai)* ← BLACK AND WHITE ← RIDE, Terry Kinney *(Roy Johnson)*, Bianca Lawson *(Nikki)* ← the TEMPTATIONS ← PRIMARY COLORS / → BONES, Vince Green *(Snookie)*, Garland Whitt *(Kenny)*, Elisabeth Oas *(Diggy)*

Storyline: After the death of her mother, Sara Johnson moves in with her father in a downtown ghetto apartment in Chicago. She finds trouble adjusting to her new life (she's the only white person in class) until she befriends Chenille and her brother Derek. Derek is a talented dancer like Sara but is still involved in the gang culture of the area. Can Sara change Derek's ways and will she finally be accepted by the community? *JZ*

Movie rating: *6

Visual: dvd

Off the record: Fredro Starr is a member of hip hop outfit, Onyx.

—

Various Artists (score: Mark Isham)

Dec 00. (cd/c) *Hollywood; <0927-42431-2/-4> (01254-2/-4 HWR)* 3 Apr01 5
– Shining through (theme from "Save The Last Dance") (FREDRO STARR & JILL SCOTT) / You (LUCY PEARL feat. SNOOP DOGG & Q-TIP) / Bonafide (X-2-C) / Crazy (K-CI & JOJO) / You make me sick (PINK) / U know what's up (DONELL JONES) / Move it slow (KEVON EDMONDS) / Murder she wrote (CHAKA DEMUS & PLIERS) / You can do it (ICE CUBE feat. MACK 10 & MS. TOI) / My window (SOULBONE) / Only you (112 feat. the NOTORIOUS B.I.G.) / Get it on tonite (MONTELL JORDAN) / All or nothing (ATHENA CAGE).

S/track review: Lifting the hook from Cyndi Lauper's 'True Colors', 'Shining Through' – the theme from this teen-focused fusion of 'DIRTY DANCING' and 'Romeo & Juliet' – sets its stall out early, confirming a melding of accessible R&B soul pop with hip hop big hitters. And there is no shortage of the latter, it would seem, with the NOTORIOUS B.I.G., ICE CUBE, Q-TIP and SNOOP DOGG all on hand to toss in a verse. Elsewhere, R&B crooners K-CI & JOJO unearthed a not completely unpleasant weird heavy metal ballad to assault, with their vocodered vocal warbles, while PINK rhymes "you make me sick" with "candle stick" on her woeful contribution. Thank God then for the likes of DONELL JONES who out-Luthers Mr Vandross with a silky seduction theme 'U Know What's Up'. In joyful contrast, Jamaica's mighty CHAKA DEMUS & PLIERS bust the whole case open with gently suggestive sway of 'Murder She Wrote'; Angela Lansbury never sounded so frisky. The song may sound incongruous in this US-centric mix, but shows just how less can definitely mean more. A painfully scant verse from the NOTORIOUS B.I.G. on 112's 'Only You' also serves to remind us what we're missing here, more lyrical innovation. Even the normally reliable MONTELL JORDAN phones in more of his signature smooth-talking funk. The finest moment here, however, remains ICE CUBE's interminably funky 'You Can Do It', a certified hip hop classic, and about dancing, sort of. How appropriate. *MR*

Album rating: *6.5 / More . . . *5

– spinoff hits, etc. –

PINK: You Make Me Sick (mixes)

Jan 01. (c-s/cd-s/12") *LaFace-Arista; <24556> (74321 82870-4/-2/-1)* 9 33

Various Artists: More music from the motion picture . . .

May 01. (cd) *<162323> (012998-2 HWR)* Jul01
– Da rockwilder (METHOD MAN & REDMAN) / Let's get crunk (SHAWTY REDD) / So special (WORLD BEATERS) / Hate the playaz (AUDREY MARTELLS) / Dance floor (TA-GANA) / I can tell (JESSE POWELL) / When it doesn't matter (ANGELA AMMONS) / Do things (SY SMITH) / Where ya at (FAT MAN SCOOP) / Bust off (MEDINA GREEN) / You don't really want some (BLAQOUT) / Bounce (JR YOUNG) / In for cream (BLAQOUT).

K-CI & JOJO: Crazy

Jun 01. (cd-s) *Universal; <155805> M.C.A.; (MCSTD 40253)* 11 Apr01 35

SAVE THE LAST DANCE 2

2006 (US 90m) MTV Studios / Paramount Home (PG-13)

Film genre: romantic teen/Dance Musical drama

Top guns: dir: David Petrarca / s-w: Kwame Nyanning

Stars: Izabella Miko *(Sara Johnson)* ← BYE BYE BLACKBIRD ← COYOTE UGLY, Columbus Short *(Miles Sultana)* ← YOU GOT SERVED / → STOMP THE YARD, Jacqueline Bisset *(Monique Delacroix)* ← AMO NON AMO, Maria Brooks *(Katrina)*, **Ne-Yo** *(himself)*, Aubrey Dollar *(Zoe)*, Ian Brennan *(Franz)*, Tracey 'Tre' Armstrong *(Candy)* ← HONEY / → HOW SHE MOVE, Matthew Watling *(Marcus)*, Robert Allan *(Paul)*

Storyline: Sara Johnson is an up-and-coming ballet student at the famous Juilliard dance school. Life there isn't easy and she finds herself well down the pecking order with the other students and her tetchy tutor Miss Delacroix. It's only when she meets guest lecturer, Miles, who introduces her to hip-hop dance, that she starts enjoying herself and can see an alternative future to the relentless hard work of ballet lessons. *JZ*

Movie rating: *4

Visual: dvd

Off the record: Ne-Yo (b. Shaffer Smith, 18 Oct'82, Camden, Arkansas; raised in Las Vegas) was initially an R&B songwriter, mainly for Youngstown, Mario and Cassidy. In early 2006, on the strength of his No.1 single, 'So Sick', his first "official" long-player also scaled the US charts. He subsequently went on to guest on sets by Ghostface Killah ('Fishscale') and Remy Ma ('There's Something About Remy'). *MCS*

—

Various Artists

Nov 06. (cd) *Mass Appeal; <MAE-0004>* –
– Dance floor (T-PAIN feat. PITBULL) / Clap for that (NOEL feat. GHOSTFACE KILLAH) / Watch you dance (NE-YO) / Just my thang (RYAN TOBY) / The hotness (RIHANNA feat. SHONTELLE) / Dance alone (DEBRECA) / It's on you (JOE) / You and me (CANDACE JONES) / All I need (JALEN) / Kiss me (CASSIE) / Feel beautiful (RUBEN STUDDARD) / Escape (JAIDEN) / Bridging the gap (BOXIE).

S/track review: How you can have a last dance for a second time, we're not exactly sure, but semantics aside, this sequel arrived six years on, and the smooth 90s funk of the first film's soundtrack has been unceremoniously shunted aside in favour of more economic, near-the-knuckle sounds, heavily influenced by southern hip hop's raspy minimalism. The flirtatious innocence of the first movie soundtrack has also been replaced with an aggressive, heavily sexualised undertone that kind of undermines the whole notion of assertive young females within the film. RIHANNA's sublime wink-and-a-nod 'The Hotness' is a product of such backward thinking. Damn good tune though. As if we didn't realise subtlety was not a concern already, NOEL & GHOSTFACE KILLAH's unashamed tribute to ladies' wobbly posteriors is both unsettling and hilarious. "It must be jelly/'cos cake don't shake like that" might not be something Germaine Greer will be printing up on a T-shirt anytime soon, but it disturbs, mainly because GHOSTFACE remains one of the finest living MCs who can bring a sheen to even the most shallow of material. The rest are left foundering though. NE-YO does his best with what was clearly a sub-standard Justin Timberlake cast-off in 'Watch You Dance', while RYAN TOBY brings a more lively prospect to the table with 'Just My Thang', a pop take on the Mayfield/Wonder/Gaye soul blueprint. Similarly, DEBRECA's Latin-tinged story of pop empowerment is understated and sophisticated. While momentarily catchy, this is a truly patchy, unfocused collection. *MR*

Album rating: *5.5

SCENES FROM THE GOLDMINE

1987 (US 99m) Hemdale Film Corporation (R)

Film genre: Rock-music drama

Top guns: s-w: (+ dir) Marc Rocco, Danny Eisenberg, John Norvet

Stars: Catherine Mary Stewart *(Debi DiAngelo)* ← the APPLE / → DUDES, Cameron Dye *(Niles Dresden)* ← BODY ROCK, Steve Railsback *(Harry Spiros)* → the DEVIL'S REJECTS, Jewel Shepard *(Dana)* ← the RETURN OF THE LIVING DEAD, Joe Pantoliano *(Manny)* ← EDDIE AND THE CRUISERS ← RISKY BUSINESS ← the IDOLMAKER / → LA BAMBA → ROCK'N'ROLL MOM → the IN CROWD → BLACK AND WHITE, **John Ford Coley** *(Kenny Bond)*, **Timothy B. Schmit** *(Dennis)* → NASHVILLE SOUNDS, Alex Rocco *(Nathan DiAngelo)* ← VOICES ← THREE THE HARD WAY / → THAT THING YOU DO!, Pamela Springsteen *(Stephanie)*, **Lee VING** *(Ian Weymouth)*, Lesley-Anne Down *(herself)* ← ALL THE RIGHT NOISES, **Nick Gilder**

Storyline: A love affair strikes up between an up and coming songwriter and the leader of an L.A. rock band. Tagged, "She let him steal her heart. But no one was going to mess with her music", just about says it all. *MCS*

Movie rating: *3.5

Visual: Transvideo (Brazil)

Off the record: **Timothy B. Schmidt** was a member of Poco before becoming a rock legend with Eagles. In similar country-rock style was the man **John Ford Coley**, one half of a singing-songwriter duo alongside England Dan; 'I Really Want To See You Tonight' was their first and biggest hit, reaching No.2 in summer 1976. London-born/Canadian-raised **Nick Gilder** had a US chart-topper in 1978 with 'Hot Child In The City'. **Lee Ving** was a member of hardcore punk outfit, the Fear. Also of note:- Cameron Dye wrote and performed some of the songs for the movie – one metal track I recognised was Precious Metal's 'Twist And Shout'. Pamela Springsteen is the younger sister of "The Boss" Bruce. *MCS*

□ Zander SCHLOSS
(⇒ CIRCLE JERKS)

SCHOOL DAZE

1988 (US 121m) Forty Acres and a Mule / Columbia Pictures (R)

Film genre: political R&B/Pop Musical comedy

Top guns: s-w + dir: Spike Lee as below + → HE GOT GAME

Stars: Laurence Fishburne *(Vaughn "Dap" Dunlap)* ← DEATH WISH II ← FAST BREAK ← CORNBREAD, EARL AND ME / → WHAT'S LOVE GOT TO DO WITH IT → EVENT HORIZON → the SOUL OF A MAN, Giancarlo Esposito *(Julian "Big Brother Almighty" Eaves)* ← MAXIMUM OVERDRIVE / → NIGHT ON EARTH → KLA$H → FEEL THE NOISE, Tisha Campbell *(Jane Toussaint)* ← LITTLE SHOP OF HORRORS / → HOUSE PARTY → HOUSE PARTY 2 → HOUSE PARTY 3, Spike Lee *(Half-Pint)* → JUNGLE FEVER → CROOKLYN → GIRL 6, Kyme *(Rachel Meadows)*, Joe Seneca *(President McPherson)* ← CROSSROADS, Ellen Holly *(Odrie McPherson)*, Art Evans *(Cedar Cloud)* ← YOUNGBLOOD ← BIG TIME ← LEADBELLY ← CLAUDINE / → TRESPASS → CB4: THE MOVIE → the STORY OF US, Ossie Davis *(Coach Odom)* ← COUNTDOWN AT KUSINI ← LET'S DO IT AGAIN / → JUNGLE FEVER → BUBBA HO-TEP, Bill Nunn *(Grady)* → HE GOT GAME → IDLEWILD, **Branford MARSALIS** *(Jordam)*, Joie Lee *(Lizzie Life)* → CROOKLYN → GIRL 6 → COFFEE AND CIGARETTES, Cinque Lee *(Buckwheat)* → MYSTERY TRAIN → COFFEE AND CIGARETTES, Samuel L. Jackson *(Leeds)* ← MAGIC STICKS / → JUNGLE FEVER → JUICE → PULP FICTION → JACKIE BROWN → KILL BILL: VOL.1 → KILL BILL: VOL.2 → BLACK SNAKE MOAN, Eric A. Payne *(Booker T.)*, Leonard L. Thomas *(Big Brother Gen. George Patton)* → GIRL 6, Jasmine Guy *(Dina)* → KLA$H → TUPAC: RESURRECTION, Tyra Ferrell *(Tasha)* → TAPEHEADS → JUNGLE FEVER, Kirk Taylor *(Sir Nose)*, Roger Smith *(Yoda)* → HE GOT GAME, Adrienne-Joi Johnson *(Cecilia)* → HOUSE PARTY, Laurnea Wilkerson *(Laurnea)* → SING, Rusty Cundieff *(Big Brother Chucky)* → FEAR OF A BLACK HAT, Kadeem Hardison *(Edge)* ← RAPPIN', Kasi Lemmons *(Perry)* → the FIVE HEARTBEATS → FEAR OF A BLACK HAT, James Bond III *(Monroe)*

Storyline: Dap and Half-Pint are cousins studying at a mainly black university in America's South. While Dap is a political animal, young Half-Pint just wants to be accepted as one of the boys. Meanwhile, the girls on campus are divided according to skin colour and hairstyle into the Wannabes and the Jigaboos. They have a permanent hate-hate relationship. At last Half-Pint has a chance to play with the big boys – but only after undergoing an unusual initiation ceremony. *JZ*

Movie rating: *5.5

Visual: video + dvd

Off the record: nothing

Various Artists (composer/producer: Bill Lee *)

Mar 88. (cd)(c/lp) *EMI-Manhattan; <(72438-19970-2)>(TC+/ MTL 1031)* **81** Jul88 □

– Da'butt (E.U.) / Perfect match (TECH AND THE EFFX) / Be alone tonight (the RAYS) / Straight and nappy (JIGABOOS & WANNABEES CHORUS – lead vocals by KYME & TISHA CAMPBELL) * / One little acorn (KENNY BARRON and TERENCE BLANCHARD) * / I'm building me a home (the MOREHOUSE COLLEGE GLEE CLUB – soloist: TRACY COLEY) / I can only be me (KEITH JOHN) / One little acorn – piano solo (KENNY BARRON) * / Be one (PHYLLIS HYMAN) * / Wake up suite (the NATURAL SPIRITUAL ORCHESTRA) * / We've already said goodbye (before we said hello) (PIECES OF A DREAM – lead vocals by PORTIA GRIFFIN – tenor saxophone solo by BRANFORD MARSALIS).

S/track review: Spike Lee knows getting an education should be a whole rainbow of experience. This wildly eclectic soundtrack attempts to reflect that and in doing so reveals everything from the sublime to the ridiculous. EU's 'Da'butt' kicks things off with a chunky Cameo-style groove of pop funk, segueing into TECH AND THE EFFX's 'Perfect Match' a surreal soul poem about potential suitors intoned by a posh English woman! Before you've had a chance to recover from this slightly creepy outing, some sub-Billy Ocean Caribbean pop comes your way, followed hastily by a fun, if cheesy 30s jive pastiche. This battery is quite a beginning, especially when followed with some plaintive, touching trumpet and piano balladry courtesy of TERENCE BLANCHARD and KENNY BARRON which adds a tad of gravitas to the proceedings. Throw in some creditable southern spirituals from the NATURAL SPIRITUAL ORCHESTRA and top it off with PHYLLIS HYMANS' immense and powerful 'No One' to complete this already stuffed programme. Lee runs the gamut of musical styles here but except for a few occasions, he struggles to find a truly satisfying hunk of anything one thing. 'SCHOOL DAZE' is also like real time in formal education in that it's untidy and unpredictable, and while you know you'll get something out of it, just not always what you expect. *MR*

Album rating: *6

– spinoff hits, etc. –

E.U.: Da'butt / (dub version)

Apr 88. (7"/12") *<50115> (MT/12MT 43)* **35** May88 □

SCHOOL OF ROCK

2003 (US/Ger 108m) New Century / Paramount Pictures (PG-13)

Film genre: Hard Rock-music teen comedy

Top guns: dir: Richard Linklater ← SUBURBI@ / s-w: Mike White

Stars: Jack Black *(Dewey Finn)* ← HIGH FIDELITY ← DEAD MAN WALKING / → the PICK OF DESTINY → WALK HARD: THE DEWEY

COX STORY, Joan Cusack *(Rosalie Mullins)* ← HIGH FIDELITY ← WORKING GIRL, Mike White *(Ned Schneebly)*, Sarah Silverman *(Patty Di Marco)* → RENT, Miranda Cosgrove *(Summer Hathaway)*, Joey Gaydes Jr. *(Zach Mooneyham)*, Jordan-Claire Green *(Michelle)*, Veronica Afflerbach *(Eleni)*, Robert Tsai *(Lawrence)*, Angelo Massagli *(Frankie)*, Adam Pascal *(Theo)* ← SLC PUNK! / → TEMPTATION → RENT, Kevin Clark *(Freddy Jones)*, Nicky Katt *(Razor)* ← SUBURBI@ ← STRANGE DAYS, Suzzanne Douglass *(Tomika's mother)*

Storyline: Dewey Finn is the archetypal "heavy" metal wannabe lead guitarist who, after being sacked by his band for self-indulgent solos and embarrassing stage-diving, steals his roommates job – as a supply teacher at an upper class pre-teen school. Bored, but still with the enthusiasm to win the annual Battle-Of-The-Bands competition (his old group always compete in), he devises a plan to teach his fresh-faced pupils lessons on how to become his ROCK protogees. But only if he/they keep an eye out for suspicious headmistress, Principal Mullins. *MCS*

Movie rating: *9

Visual: dvd

Off the record: Jack Black is of course, the man behind legends of their lunchtime, Tenacious D, doing the rounds as we speak, in the movie, 'The PICK OF DESTINY'. *MCS*

—

Various Artists (score: Craig Wedren)

Sep 03. (cd) *Atlantic; <(7567 83694-2)>* [95] Oct03 [ ]
– School of rock (SCHOOL OF ROCK) / Your head and your mind and your brain . . . – dialogue / Substitute (the WHO) / Fight (NO VACANCY) / Touch me (the DOORS) / I pledge allegiance to the band . . . – dialogue / Sunshine of your love (CREAM) / Immigrant song (LED ZEPPELIN) / Set you free (BLACK KEYS) / Edge of seventeen (STEVIE NICKS) / Heal me, I'm heartsick (NO VACANCY) / Growing on me (the DARKNESS) / Ballrooms of Mars (T. REX) / Those who can do . . . – dialogue / My brain is hanging upside down (Bonzo goes to Bitburg) (RAMONES) / T.V. eye (WYLDE RATTTZ) / It's a long way to the top (SCHOOL OF ROCK).

S/track review: With JACK BLACK virtually stealing the show courtesy of his manic (Tenacious D-like) performances in the movie, it's no surprise the album leads off with the infectious title track by his wee act, SCHOOL OF ROCK. JACK's other contributions, 'Fight' by NO VACANCY (his former band in the movie) and the "SCHOOL . . ." version of Ac/Dc's 'It's A Long Way To The Top' are the fun parts squeezed on the either side of Rock standards such as the WHO's 'Substitute', the DOORS' 'Touch Me', CREAM's 'Sunshine Of Your Love' and LED ZEPPELIN's 'Immigrant Song'. The more ambitious tracks come in the shape of newbie garage-act, the BLACK KEYS ('Set You Free'), er, the AOR/FM-friendly 'Edge Of Seventeen' by STEVIE NICKS, glam-metal/rock double-header ('Growing On Me' and 'Ballrooms Of Mars') by the DARKNESS and T. REX respectively, 'My Brain Is Hanging Upside Down (Bonzo Goes To Bitburg)' by the RAMONES and the obligatory Stooges cover, 'T.V. Eye', by grunge supergroup, WYLDE RATTTZ; the latter featured an old Stooge, Ron Asheton, Mike Watt (ex-Minutemen), Mark Arm (ex-Mudhoney), Don Fleming (ex-Velvet Monkeys/Gumball) and two Sonic Youth mainstays, Thurston Moore and Steve Shelley. *MCS*

Album rating: *8

SCHULTZE GETS THE BLUES

2004 (Ger 114m) United International Pictures (PG)

Film genre: Cajun Zydeco/Blues-music docu-drama/comedy

Top guns: s-w + dir: Michael Schorr

Stars: Horst Krause *(Schultze)*, Harald Warmbrunn *(Jurgen)*, Karl-Fred Muller *(Manfred)*, Ursula Schucht *(Jurgen's wife)*, Hannelore Schubert *(Manfred's wife)*, Rosemarie Deibel *(Frau Lorant)*, Wilhelmine Horschig *(Lisa)*, Alozia St. Julien *(Josephine)*, Wolfgang Boos *(gatekeeper)*, **Bobby Jones Czech Band** *(performers)*, **Jackie Caillier** *(performer)* & the **Cajun Cousins** *(performers)*, **Elton "Bee" Cormier** *(performer)*, **Kerry Christensen** *(yodeller)*

Storyline: When old timer Schultze is forced to retire he takes solace in playing the accordion in a polka band. One night he hears Cajun zydeco music on the radio and soon he's hooked. To the horror of his old cronies in the band he starts cooking jambalaya and playing zydeco to anyone who'll listen. What will the citizens of the Deep South make of the portly German when he goes on the trip of a lifetime to the States and gives them a taste of their own music? *JZ*

Movie rating: *7

Visual: dvd

Off the record: (see below)

—

Various Artists (score: THOMAS WITTENBECHER *)

Mar 07. (cd) *Normal; (N 255)* [–] German [–]
– Intro / Long temps passe (SUNPIE AND THE LOUISIANA SUNSPOTS) / Gluck auf, der Steiger kommt (CHORGEMEINSCHAFT "SANG & KLANG" ANGERDORF) / Schultze polka (*) / Zydeco from 1988 (ZYDECO FORCE) / Chere ici, chere la bas (the CREOLE CONNECTION) / Johnny can't dance (CARRIERE BROTHERS) / Mon bon vieux mari (CLEOMA B. FALCON) / Schultze ballade – live version (*) / Kein schoner land (CHORGEMEINSCHAFT "SANG & KLANG" ANGERDORF) / Bei allen beliebt (Volksmusik-medley) (BRACHSTEDTER MUSIKANTEN) / Valse qui me porte en terre (JOSEPH & CLEOMA B. FALCON) / Mei vata is a appenzeller (KERRY CHRISTENSEN MASTER YODELER) / Shiner song (BOBBY JONES CZECH BAND) / Carolyn, Carolyn (ELTON "BEE" CORMIER) / Le chemin de Gravois (Gravel road) (JACKIE CAILLIER & THE CAJUN COUSINS) / Zydeco from 1988 – live version (ZYDECO FORCE) / Schultze ballade (brass band) (BRACHSTEDTER MUSIKANTEN) / Schultze ballade (*).

S/track review: A German film about an accordion player integrating with French speaking Zydeco/Cajun performers from down south Louisiana, USA – now how cosmopolitan is that? 'SCHULTZE GET THE BLUES' documents (quite literally) the most important figures of the Zydeco genre and fits them into a bayou tapestry of sheer delight. Kicking off the OST is 'Long Temps Passe' by former American pro footballer turned accordion/harmonica-player, Bruce "Sunpie" Barnes and his early 90s outfit, SUNPIE AND THE LOUISIANA SUNSPOTS. Like R&B meeting "DELIVERANCE" (with a twist of 'Southern Comfort'!), SUNPIE and each subsequent artist raise their proud heads from the swamps of the south into the hearts and minds of the listener. DJ Mark Kershaw, and probably the team of John Peel and John Walters would love this exhibition of "un'eard" musicianship. Bar some novelty interludes (and I would if I could!) from the likes of beer-buddy choir, CHORGEMEINSCHAFT "SANG & KLANG" ANGERDORF, the Captain Pugwash-sounding scoremeister, THOMAS WITTENBECHER, brass band BRACHSTEDTER MUSIKANTEN and a master yodeller named KERRY CHRISTENSEN, the set is full of Zydeco merchants at the top of their musical trade. Dancehall exponents, ZYDECO FORCE (from Opelosaus, Louisiana and featuring bandleader Robbie "Mann" Robinson, voxman/guitarist Jeffrey Broussard, rub-boarder Herbert Broussard, guitarist Shelton Broussard and drummer Raymond Thomas) propel two versions of 'Zydeco From 1988' striking high over the smokestacks. The CREOLE CONNECTION (featuring MoC, Keith Frank, on 'Chere Ici, Chere La Bas') and CARRIERE BROTHERS (namely recently deceased fiddler, Joseph "Bebe" & brother Eraste) were masters of the traditional, the latter on a rendition of Clifton Chenier's 'Johnny Ne Peut Pas Danser'. Females were rare in the trade of Cajun music, but CLEOMA B. FALCON (aka pioneer Cleoma Breaux) was the exception to the rule. 'Mon Bon Vieux Mari' highlighted her simplistic guitar plucking and emotional singing; she died in 1941. With her hubby JOSEPH FALCON (born Rayne, 1900), CLEOMA shines again via 1928 recording 'Valse Qui Me Porte En Terre'; he died in Crowley, Louisiana, 1965. We can round off the album with movie cameos by: one of the CORMIER kin, ELTON "BEE" on the fiddle with 'Carolyn, Carolyn', JACKIE CAILLIER & THE CAJUN COUSINS (steel guitars a speciality) on 'Le Chemin De Gravois' and BOBBY JONES CZECH BAND on 'Shiner Song'. So, a good night out at the old "SCHULTZE & Dragon", taking you back in time to a place where you can drink all the Southern Comfort you want. Sounds too close. In fact, I'm away, see you . . . *MCS*

Album rating: *6.5

□ SCREAMERS segment
(⇒ POPULATION: ONE)

□ SEASIDE SWINGERS alt.
(⇒ EVERY DAY'S A HOLIDAY)

SEEING DOUBLE

aka S CLUB: SEEING DOUBLE

2003 (UK/Spain 91m) Columbia TriStar (PG-13)

Film genre: Pop Musical comedy

Top guns: dir: Nigel Dick / s-w: Paul Alexander, Kim Fuller ← SPICEWORLD / → FROM JUSTIN TO KELLY

Stars: S Club:- Jo O'Meara, Tina Barrett, Rachel Stevens, Hannah Spearritt, Jon Lee, Bradley McIntosh *(themselves/performers)*, David Gant *(Victor)* ← the WICKED LADY, Joseph Adams *(Alistair)*, Cristina Piaget *(Susan Sealove)*, **Gareth Gates** *(Gareth Gates clone)*

Storyline: Mad scientist Victor hatches a plot to kidnap the world's leading pop stars and replace them with clones (is that really so bad?). Next on the list is S Club, who are left stranded in Spain while their clones have a rollicking time on tour in the States. However, our heroes soon escape and meet up with their doubles, and the scene is set for a showdown with villainous Victor in his lab. *JZ*

Movie rating: *2

Visual: video (no "proper" audio OST)

Off the record: S Club (now without S Club 7 member, Paul Cattermole) would split not long after the film was made. Stammering **Gareth Gates** was runner-up to Pop Idol winner Will Young in 2001. *MCS*

– associated releases –

S CLUB: Alive (mixes)

Nov 02. (cd-s) *Polydor; (065891-2)* [5] [–]
(cd-s) *(065890-2)* – ('A') / ('A'-remixes).

S CLUB: Seeing Double

Nov 02. (cd) *Polydor; (065496-2)* [17] [–]
– Alive / Whole lotta nothing / Love ain't gonna wait for you / Bittersweet / Straight from the heart / Gangsta love / Who do you think you are? / Do it 'till we drop / Hey kitty kitty / Dance / Secret love / The greatest / In too deep / Let me sleep / Every kind of people *[UK-only]* / Alive (almighty mix).

SELENA

1997 (US 127m) Warner Bros. Pictures (PG)

Film genre: Latin-Pop Musical bio-pic drama

Top guns: s-w + dir: Gregory Nava → WHY DO FOOLS FALL IN LOVE

Stars: Jennifer Lopez *(Selena Quintanilla-Perez)*, Edward James Olmos *(Abraham Quintanilla)* ← EVEN COWGIRLS GET THE BLUES ← BLADE RUNNER / → the ROAD TO EL DORADO, Jon Seda *(Chris Perez)*, Constance Marie *(Marcela Quintanilla)*, Jacob Vargas *(Abie Quintanilla)* ← GAS, FOOD LODGING, Rebecca Lee Meza *(young Selena)*, Lupe Ontiveros *(Yolanda Saldivar)*, Jackie Guerra *(Suzette Quintanilla)*, Sal Lopez *(Juan Luis)* → the BANGER SISTERS, **Selena** *(archive footage)*

Storyline: The rise, reign and cruel fate of Tejano superstar Selena Quintanilla, from her childhood as a precocious member of her family's vocal group, the Dinos, to her conquering of the crossover Latino market under an archetypally domineering father, and her untimely demise at the hands of a disgruntled employee. *BG*

Movie rating: *6

Visual: video + dvd

Off the record: Selena (b. Selena Quintanilla, 16 Apr'71, Lake Jackson, Texas, USA. Although born to Mexican-American parents with English as her mother tongue, Selena's versatile, chameleon-esque take on Latino pop – backed by her father's old band Los Dinos – went down a storm on the Tejano scene, obliging her to learn Spanish as a career requirement. By the early 90s she'd signed to EMI Latin and begun picking up Grammys, the signal for her screen debut (as a singer) in Johnny Depp feature, 'Don Juan De Marco' (1994). Tragically, her death (in Corpus Christi, Texas on 31st March, 1995) at the hands of the president of her fan club, Yolanda Saldivar, cut short both her film career and her imminent pop breakthrough; her next feature appearance was to be posthumous, 'SELENA'. Incidentally, Edward James Olmos had a career in 60s garage bands such as the Pacific Ocean. *BG*

—

SELENA (score: Dave Grusin)

Mar 97. (cd/c) *EMI International; <55535>* [7] [–]
– Disco medley (part 1):- I will survive – Funky town / Where did the feeling go? / Disco medley (part 2):- Last dance – The hustle – On the radio / Is it the beat? / Only love / Oldies medley:- Blue moon – We belong together (VIDAL BROTHERS) / Dreaming of you / A boy like that / I could fall in love / Cumbia medley:- Como la flor – La carcacha – Bidi bidi bom bom – Baila esta Cumbia / Viviras Selena (PETE ASTUDILLO, GRACIELA BELTRAN, BARRIO BOYZZ, EMILIO, JENNIFER PENA & BOBBY PULIDO) / One more time (LIL' RAY).

S/track review: Given that popular culture hasn't turned up so many Mexican-American icons in its time, Jennifer Lopez's filling of the void left by SELENA's death could be viewed as inevitable, fateful, karmic or a combination of all three. Happily, with Hispanic hip hop not quite the marketing tool it is now, SELENA preferred disco, the genre synonymous with role model Donna Summer. So we get not one, but two live 'Disco Medley's, one pairing Gloria Gaynor's 'I Will Survive' and that 80s synth-pop parable beloved of Latin American market tapes, 'Funky Town', and the other reprising minor Summer classics, 'Last Dance' and 'On The Radio'. Unless you have a soft spot for slushy balladry, they're by far the best thing about this soundtrack. SELENA may have been the perro's bollocks in her core Tejano market, and well capable of cleaning up in the Billboard charts, but most of this stuff is very much of its time. The likes of 'Where Did The Feeling Go', 'Dreaming Of You', 'Only Love' and the classier 'I Could Fall In Love' (bit of a theme emerging here) are consummate, pre-R&B warblers in the Celine Dion mould; as with Dion, any distinguishing ethnicity is buried in the powder-puff production. Unless you've seen the film, or you fast forward to the live 'Cumbia Medley', the preponderance of English language tracks means there's no almost indication whatsoever – apart from some slobbering-tongue-in-lug whispering – of SELENA's Mexican heritage. Her jazzy West Side Story tribute, 'A Boy Like That', is much more hot-blooded, like a spicier Paula Abdul, but an equally dated Italio-house production, LIL RAY's conspicuously Billy Ocean-esque 'One More Time', and a limp, all-star tribute contribute to an underwhelming epitaph. *BG*

Album rating: *5.5

SEX, CHIPS AND ROCK N' ROLL

1999 (UK 50 x 6 epi TV-mini) BBC

Film genre: Rock'n'roll-music comedy drama

Top guns: dir: John Woods / s-w: Debbie Horsfield

Stars: Gillian Kearney *(Ellie Brookes)* → IN HIS LIFE: THE JOHN LENNON STORY, Emma Cooke *(Arden Brookes)*, Sue Johnston *(Irma Brookes)*, Phil Daniels *(Larry Valentine)* ← STILL CRAZY ← BREAKING GLASS ← QUADROPHENIA, James Callis *(the Wolf; Justin DeVere Montague)*, Julian Kerridge *(Tex Tunnicliffe)*, Joseph McFadden *(Dallas McCabe)*, David Threlfall *(Norman Kershawe)*, Nicholas Farrell *(Howard Brookes)*, Brian Poyser *(Alphonse)*, Michelle Abrahams *(Hayley)*, Jim Hooper *(Clifford)*

Storyline: It's 1965 and times are changing – fast! Ellie and Arden are twin sisters who until now have lived under the thumb of their overbearing grandmother. However, on their 18th birthday they begin to break free of their shackles when Arden gets engaged to older cousin Norman, but things really take off when the girls meet up-and-coming rock group the Ice Cubes and follow them to London. Ellie becomes pregnant, but which of the Ice Cubes will turn out to be the father? Aired between 5th September to 10th October, 1999. *JZ*

Movie rating: *7

Visuals: dvd

Off the record: Phil Daniels & The Cross (now a member of the cast of 'Eastenders') had a couple of flop of post-'QUADROPHENIA' singles during 1979/80: 'Kill Another Night' & 'Welcome To The Party'. *MCS*

—

Various Artists & Cast (*)

Oct 99. (d-cd) *Virgin Television; (VTDCD 264)*
– Do wah diddy diddy (MANFRED MANN) / Just one look (the HOLLIES) / The young ones (CLIFF RICHARD) / Apache (the SHADOWS) / House of the rising sun (the ANIMALS) / Waterloo sunset (the KINKS) / (If paradise is) Half as nice (AMEN CORNER) / Silence is golden (the TREMELOES) / Itchycoo park (the SMALL FACES) / Hippy hippy shake (the SWINGING BLUE JEANS) / Friday on my mind (the EASYBEATS) / I want doesn't get (JOSEPH McFADDEN *) / Words in my mouth (JOSEPH McFADDEN *) / Sha-la-la-la-lee (the SMALL FACES) / I'm alive (the HOLLIES) / I'm into something good (HERMAN'S HERMITS) / Do you want to know a secret (BILLY J. KRAMER & THE DAKOTAS) / Sweets for my sweet (the SEARCHERS) / Good vibrations (the BEACH BOYS) / Mony mony (TOMMY JAMES & THE SHONDELLS) / Walkin' back to happiness (HELEN SHAPIRO) / The locomotion (LITTLE EVA) / Do you love me (the TREMELOES) / Why oh why (PHIL DANIELS *) / The wanderer (DION) / Summertime blues (EDDIE COCHRAN) / Tulsa (GENE PITNEY) // The crying game (DAVE BERRY) / Wishing and hoping (DUSTY SPRINGFIELD) / She's not there (the ZOMBIES) / You'll never walk alone (GERRY & THE PACEMAKERS) / Don't throw your love away (the SEARCHERS) / I'll never find another you (the SEEKERS) / I'll never fall in love again (BOBBIE GENTRY) / Go now (the MOODY BLUES) / The first cut is the deepest (P.P. ARNOLD) / Will you love me tomorrow (the SHIRELLES) / One fine day (the CHIFFONS) / Baby, now that I've found you (the FOUNDATIONS) / The boy next door (*) / A groovy kind of love (the MINDBENDERS) / Something's gotten hold of my heart (GENE PITNEY) / (There's) Always something there to remind me (SANDIE SHAW) / Downtown (PETULA CLARK) / Concrete and clay (UNIT 4 + 2) / Out of time (CHRIS FARLOWE) / Got to get you into my life (CLIFF BENNETT) / We've gotta get out of this place (the ANIMALS) / Hi ho silver lining (JEFF BECK) / On the road again (CANNED HEAT) / Look through any window (the HOLLIES) / Everything changed (JOSEPH McFADDEN *).

S/track review: "52 Hits from the 60s and Original Songs from the BBC Series" – as it says on the sleeve – just about sums up this fantastic array of classic cross-Atlantic pop talent. The original songs from the TV movie come via three by Scots actor JOSEPH McFADDEN: 'I Want Doesn't Get', 'Words In My Mouth' & 'Everything Changed', one by Cockney lad-turned-Blur associate PHIL DANIELS, via 'Why Oh Why' and Cast number, 'The Boy Next Door'. Although, if there's one album (albeit a double-CD!) that encompasses the best of the 60s contemporary music, 'SEX, CHIPS . . .' has to be a worthy contender. Some artists such as the HOLLIES, GENE PITNEY, the TREMELOES, the ANIMALS (with two classics 'House Of The Rising Sun' & 'We've Gotta Get Out Of This Place') and the SMALL FACES (ditto 'Sha-La-La-La-Lee' & 'Itchycoo Park') are not limited to just one track, the reason must be on the strength of each individual song and its relevance to the film's plot line. The musical gap between CANNED HEAT's 'On The Road Again' and PETULA CLARK's 'Downtown' is of Grand Canyon scale, but the hits are equally effective in their own right, as is 'Hi Ho Silver Lining' (by JEFF BECK), 'Friday On My Mind' (the EASYBEATS), 'Waterloo Sunset' (the KINKS), 'Apache' (the SHADOWS), 'She's Not There' (the ZOMBIES), 'Go Now' (the MOODY BLUES) and 'Good Vibrations' (the BEACH BOYS). One could go on forever. Research, however, just might've told the film's makers that 'Summertime Blues' by EDDIE COCHRAN was indeed released in 1958, although he did die in 1960. *MCS*

Album rating: *7.5

□ Charlie SEXTON segment
(⇒ MASKED AND ANONYMOUS)

SGT. PEPPER'S LONELY HEARTS CLUB BAND

1978 (US 111m) RSO / Universal Pictures (PG)

Film genre: Pop-Rock Musical comedy

Top guns: dir: Michael Schultz ← CAR WASH / → the LAST DRAGON → KRUSH GROOVE → ROCK'N'ROLL MOM / s-w: Henry Edwards

Stars: Peter Frampton *(Billy Shears)* ← SON OF DRACULA / → ALMOST FAMOUS, **the BEE GEES:- Barry Gibb** *(Mark Henderson)*, **Robin Gibb** *(Dave Henderson)* **Maurice Gibb** *(Bob Henderson)* / Frankie Howerd *(Mean Mr. Mustard)* ← CUCUMBER CASTLE, **Paul NICHOLAS** *(Dougie Shears)*, George Burns *(Mr. Kite)*, Donald Pleasence *(B.D. Hoffler)* ← PIED PIPER / → the MONSTER CLUB → PHENOMENA, Sandy Farina *(Strawberry Fields)*, Steve Martin *(Dr. Maxwell Edison)* → the KIDS ARE ALRIGHT → LITTLE SHOP OF HORRORS, **Alice COOPER** *(Father Sun)*, **AEROSMITH:- Steven Tyler, Joe Perry, Tom Hamilton, Brad Whitfield, Joey Kramer** *(Future Villain Band)*, **Billy PRESTON** *(Sgt. Pepper)*, Dianne Steinberg *(Lucy)*, Jay W. MacIntosh *(Mrs. Fields)* → ELVIS AND THE BEAUTY QUEEN, **Linda McCartney** *(Heartland guest)* ← ONE HAND CLAPPING ← LET IT BE / → ROCKSHOW → CONCERTS FOR THE PEOPLE OF KAMPUCHEA → GIVE MY REGARDS TO BROAD STREET → GET BACK, Barry Humphries *(Heartland guest)* ← SIDE BY SIDE / → SHOCK TREATMENT → SPICEWORLD, Wolfman Jack *(Heartland guest)* ← DEADMAN'S CURVE ← AMERICAN GRAFFITI / → MORE AMERICAN GRAFFITI, **John Mayall** *(Heartland guest)* ← DON'T LOOK BACK / → BAJA OKLAHOMA → RED, WHITE & BLUES → the SOUL OF A MAN, Sheryl Cooper *(dancer)* ← WELCOME TO MY NIGHTMARE ← the NIGHTMARE / → ROADIE, **Leif Garrett** *(Heartland guest)* → the SPIRIT OF 76 → POPSTAR, **Peter Noone** *(Heartland guest)* <= HERMAN'S HERMITS =>, **Yvonne Elliman** *(Heartland guest)* ← JESUS CHRIST SUPERSTAR

Storyline: Possibly the most derided film of all time and certainly the most critically savaged musical of all time, Robert Stigwood's BEATLES tribute boasts a ludicrously threadbare plot following the efforts of Billy Shears as he battles evil music biz bigwig B.D. Brockhurst. *BG*

Movie rating: *3.5

Visual: video + dvd

Off the record: A star-studded movie, but there are surprises: ex-Bluesbreakers guitar giant, **John Mayall** for one.

—

Various Artists (composers: the BEATLES)

Aug 78. (d-lp; pink) *R.S.O.; <4100> A&M; (AMLZ 66600)* [5] [38]
– Sgt. Pepper's lonely hearts club band – With a little help from my friends (the BEE GEES, PAUL NICHOLAS & PETER FRAMPTON) / Here comes the sun (SANDY FARINA) / Getting better (PETER FRAMPTON & the BEE GEES) / Lucy in the sky with diamonds (DIANNE STEINBERG & STARGARD) / I want you (she's so heavy) (the BEE GEES, DIANNE STEINBERG, PAUL NICHOLAS, DONALD PLEASANCE & STARGARD) / Good morning, good morning (PAUL NICHOLAS, PETER FRAMPTON & the BEE GEES) / She's leaving home (the BEE GEES, JAY MacINTOSH & JOHN WHEELER) / You never give me your money (PAUL NICHOLAS & DIANNE STEINBERG) / Oh! darling (ROBIN GIBB) / Maxwell's silver hammer (STEVE MARTIN & CHORUS) / Polythene Pam – She came in through the bathroom window – Nowhere man – Sgt. Pepper's lonely hearts club band (reprise) (the BEE GEES & PETER FRAMPTON) / Got to get you into my life (EARTH, WIND & FIRE) / Strawberry fields forever (SANDY FARINA) / When I'm sixty-four (FRANKIE HOWERD & SANDY FARINA) / Mean Mr. Mustard (FRANKIE HOWERD) / Fixing a hole (GEORGE BURNS) / Because (ALICE COOPER & the BEE GEES) / Golden slumbers – Carry that weight (PETER FRAMPTON & the BEE GEES) / Come together (AEROSMITH) / Being for the benefit of Mr. Kite (MAURICE GIBB, PETER FRAMPTON, GEORGE BURNS & the BEE GEES) / The long and winding road (PETER FRAMPTON) / A day in the life (BARRY GIBB & the BEE GEES) / Get back (BILLY PRESTON) / Sgt. Pepper's lonely hearts club band (the Cast). *<d-cd-iss. Apr98; 557076-2>*

S/track review: Possibly the most derided ... well you get the picture. With the plot so obviously a paper-thin vehicle for the music, you'd expect the soundtrack to at least have some staying power, but – with notable exceptions from EARTH, WIND & FIRE ('Got To Get You Into My Life') and AEROSMITH ('Come Together') – you'd be wrong. BEATLES classics are determinedly mangled right, left and centre as PETER FRAMPTON does his best BEE GEES impression on 'The Long And Winding Road', the BEE GEES themselves stumble cack-handedly through 'A Day In The Life' and GEORGE BURNS injects a whole new meaning into 'FIXING A HOLE'. A roll call of rock aristocracy cameos from ROBERT PALMER and TINA TURNER to BOBBY WOMACK and CURTIS MAYFIELD failed to rescue the movie from eternal damnation. *BG*

Album rating: *4

– spinoff hits, etc. –

EARTH, WIND & FIRE: Got To Get You Into My Life

Jul 78. (7") *Columbia; <10796> C.B.S.; (6553)* [9] Sep78 [33]

AEROSMITH: Come Together

Jul 78. (7") *Columbia; <10802> C.B.S.; (6584)* [23] Sep78 [ ]

ROBIN GIBB: Oh! Darling! / BEE GEES, JAY MacINTOSH & JOHN WHEELER: She's Leaving Home

Aug 78. (7") *<907> (RSO 19)* [15] Sep78 [ ]

BILLY PRESTON: Get Back

Oct 78. (7") *A&M; <2071> (AMS 7418)* [86] Mar79 [ ]

☐ the SHADOWS
(⇒ Cliff RICHARD)

SHAG: THE MOVIE

1989 (UK/US 98m) Hemdale Film Corporation (PG)

Film genre: coming-of-age romantic Dance-music comedy

Top guns: dir: Zelda Barron / s-w: Robin Swicord, Lanier Laney (+ story), Terry Sweeney (+ story)

Stars: Phoebe Cates *(Carson McBride)* ← FAST TIMES AT RIDGEMONT HIGH, Scott Coffey *(Chip Guillyard)* ← SATISFACTION / → SHOUT → WAYNE'S WORLD 2, Bridget Fonda *(Melaina Buller)* → SINGLES → GRACE OF MY HEART → TOUCH → JACKIE BROWN → FINDING GRACELAND → SOUTH OF HEAVEN, WEST OF HELL, Annabeth Gish *(Caroline "Pudge" Carmichael)*, Page Hannah *(Luanne Clatterbuck)* ← the IN CROWD, Robert Rusler *(Buzz Ravenel)*, Tyrone Power III *(Harley Ralston)*, Jeff Yagher *(Jimmy Valentine)* → MADONNA: INNOCENCE LOST, Shirley Ann Field *(Mrs. Clatterbuck)*, Leilani Sarellke *(Suette)* ← NEON MANIACS

Storyline: Set in Myrtle Beach in the 1960s, three girls take their friend Carson for a last hurrah before she gets married and is consigned to oblivion away from the beach-lovers forever. Amidst the dancing, romancing and drinking, the girls begin to let their true characters come to the fore and achieve their secret lifelong ambitions – live the dream, not be fat, shed the spectacles etc. It's a time of innocent enjoyment before the spectre of Vietnam takes over America. *JZ*

Movie rating: *6

Visual: video

Off the record: (see below)

—

Various Artists (composers: Various)

Nov 88. (lp/c)(cd) *Warners; (WX 208/+C)(2 543892-2) Sire; <9 25800-1/-4/-2>* [ ] Aug89 [ ]
– The Shag (TOMMY PAGE) / I'm in love again (RANDY NEWMAN) / Our day will come (k.d. LANG & the RECLINES with TAKE 6) / Ready to go steady (the CHARMETTES) / Shaggin' on a grandstand (HANK BALLARD) / Oh what a night (the MOONLITERS) / Saved (LA VERN BAKER) / I'm leaving it all up to you (LA VERN BAKER and BEN E. KING) / Surrender (LOUISE GOFFIN) / Diddley daddy (CHRIS ISAAK).

S/track review: It's 1963, the Twist was dead and the Shag is the dance that's sweeping the nation – or so it declares on the front cover. But there's no getting away from it, no matter how you say the word "shag" in any American reference, it still means something completely different in Britain (think of another four-letter word beginning with F). It's no secret that until, possibly, the years leading up to 'Austin Powers: The Spy Who Shagged Me', the S word was the biggest euphemism to raise a snigger between cross-Atlantic cousins. Anyway, 'SHAG' (the movie) – tee hee hee! – was intended to be a taste of retrofied music history in the tradition of 'GREASE', 'DIRTY DANCING' or even 'HAIRSPRAY'. Opening song 'The Shag' ("Sha-a-a-a-a-ag") – no relation to Billy Graves' 1959 hit – by fresh-faced, teenage sensation from New Jersey, TOMMY PAGE, was very much in the "True" Spandau Ballet/ABC mould. RANDY NEWMAN (already a film composer in his own right) was next in line, and who could fault his interpretation of Fats Domino's 1956 hit 'I'm In Love Again'. The dreamy, 'Our Day Will Come' (a cover of Ruby & The Romantics' 1963's chart-topper), was an exclusive number performed by k.d. LANG & The RECLINES (with vocal backing group, TAKE 6); the butter to PAGE's margarine. A proper throwback to 1963, 'Ready To Go Steady' (by the re-formed female trio the CHARMETTES), was basically a souped-up 'Where Did Our Love Go' by the Supremes, er ... without the charm. Partly responsible for a handful of the songwriting credits, producer Andy Paley, 'Sire' label boss Seymour Stein and Detroit's recently revived "Twist" man himself, HANK BALLARD, collaborated on a second "dance"-themed song, 'Shaggin' On The Grandstand' –

not really recommended if one suffers from vertigo-go. Bypassing the MOONLITERS' 'Oh What A Night' (masked as "The Great Pretender") and CHRIS ISAAK's 'Diddley Daddy', there were two entries from R&B icon, LA VERN BAKER, the Leiber-Stoller uptempo gospel hit from 1961, 'Saved' and a new duet with BEN E. KING, 'I'm Leaving It All Up To You' (a cover of the 1963 Dale & Grace No.1). That leaves the burgeoning LOUISE GOFFIN (daughter of "Brill Building" songwriters Gerry Goffin & Carole King), who threw in her own and Dominic King's composition, 'Surrender', a case of being more like Diana Ross than her famous mum. *MCS*

Album rating: *5

SHAKE, RATTLE AND ROCK!

1956 (US 73m b&w) Sunset Pictures / American International Pictures

Film genre: Rock Musical comedy drama

Top guns: dir: Edward L. Cahn / s-w: Lou Rusoff → HOT ROD GANG → BEACH PARTY

Stars: Touch Connors *(Garry Nelson)*, Lisa Gaye *(June Fitzdingle)* ← ROCK AROUND THE CLOCK, Sterling Holloway *(Albert 'Axe' McAllister)* ← LIVE A LITTLE, LOVE A LITTLE, Raymond Hatton *(Horace Fitzdingle)*, Douglas Dumbrille *(Eustace Fentwick III)*, Margaret Dumont *(Georgianna Fitzdingle)*, Paul Dubov *(Bugsy Smith)*, Percy Helton *(Hiram, the funeral director)* → JAILHOUSE ROCK → WHERE THE BOYS ARE → GET YOURSELF A COLLEGE GIRL → HEAD, Clarence Kolb *(Judge McCombs)*, **Fats DOMINO** *(performer)*, **Joe Turner** *(performer)*, **Tommy Charles** *(performer)*, Annitta Ray *(Annita; singing slum teen)*

Storyline: A body of old fuddie-duddies ("into" Chopin) attempt to impose a ban on rock'n'roll music, which they say is corrupting the teenagers and making them juvenile delinquents. In comes hip disc jockey and TV producer, Garry Nelson, to save the day, as a showcase of musical talent is aired and debated for the small screen. A trial by TV is arranged and the rock'n'roll line-up includes Fats Domino and Tommy Charles. Will the town's youngsters descend into anarchy or will rock music be proved to be harmless entertainment? *MCS & JZ*

Movie rating: *5

Visual: video (no audio OST)

Off the record: Besides the legendary **FATS DOMINO** (on three songs 'Ain't That A Shame', 'Honey Chile' and 'I'm In Love Again'), the movie features TOMMY CHARLES & ANNITTA RAY singing 'Sweet Love On My Mind' and 'Rockin' On Saturday Night', while BIG JOE TURNER (the bluesman who scored first with 'Shake, Rattle & Roll') entertains us with 'Lipstick, Powder And Paint' and 'Feelin' Happy'. *MCS*

SHAKE, RATTLE & ROCK!

1994 (US 83m TV) Spelling Films International (PG-13)

Film genre: Rock Musical teen drama

Top guns: dir: Allan Arkush ← GET CRAZY ← ROCK'N'ROLL HIGH SCHOOL / → the TEMPTATIONS / s-w: Trish Soodik

Stars: Renee Zellweger *(Susan)* ← REALITY BITES / → EMPIRE RECORDS → COLD MOUNTAIN, Howie Mandel *(Danny Klay)*, Patricia Childress *(Cookie)*, Max Perlich *(Tony)* ← RUSH / → GEORGIA, Lantanyia Baldwin *(Sireena)* → GRACE OF MY HEART, & the Sirens:- Necia Bray, Wendi Williams & Josina Elder *(performers)* → GRACE OF MY HEART, **John DOE** *(Lucky)*, Gerrit Graham *(Lipsky)* ← WALKER ← PHANTOM OF THE PARADISE, **James Intveld** *(Bubber)* ← CRY-BABY, Riki Rachtman *(Eddie Cochran)*, Nora Dunn *(Margo)* ← WORKING GIRL, Mary Woronov *(E. Joyce Togar)* ← DICK TRACY ← ROCK'N'ROLL HIGH SCHOOL FOREVER ← GET CRAZY ← ROCK'N'ROLL HIGH SCHOOL ← the VELVET UNDERGROUND AND NICO, Dey Young *(Kate Rambeau Sr)* ← ROCK'N'ROLL HIGH SCHOOL / → the DAVID CASSIDY STORY, P.J. Soles *(Evelyn Randall)* ← SWEET DREAMS / → the DEVIL'S REJECTS, Jenifer Lewis *(Amanda)* ← WHAT'S LOVE GOT TO DO WITH IT ← BEACHES / → GIRL 6 → the PREACHER'S WIFE → the TEMPTATIONS → JACKIE'S BACK! → LITTLE RICHARD, **Ruth Brown** *(Ella)* ← HAIRSPRAY ← ROCK'N'ROLL REVUE ← RHYTHM AND BLUES REVUE / → LIGHTNING IN A BOTTLE, Stephen Furst *(Frank)* ← ANIMAL HOUSE, **Julianna Raye** *(Eggroll's guitar girl)*, Dick Miller *(officer Paisley)* ← GET CRAZY ← ROCK'N'ROLL HIGH SCHOOL ← I WANNA HOLD YOUR HAND ← TRUCK TURNER ← the TRIP ← the WILD ANGELS ← WILD, WILD WINTER ← BEACH BALL ← SKI PARTY ← the GIRLS ON THE BEACH ← ROCK ALL NIGHT ← CARNIVAL ROCK, **Paul Anka** *(cameo)* ← LET'S ROCK!

Storyline: Music-mad Susan dreams of appearing on Danny Klay's TV show to sing her rock'n'roll heart out in front of the nation. Her mum Margo, who rules with an iron fist inside her iron glove, has different ideas for her delinquent daughter, and together with the upright citizens of the town she tries to stop Susan and her friends from opening a club (in those days this was one step away from devil-worship). Cue rebellions, riots and rock'n'roll music. *JZ*

Movie rating: *4.5

Visual: Buena Vista video + Dimension dvd (no audio OST)

Off the record: **Julianna Raye** had already released her debut Jeff Lynne-produced set, 'Something Peculiar' (1992) for 'Warner Bros.'. *MCS*

SHAKE, RATTLE & ROLL: AN AMERICAN LOVE STORY

1999 (US 2x120m TV-mini) Morling Manor Media / Phoenix Pictures / CBS

Film genre: Rock'n'roll-music drama

Top guns: s-w: (+ dir) Mike Robe, Bill Kerby ← the ROSE / → LITTLE RICHARD

Stars: Bonnie Somerville *(Lyne Danner)*, Brad Hawkins *(Tyler Hart)* → DON'T LET GO → CRAZY, Samaria Graham *(Marsha Stokes)*, Travis Fine *(Mookie Gilliland)*, Kai Lennox *(Dotson)* ← SUGAR TOWN / → THINGS BEHIND THE SUN, Dana Delany *(Elaine Gunn)*, James Coburn *(Morris Gunn)* ← AFFLICTION ← YOUNG GUNS II ← WHITE ROCK ← PAT GARRETT & BILLY THE KID ← CANDY, Frank Whaley *(Allen Kogan)* ← WENT TO CONEY ISLAND ON A MISSION FROM GOD ... BE BACK BY FIVE ← PULP FICTION ← the DOORS / → CHELSEA WALLS → the HOTTEST STATE, Kathy Baker *(Janice Danner)* ← PERMANENT RECORD / → COLD MOUNTAIN, Gerald McRaney *(Howard Danner)*, Troy Donahue ← SHOCK 'EM DEAD ← CRY-BABY ← HARD ROCK NIGHTMARE ← SUMMER LOVE, Maggie Gyllenhaal, Leo Burmester ← the LAST TEMPTATION OF CHRIST ← FLY BY NIGHT, Edd Byrnes ← BACK TO THE BEACH ← GREASE ← STARDUST ← BEACH BALL, **Billy Porter** *(Little Richard)*, Mark Christopher Lawrence *(Fats Domino)* ← FEAR OF A BLACK HAT, Shawn Wayne Klush *(young Elvis Presley)*, Gary Allan *(Eddie Cochran)*, **Dicky Barrett** *(Bill Haley)* → TOO TOUGH TO DIE: A TRIBUTE TO JOHNNY RAMONE → AMERICAN HARDCORE, Cornelius Bates *(Chuck Berry)*, **Terence Trent D'Arby** *(Jackie Wilson)* ← CLUBLAND, Quint Von Canon *(Neil Sedaka)*, **Thomas DeLonge** *(Jan Berry)* ← RELEASE, **Mark Hoppus** *(Dean Torrence)* ← RELEASE / → GIGANTIC (A TALE OF TWO JOHNS), Keith Flippen *(Jerry Capeheart)*, **B.B. KING** *(the bluesman)*, **Chante Moore** *(Candy)*, **Christopher Fennell** *(Stevie)* → COLD MOUNTAIN, the Velvet 4:- **K-Ci** *(Nate)*, **JoJo** *(Michael)*, **Rashaan Patterson** *(Willie)*, **Jesse Powell** *(Shugg)*, Corri English → STUCK IN THE SUBURBS

Storyline: When rock'n'roll was still emerging from its cocoon, a group called the HartAches was making its way into the limelight. Lead singer Tyler only had eyes for fellow band member Lyne, but as success followed success their swelling popularity was matched only by the swelling of Tyler's head. Lyne eventually had enough and went her own way, but will Tyler conquer his egomania and win her back? *JZ*

Movie rating: *6

Visual: dvd

Off the record: R&B balladeer **Billy Porter** had a brief career in music in the mid-90s ('Untitled' set for 'A&M') having built up a CV on Broadway. (for others see below) *MCS*

—

Various Artists/Cast (aka the HARTACHES *)

Oct 99. (cd) *M.C.A.; <(5 45085-2)>* ☐ Dec99 ☐
– Sh-boom (the CHORDS) / One bad stud (*) / Baby, here I am (*) / Shake, rattle & roll (DICKY BARRETT w/ DAN WILSON) / Fur slippers (B.B. KING) / Ain't that a shame (RANDY JACKSON) / Tears on my pillow (the VELVET 4; K-CI & JOJO, RASHAAN PATTERSON & JESSE POWELL) / Side by side (*) / Wall around my heart (the EMERALDS feat. CHANTE MOORE) / My back seat (*) / Slippin' and slidin' (*) / Summertime blues (GARY ALLAN) / To be loved (TERENCE TRENT D'ARBY) / Detour (*) / Long tall Sally (BILLY PORTER) / A touch of heaven (*) / Break out (*) / Just one dance with you (*) / Dead man's curve (MARK HOPPUS & THOMAS DeLONGE) / Only you (and you alone) (the PLATTERS) / Side by side (original cast).

S/track review: We were nearly into the new millennium, when this retrofied study at what presumably happened to 50s teenagers, hit your TV screens. Split into two camps, we have mediocre movie group, the HARTACHES, doo wop-ing their way through 9 of the 21 numbers, while the other tracks are by modern-day various artists and cast members. The strangest by far has to be the pairing of Blink-182's MARK HOPPUS & THOMAS DeLONGE on Jan & Dean's 'Dead Man's Curve', while other good "rock" combinations included DICKY BARRETT and DAN WILSON (of the Mighty Mighty Bosstones and Semisonic respectively) on Bill Haley's 'Shake, Rattle & Roll'; can't really count 'Tears On My Pillow' by the VELVET 4: K-CI & JOJO, RASHAAN PATTERSON & JESSE POWELL – can we? BILLY PORTER's take of 'Long Tall Sally' and CHANTE MOORE (augmented the EMERALDS) on 'Wall Around My Heart' are nice enough for a great karaoke night, but that's for someone else to judge. One-time session bassist and music producer – now "judge" in American Idol – RANDY JACKSON, is also on board here via Fats Domino's 'Ain't That A Shame', while back from the musical wilderness comes TERENCE TRENT D'ARBY on 'To Be Loved'. Two golden oldies virtually bookended the soundtrack, the CHORDS' 'Sh-Boom' and the PLATTERS' 'Only You (And You Alone)', while there was an encore of sorts by the original cast for a rendition of 'Side By Side'. *MCS*

Album rating: *5

☐ SHINING STAR alt.
(⇒ THAT'S THE WAY OF THE WORLD)

SHIRLEY THOMPSON VERSUS THE ALIENS

1972 (Aus 104m w/b&w; cut to 79m) Kolossal Piktures (R)

Film genre: psychological sci-fi thriller cum 50s Rock Musical

Top guns: s-w: (+ dir) Jim Sharman → the ROCKY HORROR PICTURE SHOW → SHOCK TREATMENT, Helmut Bakaitis

Stars: Jane Harders *(Shirley Thompson)*, June Collis *(Dr. Leslie Smith)*, Tim Elliott *(Dr. George Talbot)*, Marion Johns *(Rita Thompson)*, John Llewellyn *(Reg Thompson)*, Marie Nicholas *(Narelle Thompson)*, Helmut Bakaitis *(Harold)*, John Ivkovitch *(Bruce)*, Bruce Gould *(Blake)*

Storyline: On a visit to Luna Park, teenage rebel Shirley has a close encounter with aliens who "speak" to her through a statue of the Duke of Edinburgh. Over the next ten years, Shirley tries to convince people that the park is really the aliens' HQ on Earth, but no one will believe her. Finally she is committed to an asylum as a hopeless case, driven over the edge by everyone's refusal to take her seriously. *JZ*

Movie rating: *6.5

Visual: none (no audio OST; score: Ralph Tyrell)

Off the record: Australian **Jeannie Lewis** was the lady behind the voice of Shirley Thompson. Lewis started off in the folk and jazz scene performing with the Alan Lee Quintet and the Ray Price Jazz Quintet. Prior to her work on 'SHIRLEY THOMPSON..', she sang with Sydney-based Gypsy Train; her subsequent albums including 'Free Fall Through Featherless Flight' – like a mix between Sandy Denny and Kate Bush – were well received in her homeland. *MCS*

SHOCK 'EM DEAD

aka ROCK 'EM DEAD

1991 (US 93m) Academy Entertainment (R)

Film genre: Rock-music horror thriller

Top guns: s-w: (+ dir) Mark Freed, Andrew Cross, Dave Tedder

Stars: Stephen Quadros *(Martin Paxton)*, Traci Lords *(Lindsay Roberts)* ← CRY-BABY, Troy Donahue *(record exec)* ← CRY-BABY ← HARD ROCK NIGHTMARE ← SUMMER LOVE / → SHAKE, RATTLE & ROLL: AN AMERICAN LOVE STORY, Aldo Ray *(Tony)* ← DYNAMITE BROTHERS ← RIOT ON SUNSET STRIP, Tim Moffett *(Greg)*, Markus Grupa *(Jonny)*, Karen Russell *(Michelle)*, Gina Parks *(Marilyn)*, Christopher Maleki *(Dustin)*, Laurel Wiley *(Monique)*, Frank Gallagher *(production manager)* → the YOUNG PERSON'S GUIDE TO BECOMING A ROCK STAR

Storyline: Martin is one of life's losers, with a dead-end job in a pizza parlour, and a nonentity as far as women are concerned. What to do? Simply look up the Yellow Pages ad for the local voodoo priestess, cross her palm with silver and sell your soul to Satan. Next morning Martin has become Angel, (ahem) a musician par excellence who the women drool over, and happy days seem to be here again. The catch is, when Martin feels hungry his new diet is rather different from pepperoni pizza . . . *JZ*

Movie rating: *3.5

Visual: video (no audio OST; score: Robert Decker)

Off the record: Traci Lords went on to have a minor UK hit, 'Fallen Angel', in 1995.

SHOCK TREATMENT

1981 (US 94m) 20th Century Fox (PG)

Film genre: Pop-Rock Musical fantasy comedy

Top guns: s-w: Jim Sharman (+ dir) ← the ROCKY HORROR PICTURE SHOW ← SHIRLEY THOMPSON VERSUS THE ALIENS, Richard O'Brien ← the ROCKY HORROR PICTURE SHOW

Stars: Cliff De Young *(Brad Majors / Farley Flavors)*, Jessica Harper *(Janet Majors)* ← SUSPIRIA ← PHANTOM OF THE PARADISE, Richard O'Brien *(Cosmo McKinley)* ← FLASH GORDON ← JUBILEE ← the ROCKY HORROR PICTURE SHOW / → SPICEWORLD, Patricia Quinn *(Nation McKinley)* ← the ROCKY HORROR PICTURE SHOW, Charles Gray *(Judge Oliver Wright)* ← the ROCKY HORROR PICTURE SHOW, Ruby Wax *(Betty Hapschatt)*, Nell Campbell *(Ansalong)* ← JUBILEE ← ROCK FOLLIES OF '77 ← LISZTOMANIA ← the ROCKY HORROR PICTURE SHOW / → the WALL → the KILLING FIELDS, Rik Mayall *('Rest Home' Ricky)* → EAT THE RICH → BRING ME THE HEAD OF MAVIS DAVIS, Darlene Johnson *(Emily Weiss; mom)*, Manning Redwood *(Harry Weiss; dad)*, Betsy Brantley *(Neely Pritt)*, Barry Dennen *(Irwin Lapsey)* ← JESUS CHRIST SUPERSTAR, Barry Humphries *(Bert Schnick)* ← SGT. PEPPER'S LONELY HEARTS CLUB BAND ← SIDE BY SIDE / → SPICEWORLD, Christopher Malcolm

(Vance Parker) → LABYRINTH, **Sinitta Renet** *(Frankie)*, Gary Shail *(Oscar Drill)* ← QUADROPHENIA ← the MUSIC MACHINE / → GIVE MY REGARDS TO BROAD STREET, David John *('Bit' drummer)*, Garry Martin *('Bit' guitarist)*, Imogen Claire *(wardrobe mistress)* ← FLASH GORDON ← the ROCKY HORROR PICTURE SHOW ← LISZTOMANIA ← TOMMY / → HAWKS

Storyline: Brad and Janet return from the Rocky Horror Picture Show as a not-very-happily married couple in the TV town of Denton, where everyone is either on a show or watching it. However, a sinister plot is afoot – Brad finds himself given a bit-part as a patient in the sanatorium (and the key to his padded cell may be thrown away), while Janet becomes the new town superstar who's never off the screens. Who's pulling all the strings, and why? *JZ*

Movie rating: *4

Visual: video + dvd

Off the record: Cliff De Young (b.12 Feb'45) was in a band named Clear Light who formed 1967 in Los Angeles, California, USA. A basic heavy-rock outfit, their eponymous album for 'Elektra' only reached the lower regions of the American Top 200. The single, 'Black Roses,' was definitely the highlight of the album, its flip side 'She's Ready To Be Free' was subsequently used in the film, 'The President's Analyst' (1967). *MCS*

Various Cast (score: Richard Hartley & Richard O'Brien)

Nov 81. (lp/c) *Ode; <OSV/+C 21654> Warners; (K 56957)* ☐ ☐
– Overture / Denton, U.S.A. (NEELY, DAD, MOM, VANCE, MACY, RALPH, cheerleaders & chorus) / Bitchin' in the kitchen (BRAD & JANET) / In my own way (JANET) / Thank God I'm a man (DAD & CHORUS) / Farley's song (FARLEY, MAC, NATION, RICKY & ANSALONG) / Lullaby (MAC, NATION, JANET, RICKY & ANSALONG) / Little black dress (MAC, JANET, NATION & BERT) / Me of me (JANET & cheerleaders) / Shock treatment (MAC, NATION, ANSALONG, DAD, MOM, JANET & BERT) / Carte blanche (JANET) / Looking for trade (JANET & BRAD) / Look what I did to my id (MOM-DAD, RALPH-MACY, COSMO-NATION & RICKY-ANSALONG) / Breaking out (OSCAR DRILL & the BITS) / Duel duet (BRAD & FARLEY) / Anyhow, anyhow (BRAD, JANET, BETTY, OLIVER & chorus). *<cd-iss. 1990 on 'Ode-Rhino'; R2 71687>*

S/track review: 'SHOCK TREATMENT' is Richard O'Brien's sort of sequel to 'The ROCKY HORROR PICTURE SHOW' and like most sequels the old adage lightning doesn't strike twice immediately springs to mind. It lacks the audacity, vibrancy and sheer burlesque excess of its predecessor, not to mention the tunes. There aren't any songs that could be classed as sing-a-longs or any that grab you by the balls as being show hits like 'Time Warp'. It's easy to tell that the soundtrack is trying to be a slick and dirty rock'n'roll extravaganza but instead turns out like AOR for nuns. Songs like 'Bitchin' In The Kitchen', 'Little Black Dress' and 'Looking For Trade' are not the funny, sleazy parodies they promise to be, while 'Thank God I'm A Man' is a poor attempt at simply bleating the obvious. The main theme, 'Denton U.S.A.' is fingers-down-the-throat stuff that would probably even fail to make it on to the 'HAIRSPRAY' soundtrack and the opening 'Overture' lacks any kind of drama or energy to whet your appetite. In short, 'SHOCK TREATMENT' is a disappointment to say the least; any 'ROCKY HORROR . . .' fans should just stick to the original, at least they'd get to do the 'Time Warp' again! *CM*

Album rating: *4

☐ SHORT FUSE alt.
(⇒ GOOD TO GO)

SHOUT

1991 (US 89m) Universal Pictures (PG-13)

Film genre: Pop/Rock Musical teen drama

Top guns: dir: Jeffrey Hornaday / s-w: Joe Gayton

Stars: John Travolta *(Jack Cabe)* ← STAYING ALIVE ← ← URBAN COWBOY ← GREASE ← SATURDAY NIGHT FEVER / → PULP FICTION → PRIMARY COLORS → SWORDFISH → BE COOL → HAIRSPRAY re-make, **James Walters** *(Jesse Tucker)*, Heather Graham *(Sara Benedict)* → EVEN COWGIRLS GET THE BLUES → BOOGIE NIGHTS → COMMITTED, Richard Jordan *(Eugene Benedict)* ← DELUSION ← DUNE, Linda Fiorentino *(Molly)* → ORDINARY DECENT CRIMINAL, Scott Coffey *(Bradley)* ← SHAG: THE MOVIE ← SATISFACTION / → WAYNE'S WORLD 2, Glenn Quinn *(Alan)* → AT ANY COST, Gwyneth Paltrow *(Rebecca)* → DUETS, **Linda M. Womack** *(singer)*, **Cecil D. Womack** *(lead singer)*

Storyline: Jack Cabe is a music teacher on the run from the law in 1950s Texas. Wanted for murder, he joins a Boy's Institute and begins teaching music – but not the music he's supposed to. He encourages the boys to listen to rock'n'roll to the annoyance of school director Benedict, but when the kids respond to their new teacher Cabe has a decision to make: to stay for the big concert or to hit the road as the police are closing in fast. *JZ*

Movie rating: *4

Visual: video

Off the record: James aka **Jamie Walters** was to soon star in TV show/band, 'The Heights' (1992), when they had a No.1 single with 'How Do You Talk To An Angel'; three years later he had a solo hit, 'Hold On'. Husband & wife duo, Womack & Womack, aka **Cecil D. Womack** (brother of Bobby Womack) and **Linda M. Womack** (daughter of Sam Cooke) had a handful of UK hits in the mid-to-late 80s: 'Love Wars', 'Teardrops' & 'Celebrate The World'. *MCS*

Various Artists (score: RANDY EDELMAN *)

Oct 91. (cd) *Milan; <262 371>* ☐ ☐-
– Up against the sky (JOHN HIATT) / Alimony (WOMACK & WOMACK) / Devil call me back home (OTIS RUSH) / I was a fool (ELMORE JAMES) / Main title theme (*) / More than a kiss (TOMMY CONWELL) / Get with the band (WOMACK & WOMACK) / Rockin' the pad (JAMES WALTERS) / Sara and Jesse (*).

S/track review: "What we have here is a failure to communicate" was a poignant line once spoken by the warden in the movie, 'Cool Hand Luke'. 'SHOUT' has an all-round communication problem in the fact there's just too many duff tracks. Sounding like a long-lost Neville Brother (who's just joined U2), JOHN HIATT opens the set with 'Up Against The Sky', although film composer Randy Newman might be a closer comparison. Up next, WOMACK & WOMACK (albeit through a few music cameos from CECIL & LINDA) get the Chuck Berry vibes through two numbers, 'Alimony' and 'Get With The Band'. On the same Berry trail, arrives OTIS RUSH and the bluesy 'Devil Call Me Back Home', while original ELMORE JAMES (and 'I Was A Fool') had its own roots. If there had been more blues numbers, the listener just might've withstood the barrage of subsequent tracks by weaker artists. RANDY EDELMAN (he of 'Uptown, Uptempo Woman' fame) was now a fully-fledged scoresmith, but two long-ish film excerpts next to the aforementioned rock standards just didn't come up trumps. Finally, blue-eyed soul boy, TOMMY CONWELL (with 'More Than A Kiss') and the movie's co-star JAMES WALTERS (who sounds like Shakin' Stevens fronting the Stray Cats) were just basically woeful. *MCS*

Album rating: *3.5

SHOUT!: THE STORY OF JOHNNY O'KEEFE

1985 (Aus 100m TV) 7 Network / View Pictures Limited

Film genre: Rock'n'roll-music bio-pic/drama

Top guns: dir: Ted Robinson / s-w: Robert Caswell ← ABBA: THE MOVIE

Stars: Terry Serio *(Johnny O'Keefe)*, John McTiernan *(Lee Gordon)*, Marcelle Schmitz *(Marianne O'Keefe)*, Candy Raymond *(Maureen O'Keefe)*, Tony Barry *(Alan Heffernan)*, Melissa Jaffer *(Thelma O'Keefe)* ← STARSTRUCK, John Paramor *(Bill Haley)*, Greg Stone *(Deejay double bass)*, John Polson *(Deejay saxophone)*, Chuck McKinney *(Little Richard)* ← the PIRATE MOVIE, Nique Needles *(Col Joye)* → DOGS IN SPACE

Storyline: The man who took Aussie rock'n'roll music onto the world stage is portrayed here performing some of his greatest hits, including the film title. However, the downside of his career is given equal (if not more) prominence, including his nervous breakdowns and his time in a psychiatric ward in Sydney, not to mention his early death from a drugs overdose aged just 43. Features original footage from the 50s and 60s. *JZ*

Movie rating: *6.5

Visual: video (no audio OST)

Off the record: Johnny O'Keefe (b.19 Jan'35, Sydney, Australia) was his country's only major rock'n'roll singer and export in the late 50s. The former furniture salesman single-handedly took the genre (like a fusion of Elvis & Johnnie Ray) into fresh rural territory and had hit after hit, but not in UK or US. He'll be best remembered for one song at least, 'I'm The Wild One', subsequent acquisitions of JERRY LEE LEWIS and IGGY POP, the latter renaming it 'Wild One (Real Wild Child)'. O'Keefe died of a heart attack on the 6th of October, 1978. *MCS*

SID & NANCY

1986 (UK 111m) Universal Pictures (R)

Film genre: Punk rock-music bio-pic drama

Top guns: s-w: Alex Cox (+ dir) ← REPO MAN / → STRAIGHT TO HELL → WALKER → FEAR AND LOATHING IN LAS VEGAS → REVENGERS TRAGEDY, Abbe Wool → ROADSIDE PROPHETS

Stars: Gary Oldman *(Sid Vicious)*, Chloe Webb *(Nancy Spungen)*, Andrew Schofield *(Johnny Rotten)* → REVENGERS TRAGEDY, David Hayman *(Malcolm McLaren)* → WALKER → ORDINARY DECENT CRIMINAL → the LAST GREAT WILDERNESS, Debbie Bishop *(Phoebe)*, Xander Berkeley *(Bowery Snax; drug dealer)* → STRAIGHT TO HELL → WALKER → TAPEHEADS → STORYTELLING, Tony London *(Steve Jones)*, Perry Benson *(Paul Cook)* ← BIRTH OF THE BEATLES / → THIS IS ENGLAND, Anne Lambton *(Linda)*, Kathy Burke *(Brenda Winczor)* → EAT THE RICH → STRAIGHT TO HELL → WALKER → KEVIN & PERRY GO LARGE, Mark Monero *(Jah Clive)* ← BABYLON, Sandy Baron *(hotelier in New York)* ← BIRDY, Sy Richardson *(methadone caseworker)* ← REPO MAN ← PETEY WHEATSTRAW / → STRAIGHT TO HELL → WALKER → TAPEHEADS → MYSTERY TRAIN, Milton Selzer *(granpa)* ← LADY SINGS THE BLUES / → WALKER → TAPEHEADS, **Keith Morris** * *(Riker's junky)*, **Coati Mundi** *(desk clerk)* <= KID CREOLE & THE COCONUTS =>, **Eddie Tenpole Tudor** *(hotelier in London)* ← ABSOLUTE BEGINNERS ← the GREAT ROCK'N'ROLL SWINDLE / → STRAIGHT TO HELL → WALKER, Biff Yeager *(detective)* ← REPO MAN ← DYNAMITE BROTHERS / → STRAIGHT TO HELL → WALKER → ROADSIDE PROPHETS, John Snyder *(Vito)* → ROADSIDE PROPHETS, **Courtney Love** *(Gretchen)* → STRAIGHT TO HELL → TAPEHEADS → MAN ON THE MOON → MAYOR OF THE SUNSET STRIP, Andy Bradford *(Dick Bent)* ← FLASH GORDON ← the FAMILY WAY, John M. Jackson *(Lance Boyles, MD)* ← LOCAL HERO / → BAJA OKLAHOMA → DEAD SOLID PERFECT → GINGER ALE AFTERNOON, **Iggy POP** *(prospective guest)*, **CIRCLE JERKS w/** * *(Kittens)*, Miguel Sandoval *(record company executive)* ← HOWARD THE DUCK ← REPO MAN / → STRAIGHT TO HELL → WALKER → JUNGLE FEVER, **Pray For Rain** *(band)*, **Dick Rude** *(Riker's guard)* ← REPO MAN / → STRAIGHT TO HELL → WALKER → ROADSIDE PROPHETS → LET'S ROCK AGAIN!, Graham Fletcher-Cook *(Wally hairstyle)* ← ABSOLUTE BEGINNERS / → STRAIGHT TO HELL → SIESTA

Storyline: In this fact-based depiction of the Romeo & Juliet of punk, Sid Vicious and American groupie Nancy Spungen embark upon a messy, violent and fatally flawed love affair at the fag end of the Sex Pistols' career. Things reach a bloody conclusion as the couple's heroin dependency spirals out of control. *BG*

Movie rating: *6.5

Visual: video + dvd

Off the record: Facts Told The Pub No.346!: Gary Oldman's sister is Eastenders soap actress Laila Morse (real name Maureen Oldman) who plays the unwielding character of Mo Harris, grandma of the Slater family. *MCS*

—

Various Artists: Love Kills *(score: PRAY FOR RAIN *)*

Aug 86. (lp/c) *M.C.A.; (MCG/+C 6011)* [ ] [–]
– Love kills – title track (JOE STRUMMER) / Haunted (the POGUES) / Pleasure And Pain (STEVE JONES) / Chinese choppers (*) / Love kills (CIRCLE JERKS) / Off the boat (*) / Dum dum club (JOE STRUMMER) / Burning room (*) / She never took no for an answer (JOHN CALE) / Junk (the POGUES) / I wanna be your dog (GARY OLDMAN) / My way (GARY OLDMAN) *[US-only]* / Taxi to Heaven (*). *(<cd-iss. Mar03; 112413>)*

S/track review: A classy set-list combines memorable tracks from JOE STRUMMER – who composed the excellent title track 'Love Kills' and 'Dum Dum Club', the POGUES (although the band's Cait O'Riordan rather than Shane MacGowan, sings on 'Haunted') and JOHN CALE, who contributes the eddying melancholy of 'She Never Took No For An Answer'. Add to this the unsettling atmospherics of PRAY FOR RAIN's score, Gary Oldman's professionally sloppy covers of 'My Way' and Iggy's 'I Wanna Be Your Dog', and you have a killer soundtrack all the more praiseworthy for not relying purely on the Sex Pistols (STEVE JONES' 'Pleasure And Pain' aside) and other period rehashes from the likes of the CIRCLE JERKS. Alex Cox's musical brain/knowledge had already expanded to a certain degree with 'REPO MAN' (1984) – featuring Iggy and the Circle Jerks; in the subsequent can – so to speak – 'STRAIGHT TO HELL' (1986) by the POGUES and PRAY FOR RAIN, plus Strummer's 'WALKER' (1988) score. *MCS & BG*

Album rating: *7

– spinoff hits, etc. –

the POGUES: Haunted / Junk

Aug 86. (7") *(MCA 1084)* [42] [–]
(12"+=) *(MCAT 1084)* – Hot dogs with everything.

JOE STRUMMER: Love Kills / Dum Dum Club

Oct 86. (7"/12") *C.B.S.; (A/TA 7244)* [69] [–]

SIDE BY SIDE

1975 (UK 84m) G.T.O.

Film genre: Glam-Pop Musical comedy

Top guns: s-w: (+ dir) Bruce Beresford → TENDER MERCIES, Garry Chambers, Ron Inkpen ← NEVER TOO YOUNG TO ROCK ← REMEMBER ME THIS WAY, Peter James

Stars: Barry Humphries *(Rodney)* → SGT. PEPPER'S LONELY HEARTS CLUB BAND → SHOCK TREATMENT → SPICEWORLD, Terry-Thomas *(Max Nugget)*, **Stephanie De Sykes** *(Julia)*, Billy Boyle *(Gary)* ← GROUPIE GIRL, Frank Thornton *(Inspector Crumb)* ← the MAGIC CHRISTIAN ← GONKS GO BEAT ← IT'S TRAD, DAD!, **Dave Mount** *(Flip)*, Jennifer

Guy *(Violet)*, Sheila Collings *(Bessie)* → RETURN TO WATERLOO, **the Rubettes:- Alan Williams, Tony Thorpe, Mick Clarke, Peter Arnesen, Bill Hurd** *(performers)* ← NEVER TOO YOUNG TO ROCK, **Mac & Katie Kissoon** *(performers)*, **the Second Generation** *(performers)*, **Fox:- Noosha Fox** *(performers)*, **Mud:- Les Gray, Ray Stiles, Bob Davis + Mount** *(performers)* ← NEVER TOO YOUNG TO ROCK, **Hello:- Bob Bradbury, Keith Marshall, Vic Faulkner, Jeff Allen** *(performers)*, **Disco Tex** *(performer)*, **Billy Ocean** *(performer)*, **Desmond Dekker** *(performer)*, Eric Idle *(himself)* → the RUTLES → SOUTH PARK: BIGGER LONGER & UNCUT

Storyline: Two rival club owners go head-to-head trying to fix up some sappy pop groups to re-establish their credibility and finances. *MCS*

Movie rating: *2

Visual: none (no audio OST; score by **John Shakespeare** & Derek Warne)

Off the record: Stephanie De Sykes (b. Stephanie Ryton) kicked off her pop career in the summer of '74 with a near chart-topping UK hit, 'Born With A Smile On My Face' (showcased in the film); she would have only one more Top 20 hit, 'We'll Find A Day', the following year. She subsequently co-wrote (with 70s pop star, Barry Blue) the theme to ITV's 'The Golden Shot' and Britain's unsuccessful 1978 Eurovision Song Contest entry for Co-Co, 'Bad Old Days'. Reggae man, **Desmond Dekker**, turned up to sing 'The Israelites', while **Hello** ('Game's Up' and 'Bend Me, Shape Me'), **the Rubettes** ('I Can Do It'), **Fox** ('Only You Can') & **Mud** ('Side By Side'), also provide the film some of their recent glam-rock blockbusters; wannabe actor, **Dave Mount**, was the drummer with Mud. **John Shakespeare** was a singer with the Ivy League, who had hits in the mid-60s, including 'Tossin' And Turning'. **Disco Tex & The Sex-O-Lettes** (aka Joseph Montanez) had two Top 10'ers, 'Get Dancing' and 'I Wanna Dance Wit Choo (Doo Dat Dance) – Part 1', while **Billy Ocean** (b. Leslie Charles) was about to break through early in 1976 with 'Love Really Hurts Without You'; he would have a No.1 hit a decade later with 'When The Going Gets Tough..' from the movie 'Jewel Of The Nile'. *MCS*

SIDE BY SIDE: THE TRUE STORY OF A MAGICAL FAMILY

1982 (US 100m TV) Comworld / Osmond Communications

Film genre: Pop-music bio-pic & family docu-drama

Top guns: dir: Russ Mayberry / s-w: E.F. Wallengren (+ story w/ Tom Lazarus → STIGMATA)

Stars: Joseph Bottoms *(George Osmond)*, **Marie Osmond** *(Olive Osmond)* ← GOIN' COCONUTS / → INSIDE THE OSMONDS, Karen Alston *(Belva)*, Cheryl Hudock *(Marianne)*, Scott Wilkinson *(Lt. Gontz)*, H.E.D. Redford *(Tom Davis)* → FOOTLOOSE, Oscar Rowland *(Howard Corbin)* → FOOTLOOSE, George & Olive Osmond *(themselves)* → INSIDE THE OSMONDS, Amy Osmond *(young Marie)*, Justin Osmond *(young Tom)*, Jason Sanders *(young Jay)*, Jamon Rivera *(young Donny)*, Spencer Alston *(young Merrill)*, Daryl Bingham *(young Alan)*, Brian Poelman *(young Wayne)*, Travis Osmond *(young Virl)*, Shane Wallace *(Merrill)*, Todd Dutson *(Alan)*, Jeremy Haslam *(Jay)*, Vinc Massa *(Wayne)*

Storyline: The story of the Osmonds from the early days till the late 70s, as seen through the eyes of mother Olive (possibly also through rose-tinted glasses). Authoritarian dad, George, is really just trying to do the best for the kids, and doesn't bully them along at all, honest. The kids all love each other, never argue and have no idea about nasty things like drink or sex. And of course their eventual decline was, well, just one of those things. *JZ*

Movie rating: *3.5

Visual: video (no audio OST; score: George Aliceson Tipton)

Off the record: The Osmonds, and more in particular, **Marie Osmond** had recent film experience via 'GOIN' COCONUTS' (1978).

□ SIEBZEHN JAHR, BLONDES HAAR alt.
(⇒ la BATTAGLIA DEI MODS)

Beanie SIGEL

Born: Dwight Grant, 6th March '74, Philadelphia, Pennsylvania, USA; named after Sigel Street. A relative newcomer to the East Coast Gangsta rap scene, Beanie has gradually found a market since his post-millennium Top 5 breakthrough set, 'The Truth'. Subsequent albums, 'The Reason' (2001) and 'The B. Coming' (2005) followed in much the same direction, the latter released while his freedom was still in tact; he was arrested in 2003 on drugs charges, illegal gun possession and an attempted murder. While on bail and a possible prison sentence, Beanie featured in several films, 'BACKSTAGE' (2000), 'State Property' (2002) – with his group State Property – 'PAPER SOLDIERS' (2002), a cameo in 'BROWN SUGAR' (2002), 'DEATH OF A DYNASTY' (2003), 'FADE TO BLACK' (2004) – a second with pal Jay-Z – & 'State Property 2' (2005). *MCS*

- **filmography** {actor/performance} (composer) –

Backstage *(2000 {p} on OST =>)* / State Property *(2002 {*} on OST w/ V/A =>)* / **Paper Soldiers** *(2002 {*} =>)* / **Brown Sugar** *(2002 {c} =>)* / **Death Of A Dynasty** *(2003 {a} =>)* / **Fade To Black** *(2004 {c} =>)* / State Property 2 *(2005 {*} score w/ Kerry Muzzey =>)*

□ Gene SIMMONS
(⇒ KISS)

SING

1989 (US 98m) TriStar Pictures (PG-13)

Film genre: coming-of-age/teen drama

Top guns: dir: Richard J. Baskin / s-w: Dean Pitchford ← FOOTLOOSE

Stars: Lorraine Bracco *(Miss Lombardo)* → EVEN COWGIRLS GET THE BLUES → the BASKETBALL DIARIES → DEATH OF A DYNASTY, Peter Dobson *(Dominic)* → LAST EXIT TO BROOKLYN, Jessica Steen *(Hannah Gottschalk)*, Louise Lasser *(Rosie)*, **Patti LaBelle** *(Mrs. DeVere)* → IDLEWILD, George DiCenzo *(Mr. Markowitz)* ← ACROSS 110th STREET, Susan Peretz *(Mrs. Tucci)*, Laurnea Wilkerson *(Zena)* ← SCHOOL DAZE, **Rachel Sweet** *(Cecelia)*, Cuba Gooding Jr. *(Stanley)* → JUDGMENT NIGHT → the FIGHTING TEMPTATIONS, Lori Ann Alter *(singer/dancer)* → the CHEETAH GIRLS → the CHEETAH GIRLS 2

Storyline: New teacher Miss Lombardo is in charge of this year's Sing event at high school. While there's no surprise at her choice of Hannah as leading lady, heads are turned when she picks tough guy Dominic as her partner. But Miss Lombardo is convinced he's got talent in his voice as well as his fists, and the happy couple are soon warbling their songs together. But disaster looms as the Sing is cancelled by the Board – never mind, the kids will sing anyway to save the day. *JZ*

Movie rating: *4.5

Visual: video

Off the record: Rachel Sweet (b.28 Jul'62, Akron, Ohio, USA) cut her teeth as a pre-pubescent, 12-year-old country singer. Subsequently signing to UK indie imprint, 'Stiff', she finally had a Top 40 hit in 1979 via 'B-A-B-Y'. In 1981, her duet of 'Everlasting Love' with Rex Smith hit Top 40 again, but this time also in America. Her singing voice was further used on John Waters films, 'HAIRSPRAY' (1988) and 'CRY-BABY' (1990). *MCS*

—

Various Artists (score: Jay Gruska)

Apr 89. (lp/c/cd) *Columbia; <45086-1/-4/-2> C.B.S.; (463455-1/-4/-2)* □ Jun89 □
– Sing (MICKEY THOMAS) / Birthday suit (JOHNNY KEMP) / Romance (love theme from "Sing") (PAUL CARRACK and TERRI NUNN) / You don't have to ask me twice (NIA PEEPLES) / One more time (MICHAEL BOLTON with the cast of Sarafina) /

Somethin' to believe in (BILL CHAMPLIN) / Total concentration (PATTI LaBELLE) / (Everybody's gotta) Face the music (KEVIN CRONIN of REO SPEEDWAGON) / What's the matter with love? (LAURNEA WILKERSON) / We'll never say goodbye (ART GARFUNKEL).

S/track review: The first thing one notices when looking at the 'SING' credits is that all are by solo artists, albeit two of them (Mike & The Mechanics' PAUL CARRACK and Berlin's TERRI NUNN) being pared up for the film's "Love Theme", 'Romance'. Co-penned by Patrick Leonard & main 'SING' songwriter, Dean Pitchford (the latter lyricist/songwriter on 'Fame', 'Footloose', 'D.A.R.Y.L.', 'Quicksilver' and Disney's 'Oliver And Company'), this AOR-ballad is typical 80s mush; Pitchford subsequently collaborates with a permutation ("perm" being the appropriate word!) including Jonathan Cain, Martin Page, Rhett Lawrence, Desmond Child, Dianne Warren, Tom Kelly & Richard Marx. Dean's most productive partnership is alongside Tom Snow, who supply four songs, 'You Don't Have To Ask Me Twice' (by singer/actress NIA PEEPLES), 'One More Time' (by hit of the moment, MICHAEL BOLTON with the cast Of Sarafina), 'What's The Matter With Love? (by LAURNEA WILKERSON) and 'We'll Never Say Goodbye' (by ART GARFUNKEL), all of them run-of-the-mill pop. Non-Premier League belters such as MICKEY THOMAS ('Sing'), JOHNNY KEMP (with film hit, 'Birthday Suit'), BILL CHAMPLIN ('Somethin' To Believe In'), PATTI LaBELLE ('Total Concentration') and the obligatory rock-ish number by KEVIN CRONIN of Reo Speedwagon ('(Everybody's Gotta) Face The Music'. Nearly a dozen artists on show here and not one of "stepping out" on their own musically. Thankfully the 90s and grunge was just around the proverbial corner. *MCS*

Album rating: *3

– spinoff hits, etc. –

JOHNNY KEMP: Birthday Suit / (instrumental)

Feb 89. (7") *<68569-7> (654838-7)* 36 May89
(12"+=/cd-s+=) *(654838-0/-2)* – (extended & club mixes).

□ SING AND SWING alt.
(⇒ LIVE IT UP)

SING BOY SING

1958 (US 91m b&w) 20th Century-Fox Cinemascope

Film genre: Rock'n'roll Musical drama

Top guns: dir: Henry Ephron / s-w: Claude Binyon (au: Paul Monash)

Stars: Tommy Sands *(Virgil Walker)*, Edmond O'Brien *(Joseph Sharkey)* ← the GIRL CAN'T HELP IT, Lili Gentle *(Leora Easton)*, John McIntire *(Rev. Walker)* → FLAMING STAR → HONKYTONK MAN, Nick Adams *(C.K. Judd)*, Josephine Hutchinson *(Caroline Walker)*, Diane Jergens *(Pat)* → HIGH SCHOOL CONFIDENTIAL! → TEENAGE MILLIONAIRE

Storyline: Rock star Virgil Walker enjoys his life as a popular singer, even though he knows he's being ripped off by his agent Joe Sharkey. His poorly grandfather, who belongs to the fire and brimstone school of preaching, is forever warning him about his lax lifestyle, and when the old boy dies guilt-ridden Virgil changes his ways and becomes a preacher himself. However, he is still torn in two between "sinful" rock music and the church version – will he choose a halo or a pair of horns? *JZ*

Movie rating: *5

Visual: none

Off the record: TOMMY SANDS (see below)

—

TOMMY SANDS (score: Lionel Newman)

Feb 58. (lp) *Capitol; <(T 929)>* 17 Apr58
– I'm gonna walk and talk with my Lord / Who baby / A bundle of dreams / Just a little bit more / People in love / Crazy 'cause I love you / Your daddy wants to do right / That's all I want from you / Soda-pop pop / Would I love you / Rock of ages / Sing boy sing.

S/track review: It seemed anybody who could croon in tune got a chance to whine and shine in a major rock'n'roll movie of the day – there was no doubt clean-cut good looks also helped. Chicago-born TOMMY SANDS, famous for nearly topping the charts a year earlier with 'Teen-Age Crush', was no exception – he was also married to Nancy Sinatra at the time. If there was talk of Elvis being drafted into the army, executive record producers wanted to come up with a new boy on the block. From uptempo rock'n'roll cues such as 'I'm Gonna Walk And Talk With My Lord' (complete with hand-clapping gospel intro), 'A Bundle Of Dreams' and 'Crazy 'Cause I Love You', to the soft'n'smoove, 'Who Baby', 'Just A Little Bit More' and 'People In Love', here we had the poor man's Elvis – but God loves a trier. Doesn't he just. Side two kicks off in the same vein, 'Your Daddy Wants To Do Right' giving the impression SANDS had just played 'Hound Dog' before he took to the studio. Ditto 'Soda-Pop Pop', but only this time it's 'Don't Be Cruel' that comes up for grabs. The uptempo/downtempo formula continues unabated for a further three numbers including 'That's All I Want From You' and the Southern country boy Top 30 title track. Thank the Lord for the Beatles. *MCS*

Album rating: *4

– spinoff hits, etc. –

TOMMY SANDS: Sing Boy Sing / Crazy 'Cause I Love You

Feb 58. (7") *<3867> (CL 14834)* 24

the SINGING DETECTIVE

2003 (US 109m) Paramount Pictures (R)

Film genre: Pop-Rock Musical & psychological drama

Top guns: dir: Keith Gordon / s-w: Dennis Potter ← LIPSTICK ON YOUR COLLAR ← BRIMSTONE & TREACLE

Stars: Robert Downey Jr. *(Dan Clark)* ← BLACK AND WHITE ← NATURAL BORN KILLERS, Robin Wright Penn *(Nicola / Nina / blonde)* ← the PRINCESS BRIDE / → BREAKING AND ENTERING, Mel Gibson *(Dr. Gibbon)* ← the MILLION DOLLAR HOTEL, Jeremy Northam *(Mark Binney)*, Adrien Brody *(first hood)*, Katie Holmes *(nurse Mills)* → PIECES OF APRIL, Jon Polito *(second hood)* ← the CROW, ← HOMEBOY, Carla Gugino *(Betty Dark / hooker)*, Saul Rubinek *(skin specialist)*, Alfre Woodard *(Chief of Staff)* ← CROOKLYN / → TAKE THE LEAD, Amy Aquino *(nurse Nozhki)* ← WORKING GIRL

Storyline: Novelist Dan Dark is in a hospital bed with acute psoriasis. Feverish and in great pain, he reviews one of his old books in his head with himself as the hero detective who sings musical numbers while solving murders. As he drifts in and out of consciousness he comes to realize that his psoriasis, like his daydreams, is all in the mind and he must resolve his own inner conflicts to heal himself properly. *JZ*

Movie rating: *6

Visual: dvd

Off the record: The original TV series in 1986 starring Michael Gambon in the lead role has been regarded as a classic – it features pre-rock'n'roll musical numbers. *MCS*

—

Various Artists

Oct 03. (cd) *Doc Hollywood; <DHS 2045>* [ ] [-]
– In my dreams (GENE VINCENT) / Just walking in the rain (JOHNNIE RAY) / Mr. Sandman (the CHORDETTES) / It's all in the game (TOMMY EDWARDS) / Poison Ivy (the COASTERS) / Important words (GENE VINCENT) / Harlem nocturne (the VISCOUNTS) / At the hop (DANNY & THE JUNIORS) / Woman love (GENE VINCENT) / When (the KALIN TWINS) / Flip flop and fly (BIG JOE TURNER) / Three steps to Heaven (EDDIE COCHRAN) / It's only make believe (CONWAY TWITTY) / In my dreams (ROBERT DOWNEY JR.).

S/track review: What English dramatist Dennis Potter would have made of the all-new American film version and soundtrack of 'The SINGING DETECTIVE' is anybody's guess. Judging on the jump from 1940s era nostalgia (in the original 1986 BBC-TV play) to 1950s rock'n'roll, one thinks he might've been a little perturbed had he still been alive (he died 7th June, 1994). Maybe 1950s staples, 'When' (by the KALIN TWINS) and the dreamy, powder-puff of 'Mr. Sandman' (by the CHORDETTES), would've been given pass marks by the playwright, but as for the rest of the R&B/R&R bunch, possibly not. The fact that rock'n'roller, GENE VINCENT, is afforded three lesser-known numbers here ('In My Dreams', 'Important Words' & 'Woman Love'), while his old mucker EDDIE COCHRAN gets only one ('Three Steps To Heaven'), may surprise many music buffs, although GENE shines through as always. Smash hits from DANNY & THE JUNIORS ('At The Hop'), the COASTERS ('Poison Ivy') and JOHNNIE RAY ('Just Walking In The Rain') take pride of place here, while the unearthing of non-hit 'Flip, Flop & Fly' (by BIG JOE TURNER) underpins the whole set. Bypassing CONWAY TWITTY, TOMMY EDWARDS and the VISCOUNTS, we come to finale track 'In My Dreams' (penned by GENE VINCENT, incidentally) from "the Singing Detective" himself, ROBERT DOWNEY, JR. This was certainly not the greatest crooning effort by any manner of means, but it did show the actor's versatility and nerve. *MCS*

Album rating: *6

SINGLES

1992 (US 100m) Warner Bros. Pictures (PG-13)

Film genre: romantic/urban comedy

Top guns: s-w + dir: Cameron Crowe → ALMOST FAMOUS

Stars: Bridget Fonda *(Janet Livermore)* ← SHAG: THE MOVIE / → GRACE OF MY HEART → TOUCH → JACKIE BROWN → FINDING GRACELAND → SOUTH OF HEAVEN, WEST OF HELL, Campbell Scott *(Steve Dunne)* → MUSIC AND LYRICS, Kyra Sedgwick *(Linda Powell)*, Sheila Kelley *(Debbie Hunt)*, Jim True *(David Bailey)*, Matt Dillon *(Cliff Poncier)* → GRACE OF MY HEART → ALBINO ALLIGATOR → the FUTURE IS UNWRITTEN, Bill Pullman *(Dr. Jeffrey Jamison)* → the END OF VIOLENCE, Ally Walker *(Pam)*, Eric Stoltz *(the mime)* ← FAST TIMES AT RIDGEMONT HIGH / → PULP FICTION → GRACE OF MY HEART → THINGS BEHIND THE SUN, Jeremy Piven *(Doug Hughley)* → JUDGMENT NIGHT, Tom Skerritt *(Mayor Weber)* ← UP IN SMOKE ← HAROLD AND MAUDE, **Pat Di Nizio** *(Sid)*, **Pearl Jam:- Eddie VEDDER *, Stone Gossard, Jeff Ament** *(themselves)* / **Soundgarden:- Chris Cornell, Matt Cameron, Kim Thayil, Ben Shepherd** * *(themselves)* → HYPE! / Bruce Pavitt *(Bruce)* → HYPE!, Cameron Crowe *(club interviewer)* ← AMERICAN HOT WAX, Peter Horton *(Jamie)* → the END OF VIOLENCE, Debi Mazar *(Brenda)* ← JUNGLE FEVER ← the DOORS ← DOWNTOWN 81 / → GIRL 6 → EMPIRE RECORDS → the INSIDER → BE COOL, Tim Burton *(Brian)*, Paul Giamatti *(kissing man)* → PRIVATE PARTS → MAN ON THE MOON → DUETS → STORYTELLING, **Alice In Chains:- Jerry Cantrell, Layne Staley, Michael Starr, Sean Kinney** *(themselves)*

Storyline: Proto-'Friends' japery in Seattle as a group of twenty-something block-mates negotiate life and love, pouring out their personal joys and woes along with the lattes at the local coffee shop. Thinking man's block-mate, Steve, has the dubious honour of meeting his true amour, Linda, at an Alice In Chains gig. After being given the run-around by a slimey Spanish student, however, she's wary of getting involved. Cliff Poncier is the Joey character, a solipsistic, lovably dumb longhair who plugs away with his band despite disparaging reviews. To his waif-ish girlfriend, Janet, he can do no wrong, even when he confesses to occasionally wishing her breasts were bigger. Of the grunge star cameos, the girthsome Tad steals the show but gets passed over on the soundtrack. *BG*

Movie rating: *6.5

Visual: video + dvd

Off the record: Among the grunge band was **Pat Di Nizio** of the Smithereens.

Various Artists (songs: PAUL WESTERBERG *)

Jun 92. (cd/c/lp) *Epic; <EK/ET 52476> (471438-2/-4/-1)* [6] Jul92 [ ]
– Would? (ALICE IN CHAINS) / Breath (PEARL JAM) / Seasons (CHRIS CORNELL) / Dyslexic heart (*) / Battle of Evermore (the LOVEMONGERS) / Chloe dancer – Crown of thorns (MOTHER LOVE BONE) / Birth ritual (SOUNDGARDEN) / State of love and trust (PEARL JAM) / Overblown (MUDHONEY) / Waiting for somebody (*) / May this be love (JIMI HENDRIX) / Nearly lost you (SCREAMING TREES) / Drown (SMASHING PUMPKINS).

S/track review: To the untrained ear, the first three tracks of this album could almost be the same band. For critics and a Friends Reunited generation who spent the early late 80s/early 90s hanging on 'Sub Pop's every 45, 'SINGLES' is often fetishised as some kind of holy grail; for a younger generation to whom grunge means zilch, it's not the greatest place to get started, stuffed as it is with the kind of dinosaur metallurgy that eventually dragged the whole thing down. Presumably John Coltrane, Muddy Waters, Sly & The Family Stone and Public Enemy weren't heavy – or white – enough to make the final cut. Shrewd timing ensured zeitgeist status even without Nirvana, yet MUDHONEY's Mark Arm, ringleader of perhaps the greatest – and definitely the least Led Zeppelin-obsessed – of Seattle's class of '92, says it all: "It's so overblown". At least the LOVEMONGERS (aka recovering hair-metallers ANN & NANCY WILSON) are honest enough to just come out and do a 'Zep cover version, 'The Battle Of Evermore'; ALICE IN CHAINS, PEARL JAM and MOTHER LOVE BONE (who've even perfected the Plant-patented "Wooomaaan . . .") howl away oblivious, and at times it can feel like one long, ceaseless dirge. Only SOUNDGARDEN do the quasi-Zeppelin bit with any real style; the pneumatic throb of 'Birth Ritual' is a lesson in how to flatter without imitating. When he wasn't indulging his own 70s fantasies, Billy Corgan always had an ear for a gorgeous melody and SMASHING PUMPKINS' 'Drown' is worth the price alone; it's not exactly Seattle, but it is some kind of wonderful, the kind that a checked shirt can't buy. Of a different timeline entirely, PAUL WESTERBERG isn't best served by his inclusions here (although 'Dyslexic Heart' and 'Waiting For Somebody' are catchy in a pop sense), and the JIMI HENDRIX track is transcendental in its incongruity, proof of just how pedestrian major-label rock music had become in the two decades since his death. If you want to know what grunge was all about, hunt down MUDHONEY's 'Superfuzz Bigmuff' instead. *BG*

Album rating: *6.5

SIR DRONE

1989 (US 57m video) Provisional Video

Film genre: Punk-Rock music comedy

Top guns: s-w + dir: Raymond Pettibon ← WEATHERMAN '69

Stars: Mike Kelley *(Jinx)*, **Mike Watt** *(Duane)* ← WEATHERMAN '69 / →

RISING LOW → WE JAM ECONO: THE STORY OF THE MINUTEMEN, Ricky Lee *(Skooter)*, Angela Taffe *(Goo)*, **Crane** *(Geezer)* ← WEATHERMAN '69, Chris Wilder *(Bizz)*, Joe Cole *(Drumbo)* ← WEATHERMAN '69 ← REALITY 86'D / → 1991: THE YEAR PUNK BROKE, Raymond Pettibon as Lance *(Vomit)*

Storyline: Jinx and his pals decide to leave the suburbs of Los Angeles and form a punk band along the road in Hollywood. They do all the things you would expect of a young punk band – play bad music, be drunk all day and chase after various groupies unfortunate enough to tag along with them. How will they get on with the other punk bands on the L.A. scene, who play bad music, get drunk all day etc., etc. *JZ*

Movie rating: *6

Visual: video (no audio OST)

Off the record: **Mike Watt** was ex-Minutemen.

the 6.5 SPECIAL

1958 (UK 85m b&w) Anglo-Amalgamated Productions

Film genre: Rock'n'roll Musical comedy

Top guns: dir: Alfred Shaughnessy / s-w: Norman Hudis ← the DUKE WORE JEANS ← the TOMMY STEELE STORY

Stars: Diane Todd *(Ann)*, Avril Leslie *(Judy)*, **Lonnie Donegan** *(performer)* → the COMPLEAT BEATLES → RED, WHITE & BLUES, **Dickie Valentine** *(performer)*, **Jim Dale** *(performer)*, **Russ Hamilton** *(performer)*, **Petula Clark** *(performer)* → the BIG T.N.T. SHOW, **Joan Regan** *(performer)*, **Don Lang and his Frenetic Five** *(performer/s)*, **Johnny Dankworth and his Orchestra with Cleo Laine** *(performer/s)*, **John Barry Seven** *(performers)*, Pete Murray *(himself)* → IT'S TRAD, DAD!, Freddie Mills *(himself)*, Mike & Bernie Winters *(themselves)*, Victor Soverall *(himself)*, Jimmy Lloyd *(himself)*, Jo Douglas *(herself)*, Finlay Currie *(himself)* → BUNNY LAKE IS MISSING

Storyline: A spin-off from the popular BBC-TV series ('Six-Five Special') a year earlier, and contrary to popular belief, this had a narrative. A teenage wannabe singer, Ann, is persuaded by a friend to find her popstar dreams and hops onto the "6.5 Special" overnight train to London. They find a plethora of British pop singers and television presenters heading the same way, so, she just might have a chance on the aforementioned telly show. Re-issued and shortened (to 58m) in 1962 as 'CALLING ALL CATS'. *MCS*

Movie rating: *4

Visual: Warner Home video (1991)

Off the record: Stand-up comedian, **Jim Dale**, nearly hit the top of the UK charts in 1957 with 'Be My Girl' – three Top 30 entries followed but he would subsequently make his fame in a dozen or so "Carry On" films. **Don Lang** actually sang the theme to the TV series and had the Top 5 hit 'Witch Doctor', when this film was in the pictures; he died 3rd August, 1992. **Lonnie Donegan** was the Scottish-born skiffle king who had a plethora of Top 10 hits including 'Rock Island LIne', 'Cumberland Gap' and 'Puttin' On The Style', before he branched out in novelty bubblegum (or chewing gum!) chart entries; he died of heart related problems on 2nd November 2002. **Petula Clark** was a pre-Rock'n'Roll music hall singer who went on to worldwide success on the back of hits like 'Sailor' and the classic 'Downtown'. **Dickie Valentine** was the singer with the Ted Heath orchestra and had two No.1 old-style hits, 'The Finger Of Suspicion' and 'Christmas Alphabet'. **Joan Regan** was of the same ilk and was mostly out of chart contention – having scored with 'If I Give My Heart To You' – by the time of this movie. **Jackie Dennis** had recently hit No.4 via single, 'La Dee Dah', while Everton-born **Russ Hamilton** nearly hit the top with 'We Will Make Love' in 1957. **Johnny Dankworth** and **John Barry** went on to greater orchestral things with numerous, and I mean numerous orchestral-based soundtracks (see future Scores edition). *MCS*

– spinoff releases, etc. –

PETULA CLARK: Baby Lover / (non-OST song)

Feb 58. (7"/78) *Pye Nixa; (N 15126)* [12] [–]

DIANE TODD: It's A Wonderful Thing To Be Loved / You Are My Favourite Dream

Mar 58. (7"/78) *Decca; (F 10993)* [ ] [–]

Various Artists

Mar 58. (7"ep) *Decca; (DFE 6485)* [ ] [–]
– (tracks by JACKIE DENNIS, JOAN REGAN, DIANE TODD & DICKIE VALENTINE).

SIX-STRING SAMURAI

1998 (US 91m) HSX Films / Palm Pictures (PG-13)

Film genre: sci-fi Rock Musical comedy adventure

Top guns: s-w: (+ dir) Lance Mungia, Jeffrey Falcon

Stars: Jeffrey Falcon *(Buddy)*, Justin McGuire *(the kid)*, Stephane Gauger *(Death)*, John Sakisian *(Russian general)*, Gabrielle Pimenter *(little man)*, Kim De Angelo *(mother)*, Clifford Hugo *(Psycho)*, Zuma Jay *(Clint)*, Monti Ellison *(head pin pal)*, **Red Elvises:- Igor Yuzov, Oleg Bernov, Avi Sills, Zhenya Kolykhanov** *(themselves/performers)*

Storyline: In a back-to-the-future, post-apocalyptic America decimated by Russian nukes, "Lost Vegas" is the dystopian desert capital. With Elvis dead, warrior guitarist-with-a-rock'n'roll-name Buddy fancies himself as a replacement ruler, finding himself a sidekick in the shape of an orphaned "Kid" as he cuts a Samurai swathe through the dunes. *BG*

Movie rating: *6

Visual: video + dvd

Off the record: The **RED ELVISES** (see below)

—

Various Artists (score: BRIAN TYLER * / + "dialogue")

Aug 98. (cd) *Ryko/Palm; <PALMCD 2003>* [ ] [–]
– United States of Russia (the RED ELVISES w/ "dialogue" & *) / Neverland (*) / Love pipe (the RED ELVISES) / A mother's hand – Buddy (*) / Fly away little butterfly (* w/ "dialogue") / "Kill 200 men" / Boogie on the beach (the RED ELVISES) / "I do not like rock and roll" / Hungarian dance #5 (the RED ELVISES) / "Arrowed kid" – Bowlers on the floor (*) / "Rock n' rolling ourselves to death" – Jerry's got the squeeze box (the RED ELVISES) / "Lonely highway of love" – Scorchi chronie (the RED ELVISES) / My darling Lorraine (the RED ELVISES) / Astro (*) / "Follow the yellow brick road" – Leech (the RED ELVISES) / "See you around kid" – Siberia (the RED ELVISES) / Good golly Miss Molly (the RED ELVISES) / My love is killing me (the RED ELVISES) / Sacred funeral (*) / Relentless sun (*) / Over the hill (*) / "Bring his guitar to me" – Sahara burn (*) / A boy and his spirit (*) / "If you were me, you'd be good-looking" – Surfing in Siberia (the RED ELVISES) / Dragging a fallen hero (*) / "Nice tuxedo" – Showdown at not okay corral (*) / "Bend before the ways of heavy metal" – Duelling guitars (*) / Dream march (*) / The great battle (*) / End of a hero – Finale (*) / On my way to Vegas (JA WAH).

S/track review: Yet another bunch of surf slingers neck deep in brylcreem, reverb and a Tarantino fixation? So what's new you cry? Well, the RED ELVISES just happen to hail from Siberia ("Land of cottage cheese and happy smiles" says their cod-chorale tribute), joining the polka dots from the Greek folk origins of Dick Dale's 'Miserlou' all the way back to Mother Russia. Cue copious wiry trilling, KGB interrogation-chamber/Cossack-esque chants/vocals and enough deadpan humour to crack up the Kremlin; the kind of soundtrack that'd have Borat slavering at the mouth. Their inimitable take on the iconography of their Cold War cousins is inevitably worth a tone-deaf titter: "Let's take a Greyhound bus to California, all that fancy food will make us hornier". The lads can even scat, although it sounds more like a bad case of indigestion. And you've got to hand it to a band who can sing the Monty Python/Weird Al Yankovic-esque lyrics of Chris Isaak take-off, 'My Love Is Killing Me' (sample: "She loves me too much when she kisses my ear, it sounds f**king loud, that's why I can't hear") with such straight-faced misery, over such an evocatively tragic balalaika melody. Don't get too excited, though, when just occasionally they come up with something that eschews novelty for Morricone-esque mood; read the small print and you'll discover it's actually composer Brian Tyler behind the schlepping tabla and tombstone guitar of 'Astro', the death-flange rattle of 'Sacred Funeral' and the Steppes-symphonic pieces which steer the whole mess to some kind of final showdown. Worth hearing at least once, preferably accompanied by a fistful of hamburgers on rye. *BG*

Album rating: *6.5

SKI PARTY

1965 (US 90m) Alta Vista / American International Pictures

Film genre: romantic Pop-Rock Musical comedy

Top guns: dir: Alan Rafkin / s-w: Robert Kaufman → the COOL ONES

Stars: Frankie AVALON *(Todd Armstrong)*, Dwayne Hickman *(Craig Gamble)* → HOW TO STUFF A WILD BIKINI, Deborah Walley *(Linda Hughes)* ← the GHOST IN THE INVISIBLE BIKINI ← BEACH BLANKET BINGO / → SPINOUT → IT'S A BIKINI WORLD, Yvonne Craig *(Barbara Norris)* ← ADVANCE TO THE REAR ← KISSIN' COUSINS ← IT HAPPENED AT THE WORLD'S FAIR, Robert Q. Lewis *(Donald Pevney)*, Bobbi Shaw *(Nita Elksberg)* ← BEACH BLANKET BINGO ← PAJAMA PARTY / → HOW TO STUFF A WILD BIKINI → the GHOST IN THE INVISIBLE BIKINI → PIPE DREAMS, Aron Kincaid *(Freddie Carter)* ← the GIRLS ON THE BEACH / → BEACH BALL → the GIRL IN THE INVISIBLE BIKINI, Steve Rogers *(Gene)* ← the GIRLS ON THE BEACH / → WILD, WILD WINTER, Patti Chandler *(Janet)* ← BEACH BLANKET BINGO ← PAJAMA PARTY ← BIKINI BEACH / → HOW TO STUFF A WILD BIKINI, Mike Nader *(Bobby)* ← BEACH BLANKET BINGO ← PAJAMA PARTY ← BIKINI BEACH ← MUSCLE BEACH PARTY ← BEACH PARTY / → HOW TO STUFF A WILD BIKINI → the TRIP, Salli Sachse *(Indian)* ← BEACH BLANKET BINGO ← PAJAMA PARTY ← BIKINI BEACH ← MUSCLE BEACH PARTY / → HOW TO STUFF A WILD BIKINI → the GHOST IN THE INVISIBLE BIKINI → THUNDER ALLEY → the TRIP → WILD IN THE STREETS, Mikki Jamison *(Mikki)* → BEACH BALL, Mary Hughes *(Mary)* ← BEACH BLANKET BINGO ← PAJAMA PARTY ← BIKINI BEACH ← MUSCLE BEACH PARTY / → HOW TO STUFF A WILD BIKINI / → THUNDER ALLEY, Mickey Dora *(Mickey)* ← BEACH BLANKET BINGO ← BIKINI BEACH ← MUSCLE BEACH PARTY ← SURF PARTY ← BEACH PARTY / → HOW TO STUFF A WILD BIKINI, Luree Holmes *(Luree)* ← BEACH BLANKET BINGO ← PAJAMA PARTY ← BIKINI BEACH ← MUSCLE BEACH PARTY ← BEACH PARTY / → HOW TO STUFF A WILD BIKINI → the GHOST IN THE INVISIBLE BIKINI → THUNDER ALLEY → the TRIP, **James BROWN** *(performer)*, **Lesley Gore** *(performer)* ← the GIRLS ON THE BEACH ← the T.A.M.I. SHOW, **ANNETTE Funicello** *(cameo)*, + Dick Miller ← the GIRLS ON THE BEACH ← ROCK ALL NIGHT ← CARNIVAL ROCK / → BEACH BALL → WILD, WILD WINTER → the WILD ANGELS → the TRIP → TRUCK TURNER → I WANNA HOLD YOUR HAND → ROCK'N'ROLL HIGH SCHOOL → GET CRAZY → SHAKE, RATTLE & ROCK! tv, **Marvin Hamlisch** *(himself)*

Storyline: Beach Party movie which centers around two college friends, Todd and Craig, who fancy a pair of English girls, Jane and Nora. They decide on gate-crashing a girls-only ski lodge. *MCS*

Movie rating: *4.5

Visual: dvd double feature w/ 'MUSCLE BEACH PARTY'

Off the record: Songs featured in the film are:- **FRANKIE AVALON** ('Ski Party', 'Lots, Lots More', 'Paintin' The Town' – with DEBORAH WALLEY, DWAYNE HICKMAN & YVONNE CRAIG) plus 'We'll Never Change Them' by DEBORAH WALLEY and 'The Gasser' by the HONDELLS. **Lesley Gore** (b. Lesley Sue Goldstein, 2 May'46, Brooklyn, New York City, NY) was discovered by Quincy Jones and had already a string of US Top 5 hits behind her including 'It's My Party', 'Judy's Turn To Cry', 'She's A Fool' and 'You Don't Own Me' – all when she was still a teenager. *MCS*

– spinoff hits, etc. –

LESLEY GORE: Sunshine, Lollipops And Rainbows / (non-OST-song)

Jun 65. (7") *Mercury; <72433> (MF 862)* [13] [ ]

JAMES BROWN & THE FAMOUS FLAMES : I Got You (I Feel Good) / (non-OST song)

Oct 65. (7") *King; <6015> Pye Int. (7N 25350)* [3] [29]

□ SLADE segment
(⇒ FLAME)

SLAVES TO THE UNDERGROUND

1997 (US 93m) NEO Motion Pictures (R)

Film genre: romantic Rock music-based comedy/drama

Top guns: dir: Kristine Peterson / s-w: Bill Cody

Stars: Molly Gross *(Shelly)*, Marisa Ryan *(Suzy)*, Jason Bortz *(Jimmy)*, **B. Neuwirth** *(Big Phil)* ← RENALDO AND CLARA ← DON'T LOOK BACK / → NO DIRECTION HOME, Natacha LaFerriere *(Zoe)*, Claudia Rossi *(Brenda)*, **James Garver** *(Brian)*, Bill Johns *(Joe Burke)* ← GEORGIA

Storyline: Shelly and Suzy are leaders of an all-girl punk band, No Exit. Just when they are about to hit the big time, Shelly's ex-boyfriend Jimmy arrives on the scene and causes trouble between the girls, who have begun a lesbian affair. Now Shelly finds herself in love with both Suzy and Jimmy and the future of the band is in doubt as issues of feminism and sexuality threaten to ruin the girls' relationship. *JZ*

Movie rating: *4.5

Visual: video (no audio OST by Mike Martt)

Off the record: James Garver was the guitarist with Garth Brooks. Tracks – mainly of the Grunge variety – featuring "No Exit" (aka Red Five & stars Molly &/or Marisa):- 'Ego', 'Little Mind', 'Sometimes The Truth', 'Lisa', 'Cover Me'. Other artists on the soundtrack are MIRIAM CUTLER ('TV Que'), LO BALL ('Airsick'), JOAN JETT/EVIL STIG ('Activity Grrrl' & You Got A Problem'), FLUFFER ('The Ballad Of Larry Csonka'), TEEN ANGELS ('Rawhead'), DECAL ('So Long'), STARFISH ('Runaround' & 'Princeton Reverb'), POLARA ('Taupe'), ABBY TRAVIS with MOMMY ('Give Me Just A Little More Time'), LIFTER 'Sullen Wood'), STONE FOX ('Tiny Box Of Lies'), NOISE ADDICT ('My Pathetic Friend' & 'Poison 1080'), JOHN MASSARI ('America Tonight'), SUZI GARDNER & MIKE MARTT ('Downtown Lights'); latter w/ 'Who's Sorry Now', BUTT TRUMPET ('Love/Hate'), ANI DiFRANCO ('Buildings And Bridges'). *MCS*

a SLIPPING-DOWN LIFE

1999 (US 111m) DVC Entertainment / Lions Gate Films (R)

Film genre: romantic showbiz/Pop-music comedy/drama

Top guns: s-w + dir: Toni Kalem (au: Anne Tyler)

Stars: Lili Taylor *(Evie Decker)* ← I SHOT ANDY WARHOL ← FOUR ROOMS / → HIGH FIDELITY, Guy Pearce *(Drumstrings Casey)* → RAVENOUS → the PROPOSITION, John Hawkes *(David Elliot)* ← HEARTBREAK HOTEL, Irma P. Hall *(Clotelia)* ← STRAIGHT TALK ← BOOK OF NUMBERS / → DON'T LET GO, Sara Rue *(Violet)* → GYPSY 83, Veronica Cartwright *(Mrs. Casey)*, Tom Bower *(Mr. Decker)* → the MILLION DOLLAR HOTEL, Marshall Bell *(Mr. Bell)* ← AIRHEADS ← DICK TRACY ← TUCKER: THE MAN AND HIS DREAM ← BIRDY, Shawnee Smith *(Faye-Jean Lindsay)*, Clea DuVall *(nurse)* ← GIRL / → COMMITTED → the SLAUGHTER RULE, Bruno Kirby *(kiddee arcades manager)* ← the BASKETBALL DIARIES ← GOOD MORNING, VIETNAM ← BIRDY ← THIS IS SPINAL TAP ← WHERE THE BUFFALO ROAM ← ALMOST SUMMER

Storyline: Evie is a lonely young woman whose sole enjoyment is listening to late night radio in her home in Carolina. One night her whole life changes when she hears a singer called Drumstrings Casey and becomes infatuated with him, to the extent of tattooing his name on her forehead. She goes to his concerts and her "headware" draws the attention of the media and Casey himself. But while Evie falls head over heels in love, Casey's career problems start to overshadow their romance. *JZ*

Movie rating: *6

Visual: dvd

Off the record: GUY PEARCE (see below)

—

GUY PEARCE (score: Peter Himmelman)

Jun 04. (cd) *Commotion / Koch; <CR 002 / KOC CD 5755>* [ ] [-]
– One grey morning / You've got a sweet mouth on you baby / You alone / Fuse / This cruel thing / Dirty windows / Elizabeth Jade / Monkey / In this love / Want too much / Start again.

S/track review: 'A SLIPPING-DOWN LIFE' offers a pleasant surprise in that GUY PEARCE is an actor who can actually sing a bit without sounding forced. Okay so he's no Frank Sinatra, but he can carry off the songs here, which are mostly blues-influenced soft-rock, without any pretentiousness or flat attempt at unattainable perfection. His voice is rough and he doesn't hit every note but he at least sounds like he means it and there is enough intensity and energy to make it worth a listen. The songs are all written by a variety of highly-respected singer-songwriters such as Ron Sexsmith, Joe Henry, Robyn Hitchcock and Vic Chesnutt (Guy's backing band feature RANDY JACOBS – guitar, bass; CURT BISQUERA – drums; JENNIFER CONDOS – bass; CRAIG ROSS – bass, organ, additional guitar), and add depth to the soundtrack, creating something that is not merely a superficial accompaniment to the film. The album could easily stand alone as a body of work that is at least the equal of many artists out there. Not all the songs are great but there are some gems hidden here. Opening track 'One Grey Morning' is a mid-paced blues rock number with a funky guitar riff and 'You Alone' is a good acoustic love song. Arguably the best tracks though are 'Fuse' and 'Elizabeth Jade', the former a dark, taut piece, reminiscent of the likes of James Grant and Tom Waits, while the latter is just a good ole rock'n'roll stomper that could easily hark back to Them or the 13th Floor Elevators. However, a few of the tracks are a bit weak; 'You've Got A Sweet Mouth On You Baby', 'This Cruel Thing' and 'Start Again' are tedious affairs that place a large blot in the copybook. On the whole, though, this soundtrack is a decent album, without being spectacular. *CM*

Album rating: *5.5

SLUMBER PARTY MASSACRE II

1987 sequel (US 75m) Concorde Pictures (R)

Film genre: slasher/horror comedy rock Musical

Top guns: s-w + dir: Deborah Brock → ROCK'N'ROLL HIGH SCHOOL FOREVER

Stars: Crystal Bernard *(Courtney Bates)*, Kimberly McArthur *(Amy)*, Juliette Cummins *(Sheila Barrington)*, Patrick Lowe *(Matt Arbicost)*, Heidi Kozak *(Sally Burns)*, Atanas Ilitch *(the driller killer)*, Cynthia Eilbacher *(Valerie Bates)*, Hamilton Mitchell *(officer Voorhies)* ← CADDYSHACK, Jennifer Rhodes *(Mrs. Bates)*

Storyline: Singer Courtney and her all-girl rock group decide to enjoy a weekend of music and geeky boyfriends in a disused condominium. Poor Courtney's still behaving strangely after the first massacre, and her dreams consist not of hunky boyfriends and cuddly bunnies but of a drill-wielding maniac who's out to get her. Massacre number two begins when her dreams merge with reality and the driller killer really gets the bit between his teeth. *JZ*

Movie rating: *2

Visual: video + dvd (no audio OST; score: Richard Cox)

Off the record: Songs include 'Tokyo Convertible' (penned by John Coinman), 'If Only' (WEDNESDAY WEEK; written by Kristi & Kelly Callan), 'Don't Let Go' (penned by Michael Monagan), 'Hell's Cafe' (HELL'S CAFE; Gregory Lee Schilling), 'Why' (WEDNESDAY WEEK; penned by Heidi Rodewald and another from their one and only set, 'What We Had'), 'Let's Buzz' (by John Juke Logan) & 'Can't Stop (Lovin' You)' (by Sterling E. Smith). Crystal Bernard (b.30 Sep'61, Garland, Texas) was literally born to sing having performed with her father and sister as the Bernard Trio from an early age (over a dozen gospel LPs). She subsequently wrote songs for Paula Abdul ('If I Were Your Girl'), etc., while she also sang duet with Peter Cetera ('I Wanna Take Forever Tonight'). *MCS*

SMASHING TIME

1967 (UK 96m) Paramount Pictures (PG-13)

Film genre: Mod/Pop Musical comedy

Top guns: dir: Desmond Davis / s-w: **George Melly**

Stars: Rita Tushingham *(Brenda)* → the GURU → SWING, Lynn Redgrave *(Yvonne)*, Michael York *(Tom Wabe)* → the GURU → 54, Ian Carmichael *(Bobbi Mome-Rath)*, Anna Quayle *(Charlotte Brilling)* ← a HARD DAY'S NIGHT, Irene Handl *(Mrs. Gimble)* ← JUST FOR FUN / → WONDERWALL → the GREAT ROCK'N'ROLL SWINDLE → ABSOLUTE BEGINNERS, Jeremy Lloyd *(Jeremy Tove)* ← JUST FOR FUN, Arthur Mullard *(cafe boss)*, Peter Jones *(Dominic)* → CONFESSIONS OF A POP PERFORMER, Toni Palmer *(Toni)* ← WHAT A CRAZY WORLD, Arthur Mullard *(cafe boss)* ← CUCKOO PATROL ← IT'S TRAD, DAD!, **Tomorrow:- John Alder, Steve Howe** *, **John Pearce, Keith West** *(the Snarks)* → YESSONGS *, **David Essex** *(beatnik)* → THAT'LL BE THE DAY → STARDUST → SILVER DREAM RACER

Storyline: Yvonne and Brenda are two innocent girls from "oop north" who decide to sample life in swinging sixties London. The two girls soon go their separate ways, one as a singer and the other as a fashion model, each managing to leave a trail of mayhem on their travels. Be prepared for chip shop riots and a pie fight straight from a Mack Sennett film as well as a round-the-town tour of London. *JZ*

Movie rating: *6

Visual: video + dvd

Off the record: **TOMORROW** were a pop-rock from London and formed in 1967 out of the In-Crowd by singer Keith West, guitarist Steve Howe, drummer Twink (John Adler) and bassist John Pearce. With psychedelia all the rage, their first single, 'My White Bicycle', was surely in the one-that-got-away category, although it did surface six years later as a UK Top 10 smash for Nazareth. Another flop 45 surfaced later in the year, tailed by an eponymous album which did little or nothing except become a subsequent collector's item. Meanwhile, Keith West's 'Excerpt From A Teenage Opera' (aka "Grocer Jack") had made him a star overnight when it peaked at No.2 – it hadn't all been bad then. Suddenly requests for Keith and Tomorrow to tour were so demanding, that they even wanted the 4-piece to play the hit, although it was originally recorded in the studio with a full orchestra! It was inevitable that they would disband after the album's release. West continued for a short spell as a solo artist, while Twink joined the Pretty Things; Howe formed Bodast before joining Yes. *MCS*

—

RITA TUSHINGHAM &/or LYNN REDGRAVE (composer: John Addison w/ instrumentals *)

Feb 68. (lp) *Stateside; (SSL 10224) A.B.C.; <ABC/S-OC 6>* [ ] Apr68 [ ]
– Smashing Time (main title) / Carnaby Street / Waiting for my friend / Aerosol knock-about (*) / New clothes / It's always your fault / While I'm still young / Day out / Trouble / The morning after / Jabberwock march (*) / Baby don't go / Can't help laughing (*) / Swinging thru London / Pie fight (*) / Smashing Time (end title).

S/track review: "Two girls go stark Mod!" and by accounts Brenda (RITA TUSHINGHAM of a 'A Taste Of Honey' fame) and Yvonne

(LYNN REDGRAVE of 'Georgy Girl' renown) were indeed having a 'SMASHING TIME'. From the opening (and closing) title track to the colourful 'Carnaby Street', etc, etc, the girls sing like there was no Tomorrow (that particular quartet didn't feature on the LP). You can hear the twee innocence of the mid-20-ish actresses, although their shortcomings were the record's appeal. "Going Down To London/Going Down To London/We Hope To Make A Splash In Time . . ." are examples of the lyrical folly supplied by trad jazzman George Melly (who incidentally co-wrote the screenplay), while the vaudeville-ian score was the work of (part-lyricist) JOHN ADDISON who conducted the London Sinfonia Group. Cheeky and chirpy best describe his playful tunes spread all over the set (and complemented by concertina and banjo!), his best cue stemming from 'Aerosol Knock-About'. While there were goddamn embarrassing moments (TUSHINGHAM's 'New Clothes' for one, and REDGRAVE's 'Baby Don't Go' for another), there were a few choice cuts. Without doubt, three teen anthems stand out from the pack, Rita's 'Trouble', Lynn's 'While I'm Still Young' and the girls' duet 'Day Out'. A question that crops up is: was there a Slits-like cover of the former song? – the whispered lyrics are "Oh Oh Oh/Got To Get Her Out Of Trouble/Oh Oh Oh/Now She's Nearly Seeing Double". The aforementioned gems are worthy of the admission price alone. What about a "40th Anniversary" CD re-issue? *MCS*

Album rating: *6.5

– spinoff singles, etc. –

RITA TUSHINGHAM & LYNN REDGRAVE: Smashing Time / RITA TUSHINGHAM: Waiting For My Friend

Jan 68. (7") *(SS 2081)* ☐ [-]

☐ Keely SMITH segment
(⇒ HEY BOY! HEY GIRL!)

SMITHEREENS

1982 (US 89m) Domestic Productions (R)

Film genre: urban drama

Top guns: s-w: Susan Seidelman (+ dir), Peter Askin, Ron Nyswaner (+ story)

Stars: Susan Berman *(Wren)*, Brad Riin *(Paul)*, **Richard HELL** *(Eric)*, Nada Despotovich *(Cecile)* → SERIES 7, Roger Jett *(Billy)*, Kitty Summerall *(Eric's wife)*, **X-Sessive** *(lead singer)*, Amos Poe *(bar hustler)* ← SUBWAY RIDERS ← DOWNTOWN 81 ← the FOREIGNER, Roma Maffia *(prostitute)* → the DAVID CASSIDY STORY

Storyline: Untalented herself, Wren, decides to promote herself through potential NY scene punk rock stars, Paul and Eric. However, her plans go somewhat awry when she and Eric scam money in order to pursue their dream in California. *MCS*

Movie rating: *6.5

Visual: video + dvd

Off the record: RICHARD HELL (on two songs, 'Another World' & 'The Kid With The Replaceable Head') had already starred in the film, 'BLANK GENERATION', while singer **X-Sessive** was unknown. Singer/guitarists, GLENN MERCER and BILL MILLION (of the Feelies), contributed the music to the unreleased soundtrack ('The Boy With The Perpetual Nervousness', 'Loveless Love' & 'Original Love'). The band had been around the New York scene since 1976, releasing a handful of 45s (for 'Rough Trade' UK) and a 1980 LP, 'Crazy Rhythms' (for 'Stiff' records). After the pair reunited for 'SMITHEREENS', the Feelies were back in circulation and subsequently featured in the soundtrack to the film, 'Something Wild', in 1986. Other tracks included 'I Never Felt' (the NITECAPS), 'Guitar Beat' (the RAYBEATS), 'Out Of Baby's Reach' (DAVE WECKERMAN), 'Devious Woman' (SINGERS AND PLAYERS) and 'Moody' (ESG). *MCS*

SNOOP DOGG

Born: Calvin Cordozar Broadus, Jr., 20 Oct'71, Long Beach, California, USA. There are few more distinctive images in hip hop than the trademark braids and deceptively sleepy visage of bad boy extraordinaire and impressively enduring hip hop godfather, SNOOP (DOGGY) DOGG. A fully paid up gangsta who co-founded the West Coast G-Funk sound with mentor Dr Dre, he went on to maintain a prolific sideline in acting (and a consistently high TV/media profile) Ó la ICE's CUBE and T. As fate would have it, his first collaboration with Dre was a theme for Bill Duke's drug noir, 'Deep Cover' (1992), recorded the same year as Dre's seminal debut, 'The Chronic'. While SNOOP's equally influential 'Doggstyle' (1993) made him one of the hottest stars in hip hop, a Dre-directed short film/soundtrack, 'MURDER WAS THE CASE' (1994), was released in the midst of a real life murder trial relating to the death of a gang member; SNOOP was acquitted but the legal complexities rumbled on until 1996. In the meantime, he'd contributed to another Dre-produced 'Death Row' landmark with the soundtrack for Jeff Pollack's basketball drama, 'Above The Rim' (1994). After acrimoniously departing 'Death Row', he pitched up at Master P's Southern-fried 'No Limits' outfit, contributing the track 'Hooked' for P-scripted mobile phone farce, 'I Got The Hook Up!' (1998), adding a cameo to that year's healthy quota of screen credits for similar P-scripted fare like 'MP Da Last Don' and 'Da Game Of Life' (his first full length starring role), as well as a cameo alongside the likes of WILLIE NELSON in Dave Chappelle-written comedy, 'Half Baked' and a part in 'Menace II Society'-producer Darin Scott's crime thriller, 'Caught Up'. He was back on top of a P script in 1999's 'Hot Boyz', also starring alongside ICE-T in low budget Albert Pyun actioners, 'Urban Menace' and 'The Wrecking Crew', alongside Doug E. Fresh in Marc Levin's 'WHITEBOYS' (1999) and – alongside a regrouped NWA – on the soundtrack to ICE CUBE comedy, 'Next Friday'. SNOOP kicked off the new millennium by producing and starring in his own gang-based crime drama, 'The Eastsidaz' (2000), and again appeared alongside ICE-T – and Ja Rule – in Donald Goines adaptation, 'Crime Partners' (2001). As well as moving into porn – paving the way for his peers to do the same – with the Larry Flynt-produced 'Snoop Dogg's Doggystyle' and starring alongside Pam Grier in blaxploitation-cum-horror-spoof 'BONES' (he also supplies several songs for the soundtrack), 2001 saw a number of higher profile credits including John Singleton's 'Baby Boy' and – alongside Denzel Washington and Ethan Hawke – Antoine Fuqua's Oscar-winning 'Training Day'. He also executively produced and starred – in tandem with Dr Dre – in ensemble comedy, 'The Wash' (2001), likewise supplying its title theme as well as the theme for the Eddie Murphy-starring 'Dr. Doolittle 2' (2001). The following year he was in the rarefied company of Bootsy Collins and Fred Wesley on the soundtrack to blaxploitation spoof, 'Undercover Brother' (2002), going on to surpass himself as Huggy Bear alongside Ben Stiller, Owen Wilson and Fred Williamson in the inevitable remake of 'Starsky & Hutch' (2004). Less well remembered is his part as Captain Mack in Mile High comedy, 'Soul Plane' (2004), while a narration credit – alongside the likes of Mandy Moore and Whoopi Goldberg – in talking animal family feature, 'Racing Stripes' (2005), suggested the ageing gangsta was beginning to mellow. His continuing brushes with the law notwithstanding, it was an impression compounded by an uncharacteristically bohemian role in retro race drama, 'The Tenants' (2005) and another narration credit in Luc Besson's 'Arthur Et Les Minimoys' (2006), if not by a pimping lead part in another blaxploitation tribute, 'BOSS'N UP' (2005), the debut feature of his production company 'Snoopadelic Films' and itself inspired by his multi-platinum Neptunes-produced album, 'R&G

(Rhythm And Gangsta): The Masterpiece' (2004). Comic book-inspired trilogy 'Hood Of Horror', served as the company's 2006 follow-up with SNOOP taking a demonic starring role. *BG*

- **filmography** {acting} (composer) –

the Show *(1995 {p} OST by V/A =>)* / Half-Baked *(1998 {b} OST by V/A)* / Caught Up *(1998 {a} future edition)* / **Ride** *(1998 {a} on OST w/ V/A =>)* / I Got The Hook Up *(1998 {b} on OST by V/A; future edition)* / the Wrecking Crew *(1999 {a})* / Hot Boyz *(1999 {*})* / Urban Menace *(1999 {*})* / **Whiteboys** *(1999 {c})* / tha Eastsidaz *(2000 {*})* / Crime Partners 2000 *(2001 {*})* / Baby Boy *(2001 {a} on OST by V/A =>)* / Training Day *(2001 {a} OST by V/A; see future edition)* / **Bones** *(2001 {*} on OST by V/A =>)* / the Wash *(2001 {a} on OST by V/A; see future edition)* / Whasango *(2001 {v})* / **Thug Angel – The Life Of An Angel** *(2002 {c} OST by V/A =>)* / Old School *(2003 {c})* / **Malibu's Most Wanted** *(2003 {v} on OST by V/A =>)* / Starsky & Hutch *(2004 {*} OST by V/A; see future edition)* / Soul Plane *(2004 {*} on OST by V/A; future edition)* / the Tenants *(2005 {*})* / Racing Stripes *(2005 {v} OST see; future editions =>)* / the L.A. Riot Spectacular *(2005 {n})* / **Boss'n Up** *(2005 {*})* / Hood Of Horror *(2006 {*})*

SNOW

1996 (US 81m b&w) Winter Light Films LLC

Film genre: romantic urban drama

Top guns: s-w + dir: Eric Tretbar

Stars: Shane Barach *(Thomas)*, Rose Mailutha *(Sabina)*, Lara Miklasevics *(Jessica)*, Erika Remillard *(Robbie)*, John Crozier *(Spike)*, Khalil Jamal Battle *(Marcus)*

Storyline: Rock musician Thomas wakes up one morning to find that he is no longer top dog of the Minneapolis music scene. Things get even worse when his girlfriend Jessica leaves him. Feeling sorry for himself, he heads for a coffee shop where by chance he meets out-of-luck Sabina, and they decide to spend 24 hours together to relive the good times of their youth. But Sabina has a young child to look after, and Thomas no longer has a job to go to. *JZ*

Movie rating: *6

Visual: none (no audio OST by Chan Poling)

Off the record: nothing

SOME PEOPLE

1962 (UK 93m b&w) Vic Films / Anglo-Amalgamated

Film genre: Pop-music melodrama

Top guns: dir: Clive Donner → HERE WE GO ROUND THE MULBERRY BUSH / s-w: John Eldridge

Stars: Kenneth More *(Mr. Smith)*, Ray Brooks *(Johnnie)* ← PLAY IT COOL, Annika Wilks *(Anne)*, David Andrews *(Bill)*, Angela Douglas *(Terry)* → IT'S ALL HAPPENING, David Hemmings *(Bert)* ← PLAY IT COOL / → LIVE IT UP → BE MY GUEST → BLOW-UP → PROFONDO ROSSO → la VIA DELLA DROGA, Harry H. Corbett *(Johnnie's father)* → WHAT A CRAZY WORLD → SILVER DREAM RACER, Fanny Carby *(Johnnie's mother)* → WHAT A CRAZY WORLD → the FAMILY WAY, Frankie Dymon *(Black Power militant)* → SYMPATHY FOR THE DEVIL

Storyline: "Some people think that kids today have gone astray", is the opening line from a film that tackle the issues of being a bored youth in the early 60s. A group of delinquents living in Bristol get into all sorts of trouble, before being persuaded to form a rock band by local choirmaster, Mr. Smith. *MCS*

Movie rating: *6

Visual: video (no audio OST by Ron Grainer)

Off the record: Harry H. Corbett went on to star in the classic TV comedy, 'Steptoe & Son'. *MCS*

– spinoff releases, etc. –

VALERIE MOUNTAIN: Some People / Yes You Did

Apr 62. (7") *Pye; (7N 15450)* [ ] [-]

EAGLES: Bristol Express / Johnny's Tune

Apr 62. (7") *Pye; (7N 15451)* [ ] [-]

Various Artists: SOME PEOPLE EP

May 62. (7"ep) *Pye; (NEP 24158)* [2] [-]
– (compilation of above)

RON GRAINER: Johnny's Tune / (non-OST song)

1962. (7") *Fontana; (267232 TF)* [ ] [-]

SONGWRITER

1984 (US 94m) Tri-Star Pictures (R)

Film genre: showbiz/Country-music drama

Top guns: s-w: Alan Rudolph (+ dir ← ROADIE), Edwin (Bud) Shrake

Stars: Willie NELSON *(Doc Jenkins)*, **Kris KRISTOFFERSON** *(Blackie Buck)*, Melinda Dillon *(Honey Carder)* ← BOUND FOR GLORY / → MAGNOLIA, Rip Torn *(Dino McLeish)* ← FLASHPOINT ← ONE-TRICK PONY ← PAYDAY ← YOU'RE A BIG BOY NOW / → WHERE THE RIVERS FLOW NORTH → the INSIDER, Lesley Ann Warren *(Gilda)* ← BAJA OKLAHOMA → PURE COUNTRY, Mickey Raphael *(Arly)* ← HONEYSUCKLE ROSE / → TEATRO, Rhonda Dotson *(Corkie)*, Richard C. Sarafian *(Rodeo Rocky)* → MASKED AND ANONYMOUS, Shannon Wilcox *(Anita)* ← the BORDER, Gailard Sartain *(Mulreaux)* ← HARD COUNTRY ← ROADIE ← the BUDDY HOLLY STORY ← NASHVILLE, **Johnny Gimble** *(fiddle player)* ← HONKYTONK MAN ← HONEYSUCKLE ROSE / → ALAMO BAY, Gilda's band:- **Booker T. Jones** *(keyboard player)* ← a STAR IS BORN, **Grady Martin** *(guitarist)* ← HONEYSUCKLE ROSE, **Jody Payne** *(guitarist)* ← HONEYSUCKLE ROSE, **Bobbie Nelson** *(pianist)* ← HONEYSUCKLE ROSE, **Bee Spears** *(bassist)* ← HONEYSUCKLE ROSE, **Paul English** *(drummer)* ← HONEYSUCKLE ROSE, Roarers Band:- **Donnie Fritts** *(performer)* ← a STAR IS BORN ← PAT GARRETT & BILLY THE KID / → the LIFE AND HARD TIMES OF GUY TERRIFICO, **Steve Fromholz** *(engineer)* ← OUTLAW BLUES, Thomas McClure, Sammy Lee Creason, Michael Reesburg *(performers)*

Storyline: The "Songwriter" in question is Doc Jenkins, a talented musician but a hopeless businessman. When he is duped into selling his assets to wide boy Rodeo Rocky, he goes to see his old pal Blackie to cry on his shoulder. Together with young singer Gilda (who likes a drink or three), they come up with a Machiavellian plan to turn the tables on Rocky. But things don't quite go to plan when an unlooked-for romance blooms between Doc and Gilda. *JZ*

Movie rating: *5.5

Visual: video

Off the record: Booker T. Jones, Grady Martin, Jody Payne, Bee Spears & Bobbie Nelson were all in Gilda's band.

WILLIE NELSON & KRIS KRISTOFFERSON: Music from Songwriter

Oct 84. (lp/c) *Columbia; <FC 39531>* [ ] [-]
– How do you feel about foolin' around / Songwriter / Who'll buy my memories / Write your own songs / Nobody said it was going to be easy / Good times / Eye of the storm (duet) / Crossing the border / Down to her socks / Under the gun / The final attraction.

S/track review: Independent thinkers, great talents and both men with a story to tell, WILLIE NELSON and KRIS KRISTOFFERSON are kindred spirits who have worked together frequently since the early 80s – to questionable effect. The truth is, NELSON is an infinitely superior performer, and the best combination of the pair is arguably on the 'Willie Nelson Sings Kris Kristofferson' album, made five years before this movie. For 'SONGWRITER', they join forces on two unremarkable duets, dividing the rest of the album between them. NELSON fares the best, turning out five excellent new songs: songs rich with a voice that manages to be both raw and intimate, beautifully measured small group arrangements with his time-served band, and his own utterly-distinctive spiky interpolations on acoustic guitar. Never before, surely, has the line "Is your head up your ass so far that you can't get it out?" (in 'Write Your Own Songs', his rebuke to the music industry) sounded like a lullaby. KRISTOFFERSON's contribution is less arresting, coloured by rock mannerisms which do nothing for a characterful but wobbly voice, and lacking any surefire additions to his impressive back-catalogue as a composer. Nominated for the Oscar for best original song score, the collection was pipped by 'PURPLE RAIN'. *ND*

Album rating: *6.5

SONNY & CHER

Formed: As one half of the neo-hippy odd couple who dominated the mid-60s charts and the early 70s TV ratings, CHER used her showbiz schooling to carve out a distinctive and highly successful acting career while her partner and mentor SONNY BONO substituted pop for politics. The pair initially hooked up when CHER was still a teenager and BONO an opportunistic Phil Spector protégé. Pitting the latter's diminutive Sicilian flamboyance against the former's dusky, statuesque physique, their visual appeal was as central to their early success as campy BONO-penned chestnuts like 'I Got You Babe' and 'Bang Bang (My Baby Shot Me Down)'. The inevitable move from Sunset Strip to Hollywood was previewed with a singing cameo appearance in teen movie, 'WILD ON THE BEACH' (1965) and 'GOOD TIMES' (1967), an all-singing fantasy vehicle for the duo's rapidly fading pop career. Despite the latter's failure at the box office, SONNY subsequently wrote the screenplay and composed the music for CHER's first major feature, 'CHASTITY' (1969), another costly dud which compounded the misery of huge tax bills and contractual problems. Although a wisecracking, early 70s TV variety show gave the couple a second wind, it was CHER who successfully forged ahead in the entertainment world following their personal and professional mid-decade divorce. And while BONO secured some TV work and occasional parts in pedestrian action movies like 'The Golden Raiders' (1979) and 'Escape To Athena' (1979), it was CHER who received all the attention for what was to all intents and purposes her screen debut proper in Robert Altman's 'Come Back To The Five And Dime Jimmy Dean, Jimmy Dean' (1982). She proved it was no fluke with sterling performances in Mike Nichols' fact based drama, 'Silkwood' (1983), and particularly Peter Bogdanovich's 'Mask' (1985), another true story in which she played the mother of a deformed boy, receiving recognition for her efforts in the shape of a Best Actress award at Cannes. Her acting credentials confirmed, CHER went on to hold down starring roles in fantasy comedy, 'The Witches Of Eastwick' (1987), courtroom drama, 'Suspect' (1987) and, as a wayward mother in domestic comedy, 'Mermaids' (1990). In contrast to most pop performers, CHER subsequently used her acting fame as a springboard back into music rather than the other way round, so successful a move in fact, that it somewhat curtailed her screen activities over much of the next decade. She nevertheless continued to make the odd appearance, popping up as her unfeasibly young looking self in Robert Altman films, 'The Player' (1992) and 'Pret-a-Porter' (1994), as a suicidal wife in Robert Mazursky's black comedy, 'Faithful' (1996) and, in her most acclaimed role in years, as a feisty American abroad opposite Judi Dench and Lily Tomlin in 'Tea With Mussolini' (1999). As for her former squeeze SONNY, he'd combined the occasional acting appearance in the likes of 'Airplane II: The Sequel' (1982), 'Troll' (1985) and 'Under The Boardwalk' (1989) with a move into business and politics. If his beliefs weren't quite as conservative as the character he played in John Waters' acclaimed musical comedy, 'HAIRSPRAY' (1988), BONO nevertheless made a name for himself as an uncompromising Republican following his rather unlikely nomination as Mayor of Palm Springs and even more unlikely 1994 election to the US Congress. Yet in one of rock'n'roll's more bizarre deaths, SONNY's burgeoning political career was tragically cut short when he was killed in a skiing accident on 5th January 1998. *BG*

- **filmography** {acting} (composer) –

Wild On The Beach *(1965 {c SONNY} {c CHER})* / **Good Times** *(1967 {* SONNY} {* CHER} OST by SONNY & CHER =>)* / **Chastity** *(1969 {s-w SONNY} {* CHER} single by CHER on OST by SONNY =>)* / Murder On Flight 502 *(1975 {a SONNY})* / the Golden Raiders *(1979 {a SONNY})* / Murder In Music City *(1979 TV {a SONNY})* / Escape To Athena *(1979 {a SONNY})* / the Top Of The Hill *(1980 TV {a SONNY})* / Balboa *(1982 TV {a SONNY})* / Come Back To The Five And Dime Jimmy Dean, Jimmy Dean *(1982 {* CHER})* / Airplane II: The Sequel *(1982 {a SONNY})* / Silkwood *(1983 {* CHER})* / the Vals *(1985 {a SONNY})* / Mask *(1985 {* CHER})* / Troll *(1985 {* SONNY})* / Dirty Laundry *(1987 {* SONNY})* / the Witches Of Eastwick *(1987 {* CHER})* / Suspect *(1987 {* CHER})* / Moonstruck *(1987 {* CHER})* / **Hairspray** *(1988 {* SONNY})* / Under The Boardwalk *(1989 {a SONNY})* / Thanksgiving Day *(1989 TV {a})* / Mermaids *(1990 {* CHER} hit by CHER on V/A OST see; future editions)* / the Player *(1992 {c CHER})* / Pret-a-Porter *(1994 {c CHER})* / First Kid *(1996 {*c SONNY})* / If These Walls Could Talk *(1996 TV {dir/* CHER})* / Faithful *(1996 {* CHER})* / Tea With Mussolini *(1999 {* CHER})* / Stuck On You *(2003 {c CHER})*

SONS OF PROVO

2004 (US 93m) Fresh-Mex Productions / Halestorm Entertainment

Film genre: Pop-music mockumentary/comedy

Top guns: s-w: (+ dir) Will Swenson, Peter Brown

Stars: Will Swenson *(Will Jensen)*, Kirby Heyborne *(Kirby Laybourne)*, Danny Tarasevich *(Danny Jensen)*, Jennifer Erekson *(Jill Keith)*, Peter Brown *(Grayson Jensen)*, Maureen Eastwood *(Yvonne Bolschweiler)*, Robert Swenson *(singing Zak)*

Storyline: "Three guys.. One dream.. No clue." – "The spiritual sound barrier is about to be broken". Will and Danny Jensen are the founder-members of LDS boy band Everclean. In their quest for stardom, they recruit a third member Kirby as well as a manager and a choreographer. Accidents and disasters follow the group as they perform gigs around the State, and their first album gets damning reviews from all sides. Their tour goes from bad to worse when Kirby falls out with the brothers before their big show. Will this be Everclean's last performance, or will Kirby get his own way and be lead vocalist? *JZ*

Movie rating: *6

Visual: dvd (no audio OST)

Off the record: WILL SWENSON wrote nine of the ten songs for the film, 'Everclean', 'Word Of Wizzum', 'Love Me, But Don't Show Me', 'Diddly Wack Mack Mormon Daddy', 'Wait For Me', 'Spiritchal As Me', 'Sweet Spirit', 'Nourish And Strengthen', 'Dang, Fetch, Oh My Heck' & 'Beautiful Inside', the latter was penned by KIRBY HEYBORNE; note that all the actors actually sing the songs. *MCS*

SONS OF STEEL

1989 (Aus 104m) Big Island Pictures / Jet Films (M)

Film genre: sci-fi Rock Musical comedy

Top guns: s-w + dir: Gary L. Keady

Stars: Rob Hartley *(Black Alice)*, Roz Watson *(Hope)*, Ralph Cotterill *(Karzoff)* ← RIKKY AND PETE / → the PROPOSITION, Jeff Duff *(Secta)*, Dagmar Blahova *(Honor)*, Elizabeth Richmond *(Djard)*, Wayne Snell *(Ex)*, Mark Hembrow *(Mal)*

Storyline: Heavy-metal headbanger dude, Black Alice and his girlfriend, are assigned by a futuristic Australia to time travel back in time to save Sydney Harbour (and it's Opera House!) from a nuclear holocaust bomb plot. *MCS*

Movie rating: *3.5

Visual: none (no audio OST)

Off the record: Gary L. Keady not only scripted and directed his only ever venture into the movies, he co-wrote the score with Rod Keady and John Vallins. *MCS*

SOUL SURVIVOR

1995 (UK 2x90m mini TV; US 115m) BBC-TV (PG-13)

Film genre: Pop/Rock-music comedy

Top guns: dir: Sandy Johnson / s-w: **Barry Devlin**

Stars: Ian McShane *(Otis Cooke)* → SEXY BEAST, Margi Clarke *(Connie)* → 24 HOUR PARTY PEOPLE → REVENGERS TRAGEDY, **Isaac HAYES** *(Vernon Holland)*, Derek O'Connor *(Dave)*, Antonio Fargas *(Leroy James)* ← FIRESTARTER ← CAR WASH ← CORNBREAD, EARL AND ME ← FOXY BROWN ← CLEOPATRA JONES ← ACROSS 110th STREET ← SHAFT, Taurean Blacque *(Eddie)*, Scott Wilson *(Bradley Facemeyer)* ← GERONIMO: AN AMERICAN LEGEND ← ELVIS AND THE COLONEL: THE UNTOLD STORY ← YOUNG GUNS II ← JOHNNY HANDSOME ← BLUE CITY / → DEAD MAN WALKING → SOUTH OF HEAVEN, WEST OF HELL → DON'T LET GO → MONSTER, Al Matthews *(Grover Cleveland)*

Storyline: Faced with the cancellation of his late night radio show, soul DJ Otis Cooke decides to head to the States to re-unite his favourite band, the Tallahassees. Cooke tracks down the band members one by one and persuades them to get together for one last tour, and finds a new sense of purpose in his own life which was missing before. *JZ*

Movie rating: *5.5

Visual: video (no audio OST)

Off the record: Screenwriter, **Barry Devlin** (b.27 Nov'48, Ardboe, Co. Tyrone, N. Ireland), first found fame as bassist/vocalist with 70s Dublin-based, folk-rock outfit, Horslips. After many hits in their homeland, they finally tasted the sweet smell of success in Britain (Top 40) via 1977's 'The Book Of Invasions – A Celtic Symphony'. When they disbanded, Devlin issued a solo set, 'Breaking Star Codes', before getting into writing (his sister Marie is the wife of top poet, Seamus Heaney) with television play, 'Lapsed Catholics' (1987). Actor Ian McShane (he of 'Lovejoy' & 'Deadwood') fancied himself as a singer, and in 1992, he cracked the UK Top 40 with a TV-financed covers album, 'From Both Sides Now'. Al Matthews was a part-time lyricist. *MCS*

SOUTH PARK: BIGGER, LONGER & UNCUT

1999 (US 81m) Paramount Pictures (R)

Film genre: animated Pop/Rock Musical satire/comedy

Top guns: s-w: Trey Parker (+ dir), Matt Stone, Pam Brady

Voices: Trey Parker *(Eric Cartman / Stan Marsh / Officer Barb / Satan / Mr. Garrison / Mr. Hat / Phillip Niles Argyle / Randy Marsh Ned Gerblanski / etc.)*, Matt Stone *(Kyle Broflovski / Kenny McCormick / Saddam Hussein / Bill Gates / Terrence Henry Stoot / etc.)*, Mary Kay Bergman *(Sharon Manson / Sheila Broflovski / Mrs. Cartman / Mrs. McCormick)*, **Isaac HAYES** *(Jerome "Chef" McElroy)*, Jesse Howell *(Bebe Stevens)*, Eric Idle *(Dr. Vosknocker)* ← the RUTLES ← SIDE BY SIDE, **Stewart Copeland** *(American soldier #1)* ← the RHYTHMATIST ← URGH! A MUSIC WAR / → the FILTH AND THE FURY, George Clooney *(Dr. Gouache)* ← FROM DUSK TILL DAWN / → O BROTHER, WHERE ART THOU?, Minnie Driver *(Brooke Shields)* ← TARZAN ← GOOD WILL HUNTING, Mike Judge *(voice; Kenny McCormick saying goodbye)* ← BEAVIS AND BUTT-HEAD DO AMERICA ← AIRHEADS

Storyline: Deep in smalltown Colorado, miniscule chums Kyle, Stan, Cartman and Kenny develop a penchant for expletives after watching 'Asses Of Fire', the cinematic pièce de résistance of Zippy-esque Canadian jokers Terrence and Phillip. Appalled at this state of affairs, the mothers and moral guardians of South Park place the pair under citizens arrest, demanding that the USA wages war on Canada in retaliation. Down in the fiery pit, meanwhile, Satan and his lover Saddam Hussein are planning a return to the mortal plane should Terrence and Phillip die for their sins; you really have to see it. *BG*

Movie rating: *8

Visual: dvd

Off the record: On a serious note, voiceover actress Mary Kay Bergman subsequently committed suicide by a single gunshot to the head (11th November, 1999); it was disclosed she had suffered from depression all her life. *MCS*

—

Various Cast/Artists (score: Trey Parker w/ Marc Shaiman)

Jun 99. (cd/c) *Atlantic; <(83199-2/-4)>* [28] Aug99 [9]
– Mountain town / Uncle Fucka / It's easy, Mmmkay / Blame Canada / Kyle's mom's a bitch / What would Brian Boitano do? / Up there / La resistance – medley / Eyes of a child (MICHAEL McDONALD) / I can change / I'm super / Mountain town – reprise / Good love (ISAAC HAYES) / Shut yo face (Uncle Fucka) (TRICK DADDY) / Riches to rags (Mmmkay) (NAPPY ROOTS) / Kyle's mom's a big fat bitch (JOE C.) / What would Brian Boitano do? – pt.II (DVDA) / I swear it (I can change) (the VIOLENT FEMMES) / Super (RuPAUL) / O Canada (GEDDY LEE & ALEX LIFESON).

S/track review: A soundtrack that kicks off with a reprise, a happy ending where "Americans and Canadians are friends again" before they've even fallen out? Welcome to the crazy world of 'SOUTH PARK', where most things are proverbially, and sometimes literally, arse over tit. If you ever happen to listen to this with your mother, or worse, your uncle, you'll probably want to skip the Terrence and Phillip ditty, 'Uncle F**ka', surely the most scatological, profane lyrics – and farting noises – ever set to animation. And if it doesn't at least bring a crease to your coupon, you really need to dig out that old whoopee cushion. In fact, if you've an aversion to farting or the 'F' word at all, you'd best skip the whole album, or else take comfort in the advice of your elders and just repeat "MMMKay" after them. As well as slaughtering every socially, sexually and politically correct cow they can think of, Trey Parker, Matt Stone and Marc Shaiman conceive their movie as an all-singing, all-swearing send-up of the Great American Musical, reimagining Hollywood as a toilet-humour convention, and setting it all to cymbal-crashing orchestration. Cartman scowlingly whines an outrageous number of bad words and a hilarious finale in 'Kyle's Mom's A B**ch', and Satan and MICHAEL McDONALD both croon their own power ballads, but it's the retrospectively even-more-ironic-than-intended, chipmunk-voiced Saddam Hussein who gets most satirical mileage out of the MGM mentality, wrestling with cod-Arabic frills and his conscience on 'I Can Change'. The add-ons and interpretations are an unnecessary but fleetingly interesting mixed bag: the hip-hop "interpretations" only end up parodying themselves although the D.V.D.A. reinvention of 'What Would Brian Boitano Do' successfully and simultaneously sends up the Pogues and Rage Against The Machine. The VIOLENT FEMMES lose the humour but bring out the latent gothic poesy of '. . .Change', Rush troupers GEDDY LEE and ALEX LIFESON boldly defend charges of "not even a real country" on 'O Canada' and, save for the George Clinton-esque couplet "I don't know but I been told by a playa hater, that my bedroom is a disguise for a freak incubator", ISAAC HAYES can't quite rustle up anything as tasty as 'Chocolate Salty Balls'. *BG*

Album rating: *7

SOUTHLANDER

2001 (US 80m) Propaganda Films

Film genre: experimental-music-based comedy drama

Top guns: s-w: (+ dir) Steve Hanft, Ross Harris, Robert J. Stephenson

Stars: Rory Cochrane *(Chance)* ← EMPIRE RECORDS, Ross Harris *(Ross Angeles; Bek's jam double axe)*, **Beth Orton** *(Rocket)* → I'M YOUR MAN, Lawrence Hilton-Jacobs *(Motherchild)* ← the JACKSONS: AN AMERICAN DREAM ← YOUNGBLOOD ← CLAUDINE ← DEATH WISH, **Richard Edson** *(Thomas)* ← the MILLION DOLLAR HOTEL ← STRANGE DAYS ← WHAT ABOUT ME ← TOUGHER THAN LEATHER ← GOOD MORNING, VIETNAM ← WALKER ← HOWARD THE DUCK, **Beck** *(Bek)* ← FREE TIBET / → SOUL OF A MAN → MAYOR OF THE SUNSET STRIP → HIGH AND DRY → FEARLESS FREAKS, Gregg Henry *(Lane Windbird)*, Kurt Lilly *(Steely Danzig)*, Meghan Gallagher *(Snowbunny)*, Ione Skye *(Miss Highrise)* ← WENT TO CONEY ISLAND ON A MISSION FROM GOD . . . BE BACK BY FIVE ← FOUR ROOMS ← GAS, FOOD LODGING ← WAYNE'S WORLD, Laura Prepon *(Seven Equals Five)*, **Hank Williams III** *(Hank III)* → AMERICAN HARDCORE, **Elliott Smith** *(bus driver)*, **Craig Borrell** *(swimmer)*, **Jennifer Herrema** *(record girl)*, **Future Pigeon:- Brandon Wells** *(drums)*, **Fred Martinez** *(bassist)*, **Union 13** *(skate band)*, **Eddie Ruscha** *(Bek's jam guitarist)*, **Senon Williams** *(Bek's jam drummer)*, Bill Duscha *(Steely's solo)*

Storyline: Chance is a run-of-the-mill keyboard player in downtown LA. One day he sees a 1969 Moletron keyboard and is determined to buy it. The keyboard produces magical, ethereal sounds which soon get him noticed by bands on the circuit. When the Moletron is stolen before a concert, Chance and his pal Rossangeles begin a wild goose chase around LA relying on local magazine The Southlander for clues to the keyboard's whereabouts. *JZ*

Movie rating: *6

Visual: dvd

Off the record: 'Central Reservation' girl, **Beth Orton** fronts dubmeisters, **Future Pigeon** (i.e Dada Munchamonkey aka ex-Medicine guitarist **Eddie Ruscha** ex-Maids Of Gravity & Radar Bros. – bassist here is **Senon Williams**) although a "real" FP outfit includes [not in film] Jason Mason, Jeff Cairns, Dave Scher & Grant Vanderslice; RUSCHA contributions to the soundtrack number 'Southlander Theme', 'Illumination Dub' (w/ ORTON), 'Dr. Fantasm', 'Making Out', 'Speedway Child', 'Taste It' (w/ HARRIS), 'Space Kat', 'Rust Drive', 'Elemental Blues', 'Motherchild Theme', 'Zu Zu Dubrider', 'Lane's World', 'Solar Invocation', 'Confederate Dub' & 'Motherchild Chase'; ORTON solo 'Sweetest Decline'. **Elliott Smith** sadly, not long for this world, donated 2 songs, 'Snowbunny's Serenade' & 'Splitzville'. **Hank Williams III** (grandson of the country legend) featured with 'Alone And Dying'. **BECK** meanwhile, showed up on 'Broken Train' & 'Puttin' It Down', ROYAL TRUX featuring **Jennifer Herrema** delivered 'End Of The Century' while UNION 13 dropped in via 'A Life Story'. Other tracks:- 'Green Room' (by BILLY HIGGINS, JEFFERY LITTLETON, KITO GAMBLE & AZAR LAWRENCE), 'Video City Boy' (by CRAIG BORRELL & ROSS HARRIS), latter on 'Piano Drop', 'Seven Equals Seven' (by BILL DUSCHA, etc.) and 'Gently Waves' (TAKAKO MINEKAWA). *MCS*

SPACE IS THE PLACE

1974 (US 63m) North Star (R)

Film genre: avant-Jazz Musical & sci-fi comedy

Top guns: dir: John Coney / s-w: **Sun Ra**, Joshua Smith

Stars: Sun Ra *(Sun Ra)*, Barbara Deloney *(Candy)*, Ray Johnson *(the overseer)*, Erika Leder *(Tania)*, Sinthia Ayala *(Chili Pepper)*, Christopher Brooks *(Jimmy Fey)* ← the MACK, La Shaa Stallings *(Bertha)*, Sinthia Ayala *(Chili Pepper)*, Clarence Brewer *(Bernard)*, **Arkestra:- John Gilmore, June Tyson, Marshall Allen, Danny Davis, Eloe Omoe, Tommy Hunter, Danny Thompson, Lex Humphries, Ken Moshesh, Larry Northington, Kwame Hadi**, Morgan Upton *(agent #2)* ← STEELYARD BLUES / → MORE AMERICAN GRAFFITI → TUCKER: THE MAN AND HIS DREAM → the SPIRIT OF '76

Storyline: The weird and invariably wonderful world of Sun Ra makes it to the big screen, charting Ra's efforts to outsmart the pimp suited, Man-like Overseer, educate black inner city youth, recruit fellow space cadets for relocation to a new planet and generally spread positive vibes through his moog-centric jazz. Along the way, there's plenty of blaxploitation style gratuitous nudity, fascinating period detail and political subtext, as sinister government agents tie our hero to a warehouse chair and grill him with such crucial national security-dependent questions as "what does trans-molecularisation mean?" and "how do you convert your harmonic progressions to energy?" Fair point. *BG*

Movie rating: *7

Visual: video + dvd

Off the record: SUN RA (see below)

—

SUN RA & HIS ASTRO INTERGALACTIC INFINITY ARKESTRA

Nov 93. (cd) *Evidence; <ECD 22070-2>* ☐ ☐
– It's after the end of the world / Under diferent stars / Discipline 33 / Watusi / Calling planet Earth / I am the alter-destiny / The satellites are spinning (take 1) / Cosmic forces / Outer spaceways incorporated (take 3) / We travel the spaceways / The overseer / Blackman – Love in outer space / Mysterious crystal / I am the brother of the wind / We'll wait for you / Space is the place.

S/track review: Recorded in 1972 (a great year for composing, a bad year for moustaches), shelved for more than two decades and easily confused with the 'Impulse' release of the same name, the soundtrack to SUN RA's celluloid allegory finally saw the light of day on 'Evidence' in 1993. In its often definitive, deep-space survey of compositions which the ARKESTRA toured during the mid-70s, some of which had been staples for years and many of which they continued to interpret in later decades, the CD re-issue filled one of the more glaring gaps in the man's gargantuan back catalogue. It's also a great place for RA neophytes to get their cosmic wings, what with such essential but comparatively accessible material as the title track and 'Outer Spaceways Incorporated', one of JUNE TYSON's most joyous vocal incantations. RA's right-hand woman also channels the root essence of her mytho-siren soulfulness through the modal drones and percussive frenzy of 'Blackman', tenderly carries a hushed, all too short 'We Travel The Spaceways' (a galactic spiritual almost as old as her mentor's recording career) and leads the collective chant, 'Calling Planet Earth'. The closest the record comes to conventional jazz is 'Watusa', another 50s vintage swing number which morphs into an Afro-centric, jaw-rattling marathon of bongos, conga and cowbell. But it's SUN RA's arsenal of vintage keyboards (including mini-moog, farfisa organ, clavinet and his trusty "Rocksichord") which forms the thrust of the soundtrack's most challenging and exploratory forays, and which reveals the extent of his influence on latter-day moog merchants. On the likes of 'The Overseer' and 'We'll Wait For You', his cosmic tones accelerate and decelerate, thrash and splinter like brittle bones, all the while lashed by the dialectic fury of saxophonists Marshall Allen and John Gilmore. Ironically, the only track which disappoints is 'Space Is The Place' itself, a skeletal, abbreviated take bereft of RA's klaxon-like farfisa splurges, as well as the depth, richness and sheer speaking-in-tongues madness of the twenty-minute-plus version on the aforementioned 'Impulse' album, even if does retain something of its lumbering, gloriously chaotic swing. Funk, Jim, but not as we know it. *BG*

Album rating: *8

SPARKLE

1976 (US 98m) RSO / Warner Bros. Pictures (PG)

Film genre: R&B/Pop Musical drama

Top guns: dir: Sam O'Steen / s-w: Joel Schumacher → CAR WASH → the WIZ (au: Zvi Howard Rosenman)

Stars: Philip Michael Thomas *(Stix)* ← BOOK OF NUMBERS ← COME BACK, CHARLESTON BLUE, Irene Cara *(Sparkle)* ← AARON LOVES ANGELA / → FAME, **Lonette McKee** *(Sister)* → JUNGLE FEVER → HE GOT GAME → HONEY, Dwan Smith *(Dolores)* → BROTHERS, Mary Alice *(Effie)* ← the EDUCATION OF SONNY CARSON / → BEAT STREET, Beatrice Winde *(Mrs. Waters)* → SHE'S THE ONE, Dorian Harewood *(Levi)* → HENDRIX → GLITTER, Tony King *(Satin)* ← BUCKTOWN ← HELL UP IN HARLEM ← GORDON'S WAR ← SHAFT, **DeWayne Jessie** *(Ham)* → CAR WASH → THANK GOD IT'S FRIDAY → ANIMAL HOUSE → WHERE THE BUFFALO ROAM, Ren Woods *(Jim Dandy singer)* → CAR WASH → YOUNGBLOOD → HAIR → XANADU

Storyline: Rags to riches clichés abound as a trio of singing sisters from Harlem attempt to make it in the music business. Eldest sibling sister (as in her uh, name . . .) becomes romantically involved with crime boss Satin Struthers, although all is not lost as the gals ultimately wind up opening for brother Ray Charles. *BG*

Movie rating: *4.5

Visual: video

Off the record: ARETHA FRANKLIN (see below)

—

ARETHA FRANKLIN (composer: CURTIS MAYFIELD)

Jun 76. (lp/c) *Atlantic; <SD 18176> (K/K4 56248)* 18 Apr77 ☐
– Sparkle / Something he can feel / Hooked on your love / Look into your heart / I get high / Jump / Loving you baby / Rock with me. *<(cd-iss. Jun00 on 'Rhino'; 8122 71148-2)>*

S/track review: 'SPARKLE' is often trumpeted as ARETHA FRANKLIN's great return to form after a mid-70s slump. In reality it was a fairly tepid last gasp before almost a decade in the wilderness. On paper, the prospect of CURTIS MAYFIELD and the Queen of Soul was irresistible, especially after the earthy magic MAYFIELD had worked on a backsliding Staple Singers with 'LET'S DO IT AGAIN' (1975). The former Impressions man was on a roll for sure, but somehow his Midas touch failed him here. His arrangements are far too slick for a start, with all the polish but little of the bite of his earlier soundtracks – both he and FRANKLIN sound like they're going through the motions. Part of the problem is that his airy compositions oblige her to sing at the upper end of her range, to the extent that it becomes wearing. Technically, she's flawless, but what this album lacks is root-down, diaphragm-busting grit of the kind which defined past glories like 'Baby, I Love You' and 'Think'. The listless 'Something He Can Feel' scraped into the US Top 30, but the neo-Southern soul of 'Loving You Baby' or even the title track might well have been better bets for a single release. They're among the few moments when FRANKLIN's stratospheric vocal and Rich Tufo's strings really sting – for the most part, Tufo's orchestrations are syrupy rather than rhythmic. And only with 'I Get High' do he and his famous partner hint at the conscious soul of yore and how great this album could have been, while 'Jump' at least has a funky, neo-disco kick to it. MAYFIELD would subsequently reassert himself with the powerful 'SHORT EYES' (1977), but he and FRANKLIN's curious lack of chemistry was all too evident on her 1978 studio album, 'Almighty Fire'. *BG*

Album rating: *5.5

– spinoff hits, etc. –

ARETHA FRANKLIN: Something He Can Feel / Loving You Baby
Jun 76. (7") *<3326> (K 16765)* 28 Sep76 ☐

ARETHA FRANKLIN: Jump / Hooked On Your Love
Sep 76. (7") *<3358>* 72 –

ARETHA FRANKLIN: Look Into Your Heart / Rock With Me
Jan 77. (7") *<3373>* 82 –

SPEEDWAY

1968 (US 90m) Metro-Goldwyn-Mayer (G)

Film genre: Rock'n'roll Musical sports drama

Top guns: dir: Norman Taurog ← DOUBLE TROUBLE ← SPINOUT ← TICKLE ME ← IT HAPPENED AT THE WORLD'S FAIR ← GIRLS! GIRLS! GIRLS! ← BLUE HAWAII ← G.I. BLUES / → LIVE A LITTLE, LOVE A LITTLE / s-w: Phillip Shuke

Stars: Elvis PRESLEY *(Steve Grayson)*, **Nancy Sinatra** *(Susan Jacks)* ← the WILD ANGELS ← the GHOST IN THE INVISIBLE BIKINI ← GET YOURSELF A COLLEGE GIRL / → MAYOR OF THE SUNSET STRIP, Bill Bixby *(Kenny Donford)* ← CLAMBAKE, Gale Gordon *(R.W. Hepworth)*, William Schallert *(Abel Esterlake)*, Victoria Paige Meyerink *(Ellie Esterlake)*, Ross Hagen *(Paul Dado)* → MELINDA, Carl Ballantine *(Birdie Kebner)*, Miss Beverly Hills *(Mary Ann)* ← KISSIN' COUSINS

Storyline: Steve Grayson, a singing racecar driver (haven't we heard this one before?..), attempts to rescue his gambling manager Kenny Donford from financial ruin and the wrath of the American Inland Revenue. *BG*

Movie rating: *5

Visual: video + dvd

Off the record: Nancy Sinatra (b. 8 Jun'40, Jersey City, New Jersey, USA) had already two chart-toppers under her belt (whew!): 'These Boots Are Made For Walkin'' in '66 and 'Somethin' Stupid' with her father Frank a year later, *MCS*

—

ELVIS PRESLEY (composers: Jeff Alexander, etc.)

Jun 68. (lp; mono/stereo) *R.C.A.; <LSP 3989> (RD/SF 7957)* 82 Aug68 ☐
– Speedway / There ain't nothing like a song / Your time hasn't come yet baby / Who are you (who am I?) / He's your uncle, not your dad / Let yourself go / Your groovy self (NANCY SINATRA) / Five sleepyheads / Western union / Mine / Goin' home / Suppose. *(re-iss. Aug81 on 'RCA International'; INTS 5041) (re-iss. Jan84 lp/c; NL/NK 85012)*

S/track review: Having already reached rock bottom, there wasn't much creative freefall left for PRESLEY's soundtracks and this – the last of his career – ends a dodgy decade, if not exactly on a high, then at least higher than recent years. Mandatory instalment of drivel ('He's Your Uncle Not Your Dad') aside, there are some memorable moments here, and the presence of NANCY SINATRA livens things up. She adds her satisfyingly off-hand, half-spoken vocal to the otherwise forgettable 'There Ain't Nothing Like A Song' and makes the most of a solo spot (the brassy, deliciously slinky 'Your Groovy Self'), the first and only time another artist was afforded such a luxury on an ELVIS soundtrack. PRESLEY at least sings it from the heart on the poignant 'Suppose', inexplicably left out of the film but resurrected in both its original and alternate versions on the CD re-issue. He's also in fine form on the gentle, semi-acoustic scribble, 'Your Time Hasn't Come Yet, Baby', an easygoing highlight with some endearingly unusual arrangements. Within months of this record's release, ELVIS would resurrect his ailing career with one of the most celebrated live comebacks ever, consigning forever his ill-starred soundtrack efforts to the annals of rock history. *BG*

Album rating: *4

– spinoff hits, etc. –

ELVIS PRESLEY: Your Time Hasn't Come Yet Baby / Let Yourself Go

Jun 68. (7") *<47-9547> (RCA 1714)* 72 / 71 Jul68 22

ELVIS PRESLEY: Easy Come, Easy Go / Speedway

Mar 95. (cd) *<(07863 66558-2)>*

SPICEWORLD

1997 (UK 92m) Polygram / Icon Entertainment (PG)

Film genre: Pop Musical comedy

Top guns: dir: Bob Spiers / s-w: Kim Fuller → SEEING DOUBLE → FROM JUSTIN TO KELLY, Jamie Curtis

Stars: the Spice Girls:- Melanie Brown *(Scary Spice)*, **Emma Bunton** *(Baby Spice)*, **Geri Halliwell** *(Ginger Spice)*, **Victoria Adams** *(Posh Spice)*, **Melanie Chisholm** *(Sporty Spice)* / Richard E. Grant *(Clifford)*, Alan Cumming *(Piers Cuthbertson-Smyth)* → JOSIE AND THE PUSSYCATS, George Wendt *(film producer)* ← BYE BYE BIRDIE re-make / → GARAGE: A ROCK SAGA → MY DINNER WITH JIMI, Claire Rushbrook *(Deborah)*, Mark McKinney *(Graydon)*, Richard O'Brien *(Damien)* ← SHOCK TREATMENT ← FLASH GORDON ← JUBILEE ← the ROCKY HORROR PICTURE SHOW, Naoko Mori *(Nicola)*, Roger Moore *(chief)*, Barry Humphries *(Kevin McMaxford)* ← SHOCK TREATMENT ← SGT. PEPPER'S LONELY HEARTS CLUB BAND ← SIDE BY SIDE, Jason Flemyng *(Brad)* → ROCK STAR, Michael Barrymore *(Mr. Step)*, **MEAT LOAF** *(Dennis)*, Bill Paterson *(Brian)* ← the KILLING FIELDS, Richard Briers *(bishop)* ← FLASH GORDON ← JUBILEE ← the ROCKY HORROR PICTURE SHOW, Stephen Fry *(judge)*, **Jools Holland** *(musical director)* ← EAT THE RICH ← URGH! A MUSIC WAR / → CONCERT FOR GEORGE, **Elton JOHN** *(himself)*, **Elvis COSTELLO** *(himself)*, Dominic West *(photographer)* → ROCK STAR, **Bob Geldof** *(himself)* ← the WALL ← PUNK IN LONDON / → NEW YORK DOLL, Bob Hoskins *(Geri's disguise)* ← the SECRET POLICEMAN'S THIRD BALL ← the WALL / → BEYOND THE SEA → DANNY THE DOG, Hugh Laurie *(Poirot)*, Kevin McNally *(policeman)*, Jonathan Ross *(himself)*, Jennifer Saunders *(fashionable woman)* ← EAT THE RICH, Neil Fox *(radio DJ)*

Storyline: Spice dames Scary, Sporty, Ginger, Baby and Posh get the slapstick treatment á la 'A Hard Day's Night', braving the rigours of celebrity with girl humour and lashings of celebrity cameos. *BG*

Movie rating: *4

Visual: video + dvd

Off the record: the Spice Girls (see below)

---

the SPICE GIRLS (composers: Various)

Nov 97. (cd/c/lp) *Virgin; (CD/TC+/V 2850) <45111>* 1 3
– Spice up your life / Stop / Too much / Saturday night divas / Never give up on the good times / Move over / Do it / Denying / Viva forever / The lady is a vamp.

S/track review: Girl Power? Viewed against the points-make-prizes pop warbled in their wake, the SPICE GIRLS look like PJ Harvey. Already four UK No.1 singles under their belts ('Wannabe', 'Say You'll Be There', '2 Become 1' and 'Mama'), the five were content in telling everybody on the planet what they "really, really wanted" – fame and fortune. This soundtrack-cum-second-album shipped in record-breaking quantities in 1997; ten years later it hasn't aged so badly, especially given that their legacy as a cultural brand still overshadows the music, and the film hasn't exactly gone down as a youth culture classic. No-one can accuse them of being short on irony; 'Saturday Night Divas' Quo-tes one of Francis Rossi and Co's hairiest headbangers, recycling the hook with chat-show camp. It's indicative of the kind of playfulness, pop nous and craft which is absent from the reality show brigade, and – rote production notwithstanding – points the way to hidden depths. Puta madre! Never mind Madonna – who would've imagined Sandy Denny (see the otherwise hackneyed 'Lady Is A Vamp') as a Girl Power inspiration? 'Never Give Up' brilliantly manages to play to the 70s revival of the 90s, while anticipating the 80s revival of the 00s, referencing both Matthew Wilder's 'Break My Stride' and Earth, Wind & Fire's 'Let's Groove'. 'Do It' cleverly harnesses the easy exhilaration of prime Jackson 5 and 'Stop' remains one of the most capable pop reprises of classic 'Motown' since the 80s. Post-"Cool-Britannia", the SPICE GIRLS lost direction (this album was the beginning of the end), but at least they knew where they were coming from. *BG*

Album rating: *6

– spinoff hits, etc. –

the SPICE GIRLS: Spice Up Your Life / (mixes)

Oct 97. (7"/c-s/cd-s/cd-s) *(VSLH/VSC/VSCDT/VSDG 1660)* *<38620>* 1 18

the SPICE GIRLS: Too Much / (mix)

Dec 97. (7"/c-s/cd-s) *(VSLH/VSC/VSCDX 1669) <38630>* 1 Jan98 9
(cd-s) *(VSCDT 1669)* – ('A') / Spice up your life.

the SPICE GIRLS: Stop

Mar 98. (7"/c-s) *(VSLH/VSC 1679)* 2 Jun98 16
(cd-s+=) *(VSCDT 1679) <38641>* – Mama.
(cd-s) *(VSCDX 1679) <39642>* – ('A') / (3 other mixes).

the SPIDERS

Formed: Tokyo, Japan . . . 1961, although at this time they were a C&W-orientated group led by a female singer. A subsequent change of direction from "eleki"/instrumental style and personnel in the mid-60s, saw the Spiders (now Jun Inoue – vocals, Masaaki Sakai – vocals, flute, Hiroshi "Monsieur" Kamatastu – guitar, vocals, Takayuki Inoue – guitar, Katsuo Ohno – keyboards, steel guitar, Mitsuru Kato – bass, Shochi Tanabe – drums) hit the homeland charts with both singles and LPs. The Japanese equivalent of the Fab Four (after the BEATLES' arrival at the Budokan in 1966), this mod/garage-beat outfit had seven members. The SPIDERS were considered the best of the "Group Sounds" (GS) outfits, a term used instead of "rock'n'roll", because the people could not pronounce their R's. Unfortunately, their brand of copycat pigeon-English R&B (think the Animals, the Yardbirds and the Beatles) didn't go down too well Stateside, although the septet issued a rare – and pricy! – single in the UK ('Sad Sunset' / 'Hey Boy'), promoting it on British pop show, 'Ready Steady Go' (1966); check out CD compilation below. Their debut film, 'WILD SCHEME A-GO-GO' (1967), saw the SPIDERS arrive at Tokyo airport to overwhelming audience reaction. This leads to a media barrage, a press conference and ultimately – spliced between the odd Help!-style camera work – a concert, where the beat group perform several numbers alongside go-go dancers. 'Go Forward!!' (1968) was also Richard Lester/ 'HELP!'-inspired, goofy, psychedelic and basically a lot of nonsense, if you're say . . . not Japanese. 'Big Commotion!' (1968) is another in similar loopy vein, the multi-legged ones breaking free from screaming fans and landing themselves in a psychedelic hospital. 'The Road To Bali' (1968) ended a busy year with a Monkees/ 'HEAD'-orientated movie that took them everywhere from Hong Kong to Sydney. The group disbanded in 1971, although Takayuki and Katsuo (with various other names) subsequently resurfaced in the band PYG, while the former wrote for TV and film. *MCS*

- filmography (composers)

Wild Scheme A-Go-Go *(1967 {*/p})* / Go Forward!! *(1968 {*/p})* / Big Commotion! *(1968 {*/p})* / the Road To Bali *(1968 {*/p})*

- associated release –
the SPIDERS: Let's Go Spiders!

Dec 00. (cd) *Big Beat; (<WIK 202>)*
– Furi furi '66 / Upside down / Go go / Johnny B. Goode / Teardrops / Hey boy / Mr. Tax / Yves / Once again / Ban ban / Yogiri no London / Kuroyuri no uta / Koi no doctor / Akai dress no onna no ko / Robby Robby / End of love / Lucky rain / Thinking of you baby / Little Robby / Kaze ga naiteriru / Mo ichido mo ichido / S.P.I. / Inside looking out / Summer girl / No no boy / Ano niji wo tsukamo / Mr. Monkey / Sad sunset.

□ SPINAL TAP segment
(⇒ THIS IS SPINAL TAP)

SPINOUT

aka CALIFORNIA HOLIDAY

1966 (US 93m) Metro-Goldwyn-Mayer (G)

Film genre: Rock'n'roll Musical sports drama

Top guns: dir: Norman Taurog ← TICKLE ME ← IT HAPPENED AT THE WORLD'S FAIR ← GIRLS! GIRLS! GIRLS! ← BLUE HAWAII ← G.I. BLUES / → DOUBLE TROUBLE → SPEEDWAY → LIVE A LITTLE, LOVE A LITTLE / s-w: Theodore J. Flicker, George Kirgo

Stars: Elvis PRESLEY *(Mike McCoy)*, Shelley Fabares *(Cynthia Foxhugh)* ← HOLD ON! ← GIRL HAPPY ← RIDE THE WILD SURF ← SUMMER LOVE ← ROCK, PRETTY BABY / → CLAMBAKE / → a TIME TO SING, Carl Betz *(Howard Foxhugh)*, Diane McBain *(Diana St. Clair)*, Dodie Marshall *(Susan)* → EASY COME, EASY GO, Deborah Walley *(Les)* ← the GHOST IN THE INVISIBLE BIKINI ← SKI PARTY ← BEACH BLANKET BINGO / → IT'S A BIKINI WORLD, Cecil Kellaway *(Bernard Ranley)*, Jack Mullaney *(Curly)* ← TICKLE ME / → LITTLE BIG MAN, Will Hutchins *(Lt. Tracy Richards)* → CLAMBAKE, Una Merkel *(Violet Ranley)*, Deanna Lund *(gorgeous redhead)* ← OUT OF SIGHT, Nancy Czar *(platinum beauty)* ← WINTER A-GO-GO ← GIRL HAPPY ← WILD GUITAR

Storyline: Racecar driver, sorry, singing racecar driver (of course..), Mike McCoy has his pick of the women although he's more interested in Howard Foxhugh's experimental motor which he agrees to test drive in the Santa Fe Road Race. *BG*

Movie rating: *4

Visual: video + dvd

Off the record: nothing

—

ELVIS PRESLEY (composers: George Stoll, etc.)

Nov 66. (lp; mono/stereo) *R.C.A.; <LSP 3702> (RD/SF 7820)* [18] [17]
– Stop, look and listen / Adam and evil / All that I am / Never say yes / Am I ready / Beach shack / Spinout / Smorgasbord / I'll be back / Tomorrow is a long time / Down in the alley / I'll remember you. *(re-iss. Aug80 on 'RCA Int.' lp/c; INT S/K 5038) (cd-iss. May04 on 'Follow That Dream'+=; FTD 1008) – (extra takes).*

S/track review: Incredibly, this was the fourth ELVIS PRESLEY soundtrack inside ten months. Even more incredibly, it didn't sound as tired as might be expected given such a punishing schedule. Doc Pomus once again outflanks the competition with 'Never Say Yes' (although it's not difficult to recognise rhythmic similarities with Buddy Holly's 'Not Fade Away'), while the Grammy-nominated 'I'll Be Back' is a decent, if rather turgid blues number. 'Beach Shack' plays as an enjoyably dizzy, Ritchie Valens-lite pop confection, and if it's goofy biblical allusions, ominous backing vocals, a ridiculous snake-charming sax melody and high camp you're after, look no further than 'Adam And Evil'. As ever, the King is in suitably smoking vocal form on the ballads; 'All That I Am', incidentally, was a taste of things to come in that it was PRESLEY's first track to feature strings. In neglecting to include the original soundtrack's three bonus cuts on the 1994 CD re-issue, however, the good folks at 'R.C.A.' deprived ELVIS novices and younger fans of 'SPINOUT's best tracks: the Bob Dylan cover (the only one of PRESLEY's career), 'Tomorrow Is A Long Time' and the original version of 'I'll Remember You'. *BG*

Album rating: *6

– spinoff hits, etc. –

ELVIS PRESLEY: Spinout / All That I Am

Oct 66. (7") *<47-8941> (RCA 1545)* [40] B-side [17]

ELVIS PRESLEY: Spinout / Double Trouble

Jun 94. (cd) *<(07863 66361-2)>*

the SPIRIT OF '76

1990 (US 82m) Commercial Pictures / Columbia Pictures (PG-13)

Film genre: retro sci-fi comedy

Top guns: s-w: (+ dir) Lucas Reiner, Roman Coppola

Stars: David Cassidy *(Adam-11)* → POPSTAR, Olivia D'Abo *(Chanel-6)* → WAYNE'S WORLD 2, Geoff Hoyle *(Heinz-57)* ← POPEYE, Liam O'Brien *(Rodney Snodgrass)*, **Leif Garrett** *(Eddie Trojan)* ← SGT. PEPPER'S LONELY HEARTS CLUB BAND / → POPSTAR, **REDD KROSS:- Steve McDonald** *(Tommy Sears)* + **Jeff McDonald** *(Chris Johnson)* / Carl Reiner *(Dr. Von Mobil)*, **DEVO:- Mark Mothersbaugh** *(Chevron-17)*, **Gerald V. Casale** *(Yale-44)*, **Bob Casale** *(Ron-29)*, **David Kendrick** *(Ron-31)* / **Tommy Chong** *(Stoner)* <= CHEECH & CHONG =>, Julie Brown *(Ms. Liberty)* ← EARTH GIRLS ARE EASY / → MEDUSA: DARE TO BE TRUTHFUL, **Moon Zappa** *(Cheryl Dickman)*, Morgan Upton *(teacher)* ← TUCKER: THE MAN AND HIS DREAM ← BUCKTOWN ← SPACE IS THE PLACE ← STEELYARD BLUES

Storyline: In 2176, a magnetic storm obliterates all recorded history. Adam-11 invents a time machine and is sent back to 1776 to meet the Founding Fathers and retrieve a copy of the Constitution. The time machine malfunctions and Adam-11 and his buddies unknowingly end up in 1976 instead. Chased by UFO buffs, they must overcome the culture shock of flowery shirts, platform shoes and stoned hippies and try and find the Constitution, even if it happens to be printed on a T-shirt. *JZ*

Movie rating: *4.5

Visual: video + dvd

Off the record: (see below)

—

Various Artists (score: David Nichtern)

1991. (lp/c/cd) *Rhino; <R1/R4/R2 70799>* [–]
– Spirit of '76 (the DICKIES) / We're an American band (GRAND FUNK) / Love's theme (the LOVE UNLIMITED ORCHESTRA) / Takin' care of business – live (BACHMAN-TURNER OVERDRIVE) / The hustle (VAN McCOY & The SOUL CITY SYMPHONY) / Kung fu fighting (CARL DOUGLAS) / Turn the beat around (VICKI SUE ROBINSON) / Rock the boat (the HUES CORPORATION) / Boogie fever (the SYLVERS) / Disco inferno (the TRAMMPS) / A fifth of Beethoven (WALTER MURPHY & The BIG APPLE BAND) / Saturday night (BAY CITY ROLLERS) / 1976 (REDD KROSS).

S/track review: One look at the line-up on this disco-cum-rock-orientated OST is the oversight of two thespian pop stars, David Cassidy and the younger Leif Garrett, 70s Smash Hits icons both. But having said that, campy dancefloor-fillers such as 'Rock The Boat', 'The Hustle', 'Disco Inferno', 'Boogie Fever', 'Turn The Beat

Around', 'A Fifth Of Beethoven' and er . . . 'Kung Fu Fighting', charge up this time-travelling farce of a film. If 'SATURDAY NIGHT FEVER' was your bag (not really 'Saturday Night' by BAY CITY ROLLERS), this soundtrack takes it right through to drive-in-Sunday afternoon via the wheelspinning, 'Takin' Care Of Business' (by BACHMAN-TURNER OVERDRIVE) and 'We're An American Band' (by GRAND FUNK). The punks among you might recall a certain DICKIES outfit, who supply the boisterous title theme, while punk-retro comes via another soundtrack exclusive, '1976' by REDD KROSS. A boogie wonderland for some, a hangover for others. *MCS*

Album rating: *6

SPLENDOR

1999 (US/UK 93m) Desperate / Dragon / Newmarket Films / Summit (R)

Film genre: romantic seXual comedy drama

Top guns: s-w: (+ dir) Gregg Araki → MYSTERIOUS SKIN

Stars: Kathleen Robertson *(Veronica)* → PSYCHO BEACH PARTY → I AM SAM, Johnathon Schaech *(Abel)* ← FINDING GRACELAND ← THAT THING YOU DO!, Matt Keeslar *(Zed)* → PSYCHO BEACH PARTY, Kelly MacDonald *(Mike)* ← TRAINSPOTTING, Eric Mabius *(Ernest)* ← I SHOT ANDY WARHOL, **Dan Gatto** *(Mutt)*, Linda Kim *(Alison)*, Mink Stole *(casting director)* ← PINK AS THE DAY SHE WAS BORN ← MONSTER MASH: THE MOVIE ← CRY-BABY ← HAIRSPRAY

Storyline: Actress Veronica starts dating again, but immediately runs into a problem – she can't choose between the two guys she's seeing. Caught between Abel's mind and Zed's body (rock critic and rock drummer respectively), Veronica quickly finds the solution by introducing the boys to each other and forming a threesome. The plan works for a while until film director Ernest comes along and offers her the chance of a normal life with him – along with her unborn baby, father unknown. *JZ*

Movie rating: *5

Visual: dvd

Off the record: **Dan Gatto** is the lead singer of L.A. junk punk act, Babyland, who debutted in 1994 with the album, 'You Suck Crap' (released on the 'Flipside' imprint). *MCS*

Various Artists (score: Daniel Licht)

Sep 99. (cd) *Astralwerks; <(ASW 6282)>* ☐ ☐
– Sho' nuff (FATBOY SLIM) / Shine – Splendiferous Locust mix (SLOWDIVE) / The chemistry between us – Lionrock remix (SUEDE) / Before today – Chicane remix (EVERYTHING BUT THE GIRL) / I don't know why I love you – 7" Drip Of Rockman mix (HOUSE OF LOVE) / Kelly watch the stars – Moog Cookbook remix (AIR) / The jag (the MICRONAUTS feat. JOYCE SIMS) / Elektrobank – radio edit (the CHEMICAL BROTHERS) / Beetlebum – Moby's mix (BLUR) / Mesmerise – the mesmerising vocal mix (CHAPTERHOUSE) / Only the strongest will survive – James Lavelle remix (HURRICANE #1) / Sweetness & light – the Orange Squash mix (LUSH) / Flowerz – radio edit (ARMAND VAN HELDEN feat. ROLAND CLARK) / Bizarre love triangle (NEW ORDER).

S/track review: Remixes, like cover versions, are a very, very tricky business. The central question remains the same. Do you tweak the song a little to update it or do you create something completely different? The main difference being that with a remix you are using the actual original recordings as all, or at least part of the new song you are creating. Both ways will either work or they won't. The majority of 'SPLENDOR' is made up of remixes, some of them are unrecognisable from the originals while little has changed in others. Take Moby's remix of BLUR's 'Beetlebum', using only snippets of Damon Albarn's falsetto vocals and the basic bass melody, he adds strings and synths to produce a exceptional chill out track from what was originally a straightforward rock'n'roll piece. On the other hand, you have Moog Cookbook's take on 'Kelly Watch The Stars' from AIR, which remains relatively true to the original but turns it into more of a funk stomper by bringing out the bass and drums and adding a hefty dose of wah-wah infused guitar. It works remarkably well. Atlas provide another remix that doesn't stray too far with HOUSE OF LOVE's 'I Don't Know Why I Love You', however it somehow loses the alt/indie edge of the original leaving it a bit flat while Chicane fashion a slightly more atmospheric, if that was possible, version of 'Before Today' by EVERYTHING BUT THE GIRL. The London SUEDE, Brett Anderson and Bernard Butler's US moniker, are given a once over by Lionrock on 'The Chemistry Between Us' and 'Only The Strongest Will Survive' by HURRICANE #1 is given a facelift by James Lavelle, while My Bloody Valentine give LUSH's 'Sweetness And Light' a complete makeover. It's not all about the remixes though as there are some fantastic original recordings on here as well. FATBOY SLIM, normally the king of the remixes, settles for one of his own compositions, 'Sho' Nuff', while the CHEMICAL BROTHERS add the thumping 'Elektrobank'. Rounding up the album is the splendid 'Bizarre Love Triangle' from NEW ORDER, a forlorn ballad that sounds like, well, NEW ORDER. 'SPLENDOR' is indeed an outstanding soundtrack that showcases the talents of the artists involved and offers an alternative perspective on what were already top notch songs. *CM*

Album rating: *7.5

☐ Rick SPRINGFIELD segment
(⇒ HARD TO HOLD)

STADT DER VERLORENEN SEELEN

aka City Of The Lost Souls

1983 (W.Ger 90m) Hessischer Rundfunk / Sender Freies Berlin (R)

Film genre: seXual Rock Musical comedy

Top guns: s-w + dir: Rosa von Praunheim

Stars: Angie Stardust *(himself)*, Judith Flex *(Judith)*, Joaquin La Habana *(himself)*, **Wayne County** *(Leila)* ← the PUNK ROCK MOVIE ← JUBILEE ← PUNK IN LONDON ← the BLANK GENERATION / → END OF THE CENTURY, Manfred Finger *(himself)*, Helga Goetze *(herself)*, Gary Miller *(Gary)*, Tara O'Hara *(herself)*, Tron von Hollywood *(Tron)*, Gerhard Helle *(Gerhard)*, Rosa von Praunheim *(himself)*

Storyline: German gay rights activist, Rosa von Praunheim, delivered his quasi-musical slant towards the eccentric American transvestites and drag queens living in Berlin. The Hamburger Konigin restaurant takes center stage as the place all of them want to er, hang out. All this comes to you nearly two decades before "Hedwig". *MCS*

Movie rating: *6

Visual: video (no audio OST; score: Alexander Kraut)

Off the record: Prior to the movie (1980), New Wave/Punk icon **Wayne County** (b. Wayne Rogers, 1947, Dallas, Georgia) had returned to his/her stamping ground in New York – only this time as transexual Jayne County. But who could forget her time with the Electric Chairs when she "dragged" herself on stage to perform such gems as 'Max's Kansas City', 'Stuck On You' and the banned 'Fuck Off'. *MCS*

☐ Lisa STANSFIELD segment
(⇒ SWING)

a STAR IS BORN

1976 third re-make (US 140m) Warner Bros. (R)

Film genre: showbiz/Pop/Rock Musical drama

Top guns: s-w: Frank Pierson (+ dir), Joan Didion, John Gregory Dunne (au: Robert Carson)

Stars: Barbra Streisand *(Esther Hoffman)* ← the OWL AND THE PUSSYCAT, **Kris KRISTOFFERSON** *(John Norman Howard)*, Paul Mazursky *(Brian)* ← BLACKBOARD JUNGLE / → DOWN AND OUT IN BEVERLY HILLS → HEY HEY WE'RE THE MONKEES → TOUCH → WHY DO FOOLS FALL IN LOVE, Gary Busey *(Bobby Ritchie)* → the BUDDY HOLLY STORY → CARNY → FEAR AND LOATHING IN LAS VEGAS, Oliver Clark *(Gary Danziger)* ← the LANDLORD, **Montrose:- Ronnie Montrose, Sammy Hagar, Bill Church, Denny Carmassi** *(themselves)*, Sally Kirkland *(photographer)* ← PIPE DREAMS ← HEY, LET'S TWIST / → HUMAN HIGHWAY → THANK YOU, GOOD NIGHT, **Tony Orlando** *(himself)*, **Rita Coolidge** *(herself)* ← PAT GARRETT & BILLY THE KID ← VANISHING POINT ← MAD DOGS & ENGLISHMEN, **Booker T. Jones** *(speedway)* → SONGWRITER, Robert Englund *(Marty)* → the ADVENTURES OF FORD FAIRLANE, **Donnie Fritts** *(speedway)* ← PAT GARRETT & BILLY THE KID / → SONGWRITER → the LIFE AND HARD TIMES OF GUY TERRIFICO, M.G. Kelly *(Bebe Jesus)* → the BUDDY HOLLY STORY → ROLLER BOOGIE → VOYAGE OF THE ROCK ALIENS → UHF, Bill Graham *(himself)* ← FILLMORE ← MUSCLE BEACH PARTY / → the RETURN OF BRUNO → the DOORS

Storyline: The world of Rock and Pop music take over from the glitz that was Hollywood in the original versions, but there's no business like showbusiness in any shape or form. Rock singer John Norman Howard has seen better days, but when he walks into a nightclub and spots the talent of Esther Hoffman, he's instantly smitten. Through his help, she becomes a pop star (and his lover), but as she rises to the top, his career takes a boozy tumble. *MCS*

Movie rating: *5

Visual: video

Off the record: Hard-rock outfit, **Montrose**, were a strange choice to appear in the movie. From 1974, they appeared in the lower rungs of the US album charts courtesy of 'Montrose', 'Paper Money', 'Warner Bros. Presents Montrose!' & 'Jump On It' (1976). *MCS*

BARBRA STREISAND & KRIS KRISTOFFERSON *)

Nov 76. (lp/c) *Columbia; <JS/JC 34403> C.B.S.; (CBS/40 86021)* [1] Mar77 [1]
– Watch closely now (*) / Queen bee / Everything / Lost inside of you / Hellacious acres (*) / Love theme from 'A Star Is Born' (Evergreen) / The woman in the moon / I believe in love / Crippled crow (*) / Finale: With one more look at you – Watch closely now / Reprise: Love theme from 'A Star Is Born' (Evergreen). *(re-iss. Jan89 lp/c; ACS/BT 8740) <(re-iss. Apr95 on 'Columbia' cd/c; 474905-2/-4)> <cd re-mast.2003; CK 86119>*

S/track review: At times, this is like wading through waist-deep treacle. Musically, it's so indeterminate it defies categorisation. Whether its BABS or KRIS manning the mike, the record chunders along at a truly somnolent tempo, STREISAND warbles away like a Broadway-sick, rock-chick cliché and KRISTOFFERSON barks like he's gargling piranha teeth, singing lyrics that aren't his own, more often than not on the wrong side of trite ("You're coming closer lady, don'tcha leave me now, We're gonna make it, don't look down", etc, etc). To be fair, the man's onscreen demons were propping up a mirror to his real life travails, and his tortuous, hangdog trawl through 'Crippled Crow' is real car-crash stuff, coming close to the ghoulish fascination of Neil Young's 'Tonights The Night'; it sounds like the last thing KRISTOFFERSON's ever going to bring himself to sing. Rupert Holmes was in better shape; before he saw out the 70s with 'The Pina Colada Song', he was a STREISAND protégé, supplying the wordy but forgettable 'Queen Bee' and the corny ballad, 'Everything'. He didn't pen 'Evergreen', though, the film's "Love Theme", and, being a mega-selling, Oscar-winning US No.1 (UK Top 3), the song that everyone remembers. Here it sounds more anonymous than it did as a single, blending into the often staggering blandness, a mood that only breaks with the variety-show disco of 'I Believe In Love' (music by.. Kenny Loggins!!). If ever a 70s dinosaur needed slaying, this, verily, offered its bloated head for the block. *BG*

Album rating: *3.5

– spinoff hits, etc. –

BARBRA STREISAND: Love Theme From 'A Star Is Born' (Evergreen) / I Believe In Love
Nov 76. (7") *<10450> (A 4855)* [1] Mar77 [3]

STARDUST

1974 sequel (UK 111m) Goodtimes / Anglo-EMI (AA)

Film genre: Pop/Rock'n'roll Musical drama

Top guns: dir: Michael Apted → COAL MINER'S DAUGHTER → BRING ON THE NIGHT / s-w: Ray Connolly ← THAT'LL BE THE DAY

Stars: David Essex *(Jim Maclaine)* ← THAT'LL BE THE DAY ← SMASHING TIME / → SILVER DREAM RACER, **Adam Faith** *(Mike)* → McVICAR, Larry Hagman *(Porter Lee Austin)* → PRIMARY COLORS, Ines Des Longchamps *(Danielle)*, Rosalind Ayres *(Jeanette)* ← THAT'LL BE THE DAY, **Marty Wilde** *(Colin Day)* ← WHAT A CRAZY WORLD, **Keith Moon** *(J.D. Clover)* <= the WHO =>, **Dave Edmunds** *(Alex)* → CONCERT FOR KAMPUCHEA, **Paul NICHOLAS** *(Johnny)*, Peter Duncan *(Kevin)*, Karl Howman *(Stevie)* ← THAT'LL BE THE DAY / → BABYLON, Edd Byrnes *(TV interviewer)* ← BEACH BALL / → GREASE → BACK TO THE BEACH → SHAKE, RATTLE & ROLL: AN AMERICAN LOVE STORY, James Hazeldine *(Brian)*, David Daker *(Ralph Woods)* ← O LUCKY MAN!, Charlotte Cornwell *(Sally Potter)* → ROCK FOLLIES → ROCK FOLLIES OF '77, David Jacobs *(disc jockey)* ← JUST FOR FUN ← IT'S TRAD, DAD! ← the GOLDEN DISC, Michael Elphick ← O LUCKY MAN! / → QUADROPHENIA → BUDDY'S SONG, **Nick Lowe**

Storyline: Jim Maclaine is the lead singer of rock group the Stray Cats. When the group suddenly hit the big time Jim finds things too much to handle. Faced with unscrupulous hangers-on, a greedy, egotistical manager and a string of dodgy business deals, he starts on a rollercoaster of drink, sex and drugs which inevitably leads to his self destruction. Jim knows deep down there may be only one way to escape from all his problems. *JZ*

Movie rating: *6

Visual: video + dvd

Off the record: (see below)

Various Artists (md/songs: DAVE EDMUNDS *)

Nov 74. (d-lp) *Rockfield; (RG 2009-10)* [ ] [-]
– Happy birthday sweet 16 (NEIL SEDAKA) / Oh no not my baby (MAXINE BROWN) / Take good care of my baby (BOBBY VEE) / She's not there (the ZOMBIES) / Dream lover (BOBBY DARIN) / Do you want to know a secret (BILLY J. KRAMER & THE DAKOTAS) / Da doo ron ron (*) / I get around (the BEACH BOYS) / Up on the roof (the DRIFTERS) / One fine day (the CHIFFONS) / Loco-motion (LITTLE EVA) / You've got your troubles (the FORTUNES) / It might as well rain until September (CAROLE KING) / Don't let the sun catch you cryin' (GERRY & THE PACEMAKERS) / Surf city (JAN & DEAN) / Matthew and son (CAT STEVENS) / Make me your baby (BARBARA LEWIS) / Will you love me tomorrow (the SHIRELLES) / The letter (the BOX TOPS) / Monday, Monday (the MAMAS & THE PAPAS) // Summer in the city (the LOVIN' SPOONFUL) / I'm a believer (the MONKEES) / The house of the rising sun (the ANIMALS) / Carrie Anne (the HOLLIES) / I've gotta get a message to you (the BEE GEES) / You've lost that lovin' feelin' (RIGHTEOUS BROTHERS) /

Eve of destruction (BARRY McGUIRE) / White rabbit (JEFFERSON AIRPLANE) / (You make me feel like) A natural woman (ARETHA FRANKLIN) / When will I be loved (*) / A shot of rhythm and blues (*) / Make me good (*) / You keep me waiting (DAVID ESSEX) / Let it be me (*) / Some other guy (*) / Take it away (DAVID ESSEX) / C'mon little Dixie (*) / Americana Stray Cat blues (DAVID ESSEX) / Dea sancta (DAVID ESSEX) / Stardust (DAVID ESSEX).

S/track review: A breadth of 60s sounds (bar some new-ish 'STARDUST' gems from 70s stars, DAVID ESSEX and DAVE EDMUNDS), featured here. Brill Building-type classics from the likes of the DRIFTERS, NEIL SEDAKA, the CHIFFONS, LITTLE EVA, BOBBY VEE, ARETHA FRANKLIN, BOBBY DARIN, CAROLE KING and the SHIRELLES were all present and correct alongside surf hits from the BEACH BOYS, JAN & DEAN, British Invasion blockbusters from the ZOMBIES, BILLY J. KRAMER & THE DAKOTAS, GERRY & THE PACEMAKERS, the ANIMALS, the HOLLIES and even CAT STEVENS. The aforementioned DAVID ESSEX, a teenage pin-up at the time and star of the film and OST, delivered the priceless closing title track which hit the UK Top 10. The true strength of this double-set is its easy flow into the flower-power movement via the MAMAS & THE PAPAS ('Monday, Monday'), the LOVIN' SPOONFUL ('Summer In The City'), BARRY McGUIRE ('Eve Of Destruction') and JEFFERSON AIRPLANE ('White Rabbit'). DAVE EDMUNDS surpassed ESSEX's five entries with seven titles, the bulk of the show by far, his rendition of a few oldies such as 'When Will I Be Loved' & 'A Shot Of Rhythm & Blues', gelled this timepiece collection together. *MCS*

Album rating: *7

– spinoff hits, etc. –

DAVE EDMUNDS: A Shot Of Rhythm And Blues / Let It Be Me

Sep 74. (7") *Rockfield; (ROC 4)* [ ] [–]

DAVID ESSEX: Stardust

Nov 74. (7") *C.B.S.; (2828)* [7] [–]

□ Ringo STARR
(⇒ the BEATLES)

STARSTRUCK

1982 (Aus 105m) AFC / Palm Beach Pictures (PG)

Film genre: showbiz/Pop/Rock Musical comedy

Top guns: dir: Gillian Armstrong / s-w: Stephen MacLean

Stars: Jo Kennedy *(Jackie Mullens)*, Ross O'Donovan *(Angus Mullens)*, Margo Lee *(Pearl)*, Pat Evison *(Nana)*, Max Cullen *(Reg)*, John O'May *(Terry Lambert)*, Ned Lander *(Robbie)*, Melissa Jaffer *(Mrs. Booth)* → SHOUT!: THE STORY OF JOHNNY O'KEEFE, Mark Little *(Carl)*, Geoffrey Rush *(floor manager)* → LANTANA → the BANGER SISTERS, **the Swingers:- Philip Judd, Dwayne 'Bones' Hillman, Ian 'Killjoy' Gilroy** *(performers)*, Ben Franklin *(young policeman)* → ROCK N' ROLL COWBOYS, Kaarin Fairfax *(ice cream girl)* → ONE NIGHT THE MOON

Storyline: Jackie and Angus are cousins who will do anything to make it big. However, at the moment they're stuck with the family-run hotel in downtown Sydney. After some failures and fiascos they see a talent competition advertised with a $25,000 first prize. The pair are determined to win, especially after the hotel takings disappear from the safe, but they'll have to come up with something better than a singing kangaroo at the Sydney Opera House. *JZ*

Movie rating: *7

Visual: video + dvd

Off the record: The Swingers were a Aussie supergroup of sorts consisting of ex-Split Enz personnel **Philip Judd**, bass player **Dwayne 'Bones' Hillman** and drummer **Ian 'Killroy' Gilroy**. *MCS*

—

Various Cast (composers: the SWINGERS * & JO KENNEDY **)

Jan 83. (lp) *A&M; <SP 4938>* [–] [ ]
– Starstruck overture (*) / Starstruck (*) / Gimme love (*) / Temper temper (**) / It's not enough (**) / Tough (JOHN O'MAY & **) / Humming a tune (MENTAL AS ANYTHING) / I want to live in a house (ROSS O'DONOVAN) / Body and soul (**) / My belief in you (**) / Turnaround (TURNAROUND) / Monkey in me (**) / Starstruck finale (*).

S/track review: There is a certain level of apprehension when faced with the soundtrack to an Australian film that is made up of artists from down-under, just because the music that has emanated from our Southern Hemisphere neighbours can be a bit touch and go at times. While there have been some decent bands, there have also been a lot of not so decent ones. The soundtrack to 'STARSTRUCK' reflects both sides of this predicament. The SWINGERS are one band that are not too bad, with songs such as 'Starstruck' and 'Gimme Love' sounding a bit like glam rockers the Sweet, while ska-punk band MENTAL AS ANYTHING's 'Humming A Tune' could easily pass for Madness at their peak. Unfortunately, the rest of the album is sung by a mixture of other artists and actors from the film. Tracks like 'Temper Temper', 'It's Not Enough', 'I Want To Live In A House' and 'Monkey In Me' are dull, tepid 80s pop affairs and better off left alone, unless you want to use them as an anaesthetic. There are a couple of decent tracks here but nothing to write home about and certainly not worth buying this album for. *CM*

Album rating: *3.5

STAY AWAY, JOE

1968 (US 99m) Metro-Goldwyn-Mayer (PG)

Film genre: western comedy/drama

Top guns: dir: Peter Tewksbury / s-w: Michael A. Hoey (novel: Dan Cushman)

Stars: Elvis PRESLEY *(Joe Lightcloud)*, Burgess Meredith *(Charlie Lightcloud)* → SKIDOO, Joan Blondell *(Glenda Callahan)* ← ADVANCE TO THE REAR / → the PHYNX → GREASE, Katy Jurado *(Annie Lightcloud)* → PAT GARRETT & BILLY THE KID, Thomas Gomez *(Grandpa)*, L.Q. Jones *(Bronc Hoverty)* → TIMERIDER: THE ADVENTURE OF LYLE SWANN, Quentin Dean *(Mamie Callahan)*, Anne Seymour *(Mrs. Hawkins)*

Storyline: Mixed-blood rodeo rider Joe Lightcloud goes back to his roots on an Indian reservation, plying his luck with local ladies and attempting to secure the benefits of a government scheme. *BG*

Movie rating: *2.5

Visual: video + dvd

Off the record: nothing

—

ELVIS PRESLEY: Kissin' Cousins / Clambake / Stay Away, Joe

Jun 94. (cd) *R.C.A.; <(07863 66362-2)>* [ ] [ ]
– (KISSIN' COUSINS tracks) / (CLAMBAKE tracks) / STAY AWAY, JOE:- Stay away, Joe / Dominic / All I needed was the rain / Goin' home / Stay away.

S/track review: A strange one this, a clutch of Americana-rooted tracks kicking off with the hand-clapping, furrowed-brow R&B stomp/high country camp of the title track. Even ELVIS can't help from laughing at the Birdy-song-like sound effects on the tedious 'Dominic' but 'All I Needed Was The Rain' is a coolly rendered confession, coming from that same depression in the Deep South landscape as Bobbie Gentry's 'Ode to Billie Joe'. 'Goin' Home', meanwhile, is downright irresistible, a slice of rollicking, un-saddled country-rock in the best late 60s tradition. Listening to this, it feels almost as if PRESLEY has been waiting the whole decade to discover what he should've been doing all along; he also scales those lusty canyon heights on the Western, Bonanza-esque theatrics of closer 'Stay Away'. Originally never issued as a soundtrack, these songs appeared as various b-sides and album add-ons, although they were finally collected together (with the glaring omission of Jerry Reed's 'U.S. Male' and 'Dominique', unreleased at PRESLEY's request) as part of a three-on-one (with 'KISSIN' COUSINS' and 'CLAMBAKE') CD re-issue. *BG*

Album rating: *4

– spinoff hits, etc. –

ELVIS PRESLEY: Stay Away

Mar 68. (7") *<47-9465> (RCA 1688)* 67 May68 15

STAYING ALIVE

1983 (US 94m) Paramount Pictures (PG)

Film genre: showbiz/Pop-music drama

Top guns: s-w (+ dir): Sylvester Stallone → RHINESTONE → HARD TO HOLD, Norman Wexler ← SATURDAY NIGHT FEVER ← JOE

Stars: John Travolta *(Tony Manero)* ← URBAN COWBOY ← GREASE ← SATURDAY NIGHT FEVER / → SHOUT → PULP FICTION → PRIMARY COLORS → SWORDFISH → BE COOL → HAIRSPRAY re-make, **Cynthia Rhodes** *(Jackie)* ← FLASHDANCE / → DIRTY DANCING, Finola Hughes *(Laura)* ← the APPLE, Steve Inwood *(Jesse)* ← FAME, Julie Bovasso *(Mrs. Manero)* ← SATURDAY NIGHT FEVER, **Frank Stallone** *(Carl)*, Norma Donaldson *(Fatima)* ← WILLIE DYNAMITE ← ACROSS 110th STREET / → HOUSE PARTY → the FIVE HEARTBEATS, Cindy Perlman *(Cathy)* → RHINESTONE → HARD TO HOLD, Kurtwood Smith *(choreographer)* ← ROADIE / → FLASHPOINT

Storyline: Sylvester Stallone took an ill-advised seat in the director's chair for this universally slated follow-up to 'SATURDAY NIGHT FEVER'. Six years on, our Tony (Manero) is older but not necessarily wiser as he attempts to make his name on Broadway, accepting a bit part in a show improbably titled 'Satan's Alley' . . . *BG*

Movie rating: *3.5

Visual: video

Off the record: (see below)

---

the BEE GEES // Various Artists)

Jul 83. (lp/c)(cd) *R.S.O.; (RSBG/TRSBG 3)(<813 269>)* 6 14
– The woman in you / I love you too much / Breakout / Someone belonging to someone / Life goes on / Stayin' alive / Far from over (FRANK STALLONE) / Look out for number one (TOMMY FARAGHER) / Finding out the hard way (CYNTHIA RHODES) / Moody girl (FRANK STALLONE) / (We dance) So close to the fire (TOMMY FARAGHER) / I'm never gonna give you up (FRANK STALLONE & CYNTHIA RHODES).

S/track review: While the platinum-selling, BEE GEES-dominated score to this Travolta turkey wasn't exactly ignored, it didn't generate nearly as much interest as its big brother, 'SATURDAY NIGHT FEVER'. Which is probably as much as it deserved given that the film's creators couldn't even come up with an original title track. If anything, the inclusion of the classic, 1977-vintage 'Stayin' Alive' merely emphasises how much musical fashion had changed – for the worse – in the interim. Gone is the debonair, falsetto funk of old; in its place are a clutch of half-decent BEE GEES songs tainted by 80s production values. The only track strong enough to really rise above the malaise is 'Someone Belonging To Someone', a classy ballad which admittedly deserved more than its transatlantic Top 50 chart placing. 'The Woman In You', the other single lifted from this album, actually charted higher. Of course, part of the problem is that disco had long since fallen out of fashion, and the BEE GEES struggled to re-adjust their sound accordingly. The fact is that these songs were still stronger than much of the pop competition of the day, yet they're shoehorned into a kind of halfway house between disco and 80s artifice. Then again, they're streets ahead of the rancid, sub-SURVIVOR contributions from FRANK STALLONE (yes, Sly's brother!) and TOMMY FARAGHER. Animotion singer CYNTHIA RHODES' soul-lite efforts are marginally more palatable, although just when you think things can't get any worse, you're faced with a "tasteful" FRANK 'n' CYTNHIA duet . . . Aaarrggh! *BG*

Album rating: *3.5

– spinoff releases, etc. –

the BEE GEES: The Woman In You / Stayin' Alive

May 83. (7") *<813 713-7> (RSO 94)* 24 Jul83
(12") *(RSOX 94)* – ('A') / Saturday Night Fever segue.

FRANK STALLONE: Far From Over

Jul 83. (7") *<815 023-7> (RSO 95)* 10 Oct83 68

the BEE GEES: Someone Belonging To Someone / I Love You Too Much

Aug 83. (7") *<815 235-7> (RSO 96)* 49 Sep83 49
(12") *(RSOX 96)* – ('A') / Saturday Night Fever medley.

Tommy STEELE

Born: Thomas Hicks, 17 Dec'36, Bermondsey, London, England. Long before his 60s song and dance musical appearances in the likes of 'Half A Sixpence' & 'Finian's Rainbow', TOMMY STEELE was the quintessentially cheeky cockney barrow boy, and of course the first manufactured rock'n'roll pop singer. In 1956 (discovered by Larry Parnes), he had two major hits, 'Rock With The Caveman' and 'Singing The Blues', the latter his only chart-topper. During a period between his two No.1 film soundtracks ('The TOMMY STEELE STORY' & 'The DUKE WORE JEANS' – both 10", by the way), STEELE & His Steelmen notched up several more including 'Water Water' & 'Nairobi'. He abandoned rock for child-like novelty on 'Little White Bull' (a Top 10 hit from the 'Tommy The Toreador' film in '59), and it wasn't long before he disappeared from the music charts. His last movie in 1979, 'Quincy's Quest', was another to appeal to the festive family audience. *MCS*

- **filmography** {acting} –

The Tommy Steele Story *(1957 {*} OST to STEELE =>)* / Kill Me Tomorrow *(1957 {*})* / **the Duke Wore Jeans** *(1958 {*} OST to STEELE =>)* / Tommy The Toreador *(1959 {*} & theme)* / Light Up The Sky! *(1960 {*})* / **It's All Happening** *(1963 {*} on OST by V/A =>)* / Half A Sixpence *(1967 {*} OST to STEELE & V/A see; future editions =>)* / the Happiest Millionaire *(1967 {*})* / Finian's Rainbow *(1968 {*})* / Twelfth Night *(1969 TV {a})* / Where's Jack *(1969 {*})* / the Yeomen Of The Guard *(1978 TV {*})* / Quincy's Quest *(1979 {*})*

STEP UP

2006 (US 103m) Buena Vista / Touchstone Pictures (PG-13)

Film genre: romantic teen Dance-music comedy drama

Top guns: dir: Anne Fletcher / s-w: Duane Adler (+ story) ← the WAY SHE MOVES ← SAVE THE LAST DANCE, Melissa Rosenberg

Stars: Channing Tatum *(Tyler Gage)*, Jenna Dewan *(Nora Clark)* ← TAKE THE LEAD, Damaine Radcliff *(Mac Carter)* ← MARCI X, De'Shawn Washington *(Skinny Carter)*, **Mario** *(Miles Darby)*, Drew Sidora *(Lucy Avila)*, Rachel Griffiths *(director Gordon)* ← AMY ← TO HAVE AND TO HOLD, Josh Henderson *(Brett Dolan)* → BROKEN BRIDGES, Tim Lacatena *(Andrew)*, Alyson Stoner *(Camille)*, **Heavy D** *(Omar)* ← RHYME & REASON ← WHO'S THE MAN?

Storyline: Street dancer Tyler can't keep himself out of trouble and finally he's given community service by the judge at Maryland School of Arts. There he meets ballet artiste Nora, who is desperate for a suitable partner, but it seems no-one in her class is up to scratch. When she sees Tyler's amazing dance skills she tries to convince her teachers that he's the right man for the part, but can she shape her rough diamond into a sparkling gem? – "Two dancers, Two worlds, One dream". *JZ*

Movie rating: *5

Visual: dvd

Off the record: Mario (b. Mario Barrett, 27 Aug'86, Baltimore, Maryland, USA) was an R&B singer with several hits for 'J' records including No.1 'Let Me Love You' in 2004.

—

Various Artists (score: Aaron Zigman)

Aug 06. (cd) *Zomba-Jive; <(82876 88063-2)>* [6] Oct06 [ ]

– 'Bout it (YUNG JOC feat. 3LW) / Get up (CIARA feat. CHAMILLIONAIRE) / (When you gonna) Give it up to me (SEAN PAUL feat. KEYSHIA COLE) / Show me the money (PETEY PABLO) / 80s joint (KELIS) / Step up (SAMANTHA JADE) / Say goodbye (CHRIS BROWN) / Dear life (ANTHONY HAMILTON) / For the love (DREW SIDORA feat. MARIO) / Ain't cha (CLIPSE feat. RE-UP GANG and ROSCOE P. GOLDCHAIN) / I'mma shine (YOUNGBLOODZ) / Feelin' myself (DOLLA) / 'Til the dawn (DREW SIDORA) / Lovely (DEEP SIDE) / U must be (GINA RENE) / Made (JAMIE SCOTT).

S/track review: Opener, ''Bout It', by YUNG JOC and 3LW, is the expected bombastic boy-girl collaboration that is the current Zeitgeist in the world of RnB, whilst CIARA and CHAMILLIONAIRE's 'Get Up' is more minimalist, focussing on CIARA's alternating rough and smooth vocals. The ubiquitous SEAN PAUL is up next, featuring the obligatory guest appearance, this time from KEYSHIA COLE, with his usual brand of smooth dancehall on '(When You Gonna) Give It Up To Me' which has nowhere near the level of irritating infectiousness present in his chart hits, rather it is just irritating. PETEY PABLO's 'Show Me The Money' is fairly derivative gangsta rap, much like CHRIS BROWN and DEEP SIDE's efforts are third rate copies of Usher-type ballads. Meanwhile, KELIS' 80s Joint' is enjoyable chilled out floating funk, though SAMANTHA JADE's title track, despite being co-written by Wyclef Jean, cannot be saved from becoming routine cloying dance-orientated hip-hop. The Spanish guitars and affecting violins on ANTHONY HAMILTON's 'Dear Life' lend it an air of quality that sets it apart from the pack until it inevitably slips back into the comfort zone. Unfortunately, 'For The Love' by DREW SIDORA and MARIO is so slick and smooth that any semblance of a song is actually lost and 'Ain't Cha' by CLIPSE featuring RE-UP GANG and ROSCOE P GOLDCHAIN may be leaning towards old-school rap, but that doesn't mean it leaves any kind of impression. YOUNGBLOODZ' 'I'mma Shine' is only slightly better with its aggressive in-your-face modern hip-hop which is outdone by the bass-heavy crunk of DOLLA's 'Feelin' Myself'. GINA RENE then brings a touch of 70s string-laden soul to the proceedings on 'U Must Be', before JAMIE SCOTT is another to "step up", building the short and snappy funky racket that is 'Made' around a dirty guitar riff. *LF*

Album rating: *6

– spinoff releases, etc. –

PETEY PABLO: Show Me The Money

Aug 06. (cd-s) *<radio>* [58] [–]

STILL CRAZY

1998 (UK 120m) Columbia TriStar (R)

Film genre: showbiz/Rock-music comedy drama

Top guns: dir: Brian Gibson ← WHAT'S LOVE GOT TO DO WITH IT ← BREAKING GLASS / s-w: Dick Clement → ACROSS THE UNIVERSE, Ian La Frenais ← the TOUCHABLES / → ACROSS THE UNIVERSE

Stars: Stephen Rea *(Tony Costello)*, **Billy Connolly** *(Hughie)* ← the CONCERTS FOR THE PEOPLE OF KAMPUCHEA / → OVERNIGHT → OPEN SEASON, **Jimmy NAIL** *(Les Wickes)*, Timothy Spall *(David 'Beano' Baggot)* ← GOTHIC ← QUADROPHENIA / → ROCK STAR, Bill Nighy *(Ray Simms)*, Juliet Aubrey *(Karen Knowles)*, Helena Bergstrom *(Astrid Simms)*, Hans Matheson *(Luke Shand)* ← MOJO, Phil Daniels *(Neil Gaydon)* ← BREAKING GLASS ← QUADROPHENIA / → SEX, CHIPS AND ROCK N' ROLL, Philip Davis *(Chalky)* ← the WALL ← QUADROPHENIA, Brian Capron *(senior exec)* ← CROCODILE SHOES, Lee Williams *(young Keith)* → IN HIS LIFE: THE JOHN LENNON STORY, Frances Barber *(lady in black)* ← YOUNG SOUL REBELS ← WHITE CITY, Sabina Michael *(Dutch receptionist)* ← RADIO ON

Storyline: A bittersweet Spinal Tap-esque comedy about the reunion of a fictional 70s band ('Strange Fruit') after a chance meeting between the keyboard player and their old festival promoter's son. As they gradually track down the remaining group, the film hones in on the individual member's personal lives twenty years since the split. The interminable tensions and squabbling which originally tore them apart resurface as the group warm up for the big comeback concert. *KM*

Movie rating: *7

Visual: video + dvd

Off the record: Billy Connolly was in a band long before he was a stand-up comedian. The Humblebums (late 60s to early 70s) also featured a young Gerry Rafferty. This and everything more about their Caledonian roots can be found in The Great Scots Musicography by er . . . *MCS*

—

Various Cast (composers: CLIVE LANGER * / JEFF LYNNE & IAN LA FRENAIS ** / MICK JONES, FREDERIKSEN, & CHRIS DIFFORD *** / etc.)

Nov 98. (cd/c) *London; (<556055-2/-4>)* [ ] Feb99 [ ]

– The flame still burns (STRANGE FRUIT with JIMMY NAIL) *** / All over the world (STRANGE FRUIT) *** / What might have been (JIMMY NAIL) / Brian's theme – acoustic (STEVE DONNELLY) * / Dirty town (STRANGE FRUIT) ** / Stealin' (BILLY CONNOLLY) / Black moon (STRANGE FRUIT) / Live for today (HANS MATHESON) * / Bird on a wire (STRANGE FRUIT with JIMMY NAIL) *** / Ibiza theme (22.33.44) * / Scream freedom (STRANGE FRUIT) *** / A woman like that (BERNIE MARSDEN) ** / Dangerous things (STRANGE FRUIT) * / Brian's theme – reprise (STEVE DONNELLY) *. *(cd re-iss. Sep99; 3984 28235-2)*

S/track review: Enlisting Foreigner's MICK JONES and Squeeze's CHRIS DIFFORD to compose the soundtrack (alongside JEFF LYNNE) about an imaginary late 70s band turned out to be a wise move as they succeeded in capturing the essence of a time when rock went mainstream. Kicking off with the earnest 'The Flame Still Burns' (also a minor UK hit), JIMMY NAIL's vocal does justice to this textbook Foreigner power ballad. With all the hallmarks of a soft rock classic (the lighters aloft chorus, the twiddly over-synthesized solo and the one semi-tone up finally) this song fits neatly into the era like it was always there. The production is stripped down for NAIL's next ballad, 'What Might

Have Been', which unfortunately leaves his voice open for closer scrutiny. Although out of his depth slightly, the strings, mandolin and harpsichord (probably synthesized) add a pleasant backdrop to this painfully sad song. Happier times come courtesy of the STRANGE FRUIT recordings like 'Scream Freedom's Sabbath-like grunge and the stomp rock homage to pushers and prostitutes in 'Dirty Town'. Ex Whitesnake boogie-man, BERNIE MARSDEN attempts to keep up the momentum with 'A Woman Like That', but, coming on like a 'Quo covers band, the weedy vocal shows exactly why his solo career never took off. More interesting is new wave producer CLIVE LANGER's composition, 'Live For Today', with a production emulating the Beatles' psych era in its string arrangement and sustained guitar. Only the 'Ibiza Theme' and the BILLY CONNOLLY song seem out of place here, but at least the latter makes a welcome change to the sometimes overwhelming Rawk seriousness. *KM*

Album rating: *5.5

– spinoff releases, etc. –

JIMMY NAIL with STRANGE FRUIT: The Flame Still Burns / Bird On A Wire / ('A'-version)

Nov 98. (cd-s) *(LONCD 420)* [47] [–]

STOMP THE YARD

2007 (US 115m) Rainforest Films / Screen Gems (PG-13)

Film genre: teen/Dance Musical drama

Top guns: dir: Sylvain White / s-w: Robert Adetuyi ← TURN IT UP, Gregory Ramon Anderson

Stars: Columbus Short *(DJ Williams)* ← SAVE THE LAST DANCE 2 ← YOU GOT SERVED, Meagan Good *(April)* ← ROLL BOUNCE ← YOU GOT SERVED, **Ne-Yo** *(Rich Brown)* ← SAVE THE LAST DANCE 2, Darrin Henson *(Grant)* ← LONGSHOT, Brian J. White *(Sylvester)*, Laz Alonso *(Zeke)*, Jermaine Williams *(Noel)* ← the BEAT, Valarie Pettiford *(Jackie)* ← GLITTER, Harry J. Lennix *(Nate)* ← RAY ← the FIVE HEARTBEATS, **Chris Brown** *(Duron)*

Storyline: Street dancer DJ finds life hard when he first enrols at Truth University. Having already been in jail, and his young brother a murder victim, DJ's life has not been easy and now he must adapt to the academic world. However, his dance skills draw the attention of two rival campus groups who each want to sign him for the big competition, and DJ finds himself fitting in at last with the college crowd. *JZ*

Movie rating: *3

Visual: dvd

Off the record: Chris Brown (b. 5 May'89, Tappahannock, Virginia, USA) is the youngest R&B kid on the block, having had his first No.1 hit, 'Run It', in 2005 at only 16. *MCS*

Various Artists (score: Tim Boland & Sam Retzer)

Jan 07. (cd) *Artists' Addiction; <90016>* [ ] [–]
– Go hard or go home (E-40 feat. the FEDERATION) / Vans (the PACK) / Poppin' (CHRIS BROWN) / Sign me up (NE-YO) / The champ (GHOSTFACE KILLAH) / Walk it out (UNK) / Pop, lock & drop it (HUEY) / The deepest hood (AL KAPONE aka KAPEEZY) / Come on (BONECRUSHER feat. ONSLAUGHT) / Supermixx's black in the building (PUBLIC ENEMY) / Storm (CUT CHEMIST feat. EDAN & MR. LIF) / In the music (the ROOTS feat. MALIK B. & PORN) / Ain't nothing wrong with that (ROBERT RANDOLPH & the FAMILY BAND) / Bounce wit me (R.E.D. 44).

S/track review: Step dancing remains an almost exclusively American high school phenomenon, but that doesn't mean the music need be something to soundtrack the prom. The film is essentially an excuse to show off expertly choreographed dance routines, so the soundtrack is a driven collection of tunes to throw out some serious moves to. There's no space for slow jams or gloopy balladry, this is full-on, high-octane beats that bounce. Deliberate, throbbing cuts, filled with chant-a-longs and choruses you can see coming a mile off but are still electrifying. The highlights are plentiful. NE-YO's excellent 'Sign me up' is the right side of classic Michael Jackson pop, underpinned with a syncopated handclap beat. The PACK's sublimely quirky tribute to the original skate sneaker 'Vans' shows that less (this barely even has a drumbeat!) is often more. In contrast, BONECRUSHER and ONSLAUGHT even throw in some chunky metal guitar riffs on 'Come on' and HUEY, UNK and E-40 all drink down Lil Jon's finest crunk juice recipe for inspiration but still sound like their own men. Things get spooky when the ROOTS unfurl 'In The Music', a doomy late night cruise under fluorescent streetlights. The cherry on top here, however, is both sublime and ridiculous. 'The Champ', from the supremely skilled GHOSTFACE KILLAH, may sound goofy initially with its 'Rocky III' take-offs but as always his rhymes are complex and wildly vivid. This is a stroke of genius in an already strong field. After 53 minutes of rallying cries and inspirational jump-up just try and not end up leaping up and down on the couch, pumping your fists. *MR*

Album rating: *7.5

STONED

2005 (UK 102m) Vertigo Films (15)

Film genre: Rock-music bio-pic/drama

Top guns: dir: Stephen Woolley / s-w: Neal Purvis, Robert Wade

Stars: Leo Gregory *(Brian Jones)* ← OCTANE, Paddy Considine *(Frank Thorogood)* ← 24 HOUR PARTY PEOPLE, Monet Mazur *(Anita Pallenburg)*, Tuva Novotny *(Anna Wohlin)*, David Morrissey *(Tom)*, Amelia Warner *(Janet)*, Will Adamsdale *(Andrew Loog Oldham)*, Ben Whishaw *(Keith Richards)* → I'M NOT THERE, Luke de Woolfson *(Mick Jagger)*, James D. White *(Charlie Watts)*, Ralph Brown *(Gysin)* ← WAYNE'S WORLD 2

Storyline: Charting the last few months of Brian Jones' life: working class builder Frank Thorogood is sent to repair Jones' country house and to keep an eye on him at the same time. But it's impossible for Jones to keep on the straight and narrow for long and Thorogood soon becomes drawn into Jones' world of booze, sex and drugs. As the money begins to dry up, tragedy is just around the corner. *JZ*

Movie rating: *6

Visual: dvd

Off the record: *Brian Jones* was guitarist with the Rolling Stones up until he was sacked in June '69; he died on the 3rd of July '69, mysteriously drowning in his swimming pool. *MCS*

Various Artists (score: DAVID ARNOLD *)

Nov 05. (cd) *Milan-WEA; (5913 01731-5) <36147-2>* [ ] May06 [ ]
– Little red rooster (the COUNTERFEIT STONES) / Stop breaking down (the BEES) / Lazy Sunday (the SMALL FACES) / White rabbit (JEFFERSON AIRPLANE) / Paper sun (TRAFFIC) / Devil in me (22-20s) / Love in vain (HALEY GLENNIE-SMITH) / Brian's joint (*) / Ballad of a thin man (KULA SHAKER) / Out of control (*) / Come on in my kitchen (HALEY GLENNIE-SMITH) / The last time (the BEES) / Pool fight (*) / Love in vain (PAUL BUTLER & LITTLE BARRIE) / Angel-Devil (*) / Not fade away (the BEES) / Time is on my side (the BEES) / Stop breakin' down blues (ROBERT JOHNSON).

S/track review: With a complete absence of material from the Rolling Stones themselves, the bulk of the soundtrack relies on the

BEES, and the hirsute combo are more than capable of shouldering the burden. From the psychedelic washes of organ that adorn 'Stop Breaking Down', through to the pounding rendition of 'Not Fade Away', they provide the perfect aural experience for the backwards-looking, as well as revisionist, retro aesthetic that the film espouses. If imitation is the sincerest form of flattery, Mick Jagger must blush at the note-and-tone-perfect rendition of the COUNTERFEIT STONES' Steve Elson on 'Little Red Rooster', and its bluesy slide guitar is impressively rendered. But it's not all about recreation; the SMALL FACES classic 'Lazy Sunday' with its joyful, breezy Cockney music hall stylings, JEFFERSON AIRPLANE and 'White Rabbit's drug-induced foreboding, and TRAFFIC's 'Paper Sun', a hazy psychedelic excursion replete with sitar and flute, are all present and correct. Things are brought up to speed with the 22-20s' slice of neo-psychedelic rock'n'roll, 'Devil In Me', but the glossy sheen only just elevates it above the advertorial music it truly is. The movie's composer DAVID ARNOLD contributes a few choices of stirring and menacing strings to orchestrate the film's posited murder scenario. HALEY GLENNIE-SMITH's 'Come On In My Kitchen' comes over as badly as KT Tunstall, and her version of 'Love In Vain' is simply outclassed by the primal blues workover of the same track performed by PAUL BUTLER and LITTLE BARRIE. It seems almost inevitable that on such a retro album KULA SHAKER should raise their heads, some ten years after beginning to plough the retro-psych furrow. All in all it's a welcome relief when one gets the real deal, and it doesn't get more real or authentic than ROBERT JOHNSON and 'Stop Breakin' Down Blues', which takes us straight back to the source, crackling Mississippi blues from one of its first progenitors. *DF*

Album rating: *6.5

STRAIGHT TO HELL

1987 (UK/Spain 86m) Commies From Mars / Initial / Island (15)

Film genre: western crime caper/comedy

Top guns:s-w: Alex Cox (+ dir) ← SID & NANCY ← REPO MAN / → WALKER → FEAR AND LOATHING IN LAS VEGAS → REVENGERS TRAGEDY, **Dick Rude**

Stars: Dick Rude *(Willy)* ← SID & NANCY ← REPO MAN / → WALKER → ROADSIDE PROPHETS → LET'S ROCK AGAIN!, Sy Richardson *(Norwood)* ← SID & NANCY ← REPO MAN ← PETEY WHEATSTRAW / → WALKER → TAPEHEADS → MYSTERY TRAIN, **Joe STRUMMER** *(Simms)*, **Courtney LOVE** *(Velma)*, Dennis Hopper *(I.G. Farben)* ← RUNNING OUT OF LUCK ← WHITE STAR ← HUMAN HIGHWAY ← EASY RIDER ← HEAD ← the TRIP, **Elvis COSTELLO** *(Hives, the butler)*, Jim Jarmusch *(Mr. Amos Dade)* → CANDY MOUNTAIN → LENINGRAD COWBOYS GO AMERICA → SLING BLADE → YEAR OF THE HORSE → I PUT A SPELL ON ME → the FUTURE IS UNWRITTEN, **Zander Schloss** *(Karl)* <= the CIRCLE JERKS =>, **Grace Jones** *(Sonya)* ← GORDON'S WAR / → SIESTA, Biff Yeager *(Frank McMahon)* ← SID & NANCY ← REPO MAN ← DYNAMITE BROTHERS / → WALKER → ROADSIDE PROPHETS, Jennifer Balgobin *(Fabienne)* ← REPO MAN / → TAPEHEADS → ROADSIDE PROPHETS, Frank Murray *(Biff MacMahon)*, **the POGUES:- Shane MacGowan** *(Bruno McMahon)*, **Spider Stacey** *(Angel Eyes McMahon)*, **Cait O'Riordan** *(Slim McMahon)*, **Philip Chevron** *(Ed McMahon)*, **Jem Finer** *(Granpa McMahon)*, **James Fearnley** *(Jimmy McMahon)*, **Andrew Ranken** *(Lance McMahon)*, **Terry Woods** *(Tom McMahon)* / Miguel Sandoval *(George)* ← SID & NANCY ← HOWARD THE DUCK ← REPO MAN / → WALKER → JUNGLE FEVER, Kathy Burke *(Sabrina)* ← SID & NANCY ← EAT THE RICH / → WALKER → KEVIN & PERRY GO LARGE, **Xander Berkeley** *(Preacher McMahon)* ← SID & NANCY / → WALKER → TAPEHEADS → STORYTELLING, **Edward Tudor-Pole** *(Rusty Zimmerman)* ← SID & NANCY ← ABSOLUTE BEGINNERS ← the GREAT ROCK'N'ROLL SWINDLE / → WALKER, Graham Fletcher-Cook *(Whitey/Jeeves)* ← SID & NANCY ← ABSOLUTE BEGINNERS / → SIESTA

Storyline: After burning their underworld bridges, a trio of coffee guzzling gangsters and their proxy moll retreat to the dodgy environs of Blanco Town, a godforsaken last chance saloon populated by deadbeats and a resident cocktease. The McMahon Gang run what little of a show there is, and despite initially frosty relations, the two criminal fraternities indulge in mucho dusty and booze-sodden bonding before it all ends in ketchup splattered tears. *BG*

Movie rating: *5.5

Visual: video + dvd

Off the Record: (see below)

the POGUES // Various Artists (w/ PRAY FOR RAIN **)

Jun 87. (cdc/lp) *Hell-Stiff; (C/Z/+DIABLO 1) Enigma; <D2/4XJE 73308>* ☐ Nov87 ☐
– The good, the bad and the ugly / Rake at the gates of Hell / If I should fall from grace with God / Rabinga / Danny boy // Evil darling (JOE STRUMMER) / Ambush at Mystery Rock (JOE STRUMMER) / Money, guns and coffee (**) / Killers (**) / Salsa y ketchup (ZANDER SCHLOSS) / Big nothing (McMANUS GANG). *(cd re-iss. Aug91 on 'Repertoire'; REP 4224-WY)*

S/track review: When the rest of Britain was still following the herds down to the Costa Del Sol, London Irish rebel rousers the POGUES and their pals headed for a pre-easyJet Almería. In lieu of a Nicaraguan solidarity tour and in the same badlands which once hosted Eastwood, Van Cleef, Bronson et al, SHANE MacGOWAN, ELVIS COSTELLO, a pre-Hole COURTNEY LOVE and JOE STRUMMER exposed their milkbottle-white coupons to the ferocity of an Andalucían sun. The reward for their undoubtedly sweaty labours was a fistful of pejoratives from critics unimpressed with the lack of narrative and general anarchy. Two decades on, and Tarantino has made his name with satirical, sharp-suited hoods, Mojo has dubbed the movie "the apotheosis of gonzo cinematography", and the belated release of the full length soundtrack has further whetted revisionist appetites. Previously unreleased material by the POGUES, especially, is worthy of more than a backward glance, and not merely to hear guitarist JEM FINER playing out his Ennio Morricone fantasies. "We responded compulsively to our environment", claims producer PHIL CHEVRON in his sleevenotes, and while most of the instrumental sketches are bone-dry evocations (and the great 'Night On Bald Mountain' pure tack piano ham), there's just enough of the black stuff to lubricate the likes of 'Rabinga', 'Big Question Mark' and the gorgeous 'L'Amoria', roping a lasso between Celtic and Hispanic tradition. You also get the more well known 'If I Should Fall From Grace..', the Cajun-flavoured 'Rake At The Gates Of Hell' and a spine-massaging, CAIT O'RIORDAN (sorely missed from the band's subsequent albums)-led 'Danny Boy'. It's more obvious that PRAY FOR RAIN do this kind of stuff for their day job, with no hesitation in giving it some welly with the mariachi horns, terrace chants and chimes of doom. The excellent main title was obviously on the original soundtrack but Spaghetti fiends will relish previously unreleased cues like 'Spoils', where the church organ interlude is the most blatant Morricone reference on the whole record. Even STRUMMER tries his hand at some sinister Spanish mutterings on the militant 'Ambush At Mystery Rock', while, as the sleevnotes suggest, opener 'Evil Darling' predicted his Mescaleros years. At 28 tracks, the expanded CD is well worth a punt, even for film-score buffs who've never owned a Clash album or indeed never felt the urge to watch a grown man bang himself over the head with a tin tray. *BG*

Album rating: *6 / re-CD *7.5

– spinoff releases, etc. –

Various Artists (the POGUES * & PRAY FOR RAIN **): Straight To Hell – Returns

Jun 04. (cd) *Big Beat; (<CDWIKD 239>)* ☐ ☐
– Evil darling (JOE STRUMMER) / Long cool day in Hell (*) / The killers (**) / Three deadly cars (**) / Spoils (**) / Bolero del perro listo (aka Bolero) (*) / Fabienne (MIGUEL SANDOVAL) / Night on Bald Mountain (*) / Blood sausage (ZANDER SCHLOSS) / Ambush at Mystery Rock (JOE STRUMMER) / Harmonicas (*) / Windle binky boo (ZANDER SCHLOSS) / Rabinga (*) / Big question mark (*) / L'amoria (*) / Obsession (*) / Salsa y ketchup (ZANDER SCHLOSS) / Quiet day in Blanco town (*) / Sadistic sausage (aka Sado sausage) (ZANDER SCHLOSS) / If I should fall from grace with God (*) / Danny boy (*) / Insipid sausage (ZANDER SCHLOSS & **) / Shoot out (**) / Fan out (**) / Big nothing (McMANUS GANG) / Taranta del fuente (*) / High fives (ZANDER SCHLOSS) / Rake at the gates of Hell (*).

☐ George STRAIT segment
(⇒ PURE COUNTRY)

STRANGE DAYS

1995 (US 145m) 20th Century Fox (R)

Film genre: sci-fi thriller

Top guns: dir: Kathryn Bigelow / s-w: James Cameron (+ story), Jay Cocks

Stars: Ralph Fiennes *(Lenny Nero)*, Angela Bassett *(Lornette "Mace" Mason)* ← WHAT'S LOVE GOT TO DO WITH IT ← the JACKSONS: AN AMERICAN DREAM / → MASKED AND ANONYMOUS, Juliette Lewis *(Faith Justin)* ← the BASKETBALL DIARIES ← NATURAL BORN KILLERS ← the RUNNIN' KIND / → FROM DUSK TILL DAWN → the FEARLESS FREAKS → CATCH AND RELEASE, Tom Sizemore *(Max Peltier)* ← NATURAL BORN KILLERS, Michael Wincott *(Philo Gant)* ← DEAD MAN ← the CROW ← the DOORS, Vincent D'Onofrio *(Burton Steckler)* → CHELSEA WALLS → OVERNIGHT → THUMBSUCKER, Glenn Plummer *(Jeriko One)* ← TRESPASS ← WHO'S THAT GIRL, **Richard Edson** *(Tick)* ← WHAT ABOUT ME ← TOUGHER THAN LEATHER ← GOOD MORNING, VIETNAM ← WALKER ← HOWARD THE DUCK / → the MILLION DOLLAR HOTEL → SOUTHLANDER, William Fichter *(Dwayne Engelman)* → ALBINO ALLIGATOR, Josef Sommer *(Palmer Strickland)*, Nicky Katt *(Joey Corto)* → SUBURBI@ → SCHOOL OF ROCK, Michael Jace *(Wade Beemer)*, David Packer *(Lane)* ← the RUNNIN' KIND, Kelly Hu *(anchor woman)* ← the DOORS, **Season To Risk:- Paul Malinowski, Duane Trower, Steve Tulipana, Chad Sabin** *(warehouse party band)*

Storyline: Wouldn't it be amazing to be able to read somebody else's mind! In turn of the century L.A. a device called a "squid" enables you to do just that, and it's the hottest thing on the black market. Lonely ex-cop Lenny Nero uses his squid to play clips of his old girlfriend, who's now seeing top music boss Philo Grant. When a clip shows the police murdering one of Grant's stars, Nero finds himself in trouble from both sides of the law. *JZ*

Movie rating: *7

Visual: video + dvd

Off the record: Season To Risk (from Kansas City. Missouri, USA) have been on the go since 1989, releasing albums such as 'Season To Risk' (1992), 'In A Perfect World' (1995), 'Men Are Monkeys, Robots Win' (1998) and 'The Shattering' (2001) – think Jesus Lizard and Bad Brains. *MCS*

Various Artists (score: GRAEME REVELL *)

Oct 95. (cd/c) *Epic; <67226> (480984-2/-4)* ☐ Jan96 ☐
– Selling Jesus (SKUNK ANANSIE) / The real thing (LORDS OF ACID) / Overcome (TRICKY) / Coral lounge (DEEP FOREST) / No white clouds (STRANGE FRUIT) / Hardly wait (JULIETTE LEWIS) / Here we come (ME PHI ME & JERIKO ONE) / Feed (SKUNK ANANSIE) / Strange days (PRONG feat. RAY MANZAREK) / Walk in freedom (SATCHEL) / Dance me to the end of time (KATE GIBSON) / Fall in the light (LORI CARSON & *) / While the earth sleeps (PETER GABRIEL & DEEP FOREST).

S/track review: Put together in 1995 as the grunge rock revolution was subsiding, and just before the big beat explosion of the Prodigy and their ilk, the soundtrack to Kathryn Bigelow's millennial dystopia is a curious blend of hard-edged alternative rock and electronica, with industrial flavourings. And some awful new age techno. SKUNK ANANSIE fare well (they appear in the film), baiting the corporate "man" with a raging, churning 'Selling Jesus', and a more intriguing contribution with 'Feed' in which a thrashy ascending riff, overlaid with a rich solo guitar sound, gives way to a pounding breakdown that sits back on the groove with lashings of wah-wah histrionics. LORDS OF ACID's nondescript take on NIN and late Depeche Mode fails to catch alight, but TRICKY's deeply sexy, minimalist programming suits the dirty back streets vibe of the film (sampling Shakespear's Sister's 'Moonchild' as it does). The military snare patterns and ominous bassline of STRANGE FRUIT's 'No White Clouds' loll into a louche saxophone melody before breaking into a solid muscular riff, although it drags along for too long before it descends into a spiralling percussion-heavy freakout. Before she had committed herself to a parallel career as a rawk chick with the Licks, JULIETTE LEWIS covers PJ Harvey's 'Hardly Wait' with some success. The most arresting collaboration is between proto-Nu Metal industrialists PRONG and RAY MANZAREK, covering the latter's Doors classic, 'Strange Days'. The intended effect of re-interpreting the song with the black sheen of the film's futuristic urban aesthetic is clear, but the march of the replicants drumbeat and down-tuned riffage never really meld with MANZAREK's organic keyboards. It's a bit of a mess. That said it's not a patch on the travesty of PETER GABRIEL's link-up with DEEP FOREST on 'While The Earth Sleeps', which is the sort of dance music-inflected world music crap that sounds like it was recorded for a travel agency advert. It samples the Tsianandali choir for ethnic kudos, but singly fails to do anything but sound generic as GABRIEL strains his ageing vocal chords through a vocal processor turned up to the maximum. *DF*

Album rating: *6

STRANGELAND

1998 (US 86m) Raucous Releasing (R)

Film genre: psychological/occult horror

Top guns: dir: John Pieplow / s-w: **Dee Snider**

Stars: Kevin Gage *(Mike Gage)*, Elizabeth Peña *(Toni Gage)* ← LA BAMBA ← DOWN AND OUT IN BEVERLY HILLS ← TIMES SQUARE / → THINGS BEHIND THE SUN, Brett Harrelson *(Steve Christian)*, Robert Englund *(Jackson Roth)* ← the ADVENTURES OF FORD FAIRLANE ← a STAR IS BORN, Linda Cardellini *(Genevieve Gage)*, Tucker Smallwood *(Captain Churchill Robbins)*, Amy Smart *(Angela Stravelli)*, Ivonne Coll *(Rose Stravelli)*, **Dee Snider** *(Captain Howdy / Carleton Hendricks)* ← PRIVATE PARTS / → METAL: A HEADBANGER'S JOURNEY

Storyline: There's an internet psycho on the loose, and when his daughter Genevieve is posted missing, Detective Mike Gage tracks down the culprit, Captain Howdy. When redneck vigilantes subsequently take it on themselves to dish out a hanging to the perpetrator, the reincarnated Howdy (now as Carleton Hendricks), wreaks his revenge by once again kidnapping Gage's daughter. *MCS*

Movie rating: *4.5

Visual: video + dvd

Off the record: Dee Snider (see below)

Various Artists (score: Anton Sanko)

Sep 98. (cd) *T.V.T.; <8270> (16581 8370-2)* ☐ ☐
– Inconclusion (DEE SNIDER) / Breathe (SEVENDUST) / A secret place (MEGADETH) / Where you come from (PANTERA) /

P & V (ANTHRAX) / Absent (SNOT) / Street justice (DAYINTHELIFE . . .) / Not living (COAL CHAMBER) / In league (BILE) / Sweet touch (MARILYN MANSON) / Eye for an eye (SOULFLY) / Serpent boy (HED P.E.) / Fxxk off (KID ROCK) / Awake (the CLAY PEOPLE) / Marmalade (SYSTEM OF A DOWN) / I'm the man (NASHVILLE PUSSY) / Captain Howdy (CRISIS) / Heroes are hard to find (TWISTED SISTER).

S/track review: In terms of soundtracks, it doesn't get any heavier than 'STRANGELAND'. Led by former Twisted Sister, DEE SNIDER, who also wrote and starred in the movie, the album is almost like a who's who of heavy metal. MEGADETH, PANTERA, ANTHRAX, COAL CHAMBER, MARILYN MANSON and SYSTEM OF A DOWN all contribute old or new tracks to the proceedings and the stature of the artists involved makes it stand out from many other metal soundtracks (example the mind-numbingly wicked 'Eye For An Eye' by Sepultura offshoot, SOULFLY). There are also some vital additions from lesser-known acts, which reinforce the album's unique quality. 'In League' by BILE and DAYINTHELIFE's cover of the Twisted Sister track, 'Street Justice', are all lethal riffage and growling vox. Only KID ROCK (who just can't seem to do anything good) and NASHVILLE PUSSY (the less said the better) let the album down by way of 'Fxxk Off' and 'I'm The Man', two tracks that can only be described as pointless nonsense. Possibly the highlight for many a metal fan will be the re-formation of TWISTED SISTER for the excellent 'Heroes Are Hard To Find', a balls-out, 80s throwback anthem that ties a fantastic album up perfectly. *CM*

Album rating: *8

the STRAWBERRY STATEMENT

1970 (US 109m) Metro-Goldwyn-Mayer (R)

Film genre: political drama/comedy

Top guns: dir: Stuart Hagmann / s-w: Israel Horovitz (au: James Kunen)

Stars: Bruce Davison *(Simon)* → SHORT EYES → DEADMAN'S CURVE → CRIMES OF PASSION → an AMBUSH OF GHOSTS → GRACE OF MY HEART, Kim Darby *(Linda)* → NORWOOD, James Coco *(grocer)*, Murray MacLeod *(George)*, Bud Cort *(Elliot)* → BREWSTER McCLOUD → GAS-S-S-S! → HAROLD AND MAUDE → ELECTRIC DREAMS → SOUTH OF HEAVEN, WEST OF HELL → the MILLION DOLLAR HOTEL → COYOTE UGLY → the LIFE AQUATIC WITH STEVE ZISSOU, Michael Margotta *(Swatch)* ← WILD IN THE STREETS / → TIMES SQUARE, Israel Horovitz *(Dr. Benton)*, Danny Goldman *(Charlie)* → WHERE THE BUFFALO ROAM, Tom Foral *(Coach)*, Booker Bradshaw *(Lucas)* → COFFY, Bert Remsen *(policeman)* → NASHVILLE → FAST BREAK → DICK TRACY, Bob Balaban *(Elliott)* ← MIDNIGHT COWBOY / → a MIGHTY WIND, Robin Menken *(w/ Guerilla Theatre Group)* ← FOOLS / → THANK GOD IT'S FRIDAY → THIS IS SPINAL TAP → BODY ROCK

Storyline: Simon is a student at Columbia University in San Francisco. He's fed up being in the rowing team when all the good looking gals are in the campus revolution movement. He sits in at a meeting and meets Linda, who soon gets him much more involved in student protests and it's not long before Simon is marching against Vietnam, the police, and society in general. The big showdown looms when Simon, Linda and their comrades stage a sit-in and the cops come to break it up. *JZ*

Movie rating: *5.5

Visual: video

Off the record: (see below)

Various Artists (score: IAN FREEBAIRN-SMITH *)

Aug 70. (d-lp) *M.G.M.; <2SE 14ST>* [91] [–]
– The circle game (BUFFY SAINTE-MARIE) / Our house (CROSBY, STILLS, NASH & YOUNG) *[on some copies only]* / Market basket (theme from "The Strawberry Statement") (*) / Down by the river (NEIL YOUNG) / Long time gone (CROSBY, STILLS and NASH) / Cyclatron (theme from "The Strawberry Statement") (*) / Something in the air (THUNDERCLAP NEWMAN) // Also Sprach Zarathustra (KARL BOHM conducting the BERLIN PHILHARMONIC ORCHESTRA) / The loner (NEIL YOUNG) / Coit tower (theme from "The Strawberry Statement") (*) / Fishin' blues (the RED MOUNTAIN JUG BAND) / Concerto in D minor (conducted by *) / Helpless (NEIL YOUNG) / Pocket band (theme from "The Strawberry Statement") (*) / Give peace a chance (the Cast in the film). *<(re-iss. Apr90 cd/c/lp; CD/TC/LP MGM 19)>*

S/track review: The 60s were coming to an end, the peace and love movement was being trampled on by the riot police, but protest music just-a kept on a-comin' brother and sister. 'The STRAWBERRY STATEMENT' was an ambitious double-LP (at around an hour running time), and one man stood head-n-shoulders above the pack – NEIL YOUNG. The croaky one delivers three numbers, the 9-minute-long classic, 'Down By The River', 'The Loner' and his CROSBY, STILLS, NASH & YOUNG collaboration, 'Helpless'; without YOUNG the trio contributed the harmony-fuelled 'Long Time Gone' (and on some rare copies, 'Our House'!). Of the other various artists (all pieced together by record exec, Mike Curb), there's only really three, BUFFY SAINTE-MARIE with her rendition of Joni Mitchell's 'The Circle Game', THUNDERCLAP NEWMAN's 'Something In The Air' and a self-explanatory, public domain chestnut ('Fishin' Blues') from the RED MOUNTAIN JUG BAND. If you're looking for more golden nuggets, don't hold your breath. A handful of themes by IAN FREEBAIRN-SMITH, an orchestral '2001 Odyssey' excerpt, 'Also Sprach Zarathustra' (by Karl Bohm and the Berlin Philharmonic Orchestra) and a closing cast performance of Lennon & McCartney's 'Give Peace A Chance' fill out the gaps. *MCS*

Album rating: *6.5

STREETS OF FIRE

1984 (US 94m) Universal Pictures (PG-13)

Film genre: Rock Musical drama

Top guns: s-w: Walter Hill (+ dir) ← the LONG RIDERS / → BLUE CITY → JOHNNY HANDSOME → TRESPASS → GERONIMO: AN AMERICAN LEGEND → LAST MAN STANDING, Larry Gross → GERONIMO: AN AMERICAN LEGEND

Stars: Michael Pare *(Tom Cody)* ← EDDIE AND THE CRUISERS / → EDDIE AND THE CRUISERS II: EDDIE LIVES! → the VIRGIN SUICIDES, Diane Lane *(Ellen Aim)* ← LADIES AND GENTLEMEN, THE FABULOUS STAINS, Rick Moranis *(Billy Fish)* → CLUB PARADISE → LITTLE SHOP OF HORRORS → BROTHER BEAR, Amy Madigan *(McCoy)* → PLACES IN THE HEART → ALAMO BAY → CROCODILE SHOES, Willem Dafoe *(Raven Shaddock)* → TO LIVE AND DIE IN L.A. → the LAST TEMPTATION OF CHRIST → CRY-BABY → WILD AT HEART → AFFLICTION → OVERNIGHT → the LIFE AQUATIC WITH STEVE ZISSOU, Deborah Van Valkenburgh *(Reva Cody)* ← the WARRIORS / → CHASING DESTINY → the DEVIL'S REJECTS, Richard Lawson *(officer Ed Price)* ← WILLIE DYNAMITE, Rick Rossovich *(officer Cooley)*, Ed Begley Jr. *(Ben Gunn)* ← THIS IS SPINAL TAP ← GET CRAZY ← ELVIS: THE MOVIE ← RECORD CITY / → EVEN COWGIRLS GET THE BLUES → a MIGHTY WIND, Bill Paxton *(Clyde the bartender)* → NEAR DARK → TRESPASS → DERAILROADED, **Lee VING** *(Greer; Bomber)*, Stoney Jackson *(Bird; the Sorels)* ← ROLLER BOOGIE / → SWEET DREAMS → KNIGHTS OF THE CITY → TRESPASS → CB4: THE MOVIE, Robert Townsend *(Lester, the Sorels)* → the FIVE HEARTBEATS, Elizabeth Daily *(Baby Doll)* ← LADIES AND GENTLEMEN, THE FABULOUS STAINS / → the COUNTRY BEARS ← the DEVIL'S REJECTS, Mykel T. Williamson *(B.J.; the Sorels)* → PRIMARY COLORS, Matthew Laurance *(Ardmore cop)* ← EDDIE AND

THE CRUISERS / → EDDIE AND THE CRUISERS II: EDDIE LIVES!, John Dennis Johnston *(Pete the mechanic)* ← the ROSE ← KISS MEETS THE PHANTOM OF THE PARK, **the Blasters:- Dave Alvin** *(performer)* → BORDER RADIO, **Philip Alvin, Lee Allen, William Bateman, Steve Berlin, John Bazz, Eugene Taylor** / Lynne Thigpen *(subway motorwoman)* ← GODSPELL / → the INSIDER

Storyline: The lead singer of a successful group is kidnapped during a concert by the leader of a sinister biker gang. Her manager, Billy Fish, hires her ex-boyfriend, Tom Cody, a former mercenary to rescue her from the biker's nightclub. Accompanied by a female ex-soldier, McCoy, who he meets in a bar, they head in to the gang's neighbourhood to confront the gang. Set in a surreal urban landscape, this was indeed a bombastic, comic-book of a Rock Musical. *KM & MCS*

Movie rating: *5.5

Visual: video + dvd

Off the record: The **Blasters** were formed in Downey, Los Angeles, California, USA. Taking their name from blues artist Jimmy McCracklin's Blues Blasters, the band traded off the music brothers **Phil** and **Dave Alvin** had soaked up in their youth; urban blues, stone country, greasy rockabilly and classic R&B were the base ingredients, the vibrancy of the local punk/hardcore scene the glue binding the whole thing together. Initially erm, blasting out a set comprised largely of cover versions at any establishment that would have them, the band had soon sufficiently honed their skills to undertake a debut album in 1980, 'American Music'. One of the most sought after artefacts of the early 80s "cowpunk" scene, this independently released record featured a couple of songs ('Marie, Marie' and the title track) which would resurface on their eponymous major label debut for 'Slash/Warners'. Don't let the fact that 'Marie, Marie' was covered by Shakin' Stevens put you off, the album (enhanced by **Bill Bateman** and **John Bazz** plus pianist **Gene Taylor** and saxophonists **Lee Allen & Steve Berlin**) remains a thrilling and satisfying journey through the weatherbeaten terrain of US tradition, as consummate as it is kick-ass. The band endeavoured to widen their musical horizons with mixed results on 'Non Fiction' (1983), Dave's songwriting was beginning to outgrow the confines of the Blasters' trad-rock format; the subsequent 'Hard Line' (1985) set would be the last recorded with the original line-up. Following Dave's departure, the band limped on for another year before finally splitting early in 1986. This was due to the untimely death (heart attack) of Dave's replacement, Michael "Hollywood Fats" Mann, aged only 32. While Phil recorded a one-off solo set, 'Unsung Stories', before going back to university, Dave undertook a more long term solo career, recording a string of albums between 1987 and 1994 as well as scoring the music for a minor budget movie, 'BORDER RADIO' (1987). *BG & MCS*

Various Artists (score: RY COODER *)

May 84. (lp/c) *M.C.A.; <MCA/MCC 5492> (MCF/+C 3221)* [32] [ ]
– Nowhere fast (FIRE INC) / Sorcerer (MARILYN MARTIN) / Deeper and deeper (the FIXX) / Countdown to love (GREG PHILLINGANES) / One bad stud (the BLASTERS) / Tonight is what it means to be young (FIRE INC) / Never be you (MARIA McKEE) / I can dream about you (DAN HARTMAN) / Hold that snake (*) / Blue shadows (the BLASTERS). *<(cd-iss. Jun88; MCAD 5492)> (cd re-iss. Feb95 on 'Beat Goes On'; BGOCD 220)*

S/track review: With the absence of Meat Loaf, JIM STEINMAN's two typically histrionic compositions – performed by FIRE INC. – are disappointingly weak, relying far too heavily on vocal overdubs. Keeping up with the times, he adds an uncharacteristically Erasure-esque middle 8 to 'Tonight Is What It Means To Be Young', yet it's not enough to rescue these fire-free performances. More promising are the Stevie Nicks-penned 'Sorcerer' by MARILYN MARTIN and a pre-'Show Me Heaven' MARIA McKEE's rootsy pop tune, 'Never Be You', written and produced by Tom Petty. Where these songs have stood up to the passage of time, UK new wavers the FIXX remind us how far we've come with their tinny, technologically reliant confections, one of which – 'Countdown To Love' – at least deserves credit for bravely (crazily?) attempting a doo wop/80s pop fusion. More successful was one-time Edgar Winter Group keyboardist turned disco don DAN HARTMAN, shrewdly drawing on the blue eyed soul of Hall & Oates with his blow-dried anthem, 'I Can Dream About You'. Less credit was given to RY COODER, who, with the exception of the BLASTERS' two bland rockabilly tunes, provided the rest of the music yet only saw one track – 'Hold That Snake' – make it onto the soundtrack. *KM*

Album rating: *4.5

– spinoff hits, etc. –

DAN HARTMAN: I Can Dream About You / FIRE INC.: Blue Shadows

Apr 84. (7"/12") *<52378> (MCA/+T 895)* [6] Jun84 [ ]

FIRE INC.: Tonight Is What It Means To Be Young / RY COODER: Hold That Snake

May 84. (7") *<52377> (MCA 889)* [80] May84 [ ]

DAN HARTMAN: I Can Dream About You

Aug 85. (7"/12"/12") *(MCA/+T/X 988)* [–] [12]

STUCK IN THE SUBURBS

2004 (US 82m TV) Richard Fischoff Productions / Disney Channel

Film genre: family/teen Pop Musical comedy

Top guns: dir: Savage Steve Holland / s-w: Dan Berendsen, Wendy Engelberg (+ story), Amy Engelberg (+ story)

Stars: Danielle Panabaker *(Brittany Aarons)*, Brenda Song *(Natasha Kwon-Schwartz)*, Taran Killam *(Jordan Cahill)*, CiCi Hedgpeth *(Ashley Simon)*, Jennie Garland *(Olivia Hooper)*, Ryan Belleville *(Eddie)*, Todd Stashwick *(Len)*, Kirsten Nelson *(Susan Aarons)*, Amanda Shaw *(Kaylee Holland)*, Corri English *(Jessie Aarons)* ← SHAKE, RATTLE AND ROLL: AN AMERICAN LOVE STORY

Storyline: A couple of young teens, Brittany and her newfound friend Natasha, accidentally swop cell phones with their fave pop star, Jordan Cahill. The girls proceed to have as much fun at his expense through the odd practical joke. However, they find out it's not an easy life being Jordan, as the world of manufactured pop mainly through his record company put a stop to his every bit of his creativity. *MCS*

Movie rating: *4.5

Visual: dvd

Off the record: nothing

Various Artists (incl. JORDAN CAHILL *)

Jul 04. (cd) *Disney; <861106>* [ ] [–]
– A whatever life (HAYLIE DUFF) / Good life (JESSE McCARTNEY) / Stuck (STACIE ORRICO) / Over it (ANNELIESE VAN DER POL) / Stuck in the middle with you (STEALERS WHEEL) / Take me back home (GREG RAPOSO) / More than me – acoustic version (*) / On top of the world (*) / Make a wish (*) / More than me – pop version (*).

S/track review: Opening with standard teen-movie breezy guitar-pop, akin to a mix of Alanis Morissette and Pink, HAYLIE DUFF's 'A Whatever Life' has an ambitious life-affirming message which is very American, but surprisingly pleasant – which can't be said of JESSE McCARTNEY's girning over the patchwork funk that is 'Good Life'. Meanwhile 'Stuck' by STACIE ORRICO is a passable attempt at marrying contemporary RnB with rock, though ANNELIESE VAN DER POL's 'Over It' fares much worse due to its unpalatable plethora of lyrical clichés. The dad-rock of STEALERS WHEEL's 'Stuck In The Middle With You' is completely out of place amongst the teeny bopping and faux emoting with its plodding MOR rock, but sounds like a masterpiece next to GREG RAPOSO's unconvincing self-pitying and posturing on 'Take Me Back Home' with its ridiculous attempts to tackle heavyweight topics beside slick and lightweight music. The last three tracks are left to JORDAN

CAHILL (or rather Taran Killam under his character's name) to provide us with the forgettable 'More Than Me', the vacuous 'On Top Of The World' and the earnest 'Make A Wish'. *LF*

Album rating: *3

STUNT ROCK

aka SORCERY

1978 (Aus/Neth 86m) Corona Films (AL)

Film genre: Hard-Rock-music thriller/pseudo-documentary

Top guns: s-w: (+ dir) Brian Trenchard-Smith, Paul-Michel Mielche Jr.

Stars: Grant Page *(himself; stuntman)*, Monique Van de Ven *(TV star)*, Margaret Gerard *(newspaper reporter)*, **Richard Taylor** *(guitarist)* → ROCKTOBER BLOOD, Curtis Hyde *(the Devil)*, Paul Haynes *(Merlin)*, Greg Magie *(himself)*, **Greg McGee** *(vocalist)*, **Doug Locke** *(keyboard player)*, **Richie King** *(bass player)* → ROCKTOBER BLOOD, **Perry Morris** *(drummer)* → ROCKTOBER BLOOD

Storyline: Fearless Aussie stuntman Grant Page lands a television co-ordinator job in L.A., meeting up with friend and fellow stuntman Curtis Hyde along the way. While the latter shows off his magical tricks in front of cod-heavy, hard-rock band, Sorcery, the pair get to grips with some backstage pyrotechnics. Meanwhile, Page gets into party mode and hooks up with two lovely career girls. *MCS*

Movie rating: *5

Visual: dvd

Off the record: Tagged "Death Wish At 120 Decibels".

—

SORCERY (composer: RICHARD "SMOKEY HUFF" TAYLOR)

1978. (lp) *Groovy 19; (GRL 25087)* [–] Nether [–]
– Sacrifice / Wizards council / Talking to the Devil / Burned alive / Book of magic / Stuntrocker / Mark of the beast / Bird song / Wicked city / Woman city / Power mad. *(cd-iss. Jun00 on 'Moving Image Entertainment' Italy; MIE 006-2)*

S/track review: Combining mystical magic, stunning stunts and muscular hard rock, California outfit SORCERY were years ahead of mockumentary faves-to-be SPINAL TAP. With future 'ROCKTOBER BLOOD' axeman on board, Richard Taylor, their blend of Uriah Heep-meets-Kiss rock showcased the "forgotten" cult movie, 'STUNT ROCK'. With tracks such as 'Stuntrocker', the album is quite a catch for the odd collector, thus its er, heavy price-tag. Merlin on stage battling with the Devil as the band plays on, while a myriad of stunts take place, is a sight to behold, while the music itself can stand on its own two feet. Other tracks that stick in the throat – so to speak – include 'Sacrifice', 'Burned Alive' and 'Mark Of The Beast'. SORCERY, now featuring David Glen Eisley, ex-Giuffra (replacing Greg McGee), went on to achieve a modicum of cult success in the early 80s . . . and beyond. *MCS*

Album rating: *6

SUBURBIA

aka The WILD SIDE

1984 (US 99m) New World Pictures (R)

Film genre: coming-of-age drama

Top guns: s-w + dir: Penelope Spheeris ← the DECLINE OF WESTERN CIVILIZATION / → DUDES → the DECLINE OF WESTERN CIVILIZATION 2: THE METAL YEARS → WAYNE'S WORLD → the DECLINE OF WESTERN CIVILIZATION PART III → WE SOLD OUR SOULS FOR ROCK'N'ROLL

Stars: Bill Coyne *(Evan Johnson)*, Chris Pederson *(Jack Diddley)*, Jennifer Clay *(Sheila)*, Timothy O'Brien *(Skinner)*, **Wade Walston** *(Joe Schmo)*, **Mike B. The FLEA** *(Razzle)*, Grant Miner *(Keef)*, Maggie Ehrig *(Mattie)*, Christina Beck *(T'resa)*, Andrew Pece *(Ethan Johnson)*, Jeff Prettyman *(Bob Stokes)* → PURE COUNTRY, **D.I.:- Casey Royer** *(vocals)*, **Tim Maag** *(guitar)*, **Derek O'Brian** *(drums)* / **T.S.O.L.:- Jack Grisham** *(vocals)*, **Ron Emory** *(guitar)*, **Mike Roche** *(bass)*, **Greg Kuehn** *(keyboards)*, **Todd Barnes** *(drums)* / **the Vandals:- Steve O** *(vocals)*, **Jan Ackerman** *(guitar)*, **Steve Pfauter** *(bass)*, **Joseph Escalante** *(drums)*, **Frank Gargani** *(himself)* ← the DECLINE OF WESTERN CIVILIZATION / → the UNHEARD MUSIC

Storyline: Evan Johnson is an L.A. teenager fed up with the world he sees around him, so he joins up with a group of punk rocker misfits who call themselves the Rejected. They hang out in the local neighbourhood looking for aggro and violence, and they find it! However, the kicks they get out of their lifestyle come at a price and tragic consequences are inevitable. *JZ*

Movie rating: *7

Visual: video + dvd

Off the record: **Wade Walston** was the US Bombs bassman; **Flea** was future Red Hot Chili Peppers bassist; other L.A. punks included **D.I., T.S.O.L. & the Vandals** (see below)

—

Various Artists // ALEX GIBSON (score)

1990. (cd/c/lp) *Restless; <7 71093-2/-4/-1>* [–] [–]
– Richard hung himself (D.I.) / Wash away (T.S.O.L.) / Darker my love (T.S.O.L.) / Legend of Pat Brown (the VANDALS) // Picking up Joe / Ethan's rescue / Punk parade / Sheila's song / Keep off the grass / Garage raids / T.R. revisited / Suburbia.

S/track review: There isn't a lot to choose from 'SUBURBIA', containing only four "proper" tracks propped up by ALEX GIBSON's instrumental score. If you like raw, straightforward, angst-ridden punk then the first four tracks are for you. 'Richard Hung Himself' by D.I. is a mid-paced tune with a memorable chorus, while the VANDALS' 'Legend Of Pat Brown' was made purely for pogoing and head banging. There are also two excellent tracks from little known band at the time, T.S.O.L., 'Wash Away' and 'Darker My Love', reminiscent of the Damned or Jonathan Richman, than any hardcore outfit. Serial soundtracker, ALEX GIBSON, makes up the rest of the set with a series of instrumentals that combine distorted guitars and heavy drums over atmospheric synths and stark sound effects. He does deviate from this format though on the piano ballad, 'Sheila's Song' but there isn't much to get excited about as the instrumentals fail to capture the urgency or indeed the spirit of the scene. 'SUBURBIA' is worth it for the first four tracks (and a smidgen of GIBSON), although the question has to be: why more punk songs were not used for this type of film; making the outcome a rather mediocre listen overall. *CM*

Album rating: *4.5

SUBURBI@

1996 (US 121m) Castle Rock / Detour / Carlton (R)

Film genre: coming-of-age comedy/drama

Top guns: dir: Richard Linklater → SCHOOL OF ROCK / s-w: Eric Bogosian (+ play)

Stars: Jayce Bartok *(Pony)*, Amie Carey *(Sooze)*, Nicky Katt *(Tim)* ← STRANGE DAYS / → SCHOOL OF ROCK, Ajay Naidu *(Nazeer Chaldi)*, Parker Posey *(Erica)* → JOSIE AND THE PUSSYCATS → a MIGHTY WIND, Giovanni Ribisi *(Jeff)* → THAT THING YOU DO! → FIRST LOVE, LAST

RITES → the VIRGIN SUICIDES → MASKED AND ANONYMOUS → LOST IN TRANSLATION → COLD MOUNTAIN, Samia Shoaib *(Pakeesa Chaldi)*, Steve Zahn *(Buff)* ← THAT THING YOU DO! ← REALITY BITES / → CHELSEA WALLS, Dina Spybey *(Bee-Bee)*

Storyline: A group of bored teenagers hang out at a convenience store, the highlight of their lives. Shop owner Nazeer is fed up with listening to their dreams which will never be realized. However tonight something special is going to happen: the only successful member of the gang is returning home after making it as a rock star. Will the others be inspired by his success or will they sink further into their world of drugs and alcohol? *JZ*

Movie rating: *4

Visual: video + dvd

Off the record: Based on the life of Armenian scriptwriter Eric Bogosian, a stand-up monologuist (with two sets) who collaborated with Frank Zappa on 1986's 'Blood On The Canvas'. *BG*

Various Artists (score: SONIC YOUTH *)

Feb 97. (cd) *Geffen; <(GED 25121)>* ☐ Jul97 ☐
– Unheard music (ELASTICA feat. STEPHEN MALKMUS) / Bee-Bee's song (*) / Bullet proof Cupid (GIRLS AGAINST BOYS) / Feather in your cap (JOEY WARONKER) / Berry meditation (UNKLE) / I'm not like everybody else (BOSS HOG) / Cult (SKINNY PUPPY) / Does your hometown care? (SUPERCHUNK) / Sunday (*) / Human cannonball (BUTTHOLE SURFERS) / Tabla in suburbia (*) / Hot day (the FLAMING LIPS) / Psychic hearts (THURSTON MOORE) / Town without pity (GENE PITNEY).

S/track review: By the mid-late 90s, the zeitgeist which had raised SONIC YOUTH to godfathers-of-grunge status and even gifted them a Top 10 album (1992's 'Dirty'), had begun to flag. So had the fascination with slackerdom which had forged Richard Linklater's uber-hip reputation. Still, this is a decent effort, filtering the small solace of angry music through a cast of alternative sharpshooters past and present. From the 'Youth's score we get delicious avant-groove oddities like 'Tabla Suburbia' and the Kim Gordon-sung 'Bee-Bee's Song' as well as a prototype 'Sunday', creating the headspace for their move back into more freeform material on the underrated 'A Thousand Leaves' (1998). THURSTON MOORE's solo turn, 'Psychic Hearts', is more in the vein of the band's 'Geffen' work, a spleen-venting trawl through botched adolescence and broken homes. ELASTICA and STEPHEN MALKMUS twist and heave their way through an impresively dissonant cover of the old X song, 'Unheard Music,' but making themselves heard louder and even clearer are the reliably demented BOSS HOGG, who spit home their originality over a funeral-parlour organ freakout on an evil version of the Kinks' 'I'm Not Like Everybody Else'. The BUTTHOLE SURFERS splurge through some old skool punk on 'Human Cannonball', UNKLE offer some passable psycho-analytic ambience on 'Berry Meditation' and GENE PITNEY wrings the pathos from 'Town Without Pity', but it's the FLAMING LIPS who show the young pretenders how to barn-dance with the bass turned up to eleven on the cruelly brief 'Hot Day'. And if nothing else, this soundtrack's worth picking up for the rare Beck track, 'Feather In Your Cap' (credited to the man's drummer, JOEY WARONKER). Like, dig those 'burbs dude. *BG*

Album rating: *6.5

SUBWAY RIDERS

1981 (US 119m) River Lights Pictures Inc. (15)

Film genre: mystery/crime/detective thriller

Top guns: dir (+ s-w): Amos Poe ← the FOREIGNER ← the BLANK GENERATION / → JUST AN AMERICAN BOY

Stars: Robbie Coltrane *(Det. Fritz Langley)* ← FLASH GORDON / → GHOST DANCE → ABSOLUTE BEGINNERS → EAT THE RICH → TUTTI FRUTTI, **John LURIE** *(the saxophonist)*, Charlene Kaleina *(Claire Smith)*, Cookie Mueller *(Penelope Thrasher)* ← DOWNTOWN 81 / → SMITHEREENS, Amos Poe *(Writer Ant)* ← DOWNTOWN 81 ← the FOREIGNER / → SMITHEREENS, Susan Tyrell *(Eleanor Langley)* ← FORBIDDEN ZONE ← CATCH MY SOUL / → TAPEHEADS → ROCKULA → CRY-BABY → PINK AS THE DAY SHE WAS BORN → MASKED AND ANONYMOUS, William Rice *(Mr. Gollstone)* ← the OFFENDERS / → COFFEE AND CIGARETTES, Tom Wright *(On The Waterfront)*, **Lance Loud** *(1st client)* → LANCE LOUD!: A DEATH IN AN AMERICAN FAMILY → MAYOR OF THE SUNSET STRIP, **Lydia Lunch**

Storyline: In New York, a mental sax player entices people into alleyways with his music and unceremoniously guns them down. Detective Fritz Langley (not Fitz!) gets on the case. *MCS*

Movie rating: *3

Visual: nothing yet

Off the record: **Lance Loud** was the subject of a TV documentary, 'An American Family' and subsequently joined punk band, the Mumps; a reunion film of sorts, 'Lance Loud!: A Death In An American Family' was shown in 2003 after the man dies of AIDS a few years earlier. Punkette, **Lydia Lunch**, solo artist and singer of numerous New Wave outfits – including Teenage Jesus & The Jerks – also appeared in the film. **John Lurie** (ex-Lounge Lizards) co-wrote the score and has his own biographical entry elsewhere. *MCS*

SUGAR TOWN

1999 (US 92m) Film 4 International / October Films (R)

Film genre: showbiz/Rock-music comedy/drama

Top guns: s-w + dir: Allison Anders ← GRACE OF MY HEART ← FOUR ROOMS ← GAS, FOOD LODGING ← BORDER RADIO / → THINGS BEHIND THE SUN + Kurt Voss ← DELUSION ← BORDER RADIO / → THINGS BEHIND THE SUN → DOWN AND OUT WITH THE DOLLS

Stars: Jade Gordon *(Gwen)* ← GRACE OF MY HEART / → THINGS BEHIND THE SUN, **John Taylor** *(Clive)*, **Michael Des Barres** *(Nick)* → MAYOR OF THE SUNSET STRIP, **Martin Kemp** *(Jonesy)*, **Larry Klein** *(Burt)* ← GRACE OF MY HEART / → CRAZY, **John DOE** *(Carl)*, Lucinda Jenney *(Kate)* ← GRACE OF MY HEART / → the MOTHMAN PROPHECIES, Ally Sheedy *(Liz)* ← HIGH ART ← BLUE CITY, Rosanna Arquette *(Eva)* ← BUFFALO '66 ← PULP FICTION ← MORE AMERICAN GRAFFITI / → THINGS BEHIND THE SUN, **Jeffrey McDonald** *(Kevin)* <= REDD KROSS =>, Beverly D'Angelo *(Jane)* ← COAL MINER'S DAUGHTER ← HAIR, **Simon Bonney** *(band member #1)*, Kelly Jones *(band member #2)*, Kai Lennox *(Alex)* → SHAKE, RATTLE AND ROLL: AN AMERICAN LOVE STORY → THINGS BEHIND THE SUN, Chris Mulkey *(Aaron)* ← GAS, FOOD LODGING ← HEARTBREAK HOTEL ← TIMERIDER: THE ADVENTURE OF LYLE SWANN / → MYSTERIOUS SKIN, **Bijou Phillips** *(autograph girl)* → BLACK AND WHITE → ALMOST FAMOUS → OCTANE

Storyline: Film assistant Gwen is determined to make it all the way to the top, and she'll do anything to get there. In her quest for success she meets Burt, a music producer who is orchestrating a comeback for an ageing British glam-rock band. The deal depends on millionairess Jane, who will only bankroll the venture for certain favours in return. *JZ*

Movie rating: *6

Visual: dvd (no audio OST; score Larry Klein)

Off the record: **John Taylor** was the bass player of Duran Duran and a member of DD offshoot act, the Power Station, with ex-Detective vocalist turned actor, **Michael Des Barres**. Fellow new romantics, Spandau Ballet was the stamping ground for future Eastenders actor, **Martin Kemp**. **Simon Bonney** was of Crime & The City Solution and the Kelly Jones is not the leader of Stereophonics. *MCS*

SUMMER DREAMS: THE STORY OF THE BEACH BOYS

1991 (US 97m TV) Leonard Hill Films

Film genre: Pop/Rock-music bio-pic/drama

Top guns: dir: Michael Switzer / s-w: Charles Rosin (story: Steven Gaines)

Stars: Bruce Greenwood *(Dennis Wilson)*, Greg Kean *(Brian Wilson)*, Casey Sander *(Mike Love)*, Bo Foxworth *(Carl Wilson)*, Andrew Myler *(Al Jardine)*, Arlen Dean Snyder *(Murry)*, Linda Dona *(Karen Lamm)* ← DEAD SOLID PERFECT ← BAJA OKLAHOMA, Robert Lee *(Bruce Johnston)*, Billy Vera *(Sal)* ← BAJA OKLAHOMA / → the DOORS, Michael Reid MacKay *(Charles Manson)*

Storyline: The film, it has to be said, is more interested in the downs of the group's rollercoaster career, for example over-emphasising Dennis' problems with drugs and his flirtation with the Manson set. It also details the power struggle between Brian and dad Murry for the ultimate control of the band. Some – though by no means all – of their best music is included. *JZ*

Movie rating: *5.5

Visual: dvd (no audio OST)

Off the record: There are a couple of BEACH BOYS ('Summer Dreams') compilations with several of the quintet's faves.

SUMMER HOLIDAY

1963 (UK 109m) Warner-Pathe (U)

Film genre: Rock'n'roll Musical comedy

Top guns: dir: Peter Yates / s-w (+ story): Ronald Cass & Peter Myers ← the YOUNG ONES / → WONDERFUL LIFE

Stars: Cliff RICHARD *(Don)*, Lauri Peters *(Barbara)*, Melvyn Hayes *(Cyril)* ← the YOUNG ONES / → WONDERFUL LIFE, Una Stubbs *(Sandy)* ← WONDERFUL LIFE, Teddy Green *(Steve)* ← the YOUNG ONES, **the Shadows:- Hank B. Marvin, Brian Bennett, Bruce Welch, Brian Locking** *(themselves)* ← the YOUNG ONES / → WONDERFUL LIFE → FINDERS KEEPERS, Ron Moody *(The Great Orlando)* → EVERY DAY'S A HOLIDAY, Lionel Murton *(Jerry)*, Jeremy Bullock *(Edwin)* ← PLAY IT COOL / → O LOCKY MAN!, David Kossoff *(magistrate)*, Tom Oliver → ABBA: THE MOVIE

Storyline: Don and his mechanic pals do a deal with the boss and begin a tour of Europe in a red London bus doubling as a hotel (with outside toilet only). High drama unfolds as they pick up a young American "boy" whom Don finds increasingly attractive as the journey progresses. Not to worry, the boy turns out to be a stowaway girl in disguise but her money-grabbing mother has reported her as being kidnapped. The first stop in Athens, then, could well be the town jail. *JZ*

Movie rating: *6

Visual: video + dvd

Off the record: nothing

—

CLIFF RICHARD AND THE SHADOWS (composer: Stanley Black)

Jan 63. (lp) *Columbia; (33SX 1472/SCX 3462) Epic; <BN 26063>* [1] [ ]
– Seven days to a holiday / Summer holiday / Let us take you for a ride / Les girls (the SHADOWS) / Round and round (the SHADOWS) / Foot tapper (the SHADOWS) / Stranger in town / Orlando's mine (A.B.S. ORCHESTRA) / Bachelor boy / A swingin' affair (with GRAZINA FRAME) / Really waltzing / All at once / Dancing shoes / Yugoslav wedding (A.B.S. ORCHESTRA) / The next time / Big news. *(re-iss. Apr83 on 'E.M.I.' lp/c; EMS/TCEMS 1009) (re-iss. Apr88 on 'Music for Pleasure' lp/c; MFP/TC-MFP 5824) (cd-iss. ; CDMFP 6021) (40th anniversary cd re-mast.Jan03 on 'E.M.I.'+=; 543999-2)* – (bonus tracks).

S/track review: A box office record-breaker, 'SUMMER HOLIDAY' was the biggest showcase of CLIFF RICHARD's career, extending the big-budget musical blueprint of 'The YOUNG ONES'. Yet while the latter leavened its MGM-inspired whimsy with some great songs, '. . .HOLIDAY' lays on the showbiz snazz with a trowel. If the famous title track (another UK No.1, alongside 'The Next Time') admittedly benefits from sparingly applied orchestration, an excess of cheesy show tune numbers like 'Seven Days To A Holiday' and 'A Stranger In Town' make this a far less attractive and enduring album than its predecessor, unless you're a fan of Broadway musicals. As an attempt at Sinatra-style sophistication, 'A Swingin' Affair' falls fairly flat and even unadorned chestnuts like 'Bachelor Boy' have a whiff of novelty about them. Cliff sounds far more comfortable and natural singing homegrown rock'n'roll like 'Dancing Shoes', and as a stand-alone listening experience, this soundtrack would've considerably improved its shelflife by including a few more in a similar vein. *BG*

Album rating: *6.5

– spinoff hits, etc. –

CLIFF RICHARD AND THE SHADOWS: Bachelor Boy / The Next Time
Dec 62. (7") *(DB 4950)* [1] [–]

CLIFF RICHARD AND THE SHADOWS: Summer Holiday / Put Your Dancing Shoes On
Feb 63. (7") *(DB 4977)* [1] [–]

CLIFF RICHARD AND THE SHADOWS: Hits From 'Summer Holiday'
Jun 63. (7"ep) *(SEG 8250)* [ ] [–]
– Summer holiday / The next time / Dancing shoes / Bachelor boy.

CLIFF RICHARD AND THE SHADOWS: More Hits From 'Summer Holiday'
Sep 63. (7"ep) *(SEG 8263)* [ ] [–]
– Seven days to our holiday / Stranger in town / Really waltzing / All at once.

SUMMER LOVE

1958 sequel (US 85m b&w) Universal Pictures (PG)

Film genre: Rock'n'roll Musical comedy

Top guns: dir: Charles F. Haas / s-w: Herbert H. Margolis ← ROCK BABY: ROCK IT ← ROCK, PRETTY BABY, William Raynor ← ROCK BABY: ROCK IT ← ROCK, PRETTY BABY

Stars: John Saxon *(Jim Daley)* ← ROCK, PRETTY BABY / → FROM DUSK TILL DAWN, **Molly Bee** *(Alice)* → the YOUNG SWINGERS, **Rod McKuen** *(Ox Bentley)* → ROCK, PRETTY BABY, Judi Meredith *(Joan Wright)*, Jill St. John *(Erica Landis)*, Edward Platt *(Dr. Thomas Daley)* ← ROCK, PRETTY BABY, Fay Wray *(Beth Daley)* ← ROCK, PRETTY BABY, John Wilder *(Mike Howard)* ← ROCK, PRETTY BABY, George Winslow *(Thomas Daley III)* ← ROCK, PRETTY BABY, Troy Donahue *(Sax Lewis)* → HARD ROCK NIGHTMARE → CRY-BABY → SHOCK 'EM DEAD → SHAKE, RATTLE & ROLL: AN AMERICAN LOVE STORY, Bob Courtney *("Half-Note" Harris)* ← ROCK, PRETTY BABY, Shelley Fabares *(Twinkle Daley)* ← ROCK, PRETTY BABY / → RIDE THE WILD SURF → GIRL HAPPY → HOLD ON! → SPINOUT → CLAMBAKE → a TIME TO SING

Storyline: In this sequel to 'ROCK, PRETTY BABY', Jim Daley and the band are back, this time hired to play at a summer camp. Soon all that sunshine and fresh air has its predictable effect on the guys and gals and Jim can't make up his mind between sun-worshippers Joan and Erica. Band member Alice finds herself the apple of Mike's eye and Jim's tut-tutting parents Tom and Beth are also on the scene. There's even time for some pop music amidst all the campsite canoodling. *JZ*

Movie rating: *6

Visual: none

Off the record: nothing

—

Various Artists: featuring JIMMY DALEY AND THE DING-A-LINGS (**) *(composer: Henry Mancini *)*

Mar 58. (lp) *Decca; <DL 8714>* ☐ ☐
– Main title – Summer Love (KIP TYLER & **) * / Beatin' on the bongos (MOLLY BEE & **) * / Sox hop (**) * / Love is something (the magic penny) (MOLLY BEE & **) / Walkin' the rock (**) * / Ding-a-ling (**) * / Night walk (**) * / To know you is to love you (ROD McKUEN & MOLLY BEE) * / Boppin' at the bash (**) * / To know you is to love you (**) * / Calypso rock (ROD McKUEN with **) / Joannie (**) * / The rock talks (**) * / Theme for a crazy chick (**) * / Soft touch (**) * / Sad sax (**) * / Kool breeze * / So, good night (**). *<cd-iss. 1995 on 'M.C.A.' Japan; MVCM 22055>*

S/track review: Who'd have thought it: Henry Mancini (who'd go on to score for movies 'Breakfast At Tiffanys' and 'The Pink Panther') composing a rock'n'roll flick. Yes, it's true, the man who penned 'Peter Gunn' (a hit for Duane Eddy in 1960) was behind this nostalgic slice of historic irreverence. From the 'Main Title' opening theme (featuring KIP TYLER on vocal with instrumental accompaniment by JIMMY DALEY AND THE DING-A-LINGS), one knows one'll be hearing Bill Haley's 'Rock Around The Clock' till one's ears drop off – example 'Beatin' On The Bongos', 'Sox Hop', 'Ding-A-Ling', etc., for an overdose of Comet-like sax-playing. Fifty years is a long way away, and one can easily criticise this LP for being very dated and derivative of the time. But this is definitely candyfloss dross, cheap rock'n'roll that was akin to some lounge-jazz performers on a cruise ship. Maybe musical director Joseph Gershenson had more than his fair share of critics at the time, its release went somewhat unnoticed in Britain. If there's any variety squeezed into the er . . . "value-for-money" OST, it comes by way of the self-explanatory 'Calypso Rock', sung by a young ROD McKUEN before his days as a poet and folk singer. 'So, Good Night' ends proceedings as narcolepsy sets in – the only trouble is it's the afternoon . . . zzzz. *MCS*

Album rating: *3

SURF PARTY

1964 (US 68m b&w) 20th Century Fox (PG)

Film genre: romantic Pop-music comedy/drama

Top guns: dir: Maury Dexter ← the YOUNG SWINGERS / → WILD ON THE BEACH / s-w: Harry Spalding ← the YOUNG SWINGERS ← TEENAGE MILLIONAIRE / → WILD ON THE BEACH

Stars: Bobby Vinton *(Len Marshall)*, Patricia Morrow *(Terry Wells)*, **Jackie De Shannon** *(Junior Griffith)* → C'MON, LET'S LIVE A LITTLE, Kenny Miller *(Milo Talbot)*, Lory Patrick *(Sylvia Dempster)*, Martha Stewart *(Pauline Lowell)*, **Jerry Summers** *(Skeet Wells)* ← the YOUNG SWINGERS, Richard Crane *(Sgt. Wayne Neal)*, **the Astronauts:- Rich Fifield, Jim Gallagher, Dennis Lindsey, Stormy Patterson, Bob Demmon** *(performers)* → WILD, WILD WINTER → OUT OF SIGHT / **the Routers:- Tommy Tedesco, Leon Russell, Hal Blaine, Scott Walker * + Sid Sharp** *(performers)*, Mickey Dora → BEACH PARTY * → 30 CENTURY MAN * / → MUSCLE BEACH PARTY → BIKINI BEACH → BEACH BLANKET BINGO → SKI PARTY → HOW TO STUFF A WILD BIKINI

Storyline: "It's fun, fun, fun all the way" (except for the grumpy police sergeant) as Malibu Beach is invaded by a swinging, surfing bunch of youngsters who break into song at every opportunity. Terry and her friends arrive to visit her brother Skeet and in a series of sand-packed adventures (wow, surfing under the pier) the glamorous gliders discover that a life on the ocean wave is not all sand, sea and surf. *JZ*

Movie rating: *3

Visual: none

Off the record: Bobby Vinton had already three chart-toppers to his name: 'Roses Are Red My Love', 'Blue Velvet' (later revived for the 'Blue Velvet' movie in '86) & 'There! I've Said It Again'. *MCS*

Various Artists/Cast incl. JIMMIE HASKELL (*)

1964. (lp; mono/stereo) *20th Century Fox; <TFM 3131/TFS 4131> Stateside; (SL 10089)* ☐ ☐
– If I were an artist (KENNY MILLER) / Pearly shells (KENNY MILLER) / That's what love is (PATRICIA MORROW) / Never comin' back (JACKIE DE SHANNON, PATRICIA MORROW & LORY PATRICK) / Firewater (the ASTRONAUTS) / Glory wave (JACKIE DE SHANNON) / Surf party (the ASTRONAUTS) / Symphony of sorrow (*) / Great white water (*) / Crack-up (the ROUTERS) / The big wheel (*) / Racing wild (*).

S/track review: The "surf sound" was everywhere in 1964, the Beach Boys, Jan & Dean and Dick Dale having a lot to answer for, especially on this second division piece of nostalgic rock'n'roll. Up first, KENNY MILLER (or Ken to his friends) who was born in Springfield, Ohio – doh! – and was in his early 30s when 'SURF PARTY' was placed on the B-movie conveyor belt. After a plethora of acting roles and a time performing country music, Kenny decided to write a few Hollywood-orientated novels and soak up the sun in his Palm Springs home. His contributions here ('If I Were An Artist' & 'Pearly Shells') were romantic, clean-cut, Neil Sedaka/Paul Anka-like croons. Like so many of the cues, all were penned by B. Dunham & B. Beverly, while the former songwriter teams up with JIMMIE HASKELL for the "Da-Doo-Ron-Ron"-esque 'Never Comin' Back' by the all-girl trio of JACKIE DE SHANNON, PATRICIA MORROW and LORY PATRICK; both JACKIE and PATRICIA also contributed two solo numbers, the gospel-ish 'Glory Wave' and 'That's What Love Is' respectively. The undeniable highlight of the show is two instrumentals ('Firewater' & 'Surf Party') by the ASTRONAUTS – think Dick Dale and the Ventures, while the ROUTERS (featuring a young-ish Scott Walker) produce a Champs-esque ditty via 'Crack-Up'. The aforementioned JIMMIE HASKELL (who subsequently scored 'WILD ON THE BEACH' 1965, 'ZACHARIAH' 1971 and 'JOYRIDE' 1977) tackles side two almost single-handedly courtesy of four surf-rock-meets-orchestral instrumentals, 'Symphony Of Sorrow', 'Great White Water', 'The Big Wheel' & 'Racing Wild'. All'n'all, a bit eclectic, a bit simplistic, but mostly you get a lot packed into a short space of time – 27 minutes to be exact! *MCS*

Album rating: *4.5

☐ SWANKY MODES segment
(⇒ TAPEHEADS)

☐ Rachel SWEET segment
(⇒ SING)

SWEET COUNTRY ROAD

aka 'SWEET COUNTRY MUSIC'

1981 (Can 95m) New World Films

Film genre: Country-music drama

Top guns: dir: Jack McCallum / s-w: Gordie Tapp

Stars: Buddy Knox *(Buddy Sutton)* ← JAMBOREE, Jack McCallum *(disc jockey)*, Kary Lynn McCallum *(Buddy's girlfriend)*, Gordie Tapp *(host)*, Myrtle McCallum *(Miss Wilson)*, **Johnny Paycheck** *(performer)*, **Jeanne Pruett** *(performer)*, **Faron Young** *(performer)* ← NASHVILLE REBEL ← COUNTRY MUSIC HOLIDAY / → WHAT AM I BID? → ROAD TO NASHVILLE, **Boots Randolf** *(performer)*

Storyline: A fading rock'n'roll star decides to change direction and go for that good ole' country boy Nashville sound. A story not too far removed from that of "real-life" singer, Buddy Knox, who plays Buddy Sutton. *MCS*

Movie rating: *3

Off the record: Jack McCallum had been responsible for two more similarly-themed movies, 'Sing A Country Song' (1973) and 'Travelin' Light' (1971), the latter featuring R&R "Party Doll" hitmaker, **Buddy Knox**; both films are too rare to review. Singer/steel-guitarist, **Johnny Paycheck**, was a Nashville country rebel whose other film work included singing the "blue collar" anthem/theme to the 1981 movie, 'Take This Job And Shove It' – surprisingly never a hit! Others on show were **Jeanne Pruett**, a long-standing C&W singer with one hit, the classic 'Satin Sheets', and Nashville session sax player, **Boots Randolph**, who reached the Top 40 via a version of 'Yakety Yak/Sax' in 1963. *MCS*

SWEET DREAMS

1985 (US 115m) HBO Pictures (PG-13)

Film genre: Country-music bio-pic drama

Top guns: dir: Karel Reisz / s-w: Robert Getchell ← BOUND FOR GLORY

Stars: Jessica Lange *(Patsy Cline)* → FAR NORTH → MASKED AND ANONYMOUS, Ed Harris *(Charlie Dick)* ← ALAMO BAY ← PLACES IN THE HEART / → WALKER → MASKED AND ANONYMOUS, Ann Wedgeworth *(Hilda Hensley)* ← ELVIS AND THE BEAUTY QUEEN / → FAR NORTH, David Clennon *(Randy Hughes)* ← LADIES AND GENTLEMEN, THE FABULOUS STAINS ← BOUND FOR GLORY / → GRACE OF MY HEART, James Staley *(Gerald Cline)*, Gary Basaraba *(Woodhouse)* ← ALAMO BAY / → WHO'S THAT GIRL → the LAST TEMPTATION OF CHRIST, John Goodman *(Otis)* → TRUE STORIES → BLUES BROTHERS 2000 → O BROTHER, WHERE ART THOU? → COYOTE UGLY → the EMPEROR'S NEW GROOVE → STORYTELLING → MASKED AND ANONYMOUS → OVERNIGHT → BEYOND THE SEA, P.J. Soles *(Wanda)* ← ROCK'N'ROLL HIGH SCHOOL / → SHAKE, RATTLE & ROCK! tv → the DEVIL'S REJECTS, Bruce Kirby *(Arthur Godfrey)* → the IN CROWD, **Boxcar Willie** *(jailbird)*, Tony Franks *(bartender)* ← ALAMO BAY / → YOUNG GUNS II → RUSH, Stonewall Jackson *(Opry announcer)* ← STREETS OF FIRE ← ROLLER BOOGIE / → KNIGHTS OF THE CITY → TRESPASS → CB4: THE MOVIE, Toni Sawyer *(baby nurse)* ← DOWN ON US, **Kracker Band:- Odie Palmer, Walter Caton, Fred Paul Tenly, James Bartley Young, Dennis Donaldson, Jimmy Mack Hodge Jr. / Patsy's band:- John R. Smart, William Byrd, Curtis Young, Michael David Black, Fred K. Young, Gary W. Pigg** *(Opry Band singer)* → HEART OF GOLD

Storyline: This life story of Patsy Cline concentrates mainly on her marriage to Charlie Dick. Charmed by his good looks and cocky self-assurance, Patsy falls in love with him and they wed, but she soon finds out that she's going to be the breadwinner of the family. Charlie hits the bottle and battle commences (literally) between Patsy's career and Charlie's jealousy of her success, until a tragic plane crash puts an end to her troubled marriage for ever. *JZ*

Movie rating: *7

Visual: video

Off the record: *Patsy Cline* will always be known for at least three classics (all Top 20 hits), 'Walkin' After Midnight', 'I Fall To Pieces' & 'Crazy'. *MCS*

PATSY CLINE (& Various songwriters)

Nov 85. (lp/c)(cd) *M.C.A.; <MCG/+C 6003> (MCAD 6149)* 29 Feb86

– San Antonio rose / Seven lonely days / Your cheatin' heart / Lovesick blues / Walking after midnight / Foolin' around / Half as much / I fall to pieces / Crazy / Blue moon of Kentucky / She's got you / Sweet dreams. *<(cd-iss. Mar03; AAMCAD 6149)>*

S/track review: Neither a true greatest hits nor a representative history (many PATSY CLINE aficionados deplore the absence of material from her Honky Tonk/rockabilly recordings of the 50s) this nevertheless sold extremely well on both sides of the Atlantic. Legendary producer Owen Bradley was brought in (like many of the production crew) to reprise the job he'd done on the hugely-successful 'COAL MINER'S DAUGHTER', and it's possible to hear the result as both a great-sounding sampler of CLINE's most successful period and a monument to destructive revisionism. Reassembling many of the musicians he'd produced a quarter-century before, Bradley remastered and remodelled the original recordings, even recruiting country singer Jamey Ryan (who had married CLINE's widower after the star's death) as a Patsy sound-a-like on a couple of tracks. This Frankenstein-work trims the choral and orchestral upholstery of the originals and produces a polished bass-heavy sound, with a jazzy arrangement of 'Walking After Midnight' the most obvious remould. Jamey Ryan's contribution is thankfully omitted, and crystal-clear, CLINE's personality-filled voice remains irresistible; the singer was an impressive lady – probably more than the soapy biopic allows – and her commanding alto embodies emotion as well as attitude. What you get, then, are a dozen songs drawn from the famous three years before her death, including less familiar country covers like her magnificent, stately reading of 'Your Cheatin' Heart', and those indisputable classics of popular music: 'Crazy', 'Sweet Dreams' and 'I Fall To Pieces' – even if these can't be considered the definitive versions. *ND*

Album rating: *8

SWEETWATER: A TRUE ROCK STORY

1999 (US 96m TV) Wilshire Court Productions / VH-1 Television (PG-13)

Film genre: Rock-music bio-pic/drama

Top guns: dir: Lorraine Senna / s-w: Victoria Wozniak

Stars: Amy Jo Johnson *(Nansi Nevins)*, Kelli Williams *(Camo Carlson)*, Kurt Max Runte *(Alex Del Zoppo)* → JOSIE AND THE PUSSYCATS, Robert Moloney *(Fred Herrera)*, Nancy Moonves *(Mrs. Nevins)*, Michael Anthony Rawlins *(Ian)*, **Adam Aant** *(Todd Badham)* ← DROP DEAD ROCK ← JUBILEE, **Michelle Phillips** *(Nansi Nevins; present day)* ← MONTEREY POP / → MAYOR OF THE SUNSET STRIP, Frederic Forrest *(Alex Del Zoppo; present day)* ← the END OF VIOLENCE ← TUCKER: THE MAN AND HIS DREAM ← ONE FROM THE HEART ← the ROSE, Trevor Roberts *(Alan Malarowitz)* ← HARD CORE LOGO, Peter Williams *(Albert Moore)*, John Burgess-Murray *(August Burns)*, Zak Alam *(Jorge)* → LATE NIGHT SESSIONS → JOSIE AND THE PUSSYCATS, Erin Wright *(Janis Joplin)* → DUETS → BONES, Mark Brandon *(J.D. Simon)* ← MIKE'S MURDER, Lynda Boyd *(Alice Belzer)* → BONES

Storyline: Cable TV reporter Cami Carlson is assigned to track down 1960s band Sweetwater and its lead vocalist Nancy Nevins. Nothing has been heard from the band since they opened the Woodstock festival in 1969, and Cami makes little headway in her search until she finally tracks down Nancy. Then she learns that a tragic car accident has permanently scarred Nancy's vocal chords and the trauma of this has led her to a life of drink and near destitution. *JZ*

Movie rating: *5.5

Visual: video (no audio OST; see below)

Off the record: Psychedelic folk-rockers, **SWEETWATER** released only one LP before tragedy struck Nansi, the eponymous 'Sweetwater' (1969). The band consisted of the aforementioned Nansi Nevins (vocals), R.G. Carlyle (guitar), Albert Moore (flute), Alex Del Zoppo (keyboards), Alan Malarowitz (drums), Elpidio Cobain (conga) and August Burns (cello). Two sets, 'Just For You' (1970) and 'Melon' (1971), were nothing without their lead singer and they folded soon afterwards. Nevins (on the mend) was to augment Zoppo and bassist Fred Herrera on a reunion gig in 1997. Actress, Amy Jo Johnson, sings lead in part-time outfit, Valhalla; she also released a solo set, 'The Trans-American Treatment' (2001) on the 'Sneaky Alligator' imprint. **Michelle Phillips** was part of 60s psych/bubblegum act, the Mamas & The Papas; **Zak Santiago Alam** is a decks DJ who tours Europe. *MCS*

– associated release –

SWEETWATER: Cycles: The Reprise Collection

Sep 99. (cd) *Rhino Handmade; <7702>*
– Motherless child / Here we go again / What's wrong / In a rainbow / My crystal spider / Rondeau / Two worlds / Through an old storybook / Why oh why / What's wrong (live) / Just for you / Day song / Song for Romeo / Look out / God rest ye merry gentlemen / Get it while you can / Don't forget / Join the band / Home again. *<re-iss. Nov03; same>*

SWING

1999 (UK 98m) Tapestry Films & The Kushner-Locke Company (PG-13)

Film genre: Pop/Rock-musical comedy/melodrama

Top guns: s-w: (+ dir) Nick Mead ← CROCODILE SHOES II (story: Su Lim)

Stars: Lisa Stansfield *(Joan Woodcock)*, Hugo Speer *(Martin)*, Paul Usher *(Liam Luxford)* → IN HIS LIFE: THE JOHN LENNON STORY, Tom Bell *(Sid Luxford)* ← ALL THE RIGHT NOISES ← BALLAD IN BLUE, Rita Tushingham *(Mags Luxford)* ← the GURU ← SMASHING TIME, Danny McCall *(Andy)*, Alexei Sayle *(Mighty Mac)* ← SIESTA, **Clarence Clemons** *(Jack)* ← BLUES BROTHERS 2000 ← BILL & TED'S EXCELLENT ADVENTURE, Nerys Hughes *(Maria)*, **Jimmy NAIL** *(Arthur)*, Scot Williams *(Buddy)* ← BACKBEAT / → IN HIS LIFE: THE JOHN LENNON STORY

Storyline: Martin Luxford learns the sax while serving two years inside for fraud. When he's released he puts his new skills to good use and forms a swing band. He knows the one person who can really make the band a success is ex-girlfriend Joan, who is now married to (of all people) Martin's arresting officer. This man Andy takes great delight in fouling things up for Martin any way he can, and he won't be happy until the band and Martin are both a thing of the past. *JZ*

Movie rating: *4

Visual: video + dvd

Off the record: Lisa Stansfield (see below)

—

LISA STANSFIELD (score: Ian Devaney)

May 99. (cd) *B.M.G.; (74321 66923-2) R.C.A.; <63541-2>* Jul99
– Baby I need your loving *[re-track 3]* / The best is yet to come *[re-track 11]* / I thought that's what you liked about me (GEORGIE FAME) *[re-track 9]* / Two years too blue *[re-track 14]* / Why do we call it love / It ain't what you do *[re-track 1]* / Gotta get on this train (GEORGIE FAME) *[re-track 4]* / Martin's theme *[re-track 5]* / Ain't nobody here but us chickens *[re-track 2]* / Our love is here to stay *[re-track 7]* / Love theme *[re-track 8]* / Watch the birdie *[re-track 10]* / Martin's theme (reprise) *[re-track 12]* / Blitzkrieg baby *[re-track 13]* / Mack the knife. *(re-iss. 2003 new track listing see above; 82876 52245 2)*

S/track review: Northern lass, LISA STANSFIELD (b.11 April '66, Rochdale, England) was the obvious choice to star and perform in Brit-flick musical, 'SWING'. Having a string of cooler than cool UK Top 20 hits behind her, including 'People Hold On' (with Coldcut), 'This Is The Right Time' (her 1989 solo debut), 'All Around The World' (her only solo No.1), 'Change', 'All Woman', 'In All The Right Places' & 'The Real Thing' (her most recent in '97), her credentials were second to none for the part of swing singer, Joan Woodcock. From 30s standards to big band traditional numbers, LISA with an S – not Liza with a Z – took command of anything from Jimmie Lunceford's 'It Ain't What You Do' to Louis Jordan's 'Ain't Nobody Here But Us Chickens' to the Gershwins' 'Our Love Is Here To Stay'. From the world of R&B/pop, Lisa (and her songwriting hubby, Ian Devaney) even re-created the Four Tops' Motown nugget 'Baby I Need Your Lovin'', while she also took on Mabel Mercer's 'The Best Is Yet To Come', Kurt Weill's 'Mack The Knife' and pre-WWII number 'Hellzapoppin'' number 'Watch The Birdie'. While the aforementioned DEVANEY was afforded three of his own compositions, however brief, both he and Lisa collaborated on new songs, 'Why Do We Call It Love' and 'Two Years Too Blue'. GEORGIE FAME (known for recent dual sets with Van Morrison) was also given license to kill: 'Gotta Get On This Train' & 'I Thought That's What You Liked About Me', not really "yeh yeh", rather the opposite. There's no denying LISA STANSFIELD is a great modern-day singer, but 'SWING' might not be to everyone's taste. *MCS*

Album rating: *4.5

SWINGIN' ALONG

original: 'DOUBLE TROUBLE'

1962 (US 74m) 20th Century Fox

Film genre: Rock'n'roll/Pop Musical comedy

Top guns: dir: Charles Barton / s-w: Jameson Brewer

Stars: Tommy Noonan *(Freddy Merkel)*, Pete Marshall *(Duke)*, Barbara Eden *(Carol Walker)* → RIDE THE WILD SURF, Connie Gilchrist *(Aunt Sophie)* → TICKLE ME, **Ray CHARLES** *(himself)*, **Bobby Vee** *(himself)* → PLAY IT COOL → JUST FOR FUN → C'MON, LET'S LIVE A LITTLE, **Roger Williams** *(himself)*, Tommy Farrell *(Georgie)* → KISSIN' COUSINS → GIRL HAPPY, Ted Knight *(priest)* → CADDYSHACK, Carol Christensen *(Ginny)*, Alan Carney *(Officer Sullivan)*, Art Baker *(television announcer)* → the WILD ANGELS

Storyline: Accident prone delivery boy, Freddy Merkel, muses the day he will be a top pop star. When his trusty motor scooter bites the proverbial dust, he starts to write songs, which, in turn, leads him to meet scam merchant, Duke. One song in particular is entered for a contest, although rather mischievously, it blows into the hands of a priest, who likes it so much he has a go with it himself. *MCS*

Movie rating: *2.5

Visual: none (no audio OST; score: Arthur Morton)

Off the record: RAY CHARLES performs a few numbers in the film: 'What'd I Say' & 'Sticks And Stones', **Bobby Vee** delivered 'More Than I Can Say'. **Roger Williams** (b. 1 Oct'24, Omaha) was a big-time recording pop artist from the time he topped the US charts in 1955 with 'Autumn Leaves' (his only No.1). I think he was the one who sang, 'Swingin' Along' & 'Song Of The City'. *MCS*

□ the SWINGIN' SET alt.
(⇒ GET YOURSELF A COLLEGE GIRL)

a SWINGIN' SUMMER

1965 (US 80m) National Talent consultants / United Screen Arts

Film genre: Pop-Rock Musical teen comedy

Top guns: s-w: (+ dir) Robert Sparr, Leigh Chapman → TRUCK TURNER

Stars: James Stacy *(Rickey)* → WINTER A-GO-GO, William A. Wellman, Jr. *(Rick)* ← HIGH SCHOOL CONFIDENTIAL! / → WINTER A-GO-GO → BLACK CAESAR, Quinn O'Hara *(Cindy)* → the GHOST IN THE INVISIBLE BIKINI, Martin West *(Turk)* → the GIRLS ON THE BEACH, Raquel Welch *(Jeri)* ← ROUSTABOUT / → the MAGIC CHRISTIAN, Mary Mitchell *(Shirley)* ← TWIST AROUND THE CLOCK / → the GIRLS ON THE BEACH, **the Righteous Brothers:- Bill Medley & Bobby Hatfield** *(performers)* → BEACH BALL, **Gary Lewis & the Playboys:- Gary Lewis, Al Ramsey, John West, David Walker, David Costell** *(performers)* → OUT OF SIGHT, **the Rip Chords:- Terry Melcher, Bruce Johnston, Arnie Marcus, Rich Rotkin** *(performers)*, **Donnie Brooks** *(performer)* ← GET YOURSELF A COLLEGE GIRL, **the Dovells:- Len Barry, Arnie Satin, Mike Dennis, Jerry Summers** *(performers)* ← DON'T KNOCK THE TWIST, Gypsy Boots *(himself)* → MONDO HOLLYWOOD, Lori Williams *(dancer)* → IT'S A BIKINI WORLD

Storyline: Famous for being the movie debut of screen goddess, Raquel Welch, although her various bikini appearances are often er, all too brief – phew! The beach at Lake Arrowhead is the setting for all the teenage romp-age shenanigans, and the kids who frequent the resort are trying to obtain money to finance through putting on a pop concert. *MCS*

Movie rating: *3.5

Visual: none (no audio OST; score: Harry Betts)

Off the record: A handful of pop acts are featured in the film, including **the Righteous Brothers** (famous for massive hits, 'You've Lost That Lovin' Feelin'' & 'Unchained Melody'), **the Rip Chords** (No.4 early in 1964 with 'Hey Little Cobra', and boasting the son of Doris Day, Terry Melcher), **Gary Lewis & the Playboys** (already registering a US chart-topper, 'This Diamond Ring'), Philadelphia's **the Dovells** (two Top 3 hits, 'Bristol Stomp' & 'You Can't Sit Down') and **Donnie Brooks** (b. John Abahosh, Dallas; raised Ventura, California) who was first of the bunch to breakthrough with 1960s Top 10'er, 'Mission Bell'. Raquel Welch sings one one in the film, 'Ready To Groove'. *MCS*

– spinoff hits, etc. –

the RIGHTEOUS BROTHERS: Justine / In That Great Gettin' Up Mornin'

Jun 65. (7") *Moonglow; <242>* [85] [–]

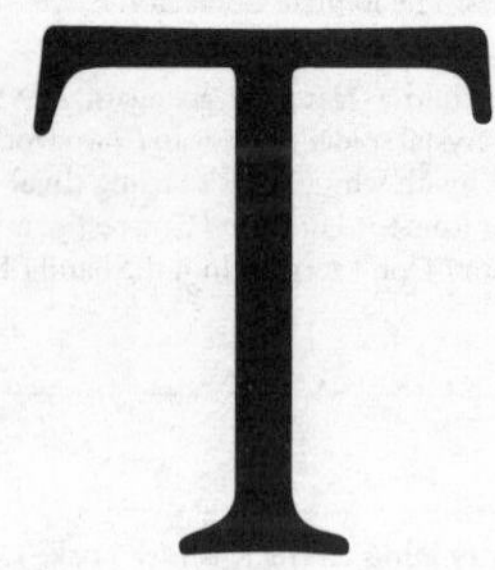

TAKE ME HIGH

1973 (UK 90m) Anglo-EMI Films (U)

Film genre: Pop/Rock Musical drama

Top guns: dir: David Askey / s-w: Christopher Penfold

Stars: Cliff RICHARD *(Tim Matthews)*, Debbie Watling *(Sarah)* → THAT'LL BE THE DAY, Hugh Griffith *(Sir Harry Cunningham)*, George Cole *(Bert Jackson)*, Anthony Andrews *(Hugo Flaxman)*, Richard Wattis *(Sir Charles Furness)* ← WONDERWALL ← BUNNY LAKE IS MISSING ← UP JUMPED A SWAGMAN ← PLAY IT COOL, Ronald Hines *(Sam)*, Madeline Smith *(Vicki)*, Jimmy Gardner *(Hulbert)* ← the COMMITTEE / → FLAME, Moyra Fraser *(Molly)* ← HERE WE GO ROUND THE MULBERRY BUSH

Storyline: A grand tour of Britain's second city as office worker Tim discovers that money can't always buy you happiness – but it helps. Instead, the secret for success is to open a restaurant selling nothing but Brumburgers (never mind the calories) and convert your mouldy old barge into a floating palace off the proceeds. Also watch for Tim's virtuoso map-reading skills in his attempt to find Gas Street – he obviously wasn't in the Scouts. *JZ*

Movie rating: *3.5

Visual: video

Off the record: As everyone will know in Britain, George Cole subsequently became Arthur Daley in TV comedy drama series, 'Minder'.

CLIFF RICHARD (composer: Tony Cole)

Jan 74. (lp) *E.M.I.; (EMC 3016)* [41] [–]
– It's only money / Midnight blue / Hover / Why (w/ ANTHONY ANDREWS) / Life / Driving / The game / Brumberger duet (w/ DEBBIE WATLING) / Take me high / The anti-brotherhood of man / Winning / Join the band / The word is love.

S/track review: At a time when CLIFF RICHARD was supporting Mary Whitehouse in her moral crusades, it's difficult to believe that he'd star in a film with as ambiguous a title as 'TAKE ME HIGH'. Be assured though, the movie has absolutely nothing to do with drugs, and, unfortunately, everything to do with hamburgers. Still, if the woeful plot finally put an end to Cliff's screen career, at least the music is worth revisiting. If the axe-wielding intro to 'It's Only Money' is disturbingly reminiscent of Robbie Williams' 'Let Me Entertain You', the song itself deals in the kind of feelgood rock which the Doobie Brothers used to write in their sleep. The rest of the soundtrack runs the gamut of 70s stylistic bases, from glam rock to neo-rock'n'roll to singer-songwriter to the Beatles/Abba-esque pop of the title track (a Top 30 hit), in a rarely less than entertaining if never exactly thrilling fashion. Cliff arguably recorded some of his best work in the 70s, not least 'Devil Woman' and 'We Don't

Talk Anymore', and this album – minus embarrassing rubbish like 'Brumburger Duet' – is a pointer towards it. *BG*

Album rating: *3.5

– spinoff hits, etc. –

CLIFF RICHARD: Take Me High / (non-OST song)

Nov 73. (7") *(EMI 2088)* 27 –

TAKE ME HOME: THE JOHN DENVER STORY

2000 (US 90m TV) Granada Entertainment USA

Film genre: country/pop-Music biopic drama

Top guns: dir: Jerry London / t-p: Stephen Harrigan (book: **John Denver** + Arthur Tobier)

Stars: Chad Lowe *(John Denver)*, Kristin Davis *(Annie Denver)*, Gerald McRaney *(Dutch)*, Brian Markinson *(Hal Thau)* ← PRIMARY COLORS, Susan Hogan *(Irma)*, Wezley Morris *(Zak)*, Stefanie Walmsley *(Anna Kate)*, Clare Lapinskie *(Cassandra)*, Gary Chalk *(Milt)*

Storyline: The film begins with young John going against the wishes of his army-type father and starting his music career. After a lot of hard work he eventually climbs to the top of the tree, on the way marrying Annie. But our quiet, bespectacled crooner finds it all a bit too much and turns to the bottle, and while Annie sits and suffers we see the Denver Chainsaw Massacre as he destroys his living room in anger. *JZ*

Movie rating: *5

Visual: video

Off the record: JOHN DENVER was born John Henry Deutschendorf, Jnr., 31st December '43, Roswell, New Mexico, USA. The son of a record-breaking aviator and US airforce instructor, his childhood was characterised by a rootless existence that saw him shuttled between various states in the American southwest and even a spell in Japan (no doubt a clue to the recurring theme of "home" – leaving and especially returning – in DENVER's later work). Famously given a Gibson acoustic guitar by his grandmother as he entered his teens, it was only after he was rejected by the airforce for shortsightedness that the budding singer/songwriter began to seek out a career as a musician. Although he attended an architectural course in Texas, John soon headed for L.A. where he immersed himself in the thriving folk scene. At the suggestion of the NEW CHRISTY MINSTRELS' Randy Sparks, he subsequently changed his name to JOHN DENVER which best suited his passion for the mountains and all things natural. After rumours that he was to join the Byrds, DENVER enlisted with the Chad Mitchell Trio instead, helping to revitalise their flagging fortunes. Finally gaining the confidence to strike out on his own, John signed to 'R.C.A.' in 1969 with the help of veteran folk producer, Milt Okun, who was to have a long and fruitful relationship with the singer. DENVER's exquisite 'Leaving, On A Jet Plane', originally recorded by the 'Trio in 1967, furnished Peter, Paul & Mary with a US No.1 the same year and suddenly DENVER's name was on the map. A hangover from his Chad Mitchell days, DENVER moved unequivocally into the mould of sensitive, sentimental country-folk balladeer over the course of his next two albums. Yet it was only with the release of his 'Poems, Prayers And Promises' (1971) 4th album and its massive 'Take Me Home, Country Roads' single that DENVER became a household name. 'Rocky Mountain High' (1972) cemented his position as eco-friendly blonde warrior with the title track (US Top 10) waxing lyrical about his "rebirth" in the surroundings of his beloved Colorado. By 1974/5, DENVER was a bonafide superstar partly as a result of his hugely successful US TV show, 'An Evening With John Denver' and partly down to the No.1 album, 'Back Home Again' (1974). The latter set featured the transatlantic No.1 tribute to his wife, 'Annie's Song', a track that perhaps more than any other is identified with DENVER in his heyday and surprisingly, remains his only UK Top 40 hit. The fact that the execrable 'Thank God I'm A Country Boy' made No.1 in the States was possibly a sign that DENVER fever was getting out of hand; the governor of Colorado even proclaimed him poet laureate of the state (!). He also started his own label ('Windsong') and branched into acting (alongside George Burns in 1977's 'Oh God!'), becoming an all round showbiz personality. He even cut an album with the Muppets (1979's 'A Christmas Together With . . .'), oh God right enough. By the early 80s, DENVER had separated from his wife and was focusing his energies on ecological, anti-nuclear and humanitarian causes, even touring the Eastern Bloc and China. Albums such as 'Autograph' (1980), etc, saw his commercial returns progressively diminish. Worse was to come in 1993 when his wholesome image was tarnished with a drunk-driving charge. Nevertheless, the man's basic philosophy remained the same and he picked up the Albert Schweitzer Music Award for lifetime humanitarianism that same year before publishing his autobiography in 1994. In one of popular music's stranger fatal accidents (and there've been more than a few), DENVER died tragically on October the 12th, 1997 at the age of 53 when the light plane he was flying suddenly dropped out of the sky, killing him instantly. *BG*

—

JOHN DENVER

Apr 00. (cd) *R.C.A.; <07863 67950-2>* –

– Annie's song / Leaving, on a jet plane / Back home again / My sweet lady / Rocky mountain high / Take me home, country roads / This old guitar / Love again / Thank God I'm a country boy (live) / For baby (for Bobbie) / Follow me / Calypso / Poems, prayers and promises / Perhaps love / Sunshine on my shoulders / Flying for me.

S/track review: 'TAKE ME HOME . . .' is basically another in a long line of JOHN DENVER compilations, albeit this one's a made-for-TV biopic. The fact that guitar-strumming singer-songwriter DENVER had tragically died in an airplane crash in '97 gives the set a certain poignancy, not least on his re-vamped rendition of 'Leaving, On A Jet Plane'. This is an easy-listening and family-friendly CD in many respects, and his loving wife was the inspiration to many a tune, the bespectacled JD coming off best on album opener and former hit, 'Annie's Song' (forget James Galway & flute, if you can). Ditto love ballads 'My Sweet Lady', 'Back Home Again' and 'This Old Guitar'. With most of his songs not the originals! (re-recorded for his label 'Windsong' in '96), the CD fails to be a bona fide compilation, although who could argue that any versions here of his much-loved standards (such as 'Take Me Home, Country Roads', 'Rocky Mountain High', etc.) are not up to scratch; the latter is one for the environmentalists and ageing hippies. A picturesque songbook of sorts, one can imagine him flying high across the setting sun in the Colorado barrens (John's love of air-travel exceeded to simulation NASA space-shuttle trials). Not content with birdly pursuits, DENVER wrote the song 'Calypso' on the deck of a boat he sailed with deep-sea filmmaker, Jacques Cousteau. Live highlights come by way of 'Thank God I'm A Country Boy' (written by John Martin Sommers), a sort of unintentional sing-a-long for rednecks and Opry-loving truckers everywhere. With another highlight, 'Sunshine On My Shoulders' (the penultimate number on the CD), and finale 'Flying For Me' getting overtly sentimental, DENVER completes the soundtrack from a distance – so to speak. All 'n' all, the hour-long OST is like a stroll in the park, never too exciting but worthwhile nevertheless. *MCS*

Album rating: *6

TAKE THE LEAD

2006 (US 109m) Tiara Blu Films / New Line Cinema (PG-13)

Film genre: Dance/Pop-Rock Musical bio-pic/drama

Top guns: dir: Liz Friedlander / s-w: Dianne Houston

Stars: Antonio Banderas *(Pierre Dulaine)* ← EVITA ← FOUR ROOMS ← TRUTH OR DARE, Rob Brown *(Rock)*, Yaya DaCosta *(LaRhette)*, Alfre Woodard *(Principal Augustine James)* ← the SINGING DETECTIVE ← CROOKLYN, Dante Basco *(Ramos)* ← MOONWALKER, Marcus T. Paulk *(Eddie)* ← ROLL BOUNCE, Jenna Dewan *(Sasha)* → STEP UP, **Jonathan**

Malen *(Kurd)*, John Ortiz *(Joe Temple)*, Laura Benanti *(Tina)*, Lauren Collins *(Caitlin)*, Lyriq Bent *(Easy)* ← the LIFE AND HARD TIMES OF GUY TERRIFICO ← HONEY, Elijah Kelley *(Danjou)* → HAIRSPRAY re-make

Storyline: Ballroom dancer Pierre Dulaine complains to a high school Principal about some students vandalising a car. The Principal is at her wit's end with her charges and challenges Dulaine to see if he can make a difference by teaching her detention class some of his dance moves. Dulaine gradually starts to win the kids over and even creates a new dance style, so it looks like he'll get to park his car outside school after all. *JZ*

Movie rating: *6.5

Visual: dvd

Off the record: Jonathan Malen sings and plays guitar for Toronto band, StillSoul. Laura Benanti's musical connections are quite considerable: her cousin is Steve Hansgen, bassist of Minor Threat, while she recently (July 2005) married Chris Barron, frontman of the Spin Doctors. *MCS*

Various Artists (producer: Swizz Beatz)

Apr 06. (cd) *Republic-Universal; <0006372>*
– I got rhythm – Take The Lead remix (LENA HORNE & Q-TIP) / Take the lead (wanna ride) (BONE THUGS-N-HARMONY & WISIN Y YANDEL feat. FATMAN SCOOP) / Feel it (BLACK EYED PEAS) / I like that (stop) (JAE MILLZ) / These days (RHYMEFEST) / Here we go (DIRTBAG) / Whuteva (REMY MA) / Ya ya – Al Stone mix (the EMPTY HEADS) / Never gonna get it (SEAN BIGGS feat. TOPIC & AKON) / I like that you can't take that away from me (JAE MILLZ, JUNE CHRISTY, ERIC B & RAKIM, MASHONDA) / Fascination (KEM) / Que sera, sera (whatever will be, will be) (SLY & THE FAMILY STONE).

S/track review: Fusing contemporary hip hop and classic ballroom has to be a recipe for disaster but the odd bedfellows sit together remarkably well on this urban dance film soundtrack. However, the clever production does not help to endear you to many of the tunes themselves. The soundtrack, though distinctly hip hop heavy, is also peppered with elements of ska, gospel and R&B. 'I Got Rhythm' by LENA HORNE with additional vocals by Q-TIP, begins with the original tune until it, frighteningly at first, zips into a jazz infused rap. The rather seamless result is nothing overly interesting. Meanwhile, 'Take The Lead (Wanna Ride)' by BONE, THUGS-N-HARMONY, has a thumping salsa beat complete with bells and whistles, FATMAN SCOOP rhyming in Spanish and as a contrast the soulful vocals of Melissa Jiménez. One of the more exciting numbers on the soundtrack, this tune is spoiled by a lack of flow from the desire to squeeze too many styles onto the one track. BONE and his crew should have taken advice from the BLACK EYED PEAS with 'Feel It', a slice of catchy hip "pop" hop and indeed evidence of why the band went on to chart success. Similarly, the straight up ska of 'Ya Ya' by the EMPTY HEADS is hands and feet, heads and shoulders above the rap on the album. Fast paced with trumpets pumping throughout and samples, the tune is cleverly mixed by producer of choice Al Stone who has worked with the likes of Bjork. 'I Like That You Can't Take That Away from Me' by JAE MILLZ remixes the classic JUNE CHRISTY track with a bass heavy team of rappers including legends ERIC B and RAKIM and speeds up the tempo, though instead of being pioneering as it should be is just irritating. Bonus track 'Que Sera, Sera' by SLY AND THE FAMILY STONE, from their 1973 album 'Fresh', is the jewel in a more or less unimpressive crown. Sly forgets the funk and takes the beat down a key with a smooth vocal teamed with a dramatic gospel organ. Hallelujah. Give praise to the few saviours on this soundtrack, which is otherwise a sinful creation. *SM*

Album rating: *4.5

TAPEHEADS

1988 (US 93m) Front Films / Avenue Pictures Productions (R)

Film genre: showbiz/Rock-music satire

Top guns: s-w: Bill Fishman (+ dir) → MY DINNER WITH JIMI, Peter McCarthy (+ story: James Herzfeld, Ryan Rowe)

Stars: John Cusack *(Ivan Alexeev)* → ROADSIDE PROPHETS → HIGH FIDELITY → the FUTURE IS UNWRITTEN, Tim Robbins *(Josh Tager)* ← HOWARD THE DUCK / → JUNGLE FEVER → HIGH FIDELITY → the PICK OF DESTINY, Mary Crosby *(Samantha Gregory)*, Clu Gulager *(Norman Mart)* ← the RETURN OF THE LIVING DEAD ← LIVING PROOF: THE HANK WILLIAMS JR. STORY / → EDDIE PRESLEY, Katy Boyer *(Belinda Mart)*, Jessica Walter *(Kay Mart)*, **Sam Moore** *(Billy Diamond)* ← ONE-TRICK PONY / → BLUES BROTHERS 2000, **Junior Walker** *(Lester Diamond)*, Susan Tyrrell *(Nikki Morton)* ← SUBWAY RIDERS ← FORBIDDEN ZONE ← CATCH MY SOUL / → ROCKULA → CRY-BABY → PINK AS THE DAY SHE WAS BORN → MASKED AND ANONYMOUS, Doug McClure *(Sid Tager)*, Connie Stevens *(June Tager)* → BACK TO THE BEACH ← GREASE 2, **King Cotton** *(Roscoe)*, Milton Selzer *(Merlin Hinkle)* ← WALKER ← SID & NANCY ← LADY SINGS THE BLUES, Don Cornelius *(Mo Fuzz)* ← ROADIE ← NO WAY BACK ← CLEOPATRA JONES / → JACKIE'S BACK!, **Zander Schloss** *(heavy metal fan)* <= the CIRCLE JERKS =>, Xander Berkeley *(Ricky Fell)* ← WALKER ← STRAIGHT TO HELL ← SID & NANCY / → STORYTELLING, **Stiv Bators** *(Dick Slammer)* ← D.O.A., **Coati Mundi** *(bald executive)* <= KID CREOLE & THE COCONUTS =>, **Jello BIAFRA** *(FBI man #1)*, **Sy Richardson** *(bartender)* ← WALKER ← STRAIGHT TO HELL ← SID & NANCY ← REPO MAN ← PETEY WHEATSTRAW / → MYSTERY TRAIN, **Ted Nugent** *(rock star)* → PRIVATE PARTS, **Michael Nesmith** *(water man)* <= the MONKEES =>, **"Weird Al" Jankovic** *(himself)* → UHF → DERAILROADED, **Brie Howard** *(flygirl)* → the RUNNIN' KIND, Jo Harvey Allen *(Madame Olga)* ← TRUE STORIES / → ALL THE PRETTY HORSES, **Doug E. Fresh** *(record executive)* ← BEAT STREET / → WHITEBOYS → BROWN SUGAR → AWESOME: I FUCKIN' SHOT THAT! / **Fishbone:- Angelo Moore** → BACK TO THE BEACH / → IDLEWILD, **Kendall Jones, Norwood Fisher, Walter Kibby II, Christopher Dowd, Phillip Fisher** *(band; Ranchbone)* / **Jim Keltner** *(Swanky Modes musician)* ← the CONCERT FOR BANGLADESH / → CONCERT FOR GEORGE, **Billy Bremner** *(Swanky Modes musician)* ← CONCERT FOR KAMPUCHEA, Tyra Ferrell *(Flygirl)* ← SCHOOL DAZE / → JUNGLE FEVER, **Courtney LOVE** *(Norman's spanker)*, **Billy Ferrick** *(Cube Squared)* → ROADSIDE PROPHETS, Jennifer Balgobin *(calypso dancer)* ← STRAIGHT TO HELL ← REPO MAN / → ROADSIDE PROPHETS, Martha C. Quinn *(RVTV-VJ)* → EDDIE AND THE CRUISERS II: EDDIE LIVES! → BAD CHANNELS, Bobcat Goldthwait as Jack Cheese *(Don Druzel)* → MEDUSA: DARE TO BE TRUTHFUL, John Fleck *(critic #1)* ← HOWARD THE DUCK ← HARD ROCK ZOMBIES / → CRAZY

Storyline: Josh and Ivan are two buddies who decide to form their own video production company when they lose their jobs as security guards. Soon Video Aces hits the market place and some wacky assignments come their way, most of them ending in disaster. However their luck turns when they get to direct a heavy metal video which suddenly becomes a smash hit. Will they notice the Secret Service boys on their tail amidst their excitement? *JZ*

Movie rating: *6

Visual: video + dvd

Off the record: SWANKY MODES (see below), etc.

SWANKY MODES (*) & Various (score: MARK MOTHERSBAUGH **)

Oct 88. (lp/c/cd) *Polygram; <842890-1/-4/-2>*
– An ordinary man (*) / Roscoe's rap (KING COTTON) / Surfer's love chant (BO DIDDLEY) / You hooked me baby (*) / Betcher bottom dollar (*) / Baby doll – Swedish version (DEVO) ** / Slow bus movin' – Howard's beach party mix (FISHBONE) / Audience for my pain (*) / Language of love (*) / An ordinary man – Can't keep a good man down mix (*).

S/track review: If you've seen the 'TAPEHEADS' movie you'll know SWANKY MODES are in fact vocalist SAM MOORE (of Sam & Dave fame) and vocalist/sax-player, JR. WALKER. In the mid-60s, over two decades previously, these soul-stirrers had a plethora of US hits, SAM (& Dave) with 'Hold On! I'm A Comin'' & 'Soul Man', JR WALKER via 'Shotgun' & '(I'm A) Road Runner'. Together with a large backing ensemble (including ex-Rockpile musician, BILLY BREMNER), the fictitious movie duo are billed as SWANKY MODES on the soundtrack set. In reality, the pair are credited with 6 out of the 10 tracks; opening and closing track 'An Ordinary Man' . . . "would have given it up by now" (as the HITMEN in the film) has two versions. Worshipped by Ivan and Josh (John Cusack and Tim Robbins respectively), the show-stopping, 50-something duo feature on four other songs: 'You Hooked Me Baby', 'Betcher Bottom Dollar', 'Audience For My Pain' & 'Language Of Love', all rather dated R&B/soul but nevertheless hi-energy in all the right places. Sadly, WALKER was to die of cancer in his Battle Creek, Michigan home, on 23rd November, 1995. The four various artists' tracks (and there could've been so many more; DEAD KENNEDYS, CIRCLE JERKS, THEY MIGHT BE GIANTS, etc.), stem from the likes of the Beastie Boys-like KING COTTON on 'Roscoe's Rap' (complete with all-girl trio), BO DIDDLEY's 'Surfer's Love Chant', FISHBONE's 'Slow Bus Movin'' (a Rawhide-styled, C&W number) and DEVO's 'Baby Doll', the latter sung in Swedish and mimed by a trio of new romantic idiots in the movie. On reflection, the combination of both SWANKY MODES-versus-V/A "parties" (and their correlation to the movie) sends out a fun message, although the fun part is removed when you see the price tag of over $200 for the rare CD and/or LP. *MCS*

Album rating: *6

TEENAGE MILLIONAIRE

1961 (US 84m w/b&w) Clifton & Ludlow Productions / United Artists

Film genre: R&B/Rock'n'roll Musical comedy

Top guns: s-w: (+ dir) Lawrence Doheny, Harry Spalding → the YOUNG SWINGERS → SURF PARTY → WILD ON THE BEACH

Stars: Jimmy Clanton *(Bobby Chalmers)* ← GO, JOHNNY, GO!, Rocky Graziano *(Rocky)* ← COUNTRY MUSIC HOLIDAY ← MISTER ROCK AND ROLL, Zasu Pitts *(Aunt Theodora)*, Diane Jergens *(Bambi)* ← HIGH SCHOOL CONFIDENTIAL! ← SING BOY SING, Joan Tabor *(Adrienne)*, Sid Gould *(Sheldon Vale)*, Maurice Gosfield *(Ernie)*, Eileen O'Neill *(Desidieria)*, **Chubby Checker** *(performer)* → TWIST AROUND THE CLOCK → IT'S TRAD, DAD! → DON'T KNOCK THE ROCK → LET THE GOOD TIMES ROLL → PURPLE PEOPLE EATER → TWIST, **Dion** *(performer)* → TWIST AROUND THE CLOCK, **Bill Black's Combo** *(performers)*, **Marv Johnson** *(performer)*, **Vicki Spencer** *(performer)* ← TWIST AROUND THE CLOCK, **Jackie Wilson** *(performer)* ← GO, JOHNNY, GO!, Jack Larson *(performer)* → the YOUNG SWINGERS

Storyline: Teenager Bobby Chalmers inherits his parents' fortune after their death, but he also inherits his mollycoddling Aunt Theodora and a tough bodyguard to keep him honest. At last, however, he gets a chance to go wild and sneaks down to his father's radio station where he anonymously cuts a single while chatting up new friend Bambi. When the single is a success, the hunt is on to find the mystery voice. *JZ*

Movie rating: *3.5

Visual: video + dvd

Off the record: Jimmy Clanton etc. (see below)

—

Various Cast starring JIMMY CLANTON (*)

Aug 61. (lp) *Ace; <LP 1014>*
– Teenage millionaire (*) / Possibility (*) / Smokey (BILL BLACK'S COMBO) / Yogi (BILL BLACK'S COMBO) / Kissin game (DION) / Somebody nobody wants (DION) / Back to school blues (JACK LARSON) / Hello Mister Dream (VICKI SPENCER) / Greenlight (*) / Happy times (*) / Lets twist again (CHUBBY CHECKER) / The jet (CHUBBY CHECKER) / The way I am (JACKIE WILSON) / Lonely life (JACKIE WILSON) / Show me (MARV JOHNSON) / Oh Mary (MARV JOHNSON) / I wait (VICKI SPENCER).

S/track review: Quite a package here on 'TEENAGE MILLIONAIRE' if the money's-worth 17 songs is anything to go by. JIMMY CLANTON gets star-billing with four numbers, the opening title track, the nostalgic 'Possibility', 'Greenlight' & 'Happy Times', not nearly as great as his earlier smashes, 'Just A Dream' & 'Go, Jimmy, Go'. The Baton Rouge boy (who'd only just turned 21 when this OST was in the shops) had several other hits and was about to have one of his biggest a year later in 1962, with his version of Neil Sedaka's 'Venus In Blue Jeans'. The rest of the cast are afforded two numbers each, notably teenage idol DION on 'Kissin Game' & 'Somebody Nobody Wants', the dance-craze R&B crooner CHUBBY CHECKER on 'Lets Twist Again' (a current Top 10 entry) & 'The Jet', the "Reet Petite" man JACKIE WILSON on 'The Way I Am' & 'Lonely Life', plus "You Got What It Takes" rootsy R&B singer MARV JOHNSON on the wonderful 'Show Me' & 'Oh Mary'. Exclusive tracks also come via the ex-Elvis bassman BILL BLACK'S COMBO on 'Smokey' & 'Yogi' (the latter a B-side of Top 30 hit, 'Ole Buttermilk Sky') and who could forget teenager VICKI SPENCER on 'Hello Mister Dream' & 'I Wait'. It seemed everybody did according to every history book on the planet. *MCS*

Album rating: *4

TEMPTATION

2004 (US 90m*) unknown

Film genre: Rock Musical drama

Top guns: dir: Mark Tarlov / s-w: Sydney Forest, Jon Taylor

Stars: Zoe Saldana *(Annie)* ← GET OVER IT ← CENTER STAGE, Adam Pascal *(Nicholi)* ← SCHOOL OF ROCK ← SLC PUNK! / → RENT, Michael Cerveris *(Pablo)* ← ROCK'N'ROLL HIGH SCHOOL FOREVER, Deven May *(Matt)*, Alice Ripley *(Sabrina)*, Orfeh *(Yvonne)*, **Annie Golden** *(Nora)* ← THIS IS MY LIFE ← HAIR, Manley Pope *(Billy)*, Anika Noni-Rose *(Fog)* ← FROM JUSTIN TO KELLY / → DREAMGIRLS, Felicia Finley *(Sally)* ← HE GOT GAME, David St. Louis *(Marco; bartender)*

Storyline: Be careful what you wish for, is the message of the movie, especially when you're dealing with the Devil. Like the Faust fable of old, this modern musical set in the Big Apple is told with a flowing plotline that was also the toast of Broadway a few years earlier. *MCS*

Movie rating: *6

Visual: none (no audio OST)

Off the record: Annie Golden was the singer with the Shirts, a new wave act of the late 70s.

the TEMPTATIONS

1998 (US 75m x2 mini-TV) De Passe / Hallmark Entertainment / ABC

Film genre: R&B/Soul-music bio-pic/drama

Top guns: dir: Allan Arkush ← SHAKE, RATTLE AND ROCK tv ← GET CRAZY ← ROCK'N'ROLL HIGH SCHOOL / s-w: Robert Johnson, Kevin Arkadie

Stars: Charles Malik Whitfield *(Otis Williams)*, D.B. Woodside *(Melvin Franklin)*, Terron Brooks *(Eddie Kendricks)*, Christian Payton *(Paul*

Williams), Leon *(David Ruffin)* ← the FIVE HEARTBEATS / → LITTLE RICHARD → GET RICH OR DIE TRYIN', Tina Lifford *(Haze)* → CATCH AND RELEASE, Jenifer Lewis *(Mama Rose)* ← the PREACHER'S WIFE ← GIRL 6 ← SHAKE, RATTLE AND ROCK! tv ← WHAT'S LOVE GOT TO DO WITH IT ← BEACHES / → JACKIE'S BACK! → LITTLE RICHARD, Alan Rosenberg *(Shelly Berger)* ← MIRACLE MILE ← the LAST TEMPTATION OF CHRIST, Erik Michael Tristan *(Smokey Robinson)*, Charles Ley *(Dennis Edwards)*, J. August Richards *(Richard Street)* ← WHY DO FOOLS FALL IN LOVE, Obba Babatunde *(Berry Gordy)* → HOW HIGH, Vanessa Bell Calloway *(Johnnie Mae Matthews)* ← WHAT'S LOVE GOT TO DO WITH IT, Mel Jackson *(Norman Whitfield)* → LITTLE RICHARD, **Christopher Reid** *(Joltin' Joe)* ← HOUSE PARTY 3 ← CLASS ACT ← HOUSE PARTY 2 ← HOUSE PARTY, Bianca Lawson *(Diana Ross)* ← PRIMARY COLORS / → SAVE THE LAST DANCE → BONES, Melissa Mercedes Cardello *(Florence Ballard)*, Taifa Harris *(Mary Wilson)*, N'tasha A. Pierre *(Martha Reeves)*, Ricky Fante *(Marvin Gaye)*, Lamman Rucker *(Jimmy Ruffin)* ← the JACKSONS: AN AMERICAN DREAM, Nyjah Moore *(Tammi Terrell)*, Jonnie Brown *(Damon Harris)*, **Smokey Robinson** *(himself)* ← KNIGHTS OF THE CITY ← the T.A.M.I. SHOW

Storyline: Last survivor of the original Temptations, Otis Williams, recollects the life and turbulent times of the Motown group. From their first hit in 1964 till 1968 they go from triumph to triumph, but after David Ruffin "leaves" and Paul Williams commits suicide three years later, the Temptations split up into rival bands. It's not until several years later that a reunion tour takes place and a well-deserved spot in the Hall Of Fame is reserved for them. *JZ*

Movie rating: *7

Visual: dvd

Off the record: The **TEMPTATIONS** were formed initially as the Elgins in Birmingham, Alabama, USA in 1960, by Eddie Kendricks and Paul Williams (from the Primes), plus Melvin Franklin and Otis Williams (from the Distants). After moving to Detroit the following year and securing a deal with the Berry 'Gordy' label (aka 'Tamla Motown'), the vocal group finally delivered their first hit in 1964 with 'The Way You Do The Things You Do'. By early 1965, 'My Girl' had given them their first chart topper, a classic ballad penned by SMOKEY ROBINSON, who dominated most of the band's songwriting during this period; an incredible run of chart hits followed including 'It's Growing', 'Since I Lost My Baby' and 'My Baby', all released in 1965. Though the act were "manufactured" to a certain degree, the TEMPTATIONS possessed an impressive three-pronged vocal attack in David Ruffin's gravel-flecked rasp, Eddie Kendricks' high tenor and Paul Williams' heavy baritone. As the band enjoyed a further string of hits such as 'Ain't Too Proud To Beg', '(I Know) I'm Losing You' (1966), 'You're My Everything' (1967) and 'I Wish It Would Rain' (1968), Ruffin became increasingly jealous of the way DIANA ROSS was being nurtured for solo stardom by 'Motown', things coming to a head when the man failed to show for a gig. The group duly sent him packing, recruiting Dennis Edwards and with the 'Cloud Nine' (1969) single, hitched a ride on the magic roundabout of "psychedelic soul" pioneered by Sly Stone's thrilling honky hybrids. With Whitfield and his writing partner Barrett Strong penning most of the material, the band released a clutch of hard-hitting, socially aware classics like 'Psychedelic Shack' (1970), 'Ball Of Confusion' (1970), the funk getting dirtier and nastier with the hard-bitten tale of a broken home, 'Papa Was A Rolling Stone' (1972). Kendricks departed in 1971 after his swansong for the band, 'Just My Imagination (Running Away With Me)'. Paul Williams left later the same year, the band drafting in replacements Damon Harris and Richard Street. While the singles dried up, in the pop charts at least, the band still shifted albums up until the late 70s. As their creative muse began to falter, the band extricated itself from 'Motown' and despite a well-received self-produced album, 'The Temptations Do The Temptations' (1976), their two albums for 'Atlantic', 'Hear To Tempt You' (1978) and 'Bare Back' (1978) were marred by insipid disco stylings. Edwards had been absent for these albums (replaced by Louis Price), although he returned towards the end of the decade when the band hooked up with 'Motown' again for a comeback single, 'Power' (1980). Ruffin and Kendricks returned to the fold for a short-lived reunion in 1982 and following their departure, Otis Williams and Melvin Franklin carried the TEMPTATIONS flame through the 80s and beyond, completing studio and live work with a changing cast of musicians. With Kendricks dying of cancer in 1992 and Franklin dying three years later, Otis is the sole remaining member from the original group. *BG & MCS*

□ TENACIOUS D segment
(⇒ the PICK OF DESTINY)

TENDER MERCIES

1983 (US 100m) Antron Media Productions / EMI Films (PG)

Film genre: Country-music-based melodrama

Top guns: dir: Bruce Beresford ← SIDE BY SIDE / s-w: Horton Foote

Stars: Robert Duvall *(Mac Sledge)* → GERONIMO: AN AMERICAN LEGEND → a SHOT AT GLORY, Tess Harper *(Rosa Lee)* → FLASHPOINT → FAR NORTH → BROKEN BRIDGES, **Betty Buckley** *(Dixie)*, Wilford Brimley *(Harry)* ← the ELECTRIC HORSEMAN, Ellen Barkin *(Sue Anne)* ← UP IN SMOKE / → EDDIE AND THE CRUISERS → DOWN BY LAW → SIESTA → JOHNNY HANDSOME → FEAR AND LOATHING IN LAS VEGAS, Allan Hubbard *(Sonny)*, Lenny von Dohlen *(Robert)*

Storyline: Washed-up country and western singer, Mac Sledge, finds himself in the last chance saloon (or motel) when he wakes up jobless and penniless with a raging hangover. Motel owner, Rosa Lee, takes pity on him and has him doing hotel work for peanuts per hour and no whisky. Suddenly he starts to get back his self-esteem through doing the simple things, and before long he and Rosa Lee tie the knot and he even resurrects his old singing career – this time without the demons of the past. *JZ*

Movie rating: *8

Visual: video

Off the record: **Betty Buckley** sang a Charlie Craig song in the movie, 'The Best Bedroom In Town'.

—

Various Artists (composers: various)

Mar 83. (lp/c) *Liberty; <LO/4LO 51147> (LBG7 51147-1)* □ Aug83 □
– Off on Wednesdays (vocal: CHARLIE CRAIG feat. SHERRY GROOMS) / If you'll hold the ladder (I'll climb to the top) (vocal: ROBERT DUVALL) / It hurts to face reality (vocal: ROBERT DUVALL) / Makin' love and makin' out (vocal: CHARLIE CRAIG) / Overnight sensations (vocal: CRAIG BICKHARDT) / Midnight Tennessee woman (vocal: CHARLIE CRAIG) / Over you (LANE BRODY) / I've decided to leave here forever (vocal: ROBERT DUVALL) / Wings of a dove (vocal: ROBERT DUVALL feat. GAIL YOUNGS) / You are what love means to me (vocal: CRAIG BICKHARDT).

S/track review: This is workaday genre stuff largely written and executed by contract songwriters including CHARLIE CRAIG (who sings on three of the songs, and impressively attempts to rhyme "Wednesdays" with "business") and CRAIG BICKHARDT, whose two songs are almost anachronistically polished. The formulaic but expertly-executed tearjerker 'Over You', a straight pop ballad co-written by the Monkees' songwriter Bobby Hart and sung by LANE BRODY, who had previously been best known for her work on commercials, was nominated for an Oscar. But the greatest fascination is in listening to ROBERT DUVALL's heroic efforts to make something workable of vocal resources that – with apologies – were clearly not designed with singing in mind. His four songs include familiar country hokum like 'If You'll Hold The Ladder' (more famously covered by David Allan Coe) and Lefty Frizell's 'It Hurts To Face Reality', and two more that were re-recorded after the film, to no discernible advantage. It's hard to know whether to be amused or awestruck; but, successfully conveying his screen character's aspirations and frailties, this must go down as one of the great actor's most valiant performances. Truly, Robert Duvall earned his Oscar. *ND*

Album rating: *5.5

TERMINAL CITY RICOCHET

1990 (Can 107m) E.Motion Films / Festival Films (R)

Film genre: sci-fi punk thriller

Top guns: dir: Zale Dalen / s-w: Phil Savath, John Conti, Ken Lester, Al Thurgood, Bill Mullan

Stars: Peter Breck *(Ross Gilmore)* ← HOOTENANNY HOOT ← the BEATNIKS / → HIGHWAY 61, Germain Houde *(Ace "the Savior" Tomlinson)*, **Jello BIAFRA** *(Bruce Coddle)*, Gabe Khouth *(Jim Gilmore)*, Marcel Masse *(wino)*

Storyline: Imagine a decaying world sometime in the future. Terminal City is that place, a place where television is king and the consumer is its slave, where the need for technology has outweighed any space to put it, therefore junk is raining down on its people. Will the campaigning Ross Gilmore, get re-elected to be mayor once again, or will someone save the land from this modern day evil. *MCS*

Movie rating: *6

Visual: video

Off the record: Jello BIAFRA (see below + own entry)

Various Artists (score: J. Douglas Dodd)

Nov 89. (lp/cd) *Alternative Tentacles; <(VIRUS 75/+CD)>* ☐ ☐
– Behind the smile (D.O.A.) / Television (the BEATNIGS) / Falling space junk (hold the anchovies) (JELLO BIAFRA w/ NOMEANSNO) / Modern man (I, BRAINEATER) / Living with the lies GERRY HANNAH) / War party (ART BERGMANN) / That's progress (JELLO BIAFRA w/ D.O.A.) / Madhouse (EVAN JOHNS & THE H-BOMBS) / It's catching up (NOMEANSNO) / Pull the trigger, sunshine! (the GROOVAHOLICS) / Concrete beach (D.O.A.) / Message from our sponsor – Object-subject (KEITH LeBLANC / JELLO BIAFRA).

S/track review: 'Alternative Tentacles' records (the San Franciscan-based label that brought you this movie) had been around now for over a decade since signing iconic hardcore punk group, Dead Kennedys. Its leader JELLO BIAFRA was now a solo artist in his own right who also spread the punk gospel through his spoken word gigs/recordings and his manic appearances on celluloid. Originating a little north-east of Frisco (Vancouver, Canada, to be exact), were fellow hardcorists, D.O.A., starring Joe Keithley they protracted three cuts for ' . . . RICOCHET': opener 'Behind The Smile', the NY Dolls-like sing-a-long 'Concrete Beach' and the BIAFRA-fronted 'That's Progress'. That man BIAFRA was found on two other collaborative songs, 'Message From Our Sponsor / Object-Subject' with Tackhead dubmeister KEITH LeBLANC and 'Falling Space Junk (Hold The Anchovies)' with NOMEANSNO; the latter Canadians also checked in with metallic-funk-punk, 'It's Catching Up'. The former's holocaustic 'Message From Our Sponsor' was typical LeBLANC, the producer combining elements of doom and gloom over BIAFRA's effective disaster-tone "You Will Be Shot" narration. Certainly the most intriguing piece was the bombastic embryonic version of 'Television' by the BEATNIGS, pre-dating the group's/Michael Franti's "Gil Scott-Heron-esque" Disposable Heroes Of Hiphoprisy classic take a few years later. Of the remaining five acts, bar-room blues D.C. act EVAN JOHNS & THE H-BOMBS ('Madhouse') was worthy of the admission charge alone, a record that was recorded several years previously but only dispatched on 1986's 'Rollin' Through The Night'. If you thought Eric Burdon, Jim Morrison and Howlin' Wolf were whiskey-soaked gruff then listen to this 6-minute journey of earthy vox and trippy lead guitar excellence. I, BRAINEATER (featuring Jim Cummins on 'Modern Man') were a little too obscure and Cramps-ish for my liking, although it might be worth checking out early LPs such as 'I, Here – Where You!' & 'Artist Poet Thief'. Once again, Vancouver was a direct source for yet another former punk, GERRY HANNAH, it seemed the ex-Subhumans bassist had a penchant for "Peaceful, Easy, Feeling" on his Eagles-esque 'Living With The Lies'. Guess where ART BERGMANN came from? No don't bother, especially when you find out he played in a band called the the Young Canadians. ART was behind the Warren Zevon-ish, 'War Party', the man featuring in films 'HIGHWAY 61' & 'HARD CORE LOGO', while also releasing albums for the 'Duke Street' imprint. Brighter than anything on this time-eclipsing set was the GROOVAHOLICS' 'Pull The Trigger, Sunshine!', all electric fuzz guitars and retro funk. 'TERMINAL CITY RICOCHET' represents more than just a run-of-the-mill punk-cum-socially-conscious long-player, it defines the end of the 80s, before a time when Green Day were only an indie band. *MCS*

Album rating: *7.5

TERROR ON TOUR

1980 (US 90m) Four Feathers Partners / Intercontinental (18)

Film genre: horror/mystery/crime thriller

Top guns: dir: Don Edmonds / s-w: Dell Lekus

Stars: Chip Greenman *(Ralph)*, Rich Pemberton *(Henry)*, Dave Galluzzo *(Cherry)*, Rick Styles *(Fred)*, Larry Thomasof *(Tim)*, Jeff Ray Morgan *(Herb)*, Dave Thompson *(Jeff)*, Johnny Green *(Lt. Lambert)* → RUDE BOY, Lisa Rodriguez *(Jane)*, Sylvia Wright *(Carol)*, Lindy Leah *(Nancy)*

Storyline: The Clowns are the freshest band in theatrical rock'n'roll, their stage shows full of simulated violence and macabre. However, when a real murder appears at their doorstep (the alley outside, actually), and several groupies are mutilated, suspicion lies somewhere between the road crew and the band. An Insane Clown Posse, indeed.

Movie rating: *3

Visual: video on Media Home Entertainment

Off the record: The Names wrote the songs (although they were not the Belgian post-punk act).

THANK GOD IT'S FRIDAY

1978 (US 89m) Casablanca Filmworks / Columbia Pictures (PG)

Film genre: Dance/Pop Musical comedy

Top guns: dir: Robert Klane / s-w: Armyan Bernstein → ONE FROM THE HEART

Stars: Donna Summer *(Nicole Sims)*, Valerie Landsburg *(Frannie)* → ROCK STAR, **Terri Nunn** *(Jeannie)*, Jeff Goldblum *(Tony Di Marco)* ← NASHVILLE ← DEATH WISH / → EARTH GIRLS ARE EASY → BARENAKED IN AMERICA, Ray Vitte *(Bobby Speed)* ← CAR WASH, Chick Vennera *(Marv Gomez)*, Debra Winger *(Jennifer)* → URBAN COWBOY → MIKE'S MURDER, Robin Menken *(Maddy)* ← the STRAWBERRY STATEMENT ← FOOLS / → THIS IS SPINAL TAP → BODY ROCK, **Paul Jabara** *(Carl)*, John Friedrich *(Ken)* → ALMOST SUMMER, Mark Lonow *(Dave)*, Andrea Howard *(Sue)*, **DeWayne Jessie** *(Floyd)* ← CAR WASH ← SPARKLE / → ANIMAL HOUSE → WHERE THE BUFFALO ROAM, Marya Small *(Jackie)* → AMERICAN POP → MAN ON THE MOON, Judith Brown *(badmouth in bar)* ← WILLIE DYNAMITE ← SLAUGHTER'S BIG RIP-OFF, **the Commodores:- Lionel Richie** *(himself)* → the PREACHER'S WIFE, **Walter Orange, William King, Ronald LePread, Milan Williams, Thomas McClary** *(themselves)*

Storyline: Thank God for the 70s, and the chance to wallow in frothy nostagia like this. Funnier and less self conscious than 'Saturday Night Fever', the film follows the motley clientele of Zoo, a state of the art disco where the DJ's called

Bobby Speed and where the Commodores still have some mean funk chops. *BG*

Movie rating: *3.5

Visual: video + dvd

Off the record: Terri Nunn was later of 'Top Gun' ('You Take My Breath Away') hitmakers, Berlin; **Donna Summer** (see below).

—

Various Artists (score: PAUL JABARA *)

Apr 78. (lp/c) *Casablanca; <7099> (K 66076)* [10] May78 [40]
– Thank God it's Friday (LOVE AND KISSES) / With your love (DONNA SUMMER) / After dark (PATTI BROOKS) / Last dance (DONNA SUMMER) / Disco queen (*) / Find my way (CAMEO) / Too hot ta trot (COMMODORES) / I wanna dance (MARATHON) / Sevilla nights (SANTA ESMERALDA) / You're the most precious thing in my life (LOVE AND KISSES) / Do you want the real thing (D.C. LaRUE) / Lovin', livin' and givin' (DIANA ROSS). *<US w/ 12"ep+=>* – Leatherman's theme (WRIGHT BROS. FLYING MACHINE) / Take it to the zoo (SUNSHINE) / Trapped in a stairway (*) / Floyd's theme (NATURAL JUICE) / Love masterpiece (THELMA HOUSTON) / Je t'aime (moi non plus) (DONNA SUMMER). *<cd-iss. Mar97 on 'Polygram'++=; 534606>* – (see 12" tracks) / Last dance – reprise (DONNA SUMMER).

S/track review: Together with DONNA SUMMER and Giorgio Moroder, Neil Bogart's legendary 'Casablanca' label effectively launched disco with 1975's 'Love To Love You Baby'. John Travolta and the Bee Gees took it worldwide two years later, but Bogart's fiefdom finally got a piece of the big screen action with this last-gasp, night-in-the-life disco movie. Missing both the film's gags and most of the label's classic singles, the soundtrack isn't one of their more essential releases, but it has its moments, most of them involving SUMMER. In 1978, her mercurial partnership with Moroder was still massaging the parts other producers couldn't reach: 'With You Love' and 'Lovin' Livin' And Givin' serve up Euro-disco dark and squelchy enough to stain your flares (and influence Goldfrapp), while the more soulful 'Last Dance' won a Grammy for both her and writer PAUL JABARA (who also makes a solo appearance with the Bee Gees-alike 'Disco Queen'). And the CD-reissue seriously short-changes SUMMER fans by dropping her sensational romp through Serge Gainsbourg's 'Je T'Aime (Moi Non Plus)'. CAMEO and the COMMODORES are the other big names ('Motown' were also involved in the movie), the former with their forgettable, pre-monster-funk debut single, 'Find My Way', the latter pre-figuring their move into soul-pop with the late decade dance-funk of 'Too Hot To Trot'. If it wasn't so derivative of their dancefloor classic, 'Don't Let Me Be Misunderstood', SANTA ESMERALDA's 'Sevilla Nights' would be a decent Chicano-disco instrumental, while the electro-percussive breakdown of PATTI BROOKS' 'After Dark' predicts the rise of house. There are better compilations out there, but 'THANK GOD IT'S FRIDAY' frames a Bacchanalian moment in time: the real last days of disco. *BG*

Album rating: *5.5

– spinoff hits, etc. –

LOVE AND KISSES: Thank God It's Friday / You're The Most Precious Thing In My Life

Apr 78. (7") *<925> (TGIFS 1)* [22] May78 [ ]

DONNA SUMMER: Last Dance / With Your Love

Apr 78. (7") *<926> (TGIFS 2)* [3] May78 [51]

THANK YOU, GOOD NIGHT

2001 (US 89m) Burkhardt-Griffith Productions / Deeper Magic

Film genre: Grunge-Rock music comedy drama

Top guns: s-w: (+ dir) Chuck Griffith, Chris Provenzano, Robert Zimmer Jr.

Stars: Christian Campbell *(Lee)*, Lara Boyd Rhodes *(Trixie)*, John Paul Pitoc *(Donnie)*, Jay Leggett *(Big Frank)*, Scott Burkhardt *(Mike)*, Mark Hamill *(Karl; Lee's father)*, Sally Kirkland *(Doreen)* ← HUMAN HIGHWAY ← a STAR IS BORN ← PIPE DREAMS ← HEY, LET'S TWIST, Nicole Eggart *(Janine)* ← PINK AS THE DAY SHE WAS BORN, Brett Domrose *(Jim)*, **Billy Davis Jr.** *(music store clerk)*, Gedde Watanabe *(cafe owner)* ← THAT THING YOU DO! ← UHF / → ALFIE re-make, Diva Zappa *(fan)* ← BABY SNAKES, Erik Passoja *(bingo caller)* ← the BEACH BOYS: AN AMERICAN FAMILY

Storyline: Four years in the making, New Jersey alt-rock band the Handy Kaufmans, are in shock when they hear that their grunge hero, Kurt Cobain, has committed suicide (April 1994). Drummer and spokesman, Lee, guitarist Mike, lead singer Donnie and bassist Jim (not forgetting manager, Big Frank), plan a final make-or-break American tour. Things get off to a bad start when the drunken Jim gets electrocuted while pissing too high; his last-minute replacement, Trixie, is perfect fodder for womaniser Lee. *MCS*

Movie rating: *4.5

Visual: dvd in 2006 – re-scored by Orange County Senza Motiva.

Off the record: Diva Muffin Zappa is the youngest daughter of the late, great Frank Zappa; she appeared on the track, 'Chana In De Bushwop' from his 1989 collection, 'You Can't Do That On Stage Anymore, Vol.3'. Chuck Griffith, Robert Zimmer Jr. & Andre Devon Magone wrote three songs for the film, 'Wish You Were Dead', 'Not In High School Anymore' & 'Fifth Of July'; the rest of the unreleased original score was by Christopher Hoag. **Billy Davis Jr.** was part of 60s pop act, the Fifth Dimension; memorable hits included 'Up – Up And Away', 'Stoned Soul Picnic', 'Aquarius – Let The Sunshine In' & 'Wedding Bell Blues'. He subsequently formed spinoff duo with Marilyn McCoo; they had a 1976 US chart-topper, 'You Don't Have To Be A Star (To Be In My Show'. *MCS*

THAT DARN PUNK

2000 (US 90m straight-to-video; +5m dvd) Kung Fu Films

Film genre: sci-fi comedy drama

Top guns: s-w: (+ dir) Jeff Richardson, Robert Stinson

Stars: Joseph Escalante *(Dirk Castigo)* ← DUDES ← SUBURBIA / → PUNK ROCK HOLOCAUST → CAKE BOY → PUNK'S NOT DEAD, **Kara Wetington/Katalina** *(Merla)*, Mia Crowe *(Claire Won)* → CAKE BOY, Kandis Scalise *(Lina)*, **Zander Schloss** *(Benny Harper)* <= the CIRCLE JERKS =>, Lisa Hannon *(Doll Part girl)*, **Warren Fitzgerald** *(Billy)* ← GODMONEY ← DUDES / → CAKE BOY → PUNK'S NOT DEAD, **Kyle Gass** *(Mr. Jailbait)* → CAKE BOY → the PICK OF DESTINY, Scott Aukerman *(Mr. Hollywoodpants)* → CAKE BOY, Akemi Royer *(Jackie)* → CAKE BOY, **Dave Quackenbush** *(Big Tipper's singer)* ← DUDES / → PUNK'S NOT DEAD, **Josh Freese** *(Big Tipper's drummer)*, **Mark Adkins** *(Guttermouth)*

Storyline: Kicked out by his girlfriend with only a pair of boxer shorts to his name, punk rock musician, Dirk Castigo, finds himself in an even worse situation when he's kidnapped by aliens from outer space. His escape and perilous journey back into the "real" world is the film's "real" purpose. *MCS*

Movie rating: *5

Visual: video + dvd

Off the record: Joe Escalante, Warren Fitzgerald, Dave Quackenbush, Josh Freese are all of the Vandals, while **Mark Adkins** is in the group Guttermouth; **Zander Schloss** was ex-CIRCLE JERKS. Solo dance artist, **Katalina** (aka Kara Wetington), guested for the punk revival band, the Bouncing Souls. *MCS*

—

Various Artists

Mar 01. (cd) *Kung Fu; <78780>* [ ] [–]
– "Well, that's queer" – Joey & Lenny / Siegfried and Roy (NERF HERDER) / Still (BIGWIG) / "Palookaville" – Johnny Puke / After you my friend (LAGWAGON) / Right on Q (the VANDALS) / "Good vs. great" – Mr. Hollywoodpants / Domino effect (OZMA) / Alien (PENNYWISE) / "It's not like that" – Dirk Castigo / Ben Lee (ATARIS) / Dream of waking (AFI) / "Sex with a man" – Doll Part girl / The ides (ANTIFREEZE) / Only you (NO MOTIV) / "He touched me daddy" – Daddy & Jailbait / Jabberjaw (MI6) / "My property" – Officer Shithead / GGF (RANCID) / Pic 'n' save (ASSORTED JELLY BEANS) / "Bad boyfriend" – Pink Lady / Queen of Outer Space (SLOPPY SECONDS) / The lonely (SWINGIN' UTTERS) / "Funky see, funky do" – the Drummer / Why won't Left Eye get with me? (JOSH FREESE) / "Potent potables" – Merla / My heart will go on (the VANDALS feat. KATALINA) / Theme from That Darn Punk (the VANDALS).

S/track review: The 'Kung Fu' imprint were responsible for a plethora of power-pop-punk acts, led of course by Warren Fitzgerald's VANDALS, who are afforded a few cuts here, 'Right On Q', a goddamn awful rendition of Celine Dion's 'My Heart Will Go On' (featuring KATALINA), and their theme from 'THAT DARN PUNK'. Further exclusive numbers stem from the similar NERF HERDER ('Siegfried And Roy'), NO MOTIV ('Only You'), etc., all fast, furious and for the most part, fun. Big names come courtesy of RANCID ('GGF'), PENNYWISE (the 4-minute! 'Alien'), LAGWAGON ('After You My Friend'), AFI ('Dream Of Waking') and the Vandals' JOSH FREESE ('Why Won't Left Eye Get With Me?'), the latter a reference to former TLC siren, Lisa "Left Eye" Lopes, who sadly died a year after the movie was released. The dialogue snippets might well've been left at the cutting stage, although they do offer a break between the derivative bands on show here – Green Day and Foo Fighters had a lot to answer for. As for ASSORTED JELLY BEAN ('Pick 'n' Save'), what we have here is a failure to register anything fresh, and that could be anything between the Red Hot Chili Peppers jamming with the Mighty Mighty Bosstones. Never mind the bollocks – next to impossible to do! – 'cause this is a case for quantity over quality. *MCS*

Album rating: *4

THAT THING YOU DO!

1996 (US 108m) 20th Century Fox (PG)

Film genre: Pop/Rock musical comedy/drama

Top guns: s-w + dir: Tom Hanks

Stars: Tom Everett Scott *(Guy Patterson; drummer)*, Liv Tyler *(Faye Dolan)* ← EMPIRE RECORDS ← HEAVY / → DR. T & THE WOMEN, Johnathon Schaech *(Jimmy Mattingly; vocalist)* → FINDING GRACELAND → SPLENDOR, Steve Zahn *(Lenny Haise; guitarist)* ← REALITY BITES / → SUBURBI@ → CHELSEA WALLS, Ethan Embry *(the bass player)* ← EMPIRE RECORDS, Tom Hanks *(Mr. White)*, Charlize Theron *(Tina)*, Giovanni Ribisi *(Chad)* → SUBURBI@ → FIRST LOVE, LAST RITES → the VIRGIN SUICIDES → MASKED AND ANONYMOUS → LOST IN TRANSLATION → COLD MOUNTAIN, **Chris Isaak** *(Uncle Bob)* ← GRACE OF MY HEART, Alex Rocco *(Sol Siler)* ← SCENES FROM THE GOLDMINE ← VOICES ← THREE THE HARD WAY, Bill Cobbs *(Del Paxton)* ← the BODYGUARD ← ROADSIDE PROPHETS ← a HERO AIN'T NOTHIN' BUT A SANDWICH / → a MIGHTY WIND, Kevin Pollak *(Victor Kosslovich)* ← WAYNE'S WORLD 2 / → BUFFALO 66, Robert Wisdom *(Bobby Washington)* → STORYTELLING → MASKED AND ANONYMOUS → KILLER DILLER → RAY, Clint Howard *(KJZZ disc jockey)* ← GET CRAZY ← ROCK'N'ROLL HIGH SCHOOL ← COTTON CANDY / → CURIOUS GEORGE, Gedde Watanabe *(Play-Tone photographer)* ← UHF / → THANK YOU, GOOD NIGHT → ALFIE re-make, Rita Wilson *(Marguerite)* → the STORY OF US → RAISE YOUR VOICE, Holmes Osborne Jr. *(Mr. Patterson)* → AFFLICTION, Marc McClure *(Hollywood showcase director)* ← I WANNA HOLD YOUR HAND, Robert Ridgely *(Hollywood showcase announcer)* ← BOOGIE NIGHTS

Storyline: Budding jazz musician Guy Patterson gets his chance to shine when local rock band the One-Ders recruit him as a drummer. When Guy changes the tempo of their signature tune the band suddenly find themselves in demand and raise enough money to release a 45. The song becomes a big hit and stardom seems just around the corner, but Guy finds himself attracted to lead singer Jimmy's girlfriend and still there are no plans laid for a second follow-up hit. *JZ*

Movie rating: *6.5

Visual: video + dvd

Off the record: Chris Isaak was no stranger to the odd film theme having hit the charts in 1990 with 'Wicked Game' from the 'WILD AT HEART' movie.

—

Various Artists incl. the WONDERS * (score: Howard Shore)

Sep 96. (cd/c) *Play-Tone Epic; <EK/ET 67828> (486551-2)* [21] Feb97 [ ]
– Lovin' you lots and lots (the NORM WOOSTER SINGERS) / That thing you do! (*) / Little wild one (*) / Dance with me tonight (*) / All my only dreams (*) / I need you (that thing you do) (*) / She knows it (the HEARDSMEN) / Mr. Downtown (FREDDY FREDRICKSON) / Hold my hand, hold my heart (the CHANTRELLINES) / Voyage around the Moon (the SATURN 5) / My world is over (DIANE DANE) / Drive faster (the VICKSBURGS) / Shrimp shack (CAP'N GEECH & SHRIMP SHACK SHOOTERS) / Time to blow (DEL PAXTON) / That thing you do! – live at the Hollywood Television Showcase (*).

S/track review: Not content with winning Oscars a-plenty, TOM HANKS showed his versatility by writing four of the songs for this soundtrack, while also directing and writing the movie. HANKS' opening salvo/parody, 'Lovin' You Lots And Lots' (by the fictional NORM WOOSTER SINGERS), evokes the insipid, easy-listening/easy-going, pre-60s nostalgia when the Ray Coniff Singers and Marty Robbins were top guns. One of HANKS' three other pseudonymous contributions (alongside co-writers Gary Goetzman and Mike Piccirillo) find him as FREDDY FREDRICKSON in crooning/bombastic mood for the swinging "Batman"-esque, 'Mr. Downtown'. HANKS gets Phil Spector-ish for all-girl group the CHANTRELLINES, their 'Hold My Hand, Hold My Heart', a song that projected back to the Chiffons, the Crystals or even Lulu. The SATURN 5 (and 'Voyage Around The Moon') was HANKS' up-tempo, surf-instrumental er ... Venture(s), with a side-salad of the Tornados or Dick Dale revisiting Del Shannon's 'Runaway'. The aforementioned songwriter Piccirillo gets two follow-on solo credits courtesy of the Bacharach & David-like 'My World Is Over' (by DIANE DANE; where's Dusty & Cilla?) and the Champs-like 'Shrimp Shack' (by CAP'N GEECH & THE SHRIMP SHACK SHOOTERS – do not say that too fast!). Of course, mock-pop outfit, the WONDERS, capture the essence (and half the album!) of the film's early '64 era, a time when the Beatles were conquering the world of music. Bridging the gap between the clean-cut Merseybeat sound, R&R and the subsequent power-pop of the late 70s, the WONDERS – like the early Beatles fronted by Nick Lowe – branch out on several cuts including fab movie spin-off single, 'That Thing You Do!'; a timeless song incidentally written by Fountains Of Wayne frontman, Adam Schlesinger. Ditto for 'Little Wild One', 'Dance With Me Tonight', 'All My Own Dreams' and the Byrds-meets-Bryan Adams-esque 'I Need You (That Thing You Do)', half supplied by songwriters Scott Rogness & Rick Elias, who also gave us the similar 'She Knows It' (by the HEARDSMEN) and the surf-rock 'Drive Faster' (by the VICKSBURGS). A little out of context is DEL PAXTON's jazz number, 'Time To Blow', but HANKS gets to have his wee foibles now and then. He deserves them. *MCS*

Album rating: *7.5

– spinoff hits, etc. –

the WONDERS: That Thing You Do! / the SATURN 5: Voyage Around The Moon

Sep 96. (c-s) *<78401> (664055-4)* [41] Jan97 [22]
(cd-s+=) *(664055-2)* – the VICKSBURGS: Drive Faster

THAT'LL BE THE DAY

1973 (UK 91m) Goodtimes Enterprises / Anglo-EMI Films (15)

Film genre: coming-of-age Rock'n'roll Musical drama

Top guns: dir: Claude Whatham → BUDDY'S SONG / s-w: Ray Connolly → STARDUST

Stars: David Essex *(Jim MacLaine)* ← SMASHING TIME / → STARDUST → SILVER DREAM RACER, **Ringo Starr** *(Mike)* <= the BEATLES =>, Rosemary Leach *(Mrs. MacLaine)*, **Billy Fury** *(Stormy Tempest)* ← I'VE GOTTA HORSE ← PLAY IT COOL, James Booth *(Mr. MacLaine)* → the JAZZ SINGER, **Keith Moon** *(J.D. Clover)* <= the WHO =>, Robert Lindsay *(Terry)*, Rosalind Ayres *(Jeanette)* → STARDUST, Deborah Watling *(Sandra)* ← TAKE ME HIGH, Patti Love *(Sandra's friend)*, Beth Morris *(Jean)* → SON OF DRACULA, **Graham Bond** *(sax player)* ← GONKS GO BEAT, **Viv Stanshall** *(cameo)* ← MAGICAL MYSTERY TOUR, Johnny Shannon *(Jack)* ← PERFORMANCE / → FLAME → ABSOLUTE BEGINNERS, Sara Clee *(girl with baby)* → FLAME, Karl Howman *(Johnny)* → STARDUST → BABYLON, Eugene Wallace *(Stuart)*

Storyline: Jim MacLaine is a young man growing up in working class 1950s Britain. Bored with school, he drops out and moves away from his parents, making a living of sorts with a variety of dead-end jobs. It's while he's selling deck chairs on a lonely stretch of coast that wide boy Mike gets to know him and teaches him how to survive in the big world. Soon Jim's introverted character is changed completely as he takes Mike's lessons to heart. *JZ*

Movie rating: *6.5

Visual: video + dvd on Warners

Off the record: (see below)

—

Various Artists: 40 Smash Hits based on the film . . .

Jun 73. (d-lp) *Ronco; (MR 2002/3)* [1] [–]
– Bye bye love (EVERLY BROTHERS) / Poetry in motion (JOHNNY TILLOTSON) / Little darlin' (the DIAMONDS) / Smoke gets in your eyes (the PLATTERS) / Chantilly lace (BIG BOPPER) / Runaround Sue (DION and the BELMONTS) / Great balls of fire (JERRY LEE LEWIS) / Running bear (JOHNNY PRESTON) / Tequila (the CHAMPS) / Tutti frutti (LITTLE RICHARD) / (Till) I kissed you (EVERLY BROTHERS) / I love how you love me (PARIS SISTERS) / Runaway (DEL SHANNON) / Bony Moronie (LARRY WILLIAMS) / Honeycombe (JIMMY RODGERS) / Why do fools fall in love (FRANKIE LYMAN) / Party doll (BUDDY KNOX) / Linda LOu (RAY SHARP) / Red river rock (JOHNNY and the HURRICANES) // That'll be the day (BOBBY VEE and the CRICKETS) / Born too late (the PONITAILS) / Wake up little Suzy (EVERLY BROTHERS) / Sealed with a kiss (BRIAN HYLAND) / Book of love (MONOTONES) / (You've got) Personality (LLOYD PRICE) / Well all right (BOBBY VEE and the CRICKETS) / At the hop (DANNY and the JUNIORS) / Ally oop (DANTE and the EVERGREEN) / Raunchy (BILL JUSTIS) / Rock on (DAVID ESSEX) / A thousand stars (BILLY FURY) / Real leather jacket (VIV STANSHALL) / Long live rock (BILLY FURY) / What in the world (shoop) (STORMY TEMPEST) / That's all right mama (BILLY FURY) / Slow down (EUGENE WALLACE) / Get yourself together (BILLY FURY) / What did I say (BILLY FURY) / It'll be me (WISHFUL THINKING).

S/track review: As Mick Jagger was to subsequently sing, "I know it's only rock'n'roll, but I like it", words that could fit hand in glove for 'THAT'LL BE THE DAY' (actually, "40 Smash Hits based on the film . . ." as it's billed on the sleeve). The double-LP (or at least 3 sides) highlights the latter half of the rock'n'roll 50s and the early 60s, the EVERLY BROTHERS soaking up four of the credits ('Bye Bye Love', 'Devoted To You', '(Till) I Kissed You' & 'Wake Up Little Suzy'), alongside choice cuts from DEL SHANNON, LITTLE RICHARD, JERRY LEE LEWIS, DION, DANNY AND THE JUNIORS, the PLATTERS and the CHAMPS. Timeless. Virtual one-hit wonders, the PONITAILS ('Born Too Late'), BIG BOPPER ('Chantilly Lace') and BILL JUSTIS ('Raunchy'), all find their rightful place in amongst this hall of fame, while the Buddy Holly title track is hijacked by BOBBY VEE & THE CRICKETS; the latter also pay Holly a tribute via 'Well All Right'. However, it's side 4 that's of special interest to collectors and film fans alike, seeing the emergence of a new star, DAVID ESSEX, who had yet to have a hit; 'Rock On' was his first of many. Co-star, BILLY FURY (a hitmaker in the early 60s – 'Halfway To Paradise', etc), virtually took over from then on, chalking up no fewer than five varying solo numbers, among them Pete Townshend's 'Long Live Rock', Arthur Crudup's 'That's All Right Mama' (yes, the Elvis one) and Ray Charles' 'What Did I Say'. As STORMY TEMPEST, FURY and his band deliver 'What In The World (Shoop)', a song written by ex-Bonzo Dog Band space cadet, VIV STANSHALL, the latter also cameoing with the RnR pastiche, 'Real Leather Jacket'. But for tracks such as fillers, 'Slow Down' by actor EUGENE WALLACE and 'It'll Be Me' by WISHFUL THINKING (spelt with two L's on the sleeve!), this side 4 and the rest of the album would have been near faultless. We await the CD. *MCS*

Album rating: *7.5

– spinoff releases, etc. –

BILLY FURY: Long Live Rock

Jul 73. (7"ep) *Ronco; (MREP 001)* [ ] [–]
– Long live rock / No other love like yours / etc.

DAVID ESSEX: Rock On / (non-OSTrack)

Aug 73. (7") *C.B.S.; (1693) Columbia; <45940>* [3] Oct73 [5]

THAT'S THE WAY OF THE WORLD

alt. SHINING STAR

1975 (US 99m) United Artists Pictures (PG)

Film genre: R&B/Pop Musical Mockumentary/drama

Top guns: dir: Sig Shore / s-w: Robert Lipsyte (+ story)

Stars: Harvey Keitel *(Coleman Buckmaster)* → the BORDER → the LAST TEMPTATION OF CHRIST → RESERVOIR DOGS → PULP FICTION → FROM DUSK TILL DAWN → FINDING GRACELAND → BE COOL, Ed Nelson *(Carlton James)* ← ROCK ALL NIGHT ← CARNIVAL ROCK, Bert Parks *(Franklyn Page)*, Cynthia Bostick *(Velour Page)*, Jimmy Boyd *(Gary Page)* ← NORWOOD, Murray Moston *(Buck's father)* → SATURDAY NIGHT FEVER, Frankie Crocker *(himself)* ← FIVE ON THE BLACK HAND SIDE ← JIMI HENDRIX ← CLEOPATRA JONES / → BREAKIN' 2: ELECTRIC BOOGALOO, Charles MacGregor *(Mantan)* ← THREE THE HARD WAY ← ACROSS 110th STREET ← SUPERFLY / → AARON LOVES ANGELA, **Earth, Wind & Fire** *(themselves; see below)*, Michael Dante *(Mike Lemongello)* ← KID GALAHAD, **Doris Troy** *(the pianist)*

Storyline: Yet another tale of corruption and dirty dealings in the music biz, centring on the shady activities of producer Coleman Buckmaster and heroin-addicted singer Velour Page. *BG*

Movie rating: *3.5

Visual: dvd

Off the record: **Earth, Wind & Fire** (see below)

—

EARTH, WIND & FIRE

Mar 75. (lp/c) *Columbia; <33280> C.B.S.; (CBS/40 80575)* [1] Apr75 [ ]
– Shining star / That's the way of the world / Happy feelin' / All about love / Yearnin', learnin' / Reasons / Africano / See the light. *(re-*

iss. Nov81 on 'CBS-Embassy'; 32054) (cd-iss. May87; CD 80575) (cd re-iss. Feb97 on 'Columbia'; 484467-2) <US cd-iss. 1999 on 'Legacy'+=; 65920> – (extra mixes).

S/track review: By the mid-70s, the EARTH, WIND & FIRE that had fleshed out Melvin Van Peebles' underground ravings five years earlier was all but unrecognisable. In creating the conscious, cleaned-up soul which made them famous, founder and former 'Chess' sessioneer MAURICE WHITE had retained only his brother VERDINE. In a rare case of life imitating art, his streamlined EW&F hit paydirt on the back of a soundtrack to a rags-to-riches music biz feature. The film itself stiffed but, as San Francisco funk authority Rickey Vincent tells it (in his excellent book, 'Funk – The Music, the People, and the Rhythm of The One'), 'THAT'S THE WAY OF THE WORLD' "opened doors for the band's imagination and paved the way for a live tour that expanded the realm of black popular music". The WHITE brothers had helped initiate blaxploitation but they'd become the antithesis of it, envisioning black culture as a spiritual continuum rather than celebrating it through sharp-suited caricature. 'Shining Star' lit upon their self-help ethos and reflected it back from the top of the American charts. Powered by hard-pecking chicken scratch and scalpel-sharp horn charts, it's about as earth-bound as EW&F Mk.II ever came; ironically, it was their only No.1 single. The title track and 'Reasons' explore higher ground: flawless cosmic soul just on the right side of muzak, lulled into the lotus position by PHILIP BAILEY's falsetto. Love yourself, love everybody else, stay young, hug trees, go with the flow, channel the right vibes: these were the band's mantras, as 70s as the dashikis they wore on stage. WHITE even played a kalimba, the African thumb piano beloved of avant-garde jazzers and Congo alchemists. He shows off its brittle charms on 'Happy Feelin', and the choppy ethno-funk of 'Africano' (when you suddenly remember you're listening to a soundtrack), as worthy highlights as the jazzy, Sly Stone-esque 'Yearnin', Learnin'. If it was all a bit much for some – most infamously George Clinton, who dubbed them "Earth, Hot Air and No Fire" – this album at least remains one of the benchmarks of prog-soul, and an influence on the likes of early-period Lenny Kravitz and Lauryn Hill amongst others. *BG*

Album rating: *7.5

– spinoff hits, etc. –

EARTH, WIND & FIRE: Shining Star / Yearnin', Learnin'

Feb 75. (7") *<10090> (CBS 3137)* [1] Apr75 [ ]

EARTH, WIND & FIRE: That's The Way Of The World / Africano

Jun 75. (7") *<10172> (CBS 3519)* [12] Jul75 [ ]

THICKER THAN WATER

1999 (US 89m) Palm Pictures (R)

Film genre: urban crime/gangster drama

Top guns: dir: Richard Cummings Jr. / s-w: Ernest Nyle Brown (story: Julie Shannon)

Stars: **Mack 10** *(DJ)* ← RHYME & REASON / → BEEF, **Fat Joe** *(Lonzo)* → WHITEBOYS → PRISON SONG, **ICE CUBE** *(Slink)*, **MC Eiht** *(Lil' Ant)* ← RHYME & REASON, **CJ Mac** *(Gator)*, **Big Punisher** *(Punny)* → WHITEBOYS, **K-Mack** *(Tyree)*, Tom'ya Bowden *(Leyla)*, Kidada Jones *(Brandy)* → BLACK AND WHITE, **B-Real** *(himself)* ← RHYME & REASON ← WHO'S THE MAN? / → HOW HIGH, **Krayzie Bone** *(himself)* → BEEF, **Flesh-N-Bone** *(himself)* → BEEF, **Bad Azz** *(himself)*, **WC** *(himself)*

Storyline: Gangsters DJ and Lonzo become allies when their first efforts to break into the rap scene end in financial disaster. The uneasy bedfellows visit drugs baron Gator to persuade him to bankroll their new joint venture, and at first all goes well. But when an informer tells all to the cops, suspicion rears its ugly head and DJ and Lonzo are soon back at each other's throats – and the subsequent death of a gang member could lead to a street war between the pair. *JZ*

Movie rating: *5

Visual: dvd

Off the record: (see below)

——

Various Artists (score: QDIII)

Oct 99. (d-cd/d-c/d-lp) *Hoo Bangin' – Priority; <P2 50016>* [64] [–]
– Let it reign (WESTSIDE CONNECTION) / LB 2000 (TECHNIEC feat. SOULTRE) / Live life 2 tha fullest (MEMPHIS BLEEK) / Gang bang s*** (ROAD DAWGS feat. MACK 10 & SQUEAK RU, AND THE HOO BANGIN' AFFILIATES) / Thicker than blood (FAT JOE feat. TERROR SQUAD) / The belly of the beast (EIGHTBALL & BIG DUKE) / Thicker than water (MC EIHT feat. VAL) / I don't wanna die (KING T) / It's time to roll (CHILDRIN OF DA GHETTO feat. MACK 10) / King of L.A. (CJ MAC) / Who got some gangsta s*** (MACK 10 feat. BAD AZZ, CJ MAC, K-MAC, ROAD DAWGS, TECHNIEC and BINKY MAC) / Survival of the fittest (DRESTA feat. W.C. and YOUNG SHANE) / Planet rock (TECH N9NE) // Wanna be gangsta (COMRADS feat. SOULTRE) / Me & my b**** (MC EIHT feat. TECHNIEC) / Half a million (SOULTRE) / Flagrant (CHOCLAIR) / Hate (CJ MAC) / Drug lord (CHILDRIN OF DA GHETTO) / Partners in crime (MR. MIKE) / Do you wanna get with this (SOULTRE feat. TECHNIEC) / Police rush the spot (THUGGED OUT feat. NOREAGA, MAZE and MUSOLINI) / Gangsta gangsta (MACK 10) / Flex with you (MECHALIE JAMISON feat. WILD STYLE) / Blue liquid (BEEFY) / Mashin'-n-smashin' (BOO KAPONE & TECHNIEC) / U know (GANGSTA) / Freeze (MMO).

S/track review: Underground hip hop cinema too frequently short-changes fans with barely-there genre movies and afterthought soundtracks. For once, it seemed that someone had finally given punters some bang for their buck with an epic 28 tracks here. Appearances can be deceptive, it would seem. This two-CD collection barely covers even a few of the bases in rap. By far the dominant force is pure, unfiltered, hardcore gangsta flavour. Unsurprisingly perhaps, the quality varies. To their compiler's credit, they rely less on big names and more on MCs attempting to stake out their own pitch. Some do, but others struggle. Sonically, two of the insurmountable forces in hip hop production at the dog-end of the 90s were still DR DRE's bouncy, George Clinton-inspired, G-funk sound and RZA of Wu-Tang Clan style with his fondness for stripped-back emotive cinematic samples, primitive musical figures and martial art movie dialogue. One of the strongest cuts here is FAT JOE's excellent 'Thicker Than Blood', which digs out a rusty Giorgio Moroder synth line a la 'Scarface' to inspire visceral thrills akin to the former, as does KING TEE with 'I Don't Wanna Die', while MEMPHIS BLEEK's tremendous 'Live Life 2 Tha Fullest' is a coruscating track inspired by the latter's aural trickery. The problem here, however, is too many artists are just content to follow, trundle out clichés and hope no one notices and, despite occasional interludes of inspiration, this collection drags on as it struggles to find its own sonic peaks and troughs. *MR*

Album rating: *5

the THING CALLED LOVE

1993 (US 116m) Paramount Pictures (PG-13)

Film genre: romantic showbiz/Country-music drama

Top guns: dir: Peter Bogdanovich / s-w: Carol Heikkinen → EMPIRE RECORDS → CENTER STAGE

Stars: River Phoenix *(James Wright)*, Samantha Mathis *(Miranda Presley)* ← THIS IS MY LIFE ← PUMP UP THE VOLUME, Dermot Mulroney *(Kyle Davidson)*, Sandra Bullock *(Linda Lue Linden)*, K.T. Oslin *(Lucy)*, Anthony Clark *(Billy)*, **Webb Wilder** *(Ned)*, **Earl Poole Ball** *(Floyd)*, Micole Mercurio *(Mary)* ← FLASHDANCE / → ELVIS AND THE COLONEL: THE UNTOLD STORY, **Deborah Allen** *(herself)*, **Trisha Yearwood** *(herself)*, **Jimmie Dale Gilmore** *(himself)* → LUBBOCK LIGHTS, **Katy Moffatt** *(herself)* ← HARD COUNTRY, **Pam Tillis** *(herself)*, **Jo-El Sonnier** *(himself)*, **Kevin Welch** *(himself)*, Tom Nolan *(desk cop)* ← VOYAGE OF THE ROCK ALIENS ← FAST TIMES AT RIDGEMONT HIGH ← CHASTITY

Storyline: Newly arrived in Nashville from New York, country wannabe Miranda Presley finds the lyrics of Dolly Parton's 'Down On Music Row' still apply two decades on, as she struggles to have her talents recognised. Picking up a job as a waitress in scene hotspot the Bluebird Café, she makes connections with her contemporaries and finds ample heartbreak material for her songs. *BG*

Movie rating: *6

Visual: video + dvd

Off the record: RIVER PHOENIX (b.23 Aug'70, Madras, Oregon) sang several songs in the film:- 'Standing On A Rock', 'Until Now' (both of these performed by RODNEY CROWELL on the OST), 'Blame It On Your Heart' (DEBORAH ALLEN on OST), 'Lone Star State Of Mind', 'Ol' John And Jimmy', 'Lost Highway' and 'Love Is'. His penultimate movie prior to his untimely death (o.d.'d; 31 Oct'93 in Hollywood, California), his final role was in the posthumous, 'Silent Tongue' (1994). Other cast singers mysteriously not on OST were:- DERMOT MULRONEY ('Someone Else's Used Guitar', 'Hey, Porter', 'Ain't No Train Outta Nashville' & 'Streets Of Love'; latter performed by KEVIN WELCH on OST), SAMANTHA MATHIS ('Big Bar Hair', 'Crazy' & 'Big Dream') and SANDRA BULLOCK ('Heaven Knocking On My Door'); latter co-wrote the song! **Earl Poole Ball** (film contribution 'Plenty Of Too Little') was a session man for numerous country acts and for around two decades played piano for Johnny Cash. Texas' retro-fied honky-tonk solo star, **Jimmie Dale Gilmore** (contributed three songs, 'Stop Saying Goodbye', 'What Kind Of Love' & 'Big Bad Love'), was an integral part of early 70s Lubbock outfot, the Flatliners (alongside Joe Ely); of interest film-wise was their reunion track for the 1998 movie 'The Horse Whisperer'. Louisiana Cajun artist, **Jo-El Sonnier** (songs in film, 'Plenty Of Too Little' & 'Never Did Say Goodbye') drifted easily into the country scene, his album 'Come On Joe' (1987), spreading his neo-traditionalist repertoire all over America, and beyond. Oklahoma kid, **Kevin Welch** was a gifted songwriter for a plethora of artists (Ricky Scaggs, Waylon Jennings) before he finally delivered his eponymous solo set for 'Reprise' records in 1990. Joker in the pack, **Webb Wilder** (a name taken from a short detective movie character of the 50s!) came out of the backwoods and into the rock'n'roll country limelight via debut 'Island' records album, 'Hybrid Vigor' (1989); follow-up sets, 'Doo Dad' (1991) and the twang-tastic 'It Came From Nashville' (1993), were easily plucked from Nashville's eccentric side. Four ladies of neo-country took up the slack on both the film and the OST: "Homeward Looking Angel" **Pam Tillis** (daughter of Mel Tillis) secured numerous country hits and a couple of splendid albums, 'Put Yourself In My Place' (1991) and the aforementioned 'Homeward . . .' (1992). **Trisha Yearwood** was by far – and still is! – one of country music's brightest stars, having kicked off her career with three Top 50 albums, 'Trisha Yearwood' (1991), 'Hearts In Armor' (1992) and 'The Song Remembers When' (1993); she was subsequently praised for her glorious hit, 'How Do I Live', in 1997. Country-pop acts, **Deborah Allen** and **Katy Moffatt** were also the genre's best-loved but not generally known acts outside the USA. *MCS*

—

Various Artists (score: G. Marq Roswell)

Sep 93. (cd/c) *Giant-Warners; <24497-2/-4>* ☐ ☐
– Dreaming with my eyes open (CLAY WALKER) / You'd be home by now (DARON NORWOOD) / I can't understand (TRISHA YEARWOOD) / I don't remember your name (but I remember you) (K.T. OSLIN) / Diamonds and tears (MATRACA BERG) / Ready and waiting (DEBORAH ALLEN) / Until now [*] (RODNEY CROWELL) / Looking for a thing called love (DENNIS ROBBINS) / Street of love [*] (KEVIN WELCH) / Partners in wine (RANDY TRAVIS) / Blame it on your heart (DEBORAH ALLEN) / Standing on a rock (RODNEY CROWELL). *[* not movie versions]*

S/track review: River Phoenix's last full-length feature is remembered with a lot of affection by his fans; the same, alas, can't be said of the soundtrack. Arbitrarily omitting valiant performances from the main actors – as well as a self-penned Phoenix composition – in favour of a bloodless New Country roundup, it brought down the wrath of film fans sick of soundtrack producers/ supervisors making a mockery of their intelligence. If the generally hackneyed standard of songwriting presented here is really what making it in Nashville is all about, can there be any real point? The evocative 'Partners In Wine' at least puts a semi-novel spin on the perennial theme of drowning your sorrows, with RANDY TRAVIS lamenting lyrics like "sailing a whiskey sea" and "George on the jukebox", in a smokehouse baritone that – uniquely on this album – kindles the blush of nostalgia. 'Streets Of Love' is one of the tracks berated for its re-recording but – vagabond clichés aside – KEVIN WELCH at least bears the gait of a genuine lone-wolf traditionalist. CLAY WALKER's 'Dreaming With My Eyes Open' is country-pop at its brightest, spiced with the bass counterpoint favoured by early-era Steve Earle, and onetime Guy Clark associate KT OSLIN supplies some on-screen country soul, but overall this is a case of too many hats spoiling the sorrow. *BG*

Album rating: *5.5

THINGS BEHIND THE SUN

2001 (US 118m TV) Echo Lake Productions / Sidekick Entertainment (R)

Film genre: psychological Rock music-based drama

Top guns: s-w: (+ dir) Allison Anders ← SUGAR TOWN ← GRACE OF MY HEART ← FOUR ROOMS ← GAS, FOOD LODGING ← BORDER RADIO, Kurt Voss ← SUGAR TOWN ← DELUSION ← BORDER RADIO / → DOWN AND OUT WITH THE DOLLS

Stars: Kim Dickens *(Sherry McGrale)* ← COMMITTED, Gabriel Mann *(Owen Richardson)* ← HIGH ART ← I SHOT ANDY WARHOL / → JOSIE AND THE PUSSYCATS, Eric Stoltz *(Dan)* ← GRACE OF MY HEART ← PULP FICTION ← SINGLES ← FAST TIMES AT RIDGEMONT HIGH, Rosanna Arquette *(Pete)* ← SUGAR TOWN ← BUFFALO '66 ← PULP FICTION ← MORE AMERICAN GRAFFITI, Don Cheadle *(Chuck)* ← BOOGIE NIGHTS ← ROADSIDE PROPHETS / → SWORDFISH, Elizabeth Pena *(Carmen)* ← LA BAMBA ← DOWN AND OUT IN BEVERLY HILLS ← TIMES SQUARE, Patsy Kensit *(Denise)* ← GRACE OF MY HEART ← ABSOLUTE BEGINNERS, Kai Lennox *(Colin)* ← SHAKE, RATTLE & ROLL: AN AMERICAN LOVE STORY ← SUGAR TOWN, the Sherry McGrale Band:- **J. Mascis** *(Erik)* ← GRACE OF MY HEART ← GAS, FOOD LODGING ← 1991: THE YEAR PUNK BROKE, **Jeff McDonald** *(Martin)* & **Steve McDonald** *(Fred)* <= REDD KROSS =>, Tom Caffey *(Alex)* // L.A. club band:- Cowboys & Indians:- Chad King & Josh Maynard / **Kristen Vigard** *(Sherry McGrale; singing voice)* ← GRACE OF MY HEART, Jade Gordon *(Sam)* ← SUGAR TOWN ← GRACE OF MY HEART

Storyline: Rock journalist Owen Richardson convinces his editor to do an article on troubled singer Sherry McGrale. Her personal life is dominated by drink and drugs although her music is beginning to be recognised nationally, especially her signature song about the horrific rape of a young woman. As Owen heads out for the interview, he knows that he is much more deeply involved with Sherry, and her song, than he has revealed. *JZ*

Movie rating: *7

Visual: dvd (no audio OST by SONIC YOUTH/JIM O'ROURKE)

Off the record: The Sherry McGrale Band were made up of "real" musicians, **J. Mascis** (Dinosaur Jr.), **Jeff & Steve McDonald** (REDD KROSS); Tom Caffey is the brother of Go-Go's musician Charlotte Coffey. *MCS*

30 DAYS UNTIL I'M FAMOUS

2004 (US 90m TV) Madacy Entertainment Group / VH-1 Television

Film genre: romantic showbiz/Pop-music comedy

Top guns: dir: Gabriela Tagliavini / s-w: Laura Angelica Simon

Stars: Camille Guaty *(Maggie Moreno)*, Sean Patrick Flanery *(Cole)* ← OVERNIGHT ← GIRL, Alanna Ubach *(Daisy Fresh)* ← PINK AS THE DAY SHE WAS BORN, Mindy Sterling *(Lupe Horowitz)*, Udo Kier *(Barry)* ← PIGS WILL FLY ← DANCER IN THE DARK ← NINA HAGEN = PUNK + GLORY ← the END OF VIOLENCE ← EVEN COWGIRLS GET THE BLUES ← SUSPIRIA, David Shackelford *(Christian)*, Carmen Electra *(cameo)*, **Scott Stapp** *(cameo)* ← WOODSTOCK '99

Storyline: Music talent-spotter Cole bets that he can turn anyone into a singer in a month. Enter Maggie, who'll get $40,000 if she becomes the next Latin pop star in the time allowed. When Cole decides she's not "Latin enough" his coaching makes her more "ethnic" and improves her singing and dancing. Meanwhile, rival Daisy Fresh is also out for the money and the pressure is on Maggie to adjust to her new persona and deal with Cole's increasingly romantic lessons before the deadline. *JZ*

Movie rating: *5

Visual: dvd (no audio OST; score: Douglas J. Cuomo)

Off the record: Scott Stapp is the frontman for post-grunge outfit, Creed, a band from Tallahassie, Florida who topped the chart in 1999 with 'With Arms Wide Open', taken from similarly-feted parent set, 'Human Clay'. *MCS*

THIS IS ELVIS

1981 (US 88m) Warner Bros. Pictures (PG)

Film genre: Rock'n'roll Musical biopic

Top guns: s-w + dir: Andrew Solt → IMAGINE: JOHN LENNON, Malcolm Leo → an AMERICAN BAND

Stars: David Scott *(Elvis at 18)*, Paul Boensch II *(Elvis at 10)*, Johnny Harra *(Elvis at 42)*, Dana MacKay *(Elvis at 35)*, Lawrence Koller *(Vernon Presley)*, Rhonda Lyn *(Priscilla Presley)*, Debbie Edge *(Gladys Presley)*, Larry Raspberry *(Dewey Phillips)*, **Furry Lewis** *(bluesman)*, Liz Robinson *(Minnie Mae Presley)*, Knox Phillips *(Sam Phillips)*, Jerry Phillips *(Bill Black)*, Emory Smith *(Scotty Moore)*, Andrea Cyrill *(Ginger Alden)*, Ral Donner *(voice; Elvis)*

Storyline: Elvis Presley biopic retelling the singer's life via a combination of acted reconstruction – including reminiscences from childhood – and original footage, all the way through his snake-hipped early appearances, post-war movie era, Vegas years and ignominious, self-destructive end. *MCS*

Movie rating: *7

Visual: video

Off the record: Furry Lewis was immortalised in song ('Furry Sings The Blues') by Joni Mitchell on her 1976 set, 'Hejira'. He died shortly after appearing in this movie; 14 Sep'81, Memphis, Tennessee. Knox Phillips played the part of his record producer dad, Sam Phillips, who instigated 'Sun' records. *MCS*

ELVIS PRESLEY (score: Walter Scharf)

Apr 81. (d-lp/d-c) *R.C.A.; <CPL 4031> (RCA LP/K 5029)* ☐ May81 47
– (Marie's the name) His latest flame / Moody blue / That's all right / Shake, rattle & roll, flip, flop & fly / Heartbreak hotel / Hound dog / (excerpt from Hy Gardner interview) / My baby left me / Merry Christmas baby / Mean woman blues / Don't be cruel / (Let me be your) Teddy bear / Jailhouse rock / (army swearing in) / G.I. blues / (excerpt from Departure For Germany press conference ("Elvis sails") / (excerpt from Home From Germany press conference) // Too much monkey business / Love me tender / I've got a thing about you baby / I need your love tonight / Blue suede shoes / Viva Las Vegas / Suspicious minds – (excerpt from J.C.'s Award To Elvis) / Promised land / (excerpt from Madison Square Garden press conference) / Always on my mind / Are you lonesome to-night? / My way / An American trilogy / Memories. *(re-iss. May84 d-lp/d-c; BL/BK 84031)*

S/track review: A double set of ELVIS greats from his 50s work right through to his final No.1, 'Moody Blue', which appears here as the second track! This is certainly an overview of ELVIS at his best and programmed randomly to counteract his chronologically-tracked '40 Greatest Hits' – a UK chart-topper in 1975 – or indeed the botched-up, Ronnie McDowell-voxed 'ELVIS' the movie of 1979. Complete with sharper than sharp TV introductions (from Ed Sullivan, Milton Berle and the Dorsey show) plus press conferences, 'THIS IS ELVIS' pulls no punches in getting to know the "real" ELVIS PRESLEY, not just the man shaking his pelvis behind a stand-up mic. With a plethora of ELVIS compilations flooding the market, this 4-sided posthumous contribution also unearthed some previously unheard song versions including 'Too Much Monkey Business' (from January 1968), 'Mean Woman Blues' (the unreleased movie version), 'Hound Dog' (from 1956), 'Don't Be Cruel' (featuring the Jordanaires), 'Shake, Rattle & Roll' (from '56), 'Heartbreak Hotel' (ditto) and 'Blue Suede Shoes' (from his 1968 TV special). Add to the pot 'Always On My Mind' (with J.D. Sumner and the Stamps on vocal accompaniment), 'Suspicious Minds' & 'An American Trilogy' (augmented as above, plus Kathy Westmoreland and the Sweet Inspirations), and you had something brilliant for collectors' or indeed any ELVIS buff. But by all accounts 'THIS IS ELVIS' is a compilation, as originals such as 'His Latest Flame', 'G.I. Blues', 'Viva Las Vegas', 'Are You Lonesome To-night?', 'Love Me Tender', 'Jailhouse Rock' and 'That's All Right' (his first recorded song for 'Sun' records in 1954) can testify. One can only hope for the CD version to be issued soon. *MCS*

Album rating: *6.5

THIS IS ENGLAND

2007 (UK 101m) Film Four / Optimum / Universal (18)

Film genre: coming-of-age drama

Top guns: s-w + dir: Shane Meadows ← TWENTYFOURSEVEN

Stars: Thomas Turgoose *(Shaun)*, Stephen Graham *(Combo)* ← REVENGERS TRAGEDY, Jo Hartley *(Cynthia Fields)*, Andrew Shim *(Milky)*, Joe Gilgun *(Woody)*, Vicky McClure *(Lol)*, Perry Benson *(Meggy)* ← SID & NANCY ← BIRTH OF THE BEATLES, George Newton *(Banjo)*, Frank Harper *(Lenny)* ← KEVIN & PERRY GO LARGE ← TWENTYFOURSEVEN

Storyline: Set in 1983, 12 year-old Shaun wanders the streets at the start of the school holidays. Still recovering from the loss of his dad in the Falklands War, he bumps into a group of skinheads who laugh and jeer at him for wearing old flares. But Shaun gives as good as he gets and impresses gang leader Woody who takes him under his wing. But the good times come to an end when vicious Combo is released from prison and steers the gang towards racial violence. *JZ*

Movie rating: *8

Visual: dvd

Off the record: Thomas Turgoose had never acted previously and was even banned from a school play for disruptive behaviour.

Various Artists (w/ "dialogue")

May 07. (cd) *Universal; (9848363)* ☐ –
– 54-46 was my number (TOOTS & THE MAYTALS) / Come on Eileen (DEXYS MIDNIGHT RUNNERS) / Tainted love (SOFT CELL) / "Underpass – Flares" / Nicole – instrumental (GRAVENHURST) / "Cynth – Dad" / Morning sun (AL BARRY & THE CIMARONS) / "Shoe shop" / Louie Louie

(TOOTS & THE MAYTALS) / Pressure drop (TOOTS & THE MAYTALS) / "Hair in cafe" / Do the dog (the SPECIALS) / Ritonare (LUDOVICO EINAUDI) / "This is England" / Return of Django (the UPSETTERS) / Warhead (UK SUBS) / Fuori dal mondo (LUDOVICO EINAUDI) / Since yesterday (STRAWBERRY SWITCHBLADE) / "Tits" / The dark end of the street (PERCY SLEDGE) / Oltremare – edit (LUDOVICO EINAUDI) / Please please please let me get what I want (CLAYHILL) / Dietro casa (LUDOVICO EINAUDI). *(bonus from film trailer +=)* – Never seen the sea (GAVIN CLARK).

S/track review: More than just an exercise in nostalgia, the soundtrack for Shane Meadows' 'THIS IS ENGLAND' attempts to reflect the diversity of 80s youth culture, with all its tribal divisions and their distinct musical identities, while re-evaluating the belief that skinheads were no more than right-wing thugs. As Meadows states in the liner notes, original skinheads "listened to a lot of black music", and they certainly must have good taste if the three TOOTS & THE MAYTALS tracks here are representative. Any soundtrack that includes their 'Pressure Drop' already has a head start, and opening with their '54-46 Was My Number' sets the bar estimably high. Thankfully, the quality is maintained throughout, Meadows never sacrificing visceral pop thrills for diversity's sake alone. So although famous pop tracks by DEXYS MIDNIGHT RUNNERS and SOFT CELL are easy shorthand for establishing the right milieu (used time and time again for instant 80s atmosphere), this soundtrack is more than just another synergistic collection. In the grand tradition of 'QUADROPHENIA' and 'TRAINSPOTTING', 'THIS IS ENGLAND' can seem guilty of packaging and/or fetishising the skinhead culture for new generations, but the melancholy piano pieces by LUDOVICO EINAUDI do a good job of qualifying any unchecked nostalgia, just as Meadows' film ultimately undermines the attraction of the emergent right-wing ideology. EINAUDI's music, created for the film, is pared down but still melodically strong, understated but affecting. The minimalist piano of his 'Fuori Dal Mondo' ('Outside From the World') has a refrain which brings to mind Radiohead's 'Street Spirit (Fade Out)' and his 'Oltremare' ('Overseas') seems to subtly quote the melody from David Bowie's 'Ashes to Ashes'. Whether or not this is true, it does reflect the hidden charms that reward repeated listens. Choosing a less overused SPECIALS track with 'Do The Dog' is a wise move, while Scottish duo STRAWBERRY SWITCHBLADE's 'Since Yesterday' is a good one-hit wonder to revisit (although it came out two years after the movie was set). Including clips of dialogue is always a risky move, and while it's sometimes interesting to hear the songs in the context of the movie, and the script is full of gems like "I only didn't suck your tits cause I've never done it before", with repeated listens they become distracting and irritating. The only other serious misstep in an otherwise great soundtrack is CLAYHILL's lumpen cover of 'Please Please Please Let Me Get What I Want', which substitutes sublime melancholia for James Morrison-esque warblestrum. All in all a brilliant reflection of a time before the commodification/americanisation of youth culture, and full of unmistakably great tunes too. *SW*

Album rating: *8

THIS IS SPINAL TAP

1984 (US 82m) Mainline / Embassy (R)

Film genre: Hard rock-music mockumentary/comedy

Top guns: s-w: Rob Reiner (+ dir) → the PRINCESS BRIDE → the STORY OF US, Michael McKean, Christopher Guest, Harry Shearer

Stars: Christopher Guest *(Nigel Tufnel)* ← the LONG RIDERS ← DEATH WISH / → LITTLE SHOP OF HORRORS → the PRINCESS BRIDE → a MIGHTY WIND, Michael McKean *(David St. Hubbins)* → LIGHT OF DAY → EARTH GIRLS ARE EASY → AIRHEADS → GIGANTIC (A TALE OF TWO JOHNS) → a MIGHTY WIND, Harry Shearer *(Derek Smalls)* ← ONE-TRICK PONY ← ANIMALYMPICS / → WAYNE'S WORLD 2 → GHOST DOG: THE WAY OF THE SAMURAI → GIGANTIC (A TALE OF TWO JOHNS) → a MIGHTY WIND, Rob Reiner *(Marty DiBergi)* → PRIMARY COLORS → the STORY OF US, R.J. Parnell *(Mick Shrimpton)*, Tony Hendra *(Ian Faith)*, David Kaff *(Viv Savage)*, Bruno Kirby *(Tommy Pischedda)* ← WHERE THE BUFFALO ROAM ← ALMOST SUMMER / → BIRDY → GOOD MORNING, VIETNAM → the BASKETBALL DIARIES → a SLIPPING-DOWN LIFE, Ed Begley, Jr. *(John "Stumpy" Pepys)* ← GET CRAZY ← ELVIS: THE MOVIE ← RECORD CITY / → STREETS OF FIRE → EVEN COWGIRLS GET THE BLUES → a MIGHTY WIND, **Danny Kortchmar** *(Ronnie Pudding)*, **Russ Kunkel** *(Eric "Stumpy Joe" Childs)*, Fran Drescher *(Bobbi Flekman)* ← AMERICAN HOT WAX ← SATURDAY NIGHT FEVER / → ROCK'N'ROLL MOM → UHF, Dana Carvey *(mime waiter)* → WAYNE'S WORLD → WAYNE'S WORLD 2, Anjelica Huston *(Polly Deutsch)* → GOOD TO GO → BUFFALO 66, Robin Mencken *(Angelo's associate)* ← THANK GOD IT'S FRIDAY ← FOOLS ← the STRAWBERRY STATEMENT / → BODY ROCK, Fred Willard *(Lt. Hookstratten)* ← MODEL SHOP / → HOW HIGH → a MIGHTY WIND → KILLER DILLER, Billy Crystal *(Morty the Mime)*, Charles Levin *(Disc'n'Dat manager)* ← HONEYSUCKLE ROSE, Howard Hesseman *(Terry Ladd)* ← STEELYARD BLUES

Storyline: The trials and tribulations of life as a struggling British metal band undertaking a ruinous US 'Smell The Glove' tour. Stonehenge stage props, cucumbers down trousers, amps that went up to 11 (!), drummers dying in "bizarre gardening accidents" – in fact every metal cliché in the book (and some that weren't) are exploited in such hilariously deadpan style that many moviegoers were convinced they were watching a real-life rockumentary. *MCS*

Movie rating: *9

Visual: video + dvd

Off the record: SPINAL TAP er ... the "real" story. Formed – not in London's Squatney District out of mid-60s skiffle acts, the Creatures and the Lovely Lads – but the late 70s as a razor-sharp satire on the inherent absurdity of the metal scene by American comedy writers (see above & below). Initially activated for a TV sketch, the idea was transformed into this celebrated full-length feature film. Although the movie was a relative failure at the time, 'TAP have since become a rock'n'roll institution and a comeback set was inevitable. Featuring such luminaries as JEFF BECK, Slash, Joe Satriani and CHER (along with new recruits C.J. Vanston on keyboards and Ric Shrimpton on drums), 'Break Like The Wind' (1992), brought the band belated chart success, scraping into the lower regions of the UK and US charts. Although there wasn't a movie sequel as such to complement the album, fans could relive those spandex-clad 80s days with such wonderfully unreconstructed fare as 'Bitch School', incredibly a UK Top 40 hit. Check out the accompanying tour video, 'Return Of Spinal Tap', essential viewing for anyone with delusions of metal grandeur. Many will recognise them and their shenanigans in a further bout of mockumentary madness, 'a MIGHTY WIND' (2003). *MCS*

—

SPINAL TAP

Apr 84. (lp/c) *Polydor; <(817 846-1/-4)>* ☐ Sep84 ☐
– Hell hole / Tonight I'm gonna rock you tonight / Heavy duty / Rock and roll creation / America / Cups and cakes / Big bottom / Sex farm / Stonehenge / Gimme some money / (Listen to the) Flower people. *(UK-iss.Mar89 on 'Priority' lp/c; LUS LP/MC 2) (cd-iss. Aug90; 817 846-2) <(cd re-iss. Oct00 +=; 549075-2)>* – Christmas with the Devil (2 versions).

S/track review: To many the funniest movie of all time, it still surprises me to this day, how – next to every "real" hard-rock & metal act around at the time – this album stands head and shoulders above them all, bar of course a few Iron Maiden and Def Leppard sets. It surprises one more that the screenwriter/director (Rob Reiner) and 3/4 of the main cast (MICHAEL McKEAN, CHRISTOPHER GUEST and HARRY SHEARER) wrote and performed all the songs – now that's talent! The lads were indeed "having a laugh", as the OTT lyrics suggest. Take opener, 'Hell Hole', a strange kind of Deep Purple track in everything but name, Gillan, Blackmore & Co would've probably sued – if they'd stop laughing. 'Tonight I'm Gonna Rock You Tonight' (love the grammar) probably unmasks, Kiss-like, SPINAL TAP's Stateside credentials big time, that ZZ guitar riff and wailing organ worth getting out your old leather breeks from the side of the wardrobe. Getting back to reality, tongue-in-proverbial-cheek-wise at least, 'Heavy Duty' could well have graced an Alice Cooper or Johnny Winter set; fictitiously it was from SPINAL TAP's 1975 LP, 'Bent For The Rent'. 'Rock And Roll Creation' harked back to the darker days of Black Sabbath; a segue'd Who/'Tommy'-like interlude giving it that subtle-as-a-sledgehammer appeal. Track five, 'America', is lyrically all of that country rolled into one Big bad Apple pie, while 'Cups And Cakes' (supposedly Tap-ped back to the 60s) sounds remarkably like Status Quo when they were a bubblegum Traffic Jam. The funniest track for me is undoubtably 'Big Bottom', verses such as " . . . Drive me out of my mind, How can I leave this behind?" and "My baby fits me like a flesh tuxedo, I love to sink her with my pink torpedo", pure unadulterated aural slapstick. 'Sex Farm', as you can imagine was more of the same, "Getting out my pitchfork, poking your hedge", just about said it all. The mystical 'Stonehenge' was the visual highlight of the movie and best experienced in front of a TV monitor. Having said that, the mind's eye takes you there with all its comical little-people imagery, prog-folk, et al (er, see the film first). To end the show, hard-rock and make-shift metal makes way for SPINAL TAP and their 60s beat-sound on 'Stones-esque 'Gimme Some Money' and the Gene Pitney-cloned '(Listen To The) Flower People'. Truly the greatest band that never was – or was it? Forget Ten-acious D, and turn the volume up a notch to Eleven-acious D. *MCS*

Album rating: *8.5

□ Rufus THOMAS segment
(⇒ MYSTERY TRAIN)

□ Jon Mikl THOR segment
(⇒ ROCK'N'ROLL NIGHTMARE)

THUNDER ALLEY

1967 (US 90m) American International Pictures (PG-13)

Film genre: sports drama

Top guns: dir: Richard Rush / s-w: Sy Salkowitz

Stars: FABIAN *(Tommy Callahan)*, **ANNETTE Funicello** *(Francie Madsen)*, Diane McBain *(Annie Blaine)*, Warren Berlinger *(Eddie Sands)*, Jan Murray *(Pete Madsen)*, Stanley Adams *(Mac Lunsford)*, Maureen Arthur *(Babe)*, Kip King *(Don)*, Sandy Reed *(announcer)*, Michael T. Mikler *(Harry Wise)*, **Frankie AVALON** *(himself)*, Luree Holmes *(Luree)* ← the GHOST IN THE INVISIBLE BIKINI ← HOW TO STUFF A WILD BIKINI ← SKI PARTY ← BEACH BLANKET BINGO ← PAJAMA PARTY ← BIKINI BEACH ← MUSCLE BEACH PARTY ← BEACH PARTY / → the TRIP, Salli Sachse ← the GHOST IN THE INVISIBLE BIKINI ← HOW TO STUFF A WILD BIKINI ← SKI PARTY ← BEACH BLANKET BINGO ← PAJAMA PARTY ← BIKINI BEACH ← MUSCLE BEACH PARTY / → the TRIP → WILD IN THE STREETS, Mary Hughes ← HOW TO STUFF A WILD BIKINI ← SKI PARTY ← BEACH BLANKET BINGO ← PAJAMA PARTY ← BIKINI BEACH ← MUSCLE BEACH PARTY / → DOUBLE TROUBLE

Storyline: Stock car racer Tommy Callahan's career comes unstuck when he suffers a blackout on the track and causes a fatal accident. Reduced to working as a circus stunt driver, Tommy soon falls for fiery Francie, the circus owner's daughter, to the annoyance of ex-girlfriend Annie, who promptly dates rival driver Eddie. The two jealous speedsters vie for supremacy on and off the track but Tommy knows another blackout may be just around the corner. *JZ*

Movie rating: *4.5

Visual: video

Off the record: (see own entries)

Various Artists (md: MIKE CURB) (& the SIDEWALK SOUNDS *)

Mar 67. (lp; mono/stereo) *Sidewalk; <T/ST 5902>* □ [-]
– Theme from Thunder Alley (the BAND WITHOUT A NAME) / Riot in Thunder Alley (EDDIE BERAM) / What's a girl to do (ANNETTE) / Pete's orgy (*) / Mud fight (*) / Time after time (I keep lovin' you) (the BAND WITHOUT A NAME) / Calahan's theme (the LORRAINE SINGERS) / Calahan's march (*) / When you get what you want (ANNETTE) / Calahan's vision (*) / Annie's theme (*) / Theme from Thunder Alley (*).

S/track review: 'THUNDER ALLEY' was under the direction of MIKE CURB, who'd recently supplied another road-themed movie, 'The WILD ANGELS'. The first to come out from under his wing were the BAND WITHOUT A NAME, a thrilling quintet (featuring songwriters Guy Hemric & Jerry Styner) who contributed the Searchers/Hollies-like 'Theme From . . .' and 'Time After Time (I Keep Lovin' You)'. Bypassing the long-forgotten ANNETTE (on flop single, 'What's A Girl To Do' and its dreamy B-side 'When You Get What You Want') plus the smoove Fifth Dimension-esque LORRAINE SINGERS ('Calahan's Theme'), exactly half of the LP is snatched by the SIDEWALK SOUNDS, aka CURB and session people. While 'Mud Fight' is both clumsy and saxy and 'Calahan's March' is full of pomp and circumstance, 'Pete's Orgy' – frenzied fuzz guitar precursing Iron Butterfly – is the faceless outfit at its best; they close the show with their take on the 'Theme From . . .'. Before you think, there's one act I've not mentioned, it's because I've saved the best till last. The unknown EDDIE BERAM. The off-kilter gem 'Riot In Thunder Alley' (a sort of surf-rock-cum-hot-rod instrumental with a twist of Sandy Nelson!) is worth the ticket-price alone, with its raging guitars, psychedelic sitar and oh boy 'Let There Be Drums'). While BERAM (one is told) sessioned for the Mike Curb-managed October Country, little did he know that Quentin Tarantino – searching for that elusive, exclusive obscurity – stuck the track on his 'Death Proof' movie in 2007. *MCS*

Album rating: *4.5

– spinoff hits, etc. –

ANNETTE: What's A Girl To Do / When You Get What You Want
Mar 67. (7") *Tower; <T 326>* □ [-]

THUNDERSTRUCK

2004 (Aus 98m) AFFC / Icon / Eddie Wong / Wildheart Films (M)

Film genre: coming-of-age comedy drama

Top guns: s-w: (+ dir) Darren Ashton, Shaun Angus Hall

Stars: Damon Gameau *(Sonny)*, Stephen Curry *(Ben)*, Ryan Johnson *(Lloyd)*, Callan Mulvey *(Sam)*, Sam Worthington *(Ronnie)* → SOMERSAULT, Rachel Gordon *(Molly)*, Kestie Morassi *(Amy)*, Saskia Burmeister *(Chloe)*, Boyana Novakovitch *(Anna)*, Jason Gann *(Robbo)*, Shaun Angus Hall *(Simmo)*, Al Clark *(Gary Geffen)* → 30 CENTURY MAN, **Ella Hooper** *(herself)*

Storyline: Set in 1991, five Ac/Dc fans (after witnessing a gig on the Sydney leg of the Razor's Edge tour) survive a near-death experience. This prompts them to sign a pledge which would enable the surviving four to bury the first to die, beside the graveside of their Ac/Dc icon, Bon Scott. Twelve years on, putting mundane jobs and activities aside, they hold to their motto of "Break every rule but never break a promise" when one is er "Thunderstruck" by a bolt of lightning. *MCS*

Movie rating: *6

Visual: Warner Home Video/DVD

Off the record: Ironically, one of the members of the fan group, Callan Mulvey, was nearly killed in a car accident after filming this movie; he's since returned to acting (early 2007) in a couple of episodes of Australian TV soap 'Home And Away'. **Ella Hooper** fronts the post-grunge band Killing Heidi, alongside her guitarist (older) brother, Jesse. At the turn of the millennium the youngsters had a massive Australian No.1 with their second single, 'Mascara', taken from their platinum-selling debut set, 'Reflector' (2000); a bit of a "killing joke" outside of their antipodean roots. *MCS*

—

Various (score: DAVID THRUSSELL & FRANCOIS TETAZ *)

May 04. (cd) *Columbia; (5160072000)* [–] Aus [–]
– Long way to the top (the JACK) / Run to paradise (DAVID CAMPBELL) / Living in the city (the CASANOVAS) / Smoke on the water (SEÑOR COCONUT AND HIS ORCHESTRA) / Hello how are you (AUDIUS AND CARMEL MERCITI) / Take it (KILLING HEIDI) / TNT (HAYSEED DIXIE) / The quest (*) / Spousal abuse (PEGGY SCOTT ADAMS) / Total eclipse of the heart (the THUNDERSTRUCK BOYS) / Total eclipse of the heart (BONNIE TYLER) / Good times medley (*) / Final countdown (EUROPE) / High test love (SCOOTER LEE) / Drop kick me Jesus (the BLACKEYED SUSANS) / Boys in action (*) / Jupiter's landscape (BON SCOTT AND FRATERNITY) / Robbo and Simmo (*) / Crash and burn (the JACK).

S/track review: There are two things fundamentally wrong with 'THUNDERSTRUCK'. Firstly, for a movie about a group of Ac/Dc lovin' guys, there is a distinct lack of actual Ac/Dc songs. Unless you count the version of 'Long Way To The Top' performed by the movie's fictional band, the JACK, which, based on the available evidence, suggests that the way to the top for this band (if they are in fact real) just got a whole lot longer. The second problem is that the dubious award of best track on the album could be a tie between EUROPE's 'Final Countdown' and BONNIE TYLER's 'Total Eclipse Of The Heart', a fact that is rather embarrassing, especially for an album that is supposed to be "rock'n'roll". There are one or two highlights though, including the CASANOVAS' 'Living In The City' and 'Jupiter's Landscape' by BON SCOTT with his pre-Ac/Dc band, the FRATERNITY. The former is a straightforward RnR number heavily inspired by you-know-who, while the latter is a luscious piece of folk-rock with an irresistible piano melody. As for the rest, the less said the better. However, there are several comic redneck-type tracks such as 'TNT' (yes, Ac/Dc's classic) by, say it fast now, HAYSEED DIXIE and 'High Test Love' by SCOOTER LEE – just downright weird. A special mention in the surreal stakes has to go to the quite frankly bizarre version of 'Smoke On The Water' from SEÑOR COCONUT AND HIS ORCHESTRA (a German, surprisingly enough), who manages to turn the Deep Purple staple into something that could inspire a samba. But overall, 'THUNDERSTRUCK' is a bit under the weather. *CM*

Album rating: *4.5

TICKLE ME

1965 (US 90m) Allied Artists Pictures (PG)

Film genre: Pop/Rock Musical – western comedy

Top guns: dir: Norman Taurog ← IT HAPPENED AT THE WORLD'S FAIR ← GIRLS! GIRLS! GIRLS! ← BLUE HAWAII ← G.I. BLUES / → SPINOUT → DOUBLE TROUBLE → SPEEDWAY → LIVE A LITTLE, LOVE A LITTLE / s-w: Elwood Ullman → the GHOST IN THE INVISIBLE BIKINI, Edward Bernds

Stars: Elvis PRESLEY *(Lonnie Beale)*, Julie Adams *(Vera Radford)* → BLACK ROSES, Jocelyn Lane *(Pam Merritt)*, Jack Mullaney *(Stanley Potter)* → SPINOUT → LITTLE BIG MAN, Merry Anders *(Estelle Penfield)*, Connie Gilchrist *(Hilda)* ← SWINGIN' ALONG, Barbara Werle *(Barbara)* → HARUM SCARUM → CHARRO!, Linda Rogers *(Clair Kincannon)* ← PAJAMA PARTY ← BIKINI BEACH ← BEACH PARTY / → WINTER A-GO-GO → WILD, WILD WINTER, Merry Anders *(Estelle Penfield)* ← CALYPSO HEAT WAVE, Laurie Burton *(Janet)* → BLACK MAMA, WHITE MAMA

Storyline: A singing rodeo star finds unlikely employment on an all-female health ranch. While his womanising ways see him served with the boot, he subsequently helps one of the dames escape from baddies on the hunt for hidden loot. *BG*

Movie rating: *4

Visual: video + dvd

Off the record: nothing

—

ELVIS PRESLEY

Aug 05. (cd) *Sony; (8287670305-2)* [ ] [–]
– I feel that I've known you forever / Slowly but surely / Night rider / Put the blame on me / Dirty, dirty feeling / It feels so right / (Such an) Easy question / Long lonely highway / I'm yours (undubbed) / Something blue / Make me know it / Just for old time sake / Gonna get back home somehow / There's always me / Allied Artists' radio trailer (version 1) / Slowly but surely (take 1) / It feels so right (take 2) / I'm yours (LP master) / Long lonely highway (LP master) / I feel that I've known you forever (take 3) / Night rider (take 5) / Dirty, dirty feeling (take 1) / Put the blame on me (take 1 & 2) / Easy question / Allied Artists' radio trailer (version 2).

S/track review: Compiled from two extended EP's (9 songs) released in 1965, plus a plethora of alternate cues and film outtakes, ELVIS' 'TICKLE ME' was finally marketed by 'Sony-BMG/RCA', who also housed the soundtrack in a 7"x7" cover/sleeve. The CD opens with slow crooner, 'I Feel That I've Known You Forever', while follow-on number 'Slowly But Surely' raises the pulse a little via a rock'n'roll fuzz guitar. What one's got to remember here, is that most of the 'TICKLE ME' tracks were recorded between 1960-1963, lying dormant until thought neccessary to unleash to the ELVIS fanbase. Having provided the opening song, songwriters Doc Pomus & Mort Shuman supplied a further two cuts, the upbeat 'Night Rider' and the single master of '(It's A) Long Lonely Highway'; the bonus track, 'Gonna Get Back Home Somehow', might've found its way onto a suggested Colonel Tom Parker LP, alongside the likes of 'Something Blue', 'Make Me Know It', 'Just For Old Time Sake' and 'There's Always Me'. Nearly a US Top 50 hit in its own right and first track on the 'Vol.2' EP, 'It Feels So Right' (the B-side to hit 45, '(Such An) Easy Feeling'), is one of ELVIS's better songs here, its cool twang something of a relief that the King had not lost his rock'n'roll crown. It's a pity this wasn't released as an LP in '65, because it's certainly one of ELVIS's best soundtracks. While Leiber-Stoller got their usual two-penneth in via 'Dirty, Dirty Feeling', there's also the sedate and melancholy side of the man on 'I'm Yours'. *MCS*

Album rating: *6

– spinoff hits, etc. –

ELVIS PRESLEY: (Such An) Easy Question / It Feels So Right

Jun 65. (7") *<47-8585>* [11] [55] [–]

ELVIS PRESLEY: Tickle Me Volume 1

Jul 65. (7"ep) *R.C.A.; <EPA 4383> (RCX 7173)* [70] [ ]
– I feel that I've known you forever / Night rider / Slowly but surely / Dirty, dirty feeling / Put the blame on me.

ELVIS PRESLEY: I'm Yours / (It's A) Long, Lonely Highway

Aug 65. (7") *<47-8657>* [11] [–]

ELVIS PRESLEY: Tickle Me Volume 2

Aug 65. (7"ep) *R.C.A.; (RCX 7174)* [–] [ ]
– I'm yours / (It's a) Long, lonely highway / It feels so right / (Such an) Easy question.

ELVIS PRESLEY: Tickle Me – Original Soundtrack (re-mastered)

Jun 02. (lp) *Castle; (ELVIS 113)* [–] [ ]
– (9 tracks from above re-organised + 11 other takes).

a TIME TO SING

1968 (US 91m) Metro-Goldwyn-Mayer (PG-13)

Film genre: Country/C&W Musical drama

Top guns: dir: Arthur Dreifuss ← RIOT ON SUNSET STRIP / s-w: Robert E. Kent ← the FASTEST GUITAR ALIVE ← WHEN THE BOYS MEET THE GIRLS ← GET YOURSELF A COLLEGE GIRL ← HOOTENANNY HOOT ← DON'T KNOCK THE TWIST ← TWIST AROUND THE CLOCK ← DON'T KNOCK THE ROCK ← ROCK AROUND THE CLOCK, Orville H. Hampton ← RIOT ON SUNSET STRIP ← CALYPSO HEAT WAVE / → FRIDAY FOSTER

Stars: Hank WILLIAMS Jr. *(Grady Dodd)*, Shelley Fabares *(Amy Carter)* ← CLAMBAKE ← SPINOUT ← HOLD ON! ← GIRL HAPPY ← RIDE THE WILD SURF ← SUMMER LOVE ← ROCK, PRETTY BABY, Ed Begley *(Kermit Dodd)* ← WILD IN THE STREETS, Charles Robinson *(Shifty Barker)*, D'Urville Martin *(Luke Harper)* → WATERMELON MAN → the FINAL COMEDOWN → HELL UP IN HARLEM → BOOK OF NUMBERS → BLACK CAESAR → the SOUL OF NIGGER CHARLEY → FIVE ON THE BLACK HAND SIDE → SHEBA, BABY → DOLEMITE → DISCO 9000, Donald Woods *(Vernon Carter)* ← KISSIN' COUSINS, **Clara Ward** *(herself)* → IT'S YOUR THING, Dick Haynes *(M.C.)*

Storyline: With a dictatorial uncle called Kermit, it's not surprising Grady Dodd has dreams of a music biz escape route. When Kermit squanders the housekeeping in a card game, it's left to Grady – fresh from scooping first prize in a supermarket-sponsored talent contest – to earn some money by singing on local TV show. Moving on to Nashville, Dodd ultimately secures a record deal and hits the big time. *BG*

Movie rating: *4

Visual: video

Off the record: Clara Ward was a gospel singer.

HANK WILLIAMS JR. (composer: Fred Karger)

Oct 68. (lp) *M.G.M.; <SE 4540ST>* [ ] [–]
– A time to sing / Next time I say goodbye I'm leaving / Old before my time / Rock in my shoe / Money can't buy happiness / Man is on his own / There's gotta be much more to life than you / It's all over but the crying / Give me the hummingbird line / A time to sing.

S/track review: With a soundtrack for 'YOUR CHEATIN' HEART' (1964) already under his belt, HANK WILLIAMS JR. wasn't long in being earmarked for an 'M.G.M.' extravaganza of his own. On the same basic premise they'd rehashed countless times with Elvis, WILLIAMS JR was transformed from country hick to major label star, a plot which rang fairly true in Elvis' case but not in HANK's. Unlike PRESLEY, he'd been destined for the Grand Ole Opry since birth; 'a TIME TO SING' was the culmination of a youth spent in his father's tortured footsteps. While he and Presley shared both a lugubrious baritone and a similar turn of phrase (and even the same leading lady in Shelley Fabares, fresh from playing the King's bit of rich in 'SPINOUT'), their careers were heading in opposite directions, almost meeting in the middle as Elvis progressed from rocker-gone-Hollywood to Vegas crooner and WILLIAMS JR. went from pliable country heir to expectation-busting Southern rocker. As a genre, the pop musical was way past its sell-by date in 1968, but their respective soundtracks from that year are more listenable than they have a right to be, especially HANK's. If you're more familiar with the man's 70s/80s outlaw persona, you might have a hard time recognising these ballads as sung by the same guy, yet ignore the obligatory cod-celestial backing singers/strings – as well as the generic Fabares-sung number – and there are a few weeping glories here. While 'Old Before My Time' verges on country rock and 'Money Can't Buy Happiness' parlays the kind of above-average honky tonk of which papa would've approved, the self-penned 'It's All Over But The Crying' proves WILLIAMS JR. is more than just a contrary chip off the old block; it's his movie character's breakthrough and – in another case of life mirroring art – stands as one of his biggest hits of the decade. Over guitar and pedal steel, 'A Man Is On His Own' articulates both his story so far and his identity crisis to come, while 'Give Me The Hummingbird Line' not altogether successfully combines bluegrass ramble and Nashville Sound gloss. Unsurprisingly, the most Presley-esque presentation is reserved for the title track; fans of Hollywood Elvis will be singing it in the shower. *BG*

Album rating: *5.5

TIMES SQUARE

1980 (US 111m) Robert Stigwood Productions (R)

Film genre: coming-of-age/teen Rock-music movie

Top guns: dir: Allan Moyle → PUMP UP THE VOLUME → EMPIRE RECORDS → MAN IN THE MIRROR: THE MICHAEL JACKSON STORY(+ story w/ Leanne Unger) / s-w: Jacob Brackman

Stars: Tim Curry *(Johnny LaGuardia)* ← ROCK FOLLIES OF '77 ← the ROCKY HORROR PICTURE SHOW / → LEGEND → the WALL: LIVE IN BERLIN → JACKIE'S BACK!, Trini Alvarado *(Pamela Pearl)* → SATISFACTION, Robin Johnson *(Nicky Marotta)*, Peter Coffield *(David Pearl)*, David Margulies *(Dr. Zymabsky)* → MAGIC STICKS → CANDY MOUNTAIN → LOOKING FOR AN ECHO, Herbert Berghof *(Dr. Huber)*, Anna Maria Horsford *(Rosie Washington)* → HOW HIGH → BROKEN BRIDGES, Michael Margotta *(JoJo)* ← the STRAWBERRY STATEMENT ← WILD IN THE STREETS, J.C. Quinn *(Simon)* → MAXIMUM OVERDRIVE, Elizabeth Pena *(disco hostess)* → DOWN AND OUT IN BEVERLY HILLS → LA BAMBA → STRANGELAND → THINGS BEHIND THE SUN, Steve James *(dude)* → TO LIVE AND DIE IN L.A.

Storyline: Angst-ridden teen drama as two adolescent inmates of a mental institution escape to the mean streets of New York against the backdrop of an insurgent US punk scene. *BG*

Movie rating: *4.5

Visual: video + dvd

Off the record: (see below)

Various Artists

Sep 80. (d-lp) *R.S.O.; <RS-2-4203> (2685 145)* [37] Oct80 [ ]
– Rock hard (SUZI QUATRO) / Talk of the town (the PRETENDERS) / Same old scene (ROXY MUSIC) / Down in the park (GARY NUMAN) / Help me! (MARCY LEVY & ROBIN GIBB) / Life during wartime (TALKING HEADS) / Pretty boys (JOE JACKSON) / Take this town (XTC) / I wanna be sedated (the RAMONES) / Damn dog (ROBIN JOHNSON) // Your daughter is one (ROBIN JOHNSON & TRINI ALVARADO) / Babylon's burning (the RUTS) / You can't hurry love (D.L. BYRON) / Walk on the wild side (LOU REED) / The night was not (DESMOND CHILD & ROUGE) / Innocent, not guilty (GARLAND JEFFREYS) / Grinding halt (the CURE) / Pissing in the river (PATTI SMITH GROUP) / Flowers in the city (DAVID JOHANSEN & ROBIN JOHNSON) / Damn dog – reprise – the Cleo club (ROBIN JOHNSON).

S/track review: Another Robert Stigwood effort and a damn sight more palatable than his Beatles debacle of two years previous ('SGT.

PEPPER'S LONELY HEARTS CLUB BAND'). An impressive cast of new wave and punky scenesters (the likes of GARLAND JEFFREYS, MARCY LEVY & ROBIN GIBB notwithstanding) were lined up across four sides of the original vinyl, with highlights from TALKING HEADS ('Life During Wartime'), GARY NUMAN ('Down In The Park'), the RAMONES ('I Wanna Be Sedated'), the CURE ('Grinding Halt') the RUTS ('Babylon's Burning') and LOU REED ('Walk On The Wild Side'). Although JOE JACKSON's 'Pretty Boys' was not his greatest 3-mins by any manner of means, there were a few "pretty girls" on show: SUZI QUATRO ('Rock Hard'), Chrissie Hynde's PRETENDERS ('Talk Of The Town'), er . . . PATTI SMITH Group ('Pissing In The River') and actress ROBIN JOHNSON ('Damn Dog', 'Your Daughter Is Gone' w/ fellow actress TRINI ALVARADO and 'Flowers In The City' w/ ex-New York Doll DAVID JOHANSEN). Alongside XTC ('Take This Town') and a revamped ROXY MUSIC ('Same Old Scene'), 'TIMES SQUARE' turkeys go to D.L. BYRON covering 'You Can't Hurry Love' and DESMOND CHILD & ROUGE (augmented by three female singers) with 'The Night Was Not'; the latter was the shape of things to come in the mediocre 80s. *MCS*

Album rating: *6.5

– spinoff hits, etc. –

MARCY LEVY & ROBIN GIBB: Help Me! / (instrumental)

Oct 80. (7") *<1047> (RSO 65)* [50] Nov80 [ ]

XTC: Take This Town / the RUTS: Babylon's Burning

Dec 80. (7") *(RSO 71)* [–] [ ]

TO HELL AND BACK

MEAT LOAF: TO HELL AND BACK

2000 (US 87m TV) VH-1 Television / Viacom (PG-13)

Film genre: Pop-Rock drama/biopic

Top guns: dir: Jim McBride ← GREAT BALLS OF FIRE! / s-w: Ron McGee ← DAYDREAM BELIEVERS: THE MONKEES STORY

Stars: W. Earl Brown *(Meat Loaf)* → KILLER DILLER, Dedee Pfeiffer *(Leslie)*, Zachary Throne *(Jim Steinman)*, Tom Wood *(Kevin Frears)*, Lisa Jane Persky *(Wilma Aday)* ← GREAT BALLS OF FIRE! ← AMERICAN POP ← KISS MEETS THE PHANTOM OF THE PARK, Kim Robillard *(Wes Aday)*, **Scott Baldyga** *(guitarist)*, Emmy Collins *(Gregg Allman)* → ALMOST FAMOUS → ROCK STAR, Jesse Lenat *(Todd Rundgren)* ← WENT TO CONEY ISLAND ON A MISSION FROM GOD . . . BE BACK BY FIVE, Keith Allan *(Tim Curry)*

Storyline: Meat Loaf (aka Marvin Lee Aday) gets the biopic star treatment here. From an obese child raised by his mother (who was dying of cancer) and bullied by his alcoholic dad, Dallas-born Marvin catapults to stardom via a meeting with gothic-rock songwriter, Jim Steinman. His classic, anthemic rock opus, 'Bat Out Of Hell' (produced by another great, Todd Rundgren), made Meat Loaf the star he was destined to be. *MCS*

Movie rating: *6

Visual: dvd (no audio OST)

Off the record: Meat Loaf lookalike, W. Earl Brown, performed in a band billed as the Sacred Cowboys, with amongst others, director Peter Spirer. **Scott Baldyga** played keyboards with Ziggy Marley (son of Bob). Emmy Collins is the son of top author, Jackie Collins. See **MEAT LOAF** entry for his bio/filmography. *MCS*

TOKYO POP

1988 (Japan/US 99m) Kuzui Enterprises / Lorimar Films (R)

Film genre: Rock-music based comedy drama

Top guns: s-w: (+ dir) Fran Rubel Kuzui, Lynn Grossman

Stars: Carrie Hamilton *(Wendy Reed)*, Yatuka Tadokoro *(Hiro Yamaguchi)* → LOST IN TRANSLATION, Hiroshi Kobayashi *(Kaz)*, **X Japan:- Toshimitsu Deyama, Hideto Matsumoto, Yoshiki Hayashi, Tomoaki Ishizuka** *(performers)*, ex-member **Taiji Sawada** *(performer)*

Storyline: Unappreciated by her post-New Wave-styled band, female rock singer, Wendy, borrows/steals their money and takes an invitation from a male friend to visit Tokyo, Japan. There, she embarks on a romance with the leader of her friend's all-male band (the Red Warriors), but with language difficulties, etc., she finds it a little hard going. *MCS*

Movie rating: *5.5

Visual: Warner video

Off the record: X *Japan* (not to be confused with X of the USA). *MCS*

CARRIE HAMILTON (*) & YUTAKA TADOKORO (**)

1988. (cd/c/lp) *RiC; <RCC 1850>* [–] Japan [–]
– Never forget (*) / Monkey dancin' (RED WARRIORS: vocal **) / You! (MICHAEL CERVERIS) / Hearts and diamonds (**) / Hiro's song (RED WARRIORS: vocal – **) / Blue suede shoes (**) / (You make me feel like a) Natural woman (* & **) / Homesick blues / Do you believe in magic? (* & **) / Rakuen, rakuen (Paradise, paradise) (PAPAYA PARANOIA) / Home on the range (*).

S/track review: 'TOKYO POP' was musically devised by female filmmaker, Fran Rubel Kuzui (director of 'Buffy The Vampire Slayer' movie), having travelled many times between Tokyo and New York. From the Japanese camp there was youthful rock-pop star, Diamond Yukai (aka YUTAKA TADOKORO) and his RED WARRIORS, while from America there was CARRIE HAMILTON, both singer/songwriters with their own distinctive styles and fashion attire (or at least for the film). Embedded firmly in the late 80s, this soundtrack begins to grate somewhat when YUTAKA attempts something akin to a karaoke version of Carl Perkins' 'Blue Suede Shoes', while the pair soon try to hit it off by way of duet renditions of Lovin' Spoonful's 'Do You Believe In Magic?' and the Goffin-King-Wexler standard, '(You Make Me Feel Like A) Natural Woman'. It must be said, CARRIE sounds very comfortable in her role as singer, while YUTAKA – by the very nature and title of the latter cue – embarrassingly interrupts. The whole project had kicked off reasonably well courtesy of CARRIE (ex-Big Business) and her self-penned 80s AOR ballad, 'Never Forget', a mixture of Roxette meets Heart meets Roxette again. With his RED WARRIORS, TADOKORO gets into the funky and downbeat mode respectively via 'Monkey Dancin'' and 'Hiro's Song'; a solo instrumental 'Hearts And Diamonds' was a good attempt at reviving John Lennon. Composer ALAN BREWER supplies the OST with two cuts, one vocal 'You!' by MICHAEL CERVERIS and the instrumental 'Homesick Blues' (very Elton meets Hornsby). If you're looking for something truly Japanese check out 'Rakuen, Rakuen' by PAPAYA PARANOIA, whose singer is young enough to have pig-tails! – Tarantino were you watching. The finale takes CARRIE – whose mother just happens to be actress Carol Burnett – to new "napalm depths" on a hardcore version of 'Home On The Range'. File under 80s junk. *MCS*

Album rating: *3.5

TOMMY

1975 (UK 109m) Robert Stigwood Organisation / Hemdale (AA)

Film genre: Rock opera/Musical drama/comedy

Top guns: dir (+ s-w): Ken Russell → LISTZOMANIA → CRIMES OF PASSION → GOTHIC / opera/s-w: **Pete Townshend**

Stars: Roger Daltrey *(Tommy Walker)* <= the WHO =>, **Ann-Margret** *(Nora Walker Hobbs)* ← VIVA LAS VEGAS ← BYE BYE BIRDIE, Oliver Reed *(Frank Hobbs)* → LISZTOMANIA → CAPTIVE, **Elton JOHN** *(Pinball Wizard)*, **Keith Moon** *(Uncle Ernie)* <= the WHO =>, **Eric CLAPTON** *(the preacher)*, Jack Nicholson *(A. Quackson)* ← EASY RIDER ← HEAD ← PSYCH-OUT / → the BORDER → BATMAN, **Paul NICHOLAS** *(cousin Kevin)*, Robert Powell *(Capt. Walker)*, **Tina TURNER** *(the Acid Queen)*, Barry Winch *(young Tommy)*, Victoria Russell *(Sally Simpson)*, Eddie Stacey *(bovver boy)* → FLASH GORDON → 1984, **Arthur Brown** *(the preacher)* ← the COMMITTEE / → CLUB PARADISE → JAILBIRD ROCK → I PUT A SPELL ON ME, **Pete Townshend** *(himself)* <= the WHO =>, **John Entwistle** *(himself)* <= the WHO =>, Imogen Claire *(nurse)* → the ROCKY HORROR PICTURE SHOW → LISZTOMANIA → FLASH GORDON → SHOCK TREATMENT → HAWKS, Jennifer Baker *(nurse #1)* ← EVERY DAY'S A HOLIDAY, Susan Baker *(nurse #2)* ← EVERY DAY'S A HOLIDAY, **Simon Townshend** *(newsboy; voice)* → BRITISH ROCK SYMPHONY

Storyline: Maverick director Ken Russell lived up to his visually arresting reputation in this film adaptation of the Who's Rock Opera. Tommy is the "deaf, dumb and blind kid" who goes into emotional shutdown after the death of his father. While doctors struggle to bring him out of his shell, Tommy's salvation eventually arrives in the form of a pinball machine. After wresting the crown from the Pinball Wizard, Tommy forms a religious cult from the ranks of his adoring fans. *BG*

Movie rating: *6

Visual: video + dvd

Off the record: (see below)

—

the WHO (featuring . . . Various Artists)

Aug 75. (d-lp/d-c) *Polydor; (2657/5326 002) <9502>* [30] Mar75 [2]
– Overture / Prologue – 1945 / Captain Walker – It's a boy / Bernie's holiday camp / 1951 – What about the boy? / Amazing journey / Christmas / Eyesight to the blind / The Acid queen / Do you think it's alright / Cousin Kevin / Do you think it's alright / Fiddle about / Do you think it's alright / Sparks / Extra, extra, extra / Pinball wizard / Champagne / There's a doctor / Go to the mirror / Tommy can you hear me / Smash the mirror / I'm free / Mother and son / Sensation / Miracle cure / Sally Simpson / Welcome / T.V. studio / Tommy's holiday camp / We're not gonna take it / Listening to you – See me, feel me.

S/track review: The WHO's "rock opera" sits uncomfortably alongside their reputation as the Great Modfathers of Britpop. Today, they prefer the Union Jack aesthetic and Oasis-friendly dimension of their back catalogue. The 1975 film version, directed by Ken Russell, features a superb cast, a strongly psychedelic visual element, and filled the narrative and cognitive gaps deliberately left out of the album. What was most striking was the sonic spareness of the original album, the music was uncluttered and insistent, whereas the film is awash with sound, bolstered by synthesizers. PETE TOWNSHEND's limitations as a guitar player find expression in Tommy's deprived world, he is a musician in thrall to touch and sensation rather than natural gifts, and he relies on his strengths as a composer here. The music also benefits from a much stronger sense of character than the major players invest in it. It was KEITH MOON's idea to set the film in Bernie's holiday camp, and the song of the same name sees OLIVER REED as Frank playing it up for all he's worth, as a busy synth melody whirls around the tune, and an insistent 1-2-1-2 drum beat drives things forward at a slightly uncomfortable pace. ANN-MARGRET as Nora adds a wistful romanticism to proceedings as the song slows to a woozy conclusion. 'Amazing Journey' sets the quasi-mysticism of TOWNSHEND's guru Meher Baba within the psych-pop of the end of the sixties, the phasing effects enacting its supersonic flight. 'Christmas' sees the "opera" really get into its stride with one of the album's best vocal melodies, inquiring whether without sensation one is also bereft of spiritual guidance, and introduces the superb and classic melody of the 'See Me Feel Me' refrain which ROGER DALTREY later depicts in full-on Jesus sex-rock mode, though here it's disturbingly rendered by a young child. Is this exhortation somehow summoning a dark note of invitation in the abuse he suffers? The role call of guest musicians is superb. ERIC CLAPTON is on well-known ground with his rendition of Sonny Boy Williamson's 'Eyesight To The Blind', a heavy blues ode to the curative power of sex, and sensation. TINA TURNER excels as 'The Acid Queen' (though legend has it David Bowie was first choice for the role, whilst RON WOOD works his magic on guitar), her promise to "tear your soul apart" sends a stark warning against the indulgences of hallucinogens as a means of escaping mental entrapment. JOHN ENTWISTLE's writing skills are enlisted to depict the two most unnerving characters of the song cycle. 'Cousin Kevin' (sung by PAUL NICHOLAS) is a miasma of minor melodic figures, a mini-universe of Floyd-ish unease where the mental and physical abuse Tommy is subjected to takes shape. 'Fiddle About's braying horns and incantations make for a strange psych menace, a terrifying slice of nursery rhyme avant-pop, and who could best embody the character but a deranged KEITH MOON. 'Pinball Wizard', written in response to critic Nic Cohn's lukewarm reception to the original album during recording, played up to his love of pinball. It's a Rock classic and became the anthem around which the story's narrative was amended. ELTON JOHN (stilts and all) belts it out, laying piano arpeggios all over the iconic chordal stabs, though the wall-of-sound orchestration might be said to diminish the original's clarity and immediacy. Despite its well-deserved conceptual credentials, some of TOMMY's tracks occupy a tame, 60s rock-pop middle ground, cobbled together from a variety of different elements that TOWNSHEND was grabbing at: some flamenco guitar here, baroque flourishes there, a large dose of 60s power pop. 'Smash The Mirror' seems a decidedly conventional musical excursion for such a decisive moment in the narrative, and pales to the surprisingly rich voice of JACK NICHOLSON as the Specialist, supported by the sound of CALEB QUAYE's guitar gently weeping. 'Champagne', 'Extra, Extra, Extra' and 'T.V. Studio' were written for the film, and adumbrate the story of celebrity in an emergent Television age. 'Sally Simpson' has always seemed a lengthy digression, for what amounts to a patronising message to groupies of messiah figures and rock bands alike: know your place – "Never mind your part . . . / Is to be what you'll be . . .". In contrast, 'I'm Free' is a gloriously langurous, guitar-heavy excursion. "Freedom tastes of reality" we are told. But what reality is this in the end? One where we are invited to "Come to our house" in the lilting, folky 'Welcome', but then ushered into 'Tommy's Holiday Camp' by a visibly cracked and insane Uncle Ernie. 'We're Not Gonna Take It' on the face of it is an anti-establishment proclamation, but what community is this that seems steeped in hypocrisy ("Don't want no religion" when it reeks of the cult)? Where errant behaviour is crushed (those "gettin' drunk" and "smokin' mother nature")? Where non-believers are threatened with "rape"? It's a proto-fascist state, deprived of sensation, where Tommy is your führer, you're strapped to a pinball machine and Uncle Ernie is fiddling about . . . *DF*

Album rating: *5.5

– spinoff hits, etc. –

TINA TURNER: The Acid Queen

Jan 76. (7") *United Artists; (UP 36043)* [ ] [–]

ELTON JOHN: Pinball Wizard

Mar 76. (7") *D.J.M.; (DJS 652)* [7] [–]

– inspirational release –

the WHO: Tommy

May 69. (d-lp) *Reaction; (613 013-014) Decca; <7205>* [2] [4]
– Overture / It's a boy / 1921 / Amazing journey / Sparks / Eyesight for the blind / Miracle cure / Sally Simpson / I'm free / Welcome / Tommy's holiday camp / We're not gonna take it / Christmas / Cousin Kevin / The acid queen / Underture / Do you think it's alright / Fiddle about / Pinball wizard / There's a doctor / Go to the mirror / Tommy can you hear me / Smash the mirror / Sensation. *(re-iss. Jul84 on 'Polydor'; 2486 161/2) (d-cd-iss. Apr89; 800 077-2)*

the TOMMY STEELE STORY

aka ROCK AROUND THE WORLD

1957 (UK 71m b&w) Anglo Amalgamated

Film genre: Pop/Rock'n'roll Musical & er . . . biopic!

Top guns: dir: Gerard Bryant / s-w: Norman Hudis → the DUKE WORE JEANS → the 6.5 SPECIAL

Stars: Tommy STEELE *(himself)*, Patrick Westwood *(Brushes)*, Hilda Fenemore *(Mrs. Steele)*, Charles Lamb *(Mr. Steele)*, Lisa Daniely *(hospital nurse)*, Cyril Chamberlain *(chief steward)*, John Boxer *(Paul Lincoln)*, Peter Lewiston *(John Kennedy)* → the DUKE WORE JEANS, musicians:- **Dennis Price** *(pianist)*, **Alan Stuart** *(saxophonist)*, **Alan Weighell** *(bassist)*, **Leo Pollini** *(drummer)*, **Charles McDevitt Skiffle Group** *(performers)*, with **Nancy Whiskey** *(performer)* → the GOLDEN DISC, Humphrey Lyttelton *(performer)* → RED, WHITE & BLUES

Storyline: From the rocker's early days up to the present (1957), the film tells the story of merchant seaman Thomas Hicks, who is granted leave to look after his sick mother. To pass the evenings he and his guitar visit the 2I's club and are soon noticed by promoter John Kennedy. Within weeks, Thomas Hicks has become Tommy Steele and the nice man of British rock'n'roll music is born (despite his manager wanting him to be tough like Elvis). *JZ*

Movie rating: *3.5

Visual: none

Off the record: Songs not included on the OST: 'Bermonsey Bounce' (HUMPHREY LYTTELTON), 'Freight Train' (the CHARLES McDEVITT SKIFFLE GROUP featuring NANCY WHISKEY).

TOMMY STEELE AND THE STEELMEN

May 57. (10"lp) *Decca; (LF 1288)* [1] [–]
– Take me back, baby / Butterfingers / I like / A handful of songs / You gotta go / Water, water / Cannibal pot / Will it be you / Two eyes / Build up / Time to kill / Elevator rock / Doomsday rock / Teenage party.

S/track review: Whether it was pretentious or indeed just prophetic, a biopic about a singer filmed only around four or five months after their career took off is something of a misnomer. Okay, TOMMY STEELE was big at the time (although only 5'7" in stature), but surely three hits down the line ('Rock With The Caveman', No.1 'Singing The Blues' and 'Knee Deep In The Blues') did not warrant some kind of celluloid and vinyl congratulatory "This Is Your Life". The combination of Lionel Bart, Michael Pratt and STEELE himself was responsible for nearly all of the 14 cues on the chart-topping 'TOMMY STEELE STORY', which, incidentally, carved out another hit in crooning ballad 'Butterfingers'. This was a guy hopping on board the rock'n'roll bandwagon, and as it was to prove a little later, a man only too eager to hop back off. If Bill Haley & Co had heard 'Take Me Back, Baby' (a rip-off of 'Rock Around The Clock'), why no phone call to their legal department, although I suppose listening to the record half a century on could be misleading. Ditto the sax-riddled 'You Gotta Go', 'Two Eyes', 'Build Up' and 'Elevator Rock', although the latter portrays more 'See You Later, Alligator'. STEELE was a wannabe Elvis, but always quintessentially English through-and-through, cues such as 'Water, Water' (tea, fish & chips, etc) being prime examples of why the cockney lad never crossed over. Ditto Cliff. *MCS*

Album rating: *3.5

– spinoff releases, etc. –

CHARLES McDEVITT featuring NANCY WHISKEY: Freight Train

Mar 57. (7") *Oriole; (CB 1352)* [5] [ ]

TOMMY STEELE & THE STEELMEN: Butterfingers / Cannibal Pot

Apr 57. (7") *(F 10877)* [8] [–]

TOMMY STEELE & THE STEELMEN: The Tommy Steele Story No.1

Jun 57. (7"ep) *(DFE 6398)* [ ] [–]

TOMMY STEELE & THE STEELMEN: Water, Water / A Handful Of Songs

Aug 57. (7") *(F 10923)* [5] [–]

TOMMY STEELE & THE STEELMEN: The Tommy Steele Story No.2

Aug 57. (7"ep) *(DFE 6424)* [ ] [–]
– A handful of songs / Cannibal pot / Time to kill / You gotta go.

□ TOMORROW segment
(⇒ SMASHING TIME)

TOO LEGIT: THE MC HAMMER STORY

2001 (US 89m TV) VH-1 Television

Film genre: Rap/Hip Hop-music biopic

Top guns: dir: Artie Mandelberg / s-w: Eugene Corr (+ story), John Wierick

Stars: Romany Malco *(MC Hammer)*, Robert Bailey Jr. *(young MC Hammer)* ← JACKIE'S BACK!, Lamont Bentley *(Tupac Shakur)*, Tangi Miller *(Stephanie)*, Tony Norris *(Marion "Suge" Knight)*, Brent Anderson *(Michael Fiebish)*, Jesse Adams *(Chris)* ← AT ANY COST

Storyline: Hip hopper MC Hammer takes center stage in this biopic of the man's early life and rise to stardom. As Stanley Burrell, the young MC struggled as a batboy for baseball superstar Henry Aaron. Cue director to church rapper (as most of the film flicks through), Hammer eventually finds his niche in the music business. However, after earning over $30 million and a plethora of hits behind him, he filed for bankruptcy. *MCS*

Movie rating: *4

Visual: dvd (no audio OST by Jay Ferguson)

Off the record: Lamont Bentley was a member of hip hop duo, Uprise, before he sadly died in a car crash on the 18th of January 2005, aged 31. *MCS*

TOOMORROW

1970 (UK 95m) Rank Films (PG)

Film genre: Pop/Rock sci-fi Musical

Top guns: s-w + dir: Val Guest

Stars: Olivia Newton-John *(Olivia)* → GREASE → XANADU, **Vic Cooper**

(Vic), **Benny Thomas** *(Benny)*, Roy Dotrice *(John Williams)*, **Karl Chambers** *(Karl)*, Roy Marsden *(Alpha)*, Tracey Crisp *(Suzanne Gilmore)* → PERCY, Imogen Hassall *(Amy)*, Margaret Nolan *(Johnson)* ← FERRY 'CROSS THE MERSEY ← a HARD DAY'S NIGHT

Storyline: Olivia Newton-John and her bandmates (who star under their own names) literally find themselves beamed-up to perform for an audience of aliens after sending out some cosmic frequencies from a newly invented musical instrument. *BG*

Movie rating: *5.5

Visual: none

Off the record: TOOMORROW (see below)

—

TOOMORROW (score/composer: Hugo Montenegro)

Aug 70. (lp) *RCA Victor; (LSA 3008)*
– You're my baby now / Taking your own sweet time / Toomorrow (instr.) / Let's move on / Walkin' on air (instr.) / If you can't be hurt / Toomorrow / Walkin' on air / Spaceport / Happiness valley / Let's move on (instr.) / Goin' back.

S/track review: HUGO MONTENEGRO – in conjunction with Ritchie Adams and Mark Barkan – was the man behind the score for this most strange of 70s musicals, with OLIVIA NEWTON-JOHN committed to vinyl for the very first time. Less far-fetched than the plot, the music grooves on an earthier plane with some fine, brassy pop and serious moog business. The fact is, MONTENEGRO (the man who took Morricone's 'The Good, The Bad & The Ugly' to No.2 in the UK singles charts) only gets in one cue, the breakbeat, Schifrin-cloned 'Spaceport'. If you're a lover of 'Hair' and anything by Don Kirshner's other creations, the Monkees and the Archies, you'll like this. Australian-born NEWTON-JOHN (only just turned 21 at the time) is the real star of the show, while other places as musicians are taken up by BENNY THOMAS, VIC COOPER and KARL CHAMBERS. Note that 60s session man, CHRIS SLADE (later of Manfred Mann's Earth Band, Ac/Dc, Asia, etc) was the real drummer here. Be prepared to pay over £100 for the LP; the accompanying single 'You're My Baby Now' (+ the 'Decca' follow-up, 'I Could Never Live Without Your Love' / 'Roll Like A River' will set you back £50 each. *BG & MCS*

Album rating: *4.5

– spinoff releases, etc. –

TOOMORROW: You're My Baby Now / Goin' Back

Aug 70. (7") *(RCA 1978) Kirshner; <63-5005>*

TOP SECRET!

1984 (US 90m) Paramount Pictures (PG)

Film genre: romantic Rock'n'roll spy spoof/comedy

Top guns: s-w + dir: David Zucker, Jim Abrahams, Jerry Zucker

Stars: Val Kilmer *(Nick Rivers)* → the DOORS → MASKED AND ANONYMOUS, Lucy Gutteridge *(Hillary Flammond)*, Peter Cushing *(bookstore propietor)*, Jeremy Kemp *(General Streck)*, Christopher Villiers *(Nigel "The Torch"; resistance leader)*, Warren Clarke *(Colonel von Horst)* ← O LUCKY MAN! ← a CLOCKWORK ORANGE, Michael Gough *(Dr. Paul Flammond)* → BATMAN, Jim Carter *(Déjà Vu; resistance member)* ← FLASH GORDON / → LIPSTICK ON YOUR COLLAR → HEARTLANDS, Eddie Tagoe *(Chocolate Mousse; resistance member)* ← the WALL, Harry Ditson *(Du Quois; resistance member)* ← BIRTH OF THE BEATLES, Omar Sharif *(agent Cedric)* ← GREEN ICE, Ian McNeice *(blind souvenir vendor)*

Storyline: Elvis look-alike Nick Rivers goes to East Germany for a goodwill concert, but soon finds there's a lot more going on behind the Curtain than meets the eye. Luscious Hillary Flammond's dad, the brainiest scientist in the world, is in the clutches of some nasty Nazis (who seem to have emigrated east since 1945) and it's up to Nick and Hillary to save him from torture, death and worse before it's too late. *JZ*

Movie rating: *6.5

Visual: video + dvd

Off the record: The Royal Philharmonic Orchestra performs the Maurice Jarre score for the other 'TOP SECRET!' OST.

—

VAL KILMER (composers: various)

Dec 84. (m-lp) *Passport; <PB 3603>*
– Skeet surfing / Are you lonesome tonight? / How silly can you get / Straighten out the rug / Tutti frutti / Spend this night with me.

S/track review: There's not many chances of hearing VAL KILMER singing – even on the subsequent 'The DOORS' movie when he played the role of Jim Morrison. And with this rare-as-hen's-teeth, 15-minute mini-set, it's all too brief. There are tribute segments spread out everywhere on this rare and hard-to-get 12", KILMER parodying the Beach Boys on 'Skeet Surfing', a con-fusion of 'Surfin' USA', 'Fun, Fun, Fun', 'Little Honda', 'California Girls', 'The Girls On The Beach' & 'Hawaii'. For 'Are You Lonesome Tonight', Val goes Elvis, while 'Tutti Frutti' goes rock'n'roll. With former Turtles, Flo & Eddie (Mark Volman & Howard Kaylan), on board, KILMER shakes his pelvis on three further cues, 'How Silly Can You Get', 'Straighten Out The Rug' and 'Spend This Night With Me'. Short and sweet maybe, but an enjoyable plough through what could have been KILMER's long-lost vocation. *MCS*

Album rating: *4

the TOUCHABLES

1968 (UK 88m) 20th Century-Fox (18)

Film genre: showbiz/Rock-music melodrama

Top guns: dir: Robert Freeman / s-w: Ian La Frenais → STILL CRAZY → ACROSS THE UNIVERSE

Stars: David Anthony *(Christian)*, Esther Anderson *(Melanie)*, Judy Huxtable *(Sadie)*, Monika Ringwald as Marilyn Rickard *(Busbee)*, Kathy Simmonds *(Samson)*, Harry Baird *(Lillywhite)*, James Villiers *(Twyning)*, William Dexter *(Quayle)*, Michael Chow *(Denzil)*, Joan Bakewell *(interviewer)*

Storyline: Rock singer Christian is (sort of) worried when he is kidnapped by four lusty maidens and tied to a large turntable. Dressed as nuns, they find the bemused singer guilty of liking women too much and leniently decide merely to shoot him. At this point Christian has had enough of the bondage session and escapes into the woods. With the nuns, a gay wrestler and gangsters all in pursuit, we'll see if Christian is finally converted. *JZ*

Movie rating: *3.5

Visual: none

Off the record: Director Robert Freeman had earlier worked on the Beatles' LP sleeves including 'Rubber Soul'.

—

Various Artists / KEN THORNE (*)

Feb 69. (lp) *Stateside; (SSL 10271) 20th Century-Fox; <TFS 4206>*
– The Touchables theme (All of us) (NIRVANA) / Dancing frog (WYNDER K. FROG) / The chase (*) / Blues for a frog (WYNDER K. FROG) / Respect (FERRIS WHEEL) / Good day sunshine (ROY REDMAN) / Sadies theme (*) / Christian & Melanie (*) / Samson's theme (*) / The dome (*) / Jalousie (*) / The Touchables theme (All of us) (NIRVANA).

S/track review: A game of two halves you could say (well, nearly); on side A: Various Artists, on side B: the KEN THORNE score. Compiled by 'Island' records boss, Chris Blackwell, and this basically answers the question to why a few artists were involved. "Rainbow Chasers" NIRVANA (aka Alex Spyropoulos & Patrick Campbell-Lyons – not Cobain, Grohl & co!) opened proceedings with 'All Of Us' a delicate psychedelic/bubblegum pop anthem; another version closed the LP. Another of Blackwell's recent 'Island' signings, er . . . WYNDER K. FROG (featuring ex-Fairies guy, Mick Weaver and future Grease Band musicians) delivered two organic numbers, 'Dancing Frog' & 'Blues For A Frog', reminiscent of Chris Barber or Booker T & The MG's. Surely these tracks do not merit the LP asking price of $149.00. Anyway, just when you thought it couldn't get any worse, up pops poor-man's club act, the FERRIS WHEEL (a 'Pye' records outfit featuring singers Diana Ferris and future solo star Linda Lewis), sanitising the late, great Otis Redding's 'Respect'. Maybe they should've swapped songs with soulful R&B singer, ROY REDMAN, who, on the follow-on track, crucified Lennon & McCartney's staple, 'Good Dat Sunshine'. On then to Norfolk-born composer KEN THORNE, a man in his forties who'd been involved with other "Rock" movies, 'IT'S TRAD, DAD!' (1962), the Beatles' 'HELP!' (1965) and subsequently 'The MAGIC CHRISTIAN' (1969). His score was indeed "thorny", essentially avant-jazz at its most eerie ('Sadie's Theme'), although at times it slipped into romantic or bombastic, string-led, John Barry-type orchestrals ('Samson's Theme' & 'The Dome'). With only about a quarter of an hour at his disposal, THORNE might've thought better than to include old-time waltzer, 'Jalousie' – and on that word . . . *MCS*

Album rating: *3.5

– spinoff singles, etc. –

NIRVANA: All Of Us (The Untouchables) / (non-OST song)

Nov 68. (7") *(WIP 6045) <739>* [ ] Dec68 [ ]

TOUGHER THAN LEATHER

1988 (US 92m) Def Pictures / New Line Cinema (R)

Film genre: Rap & Hip-Hop-music crime drama

Top guns: s-w: (+ dir) **Rick Rubin**, Ric Menello → DROP DEAD ROCK

Stars: RUN-D.M.C.:- Darryl McDaniels *(Darryl 'D.M.C.' McDaniels)*, **Joseph Simmons** *(Joseph 'Run' Simmons)*, **Jason Mizell** *(Jason 'Jam Master Jay' Mizell)*, Daniel Simmons *(prison warden)* ← KRUSH GROOVE / **Richard Edson** *(Bernie Carteez)* ← GOOD MORNING, VIETNAM ← WALKER ← HOWARD THE DUCK / → WHAT ABOUT ME → STRANGE DAYS → the MILLION DOLLAR HOTEL → SOUTHLANDER, George Godfrey *(Nathan Burdette)*, **Russell Simmons** *(himself)* ← KRUSH GROOVE / → the SHOW → BROWN SUGAR → BEEF → DEATH OF A DYNASTY, **the BEASTIE BOYS:- Adam Yauch, Mike D, Adam Horovitz** *(themselves/performers)*, Raymond White *(Raymond 'Runny Ray' Walker)* ← KRUSH GROOVE, Lois Ayres *(Charlotte Hopper)*, **Slick Rick** *(MC Ricky D)* → the SHOW → WHITEBOYS → BROOKLYN BABYLON → BROWN SUGAR → FADE TO BLACK

Storyline: Rap band Run-DMC are "pushed too far" when their roadie is murdered after witnessing a drugs-related killing. It turns out that the baddies are some record company executives (and, of course, white) who try to put the blame on the rappers to cover themselves. Mindless violence ensues as our heroes take on rednecks, drug barons, gays, whites and anyone else who crosses their path except women, who have a different but predictable fate in store for them. *JZ*

Movie rating: *3

Visual: video (no "proper" audio OST)

Off the record: Richard Edson was the original Sonic Youth drummer (and later rhythmic dance act, Konk)

– associated releases, etc. –

RUN-D.M.C.: Run's House / Beats To The Rhyme

Apr 88. (7"/7"pic-d) *(LON/+P 177)* [–] [37]
(12"+=/cd-s+=) *(LON X/CD 177)* – ('A'&'B'instrumental).

RUN-D.M.C.: Tougher Than Leather

May 88. (lp/c)(cd) *London; <1265> (LON LP/C 38)(828070-2)* [9] Jun88 [13]
– Run's house / Mary, Mary / They call us Run DMC / Beats to the rhyme / Radio station / Papa crazy / Tougher than leather / I'm not going out like that / How d'ya do it Dee? / Miss Elaine / Soul to rock and roll / Ragtime. *(re-iss. Nov92 on 'Profile' cd/c; PCD/PCT 1265) (cd re-iss. Sep99 on 'Arista'; 07822 16409-2)*

RUN-D.M.C.: Mary, Mary / Rock Box

Jul 88. (7") *<5211>* [75] [–]

RUN-D.M.C.: Mary, Mary / Raising Hell

Aug 88. (7"/7"s) *(LON/+S 191)* [–] [ ]
(12"+=) *(LONX 191)* – ('A'instrumental).

à TOUT CASSER

1968 (Fra 90m) CCFC / Finistère Films / United Pictures (15)

Film genre: crime comedy/caper

Top guns: s-w: (+ dir) John Berry (+ story) → CLAUDINE, Guy Lionel, Christian Plume (+ story)

Stars: Eddie Constantine *(Ric)*, **Johnny Hallyday** *(Frankie)* ← D'OU VIENS-TU, JOHNNY?, Annabella Incontrera *(Eva)*, Michel Serrault *(Aldo Moreni)*, Hélène Soubielle *(Jacqueline)*, Catherine Allégret *(Mimi)*, Robert Lombard *(Reggie)*

Storyline: The strongest drink you can get in Frankie's bar is sasparilla, which isn't to the taste of the hippy bikers who stop off for some refreshments. The gang leader is so desperate for a drop of the hard stuff he even offers to buy the whole joint from Frankie and restock it. Frankie politely refuses and gets a knuckle sandwich for his troubles – luckily for him his pal Ric is on hand to take on the thirsty bikers and woo any damsel in distress in the passing. *JZ*

Movie rating: *3

Visual: none (no OST; score: JOHNNY HALLYDAY & MICKEY JONES)

Off the record: Eddie Constantine (b.29 Oct 1917, Los Angeles, Calif.) was an actor and singer who was taken under the wing of the iconic Edith Piaf. He subsequently became the "Humphrey Bogart" of French films, when he took on the role of Lemmy Caution in numerous 60s Gallic detective flicks. Germany was to be his next port of call, Jean-Luc Godard reviving the Lemmy character for 1991's 'Allemagne 90 Neuf Zéro'. Sadly, he was to die of a heart attack on 25th February, 1993. *MCS*

TOYAH

Born: Toyah Willcox, 16 May'58, Kings Heath, Birmingham, England. Following a stint in drama school, TOYAH's big break came when Derek Jarman offered her a prestigious role in his influential punk flick, 'JUBILEE' (1978); she was later to star in the filmmaker's gothic 1979 version of Shakespeare's 'The Tempest'. Through a singing partnership (as movie band the Maneaters) with budding singer, Adam Ant, the petite punkette already found herself as a rising star among the underground New Wave movement; Siouxsie & The Banshees was already at the top of the tree. Wisely perhaps, TOYAH continued to juggle an acting career via 'The Corn Is Green' (1979) – starring Katharine Hepburn – and the forming of her new band, aptly titled TOYAH. Securing a record deal with burgeoning indie label, 'Safari', they released their debut single, 'Victims Of The Riddle', in the summer of '79. Unsurprisingly for such a cringe-inducingly titled track, it failed to break the chart, with an accompanying album, ahem . . . 'Sheep Farming In Barnet'

(1979), meeting a similar fate. Compensation was at hand with another esteemed cheeky role in PETE TOWNSHEND's seminal mod-revisionist movie, 'QUADROPHENIA' (1979). Though a sophomore LP, 'The Blue Meaning' (1980), and a live effort, 'Toyah! Toyah! Toyah!' (1981), gave the singer her first Top 40 action, it was only with the release of the 'Four From Toyah' EP (in 1981) that the modern-day, dead-end kids found appealing. The lead track, 'It's A Mystery', was uniquely lispy and "infect-t-tious" enough to take her into the Top 5, though it was her aggressively-hyped image – dauntingly flame-haired or quintessentially post-apocalyptic ice-queen – which turned her into an unlikely pop star. While TOYAH and group had already featured in the performance movie, 'URGH! A MUSIC WAR!' (1981), it just got even better when 'I Want To Be Free' – a rebel song up there with Cliff's 'Summer Holiday' in terms of anti-establishment ire – hit Top 10. TOYAH's third and final Top 10 single was 'Thunder In The Mountains', a song as majestically bombastic as the title suggests. The singer continued her mythical/futuristic lyrical musings with further releases, although her acting had now moved into the back seat. Taking a musical sabbatical in the mid-80s, during which she married ex-King Crimson guitar maestro Robert Fripp, TOYAH eventually returned to the fold via some low-key thespian roles and studio albums (1987-1994). Mrs Fripp subsequently sidelined into appearing in a plethora of TV shows, one of them presenting BBC1's 'Holiday' programme. In 1999, now into her forties, she played a part-singing role in the British flop, 'JULIE AND THE CADILLACS' (1999). *MCS*

- **filmography** {acting} –

Jubilee *(1977 {*} OST by BRIAN ENO & V/A =>)* / the Quatermass Conclusion *(1979 {a})* / the Corn Is Green *(1979 TV {a})* / the Tempest *(1979 {*})* / **Quadrophenia** *(1979 {a} OST by the WHO & V/A =>)* / **Urgh! A Music War** *(1981 {p} OST by V/A =>)* / Dr. Jekyll And Mr. Hyde *(1981 TV {a})* / Murder: Ultimate Grounds For Divorce *(1984 {a})* / the Ebony Tower *(1984 TV {a})* / the Disputation *(1986 TV {a})* / Midnight Breaks *(1990 {a})* / Anchoress *(1993 {*})* / the Most Fertile Man In Ireland *(1999 {a})* / **Julie And The Cadillacs** *(1999 {a} on OST by Various Cast =>)*

TRAIN RIDE TO HOLLYWOOD

1975 (US 85m) Billy Jack Enterprises / Crystal Jukebox Films (G)

Film genre: showbiz/R&B-music comedy fantasy

Top guns: dir: Charles R. Rondeau / s-w: Dan Gordon

Stars: Bloodstone:- Harry Williams, Willis Draffen Jr., Charles Love, Charles McCormick *(themselves)* / Guy Marks *(Humprey Bogart)*, Michael Payne *(Eric; producer)*, Jay Robinson *(Dracula)* ← THREE THE HARD WAY, Jay Lawrence *(Rhett Butler aka Clark Gable)*, Phyllis Davis *(Scarlett O'Hara)*, Bill Oberlin *(W.C. Fields)*, Roberta Collins *(Jean Harlow)*, Peter Ratray *(Nelson Eddy)*, Tracy Reed *(stupid bimbo)* ← TROUBLE MAN / → NO WAY BACK → CAR WASH ← a PIECE OF THE ACTION

Storyline: 70s soul-pop'ers Bloodstone (formerly the Sinceres) starred in this fantasy musical wherein lead singer Harry Williams, after sustaining a knock to the head, imagines he's on a celebrity-packed train. Among the legends accompanying him and his singing bandmates/conductors are Dracula, Laurel & Hardy and Marlon Brando (all played by actors), the latter of whom supplies a bit of wafer thin plot by bumping off his fellow passengers. *BG*

Movie rating: *3.5

Visual: video + dvd

Off the record: **BLOODSTONE** (see below)

—

BLOODSTONE

Jan 76. (lp) *London; <PS 665>* [ ] [–]
– As time goes by / Yakety yak / Train ride / What do I have to do? / Hooray for romance / Rock'n'roll choo choo / Go to sleep / Toot! toot! Tootsie! (goodbye) / I'm in shape / Sh-boom (life could be a dream) / Money (that's what I want). *<cd-iss. Oct99 on 'Collectables'; 5872>*

S/track review: Funky like a train? Not exactly. It's difficult to imagine what kind of audience – outside of BLOODSTONE's fanbase and those who successfully suffered the film – this soundtrack would've been marketed to in 1975. The cover art and the band's soul pedigree suggest blaxploitation but the reality is more Broadway cast, parlaying the legacy of popular song and black harmony styles from pre-war to doo-wop, paying tribute to Hollywood heroes en route. Supremely talented falsetto HARRY WILLIAMS and his fellow BLOODSTONE travellers (WILLIS DRAFFEN Jr, CHARLES LOVE and CHARLES McCORMICK) high-step through an unrepentently theatrical title theme, wheel out the mouldering standard, 'As Time Goes By' and charge through 'Rock'n'Roll Choo Choo' like a black Status Quo. Even the WILLIAMS-penned funk jam, 'I'm In Shape', is ruined by a mocked-up mid-section, aaaaarghhh! Alongside the unshackled joy of WILLIAMS' falsetto on the Jackson 5-esque 'Hooray For Romance', one of the few credible moments is an armour-plated funk-rock cover of Berry Gordy's 'Money (That's What I Want)', as tight and hypnotic as prime Kool & The Gang but way out of context next to the kazoo-impersonating doo-wop of 'Sh-Boom (Life Could Be A Dream)'. It's almost worth picking up for 'Money' alone but at barely half an hour's worth of music in total, not to mention rudimentary sleevenotes which devote a grand total of one paragraph to the soundtrack they're supposedly trying to comment on, this is a journey almost as inconsequential as the destination. *BG*

Album rating: *4.5

TRAINSPOTTING

1996 (UK 94m) Channel 4 / Polygram / Noel Gay Motion Pictures (18)

Film genre: buddy/urban comedy

Top guns: dir: Danny Boyle / s-w: John Hodge (au: Irving Welsh → the ACID HOUSE)

Stars: Ewan McGregor *(Mark Renton)* ← LIPSTICK ON YOUR COLLAR / → VELVET GOLDMINE → MOULIN ROUGE → YOUNG ADAM, Ewen Bremner *(Spud)* → MOJO → the ACID HOUSE → HALLAM FOE, Jonny Lee Miller *(Sick Boy)*, Kevin McKidd *(Tommy)* → the ACID HOUSE, Robert Carlyle *(Francis Begbie)* → RAVENOUS, Kelly Macdonald *(Diane)* → SPLENDOR, Peter Mullan *(Swanney)* → ORDINARY DECENT CRIMINAL → YOUNG ADAM, Irvine Welsh *(Mikey Forrester)* → the ACID HOUSE, Finlay Welsh *(sheriff)*, James Cosmo *(Mr. Renton)*, Shirley Henderson *(Gail)* → 24 HOUR PARTY PEOPLE, Stuart McQuarrie *(Gavin; American tourist)* → YOUNG ADAM, Keith Allen *(dealer)* → the YOUNG PERSON'S GUIDE TO BECOMING A ROCK STAR → 24 HOUR PARTY PEOPLE, Dale Winton *(game show host)*

Storyline: While not coming close to the chaotic nihilism and scabrous search for working class Scottish identity which characterised Irvine Welsh's novel, or even the sheer physicality of the theatre production, Danny Boyle's stylised film adaptation is nevertheless a queasy, rollercoaster ride through Edinburgh's dark side. It follows the misadventures of easy going heroin addict (and narrator of the action), Mark Renton and his motley crew of pals – the guileless Spud, the vain Sick Boy and the disturbingly unhinged Begbie – as they stumble through life in search of something more than just the next shot of smack or pint of lager. *BG*

Movie rating: *10

Visual: video + dvd

Off the record: In the same year as his debut screenplay movie, Irvine Welsh (alongside Primal Scream & On-U Sound), hit the UK Top 20 with 'The Big Man And The Scream Team Meet The Barmy Army Uptown'. *MCS*

—

Various Artists

Feb 96. (cd) *E.M.I.; (CDEMC 3739) Capitol; <37190>* 2 Jul96 48
– Lust for life (IGGY POP) / Deep blue day (BRIAN ENO) / Trainspotting (PRIMAL SCREAM) / Atomic (SLEEPER) / Temptation (NEW ORDER) / Nightclubbing (IGGY POP) / Sing (BLUR) / Perfect day (LOU REED) / Mile end (PULP) / For what you dream of – full on renaissance mix (BEDROCK + KYO) / 2:1 (ELASTICA) / A final hit (LEFTFIELD) / Born slippy (nuxx) (UNDERWORLD) / Closet romantic (DAMON ALBARN).

S/track review: The 'TRAINSPOTTING' soundtrack came to define the 90s as much as – albeit in a completely different way – 'SATURDAY NIGHT FEVER' defined the late 70s. With an evocative (and largely exclusive) tracklist of Britpop, techno and cult classics from the likes of LOU REED and IGGY POP, the record caught the mood of the times and preserved it for posterity. Among the older tracks, BRIAN ENO's 'Deep Blue Day' captured the zoned-out high of a heroin hit, while IGGY POP's 'Lust For Life' played against Renton's opening Princes Street sprint was a stroke of genius. PRIMAL SCREAM – who also worked with Welsh on the unofficial and enjoyably controversial theme to Scotland's doomed Euro '96 soccer campaign – contributed the dubby, claustrophobic title cut, summoning (intentionally or otherwise) the desolation of the novel's encounter between Begbie and his drunken father in Leith's old train depot. BLUR and PULP lent a bit of geezer credibility to the London scenes while throbbing techno from LEFTFIELD and UNDERWORLD contextualised the film's mid-90s genesis. All in, it was and is – like the movie itself – a freewheeling, white-knuckle ride and one which inspired a second volume of tracks used in the film but not included on the original, together with songs Boyle intended for the film but which never made the final cut. *BG*

Album rating: *9 / Trainspotting #2: *8

– spinoff hits, etc. –

UNDERWORLD: Born Slippy

Jul 96. (cd-s) *Junior Boy's Own; (JBO 44CDS)* 2 –

IGGY POP: Lust For Life

Nov 96. (cd-s) *Virgin America; (VUSCD 116)* 26 –

Various Artists: Trainspotting #2

Sep 97. (cd) *Premier; (PRMDCD 36) Capitol; <21686>* 11 Oct97
– Choose life (PF PROJECT featuring EWAN McGREGOR) / The passenger (IGGY POP) / Dark & long – dark train mix (UNDERWORLD) / Habanera – from "Carmen" suite (Bizet) / Statuesque (SLEEPER) / Golden years (DAVID BOWIE) / Think about the way (ICE MC) / A final hit – full length version (LEFTFIELD) / Temptation (HEAVEN 17) / Nightclubbing – Baby Doc remix (IGGY POP) / Our lips are sealed (FUN BOY THREE) / Come together (PRIMAL SCREAM) / Atmosphere (JOY DIVISION) / Inner city life (GOLDIE) / Born slippy – Darren Price mix (UNDERWORLD).

PF PROJECT featuring EWAN McGREGOR: Choose Life

Nov 97. (cd-s) *Positiva; (CDTIV 84)* 6 –

TRICK OR TREAT

1986 (US 97m) De Laurentis Entertainment (R)

Film genre: occult horror comedy/satire

Top guns: dir: Charles Martin Smith / s-w: Michael S. Murphey, Joel Soisson, Rhet Topham

Stars: Marc Price *(Eddie Weinbauer)*, Tony Fields *(Sammi Curr)*, Lisa Orgolini *(Leslie Graham)*, Doug Savant *(Tim Hainey)*, Elaine Joyce *(Angie Weinbauer)*, Glen Morgan *(Roger Mockus)*, **Gene Simmons** *(Nuke)* <= KISS =>, **Ozzy Osbourne** *(Rev. Aaron Gilstrom)* → the DECLINE OF WESTERN CIVILIZATION 2: THE METAL YEARS → PRIVATE PARTS → MOULIN ROUGE! → WE SOLD OUR SOULS FOR ROCK'N'ROLL, Elise Richards *(Genie Wooster)*, Clare Nono *(Maggie Wong-Hernandez)* ← the DYNAMITE BROTHERS, Charles Martin Smith *(Mr. Wimbley)* ← MORE AMERICAN GRAFFITI ← COTTON CANDY ← the BUDDY HOLLY STORY ← AMERICAN GRAFFITI ← PAT GARRETT & BILLY THE KID, Alice Nunn *(Mrs. Sylvia Cavell)* → WHO'S THAT GIRL → THREE O'CLOCK HIGH, Steve Boles *(cop #3)* → DEAD MAN WALKING → the BASKETBALL DIARIES

Storyline: High school student Eddie is a great fan of devil-worshipping rock star, Sammi Curr, who burned to death in a hotel fire. When Eddie comes into possession of one of Sammi's rare demo tapes, he is amazed to discover he can communicate with the dead Sammi when the record is played backwards. Eddie follows Sammi's instructions from beyond the grave to settle a few old scores, but Sammi has many more evil plans afoot for Eddie and the whole town. *JZ*

Movie rating: *4.5

Visual: video + dvd

Off the record: FASTWAY were formed in and around London, England . . . mid '82 by ex-Motorhead guitarist, "Fast" Eddie Clarke and ex-UFO bassist Pete Way. Together with newbie Irishman Dave King on vocals and ex-Humble Pie sticksman, Jerry Shirley, they signed to 'C.B.S.' records and even nudged into the UK Top 75 via debut single 'Easy Livin'' the following spring; an eponymous album nearly cracked the US Top 30. Comparisons with the mainlining scuzz-rock of Motorhead were inevitable and FASTWAY's rather unadventurous Brit-rock approach emerged looking pretty lame. The fact that Way had left just prior to the LP's release (he subsequently formed Waysted) didn't help matters, although FASTWAY put their faith in their encouraging US reception and began work on another album, 'All Fire Up' (Charlie McCracken, ex-Taste, filled in). Sticking to the same basic formula as the debut, the record struggled to make it into the US Top 60, while in Britain and Europe, FASTWAY found it difficult to make any significant headway at all. Disillusioned with this state of affairs, McCracken and Shirley departed, their replacements being Shane Carroll and Alan Connor respectively. Following another listless album in 1986, 'Waiting For The Roar', FASTWAY enjoyed a bit of belated success with their soundtrack for cheesy metal/horror comedy, 'TRICK OR TREAT'. Despite this surprise exposure, the band subsequently broke up, with Eddie heading back to Britain and enlisting a complete new line-up headed by ex-Joan Jett man, Lea Hart, along with Paul Gray and Steve Clarke. Now signed to 'G.W.R.' (also home to LEMMY's Motorhead), this revamped FASTWAY took another shot at rock fame with 'On Target' (1988), although predictably their aim was poor and the album missed by a mile. Surely flogging the proverbial dead horse, Eddie and Hart lined up yet another variation on the FASTWAY theme (including members of Girlschool) for a final effort, 'Bad Bad Girls' (1990), before finally calling it a day. Clarke subsequently pursued a low-key solo career. *MCS*

FASTWAY

Nov 86. (lp/c/cd) *Columbia; <40549> C.B.S.; (450444-1/-4/-2)* May87
– Trick or treat / After midnight / Don't stop the fight / Stand up / Tear down the walls / Get tough / Hold on to the night / Heft / If you could see me.

S/track review: Not the most successful in soundtrack genres, horror-themed Hard-Rock and/or Heavy-Metal scores scared the pants off many an unaffiliated member of the Kerrang! club. Hitting the cinema only a few months after another metallic flop, Ac/Dc's 'MAXIMUM OVERDRIVE', it was hardly rocket-science that 'TRICK OR TREAT' died several deaths – even "Bat-man" Ozzy couldn't save its soul. In fact, one could be forgiven if one thought they had mistakenly picked up an Ac/Dc LP. There's no denying FAST EDDIE CLARKE is a phenomenal axeman and DAVE KING had found his voice, but the anthemic lyrics were just too clichéd – however intentional. From 'Trick Or Treat', 'After Midnight', 'Stand Up' and 'Tear Down The Walls' (fuse Ac/Dc, Judas Priest and/or Quiet Riot) to 'Don't Stop The Fight' and 'Get Tough' (fuse Ozzy, Iron Maiden and Rainbow), they all seemed a bit simplistic and bombastic without being too "hair-raising!". Track seven, 'Hold On To The Night', gets a little better, but it was probably down to the unbeatable 'Radar Love'-esque rhythm and beat, while follow-on cues, 'Heft' and 'If You Could See Me', intro like some classic Led Zeppelin number. Too little too late. No shocks here then, just a lot of metallic hokum. *MCS*

Album rating: *3

the TROUBLE WITH GIRLS

1969 (US 105m) Metro-Goldwyn-Mayer (PG)

Film genre: Rock Musical comedy/drama

Top guns: dir: Peter Tewksbury ← STAY AWAY, JOE / s-w: Arnold & Louis Peyser (au: 'The Chautauqua' by Day Keene, Dwight Babcock, Mauri Grashin)

Stars: Elvis PRESLEY *(Walter Hale)*, Marlyn Mason *(Charlene)*, Nicole Jaffe *(Betty)*, Sheree North *(Nita Bix)*, Edward Andrews *(Johnny)*, John Carradine *(Mr. Drewcolt)* → the MONSTER CLUB, Vincent Price *(Mr. Morality)* ← BEACH PARTY / → CUCUMBER CASTLE → the NIGHTMARE → WELCOME TO MY NIGHTMARE → the MONSTER CLUB, Joyce Van Patten *(Maude)*

Storyline: Walter Hale is the manager of a 1920s chautauqua, a travelling medicine show with a bit of education thrown in. Things get complicated as Hale confronts the militant Union organiser Charlene. *BG*

Movie rating: *4.5

Visual: video + dvd

Off the record: nothing

ELVIS PRESLEY: Live A Little, Love A Little / Charro! / The Trouble With Girls / Change Of Habit

Mar 95. (cd) *R.C.A.; <(07863 66559-2)>* ☐ ☐
– (LIVE A LITTLE, LOVE A LITTLE tracks) / (CHARRO! tracks) / Clean up your own backyard / Swing down, sweet chariot / Signs of the zodiac (by MARLYN MASON) / Almost / Whiffenpoof song / Violet / Clean up your own backyard (undubbed version) / Almost (undubbed version) / (CHANGE OF HABIT tracks).

S/track review: Originally released as a brass-overdubbed single in the wake of ELVIS' dramatic 1968 resurgence, 'Clean Up Your Own Backyard' is the only track worth mentioning among those posthumously collected for this soundtrack's CD re-issue (alongside 'LIVE A LITTLE, LOVE A LITTLE', 'CHARRO!' and 'CHANGE OF HABIT'). Bluesy, funky and gritty in a way that most of PRESLEY's Hollywood stuff wasn't, it bears the mark of a man back in the ascendance. The same can't be said of the other stuff, especially previously unreleased (there was a reason guys..) dross like 'Signs Of The Zodiac' and the unfortunately named 'Whiffenpoof Song'. Arrgghhh!! *BG*

Album (CD compilation) rating: *4

– spinoff hits, etc. –

ELVIS PRESLEY: Clean Up Your Own Backyard

Jul 69. (7") *R.C.A.; <47-9747> (RCA 1869)* 35 Aug69 21

TRUE STORIES

1986 (US 89m) Warner Bros. Pictures (PG)

Film genre: Americana spoof/satire/Rock Musical

Top guns: s-w: **David BYRNE** (+ dir), Beth Henley

Stars: David BYRNE *(narrator/singer)*, John Goodman *(Louis Fyne)* ← SWEET DREAMS / → BLUES BROTHERS 2000 → O BROTHER, WHERE ART THOU? → COYOTE UGLY → the EMPEROR'S NEW GROOVE → STORYTELLING → MASKED AND ANONYMOUS → OVERNIGHT → BEYOND THE SEA, Swoosie Kurtz *(Miss Rollings)* → BAJA OKLAHOMA → REALITY BITES, Spalding Gray *(Earl Culver)* ← the KILLING FIELDS / → BEACHES → STRAIGHT TALK → HOW HIGH, Annie McEnroe *(Kay Culver)* → the DOORS → S.F.W., Alix Elias *(the cute woman)* ← ROCK'N'ROLL HIGH SCHOOL, Jo Harvey Allen *(the lying woman)* → TAPEHEADS → ALL THE PRETTY HORSES, John Ingle *(the preacher)*, **Roebuck "Pops" Staples** *(Mr. Tucker)* <= the STAPLE SINGERS =>, **Tito Larriva** *(Ramon)* ← ROAD HOUSE / → FROM DUSK TILL DAWN → the MILLION DOLLAR HOTEL, rest of **Talking Heads:- Tina Weymouth, Jerry Harrison & Chris Frantz** *(musicians)* ← STOP MAKING SENSE, Louis Black *(marching accordion band member)* → JANIS JOPLIN SLEPT HERE → HOME OF THE BLUES → the DEVIL AND DANIEL JOHNSTON

Storyline: The little-known town of Virgil, Texas is ready to celebrate its 150th anniversary. David Byrne dresses himself like the natives and, driving a red convertible, introduces us to a few of the locals who at the very least should all be receiving some sort of psychiatric treatment or counselling. Meet the laziest woman ever, the soothsayer and the vegetable-driven dignitary Earl Culver amongst others. *JZ*

Movie rating: *6.5

Visual: video + dvd

Off the record: Jo Harvey Allen is the wife of country singer, Terry Allen, who actually sings on the soundtrack below.

DAVID BYRNE: Sounds From True Stories *(w/ Various Artists)*

Nov 86. (lp/c) *Sire; <25515> E.M.I.; (ENC/TCENC 3520)* ☐ ☐
– Cocktail desperado (TERRY ALLEN & THE PANHANDLE MYSTERY BAND) / Road song (MEREDITH MONK) / Freeway son / Brownie's theme / Mall muzak: a) Building a highway, b) Puppy polka, c) Party girls / Dinner music (the KRONOS QUARTET) / Disco hits! / City of steel (TALKING HEADS) / Love theme from True Stories / Festa para um Rei Negro (BANDA ECLIPSE) / Buster's theme (CARL FINCH) / Soy de Tejas (STEVE JORDAN) / I love metal buildings / Glass operator. *(some cd's w/ bonus +=)* – People like us (JOHN GOODMAN) / Puzzlin' evidence (JOHN INGLE) / Papa Legba (POP STAPLES) / Hey now (ST THOMAS AQUINAS SCHOOL CHOIR) / Radio head (TITO LARRIVA).

S/track review: A mile or so away from DAVID BYRNE's 1986 Talking Heads album project of the name, 'Sounds From TRUE STORIES' misleads us on a road to nowhere, to a big country where rural Americana finds solace. Like something from a Danny Elfman score (mainly 'FORBIDDEN ZONE'), the movie soundtrack opens its musical account with the TERRY ALLEN-sung, 'Cocktail Desperado', a novelty tune like several of the subsequent dirges. There are glimpses of TALKING HEADS (in fact a whole song 'City Of Steel'), but this is solo BYRNE's brainchild, and definitely no 'Catherine Wheel'. The Nu Yoik musician (once saviour of the New Wave scene) gets his maracas out on 'Freeway Son' (so to speak), the first of many meetings between hand-held instrument, Hawaiian guitar and orchestra. Bypassing a few lounge instrumentals, BYRNE takes us Contempi-rary-style into the world of 'Mall Muzak' (a medley); stand-up comic John Shuttleworth would get his inspiration here (we think). When one thinks of BYRNE you immediately 'STOP MAKING SENSE', or you think of that big white suit he wore in that docu-film. His choice of various artists for the film and soundtrack is either genius or downright mystifying; MEREDITH MONK's 'Road Song' could well be the Penguin Cafe Orchestra, while the KRONOS QUARTET's inclusion baffles mere mortals. If you love the bossa nova, Mexican polka (via STEVE JORDAN's 'Soy De Tejas') and anything worldly, this one's for you, kid, the sad one that loves anything BYRNE does. If it wasn't for his 'Glass Operator' finale, complete with symphony, straining violins and a brief peak of climactic crescendo, this would be one of the most over-indulgent albums ever. *MCS*

Album rating: *5

– associated releases, etc. –

TALKING HEADS: Wild Wild Life / People Like Us – movie version

Aug 86. (7") *<28629> (EMI 5567)* [25] [43]
(12"+=/12"pic-d+=) *(12EMI/+P 5567)* – ('A'extended).

TALKING HEADS: True Stories

Sep 86. (lp/c)(cd) *Sire; <25512> E.M.I.; (EU/TCEU 3511)(CDP 746345-2)* [17] [7]
– Love for sale / Puzzlin' evidence / Hey now / Papa Legba / Wild wild life / Radio head / Dream operator / People like us / City of dreams. *(cd+=)* – Wild wild life (Eric 'E.T.' Thorngren mix). *(re-iss. Sep89 on 'Fame' cd/c/lp; CD/TC+/FA 3231)*

TALKING HEADS: Love For Sale / Hey Now

Nov 86. (7") *<28497>* [ ] [–]

TALKING HEADS: Radio Head / Hey Now – movie version

Apr 87. (7") *(EM 1)* [–] [52]
(d7"+=)(12"+=/cd-s+=) *(EMD 1)(12/CD EM 1)* – ('A'-remix) / ('B'-Milwaukee remix).

TURN IT UP

2000 (US 86m) MadGuy Films / Paris Brothers / New Line Cinema (R)

Film genre: urban Hip-Hop-music/showbiz crime drama

Top guns: dir: (+ s-w) Robert Adetuyi → STOMP THE YARD (story: Ray 'Cory' Daniels, Chris Hudson, Kelly Hilaire)

Stars: Pras Michel *(Denzel/Diamond)* → BLOCK PARTY → FEEL THE NOISE, **Ja Rule** *(David 'Gage' Williams)* → BACKSTAGE → BEEF → BEEF III, Jason Statham *(Mr. B)*, Vondie Curtis-Hall *(Cliff)* ← CROOKLYN ← the MAMBO KINGS ← MYSTERY TRAIN, Tamala Jones *(Kia)* ← LITTLE RICHARD, John Ralston *(Mr. White)*, Chris Messina *(Baz)*, Eugene Clark *(Marshall)* → MAN IN THE MIRROR: THE MICHAEL JACKSON STORY, **Faith Evans** *(Natalie)* → TUPAC: RESURRECTION → the FIGHTING TEMPTATIONS, **Shinehead** *(Smiley)* ← the REGGAE MOVIE, Chang Tseng *(Mr. Chang)*, **Lauryn Hill** (cameo) → BLOCK PARTY, Patricia Velasquez → COMMITTED

Storyline: It's been quite a week for rap musician Diamond. His mother's just died, his long-lost dad Cliff appears and starts giving him grief, and Kia his girlfriend tells him she's pregnant. Added to this triple whammy is the fact that his manager and friend Gage has unwittingly stolen $100,000 from drugs baron Mr B to finance Diamond's new album. As the body count rises and the net closes in, the two rappers take things into their own hands to save their lives. No pressure eh? *JZ*

Movie rating: *3.5

Visual: video (no audio OST; score: Frank Fitzpatrick)

Off the record: Pras Michel was a member of the Fugees.

Tina TURNER

Born: Anna Mae Bullock, 26 Nov'38, Brownsville, Texas, USA; she was raised in Nutbush, Tennessee and became a local choir singer. In the late 50s and eight years her senior, she met up with R&B musician, Ike Turner, and they were to strike up a working and loving partnership (after she persuaded him to let her have a go at fronting his band). In 1960, now billed as Ike & Tina Turner, they hit the US Top 30 with 'A Fool In Love'. As well as presenting a much feted stage show (which served to highlight both Ike's musical and choreographic skills alongside Tina's raunchy vocals and stunning appearance), the duo proceeded to notch up a string of R&B hits, even hitting the pop charts the following year with their Top 20 smash hit, 'It's Gonna Work Out Fine'. Things virtually dried up until the mid-60s, when they were introduced to the legendary Phil Spector. He produced their magnum opus, 'River Deep Mountain High', a "wall of sound" soul classic which, although a relative flop in the States, peaked at No.3 in the UK. With varying degrees of fortune, the pair moved from one label to another, finally scoring a massive Top 5 US hit on 'Liberty' in early '71 with an earthy cover of John Fogerty's classic 'Proud Mary'. The enthusiastic patronage by the ROLLING STONES did much to raise their profile (the pair performed at the ill-fated Altamont gig in 1969; filmed as 'GIMME SHELTER') and they finally broke out again in 1973 when Tina's autobiographical composition, 'Nutbush City Limits', was a massive seller on both sides of the Atlantic. In 1974, she landed the part of "The Acid Queen" in the WHO's rock opera, 'TOMMY' (1975), her new-found independence giving her time to reflect on her well-documented ill-treatment by husband Ike. In 1976, after converting to Buddhism, she finally divorced him, in effect ending not only their marriage but their lucrative musical partnership. After a time on welfare, she began to make tentative moves to carve out a solo career, already having released an impressive album of covers, 'Acid Queen', the previous year. Yet although she remained a star attraction on the live club circuit scene, she still found it hard to sell records. Until, that is, 'Capitol' contracted her late in '82 following some show-stopping support slots for the 'Stones. Following the surprise international success of her Al Green cover, 'Let's Stay Together', in late '83, the multi-million 'Private Dancer' album was rush-recorded and released in summer '84. The record included her recent Grammy winner and US No.1, 'What's Love Got To Do With It', while it also showcased a more sophisticated, smoother approach, although TURNER's range was as impressive as ever and, incredibly she was looking better than many female stars half her age. In '85, she starred in the film 'Mad Max: Beyond The Thunderdome' (for which she provided the theme tune, 'We Don't Need Another Hero'), receiving an award by NAACP for best actress; TURNER was also reputed to have turned down the offer of a major part in the film, 'The Color Purple'. She was now arguably the most famous female Rock & Pop singer on earth, a claim to which the 180,000 audience attending the Rio De Janeiro January '86 concert would testify. Tina went on to release further million-selling 80s albums, 'Break Every Rule' (1986) and 'Foreign Affair' (1989), while the troubled history of Ike and Tina's former partnership was documented in the 1993 biopic, 'WHAT'S LOVE GOT TO DO WITH IT' (based on Tina's book, 'I, Tina'); the accompanying soundtrack topped the UK charts. In 1995, she became another in the long list of James Bond theme ladies, when she sang the title track to 'GoldenEye'. *BG & MCS*

- filmography {acting} etc.-

Gimme Shelter *(1970 {p w/ IKE})* / **Soul To Soul** *(1971 {p w/ IKE} OST by V/A =>)* / Taking Off *(1971 {c})* / **Cocksucker Blues** *(1972 {p})* / **Tommy** *(1975 {a/p} on OST by the WHO & V/A =>)* / **All This And World War II** *(1976 on OST by V/A =>)* / **Sgt. Pepper's Lonely Hearts Club Band** *(1978 {c} OST by V/A =>)* / Mad Max Beyond Thunderdome *(1985 {*} hit theme on OST)* / Last Action Hero *(1993 {a} OST by V/A)* / **What's Love Got To Do With It?** *(1993 hits + OST =>)* / GoldenEye *(1995 hit theme on OST)* / the Goddess *(2005 {*})*

□ the TURTLES segment
(⇒ MY DINNER WITH JIMI)

TUTTI FRUTTI

1987 (UK 6x50m mini-TV) BBC Scotland

Film genre: Rock'n'roll Musical comedy/drama

Top guns: dir: Tony Smith / s-w: John Byrne → YOUR CHEATIN' HEART tv

Stars: Robbie Coltrane *(Danny McGlone)* ← EAT THE RICH ← ABSOLUTE BEGINNERS ← GHOST DANCE ← SUBWAY RIDERS ← FLASH GORDON, Emma Thompson *(Suzi Kettles)* → PRIMARY COLORS, Maurice Roëves *(Vincent Driver)* → the ACID HOUSE → HALLAM FOE, Richard Wilson *(Eddie Clockerty)*, Stuart McGugan *(Bomba MacAteer)*, Jake D'Arcy *(Fud O'Donnell)*, Katy Murphy *(Janice Toner)* → YOUR CHEATIN' HEART, Ron Donachie *(Dennis Sproul)*, Barbara Rafferty *(woman at infirmary)* ← the WICKER MAN / → the ACID HOUSE → the YOUNG PERSON'S GUIDE TO BECOMING A ROCK STAR, **Tam White** *(voice; Big Jazza McGlone)*

Storyline: Scottish singers the Majestics' plans for their 25th anniversary tour go up in smoke when lead singer Big Jazza is killed in a car crash. The show must go on and Jazza's tubby young brother Danny and his old girlfriend Suzi are recruited to the band as replacements. Meanwhile, grumpy manager Mr Clockerty and sarky secretary Janice try to keep the tour going as tempers fray and difficulties arise. The series was aired on 3rd March – 7th April, 1987. *JZ*

Movie rating: *7.5

Visual: video

Off the record: Tam White occasionally recorded under the more Anglo-friendly Tom White – but in 1975 Tam had a rare Top 40 hit with 'What In The World's Come Over You'. The latter was released on Mickie Most's 'Rak' label, the famed producer picking White up after judging in his favour in a TV talent contest. *MCS*

——

the MAJESTICS: Tutti Frutti

Mar 87. (lp/c) *B.B.C.; (REN/ZCN 629)* 64 –
– Almost grown / Rockin' through the rye / No particular place to go / Promised land / Rip it up / Bye bye love / Great balls of fire – Tutti frutti / Love is strange / That'll be the day / You're sixteen (you're beautiful and you're mine) / Love hurts / Almost grown (Tutti Frutti).

S/track review: Rock'n'roll outfit, the MAJESTICS, were supposedly doing the Glasgow "toilet" circuit since the early 60s (and, going by the LP liner notes, even further back!). The actual truth of the matter – as everybody and their wee granny knows – they were indeed a bunch of up and coming thespians awaiting their big break in showbiz – the relatively young, London-born EMMA THOMPSON was one who subsequently succeeded, while "leader of the pack" ROBBIE COLTRANE was growing in stature in more ways than one (Hagrid in 'Harry Potter'). The 'TUTTI FRUTTI' TV series aside, the soundtrack – featuring Danny (COLTRANE), Fud, Vincent, Bomba and at times Suzi (THOMPSON) – was a bit of a social club night out, all cover versions et al. The catalogue of R&B legend Chuck Berry is pilfered the most, songs such as 'Almost Grown' (which bookends the album), 'No Particular Place To Go' & 'Promised Land' are pure novelty. The works of the Everly Brothers ('Bye Bye Love' & 'Love Hurts') and Little Richard ('Rip It Up' & 'Tutti Frutti') also show up, or indeed show us all up. People well into middle-age will probably love the banter and that – as they say in posher Glasgow residencies – but then again 'Love Is Strange'. One recommends you try to obtain the DVD TV series, which, after some legal wrangles, might finally be released. *MCS*

Album rating: *3.5

20th CENTURY OZ

original Australian title 'OZ'

1976 (Aus 103m; cut US 85m) Australian Film Commission / Z (R)

Film genre: Rock'n'roll road movie Musical fantasy/comedy

Top guns: s-w + dir: Chris Lofven (nov: 'The Wonderful Wizard Of Oz' by L. Frank Baum)

Stars: Joy Dunstan *(Dorothy)*, Graham Matters *(the Wizard / Wally / etc.)* / Bruce Spence *(Blondie the surfie & bass player)* → SWEET TALKER → RIKKY AND PETE → QUEEN OF THE DAMNED, Garry Waddell *(Killer the bikie & guitarist)* → SWEET TALKER → CHOPPER → the PROPOSITION, Michael Carman *(Greaseball the mechanic & drummer)*, Robin Ramsey *(Glin; the Good Fairy)*, Paula Maxwell *(Jane)*, Ned Kelly *(bouncer / trucker)*

Storyline: When teenage groupie Dorothy is knocked unconscious in a road accident, she dreams she is in a fantasy world on her way to the last concert of 'The Wizard'. However, she learns that during her transition from Earth to Oz she has killed a young hoodlum, whose brother is out for revenge. Help is at hand in the form of a dumb surfboarder, a heartless mechanic and a cowardly biker, who accompany her on her imaginary journey. *JZ*

Movie rating: *5

Visual: video + dvd (2004)

Off the record: Chris Lofven was also a noted session man who subsequently (from 1987 . . .) went on to play bass (& sing) with the Ragged Band, an Australian Celtic trad/folk-styled quintet who've so far delivered three CD-albums, 'Up The Sides And Down The Middle', 'Distant Shores' & 'Cousin Jack And Other Celtic Stories'. ROSS WILSON had been part of the Australian rock scene for over a decade having sang and played guitar for Ross Wilson & The Pink Finks (in the mid-60s), the Party Machine (in the late 60s), Sons Of The Vegetal Mother (late 60s-early 70s) and the long-standing Daddy Cool (until 1975); he subsequently formed Mondo Rock in '79 and had a minor US hit in 1987 via 'Primitive Love Rites'. *MCS*

——

Various Cast (composer: ROSS WILSON *)

1977. (lp) *Celestial; <OZ-4001>* –
– Living in the land of Oz (*) / The mood (*) / Beatin' around the bush (JO JO ZEP & THE FALCONS) / Our warm tender love (JOY DUNSTAN) / You're driving me insane (GRAHAM MATTERS as WALLY) / Living in the land of Oz – reprise 1 (*) / Greaseball (*) / Glad I'm living here (JO JO ZEP & THE FALCONS) / Who's gonna love you tonight? (*) / You're driving me insane (GRAHAM MATTERS as WIZARD) / Living in the land of Oz – reprise 2 (*) / Atmospherics (instrumental).

S/track review: If one loved the music of Little Feat, then the funky-tonk ' . . .OZ' soundtrack is worth the finding. Featuring former Daddy Cool frontman, ROSS WILSON (the Australian Lowell George!), on more than half the cues, opener 'Living In The Land Of Oz' surfaces three times, the second a Zappa/Turtles-esque reprise, the third just short'n'sweet. The raunchy and risqué 'Greaseball' (think Bachman-Turner Overdrive) is superhighway-fuelled rock'n'roll, whilst 'Who's Gonna Love You Tonight?' is falsetto to the point of mystery – it does sound like a female vocalist. Under the production of Wilson, recent Aussie acquisitions JO JO ZEP & THE FALCONS (featuring vocalist Joe Camilleri, guitarists Jeff Burstin & Wayne Burt, bassist John Power and drummer Gary Young) contributed two tracks of the pub-rock variety, the Chuck Berry-esque 'Beating Around The Bush' and the Mick Jagger-cloning 'Glad I'm Living Here'. JOY DUNSTAN ('Our Warm Tender Love'), on the other hand, is like a fusion of Dolly Parton and Bonnie Tyler, while fellow rock-thespian GRAHAM MATTERS ('You're Driving Me Insane' – 2 versions) virtually transgresses respectively from Iggy & The Stooges to the original Aussie mid-60s pensmiths, the Missing Links. The weird and instrumental 'Atmospherics' brings the curtain down to its dour climax, and on reflection the LP is nothing startling, just colourful. *MCS*

Album rating: *5

– spinoff singles, etc. –

JO JO ZEP & THE FALCONS: Beating Around The Bush

Jul 76. (7") *Oz;* [–] Austra [–]

24 HOUR PARTY PEOPLE

2002 (UK 113m) Pathe / Film Consortium / Film Four (R)

Film genre: showbiz/Rock/Pop-music bio-pic comedy

Top guns: dir: Michael Winterbottom → 9 SONGS / s-w: Frank Cottrell Boyce → REVENGERS TRAGEDY

Stars: Steve Coogan *(Tony Wilson)* → COFFEE AND CIGARETTES, Shirley Henderson *(Lindsey)* ← TRAINSPOTTING, Lennie James *(Alan Erasmus)*, Paddy Considine *(Rob Gretton)* → STONED, Andy Serkis *(Martin Hannett)* ← MOJO, Sean Harris *(Ian Curtis)* → BROTHERS OF THE HEAD, Danny Cunningham *(Shaun Ryder)*, John Simm *(Bernard Sumner)* ← HUMAN TRAFFIC / → BROTHERS OF THE HEAD, Ralf Little *(Peter Hook)*, Keith Allen *(Roger Ames)* ← the YOUNG PERSON'S GUIDE TO BECOMING A ROCK STAR ← TRAINSPOTTING, Chris Coghill *(Bez)*, Paul Popplewell *(Paul Ryder)*, Raymond Waring *(Vini Reilly)*, John Thomson *(Charles, producer)*, Rob Brydon *(Ryan Letts)*, Keiran O'Brian *(Nathan McGough)* → 9 SONGS, Martin Hancock *(Howard Devoto)*, Dave Gorman *(John, the postman)*, Christopher Eccleston *(Boethius)* ← the INVISIBLE CIRCUS / → REVENGERS TRAGEDY, Peter Kay *(Don Tonay)*, Ron Cook *(Derek Ryder)*, Darren Tighe *(Mike Pickering)*, Kate Magowan *(Yvette Wilson)* → IT'S ALL GONE PETE TONG, **Paul Ryder** *(Pel)*, **Martin Coogan** *(Chris Nagle)*, **Mark E. Smith** *(punter)*, **Howard Devoto** *(cleaner)*, Mark Windows *(Johnny Rotten)*, **Mike Pickering** *(Hacienda DJ)*, **Mani** *(sound engineer)* → 9 SONGS, **Martin Moscrop** *(partygoer)*, Sam Riley *(Mark E. Smith)* → CONTROL, **Clint Boon** *(railway guard #2)*, **Tony Wilson** *(studio director)*, Margi Clarke *(actor in corridor)* ← SOUL SURVIVOR / → REVENGERS TRAGEDY, **Roweta** *(herself)*, footage:- **Siouxsie** *(herself)* ← the FILTH & THE FURY ← WESTWAY TO THE WORLD ← the PUNK ROCK MOVIE ← JUBILEE / → PUNK: ATTITUDE

Storyline: The life and cultural times of Granada TV journalist Tony Wilson and his beloved Manchester converge as the Sex Pistols hit town. When not filing a report from some dung cluttered farm yard, the witty, debonair Wilson is philosophising on the city's zealous love affair with punk. His label, 'Factory' records, serves as a chaotic refuge for Joy Division on down, while his 'Hacienda' nightclub becomes the epicentre of an ecstasy fuelled spin on American house music. *BG*

Movie rating: *7.5

Visual: dvd

Off the record: A plethora of indie rock stars appear on film: **Mark E. Smith** (of the Fall), **Clint Boon** (Inspiral Carpets), **Martin Coogan** (Mock Turtles; and older brother of Steve), **Mike Pickering** (ex-Quando Quango before joining M People), **Martin Moscrop** *(A Certain Ratio)*, ***Howard Devoto*** (ex-Buzzcocks and Magazine), **Mani** (ex-Stone Roses, now Primal Scream), **Paul Ryder** (Happy Mondays) and **Roweta** Satchell (ex-backing singer for the Happy Mondays and finalist of ITV's X Factor in 2004). **Tony Wilson** made a guest appearance in the film, sadly he died of cancer on 10th August, 2007 at the age of 57, having just co-produced the Ian Curtis biopic, 'CONTROL'. *MCS*

Various Artists

Apr 02. (cd) *London; (0927 44930-2) ffrr; <78136-2>* [15] Aug02 [ ]
– Anarchy in the UK (SEX PISTOLS) / 24 hour party people – Jon Carter mix (HAPPY MONDAYS) / Transmission (JOY DIVISION) / Ever fallen in love (BUZZCOCKS) / Janie Jones (CLASH) / New dawn fades (MOBY & NEW ORDER) / Atmosphere (JOY DIVISION) / Otis (DURUTTI COLUMN) / Voodoo Ray (A GUY CALLED GERALD) / Temptation (NEW ORDER) / Loose fit (HAPPY MONDAYS) / Pacific state (808 STATE) / Move your body (MARSHALL JEFFERSON) / She's lost control (JOY DIVISION) / Hallelujah (club mix) (HAPPY MONDAYS) / Here to stay (NEW ORDER & CHEMICAL BROTHERS) / Love will tear us apart (JOY DIVISION).

S/track review: Historically, the Bee Gees were about the best Manchester could offer, and even then the Gibb brothers had emigrated to Australia before actually forming their band. That a one-off SEX PISTOLS gig could force such an unlikely cultural revolution is the basic premise for the film and for the soundtrack. We're still waiting for 'Anarchy In The UK' but at least Manchester's music scene – for a while at least – was as close to organised anarchy as the industry had dared go. Despite the fact it hadn't even been written at the time Johnny Rotten and Co played to a half-empty hall, 'Anarchy..' serves as the soundtrack's year zero, JOY DIVISION its new dawn fading. The unquiet art of Ian Curtis is still the most extraordinary to have come out of that city, out of any British city. His band gets the most space on this soundtrack, and justify it with convulsive epistles like 'Transmission' and 'Love Will Tear Us Apart'. Contemporaries like the BUZZCOCKS couldn't hope to compete, but made great, infatuated music anyway. NEW ORDER are the window into the next generation, Peter Hook's turbine bass lines driving the lemming-like rush to the dancefloor; there's no 'Blue Monday', but the spastic modulations of A GUY CALLED GERALD's 'Voodoo Ray', are the next best thing. HAPPY MONDAYS take it from the dancefloor into the studio (Martin Hannett's worst nightmare) and back onto the dancefloor again. After the austerity which coloured Manchester's coming of age, Shaun Ryder brought back the hedonism with a vengeance which even the movie doesn't do justice: 'Hallelujah' and the title track are classic 70s records dressed in outsized late 80s fashion. With key Northern players like the Fall, the Smiths and the Stone Roses missing, this doesn't claim to be a complete document but it's as close to one as we're likely to get. *BG*

Album rating: *8.5

– spinoff hits, etc. –

NEW ORDER & THE CHEMICAL BROTHERS: Here To Stay (mixes)

Apr 02. (cd-s) *(NUOCD 11)* [15] [–]
(cd-s) *(NUCDP 11)* – ('A'mixes; radio / Felix Da Housecat – thee extended glitz / the scumfrog dub).
(12") *(NUOX 11)* – ('A'mixes).

HAPPY MONDAYS: 24 Hour Party People

May 02. (12") *(LONX 466)* [ ] [–]

☐ 22 PISTEPIRKKO segment
(⇒ DOWNHILL CITY)

☐ TWIST ALL NIGHT alt.
(⇒ the CONTINENTAL TWIST)

TWIST AROUND THE CLOCK

1961 (US 86m b&w) Four Leaf Productions / Columbia Pictures

Film genre: Rock'n'roll/Dance Musical drama

Top guns: dir: Oscar Rudolph → DON'T KNOCK THE TWIST / s-w: James B. Gordon ← DON'T KNOCK THE ROCK ← ROCK AROUND THE CLOCK / → DON'T KNOCK THE TWIST → HOOTENANNY HOOT → GET YOURSELF A COLLEGE GIRL → WHEN THE BOYS MEET THE GIRLS → the FASTEST GUITAR ALIVE → a TIME TO SING

Stars: Chubby Checker *(performer)* ← TEENAGE MILLIONAIRE / → IT'S TRAD, DAD! → DON'T KNOCK THE TWIST → LET THE GOOD TIMES ROLL → PURPLE PEOPLE EATER → TWIST, **Dion** *(performer)* ← TEENAGE MILLIONAIRE / → MAYOR OF THE SUNSET STRIP, **the Marcels:- Allen Johnson, Fred Johnson, Richard Knauss, Cornelius Harp,**

Gene Bricker, Ronald Mundy *(performers)*, **Vicki Spencer** *(performer)* ← TEENAGE MILLIONAIRE, **Clay Cole** *(performer)*John Cronin *(Mitch Mason)*, Mary Mitchell *(Tina Louden)* → a SWINGIN' SUMMER → the GIRLS ON THE BEACH, Maura McGiveney *(Debbie Marshall)*, Tol Avery *(Joe Marshall)*, Alvy Moore *(Dizzy Bellew)*

Storyline: see ROCK AROUND THE CLOCK for details – because this is an update of the original, albeit with Twist dance fever the subject. *MCS*

Movie rating: *4.5

Visual: video (no audio OST)

Off the record: Chubby Checker + Dion were already off the movie mark with appearances in 'The HAPPIEST MILLIONAIRE'. **the Marcels** were a doo-wop outfit from Pittsburgh who shot onto the scene in 1961 with US chart-topper, 'Blue Moon'; the movie also featured relatively unknowns **Vicki Spencer + Clay Cole.** *MCS*

TWO A PENNY

1968 (UK 98m) World Wide (A)

Film genre: religious-Pop-music drama

Top guns: dir: James F. Collier / s-w: Stella Linden

Stars: Cliff RICHARD *(Jamie Hopkins)*, Dora Bryan *(Ruby Hopkins)*, Ann Holloway *(Carol Turner)*, Avril Angers *(Mrs. Burry)* ← the FAMILY WAY ← BE MY GUEST, Peter Barkworth *(vicar)* ← PLAY IT COOL, Geoffrey Bayldon *(Alec Fitch)* → TO SIR, WITH LOVE → BORN TO BOOGIE → the MONSTER CLUB, Mona Washbourne *(Mrs. Duckett)* ← FERRY 'CROSS THE MERSEY / → MRS. BROWN, YOU'VE GOT A LOVELY DAUGHTER → O LUCKY MAN!, Charles Lloyd Pack *(Rev. Allison)* ← EVERY DAY'S A HOLIDAY, Richard Vanstone *(David)* → MADE, Rev. Billy Graham *(himself)*

Storyline: Jamie Hopkins has strayed from the straight and narrow and makes a penny or two nicking prescription drugs from his mum's employer (a doctor). Girlfriend Carol is also not averse to a spot of law-bending herself until, that is, she attends a Billy Graham crusade meeting and is shown the error of her ways by the egregious evangelist. Her mission is now to convert Jamie to the saintly life but he still has a cross or two to bear. *JZ*

Movie rating: *2

Visual: video + dvd

Off the record: Rev. Billy Graham . . . was a christian mentor to many a pop star including Pat Boone, Johnny Cash and of course, Cliff. *MCS*

CLIFF RICHARD (composer: Mike Leander)

Jul 68. (lp; mono/stereo) *Columbia; (SX/SCX 6262)* [ ] [-]
– Two a penny / I'll love you forever today / Questions / Long is the night (instrumental) / Lonely girl / And me (I'm on the outside now) / Daybreak (instrumental) / Twist and shout / Celeste (instrumental) / Wake up, wake up / Cloudy / Red rubber ball / Close to Kathy / Rattler.

S/track review: With the Shadows now out of the picture, CLIFF RICHARD was once again paired with a studio orchestra although thankfully there was no return to the stage theatrics of old. In fact, with only four featured songs and a more serious plot line, the film was a conscious move away from the commerically ailing boy-meets-girl musical. The man even got to write some of his own songs, even if he only performed one of them in the film itself (a stodgy version of 'Twist And Shout'). His voice was also maturing and, framed by funky, Swinging London brass arrangements, RICHARD sounds like a different man from the one who coyly crooned 'Living Doll' all those years ago. As if to underline how seriously he was now taking his artistry, 'Questions' finds him wrestling with the existence of the big man upstairs; as metaphysical material goes, it's at least more engaging than 'Saviour's Day' . . . *BG*

Album rating: *4

– spinoff hits, etc. –

CLIFF RICHARD: I'll Love You Forever Today

Jun 68. (7") *(DB 8437)* [27] [-]

TWO OF US

2000 (US 89m cable-TV) Viacom Productions Inc. / VH-1 (PG-13)

Film genre: Pop/Rock-music docudrama

Top guns: dir: Michael Lindsay-Hogg ← ROCK AND ROLL CIRCUS ← LET IT BE / s-w: Mark Stanfield

Stars: Adian Quinn *(Paul McCartney)*, Jared Harris *(John Lennon)* ← I SHOT ANDY WARHOL ← DEAD MAN ← NATURAL BORN KILLERS, Ric Reid *(TV interviewer)*, Martin Martinuzzi *(limo driver)*, Jeremy Tracz *(political activist)* → HENDRIX, Joe Bostick *(elevator attendant)* → HENDRIX, Neil Foster *(concierge)*, Ian Ryan *(dreadlocked man)*, Derek Aasland *(young man)* → HENDRIX

Storyline: Fictional account of a McCartney (Wings had taken off again) and Lennon (then a house-hubby) meeting in New York in 1976 at the latter's Dakota apartment. Little did Saturday Night Live comedian Lorne Michaels know when he prophetically announced that NBC-TV would pay a re-formed Beatles $3,000 to perform live on the show, that the two were in the Big Apple – but did they discuss the ramifications of such an act – and of course, everything else under the sun. *MCS*

Movie rating: *6

Visual: video + dvd (no audio OST; score: David Schwartz)

Off the record: Jared Harris is the son of the late, great Irish actor, Richard Harris. *MCS*

TWO TICKETS TO PARIS

1962 (US 78m b&w) Columbia Pictures

Film genre: Rock'n'roll Musical comedy

Top guns: dir: Greg Garrison ← HEY, LET'S TWIST / s-w: Hal Hackady ← HEY, LET'S TWIST ← LET'S ROCK

Stars: Joey DEE *(Joey)*, Gary Crosby *(Gary)* → GIRL HAPPY, Jeri Lynne Fraser *(Piper)*, Kay Medford *(Aggie)* ← JAMBOREE, Lisa James *(Coco)*, Charles Nelson Reilly *(Claypoole)* → ROCK-A-DOODLE, Jeri Archer *(Mrs. Patten)*, Richard Dickens *(Tony)* ← HEY, LET'S TWIST, Sal Lombardo *(Marmaduke)* → UNCLE MEAT, **the Starliters:- Dave Brigati, Carlton Lattimore, Willie Davis, Don Martin, Larry Vernieri** *(themselves)* ← HEY, LET'S TWIST

Storyline: The rocking and rolling of a ship on the Atlantic can't stop two young lovebirds from twisting away on a pre-marriage cruise to Paris. But in the confined space of an ocean liner boys and girls can't help talking and dancing with each other and soon our twisty twosome are deep in troubled waters with different partners. Will their love pull them through their sea of troubles or will a life on the ocean wave prove their undoing? *JZ*

Movie rating: *3.5

Visual: none

Off the record: Gary Crosby is the son of crooning legend, Bing Crosby.

Various (composer: HENRY GLOVER & the Orchestra *)

Aug 62. (lp) *Roulette; <R 25182> Columbia; (33SX 1482)* [ ] [ ]
– What kind of love is this (JOEY DEE) / Willy Willy (WILLY DAVIS & THE STARLITERS) / The open sea (*) / Twistin' on a liner (JOEY DEE) / C'est la vie (GARY CROSBY) / Instant men (KAY MEDFORD) / Two tickets to Paris (ORCHESTRA & CHORUS) /

Teenage vamp (JERI LYNNE FRASER) / Left Bank blues (*) / C'est si bon (JOEY DEE) / Everytime (I think about you) (JOEY DEE & THE STARLITERS) / This boat (JOEY DEE & THE STARLITERS).

S/track review: Hot on the heels of JOEY DEE's first feature film, 'HEY, LET'S TWIST!', comes a second instalment of "Peppermint Lounge", rock'n'roll, 'TWO TICKETS TO PARIS'. However, it's not all plain sailing aboard the album's proverbial love-boat, as DEE (& his STARLITERS) only feature on a handful of cues, including Top 20 Johnny Nash-penned hit, 'What Kind Of Love Is This'. His solo 'Twistin' On A Liner' and 'C'est Si Bon', paddle up the same stream, while he finally gets back to his twistin', RnR roots by way of JOEY DEE & THE STARLITERS (Dee-Glover-Levy/-Taylor) songs, 'Everytime (I Think About You)' and 'This Boat'. The STARLITERS (WILLIE DAVIS deputising for DEE), also come up trumps courtesy of Coasters-esque 'Willy Willy', by far the best thing here and pure unadulterated R&B. Orchestra leader HENRY GLOVER lets float his nostalgic world of sexy lounge musak by way of two easy-listening numbers, 'The Open Sea' & 'Left Bank Liner'; the title track – with a hint of the French National anthem – is also conducted by Marty Manning, complete with additional chorus. Actor GARY CROSBY takes croon to a new level via his Dean Martin-ish, 'C'Est La Vie', while newbie actress, JERI LYNNE FRASER bursts out on 'Teenage Vamp'. Veteran of dry humour and of course acting, KAY MEDFORD used her sardonic, Brooklyn wit on the novelty song, 'Instant Men', a plea for all kitchen-sink housewives dreaming for that perfectly made male. *MCS*

Album rating: *5

– spinoff hits, etc. –

JOEY DEE: What Kind Of Love Is This / Wing-Ding

Aug 62. (7") *<4438> (DB 4905)* [18] [ ]

200 MOTELS

aka FRANK ZAPPA'S 200 MOTELS

1971 (US 98m) Bizarre Productions / United Artists (R)

Film genre: Rock Musical fantasy/road movie

Top guns: dir: (+ s-w + story) **Frank ZAPPA**, visual dir: Tony Palmer (+ s-w), cartoons: Charles Swenson (special material: **Mark Volman + Howard Kaylan** * → MY DINNER WITH JIMI *

Stars: Frank ZAPPA *(himself)*, **Mothers Of Invention:- Jimmy Carl Black** *(+ Lonesome Cowboy Burt)* ← MONDO HOLLYWOOD / → UNCLE MEAT → ROCK SCHOOL, **Ian Underwood** *(himself)* → UNCLE MEAT, **Don Preston** *(himself)* → UNCLE MEAT, **George Duke** *(himself)*, **Aynsley Dunbar** *(himself)* ← AMOUGIES / → UNCLE MEAT, **Howard Kaylan** *(himself)* → GET CRAZY, **Mark Volman** *(himself)*, **Martin Lickert** *(Jeff Simmons)*, **'Motorhead' Sherwood** *(himself)* → UNCLE MEAT, **Ruth Underwood** *(fake drummer)*, Theodore Bikel *(Rance Muhammitz)*, **Keith Moon** *(the hot nun)* <= the WHO =>, **Ringo Starr** *(Larry The Dwarf / Frank Zappa)* <= the BEATLES =>, Dick Barber *(Bif Debris – the vacuum cleaner)* → UNCLE MEAT, **Pamela Miller** *(interviewer)* → SLAUGHTER'S BIG RIP-OFF → MAYOR OF THE SUNSET STRIP → FALLEN ANGEL → METAL: A HEADBANGER'S JOURNEY

Storyline: A discordant montage of impenetrable weirdness from Frank Zappa. While the film ostensibly follows Zappa and his Mothers Of Invention in a gonzoid portrayal of touring life, the almost complete absence of any plot and profusion of oblique humour renders any semblance of storyline secondary to the impressive (mostly live) musical performances. *BG*

Movie rating: *5.5

Visual: video

Off the record: Several Mothers feature here including ex-Turtles, **Howard Kaylan & Mark Volman.**

FRANK ZAPPA's 200 Motels

Oct 71. (d-lp) *United Artists; <9956> (UDF 50003)* [59] [ ]

– Semi-fraudulent – Direct-from-Hollywood overture / Mystery roach / Dance of the rock & roll interviewers / This town is a sealed tuna sandwich (prologue) / Tuna fish promenade / Dance of the just plain folks / This town is a sealed tuna fish sandwich (reprise) / The sealed tuna bolero / Lonesome cowboy Burt / Touring can make you crazy / Would you like a snack? / Redneck eats / Centerville / She painted up her face / Janet's big dance number / Half a dozen provocative squats / Mysterioso / Shove it right in / Lucy's seduction of a bored violinist & postlude / I'm stealing the towels / Dental hygeine dilemma / Does this kind of life look interesting to you? / Daddy, daddy, daddy / Penis dimension / What will this evening bring me this morning / A nun suit painted on some old boxes / Magic fingers / Motorhead's midnight ranch / Dew on the newts we got / The lad searches the night for his newts / The girl wants to fix him some broth / The girl's dream / Little green scratchy sweaters & corduroy ponce / Strictly genteel (the finale). *(re-iss. Jan89 on 'M.C.A.' d-lp/c; MCA/+C 24183) <(d-cd-iss. Oct97 on 'Rykodisc'+=; RCD 10513)>* – cut 1: Coming soon! / cut 2: The wide screen erupts / cut 3: Coming soon! / cut 4: Frank Zappa's 200 Motels / Magic fingers (single edit).

S/track review: With added symphonic muscle from the Royal Philharmonic Orchestra, FRANK ZAPPA, still echoing the artistic breakthrough of his earlier pastiche landmark, 'UNCLE MEAT', and as ambitious as ever, frantically see-saws between rock, neo-jazz and classical idioms while liberally anointing the whole with wacked-out snippets of dialogue and libidinous humour. Initially a double LP (released by 'Rykodisc' on 2-CDs in 1997), '200 MOTELS' is definitely not for non-ZAPPA fanatics, or who take themselves too seriously. ZAPPA and his MOTHERS of the moment (JIMMY CARL BLACK, GEORGE DUKE, AYNSLEY DUNBAR, IAN UNDERWOOD, HOWARD KAYLAN, MARK VOLMAN, RUTH UNDERWOOD and JIM PONS) concocted a real mothership of a record, musically like something resembling a Marx Brothers movie or a Dada-ist opera. With augmentation from THEODORE BIKEL (the narrator) and RINGO STARR (of some weird dialogue who incidentally mentions a train!), the music on its own needs the film so badly. The strained orchestra gets in the way – a lot, while "proper" songs struggle to the surface, and when they do its mostly down to the lewdness and crudeness of messers FLO & EDDIE (aka the aforementioned ex-Turtles VOLMAN and KAYLAN repectively). The highlights – and there ain't many – are faux country number, 'Lonesome Cowboy Burt', vocalist JIMMY CARL BLACK wanting a waitress to "sit on his face", was boy-ish, unadulterated humour, and "does humor belong in music?". 'Mystery Roach' carried off ZAPPA's approach to standard R&R, while 'Magic Fingers' and the psychedelic 'She Painted Up Her Face', play a different tune. Incidentally, former Mother, JEFF SIMMONS (whose real-life antics were portrayed in the movie) took off for other other pastures during the filming. Good judgement I say. *BG & MCS*

Album rating: *4.5

– spinoff releases, etc. –

FRANK ZAPPA: Magic Fingers / Daddy, Daddy, Daddy

Oct 71. (7") *<50857>* [–] [ ]

FRANK ZAPPA: What Will This Evening Bring Me This Morning? / Daddy, Daddy, Daddy

Nov 71. (7") *(UP 35319)* [ ] [–]

UHF

1989 (US 97m) Orion Pictures (PG-13)

Film genre: screwball showbiz/media satire/comedy

Top guns: s-w: Jay Levey (+ dir), **"Weird Al" Yankovic**

Stars: "Weird Al" Yankovic *(George Newman)* ← TAPEHEADS / → DERAILROADED, Michael Richards *(Stanley Spadowski)*, Kevin McCarthy *(R.J. Fletcher)*, Victoria Jackson *(Teri)*, David Bowe *(Bob)*, Stanley Brock *(Uncle Harvey)*, Anthony Geary *(Philo)*, Trinidad Silva *(Raul Hernandez)*, Geddy Watanabe *(Kuni)* → THAT THING YOU DO! → THANK YOU, GOOD NIGHT → ALFIE re-make, Fran Drescher *(Pamela Finklestein)* ← ROCK'N'ROLL MOM ← AMERICAN HOT WAX ← SATURDAY NIGHT FEVER, Sue Ann Langdon *(Aunt Esther)*, Emo Philips *(Joe Earley)*, Jay Levey *(Gandhi)*, Billy Barty *(Noodles MacIntosh)* ← LEGEND ← HARUM SCARUM ← ROUSTABOUT, Belinda Bauer *(mud wrestler)* ← FLASHDANCE ← TIMERIDER: THE ADVENTURE OF LYLE SWANN, **Dr. Demento** *(whipped cream eater)* → DERAILROADED, M.G. Kelly *(promo announcer)* ← VOYAGE OF THE ROCK ALIENS ← ROLLER BOOGIE ← the BUDDY HOLLY STORY ← a STAR IS BORN

Storyline: George Newman gets fired from yet another job but lands on his feet when he's left in charge of his uncle's failing TV station (which he won in a poker game). George tries his best but the debts keep piling up and the ratings keep plummeting down. Finally he stomps off the set of a children's show leaving screwball janitor Stanley Spadowski in charge of the kids – and the ensuing mayhem turns a recipe for disaster into an overnight success. *JZ*

Movie rating: *6

Visual: video

Off the record: "Weird Al" Yankovic (see below)

"WEIRD AL" YANKOVIC

Aug 89. (lp/c/cd) *Rock'n'roll; <45265>* [ ] [–]
– Money for nothing – Beverly Hillbillies / Gandhi II / Attack of the radioactive hamster from a planet near Mars / Isle thing / The hot rocks polka / UHF / Let me be your hog / She drives like crazy / Generic blues / Spatula city / Fun zone / Spam / The biggest ball of twine in Minnesota. *<cd re-iss. 2000s on 'Volcano'; 61422-32013-2>*

S/track review: Without going into a great deal of detail, novelty pop parodiest "WEIRD AL" YANKOVIC (b.23 Oct '59, Lynwood, California) was famous/infamous for a handful of hits including his funniest, 'Eat It' and 'Like A Surgeon'. This soundtrack album goes one step beyond unadulterated humour, and ultimately smells like teen something or other. Adept too at playing the accordion, YANKOVIC sets out to ridicule anything that was reasonably catchy the first time around. He sets out his stall straight from the start, combining Dire Straits' 'Money For Nothing' (featuring KNOPFLER himself) with the 'Beverly Hillbillies' theme, demonstrating his post-National Lampoon warped comedy to the Nth degree. One did snigger a bit it must be stated. Maybe it's the polka thing on many of the subsequent ditties, but it just doesn't work; then again it could be a bad hair day 80s thing (AL has a Michael Bolton-esque poodle perm). With his real band and a few session people in tow, including guitarist/producer RICK DERRINGER, AL strikes out at some deserved targets such as Fine Young Cannibals ('She Drives Like Crazy' – another play on words), R.E.M. ('Spam' – instead of 'Stand') and Tone Loc ('Isle Thing'). His poke at the Rolling Stones in a 'Hot Rocks Medley' just doesn't cut it, but I suppose "It's Only Rock'n'Roll, and I like it" . . . NOT. When he isn't taking the pish out of some iconic rock act, the man takes the P out of himself, surely 'Attack Of The Radioactive Hamster From A Planet Near Mars' and 'The Biggest Ball Of Twine In Minnesota' (although I can think of another Ball Of something!) are for the bumpkins among us. One saviour, it must be said, is his mock movie trailers, YANKOVIC at last justifying his OTT credentials via 'Gandhi II'. But then again, National Lampoon's 'Kentucky Fried Movie' covered this genre several times over a decade or so previously. *MCS*

Album rating: *3.5

□ UNCLE MEAT
(⇒ Rockumentaries/Performance Movies)

UNDER THE CHERRY MOON

1986 (US 99m b&w) Warner Bros. Pictures (PG-13)

Film genre: R&B/Rock Musical drama

Top guns: dir: **PRINCE** / s-w: Becky Johnston

Stars: PRINCE *(Christopher Tracy)*, Steven Berkoff *(Mr. Sharon)* ← ABSOLUTE BEGINNERS ← McVICAR, Francesca Annis *(Mrs. Wellington)* ← DUNE ← MACBETH, Kristin Scott Thomas *(Mary Sharon)*, Jerome Benton *(Tricky)* ← PURPLE RAIN / → GRAFFITI BRIDGE, Emmanuelle Sallet *(Katy)*, Victor Spinetti *(the Jaded Three #1)* ← MAGICAL MYSTERY TOUR ← HELP! ← a HARD DAY'S NIGHT / → JULIE AND THE CADILLACS, Pamela Ludwig *(the girlfriend)*, Alexandra Stewart *(Mrs. Sharon)*

Storyline: Basically Prince poncing around on the French Riviera as ego-swollen gigolo Christopher Tracy. The only thing which saves this is the music and unfortunately there's not enough of it, as our jump-suited hero spends most of his time trying to cop off with rich chick Mary Sharon. His bosom buddy Tricky is none too pleased with this, being keen on the lass himself. Predictably, it all ends in crocodile tears. *BG*

Movie rating: *2

Visual: video + dvd

Off the record: (see below)

PRINCE & THE REVOLUTION: Parade

Apr 86. (lp,pic-lp/c/cd) *Paisley Park; <(9 25395-1/-4/-2)>* [3] [4]
– Christopher Tracy's parade / New position / I wonder U / Under the cherry moon / Girls and boys / Life can be so nice / Venus de Milo / Mountains / Do U lie? / Kiss / Anotherloverholenyohead / Sometimes it snows in April.

S/track review: The last gasp of a REVOLUTION-era PRINCE, 'Parade' attracted a dodgy reputation only because of its association with the movie and its subsequent rejection as a "disaster" by the Purple One himself. PRINCE has presided over his fair share of disasters, to be sure, but this isn't one of them; in spurts, it's as seductively funky as anything in his catalogue, earthing the psyche-spiritual residue from 'Around The World In A Day' (1985). While we can only salivate at the prospect of the kind of organic grooves he might've concocted had he started his recording career in 1970 rather than 1977, the fact that he produced as much smoking funk as he did, in such a seriously funk d'void decade as the 80s, is a minor miracle in itself. The falsetto whump of 'Kiss' remains one of the most audacious examples of digitised funk ever recorded, svelte enough even to accommodate Tom Jones. 'Girls & Boys' isn't far behind; equal parts trombone-honking haute couture and erotic, Siamese swing, it reeks of exactly the kind of post-modern Gauloise fog that the film so dismally failed to deliver. Even when he falls back on four-to-the-floor drum machine clatter, his arrangements – 'Mountain's horn charts, the bass and Trinidadian steel of 'New Position'; the whistling woodwinds in 'Life Can Be So Nice' – are inventive enough to hypnotise. And while the likes of 'Venus De Milo', 'Sometimes It Snows In April' and 'Under The Cherry Moon' itself find the androgynous valentino toying with ballad hybrids and baroque pop, it's the funk – naked, cosmopolitan, Caribbean; take your pick – which drives this album and renders its much-touted stylistic eclecticism – more convincingly realised on 'SIGN 'O' THE TIMES' (1987) – a secondary consideration at best. *BG*

Album rating: *7.5

– spinoff hits, etc. –

PRINCE & THE REVOLUTION: Kiss

Feb 86. (7"/7"pic-d/ext-12") *<28751> (W 8751/+P/T)* [1] [6]

PRINCE & THE REVOLUTION: Mountains

May 86. (7"/10"white/12") *<28711> (W 8711/+TW/T)* [23] [45]

PRINCE & THE REVOLUTION: Girls And Boys / Under The Cherry Moon

Aug 86. (7"/7"sha-pic-d/12"/d7") *(W 8586/+P/T/F)* [–] [11]

PRINCE & THE REVOLUTION: Anotherloverholenyohead / Girls And Boys

Oct 86. (7") *<28620>* [63] [–]

PRINCE & THE REVOLUTION: Anotherloverholenyohead / Mountains

Oct 86. (7"/ext-12"/ext-12"pic-d/d7") *(W 8521/+T/TP/F)* [–] [36]

UNTAMED YOUTH

1957 (US 80m w/b&w) Warner Bros.

Film genre: prison Rock Musical drama

Top guns: dir: Howard W. Koch → BOP GIRL / s-w: John C. Higgins (au: Stephen Longstreet)

Stars: Mamie van Doren *(Penny Lowe)* → HIGH SCHOOL CONFIDENTIAL! → LAS VEGAS HILLBILLYS, Lori Nelson *(Jane Lowe)*, John Russell *(Ross Tropp)* → HONKYTONK MAN, Don Burnett *(Bob Steele)* → JAILHOUSE ROCK, **Eddie Cochran** *(Bong)* ← the GIRL CAN'T HELP IT / → HOT ROD GANG → GO, JOHNNY, GO! → BLUE SUEDE SHOES → the COMPLEAT BEATLES, Glenn Dixon *(Jack Landis)*, Lurene Tuttle *(Judge Cecilia Steele Tropp)*, Jerry Barclay *(Ralph)* → BOP GIRL, Yvonne Lime *(baby)* → LOVING YOU

Storyline: Cotton grower Ross Tropp is in cahoots with the town judge Mrs Steele in a fiendish plot to make convicts work on Tropp's farm for slave wages. The latest arrivals are Jane and Penny, two entertainers who have fallen foul of the sneaky judge. Salvation is at hand in the form of Bob, Mrs Steele's son, who has gone undercover at the farm to expose his mom's malicious scheme. *JZ*

Movie rating: *3

Visual: none

Off the record: **Eddie Cochran** performed one song ('Cottonpicker') in the movie.

– spinoff releases, etc. –

MAMIE VAN DOREN (composer: Les Baxter, etc.)

Aug 57. (7"ep) *Prep; <M 1-1>* [ ] [–]
– Salamander / Go, go calypso / Rolling stone / Oobala baby.

☐ the UNTOUCHABLES segment (⇒ REPO MAN)

UP IN SMOKE

aka CHEECH & CHONG'S UP IN SMOKE

1978 (US 86m) Warner Bros. Pictures (R)

Film genre: screwball buddy film/comedy

Top guns: dir: Lou Adler → LADIES AND GENTLEMEN, THE FABULOUS STAINS / s-w: **CHEECH & CHONG**

Stars: CHEECH Marin *(Pedro De Pacas)* + **Tommy CHONG** *(Anthony 'Man' Stoner)*, Stacy Keach *(Sgt. Stedenko)*, Edie Adams *(Mrs. Tempest Stoner)*, Strother Martin *(Arnold Stoner)*, Tom Skerritt *(Strawberry)* ← HAROLD AND MAUDE / → SINGLES, Zane Buzby *(Jade East)*, **the Dills, Berlin Brats, the Whores**, Rodney Bingenheimer *(himself)* → REPO MAN → UNCLE MEAT → BACK TO THE BEACH → MAYOR OF THE SUNSET STRIP, David Nelson *(Roxy doorman)* → CRY-BABY, Louisa Moritz *(officer Gloria Whitey)* → NEW YEAR'S EVIL, Ellen Barkin *(guitarist)* → TENDER MERCIES → EDDIE AND THE CRUISERS → DOWN BY LAW → SIESTA → JOHNNY HANDSOME → FEAR AND LOATHING IN LAS VEGAS

Storyline: Two doped-up buddies go on the road trip of a lifetime in their endless search for more weed. Disaster strikes when they are deported across the border only hours before they're due to perform in a gig. However with the help of two equally stoned female hitchhikers and a car built entirely out of marijuana they race against the clock (and the local cops) to get to their show on time. *JZ*

Movie rating: *5.5

Visual: video + dvd

Off the record: Three unknown acts appear here.

CHEECH & CHONG * (w/ Various Artists/Aliases)

Nov 78. (lp/c) *Warners; <(BSK/MS 3249)>* [ ] Feb79 [ ]
– The Finkelstein shit kid (MR. STONER) / Up in smoke (*) / Low rider (WAR) / 1st gear, 2nd gear (PEDRO AND MAN) / Framed (*) / Searchin' (SEARCH BOYS) / The Ajax lady (MAN AND THE AJAX LADY) / Strawberry's (YESCA) / Here come the mounties to the rescue (YESCA) / Sometimes when you gotta go, you can't (PEDRO AND SGT. STEDENKO) / Lost due to incompetence (theme for a big green van) (YESCA) / Lard ass (PEDRO, MAN, OFFICER CLYDE & SGT. STEDENKO) / Rock fight (*) / I didn't know your name was Alex (MAN, JADE EAST, PEDRO) / Earache my eye (ALICE BOWIE) / Up in smoke reprise (*). *<cd-iss. 1990; 3249-2>*

S/track review: Stoners (in every sense of the word!) CHEECH & CHONG secure a major motion picture deal and er . . . blow it. After a string of platinum-selling LP's, 'Cheech & Chong' (1971), 'Big Bambu' (1972), 'Los Cochichos' (1973), 'Cheech & Chong's Wedding Album' (1974) and 'Sleeping Beauty' (1976), featuring many of the movie's far-out characters, the rockin' comedy duo of CHEECH MARIN and TOMMY CHONG tripped up rather than tripped-out. Yes, this set is a prime example of what works on the big screen doesn't neccessarily project onto vinyl. Forgetting their National Lampoon-like 'Finkelstein Kid Shit' skit, their opening country-angled title song was basic unadultered humour, and who let Nick Cave into the studio when he was only an Australian Boy Next Door waiting for his Birthday Party to come! Thankfully, WAR's classy 1975 smash, 'Low Rider' comes to the rescue with its funky, gruff stylings better than any toke around. The speeding narrative of sorts, '1st Gear, 2nd Gear', by the pseudonymous PEDRO AND MAN is one the funniest things from their boistrious repertoire, the dialogue between rider and hitchhiker about toothpick joints and mighty burger dogshit reefers is heavy shit man, and the acid's heavy too, man. Just when it's picking up big time, C&C leave you on a downer via two Leiber & Stoller pearls, 'Framed' (complete with "stoned" lyrics) & 'Searchin'', the former was already a staple of Alex Harvey, while the latter was tinged here by the reggae-fuelled SEARCH BOYS. Ten minutes and three songs (the funked-up 'Strawberry's', the Little Feat-esque 'Here Come The Mounties To The Rescue' & the Osibisa-like 'Lost Due To Incompetence (Theme For A Big Green Van)') are allocated to sessionmen supergroup, YESCA. Most Funky Nassau aficionados will cream their pants when they hear the line-up of DANNY "KOOTCH" KORTCHMAR (guitar), WADDY WACHTEL (guitar), RICK MAROTTA (drums), JAI WINDING (keyboards), DAVID SANBORN (saxophone) and GENE PAGE (horn arrangements), etc., most others, like myself, just marked time – slowly. Main writers KORTCHMAR and WACHTEL get all punky rather than funky when they augment C&C for their ode to the new wave movement on their 'Rock Fight', a taster one supposes for another "rock fight" by way of ALICE BOWIE's excellent 'Earache My Eye'; a Zappa-meets-Cooper-meets-Kiss number CHEECH & CHONG had already given us on their aforementioned 'Wedding Album'. Toke off! *MCS*

Album rating: *5

UP JUMPED A SWAGMAN

1965 (UK 87m) Elstree Pictures

Film genre: Pop Musical comedy

Top guns: dir: Christopher Miles / s-w: Lewis Greifer

Stars: Frank Ifield *(Dave Kelly)*, Annette Andre *(Patsy)*, Ronald Radd *(Harry King)*, Suzy Kendall *(Melissa Smythe-Fury)* → UP THE JUNCTION, Richard Wattis *(Lever; music publisher)* ← PLAY IT COOL / → BUNNY LAKE IS MISSING → WONDERWALL → TAKE ME HIGH, Donal Donnelly *(Bockeye)*, Bryan Mosley *(Jo-Jo)*, Martin Miller *(Herman)*

Storyline: Aussie singer Dave Kelly jumps off the boat at London docks to start a new life in the old country. He falls in love with the first girl he sees (even though she's painted on a billboard) and so begins a series of adventures for our singing version of Crocodile Dundee involving gangsters, shootings and femmes fatales. Can Dave overcome his problems and pave the way for Jason and Kylie or will he be shipped back to Oz in disgrace like his ancestors? *JZ*

Movie rating: *4.5

Visual: video

Off the record: Frank Ifield was born in Coventry, England on the 30th November '37. Raised in Dural. nr. Sydney, Australia by his emmigrant parents since the age of 11 (his dad invented the Ifield pump used for jet aircrafts!), the young Frank established himself as a teen sensation on Bonnington's Bunkhouse radio show, before landing a spot on the travelling Ted Quigg Show. This resulted in a deal with the Aussie branch of 'E.M.I.', who issued two subsequent hit singles, one of them 'There's A Love In My Lariat' topped the charts down under. With yodelling all the rage in the early 60s and two minor UK hits under his belt, IFIELD returned to English shores on a permanent basis. IFIELD never looked back and in summer 1962, the C&W crooner/yodeller was top of the charts with 'I Remember You'; the start of three consecutive No.1's (along with 'Lovesick Blues' & 'The Wayward Wind') – and a smash in the States of all places. 1962 also saw him being entered for United Kingdom in the Eurovision Song Contest, although his 'Alone Too Long' only managed 2nd place to Ronnie Carroll (IFIELD tried again 1976 and was last!). His career was on a downward spiral by the time of 'UP JUMPED THE SWAGMAN', and with critics panning both the film and the soundtrack, the man took off in 1966 to find more sympathetic pastures in Nashville (he became an Honorary Tennessean in the process). With 50 odd years behind him in 1991 and still touring the globe, FRANK IFIELD (and the Backroom Boys) squeezed into the UK Top 40 courtesy of novelty record, 'She Taught Me How To Yodel'. *MCS*

FRANK IFIELD (with Norrie Paramor and his Orchestra . . .)

1965. (lp) *Columbia; (33SX 1751/SCX 3559)* [ ] [–]
– Once a jolly swagman / Look don't touch / I remember you / I've got a hole in my pocket / I'll never feel this way again / Cry wolf / Wild river / Make it soon / Botany Bay / Lovin' on my mind / I guess / Waltzing Matilda.

S/track review: Quite frankly, where do you start with this record. As previously mentioned above, the easy-listening FRANK IFIELD – looking remarkably like a young Burt Lancaster – was going nowhere fast when he and his partner in musical crime, Norrie Paramor (who'd worked with Cliff & the Shadows on a handful of movies) came up with this poor effort; they'd even had the cheek to throw in IFIELD's most memorable couple of minutes, 'I Remember You'. If you're a lover of traditional folk music and you must listen to this (I had to!), strap yourself to the chair for his sprightly renditions of 'Wild Rover', 'Botany Bay' & 'Waltzing Matilda'. There's no doubting IFIELD's ability to hit the yodelling high points, but 40-odd years on it's very dated. If you're looking for highlights – and there aren't many on show from the dozen songs – maybe Salvador & Engvick's 'Make It Soon' is one, it's just a pity about the derivative Buddy Holly-type arrangement. When they made 'UP JUMPED A SWAGMAN', little did they know that the title more or less described anyone who earned a Swiss franc from this – daylight robbery indeed! *MCS*

Album rating: *2

URBAN COWBOY

1980 (US 135m) Paramount Pictures (PG)

Film genre: romantic drama

Top guns: s-w: James Bridges (+ dir) → MIKE'S MURDER, Aaron Latham (+ story)

Stars: John Travolta *(Buford 'Bud' Uan Davis)* ← GREASE ← SATURDAY NIGHT FEVER / → STAYING ALIVE → SHOUT → PULP FICTION → PRIMARY COLORS → SWORDFISH → BE COOL → HAIRSPRAY re-make, Debra Winger *(Sissy Davis)* ← THANK GOD IT'S FRIDAY / → MIKE'S MURDER, Scott Glenn *(Wes Hightower)* ← MORE AMERICAN GRAFFITI ← NASHVILLE / → the VIRGIN SUICIDES, Madolyn Smith *(Pam)*, Barry Corbin *(Bob Davis)* → the BEST LITTLE WHOREHOUSE IN TEXAS → HONKYTONK MAN → PERMANENT RECORD, Brooke Alderson *(Aunt Corene)* → MIKE'S MURDER, Cooper Huckabee *(marshall)*, James Gammon *(Steve Strange)* → the COUNTRY BEARS → COLD MOUNTAIN, **Bonnie RAITT** *(performer)*, **Mickey Gilley** *(performer)*, **Johnny Lee** *(performer)*, **Charlie Daniels band** *(performer/s)* → HEARTWORN HIGHWAYS, Jerry Hall *(sexy sister)* → LET'S SPEND THE NIGHT TOGETHER → RUNNING OUT OF LUCK → BATMAN → 25X5: THE CONTINUING ADVENTURES OF THE ROLLING STONES → the WALL: LIVE IN BERLIN

Storyline: Wimpish Texas lad, Bud, finds himself jealous of a mechanical bull in the local night spot, when his wife Sissy spends more time on it with ex-con Wes than she does with him. Wise old Uncle Bob begins to teach Bud all about what it takes to be a real man after he dumps Sissy for pouting Pam, and helps him master the mechanical moo in the process. *JZ*

Movie rating: *7.5

Visual: video + dvd

Off the record: (see below)

Various Artists (score: Ralph Burns)

May 80. (d-lp/d-c) *Full Moon – Asylum; <D/D5 90002> (K/K4 99101)* 3 Jul80

– Hello Texas (JIMMY BUFFET) / All night long (JOE WALSH) / Times like these (DAN FOGELBERG) / Nine tonight (BOB SEGER AND THE SILVER BULLET BAND) / Stand by me (MICKEY GILLEY) / Cherokee fiddle (JOHNNY LEE) / Could I have this dance (ANNE MURRAY) / Lyin' eyes (EAGLES) // Lookin' for love (JOHNNY LEE) / Don't it make you want to dance (BONNIE RAITT) / The Devil went down to Georgia (CHARLIE DANIELS BAND) / Here comes the hurt again (MICKEY GILLEY) / Orange blossom special – Hoedown (GILLEY'S "URBAN COWBOY" BAND) / Love the world away (KENNY ROGERS) / Falling in love for the night (CHARLIE DANIELS BAND) / Darlin' (BONNIE RAITT) / Look what you've done to me (BOZ SCAGGS) / Hearts against the wind (LINDA RONSTADT / J.D. SOUTHER). *<cd-iss. Mar95 on 'Elektra'; 60690>*

S/track review: The phenomenally-successful EAGLES had laid a bad-smelling egg, and racing for the country rock hatchery to grab what it can, this double album scoops up more po-faced mid-tempo middle-of-the-road mediocre music than should legally be allowed in one room. Here are those who rode the late-70s wave of country-flavoured opiate – MICKEY GILLEY (whose Stetson-wearing take on 'Stand By Me' is the nadir) JOHNNY LEE, KENNY ROGERS, ANNE MURRAY. But it's even more depressing to discover them backed by a host of musicians who should have known better (bow your heads, LARRY CARLTON, SNEAKY PETE KLEINOW, BYRON BERLINE, JAMES BURTON). On screen this bland kitsch might work every bit as ironically as the Blues Brothers' take on 'Stand By Your Man', but short of pictures it's just grating; 'Here Comes The Hurt Again' indeed. The EAGLES themselves are represented by 1973's airbrushed 'Lyin' Eyes', and there's also a heap of unremarkable AOR (much of it from musicians managed by the film's producer Irving Azoff): JOE WALSH, DAN FOGELBERG, BOB SEGER. Amazingly, like pearls in the dirt, there are two fine songs, too – CHARLIE DANIELS' showboating 1979 hit 'The Devil Went Down To Georgia', and even more unexpectedly, a lovely acoustic ballad from LINDA RONSTADT and J.D. SOUTHER, 'Hearts Against The Wind' (later covered by Diamond Rio, and featured on the 'Linda Ronstadt Boxed Set'). *ND*

Album rating: *4.5 / Urban Cowboy II (*4)

– spinoff hits, etc. –

JOE WALSH: All Night Long / GILLEY'S "URBAN COWBOY" BAND: Orange Blossom Special – Hoedown

May 80. (7") *<46639> (K 79146)* 19 Jun80

MICKEY GILLEY: Stand By Me / UNSTRUNG HEROES: Cotton Eyed Joe

May 80. (7") *<46640>* 22 –

KENNY ROGERS: Love The World Away / (non-OST song)

Jun 80. (7") *United Artists; <1359>* 14 –

JOHNNY LEE: Lookin' For Love / EAGLES: Lyin' Eyes

Jun 80. (7") *<47004> (K 79153)* 5 Sep80

BOZ SCAGGS: Look What You've Done To Me / (non-OST song)

Aug 80. (7") *Columbia; <11349>* 14 –

ANNE MURRAY: Could I Have This Dance / (non-OST song)

Aug 80. (7") *Capitol; <4920> (CL 16175)* 33 Nov80

MICKEY GILLEY: Stand By Me / Here Comes The Hurt Again

Oct 80. (7") *(K 79181)* –

BOZ SCAGGS: Look What You've Done To Me / (diff. non-OST song)

Oct 80. (7") *C.B.S.; (9034)* –

Various Artists: Urban Cowboy II

Jan 81. (lp/c) *Full Moon; <36921>* –

– Rode hard and put up wet (JOHNNY LEE) / Texas (CHARLIE DANIELS BAND) / Mammas don't let your babries grow up to be cowboys (MICKEY GILLEY & JOHNNY LEE) / Cotton eyed Joe (BAYOU CITY BEATS) / Honky tonk wine (MICKEY GILLEY) / The moon just turned blue (J.D. SOUTHER) / Rockin' my life away (MICKEY GILLEY) / Jukebox argument (MICKEY GILLEY) / Orange blossom special (CHARLIE DANIELS BAND).

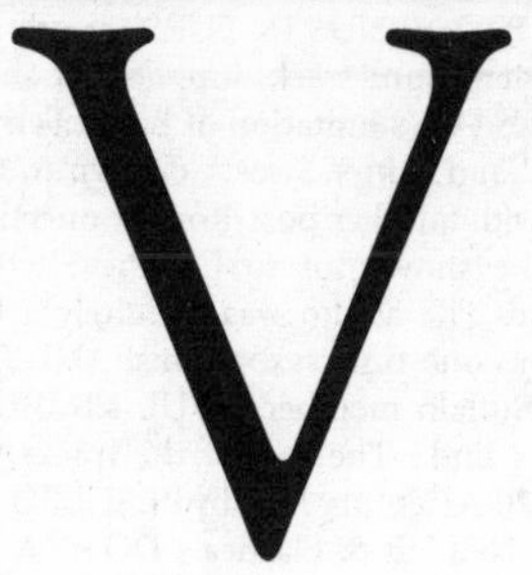

□ Ritchie VALENS segment
(⇒ LA BAMBA)

□ Gus VAN SANT segment
(⇒ LAST DAYS)

□ Kenny VANCE segment
(⇒ LOOKING FOR AN ECHO)

□ VANILLA ICE segment
(⇒ COOL AS ICE)

VANISHING POINT

1971 (US 107m) Twentieth Century-Fox Films (R)

Film genre: road/chase movie

Top guns: dir: Richard C. Sarafian / s-w: G. Cabrera Infante as Guillermo Cain ← WONDERWALL (story: Malcolm Hart)

Stars: Barry Newman *(Kowalski)*, Cleavon Little *(Super Soul)* ← COTTON COMES TO HARLEM / → FM, Dean Jagger *(prospector)* ← KING CREOLE ← BERNARDINE, Victoria Medlin *(Vera Thornton)*, Paul Koslo *(Charlie; young cop)* → CLEOPATRA JONES, Robert Donner *(Collins; older cop)* ← SKIDOO ← CATALINA CAPER, Timothy Scott *(Angel)* → FOOTLOOSE, **Rita Coolidge** *(performer)* → MAD DOGS & ENGLISHMEN → PAT GARRETT & BILLY THE KID → a STAR IS BORN, Severn Darden *(J. Jessie Hovah)* ← MODEL SHOP / → the HIRED HAND, **Delaney** * & **Bonnie Bramlett** (J. Hovah's singers) → MEDICINE BALL CARAVAN → CATCH MY SOUL → the DOORS * → FESTIVAL EXPRESS, **David Gates** *(piano player)*, John Amos *(Super Soul's engineer)* → SWEET SWEETBACK'S BAADASSSSS SONG → LET'S DO IT AGAIN → DISAPPEARING ACTS

Storyline: Ex-road racer, cop and Vietnam vet, Kowalski, leads the "deep blue meanies" a high octane, cross-state dance as he mercilessly barrels his white Dodge Challenger from Denver to San Francisco. Wired on Benzedrine and battling his private demons as much as the clock, he becomes a counter cultural cause celebre as blind radio jock Super Soul's running commentary raises his journey to grand allegory. *BG*

Movie rating: *8

Visual: video + dvd

Off the record: **David Gates** was a member of the highly-regarded soft-rock band, Bread.

—

Various Artists (score: JIMMY BOWEN ORCHESTRA *)

Jul 71. (lp) *Amos; <AAS 8002> London; (SH-U 8420)* □ □
– Super Soul theme (J.B. PICKERS) / The girl done got it together (BOBBY DOYLE) / Where do we go from here (JIMMY WALKER) / Welcome to Nevada (JERRY REED) / Dear Jesus God (SEGARINI & BISHOP) / Runaway country (DOUG DILLARD EXPEDITION) / You got to believe (DELANEY & BONNIE & FRIENDS) / Love theme (*) / So tired (EVA) / Freedom of expression (J.B. PICKERS) / Mississippi queen (MOUNTAIN) / Sing out for Jesus (BIG MAMA THORNTON) / Over me (SEGARINI & BISHOP) / Nobody knows (KIM & DAVE). *<(re-iss. Apr03 on 'Harkit' cd/lp; HRK CD/LP 8050)>*

S/track review: Part apocalyptic preacher, part jive-talking soul brother, Cleavon Little's DJ Super Soul and his down-home taste in music remain central to 'Vanishing Point's cult mythology – this is one of the few instances where dialogue would've enhanced and contextualised the soundtrack rather than marring it. Yet even without Super Soul's holy-rolling harangues and staccato intros, this ragbag of funk, rock, country and soul works up the kind of righteous early 70s fervour that's hard to resist. JIMMY BOWEN, more famous for his 50s easy-listening productions, is the unlikely choice of music supervisor and score composer although heavy-duty psych-funk freak-outs like Freedom Of Expression – performed by his instrumental aggregate the J.B. PICKERS – lay any Bing Crosby associations soundly to rest; both this and the opening 'Super Soul Theme' could've easily graced a blaxploitation flick. Among BOWEN's motley pool of contributing artists, sludge rockers MOUNTAIN carry the biggest rep, and their grizzled Top 30 hit, 'Mississippi Queen', is by far the most famous thing here. 'VANISHING POINT's essence, however, is in the small print, in gratifyingly obscure entries like SEGARINI & BISHOP. Bob Segarini had previously played with Quicksilver Messenger Service guitarist Gary Duncan and had been a founding member of cult West Coast act Family Tree. Together with Randy Bishop, he composed two songs especially for Richard Sarafian's movie, 'Over Me' and the dirt-under-the-fingernails spiritual, 'Dear Jesus God'. Up to a point, Segarini shares a scuffed pew with ubiquitous roots-rock acolytes, DELANEY & BONNIE, whose bongo-hollering, sub-'Exile On Main Street' sermonising preaches live in the desert to the J. Hovah converted during one of the movie's more bizarre scenes. Nor is Willie Mae 'BIG MAMA' THORNTON – who took the original version of 'Hound Dog' to the top of the US R&B charts back in 1953 – in danger of losing her religion as she loses her ravaged chords on the gospel-charged, Kim Carnes-penned 'Sing Out For Jesus'. Given 'Vanishing Point's B-movie brew of white-line existentialism, hip cultural references and raw, redemptive music, it's not difficult to see why Primal Scream were sufficiently enamoured to name an album after it. Full marks to 'Harkit' for finally re-issuing a CD, although blues fans will no doubt have spotted the erroneous listing of Jerry Reed as Jimmy Reed. Super Soul would've been horrified. *BG*

Album rating: *6.5

VELVET GOLDMINE

1998 (UK/US 123m) Film Four / Goldwyn / Miramax Films (18/R)

Film genre: alt/Glam-Rock Musical drama

Top guns: s-w + dir: Todd Haynes → I'M NOT THERE (+ story w/ James Lyons)

Stars: Ewan McGregor *(Curt Wild)* ← TRAINSPOTTING ← LIPSTICK ON YOUR COLLAR / → MOULIN ROUGE! → YOUNG ADAM, Jonathan Rhys-Meyers *(Brian Slade)* → OCTANE → ELVIS, Toni Collette *(Mandy Slade)* → ABOUT A BOY, Christian Bale *(Arthur Stuart)* ← METROLAND / → LAUREL CANYON → I'M NOT THERE, Eddie Izzard *(Jerry Devine)* → REVENGERS TRAGEDY → ROMANCE & CIGARETTES → ACROSS THE UNIVERSE, Emily Woof *(Shannon)*, Michael Feast *(Cecil)* ← McVICAR, Janet McTeer *(narrator)* ← HAWKS, Osheen Jones *(Jack Fairy at 7)*, **Micko Westmoreland** *(Jack Fairy)*, Don Fellows *(Lou)* ← ELECTRIC DREAMS, Flaming Creatures:- **Brian Molko** *(Malcolm)*, **Steve**

Hewitt *(Billy)*, **Antony Langdon** *(Ray)*, **Xavoir** *(Pearl)*, Polly Small's Band:- **Donna Matthews** *(Polly Small)*, Ritz *(lead guitarist)*, **Stefan Olsdal** *(bassist)*, Trevor Sharpe *(drummer)*, the Venus In Furs:- Guy Leverton *(Trevor)*, Justin Salinger *(Rodney)* → REVENGERS TRAGEDY, Vinney Reck *(Reg)*, Ray Shell *(Murray)* ← the APPLE, Keith Lee-Castle *(Harley)*, the Wilde Rattz:- Jono McGrath *(lead guitarist)*, Alan Fordham *(bass guitarist)*, Perry Clayton *(drummer)*, Lindsay Kemp *(pantomime dame)* ← JUBILEE ← the WICKER MAN

Storyline: Set in 1984, a UK journalist (working for a New York paper) Arthur Stuart tries to trace the wherabouts of 70s glam rock star, Brian Slade, who, at the peak of his glittering career and unable to cope with fame, faked his own death. *MCS*

Movie rating: *6.5

Visual: video + dvd

Off the record: Osheen Jones is the son of 80s electro-pop star, Howard Jones. Look out too for appearances by members of Placebo (**Brian Molko, Stefan Olsdal & Steve Hewitt**), Spacehog (**Antony Langdon**), and Elastica (**Donna Matthews**). Producer **Micko Westmoreland** played bass, keyboards & guitar with the Bowling Green. **Xavoir** (aka Belfast-born Paul Wilkinson) went from club act DexDexTer and subsequently played keyboards on Placebo's 2003 tour. *MCS*

Various Artists (score: CARTER BURWELL *)

Sep 98. (cd) *Deram; (<556035-2>)* ☐ Nov98 ☐
– Needle in the camel's eye (BRIAN ENO) / Hot one (SHUDDER TO THINK) / 20th Century boy (PLACEBO) / 2HB (VENUS IN FURS) / T.V. eye (WYLDE RATTTZ) / Ballad of Maxwell Demon (SHUDDER TO THINK) / The whole shebang (GRANT LEE BUFFALO) / Ladytron (VENUS IN FURS) / We are the boys (PULP) / Virginia plain (ROXY MUSIC) / Personality crisis (TEENAGE FANCLUB & DONNA MATTHEWS) / Satellite of love (LOU REED) / Diamond meadows (T. REX) / Bitter's end (PAUL KIMBLE & ANDY MACKAY) / Baby's on fire (VENUS IN FURS) / Bitter-sweet (VENUS IN FURS) / Velvet spacetime (*) / Tumbling down (VENUS IN FURS) / Make me smile (come up and see me) (STEVE HARLEY).

S/track review: Glam rock is the obvious stamping ground here for a combination of iconic 70s songs/stars and 90s alt-rockers, showing that there isn't much distance between the two generations. The OST kicks into gear courtesy of a rare 1974 gem from BRIAN ENO ('Needle In The Camel's Eye'), his post-Roxy Music number performed at a time when the synthetic knob-twiddler sang. Other 70s originals featured are ROXY MUSIC's classic, 'Virginia Plain' (listen out for ENO again), 'Satellite Of Love' from Noo Yoik punk LOU REED, 'Diamond Meadows' from King of glam Marc Bolan and his T. REX and probably the surprise package here, 1975 UK chart-topper 'Make Me Smile (Come Up And See Me)' by STEVE HARLEY surely at a time when the glitter had faded. There's probably no apology for the omission of glam-pop icons, Slade, Mott The Hoople, Gary Glitter and Sweet, the latter of which was nowhere to be heard or seen in the actual film; 'Coz I Luv You' and the now cringeworthy 'Do You Want To Touch Me (Oh, Yeah)' might well have been embarrassing but they're essential to the cult of glam. And where the fig was Bowie . . . I mean Ziggy played guitar for fig's sake. Instead, 90s poseurs SHUDDER TO THINK (with two songs, 'Hot One' & 'Ballad Of Maxwell Demon'), GRANT LEE BUFFALO ('The Whole Shebang') and PULP ('We Are The Boyz'), showed a disrespect to a person say . . . brought up to the sounds of the aforementioned 70s icons. Having said that, these self-penned nu-glam tracks were an incarnation of anything from Bowie's 'Hunky Dory', for me a poor substitute. Nu-glam covers were a-plenty, most of them stemming from the movie's undercover band, VENUS IN FURS (featuring Brits, THOM YORKE of Radiohead and BERNARD BUTLER of Suede) and the WILDE RATTTZ (with Americans, THURSTON MOORE and STEVE SHELLEY of Sonic Youth, MARK ARM of Mudhoney and RON ASHETON of the Stooges), the latter tribute band understandably taking on Iggy Pop's 'T.V. Eye'. VENUS IN FURS (clearly named after that classic Velvet Underground track) supplied the shock of the album, THOM YORKE and Co's imitation of Bryan Ferry/Roxy Music on '2HB', 'Ladytron' and 'Bitter-Sweet', déjà vu to the extreme max; two others, one with another post-Roxy connection, Eno's 'Baby's On Fire' stole the show, not so Cockney Rebel/Steve Harley's 'Tumbling Down'. The album was definitely a Roxy Music OST in all but name, as one-time saxophonist ANDY MACKAY along with Grant Lee Buffalo member, PAUL KIMBLE, took on Ferry and Co's 'Bitter's End'. The rest of the tracks were a "straight" cover of Bolan's '20th Century Boy' by PLACEBO, a weird collective of TEENAGE FANCLUB & Elastica's DONNA MATTHEWS on solitary New York Dolls entry, 'Personality Crisis', and one score piece, 'Velvet Spacetime' by CARTER BURWELL. All in all, an album with its moments, although not with its moments in time – "Bitter-Sweet" but NOT "The Whole Shebang". *MCS*

Album rating: *7

VIBRATIONS

1996 (US 103m) Tanglewood Films (R)

Film genre: Rock Musical drama

Top guns: s-w (+ dir): Michael Paseornek

Stars: James Marshall *(T.J. Cray)*, Christina Applegate *(Anamika)* ← BEATLEMANIA / → GRAND THEFT PARSONS, Faye Grant *(Zina)*, Scott Cohen *(Simeon)* ← the MAMBO KINGS / → PRIVATE PARTS, Paige Turco *(Lisa)*, Bruce Altman *(Barry)*

Storyline: T.J. Cray is an up and coming rock star and keyboard player when tragedy strikes him on the way to an audition. He loses both his hands and subsequently ends up in the gutter begging for hand-outs. Then he befriends New Age beauty, Anamika, who, with the help of computer friends, sets about rebuilding prosthetic hands and a metallic suit – and Cyberstorm is born. *MCS*

Movie rating: *3.5

Visual: straight-to-video (score by Bob Christianson)

Off the record: "Married With Children" TV sitcom actress, Christina Applegate, was the daughter of record producer, Robert Applegate and singer/actress, Nancy Priddy; Nancy was long-term partner of Stephen Stills. Christina subsequently proved she could sing a bit herself, when she starred in the theater production of 'Sweet Charity'; a cast recording CD was released in 2005. *MCS*

☐ Sid VICIOUS segment
(⇒ SID & NANCY)

☐ the VILLAGE PEOPLE segment
(⇒ CAN'T STOP THE MUSIC)

Lee VING

Born: Lee Capellaro, 10 Apr'50, Minneapolis, Minnesota, USA. He upped sticks to San Francisco in 1978 and formed the Fear, one of the first bands to emerge from the US West Coast punk/proto-hardcore scene. The Fear had already become infamous for their raucous stage show by the time they made their vinyl debut on the soundtrack to Penelope Spheeris' acclaimed punkumentary, 'The DECLINE OF WESTERN CIVILIZATION' (1981); 'The SLOG MOVIE' was in a similar vein. Subsequently signing a full deal with 'Slash' records, these defiantly un-PC reprobates (including Derf Scratch, etc.) eventually issued a single in their own right via 1982's 'The Record', a mini-set rammed with brief bursts of full-throttle hardcore-punk that even stretched to a fine trashing of the Animals' 'We Got To Get Out Of This Place'. By the time of the record's release, Stix had already been replaced by Johnny Backbeat while a certain FLEA (of subsequent hyperactive RED HOT CHILI PEPPERS fame) honed his bass playing on 1983's yuletide extravaganza, the 'Fuck Christmas' EP. 1985's 'More Beer' album was the band's first release for new label, 'Restless', while VING himself had carved out an acting career in movies such as 'FLASHDANCE' (1983), 'GET CRAZY' (1983), 'STREETS OF FIRE' (1984), 'SUBURBIA' (1984) and 'DUDES' (1987). Save for a 1991 live album, the ensuing decade saw the Fear keep a low profile, most fans having long forgotten about them by the release of 1995's belated 'Have Another Beer With Fear'. *MCS*

- **filmography** {acting} –

the Decline Of Western Civilization *(1981 {p w/ the FEAR} on OST by V/A =>)* / **the Slog Movie** *(1982 {p w/ the FEAR} =>)* / **Flashdance** *(1983 {a} OST by V/A & Giorgio Moroder =>)* / **Get Crazy** *(1983 {a} =>)* / **Streets Of Fire** *(1984 {a} OST by RY COODER & V/A =>)* / **Suburbia** *(1984 {b} OST by V/A & EDDIE VAN HALEN; see future edition =>)* / the Ratings Game *(1984 TV {b})* / Clue *(1985 {a})* / Black Moon Rising *(1986 {a})* / Oceans Of Fire *(1986 TV {a})* / **Dudes** *(1987 {*} =>)* / Grave Secrets *(1989 {a})* / Masters Of Menace *(1990 {a})* / the Taking Of Beverly Hills *(1991 {a})* / Fast Sofa *(2001 {a})*

VIVA LAS VEGAS

UK title 'LOVE IN LAS VEGAS'

1964 (US 85m) Metro Goldwyn Mayer (PG)

Film genre: romantic Rock'n'roll Musical drama

Top guns: dir: George Sidney ← BYE BYE BIRDIE / s-w: Sally Benson

Stars: Elvis PRESLEY *(Lucky Jackson)*, **Ann-Margret** *(Rusty Martin)* ← BYE BYE BIRDIE / → TOMMY, Cesare Danova *(Count Elmo Mancini)*, William Demarest *(Mr. Martin)*, Nicky Blair *(Shorty Farnsworth)*, Jack Carter *(himself)*, **the Jubilee Four** *(themselves)*, Terri Garr *(showgirl)* ← the T.A.M.I. SHOW ← KISSIN' COUSINS ← FUN IN ACAPULCO / → PAJAMA PARTY → ROUSTABOUT → the COOL ONES → CLAMBAKE → HEAD → ONE FROM THE HEART

Storyline: Lucky Jackson is a singing sports car racer who takes a waiting job to fund his entry into the Las Vegas Grand Prix. Among his many female interests, Rusty Martin is the one who really revs his motor and with whom he indulges in some choice duets. *BG*

Movie rating: *6

Visual: video + dvd

Off the record: Ann-Margret (b. Ann-Margret Olsson, 28 Apr'41, Stockholm, Sweden) had at least one Top 20 hit, 1961's 'Just Don't Understand'. **the Jubilee Four** were gospel singers. *MCS*

—

ELVIS PRESLEY: Viva Las Vegas / Roustabout

Mar 93. (cd) *<(74321 13432-2)>* [ ] [ ]
– Viva Las Vegas / If you think I don't need you / I need somebody to lean on / You're the boss (with ANN-MARGRET) / What'd I say / Do the vega / C'mon everybody / The lady loves me (with ANN-MARGRET) / Night life / Today, tomorrow and forever / Yellow rose of Texas – The eyes of Texas / Santa Lucia / (+ Roustabout tracks).

S/track review: The sizzling chemistry between ELVIS and his leading lady, Ann-Margret, went some way towards this campy success story, as did the surprisingly high standard of song material, at least in terms of the King's overall movie career. The Doc Pomus/Mort Shuman-penned title track remains one of the most famous and evergreen of all ELVIS film songs, one that functions equally as a tongue-in-cheek, high camp romp and a bluesy, rhythmically complex rock classic later covered by ZZ Top. It was originally released as a single backed with a spirited cover of Ray Charles' 'What'd I Say' while a soundtrack EP featuring the Pomus/Shuman ballad 'I Need Somebody To Lean On' as well as the ballsy 'If You Think I Don't Need You', and the lesser 'C'mon Everybody' and 'Today, Tomorrow And Forver', appeared a month later. It's nevertheless surprising that the slinky Leiber/Stoller duet (with ANN-MARGRET), 'You're The Boss' was left off the movie's final print at the expense of the more staid 'The Lady Loves Me'. Oh, and ELVIS even sings (impressively) in Italian on the traditional 'Santa Lucia'. *BG*

Album rating: *4

– spinoff releases, etc. –

ELVIS PRESLEY: Viva Las Vegas / What'd I Say

Apr 64. (7") *<47-8360> (RCA 1390)* [29]
[21] Mar64 [17]

ELVIS PRESLEY: Love In Las Vegas

Jun 64. (7"ep) *R.C.A.; <EPA 4382> (RCX 7141)* [92] Apr64 [ ]
– If you think I don't need you / I need somebody to lean on / C'mon everybody / Today, tomorrow and forever.

– other bits & pieces, etc. –

ZZ TOP: Viva Las Vegas

Mar 92. (7"/12"/cd-s) *Warners; (W 0198/+T/CD)* [–] [10]

VIVIR INTENTANDO

alt. video title 'CINCO AMIGAS'

2003 (Arg 95m) Patagonik Film Group / Buena Vista International

Film genre: family Pop/Rock-Musical comedy

Top guns: s-w: (+ dir) Tomas Yankelevich, Caroline Hughes, Alejandro Sapognikoff

Stars: Bandana:- Lissa Vera, Lourdes Fernandez, Valeria Gastaldi, Virginia Da Cunha, Ivonne Guzman *(themselves/performers)*, Gino Renni *(Tomas Copito)*, Valeria Britos *(Clara)*, Alejandra Rubio *(Madre de Lissa)*, Coco Sily *(uncle of Lissa)*, Daniela Brignola *(Natacha)*

Storyline: Five adventurous career girls, with varying degrees of ambition and drive, seek fame and fortune in a looks and fashion-conscious world (or indeed, Argentina). *MCS*

Movie rating: *5

Visual: dvd

Off the record: BANDANA (see below)

—

BANDANA (score: Diego Grimblat & Fernando Lopez Rossi)

Apr 03. (cd) *Sony; <6 52625-2>* [–] Argent [–]
– Sigo dando vueltas / Que pasa con vos / Hasta el dia de hoy / Y asi fue / Dame una razon / Con eso tengo seguro to amor / No me importa esperar / Andando las calles del sol / Me voy a caminar / Hay dias / Bailar / Canto con vos.

S/track review: BANDANA were Argentina's answer to Girls Aloud, having just won 'Popstars', their country's equivalent to 'Pop Idol' in 2001. Manufactured teen-pop that one just can't shake from the bottom of one's dancing shoes, South America must be thanking us Brits for giving this 5-piece group (not a band-ana in sight) so many inspirators. Having said this, million-sellers BANDANA, who were now into their third album, were great if you were a petite wee lassie with pigtails. If you stay outside Argentina, 'VIVIR INTENTANDO' will cost you an arm and a leg. With each song ('Sigo Dando Vueltas' to 'Canto Con Vos') as colourful as their franchise clothing, these girls have yet to break through Stateside or even pop-smart Britain. *MCS*

Album rating: *4

VOICES

1979 (US 106m) Metro-Goldwyn-Mayer (PG)

Top guns: dir: Robert Markowitz / s-w: John Herzfeld

Stars: Michael Ontkean *(Drew Rithman)*, Amy Irving *(Rosemarie Lemon)*, Alex Rocco *(Frank Rothman)* ← THREE THE HARD WAY / → SCENES FROM THE GOLDMINE → THAT THING YOU DO!, Barry Miller *(Raymond Rothman)*, Viveca Lindfors *(Mrs. Lemon)*, Herbert Berghof *(Nathan Rothman)*, Allan Rich *(Montrose Meier)*

Storyline: When delivery man, Drew, meets deaf schoolteacher Rosemarie it's love at first sight. Drew wants to deliver songs instead of packages and Rosemarie wants to be a dancer. However, both seem to belong to Families From Hell who want to stop the romance at all costs, but this just makes the pair even more determined to see things through as Drew slowly becomes accustomed to Rosemarie's deafness. *JZ*

Movie rating: *5

Off the record: (see below)

JIMMY WEBB (songs & score) (& Various Artists)

Apr 79. (lp) *Planet; <P 9002>* ☐ ⊟

– I will always wait for you (theme from Voices) (vocals: BURTON CUMMINGS) / Rosemarie's theme / Disco if you want to / The children's song (ANDREW and DAVID WILLIAMS) / Family theme / Anything that's rock'n'roll (TOM PETTY AND THE HEARTBREAKERS) / I will always wait for you (instrumental) / On a stage (vocals: BURTON CUMMINGS) / Across the river / Bubbles in my beer (TOMMY DUNCAN, CINDY WALKER and BOB WILLS) / Rosemarie and Drew / Drunk as a punk (vocals: BURTON CUMMINGS) / The children's song (instrumental) / Rosemarie's dance – I will always wait for you (reprise).

S/track review: Ten years after the likes of 'MacArthur Park', 'Wichita Lineman' and 'Galveston' had set the seal on his songwriting reputation, JIMMY WEBB had been concentrating on his own performing and recording when he took on the score for this little-celebrated weepie. One of those gifted writers (THINK Bacharach, Kristofferson, etc.) whose success gives them a regrettable license to sing, he thankfully passed the mike here to BURTON CUMMINGS. And the Canadian singer's syrupy rendering of 'I Will Always Wait For You' ("The future surrounds me/The moment has found me") may come as some surprise to those who remember him bawling out 'American Woman' with the Guess Who – though he does get to growl a bit on the truly terrible 'Drunk As A Punk', whose rocky bluster is as wide of the mark as its title. The tired story doesn't bring the best out of WEBB; hard-hearted listeners will struggle to keep a straight face during the quavery 'Children's Song', and though the incidental music is polished pop-jazz, it makes a truly surreal setting for WILLIE NELSON's jaunty cover of 'Bubbles In My Beer' and TOM PETTY's posturing 'Anything That's Rock'n'Roll' (recycled from 1973 and 1976 respectively). The resulting mess is probably only of interest to those whose Kleenex are still damp from a night with the movie. *ND*

Album rating: *3.5

VOYAGE OF THE ROCK ALIENS

1984 + 1988 (US 97m) KGA / Interplanetary-Curb Communications (PG)

Film genre: sci-fi Rock Musical comedy

Top guns: dir: James Fargo / s-w: Edward Gold, Charles Hairston, S. James Guidotti

Stars: Pia Zadora *(Dee Dee)* → HAIRSPRAY, Craig Sheffer *(Frankie)*, Tom Nolan *(Absid/ABCD)* ← FAST TIMES AT RIDGEMONT HIGH ← CHASTITY / → the THING CALLED LOVE, Ruth Gordon *(sheriff)* ← HAROLD AND MAUDE, Jeffrey Casey *(F-Gee/FGHI)*, Michael Berryman *(Chainsaw)* → the DEVIL'S REJECTS, Alison La Placa *(Diane)*, Gregory Bond *(Jaklem/JKLM)*, Craig Quiter *(Nopquir/NOPQR)*, Patrick Byrnes *(Stovitz/STUVWXYZ)*, Marshall Rohner *(Crusades)* → ROAD HOUSE, **Jermaine Jackson** *(Rain)* ← SAVE THE CHILDREN / → LONGSHOT, M.G. Kelley *(radio DJ)* ← ROLLER BOOGIE ← the BUDDY HOLLY STORY ← a STAR IS BORN / → UHF

Storyline: A bunch of aliens – dressed a lot like new wave act Devo – receive signals from Earth (mainly the video of a Jermaine Jackson & Pia Zadora/Dee Dee tune!) into their guitar-shaped spaceship. Complete with a robot-monster, they land in the town of er, Speelberg, and one of them, Absid, falls for teenager Dee Dee, who is fed up with her tough rocker boyfriend, Frankie. *MCS*

Movie rating: *2.5

Visual: video + (recent) dvd

Off the record: Supposedly a follow-up to child actress, Pia Zadora's debut 1964 film, 'Santa Claus Conquers The Martians', 'VOYAGE OF THE ROCK ALIENS' was actually scheduled to be premiered in America at the back end of 1984 (only parts of Europe were "landed" with this kitchy trash!). New Jersey-born actress and singer, Zadora – just turned 30, married to a multi-millionaire, Meshulam Riklis and with a couple of raunchy starring roles behind her ('Butterfly' and 'The Lonely Lady' – had already cracked the US charts via two 1982 Top 50 entries, 'I'm In Love Again' & 'The Clapping Song'. A further US hit single, the aforementioned duet with Jacksons singer, **Jermaine Jackson** and the untimely failure for ' . . . ROCK ALIENS' to be released at the cinema, led to Zadora's musical demise, although a step away from ballad-styled pop albums into uptempo work in 1988 alongside Jam & Lewis on her album, 'When The Lights Go Out' (featuring Pia's UK hit, 'Dance Out Of My Head'), snatched back some credibility; she also featured in the "Rock" movie, 'HAIRSPRAY', directed by fan, John Waters. *MCS*

Various Cast/Artists (score: Jack White)

Nov 84. (cd) *Curb International; (147.715)* ⊟ German ⊟

– When the rain begins to fall (JERMAINE JACKSON & PIA ZADORA) / A little bit of Heaven (PIA ZADORA & MARK SPIRO) / Real love (PIA ZADORA) / Nature of the beast (MICHAEL BRADLEY) / Let's dance tonight (PIA ZADORA) / Back on the street (3 SPEED) / Openhearted (REAL LIFE) / She doesn't mean a thing to me (MARK SPIRO) / 21st Century (RHEMA) / Justine (JIMMY & THE MUSTANGS) / My world is empty without you babe (JOHN FARNHAM & RAINEY).

S/track review: As mentioned previously, and going much the same way as the movie, the CD was never released in the US, only the JERMAINE JACKSON & PIA ZADORA duet picked up sales, firstly in the UK at the end of '84. In Germany (and other European countries) the single hit No.1, and therefore demand was fulfilled for the Baywatch/David Hasselhoff-loving, Euro-pop market. To confuse matters even more, all of the tracks featured in the movie (including one not featured on the OST, 'You Bring Out The Lover In Me'), were chosen to fill her 1984, part-compilation set, 'Let's Dance Tonight'. (Thankfully) unheard for many outside the European union, 'VOYAGE OF THE ROCK ALIENS', featured a further string of continental ZADORA hits such as 'A Little Bit Of Heaven' (with MARK SPIRO; who also contributed his solo 'She Doesn't Mean A Thing To Me'), 'Real Love' and 'Let's Dance Tonight', cornered what could only be described as overdubbed, dance-pop drivel. Of the other non-ZADORA tracks, only MICHAEL BRADLEY's 'Nature Of The Beast' was worthy of its inclusion, while Little River Band and solo-'You're The Voice'-man JOHN FARNHAM mustered up all he could on the lacklustre, 'My World Is Empty Without You Babe'. Label bands, REAL LIFE (i.e. Melbourne stars, David Sterry, Richard Zatorski, Allan Johnson & Danny Simcic – with two US Top 40 hits under their belts!) and JIMMY & THE MUSTANGS (i.e. Jimmy Haddox, Marshall Rohner, Jeff Cranford & Troy Mack), were also aboard the 'VOYAGE . . .', the former delivering their post-New Romantic-styled 'Openhearted', the latter space-age rockers contributing a version of Don & Dewey's R&B song, 'Justine', from their one-off eponymous mini-set. And just who the hell were unknowns RHEMA and 3 SPEED? *MCS*

Album rating: *3

– spinoff hits, etc. –

JERMAINE JACKSON & PIA ZADORA: When The Rain Begins To Fall / PIA ZADORA: Substitute

Jan 85. (7"/12") *Curb-MCA; <52521> Arista; (ARIST/12ARIST 584)* 54 Oct84 68

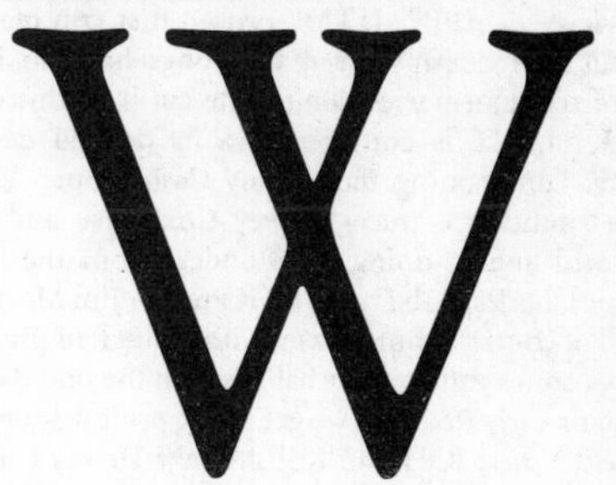

WALK HARD: THE DEWEY COX STORY

2007 (US 96m) Columbia Pictures (R)

Film genre: Rock'n'roll Musical comedy/satire

Top guns: s-w: (+ dir) Jake Kasdan, Judd Apatow ← KNOCKED UP

Stars: John C. Reilly *(Dewey Cox)* ← the PICK OF DESTINY ← MAGNOLIA ← BOOGIE NIGHTS ← GEORGIA, Jenna Fischer *(Darlene Madison)*, Raymond J. Barry *(Pa Cox)* ← DEAD MAN WALKING, Margo Martindale *(Ma Cox)* ← DEAD MAN WALKING, Kristen Wiig *(Edith)* ← KNOCKED UP, Tim Meadows *(Sam)* ← WAYNE'S WORLD 2, Chip Hormess *(Nate Cox)*, Conner Rayburn *(Dewey Cox; age 8)*, **David "Honeyboy" Edwards** *(old bluesman)* ← LIGHTNING IN A BOTTLE, Harold Ramis *(L'Chai'm)* ← KNOCKED UP ← AIRHEADS ← HEAVY METAL, Martin Starr *(Schmendrick)* ← KNOCKED UP, Frankie Muniz *(Buddy Holly)*, **Jack White** *(Elvis)* ← TWO HEADED COW ← the FEARLESS FREAKS ← COLD MOUNTAIN ← COFFEE AND CIGARETTES, John Ennis *(The Big Bopper)*, **the Temptations: Otis Williams *, Ron Tyson, Joe Herndon, Terry Weeks, Bruce Williamson** *(themselves)* ← SAVE THE CHILDREN *, **Eddie VEDDER** *(himself)*, **Jackson Browne** *(himself)* ← ENDLESS HARMONY: THE BEACH BOYS STORY ← NICO ICON ← BLACK & WHITE NIGHT ← NO NUKES, **Lyle LOVETT** *(himself)*, **Ghostface Killah** *(himself)* ← FADE TO BLACK ← BLACK AND WHITE, **Jewel Kilcher** *(herself)* ← WOODSTOCK '99, Paul Rudd *(John Lennon)* ← KNOCKED UP, Jack Black *(Paul McCartney)* ← the PICK OF DESTINY ← SCHOOL OF ROCK ← HIGH FIDELITY ← DEAD MAN WALKING, Justin Long *(George Harrison)*, **Justin Schwartzman** *(Ringo Starr)*, Adam Herschman *(Jerry Garcia)*

Storyline: Dewey Cox is an enigmatic rock legend who's bedded over 400 ladies, married three of them and has kids all over the place – one thing is missing though . . . the love of a good woman, backing-singer Darlene. His rollercoaster lifestyle (drugs and more drugs!) has also saw him befriend Elvis, the Beatles, etc. *MCS*

Movie rating: *7

Visual: dvd

Off the record: Jason Schwartzman is a cousin of Nicolas Cage and was the drummer with indie-rock band, Phantom Planet; one UK Top 10 hit, 'California' (from US TV show, 'The O.C.'). Born in 1915, **David Honeyboy Edwards** carried on the Delta blues tradition well into his 90s. *MCS*

JOHN C. REILLY (songwriters: Dan Bern, Mike Viola, etc.)

Dec 07. (cd) *Columbia: <88697 18248-2>* – –

– Walk hard / Take my hand / (Mama) You got to love your negro man / A life without you (is no life at all) / Let's duet (w/ ANGELA CORREA) / Darling / (I hate you) Big daddy / Guilty as charged / Dear Mr. President / Let me hold you (little man) / Royal jelly / Black sheep / Starman / Beautiful ride / (Have you heard the news) Dewey Cox died.

S/track review: '. . .SPINAL TAP' proved that you may be taking the piss but that doesn't mean the songs have to be bad. So many spoof rockumentaries don't quite cut it in this department but 'WALK HARD' is convincing in its dogged dedication to authenticity. Lampooning the Johnny Cash biopic 'WALK THE LINE', the soundtrack traces Dewey Cox's rise and fall in the musical world and in doing so, plunders from the musical log books of Ray Charles, Bob Dylan, Elvis Presley, Jim Morrison, Brian Wilson and of course, Johnny Cash, with a clutch of predominantly acoustic folk songs and country ballads with the odd dash of blues, psychedelia or early R&B. So we get mock protest songs like 'Dear Mr President' where JOHN C. REILLY (aka Dewey Cox) manages to offend every racial and social cultural group in the US of A, from native Americans to the clinically insane, all played deadly straight. Another terrifying turn of events is the genteel disco reworking of Bowie's 'Starman' which might make sense in the context of the film but is just plain terrifying here. The majority of the tracks were by duo Dan Bern and Mike Viola of the Candy Butcher with the indefatigable Van Dyke Parks writing the psychedelic odyssey 'Black Sheep' and power pop legend Marshall Crenshaw penning the Johnny Cash-aping 'Let's Duet'. The song was also nominated for an Academy Award for Best Song. The lyrics are a string of smutty double entendres about "beating off . . . my demons' and 'In my dreams your blowing me . . . some kisses'. The whole thing is insanely tongue-in-cheek but extremely skillfully done. The arrangements and attention to detail are phenomenal, though whether it justifies many repeated listens is another thing. If anything you crave the real thing. *MR*

Album rating: *7

WALK THE LINE

2005 (US 136m) Twentieth Century-Fox (PG-13)

Film genre: Country-music bio-pic/drama

Top guns: s-w: James Mangold (+ dir) ← HEAVY, Gill Dennis

Stars: Joaquin Phoenix *(Johnny Cash)* ← BROTHER BEAR, Reese Witherspoon *(June Carter)* ← S.F.W., Ginnifer Goodwin *(Vivian Cash)*, Robert Patrick *(Ray Cash)* ← ALL THE PRETTY HORSES ← WAYNE'S WORLD / → ELVIS, Dallas Roberts *(Sam Phillips)*, **Dan John Miller** *(Luther Perkins)*, Larry Bagby *(Marshall Grant)*, **Shelby Lynne** *(Carrie Cash)*, Tyler Hilton *(Elvis Presley)*, **Waylon Malloy Payne** *(Jerry Lee Lewis)* → CRAZY, Shooter Jennings *(Waylon Jennings)*, Sandra Ellis Lafferty *(Maybelle Carter)*, Jonathan Rice *(Roy Orbison)*, **Johnny Holiday** *(Carl Perkins)*, Clay Steakley *(W.S. 'Fluke' Holland)* → ELVIS, James Keach *(warden)* ← the LONG RIDERS ← FM, Amy Kudela *(Wanda)* → BLACK SNAKE MOAN

Storyline: The inevitable Hollywood biopic of the late Johnny Cash, recreating his life from the pain of his brother's premature death and tortured relationship with his father (criticised as overcooked) to the centrifugal force of his love for June Carter. Along the way he ploughs a fiercely individual course through early rock'n'roll and country music, pushes his mind and body to the limit with booze and pills, and forever sets in stone his outsider art with performances at San Quentin and Folsom prisons. *BG*

Movie rating: *8.5

Visual: dvd

Off the record: Actor Robert Patrick (aka T-1000 from Terminator 2: Judgment Day) is the brother of Richard Patrick (of Filter and ex-Nine Inch Nails guitarist). **Dan John Miller** was a member of Goober & The Peas, Blanche, etc. **Shelby Lynne** was a country-singer, Waylon Malloy Payne is son of country artists Sammi Smith and Jody Payne, Shooter Jennings is actually the son of Waylon Jennings whom he portrays in the film. **Johnny Holiday** is a young blues guitarist with one album (not the jazz artist). *MCS*

—

Various Cast (score: T-Bone Burnett)

Nov 05. (cd) *Wind-Up*; <(60150 13109-2)> [9] Jan06 [ ]
– Get rhythm (JOAQUIN PHOENIX) / I walk the line (JOAQUIN PHOENIX) / Wildwood flower (REESE WITHERSPOON) / Lewis boogie (WAYLON MALLOY PAYNE) / Ring of fire (JOAQUIN PHOENIX) / You're my baby (JONATHAN RICE) / Cry cry cry (JOAQUIN PHOENIX) / Folsom Prison blues (JOAQUIN PHOENIX) / That's all right (TYLER HILTON) / Juke box blues (REESE WITHERSPOON) / It ain't me babe (JOAQUIN PHOENIX & REESE WITHERSPOON) / Home of the blues (JOAQUIN PHOENIX) / Milk cow blues (TYLER HILTON) / I'm a long way from home (SHOOTER JENNINGS) / Cocaine blues (JOAQUIN PHOENIX) / Jackson (JOAQUIN PHOENIX & REESE WITHERSPOON).

S/track review: Few will disagree that JOACHIN PHOENIX's portrayal of Johnny Cash is one of the most compelling in the long, chequered history of rock biopics. Mangold's decision not to use the original recordings was a brave one, just as his request that PHOENIX "find the man inside" (as recounted by David Wild in the sleevenotes) was a canny one. PHOENIX doesn't sound identical to Cash, nor does he attempt to completely replicate his phrasing and gravitas. But even without the movie's stage mannerisms and attention to physical detail, his affinity with the role is uncanny, ghosting out of these recordings like a premonition and at least approaching something of the man's root essence. Hardly suprising then, that the prophetic, basso profundo vibrations of performances like 'I Walk The Line' and 'Ring Of Fire', increased sales of Cash's back catalogue by over 500%. It didn't hurt that original 'Sun' engineeer and subsequent Outlaw associate Cowboy Jack Clement was on hand, or that T-BONE BURNETT – who'd worked such magic on 'O Brother, Where Art Thou?' (2000) – was executive producer. And while June Carter was probably more difficult to depict, REESE WITHERSPOON acquits herself well, especially on the duets. PHOENIX himself sounds like he's having most fun on the mad, bad and dangerous likes of 'Cocaine Blues'; more of the same would've been preferable to lesser efforts from his supporting cast (SHOOTER JENNINGS – playing his late, great dad, Waylon – and his haunting, Jeff Tweedy-esque 'I'm A Long Way From Home' excepted) but then this is a soundtrack, not a proxy Cash anthology. *BG*

Album rating: *7

the WALL

aka PINK FLOYD: THE WALL

1982 (UK 95m w/anim.) Goldcrest / Metro-Goldwyn-Mayer (15)

Film genre: psychological Rock Musical drama

Top guns: dir: Alan Parker ← FAME / → BIRDY → the COMMITMENTS → EVITA / s-w: **Roger Waters** <= PINK FLOYD =>

Stars: Bob Geldof *(Pink)* ← PUNK IN LONDON / → SPICEWORLD → NEW YORK DOLL, Christine Hargreaves *(Pink's mother)* → 1984, James Laurenson *(Pink's father)* ← thye MONSTER CLUB / → HEARTBREAKERS → the MAN INSIDE, Eleanor David *(Pink's wife)*, Bob Hoskins *(rock'n'roll manager)* → SPICEWORLD → BEYOND THE SEA → DANNY THE DOG, Kevin McKeon *(young Pink)*, Jenny Wright *(American groupie)* YOUNG GUNS II, Peter Jonfield *(roadie)* ← McVICAR, Joanne Whalley (groupie), Nell Campbell *(groupie)* ← SHOCK TREATMENT ← JUBILEE ← ROCK FOLLIES OF '77 ← LISZTOMANIA ← the ROCKY HORROR PICTURE SHOW / → the KILLING FIELDS, Philip Davis *(roadie)* ← QUADROPHENIA / → STILL CRAZY, **Roger Waters** *(Pink's best man)* <= PINK FLOYD =>, Gary Olsen *(roadie)* ← BREAKING GLASS ← BIRTH OF THE BEATLES, Eddie Tagoe *(minder)* → TOP SECRET!

Storyline: Alan Parker's semi-animated film adaptation of Pink Floyd's Rock

Opera examines the tormented life of central character Pink, from the death of his father in the second world war to his disillusionment with life as a rock star and his inexorable descent into madness. *BG*

Movie rating: *6

Visuals: video + dvd

Off the record: Although there was not a soundtrack as such to accompany the 1982 film, PINK FLOYD's original double set which inspired the film remains a dark triumph of sorts. The autobiographical brainchild of ROGER WATERS, 'The WALL' renders its unremittingly bleak themes and convoluted lyrics palatable through a handful of career best songs and state of the art production. 'Another Brick In The Wall (Part II)' topped the charts in both America and Britain, haunting and sinister with a disco-inspired bassline, while 'Comfortably Numb' (a recent hit for the Scissor Sisters), another touchstone, was partly written by DAVID GILMOUR and represented the last gasp efforts of the WATERS/GILMOUR creative partnership. *BG*

– spinoff hits, etc. –

PINK FLOYD: When The Tigers Broke Free / Bring The Boys Back Home

Jul 82. (7") *Harvest; (HAR 5222)* [39] [–]

PINK FLOYD: Pink Floyd – The Wall

Jan 84. (video) *Thorn-EMI; (1VA 90 1431-2)* [–] [–]
– When the tigers broke free / Another brick in the wall (pt.2) / The happiest days of our lives / Empty spaces / One of my turns / Don't leave me now / Another brick in the wall (pt.3) / Goodbye cruel world / Is there anybody out there? / Nobody home / Vera / Waiting for the worms / Outside the wall / In the flesh / Stop / Thin ice / Another brick in the wall (pt.2) / Mother / Goodbye blue sky / Bring the boys come home / Young lust / Comfortably numb / Run like hell / The trial. *(re-iss. Sep89 on 'Channel 5'; CFV 08762)*

– inspirational release –

PINK FLOYD: The Wall

Dec 79. (d-lp/d-c) *Harvest; (SHWD/TC2SHWD 411) Columbia; <36183>* [3] [1]
– In the flesh / The thin ice / The happiest days of our lives / Another brick in the wall (part 2) / Mother / Goodbye blue sky / Empty spaces / Young lust / One of my turns / Don't leave me now / Another brick in the wall (part 3) / Goodbye cruel world / Hey you / Is there anybody out there? / Nobody home / Vera / Comfortably numb / The show must go on / Run like hell / Waiting for the worms / Stop / The trial / Outside the wall. *(d-cd-iss. Sep84; CDS 746036-2) (re-iss. Oct94 on 'E.M.I.' cd/c; CD/TC EMD 1071)*

PINK FLOYD: The Wall

1999. (dvd) *S.M.V.; (501989) <VFC 13391>* [–] [–]
– + (a 25 minute making of the film) / (a 45 min documentary of interviews with Roger Waters, Gerald Scarfe, Alan Parker, Peter Biziou, Alan Marshall & James Guthrie) *(re-iss. Jun06 on 'Sony Music Video'; 501986)*

– other bits & pieces, etc. –

SCISSOR SISTERS: Comfortably Numb / (extended mixes) / (video)

Jan 04. (cd-s/12"/12") *Polydor; (981588-3/-4/-5)* [10] [ ]

the WARRIORS

1979 (US 94m) Paramount Pictures (R)

Film genre: gangster/crime drama

Top guns: dir: Walter Hill / s-w: David Shaber → NIGHTHAWKS (au: Sol Yurick)

Stars: Michael Beck *(Swan)*, Thomas G. Waites *(Fox)*, James Remar *(Ajax)* → the LONG RIDERS, Marcelino Sanchez *(Rembrandt)*, Deborah Van Valkenburgh *(Mercy)* → STREETS OF FIRE → CHASING DESTINY → the DEVIL'S REJECTS, Mercedes Ruehl *(policewoman)*, Brian Tyler *(Snow)*, David Harris *(Cochise)*, Tom McKitterick *(Cowboy)*, David Patrick Kelly *(Luther)*, Dorsey Wright *(Cleon)*, Terry Michos *(Vermin)*, Roger Hill *(Cyrus)*, Lynn Thigpen *(D.J.)*

Storyline: Still the quintessential street gang flick, this notoriously violent movie centres around the unenviable predicament of Long Island gang the Warriors, as they attempt to negotiate a bloody passage home after being framed for murdering gangland peacemaker Cyrus. The incident happens in a Bronx park as the latter attempts to unite New York's warring factions, leaving the Warriors to battle it out on the city's subways. *BG*

Movie rating: *7

Visual: video + dvd

Off the record: nothing

Various Artists (score: BARRY DE VORZON *)

Apr 79. (lp) *A&M; <(SP 4761)>* [ ] Jun79 [53]
– Theme from The Warriors (*) / Nowhere to run (ARNOLD McCULLER) / In Havana (KENNY VANCE & ISMAEL MIRANDA) / Echoes in my mind (MANDRILL) / The fight (*) / In the city (JOE WALSH) / Love is a fire (GENYA RAVAN) / Baseball furies chase (*) / You're movin' too slow (JOHNNY VASTANO) / Last of an ancient breed (DESMOND CHILD). *(re-iss. Apr89 lp/c/cd; SP/CS/CDA 3151) (cd re-iss. Sep95 on 'Spectrum'; 551169-2) <(cd re-iss. Nov05 on 'Universal'; B000 5727-02)>*

S/track review: Composer BARRY DE VORZON stoked up the pressure-cooker atmosphere of a gang-ravaged NYC through a volatile strain of dark, lumbering, late-decade funk-rock ('Theme From The Warriors', 'The Fight' & 'Baseball Furies Chase'), while the likes of MANDRILL and KENNY VANCE & ISMAEL MIRANDA provide more soulful late 70s relief. Future 80s hair-metal guru DESMOND CHILD even makes an unlikely appearance via 'Last Of The Ancient Breed', although it's Eagles man JOE WALSH who leaves the deepest impression with the ballsy 'In The City'. Of the others, Polish-born GENYA RAVAN (formerly of bluesy jazz-rockers Ten Wheel Drive in the 70s and Goldie & The Gingerbreads in the 60s) was most interesting as she attempted a comeback of sorts with 'Love Is A Fire'. *BG & MCS*

Album rating: *6

WASSUP ROCKERS

2006 (US 111m) Capital Entertainment / Glass Key / Wildcard (R)

Film genre: urban/coming-of-age comedy/drama

Top guns: s-w + dir: Larry Clark ← KIDS (+ story w/ Matthew Frost)

Stars: Jonathan Velasquez *(Jonathan)*, Francisco Pedrasa *(Kiko)*, Milton Velasquez *(Milton/Spermball)*, Yunior Usualdo Panameno *(Porky)*, Eddie Velasquez *(Eddie)*, Luis Rojas-Salgado *(Louie)*, Carlos Velasco *(Carlos)*, Iris Zelaya *(Iris)*, Ashley Maldonado *(Rosalia)*, Jessica Steinbaum *(Nikki)*, Laura Cellner *(Jade)*

Storyline: A group of streetwise, mainly Hispanic youths – played by first-time actors – have a passion for skateboarding and punk-rock which alienates their South Central, Los Angeles, hip-hop neighborhood. Disillusioned, they try to find solace (and girls!) in and around the Beverly Hills area, although their presence is either wanted or tolerated from the local Anglos and the cops. *MCS*

Movie rating: *6

Visual: dvd

Off the record: (see below review).

Various Artists (score: Harry Cody)

Sep 06. (cd) *Record Collection; <44414-2>* [ ] [–]
– Politica corrupta (LA'S MORAL DECAY) / SC drunx (SOUTH

CENTRAL RIOT SQUAD) / SCRS (SOUTH CENTRAL RIOT SQUAD) / No future, no hope (DEFIANCE) / Stop these wars (the REVOLTS) / It's my life (the RETALIATES) / Youth in the streets (LA'S MORAL DECAY) / Unfinished story (LA'S MORAL DECAY) / La guerre de la muerte (the REMAINS) / Disgrace (SOUTH CENTRAL RIOT SQUAD) / No justice (the RETALIATES) / War on society (the REMAINS) / High school riot (the RETALIATES) / No control (the REVOLTS).

S/track review: Not a hip-hop track in sight, the record features six hardcore-punk bands of South Central L.A., including the loudest and wildest of the bunch, MORAL DECAY and SOUTH CENTRAL RIOT SQUAD. Larry Clark's movies are well known to be raw and unflinching studies of adolescent life and it's these qualities that make his work stand out. For this study of poor L.A. teen skate punks the soundtrack is suitably gnarly, an untidy compilation of hardcore thrash outs. There is a universally bleak lyrical outlook from all five bands featured. Its fair to say given their socio-economic backgrounds, there aren't too many tracks here about puppies, ice cream or going to the prom. Clark uses real bands playing real punk music and the lack of musicianship and polish only adds to the effect. Heavily influenced by the big three – Black Flag, Minor Threat and Bad Brains – and their successors, these bands sound like they would have imploded mere minutes after their demos were crudely laid to tape such is the vitriol and fury. The skill in great hardcore however, is judging the violence and energy of the music against the actual songcraft and only a few manage to strike the right balance of mania and message. DEFIANCE offer a degree of music deftness with 'No Future, No Hope' which apes the Skids' 'Into The Valley' and the Only Ones' 'Another Girl, Another Planet' in a comparatively slick anthem which is head and shoulders above anything else here. Others like the RETALIATES' 'High School Riot' and 'It's My Life' are valiant efforts but without the adrenalised visuals of teen punks on skateboards wooing rich Beverly Hills girls with their abrasive charms it sounds like what it could be: a pretty bog standard mixtape made in 1983. *MR*

Album rating: *4

☐ WAVELENGTH: Tangerine Dream (⇒ Pop/Rock Scores)

WAYNE'S WORLD

1992 (US 95m) Paramount Pictures (PG-13)

Film genre: showbiz satire / buddy film

Top guns: dir: Penelope Spheeris ← the DECLINE OF WESTERN CIVILIZATION 2: THE METAL YEARS ← DUDES ← SUBURBIA ← the DECLINE OF WESTERN CIVILIZATION / → the DECLINE OF WESTERN CIVILIZATION PART III → WE SOLD OUR SOULS FOR ROCK'N'ROLL / s-w: Mike Myers → WAYNE'S WORLD 2, Bonnie Turner+ Terry Turner → WAYNE'S WORLD 2

Stars: Mike Myers *(Wayne Campbell)* → as above + → 54, Dana Carvey *(Garth Algar)* ← THIS IS SPINAL TAP / → WAYNE'S WORLD 2, Rob Lowe *(Benjamin Oliver)*, Tia Carrere *(Cassandra Wong)* → WAYNE'S WORLD 2, Lara Flynn Boyle *(Stacy)*, Brian Doyle-Murray *(Noah Verderhoff)* ← CLUB PARADISE ← CADDYSHACK, Michael DeLuise *(Alan)*, Colleen Camp *(Mrs. Vanderhoff)*, Dan Bell *(Neil)* ← CATCH ME IF YOU CAN / → WAYNE'S WORLD 2, **MEAT LOAF** *(Tiny)*, Ed O'Neill *(Glen; Mikita's manager)* ← the ADVENTURES OF FORD FAIRLANE / → WAYNE'S WORLD 2, Robert Patrick *(bad cop/T-1000)* → ALL THE PRETTY HORSES → WALK THE LINE → ELVIS, Ione Skye *(Elyse)* → GAS, FOOD LODGING → FOUR ROOMS → WENT TO CONEY ISLAND ON A MISSION FROM GOD . . . BE BACK BY FIVE → SOUTHLANDER, Chris Farley *(security guard)* → WAYNE'S WORLD 2 → AIRHEADS Alice **COOPER** *(himself)*, Sean Gregory Sullivan *(Phil)* ← the IN CROWD ← WHO'S THAT GIRL? / → 54, Penelope Spheeris *(cameo)* ← NAKED ANGELS

Storyline: Nutty nice guys Wayne and Garth run a cable TV talk show from their basement. When the show is spotted by sleazeball executive Ben Oliver, he signs up the boys and promotes them to his own Chicago network station. Fame and fortune beckon and soon Wayne falls in love with lead singer Cassandra, but just when things look fine and peachy the guys realize Oliver has another agenda – as well as the TV rights, he wants Cassandra too. *JZ*

Movie rating: *8

Visual: video + dvd

Off the record: What no UGLY KID JOE on the OST/soundtrack.

Various Artists (score: J. Peter Robinson)

Feb 92. (cd/c) *Reprise; <(7599 26805-2/-4)>* [1] May92 [5]
– Bohemian rhapsody (QUEEN) / Hot and bothered (CINDERELLA) / Rock candy (BULLETBOYS) / Dream weaver (GARY WRIGHT) / Sikamikanico (the RED HOT CHILI PEPPERS) / Time machine (BLACK SABBATH) / Wayne's World theme (MIKE MYERS & DANA CARVEY) / Ballroom blitz (TIA CARRERE) / Foxey lady (JIMI HENDRIX) / Feed my Frankenstein (ALICE COOPER) / Ride with yourself (RHINO BUCKET) / Loving your lovin' (ERIC CLAPTON) / Why you wanna break my heart (TIA CARRERE).

S/track review: The film responsible for the resurgence in popularity of QUEEN's 'Bohemian Rhapsody' and it taking up residence at No.1 for weeks on end in the early 90s, 'WAYNE'S WORLD' changed the way the whole song is experienced; the heavy metal section can't be heard without the re-creation of the iconic headbanging-in-a-car sequence. We then get all 'Hot And Bothered' with CINDERELLA, as Tom Keifer does his best Brian Johnson impression, giving way to the fiery lead and slow-moving excess of 'Rock Candy' by BULLETBOYS, which grooves deliciously on a grinding riff. What it lacks in taste GARY WRIGHT's 'Dream Weaver' makes up for in sheer dry ice spectacle: it's a funky and defiantly overblown slab of cheese. Before they became stadium giants and mellowed out considerably, the RED HOT CHILI PEPPERS were the hyperactive, over-sexed purveyors of angular funk metal of which 'Sikamikanico' is a prime example, which sitting alongside BLACK SABBATH's latter day 'Time Machine' makes the Dio-fronted Sabbs seem all the more monolithic. The 'Wayne's World Theme' is the album's dumb highlight, monkeys flying out of butts, and the rest. Proving her vocal capabilities, TIA CARRERE's rendition of 'Ballroom Blitz' is exciting enough, but a HENDRIX classic like 'Foxey Lady' in this context can only invoke images of Garth's hilarious hounding at the feet of Kim Basinger. If you book them they will come, so other notable contributions come in the form of ALICE COOPER's bombastic 'Feed My Frankenstein' and ERIC CLAPTON's execrable 'Loving Your Lovin' which is a long way from relighting past glories. "We are not worthy". *DF*

Album rating: *7

– spinoff hits, etc. –

UGLY KID JOE: Everything About You

Mar 92. (7"/c-s/12"/cd-s) *Mercury; <866632> (MER/+MC/X/CD 367)* [9] May92 [3]

ALICE COOPER: Feed My Frankenstein / (non OST songs)

Jun 92. (7"/c-s/12"pic-d/cd-s/cd-s) *Epic; (658092-7/-4/-6/-2/-5)* [–] [27]

WAYNE'S WORLD 2

1993 (US 95m) Paramount Pictures (PG-13)

Film genre: Rock-music comedy

Top guns: dir: Stephen Surjik / s-w: Mike Myers ← WAYNE'S WORLD, Bonnie Turner ← WAYNE'S WORLD, Terry Turner ← WAYNE'S WORLD

Stars: Mike Myers *(Wayne Campbell)* → as above + → 54, Dana Carvey *(Garth Algar)* ← WAYNE'S WORLD ← THIS IS SPINAL TAP, Tia Carrere *(Cassandra Wong)* ← WAYNE'S WORLD, Christopher Walken *(Bobby Cahn)* ← HOMEBOY / → PULP FICTION → LAST MAN STANDING → TOUCH → the COUNTRY BEARS → ROMANCE & CIGARETTES → HAIRSPRAY re-make, Chris Farley *(Milton)* ← WAYNE'S WORLD → AIRHEADS, Michael A. Nickles *(Jim Morrison)*, Kim Basinger *(Honey Hornee)* ← BATMAN ← HARD COUNTRY / → 8 MILE, Charlton Heston *(good actor)*, Drew Barrymore *(Bjergen Kjergen)* ← FIRESTARTER / → the WEDDING SINGER → RAMONES: RAW → CURIOUS GEORGE → MUSIC AND LYRICS, Heather Locklear *(herself)* ← ROCK'N'ROLL MOM ← FIRESTARTER, Kevin Pollak *(Jerry Segel)*, → THAT THING YOU DO! → BUFFALO 66, Dan Bell *(Neil)* ← WAYNE'S WORLD ← CATCH ME IF YOU CAN, Harry Shearer *(Handsome Dan)* ← THIS IS SPINAL TAP ← ONE-TRICK PONY ← ANIMALYMPICS / → GHOST DOG: THE WAY OF THE SAMURAI → GIGANTIC (A TALE OF TWO JOHNS) → a MIGHTY WIND, Ed O'Neill *(Glen; Mikita's manager)* ← WAYNE'S WORLD ← the ADVENTURES OF FORD FAIRLANE, Jay Leno *(himself)*, Tim Meadows *(Sammy Davis Jr.)* → WALK HARD: THE DEWEY COX STORY, **AEROSMITH:- Steven Tyler, Joe Perry, Brad Whitfield, Tom Hamilton, Joey Kramer** *(performers)* / Olivia D'Abo *(Betty Jo)* ← the SPIRIT OF '76, Scott Coffey *(heavy metaller)* ← SHOUT ← SHAG: THE MOVIE ← SATISFACTION, James Hong *(Jeff Wong)* ← the KAREN CARPENTER STORY ← BLADE RUNNER ← BOUND FOR GLORY ← DYNAMITE BROTHERS / → EXPERIENCE, Ralph Brown *(Del Preston)* → STONED

Storyline: Just like Scrooge, Wayne is visited during the night by a ghost from the past, on this occasion Jim Morrison. He tells Wayne to set up a rock concert (Waynestock), which he does. Meanwhile, Garth finally meets the girl of his dreams and is promptly seduced by her, but it's Cassandra who's causing all the trouble when she is wined and dined by new manager Bobby. Just as Wayne is settling down at the concert he learns that Cass is about to be dragged down the aisle. Stop that wedding! *JZ*

Movie rating: *5

Visual: video + dvd

Off the record: (see below)

—

Various Artists (score: Carter Burwell)

Dec 93. (cd/c) *Reprise; <(7599 45485-2/-4)>* [78] Feb94 [17]
– Louie, Louie (ROBERT PLANT) / Dude (looks like a lady) (AEROSMITH) / Idiot summer (GIN BLOSSOMS) / Superstar (SUPERFAN) / I love rock'n'roll (JOAN JETT & THE BLACKHEARTS) / Spirit in the sky (NORMAN GREENBAUM) / Out there (DINOSAUR JR.) / Mary's house (4 NON BLONDES) / Radar love (GOLDEN EARRING) / Can't get enough (BAD ENOUGH) / Frankenstein (EDGAR WINTER) / Shut up and dance (AEROSMITH) / Y.M.C.A. (the VILLAGE PEOPLE).

S/track review: Let's get one thing sorted from the start. There is only one way that 'Louie Louie' should be performed and that is in the style commonly referred to as a drunken shambles. So what, we politely ask, was ROBERT PLANT thinking when he made this limp, half-arsed pop rock nonsense version that even dispenses with the customary, "aye aye aye aye", refrain. For this travesty he should, were it not for its past glories, be beaten to death with his own shoe. Sadly, it seems to set the tone for the rest of the album, which is packed with rock standards. Like many sequels, 'WAYNE'S WORLD 2' has been played safe, lacking flair and originality. There is no 'Bohemian Rhapsody' moment here. AEROSMITH take ALICE COOPER's place from the first film in providing the live music and it is not for the better as there is only so long you can listen to Joe Perry noodling away at a guitar solo on both 'Dude (Looks Like A Lady)' and 'Shut Up And Dance'. Lovers of MOR rock will have a field day here with JOAN JETT AND THE BLACKHEARTS's 'I Love Rock'n'Roll', 'Can't Get Enough' by BAD COMPANY and GOLDEN EARRING's 'Radar Love' among several others. Its not that the songs are bad, it's just that they are nothing new either. DINOSAUR JR do break up the monotony with 'Out There', a swirling, post-grunge meltdown that at least makes good use of a guitar solo. However, perhaps the saddest indictment of this soundtrack is that, by the time you get to the last track, you are almost delighted when you hear the VILLAGE PEOPLE's 'Y.M.C.A.' If only so you can reminisce about the hilarious scene in the film. Ready? 1, 2, 3, "its fun to stay at the . . ." *CM*

Album rating: *5

the WEDDING SINGER

1998 (US 95m) New Line Cinema (PG-13)

Film genre: romantic comedy

Top guns: dir: Frank Coraci / s-w: Tim Herlihy

Stars: Adam Sandler *(Robbie Hart)* ← AIRHEADS, Drew Barrymore *(Julia Sullivan)* ← WAYNE'S WORLD 2 ← FIRESTARTER / → RAMONES: RAW → CURIOUS GEORGE → MUSIC AND LYRICS, Christine Taylor *(Holly)* → AWESOME: I FUCKIN' SHOT THAT!, Allen Covert *(Sammy)* ← AIRHEADS, Matthew Glave *(Glen Gulia)* → ROCK STAR, Ellen Albertini Dow *(Rosie)* → 54 → LONGSHOT, Christina Pickles *(Angie Sullivan)* ← GRACE OF MY HEART, Kevin Nealon *(Mrs. Simms)*, **Billy IDOL** *(himself)*, Steve Buscemi *(Dave Veltri)* ← AIRHEADS ← PULP FICTION ← RESERVOIR DOGS ← MYSTERY TRAIN ← the WAY IT IS → COFFEE AND CIGARETTES → ROMANCE & CIGARETTES → the FUTURE IS UNWRITTEN, Alexis Arquette *(George Stitzer)* ← LAST EXIT TO BROOKLYN / → CLUBLAND, Jason Cottle *(Scott Castellucci)* ← WAG THE DOG ← FALL AND SPRING, Teddy Castellucci, Randy Razz & John Vana *(Robbie Hart band musicians)*

Storyline: Successful Rom-Com set in 1985 in which wedding singer Robbie meets waitress Julia at the last gig before his own wedding. While his affections switch towards the lady after being left standing at the altar by his fiancée, Julia herself must realise that she is engaged to a womanising cheat before the film can come to its natural conclusion. *KM*

Movie rating: *7

Visual: video + dvd

Off the record: (see below)

—

Various Artists (score: Teddy Castellucci)

Feb 98. (cd/c) *Maverick – Warners; <(9362 46840-2/-4)>* [5] Jun98 [15]
– Video killed the radio star (the PRESIDENTS OF THE UNITED STATES OF AMERICA) / Do you really want to hurt me (CULTURE CLUB) / Every little thing she does is magic (the POLICE) / How soon is now? (the SMITHS) / Love my way (PSYCHEDELIC FURS) / Hold me now (THOMPSON TWINS) / Everyday I write the book (ELVIS COSTELLO) / White wedding (BILLY IDOL) / China girl (DAVID BOWIE) / Blue Monday (NEW ORDER) / Pass the dutchie (MUSICAL YOUTH) / "Have you written anything lately?" / Somebody kill me (ADAM SANDLER) / Rapper's delight – medley (ELLEN DOW & SUGARHILL GANG).

S/track review: Entries from the POLICE, CULTURE CLUB and BILLY IDOL make this album read more like a best of the 80s compilation than a soundtrack. Would you stick with it until death do you part? Probably not. With the exception of a couple of tracks including the barely bearable PRESIDENTS OF THE UNITED STATES cover of Buggles' 'Video Killed The Radio Star', all selections are from the decade that sense forgot. A few pleasant surprises do crop up, notably spliffy schoolboys, MUSICAL YOUTH, with their mischievous 'Pass The Dutchie' and the SMITHS phd in floppy fringed alienation, 'How Soon Is Now'. BILLY IDOL's raucous 'White Wedding' could never have been far from the soundtrack creator's mind especially with his cameo at the end of the film; nominally annoying after a decade of death-by-rotation, here – on the back of ELVIS COSTELLO's whingeing 'Everyday I Write The Book' – it's actually blessed relief. New wave and post punk inevitably had to feature strongly on a soundtrack wallowing in the mid-80s and predictably, NEW ORDER's 'Blue Monday' covers the former while PSYCHEDELIC FURS' 'Love My Way' remains a frowning cult classic. On the other side of the Atlantic, hip hop was becoming mainstream and 'THE WEDDING SINGER' just about manages to acknowledge the genre with a bizarre, quasi-humorous coda of SUGARHILL GANG's 'Rapper's Delight' (a second batch of 80s throwaways on 'WEDDING SINGER 2', also found their way to your hearts). For New Romantics everywhere. *KM*

Album rating: *6 (volume 2; *5)

– spinoff hits, etc. –

the PRESIDENTS OF THE UNITED STATES OF AMERICA: Video Killed The Radio Star / ELLEN DOW & SUGARHILL GANG: Rapper's Delight – medley / CULTURE CLUB: Do You Really Want To Hurt Me

Jul 98. (c-s/cd-s) *(W 0450 C/CD)* [–] [52]

Various Artists: The Wedding Singer volume 2

Jul 98. (cd/c) *<(9362 46984-2/-4)>* [22] Aug98 [ ]
– Too shy (KAJAGOOGOO) / It's all I can do (the CARS) / True (SPANDAU BALLET) / Space age love song (A FLOCK OF SEAGULLS) / Private Idaho (the B-52'S) / Money (that's what I want) (the FLYING LIZARDS) / You spin me 'round (like a record) (DEAD OR ALIVE) / Just can't get enough (DEPECHE MODE) / Love stinks (J. GEILS BAND) / You make my dreams (HALL & OATES) / Holiday (MADONNA) / Grow old with you (ADAM SANDLER).

☐ Chuck E. WEISS segment
(⇒ DU-BEAT-E-O)

☐ WHALE MUSIC
(⇒ Rock/Pop Scores)

WHAT A CRAZY WORLD

1963 (UK 88m b&w) Capricorn Production / Warner-Pathe

Film genre: Rock'n'roll Musical comedy

Top guns: dir: Michael Carreras / s-w: Alan Klein (+ play)

Stars: Joe Brown *(Alf Hitchens)* → JUST FOR FUN → CONCERT FOR GEORGE, **Susan Maughan** *(Marilyn)* → POP GEAR, **Marty Wilde** *(Herbie Shadbolt)* → STARDUST, Harry H. Corbett *(Sam Hitchens)* ← SOME PEOPLE / → SILVER DREAM RACER, Avis Bunnage *(Mary Hitchens)* → MRS. BROWN, YOU'VE GOT A LOVELY DAUGHTER, Grazina Frame *(Doris Hitchens)* → EVERY DAY'S A HOLIDAY, Monty Landis *(Solly Gold)* ← PLAY IT COOL / → DOUBLE TROUBLE, Michael Ripper *(the common man)* → EVERY DAY'S A HOLIDAY, **Freddie & The Dreamers:- Freddie Garrity, Peter Birrell, Roy Crewsdon, Derek Quinn, Bernie Dwyer** *(performers)* → JUST FOR YOU → EVERY DAY'S A HOLIDAY → CUCKOO PATROL → DISK-O-TEK HOLIDAY → OUT OF SIGHT, Fanny Carby *(Dolly)* ← SOME PEOPLE / → the FAMILY WAY, Harry Locke *(George)* → the FAMILY WAY, Bill Fraser *(Milligan)* → I'VE GOTTA HORSE, Billy Murray *(youth at dance)* → UP THE JUNCTION → PERFORMANCE → ROCK FOLLIES → McVICAR, Jessie Robins *(fat woman)* → MAGICAL MYSTERY TOUR → UP THE JUNCTION, Toni Palmer *(waitress)* → SMASHING TIME

Storyline: Cheeky chappie Alf has a smile on his face despite living in an impoverished area of London's East End. That's because he knows success is just around the corner although Ma and Pa would prefer he kept away from corners altogether, as that's where all the bad guys hang out. Instead of settling down and finding a steady job, Alf writes a song which impresses a local producer, and suddenly London's streets might be paved with gold after all for the Cockney crooner. *JZ*

Movie rating: *5

Visual: dvd

Off the record: Joe Brown and Co (see below)

—

Various Artists (composer: Stanley Black)

Oct 63. (lp) *Piccadilly; (NPL/NSPL 38011)* [ ] [–]
– What a crazy world (we're livin' in) (JOE BROWN AND THE BRUVVERS, MARTY WILDE) / A layabout's lament (MARTY WILDE, JOE BROWN) / I sure know a lot about love (MICHAEL GOODMAN) / Bruvvers (GRAZINA, JOE BROWN, MICHAEL GOODMAN) / Oh, what a family (MARTY WILDE, JOE BROWN) / Alfred Hitchins (SUSAN MAUGHAN) / Sally Ann (JOE BROWN AND THE BRUVVERS) / Wasn't it a handsome punch-up (JOE BROWN, MARTY WILDE) / Please give me a chance (SUSAN MAUGHAN) / Independence (JOE BROWN, MARTY WILDE, the BRUVVERS) / I feel the same way too (SUSAN MAUGHAN, JOE BROWN) / Just you wait and see (JOE BROWN) / Things we never had – Reprise of Crazy World (HARRY H. CORBETT). *(re-iss. 1964 on 'Golden Guinea'; GGL 0272) (re-iss. Jan84 on 'President'; PLE 512) (cd-iss. Nov01 on 'Castle'+=; CMRCD 396)* – Sally Ann (FREDDIE & THE DREAMERS) / Camptown races (FREDDIE & THE DREAMERS) / Lonely boy (FREDDIE & THE DREAMERS) / Short shorts (FREDDIE & THE DREAMERS).

S/track review: Based on a JOE BROWN AND THE BRUVVERS minor hit, 'What A Crazy World We're Living In' (from early '62), the film and soundtrack were basically a vehicle for the cheeky Cockney, who was actually born in Swarby, Lincolnshire. Formerly a lead guitarist for BILLY FURY, JOE and his backing band had three Top 10 hits, 'A Picture Of You', 'It Only Took A Minute' & 'That's What Love Will Do', prior to appearing in this movie. 'WHAT A CRAZY WORLD' only produced one Top 30 entry, the song and dance number, 'Sally Ann', and this was the combination's final hit together, while the newly recorded title track credited them alongside movie co-star, MARTY WILDE. The latter had been around in the pop music business since the late 50s ('Endless Sleep', 'Donna', 'A Teenager In Love', 'Sea Of Love' & 'Bad Boy'); however, his hits had dried up and he'd been unsuccessful during all of '63. Alongside JOE BROWN, the duo contributed a handful of cues here, 'A Layabout's Lament', 'Oh, What A Family', 'Wasn't It A Handsome Punch-Up' and 'Independence' (with the BRUVVERS), all of them good ol' Cockney rock'n'roll with a hint a naughtiness. Things are brought to a grinding halt, rock-wise at least, when SUSAN MAUGHAN smooches her way through a few solo numbers, 'Alfred Hitchins' & 'Please Give Me A Chance', while she also duets with JOE BROWN (who else!) for a third effort, 'I Feel The Same Way Too'. 'WHAT A CRAZY WORLD' was a bit of a blast for BROWN and the cast, even Steptoe & Son actor HARRY H CORBETT got his two-penneth in via 'Things We Never Had . . .'. The re-issued CD fares even better with the inclusion of four FREDDIE & THE DREAMERS tracks, including their take of 'Sally Ann' and the perennial 'Short Shorts'. Now I'm off down the apples and pears to the rub-a-dub-dub to down a few Mick Jaggers. *MCS*

Album rating: *5 (cd *5.5)

– spinoff hits, etc. –

JOE BROWN & THE BRUVVERS: Sally Ann

Sep 63. (7") *(7N 35138)* [28] [–]

FREDDIE AND THE DREAMERS: Songs From 'What A Crazy World'

1963. (7"ep) *Columbia; (SEG 8287)* [ ] [–]

WHAT ABOUT ME

1993 (US 87m b&w) unknown

Film genre: urban drama

Top guns: s-w + dir: Rachel Amodeo

Stars: Rachel Amodeo *(Lisa Napolitano)*, **Richard Edson** *(Nick)* ← TOUGHER THAN LEATHER ← GOOD MORNING, VIETNAM ← WALKER ← HOWARD THE DUCK / → STRANGE DAYS → the MILLION DOLLAR HOTEL → SOUTHLANDER, Nick Zedd *(Tom)* → JOE'S APARTMENT, **Richard HELL** *(Paul)*, Judy Carne *(homeless woman)* ← ALL THE RIGHT NOISES, **Johnny Thunders** *(Vito Napolitano)* <= NEW YORK DOLLS =>, **Jerry Nolan** *(Joey)* <= NEW YORK DOLLS =>, **Dee Dee Ramone** *(Dougie)* <= RAMONES =>), Gregory Corso *(hotel desk clerk)*, Rockets Redglare *(Frank; the rapping landlord)* ← MYSTERY TRAIN ← CANDY MOUNTAIN ← DOWN BY LAW

Storyline: Set in New York's tough East Side, Lisa Napolitano finds her life upended after a bike accident and the death of her parents. She goes to live with her elderly aunt, but when she dies as well, the landlord rapes her and evicts her the next day. Now homeless and jobless, Lisa is befriended by Vietnam veteran Nick, but their struggle to survive on the streets isn't helped by Nick's own problems and the onset of the cold winter. *JZ*

Movie rating: *6

Visual: dvd rel. 2003 (no audio OST)

Off the record: JOHNNY THUNDERS (d.23 Apr'91, New Orleans, Louisiana; o.d.) was the man behind five of the tracks, 'So Alone' (w/ the HEARTBREAKERS), Bob Dylan's 'Joey Joey', 'You Can't Put Your Arms Around A Memory', 'Bird Song' & 'In God's Name'; other various include 'Another Girl, Another Planet' (the ONLY ONES) and 'Aisha' (VACUUM BAG). *MCS*

WHAT AM I BID?

1967 (US 92m) Liberty International

Film genre: showbiz/Country & Western Musical drama

Top guns: s-w + dir: Gene Nash

Stars: **LeRoy Van Dyke** *(Pat Hubbard)*, Kristin Nelson/Harmon *(Beth Hubbard)*, Stephanie Hill *(Maggie Hendricks)*, Bill Craig *(Mike Evans)*, Billy Benedict *(Clem)*, Jack McCall *(Hal Cook)*, **Tex Ritter** *(performer)* ← NASHVILLE REBEL / → the NASHVILLE SOUND, **Faron Young** *(performer)* ← SECOND FIDDLE TO A STEEL GUITAR ← NASHVILLE REBEL ← COUNTRY MUSIC HOLIDAY / → ROAD TO NASHVILLE, **Al Hirt** *(performer)*, Johnny Sea *(himself)*, Ray Sims *(auctioneer)*

Storyline: Pat Hubbard leaves the navy and settles down as a cattle auctioneer, the career he has always wanted. However his manager and fans have other plans – they would rather he use his singing talents in the world of showbiz like his famous father. But Pat knows how that career ruined his father and doesn't want to go down the same path in case the same thing happens to him. *JZ*

Movie rating: *5

Visual: none

Off the record: **LeROY VAN DYKE** (see below)

—

LeROY VAN DYKE

Nov 66. (lp) *M.G.M.; <E/SE 4506ST>* [ ] [–]
– What am I bid? / Time is the only thing I'm after / Don't look back / I never got to kiss the girl / I'll make it up to you / Auctioneer / When a boy becomes a man (JOHNNY SEA) / Big, wide, wonderful world of country music / Life gets a little more mixed up ev'ry day / We've got the best there is.

S/track review: Country music's slide into TV-led showbusiness – a journey that all but submerged the music's rural folk roots in formulaic commercial pap – had reached its nadir in the 1960s, and LeROY VAN DYKE was a pivotal figure in the process. Catapulted to prominence in 1956 by his own song 'Auctioneer', VAN DYKE went on to sell three million copies of another composition, 'Walk On By' (definitely not the Bacharach and David classic, though named by Billboard in 1994 as the biggest-selling country single of all time). A Grand Old Opry regular, he was also the first man to take a choreographed "country" show to Las Vegas, and duly earned this little-remembered Hollywood vehicle at the height of his fame. The songs by director/screenwriter GENE NASH are Identikit big-screen musical fare at the fag-end of the Rodgers & Hammerstein tradition, and though both FARON YOUNG and TEX RITTER take an honourable stab at a song, and VAN DYKE's own vocals are not without charm, any relation to rootsy traditions ('Big, Wide Wonderful World of Country Music') is strictly titular. A retread of 'Auctioneer', complete with country fair calling, somehow retains its novelty appeal amidst this hapless gaucherie; "the world's most famous auctioneer" would continue to perform for decades afterwards at country fairs and livestock events. *ND*

Album rating: *3

WHAT'S LOVE GOT TO DO WITH IT

1993 (US 118m) Touchstone Pictures (R)

Film genre: R&B/Pop-music biopic/drama

Top guns: dir: Brian Gibson ← BREAKING GLASS / → STILL CRAZY / s-w: Kate Lanier → GLITTER (au: Kurt Loder, Tina Turner 'I, Tina')

Stars: Angela Bassett *(Tina Turner)* ← the JACKSONS: AN AMERICAN DREAM / → STRANGE DAYS → MASKED AND ANONYMOUS, Laurence Fishburne *(Ike Turner)* ← SCHOOL DAZE ← DEATH WISH II ← FAST BREAK ← CORNBREAD, EARL AND ME / → EVENT HORIZON → the SOUL OF A MAN, Jenifer Lewis *(Zelma Bullock)* ← BEACHES / → SHAKE, RATTLE & ROCK! tv → GIRL 6 → the PREACHER'S WIFE → the TEMPTATIONS → JACKIE'S BACK! → LITTLE RICHARD, Phyllis Yvonne Stickney *(Alline Bullock)* ← JUNGLE FEVER, Vanessa Bell Calloway *(Jackie)* → the TEMPTATIONS, Khandi Alexander *(Darlene)* ← CB4: THE MOVIE / → HOUSE PARTY 3, Rae'ven Kelly *(young Anna Mae)*, Penny Johnson *(Lorraine)*, Richard T. Jones *(Ike Turner, Jr.)* → EVENT HORIZON, **Chi** *(Fross)* → ROLL BOUNCE, Virginia Capers *(choir mistress)* ← HOWARD THE DUCK ← FIVE ON THE BLACK HAND SIDE ← TROUBLE MAN ← LADY SINGS THE BLUES ← NORWOOD, **Tina Turner** *(singing voice)* ← TOMMY ← SOUL TO SOUL, **Gene 'Groove' Allen** *(MC announcer)* ← HOUSE PARTY 2 ← HOUSE PARTY, Michael Colyar *(Apollo announcer)* → HOUSE PARTY 3

Storyline: The famously troubled life of Tina Turner gets the rock bio-pic treatment, focusing largely on the abusive relationship she endured with mentor, singing partner and husband Ike. *BG*

Movie rating: *6

Visual: video + dvd

Off the record: **Gene 'Groove' Allen** was of Groove B. Chill duo.

—

TINA TURNER (score: Stanley Clarke)

Jun 93. (cd/c/lp) *Virgin; <88189> Capitol; (CD/TC+/PCSD 128)* [17] [1]
– I don't wanna fight / Rock me baby / Disco inferno / Why must we wait until tonight? / Nutbush city limits / (Darlin') You know I love you / Proud Mary / A fool in love / It's gonna work out fine / Stay awhile / Shake a tail feather *[UK-only]* / I might have been Queen / What's love got to do with it (live) / Tina's wish *[UK-only]*.

S/track review: Unlike the more recent Ray Charles biopic, 'RAY', 'WHAT'S LOVE GOT TO DO WITH IT' is comprises of re-recordings rather than originals. When faced with trawling through her back catalogue, TINA TURNER admits that "the thought did not thrill me". It's a thought which can't have thrilled her fans much either. Mercifully, her R&B classics are regurgitated pretty faithfully, and show up newer tracks like 'Why Must We Wait Until Tonight?' for the flaccid, Bryan Adams-penned fillers that they are. And they turn out some of the most soulful performances from TURNER in years. She might have reinvented herself as an airbrushed 80s pop diva, yet – as an old cliché doubtless goes – you can take the girl out of the South, but you can't take the Southern Soul out of the girl. Her 80s efforts have held up better than almost all of her peers, and there aren't many singles as redolent of their era as the definitive, Grammy-winning title track. But filed alongside chitlin time capsules like 'It's Gonna Work Out Fine' and 'A Fool In Love', they lose some of their moody lustre, even if these recordings themselves can't hope to measure up to the Phil Spector-produced versions on 'River Deep Mountain High' from 1966. The omission of 'River Deep Mountain High' itself is unforgivable, but a couple of sizzling B.B. King covers, and a decent run through her Creedence calling card, 'Proud Mary', go some way to making up for it. A TINA virgin might get some mileage out of this soundtrack but given that there are far more comprehensive anthologies on the market – and the fact that Stanley Clarke's score is passed over completely – its only real selling point is the onetime hardest-working woman in showbusiness redoing her back catalogue. *BG*

Album rating: *6

– spinoff hits, etc. –

TINA TURNER: I Don't Wanna Fight / The Best

May 93. (7"/c-s) *(R/TCR 6346)* [–] [7]
(cd-s+=) *(CDR 6346)* – I don't wanna lose you / What's love got to do with it.
(cd-s) *(CDRS 6346)* – ('A') / Tina's wish / ('A'-urban mix).

TINA TURNER: I Don't Wanna Fight / Tina's Wish

May 93. (c-s,cd-s) *<12652>* [9] [–]

TINA TURNER: Disco Inferno / I Don't Wanna Fight

Aug 93. (7"/c-s) *(R/TCR 6357)* [–] [12]
(12"+=/cd-s+=) *(12R/CDR 6357)* – ('A'-mixes).

TINA TURNER: Why Must We Wait Until Tonight? / Shake A Tail Feather

Oct 93. (7"/c-s) *(R/TCR 6366) <12683>* [97] [16]
(cd-s+=) *(CDR 6366)* – The best.
(cd-s++=) *(CDRS 6366)* – ('A'-remix).

WHEN THE BOYS MEET THE GIRLS

1965 (US 97m) Metro-Goldwyn-Mayer (PG)

Film genre: Pop/Rock Musical comedy

Top guns: dir: Alvin Ganzer ← COUNTRY MUSIC HOLIDAY / s-w: Robert E. Kent ← GET YOURSELF A COLLEGE GIRL ← HOOTENANNY HOOT ← DON'T KNOCK THE TWIST ← DON'T KNOCK THE ROCK ← ROCK AROUND THE CLOCK / → the FASTEST GUITAR ALIVE → a TIME TO SING

Stars: Connie FRANCIS *(Ginger Gray)*, Harve Presnell *(Danny Churchill)*, Sue Ane Langdon *(Tess Rawley)* ← ROUSTABOUT / → FRANKIE AND JOHNNY → HOLD ON!, Joby Baker *(Sam)* ← GIRL HAPPY ← LOOKING FOR LOVE ← HOOTENANNY HOOT, Fred Clark *(Bill Denning)* → SKIDOO, Hortense Petra *(Kate)* ← YOUR CHEATIN' HEART ← GET YOURSELF A COLLEGE GIRL ← KISSIN' COUSINS ← DON'T KNOCK THE TWIST / → HOLD ON! → RIOT ON SUNSET STRIP, plus **Louis Armstrong** *(performer)* → RED, WHITE & BLUES, **HERMAN'S HERMITS:- Peter Noone, Karl Green, Keith Hopwood, Derek Leckenby, Barry Whitman** *(performers)* / Liberace *(performer)*, **Sam The Sham:- Domingo Samudio** *(performer)* → the FASTEST GUITAR ALIVE, **& the Pharoahs:- Dave Martin, Jerry Patterson, Butch Gibson, Ray Stinnet** *(performers)*, Susan Holloway *(Delilah)*

Storyline: Young millionaire Danny Churchill comes to the rescue of sweet little Ginger, whose daddy's Nevada ranch is on its last legs. He decides the only way to make money is to turn the ranch into a hotel for would-be divorcees (no double bedrooms, we assume) and pay off dad's debts. All goes well until fly in the ointment Tess appears on the scene, desperate to get her mitts on Danny and his dosh. This will surely drive Ginger nuts. *JZ*

Movie rating: *5.5

Visual: none

Off the record: Sam The Sham (see below)

Various Artists (composers: George & Ira Gershwin *, etc.)

Jan 66. (lp; mono/stereo) *M.G.M.; <E/ES 4334>* [61] [–]
– When the boys meet the girls (CONNIE FRANCIS) / Monkey see, monkey do (SAM THE SHAM AND THE PHAROAHS) / Embraceable you (HARVE PRESNELL) * / Throw it out your mind (LOUIS ARMSTRONG & ORCHESTRA) / Mail call (CONNIE FRANCIS) / I got rhythm (HARVE PRESNELL & CONNIE FRANCIS) * / Listen people (HERMAN'S HERMITS) / Bidin' my time (HERMAN'S HERMITS) * / Embraceable you (CONNIE FRANCIS) * / Aruba Liberace (LIBERACE) / But not for me (CONNIE FRANCIS & HARVE PRESNELL) * / I got rhythm (LOUIS ARMSTRONG & ORCHESTRA) *. *(UK-iss.Jan89 on 'M.C.A.' lp/c; MCA/+C 25013)*

S/track review: A hotch-potch of the day's "pop" stars, namely stars of the 'M.G.M.' movie, CONNIE FRANCIS, HARVE PRESNELL, HERMAN'S HERMITS, SAM THE SHAM AND THE PHARAOHS, LIBERACE and LOUIS ARMSTRONG. Where does one start, indeed. CONNIE was undoubtedly the biggest female attraction at the time, a plethora of Top 20 hits (including 'Stupid Cupid' & 'Lipstick On Your Collar') in the early 60s had guaranteed her place in the rock'n'roll hall of fame, while her previous movies, 'WHERE THE BOYS ARE' (1960), 'FOLLOW THE BOYS' (1963) and 'LOOKING FOR LOVE' (1964) had shown her acting/performing versatility. I suppose she was the female equivalent of Elvis, movie-wise at least. Here, the bouffant CONNIE gets five bites at the musical cherry, three solo numbers ('When The Boys Meet The Girls', 'Mail Call' and the sensual 'Embraceable You') plus two balladeer duets (trad-jazz standard 'I Got Rhythm' & 'But Not For Me') with clean-cut crooning co-star, HARVE PRESNELL. The Gershwin name (famous for old-style musicals from way back) was all over the place, the Johnny Mathis-esque PRESNELL (of 'The Unsinkable Molly Brown' fame) producing the worst of the batch with his rendition of 'Embraceable You'. Names of the past, jazzman LOUIS ARMSTRONG (celebrating his 50th anniversary as an entertainer!) and the gold-sequinned LIBERACE, should've known better, but as they say in showbiz, anything goes! The latter's 'Aruba Liberace' was all too much samba, rumba, marimba, baba . . . but no one can doubt that he was a total pianist. The set really kicks in when Dallas-raised 'Wooly Bully' guys SAM THE SAM AND THE PHARAOHS take a leaf out of the Bo Diddley style book for the "magical" 'Monkey See, Monkey Do'. Produced by svengali Mickie Most, Manchester boys, HERMAN'S HERMITS (who were recently "Into Something Good"), surfaced on side 2 courtesy of US Top 3 smash, 'Listen People' and Gershwin's 'Bidin' My Time'. All'n'all, very dated and very, very manufactured. *MCS*

Album rating: *3.5

– spinoff hits, etc. –

HERMAN'S HERMITS: Listen People / (non-OST song)

Feb 66. (7") *<13462>* [3] [–]
(above on the UK B-side of Top 20 hit, 'You Won't Be Leaving')

WHERE THE BOYS ARE

1960 (US 99m) Metro-Goldwyn-Mayer (PG-13)

Film genre: romantic teen drama

Top guns: dir: Henry Levin ← APRIL LOVE ← BERNARDINE / s-w: George Wells (nov: Glendon Swarthout)

Stars: George Hamilton *(Ryder Smith)* → LOOKING FOR LOVE → YOUR CHEATIN' HEART, Dolores Hart *(Merrit Andrews)*, Yvette Mimieux *(Melanie Coleman)*, Jim Hutton *(TV Thompson)* → LOOKING FOR LOVE, Paula Prentiss *(Tuggle Carpenter)*, **Connie FRANCIS** *(Angie)*, Barbara Nichols *(Lola)*, Frank Gorshin *(Basil)* → SKIDOO → RECORD CITY, Chill Wills *(police captain)*, Percy Helton *(Fairview hotel manager)* ← JAILHOUSE ROCK ← SHAKE, RATTLE AND ROCK! / → GET YOURSELF A COLLEGE GIRL → HEAD

Storyline: Four teenage co-eds on their spring vacation escape from the bleak mid-west and head for the sunny climes of Fort Lauderdale because – that's where the boys are. Merritt, Tuggle, Melanie and Angie soon get down to business but while it's love and marriage they're after, their boyfriends only have one thing on their minds. JZ

Movie rating: *4.5

Visual: video + dvd

Off the record: no full-length score (by George Stoll & Pete Rugolo); other songwriters: Stella Unger, Howard Greenfield, Victor Young + title track – Neil Sedaka.

– spinoff releases, etc. –

CONNIE FRANCIS: Where The Boys Are

Jan 61. (7") *M.G.M.; <12964>* 4 –

CONNIE FRANCIS: Where The Boys Are / (diff. B-side)

Mar 61. (7") *M.G.M.; (1121)* – 5

□ Tony Joe WHITE segment (⇒ CATCH MY SOUL)

WHITE CITY

1985 (UK 60m video) Eel Pie / Midnight Films (15)

Film genre: romantic Rock Musical docudrama

Top guns: s-w: (+ dir) Richard Lowenstein → AUSTRALIAN MADE: THE MOVIE → DOGS IN SPACE, **Pete Townshend**

Stars: Pete Townshend *(Pete Fountain)* <= the WHO =>, Frances Barber *(Alice)* → YOUNG SOUL REBELS → STILL CRAZY, Andrew Wilde *(Jim)* ← 1984, Cecily Hobbs *(clerk)*, Barbara Young *(mother)*, Gwyneth Strong *(girlfriend)*, Ewan Stewart *(Scotsman)* → the LAST GREAT WILDERNESS → YOUNG ADAM

Storyline: Jim and Alice are a young London couple whose marriage is on the rocks. When best friend Pete turns up he tries to sort things out between the pair while setting up a concert at the White City Hall at the same time. But as time goes on it seems as though Pete will have more success as a music maker than as a marriage guidance counsellor. JZ

Movie rating: *5

Visual: video on 'Vestron'

Off the record: Glasgow-born Ewan Stewart is the son of traditional-folk singer, Andy Stewart. MCS

PETE TOWNSHEND: White City – a novel

Nov 85. (lp/c/cd) *Atco; (252392-1/-4/-2) <90473>* 70 26
– Give blood / Brilliant blues / Face the face / Hiding out / Secondhand love / Crashing by design / I am secure / White City fighting Come to mama. *(re-iss. cd Nov93; same)*

S/track review: No stranger to soundtracks, PETE TOWNSHEND, along with his band the Who had already scored the likes of 'QUADROPHENIA' and 'TOMMY', to name but two. 'WHITE CITY', is a novel, film and album, all written by TOWNSHEND and set in the area of the same name in London near to where he grew up. In the absence of his band, TOWNSHEND has surrounded himself with a group of accomplished musicians to create the soundtrack. MARK BRZEZICKI and TONY BUTLER of Big Country contribute drums and bass respectively while Blondie's CLEM BURKE also plays drums. Long-time WHO keyboardist JOHN BUNDRICK appears along with a wealth of well-travelled session musicians including PINO PALLADINO and the Kick Horns. The music itself though is a far cry from TOWNSHEND's best work, either with or without the WHO, lacking any discernible spark or inspiration that might make the album worth listening to. The lyrics seem forced and bland, lacking TOWNSHEND's renowned razor sharp wit and ability to articulate his worldly observations. It's as though he's struggling to speak for his own generation now that they've all grown up. In saying that, opening track 'Give Blood' and 'Face The Face' are good tracks, the former a rousing call for solidarity while the latter is a synth-infused rockabilly tune. The only other song worth mention is 'White City Fighting', simply a track written by David Gilmour of Pink Floyd. It's difficult listening to 'WHITE CITY' because you know that TOWNSHEND is capable of so much more, but nobody's perfect, as this proves. CM

Album rating: *4

– spinoff releases, etc. –

PETE TOWNSHEND: Face The Face / Hiding Out

Oct 85. (7"/12") *(U/UT 8859) <99590>* □ 26

PETE TOWNSHEND: Secondhand Love / White City Fighting

Jan 86. (7") *<99553>* – □

WHITE "POP" JESUS

1980 (Ita 94m) Sirus Film (18)

Film genre: Pop/Rock Musical comedy

Top guns: s-w + dir: Luigi Petrini

Stars: Awana-Gana *(Jesus)*, Stella Carnacina *(Lattuga Pop)*, Gianni Magni *(Commissario Vito)*, Gisela Hahn *(Stella Young)* → CONTAMINATION, Grippy Jocard *(Playboy Smith)* ← MR. MEAN, Tony Schneider *(Gabriele)*

Storyline: Disco-loving Jesus comes down from Heaven to sort out the Mafia, but will his second coming see him "sleep with the fishes" (5,000 of them) at the bottom of the Mediterranean? MCS

Movie rating: *3.5

Visual: video

Off the record: GOBLIN (see own entry)

FRANCO BIXIO, VINCE TEMPERA & GOBLIN

1980. (lp) *E.M.I.;* – Italy –
– W.P. Jesus / Amare ma / Come un navigante / Overdose / Via con te / Vivi! / Osanna / Jesus Jesus / Unisex / W.P. Jesus.

S/track review: FRANCO BIXIO was the composer of this VERY rare one; VINCE TEMPERA and cohorts take on the music with the aid of MASSIMO LUCA, ELLADE BANDINI, TONY CICCO and MINO FABIANO, alongside GOBLIN musicians CARLO PENNISI, AGOSTINO MARANGOLO and FABIO PIGNATELLI. Reports are it's not great and it must be expensive – just couldn't find but there must be some Italian person out there to properly review it? *MCS*

Album rating: *3

WHITE STAR

US title/video 'LET IT ROCK'

1983 (W.Ger 75m) Media Home Entertainment US 1986

Film genre: Rock-music comedy/drama

Top guns: s-w + dir: Roland Klick

Stars: Dennis Hopper *(Kenneth Barlow)* ← HUMAN HIGHWAY ← EASY RIDER ← HEAD ← the TRIP / → RUNNING OUT OF LUCK → STRAIGHT TO HELL, Terrance Robay *(Moody Mudinsky)*, **David Hess** *(Frank)*, **Klaus Voormann** *(Tonmeister)* ← POPEYE ← SON OF DRACULA ← the CONCERT FOR BANGLADESH / → CONCERT FOR GEORGE, Ramona Sweeny *(Mascha)*, Peter Kybart *(Frank)*, Ute Cremer *(Eurosound Sekretärin)*

Storyline: Kenneth Barlow is a veteran of the music business who sells his new musical finds to the public by fair means and foul. His latest acquisition is Moody Mudinsky, who is soon renamed White Star. Stage-managed riots, failed death threats and forged cheques are all part of the hype, but as Kenneth becomes more and more impassioned, White Star starts to think that Mr Barlow may be barking up the wrong street. Tagged "Music, madness and a quest for the ultimate rock'n'roll power-trip!". *JZ*

Movie rating: *3.5

Visual: video (see above) – no audio OST

Off the record: New York City-born, **David Hess** recorded under the pseudonym of David Hill and had two minor hits in the late 50s (having penned 'Hound Dog' for Elvis), 'Two Brothers' & 'Living Doll'. Elvis and the Colonel retained his services for further work, while Pat Boone was next to utilise Hill with his 1963 Top 10'er, 'Speedy Gonzales'. RAMONA SWEENY sang 'Rock Me' in the film. *MCS*

WHITEBOYS

aka WHITEBOYZ

1999 (US 92m) Bac Films / Fox Searchlight / Maes Films (R)

Film genre: urban comedy

Top guns: s-w: Marc Levin (+ dir) → BROOKLYN BABYLON → GODFATHERS AND SONS, Danny Hoch (+ story), Garth Belcon (+ story) → FRONTERZ, Richard Stratton

Stars: Danny Hoch *(Flip)* → PRISON SONG, Dash Mihok *(James)*, Mark Webber *(Trevor)* → STORYTELLING → CHELSEA WALLS → the HOTTEST STATE, Piper Perabo *(Sara)* → COYOTE UGLY, Eugene Byrd *(Khalid)* ← DEAD MAN / → WENT TO CONEY ISLAND ON A MISSION FROM GOD . . . BE BACK BY FIVE → 8 MILE, Bonz Malone *(Darius)* → BROOKLYN BABYLON, **Dr. Dre** *(Don Flip Crew #1)* ← RHYME & REASON ← the SHOW ← MURDER WAS THE CASE, **SNOOP DOGG** *(himself)*, **Fat Joe** *(Don Flip Crew #2)* ← THICKER THAN WATER / → PRISON SONG, **Big Pun** *(Don Flip Crew #3)* ← THICKER THAN WATER, **Slick Rick** *(parking lot rapper #1)* ← the SHOW ← TOUGHER THAN LEATHER / → TRUE VINYL → BROOKLYN BABYLON → BROWN SUGAR → FADE TO BLACK, **Doug E. Fresh** *(parking lot rapper #2)* ← TAPEHEADS ← BEAT STREET / → BROWN SUGAR → AWESOME: I FUCKIN' SHOT THAT!, **Dead Prez** *(cornfield rappers)* → BLOCK PARTY, Reno Wilson *(Mace)* → FRONTERZ, Garth Belcon *(Chilly B)* → FRONTERZ

Storyline: Flip has the moves and the rhymes to blow many a rap superstar off the stage. There's one problem though, he's a middle-class white kid from a farm town in Iowa. When Khalid, an African-American teen from Chicago transfers to Flip's school, despite the obvious suspicion on Khalid's part, a friendship emerges, and when the pair head to Chicago on Flip's request, they get to see hip hop culture like they never had before, both good and bad. *MR*

Movie rating: *4.5

Visual: dvd

Off the record: (see below)

—

Various Artists

Jul 99. (cd/c) *T.V.T.; <(16581 8310-2)>* ☐ ☐
– Who is a thug (BIG PUNISHER feat. 6430) / Come get it (DJ HURRICANE feat. FLIPMODE SQUAD's RAH DIGGA, RAMPAGE and LORD HAVE MERCY) / Hell ya (SOOPAFLY feat. DAZ DILLINGER, TRAY DEEE and KURUPT) / White boyz (SNOOP DOGG feat. T-BO) / Respect power (RAEKWON) / Watch who you beef wid (CANIBUS) / Paper chasers (up north) (TOMMY FINGER) / Don't come my way (SLICK RICK and COMMON feat. RENEE NEUFVILLE) / Wanna be's (THREE 6 MAFIA) / Perfect murda (DO OR DIE) / Real hustlers (GOTTA BOYZ) / Get rowdy (the WHORIDAS) / For the thugs (TRICK DADDY) / Intrigued (COCA BROVAZ feat. BUCKSHOT) / I can relate (BLACK CHILD) / What's up Jack (WILDLIFFE SOCIETY) / Pimps VIP (12 GAUGE).

S/track review: There's little here to attract mainstream rap fans here aside from a C-grade contribution from the only A-list name here, SNOOP DOGG on 'White Boyz'. But that's not to say this is all filler and no thriller. There may be few superstars here but it's all the better for it, a varied mix of styles and sonics. Okay, so the gangsta gurning gets wearing after a while. You've got to wonder if there are really this many pimps in America? This is especially true two thirds of the way through when the quality takes a dip with BLACK CHILD, 12 GAUGE and the WHORIDAS providing a regular who's not of gangsta rap. For the first 10 tracks however, 'WHITE BOYS' is a compelling enough collection. The real standouts are RAEKWON's 'Respect Power', his spiralling rhymes tumbling out over minimal signature Wu-Tang beat, while 'Don't Come My Way' continues the influx of quality names with old school vet SLICK RICK teaming up with the unflappable COMMON for a supremely eloquent track that is tough but still soulful. These, along with DJ HURRICANE's 'Come Get It' are worth the admission alone, Hurra's beat, a skeletal funker that Massive Attack would be proud of, has the FLIPMODE SQUAD busting out all over like a rash. Well, a big, boisterous, shouty rash, if such a thing actually exists. *MR*

Album rating: *6.5

the WHO

Formed: Chiswick & Hammersmith, London, England . . . 1964 as the Detours by ROGER DALTREY, PETE TOWNSHEND, John Entwistle and Doug Sandom. Drummer Keith Moon soon replaced the latter and completed the classic line-up which would court more controversy and flaunt more attitude than any band save perhaps the ROLLING STONES and later the SEX PISTOLS. After initially hanging on the fish tails of the mod scene, the WHO rubber stamped their own identity through sheer force of will. By regularly trashing their own equipment on stage, they effectively destroyed and renewed their own means of expression, always keeping it fresher than the competition. It showed in their records; singles and albums which constantly challenged the received wisdom of how an R&B/rock band should approach their subject. In 1966, TOWNSHEND penned a near ten minute mini-opus entitled 'A Quick One (While He's Away)'. Consisting of separate songs with thematic and narrative links, the track was a primitive version of the concept he'd go on to pioneer as the 60s drew to close. 'Tommy' (1969) was the end result of TOWNSHEND's experiments, a full length drama in song recounting the unlikely tale of a "deaf, dumb and blind kid" who finds a window out of his sensual deprivation through pinball and the religious fanaticism of his admirers. Dubbed the first "rock opera", the project was subsequently made into a typically flamboyant film by British maverick Ken Russell, who cast DALTREY as the mute pinball wizard. While the soundtrack was a poor relation to the original album, the likes of ELTON JOHN, ERIC CLAPTON, TINA TURNER and erm ... Oliver Reed at least got to show their appreciation. By the time of the film's release in 1975, TOWNSHEND had already abandoned one opera (the 'Lifehouse' project, whose songs were subsumed into 1971's 'Who's Next' album) and completed another, 'Quadrophenia' (1973). A more coherent work than its predecessor, centering on the mod culture TOWNSHEND had always identified so closely with, the project was made into a film in 1979. Although none of the band actually appeared in the movie as they had in 'TOMMY', DALTREY in particular had been maintaining a sideline in acting. Russell had cast him as Franz Liszt in his critically lambasted, 1975 high camp re-invention of the classical composer's life, in which the WHO frontman also contributed some vocals to RICK WAKEMAN's score. DALTREY also appeared in Richard Marquand's second division chiller, 'The Legacy' (1978), and landed one of his most accomplished screen roles in 'McVICAR', a 1980 bio-pic of the reformed gangster which saw him both acting and handling the soundtrack (backed up by the remaining members of the WHO – Keith Moon having died of an overdose in 1978 – even though it wasn't billed as a WHO album). Prior to his death, Moon had also notched up a string of big screen appearances, true to type playing skewed comic roles alongside pal RINGO STARR in the likes of nostalgic rock'n'roll pastiche, 'THAT'LL BE THE DAY' (1973), and the Harry Nilsson-starring horror comedy, 'SON OF DRACULA' (1974) as well as, more bizarrely, Mae West's final, failed movie, 'Sextette' (1978). Following the the WHO's split in 1983, DALTREY continued to concentrate on acting with roles in various minor movies, including 'Mack The Knife' (1989), 'BUDDY'S SONG' (1991), 'Teen Agent' (1991), 'Lightning Jack' (1994) and 'CHASING DESTINY' (2000). Like that other ageing rebel, John Lydon, he's recently taken to adventurous, hands-on presentation of ostensibly educational TV shows like 'Extreme History'. *BG*

- **filmography** (TOWNSHEND composer) {acting} –

Monterey Pop *(1968 {****p} OST by V/A =>)* / **the Magic Christian** *(1969 {a KEITH} =>)* / *Double Pisces, Scorpio Rising (1970 by TOWNSHEND & SPEEDY KEEN)* / **Woodstock** *(1970 {****p} on OST by V/A =>)* / **the Who: Live At The Isle Of Wight Festival 1970** *(1970 {****p} OST =>)* / **200 Motels** *(1971 {a KEITH} =>)* / **That'll Be The Day** *(1973 {a KEITH})* / **Son Of Dracula** *(1974 {a KEITH} =>)* / **Stardust** *(1974 {a KEITH} =>)* / **Tommy** *(1975 {* ROGER + KEITH} {c PETE + JOHN} OST w/ V/A =>)* / **Lisztomania** *(1975 {* ROGER} + on OST by RICK WAKEMAN =>)* / Legacy *(1975 {a ROGER})* / **All This And World War II** *(1976 {a KEITH} =>)* / the Legacy *(1978 {* ROGER})* / Sextette *(1978 {a KEITH})* / **the Kids Are Alright** *(1979 {****p} OST =>)* / **Quadrophenia** *(1979 OST by the WHO & V/A =>)* / the Secret Policeman's Ball *(1979 {*p PETE} OST by V/A =>)* / **McVicar** *(1980 {* ROGER} OST by DALTREY =>)* / **Concert For Kampuchea** *(1980 {* all} on OST by V/A =>)* / the Secret Policeman's Other Ball *(1982 {*p PETE} OST by V/A =>)* / **the Who Rocks America** *(1983 {****p} =>)* / the Secret Policeman's Private Parts *(1984 {*p PETE})* / Murder: Ultimate Grounds For Divorce *(1985 {* ROGER})* / **White City** *(1985 {* PETE} OST by TOWNSHEND =>)* / **Deep End** *(1986 {*p PETE} OST by TOWNSHEND =>)* / the Little Match Girl *(1987 {* ROGER})* / Cold Justice *(1989 {* ROGER})* / Mack The Knife *(1989 {* ROGER})* / Forgotten Prisoners: The Amnesty Files *(1990 TV)* / **Buddy's Song** *(1991 {* ROGER} =>)* / **Psychoderelict** *(1993 TV {*p PETE} =>)* / Lightning Jack *(1994 {a ROGER})* / **Thirty Years Of Maximum R&B Live** *(1994 TV {****p} =>)* / Vampirella *(1996 {* ROGER})* / **Message To Love: The Isle Of Wight Festival** *(1997 {****p} on OST by V/A =>)* / Like It Is *(1998 {* ROGER})* / the Magical Legend Of The Leprechauns *(1999 TV {* ROGER})* / **British Rock Symphony** *(1999 {p ROGER} OST by V/A =>* / Best *(2000 {a ROGER})* / Dark Prince: The True Story Of Dracula *(2000 {a ROGER})* / **Lifehouse** *(2000 {*p PETE} =>)* / **My Generation** *(2000 {****p} =>)* / **the Who Live At The Royal Albert Hall** *(2000 {****p} OST 2003 =>)* / **Chasing Destiny** *(2001 TV {a ROGER} =>)*

WHO IS HARRY KELLERMAN AND WHY IS HE SAYING THOSE TERRIBLE THINGS ABOUT ME?

1971 (US 108m) Cinema Center 100 / National General Pictures (PG)

Film genre: showbiz/Pop-music drama/fantasy

Top guns: dir: Ulu Grosbard → GEORGIA / s-w: Herb Gardner (+ story)

Stars: Dustin Hoffman *(Georgie Soloway)* ← the POINT! ← LITTLE BIG MAN ← MIDNIGHT COWBOY ← the GRADUATE / → DICK TRACY → WAG THE DOG, Gabriel Dell *(Sidney Gill)*, Jack Warden *(Dr. Solomon F. Moses)*, Barbara Harris *(Allison Densmore)* → NASHVILLE, David Burns *(Leon Soloway)*, Betty Walker *(Margot Soloway)*, Rose Gregorio *(Gloria Soloway)*, Dom DeLuise *(Irwin Marcy)* ← NORWOOD → the BEST LITTLE WHOREHOUSE IN TEXAS, Regina Baff *(Ruthie Tresh)*, Ed Zimmermann *(Peter Holloran)*, Amy Levitt *(Susan)* → AMERICAN POP, **Shel SILVERSTEIN** *(Bernie)*, **Dennis Locorriere** *(himself)*

Storyline: As the approach of mid-life, the umpteenth romantic knockback and the loss of his marbles ("they are spilling; they're rolling out on the floor and behind the refrigerator") gets too much to bear, moustachioed folk superstar Georgie Soloway cocoons himself in an archetypal artistic bubble, flying his troubles – and the unwanted slandering of the mysterious Harry Kellerman – away in his private plane. *BG*

Movie rating: *4.5

Visual: video

Off the record: Dennis Locorriere (see below)

SHEL SILVERSTEIN (& Various Artists)

1971. (lp) *Columbia; <S 30791>* ☐ ☐
– The last morning (DR. HOOK & THE MEDICINE SHOW) / Don't tell me your troubles (RAY CHARLES) / Bunky and Lucille (DR. HOOK & THE MEDICINE SHOW) / Happy dancing fingers / Goodbye to goodbye / Free as a bird / Calypso / The Ricky Ticky song / Georgie Porgie / The last morning.

S/track review: Dudley Moore might've maintained a more than respectable sideline as a jazz pianist but it's probably for the best that Dustin Hoffman didn't take up folk singing. His few flat-toned, deadpan ditties – performed at the legendary Fillmore East no less – are amiable but hardly enduring soundtrack material, while the reams of ultimately tiresome dialogue and stingy quota of conventional songs really don't amount to an album worthy of the price tag or the time to hunt it down. A shame, as the early period DR HOOK AND THE MEDICINE SHOW (featuring Dennis Locorriere) tracks show a different side to the band from the nudge-nudge wink-wink novelty hits which made their name. Opener 'Last Morning' is fine urban Americana sung in a gin-soaked croak that sounds as if it's come down hard on a lifetime of mornings, while 'Bunky And Lucille' plays as a bluesy adjunct to the brief, SHEL SILVERSTEIN-fronted 'One More Ride'. While a few blasts of percussive mayhem, 30 seconds of prime RAY CHARLES and some audition crooning – and an inspired, end-of-tether monologue ("time, mister, it's not a thief at all like they say, it's something much sneakier; it's an embezzler, up nights juggling the books so you don't know anything's missing") – from Barbara Harris are really only small change, the whole thing just about redeems itself with the SILVERSTEIN-composed 'Happy Dancing Fingers (Kellerman's Theme)', orchestrated folk-pop that dances on air, magically surfing the thermals of Hoffman's neurosis. *BG*

Album rating: *5

WHO'S THAT GIRL

1987 (US 94m) Warner Bros. Pictures (PG)

Film genre: romantic screwball comedy/mystery

Top guns: dir: James Foley / s-w: Andrew Smith (+ story), Ken Finkleman ← GREASE 2

Stars: MADONNA *(Nikki Finn)*, Griffin Dunne *(Loudon Trott)* → STRAIGHT TALK, Haviland Morris *(Wendy Worthington)*, John McMartin *(Simon Worthington)*, Robert Swan *(detective Bellson)*, Bibi Besch *(Mrs. Worthington)*, Sir John Mills *(Montgomery Bell)* ← WHEN THE WIND BLOWS ← the FAMILY WAY, Drew Pillsbury *(detective Doyle)*, **Coati Mundi** *(Raoul)* <= KID CREOLE & THE COCONUTS =>, Dennis Burkley *(Benny)* ← BUMMER! / → LAMBADA → the DOORS → RUSH → TOUCH, Albert Popwell *(parole chairman)* ← the BUDDY HOLLY STORY ← CLEOPATRA JONES, Mike Starr *(shipping co-worker)* ← MAGIC STICKS / → the BODYGUARD, Alice Nunn *(woman parole person)* ← TRICK OR TREAT / → THREE O'CLOCK HIGH, Glen Plummer *(Harlem kid #1)* → TRESPASS → STRANGE DAYS, Gary Basaraba *(shipping clerk)* ← SWEET DREAMS ← ALAMO BAY / → the LAST TEMPTATION OF CHRIST, Sean Gregory Sullivan *(gun dealer)* → the IN CROWD → WAYNE'S WORLD → 54

Storyline: Big Apple tax lawyer Louden Trott has more than a bad day at the office when his future father-in-law charges him with collecting newly released con Nikki Finn from jail. Squawking like a clockwork toy, the bleached blonde Finn turns Trott into a gibbering idiot before he can say "where's my Cartier", involving him in a "madcap" race to prove her innocence before the father-in-law's evil henchmen can bump her off. Oh dear. *BG*

Movie rating: *3

Visual: video + dvd

Off the record: (see below)

MADONNA (& Various Artists) (music: Stephen Bray)

Jul 87. (lp/c)(cd) *Sire; <1-/4-/2-25611> (WX 102/+C)(925611-2)* [7] [4]
– Who's that girl / Causing a commotion / The look of love / 24 hours (DUNCAN FAURE) / Step by step (CLUB NOUVEAU) / Turn it up (MICHAEL DAVIDSON) / Best thing ever (SCRITTI POLITTI) / Can't stop / El coco loco (so so bad) (COATI MUNDI). *(cd re-iss. Feb95; same)*

S/track review: By the release of this nigh-on unwatchably bad "comedy" in 1987, MADONNA was already something of a screen trooper, propelled to ever greater heights with chart-scaling movie spin-offs. This was her first soundtrack in her own name, even if she only performed four of the nine songs, and even if none were anywhere near the standard of what had come before. Sounding for all the world like a 'True Blue'-outtake – right down to the Spanish lyrics – the title cut is a ho-hum spin on 'La Isla Bonita'; released a matter of months later, it likewise took the A-train to No.1. 'Causing A Commotion' was the other hit, hobbled by that same strange monotony, strange because it punctuated some of MADONNA's best material of the decade. Her other two songs, 'The Look Of Love' and 'Can't Stop', are forgotten as soon as they fade out, and the less said about the other contributions the better; recorded at the nadir of 80s production folly – Stock, Aitken & Waterman among the credits – they are, verily, the revenge of disco. Even SCRITTI POLITTI had lost their patter by 1987; it's unlikely they'll want to be remembered for 'Best Thing Ever'. Come to think of it, it's unlikely MADONNA will want to remember this "half-wit" (in the words of Rolling Stone) soundtrack – or film – at all. *BG*

Album rating: *3.5

– spinoff hits, etc. –

MADONNA: Who's That Girl

Jul 87. (7"/12"/12"pic-d/12") *<28341> (W 8341/+T/TP/TX)* [1] [1]
(ext.12") *(W 8341TX) <20692>* – ('A'dub version).

MADONNA: Causing A Commotion

Sep 87. (7"/12"/12"pic-d/c-s) *<28224> (W 8224/+T/TP/C)* [2] [4]

MADONNA: The Look Of Love

Dec 87. (7"/12"/12"pic-d) *(W 8115/+T/TP)* [–] [9]

WHO'S THE MAN?

1993 (US 124m) New Line Cinema (R)

Film genre: cop/detective comedy

Top guns: dir: Ted Demme / s-w: Seth Greenland (+ story w/: Doctor Dre & Ed Lover)

Stars: Doctor Dre *(himself)* ← JUICE / → RIDE → DEATH OF A DYNASTY, Ed Lover *(himself)* ← JUICE / → RIDE → DOUBLE PLATINUM → DEATH OF A DYNASTY → TUPAC: RESURRECTION, Badja Djola *(Lionel Douglas)*, **Cheryl 'Salt' James** *(Teesha Braxton)*, Jim Moody *(Nick Crawford)* ← the LAST DRAGON ← FAME, **ICE-T** *(Chauncey 'Nighttrain' Jackson)*, Denis Leary *(Sgt. Cooper)* → JUDGMENT NIGHT → WAG THE DOG, Richard Bright *(Demetrius)* ← the IDOLMAKER ← HAIR ← RANCHO DELUXE ← PAT GARRETT & BILLY THE KID, Bill Bellamy *(K.K.)*, Bernie Mac *(G-George)* → HOUSE PARTY 3, Vincent Pastore *(Tony 'Clams' Como)* ← BLACK ROSES / → the BASKETBALL DIARIES → WALKING AND TALKING → JOE'S APARTMENT, **Bow-Legged Lou** *(Forty)* ← HOUSE PARTY 2 ← HOUSE PARTY / → LONGSHOT, **B-Fine** *(club guy #1)* ← HOUSE PARTY 2 ← HOUSE PARTY ← KRUSH GROOVE / → LONGSHOT, **Fab 5 Freddy** *(himself)* ← JUICE ← WILD STYLE ← DOWNTOWN 81 / → TUPAC: RESURRECTION, **T-Money** *(Bubba)*, **Apache** *(Bubba worker #1)*, **Smooth B** *(Bubba worker #2)*, **Pete Rock** *(robber #1)* → BROWN SUGAR, **C.L. Smooth** *(robber #2)*, **Eric B.** *(robber #5)*, **Flavor Flav** *(himself)* ← CB4: THE MOVIE / → PRIVATE PARTS → DEATH OF A DYNASTY, **Busta Rhymes** *(Jaween)* → RHYME & REASON → DEATH OF A DYNASTY, **Heavy D** *(himself)* → RHYME & REASON → STEP UP, **Kid Capri** *(himself)* → FLY BY NIGHT → the SHOW → DEATH OF A DYNASTY, **Queen Latifah** *(herself)* ← JUICE ← HOUSE PARTY 2 ← JUNGLE FEVER / → the COUNTRY BEARS → BROWN SUGAR → HAIRSPRAY re-make, **Sandra 'Pepa' Denton** *(Sherise)* → WOODSTOCK 94 → JOE'S APARTMENT, **KRS-One** *(Rashid)* → RHYME & REASON → BEEF, **Paul A. George** *(club guy #2)* ← HOUSE PARTY 2 ← HOUSE PARTY, Terrence Dashon Howard *(customer)* ← the JACKSONS: AN AMERICAN DREAM / → GLITTER → RAY → HUSTLE & FLOW → GET RICH OR DIE TRYIN' → IDLEWILD, **Everlast** *(Billy)* → JUDGMENT NIGHT → WOODSTOCK '99, **D-Nice** *(male nurse)*, **Yolanda Whitaker** *(woman)* → LONGSHOT → PAPER SOLDIERS, Kurt Loder *(hitman)* ← the ADVENTURES OF FORD FAIRLANE / → AIRHEADS → FEAR OF A BLACK HAT → TUPAC: RESURRECTION → RAMONES: RAW → LAST DAYS, **Darryl 'DMC' McDaniels** *(D.M.C.)* <= RUN-D.M.C. =>, **Kris Kross** *(Karim)*, **Phife Dawg** *(Gerald)* → FREE TIBET, **Kool G Rap** *(guy in barbershop chair)* → BROWN SUGAR → BLOCK PARTY, **Bushwick Bill** *(bar vagrant)*, **Humpty Hump** *(club doorman)*

Storyline: Ed Lover and Doctor Dre (not Dr Dre of NWA fame, but the goofy MTV hip hop host) are eking out a living as barbers when they decide a change in career is in order. They join the police force and despite being the most inept detectives ever and constantly under the cosh from their sadistic desk sergeant, Sgt. Cooper, they manage to uncover a murder plot, while fighting through the hordes of hip hop star cameos. *MR*

Movie rating: *4

Visual: video + dvd

Off the record: Doctor Dre is not the ex-NWA rapper and top producer (Dr. Dre), this one used to DJ for the Beastie Boys before acting in the film 'Juice'. **Cheryl James** (is the Salt out of Salt-N-Pepa) while **Sandra 'Pepa' Denton,** is the other half. Other rappers include **Full Force, T-Money** (R&B rapper); **Apache, Smooth B, Pete Rock & C.L. Smooth; Eric B. , Humpty Hump** (Shock G of Digital Underground); **Everlast** (ex-House Of Pain); **D-Nice** ; Yolanda Whitaker is **Yo-Yo; Kris Kross** (aka Chris Kelly) & **Bushwick Bill** (the Geto Boys). *MCS*

Various Artists (score: Nic.tenBroek)

Apr 93. (cd/c/lp) *Uptown-M.C.A.; <MCD/MCC/MCA 10794)>* 32 May93
– Party and bullshit (BIG) / Let's go through the motions (JODECI) / What's next on the menu? (PETE ROCK & C.L. SMOOTH) / You don't have to worry (MARY J. BLIGE) / Hittin' switches (ERICK SERMON) / Hotness (HEAVY D & BUJU BANTON) / Who's the man? (HOUSE OF PAIN) / Lovin' you (CRYSTAL J. JOHNSON) / Pimp or die (FATHER M.C.) / Hello, it's me (SPARK 950 & TIMBO KING) / Ease up (3RD EYE & THE GROUP HOME).

S/track review: For such a silly little movie the soundtrack is pretty flavoursome. It helps that it eschews that staple of the hip hop comedy – the spoof rap – in favour of an eclectic mix of hardcore rap, seasoned with dancehall ragga, finely-planed soul and thick R&B and that it also contains two of the greatest names in modern black music: MARY J. BLIGE and the NOTORIOUS B.I.G. Mary was a mere pup when she supplied the silky smooth stylings of 'You Don't Have To Worry', which is a slice of sugary, funked up soul but she makes a big impression, as does the Big Poppa himself, B.I.G., whose 'Party And Bullshit' is without question a classic of the genre and reminds us why he was so often lauded as the finest rapper of all time. With these two diamonds on show everything else may have looked like pebbles but PETE ROCK & C.L. SMOOTH and ERICK SERMON keep the pot boiling with some dextrous lyrical turns. The only incongruous entries in this officer's notepad are the eponymous title track by everyone's favourite clover-wielding, jumping-around faux Irishmen HOUSE OF PAIN. 'Who's The Man?' has all the bluster and some decent beats but some truly corny rhymes. Similarly, 'Pimp Or Die' by FATHER M.C. is a hamfisted shot at flexing some gangster muscle which is nothing more than a pigeon-chested lightweight blowing off steam. *MR*

Album rating: *6

– spinoff hits, etc. –

JODECI: Let's Go Through The Motions

Apr 93. (c-s/cd-s) *<54602>* 65

HOUSE OF PAIN: Who's The Man? / (non-OST song/s)

May 93. (c-s/cd-s) *Tommy Boy; <556>* 96

MARY J. BLIGE: You Don't Have To Worry / (rap version)

Nov 93. (c-s/12"/cd-s) *<54701> (MCS C/T/TD 1948)* 63 36

WHY DO FOOLS FALL IN LOVE

1998 (US 115m) Rhino Films / Warner Bros. Pictures (R)

Film genre: R&B/Rock'n'roll Musical bio-pic drama

Top guns: dir: Gregory Nava ← SELENA / s-w: Tina Andrews

Stars: Halle Berry *(Zola Taylor)* ← GIRL 6 ← CB4: THE MOVIE ← JUNGLE FEVER / → SWORDFISH, Vivica A. Fox *(Elizabeth 'Mickey' Waters)* → HENDRIX → KILL BILL: VOL.1, Lela Rochon *(Emira Eagle)* ← BREAKIN' 2: ELECTRIC BOOGALOO ← BREAKIN', Larenz Tate *(Frankie Lymon)* → RAY, Paul Mazursky *(Morris Levy)* ← TOUCH ← HEY HEY WE'RE THE MONKEES ← DOWN AND OUT IN BEVERLY HILLS ← a STAR IS BORN ← BLACKBOARD JUNGLE, Pamela Reed *(Judge Lambrey)* ← the LONG RIDERS, Alexis Cruz *(Herman Santiago),* **LITTLE RICHARD** *(himself),* David Barry Gray *(Peter Markowitz)* ← S.F.W., Lane Smith *(Ezra Grahme)* ← PLACES IN THE HEART ← HONEYSUCKLE ROSE, Ben Vereen *(Richard Barrett)* ← GAS-S-S-S! / → IDLEWILD, Clifton Powell *(Lawrence Roberts)* ← HOUSE PARTY / → BONES → RAY, Paula Jai Parker *(Paula King)* → HUSTLE & FLOW → IDLEWILD, Kevin Fry *(MP)* → DILL SCALLION, Joe Huertas *(Joe Negroni of the Teenagers),* J. August Richards *(Sherman Garnes of the Teenagers)* → the TEMPTATIONS, Norris Young *(Jimmy Merchant of the Teenagers),* Miguel A. Nunez Jr. *(young Little Richard)* ← the RETURN OF THE LIVING DEAD

Storyline: Three women, each armed with a lawyer, contest the estate of the late Frankie Lymon. Each has some sort of claim on his royalties and their involvement with the troubled young singer is told in flashback. However, manager Morris Levy hasn't yet paid a cent to any of them and so it's up to Judge Lambrey to decide whether it's first love Zola, shoplifter-turned-prostitute Elizabeth or churchy Emira who gets the loot. *JZ*

Movie rating: *5.5

Visual: video + dvd

Off the record: FRANKIE LYMON & THE TEENAGERS were formed in 1955 out of The Bronx in New York, when 13 year-old Lymon, joined school group the Premiers (made up of Puerto Rican & African/Americans, Herman Santiago, Joe Negroni, Jimmy Merchant and Sherman Garnes). The boys changed their name to the Teenagers but also credit Frankie Lymon, and through Valentinos singer, Richard Barrett, they gain break with 'Gee' records label owner George Goldner; he also helped choreograph their new dance routines. Their first cut 'Why Do Fools Fall In Love' was released early 1956 and was soon inside the Top 10. On their follow-up singles, Frankie is afforded top billing since he was fast becoming the latest and youngest teenybop idol. However, things took a nosedive and after only three more major hits, their popularity dwindled. By 1960, Frankie had now turned to drugs, and by 28 February, 1968, he was dead. Tragedy found its way in again when Garnes and then Negroni died in 1977 and '78 respectively, two guys still in their late thirties. *MCS*

Various Artists (score: Stephen James Taylor)

Sep 98. (cd/c) *East West; <7559 62265-2/-4>* 55 –
– Why do fools fall in love (GINA THOMPSON feat. MOCHA) / Get on the bus (DESTINY'S CHILD feat. TIMBALAND) / He be back (COKO feat. MISSY "MISDEMEANOR" ELLIOTT) / No fool no more (EN VOGUE) / Get contact (MISSY "MISDEMEANOR" ELLIOTT & BUSTA RHYMES) / Five minutes (LIL' MO feat. MISSY "MISDEMEANOR" ELLIOTT) / I want you back (MELANIE B. feat. MISSY "MISDEMEANOR" ELLIOTT) / About you (MISTA) / Love is for fools (MINT CONDITION) / Without you (NICOLE) / Splash (NEXT) / What the dealio (TOTAL feat. MISSY "MISDEMEANOR" ELLIOTT) / Crazy love (ENVYI feat. BABY SHAM of the FLIPMODE SQUAD). *(bonus track +=)* – Keep a knockin' (LITTLE RICHARD).

S/track review: It may be an exercise in pure pedantry to complain about the fact that 'WHY DO FOOLS FALL IN LOVE' isn't actually a statement (would a question mark have been such a terrible thing now, people?) but it doesn't change the fact that this collection is still a mangy, collection of jittery R&B pop barely worth your attention. With MISSY "MISDEMEANOR" ELLIOTT and TIMBALAND as executive producers, hopes were high but this was wishful thinking. Considering what the pair are capable of, this dog's dinner of tepid balladry is a travesty. The normally reliable DESTINY'S CHILD and BUSTA RHYMES weigh in with below par tracks but way more alarming is the grim Missy collaboration with Spice Girl MELANIE (née Mel) B. Worth hearing if only for the truly ludicrous spoken word middle eight from Miss B who succeeds in making herself sound like the thick one among a bunch of lyrical clichés. EN VOGUE do deserve credit for keeping things simple and pushing their collected vocals to the fore on 'No Fool No More' and MISTA's understated 'About You' makes a decent stab at decadent R&B, but these are rare moments of interest in a messy afterthought of a soundtrack. The original film itself is filled with 50s and 60s pop classics on it – LITTLE RICHARD's 'Keep A Knockin'' is incongruously tacked on at the end here, but the rest of this motley collection is strictly for the fools. *MR*

Album rating: *3.5 / oldies *7

– spinoff releases, etc. –

EN VOGUE: No Fool No More / MISSY "MISDEMEANOR" ELLIOTT & BUSTA RHYMES: Get Contact

Sep 98. (c-s/cd-s) *Elektra; <64082>* [57] [–]

MELANIE B feat. MISSY "MISDEMEANOR" ELLIOTT: I Want You Back

Sep 98. (c-s/12"/cd-s) *Virgin; (VS C/T/CDT 1716)* [–] [1]

Various Artists:

Sep 98. (cd/c) *Rhino; <75564-2/-4>* [ ] [–]
– Why do fools fall in love (the TEENAGERS featuring FRANKIE LYMON) / Tutti frutti (LITTLE RICHARD) / The great pretender (the PLATTERS) / Baby, baby (FRANKIE LYMON & THE TEENAGERS) / Long lonely nights (CLYDE McPHATTER) / Smoke gets in your eyes (the PLATTERS) / Little bitty pretty one (FRANKIE LYMON) / California dreamin' (the MAMAS & THE PAPAS) / All day and all of the night (the KINKS) / The ABC's of love (FRANKIE LYMON & THE TEENAGERS) / Will you love me tomorrow (the SHIRELLES) / Try a little tenderness (OTIS REDDING) / California dreamin' (BOBBY WOMACK) / Goody goody (FRANKIE LYMON & THE TEENAGERS).

the WILD ANGELS

1966 (US 85m) American International Pictures (R)

Film genre: biker/road movie

Top guns: dir: Roger Corman ← ROCK ALL NIGHT ← CARNIVAL ROCK / → the TRIP → GAS-S-S-S! / s-w: Charles B. Griffith ← ROCK ALL NIGHT / → LITTLE SHOP OF HORRORS

Stars: Peter Fonda *(Heavenly Blues)* → the TRIP → EASY RIDER → the HIRED HAND → GRACE OF MY HEART → SOUTH OF HEAVEN, WEST OF HELL, **Nancy Sinatra** *(Mike)* ← the GHOST IN THE INVISIBLE BIKINI ← GET YOURSELF A COLLEGE GIRL / → SPEEDWAY → MAYOR OF THE SUNSET STRIP, Bruce Dern *(Loser Joey Kerns)* → the TRIP → PSYCH-OUT → LAST MAN STANDING → ALL THE PRETTY HORSES → MASKED AND ANONYMOUS, Michael J. Pollard *(Pigmy)* → LITTLE FAUSS AND BIG HALSY → DICK TRACY, Diane Ladd *(Gaysh)* → WILD AT HEART → PRIMARY COLORS, Gayle Hunnicutt *(Suzie)*, Coby Denton *(Bull Puckey)* ← OUT OF SIGHT, Norman Alden *(medic)* → GOOD TIMES, Dick Miller *(rigger)* ← WILD, WILD WINTER ← the GIRLS ON THE BEACH ← SKI PARTY ← BEACH BALL ← ROCK ALL NIGHT ← CARNIVAL ROCK / → the TRIP → TRUCK TURNER → I WANNA HOLD YOUR HAND → ROCK'N'ROLL HIGH SCHOOL → GET CRAZY → SHAKE, RATTLE & ROCK! tv, Lou Procopio *(Joint)* → GAS-S-S-S, Joan Shawlee *(Momma Monahan)* → LIVE A LITTLE, LOVE A LITTLE, Barboura Morris *(mother)* ← ROCK ALL NIGHT / → the TRIP, Jack Bernardi ← BEACH BALL / → IT'S A BIKINI WORLD → WILLIE DYNAMITE → FOXY BROWN, Art Baker *(Thomas)* ← SWINGIN' ALONG

Storyline: Hell's Angel, Loser, lives up to his name when his bike gets stolen by some malicious Mexicans. He calls up the rest of the gang and vengeance is swift, but the cops arrive before he can get his bike back. Loser even botches his getaway on a policeman's motorcycle when he manages to get shot. When the gang bust him out of hospital (probably on Friday 13th) his life support blood drip is broken and poor Loser goes off to join the more heavenly sort of angels. *JZ*

Movie rating: *6

Visual: video + dvd

Off the record: DAVIE ALLAN & THE ARROWS (see below)

—

Various Artists (incl. DAVIE ALLAN AND THE ARROWS *)

Sep 66. (lp; mono/stereo) *Tower; <T/DT 5043>* [17] [–]
– Theme from the "Wild Angels" (the VISITORS feat. BARBARA) / The chase (*) / Lonely in the chapel (the HANDS OF TIME) / Bongo party (*) / Blue's theme (*) / Theme from "The Wild Angels" (*) / Midnight rider (the HANDS OF TIME) / Rockin' angel (*) / The lonely rider (*) / The unknown rider (*) / The Wild Angels ballad (dirge) (*).

S/track review: This is where the young MIKE CURB (21 years old here and already an L.A. producer) made his LP soundtrack debut; the latter half of the 60s also saw 'THUNDER ALLEY' (1967), 'IT'S A BIKINI WORLD' (1967), 'MONDO HOLLYWOOD' (1967), 'The SAVAGE SEVEN' (1968), etc. While CURB might be the star of the mixing desk, 'The WILD ANGELS' top credits go to hot-rod, surf-rock outfit, DAVIE ALLAN AND THE ARROWS. Formerly a session lead guitarist with CURB, Davie formed the ARROWS in 1964 (alongside bassist Drew Bennett, drummer Larry Brown and Jared Hendler on keyboards), a sort of US answer to the Shadows; in fact their first hit was 'Apache '65'. With eight numbers, DAVIE ALLAN AND THE ARROWS surprisingly found their way into the Top 20 via 'The WILD ANGELS', while two 45s also saw chart action, 'Blue's Theme' reaching the Top 40. While a handful of the instrumental tracks were novelty and throwaway ('Rockin' Angel' & 'The Lonely Rider' were two examples), their choice cut was unquestionably 'The Chase' – a precursor to the psychedelic sound of Pink Floyd. 'Bongo Party' speaks for itself, while the 'Theme From . . .' (also a minor hit) creates something akin to a meeting of Johnny & The Hurricanes and the Ventures (or the Rah Band – anybody?). You can't escape the roaring bikes, while the opening vocal equivalent by the VISITORS featuring BARBARA (we think surname Kelly), cruising easily ahead of the pack. CURB gets in his two-penneth worth with a cheeky impersonation of Elvis under the guise of the HANDS OF TIME and 'Lonely In The Chapel', while the same pseudonymous outfit carried off the Jan & Dean/Beach Boys vibe by way of 'Midnight Rider'. All'n'all, short'n'sweet at just over 22 minutes, a sort of compact disc, although there is a 'Vol.II'. *MCS*

Album rating: *5.5 / Vol.II *4

– spinoff hits, etc. –

DAVIE ALLAN AND THE ARROWS: Theme From The "Wild Angels"

Oct 66. (7") *<T 267>* [99] [–]

DAVIE ALLAN AND THE ARROWS: Blue's Theme / Bongo Party

Apr 67. (7") *<T 295>* [37] [–]

DAVIE ALLAN AND THE ARROWS: The Wild Angels Vol.II

Apr 67. (lp; mono/stereo) *<T/DT 5056>* [94] [–]

DAVIE ALLAN AND THE ARROWS: The Wild Angels And Other Themes

1996. (cd) *Curb; <D2-77866>* [ ] [–]

WILD AT HEART

1990 (US 125m) Propaganda / Samuel Goldwyn Company (R)

Film genre: romantic crime thriller + road movie/comedy

Top guns: s-w + dir: David Lynch ← DUNE (story: Barry Gifford)

Stars: Nicolas Cage *(Sailor Ripley)* ← BIRDY ← FAST TIMES AT RIDGEMONT HIGH, Laura Dern *(Lula Pace Fortune)* ← LADIES AND GENTLEMEN, THE FABULOUS STAINS / → DR. T & THE WOMEN → I AM SAM, Diane Ladd *(Marietta Fortune)* ← the WILD ANGELS / → PRIMARY COLORS, Willem Dafoe *(Bobby Peru)* ← CRY-BABY ← the LAST TEMPTATION OF CHRIST ← TO LIVE AND DIE IN L.A. ← STREETS OF FIRE / → AFFLICTION → OVERNIGHT → the LIFE AQUATIC WITH STEVE ZISSOU, Isabella Rossellini *(Perdita Durango)* ← SIESTA, Harry

Dean Stanton *(Johnnie Farragut)* ← the LAST TEMPTATION OF CHRIST ← PRETTY IN PINK ← PARIS, TEXAS ← REPO MAN ← ONE FROM THE HEART ← the ROSE ← RENALDO AND CLARA ← RANCHO DELUXE ← PAT GARRETT & BILLY THE KID / → FEAR AND LOATHING IN LAS VEGAS, Crispin Glover *(Dell)* → the DOORS → EVEN COWGIRLS GET THE BLUES → DEAD MAN, Grace Zabriskie *(Juana)* → EVEN COWGIRLS GET THE BLUES, Calvin Lockhart *(Reggie)* ← LET'S DO IT AGAIN ← MELINDA ← COTTON COMES TO HARLEM, David Patrick Kelly *(Dropshadow)* ← the ADVENTURES OF FORD FAIRLANE / → the CROW → CROOKLYN → HEAVY → LAST MAN STANDING, Freddie Jones *(George Kovich)* ← DUNE ← NEVER TOO YOUNG TO ROCK ← SON OF DRACULA, Pruitt Taylor Vince *(Buddy)* ← SHY PEOPLE / → NATURAL BORN KILLERS → HEAVY → the END OF VIOLENCE → MONSTER, Jack Nance *(00 Spool)* ← DUNE ← FOOLS / → the HOT SPOT, Sherilyn Fenn *(girl in accident)*, **John LURIE** *(Sparky)*, Charlie Spradling *(Irma)* → the DOORS → BAD CHANNELS, **Koko Taylor** *(singer at Zanzibar)* ← CHICAGO BLUES / → PRIDE AND JOY → BLUES BROTHERS 2000 → GODFATHERS AND SONS, **Billy Swan** *(himself)*

Storyline: Lula's madcap mother can't bear the thought of her daughter going out with ex-con Sailor. The two lovers head for the hills when they find themselves the target of a detective, a bounty hunter and worst of all, mum herself. Staying one step ahead, Lula and Sailor encounter a variety of bizarre people on their travels and get involved in a make or break bank heist. *JZ*

Movie rating: *8

Visual: video + dvd

Off the record: **Billy Swan** was a producer-turned-singer-songwriter when he topped the charts in 1974 with 'I Can Help'. *MCS*

Various Artists (score: ANGELO BADALAMENTI & KINNY LANDRUM *)

Aug 90. (cd/c/lp) *Polydor; <845098-2/-4> London; (845128-2/-4/-1)* ☐ Sep90 ☐
– Im abendrot – excerpt (GEWANDHAUSORCHESTER) / Slaughterhouse (POWERMAD) / Cool cat walk (*) / Love me (NICOLAS CAGE) / Baby please don't go (THEM) / Up in flames (KOKO TAYLOR) * / Wicked game (CHRIS ISAAK) / Be-bop a lula (GENE VINCENT & THE BLUE CAPS) / Smoke rings (GLEN GRAY AND THE CASA LOMA ORCHESTRA) / Perdita (RUBBER CITY) / Blue Spanish sky (CHRIS ISAAK) / Dark Spanish symphony – string version (*) / Dark Spanish symphony – 50s version (RUBBER CITY) / Dark Lolita (*) / Love me tender (NICOLAS CAGE). *(cd re-iss. Nov99 on 'Spectrum'; 551318-2) <cd re-iss. Mar03 on 'Universal'; AA 845098-2)>*

S/track review: One of the most interesting things about the soundtrack to David Lynch's 'WILD AT HEART' is the breadth of musical styles and their juxtaposition to one another. An excerpt from the classical piece 'Im Abendrot' performed by the GEWANDHAUSORCHESTER is quickly followed by the ferocious speed metal of 'Slaughterhouse' by POWERMAD, itself preceding the finger clicking jazz of ANGELO BADALAMENTI and KINNY LANDRUM's 'Cool Cat Walk'. The fact that nothing sounds out of place or disorientating is a spectacular achievement in itself. CHRIS ISAAK provides the effortlessly cool 'Wicked Game' and 'Blue Spanish Sky', his sonorous voice wrapping itself around velvet smooth guitar melodies is as seductive as ever. THEM's 'Baby Please Don't Go' and 'Be-Bop A Lula' by GENE VINCENT AND THE BLUE CAPS increase the rock'n'roll presence, the former a blues rooted stomp with Van Morrison wailing over jangling guitars and screeching harmonica with the latter being one for the Teddy Boys to shuffle their feet to. Sandwiched in between is 'Up In Flames', a haunting jazz track of muted brass written by the director and performed by KOKO TAYLOR. Lynch is also involved in the writing of another jazz based song, 'Perdita', while leading man NICOLAS CAGE takes on 'Love Me' and the Elvis classic 'Love Me Tender'. It's always a risky business when actors try to sing for the soundtrack but CAGE handles it well, showing himself to be something of a crooner and both songs are better than anything you'll ever hear on the X Factor or Pop Idol. The songs on 'WILD AT HEART' are miles apart in terms of sound and style but somehow they manage to complement each other and create a fascinating sonic journey. *CM*

Album rating: *7

– spinoff hits, etc. –

CHRIS ISAAK: Wicked Game / (instrumental)

Nov 90. (c-s) *Reprise; <19704>* 6 –

CHRIS ISAAK: Wicked Game / ANGELO BADALAMENTI: Cool Cat Walk

Nov 90. (7"/c-s) *(LON/+CS 279)* – 10
(12"+=/cd-s+=) *(LON X/CD 279)* – ANGELO BADALAMENTI: Dark Spanish Symphony – edited string version.

WILD GUITAR

1962 (US 92m b&w) Fairway International Pictures

Film genre: romantic Rock'n'roll Musical melodrama/comedy

Top guns: dir: Ray Dennis Steckler → RAT PFINK A BOO-BOO / s-w: Nicholas Merriweather (i.e. Arch Hall Sr.) → EEGAH, Robert O. Wehling ← EEGAH

Stars: **Arch Hall Jr.** *(Bud Eagle)* ← EEGAH, Nancy Czar *(Vickie Wills)* → GIRL HAPPY → WINTER A-GO-GO → SPINOUT, Arch Hall Sr. as William Watters *(Mike McCauley)* ← EEGAH, Ray Dennis Steckler as Cash Flagg *(Steak)*, ← EEGAH, Marie Denn *(Marge)*, Robert Crumb *(Don Proctor)*, Al Scott *(Ted Eagle)*, William Lloyd *(Weasel)* ← EEGAH, Carolyn Brandt *(dancer on ramp)* ← EEGAH / → RAT PFINK A BOO-BOO

Storyline: Guitarist/singer, Bud Eagle, rides into Hollywood on his motorscooter and becomes an overnight sensation. However, when he is taken under the wings of unscrupulous manager, Mike McCauley, the squeeze is on to make money at all costs. *MCS*

Movie rating: *2

Visual: video + dvd (no audio OST)

Off the record: **Arch Hall Jr.** is the son of the director, who, of course, is also in this terrible movie. *MCS*

– associated release –

ARCH HALL, JR. and the ARCHERS: Wild Guitar!

May 05. (cd) *Norton; <CED 307>* ☐ –
– (featuring hits from 'Wild Guitar' / 'Eegah' / 'The Sadist' / 'The Choppers').

WILD IN THE COUNTRY

1961 (US 114m) 20th Century Fox (PG)

Film genre: Romantic drama

Top guns: dir: Philip Dunne / s-w: Clifford Odets (nov: 'The Lost Country' by J.R. Salamanca)

Stars: **Elvis PRESLEY** *(Glenn Tyler)*, Hope Lange *(Irene Sperry)* → DEATH WISH, Tuesday Weld *(Noreen)* ← ROCK, ROCK, ROCK! / → I WALK THE LINE → THIEF → HEARTBREAK HOTEL → CHELSEA WALLS, Millie Perkins *(Betty Lee Parsons)* → WILD IN THE STREETS, John Ireland *(Phil Macy)*, Gary Lockwood *(Cliff Macy)* → IT HAPPENED AT THE WORLD'S FAIR → MODEL SHOP, Rafer Johnson *(Davis)*, William Mimms *(Uncle Rolfe)*

Storyline: Glenn Talbot is a troubled but talented country bumpkin given to drinking and brawling. Despite finding help in battling his inner demons, the pivotal relationship with his psychiatrist comes under fire from the small minded local community. *BG*

Movie rating: *5.5

Visual: video + dvd (no audio OST)

Off the record: nothing

—

ELVIS PRESLEY: Flaming Star / Wild In The Country / Follow That Dream

Mar 95. (cd) *R.C.A.; <66557> (74321 90612-2)* ☐ ☐
– (FLAMING STAR tracks) / Wild in the country / I slipped, I stumbled, I fell / Lonely man / In my way / Forget me never / Lonely man (solo) / I slipped, I stumbled, I fell / (FOLLOW THAT DREAM tracks).

S/track review: Like its predecessor 'FLAMING STAR', this film again paired ELVIS rather uneasily with an overly ambitious concept. And, like that movie, it also featured a minimum of ELVIS performances, cutting two ballads, 'Forget Me Never' and 'Lonely Man', from the final print. The spare, poignant acoustic version of the latter, in particular, suggests that this wasn't the best of decisions, especially given the sentimental indulgence of the title song. Among the numbers deemed suitable for inclusion, Wise/Weisman's endearing rock'n'roll pastiche, 'I Slipped, I Stumbled, I Fell', is the most memorable, although it has to be said its queasy, sonorous backing vocals give the impression that poor old ELVIS has actually slipped, stumbled and fallen into something rather unpleasant . . . While the title tune was only released as an a-side in the UK, the remaining songs from the film surfaced sporadically, and a CD soundtrack of sorts featuring all the songs and variations, was eventually cobbled together alongside 'FLAMING STAR' and 'FOLLOW THAT DREAM'. *BG*

Album rating: *4

ELVIS PRESLEY: Surrender / Lonely Man

Feb 61. (7") *R.C.A.; <47-7850> (RCA 1227)* 1 / 32 May61 4

(re-iss. May77; PB 2701)

ELVIS PRESLEY: Wild In The Country / I Feel So Bad

May 61. (7") *R.C.A.; <47-7880> (RCA 1244)* 26 / 5 Aug61 1

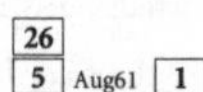

WILD IN THE STREETS

1968 (US 97m) American International Pictures (GP)

Film genre: political showbiz/Rock-music drama

Top guns: dir: Barry Shear → ACROSS 110th STREET / s-w: Robert Thom (story: 'The Day It All Happened, Baby') → ANGEL, ANGEL, DOWN WE GO

Stars: Christopher Jones *(Max Flatow/Frost)*, Shelley Winters *(Mrs. Flatow)* → CLEOPATRA JONES → ELVIS: THE MOVIE → PURPLE PEOPLE EATER → HEAVY, Diane Varsi *(Sally LeRoy)*, Hal Holbrook *(Sen. John Fergus)* → JONATHAN LIVINGSTON SEAGULL → INTO THE WILD, Ed Begley *(Senator Allbright)* → a TIME TO SING, Millie Perkins *(Mrs. Fergus)* ← WILD IN THE COUNTRY, Richard Pryor *(Stanley X)* → the PHYNX → YOU'VE GOT TO WALK IT LIKE YOU TALK IT . . . → LADY SINGS THE BLUES → WATTSTAX → the MACK → ADIOS AMIGO → CAR WASH → the WIZ → BUSTIN' LOOSE, Larry Bishop *(the Hook; Abraham)* → the SAVAGE SEVEN, Michael Margotta *(Jimmy Fergus)* → the STRAWBERRY STATEMENT → TIMES SQUARE, **Peter Tork** *(ticket buyer)* <= the MONKEES =>, Salli Sachse *(hippie mother)* ← the TRIP ← THUNDER ALLEY ← the GHOST IN THE INVISIBLE BIKINI ← HOW TO STUFF A WILD BIKINI ← SKI PARTY ← BEACH BLANKET BINGO ← PAJAMA PARTY ← BIKINI BEACH ← MUSCLE BEACH PARTY, Paul Frees *(narrator)* → the POINT!, Dick Clark *(himself)* ← JAMBOREE / → the PHYNX → DEADMAN'S CURVE, Bill Mumy *(boy)* → HARD TO HOLD → DERAILROADED

Storyline: "Never trust anyone over 30" is the watchword of rock superstar Max Frost. When shifty senator Johnny Fergus uses Frost to get the voting age lowered to 14, the forthcoming elections are a walkover and soon Fergus is sitting in the White House. His first presidential decree sees all thirty-somethings (and upwards) packed off to retirement camps and fed LSD instead of porridge. Meanwhile Max and the youngsters go from strength to strength. *JZ*

Movie rating: *5.5

Visual: video

Off the record: Folk troubadour PHIL OCHS was said to be first choice for the main role – now that would've been interesting! *MCS*

—

Various Artists (songs: Barry Mann and Cynthia Weil) (score: Les Baxter *)

Jun 68. (lp) *Tower; <(SKAO 5099)>* 12 Oct68 ☐
– Love to be your man (the 13th POWER) / Free lovin' (the 13th POWER) / Fifty two per cent (the 13th POWER) / Shape of things to come (the 13th POWER) / Psychedelic senate (the SENATORS) * / Fourteen or fight (the 13th POWER) / Wild in the streets (JERRY HOWARD) * / Listen to the music (the SECOND TIME) / Sally Le Roy (the SECOND TIME) / Shelly in camp (the GURUS) *.

S/track review: 'WILD IN THE STREETS' preceded the similarly-themed Brit movie, 'PRIVILEGE' by a couple of months. Many might've thought the revolutionary, political pop message was getting more intense and indeed global, although the latter was interjected by an overpowering religious and moral element. While "real" pop star (Paul Jones) took on the premier role in 'PRIVILEGE', rookie actor Christopher Jones (no relation – obviously!) was given the opportunity to shine as pop star turned Presidential candidate, Max Frost. Indeed, his group MAX FROST AND THE TROOPERS were accredited on the vinyl insert (and a hit 45, 'Shape Of Things To Come'), but not however on the inner sleeve – that went to in-house band, the 13th POWER. Contract songwriters, Barry Mann and Cynthia Weil (behind a plethora of mid-60s bubblegum-pop hits) were possibly too sugary to take on such a complex musical basis. If their past writing credits had been a tad manufactured and "music by numbers", they went OTT with some of these er . . . numbers, the Seeds-esque 'Fifty Two Per Cent' (a reference to 52% of the population being under 25) and the anthemic 'Fourteen Or Fight' (a ref to the plot theme of lowering the voting age to 14). To confuse matters worse, the 13th POWER had five cuts here, including 'Free Lovin'', a song not scribed by Mann & Weil, who also provided two others ('Listen To The Music' & 'Sally Leroy') for another fictitious house outfit, the SECOND TIME. One has to find one's calculator soon. Not all the blame can be attributed to MAX and Co, scoresmith Les Baxter (with arranger and conductor Mike Curb) also served up some freaky calculus via the pseudonymous and groov-eee 'Psychedelic Senate' (by the SENATORS), 'Wild In The Streets' (by JERRY HOWARD) and 'Shelly In Camp' (by the GURUS). The kids must've loved it at the time as the album nearly reached the Top 10, now, though, it all seems dated and remotely fantastical. *MCS*

Album rating: *5

– spinoff hits, etc. –

MAX FROST AND THE TROOPERS: Shape Of Things To Come / Free Lovin'

Aug 68. (7") *<419> Capitol; (CL 15565)* 22 Oct68 ☐

WILD ON THE BEACH

1965 (US 77m b&w) Lippert / 20th Century Fox (PG-13)

Film genre: Pop-Rock teen Musical comedy

Top guns: dir: Maury Dexter ← SURF PARTY ← the YOUNG SWINGERS / s-w: Harry Spalding ← SURF PARTY ← the YOUNG SWINGERS ← TEENAGE MILLIONAIRE (story: Hank Tani)

Stars: Frankie Randall *(Adam Miller)*, Sherry Jackson *(Lee Sullivan)*, **Gayle Caldwell** *(Marsie Lowell)* → WILD, WILD WINTER, **Jackie Miller** *(Toby Carr)* → WILD, WILD WINTER, Russ Bender *(Shep KIrby)* ← HOT ROD GANG, **Sonny & CHER** *(performers)*, **Sandy Nelson** *(performer)*, Justin Smith *(Mort Terwilliger)* ← the YOUNG SWINGERS

Storyline: Male and female college students fight over a plush beach house – a type of "battle of the sexes" – and have parties at the weekend frequently by surf groups and pop singers. Yahoo! – not. *MCS*

Movie rating: *2.5

Visual: video

Off the record: (see below)

—

Various Artists (arranged: Jimmie Haskell)

Aug 65. (lp;mono/stereo) *RCA Victor; <LPM/LSP 3441>* ☐ ☐
– The yellow haired woman (FRANKIE RANDALL) / Rock the world (the ASTRONAUTS) / Run away from him (CINDY MALONE) / Drum dance (SANDY NELSON) / The gods of love (FRANKIE RANDALL) / It's gonna rain (SONNY & CHER) / Little Speedy Gonzales (the ASTRONAUTS) / Pyramid stomp (the ASTRONAUTS) / The house on the beach (FRANKIE RANDALL) / Snap it (the ASTRONAUTS) / Winter nocturne (JACKIE & GAYLE).

S/track review: Instructively prescribing: "Teens: Listen to Your Favorites in this Musical Celebration" on the back cover, 'WILD ON THE BEACH' is hardly speaking from the hip or for the youth. For a start, kicking off with a clean-cut crooner such as FRANKIE RANDALL doesn't smell like teen spirit to me. 'The Yellow Haired Woman' (not actually sung by RANDALL in the movie!) stinks of nostalgia, novelty and nonsense, epitomised by the chorus-line of "My Heart Went Tick Ticka Ticka Tack . . ."; the night-club recording sensation (as it boasts on the sleeve) with no hits to his name was afforded two other cues, 'The Gods Of Love' and 'The House On The Beach'. Other pop wannabe's, too, found this musical umbrella their albatross: CINDY MALONE ('Run Away From Him') and ex-Christy Minstrels JACKIE Miller & GAYLE Caldwell ('Winter Nocturne'). Okay, there were stars here, although recent breakthrough act SONNY & CHER could only supply the B-side ('It's Gonna Rain') to their multi-selling, chart-topping smash 'I Got You Babe'. Rock'n'roll "Teen Beat" man himself, SANDY NELSON (remember 'Let There Be Drums'), had been stuck for a hit since his late-50s/early-60s heyday – 'Drum Dance' was no comeback. Talking of instrumentalists, the ASTRONAUTS quartet were given priority, possibly because they had now found their voice. 'Rock The World' (cloning Elvis in '65!) and the Pat Boone rip-off 'Little Speedy Gonzales' sit uncomfortably with two run-of-the-mill instrumentals, 'Pyramid Stomp' and 'Snap It'. All'n'all, 'WILD ON THE BEACH' is under 23 minutes of unadulterated pot-pourri – "wild" no, "tame" yes. *MCS*

Album rating: *3

☐ WILD SCHEME A-GO-GO
(⇒ the SPIDERS)

☐ the WILD SIDE alt.
(⇒ SUBURBIA)

WILD STYLE

1983 (US 82m) First Run Features (R)

Film genre: urban music docudrama

Top guns: s-w + dir: Charlie Ahearn

Stars: 'Lee' George Quinones *(Raymond 'Zoro')* ← DOWNTOWN 81, Patti Astor *(Virginia)* ← the FOREIGNER, Andrew 'Zephyr' Witten *(Zroc)*, Sandra Fabara *(Rose)*, Frederick Braithwaite *(Phade)*, Carlos Morales *(Raymond's brother)*, Glenn O'Brien *(museum currator)* ← DOWNTOWN 81, **Fab Five Freddy** *(performer)* ← DOWNTOWN 81 / → JUICE → WHO'S THE MAN?, **Grandmaster Flash** *(performer)*, **Kool Moe Dee** *(performer)* → BEAT STREET → BEEF, **Grandmaster D.St** *(performer)* → SCRATCH, **Busy Bee** *(performer)*, **Cold Crush Bros.:- Grand Master Caz, Tony Tone, J.D.L., Charlie Chase, Easy A.D. & Almighty K.G.** *(performers)*, **Rock Steady Crew:- Frosty Freeze, Mr. Freeze *, Crazy Legs & Prince Ken Swift** *(performers)* → FLASHDANCE → KNIGHTS OF THE CITY *, **DJ AJ** *(himself)*, **Lisa Lee** *(performer)* → BEAT STREET, **Double Trouble:- Lil' Rodney Cee, Kevie Kev Rockwell** *(performers)*, **Fantastic Freaks:- Grand Wizard Theodore** *(performer)* → SCRATCH, **Prince Whipper Whip, Master Rob, Ruby Dee & Dot-a-Rock** *(performers)*

Storyline: The original hip hop document, oblivious to the flaccid imitators it'd inspire, with a loose plot and even looser-tongued spirit peopled by paid-up rappers, graffiti artists, DJs, breakdancers and hangers-on. Graffiti artist Zoro and promoter Phade both negotiate the gulf between unforgiving Bronx slumscapes and uptown wealth, representative of the genre's unlikely cross-pollination with New York's art/new wave scene, and providing the lens within which hip hop's genesis is brought into focus. Minus points for the DVD reissue's messing with Grandmaster Flash and his flying fingered sorcery on Bob James' 'Take Me To The Mardis Gras'. *BG*

Movie rating: *5

Visual: video + dvd

Off the record: The pick here is **Grandmaster Flash** (for other Grandmasters – see below), responsible for at least two hip hop classics, 'The Message' or 'White Lines (Don't Don't Do It)'. *MCS*

—

Various (score: FAB FIVE FREDDY * & CHRIS STEIN **)

Oct 83. (lp/c) *Animal-Chrysalis; (CHR/ZCHR 1453)* ☐ ☐
– Military cut – scratch mix (GRAND WIZARD THEODORE & K.K. ROCKWELL) / M.C. battle (BUSY BEE, LIL' RODNEY CEE & GRAND WIZARD THEODORE) / Basketball throwdown (COLD CRUSH BROS. & FANTASTIC FREAKS) / Fantastic Freaks at the Dixie (FANTASTIC FREAKS & GRAND WIZARD THEODORE) / Subway theme (DJ GRAND WIZARD THEODORE) / Cold Crush Bros. at the Dixie (COLD CRUSH BROS.) / Cuckoo clocking (* & **) / Stoop rap (DOUBLE TROUBLE) / Double Trouble at the Amphitheatre (DOUBLE TROUBLE & DJ STEVIE STEVE) / South Bronx subway rap (GRAND MASTER CAZ) / Chief Rocker Busy Bee – the DJ AJ at the Amphitheatre (BUSY BEE & DJ AJ) / Gangbusters (GRAND MASTER THEODORE & KEVIE KEV ROCKWELL) / Rammellzee and Shock Dell at the Amphitheatre (RAMMELLZEE, SHOCK DELL & GRANDMIXER D.ST). *<US cd-iss. Aug97 on 'Rhino'+=; RCD 72892>* – Street rap (BUSY BEE) / Down by law (*) / Wild Style theme rap 1 (GRAND MASTER CAZ & **) / Wild Style subway rap 2 (GRAND MASTER CAZ & **).

S/track review: Hip hop as secular religion, proselytising across national and cultural boundaries like the last decadent days of the Roman Empire, and 'WILD STYLE' as is its creation myth. Or at least it should be. Its beats, its quotes, its funky tropes, have informed the art of countless American icons, from Public Enemy to the Beastie Boys to Beck, and thousands of rappers and (ostensibly) evolutionary production leaps in between. And if it wasn't a myth already, the stubborn lack of a CD reissue for more than two decades made it into one; rap bible 'Vibe' dubbed it "one of the ten best movie soundtracks of all time". Listening to BUSY BEE's "sex, cheeba and cash money" mantra, you can just about see how the large part of an art form so exciting, vital and resourceful degenerated into so much violence, corporate celebrity and general meaninglessness. And just try and resist that sneaking suspicion that it's all about the bass and the beats: 'WILD STYLE' is live and organic, played on real instruments by guys like LENNY FERRARI, masterminded by FAB 5 FREDDY and Blondie's CHRIS STEIN, scratched over by GRAND WIZARD THEODORE and rapped over by GRAND MASTER CAZ. It's the sound of the Funk reclaimed from the worst excesses of disco, and it's something else entirely from a beat looped into spirit-crushing monotony, or a so-called rock band filching all the style and none of the substance from a long dead scene. The music is not only live, it's alive, it not only moves – to paraphrase George Clinton – it removes. It does not furnish a fur-lined backdrop for blood diamonds or outsized cars. What it does do is create a febrile context for transforming social malaise into witty, conscious, cathartic art, and capturing the imagination of millions, black and white, rich and poor. It channels the wasteland ambience of a post-70s, back-from-the-brink-of-bankruptcy New York into hugely atmospheric tone poems like THEODORE's 'Subway Theme' and 'Cuckoo Clocking', and – on the likes of 'Cold Crush Bros. At The Dixie' – it trademarks the rasping, declamatory MC-style fellow NY pioneers like the Beastie Boys would themselves get so much purchase from. With FREDDY's 'Down By Law' (guitar courtesy of STEIN), it also births the grimy rock-rap hybrid the Beasties, RUN DMC and 'Def Jam' in general would run with through the 80s. Part of 'WILD STYLE's enduring genius is that, despite not featuring any of the big Grandmaster Flash or Afrika Bambaataa anthems of its day, it's as consistent an old skool record as the era threw up, with a unique sonic architecture even clearer on the collection of instrumental excerpts issued a few years back by 'Mr Bongo'. Oh for the inconsequence of a basketball battle. *BG*

Album rating: *9

WILD, WILD WINTER

1966 (US 80m w/b&w) Universal Pictures

Film genre: Pop/Rock Musical comedy

Top guns: dir: Lennie Weinrib ← BEACH BALL / → OUT OF SIGHT / s-w: David Malcolm ← BEACH BALL ← the GIRLS ON THE BEACH

Stars: Gary Clarke *(Ronnie)*, Chris Noel *(Susan)* ← BEACH BALL ← GIRL HAPPY ← GET YOURSELF A COLLEGE GIRL, Don Edmonds *(Burt)* ← BEACH BALL, Suzie Kaye *(Sandy)* → C'MON, LET'S LIVE A LITTLE → IT'S A BIKINI WORLD → CLAMBAKE, Les Brown Jr. *(Perry)*, Steve Franken *(John)*, James Wellman *(Dean)* ← BEACH BALL, Steve Rogers *(Benton)* ← SKI PARTY ← the GIRLS ON THE BEACH, Dick Miller *(Rik)* ← BEACH BALL ← SKI PARTY ← the GIRLS ON THE BEACH ← ROCK ALL NIGHT ← CARNIVAL ROCK / → the WILD ANGELS → the TRIP → TRUCK TURNER → I WANNA HOLD YOUR HAND → ROCK'N'ROLL HIGH SCHOOL → GET CRAZY → SHAKE, RATTLE & ROCK! tv, Linda Rogers *(Trisha)* ← WINTER A-GO-GO ← TICKLE ME ← PAJAMA PARTY ← BIKINI BEACH ← BEACH PARTY, Buck Holland *(McGee)* ← WINTER A-GO-GO, **the Beau Brummels:- Sal Valentino *, Ron Meagher, Ron Elliott, John Peterson** *(performers)* → MEDICINE BALL CARAVAN, **Dick and DeeDee** *(performers)*, **Jay & The Americans** *(performers)*, **the Astronauts:- Bob Demmon, Dennis Lindsey, Storm Patterson, Rich Fifield + Jim Gallagher** *(performers)* ← SURF PARTY / → OUT OF SIGHT, **Jackie Miller & Gayle Caldwell** *(performers)* ← WILD ON THE BEACH

Storyline: California beach bum, Ronnie, and other students at a ski college attempt to seduce sexy secretary Susan – but it's the music that steals the show. *MCS*

Movie rating: *4

Visual: video

Off the record: Here's a briefing of all concerned:- **the Beau Brummels** were a folk-rock act formed 1964 in San Francisco and had three massive US hits the following year, 'Laugh, Laugh', 'Just A Little', and 'You Tell Me Why'. **Jackie Miller and Gayle Caldwell** were ex-New Christy Minstrels folk-duo. Another folk-pop duo, **Dick And Dee Dee** (aka Dick St. John and his childhood friend Dee Dee Sperling), had a string of US hits, kicking off in 1961 with near chart-topper, 'The Mountain's High'. Surf-rock quintet **the Astronauts** (from Boulder, Colorado) only scraped into the US Top 100 in 1963 with novelty instrumental, 'Baja'. **Jay And The Americans** (from Brooklyn, New York) and featuring Jay Black, broke through in 1962 via a stack o' hits including US Top 10 smashes, 'She Cried', 'Come A Little Bit Closer' and 'Cara, Mia'. *MCS*

Various Artists // JERRY LONG (score)

Jan 66. (lp; mono) *Decca; <DL 74699>* □ [-]
– Two of a kind (JAY AND THE AMERICANS) / A change of heart (the ASTRONAUTS) / Just wait and see (the BEAU BRUMMELS) / Heartbeats (DICK AND DEE DEE) / Our love's gonna snowball (JACKIE AND GAYLE) // Main title / Latin source / Wild watusi / Hawaii to military / The chase / End title.

S/track review: To give this sort of soundtrack LP a fair critique four decades after its initial release, was somewhat difficult. The climate in 1966 (no pun intended) is indeed a little different. Like so many 60s OST's, there were two sides to the story, one side Various artists tracks, the other belonging to the score composer – in this case, newbie JERRY LONG. The latter's six-strong instrumentals on side two can best be desribed as lounge-R&B for the swinging set. Side one (only 5 tracks at just under 12 minutes!) is hardly money well spent, especially when the bubblegum-pop provided by clean-cut acts such as JAY AND THE AMERICANS (who feature KENNY VANCE) on 'Two Of A Kind' fell well short of rock'n'roll. 'A Change Of Heart' by the ASTRONAUTS, who'd found a vocalist since their early 60s surf-rock heyday, and the Beatles-esque BEAU BRUMMELS (with 'Just Wait And See'), are poor beyond anybody's standards. The squeaky DICK AND DEE DEE ('Heartbeats') were verging on Northern Soul, although former mods would be up in arms with this description – so would DICK. Also written by Al Capps & Mary Dean – and the only wintery record on show! – is 'Our Love's Gonna Snowball' by bikini-clad blonde/brunette girl-duo, JACKIE AND GAYLE; lyrically cheesy and out of sync with the instrumental accompaniment. Get me outta here! *MCS*

Album rating: *3

□ Hank WILLIAMS segment
(⇒ YOUR CHEATIN' HEART)

Hank WILLIAMS Jr.

Born: Randall Hank Williams, 26 May'49, Shreveport, Louisiana, USA. The living heir to the godfather of country music, HANK WILLIAMS Jr. inevitably started out singing his daddy's songs, appearing on the Grand Ole Opry before he'd even reached his teens. In 1964, he duly took the place of his father on the soundtrack to the Sam Katzman-produced biopic, 'YOUR CHEATIN' HEART', although in the movie George Hamilton actually played the part of Hank Sr., HANK JR. got his chance in a lead role four years later, playing a country singer struggling to make it big in the Arthur Dreifuss musical, 'A TIME TO SING' (1968). While the man subsequently found his own rough'n'tumble outlaw-orientated style come the 70s, his only other feature appearance was a part in Alan Rudolph's music biz comedy, 'Roadie' (1980), in which he appeared as himself and also featured on the soundtrack. He was eventually the subject of his own TV biopic in 1983, a film based on his own autobiography and notable for an early appearance by Christian Slater. *BG*

- **filmography** (composer) {acting} –

Your Cheatin' Heart *(1964 OST =>)* / **a Time To Sing** *(1968 {*} OST =>)* / Willa *(1979 {a})* / **Roadie** *(1980 {a} on OST by V/A =>)*

□ Paul WILLIAMS segment
(⇒ PHANTOM OF THE PARADISE)

□ Anthony WILSON segment
(⇒ 24 HOUR PARTY PEOPLE)

WINTER A-GO-GO

1965 (US 88m) Columbia Pictures Corporation

Film genre: Pop-Rock Musical teen comedy

Top guns: dir: Richard Benedict / s-w: Bob Kanter (story: Reno Carell)

Stars: James Stacy *(Danny Frazer)* ← a SWINGIN' SUMMER, William Wellman, Jr. *(Jeff Forrester)* ← a SWINGIN' SUMMER ← HIGH SCHOOL CONFIDENTIAL! / → BLACK CAESAR, Beverly Adams *(Jo Ann Wallace)* ← HOW TO STUFF A WILD BIKINI ← GIRL HAPPY ← ROUSTABOUT, John Anthony Hughes *(Burt)* ← RIDE THE WILD SURF, Tom Nardini *(Frankie)*, Jill Donohue *(Janine)*, Duke Hobbie *(Bob)* → MODEL SHOP, Julie Parrish *(Dee Dee)* → PARADISE, HAWAIIAN STYLE, Buck Holland *(Will)* → WILD, WILD WINTER, Linda Rogers *(Penny)* ← TICKLE ME ← PAJAMA PARTY ← BIKINI BEACH ← BEACH PARTY / → WILD, WILD WINTER, Nancy Czar *(Gloria 'Jonesy' Jones)* ← GIRL HAPPY ← WILD GUITAR / → SPINOUT

Storyline: The mid-60s were responsible for two temperature-baiting, weathery films, either the hot "Beach Party" movies, or the cold "Ski Party" sort – this film was of the freezing-down-a-slippery- slope variety. Goody-two-shoe ski-teens are resident at the newly inherited Snow Mountain Lodge in whereverland, and it looks fun and jolly when it's turned into a dance club – but only for rich kids. Oh, shucks! *MCS*

Movie rating: *2.5

Visual: none (no audio OST; score: Harry Betts)

Off the record: Main actor, JAMES STACY ('Columbia's answer to 'Beach Party' star, Frankie Avalon), performed one song, 'Hip Square Dance', while future Monkees songsmiths Tommy Boyce & Bobby Hart also supplied 'Do The Ski (With Me)' for the NOONEY RICKETT FOUR & JONI LYMAN. The latter singer was chosen for 'King Of The Mountain' and the former quartet performed 'Ski City'; the moody REFLECTIONS were behind '(I'm) Sweet On You', while the opening/closing title theme (the movie's third penned by Howard Greenfield & Jack Keller) saw hitmakers of 'Little Honda, the HONDELLS, shake it on down. *MCS*

□ WIR KINDER VOM BAHNHOF ZOO alt.
(⇒ CHRISTIANE F.)

□ Jimmy WITHERSPOON segment
(⇒ GEORGIA)

the WIZ

1978 (US 134m) Motown / Universal Pictures (G)

Film genre: R&B/Rock Musical fantasy adventure

Top guns: dir: Sidney Lumet / s-w: Joel Schumacher ← CAR WASH ← SPARKLE (au: L. Frank Baum)

Stars: Diana ROSS *(Dorothy)*, **Michael Jackson** *(Scarecrow)* ← SAVE THE CHILDREN / → MOONWALKER, Nipsey Russell *(Tin Man)*, Ted Ross *(Lion)*, Lena Horne *(Glinda the Good)*, Richard Pryor *(Herman Smith / The Wiz)* ← CAR WASH ← ADIOS AMIGO ← the MACK ← WATTSTAX ← LADY SINGS THE BLUES ← YOU'VE GOT TO WALK IT LIKE YOU TALK IT . . . ← the PHYNX ← WILD IN THE STREETS / → BUSTIN' LOOSE, Mabel King *(Evillene)* ← DON'T PLAY US CHEAP, Theresa Merritt *(Aunt Em)* ← DON'T PLAY US CHEAP, Stanley Greene *(Uncle Henry)* ← COTTON COMES TO HARLEM ← the LANDLORD, Clarice Taylor *(Addaperle; the Good Witch of the North)* ← FIVE ON THE BLACK HAND SIDE, **Patti Austin** *(the Wiz Singers . . .)* ← IT'S YOUR THING / → ONE-TRICK PONY → TUCKER: THE MAN AND HIS DREAM → JACKIE'S BACK!

Storyline: Oz gets a socially conscious Harlem makeover as timid primary teacher Dorothy and her dog are whipped up in a blizzard and carried to a graffitied urban netherworld. A posse of skateboarding munchkins aren't much help but – after shooing away some Groucho Marx-style crows – she soon finds solace in a brainless Scarecrow. The Tin Man and cowardly Lion join them as they encounter a parade of ten brilliantly surreal creatures: Fu Manchu voodoo dolls, gnashing litter bins and a posse of simean hells angels. The Wiz himself turns out to be a dodgy politician. *BG*

Movie rating: *6.5

Visual: video + dvd

Off the record: Lena Horne was a pre-R'n'R popular music singer who had a Top 20 hit in 1955 with 'Love Me Or Leave Me'. *MCS*

—

Various Cast (score: Quincy Jones / songs: Charlie Smalls)

Oct 78. (d-lp/d-c) *M.C.A.; <14000> (MCSP/+C 287)* [40] Feb79 [ ]
– Main title from "The Wiz" (overture pt.1) / (Overture pt.2) / The feeling that we have / Can I go on? / Glinda's theme / He's the wizard / Soon as I get home – Home / You can't win / Ease on down the road / What would I do if I could feel? / Slide some oil to me / Ease on down the road / (I'm a) Mean ole lion / Ease on down the road / Poppy girls / Be a lion / End of the yellow brick road / Emerald City sequence / So you wanted to see the wizard / Is this what feeling gets? (Dorothy's theme) / Don't nobody bring me no bad news / Liberation agitato / A brand new day (everybody rejoice) / Believe in yourself / Liberation ballet / The good witch Glinda. *<d-cd iss.Dec99; AAMCAD2 11649> (UK d-cd iss.Mar03; same)*

S/track review: The Sidney Lumet-QUINCY JONES partnership stretches back to 'The Pawnbroker' (1964), but 'THE WIZ' was something different. JONES was hired as a de facto musical director rather than just a composer, taking Charlie Smalls' Broadway songs and adapting them for a small army of musicians and singers; A-list among them: Ron Carter, Hubert Laws, Patti Austin, Luther Vandross, Toots Thielmans, Michael Brecker, Eric Gale, Steve Gadd, Ralph McDonald, Bob James, Dick Hyman, Richard Tee and Dave Grusin; chief among them: Motown graduate MICHAEL JACKSON and first lady DIANA ROSS. Regardless of the movie's merits, the soundtrack's a fascinating curio of a late-teen JACKSON, suspended between the sibling disco of the Jacksons and his reinvention as a self-contained solo act. 'Ease On Down The Road' is his showcase, a pull-yourself-up-by-the-bootstraps anthem that should've been a bigger hit. JACKSON throws himself into the song with the kinetic conviction of a faith-healer, bouncing over JONES' arrangements and breathlessly stealing ROSS' thunder. It worked so well that JONES eased JACKSON on down the road to superstardom by producing 'Off The Wall' (1979). The Big Band Bossa man is in his element here – happily, his orchestrations aren't as effusive as his sleevenotes. His sources are sometimes a little familiar ('Poppy Girls' sounds uncannily similar to the O'Jays' 'Love Of Money', and he doesn't mind slipping in a few bars of classic Brazilian samba), but his holistic grasp of his trade means he can navigate pretty seamlessly between thespian melodrama, Thielmans-abetted 'Midnight Cowboy'-goes-Broadway and all-out disco evangelism. And you really don't have to be a fan of musicals to appreciate 'The WIZ'. Even the pantomine-funk of the main title is great fun – give it the slightest leeway and it'll have you yak-yakking along in the shower. *BG*

Album rating: *6.5

– spinoff hits, etc. –

DIANA ROSS & MICHAEL JACKSON: Ease On Down The Road / QUINCY JONES: Poppy Girls

Sep 78. (7") *<40947> (MCA 396)* [41] Nov78 [45]

MICHAEL JACKSON: You Can't Win / (part 2)

Feb 79. (7"pic-d/12") *Epic; <50654> (EPC/+13 7135)* [81] May79 [ ]

WONDERFUL LIFE

1964 (UK 113m) ABPC / Warner-Pathe (U)

Film genre: romantic Pop/Rock Musical comedy

Top guns: dir: Sidney J. Furie ← the YOUNG ONES / → LITTLE FAUSS AND BIG HALSY → LADY SINGS THE BLUES / s-w: Peter Myers & Ronald Cass ← SUMMER HOLIDAY ← the YOUNG ONES

Stars: Cliff RICHARD *(Johnnie)*, Walter Slezak *(Lloyd Davis)*, Susan Hampshire *(Jenny)*, Melvyn Hayes *(Jerry)* ← SUMMER HOLIDAY ← the YOUNG ONES, **the Shadows** *(musicians)* ← SUMMER HOLIDAY ← the YOUNG ONES / → FINDERS KEEPERS, Richard O'Sullivan *(Edward)* ← the YOUNG ONES / → EVERY DAY'S A HOLIDAY, Una Stubbs *(Barbara)* ← SUMMER HOLIDAY, Derek Bond *(Douglas Leslie)*, Gerald Harper *(Scotsman / sheik / Harold)* ← the YOUNG ONES, Joe Cuby *(Miguel)*

Storyline: Johnny is in charge of a group of singing sailors, who are so inept they manage to scupper their ship and end up drifting along to the Canaries. The only way back home is to go banana-picking to raise some money (honestly) but on their way to the trees they bump into a film crew and budding starlet Jenny. Johnny and the gang secretly help her make a film behind the back of nasty director, Lloyd, in a desperate effort to get home and save the banana crop from extinction. *JZ*

Movie rating: *5.5

Visual: video + dvd

Off the record: nothing

CLIFF RICHARD AND THE SHADOWS (composer: Stanley Black)

Jul 64. (lp) *Columbia; (SX 1628/SCX 3515) Epic; <BN 26145>* [2] [ ]
– Wonderful life / A girl in every port / Walkin' (the SHADOWS) / Home / A little imagination / On the beach / In the stars / We love a movie / Do you remember / What've I got to do / Theme for young lovers (the SHADOWS) / All kinds of people / A matter of moments / Youth and experience.

S/track review: The studio schmaltz continued with CLIFF RICHARD's third and final all-singing all-dancing extravaganza, boasting a title song which could easily take pride of place on 'The Sound Of Music'. Some of this soundtrack really is gormless Broadway by numbers, and it makes you pine for the SHADOWS' patented twang. Yet with Merseyside's finest breathing down CLIFF's neck and making him look more than a bit passé by this point, RICHARD was savvy enough to perform a few neo-Beatles pop songs and at least attempt to claw back some of his fading street cred: despite blatant inspiration from 'Twist And Shout', 'On The Beach' isn't half bad, a spin-off Top 10 and the toughest track RICHARD had done in years. 'What've I Gotta Do' isn't so hot, but it's at least more animated than most of the dreary ballads. *BG*

Album rating: *4

– spinoff hits, etc. –

CLIFF RICHARD AND THE SHADOWS: On The Beach / A Matter Of Moments

Jun 64. (7") *(DB 7305)* [7] [–]

CLIFF RICHARD AND THE SHADOWS: Wonderful Life

Aug 64. (7"ep; mono/stereo) *(SEG 8338/ESG 7902)* [ ] [–]
– Wonderful life / Do you remember / What I've gotta do / Walkin'.

CLIFF RICHARD AND THE SHADOWS: Wonderful Life No.2

Oct 64. (7"ep; mono/stereo) *(SEG 8354/ESG 7903)* [–]
– A matter of moments / A girl in every port / A little imagination / In the stars.

CLIFF RICHARD AND THE SHADOWS: Hits From 'Wonderful Life'

Dec 64. (7"ep; mono/stereo) *(SEG 8376/ESG 7906)* [ ] [–]
– On the beach / We love a movie / Home / All kinds of people.

XANADU

1980 (US 93m) Universal Pictures (PG)

Film genre: Dance/Pop-Rock Musical fantasy

Top guns: dir: Robert Greenwald / s-w: Richard Christian Danus, Marc Reid Rubel ← ALMOST SUMMER

Stars: Olivia Newton-John *(Kira)* ← GREASE ← TOOMORROW, Gene Kelly *(Danny McGuire)*, Michael Beck *(Sonny Malone)*, James Sloyan *(Simpson)*, Dimitra Arliss *(Helen)*, Katie Hanley *(Sandra)* ← GODSPELL, Fred McCarren *(Richie)*, Ren Woods *(Jo)* ← HAIR ← YOUNGBLOOD ← CAR WASH ← SPARKLE, Coral Browne *(voice; Hera)*, Wilfred Hyde-White *(voice; Zeus)* ← the MAGIC CHRISTIAN, Matt Lattanzi *(young Danny McGuire)* → GREASE 2 → CATCH ME IF YOU CAN, **the Tubes:- Fee Waybill** *(performer)* → LADIES AND GENTLEMEN, THE FABULOUS STAINS → BILL & TED'S EXCELLENT ADVENTURE, **Vince Welnick** *(performer)* → LADIES AND GENTLEMEN, THE FABULOUS STAINS, **Prairie Prince, Bill Spooner, Roger Steen, Rick Anderson, Michael Cotten** *(themselves)* / Adolfo Quinones *(dancer)* → BREAKIN' → BREAKIN' 2: ELECTRIC BOOGALOO → LAMBADA, Miranda Garrison *(dancer)* → DIRTY DANCING → SALSA → the FORBIDDEN DANCE

Storyline: Kira, resident of Mt Helicon and daughter of Zeus, gets zapped down to L.A., where she excites the interest of hulking, lantern-jawed artist Sonny Malone. Frustrated in his job blowing up album sleeves, he agrees to partner silver fox Danny McGuire in his new club venture. Come opening night, McGuire glides around his club like a roller-skating Jools Holland, Kira performs some cosmic routines and Malone doesn't quite get the girl. As Sonny himself puts it: "this is the 80s". *BG*

Movie rating: *4

Visual: video + dvd

Off the record: the Tubes were in attendance here, a band responsible for the classic New Wave hit, 'White Punks On Dope'.

OLIVIA NEWTON-JOHN * // ELECTRIC LIGHT ORCHESTRA ** (score: Barry De Vorzon)

Jun 80. (lp/c) *M.C.A.; <6100> Jet; (JET LX/CX 526)* [4] Jul80 [2]
– Magic (*) / Suddenly (* & CLIFF RICHARD) / Dancin' (*) / Suspended in time (*) / Whenever you're away from me (* & GENE KELLY) // I'm alive (**) / The fall (**) / Don't walk away (**) / All over the world (**) / Xanadu (* & **). *<(cd-iss. Dec03 on 'Epic'; 486620-2)>*

S/track review: The credits and artwork trumpet an ELO album with OLIVIA NEWTON-JOHN guesting. What you actually get is a side's worth of mush from ONJ producer JOHN FARRAR, with JEFF LYNNE restricted to five songs (most of which wipe the floor with FARRAR's efforts). The bordering-on-mercenary single release schedule told its own story: six LYNNE efforts to FARRAR's two, one of which, 'Magic', was a half decent, Pat Benatar-goes-MOR No.1, the other a slushy collaboration with CLIFF RICHARD. There's also a grim chance to hear Fee Waybill and his TUBES go heavy metal; in the movie, the performance of 'Dancin' is at least self contained, on the soundtrack it alternates (in the same song) with a big band, perhaps Zeus' idea of a cosmic joke. ELO, for their part, carried over the symphonic disco which made the underrated 'Discovery' (1979) a guilty pleasure. 'XANADU' itself takes more than a few cues from Abba, but the combination of ONJ and ELO is an abbreviation made in fluffy pink heaven. It hovered ethereally around the top of the British charts for oh.. ages, making up for the unmitigated disaster that was the movie, a film with such a fearfully bad, beyond-kitsch reputation that the rest of LYNNE's efforts have rarely been afforded a second glance since. The truth is they're none too shabby, and if anyone can resist such shamelessly, seamlessly processed disco-pop as 'All Over The World', they're a better man/woman than me. A vocoder and chorus to die for made 'All Over The World' the campy hit that 'Last Train To London' should've been a year earlier. 'I'm Alive' was a respectable prologue to 'Livin' Thing', 'The Fall' a moody, multi-layered epic to match LYNNE's best late 70s ballads. Half a decent ELO album. *BG*

Album rating: *6

– spinoff hits, etc. –

ELECTRIC LIGHT ORCHESTRA: I'm Alive / Drum Dreams
May 80. (7") *<41246> (JET 179)* [16] [2]

OLIVIA NEWTON-JOHN: Magic / Whenever You're Away From Me
May 80. (7") *<41247> (JET 196)* [1] Aug80 [32]

OLIVIA NEWTON-JOHN & ELECTRIC LIGHT ORCHESTRA: Xanadu / OLIVIA NEWTON-JOHN: Fool Country
Jun 80. (7"/10"pink) *(JET/+10 185)* [–] [1]

OLIVIA NEWTON-JOHN & ELECTRIC LIGHT ORCHESTRA: Xanadu / OLIVIA NEWTON-JOHN & GENE KELLY: Whenever You're Away From Me
Jul 80. (7") *<41285>* [8] [–]

ELECTRIC LIGHT ORCHESTRA: All Over The World
Jul 80. (7"/10"blue) *(JET/+10 195)* [–] [11]

ELECTRIC LIGHT ORCHESTRA: All Over The World / Drum Dreams
Jul 80. (7") *<41289>* [13] [–]

OLIVIA NEWTON-JOHN & CLIFF RICHARD: Suddenly / OLIVIA NEWTON-JOHN: You Made Me Love You
Oct 80. (7") *<51007> <JET 7002)* [20] [15]

ELECTRIC LIGHT ORCHESTRA: Don't Walk Away
Nov 80. (7") *(JET 7004)* [–] [21]

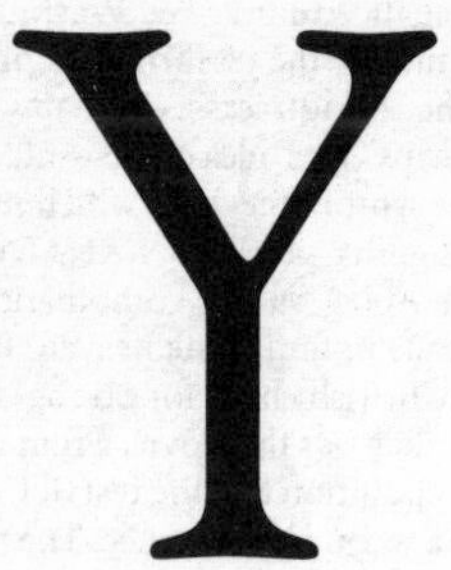

☐ "Weird Al" YANKOVIC segment
(⇒ UHF)

YELLOW SUBMARINE

1968 (UK 87m) Apple Corps / United Artists Pictures (U)

Film genre: animated Rock Musical fantasy

Top guns: dir: George Dunning / s-w: Erich Segal, Al Brodax, Jack Mendelsohn, Lee Minoff (+ story)

Voices: John Clive *(John Lennon)* ← SMASHING TIME / → NEVER TOO YOUNG TO ROCK, Geoffrey Hughes *(Paul McCartney)*, Peter Batten *(George Harrison)*, Paul Angelis *(Ringo Starr + Chief Blue Meanie)*, **the BEATLES:- John Lennon, Paul McCartney, George Harrison, Ringo Starr** *(singing voices)*, Dick Emery *(Nowhere Man + Max + Lord Mayor)* ← JUST FOR FUN / → LOOT, Lance Percival *(old Fred)* ← MRS. BROWN, YOU'VE GOT A LOVELY DAUGHTER ← IT'S ALL OVER TOWN

Storyline: Dazzling, technicolour psychedelic animation with a symbolic plot centering around Pepperland and the Blue Meanies' attempts to stifle musical expression, turn innocent people to stone and the generally spoil the peace'n'love vibe. Pepperland's Lord Admiral subsequently heads off in his submarine on a mission to London to enlist the help of, you guessed it, the Beatles. *BG*

Movie rating: *7.5

Visual: video + dvd

Off the record: Paul Angelis found fame in TV drama, Boys From The Black Stuff, while Geoffrey Hughes became Eddie Yeats in Brit Soap, Coronation Street.

—

the BEATLES (with GEORGE MARTIN *)

Jan 69. (lp; mono/stereo) *Apple; (PMC/PCS 7070) <153>* [4] [2]
– Yellow submarine / Only a northern song / All together now / Hey bulldog / It's all too much / All you need is love / Pepperland (*) / Sea of time (*) / Sea of holes (*) / Sea of monsters (*) / March of the Meanies (*) / Pepperland laid waste (*) / Yellow submarine in Pepperland. *(re-iss. Aug87; CDP 746445-2); hit UK 60) (re-iss. Nov88 lp/c; PCS/TC-PCS 7070)*

S/track review: The BEATLES themselves had nothing to do with the film, and their contribution to the soundtrack wasn't that much more substantial. Of the four new songs, only two – 'Hey Bulldog', a great, winding semi-snarl traceable in Oasis, and the 'Sesame Street'-style 'All Together Now' – were credited to Lennon/McCartney. The other two were Harrison's: 'It's All Too Much' is as convincing an excuse as any for 'YELLOW SUBMARINE's existence, a six-minute splurge using most of the psychedelic tricks in the band's book and some more besides. The less exuberant, equally lysergic 'Only A Northern Song' stands as the only BEATLES track to reference free jazz. Together with the whimsical title song, 'All You Need Is Love', and George Martin's makeweight score, they constitute what is still universally regarded as the weakest album in the band's canon. But then a weak BEATLES album is a strong album in almost any other terms. To tie in with the film's re-release in 1999, the good folks at 'E.M.I.' dreamed up the concept of a 'Songtrack' (actually a pretty accurate description of most modern soundtracks), substituting Martin's score for the rest of the previously released BEATLES material originally heard in the movie, and subtly remixing the original part-mono recordings. What you get, then, is a halfway house between a spruced-up, alternative best of and a soundtrack. Dandy for BEATLES beginners and novice Submariners, less than essential for fans, unless you really must hear those 'Eleanor Rigby' strings in stereo. *BG*

Album rating: *6 / Songtrack: *7

– spinoff releases, etc. –

the BEATLES: Yellow Submarine (Songtrack)

Sep 99. (cd/c/lp) *Parlophone; (<5 21481-2/-4/-1>)* [8] [15]
– Yellow submarine / Hey bulldog / Eleanor Rigby / Love you to / All together now / Lucy in the sky with diamonds / Think for yourself / Sgt. Pepper's lonely hearts club band / With a little help from my friends / Baby you're a rich man / Only a northern song / All you need is love / When I'm sixty-four / Nowhere man / It's all too much.

☐ YO LA TENGO segment
(⇒ I SHOT ANDY WARHOL)

YOU GOT SERVED

2004 (US 95m) Screen Gems (PG-13)

Film genre: teen/Dance Musical comedy drama

Top guns: s-w + dir: Chris Stokes

Stars: Marques Houston *(Elgin)* ← HOUSE PARTY 3, **Omari(on) Grandberry** *(David)* → FEEL THE NOISE, **J-Boog/Jarell Houston** *(Rico)*, **Raz-B/DeMario Thornton** *(Vick)*, **Lil' Fizz/Dreux Frederic** *(Rashaan)*, Jennifer Freeman *(Liyah)*, Marty Dew *(Marty)*, **Jerome Jones** *(Sonny)* ← HOUSE PARTY 3 / → FEEL THE NOISE, Steve Harvey *(Mr. Rad)* ← the FIGHTING TEMPTATIONS, Meagan Good *(Beautifull)* → ROLL BOUNCE → STOMP THE YARD, Christopher Jones *(Wade)*, **Lil' Kim** *(herself)*, Garland Spencer *(B-Boy)* ← MOONWALKER, Christopher Short *(dancer)* → SAVE THE LAST DANCE 2 → STOMP THE YARD

Storyline: Teen homies Elgin and David are thick as thieves, whether delivering the local kingpin's gear or busting their moves in "street" dancing competitions with their double jointed posse. They quickly "lose the love", though, when Elgin – left to deliver the goods on his own as David canoodles with his little sis – gets his coupon busted instead. Will they make up in time to impress star judge Lil' Kim at the televised Big Bounce contest? Do we care? *BG*

Movie rating: *3

Visual: dvd

Off the record: Prior to their time in B2K, **Jerome Jones & Marques Houston** were part of Immature, an R&B trio with several hits including 'Never Lie', 'We Got It' & 'Please Don't Go'. *MCS*

—

B2K & Various Artists (score: Tyler Bates)

Dec 03. (cd) *Urban-Epic; <EK 90744> (514975-2)* [34] [ ]
– Badaboom (w/ FABOLOUS) / Do that thing (w/ LIL' KIM) / Take it to the floor / Sprung / Out the hood / Streets is callin' / Fizzo got flow / Happy (w/ JHENE) / Smile (MARQUES HOUSTON) / Smellz like a party (O'RYAN & RUFUS BLAQ) / The one (ATL & THE

SERIOUS CREW) / Can I get it back (XSO DRIVE & RED CAFE) / Ante up (Robbin Hoodz theory) (M.O.P. & FUNKMASTER FLEX). *(UK+=)* – Uh huh – Ron G remix.

S/track review: Just as the movie was a rug-cutting masterclass adrift in a sub-'Home And Away' soap opera, the album is an unabashed B2K showcase rather than a genuine soundtrack. No DMX or De La Soul then, but plenty of tightly marshalled odes to the female posterior, on the strength of which it's difficult to imagine B2K's passing being mourned too seriously ('YOU GOT SERVED' turned out to be their epitaph). The likes of 'Badaboom', 'Take It To The Floor' and the L'il Kim-supported 'Do That Thing' may be the epitome of MTV boys trying to be ghetto lovermen, but they're infinitely more listenable than the glut of bumfluff ballads. Those looking for heavy-duty hip hop are going to be disappointed: only 'Ante Up' by M.O.P. (with FUNKMASTER FLEX) rhymes with any real conviction. Smellz like a cop-out. *BG*

Album rating: *4

– spinoff hits, etc. –

B2K: Badaboom (w/ FABOLOUS) / Take It To The Floor
Dec 03. (12") *<76716>* [59] [–]

B2K: Badaboom (w/ FABOLOUS) / (mixes) / Do That Thing (mixes)
Mar 04. (12"/cd-s) *(674751-6/-2)* [–] [ ]

B2K: Do That Thing (w/ LIL' KIM) / Out The Hood
Mar 04. (12") *<76691>* [ ] [ ]

YOU LIGHT UP MY LIFE

1977 (US 90m) Columbia Pictures

Film genre: romantic showbiz/Pop-music drama

Top guns: dir + s-w: Joseph Brooks

Stars: Didi Conn *(Lauri Robinson)* → GREASE → ALMOST SUMMER → GREASE 2, Joe Silver *(Sy Robinson)* → MAGIC STICKS, Michael Zaslow *(Cris Nolan)*, Stephen Nathan *(Ken Rothenberg)*, Melanie Mayron *(Annie Gerrard)* ← CAR WASH, **Jerry Keller** *(conductor)*, **Joseph Brooks** *(creative director)*

Storyline: Lauri Robinson is an aspiring actress who tries her hand at comedy to please her father. But she's not cut out for stand-up gags and starts going to film auditions. Although engaged to Ken, she has a one night stand with director Chris and think's she's a cert to get the part in Chris' next film. Lo and behold Chris gives the part to his latest amour, leaving Lauri in the lurch with her love life even more confused. *JZ*

Movie rating: *3.5

Visual: video + dvd

Off the record: **Jerry Keller** composed music for the movie 'Angel In My Pocket', while he also had a hit in 1959, 'Here Comes Summer'. *MCS*

JOSEPH BROOKS (composer)

Oct 77. (lp) *Arista; <AB 4159> (SPART 1038)* [17] Jan78 [ ]
– You light up my life / The morning of my life / It's a long way from Brooklyn / Phone call / You light up my life (instrumental) / Rolling the chords / Do you have a piano / Ride to Chris' house / California daydreams / You light up my life. *<cd-iss. 2002 on 'Homeland'; 189>*

S/track review: 'YOU LIGHT UP MY LIFE' will be remembered for several things, but not filmmaker JOSEPH BROOKS' score; composed, arranged and conducted by, as it says on the sleeve. Okay, the title track won an Oscar at 1978's prestigious awards ceremony, but it wasn't (the LP version sung by) KASEY CISYK that held the trophy high, but DEBBY BOONE, daughter of RnR crooner Pat Boone, who indeed stole the show. No.1 in America for 10 weeks while the film was being premiered, 'You Light Up My Life', was apparently "borrowed" (from BROOKS) by film/music label mogul, Mike Curb, who literally cashed in on the slightly more identifiable DEBBY BOONE. For some in the business, tears of joy, for one person tears of rage, but that's Hollywood for you. One could just close the book right there, but unfortunately there was more than one song (although that one was repeated three times, including a JOE BROOKS instrumental). BROOKS also lent a hand to some vocalising, along with the aforementioned KASEY, JERRY KELLER, LESLEY MILLER, KENNY KAREN and RON DANTE, all spread their uplifting messages across both sides of the Top 20 album. 'The Morning Of My Life' would've been perfect for the likes of Abba, but here it lacks the climactic punch, while the country-vs-orchestral 'It's A Long Way From Brooklyn' must've got right up Barry Manilow's nose. Working around some of BROOKS' light-weight instrumentals, were Abba/Carpenters/Manilow-type cuts (albeit country-fied) such as 'Rolling The Chords' and 'Do You Have A Piano'. Even his own troubadour-like vocals on the melancholy, Cohen-esque 'California Daydreams', were out of place here. It'd all been done many times before. *MCS*

Album rating: *3

– spinoff hits, etc. –

DEBBY BOONE; You Light Up My Life / (non-OST song)
Jul 77. (7") *Curb-Warners; <8446>* [ ] [–]

DEBBY BOONE: You Light Up My Life / (non-OST song)
Aug 77. (7") *Curb-Warners; <8455> (K 17043)* [1] Dec77 [48]

KACEY CISYK: You Light Up My Life / JOSEPH BROOKS: You Light Up My Life
Oct 77. (7") *<0287>* [80] [–]

YOUNG, HOT 'N' NASTY TEENAGE CRUISERS

1977 (US 83m) Marden Films (X)

Film genre: hardcore seXual Rock'n'roll Musical comedy/spoof

Top guns: s-w + dir: **Johnny Legend**, Tom Denucci

Stars: Serena *(Serena)*, Lynne Elaine/Margulies), **Tony Conn** *(Willy)*, Christine Shaffer *(Babsy Beaudine)*, Jerry Sokorski *(Whitey)*, **Rollin' Colin Winsky** *(himself)*, **Johnny Legend** *(Mambo Reaves)* → MAN ON THE MOON, **Chuck Higgins** *(performer)*, **Mac Curtis** *(performer)*, **Alvis Wayne** *(performer)*, **Charlie Feathers** *(performer)*, **Ray Campi** *(performer)* → BLUE SUEDE SHOES, **Jackie Lee** *(performer)*, **Kid Thomas** *(performer)*, John Holmes *(Moby)*

Storyline: Babsy Beaudine escapes from jail and goes on the hunt for men in and around the Modesto, California area. Others cruise around and get naked at every opportunity on one uneventful but crazee night. Not for the young or fans of American Graffiti. *MCS*

Movie rating: *3

Visual: none (no audio OST)

Off the record: Rockabilly tracks in the film include:- CHUCK HIGGINS ('Bip Bop Boom' & 'Don't Touch Me'), BILLY ZOOM AND THE BAD BOYS ('Bad Boy', 'Crazy, Crazy Lovin' & 'Say When'), 'Slip, Slip, Slippin' In' (MAC CURTIS), 'I Wanna Eat Your Pudding' (ALVIS WAYNE), 'That Certain Female' (CHARLIE FEATHERS), 'Well, Baby' (KID THOMAS), 'Eager Boy' (RAY CAMPI), 'Hungry Hill' (JACKIE LEE), 'Birmingham Mama' (TONY CONN), 'Red Hot Mama' (ROLLIN' COLIN WINSKY), **Johnny Legend** ('Hot Rocks' & 'Are You Up To It?'); this man scored two hardcore sex films, 'Tower Of Love' & 'Sexual Sensory Perception' – both 1975 – former as Martin Margulies. *MCS*

the YOUNG ONES

aka WONDERFUL TO BE YOUNG!

1961 (UK 108m) Warner-Pathe (U)

Film genre: Rock'n'roll Musical comedy

Top guns: dir: Sidney J. Furie → WONDERFUL LIFE → LITTLE FAUSS AND BIG HALSY → LADY SINGS THE BLUES / s-w: Ronald Cass + Peter Myers → SUMMER HOLIDAY → WONDERFUL LIFE

Stars: Cliff RICHARD *(Nicky Black)*, Robert Morley *(Hamilton Black)* → FINDERS KEEPERS, Carole Gray *(Toni)*, Richard O'Sullivan *(Ernest)* → WONDERFUL LIFE → EVERY DAY'S A HOLIDAY, Melvyn Hayes *(Jimmy)* → SUMMER HOLIDAY → WONDERFUL LIFE, Teddy Green *(Chris)* → SUMMER HOLIDAY, Gerald Harper *(Watts)* → WONDERFUL LIFE, **the Shadows:- Hank B. Marvin** *(lead guitar)* → SUMMER HOLIDAY → WONDERFUL LIFE → FINDERS KEEPERS, **Bruce Welch** *(rhythm guitar)* → SUMMER HOLIDAY → WONDERFUL LIFE → FINDERS KEEPERS, **Jet Harris** *(bass)* → JUST FOR FUN, **Tony Meehan** *(drummer)* → JUST FOR FUN

Storyline: Property developer Hamilton Black has his greedy eyes set on a piece of land containing only that den of juvenile delinquency, the youth club. Unless Nicky and his chums can find the money to pay off Hamilton (who's also Nicky's dad) the bulldozers will soon be moving in. Enter the "Mystery Singer" who touts his first concert on pirate radio to raise the cash. I wonder who on earth the singer could be? *JZ*

Movie rating: *5.5

Visual: video + dvd

Off the record: The SHADOWS (see below)

—

CLIFF RICHARD AND THE SHADOWS (composer: Stanley Black)

Dec 61. (lp) *Columbia; (33SX 1384/SCX 3397)* [1] [–]
– Friday night (w/ orchestra) / Got a funny feeling / Peace pipe (the SHADOWS) / The young ones / Nothing's impossible (CLIFF RICHARD & GRAZINA FRAME) / All for one / Lessons in love / No-one for me but Nicky (GRAZINA FRAME) / What d'you know, we've got a show – Vaudeville routine: Have a smile for everyone you meet / When the girl in your arms (is the girl in your heart) / Mambo: Just dance – Mood mambo (orchestra) / The savage (the SHADOWS) / We say yeah! *(re-iss. Apr83 on 'E.M.I.' lp/c; EMS/TCEMS 1008) (re-iss. Apr88 on 'Music for Pleasure' lp/c; MFP/TC-MFP 5823) (cd-iss. ; CDMFP 6020) <US cd-iss. 2000 on 'E.M.I.'; 52057>*

S/track review: If the first of Cliff's full-tilt, technicolour musicals entailed the hiring of various studio orchestras to fill out the arrangements, resulting in cloying, cockney-sparrar music hall trifles like 'Friday Night', the best parts of this soundtrack hinge on the haunting synergy – by this point finely honed – between the SHADOWS' vibrato charm and RICHARDS' sultry, nostalgic vocals, not least in the career-defining title track, one of the man's biggest No.1 hits and subsequent titular mascot of one of the most pioneering alternative comedy shows of the 80s. And if he'd finally given up ambitions of becoming the British Elvis, Presley was still the man's closest creative peer: the Stateside influence hangs heavy over the likes of 'Got A Funny Feeling', the gutsy 'We Say Yeah' and especially 'When The Girl In Your Arms', in which Cliff abandons his slightly fey ballad style in favour of a smouldering croon. Throw in the gorgeous '(It's) Wonderful To Be Young' and you have a seriously good record which at least competes with ELVIS' contemporary Hollywood offerings and arguably outstrips them. *BG*

Album rating: *5

– spinoff hits, etc. –

CLIFF RICHARD AND THE SHADOWS: The Young Ones / We Say Yeah!

Jan 62. (7") *(DB 4761)* [1] [ ]

CLIFF RICHARD AND THE SHADOWS: Hits From 'The Young Ones'

May 62. (7"ep) *(SEG 8159)* [ ] [–]
– The young ones / Got a funny feeling / Lessons in love / We say yeah!

the YOUNG PERSON'S GUIDE TO BECOMING A ROCK STAR

1998 (UK 35m x 6 epi TV-mini) Company / Bronco Films – Channel 4

Film genre: Pop/Rock-music/Showbiz comedy drama

Top guns: dir: Sheree Folkson, Kieron J. Walsh / s-w: Bryan Elsley

Stars: Ciaran McMenamin *(Jez MacAllister)*, Simone Lahbib *(Fiona Johnstone)*, Nicola Stapleton *(Joe Nardone)*, Stephen McCole *(Wullie Macboyne)* ← the ACID HOUSE, Duncan Marwick *(Psycho MacPhail)*, Gerard Butler *(Marty Claymore)*, Eric Barlow *(Kenny Dick)*, Frank Gallagher *(Ossie)* ← SHOCK 'EM DEAD, Forbes Masson *(Art Stilton)*, Barbara Rafferty *(Alice)* ← the ACID HOUSE ← TUTTI FRUTTI ← the WICKER MAN, Keith Allen *(Slick Sloan)* ← TRAINSPOTTING / → 24 HOUR PARTY PEOPLE

Storyline: Following the life and times of Glaswegian rock band, Jocks-Wa-Hey, as they try to break through into the big time. As things fail to progress the group try everything from changing their style of music to finding more talented players, and finally with the help of shady manager Art Stilton they release a top ten single. But who's going to foot the huge bills they've run up along the way? The Americans bought the show and named it 'MY GUIDE TO BECOMING A ROCK STAR'. *JZ*

Movie rating: *7.5

Visual: video

Off the record: Keith Allen is the father of cheeky cockney singer, Lily Allen, who's recently topped the UK charts (2006) with 'Smile'. GUY PRATT was basically a high-profile session bassman with the likes of Killing Joke, Icehouse and PINK FLOYD on his CV. *MCS*

—

Original Cast (co-songwriter: Guy Pratt)

Nov 98. (cd) *Channel 4 – Virgin; (VTCD 231)* [ ] [–]
– Lassie / No.1 (live) / Righteous / I can't stop singing / We love Cowdenbeath / Fiona / Shake / Happy / Martin the marmaset / Why won't you shag me? / Masquerade / The jokes on you / I want to die / Wahey / No.1 (demo).

S/track review: Released rather anachronistically as the powers of lad-rock and Britpop waned 'The YOUNG PERSON'S GUIDE TO BECOMING A ROCK STAR' took its lead more from the Manchester scene (Oasis, Stone Roses, Happy Mondays, etc.) and the likes of Primal Scream, despite the fictional band 'Jocks-Wa-Hey' supposedly emanating from Glasgow. Does anyone remember the Gyres. 'Lassie' is a decent stomping opener, but is symptomatic of the album as a whole in suffering from embarrassingly mawkish lyrics and delivery that miss the mark in capturing what it actually feels like to be a "Young Person". Indeed, the writing team of Robbie Williams and Guy Chambers on 'Righteous' tell you all you need to know about this record's rock credentials, with its unashamed Oasis mimicry, also unavoidably present on the tedious knock-off acoustic ballad 'Happy'. More unimaginative dross follows, like 'No.1' and 'Shake', with their strained sneering vocals now completely in a Manchester register. 'The YOUNG PERSON'S GUIDE . . .' finally hits its stride with 'Why Won't You Shag Me?' an undeniably catchy slice of Brit-rock by anyone's standards, and the decent slow-burning 'I Want To Die'. You can even catch glimpses of the second wave of Oasis-influenced bands here as there are future echoes of the likes of Stereophonics, Feeder and even the Kaiser Chiefs. Meanwhile 'This Masquerade' is an attempt at a mature piano-led lament, which could even pass as a half-decent

Tom Waits recital if wasn't for the piss-poor, clichéd angsty and earnest lyrics. One moment of true class is the out of place 'Fiona' with its sinister Chemical Brothers' beats. 'We Love Cowdenbeath' is a contradictory smug, Wet Wet Wet satirising attempt at humour, but ultimately this is an abysmally weak record and we can all rest safe in the knowledge that Jocks-Wa-Hey were only fictional. *LF*

Album rating: *5.5

the YOUNG SWINGERS

1963 (US 71m b&w) 20th Century Fox

Film genre: Rock'n'roll Musical teen comedy

Top guns: dir: Maury Dexter → SURF PARTY → WILD ON THE BEACH / s-w: Harry Spalding ← TEENAGE MILLIONAIRE / → SURF PARTY → WILD ON THE BEACH

Stars: Rod Lauren *(Mel Hudson)*, **Molly Bee** *(Vicki Crawford)* ← SUMMER LOVE, **Gene McDaniels** *(Fred Lewis)* ← IT'S TRAD, DAD!, Jack Larson *(Pete Mundy)* ← TEENAGE MILLIONAIRE, Jack Younger *(Irving Bird)*, Jo Helton *(Roberta Crawford)*, Justin Smith *(Bruce Webster)* → WILD ON THE BEACH, Jerry Summers *(Roger Kelly)* → SURF PARTY

Storyline: Land magnate Roberta Crawford has her eyes on a juicy spot for a new high rise office block – which also happens to be the local cool dudes' hangout. When singer Mel Hudson refuses to sell, things take a disastrous turn when the club is mysteriously burned to the ground, and Roberta's niece Vicki is the prime suspect. But all's well that ends well and as romance blooms between Mel and Vicki a change of heart saves the day. *JZ*

Movie rating: *2.5

Visuals: video + dvd (no audio OST)

Off the record: Rod Lauren released one LP, 'I'm Rod Lauren', in 1961 for 'RCA Victor'.

YOUR CHEATIN' HEART

1964 (US 100m b&w) M.G.M. Films (PG-13)

Film genre: Country-music biopic drama

Top guns: dir: Gene Nelson ← KISSIN' COUSINS ← HOOTENANNY HOOT / → HARUM SCARUM → the COOL ONES / s-w: Stanford Whitmore

Stars: George Hamilton *(Hank Williams)* ← LOOKING FOR LOVE ← WHERE THE BOYS ARE, Susan Oliver *(Audrey Williams)* ← LOOKING FOR LOVE, Red Buttons *(Shorty Younger)* → the STORY OF US, Arthur O'Connell *(Fred Rose)* ← KISSIN' COUSINS ← FOLLOW THAT DREAM ← HOUND-DOG MAN ← APRIL LOVE, Shary Marshall *(Ann Younger)*, Rex Ingram *(Teetot)*, Chris Crosby *(Sam Priddy)*, Donald Losby *(young Hank Williams)*, Hortense Petra *(Wilma; the cashier)* ← GET YOURSELF A COLLEGE GIRL ← KISSIN' COUSINS ← DON'T KNOCK THE TWIST / → WHEN THE BOYS MEET THE GIRLS → HOLD ON! → RIOT ON SUNSET STRIP, Rex Holman *(Charley Bybee)*, Phil Arnold *(pie eating contest person)* ← GO, JOHNNY, GO! / → HOLD ON → GOOD TIMES → SKIDOO, Bruno VeSota *(Joe)* ← DADDY-O ← ROCK ALL NIGHT ← CARNIVAL ROCK / → the GIRLS ON THE BEACH

Storyline: B&W biopic of singing legend Hank Williams, country music's original live fast/die young genius. Tracing his life from a deep south childhood, to his Fred Rose-nurtured arrival on the stage of the Grand Ole Opry and his alcohol and drug-fuelled demise. *BG*

Movie rating: *5.5

Visual: video

Off the record: *HANK WILLIAMS* (b. Hiram King Williams, 17 Sep'23, Garland, Alabama, USA). After a troublesome upbringing, he subsequently formed his first band, the Drifting Cowboys, who toured the Honky Tonk saloon bars as the 30s turned into the 40s. When the US of A decided to join the Second World War, Hank was fortunate enough not to be called up due to his bad back and he soon met soon-to-be divorced Audrey, whom he married in 1944; it was she who pestered publisher Fred Rose to listen to him singing in a hotel lobby. The famous partner of Roy Acuff was duly impressed and in 1946, after the war had ended, he was asked to scout out a new country star by 'Sterling' records. Rose, of course, sent them Hank, who cut his first discs shortly afterwards. Three singles later, he was taken by Frank Walker to the new 'M.G.M.' stable in 1947, where they released 'Move It On Over'. Walker then had him booked into the Louisiana Hayride, a weekly country radio show that was second only to the Grand Ole Opry. Troubles at home took precedence, however, as his wife and mother argued about his late night drinking binges. Early in 1949, he entered the country charts with standard, 'Lovesick Blues', propelling him overnight to Opry status. Following the birth of his son, HANK WILLIAMS, JNR., he brought the house down at the Opry and made history with six encores. In 1952 his relationship with Audrey had deteriorated to such an extent that he was drinking himself into oblivion and turning up on stage completely out of it. When Audrey and Hank Jnr. moved out of the family home, his drinking took over completely. By the time he returned to the studio in June of that year, however, the songs were coming thick and fast; classics 'Jambalaya', 'Your Cheatin' Heart' and 'You Win Again' were all recorded during these sessions, demonstrating the troubled Williams at his heartbreaking best. He tried desperately to beat his alcoholism (he married for a second time) by spending time at a detox sanitarium, all to no avail. Tragically, in the early hours of the 1st January 1953, his 17 year-old chauffeur found him dead in the back seat. Two days previously, while his plane was being delayed due to bad weather, he had downed a bottle of spirits while taking morphine in his Knoxville hotel room. Desperate to make an Ohio gig, he had phoned the chauffeur to pick his Cadillac up and drive him there. Mystery then, shrouded his death, when a rushed coroner gave a verdict as heart failure, although many still think it was an attempted suicide slow to hit fatal impact. Meanwhile, his record company 'M.G.M.' announced he was killed in a car crash! It wasn't laid to rest there, as even at his well attended funeral (estimated 20,000+), he wasn't even buried in his plot as it was too small!. Instead they dug up two nearby graves and put him in there!. A few days later, legal battles ensued between the unusual alliance of his ex-wife Audrey and his mother Lily, who fought out court battles with his recent wife Billie Jean. After around 20 painstaking years (although not for their lawyers), Billie Jean won his estate. To make matters even crazier, a biopic film 'YOUR CHEATIN' HEART' was released late in '64; his son HANK WILLIAMS Jnr. sang the soundtrack of his fathers' material. Billie Jean duly sued 'M.G.M.', claiming the movie portrayed her as a slut, although this was hardly surprising as ex-wife Audrey was employed as the film's technical advisor! Hank Jnr. carried on with his own solo career over the next 30 years, recording many of his fathers' classics. *MCS & BG*

—

HANK WILLIAMS JR. (composer: Hank Williams)

Dec 64. (lp) *M.G.M.; <SE 4260> (MGM-CS 6081)* 16 Mar65 ☐
– Your cheatin' heart / Long gone lonesome blues / I saw the light / I can't help it (if I'm still in love with you) / Jambalaya (on the bayou) (with saxophone) / Cold cold heart / Jambalaya (on the bayou) (with electric guitar) / Hey good lookin' (with saxophone) / Hey good lookin' (with electric guitar) / I'm so lonesome I could cry / Kaw-liga / You win again / Ramblin' man. *(cd-iss. Apr90 on 'M.G.M.'+=; CDMGM 18)* – The FASTEST GUITAR ALIVE (Roy Orbison) *<(cd-iss. May02 on 'Rhino'+=; 8122 72733-2)>* – Acoustic versions:- I saw the light / Jambalaya (on the bayou) / Kaw-liga / I'm so lonesome I could cry / Long gone lonesome blues / Cold cold heart / You win again / There'll be no teardrops tonight / I saw the light / I can't help it (if I'm still in love with you) / Ramblin' man.

S/track review: On first listen, it's difficult to believe that the soundtrack to 'YOUR CHEATIN' HEART', a biopic about Hank Williams, was sung by his 15-year-old son, HANK WILLIAMS, JNR. Such is the maturity in his voice and its similarity to his father's that it makes the comprehension almost impossible. The title track is performed with an understanding that belies HANK JNR's years while songs like 'I Can't Help It (If I'm Still In Love With You)', 'I Saw The Light' and 'You Win Again' are all sung with emotion and intensity. 'Long Gone Lonesome Blues', a track which both father and son had hits with some fourteen years apart, and before the film was made, is also given a good airing while 'Cold, Cold Heart' is sublime. Two versions of both 'Jambalaya (On The Bayou)' and 'Hey Good Lookin'' are offered, one each with saxophone and one each with electric guitar, the latter version of each being better, with the former versions and sounding more like television commercials. Overall it was a good effort from HANK WILLIAMS JNR. with some good renditions of his father's songs but it isn't anything special and you would probably be better off just buying a Hank Williams compilation. *CM*

Album rating: *6

Z

ZABRISKIE POINT

1970 (US 112m) Metro-Goldwyn-Mayer (R)

Film genre: ensemble/road movie

Top guns: s-w: Michelangelo Antonioni (+ dir) ← BLOW-UP, **Sam Shepard** → RENALDO AND CLARA → PARIS, TEXAS → FAR NORTH, Franco Rossetti (as Fred Gardner), Tonino Guerra, Clare Peploe

Stars: Mark Frechette *(Mark)*, Daria Halprin *(Daria)* ← REVOLUTION, Rod Taylor *(Lee Allen)*, Paul Fix *(cafe owner)* → PAT GARRETT & BILLY THE KID, G.D. Spradlin *(Lee's associate)* → ONE ON ONE, Bill Garaway *(Morty)*, Kathleen Cleaver *(Kathleen)*, Harrison Ford *(airport worker)* → AMERICAN GRAFFITI → MORE AMERICAN GRAFFITI → BLADE RUNNER → WORKING GIRL

Storyline: Michelangelo Antonioni's stylish and visually breathtaking yet ultimately flawed attempt to document America's counter-cultural ferment. Rather than treking to Woodstock, hippy rebel Mark hijacks a plane and flies into the arid expanse of the California desert where he couples with fellow free spirit Daria amidst considerable sexual license and clichéd anti-establishment activity. *BG*

Movie rating: *5.5

Visual: video

Off the record: Actor Mark Frechette was arrested on armed robbery charges not long after the film was completed; he'd donated $60,000 earnings to a commune. His accomplice was killed in the process of the alleged crime and Mark was sentenced to 15 years; he died in prison under suspicious circumstances in September '75, the result of a 150-pound weight on his throat.

Various Artists (feat. PINK FLOYD *)

Mar 70. (lp) *Polydor; (2315 002)* [–] [ ]

– Heart beat, pig meat (*) / Brother Mary (KALEIDOSCOPE) / Dark star (the GRATEFUL DEAD) / Crumbling land (*) / Tennessee waltz (PATTI PAGE) / Sugar babe (the YOUNGBLOODS) / Love scene (JERRY GARCIA) / I wish I was a single girl again (ROSCOE HOLCOMB) / Mickey's tune (KALEIDOSCOPE) / Dance of death (JOHN FAHEY) / Come in number 51, your time is up (*). *(re-iss. Jan89 on 'M.C.A.' lp/c; MCA/+C 25032) (re-iss. Apr90 on 'M.G.M.' lp/c; GO/TCGO 2029) (cd-iss. Apr90; CZ 285) <US cd-iss. 1992 on 'Sony'; 52417> <d-cd re-iss. 1997 on 'Rhino'+=; R2 72462> (d-cd-iss. Oct97 on 'Premier'+=; R 23364-2)* – Love scene improvisations (takes 1-4) (JERRY GARCIA) / Country song (*) / Unknown song (*) / Love scene (version 4) (*) / Love scene (version 6) (*). *<lp re-iss. 2003 on '4 Men With Beards'; 123>*

S/track review: The 60s had long stopped swinging by the time Antonioni got round to his controversial 'Blow Up' follow-up yet this soundtrack evoked the desert landscapes and counter-cultural disillusionment as acutely as Herbie Hancock's playful soul-jazz had evoked Swinging London. Despite its entire score originally being pencilled in for PINK FLOYD and even having a glaringly incongruous Roy Orbison song tacked on by 'M.G.M.' at the last minute, the finished sequence of music for 'ZABRISKIE POINT' stands as one of the era's more interesting aural collages. 'FLOYD may have bookended the soundtrack with the ominous heartbeat and organ-jamming broadcast detritus of 'Heart Beat, Pig Meat', and the infernal psychedelia of 'Come In Number 51, Your Time Is Up', but – in the final instance – this record suggests hippies getting back to basics, taking solace in country blues, country harmonies and the pensive, mystical angularity of neo-folk minimalism. JOHN FAHEY supplied the latter, although it was an excerpt from his haunting mid-60s classic, 'Dance Of Death', rather than the solo-guitar material he wrote at Antonioni's behest. While both 'FLOYD and KALEIDOSCOPE also fell afoul of the director's notoriously stringent requirements, FAHEY actually ended up coming to blows with him. JERRY GARCIA seems to have had an easier ride, reeling off a series of remarkable solo acoustic improvisations on the 'M.G.M.' soundstage rather than jetting off to Rome. His ringing, impressionistic sketches – detailed on the second disc of the 'Turner Classics' CD re-issue – were pooled to create the version of 'Love Scene' which appeared on the original album. As for the record's somewhat eccentric programming, it's seemingly down in large part to underground FM radio DJ Don Hall, employed by Antonioni as music co-ordinator. Quoted in the reissue's bulging sleevenotes, he maintains "There was no idea, when we were doing the film, that a rock soundtrack meant everything had to be hard, intense, electric music". If the Byrds, whose 'Notorious Byrd Brothers' psych-country era the 'FLOYD, fascinatingly enough, approximated – layered harmonies and all – on 'Crumbling Land', were one of the first bands to look to Nashville, even psychedelic pioneers like the YOUNGBLOODS and KALEIDOSCOPE got in on the action-'Sugar Babe' and 'Brother Mary' remain as vacuously pleasurable 3-minute snatches of country rock as you'll hear this side of the Joshua Tree Parkway. PATTI PAGE's 'Tennessee Waltz' and ROSCOE HOLCOMB's 'I Wish I Was A Single Girl Again' take the sepia country nostalgia even further back in time. All that's missing is a Carter Family classic. Save for The GRATEFUL DEAD's 'Dark Star' excerpt, it's PINK FLOYD who provide the "intense, electric" stuff although even then, the out-takes featured on the re-issue's bonus disc err on the rootsy side. The late '69 recording dates position the material between 'Umma Gumma' (1969) and 'Atom Heart Mother', and inevitably the likes of 'Country Song' and the finger-picking 'Unknown Song' pertain to that soft-focus psych-ballad mode which served them so well in their transitional, post-Syd Barrett phase; neither of these compositions would've been out of place on 'MORE' (1969), or even 'LA VALLEE – Obscured By Clouds' (1972). PINK FLOYD's own attempts at scoring the infamous 'Love Scene' are also documented, one an uncharacteristically forthright electric blues and the other an equally unusual – at least in the context of the 'FLOYD – and rather elegant jazz piano piece. With so many 60s rock soundtracks taking the decibel count to distraction, 'ZABRISKIE POINT' remains not only an engrossing artefact but proof that sometimes it's the quiet revolutions which endure. *BG*

Album rating: *7.5

ZACHARIAH

1971 (US 92m) Cinerama / ABC Pictures (R)

Film genre: hybrid western Rock-music drama

Top guns: dir: George Englund / s-w: Joe Massot, Peter Bergman, Philip Proctor, David Ossman, Philip Austin *(latter 4 with FIRESIGN THEATER)*

Stars: John Rubinstein *(Zachariah)*, Don Johnson *(Matthew)* → ELVIS AND THE BEAUTY QUEEN → the HOT SPOT, Patricia Quinn *(Belle Starr)* ← ALICE'S RESTAURANT, **Doug Kershaw** *(fiddler)* → MEDICINE BALL CARAVAN, Dick Van Patten *(the dude)* ← CHARLY, William Challee *(old man)*, **Country Joe & The Fish:- Country Joe McDONALD, Barry Melton** *(the Cracker band)* / **White Lightnin'** *(old man's band)*, **Elvin Jones** *(Job Cain)*, **the James Gang:- Joe Walsh** *(vocalist/guitarist)* → the BLUES BROTHERS

Storyline: A drum kit, speaker stacks and the bleached terrain of the American west: 'Zachariah's striking opening sequence has a windmilling Joe Walsh redefining desert rock, before the action switches to include the pre-electricity trappings of horses, carts and blacksmiths. The handsome-verging-on-the-homoerotic pairing of Zachariah and his salon-fresh blonde sidekick Matthew (a dead ringer for a young Gram Parsons) end up joining local rockers-cum-outlaws the Crackers after Zac fatally draws on a local loudmouth in a barfight. While Crackers leader Country Joe gets carried away to the point of fantasising about gig-robberies in Clapham Junction and Madagascar, the restless cowboys end up at a skull-hammered saloon in the high desert where black sharp-shooter Job Cain is the fastest draw in Christendom (not only that, he's an ace drummer who wears silver-spangled tops – now that's revisionist!). Disillusioned by the whole scene, Zac departs for the fleshpots of Camino, stopping off en-route to absorb the wisdom of a solitary Grizzly Adams/Carlos Castaneda type, and again on the way back after having his fun with prized prostitute, Belle Starr in a Ken Russell-strength, Siddartha-referencing slice of rock opera. What little plot there is proceeds to work itself into a laughably underwritten finale. *BG*

Movie rating: *6

Visual: video + dvd

Off the record: White Lightnin' (a very obscure band indeed) also featured in another movie, 'The Legend Of Hillbilly John' (1974). *MCS*

Various Artists (score: JIMMIE HASKELL *)

Jan 71. (lp) *A.B.C.; <ABCS-OC 13> Probe; (SPB 1026)* ☐ Mar71 ☐
– Zachariah – main title (*) / Laguna salada (the JAMES GANG) / We're The Crackers (COUNTRY JOE & THE FISH) / William Tell overture (*) / All I need (COUNTRY JOE & THE FISH) / Ballad of Job Cain (DOUG KERSHAW) / Country fever (the JAMES GANG) / The lonely ride (*) / Camino – Used horse salesman (*) / Camino waltz (JOHN RUBENSTEIN) / Gravedigger (NEW YORK ROCK ENSEMBLE) / Shy Ann (WHITE LIGHTNIN') / Matthew (*) / Zachariah – end title (*). *(re-iss. Mar87 on 'See For Miles'; SEE 91)*

S/track review: "Never before has music been so vitally integrated into the acting of a film", claimed director George Englund, "Instead of underscoring the action, the musicians are brought on to the screen and music becomes an extension of each character". Probably just as well given the groaning one-liners which often fill the gaps. Billing itself as an "electric western", this kitschy, underviewed – and, if you take Englund's points on board, revolutionary – cult classic has its roots in the counter-cultural retreat of the early 70s, when hippies realised flower power wasn't going to change the Man's mind, never mind the world. As in 'Vanishing Point' and 'Zabriskie Point' (even 'Sweet Sweetback's Baadasssss Song'), the desert is where it all comes out in the wash. Having resisted louder, longer and more rudely than most of their peers, COUNTRY JOE & THE FISH were the archetypal hippies on the run, and – alongside the JAMES GANG – they get their fair share of dues on this soundtrack. They'd already split, in fact, by the time this album was released and – while not even beginning to predict a solo COUNTRY JOE's mesmerising work on 'QUIET DAYS IN CLICHY' (1973) – the droll 'All I Need' and Doors-y calling card, 'We're The Crackers', don't make for such a bad epilogue. Joe Walsh's peaceful, easier feelin' side might have been more in step here than the incongruously raging JAMES GANG cuts: 'Laguna Salada' is a power-chord thrash plugged into the bush telegraph, while the chugging 'Country Fever' comes down like the 'Cat Scratch..' variety; they do rock, oh yes sirree they do. As do the NEW

YORK ROCK ENSEMBLE. A sensation upon their conception, now almost completely forgotten/ignored, the Juilliard-trained prog-classical fusionists (co-founded by none other than late Hollywood composer Michael Kamen) weigh in with 'Gravedigger'; like the JAMES GANG, it sounds – at least initially – as if it ain't from round these parts (renaissance horns out west?), and about to be run out of town for being too damn highfalutin; a Southern-tinged piano groove redeems the Big Apple origins. Composer/arranger JIMMIE HASKELL's main theme is an archetypal brokeback cowboy lullaby (and the film a distant, playful predecessor to 'Brokeback Mountain') crooned on acoustic guitar, woodwind and strings (and inevitably a snatch – only a snatch, mind – of mariachi horn), but the exotica pioneer only really saddles up with 'Camino', just under two minutes of fuzz/bass/sitar cactus-funk brilliance ultimately degenerating into backporch novelty. Talking of which, arguably the most endearing contributor is veteran Cajun revivalist/bluegrass fiddler DOUG KERSHAW, whose wry, deadpan delivery finds expression in 'Ballad Of Job Cain'. More honest-to-goodness country-rock might've been in order here ('A.B.C.' weren't exactly blessed on that front), but while the lasting impression is something of a tongue-in-cheek 'ZABRISKIE POINT' without the Death Valley mysticism (and, shamefully, without a note from ELVIN JONES – surely HASKELL's tedious 'William Tell Overture' could've made way for his blues piece, or even his drum solo), 'ZACHARIAH' is a record which just couldn't/wouldn't happen today – so cherish it. *BG*

Album rating: *7

ZOMBIE JA KUMMITUSJUNA

US title 'ZOMBIE AND THE GHOST TRAIN'

1991 (Fin 88m) Marianna Films / Villealf Film Productions

Film genre: Rock-music comedy/drama

Top guns: s-w + dir: Mika Kaurismaki (+ story w/ **Sakke Jarvenpaa** ← see below →, Pauli Pentti)

Stars: Silu Seppala *(Antti "Zombie" Autiomaa)* <= LENINGRAD COWBOYS =>, Marjo Leinonen *(Marjo)*, Matti Pellonpaa *(Harri)* ← LENINGRAD COWBOYS GO AMERICA / → NIGHT ON EARTH → LENINGRAD COWBOYS MEET MOSES, Vieno Saaristo *(Aiti)*, Juhani Niemela *(Isa)*, **the Mulefukkers:- Sakke Jarvenpaa + Mato Valtonen + Mauri Sumen, Jyri Narvanen + Jami Haapanen** *(performers)* <= LENINGRAD COWBOYS =>, Kari Vaananen *(cameo)* ← LENINGRAD COWBOYS GO AMERICA / → LENINGRAD COWBOYS MEET MOSES, Kauko Laurikainen *(Laakan)*

Storyline: Zombie is a bass playing alcoholic who looks as grey and miserable as the Finnish countryside where he lives. He can't hold down a proper job and his life seems to be a long, unending struggle, despite the best efforts of girlfriend Marjo to cheer him up. When his band the Ghost Train swap the bleak plains of freezy Finland for the bleak plains of Turkey, it can only be hoped the change of scenery (!) will do him some good. *JZ*

Movie rating: *7

Visual: video + dvd (no audio OST by MAURI SUMEN)

Off the record: There are a few LENINGRAD COWBOYS on show here.

Section 2

Rockumentaries and Performance Movies

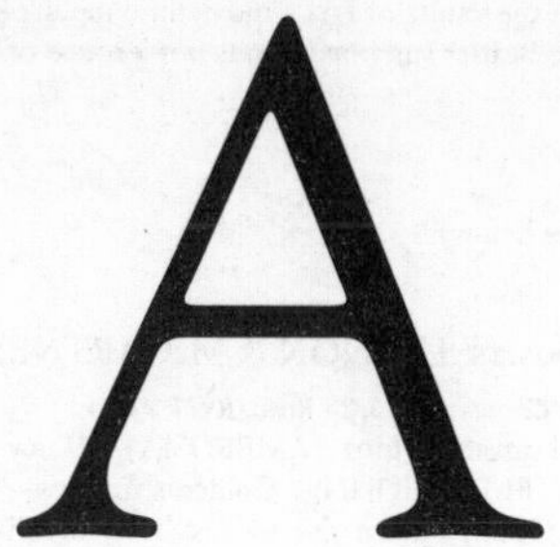

ABBA: THE MOVIE

1977 (Swe/Austra 94m) Polar Music Int. / Reg Grundy Productions

Film genre: Pop-music concert/documentary

Top guns: s-w: (+ dir) Lasse Hallstrom, Robert Caswell → SHOUT! THE STORY OF JOHNNY O'KEEFE

Stars: Abba:- Bjorn Ulvaeus, Benny Andersson, Agnetha Faltskog, Anni-Frid "Frida" Lyngstad *(performers/themselves)*, Robert Hughes *(Ashley Wallace, disc jockey)*, Bruce Barry *(radio station manager)* ← NED KELLY / → PATRICK, Stig Anderson *(himself/Abba manager)*, Tom Oliver *(bodyguard/bartender/taxi driver)* ← SUMMER HOLIDAY

Storyline: Not much of a plot really – a young radio DJ tenaciously tries to interview Swedish pop stars, Abba, on their triumphant tour of Australia. Abba supply their biggest hits to date. *MCS*

Movie rating: *6

Visual: video + dvd

Off the record: Abba – the group – shot to worldwide fame after they won the 1974 Eurovision Song Contest with the song 'Waterloo' (also included in the film, as well as 17 other songs). The Swedish "Fab Four" subsequently hit the No.1 spot on numerous occasions, although couples Bjorn and Agnetha, and Benny and Anni-Frid were to separate a few years later; the group split in 1982. *MCS*

– associated releases, etc. –

ABBA: The Name Of The Game / I Wonder (Departure)

Oct 77. (7") *(EPC 5750)* <3449> [1] Dec77 [12]

ABBA: Take A Chance On Me *[not in film]* / I'm A Marionette

Jan 78. (7") *(EPC 5950)* <3457> [1] Apr78 [3]

ABBA: The Album *[some tracks not in film]*

Jan 78. (lp/c) *(EPC/40 86052)* <19164> [1] Feb78 [14]
– Eagle / Take a chance on me *[not in film]* / One man, one woman *[not in film]* / The name of the game / Move on *[not in film]* / Hole in your soul / The girl with the golden hair (three scenes from a mini musical): Thank you for the music – I wonder (departure) *[not in film]* – I'm a marionette. *(re-iss. Mar84 lp/c; EPC/40 32321) (cd-iss. 1986; CD86052) (cd re-iss. Jun89; CD 32321) (re-iss. Sep92 on 'Polydor' cd/c; 821217-2/-4) <cd re-iss. Oct01; 549954-2>*

— note: 'Greatest Hits' packages have included several other hit songs featured in the film including, 'Dancing Queen', 'When I Kissed The Teacher', 'Money, Money, Money', 'Why Did It Have To Be Me', 'Tiger', 'Fernando', 'Ring Ring', 'Waterloo', 'Mamma Mia', 'S.O.S.', 'Rock Me', 'Intermezzo No.1', 'I've Been Waiting For You', 'So Long', 'Get On The Carousel' and 'Please Change Your Mind'.

☐ Derroll ADAMS segment
(⇒ DON'T LOOK BACK)

AEROSMITH

Formed: Sunapee, New Hampshire, USA . . . summer 1970, by JOE PERRY and STEVEN TYLER, who, with others (Brad Whitford, Tom Hamilton and Joey Kramer), moved to Boston, Massachusetts. By 1972, through a Max's Kansas City gig, they were signed to 'Columbia' by Clive Davis for a six figure sum. The band released their eponymous debut album the following year and the Rolling Stones comparisons were inevitable from the off. While the Stones had taken American music, translated it and shipped it back across the water, AEROSMITH took the Stones' interpretation of the Blues and customized it for a younger generation. Comparisons with Led Zeppelin were somewhat off the mark, the PERRY/TYLER partnership closely mimicking that of Jagger and Richards, and while the latter two proclaimed themselves the "Glimmer Twins", so it came to pass that TYLER and PERRY were duly christened the "Toxic Twins" in recognition of their legendary mid-70s decadence. The follow-up album, 'Get Your Wings' (1974), consolidated the band's rock'n'raunch but it wasn't until the release of 'Toys In The Attic' the following year that the band staked their claim as one of America's biggest and sexiest rock acts. Quintessentially American, the band cut little ice in Britain where punk was the order of the day. While Britain was pogoing to the strains of 'Anarchy in the UK', American heavy metal kids were skinning up to AEROSMITH's 'Rocks' (1976), a seminal record that saw the band at the peak of their powers. An appearance in the Beatles-penned "disaster" movie, 'SGT. PEPPER'S LONELY HEARTS CLUB BAND' in 1978, did nothing for the band's credibility, and when 'Draw The Line' (1978) and 'Night In The Ruts' (1980) fell woefully short of the band's capabilities, tension between TYLER and PERRY eventually led to a split. Despite a near-fatal road accident, Tyler soldiered on with a revamped line-up for the equally uninspired 'Rock In A Hard Place' (1982). Just as it looked like the end of the road for the band, the pair settled their differences and the original AEROSMITH line-up signed to 'Geffen', getting it together for the 'Done With Mirrors' (1985) album, their best effort since the 70s heyday. AEROSMITH always had the funk and it seemed fitting that their miraculous commercial and creative rebirth was kickstarted by black hip hop crew RUN DMC. Their reworking of 'Walk This Way' was released at the height of the rock/rap crossover in 1986 when 'Def Jam' was a force to be reckoned with and VW badges were in short supply, duly exposing AEROSMITH to a generation of kids who had never even heard of the band. Bang on cue, the band released 'Permanent Vacation' (1987), a masterful return to form which spawned a classic slice of AEROSMITH sleaze in 'Dude (Looks Like A Lady)'. Moreover, the band had almost singlehandedly inspired a whole scene; almost every band in the late 80s glam-metal movement modelled themselves on prime 70s AEROSMITH (i.e. Guns N' Roses, L.A. Guns, etc.). Prior to releasing the adventurous and critically acclaimed 'Pump' (1989), TYLER, PERRY and Co were featured in Penelope Spheeris' "Metal Years" instalment of 'The DECLINE OF WESTERN CIVILIZATION' (1988); cameos in 'WAYNE'S WORLD 2' (1993) kept them in celluloid profile. If 'Get A Grip' (1993) sounded somewhat formulaic, it was another massive hit nevertheless. After just more than three years away, they returned to 'Columbia', appeared at 'WOODSTOCK '94' and had yet another massive-selling opus, 'Nine Lives' (1997). AEROSMITH unplugged their amps to power-ballad to hit the top of the Hot 100 with 'I Don't Want To Miss A Thing'. Almost as sentimental as the film it was lifted from ('Armageddon'), TYLER and his cohorts crooned through every filled-up wrinkle whilst leaving a few mascara stains on their female fans; TYLER's daughter Liv had also come-of-age as a leading actress. Come the new millennium, the veteran campaigners were back to the hard stuff (music, that is) with 'Just Push Play' (2001), the Boneyard Boys (aka producers Mark Hudson and Marti Frederiksen) helping tease out a set which many believed was AEROSMITH's best since 'Pump'. Three years on, the Toxic Twins were 'Honkin' On Bobo'; no, not some dodgy new drug craze, but a full-scale covers set in the grand tradition of 'Train Kept A-Rollin'', etc. Having already contributed to the 'MY GENERATION' documentary, TYLER and PERRY were also seen and heard in the films 'LIGHTNING IN A BOTTLE' (2004) and 'BE COOL' (2005). *BG & MCS*

- **filmography** {acting/performance} –

Sgt. Pepper's Lonely Hearts Club Band *(1978 {p/a} on OST by V/A =>)* / **the Decline Of Western Civilization Part II: The Metal Years** *(1988 {p} on OST by V/A =>)* / **Wayne's World 2** *(1993 {c STEVEN + JOE} on OST by V/A =>)* / **Woodstock '94** *(1995 {p} on OST by V/A =>)* / Armageddon *(1998 theme/hit on OST; see future edition)* / **My Generation** *(2000 {p} =>)* / **Lightning In A Bottle** *(2004 {p} on OST by V/A =>)* / **Be Cool** *(2005 {c STEVEN + JOE} OST by V/A =>)*

ALL KINDSA GIRLS

2003 (US 66m w/b&w) BFVF

Film genre: New Wave/Punk-rock music documentary

Top guns: dir: Cheryl Eagan-Donovan

Stars: the Real Kids:- John Felice *(himself/performer)* + **Billy Borgiolo, Howard Ferguson, Allen 'Alpo' Paulino** *(archive performers)*, **the Explosion:- Matt Hock, Dave Walsh, Damian Genaurdi, Dan Colby, Sam Cave** *(performers)*

Storyline: Who better to take on the task of putting together footage of garage-rock's most understated (and certainly underachieving) combos, than Boston-based filmmaker and fan of the Real Kids, Cheryl Eagan-Donovan. She enters the eccentric world of frontman, John Felice, as he traces his rock'n'roll footsteps to his childhood days in Natick, Massachusetts. Then it's off to France and Japan, where the band were revered to the point of being "Rock Gods". *MCS*

Movie rating: *6

Visual: dvd (no audio OST; try debut album now on CD)

Off the record: The **Real Kids** were formed in Boston, Massachusetts, 1975 by songwriter **John Felice** who enlisted other like-minded, Ramones-influenced punks, **Allen 'Alpo' Paulino**, **Billy Borgiolo** and **Howard Ferguson**. With the New Wave explosion providing a perfect platform for Felice's brand of slap-dash high-octane rock'n'roll, the band were regulars at New York's CBGB's. Bizarrely enough, the quartet became a leading light of the Paris punk scene after issuing their debut single, 'All Kindsa Girls', as a French-only release in '77. American and UK fans had to wait for 1978's eponymous LP which featured the song as its opening track, the record subsequently achieving underground cult status for its combination of raw beer-drenched originals and spirited covers of material by Buddy Holly and Eddie Cochran. The band was put on hold however, as Felice became part of the Ramones' road crew, the man (along with a new cast of musicians) later releasing an EP as the Taxi Boys, taking the moniker from an old Real Kids track. A near original line-up of the latter combo regrouped in '82, signing to French label 'New Rose' for a trio of albums, 'Outta Place' (1982), the live 'All Kindsa Jerks' (1983) and 'Hit You Hard' (1983). With the band again put on ice, John Felice & His Lowdowns returned in '88 with a collection of songs entitled 'Nothing Pretty'; the Real Kids were subsequently back on the block one last time in 1999 with a new EP, 'Down To You'. Forming in 1998, **the Explosion**, drew inspiration from their now ageing counterparts, and signed to 'Virgin' for their third album, 'Black Tape' (2004). *MCS*

ALL THIS AND WORLD WAR II

1976 (US 88m w/ b&w) 20th Century Fox

Film genre: war documentary

Top guns: dir: Susan Winslow

Stars: none

Storyline: Here we have the culminative history of World War II, edited in no small part from the vaults of Fox's movietone newsreels and augmented by the music of the Beatles sung by various pop groups of the day. *MCS*

Movie rating: *5

Visual: video

Off the record: (see below)

—

Various (composers: LENNON & McCARTNEY)

Nov 76. (d-lp) *20th Century; <2T 522> Riva; (RVLP 2)* [48] [ ]
– Magical mystery tour (AMBROSIA) / Lucy in the sky with diamonds (ELTON JOHN) / Golden slumbers – Carry that weight (the BEE GEES) / I am the walrus (LEO SAYER) / She's leaving home (BRYAN FERRY) / Lovely Rita (ROY WOOD) / When I'm sixty-four (KEITH MOON) / Get back (ROD STEWART) / Let it be (LEO SAYER) / Yesterday (DAVID ESSEX) / With a little help from my friends – Nowhere man (JEFF LYNNE) / Because (LYNSEY DE PAUL) / She came in through the bathroom window (the BEE GEES) / Michelle (RICHARD COCCIANTE) // We can work it out (the FOUR SEASONS) / The fool on the hill (HELEN REDDY) / Maxwell's silver hammer (FRANKIE LAINE) / Hey Jude (the BROTHERS JOHNSON) / Polythene Pam (ROY WOOD) / Sun king (the BEE GEES) / Getting better (STATUS QUO) / The long and winding road (LEO SAYER) / Help (HENRY GROSS) / Strawberry fields forever (PETER GABRIEL) / A day in the life (FRANKIE VALLI) / Come together (TINA TURNER) / You never give me your money (WILL MALONE & LOU REIZNER) / The end (the LONDON SYMPHONY ORCHESTRA).

S/track review: Nowadays, you'd probably stifle a yawn at the thought of an album of Lennon & McCartney covers by a host of big name artists. However, in 1976, seven years after the Fab Four split, this was a bit more of a novelty, especially when the line-up includes ELTON JOHN, PETER GABRIEL, BRYAN FERRY, ROD STEWART, DAVID ESSEX, KEITH MOON and TINA TURNER. Unfortunately, reading the name LEO SAYER is all it takes to stop you salivating. Indeed, that is the central problem with the soundtrack to 'ALL THIS AND WORLD WAR II', it is too disjointed with some wonderful cover versions spoiled by the inclusion of some truly awful ones. ELTON JOHN's 'Lucy In The Sky With Diamonds' remains psychedelic but is tempered by an almost country-rock feel with some excellent harmonies thrown in to boot. KEITH MOON's chuckling version of 'When I'm Sixty-Four' is George Formby meets Eric Idle while an excellent rendition of 'Yesterday' from DAVID ESSEX is brought to life with the backing of the London Symphony Orchestra, who accompany many of the tracks on the album. 'Get Back' is ROD STEWART going back to some Faces era rock'n'roll that really gives the song an edge and TINA TURNER digs up 'Come Together' and re-roots it deep in the blues. BRYAN FERRY and PETER GABRIEL also deserve a mention for excellent versions of 'She's Leaving Home' and 'Strawberry Fields Forever' respectively, while the FOUR SEASONS' attempt to give 'We Can Work It Out' a disco soul spin actually works to some degree. On the other side of the coin, the aforementioned SAYER manages to destroy not just one, nor two, but three songs. 'I Am The Walrus', 'Let It Be' and 'The Long And Winding Road' are awful and will never be remembered in quite the same way ever again. Whoever let him loose in the studio had obviously been seeing too much of Lucy and her diamonds. 'Golden Slumbers' / 'Carry That Weight' and 'Sun King' are turned into something approaching nursery rhymes by the BEE GEES, while FRANKIE LAINE should never have chosen 'Maxwell's Silver Hammer' – it just doesn't work. Out of the 28 covers spread over 2 discs maybe just over half are worth a listen and would make up a good single album. As for the rest, well, the politest thing would be to say that there are better covers of BEATLES songs out there. *CM*

Album rating: *6.5

– spinoff hits, etc. –

ROD STEWART: Get Back
Nov 76. (7") *(Riva 6)* [–] [11]

AMBROSIA: Magical Mystery Tour
Feb 77. (7") *<2327>* [39] [–]

□ GG ALLIN & THE MURDER JUNKIES segment (⇒ HATED)

AMANDLA! – A REVOLUTION IN FOUR-PART HARMONY

2002 (S.Africa/US 108m) ATO Pictures / Kwela Productions / Artisan

Film genre: Roots/World-music concert/documentary

Top guns: dir: Lee Hirsch

Stars: Vusi Mahlesela *(performer)*, **Hugh Masekela)** ← MONTEREY POP, **Miriam Makeba** *(performer)*, **Abdullah Ibrahim** *(performer)*, **Thandi Modise** *(performer)*, **Dolly Rathebe** *(performer)*, **Sophie Mgcina** *(performer)*, **Lindiwe Zulu** *(performer)*, **Sibongile Khumalo** *(performer)*, **Duma Kandlovu** *(performer)*, **Sifiso Ntuli** *(performer)*, Walter Cronkite *(voice)*

Storyline: Winner of the 2002 Sundance Festival, opening with the emotional exhumation of murdered activist/composer Vuyisile Mini's bones ("even a dog you don't bury this way" comments one of the onlookers) and going on to tell black South Africa's anti-apartheid story through the recollections of major and minor players, monochrome stills and often disturbing, usually colourful anecdote. *BG*

Movie rating: *8

Visual: dvd

Off the record: Jazz singer, **Dolly Rathebe**, died on 16th September 2004, **Sophie Mgcina** over a year later.

—

Various Artists

Feb 03. (cd) *ATO-BMG; <21510>* [ ] [ ]
– Amandla! (AMANDLA!) / When you come back (VUSI MAHLASELA) / Lizobuya (MBONGENI NGEMA) / Meadowlands (NANCY JACOBS & SISTERS) / Sad times, bad times (ORIGINAL CAST OF KING KONG) / Senzeni na? (HARMONIOUS SERADE CHOIR) / Beware verwoerd (Naants' Indod'Emnyama) (MIRIAM MAKEBA) / Y'zinga (ROBBEN-ISLAND PRISON SINGERS) / Stimela (HUGH MASEKELA) / Injambo – Hambani kunye nevangeli (the stomps ... carry the word of God) (PRETORIA CENTRAL PRISON) / Mannenberg (ABDULLAH IBRAHIM) / Nkosi sikelei (SOWETO COMMUNITY HALL) / Thina lomhlala slwugezi (we have cleansed this soil) (VUSI MAHLASELA) / Mayibuye (VUSI MAHLASELA) / Thina sizwe (SABC CHOIR) / Folk vibe No.1 (TANANAS) / Dubula nges'bam (shoot with the guns ...) (SOWETO COMMUNITY HALL) / Sobashiya abazale (AMANDLA GROUP) / Bring him back home (Nelson Mandela) (HUGH MASEKELA) / Did you hear that sound (dreamtime improv) (ABDULLAH IBRAHIM) / S'Bali (JOE NINA) / Makuliwe (SOWETO COMMUNITY HALL) / Bahleli bonke (MIRIAM MAKEBA) / Kuzobenjani na? (VUSI MAHLESELA) / "You strike the rock ..." (SOPHIE MGCINA) / The untold story (SIBONGILE KHUMALO) / Iyo (HARMONIOUS SERADE CHOIR) / Usi letela uxdlo (Nelson Mandela brings us peace) (AFRICAN NATIONAL CONGRESS CHOIR) / Toyi-toyi – Kramat (ABDULLAH IBRAHIM).

S/track review: "Amandla!" translates as "Power!", and in the context of this inspirational docu-soundtrack, it's a call to arms for a country in which music and politics were – and to a certain degree still are – necessarily one and the same. Compilations of South African music are ten a penny but this one bleeds authenticity, the combined voices of artists who struggled against apartheid through their songwriting. MIRIAM MAKEBA, HUGH MASAKELA, ABDULLAH IBRAHIM, all were either self-exiled or persona non grata for much of their careers, conducting what IBRAHIM dubbed "a revolution in four-part harmony" from Europe, the States and West Africa. And it's the artist formerly known as Dollar Brand who supplies the album's most familiar moment, the mellow-rolling, Afro-Cuban-American piano chords of 'Mannenberg'. But it's a specially recorded, seriously abbreviated version, freeing up space for a parade of lesser-known artists, local a capellas and 50s jazz nuggets. Best of all is 'Meadowlands', a glorious ode to a disappeared community, so at one with harmony and rhythm that it renders illusory the sonic complexity of South African music. The sleevenotes describe the track as a "lament", but it's the most rapturous lament this writer's ever heard. From the same era (and the African musical that introduced MIRIAM MAKEBA to the wider world, 'King Kong'), 'Sad Times, Bad Times' is an Ellingtonian elegy for Sophiatown, the connecting thread of a blossoming MAKEBA as deep in her pain as 'Meadowlands' is in her joy and defiance. 'Beware Verwoerd' (admonishing against big bad Prime Minister Hendrik Verwoed) displays that same, astonishing ability to turn anger into exuberance and elation, the essence of non-violent protest; it's impossible to listen to this stuff without breaking into a cheesy grin. And those harmonies, my God! MASAKELA's methods were different but his sound just as addictive, deep, spiritual Afro-funk sun-kissed by his L.A. exile (where he sessioned for the likes of the Byrds); it's a crime against jazz that his early-mid 70s 'Blue Thumb' albums have yet to be reissued, but at least we get a digitised 'Stimela', a near 7-minute migrant worker lament (one that actually sounds like a lament) from 'I Am Not Afraid' (1974). VUSI MAHLASELA isn't as widely recognised outside South Africa but he's famous at home, where his rustic-angelic tenor has earned him the nickname 'The Voice'; on the strength of the keening, Paul Simon-esque 'Mayibuye' it's well earned. There's even a timber-shivering, goosestepping recording from prisoners at the notorious Robben Island, and as the whole thing swings towards the victorious hurrah of ANC anthem, 'Usilethela Uxolo (Nelson Mandela Brings Us Peace)', about the only gripe is the relative insipidness of a contemporary artist like JOE NINA, but then is it really fair to blame him for languishing in the shadow of MASAKELA et al? For the most part, the most important part, 'AMANDLA!' is an ecstatic riposte to those who insist music and politics shouldn't mix, a genuine revolution of the mind. *BG*

Album rating: *8.5

□ an AMERICAN BAND alt. (⇒ the BEACH BOYS: AN AMERICAN BAND)

AMOUGIES

aka 'MUSIC POWER

1970 (Fra 215m; unreleased until ?) Capital Films

Film genre: Jazz-rock/Avant-Rock music concert/documentary

Top guns: dir: Jerome Laperrousaz ← CONTINENTAL CIRCUS / → PRISONER IN THE STREET → MADE IN JAMAICA, Jean-Noel Roy

Stars: PINK FLOYD:- Roger Waters, David Gilmour, Richard Wright, Nick Mason *(performers)*, **Frank ZAPPA** *(MoC/performer)*, **Captain Beefheart & His Magic Band:- Captain Beefheart/Don Van Vliet, Zoot Horn Rollo/ Bill Harkleroad, Rockette Morton/Mark Boston, The Mascara Snake/**

Victor Hayden, Jeff Bruchell *(performers)*, **Aynsley Dunbar's Retaliation** *(performers)* → 200 MOTELS → UNCLE MEAT, **Caravan:- Pye Hastings, Richard Sinclair, David Sinclair, Richard Coughlan, Steve Miller** *(performers)*, **Blossom Toes:- Brian Godding, Jim Cregan, Brian Belshaw, Kevin Westlake** *(performers)*, **Sam Apple Pie:- Sam Sampson, Mike Johnson, Andy Johnson, Bob Rennie, Dave Charles** *(performers)*, **Steve Lacy** *(performer)*, **Archie Shepp** *(performer)*, **Don Cherry** *(performer)*, **the Soft Machine:- Robert Wyatt *, Hugh Hopper, Mike Ratledge** *(performers)* → LOVE AND MUSIC → the ANIMALS FILM, **East Of Eden:- Geoff Nicholson, Geoff Britton, Dave Arbus, Ron Caines, Andy Sneddon** *(performers)*, **the Pretty Things:- Phil May, Skip Allan, John Povey, Peter Tolson** *(performers)*, **Gong:- Daevid Allen** *(performers)* ← CONTINENTAL CIRCUS, **Art Ensemble Of Chicago** *(performers)*

Storyline: America had just wiped its muddy boots on the proverbial rock cornerstone via Woodstock, and now it was Belgium's turn to set the outdoor concert scene alight courtesy of a 5-day free-jazz rock festival at Actuel, 24th-28th October, 1969. Among the highlights were Pink Floyd (sadly without Syd Barrett) and 'Trout Mask Replica'-period Captain Beefheart & His Magic Band – all in uniform (the latter introduced by Frank Zappa). I think there's two versions of the film which confuses the odd punter. *MCS*

Movie rating: *5

Visual: none (two audio bootlegs have surfaced, 'Inter-Zappa Overdrive' & 'Pink Floyd Meets Frank Zappa')

Off the record: The film(s) feature a PINK FLOYD set (25th – Day 2) on 'Astronomy Domine', 'Green Is The Colour', 'Careful With That Axe, Eugene', 'Tuning Up With Frank Zappa', 'Interstellar Overdrive' (w/ ZAPPA on guitar; but not in the movie!), 'Set The Controls For The Heart Of The Sun' and 'A SAucerful Of Secrets'. CAPTAIN BEEFHEART & HIS MAGIC BAND contributed a handful of rarely-performed 'Trout Mask Replica' songs, 'She's Too Much For My Mirror', 'My Human Gets Me Blues', 'Wild Life', 'Hobo Chang Ba', 'When Big Joan Sets Up' and 'Who Will Be The Next?' (the latter jam with guest ZAPPA on guitar). Among other tracks and highlights were:- (AYNSLEY DUNBAR'S RETALIATION):- 'Improvisation', (CARAVAN):- 'If I Could Do It All Over Again, I'd Do It All Over you', (BLOSSOM TOES):- 'Improvisation', (SAM APPLE PIE):- 'Moonlight Man', (the SOFT MACHINE):- 'Moon In June', 'Eamon Andrews' & 'Hibou, Anemone And Bear', (EAST OF EDEN):- 'Confusion', (the PRETTY THINGS):- 'Blow Your Mind' & 'Alexander', (GONG):- 'Rational Anthem' & (the ART ENSEMBLE OF CHICAGO):- 'Rock Out'. *MCS*

□ Laurie ANDERSON segment
(⇒ HOME OF THE BRAVE)

ANOTHER STATE OF MIND

1984 (US 78m) Coastline Films

Film genre: Punk rock-music documentary

Top guns: s-w (+ dir): Adam Small → MALIBU'S MOST WANTED, Peter Stuart

Stars: Youth Brigade:- Sean Stern, Adam Stern, Mark Stern *(themselves/performers)* → PUNK'S NOT DEAD → AMERICAN HARDCORE, **Social Distortion:- Mike Ness, Dennis Danell, Brent Liles, Derek O'Brien** *(themselves/performers)* → PUNK'S NOT DEAD, **Minor Threat: Ian MacKaye** *(themselves/performers)* → INSTRUMENT → the SHIELD AROUND THE K → WE JAM ECONO: THE STORY OF THE MINUTEMEN → PUNK'S NOT DEAD → AMERICAN HARDCORE, **Keith Morris** *(himself)* <= CIRCLE JERKS =>

Storyline: Two punk rock groups decide to tour America to promote their music and their 'Better Youth Organisation', a non-profiteering indie label. They fix up an old school bus and set off on a shoestring budget, and sure enough it's not long before the bus breaks down and relations between the bands take a nosedive. Finally, after many ups and downs, they call it a day when their tour causes more problems than it's worth. *JZ*

Movie rating: *6

Visual: video + dvd on 'Timebomb' 1995 + 2004 (no audio OST)

Off the record: Youth Brigade were America's answer to Sham 69 (example 1984's 'Sound & Fury' LP). **Social Distortion** supplied a track called 'Another State Of Mind'; when the signed to 'Epic' in the 90s, the L.A. punks hit paydirt with 'Social Distortion' (1990), 'Somewhere Between Heaven And Hell' (1992) and 'White Light White Heat White Trash' (1996). **Keith Morris** was ex-Black Flag and CIRCLE JERKS. **Ian MacKaye** subsequently formed Fugazi (see 'INSTRUMENT'). *MCS*

AT THE MAX

aka ROLLING STONES LIVE AT THE MAX

1991 (Ire/Can/US 89m) The BCL Group / IMAX Corporation

Film genre: Rock-music concert documentary

Top guns: dir: Julien Temple ← EARTH GIRLS ARE EASY ← RUNNING OUT OF LUCK ← ABSOLUTE BEGINNERS ← the GREAT ROCK'N'ROLL SWINDLE / → the FILTH AND THE FURY → the FUTURE IS UNWRITTEN → GLASTONBURY, Noel Archambault, David Douglas, Roman Kroiter, Christine Strand

Stars: the ROLLING STONES:- Mick Jagger, Keith Richards, Ron Wood, Bill Wyman, Charlie Watts *(performers)*, **Chuck Leavell** *(musician)* ← HAIL! HAIL! ROCK'N'ROLL, **Bobby Keys** *(musician)* ← HAIL! HAIL! ROCK'N'ROLL ← LET'S SPEND THE NIGHT TOGETHER ← LADIES AND GENTLEMEN ← MAD DOGS & ENGLISHMEN, **the Uptown Horns:- Bob Funk, Crispin Cioe, Arno Hecht, Hollywood Paul Litteral** *(musician)*, **Bernard Fowler, Sophia Jones, Lorelei McBroom** *(vocals)*

Storyline: The Rolling Stones are profiled in this IMAX concert documentary of their 'Steel Wheels' tour of Europe (the images on 35mm film were projected onto a 50x70-foot screen with surround sound). *MCS*

Movie rating: *7

Visual: video 1995 / DVD (no audio OST)

Off the record: The **ROLLING STONES** performed over a dozen tracks:- 'Continental Drift', 'Start Me Up', 'Sad Sad Sad', 'Tumbling Dice', 'Ruby Tuesday', 'Rock And A Hard Place', 'Honky Tonk Woman', 'You Can't Always Get What You Want', 'Happy', 'Paint It Black', '2000 Light Years From Home', 'Sympathy For The Devil', 'Street Fighting Man', It's Only Rock'n'Roll', 'Brown Sugar' & '(I Can't Get No) Satisfaction'. *MCS*

ATHENS, GA. – INSIDE/OUT

1987 (US 82m) I.R.S. Pictures

Film genre: alt-Rock-music concert/documentary

Top guns: dir: Tony Gayton → TWO HEADED COW

Stars: R.E.M.:- Michael Stipe, Bill Berry, Mike Mills, Peter Buck *(performers)* / **the B-52's:- Fred Schneider, Kate Pierson, Cindy Wilson, Ricky Wilson, Keith Strickland** *(performers)* ← ONE-TRICK PONY / **Bar-B-Q Killers:- Arthur Johnson / Time Toy:- Bryan Cook, Paul Hammond, Danny Kottar, Rob McMahon** / Jim Herbert / **Flat Duo Jets:- Dexter Romweber, Curtis Crowe** *(performers)* → TWO HEADED COW / **Dreams So Real:- Barry Marler, Trent Allen, Drew Worsham / Love Tractor:- Michael Richmond, Armistead Wellford, Kit Schwartz, Mark Cline** / Rev. John D. Ruth, J.J. Ort / **Kilkenny Cats:- Tom Cheek, Sean O'Brien, John Seawright, Rev. Howard Finster** + 1 / **the Squalls:- Bob Hay, Ken Starratt, Diana Torrell, Mark Cooper Smith, Juan Molina, Paul Hammond / Pylon:- Randy Bewley, Michael Lachowski, Curtis Crowe, Vanessa Briscoe**

Storyline: A trip down to Athens, Georgia, for this insight into the local indie/alt-rock movement, a scene that created the likes of R.E.M. among others. *MCS*

Movie rating: *6

Visual: video + dvd

Off the record: the **B-52's** were featured in the film, but sadly, not the soundtrack below.

—

Various Artists

May 87. (lp/c) *I.R.S.; <IRS/+C 6185> Illegal; (ILP 017)* ☐ ☐
– Na, na, na, na (the SQUALLS) / Crazy hazy kisses (FLAT DUO JETS) / (All I've got to do is) Dream (R.E.M.) / Pretty (LOVE TRACTOR) / Nightfall (KILKENNY CATS) / Window sill (TIME TOY) / Stop it (PYLON) / Hi (TIME TOY) / His and hearse (BAR-B-Q KILLERS) / Golden (DREAMS SO REAL) / Swan swan H (R.E.M.) / Jet tone boogie (FLAT DUO JETS) / Elephant radio (the SQUALLS).

S/track review: Mostly live in early '86 at various venues in Athens, Georgia (40 Watt Club, SAE House, Lucy Cobb Chapel and Uptown Lounge), this OST highlighted the area's local alt-rock groups. Afforded two tracks apiece (and all from Miles Copeland's 'I.R.S.' stable) were headliners R.E.M., plus FLAT DUO JETS, TIME TOY and the SQUALLS. The latter act open the set with 'Na, Na, Na, Na', and close with 'Elephant Radio', both songs coming across as something you might've heard on a Talking Heads B-side. The short'n'sweet TIME TOY tunes, 'Window Sill' & 'Hi' (both under 2 minutes), screech and grind in a staccato, stop-start kind of way, and it's easy to see why they failed to generate any passion outside their hometown. The FLAT DUO JETS on the other hand, exemplify what's best in good old rock'n'roll, via a couple of exciting punk-abilly cues, 'Crazy Hazy Kisses' & the instrumental speedball, 'Jet Tone Boogie' – Eddie Cochran, Gene Vincent and Elvis are alive and well and kicking ass in Athens. On 'Life's Rich Pageant' one could say, R.E.M. deliver the soundtrack's most playlisted tune, 'Swan Swan H', together with their rare, cheesy rendition of the Everlys '(All I Have To Do Is) Dream'. Courtesy of 'Big Time' records, LOVE TRACTOR ('Pretty') were certainly the most "wigged-out" act on show (like an instrumental Pere Ubu), while 'Coyote/Twin Tone' outfit KILKENNY CATS opted for a more Steppenwolf-meets-Hawkwind approach via 'Nightfall'. With no B-52s on parade (except on film), two studio cuts completed the ' ... INSIDE/OUT' side of things, 'Golden' from the R.E.M.-like, 'Arista' records-bound DREAMS SO REAL and 'Stop It' from premier "Gyrate"-ors, PYLON – think Lulu fronting Devo! *MCS*

Album rating: *7.5

AUSTRALIAN MADE: THE MOVIE

aka AUSTRALIAN MADE *** FEATURING *** INXS LIVE

1987 (Aus 52m) Captured Live / Hoyts Distribution

Film genre: Pop/Rock-music concert/documentary

Top guns: dir: Richard Lowenstein ← WHITE CITY / → DOGS IN SPACE

Stars: Inxs:- Michael Hutchence *, Tim Farriss, Andrew Farriss, Jon Farriss, Garry Beers, Kirk Pengilly *(performers)* → DOGS IN SPACE *, **Models** *(performers)*, **the Divinyls** *(performers)*, **the Saints** *(performers)*, **I'm Talking** *(performers)*, **Jimmy Barnes** *(performer)*, **Mental As Anything** *(performers)*

Storyline: The title refers to the January 1987 Australian Made tour (and book!) which was headed by Inxs and supposed to have over a total of 200,000 people in attendance. *MCS*

Movie rating: *5.5

Visual: dvd (no audio OST)

Off the record: INXS contributed the tracks:- 'Melting In The Sun', 'Don't Change', 'The Loved One', 'What You Need', 'Burn For You' & 'Mystify'; others by I'M TALKING ('Lead The Way'), the SAINTS ('Ghost Ships'), MODELS ('Let's Kiss' & 'Out Of Mind Out Of Sight'), the DIVINYLS ('Temperamental' & 'Only Lonely'). *MCS*

AWESOME: I FUCKIN' SHOT THAT!

2006 (US 89m w/b&w) Oscilloscope Films / ThinkFilm (R)

Film genre: Rap/Hip Hop-music concert/documentary

Top guns: dir: **Adam Yauch** as Nathaniel Hornblower

Stars: BEASTIE BOYS:- Mike D, Ad Rock/Adam Horovitz, MCA/Adam Yauch *(themselves/performers)*, **Mix Master Mike** *(himself/performer)* ← MOOG ← 5 SIDES OF A COIN ← SCRATCH, **Money Mark** *(himself)* ← MOOG, **Doug E. Fresh** *(himself)* ← BROWN SUGAR ← WHITEBOYS ← TAPEHEADS ← BEAT STREET, Ben Stiller *(himself)* → the PICK OF DESTINY, Christine Taylor *(herself)* ← the WEDDING SINGER

Storyline: Naughty lads the Beastie Boys, letting their loyal fans do the work of cameramen on their 2004 "Challah At Your Boy" tour (aka the concert at Madison Square Garden). Supervising editor Neal Usatin and director Nathaniel Hornblower have the final say in what is quite a unique insight into an ever-evolving band. *MCS*

Movie rating: *6.5

Visual: dvd = 'AWESOME; I SHOT THAT!' (no audio OST)

Off the record: see BEASTIE BOYS entry

B

BABY SNAKES

1979 (US 183m w/ anim.) Intercontinental Absurdities

Film genre: avant-Rock-music concert/documentary

Top guns: s-w + dir: **Frank ZAPPA**

Stars: Frank ZAPPA *(himself/performer)*, Ron Delsener *(himself)*, Johnny Psychotic *(himself)*, Donna U. Wanna *(herself)*, Diva Zappa *(herself)* → THANK YOU, GOOD NIGHT, **Adrian Belew** *(performer)* → HOME OF THE BRAVE, **Terry Bozzio** *(performer)*, **Roy Estrada** *(performer)* → UNCLE MEAT, **Patrick O'Hearn** *(performer)*, **Ed Mann** *(performer)*, **Dale Bozzio** *(performer)*, **Peter Wolf** *(performer)*, Bruce Bickford, Christopher Martin, Bill Harrington, Phil Parnet, Klaus Hundsbichler, Angel, Tommy Mars, Phil Kaufman → GRAND THEFT PARSONS → FALLEN ANGEL → the LIFE AND HARD TIMES OF GUY TERRIFICO, John Smothers, Jennifer James

Storyline: In 1977 zany composer and bandleader Frank Zappa holds a hallowe'en concert in New York. Songs include 'Disco Boy', 'Curse of the Knick Knack People' and 'City of Tiny Lights', and the film includes backstage footage of the group and Bill Bickford's claymation sequences. Zappa also mixes in some audience participation and comedy sketches in his own inimitable style. *JZ*

Movie rating: *5

Visual: video on MPI 1987

Off the record: Peter Wolf was lead singer with the J. Geils Band, and like **Patrick O'Hearn**, is now a film composer in his own right. *MCS*

FRANK ZAPPA

Mar 83. (lp) *Barking Pumpkin; <1115>*
– Intro rap / Baby snakes / Titties and beer / Black page No.2 / Jones crusher / Disco boy / Dinah-Moe Humm / Punky's whips. *<(cd-iss. Jan89 on 'Zappa'; CDZAP 16)* *<(cd re-iss. May95 on 'Rykodisc'; RCD 10539)>*

S/track review: In the 'Intro Rap' it is put to FRANK ZAPPA that the New York crowd is all about the madman element, they expect the craziness in his performance, but not necessarily the skill. But here, ZAPPA delivers both. In spades. This live recording is a demonstration of intricately constructed chaos, where the fine line between madman and genius is erased. Billed as "A movie about people who do stuff that is not normal", 'BABY SNAKES' showcases an extraordinary band, virtuosic performances and dubious sexual politics. 'BABY SNAKES' is heavy, funky, with an awesome vocal, and the effect it would have on later mavericks such as Mike Patton (Faith No More, Mr. Bungle, Fantomas) is patent, as it coils and twists, warping from heavy funk to soul. 'Titties 'n' Beer' showcases more vocal gymnastics and ZAPPA's narrative skills in full flight. What we are to make of his love of lager and mammaries today, and the lovely image of "titty skin" underneath his fingernails is uncertain. Is this irony or rampant objectification? Perhaps both. A dialogue ensues with Satan; it's the encounter with the devil of "Black Sabbath" re-interpreted as an amusing improvisation questioning Zappa's style credentials to get into Hell. He isn't too concerned, he slavers for it to be "titty-squeezin' time", and as for Hell, no problem, since he was "signed to Warners for eight fuckin years". At the end of this warped vision his Chrissy ("titties plop-poppin") re-emerges only to decide to leave him after all. Hmph! Women! 'The Black Page #2' showcases some anthemic synths, awesome bass and drum interplay (the masterful TERRY BOZZIO would somehow go on to play in Korn for a while) and xylophone playing, all so accomplished, all so funky. 'Jones Crusher' takes ZAPPA's favourite subject, his dick, and works it into a riotous, rock n roll workout, getting to grips with a woman who's trying to "grind up [his] jones", and there's more choice metaphors as "steam shoots out from sprinklers on the lawns". After a funky breakdown, the song winds up with a searing guitar solo. 'Disco Boy' (from 'Zoot Allues') succeeds in lampooning the John Travoltas of the era gripped by 'SATURDAY NIGHT FEVER'. There are echoes of TOMMY in its operatic treatment of vocals, the tune morphs into rock and rolla 50s swing, complemented by ZAPPA's low breathy vocals. Ostensibly this is a tribute to the consolation of masturbation, about a guy who fails to get off with a girl, who then walks off with his friend, leaving him to thank the Lord he still has hands to "do that jerkin' that'll blot out yer disco sorrow". It's spot on and very funny. 'Dinah-Moe Humm' (from his 'Over-nite Sensation' set) grapples again with the female of the species in his oh so subtle style. ZAPPA is challenged to make a girl cum, but failing that does her sister instead, it's a mentalist concoction, again with superb ensemble playing. ZAPPA is narratorial ring master of this circus funk rock, hosting a ZAPPA-alike performance contest in the middle, coming on like a circus troupe James Brown. 'Punky's Whips' stars PUNKY MEADOWS, lead singer of Nagel, his pouty rictus stretched across his face, as ZAPPA dissects the pitfalls of rock celebrity obsessions, veering from heavy rock to louche funk which hits a thrilling, heavy groove in its latter stages, making a vibrant musical cornucopia and collage. A glorious jam ends the album with distorted guitar and a trumpeting synthesizer conclusion. FRANK ZAPPA might not make much hay with the women's lib movement, but much is done with his tongue fully in his cheek, and he cooks up a complete crazy storm doing so. *DF*

Album rating: *5.5

BACKSTAGE

2000 (US 86m) Dimension Films (R)

Film genre: Hip Hop/Rap-music concert documentary

Top guns: dir: Chris Fiore

Stars: JAY-Z *(performer)*, **DMX** *(performer)* → BEEF, **Method Man** *(performer)* ← RHYME & REASON ← the SHOW ← BLACK AND WHITE / → HOW HIGH → BROWN SUGAR, **Redman** *(performer)* ← RIDE ← RHYME & REASON / → HOW HIGH, **Beanie SIGEL** *(performer)*, **Memphis Bleek** *(performer)* → PAPER SOLDIERS → DEATH OF A DYNASTY → FADE TO BLACK, **DJ Clue** *(performer)*, **Ja Rule** *(performer)* ← TURN IT UP / → BEEF → BEEF III, **Amil** *(performer)*, **Damon Dash** *(himself)* → PAPER SOLDIERS → FADE TO BLACK, Tyran 'Ty-Ty' Smith *(himself)*

Storyline: Roc-A-Fella records and Jay-Z (he of 'Hard Knock Life') and all his hip-hop buddies such as Method Man, Redman, DMX, etc get together for a documented road trip that sold out 54 venues and grossed an enormous amount of k-ching for their bling. *MCS*

Movie rating: *5

Visual: dvd

Off the record: (see below for numerous rap artists)

—

Various Artists: DJ Clue Presents: Backstage – Mixtape

Aug 00. (cd) *Roc-A-Fella; <(546641-2)>* ☐ Sep00 ☐
– (intro skit) / Best of me part 2 (MYA & JAY-Z) / In the club (BEANIE SIGEL) / Keep it thoro (PRODIGY) / My mind right (MEMPHIS BLEEK) / Who did you expect (the LOX) / Wanna take me back (T-BOZ) / Just leave your love (CHRISTION) / Darlin' (RELL) / Millionaire (HOT BOYS feat. BIG TYMERS) / Road dawgs (AMIL, EVE & DA BRAT feat. JAY-Z) / Funkanella (OUTKAST feat. SLIMM CALHOUN & KILLER MIKE) / Come and get it (REDMAN & LADY LUCK) / Hate music (CAM'RON feat. JUELZ SANTANA) / Gotta be a thug (FABULOUS) / Don't wanna beef (CAPONE-N-NOREAGA) / Crime life (MEMPHIS BLEEK, LIL' CEASE & JA RULE) / Say what U say (DA RANJAHZ feat. JA RULE) / People's court (JAY-Z).

S/track review: Soundtrack compilers have one real Get-Out-Of-Jail-Free-card when getting a disc fit for our delectation with the disclaimer "music inspired by the film". This, in truth, means the album can have virtually anything on it as long as it can claim to be inspired by said flick. This documentary follows the fortunes of JAY-Z, Method Man, Redman and DMX on the road on the former's 'Hard Knock Life' Tour. JAY-Z drops in for a couple of cuts here which bookend Clue's 18-track mix, but otherwise it's a random mix of what DJ CLUE fancies. Mix is maybe a misnomer too as CLUE is famed for not mixing tracks on his mixtapes. What we do get is a comp that leans towards the rougher end of the rap spectrum. MEMPHIS BLEEK, PRODIGY, CAPONE-N-NOREAGA and REDMAN are among those who commit themselves well, dealing in hard-hitting street rhymes. T-BOZ is on hand to add a bit of feminine wile to the testosteroned line-up, 'Wanna Take Me Back' is sleek and fresh-sounding, as is CHRISTION's take on the R&B soul boy. Only RELL's insipid 'Darlin'' lets down this more introspective interlude. The remainder are more gnarly gangsterisms aside from the mighty OUTKAST. Taking this even further away from the notion of a film soundtrack, CLUE insists on peppering the collection with endless shout-outs that only detract from the music. At the heart of this disc though, there's enough of the good stuff to chew on. Not amazing, but respectable. *MR*

Album rating: *6.5

BADSVILLE

2001/2 (US/Can 84m; str8-to-vid) Cinema Diablo

Film genre: alt-Rock'n'roll-music documentary

Top guns: dir: P.J. Wolff

Stars: the SuperBees:- Dave James, Dat Bgo, Scott Carlson, Johnny Sleeper *(performers)*, **Coyote Shivers** *(performer)* ← DOWN & OUT WITH THE DOLLS ← EMPIRE RECORDS, **the Newlydeads:- Taime Downe, Kyle, Meghan, Xristian** *(performers)*, **Lo-Ball:- Pauley P. *, J.C., Lissa, Katie, Claudia** *(performers)* ← ALMOST FAMOUS / → BROTHER BEAR

Storyline: As it says on the tin, part concert film, part documentary, all rock n' roll. L.A.'s up and coming alt-rock acts in all their warts'n'all glory. *MCS*

Visual: video + dvd <7009> (no audio OST)

Off the record: The **SuperBees** had been around for a couple of years, releasing an eponymous EP and the MC5-influence single, 'Got This Feeling', before getting around to their debut long-player, 'High Volume' (2002), for 'Acetate' records. Industrial goth-rockers, the **Newlydeads** (comprising of ex-Faster Pussycat and Bang Tango members) have delivered three sets, 'The Newlydeads' (1997), the re-mixed 'Re-Bound' (1999) and 'Dead End' (2001); they've since disbanded. The all-grrrl glam-punk quintet, **Lo-Ball** (featuring New Orleans-born actress/poet/singer, **Pauley P./Perrette**), were had all the right credentials – if they had been around a decade ago! – to make the big time; a CD is on sale at www.loballrocks.com. Up until early 2006, Pauley was the spouse of actor/singer, **Coyote Shivers** (b. Toronto, Canada) who featured in the rock band, Sharkskin, and was the producer of Shadowy Men On A Shadowy Planet (check out his 2004 solo double-set, 'Gives It To Ya, Twice'. *MCS*

Joan BAEZ

Born: 9 Jan'41, Staten Island, New York, USA. The preeminent female figurehead of the 60s folk-protest movement and a romantic and professional foil to BOB DYLAN, JOAN BAEZ wielded her potent soprano with unstinting earnestness even as the idealism of the 60s gave way to the self absorption of the 70s. Screenwise, BAEZ made at least one memorable film score contribution and also appeared in a number of features, notably D.A. Pennebaker's Dylan document, 'Don't Look Back' (1967), Michael Wadleigh's epic 'WOODSTOCK' (1970) and 'CARRY IT ON' (1970), a rockumentary focusing on BAEZ and her then draft evading husband, David Harris. She also popped up alongside the likes of JOHN LENNON in quasi-documentary, 'Dynamite Chicken' (1972). Leading a classic Ennio Morricone score, her haunting theme to Giuliano Montaldo's 'Sacco E Vanzetti' (1971) suggested her singular talents could indeed be applied to the big screen, and strikingly so. Admittedly, the film's politically slanted account of one of America's most infamous courtroom dramas was prime BAEZ material, although it remains disappointing that she never really pursued this avenue further. Perhaps her most high profile screen role outside of the earlier musical documents was DYLAN's commercially and critically disastrous art film, 'RENALDO AND CLARA' (1978), in which she appeared, rather queasily, alongside DYLAN's ex-wife, Sara. *BG*

- filmography {performer} (composer) –

the Big T.N.T. Show *(1966 {p})* / **Don't Look Back** *(1967 {*})* / **Festival** *(1967 {p})* / **Woodstock** *(1970 {p} on OST by V/A =>)* / Scruggs *(1970 {p})* / **Carry It On** *(1970 {*} OST =>)* / **Celebration At Big Sur** *(1971 {p} =>)* / Silent Running *(1971 theme on OST by Peter Schikele)* / Sacco And Vanzetti *(1971 single/theme on OST by Ennio Morricone)* / Dynamite Chicken *(1972 {p})* / **Sing Sing Thanksgiving** *(1974 {p} =>)* / **Banjoman** *(1975 {p} OST by EARL SCRUGGS =>)* / **Renaldo And Clara** *(1978 {*} =>)* / Sag Nein! *(1983 {p})* / Choices Of The Heart *(1983 TV by BAEZ & John Rubinstein)* / In Our Hands *(1984 {p})* / Berkeley In The Sixties *(1990 {p})*

the BALLAD OF RAMBLIN' JACK

2000 (US 112m) Journeyman Pictures / Plantain Films

Film genre: Blues/Folk-music concert/documentary bio-pic

Top guns: s-w: Aiyanna Elliott (+ dir), Rick Dahl

Stars: Jack Elliott *(himself)* ← ROADIE ← RENALDO AND CLARA ← BANJOMAN, **Pete SEEGER** *(himself)*, **Kris KRISTOFFERSON** *(himself)*, **Arlo Guthrie** *(himself)* ← ROADSIDE PROPHETS ← RENALDO AND CLARA ← WOODSTOCK ← ALICE'S RESTAURANT, **Odetta** *(herself)* ← CHORDS OF FAME ← FESTIVAL / → LIGHTNING IN A BOTTLE → BLUES DIVAS → NO DIRECTION HOME, **Dave Van Ronk** *(himself)* ← CHORDS OF FAME / → NO DIRECTION HOME, **Harold Leventhal** *(himself)* → NO DIRECTION HOME, Alan Lomax, Gil Gross, D.A. Pennebaker *(himself)* → NO DIRECTION HOME, June Shelley, Victor Maymudes

Storyline: Winner of the Special Jury Prize at the 2000 Sundance Film Festival, Aiyana Elliott's fond portrait of her rootless Ramblin' pop recounts a colourful life through rare footage, on-the-road anecdote and the reminiscences of famous pals (Johnny Cash introduces him as a man with "a song and friend for every mile behind him"). From the urban jungle of New York, the teenage Jack Elliott runs away to join a rodeo (the soundtrack sleeve features an official missing persons notice with the priceless caveat "Parents not opposed to his staying on ranch"), initiating an itinerant itch in need of lifelong scratching. *BG*

Movie rating: *8

Visual: dvd

Off the record: RAMBLIN' JACK ELLIOTT (see below)

—

RAMBLIN' JACK ELLIOTT

Jul 00. (cd) *Vanguard; <(VCD 79575)>* ☐ Feb01 ☐
– (Introduction by Johnny Cash) / Mule skinner blues / Cuckoo / Hard travelin' / Railroad Bill (w/ WOODY GUTHRIE) / Buskin' / Pastures of plenty / Rake and Ramblin' boy / San Francisco Bay blues / Candy man – Talkin' sailor blues / Acne (w/ BOB DYLAN) / Don't think twice, it's all right / Take me home (w/ JOHNNY CASH) / If I were a carpenter / Car song / 900 miles / Cup of coffee / (introduction by President Clinton) / 1913 massacre / Cuckoo – reprise.

S/track review: "Jack sounds more like me than I do myself"- from the lips of Woody Guthrie, this was doubtless the highest of compliments, not in an egotistical sense but in the sense of embodying a state of mind. For those who haven't seen the film, Aiyana Elliott's sleevenotes hint at the extent to which Guthrie was a role model for her father, and ELLIOTT a protégé to him. It's a relationship illuminated on the previously unreleased 'Railroad Bill' (a traditional hobo tune which Anne Briggs adapted as the haunting 'Ride, Ride'), with Guthrie's foghorn of a voice coaxing relatively slight yet quietly soulful and tenacious lines out of his younger partner. When Guthrie passed away from Huntington's disease shortly after, RAMBLIN' JACK ELLIOTT took the American troubadour tradition into the modern era; Aiyana's best anecdote has got to be the one about her father and banjo player Derroll Adams "rambling" through Europe on Vespa scooters. RAMBLIN' JACK's not the most gifted of vocalists but he's always made the best of what he has, a garrulous, self-perpetuated myth of a singer capable of emulating Guthrie's talking blues and children's songs, comic doo-wop duetting with his own protégé "BOBBY" DYLAN ('Acne') and poignantly making Dylan's 'Don't Think Twice ...' his own with a bristled, folk-blues drawl betraying every unsympathetic audience, small victory and cracked pavement on his lifelong travels. The Townes Van Zandt-like phrasing and picking of 'Cuckoo (reprise)' (from his classic 1980 set, 'Kerouac's Last Dream') aside, it's this latter-day incarnation of ELLIOTT's voice which cuts deepest, and it's possible to trace the making of it through the rare and familiar Alan Lomax recordings, spoken word intros and asides, Cowboy Poetry Festival performances, TV show excerpts and album tracks lined up here, even if they aren't sequenced in chronological order. Taken together, they're cohesive in the way ELLIOTT's haphazard career never was, and there isn't a finer introduction to the man and his work on the market. *BG*

Album rating: *8

the BAND

Formed: Toronto, Ontario, Canada ... 1967 by expatriate American LEVON HELM along with Canadians ROBBIE ROBERTSON, Richard Manuel, Garth Hudson and Rick Danko. Worshipped by critics for their luminous distillation of American myth, and revered by fellow musicians for their vocal and instrumental potency, the BAND – and particularly their late 60s recordings – inspire the kind of devotion normally reserved for the likes of the BEATLES or literary songsmiths such as VAN MORRISON and, of course, BOB DYLAN. As it turned out, DYLAN – as he was in so many cases during the 60s – was the lynchpin behind the group's ascendance, intially hiring them as his backing band when they were still called the Hawks, and collaborating with them on the mid-60s sessions which would be belatedly released almost a decade on as 'The Basement Tapes' (1975). The BAND's own debut album 'Music From The Big Pink' (1968) quickly became the holy grail of a movement away from the kind of psychedelic excess so fashionable just a year before, a movement bolstered by landmark releases from the Byrds, the GRATEFUL DEAD and DYLAN himself. An eponymous second album perfected their traditionalist vision and secured their legendary status. By the early 70s, as even the ROLLING STONES were getting back to their roots, the BAND began to falter amid the usual rock'n'roll ailments of drugs, in-fighting and assorted personal problems. Buckling under the weight of adulation and expectation, they finally decided to pack it in mid-decade, although not before one of the most lavish send-offs in rock history. 'The LAST WALTZ' (1978) was the Martin Scorsese directed document of the group's final concert, featuring an unprecedented line-up of rock's good and great (including DYLAN, VAN MORRISON, NEIL YOUNG, JONI MITCHELL, ERIC CLAPTON and Muddy Waters) and, given its Thanksgiving 1976 date, a symbolic curtain closer on a generation soon to be overtaken by the dawn of punk and new wave. While most of the BAND's members would remain pretty much out of the limelight for much of the ensuing decade, principal songwriter ROBBIE ROBERTSON went on to develop his relationship with Martin Scorsese, becoming the director's right hand composer for a series of early 80s classics. While no soundtrack was ever released from grainy boxing epic, 'Raging Bull' (1980), ROBERTSON's sterling work on sideshow drama, 'CARNY' (1980) and searing media satire, 'The King Of Comedy' (1983), were testament to a talent undimmed by the trials of rock stardom. He also scored Scorsese's 'Hustler' follow-up, 'The Color Of Money' (1986), complementing contributions from old pals like CLAPTON. Tragically, fellow songwriter and highy regarded singer Richard Manuel hanged himself the same year (he was found dead in his Florida hotel room on 4th of March) in the midst of a ROBERTSON-less BAND reunion. While he'd made a one-off acting appearance (as, appropriately enough, a composer) in Canadian romantic fantasy, 'Eliza's Horoscope' (1975), his post-BAND years had been plagued by alcoholism. LEVON HELM had been more successful, receiving encouraging notices for his acting debut in Loretta Lynn biopic, 'COAL MINER'S DAUGHTER' (1980), and continuing to work in film in tandem with the BAND's 1983 reunion. A part in Philip Kaufman's space exploration history, 'The Right Stuff', followed in 1983 although save for some TV work, it'd be 1988 before he appeared in another feature, 'Man Outside', playing a sheriff in his native Arkansas alongside BAND members Garth Hudson, Rick Danko (who'd previously appeared in 1979 WHO documentary, 'The KIDS ARE ALRIGHT') and, posthumously, Richard Manuel. By this juncture, ROBERTSON was enjoying a successful solo recording career, releasing a couple of well received albums on 'Geffen' before returning to film scoring with Barry Levinson's showbiz satire, 'Jimmy Hollywood' (1994), the documentary 'The NATIVE AMERICANS' and Oliver Stone's American Football drama, 'Any Given Sunday' (1999). HELM had also kept up his acting career, starring in another Arkansas-set drama, 'End Of The Line' (1988) and low key comedy 'Staying Together' (1989). While the 90s saw yet another successful BAND reunion (still minus ROBERTSON) and a clutch of well received albums, HELM continued to sideline in acting with parts in bigger budget features such as 'Feeling Minnesota' (1996) and 'Fire Down Below' (1997). Sadly, American rock's greatest curators finally reached the end of the line with the death of Danko at his Woodstock home on 10th December 1999. *BG*

- **filmography** scores & {acting} –

Eliza's Horoscope *(1975 {a RICHARD})* / **the Last Waltz** *(1978 {p* all} OST by the BAND =>)* / **the Kids Are Alright** *(1979 {c RICK} =>)* / **Coal Miner's Daughter** *(1980 {* LEVON} OST by Cast =>)* / **Carny** *(1980 {* ROBBIE} OST by ROBERTSON & Alex North =>)* / Raging Bull *(1980 score by ROBERTSON / OST by V/A see; future editions =>)* / Visiting Hours *(1982 {b ROBBIE})* / the King Of Comedy *(1983 OST by ROBERTSON & V/A see; future editions =>)* / the Right Stuff *(1983 {b LEVON})* / **Best Revenge** *(1983 {* LEVON} OST by KEITH EMERSON =>)* / the Dollmaker *(1984 TV {a LEVON})* / Smooth Talk *(1985 TV {* LEVON})* / the Color Of Money *(1986 OST by ROBERTSON & V/A see; future editions =>)* / Elvis '56: In The Beginning *(1987 {n LEVON})* / End Of The Line *(1988 {* LEVON})* / Man Outside *(1988 {* LEVON} {b RICHARD} {b GARTH} {b RICK})* / Staying Together *(1989 {a LEVON})* / Jimmy Hollywood *(1994 OST by ROBERTSON & V/A see; future editions =>)* / **the Native Americans** *(1994 OST by ROBERTSON =>)* / the Crossing Guard *(1995 {b ROBBIE})* / Feeling Minnesota *(1996 {a LEVON} OST by V/A see; future editions =>)* / Fire Down Below *(1997 {a LEVON})* / Any Given Sunday *(1999 songs on OST Volume II by ROBERTSON & V/A / score by RICHARD HOROWITZ & Paul Kelly + other OST by V/A; see future editions)*

the BAND THAT WOULD BE KING

aka HALF JAPANESE: THE BAND THAT WOULD BE KING

1993 (US 90m) unknown

Film genre: Indie/Rock-music documentary

Top guns: s-w + dir: Jeff Feuerzeig → the DEVIL AND DANIEL JOHNSTON

Stars: Half Japanese:- David Fair & Jad Fair *(themselves)* → the DEVIL AND DANIEL JOHNSTON, Penn Jillette *(himself)* ← ROCK & ROLL HEART → FEAR AND LOATHING IN LAS VEGAS, **Maureen Tucker** *(herself)* ← the VELVET UNDERGROUND AND NICO / → ROCK & ROLL HEART

Storyline: Described as "The funniest rock'n'roll movie since This Is Spinal Tap" (by the Chicago Tribune), although by all accounts this is not a mockumentary, this is the true-ish story of cult indie faves, Half Japanese; it "has the feel of a complete put on" (said NY Times). *MCS*

Movie rating: *7

Visual: video + dvd

Off the record: The original LP was issued on Half Japanese's own label in April '89 (cat.no. <HALF 8>) and updated to coincide with the documentary release, although it's clear that both the re-issued CD version (with extra tracks!) is different to the movie. **Half Japanese** were formed in Uniontown, Maryland, USA . . . 1977 by San Franciscan-born brothers **Jad & David Fair**; a debut EP, 'Calling All Girls . . .' was released that year, its deliberate amateurism and wilful experimentation heralding a long and chequered career for the Fair siblings. After they issued a further EP in 1979, 'No Direct Line From My Brain To My Heart', the pair decided to recruit two other brothers, Ricky and John Dreyfuss, their inaugural appearance coming in the shape of 1980s UK-only single, 'The Zombies Of Mora-Tau'. By 1981, they had amassed enough material to fill a triple album, 'Half Gentlemen, Not Beasts', a schizoid trip through the brothers' warped muse featuring numerous crazed cover versions (see below) alongside defiantly DIY creations which set the tone for homemade US underground music throughout the 80s. From then on they assembled various musicians to augment them on each album project, Jad simultaneously juggling a prolific solo career with Half Japanese albums such as 'Loud' (1981), the Kramer-produced 'Music To Strip By' (1987), 'Charmed Life' (1988) and 'The Band That Would Be King' (1989); David would now be just part-time in '88. Jad subsequently worked with the likes of Don Fleming, John Zorn and Fred Frith (ex-Henry Cow), to mention but a few. At the turn of the decade, Jad collaborated with fellow maverick, Daniel Johnston on their demon-exorcising 1989 album and went on to work with Scottish spiritual cousins, the Pastels. In 1993, a feature-length film, 'HALF JAPANESE: THE BAND THAT WOULD BE KING' was being screened in art-house cinemas, while the band came perilously close to fame as fans: Nirvana invited them as support on tour. Penn Jillette, from magic duo Penn & Teller was one of their biggest fans. Other noteable fans have included **Maureen Tucker** (former drummer with the Velvet Underground), **Don Fleming** (who's been associated with B.A.L.L., Velvet Monkeys, Gumball, etc.), while director Jeff Feuerzeig was in the band Kickstand. *MCS*

– associated release –

HALF JAPANESE: The Band Who Would Be King

1994. (cd) *50 Skidillion Watts; <80008> / Paperhouse; (PAPCD 018)* ☐ Jul93 ☐
– Open your eyes – Close your eyes / Daytona beach / Lucky star / Some things last a long time / My most embarrassing moment / Buried treasure / Open book / Little records / Deadly alien spawn / Postcard from far away / Ventriloquism made easy / Something in the wind / Bingo's not his name-o / Put some sugar on it / What more can I do? / Brand new moon / Another world / Every word is true / I live for love / Werewolf / Ride ride ride / Sugar cane / I wish I may / Ashes on the ground / Curse of the doll people / Horse shoes / Bluebirds / Frankenstein meets Billy The Kid / My bucket's got a hole in it / Africans built the pyramids. *(re-iss. +=)* – Better than before / Daytona / Back home / Mule skinner blues / Sugar cane / Jump up / Postcard from far away / Big wheels / Ordeal / Jump down / Cowboys / Man without a head.

BANJOMAN

1975 (US 105m) Blue Pacific

Film genre: Folk-rock-music concert/documentary

Top guns: dir: Richard Gilbert Abramson, Michael Varhol

Stars: Earl Scruggs *(performer)* ← the NASHVILLE SOUND, **Joan BAEZ** *(performer)*, **the Byrds:- Roger McGuinn, Gene Parsons, Skip Battin, Clarence White** *(performers)*/ **Ramblin' Jack Elliott** *(performer)* → RENALDO AND CLARA → ROADIE → the BALLAD OF RAMBLIN' JACK, **Doc Watson** *(performer)* → DISCO GODFATHER & **Merle Watson** *(performer)*, **Tracy Nelson** *(performer)*, **David Bromberg** *(performer)*, **the Nitty Gritty Dirt Band:- Jeff Hanna, John McEuan** *(performers)*, **Lester Flatt** *(performer)*

Storyline: On a snowy night on the 23rd of January 1973, several major roots artists paid tribute to legendary bluegrass co-founder, Earl Scruggs, who also performs here. The concert footage is interspersed with rare interviews and testimonials from friends and associates. The actual gig itself took place in Manhattan, Kansas, starting at 7 o'clock at night until the same hour the next morning! *MCS*

Movie rating: *7

Visual: video

Off the record: Earl Scruggs (b. 6 Jan'24, Flint Hill, North Carolina, USA) was the "Banjoman" in question. With fellow bluegrass and Nashville player, **Lester Flatt**, he was part of the Foggy Mountain Boys from the late 40s to 1969. *MCS*

Various Artists

1977. (lp) *Sire; <SA 7527> (SRK 6026)* ☐ Feb79 ☐
– Lonesome Ruben (the EARL SCRUGGS REVUE) / Battle of New Orleans (the NITTY GRITTY DIRT BAND) / You ain't goin' nowhere (JOAN BAEZ) / Freight train boogie (DOC & MERLE WATSON) / T for Texas (blue yodel #1) (the EARL SCRUGGS REVUE) / Roll over Beethoven (the BYRDS) / Me and Bobby McGee (RAMBLIN' JACK ELLIOTT) / Mr. Tambourine man (the BYRDS) / Black mountain rag (DOC & MERLE WATSON) / The night they drove old Dixie down (JOAN BAEZ) / Diggy liggy lo (the NITTY GRITTY DIRT BAND) / Blowin' in the wind (JOAN BAEZ) / Foggy

mountain breakdown (the EARL SCRUGGS REVUE) / Billy Fehr (RAMBLIN' JACK ELLIOTT).

S/track review: While there's an apology inside the inner sleeve, regretting the fact there was no room for David Bromberg, Tracy Nelson & Mother Earth, the 'BANJOMAN' concert OST is still a worthy introduction to electric bluegrass music. Yes, the banjo is king here, and one of its top exponents is EARL SCRUGGS (and his REVUE, featuring sons GARY, RANDY & STEVE plus drummer JODY MAPHIS), who is awarded no less than three numbers here: the plucky 'Lonesome Ruben', 'T For Texas' and that old chestnut, 'Foggy Mountain Breakdown'. In a similar vein, the NITTY GRITTY DIRT BAND performed two songs, Jimmy Driftwood's perennial 'Battle Of New Orleans' (a minor hit for the band in '74) and J.D. Miller's fun cajun cue 'Diggy Liggy Lo'. SCRUGGS' long-time friends, JOAN BAEZ, RAMBLIN' JACK ELLIOTT and DOC WATSON (with son MERLE), were also invited to shine on that eventful snowy evening, while surprise package the BYRDS (featuring guitarist Clarence White – who was tragically killed in a car crash six months later) also showed up. The latter folk-rock quartet contributed two songs, a rollickin' rendition of Chuck Berry's 'Roll Over Beethoven' and a Dylan-ish take of er . . . Dylan's 'Mr. Tambourine Man'. Two further Bobby Zimmerman standards came via the aforementioned BAEZ, the long-standing "lady of folk" tackling 'You Ain't Goin' Nowhere' (featuring a cheeky impersonation of the bard himself!) and 'Blowin' In The Wind' (with chorus partly sung in French), plus Robbie Robertson's 'The Night They Drove Old Dixie Down'. DOC & MERLE WATSON (the former, another flat-picking pioneer of old-timey, trad-folk artists) chug along nicely with 'Freight Train Boogie' and 'Black Mountain Rag', the latter instrumental showing great guitarists don't have to come via the world of rock. Subject of a subsequent film documentary himself in 2000, RAMBLIN' JACK ELLIOTT gets his two-penneth worth courtesy of the admittedly croaky and brave versions of Kris Kristofferson's 'Me And Bobby McGee' and his own 'Billy Fehr' – he really shouldn't have bothered. Incidentally, if one wants to find out about the origins and history of the banjo itself (and its popular master, Joel Sweeney), look no further than the album's inner sleeve notes. *MCS*

Album rating: *7

BARENAKED IN AMERICA

1999 (Can/US 89m) Nettfilms

Film genre: alt-Rock-music concert/documentary

Top guns: dir: Jason Priestley

Stars: Barenaked Ladies:- Ed Robertson, Steven Page, Jim Creegan, Tyler Stewart, Kevin Hearn *(themselves/performers)*, Jason Priestley *(himself)*, Jeff Goldblum *(himself)* ← EARTH GIRLS ARE EASY ← THANK GOD IT'S FRIDAY ← NASHVILLE ← DEATH WISH, Jon Stewart *(himself)* → GIGANTIC (A TALE OF TWO JOHNS), Moses Znaimer *(himself)* ← BEST REVENGE, Andy Richter *(himself)* → GIGANTIC (A TALE OF TWO JOHNS), Conan O'Brien *(himself)* → STORYTELLING → GIGANTIC (A TALE OF TWO JOHNS)

Storyline: Canadian all-male band Barenaked Ladies are filmed on their US tour after the success of their fifth album, 'Stunt'. As well as seeing them perform on stage, they are shown talking together as they travel on their tour bus about how they formed and made it big. They aren't overawed by their success despite being one of Canada's biggest pop acts. *JZ*

Movie rating: *6.5

Visual: video (no audio OST)

Off the record: Barenaked Ladies were formed in Scarborough, Toronto, Canada, 1988 by songwriting college students Ed Robertson and Steven Page, both having cut their teeth in a Rush covers band; Jim Creegan, his brother Andrew and Tyler Stewart later completed the line-up. Their first album proper 'Gordon' (a Canadian No.1) fused structured melodies and graceful pop with 'Sgt. Pepper'-esque dizziness and a little touch of Brian Wilson-ish psychedelic rock; it went on to stay a further 8 weeks at the top of the charts. Sophomore set, 'Maybe You Should Drive' (1994), climbed into the US Top 60, and by the timely release of their third studio album, 'Rock Spectacle' (1997), the band were now reaching out to the mainstream by selling out dates across America and Europe. The group embarked on what was to become their breakthrough instalment, 'Stunt' (1998), a record which was released hot on the heels of their definitive smash hit single, 'One Week'. The group subsequently deposited a track to the 'Ed TV' soundtrack, and also roped in production maverick Don Was for 2000s 'Maroon'. *MCS*

BE GLAD FOR THE SONG HAS NO ENDING

1970 (UK 50m) independent

Film genre: Folk-rock-music documentary

Top guns: dir: Peter Neal → EXPERIENCE / → GLASTONBURY FAYRE → YESSONGS

Stars: the Incredible String Band:- Robin Williamson, Mike Heron, Licorice McKechnie, Rose Simpson *(themselves/performers)*

Storyline: "My name's Robin Williamson, genius of this parish; how do you do?" Engagingly haphazard portrait imparting the impression of two impossibly nice chaps with not a rock'n'roll bone in their respective bodies. Footage includes Mike Heron – strangely reminiscent of a young Gordon Brown – shyly deflecting the questions of a Newsweek reporter ("How would you describe them [the songs]?"; "If I could describe them I wouldn't sing them"), Robin Williamson visiting the home of a guitar maker to procure a hurdy gurdy and various sun-dappled shots of the lads in rural bliss, with some fascinating glimpses of '60s Edinburgh and nearby Pentland Hills. Performances – many of which don't feature on the soundtrack – include a wonderful 'All Writ Down' and 'The Iron Stone', with the last quarter of an hour or so given over to 'The Pirate & The Crystal Ball – A Fable', a theatrical, silent film (with title montage over the top) enactment of a Groucho Marx-cum-shiver-me-timbers type mystically brought to book (great facial expressions). A film which leaves you all warm and fuzzy inside. *BG*

Movie rating: *6.5

Visual: video + 80m dvd w/ Peter Neal interviews

Off the record: The **Incredible String Band** were founded in Glasgow, Scotland . . . early 1966 by **Robin Williamson**, **Mike Heron** and London-born Clive Palmer. After months tracking them down, American producer Joe Boyd finally found them and duly signed them to 'Elektra'. He almost immediately took them to London, where they recorded their eponymous debut album (in summer '66), an LP which was well-received, although it didn't stop Palmer leaving for a trip to Afghanistan. Upon Robin's return from a similar trip to Morocco, he and Mike (augmented by some friends but not Clive), delivered a second album, 'The 5000 Spirits Or The Layers Of The Onion', a record which made the UK Top 30 in 1967. In spring '68, they surprisingly crashed into the UK Top 5 with their third set, 'The Hangman's Beautiful Daughter', a record with witty lyrics (alternately penned by Heron or Williamson) and ethnic multi-instrumentation embellished with the "out-there" vocals of the duo's girlfriends, **Licorice** and **Rose**. Later that same year, the ISB issued two single LP's as a double-set, 'Wee Tam' & 'The Big Huge', however, this brilliant but confused package failed to sell. Over the next two years, the ensemble released three UK Top 40 albums, 'Changing Horses' (very sub-standard and OTT), 'I Looked Up' (a collection of baroque eclecticism and 'U' (verging on pantomine), and of course, this film, their first release for 'Island' records. *MCS*

—

the INCREDIBLE STRING BAND

Apr 71. (lp) *Island; (ILPS 9140)* ☐ –
– Come with me / All writ down / Vishangro / See all the people /

Waiting for you / Be glad for the song has no ending. *(cd-iss. Jun98 on 'Edsel'+=; EDCD 564)* – Song has no ending (pts.2-9).

S/track review: Ah, the good ship INCREDIBLE STRING BAND, don't you just love their gnomish, gnomic little world? Looking back, it's surprising that more 60s filmmakers didn't hire out their bizarro meta-folk. Despite being something of a grab-bag of late 60s offcuts to an all but shelved movie, this underrated quasi-soundtrack suited their own capricious purposes just fine, and threw up a clutch of unlikely ISB classics. WILLIAMSON's 'Come With Me' and HERON's 'All Writ Down' makes for one of the strongest openings to any ISB album. HERON's song is one of the few moments the album approaches conventional melodic folk-pop, and therein lies the enduring nub of the whole ISB project. When MIKE HERON and ROBIN WILLIAMSON deigned to write straightforwardly, the results were rarely less than indestructible; most of the time they decided not to . . . Their back catalogue is a proverbially wyrd and wonderful, often magnificent, often maddeningly whimsical flight into the arcane; we can only guess how much less nebulous it would all have been, and perhaps how much bigger their legend would be, if they'd recorded more simple acoustica and less deliberate attempts to "devastate your synaesthesia". But then they wouldn't have been the INCREDIBLE STRING BAND, a troupe whose influence on the current crop of neo-folkies is incalculable. Assembled just as Joe Boyd sold up to 'Island', 'BE GLAD . . .' does, ironically, signify an ending of sorts, before the duo increasingly fell into line with the folk scene's rock inclinations. And as such, it's a record to be treasured rather than passed over, imparting an unforgettable flavour of mid-period ISB's many-cloaked personality. 'Veshengro' is typical WILLIAMSON dream diary, recounting a colourful assortment of incarnated lives ("swineherd at the court of Finn", "a monk repelled by a woman's smell", "a mouse that gnawed the grain", etc.) in that portentous Edinburgh whine. The slight 'See All The People' derives from the movie's Festival Hall clip, while 'Waiting For You' indulges the band's penchant for theatre and music hall, reeling off more of WILLIAMSON's extra-curricular guises and Cole Porter-like asides over a wheezing steam organ. Acquired listening for sure, but it's impossible not to be charmed by the casual absurdity; WILLIAMSON's Etonian intros are priceless ("On the pounding batterie and coterie we have that well known bricklayer's labourer from Pilton" . . .). Most of this soundtrack – almost a full half hour's worth and a whole side of the original vinyl – is taken up with the title piece, which backs the piratical capering informing much of the movie and is probably best heard in that context. Stylistically, it could almost be a microcosm of the ISB's career, breaking their polymath influences into constituent parts, feverishly jumping from Nino Rota-esque Sicilian folk and gorgeous, chordal-strum lament to Third Ear Band-style medieval quacking, droning and cymbal-bashing to pealing wind chimes to Indo-Caucasian classicism to choral chant to high register orientalism and on across borders and centuries . . . It's been said before but it's worth saying again: along with the jazz avant-garde, the INCREDIBLE STRING BAND were playing world music decades before record shops supplied a section for it. *BG*

Album rating: *6.5 / re-CD *7

BE HERE TO LOVE ME

. . . A FILM ABOUT TOWNES VAN ZANDT

2004 (US 99m) Rake Films / Palm Pictures

Film genre: Roots-Rock-music documentary/bio-pic

Top guns: dir: Margaret Brown

Stars: Townes Van Zandt *(archive; himself/performer)* ← HEARTWORN HIGHWAYS, **Guy Clark** *(himself)* ← HEARTWORN HIGHWAYS, **Steve Earle** *(himself)* ← JUST AN AMERICAN BOY ← HEARTWORN HIGHWAYS, **Emmylou HARRIS** *(herself)*, **Kris KRISTOFFERSON** *(himself)*, **Willie NELSON** *(himself)*, **Steve Shelley** *(himself)* <= SONIC YOUTH =>

Storyline: For all his embrace of live-smashed-die-young cliché, Townes Van Zandt existed far from rock'n'roll caricature. The publicity shot – all laconic glance and aviator shades – has him resembling a young Richard Ashcroft of all people, but the film reveals a troubled life closer to Gram Parsons: a relatively privileged Southern upbringing with a grand family heritage from which Townes more or less divorced himself, compelled to take to a life of wine, women and heart-ripping song instead. One of the movie's most dryly ironic moments comes as his first wife recalls him shutting himself away in a cupboard after they're first married and penning 'Waitin' Around To Die'; with rueful humour, she admits it wasn't quite what she was expecting. Refused entry to the military on mental health grounds, Van Zandt – a "migratory beast", as Earle casts him – hits the road and never really comes back, trying to regain his ECT-erased childhood memory through song and an unparalleled talent for pathos. Joe Ely remembers a "long, tall, scarecrow lookin' guy" and – through 70s footage of trailer parks and bearded pow wows – the young Townes certainly cuts a rakish figure. Revelations of schoolboy glue sniffing, leisure-time Russian Roulette and jumping from a fourth floor balcony "just to see what it felt like" don't quite fit with the reclusive sadness of his writing, and the sadness of his writing doesn't quite fit with the witty, gregarious persona portrayed in the washed-out celluloid. Poignant anecdote after poignant anecdote (Townes finally topping the country charts and jubilantly offering the fact as a prelude to a possible reunion with his first wife, just after she's newly married again; Sonic Youth's Steve Shelley recounting the breakdown of a final session in Memphis) offer clues, but ultimately Van Zandt remains the proverbial mystery wrapped up in an enigma. *BG*

Movie rating: *7.5

Visual: dvd

Off the record: Townes Van Zandt was born on 7th March '44, Fort Worth, Texas, USA. Steve Earle called him the "greatest songwriter in the world", but Townes Van Zandt's parcel of demons also made him one of the most elusive. As far as screen footage goes, he left less to posterity than your average genius, most of it crammed into the excellent 'BE HERE TO LOVE ME . . .'. Even if the only official existing video concert set is the late period 'Houston 1988 – A Private Concert' (1988), the man's mercurial life and times is surely a biopic waiting to happen. Until then, fans of his fateful parables will have to content themselves with Margaret Brown's aforementioned documentary or else James Szalapski's equally fascinating (and recently reissued) snapshot of the Texas songwriting scene, 'HEARTWORN HIGHWAYS' (1981). *BG*

TOWNES VAN ZANDT

Aug 05. (d-cd) *Tomato; <50 3015-2>* ☐ ☐
– "I've designed it that way" (film excerpt) / At my window / Be here to love me / Black crow blues / Brand new companion / Delta momma blues / Dollar bill blues / Don't you take it too bad / Flyin' shoes / Highway kind / High, low and in between / If I needed you / Marie / Mr. Mudd and Mr. Gold // My proud mountains / No place to fall / Nothin' / Pancho and Lefty / Rake / Rex's blues / Snake song / St. John the gambler / To live's to fly / Waitin' round to die / When she don't need me / Where I lead me.

S/track review: "They're not all sad; some of them are hopeless". Questioned on his songs, TOWNES VAN ZANDT displayed all the coal-black wit, brutal honesty and congenital pathos that delivered his writing to a plain far beyond C&W cliché. Not since Hank Williams did a Southern songwriter embrace the totem of tortured artist as recklessly and as wholeheartedly; in terms of unfathomable self-destructiveness, no-one – not Gram Parsons, not Steve Earle – can hold a candle to the man. So for his suffering – and that of those who loved him – we get music of an often terrible beauty, which hardly seems fair but there you go; VAN ZANDT doubtless would've appreciated the irony. By all accounts, he was always convinced his time wasn't long, and he wrote accordingly.

'Waitin' Around To Die' is still the ultimate statement of country existentialism, here rendered in its original, gulch-echo, Morricone-esque production. And of course he was being gratuitously disingenuous when he said his songs were either sad or hopeless: the finely plucked gentle rain and madrigal chorus of 'At My Window' render it too poignant, too perfect to be anything but inspirational; 'Be Here To Love Me' itself strums a desert air emolliated by the same jazz-sprite arrangements Van Morrison called down on 'Astral Weeks'; and 'To Live's To Fly' actually celebrates the joy of itinerant life and hope of return. Excepting a handful of orchestrated numbers, the rest of the material on this soundtrack-cum-career overview is more familiarly stark, just TOWNES finger-picking the cardinal points of the soul. For those untouched by his genius, it's as good a place as any to pick up the thread, and – with the inclusion of several latter period numbers (including the harrowing 'Marie') sung in the voice of a craggy pensioner, somewhere between Kris Kristofferson and the grim reaper – at least you'll get a sense of the magnitude of the loss that his drinking wreaked on his talent. The pinnacle of which was poured into 'Pancho And Lefty', an outlaw ballad popularised by Emmylou Harris and Willie Nelson, still staking a claim as the most evocative ever penned, and included here as a pared-to-the-quick live version. Other highlights include a live 'If I Needed You' and the lovely 'No Place To Fall', while lesser heard oddities like Dylan-esque gambling allegory, 'Mr Mudd And Mr Gold' and an out of focus, painfully intimate 'Black Crow Blues' (hailed with only the meanest scattering of applause) will satisfy the hardcore. But the most affective, loaded moment on any VAN ZANDT anthology has to be 'Flying Shoes', an aching treatise on a corrosive wanderlust, which, in TOWNES' case, proved terminal. *BG*

Album rating: *8.5

the BEACH BOYS

Formed: Hawthorne, Los Angeles, California, USA . . . 1961 by the Wilson brothers Brian, Dennis and Carl, plus cousin Mike Love and neighbour Al Jardine. The quintet went through a series of cringe-inducing names before being individually christened the BEACH BOYS by a local DIY studio, who had released their first single 'Surfin'' on their small 'Candix' label. As sales of the record mushroomed, the band decided to keep the name. Murray Wilson, the brothers' tyrannical father, seized the opportunity to become their manager, producer and song publisher; not exactly a healthy combination and one which the band would come to regret when financial troubles dogged them throughout the next decade and beyond. For the moment, however, on the surface at least, everything was hunky dory, the band riding the commercial crest of their surfing wave as they signed to 'Capitol' in 1962 and became the very essence of the sun-tanned, Californian dream. The hits came thick and fast with the prodigiously talented Brian writing most of the material. Songs like 'Surfin Safari' and 'Surfin U.S.A.' were effervescent feelgood anthems, their jaw-dropping vocal harmonies framing images of surf, sea and beautiful girls. Early glimpses of Brian's penchant for introspection are evident on tracks like the poignant 'In My Room', co-written with Gary Usher, the first of many songwriters Brian would collaborate with during the course of his career. By Christmas 1964, however, the strain of their horrendous recording/touring treadmill was too much for Brian and he suffered a series of nervous breakdowns. Producing and arranging six albums in just over 2 years as well as writing over 60 songs in the same period would've been too much for the hardiest of souls, let alone the painfully shy and sensitive Brian. This episode signalled the end of Brian's live commitment to the band, allowing him to concentrate solely on composing and recording. In the meantime, the 'Boys were always ready for the odd cameo, and the "BEACH PARTY" movies saw them branch out into the flicks. BRIAN WILSON had become obsessed with outdoing the BEATLES who he saw as a threat, a paranoia that grew stronger after his first forays into the world of LSD. He first took the drug in the summer of '65 and it changed his approach to music, to his whole life in fact, with Brian later stating that his mind was opened and it scared the shit out of him. He then enlisted the unlikely help of erstwhile ad sloganeer Tony Asher to express the lyrical mood of these new pieces, and the result was 'Pet Sounds'. Released in May '66, it still holds the coveted "best album of all time" position among many critics, with fragile highlights being 'God Only Knows', 'Wouldn't It Be Nice' and 'Caroline No', which perfectly evoked Brian's turbulent emotional state. Reportedly devastated at the album's lack of success in his home country (yes, it did hit Top 10) and feeling outdone by the Beatles' 'Revolver' and Dylan's 'Blonde On Blonde', he upped his drug use and vowed to go one better, dreaming of the ultimate studio masterpiece. Initially pencilled in for inclusion on 'Pet Sounds' in its earliest incarnation, 'Good Vibrations' was released in October that year and soon became their biggest ever selling single. With its pioneering use of the theramin and complex vocal arrangements, its success vindicated Brian's vision of grand sonic tapestries over the formulaic pop that other members (most notably Mike Love and his father) wanted to churn out. Around this time, Brian began working on his masterpiece (with self-styled L.A. boho scenester/songwriter Van Dyke Parks), which had a working title of 'Dumb Angel', later changing to 'Smile'. The sessions that resulted are the stuff of legend with Brian's mental condition deteriorating rapidly under the weight of his own expectation. Among his more whimsical foibles were having a box filled with sand so he could play piano barefoot "like on the beach, man" (Surf's Up, indeed). More worrying was the pathological superstition which saw him attempt to destroy tapes of the abandoned 'Smile' album, although these did surface later on albums 'Smiley Smile', 'Heroes And Villains' and 'Surf's Up'. From this point on, Brian retreated even further from the world at large and spent much of the following decade in bed. A string of average, occasionally good albums followed with Dennis emerging as a fairly talented songwriter. Recorded after the band's acrimonious split with 'Capitol', the aforementioned 'Surf's Up' (1971) was the highlight of this period with its 'Smile'-era title track and spirited contributions from other band members. Dennis Wilson's association with the infamous Charles Manson, albeit before he went on his killing spree in 1969, probably brought more attention than any music the band released at this time. With the exception of one outstanding Brian-penned song 'Sail On Sailor' from the disappointing 'Holland' set, much of the 70s material was creatively bland to say the least. On the 4th June 1973, their father died and eventually Mike Love's brothers Stan and Steve were removed from management after the latter was found guilty of embezzling around $1 million. 1977's 'Beach Boys Love You' album saw Brian return to take the reins again for the first time in 10 years, and included some fine material. From there on in, the BEACH BOYS became nothing more than a nostalgic novelty act, living on past glories while producing stagnant albums for the over-40s. One supposes in retrospection that MIKE LOVE's foray into film soundtracks, via 1978's 'ALMOST SUMMER' (with his band Celebration) was another that might've been overlooked had it not been recorded by a Beach Boy. On the 28th December '83, tragedy struck when Dennis drowned during a diving trip in Marina Del Ray. The band struggled on, minus Brian who'd been sacked a year earlier. The band scored a surprise US No.1 hit in 1988 with the soppy 'Kokomo' (from the movie 'Cocktail'), which was co-written with former Mamas & The Papas singer John

Phillips. Meanwhile, Brian released a competent, not to mention long-awaited, solo album under the guidance of his controversial therapist Eugene Landy. He even recorded a second album, which was strangely turned down by his new label 'Sire', despite garnering rave reviews from critics who'd heard the pre-release tapes. 1995 saw the release of BRIAN's 'I JUST WASN'T MADE FOR THESE TIMES', an album and film documentary project combining re-working of older and rare material. A year later the BEACH BOYS scraped the barrel of banality when they did a nauseating run-through of their 60s hit 'Fun, Fun, Fun' with Status Quo. This was surely the end of the sandy road for the once inspirational outfit; tragedy struck with the lung cancer death (on the 6th of February, 1998) of Carl. Remaining brother Brian carried on, his 'Imagination' (1998) set receiving rave reviews from the "old fogey" brigade while reaching the Top 100 (Top 30 in Britain); he subsequently teamed up with Brian Setzer (ex-Stray Cats) to record 'Little Deuce Coupe' for a V/A "save our beaches" benefit album, 'Music For Our Mother Ocean'. Brian's musical rehabilitation went from strength to strength in the new millennium: a live solo album from the troubled genius would've been unimaginable only a decade earlier yet 'Live At The Roxy Theatre' (2000) was just that, an internet-only release delving into at least some of the kind of difficult, introspective material which the BEACH BOYS steered clear of on stage. When the man went the whole hog and performed 'Pet Sounds Live' (2002) over a four-night run at London's Royal Festival Hall, it was, understandably, the cue for grown men to weep in the aisles. Though the album was hardly a substitute for the living history of actually being there, critics were generally kind to it, and to BRIAN WILSON's weathered vocals/erratic stage presence. 'Gettin' In Over My Head' (2004) took the same troupe of sympathetic and dedicated musicians into the studio alongside guests like PAUL McCARTNEY, ELTON JOHN and – with the help of studio technology – his late brother Carl. An obsession with studio possibilities had originally helped put the lid on 'SMILE' (2004), the would-be masterpiece he abandoned in 1967. Re-recorded and finally released in full, as a gloriously seamless whole, the DVD and album was final proof that WILSON was more than capable of making up for vanished years and genius overreached. The chart positions – UK Top 10, US Top 20 – were the best he'd scored in decades. Over the years, we've witnessed the odd biopic, two especially come to mind, 'The BEACH BOYS: AN AMERICAN BAND' (1985) and 'ENDLESS HARMONY: THE BEACH BOYS STORY' (1998), while Brian and Co have contributed to many a rockumentary flick. *BG & MCS*

- **filmography** {performers} (composers) –

Beach Party *(1963 {b BRIAN} OST by ANNETTE =>)* / **the T.A.M.I. Show** *(1964 {p} =>)* / **Beach Blanket Bingo** *(1965 {b BRIAN} OST by DONNA LOREN =>)* / **the Girls On The Beach** *(1965 {p} =>)* / **How To Stuff A Wild Bikini** *(1965 {b BRIAN} OST by the KINGSMEN & V/A =>)* / **Almost Summer** *(1978 OST by CELEBRATION =>)* / **Deadman's Curve** *(1978 {b MIKE} =>)* / **the Beach Boys: An American Band** *(1985 {c} =>)* / My Own Private Idaho *(1991 {b BRIAN})* / **I Just Wasn't Made For These Times** *(1995 TV {p} OST by WILSON =>)* / **Nashville Sounds** *(1996 {c BRIAN} OST =>)* / **Imagination** *(1998 TV {*p BRIAN} OST =>)* / **Endless Harmony: The Beach Boys Story** *(1998 TV {*} OST =>)* / **Blues Odyssey** *(2001 TV {p MIKE} =>)* / **Mayor Of The Sunset Strip** *(2003 {c BRIAN} OST by V/A =>)* / **Beautiful Dreamer: Brian Wilson And The Story Of 'Smile'** *(2004 {p* BRIAN} =>)* / **Who Is Harry Nilsson (And Why Is Everybody Talkin' About Him?)** *(2006 {c BRIAN} =>)* / Tales Of The Rat Fink *(2006 {v BRIAN})*

the BEACH BOYS: AN AMERICAN BAND

1985 (US 103m w/b&w) High Ridge Productions / ABC (PG-13)

Film genre: Pop/Rock-music concert/documentary bio-pic

Top guns: s-w + dir: Malcolm Leo ← THIS IS ELVIS

Stars: the BEACH BOYS:- Brian Wilson, Carl Wilson, Dennis Wilson, Mike Love, Bruce Johnston, Al Jardine *(themselves/performers)*, **Jimi HENDRIX** *(archive performer)*, **Paul McCartney** *(performer)* <= the BEATLES =>, **Van Dyke Parks** *(himself)* ← POPEYE / → BEAUTIFUL DREAMER: BRIAN WILSON AND THE STORY OF 'SMiLE', Bob Hope *(archive)*, Jack Benny *(archive)*

Storyline: The authorized Beach Boys story complete with live TV footage and special shows, alongside rare interviews with Brian Wilson (in his bed!) and even movie clips they featured in. *MCS*

Movie rating: *7.5

Visual: video on Vestron / dvd on Artisan (no audio OST)

Off the record: Track listing on film is as follows:- 'Surf's Up', 'Surfin' U.S.A.', 'Be True To Your School', 'Surfin'', 'Surfer Girl', 'Fun, Fun, Fun', 'I Get Around', '409', 'Little Honda', 'California Girls', 'Help Me, Rhonda', 'In My Room', 'Student Demonstration Time', 'Dance, Dance, Dance', 'Please Let Me Wonder', 'Wouldn't It Be Nice', 'That's Not Me', 'Sloop John B.', 'God Only Knows', 'Good Vibrations', 'Heroes And Villains', 'Fire', 'Do It Again', 'I Can Hear Music', 'Break Away' & 'Barbara Ann'. *MCS*

BEASTIE BOYS

Formed: Greenwich Village, New York, USA . . . 1981 by Adam Yauch and Mike Diamond; Adam Horowitz was soon brought in to replace two others (Kate Schellenbach and John Berry). The trio signed to 'Def Jam', the label run by their friend and sometime DJ, Rick Rubin, while the VW-stealing lads were also viewed in the film, 'KRUSH GROOVE' (1985). The BEASTIE BOYS' debut album 'Licensed To Ill' (1986) was the first real attempt to create a white, rock-centric take on Afro-American Hip Hop. At turns hilarious and exhilarating, Rubin and the BEASTIEs shared taste in classic metal was evident with samples from the likes of Ac/Dc and Led Zeppelin along with the theme tune from American TV show 'Mr. Ed'. With snotty rapping and riff-heavy rhymes, tracks like 'Fight For Your Right (To Party)' and 'No Sleep Till Brooklyn' stormed the charts on both sides of the Atlantic. The record turned the band into a phenomenon and in 1987 they undertook a riotous headlining tour, while courting controversy wherever they played, even on Run-DMC's 'TOUGHER THAN LEATHER' (1988) movie. Despite all the upheaval, by the release of 'Paul's Boutique' (1989), the trio's profile was negligible and the album was more or less passed over. A tragedy, as it remains one of hip hop's lost gems, a widescreen sampladelic collage produced by the ultra-hip Stateside Dust Brothers. After another extended sabbatical during which the group relocated to California, the BEASTIE BOYS returned in 1992 with 'Check Your Head', while Horowitz (Ad Rock to his mates) co-starred in the cult Abbe Wool movie, 'ROADSIDE PROPHETS' (1992). 'Ill Communication' (1994) was the group's most mature and accomplished work to date; the hardcore was still there but it was offset by some sombre strings and the screechingly brilliant 'Sabotage' (complete with entertaining cop-pastiche video). From the artwork to the meditative feel of the music, it was no surprise that Yauch had become a Buddhist – the band subsequently played a high profile benefit for the oppressed nation of Tibet, made into a docu-film, 'FREE TIBET' (1998). Ever industrious, the group also started their own label and fanzine 'Grand Royal', while

1998's 'Intergallactic' single (along with bizarre Power-Rangers-esque video) led the way for the release of the eagerly-awaited 5th set proper, 'Hello Nasty'. When the original Caucasian B-Boys finally got around to releasing a follow-up some six years later, Eminem had long since had the monopoly on petulant sneer, and the American cultural landscape had changed almost beyond recognition. Rather than kowtowing to contemporary production – not that they'd ever done that anyway – 'To The 5 Boroughs' (2004) found the BEASTIEs reliving the thrill of misspent youth through the prism of middle age. It was inevitable some sort of BEASTIE BOYS movie would be released, what was more surprising is that 'AWESOME; I FUCKIN' SHOT THAT' (2006) was filmed by their fans. *BG & MCS*

- **filmography** {acting/performance} (composers) –

Over Exposed *(1984 {b ADAM H})* / **Krush Groove** *(1985 {p} OST by V/A =>)* / **Tougher Than Leather** *(1988 {p} =>)* / Lost Angels *(1989 {* ADAM H})* / Long Road Home *(1991 TV {b ADAM H})* / a Kiss Before Dying *(1991 {a ADAM H})* / **Roadside Prophets** *(1992 {a ADAM H} OST by PRAY FOR RAIN & V/A =>)* / Cityscrapes: Los Angeles *(1994 {b})* / **Free Tibet** *(1998 {p} =>)* / Keep Your Eyes Open *(2002 score)* / **Fade To Black** *(2004 {p ADAM H} =>)* / **Awesome; I Fuckin' Shot That** *(2006 {p} score =>)*

BEAUTIFUL DREAMER: BRIAN WILSON AND THE STORY OF 'SMiLE'

aka Brian Wilson presents SMiLE

2004 (US 120m TV) Chautauqua Entertainment / LSL Productions Inc.

Film genre: Pop/Rock-music documentary & concert

Top guns: dir: David Leaf → the U.S. vs. JOHN LENNON

Stars: Brian Wilson *(himself/performer)* <= the BEACH BOYS =>, **Van Dyke Parks** *(himself)* ← POPEYE, **Elvis COSTELLO** *(himself)*, George Martin *(himself)* ← IN MY LIFE, **Paul McCartney** *(himself)* <= the BEATLES =>, **Roger Daltrey** *(himself)* <= the WHO =>, **Natalie Imbruglia** *(herself)*, **Hal Blaine** *(himself)* ← the DR. JEKYLL & MR. HYDE ROCK 'N ROLL MUSICAL ← MAN ON THE MOON ← GIRLS! GIRLS! GIRLS!, **Carol Kaye** *(herself)*, Michael Vosse *(himself)*

Storyline: 'Smile' was scheduled to supersede the inspirational Beach Boys LP, 'Pet Sounds', of '66. Sadly, due to overwhelming conflicts with the record company, his drug habit, depression and the rest of the group, the extremely fragile Brian Wilson was forced to shelve the record. After a gap of 37 years, the album was finally unleashed, while this accompanying documentary of interviews, etc., tells the story. *MCS*

Movie rating: *8

Visual: dvd w/ 'SMiLE' in May'05

Off the record: Carol Kaye was a session bassist for the Beach Boys, Phil Spector, Motown, etc. *MCS*

– associated release –

BRIAN WILSON: Brian Wilson presents SMiLE

Sep 04. (cd) *Nonesuch; <(7559 79846-2)>* [13] [7]
– Our prayer – Gee / Heroes and villains / Roll Plymouth rock / Barnyard / Old master painter – You are my sunshine / Cabin essence / Wonderful / Song for children / Child is father of the man / Surf's up / I'm in great shape – I wanna be around – Workshop / Vega-tables / On a holiday / Wind chimes / Mrs. O'Leary's cow / In Blue Hawaii / Good vibrations. *(d-lp iss.Nov04 + dvd+=; 7559 79846-1)* – (instrumentals):- Heroes and villains / Cabin essence / On a holiday / Wind chimes.

BRIAN WILSON: Wonderful / Wind Chimes

Sep 04. (7"green/blue/yellow) *Must Destroy; (MDA 001/+X/XX)* [–] [29]

BRIAN WILSON: Good Vibrations / In Blue Hawaii

Dec 04. (7"/cd-s) *Nonesuch; (NS 001/+CD)* [–] [30]

BEEF

2003 (US *90m) Open Road Films / Image Entertainment (R)

Film genre: Hip-Hop/Rap-music concert documentary

Top guns: s-w: Peter Spirer (+ dir) ← THUG ANGEL ← RHYME & REASON, Peter Alton

Stars: Ving Rhames *(narrator)* ← PULP FICTION / → IDLEWILD, **50 Cent** *(himself)* → GET RICH OR DIE TRYIN', **ICE CUBE** *(himself)*, **Common** *(himself)* ← GODFATHERS AND SONS ← BROWN SUGAR / → FADE TO BLACK → BLOCK PARTY, **DMX** *(himself)* ← BACKSTAGE, **JAY-Z** *(himself)*, **Ja Rule** *(himself)* ← BACKSTAGE ← TURN IT UP / → BEEF III, **Nas** *(himself)* ← RHYME & REASON, **Mack 10** *(himself)* ← THICKER THAN WATER ← RHYME & REASON, **KRS-One** *(himself)* ← RHYME & REASON ← WHO'S THE MAN?, **Mobb Deep** *(themselves)*, **Tupac SHAKUR** *(archive footage)*, **Kool Moe Dee** *(himself)* ← BEAT STREET ← WILD STYLE, **Bone Thugs-N-Harmony:- Krayzie Bone, Flesh-N-Bone, Layzie Bone** *(themselves)* ← THICKER THAN WATER, **Russell Simmons** *(himself)* ← DEATH OF A DYNASTY ← BROWN SUGAR ← the SHOW ← TOUGHER THAN LEATHER ← KRUSH GROOVE, **the Notorious B.I.G.** *(archive performer)* ← THUG ANGEL ← TUPAC: RESURRECTION ← BIGGIE AND TUPAC ← RHYME & REASON ← the SHOW, Jessica Hagan *(newscaster)*

Storyline: Bitching and infighting has become an art form in the hip hop world and this documentary traces the most famous fall outs in the rap community, examining their roots and the manufactured nature of some and their effect on the people and their music. Most significantly perhaps the ones that end in bloodshed, and even death. *MR*

Movie rating: *6.5

Visual: dvd

Off the record: Along with rap stars **ICE CUBE, KRS-One** and **TUPAC SHAKUR** the movie featured relative new rappers **50 Cent, Common, DMX, Jay-Z, Ja Rule, Nas** alongside **Mobb Depp** (aka Prodigy/Albert Johnson & Havoc/Kejuan Muchita), **Bone Thugs-N-Harmony** and **Kool Moe Dee**.

Various Artists: Beef – Music From And Inspired . . .

Oct 03. (cd) *Strange Music – M.S.C.; <MSC 10092>* [ ] [–]
– No vaseline (ICE CUBE) / Beef (TECH N9NE feat. BIG KRIZZ KALIKO) / You don't really want it (KRS-ONE) / Westside slaughterhouse (WESTSIDE CONNECTION) / Murder by #'s (SKATTERMAN & SNUG BRIM feat. RICKY SKARFO) / Drama (PRODIGY feat. TWIN) / Real muthaph****in' G's (EAZY-E feat. B.G. KNOCKOUT) / Caution (BLACK CHILD) / When the rain drops (KUTT CALHOUN feat. SNUG BRIM) / That's it (KRS-ONE feat. MAD LION) / Postman (POVERTY) / Now I see (M C SHAN) / Snake ya (TECH N9NE feat. BIG KRIZZ KALIKO) / Let's go (it's a movement) (WARREN G. feat. KRS-ONE & LIL' AI) / Witness protection (JAYO FELONY) / Day I die (TRU-LIFE) / F*** tha police (N.W.A). *// (+ bonus CD footage)*

S/track review: For the soundtrack to a film about feuds in the rap world, two men are hugely conspicuous by their absence. Notorious B.I.G. and Tupac Shakur. For they were two parties in the most famous falling out in rap's short history, a tiff that ended in both men dead, gunned down in separate incidents before their respective 25th and 26th birthdays. Instead, we get a relentless 15 tracks of serious aggro. Even that advocate of smart thinking KRS-ONE shows his teeth on sage but shirty, Nelly-baiting 'You Don't Really Want It'. There are a couple of the most famous "beef" tracks ever included here, NWA's rather direct denigration of the LAPD, 'Fuck Tha Police' and ICE CUBE's, now legendary brush off of his former NWA band members 'No Vaseline'. Beyond that, there is an incomplete picture of the whole "beef as track" idea. There's also a couple of choice cuts: the hooky, poppy grump of MC SHAN's 'Now I See' and TECH N9NE's thumping infidelity rant 'Snake Ya'. This soundtrack is defined however, by what's missing: Nas, Jay-Z, LL Cool J and DMX. The stuff of legend. What's here is a hotch potch of 70s funk sampling sub-Dre bouncing and brawling. The effect is one where the lyrical flows just aren't strong enough to justify prolonged attention. The genius of insulting another on record is that it's witty and it works. Too many of the hamfisted insults traded across verses here are not worthy of repeating. *MR*

Album rating: *5

BELOVED INVADERS

aka BELOVED INVADERS: THE VENTURES

1965 (Japan/US 56m b&w) InterFilm

Film genre: Pop/Rock-music concert/documentary

Top guns: dir: George M. Reid / s-w: Junko Terayama (story: Robert Hunter)

Stars: the Ventures:- Nokie Edwards *(performer)*, **Bob Bogle** *(performer)*, **Don Wilson** *(performer)*, **Mel Taylor** *(performer)*, + dancers, etc.

Storyline: Low-key documentary on the "Venture-mania" that was hitting America, and more so, Japan (where they are featured live! on tour); something like the Beatles' 'A Hard Day's Night', a year earlier. *MCS*

Movie rating: *6

Visual: video (no audio OST, but see below)

Off the record: The **Ventures** were formed in Seattle, Washington, USA . . . 1959 by rhythm guitarist **Don Wilson** and lead guitarist **Bob Bogle**, initially as the Versatones; bassist **Nokie Edwards** and drummer Howie Taylor joined not long after (although **Mel Taylor** became the new drummer in 1961). In 1960, licensed to Bob Reisdorff's 'Dolton' label, they hit No.2 with 'Walk – Don't Run' (a song written by jazz guitarist Johnny Smith. Hot on its heels was the equally impressive, 'Perfidia', which reached the Top 20, while the instrumentalists ("the American Shadows") poached a few subsequent hits from the odd feature flick ('Lolita', etc.). By the mid-60s, after numerous US chart entries, the Ventures concentrated on the burgeoning Japanese market. *MCS*

– associated release –

the VENTURES: The Ventures On Stage

Jun 65. (lp; stereo/mono) *Dolton; <BST 8035> Liberty; (S+/LBY 1270)* [27] Nov65 [ ]
– Wipe out / Journey to the stars / Slaughter on Tenth Avenue / Caravan / Pedal pusher / Apache '65 / Bumble bee / Driving guitars / Walk, don't run – Perfidia – Lullaby of the leaves / Yellow jacket.

BENJAMIN SMOKE

2000 (US 73m w/b&w) Cowboy Booking International / Plexifilm

Film genre: Rock-music documentary bio-pic

Top guns: dir + s-w: Jem Cohen ← INSTRUMENT, Peter Sillen

Stars: Smoke:- Benjamin Dickerson *(himself)*, **Coleman Lewis** *(guitar)*, **Bill Taft** *(trumpet/banjo)*, **Brian Halloran** *(cello)*, **Tim Campion** *(perkussion)*, **Patti Smith** *(herself)* ← ROCK & ROLL HEART ← the BLANK GENERATION / → YOU'RE GONNA MISS ME, **Deacon Lunchbox** *(archive footage)*, Blondie Strange *(herself)*

Storyline: Documentary subject matter, Benjamin Smoke (drag queen and frontman for two infamous Atlanta-based bands, Opal Foxx Quartet and Smoke), and his losing battle with drug-addiction, HIV/AIDS; he died of Hepatitis C and liver failure in January 1999. *MCS*

Movie rating: *6

Visual: dvd (no audio OST)

Off the record: Smoke, in particular, **Benjamin Smoke** (b. Robert Dickerson, 28 Jan'60), was the gruff-voxed spokesman for the queercore punk generation that frequented the streets and clubs of Cabbagetown, Atlanta. Two of his bands (featuring some musicians in the film) surfaced in the mid-90s, releasing a couple of weird albums, 'The Love That Won't Shut Up' (by Opal Foxx Quartet; a 10-piece outfit!) and 'Another Reason To Fast' (by Smoke; members above). The former featured Benjamin reciting versions of the 'Mary Tyler Moore theme' and a medley of musical standards, 'I Don't Know How To Love Him' and 'Strange Fruit', while **Deacon Lunchbox** (b. Timothy Tyson Ruttenber, 1950, Washington, DC) – of the Jody Grind – contributed a couple of his compositions; he also died, killed in a car crash on 19th April, 1992. *MCS*

Chuck BERRY

Born: Charles Berry, 18 Oct'26, St. Louis, Missouri, USA. Having learned the guitar while at school, BERRY had his first run-in with the law in his late teens, when he was sent to reform school for a 3-year stretch after being convicted of attempted armed robbery. Upon his release, he worked blue collar jobs by day, perfecting his playing and songwriting by night; BERRY's first professional combo (with pianist Johnnie Johnson and drummer Ebby Hardy) became a regular local attraction during the early to mid-50s with their upbeat blend of R&B/C&W. During a trip to Chicago ("home of the blues"), BERRY enjoyed an opportunistic encounter with the legendary Muddy Waters, who in turn, put him in touch with 'Chess' records. By the summer of '55, his first recording, 'Maybellene' (an adaptation of an old country standard), was riding high in the US singles chart; this rock'n'roll template would be successfully utilised by BERRY right through to the end of the decade on such definitive R&B gems as 'Too Much Monkey Business', 'Roll Over Beethoven', 'Rock And Roll Music', 'Sweet Little Sixteen' and 'Johnny B. Goode'. As well as inventing his inimitable stage party piece, the "duck-walk", BERRY injected a quintessentially Afro-American element of humour, wit and innuendo into the concept of pop music as teen rebellion, reclaiming the rock'n'roll crown from white pretenders such as Bill Haley and ELVIS. His showman antics were witnessed in such celluloid flicks such as 'ROCK, ROCK, ROCK!' (1956), 'MISTER ROCK AND ROLL' (1957), 'GO, JOHNNY, GO!' (1959), etc. (see below filmography). However, the position of a famous black, anti-establishment star was a precarious one and BERRY fell foul of the authorities after employing a 14-year old Apache Indian as a hat-check girl in his nightclub. Unbeknown to BERRY, the girl had allegedly worked as a prostitute, and he was subsequently found guilty of contravening the "Mann act" by bringing an under-age child across the Texas-Missouri border. In October '61, he was sentenced to jail for five years, although due to the judge's racist remarks, he was given a retrial. He was later successfully tried and sentenced to three years, although with good behaviour, he was out early in '64. While in jail, BERRY's work was being successfully reappraised, with many British-invasion artists, including the BEATLES and the ROLLING STONES, covering his early material as a sizeable part of their repertoire. Inspired, "Crazy Legs" (as he was nicknamed) returned to the studio to record a new song, 'Nadine', the single becoming a Top 30 hit on both sides of the Atlantic. BERRY also set foot in Britain for the first time, wowing audiences with a further brace of recent hits including 'No Particular Place To Go' and 'You Never Can Tell'. In June 1966, with flower-power just over the horizon, he signed to 'Mercury', although this ill-advised partnership proved commercially fruitless. In 1972, following a return to the 'Chess' label three years previous, he scored a UK No.1 novelty hit with the embarrassing 'My Ding-A-Ling'. Its double entendre lyrical content sufficiently enraged morality pest, Mary Whitehouse, for her to press for a media ban. In June 1979, BERRY was again imprisoned (100 days this time) for tax evasion, although during this period he signed a deal with 'Atlantic'. Throughout the 80s, he continued to work sporadically. A docu-film 'HAIL! HAIL! ROCK'N'ROLL' was released early in '88, featuring footage from his 60th birthday concert (Keith Richards – his biggest fan – along with other star names formed his backing band at the time). BERRY subsequently retired from recording, choosing to live in his own amusement park in Wentzville, Missouri. He did, however, play live again in a November '89 revival concert alongside BO DIDDLEY, the Coasters, etc. The following month, more controversy surrounded him when it was claimed he had been videoing a ladies rest-room for immoral purposes! In June 1990, his house was raided by the drugs squad, who seized marijuana, guns and homemade pornography. He was later charged with possession of drugs and child abuse, although he was cleared of the latter and handed a fine and a 6-month suspended prison sentence for the drugs misdemeanour. Hail! hail!, rock'n'roll! right enough! *BG & MCS*

- **filmography** {acting} –

Rock, Rock, Rock! *(1956 {p} on OST by V/A =>)* / **Mister Rock And Roll** *(1957 {p})* / This Could Be The Night *(1957 {c})* / **Go, Johnny, Go!** *(1959 {p} on OST by V/A =>)* / Jazz On A Summer's Day *(1960 {p} on OST by V/A; see future edition)* / **the T.A.M.I. Show** *(1965 {p})* / **Keep On Rockin'** *(1969 {p})* / Summer In The City *(1970 score w/ the TROGGS & GENE VINCENT)* / **Let The Good Times Roll** *(1973 {p} on OST by V/A =>)* / **the London Rock And Roll Show** *(1973 {p} on OST by V/A =>)* / Alice In Den Stadten *(1974 {c})* / **American Hot Wax** *(1978 {c} on OST by V/A =>)* / Class Reunion *(1982 {c})* / **the Compleat Beatles** *(1984 {p/f} OST by the BEATLES =>)* / **Hail! Hail! Rock'n'Roll** *(1987 {*c/p} on OST w/ V/A =>)* / Bluesland: A Portrait In American Music *(1993 {p})*

BETTER LIVING THROUGH CIRCUITRY

1999 (US 86m) Cleopatra Pictures

Film genre: Electronica/Techno-music documentary

Top guns: dir: Jon Reiss

Stars: MOBY *(himself)*, **Lords Of Acid:- Lord T. Byron, Lady Galore, McGuinnes & Shai De La Luna** *(performers)*, **Roni Size** *(performer)*, **DJ Spooky** *(performer)* ← MODULATIONS / → MOOG, **Genesis P-Orridge** *(performer)* ← MODULATIONS / → DIG!, **Frankie Bones** *(performer)*, **BT aka Brian Transeau** *(himself)*, **Uberzone** *(performer)*, **the Crystal Method:- Scott Kirkland & Ken Jordan** *(performers)*, **Meat Beat Manifesto:- Jack Dangers & Jonny Stevens** *(performers)*, **Electric Skychurch:- Alex Spurkel, James Lumb & Roxanne** *(performers)*, **Wolfgang Flur** *(himself)*, **Jason Bentley** *(performer)*, **DJ Keoki** *(performer)*, **Robin Rimbaud** *(himself)*, **Atomic Babies:- P-Smooth & Joey Jupiter, Medicine Drum:- Chris Deckker, Andy Guthrie & DJ Christo** *(performers)*, **System 7:- Steve Hillage & Miquette Giraudy** *(performers)*, **Loop Guru:- Jamuud & Salman Gita** *(performers)*, **Phillip Blaine** *(performer)*, **Mike Szabo** *(himself)*, **Simply Jeff** *(himself)*, **Juno Reactor:- Ben Watkins, Stefan Holweck & Mike Maguire** *(performers)*, **Adam X** *(performer)*, **Heather Heart** *(performer)*

Storyline: From acid-house rave to techno/electro and jungle drum'n'bass, this film takes on a journey to find the source of the underground dance culture(s) that inspired a whole new generation – look out for ex-Throbbing Gristle mainman Genesis P-Orridge and his Psychic TV. *MCS*

Movie rating: *6

Visual: dvd

Off the record: Robin Rimbaud aka Scanner, might not be a household name, while **Wolfgang Flur** (ex-Kraftwerk), certainly isn't – outside Germany. *MCS*

—

Various Artists

Apr 00. (cd) *Moonshine; <(MM 80127-2)>*
– Truth in the eyes of a spaceship – edit (SPACESHIP EYES) / Expander – remix (FUTURE SOUND OF LONDON) / Now is the time – millennium remix (CRYSTAL METHOD) / Endor fun – edit (LCD) / Money for E (PSYCHIC TV) / Peace in Zaire (DJ SPOOKY) / Brown paper bag (RONI SIZE) / Parts 1-4 (MEAT BEAT MANIFESTO) / Cetch da monkey (ATOMIC BABIES) / Freaks (UBERZONE) / Caterpillar (KEOKI) / Deus (ELECTRIC SKYCHURCH).

S/track review: As it says on the tin: "A Digital Odyssey Into The Electronic Dance Underground", 'BETTER LIVING THROUGH CIRCUITRY' has exactly a dozen of the 90s top purveyors of techno-rock. From old school knob-twiddlers PSYCHIC TV via 1987's acid-house-esque 'Money For E' ('Ebeneezer . . .' was conceived here!) to something up-to-date by Jack Dangers' MEAT BEAT MANIFESTO ('Parts 1-4'), the soundtrack encompasses everything in this field, bar the big guns, the Prodigy, Orbital, Leftfield and the Chemical Brothers. There are a few acts similar to the aforementioned giants of rave and dance music, FUTURE SOUND OF LONDON with their hypnotic dancefloor cruncher from '92, 'Expander' (a minor UK hit in '94), America's CRYSTAL METHOD by way of a Millennium remix of 'Now Is The Time' and LCD's 'Endor Fun' edit. Another success from across the pond, DJ SPOOKY (aka Paul D. Miller), sets off on his synthetic rumble-in-the-jungle breeze, courtesy of 'Peace In Zaire', 8 minutes of powerful drum'n'bass turntablism. While the track is effective on many levels, it's somewhat eclipsed by Bristolian equivalent, 'Brown Paper Bag', penned by Mercury Prize-winner RONI SIZE – in a word, class. The remainder of the derivative dance-by-numbers soundtrack fails in comparison, the repetitive ATOMIC BABIES ('Cetch Da Monkey'), the Kraftwerk-ish UBERZONE and, just "who let the dogs out" for Panama-born, Keith Flint-like KEOKI Franconi on 'Caterpillar'? With only one minute allocated to opening track, 'Truth In The Eyes Of A Spaceship' by SPACESHIP EYES, why nearly 12 minutes to the finale, 'Deus', by L.A.-based trio, ELECTRIC SKYCHURCH? Better living through Tangerine Dream, I say. *MCS*

Album rating: *6.5

BETTY BLOWTORCH AND HER AMAZING TRUE LIFE ADVENTURES

2003 (US 98m) FoodForTwelve LLC (R)

Film genre: Punk-rock music concert/documentary drama

Top guns: s-w + dir: Anthony Scarpa

Stars: Betty Blowtorch:- Bianca Butthole, Blare N' Bitch, Sharon Needles, Judy Molish *(themselves/performers)*, **Vanilla Ice** *(himself)* ← COOL AS ICE / → the BROS., **Duff McKagan** *(himself)* → LIVE 8 → AMERICAN HARDCORE, **Kevin Baldes** *(himself)* ← WOODSTOCK '99, **Dez Cadena** *(himself)* ← DESPERATE TEENAGE LOVEDOLLS ← the SLOG MOVIE / → AMERICAN HARDCORE, Thom Bone *(himself)*, **Jennifer Finch** *(herself)* ← NOT BAD FOR A GIRL ← the CENSUS TAKER, Dave Gara *(himself)*, Kelly Spencer *(herself)*, **Johnny Angel** *(himself)*, Lina Lecaro *(herself)*, **Flames Evil** *(himself)*

Storyline: Two years on the road with "rock'n'roll hussies" Betty Blowtorch, an all-girl heavy-metal/glam band from L.A. with a streetwise reputation second-to-none. Sadly, the film also depicts the highs and lows that preceded the high speed car crash that killed the confrontational Bianca. *MCS*

Movie rating: *7

Visual: dvd (no audio OST; see below)

Off the record: Betty Blowtorch were the short-lived heavy/hardcore glam-punk outfit formed in Hollywood 1998 (see above line-up). Only a few albums were released, 1999's 'Get Off' and 2001's 'Are You Man Enough?', while a single, 'Size Queen', featured white rapper **Vanilla Ice. Jennifer Finch** was the bassist of L7 before joining BB (she deputised for car-crash victim, Bianca Halstead, who died 15th December, 2001). **Duff McKagan** is ex-Guns N' Roses & now of Velvet Revolver. **Kevin Baldes** is bass player for alt-rock quartet, Lit. **Johnny Angel** (b. John Carmen) fronted for bands, City Thrills, the Blackjacks and the Swinging Erudites. *MCS*

– associated release –

BETTY BLOWTORCH: Last Call

May 03. (cd) *Foodchain; <7>*
– Rock my world (live) / Party 'til ya puke / I wanna be on Epitaph (unreleased demo) / Fish taco / Shrinkwrap (unreleased demo) / Limousines (interview clip) / Van (unreleased demo) / Dresses (unreleased demo) / Shut up and fuck (alternate version) / Diarrhea (outtake) / Changing underwear (interview clip) / Yesterday II, the sequel (B-side) / Frankie (live) / I wanna be your sucker (live) / Ode to dickhead (acoustic) / Dickhead on the radio (interview clip) / Get off / Kill the butcher (unreleased demo) / Teenage whore (unreleased demo) / Funeral crashing tonite (acoustic) / T.I.T. (interview clip) / Rock'n'roll '85 / Love-hate / I've been so mad lately (rehearsal) / Johnny Depp (interview clip) / Size queen (live) / I'm ugly and I don't know why (live) / Betty Blowtorch anthem (live) / Hell on wheels (live).

Jello BIAFRA

Born: Eric Boucher, 17 Jun'58, Boulder, Colorado, USA. Inspired by British punk rock, the 19-year-old BIAFRA formed San Franciscan-based punks, Dead Kennedys (with Klaus Flouride and East Bay Ray), primarily as a vehicle for his raging, razor-sharp satire of America and everything it stood for. Public enemy #1 from the off, major labels steered well clear of the band. BIAFRA and Co subsequently formed their own label, the legendary 'Alternative Tentacles', releasing 'California Über Alles' as their debut 45 in late 1979. A scathing critique of California governor, Jerry Brown, the record introduced the singer's near-hysterical vocal undulations set against a pulverising punk/hardcore musical backdrop. Released on the independent 'Fast' imprint in Britain, the record's initial batch of copies sold like proverbial hotcakes. The 1980 follow-up, 'Holiday In Cambodia' (released on Miles Copeland's 'Faulty' label; 'Cherry Red' in the UK), remains the group's most viciously realised moment, a dark, twisting diatribe on American middle-class liberal trendies. Later in the year, the group kept up their aural assault with a debut album, 'Fresh Fruit For Rotting Vegetables', an unexpected Top 40 entry in the seemingly "Punk Is Dead" Britain, which contained the aforesaid 45s plus perennial favourites, 'Let's Lynch The Landlord', 'Drug Me' and the UK hit, 'Kill The Poor'. Their early antics are on show via live concert excerpt movie, 'URGH! A MUSIC WAR' (1981). In 1982, Dead Kennedys released their second album proper, 'Plastic Surgery Disasters', and spent the ensuing few years touring. They resurfaced in 1985 with 'Frankenchrist', an album that finally saw BIAFRA's upstanding enemies closing in (i.e. the PMRC, the US government, etc.) due to the album's free "penis landscape" poster by Swiss artist HR Giger. Although BIAFRA and Co (including some senior label staff) were tried in court for distributing harmful material to minors (a revised obscenity law), the case was subsequently thrown out after a hung jury. Nevertheless, the cost of the trial effectively put the band out of business, the band's poignantly-titled finale, 'Bedtime For Democracy', being issued late in 1986. The ever-prolific BIAFRA vociferously protested against his treatment on spoken-word sets, 'No More Cocoons' (1987) and 'The High Priest Of Harmful Matter' (1989), while also featuring in independent movies such as 'LOVEDOLLS SUPERSTAR' (1986), 'TAPEHEADS' (1988), 'TERMINAL CITY RICOCHET' (1990) and 'HIGHWAY 61' (1991). He also collaborated with a wide range of hardcore/industrial acts such as D.O.A., No Means No, Tumor Circus and Lard and in 1994, he hooked up with another likeminded hillbilly punk, Mojo Nixon, releasing one album, 'Prairie Home Invasion' (the title possibly a parody of an ICE-T album). BIAFRA continues to work at 'Alternative Tentacles', supplying the country with suitably deranged hardcore and occasionally taking time out to appear in the odd punk documentary/project (see below). *BG & MCS*

- **filmography** {acting} –

Urgh! A Music War *(1981 {p w/ DEAD KENNEDYS}* / Anarchism In America *(1983 {p})* / **the Unheard Music** *(1986 {c} =>)* / **Lovedolls Superstar** *(1986 {c} OST by V/A =>)* / **Tapeheads** *(1988 {b})* / **Terminal City Ricochet** *(1990 {*} OST by V/A =>)* / **Highway 61** *(1991 {a} OST by NASH THE SLASH =>)* / Skulheadface *(1994 {c} =>)* / Mary Jane's Not A Virgin Anymore *(1997 {*})* / the Widower *(1999 {a})* / Virtue *(1999 {*})* / Trade Off *(2000 {*p})* / **Rage: 20 Years Of Punk Rock West Coast Style** *(2001 {p} =>)* / Plaster Caster *(2001 {c})* / **Mayor Of The Sunset Strip** *(2003 {p} on OST by V/A =>)* / Death & Texas *(2004 {a})* / **Punk: Attitude** *(2005 {p} =>)* / **Punk's Not Dead** *(2007 {p w/ DEAD KENNEDYS} =>)*

the BIG T.N.T. SHOW

1966 (US 93m b&w) American International Pictures

Film genre: R&B/Pop-music concert documentary

Top guns: dir: Larry Peerce → GOODBYE, COLUMBUS → HARD TO HOLD

Stars: Roger Miller *(performer)*, **Joan BAEZ** *(performer)*, David McCallum Jr. *(conductor/host)*, **Bo DIDDLEY** *(performer)*, **Ike Turner** *(performer)* → IT'S YOUR THING → GIMME SHELTER → SOUL TO SOUL → BLUES ODYSSEY → the ROAD TO MEMPHIS → GODFATHERS AND SONS & **Tina TURNER** *(performer)*, **Ray CHARLES** *(performer)*, **the LOVIN' SPOONFUL:- John Sebastian, Zal Yanovsky, Joe Butler, Steve Boone** *(performers)*, **the Ronettes:- Ronnie Spector, Estelle Bennett, Nedra Talley** *(performers)*, **the Byrds:- Roger McGuinn, David Crosby, Chris Hillman, Gene Clark, Mike Clarke** *(performers)* → BANJOMAN, **the Modern Folk Quartet:- Chip Douglas *, Jerry Yester, Cyrus Faryar, Heney Diltz** *(performers)* → HEY HEY WE'RE THE MONKEES, **DONOVAN** *(performer)*, **Petula Clark** *(performer)* ← the 6.5 SPECIAL

Storyline: Originally billed as the T.A.M.I. Show II, Phil Spector produces a concert filled with the biggest stars of the 1960s. Tina Turner, Ray Charles and Bo Diddley all perform, and Spector himself plays piano for Joan Baez singing 'You've Lost That Lovin' Feeling'. Filmed at the Hollywood Palace, the concert is a snapshot of the American music scene in the mid 60s. *JZ*

Movie rating: *6

Visual: video as 'THAT WAS ROCK' compilation (no audio OST)

Off the record: Tracks featured:- the MODERN FOLK QUARTET: 'This Could Be The Night', RAY CHARLES: 'It's All Right', 'Georgia On My Mind' & 'Let The Good Times Roll', PETULA CLARK: 'Downtown', 'You're The One' & 'My Love', the LOVIN' SPOONFUL: 'Do You Believe In Magic?' & 'You Didn't Have To Be So Nice', BO DIDDLEY: 'Bo Diddley', JOAN BAEZ: 'A Hundred Miles', 'There But For Fortune' & 'You've Lost That Lovin' Feeling', the RONETTES: 'Be My Baby' & 'Shout', ROGER MILLER: 'Dang Me', 'Engine Engine #9', 'King Of The Road' & 'England Swings', the BYRDS: 'Turn! Turn! Turn!' & 'Mr. Tambourine Man', DONOVAN: 'Universal Soldier', 'A Reflection On A Summer's Day', 'Bert's Blues' & 'Sweet Joy', IKE & TINA TURNER: 'It's Gonna Work Out Fine' & 'Tell The Truth', concert band conducted by DAVID McCALLUM: '(I Can't Get No) Satisfaction' & 'One, Two, Three (1-2-3)'. *MCS*

BIG TIME

1988 (US 87m) Island Visual Arts (PG)

Film genre: Roots/Rock-music concert/documentary

Top guns: s-w: Chris Blum (+ dir), **Tom WAITS**, Kathleen Brennan

Stars: Tom WAITS *(performer/himself)*, other musicians:- **Michael Blair** *(performer)*, **Marc Ribot** *(performer)* → the SOUL OF A MAN, **Ralph Carney, Greg Cohen, Willie Schwarz, Roxanne Hart, Jayne Kennedy, Paul Guilfoyle**

Storyline: There's no doubt Tom Waits is way-out-there; this gig at L.A.'s Wiltern Theatre (featuring the man taking the roles of his fictional characters) proves it beyond doubt. *MCS*

Movie rating: *7.5

Visual: video

Off the record: see below

TOM WAITS

Sep 88. (lp/c/cd) *Island; <90987> (ITW/+C/CD 4)* [ ] [84]
– 16 shells from a 30.6 / Red shoes / Underground *[cd-only]* / Cold cold ground / Straight to the top *[cd-only]* / Yesterday is here *[cd-only]* / Way down in the hole / Falling down / Strange weather / Big black Mariah / Rain dogs / Train song / Johnsburg, Illinois *[cd-only]* / Ruby's arms *[cd-only]* / Telephone call from Istanbul / Clap hands *[cd-only]* / Gun street girl / Time. *(cd-iss. Mar97; IMCD 249)*

S/track review: Divorced from the queasy visuals, 'BIG TIME' is more an extended precis of TOM WAITS' 'Island' wild years than a soundtrack. As a stand-alone document, it's also a gruffly spirited insight into the – increasingly rare – phenomenon of WAITS in the raw. The fact that some of the material was drawn from Swedish and German gigs might account for the relative lack of banter, but that just means more focus on the music and the growling. If Captain Beefheart cultivated his bark with deliberately caught head colds, WAITS sounds as if he's had chronic bronchitis since birth; has anyone else in popular music drawn quite as much phonetic mileage from as relatively innocuous a word as "Down"?; a back to back, near definitive version of 'Way Down In The Hole' and 'Falling Down' (the obligatory unreleased studio track) has WAITS taking the proverbial rough with the smooth. The latter actually stands as one of his more unsung ballads, differentiated from the rest of the album by its personnel – including Little Feat alumni FRED TACKETT and RICHIE HAYWARD – and elegiac pump organ. WILLIE SCHWARZ evokes a similar tone with his accordion on a delicious 'Cold Cold Ground', even if his stage-mates are all jutting elbows and bulging veins. Restricting himself to a casually shredded solo on '16 Shells From A Thirty-Ought-Six', veteran NY hipster MARC RIBOT, in particular, is a model of discordant economy. Together with GREG COHEN, RALPH CARNEY and MICHAEL BLAIR, he connives with WAITS in re-animating many of the man's creations for the psycho-dramatic headspace of the stage: 'Telephone Call From Istanbul' shuffles and spasms like a slavering idiot savant gone to the hop, 'Yesterday Is Here' menaces by stealth and – even if the idea of an audience clapping along to a TOM WAITS song is somehow ridiculous – 'Clap Hands' is sheer reptilian, RIBOT-strafed incantation. Even if you prefer the man sequestered in his studio, get this album for his priceless anecdote on the American Civil War; Cold Mountain it ain't. *BG*

Album rating: *7.5

– spinoff releases, etc. –

TOM WAITS: 16 Shells From A Thirty-Ought-Six / Big Black Mariah

Sep 88. (7") *(IS 370)* [–] [ ]
(12"+=) *(12IS 370)* – Ruby's Arms.

BIGGIE AND TUPAC

2002 (UK 108m) FilmFour / Roxie Releasing (18)

Film genre: hip-hop/rap-Music documentary

Top guns: dir: Nick Broomfield ← KURT & COURTNEY

Stars: the Notorious B.I.G./Biggie *(himself; archive)* ← RHYME & REASON ← the SHOW / → THUG ANGEL → TUPAC: RESURRECTION → BEEF, **Tupac SHAKUR** *(himself; archive)*, **Sean "P. Diddy" Combs** *(archive)* ← RHYME & REASON ← the SHOW / → TUPAC: RESURRECTION → FADE TO BLACK, **SNOOP DOGG** *(archive)*, Marion "Suge" Knight *(himself)* → THUG ANGEL → TUPAC: RESURRECTION, **Lil' Cease** *(himself)* → BLOCK PARTY, **Mopreme** *(himself)*, Voletta Wallace *(herself; mother of Biggie)*, Billy Garland *(himself; father of Tupac)*

Storyline: English documentary maker, Nick Broomfield (again with a controversial subject matter), investigates the brutal murders of top rappers, Christopher Wallace (Biggie) and Tupac Shakur. *MCS*

Movie rating: *6

Visual: dvd (no audio OST; score by Christian Henson)

Off the record: Excerpts of some songs include:- several by the NOTORIOUS B.I.G.: 'Hypnotize', 'Miss U', 'Unbelievable', 'The Notorious B.I.G.' & 'Juicy', while objections made it nigh-on impossible for 2PAC's tracks to get on board (his version of 'Superfreak' the exception). Others featured:- 'Play Around' (LIL' CEASE), 'Return Of The Outlawz' (MOPREME; Tupac's step-brother), 'Total Eclipse' (KLAUS NOMI), 'The Militia' & 'The Rep Grows Bigger' (both by GANGSTARR). *MCS*

BILLY CHILDISH IS DEAD

2005 (US 70m) Cherry Red

Film genre: Garage/Indie-rock documentary/concert movie

Top guns: dir: Graham Bendel

Stars: Billy Childish *(himself/performer)*, **Holly Golightly** *(herself/performer)*, **Shane MacGowan** *(himself)* <= the POGUES =>, Bevis Hillier *(himself)*, Miranda Sawyer *(herself)*, Matthew Collings *(himself)*

Storyline: Documentary which charts the career of Billy Childish (aka William Lovejoy). Creator of over 2000 paintings, novelist, poet and prolific musician, this extraordinary man talks about his childhood and personal life and lets the cameras go behind the scenes with his band the Buff Medways. There are also comments and tributes from stars such as Shane MacGowan and Holly Golightly. *JZ*

Movie rating: *5

Visual: dvd (no audio OST by BILLY CHILDISH)

Off the record: Billy Childish was born Stephen John Hamper, 1 Dec'59, Chatham, Kent, England. Having formed the Pop Rivets in 1977 – they only lasted a few years and a couple of albums – he went on to form the Milkshakes (subsequently known as Thee Milkshakes) with original guitarist, Bruce Brand (who was relegated to the drum stool when Childish became 6-string proficient). This psychobilly/garage outfit toured alongside fellow Medway bands, the Prisoners and the Dentists, while Billy also turned his hand to poetry (his published works are now in double figures, something of an achievement in itself bearing in mind the man's chronic dyslexia!). In the early 80s, the Milkshakes released numerous albums, combining a plethora of R&B cover versions somewhat akin to what the Count Bishops had been doing several years earlier. In 1985, the hard-drinking Wild Billy formed another outlet for his irrepressible creativity, Thee Mighty Caesars, while also combining a solo career(!). Towards the end of the 80s, he virtually re-formed Thee Milkshakes, although this time around they were known as Thee Headcoats. In 1990, the group (featuring Mickey Hampshire, Russ Wilkins and Bruce Brand) were back on form with third set, 'Beach Bums Must Die', followed almost immediately by 'Heavens To Murgatroyd . . .' (1991), a set that would find its way on to US grunge bastion 'Sub Pop'. While Childish also undertook solo work, he worked with yet another associated project, Thee Headcoatees (featuring Holly Golightly), and in 1995, Childish celebrated by inviting all his previous musical incarnations to farewell gigs at London's 'Wild West Rooms'. With a neolithic plethora of recordings behind him and his cohorts (a bloody discographical nightmare, to be blunt!), BILLY formed the post-millennial trio, Buff Medways, a harder-edged garage-rock act who've so far released a couple of albums. It's no wonder, the man has been cited as the inspiration to a string of Detroit outfits, top of them being the White Stripes. *MCS*

BITTERSWEET MOTEL

aka PHISH: BITTERSWEET MOTEL

2000 (US 83m) Stranger Than Fiction Films

Film genre: alt-Rock-music concert/documentary

Top guns: dir: Todd Phillips ← HATED

Stars: Phish:- Trey Anastasio, Jon Fishman, Page McConnell, Mike Gordon * *(performers)* → OUTSIDE OUT → RISING LOW → ELECTRIC APRICOT: QUEST FOR FESTEROO

Storyline: Basically a year in the life (August 1997-1998) of young "jam" rock band Phish, from a concert at The Great Went (Limestone, ME) and on their long sojourn along the East Coast. Grateful Dead for a new generation. *MCS*

Movie rating: *7

Visual: video + dvd (no audio OST)

Off the record: Phish were formed in Burlington, Vermont in 1983 by **Trey Anastasio**, **Jon Fishman** and **Mike Gordon** while they were students at the local university. Following the addition of **Page McConnell**, the band began touring in earnest, playing gigs across the States and in the process building up a grassroots fanbase and a reputation gained largely by word of mouth. An archetypal "Great American Band", Phish have undoubtedly tapped into the same constituency of MOR-friendly, liberal/hippy Americans who once followed (and probably still do) the Grateful Dead and now dig Hootie & The Blowfish. With two independently released albums, 'Junta' (1988) and 'Lawn Boy' (1990), and packing out venues in almost every state, it was only a matter of time before the band were picked up by a major; 'Elektra' won out and released 'A Picture Of Nectar' (1992). 'Rift' (1993) was Phish's first major chart entry, the band subsequently gaining further ground with each successive album, including three live efforts, 1997's 6-pack 'Hampton Comes Alive' (a reference to hippie guitar-slinger, Col. Bruce Hampton, not neccessarily a Peter Frampton live-set) being the most arrogantly retrofied. Perhaps this was a ploy to placate diehard fans before the release of 'Farmhouse' (2000), a record that – as its title might've suggested – veered closer to the dusty paths of country rock than exploratory jams. This documentary would be their next project. **Mike Gordon** directed a handful of short films, culminating in his first feature, 'OUTSIDE OUT' (2000). *MCS*

BLACK & WHITE NIGHT

1988 (US 64m TV b&w) HBO

Film genre: Country/Pop concert/documentary

Top guns: dir: Tony Mitchell

Stars: Roy ORBISON *(performer)*, **Tom WAITS** *(performer)*, **James Burton** *(performer)* ← ELVIS ON TOUR ← ELVIS: THAT'S THE WAY IT IS, **Glenn D. Hardin** *(performer)* ← ELVIS ON TOUR ← ELVIS: THAT'S THE WAY IT IS, **Jerry Scheff** *(performer)* ← ELVIS ON TOUR ← ELVIS: THAT'S THE WAY IT IS, **Ronnie Tutt** *(performer)* ← ELVIS ON TOUR ← ELVIS: THAT'S THE WAY IT IS, **J. Steven Soles** *(performer)*, **Mike Utley** *(performer)*, **Jackson Browne** *(performer)* ← NO NUKES / → NICO ICON → ENDLESS HARMONY: THE BEACH BOYS STORY → WALK HARD: THE DEWEY COX STORY, **T-Bone BURNETT** *(performer)*, **Elvis COSTELLO** *(performer)*, **k.d. LANG** *(performer)*, **Bonnie RAITT** *(performer)*, **J.D. Souther** *(performer)*, **Bruce SPRINGSTEEN** *(performer)*, **Jennifer Warnes** *(performer)*

Storyline: On the night in September 1988, Roy Orbison and his "Friends" get together in the Cocoanut Grove Nightclub in L.A. (40s style) to celebrate his life and work. Sadly, three months later (6th December), Roy O suffered a heart attack and died in Madison, Tennessee. *MCS*

Movie rating: *8.5

Visuals: dvd rel. Sony BMG Video

Off the record: Nearly every performer here has his/her own entry.

—

ROY ORBISON

Nov 89. (cd/c/lp) *Virgin; <91295> (CD/TC+/V 2601)* 51
– Only the lonely / In dreams / Dream baby (how long must I dream) / Leah / Move on down the line / Crying / Mean woman blues / Running scared / Blue bayou / Candy man / Uptown / Ooby dooby / The comedians / (All I can do is) Dream you / It's over / Oh, pretty woman. *(re-iss. c+cd.Aug91; same) <cd re-iss. 1999 on 'Orbison-Legacy' diff.track order +=; 82876 78150-2>* – Go, go, go (down the line) / Claudette. *(cd re-iss. Mar03 on 'Orbison'+=; ROBW 7891)* – Claudette.

S/track review: Few pop stars have had as caring or affectionate a makeover as ROY ORBISON, who was languishing on the nostalgia circuit when 'In Dreams' popped up in David Lynch's 'Blue Velvet' to remind everyone of the one-time 'Sun' records star's arcane charms. This TV special delivers the rediscovered, Traveling Wilburys-era ORBISON, with younger (and by then more famous) celebrities like BRUCE SPRINGSTEEN, k.d. LANG and ELVIS COSTELLO crowding the stage of the Cocoanut Hotel in Los Angeles to pay tribute. It sounds like the recipe for a shiny-eyed shambles, but T-BONE BURNETT's tight production keeps the arrangements firmly focused on the singer and his real sidemen – the exemplary TCB BAND (including JAMES BURTON), who had been with Elvis for his last eight years. The set list is unusual for latter-day ORBISON in its emphasis on his classic late-50s/early-60s hits, from 'Only The Lonely' and 'Dream Baby' to 'Crying' and 'It's Over'. The world is divided into those who are touched by the tenor's vibrato-laden keening – an evocation of suffering as stylised as Billie Holiday's – and those who are resistant to its histrionics; but the former will find this an appealing synthesis of classic and late-period ORBISON. *ND*

Album rating: *7.5

– spinoff releases, etc. –

ROY ORBISON: California Blue *[not in film]* / ROY ORBISON with k.d. LANG: Blue Bayou

Jul 89. (7") *<99202> (VS 1193)*
(12"+=) *(VST 1193)* – Leah.
(3"cd-s++=) *(VSCD 1193)* – In dreams.

ROY ORBISON: Oh, Pretty Woman / Claudette

Nov 89. (7") *<99159> (VS 1224)*
(12"+=/cd-s+=) *(VS T/CD 1224)* – ('A'-lp version).

the BLACK MOSES OF SOUL

1974 (US 80m) Aquarius Releasing (G)

Film genre: R&B/Soul-music concert documentary

Top guns: dir: Chuck Johnson

Stars: Isaac HAYES *(performer)* & **the Movement** *(performers)*, Terry Levene *(presenter)*

Storyline: A live concert by the one and only Isaac Hayes in Atlanta, Georgia. Superbad is wicked to the core. *MCS*

Movie rating: *7

Visual: video on 'More Music' / dvd on 'Sofa' (no audio OST)

Off the record: ISAAC HAYES smooths out his takes on the Doors' 'Light My Fire', Dusty Springfield's 'I Don't Know What To Do With Myself', Mac Davis' 'Never Can Say Goodbye', Jimmy Webb's 'By The Time I Get To Phoenix', Bacharach & David's 'The Look Of Love' & Jerry Butler's 'I Stand Accused'. *MCS*

□ Ronee BLAKELY segment
(⇒ I PLAYED IT FOR YOU)

the BLANK GENERATION

1976 (US 55m b&w) Bohemia Films / Czech Television (15)

Film genre: Punk-rock-music documentary

Top guns: dir: Amos Poe → the FOREIGNER → SUBWAY RIDERS → JUST AN AMERICAN BOY, **Ivan Kral**

Stars: RAMONES *(performers)*, **Television:- Tom Verlaine, Richard Lloyd, Billy Ficca, Richard HELL** *(performers)*, **Talking Heads:- David BYRNE, Tina Weymouth, Jerry Harrison, Chris Frantz** *(performers)*, **Patti Smith (Group):- Patti Smith + Lenny Kaye** * *(performers)* * → the COMPLEAT BEATLES / → ROCK & ROLL HEART → BENJAMIN SMOKE → YOU'RE GONNA MISS ME, **BLONDIE:- Debbie Harry, Chris Stein** *(performers)*, **Heartbreakers/Johnny Thunders** *(performers)* → the PUNK ROCK MOVIE → BORN TO LOSE: THE LAST ROCK AND ROLL MOVIE → END OF THE CENTURY → HEY IS DEE DEE HOME, **Wayne County** *(performer)* → PUNK IN LONDON → JUBILEE → the PUNK ROCK MOVIE → STADT DER VERLORENEN SEELEN → END OF THE CENTURY, **the Shirts** *(performers)*, **the Dolls** *(performers)*, **Harry Toledo** *(performer)*, **the Marbles** *(performers)*, **Miamis** *(performers)*, **Tuff Darts/Robert Gordon** *(performers)*

Storyline: Czech exile, Ivan Kral (also guitarist with the Patti Smith Group) teamed up with underground filmmaker Amos Poe to establish a New Wave of celluloid moviemaking of the New Wave music scene in New York – mainly the CBGB's. *MCS*

Movie rating: *6

Visual: video + dvd (no audio OST)

Off the record: Richard HELL was also in this film as part of Television. RICHARD HELL & THE VOID-OIDS released an LP for 'Sire', 'Blank Generation', in 1977. *MCS*

– associated/related, etc. –

Various Artists: D.I.Y. – Blank Generation – The New York Scene (1975-1978)

Jan 93. (cd) *Rhino; <RND 71175>* □ □

Blank Generation / Dancing Barefoot

Aug 01. (dvd) *Music Video; <4321>* [-] [-]
– (compilation of two films)

BLOCK PARTY

aka DAVE CHAPPELLE'S BLOCK PARTY

2006 (US 102m) Focus Features / Rogue Pictures (R)

Film genre: comedy/Hip-Hop music concert/documentary

Top guns: dir: **Michel Gondry / s-w: Dave Chappelle**

Stars: Dave Chappelle *(host)*, **Kanye West** *(performer)* ← FADE TO BLACK, **Dead Prez:- Stick Man, M1** *(performers)* ← WHITEBOYS, **Blackstar:- Mos Def** *(performer)* ← BROWN SUGAR ← CARMEN: A HIP HOPERA + **Talib Kweli** *(performer)* ← BROWN SUGAR / **Common** *(performer)* ← FADE TO BLACK ← BEEF ← GODFATHERS AND SONS ← BROWN SUGAR, **the Fugees:- Lauryn Hill** *(performer)* ← TURN IT UP, **Wyclef Jean** *(performer)* ← BE COOL ← the COUNTRY BEARS ← CARMEN: A HIP HOPERA ← RHYME & REASON, **Prakazrel "Pras" Michel** *(performer)* ← TURN IT UP / → FEEL THE NOISE, **Jerry "Wonda" Duplessis** *(performers)* / **the Roots:- Tariq "Black Thought" Trotter, Ahmir "?ustlove" Thompson, Leonard 'Hub' Hubbard, Kiek "Make Your Body Work" Douglas, Frank "Knuckels" Walker, James 'Kamal' Gray** *(performers)* ← FADE TO BLACK ← BROWN SUGAR ← BROOKLYN BABYLON ← WOODSTOCK '99, **Erykah Badu** *(performer)*, **Jill Scott** *(performer)*, **Bilal Oliver** *(performer)* ← the FIGHTING TEMPTATIONS ← MOONWALKER, **Big Daddy Kane** *(performer)* ← BROWN SUGAR, **Kool G Rap** *(performer)* ← WHO'S THE MAN?, **Cody ChesnuTT** *(performer)*, **Lil' Cease** *(performer)* ← BIGGIE AND TUPAC, **Keyshia Cole** *(performer)*, **John Legend** *(performer)*, **Pharoahe Monch** *(performer)*, **Martin Luther** *(performer)* → ACROSS THE UNIVERSE, **Chairman Fred Hampton Jr.** *(performer)*

Storyline: A cockle-warming tonic to excess for the sake of it, as eccentrically loveable comedian/MC/scenester Dave Chappelle throws a free neighbourhood bash in Brooklyn NYC, with nary a violent/misogynist boast in sight (although Chappelle and Mos Def do trade a few dirty jokes). Afros are out in force (Erykah Badu's wig looks like it's been lifted in by hydraulic crane), fans – many of them women, and all there through word of mouth – wear 'Free Tibet' t-shirts and – in front of funky live backing, complete with brass section – the performers rap on unity, harmony and resistance. With naturalistic ease, the film not only canvases the constituent parts of such an event – including many scenes in the local day care centre and surrounding environs, where many folks were, once upon a time, on first name terms with slain star Biggie Smalls – but underscores the raw power of black music rather than watering it down with adolescent pop. Highlights include Jill Scott bending it like Hendrix, Scott and Badu riffing on a Roots chorus, and Wyclef Jean galvanising a university marching band, as well as a rare Lauryn Hill interview. *BG*

Movie rating: *7.5

Visual: dvd

Off the record: Michel Gondry was the drummer in early 90s pop-rock act, Oui-Oui (two albums, 'Chacun Tout Le Monde' and 'Formidable') before he progressed into pop video promos for the likes of Bjork ('Human Behavoir'), the Chemical Brothers, Massive Attack and of course, the odd TV commercial. His career hit a peak when he directed the cult movie, 'Eternal Sunshine Of The Spotless Mind' (2004). **Mos Def + Talib Kweli** were members of Blackstar. *MCS*

Various Artists (score: Cory Smith)

Mar 06. (cd) *Geffen; <63660-2>* [44] □
– Hip hop (DEAD PREZ) / Definition (BLACKSTAR) / Golden (JILL SCOTT) / Universal magnetic (MOS DEF) / The blast (TALIB KWELI feat. ERYKAH BADU) / The light (COMMON feat. ERYKAH BADU & BILAL) / Boom (the ROOTS feat. BIG DADDY KANE & KOOL G RAP) / Back in the day (ERYKAH BADU) / The way (JILL SCOTT) / Umi says (MOS DEF) / You got me (the ROOTS feat. ERYKAH BADU & JILL SCOTT) / Born & raised (BLACKSTAR).

S/track review: "Nigger, all a' your records sound the same, I'm sick of that fake thug R&B rap scenario all down the radio, same scenes in the video, monotonous material"; "you rather have a Lexus or justice, a dream or some substance?" This is one party that has to be seen as well as heard, but the album's a conscious keepsake, with more soul in one line than the average MTV pimp has stockpiled in his entire bling bling arsenal. As one of the few high profile examples channelling and challenging the positive legacy of cosmic black music, the importance of CHAPPELLE's little get-together is underestimated. You won't find much sex, violence or empty glamour but you will find humour, intellect, politics, and an art that recognises both its heritage and the awesome power it still harnesses. The guest list may be the usual suspects – JILL SCOTT, ERYKAH BADU, the ROOTS, TALIB KWELI, COMMON, etc. – but they present their case for the defence as an inspirationally united front, dazzling in its scope and impact. DEAD PREZ's godzilla-bass opener, 'Hip Hop' (see above), is nothing less than a manifesto for musical and lyrical liberation, slating the fakers and "crackers in the city hall". A maelstrom of jazz, rock, funk and soul-psychedelic references and possibilities whirl around the likes of 'You Got Me' and 'The Way', while 'Boom' pays respect to a pioneer in BIG DADDY KANE, rushing on an old skool bedrock that's harder, faster and funkier than any contemporary comparison. MOS DEF delivers his own message to the would-be playas ("most of y'all brothers is livin' wit your mothers, your boogie man yanking up your covers"), and – in tandem with KWELI and COMMON – exhorts the spirit of Cymande, Bob Marley and the Last Poets with the brilliant 'Umi Says', prompting the tightest live backing of the whole show. Whether it captures the spirit of the original block parties is something only a Brooklyn veteran could gauge, but one thing's for sure: it preaches the gospel of evolution, and long may it sound. *BG*

Album rating: *7.5

☐ Vicky BLUE / Victory Tischler-BLUE segment
(⇒ the RUNAWAYS)

BLUE SUEDE SHOES

1980 (UK 95m w/b&w) Kendon Films

Film genre: Rock'n'roll-music concert/documentary

Top guns: dir: Curtis Clark

Stars: Bill HALEY & the Comets:- Ray Parsons, Jim Lebak, Geoff Driscoll, Steve Murray, Pete Spencer, Jerry Tilley *(performers)*, **Ray Campi** *(performer)* ← YOUNG, HOT 'N' NASTY TEENAGE CRUISERS, **Freddie Fingers Lee** *(performer)*, **Matchbox:- Graham Fenton, Gordon Scott, Steve Bloomfield, Wiffle Smith, Fred Poke, Jimmy Redhead, Rusty Lipton, Bob Burgos** *(performers)*, **Gene Vincent** *(archive performer)* ← LIVE IT UP ← IT'S TRAD, DAD! ← HOT ROD GANG ← the GIRL CAN'T HELP IT / → NO DIRECTION HOME, **Eddie Cochran** *(archive performer)* ← HOT ROD GANG ← GO, JOHNNY, GO! ← the GIRL CAN'T HELP IT ← UNTAMED YOUTH / → the COMPLEAT BEATLES, **Cliff RICHARD** *(archive performer)*, **Tommy STEELE** *(archive performer)*,

Storyline: Great Yarmouth holiday camp was the setting for part of this piece of rock history, Bill Haley & the Comets (and various footage of other R&R icons) getting the star treatment at a gig in London, circa 1978. *MCS*

Movie rating: *6

Visual: video in US (no audio OST)

Off the record: BILL HALEY & THE COMETS performed a handful of songs in the film, including:- 'Shake, Rattle And Roll', 'See You Later Alligator', 'Rock Around The Clock', 'Rock-a-Beatin' Boogie' & 'Rockin' Robin' (latter with vocals by RAY PARSONS). British retro rock'n'rollers, **Matchbox** (named after a Carl Perkins track), were on a high at the time of the film's release, having had a string of hits including 'Rockabilly Rebel', 'Buzz Buzz A Diddle It' and 'Midnite Dynamos'; actually in 1978 they were still in the musical backwoods with a failed LP on 'Chiswick'. *MCS*

☐ the BLUES:
A MUSICAL JOURNEY mini series
(⇒ FEEL LIKE GOING HOME)
(⇒ GODFATHERS AND SONS)
(⇒ PIANO BLUES)
(⇒ RED, WHITE & BLUES)
(⇒ the ROAD TO MEMPHIS)
(⇒ the SOUL OF A MAN)
(⇒ WARMING BY THE DEVIL'S FIRE)

BLUES DIVAS

2005 (US 116m) Blue M Productions

Film genre: Blues/Soul/Gospel-music concert documentary

Top guns: dir: Robert Mugge ← LAST OF THE MISSISSIPPI JUKES ← HELLHOUNDS ON MY TRAIL ← PRIDE AND JOY ← DEEP BLUES ← COOL RUNNINGS: THE REGGAE MOVIE

Stars: Morgan Freeman *(himself)* ← DANNY THE DOG ← LAST OF THE MISSISSIPPI JUKES ← JOHNNY HANDSOME, **Renee Austin** *(performer)*, **Deborah Coleman** *(performer)*, **Denise La Salle** *(performer)*, **Bettye Lavette** *(performer)*, **Odetta** *(performer)* ← LIGHTNING IN A BOTTLE ← the BALLAD OF RAMBLIN' JACK ← CHORDS OF FAME ← FESTIVAL / → NO DIRECTION HOME, **Ann Peebles** *(performer)* ← ONLY THE STRONG SURVIVE, **Mavis Staples** *(performer)* ← the STAPLE SINGERS =>, **Irma Thomas** *(performer)* → MAKE IT FUNKY!

Storyline: Ground Zero Blues Club (in Clarksdale, Mississippi, and co-owned by host, Oscar-winning actor Morgan Freeman) is at the centre of this 3-day showcase featuring eight golden oldies of America's Blues heritage. "Sisters are still, indeed, doin' it for themselves". *MCS*

Movie rating: *6

Visual: dvd (no audio OST)

Off the record: Highlights of the film stem from:- Soul Queen of New Orleans, IRMA THOMAS ('Chains Of Love', etc.), blues-rock singer/guitarist DEBORAH COLEMAN (KoKo Taylor's 'I'm A Woman'), soul/gospel legend MAVIS STAPLES ('God Is Not Sleeping'), BETTYE LAVETTE ('Your Turn To Cry (Your Time To Cry)'), blues/protest singer – now in her 70s – ODETTA ('Careless Love'), ANN PEEBLES ('I Can't Stand The Rain'; her only big hit from the 70s), RENEE AUSTIN ('Fool Moon'; a tribute to Ella Fitzgerald) and Queen of the Southern Soul Blues DENISE LA SALLE ('Still The Queen'). *MCS*

BLUES ODYSSEY

aka BILL WYMAN'S BLUES ODYSSEY

2002 (US 110m TV) Ripple Productions

Film genre: Blues/Rock-music concert/documentary

Top guns: dir: Chris Watson, Barry Eyre

Stars: Bill Wyman *(presenter)* <= the ROLLING STONES =>, **Mick Fleetwood** *(himself)* ← MR. MUSIC / → RED, WHITE & BLUES, **B.B. KING** *(himself)*, **Buddy Guy** *(himself)* ← CHICAGO BLUES ← SUPERSHOW / → GODFATHERS AND SONS → LIGHTNING IN A BOTTLE, **Georgie Fame** *(himself)* → RED, WHITE & BLUES, **Gary Brooker** *(himself)* ← EVITA / → CONCERT FOR GEORGE, **Albert Lee** *(himself)* → CONCERT FOR GEORGE, **Taj MAHAL** *(himself)*, **Wilson PICKETT** *(himself)*, **Mike Love** *(himself)* <= the BEACH BOYS =>, **Bruce Johnston** *(himself)* <= the BEACH BOYS =>, **Ike Turner** *(himself)* ← SOUL TO SOUL ← GIMME SHELTER ← IT'S YOUR THING ← the BIG T.N.T. SHOW / → the ROAD TO MEMPHIS → GODFATHERS AND SONS, **Otis Rush** *(himself)*, Mike Vernon *(himself)*, **Sam Phillips** *(himself)* → the ROAD TO MEMPHIS

Storyline: "A Journey To Music's Heart & Soul" suffixed the title and suggested just about what this historical document was all about. Bill Wyman takes us to the roots (and routes) of blues music, from its inception in the Mississippi Delta and Deep South, to Chicago, New Orleans and eventually across the big pond to Britain. *MCS*

Movie rating: *7

Visual: dvd on Image Entertainment

Off the record: Bill Wyman was now a "Stone Alone" (the title of the bassman's biography), having left the ROLLING STONES early in 1993.

—

Various Artists

Nov 01. (d-cd) *Document; <(DOCD-32-20-2)>* ☐ ☐
– Goin' crazy with the blues (MAMIE SMITH) / Lock and key (BESSIE SMITH) / All I want is a spoonful (PAPA CHARLIE JACKSON) / Black snake moan (BLIND LEMON JEFFERSON) / Church bell blues (LUKE JORDAN) / Southern rag (BLIND BLAKE) / What's the matter blues (FRANK STOKES) / Stack o' Lee blues (MISSISSIPPI JOHN HURT) / Pine Top's boogie woogie (PINE TOP SMITH) / Indiana avenue stomp (MONTANA TAYLOR) / The duck yas yas yas (TAMPA RED & GEORGIA TOM) / Shake it and break it (but don't let it fall mama) (CHARLEY PATTON) / Come on mama, do that dance (FRANKIE 'HALF-PINT' JACKSON) / Blue goose blues (JESSE 'BABYFACE' THOMAS) / The dirty dozens (SPECKLED RED) / South Carolina rag (BLIND WILLIE WALKER) / Pussy cat blues (BO CARTER) / Searching the desert for the blues (BLIND WILLIE McTELL) / Cows, see that train comin' (JOE PULLUM) / West Dallas drag (ROB COOPER) / Ramblin' with that woman (BUMBLE BEE SLIM) / W.P.A. blues (CASEY BILL WELDON) / Honky tonk train blues (MEADE 'LUX' LEWIS) // Terraplane blues (ROBERT JOHNSON) / Ice pick mama (WALTER 'COWBOY' WASHINGTON) / Gamblin' jinx blues (BLACK BOY SHINE) / Peetie Wheatstraw blues (PEETIE WHEATSTRAW) / Good boy (BIG BILL BROONZY) / Alley boogie (GEORGIA WHITE) / Meat shakin' woman (BLIND BOY FULLER) / Railroad blues ('COW COW' DAVENPORT) / Special agent (railroad police blues) (SLEEPY JOHN ESTES) / Roll 'em Pete (JOE TURNER) / Jersey belle blues (LONNIE JOHNSON) / Brown skin girl (TOMMY McCLENNAN) / Beer drinkin' woman (MEMPHIS SLIM) / Me and my chauffeur blues (MEMPHIS MINNIE) / Baby please don't go ('BIG' JOE WILLIAMS) / Dive bomber (PETE JOHNSON) / Carolina blues (SONNY TERRY & BROWNIE McGHEE) / Kid man blues (BIG MACEO) / Boogie chillen (JOHN LEE HOOKER) / You're gonna miss me (when I'm dead and gone) (MUDDY WATERS) / Rockin' and rollin' (LIL SON JACKSON) / 3 o'clock blues (B.B. KING) / Dust my broom (ELMORE JAMES).

S/track review: This pleasingly eccentric compilation sets aside the documentary film's preoccupation with the 60s British blues boom to concentrate on a narrow 26-year period from the first days of the recorded blues. Out go the Rolling Stones and Fleetwood Mac, in favour of a rich exploration of American blues roots and particularly pre-war acoustic music. Among the 46 tracks stretched over 2 CDs there's a song by each of the genre's famous names, and plenty that explore the foundations of rock – but for every Elmore James or Muddy Waters there are two or three lesser-known musicians whose songs fully earn their place. Blues fans who have never heard BLIND WILLIE WALKER's rich clear baritone (he only cut four sides before his death from syphilis in 1933) or smooth-voiced BLACK BOY SHINE (who came from nobody-knows-where to Fort Worth in 1935 and disappeared the same route soon after) are in for a treat. Outfits like Fat Possum records and Music Maker Relief Foundation have shown that rural blues culture is still alive and well on the margins today – but in the meantime this is terrific archaeology, repaying some of the debt Bill Wyman owes to the music that has provided his living. He may not have been able to spare the first generation of bluesmen and women their adversities, but he's done an admirable job of redeeming their obscurity. *ND*

Album rating: *8

the BOB MARLEY STORY; CARIBBEAN NIGHTS

BOB MARLEY AND THE WAILERS: THE BOB MARLEY STORY – CARIBBEAN NIGHTS

1984 (US 90m) Island Visual Arts

Film genre: Reggae-music documentary/bio-pic compilation

Top guns: dir: Jo Mendel

Stars: Bob Marley and the Wailers:- Bob MARLEY *(himself/performer)*, **Peter Tosh** *(himself/performer)* ← HEARTLAND REGGAE ← REGGAE SUNSPLASH ← ROCKERS / → STEPPING RAZOR RED X, **Bunny Wailer** *(himself/performer)* ← ROCKERS, **Rita Marley** *(herself/performer)*, **Judy Mowatt** *(herself/performer)* ← COOL RUNNINGS: THE REGGAE MOVIE ← HEARTLAND REGGAE, Chris Blackwell *(himself)*, Darcus Howe *(narrator)*

Storyline: The King of Reggae, Bob Marley, is the focus of this informent document of Rastafarian and Jamaican culture. The film takes us back to 1966 and the visit of Ethiopian leader Haile Selassie to Bob's hometown Jamaica and then on to the latter star's musical life. Look out for footage of a young Jimmy Cliff as well as the Wailers. *MCS*

Movie rating: *8

Visual: video 1990 (no audio OST)

Off the record: BOB MARLEY AND THE WAILERS perform live versions of his songs:- 'No Woman, No Cry', 'Bad Card', 'Stir It Up', 'Trenchtown Rock', 'Slave Driver', 'Rasataman Chant', 'Concrete Jungle', 'Lively Up Yourself', 'War', 'Jammin', 'Zimbabwe', 'Redemption Song' & 'Could You Be Loved'. *MCS*

☐ Marc BOLAN & T. REX segment
(⇒ BORN TO BOOGIE)

☐ BONO
(⇒ U2)

BORN TO BOOGIE

1972 (UK 66m) Apple Films Ltd.

Film genre: Glam-rock-music concert/documentary

Top guns: dir: **Ringo Starr** <= the BEATLES =>

Stars: Marc Bolan *(performer)* → GLASTONBURY, **Ringo Starr** *(performer)* <= the BEATLES =>, **Elton JOHN** *(performer)*, **Mickey Finn** *(himself / the vampire)*, George Claydon *(the dwarf, eater of cars)* ← MAGICAL MYSTERY TOUR, Geoffrey Bayldon *(waiter)* ← TO SIR, WITH LOVE ← TWO A PENNY / → the MONSTER CLUB, Miss Chelita Secunda *(nun)*

Storyline: Ringo Starr directs his first movie, a mixture of surreal, homemade-style vignettes and live concert footage of glam-rock idol, Marc Bolan and his band, T. Rex. *MCS*

Movie rating: *5.5

Visual: (see below album)

Off the record: Marc Bolan was born Marc Feld, 30th Sep '47, London, England. He began his performing career under the improbable moniker of Toby Tyler, before ditching it and signing to 'Decca'. After three flop singles, he enjoyed a brief stint with John's Children ('Desdemona' era) before teaming up with bongo player Steve Peregrine Took to form Tyrannosaurus Rex in 1967. Far from the hoary, chest-beating proto-metal that name might imply, the band's sound was a folky melange of acoustic guitar, manic bongos and pop melodies. A bit of a hippy himself at the time, Radio One DJ, John Peel, championed their first single 'Debora', as well as material from their four subsequent LPs. Marc's ex-model features and effeminate charisma did no harm in making him an object of hippy chick lust, and it was about time the band had a sexier name to match; Took was also replaced by percussionist Mickey Finn as they gradually adopted an all-electric sound. The change done them good, as they say, and after three top hits and a well-received album, 'Electric Warrior' (1971), BOLAN then set up his own label through 'E.M.I.'. He almost single-handedly invented the "glam-rock" phenomenon, achieving even more success with 45s 'Telegram Sam', 'Metal Guru' and the evergreen '20th Century Boy' – these are still guaranteed to get you dusting down your 6-inch platforms a quarter of a century on. After splitting with his then wife, June Child, BOLAN brought in his new girlfriend Gloria Jones to become a fully-fledged member of T.REX. With his creativity ebbing somewhat, he moved to America to record some lacklustre formulaic material. BOLAN was beginning to embrace the punk movement (he had his own TV show at the time) and had set up a new deal with 'R.C.A.', when he met his untimely end on 16th September 1977. In yet another bizarre rock'n'roll death, his girlfriend crashed their car into a tree near Barnes Common. It's since become a shrine. On another sad note, Finn died of apparent kidney and liver failure on the 12th of January, 2003; he was 55. *BG & MCS*

—

MARC BOLAN / T.REX (w/ "spoken word")

May 05. (d-cd) *Sanctuary; (SMEDD 0215) <86382>* [ ] Jun05 [ ]
– "Intro" / Jeepster / Baby strange / "Electric wind" (poem) / Tutti frutti (ELTON, RINGO & T.REX) / Children of the revolution (ELTON, RINGO & T.REX) / "Look to the left" (MARC & RINGO) / Spaceball ricochet / "Some people like to rock" (MARC & RINGO) / Telegram Sam / "Some people like to roll" (MARC & RINGO) / Cosmic dancer / "They've come, tis said" / Tea party medley: a) Jeepster, b) Hot love, c) Get it on, d) The slider / "Union hall" (poem) / Hot love / Get it on / Children of the revolution – reprise / "BBC interview with Marc Bolan from late 1971". *// (T.REX IN CONCERT 18th MARCH 1972) (dvd-iss.May06 on 'Sanctuary Visual Entertainment'; SVEM 0306)*

S/track review: MARC BOLAN & T.REX were at the giddy heights of a glittering career, when he/they made the 'BORN TO BOOGIE' movie soundtrack. After his late 60s psychedelic ramblings as leader of Tyrannosaurus Rex, BOLAN and his new sidekick, MICKEY FINN, shortened the billing to T.REX and had massive early 70s hits with 'Ride A White Swan', 'Hot Love', 'Get It On', etc. At the behest of former Beatles drummer RINGO STARR, then MD of Apple Films Ltd, the movie was shot in 1972 and featured cameos from RINGO (also the director!) and ELTON JOHN; it premiered on the 14th December 1972 at Oscar's in Brewer Street, Soho, London. No album was released at the time and for thirty years it was thought that only shabby copies of the reels existed, that was until numerous cans of long-lost footage were found in a West London warehouse. The result was the double CD before you (complete with the unearthed Wembley concert from the 18th March 1972 – "the day that pop came back") and the DVD movie release. The re-birth of 'BORN TO BOOGIE' was complete. For the opening 25-second "intro" you might be forgiven that the tapes were mixed up with Pink Floyd's 'Dark Side Of The Moon' outtakes, but then it's "a 1 & a 2 & a 3 & a 4" for a screaming live version of 'Jeepster'. Later in the set, the song is acoustically reprised (accompanied by a string quartet) for 'Tea Party Medley' alongside 'Hot Love' – 'Get It On' – 'The Slider'; BOLAN was indeed a true, top "Mad Hatter". Exclusive screaming versions of non-hits such as 'Baby Strange', 'Spaceball Ricochet' and 'Cosmic Dancer' showed the man was on another planet musically, Bowie the only man who could match him at the time. As you'd expect on such a diverse project, the album is interspersed with short poems, fun (but not funny) dialogue alongside RINGO and a closing BBC interview with BOLAN from late '71. ELTON was added for two joint (in-the-basement) renditions of Little Richard's 'Tutti Frutti' and chart-topper of the time 'Children Of The Revolution'. Other smash hits – live, 'Telegram Sam', 'Hot Love' and an 11-minute version of 'Get It On' proved that BOLAN was not just a pop teen-idol phenomenon, but a bona fide rock'n'roll superstar. *MCS*

Album rating: *7.5

BRING ON THE NIGHT

1985 (UK/US 97m) A&M Films / Samuel-Goldwyn Company (PG-13)

Film genre: Jazz/Pop-music concert/documentary

Top guns: dir (+ s-w): Michael Apted ← COAL MINER'S DAUGHTER ← STARDUST

Stars: **STING** *(performer)*, **Kenny Kirkland** *(keyboardist)*, **Branford MARSALIS** *(musician)*, **Darryl Jones** *(musician)*, **Omar Hakim** *(musician)*, Miles Copeland III *(himself)* → EAT THE RICH, **Dolette McDonald** *(backing vocalist)* → HOME OF THE BRAVE, **Janice Pendarvis** *(backing vocalist)* → HOME OF THE BRAVE, Trudie Styler *(herself)*

Storyline: Former Police man Sting is in the spotlight here, songs from his solo debut 'The Dream Of The Blue Turtles' (1985) and others from his group days prove his worth. The singer's settled-down family life also finds a place here as the man shows he's just a down-to-earth kind of guy with a sharp sense of humour. *MCS*

Movie rating: *5

Visual: video

Off the record: see STING entry

—

STING

Jul 86. (d-lp/c/cd) *A&M; (BRIN G/C/D 1)* [16] [–]
– Bring on the night – When the world is running down you make the best of what's still around / Consider me gone / Low life / We work the black seam / Driven to tears / The dream of the blue turtles – Demolition man / One world (not three) – Love is the seventh wave / Moon over Bourbon Street / I burn for you / Another day / Children's crusade / Down so long / Tea in the Sahara.

S/track review: After starting out as a jazz bassist and flirting with it several times with the Police, it was only natural that STING would release a jazz-orientated album. 'BRING ON THE NIGHT' is that album, a live one at that, and is the veritable hit and miss attempt. There are some neat tunes on the set, mostly when the band retain the focus of a four-to-five minute song (no song is shorter than four minutes) and incorporate some of the African and Latin flavours which characterised much of STING's solo career. Songs such as 'Consider Me Gone', 'Moon Over Bourbon Street' and 'Down So Long' are excellent and showcase STING's skills as a songwriter and arranger. However, on the medleys (three in all) and some of the more expansive tracks, the band and their arrangements lose their tightness, succumbing to some chronic bouts of overindulgence, which lets the album down severely. There is also a sense that this is more about showing off STING as someone who can "do" jazz, with the focus on him, rather than just trying to make a great album. *CM*

Album rating: *5.5

BRITISH ROCK SYMPHONY

1999 (UK 88m TV) Mission Television Productions / WLIW-21

Film genre: Orchestral-Rock music concert/documentary

Top guns: dir: Aubrey Powell

Stars: **Eric Burdon** *(performer)* <= the ANIMALS =>, **Alice COOPER** *(performer)* ← SGT. PEPPER'S LONELY HEARTS CLUB BAND, **Roger Daltrey** *(performer)* <= the WHO =>, **Thelma Houston** *(performer)* ← 54, **Nigel Kennedy** *(performer)*, **Paul Rodgers** *(performer)* ← MESSAGE TO LOVE: THE ISLE OF WIGHT FESTIVAL ← WOODSTOCK '94, **Tommy Shaw** *(performer)*, **Ann Wilson** *(performer)*, **Gary Brooker** *(performer)* ← EVITA / → BLUES ODYSSEY → CONCERT FOR GEORGE, **Darlene Love** *(performer)*, **Zak Starkey** *(performer)* → the WHO LIVE AT THE ROYAL ALBERT HALL, **Simon Townshend** *(performer)*, **Geoff Whitehorn** *(performer)*

Storyline: With the Who's Roger Daltrey at the helm, 'British Rock Symphony' is the brainchild of producer/promoter David Fishof. It's an attempt to unite some of pop culture's greatest songs with the full orchestral backing they'd always been deprived of, live in a concert tour. Filmed on the opening night at the Albert Hall, Daltrey is joined on stage by a bizarre lottery of ex-stars (see above) attempting to breathe new life and a different perspective into old the classics. It was also sub-titled ".. A Musical Tribute To the Rolling Stones, the Beatles, the Who, Led Zeppelin, and others . . . ." the others were Pink Floyd, Queen, etc . . . *KM*

Movie rating: *5

Visual: video + dvd Oct'00

Off the record: Posh-lad-cum-cheeky-cockney **Nigel Kennedy** plays violin here alongside ex-Procol Harum singer **Gary Brooker** and **Tommy Shaw** of Styx. *MCS*

——

Various Artists (with orchestra)

Oct 99. (cd) *Polygram; <538006-2>* [–] [ ]
– Kashmir (ROGER DALTREY & ANN WILSON) / While my guitar gently weeps (NIGEL KENNEDY) / Comfortably numb (THELMA HOUSTON) / Norwegian wood (PAUL RODGERS & ANN WILSON) / Ruby Tuesday (THELMA HOUSTON) / Peace suite: Imagine – Penny Lane – Blackbird – Give peace a chance – Come together (PAUL RODGERS) / Another brick in the wall, part II (ERIC BURDON) / Stairway to Heaven (ANN WILSON) / Let it be (ROGER DALTREY & THELMA HOUSTON) / Celebration suite: Start me up – A hard day's night – 5:15 – See me, feel me – Listening to you (ALICE COOPER & TOMMY SHAW).

S/track review: An inspired choice of opener, ROGER DALTREY's duet of 'Kashmir' with Heart's ANN WILSON offers an encouraging declaration of intent: the orchestra's dramatic reconstruction of the original resonates superbly with WILSON's surprisingly Robert Plant-like vocal although the song is needlessly marred by her partner in rhyme who fails to muster enough skill to match the effort he obviously put in. Clearly in a Zeppelin mood, WILSON returns with a pallid version of 'Stairway To Heaven', which, lacking the support of a band who cares or an orchestra who've even heard the original, is unsalvageable even with her intrinsic ability. Teaming up with PAUL RODGERS on 'Norwegian Wood', WILSON makes a natural connection: loosely conforming to the original's arrangement, they duet a near flawless vocal tainted only by the song's general blandness. A more challenging prospect is listening to spiky topped rebel, NIGEL KENNEDY, turning George Harrison's 'While My Guitar Gently Weeps' into one of those painfully banal Beatles instrumentals more commonly associated with the panpipes. The Beatlemania continues as RODGERS returns to perform his so-called 'Peace Sweet' medley where he turns 'Imagine' into a gospel celebration before rushing through 'Penny Lane' to briefly shine with 'Blackbird'. Further Beatles' numbers follow as ROGER DALTREY enlists the help of ex-disco diva, THELMA HOUSTON to shamefully butcher McCartney's 'Let It Be' where the pair laughably jostle to out-soul each other. No mistress of the understatement, HOUSTON belts her way through Pink Floyd's 'Comfortably Numb' before succumbing to restrained orchestration on the Stones' 'Ruby Tuesday'. Her seeming lack of understanding for the subject matter of these songs epitomises the misguided nature of this project which, with all its good intentions, lacks the necessary skills, professionalism or rehearsal to succeed. *KM*

Album rating: *4.5

☐ Chris BROKAW segment
(⇒ I WAS BORN, BUT . . .)

☐ Herman BROOD segment
(⇒ ROCK'N'ROLL JUNKIE)

BUENA VISTA SOCIAL CLUB

1999 (Ger/US 105m) Senator Films

Film genre: World-music concert/documentary

Top guns: dir (+ s-w): Wim Wenders ← TEATRO ← the END OF VIOLENCE ← PARIS, TEXAS / → the MILLION DOLLAR HOTEL → the SOUL OF A MAN

Stars: **Ry COODER** *(performer)*, **Compay Segundo, Ruben Gonzalez, Ibrahim Ferrer, Eliades Ochoa, Omara Portuondo, Manuel "Guajiro" Mirabel, Orlando Lopez "Cachaito", Barbarito Torres, Manuel "Puntillita" Licea, Raul Planes, Felix Valoy, Richard Eques, Joaquim Cooder, Maceo Rodriguez** *(performers)*

Storyline: A case of the album (see below) inspiring the documentary rather than the other way around, this life affirming Wim Wenders film accompanies Ry Cooder on a return visit to Cuba in 1998. The Buena Vista musicians guilelessly and charmingly recount their life stories, as Wenders cuts between personal anecdote and concert footage shot in Amsterdam and New York. *BG*

Movie rating: *7.5

Visual: dvd

Off the record: (see below)

——

BUENA VISTA SOCIAL CLUB (score: RY COODER, etc.)

Jun 97. (cd) *World Circuit; (WCD 050) Nonesuch; <79478-2>* [44] Sep97 [80]
– Chan chan / De camino a la vereda / El cuarto de tula / Pueblo nuevo / Dos gardenias / Y tu que has hecho? / Viente anos / El carretero / Candela / Amor de loca juventud / Orgullecida / Murmullo / Buena Vista social club / La bayamesa. *(lp-iss.Dec98 on 'Rock The House'; RTH 79468)*

S/track review: The pinnacle of RY COODER's restless global explorations and beginning of the resurgence in interest in not only Cuban music but the wider genre of World Music; this album still tops sales charts six years on from its original release. More, it recorded for posterity and announced to the outside world an aged but peerless group of musicians who'd never before been given such a platform and at least two of whom would pass away within a few years. As such, it plays like a history lesson in what non-Cubans had been missing all these embargo-blocked years, a joyous, free spirited journey through the past musical lives of the island's great musicians and composers; music which, in COODER's words, "rebuilds you from the inside out". From the plangent opening chords of 'Chan Chan' to the final sustained notes of 'La Bayamesa', this record is rarely less than beguiling. Most of Cuba's major musical styles are covered, including son, bolero and danzon, while COODER's bluesy guitar lines fall into place as naturally as if he'd been playing with these people all his life. Even his son JOACHIM gets in on the action, continuing COODER Sr.'s cultural splicing by introducing – surprisingly effective – Asian and African percussion to proceedings. But it's the native Cubans who steal the show, people like IBRAHIM FERRER, COMPAY SEGUNDO, RUBEN GONZALES, ELIADES OCHOA, ORLANDO 'CACHAITO' LOPEZ and OMAR PORTUONDO, veteran performers who'd all go on to release acclaimed solo albums off the back of 'BUENA VISTA's huge impact. Highlights? There are too many to list, although the late GONZALES' mesmerising piano deserves special mention. Such vitality, fluidity, passion and humour are rare in the playing of a man in his late 70s, and anyone lucky enough to witness him in concert before his death will have realised just how much of a one-off GONZALES really was (and how reluctant he was to leave the world's stage, both metaphorically and literally!). The trumpet of MANUEL 'GUAJIRO' MIRABAL is perhaps even more crucial to this record's power; there are any number of moments where his sad, singing lines swoop into songs unexpectedly, alchemising the music and raising goosebumps on the skin. If you haven't heard this record, buy it. If you can't afford it, beg, borrow or steal a copy. *BG*

Album rating: *9

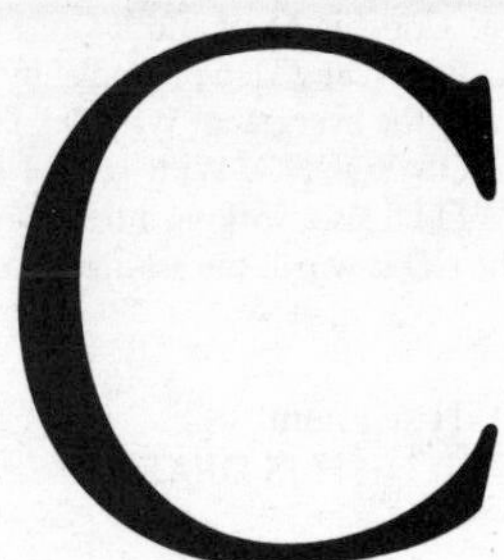

□ Glen CAMPBELL
(⇒ Rock Movies & Musicals)

CARRY IT ON

1970 (US 80m b&w) New Film Company / Maron Films (GP)

Film genre: Folk-rock concert documentary

Top guns: s-w + dir: James Coyne

Stars: Joan BAEZ *(herself)*, **David Harris, Jeffrey Shurtleff**

Storyline: Documentary focusing on the anti-Vietnam war activism of Joan Baez and then student protest leader David Harris, whom she married in 1968. On the verge of a lengthy prison sentence for draft evasion, Harris expounds on his radical philosophies while Baez keeps her fans updated after he's jailed. *BG*

Movie rating: *4

Visual: none

Off the record: see below

JOAN BAEZ *(w/ spoken word *)*

Dec 71. (lp) *Vanguard; <(VSD 79313)>* □ Jul72 □
– Oh, happy day / Carry it on / In forty days (* w/ DAVID HARRIS) / Hickory wind / The last thing on my mind / Life is sacred (* DAVID HARRIS) / Joe Hill / I shall be released / Do right woman, do right man / Love is just another four-letter word / Suzanne / Idols and heroes (* DAVID HARRIS) / We shall overcome (DAVID HARRIS). *<(cd-iss. Sep99; VCD 79313)>*

S/track review: Well intentioned and historically insightful as they are, the political harangues, interview snippets and intellectual musings which punctuate this soundtrack get tired pretty quickly – BAEZ is more convincing when she's communicating her sentiments in song. Surprisingly, given the fact that most of them are lifted from benefit gigs, the "organising" songs, as she terms them, are kept to a minimum here. Instead, folk's grand dame plays a selection of her recent covers, with the same country slant which had characterised her releases since the late 60s (hubby DAVID HARRIS was a keen country fan, apparently) and which culminated in her hit version of the Band's 'The Night They Drove Old Dixie Down' (from this record's 1971 predecessor, 'Blessed Are'). She doesn't perform it here, although she does revisit Gram Parsons' 'Hickory Wind' and gamely has a shot at the Dan Penn/Chips Moman classic, 'Do Right Woman, Do Right Man'. That vestal, vibrato-quivering soprano really doesn't chime with such earthy southern mores, but it's a brave try. As ever, both in diction and atmosphere, she sounds much more comfortable on the Dylan material, bringing her unequivocal interpretative faculties to bear on both 'I Shall Be Released' and 'Love Is Just A Four-Letter Word'. Likewise, while BAEZ's relatively narrow stylistic reach precludes her from possessing a song in the manner of say, Nina Simone, she brings her own brand of glacial elegance to Leonard Cohen's 'Suzanne'. And if the likes of 'Joe Hill' and 'We Shall Overcome' are inevitable inclusions, BAEZ's most politically charged – and impassioned – work of the early 70s is actually hidden away on another soundtrack, Ennio Morricone's 'Sacco E Vanzetti' (1971). *BG*

Album rating: *5.5

CELEBRATION AT BIG SUR

1971 (US 82m) Tedd Mann Productions / 20th Century Fox

Film genre: Roots-music concert documentary

Top guns: dir: Baird Bryant, Johanna Demetrakas

Stars: Joan BAEZ *(performer)*, **CROSBY, STILLS, NASH & YOUNG** *(performers)*, **Joni Mitchell** *(performer)* → RENALDO AND CLARA → the LAST WALTZ → MESSAGE TO LOVE: THE ISLE OF WIGHT FESTIVAL 1970, **John Sebastian** *(performer)* <= the LOVIN' SPOONFUL =>, **Dorothy Morrison** *(performer)*, **Edwin Hawkins' Singers** *(performers)* ← IT'S YOUR THING, **Carol Ann Cisneros** *(performer)*, **the Struggle Mountain Resistance Band** *(performers)*, **the Combs Sisters** *(performers)*, **Julioe Payne** *(performer)*, **Mimi Farina** *(performer)* ← FOOLS ← FESTIVAL / → SING SING THANKSGIVING, **Chris Ethridge** *(performer)* → HONEYSUCKLE ROSE, Johanna Demetrakas *(herself)*, **Gram Parsons** *(himself)* ← GIMME SHELTER

Storyline: The Big Sur Festival 1969 – "It happened one weekend by the sea" – "Everyone did it . . . for the sheer love of it." The 60s, and hippie folk music in particular, bowed out just about here. *MCS*

Movie rating: *5

Visual: video (no audio OST)

Off the record: All the Big Surs are here, **Crosby, Stills, Nash & Young, John Sebastian**, plus lovely ladies, **Joni Mitchell** and **Joan Baez** (singing 'Song For David' and 'I Shall Be Released'), her sister **Mimi Farina. Dorothy Morrison** was of the **Edwin Hawkins Singers**, who had a massive hit with 'Oh Happy Day'. *MCS*

CHARLIE IS MY DARLING

1966 (UK 60m b&w) producer: Andrew Loog Oldham

Film genre: Rock-music documentary

Top guns: dir: Peter Whitehead → TONITE LET'S ALL MAKE LOVE IN LONDON

Stars: the ROLLING STONES:- Charlie Watts, Mick Jagger, Keith Richards, Brian Jones + Bill Wyman *(themselves)*

Storyline: A tourist's eyeview of the London's finest exports, the Rolling Stones, on a two-day stint in Ireland. Charlie Watts gets top billing (the title, a reference by one female fan's shout of admiration to the drummer) and exorcises his philosophical demons, while the soon-to-be dead Brian Jones thinks he's the b's and e's. *MCS*

Movie rating: *6.5

Visual: video (no audio OST)

Off the record: the ROLLING STONES perform several songs:- 'Get Off My Cloud', 'The Last Time', 'Play With Fire', 'Heart Of Stone', 'I'm Alright', '(I Can't Get No) Satisfaction' and surprisingly enough, 'Maybe It's Because I'm A Londoner', while MICK JAGGER covered the Beatles' 'I Feel Fine'. *MCS*

CHICAGO BLUES

1972 (US 50m) Rhapsody films (R)

Film genre: Blues-music concert/documentary

Top guns: dir: Harley Cokliss

Stars: Buddy Guy *(performer)* ← SUPERSHOW / → BLUES ODYSSEY → FESTIVAL EXPRESS → GODFATHERS AND SONS → LIGHTNING IN A BOTTLE, **Junior Wells** *(performer)* → BLUES BROTHERS 2000, **Johnny Young** *(performer)*, **Muddy Waters** *(performer)* → the LAST WALTZ → ERIC CLAPTON AND HIS ROLLING HOTEL → FEEL LIKE GOING HOME, **Mighty Joe Young** *(performer)*, **KoKo Taylor** *(performer)* → WILD AT HEART → PRIDE AND JOY: THE STORY OF ALLIGATOR RECORDS → BLUES BROTHERS 2000, **J.B. Hutto** *(performer)*, **Johnie Lewis** *(performer)*

Storyline: Mid-20s director, Harley Cokliss, stumbled upon a plethora of ageing blues singers down at the 'Arhoolie' record imprint. Chicago – although still relatively poor and er, windy – was once again a burgeoning place to be if you wanted to hear the electric blues of Muddy Waters and Co. *MCS*

Movie rating: *6

Visual: video + dvd

Off the record: Junior Wells was born Amos Blackmore in Memphis, Arkansas, 1934 (died 1998). Became one of the greatest blues harmonica players after he settled in Chicago after the war. He fronted the Aces, which also included **Buddy Guy**. George Guy (b. 1936) grew up in Lettsworth, Louisiana, and has been a part of the blues and rock world from the 50s onwards. **Johnny Young** (b. 1918) was one of the pioneers of the Blues, writing several seminal tunes including 1947 classic, 'Money Talking Women' (unfortunately not included on the OST). Adept at guitar and vocals, he was also renowned for his mandolin playing – who else can say that in the Blues world. Sadly, he was to die a few years after the making of the movie in 1974. **Muddy Waters** was born around the same time (as McKinley Morganfield, 1915) in Rolling Fork, Mississippi (died of a heart attack in 1983). A legend and Father of Chicago Blues (having moved there in 1943), he was the influence to thousands of aspiring bluesmen including Chuck Berry, the Rolling Stones, etc. **Mighty Joe Young** (b. 1927; d. 1999) came from the depths of Milwaukee via Louisiana, moving to the north side of Chicago during the mid 50s. Became a prolific recording artist – mainly singles – and subsequently took on the role of backing guitarist for Otis Rush and session man in the late 60s. **Koko Taylor** was another born in Memphis, Tennessee (1935). Due to her brassy, larger than life persona and voice (check out 'Wang Dang Doodle'), she was rightly dubbed "the Queen of Chicago Blues". **J.B. Hutto** (b. 1926, Blackville, South Carolina, d. 1983, Harvey, Illinois) moved to the Windy City in the mid-40s, while in 1954 formed the original Hawks. Along with Hound Dog Taylor, he was probably the greatest Blues exponent of the slide guitar. **Johnie Lewis** (b. 1908, Eufaula, Alabama) was a painter/decorator by trade and only took up performing the blues (with his slide guitar) as a part-time affair. *MCS*

—

Various Artists

Jul 95. (cd) *Drive; <3201>* ☐ [-]
– BUDDY GUY & JUNIOR WELLS: We're ready / First time I met the blues *[track 16]* / Country girl *[track 8]* / Hoodoo man blues *[track 13]* / We're ready 2 *[track 18]* / In my younger days *[track 3]* / JOHNNY YOUNG: Driving wheel *[track 11]* / Walking groundhog *[track 12]* / MUDDY WATERS: She's 19 years old *[track 15]* / Hoochie coochie man *[track 2]* / I got my mojo working *[track 6]* / MIGHTY JOE YOUNG: Why you want to hurt me *[track 7]* / KOKO TAYLOR: Wang dang doodle *[track 10]* / J.B. HUTTO: Speak my mind *[track 4]* / Come on back home *[track 5]* / JOHNIE LEWIS: You're gonna miss me *[track 17]* / Uncle Sam ain't no woman *[track 14]* / Hobo blues *[track 9]*. *<re-iss. Feb99 as '18 Tracks From The Film Chicago Blues' on 'M.I.L.';>* – [tracks in different order] *(lp-iss.Mar05 on 'Red Lightnin';)*

S/track review: Why it took so long for a proper release, God only knows, and why a second release with a different track order? Sounds a bit rusty due to earthy live recordings, the album was nonetheless a document (albeit in the early 70s) of what it might've been like in Chicago post-2nd World War. Most of the classics were here, 'Hoochie Coochie Man' and 'I Got My Mojo Working' by MUDDY WATERS, 'Wang Dang Doodle' by "Queen of Loud" KOKO TAYLOR and the evergreen 'Why Do You Want To Hurt Me' by MIGHTY JOE YOUNG. With several songs by BUDDY GUY & JUNIOR WELLS also working a treat, and that slide guitar of J.B. HUTTO, the CD is worth the asking price. *MCS*

Album rating: *6

☐ Billy CHILDISH segment
(⇒ BILLY CHILDISH IS DEAD)

CHORDS OF FAME

1984 (US 88m) Pretty Smart Co.

Film genre: Folk-music concert/documentary/bio-pic

Top guns: s-w: (+ dir) Michael David Korolenko, Mady Schutzman

Stars: Phil Ochs *(archive/performer)* ← TEN FOR TWO, Bill Burnett *(Phil Ochs)*, Martha Wingate *(Alice Ochs)*, Abbie Hoffman *(himself)*, **Odetta** *(herself)* ← FESTIVAL / → the BALLAD OF RAMBLIN' JACK → LIGHTNING IN A BOTTLE → BLUES DIVAS → NO DIRECTION HOME: BOB DYLAN, Jerry Rubin *(himself)* ← TEN FOR TWO / → the U.S. vs. JOHN LENNON, Oscar Brand *(himself)*, **Tom Paxton** *(himself)*, **Dave Van Ronk** *(himself)* → the BALLAD OF RAMBLIN' JACK → NO DIRECTION HOME, Mike Porco *(himself)*

Storyline: Legendary folk singer/political activist, Phil Ochs, gets the documentary biography treatment here, filmmaker Michael David Korolenko taking us through the man's complex but brilliant career. *MCS*

Movie rating: *7

Visual: video (no audio OST; but see below)

Off the record: Phil OCHS (b.19 Dec'40, El Paso, Texas, USA) was raised by Scottish/Polish parents, his family finally settling in Perrysburg; he subsequently studied journalism at Ohio State University and became part of the emerging folk scene in New York's Greenwich Village. Throwing himself headlong into radical politics, OCHS soon built up a grassroots following, playing many benefit gigs as well as the prestigious Newport Folk Festival (1963, 1964 & '66). 'Elektra' records released his acoustic folk set, 'All The News That's Fit To Sing' (1964), a strident set of protest songs, OCHS had now proved himself an intelligent, witty and inspring voice of dissent on such topical issues as the Cuban crisis and the spiralling Vietnam war. The title track of his next album, 'I Ain't Marching Anymore' (1965) became an anthem for the 60s anti-war movement, although further recordings were far too eclectic to fit into an ever-progressive folk-rock scene. Severely troubled by the assassination of Bobby Kennedy and the ensuing riots at the 1968 democratic convention, OCHS became increasingly disillusioned; he had also just moved to L.A, having signed a deal with 'A&M'. OCHS dreamed up the ill-advised idea of creating a persona which combined the rock'n'roll showmanship of ELVIS and the political fire of Che Guevara. Nevertheless, the self-deprecatingly titled 'Phil Ochs Greatest Hits' (1970) remains arguably his most affecting release and to promote the album, the mangled genius wore a gold lamé suit onstage – his audience remained unimpressed. OCHS went into semi-retirement, losing his self-belief as an artist, although he did travel to South America, playing a benefit gig in aid of the (then) recently overthrown Chilean leader. His vocal chords were seriously damaged after a mysterious attack in Africa and this plunged the man further into depression and bouts of alcoholism. Finally, on the 9th of April 1976, OCHS hanged himself at his sister's home, tragically ending a career that had begun so buoyantly and full of hope. *BG & MCS*

– associated/inspired release –

PHIL OCHS: Chords Of Fame

1974. (d-lp) *A&M; <4599> (AMLM 64599)* ☐ Jan77 ☐
– I ain't marchin' anymore / No more parades / Draft dodger rag /

Here's to the state of Richard Nixon / The bells / Bound of glory / Too many martyrs / There but for fortune / I'm going to say it now / Santo Domingo / Changes / Is there anybody here? / Love me, I'm a Liberal / When I'm gone / Outside of a small circle of friends / Pleasures of the harbor / Tape from California / Chords of fame / Crucifixion / War is over / Jim Dean of Indiana / The power and the glory / Flower lady / No more songs. *<re-iss. 1976 lp/c; 75021-6511-1/-4>*

CIRCLE JERKS

Formed: Los Angeles, California, USA . . . 1980 by former Black Flag frontman, Keith Morris, ex-REDD KROSS guitarist Greg Hetson, along with Roger Rogerson and Lucky Lehrer. Holed up in their Hawthorne, California garage, they set the tone for the rest of their career by recording their debut album, 'Group Sex' (1981), a frenetic burst of primal hardcore and adolescent humour. After appearing in that year's docu-film 'The DECLINE OF WESTERN CIVILIZATION', the guys were brought to the attention of Police manager, Miles Copeland, his 'Faulty' label (licensed to 'Step Forward' in the UK) delivering the follow-up 'Wild In The Streets' (1982). By this point, ex-DOA drummer, Chuck Biscuits replaced Lehrer; he was in turn replaced by John Ingram prior to a mini compilation album, 'Golden Shower Of Hits', featuring the title track medley of crooning standards by Paul Anka, Bacharach & David, etc. Other notable tracks included 'Coup D'Etat' and 'When The Shit Hits The Fan', surprise inclusions to the soundtrack of cult 1984 movie, 'REPO MAN'. Like many of their hardcore/punk peers, CIRCLE JERKS changed direction into heavy Twisted Sister/Dictators-like metal as the thrash and speed scene began to gather momentum in the mid to late 80s. With ZANDER SCHLOSS and Keith Clark now coming in as the new rhythm section, the 'Jerks made two further albums, 'Wonderful' (1985) and 'VI' (1987) for metal labels 'Combat' and 'Roadrunner' respectively. While they continued to tour the States, they virtually abandoned studio work, that is, until 1995's major label debut, 'Oddities, Abnormalities And Curiosities', infamous for its cover of the Soft Boys' 'I Wanna Destroy You' featuring pop starlet Debbie Gibson on lead vocals. The CIRCLE JERKS (in many shapes and formations) have featured on a plethora of rockumentaries, while the group themselves have acted (and performed) in 'SID & NANCY', 'STRAIGHT TO HELL' and the aforementioned 'REPO MAN'. *MCS*

- **filmography** (composer) {acting} –

the Decline Of Western Civilization *(1981 {p} on OST =>)* / **the Slog Movie** *(1982 {p} =>)* / **Repo Man** *(1984 {b+p ZANDER} on OST by V/A =>)* / **Another State Of Mind** *(1984 {c KEITH} =>)* / Space Rage *(1985 score by SCHLOSS w/ Billy Ferrick)* / **Sid & Nancy** *(1986 {p} on OST by V/A =>)* / **Straight To Hell** *(1987 {a ZANDER} on OST w/ the POGUES, PRAY FOR RAIN, JOE STRUMMER & V/A =>)* / **Walker** *(1987 {b ZANDER} OST by JOE STRUMMER =>)* / Feds *(1988 {b KEITH})* / **Tapeheads** *(1988 {b ZANDER} OST by V/A =>)* / Highway Patrolman *(1993)* / Floundering *(1994 {b ZANDER} score by PRAY FOR RAIN & V/A; see future edition)* / the Winner *(1996 score by SCHLOSS w/ PRAY FOR RAIN)* / Don't Be A Menace To South Central While Drinking Your Juice In The Hood *(1996 {b KEITH})* / **the Beat Nicks** *(2000 score by SCHLOSS =>)* / **Rage: 20 Years Of Punk Rock West Coast Style** *(2001 {p} =>)* / **That Darn Punk** *(2001 {a GREG} OST by V/A =>)* / Loren Cass *(2006 {v KEITH} =>)* / **American Hardcore** *(2006 {p GREG} =>)* / **Punk's Not Dead** *(2007 {p} =>)*

□ the CLASH

(⇒ Joe STRUMMER / the CLASH)

Joe COCKER

Born: John Robert Cocker, 20 May'44, Sheffield, England. COCKER's first musical influence was Ray Charles after hearing the track 'What'd I Say'; also taking in the blues sounds of Lightning Hopkins, Muddy Waters and John Lee Hooker. Pipefitter by day and pub singer by night, his band, Vance Arnold & The Avengers, were signed to 'Decca' in 1965, cutting the Beatles cover, 'I'll Cry Instead'. Although the single failed to achieve any real success, COCKER gave it a second bash in '67, making a demo tape for the influential Denny Cordell, the producer of Procol Harum's 'A Whiter Shade Of Pale'. This proved a shrewd move, his subsequent single (cut by Cordell), 'Marjorine', leading to a deal with A&M. '68 saw COCKER catapulted to fame with a cover of the Beatles' 'With A Little Help From My Friends', featuring JIMMY PAGE on guitar. Reaching No.1 in Britain, the song showcased COCKER's powerful, gravel-throated voice and his ability to make a song his own. With heavyweight fame looming large, COCKER hired manager Dee Anthony, who promptly booked him for gigs in America with his group, the Grease Band, and in '69, the Cordell-produced album 'With A Little Help From My Friends' was issued to critical success. With the festival scene buzzing (he'd already cameoed in the UK docu-movie, 'POPCORN'), COCKER and the Grease Band appeared in America on a series of five gigs, the last being the 'WOODSTOCK' Music and Arts Fair in Bethal, New York, where his full-on performance of 'With A Little Help . . .' summed up the mood of the weekend. His second long-player, 'Joe Cocker!', produced a Top 10 hit in the UK via the Leon Russell-penned 'Delta Lady', the album characterised by COCKER's primordial, blasting vocals. Dismantling the Grease Band in 1970 after a hectic two years on the road, the newly-formed Mad Dogs band were made up of Leon and a full horn section from the recently disbanded Delaney & Bonnie & Friends. A live 70s recording for a movie, 'MAD DOGS & ENGLISHMEN' (cut at Fillmore during the tour of the same name), solidified COCKER's fame. The album rocketed to No.2 on the Billboard chart and the film was premiered at Cannes in '71. Ironically, the tour left COCKER a wreck and led to his withdrawal from the music business. A half-hearted comeback in '72 saw the release of 'Joe Cocker' (without the exclamation mark, which is exactly what it was) while another comeback set in May '74, 'I Can Stand A Little Rain', was equally disastrous. Although 'You Are So Beautiful' (taken from the LP of the same name) charted in March '75, the personal turmoil continued, painfully illustrated by John Belushi's hilarious impersonation of COCKER on 'Saturday Night Live'. COCKER subsequently switched labels, borrowing the talents of reggae/dub stars, Sly & Robbie, for 1978's 'Sheffield Steel' (1978), although only to lukewarm effect. The comeback that had threatened to happen with the release of another album actually came a year later with 'Up Where We Belong', a chart-topping duet sung with Jennifer Warnes and the love theme to the movie, 'An Officer And A Gentleman' (1982). COCKER was on the move again in '84, signing to 'Capitol', where he released albums largely aimed at the AOR market, while another theme, 'Edge Of A Dream', featured in the movie 'Teachers'. The 90s saw more AOR sets, plus the rehashing of two of his most celebrated recordings, 'With A Little Help From My Friends' and 'Feelin' Alright', for the commercial re-run of 'WOODSTOCK 94'. Now with Sony's '550' label, he continues to tour the globe and confound the critics with his durability; his soulful rasp seems to be maturing like a fine malt: smoky, peaty and designed to put hairs on your chest. in 2007, COCKER turned his hand at acting in Beatles-scored movie, 'ACROSS THE UNIVERSE'. *BG & MCS*

- filmography {performance} –

Popcorn *(1969 {p} =>)* / **Woodstock** *(1970 {p} on OST by V/A =>)* / **Groupies** *(1970 {p} =>)* / **Mad Dogs & Englishmen** *(1971 {*p} OST by COCKER =>)* / Sound Of The City: London 1964-73 *(1981 {p} =>)* / an Officer And A Gentleman *(1982 hit theme on OST by V/A; see future edition)* / Teachers *(1984 hit single on OST by V/A; see future edition)* / **Woodstock '94** *(1995 {p} =>)* / **My Generation** *(2000 {p} =>)* / **Across The Universe** *(2007 {a} on OST by V/A =>)*

COCKSUCKER BLUES

1972 (US 94m w/b&w) independent (X)

Film genre: Rock-music documentary

Top guns: dir: Robert Frank → CANDY MOUNTAIN

Stars: the ROLLING STONES:- Mick Jagger, Keith Richards, Mick Taylor, Bill Wyman, Charlie Watts *(themselves/performers)*, **Nicky Hopkins** *(performer)* ← ROCK AND ROLL CIRCUS ← SYMPATHY FOR THE DEVIL / → LADIES AND GENTLEMEN, THE ROLLING STONES, **Bobby Keyes** *(performer)* MAD DOGS & ENGLISHMEN / → LET'S SPEND THE NIGHT TOGETHER → HAIL! HAIL! ROCK'N'ROLL, **Jim Price** *(performer)* → MAD DOGS & ENGLISHMEN, **Tina TURNER** *(performer)*, **Stevie WONDER** *(performer)*, Dick Cavett *(himself)* → IMAGINE → JIMI HENDRIX → JANIS, Terry Southern *(himself)*, Marshall Chess *(himself/producer)* → DOWNTOWN 81 → GODFATHERS AND SONS, Truman Capote *(himself)*, Andy Warhol *(himself)* ← the VELVET UNDERGROUND AND NICO / → IMAGINE → BLANK GENERATION → NICO-ICON → ROCK AND ROLL HEART → DETROIT ROCK CITY → END OF THE CENTURY, Bianca Jagger *(herself)* → the RUTLES → 25X5: THE CONTINUING ADVENTURES OF THE ROLLING STONES

Storyline: Okay, it's a bootleg, but it's the one that everyone talks about. 'Cocksucker Blues' (directed by photographer Robert Frank) was suppressed by the Rolling Stones, although in later years they sanctioned a few snippets for various compilations. A behind-the-scenes look at the band on their 1972 American tour, all the booze and birds parties, but after all the commotion, not really much to write home about. *MCS*

Movie rating: *6

Visual: none

Off the record: Also known as 'CS Blues'.

– associated bootleg –

the ROLLING STONES

1977. (lp) *Blank; <1822>* [–] bootleg [–]
– Cocksucker blues / Brown sugar / Jumpin' Jack Flash / Love in vain / Sweet Virginia / As tears go by / Exile on Main Street blues / You can't always get what you want / All down the line / Midnight rambler.

Leonard COHEN

Born: 21 Sep'34, Montreal, Quebec, Canada. The high priest of world-weary romantic miserabilism, LEONARD COHEN has grappled with life's big and small questions, contradictions, surrender, sacredness and profanity, as engagingly and enduringly as any living artist. A voraciously literate, incorrigible ladies' man turned Zen Buddhist monk, COHEN started out writing poetry, the oblique subtleties, luminous imagery and metaphorical possibilities of which have always been the focal point for his art. Turning his hand to prose, he wrote a series of novels including 'Beautiful Losers' (1966), a book which scandalised opinion in its day but is now regarded as one of the decade's key texts. While COHEN also read from the book in experimental short film, 'Poem' (1966), and appeared in another Canadian short, 'Angel' (1966), his debut screen appearance had actually come a year earlier. Even as he lived a semi-reclusive existence on the Greek Island of Hydra, the young literary star was the subject of a documentary, 'LADIES AND GENTLEMEN, MR. LEONARD COHEN' (1965). His metamorphosis into a folk singer began after he sang a couple of his poems at a New York reading in 1966. One of the song-poems, 'Suzanne', was picked up by folk singer Judy Collins (to whom he'd originally sang the song down a telephone line and who first persuaded him to sing it live) and has since become one of the most covered in his repertoire. Signed to 'Columbia' by the legendary John Hammond, COHEN became a cult singer-songwriter, defining his besuited griot-noir persona over a series of brooding, bleakly charming albums full of biblical allegory and obscure wisdom. While the cinematic bent of the arrangements on these records might well have facilitated a move into film scoring had he so desired, the man has accumulated a mere scattering of credits including obscure Italian movie, 'Satellite' (1968), and Robert Altman's revisionist western 'McCabe & Mrs. Miller' (1971), the latter of which generated a soundtrack EP. The early 70s (an era which saw COHEN play Israeli military bases during the buildup to the Yom Kippur war) also found the man appearing in media satire 'Dynamite Chicken' (1972) alongside various countercultural personnel. Later in the decade, he followed the infamous Phil Spector-produced 'Death Of A Ladies' Man' (1977) via one of his first serious engagements with Zen Buddhism. While the early 80s found COHEN – in common with many of his peers – in something of a commercial wilderness, he picked up a Golden Rose award in Montreux for 'I And A Hotel' (1983), a TV short written, scored and directed by the man himself, in which he also acted. Just prior to his Jennifer Warnes-inspired "comeback", COHEN also contributed lyrics to LEWIS FUREY's rock opera, 'NIGHT MAGIC' (1985). Although the man's artistic stock has been rising ever since, with an avalanche of tribute albums and the regular appearance of his songs on film soundtracks, his seclusion in the Mount Baldy Zen Center near Los Angeles has kept his public profile fairly low. He's nevertheless continued to record sporadically and has narrated a couple of Buddhist films, 'The Tibetan Book Of The Dead: A Way Of Life' (1994) and 'The Tibetan Book Of The Dead: The Great Liberation' (1994). His novel, 'The Favourite Game' (1963), was also recently adapted for a TV feature by Canadian director Bernar Hébert. *BG*

- filmography (composer) {acting} –

Ladies And Gentlemen . . . Mr. Leonard Cohen *(1965 {*p} =>)* / Satellite *(1968 score)* / McCabe & Mrs. Miller *(1971 OST EP; see future edition)* / Dynamite Chicken *(1972 {*p})* / Guitare Au Poing *(1972 {*p})* / Who's He Anyway *(1983 score)* / Other Tongues *(1984 score w/ Zone Jaune)* / **Night Magic** *(1985 [s-w] lyrics-only on OST by LEWIS FUREY & Carole Laure =>)* / Life According To Agfa *(1992 songs but no OST by Naftali Alter)* / Songs From The Life Of Leonard Cohen *(1988 {p})* / Schneeweissrosenrot *(1993 {v})* / Tibetan Book Of The Dead Part 2: The Great Liberation *(1994 {n})* / **Message To Love: The Isle Of Wight Festival** *(1997 {p} on OST by V/A =>)* / Kiss The Sky *(1999 songs)* / **Looking For Leonard** *(2001 {a/f} OST by PORTASTATIC =>)* / **I'm Your Man** *(2005 {p} =>)*

the COMPLEAT BEATLES

1982 (US 119m w/b&w) Delilah Films / MGM

Film genre: Pop/Rock-music documentary/concert bio-pic

Top guns: dir: Patrick Montgomery / s-w: David Silver

Stars: Malcolm McDowell *(narrator)* ← O LUCKY MAN! / → GET CRAZY → the DAVID CASSIDY STORY, **the BEATLES:- John Lennon, Paul McCartney, George Harrison, Ringo Starr** *(archive/performers)*, **Tony Sheridan** *(archive/performer)*, Brian Epstein *(archive)* ← I WANNA HOLD YOUR HAND / → IMAGINE: JOHN LENNON, **Yoko ONO** *(archive)*,

George Martin *(archive)* ← LET IT BE / → GIVE MY REGARDS TO BROAD STREET → IMAGINE: JOHN LENNON → BEAUTIFUL DREAMER: BRIAN WILSON AND THE STORY OF 'SMiLE', **Mick Jagger** *(archive)* <= the ROLLING STONES =>, **Eddie Cochran** *(archive/performer)* ← BLUE SUEDE SHOES ← GO, JOHNNY, GO! ← HOT ROD GANG ← UNTAMED YOUTH ← the GIRL CAN'T HELP IT, **Elvis PRESLEY** *(archive/performer)*, **Bill HALEY** *(archive/performer)*, **Chuck BERRY** *(archive/performer)*, **Fats DOMINO** *(archive/performer)*, **Jerry Lee LEWIS** *(archive/performer)*, **LITTLE RICHARD** *(archive/performer)*, **Lonnie Donegan** *(archive/performer)* ← the 6.5 SPECIAL / → the BEATLES ANTHOLOGY, **Cliff RICHARD** *(archive/performer)*, **the Everly Brothers:- Don & Phil** *(archive/performers)* → HAIL! HAIL! ROCK'N'ROLL, **Marianne FAITHFULL** *(archive)*, **Mike Love + Bruce Johnston** *(archive/performers)* <= the BEACH BOYS =>, **Billy PRESTON** *(archive/performer)*, **DONOVAN** *(archive/performer)*, Mia Farrow *(archive)* → the LAST UNICORN → PRIVATE PARTS, **Lenny Kaye** *(himself)* ← the BLANK GENERATION, **Billy J. Kramer** *(archive/performer)* ← POP GEAR ← the T.A.M.I. SHOW, **Gerry Marsden** *(archive/performer)* ← FERRY 'CROSS THE MERSEY ← the T.A.M.I. SHOW, Patti Boyd, Ed Sullivan ← the PHYNX ← BYE BYE BIRDIE / → ELVIS BY THE PRESLEYS, Maharishi Mahesh Yogi

Storyline: Just as it says on the er . . . tin, the documented history of the Fab Four, from their early incarnations to a smidgen of their solo careers (the murder of Lennon especially). *MCS*

Movie rating: *8

Visual: video in 1984 MGM/UA

Off the record: BEATLES tracks (excerpts) amounted to:- 'See You Later Alligator', 'Rock Around The Clock', 'Rock & Roll Music', 'Jack Of Diamonds', 'Rock Island Line', 'Jambalaya (On The Bayou)', 'Living Doll', 'Be-Bop-A-Lula', 'Raunchy', '20 Flight Rock', 'Venus', 'Living Doll' again!, 'My Bonnie', 'We Love You Beatles', 'When The Saints Go Marching In', 'She'll Be Comin' Around The Mountain', 'Jingle Bells', 'Rock Night Club Theme', 'Rock & Roll Music' again!, 'All My Loving', 'Mr. Moonlight', 'A Taste Of Honey', 'Kansas City', 'Some Other Guy', 'Hippy Hippy Shake', 'Long Tall Sally', 'Please Please Me', 'I Saw Her Standing There', 'She Loves You', 'Twist And Shout', 'It Won't Be Long', 'I Want To Hold Your Hand', 'From Me To You', 'A Hard Day's Night', 'I'm Happy Just To Dance With You', 'I'm A Loser', 'Things We Said Today', 'Ticket To Ride', 'Help!', 'You're Gonna Lose That Girl', 'Yesterday', 'Nowhere Man', 'If I Needed Someone', 'She's A Woman', 'Taxman', 'Tomorrow Never Knows', 'Strawberry Fields Forever', 'Penny Lane', 'A Day In The Life', 'Being For The Benefit Of Mr. Kite', 'Sgt. Pepper's Lonely Hearts Club Band', 'Lucy In The Sky With Diamonds', 'All You Need Is Love', 'Love You To', 'Magical Mystery Tour', 'Hello, Goodbye', 'Yellow Submarine', 'Hey Jude', 'Revolution', 'Glass Onion', 'Revolution #9', 'Why Don't We Do It In The Road?', 'Get Back', 'I've Got A Feeling', 'Because', 'The End', 'I'm So Tired', 'Let It Be' & 'Blackbird'.

the CONCERT FOR BANGLADESH

1972 (US 95m) Apple Corps / 20th Century Fox (G)

Film genre: Roots-music concert/documentary

Top guns: dir: Saul Swimmer ← MRS. BROWN, YOU'VE GOT A LOVELY DAUGHTER

Stars: George Harrison *(performer)* <= the BEATLES =>, **Ringo Starr** *(performer)* <= the BEATLES =>, **Ravi SHANKAR** *(performer)*, **Billy PRESTON** *(performer)*, **Leon Russell** *(performer)* ← MAD DOGS & ENGLISHMEN, **Bob DYLAN** *(performer)*, **Eric CLAPTON** *(performer)*, **Klaus Voormann** *(performer)* → SON OF DRACULA → POPEYE → WHITE STAR → CONCERT FOR GEORGE, **Jim Keltner** *(performer)* → TAPEHEADS → CONCERT FOR GEORGE, **Badfinger:- Pete Ham, Tom Evans, Mike Gibbons, Joey Molland, Jesse Ed Davis** *(performer)* → ROCK AND ROLL CIRCUS, **Jim Horn** *(performer)*, **Phil Spector** *(himself)* ← EASY RIDER ← the BIG T.N.T. SHOW ← the T.A.M.I. SHOW / → IMAGINE → IMAGINE: JOHN LENNON → MAYOR OF THE SUNSET STRIP

Storyline: Former Beatle, George Harrison (and a plethora of stars), raise much needed funds for the war-torn people of Bangladesh with a concert from Madison Square Garden, New York, 1st August 1971. *MCS*

Movie rating: *6

Visual: video + dvd

Off the record: BADFINGER also contributed three tracks to 'The MAGIC CHRISTIAN' (1969) soundtrack.

—

GEORGE HARRISON (*) & Various Artists

Jan 72. (t-lp) *Apple; <(STCX 3385)>* [2] [1]
– introduction (* & RAVI SHANKAR) / Bangla dhun (RAVI SHANKAR) / Wah wah (*) / My sweet Lord (*) / Awaiting on you all (*) / That's the way God planned it (BILLY PRESTON) / It don't come easy (RINGO STARR) / Beware of darkness (*) / While my guitar gently weeps (*) / Jumping Jack Flash – Youngblood (LEON RUSSELL) / Here comes the sun (*) / A hard rain's gonna fall (BOB DYLAN) / It takes a lot to laugh, it takes a train to cry (BOB DYLAN) / Blowin' in the wind (BOB DYLAN) / Mr. Tambourine man (BOB DYLAN) / Just like a woman (BOB DYLAN) / Something (*) / Bangla Desh (*). *<(d-cd/d-c iss.Aug91 & Jan02; 468835-2/-4)>*

S/track review: Re-released in a highly desirable, impressively remastered deluxe edition for 2005, the Grammy-winning 'The CONCERT FOR BANGLADESH' was originally issued on muddy sounding triple vinyl, hot on the afghan coat tails of GEORGE HARRISON's 'All Things Must Pass' (1970). In such a doggedly secular environment as rock music, HARRISON had triumphed in illuminating deeply held spiritual beliefs in song without getting on his soap box. At the behest of his friend RAVI SHANKAR, he subsequently made good on those beliefs by organising what biographer Geoffrey Giuliano called "the first example of the staggering philanthropic power of rock and roll". The philanthropy was in aid of refugees fleeing internecine war and natural disaster in Bangladesh, issues which, in 2005 of all years, have the bitter whiff of déjÓ vu. Back in 1971, the concept of such a large-scale benefit concert – staged at New York's Madison Square Garden over both an afternoon and evening stint – was novel enough to generate huge interest and inspire HARRISON to write a song for the occasion; it's difficult to regard 'Bangla Desh' as a hirsute precursor of 'Do They Know It's Christmas' and 'We Are The World', but that's effectively what it is; if more convincing in its urgency and fired, naturally, by the Eastern zeal and dark horse undertow of HARRISON's post-Beatles liberation music . . . music which had been recorded with the help of an inner circle coterie that included the likes of ERIC CLAPTON, RINGO STARR, BILLY PRESTON, BADFINGER and KLAUS VOORMAN. They all show up here, along with RAVI SHANKAR, LEON RUSSELL and a post-seclusion, denim-clad BOB DYLAN, with whom he'd recently played on the underrated 'New Morning' (1970). DYLAN's appearance – his first since a low-key Isle Of Wight performance in 1969, and his first American appearance for years – was something of a coup, and, given his prevarication ('Apple' promotion manager Pete Bennett allegedly had to coax him out of the toilet at the last minute), a minor miracle. His performance fills up the bulk of the second disc, falling back on his mid-60s classics rather than the looser material he'd been recording at the time. Measured against subsequent 70s live recordings, his voice is in rude health even if, through fairly straight, acoustic renditions of 'A Hard Rain's A-Gonna Fall', 'It Takes A Train..' and a bonus 'Love Minus Zero/No Limit' (not included on the original vinyl) amongst others, he moves away from the ochre Nashville tones and errs on the nasal whinny of old. HARRISON himself cherry picks the cream of 'All Things Must Pass' and latter-day Beatles classics, none of which he'd performed live before. In fact, he hadn't performed a live solo concert at all, and he was reportedly as nervous as DYLAN. Accompanied on 'Wah-Wah', 'My Sweet Lord' and 'While My Guitar Gently Weeps' by CLAPTON – who, despite allegedly being "on cloud nine throughout the whole Concert", according to Bennett, handles himself well – the quiet Beatle emerges victorious, defeating the jitters with poise and unselfish purpose. RINGO runs through an engagingly ramshackle 'It Don't Come Easy', PRESTON sounds frighteningly like a gospel-ised Kiss on 'That's The Way God Planned It' and RUSSELL redeems a stolid medley with some gutsy, Southern fried lines in HARRISON's 'Beware Of Darkness'. But it's SHANKAR who actually opens the whole shebang, famously parrying some premature applause before bravely performing the lengthy, austerely beautiful 'Bangla Dhun' to the waiting, potentially partisan masses. More dignified than Woodstock and, in terms of raising rock's perspective from the individual to the international, more important. *BG*

Album rating: *8

CONCERT FOR GEORGE

2003 (UK 104m) ArenaPlex LLC

Film genre: Pop/Rock-music concert/documentary

Top guns: dir: David Leland

Stars: George Harrison *(archival footage)* <= the BEATLES =>, **Ringo Starr** *(performer)* <= the BEATLES =>, **Billy PRESTON** *(performer)*, **Paul McCartney** *(performer)* <= the BEATLES =>, **Ravi SHANKAR** *(performer)*, **Klaus Voormann** *(performer)* ← WHITE STAR ← POPEYE ← SON OF DRACULA ← the CONCERT FOR BANGLADESH, **Tom Petty** (performer) ← FM, **Jim Keltner** *(performer)* ← TAPEHEADS ← the CONCERT FOR BANGLADESH, **Anoushka Shankar** *(performer)*, **Gary Brooker** *(performer)* ← BLUES ODYSSEY ← BRITISH ROCK SYMPHONY ← EVITA, **Jeff Lynne** *(performer)*, **Albert Lee** *(performer)* ← BLUES ODYSSEY, **Andy Fairweather-Low** *(performer)* ← PSYCHODERELICT ← the WALL: LIVE IN BERLIN, **Jools Holland** *(performer)* ← SPICEWORLD ← EAT THE RICH ← URGH! A MUSIC WAR, **Jim Capaldi** *(performer)* ← WOODSTOCK 94, **Joe Brown** *(performer)* ← JUST FOR FUN ← WHAT A CRAZY WORLD, **Sam Brown** *(performer)*, **Ray Cooper** *(performer)* ← POPEYE / → BROTHERS OF THE HEAD, Monty Python w/ Tom Hanks, **Neil Innes** *(performer)* ← the RUTLES ← MAGICAL MYSTERY TOUR, **Katie Kissoon** *(performer)* ← PSYCHODERELICT

Storyline: The death of the "quiet" Beatle, George Harrison, from lung cancer on 29th November, 2001, hit every fan (old & new) plus everyone who'd ever been connected to the man. Exactly a year later (at The Royal Albert Hall in London), his friends and associates came together to pay tribute to George; the funds collected were given to his charity organization The Material World Foundation. *MCS*

Movie rating: *6

Visual: dvd

Off the record: Gary Brooker (ex-Procol Harum), **Jeff Lynne** (ex-Electric Light Orchestra), **Andy Fairweather-Low** (ex-Amen Corner), **Albert Lee** *(ex-Heads, Hands & Feet)*, **Neil Innes** (ex-Bonzo Dog Doo Dah Band), **Jim Capaldi** *(ex-Traffic)*, ***Ray Cooper*** *(Elton John Band)*, **Sam Brown** is the daughter of **Joe Brown**.

Various Artists (composers: Ravi SHANKAR // GEORGE HARRISON)

Nov 03. (d-cd) *W.S.M.; (<8122 74546-2>)* [ ] [97]
– Sarve shaam / Your eyes – sitar solo (ANOUSHKA SHANKAR) / The inner light (JEFF LYNNE and ANOUSHKA SHANKAR) / Arpan (conducted by ANOUSHKA SHANKAR) // I want to tell you (JEFF LYNNE) / If I needed someone (ERIC CLAPTON) / Old brown shoe (GARY BROOKER) / Give me love (give me peace on Earth) (JEFF LYNNE) / Beware of darkness (ERIC CLAPTON) / Here comes the sun (JOE BROWN) / That's the way it goes (JOE BROWN) / Taxman (TOM PETTY and the HEARTBREAKERS) / I need you (TOM PETTY and the HEARTBREAKERS) / Handle with care (TOM PETTY and the HEARTBREAKERS with JEFF LYNNE & DHANI HARRISON) / Isn't it a pity (BILLY PRESTON) / Photograph (RINGO STARR) / Honey don't (RINGO STARR) / For you blue (PAUL McCARTNEY) / Something (PAUL McCARTNEY and ERIC CLAPTON) / All things must pass (PAUL McCARTNEY) / While my guitar gently weeps (PAUL McCARTNEY & ERIC CLAPTON) / My sweet Lord (BILLY PRESTON) / Wah wah (ERIC CLAPTON and band) / I'll see you in my dreams (JOE BROWN).

S/track review: Those reporting back from this tribute concert were mesmerised by 25 year-old DHANI HARRISON's on-stage resemblance to his father – a ghostly affirmation of the late Beatle's continuing presence. DHANI himself is rarely discernible on this soundtrack, but anybody who remembers GEORGE HARRISON will find it impossible to disengage the music from the man who wrote it. An English eccentric, HARRISON was a well-defined personality whose gentle but insistent philosophy pervaded his songs and his philanthropic activism (the show's title echoes his pioneering 1972 'CONCERT FOR BANGLADESH'). And his memory seems to inspire almost everybody involved here to near-mimickry, with mixed results. ERIC CLAPTON's recreation of the yearning slide guitar solos he had provided for Beatles songs more than thirty years before is undeniably poignant, while TOM PETTY's attempt to evoke HARRISON's winsome vocal earnestness is near-disastrous. But PAUL McCARTNEY's grab for a ukelele to start 'Something' is perfectly appropriate, and provides the musical highlight when the song swells into its familiar arrangement. There's no question CLAPTON does a terrific job as bandleader (there were three weeks of rehearsals) and JEFF LYNNE as producer; the music is near note-perfect and sounds wonderful. And if it's an occasionally bumpy ride, the spirit of the night shines through with warmth and charm. A sparky sitar-dominated second CD represents HARRISON's Eastern preoccupations, including a suite composed by RAVI SHANKAR. *ND*

Album rating: *6.5

CONCERTS FOR THE PEOPLE OF KAMPUCHEA

1980 (US 72m) EMI Films Ltd. / Keefco

Film genre: Rock/Pop-music concert/documentary

Top guns: dir: Keith McMillan

Stars: Paul McCartney *(performer)* <= the BEATLES =>, **Linda McCartney** *(performer)* ← ROCKSHOW ← SGT. PEPPER'S LONELY HEARTS CLUB BAND ← ONE HAND CLAPPING ← LET IT BE / → GIVE MY REGARDS TO BROAD STREET → GET BACK, **Denny Laine** *(performer)* ← ROCKSHOW ← ONE HAND CLAPPING / → CHASING DESTINY& **Rockestra:- Robert Plant, John Bonham, John Paul Jones** *(performers)* <= LED ZEPPELIN =>, **the WHO** *(performers)*, **the Pretenders:- Chrissie Hynde, James Honeyman-Scott, Pete Farndon, Martin Chambers** *(performers)* → NEW YORK DOLL, **the CLASH:- Joe STRUMMER, Paul Simonon, Mick Jones, Topper Headon** *(performers)*, **Elvis COSTELLO** *(performer)*, **Queen:- Freddie Mercury, Brian May, Roger Taylor, John Deacon** *(performers)*, **Ian DURY** *(performer)* & **the Blockheads:- Mickey Gallagher, Chaz Jankel, Norman Watt-Roy** *(performers)*, **the Specials** *(performers)* → DANCE CRAZE, **Rockpile:- Dave Edmunds** *(performer)* ← STARDUST, **Nick Lowe** *(performer)*, **Billy Bremner** *(performer)* ← TAPEHEADS, **Billy Connolly** *(performer)* → STILL CRAZY → OVERNIGHT → OPEN SEASON, **Matumbi** *(performers)*

Storyline: Between 1975-79, the Khmer Rouge leader Pol Pot and the Kampuchean (Cambodian) government were at the center of a complete radicalization of their war-torn country. With millions dead or dying of starvation and with the threat of fatal diseases, the world finally woke up to their miserable plight. With the help of UNICEF and other charity organisations, Paul McCartney and an all-star cast of rock singers/ musicians got together (post-Xmas 1979) on four separate nights at London's Hammersmith Odeon. The subsequent results helped over 5 million people from that side of the globe and no doubt guided a certain Mr Geldof to further the examples set here for Live Aid in '85. *MCS*

Movie rating: *7

Visual: video on 'Miramax' in 1988

Off the record: The video featured extra tracks by QUEEN ('Crazy Little Thing Called Love'), MATUMBI (Guide Us Jah (In Your Own Way)', the PRETENDERS ('Brass In Pocket'), WINGS ('Getting Closer' & 'Arrow Through Me') and an opening commentary by Peter Ustinov and a introduction by Billy Connolly. *BG*

Various Artists

Apr 81. (d-lp) *Atlantic; (K 60153)* [–] [39]
– (the WHO):- Baba O'Riley / Sister disco / Behind blue eyes / See me, feel me / (PRETENDERS):- The wait / Precious / Tattooed love boys / (ELVIS COSTELLO & THE ATTRACTIONS):- The imposter / (ROCKPILE):- Crawling from the wreckage / Little sister (with ROBERT PLANT) / (QUEEN):- Now I'm here / (the CLASH):- Armagideon time / (IAN DURY & THE BLOCKHEADS):- Hit me with your rhythm stick / (the SPECIALS):- Monkey man / (PAUL McCARTNEY & WINGS):- Got to get you into my life / Every night / Coming up / (ROCKESTRA):- Lucille / Let it be / Rockestra theme.

S/track review: Just as the 80s were about to commence, Christmas, charity and a feast of rock stars combined to bring to light the plight of the people of Kampuchea. On the evenings of December 26th, 27th, 28th & 29th, 1979, Hammersmith Odeon gave way to thousands of rock & pop fans who witnessed their idols under the spotlight. Whether severely malnourished children and the casualties of war were on many of their minds when these stars were on stage is indeed a topic of pub-talk speculation. On the music front, however, the WHO kick off the double-LP (if not the first night itself) with a whole side devoted to them. While 'Sister Disco' has its merits (and its 'Lifehouse' roots), the track is somewhat overshadowed by the likes of classics such as 'Baba O'Riley' ('Teenage Wasteland' to some), 'Behind Blue Eyes' and 'See Me, Feel Me'. First night headliners, QUEEN (in fact the only band who performed on the 26th), are shockingly under-represented here, as only one lengthy version of 'Now I'm Here' – featuring Mercury going OTT with the audience – testifies. Post-punk acts such as the CLASH ('Armagideon Time'), IAN DURY & THE BLOCKHEADS ('Hit Me With Your Rhythm Stick') and the SPECIALS ('Monkey Man') fill out the rest of side three. Side two, meanwhile, affords three numbers to relative newcomers, the PRETENDERS ('The Wait', 'Precious' & 'Tattooed Love Boys'); the sultry Chrissie Hynde must have had some pull on the "Brass In Pocket"-type executive producers; 'The Imposter' by ELVIS COSTELLO & THE ATTRACTIONS and two covers by Dave Edmunds' ROCKPILE: Graham Parker's 'Crawling From The Wreckage' & Pomus-Shuman's 'Little Sister' (the latter featuring ROBERT PLANT), were worthy inclusions. Naturally enough, side four was down to co-organizer, PAUL McCARTNEY, who delivered three with WINGS: the Beatles nugget, 'Got To Get You Into My Life', 'Every Night' (a hit present for Phoebe Snow) and 'Coming Up', plus three with the appropriately-billed ROCKESTRA. The latter rock congregation featured a plethora of all-star musicians (including John Bonham, Billy Bremner, Gary Brooker, Dave Edmunds, James Honeyman-Scott, Kenney Jones, John Paul Jones, Ronnie Lane, Wings, Robert Plant, Bruce Thomas, Pete Townshend, etc.), all contributing more or less to three further cues, Little Richard's 'Lucille', Lennon-McCartney's 'Let It Be' & the 'Rockestra Theme'. Although not recorded without any quality control – so to speak – the mastertapes could well do with a re-working for possibly a CD re-issue or DVD release – with all proceeds again going to UNICEF. *MCS*

Album rating: *6

– spinoff releases, etc. –

ROCKESTRA: Concerts For The People Of Kampuchea

Sep 80. (7"ep) [–] promo [–]
– Rockestra theme / Let it be / Lucille / Rockestra theme (reprise).

COOL RUNNINGS: THE REGGAE MOVIE

1983 (US/Jama 105m) Sunsplash Filmworks / Synergy Productions

Film genre: Reggae-music concert/documentary

Top guns: dir: Robert Mugge → DEEP BLUES → PRIDE AND JOY → HELLHOUNDS ON MY TRAIL → LAST OF THE MISSISSIPPI JUKES → BLUES DIVAS

Stars: Gregory Isaacs *(performer)* ← LAND OF LOOK BEHIND ← ROCKERS / → MADE IN JAMAICA, **Third World** *(performers)* ← REGGAE SUNSPLASH ← PRISONER IN THE STREET / → MADE IN JAMAICA, **Rita Marley** *(performer)* → the BOB MARLEY STORY → ONE LOVE, **Ziggy Marley and the Melody Makers** *(performers)* → the REGGAE MOVIE, **Gil Scott-Heron** *(performer)* ← NO NUKES, **Sugar Minott** *(performer)*, **Mutabaruka** *(performer)* ← LAND OF LOOK BEHIND, **Judy Mowatt** *(performer)* ← HEARTLAND REGGAE / → the BOB MARLEY STORY; CARIBBEAN NIGHTS, **the Skatalites** *(performers)*, **Anton Ellis** *(performer)*, **Musical Youth** *(performers)*, **Chalice** *(performer)*, **Bankie Banx** *(performer)*, Armand Thirard *(himself)*

Storyline: Robert Mugge's third excursion into music documentary. The 1983 Reggae Sunsplash Festival at Montego Bay in Jamaica takes centre stage here as a plethora of top stars give performances and interviews. *MCS*

Movie rating: *7

Visual: dvd Nov'05 (no audio OST)

Off the record: Birmingham reggae outfit from the school of Duddleston Manor, **Musical Youth** (led by Dennis Seaton) had a No.1 hit in 1982 with 'Pass The Dutchie'. *MCS*

Alice COOPER

Born: Vincent Damon Furnier, 4 Feb'48, Detroit, Michigan, USA. Son of a preacher man as they say, and living in Phoenix, Arizona, Vincent formed his first pro group in 1965, the Earwigs. Together with his partners in musical crime, Glen Buxton, Michael Bruce, Dennis Dunaway and Neal Smith, the singer relocated to L.A., changing their moniker to the Spiders along the way. After a few flop 45s and another brief name change to Nazz (Todd Rundgren had got there first!), the band adopted the improbable moniker of ALICE COOPER (a 17th Century witch, apparently) and signed to FRANK ZAPPA's 'Straight' records. Turgid, clumsy cod-psychedelia, the debut album, 'Pretties For You' (1969) didn't bode well, while the follow-up 'Easy Action' (1970) fared little better. Moving to Detroit in 1970, the band were inspired by the Motor City madness of MC5 and the Stooges, tightening up their sound somewhat and developing their theatrical shock tactics. Vincent simultaneously used the band name for his ghoulish, androgynous alter-ego, infamously embellishing the band's stage show with all manner of sick trickery: simulated hangings, mangled baby dolls, a live snake, mmm . . . nice. Signing to 'Warner Bros' and drafting in Bob Ezrin on production, the band actually started writing material to match the effectiveness of their live shows. This wasn't gloomy, horror soundtrack minimalism, however, it was freewheeling, revved-up rock'n'roll, often with more than a touch of tongue-in-cheek humour. While 'Killer' probably stands as COOPER's peak achievement, with the hilarious 'Under My Wheels' and the classic 'Be My Lover', the band really hit big with 'School's Out' (1972). The title track was an irrepressible blast of adolescent-style attitude that made the UK No.1 spot and propelled the album to the upper reaches of the charts on both sides of the Atlantic. The 'Elected' single was another hit and the accompanying 'Billion Dollar Babies' (1973) album made UK and US No.1. 'Muscle Of Love' (1974) was a little limp – so to speak – and cracks were beginning to show in the songwriting armoury. COOPER subsequently sacked the rest of the band in the summer of '74, hiring a cast of musicians that had previously backed up LOU REED. 'WELCOME TO MY NIGHTMARE' (1975; complete with eerie narration by the legendary Vincent Price – and a video!) was the last great vintage COOPER effort, a macabre concept album that spawned the hit single, 'Only Women Bleed'. In contrast to his superfreak, anti-hero stage character, offstage COOPER was becoming something of a celebrity, hobnobbing with the Hollywood elite and even hosting his own TV show, wherein the band shamelessly retro'd past glories. Throughout the 70s and into the early 80s, Alice (and the band) featured in several movies, noteably 'Diary Of A Mad Housewife' (1970) – performing 'Dead Babies' – the rockumentary 'MEDICINE BALL CARAVAN' (1971), his own 'GOOD TO SEE YOU AGAIN . . .' (1974), 'SGT. PEPPER'S LONELY HEARTS CLUB BAND' (1978) and 'ROADIE' (1980). By the mid-80s his musical output had degenerated into AOR mush and he spent time in rehab for alcohol addiction. It's unclear if performing in the rockumentary, 'The DECLINE OF WESTERN CIVILIZATION II: THE METAL YEARS' (1988), helped his cause, but with the aid of hair-rock writer, Desmond Child, COOPER once again became a major Top 10 player through the comeback single 'Poison' single. The accompanying album, 'Trash', fared almost as well, although it sounded about as menacing as Bon Jovi. 'Hey Stoopid' (1989) consolidated COOPER's newfound success, as did appearances in the odd horror flick; Alice the pro-am golfer continued to pop up in places where you'd least expect him, 'WAYNE WORLD' (1992), for one. With appearances from the likes of ROB ZOMBIE and Slash, 1997's 'A Fistful Of Alice' album was one of the man's better live efforts while 'Brutal Planet' (2000) finally found the grandaddy of gore back in the studio. More streetwise than schlock, the album delivered a sharp poke in the eye to those who'd already written him off for the umpteenth time. With the millennial 'Dragontown' (2001), COOPER proved that middle age hasn't mellowed him just yet, and appearances in 'MAYOR OF THE SUNSET STRIP' (2003) and 'METAL: A HEADBANGER'S JOURNEY' (2005), kept him in high esteem with his rock fanbase. *BG & MCS*

- **filmography** {acting} (composer) –

Diary Of A Mad Housewife *(1970 {c})* / **Medicine Ball Caravan** *(1971 {p} OST by V/A =>)* / Rock-A-Bye *(1973 {c})* / **Good To See You Again, Alice Cooper** *(1974 {*c} =>)* / **Alice Cooper: The Nightmare** *(1975 {*} =>)* / **Welcome To My Nightmare** *(1976 video {*p/c} =>)* / Sextette *(1978 {a})* / **Sgt. Pepper's Lonely Hearts Club Band** *(1978 {a} on OST by V/A =>)* / **Roadie** *(1980 {*c} on OST by V/A =>)* / **Monster Dog** *(1985 {*} + score w/ Grupo Dichotomy =>)* / Alice Cooper: The Nightmare Returns *(1986 {*p})* / Prince Of Darkness *(1987 {b})* / **the Decline Of Western Civilization Part II: The Metal Years** *(1988 {p} on OST by V/A =>)* / **Shocker (No More Mr. Nice Guy)** *(1989 score by COOPER on OST by V/A; see future edition)* / Freddy's Dead: The Final Nightmare *(1991 {b})* / **Wayne's World** *(1992 {c} on OST by V/A =>)* / Halloween . . . The Happy Haunting Of America! *(1997 {c})* / Dario Argento: An Eye For Horror *(2000 TV {c})* / the Attic Expeditions *(2001 {a})* / **Mayor Of The Sunset Strip** *(2003 {c})* / **Metal: A Headbanger's Journey** *(2005 {p} on OST by V/A =>)* / Unauthorized And Proud Of It: Todd Loren's Rock'n'roll Comics *(2006 {c})*

CROSBY, STILLS & NASH

Formed: Los Angeles, California, USA . . . summer 1968 by (David) Crosby, (Stephen) Stills and (Graham) Nash. The Indian summer of love was getting less loving by the day when this superhippy trio teamed up to croon about Morrocco and close shaves with barbers. But they came to define the ethos of the counterculture anyway, and there was no messing with those harmonies, forever defining the Laurel Canyon agenda with brilliant, doobie-scat flights of fancy like 'Suite: Judy Blue Eyes'. A kind of Southern Californian Grateful Dead, in generational appeal if not musical approach, who're rarely credited for some of the Isley Brothers' most stinging performances. Inevitably, they became flagbearers for 'WOODSTOCK' (1970), only their second gig as a band, and by which point they'd souped up their supergroup with the not inconsiderable talents of NEIL YOUNG. The actual film only featured one performance, but the soundtrack was more generous, including YOUNG's rare 'Sea Of Madness'. As well as appearing in 'CELEBRATION AT BIG SUR' (1971) and, more ironically, at the ROLLING STONES' infamous Altamont freebie (although they weren't featured in the original print of the Maysles Bros' 'GIMME SHELTER', they made the restored release in 2000) the group were also sighted in YOUNG's directorial debut, 'JOURNEY THROUGH THE PAST' (1972), with a couple of CSN&Y songs making the soundtrack. A decade on, amid the usual intermittent reformations, the ageing hippies tried to change the world one last time at old guard benefit, 'NO NUKES' (1980). *BG*

- **filmography** {performers/acting} (composers) –

It's All Over Town *(1963 {p GRAHAM w/ the Hollies} on OST by V/A =>)* / **the Big T.N.T. Show** *(1966 {p DAVID w/ the Byrds} =>)* / **You Are What You Eat** *(1968 {p DAVID} OST by V/A =>)* / **Supershow** *(1969 {p STEPHEN} =>)* / **Woodstock** *(1970 {p CS&N} on OST by V/A =>)* / **Celebration At Big Sur** *(1971 {p CSN & YOUNG} =>)* / **Love And Music** *(1971 {p DAVID w/ the Byrds} =>)* / **Journey Through The Past** *(1972 {p by CSN&Y} OST by NEIL YOUNG =>)* / **No Nukes** *(1980 {p CS&N} on OST by V/A =>)* / the Return Of Bruno *(1988 {p STEPHEN & GRAHAM})* / To Cross The Rubicon *(1991 {a DAVID})* / Backdraft *(1991 {b DAVID})* / Hook *(1991 {b DAVID})* / Perry Mason: The Case Of The Heartbroken Bride *(1992 TV {b STEPHEN})* / Thunderheart *(1992 {b DAVID})* / **Woodstock '94** *(1995 {p CS&N} on OST by V/A =>)* / Suddenly *(1996 TV {a DAVID})* / **My Generation** *(2000 {p CSN & YOUNG} =>)* / New Gladiators *(2002 score by CROSBY & NASH)* / Can't Buy Me Lunch: The Rutles 2 *(2002 TV {c GRAHAM})* / Autism: The Musical *(2007 {c STEPHEN})*

□ Cherie CURRIE segment
(⇒ the RUNAWAYS)

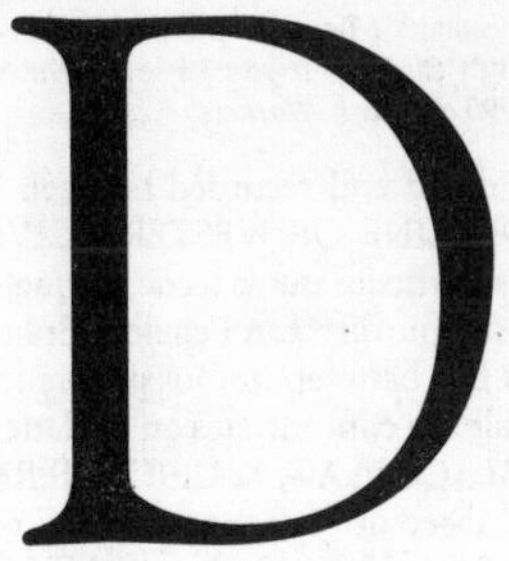

D.O.A.

1980 (US 99m) Lightning Films

Film genre: Punk Rock-music documentary/concert

Top guns: dir: Lech Kowalski → BORN TO LOSE: THE LAST ROCK AND ROLL MOVIE → HEY! IS DEE DEE HOME, S. Chris Salewicz

Stars: the SEX PISTOLS:- Johnny Rotten, Steve Jones, Paul Cook, Sid Vicious *(performers)*, **the Dead Boys:- Stiv Bators** *(performers)* → TAPEHEADS, **Generation X:- Billy IDOL, Tony James** *(performers)*, **Gene October** *(performer)* ← JUBILEE ← PUNK IN LONDON / URGH! A MUSIC WAR / **X-Ray Spex:- Poly Styrene** *(performers)*, **Sham 69:- Jimmy Pursey** *(performers)* → PUNK'S NOT DEAD, **Rich Kids:- Glen Matlock** *(performers)* <= the SEX PISTOLS =>, **the Clash:- Joe STRUMMER, Mick Jones, Paul Simonon, Topper Headon** *(performers)*, **Terry (Chimes) & The Idiots** *(performers)* <= Joe STRUMMER/the CLASH =>, **Iggy POP** *(performer)*, **Augustus Pablo** *(performer)*, Nancy Spungen *(herself)* ← the GREAT ROCK'N'ROLL SWINDLE / → the FILTH AND THE FURY

Storyline: A warts'n'all document on the punk rock movement, from its rise in 1976 to its impending fall late in 1978. Throw in footage of the last days of the Sex Pistols and archive in-bed interviews with catalysts (and soon-to-be dead) Sid Vicious and his girlfriend Nancy Spungen and you have a spiky-topped cocktail of sex and drugs and rock and roll. *MCS*

Movie rating: *6

Visual: video

Off the record: Punk rock groups such as **Sham 69** and **X-Ray Spex** had become big major label property during filming in 1978, the former having three UK Top 20 hits, 'Angels With Dirty Faces', 'If The Kids Are United' and 'Hurry Up Harry', while the latter charted Top 30 via 'The Day The World Turned Dayglo', 'Identity' and 'Germ Free Adolescence'. *MCS*

DANCE CRAZE

1981 (UK 50m) UFO Productions

Film genre: Ska-music concert/documentary

Top guns: dir: Joe Massot ← the SONG REMAINS THE SAME ← WONDERWALL

Stars: the Specials:- Terry Hall, Jerry Dammers, Lynval Golding, Neville Staples, Roddy Radiation, Sir Horace Gentleman, John Bradbury *(performers)* ← CONCERTS FOR THE PEOPLE OF KAMPUCHEA / **Madness:- Graham "Suggs" McPherson, Mike Barson, Chris Foreman, Lee Thompson, Mark Bedford, Chas Smash, Dan Woodgate** *(performers)* / **the Beat:- Dave Wakeling, Ranking Roger, Andy Cox, Dave Steel, Everett Moreton, Saxa** *(performers)* / **Bad Manners:- Buster Bloodvessel, Louis Cook, Martin Stewart, David Farren, Brian Tuitti, Gus Herman, Andrew Marson, Chris Kane** *(performers)* / **the Selecter:- Pauline Black, Compton Amanour, Charley "H" Bembridge, Charlie Anderson, Desmond Brown, Arthur "Gaps" Hendrickson** *(performers)* / **the Bodysnatchers:- Rhoda Dakar** *(performers)*

Storyline: The whole of Britain was taken over at the turn of the 80s by the second wave of ska. This film compiles footage of six of the genre's finest (indeed only) outfits from the 2-Tone days of yore. So grab your pork-pie hat and re-live these fun-tastic times. *MCS*

Movie rating: *7

Visual: video

Off the record: (see below)

Various Artists

Feb 81. (lp/c) *2-Tone-Chrysalis; (CHRTT/ZCCHRTT 5004)* *<21783>* [5] 1983 [ ]
– Concrete jungle (the SPECIALS) / Mirror in the bathroom (the BEAT) / Lip up fatty (BAD MANNERS) / Razor blade alley (MADNESS) / Three minute hero (the SELECTER) / Easy life (the BODYSNATCHERS) / Big shot (the BEAT) / One step beyond (MADNESS) / Ranking full stop (the BEAT) / Man at C&A (the SPECIALS) / Missing words (the SELECTER) / Inner London violence (BAD MANNERS) / Night boat to Cairo (MADNESS) / Too much pressure (the SELECTER) / Nite club (the SPECIALS).

S/track review: At the end of the pecked-out punk movement, and with arguably the same enthusiasm, the British ska revival (under the auspices of the SPECIAL A.K.A. and 'Two-Tone' records) provided teenage kids with another "DANCE CRAZE". Observed "live" – as in this film soundtrack – the SPECIALS, MADNESS, the SELECTER, et al, went 'One Step Beyond' the boundaries of conventional rock'n'roll and brought back excitement and fun back into popular music. 'DANCE CRAZE' (sub-titled "The Best Of British Ska . . . Live!", highlighted six bands and 15 hits from the turn of the 80s. Coventry's finest, the SPECIALS, fire in three classic cues, 'Concrete Jungle', 'Man At C&A' & 'Nite Club', while MADNESS, the SELECTER and the BEAT are afforded the same number. The "Nutty Boys" from Camden, MADNESS, are inspirational when delivering 'Night Boat To Cairo' and 'One Step Beyond', although the inclusion of 'Razor Blade Alley' is questionable. The SELECTER choose their best of all-time, 'Three Minute Hero', 'Too Much Pressure' & 'Missing Words', while the English BEAT (as they were known Stateside) nearly follow suit with 'Mirror In The Bathroom', 'Ranking Full Stop' and er.. 'Big Shot'. The weakest tracks stem from all-girl Ska act, the BODYSNATCHERS ('Easy Life') and bloated fun act, BAD MANNERS (featuring Buster Bloodvessel – the Homer Simpson of the 80s) on 'Inner London Violence'; 'Lip Up Fatty' aside, the latter were never taken too seriously. So look out and put on your old Ben Sherman shirt, stay-press drainpipes, two-tone spats and pork-pie hat, and relive the memories of 'DANCE CRAZE' – or better still, go down the pub. *MCS*

Album rating: *7.5

DANIELSON: A FAMILY MOVIE (OR, MAKE A JOYFUL NOISE HERE)

2006 (US 96m w/b&w) Creative Arson Productions

Film genre: Alt/Indie Rock-music documentary

Top guns: dir: J.L. Aronson

Stars: Daniel Famile:- Daniel Smith, Rachel Smith, Andrew Smith, Megan Smith, Lenny Smith, Elin K. Smith, Lilly Smith, David Smith, Chris

Palladino, Melissa Palladino *(performers)*, ***Sufjan Stevens*** *(performer)*, **Steve Albini** *(himself)*, **Daniel Johnston** *(performer)* ← the DEVIL AND DANIEL JOHNSTON, David Garland *(himself)*, **Kramer** *(himself)*, **Alan Sparhawk** *(himself)*, Rick Moody *(himself)*

Storyline: The talented Daniel Smith (an eccentric christian musician) and his famile/entourage are the lynchpins of this feature-length documentary. Also worthy of note is the movie's animation and its introduction to Daniel's (then) unknown protege/solo star, Surjan Stevens. *MCS*

Movie rating: *7

Visual: dvd 110m (no audio OST)

Off the record: Danielson Famile were formed in Clarksboro, New Jersey, around 1993. A real family affair indeed, the group was comprised of falsetto singer-songwriter Daniel Smith and his spouse Elin K., both his sisters Megan Slaboda and Rachel Galloway, brothers David and Andrew plus extended family members Chris and Melissa Palladino. This bunch of Christian indie-rockers released their debut 'A Prayer For Every Hour' (1995), actually handed into Rutgers Uni as Daniel's senior thesis project. Follow up, 'Tell Another Joke At The Ol' Choppin Block' (1997), was further proof that rock and roll should've remained the Devil's domain. However, the Danielson Famile continued to plug away (a trio of "Tri-Danielson" albums were issued), finally moving from 'Tooth & Nail' records to 'Secretly Canadian' for three post-millennium efforts, 'Fetch The Compass Kids' (2001), the Br. Danielson (solo) 'Brother Is To Son' (2004) and the latest 'Ships' (2006). **Surjan Stevens** (b. 1 Jul'75, Detroit, Michigan) was already an established folk/indie-pop star with several albums to his name including his debut 'A Sun Came' (2000) and his recent breakthrough 'Illinoise' (2005). *MCS*

□ DEAD CAN DANCE segment
(⇒ Lisa GERRARD)

the DECLINE OF WESTERN CIVILIZATION

1981 (US 100m) Spheeris Films Inc. (R)

Film genre: Punk rock-music documentary

Top guns: s-w + dir: Penelope Spheeris → SUBURBIA → DUDES → the DECLINE OF WESTERN CIVILIZATION PART II: THE METAL YEARS → WAYNE'S WORLD → the DECLINE OF WESTERN CIVILIZATION PART III → WE SOLD OUR SOULS FOR ROCK'N'ROLL

Stars: (performers) **Black Flag:- Ron Reyes, Greg Ginn *, Gary McDaniel, Robo** *(performers)* → WE JAM ECONO: THE STORY OF THE MINUTEMEN → AMERICAN HARDCORE / **the Germs:- Darby Crash, Pat Smear, Lorna Doom, Don Bolles / Catholic Discipline:- Claude Bessey, Phranc, Rick Jaffe, Robert Lopez, Craig Lee** *[also guitar w/ Alice Bag]* / **X:- Exene Cervenka, John DOE, Frank Gargani, Billy Zoom** *(performers)* / **CIRCLE JERKS:- Keith Morris, Greg Hetson, Roger Dowding, Lucky Lehrer** *(performers)* / **Alice Bag Band** *(performers)* / **the Fear:- Lee VING, Philo Cramer, Derf Scratch** * → the SLOG MOVIE * → GET CRAZY * → DU-BEAT-E-O *

Storyline: L.A. was the epicentre of America's hardcore punk scene towards the end of the 70s. Newbie filmmaker Penelope Spheeris played her part in documenting – via concert footage and interviews – every band who had a place in its controversial history. *MCS*

Movie rating: *7

Visual: video + dvd

Off the record: Lee VING went on to act in movies, 'GET CRAZY', 'FLASHDANCE', 'STREETS OF FIRE' and 'DUDES'. **Pat Smear** was later a member of Nirvana and Foo Fighters. *MCS*

—

Various Artists

Dec 81. (lp) *Slash; <SR 105>* □ [-]
– BLACK FLAG: White minority / Depression / Revenge / the GERMS: Manimal / CATHOLIC DISCIPLINE: Underground babylon / X: Beyond and back / Johny hit and run Paulene / We're desperate / CIRCLE JERKS: Red tape / Back against the wall / I just wanna some skank / Beverly Hills / ALICE BAG BAND: Gluttony / FEAR: I don't care about you / I love livin' in the city / Anthem. *<cd-iss. Sep93 on 'Slash-Warners'; 8 28812-2>*

S/track review: Filmed and recorded between December '79 and May '80, 'The DECLINE OF WESTERN CIVILIZATION' is an insight into L.A.'s hardcore punk scene through the lens (+ audio equipment) of first-time director, Penelope Spheeris. While the no-holds-barred film flits between riotous punk audiences and the top notch music, the album concentrates on the latter. The cream of the crop stem from BLACK FLAG, X, CIRCLE JERKS and FEAR, who are each afforded three or four songs, not all of them transferred from film to LP. A pre-Henry Rollins BLACK FLAG – fronted by Puerto Rican, Ron Reyes – kick off the set via 'White Minority', as cutting edge and offensive as one could get in these heady, spit-on-my-face times; the band's equally hostile, 'Depression' & 'Revenge' followed suit. It was no surprise the GERMS were apportioned only one track, 'Manimal', as their extremely inebriated spokesman, Darby Crash – influenced by the late Sid Vicious, no doubt – was too drunk to f*** on LP outtake, 'Shutdown'. 'Slash' fanzine/paper editor, Frenchman Claude Bessey (aka Kickboy Face), is certainly the weak link on show here; the punk poet and his act, CATHOLIC DISCIPLINE (with future soloist Phranc in their ranks), come off worse via the Doors-esque 'Underground Babylon'; a second track, 'Barbee Doll Lust', was on celluloid only. Ditto, ALICE BAG BAND and the Siouxsie-like, 'Prowler In The Night', although 'Gluttony' did make it on to the LP. While 'Nausea' from X opened the movie, Exene & Co's concert fave didn't merit a place on the LP, although the likes of 'Beyond And Back', 'Johny Hit And Run Paulene' (sung by JOHN DOE) and early gem, 'We're Desperate', did fit the bill. The wonderful CIRCLE JERKS, meanwhile, fire out four tracks in quick succession, 'Red Tape', 'Back Against The Wall', 'I Just Want Some Skank' and 'Beverly Hills', all as one might suspect, menacing and confrontational; their fifth film cut, 'Wasted', was not included. That just left the antagonist FEAR (led by humorous, homo-baiting Lee Ving), who concluded the 16-song LP with 'I Don't Care About You', 'I Love Livin' In The City' & 'Anthem', although, shamefully, not two of their best-loved numbers, 'Let's Have A War' & 'Beef Bologna'. Yes, it could've been even better. *MCS*

Album rating: *7.5

the DECLINE OF WESTERN CIVILIZATION PART II: THE METAL YEARS

1988 (US 93m) Spheeris Films Inc. (R)

Film genre: Hard rock-music documentary

Top guns: dir: Penelope Spheeris ← DUDES ← SUBURBIA ← the DECLINE OF WESTERN CIVILIZATION / → WAYNE'S WORLD → the DECLINE OF WESTERN CIVILIZATION PART III → WE SOLD OUR SOULS FOR ROCK'N'ROLL

Stars: AEROSMITH:- Steven Tyler, Joe Perry, Joey Kramer, Tom Hamilton, Brad Whitfield *(performers)*, **Alice COOPER** *(performer)*, **KISS:- Gene Simmons, Paul Stanley, Ace Frehley, Peter Criss** *(performers)*, **Ozzy Osbourne** *(performer)* ← TRICK OR TREAT / → PRIVATE PARTS → MOULIN ROUGE, **Poison** *(performers)*, **Faster Pussycat** *(performers)*, **Motorhead:- incl. LEMMY** *(performers)*, **Megadeth:- Dave Mustaine *, Marty Friedman, Dave Ellefson, Nick Menza** *(performers)* → WOODSTOCK '99 → SOME KIND OF MONSTER *, **Lizzy Borden:- Lizzy Borden, Gene**

Allen, Mike Davis, Joey Scott *(performers)*, **Armored Saint:- John Bush, Phil Sandoval, Joey Vera, Gonzo** *(performers)*, **Queensryche:- Geoff Tate, Chris DeGarmo, Michael Wilton, Eddie Jackson, Scott Rockenfield** *(performers)*, **Metal Church:- David Wayne, Craig Wells, Kurdt Vanderhoof, Duke Erikson, Kirk Arrington** *(performers)*, **Rigor Mortis:- Bruce Corbitt, Harden Harrison, Casey Orr, Mike Scaccia** *(performers)*, **Seduce:- Mark Andrews, David Black, Chuck Burns** *(performers)*

Storyline: Penelope Spheeris' documentary charts the rise of heavy metal music from its R&B roots to the present. Commentaries from Alice Cooper, Ozzy Osbourne and a host of other big names are interspersed with music from up and coming metal bands. There are touches of humour throughout the film, especially Ozzy's miserable attempt to make himself breakfast, as well as a look at the "dark side" of drugs and satanism. *JZ*

Movie rating: *7

Visual: video + dvd

Off the record: (see below).

—

Various Artists (w/ dialogue *)

May 88. (cd/c/lp) *Capitol; <C2/C4/C1 90205> (CD/TC+/EST 2065)* ☐ Jul88 ☐

– (GENE SIMMONS speaks *) / Under my wheels (ALICE COOPER w/ AXL ROSE, SLASH and IZZY of GUNS N' ROSES) / The bathroom wall (FASTER PUSSYCAT) / Cradle to the grave (MOTORHEAD) / You can run but you can't hide (ARMORED SAINT) / Born to be wild (LIZZY BORDEN) / (ALICE COOPER speaks *) / (RIKKI ROCKETT speaks *) / In my darkest hour (MEGADETH) / The prophecy (QUEENSRYCHE) / The brave (METAL CHURCH) / Foaming at the mouth (RIGOR MORTIS) / Colleen (SEDUCE) / (STEVEN TYLER speaks *).

S/track review: "I think the head bangers go back to Elvis. Any time you get that kind of music that makes people go totally out of their minds they're head banging." The surprisingly profound words of Vincent Furnier, better known by the moniker ALICE COOPER, in one of the short interview extracts on the " . . .METAL YEARS" soundtrack. Just like dancing, pogoing or moshing, headbanging is another derivative of the way we enjoy certain types of music, even if it does look a bit ridiculous at times, as that "Bohemian Rhapsody" scene in 'WAYNE'S WORLD' goes to show. Headbanging will always be associated with heavy metal and this collection of ten songs showcases all that was good and, alas, all that was bad about 80s heavy metal. To begin we have the aforementioned COOPER accompanied by AXL, SLASH and IZZY of Guns N' Roses for a rockin' version of 'Under My Wheels', while 'Cradle To The Grave' from MOTORHEAD is as raw as you'll get from Lemmy and Co. LIZZY BORDEN's cover of 'Born To Be Wild' is good if not exactly mind-blowing and QUEENSRYCHE's 'The Prophecy' is a perfect example of the epic grandeur that this kind of music can achieve when handled properly. However, the but is as big as the hair. ARMORED SAINT's 'You Can Run But You Can't Hide', METAL CHURCH's 'The Brave' and 'Foaming At The Mouth' from RIGOR MORTIS are just downright nasty, full of the unimaginative slaverings and sluggish riffs that are the downfall of so many metal bands. "THE METAL YEARS" does document and explore one of the biggest music scenes ever established, in all its big hair and tight leather splendour, and, whether intentionally or not, also shows what makes it laughable at times. *CM*

Album rating: *6.5

the DECLINE OF WESTERN CIVILIZATION – PART III

1998 (US 86m) Spheeris Films Inc. (R)

Film genre: Metal/Punk rock-music documentary

Top guns: dir: Penelope Spheeris ← WAYNE'S WORLD ← the DECLINE OF WESTERN CIVILIZATION 2: THE METAL YEARS ← DUDES ← SUBURBIA ← the DECLINE OF WESTERN CIVILIZATION / → WE SOLD OUR SOULS FOR ROCK'N'ROLL

Stars: Naked Aggression *(performers)*, **Litmus Green** *(performers)*, **Final Conflict** *(performers)*, **the Resistance** *(performers)*, **Rick Wilder** *(himself)*, Gary Fredo *(himself/LAPD)*, Stephen Chambers *(himself)*, **FLEA** *(himself)*

Storyline: With two "Decline Of . . ." documentaries behind her (and now numerous feature films), Penelope Spheeris completes her L.A.-based rock trilogy with "Part III" of the series. Now concentrating on the plight of the homeless (the why's and wherefore's) with music from four local rock bands, she discovers that living on the streets as an alienated youth can be socially demoralising for all parties concerned (the LAPD included). *MCS*

Movie rating: *6

Visual: video (no audio OST)

Off the record: Naked Aggression (fronted by Kirsten Patches/Suchomel) were arguably the most well known of the pack, having released a clutch of sets, 'Bitter Youth' (1994 on 'Broken Rekids'), 'March March Along' (1995) – featuring a version of Kim Wilde's 'Kids In America' – & 'March March Alive' (1996); post-'DECLINE . . .'; they issued 'Gut Wringing Machine' (2000 on 'Grilled Cheese') and the compilation, 'Heard It All Before' (2005). **Final Conflict** delivered only one CD, 'American Scream' (1995) on 'Nemesis' records, **Litmus Green** were responsible for two sets, 'It Must Suck To Be You' (1998) and 'Cockring' (2000), while the **Resistance** went on to release 'Plague The Nation' (2003). **Rick Wilder** played with the Mau-Maus, and **FLEA** was of course bassist for the Red Hot Chili Peppers. *MCS*

DEEP BLUES

1992 (US 91m) Oil Factory / Radio Active Films / Tara Releasing

Film genre: Blues-music documentary bio-pic

Top guns: dir: Robert Mugge ← COOL RUNNINGS: THE REGGAE MOVIE / → PRIDE AND JOY → HELLHOUNDS ON MY TRAIL → LAST OF THE MISSISSIPPI JUKES → BLUES DIVAS / s-w: Robert Palmer

Stars: Big Jack Johnson *(performer)*, **R.L. Burnside** *(performer)* → HILL STOMP HOLLAR → HELLHOUNDS ON MY TRAIL → YOU SEE ME LAUGHIN', **Roosevelt "Booba" Barnes** *(performer)* → HELLHOUNDS ON MY TRAIL, **Junior Kimbrough** *(performer)* → HELLHOUNDS ON MY TRAIL → YOU SEE ME LAUGHIN', **Jessie Mae Hemphill** *(performer)*, **Booker T. Laury** *(performer)* ← GREAT BALLS OF FIRE!, **Wade Walton** *(performer)*, **Jack Owens** *(performer)*, **Lonnie Pitchford** *(performer)*, **Bud Spires** *(performer)*, Robert Palmer *(narration)*

Storyline: Conceived by writer/critic Robert Palmer (not the same guy) and inspired by his book of the same name; executively produced by Dave Stewart (the same guy) and directed by Robert Mugge, this magnetic, historically priceless work of modern day musicology trawls the Mississippi back roads and byways for the "blues reality" Palmer cites in his soundtrack sleevenotes, excavating the grimiest art and most colourful practitioners, filming them in their rural locale and on-stage in the cauldron of their favourite juke joints. *BG*

Movie rating: *7

Visual: video + dvd

Off the record: (see below)

—

Various Artists

Oct 92. (cd) *Atlantic; <7 82450-2>* ☐ [–]
– Jumper on the line (R.L. BURNSIDE) / Jr. blues (JUNIOR KIMBROUGH) / Catfish blues (BIG JACK JOHNSON) / Daddy, when is momma coming home (BIG JACK JOHNSON) / Big boy now (BIG JACK JOHNSON) / Midnight prowler (FRANK FROST) / You can talk about me (JESSIE MAE HEMPHILL) / Shame on you (JESSIE MAE HEMPHILL) / Long haired doney (R.L. BURNSIDE) / Heartbroken man (ROOSEVELT "BOOBA" BARNES) / Ain't gonna worry about tomorrow (ROOSEVELT "BOOBA" BARNES) / Love like I wanna (ROOSEVELT "BOOBA" BARNES) / Terraplane blues (LONNIE PITCHFORD) / If I had possession over judgement day (LONNIE PITCHFORD) / Devil blues (JACK OWENS & BUD SPIRES).

S/track review: A good few hundred days and nights before Jon Spencer made the likes of R.L. BURNSIDE (whose 'Jumper On The Line', like much of his work, suggests a Saharan Skip James) acceptable to the alternative music press, and even before 'Fat Possum' Records started recording him, Robert Mugge's film showcased exactly the kind of deepest Mississippi mud that lit Spencer and co's fire. As Palmer makes clear in his brilliant notes, the music on this soundtrack isn't quite as heard in the film, neither in content nor sound mix, but it easily lives up to the voodoo trimmings and tales of inexplicably-erased reels he delights in conjuring. For the most part it isn't blues as celebrated in the Martin Scorsese series, as interpreted by pedestrian blues-rockers or as portrayed by any number of Hollywood clichés. It's a dark, trance-inducing rumble, not too keen on anything as elaborate as chord changes and resultantly far closer in spirit and function to the music of North and West Africa, lined with an agitated fuzz of crowd debris and spiked with spontaneous outbursts of solidarity rather than any deliberately solicited call and response. As good as Mugge's subsequent juke joint survey ('LAST OF THE MISSISSIPPI JUKES') was, 'DEEP BLUES' communicates an atmosphere so electric, tribal and arcane ("recorded", according to Palmer, "in circumstances where life and property are perpetually at risk"), you can hardly believe it existed in 1990, which makes you envious no club in Europe could come anywhere close. But if you'd want to breathe liquid sweat at any of the boltholes purveyed here it'd probably be Jr. Kimbrough's Joint in Holly Springs, the showcase for both JESSIE MAE HEMPHILL and KIMBROUGH himself, both of whom have been belatedly feted by the British press in recent years. KIMBROUGH's bass-heavy echo-drone – which Palmer counts as a "formative influence" on the likes of 'Sun' sessioner Stan Kesler and Tarantino favourite, Charlie Feathers – is a thing of atavistic power, determinedly, triumphantly not of the modern world. HEMPHILL is more subdued but no less potent, granddaughter of SID and natural born inheritor of the HEMPHILL clan's legacy. Parlaying repetition as shamanism, and phrasing 'Shame On You' like a quavering high priestess, she exorcises the ghosts of a broken relationship. Palmer loves to play with the mythology of the blues, but his description of the recording of LONNIE PITCHFORD's Robert Johnson covers is almost as compelling as the performances themselves, likewise his anecdote about JACK OWENS and BUD SPIRES' 'Devil Blues', and the forbidding terrain – not merely the preserve of Skip James, as it turns out – its haunted whine emanates from. With BIG JACK JOHNSON (still delivering heating oil as a day job at the time) tearfully mellowing out for at least one track, though, it's not all crossroads and demons; difficult to believe Lenny Kravitz (you really have to hear it . . .) didn't cop an earful prior to his 'Mama Said' album, even if he can't hold a voodoo candle to these guys. God knows their collective age when 'DEEP BLUES' was recorded – it must have been more than just several hundred years, at once it's genius and tragedy; with most of them now dead, are there really any young players who'll be able to make music as bled-raw vital as this in fifty years' time? *BG*

Album rating: *9

DEEP END

aka PETE TOWNSHEND'S DEEP END LIVE!

1986 (UK 87m) Warner Bros. / Atlantic

Film genre: Rock-music concert/documentary

Top guns: dir: Keef (aka Keith MacMillan)

Stars: Pete Townshend *(performer)* <= the WHO =>, **David Gilmour** *(musician)* <= PINK FLOYD =>, **John 'Rabbit' Bundrick** *(musician)* → PSYCHODERELICT → THIRTY YEARS OF MAXIMUM R&B LIVE → LIFEHOUSE → the WHO LIVE AT THE ROYAL ALBERT HALL, **Peter Hope Evans** *(musician)* → PSYCHODERELICT, **Simon Phillips** *(musician)* ← PSYCHODERELICT

Storyline: A performance in Brixton, London, sees the Who guitarist Pete Townshend (and a plethora of musicians) play their socks off. *MCS*

Movie rating: *7

Visual: video <50110> mini-video (318)

Off the record: Pete Hope Evans was a member of early 70s outfit, Medicine Head.

PETE TOWNSHEND: Pete Townshend's Deep End Live!

Oct 86. (lp/c/cd) *Atco; <90553-1/-4/-2>* [–] [98]
– Barefootin' / After the fire / Behind blue eyes / Stop hurtin' people / I'm one / I put a spell on you / Save it for later / Pinball wizard / A little is enough / Eyesight to the blind.

S/track review: PETE TOWNSHEND was joined by DAVID GILMOUR on guitar, SIMON PHILLIPS on drums and PETER HOPE-EVANS on blues harp for this concert in Brixton in 1985. It features a handful of Who classics, a couple of blues standards and some TOWNSHEND originals. What strikes the listener now is the 80s sheen: the horns on accompaniment and the tone of the instruments evoke cheap hairspray and bad suits, and enervates the earlier Who-era material, which thrived on the rawness and frustration of its inception. 'Barefootin'' is an upbeat number, replete with big horns, popping bass, Hammond synth, though it is slightly tepid. Written in the wake of the recent Live Aid concert, 'After The Fire' features a quasi-religious, exultant vocal from TOWNSHEND, a solid solo, but gains pace like a keyboard programmed beat when you increase the tempo; there's something unavoidably synthetic about the listening experience. 'Behind Blue Eyes' is a stone cold classic played too fast, but it's interesting listening to how TOWNSHEND's slightly strained vocal holds its own compared to Roger Daltrey's original rendition. 'Stop Hurting People', however, is pretty wretched. TOWNSHEND seems unable to bring himself to fully sing it, instead relying on an almost spoken vocal, with a strange transatlantic enunciation, and the sentiment that "love smashes stances" seems anachronistic in the callous mid-80s. 'I'm One' works better, it is stripped down to bare essentials, and plays on TOWNSHEND's weakness, his "fingers so clumsy, voice too loud", defiant in its vulnerability. Then follows a good version of Screamin' Jay Hawkins' 'I Put A Spell On You', with a grooving harmonica solo, and a supremely tasteful GILMOUR solo. 'Pinball Wizard' elicits a near ecstatic response from the audience, even stripped down to a solo guitar spot, the opening guitar stabs are legendary and undeniably great. The less said about 'A Little Is Enough' the better, it feels like another 80s abomination, pumping bass and synths galore, though the proceedings are redeemed with that perennial tale of the power of sex 'Eyesight To The Blind', and a playful rendition of 'Magic Bus'. The flower power sentiment of

'Won't Get Fooled Again', and "smelling green at the change all round" is full-on; a scorching rendition with an extended outro. TOWNSHEND's resurgence as part of the Who no doubt assuages the guilt of this excursion. *DF*

Album rating: *5

– spinoff releases, etc. –

PETE TOWNSHEND: Give Blood / Magic Bus

Apr 86. (7") *(U 8744)* ☐ ☐
(12"+=) *(UT 8744)* – Won't Get Fooled Again.

PETE TOWNSHEND: Behind Blue Eyes / Barefootin'

Oct 86. (7") *<99499>* ☐ ☐

☐ DEPECHE MODE segment
(⇒ 101)

DERAILROADED

2005 (US 86m) Ubin Twinz Productions

Film genre: avant-Rock-music documentary

Top guns: dir: Josh Rubin

Stars: Wild Man Fischer *(himself/performer)*, **Frank ZAPPA** *(archival/ performer)*, **Solomon Burke** *(himself)* ← LIGHTNING IN A BOTTLE ← COOL BREEZE (s/t), **Mark Mothersbaugh** *(himself)* <= DEVO =>, **Dr. Demento** *(himself)* ← UHF, Miguel Ferrer *(himself)* ← FLASHPOINT, Bill Mumy *(himself)* ← HARD TO HOLD ← WILD IN THE STREETS, Richard Foos *(himself)*, Harold Benson *(himself)*, **"Weird Al" Yankovic** *(himself)* ← UHF ← TAPEHEADS, Bill Paxton *(himself)* ← TRESPASS ← NEAR DARK ← STREETS OF FIRE, Gail Zappa *(herself)*, Dan Rowan *(himself)*

Storyline: This docu-film takes us "Inside the Mind of Larry 'Wild Man' Fischer" (as it says on the sleeve), a manic depressive, paranoid schizophrenic or just another tortured rock'n'roll artist – delete as appropriate, you decide. *MCS*

Movie rating: *6.5

Visual: dvd (no audio OST)

Off the record: Wild Man Fischer (b. Lawrence Wayne Fischer, 6 Nov'45, Los Angeles, California, USA). Larry's musical origins stemmed from the street corners of L.A.'s Sunset Strip, where he sang made-to-order songs in return for dimes. A near acid (LSD) casualty, he spent time in a mental institution, before he met up with Frank ZAPPA, who produced his 1969 double debut album 'An Evening With Wild Man Fischer'. Critics were split in opinion to his eccentric 50s-style compositions, some thought it voyeuristic, while others saw it's artistic merit. However, this was his only recording for some time, as he took off around America, singing occasional for the faithful cult disciples. In 1975, he re-appeared with a single 'Go To Rhino Records', a song inspired by the record store of that name, which was the only one never to have thrown him out. It sold over 2,000 copies, which led to the owner Richard Foos and Harold Benson, starting their own label, which has become a major source for re-issues and compilations still to this day. The first release on the label was Fischer's 1977 follow-up album 'Wildmania', which reconsolidated his weirdo status. Two more albums appeared in the first half of the 80s, although his whereabouts have always been the source of jest. 'DERAILROADED' should set the record straight, so to speak. Others on show, **Mark Mothersbaugh** formerly of robotic-rock outfit, DEVO, is now a film composer with numerous scores/OST's behind him (see; future edition). *MCS*

the DEVIL AND DANIEL JOHNSTON

2004 (US 110m w/ b&w) This Is That / Complex (PG-13)

Film genre: Indie-Rock-music documentary/bio-pic

Top guns: s-w + dir: Jeff Feuerzeig ← the BAND THAT WOULD BE KING

Stars: Daniel Johnston *(humself)* → DANIELSON: A FAMILY MOVIE (OR, MAKE A JOYFUL NOISE HERE), Bill Johnston *(himself)*, Mabel Johnston *(herself)*, Louis Black *(himself)* ← HOME OF THE BLUES ← JANIS JOPLIN SLEPT HERE ← TRUE STORIES, **Kathy McCarthy** *(herself)*, Jeff Tartakov *(himself)*, **Gibby Haynes** *(himself)* ← DEAD MAN / → YOU'RE GONNA MISS ME, **David Fair** *(himself)* ← the BAND THAT WOULD BE KING, **Jad Fair** *(himself)* ← the BAND THAT WOULD BE KING, Dick Johnston *(himself)*, Margie Johnston *(herself)*, Matt Groening *(himself)*

Storyline: The film – through footage and interviews – follows the life of manic depressive, singer-songwriter, Daniel Johnston, a multi-talented but tortured genius who's been praised by the likes of Kurt Cobain. Premiered at the Sundance Film Festival, the film finally gained universal by 'Sony' release in 2006. *MCS*

Visual: dvd (see below)

Movie rating: *8.5

Off the record: Daniel Johnston was born 22 January, 1961 in Sacramento, California. A tortured but incredibly prolific legend of the US underground music scene, Daniel has spent a lifetime balancing the unpredictable demands of mental illness with a recording career. Presumably self-taught, Johnston issued a series of early cassette-only releases on his 'Stress' label, beginning with 1980s self-explanatory 'Songs Of Pain'. Hardly a musical genius, the appeal lay in the heart-rending emotional nakedness of Johnston's amateur guitar strumming, keyboard plonking and singing, his lyrics focusing on the day to day difficulties, heartaches and small victories of Johnston's world. Having based himself in Austin, Texas, he finally broke from obscurity after MTV filmed him as part of a profile on the city's thriving indie/alt-Rock scene. While his name soon became more famous than his music, 'Homestead' redressed the balance in the late 80s by re-issuing 'Yip Jump Music', an acclaimed set featuring heartfelt tributes to the BEATLES and cartoon legend, 'Caspar The Friendly Ghost' against a backdrop of skeletal organ. The late 80s also found Daniel collaborating with fellow maverick, Jad Fair, on an eponymous album for the latter's '50 Skidillion Watts' label. By this point, Johnston had already survived two periods of hospitalisation yet his work rate showed no sign of slowing. A move to Kramer's 'Shimmy Disc' in the early 90s resulted in the appropriately titled '1990' and 'Artistic Vice' (1992). Against all the odds, the irrepresible troubadour subsequently signed a major label deal with 'Atlantic', releasing the well received 'Fun' in 1994. With production assistance from Butthole Surfer, Paul Leary, the record displayed a marked leap in confidence with a strong set of songs which brought widespread critical plaudits. Johnston, who was unceremoniously dropped by the major, spent several years in the wilderness overcoming his battle with chronic depression and writing material for his comeback album 'Rejected Unknown' (2001). The set, which consisted of Johnston's trademark lo-fi ramblings, coupled with a shambolic production and some nifty musical noodlings, once again established a true American songwriting genius. **Kathy McCarthy** (is ex-Glass Eye, the band), while Louis Black is the brainchild behind the South By Southwest Music Festival and Matt Groening is the man behind the Simpsons. *BG & MCS*

DANIEL JOHNSTON

Aug 06. (dvd) *Tartan Video; (TVD 3600)* ☐ ☐
– (scenes):- 1. A Bright Beginning / 2. Star Art Guys / 3. Problems And Persecution / 4. Laurie The Muse / 5. Sorry Films / 6. Leaving The Nest / 7. Arrival In Austin / 8. MTV And LSD / 9. Famous In NYC / 10. Take Me Home, West Virginia / 11. Ups And Downs / 12. World's Greatest Manager / 13. Life In Water / 14. Art Can Save You / 15. True Love Will Find You / 16. Casper Lives.

– associated compilation –

DANIEL JOHNSTON: Welcome To My World – The Music Of Daniel Johnston

Apr 06. (cd) *Eternal Yip Eye Music; <110>* ☐ ☐
– Peek a boo / Casper the friendly ghost / Some things last a long time / Walking the cow / I'm nervous / Man obsessed / Don't let the sun go down on your grievances / Never before never again / Sun shines down on me / Chord organ blues / Living life (full repaired version) / Speeding motorcycle / True love will find you in the end / Never relaxed / Sorry entertainer / Ain't no woman gonna make a George Jones outta me / Lennon song / Devil town / Laurie / Story of an artist / Funeral home.

the DEVIL'S MUSIC

1976 (UK 50m x 5 epi TV-mini) BBC

Film genre: Blues-music documentary (+ concert)

Top guns: dir: Giles Oakley

Stars: Sam Chatmon *(performer)*, **Big Joe Williams** *(performer)*, **Houston Stackhouse** *(performer)*, **Bukka White** *(performer)*, **Mose Vinson** *(performer)*, **Joe Willie Wilkins** *(performer)*, **Billy Boy Arnold** *(performer)*, **the Aces** *(performers)*, **Joe Carter** *(performer)*, **Fenton Robinson** *(performer)*, **Sonny Blake** *(performer)*, **Laura Dukes** *(performer)*, **Good Rockin' Charles** *(performer)*, **Little Brother Montgomery** *(performer)*, **Edith Wilson** *(performer)*, **James DeShay** *(performer)*

Storyline: Writer/producer Giles Oakley and an intrepid BBC team undertake what in the mid-70s was still a relatively adventurous and unusual project (at least for a bunch of Brits), travelling the length of the USA in search of unsung and not-sung-enough bluesmen and women, acoustic and electric, black and white, and filming and recording them in their natural born backyards. *BG*

Movie rating: *6

Visual: dvd to come

Off the record: Sam Chatmon etc. (see below)

—

Various Artists

1976. (d-lp) *Red Lightnin'; (RL 0033)* ☐ [-]
– Stop and listen (SAM CHATMON) / Highway 49 (BIG JOE WILLIAMS) / Cool drink of water (HOUSTON STACKHOUSE) / Sam's rag (SAM CHATMON) / Watergate blues (BIG JOE WILLIAMS) / Who gonna love you tonight (SAM CHATMON) / Aberdeen, Mississippi (BUKKA WHITE) / When you got rid of my mule (MOSE VINSON) / One room country shack (SONNY BLAKE) / Bring it on home (SONNY BLAKE) / Mr. Downchild (JOE WILLIE WILKINS) / Mean red spider (HOUSTON STACKHOUSE) / Bugle call blues (MOSE VINSON) / Crawdad (LAURA DUKES) / Take a little walk with me (the ACES) / Somebody help me (BILLY BOY ARNOLD) / Somebody loan me a dime (FENTON ROBINSON) / Don't start me talkin' (GOOD ROCKIN' CHARLES) / You don't know what love is (FENTON ROBINSON) / It hurts me too (JOE CARTER) // She fooled me (BILLY BOY ARNOLD) / Blue shadows (the ACES) / Shake your boogie (GOOD ROCKIN' CHARLES) / Vicksburg blues (LITTLE BROTHER MONTGOMERY) / Yankee doodle blues (EDITH WILSON) / I ain't got no special rider now (LITTLE BROTHER MONTGOMERY). *<US 3xcd-box iss.Aug03 on 'Sanctuary'+=; 8131-2> (UK 3xcd-box iss.Aug03 on 'Indigo'+=; IGOTCD 25371>* – (CD Disc 2 + 3 = 6 live tracks by JAMES DeSHAY) + other rare live tracks from a 1963 European Blues Festival featuring MEMPHIS SLIM, SONNY BOY WILLIAMSON & MATT MURPHY).

S/track review: Don't be put off by the walking cliché of a title – it was dreamt up three decades ago to frame a BBC TV series, or rather field recording trip, at a time when Robert Johnson, crossroads and demonic bargains hadn't carved out such a hold on mainstream popular culture. Punk held sway instead; "I am the anti-Christ" Johnny Rotten declared, as the good folks at the Beeb trawled the Deep South and urban north for living examples of a genre which had long been regarded – at least by religious types – as, if not always, anti-Christian, at least morally suspect. Like most of the serious attempts to document the genre since interest in it – at least among white audiences – was "revived" by the 60s blues-rock boom, the historical value of 'The DEVIL'S MUSIC' can at least partly be measured in how many of its artists have since passed away. And that'll be most of them. Naturally, the first disc starts out in deepest Mississippi with a gnarled, playful representative of a bespoke blues clan in SAM CHATMON; opener 'Stop And Listen' has him pulling on his bass strings like a capering bullfrog, and cutting a vintage jazz dash on 'Sam's Rag'. Only on the Jimmy Rogers-credited 'Who Gonna Love You Tonight', does he play it relatively straight. Other famous names include BIG JOE WILLIAMS, writer of rock stand-by 'Baby, Please Don't Go' and described in the sleevenotes as "essentially a loner and a hard man", who "devised a nine-string instrument that ended up as battered as he was". WILLIAMS had customised his guitar and his tuning so no-one could mimic him, and – a mere six years before his death – he performs a singular (and, unusually for the genre, then politically topical) 'Watergate Blues' in a voice as lived-in, phlegmatic and obscure as any on this album (with, by all accounts, a personality to match). BUKKA WHITE is the other big name; disappointingly, he only gets one track but his vintage growl isn't quite as poorly modulated as the notes make apology for, and, with his death coming as early as 1977, 'Aberdeen, Mississippi' is one of the great Delta folk-bluesman's final recordings. But any project of this scope is attractive in the way it holds out the anticipation of discovery and excavation; there's a whole raft of lesser-known musicians here, artists you'd likely only be familiar with if you'd been an afficionado for as many years as they'd been treading the boards. FENTON ROBINSON – who battled (and won) Boz Scaggs over ownership of his classic 'Somebody Loan Me A Dime' – is one of them, having, at the time of recording, not long completed his magnum opus of the same name. He's one of the few artists here availing himself of 70s signifiers like Fender Rhodes on the great blues-funk groove of 'You Don't Know What Love Is'. The evocatively named HOUSTON STACKHOUSE didn't record until he was 60, a Delta native whose credentials whine for themselves on Tommy Johnson's 'Cool Drink Of Water', Johnson – rather than his more famous namesake Robert – being the real source of the diabolic crossroads pact and whose character was recently reanimated in 'O BROTHER, WHERE ART THOU?'. MOSE VINSON is a pianist with a scruffy, Professor Longhair-esque slur of a voice who hails from Holly Springs of all places, the same nexus which spawned such belatedly appraised primitivists as R.L. Burnside and Jr. Kimbrough (see the brilliant 'DEEP BLUES' elsewhere in this section). According to the notes, VINSON spent his career in Memphis rather than New Orleans but the likes of 'When You Got Rid Of My Mule' and 'Bugle Call Blues' is the kind of material that would've slotted nicely into Clint Eastwood's entry in the Martin Scorsese series. As would LITTLE BROTHER MONTGOMERY, whose 'Vicksburg Blues' mutated into the '44 Blues' recorded by Howlin' Wolf, and was later covered by Lowell George. MONTGOMERY's boogie makes way mid-disc 2 for a raw, slatternly electric blues set – complete with chundering vintage organ – from JAMES DeSHAY, recorded in his own St. Louis club and all the more fascinating given that he never recorded commercially. Then there's the dames: LAURA DUKES isn't a woman to hide her light under a bushel, roaring like a lioness on a banjo-accompanied 'Crawdad', caring not a whit if her voice doesn't quite hold out on every note; the venerable EDITH WILSON takes inspiration from George Gershwin on the word-playfully bumptious 'Yankee Doodle Blues' ("I couldn't stay in London because I couldn't stand the fog, couldn't stay in Paris cos' I couldn't eat a frog"). Disc three turns up the volume again, comprising live sets from MEMPHIS SLIM, MATT MURPHY and SONNY BOY WILLIAMSON, recorded on a 1963 European tour which saw WILLIAMSON feted as a genius but, like too many of the geniuses on this treasure of a box set, didn't live long enough to fully reap the benefits. *BG*

Album rating: *8.5

Bo DIDDLEY

Born: Otha Ellas Bates, 30th December 1928, McComb, Mississippi, USA. As a toddler he was given the surname, McDaniel, after he was adopted by his mother's cousin. In the early 50s, BO DIDDLEY (named after a one-stringed African guitar) gave up a promising boxing career and subsequently (1955) moved from Chicago and street busking to sign for 'Checker' records. His debut recording, 'Bo Diddley', sold well enough in R&B circles to give him his first break on the 'Ed Sullivan Show'. Its flip side, 'I'm A Man', also became a standard for many 60s beat combos (the WHO, the Yardbirds, MANFRED MANN and especially the ROLLING STONES), and although DIDDLEY initially failed to achieve a Billboard Hot 100 hit, the bulk of his output ('Diddy Wah Diddy', 'Who Do You Love', 'Mona', etc.) were later embraced by countless rock acts. His umpteenth attempt at commercial success was finally rewarded with a belated minor US hit 45, 'Crackin' Up' in the summer of '59. This was almost immediately followed by an even bigger hit, 'Say Man', which saw BO flaunt his quick witted humour in a taunting match with maracas man, Jerome. DIDDLEY continued in the same fashion throughout the early 60s, scoring low-key hits with 'Road Runner' and 'You Can't Judge A Book By The Cover'. This period represented the pinnacle of his career and as the white R&B/rock bands took over, DIDDLEY and his ilk were consigned to the margins. Having featured in a number of rocku-movies after his star had faded ('LET THE GOOD TIMES ROLL' & 'The LONDON ROCK AND ROLL SHOW'), BO also found time to get in a few cameos/bit parts in movies such as 'Trading Places' (1983), 'EDDIE AND THE CRUISERS II: EDDIE LIVES!' (1989), 'ROCKULA' (1990) and 'BLUES BROTHERS 2000' (1998). Most people in the music world acknowledge the fact that "BO DIDDLEY put the Rock in Rock'n'Roll" – he shaped the music we hear nowadays from Elvis and Holly to the 'Stones and ZZ Top to Prince and Run DMC. *MCS*

- **filmography** {performance/acting} –

the Big T.N.T. Show *(1966 {p} =>)* / Crush Proof *(1972 {c})* / **Let The Good Times Roll** *(1973 {p} OST by V/A =>)* / **the London Rock And Roll Show** *(1973 {p} OST by V/A =>)* / Trading Places *(1983 {b})* / **Hail! Hail! Rock'n'Roll** *(1987 {p} OST by CHUCK BERRY =>)* / **Eddie And The Cruisers II: Eddie Lives!** *(1989 {b} OST by JOHN CAFFERTY =>)* / **Rockula** *(1990 {a})* / **Blues Brothers 2000** *(1998 {p} OST by V/A =>)* / **I Put A Spell On Me** *(2001 {c} =>)*

DIG!

2004 (US 107m; Palm Pictures / Interloper) (15)

Film genre: Punk Rock-music documentary (w/ performance)

Top guns: dir (+ s-w): Ondi Timoner

Stars: the Brian Jonestown Massacre:- Anton Newcombe, Joel Gion, Matt Hollywood, Dean Taylor, Jeff Davies, Peter Hayes → 9 SONGS *(themselves)* / Dave Deresinski *(manager)*, **the Dandy Warhols:- Courtney Taylor** *(+ narrator)*, **Peter Holmstrom, Eric Hedford, Zia McCabe** → 9 SONGS, plus **Brent DeBoer** *(himself)* / **Genesis P'orridge** *(interviewee)* ← BETTER LIVING THROUGH CIRCUITRY ← MODULATIONS, Nina Ritter, Adam Shore, Carlo McCormick, Perry Watts-Russell, **Greg Shaw** *(of Bomp! records)*, Michael Dutcher *(manager)*, **Rob Campenella** *(ex-BJM)*, **Miranda Lee Richards** *(herself)*, Nic Harcourt *(himself)*, **Sara Tucek** *(herself/ performer)*

Storyline: First-time female director Ondi Timoner's exhaustive document (several years 1996 to 2003 and over 1500 hours of footage!) on two diverse indie rock bands, the Brian Jonestown Massacre and the Dandy Warhols; showcasing bombastic frontmen Anton Newcombe and Courtney Taylor respectively. The film also focuses on the record industry and the ongoing friendship and evolving rifts between the two star-crossed factions. While Anton goes from manic to maniac, Courtney and his band grow to be a worldwide success. Watch more than once!! *MCS*

Movie rating: *8.5

Visual: (see below DVD) tartanvideo.com

Off the record: The **Brian Jonestown Massacre** were formed in San Francisco, California in 1991 by the self-styled, one-off, **Anton Newcombe**, along with **Matt Hollywood, Dean Taylor**, Mara Regal, Dawn Thomas, Brian Glaze and shamanic leader **Jel Gion**, although throughout their career they employed more than 40 different musicians. Named after, both, the ex-Rolling Stones guitarist and a mass cult suicide in America in the 1960s, the band clearly hoped to be perceived as darkly debaucherous. Their 1995 debut 'Methodrone' was a muddy cross between My Bloody Valentine and the Jesus & Mary Chain, with distorted guitars and fuzzy psychedelic atmospherics their forte. Their sophomore effort, 'Their Satanic Majesties' Second Request' (1996) borrowed more than just its name from the 'Stones. A knowing pastiche of late 60s psychedelic experiments, the album did well to carve out an identity of its own. The group released two more albums that year 'Take It From The Man' and 'Thank God For Mental Illness'; however trouble was a-brewing with old friends and sparring partners, the Dandy Warhols, who, unlike their anti-commercial, live-out-a-van compadres, were making it big time. BJM's next three releases, 'Give It Back!' (1997), 'Strung Out In Heaven' (1998) and 'Bringing It All Back Home Again' (2000), continued along the same lines, although the latter borrowed from Gram Parsons'-influenced 70s sound. Their 2001 release, 'Zero: Songs From The Album Bravery, Repetition And Noise' (featuring the Warlocks' Bobby Hecksher), was a sudden departure for the band who were now paying homage to the British post-punk groups of the 1980s. Once again the band managed to wear their influences fully on their sleeves whilst enforcing a sense of originality. The **Dandy Warhols** were from Portland, Oregon and consisted of buzzed-up guys, **Courtney Taylor-Taylor** and **Peter Holmstrom** (later Loew), who, with rhythm section, **Eric Hedford** and feisty babe, **Zia McCabe**, emerged from their recording basement in 1996. After a one-off double mini-CD, the harmony-fuelled psychedelia of 'Dandys Rule Ok', they inked a deal with 'Capitol', much to the annoyance of rock'n'roll cousins, the BJ Massacre. The Dandys also riled their bosses by failing to deliver on a promised set of songs; exposure in the Rolling Stone was subsequently mis-timed. Unsurprisingly the band gave themselves a proverbial kick up the ass and rose from their drug ashes with a fine set of songs, two of which ('Everyday Should Be A Holiday' and 'Not If You Were The Last Junkie On Earth') were UK Top 30 singles taken from their Top 20 album, '. . .Come Down' (1998). Spending just over a year in the studio – Hedford being replaced by **Brent DeBoer** – the Dandy Warhols emerged with the most accomplished set to date, 'Thirteen Tales From Urban Bohemia' (2000); catchy UK Top 5 single 'Bohemian Like You' (virtually ignored on its initial release) was used to great effect in a mobile phone ad. With Duran Duran's Nick Rhodes manning the engineering desk for 'Welcome To The Monkey House' (2003), the Dandys started to dabble in electronic machinery and other gadgets. *MCS*

– associated releases –

the DANDY WARHOLS / the BRIAN JONESTOWN MASSACRE

2004. (dvd) *Palm Pictures: <PAL VFC 81570> Tartan; (TVD 3548)* [–] [–]
– *Chapter Index:-* 1: Start / 2: Portland / 3: Capitol Records / 4: Industry Showcase / 5: New Year's Eve 1996-7 / 6: "Give It Back" Recordings / 7: Cleveland / 8: David LaChapelle / 9: Homer, Georgia / 10: The Dandy Warhols Show / 11: TVT Records / 12: London / 13: L.A. / 14: Thirteen Tales From Urban Bohemia / 15: Monkey House / 16: End Credits. *(d-DVD-iss.Apr05 +=;*

the BRIAN JONESTOWN MASSACRE: Tepid Peppermint Wonderland – A Retrospective

Nov 04. (d-cd) *Tee Pee; <(TP 059)>* [ ] [ ]
– All around you – intro / Who? / When jokers attack / Servo / Open heart surgery / If love is the drug / It girl / Sailor / Straight up and down / Anenome / Wisdom / Just for today / Stars / Vacuum boots / Prozac vs. heroin / She's gone // Nailing honey to the bee / That girl suicide / Nevertheless / Evergreen / Starcleaner / Let me stand next to your flower – live / Hide and seek – live / In my life / Mary please / Talk-action = shit / Oh Lord / This is why you love me / Not if you were the last DAndy on earth / Swallowtail – live / Feel so good / Fucker / #1 hit jam / Ballad of Jim Jones / Free and easy – take 2 / Stolen / Mansion in the sky / Sue.

DIVINE MADNESS

1980 (US 94m) The Ladd Company / Warner Bros. (R)

Film genre: Nostalgia/Pop-music concert/documentary comedy

Top guns: dir: Michael Ritchie / s-w: **Bette MIDLER**, Jerry Blatt, Bruce Vilanch

Stars: Bette MIDLER *(The Divine Miss M)*, **Jocelyn Brown, Ula Hedwig + Diva Gray** *(the Harlettes)*, Irving Sudrow *(head usher)*, band vocalists:- **Tony Berg, Randy Kerber, Joey Carbone, Jon Bonine**

Storyline: The new Mae West in many respects, the divine Miss M is under the spotlight in this mixture of "musical" mayhem and comedic routines. Risqué, with language that could strip wallpaper at four paces, Bette Midler becomes all manner of exotic people in a concert from Pasadena Civic Auditorium. *MCS*

Movie rating: *6

Visual: video + dvd

Off the record: BETTE MIDLER songs exclusive to the video include, 'The Rose', Maxwell-Sigman's 'Ebb Tide', 'Hawaiian War Chant', Paul Anka's 'My Way', Dr. John's 'Rain', 'Ready To Begin Again' and Bobby Freeman's 'Do You Want To Dance?'. *MCS*

—

BETTE MIDLER (composers: Various)

Nov 80. (lp/c) *Atlantic; <SD 16022> (K/K4 50760)* [34] Jan81 [ ]
– Big noise from Winnetka / Paradise / Shiver me timbers / Fire down below / Stay with me / My mother's eyes / Chapel of love – Boogie woogie bugle boy / E Street shuffle – Summer (the first time) – Leader of the pack / You can't always get what you want – I shall be released. *<(cd-iss. Feb92; 7567 81476-2)>*

S/track review: The previous year she starred in 'The ROSE', this new decade saw the Divine Miss MIDLER "stand up" to be counted, although here on the OST there are no comic routines, just her musical performances. Multi-talented in every respect, the new Barbra Streisand of song-and-dance (and celluloid comedy) shines through on this live show soundtrack. 'DIVINE MADNESS' combines pre-WWII nostalgia numbers such as 'Big Noise From Winnetka' and 'Boogie Woogie Bugle Boy', with doo-wop staples, 'Chapel Of Love' and 'Leader Of The Pack', while R&B standards come via the 'Stones' 'You Can't Always Get What You Want' (medleyed with Dylan's 'I Shall Be Released') and Ragovoy-Weiss' 'Stay With Me' – quite possibly comparable to Janis Joplin's version. Her 70s pillage comes courtesy of Tom Waits' 'Shiver Me Timbers', Bob Seger's 'Fire Down Below' and Springsteen's 'E Street Shuffle'. The highlight from the show is her upbeat rendition of Bobby Goldsboro's 'Summer (The First Time)', right up there with 'My Mother's Eyes' (from the pen of underrated singer-songwriter, Tom Jans) and the aforementioned 'Stay With Me'. One thing about the high-spirited Bette is that she sings from the heart and one could say she puts the motion into emotion. *MCS*

Album rating: *6.5

– spinoff hits, etc. –

BETTE MIDLER: My Mother's Eyes / Chapel Of Love – live

Nov 80. (7") *<3771>* [39] [–]

BETTE MIDLER: Big Noise From Winnetka / Rain

Jan 81. (7") *(K 11412)* [–] [ ]

BETTE MIDLER: Fire Down Below / You Can't Always Get What You Want – I Shall Be Released

May 81. (7") *(K 11592)* [–] [ ]

DR. JOHN

Born: Malcolm Rebennack, 21 Nov'40, New Orleans, Louisiana, USA. A noted session man in 1957, Mac soon branched out on his own, taking up the piano after one of his fingers was shot off in a barroom brawl. Drawn to L.A. in the mid-60s, he continued his session work and began to assume his alter ego, DR. JOHN (Creaux) The Night Tripper. Taking the name from a 19th Century New Orleans witchdoctor type, the character was a hybrid of psychedelic mysticism and Deep South voodoo. 'Gris Gris' (1968) was the first DR. JOHN release on 'Atco', a sinister series of voodoo funk meditations that combined New Orleans R&B, creole soul and psychedelia. The next three releases, 'Babylon' (1968), 'Remedies' (1970) and 'The Sun, Moon And Herbs' (1971), carried on in much the same vein without achieving quite the same foreboding effect. The Jerry Wexler-produced 'Gumbo' (1972) saw DR. JOHN (by this time, he'd given up his nocturnal tripping) return to his bayou roots. A deeply satisfying journey through New Orleans' rich musical heritage, the record saw the good doctor belting out some spirited updates of standards like 'Iko Iko' and 'Junko Partner'. With impeccable credentials (produced by Allen Toussaint and recorded with the Meters), 1973's 'In The Right Place' concentrated on downhome funk. 'Desitively Bonnaroo' (1974) offered similar rhythmical remedies. Seemingly abandoning the New Orleans (black) magic, DR. JOHN made a misguided attempt at more rocking fare on the live 'Hollywood Be Thy Name' (1975), while the man was ever present on the BAND's film concert documentary, 'The LAST WALTZ' (1978). 'City Lights' (1978) and 'Tango Palace' (1979) sounded confused and it was only with 1981's 'Dr. John Plays Mac Rebennack' that he regained his focus. 'The Brightest Smile In Town' (1983) proved that his return to form was no fluke, while a subsequent commission to co-write the score for 'CANDY MOUNTAIN' (1988) was a little misguided. DR. JOHN returned to his old stamping ground on funky 90s releases like 'Goin' Back To New Orleans' (1992) and 'Television' (1994), while his far-reaching influence was illustrated by a cameo in the movie, 'BLUES BROTHERS 2000' (1998). Signing to 'Parlophone' records in the UK, the man subsequently delivered two further sets of fine work, 'Anutha Zone' (1998) and 'Duke Elegant' (2000). After the creative diversions and belated critical rebirth of recent years, it was perhaps inevitable DR JOHN was going to return to his roots with a vengeance and so he did on 2001's 'Creole Moon'. With Fred Wesley presiding over the horn section, it was back to seriously funky New Orleans bizniz for the sexagenarian piano master, while screen performances in 'LIGHTNING IN A BOTTLE' (2004) and archive-only 'MAKE IT FUNKY!' (2005) kept the motor running. *BG & MCS*

– **filmography** {performance} (composer) –

Love And Music *(1971 {p} =>)* / **the Last Waltz** *(1978 {p} on OST w/ the BAND =>)* / **Sgt. Pepper's Lonely Hearts Club Band** *(1978 {p} OST by V/A =>)* / Pray TV *(1980 {c})* / American Tongues *(1987 score as MAC REBENNACK)* / **Candy Mountain** *(1988 {p} score w/ DAVID JOHANSEN, Leon Redbone & Rita MacNeil =>)* / Comic Book Confidential *(1988 score w/ Keith Elliott, Nicholas Stirling & Gerard Leckey)* / **Blues Brothers 2000** *(1998 {p} OST by V/A =>)* / the Big Day *(2001 score)* / **Lightning In A Bottle** *(2004 {p} OST by V/A =>)* / New Orleans Music In Exile *(2005 {p})* / **Make It Funky!** *(2005 {p} =>)*

DON'T LOOK BACK

aka BOB DYLAN: DONT LOOK BACK *(sic)*

1967 (US 96m b&w) Leacock-Pennebaker Films

Film genre: Folk Rock-music docudrama (+ performance)

Top guns: dir: D.A. Pennebaker → MONTEREY POP → ZIGGY STARDUST: THE MOTION PICTURE → 101 → DOWN FROM THE MOUNTAIN → ONLY THE STRONG SURVIVE

Stars: Bob DYLAN *(himself/performer)*, **Joan BAEZ** *(herself)*, **DONOVAN** *(himself)*, **Alan Price** *(himself)* <= the ANIMALS =>, **Marianne Faithfull** *(herself)* ← ANNA / → LUCIFER RISING → the WALL: LIVE IN BERLIN → ROCK AND ROLL CIRCUS, Allen Ginsberg *(himself)* ← CHAPPAQUA / → TONITE LET'S ALL MAKE LOVE IN LONDON → TEN FOR TWO → RENALDO AND CLARA → MY GENERATION → NO DIRECTION HOME, Albert Grossman *(himself)*, **Bob Neuwirth** *(himself)* → RENALDO AND CLARA → SLAVES TO THE UNDERGROUND → NO DIRECTION HOME, Tito Burns *(himself)*, **Derroll Adams** *(himself)*, Howard Alk *(himself)*, Jones Alk *(herself)*, **John Mayall** *(himself)* → SGT. PEPPER'S LONELY HEARTS CLUB BAND → BAJA OKLAHOMA → RED, WHITE & BLUES → the SOUL OF A MAN, **Brian Pendleton** *(himself)*, Terry Ellis *(himself)*

Storyline: Shot in 16mm before it was boosted to 35mm for the cinematic release on May 17th, 1967, the feature film concentrated on Bob Dylan's 1965 UK tour and the people backstage. Fly-on-the-wall, Dylan was at his best during the Albert Hall performances, he was also in the throes of splitting with folk diva, Joan Baez. Highlight of the movie was the opening scene when Dylan (and wrongly-spelled placards) belt out hit-at-the-time, 'Subterranean Homesick Blues'; subsequently used as a video for TV playlisting. *MCS*

Movie rating: *8

Visual: video + dvd (no audio OST)

Off the record: Derroll Adams (b. Derroll Lewis Thompson, 25 Nov'25, Portland, Oregon) was a folk musician who moved to England in the mid-50s when "skiffle" and Lonnie Donegan was the rage; he wrote 'Portland Town' around this period while his plucky banjo-playing featured in a few movies. After he emigrated to Antwerp, Belgium (shortly after 'Don't . . .') his drink dependency caused major problems in his domestic life, although friends and inspirations such as Donovan (who had recorded tribute song 'Epistle To Derroll' in 1967) and Ramblin' Jack Elliott helped him concentrate on his return to music. Sadly, Derroll passed away on the 6th of February, 2000. **Brian Pendleton** (the broken glass incident in the movie) was the rhythm guitarist with London R&B giants the Pretty Things until late 1966; he returned to his former job in insurance – performed with blues outfits until he died of lung cancer on 16th May, 2001. Terry Ellis became associated with Jethro Tull and subsequently co-founded 'Chrysalis' records. *MCS*

the DOORS ARE OPEN

1968 (UK 56m TV) Granada Television International

Film genre: Rock-music concert/documentary

Top guns: dir: John Sheppard

Stars: The **Doors:- Jim Morrison** *(performer)* → MAYOR OF THE SUNSET STRIP, **Ray Manzarek** *(performer)* ← the UNHEARD MUSIC → MAYOR OF THE SUNSET STRIP, **Robby Krieger** *(performer)* → WOODSTOCK '99 → RAMONES RAW, **John Densmore** *(performer)* → GET CRAZY → DUDES → the DOORS, + all → MESSAGE TO LOVE: THE ISLE OF WIGHT FESTIVAL

Storyline: "The Doors Are Open" – more or less – invites a TV crew and the viewers into a live 1968 concert (6th September) at the Roundhouse in London, where the iconic quartet present such gems as 'Five To One', 'Break On Through', 'When The Music's Over', Alabama Song', 'Back Door Man', 'Crawling King Snake', 'Spanish Caravan', 'Love Me Two Times', 'Light My Fire', 'Unknown Soldier', 'Soul Kitchen', 'Little Game', 'The Hill Dwellers', 'Not To Touch The Earth', 'Hello, I Love You', 'Moonlight Drive', 'Horse Latitudes' and 'Money'. It was aired on the 4th of October 1968. *MCS*

Movie rating: *6

Visual: video + dvd HMP Editora – Brazil (no audio OST)

Off the record: Jim Morrison starred as "the hitchhiker" in his own 50-minute experimental film, 'HWY: An American Pastoral' (1969). **Ray Manzarek** was responsible (at least for writing and directing!) for post-millennium golden turkey, 'Love Her Madly' (2002), an idea based on the Doors song from 1971. *MCS*

DOWN FROM THE MOUNTAIN

2001 (US 98m) Momentum Pictures

Film genre: Bluegrass-music documentary/concert movie

Top guns: dir: Nick Doob, Chris Hegedus ← 101 / → ONLY THE STRONG SURVIVE, D.A. Pennebaker ← 101 ← ZIGGY STARDUST: THE MOTION PICTURE ← MONTEREY POP ← DON'T LOOK BACK / → ONLY THE STRONG SURVIVE

Stars: the Fairfield Four *(performers)*, **John Hartford** *(performer)*, **Alison Krauss** *(performer)* → LIGHTNING IN A BOTTLE, **the Cox Family:- Evelyn Cox, Willard Cox, Suzanne Cox, Sidney Cox** *(performers)* ← O BROTHER, WHERE ART THOU?, **Gillian Welch** *(performer)* ← O BROTHER, WHERE ART THOU?, & **David Rawlings** *(performer)*, **the Whites:- Buck White, Sharon White, Cheryl White** *(performers)* ← O BROTHER, WHERE ART THOU?, **Colin Linden** *(performer)* & **Chris Thomas King** *(performer)* ← O BROTHER, WHERE ART THOU? / → LAST OF THE MISSISSIPPI JUKES → the SOUL OF A MAN → LIGHTNING IN A BOTTLE → RAY, **Emmylou HARRIS** *(performer)*, **T-Bone Burnett** *(performer)* ← a BLACK & WHITE NIGHT, **Jerry Douglas** *(house band)* ← O BROTHER, WHERE ART THOU?, Holly Hunter *(herself)*, the Coen Brothers *(themselves)*, **Ralph Stanley** *(performer)*

Storyline: Legendary rockumentarian D.A. Pennebaker trains his camera on country music, in the original sense of the term. Sub-titled "Live concert performances by the artists and musicians of O Brother, Where Art Thou", it might well have come with the proviso at least the one's who're still alive. Neither Pennebaker nor musical directors T-Bone Burnett and Bobby Neuwirth can recreate the old Alan Lomax field recordings but they can and do give a sense of how at least some contemporary country artists are indebted to history. In a pre-concert documentary segment, Gillian Welch enthuses on bluegrass illumination and a shock-haired John Hartford (who finally lost his long battle with cancer a year or so after filming) regales us with tales of his other life as a riverboatman. *BG*

Movie rating: *7.5

Visual: dvd

Off the record: (see below + 'O BROTHER, WHERE ART THOU?')

—

Various Artists (md: T-BONE BURNETT)

Jul 01. (cd) *Lost Highway – Universal; <(170221-2)>*
– Po Lazarus (the FAIRFIELD FOUR) / Big rock candy mountain (JOHN HARTFORD) / Wild Bill Jones (ALISON KRAUSS) / Blue and lonesome (ALISON KRAUSE) / I am weary (let me rest) (the COX FAMILY) / Will there be any stars in my crown (the COX FAMILY) / My dear someone (GILLIAN WELCH & DAVID RAWLINGS) / I want to sing that rock (GILLIAN WELCH & DAVID RAWLINGS) / Sandy land (the WHITES) / John Law burned down the liquor sto' (COLIN LINDEN & CHRIS THOMAS KING) / Green pastures (EMMYLOU HARRIS) / I'll fly away (GILLIAN WELCH & ALISON KRAUSS).

S/track review: "Pop stations considered the music too country and country stations considered it too . . . country". In their wry sleevenote, the Coen brothers pretty much say it all about modern day Nashville and the reason why the music from their movie struck such a high lonesome chord. But it's difficult to imagine country stations ever having played an a cappella as stark and searing as RALPH STANLEY's 'O Death'. It's one of the few performances that doesn't make the album, unfortunately, but it does make the DVD well worth seeing. Nor does STANLEY perform his arrangement of the old spiritual 'I Am A Man Of Constant Sorrow', the song which was to have audiences rolling/lamenting in the cinema aisles just a few months later. Then again, he couldn't have known how talismanic it would become; if he and his fellow performers had known, perhaps they would've been a bit more nervous. As it is, they take their cue from the confidential charm of cult folkie/traditionalist curator/emcee JOHN HARTFORD, and sing and play with that gentle, old time feeling coursing out of their lungs, through the vintage mics and up into the Ryman rafters. Highlights include HARTFORD's intimate 'Big Rock Candy Mountain' (performed in the film by its writer, Harry "Mac" McClintock, and priceless for its pronunciation of "al-kay-hol" alone), the classicist harmonies of the COX FAMILY and GILLIAN WELCH/DAVID RAWLING's modern, very un-rock'n'roll elegy for old-time country's displacement, 'I Want To Sing That Rock'n'Roll'. *BG*

Album rating: *6.5

□ Steve EARLE segment
(⇒ JUST AN AMERICAN BOY)

EDGEPLAY: A FILM ABOUT THE RUNAWAYS

2004 (US 110m) Sacred Dogs Entertainment

Film genre: Hard-rock/Punk-music concert documentary

Top guns: s-w + dir: **Victory Tischler-Blue**

Stars: the RUNAWAYS:- Vicki Blue *(herself)*, **Cherie Currie** *(herself)*, **Jackie Fox** *(herself)*, **Lita Ford** *(herself)*, **Sandy West** *(herself)* / **Suzi Quatro** *(herself)*, **Kim Fowley** *(himself)*, **Joan Jett** *(archive footage)*, **Kari Krome** *(herself)*

Storyline: Basically what it says on the tin, a documentary film about five punkettes in an underachieving rock group, the Runaways (at least, commercially). The film was written and directed by one-time member, Vicki Blue (aka Victory Tischler-Blue). *MCS*

Movie rating: *6

Visual: dvd

Off the record: (see below & own entry)

Various Artists (incl. the RUNAWAYS (*))

Aug 04. (cd) *Hip-O; <B0002790-02>* □ -
– Back to the drive (SUZI QUATRO) / Black leather heart (LITA FORD) / Cherry bomb (*) / Glycerine queen (SUZI QUATRO) / Hollywood (*) / Secrets (live version) (*) / Rock 'n' roll (live version) (*) / Stiletto (LITA FORD) / School days (*) / Wasted (*) / Waitin' for the night (*) / War of the angels (LITA FORD) / Kids of tragedy (SUZI QUATRO). *(bonus track +=)* – Dead end justice.

S/track review: One thing that's regrettable about the documentary and soundtrack for 'EDGEPLAY: A FILM ABOUT THE RUNAWAYS' is the wilful omission by original guitarist/bassist/vocalist, Joan Jett. Without getting into litigation oneself, her objection to use her (co-written?) songs in the movie stunned one-time RUNAWAYS bassist and now 'EDGEPLAY' filmmaker, Victory Tischler-Blue. However, the album itself suffered none of the legal wrangles, aided and supported as it was by another Runaway herself, lawyer Jacqueline Fuchs (aka JACKIE FOX, bassist from 1976-1977). So, armed with eight classic RUNAWAYS numbers, three solo cuts by former lead guitarist, LITA FORD, and three by the girl-band's inspiration, SUZI QUATRO, the disc finally sees the er . . . "light of day". 'EDGEPLAY' kicks off with an exclusive song ('Back To The Drive') by the aforementioned leader of the girl pack, QUATRO, announcing as she does "I'm back!" to the riffs of old nuggets, 'Devil Gate Drive' & '48 Crash'. The leather-clad "mother of glam-rock" subsequently spins out a few early tracks via 'Glycerine Queen' and 'Kids Of Tragedy', while her sexy protege of sorts, LITA FORD, also goes retro raucous for fresh cut, 'Black Leather Heart'; her others include 'Stiletto' (from 1990) and an unreleased demo version of 'War Of The Angels', the latter an emotional rock ballad aimed at the RUNAWAYS' five-year battle with chemical and verbal abuse. It's hard to imagine a RUNAWAYS collection without early classics such as 'Cherry Bomb' (from 1976's eponymous LP) and 'Hollywood' (from 1977's 'Queens Of Noise'), and thankfully both are in full glam-glory here. Live versions of 'Secrets' (Toyah must've been listening!) & Lou Reed's 'Rock 'N' Roll', plus 'Dead End Justice', can also be traced back to their glorious debut in '76, while 'Wasted', 'School Days' & 'Waitin' For The Night' stem from the RUNAWAYS' latterly-named third LP. A great soundtrack album in patches; they were not the first all-girl hard-rock group (that accolade goes to Fanny), but the RUNAWAYS were certainly the most groundbreaking influential. Pity about all the bickering. *MCS*

Album rating: *6.5

□ Ramblin' Jack ELLIOTT segment
(⇒ the BALLAD OF RAMBLIN' JACK)

ELVIS BY THE PRESLEYS

2005 (US 90m TV) Red-Eye Flight Productions / C.B.S.

Film genre: Rock'n'roll-music documentary

Top guns: dir: Rob Klug / s-w: Bill Flanagan (idea: David Saltz)

Stars: Elvis PRESLEY (himself/archive), Lisa Marie Presley *(herself)*, Priscilla Presley *(herself)*, Danielle Riley Keough *(herself)*, Benjamin Keough *(himself)*, Colonel Tom Parker *(himself/archive)*, Ed Parker *(himself)*, Paul Beaulieu *(himself)*, Ann Beaulieu *(herself)*, Michelle Beaulieu Hovey *(herself)*, Ed Sullivan *(himself)* ← the COMPLEAT BEATLES ← the PHYNX ← BYE BYE BIRDIE

Storyline: The inside story of Elvis Presley's life and love, or at least the inside story according to his unfeasibly youthful looking ex-wife, Priscilla. If anyone's qualified for such a task, she is, although her account of the early to mid-period years tends to repetition. The narrative thread tracing her status as confidante during the war years to domestic other half of a Southern-by-the-grace-of-God singer, is spun out further by her parents, as well as friends like Jerry Schilling. As well as being a believer in traditional macho values, Presley is revealed as an affectionate and incredibly generous soul, as well as an indefatigable seeker, and it's the later years which really fascinate. A voracious appetite for new age literature and Eastern religion has him seeing angels in the Gracelands garden and numerologically predicting his own demise, one which comes all too soon and shockingly so; the footage of his final days is still disturbing. Perhaps the most curious aspect of it all is how his even his nearest and dearest were at a loss to explain what exactly it was that was eating the king, no pun intended. *BG*

Movie rating: *7

Visual: dvd (extended 260m)

Off the record: Colonel Tom Parker, was of course, Elvis' manager from 1956 and head of soon-to-be defunct record label, 'Sun'. *MCS*

—

ELVIS PRESLEY

May 05. (d-cd) *Sony BMG TV; <(82876 67883-2>)* 15 13
– Trying to get to you / Heartbreak hotel / I want you, I need you, I love you / I got a woman / Got a lot o' livin' to do! / (There'll be) Peace in the valley (for me) / Trouble / Hawaiian wedding song / Indescribably blue / In the ghetto / Suspicious minds / I'll hold you in my heart (till I can hold you in my arms) / Bridge over troubled water / You've lost that loving feeling / It's over / Separate ways / Always on my mind / My way / Burning love / Welcome to my world / Steamroller blues / I got a feelin' in my body / If I can dream / A little less conversation // It wouldn't be the same without you (demo) / Jailhouse rock (alt.) / Anything that's part of you (alt.) / You'll be gone (alt.) / Too much monkey business (alt.) / Baby what you want me to do (alt.) / I'm so lonesome I could cry (alt.) / Blue Christmas (live).

S/track review: Few artists are repackaged with as much tenacity as ELVIS PRESLEY. This double set rakes over those same old coals one more time for the broken-hearted, or at least the fat-walleted. Everything's already been said about most of the tracklist, and even Chuck D – he of the endlessly quoteable soundbite "Elvis was a hero to most but he never meant shit to me" – must have been exposed to these songs ad nauseam. The concept of putting the man's family life under the microscope is fair enough on film but just doesn't carry through on soundtrack. The sleevenotes claim the songs as "a repository of our individual memories and desires, as well as a reminder of our collective pop cultural history"; perhaps, but to then also claim them as "a deeply affecting commentary on ELVIS PRESLEY's public and private life" is just too convenient. The collection's limited worth lies in a few unreleased tracks and in exposing lesser-heard material to the casual fan, notably the raw early 70s cuts backed by JD Sumner & The Stamps. On the likes of 'I Got A Feelin' In My Body' (PRESLEY's funkiest moment?) and James Taylor's 'Steamroller Blues', Sumner and co take a testifying, treacle-voiced ELVIS deep into his own Southern gospel/soul shadow. The second disc at least partly lives up to the hype by including two ramshackle private recordings: a hissing, feedback-strafed cover of Jimmy Reed's 'Baby What You Want Me To Do' and an intimate rendition of Hank Williams' 'I'm So Lonesome I Could Cry' both sound like they could've been recorded in 1933 rather than 1973. We also get a trembling, Hispanic-blooded 'You'll Be Gone', a track which stopped his fledgling writing career down in its tracks. The pre-'Sun' demo, 'It Wouldn't Be The Same Without You' is nothing new but still surprises with its utter lack of sexual magnetism, and could anyone possibly need another two takes of 'Jailhouse Rock'? *BG*

Album rating: *6

ELVIS ON TOUR

1972 (US 93m) Metro-Goldwyn-Mayer (G)

Film genre: rock'n'roll/pop-music concert/documentary

Top guns: dir: Robert Abel → LET THE GOOD TIMES ROLL, Pierre Adidge ← MAD DOGS & ENGLISHMEN

Stars: Elvis PRESLEY *(performer)*, **the Stamps:- J.D. Sumner, Donnie Sumner, Ed Wideman, Bill Baize, Ed Enoch** *(performers)*, Red West *(himself)* ← ELVIS: THAT'S THE WAY IT IS, **Jerry Scheff** *(performer)* ← ELVIS: THAT'S THE WAY IT IS / → BLACK & WHITE NIGHT, **James Burton** *(performer)* ← ELVIS: THAT'S THE WAY IT IS / → BLACK & WHITE NIGHT, **Glen D. Hardin** *(performer)* ← ELVIS: THAT'S THE WAY IT IS / → BLACK & WHITE NIGHT, **Charlie Hodge** *(performer)* ← ELVIS: THAT'S THE WAY IT IS, **Ronnie Tutt** *(performer)* ← ELVIS: THAT'S THE WAY IT IS / → BLACK & WHITE NIGHT, Joe Guerico *(conductor)* ← ELVIS: THAT'S THE WAY IT IS, **Estelle Brown** *(performer)* ← ELVIS: THAT'S THE WAY IT IS, **Kathy Westmoreland** *(performer)*

Storyline: Looking slightly beefier than his previous concert movie in 1970 (see further on), the King returns to the celluloid stage (cross-country from Texas, Ohio, Virginia to North Carolina) while there's also a behind the scenes look at the man in the white, spangled suit. *MCS*

Movie rating: *6

Visual: video in 1997 (no audio OST)

Off the record: ELVIS performs over a dozen tracks here (in no particular order):- 'Johnny B. Goode', 'Proud Mary', 'Suspicious Minds', 'Polk Salad

Annie', 'Love Me Tender', 'See See Rider', 'Separate Ways', 'Never Been To Spain', 'Bridge Over Troubled Water', 'Burning Love', 'Don't Be Cruel', 'Ready Teddy', 'That's All Right', 'Lead Me, Guide Me', 'Bosom Of Abraham', 'An American Trilogy', 'Until It's Time For You To Go', 'I John', 'Funny How Time Slips Away', 'Lawdy Miss Clawdy', 'Mystery Train', 'I Got A Woman', 'A Big Hunk O' Love', 'You Gave Me A Mountain', 'Memories' & 'Can't Help Falling In Love'.

ELVIS: THAT'S THE WAY IT IS

aka THAT'S THE WAY IT IS

1970 (US 109m) Metro-Goldwyn-Mayer (PG)

Film genre: Rock'n'roll-music concert/documentary

Top guns: dir: Denis Sanders → SOUL TO SOUL

Stars: Elvis PRESLEY *(performer)*, **James Burton** *(performer)* → ELVIS ON TOUR → BLACK & WHITE NIGHT, **Glen D. Hardin** *(performer)* → ELVIS ON TOUR → BLACK & WHITE NIGHT, **Jerry Scheff** *(performer)* → ELVIS ON TOUR → BLACK & WHITE NIGHT, **Ronnie Tutt** *(performer)* → ELVIS ON TOUR → BLACK & WHITE NIGHT, Charlie Hodge *(himself)* → ELVIS ON TOUR, Red West *(himself)* → ELVIS ON TOUR, Joe Guercio *(conductor)* → ELVIS ON TOUR, **Estelle Brown** *(performer)* → ELVIS ON TOUR

Storyline: Recently re-edited with previously unseen footage, this isn't exactly a warts'n'all job but Elvis, it has to be said, doesn't look too healthy in the rehearsal scenes, his crack band occasionally bewildered. They're fascinating gilmpses into the man's 70s comeback and while he constantly plays up for the camera, you get a sense of both his affability and his vulnerability. His stage rehearsal horseplay with the Memphis Mafia sounds an ominous note, but once showtime rolls around Elvis is jumpsuited and booted, raring to let his hairy chest hang out. When he's not wandering through the audience pressing lip flesh with his still screaming female admirers, indulging in tangential banter or jokingly squaring up to his backing singers, he puts in the kind of animal magnetic display that you can't take your eyes off. Unmissable. *BG*

Movie rating: *9

Visual: video + dvd

Off the record: James Burton, Glen D. Hardin, Jerry Scheff & Ronnie Tutt were part of Elvis' backing band.

—

ELVIS PRESLEY (composers: various)

Dec 70. (lp) *R.C.A.; <LSP 4445> (SF 8162)* [21] Jan71 [12]
– I just can't help believin' / Twenty days and twenty nights / How the web was woven / Patch it up / Mary in the morning / You don't have to say you love me / You've lost that lovin' feeling / I've lost you / Just pretend / Stranger in the crowd / The next step is love / Bridge over troubled water. *(re-iss. Jan84 lp/c; NL/NK 84114) <(cd-iss. Jul93; 74321 14690-2)> (5xlp-box iss.Aug00 on 'Castle'+= * in film; ELVIS 102)* – Love letters / When I'm over you / Something / I'll never know / Sylvia / Cindy, Cindy / Rags to riches / That's all right mama (*) / Mystery train – Tiger man (*) / Hound dog / Love me tender (*) / Just pretend / Walk a mile in my shoes / There goes my everything / Words (*) / Sweet Caroline (*) / You've lost that lovin' feelin' (*) / Polk salad Annie (*) / Heartbreak hotel (*) / One night with you (*) / Blue suede shoes (*) / All shook up (*) / Little sister – Get back (*) / I was the one / Love me / Are you lonesome tonight? / Bridge over troubled water (*) / Suspicious minds (*) / Can't help falling in love (*) / I got a woman / I can't stop loving you / Twenty days and twenty nights (*) / The next step is love (*) / You don't have to say you love me / Stranger in the crowd (*) / Make the world go away / Don't cry daddy / In the ghetto / Peter Gunn theme (instrumental) / That's all right mama (*) / Cotton fields / Yesterday / I can't stop loving you / Such a night / It's now or never / (Now and then there's) A fool such as I / Little sister – Get back / I washed my hands in muddy water / Johnny B. Goode / Mary in the morning / The wonder of you / Santa Claus is back in town / Farther along / Oh happy day. *<(3xcd-box iss.Mar01 +=; 07863 67938-2)>*

S/track review: Another ELVIS soundtrack, but not as we've known them. This one's actually about the music, pepped up with a liberal sprinkling of Vegas showmanship. The date is 1970, the man's hungry again; he's putting away the pies but he still looks great, and he's got a whole lotta something going on. There's no 'In The Ghetto' (until the boxed set!), alas, but a mutton-chopped PRESLEY prowls through some staggering performances, backed by the best band money couldn't buy. Even without that visual impact, the record imparts a heady measure of the charisma generated by a legend back, finally, in his element. As for his repertoire, it's pretty much the standard Mann-Weil/singer-songwriter/contemporary country pop roll call, but it's the way PRESLEY throws himself into the material. That, and the unexpected surge of an old school R&B-rocker like 'Patch It Up'; ELVIS calls, the Sweet Impressions respond and the years melt away like so much tawdry myth. Truth be told, it's one of only four live tracks taken from his summer '70 Vegas residence; the rest were recorded in a Nashville studio. As the B-side of 'You Don't Have To Say You Love Me', 'Patch..' also made the UK Top 10, as did PRESLEY's definitive, Southern-by-the-grace-of-God version of the BJ Thomas hit, 'I Just Can't Help Believin', released by public demand, praise the Lord! He likewise staked a claim to the definitive reading of 'You've Lost That Lovin' Feelin', a premonitory flash rendering it all the more poignant as brass and strings explode and his tar-rich timbre cracks on the payoff "something beautiful's dying". Many of the studio tracks are just as powerful. The emotional blizzard of performances like 'I've Lost You' and 'Twenty Days And Twenty Nights', the spotlessly synergetic arrangements of 'Mary In The Morning', make you wonder why these songs are all but forgotten today. Even 'Bridge Over Troubled Water's canned applause seems a minor flaw next to the belief PRESLEY displays here. More live tracks were welcome on the re-issues, and this is essential 70s ELVIS, not so long before he left the building for good. *BG*

Album rating: *7.5 / re-cd *8

– spinoff hits, etc. –

ELVIS PRESLEY: I've Lost You / The Next Step Is Love

Aug 70. (7") *<47-9873> (RCA 1999)* [32] Nov70 [9]

ELVIS PRESLEY: You Don't Have To Say You Love Me / Patch It Up

Oct 70. (7") *<47-9916> (RCA 2046)* [11] Jan71 [9]

END OF THE CENTURY

aka END OF THE CENTURY: THE STORY OF THE RAMONES

2003 (US 112m w/b&w) Gugat Films / Magnolia Pictures

Film genre: Punk-Rock music documentary/bio-pic

Top guns: Michael Gramaglia, Jim Fields

Stars: RAMONES:- Johnny/John Cummings, Joey/Jeffrey Hyman, Dee Dee/Douglas Colvin, Tommy/Thomas Erdely, Marky/Mark Bell, C.J./Christopher Ward & Richie *(themselves/performers)*, **Joe STRUMMER** *(himself/performer)* + **Paul Simonon** *(archive)*, **BLONDIE:- Deborah Harry, Chris Stein, Clem Burke** *(themselves/performers)*, **Jayne County** *(her/himself/performer)* ← STADT DER VERLORENEN SEELEN ← the PUNK ROCK MOVIE ← JUBILEE ← PUNK IN LONDON ← the BLANK GENERATION, **Rob ZOMBIE** *(himself)*, **Glen Matlock** *(himself)* + Johnny Rotten <= SEX PISTOLS =>, Walter Lure *(himself)*, Rodney Bingenheimer *(himself)* ← RAGE: 20 YEARS OF PUNK ROCK WEST COAST STYLE ← ROCKULA ← BACK TO THE BEACH ← UNCLE MEAT ← X: THE UNHEARD MUSIC ← REPO MAN ← UP IN SMOKE / → MAYOR OF THE SUNSET STRIP → PUNK'S NOT DEAD, **RED HOT CHILI PEPPERS:- Anthony Kiedis, John Frusciante** *(themselves)*, **Eddie VEDDER** *(himself)*, **Iggy POP/Stooges** *(archive performer)*, Rick Rubin *(himself)*, **Captain Sensible** *(himself)* → PUNK: ATTITUDE → PUNK'S NOT DEAD, Seymour Stein *(himself)* → TOO TOUGH TO DIE: A TRIBUTE TO JOHNNY RAMONE, **Richard**

HELL *(archive/himself)*, **Kirk Hammett** *(himself)* ← SOME KIND OF MONSTER, **Lars Frederiksen** *(himself)* ← PUNK ROCK HOLOCAUST / → PUNK'S NOT DEAD, **NEW YORK DOLLS:- David Johansen, Johnny Thunders** *(archive)*, **Thurston Moore** *(himself)* <= SONIC YOUTH =>, Arturo Vega *(himself)*

Storyline: The story of New York's first new wave punk band, Ramones, complete with all the break-ups, the hissy-fits and a lifetime of silent vendetta between Johnny and Joey. 1-2-3-4. *MCS*

Movie rating: *9

Visual: dvd

Off the record: Ex/current-bands:- **Captain Sensible** (the Damned), **Lars Frederiksen** (Rancid),

the END OF THE ROAD: THE FINAL TOUR '95

2001 (US 97m) Slow Loris Films / Joint Productions

Film genre: Roots-rock concert documentary

Top guns: dir: Brent Meeske

Stars: Babatunde Olatunji *(himself)*, Wavy Gravy *(himself)* ← MY GENERATION, **Merl Saunders** *(himself)*, **GRATEFUL DEAD:- Bob Weir, Phil Lesh, Mickey Hart, Bill Kreutzmann** *(themselves)* / **Robert Hunter** *(himself)*, **John Perry Barlow** *(himself)*

Storyline: "Mandatory viewing for all Deadheads" because just about every fan, associate, exploiter (vendor), or past member of the Grateful Dead features in this 'End Of The Road' tour – Jerry Garcia would die shortly afterwards. *MCS*

Movie rating: *7

Visual: dvd ex. (no audio OST by GARCIA & SAUNDERS)

Off the record: Babatunde Olatunji (b. 1927, Ajido, Nigeria) was a virtuoso drummer; he subsequently died (advanced diabetes) in Salinas, California, on the 6th of April, 2003. The man released numerous albums from the much heralded, 'Drums Of Passion' (1959) to further similarly-titled sets for 'Rykodisc' in the 80s & 90s. *MCS*

ENDLESS HARMONY: THE BEACH BOYS STORY

1998 (US 90m TV w/b&w) VH1 Television

Film genre: Pop/Rock-music concert/documentary bio-pic

Top guns: dir: Alan Boyd ← HEY HEY WE'RE THE MONKEES

Stars: the BEACH BOYS:- Brian Wilson, Dennis Wilson, Carl Wilson, Al Jardine, Mike Love *(performers)*, **Glen CAMPBELL** *(himself)*, **Elvis COSTELLO** *(himself)*, **Jackson Browne** *(himself)* ← NICO ICON ← BLACK & WHITE NIGHT ← NO NUKES / → WALK HARD: THE DEWEY COX STORY, **Sean Lennon** *(himself)* ← MOONWALKER ← IMAGINE: JOHN LENNON / → FREE TIBET

Storyline: The Beach Boys get their most exacting rockumentary treatment to date on an officially sanctioned film gamely raking through pretty much every awkward grain of sand in the band's controversial history, from the infamous managerial method of the Wilson clan's paterfamilias to the trauma of resident troubled genius Brian. Between promo curios and unreleased footage, all the original members (including Carl, who passed away from lung cancer shortly after the film was made) get to say their piece (predictably, Mike Love says a little more than his piece), while the likes of Elvis Costello and Jackson Browne muse on the band's unassailable pop greatness. *BG*

Movie rating: *8

Visual: video + dvd (March 2000)

Off the record: (see below)

—

the BEACH BOYS: Endless Harmony – Soundtrack

Aug 98. (cd) *E.M.I.; <(4 96391-2)>* ☐ Sep98 56

– Soulful old man sunshine (writing session excerpt) / Soulful old man sunshine / (radio concert promo 1) / Medley: Surfin' safari – Fun, fun, fun – Shut down – Little deuce coupe (live) / Surfer girl (vocal) / Help me, Rhonda (alt. single version) / Kiss me, baby (stereo remix) / California girls (stereo remix) / Good vibrations (live) / Heroes and villains (demo) / Heroes and villains (live) / God only knows (live) / (radio concert promo 2) / Darlin' (live) / Wonderful – Don't worry Bill (live) / Do it again (early version) / Break away (demo) / Sail plane song / Loop de loop (flip flop flyin' in an aeroplane) / Barbara / 'Til I die (alt. mix) / Long promised road (live) / All alone / Brian's back / Endless harmony.

S/track review: Much like Bob Dylan's 'NO DIRECTION HOME', this "soundtrack" doesn't actually correlate to the rockumentary with which it shares a title, rooting around instead in the largely untouched BEACH BOYS archive; prior to the historic release of 'SMiLE' in 2004 (longtime fans can afford themselves a wry smile at Mike Love's 'Wonderful'/'Don't Worry' intro: "Several years ago we did an album called Smile – it should be out this coming year"; that was in 1972 . . .), its almost wholly unreleased rag-bag of rarities, demos and alternate mixes was the nearest equivalent to Dylan's 'Bootleg Series'. That's where the comparison ends, though, with 'Capitol' failing to ground the album in any thematic premise save for the shakey film tie-in. But if a tracklisting veering wildly between creatively finite periods of the band's career doesn't bother you unduly, you'll find sweet harmony to spare. Unbound by trifles like chronology, the album opens with its trump card, 'Soulful Old Man Sunshine'. Co-written by Rick Henn (main man of surf also-rans the Sunrays, another band in Murray Wilson's portfolio), it beams blazing solar-soul through a scat-harmony prism of Burt Bacharach proportions, backed by L.A. jazz sessioners and sounding like fake tan lathered into a 'Motown' session; it'll have you dreaming of what might have been. As will the 1966 demo of 'Heroes And Villains', spontaneously sparking sections of both 'I'm Great Shape' and 'Barnyard', anthropomorphism courtesy of Van Dyke Parks. Between these landmarks, surfing amateurs engaged by the film will find plenty of familiar hits, and pros will find the dubious novelty of familiar hits mixed in stereo ('California Girls' and 'Kiss Me Baby'), or else rendered as phantom works in progress: 'Do It Again', 'Help Me, Rhonda' and, most remarkably, 'Break Away', with BRIAN as oracular one-man-band, offering up yet another "teenage symphony to God" more or less fully formed. There's likewise an aura of the celestial about 'Til I Die', here presented in a richly atmospheric, spook-vibes mix by 'Surf's Up' engineer, Stephen Desper, even if 'Sail Plane Song' and 'Loop De Loop' suggest that the band's limited capacity for heavy-shit psychedelia was on a par with the Rolling Stones. But all this and a Dennis Wilson ballad ('All Alone') from his unreleased sophomore album; what more could a man want? Well, yet more mixes apparently; the turn of the decade saw the release of a revamped version of the soundtrack, with sonic fine tuning surely relevant to diehard obsessives only. *BG*

Album rating: *7.5

☐ Roky ERICKSON segment
(⇒ YOU'RE GONNA MISS ME)

EXPERIENCE

1969/1998 (US 29m/68m) Douglas Music Films

Film genre: Hard-rock-music concert/documentary

Top guns: dir: Peter Neal → BE GLAD FOR THE SONG HAS NO ENDING → GLASTONBURY FAYRE → YESSONGS / co-producer: Janie Hendrix

Stars: Jimi HENDRIX (archive footage), **Mitch Mitchell** *(drums & percussion)* ← ROCK AND ROLL CIRCUS ← JIMI HENDRIX ← RAINBOW BRIDGE ← MONTEREY POP, **Noel Redding** *(bass)* ← MONTEREY POP, Fawn Reed *(Dolly Dagger)*, James Hong *(old man)* ← WAYNE'S WORLD 2 ← the KAREN CARPENTER STORY ← BLADE RUNNER ← BOUND FOR GLORY ← DYNAMITE BROTHERS

Storyline: A bit of a folly here if other sources are anything to go by. Some say this was from 1967, others vary a lot! What we do know is that 'Experience' was a short film (29 minutes) released 30 years later with added concert footage and interviews by Jimi Hendrix, etc. *MCS*

Movie rating: *6

Visual: video on 'Reprise' / dvd

Off the record: The original LP/film was released with only 4 tracks (*).

---

the JIMI HENDRIX EXPERIENCE

Jun 98. (cd) *Charly; (CDGR 246)* [–] [ ]
– Sunshine of your love (*) / Bleeding heart (*) / Fire / Little wing / Voodoo chile (slight return) / Room full of mirrors (*) / Purple haze / Wild thing / The Star-Spangled Banner & smashing of the amps (*). *(re-iss. Feb00 on 'Brilliant'; BT 33045) (<re+US-iss.Feb01/Jul01/2005 on 'Snapper'; SNAP 004CD>)*

S/track review: Recorded live on 24th of February 1969 at London's Royal Albert Hall, 'EXPERIENCE' is the sound of JIMI HENDRIX at his best. Unrestrained by the confines of a studio album, HENDRIX is able to do what he does best, play the guitar. There is plenty of experimentation and improvisation on tracks such as 'Voodoo Chile (Slight Return)', 'Room Full Of Mirrors' and Cream's 'Sunshine Of Your Love'. While many guitarists would be happy to fill a whole album noodling away, HENDRIX does not fall into that trap and mixes it up nicely. 'Fire' and 'Purple Haze' are tight affairs, all coming in under the four minute mark, while the beautifully delicate 'Little Wing' is a perfect contrast to the brash, abrasive version of 'Wild Thing'. Meanwhile, thirty-odd years before Brian May got up on top of Buckingham Palace to play 'God Save The Queen', HENDRIX was doing his own decimation of his country's national anthem. A few bars of 'The Star-Spangled' are audible before it descends into a chaotic fusion of squealing guitar, feedback and drums. Finally there is the 'Smashing Of The Amps' which, unfortunately, just doesn't work without the visuals. JIMI HENDRIX is regarded as a guitar god and rightly so because, while it is an overused cliché, he genuinely makes the thing sing and portray a variety of emotions the way no one else can, all of which is clearly evident here. The only drawback is the poor quality of the recordings in some places but with music this good, it's barely noticeable. *CM*

Album rating: *7.5

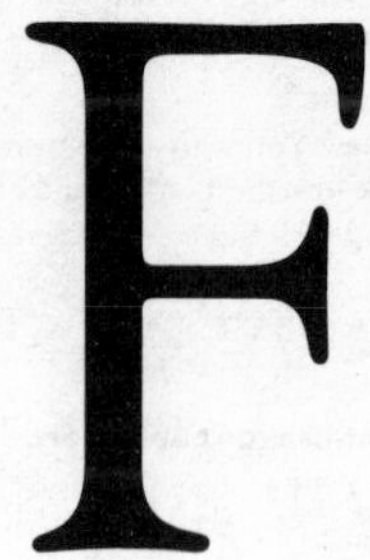

FADE TO BLACK

aka JAY-Z: FADE TO BLACK

2004 (US 109m) @radical media / Marcy Projects Productions (R)

Film genre: Rap & Hip-Hop documentary/concert movie

Top guns: dir: Patrick Paulson, Michael John Warren

Stars: JAY-Z *(performer)*, **Beyonce** *(performer)* ← the FIGHTING TEMPTATIONS ← CARMEN: A HIP HOPERA / → DREAMGIRLS, **Mary J. Blige** *(performer)* ← PRISON SONG, **R. Kelly** *(performer)*, **Foxy Brown** *(performer)*, **Common** *(performer)* ← GODFATHERS AND SONS ← BEEF ← BROWN SUGAR / → BLOCK PARTY, **Ghostface Killah** *(performer)* ← BLACK AND WHITE / → WALK HARD: THE DEWEY COX STORY, **Rick Rubin** *(performer)* ← END OF THE CENTURY ← TOUGHER THAN LEATHER ← KRUSH GROOVE / → SHUT UP & SING, **Missy 'Misdemeanor' Elliott** *(performer)* ← HONEY ← POOTIE TANG, **Funkmaster Flex** *(performer)*, **Timbaland** *(performer)*, **Kanye West** *(performer)* → BLOCK PARTY, **Slick Rick** *(performer)* ← BROWN SUGAR ← BROOKLYN BABYLON ← TRUE VINYL ← WHITEBOYS ← the SHOW ← TOUGHER THAN LEATHER, **P. Diddy** *(performer)* ← DEATH OF A DYNASTY ← TUPAC: RESURRECTION ← BIGGIE AND TUPAC ← RHYME & REASON ← the SHOW, **Q-TIP** *(performer)*, **Damon Dash** *(performer)* ← PAPER SOLDIERS ← BACKSTAGE ← STREETS IS WATCHING, **Twista** *(performer)* → BEEF 3, **Memphis Bleek** *(performer)* ← DEATH OF A DYNASTY ← PAPER SOLDIERS ← BACKSTAGE, **Young Guru** *(performer)*, **Just Blaze** *(performer)*, **Freeway** *(performer)*, **Pharrell** *(performer)*, **Beanie SIGEL** *(performer)*, **Ahmir-Khalib Thompson** *(performer)* ← BROWN SUGAR ← BROOKLYN BABYLON ← FREESTYLE: THE ART OF RHYME ← WOODSTOCK '99, **Usher Raymond** *(performer)* → IN THE MIX

Storyline: Jay-Z does two things here, perform in a sort-of hip hop all-star finale concert at New York's Madison Square Garden (November 2003) and give the viewer an insight into the making of what was to be his retirement set, 'The Black Album'. *MCS*

Movie rating: *6.5

Visual: dvd February '05 (no audio OST)

Off the record: Timbaland (aka Tim Mosley) and Magoo had a Top 20 hit in 1997 with 'Up Jumps Da' Boogie'. **Ahmir-Khalib Thompson** is a member of the Roots.

– associated release –

JAY-Z: The Black Album

Nov 03. (cd/d-lp) *<15280-2/-1> (9861121)* [1] [40]
– Interlude / December 4th / What more can I say / Encore / Change clothes / Dirt off your shoulder / Threat / Moment of clarity / 99 problems / Public service announcement (interlude) / Justify my thug / Lucifer / Allure / My 1st song.

In 1977 zany composer and bandleader Frank Zappa held a Halloween concert in New York. The riotous *Babysnakes* soundtrack includes renditions of 'Titties And beer', 'Disco Boy' and 'Dinah-Moe Humm', mixing in audience participation with virtuosic musicianship.

A case of the album inspiring the documentary, which was captured by Wim Wenders as he accompanied Ry Cooder on a return visit to Cuba in 1998. The album, released the year before, is the pinnacle of Ry Cooder's restless global explorations: a joyous, free-spirited journey through the past musical lives of Cuba's great musicians and composers, which brought the world Ibrahim Ferrer, Compay Segundo and Ruben Gonzales.

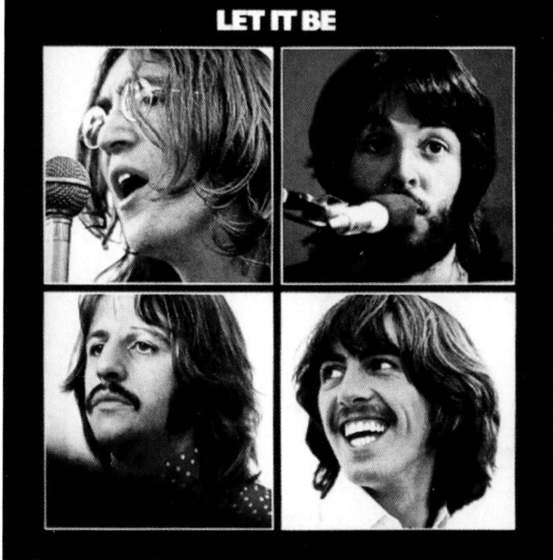

An aural document of creative fatigue and division, the Phil Spector-produced *Let It Be* album contains enough self-contained moments of genius to rank it as a classic, with Spector's controversial post-production most evident on 'Across The Universe' and 'The Long And Winding Road'. Michael Lindsay-Hogg's 1970 feature of the same name followed the tense album sessions, climaxing with the legendary final Apple building performance.

The peer popularity of 60s roots legends The Band was impressively underlined by the unprecedented wealth of talent gathered for their farewell gig at San Francisco's Winterland on Thanksgiving Day 1976. Captured in Martin Scorsese's highly regarded documentary, *The Last Waltz*, the bill included Neil Young, Joni Mitchell, Eric Clapton, Van Morrison and Bob Dylan.

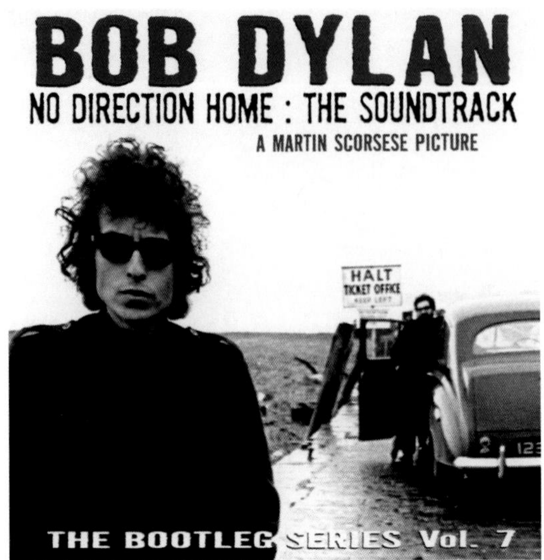

BOB DYLAN
NO DIRECTION HOME : THE SOUNDTRACK
A MARTIN SCORSESE PICTURE
HALT
TICKET OFFICE
THE BOOTLEG SERIES Vol. 7

No Direction Home is Martin Scorsese on Dylan, and the 2005 film is almost as celebrated as the man's first volume of autobiography. The insatiable appetite for completist booty means that *Bootleg Series Vol. 7* trumpets itself as the soundtrack tie-in to Scorsese's documentary, covering a finite area of Dylan's career in sonic-archaeological detail.

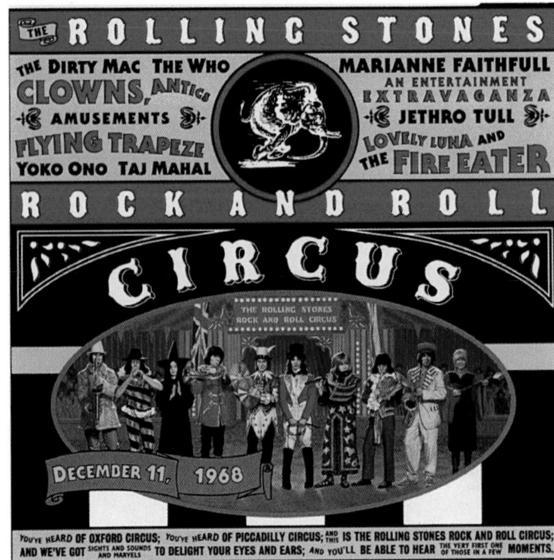

A television special – filmed on the 10th & 11th of December 1968 – this extravaganza feature was shelved because the Rolling Stones' manager at the time thought that other groups on the show (most notably The Who) upstaged them. But Jagger sounds lost to his demons on 'Sympathy For The Devil', and his surreal banter with John Lennon makes this an essential document.

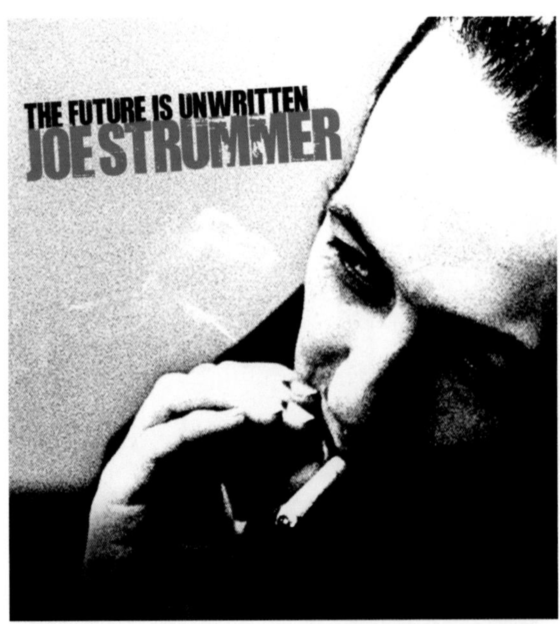

The flawed genius of Joe Strummer is explored in varied sonic terms on this expansive 18-song collection, which accompanied Julien Temple's 2007 feature. It traces the roots of Strummer's music from the stomping pub rock of the 101'ers, through the glory of The Clash to the global righteousness of The Mescaleros. Many of the tracks are rare, unreleased versions.

The Woodstock Music and Art Fair was held at Max Yasgur's 600-acre dairy farm in the rural town of Bethel, New York, 15th–18th August 1969. Around 500,000 people attended and the event is widely regarded as one of the greatest moments in music history, and the apogee of the hippie dream.

A tie-dye Joe Cocker performing with The Grease Band at Woodstock, which was immortalised in Michael Wadleigh's 1970 film of the festival. It features Cocker's seminal performance of 'With A Little Help From My Friends', a radical re-arrangement of The Beatles' original recording on *Sgt. Pepper*.

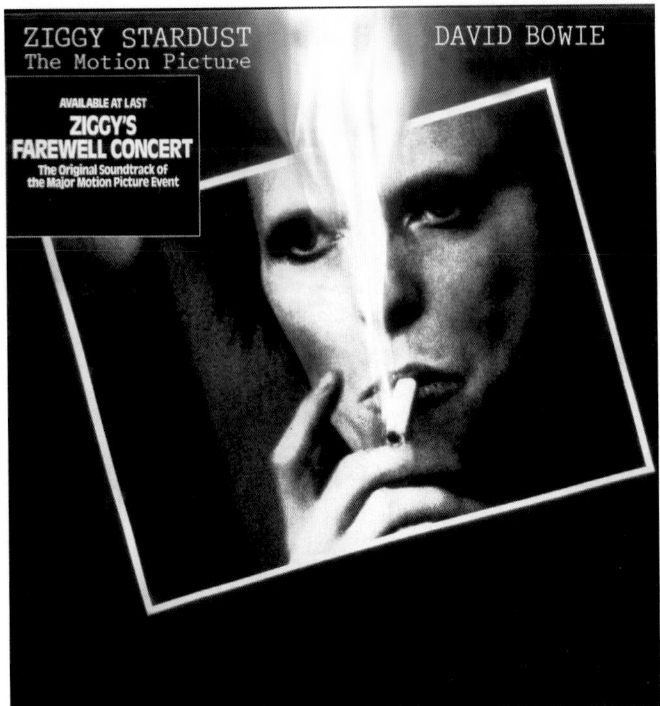

The motion picture was panned by most critics and this double-LP release (once a bootleg) was also heavily criticised. *The Rise and Fall of Ziggy Stardust and the Spiders from Mars* studio tracks are represented in full force, as well as a handful of pre-*Aladdin Sane* gems, a Rolling Stones cover, 'Let's Spend The Night Together', Velvet Underground's 'White Light/White Heat' and Jacques Brel's 'My Death'.

On 3rd July 1973 David Bowie performed his final concert at London's Hammersmith Theatre under the 'Ziggy Stardust' persona, which many fans mistook for Bowie's retirement from the music business. The concert was captured by D.A. Pennebaker, screened with behind-the-scenes footage and initially aired by America's ABC-TV shortly afterwards. It would be a decade later that the feature-length movie was put on general release.

Talking Heads' singer David Byrne in the same BIG white suit which appeared in *Stop Making Sense*. In the mid-80s his vocals sounded like ritual incantations. He wryly opined that 'Singing is a trick to get people to listen to music for longer.'

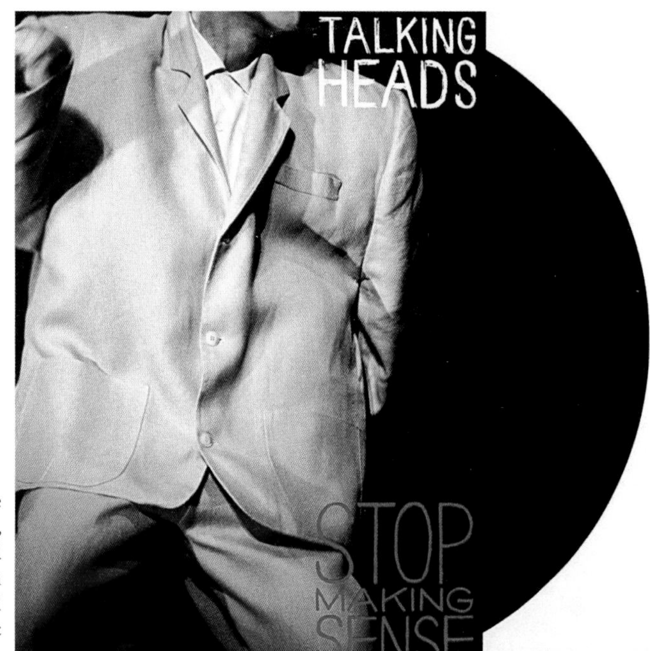

The record of Jonathan Demme's Talking Heads feature does not match up to the classic status of the film, since on initial release it cut many of the tracks and sequenced them differently, an injustice righted with the 1999 re-issue. Video or audio, both formats are still primarily remembered for the mesmeric, electro-acoustic 'Psycho Killer', an *amuse bouche* for insomniacs.

Filmed at Madison Square Garden in 1973, *The Song Remains The Same* celebrates Led Zeppelin in their glorious pomp. The band sound good – and even towering – on later material like 'The Rain Song' and 'No Quarter', but the performance suffers from eternally extended versions of 'Rock and Roll' and 'Whole Lotta Love', although the menacing, black-sky blues of 'Dazed And Confused' justifies its 26-minute running time with an electrifying display by Jimmy Page.

Robert Plant and Jimmy Page at their most iconic onstage at Madison Square Garden in 1973. The film interspersed performance footage with fantasy dream sequences, portraying Plant as a golden-maned Arthurian swordsman, and Page as an occult hermit, receding through space–time.

Released just over a year after the death of Jimi Hendrix, *Rainbow Bridge* was one of the first of several exploitation flicks (with soundtracks) to hit the market. A trio of the songs on the album were his last recordings (1st July 1970, at Electric Ladyland Studios): the funk-infused 'Dolly Dagger', Santana-esque 'Pali Gap' and album finale 'Hey Baby', which would have made it onto any of Jimi's next LP projects had he lived.

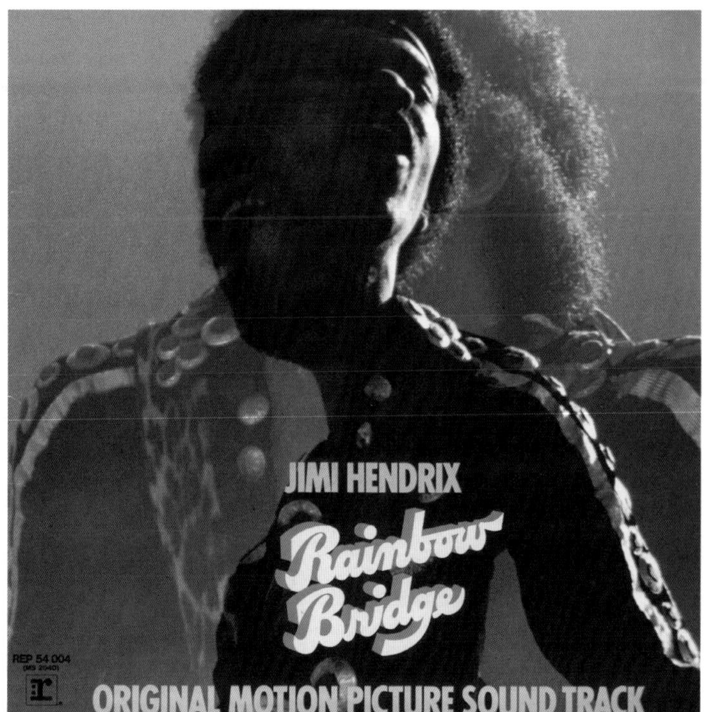

Jimi Hendrix captured at the Monterey Pop Festival, 16th–18th June 1967, immortalised in the D.A. Pennebaker rockumentary. Best remembered for burning his brightly painted, psychedelic guitar, Hendrix contributed two outstanding songs to the film's soundtrack, in the form of 'Killing Floor' and the song that broke the Experience through, 'Hey Joe'.

A five-disc trip into the heart of 'Dead Land, as accompaniment to their marathon concert/rockumentary film, showing the band just as their finances and momentum reached tipping point in the mid-70s. Many authorities agree that this sonically pristine bonanza is the pinnacle of live 'Deadheadness, recorded over a series of Winterland gigs in Autumn 1974, prior to a trucking sabbatical.

Like the film (an engaging if selective account of John Lennon's life, masterminded by Yoko Ono), this 1988 soundtrack avoids Lennon's spikier solo offerings. But there are plenty of odes to love – both romantic and filial – and the possibilities of world peace.

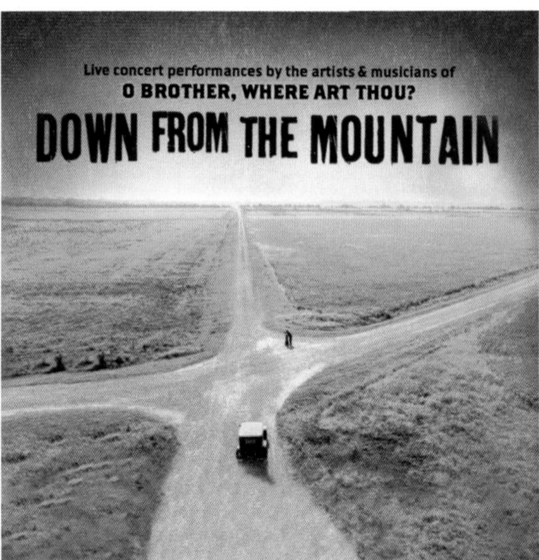

D.A. Pennebaker trains his camera on country music in his 2001 documentary/concert movie. Subtitled 'Live concert performances by the artists and musicians of *O Brother, Where Art Thou?*', it might well have come with the proviso 'at least the ones who are alive'. The soundtrack features performances by Fairfield Four, Alison Krauss, Gillian Welch, David Rawlings and Emmylou Harris.

FALLEN ANGEL

aka GRAM PARSONS: FALLEN ANGEL

2004 (Germ/UK 91m) BBC Music Entertainment / Spothouse GmbH

Film genre: Rockumentary/Performance biopic

Top guns: s-w: Gandulf Hennig (+ dir), **Sid Griffin**

Stars: Gram Parsons *(archive footage)* ← CELEBRATION AT BIG SUR ← GIMME SHELTER, **Emmylou HARRIS** *(herself)*, **Keith Richards** *(herself)* <= the ROLLING STONES =>, **Peter Buck** *(himself)* ← ATHENS, GA. – INSIDE/OUT, **Bernie Leadon** *(himself)* ← GIMME SHELTER, **Chris Hillman** *(himself)* ← GIMME SHELTER ← the BIG T.N.T. SHOW, Gretchen Parsons Carpenter *(herself)*, **Elvis COSTELLO** *(himself)*, **Dwight YOAKAM** *(himself)*, **Pamela Des Barres** *(herself)* ← MAYOR OF THE SUNSET STRIP ← SLAUGHTER'S BIG RIP-OFF ← 200 MOTELS / → METAL: A HEADBANGER'S JOURNEY, Diane Parsons *(herself)*, Phil Kaufman *(himself)* ← GRAND THEFT PARSONS ← BABY SNAKES / → the LIFE AND HARD TIMES OF GUY TERRIFICO

Storyline: Gram Parsons is the "Fallen Angel" in question, the man and the legend that helped instigate country-rock as a member the Byrds and the Flying Burrito Brothers. His controversial death on THE 19 September, 1973 – the subject of a feature film, 'GRAND THEFT PARSONS' – is now folklore, but did many people know he was to inherit over a million dollars from grandad John Snivley, owner of acres of citrus land! *MCS*

Movie rating: *7.5

Visual: dvd Feb'06 (Rhino; 970422) – (no audio OST)

Off the record: Gram Persons (b. Ingram Cecil Connor III, 5 Nov'46, Winter Haven, Florida) briefly attended Harvard University, although country music was his first love having formed the Shilos and the International Submarine Band around the mid-60s. His stint with the Byrds was also short-lived, although his contributions to the seminal country-rock set, 'Sweetheart Of The Rodeo' (1968), were all too apparent, and it might've been more had his vocals not been sacrificed due to a contractual obligation. The Flying Burrito Brothers were his next project, but with two moderately-selling albums in the can, Parsons took flight again. Subsequent friendships with Keith Richards and Emmylou Harris helped the man extend his profile somewhat, and by the time of his bizarre death and cremation under the Joshua Tree, he had released two outstanding solo LPs, 'G.P.' and 'Grevious Angel'. **Sid Griffin** had been frontman for the legendary roots rock revivalists, the Long Ryders, a band very influenced by Gram and Co; check out 'Native Sons' (1984) and 'The State Of Our Union' (1985). **Pamela Des Barres** was a member of the GTO's but more famous for being a groupie and having affairs with Mick Jagger, Jimmy Page, etc. *MCS*

□ FANIA ALL-STARS segment
(⇒ OUR LATIN THING)

□ Mimi FARINA segment
(⇒ FOOLS)

the FEARLESS FREAKS

2005 (US 100m) Shout! Factory Films

Film genre: Alt-rock concert/documentary/bio-pic

Top guns: dir: Bradley Beesley

Stars: the Flaming Lips:- Wayne Coyne, Michael Ivins, Steven Drozd *(themselves/performers)*, Bradley Beesley *(narrator)*, **the White Stripes:- Jack White** *, **Meg White** *(themselves)* * ← COLD MOUNTAIN ← COFFEE AND CIGARETTES / → TWO HEADED COW → WALK HARD: THE DEWEY COX STORY, **Liz Phair** *(herself)*, **Beck** *(himself)* ← HIGH AND DRY ← MAYOR OF THE SUNSET STRIP ← SOUL OF A MAN ← SOUTHLANDER ← FREE TIBET, Juliette Lewis *(herself)* ← FROM DUSK TILL DAWN ← STRANGE DAYS ← the BASKETBALL DIARIES ← NATURAL BORN KILLERS ← the RUNNIN' KIND / → CATCH AND RELEASE, Steve Burns *(himself)*, **Jonathan Donahue** *(himself)*, **Cat Power** *(herself)* → TWO HEADED COW, Christina Ricci *(herself)* ← MONSTER ← FEAR AND LOATHING IN LAS VEGAS ← BUFFALO 66 / → BLACK SNAKE MOAN

Storyline: "The Wondrously Improbable Story Of The Flaming Lips" (as it says on the package) just about describes the rise of one of America's great indie rock bands. Between performance footage of the Flaming Lips during the last decade or so and interviews, the appeal of Wayne Coyne and Co is clear to see. *MCS*

Movie rating: *7.5

Visual: dvd 32634 + d-dvd (no audio OST)

Off the record: The **Flaming Lips** were formed in Oklahoma City in 1983 by **Wayne Coyne** and his brother Mark, who reputedly stole instruments from a church hall to get their act off the ground. After a rare and weird EP in 1985, Mark left brother WAYNE to recruit new members for the album, 'Hear It Is' (1986). 'Oh My Gawd!!!' (1987), 'Telepathic Surgery' (1989) and 'In A Priest Driven Ambulance' (1990). Subsequently signing to 'Warners' in 1992, and between appearing at the Reading Festival, they released 'Hit To Death In The Future Head' and US breakthough album of sorts, 'Transmissions From The Satellite Heart' (1993). By the mid-90s, the Flaming Lips had secured weirdo posterity after giving birth to the drug-orientated, 'Clouds Taste Metallic' (1995) album, and the 8-song/4-disc, 'Zaireeka' (1997), the latter could be played as 1 disc or with the addition of other CD-players, a 2nd, 3rd or 4th combination. Taking a sharp detour and ended up in Dave Fridmann's upstate New York studio, the 'Lips (now consisting of only three; **Wayne Coyne, Steve Drozd** and **Michael Ivins**) recorded the spooky but highly commercial 'The Soft Bulletin' (1999). Adding the Fridmann formula, the album sounded similar to Mercury Rev's 'Deserter's Songs', although relying largely on its Yes-type chord changes/structures and Beach Boys harmonies via Coyne attempting to sing in tune (possibly for the very first time). The group returned three years later with an album just as stunning and as beautiful as the last, but now influenced by Japanese counter-culture named 'Yoshimi Battles The Pink Robots' (it's a concept album – well kind of). The 'Lips were back in 2006 with the highest charting album of their career (UK Top 10/US Top 20), 'At War With The Mystics', a groovy 'Floyd-ian psychedelia vehicle with the message, road tested at assorted vintage checkpoints. Incidentally, multi-instrumentalist, Steven Drozd, did the score for 2003 feature, 'I Love Your Work', while he also augmented actor Steve Burns on the album, 'Songs For Dustmites' 2003). *MCS & AS*

FEEL LIKE GOING HOME

1st part of Martin Scorsese presents THE BLUES

2003 (US 83m mini-TV w/b&w) Vulcan Productions / PBS (15)

Film genre: Blues-music documentary

Top guns: dir: Martin Scorsese ← the LAST TEMPTATION OF CHRIST ← the LAST WALTZ / → NO DIRECTION HOME / s-w: Peter Guralnick

Stars: Corey Harris *(performer)*, **Othar Turner** *(performer)*, **Taj MAHAL** *(performer)*, **Ali Farka Toure** *(performer)*, **Muddy Waters** *(performer)* ← ERIC CLAPTON AND HIS ROLLING HOTEL ← the LAST WALTZ, **Johnny Shines** *(performer)*, **Salif Keita** *(performer)*, **Habib Koite** *(performer)*, **Salif Keita** *(performer)*, **Willie King** *(performer)*, **Son House** *(archive performer)* ← FESTIVAL, **John Lee Hooker** *(archive performer)* ← the BLUES BROTHERS, **Keb Mo'** *(performer)* → HELLHOUNDS ON MY TRAIL / → LIGHTNING IN A BOTTLE, **Toumani Diabate** *(performer)*, **Sharde Thomas** *(performer)*

Storyline: Dean of Americana historians, Peter Guralnick, gets back to where it all began, wading through the characters, the myths and the music of the Mississippi Delta, sniffing out Celtic roots and sending contemporary bluesman Corey Harris on a mission to Mali. *BG*

Movie rating: *8.5

Visual: dvd

Off the record: Corey Harris (b.21 Feb'69, Denver, Colorado, USA) was one of a new breed of contemporary bluesmen, who picked up the guitar at the age of 12. His lengthy list of albums include debut, 'Between Midnight And Day' (1995), 'Vu-Du Menz' (2000) – both for 'Alligator' records, plus 'Downhome

Sophisticate' (2002), 'Mississippi To Mali' (2003) and 'Daily Bread' (2005) – all three for 'Rounder'. *MCS*

—

Various Artists

Sep 03. (cd) *Columbia; <90489-2> Sony; (512568-2)* ☐ Mar04 ☐
– Traveling Riverside blues (ROBERT JOHNSON) / Dynaflow blues (JOHNNY SHINES) / Hellhound on my trail (ROBERT JOHNSON) / Country blues (MUDDY WATERS) / Celebrated walkin' blues (TAJ MAHAL) / Rosalie (MUDDY WATERS with the SON SIMMS FOUR) / My black mama, pt.II (SON HOUSE) / Government fleet blues (SON HOUSE) / Gypsy woman (MUDDY WATERS) / High water everywhere, pt.I (CHARLEY PATTON) / C.C. rider (LEAD BELLY) / Terrorized (WILLIE KING & the LIBERATORS) / Oh baby (NAPOLEON STRICKLAND & the COMO DRUM BAND with OTHAR TURNER) / Lay my burden down (OTHAR TURNER & COREY HARRIS) / Mali Dje (ALI FARKA TOURE) / Tupelo blues (JOHN LEE HOOKER) / Amandrai (ALI FARKA TOURE) / Down child (JOHN LEE HOOKER) / Ananamin (it's been so long) (SALIF KEITA) / My babe (OTHAR TURNER & the RISING STAR FIFE DRUM BAND).

S/track review: Nothing in recorded music history can quite match the apocalyptic hiss of vintage country blues. It gets repackaged endlessly, although it's all but impossible to cheapen. Here at least, you know the tracks have been selected out of sheer devotion to the cause, and that has to count for something. If the casual fan will be familiar with any of the usual suspects gathered here, it'll most likely be ROBERT JOHNSON. The man's been covered and analysed so exhaustively there's not much left to say except the obvious: 'Hellhound On My Trail' is still one of the most acute evocations of impending death/madness ever performed. MUDDY WATERS is represented with the totemic, Alan Lomax-recorded 'Country Blues' and the folkier 'Rosalie', and the slate-voiced SON HOUSE performs the scratchy wake, 'Black Mama, Pt.II', a work-in-progress of what would become his mid-60s calling card, 'Death Letter', reimagined in line with his re-engagment with the blues after two decades in obscurity and subsequently covered by the likes of Diamanda Galas and the White Stripes. The mighty LEADBELLY was the only contemporary musician to rework the song, but Scorsese plumps for his classic 'C.C. Rider'. And while both HOUSE and his sometime partner CHARLEY PATTON recount the catastrophic aftermath of the 1927 Mississippi Flood, it's 'Tupelo Blues', JOHN LEE HOOKER's crepuscular interpretation of the same event, which bears the most unsettling parallels with Hurricane Katrina and its messy aftermath. Not restricting itself by either era or geography, the soundtrack also showcases late 60s-vintage TAJ MAHAL "going to get his ham bones boiled", proving that the Devil that was (is?) the blues not only had the best tunes but also the best metaphors, here framed by the unmistakable mandolin wind of RY COODER. If too many flabby modern blues practitioners fail miserably to do the form justice, WILLIE KING isn't one of them, laconically but determinedly taking issue with America's terrorism preoccupation from a black perspective. Both NAPOLEON STRICKLAND & THE COMO DRUM BAND's 'Oh Baby' and OTHAR TURNER's 'My Babe' are equally brilliant choices; are they blues? Yes they are, and utterly compelling at that, syncopated Deep South folk-funk in the raw, and revelatory examples of a clearly audible Scottish/Irish interface with Afro-American music. From there, it's but a plane ride across the Atlantic to West Africa itself, where SALIF KEITA and the late ALI FARKA TOURE cultivate(d) their own highly influential strain of desert blues. It's a journey of Odyssean scale and implication, and you won't get a more passionate guide than Scorsese, so pay attention. *BG*

Album rating: *8

FESTIVAL

1967 (US 87m w/b&w) Patchke Productions / Peppercorn-Wormser

Film genre: Folk Rock-music concert/documentary

Top guns: dir: (+ s-w) Murray Lerner → the WHO: LIVE AT THE ISLE OF WIGHT FESTIVAL 1970 → JIMI HENDRIX LIVE AT THE ISLE OF WIGHT → MESSAGE TO LOVE: THE ISLE OF WIGHT FESTIVAL

Stars: Joan BAEZ *(performer)*, **Bob DYLAN** *(performer)*, **Peter, Paul & Mary:- Peter Yarrow *, N. Paul Stookey, Mary Travers **** *(performers)* → YOU ARE WHAT YOU EAT * → WASN'T THAT A TIME ** → NO DIRECTION HOME *, **DONOVAN** *(performer)*, **Paul Butterfield** *(performer)* → YOU ARE WHAT YOU EAT → STEELYARD BLUES → the LAST WALTZ → GODFATHERS AND SONS, **Mike Bloomfield** *(performer)* → STEELYARD BLUES, **Judy Collins** *(performer)* → HARD TRAVELIN', **Mimi Farina** *(performer)* → FOOLS → CELEBRATION AT BIG SUR → SING SING THANKSGIVING, & **Richard Farina** *(performer)*, **Johnny CASH** *(performer)*, **Howlin' Wolf** *(performer)* → the ROAD TO MEMPHIS → GODFATHERS AND SONS, **Son House** *(performer)* → FEEL LIKE GOING HOME, **Mississippi John Hurt** *(performer)*, **Sonny TERRY & Brownie McGHEE** *(performers)*, **Pete SEEGER** *(performer)*, **Odetta** *(performer)* → CHORDS OF FAME → the BALLAD OF RAMBLIN' JACK → LIGHTNING IN A BOTTLE → BLUES DIVAS → NO DIRECTION HOME, **Buffy Sainte-Marie** *(performer)*, **Jim Kweskin** *(performer)*, **Theodore Bikel** *(performer)*, Ronnie Gilbert *(performer)*, **Cousin Emmy** *(performer)*

Storyline: To be precise, the Newport Folk Festival between 1963 and 1966, a showcase for the likes of Dylan, Baez, Donovan and numerous others, some from other genres such as blues and country. The highlight comes via a 1965 performance when the aforementioned Dylan plugs in his guitar, and the rest, as they say, is history. *MCS*

Movie rating: *6.5

Visual: ext.95m dvd in 2005 (no audio OST)

Off the record: New York folkies, **Peter, Paul & Mary**, were responsible for plethora of hits in the early 60s: 'If I Had A Hammer', 'Puff The Magic Dragon' (careful with that pipe, Eugene!, Dylan's 'Blowin' In The Wind' & 'Don't Think Twice, It's All Right'; and who can forget their 1969 chart-topping rendition of John Denver's, 'Leaving On A Jet Plane'. **Judy Collins** subsequently went Top 10 with Joni Mitchell's 'Both Sides Now'. **Mike Bloomfield** composed the score for 1969's political movie, 'Medium Cool'. **Buffy Sainte-Marie** contributed songs to movies such as 'Soldier Blue' – the theme at least (1970), 'Spirit Of The Wind' (1979), 'Where The Spirit Lives' (1989) and who could forget her (& hubby Jack Nitzsche's) 'Up Where We Belong' Grammy-winner from 'An Officer And A Gentleman' in '82. **Jim Kweskin** had his own jugband that was the stamping ground for Maria Muldaur, etc. **Theodore Bikel** was better as a supporting actor in films such as 'The African Queen' and 'The Enemy Below'; his folk music was witnessed on early 60s TV show, 'Hootenanny'. We can go further back to revisit **Cousin Emmy** (b. Cynthia May Carver, 14 Mar'1903) who was a country music warbler of the 40s & 50s! *MCS*

FESTIVAL EXPRESS

2003 (UK/Neth/US 90m) HanWay Films / Apollo Films / ThinkFilm (R)

Film genre: Roots/Rock-music concert/documentary

Top guns: dir: Bob Smeaton

Stars: Janis JOPLIN *(performer)* & **the Full Tilt Boogie Band** *(performers)*, **the GRATEFUL DEAD:- Jerry Garcia, Bob Weir, Phil Lesh, Mickey Hart, Ron "Pigpen" McKernan** *(performers)*, **the BAND:- Rick Danko, Richard Manuel, Robbie Robertson, Garth Hudson, Levon Helm** *(performers)*, **Buddy Guy Blues Band** *(performer/s)* ← GODFATHERS AND SONS ← BLUES ODYSSEY ← CHICAGO BLUES ← SUPERSHOW / → LIGHTNING IN A BOTTLE, **Delaney & Bonnie & Friends:- Delaney Bramlett & Bonnie Bramlett *** *(performers)* ← the DOORS * ← CATCH MY SOUL ← VANISHING POINT ← MEDICINE BALL CARAVAN, **the Flying Burrito Bros.:- Gram Parsons, Pete Kleinow, Mike Clarke, Bernie**

Leadon, Chris Hillman *(performers)* ← GIMME SHELTER, **Ian & Sylvia (Tyson) & the Great Speckled Bird** *(performers)*, **Mashmakhan:- Pierre Senecal, Jerry Mercer, Rayburn Blake, Brian Edwards** *(performers)*, **Sha Na Na:- John "Bowzer" Bauman *, Frederick "Dennis" Greene, Lennie Baker, "Dirty Dan" McBride, Jocko Marcellino, "Screamin' Scott" Simon, Donald "Donny" York, Tony Santini *, Dave "Chico" Ryan** *(performers)* ← CADDYSHACK * ← GREASE ← WOODSTOCK, **Eric Andersen** *(performer)*, Ken Walker *(himself)*, Rob Bowman *(himself)* → the LIFE AND HARD TIMES OF GUY TERRIFICO

Storyline: Woodstock was the epitomy of what a weekend festival should be, this subsequent movie – filmed in 1970 – is what a tour festival should be. Tagged "the longest party in rock-n'roll history", and the concept of music buffs Ken Walker and Thor Eaton, we follow several class acts (see above) at five venues from Toronto to Calgary. *MCS*

Movie rating: *7

Visual: dvd (no audio OST)

Off the record: Apart from the big three (see above), other lesser-known Canadian acts were featured in the movie:- **Ian & Sylvia** (Tyson & ne' Fricker, respectively) had been around the folk scene since 1959 and from 1963 to 1967, they secured six US Top 200 LPs including debut, 'Four Strong Winds' and its two 'Vanguard'-financed follow-ups, 'Northern Journey' and 'Early Morning Rain'; they married in 1964 but divorced in '73. Montreal's **Mashmakhan** was a virtual stamping ground for hard-rockers, April Wine, Mash..' musician Jerry Mercer stemming from the once dance-orientated act since the early 60s when they were billed as the Phantoms, the Dominoes and Ray Blake's Combo. Having toured in the mid-60s under the name the Triangle with soul singer, Trevor Payne, they were given their first break by producer Bob Hahn. Around the turn of the 70s and now as Mashmakhan (a reference to a hard-to-get drug), they signed to 'Columbia', where the underground quartet issued their eponymous debut. A track taken from it, 'As The Years Go By' topped the charts in Canada and even hit No.31 in the US. A second LP, 'The Family' (1971), didn't fare as well and it was down to Senecal (and future April Wine members, Brian Greenaway and Steve Laing) to keep it going for a brief time. Non-Canadian folk singer-songwriter, **Eric Andersen** (b. Pittsburgh) was found by Tom Paxton and had already released several LPs including 1965 debut, 'Today Is The Highway'. 1972's classic 'Blue River' gave him the kind of recognition he deserved, while later sets 'Memory Of The Future' (1998) and 'Waves' (2005), maintained his profile to a certain degree. *MCS*

FILLMORE

1972 (US 105m) Bill Graham Organization / 20th Century Fox (R)

Film genre: Rock-music concert/documentary

Top guns: dir: Richard T. Heffron → OUTLAW BLUES

Stars: Santana:- Carlos SANTANA, Michael Shrieve, Mike Carabello *(performers)*, **the GRATEFUL DEAD:- Jerry Garcia, Bob Weir, Keith Godchaux, Bill Kreutzmann, Robert Hunter, Ron McKernan** *(performers)*, **Hot Tuna:- Jorma Kaukonen + Jack Casady** *(performers)* ← GIMME SHELTER ← MONTEREY POP, **Quicksilver Messenger Service:- Jim Murray, John Cipollina, Gary Duncan, David Freiberg** *(performers)* ← REVOLUTION, **It's A Beautiful Day:- David LaFlamme *, Patricia Santos, Michael Holman **** *(performers)* ← * LOVE AND MUSIC / → DOWNTOWN 81, **Cold Blood:- Larry Fields** *(performers)*, **Boz Scaggs** *(performer)*, **Elvin Bishop Group:- Elvin Bishop** *(performer)* → PRIDE AND JOY, **Steve Miller** *(performer)* ← REVOLUTION, **John Chambers** *(performer)* / **New Riders Of The Purple Sage:- Garcia **, Spencer Dyden *, John Dawson** *(performers)* ← * GIMME SHELTER ← MONTEREY POP, **Lamb:- Bob Swanson, Barbara Mauritz, Ed Bogas, Bill Douglass, Rick Shlosser,** *(performers)*, Bill Graham *(himself)* ← MUSCLE BEACH PARTY / → a STAR IS BORN → the DOORS, **John Walker** *(performer)*, **Malo** *(performers)*, **Sons Of Champlin** *(performers)*, **Tower Of Power** *(performers)*, **Stoneground** *(performers)*, **Tah MAHAL** *(performer)*, **the Rowan Brothers:- Chris Rowan + Lorin Rowan** *(performers)* / **Jefferson Airplane:- Grace Slick *, Marty Balin, Paul Kantner** *(performers)* ← a NIGHT AT THE FAMILY DOG ← GIMME SHELTER ← MONTEREY POP / → JACKIE'S BACK! *

Storyline: Hippies never die and this is in evidence during the near two-hour slog through the last days of the concert arena that was Fillmore West. It closed after the last gig on the 4th of July, 1971, after opening on 6th November, 1965. *MCS*

Movie rating: *6

Visual: video + dvd

Off the record: Ed Bogas went on to score for films, 'FRITZ THE CAT' and 'HEAVY TRAFFIC'.

Various Artists: Fillmore – The Last Days

Jun 72. (t-lp;box) *Fillmore – Warner Bros.; <31390> (K 66013)* [40] [ ]
– Hello (JOHN WALKER) / Hello friends (LAMB) / So fine (ELVIN BISHOP GROUP) / Party till the cows come home (ELVIN BISHOP GROUP) / Pana (MALO) / Poppa can play (SONS OF CHAMPLIN) / White bird (IT'S A BEAUTIFUL DAY) / Fresh air (QUICKSILVER MESSENGER SERVICE) / Mojo (QUICKSILVER MESSENGER SERVICE) // Introduction (BILL GRAHAM) / Back on the streets again (TOWER OF POWER) / Baby's callin' me home (BOZ SCAGGS) / I just want to make love to you (COLD BLOOD) / Passion flower (STONEGROUND) / Henry (NEW RIDERS OF THE PURPLE SAGE) / Casey Jones (GRATEFUL DEAD) / Johnny B. Goode (GRATEFUL DEAD) // Introduction (BILL GRAHAM) / Keep your lamps trimmed and burnin' (HOT TUNA) / Incident at Neshabur (SANTANA) / In a silent way (SANTANA) / Jam session: We gonna rock (TAJ MAHAL, ELVIN BISHOP, BOZ SCAGGS) / Jam session: Long and tall (TAJ MAHAL, ELVIN BISHOP, BOZ SCAGGS) / Final night jam session / Goodbye (BILL GRAHAM). *(w/ free 7"+=; AS 1049)* – BILL GRAHAM: Words With Bill Graham *<(d-cd iss.1991 on 'Columbia-Legacy'+=; Z2K 31390)>*

S/track review: More animated, if less haunting, than the Gus Van Sant-imagined last days of Kurt Cobain, this is an elegy for a different era, when rock was still a potentially emancipatory art form. It could also conceivably be viewed as a kind of dress rehearsal for 'The LAST WALTZ', an all-star guest list sealing the end of an era. And as eras go, San Francisco circa the mid-late 60s didn't take no mess, soundtracked by names that can still strike fear into those who prefer a pop ditty to a jam session. But like the GRATEFUL DEAD themselves, the San Francisco sound was always essentially amplified roots music rather than a harbinger of heavy metal, and this album is an impressive survey of its sub-genres, justifying its existence from the opening chord by preserving the obscure LAMB for posterity (plenty of opportunity for confusion here but, as with the Charlatans, San Francisco got to the name first): 'Hello Friends' is a hugely loveable, should've-been-a-hit piece of Bay Area honky tonk sung in a Grace Slick-style holler that could've drunk your average saloon dry, or else taken Broadway by storm. There's a rare opportunity to hear erstwhile Bobby Beausoleil associate DAVID LA FLAMME extemporising on an uptempo version of his psyche classic, 'White Bird', and while the 'DEAD, SANTANA and QUICKSILVER MESSENGER SERVICE performances are suitably totemic, live documentation of these bands isn't exactly in short supply; a better reason for seeking this out – other than a keepsake for those lucky enough to be there – is the welcome excess of oddities and unknowns, many of them freely souping up funk, jazz and R&B in an age when black and white music wasn't quite as neurotically segregated. Even an obscure Latino band like MALO (also featured on the excellent 'Soul Jazz' comp, 'Chicano Power') could share the bill with rock royalty; 'Pana' is equal parts hot sauce and diesel oil. SONS OF CHAMPLIN turn out the Deep Southern-salted 'Poppa Can Play', the beyond obscure COLD BLOOD turn out a turbo-charged BS&T-esque 'I Just Want To Make Love To You' and, introduced as "that bitch of a band out of the East Bay", TOWER OF POWER turns up the heat on some of the tightest ensemble funk on the West Coast. BOZ SCAGGS (who also contributes to a fine chitlin' funk jam with TAJ MAHAL) may be a household name but his 9-minute 'Baby's Callin' Me Home', is an avant-garde symphony that renders the blue-eyed soul tag redundant, riding out on circumspect trombone and organ, going astray down oscillating blind alleys and returning in a valedictory, superflanged orgy, great soundtrack music in fact; what more could you want on what is, after all, a soundtrack? Well, you could listen to BILL GRAHAM giving the lowdown on why the "Last Days" were actually upon his legendary venue in the first place; much the same reason, it turns out, as the Isle Of Wight Festival had buckled the previous year. Rock would never be quite so hairy again. *BG*

Album rating: *7.5

– spinoff releases, etc. –

GRATEFUL DEAD: Johnny B. Goode / ELVIN BISHOP GROUP: So Fine

Aug 72. (7") *<7627>*

the FILTH AND THE FURY

. . . A SEX PISTOLS FILM

2000 (UK/US 108m) Film Four / Nitrate Films / Fine Line (15)

Film genre: Punk Rock-music concert/documentary

Top guns: dir: Julien Temple ← AT THE MAX ← EARTH GIRLS ARE EASY ← RUNNING OUT OF LUCK ← ABSOLUTE BEGINNERS ← the GREAT ROCK'N'ROLL SWINDLE / → GLASTONBURY → the FUTURE IS UNWRITTEN

Stars: the SEX PISTOLS:- Johnny Rotten/John Lydon, Steve Jones, Paul Cook, Glen Matlock *(performers)*, **Malcolm McLaren** *(himself)*, (archival footage):- **Sid Vicious** *(himself)* / **Siouxsie & The Banshees** *(performers)* ← WESTWAY TO THE WORLD ← the PUNK ROCK MOVIE ← JUBILEE / → 24 HOUR PARTY PEOPLE → PUNK: ATTITUDE, **the Police:- STING** *(performer)*, **Andy Summers** *(performer)*, **Stewart Copeland** *(performer)* ← SOUTH PARK: BIGGER, LONGER & UNCUT ← the RHYTHMATIST ← URGH! A MUSIC WAR, **Shane MacGowan** *(performer)* <= the POGUES =>, **Billy IDOL** *(performer)*, Nancy Spungen *(herself)* ← D.O.A. ← the GREAT ROCK'N'ROLL SWINDLE, Bill Grundy, Nick Kent, Stephen Fisher, Jordan + Helen Wellington-Lloyd *(herself)* ← the GREAT ROCK'N'ROLL SWINDLE ← JUBILEE

Storyline: Filmmaker Julien Temple's proper attempt at putting the real Sex Pistols' history on celluloid – never mind the bollocks that was basically Malcolm McLaren's one-sided "his story", 'The GREAT ROCK'N'ROLL SWINDLE'. This is thee definitive collection of interviews, live performances, TV appearances and newsreels. *MCS*

Movie rating: *8

Visual: dvd

Off the record: Bill Grundy is the presenter who, in December 1976 on the Today TV show, outraged the moral majority by interviewing the 'Pistols, who obliged the public by using foul and abusive language. And Punk was truly born. *MCS*

the SEX PISTOLS (& Various Artists)

May 00. (d-cd) *Virgin; (CDVD 2909) <72703>*

– God save the Queen – symphony / Shang-a-lang (BAY CITY ROLLERS) / Pictures of Lily (WHO) / Virginia plain (ROXY MUSIC) / School's out (ALICE COOPER) / Skinhead moonstomp (SYMARIP) / Glass of champagne (SAILOR) / Through my eyes (CREATION) / The Jean genie (DAVID BOWIE) / I'm eighteen (ALICE COOPER) / Submission / Don't gimme no lip child / Roadrunner / Substitute / Seventeen // Anarchy in the UK / Pretty vacant / Did you no wrong / Liar / E.M.I. / No feelings / I wanna be me / God save the Queen / Problems / Way over (in dub) (TAPPER ZUKIE) / Looking for a kiss (NEW YORK DOLLS) / Who killed Bambi (TENPOLE TUDOR) / Holidays in the sun / Bodies / My way / No fun.

S/track review: "I think most of these groups would be vastly improved by sudden death. The worst currently are the Sex Pistols and they are the antithesis of humankind". It can't be easy being a rebel in the noughties; working a Tory councillor (in the above case one Bernard Brook Partridge) into that kind of lather these days would take a Herculean effort of calculated outrage. The 'PISTOLS made it seem easy, the liberating snarl of their music even easier. In compiling their songs – the bulk of 'Never Mind The Bollocks..' plus the lesser-heard likes of 'Did You No Wrong' – against a motley selection of 60s/ 70s "rock classics", this soundtrack underscores just why their three-chord maelstrom was so explosive. As JOHN LYDON comments in the sleevenotes, "I don't think you can explain how things happen other than sometimes they just should, and the Sex Pistols should have happened and did". For all but the most raw of rock neophytes, the bulk of these tracks will be as familiar as STEVE JONES' knotted hanky headgear, but the likes of 'Anarchy In The UK' and 'Bodies' still sound like nothing else, the equivalent of aural body blows, unrivalled in their root anger and ad hoc expletives. And they still make 99.9% of contemporary alternative rock music sound eternally obsolete. While the soundtrack obviously escapes some of the criticisms levelled at the movie (the decision to film the ageing ex-PISTOLS in profile, for example), overall it's a much more contextually revealing document – especially with the waggish inclusion of the likes of the Bay City Rollers and Sailor – than Temple's original film, 'The GREAT ROCK'N'ROLL SWINDLE' (1979). Naturally, it's also a much more accurate overview of their music. Revisionist by its very nature, however, it irons out the eccentricity and self-indulgence which lent '..SWINDLE' much of its noxious charm. Where it does score is with the inclusion of great period ska/dub cuts like SYMARIP's 'Skinhead Moonstomp' and TAPPER ZUKIE's 'Way Over', less obvious influences on punk than the NEW YORK DOLLS but crucial ones nevertheless. *BG*

Album rating: *7.5

□ Wild Man FISCHER segment
(⇒ DERAILROADED)

□ the FLAMING LIPS segment
(⇒ the FEARLESS FREAKS)

FREE

1973 (US 80m) Indie-Pix

Film genre: Rock-music concert/docudrama

Top guns: dir: Bert Tenzer

Stars: Steppenwolf *(performers)*, **Jimi HENDRIX** *(performer)*, **Van MORRISON** *(performer)*, **DR. JOHN** *(performer)*, Luis Arroyo, Mel Winkler

Storyline: It's summer 1970, Woodstock was last year, but in New York City (Randall Island, to be exact) there was another rock festival going down. The director also gives the audience some re-enacted vignettes over the day's takings and receipts. Free, the band, were nowhere to be seen. *MCS*

Movie rating: *6

Visual: video

Off the record: Steppenwolf were no strangers to the world of film soundtracks, having previously contributed two gems, 'Magic Carpet Ride' and 'Rock Me' to the movie 'CANDY' (1968) and another two ('Born To Be Wild' and 'The Pusher') to 'EASY RIDER' (1969). *MCS*

FREE TIBET

1998 (US 90m) Shooting Gallery

Film genre: Rock-music documentary

Top guns: dir: Sarah Pirozek

Stars: BEASTIE BOYS:- Adam Yauch, Adam Horowitz, Mike D *(themselves/performers)*, **BECK** *(performer)*, **RED HOT CHILI PEPPERS:- Anthony Kiedis, Flea, John Frusciante, Chad Smith** *(performers)*, **Smashing Pumpkins:- Billy CORGAN, James Iha, D'arcy Wretzky, Jimmy Chamberlin** *(performers)*, **Rage Against The Machine:- Zack De La Rocha, Tom Morello, Tim Commerford, Brad Wilk** *(performers)*, **SONIC YOUTH:- Kim Gordon, Lee Ranaldo, Thurston Moore** *(performers)*, **Foo Fighters:- Dave Grohl *, Nate Mendel **, Pat Smear ***, William Goldsmith** *(performers)* ← KURT AND COURTNEY *** ← 1991: THE YEAR PUNK BROKE * ← the DECLINE OF WESTERN CIVILIZATION *** / → OUR BURDEN IS LIGHT ** → PUNK: ATTITUDE *** → the PICK OF DESTINY *, **Alanis Morissette** *(performer)* → WOODSTOCK '99, **A Tribe Called Quest:- Q-TIP, Phife Dawg *, Ali Shaheed Muhammad** *(performers)* ← WHO'S THE MAN? *, **De La Soul:- Trugoy The Dove, Posdnous, P.A. Pacemaster Mase** *(performers)* → BROWN SUGAR, **BJÖRK** *(performer)*, **Cibo Matto:- Yuka Honda, Miho Hatori, Sean Lennon** * *(performers)* * ← MOONWALKER ← ENDLESS HARMONY: THE BEACH BOYS STORY ← IMAGINE: JOHN LENNON, Dechen Wangdu *(herself)*, Robert Thurman *(himself)*

Storyline: Comprising 100,000 people and 20 bands, this concert film (produced by Buddhist convert Adam Yauch of the Beastie Boys) was shot at 1996's Tibetan Freedom Concert in San Francisco's Golden Gate Park. 'Free Tibet' is a movement to break from the shackles of the People's Republic of China and their political oppression. *MCS*

Movie rating: *5.5

Visual: video + dvd

Off the record: Dechen Wangdu is the American-Tibetan wife of **Adam Yauch** , whose aim to bring the Tibetan cause to light saw the making of the film. Professor of Indo-Tibetan studies at Columbia University in New York City, Robert Thurman (father of Uma), was also behind the campaign. *MCS*

FREEBIRD – THE MOVIE

1996 (US 103m) Cabin Fever Entertainment / Astra Cinema

Film genre: Roots/Hard-Rock-music concert/documentary

Top guns: dir: Jeff G. Waxman / s-w: Sanford Santacroce

Stars: Lynyrd Skynyrd:- Ronnie Van Zandt, Gary Rossington, Allen Collins, Artimus Pyle, Billy Powell, Leon Wilkeson, Steve Gaines, Cassie Gaines

Storyline: It's August 21st, 1976, the torrid tail end of a blistering hot summer, and those who can stand the heat are packed into the leafy environs of Knebworth Park, an unlikely venue for Southern-by-the-grace-of-God rockers Lynyrd Skynyrd. Paying little heed to the unforgiving light of late afternoon, Ronnie Van Zant and co win over a sceptical looking crowd, especially the hairier and more air guitar inclined lads. In eye popping contrast, there's also footage from Stateside gigs and 'Freebird' itself is performed in an Oakland stadium apparently bursting to capacity with nubile girls who sing along to every word. It is, truly, like punk never happened. *BG*

Movie rating: *6.5

Visual: video

Off the record: **Lynyrd Skynyrd** (see below)

—

LYNYRD SKYNYRD

Aug 96. (cd) *M.C.A.; <(MCD 1147-2)>* ☐ Sep96 ☐
– Workin' for M.C.A. / I ain't the one / Saturday night special / Whisky rock-a-roller / Travellin' man / Searching / What's your name / That smell / Gimme three steps / Call the breeze / T for Texas (blue yodel No.1) / Sweet home Alabama / Freebird / Dixie.

S/track review: This hairy nugget hails from a time when lead singers could still get away with a beer gut. The Allman Brothers invented Southern rock, but LYNYRD SKYNYRD were the archetype. No black drummers or musical miscegenation for the VAN ZANT tribe, just a barrel-load of white, countrified blooze and anti-glamour. When they weren't firing off defiant fusilades at Neil Young, they were being touted as the new Rolling Stones. 'SKYNYRD were to the 'Stones what Wild Turkey is to Famous Grouse, but the Knebworth gig gave them an opportunity to air their "smelly hillbillyisms" – to quote writer Charles Bottomley – in the Home Counties, and show up their limey idols for the "shambling parody" they were ultimately slated as. By 1976, both bands were short on songs, but the Jacksonville boys weren't yet blunted by excess. While punk was plotting rock's demise down the road in London, a newly cleaned-up LYNYRD SKYNYRD muscled through their deep south convictions in front of a sun-stroked crowd. The sound is all over place but RONNIE VAN ZANT has his bare feet planted firmly on the stage, drawling out his disillusion with the music business ('Workin' For M.C.A.'), American gun culture ('Saturday Night Special') and, most hauntingly – even though the sound quality is truly appalling, and the performance is from New Jersey rather than Hertfordshire – with drugs ('That Smell'). He's no black bluesman but – like Van Morrison – his taciturn stage presence has all the pressure cooker menace of a prison ballad. And, unavoidably in the knowledge of his plane crash demise just over a year later, the performances are poignantly, fatally loaded, even the air guitar anthems and pan-handle covers. 'One More From The Road' (1976) covers similar territory without the dodgy presentation and production, but the prospect of 'Skynyrd in their pomp is always compelling. *BG*

Album rating: *6

FRIENDS FOREVER

2002 (US 80m w/b&w) Plexifilm

Film genre: Rock-music documentary comedy bio-pic

Top guns: dir: Ben Wolfinsohn

Stars: Friends Forever:- Nate Hayden + Josh Taylor, *(themselves/performers; drums + bass)*, Jenn Keyser *(lighting girl)*, Harvey Sid Fisher *(himself/performer)*, Lloyd Kaufman *(himself)* → PUNK ROCK HOLOCAUST

Storyline: The travelogue and tour of a two-piece band, Friends Forever. Nate, Josh and female friend Jenn, go virtually anywhere and everywhere in their cars (and VW) to perform, usually for under 15 minutes – to their three dogs, onlookers and the curious passers-by. *MCS*

Movie rating: *7

Visual: dvd – has "where are they now?' piece (no audio OST)

Off the record: Friends Forever are a unique rock band who dismiss the conventional rock'n'roll trites of playing at venues to that of playing gigs in the back of their VW bus. Forming in Denver, Colorado, the hardcore punk duo of Nate and Josh have earned respect and even an award from Troma Films co-founder, Lloyd Kaufman. They've released one album to date, 'Killball' (2003) and confess to being the future of Rock'n'roll. *MCS*

☐ FUGAZI segment
(⇒ INSTRUMENT)

☐ the FUNK BROTHERS segment
(⇒ STANDING IN THE SHADOWS OF MOTOWN)

the FUTURE IS UNWRITTEN

2007 (Ire/UK 123m) Film 4 / HanWay / Sony BMG

Film genre: Punk/Reggae-music documentary bio-pic

Top guns: dir: Julien Temple ← GLASTONBURY ← the FILTH AND THE FURY ← AT THE MAX ← EARTH GIRLS ARE EASY ← RUNNING OUT OF LUCK ← ABSOLUTE BEGINNERS ← the GREAT ROCK'N'ROLL SWINDLE

Stars: the CLASH:- Joe STRUMMER, Terry Chimes, Nicky "Topper" Headon, Mick Jones *(themselves/performers)*, Martin Scorsese *(himself)*, **Bono** *(himself)* <= U2 =>, **Don Letts** *(himself)* ← NEW YORK DOLL, Bernie Rhodes *(himself)*, Johnny Depp *(himself)* ← FEAR AND LOATHING IN LAS VEGAS ← DEAD MAN ← CRY-BABY, **Anthony Kiedis + Flea** *(themselves)* <= RED HOT CHILI PEPPERS =>, **Steve Jones** *(himself)* <= SEX PISTOLS =>, Alasdair Gillis *(himself)*, Jim Jarmusch *(himself)* ← I PUT A SPELL ON ME ← YEAR OF THE HORSE ← SLING BLADE ← LENINGRAD COWBOYS GO AMERICA ← CANDY MOUNTAIN ← STRAIGHT TO HELL, Matt Dillon *(himself)* ← ALBINO ALLIGATOR ← GRACE OF MY HEART ← SINGLES, Steve Buscemi *(himself)* ← ROMANCE & CIGARETTES ← COFFEE AND CIGARETTES ← the WEDDING SINGER ← AIRHEADS ← PULP FICTION ← RESERVOIR DOGS ← MYSTERY TRAIN ← the WAY IT IS, John Cusack *(himself)* ← HIGH FIDELITY ← ROADSIDE PROPHETS ← TAPEHEADS, Harvey Weinstein *(himself)* ← OVERNIGHT

Storyline: Although there have been several Clash films, this is the first to put frontman Joe Strummer (self-described as a "mouthy little git") to the fore. With honest interviews and rare concert footage (not just of his former bands), the punk-rock icon who died on 22nd December 2002, is to many the ultimate, modern-day rock'n'roll idol. *MCS*

Movie rating: *7.5

Visual: dvd

Off the record: see Joe STRUMMER/CLASH entry

—

Various Artists (incl. JOE STRUMMER * + "dialogue")

May 07. (cd) *Sony; (88697 08832-2) <70516-2>* ☐ ☐
– "Punk rock warlord" (*) / White riot – alt. demo mix (the CLASH) * / Rock the casbah (RACHID TAHA) * / "BBC World Service" / Crawfish (ELVIS PRESLEY) / Black sheep boy (TIM HARDIN) / Kick out the jams (MC5) / Keys to your heart (the 101'ERS) * / "Mick and Paul were different" (*) / I'm so bored with the U.S.A. (the CLASH) * / Natty rebel – 2006 mix (U ROY) / Armagideon time (the CLASH) * / Nervous breakdown (EDDIE COCHRAN) / (In the) Pouring rain (the CLASH) * / Omotepe (*) / Martha Cecilia (ANDRES LANDEROS) / Minuet (ERNEST RANGLIN) / Trash city (* & LATINO ROCKABILLY WAR) / "I called him Woody" (TOPPER HEADON) / Ranger's command (WOODY GUTHRIE) / Corrina, Corrina (BOB DYLAN) / Johnny Appleseed (* & The MESCALEROS) / To love somebody (NINA SIMONE) / "Without people you're nothing" (*) / Willesden to Cricklewood (* & The MESCALEROS).

S/track review: The flawed genius of JOE STRUMMER is explored in varied sonic terms on this expansive 18-song collection, tracing the roots of his own music from the stomping, pub rock of the 101'ERS through the glory of the CLASH to the global righteousness of his MESCALEROS. The fact that many of these tracks – in particular the CLASH ones – are rare, previously unreleased versions gives even the fanatics another brief twist on the legend, especially the embryonic demo of 'I'm So Bored Of The U.S.A.' which bristles with the vitriol and energy that the band became so loved for. The thing that makes this soundtrack a more rounded experience is the inclusion of songs that STRUMMER was a fan of and inspired by, from the lyrical spark of TIM HARDIN's 'Black Sheep Boy' to the firebrand radicalism of MC5's 'Kick Out The Jams'. Similarly, U-ROY's roots rocker 'Natty Rebel' is suggestively followed here by the CLASH's own 'Armagideon Time'. Further proof, if it were ever needed, that punk's influences went far beyond the New York Dolls and Ramones. Snippets of JOE's words of wisdom, culled from interviews, on-stage diatribes and radio broadcasts now seem obligatory on any contemporary soundtrack album but some, here, out of context, make him seem more than a little preachy. But considering that the aim of the film was to show the man warts'n'all, it is maybe fitting that he comes off both sanctimonious and inspirational. *MR*

Album rating: *7.5

□ Jerry GARCIA
(⇒ GRATEFUL DEAD)

□ GARGANDI SNILLD alt.
(⇒ SCREAMING MASTERPIECE)

GENGHIS BLUES

1999 (US 88m) Roxie (PG)

Film genre: Blues-music documentary

Top guns: dir: Roko Belic

Stars: Paul Pena *(himself/performer)*, **Kongar-ol Ondar** *(himself/performer)*, **Richard Feynman** *(himself/performer)*, **B.B. KING** *(performer)*

Storyline: Charming audiences and judges at every film festival from Edinburgh to Taipei, the adventures of the late Paul Pena have something of the mythic about them, a blind hero in search of a sonic Prester John. The story is a fantastical one, rooted in the tenacity of the self-taught (he even taught himself the Tuvan language, with only Braile Tuvan-Russian/Russian-English dictionaries to help him), documenting Pena's pilgrimage to Tuva after astounding native musicians with his throat singing abilities at a San Francisco concert. Christening him "Earthquake", their invitation has him heading back east where he strikes up a friendship/partnership with champion throat singer Kongar-ol Ondar, wins first prize in a competition and – despite the disorientation of being blind (and in poor health) in a distant land – wins the solidarity of the Tuvan people. *BG*

Movie rating: *8

Visual: dvd

Off the record: Paul Pena (b.26 Jan'50, Hyannis, Massachusetts). Virtually blind since birth and plagued by illness, the guitarist subsequently released an LP, 'New Train', in 1973; Jerry Garcia is on session. The Steve Miller Band took one of its best tracks, 'Jet Airliner', and made it a massive global hit, which led to Paul "Earthquake" Pena obtaining work from B.B. King and Bonnie Raitt. Sadly after being wrongly diagnosed with pancreatic cancer and enduring a series of chemo (he actually had pancreatitis), Pena died in San Francisco on 1st October, 2005. **Kongar-ol Ondar** (b. 1962) founded the Tuva Ensemble in the mid-80s, subsequently winning many awards with his style of folk throat-singing. In the 90s, he recorded with the likes of Frank Zappa, the Kronos Quartet and had an unlikely musical partnership with the late great physicist (turned bongo-player), **Richard Feynman**. *MCS*

KONGAR-OL ONDAR & PAUL "EARTHQUAKE" PENA

Nov 00. (cd) *Six Degrees; <1038-2>* □ [-]
– What you talkin' about? / Alash hem (the Alash river) / Gonna move / Kaldak khamar (the other side of the mountain) / Tras d'Orizao (beyond the horizon) / Ondarnyng ayany (Ondar's medley) / Kargyraa moan / It's hard to lose a friend / Kongurey (where has my country gone?) / Durgen chugaa (fast talk) / Sunezin yry (soul's song) / Center of Asia / Got to move / Tuva farewell / Genghis Blues soundbites / Kaldak khamar (live) / Eki a'ttar (live).

S/track review: PAUL PENA's obvious pride in his Cape Verdean roots – he performs the traditional morna, 'Tras D'Orizão', as if he'd left Brava yesterday – might explain at least some of his wanderlust, a heritage of flight from poverty and drought to the diasporas of São Tome, Portugal, the USA and beyond. It's the story of the blues and the story of this soundtrack, taking PENA's Luso roots, impressive CV (listing T-Bone Walker, Muddy Waters and BB King as well as the credit for 'Jet Airliner', one of Steve Miller's biggest hits) and tonal experiments and delivering it even further afield, finding common currency in the folk music of an obscure Asiatic republic. By the time Ry Cooder and Ali Farka Toure's 'Talking Timbuktu' (1994) proved the creative and commercial viability of American blues as a global language, PENA had long mastered throat singing, successfully – incredibly – teaching himself from an album after hearing it on Radio Moscow. Such was his natural aptitude for it, he won a Tuvan throating singing competition; 'Kargyraa Moan' is the track which scooped him first prize, the most engrossing example of how he transposes the sub-profundo growl of the Kargyraa style (where the performer simultaneously generates "undertones" one octave or more below the main tone) into Delta blues. Dedicated to Charley Patton and Howlin' Wolf, it at least partially summons a saner, more athletic version of Captain Beefheart's barking madness, blues from the depths of a troubled soul. Singing conventionally in English, PENA's voice is gnarled in all the right places, pitched somewhere between Kris Kristofferson, Ben Harper and Jay Farrar, but it wasn't always that way. On the stomping 'Gonna Move' – a track lifted from his 1973 album, 'New Train' – he sounds like a young Lenny Kravitz fronting Brinsley Schwarz, a world away from the modal melancholy and spirit world frequencies of Tuva. On the likes of 'Alesh Hem' and 'Ondarnyng Ayany', Tuvan master KONGAR-OL ONDAR sustains otherworldy notes for inordinate passages of time; you can almost hear his face going beetroot with the effort. Compared to PENA's songs, the string accompaniment – on banjo and jaw harp – is rudimentary but the Tuvan lyrical preoccupations are remarkably similar and all too human, at least according to the sleevenotes and translations: "If they built a road over the Kaldak Hamar Pass, I could check up on my crazy girl", "The moon and snow are the only witnesses to a man dying of stab wounds after a drunken argument" etc. The most haunting moment is perhaps 'Kongurey', where PENA and ONDAR pool their pharyngeal skill on a tale of an exile returning to the ravages of communism. Not as fun, maybe, as the likes of Yat-Kha covering Kraftwerk, but a moving document and a great introduction to the cosmopolitan talents of PENA (he also does a great, thorny version of the Mississippi Fred McDowell and Rev. Gary Davis standard, 'You Gotta Move') and the thriving tradition of throat singing. *BG*

Album rating: *7.5

GET BACK

aka PAUL McCARTNEY'S GET BACK

1991 (UK/US 89m) Allied Film Makers / Front Page Films (PG)

Film genre: rock/pop-Music documentary/concert

Top guns: dir: Richard Lester ← HELP! ← a HARD DAY'S NIGHT ← IT'S TRAD, DAD!

Stars: Paul McCartney *(performer)* <= the BEATLES =>, **Linda McCartney** *(performer)*, ← GIVE MY REGARDS TO BROAD STREET ← CONCERTS FOR THE PEOPLE OF KAMPUCHEA ← ROCKSHOW ← SGT. PEPPER'S LONELY HEARTS CLUB BAND ← ONE HAND CLAPPING ← LET IT BE,

Robbie McIntosh *(performer)*, **Hamish Stuart** *(performer)*, **Chris Whitten** *(performer)*, **Wix** *(performer)*

Storyline: Paul McCartney gets a career retrospective by way of songs performed on his 1989-1990 world tour. Shot like a video by none other than Richard Lester, works from his times with the Beatles and Wings are predominant. *MCS*

Movie rating: *6

Visual: video + dvd (no audio OST)

Off the record: PAUL McCARTNEY and his band perform around 20 songs (in no particular order):- 'Yesterday', 'Band On The Run', 'Coming Up', 'The Long And Winding Road', 'Hey Jude', 'Live And Let Die', 'Get Back', 'Can't Buy Me Love', 'Let It Be', 'I Saw Her Standing There', 'Fool On The Hill', etc. *MCS*

□ GET DOWN GRAND FUNK alt. (⇒ WEEKEND REBELLION)

GIGANTIC (A TALE OF TWO JOHNS)

2002 (US 102m) Bonfire Films of America / Cowboy Pictures

Film genre: Indie/Alt-rock music documentary/concert biopic

Top guns: dir: A.J. Schnack → KURT COBAIN ABOUT A SON

Stars: They Might Be Giants:- John Flansburgh, John Linnell *(themselves/performers)*, **Frank Black** *(himself)* → FOLLOW MY VOICE: WITH THE MUSIC OF HEDWIG → loudQUIETloud: a film about THE PIXIES, **Syd Straw** *(herself)*, Dave Eggers *(himself)*, Joe Franklin *(himself)*, Janeane Garofalo *(herself)* ← TOUCH ← REALITY BITES, Michael McKean *(himself)* ← AIRHEADS ← EARTH GIRLS ARE EASY ← LIGHT OF DAY ← THIS IS SPINAL TAP / → a MIGHTY WIND, Harry Shearer *(himself)* ← GHOST DOG: THE WAY OF THE SAMURAI ← WAYNE'S WORLD 2 ← THIS IS SPINAL TAP ← ONE-TRICK PONY ← ANIMALYMPICS / → a MIGHTY WIND, **Mark Hoppus** *(himself)* ← SHAKE, RATTLE & ROLL: AN AMERICAN LOVE STORY ← RELEASE, Annette O'Toole *(narrator)* ← ONE ON ONE, Gina Arnold *(herself)*, Michael Azerrad *(himself)* ← the SHIELD AROUND THE K / → LAST DAYS, Jon Stewart *(himself)* ← BARENAKED IN AMERICA, Andy Richter *(himself)* ← BARENAKED IN AMERICA, Conan O'Brien *(himself)* ← STORYTELLING ← BARENAKED IN AMERICA, Sarah Vowell *(herself)* ← MAN IN THE SAND, David Bither *(himself)* → I AM TRYING TO BREAK YOUR HEART

Storyline: "A Movie About They Might Be Giants", an indie duo consisting of "Two Johns": John Flansburgh and John Linnell. Responsible for several quirky rock albums, this is a run through live footage and interviews plus music videos. *MCS*

Movie rating: *6.5

Visual: dvd (no audio OST; see below compilation)

Off the record: They Might Be Giants were formed in Brooklyn, New York, 1985 by former Bostonians, **John Flansburgh** and **John Linnell**, who poached the group name from an early 70s movie starring George C Scott. In true DIY fashion, this enterprising duo set up a "Dial-A-Song" service to preview their work, gathering up the cream of the material on offer for an eponymous debut album via NY indie, 'Bar None'. Licensed for the UK by 'Rough Trade', the record introduced British listeners to their quirky folk/punk hybrid and geek-appeal, drawing critical comparisons with everyone from R.E.M. to DEVO and even the RESIDENTS. Rising from relative obscurity to become college radio heroes in the space of a few years, TMBG found alternative fame with follow-up set, 'Lincoln' (1989), the band's offbeat combination of surreal/subversive lyrics and sherbet-laced melodies making them the toast of America's alternative scene. A subsequent transatlantic deal with 'Elektra' saw the duo score an unlikely UK Top 10 hit single with 'Birdhouse In Your Soul', while the accompanying album, 'Flood', made the Top 20 despite its wilful experimentation. Mainstream success was fleeting, however, further singles failing to make the grade and a third album, 'Apollo 18' (1992), proving too challenging even for many hardened fans. Things improved with the addition of four new band members in time for 'John Henry' (1994), the album pushing them to new heights back home and even securing them a soundtrack appearance on 1995 kids' movie, 'Mighty Morphin Power Rangers'. The group released two subsequent albums, 'Factory Showroom' (1997) and 'Severe Tire Damage' (1998), the latter a live set which included a new track, 'Doctor Worm' and seven untitled songs written on the night. TMBG have since issued two more quirky sets, 'Mink Car' (2001) and 'No!' (2002), and have provided the theme tune to the successful "kids?" TV sitcom, 'Malcolm In The Middle'; all together now: "you're not the boss of me now". One of their famous fans is **Mark Hoppus**, co-lead & bassist of Blink-182. *MCS*

– associated compilation –

THEY MIGHT BE GIANTS: Dial-A-Song – 20 Years Of They Might Be Giants

Sep 02. (d-cd) *Rhino; <(8122 78139-2)>* □ □
– Birdhouse in your soul / Ana Ng / Don't let's start / Boss of me / Older / Istanbul (not Constantinople) / Doctor Worm / The guitar / Dr. Evil / New York City / Particle man / Cyclops rock / Minimum wage / Man, it's so loud in here / We're the Replacements / Why does the sun shine (the sun is a mass of incandescent gas) (live) / Your racist friend / Bangs / Snail shell / Twisting / Another first kiss / They'll need a crane / The statue got me high / (She was a) Hotel detective / Put your hand inside the puppet head / I palindrome I / She's an angel / How can I sing like a girl? / James K. Polk / Meet James Ensor / Mammal / Pet name / No! / I can hear you / Spider / I should be allowed to think / Fingertips / She's actual size / Spy / Stormy pinkness / Exquisite dead guy / Robot parade / Boat of car / S-E-X-X-Y / Number three / The end of the tour / The might be giants / Hey Mr. DJ, I thought you said we had a deal / Nightgown of the sullen moon / Snowball in Hell / Purple toupee / Cowtown.

GIMME SHELTER

1970 (US 95m) Maysles Films / Cinema 5 (R)

Film genre: Rock-music concert/documentary

Top guns: Albert Maysles, David Maysles, Charlotte Zwerin

Stars: the ROLLING STONES:- Mick Jagger, Keith Richards, Charlie Watts, Bill Wyman, Mick Taylor, Ian Stewart *(themselves/performers)*, **Ike Turner** *(performer)* ← IT'S YOUR THING ← the BIG T.N.T. SHOW / → SOUL TO SOUL → BLUES ODYSSEY → the ROAD TO MEMPHIS → GODFATHERS AND SONS & **Tina TURNER** *(performer)*, **Jefferson Airplane: Grace Slick *, Marty Balin, Paul Kantner, Jorma Kaukonen, Jack Casady, Spencer Dryden** *(performers)* ← MONTEREY POP / a NIGHT AT THE FAMILY DOG → FILLMORE → JACKIE'S BACK! * / **the Flying Burrito Brothers:- Gram Parsons, Pete Kleinow, Chris Hillman, Bernie Leadon, Mike Clarke** *(performers)* → FESTIVAL EXPRESS, the GRATEFUL DEAD:- Jerry Garcia, Phil Lesh *(performers)*

Storyline: The flower-power 60s closed with a bang when a free concert at Altamont speedway track in Oakland California (on the 6th of December 1969), ended in disaster when a member of the Hell's Angels motorbike gang (who were hired as security!), stabbed and killed a spectator. A dark day indeed, although the music and Jagger's attempts at crowd control are highlights in this fly-on-the-wall feature. *MCS*

Movie rating: *8.5

Visual: video + dvd (no audio release)

Off the record: The 'Gimme Shelter' LP release was actually not the soundtrack but an exploitation compilation with live (and studio!) recordings from as far back as 1966. It tricked many fans of the 'Stones (with the live sleeve) and even the group themselves, put in a press statement against it. However, some tracks (*) do correspond to the real Altamont/'Gimme Shelter' live ones, which were probably chosen to deceive; IKE & TINA TURNER covered 'I've Been Loving You Too Long' in the movie. *MCS*

– associated release –

the ROLLING STONES: Gimme Shelter *(not the OST)*

Aug 71. (lp/c) *Decca; (SLK/KSKC 5101)* [–] [19]
– Jumpin' Jack Flash (*) / Love in vain (*) / Honky tonk women (*) / Street fighting man (*) / Sympathy for the Devil (*) / Gimme shelter (*) / Under my thumb (*) / Time is on my side / I've been loving you too long / Fortune teller / Lady Jane / (I can't get no) Satisfaction (*).

GLASTONBURY FAYRE

1972 (UK 87m) Goodtimes Enterprises (15)

Film genre: Rock-music concert documentary

Top guns: dir: Peter Neal ← BE GLAD FOR THE SONG HAS NO ENDING ← EXPERIENCE / → YESSONGS

Stars: Gong *(performers)*, Arthur Brown/Kingdom Come *(performer)*, **Linda Lewis** *(performer)*, **Fairport Convention** *(performers)*, **Traffic:- Steve Winwood** * *(performer/s)* ← CUCUMBER CASTLE ← the GHOST GOES GEAR / → WOODSTOCK 94 → BLUES BROTHERS 2000 → RED, WHITE & BLUES, **Melanie** *(performer)*, **Quintessence** *(performers)*, **Terry Reid** *(performer)* ← GROUPIES

Storyline: Down on a small Somerset dairy farm, Glastonbury Festival (1971 June 20-24) was the English equivalent to America's Woodstock. Free, yes, free to all the Stonehenge graduates, hippies and pot-headed pixies. A generation on and the yuppies had moved in. *MCS*

Movie rating: *6

Visual: video (deleted)

Off the record: David Puttnam was producer, while Nicolas Roeg ('Walkabout', etc.) worked as cinematographer. No soundtrack was officially released (a bootleg triple does exist!); the 1972 triple-LP (see below) sometimes gets mistaken for it – tracks marked * were recorded there. **Gong** were responsible for a complete soundtrack, 'CONTINENTAL CIRCUS' (1971), while **Traffic** had contributed songs to 'HERE WE GO ROUND THE MULBERRY BUSH' in 1968. *MCS*

– associated releases, etc. –

Various Artists: Revelations – A Musical Anthology For Glastonbury Fayre

Apr 72. (t-lp) *Revelation; (REV 1/2/3)* [ ] [–]
– Dark star (GRATEFUL DEAD) / Love song (BRINSLEY SCHWARTZ) / A blanket in my meusli (MIGHTY BABY) * // Sunken rags (MARC BOLAN) / Classified (PETE TOWNSHEND) / Supermen (DAVID BOWIE) / Silver machine & Welcome (HAWKWIND) / Sun music (SKIN ALLEY) / Glad stoned buried fielding flash and fresh fest footprints in my memory (DAEVID ALLEN AND GONG) * // Do it (PINK FAIRIES) * / Uncle Harry's last freak-out (PINK FAIRIES) * / Out demons out (EDGAR BROUGHTON BAND) *. *(d-cd-iss. Sep06 on 'Arkarma' Italy +=; AK 367-3)* – (w/ DVD movie).

GONG: Glastonbury Fayre 1971

Dec 02. (m-cd; ltd) *GAS; (001)* [ ] [–]
– Intro . . . / It's only the world said the girl / Dexter (electricity cut . . .) / Fun gods (Ha ha – Name game – Toe cake – Awe mantrum – Dingobox) / John Peel's judgement / Divine mother / Radio gnome (explosion) / Bambolay – Ya sunne / Applause – Dexter.

GLASTONBURY THE MOVIE

1995/6 (UK 96m) Starlight / Glastonbury (15)

Film genre: Rock-music concert/documentary

Top guns: dir: William Beaton, Robin Mahoney, Matthew Salkeld, Lisa Lake, Michael Sarne

Stars: the LEMONHEADS:- Evan Dando *(performers)*, **the Filberts: Phil Bell, Milton Johnson + Charlie Creed-Miles** *(performers)*, **Back To The Planet** *(performers)*, **Chuck Prophet** *(performer)*, **Airto Moreira** *(performer)*, **Porno For Pyros: Perry Farrell + Martin LeNoble** *(performers)* ← WOODSTOCK '94 / → MY GENERATION, **Spiritualized/Jason Pierce** *(performers)*, **McKoy:- Robin, Noel, Cornelle + Junette** *(performers)*

Storyline: From the late 60s, British institute the Glastonbury Festival has grown from strength to strength, however on these occasions (1989-1995) the spirit is mightier than the happening. *MCS*

Movie rating: *5

Visual: video + dvd (no audio soundtrack released)

Off the record: Chuck Prophet (ex-Green On Red), while Brazilian **Airto Moreira** is world music's veteran.

GLASTONBURY

2006 (US 138m) HanWay Films / Newhouse Nitrate (15)

Film genre: Rock-music concert/documentary

Top guns: Julien Temple ← the FILTH AND THE FURY ← AT THE MAX ← EARTH GIRLS ARE EASY ← RUNNING OUT OF LUCK ← ABSOLUTE BEGINNERS ← the GREAT ROCK'N'ROLL SWINDLE / → the FUTURE IS UNWRITTEN

Stars: Michael Eavis *(himself)*, **Marc Bolan/T.Rex** *(performers)* ← BORN TO BOOGIE, **David BOWIE** *(performer)*, **Radiohead** *(performers)*, **R.E.M.** *(performers)*, **Oasis** *(performers)*, **Coldplay** *(performers)*, **Blur** *(performers)*, **Pulp** *(performers)*, **the Chemical Brothers** *(performers)*, **Nick CAVE** *(performer)*, **Massive Attack** *(performers)*, **Billy Bragg** *(performer)* ← MAN IN THE SAND, **BJORK** *(performer)*, **James BROWN** *(performer)*, **Joe STRUMMER & the Mescaleros** *(performers)*, **Morrissey** *(performer)* ← NEW YORK DOLL, **Primal Scream** *(performers)*, **the Velvet Underground** *(performers)* ← the VELVET UNDERGROUND AND NICO, **New Order** *(performers)*, **Fatboy Slim** *(performer)*, **Paul McCartney** *(performer)* <= the BEATLES =>, **Van MORRISON** *(performer)*, **the Prodigy** *(performers)*, **ORBITAL** *(performers)*, **Ray DAVIES/the KINKS** *(performer/s)*, **Scissor Sisters** *(performers)*, **DR. JOHN** *(performer)*, **Richie Havens** *(performer)* ← HEARTS OF FIRE ← CATCH MY SOUL ← WOODSTOCK / → I'M NOT THERE, **Alabama 3** *(performers)*, **Stereo MC's** *(performers)*, **Alice Coltrane** *(performer)*, **Babyshambles** *(performers)*, **Skatalites** *(performers)*, **Faithless** *(performers)*, **David Gray** *(performer)*, **Melanie** *(performer)*, **Toots & The Maytals** *(performers)*, **Clint Eastwwod & General Saint** *(performers)*, **Ernest Raglin** *(performer)*, **the Wailers** *(performers)*, **the Bravery** *(performers)*, **Tinariwen** *(performer)*, **Rolf Harris** *(performer)*

Storyline: Filmmaker, Julien Temple, takes the reins for the longest-running, biggest "Rock" music festival in the world. Since summer 1970 to 2005, the farm played host to millions of folk and an eclectic taste of music styles. *MCS*

Movie rating: *6

Visual: dvd

Off the record: Glastonbury extra (see below)

Various Artists (other stuff *)

Jul 06. (d-cd) *Glastonbury Phonographic; (RECYCLE 01)* [ ] [–]
– Mud for it (*) / We have built Jerusalem (*) / Politik (COLDPLAY) / Fake plastic trees (RADIOHEAD) / Hippies! (*) / Stop that train (CLINT EASTWOOD & GENERAL SAINT) / Bring it on, Glastonbury (*) / Firestarter (the PRODIGY) / Hey boy, hey girl (the CHEMICAL BROTHERS) / It's a spiritual centre (*) / Babylon (DAVID GRAY) / Human behavoiur (BJORK) / A message for the green police (*) / Qualahila ar tesninam (TINARIWEN) / Pressure drop (TOOTS AND THE MAYTALS) / Confessions of a Devon boy (*) / Common people (PULP) / Kilimangiro (BABYSHAMBLES) / An ode to early morning (*) / The drinker's prayer (*) / Right place, wrong time (DR. JOHN) / D'accord Dakar (ERNEST RANGLIN) / Losing the dinosaurs (*) // Mud for it (*) /

It's Sunday morning (*) / First of the gang to die (MORRISSEY) / Mao Tse Tung eyes (ALABAMA 3) / An alternative nation (*) / Straight to hell (JOE STRUMMER & the MESCALEROS) / Phoenix city (the SKATALITES) / It's the vibes (*) / Someone has got to make a stand (*) / Swastika eyes (PRIMAL SCREAM) / Fearless (the BRAVERY) / He hasn't moved for 3 days (*) / Soul shakedown party (the WAILERS) / Laura (SCISSOR SISTERS) / The better the wizard (*) / We come one (FAITHLESS) / The solstice . . . is amazing (*) / Impact (ORBITAL) / Welcome to Brigadoon (*) / Journey into Satchidananda (ALICE COLTRANE).

S/track review: In what is essentially a British experience, the soundtrack eschews the large catalogue of past performances in favour of bringing the listener the more contemporary Glastonbury experience. Opening with two of the biggest bands to headline in recent times: COLDPLAY (with 'Politik') and RADIOHEAD (with 'Fake Plastic Trees') hardly evokes the joyful festival experience, rather evoking the damp, muddy days and dark, rainy nights familiar to regulars. Instead it is left to the likes of CLINT EASTWOOD & GENERAL SAINT to bring a touch of summer sunshine goodtimes with the breezy 'Stop That Train' before an incendiary rendition of the PRODIGY's 'Firestarter', one of the few highlights here, bursts forth ripping apart all that had gone before it leaving you feeling like you are really there face to face with the menacing Keith Flint. Whilst dominated by indie rock there is still time for a few dance tracks with Glastonbury essentials such as the spiritual rave-lite of FAITHLESS' crowd favourite 'We Come One', the CHEMICAL BROTHERS' 'Hey Boy, Hey Girl' and ORBITAL presenting their own block-rocking-beats in the form of the ten-minute 'Impact'. There is a fair amount of reggae here too with TOOTS & THE MAYTALS, the WAILERS and the joyful trumpeting of the SKATALITES' 'Phoenix City'. Unfortunately, the diversity almost ends there, with the presence of World Music in the form of TINAWAREN feeling like a token gesture to appease festival purists. Indeed there is a sense of trying to capture the zeitgeist here with the inclusion of Glastonbury newcomers over regular acts, so we are forced to endure the awful shite that is the BRAVERY with their embarrassingly fake English accents and it is also questionable why DAVID GRAY and SCISSOR SISTERS are included whilst the likes of DAVID BOWIE and the WHITE STRIPES are overlooked. And I'm sure they could have found a better MORRISSEY song in the archives than the plodding 'First Of The Gang To Die' and ditto the turgid version of BJORK's 'Human Behaviour'. At least BABYSHAMBLES' crowd-milking 'Kilimangiro' is purposefully ramshackle, like the perennial Glastonbury patron JOE STRUMMER whose performance of 'Straight To Hell' with the MESCALEROS is inciting and evocative. Elsewhere we are treated to a touch of jazz on the ice-cool DR JOHN's stopstart 'Right Place, Wrong Time' and the floating heavy psychedelic grooves of ALICE COLTRANE's 'Journey Into Satchidananda'. Rather irritatingly the continuity of the soundtrack is blighted by a peppering of audio clips of festival revellers' joyful exclamations, stoned mumblings and self-righteous new-age bullshit. Thankfully included is perhaps the quintessential modern Glastonbury moment, the era defining crowd sing-along that was PULP's passionate read-through of 'Common People' from 1995. Essentially, this collection could have been more eclectic, with recent recordings being favoured over an expansive archive of legendary artists and show stopping performances. Sadly it can only offer a disappointingly inconsistent snapshot of the iconic festival. *LF*

Album rating: *6.5

□ GO GO MANIA alt.
(⇒ POP GEAR)

GODFATHERS AND SONS

5th part of Martin Scorsese presents THE BLUES

2003 (US 120m w/b&w TV-mini) Vulcan Productions / PBS (15)

Film genre: Blues-music documentary

Top guns: dir: Marc Levin ← BROOKLYN BABYLON ← WHITEBOYS

Stars: Chuck D *(himself)* ← RHYME & REASON, Marshall Chess *(himself)* ← DOWNTOWN 81 ← COCKSUCKER BLUES, **Howlin' Wolf** *(archive performer)* ← FESTIVAL / → the ROAD TO MEMPHIS, **KoKo Taylor** *(performer)* ← BLUES BROTHERS 2000 ← WILD AT HEART ← CHICAGO BLUES, **Buddy Guy** *(performer)* ← the ROAD TO MEMPHIS ← BLUES ODYSSEY ← CHICAGO BLUES ← SUPERSHOW / → FESTIVAL EXPRESS → LIGHTNING IN A BOTTLE, **Magic Slim** *(performer)*, **Ike Turner** *(performer)* ← BLUES ODYSSEY ← SOUL TO SOUL ← GIMME SHELTER ← IT'S YOUR THING ← the BIG T.N.T. SHOW, **Jimmy Rogers** *(performer)*, **Jimmy Reed** *(performer)*, **Otis Rush** *(performer)* ← BLUES ODYSSEY, **Etta James** *(performer)*, **Little Walter** *(performer)*, **Common** *(performer)* ← BROWN SUGAR / → 5 SIDES OF A COIN → BEEF → FADE TO BLACK → BLOCK PARTY, **Bob DYLAN** *(performer)*, **Paul Putterfield Blues Band** *(performer)* ← the LAST WALTZ ← STEELYARD BLUES ← YOU ARE WHAT YOU EAT ← FESTIVAL, **Lonnie Brooks** *(performer)* ← BLUES BROTHERS 2000 ← PRIDE AND JOY, **Johnny Juice Rosado** *(performer)*

Storyline: A 'Chess' history with a difference, influenced by cult Rolling Stones rockumentaries 'Cocksucker Blues' (with rare footage) and 'Gimme Shelter', and taking the fruits of a link-up between militant hip hop icon Chuck D and Jewish blues godfather Marshall Chess (itself definitively laying to rest misplaced accusations of anti-semitism from the Public Enemy days) as its central thrust, with the usual archive footage and anecdote from survivors of the label's heyday. *BG*

Movie rating: *7

Visual: dvd on 'Pinnacle' (SMADVD 034)

Off the record:

—

Various Artists

Sep 03. (cd) *Hip-O; <00006270-2>* □ [-]
– Chicago bound (JIMMY ROGERS) / Mannish boy (MUDDY WATERS) / Spoonful (HOWLIN' WOLF) / I cry and sing the blues (BUDDY GUY) / Bright lights, big city (JIMMY REED) / Evil (is going on) (HOWLIN' WOLF) / Key to the highway (LITTLE WALTER) / Wang dang doodle (KOKO TAYLOR) / The red rooster (HOWLIN' WOLF) / I got what it takes (KOKO TAYLOR) / Walking the backstreets and crying – live (OTIS RUSH) / (I'm your) Hoochie coochie man (MUDDY WATERS) / Feel good doin' bad (LONNIE BROOKS) / Diddley daddy (BO DIDDLEY) / Talk to me baby (I can't hold out) (MAGIC SLIM & THE TEARDROPS) / Born in Chicago (the PAUL BUTTERFIELD BLUES BAND) / Shake your money maker (the PAUL BUTTERFIELD BLUES BAND) / Maggie's farm (BOB DYLAN) / Show 'em whatcha got (PUBLIC ENEMY) / Dooinit (COMMON) / Mannish boy (the ELECTRIK MUD KATS) / I'd rather go blind (ETTA JAMES).

S/track review: Because it tells the story of a label rather than a city, a myth or a sub-genre, this volume of the Scorsese series is the most populist of the lot, a bonanza of electric standards from the cauldron of Chicago blues. 'Chess' have compiled plenty of their own anthologies in the past and MUDDY WATERS, PAUL BUTTERFIELD and MIKE BLOOMFIELD are all veterans from the in-house early 80s project, 'Fathers And Sons' (presumably the inspiration behind Levin's title), so what makes this one different? Well, specifically the film's premise of hip-hop luminaries CHUCK D and COMMON teaming up with the band – the mighty PHIL UPCHURCH and electric era Miles Davis acolyte Pete Cosey among them – who originally backed WATERS on his psychedelic albatross, 'Electric Mud' (1968). They pile through a swirling reprise of 'Mannish Boy' guaranteed to horrify purists but likely not so alien to those attuned to the more wayward experiments of Prince. And with its siren horn and conscious rhetoric, PUBLIC ENEMY's 'Show 'Em Whatcha Got' is surprisingly congruent with the 'Chess' plunder, COMMON's 'Dooinit' less so. The soundtrack also sells itself on an OTIS RUSH track recorded at the 2001 Chicago Blues Festival, a LONNIE BROOKS cut from the same year and a shuddering contribution from Windy City flame-keepers MAGIC SLIM & THE TEARDROPS, all live and previously unreleased. Next to the ELEKTRIK MUD KATS, they're purist to the black cat bone, but work well as adjuncts to the main event of gutteral parables from HOWLIN' WOLF, amazon warrior blues from the underrated KOKO TAYLOR (the just as unsung Gene Barge blows as fiercely on her 'Wang Dang Doodle' as he does on the 'Mannish Boy' re-run) and emblematic emigration anthems from JIMMY ROGERS and REED, as well as another tribal-twang example of how BO DIDDLEY fired a metaphorical rocket up the collective arse of a Rolling Stones that hadn't even formed in 1955. The BLOOMFIELD connection even warrants the inclusion of BOB DYLAN's Newport depth-charge, 'Maggie's Farm', not so unusual when you consider that the under-written influence of the blues on DYLAN's career could've made a volume in its own right. *BG*

Album rating: *8.5

GOOD TO SEE YOU AGAIN, ALICE COOPER

1974 (US 81m w/b&w; edited) Penthouse Productions (18)

Film genre: Rock-music concert/documentary

Top guns: s-w: (+ dir) Joe Gannon, Shep Gordon, Fred Smoot

Stars: Alice Cooper:- Alice COOPER *(himself/performer)*, **Dennis Dunaway, Michael Bruce, Neal Smith, Glen Buxton** *(themselves/performers)*, **Mick Mashbir** *(guitarist)*, **Bob Dolin** *(keyboardist)*, James Randi *(dentist/executioner)*, Cindy Smith *(Dancing Tooth)*, Richard M. Dixon *(President Nixon)* → WHERE THE BUFFALO ROAM, Jefferson Kewley *(Baron Krelve/henchman)*, Pat McAllister *(producer/box office manager/rancher)*, Fred Smoot *(security guard/director/lone ranger)*

Storyline: Alice Cooper – the band! – are captured at the height of their career live on their 1973 Billion Dollar Babies tour (actually 28th & 29th April at Dallas and Houston, Texas, respectfully), all the shocking theatrics, sleazy glam-rock and even a couple of role-playing skits by the band themselves – pre-dating that Led Zep movie by a couple of years. *MCS*

Movie rating: *7.5

Visual: dvd in 2005 on 'Shout! Factory' (no audio OST)

Off the record: ALICE COOPER perform 'Never Been Sold Before', 'Hello, Hooray', 'Billion Dollar Babies', 'Elected', 'I'm Eighteen', 'Raped And Freezin'', 'No More Mr. Nice Guy', 'My Stars', 'Unfinished Sweet', 'Sick Things', 'Dead Babies', 'I Love The Dead', 'School's Out', 'Under My Wheels', 'The Lady Is A Tramp' & 'Hard Hearted Alice' on end credits. *MCS*

GOODNIGHT CLEVELAND

aka the HELLACOPTERS: GOODNIGHT CLEVELAND

2002 (Swe 48m TV; ext.114m dvd) 8th Grade Films

Film genre: Heavy-metal/Hard-rock-music concert/documentary

Top guns: dir: Jim Heneghan

Stars: the Hellacopters:- Nicke Andersson, Robert Dahlqvist, Anders "Bobba Fett" Lindstrom, Kenny Hakansson, Robert Eriksson *(themselves/performers)*, **Scott Morgon** *(performer)*, **Gaza Strippers:- Rick Sims, Darren Hooper, Mark Allen, Mike Hodgkiss** *(themselves)*

Storyline: A "fly on the wall" portrait of one of Sweden's biggest hard-rock exports in years, the Hellacopters, on their 2002 tour around America. "Goodnight Cleveland" is a THIS IS SPINAL TAP reference to the fact they mis-quoted "Hello Cleveland" in their 1984 mockumentary. *MCS*

Movie rating: *6 (ext.dvd *7)

Visual: dvd Nov'03 (no audio OST; score: Jim Heneghan)

Off the record: The **the Hellacopters** were formed in Stockholm, Sweden . . . 1994 by drummer/songwriter-turned-guitarist, **Nicke Andersson** (aka Nick Royale), as a stop-gap project while his regular band, the Entombed, tried to obtain a new record deal. Nicke enlisted the help of childhood chum, **Robert Eriksson** (bass), **Ask Dregen** (guitarist of the Backyard Babies) and drummer **Kenny Hakansson**, indulging his passion for bluesy, anthemic punk/metal in the vein of MC5 or Kiss. The mainman subsequently made this bunch a full-time project in '97 after finally leaving his beloved Entombed. It was on the 14th & 15th of June that year that the Hellacopters were to support their heroes KISS in Stockholm. Significantly more prolific than Nicke's previous outfit, the airborne metallers released a plethora of 45's (on various labels – including their own 'White Jazz') alongside three albums, 'Supershitty To The Max!' (1996), 'Payin' The Dues' (1997) and 'Disappointment Blues' (1998). Further sets, 'Grande Rock' (1999), 'High Visibility' (2000) and 'By The Grace Of God' (2002), witnessed the Swedes going from strength to strength, shaving down the rougher edges and further refining their revisionary take on 70s rock yet losing none of their sharpness or earthy power in the process. *MCS*

the GOSPEL ROAD

1973 (US 86m) 20th Century Fox (G)

Film genre: Country-music documentary drama

Top guns: dir: Robert Elfstrom ← NASHVILLE SOUND ← the MAN, HIS WORLD, HIS MUSIC / s-w: **Johnny CASH**, Larry Murray

Stars: Johnny CASH *(himself/narrator)*, Robert Elfstrom *(Jesus Christ)*, **June Carter Cash** *(Mary Magdalene)* ← JOHNNY CASH AT SAN QUENTIN ← the MAN, HIS WORLD, HIS MUSIC ← ROAD TO NASHVILLE ← COUNTRY MUSIC HOLIDAY / → THAT'S COUNTRY, Larry Lee *(John the Baptist)*, Paul Smith *(Peter)* → POPEYE, Alan Dater *(Nicodemus)*

Storyline: Shot in Israel, the man in black, Johnny Cash (now deep into religious gospel music), swops his cowboy boots for sandals in this Jesus Christ narrative. Praise the Lord it wasn't longer. *MCS*

Movie rating: *3.5

Visual: video + dvd in 2006

Off the record: Johnny CASH described the film as "my life's proudest moment". *MCS*

JOHNNY CASH

Jun 73. (d-lp) *Columbia; <KG2 32253> (CBS 68243)* ☐ ☐
– Praise the Lord (introduction) / Gospel road – part 1 (Jesus' early years) / Gospel road – part 2 (John the Baptist) – (baptism of Jesus) / Gospel road – part 3 (wilderness temptation) / He turned the water into wine (the first miracle) / I see men as trees walking (the state of the nation) / Jesus was a carpenter (choosing of twelve disciples) / Help – part 1 (Jesus teachings: parables of the good shepherd) / Help – part 2 (sermon on the mount) / Follow me (with JUNE CARTER) (Mary Magdalene speaks) // He turned the water into wine (crossing the Sea of Galilee) / He turned the water into wine – part 2 (feeding the multitude) / He turned the water into wine – part 3 / Gospel road (the raising of Lazarus) / Help (song of the children) / The burden of freedom / Lord, is it I? (the feast of the passover) / The last supper / The burden of freedom (he is risen) / Jesus was a carpenter.

S/track review: JOHNNY CASH was sliding towards rock'n'roll obscurity when he made this double-set document of the life and times of Jesus Christ; for several years the man in black had been into the man in white. Courageous to a fault, this Jesus CASH-in was too much for pure C&W fans, its endless narration too monotonous for his long-time audience. However, the record did feature several like-minded songwriters, KRIS KRISTOFFERSON, JOHN DENVER, JOE SOUTH, CHRISTOPHER WREN and of course, CASH himself. I suppose if I had to pick one track from the bunch it would be his duet-of-sorts, 'Follow Me' (Mary Magdalene speaks) with wife JUNE CARTER. It was no surprise when the ambitious set only hit No.12 in the Country music charts. *MCS*

Album rating: *3

GRATEFUL DAWG

2000 (US 81m) 11th Hour Productions./ Acoustic Disc

Film genre: Bluegrass-music concert/documentary

Top guns: dir: Gillian Grisman

Stars: **Jerry Garcia** *(performer)* <= the GRATEFUL DEAD =>, **David Grisman** *(performer)*, **Joe Craven** *(performer)*, **Ricky Jay** *(performer)*, **Jim Kerwin** *(performer)*

Storyline: "Beards of a feather" is Gillian Grisman's waggish description of her husband's longstanding bond with the late Jerry Garcia, a relationship which dates back to a chance meeting at a 1964 Bill Monroe gig. Here, she traces its serpentine course through early clips of a short-haired, shirt and tied Garcia brooding on a violin, fond memories of the pair's 70s bluegrass ensemble Old & In The Way and enough informal latter day jamming and rare footage (including a previously unreleased video for 'The Thrill Is Gone') to satsify most roots fans and stray Deadheads. As Mrs Grisman makes clear in her notes, this is a film "about the music, not about people talking about the music". *BG*

Movie rating: *7.5

Visual: dvd

Off the record: Although mandolinist **David Grisman** (b.23 Mar'45, Hackensack, New Jersey, USA) has been an ever present – if commercially marginal – figure in American popular music since the early 60s, the difficulty in pigeonholing his art means you won't find him in many music encyclopedias. And while his most famous outing remains the Grateful Dead's roots masterpiece, 'American Beauty' (1970), Grisman has straddled the mutually exclusive genres of bluegrass and jazz with freewheeling ease, playing with everyone from Stephane Grappelli and Béla Fleck to a solo Jerry Garcia, and virtually inventing the new-acoustic genre (or "Dawg Music", as the man himself christened it). He also made a brief diversion into film scoring with such unlikely low-buget efforts as 'Big Bad Mama' (1974), 'Capone' (1975) and 'Eat My Dust!' (1976), as well as Frank Pierson's Romany melodrama, 'King Of The Gypsies' (1978). *BG*

—

JERRY GARCIA & DAVID GRISMAN (& Various Artists)

Sep 01. (cd) *Acoustic Disc; <(ACD 46)>* □ □
– Intro / Grateful dawg (live) / Wayfaring stranger (BILL MONROE) / Sweet sunny south / Old & In The Way intro (PETER ROWAN) / Pig in a pen (OLD & IN THE WAY) / Dawg's waltz / Sitting here in limbo / Off to sea once more (EWAN MacCOLL) / Off to sea once more / Jenny Jenkins / Arabia / The thrill is gone / Friend of the Devil / Grateful dawg (studio).

S/track review: This wasn't JERRY GARCIA's first soundtrack appearance (an honour that goes to 'ZABRISKIE POINT') but it's the only one he had all to himself, well almost. The title – and opening track – refers to the joyful splicing of JERRY GARCIA and his impressively hirsute pal DAVID GRISMAN's respective styles: the former's jazzy, wide-horizon guitar playing and the latter's fleet-fingered mandolin picking. Jazz bible Downbeat dubbed it "a hippie equivalent to.. Stephane Grappelli and Django Reinhardt", and it's a combination that lends itself equally well to pure bluegrass, ethnic-tinged improvisation and folk-soul-reggae. Afficionados of either artist will likely be familiar with most of the studio material, but the rare live performances – the bulk of them recorded at San Francisco's Warfield Theater – make it worth searching out. If JERRY occasionally toils a bit vocally (hardly surprising given his ailing health), he pours days, weeks, months and years of hard-truckin' into Jimmy Cliff's 'Sitting In Limbo', a revelatory cover and as tender a memento as you'll hear anywhere. 'Arabia' is another unexpected highlight, an extended imaginary tour of North Africa and the Middle East, strung out on pendulous arpeggios and rattling percussion. While the inclusion of both BILL MONROE's 'Wayfaring Stranger' and EWAN MacCOLL's 'Off To Sea Once More' (back to back with the faithful Dawg version), sets the GARCIA/GRISMAN trip in some kind of historical context, they take up space that might've been filled with more live material, and 'GRATEFUL DAWG' ends up more as an excellent primer for the curious than a must-have for diehards. *BG*

Album rating: *7

GRATEFUL DEAD

Formed: San Francisco, California, USA . . . 1965 initially as the Warlocks, by JERRY GARCIA, lyricist Robert Hunter, Bob Weir, Ron McKernan (aka Pigpen), bolstering the sound with drummer Bill Kreutzmann and bassist Phil Lesh. In 1966, the GRATEFUL DEAD issued a one-off 45, 'Don't Ease Me In' for 'Fantasy' off-shoot label 'Scorpio', which led to 'Warners' signing them up the following year. Recorded in three amphetamine-fuelled days, 'The Grateful Dead' was released to the expectant hippy faithful that December, an admirable but untimately doomed attempt to recreate their fabled live sound in the studio. After an impromptu guest spot at one of their early shows, drummer Mickey Hart augmented the band's rhythm section, creating a more subtly complex rather than powerful sound. The group also recruited keyboardist Tom Constanten, whose avant-garde influences included John Cage and Stockhausen. Adding to the Dead's psychedelic stew, these two further inspired the band's live improvisation, partly captured on 'Anthem Of The Sun' (1968). An ambitious collage of live and studio pieces, the album was another flawed attempt to seize the essence of the elusive beast that was the band's live show. The experimentation continued with 'Aoxomoxoa' (1969), GARCIA's old mate Robert Hunter marking his first collaboration with the band and helping to contain the explorations inside defined song structures. With the release of 'Live Dead' in 1970, the GRATEFUL DEAD finally did itself justice on vinyl, silencing the critics of their previous output who couldn't understand why the band were held in such high esteem by their fiercely loyal San Franciscan fanbase. On the track 'Dark Star', the band crystallised their free-flowing improvisation in breathtaking style. Attracting multitudes of tye-dyed freaks, affectionately nicknamed "Deadheads", the band's gigs became communal gatherings, where both the crowd and band could lose themselves in the spaced-out jams which would often stretch songs over an hour or more. Forget 15 minutes of fame (as Andy Warhol once gave us all), the 'Dead needed 15 minutes just for the intro! Ironically the band's next two studio albums marked a radical new direction with pared-down sets of harmony laden country-folk. With Constanten out of the picture by early 1970 and mounting debts, the group went for a simpler sound, clearly influenced by CROSBY, STILLS & NASH and GARCIA's part-time dabblings with the New Riders Of The Purple Sage. 'Workingman's Dead' (1970) was symptomatic of the times as bands began to move away from the psychedelic claustrophobia of the late 60s (note 'New Speedway Boogie' about the end of the hippy dream; the Altamont Festival at which a ROLLING STONES fan was killed by a drug-crazed Hell's Angel). 'American Beauty' (1970) carried on where the previous album left off, 'Sugar Magnolia' and 'Ripple' being the highlights of this highly regarded piece of roots rock. By 1971, Hart had departed and the band were reduced to five core members. Two live albums followed, the double 'Grateful Dead' and 'Europe 72', the latter stretching to three slabs of vinyl. Years of alcohol abuse led to Pigpen dying on 6th of May '73, liver failure was the coroner's verdict – he was only 27. He was subsequently replaced by Keith Godchaux, who had toured with them the previous year; his wife Donna also joined, taking up vocal duties. Around this time the band set up their own label, imaginatively titled 'Grateful Dead' records, releasing 'Wake Of The Flood' in July '73. The album was their most successful to date, although ironically, profits were lost to bootleggers. 'Blues For Allah' (1975), signalled a jazzier, fuller sound, though by this juncture the band were in financial deep water, the result was their reluctant signature with 'United Artists'. The source of much of their money problems was a concert movie which ate up most of their resources. 'Steal Your Face' was next in line and was intended for 'The GRATEFUL DEAD (MOVIE)', although the film went straight-to-video due to the double album's relative critical failure. Signing to 'Arista' and drafting in Keith Olsen on production duties they released 'Terrapin Station' (1977), while 'Shakedown Street' (1978), was a pale reflection of what the 'Dead were capable of. Despite the inconsistent quality of their studio work, the Dead were always a safe live bet and they played the gig to surely top all gigs with their series of dates at the Pyramids in Egypt. Still carrying a hippy torch (even through the punk days), they filled large venues wherever they played and became a multi-million dollar industry in their own right. However, as they concentrated on live work, their studio outings suffered, their 1980 album 'Go To Heaven' being particularly disappointing although it spawned their first success in the US singles chart with 'Alabama Getaway'. Another two live sets followed in 1981, 'Dead Set' and the acoustic 'Reckoning'. Soon after their release, GARCIA became a full blown heroin addict, narrowly escaping death when he fell into a diabetic coma in in 1986. Once he rehabilitated, the 'Dead came back to life with 'In The Dark', a spirited set that reached the Top 10 in the US chart, even resulting in top selling 45, 'Touch Of Grey'. Their tribute to growing old with pride, it was a first when the band agreed to make a video for MTV. The awful 'Dylan & The Dead' (yes with Mr. Zimmerman) was muted and dull, as was the studio 1989 offering, 'Built To Last'. Tragedy hit the band yet again, when keyboardist Brent Mydland (who'd replaced Keith in '79) was killed by a hard drugs cocktail. Bruce Hornsby (yes that solo geezer) was drafted in temporarily for touring commitments, while Vince Welnick joined full-time. The band released yet another live album the same year, the hardly dangerous 'Without A Net' and also started issuing the "Dick's Picks" series of archive recordings from great days of yore. On the 9th August, 1995, the ailing JERRY GARCIA died of heart failure in a rehab unit after his arteries clogged up. It seemed inevitable that the long strange trip of the GRATEFUL DEAD had come to an end, GARCIA's guiding light relocating to find his "Dark Star" once again. The Dead left behind a rich musical legacy, including numerous solo outings and off-shoot projects, but will always be remembered, by the Deadheads at least, for their transcendental live performances. The posthumously released film, 'GRATEFUL DAWG' (alongside DAVID GRISMAN), saw GARCIA performing at his very best, a testament to the man with the big beard. *BG & MCS*

- **filmography** (composers) {performers} –

Petulia *(1968 {c}; see future edition)* / **Gimme Shelter** *(1970 {p} =>)* / **Zabriskie Point** *(1970 GARCIA on OST by PINK FLOYD & V/A =>)* / **Fillmore** *(1972 {p} on OST w/ V/A =>)* / **the Grateful Dead Movie** *(1977 OST rel.2005 =>)* / Heartbeeps *(1981 {v JERRY}; see future edition)* / Hell's Angels Forever *(1983 {c JERRY})* / Gang Related *(1997 score HART)* / **Grateful Dawg** *(2000 {p JERRY} OST by GARCIA & DAVID GRISMAN =>)* / **Hellhounds On My Trail** *(2000 {c BOB} =>)* / **the End Of The Road: The Final Tour 2001** *(2001 {p} GARCIA & MERL SAUNDERS score =>)* / the Journey *(2001 {c JERRY})* / **Festival Express** *(2003 {p} =>)* / Go Further *(2003 {c BOB})* / **Electric Apricot** *(2006 {c BOB} =>)* / Wetlands Preserved: The Story Of An Activist Rock Club *(2006 {c BOB} =>)*

the GRATEFUL DEAD "movie"

1977 (US 131m) Electrascope / Monarch Films / Noteworthy

Film genre: Rock-music concert/documentary

Top guns: dir: **Jerry Garcia**, Leon Gast ← OUR LATIN THING

Stars: the GRATEFUL DEAD:- Jerry Garcia, Bob Weir, Phil Lesh, Bill Kreutzmann, Keith Godchaux, Donna Godchaux + Mickey Hart *(themselves/performers)*, Betty Cantor *(herself)*, John Perry Barlow *(himself)*

Storyline: A labour of love for the late Jerry Garcia, this marathon concert/rockumentary was snipped from a rumoured five hours of footage, shining a lovelight on America's stoned-est band just as their finances and momentum reached tipping point in the mid-70s. Preaching to the faithful over the course of a mini-residency at San Francisco's Winterland Ballroom, they bid intrepid adieu to the road with typically elongated versions of freak flag-waving anthems old and new, shot through with lurid, American icon-busting animation, the anatomy of which, for those straight enough to pay attention, is explained on the DVD's inevitable bonus disc. *BG*

Movie rating: *7.5

Visual: video by Monterey + 2005 expanded dvd

Off the record: (see below)

—

the GRATEFUL DEAD: The Grateful Dead Movie Soundtrack

Mar 05. (5xcd-box) *Rhino; <(8122 79583-2)>*
– U.S. blues / One more Saturday night / China cat sunflower / I know you rider / Eyes of the world / China doll / Playing in the band // Scarlet begonias / He's gone / Jam / Weirdness / The other one / Spanish jam / Mind left body jam / Other jam / Stella blue / Casey Jones // Weather Report suite / Jam / Dark star / Morning dew / Not fade away / Goin' down the road feeling bad // Uncle John's band / Big railroad blues / Tomorrow is forever / Sugar magnolia / He's gone / Caution jam / Drums / Space / Truckin' / Black Peter / Sunshine daydream // Playing in the band / Drums / Not fade away / Drums / The other one / Wharf rat / Playing in the band / Johnny B. Goode / Mississippi half-step uptown toodeloo / We bid you goodnight.

S/track review: Hang on to your headband and gird your inner loins – a five disc trip into the heart of 'Dead-land isn't to be taken lightly, at least not on an empty brain. Measured by today's 3-second attention span, it equates to a mental circumnavigation of the globe. Longtime 'Heads know the formula by now: double/triple/quadruple/Dick's Picks/God Knows How Many More From The Vault, jams extended to the point of no return. Many venerable authorities are agreed, however, that this sonically pristine bonanza is the pinnacle of live 'Deadheadedness, recorded over a series of Winterland gigs in autumn '74, prior to a two year truckin' sabbatical. And if you're of the opinion that, in this band's case, quantity is all, you'll be glad to hear it has significantly more material than the DVD. Conversely, if the name GRATEFUL DEAD strikes hoary old fear into your pop-picking heart, chances are there's something here for you as well. San Francisco's legendary jam-cadets are arguably one of the most misrepresented bands of all time; it's surprising how many people don't actually realise they recorded their fair share of pop-psych ditties (check out 'The Golden Road To Unlimited Devotion' from their first album) and – strapped for cash and down on their luck – sublime country-rock, songs short and hooky enough for mainstream radio. Perversely, their only hit came in 1987 (1987!!!) with the droll 'Touch Of Grey', but anyone can appreciate the likes of the spirit-surging 'Playing In The Band' (so good they packaged it thrice, twice on disc five . . .) or at least the first three minutes of it. It's also just about the best example of JERRY GARCIA's soulful if slight singing and hairpin phrasing/harmonies (in tandem with DONNA GODCHAUX, who weighs in with some great, industrial-strength wailing herself) on the whole five discs, and if you're going to get to grips with the jam mentality, this – or else the keening 'Scarlet Begonias' (more GODCHAUX) on disc two – is a good place to start (with relatively abbreviated versions of 'US Blues', 'One More Saturday Night' and the tender, eerie ballad, 'China Doll', as well as the uncharacteristically featherweight 'Eyes Of The World', the whole of disc one is fairly accessible): just imagine you're listening to a simpler, one-chord variable jazz record. Failing that, fast forward to the wavy gravy, cocaine-train thrill of 'Casey Jones' (a mere five minutes), and then go out and buy 'Workingman's Dead' instead. Intermediates can get stuck in to the gorgeous 'Weather Report Suite' and 'Morning Dew', both exquisitely structured quarter of an hour marathons circumscribing blues, folk, country and jazz as only this band could, and both highlights of a consistently strong disc three which makes a case for being one of the best concert sides in the band's archive. It's where the iconic 'Dark Star' nestles, fielding GARCIA's space-dust picking and PHIL LESH's seer-like bass lines in a sequence of arcs, crescents and solar flares between '. . .Dew' and some conspicuously 'In A Silent Way'-esque keyboard jamming. Surprisingly, it doesn't represent the real hard stuff (although at almost half an hour, it's no nod in the park); for that, hark the seemingly interminable series of roaming, mid-length improvisations spanning most of disc two: the scrabbling progressions in the mid-section of 'Weirdness' knocking on the intensity of Miles Davis' 'Live Evil'; the scant vocal relief coming courtesy of a single verse and chorus in 'The Other One'. Disc four takes it right back to beginner's territory with upbeat, melodic sashays through 'Uncle John's Band', the peerless 'Sugar Magnolia' (still the band's best song, if not the best rendition) and its soaring coda, 'Sunshine Daydream', as well as their talismanic road anthem, 'Truckin', and a decent cover of Dolly Parton's 'Tomorrow Is Forever'. If you make it to disc five you can congratulate yourself for passing your own mini acid test, before steeling yourself for the much-touted return of percussion high priest MICKEY HART after his own near four year sabbatical. As well as mandatory drum solos (two, at five minutes a pop) from both HART and BILL KREUTZMANN, the disc focuses on the band's questionable fondness for extemporising on mouldy old rock'n'roll/R&B chestnuts. As such, it's arguably the most negligible of the lot. But if there's a real gripe with this box set, it's that the normally exhaustive 'Rhino' have neglected to furnish any sleevenotes in favour of trippy stills/live shots. Fair enough, music as singular as this probably speaks for itself but some background info on the gigs would've been nice. Still, if "classic", live, improvisatory rock music is your cup of pipe and slippers, you'll be smoking this till your lungs burst and your hush puppies burn from your soles. *BG*

Album rating: *8

– associated release – (*)

GRATEFUL DEAD: Steal Your Face! *(live 16-20 October 1974)*

Jun 76. (d-lp) *United Artists; <LA 620> (UAD 60131-2)* 56 42
– The promised land / Cold rain and snow / Around and around / Stella blue (*) / Mississippi half-step uptown toodeloo / Ship of fools / Beat it down the line (*) / Big river / Black-throated wind / U.S. blues (*) / El Paso / Sugaree / It must have been the roses (*) / Casey Jones (*). *(re-iss. Mar89 on 'Grateful Dead' lp/c/cd; GDV2/GDTCGDCD2 4006) (pic-cd Feb90; GDPD2 4006)*

□ the GREAT ROCK'N'ROLL SWINDLE
(⇒ Rock Movies/Musicals..)

□ David GRISMAN segment
(⇒ GRATEFUL DAWG)

GROUPIES

1970 (US 84m) First International Television Song Festival (18)

Film genre: Rock-music documentary

Top guns: dir: Ron Dorfman, Peter Nevard

Stars: Joe COCKER *(performer)*, **Ten Years After:- Alvin Lee, Ric Lee, Leo Lyons, Chick Churchill** *(performers)* ← WOODSTOCK / → MESSAGE TO LOVE: THE ISLE OF WIGHT FESTIVAL, **Spooky Tooth** *(performers)*, **Terry Reid** *(performer)*, **Dry Creek Road** *(performers)*, Cynthia Albritton *(Cynthia Plaster Caster)*, Miss Harlow *(herself)*, Patty Cakes *(herself)*, Lixie *(herself)*, Goldie Glitters *(himself)*, Chaz *(himself)*,

Storyline: Described and billed as "A wild experience, an eye-and-ear blowing trip into Weirdsville USA", this rock doc centres around the people (female and male!) behind the bands: the groupies. *MCS*

Movie rating: *4

Visual: video + dvd (no audio OST)

Off the record: TEN YEARS AFTER contributed a couple of Sonny Boy Williamson-penned tracks, 'Good Morning Little Schoolgirl' and 'Help Me Baby', JOE COCKER performed Leon Russell's 'Delta Lady', TERRY REID covered Sonny Bono's 'Bang Bang', and SPOOKY TOOTH delivered 'Fillmore Rehearsal Sessions'. *MCS*

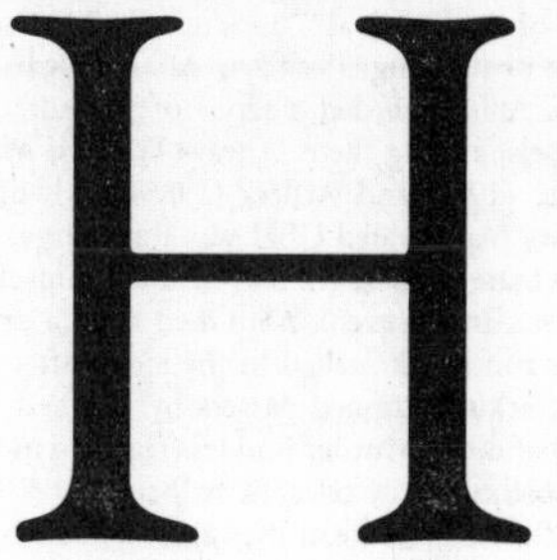

□ Nina HAGEN segment
(⇒ NINA HAGEN = PUNK + GLORY)

HAIL! HAIL! ROCK'N'ROLL

aka CHUCK BERRY: HAIL! HAIL! ROCK'N'ROLL

1987 (US 121m) Universal Pictures (PG)

Film genre: R&B/Rock'n'roll-music concert/documentary

Top guns: dir: Taylor Hackford ← the IDOLMAKER / → RAY

Stars: Chuck BERRY *(performer)*, **Eric CLAPTON** *(performer)*, **Robert Cray** *(performer)* ← ANIMAL HOUSE, **Etta James** *(performer)*, **Keith Richards** *(performer)* <= the ROLLING STONES =>, **Linda Ronstadt** *(performer)* ← UNCLE MEAT ← FM / → MAYOR OF THE SUNSET STRIP, **LITTLE RICHARD** *(performer)*, **Julian Lennon** *(performer)* → IMAGINE: JOHN LENNON, **the Everly Brothers:- Phil & Don** *(performers)* ← the COMPLEAT BEATLES, **Jerry Lee LEWIS** *(performer)*, **Bo DIDDLEY** *(performer)*, **Roy ORBISON** *(performer)*, **Bruce SPRINGSTEEN** *(himself)*, **Chuck Leavell** *(performer)* G→ AT THE MAX, **Bobby Keys** *(performer)* ← LET'S SPEND THE NIGHT TOGETHER ← LADIES AND GENTLEMEN, THE ROLLING STONES ← MAD DOGS & ENGLISHMEN / → AT THE MAX, **Johnnie Johnson** *(performer)*, **Steve Jordan** *(performer)* → LIGHTNING IN A BOTTLE → MAKE IT FUNKY!

Storyline: Chuck Berry's 60th birthday is celebrated with a concert at the Fox Theatre, St. Louis, Missouri. Keith Richards gathers a plethora of major musicians and singers to back the one-time king of R&B, while there's also added archival footage of the man dating back to his halcyon 50s days. *MCS*

Movie rating: *7.5

Visual: video

Off the record: Julian Lennon (son of Beatle, John, of course), had already a string of hits behind him, 'Valotte' & 'Too Late To Say Goodbye', among them.

—

CHUCK BERRY (w/ * guest performers)

Nov 87. (lp/c/cd) *M.C.A.; <MCA/+C/D 6217> (MCF/MCFC/DMCF 3411)* □ Feb88 □
– Maybellene / Around and around / Sweet little sixteen / Brown eyed handsome man (*: ROBERT CRAY) / Memphis Tennessee / Too much monkey business / Back in the U.S.A. (*: LINDA RONSTADT) / Wee wee hours (*: ERIC CLAPTON) / Johnny B. Goode (*: JULIAN LENNON) / Little Queenie / Rock and roll music (*: ETTA JAMES) / Roll over Beethoven / I'm through with love.

S/track review: If this was just down to a certain CHUCK BERRY and his group performing a 60th birthday concert (recorded on 16th October 1986), we all know there just wouldn't've been the movie. However, with a band that included guitarist KEITH RICHARDS (also the producer), JOEY SPAMPINATO (bass), STEVE JORDAN (drums), JOHNNIE JOHNSON (piano), CHUCK LEAVELL (keyboards) and BOBBY KEYS (saxophone) – plus the guests! – one is listening to a piece of history, much like the way Roy Orbison – & friends – completed 'BLACK & WHITE NIGHT' around the same time. On film, 'HAIL! HAIL! . . .' works a treat, on record it understandably falls a little short – to only imagine CHUCK's goose-step guitar-playing is frustrating. All his greats are here, 'Maybellene', 'Around And Around', his risqué 'Sweet Little Sixteen', 'Memphis, Tennessee', 'Too Much Monkey Business', 'Little Queenie' and 'Roll Over Beethoven', while his party guests just kept the place "reelin and a rockin". Side by side with an iconic Stone, BERRY and his guests trot out even more R&B gems such as 'Brown Eyed Handsome Man' (introducing ROBERT CRAY), 'Back In The U.S.A.' (featuring a reinvigorated and raunchified LINDA RONSTADT), 'Wee Wee Hours' (by ERIC CLAPTON), 'Johnny B. Goode' (with JULIAN LENNON) and 'Rock And Roll Music' (with ETTA JAMES). You had to be there. *MCS*

Album rating: *6.5

□ HALF JAPANESE segment
(⇒ the BAND THAT WOULD BE KING)

Emmylou HARRIS

Born: 2 Apr'47, Birmingham, Alabama, USA. With her lapis lazuli soprano and impeccable taste in songwriters, EMMYLOU HARRIS has dominated the byways of country-rock and folk since the early-mid 70s, when she played diamond to Gram Parsons' rust, and rendered BOB DYLAN's 'Desire' one of the most sensuous rock albums of its era. So entwined with the history that – relatively rare for a woman in the music business – she's routinely called upon as an interview subject, HARRIS has also performed in countless concert films and made the occasional film cameo, almost always armed with a guitar and that peerless voice. Her first major screen credit was 'The LAST WALTZ' (1978); even if her performance – like the STAPLE SINGERS – was recorded in an 'M.G.M.' studio after the event, the Robbie Robertson-penned 'Evangeline' would become one of her totems. As well as a duet with ROY ORBISON ('That Lovin' You Feelin' Again') on the soundtrack to MEAT LOAF caper, 'ROADIE' (1980), the turn of the decade saw her pitching up with another roots icon in WILLIE NELSON road movie, 'HONEYSUCKLE ROSE' (1980), going on to sing alongside the late JOHNNY CASH in American TV show, 'Johnny Cash And The Country Girls' (1981). Both NELSON and CASH – along with the likes of KRIS KRISTOFFERSON – featured in 'The Other Side Of Nashville' (1984), the first of many documentaries to also feature EMMYLOU. NELSON was her screen mate once again as she made a rare feature cameo in made-for-TV country comedy, 'BAJA OKLAHOMA' (1988), cutting 'Back In Baby's Arms' for John Candy classic, 'Planes, Trains & Automobiles', the same year. A TV tribute to Woody Guthrie and Leadbelly, 'A Vision Shared' (1988), generated covers of 'Hobo's Lullaby' and 'Deportee (Plane Wreck At Los Gatos)', as well as an ensemble 'This Land Is Your Land', all tracks save 'Deportee' appearing on a 'Folkways' compilation. Another (BBC aired) folk-based project, 'Bringing It All Back Home' (1991), saw HARRIS teaming up with Mary Black and Dolores Keane, although it was to be a partnership with producer DANIEL LANOIS that reinvigorated her career in the mid-90s, resulting in her acclaimed 'Wrecking Ball' album and her short but sweet contribution to LANOIS' score for Billy Bob Thornton's 'SLING BLADE' (1996). LANOIS, likewise, did the business for WILLIE NELSON on 'TEATRO'

(1998), the subject of a Wim Wenders-directed companion piece in which HARRIS starred alongside LANOIS. Following yet more tributes to the likes of CASH and Tammy Wynette, she was an inevitable addition to 'DOWN FROM THE MOUNTAIN' (2001), the T-Bone Burnett masterminded, concert/documentary companion piece to his all conquering 'O BROTHER, WHERE ART THOU?' soundtrack. On a different note entirely, the well travelled songstress presented a 2001 American documentary on Edinburgh's showpiece thoroughfare, the Royal Mile before the Scottish Parliament was completed. BBC4 returned the compliment with two excellent documentaries: 'Emmylous Harris: From A Deeper Well' (2003) and 'FALLEN ANGEL: GRAM PARSONS' (2004), both films putting under the microscope her formative partnership with the mercurial country-rock pioneer. Also in 2004, she was among those lining up to praise the talents of Texas legend, Townes Van Zandt in another fascinating tribute, 'BE HERE TO LOVE ME' (2004), having previously recorded what is often regarded as the definitive rendition (outside of Townes himself) of the man's badge of honour outlaw ballad, 'Pancho and Lefty'. Yet another legend, NEIL YOUNG, was the subject of Jonathan Demme's 'HEART OF GOLD' (2006), featuring HARRIS as guest vocalist on live footage of YOUNG's celebrated Ryman Auditorium performances. She also contributed that still unsullied voice to ELVIS COSTELLO and the Imposters: Live in Memphis' (2005), and featured alongside the bespectacled one (and the likes of Philip Glass, NICK CAVE and SONIC YOUTH) in 'The Old Weird America: Harry Smith's Anthology Of American Folk Music' (2006). *BG*

- **filmography** {performance} –

the Last Waltz *(1978 {p} on OST w/ the BAND =>)* / **Honeysuckle Rose** *(1980 {p} on OST by WILLIE NELSON =>)* / **Baja Oklahoma** *(1988 TV {c} =>)* / a Vision Shared *(1988 TV {p} OST by V/A =>)* / In Dreams: The Roy Orbison Story *(1988 {p} =>)* / **Teatro** *(1998 {*} on OST w/ WILLIE NELSON =>)* / **Down From The Mountain** *(2000 {p} on OST by V/A =>)* / Freedom Highway: Songs That Shaped A Century *(2001 {c} =>)* / **Fallen Angel: Gram Parsons** *(2004 {c} =>)* / **Be Here To Love Me: A Film About Townes Van Zandt** *(2004 {c} OST by TOWNES VAN ZANDT =>)* / **Heart Of Gold** *(2006 {c} =>)*

HATED

aka 'HATED: GG ALLIN & THE MURDER JUNKIES'

1994 (US 90m) Skinny Nervous Guy Productiona (18)

Film genre: Punk Rock-music documentary

Top guns: dir: Todd Phillips → BITTERSWEET MOTEL

Stars: GG Allin *(vocals for The Murder Junkies)*, **Dee Dee Ramone** *(himself)* <= RAMONES =>, Shireen Kadivar *(Razor)*, Geraldo Rivera *(himself)* → PRIMARY COLORS → the U.S. VS. JOHN LENNON, Unk *(himself)*, other **Murder Junkies:- Merle Allin** *(bass player)*, **Dino** *(drummer)*, **Bill Weber** *(guitarist)* / Unk *(fan)*, Mr. Fisher *(GG's high school teacher)*

Storyline: The life and death of America's public enemy numero uno, GG Allin, the most "hated" man to stem from the world of rock'n'roll – up until he died. We hear from the people who stuck by him, his loyal fanbase and even his high school teacher. Not for the easily offended or the squeamish – the shit definitely hits the fan here. *MCS*

Movie rating: *7

Visual: video + dvd

Off the record: GG Allin (b. Kevin Michael Allin, 29 Aug'56, Lancaster, New Hampshire, USA) was the high priest of animalistic, degenerate punk rock; his party piece was to relieve himself on stage, yes one's AND two's folks (a bit of an asshole, you could say!). Influenced by, and going one (hundred times!) uglier than IGGY POP and MC5, Allin went beyond conventional rock'n'roll outrage by indulging in increasingly more explicit acts of on-stage sex, violence, self-mutilation, drug-taking, defecation, masturbation, verbal-abuse and general depravity as his career dragged on. Public enemy No.1, the crazed Allin was continually in trouble with the law, the performance (and actual enactment!) of songs such as 'You Scum, Eat My Diarrhoea' not exactly the behaviour of an upstanding US citizen. Alternately backed by the Jabbers and the Scumfucs, Allin recorded a series of sporadic LP's for a number of independent labels, among them 'Always Was, Is, And Always Shall Be' (1980), 'Eat My Fuc' (1984) and 'Artless' (1985). Early in 1990, GG was sent down for four years (Aggravated GBH was the charge), boasting from his Michigan (Jackson State) prison cell that he'd kill himself on stage upon his return to civvy street. In the event, Allin died from a drugs overdose (28th June 1993) having run amok, naked in the street after a New York show, indiscriminately attacking stunned passers-by. He had recently completed sessions with new band, the Murder Junkies (featured in the 'HATED' flick), these recordings posthumously released as 'Brutality & Bloodshed For All'. Allin was recently (late 1998) one of the subjects of a Channel 4 (UK) series documenting the history of subversive performers in rock music. *MCS*

—

GG ALLIN & THE MURDER JUNKIES

1993. (cd) *Awareness; <AWARE 7CD>* **HATED** ☐ ☐-
– Die when you die / Bite it you scum / Carmalita / Snakeman's dance / Young little meat / Fuck authority / Gypsy motherfucker / Suck my ass it smells / Outlaw scumfuc / Cunt sucking cannibal / I wanna kill you / When I die.

S/track review: With evil cover art by imprisoned serial killer, John Wayne Gacy, and a warning not to sell to persons under 18 years of age, one thinks one knows what one's getting right from the bloody f***in' start. GG ALLIN's history is now well documented in punk's underground scene, but this film and album gets the story straight from the people who worshipped him, the MURDER JUNKIES (his brother and bassist MERLE ALLIN, drummer DINO, guitarist BILL WEBER – although not on record), No.1 fan Unk; GG's high school teacher Mr. Fisher also talks about er.. punkers and their social message. Nearly half of the songs featured here were lifted from an earlier, re-recorded "best of" LP, 'Freaks, Faggots, Drunks & Junkies' (1988), although it must be pointed out that 'Snakeman's Dance' was from his GG Allin & The Holy Men set, 'You Give Love A Bad Name', and not the former as it states in the inner sleeve. 'Die When You Die', is classic hardcore punk probably in the mould of "year of '77" bands such as Slaughter & The Dogs or Johnny Thunders & The Heartbreakers, while 'Suck My Ass It Smells', the glorious 'Outlaw Scumfuc' and 'I Wanna Kill You' are perversely overshadowed by the sickly, pro-paedo antics of 'Young Little Meat'. To quote his brother MERLE: "I think just growing up, being different and having everybody laughing at him. He didn't really get along with anyone growing up, especially at school. It probably made him hate just about everyone, you know, he pretty much does hate everyone. He started rebelling right from the beginning, I mean he'd go to high school wearing women's clothing." speaks volumes for his mental state. On a lighter note, the set does produce a rare cowpunk cover of Warren Zevon's 'Carmalita', but what the singer-songwriter made of this is anyone's guess. Ditto 'F*** Authority' (performed with the CRIMINAL QUARTET), a C&W track courtesy of Vinyl Retentive Productions. Tape recorded live (NYC late '91) on some decidedly dodgy equipment, 'Bite It You Scum', 'C*** Sucking Cannibal' and 'Gypsy Motherf***er' (the latter un-PC effort was augmented by RAMONES bassist DEE DEE), these numbers take punk rock to new lows. GG R.I.H. *MCS*

Album rating: *6 for the music

☐ Screamin' Jay HAWKINS segment
(⇒ I PUT A SPELL ON ME)

HEART OF GOLD

aka NEIL YOUNG: HEART OF GOLD

2006 (US 103m) Shakey Pictures / Paramount Classics (PG)

Film genre: Rock/Roots-music concert documentary

Top guns: dir: Jonathan Demme ← STOREFRONT HITCHCOCK ← STOP MAKING SENSE

Stars: Neil YOUNG *(himself/performer)*, **Emmylou HARRIS** *(performer)*, **Ben Keith** *(performer)* ← GREENDALE, **Spooner Oldham** *(performer)*, **Rick Rosas** *(performer)*, **Karl Himmel** *(performer)*, **Chad Cromwell** *(performer)*, **Pegi Young** *(performer)* ← GREENDALE, **Gary W. Pigg** *(performer)* ← SWEET DREAMS, **Wayne Jackson** *(performer)* ← RATTLE AND HUM, **Tom McGinley** *(performer)*, **Diana DeWitt** *(performer)*, **Grant Boatwright** *(performer)*, **Anthony Crawford** *(performer)*, **Clinton Gregory** *(performer)*, **Larry Cragg** *(performer)* ← YEAR OF THE HORSE, **Jimmy Sharp** *(performer)*

Storyline: Neil Young performs two nights in the fall of 2005 at the Ryman Auditorium in Nashville (home of the Grand Ole Opry) with the help of filmmaker Jonathan Demme. Young recorded his album 'Prairie Wind' (featured here) after being diagnosed with a brain aneurysm, although he did recover after surgery. *MCS*

Movie rating: *8

Visual: dvd (no audio OST; see below)

Off the record: Among 90% of the tracks from NEIL YOUNG's most recent set, 'Prairie Wind', the man performed old nuggets, 'I Am A Child', 'Harvest Moon', 'Heart Of Gold', 'Old Man', 'Needle And The Damage Done', 'Old King', 'Comes A Times', 'Four Strong Winds', 'One Of These Days' & 'The Old Laughing Lady'. Guitarist **Grant Boatwright** actually wrote the score for 1975's horror/slasher flick, 'Poor Pretty Eddie'. *MCS*

– associated release –

NEIL YOUNG: Prairie Wind

Sep 05. (cd/d-lp) *Reprise; <(9362 49593-2/-1)>* 11 22
– The painter / No wonder / Falling off the face of the earth / Far from home / It's a dream / Prairie wind / Here for you / This old guitar / He was the king / When God made me. *<US d-lp+=>* – (interview). *(ltd-cd w/dvd+=; 9362 49494-2)* – (DVD footage).

HEARTLAND REGGAE

aka BOB MARLEY: HEARTLAND REGGAE

1980 (Can/UK 90m/86m) Canada Offshore / Media Aides / Tuff Gong (15)

Film genre: Reggae-music concert/documentary

Top guns: dir: James P. Lewis

Stars: Jacob Miller *(performer)* ← ROCKERS, **Bob MARLEY & the Wailers** *(performer/s)*, **Peter Tosh** *(performer)* ← REGGAE SUNSPLASH ← ROCKERS / → the BOB MARLEY STORY; CARIBBEAN NIGHTS → STEPPING RAZOR RED X, **Althea & Donna** *(performers)*, **Judy Mowatt** *(performer)* → COOL RUNNINGS: THE REGGAE MOVIE → the BOB MARLEY STORY; CARIBBEAN NIGHTS, **Dennis Brown** *(performer)* → the REGGAE MOVIE, **U-Roy** *(performer)*, **Junior Tucker** *(performer)*, **Lloyd Parkes** *(performer)*, Natty Garfield, Ras Lee Morris

Storyline: Reggae music and its iconic paymaster, Bob Marley, take center stage at Jamaica's One Love Peace Concert in 1980. Suffering from cancer at the time, Marley, the Wailers & several other stars of the genre "catch a fire" so to speak. *MCS*

Movie rating: *5

Visual: video + dvd

Off the record: Apart from reggae legend **Bob Marley** (tracks in the film: 'Trench Town Rock', 'War', 'Jamming', 'Natty Dread' and 'Jah Live'), other Jamaican superstars included **Jacob Miller** (b. 4 May'56, Mandeville) also died in 1981, although his death was due to a road accident – he opened the film with 'Tired Fe Lick Week In A Bush', 'Peace Treaty', 'I'm A Natty', 'Run For Cover' and 'Jah Dread' (with Inner Circle). **Peter Tosh** ('Legalize It', '400 Years', 'African' and 'Get Up, Stand Up') **Althea & Donna** sang their chart-topping smash, 'Uptown Top Ranking' – what else! Other tracks were by **Judy Mowatt & Light Of Love** ('Black Woman'), **Dennis Brown** ('Whip Them Jah') and last, but not least, **U-Roy** ('Natty Don't Fear', 'Soul Rebel' and 'Enjoy Yourself'). **Lloyd Parkes** was ex-Impact All-Stars. *MCS*

HEARTWORN HIGHWAYS

1981 (US 92m) First Run Features

Film genre: Country/Roots-music documentary

Top guns: s-w + dir: James Szalapski

Stars: Guy Clark *(performer)* → BE HERE TO LOVE ME, **Townes Van Zandt** *(performer)* → BE HERE TO LOVE ME, **David Allan Coe** *(performer)*, **Steve Earle** *(performer)* → JUST AN AMERICAN BOY → BE HERE TO LOVE ME, **Charlie Daniels** *(performer)* ← URBAN COWBOY, **Rodney Crowell** *(performer)* → NASHVILLE SOUNDS, **Barefoot Jerry** *(performer)*, **Steve Young** *(performer)*, **Gamble Rogers** *(performer)*, Larry Jon Wilson *(himself)*, Glenn Stagner *(himself)*, Peggy Brooks *(herself)*

Storyline: Shot on a limited budget, on 16mm stock by James Szalapski in the mid-70s, with the minimum of technical equipment, the film covers y'all Americana and Country music. *SL*

Movie rating: *6.5

Visual: video 1995 on 'Rhapsody' / dvd in 2004 'Navarre'

Off the record: For **Guy Clark**, **Charlie Daniels**, etc. (see 'URBAN COWBOY')

Various Artists incl. GUY CLARK (*) (& dialogue **)

Mar 06. (cd) *Shout!; <37457> Vinyl Junkie; (VJCD 167)* Apr06
– L.A. freeway (*) / " . . . That's a lightnin' lick . . ." (**) / Ohoopee river bottomland (LARRY JON WILSON) / That old time feeling (*) / "People condemn whiskey . . ." (**) / Waitin' round to die (TOWNES VAN ZANDT) / I still sing the old songs (DAVID ALLAN COE) / intro / Desperadoes waiting for a train (*) / Bluebird wine (RODNEY CROWELL, STEVE EARLE & *) / Alabama highway (STEVE YOUNG, * & JIM McGUIRE) / Intro / Pancho and Lefty (TOWNES VAN ZANDT) / Texas cookin' (*) / Charlie's place (Gamble's story) (GAMBLE ROGERS) / The black label blues (GAMBLE ROGERS) / " . . .These guards all drive cadillacs! . . ." (**) / River (DAVID ALLAN COE) / One for the one (JOHN HIATT) / Darlin' commit me (STEVE EARLE, JOHN HIATT & JIM McGUIRE) / Ballad of Laverne and Captain Flint (*, STEVE YOUNG & JIM McGUIRE) / I'm so lonesome I could cry (BILLY CALLERY, * & SUSANNAH CLARK) / Mercenary song (BILLY CALLERY, * & SUSANNAH CLARK) / " . . .Would you do Elijah's church?" (**) / Elijah's church (BILLY CALLERY, * & SUSANNAH CLARK) / Silent night (BILLY CALLERY, * & SUSANNAH CLARK).

S/track review: Any soundtrack that kicks off with GUY CLARK's 'L.A. Freeway' – the best song about serving notice on life's grindstone ever written – has got to be confident in its ability to back it up. But with the late James Szalapski's film presenting such a long-time-comin' embarrassment of mid-70s Southern singer-songwriterly riches to pick from, it's a confidence well placed. Recorded in the field, on the stage, and always from the cusp of the soul, the album's sequence of virgin performances and asides from the likes of CLARK, TOWNES VAN ZANDT and STEVE EARLE amongst others is about as authentic and unsolicited as late 20th century Americana comes, and about as spiritually divorced from contemporary Nashville. VAN ZANDT's perfunctory explanation of his most poignant song, 'Pancho and Lefty', might shatter a few romantic illusions but it's characteristic of the record's roots-verité, the same that has GAMBLE ROGERS spinning synchronised, slyly eloquent yarns about "the most diffident of observers fraught with horn". An impossibly young STEVE EARLE – like Jay Farrar after him – sings in a good ol' voice that lies shamelessly about his age, but – in the wry 'Darlin' Commit Me' – foretells the humour and personal strife to come; the forever unsung STEVE YOUNG contributes the gypsy deep country-soul of 'Alabama Highway' and a howling cover of Hank Williams classic, 'I'm So Lonesome I Could Cry', thumping out its existentialist pain; and Georgia-proud LARRY JON WILSON's 'Ohoopee River Bottomland' exemplifies the broadness of the church called Outlaw, sung in a fermented croon somewhere between Dan Penn, Tim Hardin and Tony Joe White. Wildman DAVID ALLAN COE and even a rookie JOHN HIATT bare their art with candid intimacy. Finishing up on an ensemble rendition of 'Silent Night' would be a recipe for a fondue party in lesser hands; it's down to the integrity of both director and performers that it sounds written for the occasion, and as an insight into the original country collective, in an era before so much money and marketing strategy was at stake, 'HEARTWORN HIGHWAYS' takes the proverbial Route 66. *BG*

Album rating: *8.5

HEIMA

aka HEIMA: a film by SIGUR ROS

2007 (Ice 97m) Klikk / Truenorth

Film genre: indie/alt-rock music documentary/concert

Top guns: dir: Dean DeBlois

Stars: SIGUR ROS:- Jon Por (Jonsi) Birgisson, Kjartan (Kjarri) Sveinsson, Orri Pall Dyrason, Georg (Goggi) Holm *(performers)*

Storyline: A unique account of the magical return home ("heima") to Iceland in summer 2006 for the country's best-loved avant-rock outfit, Sigur Ros. They play about fifteen unannounced free concerts in small towns around their scenic but dark homeland (also "heima"). *MCS*

Movie rating: *9

Visual: dvd on EMI Records (no audio OST)

Off the record: SIGUR ROS perform several numbers, notably 'Vaka', acoustic versions of 'Agaetis Byrjun', 'Von' and 'Staralfur', plus the unreleased 'Gitardjamm'. Canadian director, Dean DeBlois, was responsible for Disney animations including feature-length film, 'Lilo & Stitch' (2002). *MCS*

Richard HELL

Born: Richard Myers, 2 Oct'49, Lexington, Kentucky, USA. Raised in Wilmington, Delaware, he later moved to New York in his late teens, where he wrote poetry and experimented with drugs. Along with his sidekicks, Tom Miller and Billy Ficca, Richard formed the Neon Boys in 1971. By '73, they'd metamorphosed into Television, Myers adopting his RICHARD HELL moniker (while Miller became Tom Verlaine) and helping to initiate the city's new wave/punk scene. As legend has it, a sharp eyed Malcolm McLaren was rather taken by HELL's dragged-through-a-hedge-backwards attire and mop of spiked hair, initially attempting to secure his services for his new baby, the SEX PISTOLS; when this failed, well, at least he could go back to England with a few ideas. HELL subsequently split with Verlaine and co., briefly joining Johnny Thunders in the Heartbreakers, where he co-penned (along with a RAMONE!) the seminal 'Chinese Rocks'; like Thunders, HELL was well acquainted with the pleasures of heroin, which no doubt accounted for his haphazard career. HELL subsequently formed his own outfit, RICHARD HELL & the Void-Oids, along with future LOU REED guitarist Robert Quine, Ivan Julian and Marc Bell. They hastily recorded an independently released debut EP before signing to 'Sire'; with the resulting 'Blank Generation' (1977) album (the name taken from 'The BLANK GENERATION' flick), HELL had finally succeeded in capturing his brutally nihilistic poetical/musical vision, if only fleetingly. With his drug problems reaching critical levels, HELL's only release over the next five years was 'The Kid With The Replaceable Head', a 1978 Nick Lowe-produced single. A belated follow-up album, 'Destiny Street' (1982), eventually appeared in spring '82, although the momentum had long since dissipated. HELL was absent from the music scene for the next ten years, although he did star in the film 'SMITHEREENS' as well as procuring a cameo role as MADONNA's boyfriend in 'Desperately Seeking Susan'. He finally re-emerged with art-noise veterans, THURSTON MOORE and Don Fleming, for a solo EP, before adding another SONIC YOUTH-ite Steve Stelley to record an album under the Dim Stars moniker. A fave with the rockumentary punk filmmakers, HELL has taken the role of interviewee in numerous RAMONES film outings. *BG & MCS*

- **filmography** [screenwriter] {actor} –

the Blank Generation *(1976 {p} =>)* / Final Reward *(1978 {c})* / **Blank Generation** *(1980 [s-w] {*} =>)* / **Smithereens** *(1982 {*} =>)* / Geek Maggot Bingo *(1983 {*})* / Desperately Seeking Susan *(1985 {a}; see future edition)* / No Picnic *(1987 {a})* / **What About Me** *(1993 {*} =>)* / Blind Light *(1997 {*})* / We're Outta Here! *(1997 {c} OST by RAMONES =>)* / **End Of The Century** *(2003 {a/p} =>)* / **Hey Is Dee Dee Home** *(2003 {a/p} =>)* / **We Jam Econo: The Story Of The Minutemen** *(2005 {c} =>)* / **The Story Of Punk** *(2006 TV {c} =>)*

□ the HELLACOPTERS segment
(⇒ GOODNIGHT CLEVELAND)

HELLHOUNDS ON MY TRAIL

The Afterlife of Robert Johnson

2000 (US 95m w/b&w) Nonfiction / Mug-Shot Productions

Film genre: Blues-music documentary/biopic

Top guns: dir: Robert Mugge ← DEEP BLUES ← PRIDE AND JOY ← COOL RUNNINGS: THE REGGAE MOVIE / → LAST OF THE MISSISSIPPI JUKES → BLUES DIVAS

Stars: Robert Johnson *(archive performer)*, **Bob Weir** *(performer)* <= GRATEFUL DEAD =>, **Tracy Nelson** *(performer)*, **Irma Thomas** *(performer)*, **Peter Green** *(performer)*, **Guy Davis** *(performer)*, **Billy Branch** *(performer)*, **Roosevelt Barnes** *(performer)* ← DEEP BLUES, **R.L. Burnside** *(performer)* ← HILL STOMP HOLLAR ← DEEP BLUES / → YOU SEE ME LAUGHIN', **Junior Kimbrough** *(performer)* ← DEEP BLUES / → YOU SEE ME LAUGHIN', **Chris Whitley** *(performer)* → PIGS WILL FLY, **Rob Wasserman** *(performer)*, **Rory Block** *(performer)*, **Robert Lockwood Jr.** *(performer)* ← CAN'T YOU HEAR THE WIND HOWL?, **Keb' Mo'** *(performer)* ← CAN'T YOU HEAR THE WIND HOWL? / → FEEL LIKE GOING HOME → LIGHTNING IN A BOTTLE, **David A. Stewart** *(performer)*

Storyline: Robert Johnson, the enigmatic pioneer behind the blues, the myth and the legend and the singers/musicians who were inspired by the guitar maestro. Read on . . . *MCS*

Movie rating: *4.5

Visual: video + dvd (no audio OST exists – watch out!)

Off the record: Robert Johnson was born 8th May 1911, Hazlehurst (a small industrialised railway town in the deep South of..) Mississippi, USA. The seminal blues and Delta slide hero spent the early part of his life in a migrant labour camp after a fleeting affair with a W.A.P. worker (Noah Johnson) had forced Robert's mother, Julia Dodds, to flee to Memphis. After moving back with her original husband, Charles Spencer, Dodds was incapable of raising young Robert due to the struggles of parenthood and his increasingly disturbing and arrogant behaviour. Robert and his mother subsequently moved to Robinsonville, a sleepy Northern cotton community 40 miles out of Memphis, where she married Willie Willis in 1916 and settled down to raise Robert properly. Throughout his teenage years he became fascinated with music and instruments: he experimented with his new found Jews Harp before moving on to harmonica and then finally the guitar. Heading nowhere, he acquired the help of Willie Brown, a talented local musician who introduced Johnson to a string of "Jook" houses (blues venues) throughout the decade. In 1929 and rumoured to be somewhat of a ladies man, 18-year old Robert married 16-year old Virginia Travis and they subsequently bought a farmhouse when she fell pregnant. Then tragedy struck the following April: Virginia and the baby died during childbirth. This catapulted Robert into extreme depression. The only way he felt he could cure his melancholia was to play raw-edged Delta blues which displayed a degree of fiery passion, not heard since Blind Willie Johnson's (no relation) 'Dark Was The Night . . .'. It was said that he sat alone at night in the forest, engulfed in his own thoughts, strumming his guitar with an eerie, but beautiful prowess. Two months later he followed the advice of his mentor, Willie Brown, and set off to Wisconsin to record for 'Paramount'. There he created his most vivid and stripped-down recordings with preacher-cum-bluesman, Son House, a remarkable pioneer who altered Robert's perception on standard blues playing. After a short stint on the road, he returned back to his home town of Hazlehurst, where he met Ike Zinnerman, an eccentric gothic blues guitarist, who claimed that he had self-taught himself the blues whilst sitting on gravestones in the local crematorium in the dead of night! Robert remarried in 1931 to Calletta Craft who was 10 years his senior, although he abandoned her after she had a nervous breakdown. He began playing the "Jook" houses in the early 30s and enjoyed acclaim from a huge group of people who packed out venues wherever he played. However, this attraction made Robert deranged and paranoid; he would never reveal the chords or notes to any of his songs and he could be seen frequently leaving the stage midway through a set because he claimed the audience were eyeing him too closely! He continued travelling and after a brief residency in Arkansas he was approached by Ernie Oertle, a talent scout for the deep south who took him to San Antonio to record, during which time he produced the awesome 'Terraplane Blues'. A feast of slide and fast-handed guitar, with Johnson's falsetto ramblings a highlight, the song became a huge success in America, providing this new found blues hero with instant fortune and a mass following. Tours of dancehalls, camps and "Jook" houses followed, along with the arrival of no less than eleven single 78 rpm records: a total of 41 recordings. The tour path led Robert through Detroit, New York City, New Jersey, St. Louis, Canada, Windsor and back to the south. By this time he had grown fond of drinking and was said to be the "life of a party" when drunk. His final excursion came in the summer of 1938 when he stopped off in Greenwood County to play in a bar called The Three Forks. According to sources, Robert had become infatuated with the owner's wife, which caused a bad atmosphere within the joint. He was handed an open bottle of whiskey by the proprieter which was immediately slapped out of his hand by a friend who told him: "Don't ever take a drink from an open bottle, you don't know what could be in it!". Johnson took another bottle and less than an hour later he was struggling to sing on stage. Leaving halfway through his set, he was found outside vomiting violently. It was then evident that he had been poisoned by the jealous barman. He lay sick that night in bed, contracting pneumonia before he finally passed away three days later on August the 16th, 1938. Remembered as one of the great blues guitarists of his time, Robert Johnson's influence still remains to this day. Among BOB DYLAN, Muddy Waters, Keith Richards and ERIC CLAPTON, the inexplicable artist has never failed to wow listeners and musicians alike; his warped interpretation of the blues guitar and his haunting vocals have proved timeless. If you want proof, find 'The Complete Recordings Of Robert Johnson' CD. *AS*

□ Levon HELM
(⇒ the BAND)

Jimi HENDRIX

Born: James Marshall Hendrix, 27 Nov'42, Seattle, Washington, USA. To many the greatest, most soulful and technically gifted rock guitarist of all time, JIMI HENDRIX stole the genre's defining moment, electrifying the 'WOODSTOCK' crowd (or what crowd there was left in the early hours of a Monday morning) with his infamous reincarnation of 'The Star Spangled Banner', performing a historic two-hour set despite technical problems and an under rehearsed band; his raffish style, casual charisma and provocative showmanship was made for the stage, a tripartite revelation which translated almost as well to the screen. The full cache of existing footage finally saw the light of day in 2005 as 'Jimi Hendrix – Live At Woodstock'. The 1970 festival soundtrack featured two songs from his set (three on the second volume, released in 1971), while a studio version of ' . . .Banner' appeared on the posthumous 'RAINBOW BRIDGE' (1972), the soundtrack to an experimental film with a HENDRIX performance (in a Hawaiian meditation retreat . . .) as its centrepiece. Along with satirical montage, 'Dynamite Chicken' (1970), this is about the closest the man got to a feature film, although prior to 'WOODSTOCK', the JIMI HENDRIX EXPERIENCE had made its explosive live debut in the festival's D.A. Pennebaker-directed primer, 'MONTEREY POP' (1968). Such was the incendiary visual/sonic impact of his brief, Brian Jones-introduced set that he was afforded his own spin-off film, 'Jimi Plays Monterey' (1967), released along with footage from Otis Redding's performance. The spin-off soundtrack wasn't released until 1970, the same year 'Dunhill' got around to releasing the official various artists triple album, itself featuring a couple more HENDRIX numbers (with the 1997 'Rhino' box set excavating a further three). The guitar deity was also a highlight of another iconic festival in 1970s Isle of Wight bash, appearing in the main, Murray Lerner-directed film and soundtrack, 'MESSAGE TO LOVE' (unreleased until the mid-90s), and starring in his own excerpt, 'Blue Wild Angel: JIMI HENDRIX LIVE AT THE ISLE OF WIGHT' (1970). In fact, the year prior to his untimely death a few weeks after the festival on 18th September, was a prolific one for the guitarist in terms of stage footage, and in what amounts to a kind of cottage industry in itself, recent years have seen a flurry of DVD releases reclaiming the likes of 'Jimi Hendrix: Live at the Fillmore East' (1970), Joe Boyd's posthumous tribute, 'JIMI HENDRIX' (1973) and 'JIMI PLAYS BERKELEY' (1971), often regarded as the most visceral HENDRIX performance on celluloid. *BG*

- **filmography** {performances} (composer) –

Experience *(1968 {*p} OST =>)* / **Monterey Pop** *(1968 {p} on OST by V/A =>)* / **Keep On Rockin'** *(1969 {p} =>)* / **Popcorn** *(1969 {p} =>)* / **Woodstock** *(1970 {p} on OST by V/A =>)* / **Jimi Plays Berkeley** *(1971 {*p} OST rel.2003 =>)* / **Rainbow Bridge** *(1972 {*p} OST =>)* / Dynamite Chicken *(1972 {p})* / **Jimi Hendrix** *(1973 {*p} OST =>)* / **the Day The Music Died** *(1977 {p} =>)* / Sound Of The City: London 1964-73 *(1981 {p} =>)* / **the Beach Boys: An American Band** *(1985 {p} =>)* / **Jimi Hendrix Live At The Isle Of Wight 1970** *(1991 {*p} OST rel.2002 =>)* / **Message To Love: The Isle Of Wight Festival** *(1997 {p} on OST =>)* / **My Generation** *(2000 {p} =>)* / Electric Purgatory: The Fate Of The Black Rocker *(2005 {p} =>)*

HEY, HEY WE'RE THE MONKEES

1997 (US 70m TV) 3DD Entertainment / Discovery Channel

Film genre: Pop/Rock-music documentary comedy/bio-pic

Top guns: dir: Alan Boyd ← ENDLESS HARMONY: THE BEACH BOYS STORY ← NASHVILLE SOUNDS / s-w: Chuck Harter

Stars: the MONKEES:- Davy Jones, Mickey Dolenz, Michael Nesmith, Peter

Tork *(themselves/performers)*, Paul Mazursky *(himself)* ← DOWN AND OUT IN BEVERLY HILLS ← a STAR IS BORN ← BLACKBOARD JUNGLE / → TOUCH → WHY DO FOOLS FALL IN LOVE, Ward Sylvester *(himself)*, **Peter Noone** *(himself)* <= HERMAN'S HERMITS =>, Don Kirschner *(himself)*, **Bobby Hart** *(himself)*, **Chip Douglas** *(himself)*, **Jeff Barry** *(himself)*, Bob Rafelson *(archive)*, Bert Schneider *(archive)*, **Jimi HENDRIX** *(archive)*

Storyline: A retrospective look at pop icons, the Monkees, their early pre-Monkees work, their overnight success on their own mid-60s TV show (with controversially at the time, session players behind them) and their most recent reunion set from 1996, 'Justus'. *MCS*

Movie rating: *6

Visual: video + dvd (adds 19m)

Off the record: **Bobby Hart** (along with Tommy Boyce) wrote numerous songs for the Monkees during their mid-60s heyday. Monkees producer, **Chip Douglas**, was of the Modern Folk Quartet and played bass on the Turtles' 'Happy Together'. **Jeff Barry** was already a renowned songwriter who went into film scores including 'THE IDOLMAKER' (1980). The MONKEES tracks (and associated pre-MONKEES stuff) were as follows:- '(Theme From) The Monkees' *, 'Listen To The Band', 'What Are We Going To Do?' (DAVY JONES), 'Until It's Time For You To Go' (MICHAEL NESMITH), 'Mary, Mary', 'Last Train To Clarksville' *, '(I'm Not Your) Steppin' Stone', 'I'm A Believer', 'No Time', '(What Am I Doin') Hangin' Round?', 'Randy Scouse Git', 'Circle Sky', 'Daydream Believer' & 'For Pete's Sake'. *MCS*

– associated release (not!) –

the MONKEES: Hey Hey We're The Monkees

Sep 96. (cd-rom) *DJ Specialist; <352034>* [–] [–]
– (only a few tracks correspond to songs in the film *)

HEY IS DEE DEE HOME

2003 (US 63m) Extinkt Films

Film genre: Punk Rock documentary compilation

Top guns: dir: Lech Kowalski ← BORN TO LOSE: THE LAST ROCK AND ROLL MOVIE ← D.O.A.

Stars: Dee Dee Ramone *(himself)* <= RAMONES =>, **Joey Ramone** *(archive performer)* <= RAMONES =>, **Johnny Thunders** *(archive performer)*, ← END OF THE CENTURY ← BORN TO LOSE: THE LAST ROCK AND ROLL MOVIE ← the PUNK ROCK MOVIE ← the BLANK GENERATION, **Jerry Nolan** *(archive performer)*, **Richard HELL** *(archive footage)*, **Billy IDOL** *(archive footage)*

Storyline: Punk rocker and Ramones bassist, Dee Dee, gets the full interview treatment (mainly 1992) from director, Lech Lowalski. He discusses drugs, being a drug addict and the after effects of er, drugs. Sadly, Dee Dee talks of surviving all this although died of a drug overdose on the 5th June, 2002. *MCS*

Movie rating: *5.5

Visual: dvd

Off the record: **Jerry Nolan + Johnny Thunders**were of course, main men with the New York Dolls, and sadly, both are now deceased.

HIGH AND DRY

2005 (US 80m*) Upstairs Entertainment Inc.

Film genre: alt-Rock concert/documentary

Top guns: dir + s-w: Michael Toubassi

Stars: Dan Stuart *(himself/performer)* ← BORDER RADIO, **Howe Gelb** *(himself/performer)*, **Joey Burns** *(himself/performer)*, **John Convertino** *(himself/performer)*, **Tommy Larkins** *(himself/performer)*, **Al Perry** *(himself/performer)*, **Rich Hopkins** *(himself/performer)*, **Rainer Ptacek** *(archive/performer)*, **Beck** *(himself)* ← SOUL OF A MAN ← MAYOR OF THE SUNSET STRIP ← SOUTHLANDER ← FREE TIBET / → FEARLESS FREAKS, **Bob Log III** *(himself/performer)*, Brad Denboer *(artist)*, Danny Vinik *(himself)*

Storyline: "Where The Desert Meets Rock'n'Roll" (as tagged on the dvd box) just about says it all. Tucson, Arizona shares the limelight with all it's alt-country rock musicians/singers, trailing back to the 70s and winding up at Calexico in the 90s/00s. *MCS*

Movie rating: *6.5

Visual: dvd (no audio OST)

Off the record: **Dan Stuart** formed Green On Red in Tucson way back in the late 70s, although they uprooted their shackles to slide across to L.A., where they delivered the 'Green On Red' EP and albums such as 'Gravity Talks' (1984) and 'Gas Food Lodging' (1985) – the latter incidentally, the title of an unconnected film. He also co-wrote the screenplay for 2002's 'Deadrockstar' movie. **Howe Gelb** is also one of the pioneers of desert rock, Giant Sand being the group he and **Rainer Ptacek** (now sadly deceased November '97) created way back in the early to mid 80s when their seminal LP, 'Valley Of Rain' was released; 2004's 'It's All Over The Map' is Giant Sand's most recent, while 'Sno Angel Like You' is solo Gelb's latest offering. Two of their past members **Joey Burns & John Convertino** formed Calexico, branching out of the studio with several Ennio Morricone-inspired albums including 'Spoke' (1997) and 'The Black Light' (1998) to 'Garden Ruin' (2006); look out for band in the films, 'Committed' (2000) and 'Collateral' (2004). The pair were also connected to offshoot outfit, Friends Of Dean Martinez with Giant Sand drummer **Tommy Larkins**; he wrote the score to the movie, 'A Sign From God' (2000). The "legendary" **Al Perry** has a connection to the latter, having served time as guitarist/singer with interchangeable roots-rock outfit, the Cattle; a CD with the aforementioned Dan Stuart, entitled 'Retronuevo', was issued 1999. **Rich Hopkins** (ex-Sidewinders & the Sand Rubies) formed his own project, the Luminarios, in the early 90s; they released several sets including 'Dirt Town' (1994) and 'The Fifty Percenter' (2001). Bringing us up to date is the primitive Delta blues-punk rocker, **Bob Log III**, a one-man band who plays slide guitar with a woman on his lap while also singing out of a crash helmet – this you've got to see. Bob's been around for over a decade now, having cut his avant-garde teeth in the duo, Doo Rag (two albums, 'Chuncked & Muddled' 1995 & 'What We Do' 1996), before completing solo albums, 'School Bus' (1998), 'Trike' (1999) and 'Log Bomb' (2003). *MCS*

□ Robyn HITCHCOCK segment
(⇒ STOREFRONT HITCHCOCK)

HOME OF THE BRAVE

A Film By Laurie Anderson

1986 (US 91m) Cinecom Pictures

Film genre: avant-Rock-music concert/documentary

Top guns: s-w + dir: **Laurie Anderson**

Stars: Laurie Anderson *(performer)*, **Joy Askew** *(keyboards, vocals)*, **Adrian Belew** *(guitar, vocals)* ← BABY SNAKES, **Richard Landry** *(horns, winds)*, **David Van Tieghem** *(percussion)*, **Dolette McDonald** *(backing vocalist)* → BRING ON THE NIGHT, **Janice Pendarvis** *(backing vocalist)* → BRING ON THE NIGHT, **Won Sang Park** *(kayageum, vocals)*, William S. Burroughs *(poet)* ← CHAPPAQUA / → EVEN COWGIRLS GET THE BLUES, Paula Mazur *(game show hostess)*

Storyline: A visual record of Laurie Anderson's 'Mister Heartbreak' tour of 1986, combining music and spoken word pieces. *DG*

Movie rating: *5.5

Visual: video

Off the record: A boffin-like icon of the avant-garde, **Laurie Anderson** (b. 5 Jul'47, Chicago, Illinois, USA) remains best known for her one-off UK hit, 'O Superman', a near chart-topper from the early 80s. Like most performance artists, her work encompasses a myriad of disciplines, including film composition. Her earliest screen appearance was in the art film, 'Short Pieces' alongside legendary experimental guitarist and SONIC YOUTH mentor Glenn Branca. Score wise, she composed the music to one of the first computer hacker dramas, 'System Ohne Schatten' (1983), Jonathan Demme's road movie, 'Something Wild' (1986), in collaboration with John Cale, and also Demme's Spalding Gray monologue, 'Swimming To Cambodia' (1987). While only one of these projects produced a V/A soundtrack, ANDERSON was the star of her own aforementioned theatrical concert movie, which featured avant-garde poet William S. Burroughs amongst others. She again soundtracked Spalding's ramblings on the Nick Broomfield-directed 'Monster In A Box' (1992). She was subsequently one of the baby voices in the children's feature, 'The Rugrats Movie' (1998). *BG*

—

LAURIE ANDERSON

Apr 86. (lp/c/cd) *Warners; <(7599 25400-1/-4/-2)>* ☐ ☐
– Smoke rings / White lily / Late show / Talk normal / Language is a virus / Radar / Sharkey's night / Credit racket.

S/track review: Up until this soundtrack, the ever avant-garde LAURIE ANDERSON had been making challenging music for several years; she's still doing so. Opening with simple keyboard chords and Laurie singing/speaking in English and Spanish, 'Smoke Rings' was a fine start to the proceedings, highlighting outstanding backing vocals from Dolette McDonald and Janice Pendervis. After twenty odd years, the song still sounds fresh. 'White Lily' is a spoken word piece (accompanying herself on synclavier) and basically a performance poetry piece really, and with little in the way of discernible meaning. Containing a sample of William S. Burroughs, 'Late Show' is joined at times by atonal saxophone and occasional violin. Pleasant enough, but Burroughs interjecting "listen to my heartbeat" at differing amplitudes over what sounds an underwritten tune may serve only to irritate. 'Talk Normal' has more spoken word over a lolloping beat, the augmentation of more good work from McDonald and Pendervis, giving something of a world music feel. 'Language is a Virus' takes us into more conventional territory. Dominated by a strong saxophone, this is the closest the set comes to a conventional pop song. ANDERSON gets down to playing solo synclavier on 'Radar', this barely resembles a tune and is dominated by emulated bird sounds. 'Sharkey's Night' almost plays as a reprise of 'Talk Normal' with additional intricate percussion and vocal manipulation. The brief instrumental 'Credit Racket' closes the concert, and could be dismissed by the uncharitable as a pretentious racket. Other parts of this CD could be too, but ANDERSON has a self-deprecating streak which may allow the listener to forgive her excesses. *DG*

Album rating: *5.5

– spinoff releases, etc. –

LAURIE ANDERSON: Language Is A Virus From Outer Space / White Lily
May 86. (7"/12") *(W 8701/+T)* ☐ ☐

HYPE!

. . . "Surviving the Northwest Rock Explosion"

1996 (US 87m) Lions Gate Films

Film genre: Grunge Rock-music concert/documentary

Top guns: dir: Doug Pray → SCRATCH

Stars: Bruce Pavitt *(Sub Pop records co-founder)*, Jonathan Poneman *(Sub Pop records co-founder)*, **Eddie VEDDER** *(himself)*, **Fastbacks:- Kurt Bloch, Kim Warnick, Lulu Gargiulo** *(performers)*, **Wipers:- Greg Sage, Steve Plouf** *(performers)*, **the U-Men:- Tom Price, Tony Ransom** *(performers)*, **Green River:- Mark Arm, Steve Turner, Jeff Ament, Bruce Fairweather** *(performers)*, **Soundgarden:- Chris Cornell *, Kim Thayil, Ben Shepherd *, Matt Cameron** *(performers)* ← SINGLES, **Mudhoney** *(performers)*, **Nirvana:- Kurt Cobain, Dave Grohl, Krist Novoselic** *(performers)*, **Some Velvet Sidewalk** *(performers)* → SONGS FOR CASSAVETES, **Tad:- Tad Doyle, Kurt Danielson, Josh Snider, Gary Thorstensen** *(performers)*, **Gas Huffer** *(performers)*, **Young Fresh Fellows:- Scott McCaughey *** *(performer/s)* ← ROCK'N'ROLL MOBSTER GIRLS *, **Supersuckers** *(performers)*, **7 Year Bitch** *(performers)*, **the Walkabouts** *(performers)*, **Coffin Break** *(performers)*, **Pigeonhed** *(performers)*, **the Thrown-Ups** *(performers)*, **the Mono Men** *(performers)*, **Seaweed** *(performers)*, **Van Conner** *(himself)*, **Calvin Johnson** *(himself)*, Daniel House *(C/Z records founder)*, Blake Wright *(eMpTy records founder)* Conrad Uno *(PopLlama records founder)*, Dave Crider *(Estrus records founder)*, Nils Bernstein *(himself)*

Storyline: The fertile Seattle (and Pacific Northwest) music scene comes under the spotlight, although the film's director, Doug Pray, leans towards the idea that the grunge explosion became its albatross. Check out Nirvana's first public outing for 'Smells Like Teen Spirit' – now where did I put my favourite ripped jeans? *MCS*

Movie rating: *7.5

Visual: video + dvd

Off the record: If you want more grunge-rock, try 'SINGLES' in the Rock Movies/Musicals section.

—

Various Artists

Oct 96. (cd) *Sub Pop; <SP 371>* ☐ ☐
– K street – live (FASTBACKS) / Return of the rat (WIPERS) / Dig it a hole (U-MEN) / Swallow my pride – unrel. demo (GREEN RIVER) / Nothing to say (SOUNDGARDEN) / Touch me I'm sick – live (MUDHONEY) / Negative creep (NIRVANA) / Mousetrap – live (SOME VELVET SIDEWALK) / 54/40 – live (DEAD MOON) / My hometown (GIRL TROUBLE) / Giant killer (TAD) / Hotcakes – 7" version (GAS HUFFER) / Low beat (YOUNG FRESH FELLOWS) / I say fuck – live (SUPERSUCKERS) / Knot – live (7 YEAR BITCH) / Second skin – live (the GITS) / Julie Francavilla – unrel. demo (FLOP) / Throwaway – live (POSIES) / Not for you – live on radio (PEARL JAM) / The river rise (MARK LANEGAN) / Fire's coming down (PIGEONHED) / Just say (FASTBACKS).

S/track review: Remember grunge? All flannel shirts, ripped jeans and long, greasy hair. Seattle was its utopia and Kurt Cobain something akin to God. Only, there was so much more to this scene than the rose-tinted revisionists would have you believe. The soundtrack to 'HYPE!' lays bare the real sound of grunge and the eclectic mix of styles that created it. With punk as a starting point, the music evolved to include the hardcore speed metal of bands like GREEN RIVER, SUPERSUCKERS and WIPERS as well as the pop punk of FASTBACKS, the GITS and PIGEONHED. 'My Home Town' by GIRL TROUBLE sounds like Nick Cave, while 7 YEAR BITCH could be the Yeah Yeah Yeahs jamming with Eater (but that's just an "Outside View" ed!). The big names all contribute some of their lesser known songs: NIRVANA ('Negative Creep'), PEARL JAM ('Not For You') or SOUNDGARDEN ('Nothing To Say'), perhaps to show that they were indeed underground once – still all good songs nevertheless. Arguably the best track on the album is ex-Screaming Trees frontman MARK LANEGAN's 'The River Rise', an atmospheric acoustic affair that lends a nod to Neil Young or Bruce Springsteen in their more introspective moments. There is also a rather comical hidden track, a twenty second clip of 'Smells Like Teen Spirit' being played on a keyboard accompanied by whistle and triangle. It's easy to forget the diversity of the Grunge scene at the time, and that is something that 'HYPE!' – although it might not be considered as any kind of best of compilation – does help to rectify. *CM*

Album rating: *7

I AM TRYING TO BREAK YOUR HEART

. . . A FILM ABOUT WILCO BY SAM JONES

2002 (US 92m w/b&w) Bona Fide Productions / Cowboy Pictures

Film genre: alt-Country Rock-music documentary

Top guns: dir: Sam Jones

Stars: WILCO:- Jeff Tweedy, Glenn Kotche, John Stirratt, Leroy Bach + Jay Bennett *(themselves/performers)* / **Ken Coomer** *(himself; ex-Wilco)*, Tony Margherita *(himself)*, **Fred Armisen** *(himself)* → the PICK OF DESTINY, **Josh Grier** *(himself)*, **Jim O'Rourke** *(himself)*, Bill Bentley *(himself)*, David Bither *(himself)* ← GIGANTIC (A TALE OF TWO JOHNS), David Fricke *(himself)*, Howie Klein *(himself)*, Jonathan Parker *(himself)*

Storyline: The trials and tribulations of alt-rock band Wilco and the creative tensions between songwriters Jeff Tweedy and the outgoing Jay Bennett on their album, 'Yankee Hotel Foxtrot'. The said set (which included the song, 'I Am Trying To Break Your Heart') would see the uncompromising Tweedy and Wilco move stables from Reprise to Nonesuch after the former wanted fundamental changes. *MCS*

Movie rating: *7.5

Visual: dvd (no audio OST; see below)

Off the record: WILCO (see own entry). **Fred Armisen** was drummer with 90s punk rocker, Trenchmouth (was also married to Sally Timms). **Josh Grier** fronts indie rockers, Tapes 'n Tapes. **Jim O'Rourke** is a composer/engineer/producer/etc in his own right and has been a brief 5th member of SONIC YOUTH. *MCS*

– associated release –

WILCO: Yankee Hotel Foxtrot

Apr 02. (cd) *Nonesuch; <(7559 79669-2)>* [13] [40]
– I am trying to break your heart / Kamera / Radio cure / War on war / Jesus, etc. / Ashes of American flags / Heavy metal drummer / I'm the man who loves you / Pot kettle black / Poor places / Reservations. *<(d-lp-iss.Nov02 on 'Sundazed'; SCLP 5161)>*

I JUST WASN'T MADE FOR THESE TIMES

1995 (US 69m TV w/b&w) Cro Magnon Productions / Palomar Pictures

Film genre: Pop/Rock music bio-pic/concert/documentary

Top guns: dir: **Don Was**

Stars: Brian Wilson *(himself/performer)* <= the BEACH BOYS =>, **Carl Wilson** *(himself)* <= the BEACH BOYS =>, **Carnie Wilson** *(herself)*, **Wendy Wilson** *(herself)*, Audree Wilson *(herself; Brian's mother)*, Marilyn Wilson *(herself; Brian's ex-wife)*, Daniel Harrison *(himself)*

Storyline: Don Was pays monochrome, often heart-rending homage to the art, method and inspiration of Brian Wilson, for many years the benchmark of troubled genius. As with Peter Green across the Atlantic, the efforts of friends, family and peers help ease a passage back from mental freefall into the spotlight, with revealing, still evidently troubled reminiscences from the man himself, as well as interviews with family, friends and peers, and performance clips from the sessions which resulted in the accompanying soundtrack. *BG*

Movie rating: *6.5

Visual: dvd

Off the record: Carnie & Wendy Wilson are the daughters of Brian, who achieved their own success in 1990/91 courtesy of three US chart-toppers, 'Hold On', 'Release Me' and 'You're In Love'. *MCS*

BRIAN WILSON

Sep 95. (cd) *M.C.A.; <(MCD 11270)>* [ ] [59]
– Meant for you / This whole world / Caroline, no / Let the wind blow / Love and mercy / Do it again (featuring CARNIE and WENDY WILSON) / The warmth of the sun / Wonderful / Still I dream of it (original home demo, 1976) / Melt away / 'Til I die. *(re-iss. May02; same)*

S/track review: BRIAN WILSON remains an official genius, the most feted pop composer of the modern era, but even he hasn't been immune to the natural law of solo careers – almost without exception (Neil Young being one of them) failing to scale the creative heights of the bands which preceded them. But then his obstacles to even taking up that career have been more severe than almost any other solo artist, and – given the eternal silence of the late Syd Barrett – we should be glad he's still alive and making music. Save for the catharsis of 'SMiLE' finally coming full circle, his albums have drawn largely mixed, often – understandably – polite and respectful reviews, and this was no different. Coming the same year as his cult collaboration with Van Dyke Parks, 'Orange Crate Art', this soundtrack to the documentary of the same name was masterminded by ubiquitous producer Don Was, and performed by a venerable troupe of sessioners numbering the likes of JIM KELTNER and WADDY WACHTEL, even bringing in WILSON daughters CARNIE and WENDY (comically misspelled as "Windy" on the tracklist) for the Beach Boys' 'Do It Again', nostalgic even in its year of release (1969). Most of the album, in fact, comprises intimate Beach Boys interpretations, in some ways making it even more difficult for the man to live up to past glories and laying him open to the misplaced criticisms of Beach Boys diehards. Basically, this is what it is, WILSON singing solo on downscaled, sparely arranged oldies with the voice of a man in his fifties, occasionally slightly detached but still more than capable of inhabiting adolescent meditations like 'Caroline, No' (complete with fusion-esque flute). And at least Eugene Landy-era tracks 'Love And Mercy' and 'Melt Away' are rescued from the 80s production of his solo debut, but the most compelling (and inexplicable) inclusion, closer to the unknowable soul behind the enigma of BRIAN WILSON than any number of tastefully produced re-records, is the quavering home demo, 'Still I Dream Of It', a wracked monologue from the heart of his wilderness years. *BG*

Album rating: *6.5

I PLAYED IT FOR YOU

1985 (US 70m) Ronee Blakley Productions

Film genre: Country Rock-music docudrama

Top guns: s-w + dir: **Ronee Blakley**

Stars: Ronee Blakley *(herself/performer)* ← RENALDO AND CLARA ← NASHVILLE, Wim Wenders *(himself/Howard)* → NINA HAGEN = PUNK + GLORY, Scarlet Rivera *(herself)* ← RENALDO AND CLARA, Harley Stumbaugh *(himself)*

Storyline: If you're a faded singer-songwriter (turned actress) and if you split four years previously from a two-year marriage to an iconic filmmaker, Wim Wenders, why not write, direct and produce one of your own. With the initial guidance of Wim's – or Howard's, as he was named in the movie!? – steady hand, this is exactly what Ronee Blakely did, although she also threw in over a dozen of her back catalogue performed at Venice Theater, California. *MCS*

Movie rating: *5

Visual: video (no audio OST)

Off the record: Ronee Blakley (b.24 Aug'45, Caldwell, Idaho, USA) was a talented country-folk singer, who found critical fame after the release of her excellent eponymous 'Elektra' LP in 1972; the same year she wrote a song for the movie, 'Welcome Home, Soldier Boys'. When director Robert Altman invited her to play the part of Barbara Jean (some say Loretta Lynn was the inspiration) in the movie, 'NASHVILLE', premiered in 1975, Ronee looked destined for great things. However, during this lengthy musical hiatus and the relatively poor reviews of her sophomore set, 'Welcome' (1975), her career took a nosedive. She returned to star in subsequent films such as 'The Private Files Of J. Edgar Hoover' (1977), 'The Driver' (1978), 'The Baltimore Bullet', while old pal BOB DYLAN – who's she'd earlier sung with on the classic 'Hurricane', asked her to feature in his docudrama, 'RENALDO AND CLARA' (1978). The 80s saw Ronee take on lesser roles, only 1984's 'Nightmare On Elm Street' gave her major cred. One other connection to 'I PLAYED IT FOR YOU', was her involvement – as actor and composer! – in Wim Wenders' 1980 film, 'Lightning Over Water'. *MCS*

I PUT A SPELL ON ME

aka SCREAMIN' JAY HAWKINS: I PUT A SPELL ON ME

2001 (Greece 102m) Astra Show Vision and Sound / Ideefixe Productions

Film genre: R&B/Rock'n'roll-music documentary/bio-pic

Top guns: dir: (+ s-w) Nicholas Triandafyllidis

Stars: Screamin' Jay Hawkins *(himself/performer)* ← MYSTERY TRAIN ← JOEY ← AMERICAN HOT WAX ← MISTER ROCK AND ROLL, Monique Hawkins *(herself)*, **Bo DIDDLEY** *(performer)*, **Arthur Brown** *(performer)* ← JAILBIRD ROCK ← CLUB PARADISE ← TOMMY ← the COMMITTEE, **Eric BURDON** *(performer)*, **Diamanda Galas** *(performer)*, Jim Jarmusch *(himself)* ← YEAR OF THE HORSE ← WE'RE OUTTA HERE ← SLING BLADE ← LENINGRAD COWBOYS GO AMERICA ← CANDY MOUNTAIN ← STRAIGHT TO HELL / → the FUTURE IS UNWRITTEN, Frank Ash *(himself)*

Storyline: The death of Screamin' Jay Hawkins in 2000 saddened many who appreciated and cultivated his "theatrical rock" style, although it was the disclosure of the fact he had father over 75 children, all scattered in and around America and the globe. This is a strange story of the man who could quite literally "Put A Spell On You". *MCS*

Movie rating: *7.5

Visual: dvd (no audio OST by SCREAMIN' JAY HAWKINS)

Off the record: Screamin' Jay Hawkins was born Jalacy Hawkins, 18 July 1929, Cleveland, Ohio, USA. He decided upon a musical career after being orphaned and fostered as a young boy. Unfortunately he was not suited to the operatic style of performing (he chose at the time) and began his lifelong ambitions in 1951; he was pianist on several tracks by jazz veteran, Tiny Grimes. Hawkins subsequently delivered his finest 3-minutes in 1956 with the single, 'I Put A Spell On You', a meisterwork of its time that has since achieved great things although never a hit for the man; in later years it's been used on various commercials. It could be said that the man achieved little else in his lifetime, Hawkins became more famous for his onstage antics, shaped around shock-horror voodoo R'n'R, something not practised before but has since been associated with Arthur Brown and ALICE COOPER. His antics included appearing from a coffin and also carrying Henry, a macabre flaming skull companion, while shouting his words like a demented preacher man. This eccentric flair saw him being rebuked in the early 60s, with angry parents and God-fearing Americans having a field day due to its banning on radio. It also translated well onto the cinema screen when Hawkins had minor memorable roles in a share of films: 'Two Moon Junction', 'Dance With The Devil' and cult director Jim Jarmusch's masterpiece 'MYSTERY TRAIN'. However, the man did achieve his first hit single (albeit minor) when his version of Tom Waits' 'Heart Attack And Vine' made it into the UK Top 50 in spring '93. Jay died in Neuilly-sur-Seine, France on the 12th February 2000 of an aneurysm after an operation to his brain failed. The subsequent documentary, 'I PUT A SPELL ON ME', only features a handful of his songs, interviews taking up the bulk of the movie. *MCS*

I WAS BORN, BUT . . .

2002 (US 90m) Fallen Cinema / Piecmeal Films

Film genre: Alt-Rock-music documentary

Top guns: s-w + dir: Roddy Bogawa

Stars: Barbara Seaman, **Joe STRUMMER & the Mescaleros** *(performers)*, Roddy Bogawa *(narration)*

Storyline: Borrowing a title (and taking inspiration and style/homage) from Yasujiro Ozu's 1932 silent flick, New York filmmaker Roddy Bogawa examines the draw of punk rock from its inception in the mid-to-late 70s to recent times. *MCS*

Movie rating: *5

Visual: dvd

Off the record: Chris Brokaw was born in New York, although he stretched his musical skills further afield in '89 when he joined Boston slo-core outfit, Codeine, as their drummer. Now as a guitarist, he joined femme fatale singer Thalia Zedek (a former heroin addict) in bluesy rock outfit, Come, who also included the rhythm section of 'ATHENS, GA. – INSIDE/OUT' docu/concert refugees, Sean O'Brien (ex-Kilkenny Cats) and Arthur Johnson (ex-Bar-B-Q Killers). Come released four albums, 'Eleven: Eleven' (1992), 'Don't Ask Don't Tell' (1994), 'Melting In The Dark' (1996) and 'Gently, Down The Stream' (1998), the latter two without the aid of the aforementioned bassist and drummer. It's true to say their reputation was as true guardians of the blues' dark flame. After their demise (Zedek went solo), Brokaw broke out on his own, releasing two sets, 'Red Cities' (2002) and the limited edition, 'Wandering As Water' (2003). *MCS*

—

CHRIS BROKAW

Nov 04. (cd) *Atavistic; <158> 12XU; (0242)* □ □
– Reeperbahn / Dust / The average gringo / Golfing / Damon's Hawaiian blues / Halfpipe – Gangway / Gristle / Huntington Beach sunset / GPS / On a Great Lake / Huntington Beach sunrise / Chinatown / Friendly eyes.

S/track review: CHRIS BROKAW was a highly regarded figure in the American indie rock scene of the 1990s, mostly known for his work with the bands Come and Codeine. His work on the soundtrack to Roddy Bogawa's film has led the filmmaker to gasp that "the music has its own beauty and emotional resonance that invokes thoughts of cloudy days when the light is cutting ever so slightly through the sky's blues and reds". His instrumental songsmithery is reflective and reactive in equal measure; a sparse and intuitive series of mood pieces imbued with unspoken emotional resonance. It places insistent rhythmic excursions alongside more swirling, ambient fare. So whereas opener 'Reeperbahn' is a steely stringed acoustic guitar piece with some interesting and unconventional chord progressions, 'Dust' conjures a sweeping echo-y atmosphere which is distinctly Eno-esque. 'The Average Gringo' features a guitar sound dripping with reverb, lightly distorted as amplifier feedback swirls around the chordal melody, a plaintive piece where strange chords bleed into one another. 'Golfing' is a particular triumph, its alternately humming then shimmering drone reminiscent of the "otherness" of the film's subject matter, and reminiscent of Sunn 0)))'s more reflective moments. The liner notes inform us that 'Damon's Hawaiian Blues' was the only track made to order, with its Dick Dale-esque surf guitar coming through in a series of rich slides. 'Huntingdon Beach Sunset' and 'Huntingdon Beach Sunrise' have a similar stoned vibe that fits perfectly with the atmosphere they are supposed to evoke, a wet univibe guitar sound that laps at the listener like the waves. By stark contrast, 'GPS' has a distinctly punky bass groove as a drumbeat is phased in and out of the background, and 'On A Great Lake' dispenses with the effects pedals altogether in favour of a clean electric guitar and acoustic accompaniment, making its way through a series of melodic figures which build to a satisfying resolution. 'Chinatown' reverts to the reverberating drone BROKAW particularly seems to dig, and it makes for a lengthy, haunting and uneasy exploration. 'Friendly Eyes' concludes the album in a very brief and weird bout of disjointed and awkward guitar picking. This cult punk rock hero's ear for the ambient side of sonic life is finely honed indeed, and this is a deft and poised collection of instrumental pieces. *DF*

Album rating: *7

Billy IDOL

Born: William Broad, 30 Nov'55, Stanmore, Middlesex, England. In 1976, this aspiring punk formed Generation X, and although they attracted a loyal fanbase, the quartet were never considered a dyed-in-the-wool punk band per se, their more commercial, hooky power pop at odds with the genre's inherent nihilism. Signed to 'Chrysalis', the band hit the charts with 'Your Generation', following it up with 'Wild Youth' and 'Ready Steady Go', the latter track a decidedly un-punk 60s tribute. An eponymous debut album hit the Top 30 in spring '78, while the band's sound grew increasingly commercial on successive albums, the Ian Hunter-produced 'Valley Of The Dolls' (1979) and 'Kiss Me Deadly' (1981). Following their split in '81, the bleached-blond IDOL was free to pursue his barely concealed desire for pop stardom. Relocating to New York, he met manager Bill Aucoin and producer Keith Forsey. With new guitarist Steve Stevens, he cut a cover of Tommy James & The Shondells' 'Mony Mony' (a live version later topped the US charts), while a full-length eponymous debut album followed in summer '82. 'Rebel Yell' (1984) and the attendant 'Eyes Without A Face' single gave him further Stateside success, while a re-released 'White Wedding' gave IDOL a belated UK Top 10 hit in summer '85. 'Whiplash Smile' (1986) and 'Charmed Life' (1990), were to follow, although ironically enough, Billy suffered a near fatal motorbike crash, the climax to a troubled late 80s period which had seen the singer living out the rock'n'roll lifestyle to the full in sunny Los Angeles. Bluesy and confessional, 'Cradle Of Love' (also taken from the movie, 'The ADVENTURES OF FORD FAIRLANE') nearly returned him to the top of the charts, while the less said about IDOL's cover of 'L.A. Woman' (not from 'The DOORS' movie!), the better. An ill-advised concept album, 'Cyberpunk' (1993), was even less well received, although IDOL subsequently sought out a little fame when he popped up in the movie, 'The WEDDING SINGER' (1998), alongside its star Adam Sandler. The 'Sanctuary' label was another redoubt for ageing rockers, and they signed him on for a set of bona fide new material, 'Devil's Playground' (2005). Critics weren't too keen but it did scrape into the US Top 50, while one of the tracks, 'Plastic Jesus' (written by George Cromarty), was used in the Oscar-nominated film, 'Crash'. *MCS & BG*

- **filmography** {acting/performer} –

the Punk Rock Movie *(1978 {p w/ GENERATION X} =>)* / **D.O.A.** *(1980 {p w/ GENERATION X} =>)* / **the Doors** *(1991 {a} OST by the DOORS =>)* / Mad Dog Time *(1996 {a})* / **the Wedding Singer** *(1998 {c} on OST by V/A =>)* / Heavy Metal 2000 *(2000 {*v} on OST by V/A; see future edition)* / **the Filth & The Fury** *(2000 {p w/ GENERATION X} OST by the SEX PISTOLS & V/A =>)* / **Hey Is Dee Dee Home** *(2003 {c} =>)* / **Punk's Not Dead** *(2007 {p w/ GENERATION X} =>)*

IMAGINE

aka JOHN LENNON: IMAGINE

1972 (US 55m) Joko

Film genre: Pop/Rock-music documentary

Top guns: dir: Steve Gebhardt ← TEN FOR TWO, **John Lennon, Yoko Ono**

Stars: John Lennon *(himself/performer)* <= the BEATLES =>, **Yoko ONO** *(herself/performer)*, Daniel Richter *(himself)*, Jack Palance *(himself)* ← BATMAN, **George Harrison** *(himself)* <= the BEATLES =>, Andy Warhol *(himself)* ← COCKSUCKER BLUES ← the VELVET UNDERGROUND AND NICO / → BLANK GENERATION → NICO-ICON → ROCK AND ROLL HEART → DETROIT ROCK CITY → END OF THE CENTURY, Fred Astaire *(himself)*, Dick Cavett *(himself)* ← COCKSUCKER BLUES / → JIMI HENDRIX → JANIS, **Miles DAVIS** *(cameo)*, **Phil Spector** *(cameo)* ← the CONCERT FOR BANGLADESH ← EASY RIDER ← the BIG T.N.T. SHOW ← the T.A.M.I. SHOW / → IMAGINE: JOHN LENNON → MAYOR OF THE SUNSET STRIP

Storyline: More than a day in the life of ex-Beatle, John Lennon, and his wife Yoko Ono, depicted in a half-fiction, experimental kind of way. Lennon performs his seminal 'Imagine' album (virtually in its entireity), with Yoko getting her two-penneth in courtesy of a few tracks from her weird set, 'Fly'. No dialogue speaks volumes. *MCS*

Movie rating: *7

Visual: video

Off the record: Yoko ONO provided two bonus songs for the film, 'Mrs. Lennon' and 'Don't Count The Waves'. *MCS*

IMAGINE: JOHN LENNON

1988 (US 103m) Warner Bros. Pictures (R)

Film genre: Pop/Rock concert/documentary biopic

Top guns: s-w: Andrew Solt (+ dir) ← THIS IS ELVIS, Sam Egan

Stars: John Lennon *(himself/narrator)* <= the BEATLES =>, **Yoko ONO** *(herself)*, **Paul McCartney** *(himself)* <= the BEATLES =>, **George Harrison** *(himself)* <= the BEATLES =>, **Ringo Starr** *(himself)* <= the BEATLES =>, **Phil Spector** *(himself)* ← IMAGINE ← the CONCERT FOR BANGLADESH ← EASY RIDER ← the BIG T.N.T. SHOW ← the T.A.M.I. SHOW / → MAYOR OF THE SUNSET STRIP, Cynthia Lennon *(herself)*, **Julian Lennon** *(himself)* ← HAIL! HAIL! ROCK'N'ROLL, **Sean Lennon** *(himself)* ← MOONWALKER / → ENDLESS HARMONY: THE BEACH BOYS STORY → FREE TIBET, **David BOWIE** *(himself)*, George Martin *(himself)* ← GIVE MY REGARDS TO BROAD STREET ← the COMPLEAT BEATLES ← LET IT BE / → BEAUTIFUL DREAMERS: BRIAN WILSON AND THE STORY OF 'SMiLE', Derek Taylor *(himself)* ← LET IT BE, Brian Epstein *(himself)* ← the COMPLEAT BEATLES ← I WANNA HOLD YOUR HAND, Al Capp *(himself)*, May Pang *(herself)*, **Jon Cobert** *(himself)* ← URGH! A MUSIC WAR / → the NOMI SONG

Storyline: An engaging if selective account of John Lennon's life, masterminded by Yoko Ono and concentrating heavily on the 70s. The bulk of the film is interview footage effectively recounting the man's life in his own words, words which he doesn't mince in explosive encounters with cartoonist Al Capp and a female journalist. There's also an uneasily prophetic sequence where Lennon engages with a deluded fan camped out in his garden, and assorted in-studio and concert clips. The DVD Deluxe Edition adds a superfluous bonus disc choked with earnest reminiscences from the film makers and an acoustic performance of 'Imagine'. *BG*

Movie rating: *7.5

Visual:

Off the record: May Pang was the "mistress" of JOHN LENNON, his personal assistant from late 1973 to early '75 while he and YOKO had a little time-out. It was YOKO that suggested JOHN see May as he knew he would be dating if they split. *MCS*

—

JOHN LENNON (& the BEATLES *)

Oct 88. (cd/d-c/d-lp) *Columbia; <90803> Parlophone; (CD/TC+/ PCSP 722)* [31] [64]
– Real love / Twist and shout (*) / Help! (*) / In my life (*) / Strawberry fields forever (*) / A day in the life (*) / Revolution (*) / The ballad of John & Yoko (*) / Julia (*) / Don't let me down (*) / Give peace a chance / How? / Imagine (rehearsal) / God / Mother / Stand by me / Jealous guy / Woman / Beautiful boy (darling boy) / (Just like) Starting over / Imagine.

S/track review: Like the film (criticised in some quarters for its beatification of an already mythical subject), this soundtrack pretty much avoids LENNON's spikier solo offerings. No 'Working Class Hero' or 'How Do You Sleep' then, but plenty of odes to love – both romantic and filial – and the possibilities of world peace, admittedly classics all. In terms of its functioning as an update of the mid-70s compilation, 'Shaved Fish' (1975), it's fairly tame, although it did pitch BEATLES and solo songs side by side for the first time, including the poignant 'Julia', a tribute to LENNON's mother which – prior to the mid-90s anthologies – had only been available on 'The White Album' (1968). In this sense, it at least gives some sense of the man's singing/songwriting development, from early rock'n'roll covers to the limpid psychedelia of 'Strawberry Fields Forever', the buoyant turbulence of his blossoming romance ('The Ballad Of John And Yoko') and on to peace activism and domesticity. With most fans being familiar with every track, the big draw was the previously unreleased rehearsal outtake of 'Imagine' and an acoustic demo of 'Real Love' (later fleshed out as a single on the Beatles' 'Anthology 2'), although it's hard to.. er, imagine many people shelling out for those alone. And even given its doubtful merits as a greatest hits set, it's since been trumped by the exhaustive 'Working Class Hero: The Definitive Lennon' (2005). *BG*

Album rating: *7

– spinoff hits, etc. –

JOHN LENNON: Jealous Guy / Give Peace A Chance

Oct 88. (cd-s) *<44230>* [80] [–]

JOHN LENNON: Imagine / Jealous Guy

Nov 88. (7"/7"pic-d) *(R/RP 6199)* [–] [45]
(12"+=/12"pic-d+=) *(12R/+P 6199)* – Happy Xmas (war is over).
(cd-s+=) *(CDR 6199)* – Give peace a chance.

□ IN BED WITH MADONNA alt.
(⇒ TRUTH OR DARE)

□ the INCREDIBLE STRING BAND segment
(⇒ BE GLAD FOR THE SONG HAS NO ENDING)

INSTRUMENT

1999 (US 93m w/b&w) Gravity Hill

Film genre: Punk rock-music concert/documentary

Top guns: dir: Jem Cohen → BENJAMIN SMOKE

Stars: Fugazi:- Ian MacKaye *(performer)* ← ANOTHER STATE OF MIND / → the SHIELD AROUND THE K → WE JAM ECONO: THE STORY OF THE MINUTEMEN, **Guy Picciotto** *(performer)*, **Joe Lally** *(performer)*, **Brendan Canty** *(performer)*

Storyline: Sub-titled, 'Instrument: Ten Years With The Band Fugazi', this was director/photographer Jem Cohen's attempt at setting the world straight about one of the most influential outfits of the 90s. Their unique, independent and indeed "revolutionary" approach (they performed at all-age venues for $5, didn't duly promote their albums to the press and didn't sell-out to join the majors) set this film apart from the usual run-of-the-mill music documentary. *MCS*

Movie rating: *6

Visual: video + dvd

Off the record: Fugazi were founded in Washington DC, 1987, out of other DC hardcore acts, Embrace and Minor Threat; the 'Dischord' imprint also got underway. **Ian MacKaye** and former Rites Of Spring leader, **Guy Picciotto**, wrote the bulk of their material, while a rhythm section of **Brendan Canty** and **Joe Lally**, crystallised their formation. The quartet released two HENRY ROLLINS-produced mini-sets, the eponymous 'Fugazi' (1988) and 'Margin Walker' (1989), before fully realising their aggressively economical sound on the acclaimed 'Repeater' (1990) album. Bringing to mind the once wilfully obscure vocals of Pere Ubu's David Thomas backed by the hardcore of No Means No, Fugazi delivered a second set proper, 'Steady Diet Of Nothing' (1991), their perseverance paying off with a minor placing in the UK charts. Two years later, 'In On The Killtaker' scored a deserved UK Top 30 and dominated the indie charts for months; despite persistent major label interest, Fugazi have admirably refused to play the corporate game (how many bands can you say that about?). The mid-90s saw the release of 'Red Medicine', the album taking the staunchly independent hardcore crusaders into previously uncharted territory, i.e. the UK Top 20 (appropriately enough, the commercial behemoth that is the American music industry has so far prohibited the band's domestic success). Fugazi regrouped in 1998, although 'End Hits' (not a compilation) suffered a little commercially due to their long absence. *MCS*

—

FUGAZI

Apr 99. (cd/c/lp) *Dischord; <(DIS 120 CD/C/V)>* [ ] [ ]
– Pink frosty (demo) / Lusty scripps / Arpeggiator (demo) / Afterthought / Trio's / Turkish disco / Me and Thumbelina / Floating boy (demo) / Link track / Little Debbie / H.B. / I'm so tired / Rend it (demo) / Closed captioned (demo) / Guilford fall (demo) / Swingset / Shaken all over / Slo crostic.

S/track review: Up to now, FUGAZI were one of indie music's nearly men, achieving critical acclaim, although never quite hitting the heights they so richly deserved. 'INSTRUMENTAL' – a compilation of sorts – was a prime example of the why factor. Made up of home demos and unreleased studio outtakes, the album (and in some respects the movie), gave out the impression the quartet were marking time before a make-or-break finale. This was indeed the case, as the band have been inactive since 2001's 'The Argument' set, and have since gone into outside projects. Of the demos – mostly stemming from the previous year's 'End Hits' long-player – 'Pink Frosty', 'Floating Boy' and 'Arpeggiator' came up trumps. The aforementioned opening dirge, 'Pink Frosty', could well have been influenced by Tortoise's magnum opus, 'Djed', its eerie bassy rhythms pure class. 'Floating Boy' was cool and laid-back in a jazzy kind of way, while the opposite could be said for 'Arpeggiator', an upbeat sonic klash combining the efforts of MacKAYE and PICCIOTTO's angular frets plus CANTY's riveting percussion – greatness had not deserted them. Of the fresh numbers, 'Lusty Scripps' was easily FUGAZI at their most exciting, and again the guitar interaction between mainmen MacKAYE and PICCIOTTO out of this world. Of the decidely shorter studio cuts, 'Little Debbie' (with grindcore vox!), the Pink Floyd-ish 'Swingset' ("set the controls" indeed) and the "Come As You Are"-esque 'Link Track', were worthy of repeated plays. Curios such as 'Me And Thumbelina' (sounding like Vic Reeves on a "Big Night Out"!), the minute-long run-through of Johnny Kidd's 'Shaken All Over' (yes, "Shaken") and the ballady, 'I'm So Tired' (with vocals!), were for the FUGAZI faithful only. Saving one of their best for last, 'Slo Crostic', was dirty post-grunge, reminiscent of some post-millennium anthem I can't for the sake of me remember. Fans of Husker Du, Gang Of Four and Pavement will not be disappointed. *MCS*

Album rating: *6.5

□ the ISLEY BROTHERS segment
(⇒ IT'S YOUR THING)

IT'S YOUR THING

1970 (US 120m – 31m UK) Medford Films

Film genre: R&B/Soul-music concert/documentary

Top guns: dir: Mike Gargiulo

Stars: the Isley Brothers:- Ronald, Rudolph, O'Kelly *(performers)*, Moms Mabley *(host)*, **the Edwin Hawkins Singers** *(performers)* → CELEBRATION AT BIG SUR, **the Brooklyn Bridge:- Johnny Maestro** *(performers)*, **Ike Turner** *(performer)* ← the BIG T.N.T. SHOW / → GIMME SHELTER → SOUL TO SOUL / → BLUES ODYSSEY → the ROAD TO MEMPHIS → GODFATHERS AND SONS & **Tina TURNER** *(performer)*, **the Five Stairsteps: Cubie Burke, Clarence Burke, James Burke, Kenny Burke, Dennis Burke** *(performers)*, **Clara Ward** *(performer)* ← a TIME TO SING, **Patti Austin** *(performer)* → the WIZ → ONE-TRICK PONY → TUCKER: THE MAN AND HIS DREAM → JACKIE'S BACK!

Storyline: It's the Isley Brothers and friends (including Tina Turner) performing at The Yankee Stadium, New York City on the 21st of June 1969. *MCS*

Movie rating: *5

Visual: video

Off the record: The **Isley Brothers** were formed in Cincinatti, Ohio in the early 50s by siblings Ronald, Rudolph, O'Kelly and Vernon, all experienced gospel singers. The subsequent death of the latter bro' led to the remaining members moving from Cincinnati to New York in '56, where they began their recording career. After achieving some early success with 'Shout' in '59, the Isleys recorded the enduring 'Twist And Shout' a couple of years later, a song the BEATLES would later cover to significantly greater commercial success. Eager for more creative control, the Isley Brothers took the unprecedented step of setting up their own label, 'T-Neck' (named after their new location, Teaneck in New Jersey). Their first homegrown recording, 'Testify', was largely ignored although a certain lead guitarist would go on to influence generations, the axe-man in question, Jimi HENDRIX. In an effort to achieve a higher profile, the group signed to 'Motown' in '65. Unfortunately, the label insisted on moulding the band to their formulaic "hit-factory" approach, stifling their creative input and producing only one hit, 1966's 'This Old Heart Of Mine'. The brothers' finest recordings came after they indeed split with boss Berry Gordy and Co in '68, relaunching 'T-Neck' the following year. With creative control firmly back in the hands of the outfit, they let rip with funky grooves and even funkier outfits, their evolution complete with the addition of three more members of the Isley clan, brothers Ernie and Marvin plus cousin Chris Jasper. The latter contributed the classic single, 'It's Your Thing', a record which became an instant hit and earned the band a Grammy. Touring frequently in the late 60s and early 70s, a distribution deal with 'C.B.S.' in '73 led to the release of '3 + 3', an album which showcased the roots of the "Isley Sound"; Ernie's Hendrix-influenced guitar work was a vital component in the trademark blend of dance rhythms and funk-laden grooves best sampled on the sexy 'That Lady'. Through '73 to '83, the band scored nine consecutive gold or platinum albums, their sound switching back and forth between Ronald's soulfully smooth ballads and the hard and funky stuff – they're still going strong today (2007) and are still making platinum albums. *MCS & BG*

– associated release –

the ISLEY BROTHERS: Live At Yankee Stadium (w/ Various Artists)

Oct 69. (d-lp) *T-Neck; <TNS 3004-2>* □ [-]
– the ISLEY BROTHERS:- I know who you been socking it to / (a) I turned you on, (b) It's your thing / Shout / the EDWIN HAWKINS SINGERS:- Jesus, lover of my soul / Joy joy / Oh happy day // the BROOKLYN BRIDGE:- Medley: People get ready – Talkin' about my baby – It's all right – Keep on pushin' – You must believe me – I'm so proud – Amen / FIVE STAIRSTEPS: Don't change your love / JUDY WHITE: Somebody's been messin' / SWEET CHERRIES: Love is what you make it.

□ Mick JAGGER
(⇒ the ROLLING STONES)

JANIS

1975 (US 96m w/b&w) Universal Pictures (R)

Film genre: Blues-rock-music concert/documentary bio-pic

Top guns: s-w + dir: Howard Alk, Seaton Findlay

Stars: Janis JOPLIN *(herself/performer)*, **Big Brother & The Holding Company + the Full-Tilt Boogie Band + the Kozmic Blues Band** *(themselves)* ← MONTEREY POP, Dick Cavett *(himself)* ← JIMI HENDRIX ← IMAGINE ← COCKSUCKER BLUES

Storyline: The all-too-short career of Janis Joplin, a dynamic but self-destructive blues singer who was as voluptuous and volcanic offstage as she was on. Through raw'n'rare interviews, concert footage and even family photos, the viewer is taken into the private life and loves of one of America's great ladies of rock music. *MCS*

Movie rating: *6

Visual: video: 'JANIS: THE WAY SHE WAS'

Off the record: Big Brother & The Holding Company comprised of guitarists **Sam Andrew, James Gurley**, bassist **Peter Albin** and drummer **David Getz**. After the relative success of the 1967 eponymous LP, the group had a No.1 the following year with 'Cheap Thrills'. When solo artist **JANIS JOPLIN** died of a heroin overdose on the 4th October, 1970, Big Brother released two LPs, 'Be A Brother' (1970) and 'How Hard It Is' (1971). *MCS*

JANIS JOPLIN (w/ the Full Tilt Boogie Band * / w/ the Kozmic Blues Band **)

May 75. (d-lp) *Columbia; <33345> C.B.S.; (88115)* [54] [ ]
– (Early Performances:- non-soundtrack songs) // "JANIS" soundtrack:- Mercedes Benz (*) / Ball and chain (**) / Rap on "Try" / Try (just a little bit harder) (*) / Summertime (**) / (Albert Hall interview 1969) / Cry baby (*) / Move over (*) / (Dick Cavett T.V. interview 1970) / Piece of my heart (with BIG BROTHER AND THE HOLDING COMPANY) / Port Arthur high school reunion / Maybe (**) / Me and Bobby McGee (*).

S/track review: Having read a few critiques on this soundtrack, I was surprised to find it rather OK (and we are bypassing the accompanying 'Early Performances' folk sides here). 'JANIS' was a much-maligned movie, showing the blues-rock singer in all her guises, warts'n'all. We all know of her tragic death on 4th October 1970, and following the death of HENDRIX in similar o.d. circumstances, the world of music was indeed shaken to the core. We see JOPLIN with her three backing groups here, namely and chronologically San Fran's BIG BROTHER AND THE HOLDING COMPANY, the KOZMIC BLUES BAND and the FULL TILT BOOGIE BAND, while other numbers are made up from witty dialogue chatting to Dick Cavett, etc. Due to a certain TV ad, 'Mercedes Benz', has become an integral part of JJ's canon, and here it is in all its carcastic glory, but with a demo-like appeal. The live, and I mean "live", 'Ball And Chain' (from the pen of Big Mama Thornton) and 'Try (Just A Little Bit Harder)' (written by Jerry Ragovoy & Chip Taylor) carry JANIS off into a higher cosmic world and you can believe why she was the female equivalent to Led Zeppelin's Robert Plant. To loosen the tempo ever so slightly, JOPLIN attempts Gershwin's 'Summertime' (with the KOZMIC BLUES BAND), the only blues lady to carry such a standard into the realms of Rock. Yes, she does get hoarse and raspy at times, (but not on Kris Kristofferson's 'Me And Bobby McGee' – her posthumous No.1), and JANIS twists and turns her way through at least a few more soulful nuggets, 'Move Over', 'Cry Baby' and 'Piece Of My Heart' (the latter two written by Ragovoy & Bert Berns). This lady sings the blues – with ease. *MCS*

Album rating: *6.5

JANIS JOPLIN SLEPT HERE

1994 (US 120m) Flaming Angel Films

Film genre: Blues-rock-music documentary

Top guns: dir: Tara Veneruso

Stars: Double Trouble:- Jimmy Vaughan, Tommy Shannon, Chris Layton *(themselves/performers)*, Clifford Antone *(himself)* → HOME OF THE BLUES, Richard Linklater *(himself)* → BEAVIS AND BUTT-HEAD DO AMERICA → CHELSEA WALLS, Louis Black *(himself)* ← TRUE STORIES / → HOME OF THE BLUES → the DEVIL AND DANIEL JOHNSON, **Carolyn Hester** *(herself/performer)* → NO DIRECTION HOME

Storyline: Shot by a mere 20-year old (Tara Veneruso), this is a musical legacy of Austin, Texas, which takes us back some 40 years and to the legend that was R&B/Rock singer, Janis Joplin. Tara interviews and delves into some modern aspects of Austin, including its top festival, South By Southwest. *MCS*

Movie rating: *6

Visual: Old Glory video in 2000 (no audio OST)

Off the record: Janis JOPLIN and her heady lifestyle has been well-documented elsewhere (see 'JANIS'). **Double Trouble** was the band set up to back guitarist Stevie Ray Vaughan. **Carolyn Hester** was a folk singer from Waco, Texas, and once married to Richard Farina. *MCS*

JAY-Z

Born: Shawn Carter, 4 Dec'70, Brooklyn, New York, USA. Despite being one of the most lauded yet egotistical rappers in the game, JAY-Z – who worked his way up from the slums of Brooklyn – had become one of the richest young entrepreneurs in the music industry thanks to his booming 'Roc-a-Fella' imprint. Raised in the Marcy projects of Brooklyn, the young JAY-Z (then known as 'Jazzy') began hustling on the streets in his teens until he met the aspiring rapper Big Jaz, who was signed to a small label. Influenced by Jaz, JAY-Z decided to launch his own record label with just a few well-known rap artists around Brooklyn instead of trying to break into the already expanding rap industry. He enlisted Damon Dash and Kareem Burke, and together they established 'Roc-a-Fella' records in 1995, just one year before JAY-Z issued his debut set 'Reasonable Doubt'. The following year JAY-Z ditched his gangsta efforts and went for a more pop orientated direction for his subsequent release 'In My Life: Vol 1', a Billboard chart entry at

Number 3, a huge climb from the self-produced debut. 'Vol 2: Hard Knock Life' (1998) boasted huge single 'Hard Knock Life (Ghetto Anthem)' which cleverly and bizarrely enough sampled the 'Annie' song, with piano and a chorus of orphaned children respectively. By this point JAY-Z had turned his record company into a "dynasty", by producing his own clothing line and representing a huge host of New York's finest talents. Vanity project, 'Vol 3: Life And Times Of S. Carter' (1999), was truly for only the most avid collector, while the much-improved 'The Blueprint' (2001) featured the track 'Takeover', a vicious attack on East Coasters Nas and Mobb Deep. A shared album with R Kelly, 'The Best Of Both Worlds' (2002), filled time between his follow-up, 'Black Album' (2003), JAY-Z not perhaps the first to instill the title with such meaning. His style and attitude were best witnessed on performance flicks such as 'BACKSTAGE' (2000), 'BEEF' (2003) and his own production, 'FADE TO BLACK' (2004), while cameos – however brief – cropped up in features such as 'State Property' (2002) and 'DEATH OF A DYNASTY' (2003). Towards the end of 2004, JAY-Z continued his chart domination via two collaborations, the first with R&B man R Kelly ('Unfinished Business'), the second with metal-rappers, Linkin Park ('Collision Course'). *MCS*

- filmography {acting} (composer) –

Streets Is Watching *(1998 video {*c} [s-w])* / **Backstage** *(2000 {p} on OST by V/A =>)* / State Property *(2002 {a} OST by V/A; see future edition)* / **Paper Soldiers** *(2002 {b} =>)* / **Death Of A Dynasty** *(2003 {c} =>)* / **Beef** *(2003 {p} on OST by V/A =>)* / **Fade To Black** *(2004 {*p} =>)* / Through The Fire *(2005 {c})*

☐ Joan JETT
(⇒ the RUNAWAYS)

JIMI HENDRIX

1973 (US 105m) Warner Bros. (R)

Film genre: Rock-music concert/rockumentary bio-pic

Top guns: dir: Gary Weis → the RUTLES, Joe Boyd, John Head

Stars: Jimi HENDRIX *(live footage)*, **Pete Townshend** *(performer)* <= the WHO =>, **Eric CLAPTON** *(performer)*, **Mick Jagger** *(himself)* <= the ROLLING STONES =>, **Lou REED** *(himself)*, **LITTLE RICHARD** *(himself)*, **Buddy Miles** *(performer)*, ← SUPERSHOW / → the BUDDY STORY STORY, **Mitch Mitchell** *(performer)* ← RAINBOW BRIDGE ← MONTEREY POP / → ROCK AND ROLL CIRCUS → EXPERIENCE, Eddie Kramer *(himself)*, Pat Hartley *(herself)* ← RAINBOW BRIDGE → ABSOLUTE BEGINNERS, Dick Cavett *(himself)* ← IMAGINE ← COCKSUCKER BLUES / → JANIS, Germaine Greer *(herself)*, Arthur Allen *(himself)*, Frankie Croker *(himself)* ← CLEOPATRA JONES / → FIVE ON THE BLACK HAND SIDE → THAT'S THE WAY OF THE WORLD → BREAKIN' 2: ELECTRIC BOOGALOO

Storyline: Live concert footage from an appearance at The Marquee in London 1967 to his finale at the Isle Of Wight Festival in 1970 spans this documentary; interviews from contemporaries such as Clapton, Townshend, Jagger and Mitch Mitchell pay tribute to the greatest guitarist of all time. *MCS*

Movie rating: *7.5

Visual: video + dvd

Off the record: Look out too for a dvd compilation of HENDRIX's time on 'The Dick Cavett Show: Jimi Hendrix' (2002).

—

JIMI HENDRIX: sound track recordings from the film . . .

Jul 73. (d-lp) *Reprise; <6481> (K 64017)* [89] [37]
– Rock me, baby / Wild thing / Machine gun I / * Interviews I / Johnny B. Goode / Hey Joe / Purple haze / Like a rolling stone / * Interviews II // The star spangled banner / Machine gun II / Hear my train a-comin' / * Interviews III / Red house / In from the storm / * Interviews IV.

S/track review: Any good documentary will always get beneath the skin of the artist, look behind the façade and drag everything out into the open. In terms of the music to accompany such a documentary, equal attention has to be paid to those tunes the masses all love and those which only the most ardent of anoraks will have heard. The soundtrack to this documentary about JIMI HENDRIX has managed to do just that, and they are all live tracks which is HENDRIX at his best. Staples such as 'Hey Joe', 'Purple Haze' and the best version of 'Wild Thing' ever committed to record are all present here along with a collection of songs that combine to show both how HENDRIX was influenced and the sheer magnitude of what the man could do with a guitar. His take on the Chuck Berry classic 'Johnny B. Goode' is just rock'n'roll in its purest form, full of energy and intensity, as is his impassioned version of Dylan's 'Like A Rolling Stone'. These covers aren't as completely transformed as, say, 'All Along The Watchtower' was, although they do show that he knew where his influences came from. Also showcased are those little-known tracks such as 'Machine Gun I & II', 'Red House' and 'In From The Storm', songs that reflect HENDRIX's ability to experiment and improvise on songs while in the process creating sounds that no-one else has ever made nor done so to the same extent since. Instead of just noodling away some pointless solo on his guitar, HENDRIX used it to make the song, to take it to another level and obliterate any preconceptions of what a guitar is supposed to sound like. Included are interview segments from HENDRIX's friends, family and other notables, including Little Richard wondering where he got his name. This is a mighty soundtrack that reflects the talent of a true genius. *CM*

Album rating: *6.5

JIMI HENDRIX LIVE AT THE ISLE OF WIGHT 1970

1991 (US 56m) Castle Music Pictures

Film genre: Hard-Rock-music concert

Top guns: dir: Murray Lerner ← the WHO: LIVE AT THE ISLE OF WIGHT FESTIVAL 1970 ← FESTIVAL / → MESSAGE TO LOVE: THE ISLE OF WIGHT FESTIVAL

Stars: Jimi HENDRIX *(performer)*, **Billy Cox** *(performer)* ← JIMI HENDRIX ← RAINBOW BRIDGE ← JIMI PLAYS BERKELEY / → MESSAGE TO LOVE: THE ISLE OF WIGHT FESTIVAL → RISING LOW, **Mitch Mitchell** *(performer)* ← JIMI HENDRIX ← RAINBOW BRIDGE ← JIMI PLAYS BERKELEY ← MONTEREY POP ← EXPERIENCE / → ROCK AND ROLL CIRCUS → MESSAGE TO LOVE: THE ISLE OF WIGHT FESTIVAL

Storyline: Jimi Hendrix's historical final concert performance at the Isle Of Wight Festival in August 1970 comes to life via this piece of celluloid – he died 18 days after this early misty morning showing. *MCS*

Movie rating: *7

Visual: video (+ dvd 2004)

Off the record: The original video/DVD adds a few tracks including 'Foxey Lady', 'Voodoo Child (Slight Return)'.

—

JIMI HENDRIX . . .: Blue Wild Angel

Nov 02. (cd) *M.C.A.; <(113089-2)>* ☐ ☐
– God save the Queen / Sgt. Pepper's lonely hearts club band / Spanish castle magic / All along the watchtower / Machine gun / Lover man / Freedom / Red house / Dolly dagger / Hey baby (new

rising sun) / In from the storm. *(d-cd iss.Oct05 +=)* – Midnight lightning / Foxey lady / Message to love / Ezy rider / Hey Joe / Purple haze / Voodoo child (slight return) / (+ DVD w/ all above).

S/track review: The most fascinating thing about JIMI HENDRIX's performance at the Isle of Wight Festival in 1970 is the spectacle of a guitar player of such sublime skills wrestling with technical gremlins. HENDRIX seemed in a sardonic and spikey mood, frustrated at having to take the stage so late (3 am), and at the mercy of inclement British weather conditions. He later complained he couldn't really engage with the audience through the murky atmosphere, and the opening salvo of 'God Save The Queen' and (a verse of) 'Sgt. Pepper's Lonely Hearts Club Band' fail to rekindle the fire of the iconic Woodstock performance which the former strives for, or re-enact the sharp shock of the Marquee Club in 1967 when he had taken the liberty of opening with Pepper the day after that album's release. It's only with 'Spanish Castle Magic' that the sonic juggernaut starts to get going, and his brilliant reinterpretation of 'All Along The Watchtower' still thrills though it sounds slightly thin. Rather than capitulate, 'Machine Gun' (the gig's centrepiece) is a 20-minute showdown between band and equipment, it coils and meanders, as voices from the security personnel's walkie talkies get filtered through the amplifiers, eerily evoking army two-way radio. Rarely does a song so perfectly enact the sentiment it conveys, and the joy is in the individual flourishes that different musicians bring to the table; when the song was first played in the Band of Gypsys line-up Buddy Miles' ra-ta-tat-tat-tat on the snare mimicked the instrument of death itself, whereas MITCH MITCHELL prefers a military brass band drum roll. MITCHELL and bassist BILLY COX struggle to synthesize with one another, this line up of the EXPERIENCE is a composite of two very different approaches to HENDRIX's music: the intricacy and responsiveness of MITCHELL with the back to basics, rock solid work of COX. Cumulatively, it's a great and wayward rendition: in the middle section of the song a deft wah-wah lead seems to trail off before MITCHELL slowly fills out the tune to a presumed conclusion only for HENDRIX to introduce a tricky, mellifluous, snaking riff, and MITCHELL does well to pick the song back up with some off-beat improvising and syncopation. After the tune has come to an unsteady conclusion a self-conscious HENDRIX alludes to the "difficulties" plaguing the band. He even resolves to "start again" after the swift punch of 'Lover Man'. 'Freedom' is muscular as ever but it is within the boundaries of the orthodox slow blues of 'Red House' that HENDRIX – now strapped to a flying V – really soars, molten soloing spiralling through the mist. It reinvigorates the performance and the band seems to relish the rest of the night, culminating in the torrent of laid-back heavy riffing of 'In From The Storm', which seems an extremely apt conclusion. HENDRIX's death so soon after this performance infuses his promise to return soon with poignancy, and he heralds the despondency of the 70s with his wonderfully barbed final pledge of peace and happiness and "all that other bullshit". *DF*

Album rating: *7.5 / re-d-cd+DVD (*8)

JIMI PLAYS BERKELEY

1971 (US 55m) New Line Cinema

Film genre: Hard-Rock-music documentary/concert

Top guns: dir: Peter Pilafian

Stars: Jimi HENDRIX *(performer)*, **Billy Cox + Mitch Mitchell** *(performers)* <= Jimi HENDRIX =>

Storyline: The Jimi Hendrix Experience perform several great numbers at the Berkeley Memorial Day Concert (in the community center) on the 30th May, 1970. *MCS*

Movie rating: *4.5

Visual: video + dvd 2003

Off the record: (see below)

—

the JIMI HENDRIX EXPERIENCE: Live At Berkeley

Oct 03. (d-lp) *Universal; <B 11590-1>* [–] [ ]
– Introduction / Pass it on (straight ahead) / Hey baby (new sun rising) / Lover man / Stone free / Hey Joe / I don't live today / Machine gun / Foxy lady / Star spangled banner / Purple haze / Voodoo child (slight return).

S/track review: The JIMI HENDRIX EXPERIENCE's two shows at the Berkeley Community Theatre on the 30th of May 1970 were documented on film (at the behest of Jimi's manager Michael Jeffery) as a means of generating cash and maintaining the guitarist's profile while he was in the studio. The disc records the second performance that night, and showcases an increasingly jammy and experimental EXPERIENCE, in many ways a hybrid band, melding MITCH MITCHELL's responsive drumming with the locked-down steadiness of BILLY COX's bass. HENDRIX himself is in playful mood, asking for some time for the band to "get rid of these joints" before launching into a heavy, lurching 'Pass It On (Straight Ahead)', itself a tune-in-transition, an exploratory excursion. 'Hey Baby (New Rising Sun)' is a majestic follow-up, and evinces Hendrix's confidence in unveiling new material so early in a set; his opening guitar work is extraordinary, as virtuosic and classically-influenced soloing is detailed with Spanish inflections. In its exploratory mood and movements it shows a musician ready to transcend all the constrictions of what Rock might be, surging and ebbing, a cyclonic whirl of voodoo vibe. Things return to earth with the sprightly 'Lover Man' (replete with an audacious solo take-off and trilling bass groove) and a defiant, driving 'Stone Free'. Harking back to the start of all the madness with 'Hey Joe', this rendition is dislocated, lethargic even, and the inadvertent squalls of feedback infuse it with a primal surliness. MITCHELL pounds 'I Don't Live Today' into submission, but his syncopated stylings and rolling flourishes sit less comfortably on 'Machine Gun', which was the awe-inspiring centrepiece of the New Year's Band Of Gypsys shows, and which Buddy Miles so weightily anchored. The 'Star Spangled Banner', bereft of its of-the-moment magic at 'WOODSTOCK', verges on cabaret, but 'Purple Haze' is razor-sharp and twitchy as hell. An awesome 10-minute rendition of 'Voodoo Child (Slight Return)', augmented with another work-in-progress, 'Keep On Groovin'', sees the band reaching for the skies once again, and HENDRIX claiming his place in the Pantheon. *DF*

Album rating: *6.5

□ David JOHANSEN
(⇒ NEW YORK DOLLS)

JOHNNY CASH IN SAN QUENTIN

1969 (UK 60m TV) Granada TV

Film genre: Country-music concert/documentary

Top guns: dir: Michael Darlow

Stars: Johnny CASH *(performer)*, **June Carter Cash** *(performer)* ← the MAN, HIS WORLD, HIS MUSIC ← ROAD TO NASHVILLE ← COUNTRY MUSIC HOLIDAY / → GOSPEL ROAD → THAT'S COUNTRY, **the Tennessee Three:- Bob Wootton, W.S. Holland** *(performers)* → LITTLE HAUSS AND BIG HALSY, + **Carl Perkins** *(musician)* ← the MAN, HIS WORLD, HIS MUSIC ← JAMBOREE / → LITTLE FAUSS AND BIG HALSY

Storyline: A quite remarkable and unique gig, played to a large contingent of long-term jailbirds at San Quentin prison on the 24th February 1969 – it was actually aired on UK television on the 6th September that year. *MCS*

Movie rating: *8.5

Visual: video + dvd (see below)

Off the record: JOHNNY CASH's veteran back-up musician with the Tennessee Three, Luther Perkins (no relation to Carl) had tragically died in a house fire on the 5th August, 1968. *MCS*

—

JOHNNY CASH: At San Quentin

Jun 69. (lp/c) *Columbia; <CS/PCT 9827> C.B.S.; (CBS/40 63629)* [1] Aug69 [2] – Wreck of the Old '97 / I walk the line / Darlin' companion / Starkville city jail / San Quentin / San Quentin / Wanted man / A boy named Sue / Peace in the valley / Folsom Prison blues. *<cd re-iss. Jul00 on 'Columbia-Legacy'+=; 66017> (UK cd-iss. 2006 on 'Sony-BMG'+=; 4981765003)* – Big river / I still miss someone / [tracks 1-3 above] / I don't know where I'm bound / [tracks 4-10 above] / Ring of fire / He turned the water into wine / Daddy sang bass / Old account was settled long ago / Closing medley: Folsom Prison blues – I walk the line – Ring of fire – The redemption. *<re d-cd/dvd Nov06 ++=; 75914-2> (UK same on 'Sony-BMG'++=; 88697 06092-2)* – Blue suede shoes / Flowers on the wall / The last thing on my mind / (June Carter Cash talks to the audience) / Wildwood flower / Medley: The long black veil – Give my love to Rose – Folsom Prison blues – Orange blossom special – Jackson / Break my mind / Restless / Blistered / The outside looking in / Less of me / (+ DVD material).

S/track review: At the same time as when his one-time label mate ELVIS PRESLEY was reviving his flaccid career with his '68 TV Special, JOHNNY CASH was thrilling a very different kind of audience with a series of performances behind bars. 'Live In Folsom' was the first, and it reignited Cash's career. Months later, he arrived at San Quentin Prison in California with a British TV crew in tow to make an hour-long TV special, playing to 2000 inmates. The resulting soundtrack album was just ten brief tracks, including two renditions of the brand new song he'd just written 'San Quentin' and various acerbic banter between CASH, the inmates and the guards. The recording of the show itself was raw and dynamic but hindered somewhat by some incredibly loud and harsh crowd noise use to hide the edits. A more satisfactory CD edition emerged in 2000 that threw in another 8 songs and sequenced them as they were played. The ultimate version appeared in 2006 and included the full concert – including songs by opening acts CARL PERKINS, the STATLER BROTHERS and the CARTER FAMILY to boot – as well as a DVD of the original 1969 concert. This total package is unsurprisingly a more coherent and satisfying listen and shows CASH at the peak of his powers, he had not long straightened out (for a while anyway), married June Carter, and stripped of all pomp with nothing but a bare, driving rhythm section and lead guitar for armour, CASH gives a truly memorable performance. It shows a musician eager to please and be accepted by his audience and while the original 1969 edition does enjoy a degree of swiftness, the full concert allows the listener to enjoy CASH live in all his ramshackle glory. *MR*

Album rating: *7 (re-cd *8) (re d-cd+dvd *8.5)

– spinoff hits, etc. –

JOHNNY CASH: A Boy Named Sue / San Quentin

Jul 69. (7") *<44944> (CBS 4460)* [2] Aug69 [4]

□ Robert JOHNSON segment
(⇒ HELLHOUNDS ON MY TRAIL)

□ Daniel JOHNSTON segment
(⇒ the DEVIL AND DANIEL JOHNSTON)

Janis JOPLIN

Born: 19 Jan'43, Port Arthur, Texas, USA. Overweight as a teenager, she graduated from Thomas Jefferson High, already a fan of folk and blues music in the shape of Odetta, Bessie Smith and Leadbelly. In the early 60s, JOPLIN hitched to San Francisco, where she sang in the Waller Creek Boys trio alongside future 13th Floor Elevators member R Powell St John. In 1963, she subsequently appeared opposite Jorma Kaukonen (later Jefferson Airplane) at local night spots; she'd previously cut her teeth singing in Austin, Texas Bars. A few years later, after nearly giving up singing and her hippy drug-taking ways for a life of domesticity, she returned to Texas where she briefly rehearsed with Roky Erickson and the 13th Floor Elevators. In 1966, she returned to San Francisco, this time on the request of friend Chet Helms who suggested she should join Big Brother & The Holding Company. They went on to release two albums, the second of which, 'Cheap Thrills', stayed at the top of the US charts for 8 weeks in 1968. When Big Brother temporarily folded later that year, JOPLIN went solo, although her alcohol and drug abuse was becoming increasingly controlling. After three major concerts: London's Royal Albert Hall, the Newport Festival and the New Orleans Pop Festival (in 1967, JANIS and the band appeared on the bill of the 'MONTEREY POP' festival), she unleashed her 1969 solo debut, 'I Got Dem Ol' Kosmic Blues Again', a fine record which reached the US Top 5. In May '70, she formed her new backing group, the Full-Tilt Boogie Band, beginning work on an album in the autumn of 1970. Before it was completed, however, on the 4th of October 1970, JANIS was found dead in her Hollywood hotel room. The coroner's verdict reported that her death was due to an accidental drug overdose. Early in 1971, her last recording, 'Pearl' was issued, topping the US charts for 9 weeks, also giving her a first taste of UK chart action. She again hit pole position in the States with a great version of Kris Kristofferson's 'Me And Bobby McGee'. But for her death, she would probably have become the greatest female singer of all-time, her powerful 3-octave vocals having the capacity to transform the most run-of-the-mill tune into a tour de force. A film documentary, 'JANIS', was released to a lukewarm response in 1974, while her bio-pic (of sorts) was disguised as the feature flick, 'The ROSE' (1980). *MCS*

- **filmography** {performance} –

Monterey Pop *(1968 {p} on OST by V/A =>)* / Petulia *(1968 {p w/ Big Brother & the Holding Co.} OST by John Barry)* / **Keep On Rockin'** *(1969 {p} =>)* / posthumous:- **Janis** *(1974 {*a/p} OST by JOPLIN =>)* / **My Generation** *(2000 {a/p} =>)* / **Hendrix** *(2000 TV {a/p} =>)* / **Festival Express** *(2003 {*a/p} =>)*

JOURNEY THROUGH THE PAST

1974 (US 79m w/b&w) New Line Cinema (R)

Film genre: Roots/Rock-music concert/documentary biopic

Top guns: dir: Bernard Shakey (i.e. **Neil YOUNG**)

Stars: **Neil YOUNG** *(himself/performer)*, **CROSBY, STILLS & NASH:- David Crosby, Stephen Stills, Graham Nash** *(performers)*, **Dewey Martin** *(performer)*, **Jack Nitzsche** *(performer)* ← GIRLS! GIRLS! GIRLS!, Carrie Snodgrass *(herself)*

Storyline: Neil Young's first attempt at directing his own rockumentary, tracing – in an experimental montage of live, TV and news footage – his artistic evolution from the Buffalo Springfield days, through to his early 70s stature as rock's leading troubadour. *BG*

Movie rating: *5.5

Visual: video

Off the record: Although the double-album was released late in '72, the film wasn't premiered until May 1974.

—

NEIL YOUNG

Nov 72. (d-lp) *Reprise; <2XS 6480> (K 64015)* 45 Jan73 ☐
– For what it's worth – Mr. Soul / Rock & roll woman / Find the cost of freedom / Ohio / Southern man / Are you ready for the country / Let me call you sweetheart / Alabama / Words (between the lines of age) / Relativity invitation / Handel's Messiah / The king of kings theme / Soldier / Let's go away for awhile. *<(cd-iss. Jun94; 7599 26123-2)>*

S/track review: Reportedly 'Warners' released this album against the wishes of NEIL YOUNG. It's certainly something of a hodge-podge, but YOUNG fans will find much to enjoy here. As fragmentary and confounding as the YOUNG film it accompanies, the soundtrack opens with some late 1960s television recordings of his BUFFALO SPRINGFIELD miming to three of their hits, complete with the anchorman's corny introduction and the screams of the teenybopper audience. Musically, the strongest cuts are the live recordings of CROSBY, STILLS, NASH & YOUNG. While 'Find The Cost Of Freedom' is a rather pious piece of protest folk, 'Ohio' rocks harder than the studio version. Their 'Southern Man' might miss the clangour of Nils Lofgren's piano, but YOUNG's incandescent vocals and guitar more than compensate. The bulk of the album consists of alternate takes of songs from the 'Harvest' sessions, interspersed with curious segues. A low fidelity outtake of 'Are You Ready For The Country?' is cut short to make way for children singing 'Let Me Call You Sweetheart', while the powerful 'Alabama' periodically fades into studio chatter and snippets of television news reports. Fans will relish the insight into YOUNG's working methods, as he can be heard working out harmonies and confessing to a mistake, but the other clips make little sense outwith the context of the movie. A meandering 16-minute version of 'Words' – never one of 'Harvest's better songs – will test the patience of even the most die-hard YOUNG obsessive. Side four is stranger still, opening with a spaced out YOUNG humouring a Christian hippy, followed by the Tony & Susan Alamo Christian Foundation Orchestra & Chorus's rather shakey attempts at 'Handel's Messiah' and 'King Of Kings'. It's redeemed by the desolately beautiful piano ballad 'Soldier' and the incongruous, but by no means unwelcome, exotica of the Beach Boys' instrumental 'Let's Go Away For A While'. 'JOURNEY THROUGH THE PAST' fails to cohere as an album or collage, but for those who follow YOUNG's more wayward moments with a strange fascination, it's a trip worth making. *SS*

Album rating: *5.5

JUST AN AMERICAN BOY

a film about Steve Earle

2003 (US 95m w/b&w) Cowboy Pictures

Film genre: Country Rock-music concert/documentary

Top guns: Amos Poe ← SUBWAY RIDERS ← the FOREIGNER ← the BLANK GENERATION

Stars: Steve Earle *(himself/performer)* ← HEARTWORN HIGHWAYS / → BE HERE TO LOVE ME, Justin Earle *(himself)*

Storyline: On the road with country roots star, Steve Earle, and his post-9/11 trials and tribulations; i.e. his activist stance on his country's warmongering. Named for a line in the song which cast him as the bête-noire of America's religious right, 'John Walker's Blues, and directed by Amos 'Blank Generation' Poe pre-Iraq War, this fascinating film follows an embattled but defiant Steve Earle as he fends off moral majority flak, campaigns on the death penalty through theatre and takes his contemporary protest songs to the masses. "The most important thing to remember is, no matter what anybody tells you, it is never, ever unpatriotic or un-American to question anything in a democracy": Steve Earle. *BG & MCS*

Movie rating: *7

Visual: dvd

Off the record: Steve Earle (b.17 Jan'55, Fort Monroe, Virginia) was the son of an air traffic controller and raised in Schertz, Texas, where his youth was spent immersed in guitar playing and rebelling against the authorities. At the age of 16, the long-haired would-be troubadour left home and eventually wound up in Houston where he befriended a coterie of songwriters that numbered the likes of Townes Van Zandt, Guy Clark and Jerry Jeff Walker. Following a brief foray into acting (a blink-or-you'll-miss-him part in Robert Altman's 'NASHVILLE'), Earle set about bringing together a backing band, the Dukes, who survived numerous incarnations over the first decade of his career. Earle took up a new job with publishers, 'Dea & Clark', while he also featured in country documentary, 'HEARTWORN HIGHWAYS' (1981). A Nashville music journalist, John Lomax, was quick to spot Earle's talent and offered his services as manager before helping net him a deal with 'Epic'. Unfortunately, the major label bods were at odds with Earle over his musical direction, rejecting an album's worth of songs and demanding that he recut them in a more commercial style. Finally, with the backing of a revamped Dukes, the self-styled Nashville renegade released his debut album, 'Guitar Town' (1986). 'Exit 0' (1987) continued in a similar, if slightly more countrified vein, featuring signature tune 'I Ain't Ever Satisfied' alongside the track he penned for Farm Aid, 'The Rain Came Down'. Neither of these albums, however, hinted at the hard-bitten roots-rock of 'Copperhead Road', Earle's landmark 1988 effort that firmly established him within the mainstream rock community while simultaneously alienating many of his core country fans. His chaotic personal life was also catching up with him and besides coping with spiralling alcohol and drug dependency, he had to contend with an assault conviction (on a security guard at his own show) and the bankruptcy of his label 'Uni'. 'The Hard Way' (1990) then, was his dark night of the soul, a downbeat, introspective record that ironically furnished him with his highest UK chart placing (Top 30). Yet its relative commercial failure signalled the end of Earle's tenure with his label and, burned out after a punishing few years of touring, he finally disbanded the Dukes. Things hardly improved for the beleaguered singer over the ensuing five years as he struggled with cocaine and heroin addiction, avoiding a one-year jail term by agreeing to enter a detox centre. Like the proverbial phoenix rising from the ashes, Earle released what many considered his most accomplished record to date in 1995 with 'Train A-Comin'. Critically, commercially and creatively reborn, Earle subsequently signed a new contract with 'Warners' and released another winner in 1996's 'I Feel Alright'. Older and wiser, Earle has become one of the most respected elder statesmen in the country-roots field, going on to release the acclaimed 'El Corazon' (1997) and record and tour with the Del McRoury Band with whom he delivered his next set, 'The Mountain' (1999). While that was heavily steeped in bluegrass, the new millennium found Earle taking a broader but no less worldy-wise sweep through the rugged country-rock which shaped his early career on 'Transcendental Blues' (2000). As its title suggested, the singer was still seeking redemption through music, something that continued to lend his work a bruised authenticity missing in much modern country. The live 'Together At Bluebird Cafe' (2001) marked the belated release of a mid-90s benefit gig featuring Earle and two of his musical/spiritual brethren, Texan singer-songwriters Guy Clark and Townes Van Zandt. It was a tantalising bill which lent added poignancy given Van Zandt's subsequent demise. 2002's 'Jerusalem' was a quite different beast, Earle's own personal meditation on the 9/11 tragedy and its aftermath and implications. Rather than trying to find blame, he sought explanations, even attempting to get inside the mind of the so-called "American Taliban" John Walker Lindh in 'John Walker's Blues'. Predictably, the singer came in for flack from the USA's right-wing, with the political fallout spilling over into this excellent live set, 'JUST AN AMERICAN BOY'. *BG & MCS*

—

STEVE EARLE

Sep 03. (d-cd) *Artemis; <51256> Rykodisc; (RCD 17002)* ☐ ☐
– (show start) / America V 6.0 / Ashes to ashes / Paranoia / Conspiracy theory / I remember you / Schertz, Texas / Hometown blues / The mountain / Pennsylvanian miners / Harlan man / Copperhead road / Guitar town / I oppose the death penalty / Over

yonder / Billy Austin // (opening) / South Nashville blues / Rex's blues – Ft. Worth blues / John Walker's blues / Jerusalem / The unrepentant / Christmas in Washington / Democracy / What's so funny about peace, love and understanding / Time you waste.

S/track review: The audio portion of STEVE EARLE's self-proclaimed "audio documentary" is a raging, often ramshackle window on a man with a mission inherited from a roots lineage stretching back through Joan Baez to Cisco Houston and Woody Guthrie but also inspired by the likes of Malcolm X, Bobby Seale and Abbie Hoffman. Unlucky but dogged enough to be a lefty in "the land of the free", EARLE takes his stands more overtly than the likes of Bruce Springsteen, even if it earns him the approbation of fans unwilling to engage with them. As a snare-ushered 'Copperhead Road' serves to remind, EARLE has always been concerned with America's underrepresented, the "white trash" shipped out at the first declaration of war. The non-election of Bush and attendant Iraq debacle just gave him a bit more impetus, as it did to nominally politically ambiguous figures like Neil Young. Opener 'Amerika v. 6.0', in fact, is conspicuously Young-like in sound, structure and approach, both a self-administered kick up the jacksie for would-be liberals and a rant against the founding fathers' "equal as long as we can pay" legacy. It's about as subtle as a sledgehammer and sickle, but comes into its own in the heckler-blighted cauldron of EARLE and his DUKES live, as does a similarly Young/Crazy Horse-esque 'John Walker's Blues' itself, a biblically allegorical spiel like 'Ashes To Ashes' and the just-cos-you're-paranoid-doesn't-mean-they're-not-after-you sentiments of 'Conspiracy Theory', incongruous 'Pretty Woman'-like bassline and all. Not that EARLE is a humourless ideologue; the self-deprecating wit that's painted his writing since the mid-70s is in full effect here, not least in his banter on Texas cowboys and the pitfalls of hitchhiking. But his passion is social justice, and the emotional energy he projects on miners' tribute 'Harlan Man', is what makes his art tick. Other highlights include anti-corporal punishment tract 'Billy Austin' (a cross between Springsteen's 'Nebraska' and Eddie Vedder's 'DEAD MAN WALKING'), an exhortatory cover of Brinsley Schwarz anthem, '(What's So Funny 'Bout) Peace, Love And Understanding', and a spartan, confidential closer from STEVE's son JUSTIN. *BG*

Album rating: *7.5

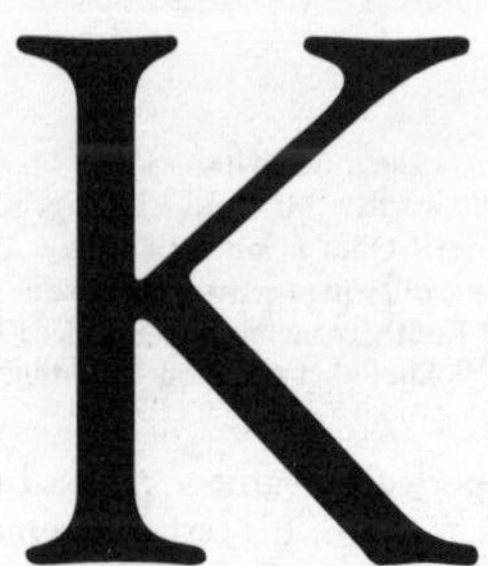

the KIDS ARE ALRIGHT

1979 (UK 99m) New World Films

Film genre: Rock-music concert/documentary bio-pic

Top guns: s-w + dir: Jeff Stein

Stars: the WHO:- Roger Daltrey, John Entwistle, Pete Townshend, Keith Moon *(performers)* / **Ringo Starr** *(performer)* <= the BEATLES =>, **Keith Richards** *(himself)*, <= the ROLLING STONES =>, **Rick Danko** *(himself)* <= the BAND =>, Steve Martin *(himself)* ← SGT. PEPPER'S LONELY HEARTS CLUB BAND / → LITTLE SHOP OF HORRORS, Tom Smothers *(himself)*, Ken Russell *(himself)*

Storyline: A film released at the tail end of the Who's career, it attempted to document their evolution and translate their genius through a combination of rare concert footage, television appearances and a segment of specially recorded live in the studio tracks, poignant for being the last time Keith Moon performed with the band. *BG*

Movie rating: *8

Visual: video + dvd

Off the record: Ken Russell was also the man behind the camera for the WHO's 'TOMMY' (1975).

---

the WHO

Jun 79. (d-lp)<US-pic-d-lp> *Polydor; (2675 179) M.C.A.; <11005>* 26 8
– My generation / I can't explain / Happy Jack / I can see for miles / Magic bus / Long live rock / Anyway, anyhow, anywhere / Young man blues / Baba O'Riley / My wife / A quick one while he's away / Tommy can you hear me? / Sparks / Pinball wizard / See me, feel me / Join together – Roadrunner – My generation blues / Won't get fooled again. *(cd-iss. Jun93; 517947-2)*

S/track review: Too random to qualify as a definitive greatest hits set, yet more compelling than the average rarities collection, the documentary's soundtrack was perhaps the most essential WHO compilation prior to the release of Polydor's 1994 box set, with riveting versions of 'My Generation', 'Magic Bus', etc. The chief draw for hardcore fans, however, was the previously unreleased performance of 'A Quick One, While He's Away', recorded as part of the Rolling Stones' 'ROCK AND ROLL CIRCUS' extravaganza and – in light of its show-stealing intensity – rumoured to be the reason why that project remained unreleased until the mid-90s. *BG*

Album rating: *7

– spinoff hits, etc. –

the WHO: Long Live Rock / I'm The Face / My Wife

Apr 79. (7"m) *(WHO 2)* 48 –

the WHO: Long Live Rock / My Wife

Jun 79. (7") *<41053>* – 54

KILL YOUR IDOLS

2004 (US 75m w/b&w) Hunger Artist.. / Palm Pictures – 2006

Film genre: Punk Rock-music documentary/bio-pic

Top guns: dir: Scott (S.A.) Crary

Stars: **SONIC YOUTH:- Kim Gordon, Lee Ranaldo, Thurston Moore, Jim Sclavunos** *(themselves/performers)*, **Yeah Yeah Yeahs:- Karen O., Nick Zinner, Brian Chase** *(themselves/performers)*, **Lydia Lunch & Teenage Jesus and the Jerks** *(herself/performer/s)* ← the OFFENDERS, **Suicide:- Martin Rev *, Alan Vega** *(himself*/performers)*, **Theoretical Girls:- Glenn Branca, Jeffrey Lohn** *(performers)*, **DNA:- Arto Lindsay, etc.** *(performers)*, **Liars:- Aaron Hemphill, Angus Andrew, Pat Noecker, Ron Albertson** *(performers)*, **Gogol Bordello:- Eugene Hutz, Sergey Rjabtzev, Oren Kaplan, Susan Donaldson, Pamela Racine, etc.** *(performers)*, **Flux Information Sciences:- Tristan Bechet, Sebastian Brault, Chris Pravdica** *(performers)*, **Black Dice:- Eric Copeland, Bjorn Copeland, Aaron Warren** *(performers)*, **Swans:- Michael Gira** *(performers)*, **A.R.E. Weapons:- Matt McAuley, Brain F. McPeck** *(performers)*, **Foetus:- J.G. Thirlwell** *(performers)*, **Lightning Bolt:- Hisham Baroocha** *(performers)*

Storyline: Inspired by the Sonic Youth track, 'Kill Yr. Idols', the documentary looks back to the rise of New York's underground New Wave scene in the mid-70s (Suicide & Lydia Lunch), and proudly represents where it's all at thirty years later (Yeah Yeah Yeahs & A.R.E. Weapons. *MCS*

Movie rating: *7.5

Visual: dvd (no audio OST)

Off the record: Too many post-No Wave outfits are involved to mention them all, although one seems to stand out from the pack: **Gogol Bordello** were originally from the Ukraine and played a type of cabaret-meets-gypsy punk rock! The ensemble's leader and one-time refugee, Eugene Hutz, subsequently starred in the 2005 movie, 'Everything Is Illuminated'. *MCS*

B.B. KING

Born: Riley B. King, 16 Sep'25, Indianola, Mississippi, USA, the cousin of respected country bluesman, Bukka White. The son of a sharecropper, as a young man KING picked cotton (through the depression) for a mere 20 dollars a week; the chances of buying a $200-$300 guitar were remote, not to mention the fact that his town didn't have any electricity! Subsequently talent-spotted, he won his own, regular 10-minute spot (The Sepia Swing Show) on a black music radio station, WDIA, and word of his prowess spread; the station's PR man dubbed him "The Beale Street Blues Boy" which was shortened to "Blues Boy" and eventually "B.B". He gradually developed his own sound on his Gibson guitar, "Lucille" (so named because of an incident after a gig in Twist, Arkansas during which a fight – caused by a woman named Lucille – ended up in the venue being evacuated). In February 1952, KING hit US/R&B number 1 for fifteen weeks with 'Three O'Clock Blues' (written by Lowell Fulson), while in November, 'You Didn't Want Me', repeated the feat. KING was to enjoy regular R&B chart success over the next five years, including two more chart toppers, 'Please Love Me' in '53 and 'You Upset Me Baby' in '54. The big man achieved his first national chart success in 1957 via 'Be Careful With A Fool' and followed it with 'I Need You So Bad' which also broke into the US Top 100. KING subsequently left 'Kent' records in 1962 for the larger 'A.B.C.' label, with whom he was to record until their absorption into 'M.C.A.' in 1979. His first ABC release was a version of Louis Jordan's 'How Blue Can You Get', while in May '62, 'Rock Me Baby' (written by Arthur "Big Boy" Crudup and recorded for 'Kent' before his move) was his first recognised pop hit, entering the US Top 40 and becoming the subject of countless cover versions by UK R&B bands. At the end of the 60s (after achieving his second US Top 40 hit with 'Paying The Cost To Be The Boss'), his version of Roy Hawkins' 'The Thrill Is Gone' gave him his biggest hit single so far, reaching the US Top 20; the accompanying album, 'Completely Well' achieved similar results. The early 70s saw KING expand his horizons into the world of performance movies, 'MEDICINE BALL CARAVAN' (1971), 'Dynamite Chicken' (1972) and 'SING SING THANKSGIVING' (1974), all showcasing the talents of one great guitar man. In 1982, KING demonstrated what a thoroughly generous guy he was when he donated his entire record collection (20,000 discs including 7,000 rare blues 78's) to the Mississippi University Centre For The Study Of Southern Culture. Alongside stadium-fillers, U2 (from their rockumentary, 'RATTLE AND HUM' – 1988), B.B. recorded 'When Loves Comes To Town', a record that made the UK Top 10 for the first and only time in his chequered history. Meanwhile, KING continued with his charity work, performing at numerous benefit concerts for the homeless, etc. Having cameo'd in the 1998 movie, 'BLUES BROTHERS 2000', while also guesting on the Paul Pena documentary, 'GENGHIS BLUES' (1999), the legend of US urban blues subsequently teamed up with the legend of white boy English blues, ERIC CLAPTON, for a one-off set, 'Riding With The King' (2000). Well past his 75th year, KING kept on trucking showing up many players half his age, while he subsequently featured on even more blues-orientatated rockumentaries including 'Bill Wyman's BLUES ODYSSEY' (2001), 'LIGHTNING IN A BOTTLE' (2004) and 'Antone's Home Of The Blues' (2004). A tireless ambassador for the blues, B.B. succeeded in bringing the form into the mainstream and remains one of the most well-known artists in the genre's history. *BG & MCS*

filmography {acting/performance} –

Medicine Ball Caravan *(1971 {p} on OST by V/A =>)* / Dynamite Chicken *(1972 {p})* / le Blues Entre Les Dents *(1973 {p} =>)* / **Sing Sing Thanksgiving** *(1974 {p} =>)* / Spies Like Us *(1985 {b})* / Amazon Women On The Moon *(1987 {c})* / **Rattle And Hum** *(1988 {p} on OST by U2 =>)* / Mr. Bluesman *(1993 {*c})* / Heart And Souls *(1993 {c})* / When We Were Kings *(1996 {c})* / **Blues Brothers 2000** *(1998 {c} OST by V/A =>)* / **Shake, Rattle And Roll: An American Love Story** *(1999 TV {p} =>)* / **Genghis Blues** *(1999 {p} on OST by PAUL PENA & KONGAR-OL ONDAR =>)* / **Blues Odyssey** *(2001 TV on OST by V/A =>)* / **Lightning In A Bottle** *(2004 {p} on OST by V/A =>)* / Antone's Home Of The Blues *(2004 {p})* / Better Late Than Never *(2005 {c} =>)*

KURT & COURTNEY

1998 (UK 95m) Strength Ltd. / Capitol Films (18)

Film genre: Grunge Rock-music documentary bio-pic

Top guns: dir: Nick Broomfield → BIGGIE AND TUPAC

Stars: Nick Broomfield *(interviewer)* → as above, **Kurt Cobain** *(archive footage)* ← 1991: THE YEAR PUNK BROKE / → KURT COBAIN ABOUT A SON, **Courtney LOVE** *(archive footage)*, **Krist Novoselic** *(himself)* ← 1991: THE YEAR PUNK BROKE, **Dylan Carlson** *(himself)*, **El Duce** *(performer)* ← POPULATION: ONE ← DU-BEAT-E-O, **Pat Smear** *(himself)* ← the DECLINE OF WESTERN CIVILIZATION / → FREE TIBET → RAGE: 20 YEARS OF PUNK ROCK WEST COAST STYLE, Hank Harrison *(himself)*, Tom Grant *(himself)*, Sam Rubin *(archive footage; newscaster)*

Storyline: English film documentarian Nick Broomfield rids the sexual "fetish" shackles of his previous flicks to investigate the once turbulent relationship between late rock superstar Kurt Cobain and his singer/actress wife Courtney Love. From Kurt's untimely death in April 1994 (and the murder conspiracies behind it), Broomfield traces the man's early years in Aberdeen, Washington and unfolds why drugs became a big part of his life. With no Courtney to speak of – quite literally – legal wrangles stopped this film from an initial BBC airing (late '97) and its premiere at the Sundance Film Festival. *MCS*

Movie rating: *6

Visual: dvd Sep'99

Off the record: Kurt Cobain/Krist Novoselic were of course iconic figures in Nirvana, while **Pat Smear** (ex-Germs) kept the Nirvana connection by joining Dave Grohl in Foo Fighters. **Dylan Carlson** was in the band, Earth. **El Duce**, was with the Mentors. *MCS*

KURT COBAIN: ABOUT A SON

2006 (US 96m) Sidetrack Films / Bonfire Films Of America

Film genre: alt-Rock-music documentary

Top guns: dir: A.J. Schnack ← GIGANTIC (A TALE OF TWO JOHNS)

Stars: Kurt Cobain *(himself/performer)* ← KURT & COURTNEY ← 1991: THE YEAR PUNK BROKE, Michael Azerrad *(interviewer)*

Storyline: Drawing from more than 25 hours of previously unreleased conversations between iconic musician Kurt Cobain and journalist Michael Azerrad (recorded on tape in March 1993 for the latter's book, 'Come As You Are: The Story Of Nirvana'), this film is down to visuals with music unlike any other rock documentary. *MCS*

Movie rating: *6

Visual: dvd

Off the record: Steve Fisk was a member of 'Sub Pop' outfits, Pell Mell and Pigeonhed as well as producer and session man. *MCS*

Various Artists ("interviews w/ Kurt") (score: BENJAMIN GIBBARD *)

Sep 07. (cd) *Barsuk; <(BARK 68)>* ☐ ☐
– Overture (STEVE FISK & *) / "Never intended" / The motorcycle song (ARLO GUTHRIE) / Eye flys (the MELVINS) / "Punk rock" / Banned in D.C. (BAD BRAINS) / Up around the bend (CREEDENCE CLEARWATER REVIVAL) / Put some sugar on it (HALF JAPANESE) / Son of a gun (the VASELINES) / Graveyard (BUTTHOLE SURFERS) / "Hardcore was dead" / Owner's lament (SCRATCH ACID) / Touch me I'm sick (MUDHONEY) / "Car radio" / The passenger (IGGY POP) / The bourgeois blues (LEAD BELLY) / New Orleans instrumental No.1 (R.E.M.) / "The limelight" / The man who sold the world (DAVID BOWIE) / Museum (MARK LANEGAN) / Indian summer (*).

S/track review: If you're looking for a certain grunge band pitched into ' . . .ABOUT A SON', forget it. As it says on the sleeve: This soundtrack does not contain the music of Kurt Cobain or Nirvana. However, it does contain *audio excerpts of the man* speaking. Many fans will already know that Nirvana's reclusive frontman had eclectic tastes: from the VASELINES, to DAVID BOWIE and CREEDENCE CLEARWATER REVIVAL, not just indie punk rock. The latter's 'Up Around The Bend' (a big hit from 1969) features here alongside LEAD BELLY's vintage folk gem 'The Bourgeois Blues', IGGY POP's 'The Passenger' and ARLO GUTHRIE's 'The Motorcycle Song' – you could indeed rhyme "motor-sickle" with "pickle" in 1972. Bypassing R.E.M.'s effective but out-of-place 'New Orleans Instrumental No.1', much of Kurt's "songs" stem from the evolving grunge and US indie-punk scenes, example MELVINS ('Eye Flys'), MUDHONEY ('Touch Me I'm Sick', BAD BRAINS ('Banned In D.C.'), BUTTHOLE SURFERS ('Graveyard'), SCRATCH ACID ('Owner's Lament'), a gem from 1984, HALF JAPANESE ('Put Some Sugar On It') and Screaming Trees frontman MARK LANEGAN's solo slo-fi 'Museum'. The UK are represented by only two artists, the aforementioned Londoner BOWIE (with 'The Man Who Sold The World') and twee Scots indie-popsters the VASELINES (with 'Son Of A Gun') – both tracks covered live by Nirvana in their halcyon days. There's also two score tracks by singer-songwriter BENJAMIN GIBBARD, the Mogwai-esque opener 'Overture' (with former Pell Mell member STEVE FISK) and closer 'Indian Summer', a bright rendition of a Calvin Johnson/Beat Happening song. *MCS*

Album rating: *7.5

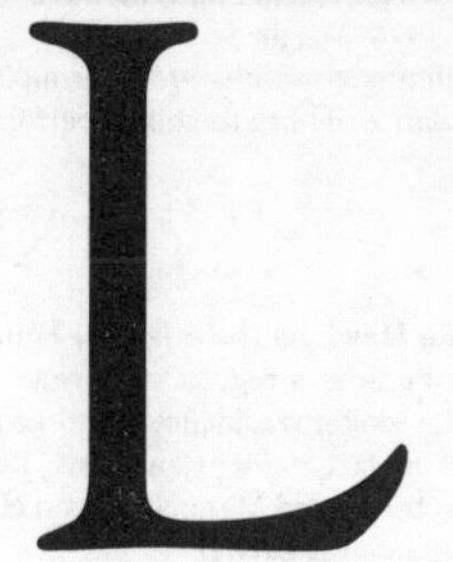

LADIES AND GENTLEMEN ... MR. LEONARD COHEN

1965 (Can 45m b&w; dvd 78m) National Film Board Of Canada

Film genre: Folk/Roots-music documentary biopic

Top guns: s-w: (+ dir) Donald Brittain, Don Owen

Stars: Leonard COHEN *(himself/performer)*, Donald Brittain *(himself)*, Irving Layton *(poet)*, Earl Birney *(poet)*, Robert Hirschhorn *(himself)*, Derek May *(himself)*, Mort Rosengarten *(himself)*, Pierre Berton *(panel interviewer)*

Storyline: Canada's favourite son, poet and novelist Leonard Cohen, gets the bio-pic treatment even before Mr. C (here, now at 30!) has even released a record. In fact, it would be another couple of years before he delivered his debut LP for 'Columbia'. The short-ish film was later made available on DVD with four "real" shorts, 'Angel' (featuring Cohen speaking to a lady), the half-animated 1988 video for 'I'm Your Man', prose from his "Beautiful Losers" novel, 'Poen', and the poem 'A Kite Is A Victim' (read by Paul Hecht). *MCS*

Movie rating: *6 / dvd *7

Visual: video/dvd (no audio OST; score: Don Douglas)

Off the record: Leonard COHEN (see own biog)

LADIES AND GENTLEMEN, THE ROLLING STONES

1974 (US 75m) Bingo-Butterfly / Dragon Aire / Musicfilm-Chessco

Film genre: Rock-music concert/documentary

Top guns: dir: Rollin Binzer

Stars: the ROLLING STONES:- Mick Jagger, Keith Richards, Charlie Watts, Mick Taylor, Bill Wyman, Ian Stewart *(performers)*, **Nicky Hopkins** *(performer)* ← COCKSUCKER BLUES ← SYMPATHY FOR THE DEVIL ← ROCK AND ROLL CIRCUS, **Bobby Keys** *(performer)* ← MAD DOGS & ENGLISHMEN / → LET'S SPEND THE NIGHT TOGETHER → HAIL! HAIL! ROCK'N'ROLL → AT THE MAX, **Jim Price** *(performer)* ← MAD DOGS & ENGLISHMEN

Storyline: This is 'Exile On Main St.'-era Rolling Stones on a 1972 North American tour to promote their classic double album; track highlights include, 'Tumbling Dice', 'Gimme Shelter' and 'Brown Sugar'. *MCS*

Movie rating: *6.5

Visual: video (no audio OST)

Off the record: Bobby Keys + Jim Price (both ex-Joe Cocker band) + **Nicky Hopkins** (multi-session man on keyboards) were featured in other ROLLING STONES flicks.

LAND OF LOOK BEHIND

1982 (US 90m) Solo Man

Film genre: Reggae-music concert/documentary

Top guns: dir: Alan Greenberg

Stars: Bob MARLEY & the Wailers *(performer/s)*, **Gregory Isaacs** *(performer)* ← ROCKERS / → COOL RUNNINGS: THE REGGAE MOVIE → MADE IN JAMAICA, Louis Lepke *(himself)*, **Mutabaruka** *(performer)* → COOL RUNNINGS: THE REGGAE MOVIE

Storyline: The poverty-stricken youth of Jamaica is poignant in this documentary – Rastafarians smoking ganja, the "political" worship of former Ethiopian emperor, Haile Selassie, and the reggae music provided by Bob Marley (and others) are also interwoven among the island's culture. *MCS*

Movie rating: *8

Visual: dvd 2006 on Subversive (no audio OST)

Off the record: Mutabaruka (b. Allan Hope, 12 Dec'52, Rae Town, Jamaica) was on the political side of reggae, his dub poetry (meta-dub) can be accessed initially on his compilation, 'The Ultimate Collection' (on 'Shanachie' records). *MCS*

LAST OF THE MISSISSIPPI JUKES

2003 (US 86m) Mug-Shot Productions / Starz! Encore Entertainment

Film genre: Blues-music concert/documentary

Top guns: dir: (+ s-w) Robert Mugge ← HELLHOUNDS ON MY TRAIL ← PRIDE AND JOY ← DEEP BLUES ← COOL RUNNINGS: THE REGGAE MOVIE / → BLUES DIVAS

Stars: Morgan Freeman *(host)* ← JOHNNY HANDSOME / → BLUES DIVAS → DANNY THE DOG, **Alvin Youngblood Hart** *(performer)* → the SOUL OF A MAN, **Chris Thomas King** *(performer)* ← DOWN FROM THE MOUNTAIN ← O BROTHER, WHERE ART THOU? / → the SOUL OF A MAN → LIGHTNING IN A BOTTLE → RAY, **Bobby Rush** *(performer)*, **Vasti Jackson** *(performer)*, **King Edward Blues Band** *(performers)*, **Patrice Moncell** *(herself)*, etc.

Storyline: A decade after his seminal 'DEEP BLUES', filmmaker Robert Mugge – a man with highly regarded portraits of Sun Ra, Gil Scott-Heron and Sonny Rollins on his CV – returns to the Deep South and its tenacious refusal to relinquish its juke joint culture, focusing on the Morgan Freeman-masterminded Ground Zero Blues Club in Clarksdale and the veteran Subway Lounge in Jackson. *BG*

Movie rating: *7.5

Visual: video + dvd

Off the record: (see below)

Various Artists

Mar 03. (cd) *Sanctuary; <06076 84596-2>* [ ] [-]
– Joe Friday (ALVIN YOUNGBLOOD HART with SAM CARR and ANTHONY SHERROD) / Every goodbye don't mean I'm gone (the DEEP CUTS) / Garbage man (BOBBY RUSH) / Subway swing (GREG "FINGERS" TAYLOR w/ CASEY PHILLIPS AND THE HOUNDS) / Stormy Monday (PATRICE MONCELL & THE HOUSE ROCKERS) / You know I've tried (LEVON LINDSEY and J.T. WATKINS with the KING EDWARD BLUES BAND) / Casino in the cottonfield (VASTI JACKSON with the KING EDWARD BLUES BAND) / John Law burned down the liquor sto' (CHRIS THOMAS KING) / Blues is alright (DENNIS FOUNTAIN and PAT BROWN with JESSE ROBINSON & CASEY PHILLIPS) / What goes around, comes around (LUCILLE with GREG "FINGERS" TAYLOR) / Hole in the wall (the KING EDWARD BLUES BAND) / Strokin' (PATRICE MONCELL and VASTI JACKSON with The HOUSE

ROCKERS) / Members only (ABDUL RASHEED & The HOUSE ROCKERS) / Juke joint jam: Last of the Mississippi jukes – Next time you see me (DAVID HUGHES and JIMMY KING with VIRGIL BRAWLEY).

S/track review: Released the same year Martin Scorsese launched his blues series, 'LAST OF THE MISSISSIPPI JUKES' counts no 'Bluebird', 'Chess' or 'Paramount' classics but it does offer no-frills proof of how the genre has survived its first hundred years in business, despite countless takeover attempts. There is, in fact, a link to Scorsese in BOBBY RUSH, the tireless road trooper featured in 'The ROAD TO MEMPHIS', arguably the most poignant and insightful film in the whole series. Here RUSH – with only a wan harmonica for company – performs a drolly rueful lament about his woman leaving him for the local garbage man, and how he'd buy himself a garbage truck if only she'd come back to him; you don't get that on MTV. And there's more, a female equivalent of RUSH in PATRICE MONCELL, a whole lotta woman with a laugh like James Brown and a serious talent for ad-libbing. She sings 'Stormy Monday' like a spiritual, before getting saucy on the nine-minute foreplay, 'Strokin'. Sharp-eyed film buffs might also recognise CHRIS THOMAS KING, previously sighted on 'O BROTHER, WHERE ART THOU?' (2000). His quietly soulful country-blues gets expression here on the anecdotal 'John Law Burned The Liquor Sto'', contemporary American folk music in its rudimentary element, the kind that doesn't need to be qualified with prefixes like "nu" or "alternative". Veterans like SAM CARR and RUSH-associate JESSE ROBINSON, and flame keepers like ALVIN YOUNGBLOOD HART and VASTI JACKSON (who rails against the menace of big money on 'Casino In The Cottonfield') will also be familiar to hardcore blues fans, yet even they – or at least those outside of the Deep South – mightn't have heard of LEVON LINDSEY, J.T. WATKINS or ABDUL RASHEED, talented men all, whose moment in the spotlight is a mutual thrill. The whole thing – all strictly live and spontaneous – is programmed to approximate a night of sweat and chicken wings, which inevitably entails a few clichés. But then whether you hear cliché or blues hardwiring is a matter of perspective. *BG*

Album rating: *7

□ the Original LAST POETS segment
(⇒ RIGHT ON!)

the LAST WALTZ

1978 (US 115m) United Artists Pictures (PG)

Film genre: Roots rock-music concert/documentary

Top guns: dir: Martin Scorsese → the LAST TEMPTATION OF CHRIST → FEEL LIKE GOING HOME → NO DIRECTION HOME

Stars: the BAND:- Robbie Robertson *(performer)*, **Rick Danko** *(performer)*, **Levon Helm** *(performer)*, **Richard Manuel** *(performer)*, **Garth Hudson** *(performer)* / **Bob DYLAN** *(performer)*, **Eric CLAPTON** *(performer)*, **Neil DIAMOND** *(performer)*, **Joni Mitchell** *(performer)* ← RENALDO AND CLARA ← CELEBRATION AT BIG SUR / → MESSAGE TO LOVE: THE ISLE OF WIGHT FESTIVAL 1970, **Neil YOUNG** *(performer)*, **Van MORRISON** *(performer)*, **Emmylou HARRIS** *(performer)*, **Paul Butterfield** *(performer)* ← STEELYARD BLUES ← YOU ARE WHAT YOU EAT ← FESTIVAL / → GODFATHERS AND SONS, **Ringo Starr** *(performer)* <= the BEATLES =>, **DR. JOHN** *(performer)*, **Muddy Waters** *(performer)* ← CHICAGO BLUES ← DYNAMITE CHICKEN / → ERIC CLAPTON AND HIS ROLLING HOTEL → FEEL LIKE GOING HOME, **Pinetop Perkins** *(pianist)* → the BLUES BROTHERS → PIANO BLUES, **Ron Wood** *(performer)* → the RUTLES → HEARTS OF FIRE, **the STAPLE SINGERS:- Mavis Staples, Roebuck 'Pops' Staples** *(performers)*, **Ronnie Hawkins** *(performer)*, Martin Scorsese *(interviewer)* → NO DIRECTION HOME

Storyline: The musicians' musicians, the peer popularity of 60s roots legends the Band was impressively underlined by the unprecedented wealth of talent gathered for their farewell gig at San Francisco's Winterland on Thanksgiving Day (25th November) 1976. Martin Scorsese's highly regarded documentary encapsulates the conflicting emotions of the group's reluctant demise and the almost defiant brilliance of both their own performance and that of their invited guests. *BG*

Movie rating: *9.5

Visual: video + dvd

Off the record: Ronnie Hawkins (b.10 Jan'35, Huntsville, Arizona) was a rockabilly singer who became a regular performer (as "Mr Dynamo") so much in Canada that he took up residence there. To back him, he employed the Hawks, who were in fact native Canadians: **Robbie Robertson, Rick Danko, Garth Hudson & Richard Manuel; (Levon Helm** was also a member early on before they became the **BAND**. *MCS*

---

the BAND

Apr 78. (t-lp) *Warners; <3WS 3146> (K 66076)* 16 39
– Theme from The Last Waltz (with orchestra) / Up on Cripple Creek / Who do you love? (w/ RONNIE HAWKINS) / Helpless (w/ NEIL YOUNG & JONI MITCHELL) / Stage fright / Coyote (w/ JONI MITCHELL) / Dry your eyes (w/ NEIL DIAMOND) / Such a night (w/ DR. JOHN) / It makes no difference / Mystery train (w/ PAUL BUTTERFIELD) / The shape I'm in / The night they drove old Dixie down / Mannish boy (w/ MUDDY WATERS) / Further on up the road (w/ ERIC CLAPTON) / The shape I'm in / Down south in New Orleans (w/ BOBBY CHARLES) / Ophelia / Tura lura lura (that's an Irish lullaby) (w/ VAN MORRISON) / Caravan (w/ VAN MORRISON) / Life is a carnival / Baby let me follow you down (w/ BOB DYLAN) / I don't believe you (she acts like we never have met) (w/ BOB DYLAN) / Forever young (w/ BOB DYLAN) / Baby let me follow you down – reprise (w/ BOB DYLAN) / I shall be released (finale w/ all guests) / The Last Waltz suite: The well – Evangeline (w/ EMMYLOU HARRIS) – Out of the blue – The weight (w/ STAPLES) – The Last Waltz refrain – Theme from The Last Waltz. *(d-cd-iss. Jul88; K 266076) <(d-cd re-iss. Oct03 on 'Rhino'; 8122 73925-2)> <(4xcd-box iss.Apr02 on 'Rhino'+=; 8122 782782-3)>* – Life is a carnival / This wheel's on fire / Caldonia (w/ MUDDY WATERS) / Rag mama rag / All our past times (w/ ERIC CLAPTON) / Four strong winds (w/ NEIL YOUNG) / Shadows and light (w/ JONI MITCHELL) / Furry sings the blues (w/ JONI MITCHELL) / Acadian driftwood / The W.S. Walcott medicine show / The genetic method – Chest fever / Hazel (w/ BOB DYLAN) / Jam #1 / Jam #2 / Don't do it / Greensleeves / King Harvest (has surely come) – concert rehearsal / Tura lura lura (that's an Irish lullaby) – concert rehearsal (w/ VAN MORRISON) / Caravan – concert rehearsal (w/ VAN MORRISON) / Such a night – concert rehearsal (w/ DR. JOHN) / Rag mama rag – concert rehearsal / Mad waltz – sketch track for "The Well" / The Last Waltz refrain – instrumental / The Last Waltz theme – sketch.

S/track review: If this didn't quite invent the tribute concert – and the tribute concert soundtrack – it patented the all-star, rock aristocratic version. A line from RONNIE HAWKINS' Bo Diddley cover stands out: "I've turned 41, I don't mind dying, who do you love?". Come the mid-70s most of these artists were getting on a bit (not least MUDDY WATERS, who still manages to upstage almost everyone with a thunderous 'Mannish Boy') and so was their definitive brand of roots music, but – even in the well documented knowledge that the BAND's decision to call it quits wasn't exactly unanimous, and even if illness and suicide put paid to even the possibility of the group sooner than they could have imagined – the most surprising thing is how so many of them convincingly reinvented themselves, eventually. NEIL YOUNG did nothing but, and it's telling that 'Helpless' is the single most moving performance here, communing with the simplicity which defined the BAND in the first place; it must be a Canadian thing. JONI MITCHELL is the one most tuned into a future baying at the ballroom doors, strumming out flanged, New Wave-y chords over the freeform road poetry of 'Coyote'; no Jaco Pastorius but there is RICHARD MANUEL, organ lines spinning through white-night-line imagery like haunted flares. MANUEL and his compadres rise to the occasion without ever really overshadowing their guests, grinding out a fault-lined 'Up On Cripple Creek', fronting RICK DANKO for an impassioned 'Stagefright' and baptising 'The Weight' with a full-tilt (if studio recorded) STAPLES vocal; the magic is in the cultural moment. With its ecstatic ensemble refrain, VAN MORRISON's 'Caravan' is often hailed as one of the gig's show-stopping performances; having credited the BAND in the past with replenishing his spiritual fire, VAN might have graced the concert with something off 'Saint Dominic's Preview' or even 'Veedon Fleece' but that's splitting hairs. By all accounts they were lucky to get him at all and the rare 'Tura Lura Lural (That's An Irish Lullaby)' is alone worth the price of this disc. BOB DYLAN's performance is as professional as it is inevitable, on a par with the contemporaneous Rolling Thunder material. The similarity between 'I Don't Believe You (She Acts Like We Never Have Met)' and the Faces' 'Cindy Incidentally' was never clearer than it is here; irony of ironies, RON WOOD solos on a poignant 'I Shall Be Released'. ROBBIE ROBERTSON's almost Jack Nitzsche-esque 'Theme From Last Waltz' sees the whole thing out, hinting at his cinematic, post-BAND métier. An inevitable 'Rhino' box set arrived in 2002, digging up the likes of NEIL YOUNG's 'Four Strong Winds', DYLAN's 'Hazel', and MUDDY WATERS' unlikely take on Louis Jordan's 'Caledonia', as well as long lamented BAND omissions 'Acadian Driftwood' and 'This Wheel's On Fire'. *BG*

Album rating: *8 / CD-boxed set *8.5

– spinoff releases, etc. –

the BAND: Theme From The Last Waltz / Out Of The Blue

Jun 78. (7") *(K 17187)* [–] [ ]

the BAND: Out Of The Blue / The Well

Nov 78. (7") *<8592>* [ ] [–]

LED ZEPPELIN

Formed: London, England . . . mid '68 as the New Yardbirds by singer Robert Plant, guitarist JIMMY PAGE, bassist JOHN PAUL JONES and drummer John Bonham. Unwitting progenitors of heavy metal and creators of some of the most bowel quaking amplified blues known to man, LED ZEPPELIN could only have been a product of the 70s. While their gargantuan sound masked a fondness for acoustic folk, the band were best known and loved (and – during the punk era – derided) for Tyrannosaurean rock monsters like 'Whole Lotta Love'. It was an approach which, unlike other, more experimental 70s giants such as PINK FLOYD, was never likely to translate to the atmospheric nuances of film scoring and indeed, the band only clocked up one soundtrack, to the rockumentary, 'The SONG REMAINS THE SAME' (1976). Nevertheless, JIMMY PAGE, although he'd previously contributed to Michelangelo Antonioni's 'Blow Up' (via a performance of one of the the Yardbirds' most impressively frenzied tracks, 'Stroll On'), unexpectedly emerged from heroin addiction and occult dabbling to score a couple of instalments of Michael Winner's 'Death Wish' franchise. While only the dark, bluesy soundtrack to 'DEATH WISH II' (1982) saw a full release, his work on 'Death Wish 3' (1985) met with an equally disparaging reception from critics and, while outliving the films themselves, neither score matched Herbie Hancock's sterling work on the original. Unsurprisingly perhaps, he duly returned to his more natural arena of rock'n'roll, although JOHN PAUL JONES even more unexpectedly succeeded him as the next ex-'Zeppelin member to try his hand at film composing. Unfortunately, the Michael Winner connection remained the same as JONES created the soundtrack for the director's dire horror, 'SCREAM FOR HELP' (1984). As one critic put it: "Over the moronic characterization, daft dialogue, inept performances and opportunistic camerawork, music has been poured like a constant stream of cold gravy" mmmm . . . Gravy or no, the man persevered, going on to create unreleased scores for dark fantasy, 'The Secret Adventures Of Tom Thumb' (1993) and romantic drama, 'Risk' (1994). *BG*

- **filmography** (composers) –

Blow-Up _(1966 {p JIMMY w/ the YARDBIRDS}; see future edition)_ / **Son Of Dracula** _(1974 {p JOHN B} =>)_ / **the Song Remains The Same** _(1976 {p****} OST =>)_ / **Concerts For The People Of Kampuchea** _(1980 {p PLANT} on OST by V/A =>)_ / **Death Wish II** _(1982 OST by PAGE =>)_ / **Scream For Help** _(1984 OST by JONES =>)_ / Death Wish 3 _(1985 score by PAGE)_ / the Secret Adventures Of Tom Thumb _(1993 score by JONES)_ / Risk _(1994 score by JONES)_

LEMMY

Born: Ian Fraser Kilmister, 24 Dec'45, Stoke-On-Trent, Staffordshire, England. A warts-n-all rock'n'roll legend if ever there was one (and son of a vicar no less . . .), LEMMY earned his stripes as roadie for the likes of JIMI HENDRIX and the Nice, passing through the ranks of forgotten bands the Rainmakers, the Motown Sect, the Rockin' Vickers, Sam Gopal and Opal Butterfly. Alas, he missed out on the opportunity of cult 70s soundtrack-dom by a greasy whisker, joining Opal Butterfly just after they'd recorded a couple of tracks for Brit B-movie 'GROUPIE GIRL' (1970). Along with 'Butterfly drummer Simon King (who did cameo in the movie!), he went on to trip the fright fantastic as bass player for Hawkwind, before forming his own speed-shredding trio, Motorhead, in the mid-70s. While most of the band's screen dalliances have been live concert films, they did contribute incidental material to the unreleased soundtrack of Orwellian fantasy, 'She' (1984), also featuring original music by the likes of Maggie Bell and Justin Hayward. LEMMY himself got to flaunt his acting chops – alongside the likes of Shane MacGowan and Jools Holland – as an arms dealer in Comic Strip satire, 'EAT THE RICH' (1987), with MOTORHEAD handling most of the soundtrack. The man is also time-served as a reliably witty, no-bulls**t interview subject whenever metal is under the microscope, adding his tuppence worth to the likes of Penelope Spheeris' cult classic, 'The DECLINE OF WESTERN CIVILIZATION PART II: THE METAL YEARS' (1988) and, more recently, adding much more than that (possibly his most entertaining and insightful commentary to date) to BBC4's excellent 'Hawkwind: Do Not Panic' (2007). *BG*

- **filmography** {acting/performance} (composer) –

Eat The Rich _(1987 {a} on OST by V/A & MOTORHEAD =>)_ / **the Decline Of Western Civilization 2: The Metal Years** _(1988 {p} on OST by V/A =>)_ / Hardware _(1990 {b})_ / **Airheads** _(1994 {b} on OST by V/A =>)_ / Tromeo And Juliet _(1996 {n})_ / Terror Firmer _(1999 {b})_ / **Nina Hagen = Punk + Glory** _(1999 {c} =>)_ / Citizen Toxie: The Toxic Avenger IV _(2000 {a})_ / **Down And Out With The Dolls** _(2001 {a} OST by V/A =>)_ / **Lemmy** _(2002 {*c/p} =>)_ / **Ramones: Raw** _(2004 {p} =>)_ / **Metal: A Headbanger's Journey** _(2005 {p} on OST by V/A =>)_ / the Curse Of El Charro _(2005 {b})_ / Poultrygeist: Night Of The Chicken Dead _(2006 {b})_

LET IT BE

1970 (UK 80m) Apple Films / United Artists

Film genre: Pop/Rock-music documentary

Top guns: dir: Michael Lindsay-Hogg → ROCK AND ROLL CIRCUS → TWO OF US

Stars: the BEATLES:- John Lennon, Paul McCartney, George Harrison, Ringo Starr *(performers)*, George Martin *(himself)* → the COMPLETE BEATLES → GIVE MY REGARDS TO BROAD STREET → IMAGINE: JOHN LENNON → BEAUTIFUL DREAMER: BRIAN WILSON AND THE STORY OF 'SMiLE', **Yoko ONO** *(herself)*, **Linda McCartney** *(herself)* → ONE HAND CLAPPING → SGT. PEPPER'S LONELY HEARTS CLUB BAND → ROCKSHOW → CONCERTS FOR THE PEOPLE OF KAMPUCHEA → GIVE MY REGARDS TO BROAD STREET → GET BACK, **Billy PRESTON** *(performer)*, Derek Taylor *(himself)* → IMAGINE: JOHN LENNON

Storyline: Michael Lindsay-Hogg's Beatles feature follows John, Paul, George and Ringo as they undergo the tense 'Let It Be' sessions amid interpersonal conflict and general fragmentation, climaxing with the legendary final performance atop the Apple building in London. *BG*

Movie rating: *7

Visual: video + dvd

Off the record: The **BEATLES** (see own biog)

—

the BEATLES

May 70. (lp/c) *Apple; (PCS/TC-PCS 7096) <34001>* [1] [1]
– Two of us / Dig a pony / Across the universe / I me mine / Dig it / Let it be / Maggie Mae / I've got a feeling / The one after 909 / The long and winding road / For you blue / Get back. *(cd-iss. Oct87; CDP 746 447-2); hit No.50) (re-iss. Nov88 lp/c; PCS/TC-PCS 7096)*

S/track review: Recorded before 'Abbey Road' but released a month after the band had split, 'LET IT BE' still plays as an aural documentation of creative fatigue and division. Yet while the album lacks the focus and cohesion which characterised the BEATLES' best work, there are enough self-contained moments of genius to rank it as a classic in any other sense: McCARTNEY finally lets it all hang out on 'Get Back', taps a deeper spiritual core with the timeless title track and – in tandem with LENNON – perhaps achieves some sense of closure on the poignant 'Two Of Us'. LENNON, for his part, contributes one of his gutsiest vocals on 'I've Got A Feeling'. 'Across The Universe' and 'The Long And Winding Road' were the most obvious subjects of Phil Spector's controversial post-production, although 2003's 'Let It Be . . . Naked' finally revealed the album in the buff as it were, minus the overdubs and whimsical interludes. *BG*

Album rating: *8.5

– spinoff hits, etc. –

the BEATLES: Let It Be / You Know My Name (Look Up The Number)

Mar 70. (7") *(R 5833) <2764>* [2] [1]
(7"pic-d iss.Mar90; RP 5833) (3"cd-s iss.Sep89; CD3R 5833)

the BEATLES: The Long And Winding Road / For You Blue

May 70. (7") *<2832>* [–] [1]

the BEATLES: Let It Be . . . Naked

Nov 03. (cd)(lp) *Capitol; (595713-2)(595438-0)* [7] [–]
– Get back / Dig a pony / For you blue / The long and winding road / Two of us / I've got a feelin / One after 909 / Don't let me down / I me mine / Across the universe / Let it be. *(cd w/ dvd+=)* – (fly on the wall outtakes). *(lp w/ free 7"+=)* – (interview).

LET THE GOOD TIMES ROLL

1973 (US 99m TV) Metromedia / Columbia Pictures (PG)

Film genre: Rock'n'roll-music concert/documentary

Top guns: dir: Robert Abel ← ELVIS ON TOUR, Sidney Levin ← MAD DOGS & ENGLISHMEN

Stars: (archive footage):- **Chubby Checker** *(performer)* ← DON'T KNOCK THE TWIST ← IT'S TRAD, DAD! ← TWIST AROUND THE CLOCK ← TEENAGE MILLIONAIRE / → PURPLE PEOPLE EATER, **Fats DOMINO** *(performer)*, **Bo DIDDLEY** *(performer)*, **Chuck BERRY** *(performer)*, **the Shirelles** *(performers)*, **LITTLE RICHARD** *(performer)*, **Bill HALEY & His Comets** *(performers)*, **the Five Satins** *(performers)*, **the Coasters** *(performers)*, **Danny & The Juniors** *(performers)*

Storyline: Combining archival footage from the 50s & 60s with a rock'n'roll revival concert in the early 70s, this rockumentary also uses a split-screen technique with films of the day, backstage and audience clips, etc. *MCS*

Movie rating: *6

Visual: none

Off the record: Don't be confused with a 1991 video/film of the same name about the New Orleans Jazz And Heritage Festival, released by 'Island Visual Arts'. CHUCK BERRY's duet with BO DIDDLEY ('Johnny B. Goode') is not included on the OST below. *MCS*

—

Various Artists

Jul 73. (d-lp) *Bell; <9002-2>* [ ] [–]
– (introduction – CHUBBY CHECKER):- Pony time / Let's twist again / The twist / (introduction – BILL HALEY & HIS COMETS):- (We're gonna) Rock around the clock / Shake, rattle & roll / (introduction – DANNY & THE JUNIORS):- At the hop / (introduction – FATS DOMINO):- My blue heaven / Blueberry hill / (introduction – SHIRELLES):- Everybody loves a lover / Soldier boy // (introduction – COASTERS):- Poison Ivy / Charlie Brown / (introduction – BO DIDDLEY):- I'm a man / Hey! Bo Diddley / (FIVE SATINS):- Save the last dance for me – Sincerely – Earth angel – In the still of the nite / I'll be seeing you / (introduction – LITTLE RICHARD):- Lucille / Good golly Miss Molly / Rip it up.

S/track review: When DANNY & THE JUNIORS (responsible here for 'At The Hop') belted out 'Rock & Roll Here To Stay', never could he/they have been more prophetic. However, what disappoints me about this double-LP of R&R giants, is the under-produced live element – which spoils the audio part – if not the film documentary itself. A rock'n'roll "Hall Of Fame" boosts this revival concert, CHUBBY CHECKER, BILL HALEY, FATS DOMINO, the COASTERS, BO DIDDLEY and LITTLE RICHARD all contribute the odd smash hit. The latter act – outrageous as ever – mesmerised a new audience with gems such as 'Lucille', 'Good Golly Miss Molly' & 'Rip It Up', while DIDDLEY definitely stole it with 'I'm A Man' & 'Hey! Bo Diddley'; but just where was his rendition of 'Johnny B. Goode' with CHUCK BERRY? *MCS*

Album rating: *5

LET THERE BE ROCK

1980 (US/Fra 96m) High Speed Productions / Sebastian / Warner Bros.

Film genre: Hard Rock-music concert/documentary

Top guns: dir: Eric Dionysius, Eric Mistler

Stars: Ac/Dc:- Bon Scott, Angus Young *, Malcolm Young *, Phil Rudd *, Cliff Williams * *(themselves/performers)* * → PRIVATE PARTS

Storyline: Australia's greatest hard rock act Ac/Dc are captured here (with accompanying backstage antics and quasi-mock interviews), performing live at the Pavillion De Paris, France, on the 9th December 1979. The concert to promote their recently released 'Highway To Hell' LP, was poignant in the fact that lead singer Bon Scott was to die a few months later. *MCS*

Movie rating: *7.5

Visual: 1991 video on Warners

Off the record: **Ac/Dc** (without Bon of course) subsequently cut the soundtrack to the 'MAXIMUM OVERDRIVE' movie: released as the album, 'Who Made Who' (1986).

—

AC/DC: Bonfire *(w/ 'Let There Be Rock – The Movie')*

Nov 97. (5xcd-box; discs 2+3) *Elektra/WEA; <62119> E.M.I.; (493273-2)* [90] [ ]
– (disc 2):- Live wire / Shot down in flames / Hell ain't a bad place to be / Sin city / Walk all over you / Bad boy boogie // (disc 3):- The jack / Highway to Hell / Girls got rhythm / High voltage / Whole lotta Rosie / Rocker / T.N.T. *[outtake]* / Let there be rock.

S/track review: It took until around Xmas 1997 for fans of AC/DC (and in particular the deceased BON SCOTT) to get their hands on the 'LET THERE BE ROCK' soundtrack. Unearthed as discs two & three inside the 5-CD, BON SCOTT-themed package 'Bonfire', 'LET THERE BE ROCK' (not to be confused with their 1977 studio set), was definitely worth the wait. AC/DC were arguably at their finest during the late 70s, pre-Brian Johnson period, SCOTT's high-pitched screeching could strip wallpaper from five paces, while the guitar-playing of pseudo-schoolboy ANGUS YOUNG was up there with the greatest. Of the 13 excellent live tracks (14, if you include worthy outtake, 'T.N.T.'), the highlights come courtesy of extended classics such as 'Live Wire', 'Bad Boy Boogie' (the longest at over 13 minutes!), 'High Voltage', 'Rocker' and 'Let There Be Rock'. If you include the cheeky-chappy, Alex Harvey-inspired gem, 'The Jack', what you have is a glimpse of the glory days of Australia's finest exports. *MCS*

Album rating (discs 2-3 only): *7.5

LET'S ROCK AGAIN!

2004 (US 67m w/b&w) Dick Rude Productions (15)

Film genre: Punk Rock-music concert/documentary

Top guns: dir: Dick Rude

Stars: **Joe STRUMMER** *(archive performer)*, Dick Rude *(himself)* ← ROADSIDE PROPHETS ← WALKER ← STRAIGHT TO HELL ← SID & NANCY ← REPO MAN, **Tymon Dogg** *(performer)*, **the Mescaleros:- Luke Bullen, Simon Stafford, Martin Slattery, Scott Shields** *(performers)*

Storyline: Somewhat of a tribute to ex-Clash frontman, Joe Strummer, and the hardships undertaken on his (late 90s/early 00s) comeback tours with backing band, the Mescaleros. *MCS*

Movie rating: *8

Visual: dvd

Off the record: Tragically, at the age of 50, **Joe STRUMMER**, died of a heart attack on the 22nd of December, 2002. *MCS*

– associated release –

JOE STRUMMER & THE MESCALEROS: Global A Go-Go

Jul 01. (cd) *Hellcat; <(0440-2)>* [ ] [68]

LET'S SPEND THE NIGHT TOGETHER

aka 'TIME IS ON OUR SIDE'

1983 (US 94m) Embassy / Raindrop Films (PG)

Film genre: Rock-music concert/documentary

Top guns: dir: Hal Ashby ← BOUND FOR GLORY ← HAROLD AND AND MAUDE ← the LANDLORD

Stars: **the ROLLING STONES:- Mick Jagger, Keith Richards, Ron Wood, Bill Wyman, Charlie Watts, Ian Stewart** *(performers)*, **Ian McLagan** *(himself)* ← TONITE LET'S ALL MAKE LOVE IN LONDON, **Bobby Keys** *(himself)* ← LADIES AND GENTLEMEN, THE ROLLING STONES ← MAD DOGS & ENGLISHMEN / → HAIL! HAIL! ROCK'N'ROLL → AT THE MAX, **Ernie Watts** *(himself)*, Jerry Hall *(dancer)* ← URBAN COWBOY / → RUNNING OUT OF LUCK → BATMAN → 25X5: THE CONTINUING ADVENTURES OF THE ROLLING STONES → the WALL: LIVE IN BERLIN

Storyline: The Rolling Stones are captured live on film for the umpteenth time, Jagger, Richards, Watts, Wood and Wyman, swaggering through a few US concert arenas in '81: the Sun Devil stadium in Tempe, Arizona and Meadowlands, New Jersey. *MCS*

Movie rating: *5.5

Visual: video + dvd (no audio OST)

Off the record: Among the classic ROLLING STONES songs were 'Black Limousine', 'All Down The Line', 'Brown Sugar', 'You Can't Always Get What You Want', 'Honky Tonk Women', 'Jumpin' Jack Flash', 'Let It Bleed', 'Let's Spend The Night Together', '(I Can't Get No) Satisfaction' and 'Under My Thumb'. Behind the scenes were **Bobby Keys** *(Joe Cocker band / the Band)*, **Ian McLagan** (the Small Faces), **Ernie Watts** *(Charlie Haden's Quartet West)*. *MCS*

LIFEHOUSE

aka Pete Townshend: Music From Lifehouse

2000 (UK 96m) EelPie Recording Productions

Film genre: Classical/Rock Musical/Opera/Concert

Top guns: dir: Hugo Currie, Toby Leslie

Stars: **Pete Townshend** *(performer)* <= the WHO =>, **John Bundrick** *(keyboards)* ← THIRTY YEARS OF MAXIMUM R&B LIVE ← PSYCHODERELICT ← DEEP END / → the WHO LIVE AT THE ROYAL ALBERT HALL, **Peter Hope Evans** *(mouth organ)* ← PSYCHODERELICT ← DEEP END, **Gaby Lester** *(violin)*, **Chucho Merchan** *(bass)*, **Phil Palmer** *(guitar)* ← PSYCHODERELICT, **Jody Linscott** *(percussion)* ← THIRTY YEARS OF MAXIMUM R&B LIVE ← GIVE MY REGARDS TO BROAD STREET, **Victoria Wood** *(oboe)*, **Chyna** *(vocals)* ← THIRTY YEARS OF MAXIMUM R&B LIVE, **Cleveland Watkiss** *(vocals)* ← THIRTY YEARS OF MAXIMUM R&B LIVE, **Billy Nicholls** *(vocals)* ← PSYCHODERELICT, Liam Bates *(conductor)* & the London Chamber Orchestra

Storyline: Pete Townshend finally brings his "Lifehouse" project to the masses after 30 years in the making – so to speak. Intended for an LP release in 1970/71, the multimedia discs (the DVD recorded live at London's Sadler's Wells Theatre on 25th February, 2000) finally saw light post-millennium. The story itself is about a reclusive Scottish farmer, Ray (unaffected by the pollution across the country), looking for his runaway, London-concert-bound daughter who might become a victim of the "suits". *MCS*

Movie rating: *6

Visual: video + dvd 2002

Off the record: The LIFEHOUSE project this time around featured tracks:- 'Fantasia Upon One Note', 'Teenage Wasteland', 'Love Ain't For Keeping', 'Greyhound Girl', 'Mary', 'I Don't Know Myself', 'Bargain', 'Pure And Easy', 'Baba O'Riley', 'Behind Blue Eyes', 'Let's See Action', 'Getting In Tune', 'Relay', 'Join Together', 'Won't Get Fooled Again', 'Can You Help The One You Really Love?', etc. *MCS*

– associated releases, etc. –

PETE TOWNSHEND: The Lifehouse Chronicles

Apr 00. (6xcd-box) *www.eelpie.com* [–] net [–]
– (CD1: The Lifehouse Demos):- Teenage wasteland / Goin' mobile / Baba O'Riley / Time is passing / Love ain't for keeping / Bargain / Too much of anything / Music must change / Greyhound girl / Mary / Behind blue eyes / Baba O'Riley – instrumental / Sister disco // (CD2: The Lifehouse Demos, cont.):- I don't know myself / Put the money down / Pure and easy / Getting in tune / Let's see action (nothing is everything) / Slip kid / Relay / Who are you / Join together / Won't get fooled again / The song is over // (CD3: Lifehouse Themes and Experiments) // (CD4: Lifehouse Arrangements & Orchestrations) / / (CD5 & 6: Lifehouse radio play).

PETE TOWNSHEND: Lifehouse Elements

May 00. (cd) *Redline; <70001>* [ ] [–]
– One note (prologue) / Baba O'Riley (orchestral) / Pure and easy / New song / Getting in tune / Behind blue eyes (new) / Let's see action (nothing is everything) / Who are you (Gateway remix) / Won't get fooled again / Baba M1 / The song is over.

– other 'Lifehouse' stuff –

the WHO: Won't Get Fooled Again / I Don't Even Know Myself

Jul 71. (7") *Track; (2094 009) Decca; <32846>* [9] [15]

the WHO: Who's Next

Sep 71. (lp) *Track; (2408 102) Decca; <79182>* [1] Aug71 [4]
– Baba O'Riley / Bargain / Love ain't for keeping / My wife / Song is over / Getting in tune / Going mobile / Behind blue eyes / Won't get fooled again. *(re-iss. Nov83 on 'Polydor' lp/c)(cd; SPE LP/MC 49)(813 651-2) (cd re-iss. Aug96; 527760-2)*

the WHO: Let's See Action / (other non 'Lifehouse' track)

Oct 71. (7") *Track; (2094 012)* [16] [–]

the WHO: Behind Blues Eyes / (other non 'Lifehouse' track)

Nov 71. (7") *Decca; <32888>* [–] [34]

the WHO: Join Together / (other non 'Lifehouse' track)

Jun 72. (7") *Track; (2094 102) Decca; <32983>* [9] [17]

PETE TOWNSHEND: Who Came First

Oct 72. (lp) *Track; (2408 201) Decca; <79189>* [30] [69]
– features:- Pure and easy / Let's see action / *(<cd-iss. Oct92 & Mar97 on 'Rykodisc'; RCD 20246>)*

the WHO: Relay / (other non 'Lifehouse' track)

Jan 73. (7") *Track; (2094 106) M.C.A.; <33041>* [21] Dec72 [39]

the WHO: Odds & Sods *(rarities collection)*

Oct 74. (lp/c) *Track; (2406/3191 116) <2126>* [10] [15]
– features:- Put the money down / Too much of anything / Pure and easy / *(cd-iss. Jun93; 517946-2)*

the WHO: The Who By Numbers

Oct 75. (lp/c) *Polydor; (2490/3194 129) M.C.A.; <2161>* [7] [8]
– features:- Slip kid / *(re-iss. Mar84 lp/c; SPE LP/MC 68) (cd-iss. Jul89; 831552-2)*

the WHO: Slip Kid / (other non 'Lifehouse' track)

Aug 76. (7") *M.C.A.; <40603>* [–] [ ]

the WHO: Who Are You? / (other non 'Lifehouse' track)

Jul 78. (7") *Polydor; (WHO 1) M.C.A.; <40948>* [18] [14]

the WHO: Who Are You?

Sep 78. (lp/c)<US-red/pic-lp> *Polydor; (WHOD/+C 5004) M.C.A.; <3050>* [6] [2]
– features:- Sister disco / Music must change / Who are you / *(re-iss. Aug84 lp/c; SPE LP/MC 77) (cd-iss. Jul89; 831557-2)*

LIGHTNING IN A BOTTLE

2004 (US 103m) Sony Pictures

Film genre: Roots/Blues-music concert/documentary

Top guns: dir: Antoine Fuqua

Stars: Steve Jordan *(performer)* ← HAIL! HAIL! ROCK'N'ROLL / → MAKE IT FUNKY!, **Levon Helm** *(performer)* <= the BAND =>, **DR. JOHN** *(performer)*, **Willie Weeks** *(performer)*, **Danny Kortchmar** *(performer)*, **Angelique Kidjo** *(performer)*, **Mavis Staples** *(performer)* <= the STAPLE SINGERS =>, **Natalie Cole** *(performer)*, **Buddy Guy** *(performer)* ← FESTIVAL EXPRESS ← GODFATHERS AND SONS ← BLUES ODYSSEY ← CHICAGO BLUES ← SUPERSHOW, **Ivan Neville** *(performer)*, **Odetta** *(performer)* ← the BALLAD OF RAMBLIN' JACK ← CHORDS OF FAME ← FESTIVAL / → BLUES DIVA → NO DIRECTION HOME, **India.Arie** *(performer)*, **Macy Gray** *(performer)*, **Keb' Mo'** *(performer)* ← HELLHOUNDS ON MY TRAIL, **Honeyboy Edwards** *(performer)* → WALK HARD: THE DEWEY COX STORY, **James Blood Ulmer** *(performer)* ← the SOUL OF A MAN, **Alison Krauss** *(performer)* ← DOWN FROM THE MOUNTAIN, **Clarence 'Gatemouth' Brown** *(performer)*, **John Fogerty** *(performer)*, **Larry Johnson** *(performer)*, **Bonnie RAITT** *(performer)*, **Gregg Allman** *(performer)* ← RUSH, **Warren Haynes** *(performer)*, **Steven Tyler + Joe Perry of AEROSMITH** *(performers)*, **the Neville Brothers** *(performers)*, **Shemekia Copeland** *(performer)* ← the SOUL OF A MAN, **Robert Cray** *(performer)*, **David Johansen** *(performer)* <= NEW YORK DOLLS =>, **Hubert Sumlin** *(performer)* ← the ROAD TO MEMPHIS, **B.B. KING** *(performer)*, **Chuck D & Fine Arts Militia** *(performers)*, **Solomon Burke** *(performer)* → DERAILROADED, **MOS DEF** *(performer)*, **Vernon Reid** *(performer)* ← the SOUL OF A MAN, **John Hammond** *(performer)*, **Kim Wilson** *(performer)*, **Chris Thomas King** *(performer)* ← the SOUL OF A MAN ← LAST OF THE MISSISSIPPI JUKES ← O BROTHER, WHERE ART THOU? ← DOWN FROM THE MOUNTAIN / → RAY, **Ruth Brown** *(performer)* ← SHAKE, RATTLE & ROCK! tv ← HAIRSPRAY ← ROCK'N'ROLL REVUE, Bill Cosby *(performer)*

Storyline: A once-in-a-lifetime, Deep Southern Social Club conglomerate of blues, jazz, soul, rock, country, gospel and hip hop luminaries converge on New York's Radio City Music Hall in February 2003, ostensibly to launch Martin Scorsese's blues project and raise money for the Blues Music Foundation, but also, naturally, to blaze off so much history, energy and mutual admiration concentrated in one place, fired by a house band which numbers, variously, Keb' Mo', Ivan Neville, Willie Weeks, Dr. John, Levon Helm, Danny Kortchmar and Steve Jordan. Stage action is intercut with rehearsals, footage documenting the songs' original musical/political context (with progenitors who didn't live long enough to see their music honoured so lavishly) along with banter and reminiscences from a lifetime of blues legends and their spiritual offspring, the most sage of whom – David "Honeyboy" Edwards, Clarence "Gatemouth" Brown and B.B. King among them – definitively prove the old cliché (as old as the blues itself), "age ain't nuthin' but a number". *BG*

Movie rating: *7

Visual: dvd

Off the record: (see below)

Various Artists (md: Steve Jordan)

Sep 04. (d-cd) *Columbia-Legacy; <C2K 92860>* [ ] [–]
– Senie Zelie (ANGELIQUE KIDJO) / See that my grave is kept clean (MAVIS STAPLES) / Gamblin' man (DAVID "HONEYBOY" EDWARDS) / Love in vain (KEB' MO') / Sittin' on top of the world (JAMES "BLOOD" ULMER with ALISON KRAUSS) / Jim Crow blues (ODETTA) / St. Louis blues (NATALIE COLE) / Men are just like street cars (NATALIE COLE, MAVIS STAPLES and RUTH BROWN) / I can't be satisfied (BUDDY GUY) / Strange fruit (INDIA.ARIE) / Hound dog (MACY GRAY) / The midnight special (JOHN FOGERTY) / Where'd you get that sound (LARRY JOHNSON) // Okie dokie stomp (CLARENCE "GATEMOUTH" BROWN) / Coming home (BONNIE RAITT) / The sky is crying (GREGG ALLMAN & WARREN HAYNES) / I'm a king bee (STEVEN TYLER & JOE PERRY) / First time I met the blues (BUDDY GUY) / Big chief (the NEVILLE BROTHERS) / I pity the fool (SHEMEKIA COPELAND & ROBERT CRAY) / Killing floor (DAVID JOHANSEN & HUBERT SUMLIN) / Turn on your love light (SOLOMON BURKE) / Down in the valley (SOLOMON BURKE) / Voodoo child (ANGELIQUE KIDJO, BUDDY GUY and VERNON REID) / Minnesota blues aka "Black Jack blues" (MOS DEF) / (No) Boom boom (CHUCK D. & THE FINE ARTS MILITIA) / Sweet sixteen (B.B. KING).

S/track review: The inside sleeve almost suggests a Southern Sgt. Pepper's, an iconic gathering of the clans which even comes with a handy little key so you can put a name to any unfamiliar faces. Not that there's many of those; the stature of Martin Scorsese means that pretty much everyone whom you'd expect to turn out for his blues series primer is present and scrubbed up. Which isn't to say it's predictable; where else would you get Beninese diva ANGELIQUE KIDJO – with BUDDY GUY and VERNON REID –

siphoning off the funk in Jimi Hendrix's 'Voodoo Child', R&B maverick MACY GRAY nonchalantly gruffing her way through 'Hound Dog' or Ornette Coleman protégé JAMES BLOOD ULMER getting traditional with nu-bluegrass dame ALISON KRAUSS? The programming of KIDJO's 'Senie Zelie' as opener is intentional, roughly shadowing the blues' forced ramble from Africa across the Atlantic, from Southern state to Northern city, acoustic to electric and ultimately into the hybridisations of rock and hip hop. In charting this odyssey, Scorsese had almost six hours of material to work with and he rarely hurries himself, content to let the music tell its own laconic story. The DVD charts a more comprehensive itinerary, but so haunted with hoary imagery are some of these songs that sometimes it's better just to listen. MAVIS STAPLES, for one, conjures some serious church on a gloweringly devout 'See That My Grave Is Kept Clean', but even more phantasmic is INDIA.ARIE's 'Strange Fruit', doubly powerful in giving voice to such an underrated talent so far outside of the dance/R&B ghetto. NINA SIMONE might've passed away when this concert was but a twinkle in Scorsese's eye but ODETTA channels her spirit, introducing a cover of Leadbelly's 'Jim Crow Blues' in that same halting, distracted style, and singing with something approaching that same cinnamon barb in her voice. And that's just the ladies. 'Men Are Just Like Street Cars', testify MAVIS STAPLES and RUTH BROWN, likely only half in jest; 'I Can't Be Satisfied', counters the peerless BUDDY GUY, thwacking out crooked notes in a sequence of percussive pops. Save for BONNIE RAITT doing Elmore James proud, and SHEMEKIA COPELAND raising the rafters, the guys get most of the second disc to themselves, building on the all-star house band and inviting the rest of the family with the NEVILLE BROTHERS' 'Big Chief', rolling out the old rockers with STEVEN TYLER and JOE PERRY (still faithful to their 'Stones fixation after all these years, a grimy 'I'm A King Bee' that's likewise harder and nastier than anything Aerosmith have done in just as many years), and DAVID JOHANSEN & HUBERT SUMLIN (the latter nursing only one lung) with a ripping 'Killing Floor' replicated on one of the best single disc soundtracks in the series. The perennially underappreciated SOLOMON BURKE delivers the soul, MOS DEF offers the clearest support for Scorsese's determined blues-to-hip hop lineage, and ultimately, CHUCK D & THE FINE ARTS MILITIA rail against Bush and his then looming Iraq war and at least partly justify a brilliantly named ensemble by reconfiguring John Lee Hooker's 'Boom Boom' as thermonuclear, blues-thrash blast (in vain, alas). *BG*

Album rating: *7.5

LITTLE RICHARD

Born: Richard Wayne Penniman, 5th Dec'35, Macon, Georgia, USA, raised in a large family by preacher parents who schooled him in the ways of gospel singing. Aged 16, the petite RICHARD was given the opportunity (through singer, Billy Wright) to record for 'RCA-Victor'. After four flop singles for the imprint, LITTLE RICHARD subsequently moved on to Don Robey's 'Peacock' label in 1953, where he sessioned for doo-wop group, the Tempo-Toppers. After fronting the Johnny Otis Orchestra in 1955, the man signed a solo deal with 'Specialty'. His first single for the label, 'Tutti Frutti', gave him his maiden entry into the US Top 20. Outrageously attired in flamboyant pink body-suits, this eccentric, clowning catalyst of rock'n'roll was like nothing the white music establishment had ever encountered; in both his image and his hollering, tongue-in-cheek assault, the effeminate RICHARD borrowed nothing from his contemporaries. Over the course of the next few years, he flounced his way through a series of classic hits which would subsequently become standards:- 'Long Tall Sally', 'Rip It Up', 'The GIRL CAN'T HELP IT' (exposure from the rock'n'roll movie of the same name gave him yet another UK hit), 'Lucille', 'Jenny, Jenny', 'Keep A Knockin'' and 'Good Golly, Miss Molly'. At the height of his fame (with a handful of other movie appearances behind him – see below), RICHARD was to publicly renounce his "evil" rock'n'roll music/lifestyle, reverting back to gospel and pledging his life to "Jeeesus". In 1960, the now Reverend LITTLE RICHARD spent a couple of years under the production of Quincy Jones, but returned to rock'n'roll in 1964. Although he had a few minor hits, including 'Bama Lama Bama Loo', his new material was overshadowed by British acts covering his earlier work. In the 70s, RICHARD released the odd album, while collaborating with the likes of Canned Heat and Delaney & Bonnie, swinging back and forth between rock'n'roll and God, homosexuality and heterosexuality. By the mid 80s, the veteran showman was back in the limelight when he took up the offer to appear in the movie, 'DOWN AND OUT IN BEVERLY HILLS' (1986). From then on in, LITTLE RICHARD has successfully kept his profile high via guest spots in TV series including 'Miami Vice', while also fraternising with top-named celebrities such as ELTON JOHN, Tanya Tucker and er, Kermit The Frog! In 2000, there was a TV movie about the man, thoughtfully titled, 'LITTLE RICHARD'. *MCS*

- **filmography** {performer/actor} –

the Girl Can't Help It *(1956 {p} theme on OST by V/A =>)* **Don't Knock The Rock** *(1956 {p})* / **Mister Rock And Roll** *(1957 {p} theme =>)* / **Catalina Caper** *(1967 {p})* / **Keep On Rockin'** *(1969 {*p})* / **Let The Good Times Roll** *(1973 {p} on OST by V/A =>)* / **Jimi Hendrix** *(1973 {p} OST by JIMI HENDRIX =>)* / **the London Rock And Roll Show** *(1973 {p} on OST by V/A =>)* / **the Little Richard Story** *(1980 {*c})* / **the Compleat Beatles** *(1984 {p/f} OST by the BEATLES =>)* / **Down And Out In Beverly Hills** *(1986 {a/p} theme on OST by V/A & ANDY SUMMERS =>)* / **Hail! Hail! Rock'n'Roll** *(1987 {p} OST by CHUCK BERRY =>)* / Goddess Of Love *(1988 TV {a})* / **Purple People Eater** *(1988 {b} OST by V/A =>)* / Mother Goose Rock'n'Rhyme *(1990 TV {a/p} OST by cast)* / Sunset Heat *(1991 {a})* / the Naked Truth *(1992 {b})* / Twist *(1992 {p})* / Last Action Hero *(1993 {c} on OST by V/A => future edition)* / the Pickle *(1993 {a})* / **Why Do Fools Fall In Love** *(1998 {c} OST by V/A =>)* / Mystery, Alaska *(1999 {p})* / the Trumpet Of The Swan *(2001 anim. {v})*

LIVE AT POMPEII

aka PINK FLOYD: Live at POMPEII

1974 (UK 59m; re-dvd 92m) Universal (E)

Film genre: Experimental Rock-music concert/documentary

Top guns: dir: Adrian Maben

Stars: PINK FLOYD:- Roger Waters, David Gilmour, Richard Wright, Nick Mason *(performers)*

Storyline: Pink Floyd perform (to an audience of camera and soundmen) at the centre of an ancient amphitheatre in the ruins of old Pompeii. Visually, the barren wastelands of the volcano-destroyed city (shot in April 1971), take equal precedence alongside the Floyd and their equipment. *MCS*

Movie rating: *6.5 / dvd w/ extras *7

Visual: (see DVD below)

Off the record: No album was forthcoming from PINK FLOYD, so it would be some time before the cinematic version hit the retail shops on video. Kicking off (and closing) with a shortened 'Echoes' from the group's 1971 album 'Meddle', PINK FLOYD dramatically set the pulse for a horizontal cocoon of experimental Prog-rock at its very best. 1968's 'Careful With That Axe Eugene' and 'A Saucerful Of Secrets' (the latter from the LP of the same name) demonstrated further that PF were prime purveyors of atmospheric rock. Track four on the video, 'One Of These Days' and 'Mademoiselle Nobs', were two further cuts lifted from the excellent 'Meddle', the latter actually being a guise for 'Seamus' with a new dog. The gong was out again for the ecliptic, 'Set The Controls For The Heart Of The Sun'; Pompeii's ghosts looked to have been awakened by FLOYD's eerie sojourn into timeless space. Percussionist NICK MASON steals the show once again. As previously mentioned, 'The Director's Cut' DVD, added a few cuts, 'Us And Them' and 'Brain Damage' (worked on in a studio in Paris) that were highlights from their 1973 multi-platinum bestseller, 'The Dark Side Of The Moon'. *MCS*

– associated releases, etc. –

PINK FLOYD

Aug 88. (video) *Channel 5; (CFV 05182)* [–] [–]
– (see above track listing) *(re-iss. Mar90; CFV 10422)*

PINK FLOYD: Live At Pompeii – The Director's Cut (+ *)

2003. (DVD) *Universal; (8201310)* [–] [–]
– Echoes (part 1) / Careful with that axe Eugene / A saucerful of secrets / Us and them (*) / One of these days / Mademoiselle nobs / Brain damage (*) / Set the controls for the heart of the sun / Echoes (part 2).

LIVE FOREVER:

. . . THE RISE AND FALL OF BRIT POP

2003 (UK 83m) Passion Pictures / BBC Film Council (R)

Film genre: Brit-Pop/Rock-music documentary

Top guns: dir (+ s-w): John Dower

Stars: Blur:- Damon ALBARN *(themselves/performers)*, **Oasis:- Liam Gallagher, Noel Gallagher** *(themselves/performers)* ← the WHO LIVE AT THE ROYAL ALBERT HALL / → MAYOR OF THE SUNSET STRIP, **Pulp:- Jarvis Cocker** *(themselves/performers)* → I'M YOUR MAN → 30 CENTURY MAN, **Sleeper:- Louise Wener** *(themselves/performers)* → MAYOR OF THE SUNSET STRIP, Ozwald Boateng, Kevin Cummings, **James BROWN** *(himself)*, **Robert "3D" del Naja/Massive Attack** *(himself)*, Peter Mandelson, Damien Hirst, Jon Savage, Phill Savidge, Toby Young, Tony Blair *(archive)*

Storyline: A chronicle of the arrival of Britpop in the 1990s, the film features Noel Gallagher's comments on society after the transition from Margaret Thatcher to Tony Blair and New Labour. Starting from the now defunct Stone Roses, the Britpop evolution is charted through bands such as Oasis, Blur and Pulp and explores their links with the political culture of the time. *JZ*

Movie rating: *7

Visual: video + dvd

Off the record: DAMON ALBARN took a diversion from his Blur activities via film (part-)scores for '101 REYKJAVIK', 'RAVENOUS' and 'ORDINARY DECENT CRIMINAL'.

—

Various Artists: The Best Of Britpop

Mar 03. (d-cd) *Virgin; (VTDCD 512) E.M.I.; <5 82049-2>* [ ] Dec03 [ ]
– Live forever (OASIS) / Common people (PULP) / Parklife (BLUR) / Alright (SUPERGRASS) / Girl from Mars (ASH) / Waking up (ELASTICA) / Mulder and Scully (CATATONIA) / Fine time (CAST) / The changing man (PAUL WELLER) / Stupid girl (GARBAGE) / Everything musy go (MANIC STREET PREACHERS) / The riverboat song (OCEAN COLOUR SCENE) / Atomic (SLEEPER) / Tattva (KULA SHAKER) / Come back to what you know (EMBRACE) / Wide open space (MANSUN) / 6 underground (SNEAKER PIMPS) / Female of the species (SPACE) / You're gorgeous (BABYBIRD) / Angels (ROBBIE WILLIAMS) // The drugs don't work (VERVE) *[UK-only]* / Protection (MASSIVE ATTACK feat. TRACEY THORN) / Street spirit (fade out) (RADIOHEAD) / Stars (DUBSTAR) *[US-only]* / The more you ignore me the closer I get (MORRISSEY) / Beautiful ones (SUEDE) / The life of Riley (LIGHTNING SEEDS) / Inbetweener (SLEEPER) / King of the kerb (ECHOBELLY) / Getting better (SHED 7) / Ready to go (REPUBLICA) / Setting song (the CHEMICAL BROTHERS) / Nancy boy (PLACEBO) / Breathe (the PRODIGY) / Weak (SKUNK ANANSIE) / Born slippy (UNDERWORLD) / Loaded (PRIMAL SCREAM) / Step on (HAPPY MONDAYS) / The only one I know (the CHARLATANS) / Champagne supernova (OASIS).

S/track review: Ten years on, it is tempting to draw comparisons between the Britpop years and the optimism and musical fecundity of the late 60s. In the summer of 1990, the Stone Roses played to over thirty thousand on an island in the Mersey Estuary. In his liner notes, 'LIVE FOREVER's director John Dower perceived this event as a "rebellious and hedonistic" counterculture in the midst of Tory rule and economic depression. It could be argued that it presaged a new age in British music which reached its zenith in 1997. Britpop became enshrined on the cover of Vanity Fair before being hijacked and manipulated by political ideology; it transmuted into "Cool Britannia" amid the hue and cry of the newly installed New Labour government. At the heart of this movement were the triumvirate of OASIS, BLUR and PULP. And what's intriguing about this soundtrack is the degree to which the other bands can or cannot lay claim to be part of this movement, and – more pertinently – whether they would want to. But what exactly was Britpop? Is it simply the OASIS-PULP-BLUR axis? The Big Three all lay claim to a working class aesthetic, and Britpop was the rejuvenation of sixties-flavoured guitar music, alloyed with the nationalistic zeal that now accompanies every major football tournament (a trend that began wholesale when England hosted Euro 96). 'LIVE FOREVER' is the lager and distortion sound of the football terraces, though I have always struggled to find any real resemblance to the BEATLES aside from those that are shared by all pop groups from the 1970s onwards. 'Common People' and 'Parklife' are the more knowing relations of the Mancunian troglodytes, "I want to live like common people" Jarvis Cocker crows from atop his art school perch and Damon Albarn even enlists Phil Daniels to instil a rugged charm to what is still a brilliant cheeky chappy anthem, replete with horns and smashing glass samples. OASIS chug on today but the other two bands have fallen to the wayside, and bands still clamour to board their Union Jack-draped bandwagon, from the WHO to Kasabian. Could it be that in actual fact one band constituted this so-called "movement"? Because the rest of this album seems to be divided into two different camps: the prototypes for Britpop, and those who had nothing to do with it, aside from the fact that they are British and (were) popular. In the former category, PAUL WELLER and MORRISSEY were both figureheads in bands that were heavily influential on the upcoming crop of indie guitar bands. PRIMAL SCREAM, HAPPY MONDAYS and the CHARLATANS were all established before the conception of the movement but have since benefitted from its afterglow; PRIMAL SCREAM have gone full circle back to the rock'n'roll of 'Loaded' having produced far more interesting work in their throbbing late 90s electronica period. There are the bands that spearheaded the parallel, though not contiguous, trip-hop and big beat explosion: MASSIVE ATTACK, the CHEMICAL BROTHERS, the PRODIGY, UNDERWORLD. There are the heavier Brit Rock acts such as MANIC STREET PREACHERS (thinking man's British rock), ASH (thinking man's British pop rock), GARBAGE (thinking woman's British rock), PLACEBO (thinking gender bender's British rock) and SKUNK ANANSIE (thinking person of mixed ethnic origin's British quasi-metal). Then there is RADIOHEAD, who transcended the whole movement (and 'Street Spirit (Fade Out)' is still a remarkable and chilling song), and ROBBIE WILLIAMS who has no place here but seems to qualify because he got twatted with OASIS at Glastonbury 1994, and 'Angels' is for some reason acceptable beered-up indie karaoke fare. In the remaining bands we begin to arrive at the fringes of Britpop proper: the chug chugging grrlll power of ELASTICA and SLEEPER, the pseudo-psychedelic stylings of KULA SHAKUR, and the superior indie rock of MANSUN. What's left is the true hollow kernel of Britpop, the watered-down lager sounds of EMBRACE ('Come Back To What You Know'), who have since been trounced by Keaneplay, the LIGHTNING SEEDS (acceptable at the time but probably most famous for their part in THAT footie song) and who can forget CAST, the Oasis clones extraordinaire, distorted guitars, shimmering melodies and nasal Liverpudlian accents (but where's 'Sandstorm'?). Britpop: three classic bands, and a host of also-rans. *DF*

Album rating: *7

the LONDON ROCK & ROLL SHOW

1973 (US 84m) Pleasant Pastures

Film genre: Rock'n'roll-music concert/documentary

Top guns: dir: Peter Clifton ← POPCORN / → the SONG REMAINS THE SAME

Stars: Bo DIDDLEY *(performer)*, **Jerry Lee LEWIS** *(performer)*, **Heinz** *(performer)* ← JUST FOR FUN ← FAREWELL PERFORMANCE ← LIVE IT UP, **LITTLE RICHARD** *(performer)*, **Chuck BERRY** *(performer)*, **Screaming Lord Sutch** *(performer)*, **Bill HALEY & the Comets** *(performer/s)*, **Roy Wood/Wizzard** *(performer/s)*, **Mick Jagger** *(commentator)* ← the ROLLING STONES =>

Storyline: On the 5th of August 1972, Wembley Stadium was host to a plethora of veteran rock'n'roll performers including "Raving Loony Party" leader Screaming Lord Sutch, who er . . . lowers the tone somewhat with bikini-clad dancers and a stripper. *MCS*

Movie rating: *7

Visual: dvd

Off the record: Roy Wood (ex-Move & ELO) had already two hits Wizzard hits under his belt, 'Ball Park Incident' & 'See My Baby Jive'.

Various Artists

Jan 01. (cd) *TKO Magnum;* [-] [ ]
– BO DIDDLEY:- Road runner / Mona / JERRY LEE LEWIS:- High school confidential / You can have her / Whole lotta shakin' goin' on / Hound dog – Good golly Miss Molly – Blue suede shoes – Whole lotta shakin' goin' on / BILL HALEY & HIS COMETS:- See you later, alligator / Rock around the clock / LITTLE RICHARD:- Lucille / Rip it up / Good golly Miss Molly / Tutti frutti / Jenny Jenny Jenny / CHUCK BERRY:- School days / Memphis Tennessee / Sweet little sixteen / Mean old 'Frisco / Wee wee hours / Carol – Little Queenie / Reelin' and rockin'. *<cd re-iss. w/ DVD in 2006 on 'Store For Music'; 009>*

S/track review: Not the best of recordings by any manner of means, but there are high points as LITTLE RICHARD, CHUCK BERRY, BO DIDDLEY and JERRY LEE LEWIS steal the show from 'Rock Around The Clock' icon, BILL HALEY (& HIS COMETS, of course). It's basically a hit parade of fantastic RnR standards such as 'Lucille', 'Rip It Up', 'Sweet Little Sixteen', 'School Days', 'Road Runner' and 'Whole Lotta Shakin' Goin' On', rip up the joint. MICK JAGGER is unfortunately only commentating on the DVD/film version, but it's still a bit of a blast. Its problem is that it was compared to the similarly-themed 'LET THE GOOD TIMES ROLL', released the same year. *MCS*

Album rating: *4

loudQUIETloud:

a film about THE PIXIES

2006 (US 85m) Cactus Three / Stick Figure Productions

Film genre: Indie/Grunge-Rock concert documentary

Top guns: dir: Steven Cantor, Matthew Galkin

Stars: Pixies:- Frank Black *(performer as Charles "Black Francis" Thompson)* ← GIGANTIC (A TALE OF TWO JOHNS), **Joey Santiago** *(performer)*, **Kim Deal** *(performer)*, **David Lovering** *(performer)*

Storyline: One of the most inspirational alt-rock bands to come out of the mediocre 80s, the Pixies, reunite after 12 years to tour the States in '04. Old clips are mixed with new footage, while a tentative rebirth of sorts provides its own problems. *MCS*

Movie rating: *6.5

Visual: dvd (no audio OST; score: DANIEL LANOIS, JIM WILSON, MARCUS BLAKE & STEVE NISTOR – + see below)

Off the record: The **Pixies** were formed in Boston, Massachusetts, 1986 by L.A.-born frontman and self-confessed UFO freak, **Black Francis** (real name, deep breath . . . Charles Michael Kitridge Thompson IV) along with guitarist **Joey Santiago**. Famously placing a newspaper ad requesting musicians with a penchant for Peter, Paul & Mary and Husker Du, the only taker was **Kim Deal** who subsequently brought in drummer **David Lovering**. Originally trading under the moniker Pixies In Panoply, the band soon trimmed this down to the punchier **Pixies** and began kicking up a storm on the Boston music scene with their spiky, angular noise-pop (that's two thirds noise, one third pop) and wilfully cryptic lyrics. Along with fellow Bostonians, Throwing Muses, the band were signed to '4 a.d.' by a suitably impressed Ivo Watts-Russell, the label releasing their debut 'Come On Pilgrim' in late '87. Stunningly different, the record galvanised the early Pixies sound, a bizarre hybrid of manic, strangulated vocals (often sung in Spanish), searing melodic noise and schizophrenic, neo-latin rhythms. The album drew an early core of believers but it wasn't until the release of 'Surfer Rosa' (1988) that the band were hailed as the saviours of indie rock. Taking the formula of the debut to its brain splintering conclusion, their blistering intensity and sheer unhinged abandon (Black Francis throwing himself into everything) the album had to be heard to be believed. Following their first headline UK tour, the band hooked up with producer Gil Norton for the 'Doolittle' (1989) album, the record showcasing a cleaner, more pop-friendly sound. Then came 'Bossanova' (1990), another breathtaking collection that had the music press in rapture. Lyrically, Black was in his element, losing himself in science fiction fantasy while the band raged and charmed in equal measure. The album reached No.3 in the UK charts and the Pixies could apparently do no wrong, consolidating their position as one of the biggest American acts in Europe. Yet the critics turned on them with the release of 'Trompe Le Monde' (1991), in keeping with the times a decidedly grungier affair and accusations of "heavy metal" were way off the mark. In reality, the record was still chokka with stellar tunes, you just had to dig deeper to find them. So without the Pixies, no Nirvana . . . but without Husker Du no Pixies. **Frank Black & Joey Santiago** scored the music for 2003's sci-fi comedy short, 'The Low Budget Time Machine'; the latter also composed 2006's Canadian documentary, 'Radiant City'. *BG & MCS*

– associated release –

PIXIES: Live In Minneapolis, MN. – 04.13.04

2004. (ltd-cd) *<none>* [-] tour [-]
– Bone machine / Wave of mutilation / U-mass / Levitate me / Broken face / Monkey gone to Heaven / Holiday song / Winterlong / Nimrod's son / La la love you / Ed is dead / Here comes your man / Vamos / Debaser / Dead / No.13 baby / Tame / Gigantic / Gouge away / Caribou / (other encores).

Courtney LOVE

Born: Courtney Michelle Harrison, 9 Jul'64, San Francisco, California, USA; daughter of hippie Hank Harrison, a GRATEFUL DEAD devotee. Courtney first worked as an exotic dancer before becoming an actress, appearing in mid-80s Alex Cox punk movies, 'SID & NANCY' (1986) & 'STRAIGHT TO HELL' (1987); her early bands included Sugar Baby Doll, alongside Jennifer Finch (L7) and Kat Bjelland (Babes In Toyland). LOVE's new outfit Hole were formed in L.A. at the turn of the decade, and in the spring of 1990 the quartet released the 'Rat Bastard' EP; they subsequently relocated to the burgeoning Seattle area. Early the following year, 'Sub Pop' issued the 'Dicknail' EP, while the band duly signed to 'Caroline' records for their debut album, 'Pretty On The Inside' (1991). Produced by Kim Gordon (of SONIC YOUTH) and Don Fleming (of B.A.L.L.), it hit the lower regions of the US charts and was voted album of the year by New York's Village Voice magazine. Around the same time, LOVE's relationship with Nirvana's Kurt Cobain was the talk of the alternative rock world, the singer subsequently marrying him in February '92, giving birth to his daughter, Frances Bean, later that summer. The following year, Hole secured a deal with the David Geffen Company ('D.G.C.'), much to the dismay of MADONNA, who wanted Hole for her newly formed 'Maverick' label. In spring 1994, LOVE finally celebrated a UK Top 20 album, 'Live Through This', although its success was overshadowed by the shocking shotgun suicide of Kurt on the 8th of April. She subsequently held a memorial two days later, hailing everyone there to call him an asshole. When she finally got over Kurt's death and indeed herself (it seemed she was never out of the news), Courtney exchanged the Seattle grunge mantle for a more respectable Hollywood career. This was largely down to her acclaimed roles in the movies 'Feeling Minnesota' (1996) and more so with the controversial 'The People Vs. Larry Flint' (1996). On the recording front, only a lone version of Fleetwood Mac's 'Gold Dust Woman' had seen light (this was included on the film soundtrack from 'The Crow II: City Of Angels'). In '98, COURTNEY (and Hole) were once again writing new material for third set, 'Celebrity Skin', this time with BILLY CORGAN of Smashing Pumpkins. With arguments about the album's writing credits, and a legal wrangle over her dead hubby's recording legacy rising its ugly head, LOVE continued to work in film, her next projects being '200 Cigarettes' (1999) and alongside Jim Carrey in the Andy Kaufman biopic, 'MAN ON THE MOON' (1999). 'Beat' (2000) – a story of poet William S. Burroughs and his fateful wife – plus 'Julie Johnson' (2001) and 'Trapped' (2002) kept LOVE busy during a hectic period in her career. On the songwriting front, ex-4 Non Blondes dame, Linda Perry, was recruited to shore up her long-vaunted solo debut, the narcissistically titled (and illustrated) 'America's Sweetheart' (2004). Various court appearances and er . . . court non-appearances didn't exactly make for a smooth promotional schedule, while underwhelming reviews helped relegate the album to the fringes of both the US and UK Top 50. She was never far away from the tabloid spotlight, though; an alleged, short-lived romance with Radio Norwich's star presenter Alan "a-ha" Partridge (alias comedian Steve Coogan) was plastered all over Britain's newspapers in August 2005 – rumours which were subsequently refuted by both parties. With no new album set for release, we await in anticipation her lead role as porn queen Linda Lovelace, scheduled for 2008 . . .

BG & MCS

- **filmography** {acting} –

Sid & Nancy *(1986 {a} OST by the POGUES, PRAY FOR RAIN & V/A =>)* / **Straight To Hell** *(1987 {*} OST by the POGUES, PRAY FOR RAIN & V/A =>)* / **Tapeheads** *(1988 {b} OST by FISHBONE & V/A =>)* / **1991: The Year Punk Broke** *(1992 {p} =>)* / **Not Bad For A Girl** *(1996 {p} =>)* / Basquiat *(1996 {a} OST by JOHN CALE & V/A; see future edition)* / Feeling Minnesota *(1996 {a} OST by LOS LOBOS & V/A; see future edition)* / the People Vs. Larry Flint *(1996 {*} OST by V/A & Thomas Newman; see future edition)* / **Kurt & Courtney** *(1998 {*c} =>)* / 200 Cigarettes *(1999 {a} OST by Mark Mothersbaugh & Bob Mothersbaugh V/A; see future edition)* / **Man On The Moon** *(1999 {*} OST by R.E.M. & V/A =>)* / Beat *(2000 {*})* / Julie Johnson *(2001 {*})* / Trapped *(2002 {*})* / **Mayor Of The Sunset Strip** *(2003 {c} OST by V/A =>)*

LULU

Born: Marie McDonald McLaughlin Lawrie, 3 Nov'48, Lennoxtown, Glasgow, Scotland. Making her first public singing appearance before she even reached her teens, Lawrie subsequently formed her own band the Glen Eagles. Soon renamed Lulu & The Luvvers, they signed to 'Decca' and had a surprise UK Top 10 hit in 1964 with a frenetic cover of the Isley Brothers' 'Shout'. Its success made the diminutive LULU a schoolgirl star, her surprisingly soulful pubescent rasp blaring out of radios and TV sets across the country. This was followed into the charts by pop ballad 'Leave A Little Love' although much of her mid-60s material consisted of rough'n'ready R&B covers such as the Rolling Stones' 'Surprise Surprise'. LULU went solo in 1966 and was soon back in the UK Top 10 the following year with a cover of Neil Diamond's 'The Boat That I Row'. 1967 also saw the lass make her critically acclaimed acting debut, co-starring alongside Sidney Poitier in the film, 'TO SIR, WITH LOVE'. The movie's title theme subsequently gave the Glaswegian a US No.1 and the success launched her into the ranks of the pop/rock aristocracy. She married Bee Gee Maurice Gibb in 1969, the same year she won the Eurovision song contest with the awful No.2 hit, 'Boom Bang-A-Bang'. This connection secured her inclusion on the BEE GEES' TV project/LP, 'CUCUMBER CASTLE' (1970). Juggling the opposing forces of TV showbiz personality and rock credibility, she made the obligatory pilgrimage to Muscle Shoals in 1970 for her blue-eyed soul effort, 'New Routes'. Released on 'Atlantic' and featuring the crack production team of Jerry Wexler, Tom Dowd and Arif Mardin, the record paired LULU with soul powerhouses like the Dixie Flyers and the Memphis Horns. 1973/74 found her working with DAVID BOWIE on a cover of his own 'The Man Who Sold The World', her first UK Top 3 hit in nearly five years. Her second foray into film theme songs was not as fruitful as her first, the Bond song 'The Man With The Golden Gun' (1974) failing to chart and a damp squid by composer John Barry's standards. For the remainder of the 70s and most of the 80s she was absent from the chart spotlight, although she did score a couple of minor US hits in 1981 and made a brief UK Top 10 comeback in 1986 with a remake of 'Shout' (an exploitative re-release of the original version also went Top 10 at the same time). A larger scale comeback/reinvention was effected early in 1993 with the club-influenced 'Independence' single (taken from the album of the same name), a near UK Top 10 hit; and how can we forget her appearances in TV sit-com, 'Absolutely Fabulous'. Her song, 'I Don't Wanna Fight' (written with her brother), also found its way on to the soundtrack of Tina Turner's 'WHAT'S LOVE GOT TO DO WITH IT'. Later that year, she set the charts ablaze in tandem with Take That on a cover of Dan Hartman's 'Relight My Fire', seeing her reach the British No.1 for the first time in her thirty-year career. She continues to be one of Scotland's most high profile celebrities; in 1999 she starred in the film, 'Whatever Happened To Harold Smith?' and a year later co-hosted the National Lottery Show. Incredibly, she still looks like a spring chicken despite about to turn 60 (November 2008).

MCS

- **filmography** {actress} –

Gonks Go Beat *(1965 {p} on OST by V/A =>)* / **To Sir, With Love** *(1967 {*} hit title theme on OST w/ Ron Grainger =>)* / **Cucumber Castle** *(1970 {p} OST by the BEE GEES =>)* / the Cherry Picker *(1972 {*})* / the Man With The Golden Gun *(1974 theme-only; see future edition)* / Alicja *(1982 {a/*p})* / Men In Love *(1990 {c})* / To Sir, With Love II *(1996 TV {a} =>)* / Whatever Happened To Harold Smith? *(1999 {*})* / **Red, White & Blues** *(2003 {p} on OST by V/A =>)* / **30 Century Man** *(2007 {c} =>)*

□ LYNYRD SKYNYRD segment
(⇒ FREEBIRD – THE MOVIE)

MAD DOGS & ENGLISHMEN

aka JOE COCKER: MAD DOGS & ENGLISHMEN

1971 (US 117m) Metro-Goldwyn-Mayer / A&M Films

Film genre: Roots-rock-music concert/documentary

Top guns: dir: Pierre Adidge → ELVIS ON TOUR, Sid Levin → LET THE GOOD TIMES ROLL

Stars: Joe COCKER *(performer)*, **Leon Russell** *(performer)* → the CONCERT FOR BANGLADESH, **Carl Radle** *(performer)*, **Chris Stainton** *(performer)*, **Bobby Keys** *(performer)* → LADIES AND GENTLEMEN, THE ROLLING STONES → LET'S SPEND THE NIGHT TOGETHER → HAIL! HAIL! ROCK'N'ROLL → AT THE MAX, **Jim Price** *(performer)* → LADIES AND GENTLEMEN, THE ROLLING STONES, **Rita Coolidge** *(performer)* ← VANISHING POINT / → PAT GARRETT & BILLY THE KID → a STAR IS BORN, Claudia Linnear *(herself)*

Storyline: Life on the road and backstage passes – so to speak – for Joe Cocker's "Mad Dogs & Englishmen" tour of the US, an expansive tour that began in Detroit and finished in San Bernardino, California. *MCS*

Movie rating: *6

Visual: video + dvd

Off the record: (see below)

—

JOE COCKER (composers: Various)

Sep 70. (d-lp) *A&M; <(AMLD 6002)>* [2] [16]
– (introduction) / Honky tonk women / (introduction) / Sticks and stones / Cry me a river / Bird on the wire / Feeling alright / Superstar / (introduction) / Let's go get stoned / Blue medley: I'll drown in my own tears – When something is wrong with my baby – I've been loving you too long / (introduction) / Girl from North Country / Give peace a chance / (introduction) / She came in through the bathroom window / Space captain / The letter / Delta lady. *(re-iss. 1983 d-lp/d-c; AMLS/CDM 6002) (cd-iss. 1988; CDA 6002) <US d-cd-iss. Jan86 on 'Mobile Fidelity'; MFCD 2-824> (cd re-iss. Jan97; 396002-2) (cd re-iss. Oct98 on 'Polydor'; 540698-2) (cd re-iss. Dec98 on 'Mobile Fidelity'; UDCD 736)*

S/track review: The Rolling Stones might've patented the concept of a "Rock'n'roll circus", but it was JOE COCKER and friends who road tested it. LEON RUSSELL wasn't as engagingly camp a ringmaster as Mick Jagger but at least his Deep South credentials were genuine. Having already covered Russell's 'Delta Lady', COCKER enlisted the big man's help in putting together the tour affectionately known as 'MAD DOGS AND ENGLISHMEN'. Despite the name, there were more yanks than Brits in the eleven strong line-up, one which infamously included three drummers. That statistic alone pretty much tells you all you need to know about this album; a full-on, often overblown, endlessly worthy attempt to spread the blue-eyed rock-gospel. RUSSELL had just clocked off from a similar crusade with Delaney & Bonnie, and carried that freewheeling spirit with him, as well as many of the same players. But it's COCKER who's the star, and there's no messing with that gas fitter's growl. Backed by a hollering "space choir", the man whom the late Ray Charles described as "my only real disciple" grinds his soul and grits his lungs through the songbooks of Lennon/McCartney, Jagger/Richards, Bob Dylan, Otis Redding, Isaac Hayes and erm ... Leonard Cohen. Inevitably, the Mad Dog treatment mercilessly leaches 'Bird On A Wire' of its ambiguity and robs 'Honky Tonk Women' of its sordidness. 'The Letter' fares better, trading off the petulant sneer of the original for a chorus of biblical intensity: gospel harmonies shout down the devil, the brass section makes like 'Moondance'-era Van Morrison, and COCKER attempts to regurgitate his small intestine. Traffic's 'Feelin' Alright' is another famous interpretation – it can't claim the sheer Caribbean joie de vivre of the Trinidad Oil Company but COCKER, RUSSELL and choir manoeuvre it into the kind of blissed-out groove only this kind of gospel grand-design could conjure. Dylan's 'Girl From The North Country' says more with less, a grits'n'gravy duet served hot with RUSSELL's chunky piano chords. His rangy Southern ivory tinkling is arguably heard to best effect on the peerless 'Superstar', ironically the only COCKER-free performance. As inextricably bound up with music biz lore as any song ever written, its pedigree stretches back to RITA COOLIDGE, who reportedly passed the groupie/rock star concept (allegedly inspired by Eric Clapton) on to RUSSELL and Bonnie Bramlett. Here COOLIDGE – the original 'Delta Lady', born of Cherokee/Scottish parentage – renders its doleful infatuation all the more fascinating; her nightly solo rendition bagged her a solo contract with 'A&M'. In many ways, the 70s began here, setting the stage for all the polyester bacchanalia, apocryphal anecdotes and inflatable pigs to come. And is it just me, or do COCKER's intros sound like Jimmy Saville? *BG*

Album rating: *7

– spinoff hits, etc. –

JOE COCKER: Cry Me A River / Give Peace A Chance

Oct 70. (7") *A&M; <1200> Fly; (BUG 3)* [11] [ ]

MADE IN JAMAICA

2006 (Fra/US 120m) Herold and Family / Lawrence Pictures

Film genre: Reggae-music documentary bio-pic

Top guns: dir: (+ s-w) Jerome Laperrousaz ← PRISONER IN THE STREETS ← AMOUGIES ← CONTINENTAL CIRCUS

Stars: Third World *(performer)* ← COOL RUNNINGS: THE REGGAE MOVIE ← REGGAE SUNSPLASH ← PRISONER IN THE STREET, **Gregory Isaacs** *(performer)* ← COOL RUNNINGS: THE REGGAE MOVIE ← LAND OF LOOK BEHIND ← ROCKERS, **Beres Hammond** *(performer)* ← the REGGAE MOVIE, **Bunny Wailer** *(performer)* ← the BOB MARLEY STORY; CARIBBEAN NIGHTS, **Toots** *(performer)*, **Bounty Killer** *(performer)*, **Lowell 'Sly' Dunbar** *(performer)*, **Robbie Shakespeare** *(performer)* ← ROCKERS, **Capleton** *(performer)*, **Lady Saw** *(performer)* ← DANCEHALL QUEEN, **Brick & Lace: Nailah & Nyanda Tharbourne** *(performers)*, **Elephant Man** *(performer)*, **Tanya Stephens** *(performer)*, **Alaine (Laughton)** *(performer)*, **Vybz Kartel** *(performer)*, **Doctor Marshall** *(performer)*

Storyline: Jamaican reggae superstars are up against the new wave dancehall artists (see below) for this exploration into the country's evolving peace vs violence culture. *MCS*

Movie rating: *6

Visual: dvd (no audio OST)

Off the record: There are a plethora of new reggae artists here:- **Bounty Killer, Capleton, Elephant Man, Lady Saw, Brick & Lace** alongside old stylers, **Third World, Gregory Isaacs, Toots, the Wailers,** etc.

MAKE IT FUNKY!

the music that took over the world

2005 (US 110m) Bottom Of The Ninth / Michael Murphy Productions

Film genre: Jazz/Funk/R&B-music documentary

Top guns: dir: Michael Murphy

Stars: Allen Toussaint *(performer)*, **the Neville Brothers:- Aaron Neville** *(performer)* ← WOODSTOCK '94, **Ivan Neville** *(performer)*, **Art Neville, Charles Neville, Cyril Neville** *(performers)*, & **funky Meters** *(performers)*, **Big Sam's Funky Nation** *(performers)*, **the Dirty Dozen Band** *(performers)*, **Earl Palmer** *(performer)*, **Irma Thomas** *(performer)* ← BLUES DIVAS, **Irvin Mayfield** *(performer)*, **Jon Cleary** *(performer)*, **Kermit Ruffins** *(performer)*, **Lloyd Price** *(performer)*, **Monk Boudreaux & the Golden Eagles** *(performers)*, **Snooks Eaglin** *(performer)*, **Troy Andrews** *(performer)*, **Walter "Wolfman" Washington** *(performer)*, **Bonnie RAITT** *(performer)*, **Keith Richards** *(performer)* <= the ROLLING STONES =>, **Steve Jordan** *(performer)* ← LIGHTNING IN A BOTTLE ← HAIL! HAIL! ROCK'N'ROLL, **Fats DOMINO** *(archive performer)*, **Henry "Professor Longhair" Byrd** *(archive performer)*, **DR. JOHN** *(archive performer)*

Storyline: New Orleans and its music culture (Crescent City, etc.) take focal point by way of archival and modern-day concert clips from the likes of Fats Domino, Dr. John, Professor Longhair, et al. *MCS*

Movie rating: *7

Visual: dvd (no audio OST)

Off the record: Tracks performed in the film/DVD (ALLEN TOUSSAINT *):- 'Trumpet Challenge' (KERMIT RUFFINS, IRVIN MAYFIELD & TROY ANDREWS), 'Skokiaan' (KERMIT RUFFINS, IRVIN MAYFIELD & TROY ANDREWS), 'My Feet Can't Fail Me Now' (the DIRTY DOZEN BAND), 'Bah Duey-Duey' (BIG SAM'S FUNKY NATION), 'Sew Sew Sew' (trad.), 'Let The Four Winds Blow' (FATS DOMINO; archive), 'Big Chief' (PROFESSOR LONGHAIR; archive), 'Tipitina' (* & JON CLEARY), 'Southern Nights' (*), 'Old Records' (* & IRMA THOMAS), 'Lawdy Miss Clawdy' (LLOYD PRICE), 'Fortune Teller' (*), 'Working In A Coalmine' (*), 'Certain Girl' (*), 'What Is Success' (BONNIE RAITT), 'Rip It Up' (IVAN NEVILLE & EARL PALMER), 'Cissy Strut' (funky METERS), 'Fire On The Bayou' (the NEVILLE BROTHERS), 'Barefootin'' (WALTER "WOLFMAN" WASHINGTON), 'Come On' (SNOOKS EAGLIN & GEORGE PORTER, JR.), 'I'm Ready' (KEITH RICHARDS, EARL PALMER & WALTER "WOLFMAN" WASHINGTON), 'Hey Pocky Way' (everybody above). *MCS*

the MAN, HIS WORLD, HIS MUSIC

aka JOHNNY CASH: THE MAN, HIS WORLD, HIS MUSIC

1969 (US 94m) Verite Production / WJRZ Radio

Film genre: Country-music documentary/performance movie

Top guns: dir (+ s-w): Robert Elfstrom → the NASHVILLE SOUND → the GOSPEL ROAD

Stars: Johnny CASH *(himself/performer)*, **June Carter Cash** *(herself)* ← ROAD TO NASHVILLE ← COUNTRY MUSIC HOLIDAY / → JOHNNY CASH AT SAN QUENTIN → the GOSPEL ROAD → THAT'S COUNTRY, **Bob DYLAN** *(himself)*, **Carl Perkins** *(himself)* ← JAMBOREE / → JOHNNY CASH AT SAN QUENTIN → LITTLE FAUSS AND BIG HALSY, **Glen CAMPBELL** *(himself)*, **Rosanne Cash** *(herself)*, **Roy Rogers** *(himself)* → MACKINTOSH & T.J., Dale Evans *(herself)*, **Helen Carter** *(herself)* ← ROAD TO NASHVILLE / → JOHNNY CASH AT SAN QUENTIN, **Mother Maybelle Carter** *(herself)* ← ROAD TO NASHVILLE, **Anita Carter** *(herself)* ← ROAD TO NASHVILLE

Storyline: The man in question is of course, country legend Johnny Cash, the people around him are his wife, June Carter, and the music featured included archive footage and a session with Bob Dylan. *MCS*

Movie rating: *7

Visual: video (no audio OST)

Off the record: JOHNNY CASH and **BOB DYLAN** perform a duet of 'One Too Many Mornings', a track featured on the latter's 'The Times They Are A-Changin'' LP. *MCS*

MAN IN THE SAND

1999 (US 89m) NVC Arts / Union Productions / BBC

Film genre: alt/Folk-Rock music performance documentary

Top guns: dir: Kim Hopkins

Stars: Billy Bragg *(himself/performer)* → GLASTONBURY, **WILCO:- Jeff Tweedy, Jay Bennett, Ken Coomer, John Stirratt** *(themselves/performers)*, Nora Guthrie *(herself + narrator)*, Corey Harris *(himself)*, **Natalie Merchant** *(herself)*, Sarah Vowell *(herself)* → GIGANTIC (A TALE OF TWO JOHNS)

Storyline: Basically the making of the 'Mermaid Avenue' studio sessions featuring unrecorded music by Woody Guthrie (found by his daughter Nora – the narrator) performed by English singer-songwriter Billy Bragg & Chicago's alt-country outfit Wilco. *MCS*

Movie rating: *6.5

Visual: video on Rykodisc + dvd (ext.120m)

Off the record: Billy Bragg & WILCO combined for two sets (see below). **Natalie Merchant** was ex-10,000 Maniacs and now a solo artist.

– associated releases –

BILLY BRAGG & WILCO: Mermaid Avenue

Jun 98. (cd/c) *Elektra; <(7559 62204-2/-4)>* [90] [34]
– Walt Whitman's niece / California stars / Way over yonder in the minor key / Birds and ships / Hoodoo voodoo / She came along to me / At my window sad and lonely / Ingrid Bergman / Christ for President / I guess I planted / One by one / Eisler on the go / Hesitating beauty / Another man's done gone / The unwelcome guest.

BILLY BRAGG & WILCO: Mermaid Avenue Vol.II

May 00. (cd/c) *Elektra; <(7559 62522-2/-4)>* [88] [61]
– Airline to Heaven / My flying saucer / Feed of man / Hot rod hotel / I was born / Secret of the sea / Stetson Kennedy / Remember the mountain bed / Blood of the lamb / Against th' law / All you fascists / Joe Dimaggio done it again / Meanest man / Black wind blowing / Someday some morning sometime.

Dave MARKEY

Born: 3 Dec'63, Burbank, California, USA. Influenced by hardcore punk, MARKEY has been at the heart of low-budget, experimental cult filmmaking and music since 1982's 'The SLOG MOVIE'. His subsequent Super-8 movies and documentaries have featured a plethora of punk outfits, REDD KROSS (in 'DESPERATE TEENAGE LOVEDOLLS' and its sequel 'LOVEDOLLS SUPERSTAR'), SONIC YOUTH ('Weatherman '69' and '1991: THE YEAR PUNK BROKE'), while he's also fronted his own bands, Sin 34 and Painted Willie (the latter on the 'S.S.T.' imprint). Having played the role of Allen Ginsberg and Yoko Ono in the aforementioned 'WEATHERMAN '69' (1989), he took the part of Bobby Beausoleil in Raymond Pettibon's bad taste homage to Charles Manson in 'The Book Of Manson' (1989). *MCS*

- **filmography** [dir + s-w] {acting/performance} -

the Slog Movie *(1982 [dir] =>)* / **Desperate Teenage Lovedolls** *(1984 [s-w*

+ dir] OST by V/A =>) / **Lovedolls Superstar** *(1986 [dir] OST by V/A =>)* / Weatherman '69 *(1989 {a})* / Citizen Tania *(1989 [dir] {*})* / the Book Of Manson *(1989 {*})* / **Reality 86'd** *(1991 {*c} =>)* / **1991: The Year Punk Broke** *(1992 [dir] {c} =>)* / **Blast Off** *(1997 [dir] =>)* / **We Jam Econo: The Story Of The Minutemen** *(2005 {c} =>)* / **American Hardcore** *(2006 {c} =>)*

Bob MARLEY

Born: Robert Nesta Marley, 2 Feb'45, Rhoden Hall, St. Ann's, Jamaica. Despite bringing reggae to worldwide prominence, influencing successive generations and ultimately attaining the status of folk hero/demigod, it's perhaps ironic that BOB MARLEY featured in neither of the genre's twin totems, 'The HARDER THEY COME' (1972) and 'ROCKERS' (1979). Instead, his first screen appearance was seminal BBC series The Old Grey Whistle Test circa 1973, a blissful 'Stir It Up' with the classic Wailers line-up (and often re-run on BBC4). MARLEY also featured – albeit only in the form of a few performance clips – in Jeremy Marre's seminal (and recently released on DVD) 'ROOTS ROCK REGGAE' (1977), the only contemporary document of the Jamaican scene. A concert film documenting MARLEY'S semi-legendary gig at London's Rainbow in 1977 reamined unseen for decades, likwise finally released to cinemas upon its 30th anniversary in June 2007. The reason MARLEY was in London in the first place was voluntary exile from the political strife in his homeland (see Marre's film for a flavour of the chaos), and 1978's 'One Love Peace Concert' was an attempt at reconciliation, the reggae icon having been coaxed back to headline. In a moment of typical spontaneity, he famously united warring political leaders Michael Manley and Edward Seaga live on stage, a hugely symbolic gesture filmed for posterity. The following year's US tour generated a concert film shot in Santa Barbara, while 'REGGAE SUNSPLASH' (1980) featured a headlining performance from the annual bash at Montego Bay. And then, on 11th May 1981, BOB MARLEY was gone, dead from cancer at the age of only 36, leaving behind a celluloid legacy which – compared to the endless reels documenting his peers in rock and pop – remains depressingly paltry. Alan Greenberg's 'LAND OF LOOK BEHIND' (1982) was one of the first posthumous documentaries, followed by the Darcus Howe-narrated 'BOB MARLEY & THE WAILERS: THE BOB MARLEY STORY' (1984) and Declan Lowney's 'TIME WILL TELL' (1992). Again it was Marre, though, who eventually put together the most high profile retrospective, following up his original documentary with the video 'Rebel Music – The Bob Marley Story' (2000). *BG*

- **filmography** {performance} –

Reggae Sunsplash *(1979 {p} =>)* / **Heartland Reggae** *(1980 {p} =>)* / **Prisoner In The Street** *(1980 {p} OST by THIRD WORLD =>)* / **Land Of Look Behind** *(1982 {*p} =>)* / **Countryman** *(1982 several songs on V/A OST =>)* / **Bob Marley & The Wailers: The Bob Marley Story** *(1984 {*p} =>)* / **Time Will Tell** *(1992 {*p} =>)*

MAYOR OF THE SUNSET STRIP

2003 (US 94m) Kino-Eye American / Caldera Productions (R)

Film genre: Rock-music documentary bio-pic

Top guns: s-w + dir: George Hickenlooper

Stars: Rodney Bingenheimer *(himself)* ← END OF THE CENTURY ← RAGE: 20 YEARS OF PUNK ROCK WEST COAST STYLE ← ROCKULA ← BACK TO THE BEACH ← UNCLE MEAT ← X: THE UNHEARD MUSIC ← REPO MAN ← UP IN SMOKE / → PUNK'S NOT DEAD, **Kim Fowley** *(himself)* <= the RUNAWAYS =>, **Phil Spector** *(himself)* ← IMAGINE: JOHN LENNON ← EASY RIDER, **Brian WILSON** *(himself)* <= the BEACH BOYS =>, **CHER** *(herself)*, **Lance Loud** *(himself)* ← LANCE LOUD!: A DEATH IN AN AMERICAN FAMILY ← SUBWAY RIDERS, **Jello BIAFRA** *(archive footage)*, **Alice COOPER** *(himself)*, **Nancy Sinatra** *(herself)* ← SPEEDWAY ← the WILD ANGELS ← the GHOST IN THE INVISIBLE BIKINI ← GET YOURSELF A COLLEGE GIRL, **David BOWIE** *(himself)*, **Neil YOUNG** *(himself)*, **Green Day:- Billie Joe Armstrong, Tre Cool, Mike Dirnt** *(themselves)* ← WOODSTOCK 94, **Oasis:- Liam & Noel Gallagher** **(themselves)* ← LIVE FOREVER ← the WHO LIVE AT THE ROYAL ALBERT HALL, **Chris Martin** *(performer)*, **X:- Exene Cervenka, John DOE** *(themselves)*, **Chris Carter** *(performer)*, **Paul McCartney** *(himself)* <= the BEATLES =>, **Pete Townshend** *(himself)* <= the WHO =>, **BLONDIE/ Deborah Harry** *(themselves)*, **Rob Zombie** *(himself)* ← AIRHEADS, **Henry Diltz** *(himself)*, **Tori Amos** *(herself)*, **Beck** *(himself)* ← SOUL OF A MAN ← SOUTHLANDER ← FREE TIBET / → HIGH AND DRY → FEARLESS FREAKS, **Dion DiMucci** *(archive)* ← TWIST AROUND THE CLOCK ← TEENAGE MILLIONAIRE, **Elvis COSTELLO** *(himself)*, **Courtney LOVE** *(herself)*, **Gwen Stefani** *(herself)*, **Cherie Currie** *(herself)* <= the RUNAWAYS =>, **Joan Jett** *(herself)* <= the RUNAWAYS =>, **Clem Burke** *(himself)* <= BLONDIE =>, **Annabella Lwin** *(herself)*, **Louise Wener** *(herself)* ← LIVE FOREVER, **Monique Powell** *(herself)*, Brooke Shields *(herself)* ← BLACK AND WHITE, **Carrie Wilson** *(herself)*, **Poe** *(herself)*, **Jim Morrison & * Ray Manzarek** *(themselves)* ← MESSAGE TO LOVE: THE ISLE OF WIGHT FESTIVAL ← X: THE UNHEARD MUSIC * ← the DOORS ARE OPEN, **Johnny Marr** *(himself)* → 30 CENTURY MAN, **Michael Des Barres** *(himself)* ← SUGAR TOWN ← TO SIR, WITH LOVE, **Pamela Des Barres** *(herself)* ← SLAUGHTER'S BIG RIP-OFF ← 200 MOTELS / → FALLEN ANGEL → METAL: A HEADBANGER'S JOURNEY, **India Dupre** *(herself)*, **Ronald Vaughan** *(himself / spaceman-at-large / Isadore Ivy)*, **Linda Ronstadt** *(herself)* ← HAIL! HAIL! ROCK'N'ROLL ← UNCLE MEAT ← FM, **Mick Jagger** *(himself)* <= ROLLING STONES =>, **John Easdale** *(himself)*, Miss Mercy *(herself)* ← RAINBOW BRIDGE, **Michelle Phillips** *(herself)* ← MONTEREY POP / → SWEETWATER: A TRUE ROCK STORY, Mackenzie Phillips *(herself)* ← MORE AMERICAN GRAFFITI ← AMERICAN GRAFFITI, **Joey Ramone** *(archive)* <= RAMONES =>, **Jerry Lee LEWIS** *(archive)*, **David Johansen** *(himself)* <= NEW YORK DOLLS =>, Paul Reubens *(himself)* ← OVERNIGHT ← ← SOUTH OF HEAVEN, WEST OF HELL ← MOONWALKER ← BACK TO THE BEACH ← the BLUES BROTHERS

Storyline: The life story of Rodney Bingenheimer, a man obsessed with the cult of celebrity and a mainstay of the LA musical scene. His breakthrough comes in the 1960s when he doubles for the Monkees' Davy Jones, and soon he becomes a club owner and a DJ. His success and fame are tempered however with the loneliness of his personal life and his difficult relationship with his parents. *JZ*

Movie rating: *6

Visual: dvd

Off the record: While many of the big names are on show here (**Kim Fowley, Phil Spector, Brian Wilson, Green Day, Chris Martin, Courtney Love, Cher, Gwen Stefani, Johnny Marr, Ray Manzarek**, etc., there were others on the fringes: **Lance Loud** (of the Mumps), **Chris Carter** (bassist of Dramarama), **Henry Diltz** (of the Modern Folk Quartet, **Annabella Lwin** (Bow Wow Wow), **Louise Wener** (of Sleeper), **Monique Powell** (Save Ferris' singer), **John Easdale** (of Dramarama), **Carrie Wilson** (of Wilson-Phillips), **Michael Des Barres** (of mid-70s hard-rockers, Detective) and **India Dupre** (whose last album was with Brit-popper, Nick Heyward). *MCS*

Various Artists (score: ANTHONY MARINELLI *)

Mar 04. (cd) *Shout! Factory; <34096>* ☐ ☐

– Let's find out about Rodney – Rodney Bingenheimer dialogue / Rodney on the ROQ (BRIAN WILSON) / Los Angeles (X) / My back pages (the BYRDS) / It was a real eye opener (PAMELA DES BARRES) / Welcome to Hollywood (LEON RUSSELL) / All the madmen (DAVID BOWIE) / Get it on (bang a gong) (T. REX) / School's out (ALICE COOPER) / What kind of music is this? – Rodney Bingenheimer dialogue / I wanna be sedated (RAMONES) / London (the SMITHS) / He picked this song – Chris Carter dialogue / Anything, anything (I'll give you) (DRAMARAMA) / Jennifer Love Hewitt (RONALD VAUGHAN) / Parklife (BLUR) / I stalked him – Courtney Love dialogue / Malibu (HOLE) / Good souls (STARSAILOR) / Yellow – live in-studio (CHRIS MARTIN of COLDPLAY) / Who is Rodney Bingenheimer? (* & CLINT BENNETT) / Mayor of the Sunset Strip (MARIZANE). *(bonus track +=)* – I hate the '90s (RODNEY & THE TUBE TOPS).

S/track review: Rodney Bingenheimer arrived in Los Angeles and became so famous in Hollywood that actor Sal Mineo dubbed him "Mayor of the Sunset Strip". However, Bingenheimer claims, "I became the talk of the town because I had the perfect Brian Jones do". He was responsible for introducing many Californians to the newest sounds, especially via his Rodney On The Roq show on local radio station KROQ, and the showcasing of talent at his 'English Disco'. He is immortalised himself by BRIAN WILSON on the opening track 'Rodney On The Roq' in glorious, surfs-up fashion, harmonies galore as Rodney "Sunday night 12 to 3 / Spins hits for my baby and me". Bingenheimer's three loves are glam, punk and Britpop, and all three are represented on this album. DAVID BOWIE's 'All The Madmen' has a great live, super-grainy intro taken from the radio show before Mick Ronson's distorted guitar announces itself, supported by a laid back groove. All in all it's "heavy as can be", with a pleasingly weird spoken word mid-section. T. REX and ALICE COOPER provide the perennial glam classics 'Get It On (Bang A Gong)' and 'School's Out'. The album is laced with some choice soundbites from Pamela des Barres and Courtney Love (HOLE are here too, with 'Malibu', co-written by Billy Corgan, which represents their later, more Hollywood-ized approach), and Bingenheimer himself poses the question "What Kind of Music Is This?" as he ushers in raucous proto-punk with RAMONES' 'I Wanna Be Sedated'. The SMITHS' 'London' is angry and edgy, "Do you think you've made the right decision this time?" Morrissey asks, striking a defining note of uncertainty in the proceedings. BLUR's classic 'Parklife' represents the Britpop era in all its glory, while STARSAILOR and COLDPLAY (with a particularly dirgy live rendition of 'Yellow') mope in its shadow. The real gems come towards the end, when the film's composer ANTHONY MARINELLI (with Clint Bennett) provides an instrumental backdrop to 'Who Is Rodney Bingenheimer?', heavy-lidded piano and organ hold sway for a series of samples of Bingenheimer in his own words, casting himself as the "designated driver between the famous and the not-so famous". It is a piece tinged with melancholy, and redolent of a man who never quite made it in the music business the way he would have wished. This sad resignation is blown apart by MARIZANE and a slamming slice of neo-glam entitled 'Mayor Of The Sunset Strip', a glorious celebration of bygone glories. But the best is saved for last, billed as RODNEY & THE TUBE TOPS, Bingenheimer fronts something of a supergroup (songwriting credits go to HOLE's Eric Erlandson and Sonic Youth's Thurston Moore), and laments how much he hates the 90s. The diminutive frontman rails against the decade defined by tattoos, piercings and grunge rock, from why bands don't produce medium and small size t-shirts anymore (only XL), to why all the cute girls are junkies. It's a primal, dirty tune, reminiscent of the Stooges, and Bingenheimer's awkward spoken word delivery is fantastic, endearing and demonstrative of a man who can't quite grasp what's going on around him anymore. *DF*

Album rating: *7

Country Joe McDONALD

Born: 1 Jan'42, Washington, D.C., USA. One of the most vocal leftist agitators in a country not exactly known for its sympathy towards socialism, COUNTRY JOE McDONALD has never been afraid to take his protest message to The Man. This he achieved initially through print in self-published magazines and then through music in his infamous psych-folk prankster vehicle, Country Joe & The Fish, most enduringly via the anti-Vietnam War "anthem", 'I-Feel-Like-I'm-Fixin'-To-Die-Rag'. A staple of the Bay Area scene, the band first appeared on screen via a couple of 1967 TV documentaries, 'A Day In The Life Of . . .' and 'How We Stopped The War'. They also played that year's famous 'MONTEREY POP' festival and later had a track featured on the 1969 film document. McDONALD's most infamous appearance, however, was at 'WOODSTOCK', where, in a solo capacity, he led the half million-strong crowd in his trademark "f-u-c-k" chant, the same one which saw him arrested for inciting lewd behaviour at a show in Worcester, Massachusetts. Prior to their 1971 demise, the group were sighted in both the Roger Corman oddity, 'GAS-S-S-S!' (1970) and rock opera western, 'ZACHARIAH' (1971), while a solo McDONALD went on to try his hand at film scoring with a trio of songs for the soundtrack to 'Stille Dage I Clichy' (1970), a warts'n'all Danish adaptation of Henry Miller's 'QUIET DAYS IN CLICHY'. American fans had to wait to hear the results, however, as, predictably, the film ran afoul of US customs and was only premiered after a court battle. McDONALD also contributed to the score and made a cameo singing appearance in Saul Landau's 'Que Hacer?' (1970), a prescient film documenting the election of doomed Chilean president Salvador Allende. An ad hoc line-up of Country Joe & The Fish subsequently appeared in Bill Norton's 'MORE AMERICAN GRAFFITI' (1979), and while McDONALD has continued to record and campaign on various issues, his only other scoring effort was for Jacki Ochs' Agent Orange documentary, 'Vietnam: The Secret Agent' (1983). *BG*

- **filmography** (composer) {acting} –

Monterey Pop *(1969 {p} on OST by V/A =>)* / **Revolution** *(1969 {p} on OST by V/A =>)* / **Woodstock** *(1970 {p} on OST by V/A =>)* / **Quiet Days In Clichy** *(1970 OST =>)* / **Gas-s-s-s!** *(1970 {p} on OST by V/A =>)* / Que Hacer? *(1970 {p})* / **Zachariah** *(1971 {p} OST by V/A =>)* / **More American Graffiti** *(1979 {p} OST by V/A =>)* / Vietnam: The Secret Agent *(1983)*

MEDICINE BALL CARAVAN

1971 (US/Fra 88m) Fred Weintraub Productions / Warner Bros. (R)

Film genre: Roots/Rock-music concert/documentary

Top guns: dir: Francois Reichenbach (story: Christian Haren)

Stars: Alice COOPER *(performer)*, **the Youngbloods** *(performers)*, **Delaney * & Bonnie** *(performers)* → VANISHING POINT → CATCH MY SOUL → the DOORS * → FESTIVAL EXPRESS, **B.B. KING** *(performer)*, **Doug Kershaw** *(performer)* ← ZACHARIAH, **Stoneground** *(performers)*, **Sal Valentino** *(performer)* ← WILD, WILD WINTER, **David Peel & The Lower East Side** *(performers)* → the U.S. vs. JOHN LENNON

Storyline: An entourage of exactly 154 hairy people take an 8,000 mile "wagon-train", month-long trip in 1970 across the States visiting the likes of San Francisco, Gallup (New Mexico), Boulder (Colorado), Sioux City (Iowa), Yellow Springs (Ohio), Moline (Illinois), Warrenton (Virginia) and Washington (D.C.). Inviting a variety of top singers and musicians along the way, this was no picnic in the park, indeed there were a few hiccups to spoil their tee(-pee) party. *MCS*

Movie rating: *5.5

Visual: video

Off the record: (see below)

Various Artists

1971. (lp) *Warners; <BS 2565>*
– Act naturally (the YOUNGBLOODS) / Medley: How blue can you get – Just a little love (B.B. KING) / Medley: Louisiana man – Battle

of New Orleans – Orange blossom special (DOUG KERSHAW) / Hippie from Olema (the YOUNGBLOODS) / Dreambo (SAL VALENTINO) / Black juju (ALICE COOPER) / Medley: Freakout – It takes a lot to laugh, it takes a train to cry (STONEGROUND) / Free the people (DELANEY AND BONNIE).

S/track review: Showing that the "WOODSTOCK" revolution had become some sort of downsized, Red Indian-ish reservation, 'MEDICINE BALL CARAVAN' failed to generate much interest outside of their tight hippie community. Opening with Johnny Russell & Vonie Morrison's redneck country song, 'Act Naturally' by the YOUNGBLOODS, one might just understand why; the same band also contributed 'Hippie From Olema', another one of their Lovin' Spoonful-like jug-band dirges. Travelling San Francisco house band, STONEGROUND (featuring ex-Beau Brummels co-leader Sal Valentino), kick "in" the jams for a gutsy Quicksilver-esque medley of their 'Freakout' and Dylan's 'It Takes A Lot To Laugh, It Takes A Train To Cry'; VALENTINO also spread his raspy drawl to full effect via 'Dreambo', easily the best song here, although many will reserve that accolade for DELANEY AND BONNIE's sing-a-long-a version of Barbara Keith's 'Free The People'. Medleys were a big part of 'MEDICINE BALL CARAVAN', revered bluesman B.B. KING taking ten minutes to spread his gospel on 'How Blue Can You Get' & 'Just A Little Love', while country-Cajun songsmith DOUG KERSHAW segued together the Buddy Holly-ish 'Louisiana Man' with versions of standards 'Battle Of New Orleans' & 'Orange Blossom Special'. Just escaping from a cameo in the feature film, 'Diary Of A Mad Housewife', ALICE COOPER (the man & group!) were again the rock in a hard place courtesy of their haunting, 'Black Juju' (written by AC's Dennis Dunaway), better served up on their 'Love It To Death' set. *MCS*

Album rating: *6

MEETING PEOPLE IS EASY

1998 (UK 98m w/b&w) Kudos Productions Ltd. / Parlophone

Film genre: alt-Rock-music documentary

Top guns: dir: Grant Gee

Stars: Radiohead:- Thom Yorke, Jonny Greenwood, Ed O'Brien, Colin Greenwood, Phil Selway *(themselves/performers)* → 30 CENTURY MAN, Nigel Godrich *(himself; manager)*, **Michael Stipe** *(himself)* <= R.E.M. =>, David Letterman *(himself)* ← BEAVIS AND BUTT-HEAD DO AMERICA ← PRIVATE PARTS / → MAN ON THE MOON → GRIZZLY MAN, Tania Scemama *(herself)*, Oliver Kube, Michael Sailer + Dirk Siepe *(journalists)*

Storyline: A dour but nevertheless entertaining insight into one of the world's biggest selling bands, Radiohead. The film concentrates on the release and accompanying world tour to promote their third set, 'OK Computer', and all-round expectations made of their lifestyles. *MCS*

Movie rating: *7

Visual: video + dvd (no audio OST)

Off the record: Of the several tracks here, 'Follow Me Around' and 'Big Boots (Man-O-War)' remain unreleased. **Radiohead**'s Thom Yorke (w/ Francois Dompierre) completed 'Betty Fisher et autres histoires' (OST shelved) in 2001, while JONNY GREENWOOD scored 'BODYSONG' (2003); watch out for him (and **Phil Selway**) in the band in 2005's 'Harry Potter And The Goblet Of Fire'. *MCS*

MESSAGE TO LOVE: THE ISLE OF WIGHT FESTIVAL 1970

1996 (US 127m) BBC for Castle Music Pictures / Pulsar

Film genre: Rock-music concert/documentary

Top guns: dir: (+ s-w) Murray Lerner ← JIMI HENDRIX LIVE AT THE ISLE OF WIGHT 1970 ← the WHO: LIVE AT THE ISLE OF WIGHT FESTIVAL 1970 ← FESTIVAL

Stars: Jimi HENDRIX *(performer)*, **Billy Cox** *(performer)*, **Mitch Mitchell** *(performer)*, **the WHO:- Roger Daltrey, Pete Townshend, John Entwistle, Keith Moon** *(performers)*, **the Doors:- Jim Morrison *, Ray Manzarek **, John Densmore, Robby Krieger** *(performers)* ← the DOORS ← the UNHEARD MUSIC ** ← the DOORS ARE OPEN / → MAYOR OF THE SUNSET STRIP *, **Joni Mitchell** *(performer)* ← the LAST WALTZ ← RENALDO AND CLARA ← CELEBRATION AT BIG SUR, **Free:- Paul Rodgers *, Paul Kossoff, Andy Fraser *, Simon Kirke** *(performers)* ← WOODSTOCK 94 * / → BRITISH ROCK SYMPHONY *, **Jethro Tull:- Ian Anderson, Martin Barre, Clive Bunker, Glenn Cornick** *(performers)* ← ROCK AND ROLL CIRCUS, **Leonard COHEN** *(performer)*, **Ten Years After:- Alvin Lee, Ric Lee, Leo Lyons, Chick Churchill** *(performers)* ← GROUPIES ← WOODSTOCK, **Emerson, Lake & Palmer:- Keith EMERSON, Greg Lake, Carl Palmer** *(performers)*, **Taste:- Rory Gallagher, John Wilson, Richard McCracken** *(performers)*, **the Moody Blues:- Justin Hayward, John Lodge, Mike Pinder, Ray Thomas, Graeme Edge** *(performers)*, **DONOVAN** *(performer)*, **John Sebastian** *(performer)* <= the LOVIN' SPOONFUL =>, **Kris KRISTOFFERSON** *(performer)*, **Tiny Tim** *(performer)* ← ONE-TRICK PONY ← YOU ARE WHAT YOU EAT / → PRIVATE PARTS, **Miles Davis** *(performer)*, **Bob DYLAN** *(performer)*, **Family:- Roger Chapman, Charlie Whitney, John Wetton, John Palmer, Rob Townsend** *(performers)*, **Joan BAEZ** *(performer)*, **Great Awakening** *(performers)*

Storyline: "The British Woodstock", "the last great event" or just a plain old "psychedelic concentration camp"? Judge for yourself as the original 1970 Isle of Wight Festival is unleashed in all its discontented, Murray Lerner-directed splendour a quarter of a century after the fact. Jimi Hendrix, Jim Morrison make their poignant last stands, the kids rail against a £3 entry fee and the dawn of guard-dog corporatism, and ELP impart a flavour of bloated, canon-firing things to come. *BG*

Movie rating: *7.5

Visual: video + dvd (also separate CD's & DVD's)

Off the record: The **WHO** had got in there first with the 1970 released 'The WHO: LIVE AT THE ISLE OF WIGHT FESTIVAL' movie.

Various Artists

Oct 96. (d-cd) *Sony; <65058> Castle; (EDF 327)* ☐ ☐
– All right now (FREE) / My Sunday feeling (JETHRO TULL) / Suzanne (LEONARD COHEN) / Foxey lady (JIMI HENDRIX) / Voodoo child (slight return) (JIMI HENDRIX) / Can't keep from cryin' (TEN YEARS AFTER) / Me and Bobby McGee (KRIS KRISTOFFERSON) / Big yellow taxi (JONI MITCHELL) / Woodstock (JONI MITCHELL) / Blue rondo a la turk – Pictures at an exhibition – Drum solo (EMERSON, LAKE & PALMER) / / When the music's over (the DOORS) / Young man blues (the WHO) / Naked eye (the WHO) / There'll always be an England (TINY TIM) / Sinner boy (TASTE) / Let it be (JOAN BAEZ) / Nights in white satin (the MOODY BLUES) / Catch the wind (DONOVAN) / Weaver's answer (FAMILY) / Red-eye express (JOHN SEBASTIAN) / Call it anything (MILES DAVIS) / Amazing grace (GREAT AWAKENING) / Desolation row (BOB DYLAN).

S/track review: With the mainstream hippy dream more or less officially dead by summer 1970, and more hardcore counter-cultural forces forging a free festival ethos around bands like Hawkwind (a seething, profanity-punctuated P.A. announcement tells its own story about the fence-trampling debacle, while various comments dictate the economics vs idealism bogeyman), this patchy double set represents a kind of hippie Waterloo while simultaneously lacking the dopey charge and unifying vision of 'WOODSTOCK'. Nor is the line-up as integrated or as free ranging, although MILES DAVIS, fresh from reinventing jazz for the second time with 'Bitches Brew' and 'JACK JOHNSON', shreds any preconceptions with 15 minutes of synapse-rattling sorcery. Even a blazing WHO and an audibly exhausted JIMI HENDRIX can't compete (the man was to pass away only a few weeks later), and while there are many fine performances, there are few great ones, or rather none that are featured here; you'll have to shell out on the DVD for the best performances (and the likes of Tony Joe White don't even make that). FREE enjoy some of the best sound of the event, LEONARD COHEN quiets the crowd with an almost studio pristine 'Suzanne' and JIM MORRISON (not long for the grim reaper himself) holds lugubrious court for a full ten minutes on a bass-heavy 'When The Music's Over' (check the disorientating similarity with TEN YEARS AFTER's 'Can't Keep From Cryin''). One artist who is on top form is JONI MITCHELL; she tells the crowd in no uncertain terms that they're "acting like tourists" but gets a cheer anyway with a fluttering 'Big Yellow Taxi' and, ironically, a starkly affective 'Woodstock' (after which she broke down in tears, although that's excised from the soundtrack). FAMILY give it up for crone-droning psych-minstrels-y, the underrated RORY GALLAGHER slides like an Irish Ron Wood, and a slow motion 'Me And Bobby McGee' sounds edited in from a different event (the cretins who booed KRIS KRISTOFFERSON go mercifully unrecorded). The whole thing is topped off with a star-spangled 'Amazing Grace' which bears all the hallmarks of prime Rod Stewart but actually hails from the mysterious GREAT AWAKENING (John Newton & co subsequently split). Music aside, among the most enduring charms of this soundtrack are the fossilized, Received Pronunciation quotes between the songs, an amusing corollary to TINY TIM's 'There'll Always Be An England': "I don't believe that you can wear long hair, long sideburns and goodness knows what and still say that you are somebody who believes in Great Britain, and it is Great Britain, whether you like it or not"; "remember this, I've been five years in the Naval Intelligence division so I know a good deal of what goes on, I mean I had connections with CID and the lot, and there is no doubt in my mind that this isn't only just hippy fun, behind it is black power and behind that is communism". Right on squire. *BG*

Album rating: *7

– associated releases, etc. –

JIMI HENDRIX: At The Isle Of Wight

Nov 71. (lp) *Polydor; (2302 016)* [–] [17]
– Midnight lightning / Foxey lady / Lover man / Freedom / All along the watchtower / In from the storm. *(re-iss. Apr84 lp/c; SPE LP/MC 71) (cd-iss. Mar89; 831 813-2)*

TASTE: Live At The Isle Of Wight

Aug 72. (lp) *Polydor; (2383 120)* [–] [41]
– What's going on? / Sugar mama / Morning sun / Sinner boy / I feel so good / Catfish. *(cd-iss. Apr94; 841 601-2)*

JIMI HENDRIX: Isle Of Wight 1970

Jul 91. (cd/c/lp) *Polydor; <(847 236-2/-4/-1)>* [ ] [ ]
– Intro – God save the Queen / Message to love / Voodoo child (slight return) / Lover man / Machine gun / Dolly dagger / Red house / In from the storm / New rising sun.

EMERSON, LAKE & PALMER: Live At The Isle Of Wight Festival 1970

Jul 02. (cd) *Castle; (CMRCD 458)* [ ] [ ]
– The barbarian / Take a pebble / Pictures at an exhibition / Nut rocker / (discussion). *(+ dvd)*

JETHRO TULL: Nothing Is Easy – Live At The Isle Of Wight 1970

Nov 04. (cd) *Eagle; (<EAGCD 281)>* [ ] [ ]
– My Sunday feeling / My God / With you there to help me / To cry you a song / Bouree / Dharma for one / Nothing is easy / Medley: We used to know – For a thousand mothers. *(+ dvd)*

METAL: A HEADBANGER'S JOURNEY

2005 (US/Can 96m) Banger Productions Inc. / 235 Films (R)

Film genre: Hard-Rock-music documentary/bio-pic

Top guns: s-w + dir: Sam Dunn, Scot McFadyen, Jessica Joy Wise

Stars: Sam Dunn *(himself)*, **Tony Iommi** *(himself/performer; Black Sabbath)* ← WE SOLD OUR SOULS FOR ROCK'N'ROLL ← ROCK AND ROLL CIRCUS, **Bruce Dickinson** *(himself/performer; Iron Maiden)*, **Dee Snider** *(himself/performer; Twisted Sister)* ← STRANGELAND ← PRIVATE PARTS, **Alice COOPER** *(himself)*, **Rob ZOMBIE** *(himself/performer; White Zombie)*, **Vince Neil** *(himself/performer; Motley Crue)*, **Ronnie James Dio** *(himself)* → the PICK OF DESTINY, **LEMMY** *(himself/performer; Motorhead)*, **Tom Araya** * + **Kerry King** *(performers; Slayer)* ← WE SOLD OUR SOULS FOR ROCK'N'ROLL, **Pamela Des Barres** *(herself)* ← FALLEN ANGEL ← MAYOR OF THE SUNSET STRIP ← SLAUGHTER'S BIG RIP-OFF ← 200 MOTELS, **James 'Munky' Shaffer** *(himself/performer; Korn)*, Donna Gaines *(herself)*, **Geddy Lee** *(himself/performer; Rush)*, **Tom Morello** *(himself/performer; Rage Against The Machine)* ← FREE TIBET, **John Kay** *(himself/performer; Steppenwolf)*

Storyline: Sam Dunn (an anthropologist!) examines the history of heavy metal from its early inception (Steppenwolf, Blue Cheer & Black Sabbath) to latter day noisefiends (Slipknot & Arch Enemy); an obsession with sex, religion and violent death are all looked at provocatively. *MCS*

Movie rating: *7.5

Visual: double dvd

Off the record: (see below)

—

Various Artists

May 06. (cd) *Universal Music Canada; <83718>* [–] [–]
– Hallowed be thy name – live (IRON MAIDEN) / Balls to the wall (ACCEPT) / Heaven and Hell (BLACK SABBATH) / Laid to rest (LAMB OF GOD) / Summertime blues (BLUE CHEER) / Working man (RUSH) / Killed by death (MOTORHEAD) / Am I evil (DIAMOND HEAD) / We're not gonna take it (TWISTED SISTER) / Blood lust (VENOM) / Disciple (SLAYER) / Silent wars (ARCH ENENY) / (sic) (SLIPKNOT) / Needled 24/7 (CHILDREN OF BODOM) / Decency defied (CANNIBAL CORPSE) / Into a satana – live (EMPEROR).

S/track review: No surprises that this film's soundtrack kicks off with IRON MAIDEN. Long have the band been the talisman of Heavy Metal's global domination. This is a live take of 'Hallowed Be Thy Name', one of the key tracks from their breakthrough 1982 'Number Of The Beast' album, and well it has served them over the years. An overwrought piece of classic metal, equal parts atmosphere and bombast, with Bruce Dickinson posturing as a man waiting to face the gallows, instilling the tune with a baroque foreboding before the song breaks into the trademark gallop and harmonics that have made 'MAIDEN the standard bearers of Heavy Metal. Just as MAIDEN were a key proponent of the New Wave of British Heavy Metal (NWOBHM) in the late 70s and early 80s, so LAMB OF GOD have spearheaded the American 21st century equivalent. LOG's firebrand metal assault is rhythmically complex and meticulous, and 'Laid To Rest' is an outstanding example of a band who have innovated within a subgenre and built a fanbase from the grass roots up, bringing quality to the masses, which has led to inevitable (though perhaps misguided) comparisons to the late, great Pantera. The rest of the first part of the album is weighted towards those bands that are held up as progenitors of the metal genre. So there is the proto-grunge of BLUE CHEER with

'Summertime Blues', classic NWOBHM act DIAMOND HEAD (seemingly present as a surrogate for Metallica, who have long since made 'Am I Evil' their own), and those other perennial t-shirt favourites – MOTORHEAD – with the rousing, mid-paced 'Killed By Death'. Most interesting is an Ozzy-less BLACK SABBATH, with 'Heaven And Hell'. Here we find 'SABBATH with Ronnie James Dio at the helm, at the height of their imperial phase. Propelled by Geezer Butler's bass and Bill Ward's steady, unfussy drums, Tony Iommi had long curbed back his bluesier excursions to engage in triumphant, shimmering power chords. Dio is probably preferred over Osbourne since he has done much to concretize metal's aesthetic (for good and ill) as preoccupied with Dungeons and Dragons, and he is also one of its stalwarts, having served the cause in Elf, Rainbow and Dio itself. And as the film testifies, he is an intelligent and articulate spokesperson for the genre. But a cut from Judas Priest would also have been welcome, a band who (with Rob Halford's barely concealed homosexuality) simultaneously cultivated and subverted the genre's redneck, biker tropes. The second part of the album is indicative of how vital and innovative metal can be, by exploring metal's extremities, and the underground acts that have really pushed the genre into new territory. VENOM and SLAYER burst onto the scene in the early 80s, both forging a more vicious assault from punk's speed and fire, and metal's muscle. 'Bloodlust' is classic VENOM, buzz-saw guitars, deliberately poorly produced, and all accomplished with a sarcastic sneer, the primitive ancestor to the even more regressive assault of grim Norwegian black metal, as practiced by Mayhem and Darkthrone. SLAYER fare less well with 'Disciple', being a more polished attempt to capture the past glories of albums such as 'Reign In Blood', which blew the doors off the rock scene in 1986. Still it burns with a white-hot fury, and Tom Araya is a poised and assured frontman who views the satanic stance of the band with a wry eye. Two of Slayer's children are present here, the Swedish ARCH ENEMY with 'Silent Wars' and Finnish CHILDREN OF BODOM with 'Needled 24/7'. The former are everything that's great about modern thrash metal, from Michael Amott's commanding axe work to Angela Gossow's astonishingly savage vocals, in the face of which COB seem decidedly pale. SLIPKNOT weigh in with '(Sic)', an extremely bland choice considering the heights that band has reached. CANNIBAL CORPSE and EMPEROR pit Death metal against Black metal, the olde enemies, and EMPEROR shine brightest with the live take of 'Inno A Satana', which exhibits their mastery of the genre and their symphonic pushing of the envelope. 'Decency defied' typifies the hilarious lyrics, and really anodyne attempts to shock, that have hampered the death metal genre, here in skin-flaying mood: "You mark your skin / It gives you pleasure / I take your precious hide / It becomes my leather". Although it leaves the impression that it could have taken more risks in its choices of bands, this album still ably exhibits what makes metal, in Jack Black's words, "ridiculous yet resplendent". *DF*

Album rating: *7.5

□ METALLICA segment
(⇒ SOME KIND OF MONSTER)

□ the MINUTEMEN segment
(⇒ WE JAM ECONO . . .)

MODULATIONS: CINEMA FOR THE EAR

1998 (US 74m) Caipirinha Productions
Film genre: Electronic-music documentary

Top guns: dir: Iara Lee

Stars: Robert Moog *(himself)* → MOOG, **Karlheinz Stockhausen** *(performer)*, **John Cage** *(performer)*, **Derrick May** *(performer)*, **Moby** *(performer)* ← JOE'S APARTMENT / → BETTER LIVING THROUGH CIRCUITRY → MY GENERATION → ALIEN SEX PARTY → AMERICAN HARDCORE, **Arthur Baker** *(performer)*, **Danny Tenaglia** *(performer)*, **DJ Spooky** *(performer)* → BETTER LIVING THROUGH CIRCUITRY → MOOG, **Afrika Bambaataa** *(performer)* ← the SHOW ← BEAT STREET / → SCRATCH, **Carl Cox** *(performer)* → BETTER LIVING THROUGH CIRCUITRY → HUMAN TRAFFIC → IT'S ALL GONE PETE TONG, **Genesis P. Orridge** *(performer)* → BETTER LIVING THROUGH CIRCUITRY → DIG!, David Kristian *(himself)*, **Mix Master Mike** *(himself)* ← SCRATCH / → AWESOME: I FUCKIN' SHOT THAT!

Storyline: From the initial experiments in potting sheds and science labs in the 1950s through the shimmer of the 60s and 70s, the rattle of the 80s, the throb of the 90s, MODULATIONS digs deep to tell the history of electronic music: avant garde classical, disco, Detroit techno, house, jungle and beyond. All the pioneers and prime practitioners converge to expound their own theories on the evolution of the genre. *MR*

Movie rating: *6

Visual: dvd

Off the record: (see below)

Various Artists (score: Karlheinz Stockhausen)

Oct 98. (cd) *Caipirinha;* <(CAI 2018)> □ Nov98 □
– I feel love (DONNA SUMMER) / Planet rock (AFRIKA BAMBAATAA) / No UFO's remix (JUAN ATKINS / MODEL 500) / Simon from Sydney (LFO) / Strings of life (DERRICK MAY) / Yeah (JESSE SAUNDERS) / Amazon 2 king of the beats (APHRODITE) / Stormbringer (PANACEA) / The shadow (GOLDIE & ROB PLAYFORD) / Luxus 1-3 (RYOJI IKEDA) / Atomic Moog 2000 (COLDCUT) / Kritische masse 1 (TO ROCOCO ROT).

S/track review: This soundtrack was quite literally, a thankless task. How on earth do you encapsulate what an entire genre of music has achieved in 40 odd years into 12 tracks? Answer is you don't, you pick out some great tracks and concede you're not going to please everyone. Electronic music, from its first earthy, primitive squelches through to the razor spliced loops of drum and bass, via the bubbling textures of Detroit techno has always been a complex, multi-faceted beast. This brief overview skips through the genre's history picking out a pretty fine-smelling bouquet. DONNA SUMMER's 'I Feel Love' was one of those truly influential tracks that laid the framework for all house and techno music. It remains one of the greatest electronic, nay, songs of all time. Starting there is a pretty high kick off point and following it with the song that made electro, AFRIKA BAMBAATAA's sensational 'Planet Rock', presented here in all its stripped down nine-minutes of instrumental madness is a smart move. Here is a song that is so simple, but so effective that it remains a dancefloor staple decades after its release. The only other bonafide classic here is 'Strings Of Life' by DERRICK MAY that shows techno in all its ragged, stuttering glory. It might sound dated as hell, but that's kind of what gives it its charm. The progressive strides made in the jungle are illustrated in three ways. APHRODITE's 'Amazon 2 – King Of Beats' shows the genre's hip hop roots but fails to go for the jugular. Unlike PANACEA's 'Stormbringer' which is as heavy as dancefloor music can get. There is however more than just brutality, 'Stormbringer is dynamic and complex and never loses that sense of groove that makes jungle so vital. GOLDIE and ROB PLAYFORD meanwhile manage the complexity and push the genre beyond the cliché, but forget to take that groove with them on 'Shadow'. A further left turn is supplied by RYOJI IKEADA whose ambient musical vapors demand repeated listening at extreme volumes. Winding up with 'Atomic Moog 2000', a sampledelic breakbeat frenzy from COLDCUT and signing off with TO ROCOCO ROT and their subtle rock shapes. This should have been a true greatest hits or a cunning showcase of unsung visionaries, instead it is a hotch-potch of tunes and styles. That doesn't mean it's not a highly listenable collection, it just could have been a whole lot better given the vast amount of music to draw on. *MR*

Album rating: *7

□ MONDO DAYTONA alt.
(⇒ WEEKEND REBELLION)

MONDO HOLLYWOOD

1967 (US 91m) Omega-Cyrano Corporations Productions / HIP (R)

Film genre: political/drugs documentary

Top guns: dir: Robert Carl Cohen

Stars: Margaretta Ramsey *(herself)*, **Frank ZAPPA** *(himself)*, Jayne Mansfield *(archival)*, **Jimmy Carl Black** *(himself)* → 200 MOTELS → UNCLE MEAT → ROCK SCHOOL, **Bobby Beausoleil** *(Cupid)*, Jay Sebring *(himself)*, Gypsy Boots *(himself)* ← a SWINGIN' SUMMER, Rudi Gernreich *(designer)*

Storyline: One for the hippies and now elderly flower children, this cultural documentary (set in Hollywood, L.A.) questions the peace and love (plus LSD) movement. Bizarrely, the film features Bobby Beausoleil (still in jail for his part in the Manson Family murders – 9th August, 1969) and Jay Sebring, one of the said victims alongside actress Sharon Tate. *MCS*

Movie rating: *6.5

Visual: dvd

Off the record: (see below)

—

Various Artists (composer/producer: MIKE CURB)

Aug 67. (lp; mono/stereo) *Tower; <T/DT 5083>* [ ] [-]
– Mondo Hollywood (city of dreams) (the MUGWUMP ESTABLISHMENT) / The magic night (MIKE CLIFFORD) / Moonfire (DAVIE ALLAN & THE ARROWS) / Last wave of the day (the RIPTIDES) / Vietnam (BOBBY JAMESON) / Great God Pan (GOD PAN) / You're beautiful (DARRELL DEE) / Magic night march (18TH CENTURY CONCEPTS) / Beast of Sunset Strip (TEDDY & DARRELL) / Mondo Hollywood freakout (the MUGWUMP ESTABLISHMENT).

S/track review: All put together by producer, MIKE CURB (he of numerous soundtracks, film work, etc.), this one can definitely be filed under W for weird. CURB worked under many pseudonymous guises around the time, here he and director/photographer/co-songwriter, ROBERT CARL COHEN were represented by the MUGWUMP ESTABLISHMENT, the RIPTIDES, 18TH CENTURY CONCEPTS (best forgotten), DARRELL DEE and, one guesses, TEDDY & DARRELL. The former collective opened and closed 'MONDO HOLLYWOOD' with some fitting mouth-organ-fired Beach Boys-esque psych title tracks, '. . . (City Of Dreams)' and the Doors-ish clash, '. . . Freakout'. Of all the various groups on board, DAVIE ALLAN & THE ARROWS, were the most well known outfit having already "surf"-aced with hot rod LPs such as 'THUNDER ALLEY' (1967) and 'The WILD ANGELS' (1966). Their exclusive 'Moonfire' instrumental showcased excellent machine-gun drums, Dick Dale-esque guitar and plodding keys (like 'Wipe Out'-meets-'Telstar') into first gear. Just when you thought the aforementioned RIPTIDES were going the same way – they sing! yes, Jan & Dean-like 'The Last Wave Of The Day'. That organ-ic moothy comes into full force again via West Coast psych-folker/veteran, BOBBY JAMESON, a man who apes Bo Diddley to a tee for a sonic attack protest of Uncle Sam's tactics in 'Vietnam'. Another L.A. guy, crooner MIKE CLIFFORD (on 'Magic Night'), was surely the Mike Flowers Pop of his day, and was he serious? – or was he just picking himself off the CURB, so to speak. Of the other acts, GOD PAN and 'Great God Pan' (fuse Burl Ives with the Incredible String Band!), left one thinking Pan alright, and another word beginning with P going down it comes to mind. 'You're Beautiful' singer, DARRELL DEE was no James Blunt, while DARRELL (one thinks?) gets another chance with TEDDY on the 'Monster Mash' hash of 'Beast Of Sunset Strip'. *MCS*

Album rating: *4.5

MONTEREY POP

1968 (US 88m) Leacock-Pennebaker Films

Film genre: Rock-music concert/documentary

Top guns: dir: D.A. Pennebaker ← DON'T LOOK BACK / → ZIGGY STARDUST: THE MOTION PICTURE → 101 → DOWN FROM THE MOUNTAIN → ONLY THE STRONG SURVIVE

Stars: Scott McKenzie *(performer)*, **the Mamas & The Papas:- Mama Cass Elliot, John Phillips, Michelle Phillips *, Denny Doherty** *(performers)* → SWEETWATER: A TRUE ROCK STORY * → MAYOR OF THE SUNSET STRIP * / **Canned Heat:- Al Wilson, Frank Cook, Bob Hite, Henry Vestine** *(performers)* / **SIMON & GARFUNKEL:- Paul Simon & Art Garfunkel** *(performers)* / **Hugh Masekela** *(performer)* → AMANDLA! – A REVOLUTION IN FOUR-PART HARMONY, **Jefferson Airplane:- Grace Slick *, Paul Kantner, Marty Balin, Jack Casady, Jorma Kaukonen, Spencer Dryden** *(performers)* → GIMME SHELTER → a NIGHT AT THE FAMILY DOG → FILLMORE → JACKIE'S BACK *, **Big Brother & The Holding Company:- Janis Joplin, Sam Andrew, Dave Getz, Peter Albin, James Gurley** *(performers)*, **Eric Burdon & The ANIMALS:- Eric Burdon, Vic Briggs, Barry Jenkins, Danny McCulloch, John Weider** *(performers)* / **the WHO:- Pete Townshend, Roger Daltrey, Keith Moon, John Entwistle** *(performers)* / **Country Joe McDONALD (& The Fish)** *(performers)*, **Jimi HENDRIX** *(performer)*, **Mitch Mitchell** *(performer)* → RAINBOW BRIDGE → JIMI HENDRIX → ROCK AND ROLL CIRCUS → EXPERIENCE, **Noel Redding** *(performer)* → EXPERIENCE, **Ravi SHANKAR** *(performer)*, **Otis Redding** *(performer)* → POPCORN

Storyline: California's 1967 (16-18 June) Monterey Pop festival lays the groundwork for Woodstock with D.A. Pennebaker's celebrated film capturing the cream of the era's musical talent and a sense of cultural sea change. The first bonafide concert film of the rock era, Monterey focuses on the festival's performances rather than its context, with the recently released DVD offering the most revealing documentation to date. *BG*

Movie rating: *8.5

Visual: video + dvd

Off the record: (see above & below)

—

RAVI SHANKAR: Ravi Shankar At The International Pop Festival

Nov 67. (lp) *World Pacific; <21442> Columbia; (SCX 6273)* [43] Oct68 [ ]
– Raga bhimpalasi / Tabla solo in Ektal / Dhun (dadra and fast teental). *(UK cd-iss. Jul93 on 'Beat Goes On'; BGOCD 147) (cd re-iss. Apr94 on 'Ravi Shankar Music Circle'; RSMCD 101) <cd re-iss. 1998 on 'Angel'; 66919>*

—

JIMI HENDRIX / OTIS REDDING: Monterey International Pop Festival

Sep 70. (lp) *Reprise; <MS 2029>* 16 –
– JIMI HENDRIX:- Like a rolling stone / Rock me, baby / Can you see me / Wild thing / OTIS REDDING:- Shake / Respect / I've been loving you too long / Satisfaction / Try a little tenderness.

—

Various Artists

1971. (t-lp) *Dunhill; <50100>* –
– San Francisco (be sure to wear flowers in your hair) (SCOTT McKENZIE) / So sad about us (the WHO) / Happy Jack (WHO) / The 59th St. Bridge song (SIMON & GARFUNKEL) / For what it's worth (BUFFALO SPRINGFIELD) / Got a feelin' (the MAMAS & THE PAPAS) / She has funny cars (JEFFERSON AIRPLANE) / D.C.B.A.-25 (JEFFERSON AIRPLANE) / Combination of the two (BIG BROTHER & THE HOLDING COMPANY) / Mystery train (PAUL BUTTERFIELD BLUES BAND) / Renaissance fair (the BYRDS) / Have you seen her face (the BYRDS) / Along comes Mary (the ASSOCIATION) / On the road again (CANNED HEAT) / Questions (BUFFALO SPRINGFIELD) / And when I die (LAURA NYRO) / Flute thing (the BLUES PROJECT) / Killing floor (JIMI HENDRIX EXPERIENCE) / Hey Joe (JIMI HENDRIX EXPERIENCE) / (Sittin' on) The dock of the bay (OTIS REDDING).

S/track review: For those without a DVD player, Rhino's four-CD box set is still the benchmark for a comprehensive aural document, with memorable tracks from the WHO (Pete Townshend's guitar abuse almost putting paid to RAVI SHANKAR's participation), the BYRDS and JANIS JOPLIN amongst others. While RAVI SHANKAR's celebrated afternoon stint was released as an album in 1967, the equally myth-making performances of the JIMI HENDRIX EXPERIENCE and OTIS REDDING were the subjects of a split US Top 20 album in 1970. 1971 saw the release of the MAMAS & THE PAPAS' performance in its own right, while JEFFERSON AIRPLANE's transitional set was documented on a 1969 album. With all this on board, one was happy to report a new double-CD version of the festival was released to mark a near 40th Anniversary. This jewel in the crown, featured several tracks from the original LP's/CD's/bootlegs (sadly, still no GRATEFUL DEAD, who allegedly objected then & now – one understands!). When you think of the range of top artists here: ERIC BURDON & THE ANIMALS, SIMON & GARFUNKEL, BOOKER T. & THE MG's to the worldly HUGH MASEKELA and the aforementioned RAVI SHANKAR, it's just absolutely staggering. 'MONTEREY POP' not only compares with the legendary 'WOODSTOCK' (1970), it at times surpasses it, tracks such as JEFFERSON AIRPLANE's 'White Rabbit' & 'Somebody To Love', the MAMAS & THE PAPAS 'California Dreamin'' and SCOTT McKENZIE's 'San Francisco (Be Sure To Wear Flowers In Your Hair'), the epitome of everything that was the summer of 1967. *BG & MCS*

Album rating: *8 / Ravi Shankar *7 / Jimi Hendrix *6 / Jefferson Airplane *6.5 / boxed set + double-CD *9 / the Mamas & The Papas *5

– others, spinoff releases, etc. –

JIMI HENDRIX: Jimi Plays Monterey

Feb 86. (lp/c/cd) *Reprise; <25358> Polydor; (827990-1/-4/-2)*
– Killing floor / Foxy lady / Like a rolling stone / Rock me, baby / Hey Joe / Can you see me / The wind cries Mary / Purple haze / Wild thing. *(re-iss. Jun91 & Mar93 cd/c/lp; 847244-2/-4/-1) (cd re-iss. Sep93 as 'Jimi Hendrix At The Monterey Pop Festival 1967' w/ tracks re-arranged on 'I.T.M.'; ITM 960008)*

JEFFERSON AIRPLANE: Live At The Monterey Festival

May 90. (cd/lp) *Thunderbolt; (CDTB/THBL 074)* –
– Somebody to love / Other side of this life / White rabbit / High flyin' bird / Today / She has funny cars / Young girl Sunday blues / The ballad of you and me and Pooneil. <*US cd-iss. 1995; same as UK*> *(cd re-iss. Feb03; same)*

the MAMAS & THE PAPAS: Monterey International Pop Festival

Jul 92. (cd) *One Way; <OW 22033>* –
– Straight shooter / Got a feelin' / California dreaming / Spanish Harlem / Somebody groovy / I call your name / Monday, Monday / Dancing in the streets.

Various Artists: The Monterey International Pop Festival June 16 17 18 – 1967

Jun 97. (4xcd-box) *Rhino; <(RCD 72825)>*
– (festival introduction by JOHN PHILLIPS) / ASSOCIATION:- Along comes Mary / Windy / LOU RAWLS:- Love is a hurtin' thing / Dead end street / Tobacco road / ERIC BURDON & THE ANIMALS:- San Franciscan nights / Hey Gyp / CANNED HEAT:- Rollin' and tumblin' / Dust my broom / Bullfrog blues / COUNTRY JOE & THE FISH:- Not so sweet Martha Lorraine / BIG BROTHER & THE HOLDING COMPANY:- Down on me / Combination of the two / Harry / Road block / Ball and chain // BUTTERFIELD BLUES BAND:- Look over younders wall / Mystery train / Born in Chicago / Double trouble / Mary Ann / STEVE MILLER:- Mercury blues / ELECTRIC FLAG:- Groovin' is easy / Wine / HUGH MASEKELA:- Bajabula bonke (the healing song) / BYRDS:- Renaissance fair / Have you seen her face / Hey Joe / He was a friend of mine / Lady friend / Chimes of freedom / So you want to be a rock & roll star / RAVI SHANKAR:- Dhun: fast teental / BLUES PROJECT:- Wake me, shake me // JEFFERSON AIRPLANE:- Somebody to love / The other side of this life / White rabbit / High flyin' bird / She has funny cars / BOOKER T. & THE MG'S:- Booker-loo / Hip hug her / Philly dog / OTIS REDDING:- Shake / Respect / I've been loving you too long / Satisfaction / WHO:- Substitute / Summertime blues / Pictures of Lily / A quick one while he's away / Happy Jack / My generation // JIMI HENDRIX EXPERIENCE:- Killing floor / Like a rolling stone / Rock me, baby / Foxy lady / Can you see me / Hey Joe / Purple haze / The wind cries Mary / Wild thing / MAMAS & THE PAPAS:- Straight shooter / Got a feelin' / California dreamin' / I call your name / Monday Monday / SCOTT McKENZIE:- San Francisco (be sure to wear flowers in your hair) / MAMAS & THE PAPAS:- Dancing in the streets.

Various Artists: Monterey International Pop Festival

Jun 07. (d-cd) *Razor & Tie; <2972>*
– Along came Mary (the ASSOCIATION) / San Franciscan nights (ERIC BURDON & THE ANIMALS) / Homeward bound (SIMON & GARFUNKEL) / The sounds of silence (SIMON & GARFUNKEL) / Down on me (BIG BROTHER & THE HOLDING COMPANY) / Ball and chain (BIG BROTHER & THE HOLDING COMPANY) / Section 43 (COUNTRY JOE & THE FISH) / Born in Chicago (PAUL BUTTERFIELD BLUES BAND) / Wine (the ELECTRIC FLAG) / Bajabula bone (HUGH MASEKELA) / Chimes of freedom (the BYRDS) / So you wanna be a rock'n'roll star (the BYRDS) / Somebody to love (JEFFERSON AIRPLANE) / White rabbit (JEFFERSON AIRPLANE) / Booker-loo (BOOKER T. & THE MG's) / Shake (OTIS REDDING) / I've been loving you (too long) (OTIS REDDING) / Dhun: fast teental (RAVI SHANKAR) / For what it's worth (BUFFALO SPRINGFIELD) / Summertime blues (the WHO) / My generation (the WHO) / The wind cries Mary (JIMI HENDRIX EXPERIENCE) / Like a rolling stone (JIMI HENDRIX EXPERIENCE) / Straight shooter (the MAMAS & THE PAPAS) / San Francisco (be sure to wear flowers in your hair) (SCOTT McKENZIE) / California dreamin' (the MAMAS & THE PAPAS).

MOOG

2004 (US 72m) Plexifilm

Film genre: Electronic-rock documentary/bio-pic

Top guns: s-w + dir: Hans Fjellestad

Stars: Robert Moog *(himself)* ← MODULATIONS, **Keith EMERSON** *(performer)*, **Rick WAKEMAN** *(performer)*, **Money Mark** *(performer)* → AWESOME: I FUCKIN' SHOT THAT!, **DJ Spooky** *(performer)* ← BETTER LIVING THROUGH CIRCUITRY ← MODULATIONS, **DJ Logic** *(performer)*, **Charlie Clouser** *(performer)*, **Bernie Worrell** *(performer)* ←

STOP MAKING SENSE, **Luke Vibert** *(performer)*, **Jean-Jacques Perrey** *(performer)*, **Pamelia Kurstin** *(herself)*, **Gershon Kingsley** *(performer)*, **Herbert Deutsch** *(performer)*, **Mix Master Mike** *(performer)* ← SCRATCH

Storyline: German inventor Bob Moog was the godfather of electronic music. He was the first to fully explore the potential of the sounds and built keyboards that would be heard everywhere from stadium rock to dancefloors worldwide. This is his story. His life, his inspirations, his inventions and luminaries from the music world converge to expound on Moog's influence on modern music. *MR*

Movie rating: *6.5

Visual: dvd

Off the record: Robert Moog (see above)

Various Artists

Sep 04. (cd) *Hollywood; <16247-1> (5050467 5716-2-4)* ☐ Nov04 ☐
– Abomination (33) / Variation one (STEREOLAB) / Bob's funk (the MOOG COOKBOOK) / You Moog me (JEAN-JACQUES PERREY & LUKE VIBERT) / The sentinel (PSILONAUT) / Unavailable memory (MEAT BEAT MANIFESTO) / When Bernie speaks (BERNIE WORRELL & BOOTSY COLLINS) / Endless horizon – I Love Bob mix (ELECTRIC SKYCHURCH) / Micro melodies (the ALBUM LEAF) / I am a spaceman (CHARLIE CLOUSER) / Sqeeble (PLASTIQ PHANTOM) / Realistic source (BOSTICH) / You have been selected (PETE DEVRIESE) / Nanobot highway (MONEY MARK) / Mixed waste 4.2 (BAIYON) / Beautiful love (TORTOISE) / Another year away (ROGER O'DONNELL). *<US+=>* – Lucky man (EMERSON, LAKE & PALMER) / Cars (GARY NUMAN) / E.V.A. (JEAN-JACQUES PERREY) / Mongoloid (DEVO) / Blue Monday (NEW ORDER) / Baroque hoedown (THEY MIGHT BE GIANTS) / Close to the edge (YES).

S/track review: That the Moog keyboard has been adopted over the years by everyone from unassuming Gallic indie kids to the hardest of technoheads in Detroit via the 70s prog gods of the Berkshire countryside, is something which is a reflection of the instrument's versatility rather than its ubiquity. You have to work to get something great out of a Moog and this selection shows just a little of the machine's potential. This 17-track collection illustrates just a part of the range of the kind of technology Bob Moog pioneered in the 60s. The focus is very much on the new generation of young experimentalists that operate outside of the Moog's hey days of the 70s (progressive rock) and the 80s and 90s (techno) like Chicago's TORTOISE and Beastie Boys collaborator MONEY MARK and English/French indie retroists STEREOLAB. This collection, given the extrovert and often emphatic potential of Bob Moog's inventions seem a little subdued to be regarded as a fair overview of the instrument's potential and while this is an obvious illustration is an indication of the subtleties that can be obtained from this analogue machinery some of it is very much style over substance. JEAN-JACQUES PERREY and LUKE VIBERT build a dreamy loping vibe with an antiquated, if sweet heart on 'You Moog Me', while one-time Funkadelic collaborators BOOTSY COLLINS and BERNIE WORRELL illustrate just how funky a little box of trick can be on the rolling 'When Bernie Speaks'. A tune which also inadvertently reminds us of how an entire sub genre of hip hop – gangsta rap – was driven by the thick bass parps of analogue bottom end from Moog's keyboards. This mix shows the subtleties and the potential of MOOG's instruments but fails to show it often enough as the aggressive star of the rock'n'roll show. That would have completed the picture. You'll find this on the expanded US version. *MR*

Album rating: *7

Van MORRISON

Born: George Ivan Morrison, 31 Aug'45, Belfast, N.Ireland. As dreamer of some of the most evocative, enigmatic and impressionistic popular music ever recorded, VAN MORRISON wrote countless metaphorical soundtracks to the mystic. It's tantalising to ponder, though, what he might have made of a real live film commission during his gypsy ecstasies of the late 60s/ early 70s. A young Wim Wenders, for one, recognised the music's imagistic power and clarity on his 1970 film, 'Three American Albums'. And if Van didn't compose a score during this period, at least – on 1973's underrated 'Hard Nose The Highway' – he namechecked his favourite screen icons. Performance-wise he was glimpsed (performing 'Come Running') in 'The Day The Music Died' (1977), a document of the 1970 Randall's Island Pop Festival, an American counter-cultural melee to rival the same year's Isle Of Wight debacle. One of the most memorable TV appearances in an era which gifted MORRISON's live double, 'It's Too Late To Stop Now' (1974), was a simultaneous BBC TV/Radio One broadcast from London's Rainbow Theatre under the aegis of the Old Grey Whistle Test, with his legendary Caledonia Soul Orchestra in full effect. Two years later he was one of the chosen few to serenade the exit of old pals the BAND, putting in what are often regarded as the most electric performances recorded for posterity on 'The LAST WALTZ' (1978). 'Van Morrison In Ireland' (1980) documented the man's homecoming Dublin gig in early 1979, while 'Coney Island Of The Mind' (1991), part of Channel 4's 'Without Walls' series, shone a rare light on the literary dimension of his art, filming him in conversation and recitation with fellow poets in both Belfast and County Wicklow. Also in 1991, BBC2's Arena presented an iconic pairing with BOB DYLAN against the suitably august backdrop of Athens' Acropolis, as well as collaborations with the likes of John Lee Hooker and Georgie Fame. According to Brian Hinton's own literary study, 'Celtic Crossroads' (1997), Van recorded his first score for 'The Schooner', a film credited to Irish national TV channel RTE. More high profile was 'Lamb' (1985), a Bernard MacLaverty adaptation starring Liam Neeson, the second and final of VAN's dalliances with film music. It wasn't however, the last of directors and soundtrack supervisors' dalliances with him; so often have his songs been featured in film, songs selected from across the spectrum of his career, that 'E.M.I.' managed to stretch them into a de facto greatest hits set and call it 'Van Morrison – At The Movies' (2007). It even featured Van's unlikely collaboration with ROGER WATERS on 'Comfortably Numb', lifted from Waters' post-communist marathon, 'The WALL: LIVE IN BERLIN' (1990), and used in Martin Scorsese's 'The Departed' (2006). Continuing an association which began with 'The LAST WALTZ', MORRISON had already offered up a rare interviewee appearance in Scorsese's look at the British blues boom, 'RED, WHITE & BLUES' (2003), a good companion piece to an unmissable appearance on a 1989 Arena documentary profiling hep-talking legend Slim Gaillard, with Van reading from Jack Kerouac's 'On The Road' over Gaillard's piano, and perhaps as poignant and revealing a MORRISON screen moment as we're going to get. *BG*

- **filmography** (composer) {performer} –

Dusty And Sweets McGhee *(1971 score w/ Jake Holmes & Ricky Nelson)* / Slipstream *(1973 score w/ Brian Ahern & Eric CLAPTON)* / **the Last Waltz** *(1978 {p} on OST by the BAND & V/A =>)* / Van Morrison In Ireland *(1980 {*p} =>)* / Shergar *1984 TV score w/ David Knopfler)* / Lamb *(1986 score)* / **the Wall: Live In Berlin** *(1990 {p} on OST by ROGER WATERS & V/A =>* / Moondance *(1995 score w/ Fiachra Trench)* / al Di La Delle Novelle *(1996 score w/ Laurent Pettigand)*

– compilations, etc. –

VAN MORRISON: At The Movies – Soundtrack Hits

Feb 07. (cd) *Manhattan-E.M.I.; (<3 844224-2>)* 17 35
– Gloria (THEM) *["the Outsiders"]* / Baby please don't go (THEM) *["Wild At Heart"]* / Jackie Wilson said (I'm in heaven when you smile) *["the Pope Of Greenwich Village"]* / Domino (live) *["Clean & Sober"]* / Moondance (live) *["an American Werewolf In London"]* / Queen of the slipstream *["Extreme Close-Up"]* / Wild night *["Thelma & Louise"]* / Caravan (live) *["the Last Waltz"]* / Wonderful remark *["the King Of Comedy"]* / Brown eyed girl *["Born On The Fourth Of July"]* / Days like these *["As Good As It Gets"]* / Into the mystic (live) *["Patch Adams"]* / Hungry for your love *["an Officer And A Gentleman"]* / Someone like you *["French Kiss"]* / Bright side of the road *["Fever Pitch"]* / Have I told you lately? *["One Fine Day"]* / Real real gone *["Donovan Quick"]* / Irish heartbeat *["the Matchmaker"]* / Comfortably numb (live) *["the Departed"]*.

☐ MUSIC POWER alt.
(⇒ AMOUGIES)

☐ MUSICAL MUTINY
(⇒ Rock Movies/Musicals..)

MY GENERATION

2000 (US/Ita/Ger 103m) Cabin Creek / Mikado Films / Schulberg

Film genre: Rock-music concert documentary

Top guns: dir: (+ s-w) Barbara Kopple ← WOODSTOCK '94 / → SHUT UP & SING, Thomas Haneke

Stars: the WHO:- Roger Daltrey, Pete Townshend, Keith Moon, John Entwistle *(performers)*, **Joe COCKER** *(performer)*, **Jimi HENDRIX** *(performer)*, **Janis JOPLIN** *(performer)*, **CROSBY, STILLS & NASH:- David Crosby, Stephen Stills, Graham Nash** *(performers)*, **Carlos SANTANA** *(performer)*, **John Sebastian** *(performer)* <= LOVIN' SPOONFUL; pt.IV: Rock scores =>, **Henry ROLLINS** *(himself)*, **Porno For Pyros:- Perry Farrell** *(himself)* ← GLASTONBURY THE MOVIE ← WOODSTOCK '94, **AEROSMITH:- Steven Tyler, Joe Perry, Tom Hamilton, Joey Kramer, Brad Whitford** *(performers)*, **Moby** *(performer)* ← BETTER LIVING THROUGH CIRCUITRY ← MODULATIONS: CINEMA FOR THE EAR ← JOE'S APARTMENT / → ALIEN SEX PARTY → AMERICAN HARDCORE, **Sheryl Crow** *(performer)* ← WOODSTOCK '99 ← DILL SCALLION; pt.I: Rock musicals ← WOODSTOCK 94, **Blues Traveler:- John Popper *, Chan Kinchla, Bobby Sheehan, Brendan Hill** *(performers)* ← BLUES BROTHERS 2000 ← PRIVATE PARTS * ← WOODSTOCK 94, Rosie Perez *(herself)* ← the ROAD TO ELDORADO ← NIGHT ON EARTH, **Peter GABRIEL** *(performer)*, **Melissa Etheridge** *(performer)* ← JACKIE'S BACK! ← WOODSTOCK 94, **Dickey Betts** *(performer)* ← SOUTHERN VOICES, AMERICAN DREAMS, Allen Ginsberg *(himself)* ← RENALDO AND CLARA ← TEN FOR TWO ← TONITE LET'S MAKE LOVE IN LONDON ← DON'T LOOK BACK ← CHAPPAQUA / → NO DIRECTION HOME, **Chris Vrenna** *(performer)* ← WOODSTOCK '94, Wavy Gravy *(host)* → the END OF THE ROAD: THE FINAL TOUR '95

Storyline: Showcasing three Woodstocks – 1969, 1994 & 1999 – and each generation from the hippies to the arsonists that individualized and ultimately tried to wreck the latter festivals. *MCS*

Movie rating: *6

Visual: dvd (no audio OST)

Off the record: Dickey Betts was of the Allman Brothers, while **Chris Vrenna** was part of Nine Inch Nails.

NASHVILLE SOUNDS

THE BEACH BOYS: NASHVILLE SOUNDS

1996 (US 110m TV) Delilah Films / The Disney Channel

Film genre: Country/Pop-music documentary

Top guns: dir: Alan Boyd → HEY HEY WE'RE THE MONKEES → ENDLESS HARMONY: THE BEACH BOYS STORY, Steven R. Monroe

Stars: the BEACH BOYS:- Mike Love, Al Jardine, Carl Wilson, Bruce Johnston, Brian Wilson *(performers)*, **Lorrie Morgan** *(performer)*, **James House** *(performer)*, **Junior Brown** *(performer)*, **Doug Supernaw** *(performer)*, **Sawyer Brown** *(performer)*, **Toby Keith** *(performer)* → BROKEN BRIDGES, **Ricky Van Shelton** *(Performer)*, **T. Graham Brown** *(performer)*, **Willie NELSON** *(performer)*, **Collin Raye** *(performer)*, **Kathy Troccoli** *(performer)*, **Timothy B. Schmit** *(performer)* ← SCENES FROM THE GOLDMINE, **Rodney Crowell** *(performer)* ← HEARTWORN HIGHWAYS, **Tammy Wynette** *(performer)*

Storyline: The Beach Boys (with Brian Wilson) and country friends perform in Nashville, recording the historic 'Stars & Stripes' set. *MCS*

Movie rating: *6

Visual: video + dvd

Off the record: Junior Brown went on to act in a few movies, 'Still Breathing' (1997), 'The Caveman's Valentine' (2001) and the voice of the balladeer in 'The Dukes Of Hazzard' (2005). **Collin Raye** subsequently starred in the film, 'Choosing Matthias' (2001). **Tammy Wynette** was famous for at least two country classics, 'Stand By Your Man' and 'D.I.V.O.R.C.E.'. *MCS*

– associated releases –

the BEACH BOYS: Stars And Stripes Vol.1

Aug 96. (cd) *River North; <514 161205-2>* ☐ -
– Don't worry baby (with LORRIE MORGAN) / Little deuce coupe (with JAMES HOUSE) / 409 (with JUNIOR BROWN) / Long tall Texan (with DOUG SUPERNAW) / I get around (with SAWYER BROWN) / Be true to your school (with TOBY KEITH) / Fun, fun, fun (with RICKY VAN SHELTON) / Help me, Rhonda (with T. GRAHAM BROWN) / The warmth of the sun (with WILLIE NELSON) / Sloop John B (with COLLIN RAYE) / I can hear music (with KATHY TROCCOLI) / Caroline no (with TIMOTHY B. SCHMIT). *(UK-iss.Jun00; same as US)*

the BEACH BOYS with KATHY TROCCOLI: I Can Hear Music

Aug 96. (cd-s) *<3011-2>* ☐ -

NEW YORK DOLL

2005 (US 75m) One Potato Productions / First Independent (PG-13)

Film genre: Punk-rock music documentary

Top guns: dir: Greg Whiteley

Stars: NEW YORK DOLLS:- Arthur Kane, David Johansen, Sylvain Sylvain, Johnny Thunders, Jerry Nolan *(themselves/archive performers)* + **Brian Koonin + Sammy Yaffa + Steve Conte** *(themselves/performers)* / Barbara Kane *(herself)*, **Morrissey** *(himself)* → GLASTONBURY, **Don Letts** *(himself)* → the FUTURE IS UNWRITTEN, Lee Black Childers *(himself)*, **Bob Geldof** *(himself)* ← SPICEWORLD ← the WALL ← PUNK IN LONDON, **Iggy POP** *(himself)*, **Mick Jones** *(himself)* <= JOE STRUMMER/the CLASH =>, **Chrissie Hynde** *(herself)* ← CONCERT FOR KAMPUCHEA, **Clem Burke + Frank Infante** *(themselves)* <= BLONDIE =>

Storyline: The New York Doll in question is recovering alcoholic and recently converted Mormon, Arthur Kane. The ups and downs are documented by fellow Mormon and filmmaker, Greg Whiteley, who is on hand to show the delight of said Kane when his New York Dolls dream reunion in 2004 becomes a reality. *MCS*

Movie rating: *7.5

Visual: dvd (no audio OST; score: Brett Boyett)

Off the record: Brian Koonin collaborated with **David Johansen** to contribute songs for the 'Mr. Nanny' movie in '93. *MCS*

NEW YORK DOLLS

Formed: New York City, New York, USA . . . late '71 by Johnny Thunders, DAVID JOHANSEN, Billy Murcia, Arthur Kane and Rick Rivets; by March the following year, Rivets left to form the Brats, replaced by Sylvain Sylvain. After a promising start as support act on a Faces British tour, the 'Dolls' first casualty was Murcia who died on the 6th of November '72 after drowning in his own bath (not, as widely believed, from a drug overdose). With Jerry Nolan to fill his shoes, they signed to 'Mercury' in March '73 and promptly began work on an eponymous debut album with Todd Rundgren producing. Released in the summer of that year, 'New York Dolls' was a proto-punk revelation, a way cool schlock of visceral rock'n'roll which combined the more essential moments of MC5, the Pretty Things, Pink Fairies and the Shangri-La's. The Rolling Stones were another obvious reference point, JOHANSEN a dead-ringer for Mick Jagger in terms of both vocal style and mascara'd looks. Inevitably, then, Thunders was the glam-punk Keith Richards, Glitter Twins to the Jagger-Richards Glimmer coupling. The 'Dolls' trashy transvestite attire also borrowed heavily from the 'Stones (circa '66: 'Have You Seen Your Mother Baby . . .'), although being American they'd obviously taken it to almost cartoon-esque proportions. The likes of 'Personality Crisis', 'Trash' and 'Jet Boy' were seminal squalls of guitar abuse, making up in attitude what they lacked in musical ability. Although the record had the critics salivating, commercial success wasn't forthcoming and, unhappy with the record's production, the band opted for Shangri-La's producer, George Morton, to work on 'Too Much Too Soon' (1974). Though the album had its moments, again the band had been paired with the wrong producer and the music press were emphatically unimpressed. The lukewarm reviews heightened inter-band tension and the Dolls' demise was swift and inevitable. Early the following year, Londoner Malcolm McLaren made a last-ditch attempt to save the band, revamping their image to no avail. Thunders was the first to leave, departing in 1975 to form the Heartbreakers, while JOHANSEN and Sylvain subsequently sacked Kane before finally calling it a day the following Christmas. While Thunders went on to most acclaim with his Heartbreakers (sadly he died from an overdose on 23rd April '91), JOHANSEN recorded a number of solo albums as well as releasing a 1988 set under the pseudonym of Buster Poindexter (he also marked out a career in acting, initially in the 1988 movie 'CANDY MOUNTAIN', for which he provided some of the score, plus 'Scrooged', 'Freejack' & 'Car 54, Where Are You'). Nolan was to also meet an untimely death (14th January, 1992), almost a year on from Thunders, the man suffering a fatal stroke while undergoing treatment for meningitis and pneumonia. The NEW YORK DOLLS have appeared in many a punk rock documentary, 'The BLANK GENERATION' (1976) to 'PUNK: ATTITUDE' (2005), while they also re-formed (with the help of long-time fan, Morrissey) around 2004. *BG & MCS*

- filmography {actors} (composers) –

the Blank Generation *(1976 {p JOHNNY} =>)* / **the Punk Rock Movie** *(1978 {p JOHNNY} =>)* / Innerspace *(1987 {b ARTHUR})* / **Candy Mountain** *(1988 {a DAVID} + JOHANSEN score w/ DR. JOHN, Leon Redbone & Rita MacNeil =>)* / Gandahar *(1988 {v DAVID})* / Married To The Mob *(1988 {a DAVID} OST by V/A & DAVID BYRNE; see future editions)* / Scrooged *(1988 {a DAVID} on OST by V/A & Danny Elfman; see future edition)* / Let It Ride *(1989 {* DAVID})* / Mona Et Moi *(1989 {a JOHNNY})* / Tales From The Darkside: The Movie *(1990 {* DAVID} OST by Chaz Jankel, etc; see future edition)* / Desire And Hell At Sunset Motel *(1992 {* DAVID})* / Freejack *(1992 {* DAVID} OST by V/A; see future editions)* / **What About Me** *(1993 {a JERRY + JOHNNY} score by THUNDERS =>)* / Naked In New York *(1993 {a DAVID})* / Mr. Nanny *(1993 {a DAVID} + JOHANSEN score w/ Brian Koonin)* / Car 54, Where Are You? *(1994 {* DAVID})* / Burnzy's Last Call *(1995 {* DAVID})* / Stand Up *(1995 TV {a DAVID})* / Nick And Jane *(1997 {* DAVID})* / Cats Don't Dance *(1997 {v DAVID} OST by Randy Newman; see future edition)* / the Deli *(1997 {* DAVID})* / 200 Cigarettes *(1999 {a DAVID} OST by Mark Mothersbaugh & Robert Mothersbaugh; see future edition)* / the Tic Code *(1999 {a DAVID} see future edition)* / **Born To Lose: The Last Rock And Roll Movie** *(1999 {p} =>)* / Campfire Stories *(2001 {a DAVID as BUSTER POINDEXTER})* / God Is On Their Side *(2002 {a DAVID as BUSTER POINDEXTER})* / Crooked Lines *(2003 {a DAVID})* / **End Of The Century** *(2003 {c} =>)* / **Hey Is Dee Dee Home** *(2003 {c JOHNNY + JERRY} =>)* / **Lightning In A Bottle** *(2004 {p DAVID} OST by V/A =>)* / **New York Doll** *(2005 {*} =>)* / **Searching For The Wrong-Eyed Jesus** *(2005 {p DAVID} OST by V/A =>)* / **Punk: Attitude** *(2005 {p DAVID} =>)*

NICO

Born: Christa Päffgen, 16 Oct'38, Cologne, Germany. When her father died in a concentration camp, the young Christa travelled throughout Europe with her mother. Developing a fondness for opera, NICO learned to play classical piano and harmonium. In 1959, while vacationing in Italy, she was introduced by new friends to film director Federico Fellini and following a bit-part in 'La Dolce Vita', she became a top model, appearing in Vogue magazine. During the early 60s, while working in various films, she became the girlfriend of French actor Alain Delon and later gave birth to his son, having already borne a daughter to actor/dancer Eric Emerson. In 1963, NICO fell in love with up-and-coming folk-star BOB DYLAN, who wrote a song for her, 'I'll Keep It With Mine'. At the rock poet's suggestion, she moved to London in '65 and signed for Andrew Loog Oldham's new label, 'Immediate', releasing a single, 'I'm Not Saying' (written by a young Gordon Lightfoot); an appearance on 'Ready Steady Go' achieved little. NICO subsequently moved to New York, where she met pop-artist Andy Warhol, who asked her to feature in an avant-garde film, 'Chelsea Girl', and ultimately to join LOU REED, John Cale, etc in his new group, the Velvet Underground. Together, the pairing made one glorious LP, 'The VELVET UNDERGROUND AND NICO' (and an accompanying cult movie); however, NICO left soon after for a return to solo work. Described as "The Edith Piaf of the Blank Generation", she was the epitome of the avant-garde songstress, anti-pop in every sense. After a liaison with Brian Jones of the ROLLING STONES, she became the opposite number of fresh-faced pensmith, Jackson Browne, who wrote a handful of songs for her debut 1968 album, 'Chelsea Girls'. Regarded as an artistic triumph, she nevertheless disagreed with producer Tom Wilson's string arrangements and subsequently moved to Los Angeles; her follow-up, 'The Marble Index', was issued soon afterwards. NICO travelled constantly between America and Europe, starring in many foreign-accent movies, including underground flicks, 'La Cicatrice Intérieure' for Philippe Garrel. Fleeing New York for France, after she was involved in a bottle fight with a female Black Panther member, NICO was to release an album for 'Island' records, 'The End', while she subsequently starred in 'Le BERCEAU DE CRISTAL' (1976). In 1981, she made a comeback album, appropriately titled 'Drama Of Exile', although afterwards she again went AWOL, shacking up in Manchester with her live-in boyfriend and comic/poet John Cooper Clarke. Tragically, on the 18th of July '88, while on a holiday in Ibiza with Clarke, she fell off her bike and subsequently died of a brain haemorrhage a few days later. *MCS*

- **filmography** {acting} (composer) –

la Tempesta *(1958 {b})* / For The First Time *(1959 {b})* / la Dolce Vita *(1960 {c})* / Un Nommé La Rocca *(1961 {a})* / Strip-Tease *(1963 {*})* / the Sandpiper *(1965 {b} OST by Johnny Mandel; see future edition)* / Chelsea Girls *(1966 {*c})* / **the Velvet Underground And Nico** *(1966 {*p} =>)* / the Closet *(1966 {*})* / I, A Man *(1967 {c})* / Imitation Of Christ *(1967 {*})* / Cleopatra *(1970 {a})* / la Cicatrice Intérieure *(1972 {*} score)* / les Hautes Solitudes *(1974 {*})* / Un Ange Passe *(1975 score {a})* / **le Berceau De Cristal** *(1976 {*})* / Voyage Au Jerdin Des Morts *(1978 {a})* / la Vraie Histoire De Gerard Lechomeur *(1979 {*} score w/ Stephen Potts, Khris Harpo, Pierre Clementi & Christian Escoude)* / le Bleu Des Origines *(1979 {*})* / Elle A Passé Tant D'Heures Sous Les Sunlights . . . *(1985 score)* / Ballhaus Barmbek *(1988 {*})* / **Nico Icon** *(1995 {p*} =>)*

NICO ICON

1995 (Ger/US 70m/67m) ZDF / Bluehorse Films

Film genre: avant-garde Rock-music documentary/biopic

Top guns: dir: (+ s-w) Susanne Ofteringer

Stars: NICO *(archive; herself/performer)*, Ari Boulogne *(himself)* ← the VELVET UNDERGROUND AND NICO, Tina Aumont *(herself)*, Edith Boulogne *(herself)*, **Jackson Browne** *(himself)* ← BLACK & WHITE NIGHT ← NO NUKES / → ENDLESS HARMONY: THE BEACH BOYS STORY → WALK HARD: THE DEWEY COX STORY, **John Cale** *(himself)* ← the VELVET UNDERGROUND AND NICO / → ROCK & ROLL HEART, **Lou REED** *(himself)*, Andy Warhol *(archive; himself)* ← BLANK GENERATION ← IMAGINE ← COCKSUCKER BLUES ← the VELVET UNDERGROUND AND NICO / → ROCK AND ROLL HEART → DETROIT ROCK CITY → END OF THE CENTURY, Danny Fields *(himself)* → END OF THE CENTURY → TOO TOUGH TO DIE: A TRIBUTE TO JOHNNY RAMONE, Viva *(herself)* ← PARIS, TEXAS ← FLASH GORDON ← FORBIDDEN ZONE, Jonas Mekas *(himself)* ← STEP ACROSS THE BORDER / → NINA HAGEN = PUNK + GLORY, Paul Morrissey *(himself)*, **Sterling Morrison** *(himself)* ← the VELVET UNDERGROUND AND NICO / → ROCK & ROLL HEART, Billy Name *(himself)* ← the VELVET UNDERGROUND AND NICO, Nico Papatakis *(himself)*, **James Young** *(performer w/ the Faction)*, **Jim Morrison** *(archive performer)* ← the DOORS ARE OPEN / → MAYOR OF THE SUNSET STRIP

Storyline: The oft tragic story of German chanteuse and supermodel/actress/ singer, Nico, told by way of film clips, songs, archival photos and interviews. *MCS*

Movie rating: *7

Visual: video + dvd (no audio OST; score: Larry Seymour)

Off the record: NICO songs featured in the film:- 'I'm Not Sayin', w/ the VELVET UNDERGROUND:- 'All Tomorrow's Parties' & 'Femme Fatale' & 'I'll Be Your Mirror' & 'I'm Waiting For The Man' & 'Venus In Furs', solo:- 'I'll Keep It With Mine', 'These Days', 'Ari's Song', 'Evening Of Light', 'Le Petit Chevalier', 'Afraid', 'Nibelungen', 'All That Is My Own', 'Vegas', 'Das Lied Der Deutschen', 'Saeta', 'Das Lied Vom Einsamen Maedchen' (w/ the FACTION), 'All Saint's Night' (w/ the FACTION), 'The End', 'Win A Few', 'Sixty-Forty', 'No One Is There', 'Reich Der Traume' (w/ LULL); JOHN CALE covered her 'Frozen Warnings'. The DOORS were seen performing (excerpts only of) 'Break On Through' and 'Light My Fire'. *MCS*

– associated release –

NICO: Nico – Icon *(recorded early 80s)*

Apr 96. (cd) *Cleopatra; <CLP 9709>* ☐ ☐
– Vegas / One more chance / The sphinx / Orly flight / Henry Hudson / Sixty-forty / Genghis Khan / Mutterlein / We've got the gold / Saeta / (29m interview w/ Nico).

a NIGHT AT THE FAMILY DOG

1970 (US 60m TV; cut from 145m!) PBS-TV

Film genre: Rock/Roots-music concert/documentary

Top guns: dir: Bob Zagone

Stars: Santana:- Carlos SANTANA, Greg Rolie, David Brown, Mike Carabello, Michael Shrieve, Jose "Chepito" Areas, Neal Schon *(performers)*, **the GRATEFUL DEAD:- Jerry Garcia, Bob Weir, Bill Kreutzmann, Phil Lesh, Mickey Hart, Ron "Pigpen McKernan** *(performers)*, **Jefferson Airplane:- Grace Slick *, Marty Balin, Jorma Kaukonen, Paul Kantner, Spencer Dryden, Jack Casady** *(performers)* ← GIMME SHELTER ← MONTEREY POP / → FILLMORE → JACKIE'S BACK! *

Storyline: Three legendary psychedelic rock outfits (Santana, the Grateful Dead and Jefferson Airplane) on one night at the Family Dog Ballroom, Haight-Ashbury, San Francisco, February 1970; first aired on US television in September 1970. *MCS*

Movie rating: *7

Visual: dvd (30122) – no audio OST

Off the record: Jefferson Airplane were still with Spencer Dryden at this stage, so the gig must've been in February 1970, not September as stated in many reviews. Track listings on the DVD:- SANTANA ('Incident At Neshabur' & 'Soul Sacrifice'), the GRATEFUL DEAD ('Hard To Handle', 'China Cat Sunflower' & 'I Know You Rider'), JEFFERSON AIRPLANE ('The Ballad Of You And Me And Pooneil' & 'Eskimo Blue Day') and all 3 bands featured on 'A Super Jam'. *MCS*

NINA HAGEN = PUNK + GLORY

1999 (Ger 102m w/b&w) BlackSUN Flower Filmproduction

Film genre: New Wave/Punk rock-music documentary

Top guns: dir: Peter Sempel → LEMMY / s-w: Tamara Goldworthy

Stars: Nina Hagen *(herself/performer)* ← ROCK'N'ROLL JUNKIE ← CHA-CHA, **Herman Brood** *(himself)* ← ROCK'N'ROLL JUNKIE ← CHA-CHA, **LEMMY** *(himself)*, Wim Wenders *(himself)* ← I PLAYED IT FOR YOU, **Dee Dee Ramone** *(himself)* <= RAMONES =>, **Blixa Bargeld** *(himself)* ← the ROAD TO GOD KNOWS WHERE ← 1/2 MENSCH, **George Clinton** *(himself)* ← MACEO ← GRAFFITI BRIDGE ← HOUSE PARTY, **Anthony Kiedis** *(himself)* <= the RED HOT CHILI PEPPERS =>, Jonas Mekas *(himself)* ← NICO ICON ← STEP ACROSS THE BORDER, **Thomas D** *(himself)*, Udo Kier *(himself)* ← the END OF VIOLENCE ← EVEN COWGIRLS GET THE BLUES ← SUSPIRIA / → DANCER IN THE DARK → PIGS WILL FLY → 30 DAYS UNTIL I'M FAMOUS, **Udo Lindenberg** *(himself)* ← PANISCHE ZEITEN, **Nam June Paik** *(himself)*

Storyline: Flamboyant German punk goddess, Nina Hagen, gets the star treatment: interviews with her and her family, overviews and rare live concert footage, make up quite a wholesome – but weird – package. *MCS*

Movie rating: *6

Visual: video (no audio OST)

Off the record: NINA HAGEN (b. Katherina Hagen, 11 Mar'55, East Berlin, East Germany. Inspired by her subsequent experience of the burgeoning London punk scene in 1976 (where she met the Slits), Nina formed her own posse of German musicians and proceeded to record an eponymous debut band album in '78. Despite the record's sizeable success on the continent, Hagen chose to temporarily neglect her budding musical career and instead moved to the Netherlands where she struck up a friendship with Herman Brood and Lene Lovich, both of whom appeared with her in the late 70s cult movie, 'CHA-CHA'. The Lovich connection ultimately proved fairly profitable as Hagen recycled her UK smash, 'Lucky Number' (having already tackled the Tubes' 'White Punks On Dope' – aka 'TV Glotzer' – on her debut) for German then American fans. A contract filling second album, 'Uunbehagen' (1980), was all the rage in her German homeland, while Austrians also developed a taste for her after allegedly witnessing the singer's simulated masturbation on TV. Having relocated to Los Angeles, she released her esoteric third set, 'NunSexMonkRock' (1982), a US Top 200 record inspired by an apparent sighting of a UFO; Hagen's newfound mysticism coincided with her decision to "sing" in English, the result being a banshee howl compared by many to a more extreme Yoko Ono. For her next project, the 1984 Giorgio Moroder & Keith Forsey-produced set, 'Fearless', Hagen moved into electro-dance territory, even roping in the fledgling RED HOT CHILI PEPPERS on the track, 'What It Is'. Hagen subsequently fused her newfound dance leanings with metal-punk, although the choice of cover material – including a punk version of Sinatra's 'My Way' – on 'In Ekstasy' (1985), suggested Nina was running out of ideas. She reunited with her old friend, Lovich on a one-off single in '87, 'Don't Kill The Animals', while the same year saw her controversially marry one of her teenage fans (Frank Chevallier). It would be 1989 before the release of another Hagen long-player, the virtually ignored eponymous 'Mercury' set being followed a few years later by 'Street' (1991); she would later star in the German musical, 'Vasilisa' (2004). Others on parade:- **Thomas D** (b. Thomas Durr, 30 Dec'68, Stuttgart) had released a solo album, called er . . . 'Solo Album' (1997) and subsequently became leader of Son Goku (one set, 'Crashkurs' 2005); he's acted in a few German movies: 'Curiosity & The Cat' (1999) and er . . . 'Soloalbum' (2003). **Udo Lindenberg** (b.17 May'46, Gronau, Germany) was the drummer with jazz-rock outfit, Passport, before becoming a singer and fully-fledged film composer. **Nam June Paik** (b.20 Jul'32, Keijo, Japan; i.e. Seoul, S.Korea – died Miami Beach, Florida, 29 Jan'06) was a celebrated avant-garde/experimental artist who has worked with (and infamously cut up the clothes of) John Cage and pianist David Tudor. *MCS*

– associated compilation –

NINA HAGEN: The Very Best Of..

Dec 00. (cd) *Sony; <467339-2>* [–] German [–]
– TV-Glotzer (White punks on dope) / Superboy / African reggae / Universelles radio / Unbeschreivilich / Smack Jack / Auf'm Bahnof zoo / Dread love / Auf'm Rummel / New York/N.Y. / Wir leben noch (Lucky number) / The change / My way / Heiss / Gott im Himmel (Spirit in the sky) / Zarah (ich weiss, es wird einmal ein wunder geschehn).

1991: THE YEAR PUNK BROKE

1992 (US 99m) We Got Power / Tara Releasing / Geffen Pictures

Film genre: Avant/Punk-Rock music documentary

Top guns: dir: **Dave MARKEY**

Stars: SONIC YOUTH:- Thurston Moore, Kim Gordon, Lee Ranaldo, Steve Shelley *(themselves/performers)* / **Nirvana:- Kurt Cobain** *(performer)* → KURT & COURTNEY → KURT COBAIN ABOUT A SON, **Dave Grohl** *(performer)* → TOUCH → FREE TIBET → the PICK OF DESTINY, **Chris Novoselic** *(performer)* → KURT & COURTNEY / **Babes In Toyland:- Kat Bjelland** *, **Lori Barbero** *, **Michelle Leon** *(performers)* → S.F.W. * → NOT BAD FOR A GIRL * / **Mudhoney:- Mark Arm** *, **Matt Lukin, Dan Peters** *(performers)* → HYPE! * → AMERICAN HARDCORE * / **Dinosaur Jr.:- J. Mascis** *, **Mike Johnson, Murph** *(performers)* → GAS, FOOD LODGING → GRACE OF MY HEART → THINGS BEHIND THE SUN / **Gumball:- Don Fleming** *, **Eric Vermillion** *(performers)* → BACKBEAT * / **Jay Spiegel** *(performer)*, **RAMONES:- Joey, Johnny, Dee Dee, Marky** *(performers)*, **Bob Mould** *(performer)*, **Courtney LOVE** *(performer)*, Joe Cole *(himself)* ← SIR DRONE ← REALITY 86'D

Storyline: Life on the road with America's biggest "underground" band, Sonic Youth (supporting Nirvana), as told by musician/filmmaker, Dave Markey. Grunge bands also provide the backdrop to that particular groundbreaking year of 1991. *MCS*

Movie rating: *7

Visual: video + dvd (no audio OST by SONIC YOUTH)

Off the record: SONIC YOUTH tracks include 'Teenage Riot', 'Brother James', 'I Love Her All The Time', 'Schizophrenia' & 'Expressway To Yr Skull'; others stem from **Babes In Toyland**, ex-Husker Du leader **Bob Mould**, etc. *MCS*

NO DIRECTION HOME

aka BOB DYLAN: NO DIRECTION HOME

2005 (UK/US 201m in 2 pts TV) Emerging Pictures / B.B.C.

Film genre: Roots/Folk/Rock-music documentary

Top guns: dir: Martin Scorsese ← FEEL LIKE GOING HOME ← the LAST TEMPTATION OF CHRIST ← the LAST WALTZ

Archive footage clips: Bob DYLAN *(performer)*, **Woody Guthrie** *(performer)* ← FREEDOM HIGHWAY ← HARD TRAVELIN', **Hank Williams** *(performer)*, **Muddy Waters** *(performer)*, **Johnnie Ray** *(performer)*, **Bobby Vee** *(performer)*, **Gene Vincent & The Blue Caps** *(performers)* ← BLUE SUEDE SHOES ← LIVE IT UP ← IT'S TRAD, DAD! ← HOT ROD GANG ← the GIRL CAN'T HELP IT, **Odetta** *(performer)* ← BLUES DIVAS ← LIGHTNING IN A BOTTLE ← the BALLAD OF RAMBLIN' JACK ← CHORDS OF FAME ← FESTIVAL, **Joan BAEZ** *(herself)*, **the Clancy Brothers, Maria Muldaur, the New Lost City Ramblers, Brother John Sellers, Peter LaFarge, Cisco Houston, Harry Belafonte, Billie Holiday, Pete Seeger, Lawrence Ferlinghetti, Peter, Paul & Mary** *(+ see below)*, **Lead Belly, the Weavers, Johnny CASH, Howlin' Wolf, the STAPLE SINGERS, the Byrds, Mike Bloomfield, the BAND**, etc. / Martin Scorsese *(interviewer)* ← the LAST WALTZ, Interviews: **Bob DYLAN, Liam Clancy**, Allen Ginsberg ← MY GENERATION ← RENALDO AND CLARA ← TEN FOR TWO ← TONITE LET'S ALL MAKE LOVE IN LONDON ← DON'T LOOK BACK ← CHAPPAQUA, **Dave Van Ronk** *(himself)* ← the BALLAD OF RAMBLIN' JACK ← CHORDS OF FAME, **Maria Muldaur, John Cohen, Bruce Langhorne, Harold Leventhal** *(himself)* ← the BALLAD OF RAMBLIN' JACK, **Mark Spoelstra**, Ruze Rotolo, Izzy Young, D.A. Pennebaker *(himself)* ← the BALLAD OF RAMBLIN' JACK, **Pete SEEGER** *(interviewee)*, **Mavis Staples** *(herself)* <= STAPLE SINGERS =>, **Joan BAEZ** *(herself)*, **Peter Yarrow** *(himself)* ← YOU ARE WHAT YOU EAT ← FESTIVAL, **Carolyn Hester** *(herself)* ← JANIS JOPLIN SLEPT HERE, Tony Glover, **Bobby Neuwirth** *(himself)* ← SLAVES TO THE UNDERGROUND ← RENALDO AND CLARA ← DON'T LOOK BACK, **Al Kooper, Paul Nelson, Mickey Jones**

Storyline: Martin Scorsese on Dylan, and almost as celebrated as the man's first volume of autobiography. Opinions are canvassed from across the spectrum, daubing lurid splashes of controversy on a roughly chronological, largely monochrome portrait of a life less ordinary. Impossibly sharp and skinny, the young Dylan wrenches out words like he's pulling nails, performing at Newport with the voice of a yodelling hag. He delivers a typically askant acceptance speech after receiving an award from the Civil Liberties Union, but it's difficult not to feel for him as he faces press conference after press conference with a combination of insouciance, humour and exasperation, turning back ridiculous questions on journalists fool enough to ask them. If it's not hacks, it's hysterical luddites/idealogues/speccy teenage girls ("he's a fake neurotic!"; "paid to see a flippin' folk singer!") berating him for daring to plug in his guitar. Scorsese cuts in a much older Dylan who disowns "jingly-jangly folk-rock", remembers Mike Bloomfield as "the best guitar player I ever heard" and, on the subject of Joan Baez, says "you can't be wise and in love at the same time" (for her part, Baez describes him as "one of the most complex human beings I've ever met"). There's a rare glimpse of Bruce Langhorne saying his piece, and some great footage of Bob and Johnny Cash at the piano, but perhaps the most fascinating reminiscences come from Beat poet Allen Ginsberg, who views Dylan as "a shaman", "focused into a single breath", yet who can also remember the young Dylan, Lennon et al in a London hotel room as "unsure of their mind and speech". After a premiere at a London theatre (for press), the two parts were shown on BBC2's Arena series on 26th/27th of Sept, 2005. *BG*

Movie rating: *8.5

Visual: dvd

Off the record: (see below)

—

BOB DYLAN: No Direction Home – The Bootleg Series Vol.7

Sep 05. (d-cd) *Sony; (520358-2) Columbia; <93937-2>* 21 16
– When I got troubles / Rambler, gambler (demo) / This land is your land (live) / Song to Woody / Dink's song (demo) / I was young when I left home (demo) / Sally gal (alt. take) / Don't think twice, it's alright (demo) / Man of constant sorrow / Blowin' in the wind (live) / Masters of war (live) / A hard rain's a-gonna fall (live) / When the ship comes in (live) / Mr. Tambourine man (alt. take) / Chimes of freedom (live) / It's all over now, baby blue (alt. take) // She belongs to me (alt. take) / Maggie's farm (live) / It takes a lot to laugh, it takes a train to cry (alt. take) / Tombstone blues (alt. take) / Just like Tom Thumb's blues (alt. take) / Desolation row (alt. take) / Highway 61 revisited (alt. take) / Leopard-skin pill-box hat (alt. take) / Stuck inside of Mobile with the Memphis blues again (alt. take) / Visions of Johanna (alt. take) / Ballad of a thin man (live) / Like a rolling stone (live).

S/track review: While the first seams of NEIL YOUNG's reputedly huge archive are only just beginning to be mined, it's getting on for a decade since the launch of BOB DYLAN's 'Bootleg Series'. An insatiable appetite for completist booty – or "unearthly unearthings" as AL KOOPER puts it – means these kind of releases are now major label bread and butter, as high – if not higher – profile as albums of newly recorded material. 'Vol.7' trumpets itself as the soundtrack tie-in to Martin Scorsese's documentary; as the sleeve proviso makes clear, though, the versions heard in the film are just "a reference point"; a simple greatest hits package was hardly going to count as "Bootleg". What we get instead is a more intensely chronological version of 'Vols.1-3', covering a finite area of DYLAN's career in sonic-archaeological detail, with an Original Hipster intro from Andrew Loog Oldham (all the way from the rock'n'roll postcode of Bogotá, Columbia, no less) and insider anecdote from chief organ grinder KOOPER. In some ways it's more of a companion piece to DYLAN's acclaimed autobiography, excavating arcane fragments most fans never knew they needed. Until now. Could that really be him singing in such cherubic tones on a no-fidelity blues from 1959? The difference between that voice and the following track – from August 1960 – is striking, a 45 degree trajectory DYLAN traced through to the late 60s. The first disc tracks it up to mid-decade, mapping his nasal take on home recorded Americana, unearthing concert x-rays of the visions it begat. In the loose vowels, bulging phrasing and aggravated intimacy of both 'Dink's Song' and 'I Was Young When I Left Home' – two tracks previously bootlegged as the 'Minnesota Hotel Tapes' (and here direct from Tony Glover's master tape for the first time) – DYLAN's latent influence on alt-country has rarely been clearer. The restatements of both Woody Guthrie's 'This Land Is Your Land' and his own 'Blowin' In The Wind' are the most plain spoken, non-rousing versions you're ever likely to hear, the first finished take of 'Mr Tambourine Man' has Ramblin' Jack Elliot raggedly trailing the famous chorus, and, on the 1964 Newport rendition of 'Chimes Of Freedom', DYLAN sounds like a mad-eyed folk muezzin, a year before his call to electric prayer was booed at the same festival. Disc two takes that negative charge and runs with it through the most manic spasm of creativity in his whole career, from the moment DYLAN's hastily assembled band followed Cousin Emmy (who?) on the Newport bill with a raucous, fully plugged 'Maggie's Farm', to the infamous 'Like A Rolling Stone' at Manchester's Free Trade Hall. In between, a succession of alternate takes analyse the anatomy of a miracle. A percussion-free, BRUCE LANGHORNE-coddled 'She Belongs To Me', an early, shuffle-shoe incarnation of 'Just Like Tom Thumb's Blues' and a 'Leopard-Skin Pill-Box Hat' as unreconstructed blues, show it wasn't all thin wild mercury, but DYLAN and his co-conspirators howl at the soundboard on bass-heavy, MIKE BLOOMFIELD-broiled versions of 'Tombstone Blues' and 'It Takes A Lot To Laugh, It Takes A Train To Cry', as well as a cowbell clanking 'Visions Of Johanna'. And Scottish fans of a certain vintage will doubtless come over all misty eyed at a GARTH HUDSON-embroidered 'Ballad Of A Thin Man', live from Edinburgh's long-gone ABC; the sound's way distorted but the atmosphere's heavy, a thick wild lead about as far from home as DYLAN went. *BG*

Album rating: *8.5

NO NUKES

1980 (US 93m) Warner Brothers

Film genre: Roots/Rock-music concert/documentary

Top guns: dir: Daniel Goldberg, Anthony Potenza, Julian Schlossberg

Stars: Jackson Browne *(performer)* → BLACK & WHITE NIGHT → NICO ICON → ENDLESS HARMONY: THE BEACH BOYS STORY → WALK HARD: THE DEWEY COX STORY, **CROSBY, STILLS, NASH & YOUNG** *(performers)*, **the Doobie Brothers** *(performers)*, **Bonnie RAITT** *(performer)*, **Carly SIMON** *(performer)*, **Bruce SPRINGSTEEN** *(performer)*, **James Taylor** *(performer)*, **Poco** *(performers)*, **Ry COODER** *(performer)*, **Nicolette Larson** *(performer)*, **Sweet Honey In The Rock** *(performers)*, **Raydio** *(performers)*, **Chaka Khan** *(performer)*, **Tom Petty & The Heartbreakers** *(performers)*, **Gil Scott-Heron** *(performer)* → COOL RUNNINGS: THE REGGAE MOVIE, **Jesse Colin Young** *(performer)*, **John Hall** *(performer)*, **Rosemary Butler** *(performer)*, Jane Fonda *(herself)*

Storyline: The great and good of 70s American rock make a politicised last stand under the banner of MUSE (Musicians United for Safe Energy), filmed over a series of gigs at New York's Madison Square Garden. *BG*

Movie rating: *6

Visual: video

Off the record: (see below)

—

Various Artists

Dec 79. (t-lp) *Asylum; <(ML 801)>* 19 May80
– Dependin' on you (the DOOBIE BROTHERS) / Runaway (BONNIE RAITT) / Angel from Montgomery (BONNIE RAITT) / Plutonium is forever (JOHN HALL) / Power (the DOOBIE BROTHERS with JOHN HALL & JAMES TAYLOR) / The times they are a-changin' (JAMES TAYLOR, CARLY SIMON & GRAHAM NASH) / Cathedral (GRAHAM NASH) / The crow on the cradle (JACKSON BROWNE & GRAHAM NASH) / Before the deluge (JACKSON BROWNE) / Lotta love (NICOLETTE LARSON & the DOOBIE BROTHERS) / Little sister (RY COODER) / A woman (SWEET HONEY IN THE ROCK) / We almost lost Detroit (GIL SCOTT-HERON) / Get together (JESSE COLIN YOUNG) // You can't change that (RAYDIO) / Once you get started (CHAKA KHAN) / Captain Jim's drunken dream (JAMES TAYLOR) / Honey don't leave L.A. (JAMES TAYLOR) / Mockingbird (JAMES TAYLOR & CARLY SIMON) / Heart of the night (POCO) / Cry to me (TOM PETTY AND THE HEARTBREAKERS) / Stay (BRUCE SPRINGSTEEN, JACKSON BROWNE & THE E-STREET BAND with ROSEMARY BUTLER) / Devil with the blue dress medley: Devil with the blue dress – Good golly, Miss Molly – Jenny take a ride

(BRUCE SPRINGSTEEN & THE E-STREET BAND) / You don't have to cry (CROSBY, STILLS & NASH) / Long time gone (CROSBY, STILLS & NASH) / Teach your children (CROSBY, STILLS & NASH) / Takin' it to the streets (the DOOBIE BROTHERS with JAMES TAYLOR). *<d-cd iss.Oct97 on 'Elektra'; 6059-2>*

S/track review: Some ten years after this album was re-issued on CD, two decades after Chernobyl and almost three decades after the original concert, the powers that be are once again sanctioning nuclear power; this time, ironically, as the answer to global warming. Not that this has spurred a younger generation of musicians into action, or even much protest. The idea of a united front on an issue as controversial (and, with global warming hogging the headlines, as relatively far down the agenda) as nuclear power is almost unthinkable in these strangest of days; even the recent 'Live Earth' concerts were received with a healthy dose of cynicism. Back in 1979, the same hippies who invented the idea of a benefit gig in the first place came together to assert their fading influence on what was then a hot topic; a lapel wasn't a lapel without a little red solar-smiley "Nuclear Power, No Thanks" badge. Even the punks agreed. And even if this terminally unfashionable aggregate of soft-rockers and Laurel Canyonites make their point with peace and harmonies rather than attitude, power chords or 'Live Aid' pizazz, they can still teach us a thing or two. Or at least the sleevenotes can, chock-full as they are with unsettling facts and reportage (as well as a certain amount of precariously earnest – and satire-ripe – quotes), much of which – in these carbon-counting times – seems to have fallen off the radar. But what about the music? As an end-of-an-era love-in, 'NO NUKES' is a pale shadow of 'The LAST WALTZ' but at least it's for a good cause and – with the likes of TOM PETTY, BRUCE SPRINGSTEEN and SWEET HONEY IN THE ROCK on board – it at least makes a token attempt to include some (relatively) new, stylistically diverse blood. GIL SCOTT-HERON is the unlikeliest and most welcome inclusion, a veteran of the anti-nuclear cause and the only artist to come ready armed with a piece of urbane, anti-nuke songwriting ("When it comes to people's safety money really wins out every time" pretty much says it all). Orleans founder/activist-turned-Congressman JOHN HALL croons his own kitschy – intentionally or otherwise – riposte to the nuclear industry with 'Plutonium Is Forever'. Introduced as "sort of a Caribbean no-nukes song", it's more fun than 'Power', the track he supplies and performs with the DOOBIE BROTHERS and JAMES TAYLOR, the kind of parody-hungry, cheesecloth session-rock that gave the new wave more of an excuse than it deserved, and which too often makes this soundtrack a back-slapping snoozeathon. Bob Dylan isn't here but 'The Times They Are A-Changin'' gets needlessly dragged out anyhow, painfully out of context given that the cultural times were surely a-changin', but definitely not in the favour of POCO, JACKSON BROWNE, CROSBY, STILLS & NASH et al. 'Honey Don't Leave L.A.' just about sums it up, even if the arrangements rock harder than almost any other performance. If you're even still awake by mid-disc 2, SPRINGSTEEN and his E STREET BAND's 'Devil With The Blue Dress Medley' will stir you out of certain lethargy, a fiery performance which still ranks with his best live work. If the commitment and solidarity of 'NO NUKES' is unrealistic today, 21st century musos might at least beware of its middle-aged spread. *BG*

Album rating: *5.5

the NOMI SONG

2004 (Ger 96m) CV Films / Filmstiftung Nordrhein-Westfalen

Film genre: avant-Pop-music documentary bio-pic

Top guns: dir (+ s-w): Andrew Horn

Stars: **Klaus Nomi** *(archive footage)* ← URGH! A MUSIC WAR, **Ann Magnuson** *(herself)* ← GLITTER, David McDermott *(himself)* ← DOWNTOWN 81, Page Wood *(himself)*, Gabriele Le Fari *(herself)*, **Man Parrish** *(himself)*, Tony Frere *(himself)*, **Kristian Hoffman** *(himself)* ← DOWNTOWN 81 ← the OFFENDERS, Kenny Scharf *(himself)*, **Jon Cobert** *(pianist Nomi Band)* ← IMAGINE: JOHN LENNON ← URGH! A MUSIC WAR, **Jay Jay French** *(himself)*, **David BOWIE** *(archive footage)*

Storyline: A documentary about the weird and wonderful opera-turned-pop singer, Klaus Nomi, and the people around him (see below). *MCS*

Movie rating: *6.5

Visual: dvd (no audio OST)

Off the record: **Klaus Nomi** (b. Klaus Sperber, 24 Jan'44, Immenstadt, Bavaria, Germany) was working as a pastry chef-cum-cabaret entertainer when he was discovered by DAVID BOWIE in 1975. Catapulted into the limelight as his backing singer in a spot on the Saturday Night Live show, NOMI also inked a deal with 'R.C.A.' records, who released a couple of LPs before his shock death of AIDS on 6th August, 1983. **Jon Cobert** (was the pianist in the Nomi band) **Ann Magnuson** (Bongwater), **Jay Jay French** (Twisted Sister), **Kristian Hoffman** (the Mumps). *MCS*

NOT BAD FOR A GIRL

1996 (US 90m) Horizon Unlimited / Spitshine

Film genre: Alt-Rock-music documentary

Top guns: dir: Lisa Rose Apramian

Stars: **L7:- Donita Sparks, Suzi Gardner, Dee Plakas, Jennifer Finch** * *(themselves/performers)* ← the CENSUS TAKER * / → BETTY BLOWTORCH AND HER AMAZING TRUE LIFE ADVENTURES *, **Babes In Toyland:- Kat Bjelland, Lori Barbero, Maureen Herman** *(themselves/performers)* ← S.F.W. ← 1991: THE YEAR PUNK BROKE, **Hole:- Courtney LOVE, Eric Erlandson, Jill Emery, Caroline Rue, Kristen Pfaff, Patty Schemel** *(themselves/performers)*, **Lunachicks:- Becky Wreck** *(performer/s)*, **Joan Jett** *(herself/performer)* <= the RUNAWAYS =>, **Mudwimmin:- Bambi Nonymous, Rachel Thoele** *(performer/s)*, **Silverfish:- Lesley Rankine** *(performer/s)*, **Bobsled:- Mia Ferraro** *(performer/s)*, **Bulimia Banquet** *(performers)*, **Calamity Jane** *(performers)*, **Chicken Milk** *(performers)*, **Choptank** *(performers)*, **Cheesecake** *(performers)*

Storyline: An analytical look back at females in the world of alternative/indie rock music (directed by psychotherapist, Dr. Lisa Rose Apramian), featuring social/political discussions and rare clips of top acts such as Joan Jett, Courtney Love and Babes In Toyland. *MCS*

Movie rating: *6

Visual: video + dvd (no audio OST)

Off the record: **L7** (look out for the group as Camel Lips in the 1994 movie, 'Serial Mom') contributed excerpts from tracks such as:- 'Fast And Frightening', '(Right On) Thru', 'Just Like Me', 'Broomstick', 'Shove', 'Freak Magnet', 'Till The Wheels Fall Off', 'Deathwish', 'Lost Cause', 'Packin' A Rod', 'Shitlist', 'Diet Pill', 'Wargasm', 'Slide', 'Pretend We're Dead', 'Monster', 'Scrap', 'Everglade', 'I Wanna Be Your Dog' & 'Bad Reputation' (the latter two w/ JOAN JETT); Other tracks stemmed from BABES IN TOYLAND:- 'Right Now', 'Spun', 'Mother', 'Real Eyes', 'Blood', 'Jungle Train', 'Swamp Pussy', 'He's My Thing', 'Ripe' & 'Catatonic'; HOLE:- 'Retard Girl', 'Baby Doll', 'Dicknail', 'Berry', 'Garbage Man', 'Drown Soda', 'Mrs. Jones', 'Pretty On The Inside', 'Beautiful Son', 'She Walks', 'Violet', 'Doll Parts' & 'Rock Star'; LUNACHICKS:- 'This Is Serious', 'Plugg', 'C.H.I.L.L.', 'Mom', '11', '2 Bad 4 U', 'Spoilt', 'Superstrong', 'Rip U' & 'Apathetic'; MUDWIMMIN:- 'Bodies', 'Cloud Rodeo', 'R-U Sleeping', 'Love Anthem', 'Have A Good Time' & 'Wild Bill'; SILVERFISH:- 'Die', 'Fat Painted Carcass' & 'Big Bad Baby Pig Squeal'; BOBSLED:- 'Puff The Starfish' & 'Latina'; BULIMIA BANQUET:- 'Loadhead Destructor'; CALAMITY JANE:- 'Magdalena'; other songs from Various include 'Male Figure Motherfucker', 'Elvis Costello Has No Soul', 'Clock', 'Before My Eyes', 'Girly Girl', 'Still Killing Us Softly', 'Quiet Room', etc. *MCS*

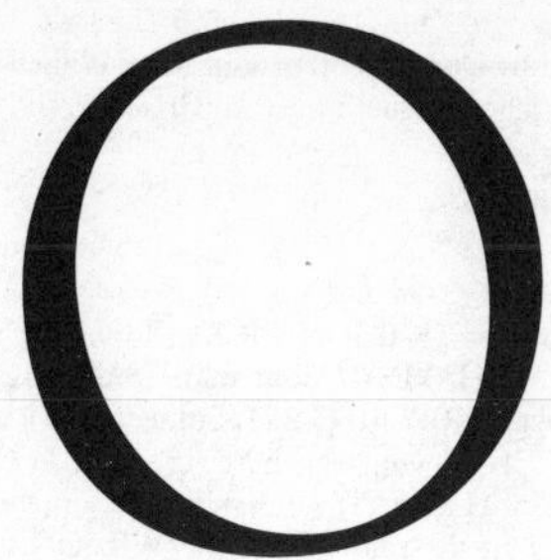

□ Phil OCHS segment (⇒ CHORDS OF FAME)

□ Kongar-ol ONDAR segment (⇒ GENGHIS BLUES)

ONE HAND CLAPPING

1974 (UK 55m; unreleased) MPL Communications

Film genre: Pop/Rock-music rehearsal/concert documentary

Top guns: dir: David Litchfield

Stars: **Paul McCartney** *(himself/performer)* <= the BEATLES =>, **Linda McCartney** *(herself/performer)* ← LET IT BE / → SGT. PEPPER'S LONELY HEARTS CLUB BAND → ROCKSHOW → CONCERTS FOR THE PEOPLE OF KAMPUCHEA → GIVE MY REGARDS TO BROAD STREET → GET BACK, **Denny Laine** *(himself/performer)* → ROCKSHOW → CONCERTS FOR THE PEOPLE OF KAMPUCHEA, **Jimmy McCulloch** *(himself/performer)* → ROCKSHOW, **Geoff Britton** *(himself/performer)*

Storyline: Paul McCartney, his wife Linda and his band, Wings, are all happily rehearsing in a studio, apparently unaware we might watch this film one day. *MCS*

Movie rating: *?

Visual: (see below CD-ROM)

Off the record: Scotsman **Jimmy McCulloch** had been an integral part of Thunderclap Newman when they hit the charts with 'Something In The Air'; sadly he subsequently died of a drug overdose on 27th of September, 1999. *MCS*

—

PAUL McCARTNEY & WINGS

1985. (d-lp) *Ur-anus and Nep-tune; <YEAH 7475>* [–] bootleg [–]
– One hand clapping / Jet / Soily / Little woman love – C moon / Let me roll it / Wild life / Jet / Soily / My love / Nineteen hundred and eighty five / Live and let die // Hi hi hi / Go now / Maybe I'm amazed / Bluebird / Junior's farm / Band on the run / Bluebird / I've just seen a face / Blackbird / Yesterday / Hi hi hi.

S/track review: If it was hard enough finding the unreleased film – unless of course you know Sir Paul and his Wings – then 'ONE HAND CLAPPING: music from the film of the same name' double-album bootleg was like finding the Holy Grail. Recorded at EMI Studios on August 16, 1974, PAUL McCARTNEY & WINGS (with newcomers to the fold, JIMMY McCULLOCH and GEOFF BRITTON) basically rehearse in Nashville (summer 1974) for the first three sides, while side 4 features excerpts of 'Band On The Run' and 'Yesterday' from the Melbourne, Australian leg of their 'Wings Over The World' tour in November 1975 (JOE ENGLISH was now on drums). Highlights on the aforementioned sides 1 to 3 included hits such as 'Jet', 'My Love', 'Live And Let Die' and a version of the old Moody Blues (featuring DENNY LAINE) chart-topper, 'Go Now'. In 2001, a CD-ROM version was issued by Apple records (unsure if it's genuine or a mock bootleg) and this saw several variations in the track listings; one was the notable cover of standard, 'Baby Face', as the group's finale. *MCS*

Album rating: *4

– spinoff releases, etc.

PAUL McCARTNEY: One Hand Clapping

2001. (cd-rom) *Apple; (ROM 74)* [–] video [–]
– One hand clapping / Jet / Soily / Little woman love – C moon / Improvisation / Billy don't be a hero / Maybe I'm amazed / My love / Bluebird / Suicide / Let's love / Sitting at the piano / All of you / I'll give you a ring / Band on the run / Live and let die (orchestra rehearsal) / Live & let die / 1985 / Baby face.

101

aka DEPECHE MODE 101

1988 (US 117m) Mute Film / Westwood One Radio

Film genre: Industrial-Rock-music/concert documentary

Top guns: dir: D.A. Pennebaker ← ZIGGY STARDUST: THE MOTION PICTURE ← MONTEREY POP ← DON'T LOOK BACK / → DOWN FROM THE MOUNTAIN → ONLY THE STRONG SURVIVE, David Dawkins, Chris Hegedus → DOWN FROM THE MOUNTAIN → ONLY THE STRONG SURVIVE

Stars: Depeche Mode:- Martin Gore *(performer)*, **David Gahan** *(performer)*, **Andrew Fletcher** *(performer)*, **Alan Wilder** *(performer)* → TRUTH OR DARE + tour entourage

Storyline: Iconic pop-music filmmaker D.A. Pennebaker and assorted crew follow synth-rock band, Depeche Mode (setting up for a sell-out concert at Pasadena's Rose Bowl), while also intertwinning a handful of their enthusiastic fanbase who've won tickets to see them in California. *MCS*

Movie rating: *6

Visual: video + dvd

Off the record: Depeche Mode found more success after the movie. Albums such as 'Violator' (1990), the transatlantic chart-topper 'Songs Of Love And Devotion' (1993) and 'Ultra' (1997), all reached the Top 10 in both Britain and the States. *MCS*

—

DEPECHE MODE

Mar 89. (d-cd/d-c/d-lp) *Sire: <25853> Mute; (CD/C+/Stumm 101)* [45] [5]
– Pimpf / Behind the wheel / Strangelove / Sacred (*) / Something to do / Blasphemous rumours / Stripped / Somebody / Things you said // Black generation / Shake the disease / Nothing (*) / Pleasure little treasure / People are people / A question of time / Never let me down again / A question of lust (*) / Master and servant / Just can't get enough / Everything counts (*). *(extended versions:- c+=*/cd+=*)*

S/track review: Next to fellow stadium-fillers, U2 (they of 'RATTLE AND HUM' fame), DEPECHE MODE were the biggest overseas attractions to hit the shores of the US. Around 80,000 fans at the Rose Bowl in Pasadena on 18th June 1988 were proof of that historic claim. With a string of consistently excellent studio albums behind them since 1981 (namely 'Speak & Spell', 'A Broken Frame', 'Construction Time Again', 'Some Great Reward', 'Black Celebration' & 'Music For The Masses'), messrs DAVID GAHAN, MARTIN GORE, ANDREW FLETCHER and ALAN WILDER broke the "rock" mould for many electro-pop outfits. Trademark anthem 'Pimpf' opened the show with dramatic, even filmatic aplomb, while 'Behind The Wheel' (a little John Barry-esque with added rpm) was one of many tried and tested hits. The rest of the songs on this exhaustive 20-track double-CD, were electro-pop classics, marred at times by screaming girlies intent on pinching the limelight from their boy-ish idols. A slightly below par "disc A" saw the band only peak a few times courtesy of 'Blasphemous Rumours' and 'Stripped', while main songwriter MARTIN GORE took his turn on vox via the melancholy 'Somebody' and the more upbeat, 'Things You Said'. In a video age (when it had indeed killed the radio star!), live records without the enhancement of the big screen (or VHS), were always going to be mediocre fare; luckily for the art of memory or this would have been complete DE-pish (er ... sorry). "Disc B" is somewhat better than its predecessor, the unrecognisable intro on 'People Are People', keeping the crowd quiet for a minute, while 'Shake The Disease' is just simply great pop. The more disterning listener could've done with a lot less techno-fied "Whey-Heys" from GORE and the boys, but then again, it was just that time when rave was kicking off. Saving the best for last, a trio of yuppie-baiting hits ('Master And Servant', 'Just Can't Get Enough' & a revamped new hit version of 'Everything Counts') end the show. "The Rich Man's Erasure", DEPECHE MODE showed they were a great live band – so watch the movie! *MCS*

Album rating: *5.5

– spinoff hits, etc. –

DEPECHE MODE: Everything Counts / Nothing

Feb 89. (7") *<40296> (7BONG 16)* ☐ 22
(12"+=/cd-s+=) *(12/CD BONG 16)* – Sacred / A question of lust.
(remix-cd-s) *(CDLBONG 16)* – Strangelove (remix).
(3"cd-s) *(LCDBONG 16)* – ('A'-Tim Simenon & M. Saunders) / ('B'-Justin Strauss remix) / Strangelove (Tim Simenon & M. Saunders remix).
(12") *(L12BONG 16)* – ('A'-Bomb The Bass) / ('B'-Hijack mix).
(10") *(10BONG 16)* – ('A'-Absolute & 1983 mix) / ('B'-US mix).

ONLY THE STRONG SURVIVE

2002 (US 96m) Pennebaker-Hegedus Films

Film genre: Blues-music concert/documentary

Top guns: dir: Chris Hegedus ← DOWN FROM THE MOUNTAIN ← 101, D.A. Pennebaker ← DOWN FROM THE MOUNTAIN ← 101 ← ZIGGY STARDUST: THE MOTION PICTURE ← MONTEREY POP ← DON'T LOOK BACK

Stars: Wilson Pickett *(performer)* ← BLUES ODYSSEY ← BLUES BROTHERS 2000 ← SGT. PEPPER'S LONELY HEARTS CLUB BAND ← SAVE THE CHILDREN ← SOUL TO SOUL, **Carla Thomas** *(performer)* ← WATTSTAX, **Sam Moore** *(performer)* ← BLUES BROTHERS 2000 ← TAPEHEADS ← ONE-TRICK PONY, **Jerry BUTLER** *(performer)*, **Mary Wilson** *(performer)*, **the Chi-Lites** *(performers)*, **Rufus Thomas** *(performer)* ← MYSTERY TRAIN ← GREAT BALLS OF FIRE! ← WATTSTAX / → the ROAD TO MEMPHIS, **Ann Peebles** *(performer)* → BLUES DIVAS, **Isaac HAYES** *(performer)*, **William Bell** *(performer)*, **Luther Ingram** *(performer)*, **Don Bryant** *(performer)*, Sir Mack Rice *(himself)*, Marshall Thompson *(performer)*, Jaye Michael Davis *(himself)*

Storyline: Following on from 'STANDING IN THE SHADOWS OF MOTOWN' (2002), this film rescues yet more pioneers from the crusty folds of oblivion and pays their dues on a Miramax-distributed stage. The film relies far less on documentary and much more on latter day performance, even if most of the renditions (Isaac Hayes' 'Theme From Shaft' among them) have been edited to fit more in. There's also enough hard knock grit to fill a quarry but it's Sam Moore (who subsequently helped bring the nostalgia ticket to the UK with all-star Soul Britannia gigs at London's Barbican) who recounts the bleakest tale, and whose soul survival is all the more compelling for it. *BG*

Movie rating: *6

Visual: dvd

Off the record: Ann Peebles (b.27 Apr'47, St. Louis, Missouri) will always be synonymous with her 1973 hit, 'I Can't Stand The Rain', a song incidentally written with her hubby Don Bryant, produced by Willie Mitchell and on the same label ('Hi') as fellow gospel singer, Al Green. *MCS*

—

Various Artists

May 03. (cd) *Koch; <KOC-CD 8655>* ☐ –
– Soul survivor (WILSON PICKETT) / Gee whiz (look at his eyes) (ISAAC HAYES) / Soul man (SAM MOORE) / For your precious love (JERRY BUTLER) / Someday we'll be together (MARY WILSON) / Have you seen her? (the CHI-LITES) / Walking the dog (RUFUS THOMAS) / Breaking up somebody's home (ANN PEEBLES) / In the midnight hour (WILSON PICKETT) / When something is wrong with my baby (SAM MOORE) / Night time is the right time (CARLA THOMAS) / Only the strong survive (JERRY BUTLER) / Don't let go (ISAAC HAYES).

S/track review: The DA Pennebaker-directed sense of occasion was never going to make it to disc wholly intact, and some of the arrangements might be too nostalgia-circuit-cluttered/polished for their own good, but there is history being made here rather than just recounted (see WILSON PICKETT's 'Soul Survivor'). Not least MARY WILSON reclaiming a Supremes classic ('Someday We'll Be Together') which Diana Ross originally recorded "behind Mary's back with two other singers"; ah, the golden age of pop chicanery. Whether it's the vindication, the memories or simply the fact she supplies the soul without the straining, Mary – along with JERRY BUTLER and ANN PEEBLES – goes a long way to justifying the whole project. BUTLER, for his part, is as ice cool and as coal-hot as he was at his post-Impressions peak; 'For Your Precious Love' rakes the spine with a voice that's embraced Old Father Time as confidante, while his Gamble & Huff-era classic supplies the film's title. ANN PEEBLES brings peerlessly-loaded Southern drama to the plight of the poor mistress in 'Breaking Up Somebody's Home' (check her late 70s nugget, 'You've Got The Papers (I've Got The Man)' for more of the same), and while he walks his dog to the point of exhaustion, at 82 it's an odds-slashing miracle to hear RUFUS THOMAS at all (he was to pass away a couple of years after these performances were recorded); his Louis Armstrong-esque scatting – like much of this soundtrack – is a joy, if not quite a substitute for the original vinyl. *BG*

Album rating: *6.5

Yoko ONO

Born: 18 Feb'33, Tokyo, Japan. Courting controversy even before the 'Two Virgins'/brown paper bag episode, one of YOKO ONO's first cinematic ventures (after appearing in b-movie, 'Satan's Bed') was the infamous 'Yoko Ono No.4' (1967), a monochrome study of bare bottoms that laughably managed to run afoul of British censors. Once she'd hooked up with JOHN LENNON, she was a fairly ubiquitous screen presence, making a memorably atonal, violin wielding appearance in the ROLLING STONES' 'ROCK AND ROLL CIRCUS' (1968), as well as cameos in cult satires, 'The MAGIC CHRISTIAN' (1969) and 'Dynamite Chicken' (1972). On a more serious note, her high profile creative and political collaborations with LENNON were amply documented in the likes of 'John Lennon And The Plastic Ono Band: Live Peace In Toronto, 1969', 'John Lennon And Yoko Ono: The Bed-In' (1969) and Jonas Mekas' 'Diaries, Notes And Sketches' (1970). So all-consuming was the zeitgeist that the pair's experimental feature, 'Rape' (1969), went under the radar, as did 'TEN FOR TWO' (1971), an ONO-produced documentary on activist John Sinclair shelved on legal reasons for almost two decades, the subject material of which informed a large part of excellent 2006 doc, 'The U.S. VS. JOHN LENNON'. Even more controversial was her presence in Michael Lindsay-Hogg's Oscar-winning BEATLES denouement, 'LET IT BE' (1970), with personal tensions infamously recorded for posterity. In the decades following LENNON's death, ONO featured prominently in both 'IMAGINE: JOHN LENNON' (1988) and Paul McGrath's 'John And Yoko: Give Peace A Song' (2005), and produced the Kevin Spacey-hosted 9/11 benefit, 'Come Together: A Night For John Lennon's Words And Music'. She also appeared in various art/film-related documentaries, notably Mekas tribute, 'Jonas In The Desert', alongside the likes of NICK CAVE, Kenneth Anger, Martin Scorsese and Al Pacino. *BG*

- **filmography** [writer + director] {performer} (composer)

Satan's Bed *(1965 {*})* / **Keep On Rockin' (1969 {p} =>)** / Honeymoon *(1969 {*} [s-w + dir])* / Diaries Notes And Sketches *(1969 {c})* / Rape *(1969 TV [s-w + dir])* / **Let It Be** *(1970 {c} OST by the BEATLES =>)* / Up Your Legs Forever *(1970 [dir])* / **Ten For Two** *(1971 {p} =>)* / Dynamite Chicken *(1972 {c})* / **Imagine** *(1972 {p} =>)* / Chelsea Girls With Andy Warhol *(1976 {c})* / **Imagine: John Lennon** *(1988 {*p} on OST w/ JOHN LENNON =>)* / the Misfits: 30 Years Of Fluxus *(1993 {c} score w/ Tom Cora)* / the Revenge Of The Dead Indians *(1993 {c})* / Jonas In The Desert *(1994 {c})* / **Rock And Roll Circus** *(1996 {p} on OST by the ROLLING STONES & V/A =>)* / Grass *(1999 {})* / **Hendrix** *(2000 TV {c} =>)* / Kiss My Grits: The Herstory Of Women In Punk And Hard Rock *(2001 {c})* / Imagine Imagine *(2003 {c})* / **Mayor Of The Sunset Strip** *(2003 {c} OST by V/A =>)* / **Who Is Harry Nilsson (And Why Is Everybody Talkin' About Him?)** *(2006 {c} =>)* / Follow My Voice: With The Music Of Hedwig *(2006 {c})* / **the U.S. vs. John Lennon** *(2006 {*c} on OST w/ JOHN LENNON =>)*

Roy ORBISON

Born: 23 Apr'36, Vernon, Texas, USA. After stints with local hillbilly groups, the Wink Westerners and the Teen Kings, ROY cut a solo single for the 'Jewel' label in 1955, before successfully auditioning for Sam Phillips' 'Sun' records. Written by two college friends, Wade Moore and Dick Penner, 'Ooby Dooby', gave him his first Top 60 hit in 1956. Subsequent 50s rockabilly/pop singles for 'Sun' and 'R.C.A.' all failed, and after moving to Nashville with his wife, ORBISON focused his attentions on songwriting. 'Claudette' (penned for his wife), was placed in the capable hands of the Everly Brothers who took the uptempo song into the US Top 30 (another, 'Distant Drums', was a massive hit for Jim Reeves, reaching No.1 after the man's untimely death in '66). In 1959, his solo career was re-activated when 'Monument' took over the reins, ORBISON embracing a more ballad-esque approach which highlighted his lyrical genius, dramatic falsetto voice and trademark tearful crescendos. It was an approach which was to make the country boy a bonafide star; the following year, 'Only The Lonely' was the first of many million sellers throughout the early to mid sixties period. Classic after classic saw Roy O become a regular chart fixture, the likes of 'Running Scared', 'Crying', 'Dream Baby', 'In Dreams', 'Blue Bayou', 'It's Over' and 'Oh Pretty Woman' transcending the era, while his contemporaries sounded somewhat dated. His ubiquitous dark glasses were initially worn in 1963 after his regular spectacles were misplaced on a plane. In November '64, at the height of his success, ORBISON divorced Claudette due to her infidelity. Reconciled, they remarried in August '65, although tragedy struck ten months later when she was killed as her motorcycle hit a truck. In 1967, Roy embarked on a short-lived acting career, his initial movie experience, 'The FASTEST GUITAR ALIVE' (1968), doing poorly at the box-office. Nevertheless his solo career was still flourishing, especially in the UK, where his more countrified material was going down reasonably well. However, another tragedy befell him on the 14th of September '68; while on tour, ORBISON's house caught fire, killing his two oldest sons, Roy Jr and Tony. Understandably, perhaps, he semi-retired in 1970 to Bielefeld, Germany with his remaining son and new German-born wife, Barbara Wellhonen; together they reared another son, Roy Kelton. ORBISON's recording career went through a minor comeback (i.e. a cameo in the film 1980, 'ROADIE') before he sued Wesley Rose (head of 'Monument') for $50m in backdated royalties. In 1987, his career finally got back on track as he signed to 'Virgin' records, while making new inroads into world popularity. The following year, he joined the Traveling Wilburys, alongside other superstars, BOB DYLAN, GEORGE HARRISON, Jeff Lynne and TOM PETTY. The team's 'Volume 1' album became a US Top 3 and UK Top 20 later in the year. Tragically, Roy was to die of a heart attack on the 6th of December. The legend had just completed a tremendous comeback album, 'Mystery Girl', which posthumously peaked in the British and American Top 5 (would've anyway!). One of the record's highlights, 'You Got It', gave the man his first entry into the US Top 10 for nearly 25 years. His 1987 concert, 'BLACK & WHITE NIGHT' (released in '88), featured guest appearances by the cream of the roots-rock aristocracy including k.d. LANG (on a duet of 'CRYING' which also became a UK Top 10 hit). *BG & MCS*

- **filmography** {acting} (composer) –

the Fastest Guitar Alive *(1968 {*} OST by ORBISON =>)* / **Roadie** *(1980 {c} on OST by V/A =>)* / **Hail! Hail! Rock'n'Roll** *(1987 {p} OST by CHUCK BERRY =>)* / She's Having A Baby *(1988 {c})* / **Black & White Night** *(1988 TV (*p} OST by ORBISON & friends =>)* / In Dreams: The Roy Orbison Story *(1999 TV {*p} =>)* / Lubbock Lights *(2003 {p} =>)*

OUR LATIN THING

(NUESTRA COSA)

1972 (US 83m) A&R Studios New York

Film genre: Salsa-music documentary/concert

Top guns: dir: Leon Gast

Stars: **Johnny Pacheco** *(md + flute)*, **Ray Barretto** *(congas)*, **Larry Harlow** *(piano)*, **Roberto Roena** *(bongos)*, **Bobby Valentin** *(bass)*, **Willie Colon** *(trombone)*, **Reynaldo Jorge** *(trombone)*, **Roberto Rodriguez** *(trumpet)*, **Barry Rogers** *(trombone)*, **Larry Spencer** *(trumpet)*, **Yomo Toro** *(cuatro)*, **Orestes Vilato** *(timbales)*, **Hector Zarzuela** *(trumpet)*

Storyline: The birth of Nuyorican salsa captured on film, with footage from the famous Cheetah gigs, interviews with the Fania big guns, rehearsal clips and an unforgettable flavour of life and bonhomie in early 70s Spanish Harlem. *BG*

Movie rating: *5

Visual: video

Off the record: The **FANIA ALL-STARS** (see below)

---

the FANIA ALL-STARS & The Spanish Speaking People Of NYC

1972. (d-lp) *Fania; <Fania 431>* [ ] [-]
– Introduction ("Cocinando") / Rehearsal & interview / Quitate tu / The producer / Anacaona / Cockfight & interview / Ponte Duro / Block party (Izzy Sanabria's impersonation of Ed Sullivan "Abran Paso") / Botanica / Abran paso pt.2 / Block party II / Lamento de un Guajiro / Descarga Fania / Bembe / Ahora vengo yo / Estrellas de Fania / Closing of movie (introduction theme). *<d-cd-iss. 1997; same>*

S/track review: The double disc soundtrack is big on atmosphere but – without the footage – low on context and not so great (occasionally appalling) on sound quality. There's not much here that isn't performed on the two classic volumes of 'Live At The Cheetah' (1971/2), but there is ramshackle charm. In big greasy buckets. Instruments tune up and tail off over random noise; a dude protests his innocence over an arrest for robbery; Puerto Rican macho talk flies thick, spicy and fast, and chicos with heavy accents hold forth on the finer points of cockfighting. When the music does take off, it's electrifiying, wide open brass and percussion arrangements ablaze with the energy of the new. RAY BARRETTO, WILLIE COLON, HECTOR LAVOE, ISMAEL MIRANDA, Fania masterminds JOHNNY PACHECO and LARRY HARLOW; all firing off the reflected energy of a New York scene suddenly finding itself at the centre of the Latin world. Highlights include the layers of ascending horns on the brief 'Abran Paso (Part 1)', the MIRANDO-led version of the old Cuban song, 'Lamento De Un Guajiro' and anthemic, all-time classic signature, 'Estrellas De Fania'. Salsa! *BG*

Album rating: *7

OVERNIGHT

2003 (US 81m) Black & White Films / ThinkFilm (R)

Film genre: showbiz/Rock-music documentary

Top guns: dir: Mark Brian Smith, Tony Montana

Stars: **Troy Duffy** *(himself/performer)*, **Jeff 'Skunk' Baxter** *(himself)* ← BLUES BROTHERS 2000, Willem Dafoe *(himself)* ← AFFLICTION ← WILD AT HEART ← CRY-BABY ← the LAST TEMPTATION OF CHRIST ← TO LIVE AND DIE IN L.A. ← STREETS OF FIRE / → the LIFE AQUATIC WITH STEVE ZISSOU, **Billy Connolly** *(himself)* ← STILL CRAZY ← the CONCERTS FOR THE PEOPLE OF KAMPUCHEA / → OPEN SEASON, **Mark Wahlberg** *(himself)* ← ROCK STAR ← BOOGIE NIGHTS ← the BASKETBALL DIARIES, Patrick Swayze *(himself)* ← ROAD HOUSE ← DIRTY DANCING / → DIRTY DANCING: HAVANA NIGHTS, Jake Busey *(himself)* ← S.F.W., Harvey (Weinstein) *(himself)* → the FUTURE IS UNWRITTEN, Billy Zane *(himself)* ← HENDRIX, Norman Reedus *(himself)* ← OCTANE ← the BEATNICKS ← REACH THE ROCK, Sean Patrick Flanery *(himself)* ← GIRL / → 30 DAYS UNTIL I'M FAMOUS, **Taylor Duffy** *(himself/performer)*, **Jimi Jackson** *(himself/performer)*, **Gordon Clark** *(himself/performer)*, John Goodman *(himself)* ← MASKED AND ANONYMOUS ← STORYTELLING ← the EMPEROR'S NEW GROOVE ← COYOTE UGLY ← O BROTHER, WHERE ART THOU? ← BLUES BROTHERS 2000 ← TRUE STORIES ← SWEET DREAMS / → BEYOND THE SEA, Vincent D'Onofrio *(himself)* ← CHELSEA WALLS ← STRANGE DAYS / → THUMBSUCKER, Matthew Modine *(himself)* ← BIRDY, Paul Reubens *(himself)* ← SOUTH OF HEAVEN, WEST OF HELL ← MOONWALKER ← BACK TO THE BEACH ← the BLUES BROTHERS / → MAYOR OF THE SUNSET STRIP, Ron Jeremy *(himself)* ← DETROIT ROCK CITY ← 54

Storyline: "Overnight success" is an overused paraphrase in today's fickle world of music and showbiz, but here it fits perfectly as the viewer witnesses the rise and fall of megalomaniacal bartender-cum-filmmaker Troy Duffy. The story goes that Miramax and Harvey Weinstein took on Troy's film script ('The Boondock Saints') with the intentions of releasing it around 1997/8, although pre-production quarrels between both parties left it in the can. Duffy's arrogance comes across in full technicolor as he just about alienates all his buddies and film colleagues. However, he did form a band . . . er, the Boondock Saints. *MCS*

Movie rating: *6.5

Visual: dvd (no audio OST; score: Jack Livesey & Peter Nashel)

Off the record: **Troy Duffy** was the man behind both the 1999 film and the group of the same name, 'The Boondock Saints' (along with brother **Taylor Duffy, Jimi Jackson & Gordon Clark**. *MCS*

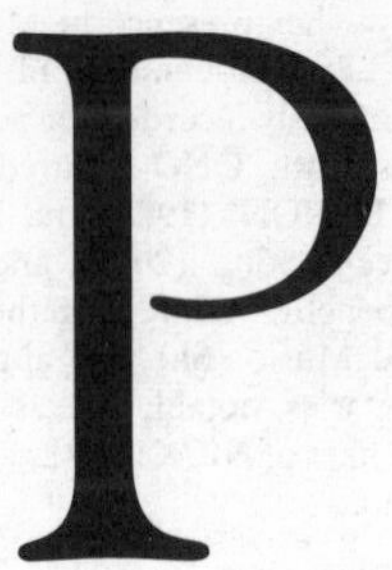

□ Gram PARSONS segment
(⇒ FALLEN ANGEL)

□ Paul PENA segment
(⇒ GENGHIS BLUES)

□ Joe PERRY
(⇒ AEROSMITH)

□ PHISH segment
(⇒ BITTERSWEET MOTEL)

PIANO BLUES

7th part of Martin Scorsese presents THE BLUES

2003 (US 120m mini TV w/b&w) Vulcan Productions / PBS (15)

Film genre: Jazz/Blues-music documentary

Top guns: dir: Clint Eastwood ← HONKYTONK MAN

Stars: Clint Eastwood *(himself)* ← HONKYTONK MAN, **Ray CHARLES** *(performer)*, **DR. JOHN** *(performer)*, **Pinetop Perkins** *(performer)* ← the BLUES BROTHERS ← the LAST WALTZ, **Jay McShann** *(performer)*, **Marcia Ball** *(performer)*, **Dave Brubeck** *(performer)*, **Fats DOMINO** *(performer)*, **Meade 'Lux" Lewis** *(archive performer)*, **Jimmy Yancey** *(archive performer)*, **Count Basie Orchestra** *(performer/s)*

Storyline: One of jazz's best loved ambassadors, Clint Eastwood, gets to grips with the influence of blues pianists on the form's development and on other Afro-American-rooted genres, from Fats Waller to the late Ray Charles, who – along with the likes of Dr. John and Jay McShann – are (or in Charles' case, were) willing and able enough to contribute anecdote and informal ivory tinkling/hammering. *BG*

Movie rating: *7

Visual: dvd

Off the record: (see below)

——

Various Artists

Sep 03. (cd) *Columbia-Legacy; <90492> Sony; (512571-2)* □ Mar04 □
– How long blues (JIMMY YANCEY) / Boogie woogie prayer, pt.1 (the BOOGIE WOOGIE BOYS) / How long blues (COUNT BASIE & HIS ORCHESTRA) / Drifting blues (JOHNNY MOORE'S THREE BLAZERS) / The fat man (FATS DOMINO) / Tatum pole boogie (ART TATUM) / Tipitina (PROFESSOR LONGHAIR) / What'd I say, parts 1 & 2 (RAY CHARLES) / Good morning Mr. Blues (OTIS SPANN) / Backward country boy blues (DUKE ELLINGTON, CHARLES MINGUS & MAX ROACH) / Blue Monk (THELONIUS MONK) / Piney brown blues (BIG JOE TURNER &

JAY McSHANN) / Mission ranch blues (JAY McSHANN & DAVE BRUBECK) / The ladder (JOE TURNER) / Honey dripper (DR. JOHN) / World full of people (HENRY TOWNSEND) / Big chief (DR. JOHN) / Carmel blues (JOE WILLIE "PINETOP" PERKINS & MARCIA BALL) / Travelin' blues (DAVE BRUBECK) / How long blues (DR. JOHN, PETE JOLLY & HENRY GRAY).

S/track review: In the sleevenotes to this pianistic jamboree, Clint Eastwood tells an anecdote about a herd of elk straining to hear an impromptu on-film set performance by FATS DOMINO. It's a wonderful image; as Clint says, "Everybody likes the blues". There are those who'd argue – not without some justification and especially given the omission of players like Jack Dupree and Memphis Slim – that this is a jazz/R&B history rather than a blues study but the stunningly fluid mischief of PROFESSOR LONGHAIR's 'Tipitina' and DR JOHN's 'Big Chief' (a new recording, but see the version on his 'Gumbo' album for maximum impish funk) laughs at labels; the sinuous, elated rhythms of New Orleans sound as inevitable as time itself, and just about as old. Eastwood nevertheless assembles a chronological playlist snaking back to BOOGIE WOOGIE BOYS ALBERT AMMONS, PETE JOHNSON and MEADE LUX LEWIS. Chicago boogie godfather JIMMY YANCEY, big band legend COUNT BASIE and DR. JOHN, PETE JOLLY & HENRY GRAY all perform singular interpretations of Leroy Carr's 'How Long Blues', even if Carr himself doesn't get a look in. But his presence also hovers over the late RAY CHARLES, whose convulsive 'What'd I Say' is the most obvious link between the blues and rock. About the closest to what most people would understand by blues is OTIS SPANN, with a late 60s recording from Copenhagen of all places, or HENRY TOWNSEND, with one of the last recordings before his death in 2006. ART TATUM, JOE TURNER and JAY McSHANN (who also pairs up with DAVE BRUBECK) keep the side up for the stride, and anyone who'd deny the centrality of the blues to either DUKE ELLINGTON (with a Charles Mingus-punctuated cut from the classic 'Money Jungle' album) or the flinty genius of THELONIOUS MONK isn't listening properly. Clint's compilation mightn't do exactly what it says on the tin, but it's a cracking record anyway, one which views seminal Afro-American music as contingent rather than finite. *BG*

Album rating: *7.5

PICTURES AT AN EXHIBITION

1973 (UK 45m) Watchgrove Limited / April Fools Production

Film genre: Prog-rock-music concert/documentary

Top guns: dir: Nicholas Ferguson

Stars: Emerson, Lake & Palmer:- Keith EMERSON *(performer)*, **Greg Lake + Carl Palmer** *(performers)* → MESSAGE TO LOVE: THE ISLE OF WIGHT FESTIVAL

Storyline: Unusual and rare movie, in the sense that, the movie followed the album – by just over a year in fact. There's no brief, just basically Prog-rock supergroup, Emerson, Lake & Palmer, adapting Mussorgsky's 1874 orchestral suite; was to have been released for television audiences having been recorded in and around March 1971. *MCS*

Movie rating: *6

Visual: video 1986 on Magnum / dvd 2005 extended

Off the record: EMERSON, LAKE & PALMER (see Keith EMERSON biog)

– associated releases –

EMERSON, LAKE & PALMER: Pictures At An Exhibition

Nov 71. (lp/c) *Island; (HELP/HELC 1) / Cotillion; <66666>* [3] Jan72 [10]
– Promenade / The gnome / Promenade / The sage / The old castle / Blues variation / Promenade / The hut of Baba Yaga / The curse of Baba Yaga / The hut of Baba Yaga / The great gates of Kiev – The end / Nutrocker. *(re-iss. Dec73 on 'Manticore' lp/c; K/K4 33501) (cd-iss. 1988 on 'Cotillion'; 19122-2) (cd re-iss. Sep89 on 'WEA'; 781521-2) (re-iss. Dec93 on 'Victory'; 828466-2) (cd re-iss. Mar96 on 'Essential'; ESMCD 342) (cd re-mast.Mar01 +=; CMRCD 167)* – studio version:- Promenade / The gnome / Promenade / The sage / The hut of Baba Yaga / The great gates of Kiev. *(cd re-iss. 2006 on 'Sanctuary'; 375)*

EMERSON, LAKE & PALMER: Nutrocker / The Great Gates Of Kiev

Mar 72. (7") *<44151>* [–] [70]

the PIED PIPER OF CLEVELAND

aka . . .: A DAY IN THE LIFE OF A FAMOUS DISC JOCKEY

1955 (US 48m; unreleased short) Polygram + Universal have the rights

Film genre: Rock'n'roll concert/documentary

Top guns: dir: Arthur Cohen

Stars: Bill Randle *(himself)*, **Elvis PRESLEY** *(performer)*, **Bill HALEY** *(performer)*, **& His Comets:- Rudy Pompilli, Johnny Grande, Al Rex, Billy Williamson, Franny Beecher** *(performers)* ← see above →, **Pat Boone** *(performer)* → BERNADINE → APRIL LOVE, **LaVern Baker** *(performer)* → ROCK, ROCK, ROCK! → MISTER ROCK AND ROLL, **Johnnie Ray** *(performer)*, **Roy Hamilton** *(performer)* → LET'S ROCK

Storyline: Biopic documentary on one of America's legendary disc jockeys, Bill Randle, who also produced the film; it was shown only once. It's accompanied by live footage of rock'n'roll giants such as Elvis (his first ever movie appearance!), Bill Haley & His Comets, Pat Boone and Johnnie Ray. Randle sold the rights to the film in 1992 and passed away around twelve years later – we await its release. *MCS*

Movie rating: *? (awaiting a showing!)

Visual: none

Off the record: Johnnie Ray (b.10 Jan'27, The Dalles, Oregon, USA) was the partially deaf singing sensation of the early 50s, who both crooned and rocked his way through emotion-fuelled hits such as 'Cry' and 'The Little White Cloud That Cried'; a role in Irving Berlin's 'There's No Business Like Show Business' propelled his profile even higher. Shortly after featuring in this film, Johnny scored with another massive single, 'Just Like Walking In The Rain'. Sadly, after "outing" his bisexuality and further scrapes with the law, the "cry guy" faded into obscurity; Morrissey of the Smiths would pay tribute to the man by wearing a hearing aid on stage. Ray died of liver failure on the 25th of February 1990, having had years of drink and barbituate abuse. **ELVIS PRESLEY** sang five songs, 'That's All Right', 'Blue Moon Of Kentucky', 'Mystery Train', I Forgot To Remember To Forget' and 'Good Rockin' Tonight'), **Haley & His Comets** contributed 'Rock Around The Clock', 'Shake, Rattle And Roll' and 'Dim, Dim The Lights'. *MCS*

☐ PIXIES segment
(⇒ loudQUIETloud)

the POGUES

Formed: North London, England . . . late 1983 by Tipperary-raised Shane MacGowan, alongside Spider Stacey and Jem Finer. MacGowan had earlier been part of punk outfit, the Nipple Erectors, through 1978-1981; this motley crew released a solitary single before shortening their name to the Nips for a further few singles and even an album. Pogue Mahone (Gaelic for "kiss my arse") were subsequently formed by MacGowan and James Fearnley (also a Nip), while also adding drinking buddies, Andrew Ranken, plus female singer/bassist Cait O'Riordan. By spring '84, they'd formed their own self-titled label, issuing a classic debut single, 'Dark Streets Of London'. Boasting all the Celtic melancholy, romance and gritted-teeth attitude which marked the best of the band's work, the track rather unfairly but predictably received an official BBC radio ban (apparently after the beeb managed to translate their name). A month later they secured a deal with 'Stiff', opting for a slight shortening of their moniker to the POGUES. Their Stan Brennan-produced debut album, 'Red Roses For Me', broke into the UK Top 100 as they acquired growing support from live audiences the length and breadth of the country. Whether interpreting trad Irish folk songs or reeling off brilliant originals, the POGUES were apt to turn from high-spirited revelry to menacing threat in the time it took to neck a pint of Guinness (in MacGowan's case, not very long at all). April '85 saw the release of perhaps their finest single (and first Top 20 hit), the misty-eyed, ELVIS COSTELLO-produced 'A Pair Of Brown Eyes'. COSTELLO also oversaw the accompanying album, 'Rum, Sodomy & The Lash' (1985), a debauched, bruisingly beautiful classic which elevated the POGUES (who'd added Philip Chevron) to the position of modern-day folk heroes. MacGowan's gift for conjuring up a feeling of time and place was never more vivid than on the likes of the aforementioned hit, the rousing 'Sally MacLennane' and the cursing malice of 'The Sick Bed Of Cuchulainn', while O'Riordan put in a spine-tingling performance as a Scottish laird on the traditional 'I'm A Man You Don't Meet Every Day' (the subsequent title of a 1994 drama starring MacGowan!). On the 16th of May '86, Cait married COSTELLO and when she left that November (after writing the Top 50 hit 'Haunted' for the Alex Cox film, 'SID & NANCY'), a vital component of POGUES chemistry went with her; Darryl Hunt and Terry Woods were subsequent additions. Around the same time, MacGowan featured in Brit-flick, 'EAT THE RICH', while the group played "The McMahon Gang" in Cox's follow-up movie 'STRAIGHT TO HELL', meeting ex-Clash singer JOE STRUMMER on the set: the veteran punk would subsequently deputise for the absent MacGowan on an early 1988 US tour. This period also saw them peak at No.3 in the album charts with 'If I Should Fall From Grace With God', an album which spawned an unlikely No.2 Xmas 1987 hit in 'Fairytale Of New York'. A drunken duet with singer Kirsty MacColl, the track was certainly more subversive than the usual Yuletide fodder and for a brief period, the POGUES were bona fide pop stars, their rampant collaboration with the Dubliners on 'Irish Rover' earlier that year having already breached the Top 10. Live, the band were untouchable, MacGowan's errant, tin-tray-wielding genius the stuff of legend. Inevitably, MacGowan's hard-drinking ways were beginning to affect his writing and 'Peace And Love' (1989) signalled a slow slide into mediocrity. 1990s 'Hell's Ditch' carried on in much the same vein, although this was to be MacGowan's final album under the POGUES banner, his failing health incompatible with the demands of a successful major label band. While the gap-toothed frontman eventually got a solo career together, the POGUES bravely soldiered on with a surprisingly impressive hit single, 'Tuesday Morning', lifted from their 1993 UK Top 20 "comeback" album, 'Waiting For Herb'. Two years on, a nostalgically-titled follow-up set, 'Pogue Mahone', failed to rekindle their former glory, while MacGowan continued to dominate the limelight. In 1999, some of the POGUES (Spider, Hunt + Ranken) got together as the Wisemen, while Finer has emerged with the band Longplayer. Following his messy departure from the POGUES in the early 90s, the Irish Keith Richards (though even Richards' mythical debauchery would struggle to match MacGowan's self-destructiveness in terms of sheer dogged determination) threatened to form his own outfit, the Popes; sceptics who doubted the man could even form an opinion were at least partly silenced by MacGowan's late '92 duet with fellow maverick, NICK CAVE, on a brilliantly skewed cover of Louis Armstrong's 'Wonderful World'. Two years on and much press rumination later, the Popes' debut single, 'The Church Of The Holy Spook', finally put an end to the speculation and announced that MacGowan's muse was as darkly fertile as ever. Released on 'Z.T.T.', the song's uptempo thrash recalled the unholy spirit of the POGUES' classic 'Sick Bed . . .', scraping into the UK Top 75. Follow-up single, 'That Woman's Got Me Drinking' (excuses, excuses), made the Top 40, while Hollywood heart-throb, Johnny Depp, played guitar on their debut Top Of The Pops appearance; Caribbean Keith Richards anyone. The accompanying album, 'The Snake', was the best album the POGUES never recorded in the last decade, finding MacGowan back at his cursing, doomed romantic best. 1997 saw the release of a disappointing follow-up set, 'The Crock Of Gold', a record that was at times easier on the ear but hardly threatened to set the pulse racing. Post-millennium, MacGowan has kept his celluloid profile down to a minimum, having appeared in a number of punk-rockumentaries, 'The FILTH & THE FURY' (2000), the CLASH's 'WESTWAY TO THE WORLD' (2000) and the misleading 'BILLY CHILDISH IS DEAD' (2005). *BG & MCS*

- **filmography** {starring} (composers) –

Sid & Nancy *(1986 OST w/ V/A =>)* / **Eat The Rich** *(1987 {a SHANE} OST by MOTORHEAD & V/A =>)* / **Straight To Hell** *(1987 {a} OST w/ PRAY FOR RAIN & V/A =>)* / **the Courier** *(1988 {* CAIT} OST by DECLAN MacMANUS =>)* / **a Man You Don't Meet Every Day** *(1994 {* SHANE} =>)* / the Informant *(1997 score by MacGOWAN)* / **the Filth & The Fury** *(2000 {c SHANE} OST by the SEX PISTOLS & V/A =>)* / **Westway To The World** *(2000 {c SHANE] =>)* / the Libertine *(2004 {b SHANE})* / **Billy Childish Is Dead** *(2005 {c SHANE} =>)*

POP GEAR

US title 'GO GO MANIA'

1965 (UK 68m + 2m US) Associated British-Pathe Limited / AIP

Film genre: Pop/Rock-music concert movie

Top guns: dir: Frederic Goode

Stars: Jimmy Saville *(host)* ← FERRY 'CROSS THE MERSEY ← JUST FOR FUN, **the BEATLES:- Paul McCartney, John Lennon, George Harrison, Ringo Starr** *(performers)*, **Billie Davis** *(performer)*, **the Honeycombs:- Dennis D'Ell, Alan Ward, Martin Murray, John Lantree, Honey Lantree** *(performers)*, **the ANIMALS:- Eric BURDON, Alan Price** *(performers)*, **the Rockin' Berries** *(performers)*, **the Nashville Teens** *(performers)* → BEACH BALL → MONTEREY POP, **the Fourmost** *(performers)*, **Peter and Gordon** *(performers)* ← JUST FOR YOU / → DISK-O-TEK HOLIDAY, **the Four Pennies:- Lionel Morton** *(performers)*, **Matt Monro** *(performer)*, **Billy J. Kramer & the Dakotas:- Billy J. Kramer, Pete Hilton, Raymond Jones, Toni Baker, Mike Maxfield, Eddie Mooney** *(performers)* ← the T.A.M.I. SHOW / → the COMPLEAT BEATLES, **Sounds Incorporated** *(performers)* ← LIVE IT UP ← JUST FOR FUN ← IT'S TRAD, DAD!, **the Spencer Davis Group** *(performers)* → the GHOST GOES GEAR → HERE WE GO ROUND THE MULBERRY BUSH, **Susan Maughan** *(performer)* ← WHAT A CRAZY WORLD, **HERMAN'S HERMITS:- Peter Noone, Keith Hopwood, Karl Green, Barry Whitbam, Derek Leckenby** *(performers)*, **Chris Farlowe** *(performer)* → TONITE LET'S ALL MAKE LOVE IN LONDON → RED, WHITE & BLUES, **Tommy Quickly** *(performer)*, **the Remo Four:- Colin Manley, Tony Ashton, Ron Dyke, Phil Rogers** *(performers)*

Storyline: None really, but legendary disc jockey, Jimmy Saville, presents the Beatles and a phenomenal amount of lip-sync singers and British Invasion pop groups. *MCS*

Movie rating: *5

Visual: dvd

Off the record: London's **the Honeycombs** were famous for their female drummer and UK chart-topper, 'Have I The Right'; lead singer **Dennis D'Ell** (died 6th July 2005). **Billy J. Kramer & The Dakotas** were one of Liverpool's biggest exports, having had a string of British hits, including 'Do You Want To Know A Secret', 'Bad To Me' and 'Little Children'. **The Four Pennies** were at the top of the charts in spring 1964 with 'Juliet', while **the Fourmost**

were in the Top 10 with 'A Little Loving'. **Susan Maughan** was virtually a one-hit wonder courtesy of 1962 smash, 'Bobby's Girl'. **Matt Monro** (b. Terrence Parsons, 1 Dec'32, London) became a singer of many a movie theme, including hits 'From Russia With Love' and 'Born Free'; he died of liver cancer on 7th Feb'85. Liverpool's **Tommy Quickly** – managed by Brian Epstein – struggled to get a major hit and also struggled with heroin addiction; he died in the late 60s. His backing band at the time, **the Remo Four** evolved into hitmakers Ashton, Gardner & Dyke ('Resurrection Shuffle'), who composed the score for 'The LAST REBEL' in 1971. *MCS*

POPCORN

aka POPCORN: An Audio-Visual Rock Thing

1969 (US 85m) United Screen Arts / Sherpix Inc. (G)

Film genre: Pop/Rock-music concert/documentary compilation

Top guns: dir: Peter Clifton → the LONDON ROCK & ROLL SHOW → the SONG REMAINS THE SAME

Stars: the ROLLING STONES:- Mick Jagger, Keith Richards, Brian Jones, Bill Wyman, Charlie Watts *(performers)*, **Jimi HENDRIX** *(performer)*, **Otis Redding** *(performer)* ← MONTEREY POP, **Joe COCKER** *(performer)*, **the BEE GEES:- Robin, Barry & Maurice** *(performers)*, **the ANIMALS:- Eric Burdon, etc.** *(performers)*, Twiggy *(herself)* → the BLUES BROTHERS → CLUB PARADISE → EDGE OF SEVENTEEN, **Vanilla Fudge:- Mark Stein, Vince Martell, Tim Bogert, Carmine Appice** *(performers)*, **John Farnham** *(himself)*, Russell Morris *(himself)*

Storyline: A rock concert movie with only compiled snippets of live footage, psychedelic photos and several interviews including one with Mick Jagger. Yes . . . drug culture, Vietnam and capitalism were rife, but did all of the subjects have to overshadow the sparse music. *MCS*

Movie rating: *3

Visual: video (no audio OST – and, no wonder!)

Off the record: Otis Redding was long gone (10th Dec'67 – plane crash) before the release of this movie; 'Dock Of The Bay' was his posthumous classic. Psychedelic blues outfit, **Vanilla Fudge**, had been on the go since they exploded on to the scene with a cover of the Supremes' 'You Keep Me Hangin' On' in '67/'68. *MCS*

POPP I REYKJAVIK

1998 (Ice 103m) Blueeyes Productions

Film genre: alt-Rock/Dance concert/documentary

Top guns: dir: Agust Jakobsson

Stars: Paul Oscar *(tour guide)*, **BJORK** *(performer)*, **GusGus** *(performers)*, **Sigur Ros:- Jon Thor Birgisson, Kjartan Sveinsson, Orri P. Dyrason, Georg Holm** *(performers)* → SCREAMING MASTERPIECE, **Bang Gang** *(performers)* → SCREAMING MASTERPIECE, **Bellatrix** *(performers)*, **Slowblow** *(performers)* → SCREAMING MASTERPIECE, **Curver** *(performers)*, **Quarashi** *(performers)* → SCREAMING MASTERPIECE, **Spitsign** *(performers)*, **Magga Stina** *(performer)*, **Ensimi** *(performer)*, **Maus** *(performers)*, **Vinyll** *(performers)* → SCREAMING MASTERPIECE, **Moa** *(performers)*, **Botnleoja** *(performers)*, **Surefni** *(performers)*, **Svanur** *(performers)*, **Vector** *(performers)*, **Pall Oskar Hjalmtysson** *(performer)*, **Stornukisi** *(performers)*

Storyline: An update of 'ROKK I REYKJAVIK' from way back in the early 80s, the music of Iceland now burgeoning since the onset of the Sugarcubes and Bjork. *MCS*

Movie rating: *5

Visual: dvd

Off the record: Sigur Ros subsequently contributed to the score of 'ENGLAR ALHEIMSIS' ('Angels Of The Universe' 2000) with fellow Icelandic composer, Hilmar Orn Hilmarsson.

—

Various Artists

Oct 98. (cd) *Dennis; (004)* [–] Icelan [–]
– Hunter (BJORK) / Very important people (GUSGUS) / A day lasts forever (LHOOQ) / Sleep (BANG GANG) / Apreggiator (ENSIMI) / Memory cloud (MOA) / Orange meadows (ARIA) / Slide off (SUREFNI) / Speedo (QUARASHI) / Flight 666 (BOTNLEDJA) / Poppaldin (MAUS) / I-Cuba (MAGGA STINA) / The harder I rock (DJ RAMPAGE, DIRTY BIX & CELL 7) / Get it on (REAL FLAVAZ) / Monkey business (DIP) / Flirt (EMILLIONU & SLOWBLOW ASAMT) / Leit ad lifi – remix (SIGUR ROS).

S/track review: 17 tracks of Iceland's best-loved "rock" bands, from BJORK, of course, new kids on the block SIGUR ROS and SLOWBLOW, to tried and tested electronica collective GUSGUS. Experimental groove machinists such as ARIA and SUREFNI also take their place alongside the Steve Albini-produced ENSIMI, the latter explode prime examples of modern-day rock versus noise. 'A Day Lasts Forever' by LHOOQ is a slight let-down, the trio incidentally – with lead female vox – didn't last long after their one and only album for 'Echo' records. The sombre and melancholic BANG GANG ('Sleep') – featuring mainman Bardi Johannsson – also struggled outside the confines of their homelands. Of the others, the award-winning MAUS (a quartet from Arbser, Iceland already into their 3rd set) stuck out of the pack via 'Poppaldin'. Not a great OST, definitely okay but be prepared to empty your pockets out to own a copy of this rarity. *MCS*

Album rating: *5.5

PRIDE AND JOY

The Story Of Alligator Records

1992 (US/UK 87m) Mug-Shot Productions

Film genre: Blues/R&B-music documentary

Top guns: dir: Robert Mugge ← DEEP BLUES ← COOL RUNNINGS: THE REGGAE MOVIE / → HELLHOUNDS ON MY TRAIL → LAST OF THE MISSISSIPPI JUKES → BLUES DIVAS

Stars: KoKo Taylor *(performer)* ← WILD AT HEART ← CHICAGO BLUES / → BLUES BROTHERS 2000 → GODFATHERS AND SONS, & Her Blues Machine *(performers)*, **Lonnie Brooks Blues Band** *(performer/s)* → BLUES BROTHERS 2000 → GODFATHERS AND SONS, **Elvin Bishop** *(performer)* ← FILLMORE, **Katie Webster** *(performer)*, **Lil' Ed & the Blues Imperials** *(performer/s)*

Storyline: Robert Mugge's "modern blues film" to follow up his earlier look at Southern juke joints, 'Deep Blues', going out on the road with the Alligator Records 20th Anniversary Tour before pitching up at the label's Chicago HQ. *BG*

Movie rating: *5.5

Visual: video

Off the record: (see below)

—

Various Artists: The Alligator Records – 20th Anniversary Tour

Apr 93. (d-cd) *Alligator; <(ALCD 107/8)>* [ ] Oct99 [ ]
– (LIL' ED & THE BLUES IMPERIALS):- Killing floor / Can't let these blues go / Pride and joy / Mean ole Frisco / (KATIE WEBSTER):- Two fisted mama / Pussycat moan / Lord, I wonder / (ELVIN BISHOP):- Stealin' watermelons / Beer drinking woman / My dog / El-Bo // (the LONNIE BROOKS BLUES BAND):- Wife for tonight / I want all my money back / Those lonely, lonely nights (with KATIE WEBSTER) / Two headed man / (KOKO TAYLOR & HER BLUES MACHINE):- Something strange is going on / I'd rather go blind / Wang dang doodle / It's a dirty job (with LONNIE BROOKS) / (ALL STAR JAM):- Sweet home Chicago.

S/track review: One of America's pre-eminent independent blues labels for well over three decades, 'Alligator' has been sweet home Chicago to successive generations of legendary and contemporary musicians since the early 70s. The 20th Anniversary Tour which served as both the inspiration for, and focus of Robert Mugge's film also gifted its soundtrack with short, fairly representative sets spread across two discs. It's a world removed from Mugge's 'DEEP BLUES' album, necessarily so given that the performances hail from the relatively less forbidding (and now defunct) environs of Philadelphia's Chestnut Cabaret, and they mostly comprise straightforward 12-bar electric blues. Not on the same level in terms of cultural impact then, but more than respectable as a live blues album. Most of the featured artists came of age in the 60s, and the emphasis is unsurprisingly on raucous electric blues, with KATIE WEBSTER and KOKO TAYLOR countering the testosterone. Even TAYLOR herself takes no mess, a lady with an epochal stint at 'Chess' behind her, who still sounds feral on her Willie Dixon calling card, 'Wang Dang Doodle', and – with help from LONNIE BROOKS – the porcupine-gargling contest, 'It's A Dirty Job'. WEBSTER's story is a different one, plying her loose-jointed swamp-groove around the South before being discovered and adopted by Otis Redding. 'Two Fisted Mama' tells her story of how her mitts became her fortune, banging out her classicist boogie woogie around the world. 'Pussycat Moan' (and her set as a whole) is arguably the highlight of the whole package, spare, gloaming piano blues serving as both wordless lamentation and mortal warning to a lover who's pushed his luck too far, earthing audible electricity from the crowd. A veteran of the 60s blues-rock boom who just happens to bear an uncanny resemblance to Nige from the Brit soap 'Eastenders', ELVIN BISHOP was on a roll in the early 90s, his playful, deep-funky style fearlessly clutching cliché to its bosom before drowning it in distilled sweat on the likes of 'Stealin' Watermelons' and the apocryphal 'Beer Drinking Woman' "We don't mean any harm/we just don't have any better sense", he says in mock apology. The cactus-voiced LIL' ED is a relative puppy compared to his co-stars but his BLUES IMPERIALS tear through a series of perennials with as much grit (and some buzzing tenor sax from EDDIE McKINLEY) as the venerable BROOKS, who himself gets a return favour – and some great banter – from WEBSTER on the old Earl King number, 'Those Lonely, Lonely Nights'. *BG*

Album rating: *6.5

PRISONER IN THE STREET

aka THIRD WORLD: PRISONER IN THE STREET

1980 (Fra/Jama 80m) Mediane Production / Island International

Film genre: Reggae-music concert documentary

Top guns: s-w + dir: Jerome Laperrousaz ← AMOUGIES ←CONTINENTAL CIRCUS / → MADE IN JAMAICA

Stars: Third World:- William Clarke, Stephen Coore, Michael Cooper, Richard Daley, Willie Stewart, Irvin Jarrett *(performers)* ← REGGAE SUNSPLASH / → COOL RUNNINGS: THE REGGAE MOVIE → MADE IN JAMAICA / **Bob MARLEY** *(performer)*

Storyline: London's long gone Rainbow Theatre is the venue for this Third World gig, filmed by French director Jérôme Laperrousaz and featuring such prestigious guests as Bob Marley. *BG*

Movie rating: *5

Visual:

Off the record: Third World were formed in Kingston, Jamaica in 1973, original members such as **Michael "Ibo" Cooper** (keyboards), **Stephen "Cat" Coore** (guitar/cello) and **Richard Daley** (bass), stemming from reggae outfit, Inner Circle. Recruiting Milton "Prilly" Hamilton (vocals), **Irvin "Carrott" Jarrett** (percussion) and Carl Barovier (drums) – the latter replaced by Cornell Marshall, the 6-piece ventured out live in the local area. After an assignation to support BOB MARLEY on his British tour in 1974, **Third World** signed to 'Island' records, who released their UK debut 45, 'Railroad Track' and their eponymous LP in '76. Now with **William Clarke** (on lead vox) and drummer **Willie "Roots" Stewart**, the band delivered their sophomore set, '96 In The Shade' (1977), a critically acclaimed record that paved the way for subsequent chart success. This came in the shape of 1978's breakthrough LP, 'Journey To Addis', a set that produced a couple of hits, 'Now That We've Found Love' (from the pens of the O'Jays) and 'Cool Meditation'. Although not as credible or fruitful as their last set, 'The Story's Been Told' (1979) and 'Rise In Harmony' (1980), continued to show every sign that they were reggae's No.1 star group. After the release of the live soundtrack, 'PRISONER IN THE STREET', they signed a fresh contract with 'C.B.S.', and charted once again. Amazingly, they're still going strong in 2007, albeit with a few personnel variations. *MCS*

THIRD WORLD

Jun 80. (lp/c) *Island; (<ILPS/ZCI 9616>)* ☐ Aug80 ☐
– Now that we've found love / Prisoner in the street / Third World man / Cold sweat / 96 in the shade / African woman / Irie ites / Street fighting. *<cd-iss. 1990; 546384>*

S/track review: The acceptable face of roots reggae, THIRD WORLD were 'Island's biggest Jamaican import after the Wailers, with the same crossover appeal if not quite as much street cred. This soundtrack captures them at the height of their late 70s/early 80s popularity, handling their lengthy jams with the slick dynamics and professionalism of a stadium rock band. Opener 'Now That We Found Love', a bass-rolling cover of the old Gamble/Huff chestnut, sounds as good here as it does on single, with STEPHEN 'CAT' COORE (son of onetime Jamaican Deputy Prime Minister David Coore) showing off his bluesy, Clapton-esque chops on the outro. 'Prisoner In The Street' itself leads in with a classic James Brown quote, but the biggest cheer of the night is reserved for the title track of their excellent sophomore album, '96 Degrees In The Shade' (1977), a vivid narrative of slavery remembered, performed with the conviction of history repeating itself. *BG*

Album rating: *6.5

PSYCHODERELICT

1993 (UK 90m* TV) Polygram Diversified Entertainment (18)

Film genre: Rock Opera/Musical concert/drama

Top guns: dir: Richard Barnes, Bruce Gowers / s-w: **Pete Townshend**

Stars: Pete Townshend *(performer)* <= the WHO =>, John Labanowski *(Ray High)*, Linal Haft *(Rastus Knight)* ← BIRTH OF THE BEATLES, Jan Ravens *(Ruth Streeting)*, Sage Carter *(Athena)*, **John Bundrick** *(musician)* ← DEEP END / → THIRTY YEARS OF MAXIMUM R&B LIVE → LIFEHOUSE → the WHO LIVE AT THE ROYAL ALBERT HALL, **Peter Hope Evans** *(musician)* ← DEEP END / → LIFEHOUSE, **Simon Phillips** *(musician)* ← DEEP END, **Phil Palmer + Billy Nicholls** *(musicians)* → LIFEHOUSE, **Andy Fairweather-Low** *(musician)* ← the WALL: LIVE IN BERLIN / → CONCERT FOR GEORGE, **Pino Palladino** *(musician)*, **Katie Kissoon** *(singer)* → CONCERT FOR GEORGE, Deirdre Harrison *(voice; Athena)*, Lee Whitlock *(voice; Spinner)*

Storyline: Basically a concert version of Pete Townshend's current CD, presented live on American television on the 29th of December, 1993. *MCS*

Movie rating: *6.5

Visual: dvd in 2006 (see below)

Off the record: Katie Kissoon was one-half of Mac & Katie Kissoon (from Trinidad) who had a handful of hits in the mid-70s, 'Sugar Candy Kisses' & 'Don't Do It Baby'. *MCS*

– associated releases, etc. –

PETE TOWNSHEND: Psychoderelict

Jul 93. (cd/c) *Atlantic; <(7567 82494-2/-4)>* □ □
– English boy / Meher Baba M3 / Let's get pretentious / Meher Baba M4 (signal box) / Early morning dreams / I want that thing / (dialogue introduction to 'Outlive the dinosaur') / Outlive the dinosaur / Flame (demo) / Now and then / I am afraid / Don't try to make me real / (dialogue introduction to 'Predictable') / Predictable / Flame / Meher Baba M5 (Vivaldi) / Fake it / (dialogue introduction to 'Now and then') (reprise) / Now and then (reprise) / Baba O'Riley (reprise) / English boy (reprise). *(cd re-iss. Jan97; same)*

PETE TOWNSHEND: English Boy / (dialogue mix)

Jul 93. (7"/c-s) *(A 7370/+C)* – □
(cd-s) *(A 7370CD1)* – ('A'-dialogue) / Fake it / Psycho Montage.
(cd-s+=) *(A 7370CD2)* – ('A') / Fake it / Flame / Early Morning Dreams (demo).

PETE TOWNSHEND: Psychoderelict – Live In New York

Feb 06. (dvd) *Universal; <(982336-9)>* □ □
– (tracks above are accompanied by Townshend/Who classics).

□ PUNK + GLORY alt.
(⇒ NINA HAGEN = PUNK + GLORY)

PUNK IN LONDON

1977 (W. Ger 111m) Hochschule fur Fernsehen.. / Stein film (15)

Film genre: Punk-Rock-music documentary

Top guns: dir: Wolfgang Buld

Stars: the Boomtown Rats/Bob Geldof *(performers)* → the WALL → SPICEWORLD → NEW YORK DOLL, **X-Ray Spex** *(performers)* → the PUNK ROCK MOVIE → PUNK: ATTITUDE, **Chelsea:- Gene October** *(performers)* → JUBILEE → D.O.A. → URGH! A MUSIC WAR, **Wayne County & the Electric Chairs** *(performers)* ← the BLANK GENERATION / → JUBILEE → the PUNK ROCK MOVIE → STADT DER VERLORENEN SEELEN → END OF THE CENTURY, **the Jam:- Paul Weller *, Bruce Foxton, Rick Buckler** *(performers)* → PUNK AND ITS AFTERSHOCKS → a SKIN TOO FEW: THE DAYS OF NICK DRAKE → the WHO LIVE AT THE ROYAL ALBERT HALL, **the Clash** *(performers)* <= Joe STRUMMER =>, **the Adverts** *(performers)*, **the Lurkers** *(performers)*, **the Jolt** *(performers)*, **Subway Sect** *(performers)*, **the Killjoys/Kevin Rowland** *(performers)*

Storyline: Aspiring moviemaker, Wolfgang Buld – complete with 16mm camera – takes us around the haunts of the local punk scene/movement and finds legends the Clash, the Jam and the Boomtown Rats creating a stir. *MCS*

Movie rating: *7.5

Visual: video + dvd (no audio OST)

Off the record: Most of the artists here, including **the Adverts** can be found on that year's 'Live At The Roxy' LP.

the PUNK ROCK MOVIE

1978 (UK 86m) Notting Hill / Punk Rock Films (12)

Film genre: Punk Rock-music documentary

Top guns: dir: **Don Letts** → DANCEHALL QUEEN → WESTWAY TO THE WORLD → ONE LOVE → PUNK: ATTITUDE

Stars: the SEX PISTOLS *(performers)*, **the Clash** *(performers)* <= Joe STRUMMER =>, **the Slits** *(performers)* → PUNK: ATTITUDE → PUNK'S NOT DEAD, **Siouxsie & The Banshees** *(performers)* ← JUBILEE / → WESTWAY TO THE WORLD → the FILTH & THE FURY → 24 HOUR PARTY PEOPLE → PUNK: ATTITUDE, **X-Ray Spex** *(performers)* ← PUNK IN LONDON / → PUNK: ATTITUDE, **Slaughter & The Dogs** *(performers)*, **Subway Sect** *(performers)*, **Wayne County** *(performer)* ← PUNK IN LONDON ← JUBILEE ← the BLANK GENERATION / → STADT DER VERLORENEN SEELEN → END OF THE CENTURY, **Generation X:- Billy IDOL** *(performer(s)*, **Eater** *(performers)*, **Johnny Thunders & The Heartbreakers** *(performers)* ← the BLANK GENERATION / → BORN TO LOSE: THE LAST ROCK AND ROLL MOVIE → END OF THE CENTURY → HEY IS DEE DEE HOME, **Alternative TV** *(performers)*, Terence Dackombe *(himself)* → WESTWAY TO THE WORLD

Storyline: With his trusty Super 8 camera, musician/filmmaker Don Letts, shoots his first documentary feature around punk clubs including the short-lived and infamous, Roxy (c. 1977). *MCS*

Movie rating: *6.5

Visual: video + dvd (no audio OST)

Off the record: After a time as a filmmaker and part-time musician, **Don Letts** joined his pal, Mick Jones, in his new, post-Clash venture, Big Audio Dynamite. *MCS*

Q

Q-TIP

Born: Jonathan Davis, 20 Nov'70, Brooklyn, New York, USA. The voice of seminal hip-hop crew A Tribe Called Quest and a mainstay of the Native Tongues collective, Q-TIP (now taking the Islamic moniker Kamaal Fareed) made his screen debut alongside Janet Jackson and TUPAC SHAKUR in John Singleton's 'Poetic Justice' (1993). A number one album, the breakup of his group and much hip hop history later, he belatedly followed up with a narration credit on forgotten romcom, 'Love Goggles' (1999). 'Prison Song' (2001) was more worthy of the man's talents; originally conceived as a musical but subsequently edited into a conventional prison film, it credited the former 'Quest MC as executive producer (alongside Robert De Niro), co-writer and – alongside Mary J Blige, with a cameo from ELVIS COSTELLO – as troubled lead. 'DEATH OF A DYNASTY' (2003) was closer to home, 'Roc-A-Fella' CEO Damon Dash's semi-autobiographical look at his own record label, in which Q-TIP made a cameo along with the likes of JAY-Z, Busta Rhymes and Russell Simmons. While he hasn't been as prolific as the likes of Native Tongues peer Mos Def, he's continued to score parts in high profile films, most recently Spike Lee's lambasted politico-sexual comedy, 'She Hate Me' (2004) and 'Downfall' director Oliver Hirschbiegel's Hollywood debut, 'The Invasion' (2007). *BG*

- **filmography** {acting} –

Poetic Justice *(1993 {a} OST by V/A =>)* / **Rhyme & Reason** *(1997 {p} on OST by V/A =>)* / **Free Tibet** *(1998 {p} =>)* / Love Goggles *(1999 {*})* / **Disappearing Acts** *(2000 TV {a} OST by V/A =>)* / Prison Song *(2001 [s-w] {*})* / **Death Of A Dynasty** *(2003 {c} =>)* / **Fade To Black** *(2004 {p} =>)* / She Hate Me *(2004 {a} OST by Terence Blanchard; see future edition)* / the Invasion *(2007 {*})*

R

R.E.M.

Formed: Athens, Georgia, USA . . . spring 1980 by Michael Stipe, Peter Buck, Mike Mills and Bill Berry. A bookish, enigmatic indie band who just happen to fill stadiums, R.E.M. remain unlikely godfathers of the US underground, a scene examined in microcosm in one of the group's first screen credits, 'ATHENS, GA. – INSIDE/OUT' (1986). While the likes of Love Tractor and Pylon remained underground, R.E.M. accompanied breakthrough albums, 'Life's Rich Pageant' (1986), 'Document' (1987) and 'Green' (1989) with groundbreaking videos, the cryptic theatricality of frontman Stipe especially, gifting the band a visual voice expressed in collections like 'R.E.M. – Succumbs' (1987) and 'R.E.M. – Pop Screen' (1987), and expressed in its own right with a low key appearance – alongside a young Steve Buscemi – in Robert Longo short, 'Arena Brains' (1988). Stipe's longtime interest in independent film had in fact taken a more concrete turn with the formation of 'C-Hundred Film Corp' with producer/director Jim McKay, partly to document R.E.M. but also with a wider remit which was to include such acclaimed material as comedic amateur cine-doc, 'American Movie: The Making Of Northwestern' (1999). In the meatime, R.E.M. entered the arena of soundtrack, albeit with a suitably visionary filmmaker, contributing 'Out Of Time' outtake, 'Fretless', to Wim Wenders' iconic 'Until The End Of The World'. The videos from 'Out Of Time' itself – including the crepuscular choreography of 'Losing My Religion' – were gathered in 'R.E.M. – This Film Is On' (1991). Mike Mills will be remembered for his backseat role in the Beatles biopic, 'BACKBEAT', playing alongside the likes of THURSTON MOORE (of SONIC YOUTH), DAVE GROHL, etc. With Andy Kaufman tribute, 'MAN ON THE MOON' – from the epochal 'Automatic For The People' (1992) – the band even lent Milos Forman the title (and title song) of a 1999 Kaufman biopic. In fact, they surpassed themselves with a full score (and one of their most memorable singles, 'The Great Beyond') successfully rising to the challenge of creating 70s incidental music, even if a surfeit of various artists and stand-up excerpts disjointed the soundtrack release. While Stipe made a few of his occasional forays into film in the 90s, in Christopher Münch's 'Color Of A Brisk And Leaping Day' (1996) alongside 'NASHVILLE' crooner Henry Gibson, and in tandem with such equally unlikely icons as Studs Terkel, Chuck D and the late Hunter S Thompson in cult road-doc, 'Anthem' (1997), it was in the back room which the self effacing rennaisance continued to make his mark, co-founding separate film production company, 'Single Cell Pictures', and racking up projects as diverse as Todd Haynes' glam-rock revision, 'VELVET GOLDMINE' (1998) and Spike Jonze mindbender, 'Being John Malkovich' (1999). Into the new millennium, he reunited with Münch on 'The Sleepy Time

Gal' (2001), and produced two slice-of-life dramas with McKay, 'Our Song' (2000) and 'Everyday People' (2004), as well Brian Dannelly's Christian satire, 'Saved' (2004). *BG*

- **filmography** (composers) {performance} -

Athens, Ga.: Inside/Out *(1987 {p} on OST by V/A =>)* / **BackBeat** *(1994 {m MIKE} =>)* / Color Of A Brisk And Leaping Day *(1996 {c MICHAEL})* / **Meeting People Is Easy** *(1998 {c MICHAEL} =>)* / **Man On The Moon** *(1999 OST w/ V/A =>)* / **Fallen Angel: Gram Parsons** *(2004 {c PETER} =>)*

□ RADIOHEAD segment
(⇒ MEETING PEOPLE IS EASY)

RAINBOW BRIDGE

1971 (US 125m) Antahkarana Production (R)

Film genre: Rock-music concert/documentary

Top guns: dir: Chuck Wein / s-w: Charlie Bacis

Stars: Jimi Hendrix Experience:- Jimi HENDRIX *(live footage)*, **Billy Cox** *(live footage)* ← WOODSTOCK / → JIMI HENDRIX, **Mitch Mitchell** *(live footage)* ← MONTEREY POP / → JIMI HENDRIX → ROCK AND ROLL CIRCUS → EXPERIENCE, Chuck Wein *(himself)*, Pat Hartley *(herself)* → JIMI HENDRIX → ROCK AND ROLL CIRCUS, Herbie Fletcher *(himself)*, Miss Mercy *(herself)* → MAYOR OF THE SUNSET STRIP, Michael Hynson *(himself)* ← the ENDLESS SUMMER

Storyline: For about 40 minutes or so, the viewer is led into the psychedelic world of the Rainbow Bridge Occult Meditation Center in Hawaii, where young folks expand their consciousness by interacting on a number of subjects. Things expand further – soundwise, at least – when the Jimi Hendrix Experience turn up and put on a show for everybody concerned. The DVD includes 12 extra minutes of previously unreleased movie trailers. *MCS*

Movie rating: *4.5

Visual: video + dvd

Off the record: Miss Mercy was a special artist/sculptress to a number of celebrities – she cast their genital organs. *MCS*

JIMI HENDRIX

Oct 71. (lp) *Reprise; <2040> (K 44159)* [15] Nov71 [16]
– Dolly dagger / Earth blues / Pali gap / Room full of mirrors / Star spangled banner / Look over yonder / Hear my train a comin' / Hey baby (new rising sun). *(cd-iss. Mar87; K2 44159) (cd re-iss. Apr89 +=; 831 312-2)* – Izabella / (I'm not your) Steppin' stone.

S/track review: It'd been just over a year since the death (18th September 1970) of iconic guitarist, JIMI HENDRIX. 'RAINBOW BRIDGE' was the first of several exploitation flicks (with soundtracks) to hit the market, high on the expectation that the HENDRIX brand name would sell the product. A mixture of his most recent studio outtakes and a live track, the LP at times shows the listener the capabilities of the greatest axeman on Earth, although that's not always the case. Augmented by MITCH MITCHELL on drums and BILLY COX on bass, a trio of songs here were indeed his last recordings (1st July 1970, at Electric Ladyland studios), the funk-infused 'Dolly Dagger', the Santana-esque 'Pali Gap' & album finale 'Hey Baby'. These three tracks, and quite possibly 'Earth Blues' (recorded 20th January 1970, and featuring the RONETTES as guest backing singers) would've made it on to any of JIMI's next LP projects had he lived. Where the man was going music-wise in the early 70s is still conjecture, but this soundtrack gives out the clues in barrowloads: spiritual funk, heavy soul, progressive R&B . . . one could go on. With BUDDY MILES on sticks (not Mitchell), November '69 recording 'Room Full Of Mirrors' and a solo HENDRIX studio practice session for his 'WOODSTOCK'/National Anthem, 'Star Spangled Banner', filled out side 1. Flipping over to the other side, we also find HENDRIX (with MITCHELL and bassist NOEL REDDING) waning slightly on 'Look Over Yonder', an outtake if ever I've heard one. The longest track by far, the live 'Hear My Train A-Comin'' (from 30th May 1970), reprised the vibrating guitar riffs of 'Voodoo Chile', very poignant if one thinks where his euphemistic train was taking him. *MCS*

Album rating: *5.5

– spinoff hits, etc. –

JIMI HENDRIX: Dolly Dagger / The Star Spangled Banner

Oct 71. (7") *<1044>* [74] [–]

Bonnie RAITT

Born: Bonnie Lynn Raitt, 8 Nov'49, Burbank, California, USA. Daughter of Broadway star John Raitt, Bonnie might've more logically followed her father onto the stage. Under the mentorship of blues revival lynchpin Dick Waterman, she took up the uncommon calling of female blues guitarist instead, yet still managed a few dramatic moments along the way. By the late 70s, she was already such a woman-about-scene that her presence was requested for one of the many cameos in Robert Stigwood debacle, 'SGT. PEPPER'S LONELY HEARTS CLUB BAND' (1978). Raised a Quaker, she was also a dedicated activist and took her place alongside the cream of 60s/70s rock on turn of the decade benefit, 'NO NUKES' (1980), going on to organise a benefit in opposition the Reagan administration's support for the Contras in Nicaragua. While the turn of the decade also saw her making a performance cameos in John Travolta-goes-Bronco drama, 'URBAN COWBOY' (1980), concert films were her most common screen conduit, numbering the likes of ROY ORBISON jamboree, 'BLACK & WHITE NIGHT' (1987) and, with her longtime involvement in the music of New Orleans, both the Neville Brothers' 'Tell It Like It Is' (1989) and the more recent 'MAKE IT FUNKY!' (2005). Aaron Neville also featured – alongside the disparate likes of SUN RA, James Taylor and TOM WAITS – on Disney tribute album, 'Stay Awake' (1988), to which Raitt contributed a version of 'Baby Mine' (from elephantine fantasy, 'Dumbo') in collaboration with then producer Don Was. A longtime association with blues legend John Lee Hooker accounted for at least one of the slew of Grammys with which RAITT was showered in the early 90s, a partnership documented on John Lee Hooker's TV/DVD 'That's My Story' (2001). Tributes to Bruce Hornsby and 'Motown' were also on her agenda, and with 2003 declared "Year of the Blues" by the US Congress, she appeared in both the all-star concert film, 'LIGHTNING IN A BOTTLE', and one of the most compelling volumes of Martin Scorsese's blues series, 'The SOUL OF A MAN' (2003). *BG*

- **filmography** {performance}

Sgt. Pepper's Lonely Hearts Club Band *(1978 {p} OST by V/A =>)* / **No Nukes** *(1980 {p} on OST by V/A =>)* / **Urban Cowboy** *(1980 {c} on OST by V/A =>)* / **Black & White Night** *(1988 TV {p} on OST by V/A =>)* / **Last Party 2000** *(2001 {p})* / **That's My Story** *(2001 TV =>)* / the Rutles 2: Can't Buy Me Lunch *(2002 {c})* / **the Country Bears** *(2002 {v} on OST by V/A =>)* / **the Soul Of A Man** *(2003 {p} on OST by V/A =>)* / **Lightning In A Bottle** *(2004 {p} on OST by V/A =>)* / Trudell *(2005 {c})* / **Make It Funky** *(2005 {p} =>)* / **Before The Music Dies** *(2006 {p} =>)*

RAMONES

Formed: Forest Hills, Queens, New York, USA in August '74 by guitarist Johnny (b. John Cummings), singer and original drummer Joey (b. Jeffrey Hyman) and Dee Dee (b. Douglas Colvin), who all took the working surname Ramone (although they were brothers only in the loosest sense of the term). One of the prime movers (many would subsequently cite them as the first) in the emergent US punk scene, the band began a residency at the legendary NY club, CBGB's, Tommy (b. Tom Erdelyi) coming in on the drum stool in order to free Joey up for suitably deranged vocal duties. In June '75, the band were dealt a slight setback when they failed an audition for Rick Derringer's 'Blue Sky' label in front of 20,000 fans at a Johnny Winter concert, although later that year manager, Danny Fields, found up-and-coming new wave label 'Sire' (run by Seymour Stein) considerably more receptive. Released around the same time as their pivotal (and highly influential) London Roundhouse gig, the band's eponymous summer '76 debut album presented a sound every bit as exhilaratingly juvenile and humorously warped as their leering, mop-topped scruffiness might suggest. Ripping out gloriously dumb, two-minute buzz-saw classics on such perennial punk subjects as solvent abuse ('I Wanna Sniff Some Glue'), girls (most of the album) and erm, chainsaws ('Chain Saw'), the RAMONES had invented themselves as larger than life, cartoon yob no-wavers well ahead of their time, their attitude alone copied by countless two-bit punk bands (and a few great ones) the length and breadth of the British Isles. Barely pausing for breath (or whatever it was these guys inhaled), the new yoik brudders followed up with 'Leave Home' (1977), another strychnine-fuelled session of primitive but tuneful terrace chant anthems, RAMONES style; from this point onwards, the words 'Gabba Gabba Hey' would be forever carved in the stone of the punk lexicon. The album even managed a minor dent in the UK charts, a full scale assault led later that year with the brilliantly throwaway 'Sheena Is A Punk Rocker'. The climax of the early RAMONES blitzkrieg came with 'Rocket To Russia' (1977), the lads easing ever so slightly off the gas pedal and taking the credo of mangled, two-minute surf-pop to its Day-Glo conclusion; the hilarious 'Cretin Hop', 'Rockaway Beach' and 'Teenage Lobotomy' remain among the most definitive moments in the RAMONES' dog-eared catalogue. A rather disappointing Top 60 placing failed to do the record justice, although by this stage the band were beginning to make some inroads into the home market. Further evidence, if any was needed, that the RAMONES' chief writer was at the peak of his powers came with the blistering 'Chinese Rocks', a Heartbreakers' track co-penned by Dee Dee. With the departure of Tommy (into production work) the following year, ex-Richard Hell cohort Marc Bell was recruited in his place, rechristened, of course, Marky Ramone. Incredibly, the tried and tested formula (with a few notable exceptions, a guitar solo (!) on 'Go Mental' and a ballad, 'Questioningly') continued to excite with 'Road To Ruin' (1978), their first album to break into the UK Top 40 and the resting place of the legendary 'I Wanna Be Sedated'. The riotous 'It's Alive' (1979) captured the RAMONES' concert experience head-on, neatly wrapping up the first stage of the boys' career, as did their attempts at breaking Hollywood with the Roger Corman movie, 'ROCK'N'ROLL HIGH SCHOOL', the same year. Every punk band coped with the scene's fragmentation in their own way, the RAMONES not so wisely choosing to indulge their love of classic 60s pop via the genre's guru, Phil Spector. The results were predictably confused, many longtime RAMONES headbangers balking at their UK Top 10 cover of The Ronettes' 'Baby I Love You'. Subsequent 80s efforts such as 'Pleasant Dreams' (1981) and 'Subterranean Jungle' (1983) lacked the ragged glory of their earlier work although with the replacement of Marky with Richie (aka Richard Reinhardt) in 1984, 'Too Tough To Die' (1985) found the band sharpening their attack and presenting a united front against the hardcore pretenders of the day. They couldn't keep it up though, and the limitations of their art really began to bite deep on the bedraggled 'Animal Boy' (1986) and 'Halfway To Sanity' (1987). Dee Dee bailed out after 'Brain Drain' (1989), replacement C.J. (b. Christopher John Ward) effecting something of a rejuvenation on 'Mondo Bizarro' (1992). The following year's 'Acid Eaters' saw the band pay tribute to the 60s sounds which had inspired them, while in turn, many of the younger bands who had actually been inspired by the RAMONES would soon be calling the shots at America's major labels. Yet despite this punk revival and the success of such acts as Green Day and the Offspring, the RAMONES finally decided to call it a day in early 1996 following the release of the 'Adios Amigos' set and the accompanying tour. Fans of all ages were shocked to hear the news of Joey's death (of lymphoma) in NY on the 15th of April, 2001. Barely a year later (5th June 2002), Dee Dee also passed away. On the 15th of September 2004, a third Ramone, Johnny, died of cancer. To mark these untimely deaths, there were a number of documentary films released, namely 'END OF THE CENTURY: THE STORY OF THE RAMONES' (2003), 'HEY IS DEE DEE HOME' (2003), 'RAMONES: RAW' (2004) and 'TOO TOUGH TO DIE: A TRIBUTE TO JOHNNY RAMONE' (2006), while the video (and CD) 'We're Outta Here' was still in the shops having been issued way back in 1997. Moviewise, JOEY was the main attraction, having cameoed in a number of weird and wonderful flicks (see below). *BG & MCS*

- filmography {acting} (composers) –

the Blank Generation *(1976 {p} =>)* / **Rock'n'Roll High School** *(1979 {*p} OST by RAMONES & V/A =>)* / **Roadkill** *(1989 {c JOEY} OST by V/A =>)* / **1991: The Year Punk Broke** *(1992 {p} =>)* / **Hated** *(1994 {c DEE DEE} OST by V/A =>)* / **Drop Dead Rock** *(1995 {c JOEY} =>)* / We're Outta Here *(1997 {p} video + CD)* / Final Rinse *(1999 {c JOEY})* / **End Of The Century: The Story Of The Ramones** *(2003 {*p} dvd-only =>)* / **Mayor Of The Sunset Strip** *(2003 {p JOEY} OST by V/A =>)* / **Hey Is Dee Dee Home** *(2003 {* DEE DEE} dvd-only =>)* / **Ramones: Raw** *(2004 {*p} dvd-only =>)* / **Punk's Not Dead** *(2006 {p} =>)* / **Too Tough To Die: A Tribute To Johnny Ramone** *(2006 {****} =>)*

RAMONES: RAW

2004 (US 105m dvd) Ramones Productions Inc.

Film genre: Punk rock-music documentary

Top guns: dir: John Cafiero ← BIG MONEY HUTLA

Stars: RAMONES:- Johnny Ramone, Joey Ramone, Dee Dee Ramone, Marky Ramone, C.J. Ramone, Tommy Ramone *(himself/performer)*, Drew Barrymore *(herself)* ← the WEDDING SINGER ← WAYNE'S WORLD 2 ← FIRESTARTER / → CURIOUS GEORGE → MUSIC AND LYRICS, **Debbie Harry** *(herself)* <= BLONDIE =>, **Chris Stein** *(himself)* <= BLONDIE =>, **Carly SIMON** *(herself)*, **LEMMY** *(himself)*, **Steve Van Zandt** *(himself)*, **Robbie Krieger** *(himself)* ← WOODSTOCK '99 ← MESSAGE TO LOVE: THE ISLE OF WIGHT FESTIVAL ← the DOORS ARE OPEN, **Bono** *(himself)* <= U2 =>, **Eddie VEDDER** *(himself)*, Kurt Loder *(archive)* ← TUPAC: RESURRECTION ← AIRHEADS ← FEAR OF A BLACK HAT ← WHO'S THE MAN? ← the ADVENTURES OF FORD FAIRLANE / → LAST DAYS, Floyd Vivino *(himself)* ← BIG MONEY HUTLA ← GOOD MORNING, VIETNAM

Storyline: "1-2-3-4 . . . I don't want to be a Pinhead no more" – well, you'll just have to be – retrospective-wise at least – for one long trip on the road with New York's greatest three-chord quartet, the Ramones, warts'n'all. *MCS*

Movie rating: *7

Visual: dvd (see below)

Off the record: Steve Van Zandt went from nearly-man rock star to 'The Sopranos'.

– (non album release) –

RAMONES: Raw

Sep 04. (dvd) *Image; <2278>* [–] [–]
– Blitzkreig bop / Teenage lobotomy / Today your love, tomorrow the world / Rockaway beach / (touring) / Cretin hop / I don't want you / Judy is a punk / I can't make it on time / Do you remember rock and roll radio / I just want to have something to do / Rock n' roll high school / Pinhead / Take it as it comes / She's the one / Sheena is a punk rocker.

RATTLE AND HUM

aka U2: RATTLE AND HUM

1988 (US 90m) Paramount Pictures (PG-13)

Film genre: Rock-music concert/documentary

Top guns: dir: Phil Joanou ← THREE O'CLOCK HIGH

Stars: U2:- Bono, the Edge, Larry Mullen Jr., Adam Clayton *(performers)* / **B.B. KING** *(performer)*, Phil Joanou *(himself)*, **Wayne Jackson** *(Memphis Horns)* → HEART OF GOLD, **Andrew Love** *(Memphis Horns)*

Storyline: Back in the 80s dark ages, before gap years existed, U2 set out in all their post-'Joshua Tree' pomp to "do" America. A recording session at 'Sun', a trip to Graceland, a jam with blues legend B.B. King, it's all here in arty back and white. Concert footage punctuates the pilgrimages as the Irish rockers attempt to create their own myth, one which still divides the critics. *BG*

Movie rating: *7.5

Visual: video + dvd

Off the record: The original cut of the movie lasts 480 minutes!

U2

Oct 88. (d-lp/c)(cd) *Island; <91003> (U2/+C 7)(CIDU 27)* [1] [1]
– Helter skelter (live) / Van Diemen's land / Desire / Hawkmoon 269 / All along the watchtower (live) / I still haven't found what I'm looking for (live) / Freedom for my people / Silver and gold (live) / Pride (in the name of love) (live) / Angel of Harlem / Love rescue me / When love comes to town / Heartland / God part II / The star spangled banner / Bullet the blue sky (live) / All I want is you. *(re-charted UK No.37 on Jun92) (re-iss. Aug93, hit UK No.34)*

S/track review: If 'The Joshua Tree' (1987) was U2's collective imagining of America, "the America of the great R&B and country performers, civil rights people like Martin Luther King and Bobby Kennedy; the new journalism of people like Truman Capote and Norman Mailer", as THE EDGE later explained, 'RATTLE AND HUM' was the reality, recorded on the road. The album's sleeve insert – a shot of the band looking studiously iconic in Memphis' Sun Studios, Elvis beaming down from the back wall and ADAM CLAYTON ramming home the point with a Sun t-shirt – says more about this album than a hundred reviews. This is the sound of U2 doing the field research after they've written the thesis, and why not. There are plenty of missteps, ill-judged covers and blind alleys, but it's often a fascinating trip, and not quite as extraneous and poorly edited as the critical consensus would have it. The live anthems are here of course, but they're not definitive, and it's in the ad hoc, the offbeat and the indulgent which this album holds its charms. With recent research highlighting a bizarre similarity between the gospel singing traditions of Gaelic speaking Scots and Southern Afro-Americans, it doesn't take too much of a leap of the imagination to consider that Irish émigrés may well have put down similarly intertwined roots, religious differences notwithstanding. There's a poignancy to THE EDGE's underrated emigrant elegy, 'Van Diemen's Land', which doesn't require Celtic citizenship to appreciate, a dedication to an obscure Fenian poet which resonates beyond mere history. And while BONO's identification with black America may actually have more substance than he realised, his own sense of spiritual kinship is more than deep enough to carry the likes of Billie Holiday tribute, 'Angel Of Harlem' and the engaging B.B. KING collaboration, 'When Love Comes To Town', huge American hits both. The ragged root and stomp of 'Desire', meanwhile, remains one of U2's most soulfully immediate singles, certainly their most soulful No.1, the gorgeous 'All I Want Is You', arguably BONO's best love song. And for all his political chest beating, the ferocious ambivalence of BONO's 'God Part II', even if it is conceived through the prism of John Lennon, gives the lie to the notion that earnestness is his bottom line. While the inevitable backlash which this record inspired led to a wholesale re-invention of the band and their sound, its grit and soul suggested that U2 and America wasn't such a bad combination. *BG*

Album rating: *8

– spinoff hits, etc. –

U2: Desire / Hallelujah (Here She Comes)

Sep 88. (7") *<99250> (IS 400)* [3] [1]
(12"+=/12"g-f+=/pic-cd-s+=) *(12IS/12ISG/CIDP 400)* – (Hollywood remix).

U2: Angel Of Harlem / A Room At The Heartbreak Hotel

Dec 88. (7") *<99254> (IS 402)* [14] [9]
(12"+=/pic-cd-s+=/US-3"cd-s+=) *(12IS/CIDP/CIDX 402)* – Love rescue me (live with KEITH RICHARDS & ZIGGY MARLEY).

U2 & B.B. KING: When Love Comes To Town / Dancing Barefoot

Mar 89. (7"/c-s) *<99225> (IS 411)* [68] Apr89 [6]
(12"+=/pic-cd-s+=/US-3"cd-s+=) *(12IS/CIDP/CIDX 411)* – ('A'-live from the kingdom mix) / God part II (the hard metal dance mix).

U2: All I Want Is You / Unchained Melody

Jun 89. (7"/7"box/c-s) *<99199> (IS/ISB/CIS 422)* [83] [4]
(ext;12"+=/12"box+=) *(12IS/+B 422)* – Everlasting love.
(pic-cd-s++=) *(CIDP 422)* – ('A'-extended).

□ Johnnie RAY segment
(⇒ the PIED PIPER OF CLEVELAND)

□ the REAL KIDS segment
(⇒ ALL KINDSA GIRLS)

REALITY 86'D

1991 (US 63m) We Got Power

Film genre: Punk Rock-music on-the-road documentary

Top guns: dir: **Dave MARKEY**

Stars: Dave MARKEY *(himself/performer)*, **Black Flag:- Henry ROLLINS, Greg Ginn, Cel Revulta, Anthony Martinez** *(themselves/performers)*, **Sim Cain** *(himself/musician)*, **Andrew Weiss** *(himself/musician)*, Joe Cole *(himself/roadie)* ← SIR DRONE / → 1991: THE YEAR PUNK BROKE, Davo Claasen *(himself)*, Dave "Ratman" Levine *(himself)*, Jordan Schwartz *(himself)* ← DESPERATE TEENAGE LOVEDOLLS ← the SLOG MOVIE / → AMERICAN HARDCORE

Storyline: Former Painted Willie mainman, Dave Markey, gets his teeth into his first rockumentary, having already supplied music features 'DESPERATE TEENAGE LOVEDOLLS' in '84 and its follow-up, 'LOVEDOLLS SUPERSTAR' a few years later. Here we see him spread the camera around the likes of Black Flag, etc. *MCS*

Movie rating: *7

Visual: video (no audio OST)

Off the record: Andrew Weiss has been a seasoned bassist for the likes of the

Rollins Band, Ween, the Butthole Surfers, Pigface, YOKO ONO, etc. Several excerpts from BLACK FLAG's current LP at the time, 'In My Head' (1985), feature in the film. *MCS*

RED HOT CHILI PEPPERS

Formed: Hollywood, California, USA ... 1983 by schoolfriends ANTHONY KIEDIS (aka Antwan The Swan), Israeli-born Hillel Slovak, Australian-born Michael "FLEA" Balzary and Jack Irons. Always the showmen, this motley bunch of funky funsters signed with 'E.M.I.' stark naked as part of a now famous publicity stunt. The exhibitionist streak was to be a mainstay of their early career, most controversially on the cover for the 'Abbey Road' EP in '88, the lads wearing nought but one sock, strategically placed (no prizes for guessing where!) in a send-up of the classic BEATLES album of the same name. With Irons and Slovak under contractual obligations to their own group, What Is This?, drummer Jack Sherman (ex-Captain Beefheart) and guitarist Cliff Martinez (ex-Teenage Jesus & The Jerks and future film composer) filled in on the 1984 eponymous debut album, a promising start which introduced the band's mutant funk-punk hybrid. Taking their cue from the cream of 70s funk (obvious reference points were Sly Stone, JAMES BROWN, the Meters, etc.) and injecting it with a bit of L.A. hardcore mayhem, the 'Chilis spotlighted their tongue-in-cheek, gonzoid grooves. The George Clinton-produced follow-up, 'Freaky Styley' (1985), sounded more cohesive; however, both these LPs were American-only affairs. Meanwhile, FLEA had been independently buzzing around Hollywood searching out some acting work, his appearances in punk movies 'SUBURBIA' (1983) and 'DUDES' (1987) upping his profile somewhat. The bassist furthered his thespian career by appearing in numerous films including 'Tough Guys' (1986), 'Less Than Zero' (1987 w/ KIEDIS), 'Let's Get Lost' (1988), 'The Blue Iguana' (1988), 'Back To The Future II' (& III), 'My Own Private Idaho' (1991), 'ROADSIDE PROPHETS' (1992), etc. The band's manic reputation was beginning to reach across the Atlantic, 'Uplift Mofo Party Plan' (1988) introducing the band to a receptive UK audience. Tougher than their earlier releases, the record consolidated the group's place at the forefront of the burgeoning funk-metal explosion, their brash, kaleidoscopic sound injecting a bit of colour and excitement to Blighty's rather dour rock scene. The party was cut somewhat short, however, with the death of Slovak on June 25th, 1988, yet another victim of a heroin overdose. With KIEDIS also a heroin addict, Irons (who subsequently formed the band, Eleven) obviously didn't like the way things were going and decided to bail out. Eventual replacements were found in guitarist JOHN FRUSCIANTE and drummer Chad Smith, while the group threw themselves into the recording of 'Mother's Milk' (1989). As well as clearly possessing red hot libidos (and indecent assault charges), by the early 90s KIEDIS, FLEA & Co had become red hot property following the release of the Rick Rubin-produced 'Blood Sugar Sex Magik' (1991). Their first release for 'Warner Bros.', at last the band had fulfilled their potential over the course of a whole album (US Top 3). With another series of striking videos, the Chili Peppers almost scored a US No.1 with the aching ballad, 'Under The Bridge' while the body-jerk funk-rock of 'Give It Away' made the UK Top 10. A multi-million seller, the album catapulted the RED HOT CHILI PEPPERS into the big league, the band subsequently securing a prestigious headlining slot on the 1992 Lollapalooza tour. Always an utterly compelling live proposition, the group's hyperactive stage show is the stuff of legend, what with KIEDIS' manic athletics and FLEA's (possibly) JIMI HENDRIX-inspired upside down bass playing, hanging feet-up by a rope!!!. By the release of 'One Hot Minute' (1995), a transatlantic Top 5, Frusciante had been replaced with Dave Navarro (ex-Jane's Addiction), adding a new dimension to the band's sound. Never the most stable of bands, rumours of a 'Peppers split were rife in 1997, although they still managed to hit the UK Top 10 with their fantastic cover of the Ohio Players' 'Love Rollercoaster' (straight from the 'BEAVIS & BUTT-HEAD DO AMERICA' flick). Talking of movies, the band featured in a handful of Rockumentaries, namely 'WOODSTOCK '94' (1995), 'The DECLINE OF WESTERN CIVILIZATION PART III' (1998), 'FREE TIBET' (1998) and 'WOODSTOCK '99', while FLEA himself chose to act in cult classics such as 'FEAR AND LOATHING IN LAS VEGAS' (1998) and 'The Big Lebowski' (1998). With the returning FRUSCIANTE out from the bench to replace Navarro, the band were back with a bang on 1999's 'Californication'. The release of 2002's 'By The Way', saw the RED HOT CHILI PEPPERS proving themselves to be one of the few acts in rock to carry off almost twenty years' worth of consistently wonderful music. Meanwhile back at the land of rock documentaries, FLEA and/or ANTHONY contributed to 'RISING LOW' (2002), 'END OF THE CENTURY' (2003), 'WE JAM ECONO: THE STORY OF THE MINUTEMEN' (2005), another RAMONES bio 'TOO TOUGH TO DIE' (2006) and 'AMERICAN HARDCORE' (2006). The quartet's global superstardom was such that they could record a sprawling double set, call it 'Stadium Arcadium' (2006) and fill it with the kind of ruminatory pop normally associated to others of their ilk. Maybe, it was time for a break. *BG & MCS*

- **filmography** {acting} (composers) –

F.I.S.T. *(1978 {b ANTHONY})* / Jokes My Folks Never Told Me *(1978 {b ANTHONY})* / **Suburbia** *(1983 {b FLEA} OST by ALEX GIBSON =>)* / Stranded *(1986 TV {b FLEA})* / Thrashin' *(1986 {p FLEA})* / Tough Guys *(1986 {p})* / **Dudes** *(1987 {* FLEA})* / Stranded *(1987 {a FLEA})* / Less Than Zero *(1987 {p FLEA + ANTHONY})* / Let's Get Lost *(1988 {p FLEA})* / the Blue Iguana *(1988 {a FLEA})* / Back To The Future II *(1989 {a FLEA})* / Back To The Future III *(1990 {a FLEA})* / Motorama *(1991 {a FLEA} no OST by ANDY SUMMERS)* / My Own Private Idaho *(1991 {a FLEA})* / Point Break *(1991 {b ANTHONY})* / **Roadside Prophets** *(1992 {p FLEA})* / Son-In-Law *(1993 {b FLEA})* / the Chase *(1994 {a FLEA + ANTHONY})* / **Woodstock '94** *(1995 {p} OST by V/A =>)* / Just Your Luck *(1996 {a FLEA})* / Gen 13 *(1998 {v FLEA})* / **the Decline Of Western Civilization Part III** *(1998 {c FLEA})* / **Free Tibet** *(1998 {c FLEA + ANTHONY})* / Small Soldiers *(1998 on OST w/ BILLY DUFFY & V/A; see future edition)* / the Big Lebowski *(1998 {a FLEA})* / **Fear And Loathing In Las Vegas** *(1998 {p FLEA} =>)* / Psycho re-make *(1998 {a FLEA})* / Mascara *(1999 {b FLEA})* / **Nina Hagen = Punk + Glory** *(1999 {c ANTHONY} =>)* / **Woodstock '99** *(1999 {p} OST by V/A =>)* / Liar's Poker *(1999 {* FLEA})* / Goodbye, Casanova *(2000 {a FLEA})* / the Wild Thornberry's Movie *(2002 {v FLEA})* / **Rising Low** *(2002 {p FLEA} =>)* / **End Of The Century** *(2003 {p ANTHONY} =>)* / Rugrats Go Wild *(2003 {v FLEA})* / **We Jam Econo: The Story Of The Minutemen** *(2005 {c FLEA} =>)* / **Too Tough To Die: A Tribute To Johnny Ramone** *(2006 {c FLEA + ANTHONY} =>)* / **American Hardcore** *(2006 {c FLEA} =>)*

RED, WHITE & BLUES

6th part Martin Scorsese presents THE BLUES

2003 (US 120m mini-TV w/b&w) Vulcan Productions / PBS (15)

Film genre: Jazz/Blues-music documentary

Top guns: dir: Mike Figgis

Stars: Jeff BECK *(performer)*, **LULU** *(performer)*, **Tom Jones** *(performer)* ← the EMPEROR'S NEW GROOVE, **John Mayall** *(performer)* ← BAJA OKLAHOMA ← SGT. PEPPER'S LONELY HEARTS CLUB BAND ← DON'T LOOK BACK / → the SOUL OF A MAN, **Eric CLAPTON** *(performer)*, **Jack Bruce/Cream** *(performer)* ← RISING LOW ← KLODEN ROKKER ← GONKS GO BEAT, **Steve Winwood** *(performer)* ← BLUES BROTHERS 2000 ← WOODSTOCK 94 ← GLASTONBURY FAYRE ← CUCUMBER CASTLE ← the GHOST GOES GEAR, **Peter Green**

(performer), **Mick Fleetwood** *(performer)* ← BLUES ODYSSEY ← MR. MUSIC, **Lonnie Donegan** *(performer)* ← the COMPLEAT BEATLES ← the 6.5 SPECIAL, **Chris Farlowe** *(performer)* ← TONITE LET'S ALL MAKE LOVE IN LONDON ← POP GEAR, **Georgie Fame** *(performer)* ← BLUES ODYSSEY, **Van MORRISON** *(performer)*, **Davy Graham** *(performer)*, **Bert Jansch** *(performer)*, **Joe Meek** *(himself)*, **Chris Barber** *(performer)* ← IT'S TRAD, DAD!, **George Melly** *(performer)*, **Ray CHARLES** *(performer)*, **Sister Rosetta Tharpe** *(archive performer)* → WARMING BY THE DEVIL'S FIRE, **Louis Armstrong** *(archive performer)* ← WHEN THE BOYS MEET THE GIRLS, **Humphrey Lyttelton** *(performer)* ← the TOMMY STEELE STORY, **Miles Davis** *(archive performer)*, **Big Bill Broonzy** *(archive performer)* ← WARMING BY THE DEVIL'S FIRE

Storyline: Like Clint Eastwood a man with a passion for black music as well as movies, Mike Figgis tells the crucial story (partly his own story, involving a pre-Roxy Music Bryan Ferry) of how jazz and blues came to Britain, and how young white musicians interpreted, hybridised and transformed them before shipping them back across the sea. Eric Clapton, John Mayall, Stevie Winwood, Chris Farlowe, Eric Burdon et al remember how they collectively shook their money maker, while the likely (Van Morrison, Jeff Beck, Peter Green) and the unlikely (Tom Jones, Lulu) are rounded up for an impromptu Abbey Road session. *BG*

Movie rating: *6.5

Visual: dvd

Off the record: The film was originally aired on American PBS TV on 3rd October, 2003.

—

Various Artists

Sep 03. (cd) *Hip-O; <00007280-2>* ☐ [-]
– Goin' down slow (TOM JONES & JEFF BECK) / Back o' town blues – live (LOUIS ARMSTRONG & ALL HIS STARS) / St. Louis man (DIXIE FOUR) / Black, brown and white blues (BIG BILL BROONZY) / Up above my head I hear music in the air (SISTER ROSETTA THARPE with MARIE KNIGHT) / Rock island line (the LONNIE DONEGAN SKIFFLE GROUP) / Cry me a river (LULU with JEFF BECK) / Generique (MILES DAVIS) / Love letters (TOM JONES with JEFF BECK) / Bad penny blues (HUMPHREY LYTTELTON) / Stormy Monday blues, parts 1 & 2 (LITTLE JOE COOK; aka CHRIS FARLOWE) / Hard times (TOM JONES & JEFF BECK) / Tell the truth – live (RAY CHARLES) / Hey darling (SPENCER DAVIS GROUP) / Shake your money maker (FLEETWOOD MAC) / Have you heard (JOHN MAYALL'S BLUESBREAKERS with ERIC CLAPTON) / Crossroads – live (CREAM) / Rollin' & tumblin' (JEFF BECK) / Lawdy Miss Clawdy (TOM JONES) / Drown in my own tears (LULU with JEFF BECK).

S/track review: With its accent on the old guard laying down new recordings of old tunes, Mike Figgis' Scorsese volume can't quite compete with the preponderance of classic material stuffing the rest of the series. You can't argue with Figgis about TOM JONES' voice, though; the fact is his half-spoken, Hooker-esque drawl sounds like it's been singing the blues since it first breached the valleys. JEFF BECK's guitar is too heavy metallic for the context (Figgis' professed aim to keep the amplification and self-indulgence to a minimum seems slightly optimistic), better reserved for his own showcase, 'Rollin' & Tumblin'', if that's your poison. Their pairing runs to a full four tracks, with JONES sounding more like his old crooning self on Ray Charles' 'Hard Times', Victor Young standard 'Love Letters', and – minus BECK – Lloyd Price's 'Lawdy Miss Clawdy'. A much more composed and economical BECK strings some exquisite lines under a torch singing LULU (and a blazing PETER GREEN) on 'Cry Me A River'. There are the inevitable CREAM and CLAPTON entries but to his credit Figgis doesn't overlook either the Deep South-voiced CHRIS FARLOWE or FLEETWOOD MAC, with PETER GREEN at full strength one of the British blues scene's most visceral, versatile talents, a band with as colourful and fascinating a history as British blues itself, and whose contribution has never really been fully acknowledged. A soulful country blues from BIG BILL BROONZY doubles as an impassioned stand against institutionalised racism, LOUIS ARMSTRONG and JACK TEAGARDEN slay New York's Town Hall, SISTER ROSETTA THARPE/MARIA KNIGHT's 'Up Above My Head I Hear Music In The Air' – despite appearing elsewhere in the Scorsese series – never ever grows old; it could turn a funeral into a festival. But the good SISTER has a rival in MARGIE HENDRIX, the earthiest (we're talking Mississippi mud) of RAY CHARLES' Raelettes, latterly ignored by mainstream narratives and consigned to the cognoscenti of the Northern Soul scene. Even other British players were a huge influence on the British players: Charles Shaar Murray's sleevenotes point out the link between HUMPHREY LYTTELTON and the Beatles' 'Lady Madonna'; well, you learn something blues every day. The most welcome surprise is 'Genérique', from MILES DAVIS' peerless French New Wave soundtrack, 'Ascenseur Pour L'Echafaud'. It's languid and porous, and half obscured in the murk of the blues. It's also the most obvious link to Figgis' own soundtrack work, and among the British material gathered here sounds as thrillingly alien as 50s Paris must've sounded to MILES. *BG*

Album rating: *7

REGGAE

1971 (UK/US 50m TV) Bamboo Records Limited / Impact Films (U)

Film genre: Reggae-music concert/documentary

Top guns: dir: Horace Ove

Stars: Andrew Salkey *(narrator)*, **Desmond Dekker** *(performer)*, **the Pioneers** *(performers)*, **Bob & Marcia** *(performers)*, **Mike Raven** *(DJ/performer)*, **Millie** *(performer)*, **John Holt** *(performer)*, **Black Faith** *(performers)*, **the Pyramids** *(performers)*, **the Maytals** *(performers)*, **Count Prince Miller** *(performer)*

Storyline: Reggae comes to England in the shape of several Jamaican pop artists at a festival at Wembley. Interspersed with interviews with disc jockey, Mike Raven, the Caribbean and the West Indies – in my humble opinion – is not best represented here. This was part of a UK television series, 'Review', aired on 26th March, 1971. *MCS*

Movie rating: *4

Visual: video (no audio OST)

Off the record: Desmond Dekker was the feature here having secured several UK hits, '007 (Shanty Town)', 'Israelites', 'It Miek' and 'You Can Get It If You Really Want'. **Millie** (Millicent Small) was famous for her No.2 hit in 1964, 'My Boy Lollipop', while groups such as **the Pyramids** had chronological chart entries via 'Train Tour To Rainbow City' (1967; No.35), **the Pioneers** 'Long Shot Kick De Bucket' (1969; No.21), **Bob and Marcia** 'Young, Gifted And Black' (1970; No.5) and **the Maytals** 'Monkey Man' (1970; No.47). **John Holt** went on to have a massive hit in 1974 with a version of Kris Kristofferson's 'Help Me Make It Through The Night'. *MCS*

the REGGAE MOVIE

1995 (US/Japan 90m) TriMedia Productions / United Artists (PG-13)

Film genre: Reggae-music concert/documentary compilation

Top guns: dir: Randy Rovins

Stars: Ziggy Marley & the Melody Makers *(performer/s)*, **Burning Spear** *(performer)* ← REGGAE SUNSPLASH ← ROCKERS, **Shaggy & Rayvon** *(performers)*, **Steel Pulse/David Hinds** *(performers)*, **Beres Hammond** *(performer)* → MADE IN JAMAICA, **Garnett Silk** *(performer)*, **Shinehead** *(performer)* → TURN IT UP, **Buju Banton & Wayne Wonder** *(performers)*, **Yami Bolo** *(performer)*, **Freddie McGregor** *(performer)*, **Apache Indian** *(performer)*, **Chaka Demus & Pliers** *(performers)*, **Inner Circle** *(performers)*,

Dennis Brown *(performer)*, **Carlene Davis** *(performer)*, **Maxi Priest** *(performer)*, **Luciano** *(performer)*, **Mystic Revealers** *(performers)*, **Dean Fraser** *(performer)*, Sandra Bernhard *(herself)* ← TRUTH OR DARE

Storyline: Basically a film of live concert clips from the world's best reggae outfits (encompassing dance-hall reggae and lovers-rock reggae), shot at exotic venues in Australia, Japan, America and, of course, Jamaica. *MCS*

Movie rating: *7

Visual: dvd on Pioneer (no audio OST)

Off the record: Tracks featured in the film:- 'Tribute' (DEAN FRASER), 'Oh Carolina' (SHAGGY & RAYVON), 'Someone Better' (BUJU BANTON & WAYNE WONDER), 'It's Growing' (GARNETT SILK) – Garnett died in a housefire on the 9th of December, 1994 – 'It's Me Jah' (LUCIANO), 'Make U Sweat' (INNER CIRCLE), 'Black Roses' (INNER CIRCLE), 'Blues Dance Raid' (STEEL PULSE), 'Jamaican In New York' (SHINEHEAD), 'Got To Be A Better Way' (MYSTIC REVEALERS), 'Putting Up Resistance' (BERESFORD HAMMOND), 'Cry Tough' (CARLENE DAVIS), 'Push Comes To Shove' (FREDDIE McGREGOR), 'Tumblin Down' (ZIGGY MARLEY & THE MELODY MAKERS), 'Peace – Loving Day' (BURNING SPEAR), 'Tease Me' (CHAKA DEMUS & PLIERS), 'Here I Come' (DENNIS BROWN), 'Love Is Dangerous' (YAMI BOLO), 'Boom Shakalak' (APACHE INDIAN & SON), 'Close To You' (MAXI PRIEST) & 'Turn Your Love Up (The Reggae Movie Theme)' (YAMI BOLO). *MCS*

REGGAE SUNSPLASH

1980 (W.Ger/Jama 107m) Arsenal Filmverleih / International Harmony

Film genre: Reggae-music concert/documentary

Top guns: s-w + dir: Stefan Paul

Stars: Bob MARLEY *(performer)*, **Peter Tosh** *(performer)* ← ROCKERS / → HEARTLAND REGGAE → the BOB MARLEY STORY; CARIBBEAN NIGHTS → STEPPING RAZOR RED X, **the Third World Band** *(performers)* ← PRISONER IN THE STREET / → COOL RUNNINGS: THE REGGAE MOVIE → MADE IN JAMAICA, **Burning Spear** *(performer)* ← ROCKERS / → the REGGAE MOVIE, **Big Youth** *(performer)*, **Marcia Griffiths** *(performer)*

Storyline: The 1979 Reggae Sunsplash II Festival in Montego Bay is at the centre of the 16mm-shot movie, featuring as it does the soon-to-be-deceased Bob Marley, Peter Tosh and several other huge names. *MCS*

Movie rating: *6.5

Visual: video (no audio OST)

Off the record: PETER TOSH contributes his version of 'Get Up Stand Up', while the 10CC's 'Dreadlock Holiday' features on the trailer. *MCS*

RELEASE

1999 (US 65m – DVD version) Sersen Park / Victory Records

Film genre: Punk rock-music documentary

Top guns: dir: Brant Sersen

Stars: Bad Religion:- Greg Graffin, Greg Hetson, Brian Baker, Jay Bentley, Bobby Schayer *(performers)* → PUNK'S NOT DEAD, **Blink-182:- Thomas DeLonge** *(performer)* → SHAKE, RATTLE AND ROLL: AN AMERICAN LOVE STORY, **Travis Barker** *(performer)*, **Mark Hoppus** *(himself/performer)* → SHAKE, RATTLE AND ROLL: AN AMERICAN LOVE STORY → GIGANTIC (A TALE OF TWO JOHNS) / **Hatebreed:- Jamey Jasta, Lou "Boulder" Richards, Sean Martin, Chris Beattie, Rigg Ross** *(performers)*, **Bouncing Souls:- Greg Attonito, Pete Steinkopf, Bryan Kienlen, Shal Khichi** *(performers)*, **Less Than Jake:- Chris Demakes, Vinnie Fiorello, Roger Manganelli, Buddy Schaub, Pete Anna** *(performers)*, **MxPx:- Mike Herrera, Tom Wisniewski, Yuri Ruley** *(performers)*, **Face To Face:- Trever Keith, Chad Yaro, Scott Shiflett, Rob Kurth** *(performers)*, **Earth Crisis:- Karl Buechner, Ian "Bulldog" Edwards, Scott Crouse, Kris Weichman, Dennis Merrick** *(performers)*, **H2o:- Toby Morse, Todd Morse, Todd Friend, Adam Blake, Rusty Pistachio** *(performers)*, **Agent Orange:- Mike Palm, James Levesque, Scott Miller** *(performers)*, **Good Riddance:- Russ Rankin, Luke Pabich, Chuck Platt, Sean "SC" Sellers** *(performers)*, **Sick Of It All:- Lou Koller, Pete Koller, Craig Setari, Arman Majidi** *(performers)*, **Home Grown:- Adam Lohrbach, John "John E. Trash" Tran, Ian Cone, Bob Herco** *(performers)*, **Atreyu:- Brandon Saller, Dan Jacobs, Chris Thomson, Travis Miguel, Alex Varkatzas** *(performers)*, **Vision Of Disorder:- Matt Baumbach, Mike Kennedy, Tim Williams, Mike Fleischmann, Brendon Cohen** *(performers)*

Storyline: Aggression and hardcore punk come under the spotlight as we witness quite an array of brutal spiky-topped acts and their crowd-surfing fans. *MCS*

Movie rating: *6.5

Visual: dvd (no audio OST)

Off the Record: Interviews include one with Blink 182's Mark Hoppus as Tom DeLonge awaits his turn to speak. Live bands include Less Than Jake, Bad Religion, etc. *MCS*

REMEMBER ME THIS WAY

1974 (UK 57m) G.T.O. / Rock Artistes Management

Film genre: Glam Rock-music concert/documentary

Top guns: dir (+ s-w): Bob Foster, Ron Inkpen → NEVER TOO YOUNG TO ROCK → SIDE BY SIDE

Stars: Gary Glitter *(himself/performer)*, **the Glitter Band:- John Rossall, Gerry Shepherd, Tony Leonard, Pete Phipps, John Springate, Harvey Ellison** *(performers)* ← NEVER TOO YOUNG TO ROCK

Storyline: Take yourself back to a time when glam rock'n'roll was all the rage – not outrageous!. It's coming up to Christmas at The Rainbow vevue in London 1973, Gary Glitter (and more so, Glittermania!) is king of the castle; at the time GG hadn't been outted as a dirty wee rascal. Shoddy production and the thinnest of plots concerning Gary being on a neo fascist hit list instead of the hit parade, was surely paranoia and/or indeed subsequent headlines: "Guilty Glitter". *MCS*

Movie rating: *2

Visual: video

Off the record: Gary GLITTER (b. Paul Gadd, 8 May'44, Banbury, England) backed by the GLITTER BAND, a group instigated by Glitter's co-writer, Mike Leander was to have appeared in 'SPICEWORLD' – scenes were deleted. *MCS*

GARY GLITTER (songwriters: Gary Glitter & Mike Leander)

Jun 74. (lp/c) *Bell; (BELL S/C 237)* [5] [–]
– I'm the leader of the gang (I am!) / Sidewalk sinner / Baby please don't go / Do you wanna touch me? (oh yeah!) / The wanderer / Rock and roll parts 1 and 2 (medley) / Hello! hello! I'm back again / I didn't know I loved you (till I saw you rock and roll) / I love you love me love / Remember me this way (studio edit).

S/track review: Pre-1999 – and GARY GLITTER's imprisonment for under-age sex – this might well've been a different review, and you would had to have been on Planet Zog to have missed all the tabloid exposure, mainly stemming from the British media. With this in mind, the album 'REMEMBER him THIS WAY' (you'll just have to!), is virtually impossible to review without both GGs entering into the equation. But let's take you back to the summer of 1974, when GLITTER was at his peak as the king of glam-rock, having already notched up several UK Top 5 hits (all included here) in a two-year span. Recorded live at the Rainbow Theatre, London with faithful backers, the GLITTER BAND (who'd just launched their own spinoff pop careers with GG's co-writer, MIKE LEANDER), 'REMEMBER ME THIS WAY' was so poignant in so many respects. One being GARY's bulging, Elvis-Vegas-like attire and his blow-dried quiff, already showing signs of receding. But how the lassies loved him. It's the very first thing you hear on the album, screaming teenage girls baying to GG's every whim, one being 'Do You Wanna Touch Me' a song that is suffixed by . . . (Oh Yeah!). The hits just keep on coming: 'Rock And Roll Parts 1 and 2', 'I Didn't Know I Loved You (Till I Saw You Rock And Roll)', 'Hello! Hello! I'm Back Again', 'I'm The Leader Of The Gang (I Am!)' and 'I Love You Love Me Love' are side by side with renditions of golden oldies such as Big Joe Williams' 'Baby Please Don't Go' and Dion's 'The Wanderer'. But it's the girls screaming at him for more that makes the listening painful and totally cringeworthy. The one time they let up is when GLITTER (real name Paul Gadd) reprises a studio version of his recent hit, 'Remember Me This Way'. It's highly unlikely some record company will release any of his original records on CD, especially this one, and with my eBay copy of the LP scratched to buggery (so to speak), I think I'll donate it to a plot in the back garden. *MCS*

Album rating: *5 (songs) *3 (the album)

RENALDO AND CLARA

1978 (US 232m + 3m UK) Lombard Street Films / Circuit Films (R)

Film genre: Folk Rock-music documentary + experimental drama

Top guns: s-w (+ dir): **Bob DYLAN, Sam Shepard** ← ZABRISKIE POINT / → PARIS, TEXAS → FAR NORTH

Stars: Bob DYLAN *(performer + Renaldo)*, Sara Dylan *(Clara)*, **Joan BAEZ** *(woman in white)*, **Ronnie Hawkins** *(Bob Dylan)* ← the LAST WALTZ / → the LIFE AND HARD TIMES OF GUY TERRIFICO, **Merle Kilgore** *(himself)* ← COAL MINER'S DAUGHTER ← NASHVILLE / → LIVING PROOF: THE HANK WILLIAMS JR. STORY, **Jack Elliott** *(Longheno de Castro)* ← BANJOMAN / → ROADIE → the BALLAD OF RAMBLIN' JACK, Harry Dean Stanton *(Lafkezio)* ← RANCHO DELUXE ← PAT GARRETT & BILLY THE KID / → the ROSE → ONE FROM THE HEART → REPO MAN → PARIS, TEXAS → PRETTY IN PINK → the LAST TEMPTATION OF CHRIST → WILD AT HEART → FEAR AND LOATHING IN LAS VEGAS, Allen Ginsberg *(the father)* ← TEN FOR TWO ← TONITE LET'S ALL MAKE LOVE IN LONDON ← DON'T LOOK BACK ← CHAPPAQUA / → MY GENERATION → NO DIRECTION HOME, Rubin "Hurricane" Carter *(himself)*, **Ronee Blakley** *(Mrs. Dylan)* ← NASHVILLE / → I PLAYED IT FOR YOU, **David Blue** *(himself)*, **Arlo Guthrie** *(mandolin player)* ← WOODSTOCK ← ALICE'S RESTAURANT / → ROADSIDE PROPHETS, **Sam Shepard** *(rodeo)* → ALL THE PRETTY HORSES → SWORDFISH → STEALTH → the ASSASSINATION OF JESSE JAMES . . ., **Joni Mitchell** *(herself)* ← CELEBRATION AT BIG SUR / → the LAST WALTZ → MESSAGE TO LOVE: THE ISLE OF WIGHT FESTIVAL 1970, **Roberta Flack** *(performer)* ← SAVE THE CHILDREN ← SOUL TO SOUL / → BUSTIN' LOOSE, Dylan's band:- **Roger McGuinn** *(performer)* ← BANJOMAN ← the BIG T.N.T. SHOW, **Mick Ronson** *(performer + bouncer)* → ZIGGY STARDUST: THE MOVIE, **David Mansfield** *(performer + angel)*, **Bob Neuwirth** *(performer + the masked tortilla)* ← DON'T LOOK BACK / → SLAVES TO THE UNDERGROUND → NO DIRECTION HOME, **T-Bone BURNETT** *(performer + the inner voice)*, **Luther Rix, Rob Stoner (*), Steven Soles, Scarlet Rivera** → I PLAYED IT FOR YOU, **Howie Wyth** *(performers + roles; Gene Vincent *)*

Storyline: Three films in one here (interpolated), the first highlights Bob Dylan and the Rolling Thunder Revue in concert 1975/76, the second a documentary about the imprisoned boxer, Ruben "Hurricane" Carter, and the third, an improvised piece of drama with Bob and his wife Sara taking on the starring roles. *MCS*

Movie rating: *4.5

Visual: video + dvd (no audio OST – just a promo EP)

Off the record: BOB DYLAN sings (among others – see below) 'When I Paint My Masterpiece' (with BOB NEUWIRTH), 'Isis', Hank Williams' 'Kaw-Liga', 'I Want You', a cover of 'Little Moses', Curtis Mayfield's 'People Get Ready', 'What Will You Do When Jesus Comes', 'If You See Her, Say Hello', 'One Too Many Mornings', 'She Belongs To Me', 'Sad-Eyed Lady Of The Lowlands', 'Patty's Gone To Laredo', 'Mississippi Blues', 'House Of The Rising Sun', 'Never Let Me Go', 'Just Like A Woman' (excerpt with Baez), etc, + other artists:- JOAN BAEZ 'Diamonds And Rust' and Leonard Cohen's 'Suzanne', while RONEE BLAKLEY performs 'Need A New Sun Rising'; other females of the species in the film:- **Joni Mitchell + Roberta Flack**. RONNIE HAWKINS covers Leadbelly's 'In The Pines', (RAMBLIN') JACK ELLIOTT performs 'Salt Pork West Virginia'. Subsequent film score composer **David Mansfield** and **Bob Neuwirth** turn up, while friends **David Blue + Mick Ronson** are not forgotten. ROGER McGUINN performs 'Eight Miles High' into 'Chestnut Mare'. Allen Ginsberg recites 'Kaddish' and William Blake's 'Nurse's Song'. *MCS*

– associated release (*) –

BOB DYLAN: Live 1975 – The Rolling Thunder Revue (The Bootleg Series Vol.5)

Nov 02. (d-cd) *Sony; <87047> Columbia; (510140-2)* 56 69
– Tonight I'll be staying here with you / It ain't me babe (*) / A hard rain's a-gonna fall (*) / The lonesome death of Hattie Carroll / Romance in Durango (*) / Isis (*) / Mr. Tambourine man / Simple twist of fate / Blowin' in the wind (with JOAN BAEZ) (*) / Mama, you been on my mind / I shall be released (with JOAN BAEZ) (*) / It's all over now, baby blue / Love minus zero – No limit / Tangled up in blue (*) / The water is wide (*) / It takes a lot to laugh, it takes a train to cry (*) / Oh, sister / Hurricane (*) / One more cup of coffee / Sara (*) / Just like a woman / Knockin' on Heaven's door (with ROGER McGUINN) (*).

REVOLUTION

1968 (US 90m) United Artists Pictures

Film genre: Rock-music documentary

Top guns: s-w: Jack O'Connell (+ dir), Norman Martin

Stars: Today Malone *(herself)*, Daria Halprin *(herself)* → ZABRISKIE POINT, **Lou Gottlieb** *(himself)*, Kurt Hirschhorn *(himself)*, **Country Joe & The Fish:- Country Joe McDONALD, Barry Melton** *(themselves)*, **the Steve Miller Band:- Steve Miller, Boz Scaggs, Tim Davis, Jim Peterman, Lonnie Turner** *(themselves)* → FILLMORE, **Mother Earth:- Tracy Nelson, Robert Cardwell, John Andrews, Andrew McMahon, Tim Drummond, Karl Himmel** *(themselves)*, **Quicksilver Messenger Service:- Gary Duncan, John Cipollina, David Freiberg, Greg Elmore** (themselves) → FILLMORE, **Dan Hicks** *(performer)*

Storyline: A vivid documentary focusing on San Francisco's hippy nexus with some predictably controversial opinions from the city's self appointed flower children (including starlet, Today Malone). Among the subjects up for discussion are sex, drugs, rock'n'roll, politics and of course, revolution. *BG*

Movie rating: *4

Visual:

Off the record: Lou Gottlieb was singer, songwriter, arranger and bassist with many a pop-folk vocal group, the Gateway Singers and the Limeliters. He was to die of intestinal cancer on the 11th of July 1996, aged 72. *MCS*

QUICKSILVER MESSENGER SERVICE * STEVE MILLER BAND ** MOTHER EARTH ***

Jul 68. (lp) *United Artists; <UAS 5185> (ULP 1226)*
– Revolution (***) / Codine (*) / Superbyrd (**) / Your old lady (**) / Babe, I'm gonna leave you (*) / Without love (***) / Mercury blues (**) / Stranger in my own home town (***).

S/track review: Unsurprisingly, it's the San Fran heavyweights who dominate here, with exclusive tracks from an early, bluesier incarnation of the STEVE MILLER BAND ('Superbyrd', the

Isleys' 'Your Old Lady' and a K.C. Douglas adaptation 'Mercury Blues'), the redoubtable acid-rockers QUICKSILVER MESSENGER SERVICE (with only two cuts, Buffy St. Marie's 'Codine' and future Zeppelin staple, 'Babe, I'm Gonna Leave You') and the lesser-known contemporary blues ensemble MOTHER EARTH (with the title track, Aretha Franklin fave 'Without Love' and Percy Mayfield's 'Stranger In My Own Home Town'). The aforementioned STEVE MILLER BAND (featuring BOZ SCAGGS at this point) paid homage to McGuinn and his funky Byrds via 'Superbyrd', an instrumental with psychedelic overtones; their discography at this point had stretched to two 1968 LPs, 'Children Of The Future' & 'Sailor'. MOTHER EARTH had drifted to the West Coast and its hippy sound via Nashville, Tennessee and Madison, Wisconsin (latter the origin of female singer TRACY NELSON), recording debut LP, 'Living With The Animals' (1968), along the way. Incidentally, if your vinyl's scratched to burglary (so to speak), the QUICKSILVER tracks feature on their 2001 CD compilation, 'Marin County Cowboys'. *MCS*

Album rating: *5.5

RHYME & REASON

1997 (US 94m) Miramax Films (R.)

Film genre: Hip-Hop/Rap-music concert/documentary

Top guns: dir: Peter Spirer → THUG ANGEL → BEEF

Stars: the Notorious B.I.G. *(performer)* ← the SHOW / → BIGGIE AND TUPAC → THUG ANGEL → TUPAC: RESURRECTION → BEEF, **Dr. Dre** *(performer)* ← the SHOW ← MURDER WAS THE CASE / → WHITEBOYS → TUPAC: RESURRECTION, **ICE-T** *(performer)*, **the RZA** *(performer)* → GHOST DOG: THE WAY OF THE SAMURAI → COFFEE AND CIGARETTES → BE COOL, **Method Man** *(performer)* ← the SHOW / → BACKSTAGE → HOW HIGH → BLACK AND WHITE → BROWN SUGAR, **Busta Rhymes** *(performer)* ← WHO'S THE MAN? / → DEATH OF A DYNASTY, **Raekwon** *(performer)* ← the SHOW / → BLACK AND WHITE, **Mack 10** *(performer)* → THICKER THAN WATER → BEEF, **Chuck D.** *(performer)* → GODFATHERS AND SONS, **Kurtis Blow** *(performer)* ← the SHOW ← KNIGHTS OF THE CITY ← KRUSH GROOVE, **Lauryn Hill** *(performer)* → TURN IT UP → BLOCK PARTY, **Wyclef Jean** *(performer)* → CARMEN: A HIP HOPERA → the COUNTRY BEARS → BE COOL → BLOCK PARTY, **KRS-One** *(performer)* ← WHO'S THE MAN? / → BEEF, **Nas** *(performer)* → BEEF, **E-40** *(performer)*, **Da Brat** *(performer)* → CARMEN: A HIP HOPERA → GLITTER, **Sean P-Diddy Combs** *(performer)* ← the SHOW / → BIGGIE AND TUPAC → TUPAC: RESURRECTION → DEATH OF A DYNASTY → FADE TO BLACK, **Erick Sermon** *(performer)* ← JUICE / → RIDE, **Master P** *(performer)*, **Q-TIP** *(performer)*, **Keith Murray** *(performer)* → RIDE, **Redman** *(performer)* → RIDE → BACKSTAGE → HOW HIGH, **L.V.** *(performer)*, **Ras Kass** *(performer)*, **Craig Mack** *(performer)* ← the SHOW, **Heavy D** *(performer)* ← WHO'S THE MAN? / → STEP UP, **MC Eiht** *(performer)* → THICKER THAN WATER, **Louis Freese** *(performer)* ← WOODSTOCK 94 ← WHO'S THE MAN? / → THICKER THAN WATER → HOW HIGH, **Senen Reyes** *(performer)* ← WOODSTOCK 94 / → HOW HIGH, **Tupac SHAKUR** *(archive footage)*

Storyline: Hip-hop and rap music take centre stage in this look-at-this "realistic" study of the genre – the gangstas, the violence, the drugs, the sex, the profanity and the inspiration. *MCS*

Movie rating: *5.5

Visual: video + dvd

Off the record: Chuck D of Public Enemy marks his territory here, while there were appearances by Wu-Tang Clan members. *MCS*

—

Various Artists

Jan 97. (cd) *Priority; <50635>* [16] [–]
– Nothin' but the Cavi hit (MACK 10 & THA DOGG POUND) / Wild hot (BUSTA RHYMES & A TRIBE CALLED QUEST) / Reason for rhyme (EIGHT BALL & MJG) / Uni-4-orm (RAS KASS, HELTAH SKELTAH & CANNIBUS) / Bogus mayn (CRUCIAL CONFLICT) / Every year (E-40) / Tragedy (RZA) / Represent (MC EIHT) / Niggaz don't want it (LOST BOYZ) / Bring it back (KRS-ONE) / Is there a heaven 4 a gangsta? (MASTER P) / Liquor store run (VOLUME 10) / The way it iz (GURU, KAI:BEE & LIL' DAP) / Business first (NYOO & DeCOCA) / No identity (DELINQUENT HABITS).

S/track review: While attempting to capture exactly what the essence and appeal of rap is, 'RHYME & REASON' gathers up a motley crew of vitriolic verbalists for the soundtrack and relies on strong verses and sharp ideas from an array of credible middleweight names rather than blow out with a couple of mammoth ones and a dozen tracks of filler. There does, however, appear to be little logic, theme or, pardon the repetition, reason to what has been put in the mix. There's little sense of history, linearity, continuity to justify the choices. Seasoned campaigners like KRS-1, RZA, A TRIBE CALLED QUEST, BUSTA RHYMES and GURU might not be espousing their finest from their book of rhymes but they commit themselves reputably, setting heads nodding in appreciation of some solid, if not startling work. That's not something that can be said for MASTER P. He may be one of hip hop's great entrepreneurs but he's also one of the genre's most ridiculous lyricists. 'Is There A Heaven 4 A Gangsta?' is punctuated with unintentionally hilarious constipated grunts, the likes of which haven't been heard since Teddy Pendergrass was smooth-talking your chicken into a basket. The finest track here, however, comes from relatively unknown VOLUME 10, who cuts in with an intoxicated gospel-funk drool 'Liquor Store Run' which sways and swaggers, propelled by an unsubtle George Clinton sample. He may sound not unlike Ice Cube enjoying a good day, but it shows you don't have to be profound, original or even sober to throw down a mean track, just inspired. *MR*

Album rating: *6.5

– spinoff hits, etc. –

MACK 10 & THA DOGG POUND: Nothin' But The Cavi Hit / **MASTER P:** Is There A Heaven For A Gangsta

Nov 96. (c-s/12"/cd-s) *<53263>* [38] [–]

RIGHT ON!

1970 (US 80m) Concept East N.Y. / Leacock-Pennebaker

Film genre: Rap-music concert/documentary

Top guns: dir: Herbert Danska

Stars: the Original **Last Poets:- Felipe Luciano, David Nelson, Gylan Kain**

Storyline: A Cannes award-winning documentary from the director of Charlie Parker-inspired drama, 'Sweet Love, Bitter' (1967). Danska films a day in life of the Original Last Poets, capturing them in full-flow in their local NY haunts. *BG*

Movie rating: *9

Visual: none as yet

Off the record: (see below)

—

the original LAST POETS

Feb 71. (lp) *Juggernaut; <STLP 8802>* [ ] [–]
– Jibard – My pretty nigger / Been done already / Hey now / Die nigga!!! / Rifle – Oracion-rifle player / Tell me brother / Black woman / James Brown / Soul / Today is a killer / Little Willie

Armstrong Jones / Puerto Rican rhythms / Poetry is black / Jazz / Shalimar / Into the streets / Alley / Library. *<cd-iss. Sep91 on 'Collectables'; COL 6500> (UK lp-iss.2004 on 'Dagored'; DAG 156)*

S/track review: Umar Bin Hassan having recently hit the Billboard singles chart with Common, and the likes of Jill Scott, Chuck D, Erykah Badu and even Doug E Fresh set to collaborate on a Last Poets tribute album, now seems as good a time as any to revisit this long lost soundtrack. The fact that Bin Hassan doesn't even appear on it matters less than the album's lyrical olympics and volcanic anger, generated by a trio who'd split from the larger ensemble they'd helped form on the anniversary of Malcolm X's birthday in May 1968. While Bin Hassan, Jalal Nuriddin (aka the mighty Lightnin' Rod) and others were the most visible faction, one which turned up on the soundtrack to Nic Roeg's 'Performance' (1970), released a series of albums on the 'Douglas' label and which itself subsequently splintered into further factions, the trio of DAVID NELSON, FELIPE LUCIANO and GYLAN KAIN billed themselves as the ORIGINAL LAST POETS and became the subject of Herbert Danska's equally long lost documentary. Prior to punk and notwithstanding the more aggressive strains of 60s free jazz, the LAST POETS (in both incarnations) were driven by an unprecedented ferocity, distilled from the germ of black pride and civil rights. If they weren't quite as eloquent as Gil Scott-Heron in directing that anger, the thrill of their art lay in its anarchy and humour. The bare, conga-accompanied routines breach comfort zones at the drop of a syllable, firing on savage imagery and flashbulb insight, and showing up contemporary hip hop for the "circus" which Hassan recently dubbed it. The social, political and spiritual predicament of the American black man (and to a lesser extent the Hispanic man; Luciano does a mean Spanish language rap) is the main agenda and KAIN, LUCIANO and NELSON don't so much mince their words as grind them into dust, raging against white intellectuals and white religion. KAIN's sermons, especially, leave a pungent aftertaste: 'Been Done Already' is a furious requiem for Afro-America set to the old spiritual, 'Swing Low, Sweet Chariot', 'Tell Me Brother / Black Woman' a harrowing contrast in horror and utopia. But it's not all glowering rhetoric; they also sing about sex, and they do it with a humour and style that's long escaped hip hop. 'Jazz' unflinchingly reclaims the term's original meaning in one long, loping stride: "jazz is a woman's tongue stuck dead in your motherf***ing mouth', and 'The Shalimar' competes for the funniest, most vivid account of a whorehouse on record, running riot with anthropomorphism and dropping a line ("the voodoo hoodoo what you don't dare do people") which the Prodigy turned into their greatest track. Righteous, sexy, vicious and hip, the 'POETS were the baying spermatozoon of rap. Be very grateful. *BG*

Album rating: *8.5

RIZE

2005 (US 85m) HSI Productions / Got Films / Lions Gate Films (PG-13)

Film genre: Hip Hop/Dance-music documentary

Top guns: dir: David LaChapelle

Stars: "Tommy The Clown" Johnson *(himself)*, **Lil'C** *(performer)*, Dragon *(himself)*, Larry Berry *(himself)*, Miss Prissy *(herself)*, Tight Eyez *(himself)*, La Nina *(herself)*

Storyline: After the Rodney King trial and the subsequent racial tensions in L.A., Tommy the Clown takes to the streets to promote his message of reconciliation through dance. Featuring African dance rituals and incredible limb gyrations, the Clown's unique style becomes known as "Krumping". Soon the craze takes off and instead of street warfare rival gangs dance against each other to see who is the best. *JZ*

Movie rating: *7

Visual: dvd

Off the record: (see below)

—

Various Artists (composers: JOSE CANCELA & AMY MARIE BEAUCHAMP *)

Jul 05. (cd) *Forster Bros; <88888> Silva Screen; (SILCD 1201)* ☐ ☐
– Rize "w/ dialogue snippet" (FLii STYLZ) * / Break it on down (battlezone) (FLii STYLZ & TENASHUS) / Fix up, look sharp (DIZZEE RASCAL) / Clownin' out (FLii STYLZ & DAP) * / I Krump "w/ dialogue snippet" * / Soar (CHRISTINA AGUILERA) / Oh! happy day (the EDWIN HAWKINS SINGERS) / Get Krumped (FLii STYLZ & LIL'C) / Make you dance (FLii STYLZ, DAP & TENASHUS) / Beaztly (FLii STYLZ) / Ready to brawl (DAP & PLANET ASIA) / Recognize (FLii STYLZ) * / By and by (FIVE BLIND BOYS OF ALABAMA) / Seek ye the Lord (the CARAVANS) / Amazing grace (ALICE RIDLEY) / Rize score suite (A&J MUSIC PRODUCTIONS, RED RONIN & FLii STYLZ) *.

S/track review: The fine art of krumping and clowning remains a cult phenomenon, even after David LaChapelle's excellent documentary about the dance craze that sent ripples across America in the mid-00s. The soundtrack, however, proved a respectable jump off point for those involved. Producer Red Ronin was on hand to help cherry-pick the best tunes from the music that had sprung up around the movement, centring on the talents of FLii STYLZ, who is the dominant force here providing a narrative voice throughout his eight tracks. His sound is that of the dirty south, low-slung, grimy magic that is simultaneously rootsy and futuristic, which compliments his deep vocal style which is reminiscent of DMX. In contrast, the remaining eight tracks cover all bases in the black musical spectrum. A couple of antique spirituals are thrown in to devastating effect, the tumultuous gospel brilliance from the EDWIN HAWKINS SINGERS performing their 1972 version of 'Oh! Happy Day' and FIVE BLIND BOYS OF ALABAMA giving a roaring rendition of 'By And By'. Less spiritual are a shrill cover of 'Seek Ye The Lord' by the CARAVANS and ALICE RIDLEY's schmaltzy 'Amazing Grace'. What is novel is the inclusion of a contemporary take on gospel pop, 'Soar' (from CHRISTINA AGUILERA). It's praise be to the genius of DIZZEE RASCAL's boisterous modern classic, the unsubtle bombast of 'Fix Up, Look Sharp', a song that, despite FLii STYLZ's name-checking of the dance moves in his tunes, generates a suitable jerky, skeletal rhythm to fully capture the dynamics of the frenzied, seemingly random dance moves. *MR*

Album rating: *7

the ROAD TO GOD KNOWS WHERE

1990 (Ger 90m b&w +23m video) DFFB / MuteFilms / uMs-productions

Film genre: alt-Rock-music documentary road movie

Top guns: s-w + dir: Uli M. Schuppel

Stars: **Nick CAVE** *(himself/performer)* & **the Bad Seeds:- Mick HARVEY** *(himself/performer)*, **Blixa Bargeld** *(himself/performer)* → NINA HAGEN = PUNK + GLORY, **Thomas Wydler** *(performer)*, **Kid Congo Powers** *(performer)*, **Roland Wolf** *(performer)* / **Lydia LUNCH** *(herself)*, Rayner Jesson *(himself)*

Storyline: Australian indie-rocker, Nick Cave (& His Bad Seeds), take to the road for a combination of videos, live footage of a US concert and a segment on a dark gothic murder – I think! *MCS*

Movie rating: *7

Visual: video + dvd (latter w/ one-hour 1992 'Paradiso' video)

Off the record: No audio OST but video has nine CAVE tracks:- 'Knocking On Joe', 'Saint Huck', 'The Mercy Seat – live', 'New Morning', 'In The Ghetto', 'Tupelo', 'The Singer', 'The Mercy Seat' and 'Deanna'; the video adds:- 'From Her To Eternity', 'Jack's Shadow', 'New Morning', 'In The Can' and 'Lost Highway'. The 'Live At The Paradiso' freebie has twelve tracks, some are different alternatives to the movie equivalents. *MCS*

the ROAD TO MEMPHIS

part 3 of Martin Scorsese presents THE BLUES

2003 (US 120m TV-mini w/b&w) Vulcan Productions / PBS (PG)

Film genre: Blues-music documentary

Top guns: dir: Richard Pearce / s-w: Robert Gordon

Stars: Bobby Rush *(performer)*, **B.B. KING** *(performer)*, **Howlin' Wolf** *(archive performer)* ← FESTIVAL / → GODFATHERS AND SONS, **Ike Turner** *(performer)* ← BLUES ODYSSEY ← SOUL TO SOUL ← GIMME SHELTER ← IT'S YOUR THING ← the BIG T.N.T. SHOW / → GODFATHERS AND SONS, **Rosco Gordon** *(performer)* ← ROCK BABY ROCK IT, **Rufus Thomas** *(performer)* ← ONLY THE STRONG SURVIVE ← GREAT BALLS OF FIRE! ← MYSTERY TRAIN ← WATTSTAX, **Hubert Sumlin** *(performer)* → LIGHTNING IN A BOTTLE, **Jim Dickinson** *(performer)*, **David JOHANSEN** *(performer)*, **Sam Phillips** *(himself)* ← BLUES ODYSSEY, **Calvin Newborn** *(himself)*, **Chris Spindel** *(performer)*, **Cato Walker II** *(performer)*, **Dr. Louis Cannonball Cantor** *(performer)*

Storyline: Richard Pearce offers up one of the warmest portraits in the series, intertwining the story of BB King (whose chagrin at being booed for playing blues at the advent of rock'n'roll is still visible decades later; "it was like being black twice" he laments) and the story of Beale Street, the famous Memphis thoroughfare which once heaved with black folks living it up in jazz and blues clubs. Now, as the late, supremely loveable Rosco Gordon laments, it's full of chain restaurants, gaudy tourist shops and blues-rockers playing so loud you can scarcely hear yourself think. Pearce accompanies the indefatigable Bobby Rush around on his endless tour, interviews the irascible and incredulous Rufus Thomas and reunites Ike Turner and a bearded Sam Phillips, who proceed to argue on the finer points of who invented rock'n'roll. The film is all the more poignant for subsequent demise of not only Gordon, but also Thomas and Philips, to whom it's dedicated. *BG*

Movie rating: *8.5

Visual: dvd on 'Pinnacle' (SMADVD 032)

Off the record: Rosco Gordon (b.10 Apr'28, Memphis, Tennessee) was a blues pianist responsible for many a tune including 'No More Doggin'', 'Do The Chicken' and 'Love You Till The Day I Die'; he died on the 11th of July 2002. *MCS*

—

Various Artists

Sep 03. (cd) *Hip-O; <B0000705-02>*
– Beale Street ain't Beale Street no more – live street recording (REV. GATEMOUTH MOORE) / Dust my broom (ELMORE JAMES) / Three o'clock blues (B.B. KING) / How many more years (HOWLIN' WOLF) / Moanin' at midnight (HOWLIN' WOLF) / Rosco's boogie (ROSCO GORDON) / Mystery train (LITTLE JUNIOR'S BLUE FLAMES) / Rocket 88 (JACKIE BRENSTON) / Precious Lord (B.B. KING) / Hoochie man – live (BOBBY RUSH) / Done got old – live (ROBERT BELFOUR) / Hen pecked (BOBBY RUSH) / Medley: Stand still, stay right here – Dance for the Devil – live (REV. CHARLES E. POLK & THE ST. LUTHER CHOIR) / I pity the fool (BOBBY BLAND) / Bring it on home (SONNY BOY WILLIAMSON) / Killing floor – live (HUBERT SUMLIN & DAVID JOHANSEN) / Now you're gone (ROSCO GORDON).

S/track review: From the fearsome exorcisms of HOWLIN' WOLF to the Rick James-goes-chitlin' gas of BOBBY RUSH's 'Hen Pecked' ("I'm not hen pecked, I've just been pecked by the right hen"), this volume of Scorsese's odyssey takes as its subject the city of Memphis, blues central ever since rural hoodoos invaded its urban space. As he's one of the stars of the film, so RUSH is the star of a soundtrack which – by repeating the likes of ELMORE JAMES' 'Dust My Broom' – doesn't correlate entirely to the movie, but blazes anyhow. RUSH is a man happy to growl about his "hoochie mama" on Saturday night and take his place in the pew on Sunday morning, digging brilliant grass roots church-funk (like all the best funk, sounding like it was recorded in a cowshed) and shouting at the Devil under the roaring eye of REV. CHARLES E. POLK; if anyone is, RUSH has to be the living embodiment of the blues, a living example of the same sacred-profane theme haunting Charles Burnett's 'WARMING BY THE DEVIL'S FIRE'. The fact that ROBERT BELFOUR laments the onset of old age in typical if compelling blues style, while RUSH is "gonna dye my hair so the girls can't see my gray", probably sums up the man's staying power. Aside from the more familiar story of BB KING, the other star is ROSCO GORDON, eclipsed by the dawn of rock'n'roll but back for more in the dusk of old age: boogie woogie piano and a primitive, single note sax-honk scrape GORDON's fag-end of a voice on a vintage 'Sun' cut, mellowed fifty years later into a shag tobacco croon with Nina Simone-esque vibrato. Even by the hard knock standards of the blues, it truly is a tragedy that this man ended up dry cleaning clothes for a living. JACKIE BRENSTON's seminal 'Rocket 88' fires off an opening salvo for rock'n'roll through an IKE TURNER-sanctioned mist of fuzz, JUNIOR PARKER rides the equally seminal 'Mystery Train' and BOBBY BLAND wails over the backbeat of legendary funk drummer JOHN "JABO" STARKS. Less pertinent but still sublime is SONNY BOY WILLIAMSON's definitive, incantatory version of Willie Dixon's 'Bring It On Home', while less pertinent still, but surprisingly feral, is HUBERT SUMLIN and newly reclaimed New York Doll DAVID JOHANSEN's take on WOLF's 'Killing Floor'. 'THE ROAD TO MEMPHIS' mightn't knit together thematically as well as some of the other collections, but musically and charismatically it's timed to perfection, stitched together so well you can hear the rough edges without seeing the joins; if you're after a soundtrack for a weekend-break to a Memphis which no longer exists, these are your men. *BG*

Album rating: *8.5

ROCK AND ROLL CIRCUS

aka The ROLLING STONES: ROCK AND ROLL CIRCUS

1996 (UK 65m) Abkco Films

Film genre: Rock-music concert/documentary

Top guns: dir: Michael Lindsay-Hogg ← LET IT BE / → TWO OF US

Stars: the ROLLING STONES:- Mick Jagger, Keith Richards, Brian Jones, Bill Wyman, Charlie Watts *(performers)*, + **Nicky Hopkins** *(keyboards)* / **John Lennon** *(performer)* <= the BEATLES =>, **Yoko ONO** *(performer)*, **the WHO:- Roger Daltrey, John Entwistle, Pete Townshend, Keith Moon** *(performers)* / **Jethro Tull:- Ian Anderson *, Clive Bunker *, Tony Iommi, Glenn Cornick *** *(performers)* * → MESSAGE TO LOVE: THE ISLE OF WIGHT FESTIVAL / **Ivry Gitlis** *(violinist)*, **Taj MAHAL** *(performer)*, **Jesse Ed Davis** *(performer)* ← the CONCERT FOR BANGLADESH, **Mitch Mitchell** *(performer)* ← JIMI HENDRIX ← RAINBOW BRIDGE ← MONTEREY POP / → EXPERIENCE, **Marianne Faithfull** *(performer)* ← the WALL: LIVE IN BERLIN ← LUCIFER RISING ← DON'T LOOK BACK ← ANNA, Donyale Luna *(herself)* ← SKIDOO ← TONITE LET'S ALL MAKE LOVE IN LONDON

Storyline: A television special – filmed on the 10th & 11th of December, 1968 – this extravaganza feature was shelved because the Rolling Stones'

manager at the time thought that other groups on show (most notably the Who) upstaged them. Performing under a psychedelic circus big top theme, the Stones and Co (co for costumes?) plough their way through some of their best tunes. *MCS*

Movie rating: *7

Visual: dvd

Off the record: Brian Jones was to quit the 'Stones a few months after recording '. . .Circus'; he'd drowned on the 3rd of July, 1969. *MCS*

---

the ROLLING STONES (& Various Artists)

Oct 96. (cd/c) *Abkco; <1268> Deram; (526771-2/-4)* 92 May99

– (Mick Jagger's introduction to Rock And Roll Circus) – Fucik's Entry of the gladiators (FUCIK) / (Mick Jagger's introduction of . . .) – Song for Jeffrey (JETHRO TULL) / (Keith Richard's introduction of . . .) – A quick one, while he's away (WHO) / Rosas' Over the waves / Ain't that a lot of love (TAJ MAHAL) / (Charlie Watts' introduction of . . .) – Something better (MARIANNE FAITHFULL) / (Mick Jagger's and John Lennon's introduction of . . .) – Yer blues (DIRTY MAC) / Whole lotta Yoko (YOKO ONO & IVRY GITLIS/DIRTY MAC) / (John Lennon's introduction of The ROLLING STONES):- Jumpin' Jack Flash / Parachute woman / No expectations / You can't always get what you want / Sympathy for the Devil / Salt of the earth.

S/track review: Shelved for nigh on three decades, this soundtrack finally saw the light of day in the mid-90s and while the feverish anticipation which foreshadowed its release suggested a lost, Royal Albert Hall-like masterpiece, the reality was a bit more ragged and, in places, a lot more compelling. Music biz lore had it that the 'STONES felt upstaged by the WHO's operatic – and admittedly bruising – contribution, 'A Quick One While He's Away'. They needn't have worried. On set climax 'Sympathy For The Devil', MICK JAGGER sounds truly lost to his own demons, "flaunting himself in narcissistic fury . . . an apparition of Lucifer awoken at a séance of the blues" according to sleevenote chronicler David Dalton. Old MICK even had a tattoo to match, baring its grisly, horned visage to the audience in the midst of his frenzy. As a piece of rock'n'roll theatre it's hard to beat and although the 'STONES steered clear of the dark side following Altamont, here they were truly in their unsavoury element, grinding out leering versions of 'Jumping Jack Flash', 'You Can't Always Get What You Want' and the rarely heard 'Parachute Woman', as well as a searing 'No Expectations'. As a historical document, it's also worth its weight in patchouli oil for the JOHN LENNON/ERIC CLAPTON/ MITCH MITCHELL/KEITH RICHARDS aggregate drolly dubbed the DIRTY MAC. As well as a coruscating, caterwauling trawl through LENNON's 'Yer Blues', the ad-hoc supergroup unveiled Yoko Ono and violinist Ivry Gitlis for 'Whole Lotta Yoko', great if you can somehow blank out Ono's bloodcurdling shrieks. Ian Anderson – whom the teenybop audience regarded in "disgusted tones" according to Dalton – sounds like an Arthurian Captain Beefheart on 'Song For Jeffrey', while TAJ MAHAL dodged Musicians Union restrictions for a driving 'Ain't That A Lot Of Love'. Factor in MICK's cocky barrow-geezer intro and surreal banter with LENNON, and you've got an essential 'STONES document, an affecting freeze frame of a band poised between the Brian Jones era and the rock legends who'd concurrently release four of the greatest albums in popular music history. *BG*

Album rating: *6

ROCK & ROLL HEART

aka LOU REED: ROCK & ROLL HEART

1998 (US 73m w/b&w) American Masters PBS / WNET Channel 13

Film genre: avant-Rock-music documentary bio-pic

Top guns: dir: Timothy Greenfield-Sanders

Stars: Lou REED *(himself/performer)*, **John Cale** *(himself/performer)* ← NICO ICON ← the VELVET UNDERGROUND AND NICO, **David BOWIE** *(himself)*, **David BYRNE** *(himself)*, **Patti Smith** *(herself)* ← the BLANK GENERATION / → BENJAMIN SMOKE → YOU'RE GONNA MISS ME, **Maureen Tucker** *(herself/performer)* ← the BAND THAT WOULD BE KING ← the VELVET UNDERGROUND AND NICO, **Jim Carroll** *(himself)*, Penn Jillette *(himself)* → FEAR AND LOATHING IN LAS VEGAS ← the BAND WHO WOULD BE KING, Mary Woronov *(herself)*, **NICO** *(archive performer)*, **Sterling Morrison** *(archive performer)* ← NICO-ICON ← the VELVET UNDERGROUND AND NICO, Andy Warhol *(archive)* ← NICO-ICON ← BLANK GENERATION ← IMAGINE ← COCKSUCKER BLUES ← the VELVET UNDERGROUND AND NICO / → DETROIT ROCK CITY → END OF THE CENTURY, **Thurston Moore** *(himself)* <= SONIC YOUTH =>, **Suzanne Vega** *(herself)*, **David A. Stewart** *(himself)*, Joe Dallesandro *(himself)* ← CRY-BABY ← JE T'AIME MOI NON PLUS, Holly Woodlawn *(herself)*

Storyline: "The definitive film on one of rock's most legendary icons", Lou Reed, this piece of celluloid collates the man's career (via concert footage and interviews) from his mid-60s days in the Primitives and the Velvet Underground to his work as a solo artist, etc. *MCS*

Movie rating: *8

Visual: video on 'Winstar' 71107 + dvd (no audio OST)

Off the record: LOU REED delivers most of his faves, 'Heroin' (live in Italy), 'Kicks', 'Sweet Jane', 'Dirty Blvd.', 'Walk On The Wild Side', 'Metal Machine Music' (excerpt), etc. All the other original VELVET UNDERGROUND members are present and correct here **John Cale, Maureen Tucker**, even the dearly departed **Sterling Morrison** and **NICO** (who released their mortal coils – so to speak – in 1995 and 1988 respectfully); a handful of VU songs appear in the film. Holly Woodlawn was born Haraldo Danhakl and part of Andy Warhol's NY drag queens; REED sang "he was a she . . ." on 'Walk On The Wild Side', while on the same song Joe Dallesandro is "Little Joe" the hustler. **Jim Carroll** was a post-New Wave solo star, whose autobiography 'The BASKETBALL DIARIES' was made into a feature movie. *MCS*

ROCK & ROLL SUPERHERO

2003 (US 89m) POD Films

Film genre: rock-Music documentary

Top guns: dir: Peter O. Devin (story: Fernanda Rossi)

Stars: Watt White *(himself/vocalist)*, **Jay Salley** *(himself/bassist)*, Asaf Shor *(himself/drummer)*, **Zak** *(himself/guitarist)*

Storyline: Over the course of three years we follow Watt White's attempts at rock superstardom (by day he sells shoes). His troubles begin when he hires two Israeli accompanists who cause major personality clashes and send the band into debt. Watt is determined to succeed come what may, as deep down he knows he was always destined to be famous. First Mr White will have to get his finances in the black again. *JZ*

Movie rating: *4

Visual: dvd (no audio OST by WATT WHITE)

Off the record: Watt White self-financed a handful of CD releases from 1993, notably 'Watt You Want' & 'Winter Blues'. Post-millennium, he was part of the SmashUp – one thinks! *MCS*

ROCK'N'ROLL JUNKIE

1994 (Neth 90m) Delta Film / Hardcore Music Films (18)

Film genre: Punk Rock-music concert/documentary bio-pic

Top guns: dir: Jan Eilander, Eugene Van Den Bosch, Frenk Van Der Stere, Ton Van Der Lee

Stars: Herman Brood *(himself/performer)* ← CHA-CHA / → NINA HAGEN = PUNK + GLORY, **Nina Hagen** *(herself)* ← CHA-CHA / → NINA HAGEN = PUNK + GLORY

Storyline: Basically, the life and times – up to 1994 – of legendary Dutch singer/pianist, Herman Brood, who personified the term sex, drugs and rock'n'roll. *MCS*

Movie rating: *6

Visual: video (no audio OST; see below)

Off the record: Herman Brood was born in Zwolle, The Netherlands, on 5th Nov'46. Having taken an early interest in rock'n'roll piano players, LITTLE RICHARD and FATS DOMINO, the teenage Herman formed his first band, the Moans (who would later evolve into Long Tall Ernie & The Shakers). In 1975, after numerous outfits came and went, he finally released his debut LP, 'Showbiz Blues'; the formation of Vitesse (with Herman van Boeyen) and one eponymous set was completed the following year. With the advent of punk-rock, Brood's career went from strength to strength and by the late 70s, he had amassed a string of homeland hits with his band, the Wild Romance; the single, 'Saturdaynight' even cracked the US Top 40 in 1979.. A subsequent movie 'CHA-CHA' (1980) – confusingly the name of a 1978 LP – with Nina Hagen and Lene Lovich as co-stars got the man an even higher profile, although little was known of the man outside Dutch quarters. Further acting work side by side with a plethora of albums and painting, took up most of the 80s and 90s. However, a life of sex, drugs and rock'n'roll – as portrayed in the '. . . JUNKIE' movie, took its toll and on the 11th of July, 2001, he jumped to his death from the top of the Amsterdam Hilton. *MCS*

– associated compilation –

HERMAN BROOD: The Hits – My Way

Oct 01. (cd) *B.M.G.; <8843921>* ☐ ☐-
– Saturday night / Love you like I love myself / Still believe / Never be clever / Hot shot / Too much grace / Blew my cool over you / Als je wint heb je vrienden / Hold on tight / Tattoo song / Checkin' out / If love is dead / All the girls 're crazy / Street / I don't need you / 50 jaar / Pijn / Sleepin' bird / Rock'n'roll junkie / Saturday night (big band version) / Back on the corner / Dance on / When I get home / My way.

ROCK SCHOOL

2005 (US 93m) A&E IndieFilms / Newmarket Films (R)

Film genre: Rock-music documentary

Top guns: dir: Don Argott

Stars: Paul Green *(himself)*, **Paul Green School Of Rock Music:- C.J. Tywoniak, Will O'Connor, Madi Diaz-Svalgard, Tucker Collins, Asa Collins, Andrea Collins** *(musicians)*, **Napoleon Murphy Brock** *(himself/performer)*, **Jimmy Carl Black** *(performer)* ← UNCLE MEAT ← 200 MOTELS ← MONDO HOLLYWOOD

Storyline: A real-life sort of 'SCHOOL OF ROCK', this documentary sees unconventional Philadelphia music buff, Paul Green, set about teaching kids (after-school students aged between 9 and 16) how to perform in a rock band. Will they hit the big time (or even the right notes) during their performance at a Frank Zappa tribute gig in Germany? *MCS*

Movie rating: *7

Visual: dvd

Off the record: Jimmy Carl Black was one-time guitarist with the sadly missed Frank Zappa.

---

the PAUL GREEN SCHOOL OF ROCK MUSIC (featuring . . .)

May 05. (cd) *Trillion; <3>* ☐ ☐-
– Black magic woman (feat. GREGG ROLIE) / I wanna be sedated (feat. MARKY RAMONE & TYSON RITTER of ALL AMERICAN REJECTS) / School's out (feat. ALICE COOPER) / Barracuda (feat. ANN WILSON) / Highway star (feat. IAN GILLAN) / L.A. woman / Heart of the sunrise (feat. JON ANDERSON) / Rebel yell (feat. BILLY IDOL) / Don't stand so close to me (feat. STEWART COPELAND) / Iron man / Peace sells (feat. DAVE MUSTAINE) / Hocus pocus.

S/track review: One for the headbanging brigade, this OST takes another step further by putting the young masterclass students of the PAUL GREEN SCHOOL OF ROCK in the spotlight next to their "professors". Yes, Classic Rock, for a whole new future generation and produced by man-in-the-know, Grammy Award-winning Phil Nicolo. The soundtrack features a dozen pieces of assorted 70s & 80s rock, mainly on the hard side but there are a few lighter pieces such as 'Black Magic Woman' (featuring Santana's GREGG ROLIE), 'Barracuda' (featuring Heart's ANN WILSON), 'Heart Of The Sunrise' (featuring Yes vocalist JON ANDERSON), 'Don't Stand So Close To Me' (featuring the Police drummer STEWART COPELAND) and the class-on-their-own version of the Doors' 'L.A. Woman'. One can't fault the sheer gusto and drive of the youngsters, who seem never in awe of the Rock God masters. With PAUL GREEN not far away, many of the kids (aged as young as 9) seem destined for greater things, while in the film at least, GREEN is a hard task-master who wants and gets results. He seems to forget there are winners and losers in this world, no matter how many of the former you create. Anyway, the new Hard-Rock kids on the block get in their element so to speak, when they perform on the likes of 'School's Out' (featuring ALICE COOPER), 'Rebel Yell' (featuring BILLY IDOL), 'Highway Star' (featuring Deep Purple's IAN GILLAN) and 'Peace Sells' (with Megadeth's DAVE MUSTAINE). For those young enough to Rock, we salute you! *MCS*

Album rating: *7

ROCKSHOW

1980 (UK 105m) MPL Communications / Miramax Films

Film genre: Ppp/Rock-music concert/documentary

Top guns: dir: **Paul McCartney**

Stars: Paul McCartney *(performer)* <= the BEATLES =>, **& Wings:- Linda McCartney** *(performer)* ← SGT. PEPPER'S LONELY HEARTS CLUB BAND ← ONE HAND CLAPPING ← LET IT BE / → CONCERTS FOR THE PEOPLE OF KAMPUCHEA → GIVE MY REGARDS TO BROAD STREET → GET BACK, **Denny Laine** *(performer)* ← ONE HAND CLAPPING / → CONCERT FOR KAMPUCHEA / → CHASING DESTINY → WINGSPAN, **Jimmy McCulloch** *(performer)* ← ONE HAND CLAPPING, **Joe English** *(performer)*, **Howie Casey** *(performer)* → THIRTY YEARS OF MAXIMUM R&B LIVE, Tony Dorsey, Steve Howard Jr., Thaddeus Richard *(themselves)*

Storyline: Paul McCartney shows the viewer what it was like on tour with his band, Wings, as they sold out and performed the last stages of a 10-country world tour in 1976; it climaxes before a 65,000+ crowd at the King Dome in Seattle. *MCS*

Movie rating: *6

Visual: video on HBO/Cannon (the film was reeled out for a week at a Boston concert hall – not a conventional movie theatre)

Off the record: Scotsman, **Jimmy McCulloch**, was a member of Thunderclap Newman, who had a hit with 'Something In The Air'. *MCS*

– associated release – (tracks *)

WINGS: Wings Over America

Jan 77. (t-lp/d-c) *Parlophone; (PCSP/TC-PCSP 720) Capitol; <11593>* 8 Dec76 1
– Venus and Mars rock show (*) / Jet (*) / Let me roll it (*) / Spirits of ancient Egypt (*) / Medicine jar (*) / Maybe I'm amazed (*) / Call me back again / Lady Madonna / The long and winding road / Live and let die (*) / Picasso's last words (drink to me) / Richard Cory / Bluebird (*) / I've just seen a face / Yesterday (*) / You gave me the answer / Magnet and titanium man (*) / Go now (*) / My love / Listen to what the man said (*) / Let 'em in (*) / Time to hide / Silly love songs (*) / Beware my love (*) / Letting go (*) / Band on the run (*) / Hi, hi, hi (*) / Soily. *(d-cd-iss. May87; CDS 746715-2) (re-iss. 1989 d-lp/d-c; ATAK/TC-ATAK 17)*

ROKK I REYKJAVIK

1982 (Ice 83m) Icelandic Film Center

Film genre: Punk Rock-music concert/documentary

Top guns: dir: Fridrik Thor Fridriksson → NICELAND

Stars: Tappi Tikarrass:- BJORK *(performer/s)*, **Vonbrigdi** *(performers)*, **Purkur Pillnikk** *(performers)*, **Ego** *(performers)*, **Beyr** *(performers)*, **Fraebbblarnir** *(performers)*, **Q4U** *(performers)*, **Baraflokkurrin** *(performers)*, **Jonee Jonee** *(performers)*, **Peyr** *(performers)*, **Bodies** *(performers)*, **Fridryk** *(performer)*, **Bruni BB** *(performer)*, **Sjalfsfroun** *(performer)*, **Spiladielf** *(performers)*, **Mogo Homo** *(performers)*, **Grylurnar** *(performers)*, **Sveinbjorn Beinteinsson** *(performer)*

Storyline: 19 "indie" acts from er . . . Iceland (c. early 80s) find an outlet for their unique brand of underground rock – but where are they now?. Frontrunners, Tappi Tikarrass, were the stamping ground for a very youthful Bjork, later of the country's mainstream breakthrough group, the Sugarcubes. *MCS*

Movie rating: *6

Visual: video

Off the record: (see below)

Various Artists

1983. (d-cd) *Smekkleysus; (SMS 02)* – Icelan –
– O Reykjavik (VONBRIGDI) / Sieg heil (EGO) / Gotta go (FRAEBBBLARNIR) / Ovaent (PURKUR PILLNIKK) / Rudolf (BEYR) / Creeps (Q4U) / Breyttir timar (EGO) / Where are the bodies (BODIES) / Hrollur (TAPPI TIKARRASS) / Moving up to a motion (BARAFLOKKURINN) / Talandi hofudq (SPILADIELF) / I kirkju (FRIDRYK) / Lifio og tilveran (START) / Gullurio (GRYLURNAR) // Sat eg inni a klepp (EGO) / Gluggagaegir (PURRKUR PILLNIKK) / Durkulisur (TAPPI TIKARRASS) / Bereft (MOGO HOMO) / Hver er svo sekur (JONEE JONEE) / Killer boogie (PEYR) / Kick us out of the country (BODIES) / Af pvi pabbi vildi pad (JONEE JONEE) / I nott (FRAEBBBLARNIR) / Gudfraedi (VONBRIGDI) / Storir strakar (EGO) / Gonna get you (Q4U) / Toys (Q4U) / Lollipops (SJALFSFROUN) / Antichrist (SJALFSFROUN) / Sjalfsfroun (SJALFSFROUN) / Af litlum neista verqur mikid mai (BRUNI BB) / Rimur (SVEINBJORN BEINTEINSSON).

S/track review: For a scene that spawned a million Identikit bands the world over, 'ROKK I REYKJAVIK' showcases a surprising diversity and level of quality within the Icelandic punk scene of the early 80s. Yes, there are a few fake English accents and some blatant Ramones rip-offs, but there is no escaping the originality and character present on those tracks delivered in their native tongue. We hear punk in all its forms; from visceral thrash-a-rounds to post-punk art-rock, and atonal yelping howls to detached laconic musings. Although most tracks are typically short sharp bursts and two-minute sprint-throughs there is still room for some expansive, experimental and even glam-leaning offerings. Performances range from the below-amateurish (see the offerings from SJALFSFROUN) to the fairly professional, and there is even room for some accomplished soloing on 'Lífio Og Tilveran' by START. The funky and spiky post-punk of BEYR would easily fit today's post-punk revival with 'Rudolf', whilst their Talking Heads-influenced 'Killer Boogie' is equally excellent; BODIES' 'Where Are The Bodies' also featured a twisted Byrne-esque delivery. Amongst the well-captured, frenzied live recordings and wilfully discordant moments we find the hook-laden catchiness of EGO's 'Sieg Heil' and 'Stórir Strákar' and the bouncing riffery of Q4U's 'Creeps' and TAPPI TIKARRASS (featuring a young pre-Sugarcubes BJORK). Continuing in this vein 'Guđfrđi' by VONBRIGÑI' is an exciting burst of bass-heavy experimental darkness reminiscent of the sound that would transform into American College Rock, whilst MOGO HOMO are progressive enough to be led by synths and drum machines on 'Bereft'. Soon Iceland would not be looking to the UK, or elsewhere, for its inspiration but would be looking inward to continue its eccentric musical journey, which is hinted at in the traditional-sounding closing track, SVEINBJORN BEINTEINSSON's 'Rímur'. *LF*

Album rating: *6

the ROLLING STONES

Formed: London, England . . . mid-1962 by Brian Jones, MICK JAGGER and Keith Richards. As the progenitors of white boy rock'n'roll as defined by its simplified, sexualised reduction of Afro-American blues, the ROLLING STONES pretty much invented youth culture as we know it, or at least its more rebellious, anti-authoritarian face. Led by ol' rubber lips himself, MICK JAGGER, with the dependably surly Keith Richards and the doomed Brian Jones bringing up the rear, and BILL WYMAN and Charlie Watts blankly comfortable in their relative anonymity, the 'Stones' unsettling chemistry was never going to translate to the big screen, at least not outside of a performance context. While there are plenty of celluloid documents of the band's mid-60s incarnation, when hits like '(I Can't Get No) Satisfaction' and 'Paint It Black' presented a sullen alternative to the BEATLES' sugary pop, the London bad boys only really got to grips with the medium in Michael Lindsay-Hogg's 'ROCK AND ROLL CIRCUS'. Conceived as a TV special and shot in late 1968, the accompanying album was almost immediately mothballed and only saw the light of day in 1996. As valuable for the performances of its various contributing artists as for the 'Stones own performance, it hangs together better than many 60s concert sets despite its rambling, amateurish feel. The band's other noteable docu from this period, 'GIMME SHELTER' (1970), was a different beast entirely, a disturbing vision of idealism turning sour amid the murder and anarchy of a poorly organised free concert. While Jean-Luc Godard had already used footage of JAGGER and Co rehearsing 'SYMPATHY FOR THE DEVIL' in his pseudo-revolutionary documentary, 'ONE PLUS ONE' (1968), the song's performance in 'GIMME SHELTER' is more far more chilling and thought provoking than anything in Godard's film. At the height of his fame and midway between the blistering triptych of 'Beggars Banquet' (1968), 'Let It Bleed' (1969) and 'Sticky Fingers' (1971), JAGGER actually turned his hand to acting, putting in a suitably gender bending role as a reclusive rock star in the Donald Cammell/Nicholas Roeg masterpiece, 'PERFORMANCE' (1970). JAGGER and Richards also wrote a song ('Memo From Turner') for the film, a sleazy, sneering monologue which, even during this period of unrivalled creativity, ranked as the best thing they'd recorded that year. JAGGER's other film role of the period, as an Irish outlaw with a faintly ridiculous accent in 'NED KELLY' (1970), isn't so well remembered. Nor – save the peerless 'Exile On Main Street' (1972) – are many of the band's 70s albums. The tour which accompanied 'Exile . . .' furnished the raw material for Robert Frank's infamous documentary, 'COCKSUCKER BLUES' (1972), a film so controversial the band employed legal means to prevent its release. Much less contentious but probably funnier was 'The RUTLES' (1978), the Neil Innes/Eric Idle-masterminded Beatles send-up, featuring MICK (and then girlfriend Bianca) in a mock interview and new 'Stones member RON WOOD as a Hells Angel. Even Richards and WYMAN took time off from interminable stadium performances, the former putting in an appearance in the the Who docu, 'The KIDS ARE ALRIGHT' (1979) and the latter composing the score for hackneyed British action flick, 'GREEN ICE' (1981). WYMAN was also the surprising subject of Robert Dornhelm's experimental, partly animated biopic, 'Digital Dream' (1983), and subsequently appeared in satirical Comic Strip effort, 'EAT THE RICH' (1987). Ron Wood also made a cameo appearance in a forgotten 80s teen comedy, 'The Wild Life' (1984). More compelling was 'Burden Of Dreams' (1982), Les Blank's documentary on the making of Werner Herzog's 'FITZCARRALDO'. Herzog had originally cast JAGGER as his leading man and Blank's docu featured the few scenes Mick shot before delays obliged him to abandon the project. Among the various members still rolling with the world's greatest rock'n'roll band, JAGGER was the only one who maintained a regular relationship with the big screen through the 80s and beyond, screenwriting 'BLAME IT ON THE NIGHT' (1984), contributing the theme song to crime farce, 'Ruthless People' (1986), and starring in all-star sci-fi effort 'Freejack' (1992), as a drag queen in Nazi drama, 'Bent' (1997) and as a male escort agency owner in 'The Man From Elysian Fields' (2001). In 2004, he finally combined his interest in film via his waning writing talent, scoring the remake of 'ALFIE' with Eurythmic David A. Stewart. *BG*

- **filmography** (composers) {acting} –

Charlie Is My Darling *(1966 {*****} =>)* / **Tonite Let's All Make Love In London** *(1967 {*****p} OST by V/A =>)* / **Rock And Roll Circus** *(1968 {*****p} OST w/ V/A 1995 =>)* / **Sympathy For The Devil** *(1968 {*****p})* / **Popcorn** *(1969 {c MICK} =>)* / **Ned Kelly** *(1970 {* MICK} =>)* / **Gimme Shelter** *(1970 {*****p})* / **Performance** *(1970 {* MICK} =>)* / **Lucifer Rising** *(1972 {c MICK} =>)* / **Cocksucker Blues** *(1972 {*****p} bootleg OST =>)* / **Ladies And Gentlemen, The Rolling Stones** *(1974 {p*****} =>)* / **Mahoney's Last Stand** *(1976 OST by WOOD & RONNIE LANE =>)* / **the Rutles** *(1978 TV {*c MICK + RON} =>)* / **the Kids Are Alright** *(1979 {c KEITH} =>)* / **Green Ice** *(1981 OST by BILL WYMAN =>)* / Burden Of Dreams *(1982 {a MICK})* / **Let's Spend The Night Together** *(1983 {*****p} =>)* / Digital Dreams *(1983 {* BILL} score by WYMAN & MIKE BATT)* / the Wild Life *(1984 {c RON})* / **Blame It On The Night** *(1984 [s-w MICK] =>)* / Willie And The Poor Boys *(1985 {***p CHARLIE, BILL + RON} video/OST by V/A =>)* / **Running Out Of Luck** *(1986 {* MICK} =>)* / **Hail! Hail! Rock'n'Roll** *(1987 {*p KEITH} on OST by CHUCK BERRY =>)* / **Eat The Rich** *(1987 {c BILL} =>)* / **25X5: The Continuing Adventures Of The Rolling Stones** *(1990 {p*****} =>)* / **At The Max** *(1991 {p*****} =>)* / Freejack *(1992 {* MICK]} on OST by V/A; future edition =>)* / Bent *(1997 {* MICK})* / Bad City Blues *(1999 score by MICK TAYLOR & MAX MIDDLETON)* / the Man From Elysian Fields *(2001 {* MICK})* / **Blues Odyssey** *(2002 {*h BILL} OST by V/A =>)* / **Alfie** re-make *(2004 OST by JAGGER & DAVE STEWART =>)* / **Fallen Angel** *(2004 {c KEITH})*

Henry ROLLINS

Born: Henry Garfield, 13 Feb'61, Washington, DC, USA. After cutting his teeth in the "straight edge" (militantly clean living) hardcore punk scene of the late 70s, ROLLINS made his name with the seminal Black Flag. Recruited in time for their 'Damaged' (1981) opus, ROLLINS added a manic intensity to the brilliant 'Six Pack' as well as new numbers like 'Life Of Pain' and the title track. So extreme was the record that MCA's top man, Al Bergamo, tried to block the record's release even though thousands of copies had already been pressed. ROLLINS honed his writing and performing talents over a further series of albums, eventually going solo after the release of 'Loose Nut' (1985); examples of his early times can be witnessed in 'The SLOG MOVIE' (1982). 'Hot Animal Machine' (1987) was a crudely visceral debut, ROLLINS indicating that, if anything, his solo career was going to be even more uncompromising than his work with Black Flag. Later the same year, the singer released the mini album, 'Drive By Shooting', under the pseudonym, Henrietta Collins And The Wife-Beating Child Haters, a taste of ROLLINS' particularly tart brand of black humour. By 1988, the Rollins Band line-up had solidified around guitarist Chris Haskett (who'd played on the earlier releases), bassist Andrew Weiss and drummer Simon Cain, releasing the Ian MacKaye (of hardcore gurus, FUGAZI)-produced 'Life Time' (1988) album later that year. An incendiary opus, the record was the band's blueprint, setting the agenda for future releases with a lyrical incisiveness and musical ferocity that would be hard to equal. Following a slot on the hugely successful 1991 Lollapalooza tour, the Rollins Band moved from cult status to a major label deal with 'Imago/RCA', releasing 'The End Of Silence' in early '92. With this set, ROLLINS had penned his most introspective work to date, leaving no stone unturned. The fact that he'd seen his best friend, Joe Cole, gunned down in cold blood had obviously deeply affected the singer and subsequently the material on the album. This intensely personal exorcism is what made ROLLINS' shows so damn compelling; for ROLLINS, this was far and beyond mere entertainment, for the most part at least, and this was no doubt a major contributing factor in the band's constant live work. As well as a punishing regime of physical exercise, ROLLINS found time to run his own publishing company, 2.13.61 (showcasing work of underground authors as well as ROLLINS' own material, including his acclaimed collection of short stories, 'Black Coffee Blues') and tour his darkly observant, often hilarious and ultimately inspiring spoken word sets. A choice selection of the latter were included on the double-set, 'Boxed Life' (1993). The Rollins Band, meanwhile, returned in 1994 with the hybrid jazz-metal 'Weight', their most commercially successful set to date, and a record which finally made inroads into the UK market, almost making the Top 20. Musically, the album was more accessible than its predecessor, firmly establishing ROLLINS & co as "alt rock" heavyweights. More recently, ROLLINS has expanded his jack-of-all-trades CV with another burst of acting (he'd made his onscreen debut alongside Lydia Lunch in 1990s 'Kiss Napoleon Goodbye' short), appearing in 'The Chase' and 'Johnny Mnemonic' as well as scoring a cameo in the much-heralded De Niro/Pacino face-off, 'Heat'. In mid '96, ROLLINS was the subject of a lawsuit (an 8-figure sum) by 'Imago' for allegedly signing with 'Dreamworks' while under contract, the singer claiming he was let go by the major distributors of the label, 'B.M.G.'. Despite all this, the singer returned to the fray in 1997 with a new album, 'Come In And Burn', the record actually appearing on 'Dreamworks'. Come the new millennium, ROLLINS had parted company with his longtime backing musicians and teamed up with Mother Superior, a three-piece unit who had already been making waves in their own right. The resulting 'Get Some Go Again' (2000) was an impressively back-to-basics effort from a man who just seems to get angrier with age. With ROLLINS becoming something of an all-round celebrity (acting in more features: 'Lost Highway', 'Jack Frost' & 'A House On A Hill') it remains to be seen whether he can retain the outsider intensity of old, though it wouldn't be an idea to argue with the man! The aforementioned album was matched by 2001's much stronger 'Nice'. On this record, ROLLINS stormed his way through the rock-steady beats and wailing heavy guitars, occasionally backed by horns or a female backing singer to great lighthearted effect. From 2003, a plethora of recordings (on his '2.13.61' label) were released, while several various artists rockumentaries (from 'WE JAM ECONO' to 'PUNK'S NOT DEAD') bore the ROLLINS brand name. *BG & MCS*

- **filmography** {acting/performance} –

the Slog Movie *(1982 {*} =>)* / **Reality 86'd** *(1991 {p} =>)* / Jugular Wine: A Vampire Odyssey *(1994 {*})* / the Chase *(1994 {*})* / **Woodstock '94** *(1995 {p} on OST by V/A =>)* / Johnny Mnemonic *(1995 {*})* / Heat *(1995 {a})* / Platinum *(1997 {c})* / Lost Highway *(1997 {a} OST by Angelo Badalamenti & V/A; see future edition)* / You Saw Me Up There *(1998 {p})* / Jack Frost *(1998 {*} OST by Trevor Rabin; see future edition)* / Morgan's Ferry *(1999 {*})* / Desperate But Not Serious *(1999 {a})* / Batman Beyond: Return Of The Joker *(2000 {v})* / **My Generation** *(2000 {p} on OST by V/A =>)* / Scenes Of The Crime *(2001 {a})* / Time Lapse *(2001 {*})* / Dogtown And Z-Boys *(2001 {c})* / Psychic Murders *(2002 {*})* / the New Guy *(2002 {a})* / Jackass: The Movie *(2002 {c})* / Shadow Realm *(2002 TV {b})* / Bad Boys II *(2003 {a} OST by V/A; see future edition)* / a House On A Hill *(2003 {*})* / Feast *(2005 {*})* / **We Jam Econo: The Story Of The Minutemen** *(2005 {c} =>)* / **Punk: Attitude** *(2005 {c} =>)* / Live Freaky Die Freaky *(2006 {v})* / the Alibi *(2006 {a})* / **Too Tough To Die: A Tribute To Johnny Ramone** *(2006 {c} =>)* / **American Hardcore** *(2006 {p} =>)* / **Punk's Not Dead** *(2007 {p} =>)* / Wrong Turn 2: Dead End *(2007 {*})*

□ RUDE BOY
(⇒ Rock Movies/Musicals..)

RUN-D.M.C.

Formed: Hollis, New York, USA . . . 1982 by Joe Simmons (aka RUN) and Daryll McDaniels (aka MC D) along with Jason Mizell (aka DJ, Jay-Master-Jay). These schoolboy friends had persuaded Joe's brother Russell (owner of 'Rush' productions and future co-chairman of the seminal 'Def Jam' label) to let them make a record, the result being the seminal 1983 single, 'It's Like That' / 'Sucker M.C.'s'. Oft quoted as the record which kickstarted modern hip-hop, 'Sucker M.C.'s' substituted the conventional live backing band of the day for stripped down, pulverising drum machine beats. RUN-D.M.C. also had attitude aplenty, their leather-clad, sneaker-obsessed B-Boy image more accurately reflecting street culture and what was going down in the underground clubs. With the help of Russell, they signed to 'Profile', releasing their eponymous debut the following year. Underscoring their uncompromising vision, the record introduced the group's pioneering marriage of metal and rap on the stinging 'Rock Box', subsequently going gold. 1985 saw the group make an appearance in the film 'KRUSH GROOVE' (based on the life of Russell), alongside the likes of Kurtis Blow and the BEASTIE BOYS as well as releasing a follow-up album, 'King Of Rock' (1985), taking their rock/rap hybrid to new extremes. But it was 'Raising Hell' (1986) which really put RUN-D.M.C. on the map, their genius collaborative effort with AEROSMITH (then in a career trough) on the latter's 'Walk This Way' making them chart stars (Top 5 UK, Top 10 US). From the style frenzy of 'My Adidas' to the vocal wordplay of 'Peter Piper' and 'It's Tricky', the record led the mid-80s hip hop zeitgeist, becoming the first rap album to go platinum. A year is a long time in hip hop, and by the release of 'TOUGHER THAN LEATHER' (1988), hard hitting young upstarts like PUBLIC ENEMY were crossing over to the lucrative white audience with a vengeance. Although tracks like 'Run's House' and 'Beats To The Rhyme' stood up among the best of their earlier work, the record lacked the fire of old, while a film of the same name failed miserably at the box office. 'Back From Hell' (1990) barely scraped into the US charts and though the record had its moments, it failed to remedy the group's critical and commercial decline. A difficult period for them, Simmons and McDaniels had undergone various personal problems, the latter suffering from alcoholism while Simmons was accused of rape. They eventually re-emerged three years later on 'Down With The King' (1993), its title a reference to their recent religious conversion. With contributions from the cream of the rap fraternity, the album was a reasonable success, their first foray into the US Top 10 in five years. However, along with the likes of the once mighty Jungle Brothers, Rakim, etc., RUN-D.M.C. have failed to re-invent themselves (like old buddies the BEASTIE BOYS), their sound now somewhat dated in a hip hop scene which thrives on constant flux. Although they did finally re-emerge in the new millennium, 'Crown Royal' (2001; although it was scheduled for '99) sounded as tired as their image looked. *MCS & BG*

- **filmography** {actors/performance}

Krush Groove *(1985 {p} OST by V/A =>)* / **Tougher Than Leather** *(1988 {*} =>)* / **Who's The Man?** *(1993 {p} OST by V/A =>)* / Freestyle: The Art Of Rhyme *(2000 {p})* / Red Dragon *(2002 {b JOSEPH})* / 5 Sides Of A Coin *(2003 {p})* / **Death Of A Dynasty** *(2003 {bx2} =>)* / **Roll Bounce** *(2005 {b DARYL} =>)* / Just For Kicks *(2005 {c})*

the RUNAWAYS

Formed: Los Angeles, California, USA . . . mid-1974 by notorious solo star-turned-record producer Kim Fowley (along with teen lyricist, Kari Krome), who set out to create a female Ramones. After successfully applying to his music paper ad, JOAN JETT became the first to join, followed soon after by Sandy West and Micky Steele. With a few gigs under their belt, Steele was replaced by CHERIE CURRIE, while the line-up was finalised with the addition of Lita Ford and Jackie Fox. This was the formation that played a rooftop session on a Los Angeles apartment block in early 1976, an event that helped secure a record deal with 'Mercury'. While their eponymous debut was hitting the shops, the girls (average age 16) made their New York debut at CBGB's in September '76 supporting Television and TALKING HEADS. Dragging glam-metal by the pubic hair and injecting it with punk energy, tracks such as 'Cherry Bomb' and 'Hollywood' saw the RUNAWAYS lumped in with the fermenting US New Wave scene. Early in '77, they released a second album, 'Queens Of Noise', and like its predecessor it too failed to capitalize on the hype. Internal tensions were coming to a head around the time of the Japanese-only (the RUNAWAYS were huge in the Far East) live set, Vicki Blue standing in for the worn out Fox, while the blonde CURRIE finally split for a solo career (JOAN JETT taking over vocal duties). Adopting a harder-edged approach, the new line-up released yet another album, 'Waitin' For The Night' (1978), the last to feature Lita Ford (another Runaway to go on to a semi-successful solo career) and Vicki Blue (who had attempted suicide). Although Laurie McCallister was brought in as a brief replacement, she didn't play on a posthumous covers set, 'And Now . . . The Runaways', the band having already split. JOAN JETT was the third and most successful member to carve out a solo niche, however, Fowley subsequently resurrected the name (minus any original members!) for a less than impressive 1987 set, 'Young And Fast'. Meanwhile, JOAN JETT (born Joan Larkin, 22 Sep'60, Philadelphia, Pennsylvania) followed her baptism by new-wave fire by relocating to London, where she hooked up with ex-SEX PISTOLS Steve Jones and Paul Cook. The results were to eventually surface in 1979 on UK indie label 'Cherry Red' as the aforementioned 'And Now . . . The Runaways'. Back in America, the singer came under the wing of veteran 60s producer/session man Kenny Laguna, who helped finance the independent US release of JETT's eponymous solo debut (issued by 'Ariola' in

Europe) in 1980. Intense interest subsequently led to a deal with Neil Bogart's 'Boardwalk' operation, the record remixed and re-released the following year as 'Bad Reputation'. With backing by the Blackhearts (Ricky Bird, Gary Ryan and Lee Crystal), the album was a heady hoedown of post-glitter raunch-pop, cruising on a hefty dose of punk energy and a healthy, two-fingered attitude to music industry convention. Culled from follow-up set, 'I Love Rock'n'Roll' (1981), the sledgehammer riffing and foot-stomping bravado of the anthemic title track saw JETT and her Blackhearts scale the US charts and stay there for nigh-on two months; the single also made a significant impact in the UK, which JETT would nevertheless find difficult to sustain. Although the album itself narrowly missed the top spot Stateside, the harder hitting set only spawned one other major hit, a cover of Tommy James & The Shondells' 'Crimson And Clover', Bogart's surprise death casting a shadow over proceedings. Moving to 'M.C.A.' for the third set, the originally titled 'Album' (1983), the record witnessed JETT expanding her musical horizons somewhat, attempting a partially successful run-through of Sly Stone's 'Everyday People'. The spunky 'Glorious Results Of A Misspent Youth' (1984) was another strong set, although by this point, JETT's commercial muscle was flagging. Despite being three years in the making, 'Good Music' (1987) did little to rectify matters, its diversions into rock-rap failing to mask a lack of inspiration. With an acting appearance alongside Michael J. Fox in 'LIGHT OF DAY' and a US Top 10 hit with 'I Hate Myself For Loving You', JETT's fortunes took a turn for the better in 1988. With Tommy Price and Casmin Sultan replacing Crystal and Ryan respectively, the accompanying album, 'Up Your Alley' (1988), saw the group benefiting from the golden pen of Desmond Child. No such help was needed on 'The Hit List' (1990), a solid covers set which took in everything from the Sex Pistols ('Pretty Vacant') to Creedence Clearwater Revival ('Have You Ever Seen The Rain'). 1992's 'Notorious' again saw Child (along with Diane Warren) share writing duties, while JETT duetted with the Replacements' Paul Westerburg on the poignant 'Backlash'. While her raw power may only surface in fits and starts, JOAN JETT remains something of a cult figurehead for female anti-rockers such as L7 and Babes In Toyland, while she's also acted in movies, 'DU-BEAT-E-O' (1984), 'Boogie Boy' (1997), 'By Hook Or By Crook' (1997), 'The Sweet Life' (2003), etc. Her former Runaway chum, CURRIE, has also acted in various movies: 'Foxes' (1980), 'WAVELENGTH' (1983) and 'Rich Girl' (1991), while Vicki Blue (see 'THIS IS SPINAL TAP') put the record straight with her "film about the Runaways", 'EDGEPLAY' (2004). *MCS & BG*

- **filmography** {actresses/performance} –

Foxes *(1980 {* CHERIE} CURRIE on OST by V/A & Giorgio Moroder; see future edition =>)* / **Urgh! A Music War** *(1981 {p JOAN} JETT & The BLACKHEARTS on OST by V/A =>)* / Parasite *(1982 {a CHERIE})* / Twilight Zone: The Movie *(1983 {a CHERIE})* / **Wavelength** *(1983 {* CHERIE} OST by TANGERINE DREAM =>)* / **Du-beat-e-o** *(1984 {c JOAN} =>)* / **This Is Spinal Tap** *(1984 {a VICKI} OST by SPINAL TAP =>)* / the Rosebud Beach Hotel *(1984 {b CHERIE})* / **Light Of Day** *(1987 {*/p JOAN} OST by JETT & Cast =>)* / the Return Of Bruno *(1988 {a VICKI})* / Rich Girl *(1991 {a CHERIE})* / Highway To Hell *(1992 {a LITA})* / **Not Bad For A Girl** *(1996 {p JOAN} =>)* / Boogie Boy *(1998 {a JOAN})* / By Hook Or By Crook *(2001 {a JOAN})* / Kiss My Grits: The Herstory Of Women In Punk And Hard Rock *(2001 {p JOAN})* / the Sweet Life *(2003 {a JOAN})* / **Mayor Of The Sunset Strip** *(2003 {c CHERIE + JOAN} OST by V/A =>)* / **Edgeplay: A Film About The Runaways** *(2004 {p} [s-w + dir VICKI] OST by the RUNAWAYS & V/A =>)* / Hollywood Trash & Tinsel *(2004 {c VICKI})* / Leather Forever *(2004 [s-w + dir VICKI] =>)* / el Camino Del Diablo *(2005 [s-w + dir VICKI] score by FORD)*

RUST NEVER SLEEPS

1979 (US 103m) Crest Productions / Shakey Pictures

Film genre: Roots/Rock-music concert documentary

Top guns: dir: **Neil YOUNG** as Bernard Shakey

Stars: Neil YOUNG *(performer)* & **Crazy Horse:- Ralph Molina, Billy Talbot, Frank 'Pancho' Sampedro** *(performers)* → YEAR OF THE HORSE

Storyline: Neil Young & Crazy Horse filmed by the man himself at a concert in the Cow Palace on 22nd October, 1978. Like any superstar worth their salt, Neil Young has always been adept at reinventing himself, or at least reinventing his image. Turned out in white kecks and braces, short haired and immaculately clean shaven, his late 70s persona is still one of his most compelling; at times in this epochal film he looks like a smalltown farmer on market day, idly ambling around the stage, busking a few tunes. The conceptual baggage then – oversized speakers/flight cases, Star Wars/Jawa-style roadies with glowing eyes (Road Eyes, duh . . .), men in white coats, that infamous Woodstock brown acid announcement etc, etc. – appears all the more superfluous. As Young moves from solo acoustica to Crazy Horse aggro, peak moments include 'After The Goldrush', a feral 'Sedan Delivery', Thrasher', 'Like A Hurricane' and 'Powderfinger', the latter's thunder stolen by a space-monk and a giant tuning fork. Billy Talbot (sporting a 'Skynyrd t-shirt) judders like a convulsive Lou Reed, the whole three of them twitch like clockwork mice and a Sun Ra-style loon does a fleeting moonstomp on 'Welfare Mothers'. "Ladies and gentlemen, please put on your rust-a-vision-let's rust!". *BG*

Movie rating: *8

Visual: video + dvd

Off the record: Bernard Shakey was the directorial nom de plume for Young, who also went on to his first feature, 'HUMAN HIGHWAY'. *MCS*

NEIL YOUNG & CRAZY HORSE: Live Rust

Nov 79. (d-lp/d-c) *Reprise; <2296> (K/K4 64041)* 15 55
– Sugar mountain / I am a child / Comes a time / After the gold rush / My my, hey hey (out of the blue) / When you dance I can really love / The loner / The needle and the damage done / Lotta love / Sedan delivery / Powderfinger / Cortez the killer / Cinnamon girl / Like a hurricane / Hey hey, my my (into the black) / Tonight's the night. *<(cd-iss. Jul93; 7599 27250-2)>*

S/track review: It's surprising how many soundtracks have borne NEIL YOUNG's signature over the last quarter century, how his neo-primitivism has so often been tied up with the visual medium. By the late 70s, Spinal Tap speaker stacks and monastic cowls were the limit of a conceptual streak which had seen his earlier film, 'JOURNEY THROUGH THE PAST', consigned to commercial obscurity. YOUNG had famously recognised a kindred spirit in punk, burning through the end of an era as his Topanga Canyon peers "faded away", rebooting and unleashing the sonic brutalism of CRAZY HORSE on some of the leanest, least sentimental writing of his career. 'RUST NEVER SLEEPS' served notice that a shorn-maned YOUNG wasn't going down quietly. Wielding his "Old Black" Gibson like a war veteran, he'd pieced some of the album together from a recent tour, the same vault which generated 'Live Rust' before the year was out. Shrewdly sticking to a folk-graduating-to-grunge template, he midwifes a gorgeous 'I Am A Child' and 'Lotta Love' before pummelling into the frantic, quasi-punk poetry of 'Sedan Delivery', a distortion-frenzied 'Hey Hey, My My (Into The Black)' and the peerless 'Powderfinger', still one of the greatest anti-war songs ever conceived. There's an even fiercer, more evocative version on 'Weld' (1992), but such is the strength of its narrative it'd take a herculean effort to squander the drama. As an encore he drags out his darkest junkie meditation, 'Tonight's The Night', sick and heaving into the harsh light of the stage. If it was all a long way from the nihilistic reality of contemporary punk – at one point big chief YOUNG instructs the crowd to think away the rain – the performances are about as terse and single- minded as he ever got, fired as a ragged, rabid reply to encroaching middle age. *BG*

Album rating: *8.5

– spinoff releases, etc. –

NEIL YOUNG & CRAZY HORSE: Cinnamon Girl / The Loner
Dec 79. (7") *<49189>* ☐ ☐-

Carlos SANTANA

Born: 20 Jul'47, Autlán de Navarro, Mexico. Still riding high on the massive, multi Grammy-winning success of his comparitively recent 'Supernatural' (1999) album, guitarist CARLOS SANTANA is one of the few oldguard rock stars to have reinvented himself in such spectacularly unexpected style. As perhaps the foremost progenitor of Latin-rock, his legacy is rich. Living in San Francisco during the city's late 60s, acid fuelled cultural ferment, he put his name to Santana the band (originally the Santana Blues Band), bucking the trend of the white, middle class dominated hippy revolution with a fiery, Afro-Latin-rooted take on blues rock in much the same way Gato Barbieri was forging a proto-world music, pan-Latin path in jazz. As well as inspiring a wave of militant Chicano rock bands, Santana made the headlines – and the soundtrack – with a dazzling appearance at the iconic 'WOODSTOCK' (1970). The exposure led to multi-platinum sales for early albums 'Santana' (1969) and 'Abraxas' (1970) and a series of high charting singles. Santana also made an unlikely but show stealing appearance in 'SOUL TO SOUL' (1971), a Denis Sanders documentary on Afro-American musicians touring Ghana. While Carlos moved in an increasingly jazz based vein in the 70s and suffered an inevitable early 80s slump, his career was on the up at the time he scored Ritchie Valens biopic, 'LA BAMBA' (1987). Unfortunately, none of his music made it to the LOS LOBOS/various artists soundtrack, while his only other cinematic involvement, Indian feature, 'Everybody Says I'm Fine' (2001) failed to generate a soundtrack at all. *BG*

- **filmography** (composer) –

Woodstock *(1970 {p} on OST by V/A =>)* / **Soul To Soul** *(1971 {p} not on OST by V/A =>)* / **Love And Music** *(1971 {p} =>)* / **Fillmore** *(1972 {p} on OST by V/A =>)* / **La Bamba** *(1987 score w/ Miles Goodman / OST by LOS LOBOS =>)* / Blue Note – A Story Of Modern Jazz *(1997 TV {p} OST by V/A; see future edition)* / Everybody Says I'm Fine *(2001 score w/ Zakir Hussain)*

SAVE THE CHILDREN

1973 (US 123m w/b&w) Stellar / Paramount Pictures (G)

Film genre: R&B/Gospel/Soul-music concert documentary

Top guns: dir: Stan Lathan → BEAT STREET / s-w: Matt Robinson (+ narrator)

Stars: Marvin Gaye *(performer)* ← TROUBLE MAN ← the T.A.M.I. SHOW, **Curtis MAYFIELD** *(performer)*, **the Temptations:- Dennis Edwards, Otis Williams *, Melvin Franklin, Richard Street, Damon Harris** *(performers)*

→ WALK HARD: THE DEWEY COX STORY, **Bill Withers** *(performer)*, **Isaac HAYES** *(performer)*, **Wilson Pickett** *(performer)* ← SOUL TO SOUL / → SGT. PEPPER'S LONELY HEARTS CLUB BAND → BLUES BROTHERS 2000 → BLUES ODYSSEY → ONLY THE STRONG SURVIVE, **the Jackson 5:- Michael Jackson *, Jermaine Jackson **, Marlon Jackson, Tito Jackson, Jackie Jackson** *(performers)* → the WIZ * → MOONWALKER * / → VOYAGE OF THE ROCK ALIENS ** → LONGSHOT **, **Roberta Flack** *(performer)* ← SOUL TO SOUL / → RENALDO AND CLARA → BUSTIN' LOOSE, **Quincy JONES** *(performer)*, **Nancy Wilson** *(performer)*, **the STAPLE SINGERS** *(performers)*, **Jerry BUTLER** *(performer)*, **Ramsey Lewis** *(performer)*, Rev. Jesse Jackson *(host)*, **Cuba Gooding** *(performer)*, **Albertina Walker** *(performer)*, **Rev. James Cleveland** *(performer)*, Sammy Davis, Jr. *(performer)*, **Cannonball Adderley** *(performer)*, **Gladys KNIGHT** *(performer)* & **the Pips** *(performers)*

Storyline: Taking the title from Marvin Gaye's brilliant song, he and other giants of soul and R&B, alongside dynamic young president of Operation PUSH (People United to Save Humanity), Rev. Jesse Jackson, performed at 1972's exposition. *MCS*

Movie rating: *6

Visual: video

Off the record: **Cuba Gooding** (b.27 Apr'44, New York; father of top actor, Cuba Gooding Jr.) was a member of the Main Ingredient, whose highest hit was (No.3 in 1972) 'Everybody Plays The Fool' – see below. He played the role of a reporter in the 1988 TV movie, 'No Means No'; further acting work 'Gedo' (2001) and 'Destination Fame' (2004). *MCS*

—

Various Artists (dialogue * – Rev. Jesse Jackson)

Apr 74. (d-lp) *Motown; <M-800 R2>*
– (*) / (narration by Matt Robinson) / Save the children (MARVIN GAYE) / Papa was a rollin' stone (the TEMPTATIONS) / Everybody plays the fool (the MAIN INGREDIENT) / Sunshine (the O'JAYS) / This child of mine (ZULEMA) / Country preacher (CANNONBALL ADDERLEY) / Sermon – Praise him with a stringed instrument (REV. JAMES CLEVELAND & THE PUSH EXPO CHOIR) / Lean on me (BILL WITHERS) / What's happening brother (MARVIN GAYE) / Give me your love (CURTIS MAYFIELD) // I've gotta be me (SAMMY DAVIS, JR.) / On a clear day (you can see forever) – Killer Joe (ROBERTA FLACK – QUINCY JONES) / I heard it through the grapevine (GLADYS KNIGHT & THE PIPS) / (They long to be) Close to you (JERRY BUTLER & BRENDA LEE EAGER) / People make the world go round (RAMSEY LEWIS TRIO) / The greatest performance of my life (NANCY WILSON) / I wanna be where you are (the JACKSON 5) / What's going on (MARVIN GAYE) / (*) / I'm too close to Heaven to turn around (JACKIE VERDELL & THE PUSH EXPO CHOIR).

S/track review: Long before Sir Bob Geldof took it on himself to give us Live Aid, there were like-minded do-gooders who could "PUSH" out a charity gig. 'SAVE THE CHILDREN' was one such project. Alongside a handful of 'Tamla Motown' artists such as MARVIN GAYE (of course), the TEMPTATIONS and JACKSON 5, the said Detroit imprint called upon a plethora of other non-affiliated soul, jazz and R&B stars, the pick of the bunch being the O'JAYS, BILL WITHERS, CURTIS MAYFIELD, ROBERTA FLACK, QUINCY JONES, GLADYS KNIGHT, JERRY BUTLER and SAMMY DAVIS, JR. The double-LP opens with the Reverend Jesse Jackson proclaiming "I am . . . somebody . . . I may be poor . . . but I am God's child", before it segues into Blaxploitation-ish narration by Matt Robinson. A powerful intro indeed, but the political rapping mercifully grinds to a halt when the groove king himself, MARVIN GAYE, pleads his own sermons by way of his magnum opus, 'Save The Children'. The man with the subsequent "sexual healing" powers sees out the day with two further early 70s gems, 'What's Happening Brother' and 'What's Going On' – one thinks: "what's better?". From the pens of Norman Whitfield & Barrett Strong, that one-time Marvin staple, 'I Heard It Through The Grapevine', gets the upbeat and funky GLADYS KNIGHT & THE PIPS treatment. The word deconstruction comes to mind. Ditto for the Bacharach-David cover duet of '(They Long To Be) Close To You' by JERRY BUTLER & BRENDA LEE EAGER. However, there was a long "conveyor-belt-like" line of classics; 'Papa Was A Rollin' Stone' by the TEMPTATIONS was one, but was somewhat spoiled by follow-on soul-pop number, 'Everybody Plays The Fool' by the MAIN INGREDIENT. Back on the right track, 'Sunshine' by the O'JAYS and 'This Child Of Mine' (not the GN'R number!) by the oft-overlooked and overshadowed ex-Lovelles singer, ZULEMA, showed it wasn't all a showcase for the big guns (or indeed, roses). The inclusion of tenor-sax legend, CANNONBALL ADDERLEY (and his rendition of Josef Zawinul's 'Country Preacher'), was a welcome balance to the proceedings, it's just a pity the man subsequently died after a stroke in 1975. If gospel and humour was your bag, the Reverend JAMES CLEVELAND's 'Praise Him . . .', showed the church wasn't all fire and brimstone. One could also put one's hands together for BILL WITHERS' perennial cut, 'Lean On Me', while CURTIS MAYFIELD's high-pitched 'Give Me Your Love', shows why he once contested soul supremacy with GAYE and Stevie Wonder. What sounds like additional canned-"clapter" from a "clap-tive" audience, side three opens with Brat-Pack icon, SAMMY DAVIS, JR. on the nostalgic, 'I've Gotta Be Me'. When jazz/scoresmith/bandleader QUINCY JONES turns up to augment soul-balladeer, ROBERTA FLACK, for cool jazz standard, 'On A Clear Day', one just knows the mums and dads are shaking their tushes in the stalls. Maintaining the cool appeal, crossover keyboard king, RAMSEY LEWIS (and Trio), mellows-out via 'People Make The World Go Round', while jazz-stylist, NANCY WILSON, tries to portray (in song, at least) 'The Greatest Performance Of "her" Life'. If there were some children that needn't be saved – well not for a while anyway – the JACKSON 5 (Michael, Jermaine, Tito, Jackie & Marlon) found favour by way of non-hit, 'I Wanna Be Where You Are'. Where better to end this feast of stars, than with this long-lost one-that-got-away. *MCS*

Album rating: *7

SCRATCH

2001 (US 91m) Firewalk Films / Palm Pictures (R)

Film genre: Rave/Dance-music documentary

Top guns: dir: Doug Pray ← HYPE!

Stars: **DJ Q-Bert** *(performer)*, **DJ Shadow** *(performer)*, **Afrika Bambaataa** *(performer)* ← MODULATIONS ← the SHOW ← BEAT STREET, **MixMaster Mike** *(performer)* → MOOG → AWESOME: I FUCKIN' SHOT THAT!, **Cut Chemist** *(performer)*, **DJ Krush** *(performer)*, **GrandMixer DXT** *(performer)* ← WILD STYLE, **DJ Jazzy Jay** *(performer)* ← BEAT STREET, **DJ Premier** *(performer)*, **Invisibl Skratch Piklz** *(performer)*, **DJ Swamp** *(performer)*, **DJ Disk** *(performer)*, **Yoga Frog** *(performer)*, **DJ Cue** *(performer)*, **Grand Wizard Theodore** *(performer)* ← WILD STYLE, **DJ Faust** *(performer)*, **the X-ecutioners:- Rob Swift** *(performers)*

Storyline: 'Scratch' explores the world of the DJ ("turntablists") and their influence and techniques behind the desks and discs that make up the expanding world of dance and techno music. *MCS*

Movie rating: *7.5

Visual: dvd

Off the record: **DJ Q-Bert** (b. Richard Quitevis) & **Yoga Frog** (b. Ritche Desuadio) were members of the award-winning San Francisco DJ team, **Invisibl Skratch Piklz**, while **DJ Premier** is one half of Gang Starr. **Cut Chemist** (aka Lucas MacFadden), meanwhile, has DJ'd for the likes of L.A. Latin-funk act, Ozomatli, and underground rappers, Jurassic 5. **DJ Swamp** was better known to Beck fans, having been an integral member of the man's backing players. Another superb turntablist, **DJ Faust** was responsible for one of the genre's best sets, 'Man Or Myth?' (1998). *MCS*

—

Various Artists

Feb 02. (d-cd) *Transparent; <(50017-2)>* ☐ May02 ☐
– Prologue (DJ FAUST scratches GRAND WIZARD THEODORE speaks) / live (MIXMASTER MIKE & DJ DISK) / Primo's x-ecution (X-ECUTIONERS feat. DJ PREMIER) / live (MIXMASTER MIKE & DJ DISK) / Re-animator (ROB SWIFT) / interlude (MIXMASTER MIKE speaks) / Rockit 2.002 (HERBIE HANCOCK feat. MIXMASTER MIKE, GRANDMIXER DXT, ROB SWIFT, Q-BERT, BABU, FAUST & SHORTEE) / interlude (CUT CHEMIST speaks) / Turntable transformer (CAT FIVE VS. SNAYK EYEZ) / interlude / live (DJ KRUSH) / Crazy 2 crazy (GRANDMIXER DXT) / interlude (DJ SHADOW speaks) / Invasion of the Octopus people (INVISIBL SKRATCH PIKLZ) / interlude (JAZZY JAY & AFRIKA BAMBAATAA speak) / All 4 one (BOOGIE BOY & KID DELIGHT feat. AFRIKA BAMBAATAA) / interlude (AFRIKA BAMBAATAA speaks again) / Skin cracked canals (DJ DISK with BUCKETHEAD) / interlude / Cut transmitter (GRANDMIXER DXT feat. JEROME "BIGFOOT" BRAILEY & JAH WOBBLE) / Universal noize maker (EDDIE DEF) / interlude (FAUST scratches Q-BERT & MIXMASTER MIKE speaks) / My style (ROB SWIFT).

S/track review: To select eleven tracks to represent the art of hip hop turntablism is, at best, a thankless task. To sum up 30 years of this now global cultural phenomenon would take a quadruple CD box-set and there would still be endless argument over that. Instead, the compilers have elected to cherry-pick some of the founders of the movement and blend them with some contemporary prime suspects, hence the obvious inclusion of the timeless track that broke scratching out of the underground clubs and into the mainstream conscious: HERBIE HANCOCK's 'Rokit', a number that, despite Grandmaster DST's cuts and blends on the track being over a quarter of a century old, still sounds fresh today. The embryonic tricks pioneered by DST and other early practitioners have been ramped up by the likes of four-man crew, the X-ECUTIONERS, and the legendary beatsmith, DJ PREMIER, both of whom commit themselves well here. Similarly, the nimble digits of INVISIBL SKRATCH PIKLZ, ROB SWIFT and EDDIE DEF impress with the rawest of techniques used to maximum effect, while tracks by DJ DISK and an all-too-brief call in from AFRIKA BAMBAATAA are truly underwhelming. Sandwiched between the tracks are snippets of dialogue from the film and clips from routines. Many of these, show hip hop turntable play at its purest and most crowd-pleasing, beats and riffs are juggled, pinched, twisted, stretched and generally abused to spectacular effect. To match the essence of many of their predictable techniques, the selections could have been a tad more energised and showy, but there are some stellar examples of the art to be found here. *MR*

Album rating: *7

SCREAMING MASTERPIECE

Icelandic title 'GARGANDI SNILLD'

2005 (Ice 87m) Zik Zak Kvikmyndir / Soda Pictures (PG)

Film genre: alt-Rock-music concert/documentary

Top guns: dir: (+ s-w) Ari Alexander Ergis Magnusson

Stars: BJORK *(performer)*, **SIGUR ROS** *(performers)*, **Mum** *(performers)*, **MUGISON** *(performer)*, **Damon ALBARN** *(himself)*, **Bang Gang** *(performers)* ← POPP I REYKJAVIK, **Minus** *(performers)*, **Slowblow** *(performers)* ← POPP I REYKJAVIK, **Hilmar Orn Hilmarsson** *(performer)*, **Ghostigital** *(performers)*, **Eivor Palsdottir** *(performer)*, **Amina** *(performers)*, **Dagur Kari Petursson** *(performer)*, **Steindor Andersen** *(performer)*, **Nilfisk** *(performers)*, **Vinyll** *(performers)* ← POPP I REYKJAVIK, **Singapore Sling** *(performers)*, **Quarashi** *(performers)* ← POPP I REYKJAVIK, **Sjon Sigurdsson** *(performer)*

Storyline: Iceland's history and traditions go back almost a thousand years when Norsemen raided Britain and sailed their longships to Newfoundland. Their music and poetry have survived and evolved through the ages and this concert is an amazing mix of folk, Norse, rock and punk featuring the best homegrown talents such as Bjork, Sigur Ros and Sugarcubes. Iceland has yet another go to tell the outside world of its thriving indie music scene. "It's Oh So Quiet" – not quite! *MCS*

Movie rating: *6.5

Visual: dvd

Off the record: (see below)

—

Various Artists (score: Por Eldon)

Nov 05. (cd) *One Little Indian; (<TPLP 703CD>)* ☐ ☐
– A fero til breioafjaroar (STEINDOR ANDERSEN & SIGUR ROS) / All is full of love (BJORK, ICELANDIC STRING OCTET & MATMOS) / #8 a.k.a. Popplagio (SIGUR ROS & AMINA) / Odi et amo (JOHANN JOHANNSSON, AUDUR HAFSTEINDOTTIR & H) / Green grass of tunnel (MUM) / Find what you get (BANG GANG) / Romantica (APPARAT ORGAN QUARTET) / Brostnar borgir (EIVOR PALSDOTTIR) / Within tolerance (SLOWBLOW) / Conversation (FINNBOGI PETURSSON) / Motorcrash (SUGARCUBES) / Bank = Faereyjar, Bruxelles, Barcelona, Reykjavik (GHOSTIGIAL, ELIS PETURSSON & FROSTI LOGASON) / I'd ask (MUGISON) / Fjarskanistan (AMINA) / Oceania (BJORK) / Hrafnagaldur – Odin's Raven Magic (STEINDOR ANDERSEN, SIGUR ROS & SCHOLA CANTORUM).

S/track review: 'SCREAMING MASTERPIECE' offers an insight into the intriguing idiosyncratic world of the Icelandic music scene. The 16 tracks showcase a land where the music is imbued with the majesty of the barren scenery and the magic of Norse mythology, skewered by the occasional mutation of contemporary western pop and rock. The presence of Icelandic heavyweights BJORK and, especially, SIGUR ROS is felt throughout, with the latter combining with STEINDOR ANDERSEN to produce the opening track, their take on the traditional 'Á ferđ til Breiđafjarđar'. If anything SIGUR ROS' musical contribution is even more funereal than usual with ANDERSEN's anachronistic vocal delivery sounding like it is drifting from a long lost sea captain reciting a surreal shanty. Next is a superior live reading of BJORK's 'All Is Full Of Love' with the music towering but never detracting from the piercing note perfect vocal delivery. Indeed the diminutive songstress' previous band the SUGARCUBES also feature here in what feels like the soundtrack's only out of place cut, with its 80s sound grating against the present-day recordings. SIGUR ROS' 'Popplagiđ' is an ethereal readthrough which spirals into an epic crescendo, whilst MUM's familiar sounding 'Green Grass Of Tunnel' is more upbeat and electronic with vocals that could only be delivered by an ice-cold Scandinavian chanteuse. Next up BANG GANG bring an unlikely hint of sunshine to the misty snow capped island with the Grandaddy-esque 'Find What You Get' and EIVOR PALSDOTTIR present typical lo-fi atmospheric minimalism that grows to a frenzied thrasharound, all wrapped up in cracked, rasping vocals. Meanwhile the APPARAT ORGAN QUARTET's 'Romantica' is an enjoyable unpretentious romp, bizarrely merging Kraftwerk and Yes's keyboard wizardry and sounding like they are gleefully trying to recreate the soundtracks to early 90s Sega computer games. MUGISON's 'I'd Ask' has a pleasant laidback 70s singer-songwriter vibe with a nautical feel, but it is the first and only time we encounter the bland mid-Atlantic vocals that blight so much of western music. Check out MUGISON's two complete soundtracks, 'NICELAND' (2004) and 'a LITTLE TRIP To Heaven' (2005). Steering us back on course, SIGUR ROS' touring partners AMINA present a piece with layered brooding strings in 'Fjarskanistan' followed by BJORK's somewhat typical, but unessential, 'Oceania'. Closing the album is a huge collaboratative effort featuring many of the artists already present on the soundtrack. 'Hrafnagaldur – Odin's Raven Magic' is an affecting piece with labyrinthine swirling, almost eerie, multiple layers of vocals and instrumentation. The track's rather drawn out, overlong conclusion gives time to reflect upon the quirky, yet high quality music produced in Iceland, where the artists, however disparate in style, are always united by their uniqueness. *LF*

Album rating: *7

□ Earl SCRUGGS segment
(⇒ BANJOMAN)

SEARCHING FOR THE WRONG-EYED JESUS

2005 (US/UK 84m) Films Transit International

Film genre: alt-Rock/Roots-music documentary

Top guns: dir: Andrew Douglas / s-w: Steve Haisman

Stars: Jim White *(narrator)*, **Johnny Dowd** *(himself)*, Harry Crews *(himself)*, **the Handsome Family** *(themselves)*, **David Eugene Edwards** *(himself)*, **David Johansen** *(himself)* <= NEW YORK DOLLS =>, **Lee Sexton** *(himself)*, **Melissa Swingle** *(herself)*

Storyline: Inspired by Jim White's debut album, 'Wrong-Eyed Jesus (The Mysterious Tale Of How I Shouted)' (1997), British director Andrew Douglas teamed up with the surfer/fashion model-turned mystic-folkster for a roadtrip through the American South. Their travels – in a battered old Chevy – are conducted at a hypnotic, tobacco-chewing pace, lingering on the minutiae of Southern life and its characters, drawing out their stories, and listening to their (invariably dark) songs. *BG*

Movie rating: *7

Visual: dvd

Off the record: Jim White was a member of the Dirty Three (a band from Australia who contributed several tracks to the 1999 feature, 'PRAISE'); the none-too-jovial **Johnny Dowd** (b. 1948) was a latecomer to the alt-country scene, his 'Wrong Side Of Memphis' released in 1998 when he was turning 50!; **the Handsome Family** were of similar weirdo ilk, having given us the unrelentless and suicidal 'Weightless Again' (also in '98); **David Johansen** was of course of the legendary NEW YORK DOLLS and an actor in numerous films; **David Eugene Edwards** is the frontman for 16 Horsepower and went on to score the music for French film, 'Blush' (2005); **Melissa Swingle** is the singer with Trailer Bride and a one-time member of all-girl trio, Pussy Teeth. *MCS*

—

Various Artists (score: JIM WHITE *)

Jun 05. (cd) *Luaka Bop; <90060> V2; (VVR 103407-2)* □ Sep05 □
– Everything was stories (HARRY CREWS poem) / Still waters (*) / My sister's tiny hands (the HANDSOME FAMILY) / Crossbones style (CAT POWER) / The last kind words (DAVID JOHANSEN & LARRY SALTZMAN) / The wound that never heals (*) / Wayfaring stranger (DAVID EUGENE EDWARDS) / Small town (MAYOR) / Black soul choir – choir (16 HORSEPOWER) / Little Maggie – live (LEE SEXTON) / First there was (JOHNNY DOWD with MAGGIE BROWN) / Coo coo bird (CLARENCE ASHLEY & DOC WATSON) / Amazing Grace (MELISSA SWINGLE) / Christmas day (*) / Essential truth (*).

S/track review: "You got to either choose Jesus or Hell. You got your choice. There's not a whole lot in between". If there's one song on this soundtrack which evokes JIM WHITE's trawl through the modern day Deep South long after the credits have rolled, it's MELISSA SWINGLE's 'Amazing Grace', an ectoplasmic hymn performed on musical saw and haunted by half-starved dogs. WHITE himself sings about sin and salvation in the pallid half-whisper of Calexico's Joey Burns, even if his dysfunctional narratives don't inhabit the South as insidiously as Burns invokes the desert. He bravely lines up his own creations against some tough competition: a creepy standout from the HANDSOME FAMILY's tombstone-country classic, 'Through The Trees' (1998), a quavering bluegrass ballad from LEE SEXTON (recorded in Kentucky's 'Convict Holler Coal Mine' no less!), a live-in-the-Louisiana-Woods 'Wayfaring Stranger' by 16 HORSEPOWER's DAVID EUGENE EDWARDS, and JOHNNY DOWD/MAGGIE BROWN's revelatory, Bonnie & Clyde-style duet, 'First There Was'. That 'SEARCHING FOR THE WRONG-EYED JESUS' is more than just another alt-country sampler is endorsed by the Beth Orton-esque purr of CAT POWER and the bourbon-soaked, post-Buster Poindexter growl of DAVID JOHANSEN. As WHITE concludes: "you wanna know the secrets of the South, you gotta get it in your blood, and you ain't gonna get a transfusion from the blood bank for it". Short of getting bitten by a bayou vampire bat, this soundtrack's as good a way as any of getting some old-cum-nu-Southern Gothic coursing through your veins. *BG*

Album rating: *7

Pete SEEGER

Born: 3 May, 1919, Patterson, New York, USA. PETE SEEGER is the archetypal folk protest singer, the son of a pacifist teacher who quit his job due to the amount of enemies his anti-WWI stance made him. On hearing the five-string banjo aged 16, Pete's life was changed forever. He dropped out of a Harvard journalism course and took a job at the Archive of American Folk Song in the Library of Congress in Washington DC. He was also founder of many folk groups including the Weavers alongside hobo hero, Woody Guthrie. SEEGER has spent his life dedicated to one political cause or another. From his early days as a communist fighting the McCarthy witch hunts of the 1950s, to an outspoken critic of the US government's shortcomings, as well as a tireless environmental campaigner for the area of northern New York state, he has always resided in the Big Apple. He kicked off a solo career aged 39 in 1958 and had commercial successes with songs such as 'If I Had A Hammer', 'Where Have All The Flowers Gone?' and 'Turn, Turn, Turn'. SEEGER became an integral part of the Greenwich Village folk revival in the 60s as well as hosting syndicated radio shows while also taking the mantle of children's storyteller. His celluloid work has seen him pen a handful of unreleased scores, while he's featured in films and documentaries such as Newport concert flick 'FESTIVAL' (1967), Arlo Guthrie's 'ALICE'S RESTAURANT' (1969), 'LEADBELLY' (1976), Phil Ochs' 'CHORDS OF FAME' (1984), 'The BALLAD OF RAMBLIN' JACK' (2000) and BOB DYLAN's 'NO DIRECTION HOME' (2005). On 16th March 2007, SEEGER, aged 88, performed with his siblings at his old workplace, the Library Of Congress. Among those who have paid tribute to SEEGER's work and life include BILLY BRAGG, Ani DiFranco and BRUCE SPRINGSTEEN, who all contributed to a double-CD album. The latter giant of rock has gone even further, recording his own entire album of songs written and made famous by SEEGER entitled 'We Shall Overcome: The Seeger Sessions' in 2006. *MR*

- filmography (composer) {performance} –

To Hear Your Banjo Play *(1947 {p})* / Indian Summer *(1960 short – score; see future editions)* / **Festival** *(1967 {p} =>)* / Gavilan *(1968 score)* / **Alice's Restaurant** *(1969 {c} on OST by ARLO GUTHRIE & V/A =>)* / Tell Me That You Love Me, Junie Moon *(1970 {p} + score w/ Philip Springer)* / a Song And A Stone *(1972 {*p})* / **Leadbelly** *(1976 {a} OST =>)* / Wasn't That A Time *(1982 {p})* / Hard Travelin' *(1984 {p} =>)* / In Our Hands *(1984 {p})* / **Chords Of Fame** *(1984 {p} =>)* / **the Ballad Of Ramblin' Jack** *(2000 {p} OST by*

RAMBLIN' JACK ELLIOTT =>) / Freedom Highway: Songs That Shaped A Century *(2001 {p})* / Strange Fruit *(2002 {p})* / **No Direction Home** *(2005 {p/c} OST by BOB DYLAN =>)* / the Power Of Song *(2007 {*p})*

the SEX PISTOLS

Formed: London, England . . . summer 1975 out of the Swankers by Paul Cook, Steve Jones and Glen Matlock, the latter two regular faces at Malcolm McLaren's 'Sex' boutique on the capital's King's Road. With the NEW YORK DOLLS already on his CV, McLaren was well qualified to mastermind the rise and fall of the SEX PISTOLS as he dubbed his new plaything, the entrepreneur/Svengali installing another 'Sex' customer, the green-haired John Lydon, as a suitably sneering frontman. Jones soon renamed the latter Johnny Rotten, informing his farting rear-end, "You're rotten, you are"; the tone of the SEX PISTOLS was set. After a few local gigs, the group supported JOE STRUMMER's 101'ers in April '76, their bedraggled, low-rent bondage chic troupe of followers including the likes of Siouxsie (later of Banshees fame) and one Sid Vicious, allegedly the perpetrator behind the infamous glass-throwing incident at the 100 Club punk all-dayer in which a girl was partially blinded. Controversy, intentional or otherwise, hung around the group like a bad smell and made the SEX PISTOLS into minor legends with barely one single under their belts. Signed to 'E.M.I.' for £40,000, their debut release 'Anarchy In The U.K.' (having already shocked those of a sensitive disposition after being aired on the 'So It Goes' TV pop show) was finally released in November '76. An inflammatory slice of primal nihilism which surpassed even the Stooges' finest efforts, the track initially climbed into the Top 40 before being unceremoniously withdrawn following the band's riotous appearance on a local chat/news programme, 'Today'. With Jones swearing copiously at presenter Bill Grundy, the tabloids had a field day, stirring up the moral majority and prompting more "must we subject our pop kids to this filth" editorials than you could shake a snotty stick at. 'E.M.I.', of course, bailed out (writing off the advance as a particularly bad debt) early the following year, while Matlock was fired around the same time for being, well, er . . . too nice. His replacement was the aforementioned Vicious (alias John Ritchie), a suitably violent and abusive character who duly became more of a punk anti-hero/caricature than McLaren could ever have dreamed. After a short period in label limbo, the 'Pistols signed to 'A&M' in March '77 for another six figure sum; the honeymoon period was probably the shortest in recording history as the band's infamous antics at the post-signing party, together with protests from other artists on the label (namely RICK WAKEMAN), saw the UK's foremost punk band once again minus a recording contract. Once again, the band retained the loot from the advance and once again, a single, 'God Save The Queen', was withdrawn (some copies did find their way into circulation and now fetch considerably more than the original 50p price tag). Arguably the SEX PISTOLS' defining moment, this jaw-clenching two-fingered salute to the monarchy and everything it represented was to truly make the band public enemy No.1, its release coinciding sweetly with Her Highness' silver jubilee year. Re-released by new label 'Virgin' (virtually the only company willing to take the band on for a meagre £15,000 advance), the single was predictably banned by the BBC, though that didn't prevent it from outselling the official No.1 at the time, Rod Stewart's 'I Don't Want To Talk About It'. That long, hot summer also saw the band hiring a boat and sailing up and down the Thames in a publicity stunt which ended in chaos; cue yet more controversy and howls of derision from the nation's moral guardians. Knuckle-headed English royalists decided to take matters into their own hands, both Cook and Rotten being attacked in separate incidents as another blankly brilliant single, 'Pretty Vacant', gatecrashed the Top 10. Previewed by the seething, squalling outrage of 'Holidays In The Sun', the legendary debut album, 'Never Mind The Bollocks, Here's The Sex Pistols', was finally released at the end of the year. While the record undeniably contained some filler, it remains the classic punk statement, the blistering 'Bodies' and the gleeful kiss-off to their former employers, 'E.M.I.', almost standing up against the intensity of the singles (included in their entirety). As ever, controversy clouded its release, the album reaching No.1 in spite of the word 'Bollocks' – a near contravention of the 1889 Indecent Advertisements Act(!) – resulting in boycotts from many major outlets. Constantly on the verge of falling apart, the band subsequently flew to America for a string of chaotic dates, the final round of blanks in the SEX PISTOLS' depleted armoury. Amid sporadic showdowns with Deep South cowboys and Sid's ever-worsening heroin problem, Rotten (bowing out on stage in San Francisco with the immortal phrase "Ever get the feeling you've been cheated") effectively ended the whole sorry affair with his departure after the final gig. While Lydon (the name he now reverted back to) went on to form Public Image Ltd., McLaren had other ideas for the splintered remains of the band, namely jetting off to Rio De Janeiro to record a single with exiled trainrobber, Ronnie Biggs. The result, 'No One Is Innocent (A Punk Prayer By Ronnie Biggs)', made the Top 10 in summer '78, although Vicious was absent from the recording, holed up in New York with his similarly addicted girlfriend, Nancy Spungeon. He did find time to record a peerless rendition of Paul Anka's 'My Way', the single taking on an added poignancy following his untimely but hardly surprising death early the following year; out on bail after being charged with the murder of Spungeon in October, Vicious succumbed to a fatal heroin overdose on the 2nd of February '79. The following month saw the belated release of McLaren's pet project, an artistically licensed celluloid account of the SEX PISTOLS' history entitled 'The GREAT ROCK'N'ROLL SWINDLE'. Widely criticised for its blatant exclusion of Matlock, the glaring absence of Rotten as an active participant and its paper-thin storyline, the movie was nevertheless an occasionally exhilarating, often hilarious trip through the misspent youth of Britain's best-loved punk band. While a perfunctory cover of Eddie Cochran's 'C'mon Everybody' (a posthumous Vicious recording) made the Top 10 later that summer and 'Virgin' continued to flog the SEX PISTOLS' dead corpse with a variety of exploitation jobs, Cook and Jones formed the short-lived Professionals. Although they didn't invent punk, the 'Pistols certainly helped popularise it and while they were at least partly responsible for an avalanche of unlistenably amateurish shit, the band's uncompromising approach permanently altered the machinations of the music industry and took three-chord rock'n'roll to its ultimate conclusion. Despite the fact original fans had long since given up on the UK ever descending into anarchy, the original 'Pistols line-up of Lydon, Matlock, Jones and Cook re-formed in summer '96 for a handful of outdoor gigs and an accompanying live album. Opinion was divided as to whether this blatantly commercial venture (billed as "The Filthy Lucre Tour") was in keeping with the original punk spirit; probably not, although few paying punters complained about what was subsequently hailed as one of the events of the summer and it was certainly a safer bet than the new Green Day album (they repeated the re-formation formula in 2007!). The feature of many a rock documentary, the SEX PISTOLS were at their punk best in Julien Temple's updated 'The FILTH & THE FURY' (2000). *BG & MCS*

- **filmography** {acting/performers} –

the Punk Rock Movie *(1978 {p})* / Mr. Mike's Mondo Video *(1979 {c SID})* / **the Great Rock'n'Roll Swindle** *(1980 {*p/a} + OST by SEX PISTOLS & V/A =>)* / Punk And Its Aftershocks *(1980 {p})* / **D.O.A.** *(1980 {p} =>)* / **Ladies**

And Gentlemen, The Fabulous Stains *(1981 {b JOHN, PAUL + STEVE})* / Order Of Death/Copkiller *(1983 {* JOHN})* / Mascara *(1999 {a STEVE})* / Four Days Playing Poker *(2000 {a STEVE])* / **the Filth & The Fury** *(2000 {*p} OST =>)* / the Independent *(2000 {a JOHN})* / **Rage: 20 Years Of Punk Rock West Coast Style** *(2001 {a/p} =>)* / **24 Hour Party People** *(2002 {a/p} =>)* / **End Of The Century** *(2003 {a/p} =>)* / **Mayor Of The Sunset Strip** *(2003 {a/p} =>)* / the Big Bounce *(2004 {b STEVE})* / the Story Of Punk *(2006 TV {a/fl} =>)*

Tupac SHAKUR

Born: Lesane Parish Crooks, 16 Jun'71, Brooklyn, New York, USA. The son of a Black Panther member, and after a successful start to his career as a member of West Coast rap act, Digital Underground, the "re-christened" Tupac Amaru Shakur signed to 'Interscope' in 1991, making his solo debut with '2Pacalypse Now' in 1991. A veritable journey into the heart of black inner city darkness, the record combined the bleak violence of gangsta with strong pro-Afro-American sentiments, as did the follow-up, 'Strictly 4 My N.I.G.G.A.Z.' (1993), 2PAC almost breaking the US Top 10 with the 'I Get Around' single. He also had a penchant for getting on the wrong side of the law, running up an incredible string of charges including shooting two off-duty police officers, forceful sodomy (not with the police officers!) and attacking the co-director of the film, 'Menace II Society', Allen Hughes (2PAC had already made appearances in 'Juice', 'Under The Rim' and an acclaimed role in 'Poetic Justice'). While the shooting charge was dropped, 2PAC was subsequently sentenced to spend some time in prison for the sexual assault, ironically beginning his sentence while his third album, the aptly titled 'Me Against The World' (1995) went to the top of the Billboard charts. The following year, the rapper was back at No.1 in defiant form with the landmark double set, 'All Eyez On Me', answering his many critics with 'Only God Can Judge Me'. The album also spawned a No.1 single in the epochal 'California Love', an utterly compelling 70s style pimp-rolling groove singing the praises of 2PAC's beloved home state, cut in collaboration with ex-Zapp frontman, Roger Troutman. But if 2PAC was pro-Cali, he was viciously anti-New York, or at least its rap contingency, as witnessed on the track 'Hit 'Em Up' (included on the CD single of 'How Do You Want It'), a ferocious litany of hate primarily directed against his one-time friend, Biggie Smalls (tried to shoot him?) but also stretching to Mobb Deep and 'Bad Boy' records, the label at the centre of the East versus West feud along with Dr Dre's 'Death Row'. It had to end in tears of course, and it came as little surprise when 2PAC was shot and killed in a drive-by incident (13 September, 1996). Although no-one was subsequently charged with the murder, the rapper's list of enemies was almost as big as his police charge sheet and it was probably inevitable that a man who lived so closely by the gun wouldn't live to see thirty. Violence and politics aside, there's no getting around the fact that 2PAC was an immensely talented artist, having scored his third US No.1 album in a row with 'The Don Killuminati: The 7 Day Theory' (1996) under the alias Makaveli. 2PAC was also a much-in-demand actor and by the time of his death, he had starred posthumously in two further features, 'Gang Related' (1997) and 'Gridlock'd' (1997). His status as an American cultural icon was underlined recently when a US college introduced a 2PAC course, exploring the man's life and work. Crazy? Well, certainly no crazier than the esteem afforded the Kray Twins in Britain, and besides, did they pen anything as groovy as 'California Love' (?!). In common with Jeff Buckley, Tupac's profile has remained high after his death through the regular release of half-finished, work in progress, the most recent being 'Until The End Of Time' (2001). Also in common with Buckley, the bulk of this material is of prime interest largely to hardcore fans who've got the time and inclination to muse over what the finished article would've sounded like. 2002's 'Better Dayz' ranked as one of the more enduring posthumous releases, a sprawling double set of largely unreleased material which attempted some kind of focus by splitting the music up into one disc of hardcore and one of more accessible tracks. Of the two, the harder material perhaps left the deepest impression, the likes of 'F*** 'Em All' – a collaboration with Outlawz – generating the kind of brooding portent that sounded all the more menacing in the light of subsequent events. One year on and fans were still being supplied with songs from beyond the grave, this time in the shape of the 'TUPAC: RESURRECTION' (2003) soundtrack. Another essential purchase for diehards, the record gathered together more obscure tracks from Tupac's bulging back catalogue, a better effort than the previous years' 'THUG ANGEL – THE LIFE OF AN OUTLAW' documentary. *BG*

- **filmography** {acting} –

Nothing But Trouble *(1991 {p} on OST by V/A =>)* / **Juice** *(1992 {*} OST by V/A =>)* / Poetic Justice *(1993 {*})* / Above The Rim *(1994 {*} OST by V/A =>)* / Bullet *(1995 {*})* / Dead Homiez *(1996 {*c})* / Gridlock'd *(1997 {*} OST by V/A)* / Gang Related *(1997 {*} OST by V/A =>)* / Thug Immortal *(1998 {*c archival})* / **Thug Angel – The Life Of An Outlaw** *(2002 {*c archival} OST by V/A =>)* / **Tupac: Resurrection** *(2003 {*p archival} OST by TUPAC =>)*

the SHOW

1995 (US 93m w/b&w) Savoy Pictures (R)

Film genre: Rap/Hip Hop-music concert/docmentary

Top guns: dir: Brian Robbins

Stars: Craig Mack *(performer)* → RHYME & REASON, **Dr. Dre** *(performer)* ← MURDER WAS THE CASE / → RHYME & REASON → WHITEBOYS → TUPAC: RESURRECTION, **Naughty By Nature** *(performers)*, **the Notorious B.I.G.** *(performer)* → RHYME & REASON → BIGGIE AND TUPAC → THUG ANGEL → TUPAC: RESURRECTION → BEEF, **Kid Capri** *(performer)* ← FLY BY NIGHT ← WHO'S THE MAN? / → DEATH OF A DYNASTY, **Afrika Bambaataa** *(performer)* ← BEAT STREET / → MODULATIONS → SCRATCH, **SNOOP DOGG** *(performer)*, **Warren G.** *(performer)* → LITTLE RICHARD, **Method Man** *(performer)* → RHYME & REASON → BACKSTAGE → BLACK AND WHITE → HOW HIGH → BROWN SUGAR, **Russell Simmons** *(performer)* ← TOUGHER THAN LEATHER ← KRUSH GROOVE / → BROWN SUGAR → BEEF → DEATH OF A DYNASTY, **Raekwon** *(performer)* → RHYME & REASON → BLACK AND WHITE, **Slick Rick** *(performer)* ← TOUGHER THAN LEATHER / → WHITEBOYS → TRUE VINYL → BROOKLYN BABYLON → → BROWN SUGAR → FADE TO BLACK, **Puff Daddy** *(performer)* → RHYME & REASON → BIGGIE AND TUPAC → TUPAC: RESURRECTION → DEATH OF A DYNASTY → FADE TO BLACK, **Kurtis Blow** *(performer)* ← KNIGHTS OF THE CITY ← KRUSH GROOVE / → RHYME & REASON, **Andre Harrell** *(performer)* ← KRUSH GROOVE, **Tripp Locc** *(performer)*, **Wayniac** *(performer)*, **Doc Ice** *(performer)*

Storyline: Russell Simmons presents . . . the culture of hip-hop and an in-depth examination (by way of interviews and music clips) into why the genre has become to popular. There's also a massive gig at The Armory in Philadelphia. *MCS*

Movie rating: *5

Visual: video + dvd

Off the record: Kid Capri (aka David Love) is a DJ/rapper from The Bronx; **Method Man** of Wu-Tang Clan; London-born **Slick Rick** had his first breakthrough in 1989 with the album, 'The Great Adventures Of . . .'; **Warren G.** had a hit with 'Regulate . . . G Funk Era'; **Andre Harrell** was half of rap duo Dr. Jekyll & Mr. Hyde; **Doc Ice** was born Christopher Harrison. *MCS*

Various Artists (score: STANLEY CLARKE *)

Aug 95. (cd/c) *R.A.L.-Def Jam; <529021>* [4] [–]
– Hip Hop is . . . (KID CREOLE, KID CAPRI & ECSTASY) / Live!!! (ONYX) / Move on . . . (SLICK RICK) / My block (2PAC) / What's up star? (SUGA) / Headbanger boogie (METHOD MAN) / How high (REDMAN / METHOD MAN) / It's entertainment . . . (DR. DRE) / Everyday thang (BONE, THUGS N HARMONY) / Everyday it rains (MARY J. BLIGE) / It's all I had (the NOTORIOUS B.I.G.) / Ol' skool (ISAAC 2 ISAAC) / Domino's in the house (DOMINO) / Summertime in the LBC (the DOVE SHACK) / The West Coast . . . (TREACH) / Sowhatusayin (SOUTH CENTRAL CARTEL PRODUCTIONS) / Zoom Zooms and Wam Wam (JAYO FELONY) / Droppin bombz (TRAY D & SO. SENTRELLE) / Save yourself (SNOOP DOGGY DOGG) / Still can't fade it (WARREN G PRODUCTIONS) / Papa luv it (L.L. COOL J) / Glamour and glitz (A TRIBE CALLED QUEST) / Nuttin' but a drumbeat . . . (RUSSELL SIMMONS) / Kill dem all (KALI RANKS) / Me and my bitch – live from Philly (the NOTORIOUS B.I.G.) / It's what I feel inside . . . (KID CREOLE, ECSTASY) / The show theme (* feat. SLICK RICK).

S/track review: The mid-90s were a fruitful time for hip hop, when it became the commercially most successful music genre in America. Many of the genre's biggest names were hitting simultaneous creative and commercial peaks, in particular the NOTORIOUS B.I.G. and 2PAC, both of whom have a showing here. The former contributes a raucous, ragged live take of 'Me And My Bitch', while 2PAC is in more reflective mood, contemplating more innocent times in his youth on the superb 'My Block'. Arch stoners METHOD MAN and REDMAN illustrate another side of their massive 'How High', while the mighty ONYX out Wu-Tang the Wu-Tang Clan with a mob-handed shout-along in the shape of 'Live!!'. There's plenty of contrasting shades and colours, MARY J BLIGE's bittersweet funk ballad, 'Everyday It Rains' is lush and hook-laden, and ISAAC 2 ISAAC's 'Ol' Skool' R&B jam might sound primitive, lifting as it does from some Run-DMC and Isley Brothers classics, but it has genuine heart. West Coasters SOUTH CENTRAL CARTEL PRODUCTIONS paint some stark pictures of Californian gang violence while nailing wailing analogue synths to dark minor chord bass riffs, making something both foreboding and downright funky. JAYO FELONY's great, if formulaic, 'Zoom Zooms And Wam Wam' also comes to similar duophonic conclusions. The idea of combining Jamaican ragga and US hip hop never quite happened like so many predicted, but KALI RANKS' 'Kill Dem All' is a prime example of ragga verbals and emphatic NYC beats in synergy suggesting again that this isn't quite the spectacular that Russell Simmons promised us, but its well worth hearing anyway. *MR*

Album rating: *7.5

– spinoff hits, etc. –

the DOVE SHACK: Summertime In The LBC / (non-OST song)

Jul 95. (12"/cd-s) *<579382> (12RAL/RALCD 5)* [54] Oct95 [ ]

REDMAN & METHOD MAN: How High / (remixes)

Aug 95. (12"/c-s) *<579924>* [13] [–]

SHUT UP & SING

2006 (US 93m) Cabin Creek Films / The Weinstein Company (R)

Film genre: Country-music documentary bio-pic

Top guns: dir: Barbara Kopple ← MY GENERATION ← WOODSTOCK '94, Cecilia Peck

Stars: Dixie Chicks:- Natalie Maines, Emily Robison, Martie Maguire *(themselves/performers)*, **Rick Rubin** *(himself)* ← FADE TO BLACK ← END OF THE CENTURY ← TOUGHER THAN LEATHER ← KRUSH GROOVE, George W. Bush *(archive)*, Simon Renshaw *(himself)*, Adrian Pasdar *(himself)* ← NEAR DARK ← MADE IN USA

Storyline: Taking a line fired at them by an irate "fan" during a concert, the Dixie Chicks (the biggest selling country act between 1998-2002) were filmed here during the recording of their 2006 set, 'Taking The Long Way'. The upstanding and brave Dixie Chicks (Natalie Maines, to be exact) had courted controversy when she/they spoke out about George W Bush's impending invasion and bombing of Iraq in March 2003. The resulting American backlash against the girls was way OTT, their records boycotted and lifted from playlists when the US of A boasts about freedom of speech – or is that as long as it's not in public? *MCS*

Movie rating: *7.5

Visual: dvd (no audio OST)

Off the record: Dixie Chicks (see TV movie '. . .On The Fly') sold millions of the debut major label set, 'Wide Open Spaces' (1998); Natalie Maines played the part of Fiona/Kmoodj in the 2002 kids movie, 'Grand Champion'. *MCS*

– associated release –

DIXIE CHICKS: Taking The Long Way

May 06. (cd) *Sony-BMG; <(8287 80739-2)>* [1] [10]
– The long way around / Easy silence / Not ready to make nice / Everybody knows / Bitter end / Lullaby / Lubbock or leave it / Silent house / Favorite year / Voice inside my head / I like it / Baby hold on / So hard when it doesn't come easy / I hope.

SIGN 'O' THE TIMES

1987 (US 85m) Purple Films / Paisley Park Films (PG-13)

Film genre: R&B/Rock-music concert/documentary

Top guns: s-w + dir: **PRINCE**

Stars: PRINCE *(performer)*, **Sheena Easton** *(performer)*, **Sheila E.** *(performer)* ← KRUSH GROOVE / → the ADVENTURES OF FORD FAIRLANE, **Mico Weaver** *(performer)* → GRAFFITI BRIDGE, **Dr. Fink** *(performer)*, **Levi Seacer Jr.** *(performer)* → GRAFFITI BRIDGE, **Boni Boyer** *(performer)* → GRAFFITI BRIDGE, **Cat** *(performer)*, **Atlanta Bliss** *(performer)* → GRAFFITI BRIDGE

Storyline: The tour of the album shoehorned into a narrative rather than a film demanding a soundtrack, comprising extended footage of shows in Rotterdam and Minneapolis (with most, but not all, of the setlist lifted from the record) spliced with typically tenuous character vignettes incorporating and linking in to the stage set. *BG*

Movie rating: *6

Visual: video (str8-to) Nov'87

Off the record: Sheena Easton (b. Sheena Shirley Orr, 27 Apr'59, Bellshill, Glasgow, Scotland) was a prolific singer and chart breaker in the 80s since her initiation test on an Esther Rantzen 'Big Time' TV talent programme; one of her hits was the title theme to the James Bond flick, 'For Your Eyes Only'. Now a multi-millionaire through real estate deals, and appreciated more in her adopted country of America, she's retained her first marriage name (spouse Sandy Easton between 1978-79). She's acted in several movies including 'Indecent Proposal' (1993) and was a voice in the animation 'All Dogs Go To Heaven 2' (1996). *MCS*

——

PRINCE

Mar 87. (cd)(d-lp) *Warners; <(9 25577-2)>(WX 88/+C)* [6] [4]
– Sign 'o' the times / Play in the sunshine / Housequake / Ballad of Dorothy Parker / It / Starfish and coffee / Slow love / Hot thing / Forever in my life / U got the look / If I was your girlfriend / Strange relationship / I could never take the place of your man / The cross / It's gonna be a beautiful night / Adore.

S/track review: A pertinent one this, given PRINCE's position at the centre of a depressingly contemporary sign o' the times, when a tabloid newspaper takes the place of a record label. Back in 1987, tabloids stuck to lurid stories and PRINCE wrestled with his habitually competing demands of the sacred and the secular, the creative and the commercial and the popular and the Funk. Despite being cobbled together from no less than three abandoned projects ('Camille', 'The Dream Factory' and 'Crystal Ball') and despite its occasional selection of the obvious over the revolutionary (with a small "r"), 'SIGN 'O' THE TIMES' is still the diminutive one's most consistent multiple album. Cut loose from the Revolution, he's stylistically all over the map, heralding the title track's end of the civilised world with uncommon detachment, reminding us he's a visionary keeper of the flame with a pointillist funk so sinuous it almost equates drug-blighted apocalypse and desire. But then the enduring appeal of his transmogrification of JB's-cum-Sly-cum-Clinton groove into 80s idioms like 'Housequake' (check the proto-'South Park' phrasing), 'Play In The Sunshine' and 'It' is, depending on how much of a purist you are, questionable. 'U Got The Look' – his shutter-speed, choreographed collabo with SHEILA's E and EASTON – lies somewhere in between, satisfying the Caucasian rockist tendencies he'd increasingly cultivated as the decade drew on. These, though, are but glittering prizes next to the eroto-spiritualdelica which PRINCE avails himself of through the album's hyperactive drift, definitively ambiguous jazz-love ballads – 'I Could Never Take The Place Of Your Man', 'Adore' and 'If I Was Your Girlfriend' – which simultaneously crown him as a Casanova of seemingly limitless imagination and possibility, and a seeker who refuses to relinquish a very personal vision of psycho-sexual intimacy. PRINCE was sitting on a raft of material just as radical but events conspired to consign it to hardcore fans willing to stick with him as he tested patience, preconceptions and, ultimately, ceded the initiative to younger bucks only too willing to play the game. *BG*

Album rating: *8

SING SING THANKSGIVING

1974 (US 78m) Varied Directions Pictures

Film genre: Folk & Blues-music concert documentary

Top guns: dir: David Hoffman ← the NASHVILLE SOUND, Harry Willard

Stars: the Voices Of East Harlem *(performers)*, **Joan BAEZ** *(performer)*, **B.B. KING** *(performer)*, **Joe Williams** *(performer)* ← JAMBOREE / → PETEY WHEATSTRAW, **Mimi Farina** *(performer)* ← CELEBRATION AT BIG SUR ← FOOLS ← FESTIVAL, Jimmie Walker *(MC)* → LET'S DO IT AGAIN → MONSTER MASH: THE MOVIE

Storyline: Johnny Cash did San Quentin and Folsom, Baez and B.B. do Sing Sing prison, New York, on er . . . Thanksgiving Day (23 November 1972). The added attraction is the documentary side by side with concert footage. *MCS*

Movie rating: *5.5

Visual: video

Off the record: Joe Williams (b. Joseph Goreed, 12 Dec'18, Cordele, Georgia) started his musical career in the mid-40s as a singer with Lionel Hampton's jazz band before he joined Count Basie's orchestra a decade later. He was still recording and touring until he died in Las Vegas of natural causes on the 29th of March, 1999. The **Voices Of East Harlem** were a gospel choir; they contributed their rousing version of 'Young, Gifted & Black', while blues legend **B.B. KING** secured his spot in the hall of prison fame with 'How Blue Can You Get'. *MCS*

a SKIN TOO FEW: THE DAYS OF NICK DRAKE

2000 – US 2002 (Neth 48m) Luijten Macrander Productions

Film genre: Folk-rock music documentary

Top guns: dir: Jeroen Berkvens

Stars: Joe Boyd *(himself)*, Gabrielle Drake *(herself)*, **Robert Kirby** *(himself)*, **Paul Weller** *(himself)* ← PUNK AND ITS AFTERSHOCKS ← PUNK IN LONDON / → the WHO LIVE AT THE ROYAL ALBERT HALL, **Nick Drake** *(archive)*

Storyline: The story of Nick Drake, the never-to-be-forgotten singer-songwriter who managed to leave three great albums behind ('Five Leaves Left', 'Bryter Layter' and 'Pink Moon'), before he fell into a deep depression and took his own life in 1974. His sister, Gabrielle Drake (a leading actress in her time in TV soap, 'Crossroads'), gives a good account of his short time in this world and there's also footage of Nick's late parents. *MCS*

Movie rating: *7.5

Visual: dvd (no audio OST)

Off the record: Robert Kirby was a brief member of 60s/70s outfit, the Strawbs.

the SLOG MOVIE

1982 (US 59m) We Got Power Films (R)

Film genre: Punk rock-music concert/documentary

Top guns: dir: **Dave MARKEY**

Stars: CIRCLE JERKS:- Greg Hetson, Keith Morris, Roger Rogerson/ Dowding, Lucky Lehrer *(performers)*, **T.S.O.L.:- Jack Greggors, Mike Roche, Ron Emory, Francis Gerald Barnes** *(performers)*, **the Fear:- Lee VING, Philo Cramer, Derf Scratch *, Spit Stix** *(performers)* ← the DECLINE OF WESTERN CIVILIZATION / → GET CRAZY → DU-BEAT-E-O, **the Cheifs** *(performers)*, **Symbol 6** *(performers)*, **Wasted Youth** *(performers)*, **Red Cross:- Steve McDonald, Jeff McDonald, Tracy** *(performers)* <= REDD KROSS =>, **Sin 34** *(performers)*, **Circle One** *(performers)*, **Black Flag:- Henry ROLLINS, Chuck Dukowski, Robo & Dez Cadena** * *(themselves)* → DESPERATE TEENAGE LOVEDOLLS * → BETTY BLOWTORCH AND HER AMAZING TRUE LIFE ADVENTURES * → AMERICAN HARDCORE *, Jordan Schwartz → DESPERATE TEENAGE LOVEDOLLS → REALITY 86'D → AMERICAN HARDCORE

Storyline: Shot on Super-8mm, this low-budget docu-flick takes the viewer to venues such as the Whiskey A Go-Go, Club 88, the Cuckoo's Nest, etc, to witness the bands (and the fans) of the So-Cal underground hardcore punk scene. *MCS*

Movie rating: *7

Visual: dvd Sep '03 (no audio OST)

Off the record: Relatively unknown acts, SIN 34 & CIRCLE ONE, can be heard on Various Artists LP, 'Buried Alive: Best From Smoke 7 Records 1981-1983' (2005), alongside contemporaries REDD KROSS; the latter heavily featured the latter and SIN 34. *MCS*

- ☐ Brian Wilson presents SMiLE alt.
(⇒ BEAUTIFUL DREAMER: BRIAN WILSON AND THE STORY OF 'SMiLE'

- ☐ Benjamin SMOKE segment
(⇒ BENJAMIN SMOKE)

SOME KIND OF MONSTER

aka METALLICA: SOME KIND OF MONSTER

2004 (US 135m) IFC Films / Paramount

Film genre: Hard Rock-music documentary

Top guns: dir: Joe Berlinger, Bruce Sinofsky

Stars: Metallica:- James Hetfield, Lars Ulrich, Kirk Hammett *, Robert Trujillo *(themselves / performers)*, **Jason Newsted** *(himself)* ← WOODSTOCK '99 ← WOODSTOCK 94 / * → END OF THE CENTURY,

Dave Mustaine *(himself)*, **Bob Rock** *(himself)*, **Cliff Burton** *(archival footage)*, Phil Towle *(himself)*, **Twiggy Ramirez** *(himself)*, **Brian Sagrafena** *(himself)* ← GREENDALE, **Dylan Donkin** *(himself)* ← GREENDALE, **Pepper Keenan** *(himself)*, **Danny Lohner** *(himself)* ← WOODSTOCK 94, etc.

Storyline: The tensions between Metallica members were coming to a head while making the album that was to become 'St. Anger'. They decide on a radical answer: to hire a group therapy psychologist (Phil Towle) as well as a film crew to shoot their every movement. The sessions (both music and therapy) are difficult, to say the least, but it shows the viewer just how modern-day rock albums are put together. *MCS*

Movie rating: *7.5

Visual: dvd

Off the record: Metallica were formed in Norvale, California, USA in 1981 by Danish-born drummer **Lars Ulrich** and guitarist/vocalist **James Hetfield**. In early '82, original second guitarist Lloyd Grant was replaced by future Megadeth mainman **Dave Mustaine**, while Ron McGovney was brought in on bass. After a brief period of relative stability, Mustaine was fired for drunkenness early the following year, being replaced by former Exodus guitarist **Kirk Hammett**; by this point, **Cliff Burton** had already joined on bass following the departure of McGovney. This was the classic early Metallica line-up that played on the first three albums, redefining the boundaries of metal. Moving to New Jersey in early '83, the band signed to John Zazula's 'Megaforce' label and unleashed their high octane debut, 'Kill 'Em All'. While it certainly wasn't without cliche, both lyrically and musically, there was a vibrancy in the speed and loudness of their sonic attack that drew on hardcore and punk, particularly in 'Seek And Destroy', a track that would come to be a staple of the band's live set. The record also featured, horror of horrors, a track that consisted entirely of a bass solo! But Metallica weren't trying to resurrect the indulgence of the 70s, their follow-up opus, 'Ride The Lightning' (1984), confirming Metallica's status as one of the most inventive, promising bands in the metal canon. The group had welded a keening sense of melody to their visceral thrash, alternating between grinding, bass-heavy, mid-tempo uber-riffing. They even came close to ballad territory with the bleakly beautiful 'Fade To Black', arguably one of the best tracks the band have ever penned. Then came 'Master Of Puppets' (1986), a masterful collection that rightfully saw Metallica hailed as one of, if not the, foremost metal act in the world, at the heavier end of the spectrum at least. The album went Top 30 in the States without the help of a hit single or even radio play, eventually achieving platinum status. The band subsequently toured with metal godfather, OZZY OSBOURNE, playing to rapturous crowds wherever they went. Disaster struck, however, when the band's tour bus crashed on 27th September '86, Burton losing his life in the accident. Metallica decided to carry on, replacing Burton with **Jason Newsted** and fulfilling their touring commitments. The following summer, the band released an EP of covers, '$5.98 EP – Garage Days Revisited', a hotch-potch of inspired reworkings from the likes of Diamond Head, Budgie and the Misfits. Their next album proper, '...And Justice For All' (1988), was marred by overly ambitious structures and complex arrangements as well as a poor production, subduing the trademark gut intensity. Nevertheless, there were moments of brilliance, most notably with 'One', a distressing first person narrative of a soldier kept alive on a life support machine. The song almost made the UK Top 10, winning the band a Grammy the following year for Best Metal Performance. With the eponymous transatlantic No.1, 'Metallica' (1991), the band entered the major league alongside the likes of U2 and R.E.M. as one of the biggest rock bands in the world. The aptly-named **Bob Rock** (ex-Payolas) had given the record a cleaner, "big rock" sound that complemented the more melodic and accessible material contained within. Not that Metallica had gone limp on the Beavis & Butthead element of their fanbase, 'Enter Sandman' was as crunchingly heavy as ever, yet the single possessed a sufficiently strong melodic hook to see it go Top 5 in the UK. With 'Nothing Else Matters', Metallica really had penned a Wishbone Ash-esque ballad, replete with strings (!) which saw the band notch up another Top 10 UK hit. After undertaking the biggest tour heavy rock has ever seen (obliterating co-headliners Guns N' Roses in the process), the band came back with another work of mature rock majesty, 'Load' (1996). From morbid metal to Lynyrd Skynyrd-style rootsy acoustics, Metallica once more developed and expanded their sonic palate, gaining widespread acclaim. The album went on to sell almost ten million copies, the band headlining the American Lollapolooza tour to promote it, again blowing most of the other acts away. In the spring of '99, **Hetfield, Ulrich** and Co were planning an orchestrated performance with composer Michael Kamen at the helm of the San Francisco Symphony Orchestra, a "best of" live album, 'S&M' hitting the bemused public later in the year. Three years into the new millennium and with more than two decades into a genre-defining career, the trio of **Hetfield, Ulrich** and **Hammett** (together with **Robert Trujillo** as a replacement for Newsted and a fill-in bassist) and producer **Bob Rock** returned with 'St. Anger' (2003), the sonic brutality and unalloyed rage that had perhaps been missing in their recent work was on show here. Judging by the fear and loathing within these pulverising grooves, Hetfield's recent stint in rehab seemed to have unlocked a fearsome closet of skeletons, the frontman raging at the world and, in the process, unleashing a momentum that had his band members caged-in from the opening bars. In 2004, the band released their warts'n'all documentary film/DVD/mini-CD, 'SOME KIND OF MONSTER' – bow to the master who is therapist, Phil Towle. **Twiggy Ramirez** is ex-bassist for Marilyn Manson and now in Nine Inch Nails; **Pepper Keenan** is of Corrosion Of Conformity & Down; **Danny Lohner** (Nine Inch Nails); **Brian Sagrafena & Dylan Donkin** are Echobrain. *BG & MCS*

– associated releases, etc. –

METALLICA: St. Anger

Jun 03. (cd/c/d-lp) *Elektra; <62853-2> Mercury; (986533-2/-4/-6)* [1] [3]
– Frantic / St. Anger / Some kind of monster / Dirty window / Invisible kid / My world / Shoot me again / Sweet amber / The unnamed feeling / Purify / All within my hands.

METALLICA: Some Kind Of Monster

Jul 04. (m-cd) *Elektra; <48838> Mercury; (9867810)* [37] Aug04 [ ]
– Some kind of monster / The four horsemen (live) / Damage, Inc. (live) / Leper messiah (live) / Motorbreath (live) / Ride the lightning (live) / Hit the lights (live) / Some kind of monster (edit & movie trailer).

the SONG REMAINS THE SAME

1976 (UK/US 132m) Warner Bros. / Swan Song (15)

Film genre: Hard-rock-music concert/documentary fantasy

Top guns: dir: Peter Clifton ← the LONDON ROCK & ROLL SHOW ← POPCORN, Joe Massot ← WONDERWALL / → DANCE CRAZE

Stars: LED ZEPPELIN:- John Bonham, John Paul Jones, Jimmy Page, Robert Plant *(performer)*, Peter Grant *(manager)*, **Roy Harper** *(himself)* ← MADE, Derek Skilton *(himself)*, Colin Rigdon *(himself)*, **Jason Bonham** *(himself)* → ROCK STAR

Storyline: One of the blueprints for Spinal Tap as thunder-metal rock gods Led Zeppelin undergo the rockumentary treatment. Alongside the Stateside live performances (from New York's Madison Square Garden, 1973), we're treated to clips of the lads in repose back in the UK. The hallucinatic dream sequences were a tad too obscure and morose, even manager Peter Grant gets in on the act by blasting everyone (1920s gangster-style) with a machine gun. The celluloid highlight has to be Page's dabble with the occult and his breathtaking climb to the top of a steep hillside, only to uncover ... er, himself, from death to birth. "I've been Dazed And Confused for so long ..." *MCS*

Movie rating: *6

Visual: video + dvd on 'Warner Bros.'

Off the record: (see below)

LED ZEPPELIN

Oct 76. (d-lp/d-c) *Swan Song; (SSK/SK4 89402) <201>* [1] [2]
– Rock and roll / Celebration day / The song remains the same / Rain song / Dazed and confused / No quarter / Stairway to Heaven / Moby Dick / Whole lotta love. *<(d-cd-iss. Feb87; 2 89402)> <(cd re-iss. Aug97 on 'Atlantic'; SK2 89402)>*

S/track review: Critics have long been in general agreement on the decidedly underwhelming nature of the accompanying soundtrack, LED ZEPPELIN's one and only live effort. ROBERT

PLANT denies us of his best vocals (well, it is live!), although the power of Zep is undeniably through the strength and overall musicianship of guitarist JIMMY PAGE, drummer JOHN BONHAM and bassist JOHN PAUL JONES; all three contribute some weird and wonderful fantasy skits for the movie. One of these (and accompanying a 26-minute version of 'Dazed And Confused') – mentioned in the synopsis – featured an electrifying PAGE with violin-bow jolting the strings of his guitar to echoing effect – surround sound, indeed. Eternally extended versions of such signature material from 'Rock And Roll' to 'Whole Lotta Love' never quite managed to lift the whole thing out of first gear, although 'No Quarter' and 'Stairway To Heaven' come close. *MCS*

Album rating: *6

SONGS FOR CASSAVETES

. . . AN ALL AGES FILM

2001 (US 91m b&w) Breadcrumb Trail Films

Film genre: Indie-rock-music concert/documentary

Top guns: dir: Justin Mitchell

Stars: Dub Narcotic Sound System *(performers)*, **the Make Up** *(performers)*, **Further** *(performers)*, **Sleater-Kinney** *(performers)*, **Henry's Dress** *(performers)*, **Some Velvet Sidewalk** *(performers)* ← HYPE!, **Unwound** *(performers)*, **Peechees** *(performers)*, **Bratmobile** *(performers)*, **Crayon** *(performers)*, **Tullycraft** *(performers)*, **Hi-Fives** *(performers)*, **Chisel** *(performers)*, **Semiautomatic** *(performers)*

Storyline: A group of friends come together for a rock show in South Bend, Indiana, 1993, basically to say goodbye to friend and musician, Brian Muller. The idea is set in concrete, an idea to re-create the early 90s underground scene of "real" indie bands. *MCS*

Movie rating: *6

Visual: dvd

Off the record: (see below)

—

Various Artists – live (& "interviews/quotes")

Oct 01. (cd) *Better Looking; <BLR 007>* ☐ ☐
– "Calvin from Dub Narcotic Sound System" / Time machine (the MAKE-UP) / I wanna be a stranger (FURTHER) / "Brent from Further" / Words and guitars (SLEATER-KINNEY) / The way she goes (HENRY'S DRESS) / "Al from Some Velvet Sidewalk" / Valley of the clocks (SOME VELVET SIDEWALK) / Arboretum (UNWOUND) / Pepper (the PEECHEES) / "Molly from the Peechees & Bratmobile" / Kiss and ride (BRATMOBILE) / Snap-tight wars (CRAYON) / Sweet (TULLYCRAFT) / You can (the HI-FIVES) / Selector Dub Narcotic (DUB NARCOTIC SOUND SYSTEM) / "Everyone" – John Cassavetes quote / Spectacles (CHISEL). *(bonus tracks +=)* – Wasted version (DUB NARCOTIC SOUND SYSTEM) / Meow for the kitty (SEMIAUTOMATIC).

S/track review: What namesake, cult actor/director, John Cassavetes, would make of this is indeed anybody's guess. With an array of indie-pop/punk artists "live" on parade (mainly from the 'K' Records & 'Kill Rock Stars' imprints), 'SONGS FOR CASSAVETES' comes across as a unique insight into a near-forgotten rock genre. The big names stem from up-and-coming, noisy girl-groups, SLEATER-KINNEY (on 'Words And Guitars') and support act BRATMOBILE ('Kiss And Ride') with two DIY, Delta 5-meets-Raincoats-type cues. The lads come up trumps by way of MAKE-UP ('Time Machine'), HENRY'S DRESS ('The Way She Goes') and They Might Be Giants-like CRAYON ('Snap-Tight Wars'). UNWOUND get the award for the longest track ('Arboretum') at nearly 7 minutes, while bands such as FURTHER, SOME VELVET SIDEWALK, TULLYCRAFT, the HI-FIVES and the PEECHEES flatter to deceive; one's heard it all before. Interspersed along with some "punk ethos" interviews with several of the artists (including Calvin Johnson), many of the tracks get bogged down to a certain degree. The soundtrack rounds off with a studio take of CHISEL's 'Spectacles', the track 'Wasted Version' by Calvin Johnson's DUB NARCOTIC SOUND SYSTEM (who also contribute 'Selector Dub Narcotic') and the female-fronted SEMIAUTOMATIC with the impressive 'Meow For The Kitty'. *MCS*

Album rating: *6

SONIC YOUTH

Formed: New York City, New York, USA . . . early 1981 by THURSTON MOORE and Kim Gordon, with a line-up solidifying around Lee Ranaldo and Richard Edson (later replaced by Steve Shelley). One of the most iconic, creative and influential American post-punk acts ever to have generated white noise for the sake of it, SONIC YOUTH, and more prominently spokesman THURSTON MOORE, have been progressively more active in film/soundtracks over the last decade or so. Their first group score effort was the unreleased (at the time) music for forgotten road movie, 'MADE IN USA' (1987), followed a decade later by two of the best cuts on the excellent soundtrack to Richard Linklater's 'SUBURBIA' (1997). MOORE, meanwhile, had contributed a mellow, acoustic-discordant score for the misadventures of Evan Dando and Liv Tyler in James Mangold's poignant, Grand Jury Prize winning drama, 'HEAVY' (1995), following it up with music for 'How To Draw A Bunny' (2002), a documentary on cult performance artist, Ray Johnson. Together with SONIC YOUTH, he also contributed another score (w/ Various Artists) for Allison Anders' fictional rock journo feature, 'THINGS BEHIND THE SUN' (2001), while the impressionistic pieces written for French techno thriller, 'DEMONLOVER' (2002), represent the band's most comprehensive soundtrack release to date. As well as saying his always worthwhile piece on rockumentary subjects as varied as the Minutemen and Sun Ra, MOORE was credited as consultant for the music on Gus Van Sant's hypnotic, harrowing portrayal of Kurt Cobain's descent into madness, 'LAST DAYS' (2005), in which wife Kim made a brief cameo. *BG*

- **filmography** (composers) {actors/performance}

Made In USA *(1987 OST rel.1995 =>)* / **Put More Blood Into The Music** *(1987 {p} =>)* / Weatherman '69 *(1989 {* KIM + THURSTON})* / **1991: The Year Punk Broke** *(1992 {*p} =>)* / Frisk *(1995 score by RANALDO)* / **Suburbi@** *(1996 on OST by V/A =>)* / **Rock And Roll Heart** *(1998 {c THURSTON} =>)* / **Free Tibet** *(1998 {p} =>)* / Fear Of Fiction *(2000 score by RANALDO & Evan Lurie)* / Kiss My Grits: The Herstory Of Women In Punk And Hard Rock *(2001 {p KIM})* / **Things Behind The Sun** *(2001 score w/ JIM O'ROURKE =>)* / **Demonlover** *(2002 OST w/ O'ROURKE =>)* / Burning Man: The Burning Sensation *(2002 score w/ OS MUTANTES)* / **End Of The Century** *(2003 {c THURSTON} =>)* / **Kill Your Idols** *(2004 {c THURSTON + LEE} =>)* / the Heart Is Deceitful Above All Things *(2004 score w/ BILLY CORGAN & Marco Castoldi)* / **Be Here To Love Me: A Film About Townes Van Zandt** *(2004 {c STEVE} OST by VAN ZANDT =>)* / **the Devil And Daniel Johnston** *(2005 {c THURSTON} =>)* / **Last Days** *(2005 {b KIM} =>)* / **We Jam Econo: The Story Of The Minutemen** *(2005 {c THURSTON} =>)* / **Punk: Attitude** *(2005 TV {c THURSTON} =>)* / **Too Tough To Die: A Tribute To Johnny Ramone** *(2006 {c THURSTON} =>)* / Noise *(2006 {p as MIRROR/DASH + TEXT OF LIGHT})* / **I'm Not There** *(2007 {b} OST by V/A =>)*

the SOUL OF A MAN

2nd part of Martin Scorsese presents THE BLUES

2003 (US 120m TV-mini w/b&w) Vulcan Productions / PBS

Film genre: Blues-music documentary

Top guns: dir (+ s-w): Wim Wenders ← the MILLION DOLLAR HOTEL ← BUENA VISTA SOCIAL CLUB ← TEATRO ← the END OF VIOLENCE ← PARIS, TEXAS

Stars: Laurence Fishburne *(narrator)* ← EVENT HORIZON ← WHAT'S LOVE GOT TO DO WITH IT ← BOYZ N THE HOOD ← SCHOOL DAZE ← DEATH WISH II ← FAST BREAK ← CORNBREAD, EARL AND ME, **Skip James** *(performer)*, **Blind Willie Johnson** *(performer)*, **J.B. Lenoir** *(performer)*, **Chris Thomas King** *(performer)* ← LAST OF THE MISSISSIPPI JUKES ← DOWN FROM THE MOUNTAIN ← O BROTHER, WHERE ART THOU? / → LIGHTNING IN A BOTTLE → RAY, **Bonnie RAITT** *(performer)*, **Nick CAVE** *(performer)*, **John Mayall** *(performer)* ← BAJA OKLAHOMA ← SGT. PEPPER'S LONELY HEARTS CLUB BAND ← DON'T LOOK BACK / → RED, WHITE & BLUES, **Cassandra Wilson** *(performer)*, **Lou REED** *(performer)*, **Lucinda Williams** *(performer)*, **Jon Spencer Blues Explosion** *(performers)* ← YOU SEE ME LAUGHIN' ← JOE'S APARTMENT / → MONKS: THE TRANSATLANTIC FEEDBACK, **Beck** *(performer)* ← SOUTHLANDER ← FREE TIBET / → MAYOR OF THE SUNSET STRIP → HIGH AND DRY → FEARLESS FREAKS, **T-Bone BURNETT** *(performer)*, **LOS LOBOS** *(performers)*, **Vernon Reid** *(performer)* → LIGHTNING IN A BOTTLE, **James "Blood" Ulmer** *(performer)* → LIGHTNING IN A BOTTLE, **Eagle-Eye Cherry** *(performer)* ← the DOORS, **Alvin Youngblood Hart** *(performer)*, **Marc Ribot** *(performer)* ← BIG TIME, **Garland Jeffreys** *(performer)*, **Shemekia Copeland** *(performer)*

Storyline: Wim Wenders, a man behind not a few great soundtracks in his time, goes in search of three bluesmen – Skip James, Blind Willie Johnson and JB Lenoir – whose old 78's inspired him and at least tangentially inspired the artists often featured on his soundtracks, people like Nick Cave, Lou Reed and T-Bone Burnett putting their typically idiosyncratic spin on things alongside narration, dramatisation and archive footage. *BG*

Movie rating: *6

Visual: dvd on 'Pinnacle'

Off the record: (see below)

Various Artists

Sep 03. (cd) *Columbia-Legacy; <90491-2> Sony; (512570-2)* ☐ Mar04 ☐
– Vietnam blues (CASSANDRA WILSON) / Down in Mississippi (EAGLE EYE CHERRY, VERNON REID & JAMES "BLOOD" ULMER) / Hard times killing floor blues (LUCINDA WILLIAMS) / Look down the road (LOU REED) / I feel so good (NICK CAVE & THE BAD SEEDS) / Devil got my woman – new recording (JON SPENCER BLUES EXPLOSION) / Slow down woman (CASSANDRA WILSON) / Don't dog your woman (T-BONE BURNETT) / Voodoo music (LOS LOBOS) / The death of J.B. Lenoir (JOHN MAYALL & THE BLUESBREAKERS) / Alabama (J.B. LENOIR) / God's word (SHEMEKIA COPELAND) / Illinois blues (ALVIN YOUNGBLOOD HART) / I'm so glad (BECK) / Special rider blues (JON SPENCER BLUES EXPLOSION) / Dark was the night, cold was the ground (MARC RIBOT) / Devil got my woman (BONNIE RAITT) / Crow Jane (SKIP JAMES) / Washington D.C., hospital center blues (GARLAND JEFFREYS) / Soul of a man (BLIND WILLIE JOHNSON) / See that my grave is kept green (LOU REED).

S/track review: It's not often you'll find the likes of CASSANDRA WILSON, JOHN MAYALL or BONNIE RAITT on the same album as NICK CAVE, JON SPENCER or BECK, but this is one blues appreciation society where day jobs are left at the door. Country blues icons BLIND WILLIE JOHNSON, SKIP JAMES and J.B. LENOIR are the common currency, but then there are almost as many ways to interpret their work as there are genres which country blues begat, and common isn't an adjective that could be applied to any of the performances. In the interests of respect and reference, each legend has a representative track slipped in among the homages, with JOHNSON's antique fervour lending the project its title, the existential dilemma at the heart of the blues and the heart of this album. LENOIR's 'Alabama' pulls no punches with its portrayal of endemic racism but it's that high whine of SKIP JAMES' 'Crow Jane' which blows the ill wind of the blues with least resistance, which gets to the nub of man's imperfection and his habitual unwillingness to ponder his inevitable fate. A large part of the album's lure is the sheer divergence in approach among the living contributors, all too willing to engage with the genre's realism; a shockingly ravaged-sounding LOU REED laughing in the face of life on a ramshackle 'Look Down The Road'; BURNETT's queasy, treated vocals getting over a trombone hump and putting a contemporary spin on SKIP JAMES' spaciness in 'Don't Dog Your Woman'; MAYALL sounding his grief on every funereal note and prison-gang cadence of 'The Death Of J.B. Lenoir'. If the JAMES cover presents him as a proto-New Man, he'd be glad to know that the likes of WILSON and SHEKEMIA COPELAND are putting the gospel soul into what's still largely a bluesman's world. Even among the avant-garde troupers, there's a gratifying gulf in perception, NICK CAVE joyfully unhinged and about to "blow his natural top", MARC RIBOT a picture of studied, finger-picking/scraping curator. *BG*

Album rating: *7.5

SOUL TO SOUL

1971 (US 96m) Ghana Arts Council / Cinerama Releasing (G)

Film genre: R&B/Soul-music concert/documentary

Top guns: dir: Denis Sanders ← ELVIS: THAT'S THE WAY IT IS

Stars: the STAPLE SINGERS:- Mavis Staples, "Pop" Staples *(performers)*, **Roberta Flack** *(performer)* → SAVE THE CHILDREN → RENALDO AND CLARA → BUSTIN' LOOSE, **Wilson Pickett** *(performer)* → SAVE THE CHILDREN → SGT. PEPPER'S LONELY HEARTS CLUB BAND → BLUES BROTHERS 2000 → BLUES ODYSSEY → ONLY THE STRONG SURVIVE, **Eddie Harris & Les McCann** *(performers)*, **Carlos SANTANA** *(performer/s)*, **Ike Turner** *(performer)* ← GIMME SHELTER ← IT'S YOUR THING ← the BIG T.N.T. SHOW / → BLUES ODYSSEY → the ROAD TO MEMPHIS → GODFATHERS AND SONS, & **Tina TURNER** *(performer)*, **Willie Bobo** *(performer)*, **Voices Of East Harlem** *(performers)*, **Amoah Azangeo** *(performer)*

Storyline: Recorded live at Black Star Square in Accra, Ghana, West Africa, this concert on the 6th March, 1971 marked the 14th anniversary of the country's independence. *MCS*

Movie rating: *7.5

Visual: video + dvd (latter w/out Flack)

Off the record: The SANTANA tracks featured in the film are:- 'Jungle Strut' & 'Black Magic Woman – Gypsy Queen'. *MCS*

Various Artists

Sep 71. (lp) *Atlantic; <SD 7207> (240 020-1)* ☐ Jan72 ☐
– Soul to soul (IKE & TINA TURNER) / Run shaker life (the VOICES OF EAST HARLEM) / Heyjorler (EDDIE HARRIS & LES McCANN with AMOA) / Freedom song (ROBERTA FLACK) / Tryin' times (ROBERTA FLACK) / Are you sure – He's alright (the STAPLE SINGERS) / I smell trouble (IKE & TINA TURNER) / Funky Broadway (WILSON PICKETT) / Land of 1000 dances (WILSON PICKETT) / Soul to soul (the VOICES OF EAST HARLEM).

S/track review: Having given us 'WOODSTOCK' a few years previously, the executives at the 'Atlantic' recording corporation (along with producer, Tom Dowd) delivered the R&B/soul/gospel equivalent, 'SOUL TO SOUL'. Although only stretching out to a mere one disc (not three like its aforementioned predecessor), the LP showcased the likes of black stars such as IKE & TINA TURNER, ROBERTA FLACK, the STAPLE SINGERS, WILSON PICKETT, etc. The concert also shaped the world of African music ("Afrobeat") after the Ghanaians witnessed Latin-rock outfit, Santana, sadly not deemed for inclusion here. Basically, in the interest of fairness (one surmises), each featured act on the 'SOUL TO SOUL' album is allocated between 5 to 10 minutes. Without a squabble in sight, married performers IKE & TINA TURNER open the LP with 'Soul To Soul', while the troubled pair also tackle Don Robey's bluesy number, 'I Smell Trouble'. WILSON PICKETT ("Soul Brother No.2" to most Africans) picked out two of his better known cuts, 'Funky Broadway' and 'Land Of 1000 Dances' (incidentally co-written by Chris Kenner & Fats Domino), although without sounding harsh or condescending he was no match for his "No.1" adversary, James Brown (who'd performed in Lagos, Nigeria, the previous year). Gospel's favourite family, the STAPLE SINGERS, put their hands together to commence side two by way of medley, 'Are You Sure' & 'He's Alright', while a few similarly-themed cuts (the upbeat and raucous, 'Run Shaker Life' & 6:45 a.m.-finale, 'Soul To Soul') stem from the VOICES OF EAST HARLEM – underrated and many times better than any Jacksons. Ghana itself was limited to only one LP track ('Heyjorler') courtesy of the weird but wrongly-spelt calabash-player, AMOA (aka Amoah Azangeo), who is credited alongside R&B jazz performers, EDDIE HARRIS & LES McCANN. The latter's protege, ROBERTA FLACK, sings her first of two cuts, 'Freedom Song', "on a portable recording machine in the dungeons of the old slave fortress in Cape Coast, Ghana" (as it says on the back cover), while her second, 'Tryin' Times', is cool jazz with a lot of soul-to-soul. *MCS*

Album rating: *6

Bruce SPRINGSTEEN

Born: 23 Sep'49, Freehold, New Jersey, USA. A brawny, blue collar carrier of his country's dying rock'n'roll flame, SPRINGSTEEN has consistently written about a different America from the one portrayed by his government and media. While the man's more bombastic songs have sometimes been adopted as miscontrued anthems, his darker, more reflective work has been compared to the likes of John Steinbeck and Woody Guthrie. Given the almost cinematic dimension of his grander arrangements and his occasional illumination of the marginal into the quasi-mythical, it's perhaps surprising that SPRINGSTEEN's filmography is fairly bare. His earliest screen appearance came via 1980s 'NO NUKES' anti-nuclear benefit, where his convictions saw him sharing a stage with the likes CROSBY, STILLS & NASH and James Taylor. Despite his age, SPRINGSTEEN was neither a contemporary of the latter nor a new wave provocateur and, having broken through in the mid-70s (with the 'Born To Run' album), he wasn't about to be sidelined just yet. The man's unassuming, almost anti-fashion image and unpretentious encapsulation of rock, pop and soul tradition endeared him to a wide audience, one which expanded massively with his mid-80s landmark, 'Born In The USA'. While the singer penned his first film theme – for Paul Schrader's kitchen sink/rock musical effort, 'LIGHT OF DAY' (1987) – around the same time, it was his wounded title tune to Jonathan Demme's AIDS drama, 'Philadelphia' (1993) which will likely go down as his lasting cinematic achievement. The theme to Tim Robbins' 'DEAD MAN WALKING' (1995) was also fertile territory for SPRINGSTEEN's narrative talent, as was the score to Sean Penn drama, 'The Crossing Guard' (1995), which he worked on with the late JACK NITZSCHE. On a lighter note, the Boss susbequently made a cameo in Stephen Frears' bittersweet Nick Hornby adaptation, 'HIGH FIDELITY'. *BG*

- filmography (composer) {performer} –

No Nukes *(1980 {p} on OST by V/A =>)* / **Light Of Day** *(1987 theme on OST by V/A =>)* / **Hail! Hail! Rock'n'Roll** *(1987 {p} OST by CHUCK BERRY =>)* / **Black & White Night** *(1988 {p} OST by ROY ORBISON =>)* / Philadelphia *(1993 hit theme on OST by Howard Shore; see future edition)* / the Crossing Guard *(1995 on score-only w/ Jack Nitzsche)* / **Dead Man Walking** *(1995 song/ theme on OST by V/A =>)* / **High Fidelity** *(2000 {c} on OST by V/A =>)*

STANDING IN THE SHADOWS OF MOTOWN

2002 (US 108m w/b&w) Artisan Entertainment (PG)

Film genre: Soul/R&B-music concert documentary

Top guns: dir: Paul Justman / s-w: Walter Dallas, Ntozake Shange (au: Alan Slutsky)

Stars: the Funk Brothers:- James Jamerson, Richard "Pistol" Allen, Jack "Black Jack" Ashford, William "Benny" Benjamin, Johnny Griffith, Robert White, Earl Van Dyke, Joe Messina, Uriel Jones, Eddie Willis, Bob Babbitt, Eddie "Bongo" Brown *(performers)*, Andre Braugher *(narrator)* ← DUETS, **Bootsy Collins** *(performer)*, **Ben Harper** *(himself)*, **Joan Osborne** *(performer)*, **Me'shell NdegeOcello** *(performer)* ← the END OF VIOLENCE, **Gerald Levert** *(performer)*, **Montell Jordan** *(performer)* → the FIGHTING TEMPTATIONS, **Chaka Khan** *(performer)* ← the BLUES BROTHERS, **Dennis Coffey** *(performer)*, **Tom Scott** *(performer)*, **Martha Reeves** *(herself)*, **Don Was** *(himself)* → the COUNTRY BEARS, **Otis Williams** *(himself)*, **the Supremes** *(archive performers)* ← BEACH BALL ← the T.A.M.I. SHOW

Storyline: Everyone knows that 'Motown' ran the tightest production line in soul history; here, finally, the human components on the factory floor get their due: guitarists Eddie "Chank" Willis and Joe Messina, keyboard players Johnny Griffith and Joe Hunter, bassist Bob Babbitt, drummers Uriel Jones and Richard "Pistol" Allen, and vibes man/percussionist Jack "Black Jack" Ashford, collectively known as The Funk Brothers. Their warm, disarmingly humble recollections and anecdotes put the heart in this documentary – annoyingly narrated in typically overdramatic, American style – and a smile on your face, tracing their disparate origins in the jazz and blues scenes, and remembering how they all ended up in Studio A, Hitsville USA, "a place where deadly grooves threatened to set the walls on fire". Old eyes shine as they reminisce on the vagaries of their deceased colleagues: James Jamerson midnight snacking on a jar of stinking pig's feet ("the dirt keeps the funk"), Eddie "Bongo" Brown reading a "nudie mag" when pretending to read sheet music. It's Allan Slutsky, though, who provides one of the film's most telling moments, recounting an incident in a restaurant where Robert White couldn't bring himself to take credit for 'My Girl' when it unexpectedly aired on the radio. Yet the permanent grin on Pistol's face, whether backing Joan Osborne or Chaka Khan, lays to rest a thousand ghosts. *BG*

Movie rating: *7

Visual: video + dvd

Off the record: The **Funk Brothers** (see below)

Various Artists & . . . the FUNK BROTHERS (live)

Sep 02. (cd) *Hip-O/Motown; <(440 064691-2)>* ☐ Jul03 ☐
– (Love is like a) Heat Wave (JOAN OSBORNE & . . .) / You've really got a hold on me (ME'SHELL NDEGEOCELLO & . . .) / Do you love me (BOOTSY COLLINS & . . .) / Bernadette (original instrumental) / Reach out I'll be there (GERALD LEVERT & . . .) / Ain't too proud to beg (BEN HARPER & . . .) / Shotgun (GERALD LEVERT feat. TOM SCOTT & . . .) / What becomes of the broken hearted (JOAN OSBORNE & . . .) / I heard it through the grapevine (BEN HARPER & . . .) / You keep me hanging on (original

instrumental) / Cool jerk (BOOTSY COLLINS & . . .) / Cloud nine (ME'SHELL NDEGEOCELLO & . . .) / What's going on (CHAKA KHAN & . . .) / Band introduction – Ain't no mountain high enough (CHAKA KHAN & MONTELL JORDAN & . . .) / The flick – original recording (EARL VAN DYKE). *<(d-cd iss.May04 +=; 066365-2)>* – Boom boom (JOHN LEE HOOKER) / (Your love keeps lifting me) Higher and higher (JACKIE WILSON) / Scorpio (DENNIS COFFEY &..) // Funk brothers in the house / Standing in the shadow of love / (dialogue: Joe Hunter – in the beginning) / The one who really loves you / Pride and joy / (dialogue: Robert White invents a classic) / My girl / Love is like an itching in my heart / Don't mess with Bill (EARL VAN DYKE QUARTET) / The hunter gets captured by the game / (dialogue: Eddie, Uriel & Jack – speaking the "language") / I second that emotion / I was made to love her / (dialogue: "Pistol" picks up the beat) / I heard it through the grapevine / Home cookin' / For once in my life / (dialogue: Jack in the club groove) / I can't get next to you / It's a shame / Ain't no mountain high enough / (dialogue: Eddie takes it to the bridge) / Mercy mercy me (the ecology) / (dialogue: Lamont Dozier – feeling the funk, brother) / You're my everything (TEMPTATIONS & JAMES JAMERSON).

S/track review: The double Grammy-winning soundtrack credits the "Departed Funk Brothers There In Spirit": guitarist ROBERT WHITE, keyboard man/artist in his own right EARL VAN DYKE, drummer WILLIAM "Benny" BENJAMIN, congo player EDDIE "Bongo" BROWN and "the greatest bass player of all time", JAMES JAMERSON. Tellingly, it offers no comment at all on the hand-picked vocalists out in front of the survivors; for once, the FUNK BROTHERS aren't playing anonymous second fiddle to the stars. Among those gathered worthies, JOAN OSBORNE is the unlikeliest, but also the one who comes up smelling of roses on an epic, Tina Turner-strength ravaging of the Jimmy Ruffin chestnut, 'What Becomes Of The Broken Hearted'. BOOTSY COLLINS is an inspired, clownish candidate for recreating mid-60s hits by the Contours and the Capitols, BEN HARPER displaces Marvin's soul with his sackcloth Southern blues and GERALD LEVERT proves he could have filled Eddie Kendricks' shoes had he been born a decade earlier, but none of these sacred Motor City cows are drastically rearranged. What is radical is that the band are on an audibly equal footing, not mixed down to highlight the singers, the live-in-the-theatre-before-a-select-audience approach lending the whole thing an MTV unplugged air, without, of course, the unplugged bit and notwithstanding the fact that some of the tracks are faded out. On almost every performance, the sheer energy of the regrouped FUNK-sters makes a mockery of their formidable collective age, and as well as Jimmy Smith-esque mascot, 'The Flick', they're afforded re-tooled versions of the jams which ended up backing the Four Tops hit, 'Bernadette' and the Supremes' 'You Keep Me Hangin' On'. For DJ's and hardcore soul and funkateers, these are the real deal and the crux of the whole exercise, forming the template for a further album's worth of sonic archaeology on the 2004 deluxe edition. Is it worth the extra expense if you've already shelled out on the original soundtrack? If you're interested in the root synergy of some of the greatest grooves ever laid down, almost certainly. With input from the surviving FUNK BROTHERS, the redoubtable Harry Weinger (the man behind the wonderful 'James Brown's Funky People' series) and Allan Slutsky (author of the book which inspired the documentary) tease out the unsung talents of each and every player, minus the distraction of the vocal overdubs. What you get, then, is the beating, racing heart of the Motown sound, cut to the funky quick, alternately isolating individual parts (JAMERSON is incredible throughout) and highlighting ensemble interaction. The wall-of-soulful-sound that is 'Standing In The Shadows Of Love' kicks it off but honourable mention has to go to the thundering 'Love Is Like An Itching In My Heart', the bass artistry and dazzling syncopation of Junior Walker's 'Home Cookin'' and the DENNIS COFFEY-bolstered 'I Can't Get Next To You'. Piqued by the poignancy of EDDIE BROWN's rather dazed recollection of the era's abrupt ending, it's also fascinating to hear the bones of Marvin Gaye's 'Mercy Mercy Me (The Ecology)', as it is to hear JAMERSON's bass singing over Eddie Kendricks and David Ruffin on 'You're My Everything', the one vocal that Weinger and Slutsky couldn't bear to leave out. The deluxe edition also throws in three bonus cuts on disc one including the full version of COFFEY's early 70s breaks classic, 'Scorpio'; how many would-be trainspotters knew this was a FUNK BROTHERS jam? The notes, meanwhile, are thorough to the point of musicological exhaustion, charting a blow by blow breakdown of almost every part the Brothers turned their hands to. But then that kind of devotion is probably why they call it soul music. *BG*

Album rating: *7.5 (deluxe *8.5)

the STAPLE SINGERS

Formed: Chicago, Illinois, USA ... 1951 as a gospel quartet by head of the family, Roebuck 'Pops' Staples (b.28 Dec'15, Winona, Mississippi) and his children, Cleotha, Pervis, Yvonne and Mavis. After a single for the 'United' label in 1954, the group signed to 'Vee-Jay' records in '56. However, it wouldn't be until the 60s that the STAPLE SINGERS made their mark, having subsequently inked a deal with 'CBS-Epic'. Two minor hits, 'Why (Am I Treated So Bad)' and a version of Stephen Stills' 'For What It's Worth', finally reached an audience. The following year 'Stax' gave them a chance to break through, although LPs 'Soul Folk In Action' & 'We'll Get Over' disappointed sales-wise. Now combining their blend of folk-gospel with soulful R&B (with the help of producer, Al Bell), the family hit paydirt in '71 via Top 30 single, 'Heavy Makes You Happy', while 'Respect Yourself' and the chart-topping 'I'll Take You There' made them household names. Their high profile was maintained when Mavis appeared in a trilogy of concert movies, 'SOUL TO SOUL' (1971), 'WATTSTAX' (1972 with all the family) and 'SAVE THE CHILDREN' (1973), while they got funky once more courtesy of Top 10 hit, 'If You're Ready (Come Go With Me)'. The STAPLE SINGERS had their second No.1 in 1975 with the CURTIS MAYFIELD-penned/produced title theme to the movie, 'LET'S DO IT AGAIN'; the LP reached Top 20 status. With the height of the sex-fuelled disco scene all the rage, the family found it hard to compete, although they were still in demand, as a place alongside the BAND in their performance movie, 'The LAST WALTZ' (1978) suggested. Sadly, Pops was to die on the 19th of December 2000, the result of a concussion. He'd shown his versatility – even though he was getting on a bit – in feature flicks, 'TRUE STORIES' (1986) and 'WAG THE DOG' (1997), while Mavis, too, was active on the big screen via 'GRAFFITI BRIDGE' (1990), 'LIGHTNING IN A BOTTLE' (2004), 'BLUES DIVAS' (2005) and 'NO DIRECTION HOME' (2005), the last three being music documentaries. *MCS*

- **filmography** {acting} –

Soul To Soul *(1971 {p MAVIS} on OST by V/A =>)* / **Wattstax** *(1972 {p} on OST w/ V/A =>)* / **Save The Children** *(1973 {p MAVIS} =>)* / the Klansman *(1974 {p})* / **Let's Do It Again** *(1975 OST by the STAPLE SINGERS =>)* / **the Last Waltz** *(1978 {p} on OST by the BAND & V/A =>)* / **True Stories** *(1986 {a POPS} OST by DAVID BYRNE & V/A =>)* / **Graffiti Bridge** *(1990 {a MAVIS} OST by PRINCE =>)* / **Wag The Dog** *(1997 {a POPS} OST by MARK KNOPFLER =>)* / **Lightning In A Bottle** *(2004 {p MAVIS} on OST by V/A =>)* / **Blues Divas** *(2005 {p MAVIS} =>)* / **No Direction Home** *(2005 {p MAVIS} on OST by BOB DYLAN =>)*

STEP ACROSS THE BORDER

1990 (Ger/Swi 90m b&w) CineNomad

Film genre: avant-Rock-music concert/documentary

Top guns: s-w + dir: Nicolas Humbert → MIDDLE OF THE MOMENT, Werner Penzel → MIDDLE OF THE MOMENT

Stars: Jonas Mekas *(Butterfly Wing)* → NICO ICON → NINA HAGEN = PUNK + GLORY, Robert Frank *(old man in train)*, **Fred FRITH** *(performer)*, **Ted Milton** *(television dancer)*, Julia Judge, Tom Walker, John Spaceley

Storyline: Fred Frith, avant-garde composer, multi-instrumentalist and all-round improv genius, is the subject matter of this musical narrative. From Japan, the States and Europe, the eccentric Englishman (one-time member of Henry Cow) performs in concert at rehearsal. *MCS*

Movie rating: *8

Visual: video + dvd

Off the record: **Ted Milton** was equally '"out-there", having released records with/as Blurt, and the solo, 'Confessions Of An Aeroplane Farter'. *MCS*

FRED FRITH

May 93. (cd/d-lp) *RecRec; (REC DEC/REC 30) East Side Digital; <ESD 80462>*

– Sparrow song / Voice of America, part III – Legs / Selluloid restaurant – The old man puts out the fire / After dinner / Houston street / Drum factory / Regardless of rain / Candy machine / Romanisches cafe / The border / Nirvana again / Scottish roppongi / Norrgarden nyvla / Birds / The as usual dance towards the other flight to what is not, part 3 / Williamsburg bridge / Same old me – Williamsburg bridge reprise / The as usual dance towards the other flight to what is not, part 7 / Lost and found / Nine by nine / Evolution / Union square / Morning song / Voice of America, part IV / Too much too little / Too late. *(cd re-iss. Jan03; ReR/FRO 03)*

S/track review: 'STEP ACROSS THE BORDER' served as both a film soundtrack and a compilation overview of composer/multi-instrumentalist FRED FRITH's best solo work during the previous decade. Throughout the 80s in particular, the former Henry Cow leader was augmented by an array of equally-talented players, including cellist (etc.) TOM CORA, bassist BILL LASWELL, drummer FRED MAHER, keys/harpist ZEENA PARKINS, bass clarinetist TIM HODGKINSON and on alto sax, JOHN ZORN (to name but a handful), all of course part of the recordings showcased here from as far afield as Japan and New York. With that unmistakable Eastern-European avant-folk beat, FRITH, CORA, PARKINS (as mid-80s outfit, Skeleton Crew) contributed two songs to the soundtrack, the quirky opener 'Sparrow Song' and the Byrne/Eno-esque gem, 'The Border'. From even earlier in his career, 'Voice Of America, part III & IV', FRITH – with synth man BOB OSTERTAG – finds heavenly solace and indeed the lost tapes from '81; the initial (part III) is segued with the fast-paced Massacre cut 'Legs' from the same year. A few of the more recent cues (also connected by a dash), the funky 'Selluloid Restaurant' & the self-descriptive 'The Old Man Puts Out The Fire', are stark but tuneful to a certain degree. The lamenting 'After Dinner' (live with the voice & piano of Japanese soloist, HACO) comes across as both inspirational and nauseating, while the latter could be said about the sawing and percussion in 'Drum Factory'. One begins to think the word experimental was termed for FRITH's foreboding arrangements, although slightly lighter cue, 'Candy Machine' (think 'The Colony Of Slippermen' by Genesis), is indeed on a lonely train to weirdsville. Fred's "Frithertronics" guitar highlight (well, King Crimson's Robert had his "Frippertronics"), the longest track on 'STEP ACROSS . . .', is the live 'Romanisches Cafe', a cellular track if ever there was one. Ditto 'Scottish Roppongi'. Previous track, 'Nirvana Again', is Beefheart with motion sickness, while the 1980-recorded 'Norrgarden Nyvla' is straight out of the Zappa musical textbook. Whether FRITH was trying to keep the prog-rock ethos alive could be questioned after listening to the Steve Hackett-esque, 'The As Usual Dance Towards The Other Flight To What Is Not' (part 3) – (the subsequent part 7 is different). Piece number 16 on parade, 'Williamsburg Bridge', seems to be congested at the moment, so we'll move on . . . straight to the excellent avant-punk cut, 'Same Old Me', which indeed segues directly to a reprise of the aforementioned traffic-noise of a track. But what's this on the 'Lost And Found' cue, a Celtic-orientated tune with no or little experimentation? Yes, FRITH could turn his guitar-hand to just about anything. One of the other highlights on this worthy FF compilation is 'Evolution', although his high-pitched voice sounds remarkably like Sting in his days with the Police as he sings "where are all the suspects". Innovative or just irritating, 'Morning Song' (accompanied by a realistic, digital alarm-clock!) shows Fred to be quite playful, as did closing novelty numbers, 'Too Much, Too Little' & 'Too Late'. Clocking in at over 74 minutes, the listener gets pure value for money on the majority of the tracks. *MCS*

Album rating: *8

STEPPING RAZOR RED X

aka PETER TOSH: STEPPING RAZOR RED X

1992 (Can 103m w/b&w) Bush Doctor Films / Northern Arts (14A)

Film genre: Reggae-music documentary/biopic drama

Top guns: s-w + dir: Nicholas Campbell

Stars: **Peter Tosh** *(archive footage)* ← the BOB MARLEY STORY; CARIBBEAN NIGHTS ← HEARTLAND REGGAE ← REGGAE SUNSPLASH ← ROCKERS, **Thunder** *(himself)*, Lloyd 'Rocky' Allen, Edward 'Bigs' Allen, Junior, Beresford Thompson, Gary Isaacs, Andrea Davis, Roy Garrick, Jahbi, Kenile, Rab Leon, Ron Headley, Bruce 'Preacher' Robinson

Storyline: The life of iconic reggae star and political activist, Peter Tosh, and the mystery and rumour surrounding his premature homicide in September 1987. Tosh's 'Red X' tapes (i.e. his personal diaries) were found after his death and reveal the real man inside. *MCS*

Movie rating: *6.5

Visual: video + dvd in Sep'02

Off the record: **PETER TOSH** was born Winston Hubert McIntosh, 19 Oct'44, Westmoreland, Jamaica. A founding member of the Wailers alongside BOB MARLEY in 1962, TOSH was equally as pivotal as his more famous peer in spreading the reggae gospel – if not more so. During his time with the Wailers, he maintained a prolific recording schedule for the famous 'Studio One' label, eventually founding his own imprint, 'Intel-Diplo H.I.M.' in 1971. This became the main outlet for TOSH's music following his break with MARLEY & Co; throughout his lengthy spell with the band, TOSH had provided them with consistently quality material, his last contribution being 'Get Up Stand Up' on the 'Burnin'' (1973) album. His career only really got off the ground again, however, when 'Virgin' signed him, his debut album proper, 'Legalize It' (1976), nearly hitting the UK Top 50. TOSH made no bones about what exactly he proposed to legalize, his hardline Rasta stance, booming baritone voice and bass-quaking reggae/dub sound winning die-hard fans across the whole musical spectrum. Recorded with backing band, Word, Sound & Power, 'Equal Rights' (1977) was an even more fiercely political set, featuring such scathing missives as 'Downpressor Man', 'Stepping Razor' and a tuffed-up revamp of the aforementioned 'Get Up Stand Up'. One of the man's more famous admirers was MICK JAGGER of the ROLLING STONES, who signed TOSH to his/their own label and even provided (clearly audible) backing vocals on his first Top 50 hit single, 'Don't Look Back'. The track was featured on the 'Bush Doctor' (1978) set, one of a trio of albums for the 'STONES label alongside 'Mystic Man' (1979) and 'Wanted Dread & Alive' (1981). After signing to 'E.M.I.' in the early 80s, he scored a further minor hit single with a cover of Chuck Berry's 'Johnny

B. Goode' and although his mainstream successes were few and far between, the man remained one of the scene's most visible figures. Tragically, 1987 protest set, 'No Nuclear War', was to become the man's swansong; TOSH was shot dead on 11th September the same year during a robbery at his Kingston home (he was only 42). Speculation that the killing was politically motivated has continued to flourish, however, TOSH having clashed with both the government and police in the past. *BG & MCS*

STONES IN THE PARK

the ROLLING STONES: STONES IN THE PARK

1969 (US 53m TV) Granada Television

Film genre: Rock-music concert/documentary

Top guns: dir: Leslie Woodhead

Stars: the ROLLING STONES:- Mick Jagger, Keith Richards, Mick Taylor, Charlie Watts, Bill Wyman *(themselves/performers)*, **Marianne Faithfull** *(herself)* ← DON'T LOOK BACK ← ANNA / → LUCIFER RISING → the WALL: LIVE IN BERLIN → ROCK AND ROLL CIRCUS, **Paul McCartney** *(himself)* <= the BEATLES =>

Storyline: Poignant piece of celluloid taking us back two days after the death of guitarist Brian Jones and a prearranged free concert by the Rolling Stones in front of an estimated 250,000 audience at London's Hyde Park (July 5th, 1969). Paul McCartney attended. Bill Wyman accounted the day in his autobiography, Stone Alone. *MCS*

Movie rating: *6

Visual: video + dvd (no audio OST)

Off the record: the ROLLING STONES perform 'Jumping Jack Flash', '(I Can't Get No) Satisfaction', 'Honky Tonk Women', 'Midnight Rambler', 'Sympathy For The Devil', etc. *MCS*

STOP MAKING SENSE

1984 (US 88m) Arnold Entertainment / Cinecom Pictures (PG)

Film genre: alt-Rock-music concert/documentary

Top guns: dir: Jonathan Demme (+ s-w) → STOREFRONT HITCHCOCK → HEART OF GOLD (← LADIES AND GENTLEMEN, THE FABULOUS STAINS ← BLACK MAMA, WHITE MAMA), **Talking Heads**

Stars: Talking Heads:- David BYRNE, Jerry Harrison, Tina Weymouth, Chris Frantz *(performers)* + guests **Bernie Worrel** *(synthesizers)* → MOOG, **Alex Weir** *(musician)*, **Steve Scales** *(musician)*

Storyline: "Singing is a trick to get people to listen to music for longer". Just one of the many nuggets of homespun philosophy ("body odor is the window to the soul" is another personal favourite) and sage advice printed on the original soundtrack's sleeve. In the case of BYRNE himself, his singing – at least in those days – sounded more like a ritual than a trick. Combined with the band's wry visual commentary and Jonathan Demme's straight-shooting camera work, it conspired to create what's still regarded as one of the best live concert films ever conceived. *BG*

Movie rating: *9

Visual: video + dvd

Off the record: (see below)

—

TALKING HEADS

Sep 84. (lp/c) *Sire; <25121> E.M.I.; (TAH/+TC 1)* [41] Oct84 [37]
– Psycho killer / Swamp / Slippery people / Burning down the house / Girlfriend is better / Once in a lifetime / What a day that was / Life during wartime / Take me to the river. *(cd-iss. Feb85; CDP 746064-2) (c+=/cd+=)* – (extra extended tracks) *(re-iss. Mar90 cd)(c/lp; CZ 289)(TC+/ATAK 147) (re-iss. Nov93 on 'Fame' cd/c; CD/TC FA 3302) (lp-iss.Apr99 on 'E.M.I.'; 499471-1) <(cd re-iss. Sep99 on 'E.M.I.'+=; 522453-2)>* – Heaven / Thank you for sending me an angel / Found a job / Making flippy floppy / This must be the place (naive melody) / Genius of love / Crosseyed and painless.

S/track review: The record didn't have it quite so easy: as well as the obvious weakness of being detached from the action, it consigned many of the tracks to the cutting room floor and also sequenced them differently, an injustice righted with the 1999 re-issue. And while this is one case where a copy of the DVD is pretty much an essential primer, the CD imparts at least some sense of the movie's minimalist largesse. Video or audio, both formats are still remembered primarily for the mesmeric, electro-acoustic 'Psycho Killer' which kicks them off, an amuse bouche for insomniacs. From there, the performance gathers a slick, gawky momentum, with former Parliament-ary aide BERNIE WORRELL firing off ever freakier synth frequencies as BYRNE makes like spasmodicus erectus. Highlights include an acoustic 'Heaven' (re-issue only), a manic 'Burning Down The House', and a body-popping, almost Harold Faltermeyer-esque 'Girlfriend Is Better'. As a livewire greatest hits, the re-issue (minus a couple of stinkers) is still a great introduction. It's also a signpost on the way to BYRNE's subsequent role as ambassador for some of the most exquisite Brazilian and African music in existence. You know it doesn't make sense. *BG*

Album rating: *7

– spinoff releases, etc. –

TALKING HEADS: Slippery People / This Must Be The Place (Naive Melody)
Oct 84. (7"/ext.12") *(EMI/12EMI 5504)* [–] [68]

TALKING HEADS: Girlfriend Is Better / Once In A Lifetime
Nov 84. (7"/ext.12") *(EMI/12EMI 5509)* [–] [ ]

TALKING HEADS: Girlfriend Is Better / Heaven
Dec 84. (7") *<29080>* [ ] [–]

TALKING HEADS: Once In A Lifetime / This Must Be The Place (Naive Melody)
Apr 86. (7") *<29163>* [91] [–]

STOREFRONT HITCHCOCK

1998 (US 77m) Orion Pictures / Metro-Goldwyn-Mayer (PG-13)

Film genre: alt-Rock-music concert/documentary

Top guns: dir: Jonathan Demme ← STOP MAKING SENSE / → HEART OF GOLD

Stars: Robyn Hitchcock *(performer)*, **Deni Bonet** *(violinist)*, **Tim Keegan** *(performer)*

Storyline: Eccentric songwriter Robyn Hitchcock performs his music for the general public in a New York shop window. Over a couple of days he stands with his back to the glass and in between songs he makes observations about himself, his work and the society he lives in, much to the bemusement of passers-by. *JZ*

Movie rating: *6.5

Visual: dvd

Off the record: Robyn Hitchcock was born 3rd March '53, East Grinstead, London, England. At age 21, he set out for Cambridge to locate the home of his idol, Syd Barrett but ended up busking instead. 1976 found him forming a string of bands including the Worst Fears, the Beetles, Maureen & The Meatpackers and, finally by the end of the year, Dennis And The Experts, an embryonic Soft Boys. In March '77, they were offered a deal with indie label, 'Raw', who almost immediately issued their debut release, 'Give It To The Soft Boys EP'. The band embarked on a UK tour supporting ELVIS COSTELLO and the Damned which, in turn, led to a contract with 'Radar' records, although after only one 45 and many disagreements, they parted company.

Taking matters into their own hands, the Soft Boys set up their own label, 'Two Crabs', and issued a debut album, 'A Can Of Bees' (1979). The record was a resounding failure although it has since been the subject of many re-issues in different versions; 1980 saw them much-improved via 'Underwater Moonlight'. Hitchcock and Co had finally managed to translate their quirky post-punk psychedelia to vinyl, pointing the way towards the direction of the frontman's erratic solo career. By the following year the Soft Boys had split, playing their final shows to more appreciative US audiences. Hitchcock subsequently completed a solo album, 'Black Snake Diamond Role' (1981), featuring the cult classics, 'Brenda's Iron Sledge' and the single, 'The Man Who Invented Himself'. Clearly the man had lost none of his Barrett-esque lyrical daftness in the interim, his tongue-in-cheek, surreal humour occasionally even outstripping Captain Beefheart. After the disastrous Steve Hillage-produced 'Groovy Decay' (1982), however, Robyn decided enough was enough. Until 1984, that is, when he returned with an affecting acoustic album, 'I Often Dream Of Trains', the record seeing him reinstate the Soft Boys rhythm section (Morris Windsor and Andy Metcalfe) under the guise of Robyn Hitchcock & The Egyptians. In 1985, their first product, 'Fegmania!', hit the shops, while a few years later his band were signed to 'A&M' (for 1988 album 'Globe Of Frogs'). His band became firm faves on the US college circuit, especially when indie idols, Michael Stipe and Peter Buck (of R.E.M.) guested on 'Queen Elvis' and 'Perspex Island'. In 1993, Robyn returned to the eccentric brilliance of old with the highly regarded, John Leckie-produced 'Respect', a creative renaissance of sorts which even inspired him to re-unite the Soft Boys early in 1994 for some Bosnia benefit concerts. A further couple of solo sets appeared in the mid-90s, 'You And Oblivion' (1995) and 'Moss Elixir' (1996), the latter with a quintessentially Hitchcock, engagingly fantastical life-after-death yarn printed on the inner sleeve. Back to the zaniness of his old self, the man was to bow out of the 90s with a low-key effort, 'Jewels For Sophia' (1999). Towards the end of 2002, Robyn delivered a whole set of Dylan tunes under the guise of 'Robyn Sings', while he also found time to re-form the Soft Boys for a one-off album 'Nextdoorland' (2002); Hitchcock, Kimberley Rew, Matthew Seligman and Morris Windsor had performed live the previous year. Had it really been over 21 years since their last? Back in 2003 with 'Luxor', Hitchcock was still plying the kind of kooky quasi-folk which moves some to label him as a wayward genius. With lyrics as engagingly impenetrable as ever, and acoustic guitar playing as wildly impressive as ever, the record was another minor classic for the man's diehard fanbase. Cue some acting work in 2004's 'The Manchurian Candidate' as an army truck driver and conspirator – eh! *BG & MCS*

—

ROBYN HITCHCOCK (w/ spoken dialogue *)

Oct 98. (cd) *Warners; <(9362 46846-2>)* ☐ Nov98 ☐
– (*) / 1974 / (*) / Let's go thundering / (*) / I'm only you / Glass hotel / (*) / I something you / (*) / The yip! song / (*) / Freeze / (*) / Alright, yeah / Where do you go when you die? / The wind cries Mary / No, I don't remember Guildford / (*) / Beautiful queen / (*).

S/track review: "Does my hair look alright?" ROBYN HITCHCOCK, erstwhile frontman of punk/new wave combo the Soft Boys, and latterly darling of the early 90s MTV generation, asks by way of introduction. Though listening to this alone can't provide an answer, and we cannot marvel at the dazzling array of bright shirts that often adorn him, what we can appreciate is a ferociously articulate songwriter, and arch raconteur, in his element. '1974' showcases his whiney, mockney, quirky vocal style, alluding to his influences: "Syd Barrett's last session", Pink Floyd and "rebel rebel". His muscular acoustic balladeering is at the fore and his lyrics traverse a popular cultural landscape of "molecules" and "inches" of time, taking in Python's last series and the Guardian's condemnation of "rotting minds". His love of the surreal, of "ghastly mellow saxophones all over the floor", is as present as his political awareness of a time when (resonantly) "you could vote Labour but not anymore". As much as the songs, a great deal of the joy in this album comes from HITCHCOCK's rigorous song introductions, at turns funny, endearing, pretentious, lucid and infuriating. He takes apart the idea of song titles before 'Let's Go Thundering' and the very idea that a mass of molecules that is a human be represented by one name. On a jaunty, all-inclusive 'Let's Go..' he is joined by DENI BONET on a plaintive violin. His introduction to 'I'm Only You' grapples with organized religion, of churches full of carcasses, and a married couple united in a bloody welt. He notes that his contempt of religion is dangerous in a time when it is risky being an infidel, but his disdain of the subjugation of belief for political purposes, what he calls 'pornography', rings as true now as it ever did. In 'I'm only you' he depicts himself as a "mirror cracked across itself", a "pattern on a china bowl", a "memory engraved upon your soul". It is a song about immersion in different selves and nature, with some great, swooping, descending and ascending, transcendent acoustic guitar work. His instrument's tone and clarity is the perfect counterpoint to his lucidity. 'Glass Hotel's use of the delay pedal adds layers of curiosity, dwelling on what "seems", as his writing departs from the symbolic order to more dreamlike, enigmatic state, verging on psych-folk. Then comes his most elaborate spoken digression: as a member of the audience extinguishes a candle, he embarks on a lengthy monologue about how he will get abducted by two minotaurs, covered in duct tape then get fired 2723 ft above sea level, lose momentum 8 feet above Leicester Square, all of which culminates in a strike on the underground. It is a bizarre vision of the apocalypse which is the best and worst of HITCHCOCK depending on your taste: brilliant, whimsical and very self-conscious. In 'I Something You', HITCHCOCK dips into the self-reflexive, reflecting how the middle bits of songs get predictable but not this one, as he disrupts the ambling chord sequence with a chugging distorted mid-section. 'The Yip! Song' which implores "Vera Lynn" to "cleanse us with your healing grin" features some silly but impressive yipping and nanananaing and receives an ecstatic reaction from the crowd. A caffeine-fuelled 'Freeze' is jittery and electrified, as HITCHCOCK stabs at his guitar. He introduces 'Alright, Yeah' as a sofa or contour-fitted chair, designed not to upset you, not even bland. It is standard alternative rock, featuring deft, melodic guitars, and just as he promised it is bright and unbothersome. On 'Where Do You Go When You Die' harmonica bolsters the slinky groove, it depicts people "praying to the void", where salvation and damnation are equally obsolescent. Again he expresses his existential concerns that everything just ends, but floats the intriguing proposition that your soul could spend time with Napoleon or Eazy-E of NWA. His fondness for fractured imagery makes 'The Wind Cries Mary', with its jacks in boxes and clowns in bed, an apt choice of cover for this acoustic-led and harmonica inflected rendition. Like HENDRIX, DYLAN and Syd Barrett, HITCHCOCK uses lyrics that pick and mix from "real life" and also reach out to another plain to reach some other truth. A song about memory lapse, 'No, I Don't Remember Guildford' only succeeds in showing that HITCHCOCK doesn't remember much about anything really. But his Intro to 'Beautiful Queen' sums him up: "If all time is eternally present all time is unredeemable, either that or it's redeemable, can't remember which". It is typical of the man: profound and playful, always full of it, but a praiseworthy exponent of cerebral alternative songwriting. *DF*

Album rating: *7

Joe STRUMMER (w/ the CLASH)

Born: John Graham Mellor, 21 Aug'52, Ankara, Turkey, son of a diplomat. Not the most conventional guy to emerge from boarding school life, London-based STRUMMER got his first taste of the limelight when he fronted mid-70s pub-rock outfit, the 101'ers. After discovering punk rock through the SEX PISTOLS in early '76, he subsequently joined the movement and formed the CLASH, alongside like-minded lovers of punk and reggae,

Mick Jones, Paul Simonon and Terry Chimes (future PiL member Keith Levene also had a brief spell early on). After a riotous tour supporting the aforementioned Pistols, their manager, Bernie Rhodes, struck a deal with major label big boys 'C.B.S.' in early '77 and subsequently unleashed the two-minute classic, 'White Riot'. A driving chantalong stomp, the record smashed into the UK Top 40 and announced the arrival of a band whose influence and impact was second only to Rotten & Co. The CLASH manipulated the energy of punk as a means of political protest and musical experimentation, and unlike others of their ilk, they needed a larger audience to get their message across. 'The Clash' (1977) was a blinding statement of intent, a finely balanced masterwork of infectious hooklines and raging conviction. 'I'm So Bored With The U.S.A.' and 'Career Opportunities' railed against inertia, while a cover of Junior Murvin's 'Police And Thieves' was the first of many sporadic forays into dub reggae. The album went Top 20, lauded by many critics as the definitive punk set, while a further two classic singles (not on the album), 'Clash City Rockers' and 'White Man In Hammersmith Palais', made the Top 40 (the latter addressing the issue of racism, a subject never far from the band's agenda). 'C.B.S.' (and no doubt the band themselves) were keen to break into America, subsequently enlisting the production services of BLUE OYSTER CULT guru, Sandy Perlman, for follow-up set, 'Give 'Em Enough Rope' (1978). The album's more rock-based, less frenetic approach met with some criticism and despite the label's best efforts, the record just failed to crack the American Top 100. It had, however, made No.2 in Britain and spawned the band's first Top 20 hit in 'Tommy Gun'. The CLASH subsequently set out to tour the States, while British fans lapped up 'The Cost Of Living' EP and its incendiary cover of Sonny Curtis' 'I Fought The Law'. Finally, in late '79, the CLASH delivered their marathon masterwork, 'London Calling'. Overseen by seasoned producer, Guy Stevens, the double set showed the band at an assured creative peak, from the anthemic echo of the title track to the brooding 'Guns Of Brixton'. A UK Top 10'er, the record finally cracked the States (Top 30), and its universal acclaim spurred them on to ever more ambitious endeavours. After the plangent dub of the 'Bankrobber' and 'The Call-Up' singles (plus their introduction into celluloid, 'RUDE BOY'), the CLASH unleashed the sprawling, triple vinyl set, 'Sandinista!' in December 1980. The record's wildly experimental material met with critical pasting, the bulk of the album's tracks failing to withstand repeated listening. Its relatively poor sales (still at single vinyl price!) forced a back-to-basics rethink for 'Combat Rock' (1982). Although the LP was a healthy seller, it sounded laboured; ironically, it became the CLASH's biggest selling album in America, where the 'Rock The Casbah' single made the Top 10. Drummer Topper Headon was already long gone by this point and was replaced by Chimes, who'd left after their 1977 debut; Jones, too, was kicked out the following year. The band stumbled on for a further album, 'Cut The Crap' in 1985, before finally disbanding the following month. While Jones enjoyed mid-80s success with Big Audio Dynamite, STRUMMER embarked on a low-key solo career before working with his pal Shane MacGowan in the POGUES. This unique collective (contributing acting and songs) also spread their musical wings on a couple of soundtracks, 'SID & NANCY' (1986) and 'STRAIGHT TO HELL' (1987), while STRUMMER himself delivered two solo scores to 'WALKER' (1987) and 'PERMANENT RECORD' (1988). The CLASH fever once again gripped the nation in 1991 when 'Should I Stay Or Should I Go' – a Top 20 hit in 1983 – hit the top of the charts after being used in a Levi jeans advert (what else!?). Come the late 90s, STRUMMER was back from music biz oblivion fronting his own band, the Mescaleros; their debut set, 'Rock Art & The X-Ray Style' (1999) ran a gamut of genres without really asserting STRUMMER's personality on any of them. 'Global A Go-Go' (2001) was significantly more focused and cohesive, the former CLASH man casting his witty, worldly-wise perspective over a series of ventures into off-kilter world-beat. Tragically, Joe was to die of heart failure at his home in Somerset on the 22nd of December, 2002. 'Streetcore' (2003) was STRUMMER's final musical will and testament, reverting back to his roots with a searing vengeance, resurrecting the dub-rock perfected by the CLASH. *BG & MCS*

- **filmography** (composer) {acting} –

Rude Boy *(1980 {p w/ the CLASH} + score w/ V/A)* / **Concerts For The People Of Kampuchea** *(1980 {p CLASH} on OST by V/A =>)* / the King Of Comedy *(1983 {c w/ the CLASH})* / **Sid & Nancy** *(1986 on OST by V/A & PRAY FOR RAIN =>)* / **Straight To Hell** *(1987 {*} on OST by the POGUES & PRAY FOR RAIN =>)* / **Candy Mountain** *(1987 {a} =>)* / **Walker** *(1987 {a} OST by STRUMMER =>)* / **Permanent Record** *(1988 OST by STRUMMER & V/A =>)* / **Mystery Train** *(1989 {a} OST =>)* / I Hired A Contract Killer *(1990 {p/a})* / When Pigs Fly *(1993 score)* / Grosse Point Blank *(1997 OST w/ V/A; see future editions =>)* / Doctor Chance *(1997 {*})* / **Westway To The World** *(2000 {p w/ the CLASH} dvd-only =>)* / Super 8 Stories *(2001 {p})* / **I Was Born But . . .** *(2002 {p} =>)* / **Let's Rock Again!** *(2004 {p} dvd-only =>)*

SUPERSHOW

1969 (UK 70m) Supershow Productions

Film genre: Rock-music concert/documentary

Top guns: dir: John Crome

Stars: Jack Bruce *(performer)*, **Eric CLAPTON** *(performer)*, **Buddy Guy** *(performer)* → CHICAGO BLUES → BLUES ODYSSEY → GODFATHERS AND SONS → FESTIVAL EXPRESS → LIGHTNING IN A BOTTLE, **Stephen Stills** *(performer)* → WOODSTOCK → JOURNEY THROUGH THE PAST → NO NUKES → WOODSTOCK '94, **Buddy Miles** *(performer)* → JIMI HENDRIX → the BUDDY HOLLY STORY, **Jon Hiseman's Colosseum** *(performers)*, **Glenn Campbell with the Misunderstood** *(performers)*, **Modern Jazz Quartet** *(performers)*, **Dick Heckstall-Smith** *(performer)*, **Chris Mercer** *(performer)*

Storyline: "The last great jam of the 60s" – well . . . by invitation only in west London, England – best described this two-day trip into power blues and jazz, celebrating pop kings such as Eric Clapton, Jack Bruce and Buddy Guy. With numerous others (see above/below) they jammed on numbers such as 'Stormy Monday', 'Visitor From Venus' and the nursery rhyme, 'Mary Had A Little Lamb'. *MCS*

Movie rating: *6

Visual: dvd 2003 on EagleVision (no audio OST)

Off the record: Concentrating slightly on the jazz-rock artists, **Buddy Miles** (b. George Miles, 5 Sep'47, Omaha, Nebraska) was famous as the legendary drummer with Electric Flag, Jimi Hendrix's Band Of Gypsys and his own Buddy Miles Express; he later collaborated with John McLaughlin and Carlos Santana. **The Modern Jazz Quartet** (Milt Jackson & Co.) were classy golden oldies from the 50s but were currently (1967-69) going through a bit of a revival, having signed to the Beatles' 'Apple' stable. **Jon Hiseman's Colosseum & Dick Heckstall-Smith** were part of a British jazz-rock boom that incorprated **Chris Mercer** who'd found fame with American one-time garage outfit, the Misunderstood, led by **Glenn Campbell** (no, not the country star!). *MCS*

SYMPATHY FOR THE DEVIL

US title 'ONE PLUS ONE'

1968 (UK 104m) Connoisseur / Cupid Productions (15)

Film genre: Rock-music documentary w/ studio rehearsal footage

Top guns: s-w + dir: Jean-Luc Godard

Stars: the ROLLING STONES:- Mick Jagger, Brian Jones, Keith Richards,

Charlie Watts + Bill Wyman *(themselves)*, Sean Lynch *(narrator)*, Frankie Dymon Jnr. *(Black Power militant)* ← SOME PEOPLE, Anne Wiazemski, Iain Quarrier, Danny Daniels, Illario Pedro, Roy Stewart, Lambert Spencer, Tommy Ansar, Michael McKay, Rudi Patterson, Mark Matthew, Karl Lewis, Bernard Boston, Nike Arighi, Francoise Pascal, Joanna David, Monica Walters, Glenna Forster Jones, Elizabeth Long, Jeanette Wild, Harry Douglas, Colin Cunningham, Graham Peet, Matthew Knox, Barbara Coleridge

Storyline: Cult French director, Jean-Luc Godard, mixes up the political medicine by piecing together overlong revolutionary/race/anti-porn vignettes to fit – with no apparent connection! – alongside several evolving studio try-outs/takes for the classic Rolling Stones number, 'Sympathy For The Devil'. Why? *MCS*

Movie rating: *3

Visuals: dvd . . .

Off the record: Not surprisingly, the **ROLLING STONES** never released the soundtrack on vinyl but the featured song appeared on the 'Beggars Banquet' album. *MCS*

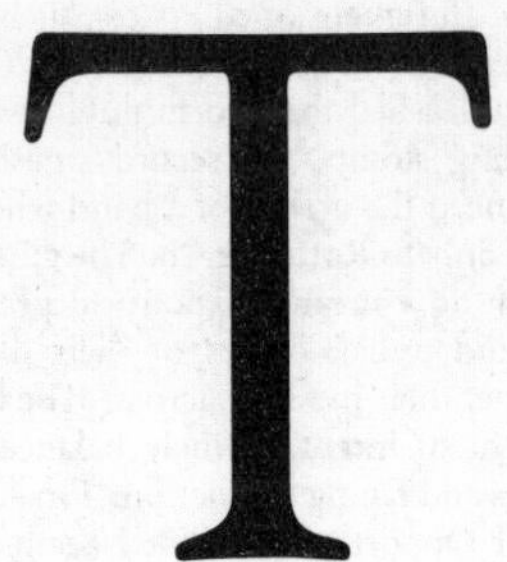

the T.A.M.I. SHOW

UK title 'TEEN AGE COMMAND PERFORMANCE'

1964 (US 123m b&w) American International Pictures

Film genre: R&B/Pop-music concert documentary

Top guns: dir: Steve Binder

Stars: Gerry & The Pacemakers:- Gerry Marsden, Freddie Marsden, Leslie Maguire, Les Chadwick *(performers)* → FERRY 'CROSS THE MERSEY → the COMPLEAT BEATLES / **Billy J. Kramer & the Dakotas:- Billy J. Kramer, Toni Baker, Pete Hilton, Raymond Jones, Eddie Mooney, Mike Maxfield** *(performer/s)* → POP GEAR → the COMPLEAT BEATLES, **Chuck BERRY** *(performer)*, **Marvin Gaye** *(performer)* → TROUBLE MAN → SAVE THE CHILDREN, **the Miracles:- Smokey Robinson *, Claudette Robinson, Bobby Rogers, Ronnie White** *(performer/s)* → KNIGHTS OF THE CITY * → the TEMPTATIONS *, **the Supremes:- Diana ROSS, Mary Wilson, Florence Ballard** *(performers)*, **Lesley Gore** *(performer)* → the GIRLS ON THE BEACH → SKI PARTY, **James BROWN & His Famous Flames** *(performer/s)*, **the ROLLING STONES:- Mick Jagger, Keith Richards, Brian Jones, Billy Wyman, Charlie Watts** *(performers)*, **the BEACH BOYS:- Brian Wilson, Dennis Wilson, Mike Love, Al Jardine** *(performers)*, **Glen CAMPBELL** *(in-house session man)*, **Jan & Dean:- Jan Berry *, Dean Torrance** *(performers)* → DEADMAN'S CURVE *, **the Barbarians:- Victor 'Moulty' Moulton, Bruce Benson, Jerry Causi, Jeff Morris** *(performers)*, **Toni Basil** *(go-go dancer)* → PAJAMA PARTY → HEAD → EASY RIDER → ROCKULA, Teri Garr *(go-go dancer)* ← KISSIN' COUSINS ← FUN IN ACAPULCO / → VIVA LAS VEGAS → PAJAMA PARTY → ROUSTABOUT → the COOL ONES → CLAMBAKE → HEAD → ONE FROM THE HEART

Storyline: Stands for "Teenage Awards Music International". America finally had a celluloid outlet for its pop music through this concert flick, filmed at Santa Monica's Civic Auditorium. A definite who's who of its time, taking in bands from both sides of the Atlantic, and indeed spectrum. *MCS*

Movie rating: *7.5

Visual: video as 'THAT WAS ROCK' compilation (no audio OST)

Off the record: Tracks featured in film (& above compilation):- CHUCK BERRY: 'Maybellene', 'Sweet Little Sixteen' & 'Nadine', JAMES BROWN: 'Out Of Sight' & 'Night Train', MARVIN GAYE: 'Stubborn Kind Of Fellow', 'Pride And Joy' & 'Hitch Hike', SMOKEY ROBINSON & THE MIRACLES: 'That's What Love Is Made Of', 'You Really Got A Hold On Me' & 'Mickey's Monkey', the ROLLING STONES: 'Around And Around', 'Off The Hook', 'Time Is On My Side', 'It's All Over Now' & 'I'm Alright', LESLEY GORE: 'Maybe I Know' & 'You Don't Own Me', JAN & DEAN: 'Sidewalk Surfin'', GERRY & THE PACEMAKERS: 'Maybellene', etc., etc. *MCS*

☐ TALKING HEADS
(⇒ David BYRNE)

TEATRO

aka: WILLIE NELSON: TEATRO

1998 (US 52m) Polygram

Film genre: Country-music documentary/concert

Top guns: s-w + dir: Wim Wenders ← the END OF VIOLENCE ← PARIS, TEXAS / → BUENA VISTA SOCIAL CLUB → the MILLION DOLLAR HOTEL → the SOUL OF A MAN

Stars: Willie NELSON *(performer)*, **Emmylou HARRIS** *(performer)*, **Daniel LANOIS** *(performer)*, **Bobby Nelson** *(performer)* ← HONEYSUCKLE ROSE, **Mickey Raphael** *(performer)* ← SONGWRITER ← HONEYSUCKLE ROSE, **Tony Mangurian** *(performer)*, **Victor Indrizzo** *(performer)*

Storyline: Filmed at the El Teatro, Oxnard, California, country icon Willie Nelson comes under the spotlight of cult director, Wim Wenders. *MCS*

Movie rating:

Visual: video on Facets

Off the record: Victor Indrizzo was a film composer in his own right, having subsequently scored 'Never Get Outta The Boat' (2002). *MCS*

—

WILLIE NELSON

Sep 98. (cd) *Island; <524548>*
– Où es-tu, mon amour? (Where are you, my love?) / I never cared for you / Everywhere I go / Darkness on the face of the Earth / My own peculiar way / These lonely nights / Home motel / The maker / I just can't let you say good-bye / I've just destroyed the world / Somebody pick up my pieces / Three days / I've loved you all over the world / Annie.

S/track review: Seven years after scattering the magic-dust on U2's 'The Joshua Tree', Daniel Lanois had overhauled and charged up Emmylou Harris's career with 1994's 'Wrecking Ball' – but his transmogrification of WILLIE NELSON under Wim Wenders' gaze looks more like a minor detour in the elder statesman's prodigious career. The noise is Identikit LANOIS: a moody, reverberating soundscape with rich clattering drums and vocals that emerge from behind the dark-shaded mix rather than standing clear of it. EMMYLOU's emotive alto is there too, quavering at the end of the echoing hallway on a handful of new songs (including LANOIS' characteristically widescreen 'The Maker') as well as some vintage NELSON standards like 'Three Days' and 'I Never Cared For You'. These Latin-tinged interpretations may not outclass earlier versions, and fans of WILLIE's traditional production will hanker for more of MICKEY RAPHAEL's harp and NELSON's own spiky, quirky acoustic guitar (a noise as distinctive as Stevie Wonder's harmonica or Billie Holiday's pipes). But the Texan has already secured his status as one of the giants of popular music, and he emerges from the LANOIS treatment – recorded in the producer's old Californian theatre – with voice unbowed by the quirky acoustics. *ND*

Album rating: *6.5

TEN FOR TWO

1971 (US 78m) Joko Film / Vaughan Films

Film genre: Rock-music concert/documentary

Top guns: dir: Steve Gebhardt → IMAGINE

Stars: John Lennon *(performer)* <= the BEATLES =>, **Yoko ONO** *(performer)*, **Stevie WONDER** *(performer)*, **Bob Seger** *(performer)*, **Phil Ochs** *(performer)* LOVE IT OR LEAVE IT → CHORDS OF FAME, Allen Ginsberg *(performer)* ← TONITE LET'S ALL MAKE LOVE IN LONDON ← DON'T LOOK BACK ← CHAPPAQUA / → RENALDO AND CLARA → MY GENERATION → NO DIRECTION HOME, Bobby Seale *(himself)* → the U.S. vs. JOHN LENNON, Jerry Rubin *(himself)* → CHORDS OF FAME → the U.S. vs. JOHN LENNON, Rennie Davis *(himself)*, John Sinclair *(himself)*, Father James Groppi *(himself)*

Storyline: A benefit concert in Ann Arbor, Michigan, set up by Ono & Lennon to highlight the injustice/punishment of leading political activist, John Sinclair, and the heavy jail sentence of "Ten" years (for possession of "Two" tokes of marijuana!). Three days after the show, the Rainbow People's Party leader was released from prison, showing at least the proof of government and/or F.B.I. intervention. *MCS*

Movie rating: *6

Visual: video (no audio OST)

Off the record: JOHN LENNON sang three songs (YOKO ONO one), while PHIL OCHS, the UP, ALLEN GINSBERG and BOB SEGER (the latter contributed 'Carol') were also featured in the movie. *MCS*

□ THAT WAS ROCK video
(⇒ the T.A.M.I. SHOW + the BIG T.N.T. SHOW)

□ THAT'S THE WAY IT IS alt.
(⇒ ELVIS: THAT'S THE WAY IT IS)

□ THEY MIGHT BE GIANTS segment
(⇒ GIGANTIC (A TALE OF TWO JOHNS))

□ THIRD WORLD segment
(⇒ PRISONER IN THE STREET)

30 CENTURY MAN

aka SCOTT WALKER: 30 CENTURY MAN

2007 (UK 95m) Missing In Action Films / Verve Pictures

Film genre: Pop/Rock-music documentary/bio-pic

Top guns: dir: Stephen Kijak

Stars: Scott Walker *(himself/performer)* ← BEACH BALL ← SURF PARTY, **David BOWIE** *(himself)*, **Radiohead:- Jonny Greenwood, Colin Greenwood, Ed O'Brien** *(themselves)* ← MEETING PEOPLE IS EASY, **Jarvis Cocker** *(himself)* ← LIVE FOREVER, **Brian ENO** *(himself)*, **Bono** *(himself)* <= U2 =>, **Damon ALBARN** *(himself)*, **STING** *(himself)*, **Johnny Marr** *(himself)* ← MAYOR OF THE SUNSET STRIP, **Alison Goldfrapp** *(herself)*, **Simon Raymonde** *(himself)*, **Rob Ellis** *(himself)*, **Dot Allison** *(herself)*, **Gavin Friday** *(himself)*, **Marc Almond** *(himself)*, **Hector Zazou** *(himself)*, **Peter Walsh** *(himself)*, **Ed Bicknell** *(himself)*, **Cathal Coughlan** *(himself)*, **LULU** *(herself)*, **Richard Hawley** *(himself)*, **Neil Hannon** *(himself)*, Angela Morley *(herself)*, David Bates *(himself)*, Al Clark *(himself)* ← THUNDERSTRUCK

Storyline: A long-awaited profile on avant-rock music's most celebrated disciple, Scott Walker, a one-time pop star and an enigmatic figure by all accounts. *MCS*

Movie rating: *7

Visual: dvd (no audio OST – as yet!)

Off the record: Scott Walker was born on 9th January, 1943, in Hamilton, Ohio, USA. As Scott Engel, he cut a few solo 45s, but it would be in 1965 with the Walker Brothers (alongside Gary Leeds and John Maus) he would make his name. Formed in Los Angeles, California, USA, they almost immediately signed to 'Smash' records, where they were advised to try their luck in London. After Scott took over on vocals the "brothers" soon hit the top spot twice via the 1965-66 cult easy-listening classics, 'Make It Easy On Yourself' (US Top 20) and 'The Sun Ain't Gonna Shine Anymore'. Scott left the trio for a lucrative solo career in '67, hitting the heights with a clutch of spaced-out crooners including 'Jackie', 'Joanna' and 'Lights Of Cincinnati'. With the release of cult album classic, 'Scott 4' (1969), however, he faded from popular stardom and languished in MOR hell for pretty much of the early 70s. The man briefly re-emerged mid-decade as part of a re-formed Walker Brothers, enjoying a UK Top 10 with a cover of Tom Rush's 'No Regrets'. Scott eschewed the lure of the beckoning nostalgia circuit, however, leading the band in a radically different direction for 1978's 'Nite Flights' (the brothers' final album together). Walker eventually resurfaced in solo mode with the tortured 'Climate Of Thunder' in 1984, hardly a record to kickstart his career. 'Virgin' were suitably unimpressed with the commercial returns and he subsequently signed to 'Fontana' in 1985. Although he recorded with BRIAN ENO, the project was never completed; similarly, Scott's collaborative work with former Japan warbler, David Sylvian-produced no concrete results. It would be a further eleven years before he came out with new work in the form of 1995's 'Tilt'. As out-there as Walker has yet ventured, fans and critics alike agreed that while he mightn't be the most prolific artist, his darkly compelling experiments are worth waiting for. More than a decade in birthing pains (albeit he did release a solo OST in '99, 'POLA X'), 'The Drift' (2006) was met with almost universal shock, horror, awe and admiration as one of the most gratuitously, beautifully unnerving listening experiences ever released. Against Dante-esque screeds of Eraserhead ambience and nerve-flaying industrio-tronics, Walker picked his metaphors with the delectation of a deranged hangman, dropping them into traumatic treatise on the likes of 9/11, Elvis' stillborn brother, and the fate of Italian dictator, Benito Mussolini. *BG & MCS*

THIRTY YEARS OF MAXIMUM R&B LIVE

aka the WHO: THIRTY YEARS OF MAXIMUM R&B LIVE

1994 (US 155m TV) Goldshower Ltd. / Profile / Universal

Film genre: Rock-music concert compilation documentary

Top guns: dir(s): various / exec producer: Bill Curbishley

Stars: the WHO:- Roger Daltrey, Pete Townshend, John Entwistle, Keith Moon, John Bundrick * *(performers)* ← PSYCHODERELICT * ← DEEP END * / → LIFEHOUSE * → the WHO LIVE AT THE ROYAL ALBERT HALL *, **Bryan Adams** *(guest)* ← the WALL: LIVE IN BERLIN / → SPIRIT: STALLION OF THE CIMARRON → the WHO LIVE AT THE ROYAL ALBERT HALL, **Eric CLAPTON** *(guest)*, **Kenney Jones** *(guest)* ← the WHO ROCKS AMERICA ← TONITE LET'S ALL MAKE LOVE IN LONDON ← DATELINE DIAMONDS, **Steve Bolton** *(musician)* ← HEARTS OF FIRE, **Roddy Lorimer** *(musician)*, **Dave Caswell** *(musician)*, **Reg Brooks** *(musician)*, **Howie Casey** *(musician)* ← ROCKSHOW, **Simon Gardner** *(musician)*, **Tim Gorman** *(musician)* ← the WHO ROCKS AMERICA, **Jody Linscott** *(musician)* ← GIVE MY REGARDS TO BROAD STREET / → LIFEHOUSE, **Tim Sanders + Neil Sidwell + Scott Halpin** *(musicians)*, **Chyna + Cleveland Watkiss** *(singers)* → LIFEHOUSE

Storyline: Okay, this is basically a compilation video of the Who live in concert(s). There's also interviews with the three surviving members at the time, while Moon fans are treated to footage of him singing 'Bell Boy', among other things of course. *MCS*

Movie rating: *7.5

Visual: video / + dvd extended to 235m

Off the record: The **WHO** tracks in the original film (and also included on the much expanded 4xCD-box) are as follows:- 'Anyway, Anyhow, Anywhere', 'So Sad About Us', 'A Quick One, While He's Away', 'Happy Jack', 'Heaven And Hell', 'I Can't Explain', 'Water', 'Young Man Blues', 'I Don't Even Know Myself', 'My Generation', 'Substitute', 'Drowned', 'Bell Boy', 'My Generation Blues, 'Dreaming From The Waist', 'Sister Disco', 'Who Are You', '5:15', 'My Wife', 'Music Must Change', 'Pinball Wizard', 'Behind Blues Eyes', 'Love Reign O'er Me', 'Boris The Spider', 'I Can See For Miles' & 'See Me, Feel Me'. *MCS*

– associated release –

the WHO: Thirty Years Of Maximum R&B Live

Jul 94. (4xcd-box) *M.C.A.; <11020> Polydor; (521751-2)* ☐ 48

THUG ANGEL – THE LIFE OF AN OUTLAW

2002 (US 92m) Image Entertainment (R)

Film genre: Rap/Hip Hop-music concert/documentary bio-pic

Top guns: s-w: Peter Spirer (+ dir) ← RHYME & REASON / – BEEF, Hafiz Farid, David Wilson

Stars: Tupac SHAKUR *(archive; himself)*, **the Notorious B.I.G.** *(archive; himself)* → BIGGIE AND TUPAC ← TUPAC: RESURRECTION ← RHYME & REASON ← the SHOW / → BEEF, **Treach** *(himself)* → TUPAC: RESURRECTION, **SNOOP DOGG** *(himself)*, **Grand Puba** *(himself)*, Marion 'Suge' Knight *(himself)* ← BIGGIE AND TUPAC / → TUPAC: RESURRECTION, **Shock-G** *(himself)*, Johnny 'J' *(himself)*

Storyline: Not so much of a "2Pac Resurrection", more an exploration into the music and politics of late iconic rapper, Tupac Shakur, through live footage and interviews with those that knew him. *MCS*

Movie rating: *6.5

Visual: dvd

Off the record: **Shock-G** (is a member Digital Underground); Marion 'Suge' Knight is behind 'Death Row' records, Johnny 'J' was/is Tupac's producer.

—

Various Artists (score: QD3 *)

Jul 02. (cd) *Image; <ID1960QD> Burning Airlines; (PILOT 190)* ☐ Sep03 ☐
– Thug Angel: Life of an outlaw (OUTLAWZ – NAPOLEON, YOUNG NOBLE & HELLRAZA') / We them gangstas (TRULIFE, MACK 10 & YOUNG DRE) / Fatal interview #1 (*) / Heavenly father (YOUNG DRE ft. GMONEY) / Keep on keepin' on (TECH N9NE) / Click clack intro (FREEJACK) / Click clack (FREEJACK) / Storm interview #1 (music: FEMI DJETUNDE) / Pain (STORM – FEMALE OUTLAW) / Storm interview #2 (*) / Soldier (KUMASI & HOPE) / Fatal interview #2 (*) / Euphanasia (OUTLAWZ – YOUNG NOBLE, EDI & NAPOLEON) / Killuminati (MAC MALL featuring BIG SKYE) / Life (TRULIFE featuring YOUNG NOBLE & NAPOLEON FROM OUTLAWZ) / The day the world ended (RAY LUV) / Ghetto lullabye (KEPLYN) / Mutulu interview from Atlanta State Penitentiary (*) / Aja (AFRICA HEARTBEAT) / Champion (TROY HORNE featuring HOPE SHORTER) / Thinking of you – tribute to Tupac (STEPCHYLDE & JOHNNY "J") / Killaz in here (OUTLAWZ – FATAL, NOBLE, EDI & NAPOLEON).

S/track review: This is a peculiar concept, a film about a rapper that contains no music by the subject. 'THUG ANGEL' has barely a sniff of Tupac Shakur's music in it, opting instead for tributes and music "inspired by". There's no shortage of punters queuing up to honor 2Pac, but that doesn't mean this is a cynical cash-in. Shakur's former band, OUTLAWZ, come correct, lending the kind of tough beats and taut rhymes that he was famed for. Elsewhere, TECH-N9NE seem keen to celebrate his friends in high places, but does so in style through some rolling lyrical tricks and a thick harmonious chorus on the excellent 'Keep On Keepin' On'. Why then follow it with 'Pain', a cumbersome beast: a killer chorus sporadically stapled into ten minutes of rambling, stuttering oration about the genius of Shakur from female vocalist STORM? KUMASI & HOPE bring things back from the brink, however, with the simple and beautiful 'Soldier'. A plaintive acoustic guitar-line is stretched over a sparse beat, with some swelling harmonies and impassioned philosophising from KUMASI. Shakur's one-time producer Johnny J teams up with STEPCHYLDE for a lyrically touching tribute. Shame it further illustrates the rap game's propensity to borrowing cheesy pop soft-rock for backing, in this time it's a section of Paul Young's 'Every Time You Go Away'. A final salvo of thugged-out gangsterisms is plated up by OUTLAWZ; 'Killaz In Here' enjoys the same fearless, deft twists that Shakur specialised in. *MR*

Album rating: *6.5

□ TIME IS ON OUR SIDE alt.
(⇒ LET'S SPEND THE NIGHT TOGETHER)

TIME WILL TELL

aka BOB MARLEY: TIME WILL TELL

1992 (UK 90m w/b&w) Island Pictures / IRS Media

Film genre: Reggae-music documentary biopic

Top guns: dir: Declan Lowney

Stars: Bob MARLEY *(archive/performer)* & **the Wailers** *(performers)*

Storyline: The life and times of Rastafarian prophet and reggae legend, Bob Marley, a man who inspired a nation and indeed the rest of the world outside Jamaica. Through interviews and archive performances, the viewer is taken in depth into Marley's world of inner peace. *MCS*

Movie rating: *7

Visual: video + dvd

Off the record: (see Bob MARLEY entry)

– associated release –

BOB MARLEY & THE WAILERS

1992. (lazer-d) *Pony Canyon; <PCLP-00335>* – Japan –
– Natural mystic / Don't rock the boat / Keep on movin' / Lively up yourself / Stop the train / Small axe / Trench town rock / Corner stone / Mr. Brown / Soul shakedown party / African herbsman / Soul almighty / Treat you right / It's alright.

TONITE LET'S ALL MAKE LOVE IN LONDON

1968 (UK 70m) Lorrimer Films

Film genre: Rock/Pop-music/showbiz documentary/footage

Top guns: dir: Peter Whitehead ← CHARLIE IS MY DARLING

Stars: Julie Christie *(herself)* → NASHVILLE → the ANIMALS FILM, Allen Ginsberg *(herself)* ← DON'T LOOK BACK ← CHAPPAQUA / → TEN FOR TWO → RENALDO AND CLARA → MY GENERATION → NO DIRECTION HOME, David Hockney *(cameo)*, Michael Caine *(cameo)*, Lee Marvin *(cameo)*, Vanessa Redgrave *(cameo)* ← BLOW-UP / → the BODY, **Eric Burdon** *(himself)* <= the ANIMALS =>, **Chris Farlowe** *(himself)* ← POP GEAR / → RED, WHITE & BLUES, **Mick Jagger** *(himself)* <= the ROLLING STONES =>, **the Small Faces:- Steve Marriott *, Ronnie Lane, Kenney Jones ***, Ian McLagan** ** ← * BE MY GUEST ← DATELINE DIAMONDS ← * LIVE IT UP / → ** LET'S SPEND THE NIGHT TOGETHER → *** THIRTY YEARS OF MAXIMUM R&B LIVE / **Andrew Loog Oldham, Vashti Bunyan, Ace Kefford, Twice As Much:- Andrew Rose & David Skinner**, Dolly Read *(herself)* → BEYOND THE VALLEY OF THE DOLLS, Donyale Luna *(herself)* → SKIDOO → ROCK AND ROLL CIRCUS, **PINK FLOYD:- Syd Barrett, Roger Waters, Nick Mason, Richard Wright** *(performers)*

Storyline: Another attempt to capture Swinging London at its height with a colourful montage of celebrity interviews (Mick Jagger, Vanessa Redgrave, Julie Christie, even Lee Marvin!), political discussion and demonstration, and rare concert footage from Brian Jones-era Rolling Stones and Syd Barrett-era Pink Floyd amongst others. *BG*

Movie rating: *4

Visual: video + dvd

Off the record: Sometimes it's better known as 'PINK FLOYD: LONDON '66'-'67' dvd + record.

Various Artists & PINK FLOYD

Oct 68. (lp) *Instant; (INLP 002)*
– Interstellar overdrive (*) / (Michael Caine interview) / (Changing of the guard – Marquess Of Kensington) / Night time girl (TWICE AS MUCH) / ("Dolly Bird" interview) / Out of time (CHRIS FARLOWE) / (Edna O'Brien interview) / Interstellar overdrive – reprise (*) / (Andrew Loog Oldham interview) / Winter is blue (VASHTI) / (ANDREW LOOG OLDHAM interview) / Winter is blue – reprise (VASHTI) / (Mick Jagger interview) / (Julie Christie interview) / (Michael Caine interview) / Paint it black (CHRIS FARLOWE) / (Alan Aldridge interview) / Paint it black – instrumental reprise (CHRIS FARLOWE) / (David Hockney interview) / Here comes the nice (SMALL FACES) / (Lee Marvin interview) / Interstellar overdrive – reprise (*) / Tonite let's all make love in London (ALAN GINSBERG). *(re-iss. Oct90 on 'See For Miles' lp/c/cd+=; SEE G/K/CD 258)<US cd-iss. 1991 on 'Columbia'+=; 47893-2> (cd re-iss. Nov93 on 'See For Miles' SFM 2)* – Interstellar overdrive – full length (*) / Nick's boogie (*) / (interviews with David Hockney & Lee Marvin).

S/track review: Contrary to what the sleevenotes claim, the songs on this soundtrack too often don't mix well with the interviews, a criticism which has more to do with the sequencing of the dialogue rather than its content. Fading an acoustic pastoral like VASHTI's 'Winter Is Blue' in and out of some blunt musings on the function of money by Andrew Loog Oldham surely misses the point, or maybe it is the point. Either way it gratuitously breaks the song's spell. (A Loog Oldham protégé who left his 'Immediate' stable after only two singles, the elusive VASHTI (BUNYAN) subsequently made a horse and cart pilgrimage to the Scottish Highlands, releasing the resulting songs she wrote in transit as the unjustly ignored 'Just Another Diamond Day' (1970). With retrospective interest in the album at an all time high – which, in turn, will no doubt generate renewed interest in this soundtrack – the Edinburgh based singer has – at the time of writing – just relaunched her career with a new album, 'Lookaftering'. Similar guerrilla tactics are employed with CHRIS FARLOWE's melodramatic, Mick Jagger-produced take on the 'Stones' own 'Paint It Black', although out of FARLOWE's two contributions, 'Out Of Time' has actually aged better anyway. Jagger himself pontificates on the politics of violence, while Michael Caine explains why he doesn't dig mini-skirts (such a hot topic that Lee Marvin also puts in his tuppence worth), but it's David Hockney who proves that brevity really is the soul of wit with a priceless 9-second snippet. And while it's difficult to believe that both Jimmy Page and John Paul Jones reportedly appear on the fey 'Night Time Girl' (credited to the hopelessly obscure TWICE AS MUCH), 'TONITE LET'S ALL MAKE LOVE IN LONDON' usually draws interest not so much for its encapsulation of the Loog Oldham psych-orchestral house style, but for the primitive, organ jamming blueprint of PINK FLOYD's 'Interstellar Overdrive'. While the 'Sony' CD re-issue adds the brooding ERIC BURDON confession, 'When I Was Young', the 'See For Miles' version is the one for 'FLOYD fanatics, featuring an extended, alternate '..Overdrive' and previously unreleased experiment, 'Nick's Boogie'. These two tracks made up the official PINK FLOYD spinoff CD and DVD, 'LONDON 1966/1967'. *BG*

Album rating: *5.5 / CD re-issue *6.5

– spinoff releases, etc. –

PINK FLOYD: London 1966/1967

Nov 95. (cd) *See For Miles; (SFMCD 3)*
– Interstellar overdrive / Nick's boogie. *(dvd-iss.2005 on 'Snapper'+=; SMADVD 049)* – (extra interviews & footage).

□ Peter TOSH segment
(⇒ STEPPING RAZOR RED X)

TOWARD THE WITHIN

1994 (UK 78m) Magidson Films

Film genre: indie/alt-Rock music documentary/concert

Top guns: dir: Mark Magidson

Stars: Dead Can Dance:- Lisa GERRARD, Brendan Perry, Robert Perry, John Bonnar, Ronan O'Snodaigh, Andrew Claxton, Lance Hogan *(performers)*

Storyline: Melbourne's finest indie export, Dead Can Dance, get the rockumentary treatment by way of several interviews and conversations plus a performance at The Mayfair Theatre, Santa Monica, California. *MCS*

Movie rating: *7

Visual: video + dvd

Off the record: DEAD CAN DANCE (see: Lisa GERRARD)

——

DEAD CAN DANCE

Oct 94. (cd)(d-lp/c) *4 a.d.; (DAD 4015CD)(DAD/+C 4015)* *<45769>* ☐ ☐
– Rakim / Persian love song / Desert song / Yulunga (spirit dance) / Piece for solo flute / The wind that shakes the barley / I am stretched on your grave / I can see now / American dreaming / Cantara / Oman / Song of the Sibyl / Tristan / Sanvean / Don't fade away.

S/track review: There's no indication that 'TOWARD THE WITHIN' is a soundtrack, but virtually the same cues appear on the video – and later DVD – equivalent, albeit in a different running order. DEAD CAN DANCE were, to some pundits, Australia's answer to Cocteau Twins, although their rich tapestry of sound boasted two singers (not one), the dark and brooding BRENDAN PERRY and ethereal warbler, LISA GERRARD. Now into their 7th set since 1984's eponymous debut, the septet (including other musicians, ROBERT PERRY on uillean pipes, etc., JOHN BONNAR and ANDREW CLAXTON on keyboards, RONAN O'SNODAIGH on percussion and LANCE HOGAN on bass) were noted for exclusive recordings when they ventured out into the concert arena (this time at Santa Monica's Mayfair Theatre). Indeed there are only three previously-heard DCD numbers on show here: from their most recent ('Into The Labyrinth') album, 'Yulunga (Spirit Dance)' and the Celtic traditional-folk song, 'The Wind That Shakes The Barley' (written incidentally by Dr. Dwyer Joyce). Needless to say, GERRARD excels abundantly on both, her Irish roots coming in handy for the latter a cappella track. From the delightful 1987 'Within The Realm Of A Dying Sun' album, we hear a much-revised live rendition of 'Cantara', where their Eastern world fusion comes into full swing. Apart from the dourly-traditional, 'Persian Love Song' and a rendition of Gottfried Von Strassburg's 'Tristan', the 16th Century Catalan chant of 'Song Of The Sibyl', is indeed atmospheric and cinematic (GERRARD was to subsequently venture into the film music); a medieval precursor perhaps to Tim Buckley's 'Song To The Siren', once delivered by a certain Cocteau Elizabeth Fraser while moonlighting with '4 a.d.' conglomerate, This Mortal Coil. BRENDAN PERRY, meanwhile, comes under the spotlight via a trio of acoustic Neil Diamond-meets-Chris Cornell songs such as 'I Can See Now', the beautiful 'American Dreaming' and 'Don't Fade Away'; his vocal range culminates with the mystical and dramatic, 'Oman' and 'I Am Stretched On Your Grave' respectively (the latter once the dominion of Sinead O'Connor). From the Perry/Gerrard-penned opening cue, 'Rakim', divided and intertwined by both vocal parties, the album shows the versatility of DEAD CAN DANCE, who were to sadly split to pursue solo careers. *MCS*

Album rating: *6.5

TRUTH OR DARE

aka MADONNA: TRUTH OR DARE (UK title 'IN BED WITH MADONNA')

1991 (US 114m w/b&w) Boy Toy Productions / Miramax Films (R)

Film genre: Pop/Dance-music concert/documentary

Top guns: dir: Alek Keshishian

Stars: MADONNA *(herself/performer)*, Warren Beatty *(himself)* ← DICK TRACY, Sandra Bernhard *(herself)* → the REGGAE MOVIE, Pedro Almodovar *(himself)*, Antonio Banderas *(himself)* → FOUR ROOMS → EVITA → TAKE THE LEAD, Kevin Costner *(himself)*, Sharon Gault *(herself)*, Al Pacino *(himself)*, **Alan Wilder** *(himself)* ← 101, + dancers (numerous)

Storyline: Madonna at her creative peak (some might say), this movie explores the world of the seXual superstar on her colourful 'Blind Ambition' tour; backstage – with her troupe of dancers – she's in glorious black & white. *MCS*

Movie rating: *6

Visual: video + dvd (no audio OST)

Off the record: MADONNA songs featured in the film include, 'Express Yourself', 'Oh Father', 'Like A Virgin', 'Promise To Try', 'Holiday', 'Live To Tell', 'Vogue', 'Causing A Commotion' and 'Family Affair – Keep It Together' (medley). Dancer GUY performed a few tracks from their repertoire 'Teddy's Jam' and 'Don't Clap Your Hands, Just Dance'. *MCS*

TUPAC: RESURRECTION

2003 (US 115m) Amaru Entertainment / Paramount Pictures (R)

Film genre: Hip-Hop/Rap documentary biopic

Top guns: s-w + dir: Lauren Lazin

Stars: (archival) **Tupac SHAKUR** *(himself)*, **Biggie Smalls/the Notorious B.I.G.** *(himself)* ← THUG ANGEL ← BIGGIE AND TUPAC ← RHYME & REASON ← the SHOW / → BEEF, **Puffy Combs/Puff Daddy** *(himself)* ← BIGGIE AND TUPAC ← RHYME & REASON ← the SHOW / → DEATH OF A DYNASTY → FADE TO BLACK, **Treach** *(himself)* ← THUG ANGEL, **Todd Bridges** *(himself)*, **SNOOP DOGG** *(himself)*, **ICE-T** *(himself)*, **Janet Jackson** *(herself)*, **KISS:- Gene Simmons, Paul Stanley, Ace Frehley, Peter Criss** *(archive performers)*, **Faith Evans** *(herself)* ← TURN IT UP / → the FIGHTING TEMPTATIONS, **Dr. Dre** *(himself)* ← WHITEBOYS ← RHYME & REASON ← the SHOW ← MURDER WAS THE CASE, **Fab Five Freddy** *(himself)* ← WILD STYLE, **Kurupt** *(himself)* ← MURDER WAS THE CASE, Will Smith *(himself)*, **Dionne Warwick** *(herself)*, Marlon Wayans *(himself)*, **Rappin' 4-Tay** *(himself)*, Ed Lover *(himself)* ← DEATH OF A DYNASTY ← DOUBLE PLATINUM ← RIDE ← WHO'S THE MAN? ← JUICE, Marion 'Suge' Knight *(himself)* ← THUG ANGEL ← BIGGIE AND TUPAC, Kurt Loder *(himself)* ← AIRHEADS ← FEAR OF A BLACK HAT ← WHO'S THE MAN ← the ADVENTURES OF FORD FAIRLANE / → RAMONES: RAW → LAST DAYS, Jasmine Guy *(herself)* ← KLA$H ← SCHOOL DAZE

Storyline: Pieced together from home movies, private photos, interviews/voice-overs, etc., this is an honest account of superstar hip-hop rapper, Tupac Shakur (2Pac), a man who was shot down in his prime. *MCS*

Movie rating: *6

Visual: dvd

Off the record: Treach is Anthony Criss of Naughty By Nature.

——

TUPAC

Nov 03. (cd) *Amaru; <154302> Interscope; (9861159)* [2] [62]
– Intro / Ghost / One day at a time [Em's version] (with EMINEM feat. the OUTLAWZ) / Death around the corner / Secretz of war / Runnin' (dying to live) (feat. the NOTORIOUS B.I.G.) / Holler if ya' hear me / Starin' through my rear view / Bury me a G / Same song / Panther power / Str8 ballin' / Rebel of the underground / The realist killaz (feat. 50 CENT).

S/track review: There was a whole new genre of rap born at the turn of the century: Pacsploitation, music which has been released posthumously from the wealth of unreleased rhymes recorded from TUPAC. EMINEM was very much the man of the moment in 2003 and he produced three tracks on this collection free of charge as a mark of respect for Shakur's mother, Afeni, who was executive producer at the helm creatively for this vivid, luxurious hagiography of her late son. With the exception of a few guest verses from the aforementioned Mr Mathers and his protege 50 CENT, the only other guest is SHAKUR's supposed rival in the coastal rap feud, the NOTORIOUS B.I.G., who reminds us again why he's regarded as the finest rapper ever. Biggie's unbeatable flow often runs at right angles to SHAKUR's thick, resonant tones and their posthumous collaboration 'Runnin'' might not have the verbal fireworks that so much of their respective back catalogues might enjoy, but hearing the pair together is still a thrill. The especially created cuts from the archive material – of which there is believed to be hundreds of hours recorded but unreleased – captures the spark of SHAKUR's original lyrical mastery. The contrast lies in the several tracks culled from SHAKUR's older albums, including the excellent sandpaper-and-syrup of 'Bury Me A G' and the dated but funky 'Panther Power' and 'Holler If Ya Hear Me'. This collection is by no means perfect, it is truly a patchy overview of the man's work, although 'TUPAC: RESURRECTION' proves that years after his death, TUPAC still sizzles and fizzles with energy like few others can muster. *MR*

Album rating: *6.5

– spinoff hits, etc. –

TUPAC & The NOTORIOUS B.I.G.: Runnin' (Dying To Live) / (versions)

Oct 03. (cd-s) *<11042> (981532-9)* [47] Jan04 [17]

25X5: THE CONTINUING ADVENTURES OF THE ROLLING STONES

1990 (UK 130m TV w/b&w) CBS/BBC

Film genre: Rock-music concert/documentary biopic

Top guns: dir: Nigel Finch

Stars: (all) **the ROLLING STONES:- Mick Jagger, Keith Richards, Charlie Watts, Bill Wyman, Brian Jones, Ron Wood, Mick Taylor** *(performers)*, Bianca Jagger *(herself)* ← the RUTLES ← COCKSUCKER BLUES, Jerry Hall *(herself)* ← the WALL: LIVE IN BERLIN ← BATMAN ← RUNNING OUT OF LUCK ← LET'S SPEND THE NIGHT TOGETHER ← URBAN COWBOY

Storyline: It's all here, the history of the longest-running and greatest rock'n'roll band ever, the Rolling Stones. Over two hours spanning a quarter of a century of live footage, archive television appearances, the death of Brian Jones, the tragic concert at Altamont (see also the movie 'SYMPATHY FOR THE DEVIL') and right up to date with their 1989 set, 'Steel Wheels'. *MCS*

Movie rating: *7.5

Visual: video + dvd (no audio OST)

Off the record: Features the ex-wife of Jagger, Bianca (1971-1980) and girlfriend and future wife, Jerry (late 1990-mid 1999). *MCS*

TWO HEADED COW

2006 (US 85m w/b&w) Cape Fear Filmworks

Film genre: alt-Rock-music documentary

Top guns: dir: Tony Gayton ← ATHENS, GA. – INSIDE/OUT

Stars: Flat Duo Jets:- Dexter Romweber, Crow *(performers)* ← ATHENS, GA. – INSIDE/OUT, **the Sadies:- Dallas Good, Travis Good, Neko Case** *(themselves)*, **Jack White** *(himself)* ← the FEARLESS FREAKS ← COLD MOUNTAIN ← COFFEE AND CIGARETTES / → WALK HARD: THE DEWEY COX STORY, **Cat Power** *(herself)* ← the FEARLESS FREAKS, **Mojo Nixon** *(himself)* ← ROCK'N'ROLL HIGH SCHOOL FOREVER ← GREAT BALLS OF FIRE!, **Exene Cervenka** *(herself)* <= John DOE/X =>, **Jason Edge** *(himself)*

Storyline: Highlighting the work of Dexter Romweber and Crow of the Flat Duo Jets, rockin' revivalists on a mission to entertain America; the indie film is not in any way a biopic, more myopic. *MCS*

Movie rating: *6

Visual: dvd

Off the record: Flat Duo Jets (from Chapel Hill, North Carolina since 1983) were of the retro-rockabilly ilk, best witnessed in the 1986 documentary, 'ATHENS, GA. – INSIDE/OUT'. Finally, their eponymous debut album saw light of day in 1990, while the rest of the 90s produced several others from 'Go Go Harlem Baby' (1991) to 'Lucky Eye' (1998). Meanwhile, former country-punk goddess and X singer, **Exene Cervenka**, is currently fronting post-millennium outfit, Original Sinners, with hubby **Jason Edge**. *MCS*

☐ 2PAC
(⇒ Tupac SHAKUR)

☐ 200 MOTELS
(⇒ Rock Musicals/Pop Fiction)

☐ Steven TYLER
(⇒ AEROSMITH)

the U.S. vs. JOHN LENNON

2006 (US 96m w/b&w) Lions Gate Pictures / VH-1 (PG-13)

Film genre: political Rock-music documentary biopic

Top guns: dir + s-w: David Leaf ← BEAUTIFUL DREAMER: BRIAN WILSON AND THE STORY OF 'SMILE', John Scheinfeld

Stars: John Lennon *(archive footage)* <= the BEATLES =>, **Yoko ONO** *(herself)*, **David Peel** *(himself)* ← MEDICINE BALL CARAVAN, Bobby Seale *(archive)* ← TEN FOR TWO, Jerry Rubin *(archive)* ← CHORDS OF FAME ← TEN FOR TWO, Angela Davis, Ron Kovic, John Sinclair, *politicians, etc:-* Richard Nixon, Walter Cronkite, J. Edgar Hoover, G. Gordon Liddy, Mario Cuomo, George McGovern, Gore Vidal

Storyline: A look at the life and activist times of ex-Beatle, John Lennon, and his controversial struggle with American politicians over Vietnam and other battles. *MCS* Kicking off with a benefit concert for imprisoned activist/MC5 associate John Sinclair (which actually resulted in Sinclair getting freed on the Monday morning – sock it to the Man..), this engrossing documentary rolls back the ex-Beatle's FBI years, when he was considered enough of a threat to slap a Strom Thurman-recommended deportation order on. Hoover-era US intelligence didn't like his support of radicals Abbie Hoffman and Jerry Rubin one bit, his solidarity with Black Panther Bobby Seale even less. Former agents give the lowdown on inside operations while usual suspects like Noam Chomsky, Tariq Ali and Gore Vidal ("Patriotism is the last refuge of a scoundrel") offer their tuppence worth in defence of fighting the good fight. Musical highlights include some rare National Steel talking blues, and don't miss the footage of a disarmingly clean-cut Lennon finally receiving his green card – he almost resembles Richard Madeley. *BG*

Movie rating: *7.5

Visual: dvd

Off the record: (see below)

—

JOHN LENNON (& the PLASTIC ONO BAND * & w/ the FLUX FIDDLERS **)

Sep 06. (cd) *Capitol/Parlophone; <(3 74912)>* ☐ ☐
– Power to the people (*) / Nobody told me / Working class hero / I found out (*) / Bed peace (w/ YOKO ONO) / The ballad of John & Yoko (BEATLES) / Give peace a chance (*) / Love (*) / Attica state – live (*) / Happy Xmas (war is over) (* w/ the HARLEM COMMUNITY CHOIR) / I don't wanna be a soldier mama (* w/ **) / Imagine (* w/ **) / How do you sleep? – instrumental (* w/ **) / New York City (* w/ ELEPHANT'S MEMORY & INVISIBLE STRINGS) / John Sinclair – live (* & YOKO ONO) / Scared (* w/ LITTLE BIG HORNS & the PHILHARMONIC ORCHESTRANGE) / God (*) / Here we go again / Gimme some truth (* w/ **) / Oh my love (* w/ **) / Instant karma! (we all shine on) (*).

S/track review: It's tempting to view this as yet another stop on the BEATLES gravy train. There's some truth in YOKO ONO's sleevenote claim that the songs "are given a whole new lease of life", but that depends which songs you're talking about. It's going to take a canvas more radical than this to really convince us that anyone needs to gather up the likes of 'Happy Xmas (War Is Over)', 'Imagine' and 'Give Peace A Chance' one more time. Painted into the bigger picture of the activism which inspired them, and the personal consequences of that activism, they resonate more than when they simply top yet another tedious 100 greatest blah blah blah countdown, but where this soundtrack really strikes a blow for LENNON's art is its championing of some of his most difficult and obdurate material. Here are songs which would probably never have been compiled on such a high profile single disc otherwise: the raging, close-mic'd grind of 'I Found Out', wherein he lays into false friends, religion and drugs, bravely cleans out his closet ("I heard something bout my ma and my pa, They didn't want me so they made me a star") and bellows the priceless couplet "Some of you sitting there with your cock in your hand, Don't get you nowhere don't make you a man". 'God' is a (musically) mellower meditation on the same thing: believe in no-one but yourself and your capacity to love another human being. U2 were to fire off an equally searing – and uncharacteristically ironic – reply on 'RATTLE AND HUM'. 'Gimme Some Truth' castigates "Short haired, yellow-bellied, son of Tricky Dicky" Nixon and "schizophrenic, ego-centric, paranoiac, prima-donnas", and we're even blessed with the six minute, 'Stonesy-purgatorial blues, 'I Don't Want To Be A Soldier Mama I Don't Wanna Die'. Then there's 'Working Class Hero', previously compiled but still one of the most biting, unflinching indictments of British society and western "civilisation" ever recorded, even more poignant in the context of this film/soundtrack than on the original 'Plastic Ono Band' album. Completists will appreciate the two unreleased acoustic tracks from the Sinclair benefit, presenting LENNON in Country Joe-sharp, roots-protest singalong mode. It's not all spit and bile, though. Some of his most controversial lyrics are excised completely from the funky score version of 'How Do You Sleep', and that chiselled wit is in full effect on the dialogue segments. Best quote? "time wounds all heels". Step lightly now. *BG*

Album rating: *7.5

U2

Formed: Dublin, Ireland . . . 1977 by BONO (b. Paul Hewson), The EDGE (b. David Evans), Adam Clayton and Larry Mullen. As the biggest band in the world and the undisputed kings of middle aged staying power, U2 require little introduction. Their global hegemony is matched only by the likes of the ROLLING STONES and to their credit they're still trying to challenge themselves musically. Like the 'Stones, they've only had fleeting encounters with the big screen and, surprisingly perhaps, it was guitarist the EDGE who first grappled with film scoring. Not exactly a stranger to more experimental work – having already collaborated with Jah Wobble and Holger Czukay on a 1983 mini-set – his soundtrack to little known thriller 'CAPTIVE' (1986) was a collaborative effort with Canadian avant garde guitarist MICHAEL BROOK and also featured a then unknown singer by the name of Sinead O'Connor. U2's own 'RATTLE AND HUM' (1988) could hardly be termed experimental although it wasn't your average U2 set. A somewhat rambling rockumentary shot on the band's landmark 'Joshua Tree' tour, and a homage of sorts to the mystery and contradictions of the country whose music had inspired them, the accompanying album came in for heavy criticism despite its random moments of genius. The band contributed their first specifically written film track to the Wim Wenders road movie, 'Until The End Of The World'

(1991), a work whose soundtrack perhaps attracted more attention and acclaim than the film itself. Wenders held over many of the contributing artists for the soundtrack to his 1993 effort, 'Faraway, So Close', including U2, whose interpretation of the title theme made the UK Top 5 towards the end of that year. 1993 also found BONO teaming up with fellow Irishman and former Virgin Prunes frontman Gavin Friday for the brooding title track to Neil Jordan's acclaimed Guildford Four drama, 'In The Name Of The Father'. The piece was as different in spirit to that year's U2 album, 'Zooropa', as 1995's 'Batman' contribution, 'Hold Me, Thrill Me, Kiss Me, Kill Me' (a No.2 hit in Britain) was to 'Original Soundtracks 1', a U2/ BRIAN ENO link-up pseudonmyously billed as Passengers. Highly experimental and organic in structure, the album was touted as a collection of songs conceived as themes for imaginary films. In actual fact, several of them turned up in real films, notably 'Always Forever Now', featured in Michael Mann's brilliant Robert De Niro/Al Pacino head-to-head, 'Heat' (1995), 'Your Blue Room' and 'Beach Sequence' in the Wim Wenders/Michelangelo Antonioni collaboration, 'Par-Dela Les Nuages / Beyond The Clouds' (1995) and 'One Minute Warning' in Japanese animation, 'Ghost In The Shell' (1995). More high profile was TINA TURNER's theme for the 1995 Bond movie, 'GoldenEye', penned by BONO and the EDGE. Adam Clayton and Larry Mullen made sure they weren't left out with their joint 1996 reinvention of the 'Mission: Impossible' theme, written for Brian de Palma's big screen version of the 60s TV series. With almost a decade's worth of soundtrack experience under his belt, BONO undertook his most ambitious celluloid project to date with 'The MILLION DOLLAR HOTEL' (2000), a Wim Wenders-directed movie conceived and partly written by the U2 frontman. He also had a major hand in the music, contributing three new U2 songs and pitching in alongside Daniel LANOIS and ENO amongst others for the score's Million Dollar Band, and even acted in the film itself. More recently, U2 penned the evocative title theme, 'The Hands That Built America', to Martin Scorsese's violent masterpiece, 'Gangs Of New York' (2002). Stop press: BONO played the role of Dr. Robert in the Beatles-esque movie, 'ACROSS THE UNIVERSE' (2007). *BG*

- **filmography** (composers) {acting} -

Captive *(1986 OST by The EDGE =>)* / **Rattle And Hum** *(1988 {****p} OST by U2 =>)* / Until The End Of The World *(1991 theme by U2 on V/A =>; see future editions)* / Faraway, So Close! *(1993 hit/theme by U2 on OST by V/A see; future editions =>)* / In The Name Of The Father *(1993 hit/theme by BONO & GAVIN FRIDAY on OST by V/A see; future editions =>)* / Batman Forever *(1995 hit/theme by U2 on OST by V/A see; future editions =>)* / Par-Dela Les Nuages – Beyond The Clouds *(1995 score w/ others =>)* / Mission: Impossible *(1996 hit/theme by ADAM CLAYTON & LARRY MULLEN on OST by V/A see; future editions =>)* / Entropy *(1999 {****p no OST w/ U2)* / **the Million Dollar Hotel** *(2000 on OST by V/A incl. BONO/U2, ENO . . . =>)* / **Across The Universe** *(2007 {a BONO} OST by V/A =>)*

– movie music compilations, etc. –

PASSENGERS: Original Soundtracks 1

Nov 95. (cd/c/lp) *Island; (CID/ICT/ILPS 8043) <524166>* 12 76
– United colours *(from the film "United Colours Of Plutonium")* / Slug *(from "Slug")* / Your blue room *(from "Par-Dela Les Nuages/ Beyond The Clouds")* / Always forever now *(end titles from "Always Forever Now")* / A different kind of blue *(from "An Ordinary Day")* / Beach sequence *(from "Par-Dela Les Nuages/Beyond The Clouds")* / Miss Sarajevo *(from the film "Miss Sarajevo")* / Ito Okashi *(from "Ito Okashi/Something Beautiful")* / One minute warning *(from "Ghost In The Shell")* / Corpse (these chains are way too long) *(from "Gibigiane/ Reflections")* / Elvis ate America *(from the film "Elvis Ate America")* / Plot 180 *(from "Hypnotize – Love Me 'Til Dawn")* / Theme from The Swan *(from "The Swan")* / Theme from Let's Go Native *(from "Let's Go Native")*.

UNCLE MEAT

1987 (US 100m shelved from 1969) independent

Film genre: Rock-music concert/documentary & sci-fi comedy

Top guns: s-w + dir: **Frank ZAPPA**

Stars: Frank ZAPPA *(himself/the imaginary director)*, **Don Preston** *(himself / Uncle Meat / Biff Debris)* ← 200 MOTELS, **Jimmy Carl Black** *(himself)* ← 200 MOTELS ← MONDO HOLLYWOOD / → ROCK SCHOOL, **Aynsley Dunbar** *(himself / Biff Junior)* ← 200 MOTELS ← AMOUGIES, **Ian Underwood** *(himself)* ← 200 MOTELS, **Euclid James 'Motorhead' Sherwood** *(himself)* ← 200 MOTELS, **Billy Mundi** *(Rollo)*, **Ray Collins** *(himself / Bill Yards)*, **Roy Estrada** *(himself)* ← BABY SNAKES, **Lowell George** *(himself)*, **Bunk Gardner** *(himself)*, **Buzz Gardner** *(himself)*, **Artie Tripp III** *(himself)*, **Linda Ronstadt** *(herself)* ← FM / → HAIL! HAIL! ROCK'N'ROLL → MAYOR OF THE SUNSET STRIP, Phyllis Altenhaus *(herself / Sheba Fleishman)*, Haskell Wexler *(himself)*, Rodney Bingenheimer *(himself)* ← the UNHEARD MUSIC ← REPO MAN ← UP IN SMOKE / → BACK TO THE BEACH → ROCKULA → RAGE: 20 YEARS OF PUNK ROCK WEST COAST STYLE → END OF THE CENTURY → MAYOR OF THE SUNSET STRIP → PUNK'S NOT DEAD, Sal Lombardo *(himself)* ← TWO TICKETS TO PARIS, Dick Barber *(himself)* ← 200 MOTELS

Storyline: Twenty years in the making (they run out of time and money!), Frank Zappa finally released the movie on video. In two parts, the first showcases the Mothers Of Invention performing at London's Albert Hall in '68. The second is an avant-garde tale of Uncle Meat, who turns into a monster at times, falls in love with the film editor (Sheba Flieschman), but ultimately – a decade later or so – has to choose between writing a hit single and the love of his life. *MCS*

Movie rating: *5

Visual: video + dvd

Off the record: During the recording of the set, drummer BILLY MUNDI went off to join/form Rhinoceros. Others too, subsequently went off to pastures new: mainly ARTIE TRIPP to Captain Beefheart and ROY ESTRADA to Little Feat. *MCS*

FRANK ZAPPA / THE MOTHERS OF INVENTION

Apr 69. (d-lp) *Bizarre; <2024> Transatlantic; (TRA 197)* 43 Sep69
– Uncle Meat: main title theme / The voice of cheese / Nine types of industrial pollution / Zolar Czakl / Dog breath, in the year of the plague / The legend of the golden arches / Louie Louie (at the Royal Albert Hall in London) / The dog breath variations / Sleeping in a jar / Our bizarre relationship / The Uncle Meat variations / Electric Aunt Jemima // Prelude to King Kong / God bless America (live at the Whisky A Go Go) / A pound for a brown on the bus / Ian Underwood whips it out (live on stage in Copenhagen) / Mr. Green genes / We can shoot you / "If we'd all been living in California" / The air / Project X / Cruising for burgers / Uncle Meat film excerpt part I * / Tengo na minchia tanta * / Uncle Meat film excerpt part II * / King Kong itself (as played by the Mothers in the studio) / King Kong (its magnificence as interpreted by Dom DeWild) / King Kong (as Motorhead explains it) / King Kong (the Gardner varieties) / King Kong (as played by 3 deranged good humor trucks) / King Kong (live on a flat bed diesel in the middle of a race track at a Miami Pop Festival.. the Underwood ramifications). *(d-cd-iss. Oct87 on 'Zappa' += *; CDZAP 3) (cd-iss. May95 on 'Rykodisc' += *; RCD 10506-7)*

S/track review: On one's first listen, this double-LP (and later double-CD) was a bit of a shambles, going in all directions but the right one. However, pieced together – much like the movie itself – 'UNCLE MEAT' probably fits into the scheme of things when recorded in a five-month spell between October 1967 and February 1968. In some respects, one could say, this was the MOTHER OF INVENTION's 'Trout Mask Replica', although many Captain Beefheart fans (and I'm one of the biggest!) would be up in arms for suggesting the connection, and anyway as I think the saying goes: "One man's Uncle Meat, is another man's poison". The main title theme kicks off the set, the xylophone & harpsichord (probably more at home in a score for TV's 'Columbo') right in the firing line of this jazz-fusion ditty; the "Suzy Cream Cheese"/funhouse interludes give 'UNCLE MEAT' that characteristic comedy that only ZAPPA was capable of. But "Does Humour Really Belong In Music?" – with 'Dog Breath, In The Year Of The Plague', 'The Dog Breath Variations' and 'The Uncle Meat Variations', the answer is yes. The inner sleeve states that "the words on this album were scientifically prepared from a random series of syllables, dreams, neuroses & private jokes that nobody except the members of the band ever laugh at . . ." – and this just about says it all. Live at the Royal Albert Hall in London, ZAPPA & the MOTHERS, with DON PRESTON on a tuba, take on – in full-blown R&B-meets-Bonzo Dog Band-pastiche – 'Louie Louie'; Richard Berry will indeed turn in his grave. Ditto 'God Bless America' – live at the Whisky A Go-Go – for Irving Berlin. 'Sleeping In A Jar' was more or less another part of 'Mom & Dad' – a track from 'We're Only In It For The Money' (1968) LP, while 'Our Bizarre Relationship' is pure dialogue by Phyllis Altenhaus, a lady with very colourful language and that goddamn awful Noo Yoik drawl. 50s doo-wop is always there or thereabouts for ZAPPA, and the Chipmunks-styled 'Electric Aunt Jemma' and 'The Air' are no exceptions. It must be stated, I hate doo wop and in my book you can't make it funny. We're treated to the first jazzy instalment of 'King Kong' on track 13, 'Prelude To . . .', while the 'Uncle Meat' theme continues in the guise of 'A Pound For A Brown On The Bus'; then we have 5 minutes of the Coltrane-esque 'Ian Underwood Whips It Out (live on stage in Copenhagen)' – oo-er. With all the conceptual weirdness behind us – not! – the more conventional 'Mr. Green Genes', is a culinary trip around the eating of beans, celery, grapes, the box, the truck & drive- mental. With 'Cruising For Burgers' – " . . .in daddy's new car", ZAPPA gets the moral message across to the self-inflicted phonies of the day. With Disc 1 out of the way, maybe one thought "Uncle" FRANK would ease up with the manic weirdness, the self-descriptive 41-minute 'Uncle Meat Film Excerpt(s) Part(s) I & II' tells us another story – quite literally. Dialogue from every MOTHER under the sun talking about the making of the film (and monsters!) is just tedious, apart from the kinky shower scene, perhaps. Best to just watch the movie – if you can handle that. Segued in between these excerpts is another piece not from the original double-LP, 'Tengo Na Minchia Tanta', pure down'n'dirty rock'n'roll and thankfully a proper song. A long time coming, 'King Kong' the variations in I to IV glorious parts, puts ZAPPA and his (inventive) Mothers back on my musical map. Jazz-rock with a busy bee stuck in the speakers, this was undoubtably the free-est, sax-iest 20 minutes of the set – real cool MOTHERS. *MCS*

Album rating: *6.5

the UNHEARD MUSIC

aka X the band: THE UNHEARD MUSIC

1986 (US 84m) Angel City / Skouras Pictures (R)

Film genre: alt-Rock-music documentary bio-pic

Top guns: s-w (+ dir): W.T. Morgan, Christopher Blakely

Stars: X the band:- Exene Cervenka, John DOE, DJ Bonebrake + Billy Zoom *(performers)*, **Frank Gargani** *(Johnny)* ← SUBURBIA ← the DECLINE OF WESTERN CIVILIZATION, **Ray Manzarek** *(himself)* ← the DOORS ARE OPEN / → the DOORS: LIVE AT THE HOLLYWOOD BOWL → MESSAGE TO LOVE: THE ISLE OF WIGHT FESTIVAL → MAYOR OF THE SUNSET STRIP, **Jello BIAFRA** *(himself)*, Rodney Bingenheimer *(himself)* ← REPO MAN ← UP IN SMOKE / → UNCLE MEAT → BACK TO THE BEACH → ROCKULA → RAGE: 20 YEARS OF PUNK ROCK WEST COAST STYLE → END OF THE CENTURY → MAYOR OF THE SUNSET STRIP → PUNK'S NOT DEAD

Storyline: Los Angeles is the place to be again in the early 80s and X were the band to love. Interviews, concert footage and even TV commercials are used to document their fight against the music moguls. *MCS*

Movie rating: *8.5

Visual: video + dvd (no audio OST)

Off the record: Frank Gargani was ex-X

URGH! A MUSIC WAR

1981 (UK 97m) Lorimar / Filmways Pictures (R)

Film genre: post-Punk Rock-music concert/documentary

Top guns: dir: Derek Burbidge

Stars: the Police:- STING *(performer)*, **Stewart Copeland** *(performer)* <= future editions =>, **Andy Summers** *(performer)*, **TOYAH Wilcox** *(performer)*, **Wall Of Voodoo:- Stan Ridgway, Chas T. Gray, Bruce Moreland, Marc Moreland, Joe Nanini** *(performers)*, **Orchestral Manoeuvres In The Dark:- Andy McCluskey, Paul Humphries, Malcolm Holmes, David Hughes** *(performers)* → PRETTY IN PINK, **Oingo Boingo:- Danny Elfman, Steve Bartek, Richard Gibbs, David Eagle, Sam Phipps, Kerry Hatch, Dale Turner, Leon Scheorman** *(rest of band)* / **Echo & The Bunnymen:- Ian McCulloch, Pete DeFreitas, Will Sergeant, Les Pattinson** *(performers)*, **Jools Holland** *(performer)* → EAT THE RICH → SPICEWORLD → CONCERT FOR GEORGE, **XTC:- Andy Partridge, Colin Moulding, Dave Gregory, Terry Chambers** *(performers)*, **Klaus Nomi w/ Jon Cobert** *(performers)* → the NOMI SONG, **Athletico Spizz '80:- Spizz, Jim Solar, C.P. Snare, Mark Coalfield, Dave Scott** *(performers)*, **the Go-Go's:- Belinda Carlisle** *(performer)*, **Jane Wiedlin** *(performer)* → BILL & TED'S EXCELLENT ADVENTURE, **Charlotte Caffey** *(performer)*, **Gina Schock** *(performer)*, **Margot Olaverra** *(performer)* / **Steel Pulse:- David Hinds** *(performers)* → the REGGAE MOVIE, **Gary Numan** *(performer)*, **Joan Jett** *(performer)* <= the RUNAWAYS =>, & the **Blackhearts** *(performers)*, **Magazine:- Howard Devoto, Barry ADAMSON, John Doyle, Dave Formula, Robin Simon** *(performers)*, **the Members:- * Nicky Tesco, Chris Payne, Adrian Lilywhite, J.C. Mainman** *(performers)* * → LENINGRAD COWBOYS . . ., **the Au Pairs:- Lesley Woods, Jane Munro, Pete Hammond, Paul Foad** *(performers)*, **the Cramps:- Lux Interior, Poison Ivy Rorschach, Nick Knox + Julien Griensnatch** *(performers)* ← the FOREIGNERS, **Invisible Sex** *(performers)*, **Pere Ubu:- David Thomas** *(performer/s)*, **DEVO:- Gerald V. Casale, Bob Casale, Mark Mothersbaugh, Robert Mothersbaugh, Alan Myers** *(performers)*, **Alley Cats:- Randy Stodola, Dianne Chai, John McCarty** *(performers)*, **John Otway** *(performer)*, **Gang Of Four:- Hugo Burnham *, Dave Allen, Jon King + Andy Gill** *(performers)* → * WON'T ANYBODY LISTEN, **999:- Nick Cash, Guy Days, Jon Watson, Pablo LaBritain** *(performers)*, **the Fleshtones:- Peter Zaremba, Keith Streng, Bill Milhizer, Jan Marek Pakulski** *(performers)*, **X:- John DOE, Exene Cervenka, DJ Bonebrake + Frank Gargani** *(performers)*, **Skafish:- Jim Skafish, Ken Bronowski, Javier Cruz, Larry Mysliewiec, Barbie Goodrich** *(performers)*, **the Dead Kennedys:- Jello BIAFRA, East Bay Ray, Klaus Flouride, Bruce Slesinger** *(performer)*, **Chelsea:- Gene October, Steve Ace, Barry Smith, Mike Howell, Chris Bashford** *(performers)* ← D.O.A. ← JUBILEE ← PUNK IN LONDON, **Surf Punks:- Dennis Dragon, Drew Steele, Mark The Shark, Pat Sullivan, Bill Dale, Ray Ban, Andrew Jackson** *(performers)*

Storyline: Thirty bands from the late 70s and 80s perform non-stop music in this alternative rock concert. Set in England, France and the USA, group styles range from punk to New Wave and other more outlandish combinations, but more conventional performances come from the Police, UB40 and Echo & The Bunnymen. *JZ*

Movie rating: *7

Visual: US video 124m

Off the record: (see below)

Various Artists

Sep 81. (d-lp) *A&M; (AMLX 64692) <6019>* ☐ ☐

– Driven to tears (the POLICE) / Back in flesh (WALL

OF VOODOO) / Dance (TOYAH WILCOX) / Enola Gay (ORCHESTRAL MANOEUVRES IN THE DARK) / Ain't this the life (OINGO BOINGO) / Respectable street (XTC) / Offshore banking business (the MEMBERS) / We got the beat (GO-GO'S) / Total eclipse (KLAUS NOMI) / Where's Captain Kirk (ATHLETICO SPIZZ '80) / Nothing means nothing anymore (ALLEY CATS) / Foolish I know (JOOLS HOLLAND) / Ku Klux Klan (STEEL PULSE) // Uncontrollable urge (DEVO) / The puppet (ECHO AND THE BUNNYMEN) / Come again (the AU PAIRS) / Tear it up (the CRAMPS) / Bad reputation (JOAN JETT & THE BLACKHEARTS) / Birdies (PERE UBU) / Down in the park (GARY NUMAN) / Shadow line (FLESHTONES) / He'd send in the army (GANG OF FOUR) / Homicide (999) / Beyond and back (X) / Model worker (MAGAZINE) / Sign of the cross (SKAFISH).

S/track review: Recorded live from various transatlantic venues in a 5-week stretch between August 15th & September 19th, 1980, this double LP was basically a showcase for alt-rock/indie bands/ acts on the 'A&M'/'I.R.S.' roster. Mostly produced, engineered and mixed by Tim Summerhayes (& acts) via California (the Whisky, Santa Monica Civic, etc.), New York (the CBGB's & the Ritz) to Paris, France (Fejus Amphitheater), London (the Lyceum Ballroom, the Rainbow Theatre & Hammersmith Palais) and er, Portsmouth (the Guild Hall), the array of post-punk talent is incredible. With Miles and Ian Copeland (A&M's Creative Consultants), who else would you have open the show than American brother Stewart's cod-reggae band, the POLICE ('Driven To Tears'); incidentally the only other reggae song is the classic 'Ku Klux Klan' by STEEL PULSE. UK "class of '77" acts are rife here, XTC, GANG OF FOUR, 999, the MEMBERS, Athletico SPIZZ '80 (with their farewell anthem, 'Where's Captain Kirk'), MAGAZINE (featuring ex-Buzzcock, Howard Devoto), poser GARY NUMAN (with the classic Tubeway Army electroid 'Down In The Park'), ex-Squeeze pianist JOOLS HOLLAND (sorry for the spelling!?), 'JUBILEE' actress TOYAH and er, cor baby JOHN OTWAY. New Brit kids on the block, numbered ORCHESTRAL MANOEUVRES IN THE DARK ('Enola Gay'), ECHO AND THE BUNNYMEN ('The Puppet') and the AU PAIRS ('Come Again'), the latter a post-feminist, tongue-in-cheeky/chappy leveller. America's New Wave was also on show, the quirky WALL OF VOODOO ('Back In Flesh'), DEVO ('Uncontrollable Urge'), the poor man's Devo, OINGO BOINGO ('Ain't This The Life'), Indiana's finest SKAFISH ('Sign Of The Cross') and out-of-place PERE UBU ('Birdies') were silly enough to hold their own, while rockabilly/cowpunks, X, FLESHTONES and the CRAMPS showed retro-rock wasn't forgotten. Fringe new-wave popsters, GO-GO'S, JOAN JETT and newbie L.A. trio ALLEY CATS were already finding their own market in America, but just where opera-rocker KLAUS NOMI stood was anyone's guess. *MCS*

Album rating: *7.5

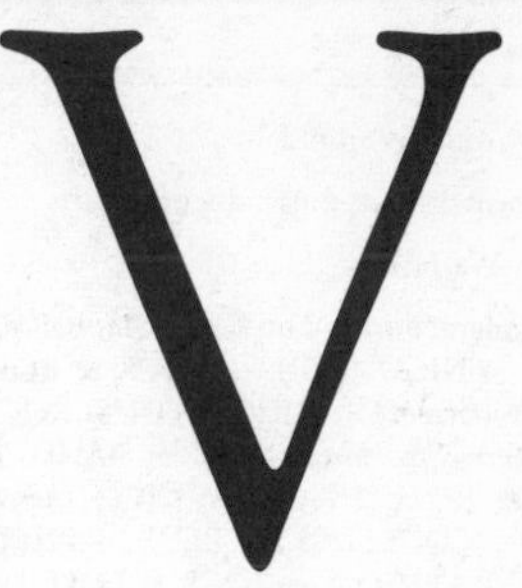

□ Townes VAN ZANDT segment
(⇒ BE HERE TO LOVE ME . . .)

Eddie VEDDER

Born: Edward Louis Severson III, 23 Dec'64, Evanston, Illinois, USA. As the gruff conscience of grunge, you can't imagine EDDIE VEDDER as a man given to dramatic trifles. His mahogany vocals and rugged good looks have nevertheless graced many a concert film, both as part of Pearl Jam and in his own right; when he has appeared in a feature film, he's unsurprisingly appeared as himself. In 1992, the first flush of commercial grunge saw him doing the obligatory 'MTV Unplugged', and appearing – as his tousled self, playing in Matt Dillon's backing band, Citizen Dick – in Cameron Crowe's scene-setting 'SINGLES', as well as contributing a couple of Pearl Jam songs to the soundtrack. Arguably at his best in a solo capacity with apocalyptic folk material, VEDDER subsequently put in the single most compelling performance (a scathing 'Masters Of War') in 'Dylan tribute shindig, 'Bob Dylan: 30th Anniversary Concert Celebration' (1993). A gentler yet equally intense humanism suffused his soundtrack contributions to Tim Robbins' capital punishment drama, 'DEAD MAN WALKING' (1995), as well as his performance at subsequent benefit gig, 'Not In Our Name: Dead Man Walking – The Concert' (1998). Come the new millennium, VEDDER was once again turning to BOB DYLAN to express himself; the choice of 'The Times They Are A-Changin' (performed live at a Ralph Nader/Green Party rally) seems, in retrospect, all the more hopelessly optimistic given the ultimate, (inevitable?) victory of the Republican campaign documented in Philip Seymour Hoffman's 'Last Party 2000' (2001). The same year, he contributed a Beatles cover ('You've Got To Hide Your Love Away') to the soundtrack of Jessie Nelson's 'I AM SAM' (2001), and subsequently composed the very VEDDER-esque 'Man Of The Hour' to Tim Burton's own humanist fantasy, 'Big Fish' (2003). 2007 saw VEDDER finally get his teeth into a full score – albeit under 33 minutes – via Sean Penn's adventure movie, 'INTO THE WILD'. *BG & MCS*

- filmography (composer) {performer} –

Singles *(1992 {p} PEARL JAM on OST by V/A =>)* / **Dead Man Walking** *(1995 on OST w/ David Robbins, etc. =>)* / **Hype!** *(1996 {p w/ PEARL JAM} on OST by V/A =>)* / **We're Outta Here!** *(1997 {c} guest on OST w/ RAMONES =>)* / **the Who Live At The Royal Albert Hall** *(2000 {p} guest on OST w/ the WHO =>)* / Last Party 2000 *(2001 {c})* / **End Of The Century** *(2003 {c} =>)* / **Too Tough To Die: A Tribute To Johnny Ramone** *(2006 {c} =>)* / **Into The Wild** *(2007 OST =>)* / **Walk Hard: The Dewey Cox Story** *(2007 {c} =>)*

the VELVET UNDERGROUND AND NICO

1966 (US 70m b&w) Andy Warhol Films

Film genre: experimental/Rock-music documentary

Top guns: dir: Andy Warhol

Stars: the Velvet Underground:- Lou REED *(himself/performer)*, **John Cale** *(himself/performer)* → NICO ICON → ROCK & ROLL HEART, **Sterling Morrison** *(himself/performer)* → NICO ICON → ROCK & ROLL HEART, **Maureen Tucker** *(herself/performer)* → the BAND THAT WOULD BE KING → ROCK & ROLL HEART & **NICO** *(herself/performer)*, Andy Warhol *(himself)* → COCKSUCKER BLUES → IMAGINE → BLANK GENERATION → NICO ICON → ROCK & ROLL HEART → DETROIT ROCK CITY → END OF THE CENTURY, Mary Woronov *(herself)* → ROCK'N'ROLL HIGH SCHOOL → GET CRAZY → ROCK'N'ROLL HIGH SCHOOL FOREVER → DICK TRACY → SHAKE, RATTLE & ROCK! tv, Gerald Malanga *(himself)*, Billy Name *(himself)* → NICO ICON, Ari *(Ari)* → NICO ICON, Stephen Shore *(himself)*

Storyline: Andy Warhol's "art for art's sakes" document of the combination of iconic rock stars, the Velvet Underground and Nico, their German-born, supermodel-cum-singer counterpart. Jamming – but not as Bob Marley knew it. *MCS*

Movie rating: *6

Visual: video (no audio OST; see below)

Off the record: 'The Velvet Underground And Nico' – the album – was produced by Andy Warhol and released towards the end of '66; his name's on the cover and he designed the "peel banana" sleeve to reveal er . . . a pink one. *MCS*

– associated release, etc. –

THE VELVET UNDERGROUND & NICO

Mar 67. (lp; stereo/mono) *Verve; <V6/V 5008> (S+/VLP 9184)* [ ] Oct67 [ ]
– Sunday morning / I'm waiting for the man / Femme fatale / Venus in furs / Run run run / All tomorrow's parties / Heroin / There she goes again / I'll be your mirror / The black angel's death song / European son. *(re-iss. Oct71 on 'M.G.M.; 2315 056) (re-iss. Aug83 on 'Polydor' lp/c; SPE LP/MC 20) (cd-iss. 1986 on 'Polydor'; 823 290-2) (cd re-iss. May96 on 'Polydor'; 531 250-2) (lp re-iss. Jun99 on 'Simply Vinyl'; SVLP 90) <(d-cd-iss. Apr02 on 'Polydor'+=; MLST 756)>* – (NICO tracks) / (mono versions) / (various versions). *(hit UK No.59)*

□ Scott WALKER segment (⇒ 30 CENTURY MAN)

the WALL: LIVE IN BERLIN

aka ROGER WATERS: THE WALL – LIVE IN BERLIN

1990 (UK/Ger 115m TV to video) Universal Pictures

Film genre: Rock-music concert/documentary

Top guns: s-w: (+ dir) **Roger Waters**, Ken O'Neil

Stars: Roger Waters *(Pink)* <= PINK FLOYD =>, **Van MORRISON** *(Pink)*, **Cyndi Lauper** *(young Pink)*, **Marianne Faithfull** *(the mother; act two)* ← LUCIFER RISING ← STONES IN THE PARK ← DON'T LOOK BACK ← ANNA / → ROCK AND ROLL CIRCUS, **Thomas DOLBY** *(schoolmaster)*, **the BAND** *(performers)*, **Sinead O'Connor** *(performer)*, **Bryan Adams** *(performer)* → THIRTY YEARS OF MAXIMUM R&B LIVE → SPIRIT: STALLION OF THE CIMARRON → the WHO LIVE AT THE ROYAL ALBERT HALL, **Paul Carrack** *(performer)*, **Joni MITCHELL** *(performer)*, **the Scorpions** *(performers)*, **Andy Fairweather-Low** *(performer)* → PSYCHODERELICT → CONCERT FOR GEORGE, James Galway *(performer)*, Tim Curry *(the prosecutor)* ← LEGEND ← TIMES SQUARE ← ROCK FOLLIES OF '77 ← the ROCKY HORROR PICTURE SHOW / → JACKIE'S BACK!, Albert Finney *(the judge)*, Jerry Hall *(the groupie)* ← 25X5: THE CONTINUING ADVENTURES OF THE ROLLING STONES ← BATMAN ← RUNNING OUT OF LUCK ← LET'S SPEND THE NIGHT TOGETHER ← URBAN COWBOY, Ute Lemper *(the mother; act one / the wife; act two)*, Group Captain Leonard Cheshire *(introduction)*

Storyline: 'The Wall' comes to "live" via a celebrity musical project performed at the Berlin Wall (Potsdamer Platz) just after the historical tearing-down of said artifact. With a cast of hundreds, the monies taken from the concert on 21st July, 1990 were donated to the World War Memorial Fund for Disaster Relief. *MCS*

Movie rating: *8

Visual: video + Polygram DVD

Off the record: Paul Carrack was a solo artist of some merit, who also sidelined with Ace, Squeeze, Mike & The Mechanics, etc.

ROGER WATERS (*) (& Various Cast/Artists)

Sep 90. (d-cd/d-c/d-lp) *Mercury; (<846611-2/-4/-1>)* [27] [56]
– In the flesh (SCORPIONS) / The thin ice (UTE LEMPER & *) / Another brick in the wall, pt.1 (*) / The happiest days of our lives (JOE CHEMAY, JOHN JOYCE, STAN FARBER, JIM HAAS & *) / Another brick in the wall, pt.2 (CYNDI LAUPER) / Mother (SINEAD O'CONNOR & The BAND) / Goodbye blue sky (JONI MITCHELL) / Empty spaces (BRYAN ADAMS & *) / Young lust (BRYAN ADAMS) / Oh my god – what a fabulous room (JERRY HALL) / One of my turns (*) / Don't leave me now (*) / Another brick in the wall, pt.3 (*) / Goodbye cruel

world (*) // Hey you (PAUL CARRACK) / Is there anybody out there? (the RUNDFUNK ORCHESTRA and choir) / Nobody home (*) / Vera (* & the RUNDFUNK ORCHESTRA and choir) / Bring the boys back home (the RUNDFUNK ORCHESTRA and choir & the MILITARY ORCHESTRA OF THE SOVIET ARMY) / Comfortably numb (VAN MORRISON, * & The BAND) / (* & the BLEEDING HEART BAND, the RUNDFUNK ORCHESTRA and choir & the MILITARY ORCHESTRA OF THE SOVIET ARMY):- In the flesh / Run like Hell / Waiting for the worms / Stop / The trial (the RUNDFUNK ORCHESTRA and choir to the end – TIM CURRY: THE PROSECUTOR, THOMAS DOLBY: TEACHER, UTE LEMPER: THE WIFE, MARIANNE FAITHFULL: MOTHER, ALBERT FINNEY: THE JUDGE) / Encore (the COMPANY) / The tide is turning (the COMPANY). *(re-iss. d-cd Sep95; same)*

S/track review: Given the politically charged heart of ROGER WATERS' opus, when the opportunity came to mark the fall of the Berlin Wall with a concert, this PINK FLOYD's 1979 behemoth seemed all too fitting. By the time this show came around WATERS hadn't performed with his old 'Floyd mates in well over a decade, but instead of reconciling with them he opened up his contacts book and called in a few friends. The story goes he wanted Rod Stewart, Bruce Springsteen, Eric Clapton and Joe Cocker to be part of the show, but for whatever reasons this never quite materialised, so instead we get the sublime – SINEAD O'CONNOR, UTE LEMPER, PAUL CARRACK – and the ridiculous – JAMES GALWAY, JERRY HALL, the SCORPIONS – in an uneven, technically fraught, epic. The concert took place on Potsdamer Platz, which sat in the no-man's-land between the two walls in Berlin. Thousands of people had died trying to traverse the space attempting to escape communism and into West Berlin and now 400,000 people would witness this show there. The new versions of the songs stay relatively true to the spirit of the originals. A few are tweaked, augmented with extra solos and choruses ('Comfortably Numb', 'Another Brick In The Wall, Part II' and 'Mother'), while others ('The Show Must Go On') are omitted completely. Despite the dramatic staging, there's little here to enhance the experience of hearing the intense and sprawling original double-album, except for a few novel vocal performances, but this recording was always more significant politically and logistically than it ever was musically. *MR*

Album rating: *6

– spinoff releases, etc. –

ROGER WATERS: Another Brick In The Wall, pt.2 / Run Like Hell (Potsdamer mix)

Sep 90. (7") *(MER 332)*
(12"+=/cd-s+=) *(MER X/CD 332)* – (full version).

ROGER WATERS: The Tide Is Turning / Nobody Home

Jan 91. (7") *(MER 336)*
(12"+=/cd-s+=) *(MER X/CD 336)* – (lp version).

WARMING BY THE DEVIL'S FIRE

4th part of Martin Scorsese presents THE BLUES

2003 (US 120m mini-TV w/b&w) Vulcan Productions / PSB (12)

Film genre: Blues-music docu-drama

Top guns: dir: (+ s-w) Charles Burnett

Stars: Carl Lumbly *(narrator)*, Nathaniel Lee Jr. *(Jr.)*, Tommy Redmond Hicks *(Uncle Buddy)* ← DELUSION ← the FIVE HEARTBEATS, **Bessie Smith** *(archive performer)*, **Dinah Washington** *(archive performer)*, **Willie Dixon** *(performer)* ← GINGER ALE AFTERNOON, **Sonny Boy Williamson** *(performer)*, **Reverend Gary Davis** *(performer)*, **Sister Rosetta Tharpe** *(archive performer)* ← the LADIES SING THE BLUES / → RED, WHITE & BLUES, **Mamie Smith** *(archive performer)*, **Lucille Bogan** *(archive performer)*

Storyline: Charles Burnett examines the spiritual complexities of the blues as performed and enjoyed alongside the moral strictures laid down by the church and its own gospel soundtrack, semi-autobiographically dramatising an eye opening Deep South summer in the company of his blues-loving uncle Buddy, alongside scratchy footage of artists – many of them female – resourceful enough to have a big sexy leg in both camps. *BG*

Movie rating: *6

Visual: dvd on 'Pinnacle'

Off the record: (see below)

——

Various Artists

Sep 03. (cd) *Sony; <90490-2> (512569-2)* Mar04
– Turtle twist (JELLY ROLL MORTON) / See see rider (MA RAINEY) / Death letter (SON HOUSE) / I'm a fool to want you (BILLIE HOLIDAY) / Big leg blues (MISSISSIPPI JOHN HURT) / K.C. moan (MEMPHIS JUG BAND) / Sweet home Chicago (ROBERT JOHNSON) / Deep blue sea blues (TOMMY McCLENNAN) / Muddy water (BESSIE SMITH) / Cross my heart (SONNY BOY WILLIAMSON) / Dust my broom (ELMORE JAMES) / You can't lose what you ain't never had (MUDDY WATERS) / Beale Street blues (W.C. HANDY) / Hang it on the wall (CHARLEY PATTON) / Up above my head (I hear music in the air) (SISTER ROSETTA THARPE) / Give me freedom (STEPHEN JAMES TAYLOR) / Mr. Thrill (MILDRED JONES) / I'll never get out of these blues alive (JOHN LEE HOOKER).

S/track review: If only in terms of profanity count, contemporary hip hop makes even the most explicit of Delta blues songs appear about as offensive as a "Pop Idol" entry. Somewhere along the way, though, black music lost the fine art of the double entendre, here given a masterclass by one MILDRED JONES; you can't imagine 'Mr Thrill' having had much mainstream radio play, unless programmers were impervious to the phallic possibilities of black cadillacs and garages. But was it really the devil's hearth she was getting hot and bothered by? Judged by the standards of her day, it probably was. Ain't it a shame, though, now we live in supposedly more tolerant times, that no-one can be bothered thinking up outrageous metaphors anymore. Surprisingly, the term "blues" itself doesn't hold any dodgy connotations, unlike "jazz"; backed up by a young Louis Armstrong and Fletcher Henderson, "Mother of the Blues" MA RAINEY performs an ancient sounding 'See See Rider', "riding" being one of blues' oldest and most enduring metaphors. JELLY ROLL MORTON even had a risqué name to go with his brothel-apprenticed "jazz stomp", and MISSISSPPI JOHN HURT quiet-spokenly sings about his preference for "black and brown". Yet as a whole this collection is less bawdy than it could have been, more a haunted window on "the veil that hides the human condition", as director Charles Burnett tells it in his sleevenotes, following the genre's dialectic between the sacred and the profane up into the urban north. As with other volumes in the series, touchstones like 'Death Letter', 'Sweet Home Chicago' and 'Dust My Broom' line up next to more obscure artists ripe for rediscovery (the carpet-tack-throated TOMMY McCLENNAN for one) and jazz and gospel equivalents performed with all the spirit and contradiction of the blues, whether aching and ravaged (late period BILLIE HOLIDAY) or ecstatic (SISTER ROSETTA THARPE's brilliant 'Up Above My Head'). Like the other albums, it also sources compelling examples of modern blues, in this case from film composer STEPHEN JAMES TAYLOR of all people; only the sound quality of the dirge-like 'Give Me Freedom', gives it away as a modern recording. But anyone still labouring under the illusion that blues is cobwebbed arcana for balding record collectors really should give MILDRED a whirl; she makes your average contemporary R&B diva sound neurotic. *BG*

Album rating: *8.5

WATTSTAX

1972 (US 98m) Columbia Pictures

Film genre: R&B/Soul-music concert documentary

Top guns: dir: Mel Stuart

Stars: the STAPLE SINGERS:- Mavis Staples, Roebuck 'Pop' Staples *(performers)* / **Isaac HAYES** *(performer)*, **the Bar-Kays** *(performers)*, **Kim Weston** *(performer)*, **Rufus Thomas** *(performer)* → GREAT BALLS OF FIRE! → MYSTERY TRAIN → ONLY THE STRONG SURVIVE → the ROAD TO MEMPHIS, **Carla Thomas** *(performer)* → ONLY THE STRONG SURVIVE, **Albert King** *(performer)*, **Little Milton** *(performer)*, **Johnnie Taylor** *(performer)* → DISCO 9000, **Luther Ingram** *(performer)*, **the Rance Allen Group** *(performers)*, **the Emotions** *(performers)*, **David Porter** *(performer)*, Richard Pryor *(himself)* ← LADY SINGS THE BLUES ← YOU'VE GOT TO WALK IT LIKE YOU TALK IT . . . ← the PHYNX ← WILD IN THE STREETS / → the MACK → ADIOS AMIGO → CAR WASH → the WIZ → BUSTIN' LOOSE, Rev. Jesse Jackson *(himself)*, Ossie Davis *(himself)*, Ruby Dee *(herself)* ← BLACK GIRL ← UP TIGHT! / → COUNTDOWN AT KUSINI → JUNGLE FEVER, Ted Lange *(himself)* → RECORD CITY ← FRIDAY FOSTER ← BLACK BELT JONES

Storyline: A concert organized by Stax Records at Los Angeles Memorial Coliseum on the 20th August, 1972 was the "Afro-American" equivalent to 'WOODSTOCK' – it commemorated the 7th anniversary of the 'Watts' riots. A dollar entrance fee for the 7-hour benefit of the Sickle Cell Anemia Foundation seemed a worthy cause, while black artists such as Isaac Hayes, the Staple Singers, etc., spread "The Living Word". *MCS*

Movie rating: *7.5

Visual: video + dvd

Off the record: (see Vol.2 below)

Various Artists: Wattstax – The Living Word

Jan 73. (d-lp) *Stax; <STS 2-3010>* [28] [–]
– (the STAPLE SINGERS):- Oh la de da / I like the things about me / Respect yourself / I'll take you there / (EDDIE FLOYD):- Knock on wood / Lay your loving on me / (CARLA THOMAS):- I like what you're doing (to me) / Gee whiz / I have a God who loves / (RUFUS THOMAS):- The breakdown / Do the funky chicken / Do the funky penguin // (the BAR-KAYS):- Son of Shaft – Feel it / I can't turn you loose / (ALBERT KING):- Killing floor / I'll play the blues for you / Angel of mercy / (the SOUL CHILDREN):- I don't know what this world is coming to / Hearsay / (ISAAC HAYES):- Ain't no sunshine. *<cd-iss. Jan90; 88007> (UK cd re-iss. Nov92; CDSXE2 079)*

S/track review: Under a hot August sun, a sporting arena in L.A. was transformed into an all-day benefit music concert to house over 100,000 black people and several of the era's top soul stars – all on one mighty fine label, 'Stax'. If Billy Preston had been invited to the 'WATTSTAX' party, he just might've sung, 'That's The Way God Planned It', an appropriately-titled number to justify the grand scale of the big gig. However, it was the STAPLE SINGERS, EDDIE FLOYD, CARLA THOMAS, her father RUFUS THOMAS, the BAR-KAYS, ALBERT KING, the SOUL CHILDREN and ISAAC HAYES who stole the show from a certain Black activist, the Rev. Jesse "I Am Somebody" Jackson. Opening with the aforementioned gospel icons, the STAPLE SINGERS and 'Oh La De Da' (incidentally, overdubbed in the studio), Mavis and Roebuck "Pops" go to work on three further songs, 'I Like The Things About Me', 'Respect Yourself' and 'I'll Take You There'; the latter two massive hits. EDDIE FLOYD continued the chartbusting flow by way of his 1966 Top 30 nugget, 'Knock On Wood', although his second cue (also re-mixed in the studio!), 'Lay Your Loving On Me', was strictly for his own fanbase. Once happy to duet with the late, great Otis Redding, faded 60s starlet CARLA THOMAS (unbeknown to the lady herself, it seemed) mixed her golden-oldie debut hit, 'Gee Whiz', squeezed between two of her lesser-known numbers, 'I Like What You're Doing (To Me)' and the boastful 'I Have A God Who Loves Me'. Her ageing father, the legendary RUFUS THOMAS (still "Walking The Dog" aged 55), displays his need to boogie-on-down with a trio of recent novelty hits, 'The Breakdown', 'Do The Funky Chicken' and the equally embarrassing 'Do The Funky Penguin' – birds of a feather beware! Disc 2 is a marked improvement on the 1st, starting and ending as it does with a Blaxploitation theme: the BAR-KAYS on the rollicking 'Son Of Shaft' (segued incidentally with 'Feel It'), while Shaft-man/Black Moses himself, ISAAC HAYES, brings down the curtain via a 17-minute rendition of Bill Withers' 'Ain't No Sunshine'. Pioneering left-handed guitarist, ALBERT KING, showed that rhythm, blues and soul could be combined courtesy of his three contributions, 'Killing Floor', 'I'll Play The Blues For You' and 'Angel Of Mercy'; the SOUL CHILDREN, meanwhile (a two-man, two-woman group), get the gospel message across via 'I Don't Know What This World Is Coming To' and their minor hit, 'Hearsay'. A volume set (also a double) was subsequently rush-released featuring "second division" artists such as the EMOTIONS, LITTLE MILTON, JOHNNIE TAYLOR and KIM WESTON, plus those comic turns by RICHARD PRYOR. The full ISAAC HAYES show was given a CD release in 2003, the same year as a 'WATTSTAX' festival & film triple-set hit the shops. *MCS*

Album rating: *6 / Vol.2 *4

– spinoff releases, etc. –

Various Artists: Wattstax 2 – The Living Word

Aug 73. (d-lp) *Stax; <STS 2-3018>* [ ] [–]
– Lift every voice and sing (KIM WESTON) / Lying on the truth (RANCE ALLEN GROUP) / Someone greater than you and I (JIMMY JONES) / Old time religion (GOLDEN 13) / Peace be still (the EMOTIONS) / Saturday night – Blue note – Backroom (RICHARD PRYOR) / Ain't that loving you (for more reasons than one) – Can't see you when I want to – Reach out and touch – (DAVID PORTER) / Finale / Arrest – Line up (RICHARD PRYOR) / Steal away – Stop doggin' me – Jody's got your girl and gone (JOHNNIE TAYLOR) / Walking the backstreets and crying (LITTLE MILTON) / Niggers – Group introduction (RICHARD PRYOR) / So I can love you – Show me how (the EMOTIONS) / Negroes (RICHARD PRYOR) / Watcha see is watcha get (the DRAMATICS) / Handshake (RICHARD PRYOR) / I may not be what you want (MEL & TIM) / Wino get a job (RICHARD PRYOR) / Rolling down a mountainside (ISAAC HAYES).

ISAAC HAYES: At Wattstax

Apr 03. (cd) *Stax; <(SCD 8804-2)>* [ ] May03 [ ]
– Theme from Shaft / Soulsville / Never can say goodbye / Part time love / Your love is so doggone good / Ain't no sunshine – Lonely avenue / I stand accused / Finale: If I had a hammer.

Various Artists: Music From The Wattstax Festival And Film

2003. (t-cd) *Stax; <4440>* [ ] [–]
– (virtually a best-of and 17 previously unreleased tracks)

WE JAM ECONO: THE STORY OF THE MINUTEMEN

2005 (US 85m w/b&w) Rocket Fuel Films

Film genre: Punk-rock music documentary/concert movie

Top guns: dir: Tim Irwin

Stars: the Minutemen:- D. Boon *(archive/performer)*, **Mike Watt** *(himself/performer)* ← RISING LOW ← SIR DRONE, **George Hurley** *(himself/performer)*, **Thurston Moore** *(himself)* <= SONIC YOUTH =>, **Ian MacKaye** *(himself)* ← the SHIELD AROUND THE K ← INSTRUMENT ← ANOTHER STATE OF MIND / → PUNK'S NOT DEAD → AMERICAN HARDCORE, **Henry ROLLINS** *(himself)*, **Flea** *(himself)* <= RED HOT CHILI PEPPERS =>,

Greg Ginn *(himself)* ← the DECLINE OF WESTERN CIVILIZATION / → AMERICAN HARDCORE, **Richard HELL** *(himself)*, **Kira Roessler** *(herself)* → AMERICAN HARDCORE, **Dave MARKEY** *(himself)*

Storyline: Taking the film's title from a 1985 comment made by bassist Mike Watt in answer to the band's economic tour and low-budget recordings, this documentary complements the achievements of SST punk outfit, Minutemen. Incidentally, it premiered at the Warner Grand Theatre in San Pedro, California. *MCS*

Movie rating: *7

Visual: dvd on Plexifilm (no audio OST by MINUTEMEN)

Off the record: Minutemen were formed in San Pedro in 1979 originally as the Reactionaries by **D Boon** and **Mike Watt** (third member **George Hurley** replaced Frank Tonche). The trio featured on Various Artists US LP's on indie labels such as 'Radio Tokyo', 'New Alliance' and 'Posh Boy', before signing for 'S.S.T.' (home base of Black Flag and Meat Puppets). For five years they committed many songs (mostly hardcore/jazz! around a minute long!) to EP and LP before having to disband late in 1985 after the untimely death of Boon (22nd December) in a van/automobile accident. From 'Paranoid Time' to '3-Way Tie (For Last)', Minutemen showcased their politically leftfield attacks on the establishment including Ronnie Reagan and Joe McCarthy. In 1986, the remaining two, Watt and Hurley, re-formed as Firehose alongside guitarist Ed Crawford. **Kira Roessler** was the bassist for Black Flag (alongside **Greg Ginn & Henry ROLLINS**) and became a sound engineer of numerous movies; she was married to Mike Watt between 1987 and 1994. **Mike Watt** now performs behind IGGY POP in the re-formed Stooges. *MCS*

– useful release –

MINUTEMEN: Introducing The . . .

Aug 98. (cd) *S.S.T.; <(SST 363CD)>* ☐ ☐
– Definitions / Joe McCarthy's ghost / Paranoid chant / Search / Punchline / Fanatics / Straight jacket / Bob Dylan wrote propaganda songs / Fake contest / Anchor / Split red / Life as a rehearsal / Cut / Dream told by Moto / I felt like a gringo / Political song for Michael Jackson to sing / Maybe partying will help / Toadies / Corona / History lesson pt.2 / This ain't no picnic / King of the hill / Tour-spiel / Price of paradise / Big stick / Courage / Spoken word piece / Just another soldier / If Reagan played disco / Cake closed / Futurism restated / Joy / Black sheep / Badges / Party with me punker.

WE SOLD OUR SOULS FOR ROCK'N'ROLL

2001 (US 90m) Divine Pictures (R)

Film genre: Hard-Rock-music documentary

Top guns: dir: Penelope Spheeris ← the DECLINE OF WESTERN CIVILIZATION – PART III ← WAYNE'S WORLD ← the DECLINE OF WESTERN CIVILIZATION 2: THE METAL YEARS ← DUDES ← SUBURBIA ← the DECLINE OF WESTERN CIVILIZATION

Stars: Black Sabbath:- Ozzy OSBOURNE *(himself/performer)*, + **Tony Iommi** *(himself/performer)* ← ROCK AND ROLL CIRCUS / → METAL: A HEADBANGER'S JOURNEY, **Geezer Butler** *(himself/performer)*, **Bill Ward** *(himself/performer)*, **Geoff Nicholls** *(himself/performer)* / **Slayer:- Tom Araya, Kerry King, Paul Bostaph, Jeff Hanneman** *(themselves/performers)* → METAL: A HEADBANGER'S JOURNEY / **Slipknot:- Corey Taylor, Paul Gray, Chris Fehn, Joey Jordison, Craig Jones, Mick Thompson, James Root, Sid Wilson, Riggs** *(themselves/performers)* / **System Of A Down:- Serj Tankian, Shavo Odadjian, Daron Malakian, Arto Tuncboyacyyan** *(themselves/performers)* / **Primus:- Les Claypool** *(himself/performer)* ← PINK AS THE DAY SHE WAS BORN ← WOODSTOCK 94 ← BILL & TED'S BOGUS JOURNEY / → RISING LOW → ELECTRIC APRICOT: QUEST FOR FESTEROO / **Brian Mantia** *(performer)* / **White Zombie:- Rob ZOMBIE** *(himself/performer)*, **Blasko** *(himself/bassist)* / **Godsmack:- Robbie Merrill, Tony Rombola, Tommy Stewart, Sully Erna** *(themselves/performers)* ← WOODSTOCK '99 / **John Tempesta** *(himself)*, Sharon Osbourne *(herself)*, Jack Osbourne *(himself)*, **Kelly Osbourne** *(herself)*, **Buckethead** *(himself/performer)*

Storyline: Sharon Osbourne (feisty wife and manager of Ozzy, if you didn't know already), produces, and even travels with the bands on the 'Ozzfest' tour/roadshows from 1994 onwards. Ozzy and Black Sabbath both in attendance as is a number of extreme metal acts such as Slayer, Slipknot and System Of A Down. *MCS*

Movie rating: *6

Visual: video (no audio OST)

Off the record: The film title actually came from a **Black Sabbath** double-compilation LP from the 70s. There were also a number of 'Ozzfest' albums on the market around 2001/2. *MCS*

WEEKEND REBELLION

aka MONDO DAYTONA, aka GET DOWN GRAND FUNK

1968 (US 85m) Mondo Productions / Craddock Films

Film genre: teen docudrama

Top guns: dir: Frank Willard

Stars: Billy Joe Royal *(narrator/performer)* → CATCH MY SOUL, **Grand Funk Railroad:- Mark Farmer, Mel Schacher, Don Brewer** *(performers)*, **Swingin' Medallions:- John McElrath, Charlie Webber, Jim Perkins, Carroll Bledsoe, Steve Caldwell, Jimbo Doares, Joe Morris, Brent Fortson** *(performers)*, **the Tams:- Charles Pope, Joseph Pope, Robert Smith, Horace Key, Floyd Ashton** *(performers)*

Storyline: Filmed with a 16mm hidden camera, we get candid shots of the partying teenagers and hippies who frequent Daytona Beach. Post-psychedelic rock music plays a big part in their lives and in the film, this spring break, 1968, was more a hot bed weather-wise than musically. *MCS*

Movie rating: *4

Visual: none (no audio OST)

Off the record: Georgia-born **Billy Joe Royal** had a handful of US hits before this movie: 'Down In The Boondocks', 'I Knew You When', 'I've Got To Be Somebody' and 'Hush' (the latter written by Joe South and covered by Deep Purple), all relatively successful for the multi-instrumentalist. **Swingin' Medallions** were an 8-piece rock band from Greenwood, South Carolina; hits included 'Double Shot (Of My Baby's Love)' & 'She Drives Me Out Of My Mind', both in 1966. The **Tams** were Atlanta's top R&B vocal quintet of the 60s. They had several hits under their belt including 'What Kind Of Fool (Do You Think I Am)' & 'Hey Girl Don't Bother Me', the latter a subsequent UK No.1 in 1971. **Grand Funk Railroad** had only just begun their rise to be one of America's biggest and loudest rock acts (see Great/Essential Rock Discography for further details). *MCS*

WELCOME TO MY NIGHTMARE

aka ALICE COOPER: WELCOME TO MY NIGHTMARE

1976 (US 84m; video) Dabill & Tommy J. Productions / PRO int.

Film genre: Rock-music concert/documentary

Top guns: dir: David Winters / s-w: Alan Rudolph ← the NIGHTMARE / → ROADIE

Stars: Alice COOPER *(performer/Alice/Steven)*, & band:- **Dick Wagner, Steve Hunter **, Jozef Chirowski, Whitey Glan **, Prakash John *** *(performers)* → the ROSE ** → BLUES BROTHERS 2000 *, Vincent Price *(voice; Spider + host)* ← the NIGHTMARE ← CUCUMBER CASTLE ← the TROUBLE WITH GIRLS ← BEACH PARTY / → the MONSTER CLUB, Sheryl Goddard *(Ethyl)* ← the NIGHTMARE / → SGT. PEPPER'S LONELY HEARTS CLUB BAND → ROADIE, Uchi Sugiyama *(frogman)* ← the NIGHTMARE, Eugene Montoya *(dancer)* ← the NIGHTMARE / → CAN'T STOP THE MUSIC, Robin Blythe *(dancer)* ← the NIGHTMARE

Storyline: Alice Cooper and back-up (including Master of Ceremonies &

horror, Vincent Price) in a 1975 concert in Britain to promote the album of the same name. *MCS*

Movie rating: *6.5

Visual: video + dvd (no "live" audio OST; see below)

Off the record: ALICE COOPER squeezed in a handful of live greats (*) into his 'Welcome To My Nightmare' set list:- 'The Awakening', 'Welcome To My Nightmare', 'Years Ago', 'No More Mr. Nice Guy' (*), 'I'm Eighteen' (*), 'Some Folks', 'Cold Ethyl', 'Only Women Bleed', 'Billion Dollar Babies' (*), 'Devil's Food', 'The Black Widow', 'Steven', 'Escape', 'School's Out' (*), 'Department Of Youth' & 'Only Women Bleed (alt. version). *MCS*

WESTWAY TO THE WORLD

aka The CLASH: WESTWAY TO THE WORLD

2000 (UK 79m uncut) Sony Music Entertainment (15)

Film genre: Punk-Rock-music concert/documentary biopic

Top guns: Don Letts ← DANCEHALL QUEEN ← the PUNK ROCK MOVIE / → ONE LOVE → PUNK: ATTITUDE

Stars: the CLASH:- Joe STRUMMER, Paul Simonon, Mick Jones, Terry Chimes + Topper Headon *(themselves/performers)*, **Siouxsie Sioux** *(footage)* ← the PUNK ROCK MOVIE ← JUBILEE / → the FILTH & THE FURY → 24 HOUR PARTY PEOPLE → PUNK: ATTITUDE, Jordan *(archive)* ← the GREAT ROCK'N'ROLL SWINDLE ← JUBILEE / → the FILTH & THE FURY, Terence Dackombe *(himself)* ← the PUNK ROCK MOVIE, **Shane MacGowan** *(himself)* <= the POGUES =>

Storyline: Clash mate, Don Letts, takes yet another look at the rise and fall of the 70s punk movement through the eyes of Joe Strummer and Co. With the help of old footage and recent interviews with the Clash, the history unfolds of a unique but factious band. *MCS*

Movie rating: *7.5

Visual: dvd (no audio OST)

Off the record: (see Joe STRUMMER/the CLASH)

the WHO: LIVE AT THE ISLE OF WIGHT FESTIVAL 1970

1970 (UK 85m TV) Pulsar Productions

Film genre: Rock-music concert/documentary

Top guns: dir: Murray Lerner ← FESTIVAL / → JIMI HENDRIX LIVE AT THE ISLE OF WIGHT 1970 → MESSAGE TO LOVE: THE ISLE OF WIGHT FESTIVAL

Stars: the WHO:- Pete Townshend, Roger Daltrey, Keith Moon, John Entwistle *(performers)*

Storyline: The third and final appearance of the Who at the massive annual Isle Of Wight Festival in 1970. *MCS*

Movie rating: *7

Visual: video + dvd

Off the record: It wasn't until the early hours of the morning that **the WHO** emerged to play their triumphant two-hour headlining set of the 1970 Isle Of Wight Festival. It saw them in the unique position of being able to enrapture an audience of anywhere between 200,000 to 600,000 people, and to define an era. The anarchists were trying to disrupt things on 'Desolation Row', and the Melody Maker summed up the mood when it lamented that the third Isle Of Wight Festival of music may well be the last occasion for a long time for which a quarter of a million kids come together to hear some rock'n'roll. *DF*

—

the WHO

Oct 96. (d-cd) *Sanctuary; (SMEDD 044) Columbia-Legacy; <65084>* ☐ ☐
– Heaven and Hell / I can't explain / Young man blues / I don't even know myself / Water / Overture / It's a boy / 1921 / Amazing journey / Sparks / Eyesight to the blind (the hawker) / Christmas // The acid queen / Pinball wizard / Do you think it's alright? / Fiddle about / Tommy, can you hear me? / There's a doctor / Go to the mirror / Smash the mirror / Miracle cure / I'm free / Tommy's holiday camp / We're not gonna take it / Summertime blues / Shakin' all over / Substitute / My generation / Naked eye / Magic bus. *(+ dvd)*

S/track review: Well, the WHO were in bullish mood. Opener 'Heaven And Hell' is rough and ready and PETE TOWNSHEND even allows himself a scorching guitar lead, before sneering at the audience: "smile you buggers, pretend it's Christmas". They continue in this raw vein, deliberately exploring their blues rock roots, early number 'I Can't Explain' giving way to the Mose Allison number 'Young Man Blues', and dedicated to all of those who had paid to get in. ROGER DALTREY excels in braying blues man mode, JOHN ENTWISTLE (dressed fetchingly as a skeleton on the night) scales up and down the fretboard with consummate ease, KEITH MOON is a blur of cymbal crashes and maverick rolling fills. The revelation is TOWNSHEND, his playing is ferocious and histrionic, as was customary for him as a musician whose frustration at his technical limitations led to angry and energised performances, but he commands a mastery of the squalls of feedback and teasing of the molten distortion that impresses. Perhaps he was spurred on by a Hendrix performance earlier in the day that didn't live up to his usual peerless standards. It's a brilliantly structured set, bookending TOMMY with choice morsels from their back catalogue, reminding everyone why they got into the WHO in the first place. Particularly refreshing is the relaxed banter back and forth between the band, clearly up for enjoying their moment. The band's centre piece performance of Tommy in almost its entirety (they excise 'Cousin Kevin' and 'Sally Simpson' in particular) draws power from its contextualisation in the band's set; the material gains from losing some of its studio cleanliness. It is instilled with new urgency and vitality, no longer at the behest of its self-conscious theatricality but in thrall to the demands of performance. If the album was becoming a millstone, in the live arena it found its voice. 'I'm Free' in particular suits a raucous live rendition, 'Pinball Wizard' elicits cheers as ever, and 'We're Not Gonna Take It' could be the anti-establishment anthem for the festival. After such a disciplined rendition of their "rock opera" the WHO go back to first principles with covers of Eddie Cochran's 'Summertime Blues' and Johnny Kidd's 'Shakin' All Over', venomous renditions that enact some kind of atavistic shakedown. The band sound, frankly, a bit knackered on the arch 'Substitute' (well, it was very late), but manage to rise to the occasion that 'My Generation' provides, engaging in an undulating and protracted improvisation, seemingly bracing themselves and a few hundred thousand people for the bleakness that the decade would hold. *DF*

Album rating: *7.5

the WHO LIVE AT THE ROYAL ALBERT HALL

aka the WHO & SPECIAL GUESTS LIVE AT THE ROYAL ALBERT HALL

2000 (UK 144m) Image Entertainment

Film genre: Rock-music concert/documentary

Top guns: dir: Dick Carruthers

Stars: the WHO:- Roger Daltrey, Pete Townshend, John Entwistle, John

"Rabbit" Bundrick **, **Zak Starkey** * *(performers)* ← BRITISH ROCK SYMPHONY * ← LIFEHOUSE ** ← THIRTY YEARS OF MAXIMUM R&B LIVE ** ← PSYCHODERELICT ** ← DEEP END **, **Paul Weller** *(performer)* ← a SKIN TOO FEW: THE DAYS OF NICK DRAKE ← PUNK AND ITS AFTERSHOCKS ← PUNK IN LONDON, **Bryan Adams** *(performer)* ← THIRTY YEARS OF MAXIMUM R&B LIVE ← the WALL: LIVE IN BERLIN / → SPIRIT: STALLION OF THE CIMARRON, **Noel Gallagher** *(performer)* → LIVE FOREVER → MAYOR OF THE SUNSET STRIP, **Eddie VEDDER** *(performer)*, **Kelly Jones** *(performer)*, **(Nigel) Kennedy** *(performer)*

Storyline: In 2000, the Who played an end of tour benefit concert (proceeds to the Teenage Cancer Trust) at London's Royal Albert Hall. *MCS*

Movie rating: *8

Visual: dvd in Nov'01 (features documentary & interviews)

Off the record: Kelly Jones was of course, frontman of the Stereophonics.

—

the WHO

Jun 03. (2xcd-box) *S.P.V.; (<093 7488-2>)* 72 Jul03 ☐
– I can't explain / Anyway anyhow anywhere / Pinball wizard / Relay / My wife / The kids are alright / Mary Anne with the shaky hand / Bargain / Magic bus / Who are you / Baba O'Riley (feat. NIGEL KENNEDY) // Drowned / A heart to hang onto / So sad about us / I'm one (feat. EDDIE VEDDER) / Getting in tune (feat. EDDIE VEDDER) / Behind blue eyes (feat. BRYAN ADAMS) / You better you bet / The real me / 5.15 / Won't get fooled again (feat. NOEL GALLAGHER) / Substitute (feat. KELLY JONES) / Let's see action (feat. EDDIE VEDDER) / My generation / See me feel me – Listening to you // *(free bonus disc +=)* – (4 tracks from a February 2002 Royal Albert Hall concert).

S/track review: It doesn't matter if its 1972 or 2002, a WHO concert will always begin with the identifiable intro of 'I Can't Explain', here quickly followed by 'Anyway, Anyhow, Anywhere'. Both are blasted out with a passion and energy that belies the age of the band members. Classics such as 'Pinball Wizard', 'Magic Bus', 'Who Are You', '5:15' and 'Baba O'Riley' have an intensity and edge while 'The Kids Are Alright' is extended to include an extra verse where PETE TOWNSHEND proclaims his own and everybody else's kids as still being alright. It shows that they know they are getting old but it's a poignant inclusion. ROGER DALTREY's voice is still ferocious and you can almost see TOWNSHEND doing the windmill on the guitar with JOHN 'THE OX' ENTWHISTLE standing almost completely still. The album is made all the more special by some well chosen guest appearances. PAUL WELLER joins in for a sublimely bitter version of 'So Sad About Us' while Pearl Jam's EDDIE VEDDER takes up vocal duties for excellent versions of 'I'm One' and 'Getting In Tune' – you can't even falter BRYAN ADAMS who pops up on 'Behind Blue Eyes'. The energy and intensity are sustained for the full two hours and closing songs 'Won't Get Fooled Again', 'Substitute' and 'See Me Feel Me' are excellent while 'My Generation' is suitably raucous. While it might lack some of the reckless abandon of earlier WHO live albums such as 'Live At Leeds', it still shows that they know exactly how to rock'n'roll. Plus it was all for charity and not to top up the pension fund which makes it even better. *CM*

Album rating: *7.5

the WHO ROCKS AMERICA

1983 (Can/US 118m) CBS/Fox

Film genre: Rock-music concert/documentary

Top guns: dir: Richard Namm

Stars: the WHO:- Roger Daltrey, Pete Townshend, John Entwistle, Tim Gorman *, **Kenney Jones** ** *(performers)* ← TONITE LET'S ALL MAKE LOVE IN LONDON ** ← DATELINE DIAMONDS ** / → THIRTY YEARS OF MAXIMUM R&B LIVE *&**

Storyline: The Who's farewell concert – well, not quite, as it subsequently turned out! – on their final leg of their North American tour at the Maple Leaf Gardens in Toronto, Canada, 1982. Kenney Jones (ex-Small Faces, Faces, etc.) had now been the Who drummer for a few years having replaced the enigmatic Keith Moon after his untimely death in '78. *MCS*

Movie rating: *6.5

Visual: video (no audio OST; score: JOHN ENTWISTLE)

Off the record: The **WHO** tracks featured are:- 'My Generation', 'I Can't Explain', 'Dangerous', 'Sister Disco', 'The Quiet One', 'It's Hard', 'Eminence Front', 'Baba O'Riley', 'Boris The Spider', 'Drowned', 'Love Ain't For Keeping', 'Pinball Wizard', 'Squeeze Box', 'Who Are You', 'Love Reign O'er Me', 'Long Live Rock', 'Won't Get Fooled Again', 'Naked Eye', 'Young Man Blues' & 'Twist And Shout' medley. *MCS*

WILCO

Formed: Belleville, Illinois, USA . . . 1994 out of Uncle Tupelo members JEFF TWEEDY, Jay Bennett, John Stirratt and veterans Max Johnston and Ken Coomer. WILCO were off the starting block with 1994's 'A.M.', an enjoyable enough set of uptempo country-rock, although it was nevertheless eclipsed by the 1996 follow-up double-set, 'Being There'. While former writing partner JAY FARRAR (now with Son Volt) continued to come up with the goods, the prospect of an Uncle Tupelo reunion was (at the time) still tantalisingly within reach. However, WILCO returned in the summer of '98, an unlikely collaboration with English bard BILLY BRAGG on a memorable Woody Guthrie tribute album, 'Mermaid Avenue', a set that was documented in the film, 'MAN IN THE SAND' (1999). The following March, the leaders of the alt-country/folk scene released their long-awaited third set, 'Summerteeth' (1999), a UK Top 40 record (Top 100 in the US) that boasted some breezy old tales, opening with minor UK hit, 'Can't Stand It'. A second volume of Guthrie re-writes, 'Mermaid Avenue Vol.2' (2000), couldn't come up with anything special, but it had its moments. WILCO's penchant for uptempo roots-rock wasn't always the best vehicle for presenting the legendary socialist's humorous protest-folk, BRAGG often stealing the limelight. TWEEDY moved even further from both his old sparring partner and his musical roots with 'Yankee Hotel Foxtrot' (2002), a record the band believed in so much they spent a hefty sum buying it back from 'Reprise'; this time documented on 'I AM TRYING TO BREAK YOUR HEART' (named after one of its tracks). Released around the same time was the soundtrack to actor Ethan Hawke's 'CHELSEA WALLS' (2002), composed in large part by TWEEDY and new WILCO drummer Glenn Kotsche. Seemingly in thrall to his newly expanded musical horizons, TWEEDY went on to cut an album's worth of off-kilter experiments with producer O'Rourke and Kotsche. An eponymous set released under the Loose Fur banner in early 2003, the record spliced the various musical personalities in intriguing and often frustrating fashion. 'A Ghost Is Born' (2004) was another thoughtful, multi-faceted meta-pop record, further proof – if needed – of TWEEDY's determination to unshackle his inner changeling (and with a US Top 10/UK Top 50 showing, proof that WILCO's new muse was better appreciated in the States). The subsequent tour saw the replacement of Leroy Bach (who replaced Jay during the 'Yankee . . .' sessions) with Pat Sansone and Nels Cline, with the latter, especially, mainlining much of the invention in concert set, 'Kicking Television: Live In Chicago' (2005). In lieu of another WILCO studio album, fans could take heart in a Loose Fur follow-up, 'Born Again In The USA' (2006), altogether a much less uptight affair. *BG & MCS*

- filmography (composers) {performance} –

Man In The Sand *(1999 {*p} =>)* / **Chelsea Walls** *(2001 OST by TWEEDY =>)* / **I Am Trying To Break Your Heart** *(2002 {*p} =>)* / Evergreen *(2004 score by STIRRATT & Patrick Sansone)* / S&Man *(2006 score by Kotsche, Darin Gray & On Filmore)*

WOODSTOCK

1970 (US 184m) Warner Bros. Pictures (R)

Film genre: Rock/Roots-music concert documentary

Top guns: dir: Michael Wadleigh

Stars: Richie Havens *(performer)* → CATCH MY SOUL → HEARTS OF FIRE → GLASTONBURY → I'M NOT THERE, **Joan BAEZ** *(performer)*, **the WHO:- Pete Townshend, Roger Daltrey, Keith Moon, John Entwistle** *(performers)*, **CROSBY, STILLS & NASH:- David Crosby, Stephen Stills & Graham Nash** *(performers)*, **Sha Na Na:- Jon 'Bowzer' Bauman, Tony Santini** * *(performers)* → GREASE → CADDYSHACK * → FESTIVAL EXPRESS, **Joe COCKER** *(performer)*, **Country Joe (McDONALD) & The Fish** *(performers)*, **Ten Years After:- Alvin Lee, Chick Churchill, Leo Lyons, Ric Lee** *(performers)* → GROUPIES → MESSAGE TO LOVE: THE ISLE OF WIGHT FESTIVAL, **John Sebastian** *(performer)* <= the LOVIN' SPOONFUL =>, **Arlo Guthrie** *(performer)* ← ALICE'S RESTAURANT / → RENALDO AND CLARA → ROADSIDE PROPHETS → the BALLAD OF RAMBLIN' JACK, **Carlos Santana/SANTANA** *(performers)*, **Sly & The Family Stone** *(performers)*, **Jimi HENDRIX** *(performer)*, Max Yasgur *(himself)*, **Jerry Garcia** *(himself)* <= GRATEFUL DEAD =>

Storyline: The seminal, iconic music festival in all its freaked out, mud spattered glory, as the hippie dream reaches its apogee down at Yasgur's farm (actually near Woodstock, New York). No plot as such but just as the label says, three days (15-17 August, 1969) of peace and music. And of course, bad acid. *BG*

Movie rating: *10

Visual: video + dvd

Off the record: (see below)

—

Various Artists

May 70. (t-lp) *Cotillion; <SD-3 500> Atlantic; (2663 001)* [1] Jul70 [35]
– I had a dream (JOHN B. SEBASTIAN) / Going up the country (CANNED HEAT) / Freedom (RICHIE HAVENS) / Rock & soul music (COUNTRY JOE & THE FISH) / Coming into Los Angeles (ARLO GUTHRIE) / At the hop (SHA-NA-NA) / I feel like I'm fixin' to die rag – The "fish" cheer (COUNTRY JOE McDONALD) / Drug store truck drivin' man (JOAN BAEZ featuring JEFFREY SHURTLEFF) / Joe Hill (JOAN BAEZ) / Suite: Judy blue eyes (CROSBY, STILLS & NASH) / Sea of madness (CROSBY, STILLS, NASH & YOUNG) / Wooden ships (CROSBY, STILLS, NASH & YOUNG) / We're not gonna take it (WHO) / With a little help from my friends (JOE COCKER) / Souls sacrifice (SANTANA) / I'm going home (TEN YEARS AFTER) / Volunteers (JEFFERSON AIRPLANE) / Medley: Dance to the music – Music lover – I want to take you higher (SLY & THE FAMILY STONE) / Rainbows all over your blues (JOHN B. SEBASTIAN) / Love march (BUTTERFIELD BLUES BAND) / Star spangled banner – Purple haze – instrumental solo (JIMI HENDRIX). *<(t-c iss.1974; K4 60001)> <(d-cd iss.Jul87; K2 60001)> <(d-cd-iss. Aug94 on 'Warners'; 7567 80593-2)>*

S/track review: Among those artists lucky enough to make the rambling, epoch defining cut of the original 'WOODSTOCK' triple album (drawn from 70+ hours of tape), highlights were many, eccentric and varied: RICHIE HAVENS furiously ad-libbing himself into the mystic on 'Freedom', Ronald Reagan getting a dedication on JOAN BAEZ's 'Drug Store Truck Drivin' Man', SLY & THE FAMILY STONE taking their psychedelic soul to the slumming middle class masses, JIMI HENDRIX mangling 'The Star Spangled Banner' and CANNED HEAT supplying an ad-hoc theme. It's a last hurrah but it doesn't know it; HENDRIX and the 'HEAT's Al Wilson (plus JANIS JOPLIN, who'd belatedly get her own 'Live At Woodstock' album) would be dead within months of each other in the autumn of 1970, SLY notoriously strung out in his Bel Air mansion. The festivals would carry on, but the sense of collective purpose obvious in the soundtrack's pie-eyed announcements would wither on the 70s vine. It's likewise rare for a festival to break a band these days, but several careers hinged upon performances up at Yasgur's farm. SANTANA hadn't even released a single, never mind an album when the ten minute splurge of 'Soul Sacrifice' slayed the crowd and birthed a third world guitar hero, one who's still making No.1 records. JOE COCKER cracked the lucrative US market and laid the groundwork for his 'Mad Dogs And Englishmen' tour via a nail-gargling, crowd pleasing 'With A Little Help From My Friends'; the WHO helped sell Pete Townshend's pioneering rock opera, 'Tommy'; and with uncanny timing, CROSBY, STILLS & NASH – who'd just released their debut album and taken on NEIL YOUNG – effectively made their live curtain-raiser with a ragged and under-rehearsed but well received set (unfairly the best represented of all the acts over the two albums). This is a far from perfect document (especially in its sound quality, for which the sleevenotes supply an apology in advance) but as a freeze frame of an inconceivably more hopeful and less cynical era (even if COUNTRY JOE's pitch-black satire could've been written for Iraq), it's out on its own. And it beats a flat pint of lager in a paper cup any day. Rather than presenting a representative cross-section or highlighting the festival's less famous acts, 'WOODSTOCK TWO' concentrates on the big names. Roughly split into acid jam and polite acoustic, the record affords JIMI HENDRIX, JEFFERSON AIRPLANE and MOUNTAIN most of the floor space on the former, CROSBY, STILLS, NASH & YOUNG (again!) on the latter. In the case of CS&N, the democracy even extends to the songs; CROSBY gets the ponderous and overrated 'Guinnevere', STILLS a luminous '4 + 20' and NASH his cloying celebration (even the band can't help stifling a yawn) of a shiny, happy, pre-Al Quaeda North Africa, 'Marrakesh Express'. MELANIE's stretched, pre-Catatonia phrasing remains an acquired taste and, despite a moving 'Sweet Sir Galahad', JOAN BAEZ is apportioned a miserly one track. Which leaves the jamming. Both HENDRIX and MOUNTAIN contributed to the vocabulary of 70s heavy metal in their own ways. While the impressively sludgy stamp of MOUNTAIN's powerchords live on, it's surprising the extent to which LESLIE WEST's mob have been sidelined in rock history. Out of all the artists on either album, its HENDRIX whose body of work continues to speak loudest, and the compilers of 'Woodstock Two' make – questionably selected – excerpts from his heroically delayed and overly analysed performance their priority. In lieu of the even more heroically belated 'Live At Woodstock' (1999), fans had to content themselves with workouts like 'Jam Back At The House', 'Get My Heart Back Together' and the more potent 'Izabella' (subsequently released as the b-side of his last single before his death). While these lose some of their feral magnetism without the footage, even HENDRIX in second gear beats the dreary JEFFERSON AIRPLANE (and their cliched drug commentary) in first. A missed opportunity for some, and one which too often sounds like an afterthought. *BG*

Album rating: *9 / Woodstock Two: *7 / Woodstock Diaries: *6.5

– spinoff releases, etc. –

Various Artists: Woodstock Two

Mar 71. (d-lp) *Cotillion; <CT-2 400> (K 6002)* [7] Jun71 [ ]
– Jam back at the house (JIMI HENDRIX) / Izabella (JIMI HENDRIX) / Get my heart back together (JIMI HENDRIX) / Saturday afternoon – Won't you try (JEFFERSON AIRPLANE) / Eskimo blue day (JEFFERSON AIRPLANE) / Everything's gonna be

alright (BUTTERFIELD BLUES BAND) / Sweet Sir Galahad (JOAN BAEZ) / Guinnevere (CROSBY, STILLS, NASH & YOUNG) / 4 + 20 (CROSBY, STILLS, NASH & YOUNG) / Marrakesh express (CROSBY, STILLS, NASH & YOUNG) / My beautiful people (MELANIE) / Birthday of the sun (MELANIE) / Blood of the sun (MOUNTAIN) / Theme for an imaginary western (MOUNTAIN) / Woodstock boogie (CANNED HEAT) / Let the sunshine in (the audience on Sunday). *<cd-iss. 1988; 781981-1)>* *<d-cd-iss. Aug94 on 'Warners'; 7567 80594-2)>*

RAVI SHANKAR: At The Woodstock Festival

Sep 72. (lp) *United Artists; (UAG 29379)* ☐ ☐

Various Artists: The Best Of Woodstock

Jun 94. (cd/c) *Atlantic; <(7567 82618-2/-4)>* ☐ ☐
– I had a dream (JOHN B. SEBASTIAN) / Going up the country (CANNED HEAT) / Freedom (RICHIE HAVENS) / The 'Fish' cheer – I feel-like-I'm-fixin'-to-die rag (COUNTRY JOE McDONALD) / Joe Hill (JOAN BAEZ) / Wooden ships (CROSBY, STILLS, NASH & YOUNG) / We're not gonna take it (the WHO) / With a little help from my friends (JOE COCKER) / Soul sacrifice (SANTANA) / Volunteers (JEFFERSON AIRPLANE) / I'm going home (TEN YEARS AFTER) / Star spangled banner – Purple haze – Instrumental solo (JIMI HENDRIX).

JIMI HENDRIX: At Woodstock

Aug 94. (cd/c) *Polydor; (523384-2/-4) M.C.A.; <11063>* [32] [37]
– (introduction) / Fire / Izabella / Hear my train a comin' / Red house / Jam back at the house (beginnings) / Voodoo child (slight return) – Stepping stone / The star spangled banner / Purple haze / Woodstock improvisation / Villanova junction / Farewell.

Various Artists: Woodstock Diary

Sep 94. (cd) *Warners; <(7567 82634-2)>* ☐ ☐
– Let's go get stoned (JOE COCKER) / The weight (BAND) / Mean town blues (JOHNNY WINTER) / Blackbird (CROSBY, STILLS & NASH) / Try (just a little bit harder) (JANIS JOPLIN) / Ball and chain (JANIS JOPLIN) / I can't make it anymore (RICHIE HAVENS) / Somebody to love (JEFFERSON AIRPLANE) / White rabbit (JEFFERSON AIRPLANE) / If I were a carpenter (TIM HARDIN) / Southbound train (MOUNTAIN) / Love city (SLY & THE FAMILY STONE) / I shall be released (JOE COCKER) / Voodoo child (slight return) (JIMI HENDRIX).

JIMI HENDRIX: Live At Woodstock

Jul 99. (d-cd/d-c) *M.C.A.; <(MCD 11987)>* [90] ☐
– (introduction) / Message to love / Hear my train a comin' / Spanish castle magic / Red house / Lover man / Foxy lady / Jam back at the house / Izabella / Fire / Voodoo child (slight return) / The star spangled banner / Purple haze / Woodstock improvisation / Villanova junction / Hey Joe.

WOODSTOCK 94

1994 (US 165m; str8-to-video) Polygram Diversified Entertainment

Film genre: Rock-music concert documentary

Top guns: dir: Bruce Gowers

Stars: Green Day:- Billie Joe Armstrong, Mike Dirnt, Tre Cool *(performers)* → MAYOR OF THE SUNSET STRIP, **AEROSMITH:- Steven Tyler, Joe Perry, Joey Kramer, Brad Whitford, Tom Hamilton** *(performers)*, **the RED HOT CHILI PEPPERS:- Anthony Kiedis, Flea, David M. Navarro, Chad Smith** *(performers)*, **Sheryl Crow** *(performer)* → 54 → DILL SCALLION → WOODSTOCK '99, **Melissa Etheridge** *(performer)* → JACKIE'S BACK! → MY GENERATION, Bob DYLAN *(performer)*, **Blind Melon:- Shannon Hoon, Roger Stevens, Christopher Thorn, Brad Smith, Glen Graham** *(performers)*, **Metallica:- James Hetfield, Kirk Hammett, Lars Ulrich, Jason Newsted** *(performers)* → WOODSTOCK '99 → SOME KIND OF MONSTER, **Salt-N-Pepa:- Cheryl 'Salt' James** *(performer)* ← WHO'S THE MAN?, **Sandra 'Pepa' Denton** *(performer)* ← WHO'S THE MAN? / → JOE'S APARTMENT, **CROSBY, STILLS & NASH** *(performers)*, with **John Sebastian** *(performer)* <= the LOVIN' SPOONFUL =>, **the Neville Brothers:- Aaron, Charles, Art, Cyril** *(performers)*, **Collective Soul:- Ed Roland, Dean Roland, Ross Childress, Will Turpin, Shane Evans** *(performers)* → WOODSTOCK '99, **Joe COCKER** *(performer)*, **Blues Traveler:- John Popper *, Chan Kinchla, Bobby Sheehan, Brendan Hill** *(performers)* → PRIVATE PARTS * → BLUES BROTHERS 2000 → MY GENERATION *, **Henry ROLLINS Band** *(performer/s)*, **Nine Inch Nails:- Trent Reznor *, Robin Finck, Danny Lohner **, Chris Vrenna** *(performers)* ← LIGHT OF DAY / → MY GENERATION → SOME KIND OF MONSTER **, **Traffic:- Steve Winwood** *(performer)* ← GLASTONBURY FAYRE ← CUCUMBER CASTLE ← the GHOST GOES GEAR / → BLUES BROTHERS 2000 → RED, WHITE & BLUES, **Jim Capaldi** *(performer)* → CONCERT FOR GEORGE / **Peter GABRIEL** *(performer)*, **Porno For Pyros:- Perry Farrell *, Stephen Perkins, Martyn LeNoble, Peter DiStefano** *(performer/s)* → GLASTONBURY THE MOVIE * → MY GENERATION *, **Paul Rodgers** * *(performer)* → MESSAGE TO LOVE: THE ISLE OF WIGHT FESTIVAL * & **Blues Revue:- Slash, Neal Schon, Andy Fraser *, Jason Bonham** *(performers)*, **Cypress Hill:- Senen Reyes, Louis Freese, Larry Muggerud, Eric Correa** *(performers)* → RHYME & REASON → HOW HIGH, **the Cranberries:- Dolores O'Riordan, Mike Hogan, Noel Hogan, Fergal Lawler** *(performers)*, **Violent Femmes:- Gordon Gano, Brian Ritchie, Victor DeLorenzo, Guy Hoffman** *(performers)*, **Live:- Ed Kowalczyk, Chad Taylor, Pat Dahlheimer, Chad Gracey** *(performers)* → WOODSTOCK '99, **Candlebox:- Kevin Martin, Peter Klett, Bardi Martin, Scott Mercado Primus:- Les Claypool *, Larry LaLonde, Tim Alexander** *(performers)* ← BILL & TED'S BOGUS JOURNEY / → PINK AS THE DAY SHE WAS BORN → WE SOLD OUR SOULS FOR ROCK'N'ROLL → RISING LOW → ELECTRIC APRICOT: QUEST FOR FESTEROO, **Jackyl:- Jesse James Dupree, Jimmy Stiff, Jeff Worley, Tom Bettini, Chris Worley** *(performers)*, others include:- **Arrested Development** *(performers)*, **King's X** *(performers)*, **Country Joe McDONALD with the Fugs** *(performers)*, **the Allman Brothers Band** *(performers)*, **the BAND with Bob Weir** *(performers)*, **Youssou N'Dour** *(performer)*, **Counting Crows** *(performers)*, **Spin Doctors** *(performers)*

Storyline: "2 More Days of Peace & Music" to celebrate the 25th anniversary of the original Woodstock Festival in 1969. Dubbed "Mudstock" – wasn't the first one muddy?! – the scheduled 2 days (August 13th & 14th, 1994) turned into 3 days at Saugerties, New York, when the organizers added the 12th due to increased ticket demand. Free it was not, sponsorship from the likes of Pepsi and the schizoid arrangement of previous Woodstock 69'ers and nu-rockers, made it more "Would-shock than Woodstock". *MCS*

Movie rating: *5

Visual: video: Nov'94 on 'Polygram'; *<633367>*

Off the record: Blind Melon's **Shannon Hoon** (b.26 Sep'67, Lafayette, Indiana) was to die of a drug overdose in New Orleans on 21st October, 1995. *MCS*

Various Artists

Nov 94. (d-cd/d-c) *A&M; <(540289-2/-4)>* [50] ☐
– Selling the drama (LIVE) / But anyway (BLUES TRAVELER) / I'm the only one (MELISSA ETHERIDGE) / Feelin' alright (JOE COCKER) / Dreams (the CRANBERRIES) / Soup (BLIND MELON) / When I come around (GREEN DAY) / Shoop (SALT-N-PEPA) / Blood sugar sex magick (the RED HOT CHILI PEPPERS) / Porno for pyros (PORNO FOR PYROS) / Those damned blue-collar tweekers (PRIMUS) / Headed for destruction (JACKYL) / Draw the line – F.I.N.E. (AEROSMITH) / Happiness in slavery (NINE INCH NAILS) // For whom the bell tolls (METALLICA) / The hunter (PAUL RODGERS & BLUES REVUE) / Come together (the NEVILLE BROTHERS) / Run, baby, run (SHERYL CROW) / Deja vu (CROSBY, STILLS & NASH) / Dance, motherfucker, dance! – Kiss off (VIOLENT FEMMES) / Shine (COLLECTIVE SOUL) / Arrow (CANDLEBOX) / How I could just kill a man (CYPRESS HILL) / Right here too much (the ROLLINS BAND) / Highway 61 revisited (BOB DYLAN) / Pearly queen (TRAFFIC) / Biko (PETER GABRIEL).

S/track review: Lightning doesn't strike twice. It's an old cliché but one that certainly rings true here. The original 'WOODSTOCK' is legendary, the perfect festival at a time of peace and love with a host of legendary performances. We have to take the word of those that were there and they aren't exactly the most reliable but for 'WOODSTOCK 94' we have evidence, unfortunately it only serves to bolster the prosecution's case. There are a host of different bands here, some good and some not, represented by one song each, which isn't always their best either. As a result the highlights are few and far between. JOE COCKER would have the whole field dancing in their wellies on 'Feelin' Alright' and 'Biko' by PETER GABRIEL is an rousing song in keeping with the original ethos of the festival. Most likely the biggest difference between this and the original festival is that the music on offer here is more eclectic. There is the folk rock of CROSBY STILLS & NASH, the funk rock of RED HOT CHILI PEPPERS and GREEN DAY's own brand of punk rock, which sit alongside the industrial metal of NINE INCH NAILS, CYPRESS HILL's hard-hittin' hip hop and the R&B of SALT-N-PEPA, all to varying degrees of success. Unfortunately, there are too many disappointments to make this a must buy. METALLICA sound sluggish on 'For Whom The Bell Tolls' while LIVE's 'Selling The Drama', BLUES TRAVELER's 'But Anyway' and 'Dance, Motherfucker, Dance' from VIOLENT FEMMES are just awful. Other tracks worth mentioning are the NEVILLE BROTHERS' cover of the Beatles 'Come Together' and 'Dreams' by the CRANBERRIES, but overall the soundtrack to 'WOODSTOCK 94' fails to give a feel for the festival or the artists who performed there. *CM*

Album rating: *5

WOODSTOCK '99

1999 (US 149m TV) Metropolitan Entertainment Group

Film genre: Rock-music concert

Top guns: no director to speak of! just a camera crew

Stars: Korn:- Jonathan Davis *, Brian 'Head' Welch, James 'Munky' Shaffer **, Fieldy, David Silveria *(performers)* ← QUEEN OF THE DAMNED * → METAL: A HEADBANGER'S JOURNEY **, **Dave Matthews Band** *(performer/s)*, **the RED HOT CHILI PEPPERS:- Anthony Kiedis, Flea, John Frusciante, Chad Smith** *(performers)*, **Sheryl Crow** *(performer)* ← DILL SCALLION ← 54 ← WOODSTOCK 94, **Kid Rock; w/ Uncle Kracker, Jimmie Bones, Joe C.** *(performer/s)*, **Metallica:- James Hetfield, Kirk Hammett, Lars Ulrich, Jason Newsted** *(performers)* ← WOODSTOCK 94 / → SOME KIND OF MONSTER, **Live:- Ed Kowalczyk, Chad Taylor, Pat Dahlheimer, Chad Gracey** *(performers)* ← WOODSTOCK 94, **Elvis COSTELLO** *(performer)*, **Alanis Morissette** *(performer)* ← FREE TIBET, **Limp Bizkit:- Fred Durst *, Wes Borland, Sam Rivers, John Otto, Leor Dimant** *(performers)* → BE COOL *, **Everlast** *(performer)* ← JUDGMENT NIGHT ← WHO'S THE MAN?, **Jamiroquai** *(performer)*, **Megadeth:- Dave Mustaine *, Marty Friedman, Dave Ellefson, Jimmy DeGrasso **** *(performers)* ← WAYNE'S WORLD ** ← the DECLINE OF WESTERN CIVILIZATION 2: THE METAL YEARS / → SOME KIND OF MONSTER, **Jewel** *(performer)* → WALK HARD: THE DEWEY COX STORY, **Everclear:- Art Alexakis, Craig Montoya, Greg Eklund** *(performers)*, **Bruce Hornsby** *(performer)*, **Rusted Root:- Mike Glabicki, John Buynak, Liz Berlin, Jim DiSpirito, Patrick Norman, Jim Donovan** *(performers)*, the **Brian Setzer Orchestra** *(performers)* ← LA BAMBA / → the COUNTRY BEARS, **Creed:- Scott Stapp, Mark Tremonti, Brian Marshall, Scott Phillips** *(performers)* with **Robby Kreiger** *(performer)* ← the DOORS ARE OPEN / → RAMONES RAW, **Willie NELSON** *(performer)*, **Rage Against The Machine:- Zack DeLa Rocha, Tom Morello, Timmy C, Brad Wilk** *(performers)*, **the Offspring:- Dexter Holland, Kevin "Noodles" Wasserman, Greg Kriesel, Ron Welty** *(performers)*, **Lit:- A.J. Popoff, Jeremy Popoff, Kevin Baldes, Allen Schellenberger** *(performers)*, **the Roots:- Tariq Trotter, Ahmir-Khalib Thompson, Malik Abdul-Basit, Leonard Hubbard** *(performers)* → BROOKLYN BABYLON → BROWN SUGAR → FADE TO BLACK → BLOCK PARTY, **Bush:- Gavin Rossdale, Nigel Pulsford, Dave Parsons, Robin Goodridge** *(performers)*, **Godsmack:- Sully Emma, Tony Rombola, Robbie Merrill, Tommy Stewart** *(performers)* → WE SOLD OUR SOULS FOR ROCK'N'ROLL, **Buckcherry:- Joshua Todd, Keith Nelson, Yogi, Jon Brightman, Devon Glenn** *(performers)* → the BANGER SISTERS, **DMX** *(performer)*, **Sevendust:- Lajon Witherspoon, Clint Lowery, John Connelly, Vinnie Hornsby, Morgan Rose** *(performers)*, **G. Love & Special Sauce:- Jim Prescott, Jeff Clemens** *(performers)*, **the Chemical Brothers:- Tom Rowlands, Ed Simons** *(performers)*, **Guster:- Adam Gardner, Ryan Miller, Brian Rosenworcel** *(performers)*, **Our Lady Peace:- Raine Maida, Mike Turner, Duncan Coutts, Jeremy Taggart** *(performers)*

Storyline: The 30th anniversary (in Rome, New York) of the legendary peace & love Woodstock Festival, but the times they were a-changin' as the inflated prices of water and food resulted in some looting and "Wicker Man"-like pyres. Oh yeah, and there were 30 acts on parade from all genres. *MCS*

Movie rating: *5

Visual: video + dvd

Off the record: JAMES BROWN opened the shorter-lengthed video with 'Sex Machine'.

—

Various Artists

Oct 99. (d-cd/d-c) *Sony; <63770-2/-4>* [32] [ ]
– Blind (KORN) / The kids aren't alright (the OFFSPRING) / Four (LIT) / Lit up (BUCKCHERRY) / Bawitdaba (KID ROCK) / Show me what you got (LIMP BIZKIT) / Bulls on parade (RAGE AGAINST THE MACHINE) / Creeping death (METALLICA) / Roadhouse blues (CREED feat. ROBBY KRIEGER) / Bitch (SEVENDUST) / Stop being greedy (DMX) / Keep away (GODSMACK) / Secret place (MEGADETH) / Everything zen (BUSH) / I alone (LIVE) / Fire (the RED HOT CHILI PEPPERS) // Tripping billies (DAVE MATTHEWS BAND) / Rock this town (the BRIAN SETZER ORCHESTRA) / Down so long (JEWEL) / Ends (EVERLAST) / Santa Monica (watch the world die) (EVERCLEAR) / If it makes you happy (SHERYL CROW) / Alison (ELVIS COSTELLO) / So pure (ALANIS MORISSETTE) / Black Capricorn day (JAMIROQUAI) / Cold beverage (G LOVE & SPECIAL SAUCE) / Block rockin' beats (the CHEMICAL BROTHERS) / Adrenaline! (the ROOTS) / Airport song (GUSTER) / Superman's dead (OUR LADY PEACE) / Ecstasy (RUSTED ROOT) / Resting place (BRUCE HORNSBY). *<re-iss. Feb00 as 2 "red" & "blue" cd's>*

S/track review: Thirty years on from the original festival, 'WOODSTOCK '99' replaced peace and love with extortionate prices and moshpit rape, culminating in the whole event going up in flames during the RED HOT CHILI PEPPERS' set, commemorated here with the spontaneous, super-frenetic cover of 'Fire'. The soundtrack divides the event into the "red" disc of alt-rock and metal, and the "blue" disc comprising everything else, from big beat to hip-hop to acoustic singer-songwriter fare. The "red" disc evinces the disjuncture between the old and the new spirit of proceedings with a plethora of agitated and seething performances, founded on (male) frustration and loathing. KORN deliver a spectacularly aggressive and chunky rendition of their classic, 'Blind', KID ROCK represents the drunken meathead contingent of the audience with a massive, grooving 'Bawitdaba', and LIMP BIZKIT soundtrack the moshpit assaults with the work-in-progress, 'Show Me What You Got'. What strikes the listener is how much these sets drip with base aggression, the seed of the violence to come borne in their agitation. But that's not to say that some of the heavier bands don't bring class to the proceedings; RAGE AGAINST THE MACHINE's political firebrand 'Bulls On Parade' is as funky and dignified in its righteous fury as ever. METALLICA imperiously slice through 'Creeping Death' and CREED subvert all expectations when ROBBY KRIEGER joins them to lick his way through a more than respectable rendition of the Doors classic 'Roadhouse Blues'. Nothing demonstrates the laughably grotesque mismatch of setting and musical circumstance than Lajon Witherspoon howling "Look at that fucking rainbow" during SEVENDUST's hateful, raging 'Bitch'. The "blue" disc is nowhere near as interesting in the context of what occurred offstage, but DAVE MATTHEWS drawls his way through 'Tripping Billies' adequately enough, the BRIAN SETZER ORCHESTRA impress, and ELVIS COSTELLO,

ALANIS MORISSETTE and SHERYL CROW are as dependable if unremarkable as ever, all once regarded as essential, now essentially past it. The CHEMICAL BROTHERS and the ROOTS bring the festival to life with end-of-the-century sounds, reminding us that EVERLAST (growling his way like a countrified Tom Waits tribute act through 'Ends') should really have stuck with House Of Pain. BRUCE HORNSBY is so middle-of-the-road he could be the markings, at least RUSTED ROOT's Spanish-inflected 'Ecstasy' sparks and parps with invention and energy. But it would be no surprise if OUR LADY PEACE's execrable 'Superman's Dead' was really responsible for sparking the riots that followed. *DF*

Album rating: *4

☐ X: the band
(⇒ John DOE)

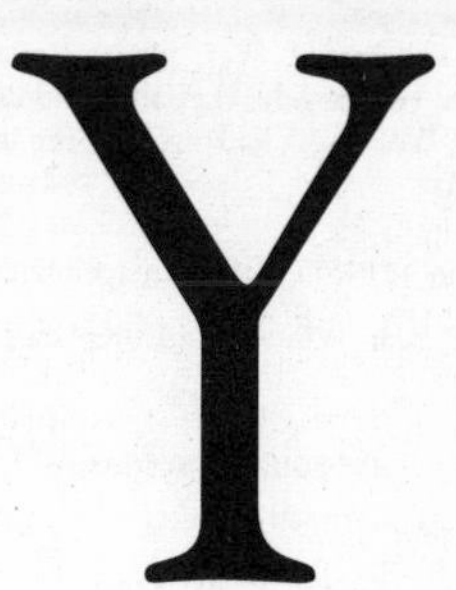

YEAR OF THE HORSE: NEIL YOUNG & CRAZY HORSE LIVE

1997 (US 106m w/b&w) Shakey Pictures (R)

Film genre: Rock-music concert/documentary

Top guns: dir: Jim Jarmusch ← DEAD MAN ← NIGHT ON EARTH ← MYSTERY TRAIN ← DOWN BY LAW / → GHOST DOG: THE WAY OF THE SAMURAI → COFFEE AND CIGARETTES

Stars: Neil YOUNG *(performer)*, **& Crazy Horse:- Frank 'Pancho' Sampedro, Billy Talbot, Ralph Molina** *(performers)* ← RUST NEVER SLEEPS, Jim Jarmusch *(himself)* ← SLING BLADE ← LENINGRAD COWBOYS GO AMERICA ← CANDY MOUNTAIN ← STRAIGHT TO HELL / → I PUT A SPELL ON ME → the FUTURE IS UNWRITTEN, Larry Cragg *(master guitar tech)* → HEART OF GOLD, Scott Young *(Neil's dad)*, Keith Wissmar *(lightning wizard)*, Elliot Roberts *(manager extraordinaire)*

Storyline: "A tale of 4 guys who like to rock" was the underwhelming tagline, the four guys being Neil Young & Crazy Horse live on tour in 1996 – a wee journey through the past also entitled the viewer to a few choice backstage clips, while up to date interviews with the band by cult director Jim Jarmusch (on his handheld Super-8) kept the documentary and music flowing. *MCS*

Movie rating: *6

Visual: video + dvd (no audio OST; but see below)

Off the record: Neil YOUNG & Crazy Horse confused many by releasing a live set of the same name, although only a handful of songs (marked * below) featured in the film; tracks not on record but in film are as follows: 'Fuckin' Up', 'Stupid Girl', 'Tonight's The Night', 'My Girl', 'Like A Hurricane' and 'Music Arcade'. *MCS*

– associated release –

NEIL YOUNG & CRAZY HORSE: Year Of The Horse

Jun 97. (cd/c/d-lp) *Reprise; <(9362 46652-2/-4/-1)>* [57] [36]
– When you dance I can really love / Barstool blues (*) / When your lonely heart breaks / Mr. Soul / Big time (*) / Pocahontas / Human highway / Slip away (*) / Scattered (let's think about livin') / Danger bird / Prisoners / Sedan delivery (*) *[not on LP]*.

YESSONGS

1975 (UK 70m) AIOK Pictures / Ellman Film Enterprises

Film genre: Prog Rock-music concert/documentary

Top guns: dir: Peter Neal ← GLASTONBURY FAYRE ← BE GLAD FOR THE SONG HAS NO ENDING ← EXPERIENCE

Stars: Yes:- Jon Anderson *(performer)*, **Steve Howe** *(performer)*, **Rick**

WAKEMAN *(performer)*, **Chris Squire** *(performer)* → RISING LOW, **Alan White** *(performer)*

Storyline: Prog-rock supergroup, Yes, play a concert to promote their recently released 'Close To The Edge' LP, at London's Rainbow Theatre late in 1972. The triple-LP, 'Yessongs', had already been issued in 1973. *MCS*

Movie rating: *7

Visual: video on 'Rhino' (2196) / dvd on Image (4209)

Off the record: Yes . . . Alan White had just replaced Bill Bruford when the gigs happened

– associated release –

YES: Yessongs *[not in film *]*

May 73. (t-lp/d-c) *Atlantic; (K/K4 60045) <SD3 100>* 1 12
– (opening excerpt from 'Firebird Suite') / Siberian Khatru [*] / Heart of the sunrise [*] / Perpetual change [*] / And you and I; (a) Cord of life – (b) Eclipse – (c) The preacher the teacher – (d) The apocalypse / Mood for a day [*] / (excerpts from 'The Six Wives Of Henry VIII') / Roundabout / I've seen all good people; Your move – All good people / Long distance runaround [*] / The fish (Shindleria Praematurus) [*] / Close to the edge (a) The solid time of change – (b) Total mass retain – (c) I get up I get down – (d) Seasons of man / Yours is no disgrace / Starship trooper (a) Life seeker – (b) Disillusion – (c) Wurm. *(d-cd-iss. Feb87; K2 60045) (re-iss. d-cd Oct94 on 'East West'; 7567 82682-2)*

YOU ARE WHAT YOU EAT

1968 (US 75m) Natoma Productions

Film genre: political/Rock-music documentary

Top guns: dir: Barry Feinstein (+ cinemaphotographer)

Stars: Peter Yarrow *(himself)* ← FESTIVAL / → NO DIRECTION HOME, **Tiny Tim** *(himself)* → ONE-TRICK PONY → MESSAGE TO LOVE: THE ISLE OF WIGHT FESTIVAL → PRIVATE PARTS, **Paul Butterfield** *(himself)* ← FESTIVAL / → STEELYARD BLUES → the LAST WALTZ → GODFATHERS AND SONS, **Barry McGuire** *(himself)*, **David Crosby** *(himself)* <= CROSBY, STILLS & NASH =>, John Simon *(himself)*, John Herald *(himself)*, (Emperor) Rosko *(himself)* → FLAME, Dave Dixon *(himself)*, **Harper's Bizarre** *(themselves)*

Storyline: Set in San Francisco during the summer of love, the film is a collection of movie clips set to the music of Tiny Tim, Pete Yarrow and other stars of the time. Capturing the innocence of the free love era (before such things as AIDS and hard drugs) we see ritual dancing, screaming Beatles fans, a pop group eating flowers (hence the title) and a never-to-be-forgotten German helmet commercial. Cool, man. *JZ*

Movie rating: *5.5

Visual: video by Ivy

Off the record: (see below)

—

Various Artists (composer: JOHN SIMON *)

1969. (lp) *Columbia; <OS 3240> C.B.S.; (70045)*
– Teenage fair – helmet commercial (ROSKO) / Moments of soft persuasion (PETER YARROW) / Silly girl (PETER YARROW) / Desert Moog music (*) / Be my baby (TINY TIM) / The family dog (JOHN HEROLD) / The nude dance (HAMSA EL DIN) / My name is Jack (*) / I got you babe (TINY TIM and ELEANOR BARUCHIAN) / You are what you eat (PAUL BUTTERFIELD) / Beach music (*) / The Wabe (PETER YARROW and *) / Don't remind me now of time (PETER YARROW) / Painting for freakout (*) / Freakout (ELECTRIC FLAG and *).

S/track review: Frustratingly omitting any of the Frank Zappa music that featured in the movie, this is a faithful companion-piece to the celluloid freak-out which gave the Stones their tongue logo. It's the real thing – which means random snatches of goofy dialogue and disjointed bits of music, plenty of tiresome self-congratulatory zaniness of the sort exemplified by TINY TIM's yodelling falsetto and a general shapelessness which is never redeemed by sufficient quantities of wit or good music. JOHN SIMON (later known for his production work for the Band, Dylan and Joni Mitchell) provides some generic instrumentals, his own 'My Name Is Jack' (which was a hit for Manfred Mann the same year) and an avalanche of quirky sounds that fail to drown out a routine jam by the ELECTRIC FLAG. There is some drippy folk by PETER YARROW that actually makes you miss Paul & Mary, the sound of somebody twiddling with the knobs on a Moog synthesizer, and a couple of snatches of PAUL BUTTERFIELD on harp and vocals. But wait, who is that backing the height-challenged one as he screeches unbearably through 'I Got You' and 'Be My Baby'? Yes brothers and sisters, that really is ROBBIE ROBERTSON, GARTH HUDSON, RICK DANKO and RICHARD MANUEL, biding their time in hippiedom before reinventing themselves as the BAND. How Levon Helm must have sniggered. *ND*

Album rating: *3.5

YOU'RE GONNA MISS ME

2007 (US 92m) Palm Pictures

Film genre: Rock-music documentary/bio-pic

Top guns: dir: Keven McAlester

Stars: Roger Kynard "Roky" Erickson *(himself/performer)*, Evelyn Erickson *(herself)*, Sumner Erickson *(himself)*, **Gibby Haynes** *(himself)* ← the DEVIL AND DANIEL JOHNSON ← DEAD MAN, **Billy Gibbons** *(himself)*, **Patti Smith** *(herself)* ← BENJAMIN SMOKE ← ROCK AND ROLL HEART ← the BLANK GENERATION, **Thurston Moore** *(himself)* <= SONIC YOUTH =>, Byron Coley *(himself)*

Storyline: The life and indeed hard-drug times of pioneering, psychedelic rock star, Roky Erickson, from his heady days in the mid-60s with his band, 13th Floor Elevators, to his mental breakdown in the 70s and now a poor recluse in a filthy apartment near Austin, Texas. *MCS*

Movie rating: *8

Visual: dvd

Off the record: Roky Erickson (b. Roger Kynard Erickson, 15 Jul'47, Dallas, Texas, USA) dropped out of school to form his first band, the Spades, in Austin, Texas, 1965. One of his/their first cuts, 'You're Gonna Miss Me', gradually found a market when released on the small 'Zero' label. The record gained national notoriety in early '66 after being picked up by the 'International Artists' label. Around this time, self-styled psychedelic explorer, Tommy Hall, had introduced Erickson to other likeminded musicians and the 13th Floor Elevators were launched into orbit, and indeed the US Top 60. The frenzied garage thrash of 'You're Gonna Miss Me' stood out from the pack by dint of Erickson's apocalyptic vocal threats and Hall's bizarre amplified jug playing. In addition to his idiosyncratic musical accompaniment, Hall penned most of the lyrics, setting out his agenda according to the chemically-enhanced evolution-of-man ethos espoused by the likes of acid guru, Timothy Leary. Debuting with 'The Psychedelic Sounds Of The 13th Floor Elevators' in '66, the band had unleashed nothing less than a musical manifesto for mind expansion. But if the idea was to promote the use of hallucinogenics, then the sirens on the DMT-tribute, 'Fire Engine', surely encouraged any sane person never to go near the stuff, sounding more like the tortured wailing of lost, limbo-locked souls. The follow-up LP, 'Easter Everywhere' (1967), was a slightly more contemplative affair, a driving tour de force of garage meets psychedelia. Inevitably, the Texan police were none too amused with the band's flagrant advocacy of drugs and after escalating harassment, Erickson found himself in court shortly after the album's release. Charged with possession of a small amount of marijuana, he was faced with a choice of jail or mental hospital. He rather ill-advisedly chose the latter. This effectively signalled the end for the band, although a disappointing live

album was released the following year and a final studio album appeared in 1969. Subjected to years of mind-numbing drugs and electro shock therapy, Roky was finally released in 1972 after a judge declared him sane. Ironically, no doubt somewhat less sane after this experience, Erickson started making music again, forming a band, Blieb Alien, and immersing himself in B-movie horror nonsense. After a stint in the studio with fellow Texan, Doug Sahm, Erickson released the inspired psychosis of the 'Red Temple Prayer (Two Headed Dog)' single in 1975. An album, 'Roky Erickson & The Aliens' surfaced in 1980 and included such wholesome fare as 'Mine, Mine, Mind', 'It's A Cold Night For Alligators' and a version of 'Two Headed Dog'. Yet this was no po-faced heavy-metal posturing, Roky actually believed what he was singing about, lending the record a certain level of intensity, despite the cliched hard-rock backing. A series of singles and compilations appeared sporadically throughout the 80s, and after Erickson was hospitalised again for a short period, 'Warner Bros.' executive and longtime 'Elevators fan, Bill Bentley, masterminded a tribute album, 'Where The Pyramid Meets The Eye', featuring the likes of the Jesus & Mary Chain and Julian Cope. Similar in some respects to Syd Barrett, history paints the man Roky as an acid casualty, and while he definitely appears to live in a world of his own making, his wayward genius continues to win the respect and admiration of fans the world over.
BG & MCS

—

ROKY ERICKSON (*)

Jul 07. (cd) *Palm Pictures; <PALMCD 2139>* [ ] [-]
– You're gonna miss me (the 13th FLOOR ELEVATORS) / Fire engine (the 13th FLOOR ELEVATORS) / Starry eyes (*) / Bloody hammer (* & the ALIENS) / Two headed dog (red temple prayer) (* & the ALIENS) / For you (I'd do anything) (*) / Mine, mine, mind (* & the ALIENS) / Unforced peace (*) / You don't love me yet (*) / The wind and more (* & the ALIENS) / It's a cold night for alligators (* & the ALIENS) / Goodbye sweet dreams (*).

S/track review: The enigmatic but fractured psychedelic soul of former 13th FLOOR ELEVATORS frontman, ROKY ERICKSON, comes under the spotlight via this lifespanning compilation soundtrack. 'YOU'RE GONNA MISS ME' ceremoniously kicks off with the 13th FLOOR ELEVATORS' storming, garage-rock title track, a mind-blowing record that sparked off the psychedelic movement in the mid-60s. ERICKSON's accented vox is drawled, screechy and indeed post-Burdon, and how can one forget the frenetic harmonica playing towards the end of the song. 'Fire Engine' keeps the motor running so to speak, but this is where, sadly, the 13th FLOOR ELEVATORS bow out, at least in terms of this OST. The remaining ten tracks were all down to either Roky solo or ERICKSON & THE ALIENS; in fact track 3, 'Starry Eyes' & track 5, 'Two Headed Dog (Red Temple Prayer)', stemmed from both sides of a comeback single in '75. The former B-side is uncharacteristically nice'n'easy, leaning as it does on Buddy Holly, while the latter A-side (this is the version with the ALIENS) chooses the route of John Fogerty for inspiration. Although you can hear hesitation and anxious tension in his expressions and manic lyrics, 'Bloody Hammer' and 'It's A Cold Night For Alligators' should please many bluesy hard-rock fans. Whether Roky had heard the work of Nick Lowe before he wrote 'Mine, Mine, Mind' (the Sponge Records version is featured here) is up for conjecture, although with ERICKSON's wayward genius it's more likely to be coincidence rather than anything untoward. Recorded, one surmises, between his stretch spent in Rusk State Hospital (c. 1971-1972), 'Unforced Peace' is a lo-fi field-recording of sorts, and therefore well ahead of its time. Another from the vaults, 'You Don't Love Me Yet', has aspirations to become a jangly Byrds track, while 'The Wind And More' is another taken from the brilliant 'Roky Erickson & The Aliens' sessions. Of the two previously unreleased cuts, the Buddy Holly-esque 'For You (I'd Do Anything)' comes off better than the unplugged and downbeat finale, 'Goodbye Sweet Dreams'. *MCS*

Album rating: *7.5

Z

Frank ZAPPA

Born: 21 Dec'40, Baltimore, Maryland, USA. The bête noire of America's moral majority and a ferociously articulate proponent of freedom of expression, FRANK ZAPPA bequeathed a recorded legacy as satirically obdurate and creatively misunderstood as it was stylistically eclectic. By the time of his death on 4th December 1993, he had amassed a back catalogue of almost 60 studio/live albums, encompassing contemporary composition and dadaist jazz, highbrow art and lowbrow humour. A cultural and social commentator par excellance, ZAPPA's unique world view was cannily disseminated through the rock idiom, even if his guiding influence was French composer Edgar Varèse and his broader frame of reference more European than American. Inevitably he also dabbled in film, composing the score and writing the title song for cult Timothy Carey B-movie, 'The World's Greatest Sinner' (1962), long before he began sending up flower power with the Mothers Of Invention. His score for the even more obscure western, 'Run Home Slow' (1965), generated the cash for his own Studio Z, anticipating the man's doggedly self-reliant ethos. He subsequently diversified into acting, reuniting with Carey in the freewheeling Bob Rafaelson-directed MONKEES vehicle, 'HEAD' (1968). The following year saw the release of 'UNCLE MEAT' (1969), nothing less than a sprawling, overdub frenzied reinvention of the rock album format, cutting and pasting everything from avant-garde composition and dadaist jazz to louche dialogue, satirical skits and mutant doo-wop. While conceived as the soundtrack to a film of the same name, the ZAPPA-directed screen version of '..MEAT' didn't see the light of day until almost two decades later. So it was that the man's cinematic entrée was actually '200 MOTELS' (1971), a gratuitously gonzoid representation of the hard touring lifestyle written and directed by ZAPPA himself. The partly orchestrated (courtesy of the Royal Philharmonic) soundtrack – a typically disjointed melee of classical gas, pyrotechnical smut and redneck baiting – was belatedly re-issued by 'Rykodisc' in the late 90s (happily leading to the same label's re-issue and remastering of the whole FZ catalogue) while the film also inspired a spin-off stage show banned from London's Royal Albert Hall. Although ZAPPA's subsequent screen ventures were confined largely to concert footage and documentary, his partnership with animator Bruce Bickford – initiated on 1979 film, 'BABY SNAKES' – found him composing the score for the clay animation 'Frank Zappa Presents: The Amazing Mr Bickford' (1988).
BG

- filmography (composer) {acting} [dir] –

the World's Greatest Sinner *(1962)* / Run Home Slow *(1965; there is a bootleg!)* / **Head** *(1968 {b} OST by MONKEES =>)* / **Amougies** *(1970 {p} =>)* / **200 Motels** *(1971 {a} [s-w + dir] OST =>)* / **Baby Snakes** *(1979 OST =>)* / the

Boy Who Left Home To Find Out About The Shivers *(1981 TV)* / the Amazing Mr. Bickford *(1987 [dir])* / **Uncle Meat: The Mothers Of Invention Movie** *(1987 [dir] {p} 1969 OST by the MOTHERS OF INVENTION =>)* / Cousteau: Alaska: Outrage At Valdez *(1989)* / Peefeeyatko *(1991 {*c})* / **Derailroaded** *(2005 {c/p} =>)*

ZIGGY STARDUST – THE MOTION PICTURE

1983 (US 91m) 20th Century Fox International (PG)

Film genre: Rock-music concert/documentary

Top guns: dir: D.A. Pennebaker ← MONTEREY POP ← DON'T LOOK BACK / → 101 → DOWN FROM THE MOUNTAIN → ONLY THE STRONG SURVIVE

Stars: David BOWIE *(performer)*+ band:- **Mick Ronson** ← RENALDO AND CLARA, **Trevor Bolder + Woody Woodmansey** / Angie Bowie *(herself)*, **Ringo Starr** *(himself)* <= the BEATLES =>

Storyline: On the 3rd of July 1973, the flamboyant David Bowie performed his "final" concert at London's Hammersmith Theatre under the "Ziggy Stardust" alter-ego/persona – some of his fans mistakenly thought Bowie himself was retiring! Rockumentary maker D.A. Pennebaker (famous for 'Don't Look Back' and 'Monterey Pop') was on hand to direct Bowie and his Spiders From Mars throughout this historic gig, screened with behind-the scenes footage and initially aired by America's ABC-TV shortly afterwards. It would be around a decade later that the feature-length movie was put on general release. *MCS*

Movie rating: *5

Visual: video + dvd

Off the record: Mick Ronson was of course BOWIE's sidekick and guitarist. Born in Hull on the 26th May, 1946, he released two LPs in the mid 70s, 'Slaughter On Tenth Avenue' & 'Play Don't Worry'. Sadly, he died of liver cancer on the 29th of April, 1993. *MCS*

—

DAVID BOWIE

Oct 83. (d-lp/d-c) *R.C.A.; <AF1/AFK1 4862> (PL/PK 84862)* [89] [17]
– Hang on to yourself / Ziggy Stardust / Watch that man / Wild eyed boy from Freecloud / All the young dudes – Oh! you pretty things / Moonage daydream / Space oddity / My death / Cracked actor / Time / Width of a circle / Changes / Let's spend the night together / Suffragette city / White light – white heat / Rock and roll suicide. *(cd-iss. Sep92 on 'E.M.I.'; CDP 780411-2)*

S/track review: With the motion picture panned by most critics for its fly-on-the-wall approach to all that surrounded the legend that was BOWIE/ZIGGY, it was not a surprise when the double-LP release (once a bootleg!) took the same flak. Important in some respects, in that it represented BOWIE in all his ZIGGY-period rock'n'roll glory, it nevertheless missed an opportunity to bridge the ever-widening gap for loyal fans who'd bought BOWIE recordings since 1973; there had also been two double-sets, 'David Live' (1975) and 'Stage' (1978) to more than compensate live concert aficionados. "The Rise And Fall Of Ziggy Stardust . . ." studio tracks (dating from '72) were represented here in full force: 'Hang On To Yourself', 'Ziggy Stardust', 'Moonage Daydream', 'Suffragette City' and 'Rock And Roll Suicide', all just short of the knock-out punch. Premiered – as was much of that year's Ziggy Stardust tour – were pre-'Aladdin Sane' gems such as 'Watch That Man', 'Cracked Actor', 'Time' and the Rolling Stones cover, 'Let's Spend The Night Together', while BOWIE and Co rehashed the Velvet Underground's 'White Light / White Heat' (a minor UK hit) and Jacques Brel's 'My Death'. Of the pre-Ziggy days, 'Space Oddity', 'Wild Eyed Boy From Freecloud', 'The Width Of A Circle' and 'Changes', were present also, although it would be his own medley arrangement of 'All The Young Dudes' & 'Oh! You Pretty Thing' – previously loaned out to friends Mott The Hoople & Peter Noone respectively, that didn't quite cut it. On a final note, this should've been a great BOWIE set, the shock is, it wasn't! Pick another bootleg to see the difference. *MCS*

Album rating: *4.5

– spinoff hits, etc. –

DAVID BOWIE: White Light – White Heat / Cracked Actor
Oct 83. (7") *<13660> (RCA 372)* [ ] [46]

Section 3

Pop/Rock Scores
and
Blaxploitation

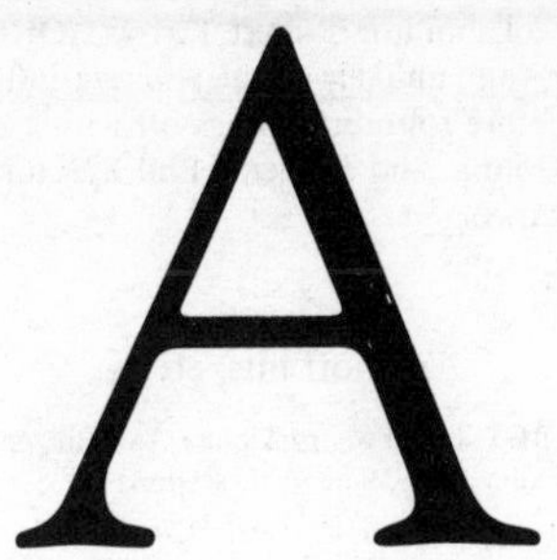

AARON LOVES ANGELA

1975 (US 99m) Aaron Angela Company / Columbia Pictures (R)

Film genre: romantic melodrama/thriller

Top guns: dir: Gordon Parks Jr. ← THREE THE HARD WAY ← SUPERFLY / s-w: Gerald Sanford

Stars: Kevin Hooks *(Aaron)* ← SOUNDER, Irene Cara *(Angela)* → SPARKLE → FAME, Moses Gunn *(Ike)* ← CORNBREAD, EARL AND ME ← SHAFT'S BIG SCORE! ← SHAFT, Robert Hooks *(Beau)* ← TROUBLE MAN, Ernestine Jackson/Feliciano *(Cleo)*, Leon Pinkney *(Willie)* → CAR WASH, **José Feliciano** *(singer)*, Charles McGregor *(Duke)* ← THAT'S THE WAY OF THE WORLD ← THREE THE HARD WAY ← ACROSS 110th STREET ← SUPERFLY, Drew Bundini Brown *(referee)* ← SHAFT'S BIG SCORE! ← SHAFT

Storyline: Aaron is black, Angela is Puerto Rican, and they're in love, a fact they decline to inform their parents about. Neither does it go down especially well in Angela's neighbourhood where Aaron gets roughed up by the local Latinos. The donation of a dying drug dealer's dollar-stuffed suitcase looks like temporary relief but vicious hoods are soon on their tail. *BG*

Movie rating: *5

Visual: none

Off the record: Blind from birth, **José Feliciano** (b.10 Sep'45, Lares, Puerto Rico) nevertheless established himself as one of the most successful Latin crossover artists of the late 60s. While a 1968 soul/bossa cover of the Doors' 'Light My Fire' (and attendant 'Feliciano!' album) marked the high water mark of his career, he continued to tour and record right through the 70s and beyond, during which time he scored 'AARON LOVES ANGELA', his one and only movie OST. Marking the debut of Puerto Rican 'Fame'/'Flashdance' star Irene Cara, the movie also saw a cameo from **Feliciano** himself. The Hispanic star subsequently appeared on a 'Fania All-Stars – Live' movie and a belated cameo in the Coen brothers' multi-Oscar winning black comedy, 'Fargo' (1996). *BG*

JOSÉ FELICIANO: Angela

1976. (lp) *Private Stock; <PS 2010>* ☐ ☐
– Angela / I've got a feeling / Sweet street / Nirvana (part 1) / Nirvana (part 2) / Why / Michaelangelo / Salsa negra / As long as I have you.

S/track review: Guitarist-crooner JOSÉ FELICIANO wasn't the only Latino artist to soundtrack a blaxploitation film, but he was the least likely. Attuned to the interracial, love across the tracks storyline, the Puerto Rican maestro actually wrote (with his wife Janna) and performed some of his most compelling material of the 70s, hot on the hi-heels of his hit theme to 'Chico And The Man', and his Steve Cropper collaboration, 'For My Love . . . Mother Music' (1974). Backed up by the likes of WILLIE 'Spanish Grease' BOBO, trumpeter CHUCK FINDLEY and future Toto belter DAVID PAICH, FELICIANO touches down at pretty much every base in his book, as well as some that aren't. Tilting a shot at Ocean Boulevard reggae-lite, 'Why', might have been tempting fate but he gets away with it, raising its stock with some Van Morrison-esque brass arrangements and a high spirited Spanish outro. Attempts at blaxploitation funk are equally difficult to dismiss: 'I've Got A Feeling' kicks in like Stevie Wonder's 'Superstition', spiralling horn charts compounding the impression, while 'Sweet Street' drawls a clavinet-enhanced take on Allen Toussaint's 'On Your Way Down', FELICIANO soaking that serenade tenor in something approaching swamp water. BOBO comes into his own on the Latin-rock of 'Salsa Negra', with FELICIANO doing his best Santana impression, but fans of the flamenco playing which ranked him among the world's best aren't short changed. While 'Michaelangelo' ably – and often beautifully – flexes those Madame Tussauds-impressed fingers, and the melodramatic title is the one which usually turns up on compilations, the most ambitious entry is 'Nirvana', an orchestrated suite in two parts, credited solely to JOSÉ. In the second part at least, he really lets his imagination run on the outside chances of classical guitar and funk, alternating preposterously portentous breakdowns and Rosinha de Valença-esque harmonic harangue over an irresistible groove. Olé! *BG*

Album rating: *6.5

ABÉLARD & HÉLOÏSE

1970 (Ger 75m* TV play) unknown

Film genre: historical romantic period animation

Top guns: s-w: Fuchs + Luca Fuchs ?

Stars: unknown (? can anyone help)

Storyline: The true and tragic love story between 12th Century French scholastic philosopher and theologian Pierre Abélard and his pupil Héloïse Fulbert, niece of the Canon at the cathedral school of Notre Dame, Paris. Their passionate relationship was doomed from the day she bore Abélard's child, while the Canon subsequently ill-treated the pair resulting in both parties becoming abbot and abbess at Saint-Gildas-en-Rhuys in Brittany. *MCS*

Movie rating: *5

Visual: none

Off the record: THIRD EAR BAND (see own entry)

THIRD EAR BAND

1999. (cd) *Blueprint; (BP 310)* ☐ ☐
– Part 1 / Part 2 / Part 3 / Part 4 / Part 5 / Part 6.

S/track review: Scheduled at one point to be THIRD EAR BAND's "third" LP (after 1969's 'Alchemy' and 1970s 'Elements'), 'ABÉLARD & HÉLOÏSE' broke new "rock" boundaries for the Prog-meets-avant-jazz outfit, although the set was shelved until 1999. With a line-up that featured percussionist GLENN SWEENEY, cellist URSULA SMITH, reedist PAUL MINNS and violinist RICHARD COFF, the quartet possessed that uneasy quality that was necessary to sustain neo-classical-like drones and pastoral mood swings. Piecing together six untitled and sombre cues in around 37 minutes, THIRD EAR BAND plucked their inspiration from the film's medieval themes of yore in a way only the band themselves know how. Not a conventional Hollywood score by any stretch of the imagination, 'ABÉLARD & HÉLOÏSE' was nevertheless melodious at times, reaching to the listener through dark atmospherics quite ahead of their time – think Popol Vuh. *MCS*

Album rating: *5.5

ABOUT A BOY

2002 (UK/US 100m) United International Pictures (12)

Film genre: romantic coming-of-age comedy drama

Top guns: s-w: Chris Weitz (+ dir) & Paul Weitz (+ dir), Peter Hedges → PIECES OF APRIL (nov: Nick Hornby ← HIGH FIDELITY)

Stars: Hugh Grant *(Will Freeman)* → MUSIC AND LYRICS, Nicholas Hoult *(Marcus)*, Toni Collette *(Fiona)* ← VELVET GOLDMINE, Rachel Weisz *(Rachel)*, Isabel Brooke *(Angie)*, Victoria Smurfit *(Susie)* ← the LAST GREAT WILDERNESS, Sharon Small *(Christine)*, Augustus Prew *(Ali)*, Mark Heap *(math teacher)* ← BRING ME THE HEAD OF MAVIS DAVIS, Murray Lachlan Young *(New Year's party guest)*

Storyline: Rich London playboy Will Freeman decides that the easiest way to pick up a girl is to pretend to be a single dad. He joins a single parents group and, complete with imaginary son, he meets Fiona and her precocious lad Marcus. The boy soon cottons on to Will's game and, through much skulduggery and bribery, gets him to date his moping mum. Just as it looks like they are settling down, however, the beautiful Rachel appears and Will's head is turned yet again. *MCS*

Movie rating: *8

Visual: dvd

Off the record: BADLY DRAWN BOY is the nom de plume for Bolton-born singer-songwriter, Damon Gough. The Lancashire lad (b. 2 Oct'69) first initiated his weird brand of gnome-ish, tea-cosy-hat psychedelia when he self-financed (with graphic designer Andy Votel) an EP on his own 'Twisted Nerve' label. 'EP1' (released in September '97) was quickly pursued by the following year's 'EP2', a contract with 'XL Recordings' (home of the Prodigy) just around the corner. In the autumn of '98, his third release, the imaginatively titled 'EP3' hit the shops, this Beck-esque trio of tracks finally making the more discerning music punter sit up and listen. Minor hits 'Once Around The Block' and 'Another Pearl' preceded a long-awaited debut set, 'The Hour Of The Bewilderbeast' (2000), the UK Top 20 entry a mixture of Nick Drake's quiet, cello-driven folk and Springsteen's poor-man's blues; the album won the coveted Mercury Prize. GOUGH subsequently put his artistry on the line by cutting a full-on soundtrack 'ABOUT A BOY' as his next release, an increasingly rare career move these days. *MCS*

BADLY DRAWN BOY

Apr 02. (cd/lp) *Twisted Nerve; (TNXL CD/LP 152) B.M.G.; <1019>* [6] [ ]
– Exit stage right / A peak you reach / Something to talk about / Dead duck / Above you, below me / I love N.Y.E. / Silent sigh / Wet, wet, wet / River, sea, ocean / S.P.A.T. / Rachel's flat / Walking out of stride / File me away / A minor incident / Delta (little boy blues) / Donna and Blitzen.

S/track review: To those who'd damn soundtracks as inconsequential promotional vehicles deleted before they've even reached the shops, BADLY DRAWN BOY (aka DAMON GOUGH) presents some incontrovertible evidence to the contrary, masterfully composing a full movie score as the unofficial follow-up to his acclaimed debut album. A John Martyn for the Ikea generation, GOUGH pretty much succeeded in making the concept of the scruffy singer-songwriter acceptable again. For that fact alone, it's probably fitting that this score accompanies an adaptation of a novel by trainspotting (with a small "t") guru, Nick Hornby. And while it's possible to pick out a roll call of classic reference points for GOUGH's buoyantly resigned style, suffice to say that he usually transcends them all to create something unique, and something uniquely British. The combination of instrumentals and handsomely skewed sketches presented here is no exception, and while the latter are hardly a departure, at their best – as on the single 'Something To Talk About' and the postcard-pretty 'Silent Sigh'- they insinuate themselves with an awkward, urban-rustic determination. And while the majority of the maddeningly brief instrumental cues are haunted by the winsome orchestral aesthetics of Nick Drake collaborator Robert Kirby, GOUGH still pulls a couple of knotty – and unlikely – funk and jazz-influenced jams out of his tea cosy before rounding things off with a rumbling festive extravaganza ('Donna And Blitzen') Phil Spector would've been proud to call his own. *BG*

Album rating: *7.5

– spinoff hits, etc. –

BADLY DRAWN BOY: Silent Sigh / Donna And Blitzen (KCRW acoustic session) / Piano Medley (KCRW acoustic session)

Mar 02. (7"/cd-s/cd-s) *(TNXL 012/+CD/CD2)* [16] [–]

BADLY DRAWN BOY: Something To Talk About

Jun 02. (7"/cd-s) *(TNXL 014/+CD)* [28] [–]
(cd-s) *(TNXL 014CD2)* – ('A') / Above you, below me (electric bedroom version).

☐ AC/DC segment
(⇒ MAXIMUM OVERDRIVE)

ACROSS 110TH STREET

1972 (US 102m) United Artists (R)

Film genre: cop/detective thriller

Top guns: dir: Barry Shear ← WILD IN THE STREETS / s-w: Luther Davis (au: Wally Ferris)

Stars: Anthony Quinn *(Capt. Frank Mattelli)* → JUNGLE FEVER, Yaphet Kotto *(Det. Lt. Pope)* ← MAN AND BOY / → TRUCK TURNER → FRIDAY FOSTER → the MONKEY HUSTLE → the PARK IS MINE, Anthony Franciosa *(Nick D'Salvio)* → DEATH WISH II, Paul Benjamin *(Jim Harris)* ← MIDNIGHT COWBOY / → the EDUCATION OF SONNY CARSON → FRIDAY FOSTER → LEADBELLY → the FIVE HEARTBEATS, Ed Bernard *(Joe Logart)* ← SHAFT / → TOGETHER BROTHERS, Richard Ward *(Doc Johnson)*, Antonio Fargas *(Henry Jackson)* ← SHAFT / → CLEOPATRA JONES → FOXY BROWN → CORNBREAD, EARL AND ME → CAR WASH → FIRESTARTER → SOUL SURVIVOR, Gloria Hendry *(Laurelene)* ← the LANDLORD / → BLACK CAESAR → SLAUGHTER'S BIG RIP-OFF → HELL UP IN HARLEM → BLACK BELT JONES, Norma Donaldson *(Gloria Roberts)* → WILLIE DYNAMITE → STAYING ALIVE → HOUSE PARTY → the FIVE HEARTBEATS, Marlene Warfield *(Mrs. Jackson)* ← JOE, Paul Harris *(Mr. C)* → the MACK → TRUCK TURNER, Charles McGregor *(Chink)* → SUPERFLY → THREE THE HARD WAY → THAT'S THE WAY OF THE WORLD → AARON LOVES ANGELA, **Adam Wade** *(patrolman)* ← COME BACK, CHARLESTON BLUE ← SHAFT / → GORDON'S WAR → CLAUDINE → PHANTOM OF THE PARADISE, Gilbert Lewis *(Shewy)* ← COTTON COMES TO HARLEM / → GORDON'S WAR, George Di Cenzo *(patrolman)* → SING, Burt Young *(Lapides)* → LAST EXIT TO BROOKLYN → CROCODILE SHOES, Thurman Scott *(Doc's guard)* → THREE TOUGH GUYS, Ken Lynch *(Tailor shop patrolman)* → WILLIE DYNAMITE

Storyline: Nervous-twitching ex-con Jim Harris and pals stage an audacious raid on the takings of a Harlem racket, sealing their fate by indiscriminately machine-gunning black and Italian gangsters. While both mobs are baying for their blood, the story hinges largely on the tense relationship between the two cops competing on the case: corrupt old pro Captain Frank Mattelli and his Afro American junior, Detective Lt Pope, an ambitious but by-the-book career man after Mattelli's job. *BG*

Movie rating: *6.5

Visual: video + dvd

Off the record: BOBBY WOMACK was born 4th March '44, Cleveland, Ohio, USA. Along with his four siblings, Cecil, Curtis, Harry and Friendly Jnr, Bobby formed the Womack Brothers as a gospel quintet in 1959. It wasn't long before he met Sam Cooke who subsequently snapped him up to play guitar in his own gospel outfit, the Soul Stirrers. In early 1960, Cooke formed the L.A.-based 'S.A.R.' label with manager J.W. Alexander and promptly added the brothers to his roster, renaming them the Valentinos. A handful of classy R&B singles followed, while two cuts, 'It's All Over Now' and 'Lookin' For A Love' became major hits for the ROLLING STONES and the J Geils Band respectively. WOMACK's songwriting and performing credentials were already well established when his group split and although he began recording for new label, 'Him', most of his time was taken up by session work for the likes of ARETHA FRANKLIN, RAY CHARLES and Wilson Pickett. As well as playing on the latter's 'Funky Broadway' single, they also became great buddies and it isn't difficult to hear similarities in their gritty soul-shout vocal style; WOMACK himself was nicknamed "The Preacher". After a brief spell at 'Chess' records, he signed to Liberty's R&B subsidiary, 'Minit', where he cut a series of fair-to-middling solo singles, none of which were big hits. The square-spectacled soul man had more success with his 'United Artists' recordings (who took over 'Liberty') which spawned his first Top 30 hit, 'That's The Way I Feel About 'Cha'. WOMACK's impressive development as both a singer and songwriter was illustrated the following year with the release of two great albums, 'Communication' and 'Understanding', the latter featuring Bobby's fond ode to his brother Harry (who was subsequently stabbed to death by his own wife in 1978), 'Harry Hippie'. 1972 was also the year of Sly & The Family Stone's seminal 'There's A Riot Goin' On', to which WOMACK added his famous wah-wah guitar; his well-documented friendship with the wayward Sly Stone led them both off the rails in the early 70s as they became increasingly dependent on drugs and the high-rolling L.A. lifestyle. Following the lead of contemporaries MARVIN GAYE and CURTIS MAYFIELD, WOMACK cut a Blaxploitation soundtrack in 1972 for the movie, 'ACROSS 110th STREET' and although the classic title track remains arguably one of the finest marriages of soul and pop ever committed to vinyl, the project failed to bring Bobby the commercial fruits he so richly deserved. That would come later. *MCS & BG*

BOBBY WOMACK / J.J. JOHNSON (*)

Jan 73. (lp) *United Artists; <UAS 5225> (UAS 29451)* 50 May73

– Across 110th Street / Harlem clavinette (*) / (If you don't want my love) Give it back / Hang on in there (*) / Quicksand / Harlem love theme (*) / Across 110th Street – instrumental (*) / Do it right / Hang on in there / If you don't want my love (*) / Across 110th Street part II. *<cd-iss. Jan98 on 'Rykodisc'+=; RCD 10706>* – (original dialogue). *(cd re-iss. May98 original on 'Charly'; CPCD 8340) <(cd re-iss. Oct03 as 'RUBARE ALLA MAFIA E'UN SUICIDIO' on 'Dagored'; RED 123CD)>*

S/track review: The iconic sleeve shot – a multi-racial gaggle of poker-faced hoods hunched over a mountain of cash money – says it all but still doesn't hint at the bittersweet triumph and desperate humanity of BOBBY WOMACK's title theme. Given the onetime Soul Stirrer's descent into his own drugs hell while working on Sly Stone's 'There's A Riot Goin' On' (1972), his talk of junkies and pushers, living and dying, was more than just idle ghetto speak. 'ACROSS 110th STREET' arguably ranks as not just the single most enduring piece of blaxploitation music ever recorded but as one of the best soul-funk singles ever released, as resonant of its era as flaming tracts of Vietnamese jungle. Quentin Tarantino, for one, recognised the song's emblematic power by making it the lead track on his own blax tribute, 'JACKIE BROWN' (1997). If the rest of the Poet's songs don't quite measure up, don't hold it against him; his California soul pedigree is intact and the likes of 'Do It Right' and 'Hang On In There' still punch above their weight, with WOMACK primal screaming like James Brown and rocking out like a black Allman brother. The venerable JJ JOHNSON supplies the ensemble score pieces, establishing the song/score pattern he'd repeat on 'WILLIE DYNAMITE' (1974). He goes for the jugular on 'Harlem Clavinette', a squelchy, winding jam which – for once – lives up to its title, and could have served as a main theme in its own right, as could the irrepressible 'Hang On . . .'. And in interpreting WOMACK's title as a rubber-burning, big band chase epic, the veteran trombonist/arranger gives a high five to the strongest partnership of any blaxploitation soundtrack. *BG*

Album rating: *8

– spinoff hits, etc. –

BOBBY WOMACK: Across 110th Street / Hang On In There

Mar 73. (7") *<196> (UP 35512)* 56 Apr73

☐ Bryan ADAMS segment
(⇒ SPIRIT: STALLION OF THE CIMARRON)

Barry ADAMSON

Born: 1 Jun'58, Manchester, England. A CV which includes stints in seminal art-punk outfit, Magazine, and NICK CAVE's backing band the Bad Seeds, formed the raw material for BARRY ADAMSON's subsequent diverson into cinematic solo work and bonafide film composing. Even the man's proto-trip hop solo debut, 'Moss Side Story' (1989), was a de facto soundtrack for a film of his own fevered imagination's making, skilfully splicing avant garde and industrial influences with jazz-noir and Bernard Herrmann/ John Barry-inspired cinematic cues. In 1991's 'DELUSION', he finally recorded his first soundtrack to a real film, an adroit road thriller tailor made for ADAMSON's brooding aesthetic. Later the same year, he was co-credited along with Dinosaur Jr's J MASCIS (plus old sparring partners NICK CAVE & The Bad Seeds), on the soundtrack to Allison Anders' acclaimed domestic drama, 'GAS FOOD LODGING'. While his scores for French neo-noir, 'Mauvaise Passe' (1999) and low-key gangster flick, 'Out Of Depth' (1999) remain unreleased, and his output has hardly been prolific, ADAMSON continues to experiment with filmic motifs in his solo work and it's wholly possible that he'll yet create a career defining soundtrack. *BG*

- **filmography** (composer) –

Delusion *(1991 OST =>)* / **Gas Food Lodging** *(1992 OST w/ J MASCIS & V/A =>)* / Mauvaise Passe *(1999)* / Out Of Depth *(1999)* / le Raid *(2002)* / the Rouge Shoes *(2004)*

ADIOS AMIGO

1976 (US 87m) Atlas Productions / Po' Boy Productions

Film genre: comedy western

Top guns: s-w (+ dir): Fred Williamson ← MEAN JOHNNY BARROWS / → NO WAY BACK → MR. MEAN

Stars: Fred Williamson *(Big Ben)* ← BUCKTOWN ← THREE THE HARD WAY ← THREE TOUGH GUYS ← the SOUL OF NIGGER CHARLEY ← BLACK CAESAR ← HELL UP IN HARLEM / → MEAN JOHNNY BARROWS → MR. MEAN → FROM DUSK TILL DAWN → RIDE → CARMEN: A HIP HOPERA, Richard Pryor *(Sam Spade)* ← the MACK ← WATTSTAX ← LADY SINGS THE BLUES ← YOU'VE GOT TO WALK IT LIKE YOU TALK IT . . . ← the PHYNX ← WILD IN THE STREETS / → CAR WASH → the WIZ → BUSTIN' LOOSE, Thalmus Rasulala *(Noah)* ← BUCKTOWN ← CORNBREAD, EARL AND ME ← FRIDAY FOSTER ← WILLIE DYNAMITE ← BLACULA ← COOL BREEZE / → LAMBADA → NEW JACK CITY, Robert Phillips, Victoria Lee, Lynn Jackson, Heidi Dobbs

Storyline: Wily, wise cracking con merchant Sam Spade has the good fortune of being able to blame failed misdemeanours on his rough hewn but naive outlaw partner, Big Ben, dragging him through an unceasing series of escapades in which he usually comes off worse. *BG*

Movie rating: *4.5

Visual: video on 'Vidmark' 1996

Off the record: **INFERNAL BLUES MACHINE** (see below)

INFERNAL BLUES MACHINE

Jan 76. (lp) *London; <PS 666>* [ ] [–]
– Adios amigo / Needing you, wanting you, loving you / When you move, you lose / Ju ju / Never turn your back on a friend / When love calls your name / Write me a letter / Ain't that love / I can make it but it would be easier with love.

S/track review: A strange one this. With the movie's cod-western capering and a kitschy Mexican bandidos sleeve, you might be entitled to expect a healthy serving of latino-funk, but no, this is, for the large part, straight down the line, conspicuously uncinematic soul, lent soundtrack status by a trio of LUCHI DE JESUS themes. 'ADIOS AMIGO', in fact, looks to be the sole legacy of the demonically monikered INFERNAL BLUES MACHINE (the catalogue number, PS 666, presumably part of the joke), an interracial "combo" comprising WARREN RAY, GREGG PARKER, MIKE CAVANAUGH and GREG MIDDLETON. To be fair, the title theme has a War-like camaraderie and an intro reminiscent of Antonio Carlos e Jocafi's early 70s Samba-funk classic, 'Kabaluere'; not quite Santana, then, but worth a spin. The A-side funk is tight enough in a glutinous kind of way, but tends to get bogged down in its own grooves. 'Needing You' plies expectant ostinato, but only on 'Ju Ju', the most blaxploitative track on the whole album, do the band really get over the hump. It's not a cover of the Wayne Shorter classic (if only . . .), but solid small group funk steering MIDDLETON's guitar from wah-wah trance to screaming lead. The rest of the album retreats into overwrought soul balladry. As for the other LDJ themes, 'Never Turn Your Back On A Friend' is good, clean, Friends Of Distinction-style fun and the long-winded 'I Can Never Make It But It Would Be Easier With Love' pulls out a harmonica and an inoffensive country-soul vibe. *BG*

Album rating: *5.5

ADVANCE TO THE REAR

1964 (US 97m b&w) Metro-Goldwyn-Mayer (PG)

Film genre: comedy western

Top guns: dir: George Marshall / s-w: William Bowers, Robert Carson, Samuel A. Peeples (nov: 'The Company Of Wolves' by William Chamberlain & Jack Schaefer)

Stars: Glenn Ford *(Capt. Jared Heath)* ← BLACKBOARD JUNGLE, Stella Stevens *(Martha Lou Williams)* ← GIRLS! GIRLS! GIRLS! / → POPSTAR, Melvyn Douglas *(Col. Claude Brackenby)*, Jim Backus *(Gen. Willoughby)* → HELLO DOWN THERE → FRIDAY FOSTER, Joan Blondell *(Easy Jenny)* → STAY AWAY, JOE → the PHYNX → GREASE, Andrew Prine *(Pvt. Owen Selous)*, Jesse Pearson *(Cpl. Silas Geary)*, Alan Hale Jr. *(Sgt. Beauregard Davis)* → BACK TO THE BEACH, James Griffith *(Hugo Zattig)*, Whit Bissell *(Capt. Queeg)*, Michael Pate *(Thin Elk)*, Yvonne Craig *(Ora)* ← IT HAPPENED AT THE WORLD'S FAIR / → KISSIN' COUSINS → SKI PARTY

Storyline: The American Civil War draws to its close and two opposing units agree to sit it out quietly until the ceasefire and hope the generals don't notice. This works fine until glory boy Captain Heath uses his initiative (always a dangerous thing to do in the army) and captures some Confederates. When the Colonel yells at him to "put them back" a series of adventures begins which sees the Union boys sent West out of harm's way to protect a gold shipment, which is when the fun really begins. *JZ*

Movie rating: *5.5

Visual: video

Off the record: The **NEW CHRISTY MINSTRELS** (see below)

—

the NEW CHRISTY MINSTRELS: Today

May 64. (lp; mono/stereo) *Columbia; <CI 2159/CS 8959>* [9] [–]
– Company of cowards / This ol' riverboat / Love theme (Today) / Whistlin' Dixie / Anything love can buy / Ladies / Charleston town / Company Q whistle march / Way down in Arkansas / Brackenby's music box / Riverboat theme / Today. *<cd-iss. 1997 on 'Collectables'+=; COL 5837>* – The NEW CHRISTY MINSTRELS: non-soundtrack set, 'Ramblin''.

S/track review: The early 60s saw a folk ballad revival and at the centre of the movement were the NEW CHRISTY MINSTRELS. Inspired by Edwin "Pops" Christy and the Christy Minstrels from the previous century (the 1840s!), one-time solo chanter RANDY SPARKS and his new West Coast troupe from Tarzana retread the boards of their travelling forefathers. Described by some as carefree, goodtime and giddy, and by others as downright nauseating, the ever-evolving 9 or 10-piece collective (including passing through members JACKIE MILLER, NICK WOODS, JERRY YESTER, GAYLE CALDWELL, BARRY McGUIRE, BARRY KANE, LARRY RAMOS and GENE CLARK) had already a handful of Top 30 albums behind them before they were commissioned to perform the folk score to 'ADVANCE TO THE REAR'. Disguising it as the more commercially-appealing 'Today' LP, the all-NEW CHRISTY MINSTRELS nearly shot themselves in the proverbial foot with this clumsy cavalry-charge of a record. From the overly exuberant opener, 'Company Of Cowards', to the RANDY SPARKS-penned (Top 20 hit!) title track finale, each has a defined cheesiness that either makes you chuckle, or indeed cry like a baby. Thankfully, the LP only lasts for around a half-hour, but it does leave one with a bitter-sweet taste of neuralgic nostalgia and deeply dippy deja vu; example 'Whistlin' Dixie' – if you must. If there's any redeeming factor it's that after a few listens you'll be subliminally whistlin' the traditional tunes until you're "blew" in the face. Now go and find 'a MIGHTY WIND' – the movie that is . . . *MCS*

Album rating: *3.5

– spinoff hits, etc. –

the NEW CHRISTY MINSTRELS: Today

Apr 64. (7") *<43000> C.B.S.; (203)* [17] Jun64 [ ]

AFFLICTION

1998 (US 113m) Lions Gate Films (R)

Film genre: psychological domestic drama

Top guns: s-w: (+ dir) Paul Schrader ← TOUCH ← the LAST TEMPTATION OF CHRIST ← LIGHT OF DAY (au: Russell Banks)

Stars: Nick Nolte *(Wade Whitehouse)* ← CLEAN ← DOWN AND OUT IN BEVERLY HILLS / → OVER THE HEDGE, James Coburn *(Glen Whitehouse)* ← YOUNG GUNS II ← WHITE ROCK ← PAT GARRETT & BILLY THE KID ← CANDY / → SHAKE, RATTLE AND ROLL: AN AMERICAN LOVE STORY, Sissy Spacek *(Margie Fogg)* ← COAL MINER'S DAUGHTER, Willem Dafoe *(Rolfe Whitehouse)* ← WILD AT HEART ← CRY-BABY ← the LAST TEMPTATION OF CHRIST ← TO LIVE AND DIE IN L.A. ← STREETS OF FIRE / → OVERNIGHT → the LIFE AQUATIC WITH STEVE ZISSOU, Mary Beth Hurt *(Lillian Whitehouse Horner)*, Jim True *(Jack Hewitt)* ← SINGLES, Marian Seldes *(Alma Pittman)* → DUETS, Holmes Osborne *(Gordon LaRiviere)* ← THAT THING YOU DO!, Brigid Tierney *(Jill)*, Sean McCann *(Evan Twombley)*, Wayne Robson *(Nick Wickham)* ← CANDY MOUNTAIN ← POPEYE

Storyline: Troubled Sheriff Wade Whitehouse has little to do in his sleepy New England patch, and so finds himself spending more and more time at the bar with girlfriend Margie, the only person who can really talk to him. As he sinks deeper into inner turmoil a businessman is killed in an alleged hunting accident and Wade pursues the truth with zealot-like vigour, the shadow of his abusive father Glen always in his mind. *JZ*

Movie rating: *7

Visual: video + dvd

Off the record: MICHAEL BROOK (see own entry/below)

—

MICHAEL BROOK

Feb 99. (cd) *Citadel; <(STC 77121)>* ☐ May99 ☐
– Opening titles / Late night phone / Crossing guard / Hunting / Flashback / Late night conspiracy / Autodentismo / Resignation / Chase / Night flashback / Wade goes wild / Worries / Homestead / Marge / Barn / Close refrain.

S/track review: MICHAEL BROOK has fast become one of the film world's most revered composers, while retaining that rock sensibility which has also assisted the likes of cohorts and friends such as PETER GABRIEL, The EDGE and BRIAN ENO. A sophomore effort in terms of his soundtrack work, having already delivered his film score debut, 'ALBINO ALLIGATOR' (in '96), 40-something Michael uses his vast experience to synthesize the movie's stark subject matter with his experimental music. Appropriately enough, 'Opening Titles' starts 'AFFLICTION', an incongruous instrumental piece that takes the listener towards the bleak and chilly backdrop of a wintry New Hampshire. Bypassing some discordant, shorter cues, BROOK and his infinite guitar, bass & keyboards gain momentum over the course of the whole album. From the plaintive 'Late Night Conspiracy' to the ethereal 'Autodentismo', BROOK sets about getting to the heart and tormented soul of the film's main character, by way of some crying strings and a pump-organ. 'Resignation', meanwhile, delivers an even darker, pitch-black sense of doom as one imagines the tumultuous emotions Wade Whitehouse is going through. Without a shadow of a doubt, the best cut stems from the manic, uptempo 'Wade Goes Wild', a track to quite literally blow your mind. Similar to the likes of John Cale or Nico (both ex-Velvet Underground), tracks 12-15, 'Worries', 'Homestead', 'Marge' and 'Barn', cross the boundaries between classical and avant-rock music. The uplifting and indeed spiritual, 'Close Refrain', brings down the curtain to a very emotional and, at times, disturbing score. *MCS*

Album rating: *6.5

AGUIRRE, WRATH OF GOD

1973 (W.Ger/Peru 90m) Filmverlag der Autoren (12)

Film genre: historical drama: people & events

Top guns: s-w + dir: Werner Herzog → HERZ AUS GLAS → NOSFERATU, THE VAMPYRE → COBRA VERDE → GRIZZLY MAN

Stars: Klaus Kinski *(Don Lope de Aguirre)* → LIFESPAN → MADAME CLAUDE → NOSFERATU, THE VAMPIRE → CODENAME: WILDGEESE → COBRA VERDE, Cecilia Rivera *(Flores)*, Helene Rojo *(Inez)*, Ruy Guerra *(Don Pedro de Ursua)*, Del Negro *(Brother Gaspar de Carvajal)*

Storyline: Conquistador extraordinaire Gonzalo Pizarro leads an ill-fated expedition to locate the fabled city of El Dorado in the Peruvian jungle, delegating a scouting party to go on ahead when supplies run low. Drunk on his own ego, the demented Don Lope de Aguirre becomes increasingly unhinged as the party descends into the proverbial heart of darkness. *BG*

Movie rating: *8.5

Visual: video + dvd

Off the record: Note: the 'AGUIRRE' LP *(on 'PDU Pld.)* didn't feature any tracks from the movie *(cd-iss. 1992 on 'Spalax'; 14219)*

—

POPOL VUH

Jan 76. (lp) *Cosmic; (840.103)* ☐ W.Ger ☐
– Aguirre I (l'acrime di rei) / Morgengruss II / Aguirre II / Agnus dei / Vergegenwartigung. *(UK cd-iss. Jan97 on 'Spalax'; 14974) (cd re-iss. May04 on 'S.P.V.'+=; SPV 085-70142CD)* – Aguirre III.

S/track review: In one of the most indelible marriages of sound and vision in cinema history, maverick German director Werner Herzog opened his seminal tale of crazed conquistadors with Klaus Kinski et al descending the mist shrouded flanks of Machu Picchu to the otherworldly siren sound of POPUL VUH. It remains an unforgettable image and a haunted, weightless music, a transmission from the beyond routed through primitive electronics. In Herzog's own words, FLORIAN FRICKE "made visible what would otherwise have remained mysterious and forever hidden in the images". Presumably a talent which every director seeks yet doesn't necessarily find, and one which FRICKE exercised to stunning effect in this, the first – and perhaps best – of his numerous collaborations with Herzog. While the combination of celestial choral and impressionistic mellotron would be a recurring feature of FRICKE's work, here developed over 'Aguirre I' and 'Aguirre II' (and on the 2004 'S.P.V.' reissue, the percussive 'Aguirre III'), POPOL VUH was as fluid a vehicle as Herzog's filmmaking, incorporating such ethnic instrumentation as Andean zampoña. The SPV version – incidentally the first time the original soundtrack has been issued on CD, despite other POPOL VUH releases under the 'AGUIRRE' title – also features the spirited semi-acoustic pastoral of 'Morgengruss II' and the hovering, twilight zone ambience of 'Vergegenwärtigung'. Sublime. *BG*

Album rating: *8

☐ AIR segment
(⇒ the VIRGIN SUICIDES)

ALAMO BAY

1985 (US 98m) TriStar Pictures (R)

Film genre: crime drama

Top guns: dir: Louis Malle / s-w: Alice Arlen

Stars: Amy Madigan *(Glory)* ← PLACES IN THE HEART ← STREETS OF FIRE / → CROCODILE SHOES, Ed Harris *(Shang)* ← PLACES IN THE HEART / → SWEET DREAMS → WALKER → MASKED AND ANONYMOUS, Donald Moffat *(Wally)* → FAR NORTH, Ho Nguyen *(Dinh)*, Rudy Young *(Skinner)*, Truyen V. Tran *(Ben)*, Cynthia Carle *(Honey)*, **Johnny Gimble** *(fiddler)*, ← SONGWRITER ← HONKYTONK MAN ← HONEYSUCKLE ROSE, Tony Frank *(Leroy)* → SWEET DREAMS → YOUNG GUNS II → RUSH, Harvey Lewis *(Tex)* → ALAMO BAY, Gary Basaraba *(Leon)* → SWEET DREAMS → WHO'S THAT GIRL → the LAST TEMPTATION OF CHRIST, other band members:- **Reese Wynans**, Wally Murphy, Ray Benson *(himself)* ← ROADIE, **Tony Anastasio**, **Richard Hormachea**

Storyline: An unusual detour into race politics for Louis Malle, focusing on local opposition to immigrant Vietnamese fisherman in Galveston, Texas. Locals Wally and Shang lock horns over the issue, with the former having no qualms about employing the incomers and the latter facing the ruin of his business. Things get complicated when Shang goes to Wally's daughter for money, while the Ku Klux Klan eventually arrive to stick their odious oar in. *BG*

Movie rating: *5.5

Visual: video

Off the record: **Reese Wynans** was the keyboard-player of Stevie Ray Vaughan & Double Trouble.

—

RY COODER (with DAVID HIDALGO, CESAR ROSAS, LEE VING, JOHN HIATT & AMY MADIGAN)

Aug 85. (lp/c) *Slash; <SLASH 3> (SLAP/SLAC 7)* ☐ Feb86 ☐
– Theme from Alamo Bay / Gooks on Main Street / Too close / Klan

meeting / Sailfish evening / The last stand (Alamo Bay) / Quatro vicios / Search & destroy / Glory. *(cd-iss. Jun06 on 'Raven' Australia +=; RVN 209)* – THE BORDER

S/track review: "A movie score is probably the last refuge of abstract music. You can't make music like this on records unless you're Brian Eno, put it out yourself and sell it to the fans. I can't do that. I need an excuse". RY COODER was perhaps being a little disingenuous when he talked about needing an excuse, or maybe just underestimating his admirers, one of whom cites his modest words in 'Raven's recent re-issue. Post-'BUENA VISTA . . .', 'Chavez Ravine' and 'My Name Is Buddy', he could probably record his own farts and go platinum. This soundtrack is more than just hot air, though, a long neglected treasure from the mid-80s, a year after he'd recorded some of the most evocative music in cinema history with 'PARIS, TEXAS'. Like that album, like most of COODER's work, 'ALAMO BAY' ceded little or nothing to its era in terms of production or arrangements. The starchy bar-room-blues of 'The Last Stand (Alamo Bay)' aside, it sounds as organic today as it must have done then, richer and fuller than ' . . .TEXAS' with a lengthy cast of sidemen – both familiar and fresh (and in addition to those credited on the sleeve): VAN DYKE PARKS, CHRIS ETHRIDGE, JIM DICKINSON and DAVID LINDLEY to name but a few. DICKINSON co-writes three of the nine tracks, including the countrified 'Too Close' and the declamatory 'Gooks On Main Street', minimal-chord rock'n'roll with JOHN HIATT barking out the redneck refrain. The word departure comes to mind, posting notice that another sundown suite wasn't going to work on a script churning with such race-related, politically subtextual aggro. Not that he abandons his slide reverie completely; ignore its gauzy orientalism and 'Klan Meeting' could almost be an outtake from ' . . .TEXAS', while the title theme's inter-woven string textures and tones, Celtic, Middle Eastern and Far Eastern tentatively circle that familiar rattlesnake vibrato and PARKS' "Chinese cowboy music on Piano", flirting with a tender kind of melancholy. A couple of traditional Hispanic arrangements complete the impression of an album casting around for a new direction, or maybe just indulging familiar pleasures, tying up the emotional and melodic threads in closer 'Glory'. Of all the music here, though – "all the buzzsaws, the boat motors", as COODER heard it – it's the Mekong Delta blues nightmare of 'Search & Destroy' that signals that new direction, the clearest intimation of the avant-garde explorations to come. *BG*

Album rating: *7

☐ ALBA PAGANA alt.
(⇒MAY MORNING)

Damon ALBARN

Born: 23 Mar'68, Whitechapel, London, England. From post-baggy debutante and Brit-pop sex symbol to film composer and world music sponsor, DAMON ALBARN has weathered the changes of the British music scene with a creative spirit as restless as it is consistently fascinating. He's nevertheless still best known as the driving force behind Blur, the band he formed at the tail end of the 80s and which he steered through cheeky pop revisionism, psychedelia, experimental noise and a much hyped joust with fellow Brit-pop contenders Oasis. While a starring role in Antonia Bird's East End crime feature, 'Face' (1997) was in keeping with ALBARN's retro-Brit preoccupations, his first scoring project was the same director's controversial cannibal tale, 'RAVENOUS' (1999). Created in collaboration with Michael Nyman of all people, his startlingly original and unsettling soundtrack suggested Randy Newman-esque Americana refracted through a particularly freakish hall of mirrors. While his soundtrack to fact-based Irish gangster pic, 'ORDINARY DECENT CRIMINAL' (1999) was more conventionally rootsy, both projects were at least vaguely similar in spirit to the pre-millennial Blur album, '13'. More indicative of ALBARN's future direction was his soundtrack to Icelandic black comedy, '101 REYKJAVIK' (2000), scored in collaboration with inimitable ex-Sugarcubes man, Einar Orn Benediktsson. Resolutely digital and evocatively dub-heavy (even if it did hark back to its author's classic-ish leanings with a gaudy reprise of the Kinks' 'Lola') with liberal use of ALBARN's beloved melodica, the record segued nicely into his cinematic, virtual reality side project, Gorillaz, not to mention his African dalliances, which themselves culminated in a melodica-blowing apperance at the 2004 'Festival In The Desert' near Timbuktu in Mali. *BG*

- **filmography** (composer) {acting} –

Face *(1997 {*})* / **Ravenous** *(1999 OST w/ MICHAEL NYMAN =>)* / **Ordinary Decent Criminal** *(2000; OST w/ V/A =>)* / **101 Reykjavik** *(2000 OST w/ EINAR ORN BENEDIKTSSON =>)* / **Screaming Masterpiece** *(2005 {c})*

ALBINO ALLIGATOR

1996 (US/Fra 97m) Electric Pictures / Miramax Films (R)

Film genre: crime thriller/drama

Top guns: dir: Kevin Spacey → BEYOND THE SEA / s-w: Christian Forte

Stars: Matt Dillon *(Dova)* ← GRACE OF MY HEART ← SINGLES / → the FUTURE IS UNWRITTEN, Faye Dunaway *(Janet)* ← the WICKED LADY ← LITTLE BIG MAN, Gary Sinise *(Milo)* → RANSOM → OPEN SEASON, William Fichtner *(Law)* ← STRANGE DAYS, Viggo Mortensen *(Guy Fouchard)* ← YOUNG GUNS II, Joe Mantegna *(Det. G.D. Browning)* ← AIRHEADS ← ELVIS: THE MOVIE, John Spencer *(Jack)* → RAVENOUS, Skeet Ulrich *(Danny Boudreaux)* → TOUCH, M. Emmet Walsh *(Dino)* ← CATCH ME IF YOU CAN ← BLADE RUNNER ← BOUND FOR GLORY ← LITTLE BIG MAN ← ALICE'S RESTAURANT ← MIDNIGHT COWBOY, Melinda McGraw *(Jenny Ferguson)*, Frankie Faison *(agent Marv Rose)* ← MAXIMUM OVERDRIVE

Storyline: Three small-time robbers botch a warehouse job and, after shooting a cop, decide to hole out in a downstairs bar, Dino's Last Chance. Soon the Feds surround the building but Law, Milo and Dova find themselves in luck – they're not the only criminals having a late drink. An international arms dealer is the Feds' real target and, seizing their chance, the three hold everyone in the bar hostage. Will there be a bloodbath or will the regulars and ageing barmaid Janet manage to find a compromise? *JZ*

Movie rating: *6

Visual: video + dvd

Off the record: **MICHAEL BROOK** (see own entry/below)

MICHAEL BROOK

Feb 97. (cd) *Warners; <46504-2> 4 a.d.; (CAD 7003)* ☐ ☐
– Arrival / Doggie dog / Slow town / Preparation / Miscalculation / Aftermath / Tunnel / Albo gator / The promise / The city / The kicker / Exit / Ill wind (you're blowing me no good). *(re-iss. Jul98 on 'Guernica – 4 a.d.'; GAD 7003CD)*

S/track review: Toronto-born MICHAEL BROOK (ex-Martha & The Muffins) and his "infinite guitar" had been at the forefront of ambient music since his early 80s collaborations with BRIAN ENO and HAROLD BUDD. His debut solo album, 'Hybrid' (1985) saw him introduce World Music to his ever-bulging CV and led him to work with the likes of Pakistani qawaali singer NUSRAT FATEH ALI KHAN. Expanding his horizons into film music, 'ALBINO ALLIGATOR' took BROOK into a comfortable zone, the territory of most of his aforementioned peers. With a backing band that included ANTON SCHWARTZ (on sax), BOB ADAMS (on bass), JASON LEWIS (on percussion), the multi-faceted guitarist took cool to a new level, smoky jazz was always in the forefront. Cymballist JAMES PINKER augmented many of the avant-ambient pieces such as 'Doggie Dog' & 'Slow Town', while 'Preparation' added second saxophonist, HAFEZ MODIRZADEH. A permutation of all tight musicians was elemental in the atmosphere 'ALBINO . . .' created and, if there were a template needed to satisfy the pigeonholers among you, maybe 'Passion' (aka 'The LAST TEMPTATION OF CHRIST' soundtrack) by PETER GABRIEL would be the closest. Playing his part (in the movie itself – and on the harmonica!), actor William Fichtner provided some "telling" dialogue for track 8, 'Albo Gator'. Star track in more ways than one, 'Ill Wind (You're Blowing Me No Good)' – written by Ted Koehler & Harold Arlen – featured R.E.M. frontman and jazzman JIMMY SCOTT on vox, while Red Hot Chili Peppers man, FLEA, turns up to play bass and co-produce. A magical finale, if not a little nostalgic. *MCS*

Album rating: *6.5

ALFIE

2004 re-make (UK/US 106m) Paramount Pictures (15)

Film genre: seXual comedy drama

Top guns: s-w: Charles Shyer (+ dir), Elaine Pope

Stars: Jude Law *(Alfie)* ← COLD MOUNTAIN / → BREAKING AND ENTERING, Marisa Tomei *(Julie)* ← FOUR ROOMS ← PLAYING FOR KEEPS, Jane Krakowski *(Dorie)* ← DANCE WITH ME / → OPEN SEASON, Omar Epps *(Marlon)* ← JUICE, Nia Long *(Lonette)* ← STIGMATA, Sienna Miller *(Nikki)*, Susan Sarandon *(Liz)* ← the BANGER SISTERS ← DEAD MAN WALKING ← the ROCKY HORROR PICTURE SHOW ← JOE / → ROMANCE & CIGARETTES, Gedde Watanabe *(Wing)* ← THANK YOU, GOOD NIGHT ← THAT THING YOU DO! ← UHF, Renee Taylor *(Lu Schnitman)*, Dick Latessa *(Joe)* ← STIGMATA

Storyline: Alfie is an Englishman in New York, Manhattan to be exact. He's a debonair, Cockney-type Don Juan who makes his living as a limousine driver, while he woos the female fraternity big time. Like its original counterpart (from '66), things get heavy when Alfie gets one of his girlfriends pregnant and faces what he's never come across before: a moral dilemma! *MCS*

Movie rating: *6

Visual: dvd

Off the record: Jude Law becomes Michael Caine!? yes, and my name is Sir Maurice Micklewhite! *MCS*

MICK JAGGER & DAVE STEWART (*) (& Various Artists)

Oct 04. (cd) *Virgin; (CDV 2992) <63934>* ☐ ☐
– Old habits die hard (*) / Blind leading the blind (live acoustic version) (*) / New York hustle (*) / Let's make it up (*) / Wicked time (JOSS STONE & NADIRAH "NADZ" SEID; additional vocals MICK JAGGER) / Lonely without you (this Christmas) (MICK JAGGER & JOSS STONE) / Darkness of your love (GARY "MUDBONE" COOPER & DAVE STEWART) / Jack the lad (*) / Oh Nikki (*) / Blind leading the blind (*) / Standing in the rain (*) / Counting the days (*) / Old habits reprise (*) / Alfie (JOSS STONE). *<US +=>* – Old habits die hard (* with SHERYL CROW).

S/track review: With a hundred or so remakes of classic movies out there, why is it time after time they get it so wrong soundtrack-wise. This is a prime example, songs such as 'Old Habits Die Hard' and 'Blind Leading The Blind' couldn't have been better titled. In fact, these two songs – with further versions late on – open the set respectively, a set that bills Head 'Stone, MICK JAGGER and Eurythmic DAVE STEWART together for the first time; Abbey Road Studios in London, to be precise. More introspective than its mid-60s predecessor, the fresh-faced 'ALFIE' (and I mean, Jude Law, et al!), also introduces the teen British R&B/pop sensation, JOSS STONE, to lend it that female touch. JAGGER's celluloid credentials are numerous, all while fronting rock's greatest band, the ROLLING STONES, longevity-wise at least, while STEWART had become one of the most prolific film composers in the business. Of the two aforementioned tracks, both are quite solid enough lyrically and both possess the quintessential JAGGER sentimentality that croaked-out 'Miss You' and 'Waiting On A Friend' many moons ago. The duo/band instrumentals, too, give the impression they had a funky time in the studio, all that wooo-ailing very Happy Mondays-meets-Area Code 615, especially on 'New York Hustle'. The aforementioned STONE (JOSS, that is) and Jamaican duet partner, the Fugees-like NADIRAH "NADZ" SEID, play their part in reprising the old "what's it all about, Alfie" theme, under the guise of hip hop-styled 'Wicked Time'; JAGGER sticks his two-pennorth in for the chorus. Why? The two STONEs are present and correct for the festive crap that was, 'Lonely Without You (This Christmas)'; at least one of them was old enough to have heard Mud's 1974 Xmas chart-topper. Yes, the subconscious can play funny "old" tricks. Many will wonder who the hell is vocalist GARY "MUDBONE" COOPER (who features on the track, 'Darkness Of Your Love'), many non-P-Funk aficionados, that is; this track very Mel & Tim or Sam & Dave (never MICK & DAVE). JOSS removes the hip hop and gets down to some Solo searching on end title track, not quite Dionne Warwick but a little better than Cilla (not so much of a "surprise, surprise" then). All n all, an average outing but too retro-fried in most departments. What would jazzman Sonny Rollins – who scored the original 1966 film – have thought about it, Alfie? *MCS*

Album rating: *5.5

– spinoff hits, etc. –

MICK JAGGER & DAVE STEWART: Old Habits Die Hard / New York Hustle

Oct 04. (cd-s) *(VSCDT 1887)* [45] [–]
(cd-s+=) *(VSCDX 1887)* – ('A'-L.A.-acoustic session) / ('A'-footage of recording session).

ALL THE PRETTY HORSES

2000 (US 117m) Miramax / Sony Pictures (PG-13)

Film genre: modern coming-of-age western drama

Top guns: dir: Billy Bob Thornton / s-w: Ted Tally (au: Cormac McCarthy)

Stars: Matt Damon *(John Grady Cole)* ← GOOD WILL HUNTING ← GERONIMO: AN AMERICAN LEGEND / → SPIRIT: STALLION OF THE CIMARRON, Henry Thomas *(Lacey Rawlins)*, Lucas Black *(Jimmy Blevins)* ← SLING BLADE / → COLD MOUNTAIN → KILLER DILLER → FRIDAY NIGHT LIGHTS, Penelope Cruz *(Alejandra de la Rocha)* → MASKED AND ANONYMOUS, **Ruben Blades** *(Rocha)* ← HOMEBOY, Robert Patrick *(Cole)* ← WAYNE'S WORLD / → WALK THE LINE → ELVIS, Julio Oscar Mechoso *(Captain)*, Miriam Colon *(Alfonsa)*, Bruce Dern *(judge)* ← LAST MAN STANDING ← PSYCH-OUT ← the TRIP ← the WILD ANGELS / → MASKED AND ANONYMOUS, **Sam Shepard** *(J.C. Franklin)* ← RENALDO AND CLARA / → SWORDFISH → STEALTH → the ASSASSINATION OF JESSE JAMES . . ., Jo Harvey Allen *(judge's wife)* ← TAPEHEADS ← TRUE STORIES, **Daniel Lanois** *(singer)* → LAUREL CANYON

Storyline: John and his best friend Lacey hit the Mexico Trail after his mother sells their Texan ranch. The cowboys seek love, adventure and wide open spaces and begin by meeting young hustler Blevins, whose horse looks suspiciously stolen. Later John and Lacey end up as cattle hands, but when John tries his hand with the beautiful Alejandra, her father has them arrested and thrown in jail. Suddenly the easy-going drifters have to survive prison life where violence and death are the norm. *JZ*

Movie rating: *5

Visual: video + dvd

Off the record: MARTY STUART (b.30 Sep'58, Philadelphia, Mississippi, USA). A man who served his teenaged apprenticeship under revered bluegrass pioneer Lester Flatt, MARTY STUART weathered the changes of country music right up until the new millennium when he began employing his hard won experience in film scoring. While his time under Flatt lasted for the most of the 70s, upon the latter's death he worked with another country legend, JOHNNY CASH, a man with whom he shared a passion for rockabilly-charged roots music. Although Stuart's solo career had begun in the early 80s, he only really began making inroads in the early 90s when – alongside the likes of Travis Tritt and DWIGHT YOAKAM – his independent streak coalesced with the rise of the neo-traditionalist movement. Although his hits dried up later in the decade, the man was to adapt his love of country tradition and Westerm myth in the score to '. . .PRETTY HORSES'. Brought on the board at the request of Thornton himself, Stuart drew almost universal critical acclaim with the Tex-Mex textures of his Golden Globe nominated score. While he went on to score Thornton's belatedly released comedy, 'Daddy & Them' (2001), as well as the Dwight Yoakam-produced, Thornton-starring 'Waking up In Reno' (2001), neither film inspired a soundtrack release. *BG*

—

MARTY STUART (score: Kristin Wilkinson & Larry Paxton)

Jan 01. (cd) *Sony; <(SK 89465)>* ☐ May01 ☐

– Cowboy's dream / Canyon sonata / All the pretty horses / Purty dad-gum good / After the rain / Mild cello blues / Malarki opus in D major / John Grady's angel / Edge of the world / Get my boots / Strawberry tango – pt.1 & 2 (SAM BACCO) / The king of horses / Far away (Alejandra's phone call) / Porque (RAUL MALO) / Waltz for hope (DANIEL LANOIS) / Ain't that a drag / My last days on Earth – What's it like to be dead? (w/ BILL MONROE) / Long journey home / Candles and lies / Rainy room / Far away / Far away – reprise / Cowboy's dream – All the pretty horses.

S/track review: The Old West of Cormac McCarthy's novel is brought to life by this fine soundtrack by country traditionalist MARTY STUART. Separated into a series of short cues, some may find the score frustrating listening, but despite the short length of each track, recurring themes lend a sense of cohesion. Acoustic guitar and mandolin are the lead instruments, reflecting STUART and collaborators LARRY PAXTON and KRISTIN WILKINSON's country and bluegrass roots. Their fluidly melodic parts are cushioned by panoramic strings, suggesting a duel between Bill Monroe and Elmer Berstein at the OK Corral. The orchestral arrangements are stirring without being bombastic, while the guitar parts create a high and lonesome mood. STUART's flat picking, always elegant but with enough edge to counter the smooth strings, makes the main theme, 'Cowboy's Dream', a wistful highlight. The versatility of the combination is deftly illustrated by 'Malarki Opus In D Major' where rapid fire mandolin darts in and out of staccato string and timpani hits to delightfully exciting effect. As the action moves south of the border, mariachi trumpet fanfares and spicy barrio rhythms strike up, recalling Ennio Morricone's peerless spaghetti western scores. This works well on both the romantic cues as well as more spirited tracks like 'Strawberry Tango'. The desert blues of Ry Cooder's brilliant 'PARIS, TEXAS' score is evoked on the atmospheric guitar piece 'After The Rain', while guest artist DANIEL LANOIS explores similar moods on his instrumental 'Waltz For Hope'. LANOIS also appears on 'Porque', a Mexican ballad sung beautifully by RAUL MALO of the Mavericks. While not quite up there with the classic Western soundtracks, 'ALL THE PRETTY HORSES' nevertheless successfully revives and reinvigorates this much missed genre. *SS*

Album rating: *6.5

ALL THE RIGHT NOISES

1969 (UK 91m) 20th Century Fox (AA)

Film genre: romantic melodrama

Top guns: s-w + dir: Gerry O'Hara (+ au)

Stars: Tom Bell *(Len Lewin)* ← BALLAD IN BLUE / → SWING, Olivia Hussey *(Val)*, Judy Carne *(Joy Lewin)* → WHAT ABOUT ME, John Standing *(Bernie)*, Gareth Wright *(Ian)*, Edward Higgens *(Ted)*, Roy Herrick *(camera operator)*, Leslie-Anne Down *(Laura)* → SCENES FROM THE GOLDMINE, Yootha Joyce *(Mrs. Byrd)* ← CATCH US IF YOU CAN

Storyline: Young electrician Len feels the spark has gone out of his marriage and begins an affair with actress Val. As Val is just fifteen he should really pull the plug on their relationship, but Val is exciting and his wife Joy is no joy at all. When Val thinks she's pregnant Len must grow up fast and take his responsibilities seriously, or else hope Val becomes less of a live wire. *JZ*

Movie rating: *4.5

Visual: none

Off the record: MELANIE was born Melanie Safka of Ukrainian-Italian parentage, 3rd February '47, Astoria, Long Island, New York, USA. In 1966, while auditioning for a bit part in a play, the shy folk singer accidentally walked into a music publisher's office where she was asked to sing and play her guitar. Fortunately, they liked what they heard and invited her back, the company in question being none other than 'Columbia' records. The budding singer-songwriter was assigned to producer, Peter Schekeryk, who was to become her husband and the father of her three children. After two flop singles, MELANIE signed to 'Buddah' records late in 1968 and her first album, 'Born To Be', revealed her to be a child-like and coy vocalist inspired by Lotte Lenya and Edith Piaf. Kafka was duly invited to play the 'WOODSTOCK' festival in 1969; her records (notably the French No.1 single, 'Bobo's Party') were already establishing themselves on the continent. In 1970, the folk-oriented Seekers had a US hit with one of her better known tracks, 'What Have They Done To My Song, Ma?', while she herself made the UK Top 10 with the melancholy 'Ruby Tuesday' (a Rolling Stones cover). Both songs were gleaned from the accompanying Top 5 album, 'Candles In The Rain', this golden period seeing the release of three further successful albums, the last of which, 'Gather Me', featured an American US No.1 (UK No.4), 'Brand New Key'. The aforementioned album appeared on her newly formed 'Neighborhood' label, an imprint she had initiated with her aforementioned husband. Despite this venture, MELANIE's commercial clout dwindled as the 70s wore on. As her record sales fell away, so her label eventually went belly-up in the mid-70s. *MCS*

—

MELANIE (w/ instrumentals *)

Jul 71. (lp) *Buddah; (2318 034) <BDS 5132>* ☐ ☐

– In the hour / Ears to the ground (*) / Save the night / All the right noises (*) / Ears to the ground / Please love me (*) / Please love me / Pebbles in the sand / In the hour (*) / My Bonnie lies over the ocean / Getting out (*) / Pebbles in the sand (*) / Getting out / In the hour (*) / Ears to the ground (*) / Please love me (*) / Pebbles in the sand / In the hour (*).

S/track review: Decades after her big-stage debut at Woodstock in 1969, New York-born MELANIE has enjoyed some critical rehabilitation (Jarvis Cocker included her alongside Iggy Pop and Motorhead in the 2007 Meltdown Festival), but she remains very much the hippie torch singer. This unexpected Brit-flick soundtrack dates from her early 70s heyday, and the artful production by manager and husband Peter Schekeryk sticks to the well-defined (and easily parodied) template that shaped a string of international hits around her impassioned sincerity and European folky inflections. There are five newly-written songs and one retread, delivering that distinctive alto loud and clear over nicely measured acoustic and orchestral arrangements. And there's undoubtedly something about MELANIE's warble that manages to wring an affecting intimacy out of the humdrum songwriting; 'Please Love Me' (both a song title and a much-repeated chorus) typifies the style. Never released on CD, this collection is a rarity that's likely to be appealing enough to MELANIE or soundtrack fans, though they could find their patience taxed by its habit of repeating every song as an instrumental – not to mention trotting out some of them three times apiece. *ND*

Album rating: *5.5

ALMOST SUMMER

1978 (US 88m) Universal Pictures (PG)

Film genre: romantic comedy

Top guns: s-w: Martin Davidson (+ dir) → EDDIE AND THE CRUISERS → LOOKING FOR AN ECHO, Marc Reid Rubel → XANADU, Judith Berg, Sandra Berg

Stars: Bruno Kirby *(Bobby DeVito)* → WHERE THE BUFFALO ROAM → THIS IS SPINAL TAP → BIRDY → GOOD MORNING, VIETNAM → the BASKETBALL DIARIES → a SLIPPING-DOWN LIFE, John Friedrich *(Darryl Fitzgerald)* ← THANK GOD IT'S FRIDAY, Lee Purcell *(Christine Alexander)*, Didi Conn *(Donna DeVito)* ← GREASE ← YOU LIGHT UP MY LIFE / → GREASE 2, Thomas Carter *(Dean Hampton)* ← the MONKEY HUSTLE, Tim Matheson *(Kevin Hawkins)* ← ANIMAL HOUSE / → the STORY OF US, Harvey Lewis *(Stanley Lustgarten)* → ALAMO BAY, **Mike Love**

Storyline: American high school drama with a brain, as wide boy Bobby DeVito assists the squeaky clean Darryl Fitzgerald to stand in the student elections against his erstwhile girlfriend. Fitzgerald subsequently resigns when he discovers the vote was rigged, and DeVito decides to go it alone in the re-run. *BG*

Movie rating: *3.5

Visual: none

Off the record: **CELEBRATION** (see below)

Various Artists (incl. CELEBRATION *) (score: CHARLES LLOYD ** & RON ALTBACH ***)

Apr 78. (lp/c) *M.C.A.; <MCA 3037> (MCF/TCMCF 2840)* ☐ Jun78 ☐
– Almost summer (*) / Sad, sad summer (*) / Cruisin' (*) / Lookin' good (***) / Summer in the city / It's o.k. (*) / Football (** & ***) / Island girl (**) / Christine and Bobby (***) / We are the future (HIGH INERGY) / She was a lady (FRESH).

S/track review: CELEBRATION were an 8-piece outfit featuring ex-Beach Boys singer MIKE LOVE, CHARLES LLOYD (sax & flute), RON ALTBACH (keyboards) and DAVE ROBINSON (bass & some lead vocals), MIKE KOWALSKI (drums, percussion), ED CARTER (guitar & bass), WELLS KELLY (bass) and GARY GRIFFIN (synths & electric piano). Released at a time when the Beach Boys were going through a lull in both their creative and commercial career, CELEBRATION's 'ALMOST SUMMER' was a lightweight substitute for anybody into the BB's girls'n'surf heyday. The opening title track (co-penned by MIKE LOVE, Brian Wilson & Al Jardine – as stated on the front cover!) managed to scrape into the US Top 30, although most of the soundtrack was mediocre, even by late 70s standards. 'It's O.K.' (written by LOVE & Wilson again) was easy-going, while a cover of the Lovin' Spoonful's 'Summer In The City' did little to distinguish it from its time lodged in the flower-power 60s. Side two was really down to non-CELEBRATION tracks by jazz-rock composers/musicians CHARLES LLOYD (check out the 7-minute 'Island Girl' if you must) and RON ALTBACH; the two closing cues stemmed from HIGH INERGY and FRESH, the former outfit straight "outta" 'Motown'. *MCS*

Album rating: *4

– spinoff releases, etc. –

CELEBRATION feat. MIKE LOVE: Almost Summer / **CELEBRATION feat.** CHARLES LLOYD: Lookin' Good

Apr 78. (7") *<40891> (MCA 365)* 28 ☐

CELEBRATION: It's O.K. / Island Girl

May 78. (7") *(MCA 379)* ☐ ☐

CELEBRATION: Cruisin' / Summer In The City

Sep 78. (7") *(MCA 391)* ☐ ☐

an AMBUSH OF GHOSTS

1993 (US 92m) Stress Fiesta Films (R)

Film genre: psychological drama

Top guns: dir: Everett Lewis / s-w: Quinton Peeples

Stars: Stephen Dorff *(George Betts)* → JUDGMENT NIGHT → BACKBEAT → S.F.W. → I SHOT ANDY WARHOL, Genevieve Bujold *(Irene Betts)*, Bruce Davison *(Bill Betts)* ← CRIMES OF PASSION ← DEADMAN'S CURVE ← SHORT EYES ← the STRAWBERRY STATEMENT / → GRACE OF MY HEART, Alan Boyce *(Christian)* ← PERMANENT RECORD, Anne Heche *(Denise)* → WALKING AND TALKING → WAG THE DOG, David Duval *(student #1)* ← SLC PUNK

Storyline: Teenager George finds himself the new man of the house ten years after his mum accidentally ran over his younger brother in a car accident. Mum is now slowly but surely going loopy and, as well as having to cope with her, he finds his friend Christian on his doorstep begging for help after killing a classmate. George hides him in the house and becomes involved with his girlfriend Denise. But how much of all this is real and how much is down to George's own traumatised mind? *JZ*

Movie rating: *5

Visual: none

Off the record: nothing

IN THE NURSERY

Nov 93. (cd) *Third Mind; <(TM 9038-2)>* ☐ ☐
– After great pain / Sedation / Lipstick / Disorientated / Archaize / White robe / Cop shed / Running scene / Christian returns / Christian decides / Silk robe / Sedation 2 / Cop house / Funeral part 1 / Funeral part 2 / Dear Grover / Casus Belli / Syntonic / The hidden fortress / Hallucinations? *(re-iss. Feb03 +=; corp 002)* – When I write to you.

S/track review: With a sound invariably described as "cinematic", and having written an album (1987's 'Stormhorse') as the soundtrack for an imaginary film, it was perhaps inevitable that IN THE NURSERY would cross into the world of film scoring. With 'An AMBUSH OF GHOSTS', identical twin brothers KLIVE and NIGEL HUMBERSTONE made their debut as film composers, approaching the project with a determination that belied their long cherished ambitions in the field. Introducing "real" live acoustic instruments (oboe, cello and flute) to their more synthetic set-up for the first time, 'AMBUSH . . .' is far more akin to classical scores than other band soundtracks. Sparse, understated, and atmospheric, ITN's score is meant to reflect the mise en scène of the film, where most of the action takes place in an old Victorian home, and the emotional turmoil of the central character, played by Stephen Dorff. All of which is apparent, but crucially the music doesn't command much interest on its own, the "real" instruments making the synth orchestration sound like a poor substitution rather than a distinctive element. ITN's score ends up sounding generic and dated due to the uncomplementary mix, while the uninspired throb of synths on almost every track is understated to the point of somnambulism. Add to this the inclusion of dramatically inert dialogue snippets, and you have a disappointingly unengaging score which aims for subtlety and hits boredom. *SW*

Album rating: *4

□ AMERICA segment
(⇒ the LAST UNICORN)

AMO NON AMO

US title 'I LOVE YOU, I LOVE YOU NOT' / re-issue 'TOGETHER?'

1979 (Ita 91m) Compagnia Europea / Titanus (18)

Film genre: domestic/romantic melodrama

Top guns: s-w: Armenia Balducci (+ dir), Ennio de Concini ← la BATTAGLIA DEI MODS

Stars: Jacqueline Bisset *(Louise)* → SAVE THE LAST DANCE 2, Maximilian Schell *(Giovanni)* ← the DEADLY AFFAIR, Terence Stamp *(Henry)*, Monica Guerritore *(Guilia)*, Gian Luca Venantini *(Luca Venantini)*, Umberto Orsini

Storyline: Set in a resort near Rome, Louise attempts to juggle a recent divorce, a boyfriend and an affair, balanced alongside a demanding son and a new career. She is a newly liberated woman seeking to define her role in the late seventies, he is facing the inevitability of age. A get out clause is needed – for her.. and the audience. *MCS & DG*

Movie rating: *3.5

Visual: video

Off the record: Screenwriter/director/actress, Armenia Balducci, appeared in the 1971 film, 'Sacco e Vanzetti'.

—

GOBLIN

1979. (lp) *Cinevox; (MDF 33.126)* [-] Italy [-]
– Amo non amo / Maniera / Both-two / Funky top / Yell * / Suspiria * / Zombi * / Profondo Rosso *. *(cd-iss. Feb02 w/out * / +=; CD MDF 347)* – Both-two / Amo non amo / Amo non amo / Amo non amo / Amo non amo / Amo non amo.

S/track review: Progressive-rock act GOBLIN (more at home with Giallo suspense thrillers than complex love stories) were simultaneously commissioned to score the Italian version of the movie while nostalgic pop songsmith, Burt Bacharach, penned the American equivalent. 'AMO NON AMO' was actually a bit of a departure for GOBLIN, seeing them embrace a number of different styles. The set opens with keyboards and synth which put you in mind of early 70s Yes, before a sustained, understated guitar line plays out. It sounds oddly like the sort of music you'd hear accompanying late night/early morning Ceefax on BBC2. 'Maniera' is an entirely different prospect, a conventional rock piece reminiscent of Deep Purple, complete with an excellent keyboard track not too high in the mix. 'Both-Two' returns us to a slower pace, acoustic guitar complemented by a light touch from the rhythm section. A languid lead solo takes us out. The Ennio Morricone-styled 'Funky Top' is possibly the stand-out track, and it does more or less what you would expect from the title. A robust bass line is topped with tidy Nile Rodgers-style riffs. Think the James Taylor Quartet playing the 'Starsky & Hutch' theme and you won't be far from the overall feel. An excellent effort, despite occasional risible "singing" following the central melody. An additional version of 'Both-Two' and five of 'Amo Non Amo' fill out the CD, which was finally released in 2002. Overall, an interesting effort. The CD also features Prog-rock classics from 'PROFONDO ROSSO', 'SUSPIRIA' and 'ZOMBI', although some copies contained alternate takes of the title track. GOBLIN at the time comprised:- FABIO PIGNATELLI, CARLO PENNISI and AGOSTINO MARANGOLO. *MCS & DG*

Album rating: *5.5

□ ANGELS OF THE UNIVERSE alt.
(⇒ ENGLAR ALHEIMSINS)

the ANIMALS FILM

1981 (UK 136m w/b&w) Beyond the Frame / Slick Pics International

Film genre: social/scientific/animal-horror documentary

Top guns: s-w: (+ dir) Victor Schonfeld, Myriam Alaux

Stars: Julie Christie *(narrator)* ← NASHVILLE ← TONITE LET'S ALL MAKE LOVE IN LONDON, Sandy Dennis *(herself)*

Storyline: A documentary by animal rights protesters showing lab experiments for research purposes. Using secret cameras, the film shows in detail what happens to the animals in the name of science. There is also a hint at the end of the film that one day it could be humans who become the guinea pigs of the future. A harrowing film not for the squeamish or faint hearted. *JZ*

Movie rating: *6

Visual: video

Off the record: **ROBERT WYATT** was born Robert Wyatt Ellidge, 28th January '45, Bristol, England. It would be while at school that he formed the Wilde Flowers alongside the Hopper brothers (Hugh and Brian), an embryonic Canterbury-scene pop act that subsequently spliced into two groups, Caravan and the Soft Machine. The latter was the band WYATT joined in 1966, but after four seminal jazz-rock albums as their drummer ('The Soft Machine', 'Volume 2', 'Third' & 'Fourth'), he departed in '71, forming his own Matching Mole outfit. The previous year, his record label, 'C.B.S.', had issued his first solo album, 'The End Of An Ear', which was assisted by fellow Soft Machine members supplying the jazz-rock feel. In the summer of '73, WYATT was paralyzed from the waist down after falling from a five-storey window during a party, convalescing for several months at Stoke Mandeville hospital. He returned the following year (now with a beard and confined to a wheelchair), his single, a version of the Monkees' 'I'm A Believer', hitting the Top 30. Richard Branson had given him a break on his 'Virgin' records, 'Rock Bottom' (1974), such gems as 'Sea Song' and 'Little Red Riding Hood Hits The Road' (in two parts), each showing just how versatile his musical and vocal interplay had reached. WYATT's second for the label, 'Ruth Is Stranger Than Richard' (1975), showed an even deeper side, WYATT covering Charlie Hayden's jazz track, 'Song For Che'. In 1977, he had another stab at the pop charts, a dire cover version of Chris Andrews' 'Yesterday Man' being his final recording for some time. He took a wide berth from the conventional and signed to indie imprint 'Rough Trade' in 1980, releasing a number of singles prior to his comeback album, 'Nothing Can Stop Us Now' (1982). This featured his classy re-working of Elvis Costello & Clive Langer's 'Shipbuilding'. In 1983, through constant airplay by Radio 1 DJ John Peel, the anti-Falklands war song gained a Top 40 placing. WYATT continued to spread his political messages through his music ('The ANIMALS FILM' was a prime example), although he was never one to preach too much, his songs retaining an intensely personal quality. *BG & MCS*

—

ROBERT WYATT

May 82. (m-lp) *Rough Trade; (ROUGH 40)* [ ] [-]
– (side 1) / (side 2). *(<cd-iss. 1999 on 'Thirsty Ear' EP-box>)*

S/track review: This isn't meant to be a comfortable listen. Seven years after making the Top 40 with his impressively cheery take on 'I'm A Believer' (and on the brink of returning to it again with his even more impressively melancholy 'Shipbuilding') the former Soft Machine drummer was setting out to disturb. Playing all the instruments himself, WYATT matches the film's method: alienation, unpleasantness and dissonance are the keynotes of a rarely-remitting 28-minute evocation of suffering. He is well served in this by early synthesisers, typically interweaving the nasty, mechanical tones and textures of several different machines over bass and drum figures that have just enough melody to retain the attention. Where there is piano it is sparse, cold and distant.

What distinguishes this from the incidental music on any low-budget British science fiction series of the period is a craft and subtlety in the development of themes that linger in the mind's ear, though there is probably just too much knob-twiddling to reward repeated discovery of these virtues. If WYATT ever felt a temptation to go the whole hog with something that tugged the heartstrings through sad beauty rather than spiky discomfort, he resisted it until 'Shipbuilding'. *ND*

Album rating: *4.5

ANIMALYMPICS

1980 (US 78m) Warner Bros. Pictures (G)

Film genre: animated children's/family sports comedy

Top guns: s-w: (+ dir) Steven Lisberger, Michael Fremer (story: Roger Allers → the EMPEROR'S NEW GROOVE, John Norton)

Voices: Billy Crystal *(Lodge "Rugs" Turkel)* → the PRINCESS BRIDE, Gilda Radner *(Barbara Warbler / Coralee Perrier / Tatiana Tushenko / Brenda Springer / Doree Turnell)* ← the RUTLES / → the WOMAN IN RED, Harry Shearer *(Keen Hackshaw)* → ONE-TRICK PONY → THIS IS SPINAL TAP → WAYNE'S WORLD 2 → GHOST DOG: THE WAY OF THE SAMURAI → GIGANTIC (A TALE OF TWO JOHNS) → a MIGHTY WIND, Michael Fremer *(Henry Hummel)*

Storyline: The cartoon feature film of the hit TV series has all the usual animated suspects competing in the inaugural Animalia Olympic Games. Current celebrities come under fire as the characters compete in the marathon, skiing and swimming. *MCS*

Movie rating: *6

Visual: video

Off the record: GRAHAM GOULDMAN (see below)

—

GRAHAM GOULDMAN

Apr 80. (lp) *A&M; <4810> Mercury; (9109 630)* ☐ ☐
– Go for it / Underwater fantasy / Away from it all / Born to lose / Kit mambo / Z.O.O. / Love's not for me (René's song) / With you I can run forever / Bionic boar / We've made it to the top.

S/track review: Taking a break from his regular band, prolific songsmith, GRAHAM GOULDMAN (ex-Mindbenders, etc.), and a handful of 10cc musicians at the time, STUART TOSH, RICK FENN, PAUL BURGESS and DUNCAN MACKAY (plus longtime affiliate, MIKE TIMONY), set about beating off OST competition from fellow 10cc stalwart, Eric Stewart. The previous year, the band in question had branched out into the movie theme world, albeit with a whimper rather than a bang, courtesy of US Top 100 entry, 'From You And I', from the 1979 film 'Moment By Moment'. 'ANIMALYMPICS' came along at an awkward period for GOULDMAN and the once-high-flying 10cc, who'd lost Godley & Creme to a spinoff outfit and nearly lost Eric Stewart in a serious car crash. GOULDMAN was said to be very dismissive of this film commission, although it certainly rates among his more adventurous projects, latter-day 10cc and their current LP, 'Look Hear', included. Kicking off with the funky-riffed 'Go For It', 'ANIMALYMPICS' slides it also gets into rock gear via follow-on number, 'Underwater Fantasy'. Although there were a few flop singles aboard such as the Parisian-esque ballad, 'Love's Not For Me (Rene's Song)' and 'Away From It All', the album wasn't at all bad. The leader's versatility on the spasmodic and pounding jungle cut, 'Kit Mambo', equalled anything from the pen of GG, while 'Bionic Boar' is just of novelty value – but why not! *MCS*

Album rating: *5

– spinoff releases, etc. –

GRAHAM GOULDMAN: Love's Not For Me (Rene's Song) / Bionic Boar
Mar 80. (7") *(MER 7)* [–] ☐

GRAHAM GOULDMAN: Away From It All / Bionic Boar
Jun 80. (7") ☐ [–]

ANTARCTICA

original title 'NANKYOKU MONOGATARI'

1983 (Japan 137m) Nippon Herald Films (G)

Film genre: nature/animal drama

Top guns: s-w: Koreyoshi Kurahara (+ dir), Toshiro Ishido, Kan Saji

Stars: Ken Takakura *(Ushioda)*, Tsunehiko Watase *(Ochi)*, Eiji Okada *(Ozawa Taicho)*, Masako Natsume *(Ozawa Keiko)*, Takeshi Kusaka *(Morishima Kyoju)*, Shigeru Koyama *(Horigome Taicho)*, Shin Kishida *(Kissaten Master)*

Storyline: Two Japanese scientists are forced to leave a team of huskies behind in the Antarctic due to terrible weather conditions. A relief mission is cancelled, and the dogs are left stranded in the desolate waste, chained to a pole with no food or shelter. In desperation, two of the huskies, Taro and Jiro, manage to break free and must somehow find enough food to survive the Antarctic winter until the scientists return next year. *JZ*

Movie rating: *6.5

Visual: video

Off the record: (see below)

—

VANGELIS

Nov 83. (lp/c/cd) *Arista; <P33P 20068>* [–] Japan [–]
– Theme from Antarctica / Antarctica echoes / Kinematic / Song of white / Life of Antarctica / Memory of Antarctica / Other side of Antarctica / Deliverance. *(UK-iss.Nov88 on 'Polydor' lp/c/cd; 815 732-1/-4/-2)*

S/track review: Those both familiar and unfamiliar with VANGELIS' work will immediately recognise how closely 'Theme From Antarctica' follows the template of his much-lauded work on 'CHARIOTS OF FIRE'. Conversely, 'Antarctica Echoes' is a pure minimalist journey with a slow-burning backbone of beautiful synths embellished by electronic bleeps and chimes. Similarly, 'Song Of White', with its oriental feel, shares the stripped down dreamy atmospherics, with moments of silence as important as the instrumentation, before climaxing with VANGELIS' trademark cascading keyboards. 'Life Of Antarctica' finds room for emotive flute lines amongst the dense synthesizers and bombastic war drums, before 'Memory Of Antarctica' pleasantly slows things down again. Meanwhile, 'Other Side Of Antarctica' is a slab of unsettling madness-inducing psychedelia reminiscent of the intro to Pink Floyd's 'Shine On You Crazy Diamond', while closer 'Deliverance' is more akin to a lighter version of Angelo Badalamenti's subsequent theme from 'Twin Peaks'. *LF*

Album rating: *6

APARTMENT HUNTING

2001 (Can 89m) Alliance Atlantis & Odeon Films

Film genre: romantic comedy

Top guns: s-w + dir: Bill Robertson

Stars: Andrew Tarbet *(Ben Riddick)*, Kari Matchett *(Sarah)*, Valerie Jeanneret *(Celine)*, Rachel Hayward *(Lola)*, Matt Gordon *(Mac McConnell)*, Arnold Pinnock *(Dean)*, **Mary Margaret O'Hara** *(homeless Helen)*

Storyline: With his marriage going through a lull and his book about to get the thumbs-down from another publisher, Ben Riddick hunts for a new apartment, his present one being above a cheeseshop in Toronto's Kensington Market. Then he meets Celine on a tele-date and immediately falls for her charm and wit – his dilemma is about to begin. *MCS*

Movie rating: *6

Visual: dvd

Off the record: **MARY MARGARET O'HARA** was born in Toronto in the Canadian province of Ontario, c. 1960. One of the most enigmatic female singer/songwriters to have emerged over the last two decades, O'HARA's slim but revered body of work has been something of a well-kept secret in a genre that appears to throw up a new starlet every other week. A graduate of Ontario art college, she began her musical career in a soul-pop outfit called Dollars before going on to join Songship, a band which soon changed its name to the equally badly-monikered Go Deo Chorus. During her time with the band, she penned much of the material which would later surface as her solo album; heard by 'Virgin' in their GDC demo form, the songs were strong enough to persuade the label to sign O'HARA as a solo artist in 1984. Despite teething problems – XTC's Andy Partridge allegedly stood down from production duties after only a day – and interminable delays, the sessions were eventually mixed and co-produced by noted Canadian guitarist, MICHAEL BROOKS, and released in 1988 as 'Miss America'. Forging her own improvisatory vocal style against a musical canvas which alternated between vintage country, jazz and even mutoid funk (on the tortured 'Not Be Alright'), O'HARA was the toast of the more discerning critic. While possessing a distinct ringing soprano, O'HARA's singing occasionally brought to mind an artier Stevie Nicks (especially on 'When You Know You're Happy') or perhaps Natalie Merchant, although few female singers have explored the fevered speaking-in-tongues territory previously mapped out by the likes of VAN MORRISON. At its most compulsive on 'Body's In Trouble', 'Miss America' was a record guaranteed to keep you second guessing. Come to that, many fans had been second guessing whether Mary would ever get round to releasing a follow-up. While the songstress parted company with 'Virgin' after the record buying Joe Public failed to get the point, she went on to work with a variety of musicians (i.e. Morrissey, This Mortal Coil, John And Mary, Gary Lucas, etc.) as well as appearing in a number of low-key movies. Her acting career already underway via 1988's 'CANDY MOUNTAIN', O'HARA played the role of Rita and provided the score for Bill Robertson's debut feature, 'The Events Leading Up To My Death' (1991). For the filmmaker's follow-up movie 'APARTMENT HUNTING' – released nine years later! – it combined as her long-awaited sophomore set. Post-millennium, the lady of leisure, so to speak, has become relatively prolific by comparison, her formative years yielding a starring role in the film noir jazz musical, 'Black Widow' (2005). *BG & MCS*

—

MARY MARGARET O'HARA (& Various Artists)

2001. (cd) *Maple; <APTCD 01>* [–] Canada [–]
– Was you / Never came back again / Rain / Dream I had (I) / Ay Candela! (KLAVE Y KONGO) / Be a man (BILL ROBERTSON) / Scary Latin love song / If you see my love (I) / I don't care / Woo-hoo (BILL ROBERTSON & RUSTY McCARTHY) / Have you gone / Apartment of cheese suite / Love will take its time / If you see my love (II) / Chez le nez suite / Dream I had (II) / Hello yellow goose (burning dog).

S/track review: Much has been reported about singer-songwriter MARY MARGARET O'HARA; the phrase "conspicuous by her absence" has never been so applicable. With the help of director/musician/composer, BILL ROBERTSON (who convinced her to take an acting part in the movie itself), O'HARA and her team of local musicians recorded the set in guitarist RUSTY McCARTHY's ever-moving basement studio. 'APARTMENT HUNTING' was no 'Miss America', but as a long-awaited follow-up, it'll do for now. The album gets underway courtesy of torch-ballad, 'Was You', a 2-minute song in the Billie Holiday/Nina Simone mould. Raising the tempo somewhat, O'HARA (alongside players McCARTHY, drummer MIKE SLOSKI, bassist RUSS BOSWELL and MATT HORNER on keyboards) majestically pulls the rabbit from the hat via funky scat-jazz cut, 'Never Came Back Again'. The inclusion of third track, 'Rain' (originally from the 1997 film, 'Erotica: A Journey Into Female Sexuality'), was indeed a masterstroke, her warbling, incoherent vox at its peak. Whether taken as a compliment or not, track 4, 'Dream I Had', has all the traits of an Annie Lennox song, while follow-on song ('Ay Candela!' by KLAVE Y KONGO) is a second cousin to the Eurythmics' 'Right By Your Side'. BILL ROBERTSON gets out of his director's chair for his one solo spot, 'Be A Man (Fallin')', while he also pairs up with McCARTHY on 1-minute ditty, 'Woo-Hoo'. There are embarrassing moments on 'APARTMENT HUNTING' (the manic 'Scary Latin Love Song' and the Eartha Kitt-like 'Chez Le Nez Suite' are indeed two such cues), but when O'HARA gets down to serious melancholy business via 'If You See My Love', 'I Don't Care' and 'Love Will Take Its Time', no one does it better. Of the best tunes, the lengthy folk-polka, 'Have You Gone', comes a close second to the quirky US-sitcom-like theme, 'Apartment Of Cheese Suite'. Now where is that elusive third set, Miss Canada? *MCS*

Album rating: *6.5

□ ASH RA TEMPEL segment
(⇒ le BERCEAU DE CRISTAL)

□ ASHTON, GARDNER & DYKE segment
(⇒ the LAST REBEL)

the ASSASSINATION OF JESSE JAMES BY THE COWARD ROBERT FORD

2007 (US 160m) Warner Bros. Pictures (R)

Film genre: outlaw western drama/biopic

Top guns: s-w + dir: Andrew Dominik ← CHOPPER (au: Ron Hansen)

Stars: Brad Pitt *(Jesse James)* ← FIGHT CLUB ← JOHNNY SUEDE, Casey Affleck *(Robert Ford)*, **Sam Shepard** *(Frank James)* ← STEALTH ← SWORDFISH ← ALL THE PRETTY HORSES ← RENALDO AND CLARA, Mary-Louise Parker *(Zee James)* ← ROMANCE & CIGARETTES, Paul Schneider *(Dick Liddil)*, Sam Rockwell *(Charley Ford)* ← LAST EXIT TO BROOKLYN, Jeremy Renner *(Wood Hite)* ← a LITTLE TRIP TO HEAVEN, **Nick CAVE** *(Bowery saloon singer)*

Storyline: Young Robert Ford is desperate to be a member of the vicious James gang, as he hero-worships its leader Jesse. Despite showing little else but contempt for Ford, Jesse invites him back to the house where he yet again berates him. Enough is enough for Ford and the tempting target of Jesse's back grows ever larger in his sights as he reaches boiling point. *JZ*

Movie rating: *8

Visual: dvd

Off the record: (see below)

—

NICK CAVE & WARREN ELLIS

Nov 07. (cd) *Mute; (CDSTUMM 294)* [ ] [–]
– Rather lovely thing / Moving on / Song for Jesse / Falling / Cowgirl / The money train / What must be done / Another rather lovely thing / Carnival / Last ride back to KC / What happens next / Destined for great things / Counting the stars / Song for Bob.

S/track review: It'd been only two years since NICK CAVE and fellow Australian WARREN ELLIS (ex-Dirty Three) had delivered their first film score collaboration, 'The PROPOSITION'; many didn't expect another so soon. 'The ASSASSINATION OF JESSE

JAMES . . .' lies basically with the virtuoso violin work of ELLIS, although CAVE does display a mean and brooding piano, but the absence of his deep vocals becomes apparent after a while. Opening with the lilting 'Rather Lovely Thing', the music slips between Ennio Morricone's romantic/outlaw western, 'Made In Heaven', and the soundtrack work of the Horse Flies. Ditto track 3, 'Song For Jesse', a flighty cue on a mission to hit the heartstrings courtesy of its tingling vibes and keys. By the time 'Moving On' plucks its way solemnly and easily into one's ears, ELLIS is in full control, while one is goaded into thinking CAVE will produce a vocal or two. It's not to be. The mood switches somewhat when the quirky 'Cowgirl' and/or 'Carnival' get into full flow, the violins here interacting with simple guitar strums, a combination of alt-country that the Handsome Family could only dream of touching. The Devil had indeed sold some of his best tunes to Messrs CAVE and ELLIS. With the Western outlaw subject matter in mind, the barren desert-bowl soundscapes do get a little bleak at times (example 'The Money Train', 'What Must Be Done' and 'Last Ride Back To KC'), but most cues come across as effective and cinematic on all levels. The drama gets intense with the addition of a full orchestra on track 11, 'What Happens Next', but the build-up peters out before it really gets going. With revisionist westerns still in vogue today ('Brokeback Mountain', 'COLD MOUNTAIN', etc.), it's great to see the odd filmmakers giving rock talent such as CAVE and Co the chance to shine. *MCS*

Album rating: *6

□ the ASSOCIATION segment
(⇒ GOODBYE, COLUMBUS)

□ ATARI TEENAGE RIOT segment
(⇒ THREAT)

□ AUDIENCE segment
(⇒ BRONCO BULLFROG)

AUSTRALIAN RULES

2002 (Aus 95m) Palace Films / AFFC / Tidy Town Pictures (M)

Film genre: coming-of-age sports drama

Top guns: s-w: Paul Goldman (+ dir), Phillip Gwynne (book: 'Deadly, Unna?')

Stars: Nathan Phillips *(Gary "Blacky" Black)* → ONE PERFECT DAY, Luke Carroll *(Dumby Red)*, Lisa Flanagan *(Clarence)*, Tom Budge *(Pickles)* → the PROPOSITION, Simon Westaway *(Bob Black)*, Celia Ireland *(Liz Black)*, Kevin Harrington *(Arks)*, Martin Vaughan *(Darcy)*, Kelton Pell *(Tommy Red)* ← ONE NIGHT THE MOON

Storyline: A kind of Antipodean equivalent to rugby, Australian rules football is the arena in which small-town claustrophobia and interracial tensions are played out in this typically straight-talking Aussie drama. Dumby Red is the Aboriginal star player, Blackie his white teamate and best pal. Both find themselves at the sharp end of racial prejudice, Dumby through the undermining of his on-field achievements, Blackie at the hands of a racist father and backward attitudes to cross-cultural romance. *BG*

Movie rating: *6.5

Visual: dvd

Off the record: (see below)

—

MICK HARVEY

Jul 03. (cd) *Ionic-Mute; (IONIC 17CD) E.M.I.; <590500>* □ □
– Opening credits / Training / Pickles rides out / Clarence and Blacky / On the boat / Darcy's gents / Fantasy line-up / Ruck training / In Pickles' bedroom / Grand final first half / Mum's tactics / Dumby at half time / Grand final second half / What I done to her (TEX, DON & CHARLIE) / Under the pier / Best on ground announcement / Pickles torches Darcy's gents / The shooting / Mourning outside the pub / Stones at house / Walking to Dumby / The funeral / End titles.

S/track review: Nominated for a Best Score award by the Australian Film Institute, this is the soundtrack which elevated MICK HARVEY on a par with the likes of RY COODER, broiling with that roots-grind key in charting the outsized wildness of non-European landscapes. If a gathering sense of that vastness shades its opening wonder, HARVEY isn't long in mapping its peril: enter scale-climbing strings, bottle-rim wood block and pounding kettle drums. It's a dichotomy he works consistently over a measured, multi-instrumental palette, all of which he arranges and the large part of which he performs personally. The spiralling, Cooder-esque reverb clang serving as his primary leitmotif is initially sounded in 'Pickles Rides Out', a tongue-in-cheek, multi-referential title for a composer whose appreciation of film music clearly runs deep. HARVEY might have developed it into an album length desert symphony; instead he toys with timbral expectations, juxtaposing mood and colour, coaxing sitar-like tones out of the blues, confounding subtextual cues with blinking pizzicato showers and the kind of orchestral hair shirts he draped over 'TO HAVE AND TO HOLD'. Unlike so many to sketch interior Australia, he's just as selective with his use of didgeridoo, so concentrated a tool he implies interracial tension with a single note. Unexpectedly, he throws it all together midway through, gelling the competing motifs into the glutinous funk of 'Grand Final Second Half', and raising the curtain on a more thematically cohesive climax, if not before recapitulating with a gorgeous piece of source music. TEX PERKINS' 'What I Done To Her' is alt-country at its most seductive: arching, aching steel and self-delusion, as evocative as anything out of America and a fitting corollary to the richest score of HARVEY's career. *BG*

Album rating: *7.5

□ Roy AYERS segment
(⇒ COFFY)

B

BT

Born: BRIAN TRANSEAU, b. 4 Oct'71, Washington DC, USA. While the acronym BT is more usually associated with phone bills (at least in Britain), those of an electronic persuasion may recall BRIAN TRANSEAU from his days as a much touted club wunderkind signed to Paul Oakenfold's 'Perfecto' imprint. Classically trained, the boy known as BT initially made his way in the dance world with the help of his pals Deep Dish, sculpting epic, airbrushed house and paving the way for such pop-techno symphonists as Robert Miles. Always more popular in the UK than his rather rave/dance-phobic home country, he racked up an impressive series of Top 40 hits over the course of the mid-to-late 90s after which time he began employing his writing and arranging skills in film. While his first commission was the score to Doug Liman's club-fuelled comedy, 'Go' (1999), only the pounding, four to the floor groove of 'Believer' made it to soundtrack, a pattern repeated with such features as Stephen Hopkins' 'Under Suspicion' (2000), Rob Cohen's high octane, illegal car racing drama, 'The Fast And The Furious' (2001), Sylvester Stallone Formula One fluff, 'Driven' (2001) and Ben Stiller's hilarious fashion satire, 'Zoolander' (2001). BT finally got to flex his film scoring muscle on 'MONSTER' (2003); two years on, TRANSEAU worked on 'STEALTH'. In 2007, a unique collaboration of BT and ex-Replacements guitarist, TOMMY STINSON, were behind the score to 'CATCH AND RELEASE'.
BG

- filmography (composer) {performer} –

Go *(1999 score on OST by V/A; see future edition)* / **Better Living Through Circuitry** *(2000 {p} on OST by V/A =>)* Under Suspicion *(2000 score; OST by V/A)* / Driven *(2001 score on OST by V/A; see future edition)* / the Fast And The Furious *(2001 score on OST by V/A; see future edition)* / **Monster** *(2003 OST =>)* / **Stealth** *(2005 OST; other by V/A =>)* / Underclassman *(2005 score / OST by V/A; see future edition)* / **Catch And Release** *(2007 OST w/ TOMMY STINSON =>)* / Look *(2007 score)*

☐ Eric BACHMANN segment
(⇒ BALL OF WAX)

☐ BAD CHANNELS
(⇒ Rock Musicals & Pop Fiction)

BAD EGGS

2003 (Aus 98m) MacQuarie / Roadshow / A Million Monkeys Films

Film genre: cop/detective comedy

Top guns: s-w + dir: Tony Martin

Stars: Mick Molloy *(Ben Kinnear)*, Bob Franklin *(Mike Paddock)*, Judith Lucy *(Julie Bale)*, Alan Brough *(Northey)*, Bill Hunter *(Ted Pratt)* ← RIKKY AND PETE ← NED KELLY, Robyn Nevin *(Eleanor Poulgrain)*, Marshall Napier *(Doug Gillespie)*, Steven Vidler *(Pendlebury)* ← FRANKIE'S HOUSE, Nicholas Bell *(Wicks)*, Shaun Micallef *(Premier Lionel Cray)*, Brett Swain *(Bartlett)*

Storyline: Two elite undercover Melbourne detectives (on the anti-corruption Zero Tolerance Unit) return to uniform duties when they are involved in headlining publicity surrounding the accidental death of a magistrate. The pair soon see a connection between this incident and a crooked casino boss, but will they get to grips with this fast-growing criminal element?
MCS

Movie rating: *6

Visual: dvd

Off the record: Australian husband and wife team, **DAVID GRANEY** and **CLARE MOORE**, first came to light in the late 70s via the Moodists after relocating from rural Mount Gambier to Melbourne; GRANEY was formerly of the short-lived Sputniks who released one single, 'Our Boys' / 'Second Chance'. Joined by Steve Miller (no, not that one), Mick Turner (later of the Dirty Three) and Chris Walsh, the Moodists enjoyed cult status in their native Australia, where the similar Birthday Party were all the rage. After a couple of homegrown 45s, GRANEY's new wave psych/garage outfit secured a UK deal with the small independent, 'Red Flame', issuing a string of releases including two mini-sets, 'Engine Shudder' (1983) and 'Double Life' (1985) either side of a full-length album, 'Thirsty's Calling' (1984). The mid-80s also saw the band (who were now without Turner) deliver a one-off single, 'Justice And Money Too', for Alan McGee's seminal 'Creation' label. GRANEY (and MOORE) went on to find commercial success with his own outfit, Dave Graney 'n' the Coral Snakes (who included former Orange Juice member, Malcolm Ross), his songwriting prowess and balladeering style seeing him elevated to the critical heights scaled by fellow countrymen, Dave McComb, NICK CAVE and Grant McLennan. Signed to UK 'Fire' imprint, GRANEY and Co delivered three albums between '89 and '92, namely 'World Full Of Daughters', 'My Life On The Plains' and 'I Was The Hunter . . . And I Was The Prey'. In 1993, he surpassed expectations with the much-lauded 'Night Of The Wolverine'. The album was given a belated UK release three years later by the astute 'This Way Up' label, who also issued a 1995 "lounge" set, 'The Soft 'n' Sexy Sound' (1996), while 'Universal' issued 'The Devil Drives' (1997). GRANEY has since formed the Dave Graney Show (a self-titled album was issued in '98), with subsequent sets such as 'Kiss Tomorrow Goodbye' (2000) and 'Heroic Blues' (2002), keeping the man and his spouse in high regard.
MCS

DAVID GRANEY and CLARE MOORE

Jul 03. (cd) *Liberation; (LIBCD 5077.2)* [–] Austra [–]
– Descent into mall / Clublock / Shortsleeves / Exactly as you left it / Ben's theme / Mr Wicks / 1989 / A brand new force / Remember our system / Three gun vendetta / XL9000 / Let's do it ladies / Million dollar question / Not going anywhere / The man in beige / Bad eggs / El finito / Boogie with Benjamin / I'm gonna release your soul (DAVE GRANEY 'N' THE CORAL SNAKES) / Bain-Marie.

S/track review: Like fellow countrymen, Nick Cave and Paul Kelly, former indie-rocker DAVID GRANEY (and wife CLARE MOORE) finally took to the world of feature film music. 'BAD EGGS' consisted of 19 instrumental tracks (all in one basket, you could say), several penned by guitarist GRANEY himself, several by MOORE and a bunch written together; the only song on board ('I'm Gonna Release Your Soul' from 1994) stems from his time spent as DAVE GRANEY 'N' THE CORAL SNAKES – think Paul Quinn & The Independent Group. The aforementioned instrumentals (featuring guitarists STUART PERERA, MATT WALKER & BILL MILLER, plus bassists NICK LOWES & ADELE PICKVANCE, saxophonist BEN GRANT and trumpeter GLYN HICKLING) open with 'Descent Into Mall', a quirky tune that precedes a slight change of tempo via follow-on track, 'Clublock'. There are a multitude of dialogue excerpts littered around the OST, mainly to complement or intro the GRANEY-MOORE lounge-lizard-styled musings.

Highlights of the album come via the Kid Loco-like 'Remember Our System', the fuzz-guitar sound of 'Not Going Anywhere' and the spiky-John Barry-esque title track. 'BAD EGGS' is indeed an acquired taste and not for fans of hard-boiled rock – so to speak. *MCS*

Album rating: *5

☐ BADFINGER segment
(⇒ the MAGIC CHRISTIAN)

☐ BADLY DRAWN BOY segment
(⇒ ABOUT A BOY)

BALL OF WAX

2003 (US 90m) Go Pictures

Film genre: psychological sports drama

Top guns: s-w + dir: Daniel Kraus

Stars: Mark Mench *(Bret Packard)*, Justin Smith *(Tod Ellis)*, Traci Dinwiddie *(Nat Packard)*, Cullen Moss *(Ricky Sparks)*, Daniel Morris *(Jimmy Ingels)*, Kevin Scanlon *(Sal Reilly)*, Larry Tobias *(Bob Tower)*, Jason Davis *(Dickie Gold)*, Stephanie Wallace *(Becky)*, Elizabeth Roberts *(June)*

Storyline: Bret Packard, best baseball player in the league, seemingly has everything – good looks, talent and money. However beneath the surface he is unhappy and bored with his millionaire lifestyle. He invents a series of cruel challenges and mind games for his unsuspecting team mates, promising them power and money if they win. The challenges soon break down friendships in the team which then starts to self-destruct, and unless something is done about power crazed Bret it's only a matter of time before the lives of all the team are completely ruined. *JZ*

Movie rating: *5

Visual: dvd

Off the record: ERIC BACHMANN formed Archers Of Loaf in Chapel Hill, North Carolina, USA in 1991 alongside Eric Johnson. Following some local attention through shared fanzine 45's and the likes, San Franciscan label, 'Alias', were suitably impressed to offer the band a deal. With its neo lo-fi, angular sound, the Archers were initially compared with Pavement, although subsequent releases revealed a band with a wide ranging array of influences inconsistent with an art-rock tag. The much anticipated debut album, 'Icky Mettle', appeared later in '93, confirming the band's credentials and putting the fertile musical breeding ground of Chapel Hill firmly on the map. Choosing to remain resolutely independent (after turning down offers from MADONNA's 'Maverick' stable), the band stuck with 'Alias' and concentrated on writing material for a follow-up album, 'Vee Vee' (1995); a third album proper, 'All The Nation's Airports', was released the following year. In 1998, to mark the end of a somewhat topsy-turvy career, AOL delivered their swansong set, 'White Trash Heroes', an album that harked back to their heady days of yore; they took their final bow in 2000. The croaking BACHMANN resurfaced a little earlier courtesy of Crooked Fingers. Their eponymous debut was followed by 'Bring On The Snakes' (2001), two sets soaked in tales of booze and blues and nothing like the sedate instrumentation of 'Short Careers' (2002). *MCS*

ERIC BACHMANN: Short Careers

Jul 02. (cd) *Merge; <(MRG 212)>* ☐ Aug02 ☐
– Good morning sleepyhead / Forks and knives / A diamond is the Devil's eye / Finding the holes filling the gaps / Jimmy the enforcer / Aspirin vs arsenic / Short careers / The mysterious death of Robert Tower / Nosebleed / Vision and execution / Reach out and touch someone / Ty Cobb.

S/track review: Subtitled, 'Short Careers: original score for the film BALL OF WAX', this was former Archers Of Loaf and Crooked Fingers man, ERIC BACHMANN's first (and so far only) foray into movie soundtracks. From the US state of North Carolina (also home to scoresmith, Mac McCaughan of PORTASTATIC), the multi-tasking BACHMANN should've been an inspired choice for the filmmakers. Veering towards sounding like a fusion of the aforementioned PORTASTATIC and STEPHIN MERRITT (of the Magnetic Fields), 'BALL OF WAX' falls into a melancholy pattern, not helped by the emotive, chamber-like augmentation from ANDREJ CURTY (violin), EUNICE KING (cello), WADE RITTENBERRY (upright bass) and EVAN THOMAS (drums). However, opener 'Good Morning Sleepyhead' contradicts this slightly with all its crowd cheering and is both uplifting and relatively sunny. 'Forks And Knives' was a lullaby of sorts, while the lilting effects of 'A Diamond Is The Devil's Eye' finally makes way for a regimented crescendo. With all the set instrumental, BACHMANN's party gets somewhat started when 'Finding Holes Filling The Gaps' also builds to neo-classical, climactic levels. If Godspeed were lo-fi, this is what they'd sound like, the uncanny thing is, GYBE! worshippers EXPLOSIONS IN THE SKY just might've been paying attention to this: example their similarly-themed baseball flick OST, 'FRIDAY NIGHT LIGHTS' (2004). 'Ty Cobb' (featuring guest MARIA TAYLOR), closes the 36-minute set with the same aplomb, sombre and sober and fit for a funeral. *MCS*

Album rating: *5.5

☐ Thomas BANGALTER segment
(⇒ IRREVERSIBLE)

☐ Tony BANKS segment
(⇒ the WICKED LADY)

BATMAN

1989 (US 126m) Warner Bros. Pictures (PG-13)

Film genre: comic-strip sci-fi fantasy

Top guns: dir: Tim Burton / s-w: Sam Hamm (+ story), Warren Skaaren

Stars: Michael Keaton *(Batman / Bruce Wayne)* ← JACKIE BROWN → a SHOT AT GLORY, Jack Nicholson *(the Joker / Jack Napier)* ← the BORDER ← TOMMY ← EASY RIDER ← HEAD ← PSYCH-OUT, Kim Basinger *(Vicki Vale)* ← HARD COUNTRY / → WAYNE'S WORLD 2 → 8 MILE, Robert Wuhl *(Alexander Knox)* ← FLASHDANCE / → GOOD MORNING, VIETNAM → the BODYGUARD, Pat Hingle *(Commissioner Gordon)* ← MAXIMUM OVERDRIVE ← ELVIS: THE MOVIE ← NORWOOD, Michael Gough *(Alfred Pennyworth)* ← TOP SECRET!, Billy Dee Williams *(D.A. Harvey Dent)* ← NIGHTHAWKS ← LADY SINGS THE BLUES ← the FINAL COMEDOWN / → the JACKSONS: AN AMERICAN DREAM, Jack Palance *(Carl Grissom)* ← IMAGINE, Jerry Hall *(Alicia)* ← RUNNING OUT OF LUCK ← LET'S SPEND THE NIGHT TOGETHER ← URBAN COWBOY / → 25X5: THE CONTINUING ADVENTURES OF THE ROLLING STONES → the WALL: LIVE IN BERLIN, Christopher Fairbank *(Nic)* → CROCODILE SHOES → CROCODILE SHOES II, Lee Wallace *(the mayor)*, Tracey Walter *(Bob the goon)* ← REPO MAN ← HONKYTONK MAN ← TIMERIDER: THE ADVENTURE OF LYLE SWANN / → YOUNG GUNS II → DELUSION → MAN ON THE MOON → HOW HIGH → MASKED AND ANONYMOUS, **Richard Strange** *(a goon)*

Storyline: Urban cowboy/philanthropist playboy Bruce Wayne kicks off Hollywood's superhero addiction, donning his cloak in the name of decency and the failings of an ineffective, D.A. Harvey Dent-led police force. Nursing an identity crisis with roots in the slaughter of his parents, Wayne's caped crusader scrapes the filth from the streets of Gotham on a nightly basis, battling his plaster painted nemesis the Joker and juggling the charms of journalist Vicky Vale. *BG*

Movie rating: *7.5

Visual: video + dvd

Off the record: Richard Strange was formerly frontman for mid-70s pre-new wave outfit, Doctors Of Madness.

—

PRINCE

Jun 89. (lp/c)(cd) *Warners; (WX 281/+C)<(9 25936-2)>* [1] [1]
– The future / Electric chair / The arms of Orion (PRINCE with SHEENA EASTON) / Partyman / Vicki waiting / Trust / Lemon crush / Scandalous / Batdance. *(re-iss. cd/c Feb95; same)*

S/track review: It's been a while since a pop icon was given carte blanche on a Hollywood blockbuster, but in 'BATMAN', a pre-symbol PRINCE excreted the kind of salty irreverence a composer just can't sweat, Danny Elfman score or no. It's his weakest album of the 80s, no argument, but given the bar-setting opuses which preceded it, that's not quite a criticism. Coming on the back of the era-capping 'Lovesexy' might have likewise clipped its batwings, but at only 42 minutes there's not much room for flab, and the Tim Burton-meets-PRINCE legacy has arguably outlasted the same era's Stevie Wonder-meets-Spike Lee document. 'The Future' throbs darkly in the knowledge that its pristine, palpitating funk carries the torch; it's PRINCE at his most soulful, stealthy and compelling. Why oh why couldn't he have have released a whole album of this stuff? 'Electric Chair' comes close, but it's PRINCE doing Sly Stone instead of himself. The epileptic 'Batdance' montage – a huge US No.1 – was his answer to the Coldcut-style mash-ups doing the rounds in the first flush of acid house, and it proved he could've cleaned up with clubby electronica if he'd fancied it, but he didn't. Oor wee SHEENA (EASTON) makes her mandatory appearance on 'The Arms Of Orion', but her talents might've been more profitably applied on falsetto confession, 'Scandalous'. 'Vicki Waiting' plies typically purple innuendo while 'Partyman' and 'Lemon Crush' funk around to no great consequence. It's not going to save the world, but as comic book funk, 'BATMAN' spins an enjoyable enough web. *BG*

Album rating: *6

– spinoff hits, etc. –

PRINCE: Batdance

Jun 89. (7"/12"pic-d/cd-s/3"cd-s) *<22924> (W 2924/+TP/CD/CDX)* [1] [2]

PRINCE: Partyman

Aug 89. (7"/12"/12"pic-d/cd-s) *<22814> (W 2814/+T/TP/CD)* [18] [14]

PRINCE with SHEENA EASTON: The Arms Of Orion

Oct 89. (7"/c-s/12"/cd-s/12"pic-d) *<22757> (W 2757/+C/T/CD/TP)* [36] [27]

BEAUTIFUL THING

1996 (UK 90m) Channel 4 Films (R)

Film genre: coming-of-age comedy drama

Top guns: dir: Hettie MacDonald / s-w: Jonathan Harvey (+ play)

Stars: Linda Henry *(Sandra Gangel)*, Glen Berry *(Jamie Gangel)*, Scott Neal *(Ste Pearce)*, Andrew Fraser *(Jayson)*, Ben Daniels *(Tony)*, Meera Syal *(Miss Chauhan)*, Julie Smith *(Gina)*, Jeillo Edwards *(Rose)*, Martin Walsh *(Mr. Bennett)*, Tameka Empson *(Leah Russell)*, Daniel Bowers *(Trevor Pearce)*, Steven M. Martin *(Ryan McBride)*, Sam Robards *(Steve Rossmore)*, Garry Cooper *(Ronnie Pearce)* ← 1984 ← QUADROPHENIA

Storyline: Life can be tough in working-class south London, and for teenager Ste it becomes even tougher when he's kicked out of the house by his drunken dad. With no other family nearby, he knocks on the door of his pal Jamie, and is allowed to spend the night there by Jamie's mum Sandra. The boys discover their feelings of friendship developing into something deeper and, still unsure of themselves, they get help and advice about adulthood from Jamie's worldly-wise mum. *JZ*

Movie rating: *7

Visual: video

Off the record: The **MAMAS & THE PAPAS** were formed as the New Journeymen in St. Thomas, Virgin Islands, USA in 1964 by Denny Doherty and two former Journeymen; JOHN PHILLIPS and Michelle Gilliam. Almost immediately, they recruited the larger-than-life MAMA CASS (ELLIOT), relocating to California where they became the MAMAS & THE PAPAS (Mama being Hell's Angels slang for girlfriend). The quartet were then introduced by 'Eve Of Destruction'-man, Barry McGuire to producer and owner of 'Dunhill' records, Lou Adler. He initially contracted the group as backing singers for McGuire's 1965 album, 'Precious Time', which included a version of PHILLIPS' 'California Dreamin''. The following year, this classic piece of harmony-orientated folk-pop became their debut 45, hitting the US Top 5. The group's follow-up, 'Monday Monday', topped the charts (No.3 in the UK), succeeded by a string of hits, abruptly halted by the split of the group in '68. This was the result of the eventual marriage break-up of John and Michelle, as well as drug busts and alleged record company rip-offs. All four took off on solo ventures, often re-uniting for one-off concerts, etc. Tragically, on the 29th of July '74, CASS died of a heart attack while choking on food. In 1982, the three remaining members re-grouped with a new singer, Spanky McFarlane (ex-Spanky & Her Gang), but little was forthcoming on the recording front. Michelle had already begun an acting career, that has since seen her in US TV dramas such as 'Knot's Landing'. Sadly, songwriter extraordinaire and film composer, JOHN PHILLIPS, died of a heart attack in March 2001. *MCS*

—

MAMA CASS / the MAMAS & THE PAPAS (*)
(& score: JOHN ALTMAN **)

Jun 96. (cd) *M.C.A.; (MCD 60013) <MCAD 11552>* [ ] [ ]
– It's getting better / One way ticket / California earthquake / Welcome to the world / Make your own kind of music / Creeque alley (*) / Dream a little dream of me (*) / Move in a little closer baby / California dreamin' (*) / Monday Monday (*) / I saw her again last night (*) / Words of love (*) / Dedicated to the one I love (*) / Look through my window (*) / Go where you wanna go (*) / Beautiful Thing medley: i. Peppermint foot lotion, ii. Beautiful thing, iii. The Gloucester, iv. Don't cry (**).

S/track review: Featuring the work of legendary Laurel Canyon scenemaker, MAMA CASS ELLIOT, 'BEAUTIFUL THING' opens with the unrelenting upbeat, brass-bolstered, duo salvo of 'It's Getting Better' and 'One Way Ticket' – tunes which could only have been borne out of naïve 60s idealism, before leading on to the funkier and hip-shakingly celebratory 'Californian Earthquake'. Many tracks feature the glorious harmonies of ELLIOT's onetime band the MAMAS & THE PAPAS, whose euphoric and sometimes psychedelic multi-layered sunshine pop is showcased on the likes of 'Creeque Alley', a satirical self-referential joyful goodtime sing-a-long, sending up the Byrds and the Californian sound of the late 60s. The class of CASS's solo work easily stands up to some of the MAMAS AND THE PAPAS' more toothless, happy-clappy numbers, such as 'Move A Little Closer Baby', 'Monday Monday' and 'Look Through My Window', though 'Go Where You Wanna Go' stands out from this pack. In fact, their best work featured here happens to be those songs written outwith the group, such as CASS's drastic and definitive take on 'Dream A Little Dream Of Me' and the Shirelles' 'Dedicated To The One I Love', which actually sees Michelle Phillips' equally dreamy and ethereal voice take the lead. However, the jewel in the crown remains the ageless and era-defining classic 'California Dreamin'' with its haunting melodies and uncharacteristically dark themes. It is then left to JOHN ALTMAN's touching 'Beautiful Thing Medley' to bookend the soundtrack, a job it does magnificently – all resonant, stirring movements and chiming pianos. *LF*

Album rating: *7.5

Jeff BECK

Born: 24 Jun'44, Wallington, Surrey, England. Unlike fellow Yardbirds graduates ERIC CLAPTON and JIMMY PAGE, guitarist JEFF BECK charted an idiosyncratic, uncertain and often underwhelming path through the 70s as his erstwhile colleagues were busy ensuring their status as rock icons. Feted as a technical genius, JEFF BECK nevertheless failed to find a galvanising band format after the relatively short-lived JEFF BECK Group, going on to dabble in heavy rock, jazz fusion and latterly, electronica, over a series of erratic, occasionally brilliant solo albums. While his earliest screen appearance was in Michelangelo Antonioni masterpeice, 'BLOW-UP' (1966), performing the blistering Yardbirds track, 'Stroll On', he also wielded his trusty axe in Ivan Reitman's odd couple comedy, 'Twins' (1988). He subsequently made a cameo as a postman in Robbie Coltrane vehicle, 'The Pope Must Die!' (1991), for which he shared scoring credits with Art Of Noise alumna Anne Dudley. His film-scoring skills even made it to disc with the soundtrack to Australian TV mini-series, 'FRANKIE'S HOUSE' (1992), an evocative, wide-ranging collaboration with keyboardist JED LEIBER. Jeff also worked with Leiber and Nile Rodgers on the William Friedkin sports drama, 'Blue Chips' (1994), although their score was passed over for a soundtrack of vintage blues, soul and R&B. *BG*

- filmography (composer) {acting} –

Blow-Up *(1966 {p w/ YARDBIRDS} OST by HERBIE HANCOCK =>)* / the Secret Policeman's Other Ball *(1982 {p} OST by V/A =>)* / Twins *(1988 {p})* / the Pope Must Die! *(1991 {b} score w/ Anne Dudley)* / **Frankie's House** *(1992 TV mini OST w/ Jed Leiber =>)* / Blue Chips *(1994 score w/ JED LEIBER / OST by Nile Rodgers & V/A; see future edition)* / **Red, White & Blues** *(2003 {p} on OST by V/A =>)* / Naked Under Leather *(2004 {p})*

□ BELLE AND SEBASTIAN segment
(⇒ STORYTELLING)

□ Einar Orn BENEDIKTSSON segment
(⇒ 101 REYKJAVIK)

BENJAMIN

1972 (W.Ger 83m) Centfox

Film genre: sports comedy

Top guns: s-w: Willy Bogner (+ dir + story), Jurgen Guett

Stars: Philip Sonntag *(Benjamin)*, Suzy Chaffee, Helmut Trunz, Art Furrer, Billy Kidd, Herman Golliner

Storyline: An expert computer program chooses Benjamin to represent his country in the big skiing championships. Obviously a slight error has occurred, as poor Benji has never set foot on a ski and has the physique of a runner bean. Nevertheless, our hero is dragged kicking and screaming to the ski slope where he must somehow achieve victory or go on a downward slide. *JZ*

Movie rating: *5

Visual: none

Off the record: GARY WRIGHT (see below)

—

GARY WRIGHT (score: Eberhard Schoener)

1974. (lp) *Ariola; (IT 86405)* [–] W.Ger [–]
– Goodbye Sunday / Ski beat / Shy love / Rodeo / Desert walk / Happy harmonica / Don Quixote / Your own song / Classical ski ballet / Aspen trees / Ski Hawaii / Ski-thesiser / Cowboys / The nun / The daydream.

S/track review: London-based GARY WRIGHT (although born in Creskill, New Jersey, USA) was soon to become a legend in the States, when, in 1976, 'Dream Weaver' hit No.2 in the singles chart. Almost immediately, the ex-Spooky Tooth singer/keys/synth-man was catapulted from relative obscurity into mainstream pop-rock stardom, although his time at the top was short. When 'BENJAMIN' was recorded in '72, WRIGHT was on/off with the aforementioned art-rockers, Spooky Tooth, while his previous Wonderwheel outfit (which backed George Harrison on his 'All Things Must Pass' sessions) had run out of steam. One of the soundtrack world's most sought-after LPs (imagine "hen's teeth" or indeed "tooth"), 'BENJAMIN' changes hands very rarely, and when it does expect to empty your bank account. Whether it's the fact that WRIGHT is the main man behind the project, or it's the fact that it features future Foreigner stalwart and ex-Wonderwheel/Spooky Tooth guitarist, MICK JONES, is anyone's guess. All friends intact, 'BENJAMIN' proved to be a closet hit for funky/Blaxploitation lovers (although the German film is in no way of that ilk!), its tight musicianship probably swinging it for those who managed to get a hold of it. If you loved mid-70s Deep Purple (between 'Stormbringer' & 'Come Taste The Band'), you'll love the funky trimmings on a lot of the numbers. Basically, the album rocks big time, although you wouldn't guess it with "apres-ski" dirges like 'Ski Beat', 'Classical Ski Ballet', 'Ski Hawaii' & 'Ski-thesizer', misleading ever so slightly. If there's one cut that stands out from the rest of the pack it's 'Aspen Trees' – you just can't get that mojo workin' or that organ funkier, man! *MCS*

Album rating: *6

le BERCEAU DE CRISTAL

1976 (Fra 80m) independent (R)

Film genre: avant-garde melodrama

Top guns: s-w + dir: Philippe Garrel

Stars: Margaret Clementi, Anita Pallenberg *(drug diva)* ← PERFORMANCE ← CANDY ← WONDERWALL, Dominique Sanda *(earth goddess)*, **NICO** *(poet/writer)*, Pierre Clementi, Philippe Garrel, Frederic Pardo

Storyline: A weird one this. An androgynous wordsmith/poet (played by Nico) takes on a oneiric, semi-mythical journey into the mind of her director/live-in partner, Philippe Garrel. Along the way, we witness other "heroin chics" and disturbing dream-like sequences, which might be a bit too trippy for some dudes out there. *MCS*

Movie rating: *6

Visual: video

Off the record: ASH RA TEMPEL were formed in Berlin, Germany in the early 70s by Manuel Gottsching and Hartmut Enke. Having been influenced by the blues and classical music from an early age, Gottsching subsequently became inspired by PINK FLOYD's psychedelic experimentation. They were joined by others, including Klaus Schulze, who had just quit TANGERINE DREAM. Their self-titled debut album, released in March '71, borrowed heavily from the trippy ambience of both said bands. In September that year, Schulze left to pursue a solo career, while the remainder completed a follow-up, 'Schwingungen', subsequently rated as their best work. A meeting with 60s acid-guru/preacher Timothy Leary in Switzerland must've paid off as the resulting acid-fried, collaborative set, 'Seven Up' (named after the fizzy drink which they lovingly spiked with LSD before each show) gave them renewed credibility. Following this, they met up with another "underground" philosopher; the painter/artist Walter Wegmuller, who collaborated on their next project 'Join Inn'. In 1976, they signed to Richard Branson's 'Virgin' (home to TANGERINE DREAM and MIKE OLDFIELD), where they made three albums under the new ASH RA tag. They were now more keyboard-orientated, breaking free from their exotic Eastern-styled psychedelia of old. On subsequent releases, Gottsching further diversified into new-age ambience. *MCS*

ASH RA TEMPEL

1993. (cd) *Spalax; (14275)* [–] French [–]
– Le Berceau de Cristal / L'hiver doux / Silence sauvage / Le sourire envole / Deux enfants sous la lune / Le songs d'or / Le diable dans la maison / . . .Et les fantomes revent aussi. *(UK-iss.Mar98; same)*

S/track review: The little-known German prog-meisters ASH RA TEMPEL (two members, MANUEL GOTTSCHING and Agitation Free's LUTZ ULBRICH) were responsible for this hour-length beaut. Think TANGERINE DREAM, PINK FLOYD and POPOL VUH – all film scorists in their own right – and you'll get the picture, so to speak. But this is minimalist and ambient at a time (1975/6) when electronic prog rock was rhythmically upbeat, Messrs TANGERINE DREAM – who had still to get off the mark with 'SORCERER' in '77 – were prime examples. Set to a pseudo-mythological backdrop with fellow German-born chanteuse (and avant-garde songstress) NICO as their cue, ASH RA TEMPEL do the POPOL VUH atmospherics to a tee. The 14-minute, title track opener certainly gets the ears ringing, ringing in a way that takes us through an inner journey of repetitous rhythms and eerie Zeeman effects. Many listeners will be watching the paint dry on the ceilings. The aforementioned POPOL VUH had already staked their claim on the atmospheric soundtrack ground with their cinematic masterpiece, 'AGUIRRE, WRATH OF GOD' (1972), and you can probably understand why ' . . .CRISTAL' took 18 years to get a release date. Track two, 'L'Hiver Doux' – also lengthy at just under 13 minutes – lets the Farfisa organ do the talking, like discovering a manic Moog-playing minister's day off practising at the cathedral, although synth-guitars do win over eventually. I've been a fan of POPOL and TD for decades now but 'TEMPEL seem too far out, cosmic with a capital C. 'Le BERCEAU DE CRISTAL', with its shifting but repetitive rhythms and soundscapes, evokes a certain degree of expectation with getting to any crescendo-like climax. And that's the pity. The pulse gets raised a few times on dirges like 'Silence Sauvage', 'Le Sourire Vole' & 'Deux Enfants Sous La Lune', the latter nearly contradicting the whole essence of my critique; I emphasise the word nearly. *MCS*

Album rating: *6

BEST REVENGE

1982 (Can 92m) Lorimar (15)

Film genre: Crime thriller

Top guns: dir: John Trent ← HOMER / s-w: David Rothberg, Rick Rosenthal, John Hunter as Logan N. Danforth

Stars: John Heard *(Charlie)* → BEACHES, **Levon Helm** *(Bo)* <= the BAND =>, Alberta Watson *(Dinah)* → HEDWIG AND THE ANGRY INCH, Moses Znaimer *(Leo Ellis)* → BARENAKED IN AMERICA, Stephen McHattie *(Brett)* ← GEROMINO: AN AMERICAN LEGEND, John Rhys-Davies *(Mustapha)*

Storyline: 60s leftovers Charlie and Bo are living the laid-back life in Spain when they get caught up in a multi-million dollar drug deal in Morocco. It becomes clear that they've been set up by a gangster intent on getting away with everything. *MCS*

Movie rating: *3.5

Visual: video

Off the record: Director John Trent's last movie; he died 3rd June, 1983. **Levon Helm** (formerly of the **BAND** =>) plays the major role of Bo, and he even contributes to the soundtrack below. *MCS*

KEITH EMERSON

Apr 85. (lp) *Chord; (CHORD 001)* [–] [ ]
– Dream runner / The runner / Wha'dya mean / Straight between the eyes / Orchestral suite to "Best Revenge" / Playing for keeps (main title theme). *(cd-iss. Nov86 +=; CDCO 3)* – MURDEROCK tracks

S/track review: KEITH EMERSON (formerly of prog giants, ELP) went for a more classical rock feel to this score, exhibiting some of the more flashy symphonics since the early 70s. However, the one-time No.1 keyboard-player – well, it's between him and RICK WAKEMAN! – couldn't quite get to grips with some forgettable and cliched AOR/pop tunes such as 'Playing For Keeps' (featuring BRAD DELP of BOSTON on vocals) and 'Straight Between The Eyes' (with LEVON HELM of the Band). The CD version added another of EMERSON's later soundtracks, 'MURDEROCK'. *MCS*

Album rating: *3 / re-CD *5

BIG TIME

1977 (US 96m) Motown Productions / WorldWide Pictures (PG)

Film genre: comedy/drama

Top guns: dir: Andrew Georgias / s-w: **Smokey Robinson**

Stars: Christipher Joy *(Eddie)* ← SHEBA, BABY ← CLEOPATRA JONES, Tobar Mayo *(Harold)*, Jayne Kennedy *(Shana)* ← LET'S DO IT AGAIN ← LADY SINGS THE BLUES, Roger E. Mosley *(J.J.)* ← LEADBELLY ← the MACK, Art Evans *(Murdock)* ← LEADBELLY ← CLAUDINE / → YOUNGBLOOD → SCHOOL DAZE → TRESPASS → CB4: THE MOVIE → the STORY OF US, Tina Dixon *(fat woman)*

Storyline: All down to a hustler looking for his next mark. *MCS*

Movie rating: *2

Visual: none

Off the record: SMOKEY ROBINSON (b. 9 Feb'40, Detroit, Michigan, USA). With his androgynous falsetto and mystifiying meditations of the vagaries of romance, Smokey forever carved a tear-stained corner in the hearts of soul afficionados. As Berry Gordy's right hand man at 'Motown', he was also critical in forging the label's overall sound as well as the careers of individual artists such as the Temptations and Mary Wells. The doyen of heartbreak hasn't been quite so crucial in cinematic terms, creating the soundtrack for this 1977 feature, and even making a few acting appearances beginning with a cameo as himself in street gang effort, 'KNIGHTS OF THE CITY' (1985). This was followed by minor roles in John McNaughton's sci-fi horror, 'The Borrower' (1989), martial arts stinker, 'Pushed To The Limit' (1992) and glib actioner, 'Hollywood Homicide' (2003). *BG*

SMOKEY ROBINSON

Sep 77. (lp/c) *Tamla Motown; <T6 355S1> (STML/CSTML 12068)* [ ] [ ]
– Theme from Big Time / J.J.'s theme / Hip trip / He is the light of the world / So nice to be with you / Shana's theme / If we're gonna act like lovers / The agony and the ecstasy / Theme from Big Time (reprise).

S/track review: As the rock dinosaurs thrashed their bloodied tails, it's surprising how many silver age soul men were still making vital records at the fag-end of the 70s. MARVIN GAYE, STEVIE WONDER and CURTIS MAYFIELD were all pushing ever more baroque concepts which needled the era's critics but were ultimately rehabilitated. SMOKEY ROBINSON was too old, shrewd and hopelessly romantic for such folly; in his own pre-coital way, though, he more or less maintained his critical stock right though the 80s. And for a man who virtually invented the American sub-genre of Quiet Storm, the well underrated dancefloor flirtations of 'BIG TIME' can be construed as his own little piece of late 70s baroque: SMOKEY does disco. Dispensing with the hard graft and hired scribes of 'Deep In My Soul' (1977), he drops an Average White Band-meets-Giorgio Moroder title bomb wired with one-track rhythm and meccano guitar; sweet Studio 54 candy, sung like a Sly Stone successor. SMOKEY's real genius, though, is to sneak in blasts of organ-awkward gospel (see 'J.J.'s Theme' and the slamming 'He Is The Light Of The World') just so we know the hedonism's blessed from on high. The man's more recognisably tearful on side two, but he sings, produces and generally turns on those sad songs like no one else; the stunning, disembodied intimacy of 'So Nice To Be With You' distills the ambience every 80s popstar-wannabe-soul-legend would try – and usually fail – to approximate. This being the decade of all things Corleone/Morricone, there's even a few minutes of trilled mandolin called 'The Agony And The Ecstasy', audaciously, absurdly fading back into that monster groove of a title reprise. Unforgivably, 'Motown' have never graced this with a reissue but vinyl cut-outs – at well under a tenner – are a bargain. *BG*

Album rating: *6.5

– spinoff releases, etc. –

SMOKEY ROBINSON: Theme From Big Time / (part 2)

Sep 77. (7") *<54288> (TMG 1085)* ☐ ☐

BIRDY

1984 (US 120m) TriStar Pictures (R)

Film genre: psychological coming-of-age drama

Top guns: dir: Alan Parker ← the WALL ← FAME / → the COMMITMENTS → EVITA / s-w: Sandy Kroopf, Jack Behr (au: William Wharton)

Stars: Matthew Modine *(Birdy)* → OVERNIGHT, Nicolas Cage *(Sgt. Al Columbato)* ← FAST TIMES AT RIDGEMONT HIGH / → WILD AT HEART, John Harkins *(Dr. Weiss)*, Sandy Baron *(Mr. Columbato)* → SID & NANCY, Karen Young *(Hannah Rourke)*, Bruno Kirby *(Renaldi)* ← THIS IS SPINAL TAP ← WHERE THE BUFFALO ROAM ← ALMOST SUMMER / → GOOD MORNING, VIETNAM → the BASKETBALL DIARIES → a SLIPPING-DOWN LIFE, Nancy Fish *(Mrs. Prevost)* ← MORE AMERICAN GRAFFITI ← STEELYARD BLUES / → HOWARD THE DUCK → CANDY MOUNTAIN, Marshall Bell *(Ronsky)* → TUCKER: THE MAN AND HIS DREAM → DICK TRACY → AIRHEADS → a SLIPPING-DOWN LIFE

Storyline: A young man returns from Vietnam so psychologically damaged he takes mental refuge in the belief that he is actually a bird rather than a human being. It's left to the best efforts of his combat buddy Al, to draw him back out of himself. *BG*

Movie rating: *7

Visual: video + dvd

Off the record: (see below)

—

PETER GABRIEL

Mar 85. (lp/cd) *Geffen; <GEF/+D 24070> Charisma; (CAS/+CD 1167)* ☐ [51]
– At night / Floating dogs / Quiet and alone / Close up / Slow water / Dressing the wound / Birdy's flight / Slow marimbas / The heat / Sketchpad with trumpet and voice / Under lock and key / Powerhouse at the foot of the mountain. *(re-iss. Apr90 on 'Virgin' lp/c; OVED/+C 283)*

S/track review: PETER GABRIEL's first foray into soundtrack work contains the following sleevenote proviso: "WARNING: This record contains recycled material and no lyrics". At least he's honest about it; most artists wouldn't feel the need to name their sources. In actual fact, just under half the tracks are textural interpretations of songs already featured on the albums 'Peter Gabriel {III}' (1980) and 'Peter Gabriel {IV}' (1982), among which 'Birdy's Flight' (a reworking of 'Not One Of Us') and 'The Heat' are probably the most compelling – both soundtracking BIRDY's on-screen attempts at flight and both building from ominous, clanking chords into daylight nightmares of grungy guitar and roiling drums, and the latter featuring some ferocious percussion from the Drummers Of Ekome. GABRIEL also showcases his increasing fondness for global instrumentation on the self explanatory 'Slow Marimbas', with barely audible bird sounds twittering around somewhere in the mix. 'Sketchpad For Trumpet And Voice' also sounds born of other climes, and Jon Hassell's contributions to the score bear comparison to his work with RY COODER. In large part an abstract and darkly contemplative work distilled in GABRIEL's keyboards and his imagination, and best expressed on opener 'At Night', this record may be recycled but it's certainly not rehashed. *BG*

Album rating: *6.5

☐ BJORK
(⇒ Rock Musicals & Pop Fiction)

BLACK BELT JONES

1974 (US 85m) Sequoin Productions / Warner Bros. Pictures (R)

Film genre: martial-arts drama

Top guns: dir: Robert Clouse / s-w: Oscar Williams ← the FINAL COMEDOWN / → TRUCK TURNER, Fred Weintraub, Alex Ross

Stars: Jim Kelly *(Black Belt Jones)* ← MELINDA / → THREE THE HARD WAY, Gloria Hendry *(Sydney)* ← HELL UP IN HARLEM ← SLAUGHTER'S BIG RIP-OFF ← BLACK CAESAR ← ACROSS 110th STREET ← the LANDLORD, Scatman Crothers *(Pop Byrd)* ← SLAUGHTER'S BIG RIP-OFF ← LADY SINGS THE BLUES / → TRUCK TURNER → FRIDAY FOSTER, Eric Laneuvulle *(Quincy)* ← DEATH WISH / → FEAR OF A BLACK HAT, Alan Weeks *(Toppy)* ← SHAFT / → TRUCK TURNER, Andre Philippe *(Don Steffano)* → DOWN AND OUT IN BEVERLY HILLS, Malik Carter *(Pinky)*, Vincent Barbi *(Big Tuna)* → DOLEMITE, Mel Novak *(Blue Eyes)* → TRUCK TURNER, Eddie Smith *(Oscar)* → TRUCK TURNER, Clarence Barnes *(Tango)* → TRUCK TURNER, Esther Sutherland *(Lucy)* ← HELL UP IN HARLEM / → FOXY BROWN → TRUCK TURNER, Earl Brown *(Jelly)* → TRUCK TURNER, Jac Emil *(Marv the Butcher)* ← WILLIE DYNAMITE / → TRUCK TURNER, Earl Maynard *(aka Junebug)* ← MELINDA / → TRUCK TURNER, Nates Esformes *(Roberts)* ← the FINAL COMEDOWN, Ted Lange *(militant)* ← WATTSTAX / → FRIDAY FOSTER → RECORD CITY

Storyline: Black Belt Jones is the meanest, high kicking, Afro-tacular martial arts expert in L.A. With their eye on some prime real estate housing Jones' karate school, mob heavy Pinky and his cronies end up killing the school's owner Pop Byrd. Wrong move; once Byrd's daughter Sidney (yes, a girl) hears of his murder, she exacts bone-crunching revenge, only to see the school's brightest rising star, Quincy, kidnapped and held to ransom. Jones – or 'Belt' to his US government superiors (he's also an undercover brother) – rounds up a posse of trampolining teenagers (seriously..) and relieves the mob of some of their own cash to pay the ransom. *BG*

Movie rating: *5

Visual: video

Off the record: Scatman Crothers is an old-style singer and guitarist! (voice of Scat Cat in Disney's 'The Aristocats') whose songwriting credits include 'Dearest One' & 'A Man's Gotta Eat'. *MCS*

—

DENNIS COFFEY and LUCHI DE JESUS

2005. (lp) *Weintraub-Heller; <WS 7771>* ☐ ☐
– Main theme / Sydney's theme / Opening theme / Main theme (version 2) / At the beach / Symphony for Jones (Warehouse battle – Pinky – Collectors theme – Drug monkey – Wrong answer) / Drama / Mafia theme (Drama part 2) / Love theme / Battle theme / Dragon style / Sexy (Love theme part 2) / Mr. Jones / Excerpts: Don't stop – One two (dialogue) – Come on in (dialogue) – Papa Bird – Turn her out – The money Pinky – Stay – Double cross / Super slick (get Pinky).

S/track review: On paper the collaboration of sometime Funk Brother DENNIS 'Scorpio' COFFEY and score don, LUCHI DE JESUS, is a marriage made in blaxtopia. On screen, it's even better, and on record, it's as good as we're going to get. For three decades, an ultra-rare 45 was the only vinyl on the market, a main theme so scandalously funky you'd sell both your grannys (and your mother-in-law) to raise the cash. A full soundtrack finally saw the light of day in 2005, so now even the poor and downtrodden can sit grinning in their parlour as preposterous Pearl & Dean strings, bassline-bubblegum scat and sub-'Frog Chorus' belching spews forth. It is, dear people, the black belt in cheese-funk, the Bushido of blaxploitation; and if you're hopelessly addicted to 70s cinema, the second version – with added "euuuggghhh!"s and "auuyyyeeeee!"s – will keep you chortling idiotically to yourself for days. The film itself is rooted in the so-terminably-bad-it's-brilliant category, something you might want to take into account given that the album lifts reams of dialogue and sound effects; be warned, it's not exactly a set of pristine remasters, but it is just about the most fun you can have with a slab of black plastic. It doesn't even matter that much of the big band blast which makes up the incidental music is all over the place, half smothered by gravelly insults – "don't start no communist shit!", "we're from the black student union you capitalistic motherfu**er!"; "who else wants to sing soprano?", "you goddamn ape, you made a monkey out of us!" etc. etc.- and the relentless crack of fist on sideburn. There are exceptions: 'Drama' works up a fair head of steam with some menacing bass runs, 'Battle Theme' matches some of the best whips, howls and yelps on the whole album and 'Mr. Jones' wins out with some long, bilious, 'French Connection'-symphonic drones. There's also a further couple of bonafide, grunt-free themes: 'Love Theme' – flip side of the original single – downgrades the vocal cheese level from critical to acceptable, replacing the monastic chant with grouchy baritone and countering it with a high stepping brass melody, while 'Opening Theme' – one and a half minutes of murderous bass, acoustic guitar and galloping bongos – leaves you wild eyed and sweaty. Did we mention the monkey gibbering? *BG*

Album rating: *8.5

– spinoff releases, etc. –

DENNIS COFFEY: Theme From Black Belt Jones / Love Theme From . . .
1974. (7") *<WB 7769>* ☐ ☐

BLACK CAESAR

aka the GODFATHER OF HARLEM

1973 (US 87m) American International Pictures (R)

Film genre: crime drama

Top guns: s-w + dir: Larry Cohen ← HELL UP IN HARLEM

Stars: Fred Williamson *(Tommy Gibbs)* ← HELL UP IN HARLEM / → the SOUL OF NIGGER CHARLEY → THREE TOUGH GUYS → THREE THE HARD WAY → MEAN JOHNNY BARROWS → ADIOS AMIGO → NO WAY BACK → MR. MEAN → FROM DUSK TILL DAWN → RIDE → CARMEN: A HIP HOPERA, **Art Lund** *(John McKinney)* → BROTHER ON THE RUN → BUCKTOWN, Gloria Hendry *(Helen Bradley)* ← ACROSS 110th STREET ← the LANDLORD / → SLAUGHTER'S BIG RIP-OFF → HELL UP IN HARLEM → BLACK BELT JONES, D'Urville Martin *(Rev. Rufus)* ← BOOK OF NUMBERS ← HELL UP IN HARLEM ← the FINAL COMEDOWN ← WATERMELON MAN ← a TIME TO SING / → the SOUL OF NIGGER CHARLEY → FIVE ON THE BLACK HAND SIDE → SHEBA, BABY → DOLEMITE → DISCO 9000, Julius Harris *(Mr. Gibbs)* ← HELL UP IN HARLEM ← TROUBLE MAN ← SUPERFLY ← SHAFT'S BIG SCORE! / → FRIDAY FOSTER → LET'S DO IT AGAIN, Minnie Gentry *(Mama Gibbs)* ← COME BACK, CHARLESTON BLUE / → CLAUDINE, James Dixon *(Bryant)* ← HELL UP IN HARLEM, Val Avery *(Cardoza)* ← KING CREOLE / → LET'S DO IT AGAIN, William Wellman Jr. *(Alfred Coleman)* ← WINTER A-GO-GO ← a SWINGIN' SUMMER ← HIGH SCHOOL CONFIDENTIAL!

Storyline: Corrupt, racist cop John McKinney suffers the karmic consequences of his actions when one of his victims grows up to be the black crime kingpin of Harlem and proceeds to exact his revenge in blackly comic style. *BG*

Movie rating: *5

Visual: video + dvd

Off the record: (see below)

JAMES BROWN (w/ co-composers: FRED WESLEY & LYN COLLINS)

Feb 73. (lp) *Polydor; <PD 6014> (2490 117)* 31 May73 ☐
– Down and out in New York city / Blind man can see it / Sportin' life / Dirty Harri / The boss / Make it good to yourself / Mama Feelgood / Mama's dead / White lightning (I mean moonshine) / Chase / Like it is, like it was. *<(re-iss. Sep98 lp/cd; 517135-1/-2)>*

S/track review: JAMES BROWN might've been an innovator in every other sense yet he was uncharacteristically late in getting hip to blaxploitation. First Minister of the New, New Superheavy Funk eventually jumped on the station wagon with Larry Cohen's 1973 revenge flick, vindicating his credentials with one of the genre's most enduring and still underrated soundtracks. As chief JB Fred Wesley remembers in Harry Weinger's sleevenotes, "At first James Brown saw movie scoring somewhat simplistically. He'd say for the love scene use Try Me, for the chase scene use Give It Up Or Turn It Loose. But once James became excited by the possibilities he had me make charts for oboes, bassoons, upright bass – very unlikely elements for him". Coming on the back of great albums like 'There It Is' (1972) and 'Get On The Good Foot' (1973), 'BLACK CAESAR' might well have paled in comparison but it's that sense of anticipation and inspiration outlined by Wesley which keeps it fresh. The pair even managed to transform a countrified demo by Bodie Chandler and Barry De Vorzon (who'd go on to score the classic soundtrack to NY gang movie, 'The Warriors') into the impassioned Top 50 hit, 'Down And Out In New York City'. 'The Boss' – an "autobiographical bulletin from the soul" according to Weinger – is BROWN at his most haunting, not an adjective often applied to Mr Showbusiness. The late great LYN COLLINS (who tragically passed away on 13th March 2005, aged only 56) weighs in with her mighty signature, 'Mama Feelgood', still one of the most compelling diva-funk tracks in existence. And then there's the instrumentals, wonderful ad-hoc sketches and quirky breakbeat manoeuvres like 'Blind Man Can See It', 'Sportin' Life' and 'White Lightning (I Mean Moonshine)', more upbeat and positive than blaxploitation material had a right to be. A resounding triumph, and one which earned BROWN the lasting sobriquet Godfather Of Soul. We are not worthy etc. *BG*

Album rating: *8

– spinoff releases, etc. –

JAMES BROWN: Down And Out In New York City / Mama's Dead
Mar 73. (7") <14168> [50] [–]

JAMES BROWN: Like It Is, Like It Was / The Boss
Mar 73. (7") <14169> [ ] [–]

□ BLACK FORCE 2 alt.
(⇒ BROTHER ON THE RUN)

BLACK GIRL

1972 (US 97m) Cinema Releasing Corporation (PG)

Film genre: domestic melodrama

Top guns: dir: Ossie Davis ← COTTON COMES TO HARLEM / → GORDON'S WAR → COUNTDOWN AT KUSINI / s-w: J.E. Franklin (+ play)

Stars: Brock Peters *(Earl)* → JACK JOHNSON → SLAUGHTER'S BIG RIP-OFF, Claudia McNeil *(Mu'Dear)*, Leslie Uggams *(Netta)*, Peggy Petit *(Billie Jean)*, Louise Stubbs *(Mama Rose)* ← the LANDLORD, Loretta Greene *(Ruth Ann)*, Gloria Edwards *(Norma)*, Ruby Dee *(Netta's mother)* ← UP TIGHT! / → WATTSTAX → COUNTDOWN AT KUSINI → JUNGLE FEVER

Storyline: Domestic melodrama focused on an extended Afro-American family and their fraught interrelationships, particularly with brainy foster kid/ college student Netta. Having taken her in out of a sense of personal failure with her own children, matriarch Mama Rose can't be too surprised when Netta's jealous step-sisters intercept the girl's mail in an effort to divert their mother's feelings for her. All hell breaks loose when absent father Earl returns to the household, closely followed by Netta herself. *BG*

Movie rating: *4

Visual: none

Off the record: (see below)

—

ED BOGAS & RAY SHANKLIN (w/ Various Artists)

1972. (lp) *Fantasy; <F 9420>* [ ] [–]
– Black girl (vocals: BETTY EVERETT) / B.J.'s step / Get me to the bridge (vocals: RODGER COLLINS) / Mother's day song / Power (trumpet solo: JOHN HUNT) / Mother's day song II / Black girl cue (sax: SONNY STITT) / No world for dreamers / I am your mailman (vocals: RODGER COLLINS) / What it is / Earl (still a pearl) / Chock-lite puddin' cue / Sister.

S/track review: Released the same year as the more famous, more frivolous and – typically – far easier to find 'FRITZ THE CAT' soundtrack, 'BLACK GIRL' was recorded by the same 'Fantasy' studio partnership of former United States of America organist ED BOGAS and arranger RAY SHANKLIN. So how did a white guy with roots in 60s prog-psychedelia and a future scoring 'Peanuts' and 'Garfield', come up with such a damn collectable blaxploitation album, wrapped in such an iconic looking, black power-esque sleeve? The fact that a bevvy of in-house soul/jazz artists were fronting the cues certainly helped, but some of the loveliest, drowsiest material here – the gentle, conciliatory vibes and gorgeous arrangement of 'Power', the organ oratorio of 'Mother's Day Song' – is largely instrumental. Unlike the uneven score/source combination of 'FRITZ . . .' and 'HEAVY TRAFFIC', BOGAS and SHANKLIN work a real internal logic into this record, easing in guest singers – the most high profile being Chicago soul diva BETTY EVERETT (a lady forever identified with a pre-Cher 'Shoop Shoop Song') – without tipping the euphonic balance. Recently reappraised Bay Area funkster RODGER COLLINS (a mainstay of the 'Galaxy' label which SHANKLIN reinstated in the early 60s) sings 'Get Me To The Bridge' over a coquettish horn part, legendary saxophonist SONNY STITT takes a long cool solo on the EVERETT-sung title and veteran bluesman J.J. MALONE looses his almost Hendrix-disdainful wisdom on 'No World For Dreamers'. Mellow yet wholesome, this is blaxploitation with a big, beating heart; given that 'FRITZ . . .' and 'HEAVY TRAFFIC' have long been on CD, it's mystifying that this has yet to see a reissue. *BG*

Album rating: *7

BLACK MAMA, WHITE MAMA

1972 (US 87m) American International Pictures (R)

Film genre: prison/crime drama/thriller

Top guns: dir: Eddie Romero / s-w: H.R. Christian (story: Joseph Viola, Jonathan Demme → LADIES AND GENTLEMEN, THE FABULOUS STAINS → STOP MAKING SENSE)

Stars: Pam Grier *(Lee Daniels)* ← BEYOND THE VALLEY OF THE DOLLS / → COOL BREEZE → COFFY → FOXY BROWN → SHEBA, BABY → BUCKTOWN → FRIDAY FOSTER → BILL & TED'S BOGUS JOURNEY → JACKIE BROWN → BONES, Margaret Markov *(Karen Brent)*, Sid Haig *(Ruben)* ← IT'S A BIKINI WORLD ← BEACH BALL / → COFFY → FOXY BROWN → the FORBIDDEN DANCE → JACKIE BROWN → HOUSE OF 1000 CORPSES → KILL BILL: VOL.2 → the DEVIL'S REJECTS, Lynn Borden *(matron Densmore)*, Zaldy Zschornack *(Ernesto)*, Laurie Burton *(warden Logan)* ← TICKLE ME, Eddie Garcia *(Captain Cruz)*

Storyline: Exploitation update of Stanley Kramer's 'The Defiant Ones', with tough talking Afro-American hooker Lee Daniels thrown into stir alongside Caucasian rich girl-turned-revolutionary Karen Brent. The ladies have to contend with a lesbian "Matron" and a spell of co-habitation in a sun-seared container before Brent's guerillas helpfully hold up the bus they're being transferred on. Subsequently putting their differences behind them, they team up and go on the lam. *BG*

Movie rating: *5

Visual: Cinema Classics video + MGM/UA on DVD 2004

Off the record: HARRY BETTS (see below)

—

HARRY BETTS

Dec 01. (cd) *Beyond; <578251>* [ ] [–]
– (JACK CONRAD: 'The Monkey Hustle' tracks) // Main title – Bus ride / Follow me / Day in the oven / Ambush / Girls exit oven / Bus stop / Police check point / Luis' work shed / Bloodhounds / Challenge and battle / Ambush, escape and roundup / End credits.

S/track review: The better half of a previously unreleased 'Soul Cinema' two-fer, 'BLACK MAMA, WHITE MAMA' is credited to HARRY BETTS, a veteran jazz trombonist/arranger who worked with the likes of RAY CHARLES, the BEACH BOYS, Frank Sinatra, Sam Cooke and Tower Of Power, and, in cult collectors' favourite, 'The Jazz Soul Of Dr. Kildare' (1962), recorded a one-off solo album with the cream of West Coast jazz sessioners. A different kettle of funk then, from the 'MONKEY HUSTLE' score which it partners. As the last track from that album fades to the silence before ' . . .MAMA's main title, fat'n'bulbous bass gives way to something altogether more ambitious: preliminary triangle, rampaging spy-jazz charts and.. spanish guitar and – rather fetching actually – panpipes!! (for the equatorial location, presumably, although they just happened to get the wrong continent). The date's 1973 but the cavalier arrangements and live-in-the-studio space – and occasionally scrambled (appalling actually) sound – makes it seem much older. BETTS is a man who knows how to use bongo, conga, güiro, maracas, gong, woodblock, African water drum and just about every other percussive device in the book for maximum close range impact; Quentin Tarantino was so taken with the dynamic tension of 'Police Check Point', he cued it into 'KILL BILL: VOL.1' (although – at a mere 40 odd seconds – it didn't make the soundtrack). In fact, rather than developing real melodic leitmotifs, BETTS keeps the mood in perpetual limbo with fraught abstraction and a succession of bony, polyrhythmic miniatures. Above all, it's the remorseless cowbell parts which dictate the pace, cutting in and out (and not just because of the sound..), down and across atonal organ and brass surges. And surprisingly given the dodgy subject matter, when he does compose with melody in mind, the mood is bossa-tender rather than sleazy, expressed in the minute-long 'Bus Stop' and infinitely nostalgic end credits, where a ghostly, gorgeous keyboard sounds transmuted from one of John Barry's arcane 60s reveries. So give it up for HARRY BETTS; he's a master of both rhythm and melody in a way that normally only becomes Brazilians, and in 'BLACK MAMA, WHITE MAMA' he composed an unjustifiably obscure, sampler's paradise of a soundtrack. A few years ago you could still pick it up for a few dollars; chances are it'll be going for a lot more than that by the time you read this. *BG*

Album rating: *7.5

BLACK MILK

aka MAVRO GALA

2000 (Greece 101m) Astra Show Vision And Sound

Film genre: romantic fantasy/comedy

Top guns: s-w: (+ dir) Nicholas Triandafyllidis → I PUT A SPELL ON ME, Christos Homenidis

Stars: Michail Marmarinos *(Alekos)*, Ieroklis Michaelidis *(Sotiris Poupalos)*, Mirto Alikaki *(Makia)*, Tania Nasibian *(Enrietta)*, Takis Spiridakis *(Mike Amitoglou)*, Marissa Triantafyllidou *(the butcher)*, Themis Panou *(Marilou)*, Panayiotis Thanassoulis *(Panoulis)*, Christos Stergioglou *(bartender)*, **Blaine Reininger** *(the pimp)* ← DOWNTOWN 81, Renos Haralambidis *(the butcher)*

Storyline: The convoluted, blackly comedic tale of Alekos, a former creative wunderkind whose life has descended into debauchery and artistic bankruptcy, and who attempts to remake his mistakes by travelling back in space and time. *BG*

Movie rating: *5

Visual: none

Off the record: **GALLON DRUNK** were formed in Turnpike Lane, London in the late 80s by James Johnston and Mike Delanian along with ex-Earls Of Suave man, Max Decharne and early drummer Nick Coombe. Replacing the latter with maestro of the maracas, Joey Byfield, GALLON DRUNK swaggered onto an indie stage dominated by the fag-end of the baggy scene and limp-wristed shoegazers; pausing only to grease back their quiffs and dust down their vintage suits, Johnston and Co proceeded to unleash the most violent, paranoid, unholy racket this side of NICK CAVE's Birthday Party. After a clutch of early singles on their manager's 'Massive' label, the band signed to London indie, 'Clawfist'. Rolling in on a crescendo of distorted bass and exploding in a howl of organ abuse and clenched-teeth threats, 'Some Fools Mess' was quintessential GALLON DRUNK (if you only ever buy one GALLON DRUNK record etc . . .). It was also a much heralded NME Single Of The Week, paving the way for a debut album, 'You, The Night And The Music' (1992). When this lot weren't spitting out their trademark cocktail of twisted blues/R&B, New Orleans voodoo and amphetamine fuelled rockabilly (Link Wray comes to mind), they were partial to a bit of low-rent lounge crooning; ok, Johnston was never going to be Neil Diamond and they never pulled it off with quite the same panache as TINDERSTICKS but covers of Lee Hazlewood's 'Look At That Woman' and Neil Sedaka's 'Solitaire' remain compulsive listening. These tasty nuggets can be found hiding on the B-side of the searing 'Bedlam' single, Terry Edwards' baritone sax adding depth to what was basically a sharpened-up, groovier take on 'Some Fools . . .'. The best track by some measure on 'From The Heart Of The Town' (1992) album, it only served to underline the impression that they couldn't quite keep the pedal to the metal over a whole album. Still, GALLON DRUNK cruising was infinitely preferable to the bloodless indie pap of the day and grimy Big Smoke sketches like 'Arlington Road' made a mockery of Blur's subsequent oi! guv! pastiche. A mark of the man's underrated talents, JOHNSTON was signed up for touring duties with NICK CAVE during the Bad Seed's Lollapalooza '94 jaunt. 1994 also saw Johnston and Edwards cut the musical accompaniment for a spoken word album ('Dora Saurez') by crime writer, Derek Raymond while GALLON DRUNK the band eventually emerged from the pub in 1995 with an EP, 'The Traitor's Gate'. By this point the line-up was Johnston, Delanian, Byfield alongside newcomers Ian Watson, Andy Dewer and Ian White, this combination working on the long-awaited third set, 'In The Long Still Night'. Released on 'City Slang' in '96, the record revealed a more sober GALLON DRUNK; while the songwriting was probably stronger, gone was the gloriously filthy sound, Johnston's mumbled menace and the delirious sense of impending chaos that characterised the band's early work. Despite overwhelmingly positive reviews, a subsequent decision that GALLON DRUNK had reached its ultimate conclusion led to the band's official dissolution in '97. Of late, Johnston has found a new outlet for his manic energy, linking up with Edwards to form J.J. Stone, who stormed the alternative dancefloors in 1998 (con)fusing unlikely elements of Spiritualized and QUINCY JONES. The Johnston/Edwards axis was to be the basis of a regrouped GALLON DRUNK (along with a new rhythm section of Jerry Cottingham and Ian White), recruited by Greek film director, Nikos Triandafyllidis, to cut the soundtrack for his 1999 thriller, 'BLACK MILK'. With their penchant for cinematic grooves and an obvious career-long fixation with Ennio Morricone, the opportunity to record a film score was never likely to be squandered. Johnston himself was to make it on to the big screen in 2001 with a part in Ken Russell's 'The Fall Of The Louse Usher' while a long awaited GALLON DRUNK studio album, 'Fire Music' (2002), confirmed that they were still one of the most potent and underrated forces in alternative music. *BG*

—

GALLON DRUNK

Mar 00. (cd) *F.M.; (FM 1134)* ☐ [-]
– Theme from Black Milk / Hurricane – new version / Every second of time / Blood is red / The funeral / Can you feel it / Now and forever / At my side / Prostitute / Hypnotised / Every second of time – Moog instrumental version / One more time / Lament.

S/track review: When JAMES JOHNSTON embarked on a solo career in the late 90s, GALLON DRUNK's sonic tomcattin' looked to have finally run out of spunk. Having definitively proved that Old Nick really did have the best tunes, the coolest cover art and the sharpest suits, there seemed no evidence left to supply. Ironically, it was that self same solo single, 'Hurricane', which bent the ear of Greek director Nicholas Triandafyllidis. Given JOHNSTON's longtime admiration for Ennio Morricone's tombstone blues, it seemed only apt that a full blown soundtrack commission announced his band's return to the fray. And having previously collaborated with Nick Cave on Jez Butterworth's 'Mojo' (1997), the 'DRUNK weren't exactly big screen virgins. BUT the results were so upwardly, digitally mobile that they were sometimes barely recognisable as the witchdoctorin' lounge hell-hounds of yore. If you can somehow ignore the Stakker Humanoid-vintage acid squelch, 'Hurricane' – and 'Can You Feel It' – are about the closest they come to their trademark seditious snarl, with TERRY EDWARDS' apoplectic tone-bashing noising things up. 'Blood Is Red' loses itself in Pop Will Eat Itself territory, where even Morricone-approved chimes of doom can't point it in the right direction. It's actually something of a relief when they pare the arrangements right down to saddle-sore bongos, spaghetti harmonica and EDWARDS' lasciviously honking baritone on 'Hypnotised', GALLON DRUNK's answer to Cave's 'Red Right Hand'. Ironically but perhaps not surprisingly, JOHNSTON is at his most cinematic – and his most soulful – when he abandons the tastefully emasculated GD template completely. Left to ponder his Morricone fantasies in peace, he comes up with the kind of hollow-eyed, multi-layered keyboard elegies ('The Funeral') and blinking orchestrations ('Prostitute') which predicted a sideline in bonafide film scoring (he went on to provide the music for Dudi Appleton's 'The Most Fertile Man In Ireland'). GALLON DRUNK would get their demonic freak back on with 'Fire Music' (2002), but 'BLACK MILK' was nowhere near as reliably curdled as the soundtrack efforts of either NICK CAVE or fellow elegant bohemians TINDERSTICKS. *BG*

Album rating: *5.5

BLACK SHAMPOO

1976 (US 83m) Dimension Pictures Inc. (R)

Film genre: crime thriller/drama

Top guns: s-w: (+ dir) Greydon Clark → the FORBIDDEN DANCE, Alvin L. Fast ← BUMMER

Stars: John Daniels *(Mr. Jonathan)* ← CANDY TANGERINE MAN, Tayna Boyd *(Brenda St. John)*, Joe Ortiz *(Mr. Wilson)*, Skip Lowe *(Artie)*, Gary Allen *(Richard)*, Anne Gaybis *(Mrs. Phillips)*, William Bonner as Jack Meoff *(Maddox)* ← CLEOPATRA JONES ← PSYCH-OUT

Storyline: Hair stylist and expert fighter Jonathan Knight swaps his scissors for a chainsaw when his pretty assistant's ex-boyfriend subtly woos her by beating up various shop staff. Taking time off from bedding rich white lady customers, Mr Knight stops horsing around and lays into the baddies with a variety of lethal weapons. Can he save his sultry secretary and be head and shoulders above every hairdresser in town? *JZ*

Movie rating: *4

Visual: VCI Home video + dvd

Off the record: Other tracks not on the set, 'Liquid Love' by ROLAND BAUTISTE and 'It Must Have Been Today ' by the GERALD LEE SINGERS featuring STEPHANA LOEB, DEBBIE JAMES & NANCY SHANKS. *MCS*

GERALD LEE *(w/ dialogue *)*

Mar 76. (lp) *Dimension Pictures Inc.; <DPI-4120>* ☐ ☐

– Mr. Jonathan / I'll get you (w/ *) / Soft / On the move / Can you feel the love / The chase / The search (w/ *) / The bust up (w/ *) / Deciding on you / Main theme / The flight / Fanfare / Can you feel the love – reprise / The BBQ (w/ *) / Love theme / Brick brief case / Deciding on you – reprise) / Mr. Jonathan – reprise (w/ *) / The rescue / Dialog: a) Get out, b) Scream, c) Know your enemy, d) Do the job, e) The boss is back.

S/track review: The blaxploitation genre made no bones about unsubtly rehashing mainstream movie ideas for black audiences and topping it with a distinct soundtrack: 'BLACK SHAMPOO' is one truly unsubtle example. The problem was that by 1976, any quality had been driven out most of these genre potboilers and the score for 'BLACK SHAMPOO', provided by jazzer GERALD LEE (and paid tribute to by hip hop outfit Wu-Tang Clan on their 1996 album, 'Wu-Tang Forever'), is hackneyed beyond belief. The problem is two-fold. Firstly, LEE is scoring a genre movie, he needs the hero's theme tune, the love theme, the chase scene (helpfully called 'The Chase'), the search (that is the spooky creeping one where the hero goes sniffing out the bad guys) plus some sundry tracks to fill in the blanks on the fight sequences. What he has also done is lifted every cliched film soundtrack in the action movie book. The upbeat strut of 'Mr Jonathan' is the strongest piece here, a nimble sub-Curtis Mayfield strut in fact. There's also a couple of down-tempo funk grooves of note but for the most part, this just rifles through the pockets of Lalo Schifrin, Quincy Jones and Isaac Hayes for melodies, style and mood. The second problem here is that the mastering on the current 'Dimension' Pictures vinyl release was clearly lifted straight from the film soundtrack itself, rather than from original master tapes of the score. So, we are treated to endless dialogue over the top of the music, including several long arguments, a spectacularly long sex scene (at least that's what one hopes it is!) and Jonathan's hairdresser being sodomised by a hairspray can. Add to this, sound quality that at best is tinny and at worst just plain distorted and you've got a whole heap of reasons as to why Blaxploitation's days were numbered. *MR*

Album rating: *3

☐ BLACK VALOR alt.
(⇒ SAVAGE!)

☐ the BLACKBYRDS segment
(⇒ CORNBREAD, EARL AND ME)

BLACULA

1972 (US 93m) American International Pictures (PG)

Film genre: horror drama

Top guns: dir: William Crain / s-w: Joan Torres, Raymond Koenig

Stars: William Marshall *(Blacula)*, Vonetta McGee *(Luva/Tina)* ← MELINDA / → SHAFT IN AFRICA → BROTHERS → REPO MAN, Denise Nicholas *(Michelle)* → the SOUL OF NIGGER CHARLEY → LET'S DO IT AGAIN → a PIECE OF THE ACTION, Thalmus Rasulala *(Gordon Thomas)* ← COOL BREEZE / → WILLIE DYNAMITE → FRIDAY FOSTER → CORNBREAD, EARL AND ME → BUCKTOWN → ADIOS AMIGO → LAMBADA → NEW JACK CITY, Charles Macauley *(Dracula)* ← HEAD, Gordon Pinsent *(Lt. Jack Peters)*, Emily Yancy *(Nancy, photographer)* ← COTTON COMES TO HARLEM, Ted Harris *(Bobby McCoy)* → the ROSE, Ji-Tu Cumbuka *(Skillet)* ← UP TIGHT / → BOUND FOR GLORY, **Ketty Lester** *(Juanita Jones; cabbie)* ← UP TIGHT! / → HOUSE PARTY 3, Elisha Cook *(Sam)* → PAT GARRETT & BILLY THE KID → CARNY

Storyline: You guessed it, a blood sucking black African Prince – originally cursed with blood lust after a run-in with Count Dracula back in 1780 – ends up reanimated in L.A. after unexpectedly emerging from his Transylvanian crypt. *BG*

Movie rating: *4.5

Visual: video

Off the record: Ketty Lester (b. Revoyda Frierson, 16 Aug'34, Hope, Arkansas) had four hits in 1962, the biggest selling was her Top 5 debut, 'Love Letters'. *MCS*

GENE PAGE (& Various Artists)

1972. (lp) *R.C.A.; <LSP 4806>* ☐ ☐

– Blacula (the stalkwalk) / Heavy changes (the 21st CENTURY LTD.) / Run, Tina, run! / There he is again (the HUES CORPORATION) / Movin' / Main chance (the 21st CENTURY LTD.) / Good to the last drop / Blacula strikes! / What the world knows (the HUES CORPORATION) / I'm gonna catch you (the HUES CORPORATION) / The call / Firebombs / Finding love, losing love / Wakeeli (Swahili farewell). *<(cd-iss. Oct98 on 'Razor & Tie'; RE 8179-2)>*

S/track review: "One of the greatest blaxploitation funk albums" according to 'blaxploitation.com', and who are we to disagree? Refreshingly free of gangsters, tricks, drugs and narcs, 'BLACULA' sinks its chops deep into classic funk and soul, and more often than not draws blood. Its chief architect, the late GENE PAGE, had been a noted industry insider since the early 60s, racking up such prestigious arranging credits as the Righteous Brothers' 'You've Lost That Lovin' Feelin', and Dobie Gray's 'The In Crowd'. He'd go on to become a key element in the Love Unlimited Orchestra (and later a solo artist in his own right), but 'BLACULA' captures him at his funkiest, after his mellower work on Robert Altman's 'BREWSTER McCLOUD' (1970) and before he colluded in Barry White's Casanovan excess. Despite a veritable arsenal of percussion, archaic synths and assorted exotica at his disposal, there's precious little of that excess here; PAGE rarely overplays his hand and the running times are kept to a minimum, even on the exquisitely arranged 'Main Chance' and experimental closer 'Wakeeli (Swahili Farewell)', where he spooks out on African water drums and harpsichord. Unlike most of the genre's main themes, 'Blacula (The Stalkwalk)' is purely instrumental, setting the tone for relentless cues like 'Good To The Last Drop' and the dissonant 'Blacula Strikes!'. It doesn't quite live up to that priceless title, being more of a loose limbed swagger than a stalkwalk, a catwalk strut set to classy horn charts. 'Run, Tina, Run!' picks up the pace before climaxing in the supernaturally funky 'There He Is Again', a genuine stalkwalk with its feet on the street, its head in the bass-bin and its foot jammed on the wah-wah pedal, agonising between danger and desire; Vincent Price with his "mojo workin". 'I'm Gonna Catch You' prowls similar territory, urged on by a supercharged, vintage soul rhythm section and screeching brass – naturally, it's all but unrecognisable from the HUES CORPORATION of 'Rock The Boat' fame. 'BLACULA's vocal tracks have come in for criticism, but technical proficiency is hardly the point here; this is soul music as primal allegory, and it's about as raw as 70s funk gets. Just don't go near it with garlic breath. *BG*

Album rating: *8

BLADE RUNNER

1982 (US 117m) Warner Bros. Pictures (R)

Film genre: sci-fi fantasy

Top guns: dir: Ridley Scott / s-w: Hampton Fancher, David Peoples (nov: Philip K. Dick 'Do Androids Dream Of Sleep?')

Stars: Harrison Ford *(Rick Deckard)* ← MORE AMERICAN GRAFFITI ← AMERICAN GRAFFITI ← ZABRISKIE POINT / → WORKING GIRL, Rutger Hauer *(Roy Batty)*, Sean Young *(Rachael)* → DUNE → EVEN COWGIRLS GET THE BLUES, Daryl Hannah *(Pris)* ← HARD COUNTRY / → KILL BILL: VOL.1 → KILL BILL: VOL.2 , Edward James Olmos *(Gaff)* → EVEN COWGIRLS GET THE BLUES → SELENA → the ROAD TO EL DORADO, M. Emmet Walsh *(Harry Bryant)* ← BOUND FOR GLORY ← LITTLE BIG MAN ← MIDNIGHT COWBOY ← ALICE'S RESTAURANT / → CATCH ME IF YOU CAN → ALBINO ALLIGATOR, William Sanderson *(J.F. Sebastian)* ← COAL MINER'S DAUGHTER / → LAST MAN STANDING, Brion James *(Leon)* ← BOUND FOR GLORY, Joe Turkel *(Tyrell)*, Joanna Cassidy *(Zhora)* ← FOOLS / → CLUB PARADISE, James Hong *(Hannibal Chew)* ← BOUND FOR GLORY ← DYNAMITE BROTHERS / → the KAREN CARPENTER STORY → WAYNE'S WORLD 2

Storyline: Ridley Scott's disturbing sci-fi classic plays out against the futuristic backdrop of L.A. circa 2019, a place of glaring inequality and capitalist-inspired technology gone haywire. Rick Deckard is a cop retired from his career as a blade runner, a specialist who goes after rogue androids (or replicants) escaped from their main occupation of colonising space. He's duly called back into action to hunt down a particularly dangerous group of replicants led by Roy Batty. Eldon Tyrell, the figure behind the shadowy corporation which invented the androids, is also in the robots' sights as the action heads towards a bloody rooftop climax. *BG*

Movie rating: *9.5

Visual: video + dvd

Off the record: (see below)

—

the NEW AMERICAN ORCHESTRA (not original soundtrack)

Nov 82. (lp) *Full Moon; <K 99262>* ☐ ☐
– Love theme / Main title / One more kiss, dear / Memories of green / End title / Blade runner blues / Farewell / End title reprise. *<(cd-iss. Jul88 on 'WEA'; 250002-2)>*

S/track review: classical/orchestral OST in future editions

Album rating: *4

—

VANGELIS (original soundtrack)

Jun 94. (cd/c) *Atlantic; <82623> East West; (4509 96574-2/-4)* ☐ [20]
– Main titles / Blush response / Wait for me / Rachel's song (with MARY HOPKIN) / Love theme from Blade Runner (with DICK MORRISSEY) / One more kiss, dear (with DON PERCIVAL) / Blade runner blues / Memories of green / Tales of the future (with DEMIS ROUSSOS) / Damask rose / Blade Runner (end titles) / Tears in rain.

S/track review: Although an orchestral re-run (by the NEW AMERICAN ORCHESTRA) of the BLADE RUNNER score was the only soundtrack on the market for more than a decade after the movie's 1982 release, VANGELIS' acclaimed original was finally made available in 1994. Glacially haunting electronica from a heart of dystopian darkness, it stands as one of the most revelatory synth scores committed to celluloid. The Greek composer's auditory imaginings of a world gone mad, leached of emotion, are occasionally warmed up by some spacey sax on the likes of 'Wait For Me' and 'Love Theme', while MARY HOPKIN contributes eerie, wordless vocals on the evocative 'Rachel's Song'. *BG*

Album rating: *8

☐ BLOOD, SWEAT & TEARS segment
(⇒ the OWL AND THE PUSSYCAT)

BLOW-UP

1966 (UK/Ita 110m) Metro-Goldwyn-Mayer (X)

Film genre: psychological seXual mystery/thriller

Top guns: s-w: Michelangelo Antonioni (+ dir) → ZABRISKIE POINT, Tonino Guerra

Stars: David Hemmings *(Thomas)* ← BE MY GUEST ← LIVE IT UP ← SOME PEOPLE ← PLAY IT COOL / → PROFONDO ROSSO → la VIA DELLA DROGA, Sarah Miles *(Patricia)*, Vanessa Redgrave *(Jane)* → TONITE LET'S ALL MAKE LOVE IN LONDON → the BODY, Peter Bowles *(Ron)*, John Castle *(painter)* → MADE, Jane Birkin *(the blonde)* → WONDERWALL → SEX POWER → MAY MORNING → CANNABIS → JE T'AIME MOI NON PLUS, Gillian Hills *(the brunette)*, **the Yardbirds:- Jimmy Page** *(rhythm guitarist)* <= LED ZEPPELIN =>, **Jeff BECK** *(lead guitarist)*, **Keith Relf** *(vocalist)*, **Chris Dreja** *(bassist)*, **Jim McCarty** *(drummer)*

Storyline: Swinging London gets perhaps its most famous cameo as the backdrop to Michelangelo Antonioni's landmark analysis of reality and illusion. Thomas is the decadent fashion photographer who accidentally captures on film what he believes to be an act of murder. Although it's a conviction strengthened when he finds a dead body in the park where he took the original photos, the reality of who is behind the killing remains unclear. *BG*

Movie rating: *8

Visual: video + dvd

Off the record: The **Yardbirds** had just run out of chart singles when 'BLOW-UP' was released, from 1964 to 1966 they had seven including four Top 3 hits: 'For Your Love', 'Heart Full Of Soul', 'Evil Hearted You' & 'Shapes Of Things' (the first featured ERIC CLAPTON not JEFF BECK). *MCS*

—

HERBIE HANCOCK (& Various Artists)

May 67. (lp; mono/stereo) *M.G.M.; (MGM-C/+S 8039) <E/SE 4447>*
– Main title "Blow-Up" / Verushka part I / Verushka part II / The naked camera / Bring down the birds / Jane's theme / Stroll on (YARDBIRDS) / The thief / The kiss / Curiosity / Thomas studies photos / The bed / End title "Blow-Up". *(cd-iss. Jan97 on 'EMI Soundtracks'+=; CDODEON 15)* – Am I glad to see you (TOMORROW) / Blow-Up (TOMORROW). *<cd-iss. 1992 on 'Sony'; 52418> (cd re-iss. Dec99 on 'Vintage Classics'+=; VCS 005)* – (extra sessions).

S/track review: A young-ish HERBIE HANCOCK used his first soundtrack commission to showcase an agility spanning the whole jazz spectrum, from greasy, beer-joint soul-jazz to strident hard bop to bass-heavy avant-garde minimalism. The score's most famous excerpt, 'Bring Down The Birds' is still an irresistibly funky club staple and was also sampled on Dee-Lite's huge 1990 hit, 'Groove Is In The Heart'. While Antonioni failed in his bid to net the Velvet Underground, he did commission two tracks from British psych band, TOMORROW, the haunting 'Am I Glad To See You' and the more prosaic, 19th Nervous Breakdown-style title cut. In the end, neither made it onto either the film's final print or the original soundtrack, although they did appear for the first time on the recent CD re-issue. Instead, the YARDBIRDS were the token rock band, running through the almost garage-punk strength 'Stroll On' in the movie's closing scene. *BG*

Album rating: *7 / re-cd *7.5

BLUE CITY

1986 (US 83m) Paramount Pictures (R)

Film genre: political/crime thriller/melodrama

Top guns: dir: Michelle Manning / s-w: Lukas Heller, Walter Hill ← STREETS OF FIRE / → LAST MAN STANDING (au: Ross MacDonald)

Stars: Judd Nelson *(Billy Turner)* → EVERYBREATH → AIRHEADS → MR. ROCK'N'ROLL: THE ALAN FREED STORY, Ally Sheedy *(Annie Rayford)* → HIGH ART → SUGAR TOWN, David Caruso *(Joey Rayford)*, Paul Winfield *(Luther Reynolds)* ← MIKE'S MURDER ← a HERO AIN'T NOTHIN' BUT A SANDWICH ← GORDON'S WAR ← TROUBLE MAN ← SOUNDER, Scott Wilson *(Perry Kerch)* → JOHNNY HANDSOME → YOUNG GUNS II → ELVIS AND THE COLONEL: THE UNTOLD STORY → GERONIMO: AN AMERICAN LEGEND → SOUL SURVIVOR → DEAD MAN WALKING → SOUTH OF HEAVEN, WEST OF HELL → DON'T LET GO → MONSTER, Anita Morris *(Malvina Kerch)* ← ABSOLUTE BEGINNERS, Julie Carmen *(Debbie Torres)*, Tommy Lister Jr. *(Tiny)* → TRESPASS → JACKIE BROWN, Willard E. Pugh *(Leroy)* → EDDIE PRESLEY → CB4: THE MOVIE, **the Textones:- Carla Olson, Phil Seymour, Tom Junior Morgan, Joe Read, George Callins** *(performers)*

Storyline: Wayward son Billy Turner returns to his Florida home only to discover that his father, the former town mayor, has been murdered. Worse, it's likely that his step-mother's new beau is the killer. *BG*

Movie rating: *4.5

Visual: video

Off the record: The **Textones** only released a couple of LPs, 'Midnight Mission' & 'Cedar Creek'; **Carla Olson** was also a solo artist with several albums under her belt, one with former Byrd Gene Clark. *MCS*

—

RY COODER

Jul 86. (lp/c) *Warners; <(9 25386-1/-4)>*
– Blue city down / Elevation 13 ft. / Marianne (TRUE BELIEVERS) / Nice bike / Greenhouse / Billy and Annie / Tell me something slick (POPS AND 'TIMER) / Blue city / Don't take your guns to town / A leader of men / Not even Key West. *<cd-iss. Jan96; 9 25386-2>*

S/track review: Released the same year as 'CROSSROADS', yet not nearly as widely heard, 'BLUE CITY' has never been reissued and will cost you more than it's probably worth second hand. But that doesn't mean it's not worth hearing. If it isn't exactly RY COODER's 80s Rock soundtrack, it's uncharacteristically more in tune with its times, front loading a peppy, jangly contribution from the TRUE BELIEVERS (the mid-80s vehicle of ESCOVEDO clan siblings JAVIER and ALEJANDRO) and a steely, mechanistic, almost 'Miami Vice' aesthetic shoved down your craw by R&B bruiser BOBBY KING on opener 'Blue City Down'. With the two JIMMYs, KELTNER and DICKINSON, present and firing on all cylinders, and the latter making his mandatory compositional contributions, it's heavy, propulsive stuff with only a trace of ethnic weave and a surprisingly profligate – at least for COODER – use of synthesizer. If it wasn't for that buckled twang, you'd never place the Toto-esque title theme (complete with DAVID PAICH and JEFF PORCARO on synth) as a COODER piece. Yet the score isn't without humour; COODER does a convincingly glowering, hugely impressive basso profundo impression of the late Johnny Cash on the man's cantering standard, 'Don't Take Your Guns To Town', and KING spits surreal comedy and pop culture quotes to match the synth-funk of POPS AND 'TIMER's 'Tell Me Something Slick'. Ultimately though, RY can't resist sneaking in a bit of what he does best, conceiving balmy closer, 'Not Even Key West', as a percussive compound of Americana, Mexicana and swarthy tropical melancholy. It's the most cinematic four and a half minutes on the album and you can't help wishing – from a purely musical point of view, demands of character and plot notwithstanding – he'd used it as a base motif for the whole score. *BG*

Album rating: *6

– spinoff releases, etc. –

RY COODER: Billy And Annie / POPS AND 'TIMER: Tell Me Something Slick

Jul 86. (7")

the BODY

1970 (UK 112m) Kestrel Films (X)

Film genre: scientific documentary

Top guns: s-w + dir: Roy Battersby (book: Anthony Smith)

Stars: Vanessa Redgrave *(narrator)* ← TONITE LET'S ALL MAKE LOVE IN LONDON ← BLOW-UP, Frank Finlay *(narrator)* → SHAFT IN AFRICA , Sadie Corre → the ROCKY HORROR PICTURE SHOW

Storyline: A pioneering, Vanessa Redgrave-narrated documentary based on Anthony Smith's best selling manual, exploring – with the aid of internal cameras and juxtaposed imagery – the functions, flaws, miracles and contradictions of the human body and humanity itself, from birth to death. *BG*

Movie rating: *6.5

Visual: video

Off the record: RON GEESIN (b.17 Dec'43, Ayrshire, Scotland). From the early 60s, GEESIN was part of Crawley-based jazz combo, the Original Downtown Syncopators, before he started to write music for documentaries and TV commercials. Living in Notting Hill, London, he built up recording equipment for his next outing; the 1967 avant-jazz album 'A Raise Of Eyebrows'. He subsequently toured alongside folkies Roy Harper and Ralph McTell, while he worked on 'The BODY', a collaboration with ROGER WATERS who had previously invited RON to augment and co-write on 'FLOYD's 'Atom Heart Mother' set the same year. After various session work for Bridget St. John, GEESIN set up his own-named label and issued three albums, although he was to drop out of the music scene until he resurfaced with the CD, 'Funny Frown' (1990); he was now living in Sussex, England. *MCS*

—

RON GEESIN & ROGER WATERS: Music From The Body

Dec 70. (lp) *Harvest; (SHSP 4008) <SW 751>* ☐ ☐
– Our song / Sea shell and stone / Red stuff writhe / A gentle breeze blew through life / Lick your partners / Bridge passage for three plastic teeth / Chain of life / The womb bit / Embryo thought / March past of the embryos / More than seven dwarfs in Penis-land / Dance of the red corpuscles / Body transport / Hand dance – Full evening dress / Breathe / Old folks ascension / Bed-time-dream-clime / Piddle in perspex / Embryonic womb-walk / Mrs. Throat goes walking / Sea shell and soft stone / Give birth to a smile. *(cd-iss. 1989 on 'E.M.I.'; CDP7 92548-2) (cd re-iss. Feb96; CZ 178)*

S/track review: A more humorous, optimistic antecedent of Jonny Greenwood's 'BODYSONG' (2003), this abstract collage is an absurdists' dream, compressing everything from farting noises, burps, hiccups, teeth-grinding, ragtime piano, genteel chamber orchestration, Spanish guitar pieces, chattering pizzicato, assorted unidentifiable sound effects and even a whistled snatch of 'The Bonnie Banks O' Loch Lomond'. It's the wayward, tape-delayed spirit of RON GEESIN – orchestrator of Pink Floyd's 'Atom Heart Mother' (1970), KPM library artist, producer and arranger of Bridget St. John's lost classic, 'Songs For The Gentle Man' (1971), all round avant-garde renaissance man and a guy who admits as much of a fondness for adjustable spanners as for Chic Murray and surrealism – which carries most of the material. Recommended to the film's producer by the late John Peel, he gets more of the credits than WATERS, and despite the fact that most of the tracks were written and recorded separately for the film, their collaborative re-recording for the album means it all flows as magnificently as Dali's moustache. 'Lick Your Partners' and 'Seven Dwarfs In Penis-Land' compete for best title, the former coming on like a spy theme gone wrong; the latter indulging a dadaist male choir (an influence on the 5.6.7.8.'s?). The funky 'Mrs Throat Goes Walking' conjures nothing less than a sectioned Slim Gaillard. As for actual songs, there are a few, and all very 'MORE'-ish. 'Breathe' exhales the kind of poisoned acoustic lullaby WATERS specialised in at the time, an eco protest number reeling off a shopping list of chemicals and an opening line which turned up on 'The Dark Side Of The Moon' (1973); 'Sea Shell And Stone' sounds like 'Grantchester Meadows part II', 'Chain Of Life' a 'Wicker Man'-esque pagan nursery rhyme. 'Give Birth To A Smile' saves the best for last, a Floyd-ian ballad (featuring the rest of the band) which segues into the kind of gospel coda which wouldn't have been out of place on a late 60s/early 70s 'Stones album. WATERS used female backing singers for the first time here – a tactic he resuscitated for his mid-70s concept opuses – and it's about as soulful as his band ever got. GEESIN has referred to at least one of these collaborations as a "big adolescent giggle"; more than anything, WATERS sounds like he at least had some fun doing this. And there ain't many Pink Floyd albums you can say that about. *BG*

Album rating: *6

BODYSONG

2003 (Neth 83m) FilmFour / Hot Property Films (18)

Film genre: avant-garde biological documentary

Top guns: s-w + dir: Simon Pummell

Stars: the visuals

Storyline: A feature from award-winning director Simon Pummell, bravely attempting to delineate the totality of the human experience from conception to death via a dense collage of archival film footage. *BG*

Movie rating: *6

Visual: dvd

Off the record: JONNY GREENWOOD (see below)

—

JONNY GREENWOOD

Oct 03. (cd) *E.M.I.; (<5 95147-0>)* ☐ ☐
– Moon trills / Moon mall / Trench / Iron swallow / Clockwork tin soldiers / Convergence / Nudnik headache / Peartree / Splitter / Bode radio – Glass light – Broken hearts / 24 hour Charleston / Milky drops from Heaven / Tehellet.

S/track review: Although 'BODYSONG's complex weave of imagery inevitably drew comparisons with Godfrey Reggio's 'Koyaanisqatsi' (1983), JONNY GREENWOOD's soundtrack is a darker, more turbulent proposition than Philip Glass' celebrated score. As an ostensible rock guitarist in the forbidding terrain of freeform composition, GREENWOOD acquits himself admirably, veering off at some fascinating tangents from the more avant-garde leanings of latter period Radiohead. The leftfield creative impulses coursing through that band's work are laid bare here, untempered by the demands of verse-chorus songwriting. Opening with the hushed piano and perambulating strings of 'Moon Trills', the record starts out familiarly enough. Closer listening reveals a disparate but rarely less than compelling series of impressions, abstract sonic fragments and morse code electronics held together by only the most tenuous of thematic premises and wont to abruptly change course at the drop of a strangulated chord yet maintaining an enigmatic continuity. As he's done in the past with his day job, GREENWOOD attempts to approximate the primal howl of Ornette Coleman via early 70s Miles Davis, and it's here where his ideas coalesce most satisfyingly: propelled by some frantically impressive drumming and scoured by Gerald Presenser's trumpet, 'Splitter' is by far the album's most solid, febrile composition, more urgent than the often amorphous string segments (performed by The Emperor Quartet) although the Davis influence also makes itself felt on the free jazz influenced 'Milky Drops From Heaven'. A brave, ambitious effort which confirms GREENWOOD as one of rock's pre-eminent intellects and which will likely continue to appeal largely to avant-garde afficionados, adventurous jazzers and hardcore Radiohead fans. *BG*

Album rating: *6.5

Ed BOGAS

Born: Edgar Noel Bogas, c. 1949, San Francisco, California, USA. United States of America was indeed the name of the short-lived band Ed augmented on their 1968 eponymous breakthrough LP, a largely psychedelic and experimental ensemble that comprised five main members Joseph Byrd, Dorothy Moskowitz, Gordon Marron, Rand Forbes and Craig Woodson; BOGAS co-wrote two numbers, 'Where Is Yesterday' & 'Stranded In Time'. In the early 70s, the pianist/organist swapped the world of heavy pop music for that of film scores, BOGAS concentrating on animation through the work of Ralph Bakshi ('FRITZ THE CAT', 'HEAVY TRAFFIC', etc.), Charles M. Schulz ('Peanuts' & 'Charlie Brown . . .') and Jim Davis ('Garfield'); the latter was of the 80s. His proper introduction into Blaxploitation movies came via 'BLACK GIRL' (1972), an Ossie Davis feature from a play by J.E. Franklin. BOGAS was also a much-in-demand session player, earning his crust through guesting on albums such as Stevie Wonder's 'Where I'm Coming From' (1971) and Cher's 'Living Proof' (2001). *MCS*

- **filmography** (composer) –

Fillmore *(1972 {p} =>)* / **Fritz The Cat** *(1972 OST w/ Ray Shanklin =>)* / **Black Girl** *(1972 OST w/ Ray Shanklin =>)* / **Payday** *(1973 score w/ others =>)* / **Heavy Traffic** *(1973 OST w/ Ray Shanklin =>)* / Silence *(1974 score)* /

Memory Of Us *(1974 score)* / Slashed Dreams *(1975 score)* / He Is My Brother *(1976 score)* / Race For Your Life, Charlie Brown *(1977 score)* / Love And The Midnight Auto Supply *(1977 score)* / etc.

□ Jon BON JOVI segment (⇒ YOUNG GUNS II)

BONES

2001 (US 96m) New Line Cinema (R)

Film genre: occult horror

Top guns: dir: Ernest R. Dickerson / s-w: Adam Simon, Tim Metcalfe

Stars: **SNOOP DOGG** *(Jimmy Bones)*, Pam Grier *(Pearl)* ← JACKIE BROWN ← BILL & TED'S BOGUS JOURNEY ← BUCKTOWN ← SHEBA, BABY ← FRIDAY FOSTER ← FOXY BROWN ← COFFY ← COOL BREEZE ← BLACK MAMA, WHITE MAMA ← BEYOND THE VALLEY OF THE DOLLS, Michael T. Weiss *(Lupovich)*, Clifton Powell *(Jeremiah Peet)* ← WHY DO FOOLS FALL IN LOVE ← HOUSE PARTY / → RAY, Ricky Harris *(Eddie Mack)*, Bianca Lawson *(Cynthia)* ← SAVE THE LAST DANCE ← the TEMPTATIONS ← PRIMARY COLORS, **Deezer D** *(Stank)* ← FEAR OF A BLACK HAT ← CB4: THE MOVIE ← COOL AS ICE / → IN THE MIX, Sean Amsing *(Maurice)*, Katharine Isabelle *(Tia)* ← JOSIE AND THE PUSSYCATS, Erin Wright *(Snowflake)* ← DUETS ← SWEETWATER: A TRUE ROCK STORY, Lynda Boyd *(Nancy Peet)* ← SWEETWATER: A TRUE ROCK STORY

Storyline: Jimmy Bones has been the long-time neighbourhood guardian, keeping away the drug pushers from his patch. When he is betrayed, murdered and buried beneath his house, the bad guys move in and the street becomes a crime ghetto. Twenty years on, and Jimmy's house is to be renovated and turned into a nightclub, but when the angry ghost of Jimmy Bones is released revenge is on the cards and no-one is safe from the enraged spook. *JZ*

Movie rating: *4

Visual: dvd

Off the record: (see below)

—

SNOOP DOGG (*) & Various Artists (score: Elia Cmiral)

Oct 01. (cd) *Priority; <50227> (CDPTY 223)* 39 □
– Birth of Jimmy Bones (*) / Legend of Jimmy Bones (* & MC REN & RBX) / Lost angels in the sky (LOST ANGELS & KOKANE) / Ballad of Jimmy Bones (LATOIYA WILLIAMS) / Dogg named Snoop (* & TREY DEEE) / This is my life (KEDRICK & C.P.O.) / It's Jimmy (KURUPT & ROSCOE) / Raise up (KOKANE) / These drugs (D12) / Death of Snow White (*, BAD AZZ, CHAN & CONIYAC) / If you came here to party (*, THA EASTSIDAZ & KOLA) / **** with us (KURUPT w/ TRAY DEEE & XZIBIT) / Jimmy's revenge (* & SOOPAFLY) / Be thankful (WILLIAM DEVAUGHN) / F-it-less (FT – **** THAT) / Gangsta wit it (*, NATE DOGG & BUTCH CASSIDY) / Memories (CYPRESS HILL) / Endo. *(bonus +=)* – Fresh and clean – remix (* & OUTKAST).

S/track review: It took until 2001 for things to come full circle for SNOOP DOGG. In the seven frantically busy years between his screen (and soundtrack) debut in 'MURDER WAS THE CASE' he lost the "Doggy" side to his moniker – it was thought to be "childish sounding" – and had become one of the biggest brand names in global hip hop. This was his first feature film as a leading man. Unsurprisingly, SNOOP's fingerprints are all over the soundtrack, overseeing its compilation as Executive Producer and throwing in a couple of his own works for good measure. True to form, there are momentary flashes of the slick, thick, tricky G-funk formula that served him so well up until this point, only 'Legend Of Jimmy Bones' and 'Death Of Snow White' explicitly appraise Dr Dre's legendary production sound in earnest. Elsewhere, we get some garish, gnarly rhymes telling the story of our eponymous undead hero, ROSCOE & KURUPT celebrate Jimmy's legend over a beat built around an accordion and flute sample, while the little-known KO KANE digs out some old analogue squelches for his excellently unhinged 'Raise Up'. While guests lined up to throw down a verse or two, including XZIBIT, D12, NATE DOGG, CYPRESS HILL and MC REN, the general vibe remains rough but playful, flitting between 70s blaxploitation and 00s refined hip hop styles. Despite claims of keeping real, this is high-gloss product. As is with all SNOOP albums, there's a reworking of a classic soul track, this time it's WILLIAM DEVAUGHN tackling 'Be Thankful', which is a fun distraction but fails to cover any new ground. Something that could be said for many of the tracks on 'BONES'. *MR*

Album rating: *5.5

BOOK OF NUMBERS

1973 (US 81m) AVCO Embassy Pictures (R)

Film genre: crime thriller

Top guns: dir: Raymond St. Jacques / s-w: Larry Spiegel (au: Robert Deane Pharr)

Stars: Raymond St. Jacques *(Blueboy Harris)* ← COME BACK, CHARLESTON BLUE ← the FINAL COMEDOWN ← COOL BREEZE ← COTTON COMES TO HARLEM ← UP TIGHT!, Philip Michael Thomas *(Dave Green)* ← COME BACK, CHARLESTON BLUE / → SPARKLE, **Freda Payne** *(Kelly Simms)*, D'Urville Martin *(Billy Bowlegs)* ← HELL UP IN HARLEM ← the FINAL COMEDOWN ← WATERMELON MAN ← a TIME TO SING / → BLACK CAESAR → the SOUL OF NIGGER CHARLEY → FIVE ON THE BLACK HAND SIDE → SHEBA, BABY → DOLEMITE → DISCO 9000, Gilbert Green *(Antoine)*, Irma P. Hall *(Georgia Brown)* → STRAIGHT TALK → a SLIPPING-DOWN LIFE → DON'T LET GO, Hope Clarke *(Pigmeat Goins)* → a PIECE OF THE ACTION → BEAT STREET

Storyline: Depression-era Arkansas, as seen through the newly uncompromising lens of 70s blaxploitation. Blueboy Harris and Dave Greene are a little and large odd couple of penniless waiters driven to throw their lot in with a numbers bank. When their operation is turned over by white rival, Luis Antoine, the boys send in their own men for a counter-raid, disguising them as Ku Klux Klan in order to terrorise Antoine's black heavies. What they don't bargain for is the local KKK sniffing out the mayhem, discovering the ruse and giving chase. *BG*

Movie rating: *5.5

Visual: none

Off the record: **Freda Payne** (b.19 Sep'42, Detroit, Michigan, USA) had a string of hits for 'Invictus' records in the early 70s, the Top 3 'Band Of Gold' (also a UK chart-topper), 'Deeper & Deeper', 'Cherish What Is Dear To You', 'Bring The Boys Home' & 'You Brought The Joy'. *MCS*

—

SONNY TERRY and BROWNIE McGHEE (score: AL SCHACKMAN)

1973. (lp) *Brut; <6002-ST>* □ □
– I walk with the Lord / Riding to Booker's / Blue's last walk / Eldorado / Stompin' at Booker's / Poor little June bug / I'm so glad / Cracker cops / Blueboy's holler / Moog montage: The clan – No way out – Chase down.

S/track review: Recorded the same year as their celebrated link-up with Earl Hooker, 'I Couldn't Believe My Eyes' (reissued by 'B.G.O.' in the late '90s), and only a couple of years before their 1975 split, 'BOOK OF NUMBERS' is an overlooked, late period oddity from the decades-long partnership of SONNY TERRY and BROWNIE McGHEE. Outside of RY COODER and TAJ MAHAL, there weren't many people scoring blues for cinema; American period pictures, Deep South or otherwise, had more often leant on jazz, specifically the kind of Dixie material heard on 'Stompin' At Booker's' (credited to a separate quintet). Yet the dislocated roots-psych of 'Blue's Last Walk' especially, proved the genre could be just as effective, McGHEE's treated vocals engulfed in a random soup of whoops, hollers and moans against TERRY's flickering harmonica, itself in the right hands as expressive a mood sculpter as any orchestra. Straighter but hardly square is the bass-heavy 'Eldorado' and Bo Diddley-esque leitmotif, 'Blueboy's Holler'. Not that the album is all blues, far from it; veteran session guitarist AL SHACKMAN – a man intrumental in the recordings of Nina Simone amongst others – is credited as both composer and arranger, and – this being the golden age of analogue electronics – he's behind the strange and wonderful 'Moog Montage', a six minute plus experimental synth/dulcimer/organ piece working up a head of funky guitar steam, with none other than BRUCE LANGHORNE manning the moog alongside him. Borne in on LANGHORNE's unmistakable, metaphysical drift, it's recommended listening for fans of his 'HIRED HAND' soundtrack. Further enriching the programme is a fine soul-gospel number by the talented and wholly unsung PAT KESSEE (part of the 'Brut'/'Buddah' stable at the time) fronting a fair-sized backing band including Steely Dan alum ELLIOT RANDALL, the man behind the famous 'Reelin' In The Years' solo, and a guy who turned down John Belushi's invitation to be musical director on 'The BLUES BROTHERS'. KESSEE's band, in fact, includes a real live Blues Brother in session-trumpeter ALLAN RUBIN, while another ubiquitous 70s sessioneer, BARBARA MASSEY, takes lead vocal on the sweet soul symphony, 'I'm So Glad'. An unlikely, profoundly satisfying piece of history. *BG*

Album rating: *6.5

□ BOOKER T. & THE MGs segment
(⇒ UP TIGHT!)

the BORDER

1982 (US 109m) Universal Pictures (R)

Film genre: cop/detective thriller/drama

Top guns: dir: Tony Richardson ← NED KELLY / s-w: Deric Washburn, Walon Green ← SORCERER, David Freeman

Stars: Jack Nicholson *(Charlie Smith)* ← TOMMY ← EASY RIDER ← HEAD ← PSYCH-OUT / → BATMAN, Harvey Keitel *(Cat)* ← THAT'S THE WAY OF THE WORLD / → the LAST TEMPTATION OF CHRIST → RESERVOIR DOGS → PULP FICTION → FROM DUSK TILL DAWN → FINDING GRACELAND → BE COOL, Valerie Perrine *(Marcy)* ← CAN'T STOP THE MUSIC / → 54, Warren Oates *(Red)* ← the HIRED HAND, Elphida Carrillo *(Maria)*, Shannon Wilcox *(Savannah)* → SONGWRITER, Manuel Viescas *(Juan)*, Jeff Morris *(J.J.)* ← the BLUES BROTHERS ← PAYDAY ← KID GALAHAD / → BLUES BROTHERS 2000, William Russ *(Jimbo)* → BIG DREAMS & BROKEN HEARTS: THE DOTTIE WEST STORY → COME ON, GET HAPPY: THE PARTRIDGE FAMILY STORY

Storyline: Charlie, a jaded, hen-pecked patrolman, gets dragged to El Paso by his rapacious, airheaded wife ("I married a fu**in' banana!"), where Cat, the husband of his sister-in-law attempts to school him in the seedy, exploitative ways of the local border police. All he wants to do is go back to the Forestry Service and feed ducks; instead, he finds himself wrestling his conscience and his colleagues' trade in "wetbacks", while his wife runs up her charge card and fantasises about TV appearances. The murder of a drug smuggling youth is the final straw, as Charlie's affection for a doe-eyed Mexicana drives him towards a final showdown. *BG*

Movie rating: *6

Visual: video + dvd

Off the record: (see below)

—

RY COODER (& Various Artists)

Mar 82. (lp) *Backstreet; <BSR 6105> M.C.A.; (MCF 3133)* □ May82 □
– Earthquake / Across the borderline (vocal: FREDDIE FENDER) / Maria / Texas bop (JIM DICKINSON) / Highway 23 / Palomita (SAM SAMUDIO) / Rio Grande / Too late (vocal: JOHN HIATT) / No quiero (SAM SAMUDIO) / Skin game (JOHN HIATT) / El scorcho / Building fires (vocal: BRENDA PATTERSON) / Nino. *(cd-iss. Jun06 on 'Raven' Australia +=; RVN 209)* – ALAMO BAY

S/track review: This Tex-Mex flavoured score served notice that COODER had begun putting the greater part of his energies into film work, using more or less the same session aggregate credited on studio set, 'The Slide Area' (1982), and providing the template for 'ALAMO BAY' (1985), right down to the racial undercurrents, the token country vocal ('Building Fires', co-written by Dan Penn) and lone experimental cue; 'Earthquake' proves that COODER picked up on Asiatic throat singing years before it came into vogue. JIM DICKINSON and JOHN HIATT contribute to the writing as well as the singing, and both get their own solo spots. COODER recreates the physical, emotional and moral borders of the movie by enfolding heart and homesick Hispanic balladry between rabid R&B and Texan swing, trailing nostalgic Norteño with hard-knock blues. For the most part, it's an effective strategy in evoking the reality of the "broken promised land", the entrapment with no return expressed so poignantly by veteran Conjunto singer and so-called "Mexican Elvis" FREDDIE FENDER on opening title, 'Across The Borderline'. The juxtaposition of JOHN HIATT and SAM SAMUDIO is especially lacerating, HIATT telling it like it is in a whiskey priest drawl, SAMUDIO pleading for honesty. At least one of COODER's solo cues, 'El Scorcho', hints at 'PARIS, TEXAS', but at root 'The BORDER' is a study in the common genes – mutually recognisable or otherwise – of American and Mexican music. 'Raven' had it spot-on releasing this as a double-header with 'ALAMO BAY'; might they surpass themselves by finally putting together a soundtrack for 'Southern Comfort'? It doesn't look like anyone else is going to do it. *BG*

Album rating: *6.5

□ Pieter BOURKE
(⇒ Lisa GERRARD)

David BOWIE

Born: David Robert Jones, 8 Jan'47, Brixton, London, England. An unassailable master of creative disguise, DAVID BOWIE started out as a second-rate 60s pop musician before reinventing himself as an androgynous, bisexual 70s superstar whose home planet just happened to be Mars. It was to be the first of many reinventions, visual, musical and conceptual; the perfect raw materials, in fact, for a sideline in acting and film composing, something which he's successfully maintained throughout most of his career. Yet even before Ziggy played guitar, BOWIE had made his tentative entrée into the movies with a blink-or-you'll-miss-it part in John Dexter's acclaimed military comedy, 'The Virgin Soldiers' (1969). While he'd long since swapped Ziggy Stardust and Aladdin Sane for the sinister Thin White Duke by the time he starred in Nic Roeg's 'The Man Who Fell To Earth' (1976), his portrayal of a discomfitingly human alien adrift on planet Earth served notice of a significant if predictably quirky screen talent. The film's downbeat, detached atmosphere was amplified in BOWIE's late 70s studio trilogy with BRIAN ENO, darkly compelling albums which fed off his fondness for West Berlin and abandoned any residual theatrics. Having already scored obscure German movie, 'Jane Bleibt Jane' (1978), his preoccupation with the then divided city extended to the next chapter in his film career, as he starred in David Hemming's

'Just A Gigolo' (1979) and appeared in concert as himself in 'CHRISTIANE F.' (1981), the grim tale of a Berlin-based teenage junkie with a soundtrack which raided the aforementioned ENO trilogy. Similarly queasy subject matter informed his role as John Merrick, the horribly deformed 'Elephant Man', in the successful Broadway show of the same name. A theme for Paul Schrader's 'Cat People' remake followed in '82, while 1983 saw the belated release of D.A. Pennebaker's rockumentary 'ZIGGY STARDUST AND THE SPIDERS FROM MARS', made up largely of concert footage from a show at London's Hammersmith Odeon a decade earlier. In fact, 1983 proved to be the most cinematically active year of his career and, in contrast with an inevitable move towards moribund MOR, BOWIE was co-credited as composer in German-made road movie, 'Hero', turned in a hypnotic performance as a prematurely ageing vampire in Tony Scott's gothic horror, 'The Hunger' and, most famously (and perhaps most disappointingly), starred as a POW in Nagisa Oshima's wartime drama, 'Merry Christmas Mr. Lawrence' (1983). While his music was also featured in French drama, 'Boy Meets Girl' (1984), the man's next major movie project was Julien Temple's ambitious musical, 'ABSOLUTE BEGINNERS' (1986), in which he played a manipulative advertising guru, and for which he composed the theme tune, actually one of his better mid-80s efforts. He was also the villainous star of the much touted George Lucas/Jim Henson fantasy, 'LABYRINTH' (1986), in which he was again co-credited for the score. As the critical stock of his recording career continued to plummet, BOWIE's most interesting artistic endeavours continued to be in the world of film, including theme work on the score to Belgian nuclear holocaust animation, 'WHEN THE WIND BLOWS' (1987), and a role as Pontius Pilate in Martin Scorsese's 'The LAST TEMPTATION OF CHRIST' (1988). It was the same in the early 90s; as his turgid Tin Machine project cranked along haplessly, BOWIE found the time to star opposite Rosanna Arquette in kinky escape artist comedy, 'The Linguini Incident' (1992), take a major part in cult David Lynch pilot, 'Twin Peaks: Fire Walk With Me' (1992) and score the BBC TV version (4 episodes) of Hanif Kureishi's novel, 'The BUDDHA OF SUBURBIA' (1993). While another ENO link-up finally attracted some mid-90s critical acclaim, he subsequently portrayed a convincing Andy Warhol in NY art world biopic, 'Basquiat' (1996) and worked on a couple of obscure Italian films, 'Passagio Per Il Paradiso' (1996) and 'Il Mio West' (1998), co-producing the former and starring as a hardened outlaw opposite Harvey Keitel in the latter. Into the new millennium, another reunion, this time with his 70s producer Tony Visconti, saw BOWIE concentrating on his studio work and making up even more lost ground with the critics although he did find time for a bit part – as his good self – in belated RUTLES follow-up, 'Can't Buy Me Lunch' (2003). *BG*

- **filmography** {acting} (composer) –

the Virgin Soldiers *(1969 {b})* / the Man Who Fell To Earth *(1976 {*})* / Jane Bleibt Jane *(1978)* / Just A Gigolo *(1979 {*})* / **Christiane F.** *(1981 {*} OST =>)* / **Cat People** *(1982 hit/theme OST by GIORGIO MORODER see; future editions =>)* / Hero *(1983 w/ MADER)* / Yellowbeard *(1983 {b})* / the Hunger *(1983 {*})* / *Merry Christmas Mr. Lawrence (1983 {*})* / **Ziggy Stardust: The Motion Picture** *(1983 {*p} OST =>)* / the Falcon And The Snowman *(1985 hit/theme OST by PAT METHENY GROUP see; future editions =>)* / Into The Night *(1985 {a})* / **Absolute Beginners** *(1986 {*} hit/theme on OST by V/A =>)* / **Labyrinth** *(1986 {*} OST w/ Trevor Jones =>)* / **When The Wind Blows** *(1987 hit/theme on OST by V/A & ROGER WATERS =>)* / **the Last Temptation Of Christ** *(1989 {*} =>)* / Twin Peaks: Fire Walk With Me *(1992 {*})* / the Linguini Incident *(1992 {*}=>)* / **the Buddha Of Suburbia** *(1993 TV-mini OST =>)* / Basquiat *(1996 {*} OST by V/A; see future edition)* / Everybody Loves Sunshine *(1998 {*})* / il Mio West *(1998 {*})* / Mr. Rice's Secret *(2000 {*})* / Zoolander *(2001 {a})* / the Rutles 2: Can't Buy Me Lunch *(2003 TV {c})* / the Prestige *(2006 {a})* / Arthur et les Minimoys *(2007 {v})*

☐ Billy BRAGG segment
(⇒ WALKING AND TALKING)

BREAKING AND ENTERING

2006 (UK/US 116m) The Weinstein Company / Miramax Films (R)

Film genre: romantic drama

Top guns: dir (+ s-w): Anthony Minghella ← COLD MOUNTAIN

Stars: Jude Law *(Will Francis)* ← ALFIE re-make ← COLD MOUNTAIN, Juliette Binoche *(Amira)*, Robin Wright Penn *(Liv)* ← the SINGING DETECTIVE ← the PRINCESS BRIDE, Martin Freeman *(Sandy)*, Ray Winstone *(Bruno)* ← the PROPOSITION ← COLD MOUNTAIN ← SEXY BEAST ← LADIES AND GENTLEMEN, THE FABULOUS STAINS ← QUADROPHENIA, Vera Farmiga *(Oana)*, Rafi Gavron *(Miro)*, Poppy Rogers *(Bea)*, Mark Benton *(Legge)*, Juliet Stevenson *(Rosemary)*

Storyline: Set in the melting pot of Kings Cross, London, an affair between an English landscape architect (Will Francis) and a Bosnian refugee (Amira) develops, when he encounters her petty thief of a son (Miro) burgarising his city office. The two contrasting and complex worlds of the two (rich-meets-poor) characters and their respective kin, can only be problematic as Will re-evaluates his life so far. *MCS*

Movie rating: *6.5

Visual: dvd

Off the record: UNDERWORLD (now the duo of Karl Hyde and Rick Smith) were possibly the right choice for the soundtrack having originated from another London suburb, Romford. Once a quartet of Smith, Hyde, Alfie Thomas and Bryn Burrows, they had all been part of Cardiff outfit Freur (which was actually a symbol translated into a word!; no, PRINCE wasn't the first!). With the more conventional moniker, UNDERWORLD had a hit in America during the late 80s having signed for Seymour Stein's 'Sire' records. After a No.1 smash, 'Radar', in Australia, they toured the States supporting EURYTHMICS, but it was clear this was not the direction for them. After ditching Thomas and Burrows and recruiting DJ Darren Emerson, the group moved to the 'Boys Own' label, releasing the seminal techno crescendo of 'Rez' in February '93 and the critically acclaimed album, 'Dubnobasswithmyheadman' (1994), a nouveau-psychedelic classic climaxing with the delirious trance-athon of 'Cowgirl'. However, their big break came with the single 'Born Slippy', and when re-released to promote 'TRAINSPOTTING' in 1996, the track stormed to No.2, boosting sales of their recently released follow-up album, 'Second Toughest In The Infants'. 1999's long-awaited 'Beaucoup Fish' brought them a US Top 100 entry, having already made Top 3 in Britain. Highlights from the set were undoubtably hit singles, 'Push Upstairs', 'Jumbo' and 'Shudder – King Of Snake', while 'Moaner' (the theme from 1997's 'Batman & Robin' feature) was its 10-star pieste de resistance. After a live album, Emerson officially departed. UNDERWORLD's next studio outing would be 'A Hundred Days Off', a strangely muted affair undoubtedly affected by the alteration in group chemistry. With the duo of Hyde and Smith getting the taste of film score work during this "comeback" soundtrack release, the pair – alongside ex-Cure man, John Murphy – were collaborating on another movie, 'Sunshine' (2007). *MCS*

—

UNDERWORLD and GABRIEL YARED

Nov 06. (cd) *V2; (VVR 104355-2) <7350>* ☐ Dec06 ☐
– A thing happens / St Pancras / Sad Amira / Monkey one / Not talking / Hungerford Bridge / We love Bea / Happy toast / Monkey two / Will and Amira / Primrose Hill / So-ree / Mending things / Broken entered / Piano modal / Counterpoint hang pulse. *(bonus Japanese track +=)* – JAL to Tokyo (Riverrun version).

S/track review: The collaborative meeting of two giants from the music business: regular film composer GABRIEL YARED and first-timers from the rave/dance/rock scene, UNDERWORLD. The former Beirut-born orchestrator was best known for his Academy-winning work on 'The English Patient' (1996) and also other nominated scores for 'The Talented Mr. Ripley' (1999) and 'COLD MOUNTAIN' (2003) – all incidentally by screenwriter/director/co-producer, Anthony Minghella – while the latter had a massive, 'TRAINSPOTTING'-fuelled smash hit via 'Born Slippy'. Other techno-orientated outfits have delved into dual film scores, noteably ORBITAL (alongside MICHAEL NYMAN) on 'EVENT HORIZON' way back in '97. After a slow beginning to the proceedings courtesy of 'A Thing Happens' and 'St Pancras', the listener is finally treated to the emotionally upbeat, 'Sad Amira', not textbook UNDERWORLD by any stretch of the imagination, and YARED just simply conducts the same thematic strings. Track 4, 'Monkey One', delivers some pizzicato guitar frets, while that haunting theme/melody recurrs to a pounding drum and bass on next piece, 'Not Talking'. Up to this point, this was indeed score Musak, a little incidental, never imposing, just effective to the point of tedium. But having listened to numerous POPOL VUH and classical works, this was just the ticket, although a poke with a sharp stick was necessary on certain occasions. The mood and theme had changed by track nine, 'Monkey Two', the take-over of acoustic guitar a welcome variation – this was arguably the best thing on the 57-minute set. The awakening was complete on follow-on cut, 'Will And Amira', the drum'n'bass gyrating to a faster rpm beat than their previous pieces. The piano takes centre stage on 'Primrose Hill', deliberately melancholy, beautifully translucent and with a few further plays, memorable. 'So-ree' was another pull on the heartstrings, and who let Mike Oldfield into the mix as it's remarkably like something he would have attempted way back in his mid-70s, 'Tubular Bells' to 'Ommadawn' period. For completists, there is a lengthy version of 'JAL To Tokyo', tagged on to the end of the Japanese CD, too long in my humble opinion. Whether 'BREAKING AND ENTERING' receives any awards is anybody's guess, but this is a collaboration that ticked many boxes, if not box A, which, in my reckoning, belongs to the world of rock. *MCS*

Album rating: *6.5

BREWSTER McCLOUD

1970 (US 101m) Lions Gate Films / MGM-EMI (R)

Film genre: fantasy comedy drama

Top guns: dir: Robert Altman / s-w: Doran William Cannon

Stars: Bud Cort *(Brewster McCloud)* ← the STRAWBERRY STATEMENT / → GAS-S-S-S → HAROLD AND MAUDE → ELECTRIC DREAMS → SOUTH OF HEAVEN, WEST OF HELL → the MILLION DOLLAR HOTEL → COYOTE UGLY → the LIFE AQUATIC WITH STEVE ZISSOU, Sally Kellerman *(Louise)*, Michael Murphy *(Frank Shaft)*, William Windom *(Weeks)*, Shelley Duvall *(Suzanne)*, Rene Auberjonois *(the lecturer)*, Stacy Keach *(Abraham Wright)*, Corey Fischer *(Officer Hines)* ← NAKED ANGELS

Storyline: The high hopes of geeky teen-dreamer Brewster McCloud involve flying into the rafters of the Houston Aerodrome he calls home. Celestial help arrives in the form of Louise (a "guardian angel who appears to have wandered in from a Dennis Potter play", as Time Out saw it), although matters are complicated with super cop Frank Shaft's mounting, bird turd body count and McCloud's ultimate weakness in the face of sexual temptation. *BG*

Movie rating: *6

Visual: video (1986)

Off the record: (see below)

—

JOHN PHILLIPS * & MERRY CLAYTON **)
(score: GENE PAGE ***)

Dec 70. (lp) *M.G.M.; <1SE-28ST>* ☐ ☐
– Rock-a-bye baby (SALLY KELLERMAN) / White feather wings (**) / Funeral (**) / Lift every voice and sing (**) / Promise not to tell (*) / Last of the unnatural acts (*) / First and last thing you do (*) / White feather wings (* & **) / The star spangled banner (MARGARET HAMILTON) / Caged (the HOUSE OF REPRESENTATIVES) / Over the rainbow (***) / Two in the bush (***) / Brewster, don't blow your mind (***) / Lost city (***) / Brewster, don't blow your mind (***). *<cd-iss. 2000 on 'Chapter III'; CHA 1004>*

S/track review: With JOHN PHILLIPS' semi-mythic solo opus, 'John, The Wolfking of L.A.' finally seeing a CD reissue, now seems as propitious a time as any to revisit his other post-Mamas & Papas oddity. Altman and Adler assembled a typically haphazard musical cast, with PHILLIPS scoring no less than six tracks, half of them sung by MERRY CLAYTON and most of them orchestrated by GENE PAGE. Don't come expecting the calamitous invocations of 'GIMME SHELTER' or 'PERFORMANCE'; CLAYTON warbles like a straight up soul diva, charming the proverbial birds from the trees, or at least willing Brewster to fly like one. She takes her star turn on a breakbeat-bolstered 'Lift Every Voice And Sing', shepherding her flock with that earth mother authority which – in a different context – so chillingly stalked the 'Stones. PHILLIPS himself is less assertive and irritatingly brief but all the more haunting for it: 'Promise Not To Tell' keeps delicately schtum against forlorn flute and a 'White Rabbit' bassline before launching into Van Morrison-pitch soul-folk, and fading out just as fast. His acoustic mini-symphony 'Last Of The Unnatural Acts' barely makes ninety seconds yet the honky-tonkin' 'First And Last Things You Do' – humdrum in comparison – hogs almost three minutes. Crate diggers looking for the PAGE that was yet to blaze through 'BLACULA' aren't going to find him at the end of Harold Arlen's ' . . .Rainbow', but he does put his name to some brassy funk-rock (performed by Adler protégés the HOUSE OF REPRESENTATIVES) and inventively groovy, syncopated orchestration. 'Brewster, Don't Blow Your Mind' is a martini-mellow chin-chin that Isaac Hayes might have served on 'THREE TOUGH GUYS' and 'Lost City' sounds like a Don Ellis cue. Oh, and you'll probably want to programme out MARGARET 'Wizard Of Oz' HAMILTON's catastrophic 'Star Spangled Banner'; it's just about funny once, if you don't have any nervous cats in the house. Like the film, the music straddles fantasy and satire so deftly that it keeps you hanging on if only to hear what comes next, a pop cultural artefact that could only have hailed from an Aquarius-age Hollywood, and one which doesn't quite deserve its bad rep. *BG*

Album rating: *6

☐ David BRIDIE
(⇒ NOT DROWNING, WAVING)

BRIGADE MONDAINE

aka VICE SQUAD

1978 (Fra 90m) Francos Films (18)

Film genre: cop/detective thriller

Top guns: dir: Jacques Scandelari / s-w: Jacques Robert (au: Gerard DeVilliers)

Stars: Patrice Valota *(Boris Corentin, the inspector)*, Odile Michel *(Micheline-Chloe)*, Florence Cayrol *(Annie)*, Michel Blanc as Patrick Olivier *(Patrick Morel)* ← JE T'AIME MOI NON PLUS, Jacques Berthier *(Paul-Henri Vaugoubert de Saint-Loup)*, Marianne Comtell *(Nada)*, Olga Georges-Picot

Storyline: Coming on like a less savoury Sweeney, the titular vice squad are on the trail of a narcotics and prostitution racket behind a series of working girl murders, one which leads to the highest echelons of officialdom. *BG*

Movie rating: *2.5

Visual: none

Off the record: CERRONE (see below)

—

CERRONE

Aug 78. (lp) *Malligator; (773.805)* [–] French [–]
– Give me love / Phonic / Cloe / Deauville / Experience / Generique / Make up / Generique / The loft / Strip tease.

S/track review: A Gallic Giorgio Moroder who started out as a Club Med A&R man (love to have seen the job description for that one), moustachioed Eurodisco pioneer Jean-Marc CERRONE is still synonymous – in the UK at least – with his 1978 Top 10, 'Supernature'. Less well known is his contribution to Kongas' 'Anikana-O', the last chanted word in hands-in-the-air Afro-Latin-disco. Perhaps even less well known than that is 'BRIGADE MONDAINE', CERRONE's first venture into cinema, recorded for an obscure French thriller and released on his own 'Malligator' label. Listening to the likes of 'Experience', the proto-deep house of 'Cloe' and the relentless, electro-gurning brilliance of 'Striptease', the 90s inheritance of Daft Punk et al becomes easier to explain. CERRONE probably should have had the same kudos in his day but at the height of punk (the real version being just a little bit daft), well, the kids just weren't 'avin' it. The record initially follows the patent of the 'Supernature' album by covering pretty much all his options, descending into cerebro-score territory on side two. Opener 'Give Me Love' is the Frenchman at his slickest, a potent, percussive homage to the hedonism of late 70s New York. But you'll like Monsieur CERRONE more when he's moody; 'Phonic' – a single originally released under the Cristal moniker – is evocative in that chromatic, continental way Kraftwerk and Moroder patented, sounding out Europe as a mysterious and seductive superstate years before open borders and budget flights proved otherwise. 'Deauville', very much on the other hand, predicts his late decade move into fusion but still sounds great, like George Benson on a flying visit (Easyjet probably) to St Tropez. A near side-2-long suite is CERRONE's grand soundtrack statement, transmitting abstract, beetling synth and sullen half melodies over monotonous, four-stuck-to-the-floor beats, dramatic rolls and trickling, dank chateau effects. It's not all doom, gloom and vice though; he ends on a high with a rhythm-free reverie, and hence to the tonal firestorm of 'Striptease'. Seminal stuff. *BG*

Album rating: *7.5

BRIMSTONE & TREACLE

1982 (UK 87m) Namara Films (18)

Film genre: religious/psychological drama

Top guns: dir: Richard Loncraine ← FLAME / s-w: Dennis Potter (+ play) → LIPSTICK ON YOUR COLLAR → the SINGING DETECTIVE

Stars: **STING** *(Martin Taylor)*, Denholm Elliott *(Thomas Bates)* ← PERCY ← HERE WE GO ROUND THE MULBERRY BUSH / → the WICKED LADY, Joan Plowright *(Norma Bates)* → DANCE WITH ME → CURIOUS GEORGE, Suzanna Hamilton *(Patricia Bates)* → 1984, Benjamin Whitrow *(businessman)* ← QUADROPHENIA, Dudley Sutton *(stroller)*, Mary MacLeod *(Valerie Holdsworth)*, ← O LUCKY MAN! ← PIED PIPER

Storyline: Smooth talking drifter Martin Taylor worms his way first into the confidence, then into the home of middle aged christian publisher, Tom Bates, and his long suffering wife, Norma. Preying on the Bates' respective weak spots, he charms and disarms them to the point that Norma unquestioningly delegates the care of her invalid daughter. Bad move; Taylor's true colours are revealed as he becomes the catalyst for the betrayal of the family's deepest, darkest secrets. *BG*

Movie rating: *7.5

Visual: video + dvd

Off the record: (see below)

—

STING (& the POLICE * / Various Artists)

Sep 82. (lp/c) *A&M; (AMLH/CAM 64915)* [67] [–]
– When the roll is called up yonder (FINCHLEY CHILDREN'S MUSIC GROUP) / Brimstone & treacle / Narration / How stupid Mr. Bates (*) / Only you / I burn for you (*) / Spread a little happiness / We got the beat (GO-GO'S) / You know I had the strangest dream / Up the junction (SQUEEZE) / Bless this house (BRIMSTONE CHORALE) / A kind of loving (*) / Brimstone 2. *<US cd/c-iss.1990s; 75021 3245-2/-4>*

S/track review: If DAVID BOWIE's contributions to the likes of 'Cat People' and 'LABYRINTH' are anything to go by, thank his 'Stella Street' trilby that he – allegedly – turned this one down. Instead, we got the pièce de résistance of STING's screen career, the kind of ambivalently sinister role which sits uneasily with his later, more charitable persona. We also got a great theme tune, 'Spread A Little Happiness', excerpted from a 1930s musical, and in perfect disharmony with the restive spirit of Dennis Potter's original play. It was STING's original solo hit (Top 20), and there's an argument that it's still the best, a devilishly irreverent, deceptively respectable show tune sung in a faux-Cole Porter accent that fans of his 'Fields Of Gold' or even 'Dream Of The Blue Turtles' phase would scarcely recognise. In fact, in a soundtrack where other dubious pleasures include a chance to hear him narrate the monotony of Mr. Bates' middle aged life (in an equally refined tone), and a dark, coiling synth experiment of a title theme, about the only track they would recognise is the seductive, Last Exit-era ballad, 'I Burn For You'. Arrangements on cues credited to the POLICE are fuller, ticking over on mechanistic 80s time along with the new wave funk of 'Only You' (cue background blustering Ó la David Byrne); setting aside the token choral intro, they link in to a surprisingly cohesive first half. With the needless inclusion of a GO GO's track and a SQUEEZE classic, as well as the gratuitously, almost unlistenably disturbing 'A Kind Of Loving' (horrific screams and hysterical shouting over a POLICE jam), it ultimately descends into more of an endurance test, yet as a de facto STING debut album, 'BRIMSTONE & TREACLE' promises an adventurousness that largely, unfortunately failed to materialise. *BG*

Album rating: *6

– spinoff hits, etc. –

STING: Spread A Little Happiness / **the POLICE:** Only You

Aug 82. (7") *(AMS 8242)* [16] [–]

BRONCO BULLFROG

1970 (UK 86m b&w) Maya Films / British Lion Film Corporation

Film genre: coming-of-age/crime drama

Top guns: s-w + dir: Barney Platts-Mills

Stars: Del Walker *(Del Quant)*, Anne Gooding *(Irene Richardson)*, Sam Shepherd *(Jo Saville aka Bronco Bullfrog)*, Roy Haywood *(Roy)*, Freda Shepherd *(Mrs. Richardson)*, Dick Philpott *(Del's father)*, Chris Shepherd *(Chris)*, Stuart Stones *(Sgt. Johnson)*, Geoff Wincott *(Geoff)*, Mick Hart *(Grimes)*

Storyline: Apprentice Del Quant and his girlfriend Irene get their kicks from small-time crime in London's East End (there's not much else to do). Del gets the chance of a bigger slice of the action when he meets Bronco Bullfrog, an ex-con, in a cafe. His plan is to break into a railyard and steal lots of goodies for resale. Del agrees and they pull off the job, but the police are soon on their trail and the trio must choose whether to stay in hiding or head for the hills. *JZ*

Movie rating: *4

Visual: none

Off the record: **AUDIENCE** was formed in 1968 in East London, England by Howard Werth (vocals & acoustic guitar), Keith Gemmell (tenor sax, flute & clarinet), Tony Connor (drums) and Trevor Williams (lyricist & bass). After their eponymous debut album for 'Polydor' and a support slot on LED ZEPPELIN's tour, AUDIENCE signed to Tony Stratton-Smith's emerging 'Charisma' label. In 1970, the art-rock quartet contributed to the unreleased film soundtrack of 'BRONCO BULLFROG', while also delivering their sophomore, 'Friend's Friend's Friend', another progressive jazz-rock hybrid that drew from Van Der Graaf Generator and the aforementioned Zeppelin. After Shel Talmy (famous for his WHO productions) had dropped out at the last minute, tunesmith Werth employed the services of Gus Dudgeon to produce their 1971 effort 'The House On The Hill'. A final album, 'Lunch', was served up in 1972, accompanying a reasonably successful tour supporting the Faces. Gemmell subsequently joined Stackridge (and later Sammy), Williams toured with the Nashville Teens, Connor joined Nice offshoot, Jackson Heights, while Werth went solo. After the eventual release of 'BRONCO . . .' (after 33 years in the can), Werth, Gemmell, Williams and newbie, John Fisher, re-formed AUDIENCE for a tour and album ('alive&kickin'&screamin'&shoutin') in 2004. *MCS*

AUDIENCE *(with "dialogue")*

Dec 03. (cd) *R.P.M.; (<RPM 511>)* ☐ Jan04 ☐

– Opening: The going song / Hut: ("'ere what 'bout that kid we done?") / Waverley stage coach / Welding – Pigeons: ("that ain't too bad") / Jo Bronco: ("what's it like inside . . .") / Up west: ("where we goin'?") / Options: ("they don't bother with us") / ("you left school yet?") / Too late I'm gone / ("what she doing 'ere?") / Tearaway: Banquet / ("'e wears boots") / Leave it unsaid / Speedway: ("do you want to come out on Friday?") / Parents advice: ("oh you silly cow") / ("you go out with that boy and . . .") / Maidens cry / Get away: (". . .wish we could get away from 'em") / ("I told her not to go with him") / Heaven was an island / ("can we come in?") / ("not going to work are you?") / Man on the box / ("do you want to get married") / ("I got to go back to work") / Caught – Closing: ("c'mon Del, get out") – Darkness all around.

S/track review: Featuring the original musical score by AUDIENCE plus additional songs from the 1969 recording sessions – as it says on the sleeve (although it's not clear which ones are which), 'BRONCO BULLFROG' finally gets a belated release after the master tapes sat on a shelf for 33 years. With cockney dialogue in abundance (over 20 minutes, albeit with group accompaniment), the up-and-coming AUDIENCE were an off-the-wall choice to score the music for such a new mod/kitchen-sink movie. From opener 'The Going Song' to finale 'Darkness All Around', one can hear elements of Eric Burdon & The Animals, the Move, the Small Faces, the Spencer Davis Group and Traffic, all iconic purveyors of British R&B and the heavy soul scene. For 'Waverley Stage Coach' (one of the many tracks also on their eponymous LP), AUDIENCE were coming-of-age with every rasp of HOWARD WERTH's vox, while '"Where We Goin'"' (music & dialogue) has all the traits of Jethro Tull, courtesy of KEITH GEMMELL's flute playing. The soulful barbershop-rock of 'Too Late I'm Gone' is something akin to the Bonzo Dog Band fronting Geno Washington's Ram Jam Band. GEMMELL again shines (this time on sax) via track 11, 'Banquet', a jazzy prog-rock precursor to, possibly, future stablemates Genesis. Whether other songs such as 'Leave It Unsaid', 'Maidens Cry' and 'Heaven Was An Island', fit better on 'BRONCO..' or on their aforementioned 1969 debut, that's for others to decide. Incidentally, the album also includes Film Trailer on Enhanced CD track. *MCS*

Album rating: *6

Michael BROOK

Born: 1952, Toronto, Canada. A central figure in the 'Real World' sponsored boom in globally sourced sound and a natural candidate for film scoring, MICHAEL BROOK started out in the same ambient/experimental orbit as BRIAN ENO, DANIEL LANOIS and HAROLD BUDD, all of whom he can count as colleagues and collaborators. His creative kinship with ENO was particularly strong, one which blossomed on BROOK's diaphanous, Eastern tinged debut album, 'Hybrid' (1985). His boffin-like creation of the much touted infinite guitar – a guitar electronically enhanced with the capacity for ringing sustain – and its use by U2's The EDGE led to the latter inviting BROOK to collaborate on his soundtrack to British thriller, 'CAPTIVE' (1986). Around the same time, the Canadian also contributed in an instrumental capacity to 'Passion: Music For The LAST TEMPTATION OF CHRIST' (1988), PETER GABRIEL's pioneering soundtrack for the Oscar-nominated Martin Scorsese epic. While BROOK went on to produce and collaborate with many of the 'Real World' stable's top stars, his first solo screen scoring project came with the IMAX documentary, 'Fires Of Kuwait' (1992), depicting the environmentally disastrous denouement to the first Gulf War. His first full solo soundtrack release, meanwhile, was Kevin Spacey's directorial debut, 'ALBINO ALLIGATOR' (1996), a noir crime thriller for which BROOK concocted a typically subtle, darkly impressionistic and intermittently rootsy and percussive score, similar in tone to RY COODER's more experimental soundtracks. His work on Paul Schrader's hard hitting 'AFFLICTION' (1998) staked out similar, if bleaker territory, zoning out on hesitant, half formed guitar fragments and dissonant synth, with unintrusive accompaniment from the Turtle Island String Quartet. While BROOK went on to score rarely seen indie, 'Getting To Know You' (1999) and again teamed with ENO for the equally obscure 'Buddy Boy' (2000), neither film generated a soundtrack, nor did acclaimed, BROOK-scored indie, 'Charlotte Sometimes' (2002). Of late, BROOK scored the music for the political Al Gore, Oscar-winning documentary, 'An INCONVENIENT TRUTH' (2006). *BG*

- filmography (composer) –

Fires Of Kuwait *(1992)* / **Albino Alligator** *(1996 OST =>)* / **Affliction** *(1998 OST =>)* / Getting To Know You *(1999)* / the Jaundiced Eye *(2000)* / Buddy Boy *(2000)* / Crime And Punishment In Suburbia *(2000 OST by V/A =>)* / Charlotte Sometimes *(2002)* / Who Killed The Electric Car? *(2006)* / **an Inconvenient Truth** *(2006 OST =>)* / Americanese *(2006)* / **Into The Wild** *(2007 score only)*

BROTHER BEAR

2003 (US 85m) Walt Disney Pictures (G)

Film genre: children's animation drama

Top guns: dir: Aaron Blaise, Bob Walker / s-w: Steve Bencich → OPEN SEASON, Ron J. Friedman → OPEN SEASON, Lorne Cameron → OVER THE HEDGE, Tab Murphy, David Hoselton → OVER THE HEDGE

Voices: Joaquin Phoenix *(Kenoia)* → WALK THE LINE, Jeremy Suarez *(Koda)*, Jason Raize *(Denahi)*, Rick Moranis *(Rutt)* ← LITTLE SHOP OF HORRORS ← CLUB PARADISE ← STREETS OF FIRE, Dave Thomas *(Tuke)*, D.B. Sweeney *(Sitka)*, Joan Copeland *(Tanana)*, Harold Gould *(old Denahi)*, Michael Clarke Duncan *(Tug)*, Greg Proops *(male lover bear)*, **Pauley Perrette** *(female lover bear)* ← BADSVILLE ← ALMOST FAMOUS

Storyline: Kenoia is a young native American boy whose father is killed by a she-bear protecting her cubs. Seeking revenge, Kenoia sets off into the forest only to find he has been magically transformed into a bear, so that he can learn about life and survival in the wilderness from the animals' point of view. In this way he will come to understand the importance of compassion and forgiveness as he grows older and appreciate the beauty of the world he lives in. *JZ*

Movie rating: *4.5

Visual: dvd

Off the record: Pauley Perrette was married to Coyote Shivers (between 2000-06) and has poetry published on CD. *MCS*

MARK MANCINA (& PHIL COLLINS *)

Oct 03. (cd) *Disney; <860127> (5046 66877-2)* [52] Nov03 [ ]
– Look through my eyes (*) / Great spirits (TINA TURNER) / Welcome (*) / No way out (theme from Brother Bear) (single version) (*) / Transformation (BULGARIAN WOMEN'S CHOIR) / On my way (*) / Welcome (BLIND BOYS OF ALABAMA & * / OREN WATERS) / No way out (theme from Brother Bear) (*) / Transformation (*) / Three brothers / Awakes as a bear / Wilderness of danger and beauty.

S/track review: The soundtrack for 'BROTHER BEAR' is all about the traditional Disney themes of friendship, love and taking care of one another in adversity. The first four tracks sum up these values while also setting the scene for the film. PHIL COLLINS (a man already with another Disney animation, 'TARZAN', to his credit) tries to add a little vitality to tracks such as 'Welcome' and 'No Way Out' but the music is bland and samey to say the least. Sadly most of the rest of the CD is an exercise in repetition of these four tracks to attract different types of listener. It is with relief that we get to the last three tracks which are purely instrumental and relatively modest. Using a combination of softer woodwind and deeper brass and violin, they give the listener an excellent sense of the natural world and its beauties and dangers. On the whole the CD is far too derivative with lyrics that have an overbearing sense of lovey-doveyness. *JZ*

Album rating: *4

– spinoff hits, etc. –

PHIL COLLINS: Look Through My Eyes / (instrumental) / BULGARIAN WOMEN'S CHOIR: Transformation

Nov 03. (cd-s) *(DISNEY 001)* [–] [61]

BROTHER ON THE RUN

1973 (US 90m) Wrightwood / Rowland-Williams (R)

Film genre: crime drama

Top guns: s-w + dir: Edward J. Lakso, Herbert L. Strock

Stars: Terry Carter *(Boots Turner)* ← NERO SU BIANCO / → FOXY BROWN, Gwenn Mitchell ← SHAFT, Kyle Johnson, **Art Lund** ← BLACK CAESAR / → BUCKTOWN, Diana Eden, James Sikking

Storyline: An oversexed high school teacher comes to the aid of one of his students, who's on the run from the law. "In the city ... you can't trust anyone – not even a cop". *BG*

Movie rating: *3

Visual: Re-issued in the US under video title, 'BLACK FORCE 2'.

Off the record: (see below)

JOHNNY PATE

May 73. (lp) *Perception; <PLP 45>* [ ] [–]
– Brother On The Run – opening / Brother (main title; ADAM WADE) / Auto chase / Maude's intro / En route to Maude's / Soulful brother on the run / Lady leaving store / Ms. Johnston's sex scene / Car bumps / Maude reminisces / Brother On The Run – closing theme. *(UK re + cd-iss. Aug01 on 'Castle'; CMRCD/CMYLP 287)*

S/track review: JOHNNY PATE was everywhere in the early 70s – arranging both Curtis Mayfield's 'SUPERFLY' and Gil Scott-Heron landmark, 'Pieces Of A Man', and composing both the classic 'SHAFT IN AFRICA' and 'BROTHER ON THE RUN' soundtracks. His contributions to blaxploitation's talismanic aesthetic are still unsung; having already worked with musicians like Wes Montgomery, Jimmy Smith and B.B. King, PATE specialised in the dynamics of black music, bringing out its dramatic potential and calibrating its impetus for the big screen. Sticking to straight soul, funk and jazz rather than the Afrodelic shades of 'SHAFT ...', he turned out what is often regarded as one of the era's peak records. 'Opening' is still one of the all-time great chase themes, ticking over with liquid percussion (courtesy of MTUME, onetime sideman to Miles Davis and son of veteran jazz saxophonist Jimmy Heath) and metronomic rhythm guitar, brass surging in formation while barely breaking sweat. PATE applies strings with the restraint of a monk, constant and punctual, while the solos bask in his reflected appreciation of both Montgomery and Smith. 'Closing Theme' is almost as rich, a grungy, dishevelled denouement. ADAM WADE sings the title song, urbane soul which echoes down to today's sample-hungry club scene. Save for the swinging 'En Route To Maude's' and rhythm frenzy of 'Autochase', the rest of the soundtrack melts into the mellower end of wee small hours soul-jazz, languid five minute marathons and tantalising liaisons which hold out the promise of more. *BG*

Album rating: *6.5

BROTHERS

1977 (US 105m) Edward Lewis Productions / Warner Bros. (R)

Film genre: prison drama

Top guns: dir: Arthur Barron / s-w: Edward Lewis, Mildred Lewis

Stars: Bernie Casey *(David Thomas)* ← CORNBREAD, EARL AND ME ← CLEOPATRA JONES / → BILL & TED'S EXCELLENT ADVENTURE, Vonetta McGee *(Paula Jones)* ← SHAFT IN AFRICA ← BLACULA ← MELINDA / → REPO MAN, Ron O'Neal *(Walter Nance)* ← SUPERFLY T.N.T. ← SUPERFLY / → YOUNGBLOOD, John Lehne *(McGee)* ← BOUND FOR GLORY / → AMERICAN HOT WAX → CARNY → LADIES AND GENTLEMEN, THE FABULOUS STAINS, Stu Gilliam *(Robinson)* ← the MACK, Renny Roker *(Lewis)* ← MELINDA ← SKIDOO, Owen Pace *(Joshua)* ← TOGETHER BROTHERS, Dwan Smith *(Kendra)* ← SPARKLE

Storyline: Gritty, factually-based portrayal of one man's struggle to survive a prison term through his relationship with a female black activist. *BG*

Movie rating: *4

Visual: video

Off the record: (see below)

TAJ MAHAL

1977. (lp) *Warners; <BS 3024>* [ ] [–]
– Love theme in the key of D / Funky butt / Brother's doin' time / Night rider / Free the brothers / Sentidos dulce (Sweet feelings) / The funeral march / Malcolm's song / David and Angela.

S/track review: "We were hitting the wall with Warner Brothers ..." TAJ MAHAL recalled years later. "They didn't know what to do with the music, or how to market it". Which is a shame, because though this is a million miles from the wondrous oddity of the 'The HOT

SPOT' soundtrack with MILES DAVIS and JOHN LEE HOOKER thirteen years later, there is nothing unappealing here. The 70s had seen TAJ moving on from the rediscovery of rootsy blues that made his name into an exploration of wider ethnic influences (his father was of Jamaican descent). And you can see how this would confuse the suits at the record company, for this is a Blaxploitation soundtrack simmered in the warm waves of the Caribbean. The standout languid ballad, 'Love Theme In D' is punctuated by the trill of steel drums, and there is an inescapable sunniness to the rest of the well-crafted songs on side one that casts a strange glow over lyrics intended to reflect urban turmoil. The truth is, the composer is probably just too much TAJ MAHAL to fit snugly into anybody else's artistic project – but that's no reason not to appreciate this quirky record's real charms (even if the 8-minute chant of 'Free The Brothers' on the instrumental second side is a test of patience). *ND*

Album rating: *6

□ Alex BROWN segment
(⇒ SHEBA, BABY)

James BROWN

Born: 3 May'33, Barnwell, South Carolina, USA. Arguably the single most influential artist in the evolution of popular music, JAMES BROWN needs little introduction. Variously known as the Godfather Of Soul, Minister Of The New Superheavy Funk and the Funky President, the man served as a magnetic, hotwired conduit for the birth of the Funk, reconnecting black music – and in its turn white music – with its most primal polyrhythmic roots. It's been said a million times before but let's say it again, loudly: without BROWN, there'd be no hip hop, modern R&B, disco, house, techno, electro, garage and virtually any other dancefloor genre you might care to mention. Whole books have been written on the subject of funk, its roots, genesis and implications but suffice to say that in the 60s/early 70s singles like 'Cold Sweat' and 'Get Up (I Feel Like Being A) Sex Machine', BROWN created one of the most compellingly physical music forms ever to emerge from American shores. Yet it was also a global phenomenon, its syncopated insistence and minimal, often chanted, gutteral lyrics requiring little translation: its continuing influence on the popular music of Africa and Brazil especially, is incalculable. After initially making his name as a peerlessly kinetic soul man with one almighty, antediluvian howl of a voice, BROWN forged the Funk through varying line-ups with the likes of guitarists Jimmy Nolen and Alphonso Kellum, sax men Maceo Parker, Fred Wesley and St. Clair Pinckney, bassist Bootsy Collins, and crucially, sticksman Clyde Stubblefield, the original Funky Drummer and the man whose famously extended drum break rendered that track so vital for future samplers. In tandem with the music came BROWN's granite self-belief and belief in the self determination of the whole African American community, expressed in anthems like 'Say It Loud – I'm Black And I'm Proud'. All of which, of course, renders if fair to say that if it wasn't for BROWN, MELVIN VAN PEEBLES' 'SWEET SWEETBACK . . .' and ISAAC HAYES' 'SHAFT' might well have never came into being. The whole blaxploitation genre, in fact, would've been pretty much unimaginable without BROWN's innovations. And while he mightn't have got in on the act until it was nearing the end of its lifespan, in his soundtrack to Larry Cohen's 'BLACK CAESAR' (1973), Mr Dynamite lived up to his rep by supplying one of the genre's most enduring and unfairly underrated documents. Quite why Cohen subsequently rejected BROWN's score for 'HELL UP IN HARLEM' (1973) as "not being James Brown enough" remains a mystery, especially given the undeniably BROWN-like monster grooves of the rejected scores's eventual incarnation, 'The Payback' (1973). BROWN's music for the Gordon Douglas-directed 'SLAUGHTER'S BIG RIP OFF' (1974) was almost as good and if selling drugs wasn't exactly what the Godfather had had in mind when he'd promoted black self-sufficiency, the portrayal of black men in positions of power, however illegal, would've been similarly unimaginable were it not at least partly for JB's unambiguous stance on race politics. While the hardest working man in showbusiness couldn't work quite hard enough to keep up with the late 70s development of what he'd begun a decade earlier, he did appear as his superbad self in both the John Landis classic, 'The BLUES BROTHERS' (1980) and, performing his sole US hit of the 80s, 'Living In America', in Sly Stallone sequel to the sequel to the sequel, 'Rocky IV' (1985). He also made a cameo in Dan Aykroyd vehicle, 'Doctor Detroit' (1983). While his latter day struggles with drugs and the law have been well documented, the indomitable BROWN eventually cleaned up his act, getting back into the studio and belatedly resuming his acting career with Duane B. Clark's 'Soulmates' (1997) and, inevitably, Landis sequel, 'BLUES BROTHERS 2000' (1998). Into the new millennium and into his seventh decade as a performer, BROWN shows little sign of slacking, appearing as himself in Malcolm D. Lee's blaxploitation parody, 'Undercover Brother' (2002) and Jackie Chan effort, 'The Tuxedo' (2002). Sadly, diagnosed with heart disease and suffering from yet another marriage break-up a few years previously, James died of pneumonia on Xmas day, 2006. *BG*

- **filmography** (composer) {acting} –

Black Caesar *(1973 OST =>)* / **Slaughter's Big Rip-Off** *(1974 OST =>)* / **the Blues Brothers** *(1980 {*} on OST by the BLUES BROTHERS & V/A =>)* / Doctor Detroit *(1983 {c})* / Rocky IV *(1985 {p} + hit theme on OST; see future edition)* / When We Were Kings *(1996 {p} on OST by V/A; see future edition)* / Soulmates *(1997 {c})* / **Blues Brothers 2000** *(1998 {a} =>)* / Undercover Brother *(2002 {c})* / the Tuxedo *(2002 {c} on OST; see future edition)*

the BROWN BUNNY

2003 (US 93m; uncut 119m) Kinetique (R)

Film genre: psychological/erotic road movie

Top guns: s-w + dir: **Vincent GALLO**

Stars: Vincent GALLO *(Bud Clay)*, Chloe Sevigny *(Daisy)* ← DEATH OF A DYNASTY ← DEMONLOVER ← KIDS, Cheryl Tiegs *(Lilly)*, Elizabeth Blake *(Rose)*, Anna Vareschi *(Violet)*, Mary Morasky *(Mrs. Lemon)*

Storyline: Bud Clay is a guy who's never gotten over the betrayal of his true love. Silently, morbidly, he clocks up the mileage across the empty quarters of the USA with only his trusty motorbike for company. Girls just can't resist that steely, penetrating gaze, but more often than not he gets cold feet before his conquests succumb. The only cure is a rendezvous with Daisy, the girl he can't forget. She proves her love with explicit (very explicit!) gusto but it's a phantom thrill. *BG*

Movie rating: *6

Visual: dvd

Off the record: VINCENT GALLO (see own entry)

Various Artists (JOHN FRUSCIANTE * non-movie tracks)

May 04. (cd) *Tulip; <TLIP 1001>* [–] Japan [–]
– Come wander with me (JEFF ALEXANDER) / Tears for Dolphy (TED CURSON) / Milk and honey (JACKSON C. FRANK) / Beautiful (GORDON LIGHTFOOT) / Smooth (MATISSE / ACCARDO QUARTET) / Forever away (*) / Dying song (*) / Leave all the days behind (*) / Prostitution song (*) / Falling (*).

S/track review: Love him or loathe him and regardless of the merits of the film, there's no denying that VINCENT GALLO is a believer; he believes. He's also good at making his public believe, and when he writes in his always entertaining sleevenotes that his working relationship with wayward 'Chili Pepper JOHN FRUSCIANTE was some kind of mystical, mutually pre-ordained inevitability, it's difficult not to believe that too. Certainly, FRUSCIANTE's five uneasy pieces have the whiff of fate about them, hermetic guitar elegies motivated by pain and written "in praise of sadness". The recurring theme is departure and loss, and if the vaulting 'Dying Song' (sic) isn't so far removed from the kind of ballad he might perform with his day band, the rest of the tracks are haunted by wordless mantras, stray fears, general studio subversion and the kind of urgent, cabalistic finger-picking which travels on frequencies other guitarists can't reach. In his own notes, FRUSCIANTE describes his contributions as "the silent music of the film . . . the part that cannot be seen", necessarily so given that they don't even feature in the movie. Is this really a soundtrack then? To the extent that GALLO apparently listened to nothing else during filming, and that his vision converged with FRUSCIANTE's score, the answer is probably yes. But why didn't the music end up on the final print? "Unexplainable", GALLO maintains. Possibly the starkness of the visuals and the music would've cancelled each other out. The sounds which GALLO did put in the film come from a different angle, elegant folk and jazz obscurities selected with typically impeccable taste; a mini soundtrack which more conventionally fits his own definition of "love story". 'Come Wander With Me' is as haunting an opening to a soundtrack as GALLO could have hoped to conjure, a hymn to the siren for speedway racers, sourced from an old episode of 'The Twilight Zone'. And surely the time is ripe for a rediscovery of JACKSON C FRANK, a one-time lynchpin of the London folk scene whose one and only album did brisker business in Britain than it ever did in America. Preaching like a white Terry Callier, with a weight of melancholy that's hard to shake off, he renders 'Milk And Honey' (popularised by his onetime girlfriend Sandy Denny) like a prophecy of his own impossibly tragic life. GORDON LIGHTFOOT's 'Beautiful' provides some light relief, onetime Charles Mingus sideman TED CURSON's 'Tears For Dolphy' some class, but 'The BROWN BUNNY' is best sampled as a whole, preferably in the wee small hours. You'll pay Japanese import prices, but it's yen well spent: this is a lesson in how to create a soundtrack that matters; it's also handsomely packaged, comes with some good stills, and of course, those sleevenotes. *BG*

Album rating: *8

BUCKTOWN

1975 (US 94m) Plitt Theaters / American International Pictures (R)

Film genre: political/crime drama

Top guns: dir: Arthur Marks ← FRIDAY FOSTER / → the MONKEY HUSTLE / s-w: Bob Ellison

Stars: Fred Williamson *(Duke)* ← THREE THE HARD WAY ← THREE TOUGH GUYS ← HELL UP IN HARLEM ← the SOUL OF NIGGER CHARLEY ← BLACK CAESAR / → ADIOS AMIGO → MEAN JOHNNY BARROWS → NO WAY BACK → MR. MEAN → FROM DUSK TILL DAWN → RIDE → CARMEN: A HIP HOPERA, Pam Grier *(Aretha)* ← SHEBA, BABY ← FOXY BROWN ← COFFY ← COOL BREEZE ← BLACK MAMA, WHITE MAMA ← BEYOND THE VALLEY OF THE DOLLS / → FRIDAY FOSTER → BILL & TED'S BOGUS JOURNEY → JACKIE BROWN → BONES, Thalmus Rasulala *(Roy)* ← CORNBREAD, EARL AND ME ← WILLIE DYNAMITE ← BLACULA ← COOL BREEZE / → FRIDAY FOSTER → ADIOS AMIGO → LAMBADA → NEW JACK CITY, Tony King *(T.J.)* ← HELL UP IN HARLEM ← GORDON'S WAR ← SHAFT / → SPARKLE, Bernie Hamilton *(Harley)*, **Art Lund** *(Chief Patterson)* ← BROTHER ON THE RUN ← BLACK CAESAR, Tierre Turner *(Steve)* ← CORNBREAD, EARL AND ME / → FRIDAY FOSTER → the CROW, Morgan Upton *(Sam)* ← SPACE IS THE PLACE ← STEELYARD BLUES / → MORE AMERICAN GRAFFITI → TUCKER: THE MAN AND HIS DREAM → the SPIRIT OF '76, Carl Weathers *(Hambone)* → FRIDAY FOSTER, Jim Bohan *(Clete)* ← AMERICAN GRAFFITI

Storyline: Small town violence, corruption and racism as cigar-smoking he-man Duke travels to his Deep South birthplace to organise the funeral of his brother, ostensibly dead from pneumonia. It's only after being talked in to opening his dead bro's night club, and subsequently forced to grease the palms of the local chief of police, that he discovers his sibling was murdered. He soon finds himself a sitting target for the same racketeers and decides to call in his old buddy, Roy, for help. The snag is that Roy's heavies, having eliminated the competition, duly claim Bucktown as their personal fiefdom, necessitating a moral stand and counter-cleanup by our sideburned hero. *BG*

Movie rating: *5

Visual: video on MGM/UA Home Entertainment

Off the record: **Art Lund** had a pop hit in 1947 with 'Mam'selle', while he was also a singer for Benny Goodman, etc.

JOHNNY PATE (w/ dialogue *)

Jul 75. (lp) *American International Records; <AIR 4477>* ☐ ☐
– Main theme / Chase / Love theme / Freeze (w/ *) / Have a good time / Check in (w/ *) / Bar fly / Stepping / Call it in / Sneaking in (w/ *) / Spin / Tank theme (w/ *) / End theme / Chase (part 2) / Love theme (reprise) / Recon / Fun for all / Pay off / End theme (reprise) / Dialogue (w/ *).

S/track review: In a kind of sonically foggy hangover from the blaxploitation mêlée of the late 90s, the last decade has witnessed a spate of never previously released soundtracks mysteriously appearing on vinyl, usually straight from the film. Quality isn't a watchword with this stuff, but if wildly vaccilating background noise and dialogue is the only way to hear JOHNNY PATE's penultimate score of the 70s, let the music play on. If there is an argument for someone to sniff out and buff down the original masters (strangely, 'BUCKTOWN' was absent from the excellent 'Soul Cinema' series), it's the revelation of a main theme: O'Jays-funky guitar and bass carving out headroom for a kerb-pounding breakbeat and inner city-anguished (as well as criminally uncredited) vocal hook. It's the kind of tune that makes a man wanna holler, the way they do his life, etc. (as Marvin Gaye kind of put it). There's also the argument that hearing the scrabbling rhythms, worming frequencies and spiteful horns of 'Chase' or the sunship synth of 'End Theme', as if they're wrapped in wire wool, makes the whole experience more visceral, especially with PATE's uncharacteristic reliance on tight, small group funk: 'Stepping' grinds out the same Stygian bass plod, keyboard and brass riff to a slumberous – if not quite ad nauseam – degree. See also the bizarre 'Spin', which sounds like a dialogue excerpt looped by mistake. 'BUCKTOWN', in places, could almost pass itself off as a conventional studio funk set, with a synth chartered, Stevie Wonder-style love theme creamed off the top. It's episodic, for sure, and the dialogue ("it's that cheap, smelly fu**in' cigar you're smoking that's makin' you talk so funny", "I don't wanna shoot you Roy, I just wanna beat the hell out of you", "that tastes like it's been flushed down the toilet" etc.) can't compete with the deranged 'BLACK BELT JONES' – which, with its similar graphics and sequencing, looks to have been pressed by the same outfit – but, even taking into account the dodgy sound, you won't regret squandering your hard earned bucks. *BG*

Album rating: *6.5

the BUDDHA OF SUBURBIA

1993 (UK 222m mini-TV 4 epi) British Broadcasting Corporation

Film genre: coming-of-age satire

Top guns: s-w: Roger Michell (+ dir), Hanif Kureishi (+ au)

Stars: Naveen Andrews *(Karim Amir)*, Roshan Seth *(Harron Amir)*, Susan Fleetwood *(Eva Kay)*, Steven Mackintosh *(Charlie Kay)*, Brenda Blethyn *(Margaret Amir)*, John McEnery *(Uncle Ted)*, Janet Dale *(Auntie Jean)*, Jemma Redgrave *(Eleanor)*, Nisha Nayar *(Jamila)*, David Bamber *(Shadwell)*, Harish Patel *(Changez)*, Surendra Kochar *(Jeela)*, Badi Uzzaman *(Anwar)*

Storyline: Karim Amir lives in a London suburb with his Indian father and English mother. He experiments with drugs and sex before finally settling down to work in fringe theatre. Meanwhile Karim's father, who teaches nonsensical, made-up philosophy, begins an affair with a rich follower and his wife walks out on him. As Karim matures, he learns how he and his family are viewed by the society in which he lives. *JZ*

Movie rating: *7

Visual: dvd

Off the record: (see below)

—

DAVID BOWIE

Nov 93. (cd/c) *R.C.A.; (74321 17004-2/-4) Virgin; <v2-40988>* [ ] Oct95 [ ]
– Buddha of suburbia / Sex and the church / South horizon / The mysteries / Bleed like a craze, dad / Strangers when we meet / Dead against it / Untitled No.1 / Ian Fish, U.K. heir / Buddha of suburbia (feat. LENNY KRAVITZ).

S/track review: Earlier in '93, a certain Mr David Jones had rescued his ailing career from the depths of a Tin Machine debacle by releasing his chart-topping comeback album, 'Black Tie, White Noise'. Once again though, the man who fell to earth stepped away from the mainstream via the subsequent release of an accompanying BBC-TV mini-series project, 'The BUDDHA OF SUBURBIA'. The album opens with fine BOWIE aplomb courtesy of the hit title track, a hark back to the pre-Ziggy days of old with even a reprise of 'All The Madmen' (from 'The Man Who Sold The World') thrown in at the "deep" end. The lyrics were certainly poignant to the TV play: "Englishmen going insane" . . . "Sometimes I fear the whole world is queer"; guitarist LENNY KRAVITZ guests on the closing version and B-side to beef things up. BOWIE gets all beatbox on track 2, 'Sex And The Church', a track that fused dance rhythms with jazzy tones and works to the point that it was the man removing boundaries once again. This paved the way for DB's venture into full-blown, Miles Davis-esque free-form jazz on 'South Horizon', the "Aladdin Sane" piano (featuring MIKE GARSON) is integral and effectively works big time. BOWIE revived yet another period in his ever-evolving life for 'The Mysteries': LP 'Low', its collaborator Brian Eno and a misty ambience come to mind. The same could be said for tracks 8 & 9, 'Untitled No.1' & 'Ian Fish, U.K. Heir' respectively, the former a romantic, smoochy number, the latter with ghostly acoustics playing over a picturesque backdrop to echo a Buddhist monastery – quite possibly. Of the others, BOWIE takes on the 'Let's Dance' role for 'Bleed Like A Craze, Dad', and even tries his hand at a bit of simple rapping. 'Strangers When We Meet' is classic BOWIE (with a hint of Roxy Music), or could have been with a bit more effort, while follow-on song 'Dead Against It' is like the man fronting OMD. A low point, indeed. All in all, not one of BOWIE's best long-players (its schizoid, filmatic direction took care of that), although with repetitive plays it could be said it was "Heart's Filthy Lesson". *MCS*

Album rating: *6.5

– spinoff hits, etc. –

DAVID BOWIE: Buddha Of Suburbia / Dead Against It

Nov 93. (7"/c-s) *(74321 17705-7/-4)* [35] [–]
(cd-s+=) *(74321 17705-2)* – South horizon / (Lenny Kravitz rock mix).

BUFFALO '66

1998 (US 120m) Lions Gate Films (R)

Film genre: road movie / crime caper

Top guns: s-w: (+ dir) **Vincent GALLO** , Alison Bagnall

Stars: Vincent GALLO *(Billy Brown)*, Christina Ricci *(Layla)* → FEAR AND LOATHING IN LAS VEGAS → MONSTER → the FEARLESS FREAKS → BLACK SNAKE MOAN, Anjelica Huston *(Janet Brown)* ← GOOD TO GO ← THIS IS SPINAL TAP, Ben Gazzara *(Jimmy Brown)* ← ROAD HOUSE, Mickey Rourke *(the bookie)* ← JOHNNY HANDSOME ← HOMEBOY / → MASKED AND ANONYMOUS, Kevin Corrigan *(Rocky the goon)* ← WALKING AND TALKING ← BANDWAGON / → DETROIT ROCK CITY → CHELSEA WALLS, Rosanna Arquette *(Wendy)* ← PULP FICTION ← MORE AMERICAN GRAFFITI / → SUGAR TOWN → THINGS BEHIND THE SUN, Jan-Michael Vincent *(Sonny)* ← HARD COUNTRY, Kevin Pollak *(TV sportscaster)* ← THAT THING YOU DO! ← WAYNE'S WORLD 2, Alex Karras *(TV sportscaster)* ← FM

Storyline: After five years in jail, Billy Brown makes facing the homeward bound music easier by kidnapping the comely Layla and pretending she's his wife. His glibly credulous parents are even taken in with a yarn about having met while working for the CIA, but it's still not enough to win the approval he so painfully craves. *BG*

Movie rating: *7

Visual: video + dvd

Off the record: (see below)

—

VINCENT GALLO (w/ Various Artists)

Jul 98. (cd/lp) *Will; <WILL 33653>* [ ] [–]
– Lonely boy / A falling down Billy Brown / Fools rush in (VINCENT GALLO, Sr.) / Moonchild (KING CRIMSON) / Drowning in brown / A somewhere place / A wet cleaner / Sixteen seconds happy / I remember when (STAN GETZ) / With smiles & smiles & smiles / Heart of the sunrise (YES) / Sweetness (YES) / A cold and grey summer day.

S/track review: "All my life I've been this lonely boy", GALLO croons in the androgynous falsetto of a catholic altar boy. It's a voice seemingly irreconcilable with his abrasive public persona and one with which we might never have been blessed had he been flush enough to afford the songs he wanted. Shoehorned into the role of director, the shock haired auteur found himself in the unique position of being able to choose the music for his own movie. As he recounts in the often hilarious sleevenotes to 'Recordings Of Music For Film' (2002), his budget (including his life savings) barely extended to the prog rock tracks, forcing him to fall back on his home studio and record some original music inside two days. Inevitably, he at least partly fell back on his earlier recordings for Eric Mitchell's 'The WAY IT IS' (1984), which – along with cleaned-up versions of his original music for 'BUFFALO . . .' – were subsequently released as part of 'Recordings . . .'. The joins aren't so obvious, though, and GALLO makes every note count. The Sunday Times called 'BUFFALO 66' "a sustained and dolorous hymn to male self pity", a description which also goes at least some way to analysing GALLO's musical impulse. Even the summer days are cold and grey in his world, but his gift is in making that world alluring, something he achieves partly through the tactile acoustics of his analogue recording techniques. The likes of 'A

Falling Down Billy Brown' suggest archival field recordings from some monochrome, long forgotten corner of the Mediterranean, while GALLO, Sr. (yes, as in Pops Gallo!) flourishes a Rat Pack-era croon on a twinkling, wax-cylinder-vintage cover of 'Fools Rush In'. And fascinatingly, unfashionably choice cuts from YES ('Heart Of The Sunrise' and 'Sweetness') and especially KING CRIMSON ('Moonchild') actually shed light on his arcane creative workings. Most encouraging of all though, the agoraphobic minimalism of his earlier recordings has gotten out more, even lifting its face to the sun 'With Smiles & Smiles & Smiles'. *BG*

Album rating: *7

Jimmy BUFFETT

Born: James William Buffett, 25 Dec'46, Pascagoula, Mississippi, USA; raised in Mobile, Alabama. To establish himself with the ever-evolving country music scene in the late 60s, Jimmy moved to Nashville, where he inked a deal with 'Barnaby' records. A debut LP, 'Down To Earth' (1970), found the singer-songwriter incorporating some socially conscious protest music – by way of 'The Christian?' – into his repertoire. Recorded and scheduled for release in '72, BUFFETT's follow-up album, 'High Cumberland Jubilee' (mostly written with the help of band member Buzz Cason), was "lost" somewhere between the defunct record label and Key West, Florida, where the man had settled the previous year; he would subsequently issue the LP in 1976 when he was a rising star. 'Dunhill/ABC' records bailed him out in '73 and, mixing a cocktail of Nashville country and beach-bum folk philosophy, Jimmy delivered a "second" LP, 'A White Sport Coat And A Pink Crustacean'. His commercial breakthrough came via Top 30 single, 'Come Monday' (written after his divorce), a song taken from the album, 'Living And Dying In 3/4 Time' (1974). His subsequent rise to fame was meteoric, mid-70s albums such as 'A1A' (1974), the 'United Artists' soundtrack, 'RANCHO DELUXE' (1975), 'Havana Daydreamin'' (1976) and 'Changes In Latitudes, Changes In Attitudes' (1977), all catapulting the happy-go-lucky singer into a pop star. The latter album featured his biggest hit to date, 'Margaritaville', a song that not only reached the Top 10, but which subsequently branched him out into the world of merchandise courtesy of an alcoholic drink, a clothing company and nightclubs littered around Key West. While the GRATEFUL DEAD had their "Deadheads" fanbase, BUFFETT had his "Parrotheads", a colourful core of followers with a neat sense of irony and self-mocking humour. From country-styled pop star to best-selling author (sample 'A Pirate Looks At Fifty'), Jimmy also found time to appear in a couple of movies, including 1978's music industry feature 'FM' and cult flick, 'REPO MAN' (1984). Although not as laudable as his previous efforts, the carefree troubadour – who acted in subsequent movies, 'Cobb' (1994) and 'Congo' (1995) – hit the album charts on numerous occasions, his 90s efforts especially ('Fruitcakes', 'Barometer Soup', 'Banana Wind', 'Don't Stop The Carnival' & 'Beach House On The Moon'), all reserving him a place in the Top 20. Just when one thought it was time for the freewheeling gentleman of country to retire to his mansion beach-hut – so to speak – he contributed several songs (and acted) in the kids' movie, 'HOOT' (2006). *MCS*

- **filmography** (composer) {acting} –

Rancho Deluxe *(1975 {c} OST =>)* / **FM** *(1978 {p} on OST by V/A =>)* / **Repo Man** *(1984 {b} =>)* / Breaking All The Rules: The Creation Of Trivial Pursuit *(1988 TV score)* / Cobb *(1994 {b})* / Congo *(1995 {b})* / **Hoot** *(2006 {a} OST w/ V/A =>)*

BUIO OMEGA

1979 (Ita 94m) D.R. Per Le Comunicazioni Di Massa (18)

Film genre: crime horror/thriller

Top guns: dir: Joe D'Amato / s-w: Ottavio Fabbri (story: Giacomo Guerrini)

Stars: Kieran Canter *(Francesco Wyler)*, Cinzia Monreale *(Anna / Elena Volkl)*, Franca Stoppi *(Iris)*, Sam Modesti *(Mr. Kale)*, Anna Cardini *(Jan, the hitchhiker)*

Storyline: When Francesco's beloved Anna dies, he swipes her from the authorities and embalms her (ah, true love). However when a passenger sees her body in his car, Francesco feels he has no choice but to murder her and has similar thoughts about the housemaid Iris who knows far too much. With a sleuthing undertaker on his trail, who should turn up next but Anna's twin sister. Will she be next on the list? *JZ*

Movie rating: *4.5

Visual: video + dvd; German/US

Off the record: (see below)

GOBLIN

Sep 97. (cd) *Cinevox; (CD-MDF 304)* [–] Italy [–]
– Buio Omega (main titles) / Quiet drops / Strive after dark / Pillage / Rush / Keen / Ghost vest / Bikini island / Buio Omega (suite 1) / Quiet drops (film version) / Strive after dark (suite) / Buio Omega (alternate version) / Strive after dark (alternate version) / Buio Omega (synth effect – alternate takes suite) / Buio Omega theme (reprise).

S/track review: GOBLIN's association with "giallo"/horror movies subsequently outlasted any expectations. 'BUIO OMEGA' would have been their 5th or 6th soundtrack (recorded in November '79, Rome) had it been released at the time. Nearly two decades on, and with a plethora of GOBLIN reissued CDs choking the market (including 'PROFONDO ROSSO', 'SUSPIRIA, etc.), 'BUIO OMEGA' takes its rightful place among them. The "main titles" track opens proceedings and starts like any other Tangerine Dream dirge – bouncy, reverberating and atmospheric – except this was GOBLIN. Yes, musicians FABIO PIGNATELLI, CARLO PENNISI, AGOSTINO MARANGOLO and MAURIZIO GUARINI had been pigeonholed many times and if this had seen the light of day, compound interest would've been added. Track 2, 'Quiet Drops', gets into the cinematic mode, although, it must be said, they could've been reading from the KEITH EMERSON (of Emerson, Lake & Palmer) music sheets. If this makes the record poor by association, rather the reverse, because GOBLIN were the subsequent masters of prog-rock. Spine-tingling keys were again present on 'Strive After Dark', while GOBLIN go funky and uptempo for 'Pillage' (and the cloning 'Rush'), similar and reminiscent of . . . here we go again!? . . . Weather Report. Jazz-rock was certainly an element of the new GOBLIN style (check out track 8, 'Bikini Island'), although many Prog groups had gradually moved into the field without really noticing the change; Genesis' PHIL COLLINS had his own Brand X for example. While the gothic-infused 'Ghost Vest' (try that on for size) passes the spooky test, tracks 9 to 15 were alternate versions of the first three numbers. *MCS*

Album rating: *6

BUNNY LAKE IS MISSING

1965 (UK 107m b&w) Columbia Pictures (15)

Film genre: psychological cop/detective mystery/thriller

Top guns: dir: Otto Preminger → SKIDOO / s-w: John Mortimer & Penelope Mortimer (au: Marryam Modell as Evelyn Piper)

Stars: Carol Lynley *(Ann Lake)* ← HOUND-DOG MAN / → NORWOOD, Laurence Olivier *(Supt. Newhouse)* → the JAZZ SINGER, Keir Dullea *(Stephen Lake)*, Martitia Hunt *(Ada Ford)*, Anna Massey *(Elvira Smollett)*, Finlay Currie *(doll-maker)* ← the 6.5 SPECIAL, Noel Coward *(Horatio Wilson)*, Clive Revill *(Sgt. Andrews)*, Lucie Mannheim *(the cook)*, Adrienne Corri *(Dorothy)*, **the Zombies:- Colin Blunstone, Rod Argent, Chis White, Paul Atkinson, Hugh Grundy** *(themselves)*, Richard Wattis *(clerk in shipping office)* ← UP JUMPED A SWAGMAN ← PLAY IT COOL / → WONDERWALL → TAKE ME HIGH, Fred Emney *(man in Soho)* ← I'VE GOTTA HORSE / → the MAGIC CHRISTIAN, Victor Maddern *(taxi driver)* → CUCKOO PATROL → the MAGIC CHRISTIAN, Delphi Lawrence *(first mother at school)* ← FAREWELL PERFORMANCE

Storyline: American Ann Lake calls in Scotland Yard when her 4-year-old daughter Bunny goes missing after her first day at nursery school. However, when Supt. Newhouse questions the school staff he discovers Bunny has never been officially enrolled and no-one can even remember seeing her. The near-neurotic Ann calls in brother Stephen to back up her story when she realizes the police don't believe her. Has Ann gone mad, or has Bunny really hopped it? *JZ*

Movie rating: *7

Visual: video + new dvd

Off the record: The **ZOMBIES** (see below)

PAUL GLASS (& the ZOMBIES *)

Oct 65. (lp) *RCA Victor; (RD 7791) <LSO 1115>* ☐ ☐
– Theme from Bunny Lake Is Missing / Chocolates for Bunny / The empty house at Frogmore End / Nothing's changed (*) / Just out of reach (*) / Remember you (*) / Bunny / A world of dolls / Wild games! / Samantha's waltz / Touching the sky / End title from Bunny Lake Is Missing.

S/track review: The ZOMBIES (aka COLIN BLUNSTONE, ROD ARGENT, CHRIS WHITE, PAUL ATKINSON and HUGH GRUNDY) were indeed quick off the mark to inject their pop-psyche into the movies, having only had a few global hits by way of 'She's Not There' and 'Tell Her No'. The quintet from St Alban's were a strange choice and just to why ambiguous filmmaker Otto Preminger, even thought it neccessary to give the band a cameo was stuff of mystery and speculation (the ZOMBIES appeared as a performing rock group on the TV hospital). Obscure in the fact that two of the songs, 'Remember You' and 'Just Out Of Reach' (fuse the Animals with Herman's Hermits), were only otherwise available on a double-headed single version in 1965/6, the soundtrack has become as rare as hens teeth, fetching over $300 in some places. The ZOMBIES' only other song, 'Nothing's Changed' (that's three songs at under 7 minutes!), is another of the blue-eyed, R&B ilk that falls flat on its face. You can also find the three tracks on the band's 'The Singles As & Bs' double CD and on the 'Repertoire' CD reissue of their 'Begin Here' set. The remainder and surplus of 'BUNNY LAKE . . .' saw composer PAUL GLASS, project some unsettling, disorientated images over a sugary sweet score, leading (at least for the viewer!) into a false sense of security (example 'A World Of Dolls' next to 'Wild Games!'). But this was no 'Psycho', more like another 'Repulsion' (by jazz drummer CHICO HAMILTON the same year). All'n'all, 'BUNNY . . .' is rather disappointing for the money, although a CD issue would be welcome with movie outtakes. *MCS*

Album rating: *4.5

– associated releases, etc. –

the ZOMBIES: Remember You / Just Out Of Reach

Jan 66. (7") *Decca; (F 12322) Parrot; <9797>* ☐ Dec65 ☐
—— (in the US, the tracks were flipped over for A&B sides)

the ZOMBIES: The Zombies EP

1967. (7"ep) *R.C.A.; <86057>* [–] ☐
– Nothing's changed / Remember you / etc.

☐ Solomon BURKE segment (⇒ COOL BREEZE)

the BURNING

1981 (US 91m) HandMade / Miramax / Orion (18)

Film genre: Slasher/Horror movie

Top guns: dir: Tony Maylam (+ story w/ Harvey Weinstein → PLAYING FOR KEEPS, Brad Grey) / s-w: Peter Lawrence

Stars: Brian Matthews *(Todd)*, Leah Ayres *(Michelle)*, Brian Backer *(Alfred)* → FAST TIMES AT RIDGEMONT HIGH, Larry Joshua *(Glazer)*, Jason Alexander *(Dave)* → BYE BYE BIRDIE re-make, Ned Eisenberg *(Eddy)*, Carrick Glenn *(Sally)*, Fisher Stevens *(Woodstock)*, Holly Hunter *(Sophie)*, Bruce Kluger *(Rod)* → PLAYING FOR KEEPS, Lou David *(Cropsy)*

Storyline: Having been the result of a practical joke that back-fired, a badly burned summer-camp caretaker with a penchant for hedgetrimmers, takes revenge on a bunch of spoilt-brat campers. *MCS*

Movie rating: *4

Visual: video

Off the record: Look out for teething appearances from Holly Hunter ('The Piano') and Jason Alexander ('Seinfeld' TV). *MCS*

RICK WAKEMAN

Jan 82. (lp) *Silva Screen; <STV 81162> Charisma; (CLASS 12)* ☐ ☐
– Theme from 'The Burning' / The chase continues (Po's plane) / Variations on the fire / Shear terror and more / The burning end title theme / Campfire story *[UK-only]* / The fire / Doin' it / Devils creek breakdown / The chase / Shear terror. *(UK re-iss. Jan89; some tracks switched; same as US)*

S/track review: RICK WAKEMAN, notable for his 70s Prog-rock masterpieces, 'The Six Wives Of Henry VIII', 'Journey To The Centre Of The Earth' and 'The Myths & Legends Of King Arthur . . .', takes the reins here for another excursion into film scores, having already delivered 'LISZTOMANIA' (1975), 'WHITE ROCK' (1976) and 'G'OLE' (1977). Slightly unusual and off-kilter, 'The BURNING' has side one (or CD first half) sub-titled as 'The Wakeman Variations', while other tracks such as 'Campfire Story' serve as a narration for star of the film, Brian Matthews. At times eerie and atmospheric-like most conventional scores such as 'Rocky' and 'Terminator', 'The BURNING' also contains two non-WAKEMAN-written pieces, the country-tinged hoedown 'Devil's Creek Breakdown' (penned by ALAN BREWER) and the jaunty fun-for-all, 'Doin' It'. Overall, RICK manages to pull off a mix'n'match set that probably reflects the man's own eclectic personal tastes. If only he'd written that 30-second ditty/segment for Channel 4's Countdown – now there's a brainy thought. *MCS*

Album rating: *5.5

BUSTIN' LOOSE

1981 (US 94m) Universal Pictures (R)

Film genre: road movie/comedy

Top guns: dir: Oz Scott → the CHEETAH GIRLS, Michael Schultz / s-w: Lonnie Elder III ← SOUNDER ← MELINDA, Roger L. Simon (story: Richard Pryor)

Stars: Richard Pryor *(Joe Braxton)* ← the WIZ ← ADIOS AMIGO ← CAR WASH ← the MACK ← WATTSTAX ← LADY SINGS THE BLUES ← YOU'VE GOT TO WALK IT LIKE YOU TALK IT . . . ← the PHYNX ← WILD IN THE STREETS, Cicely Tyson *(Vivian Perry)* ← a HERO AIN'T NOTHIN' BUT A SANDWICH ← SOUNDER / → IDLEWILD, Edwin DeLeon *(Ernesto)*, Angel Ramirez *(Julio)*, Jimmy Hughes *(Harold)*, Edwin Kinter *(Anthony)*, Tami Luchow *(Linda)*, Janet Wong *(Annie)*, Alphonso Alexander *(Martin)*, Kia Cooper *(Samantha)*, Roy Jenson *(klan leader)* ← FOOLS / → HONKYTONK MAN

Storyline: In last chance saloon after breaking his parole, likeable con Joe Braxton finds unlikely salvation in the form of some unusual community service. With his girlfriend Vivian's financially challenged care centre on the point of closure, Braxton's parole officer arranges for him to ferry the centre's special needs children across country to Vivian's farm in Washington State. While Braxton finds his true vocation, as well as predictable romance, his spurned parole officer is intent on both putting his sorry ass back inside and sending the kids back east. *BG*

Movie rating: *5

Visual: video

Off the record: **ROBERTA FLACK** was born on the 10th February 1937, Black Mountain, Asheville, North Carolina, USA. Raised in Arlington, Virginia as the daughter of a church organist, Roberta learned piano at an early age and went on to study music at Washington DC's Howard University; future collaborator DONNY HATHAWAY was one of her classmates. After graduation she began carving out a career in teaching before Hammond-organ maestro, Les McCann, discovered her singing in a club and duly recommended her to 'Atlantic' head honcho, Ahmet Ertegun. FLACK chose to cover one of McCann's own compositions ('Compared To What') as her first single in September '69, with debut album 'First Take' following a couple of months later. The record sold moderately, although her sophomore set, the appropriately-titled 'Chapter Two' (1970), edged her into the US Top 40. At her most effective interpreting the balladry of white singer/songwriters, FLACK's cover of Carole King's 'You've Got A Friend' was the first of many duets with HATHAWAY and became her first Top 30 hit as James Taylor sat atop the US chart with his version of the same song. In 1972, her version of Ewan McColl's 'The First Time Ever I Saw Your Face' (which had already gained exposure on the 1969 Clint Eastwood film, 'Play Misty For Me') became a deserved US No.1 and propelled her three-year-old debut set to a similar position on the album chart; that same year a whole album's worth of FLACK/HATHAWAY collaborations made the US Top 3. Influenced by both jazz and classical music, FLACK's cool, measured but often spine-tingling vocal cords were tailor made for 1973's 'Killing Me Softly', a track that furnished her with her second US No.1 and established her as one of America's most elegant, eloquent soul singers. In 1974 she scored her third No.1 with 'Feel Like Makin' Love', while 1975 found her guesting on BOB DYLAN's 'Rolling Thunder' revue at a special benefit night for imprisoned (and recently released) boxer, Rubin "Hurricane" Carter. The ensuing two years saw her teaching music to disadvantaged kids before returning to the chart spotlight in early 1978 with the 'Blue Lights In The Basement' album. FLACK was dealt a severe blow the following year with the death of HATHAWAY, the album they'd been working on together, 'Roberta Flack Featuring Donny Hathaway', seeing the light of day in 1980. She eventually found a new singing partner in the shape of Peabo Bryson, with whom she cut a live album in 1981 and went on to work with regularly throughout the 80s. *MCS*

—

ROBERTA FLACK (w/ MARK DAVIS: score)

Jun 81. (lp) *M.C.A.; <5141>* ☐ [-]
– Lovin' you (is such an easy thang to do) / Rollin' on / You stopped loving me / Just when I needed you / Qual E Malindrinho (Why are you so bad) / Love (always commands) / Children's song / Ballad for D. / Hittin' me where it hurts.

S/track review: Coming on the back of a Peabo Bryson-collaborative live album, 'BUSTIN' LOOSE' held over much of the same personnel – MARCUS MILLER, LUTHER VANDROSS, etc. – and at least some of the bloodlessness. BRYSON gets his oar in on 'Ballad For D.', an apparent tribute to FLACK's sometime singing partner, Donny Hathaway (who'd committed suicide a couple of years earlier), but you can't help wondering why FLACK herself doesn't get a chance to invest it with some genuine emotion. Ace Brazilian percussionist DOM UM ROMAO also gets a credit, making his influence felt on 'Qual E Malindrinho' (if you think you're going to hear FLACK practising her Portuguese, forget it, it's a fusion-y instrumental) and the cheesy but infectious 'Children's Song', probably the most engaging track on the whole album, if only because it belongs to the previous decade (feelgood shades of Stevie Wonder) rather than the one facing her. FLACK was always a smooth operator but the oil-slick arrangements she embraced in the late 70s and 80s neutralised much of that congenital melancholy. At least she still had a hand in most of the writing, contributing the sentimental main theme, 'Just When I Needed You', and ghosting back in time, framing her cultured tones with the almost Abba-esque acoustic guitar and strings of 'Love (Always Commands)'. She threatens to get earthier on the flip side's 'Hittin' Me Where It Hurts', but the passion just isn't there. As for MILLER, this was his first big screen project, almost a decade before he worked on Miles Davis' 'Siesta' (1989), and he drags FLACK into the 80s with dreary, slap bass closer, 'Lovin' You (Is Such An Easy Thang To Do)'. If only loving this soundtrack was as easy. *BG*

Album rating: *4

Jerry BUTLER

Born: 8 Dec'39, Sunflower, Mississippi, USA. While soul legend JERRY BUTLER co-founded the Impressions with CURTIS MAYFIELD, he's best remembered for his forging of the 'Sound of Philadelphia' in tandem with ace producers Kenny Gamble and Leon Huff. Having already had one track ('The Shark') featured in the 1967 movie, 'Come Spy With Me', the early 70s also saw BUTLER getting involved in film scoring with a credit on John G. Avildsen's powerful post-hippy drama, 'JOE' (1970). He followed up with 'MELINDA' (1972), an effort directed by 'Midnight Cowboy' alumni Hugh A. Robertson. BUTLER also enjoyed a short-lived acting career with a cameo in blaxploitaion era B-movie, 'The Thing With Two Heads' (1972) and a bit-part in blaxploitation western, 'Boss Nigger' (1974). *BG*

- **filmography** (composer) {acting} –

Joe *(1970 OST w/ EXUMA => / score by BOBBY SCOTT)* / the Thing With Two Heads *(1972 {c})* / **Melinda** *(1972 OST =>)* / **Save The Children** *(1973 {p} OST by V/A =>)* / Boss Nigger *(1974 {b})* / **Only The Strong Survive** *(2002 {p} =>)*

BYE BYE BLACKBIRD

2006 (Fra/Lux/UK/Ger 99m) Samsa Film / Ipso Facto (PG)

Film genre: period-costume drama

Top guns: s-w: (+ dir) Robinson Savary, Patrick Faure, Arif Ali Shah (+ story)

Stars: James Thierree *(Josef)*, Derek Jacobi *(Lord Dempsey)* ← REVENGERS TRAGEDY, Izabella Miko *(Alice)* ← COYOTE UGLY / → SAVE THE LAST DANCE 2, Jodhi May *(Nina)*, Michael Lonsdale *(Robert)*, Andrej Acin *(Roberto)*, Chris Bearne *(Lord Strathclyde)*

Storyline: After leaving his job as a construction worker (where he revelled in dancing on city top girders), Josef, finds a menial job at a circus. There he is spotted by the big top owner, who thrusts him on to the trapeze with his high-flying daughter, Alice. *MCS*

Movie rating: *6.5

Visual: dvd

Off the record: **MERCURY REV** were formed in Buffalo, New York, USA, 1988, the only lasting members from these days are Jonathan Donahue (vocals & guitar), Dave Fridmann (bass) and Grasshopper, aka Sean Mackowiak (guitars & clarinets) – all three also partly associated with the Flaming Lips; former 'Rev members numbered vocalist David Baker, drummer Jimy Chambers and flautist Suzanne Thorpe. Their early sound, which came about by playing their own soundtrack to nature TV programmes! ('Very Sleepy Rivers' indeed) was certainly deliciously deranged enough for this explanation of their secret history; they reputedly met in a mental institution. Just over two years of rehearsals passed before they finally surfaced with the classic mini-set, 'Yerself Is Steam' (1991), perhaps the most immaculate marriage of searing psychedelic noise and crystalline pop ever committed to vinyl. Sophomore set, 'Boces' (1993), their first for 'Beggars Banquet' carried on in the established schizophrenic mould and was their first record to hit the UK Top 50. The following year, the band's infamous in-fighting reached a head as the proverbial time-honoured musical differences led to the wayward Baker pursuing a noisier career of his own as Shady. It would be another two-year stretch before the release of 'See You On The Other Side' (1995), although by this time the first chapter of MERCURY REV's maverick career had already drawn to a close. While critics marvelled over the album's more accessible but wonderfully eclectic pop-jazz experiments, Donahue and Grasshopper were in the process of completing a debut album, 'Paralyzed Mind Of The Arcangel Void' (1995) for their revamped side-project, Harmony Rockets. A few years later, the pair resurrected the MERCURY REV moniker with a complete new cast (including Jeff Mercel), although the subsequent return of Thorpe, Fridmann and Chambers, resulted in a more fully-fledged reformation. Issued on Richard Branson's new 'V2' imprint, the record (which featured Garth Hudson and Levon Helm of the BAND) was widely hailed as THE album of the year as MERCURY REV enjoyed one of the critical rebirths of the decade. Older and wiser, the band (or the BAND, take your pick!) had possibly stumbled upon what Gram Parsons really meant when he dreamt of his "cosmic American music", a wistful (in a far-out sort of way) melange of quixotic pop, spacey orchestration and lullaby romanticism quite possibly unlike anything you've ever heard. After recovering from the trailblazing glory of 'Deserter's Songs', many fans and critics were pondering over the group's next release: how were they going to match the previous album? How would they write songs now that their woe and grief had disappeared thanks to their new found glory? MERCURY REV, however, answered both of these questions on the eve of the release of their fifth album, the epic 'All Is Dream' (2001). A kaleidoscope of drifting thoughts, strange orchestral lulls, and dark, uncertain things that creeped around in the shadows, the set displayed all of the usual 'Rev decorations, only with a brooding overtone. If 'Deserter's Songs' was the soundtrack to a sad children's Christmas movie, then 'All Is Dream' was pitched somewhere between a classic romantic period drama and a high-tension adventure set in a faraway land. Three years on, the Mercurial New Yorkers released one of their most intimate AOP (Adult Orientated Psychedelia/Prog) meditations to date in the shape of 'The Secret Migration' (2005), once again drawing the ubiquitous Flaming Lips comparisons. Somehow, Donahue and Co haven't quite enjoyed the same Stateside success as their LIP-py counterparts, although they always they always seemed to generate enough interest to chart in the UK. *BG & MCS*

MERCURY REV: Hello Blackbird

Oct 06. (cd) *V2; (VVR 104371-2)* ☐ ☐
– Blackbird's call / Illumination by street lamp / Waltz for Alice / Trial by wire / Daydream for Nina / Audition scene sketch (simply because) / The white birds / Josef's vision / Eye of the blackbird (travelling music II) / The last of the white birds (march funebre) / Cinema theme / First flight of the white birds / The Chimpy waltz / Dempsey's theme / Fantasia No.1 / Robert y Roberto / Travelling music / Departed angels / Simply because. *(enhanced +=)* – Making of Hello Blackbird / Grasshopper's wild ride.

S/track review: MERCURY REV (aka JONATHAN DONAHUE, DAVE FRIDMANN, GRASSHOPPER, JEFF MERCEL and relative newcomer, CARLOS ANTHONY MOLINA) were discovering how fickle the record-buying public could be, and that all was not fair in the ever-evolving world of rock music. Was it the right juncture for a somewhat risky venture into the business of film soundtracks? Only time will tell, and with still no release date on the horizon in America, MERCURY REV's 'Hello Blackbird' (faux title a mystery) could be one challenge too many. Mostly instrumental, the 19-track score had all the dreamy traits of a "real" MERCURY REV set, only without the yowl vox of frontman DONAHUE. With the circus as its theme, it's no surprise piano-led opening track, 'Blackbird's Call', slides aesthetically onto pictorial carousel soundscapes – almost beauty defined. Ditto tracks 3 and 5, 'Waltz For Alice' and the lengthy 'White Birds'. As for the short bursts of clarinet and glockenspiel diversions interspersed all around the album, they are probably too minuscule to sink the teeth into critically, nice though as they are. The remainder of the album is quite uplifting at times, eerily haunting at other times; I imagine the 'Rev listened to several movie scores by the prolific Danny Elfman or Jack Nitzsche. You can almost reach out and touch each note, played impeccably and orchestra-like by the group of players. 'The Last Of The White Birds (March Funebre)', glistens like the sun on a still river bed, while in stark contrast, 'The Chimpy Waltz' is quirky and eccentric in a light bombastic kind of way. The album closes with that old chestnut, 'Simply Because', a vocal number featuring vocals from an unknown female singer. We'll probably never hear MERCURY REV like this again, as they'll venture back to the land of rock. Like 'Departing Angels' (track 18, incidentally), hopefully their experience in film scores will stand them in good stead for further musical developments. You heard it here first – as they say. *MCS*

Album rating: *6.5

David BYRNE

Born: DAVID BYRNE certainly isn't your average son of Dumbarton (if such a thing actually exists), probably something to do with the fact that he left Scotland not long after being born on 14th May 1952. Raised in Canada and Maryland, USA, he eventually ended up in New York, where, after an unsatisfying stint at Rhode Island School of Design, he eventually teamed up with two of his former classmates to form TALKING HEADS. The band quickly established themselves as one of the mainstays of New York's nascent punk/new wave scene, signing to 'Sire' and releasing a series of albums which explored the artier, more cerebral end of edgy white-boy funk. Restlessly creative, BYRNE set the pattern of a solo career in the early 80s when, as well as recording an influential album with BRIAN ENO ('My Life In The Bush Of Ghosts'), he scored the music for choreographer Twyla Tharp's early 80s ballet, 'The Catherine Wheel'. While not too far removed from TALKING HEADS' turn of the decade material, this was fairly obscure stuff compared to the hugely successful 'STOP MAKING SENSE' (1984), a highly acclaimed, Jonathan Demme-directed concert film which threw up some of the most memorable images of the decade. BYRNE's highly developed and often whimsical sense of the absurd permeated these images, as it did both 'Music For The Knee Plays' (1985) – a score to a Robert Wilson theatre piece – and 'TRUE STORIES' (1986), to all intents and purposes the man's directorial debut. A series of eccentric Texan snapshots inspired by tabloid cuttings, the movie was written, directed, narrated and scored by BYRNE, and he carried aspects of it over to the penultimate TALKING HEADS album, also – rather confusingly – titled 'True Stories'. Following the band's mid-late 80s demise, its erstwhile frontman continued to develop his solo career through the medium of film and theatre, collaborating with Ryuichi Sakamoto and Cong

Su on the Oscar winning soundtrack to Bernardo Bertolucci's 'The Last Emperor' (1987), and scoring Demme's gangster comedy, 'Married To The Mob' (1988). Inevitably, his love of world music, and Latin and Afro-Portuguese music in particular, manifested itself in film via a compelling study of Brazilian Candomble, 'Ile Aiye' (1989), itself a great companion piece to the Brazilian compilations on his newly formed 'Luaka Bop' label. While a score for French documentary, 'Magicians Of The Earth' (1990) also tied in with his ethnic affinities, BYRNE's reputation (and one he modestly tries to play down) as a genuine renaissance man was further strengthened in 1991 with the belated release of a neo-classical score for another Robert Wilson theatre piece, 'The Forest'. While it'd be more than a decade before the release of his next major soundtrack, BYRNE's brooding ('Lead Us Not Into Temptation') score for the Alexander Trocchi adaptation, 'YOUNG ADAM' (2003), was more than worth the wait. *BG*

- **filmography** (composer) {performance} –

the Catherine Wheel *(1982 TV OST; see future edition)* / **Stop Making Sense** *(1984 {*p} OST by/w/ TALKING HEADS =>)* / **True Stories** *(1986 [s-w + dir] {*} OST by BYRNE & V/A =>)* / Dead End Kids *(1986 score)* / the Last Emperor *(1987 OST w/ Ryuichu Sakamoto; see future editions)* / a Rusting Of Leaves: Inside The Philippine Revolution *(1988 w/ Joey Ayala & Salvador Ferreras)* / Married To The Mob *(1988 OST by V/A see; future editions =>)* / Ile Aiye *(1989)* / Checking Out *(1989 TV {b})* / Magicians Of The Earth *(1990)* / Until The End Of The World *(1991 {v} see future edition)* / In The Bathtub Of The World *(2001 {c})* / In Spite Of Wishing And Wanting *(2002 OST; see future edition)* / **Young Adam** *(2003 OST as 'Lead Us Not Into Temptation' =>)*

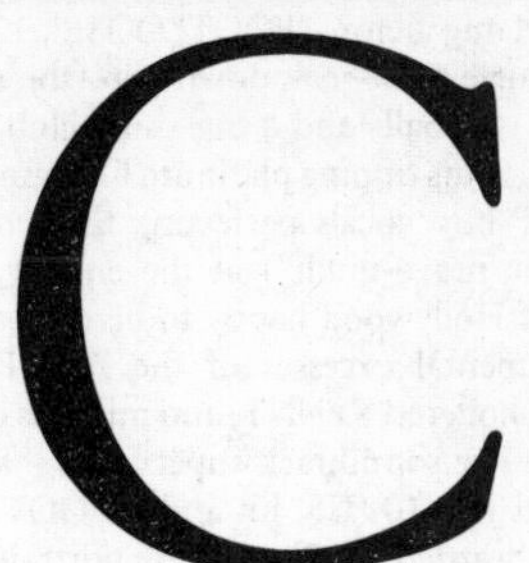

CADDYSHACK

1980 (US 99m) Orion Pictures / Warner Bros. Pictures (R)

Film genre: anarchic sports comedy

Top guns: s-w: (+ dir) Harold Ramis ← ANIMAL HOUSE / → CLUB PARADISE, Brian Doyle-Murray → CLUB PARADISE, Douglas Kenney ← ANIMAL HOUSE

Stars: Chevy Chase *(Ty Webb)*, Rodney Dangerfield *(Al Czervik)* → NATURAL BORN KILLERS, Ted Knight *(Judge Elihu Smails)* ← SWINGIN' ALONG, Michael O'Keefe *(Danny Noonan)*, Bill Murray *(Carl Spackler)* ← WHERE THE BUFFALO ROAM ← the RUTLES / → LITTLE SHOP OF HORRORS → LOST IN TRANSLATION → COFFEE AND CIGARETTES → the LIFE AQUATIC WITH STEVE ZISSOU, Sarah Holcomb *(Maggie O'Hooligan)* ← ANIMAL HOUSE, Scott Colomby *(Tony D'Annunzio)* → PORKY'S REVENGE, Cindy Morgan *(Lacey Underall)*, Dan Resin *(Dr. Beeper)*, Brian Doyle-Murray *(Lou Loomis)* → CLUB PARADISE → WAYNE'S WORLD, Henry Wilcoxon *(bishop)*, Albert Salmi *(Mr. Noonan)*, Elaine Aiken *(Mrs. Noonan)* ← the SPOOK WHO SAT BY THE DOOR, **Scott Powell** *(Gatsby)* ← WOODSTOCK / → FESTIVAL EXPRESS, Douglas Kenney *(Al Czervik's dinner guest)* ← ANIMAL HOUSE / → HEAVY METAL, Hamilton Mitchell *(Motormouth)* → SLUMBER PARTY MASSACRE II

Storyline: A sporadically mirthful few days in the life of Bushwood Country Club and its cast of schemers and eccentrics. Chief eccentric is greenkeeper Carl Spackler, a glaze-eyed, droop-lipped nutjob who claims to have caddied for the Dalai Lama and who – when he's not taking flak from his ridiculous Scottish caricature of a boss – is bent on the destruction of the club's gopher population. Judge Smails is the snobby, stingy patriarch, mentally tortured by guest-from-hell Al Czervik (who just happens to have a stereo fitted in his golf bag, and who – brave man – attempts to dance to Journey) and shown up by his slovenly grandson. Ty Webb is an idle millionaire cum cod-Zen philosopher, who regularly tells his fellow members what he doesn't think of them. Together with the teenaged caddies – among whom nice guy Noonan is vying for a scholarship – they create polite, occasionally queasy anarchy and a few decent one liners if nothing much resembling a meaningful plot. *BG*

Movie rating: *8.5

Visual: video + dvd

Off the record: Scott Powell was actually Tony Santini, founding member of 50s rock'n'roll revivalists, Sha Na Na. Co-founder of the National Lampoon and screenwriter, Douglas Kenney, was to die in a tragic clifftop accident in Kauai, Hawaii, 27th August, 1980. *MCS*

Various Artists incl. KENNY LOGGINS (*) / score: JOHNNY MANDEL **)

Aug 80. (lp/c) *Columbia; <AL/PCT 36737> C.B.S.; (70192)* 78 Oct80
– I'm alright (*) / Lead the way (*) / Make the move (*) / Mr. Night (*) / Any way you want it (JOURNEY) / There she goes (the BEAT) /

Divine intervention (**) / Mariana (**) / Something on your mind (HILLY MICHAELS) / The big bang (**).

S/track review: Long before 'FOOTLOOSE', KENNY LOGGINS had his jingle-jangle cock-rock down pap (the sleeve – a tasteless close-up of two golf balls and a big shiny club – rams home the point), his solo albums tipping platinum like punk never happened, and his good ol' boy vocals perfecting that constipated "unhh" (as in "make the move-unhh") at the end of each chorus line. It's the sound of Hollywood happy to be on less ruinous ground after the experimental excesses of the 70s: 'I'm Alright' ("I'm Alrighaaayyee"), hollered KENNY, and millions of grateful comedy fans – and not a few soundtrack supervisors – agreed. The theme was a guaranteed Top 10 (US) hit and a 'FOOTLOOSE' template, with LOGGINS' bearded, bouffant sleeve portrait doubtless shifting as many copies as Bill Murray's crazed greenkeeper. 'Make The Move' is a heavier reworking of the same formula (and a 'Danger Zone' template), 'Lead The Way' a clairvoyant combination of 'We Are The World' and post-Wham! George Michael, promising an endless decade of straining balladry. 'Mr Night' merely promises Shakin' Stevens. After all that – and not to mention a fist-pumping JOURNEY track (resistance is futile), a demented, Roy Thomas Baker-produced Queen parody and a New Wave-y number by the BEAT (NOT the English 2-Tone band) which might've been plucked from any number of post-millennial wannabes – you might expect JOHNNY MANDEL to serve up something chilled. Then again, you might not; this is a soundtrack from a movie which Time Out summed up thus: "If you're still at the age when farting and nose-picking seem funny, then Caddyshack should knock you dead". MANDEL does indeed knock us dead, stone dead, with the cod-Wagnerian 'Divine Intervention', delivering a final blow – 'The Big Bang' – just to make sure. It's enough to make a man take up golf. *BG*

Album rating: *4

– spinoff hits, etc. –

KENNY LOGGINS: I'm Alright / Lead The Way

Jul 80. (7") *<11317> (CBS 8896)* [7] Aug80 [ ]

CAL

1984 (Ire/UK 102m) Warner Bros. Pictures (15)

Film genre: political/romantic drama

Top guns: dir: Pat O'Connor / s-w: Bernard MacLaverty (+ au)

Stars: Helen Mirren *(Marcella)* ← O LUCKY MAN!, John Lynch *(Cal)*, Donal McCann *(Shamie)*, John Kavanagh *(Skeffington)*, Ray McAnally *(Dunlop)*, Stevan Rimkus *(Crilly)*

Storyline: Irish Catholic Cal tries to put the past behind him after he falls in love with the enchanting Marcella. Cal was the getaway driver when the IRA brutally murdered a policeman in his own home. Marcella's husband was also an IRA victim, so Cal says nothing as his affair with Marcella deepens. But Cal's old IRA "acquaintances" will not let him off so easily, and eventually his past comes back to haunt him as his forbidden romance is discovered. *JZ*

Movie rating: *7

Visual: video + dvd

Off the record: (see below)

——

MARK KNOPFLER

Oct 84. (lp/c)(cd) *Vertigo; (VERH/+C 17) Warners; (<822769-2>)* [65] [ ]
– Irish boy / The road / Waiting for her / Irish love / Secret place – Where will you go? / Father and son / Meeting under the trees / Potato picking / In a secret place / Fear and hatred / Love and guilt / The long road.

S/track review: A natural and haunting progression, 'CAL' finds MARK KNOPFLER at least partly realising the folk ambitions he'd so evocatively announced in 'LOCAL HERO'. By enlisting bonafide folk musicians PAUL BRADY and LIAM O'FLYNN, the Dire Straits frontman succeeded in creating an authentic and dynamic roots canvas for those plangent guitar notes, so much so that rather than carrying the melody, he often merely provides supporting texture, ingeniously working his distinctive nylon strings into the arrangements. Yet if this is true for Celtic lullabies like 'Irish Love' and 'Potato Picking', 'The Long Road' is as gorgeous a semi-acoustic ballad as KNOPFLER has yet committed to soundtrack, with Brady's tin whistle providing reedy, wispish accompaniment. Fans of Van Morrison's 80s work, especially, will appreciate this album, even if it is more mood setting than soul searching. *BG*

Album rating: *7.5

– spinoff releases, etc. –

MARK KNOPFLER: The Long Road – Theme From 'Cal' / Irish Boy

Sep 84. (7"/ext.12") *(DSTR 8/+12)* [ ] [–]

□ J.J. CALE segment
(⇒ la FEMME DE MON POTE)

John CALE

Born: 9 Mar'42, Garnant, Carmarthen, Wales. The young CALE studied classical piano and later viola at London's Guildhall School Of Music, while as an 8-year-old schoolboy prodigy, he'd already composed music for the BBC. In 1963, he moved to New York on a scholarship, and under John Cage and LaMonte Young's tuition, he experimented with avant-garde music. A few years later, he met LOU REED, and formed the legendary Velvet Underground, CALE's wailing viola and white-noise experimentation meshing with REED's pop sensibilities and dark lyrics to create their distinctive sound. After being fired by the band in 1968, CALE went solo, releasing a couple of albums for 'Columbia' records. His debut in 1970, 'Vintage Violence', saw him exhibiting a more traditional side to his enigmatic persona, with gentle folky songs; a collaboration with minimalist composer TERRY RILEY, entitled 'Church Of Anthrax', followed in 1971. CALE continued the trend towards his baroque'n'roll roots with 'Academy Of Peril', before returning once more to the songwriter format of his first album. With Little Feat members Lowell George and Richie Hayward among his backing band, he cut the classic 'Paris 1919', which infused his melancholic songwriting with a disturbing unease. This was the template for much of CALE's 70s output with 1974's 'Fear' also introducing a more aggressive element. 'Helen Of Troy' (1975), featured a version of 'Heartbreak Hotel'; guaranteed to send a shiver up anyone's spine, although the album was generally disappointing overall. In 1976, he cemented his reputation by producing the legendary Patti Smith album, 'Horses', having previously worked on the classic blast of primal noise that was the Stooges' first album. CALE's career went into a bit of a slump in the latter half of the 70s, and after an infamous incident in which he allegedly beheaded a chicken onstage (!), he had a brief dalliance with the New York punk scene. Throughout his career, CALE also sessioned for others (including ENO), while he produced the Modern Lovers (Jonathan Richman), Squeeze, etc. He regained his footing with 1982's 'Music For A New Society', an intelligent, minimalistic affair. The mid-80s saw him sign to British label 'Beggars Banquet', and release the more mainstream 'Artificial Intelligence'. 'Words For The Dying', released in 1989, was a return to the classical field which included a collaboration with BRIAN ENO; they also teamed up on the sparse 'Wrong Way Up' from 1990. 'Songs For Drella' (a tribute to mentor, Andy Warhol), saw CALE hook up once more with his old sparring partner LOU REED, together producing an album that outshone CALE's more recent solo outings. He and REED re-united with the others in the Velvet Underground for concerts, which resulted in the comeback album 'LIVE MCMXCIII'. A year later, another collaboration ('Last Days On Earth'), this time with Bob Neuwirth, was largly ignored by the public. Having scored the music for obscure flicks 'Heat' & 'Caged Heat' in the first half of the 70s, CALE found the time to compose other classically-styled soundtracks to movies such as 'Paris S'eveille' (1991), 'Primary Motive' (1992) and 'I SHOT ANDY WARHOL' (1996), to name but a few – one will go into greater detail in further editions. Meanwhile, back at the avant-rock ranch, CALE's first record of the new millennium, 'Hobosapiens' (2003), was also his most adventurous for more than a decade. With ENO returning the guest favours alongside a host of hired hands, the album was alive with spontaneous creativity and freewheeling imagination. Embracing contemporary musical trends and technology, CALE gave free rein to a muse that only seems to have become even more literate, erudite and waggish with age. Released almost simultaneously with his umpteenth soundtrack effort, 'The Process', 'Black Acetate' (2005), was another cult critical favourite evidencing CALE's refusal to grow old gracefully – he was still forging ahead with his own avant-garde impulses. *BG & MCS*

- **filmography** {performer} (composer) –

the Velvet Underground And Nico *(1966 {*p w/ the VELVET UNDERGROUND & NICO} =>)* / Heat *(1972)* / Caged Heat *(1974)* / Who Am I This Time? *(1982 TV)* / Something Wild *(1986 OST w/ LAURIE ANDERSON & V/A; see future editions)* / Paris S'eveille *(1991 OST; see future edition)* / Primary Motive *(1992 OST w/ previous effort; see future edition)* / Fragments Of A Rainy Season *(1992 {p}; see future edition)* / la Naissance De L'Amour *(1993 OST; see future edition)* / Antartida *(1995 {c} OST; see future edition)* / N'Oublie Pas Que Tu Vas Mourir *(1995 OST; see future edition)* / **Nico Icon** *(1995 {c} NICO =>)* / **I Shot Andy Warhol** (1996 OST w/ V/A =>) / Basquiat *(1996 OST w/ Bill Laswell & V/A; see future edition)* / House Of America *(1997 OST w/ V/A; see future edition)* / Rhinoceros Hunting In Budapest *(1997 {b})* / Somewhere In The City *(1998 OST w/ V/A; see future edition)* / **Rock & Roll Heart** *(1998 {c} LOU REED =>)* / the Unknown *(1999 OST for silent film; see future editions =>)* / La Vent De La Nuit *(1999 OST; see future edition)* / American Psycho *(2000 OST w/ V/A; see future editions)* / Love Me *(2000 OST =>)* / Saint-Cyr *(2002 OST; see future edition)* / Abschied *(2001)* / Paris *(2003)* / Rhinoceros Eyes *(2003)* / Process *(2004 OST; see future edition)* / See You At Regis Debray *(2005)* / a Walk Into The Sea: Danny Williams & The Warhol Factory *(2007 {c})*

CANDY

1968 (US/Fra/Ita 123m) Cinema Releasing Corporation (X)

Film genre" seXual satire/comedy

Top guns: dir: Christian Marquand / s-w: Buck Henry ← the GRADUATE / → the OWL AND THE PUSSYCAT (au: Terry Southern → EASY RIDER → the MAGIC CHRISTIAN)

Stars: Ewa Aulin *(Candy Christian)*, Richard Burton *(MacPhisto)* → 1984, Marlon Brando *(Grindl)*, **Ringo Starr** *(Emmanuel)* <= the BEATLES =>, James Coburn *(Dr. A.B. Krankheit)* → PAT GARRETT & BILLY THE KID → WHITE ROCK → YOUNG GUNS II → AFFLICTION → SHAKE, RATTLE & ROLL: AN AMERICAN LOVE STORY, Walter Matthau *(Gen. R.A. Smight)* ← KING CREOLE, John Huston *(Dr. Arnold Dunlap)*, **Charles Aznavour** *(hunchback juggler)* ← la METAMORPHOSE DES CLOPORTES, Elsa Martinelli *(Livia)*, John Astin *(T.M. Christian / Jack Christian)*, Buck Henry *(mental patient)* ← the GRADUATE / → the OWL AND THE PUSSYCAT → EVEN COWGIRLS GET THE BLUES, "Sugar Ray" Robinson *(Zero)*, Anita Pallenberg *(Nurse Bullock)* ← WONDERWALL / → PERFORMANCE → le BERCEAU DE CRISTAL, Christian Marquad *(film director)* → JE VOUS AIME

Storyline: Critically lambasted adaptation of Terry Southern's 'Candide'-inspired sex farce, with our titular heroine plagued by coitus interruptus as she naively, interminably attempts to put the big name cast of hippy-era caricatures – a poet, a guru, a zealous army general etc.- out of their lustful misery. *BG*

Movie rating: *4

Visual: video + dvd

Off the record: (see below)

—

DAVE GRUSIN (w/ Various Artists)

Jan 69. (lp) *A.B.C.; <ABCS-OC 9> Stateside; (SSL 10276)* [49] [ ]
– Child of the universe (the BYRDS) / Birth by descent / Opening night: By surgery / Spec-rac-tac-para-comm / Border town blues: A blunt instrument / Magic carpet ride (STEPPENWOLF) / Constant journey / Every mother's daughter / It's always because of this: A deformity / Marlon and his sacred bird / Ascension to virginity / Rock me (STEPPENWOLF).

S/track review: This is one of those major-label, big-name-composer (and star-studded movie) soundtracks perennially – and mystifyingly – passed over for reissue. Even more mysteriously, who could've predicted that DAVE GRUSIN would come up with 'Ascension To Virginity', the kind of freakbeat floorfiller that DJs wet-dream about? GRUSIN also surpassed himself with the rest of his score, full-on garage-psych with great, dirty, unshaven riffs, ethnic cross-currents and as many trippy effects as the soundboard could stand; 'Every Mother's Daughter' even plays like a lab-controlled 13th Floor Elevators. It's cavernous, primitive stuff, and the fact that GRUSIN approaches psychedelic rock as an orchestrator rather than a musician predicts the kind of ambitious, incongruous live arrangements that would become the norm on so much 70s soundtrack/library music; the likes of 'Spec-Rac-Tac-Para-Comm' and at least half of 'Border Town Blues' (think Morricone on mescaline), are ripe with soundclash potential. Ironically, the one track that sounds how you'd imagine a psychedelic GRUSIN to sound – and the only one that embraces full-blown pop-symphony – is 'Child Of The Universe', his collaboration with Roger McGuinn. It's a worthy addition to the BYRDS' psych-pop oeuvre, if slightly overcooked and too easily upstaged by STEPPENWOLF's 'Magic Carpet Ride', itself sounding more than ever like a hippy precursor to Lynyrd Skynyrd's 'Sweet Home Alabama' (STEPPENWOLF's other entry, 'Rock Me', went Top 10 in America). But GRUSIN doesn't need the rock stars – his score's a minor classic in its own right. It's just a pity his subsequent scores didn't use this formulaic "rock" approach, but jazz was his bag and that's why most of his future work will be reserved for a future edition. *BG*

Album rating: *7.5

– spinoff hits, etc. –

STEPPENWOLF: Rock Me

Feb 69. (7") *Dunhill-ABC; <4182>* [10] [–]

the CANDY TANGERINE MAN

1975 (US 88m) Moonstone Entertainment (R)

Film genre: crime drama

Top guns: dir: Matt Cimber / s-w: George Theakos

Stars: John Daniels *(Baron)* → BLACK SHAMPOO, Eli Haines, Mikel Angel Marilyn Joi *(Tracy King)*, Pat Wright, Tom Hankerson, Marva Farmer, George "Buck" Flower

Storyline: It isn't easy supporting a family in the oil-crisis 70s: sometimes a man just has to bite more than a few bullets to make a living. The Black Baron does just that, and then some, living it large as Sunset Strip's highest rolling kingpimp at night; ditching his luridly painted Rolls, changing back into more sober threads and becoming a dutiful husband when needs must. *BG*

Movie rating: *4

Visual: video

Off the record: SMOKE (see below)

—

SMOKE: Smoke *(w/ non-s/t songs)*

1976. (lp) *Chocolate Cities; <CCLP 2001>* ☐ ☐
– Gotta bad feeling / Screamin' / Turn this this around / There it is / I don't care (what you do) / You needn't worry now / What goes around comes around / Sunshine roses and rainbows / Freedom of the mind.

S/track review: One of the most infamous blaxploitation films just happened to use music from one of 'Casablanca's most obscure funk acts. This eponymous album – not to be confused with the Fania All-Stars latino-funk bomb of the same name – isn't a soundtrack per se, or at least it doesn't mention the film tie-in anywhere on the sleeve (although in a very un-blaxploitation move, it does thank the band's parents, aww..), but its late decade grooves are just about worth a dig. Counting five hirsute black dudes and three clean cut whiteys, the interracial ensemble that was SMOKE deal in tightly marshalled dance funk with added strings; the arrangements aren't exactly imaginative – knotty clavinet, staccato horn charts, slap bass – but the bluesy rock vocals of one ARNOLD N. RIGGS JR. are at least in harmony with 'Casablanca' policy and about the only thing which makes sure the likes of 'There It Is' and 'I Don't Care (What You Do)' aren't complete Kool & The Gang clones. They push the boat out with some treated, Miles Davis-esque horn on 'Turn This Thing Around', and sex up their sound no end with Sly Stone-style vocal arrangements and a flying female lead on excellent side two highlights 'What Goes Around Comes Around', 'Sunshine Roses And Rainbows' and the Fifth Dimension-does-disco 'Freedom Of The Mind' (and is it just me, or does the vocal melody prefigure that House-era, pop-picking "classic", 'Everybody's Free To Feel Good'?). But anyway, shouldn't a man of the Black Baron's calibre have had something just a little bit freakier in his glove compartment? *BG*

Album rating: *6

CANNABIS

1970 (Fra/Ita/W.Ger 85m) Capitole Films / C.F.D.C. – Oceanic

Film genre: cop/detective drama/thriller

Top guns: s-w: Pierre Koralnik (+ dir) ← ANNA, Franz-Andre Burguet (au: F.S. Gilbert)

Stars: Serge GAINSBOURG *(Serge)*, Jane Birkin *(Jane Swenson)*, ← MAY MORNING ← SEX POWER ← WONDERWALL ← BLOW-UP / → JE T'AIME MOI NON PLUS, **Paul NICHOLAS** *(Paul)*, Curd Jurgens *(Henri Emery)*, Gabriele Ferzetti *(Inspector Bardeche)*, Paul Albert Krumm *(Lancan)*

Storyline: If the smutty laughter on 'Histoire De Melody Nelson' (1971) was actually the sound of Jane Birkin being tickled by her brother, the sex here is real. Serge meets his real life muse on a flight from New York to Paris, where he's been sent to sort out the mob's heroin supply, but the real action and most of the character development happens between the sheets. *BG*

Movie rating: *5

Visual: video

Off the record: (see below)

—

SERGE GAINSBOURG

1970. (lp) *Bagatelle; (BAS.602)* ☐ Canada ☐
– Cannabis / Premiere blessure / Le deuxieme homme / Jane dans la nuit (JANE BIRKIN) / Danger / Chanvre Indien / Avant de mourir / Arabique / Cannabis (instrumental) / I want to feel crazy / Derniere blessure / Piege / Cannabis-bis (final). *(<cd-iss. Nov03 on 'Universal' France +=; 9809886>)* – (CE SACRE GRAND-PERE tracks w/ Michel Colombier):- Herbe tendre / Ca Sacre Grand-pere / Champetre et pop pt.1 / Nous les Jericho / Herbe tendre (instrumental) / Balade en Provence / Champetre et pop pt.2 / L'adieu.

S/track review: Who says first impressions last? 'CANNABIS' kicks off with the kind of fretboard bluster that suggests a glam-rock b-side; its descent into monumental acid-baroque, however, heralds great, great things. If you ever had any preconceptions about SERGE GAINSBOURG, leave them at the pissoir door. Even the man's subsequent conceptual masterpiece, 'Histoire De Melody Nelson', only barely hints at this soundtrack's outrageous scale and the symphonic ambition which predicted it. With Jean-Claude Vannier orchestrating his wild, vague impulses ("sometimes he'd turn up at the studio with just six bars scribbled on a piece of sheet-music", admitted director Pierre Koralnik), French Pop's ungainly enfant-terrible dreamed up one of the great lost 70s guitar riffs: hulking, salacious, majestic and undeniably, soulfully Gallic. Lest we forget SERGE is the man, he also sneaks in the suffix "par Serge Gainsbourg" to the main title. He even ventures one of his gloriously laboured vocals (as Koralnik put it, "he did his own diction") over the top; as an exercise in contrast it's up there with the KLF and Tammy Wynette. And if there was ever a convincing apology for the harpsichord in rock, this was it. Vannier's arrangements pitch it in ingenious counterpoint on the guitar pieces (and on the brief orchestral reprise, 'Dernière Blessure'), as a dramatic arabesque in 'Le Deuxième Homme' and 'Avant De Mourir', and as a conduit for stinging jazz-funk in 'Danger'. His basslines are just as prominently arranged, even louder and more inspired, and while it could be argued that the whole depends too heavily on a single motif, it's one hell of a motif; the fact that GAINSBOURG dedicated it to Jimi Hendrix and Bela Bartok speaks volumes. Regardless of its thematic singularity, 'CANNABIS' has it all: sleaze, style, Moorish mystique, sophistication, steel, savoir-faire and even a Jane Birkin cabaret number. For those about to smoke, we salute you. *BG*

Album rating: *8.5

CAPTIVE

1986 (UK/Fra 98m) Virgin Films (18)

Film genre: crime thriller

Top guns: s-w + dir: Paul Mayersberg

Stars: Irina Brook *(Rowena Le Vay)*, Oliver Reed *(Gregory Le Vay)* ← LISZTOMANIA ← TOMMY, Corrine Dacla *(Bryony)*, Xavier Deluc *(D)*, Hiro Arai *(Hiro)*, Nick Reding *(Leo)*, Annie Leon *(Pine)*, Michael Cronin *(McPherson)*

Storyline: Rich heiress Rowena Le Vay is unwittingly being watched by three kidnappers as she wanders round her father's mansion in a state of high boredom. The trio capture her and whisk her off to a secret hideaway where she is bound and gagged. As Rowena gets to know her abductors, she is groomed into their way of living and, caring less and less about returning home, she finds that taking part in a bank robbery is much more exciting – regardless of the consequences. *JZ*

Movie rating: *3.5

Visual: video

Off the record: Although raised in Dublin, Ireland, **The EDGE** was actually born (David Howell Evans, 8th August, 1961) in Barking, Essex, England. A shy, introverted lad at school, The EDGE took up the post of guitarist with U2 after answering an ad by drummer Larry Mullen. From the early 80s, the Irish quartet have become the biggest selling band in the world, helped by their early studio sets, namely 'Boy' (1980), 'October' (1981), 'War' (1983) and 'The Unforgettable Fire' (1984). During their mid-80s hiatus of sorts, and while singer BONO guested for the likes of Clannad, the infinite guitar playing of The EDGE dabbled with his experiental side on 'CAPTIVE'. *MCS*

---

the EDGE

Sep 86. (cd/c/lp) *Virgin; (CD/TC+/V 2401) Atlantic; <90609>* ☐ Jan87 ☐
– Rowena's theme / Heroine (theme from Captive) (w/ SINEAD O'CONNOR) / One foot in Heaven / The strange party / Hiro's theme I / Drift / The dream theme / Djinn (w/ MICHAEL BROOK) / Island / Hiro's theme (reprise).

S/track review: With expectations running high for U2's comeback album, 'The Joshua Tree' – an album that was to break the band into the premier league of rock in April 1987 – The EDGE approached friend and creator of his "infinite Guitar", MICHAEL BROOK, to augment him with the 'CAPTIVE' soundtrack commission. The Canadian-born composer helped co-write and co-produce the set, but his performance only stretched to one collaborative track, 'Djinn', probably the least effective track, but just might've been partly inspirational for a certain Tortoise. If The EDGE wanted to create something leftfield of U2, this mostly instrumental album certainly took him there, the core (bar one song) stemming from his guitar frets. The one theme/song in question, 'Heroine', saw the guitarist introduce 19-year-old Irish singer, SINEAD O'CONNOR, her delicate tones very much the highlight of the set; LARRY MULLEN of U2 also featured on drums. Of the rest, opener 'Rowena's Theme' (very 'Whiter Shade . . .'), 'The Strange Party' and 'Hiro's Theme I', stood out, The EDGE opting for ambient, Celtic/Eno-like soundscapes of guitar and keyboards. The aforementioned 'The Strange Party' – although very Eno/Byrne – saw a slight affinity and BROOK connection to Peter Gabriel's 'The LAST TEMPTATION OF CHRIST', albeit with "A Different Drum". *MCS*

Album rating: *5

– spinoff releases, etc. –

the EDGE feat. SINEAD O'CONNOR: Heroine / the EDGE: Heroine (mix II)
Sep 86. (7"/12") *(VS/+T 897)* ☐ [–]

CAR WASH

1976 (US 96m) Universal Pictures (PG)

Film genre: urban comedy

Top guns: dir: Michael Schultz → SGT. PEPPER'S LONELY HEARTS CLUB BAND → the LAST DRAGON → KRUSH GROOVE → ROCK'N'ROLL MOM / s-w: Joel Schumacher ← SPARKLE / → the WIZ

Stars: Franklyn Ajaye *(T.C.)* → the JAZZ SINGER → GET CRAZY → QUEEN OF THE DAMNED, Sully Boyar *(Mr. B)* → the JAZZ SINGER, Richard Pryor *(Daddy Rich)* ← ADIOS AMIGO ← the MACK ← WATTSTAX ← LADY SINGS THE BLUES ← YOU'VE GOT TO WALK IT LIKE YOU TALK IT . . . ← the PHYNX ← WILD IN THE STREETS / → the WIZ → BUSTIN' LOOSE, Ivan Dixon *(Lonnie)*, Richard Brestoff *(Irwin)*, Antonio Fargas *(Lindy)* ← CORNBREAD, EARL AND ME ← FOXY BROWN ← CLEOPATRA JONES ← ACROSS 110th STREET ← SHAFT / → FIRESTARTER → SOUL SURVIVOR, **DeWayne Jessie** *(Lloyd)* ← SPARKLE / → THANK GOD IT'S FRIDAY → ANIMAL HOUSE → WHERE THE BUFFALO ROAM, George Carlin *(taxi driver)* → BILL & TED'S EXCELLENT ADVENTURE → BILL & TED'S BOGUS JOURNEY, Bill Duke *(Duane)* → GET RICH OR DIE TRYIN', Michael Fennell *(Calvin)*, Tracy Reed *(Mona)* ← NO WAY BACK ← TRAIN RIDE TO HOLLYWOOD ← TROUBLE MAN / → a PIECE OF THE ACTION, Prof. Irwin Corey *(Mad Bomber)*, Arthur French *(Charlie)* → a HERO AIN'T NOTHIN' BUT A SANDWICH, Danny DeVito *(Joe Graziano)* → the VIRGIN SUICIDES → MAN ON THE MOON → BE COOL, Melanie Mayron *(Marsha)* → YOU LIGHT UP MY LIFE, Leonard Jackson *(Earl)* ← FIVE ON THE BLACK HAND SIDE, **the Pointer Sisters: Bonnie, Ruth, June & Anita** *(the Wilson Sisters)*, Ray Vitte *(Geronimo)* → THANK GOD IT'S FRIDAY, Timmothy Tomerson *(Kenny)* → RECORD CITY → CARNY → HONKYTONK MAN → RHINESTONE → NEAR DARK → EDDIE PRESLEY → BAD CHANNELS, Leon Pinkney *(Justin)* ← AARON LOVES ANGELA, Ren Woods *(Loretta)* ← SPARKLE / → YOUNGBLOOD → HAIR → XANADU, Garrett Morris *(Slide)* → the CENSUS TAKER → LITTLE RICHARD → HOW HIGH, Jack Kehoe *(Scruggs)* → DICK TRACY → YOUNG GUNS II, Carmine Caridi *(foolish father)* → KISS MEETS THE PHANTOM OF THE PARK

Storyline: Mr B is the owner of the De Luxe Car Wash in downtown L.A., where the crazy employees and even crazier customers ensure that mayhem is never far away. Floyd and Lloyd have a screwball double act which they perform to various dumbfounded drivers, while Lindy the drag queen gives everyone a gay old time. Amongst the visitors today are the Mad Pop Bottle Bomber and Daddy Rich, complete with gold limo and backing group. We'll all need hosed down by the end of this one. *JZ*

Movie rating: *4.5

Visual: video + dvd

Off the record: **ROSE ROYCE** (see below)

ROSE ROYCE (*) (composer: NORMAN WHITFIELD)

Sep 76. (d-lp) *M.C.A.; <2-6000> (MCSP 278)* [14] Dec76 ☐
– Car wash (*) / 6 o'clock DJ (let's rock) / I wanna get next to you (*) / Put your money where your mouth is (*) / Zig zag (*) / You're on my mind / Mid day DJ theme / Born to love you (*) / Daddy Rich (*) / (Richard Pryor dialogue – Rich reprise) / You gotta believe (POINTER SISTERS) / I'm going down (*) / Yo yo (*) / Sunrise / Righteous rhythm / Water / Crying / Doin' what comes naturally (*) / Keep on keepin' on (*). *<(cd-iss. Mar97; MCD 11502-2)>*

S/track review: Having already transcended the 'Motown' patent with his psychedelic soul outings for the Temptations, visionary producer NORMAN WHITFIELD moved on to disco-funk with this near twenty track epic. Newly independent from Berry Gordy's label and collared by the film's producers, WHITFIELD recruited an erstwhile 'Motown' backing aggregate with whom he was actually in the process of recording a debut album. Recruiting lead singer GWEN DICKEY, he renamed them ROSE ROYCE and concentrated on the soundtrack instead. While twenty tracks might have been pushing listeners' patience, the record's slick combination of soul pout, funk bottom and glitterball hedonism – not to mention its platinum sales and hit singles – successfully bridged the gap between blaxploitation and 'Saturday Night Fever'. WHITFIELD didn't even really have a film to work on as such, with the result that the soundtrack anticipated and promoted the movie as opposed to simply being a spin-off. Producer Gary Stromberg comments in the CD sleevenotes that the cast were actually in sync with the soundtrack because it was played during filming. As the Time Out film guide marvels: "The remarkable thing is the way characters, jokes and meaning are dovetailed into a single rhythmic flow". And everyone and his granny – and doubtless every poor sod who's ever grappled with a car vacuum – has, at some point in their lives, shaken their exhaust pipe to the title track, a choreographed, disco-handclap shimmy which scaled the Billboard chart the week of the film's release. 'I Wanna Get Next To You' was the other big single, a gossamer soul ballad in the mould of the Temptations and, at a push, the Isley Brothers' 'Summer Breeze'. WHITFIELD filled up the remaining hour's worth of vinyl with an engaging mix of funky score snippets, the odd ballad and assorted kinetic vocal cuts full of staccato, Kool & The Gang-style horn charts and the kind of debonair strings which had already begun creeping into funk by the mid-70s. Closer 'Keep On Keepin' On' plays like a downbeat sequel to the JJ Johnson/Martha Reeves track of the same name (from 1974's 'WILLIE DYNAMITE'), while on the evidence of the very 'Higher Ground'-esque 'Mid Day DJ Theme' and the 'Superstition'-like keyboards of 'Righteous Rhythm' – WHITFIELD wasn't averse to referencing his previous label's most forward looking stars, or giving the arrangements a neo-psychedelic tweak here and there. And it's in the less obvious stuff – cheeky instrumentals like 'Yo Yo' and 'Doin' What Comes Naturally', the mesmeric, ten minute plus 'Sunrise', the soporific 'Crying' and the moody, War-esque 'Water' – that 'CAR WASH' really gets to the sonic dirt under WHITFIELD's fingernails and earns its price of admission. *BG*

Album rating: *7

– spinoff hits, etc. –

ROSE ROYCE: Put Your Money Where Your Mouth Is / Zig Zag

Oct 76. (7") *(MCA 259)* ☐ ☐
(re-activated UK Jan77; hit No.44)

ROSE ROYCE: Car Wash / Water

Oct 76. (7") *<40615> (MCA 267)* 1 Dec76 9

ROSE ROYCE: I Wanna Get Next To You / Sunrise

Feb 77. (7") *<40662> (MCA 278)* 10 Mar77 14

ROSE ROYCE: I'm Going Down / Yo Yo

May 77. (7") *<40721> (MCA 301)* 70 Jun77 ☐

ROSE ROYCE: The Best Of Car Wash

Jun 77. (lp) *(MCF 2799)* – 59
– Car wash / I wanna get next to you / I'm going down / Put your money where your mouth is / Born to love you / Yo yo / Daddy Rich / Keep on keepin' on / Doin' what comes naturally / Crying. *(re-iss. May81 lp/c; MCL/+C 1609) (cd-iss. 1988; DMCF 3424)*

ROSE ROYCE: Car Wash

Nov 82. (lp) *Fame; (FA 3043)* – ☐
– Car wash / Zig zag / Water / Doin' what comes naturally / I'm going down / Put your money where your mouth is / I wanna get next to you / Daddy Rich / Yo yo / Sunrise.

ROSE ROYCE: Car Wash / I Wanna Get Next To You

Apr 83. (7") *Old Gold; (OG 9322)* – ☐

ROSE ROYCE: Car Wash

May 88. (7"/12") *(MCA/+T 1253)* – 20

ROSE ROYCE featuring GWEN DICKEY: Car Wash (re-recording

Oct 98. (cd-s) *(MCSTD 48096)* – 18

CARNY

1980 (US 103m) Lorimar Productions (R)

Film genre: rural/Americana romantic drama

Top guns: dir: Robert Kaylor (+ co-story w/ Phoebe Kaylor & **Robbie Robertson**) / s-w: Thomas Baum

Stars: Gary Busey *(Frankie)* ← the BUDDY HOLLY STORY ← a STAR IS BORN / → FEAR AND LOATHING IN LAS VEGAS, Jodie Foster *(Donna)* → SIESTA, **Robbie Robertson** *(Patch)* <= the BAND =>, Meg Foster *(Gerta)*, Kenneth McMillan *(Heavy St. John)* → DUNE, Elisha Cook Jr. *(On-Your-Mark)* ← PAT GARRETT & BILLY THE KID ← BLACULA, Fred Ward *(Jack)* → TIMERIDER: THE ADVENTURE OF LYLE SWANN → MASKED AND ANONYMOUS, John Lehne *(Skeet)* ← AMERICAN HOT WAX ← BROTHERS ← BOUND FOR GLORY / → LADIES AND GENTLEMEN, THE FABULOUS STAINS, Tina Andrews *(Sugaree)*, Tim Thomerson *(Doubles)* ← RECORD CITY ← CAR WASH / → HONKYTONK MAN → RHINESTONE → NEAR DARK → EDDIE PRESLEY → BAD CHANNELS, Jerry Rushing *(trucker)* → LIVING LEGEND: THE KING OF ROCK AND ROLL

Storyline: The lurid, enigmatic world of the traditional American sideshow carnival comes under the microscope in Robert Kaylor's cult drama. Frankie and Patch (the latter played by Band alumnus Robbie Robertson) have equal shares in a clownish sideshow act, part of a carnival wending its way through the Deep South. While neither have much regard for the mugs and corrupt officials which people the dead end towns they perform in, the arrival of teenage runaway Donna puts a spanner in both their partnership and general carny relations. *BG*

Movie rating: *5

Visual: none

Off the record: (see below)

—

ROBBIE ROBERTSON // ALEX NORTH

Dec 80. (lp) *Warners; <(HS 3455)>* ☐ ☐
– Midway Music:- Garden of earthly delights / Pagan knight / The fat man / Freaks' lament / Sawdust and G-strings / Rained out // Themes and Variations:- Carnival bozo / Remember to forget / Lust / I'm a bad girl / Rednecks rumble / Fear and revelation / Carny theme.

S/track review: As well as acting in the film, ROBBIE ROBERTSON – in collaboration with Hollywood composer ALEX NORTH – scored the soundtrack, a combination of conventional orchestral atmospherics and more rock-centric, New Orleans-influenced instrumentals such as the down and dirty 'Garden Of Earthly Delights'. Despite the scoring credits, the former Band guitarist only actually performed on three tracks, including the latter and a smoking, organ-heavy cover of Fats Domino's 'The Fat Man', the only vocal track on the album and only one of a handful of solo vocals he'd recorded in his entire career up to that point. *BG*

Album rating: *4

☐ Shayne CARTER segment
(⇒ FOR GOOD)

Johnny CASH

Born: 26 Feb'32, Kingsland, Arkansas, USA. Possibly the most revered and influential country singer ever and certainly the one who's enjoyed the most credible crossover success, JOHNNY CASH reversed the time honoured process of creative decline by recording some of his most compelling albums in the final decade of his life. When he made his acting debut in the obscure thriller, 'Five Minutes To Live' (1961), he had just come through the first flush of success as a feral, 'Sun'-sponsored rockabilly star. Subsequently re-released as 'Door-To-Door Maniac', the movie featured CASH as a seriously malcontented hood who pretends to be a door-to-door guitar salesman (he'd actually worked as salesman before breaking into the music business) in order to trick his way into a woman's home as part of a bank heist. It also featured him intimidating his victim with some mean guitar strumming, an apt metaphor for the reputation he was to earn as one of rock'n'roll's earliest and most infamous wildmen. Much less controversial were his appearances in the lightweight Gene Nelson musical, 'HOOTENANNY HOOT' (1963) and Music Row comedy, 'ROAD TO NASHVILLE' (1967), while CASH finally scored his first movie, the Robert Redford vehicle, 'LITTLE FAUSS AND BIG HALSY', in 1970. That year's violent John Frankenheimer crime drama, 'I WALK THE LINE', meanwhile, also used one of CASH's earliest 'Sun' singles for both its title and its soundtrack. And while that early acting potential was never developed, CASH survived his personal demons to successfully tour and record right up until his death from diabetes complications on 12th September 2003. His 90s albums on 'American' records had won him a whole new generation of admirers and sealed his legendary status, while the awards (the haunting video for his cover of NiN/Trent Reznor's 'Hurt' scooped the Best Cinematography category at the 2003 MTV Video Music Award) kept coming right until the end. The appropriately-named biopic, 'WALK THE LINE', was completed in 2005 starring Joaquin Phoenix in the CASH role. *BG*

- **filmography** (composer) {acting} –

Five Minutes To Live *(1961 {*})* / **Hootenanny Hoot** *(1963 {p} on OST by V/A =>)* / **Road To Nashville** *(1967 {*} =>)* / **The Man, His World, His Music** *(1969 {*p} =>)* / **Johnny Cash At San Quentin** *(1969 TV {*p} OST =>)* / **Little Fauss And Big Halsy** *(1970 OST by CASH, CARL PERKINS & the TENNESSEE THREE =>)* / **I Walk The Line** *(1970 OST =>)* / a Gunfight *(1971 {*})* / **the Gospel Road** *(1973 {*} OST =>)* / Thaddeus Rose And Eddie *(1978 TV {*})* / the Pride Of Jesse Hallam *(1980 TV {*})* / Murder In Coweta County *(1983 TV {*})* / the Baron And The Kid *(1984 TV {*})* / Stagecoach *(1986 TV {*})* / the Last Days Of Frank And Jesse James *(1986 {*})* / Davy Crockett: Rainbow In The Thunder *(1988 {*})*

CATCH AND RELEASE

2006 (US 124m) Columbia Pictures (PG-13)

Film genre: romantic comedy/drama

Top guns: s-w + dir: Susannah Grant

Stars: Jennifer Garner *(Gray Wheeler)*, Timothy Olyphant *(Fritz)* ← ROCK STAR, Sam Jaegar *(Dennis)* ← DOUBLE PLATINUM, Kevin Smith *(Sam)*, Juliette Lewis *(Maureen Monette)* ← the FEARLESS FREAKS ← FROM DUSK TILL DAWN ← STRANGE DAYS ← the BASKETBALL DIARIES ← NATURAL BORN KILLERS ← the RUNNIN' KIND, Joshua Friesen *(Mattie Monette)*, Fiona Shaw *(Ellen Douglas)*, Tina Lifford *(Eve the lawyer)* ← the TEMPTATIONS, Georgia Craig *(Persephone)*, Daniel A. Parker *(Deadhead singer)*, Nancy Hower *(Deadhead singer)*, Jennifer Spence *(Deadhead singer)*, Sacha Levin *(drummer)*

Storyline: Gray Wheeler's life is dramatically changed when Grady, the man she loved and was about to marry, suddenly dies before their wedding. She finds solace with Grady's friends, Sam and Dennis, but she becomes most intimate with Fritz, the one she found most obnoxious before. Through these talks she discovers there was more to Grady's life than he admitted, including a son from another relationship, and tries to come to terms with her own uncertain future as her problems mount. *JZ*

Movie rating: *5.5

Visual: dvd

Off the record: Both Juliette Lewis and Nancy Hower have their own bands, the Licks and Stella respectively. *MCS*

BT and TOMMY STINSON

Feb 07. (cd) *Varese Sarabande; <302 066 793-2> (VSD 6793)* ☐ ☐
– Bathroom intro / Mr. Yummy / Grady's house / Lawyer's office / Maureen's messages / Fritz and Gray walk the creek / Ski skates mellow / Gray removes ring / Gray overhears Maureen / Candlelight dinner / Gray's confessions / River opening / Gray ties Mattie's shoe / Gray and Fritz cook / Massage montage / Sweet nothings / Dennis and Persephone date / Farmers market / Planer fight / Fritz leaves / Not his kid / Maureen apologizes / Gray's memorial speech.

S/track review: BT (BRIAN TRANSEAU) teamed up with Replacements founder member and latter day Guns N' Roses bassist TOMMY STINSON to produce this soporific score. Almost entirely consisting of plaintive acoustic guitar-strumming on a bed of ambient electronica, the longest track here is less than three minutes long. Because of the shortness of the tracks, and the lack of any memorable or affecting quality, the first ten cues zip past without making any kind of impact. Unusually for someone with such a rock pedigree, STINSON provides the most generic and cliched guitar: sparse, wistful and completely stock. It also seems that BT has elected to take a back seat production-wise, and none of his trademark flare is apparent here, just a textbook approach to ambient noise. 'River Opening' picks up the pace a little bit with around ten seconds of percussion, and thereafter the instrumentation becomes a little more diverse, introducing slide guitar and some piano but it's not until 'Massage Montage' that the relentless vagueness is interrupted by a minute of frantic layered guitars. 'Farmers Market' again is more upbeat, injecting some manic energy that 'Planer Fight' sustains, displaying at least some of the inventiveness STINSON brought to the Replacements, which is sadly instantly dissipated by 'Fritz Leaves', another mundane strummer. The concluding 'Gray's Memorial Speech' has the promise of something that could be almost moving should it develop, but of course finishes at just over a minute. Considering himself "a student of music", BT allows his work here to be dictated by the established rules of the genre, and so is never in any danger of doing anything actually noteworthy. Rarely more than carefully poised background noise, 'CATCH AND RELEASE' is altogether a perfectly serviceable score for a terrible romantic comedy. *SW*

Album rating: *3.5

– spinoff releases, etc. –

Various Artists

Jan 07. (cd) *Legacy-Sony; <(88697 05852-2)>* ☐ ☐
– Razor (FOO FIGHTERS) / My drug buddy (the LEMONHEADS) / A nest for two (BLINKER THE STAR) / Mornings eleven (the MAGIC NUMBERS) / Pills (GARY JULES) / Electrified and ripe (STEVE DURAND) / The winding staircase (NEW RADIANT STORM KING) / Sky signal (AUDIBLE) / Leaving the ground (PETER MACLAGGAN) / What if you (JOSHUA RADIN) / These 3 sins (GOMEZ) / Resistance (ALASKA) / Let the bad times roll (PAUL WESTERBERG) / Turning blue (the SWALLOWS) / What I done (ANDREW RODRIGUEZ) / Soul meets body (DEATH CAB FOR CUTIE) / There goes the fear (DOVES).

CATCH ME IF YOU CAN

1989 (US 106m) MCEG Productions (PG)

Film genre: coming-of-age sports comedy drama

Top guns: s-w + dir: Stephen Sommers

Stars: Matt Lattanzi *(Dylan Malone)* ← GREASE 2 ← XANADU, Loryn Locklin *(Melissa Hanson)*, Grant Heslov *(Nevil)* → CLUBLAND, Billy Morrissette *(Monkey)* → PUMP UP THE VOLUME, Geoffrey Lewis *(Mr. Johnson)* → the DEVIL'S REJECTS, M. Emmet Walsh *(Johnny Phatmun)* ← BLADE RUNNER ← BOUND FOR GLORY ← LITTLE BIG MAN ← MIDNIGHT COWBOY ← ALICE'S RESTAURANT / → ALBINO ALLIGATOR, Dan Bell *(Manney)* → WAYNE'S WORLD → WAYNE'S WORLD 2, Greg Walker *(Widowmaker)*, Peter Breitmayer *(Stackowski)*

Storyline: Cathedral High School is doomed unless someone can come up with $200,000 to keep it open. Student president Melissa is desperate to save her school and so when drag racer Dylan cooks up a harebrain scheme to win money she agrees. All Dylan has to do is beat his rivals in an illegal road race and they'll collect their winnings from king of the bookies Johnny Phatmun. But will the naive schoolkids be a match for the shrewdies of the Syndicate? *JZ*

Movie rating: *4.5

Visual: video

Off the record: nothing

TANGERINE DREAM

Feb 94. (cd) *Edel America; <EDS 5413-2>* ☐ ☐
– Dylan's future / Sad Melissa / Fast Eddie's car / Back to the race / Melissa asks Dylan out / Dylan alone at home / Melissa needs help / The kiss / Racing montage / The clock is ticking / Widow maker / Dylan's dream / Taking the test / Back to the race again / One more chance / Melissa's challenge / Widow maker race / Dylan's triumph / Catch Me If You Can main theme.

S/track review: Dating from 1989, but not released for another five years, 'CATCH ME IF YOU CAN' is not one of TANGERINE DREAM's finer moments. The album may be sought after by fans, but this surely has more to do with its rarity than any artistic merit. As dated as the movie it accompanies, 'CATCH ME . . .' is a lazy piece of work by anyone's standards, let alone a group rightly considered pioneers of electronic music. As background music the pieces here do their job adequately, but no more than that. There's a unity of texture and themes, and the purpose of each cue is obvious enough. But there are none of the surprises or unusual atmospheric effects which allow their better soundtracks to stand alone. Tacky synthesizer settings – plastic digital piano, springy bass guitar – are married to cheesy themes, while the cantering rhythms, generated from splashy programmed drums and rubbery percussion, could be straight out of a 16-bit video game. *SS*

Album rating: *3.5

Nick CAVE

Born: 22 Sep'57, Warracknabeal, Victoria, Australia. One of the few talents of the post-punk generation who transcended the genre rather than stagnating, NICK CAVE is very possibly the most vital singer-songwriter working right now, and about the only real candidate talented enough to follow in the late footsteps of his own heroes JOHNNY CASH and Nina Simone. Over the course of a wildly impressive career, CAVE's sense of dark drama and poetic justice have served him well as a film composer, while his seething charisma and formidable presence have occasionally lent themselves to acting parts. Like DAVID BOWIE and LOU REED before him, a post-Birthday Party CAVE (together with his new backing troupe the Bad Seeds) found creative sustenance in the heady environs of West Berlin, a city which formed the backdrop to Wim Wenders' post-modern fairy tale, 'Wings Of Desire' (1987). A CAVE fan himself, Wenders had the Australian perform the title track of his debut solo album, 'From Her To Eternity', as part of the film's climax, while the soundtrack also featured 'The Carny', from CAVE's 1986 album, 'Your Funeral . . . My Trial'. Following a cameo in experimental German effort, 'Dandy' (1987), the man's next major celluloid project involved a very different kind of film, 'GHOSTS . . . OF THE CIVIL DEAD' (1988), one much more CAVE-esque in its subject matter and for which he'd written the screenplay some years earlier. A grim chronicle of life in an Australian prison, the movie was directed by fellow Australian, John Hillcoat, and featured CAVE as one of the inmates, while both CAVE and Bad Seeds MICK HARVEY and BLIXA BARGELD were credited on the equally unsettling soundtrack. In 1991, CAVE and Co briefly resumed their partnership with Wenders, contributing a song to the director's futuristic road movie, 'Until The End Of The World', while the Australian – as eclectic an actor as a songwriter, and proving that he didn't take himself too seriously – subsequently popped up unexpectedly as a sage, bleach blonde old rocker proferring advice to a naive Brad Pitt in Tom DiCillo's drolly stylized fantasy, 'JOHNNY SUEDE' (1991). Come the mid-90s, CAVE found time amid his regular Bad Seeds schedule to score 'Jonas In The Desert' (1994), a documentary on experimental filmaker Jonas Mekas, and – alongside the likes of LOU REED and ELVIS COSTELLO – to pay musical tribute to a German cabaret legend in the Canadian TV docu-film, 'September Songs: The Music Of Kurt Weill' (1995). In tandem with HARVEY and BARGELD, he also scored Hillcoat's torrid, Papua New Guinea-set thriller, 'TO HAVE AND TO HOLD' (1996), and even appeared alongside Ewan McGregor and Alexei Sayle in Michael Haussman's 'Rhinoceros Hunting In Budapest' (1997). Yet perhaps the most compelling piece of cinematic music CAVE has yet composed, 'Red Right Hand', wasn't even written for a film. Composed of clanking, cellar-like acoustics, with vaguely misanthopic, solidly snarled lyrics, the track was originally featured on the 1994 Bad Seeds album, 'Let Love In', although it was subsequently used in the soundtracks to both cult TV series, 'X-Files' (1996) and Wes Craven's 'Scream' (1996). CAVE and his band also contributed one of the standout songs – the seductive 'Sweetest Embrace' – to 'TRAINSPOTTING' follow-up, 'The ACID HOUSE' (1998), even if it did sit uneasily among the soundtrack's patented indie and techno selection. In fact, it's probably fair to say most of CAVE's creative output sits uneasily alongside the vast majority of modern popular music, something we should all be thankful for, but something which – in his usual contradictory fashion – doesn't prevent the man leasing out his songs (i.e. 'People Ain't No Good') to unlikely films like 'Shrek 2' (2004). CAVE's cinematic talents were about to be re-engaged more thoroughly, with shooting due to begin on a CAVE-penned Australian western, 'The PROPOSITION' (2005), to which he also composed the score with WARREN ELLIS. Ditto for 2007's 'The ASSASSINATION OF JESSE JAMES BY THE COWARD ROBERT FORD'. *BG*

- filmography {acting} (composer) –

die Stadt *(1983 {p} =>)* / Dandy *(1987 {c})* / Wings Of Desire *(1987 {c})* / **Ghosts . . .Of The Civil Dead** *(1988 {*} OST by CAVE, MICK HARVEY & BLIXA BARGELD =>)* / **the Road To God Knows Where** *(1990 {p} =>)* / Until The End Of The World *(1991 {b} see future edition)* / **Johnny Suede** *(1991 {a} =>)* / Jonas In The Desert *(1994 docu {c} w/ BLIXA BARGELD & KEVIN COYNE)* / September Songs: The Music Of Kurt Weill *(1995 TV docu {*p})* / **To Have And To Hold** *(1996 OST by BLIXA BARGELD, CAVE & MICK HARVEY =>)* / Rhinoceros Hunting In Budapest *(1997 {a})* / the Runner *(1999 score w/ Anthony Marinelli)* / Jonas At The Ocean *(2001 docu {c})* / **the Proposition** *(2005 {b} OST w/ WARREN ELLIS =>)* / **the Assassination Of Jesse James By The Coward Robert Ford** *(2007 {b} OST w/ WARREN ELLIS =>)*

☐ CELEBRATION (aka MIKE LOVE) segment
(⇒ ALMOST SUMMER)

the CELTS

1986 (UK 60m* TV mini) British Broadcasting Corporation

Film genre: historical documentary

Top guns: dir: David Richardson / s-w: Frank Delaney

Stars: Frank Delaney *(presenter)*, Dave Allen *(himself)*, **Enya** *(herself)*, Anne Ross *(herself)*, Miranda Green *(herself)*, Proinsias Mac Cana *(himself)*, Tania Grier *(Celtic princess)*

Storyline: An archeologists' dream documentary about the peoples known as the Celts, who lived in and around Europe B.C. and not, as many Scots people might think, winners of the European Cup 1967 A.D. (couldn't resist – sorry). *MCS*

Movie rating: *6

Visual: video

Off the record: Dave Allen was the Dublin-born stand-up comedian. **Enya** (see below)

ENYA: Enya

Feb 87. (lp/c/cd) *B.B.C.; (REB/ZCF/BBCCD 605) Atlantic; <81842>* [69] [ ]
– The Celts / Aldebaran / I want tomorrow / March of the Celts / Deireadh an tuath / The sun in the stream / To go beyond (I) / Fairytale / Epona / Triad: St. Patrick – Cu Chulainn – Oisin / Portrait (out of the blue) * / Boadicea / Bard dance / Dan y dwr / To go beyond (II). *(re-iss. Nov92 as 'THE CELTS' on 'WEA' hit UK No.10 – cd+= *)(lp/c; 450991167-2)(WX 498/+C)*

S/track review: ENYA's 'The CELTS' is awash with the eccentric Irish artist's idiosyncratic sound. Take, for example, the opening track with its mix of Vangelis synthesizers, and whispered multi-tracked ethereal vocals ensconced in traditional Irish and quasi-African rhythms. 'March Of The Celts' is a strange mix of dreamy synthesizers and chiming pianos, whilst 'Aldebaran' is sheer ambience, drifting by with a wondrous and almost sinister tone before building to a slight climax. 'I Want Tomorrow' follows a more straightforward song structure seeing ENYA tackle a routine ballad that even features an uncharacteristic echo-laden guitar solo. Elsewhere, 'The Sun In The Stream' features rousing bagpipes reminiscent of James Horner's subsequent work on 'Braveheart', while 'Bard Dance' is very much Mike Oldfield-flavoured; 'Epona' and 'Portrait (Out Of The Blue)' are pleasantly minimalist. Some of the slow moving ambience does become tryingly tedious, such as the pointless and ponderous 'To Go Beyond, Part 1' and 'Triad', but ENYA is at her best on the mysterious and spine-tingling 'Boadicèa', known to many as the haunting intro sample on the Fugees' hit 'Ready Or Not'. *LF*

Album rating: *7

– spinoff releases, etc. –

ENYA: I Want Tomorrow / The Celts Theme

Feb 87. (7") *(RESL 201)* [ ] [-]
(12"+=/cd-s+=) *(RESL)* – To Go Beyond I + II.
(re-iss. Nov88; same)

the CENSUS TAKER

1984 (US 95m) Argentum Productions (R)

Film genre: cop/detective horror comedy

Top guns: s-w: Bruce R. Cook (+ dir), Gordon M. Smith

Stars: Garrett Morris *(Harvey McGraw)* ← CAR WASH / → LITTLE RICHARD → HOW HIGH, Greg Mullavey *(George)*, Meredith MacRae *(Martha)* ← NORWOOD ← BIKINI BEACH ← BEACH PARTY, Timothy Bottoms *(Pete)*, Austen Taylor *(Eva)*, Troy Alexander *(Edward)*, **Jennifer Finch** *(punk girl)* → NOT BAD FOR A GIRL → BETTY BLOWTORCH AND HER AMAZING TRUE LIFE ADVENTURES, Roxanne Rolle *(woman in leopard-skin pants)* ← REPO MAN ← CLAMBAKE

Storyline: How many of you hide behind the couch when you see the man with the clipboard trudging up the drive? Perhaps that's what George and Martha should have done, but instead they answered the door and let the census taker in. The rep's questions turn increasingly personal and harassing, so much so that the not-so-happy couple shoot the inquisitive inspector dead. But how to hide the body, clipboard and pencil from the police is the next question on the list. *JZ*

Movie rating: *4

Visual: none

Off the record: Jennifer Finch was to subsequently form L7. The **RESIDENTS** (see below)

the RESIDENTS

1985. (red-lp/lp) *Episode; <(ED 21)>* [ ] [ ]
– Creeping dread / The census taker / Talk / End of home / Emotional music / Secret seed / Easter woman – Simple song / HELLno / Where is she / Innocence decayed / Romanian – Nice old man / Margaret Freeman / Lights out – Where is she / Passing the bottle / The census taker returns.

S/track review: Ah yes! the mysterious RESIDENTS (from San Mateo, California via Shreveport, Louisiana), still unknown to this day and responsible for a plethora of LPs, notably "proper" debut 'Meet The Residents' (1974), 'The Third Reich 'N Roll' (1976) and the weird but wonderful sublingual 'Eskimo' (1979). Not an obvious choice to phone up for a soundtrack commission (I mean, who you gonna call? . . .) and certainly not the first filmmaker Bruce R. Cook had in mind; it was indeed magician Penn Jillette (of Penn & Teller) who put the quartet forward to the director. To make their rushed deadline, the RESIDENTS reworked some old cuttings from previous works such as 'The Commercial Album' (1980) and 'The Mole Show' (1983), experimenting as always with newfound fundamental structures on the dark side of avant-rock. The title track (not the droning opener) was quite breezy and bright for such an uncompromising outfit, the only annoying thing about the track is some misleading ringtones. The nearest sound to anything cinematic came via 'Innocence Decayed' and 'Emotional Music', two songs precursing the film scorists-to-be, Mark Mothersbaugh and Danny Elfman, who were still working with respective new wave acts, Devo and Oingo Boingo. Arguably the most interesting pieces on the set were the short-but-sweet, 'Where Is She' (think Yello or Fad Gadget!) and 'HELLno', the latter with unknown, outsider female vox. Just to add that the RESIDENTS marketing campaign saw nearly 500 copies escape from the warehouse in red vinyl, while samples of the soundtrack-only tracks saw light on their 'Whatever Happened To Vileness Fats' reissue CD. *MCS*

Album rating: *5

□ CERRONE segment
(⇒ BRIGADE MONDAINE)

CHAPPAQUA

1966 (US 92m w/b&w) Winkler Films / Universal Pictures

Film genre: avant-garde/experimental movie

Top guns: s-w + dir: Conrad Rooks

Stars: Conrad Rooks *(Russel Harwick)*, William S. Burroughs *(Opium Jones)* → HOME OF THE BRAVE → EVEN COWGIRLS GET THE BLUES, Allen Ginsberg *(Messiah)* → DON'T LOOK BACK → TONITE LET'S ALL MAKE LOVE IN LONDON → TEN FOR TWO → RENALDO AND CLARA → NO DIRECTION HOME, Jean-Louis Barrault *(Dr. Benoit)*, Paula Pritchett *(water woman)*, **Ravi SHANKAR** *(Sun god)*, **Ornette Coleman** *(Peyote eater)*, Swami Satchidananda *(the guru)*, Moondog *(the prophet)*, **Ed Sanders** *(himself)*

Storyline: Beat scenester Conrad Rooks' stay in a Swiss sanatorium (French in the movie) is the starting point for this William Burroughs-"cut-up"-influenced, quasi-autobiographical analysis of his struggle with drugs, parlayed in a series of hallucinatory dream sequences, pseudo-documentary segments and flashbacks. *BG*

Movie rating: *3

Visual: none

Off the record: The FUGS (featuring **Ed Sanders**) performed 'I Couldn't Get High', although it wasn't used on the OST. *MCS*

RAVI SHANKAR

May 68. (lp) *Columbia; <OS 3230>* ☐ [–]
– Chappaqua / Running dear / Allah rocking / Om / Raga miniature / Back to earth / Raga / Sweet Russell / Orgy / Theme.

S/track review: Along with Jonathan Miller's BBC version of 'Alice In Wonderland', this was RAVI SHANKAR's first major western commission, and while contemporary critics have panned the hipster-studded, Venice Silver Lion-winning movie several decades after the fact, all are agreed that SHANKAR's score has aged handsomely. In his notes, Rooks recalls his first glimpse of the itinerant Indian, a "tiny little man scurrying down 57th Street in a long Nehru jacket", and how he subsequently introduced him to the likes of John Coltrane and the Modern Jazz Quartet, how in fact it was he who first "put him in touch with the jazz scene". While Rooks already had a soundtrack composer in Ornette Coleman, Coleman's orchestrated score (subsequently released as 'Chappaqua Suite') gave way to SHANKAR's by-ear/eye methods. As Rooks tells it, the sitar maestro "would create music to the absolute segment of the picture", "hum {to the guy transcribing it} the right amount of space-time-beats-everything to the image on the screen.. like pieces in a jigsaw puzzle". So it is then, that SHANKAR compresses the lengthy, rigorously structured extemporisation of Indian classical music into cue-sized mini-ragas (the frantic duel which closes side one is actually called 'Raga Miniature'). Unlike the grand orchestral arrangements of 'CHARLY', or the convulsive, sense shifting experimentalism of 'Transmigration Macabre' (i.e. 'VIOLA'), much of 'CHAPPAQUA' consists of relatively conventional dialogue between sitar and tabla, or monologues in isolation: deftly timed bass notes tear at Rooks' psychosis on 'Running Deer', plucked from the furthest reaches of an outlandish scale; syllabic cues spur breathless percussion on 'Allah Rocking', and SHANKAR addresses unknowable omnipotence on 'Om'. While pastoral reeds and puckish strings drift in and out of the pointilist canvas, most of the east-west splicing is grouped on side two: the intense percussion, bird-like woodwind whoops and almost slapstick guitar of 'Orgy' could, at a pinch, be the Incredible String Band (a troupe who themselves took more than just a leaf out of SHANKAR's parchment); opener 'Back To Earth' leavens the tabla with pentatonic piano and sylvan woodwind, while the intimate harp arrangement of 'Sweet Russell' surely betrays the contemporaneous influence of Coltrane's wife Alice. Beat grandmaster William Burroughs' owlish, nasal tones are among the spoken word fragments pasted in over the sober orchestrations which open the closing 'Theme', and while SHANKAR's score could hardly be deemed "cut-up" itself, there's a definite sense of pixelated sound constellations endlessly regrouping into a wider, inscrutable vision. *BG*

Album rating: *7

CHARIOTS OF FIRE

1981 (UK 123m) Twentieth Century-Fox / Allied Stars (PG)

Film genre: historical sports biopic/drama

Top guns: dir: Hugh Hudson / s-w: Colin Welland

Stars: Ben Cross *(Harold Abrahams)*, Ian Charleson *(Eric Liddell)* ← ROCK FOLLIES OF '77 ← JUBILEE, Nigel Havers *(Lord Andrew Lindsay)* ← BIRTH OF THE BEATLES, Nicholas Farrell *(Aubrey Montague)* → LIPSTICK ON YOUR COLLAR, Ian Holm *(Sam Mussabini)*, Daniel Gerroll *(Henry Stallard)*, Sir John Gielgud *(Master of Trinity)* → the WICKED LADY, Lindsay Anderson *(Master of Caius)* ← O LUCKY MAN!, Nigel Davenport *(Lord Birkenhead)*, Cheryl Campbell *(Jennie Liddell)* ← McVICAR, Alice Krige *(Sybil Gordon)* → BAJA OKLAHOMA, Patrick Magee *(Lord Cadogan)* ← the MONSTER CLUB, Brad Davis *(Jackson Scholz)*, Dennis Christopher *(Charles Paddock)*, Peter Egan *(Duke of Sutherland)*

Storyline: The true story of Scotsman, Eric Liddell, and English Jew, Harold Abrahams, as they prepare for the 1924 Olympics. Both have different reasons for running:- God-fearing Liddell as an act of faith (he won't even run on a Sunday) and Abrahams as proof that the Jewish race is not "inferior". The two eventually race in different events after Liddell beats Abrahams in a sprint, both knowing that failure is unacceptable both professionally and personally. *JZ*

Movie rating: *8.5

Visual: video + dvd

Off the record: (see below)

VANGELIS

Mar 81. (lp/c) *Polydor; (POLS/+C 1026) <PD1 6335>* [5] Oct81 [1]
– Titles / Five circles / Abraham's theme / Eric's theme / 100 metres / Jerusalem (the AMBROSIAN SINGERS) / Chariots of fire. *(re-iss. Apr84; POLD 5160); hit UK No.39) (cd-iss. 1983; 800020-2) <US cd-iss. 1989 on 'Polygram'; 889969> (cd re-iss. 2000; 549095-2)*

S/track review: VANGELIS became a household name (like Domestos or Dettol some might say) after the release of the Academy award-winning 'CHARIOTS OF FIRE'. Composed, arranged, produced and performed by the bearded one, the No.1 album has subsequently "run" into the millions, a feat the synth/keyboards man has never imitated. Everyone and their grannies should recognise the neo-classical theme tune, 'Titles' (which incidentally, also hit the top of the US charts), its echoey synths and melodic piano propelling visions of slow-motion athletes on a beach. It's all downhill from there on in, 'Five Circles', 'Abraham's Theme', 'Eric's Theme' and '100 Metres', saccharine and schmaltzy in equal measures. If one can criticise VANGELIS, it's just he tries so hard at times to turn full symphonic pieces into electronica noodles, while not getting organic enough to register the listener's brain above the "feel good" factor. A prime example is when he twists Hubert Parry & William Blake's jingoistic, British Empire anthem, 'Jerusalem' (complete with the AMBROSIAN SINGERS/choir), into a level of Elgar's "Pomp & Circumstance" stratum. We can either go several years in reverse for a rendition by Emerson, Lake & Palmer, or indeed fast forward several for the Fall's punkabilly version to see how it should be done. In stark contrast is the 20-minute 'Chariots Of Fire' score on the whole of side two, a lilting, piano-led suite that is as hypnotic and beautiful as it is uplifting and reflective. Verging on classical, 'CHARIOTS OF FIRE' drew in admirers such as Ridley Scott, who swiftly commissioned VANGELIS to twiddle the knobs again – so to speak – on 'BLADE RUNNER' (1982). *MCS*

Album rating: *6.5

– spinoff releases, etc. –

VANGELIS: Chariots Of Fire – Titles / Eric's Theme

Apr 81. (7") *(POSP 246) <2189>* [12] Dec81 [1]
(re-prom.UK Feb82 hit UK No.41 & re-iss. Aug84; same)

CHARLY

1968 (US 103m) Cinema Releasing Corporation (PG)

Film genre: psychological/medical drama

Top guns: dir: Ralph Nelson → a HERO AIN'T NOTHIN' BUT A SANDWICH / s-w: Stirling Silliphant → SHAFT IN AFRICA (au: Daniel Keyes 'Flowers For Algernon')

Stars: Cliff Robertson *(Charly Gordon)*, Claire Bloom *(Alice Kinnian)*, Lilia Skala *(Dr. Anna Strauss)* → FLASHDANCE, Leon Janney *(Dr. Richard Nemur)*, Richard Van Patten *(Bert)* → ZACHARIAH, Ruth White *(Mrs. Apple)* → MIDNIGHT COWBOY, Frank Dolan *(Eddie)* ← FEELIN' GOOD

Storyline: Desperate for a little more brainpower, mentally retarded bakery cleaner Charly Gordon faithfully attends nightclasses taught by the attractive, indefatigable Alice Kinian. Convinced by his potential, Kinian puts him forward for an experimental operation previously performed on mice and aimed at expanding his intellect. It works only too well and it's not long before he's left his sadistic bakery colleagues behind for a life of the mind. With his newfound mental capacity comes a sexual awakening which initially expresses itself as an assault on Kinian but – after an implied (by jarringly incongruous neo-psychedelia and split-screen experimentalism) voyage of self discovery – eventually ends in unlikely if blissful love. All that separates them from a happy ever after, of course, is a cruel twist. *BG*

Movie rating: *7

Visual: video + dvd

Off the record: (see below)

RAVI SHANKAR

Sep 68. (lp) *World Pacific; <WPS 21454>*
– Main title / Charly theme / Scenic tour / Improvisation on Charly theme – The maze – Triumph in the bakery / Turmoil / Reprise / Love montage / Variations on love theme / Self pursuit / Love theme transformation / Charly theme and resolution. *(cd-iss. 2001 on 'Moving Image Ent.' Italy; MIE 007)*

S/track review: With a Bollywood career stretching back even beyond his breathtaking music for Satyajit Ray's 'Pather Panchali', Indian sitar maestro – and much quoted "Godfather of world music" – RAVI SHANKAR was active in film long before he became fashionable in Western jazz/hippy/rock circles. After stepping into the breach for Ornette Coleman (whose work on Conrad Rooks' 'Chappaqua' – while ultimately released under Coleman's own steam – was rejected), SHANKAR was to carve out a modest niche in American/British underground filmmaking through the mid/late 60s, just as his Beatles/Monterey Pop-fired star was on the rise. His work on Oscar-winning thesp Cliff Robertson's pet project is the odd man out, a relatively big budget affair performed by a cast of top jazz sessioners including TOM SCOTT, RAY BROWN and BUD SHANK, as well as the late tabla master ALLA RAKHA ("the Einstein of rhythm", as dubbed by Grateful Dead drummer Mickey Hart). In his brief sleevenote, director Ralph Nelson – who sought out SHANKAR on the strength of the aforementioned Ray trilogy – claims they "violated every tenet of traditional scoring", and that prior to the session – having turned up minus any written music – "Ravi circulated among the musicians, talking, gesturing, determining offbeat rhythms, seeking unusual musical patterns, testing each musician for his improvisational abilities". Hardly surprising given the Hindustani tradition – improvisational by its very nature – in which he trained. With the project's Hollywood hue, though, 'CHARLY' necessarily ends up less psychedelic and more conventional than his other 60s soundtracks (particularly the – often lovely – flute and French horn arrangements, ditto the less well preserved harpsichord parts), but it's still an interesting trip, with more emphasis on the accompanists than his own playing. SHANKAR's sitar, in fact, isn't heard at all in the Middle Eastern-tinged title, making its low key entrance on the main theme instead, gently running the scale (Western rather than Eastern, at Nelson's request) over ripples of harp before fading out and reasserting itself. In the space between, SHANKAR wheels phantom tiers of reverberating woodwind in the vein of Bruce Langhorne's 'HIRED HAND', making for the most magnetic few minutes of the whole album. His experimental side is also to the fore with 'Improvisation On Charly Theme', raking over the kind of percussive shingle favoured by the era's jazz avant-garde, while RAHKA – spurred on by a violin pincer movement – takes the floor on feverish standout, 'Self Pursuit', about the only track likely to be of interest to groove diggers. 'Love Montage' and its variations marry virtuoso sitar with European whimsy, trading simultaneous melody lines in a kind of 'Norwegian Wood' inversion, and highlighting the fact that SHANKAR fans used to losing themselves in endless ragas won't necessarily appreciate this soundtrack. Yet fragmented as it is, 'CHARLY' reveals an undeniably impressive appreciation of Western pop, jazz and classical idioms, and both a willingness and a talent to engage them dramatically. *BG*

Album rating: *6.5

CHASTITY

1969 (US 82m) American International Pictures (R)

Film genre: road movie

Top guns: dir: Alessio de Paola / s-w: **Sonny Bono**

Stars: CHER *(Chastity)*, Barbara London *(Diana Midnight)* ← PSYCH-OUT, Stephen Whittaker *(Eddie)* ← UP THE JUNCTION, Tom Nolan *(Tommy)* → FAST TIMES AT RIDGEMONT HIGH → VOYAGE OF THE ROCK ALIENS → the THING CALLED LOVE, Danny Zapien *(cab driver)*, Elmer Valentine *(first truck driver)* → AMERICAN HOT WAX

Storyline: Chastity is a young hitchhiker who loves fun and adventure with various male motorists – up to a point. As soon as the men begin their amorous advances, Chastity lives up to her name and vanishes, usually with most of the guys' money. Eventually she gets a job in a Mexican brothel(?) but owner Diana wants to be more than a mother to her. Will Chastity succumb to this below-the-belt tactic or will she return to her old lover Eddie in far-off Phoenix? *JZ*

Movie rating: *5

Visual: video

Off the record: (see below + CHER entry)

SONNY BONO

Apr 69. (lp) *Atco; <S33 302>*
– Chastity's song (band of thieves) (CHER) / Chastity overture / Motel I / Chastity walk / Flowers (love of a family) / Chastity love theme / Chastity titles / Motel II / Chastity carousel / Mexico / Chastity (closing theme).

S/track review: By 1969, SONNY & CHER's huge folk-pop hits were some way behind them, and BONO's score for 'CHASTITY' never threatened to turn up another 'I Got You Babe' or 'Bang Bang'. In fact, there are only two songs here: the string-laden opener, which confirms both the power and the imprecision of CHER's famous warble, and 'Flowers (Love Of A Family)', on which SONNY's warmer voice is more endearing if only a shade more precise. The film was the pair's last roll of the dice as celebrity hippies, but none of this is hippy music. Instead, as if challenged by some cruel composing school sergeant-major, BONO fills the rest of the album with no less than seven variations on a simple and unexceptional musical theme. There's something briefly compelling about a tour of easy listening styles that takes in soaring wordless vocals and a synthetic whip-noise, a brass-led version to a ska beat, a version with concertina and maracas that evokes Italy more than the intended Mexico, a bubbling Hammond organ take and finally a funereal chorus complete with sawing violins and a church bell. It's not all bad, though: forced onto the supper-club circuit to pay the bill for this kitsch, the couple would hone the comedy act (dimwit husband outsmarted by smart-mouthed sexy wife) that would make them TV superstars in the 1970s. Their daughter may have been less impressed by their decision to name her after the movie. *ND*

Album rating: *3.5

– spinoff releases, etc. –

CHER: Chastity's Song (Band Of Thieves)

Apr 69. (7") <6684> ☐ ⊟

CHELSEA WALLS

2001 (US 109m) Lions Gate Films (R)

Film genre: urban drama

Top guns: dir: Ethan Hawke / s-w: Nicole Burdette (+ play)

Stars: Kevin Corrigan *(Crutches)* ← DETROIT ROCK CITY ← BUFFALO '66 ← WALKING AND TALKING ← BANDWAGON, Rosario Dawson *(Audrey)* ← JOSIE AND THE PUSSYCATS ← HE GOT GAME ← KIDS / → RENT, Vincent D'Onofrio *(Frank)* ← STRANGE DAYS / → OVERNIGHT → THUMBSUCKER, **Kris KRISTOFFERSON** *(Bud)*, Robert Sean Leonard *(Terry)*, Uma Thurman *(Grace)* ← PULP FICTION ← EVEN COWGIRLS GET THE BLUES / → BE COOL, Natasha Richardson *(Mary)* ← GOTHIC, Tuesday Weld *(Greta)* ← HEARTBREAK HOTEL ← THIEF ← I WALK THE LINE ← WILD IN THE COUNTRY ← ROCK, ROCK, ROCK!, Mark Webber *(Val)* ← STORYTELLING ← WHITEBOYS / → the HOTTEST STATE, Frank Whaley *(Lynny)* ← SHAKE, RATTLE & ROLL: AN AMERICAN LOVE STORY ← WENT TO CONEY ISLAND ON A MISSION FROM GOD . . . BE BACK BY FIVE ← PULP FICTION ← the DOORS / → the HOTTEST STATE, **Jimmy Scott** *(Skinny Bones)*, Steve Zahn *(Ross)* ← SUBURBI@ ← THAT THING YOU DO! ← REALITY BITES, Harris Yulin *(Bud's editor)* ← the MILLION DOLLAR HOTEL ← CANDY MOUNTAIN ← GOOD TO GO, **Isaac HAYES** *(man on elevator)*, Rick Linklater *(crony #2)* ← BEAVIS AND BUTT-HEAD DO AMERICA ← JANIS JOPLIN SLEPT HERE

Storyline: New York's fabled Chelsea Hotel has witnessed the greats of music and the arts over the decades. Our modern, less well known artistes include novelist Bud, who lives up to his name as far as booze is concerned. Grace is an aspiring poet who has to waitress to pay the bills. Frank the painter fancies Grace but she knows better, and Ross is a sex-mad rock star from out west where there are obviously no women at all to be found. A real crowd of arty oddballs to muse over. *JZ*

Movie rating: *4.5

Visual: dvd

Off the record: JEFF TWEEDY (see below + WILCO)

—

JEFF TWEEDY

Apr 02. (cd) *Rykodisc; <(RCD 10624)>* ☐ ☐
– Opening titles / Red elevator / Promising / Frank's dream / When the roses bloom again / Jealous guy / The wallman / The lonely 1 / Hello, are you there? / Softly and tenderly Jesus is calling / Finale / End credits.

S/track review: More so, perhaps, than the albums of Son Volt or Wilco, it's the soundtrack projects of JEFF TWEEDY and his former alt-country foil Jay Farrar which shed the starkest light on the divergent evolutionary arc of their respective careers. Where Farrar approximated the bleak wastes of Montana with luminous, folky acoustics in his score to 'The SLAUGHTER RULE' (2002), here TWEEDY took a far more improvisational, impressionistic approach to roots music in keeping with his inexorable gravitation towards Chicago's experimental fringe. He's partnered by GLENN KOTCHE, the industrious and hugely talented percussionist who took over the Wilco drum stool amid the brouhaha of 'Yankee Hotel Foxtrot', and who also moonlights as one third of Loose Fur alongside TWEEDY and the even more industrious Jim O'Rourke (Wilco producer and the "da Vinci of experimental music", as he's been dubbed). Anticipating their ad hoc live performances, the pair's extended percussion/guitar mantras are as ultimately oblique as their titles. Paternal kettle drums patter out a knock-kneed rhythm, strafed by feedback and stray notes; a sinuous guitar figure repeats and refines endlessly; a greasy riff grinds itself into cross-eyed submission. 'The Wallman', predicated on what sounds like harmonium – deep, blue and wheezing – and precipitate vibes, is the sound of the roots saboteurs at their most haunting, the orbiting hobo-trance of 'Hello, Are You There', representing their backwoods transmission at its ghostliest. Not until the brusquely titled 'End Credits' do they warm up their chilly aesthetic; against the syncopated chug and slap of KOTCHE's percussion, TWEEDY indulges in a cross-melodic spree of deep, resonant picking – it could almost be construed as a Chicago Underground-approved update of Uncle Tupelo's 'Screen Door'. Still, as the lilting Wilco outtake, 'Promising' – and the 'Mermaid Avenue' offcut, 'When The Roses Bloom Again' – suggest, it's all a long way from those 'No Depression' roots, a learning curve as steep as any graduate from the alt-country foundry. The permeability of TWEEDY's material also means that Ethan Hawkes' extra curricular selections bleed into it fairly inconspicuously. His thespian pal ROBERT SEAN LEONARD acquits himself well with a threadbare reading of 'The Lonely 1' (from Wilco's feted double set, 'Being There'), but the most unlikely entrant is diminutive, androgynous voiced jazz veteran, "LITTLE" JIMMY SCOTT, who adds to his cinematic credits (he's also featured on soundtracks to films as diverse as 'Twin Peaks' and 'Glengarry Glen Ross') with a rarefied arrangement of John Lennon's 'Jealous Guy'. Hawkes is no Tarantino, but, given time for its pockets of abstract beauty to assert themselves, 'CHELSEA WALLS' is a strangely addictive listen. It's also a great companion piece to Farrar's more traditional soundtrack, and a map of just how far Uncle Tupelo's legacy has panned out. *BG*

Album rating: *5.5

la CHIESA

1989 (Ita 110m) ADC Films (18)

Film genre: supernatural horror/drama

Top guns: s-w: Michele Soavi (+ dir), Dario Argento ← TENEBRE ← INFERNO ← SUSPIRIA ← PROFONDO ROSSO / → NONHOSONNO, Franco Ferrini → NONHOSONNO

Stars: Hugh Quarshie *(Father Gus)*, Tomas Arana *(Evan)*, Feodor Chaliapin Jr. *(the bishop)*, Barbara Cupisti *(Lisa)*, Antonella Vitale *(bridal model)*, Giovanni Lombardo Radice *(Reverend)*, Asia Argento *(Lotte)* → LAST DAYS

Storyline: In medieval times, a village of Devil worshippers is massacred by knights. The victims are buried in a pit on which a church is built. Hundreds of years later, a librarian discovers an ancient document and seeks to uncover the treasure it speaks of. Evil forces are unleashed and a disparate group trapped in the church must fight and seek to escape the demons unwittingly released. *DG*

Movie rating: *5.5

Visual: dvd

Off the record: Keith EMERSON (see own entry)

—

KEITH EMERSON (& GOBLIN *)

Apr 89. (lp) *Cinevox; (MDF 33/192)* ⊟ Italy ⊟
– The church (main theme) / La chiesa (*) / Prelude 24 (from well tempered clavier) / Possessione (*) / The possession / Lotte (*) / Go to hell (ZOOMING ON THE ZOO) / The wire blaze (DEFINITIVE GAZE) / The church revisted. *(cd-iss. Oct01 +=; CD-MDF 329)* – The church (single mix) / La chiesa – suite (*) / Suspence chiesa 1 (*) / Suspence chiesa 2 (*).

S/track review: Featuring five different composers and four performers, it's inevitable this comes across as a bit of a melange.

The main theme by KEITH EMERSON is all bombastic keyboards and frequent tempo changes. GOBLIN contribute 'La Chiesa', a more coherent stab which moves from a low-key trundle through neat keyboards into an eerie piece with well-judged effects, one of which you may have heard on the 'Friday the 13th' soundtrack. EMERSON then gives us a conventional rendition of J.S. Bach's 'Prelude 24', before GOBLIN return with 'Possessione', which is, frankly, a scary piece of music: whispered chants take us to a build-up of off-key chords. EMERSON's 'The Possession' sounds faintly ridiculous after this, as if he has filched parts of 'The Phantom Of The Opera'. Fortunately, GOBLIN bring things back on track with 'Lotte', the theme for one of the central characters. Then, however, we plunge headlong into stupidity with 'Go To Hell' by ZOOMING ON THE ZOO. A sort of 80s pop song, this even has a rap sequence. Entirely incongruous and not even a good tune. 'The Wire Blaze' by DEFINITIVE GAZE is equally out of place, but has the saving grace of actually being a good song, full of distorted guitar. That said, indie pop? In a "giallo" film? Additional versions of the main theme and 'La Chiesa', extended and expanded, are bonus tracks. Perhaps Michele Soavi, whose films are often incoherent, was looking for the same thing in the soundtrack. Unfortunately, it just does not work. Credit, though, to GOBLIN for holding their end up. *DG*

Album rating: *5

CHOPPER

2000 (Aus 94m) AFFC / Mushroom Pictures / Palace Films (18)

Film genre: crime bio-pic/drama/caper

Top guns: s-w + dir: Andrew Dominik → the ASSASSINATION OF JESSE JAMES . . . (au: Mark Brandon Read)

Stars: Eric Bana *(Mark "Chopper" Read)*, Vince Colosimo *(Neville Bartos)* → LANTANA, Simon Lyndon *(Jimmy Loughnan)*, David Field *(Keithy George)* ← TO HAVE AND TO HOLD ← GHOSTS . . . OF THE CIVIL DEAD / → ONE NIGHT THE MOON → SILENT PARTNER, Kate Beahan *(Tanya)*, Daniel Wyllie *(Bluey)*, Bill Young *(Det. Downie)*, Gary Waddell *(Kevin Darcy)* ← SWEET TALKER ← 20th CENTURY OZ / → the PROPOSITION, Kenny Graham *(Keith Read)*, Skye Wansey *(Mandy)* ← PRAISE

Storyline: 1978: real life criminal turned folk-legend Mark Brandon "Chopper" Read is serving a lengthy jail term for the kidnapping of a judge serving on the trial of his best mate Jimmy Loughnan. After Loughnan, co-opted by his prison enemies, makes a botched attempt at stabbing him, the fearless Read does an inverse 'Reservoir Dogs', willingly having his ear sliced off in order to get transferred from the hellish H Division wing of the maximum security prison he tried to prevent Jimmy ending up in in the first place. Finally released years later, he tracks down Jimmy and other agents of the "fairy godfathers" who've put a price on his head. *BG*

Movie rating: *7.5

Visual: dvd

Off the record: MICK HARVEY (see own entry)

Various Artists (score: MICK HARVEY *)

Jul 01. (cd) *Liberation; (LIBCD 2003.2) Dressed To Kill; <DTK 624>* [–] Austra [ ]
– The theme (*) / The plan (*) / Don't fence me in (FRANKIE LAINE) The average man (*) / Ever lovin' man (the LOVED ONES) / The stabbing (*) / / Sweet love (RENEE GEYER) / The release theme (*) / Forever now (COLD CHISEL) / The girlfriend (*) / Stuck on you (ROSE TATTOO) / The gate (*) / Release the bats (the BIRTHDAY PARTY) / The countdown (*) / Senile dementia (the SAINTS) / The threat (*) / Black & blue (the CHAIN) / The witness (*) / Bad boy for love (ROSE TATTOO) / End theme (*).

S/track review: Havin' it well large with the hard man/soft lounge aesthetic of latter day gangsterism, 'CHOPPER' boasts an undeniably ear-catching intro; another pathological plan gets the rum nod – "right.. turn 'em all into jelly sandwiches" – before FRANKIE LAINE croons classic Cole Porter: "Oh, give me land, lots of land, under starry skies above, don't fence me in".. And so it goes, ever harder and faster: profane dialogue symmetrically spliced with Aussie-rawk/punk source tracks and the barest of MICK HARVEY underscore. Cue the usual suspects: COLD CHISEL with the Journey-esque 'Forever Now'; the mighty BIRTHDAY PARTY ('Release The Bats' still sounding like an Ornette Coleman date gone just plain wrong); influential blooze-rockers ROSE TATTOO; seminal punks the SAINTS, future dreaming for the likes of the Zutons and the Strokes; all that's missing is INXS, but they wouldn't have fitted anyway. Less useful as a soundtrack than a pitstop survey of Antipodes retro, 'CHOPPER's prize is in its convincing roundup of great 60s/70s music pretty much unknown beyond down under. Like us, you've probably never heard of either the LOVED ONES or CHAIN; the latter's 'Black & Blue' serves an eye-shiner headkiss of Alex Harvey, Bon Scott and Nick Cave; the LOVED ONES are just as revelatory, nothing to do with American punk and everything to do with demented R&B. Chances are you've never heard of RENEE GEYER either, a blue-eyed soul blonde with a bible belt voice, serving up Australian funk (??!!) as tough and saucy as Betty Davis or Ann Alford. Ironically, the inverse racism of audience expectation nipped a US career in the bud; you'll swear the lady is black. All this jazz stitches up 'CHOPPER's perversely sympathetic character to a tee, and while the eerie sustain of HARVEY's theme tops and tails him, the film-scoring Bad Seed was given far more leeway on the excellent 'AUSTRALIAN RULES' three years later. *BG*

Album rating: *7

CHRISTIE MALRY'S OWN DOUBLE-ENTRY

2000 (UK/Neth/Luxem 94m) Woodline Films / Kasander (18)

Film genre: workplace drama

Top guns: dir: Paul Tickell / s-w: Simon Bent (au: B.S. Johnson)

Stars: Nick Moran *(Christie Malry)* ← BUDDY'S SONG, Neil Stuke *(Headlam)*, Kate Ashfield *(Carol)*, Mattia Sbragia *(Leonardo)*, Marcello Mazzarella *(Pacioli)*, Salvatore Lazzaro *(Giacomo)*, Sergio Albelli *(Duke Ludovice)*, Francesco Giuffrida *(Salai)*, Shirley Anne Field *(Mary)*, Peter Sullivan *(Wagner)*, Tabitha Wady *(Lucy)* ← KEVIN & PERRY GO LARGE

Storyline: Christie Malry is a young Irishman living and working in London. Fed up with his monotonous job in a bank, he decides to draw a line on his old life and begin living by the standards of double entry book-keeping. For every debit there is a credit, and vice versa. First he pays back his workmates for all their wrongdoings against him, but it doesn't stop there. When Britain and America bomb Iraq, Christie's double entry fixation leads him to much more extreme actions. *JZ*

Movie rating: *7.5

Visual: dvd

Off the Record: LUKE HAINES had been a staple with late 80s indie band, the Servants, before forming his own outfit, the Auteurs (alongside girlfriend Alice Readman) in and around Southgate in London, 1992. The band almost immediately signed a deal with 'Fire' records, although this was rather short-lived as they flitted to Virgin off-shoot label, 'Hut'. Glossy garage indie/punk merchants, fronted by the flamboyant but cynical HAINES, the Auteurs sound was characterised by the singer's brooding lyrical complexities. The addition of cellist, James Banbury produced an extra dimension to their standard guitar, bass, drums approach and the debut album's encouragingly critical reception was matched by its UK Top 40 placing. The aforementioned 'New Wave' (1993) garnered a nomination for the Mercury Music Prize.

Follow-up set, 'Now I'm A Cowboy' (1994), secured a Top 30 placing, although the group's critical acclaim continued to outweigh their commercial appeal. A remix set, 'The Auteurs Vs U-Ziq' appeared, although it wasn't until 1996 that a long-awaited third album materialised. Produced by Steve Albini, this atmospheric offering combined HAINES' downbeat tales of intrigue with grinding organs, discordant guitars and mournful strings to often hypnotic effect. Despite garnering further plaudits, the record sold poorly and after a clutch of final gigs, HAINES wound the band up, subsequently releasing an album under the moniker of Baader-Meinhof (first mentioned on their bleak 'Tombstone' track). In 1998, HAINES teamed up with two former members of Balloon, John Moore (ex-Expressway) and singer, Sarah Nixey, in the more melodic Black Box Recorder. Signing a major deal with 'Chrysalis' records, it didn't look likely that either their singles, 'Child Psychology' and 'England Made Me' (or the latterly-titled accompanying album), would return the moody HAINES to earlier heights. 1999 saw the man discarding previous projects to reincarnate the Auteurs. Comeback set, 'How I Learned To Love The Bootboys', included their nostalgic look back to 70s glam-rock in the shape of minor hit single, 'The Rubettes'. The turn of the millennium saw the turn of Black Box Recorder again, 'The Facts Of Life' (2000) hitting the Top 40 after its title track made it all the way into the Top 20. A well-received comeback shimmered with Saint Etienne-esque riffs along with jazzy piano trills that would be more at home in a fifties noir film. The ever prolific LUKE HAINES set about creating his own solo sojourn, two albums, 'CHRISTIE MALRY'S OWN DOUBLE-ENTRY' soundtrack and 'The Oliver Twist Manifesto', were both delivered in 2001. *MCS*

—

LUKE HAINES

Jun 01. (cd) *Hut; (CDHUT 65)* ☐ [-]
– Discomania / In the bleak midwinter / How to hate the working classes / The ledger / Bernie's funeral – Auto asphixiation / Discomaniax / Alchemy / Art will save the world / I love the sound of breaking glass / England, Scotland, Wales / Celestial discomania / Essexmania.

S/track review: LUKE HAINES has long been a stalwart of the UK indie scene since his days as frontman for the Auteurs; his current outfits were Baader Meinhof and Black Box Recorder. At first glance, HAINES was an unlikely candidate to be given such a high-profile film soundtrack commission, although the man really seemed at ease, taking song compositions rather than contemplating a film "score" proper. 'Discomania' (with opening line: "They're having sex to the Kids In America" – a ref. to the Kim Wilde song) sets the tone nicely, very Pulp/Disco 2000 glam or even Steve Harley & Cockney Rebel in their heyday. HAINES gets all squeeky clean and festive for the hymnal, 'In The Bleak Midwinter', accompanied by the Winchester Cathedral Choir, a song both effective and spiritual nevertheless. 'How To Hate The Working Class' carries all the hallmarks of a modern-day classic, highlighting the clever phrasing of Luke's lyrics, in particular when he gets down to "I need a holiday in Heaven" & "Let's start a party of our own". A different class, indeed. The similarly-themed instrumental, 'The Ledger', fits the film like a glove, as does follow-on piece, 'Bernie's Funeral – Auto Asphixiation'. Track 6, 'Discomaniax', gets the moody, orchestral/string treatment, a treatment less bombastic than the opening cut. The Eno-esque 'Alchemy' is probably his closest stab at typical film music, while the haunting 'Art Will Save The World' (held up banner-like by HAINES on the cover) is also of that ilk. HAINES' disruptive and cynical being gets into full flow via his fuzz terrorist re-working of Nick Lowe's 'I Love The Sound Of Breaking Glass'. A masterstroke indeed. Another barbed lullaby, 'England, Scotland, Wales' (a national anthem of sorts!?) namechecks Winston Churchill and George Orwell, while managing to keep a beat similar to Visage's early 80s gem, 'Fade To Grey'. The contrasting and thematic 'Celestial Discomania' and the upbeat rave mix of 'Essexmania' close out the album in perfect post-millennium aplomb. *MCS*

Album rating: *6.5

☐ CHUMBAWAMBA segment
(⇒ REVENGERS TRAGEDY)

Eric CLAPTON

Born: Eric Patrick Clapp, 30 Mar'45, Ripley, Surrey, England. Nicknamed, at various times, Slowhand and God, ERIC CLAPTON has always attracted the kind of manic adulation reserved only for a hardcore of rock royalty. On balance, he probably deserves it, having both reconfigured the boundaries of the electric guitar and played on many of the best rock albums ever recorded. After helping to ignite the British blues boom with the Yardbirds and John Mayall's Bluesbreakers, CLAPTON became one third of celebrated power trio Cream alongside Ginger Baker and Jack Bruce. As the 60s turned into the 70s, he recorded his greatest album, 'Layla And Other Assorted Love Songs' (1970) with the pseudonymous and woefully short-lived Derek & The Dominoes. While well documented drug problems were to delay a successful solo career, it'd be the mid-80s before he began pairing sound and image. A collaboration with Michael Kamen on the theme to a BBC TV series, 'Edge Of Darkness', marked his screen debut and while this was actually released as a single, it turned out to be the lowest charting of his career so far. Kamen was actually to prove a long term musical partner, working with CLAPTON on the bluesy scores to both the Mel Gibson vehicle, 'Lethal Weapon' (1987) and Mickey Rourke showcase, 'HOMEBOY' (1988). While the former was credited to CLAPTON, Kamen and saxophonist David Sanborn, the latter was billed as a CLAPTON solo effort. And while the CLAPTON/Kamen/Sanborn team were recalled for 1989's second instalment of 'Lethal Weapon', the guitarist's biggest soundtrack success came with his dark score for undercover cop movie, 'RUSH' (1991). The album made the US Top 30 and included CLAPTON's massive transatlantic hit, 'Tears In Heaven', a moving elegy for his son who'd died after falling from an upper story window. Although overshadowed by the huge success of his 'MTV Unplugged' set, 1992's third volume of 'Lethal Weapon' again rounded up messrs CLAPTON, Kamen and Sanborn (along with STING and ELTON JOHN) for the score, as did 1998's fourth, and thankfully final, instalment. While his score for the gritty, Gary Oldman-starring drama, 'Nil By Mouth' (1997), remains unreleased, CLAPTON's most recent film project was the soundtrack to Rob Reiner's creaky domestic study, 'The STORY OF US' (1999), scored in collaboration with Marc Shaiman. *BG*

- **filmography** (composer) {acting} –

Slipstream *(1973 w/ VAN MORRISON & Brian Ahern)* / Mean Streets *(1973)* / **Tommy** *(1975 {a} =>)* / **the Last Waltz** *(1978 {p} on OST by the BAND =>)* / Good And Bad At Games *(1983 TV w/ GEORGE HARRISON)* / Water *(1985 {c})* / Edge Of Darkness *(1985 TV mini; OST w/ MICHAEL KAMEN see; future editions =>)* / Lethal Weapon *(1987 OST w/ MICHAEL KAMEN & DAVID SANBORN see; future editions =>)* / **Homeboy** *(1988 OST w/ MICHAEL KAMEN & V/A =>)* / Lethal Weapon 2 *(1989 OST w/ MICHAEL KAMEN & DAVID SANBORN & V/A see; future editions =>)* / Communion *(1989 main theme)* / **Rush** *(1991 OST =>)* / Lethal Weapon 3 *(1992 OST w/ MICHAEL KAMEN & DAVID SANBORN & V/A see; future editions =>)* / the Van *(1996 score w/ Richard Hartley)* / Nil By Mouth *(1997 no OST)* / Lethal Weapon 4 *(1998 OST w/ MICHAEL KAMEN & DAVID SANBORN see; future editions =>)* / **Blues Brothers 2000** *(1998 {p} =>)* / the Accountant *(1999)* / **the Story Of Us** *(1999 OST w/ Marc Shaiman =>)* / **Concert For George** *(2003 {*p} OST by V/A =)*

CLAUDINE

1974 (US 92m) Twentieth Century Fox (PG)

Film genre: romantic drama

Top guns: dir: John Berry ← a TOUT CASSER / s-w: Tina & Lester Pine

Stars: Diahann Carroll *(Claudine Price)* → the FIVE HEARTBEATS → JACKIE'S BACK!, James Earl Jones *(Roop)* → a PIECE OF THE ACTION → the LION KING → PRIMARY COLORS, Tamu *(Charlene)* → a PIECE OF THE ACTION, David Kruger *(Paul)*, Lawrence Hilton-Jacobs *(Charles)* ← DEATH WISH / → YOUNGBLOOD → the JACKSONS: AN AMERICAN DREAM → SOUTHLANDER, Yvette Curtis *(Patrice)*, Eric Jones *(Francis)*, **Adam Wade** *(Owen)* ← GORDON'S WAR ← COME BACK, CHARLESTON BLUE ← ACROSS 110th STREET ← SHAFT / → PHANTOM OF THE PARADISE, Minnie Gentry *(bus woman)* ← BLACK CAESAR ← COME BACK, CHARLESTON BLUE, Stefan Gierasch *(sanitation foreman)* → CORNBREAD, EARL AND ME, Art Evans *(young brother)* → LEADBELLY → BIG TIME → YOUNGBLOOD → SCHOOL DAZE → TRESPASS → CB4: THE MOVIE → the STORY OF US, Mordecai Lawner *(process server)*

Storyline: More kitchen sink than Blaxploitation as a struggling single mother from Harlem signs on the American equivalent of the dole while working as a maid on the side. Her saviour comes in the form of bin man Roop who, despite getting cold feet at the thought of marriage, comes round in the end. *BG*

Movie rating: *5

Visual: video + dvd

Off the record: (see below)

—

GLADYS KNIGHT & THE PIPS (composer: CURTIS MAYFIELD)

Mar 74. (lp) *Buddah; <BDS 5602> (BDLP 4010)* 35 Jul74
– Mr. Welfare man / To be invisible / On and on / The makings of you / Claudine theme (CURTIS MAYFIELD) / Hold on / Make yours a happy home. *(cd-iss. Jun92 on 'Sequel'+=; NEXCD 206)* – Still Together (lp tracks). *<cd-iss. Jun99 on 'Capitol'; 9514>*

S/track review: Recorded after GLADYS KNIGHT's acrimonious departure from 'Motown' and before her descent into full blown MOR, 'CLAUDINE' suns itself in at least some of the reflected energy from contemporaneous career highlight, 'Imagination' (1973). That, and the silken drama of CURTIS MAYFIELD. Kitchen sink domesticity must have seemed a little tame after the doom mongering and druggy diorama of the man's early solo offerings, but in his identification with the underdog, he brings the trials of ordinary underclass folks to life. The main theme is about as close as CURTIS ever came to shagpile 70s screen music but 'Mr. Welfare Man' is pure MAYFIELD; GLADYS KNIGHT might be singing it, stuffing it full of all the dirt and the graft that his own, supercool tenor can't, but the effect is still champagne-socialist soul, dignifying the handouts with the cultured curlicues of Rich Tufo and refining KNIGHT's ardour, schooling it in the subtleties of his own phrasing. Why the track was never released as a single is the kind of karmic secret only 'Buddah' knows. They had themselves a huge US hit (Top 5) regardless with the unyielding 'On And On', an intimation of the MAYFIELD-Staples axis to come. They also scraped the Top 40 in Britain with the elegant 'Make Yours A Happy Home', another of those exquisitely arranged, mid-tempo mini-symphonies which made MAYFIELD a master in his field, shaping KNIGHT in his own image. He even plied her with a track, 'The Makings Of You', from his 1971 debut, and, as if to emphasise the project's mutual inspiration, went on to perform his own version of 'To Be Invisible' on the 'Sweet Exorcist' album later the same year. It's a synergy in contrast to his work with Aretha Franklin, maybe because there wasn't the same superstar expectation. Coming a couple of years after 'SUPERFLY', 'CLAUDINE' was actually the first of MAYFIELD's outsourced soundtracks, and it's still one of the best. *BG*

Album rating: *7

– spinoff hits, etc. –

GLADYS KNIGHT & THE PIPS: On And On / The Makings Of You

May 74. (7") *<423> (BDS 401)* 5 Aug74

GLADYS KNIGHT & THE PIPS: Make Yours A Happy Home

Aug 76. (7") *(BDS 447)* – 35

CLEOPATRA JONES

1973 (US 89m) Warner Bros. Pictures (PG)

Film genre: glam-spy thriller

Top guns: dir: Jack Starrett / s-w: Max Julien, Sheldon Keller

Stars: Tamara Dobson *(Cleopatra Jones)* ← COME BACK, CHARLESTON BLUE, Bernie Casey *(Reuben)* → CORNBREAD, EARL AND ME → BROTHERS → BILL & TED'S EXCELLENT ADVENTURE, Brenda Sykes *(Tiffany)*, Antonio Fargas *(Doodlebug)* ← ACROSS 110th STREET ← SHAFT / → FOXY BROWN → CORNBREAD, EARL AND ME → CAR WASH → FIRESTARTER → SOUL SURVIVORS, Bill McKinney *(Officer Purdy)* ← DELIVERANCE, Shelley Winters *(Mommy)* ← WILD IN THE STREETS / → ELVIS: THE MOVIE → PURPLE PEOPLE EATER → HEAVY, Albert Popwell *(Matthew Johnson)* → the BUDDY HOLLY STORY → WHO'S THAT GIRL, Mike Warren *(Andy)* → FAST BREAK, Esther Rolle *(Mrs. Johnson)* ← DON'T PLAY US CHEAP, Theodore Wilson *(Pickle)* ← COME BACK, CHARLESTON BLUE ← COTTON COMES TO HARLEM, Paul Koslo *(gang member)* ← VANISHING POINT, Frank Crocker *(himself)* → JIMI HENDRIX → FIVE ON THE BLACK HAND SIDE → THAT'S THE WAY OF THE WORLD → BREAKIN' 2: ELECTRIC BOOGALOO, Christopher Joy *(Snake)* → SHEBA, BABY → BIG TIME, John Garwood *(Lt. Tompkins)* ← the SAVAGE SEVEN, Don Cornelius *(himself)* → NO WAY BACK → ROADIE → TAPEHEADS → JACKIE'S BACK!, William Bonner *(cop in bust)* ← PSYCH-OUT / → BLACK SHAMPOO

Storyline: Whether traveling on turbo charged wheels or an airport baggage carousel, special agent Cleopatra Jones is as cool as a cucumber, and just about as cliched. Self-conscious 70s catchphrases abound as lesbian queenpin Mommy uses her crooked cop connections to plant heroin in Jones' lover's rehab centre and snuff out the gangling, Thunderbirds-like pimp, Doodlebug. *BG*

Movie rating: *4.5

Visual: video + dvd

Off the record: (see below)

—

J.J. JOHNSON (& Various Artists)

Jul 73. (lp) *Spring-Warners; <BS 2719>* –
– Theme from Cleopatra Jones (JOE SIMON) / The wrecking yard / Love doctor (MILLIE JACKSON) / Airport flight / Emdee / Desert sunrise (main title instrumental) / Hurts so good (MILLIE JACKSON) / Goin' to the chase / Go chase Cleo / Cleo and Reuben / Wrap up / Theme from Cleopatra Jones (instrumental). *<(cd-iss. May01; 9362 48090-2)>*

S/track review: Six months after the release of the landmark 'ACROSS 110th STREET' (1972), JJ JOHNSON proved he was no dilettante, with an intelligent, instinctive follow-up. The fact that it came packaged with two hit singles didn't exactly hurt either. What did sting just a little was MILLIE JACKSON's breakthrough single, 'Hurts So Good', rightly recognised as an – admittedly slightly dodgy – soul classic (recently described by Antony And

The Johnsons' Hegarty as "part of a long lineage of dark, playful love songs") and another example of a blaxploitation soundtrack launching a career. 'Love Doctor' wasn't too shabby either, two and a half minutes of natty old skool soul wasted as a b-side. The rippling, JOE SIMON-sung theme also hit the US charts, echoed by JOHNSON (as in JJ, not Antony) as part of an Eastern promised medley with 'Desert Sunrise'; the veteran trombonist perhaps took a few cues – if not time changes – from the 'Turkish Bath' era, big band orientalism of fellow jazzer turned film composer Don Ellis (the man behind the celebrated 'French Connection' scores). While his combined mastery of jazz and symphonic combustion fires cues like 'Airport Flight', 'Go Chase Cleo' and 'Wrap Up', unusual arrangements like fuzz guitar, wood block and sitar make this one of JOHNSON's most exploratory soundtracks; not exactly "world music-like" as the re-issue sleevenotes claim, but getting there. *BG*

Album rating: *7

– spinoff hits, etc. –

JOE SIMON featuring the MAINSTREETERS: Theme From Cleopatra Jones / JOE SIMON: Who Was That Lady

Jul 73. (7") *<138>* [18] [–]

MILLIE JACKSON: Hurts So Good / Love Doctor

Aug 73. (7") *<139> Polydor; (2066 363)* [24] Nov73 [ ]

CLUB PARADISE

1986 (US 104m) Warner Bros. (PG-13)

Film genre: anarchic workplace comedy

Top guns: s-w: (+ dir) Harold Ramis ← CADDYSHACK ← ANIMAL HOUSE, Brian Doyle-Murray ← CADDYSHACK (story: Tom Leopold, Chris Miller ← s-w ANIMAL HOUSE, Ed Roboto, David Standish)

Stars: Robin Williams *(Jack Moniker)* → GOOD MORNING, VIETNAM → GOOD WILL HUNTING, Peter O'Toole *(Gov. Anthony Cloyden Hayes)*, Rick Moranis *(Barry Nye)* ← STREETS OF FIRE / → LITTLE SHOP OF HORRORS → BROTHER BEAR, **Jimmy CLIFF** *(Ernest Reed)*, Twiggy *(Phillipa Lloyd)* ← the BLUES BROTHERS ← POPCORN / → EDGE OF SEVENTEEN, Adolph Caesar *(Prime Minister Solomon Grundy)*, Eugene Levy *(Barry Steinberg)* ← HEAVY METAL / → a MIGHTY WIND → CURIOUS GEORGE → OVER THE HEDGE, Joanna Cassidy *(Terry Hamlin)* ← BLADE RUNNER ← FOOLS, Brian Doyle-Murray *(Voit Zerbe)* ← CADDYSHACK / → WAYNE'S WORLD, Bruce McGill *(Dave the fireman)* ← ANIMAL HOUSE / → the INSIDER, Carl Bradshaw *(cab driver)* ← COUNTRYMAN ← the HARDER THEY COME / → KLA$H → DANCEHALL QUEEN → ONE LOVE, Andrea Martin *(Linda White)* → WAG THE DOG → HEDWIG AND THE ANGRY INCH, Simon Jones *(Toby Prooth)* ← ROCK FOLLIES OF '77, **Ansil "Double Barrel" Collins** *(flamboyant)*, **Arthur Brown** *(opposition leader)* ← TOMMY ← the COMMITTEE / → JAILBIRD ROCK → I PUT A SPELL ON ME

Storyline: Injured fireman Jack Moniker sinks his invalidity money into a run-down resort in the Caribbean. His first guests soon arrive and turn out to be a crazy cross-section of American society who are none too pleased at the shabbiness of the hotel. Prime Minister Solomon Grundy is also none too pleased as the hotel stands in the way of a massive real estate deal he's plotting. Will fireman Jack and his friends be shot down in flames or is it all water off a duck's back to him? *JZ*

Movie rating: *4

Visual: video

Off the record: Ansil Collins was one half of Dave & Ansil Collins, a Jamaican reggae duo from the early 70s who had two major UK hits, 'Double Barrel' (No.1) and 'Monkey Spanner' (No.7). *MCS*

—

Various Artists (incl. JIMMY CLIFF *)

Jul 86. (lp/c) *Columbia; <PK/PCT 40404> C.B.S.; (CBS/40 70298)* [ ] [ ]
– The lion awakes (*) / Seven-day weekend (* and ELVIS COSTELLO AND THE ATTRACTIONS) / You can't keep a good man down (*) / Sweetie come from America (WELL PLEASED AND SATISFIED) / Grenada (MIGHTY SPARROW) / American plan (*) / Third World people (*) / Love people (BLUE RIDDIM BAND) / Brightest star (*) / Club Paradise (*).

S/track review: Nearly fifteen years after 'The HARDER THEY COME' should have raised JIMMY CLIFF to mainstream stardom as both an actor and a musician – it didn't – the Jamaican had changed producers, record labels, religion, home country and band (collaborating with Kool & The Gang) without achieving the breakthrough made by his countryman Bob Marley. 'CLUB PARADISE' is a garish holiday postcard compared to the gritty front-line report of the earlier film, but the soundtrack is still distinguished by Cliff's talents, and enhanced by the backing of stalwarts like Sly and Robbie. Of the seven JIMMY CLIFF songs 'You Can't Keep A Good Man Down', 'American Plan' and 'Third World People' are all happy examples of the singer's gift for hook-laden melodies and concise commentary. 'Seven-Day Weekend', a punchy collaboration with ELVIS COSTELLO & THE ATTRACTIONS, is less distinctive. Of the three tracks by other artists, WELL PLEASED AND SATISFIED introduce a harder roots-reggae sound, but the stand-out is MIGHTY SPARROW's 'Grenada', a typically witty critique of the colonial atrocities in the land of his birth by the King of Calypso (his parents had emigrated to Trinidad when he was a baby). Twenty years on, JIMMY CLIFF's status as a king among reggae stars is assured – and this uneven, neglected record is due for reappraisal. *ND*

Album rating: *6.5

– spinoff releases, etc. –

JIMMY CLIFF with ELVIS COSTELLO AND THE ATTRACTIONS: Seven-Day Weekend / JIMMY CLIFF: Brightest Star

Jul 86. (7") *<06135>* [ ] [–]

JIMMY CLIFF: Club Paradise / Third World People

Sep 86. (7") *<06235>* [ ] [–]

COBRA VERDE

1987 (W.Ger 110m) De Laurentiis Entertainment Group (12)

Film genre: period-costume adventure/drama

Top guns: s-w + dir: Werner Herzog ← NOSFERATU, THE VAMPYRE ← HERZ AUS GLAS ← AGUIRRE, WRATH OF GOD / → GRIZZLY MAN (nov: 'The Viceroy Of Ouidah' by Bruce Chatwin)

Stars: Klaus Kinski *(Francisco Manoel da Silva)* ← CODENAME: WILDGEESE ← NOSFERATU, THE VAMPYRE ← MADAME CLAUDE ← LIFESPAN ← AGUIRRE, WRATH OF GOD, King Ampaw *(Taparica)*, Jose Lewgoy *(Don Octavio Coutinho)*, Salvatore Basile *(Captain Fraternidade)*, Nana Agyefi Kwame II *(Bossa Ahadee)*, Benito Stefanelli *(Captain Pedro Vincente)*

Storyline: Suspected of getting fresh with a plantation Dom's daughters, a restless Brazilian n'er do well swaps South America's dessicated outback for the fever coast of Africa. Initially at the humiliating whims of a crazed king, he eventually usurps his crown, takes up residence in an abandoned fort and grows rich from the rancid fat of slave trading. *BG*

Movie rating: *6.5

Visual: video + dvd

Off the record: (see below)

—

POPOL VUH

Feb 88. (lp/c/cd) *Milan; (A/C/CH 353)* [–] French [–]
– Der tod des Cobra Verde / Nachts: Schnee / Der marktplatz / Eine andere welt / Grab de mutter / Die singenden madchen von ho, zia vi / Sieh nicht uberm meer ist's / Ha'mut, bis dass nacht ruh' und stille kommt.

S/track review: The final chapter in the Herzog-Kinski saga and the final POPOL VUH soundtrack. For longtime fans, this had the promise of being perhaps the most fascinating of them all: a Bruce Chatwin adaptation and a locale as exotic and as terrible as 19th century Dahomey, the Bight of Benin where, as Chatwin quotes in his novel (from a "Slayer's Proverb"): "Of the one that comes out, There Are Forty Go In". The movie, though, was generally deemed to have compromised its potential with a confusing, convoluted plot, released to lukewarm reviews despite the colour, extravagance and non-ethnocentric window onto the slave trade. That final, unforgettable scene of Kinski, dead beat on the beach made for a telling adieu; he was to suffer a massive, fatal heart attack a few years later. As ever, FLORIAN FRICKE seemed hotwired to the subtext, capturing the sense of things coming full circle, Kinski finally burning himself out; the unnerving 'Sieh Nicht Überm Meer Ist's' as a requiem. The music's tone, from opener 'Der Tod des Cobra Verde' onwards, is expressly religious, rarefied by the gracious, recurring chorale of the Bavarian State Opera, possibly FRICKE's most overt example of "a mass for the heart", as he once dubbed his art. DANIEL FICHELSCHER's guitar tinkers away underneath but it's the cavernous voices which fill the space, as edifying as 'NOSFERATU' was menacing and 'HEART OF GLASS' claustrophobic. A series of shorter cues are more obviously – and surprisingly – cinematic, context-setting birdsong and swells of regal ambience from FRICKE's trusty Synclavier. There's also a vivacious African field recording (cut in Munich) from the Zigi Cultural Troupe Ho, Ziavi, and the bonus solo piano version of 'Om Mani Padme Hum' is just gorgeous. An underrated film and an underrated album, finally on CD; shame about the lurid artwork though. *BG*

Album rating: *7.5

CODENAME: WILDGEESE

aka GEHEIMCODE: WILDGANSE

1984 (Ita/W.Ger 101m) Ascot Films (18)

Film genre: military/war adventure

Top guns: dir: Antonio Margheriti as Anthony M. Dawson / s-w: Tito Carpi, Gianfranco Couyoumdijan, Michael Lester

Stars: Lewis Collins *(Cmdr. Robin Wesley)*, Lee Van Cleef *(China)*, Ernest Borgnine *(Fletcher)*, Klaus Kinski *(Charlton)* ← NOSFERATU, THE VAMPYRE ← MADAME CLAUDE ← LIFESPAN ← AGUIRRE, WRATH OF GOD / → COBRA VERDE, Manfred Lehmann *(Klein)*, Mimsy Farmer *(Kathy Robson)* ← MORE ← RIOT ON SUNSET STRIP, Thomas Danneberg *(Arbib)*, Frank Glaubrecht *(Stone)*

Storyline: Tough man Captain Wesley is ordered to the jungles of south-east Asia by his bosses Fletcher and Charlton. His mission is to blow up as much of Thailand as possible, including a heroin factory deep in the wilds. Along with his team of weapon-heavy mercenaries, Wesley blasts away at the bamboo, but the baddies fight back by bombing a local church. But there's a twist in the tale when boss Charlton's name turns up where it shouldn't and Wesley begins to wonder who's on which side. *JZ*

Movie rating: *4

Visual: video + dvd

Off the record: Former apprentice hairdresser, **Lewis Collins** (b.27 May'46, Bidston, Birkenhead, Cheshire), had played bass for many up and coming Merseybeat outfits before they eventually went into the recording studio. These included the Mojos (managed by his dad, Bill Collins), the Renegades (who became the Eyes) and the very obscure Georgians. Most will remember Lewis as Bodie, in the 1977 TV police detective series, 'The Professionals'. *MCS*

—

ELOY: Geheimcode Wildganse

Mar 85. (lp) *Milan; (MIL-CH 014)* [–] German [–]
– The patrol / Hongkong theme 1 / Hit and run / Queen of rock'n roll / Destiny / Discovery / Juke-box / Deadlock / Cha-Shoen / Sabotage / On the edge / A long goodbye / Face to face / A moment decides / Revenge / Hongkong theme 2.

S/track review: Hanover band, ELOY (named after HG Wells 'Time Machine' moniker), were not really as strange a choice as first thought for this action/war-themed film score. Their German prog-meets-heavy credentials – on a plethora of albums! – stood them in high esteem among their many filmatic progressive-rock peers such as TANGERINE DREAM, POPOL VUH, VANGELIS, RICK WAKEMAN and KEITH EMERSON. This OST was similar to the aforementioned, although sadly in a lower league division. In 1982/3 during the recording of 'CODENAME . . .', ELOY found themselves without stalwart founder, Frank Bornemann, resulting in the remaining musicians, HANNES ARKONA (on guitar), HANNES FOLBERTH (keyboards/drums) and KLAUS-PETER MATZIOL (bass/vocals) taking on the unenviable task of completing the score. 'The Patrol' opens the show Tangerine Dream-like, glistening keys, pounding drums and atmosphere to boot – what more could you ask for? 'HongKong Theme 1' (' . . .Theme 2' closes the set) gets a little bright and funky, while others, too, such as the shimmering 'Destiny' and 'Cha-Shoen' get into the oriental spirit of the film. Blatant, out'n'out hard-rock track, 'Queen Of Rock'n Roll', fused Mott The Hoople with hair-metal types such as Van Halen, while 'Juke-Box' sounded Edgar Winter (and again funky!) – ELOY were indeed, eclectic. Side 2 delivers a more sedate Popol Vuh-like approach, exampled on the cinematic and eerie 'Deadlock', a record too short by any prog standards. Of the remainder, there's little to shout about, but there are a few wee gems here. *MCS*

Album rating: *4

□ COEUR DE VERRE alt.
(⇒ HERZ AUS GLAS)

COFFY

1973 (US 91m) American International Pictures (R)

Film genre: crime thriller

Top guns: s-w + dir: Jack Hill → FOXY BROWN

Stars: Pam Grier *(Coffy)* ← COOL BREEZE ← BLACK MAMA, WHITE MAMA ← BEYOND THE VALLEY OF THE DOLLS / → FOXY BROWN → FRIDAY FOSTER → SHEBA, BABY → BUCKTOWN → BILL & TED'S BOGUS JOURNEY → JACKIE BROWN → BONES, Booker Bradshaw *(Brunswick)* ← the STRAWBERRY STATEMENT, Robert DoQui *(King George)* ← UP TIGHT! / → NASHVILLE → FAST FORWARD → GOOD TO GO, Allan Arbus *(Vittroni)* ← HEY, LET'S TWIST / → CROSSROADS, William Elliott *(Carter)*, Sid Haig *(Omar)* ← BLACK MAMA, WHITE MAMA ← IT'S A BIKINI WORLD ← BEACH BALL / → FOXY BROWN → the FORBIDDEN DANCE → JACKIE BROWN → HOUSE OF 1000 CORPSES → KILL BILL: VOL.2 → the DEVIL'S REJECTS, John Perak *(Aleva)*, Mwako Cumbako *(Grover)* → TOGETHER BROTHERS, Barry Cahill *(McHenry)*, Morris Buchanan *(Sugarman)* ← GOOD TIMES, Bob Minor *(Studs)* → FOXY BROWN, Reben Moreno *(Ramos)* ← LITTLE BIG MAN, Tracee Lyles *(Vivian)* → LADY SINGS THE BLUES, Leslie McRae *(Cindy)* ← BUMMER! / → WILLIE DYNAMITE

Storyline: Coffy moves through an early 70s milieu of unrelenting moral degradation, one in which even her 11 year old sister is in rehab. Almost without exception, the men are lecherous, corrupt, venal and murderous, not least her mayoral candidate of a boyfriend. The women aren't much better, even the lesbians. In the screen role which made her an Afro-coiffed icon, Pam Grier battles them all, a solitary blaxploitation superwoman wrestling the chicks, ensnaring the dudes through their own vanity and generally turning the genre's sexist hallmarks on their head. *BG*

Movie rating: *6

Visual: video + dvd

Off the record: **ROY AYERS** (see below)

—

ROY AYERS

1973. (lp) *Polydor; <PD 5048>* [ ] [–]
– Coffy is the color / Pricilla's theme / King George / Aragon / Coffy sauna / King's last ride / Coffy baby / Brawling broads / Escape / Shining symbol / Exotic dance / Making love / Vittroni's theme – King is dead / End of Sugarman. *<(cd-iss. Feb01 on 'Universal'; 314 529777-2)>*

S/track review: Pam Grier is "..the baddest one-chick hit squad that ever hit town!", which must make ROY AYERS the meanest one-dude vibes machine to ever hit a recording studio. Well, almost. With AYERS a few years into his Ubiquity tenure at the time this was recorded, 'COFFY' naturally leans more towards streetwise funk and R&B than it does jazz – that breezily famous vibraphone-tinkling only surfaces occasionally, most effectively on the title track, where he seamlessly blends it with cravat-elegant soul, and on 'Shining Symbol', the closest this album comes to the classic Ubiquity sound. While his band were still in their jazz-rock phase at this point, AYERS – like most of his contemporaries – jumped at the creative possibilities of a soundtrack, trying his hand at everything from an orchestrated Dee Dee Bridgewater ballad ('Coffy Baby') to bass, brass n' bongo chase music, to a deliciously dated, echo-drenched hybrid of prime Isaac Hayes and War's 'Fidel's Fantasy' entitled 'King George' (for a visual aid to this you can't go wrong with those humungous sideburns on the sleeve). The whiff of War's peace pipe is also thick on 'Exotic Dance', a mellow, low key instrumental and an unlikely highlight alongside 'Aragon', relentless funk powered by the kind of wah-wah ostinato which would shift Johnny Hammond's gears a couple of years later. Only 'Brawling Broads', tragically, doesn't quite live up to its title (how could it?!). 'COFFY' is also one the few blaxploitation albums to feature that most ubiquitous of all early 70s soundtrack accessories – the harpsichord; if it's good enough for Gainsbourg, it's good enough for ROY AYERS, and 'Vittroni's Theme-King Is Dead' – almost uniquely in black film music – strives for Morricone-esque baroque, with the closing 'End Of Sugarman' figuring as another avant-garde piece along the lines of Gene Page's 'BLACULA' (1973) denouement. 'COFFY' is the colour, classic is the vintage. *BG*

Album rating: *8

COLD MOUNTAIN

2003 (US 155m) Mirage Enterprises / Miramax Films (R)

Film genre: romantic western/civil-war drama

Top guns: s-w + dir: Anthony Minghella → BREAKING AND ENTERING (au: Charles Frazier)

Stars: Jude Law *(Inman)* → ALFIE re-make → BREAKING AND ENTERING, Nicole Kidman *(Ada Monroe)*, Renee Zellweger *(Ruby Thewes)* ← EMPIRE RECORDS ← SHAKE, RATTLE & ROCK! tv ← REALITY BITES, Eileen Atkins *(Maddy)*, Brendan Gleeson *(Stobrod Thewes)*, Philip Seymour Hoffman *(Reverend Veasey)* ← ALMOST FAMOUS ← MAGNOLIA ← BOOGIE NIGHTS, Natalie Portman *(Sara)*, Giovanni Ribisi *(Junior)* ← LOST IN TRANSLATION ← MASKED AND ANONYMOUS ← the VIRGIN SUICIDES ← FIRST LOVE, LAST RITES ← SUBURBI@ ← THAT THING YOU DO!, Donald Sutherland *(Reverend Monroe)* ← RED HOT ← ANIMAL HOUSE ← STEELYARD BLUES, Ray Winstone *(Teague)* ← SEXY BEAST ← LADIES AND GENTLEMEN, THE FABULOUS STAINS ← QUADROPHENIA / → the PROPOSITION → BREAKING AND ENTERING, Kathy Baker *(Sally Swanger)* ← SHAKE, RATTLE & ROLL: AN AMERICAN LOVE STORY ← PERMANENT RECORD, James Gammon *(Esco Swanger)* ← the COUNTRY BEARS ← URBAN COWBOY, **Jack White** *(Georgia)* ← COFFEE AND CIGARETTES / → the FEARLESS FREAKS → TWO HEADED COW → WALK HARD: THE DEWEY COX STORY, Lucas Black *(Oakley)* ← ALL THE PRETTY HORSES ← SLING BLADE / → KILLER DILLER → FRIDAY NIGHT LIGHTS, Taryn Manning *(Shyla)* ← 8 MILE / → HUSTLE & FLOW, Cillian Murphy *(Bardolph)*, Melora Walters *(Lila)* ← MAGNOLIA ← BOOGIE NIGHTS, **Chris Fennell** *(Acton Swanger)* ← SHAKE, RATTLE & ROLL: AN AMERICAN LOVE STORY, Tom Aldredge *(blind man)* ← COUNTDOWN AT KUSINI, Jena Malone *(ferry girl)* → INTO THE WILD

Storyline: Cold Mountain, North Carolina, pre-civil war ferment: terminally reticent Inman struggles to voice his affection for monied new girl in town, Ada, but somehow they manage to snog before he's whisked off to the killing fields under the confederate flag. After surviving a horrific sub-trench bombing and a neck wound, he finally decides he's had enough and sets out on an Odyssean quest for home. Back in Cold Mountain, when the sicko sheriff isn't picking off deserters and lynching their families, he's trying to worm his way into the affections of Ada and nab the farm he feels he's been cheated out of. Ada for her part, can think only of her absent sweetheart, although the tediously gung-ho support of local lass Ruby helps take her mind off things. *BG*

Movie rating: *7

Visual: dvd

Off the record: Guitarist/vocalist, **Jack White** (b. John Anthony Gillis, 9 Jul'75, Detroit, Michigan, USA), had made three albums with the White Stripes, 'The White Stripes' (1998), 'De Stijl' (2000) and 'White Blood Cells' (2002). He met actress Renee Zellweger on the 'COLD MOUNTAIN' set and dated her for just over a year until they split late in 2004. *MCS*

—

Various Artists incl. JACK WHITE ** (score: GABRIEL YARED *)

Dec 03. (cd) *Columbia; <86843> (515119-2)* [51] [ ]
– Wayfaring stranger (**) / Like a songbird that has fallen (REELTIME TRAVELERS) / I wish my baby was born (TIM ERIKSEN & RILEY BAUGUS) / The scarlet tide (ALISON KRAUSS) / The cuckoo (TIM ERIKSEN & RILEY BAUGUS) / Sittin' on top of the world (**) / Am I born to die? (TIM ERIKSEN) / Will you be my ain true love? (ALISON KRAUSE) / I'm going home (SACRED HARP SINGERS AT LIBERTY CHURCH) / Never far away (**) / Christmas time will soon be over (**) / Ruby with the eyes that sparkle (STUART DUNCAN & DIRK POWELL) / Lady Margret (CASSIE FRANKLIN) / Great high mountain (**) / Anthem (*) / Ada plays (*) / Ada and Inman (*) / Love theme (*) / Idumea (SACRED HARP SINGERS AT LIBERTY CHURCH).

S/track review: Film/soundtrack fans could've been forgiven for suffering bluegrass fatigue by the early noughties. T-BONE BURNETT, the man who masterminded the mandolin-winded 'O BROTHER, WHERE ART THOU?', returned here with another, darker Hillbilly Social Club, retaining the likes of ALISON KRAUSS and NORMAN BLAKE but sexing up the package with roots renegade JACK WHITE. The nu-bluesman not only gets to sing the talismanic 'Wayfaring Stranger' – 'COLD MOUNTAIN's equivalent to 'Man Of Constant Sorrow' – but indulges a yen for 'Beggars Banquet'-era 'Stones, hollering through 'Sittin' On Top Of The World' in a sinus-heavy whine that'd do Mick Jagger proud. It's louche, wheezing white-boy blues at its best, and as well as leading the lairy singalong, 'Christmas Time Will Soon Be Over' and linking back into 'O BROTHER . . .' with the Ralph Stanley-arranged 'Great High Mountain', WHITE transcends the show with the gentle, almost Beatles-y chamber pop of 'Never Far Away', accompanying himself on acoustic guitar. Any four out of the five songs could have furnished a great solo EP, making the soundtrack all but essential for White Stripes fans. The star count is even higher if you read the small print of the songwriting credits; Elvis Costello is behind the demurely powerful 'Scarlet Tide', KRAUSS' showcase alongside the lesser, Sting-authored 'You Will Be My Ain True Love'. It's TIM ERIKSEN, though, whose mountain song is the coldest, which isn't to say it's lacking in soul. The acclaimed punk-turned-ethno folk/classical/bluesologist chills the plasma with solo ballad, 'Am I Born To Die?', and a harmony rendition of the evergreen 'I Wish My Baby Was Born' (see Uncle Tupelo's 'March 16-20' album for an equally curdled reading). His arrangements for the SACRED HARP SINGERS are more of an acquired taste, a choral style ERIKSEN resuscitated from a 19th century songbook and later employed in an educational context; while the goose-stepping structure of 'I'm Going Home' rags against the album's flow, 'Idumea' is an ennobled finale, haunting in its bell-like harmony. The quartet of sedate score pieces from veteran collaborators Anthony Minghella and GABRIEL YARED are out of place: dispensing with them altogether (they're good enough to deserve an album in their own right) would've cut the running time back and made the record easier to digest in a single sitting. Still, BURNETT has a winning formula here, no question, convincing proof that old-timey needn't mean out of time. *BG*

Album rating: *7.5

Phil COLLINS

Born: 30 Jan'51, Chiswick, London, England. COLLINS began his career as a child-actor, his claim-to-fame for several years was his bit-part in the BEATLES' debut flick, 'a HARD DAY'S NIGHT' (1964); he also played the role of the Artful Dodger in the formative West End production of 'Oliver!'. After a period as sticksman for the short-lived Flaming Youth (one single, 'Guide Me Orion', in 1969), Phil joined prog-rockers, Genesis, replacing John Mayhew for the groundbreaking 1970 album, 'Trespass'. COLLINS' impeccable drumming anchored the Genesis sound from the early-to-mid-70s, while the enigmatic PETER GABRIEL took control of 90% of the vocals on such classic sets as 'Nursery Cryme' (1971), 'Foxtrot' (1972) and 'Selling England By The Pound' (1973). With GABRIEL subsequently leaving after the epic 'The Lamb Lies Down On Broadway' (1974), COLLINS was promoted from drummer to frontman in one fell swoop when auditions proved fruitless. Proving that he was more than capable of filling GABRIEL's hallowed shoes, COLLINS successfully steered the band through the rocky patch of late 70s punk and beyond. Mirroring his band's move into glossy AOR with the 'Duke' (1980) album, COLLINS' solo career came ready-made for the heart of the mainstream pop/rock crossover market. One must also mention his time as leader of instrumental sideline outfit, Brand X, with whom he released several albums. Trailed by overweight radio favourite 'In The Air Tonight', his debut LP 'Face Value' (1981) was a transatlantic million seller and a British No.1 to boot. Here was a man who truly polarised opinion from the start, his ubiquitous smugness and increasingly sterile pop making him a favourite target for critics. Yet his breezy melodies, cheeky chappy demeanour and soul-lite hollering made him hugely popular as the cult of the 80s coffee-table star took hold. A second set, 'Hello, I Must Be Going' (1982), was another massive seller, again blessed with an insidiously catchy No.1 single in the form of 'You Can't Hurry Love' (originally a 60s hit for the Supremes). A string of subsequent singles failed to make any commercial impression and for a while it looked like COLLINS' career was faltering. Any such doubts were cast aside with the hugely successful, Grammy-winning film soundtrack ballad, 'Against All Odds (Take A Look At Me Now)'. He was back again early the following year with the pop/funk of 'Sussidio' and his biggest album to date in 'No Jacket Required' (1985). This was the set that really broke America, the record selling faster than Michael Jackson's 'Thriller'; its success was boosted by a further two US No.1's, the American release of 'Sussidio' and the slushy ballad, 'One More Night'. Seemingly unable to get enough of the man, the Americans secured a Live Aid performance and put him back astride the US charts with the Stephen Bishop-penned 'Separate Lives', a collaborative ballad (from the film 'White Nights') with Marilyn Martin; COLLINS had earlier struck paydirt with a duet with Philip Bailey on 'Easy Lover'. Having acted as a child, COLLINS procured the star part in the film 'Buster' (1988), as well as contributing a handful of songs to the soundtrack. One of these was a nauseous cover of the Mindbenders' 'A Groovy Kind Of Love', while the asinine 'Two Hearts' (co-written with 'Motown' legend Lamont Dozier) gave him another US peak position. A transatlantic No.1 (what else?!), COLLINS' fourth studio set, '. . .But Seriously' (1989) was a lame attempt at addressing more serious issues. Many people found 'Another Day In Paradise' downright offensive, COLLINS masquerading as a friend of the street dwellers, although the man did contribute a lot of his earnings to this and certain charities. Phil continued in inimitably goal-getting fashion throughout the 90s (he played the role of Inspector Good in the 1991 feature, 'Hook'), eventually leaving Genesis in the mid-90s. Having released 'Both Sides' in '93, he returned in 1996 with 'Dance Into The Light', his first album for the unfortunately named new label, 'Face Value'. After various musical distractions and side alleys including a fleeting and unlikely appearance alongside Lil' Kim on her cover of 'In The Air Tonight', 2002's 'Testify' was back to monotonous business for COLLINS, a tired set of songs with even more well-worn themes. By this time, COLLINS had set up an alliance with Disney, co-writing two scores with Mark Mancina for animations 'TARZAN' (1999) and 'BROTHER BEAR' (2003). *MCS & BG*

- **filmography** {acting} (composer) –

a Hard Day's Night *(1964 {b} OST by the BEATLES =>)* / the Secret Policeman's Other Ball *(1982 {p} on OST by V/A =>)* / Against All Odds *(1984 hit theme on OST by Larry Carlton, Michel Colombier & V/A; see future edition)* / White Nights *(1985 hit single on OST by V/A & Michel Colombier; see future edition)* / **Playing For Keeps** *(1986 single on OST by V/A & Daniel Bechet =>)* / Buster *(1988 {*} hits on OST by V/A & Anne Dudley; see future edition)* / Hook *(1991 {*})* / And The Band Played On *(1993 TV {a})* / Frauds *(1993 {*})* / Balto *(1995 {v})* / **Tarzan** *(1999 OST by Mark Mancina & COLLINS =>)* / the Jungle Book 2 *(2003 {v})* / **Brother Bear** *(2003 OST by Mark Mancina & COLLINS =>)* / Arktos: The Internal Journey Of Mike Horn *(2005 score w/ Gareth Cousins)*

□ COMBUSTIBLE EDISON segment
(⇒ FOUR ROOMS)

COME BACK, CHARLESTON BLUE

1972 (US 100m) Warner Bros. Pictures (PG)

Film genre: cop/detective mystery

Top guns: dir: Mark Warren / s-w: Bontche Schweig, Ernest Kinoy (nov: 'The Heat's On' Chester Himes ← COTTON COMES TO HARLEM)

Stars: Godfrey Cambridge *(Gravedigger Jones)* ← COTTON COMES TO HARLEM ← WATERMELON MAN / → FRIDAY FOSTER, Raymond St. Jacques *(Coffin Ed Johnson)* ← the FINAL COMEDOWN ← COOL

BREEZE ← COTTON COMES TO HARLEM ← UP TIGHT / → BOOK OF NUMBERS, Peter De Anda *(Joe)*, Maxwell Glanville *(Caspar)* ← COTTON COMES TO HARLEM, Minnie Gentry *(Her Majesty)* ← BLACK CAESAR ← CLAUDINE, Percy Rodriguez *(Capt. Bryce)*, Jonelle Allen *(Carol)* ← COTTON COMES TO HARLEM, Leonardo Cimino *(Frank Mago)* ← COTTON COMES TO HARLEM / → DUNE, Philip Michael Thomas *(minister)* ← BOOK OF NUMBERS → SPARKLE, **Adam Wade** *(Benjy)* ← SHAFT / → ACROSS 110th STREET → GORDON'S WAR → CLAUDINE → PHANTOM OF THE PARADISE, Theodore Wilson *(cemetery guard)* ← COTTON COMES TO HARLEM / → CLEOPATRA JONES, Marcia McBroom *(girl barber)* ← BEYOND THE VALLEY OF THE DOLLS / → JESUS CHRIST SUPERSTAR → WILLIE DYNAMITE

Storyline: Based on a novel by black crime writer Chester Himes, this 'Cotton Comes To Harlem' follow-up has a crooked photographer attempting to flush out Harlem's drug-dealing competition with supernatural scare tactics. The wonderfully named Gravedigger Jones and Coffin Ed Johnson are not so easily fooled, however . . . *BG*

Movie rating: *5.5

Visual: video

Off the record: DONNY HATHAWAY (see below)

DONNY HATHAWAY (md: Quincy Jones)

1972. (lp) *Atco; <SD 7010>*
– Main theme / Basie / String segue / Vegetable wagon / Harlem dawn / Scratchy record / Explosion / Hearse to graveyard / Switch "Charleston Blue" / Come back Basie / Detective's goof / Gravedigger Jones & Coffin Ed's funeral / String seque / Little ghetto boy / Hail to the queen / Drag queen chase / Bossa nova / Tim's high / Furniture truck / Liberation / Come back Charleston Blue.

S/track review: A soul original with the voice of a sweet black angel, DONNY HATHAWAY is better known for 'The Ghetto', one of the most enduring gauges of post-civil-rights Afro-America. Almost three decades after his mysterious death in 1979, HATHAWAY's star refuses to dim, his legend kept alive in the lyrics of Nas and Amy Winehouse amongst others, popularised by unlikely American Idol performances. Less talked about is this soundtrack, released the same year as his seminal concert set, 'Live'. Rather than rarify the 60s pop Galt MacDermot had conceived for the original, the stylistically erudite singer-songwriter composed a lengthy series of cues at least partly drawn from vintage big band/jazz, not so surprising given QUINCY JONES' role as supervisor and his own unique interpretation of the jazz aesthetic. The main theme – in keeping with the title – is unadulterated ragtime in heel-kicking two-step, while both the self explanatory 'Basie' and 'Come Back Basie' pay classy homage to the legendary jazz pianist. The reason you really need this album, though, is 'Little Ghetto Boy', the studio version of a song premiered on his live set a few months earlier. It's classic HATHAWAY, conscious, imploring, redemptive, shining its wildflower possibility into the vacuum left by Martin Luther King's death four years earlier (perhaps it's a blessing HATHAWAY didn't live to hear 'The Message', Grandmaster Flash's gut-wrenching riposte to '..Ghetto Boy's potential ten years on). 'Tim's High' strains for more hallowed ground, a sinner's entreaty borne on teardrop-piano and seraphic harp. HATHAWAY also offers some wordless testifying (even his humming is soul-deep) on 'Harlem Dawn' and performs the closing title with Southern soul diva MARGIE JOSEPH, herself newly signed to 'Atlantic' alongside Aretha Franklin and HATHAWAY's sometime singing partner Roberta Flack. In between there's plenty of standard, QUINCY-patented big band chase (a predatory, recurring motif most impressive on 'Hearse To Graveyard' over some atonal, Miles Davis-esque keys), soul bossa and harmony-muted parp, but the pair really fly on 'Liberation', emancipating themselves from instrumental slavishness with a bouncing bomb of a bassline, attention-deficit flute and glad-bursting rhythm guitar in a Herbie Hancock/Bob Dorough bag; surprising this one's been missed by the funk compilers. Most of DONNY's catalogue has appeared on CD at one point or another; why oh why has '..CHARLESTON BLUE' been passed over? *BG*

Album rating: *7

COMMITTED

2000 (US 98m) Gold Circle Entertainment / Miramax Films (R)

Film genre: romantic comedy/drama/road movie

Top guns: s-w + dir: Lisa Krueger ← MANNY & LO

Stars: Heather Graham *(Joline)* ← BOOGIE NIGHTS ← EVEN COWGIRLS GET THE BLUES ← SHOUT, Casey Affleck *(Jay)* ← GOOD WILL HUNTING, Luke Wilson *(Carl)* → MASKED AND ANONYMOUS → HOOT, Goran Visnjic *(Niko/Neil)*, Patricia Velasquez *(Carmen)* → TURN IT UP, Mark Ruffalo *(T-Bo)* ← 54, Alfonso Arau *(Grampy)* ← WALKER ← el TOPO, Kim Dickens *(Jenny)* → THINGS BEHIND THE SUN, Summer Phoenix *(Meg)* ← SLC PUNK! ← GIRL, Clea Duvall *(Mimi)* ← a SLIPPING-DOWN LIFE ← GIRL / → the SLAUGHTER RULE, **Mary Kay Place** *(psychiatrist)* ← MANNY & LO ← JUST MY IMAGINATION ← MORE AMERICAN GRAFFITI ← BOUND FOR GLORY / → KILLER DILLER, **Art Alexakis** *(New York car thief)*

Storyline: Joline is the committed girl, in this case to married life with husband Carl. When Carl suddenly runs off to El Paso Joline sets off after him for an explanation, and has a series of adventures and men along the way. Eventually she finds Carl cuddling up to the curvaceous Carmen, and begins taking an interest in guy-next-door Neil. Can her ancient Mexican medicine man find a cure for Joline's marriage or will the pair go their separate ways? *JZ*

Movie rating: *5

Visual: dvd

Off the record: Art Alexakis is frontman for the Portland, Oregon band, Everclear.

Various Artists // CALEXICO

Apr 00. (cd) *Chapter III; <CHA 0200>*
– Mercy mercy (DON COVAY & THE GOODTIMERS) / Release me (and let love in) (ESTHER PHILLIPS) / Wichita lineman (GLEN CAMPBELL) / Folsom Prison blues (JOHNNY CASH) / Hello walls (FARON YOUNG) / Donna (RITCHIE VALENS) / Rueda de fuego (Ring of fire) (VAQUEROS DEL OESTE) // Bliss – Spokes / How do you know you've gone too far / Empty home / Snake magic / TBO / Chasing Carri / It was me / Tested to the limit – Spiritual vigil / A glimpse / Stealing power / Texas / Grampy / Shape shifting / Jealous / Still committed / This is what you do / El morro.

S/track review: This excellent, understated collection mixes a small, quality selection of R&B, pop and country with a full original score by Tucson, Arizona duo CALEXICO. Kicking off with 'Mercy Mercy' by DON COVAY & THE GOODTIMERS (keen ears might recognise the work of JIMI HENDRIX on bluesy guitar), 'COMMITTED' quickly establishes a tone of laid back class. Hits from ESTHER PHILLIPS and GLEN CAMPBELL follow, well known perhaps, but never overplayed. By the time the Man In Black introduces himself on 'Folsom Prison Blues', it's clear you're in good hands. A Spanglish version of CASH's 'Ring Of Fire' by VAQUEROS DEL OESTE leads into CALEXICO's original score. Mostly re-recorded, vocal-less versions of previous album tracks, the 17 short cues here are a worthwhile listen nonetheless. Recorded at the same time as their album, 'Hot Rail', CALEXICO manage to take such loaded terms as "musicianship", "improvisational" and, here, "instrumental", and make them respectable again, if only in relation to their own work. When you make music that is so inherently cinematic, too much messing with an already successful formula would be foolish, while removing the vocals doesn't detract from the songs but instead gives the already expansive music more room to breathe. Taking elements of mariachi, country and even post-rock, CALEXICO provide a spaghetti-western flavoured desert dreamscape, with shimmering guitars and jazzy, patterned drums. The standout tracks, 'Texas', 'Jealous' and 'El Morro', are so evocative of a dreamy border-town milieu that one suspects they could provide ready-made authenticity for any filmmaker smart enough to use them. Perhaps, therefore, an unnecessary purchase for CALEXICO fans, but for the uninitiated, 'COMMITTED' is a soundtrack that deserves to be considered apart from the under-performing Heather Graham vehicle from which it originates. *SW*

Album rating: *6.5

the COMMITTEE

1968 (UK 58m short b&w) Craytic / Planet (18)

Film genre: avant-garde/experimental docu-drama

Top guns: dir: Peter Sykes / s-w: Max Steuer

Stars: Paul Jones *(hitchhiker/central figure)* ← PRIVILEGE, Jimmy Gardner *(boss)* → TAKE ME HIGH → FLAME, Robert Lloyd *(Committee director)*, Pauline Munro *(girl)*, Tom Kempinski *(victim)* → MRS. BROWN, YOU'VE GOT A LOVELY DAUGHTER, **Arthur Brown** *(performer)* → TOMMY → CLUB PARADISE → JAILBIRD ROCK → I PUT A SPELL ON ME

Storyline: A hitchhiker accepts a lift from a rich businessman and, completely bored with his jargon, takes the opportunity of guillotining his "big-head" with his Mercedes car hood. Some years later, while working as a draughtsman, the central figure comes before a mysterious Committee to explain his murderous actions. *MCS*

Movie rating: *5

Visual: dvd 2005 += w/ extras (no audio OST by PINK FLOYD)

Off the record: Paul Jones (lead singer of Manfred Mann at the time) went on to star (among other films & TV plays) in 1972 horror, 'Demons Of The Mind'. Jones and Max Steuer contributed the title track (to the DVD), which was performed by the HOMEMADE ORCHESTRA (aka TIM WHITEHEAD). **Arthur Brown** (i.e. Crazy World Of . . .) highlighted their current UK chart-topper, 'Fire'. **PINK FLOYD** (their first studio outing with David Gilmour replacing Barrett!) grace the soundtrack, which is basically just incidental music, untitled and much sought after; a poor-quality bootleg has been in circulation since 1975 – complete with dialogue! We await its proper release. *MCS*

COMMUNE

2005 (US 78m w/b&w) Five Points Media

Film genre: political/social documentary

Top guns: dir: (+ s-w) Jonathan Berman ← the SHVITZ

Stars: Peter Coyote *(himself)* ← a LITTLE TRIP TO HEAVEN ← the MAN INSIDE ← BAJA OKLAHOMA ← HEARTBREAKERS ← TIMERIDER: THE ADVENTURE OF LYLE SWANN, Cedar Seeger *(himself)*, Mahaj Seeger *(herself)*, Osha Neumann *(himself)*, Rachel Neumann *(herself)*, Yeshi Neumann *(himself)*, Petey Brucker *(himself)*, Elsa Marley *(herself)*, Richard Marley *(himself)*, Geba Greenberg *(herself)*, Kenoli Oleari *(himself)*, Michael Tierra *(himself)*, Efrem Korngold *(himself)*, Harriet Beinfield *(herself)*

Storyline: This documentary charts the progress of the Black Bear communal farm, founded in 1968 and still going strong. Residents are interviewed to find out why they left mainstream society, and others who have left tell why they went back to city life. Some still remember the early days when the farm was buried under snow and survival skills came to the fore. As the FBI keeps a wary eye on the present incumbents, many now just grin and Bear it. *JZ*

Movie rating: *7

Visual: dvd

Off the record: ELLIOTT SHARP (b. 1 Mar'51, Cleveland, Ohio, USA) had been playing piano since the age of six, the protege performing only a few years later. His subsequent work was of the experimental and avant-garde factor, having studied as both a scientist and under the wing of synthesizer pioneer Robert Moog. Graduating from Buffalo, he relocated to New York City in the late 70s, already having issued a couple of LPs on his own 'Zoar' imprint. Performing at the Mudd Club, SHARP became a worthy figure in the NY underground scene, while collaborations with John Zorn kept his profile reasonably high. Influenced by free-form avant-jazz, FRANK ZAPPA and contemporary blues, multi-instrumentalist Elliott was everybody's favourite improviser and indeed, guitarist. Check out the albums, 'I/S/M' (1981) and his 'S.S.T.'-period sets, 'Tessalation Row' (1987) & 'Hammer, Anvil, Stirrup' (1989). Incidentally, songs not included on SHARP's OST are 'The Ballad Of Cedar And Mahaj' (by CEDAR SEEGER) and 'New Day Coming' (by the LILLIES). *MCS*

ELLIOTT SHARP

Jul 05. (cd) *Zoar; <ZOaR 025>* □ [-]
– Setting forth / Looking / Goin to La-La / Shadow of Shasta / Teargasser / Norther / Mountains laughin / Rural / Commune rock / BlackBear rag / That winter / Mrkana Sarkastaka / Domebuilders / Losing ground / Panic / Shivalila / Etheric.

S/track review: To unearth ELLIOTT SHARP's 'COMMUNE' has to be a reviewer's dream, albeit it does get rather horizontal at times. Released on his own 'Zoar' imprint, Elliott's album – right from opener, 'Setting Forth' – conjures up images of Hendrix, Garcia, et al. The electricity produced on this set could generate the whole of New York rather than a "commune", the underrated (well, outside the US) multi-instrumentalist, SHARP, re-creating the late 60s era in one fell swoop of a record. Track two, six and twelve, 'Looking', 'Norther' and 'Mrkana Sarkastaka' respectively, are Cooder-ish but way too short, while the longer 'Goin To La-La' takes on a Neil Young-in-Buffalo Springfield persona. One begins to think Elliott is some past-master's music forger when you hear, 'Teargasser', an explosion of Hendrix kissing the sky with feedback – or something more mystical. Guest singer, MICHELLE CASILLAS, is groovily dreamy and effective on two cues, 'Mountains Laughin' and 'Losing Ground', while 'Shadow Of Shasta' and 'Rural' are basically in the "Jefferson Airplane Takes Off"-mould – unplugged and acoustic. Things lighten up somewhat with 'BlackBear Rag' (featuring DAVID HOFSTRA on acoustic bass), a jaunty little ditty that probably fits better on film. 'That Winter' is as bleak as its title, although toke-in-hand it could be one smooth operator, in a Carlos Santana kind of way. Throughout SHARP's experimental show, drummer SIM CAIN is more than capable of letting his leader speak through his guitar, while three variously-styled tracks bookend the hour-long album, 'Panic', 'Shivalila' and 'Etheric'. *MCS*

Album rating: *7

□ Jack CONRAD segment
(⇒ the MONKEY HUSTLE)

CONTAMINATION

US title 'ALIEN CONTAMINATION' / video 'TOXIC SPAWN'

1980 (W.Ger/Ita 90m) Cannon Group (15)

Film genre: Sci-fi horror/monster movie

Top guns: s-w: Luigi Cozzi (Lewis Coates) (+ dir), Erich Tomek

Stars: Ian McCulloch *(Comm. Ian Hubbard)*, Louise Marleau *(Col. Stella*

Holmes), Marino Mase *(Lt. Tony Aris)* → TENEBRE, Siegfried Rauch *(Hamilton)*, Gisela Hahn *(Perla de la Cruz)* ← WHITE "POP" JESUS

Storyline: Alien (in part!) – without the effects. A monster from outer space (made from papier-mache!) infects a human, who in turn riddles the Earth with olive-coloured eggs, which discharge a poisonous substance to make humans explode. Will they take over the world? *MCS*

Movie rating: *3.5

Visual: video + dvd

Off the record: Director Luigi Cozzi was a protege of Dario Argento, thus the **GOBLIN** house-band connection. Before you get too excited, the Ian McCulloch here is the Glaswegian-born actor and nothing to do with the mainman of Echo & The Bunnymen – sometimes you have to point out the obvious! *MCS*

—

GOBLIN

1981. (lp) *Cinevox; (MDF 33.142)* [–] Italy [–]
– Connexion / Withy / Bikini island / Flood / Pillage / The carver / Rush / Fright / Time is on / Ogre / Quiet drops. *(cd-iss. Apr01 on 'Cinevox'+=; CD-MDF 340)* – Withy / Contamination / The carver / Fright / Contamination.

S/track review: After a somewhat poor showing for the disco-orientated 'SQUADRA ANTIGANGSTERS' (1979), GOBLIN – now down to FABIO PIGNATELLI and AGOSTINO MARANGOLO – restored their Prog-rock credentials to days when 'PROFONDO ROSSO' (1975) and 'SUSPIRIA' (1977) were all the "Giallo" rage. Opener 'Connexion' wept gothic emotion over a programmed keyboard, while track 2, 'Withy', built up an atmospheric rhythm into a powerful Genesis-like crescendo. While these and other (2 to 3 minute) tracks could certainly have withstood extended Prog-style renderings, fans of GOBLIN were in no way complaining. However, on reflection, jazz-rock numbers such as 'Bikini Island', 'Pillage' and even OTT synth exponent, 'Flood' frustrated in their attempts at musical self-indulgence. Yes, a little too schizophrenic for some (Prog-rock was all but dead in the water in most parts of Europe, especially the UK!), although 2-minute cuts such as 'Time Is On' and 'Quiet Drops' still heralded the GOBLIN of old. Guests on the album comprised of AGOSTINO's brother ANTONIO on sax, ROBERTO PULEO on guitars and M. GUARINI on keyboards. *MCS*

Album rating: *6 / cd+ *6

CONTINENTAL CIRCUS

1969 (Fra 102m) Filmanthrope

Film genre: sports documentary

Top guns: s-w + dir: Jerome Laperrousaz → AMOUGIES → PRISONER IN THE STREET → MADE IN JAMAICA

Stars: Jack Findlay *(himself)*, Giacomo Agostini *(himself)*, Terry Denehy *(himself)*, Santiago Herrero *(himself)*, Keith Turner *(himself)*, Nanou *(herself)*

Storyline: Motorcycle racing and the drivers behind such a precarious profession; the subject of impending sponsorships and money come into the equasion all too often. Australian, Jack Findlay, and playboy champion, Giacomo Agostini, are the main characters of this dangerous sport. *MCS*

Movie rating: *5.5

Visual: video

Off the record: GONG (see below)

—

GONG

1972. (lp) *Philips; (6332 033)* [ ] [–]
– Blues for Findlay / Continental circus world / What do you want? / Blues for Findlay (instrumental). *<US cd-iss.1995 on 'New Rose'; 4326> (UK cd-iss. May96 on 'Mantra'; 642089)*

S/track review: "Seems like a tropical fish to me" as GONG subsequently and so succinctly put it. The early 70s were indeed a weird and wonderful time zone to be in, psychedelia had a new home under the progressive rock roof, and one of its underlings, Australian-born guitarist/vocalist DAEVID ALLEN had found sanctuary with communal, French-based band, GONG. Alongside his new missus, GILLI SMYTH (she of spaced-out, whispering "grass" vox), saxophonist DIDIER MALHERBE, drummer PIP PYLE and bassist CHRISTIAN TRITSCH, GONG were basically way out there and from another planet – ironically, Planet Gong was a billing they took during later years – when they formed in 1968. With only the one LP ('Magick Brother, Mystic Sister') in their musical account (we could also count ALLEN's 'Banana Moon' w/ GONG if one was pushed), pot-headed pixie and main song contributor GILLI got together with French filmmaker, JEROME LAPERROUSAZ to write a few numbers (the first two) for this documentary. You could describe GONG's excursion into post-psychedelic rock as jazzed-up prog-rock with a tripped-out, playful twist that only this band could carry off. 'Blues For Findlay' kicks off the set in fine jam-rocking style, a sort of Hawkwind meets Pink Floyd, ALLEN getting into gear so to speak as he rallies off simplistic lyrics that conjure up the world of motorbike racing. Track 2, 'Continental Circus World', set the controls for the heart of the race track, revs per minute provided by the bikes themselves looped over the French National Anthem, while excerpts from the film are collaged with sparse lyrics ("Time is your life, time is your world") that belies the celluloid theme. Ditto track 3, 'What Do You Want?', totally Pink Floyd-on-'A Saucerful Of Secrets', although with repetitive mantras, gyrating glissed-out guitars, playful sax and GILLI with her come-to-me siren vox – wow. And where has one heard these lyrics, "What you want, what you really, really want"; thankfully there was no resemblance in style or fashion to another 5-piece. The downside of this timeless gem is that: Did we really need an instrumental take of 'Blues For Findlay' tagged on as the lengthy track No.4. It's not every day one recommends a bootleg, but with – even the Spalax CD being deleted and – four additional tracks, it might be worth emptying your pockets or indeed your bank accounts. If you want to sample GONG at their best and most inspirational, look out their classic LP, 'Camembert Electrique'; one could buy this new at the budget price of 49p way back in '71. A mention also has to go to why the makers of DAEVID ALLEN's unreleased film score for 1971's 'Du Cote D'Ouvet' have left it in the can, or is that Cannes. *MCS*

Album rating: *6

Ry COODER

Born: Ryland Peter Cooder, 15 Mar'47, Los Angeles, California, USA. One of American popular music's true rennaissance men, multi-instrumentalist RY COODER began his recording career as a session player, reeling off vicious slide guitar licks for the magical Captain Beefheart, the ROLLING STONES and Little Feat amongst others. A formidable talent for stringed instruments (including banjo, dulcimer, mandolin and sax), together with a seemingly insatiably eclectic music taste and reverence for his chosen metier, enabled COODER to embark on an all-encompassing, ethnographically oriented exploration of his country's popular song. Like a rock'n'roll Alan Lomax, Ry retrieved and re-appraised, rescued and re-invented, synthesized and absorbed songs from genres as varied as blues, C&W, ragtime, gospel, field hollers, vaudeville, folk and R&B. By the mid-70s, he'd expanded his vision to include foreign traditions, working with the likes of Tex-Mex accordianist Flaco Jimenez and Hawaiian slack-key guitarist Gabby Pahinui. While it'd be a further two decades before he'd fully realise his world music aspirations, COODER spent most of the 80s composing film scores, an area to which his intuitive, wide screen musical imagination was well suited, and to which he'd inexorably gravitated. Not that he was a complete novice in the field, having already contributed stinging bottleneck to the JACK NITZSCHE-scored, Donald Cammell/Nicholas Roeg masterpiece, 'PERFORMANCE' (1970), and the less highly regarded 'CANDY' (1968). More recently, he'd also collaborated with Nitzsche on the acclaimed working class drama, 'Blue Collar' (1978). Yet with his first full self-authored soundtrack, 'The LONG RIDERS' (1980), COODER announced himself as a major scoring talent, one which would outshine his conventional – and increasingly rare – studio albums of the same period. The movie soundtrack also began a lengthy association with director Walter Hill, although the two Western themed films for which he commissioned COODER were different beasts with very different soundtracks. While the score, in its fairly faithful resurrection of Civil War era song, wasn't so different from much of Ry's early material, 'GERONIMO: AN AMERICAN LEGEND' (1993) came at a time when COODER was immersing himself in the music of other cultures. As such, it echoed to the sounds of traditions as far and removed as Tuvan throat singing, as much as it did to the musical heritage of the Old West. These two records bookended an incredibly prolific and creative period which would see COODER's soundtrack work quietly garner ever more critical acclaim, even as it become increasingly experimental. While soundtracks for 'The BORDER' (1982), 'CROSSROADS' (1986) and 'BLUE CITY' were not exactly departures from COODER's trademark roots rock sound, 'ALAMO BAY' (1985) subtly incorporated elements of Asian instrumentation, while the spectral 'PARIS, TEXAS' (1983/4) was an exercise in desert minimalism which signalled a willingness to move beyond his standard musical parameters. COODER even won a Grammy for Best Recording for Children with his back porch score for the Robin Williams-narrated cable TV production, 'Pecos Bill' (1988). The menacing 'TRESPASS' (1992) and 'LAST MAN STANDING' (1996), meanwhile, were almost avant-garde in their approach, a corollary to the world music experimentation he'd instigated via his dazzling early 90s collaboration with Hindustani guitarist, V.M. Bhatt ('Meeting by the River'). Indeed, one highlight from the latter, 'Isa Lei', was subsequently used in the acclaimed Death Row drama, 'DEAD MAN WALKING' (1995), to which COODER also contributed bottleneck guitar. The man's global searching reached its apogee in 1997 with 'BUENA VISTA SOCIAL CLUB', the recording of which COODER commented as having "felt that I had trained all my life for". It made global stars of its veteran Cuban participants and inspired a wonderful Wim Wenders documentary. COODER continued to work in film, even if the success of his Cuban adventures overshadowed what was fast becoming one of the most consistent, and most consistently innovative, careers in film scoring. The late 90s found him creating music for another Wenders effort, 'The END OF VIOLENCE' (1997), and US electoral satire 'PRIMARY COLORS' (1998). Question is, whatever happened to the 'Southern Comfort' (1981) OST? You'll just have to make do with three tracks on the 1995 double soundtrack compilation, 'Music By Ry Cooder'. *BG*

- **filmography** (composer) –

the Long Riders *(1980 OST =>)* / Southern Comfort *(1981)* / **the Border** *(1982 OST =>)* / **Paris, Texas** *(1984 OST =>)* / **Streets Of Fire** *(1984 OST w/ V/A =>)* / Brewster's Millions *(1985)* / **Alamo Bay** *(1985 OST =>)* / **Blue City** *(1986 OST =>)* / **Crossroads** *(1986 OST =>)* / **Johnny Handsome** *(1989 OST =>)* / **Trespass** *(1992 OST + V/A =>)* / **Geronimo: An American Legend** *(1993 OST =>)* / **Last Man Standing** *(1996 OST =>)* / **the End Of Violence** *(1997 OST => other by Elmer Bernstein)* / **Primary Colors** *(1998 OST =>)* / **Buena Vista Social Club** *(1998/99 OST by BUENA VISTA SOCIAL CLUB =>)*

– compilations, etc. –

RY COODER: Music By Ry Cooder

Jun 95. (d-cd) *WEA; <(9362 45987-2)>* ☐ ☐
– Paris, Texas / Theme from Southern Comfort / Theme from Alamo Bay / Across the borderline / Highway 23 / Bomber bash / Greenhouse / Nice bike / I like your eyes / Main theme / See you in Hell, blind boy / Feelin' bad blues / Swamp walk / Angola / Viola Lee blues / The Long Riders / Archie's funeral (hold to God's unchanging hand) / Jesse James / King of the street / Sunny's tune / No quiero / Cruising with Rafe / Klan meeting / I can't walk this time – The prestige / East St. Louis / Goose and Lucky / Goyakla is coming / Canoes upstream / Cancion mixteca / Maria / Bound for Canaan (Sieber & Davis) / Bound for Canaan (Sieber & Davis) (The 6th cavalry) / Train to Florida / Houston in two seconds.

COOL BREEZE

1972 (US 101m) Metro-Goldwyn-Mayer (X)

Film genre: crime drama

Top guns: s-w + dir: Barry Pollack (au: W.R. Burnett)

Stars: Thalmus Rasulala *(Sidney Lord Jones)* → BLACULA → WILLIE DYNAMITE → CORNBREAD, EARL AND ME → FRIDAY FOSTER → BUCKTOWN → ADIOS AMIGO → LAMBADA → NEW JACK CITY, Judy Pace *(Obalese Eaton)* ← COTTON COMES TO HARLEM, Jim Watkins *(Travis Battle)*, Lincoln Kilpatrick *(Lt. Brian Knowles)* → TOGETHER BROTHERS, Raymond St. Jacques *(Bill Mercer)* ← COTTON COMES TO HARLEM ← UP TIGHT / → the FINAL COMEDOWN → COME BACK, CHARLESTON BLUE → BOOK OF NUMBERS, Sam Laws *(Stretch Finian)* → TRUCK TURNER → GET CRAZY, Margaret Avery *(Lark)* → HELL UP IN HARLEM → the JACKSONS: AN AMERICAN DREAM, Pamela Grier *(Mona)* ← BLACK MAMA, WHITE MAMA ← BEYOND THE VALLEY OF THE DOLLS / → COFFY → FOXY BROWN → BUCKTOWN → FRIDAY FOSTER → SHEBA, BABY → BILL & TED'S BOGUS JOURNEY → JACKIE BROWN → BONES, Paula Kelly *(Martha Harris)* → TROUBLE MAN → the SPOOK WHO SAT BY THE DOOR → THREE TOUGH GUYS, Wally Taylor *(John Battle)* ← COTTON COMES TO HARLEM / → SHAFT'S BIG SCORE! → LORD SHANGO → CROSSROADS, Stack Pierce *(Tinker)* → TROUBLE MAN → CORNBREAD, EARL AND ME → NO WAY BACK, **Bill Henderson** *(minister)* → TROUBLE MAN → CORNBREAD, EARL AND ME / → GET CRAZY, Rudy Challenger *(Roy Harris)* → SHEBA, BABY, Edmund Cambridge *(bus driver)* → the FINAL COMEDOWN → MELINDA → TROUBLE MAN → FRIDAY FOSTER → BILL & TED'S BOGUS JOURNEY, Royce Wallace *(Emma Mercer)* ← GOODBYE, COLUMBUS / → WILLIE DYNAMITE → CROSSROADS, Frank McRae *(Barry; Mercer's servant)* → SHAFT IN AFRICA → PIPE DREAMS, Charles Cyphers *(backstage police officer)* → TRUCK TURNER → ELVIS: THE MOVIE → DEATH WISH II → HONKYTONK MAN

Storyline: An Afro-American revision of 'The Asphalt Jungle', with a paroled convict, Sidney Lord Jones, hatching an L.A. jewellery heist in order to both fund his revolutionary dreams of bankrolling black business and furnish himself with a healthy pension fund. *BG*

Movie rating: *4.5

Visual: video

Off the record: SOLOMON BURKE (see below)

SOLOMON BURKE (composer: GENE PAGE)

Jul 72. (lp) *M.G.M.; <1SE 35ST>* ☐ ☐
– Cool breeze / PSR 1983 / The bus / Icbyatht W.T.? (based on

William Tell overture) / Get up and do something for yourself / Love's street and fool's road / It must be love / Fight back / Then I want to come home (instr.) / Then I want to come home (vocal) / We're almost home.

S/track review: Like many a 60s soul legend, SOLOMON BURKE fancied himself a piece of the blaxploitation action in the early 70s, with a view to kickstarting an ailing career and sweetening a new contract with 'M.G.M.'. That wasn't to be but he did leave behind this great, GENE PAGE-orchestrated soundtrack, recorded the same year as 'BLACULA' but – at least in one moment of whimsical madness – more 'BREWSTER McLOUD'; 'Icbyatht W.T.?' has BURKE chewing his teeth like a cross between Roy Rogers and Bill Murray's Hunter S. Thompson while PAGE brandishes Rossini's overture from William Tell. Have faith though, ye of little funk, the rest of the album blows cooler than a Siberian summer. Instrumentals like 'The Bus' and 'Fight Back' are pure PAGE, roiling, liquefied rhythm, full of cliff-hanging breakdowns, stop-light brass and sepentine lead guitar; 'The Bus', especially, sounds culled from 'BLACULA'. As usual, the actual musicians go uncredited, unfair given the tightness and the commitment of some of the individual performances. BURKE himself goes for the full Isaac Hayes monty on the title theme, talking up his mojo over grinding funk-rock arrangements, possibly the heaviest in the blaxploitation canon. It would've made a killer single but 'M.G.M.' went with a ballad instead, testifying proof – along with the excellent 'PSR 1983' – of just how much BURKE's soul-got-country style weighed on the art of Van Morrison, himself at the top of his game in 1972. The thunderous counsel of that voice – the man was a fully paid up preacher before he ever entered an 'Atlantic' studio – easily slips into the role of 70s ghetto crooner, and when he's not making like an earthier Hayes – best heard on the piston-pumping 'Get Up And Do Something For Yourself' – he opens his throat and rips his own lungs out on the likes of 'Love's Street And Fool's Road' (his very own 'Soulsville'), 'It Must Be Love' and epic organ hymn, 'Then I Want To Come Home', backed up, according to the liner notes, by eight of his own 20-odd children (nothing compared to his 84 grandchildren..). If soul runs in the seed, this underappreciated soundtrack's the evidence. *BG*

Album rating: *7

– spinoff releases, etc. –

SOLOMON BURKE: We're Almost Home / Fight Back

Jun 72. (7") *<14402>* ☐ ☐

SOLOMON BURKE: Get Up And Do Something For Yourself

Aug 72. (7") *<14425>* ☐ ☐

Billy CORGAN

Born: 17 Mar'67, Elk Grove, Illinois, USA. The singing, song-writing and guitar playing mastermind behind 90s alternative giants Smashing Pumpkins, BILLY CORGAN developed his own individual, complex and occasionally self indulgent take on the evolution of rock. Despite infamous personnel problems, his band released a series of landmark albums including the multi million selling 'Siamese Dream' (1993) and sprawling double set, 'Mellon Collie And The Infinite Sadness' (1995). The mid-90s also saw CORGAN (a onetime film student) branch out into film composition on the 1996 Ron Howard thriller, 'RANSOM' (itself an update of the 1956 original), bolstering James Horner's conventional score with a series of unsettling, abrasively evocative industrial cues. 'Eye', the Smashing Pumpkins' contribution to David Lynch's 'Lost Highway' (1997) was almost placid in comparison, while their theme for 'Batman & Robin' (1997), 'The End Is The Beginning Is The End', made the UK Top 10. Prior to his millennial dissolution of the 'Pumpkins, CORGAN also contributed to the score of Rupert Wainwright's 'Exorcist'-inspired chiller, 'STIGMATA' (1999). While he finally took full scoring credits in Jonas Akerlund's 'Spun' (2002), the movie's acoustic sketches have yet to make it to soundtrack. *BG*

- **filmography** (composer) –

Ransom *(1996 OST w/ James Horner =>)* / **Stigmata** *(1999 OST w/ MIKE GARSON & V/A =>)* / Spun *(2002)*

CORNBREAD, EARL AND ME

1975 (US 94m) American International Pictures (PG)

Film genre: sports/urban melodrama

Top guns: dir: Joseph Manduke → BEATLEMANIA: THE MOVIE / s-w: Leonard Lamensdorf (au: Ronald Fair)

Stars: Moses Gunn *(Benjamin Blackwell)* ← SHAFT ← SHAFT'S BIG SCORE! / → AARON LOVES ANGELA, Keith Wilkes *(Nathaniel "Cornbread" Hamilton)*, Tierre Turner *(Earl Carter)* ← FRIDAY FOSTER / → BUCKTOWN → the CROW, Bernie Casey *(Officer Larry Atkins)* ← CLEOPATRA JONES / → BROTHERS → BILL & TED'S EXCELLENT ADVENTURE, Rosalind Cash *(Sarah Robinson)* ← MELINDA / → the MONKEY HUSTLE, Madge Sinclair *(Leona Hamilton)* → LEADBELLY → the LION KING, Thalmus Rasulala *(Charlie)* ← FRIDAY FOSTER ← WILLIE DYNAMITE ← BLACULA ← COOL BREEZE / → BUCKTOWN → ADIOS AMIGO → LAMBADA, Antonio Fargas *(One-Eye)* ← FOXY BROWN ← CLEOPATRA JONES ← ACROSS 110th STREET ← SHAFT / → CAR WASH → FIRESTARTER → SOUL SURVIVOR, Lawrence Fishburne *(Wilford Robinson)* → FAST BREAK → DEATH WISH II → SCHOOL DAZE → WHAT'S LOVE GOT TO DO WITH IT → EVENT HORIZON → the SOUL OF A MAN, Charles Lampkin *(Fred Jenkins)* ← WATERMELON MAN, Stefan Gierasch *(Sgt. Danaher)* ← CLAUDINE, Stack Pierce *(Sam Hamilton)* ← TROUBLE MAN ← COOL BREEZE / → NO WAY BACK, **Bill Henderson** *(Watkins)* ← TROUBLE MAN ← COOL BREEZE / → GET CRAZY, J. Jay Saunders *(Mr. Johnson)* ← SLAUGHTER'S BIG RIP-OFF / → THIEF → HOUSE PARTY, Pamela Jones *(Diane)* ← the FINAL COMEDOWN

Storyline: A young, gifted and black basketball player, Cornbread (played by Keith Wilkes, who actually went on to play for L.A. Lakers in real life) is erroneously gunned down by police on the eve of his college scholarship. *BG*

Movie rating: *6

Visual: video + dvd

Off the record: The **BLACKBYRDS** (see below)

---

the BLACKBYRDS (composer: DONALD BYRD)

Jun 75. (lp) *Fantasy; <F 9483>* ☐ ☐
– Cornbread / The One-Eye two-step / Mother-son theme / A heavy town / One-gun salute / The gym fight / Riot / Soulful source / Mother-Son talk / At the carnival / Candy store dilemma / Wilford's gone / Mother-son bedroom talk / Courtroom emotions / Cornbread. *<(re+UK-iss.+cd.May95 on 'Beat Goes Public' cd/lp; CDBGPM/BGPD1 094)> <cd re-iss. Mar01 as 'On The Movies' on 'Prestige'+=; 24255-2>* – The DYNAMITE BROTHERS by Charles Earland

S/track review: A one-time Jazz Messenger who went on to scale the heights of academe, DONALD BYRD was the most learned funk bandleader on the block in the mid-70s. He might've been chairman of the Black Music Dept at Washington DC's Howard University (where Roberta Flack also taught before getting her big break), but he was more ebony street than ivory tower, cutting the biggest selling album in 'Blue Note' history ('Black Byrd') and leading a group of his more talented students to R&B chart domination as the BLACKBYRDS. The band eased into the scene in 1974, pissing off jazz purists with the brilliant, hypnotic grease-funk of 'Do It Fluid', and releasing a series of great albums. The best of these, 'City Life' (1975), arrived the same year they released their late period blaxploitation effort, 'CORNBREAD, EARL AND ME', and while the film, the soundtrack, and even the band themselves have been pretty much forgotten over time, this album is worth a second look, if only for the trippy, soul shuffling title track. The "man with a plan" line had already been used by Stevie Wonder, but instead of dollar bills, BYRD's character has a basketball in his mitt; it's hardly typical blaxploitaiton subject matter, or even 'He Got Game' standard, but it works. There's plenty of tight, small group instrumental funk ('The One-Eye Two-Step' and the 'The Gym Fight'), and unsurprisingly given his musical erudition and jazz background, BYRD takes the role of composer seriously enough to use full blown orchestration at will, and has few qualms about wading into the wider context of film scoring: 'One-Gun Salute's baritone sax line honks along in the spirit of Lalo Schifrin's 'Mission Impossible', 'Riot's choral parts pine lugubriously for a basketball player with no name and 'At The Carnival' sounds like one of John Barry's weirder tangents. But 'Wilford's Gone' is the one track which predicts BYRD's more holistic use of strings on his proto-disco classic, 'Places And Spaces' (1975), and this album might've held together a little better if he'd stuck to the kind of loose-limbed assignments which had already made his band such A-grade funk graduates. *BG*

Album rating: *6

☐ Don COSTA segment
(⇒ the SOUL OF NIGGER CHARLEY)

Elvis COSTELLO

Born: Declan Patrick MacManus, 25 Aug'54, Paddington, London, England. With his Irish heritage, geekish image, fiercely literate songwriting and hopeless eclecticism, ELVIS COSTELLO cut one of the more striking swathes through the new wave landscape of the late 70s and early 80s. Given his subsequent elevation to the rank of time served elder statesman, and the raft of diverse and often fairly high brow compositional collaborations under his belt, it's perhaps surprising that he he hasn't delved more deeply into the world of film scoring. The first of many big screen cameos came, appropriately enough given COSTELLO's then overt politicism, with tortuous transatlantic satire, 'Americathon' (1979), in which he performed 'Crawling To The U.S.A.' and additionally had his 1978 hit, '(I Don't Want To Go To) Chelsea' included on the soundtrack. This was followed by the man's most obscure cinematic contribution: a theme song for British teen comedy, 'Party! Party!' (1983) which languished outside the UK Top 40 in late '82. More memorable was his appearance as a harassed magician in 'No Surrender' (1986), Alan Bleasdale's blackly brilliant take on Irish sectarianism transplanted to Liverpool. He also appeared – alongside his new wife, Cait O'Riordan (of the POGUES fame), and a plethora of other music and movie hipsters – as a caffeine dispensing butler in Alex Cox's lamentable spaghetti western spoof, 'STRAIGHT TO HELL' (1987). In his role as producer of the POGUES' folk-punk masterpiece, 'Rum, Sodomy & The Lash' (1985), COSTELLO had actually been credited under his birth name, DECLAN MacMANUS and it was under this moniker that he scored his first film, 'The COURIER' (1988). An Irish crime drama with O'Riordan in a starring role, the movie came with a soundtrack which bolstered the man's score with tracks from native stars such as U2 and Hothouse Flowers. While those artists were ironically enjoying the most successful periods of their career, COSTELLO himself was in something of a creative trough. Amidst the weak albums of the 'Warners' years, perhaps his most interesting output came with the music (co-written with ex-Gryphon multi-instrumentalist Richard Harvey) for 'G.B.H.' (1991), another searing Bleasdale TV drama originally shown on Channel 4. He was to team up with Harvey again in 1995 for the music to another TV series starring Robert Lindsay, 'Jake's Progress'. Almost a decade after his last acting appearance, COSTELLO unexpectedly popped up in SPICE GIRLS vehicle, 'SPICEWORLD' (1997), a prelude to his cameo in 'Austin Powers: The Spy Who Shagged Me' (1998), wherein he extended his album length Burt Bacharach collaboration with an onscreen performance of Bacharach-David classic, 'I'll Never Fall In Love Again'. The late 90s also found him contributing the track, 'I Throw My Toys' – performed by No Doubt – to kids animation, 'The Rugrats Movie' (1998), and making a cameo in Risa Bramon Garcia's '200 Cigarettes' (1999), which also featured his version of Nick Lowe's '(What's So Funny 'Bout) Peace, Love And Understanding' on its new wave soundtrack. Come the new millennium, COSTELLO also belatedly resumed his film composing career, scoring French film, 'Sans Plomb' (2000) and Neil LaBute's psychological drama, 'The Shape Of Things' (2003). A cameo in Adam Goldberg's 'I Love Your Work', followed in 2004, as well as a performance of Cole Porter's 'Let's Misbehave' in the Irwin Winkler-directed biopic, 'De-Lovely' (2004). *BG*

- **filmography** (composer) {acting} –

Americathon *(1979 {c} + on OST)* / **Concerts For The People Of Kampuchea** *(1980 {p} on OST by V/A =>)* / Party Party *(1982 hit on V/A OST)* / No Surrender *(1986 {b})* / **Straight To Hell** *(1987 {a})* / **Black & White Night** *(1987 {p})* / **the Courier** *(1988 as DECLAN McMANUS & V/A =>)* / G.B.H. *(1991 TV-mini w/ Richard Harvey; see future edition)* / Family *(1994 TV-mini w/ John Harle)* / September Songs: The Music Of Kurt Weill *(1995 docu {p})* / Jake's Progress *(1995 TV-mini w/ Richard Harvey; see future edition)* / **Spice World** *(1998 {c})* / 200 Cigarettes *(1999 {c})* / Austin Powers: The Spy Who Shagged Me *(1999 {c})* / Oliver Twist *(1999 TV-mini additional w/ Paul Pritchard)* / Sans Plomb *(2000 {a})* / the Shape Of Things *(2003 score)* / De-Lovely *(2004 {p} see future edition)* / **Fallen Angel: Gram Parsons** *(2004 {c})* / Talladega Nights: The Ballad Of Ricky Bobby *(2006 {c})* / Delirious *(2006 {c})*

COTTON COMES TO HARLEM

1970 (US 97m) United Artists (R)

Film genre: cop/detective thriller

Top guns: s-w: Ossie Davis (+ dir) → BLACK GIRL → GORDON'S WAR → COUNTDOWN AT KUSINI, Arnold Perl (au: Chester Himes → COME BACK, CHARLESTON BLUE)

Stars: Godfrey Cambridge *(Gravedigger Jones)* ← WATERMELON MAN / → COME BACK, CHARLESTON BLUE → FRIDAY FOSTER, Raymond St. Jacques *(Coffin Ed Johnson)* ← UP TIGHT / → COOL BREEZE → the FINAL COMEDOWN → COME BACK, CHARLESTON BLUE → BOOK OF NUMBERS, Calvin Lockhart *(Rev. Deke O'Malley)* → MELINDA → LET'S DO IT AGAIN → WILD AT HEART, Judy Pace *(Iris)* → COOL BREEZE, Redd Foxx *(Uncle Bud)*, Emily Yancy *(Mabel)* → BLACULA, Theodore Wilson *(Barry)* → COME BACK, CHARLESTON BLUE → CLEOPATRA JONES, Maxwell Glanville *(Caspar)* → COME BACK, CHARLESTON BLUE, J.D. Cannon *(Calhoun)* → DEATH WISH II, Leonardo Cimino *(Tom)* → COME BACK, CHARLESTON BLUE → DUNE, John Anderson *(Bryce)* → MAN AND BOY, Cleavon Little *(Lo Boy)* → VANISHING POINT → FM, Jonelle Allen *(secretary)* → COME BACK, CHARLESTON BLUE, Wally Taylor *(2nd Black Beret)* → COOL BREEZE → SHAFT'S BIG SCORE! → CROSSROADS, **Melba Moore** *(singer at Apollo Theater)* → HAIR → the FIGHTING TEMPTATIONS, Helen Martin *(church sister)* → DEATH WISH → a HERO AIN'T NOTHIN' BUT A SANDWICH → REPO MAN → HOUSE PARTY 2, Stanley Greene *(Chep)* ← the LANDLORD / → the WIZ,

Lawrence Cook *(1st young black man)* → TROUBLE MAN → the SPOOK WHO SAT BY THE DOOR, Gilbert Lewis *(first Black Beret)* → ACROSS 110th STREET → GORDON'S WAR, Albert Hall *(background detective)* → WILLIE DYNAMITE → LEADBELLY

Storyline: Ossie Davis brings to life Chester Himes' detective duo, "Gravedigger" Jones and "Coffin Ed" Johnson, loose on the trail of a missing $87,000. Collected from poor black folks on the dubious premise of a Back To Africa campaign, the money's snatched during a Harlem rally, driven off in a gold-plated truck and hidden in a cotton bale. *BG*

Movie rating: *7

Visual: none

Off the record: (see below)

—

GALT MacDERMOT (*) (& Various Artists)

May 70. (lp) *United Artists; <UAS 5211>* ☐ ☐
– Cotton comes to Harlem (GEORGE TIPTON) / Coffin Ed and Gravedigger (*) / Going home (SHAKINAH) / Sunlight shining (LELA GALLOWAY) / Man in distress (*) / Harlem medley (*) / Black enough (MELBA MOORE) / Stockyard (*) / The loving ballad (DENISE DILLAPENA) / Deke (*) / Down in my soul (LETA GALLOWAY) / Harlem by day (*) / My salvation (MELBA MOORE) / Ed and Digger (*). *<re-iss. 1980 on 'M.C.A.'; 25133> <cd-iss. Dec01 on 'Beyond'; 578253>*

S/track review: 'COTTON COMES TO HARLEM' is rarely "credited with launching the blaxploitation film boom" as the sleevenotes claim, and its soundtrack isn't exactly typical, more in the spirit of Blue Mink-vintage soul-pop than 70s funk. But 'HAIR' window dresser GALT McDERMOT (the only man in Christendom to have run a record label called 'Kilmarnock') isn't a compadre of Bernard Purdie, Wilbur "Bad" Bascomb and Idris Muhammad for nothing, and he puts his own funky tailspin on black film music. His gutbucket title theme still sounds like it'd be more at home on a Southern stage than Hollywood celluloid, with ensemble call and response led by the sonorous tones of singer/producer/arranger George Tipton (a man who'd previously guided the genius of Harry Nilsson). Among the choir are 60s backing singer (Aretha Franklin, Ashford & Simpson, etc.)/future solo star/contemporary gospel artist MELBA MOORE and Broadway stalwart LETA GALLOWAY, both of whom take solo bows – MOORE staking the vocal high ground on 'Black Enough' and GALLOWAY taking the country-soul route, wallowing in some of that low-yo-yo stuff on the excellent 'Down In My Soul'. Instrumentally, McDERMOT swings between groovy R&B-lite ('Man In Distress' would've made a great 60s TV theme), orchestrated honky tonk and even quasi-Gallic bongo-pop, but he's at his deepest and most cinematic on 'Stockyard', recently sampled by rapper Quasimoto. Not so much Cotton comes to Harlem as McDERMOT digs Swinging London. *BG*

Album rating: *6.5

COUNTDOWN AT KUSINI

1975 (US/Nigeria 100m) Tam International Limited (PG)

Film genre: political drama

Top guns: s-w: Ossie Davis (+ dir) ← GORDON'S WAR ← BLACK GIRL ← COTTON COMES TO HARLEM, Ladi Ladebo, Al Freeman Jr. (au: John Storm Roberts)

Stars: Ruby Dee *(Leah Matanzima)* ← WATTSTAX ← BLACK GIRL ← UP TIGHT! / → JUNGLE FEVER, Ossie Davis *(Ernest Motapo)* ← LET'S DO IT AGAIN / → SCHOOL DAZE → JUNGLE FEVER → BUBBA HO-TEP, Greg Morris *(Red Salter)*, Tom Aldredge *(Ben Amed)* → COLD MOUNTAIN, Michael Ebert *(Charles Henderson)*, Thomas Baptiste *(John Okello)* ← SHAFT IN AFRICA / → the MUSIC MACHINE

Storyline: The first ever Afro-American feature filmed on location in Africa (Nigeria), recounting a typical post-colonial tale of vested corporate interests attempting to sabotage the revolutionary ideals of the fictional nation of Fahari. *BG*

Movie rating: *4

Visual: none

Off the record: MANU DIBANGO (see own entry)

—

MANU DIBANGO

Sep 75. (lp) *Delta Sigma; <LPK 1001>* ☐ ☐
– Go slow streets / Motapo / Promenade (Kusini) / Bokolo's boogie / Jam session / Marni / Bush / Leah's love theme / Blowin' western mind / Liberation's song / Red Salter.

S/track review: Maybe it's natural justice that the holy grail of blaxploitation – if it can even be classed as such – soundtracks (check your overdraft before attempting to track down this baby) brings it all back home to Africa. In the awesome cosmos of black music, the sub-genre of Afro-funk remains an umbrella term for some of the most vital and vibrant music ever recorded (if that seems like a boldly ridiculous claim, track down an earful of the Rwenzori's 'Handsome Boy (E Wara)', absolutely the last, staggering word in primordial sex-funk). Compared to its American cousin, the genre is still largely unsung; save for the efforts of a few DJs, compilers and labels, it wouldn't be sung at all. Likewise, save for a few academic tomes on Fela Kuti, a few articles and a handful of sleevenotes, it's still largely undocumented. Next to Kuti (with whom he jammed at Kuti's neo-mythical club, The Shrine), Cameroonian saxophonist MANU DIBANGO is still probably the most recognisable Afro-funk progenitor, scoring one of the first international crossover hits with the indestructible, much compiled 'Soul Makossa', and equally at home sharing an Apollo bill with the Temptations or playing Yankee Stadium with the Fania All Stars (with whom he also teamed at the famous 'Rumble In The Jungle', in Kinshasa in 1974). Those with the time, money and inclination to delve into the rest of his 70s vinyl will find countless tunes of equal merit, but 'COUNTDOWN AT KUSINI' remains the rarest, single most unheard entry in his catalogue, limited to 5000 promo copies for the film's Seattle preview. Is it worth the hype? Well, almost. It seems that the more socially/politically conscious filmmaking of Ossie Davis often spawned the best (and rarest) blaxploitation soundtracks – see 'GORDON'S WAR' and 'BLACK GIRL' – and this is no exception. And just as Hugh Masekela's L.A. exile was the catalyst for a dazzling jazz-funk-rock voodoo, DIBANGO, having left Cameroon as a private schoolboy, enjoyed a cosmopolitan life evident in his sound. Paris, Kinshasa, Yaoundé, New York, Lagos and L.A.; all those cities are audible in the rolling grooves of 'COUNTDOWN . . .', flagged by the siren-like keyboard, Kuti-esque guitar arrangement and typically whispered/chanted vocal hook of lead track 'Go Slow Streets'. It's a framework DIBANGO manipulates to varying degrees over the course, setting standard funk horn charts to the rhythms of his native Cameroon on 'Motapo', interpolating those characteristically long, wailing notes the likes of Ghanaian funkster Dan Boadi would use on his own lost Afro-disco classic, 'Money Is The Root Of Evil'. And just as the tension between the sweat of the tropics and the bite of urban America holds the key to DIBANGO's art – and the art of Afro-funk in general – so he moves stealthily through that spectrum, blowing great, greasy bubbles of sunshine brass into a Pan-African sky on the Masekela-favoured 'Bokolo's Boogie', layering screaming, distended guitar over frenzied bongos on 'Bush', reeling off the kind of cinematic, vintage 70s themes – 'Blowin' Western Mind' (that's 'Mind' singular) and the Bob James/Steely Dan-esque 'Red Salter' – which prove he could've had a soundtrack career as long and accomplished as Isaac Hayes (whom he strangely resembles, bald pate and all that), even arranging a lusciously measured love theme for Fender Rhodes and a squawking avant-garde piece which wouldn't have been out of place on a late 60s 'Impulse!' set. Yet none of this quite ascends to the mouthwatering sonic plateau the phrase "Afro-blaxploitation" promises. Only when DIBANGO condenses the spectrum does he summon a Shango-hurled thunderstone: 'Marnie' harnesses ferocious, Tony Allen-strength polyrhythms, elephantine brass headcharges and the kind of solar-gnarled guitar latterly monopolised by the likes of Tinariwen, reinforcing and releasing tension in relentless forward motion; verily, music from the centre of the world. *BG*

Album rating: *9

the COURIER

1988 (Ire/UK 85m) Euston Films / A City Vision Film (15)

Film genre: crime drama

Top guns: dir: Frank Deasy (+ s-w), Joe Lee

Stars: Padraig O'Loingsigh *(Mark)*, **Cait O'Riordan** *(Colette)* <= the POGUES =>, Gabriel Byrne *(Val)* ← SIESTA ← GOTHIC / → DEAD MAN → the END OF VIOLENCE → STIGMATA, Patrick Bergin *(Christy)* → the INVISIBLE CIRCUS, Ian Bannen *(McGuigan)*, Andrew Connolly *(Danny)*, Joe Savino *(the VJ)*, Michelle Houlden *(Sharon)*, Aidan Gillen → MOJO

Storyline: Dispatch rider Mark decides to do some investigating when he learns about the suspicious death of his old friend Danny, a drug addict. Danny's sister Colette is convinced of foul play, and sure enough Mark soon uncovers a connection between local drug dealer Val and a detective, McGuigan. Mark sets out to avenge Danny and bring down the drug ring which caused his death, but the dealers and the police are running him down. *JZ*

Movie rating: *3

Visual: video

Off the record: Cait O'Riordan (b. 4 Jan'65, Nigeria) was a member (bassist) of Irish punk band the Radiators From Space, prior to joining London-Irish outfit, the POGUES. She married a certain Declan MacManus in May 1986 (they divorced in 2002). *MCS*

—

Various Artists // DECLAN MacMANUS (i.e. ELVIS COSTELLO)

Feb 88. (cd/c/lp) *Virgin; (CD/TC+/V 2517) <90954-2/-4/-1>*
– Burn clear (SOMETHING HAPPENS) / Wild white horse (HOTHOUSE FLOWERS) / Kill the one you love (LORD JOHN WHITE) / The courier – It's a dangerous game (ASLAN) / She came from there (SOMETHING HAPPENS) *[cd-only]* / Try a little harder (TOO MUCH FOR THE WHITE MAN) *[cd-only]* / Silly dreams (CRY BEFORE DAWN) / Walk to the water (U2) // Mad dog *[cd-only]* / Painted villain / Stalking / Furinal music (piano) / Rat poison / Furinal music (sax) / Unpainted villain / Last boat leaving.

S/track review: This low budget Irish film was mostly accompanied by low budget Irish pop/rock music of the era. Several of the artists featured were just getting their big break around 1988, moving on to varying degrees of success. SOMETHING HAPPENS contribute two songs, 'Burn Clear' and 'She Came From There', both of which sound like a sedated Billy Idol while 'The Courier – It's A Dangerous Game' by ASLAN should be left in the 1980s and never be heard again. The same goes for 'Try A Little Harder' by TOO MUCH FOR THE WHITE MAN and CRY BEFORE DAWN's 'Silly Dreams', both of which could be poor Huey Lewis B-sides. 'The COURIER' does deliver (sorry, couldn't resist) a few highlights however. 'Wild White Horse' by HOTHOUSE FLOWERS sounds like a morose Irish folk ballad that's been dragged by its coat-tails from a Dublin music pub and slammed into the Doors before being ripped apart by Nick Cave. Following that is LORD JOHN WHITE, who could have been an early incarnation of Belle & Sebastian crossed with Spandau Ballet, with the deceptively jaunty 'Kill The One You Love'. Of course, an album of mid-80s Irish rock would not be complete without an appearance from U2. 'Walk To The Water' is the band at the height of their creative and experimental powers with Bono's melancholic soliloquy rising to an anguished cry over The Edge's haunting, sustained guitar. The rest of the album is made up of orchestral pieces composed by DECLAN MacMANUS that only really fit the scenes they were created for. *CM*

Album rating: *4.5

CRIMES OF PASSION

1984 (US 107m) New World (18)

Film genre: seXual/erotic thriller

Top guns: dir: Ken Russell ← LISZTOMANIA ← TOMMY / → GOTHIC / s-w: Barry Sandler

Stars: Kathleen Turner *(Joanna Crane / China Blue)* → the VIRGIN SUICIDES, Anthony Perkins *(Rev. Peter Shayne)*, John Laughlin *(Bobby Grady)* ← FOOTLOOSE, Annie Potts *(Amy Grady)* → PRETTY IN PINK, Bruce Davison *(Doony Hopper)* ← DEADMAN'S CURVE ← SHORT EYES ← the STRAWBERRY STATEMENT / → an AMBUSH OF GHOSTS → GRACE OF MY HEART, Stephen Lee *(Jerry)* → LA BAMBA, Pat McNamara *(Frank)* ← AMERICAN HOT WAX / → FIGHT CLUB, Pamela Anderson *(hooker)*, **Rick WAKEMAN** *(wedding photographer)*

Storyline: Bored with her dayjob as a sportswear designer, divorcee Joanna Crane finds sexual solace by becoming a part-time prostitute under the name of China Blue. Life gets increasingly pressurised when she comes across a repressed reverend/preacher who wants to rid her of her ungodly sins. With controversial director Ken Russell calling the shots, its no surprise that it sets out to shock and titilate rather than get a poignant message across. *MCS*

Movie rating: *3.5

Visual: video + dvd

Off the record: **Rick WAKEMAN** (see own entry)

—

RICK WAKEMAN

Dec 84. (lp/c/cd) *Edel; <CD 5404> President; (RW/+K/CD 3)* Mar87
– It's a lovely life (MAGGIE BELL) / Eastern shadows / Joanna / The stretch / Policeman's ball / Stax / Taken in hand / Paradise lost / The box / Web of love. *(cd+=)* – Dangerous woman (MAGGIE BELL). *(cd re-iss. Nov93 +=; same) (cd re-iss. Mar95 on 'Silva Screen'; CIN 2202-2)*

S/track review: RICK WAKEMAN renews his movie soundtrack partnership with Ken Russell ('LISZTOMANIA' in 1975), although the one-time keyboard king of Prog rock was not having the best of times commercially. Recruiting seasoned session men and friends of old such as drummer TONY FERNANDEZ, bassist CHARLIE CRONK, guitarist RICK FENN and saxophonist BIMBO ACOCK (from the likes of STRAWBS, 10cc, etc.), WAKEMAN and his symphonic synths – and keyboards! – get down to some no thrills basic numbers. Assisted by Scottish Blues-rock diva, MAGGIE BELL (once of Stone The Crows), the album kicks off well enough with 'It's A Lovely Life', probably the best tune on the set; she is also featured on finale, 'Dangerous Woman'. Whether it's the album – with its Dvorak's 'Ninth Symphony' overtones – or the film itself that sort of sticks in the throat, that's anybody's guess. For WAKEMAN connoisseurs only. *MCS*

Album rating: *4

☐ CROSSROADS
(⇒ Rock Music Films)

CURIOUS GEORGE

2006 (US 86m / Can 78m) Imagine / Universal Pictures (G)

Film genre: animated children's/family comedy adventure

Top guns: dir: Matthew O'Callaghan / s-w: Ken Kaufman (+ story w/ Mike Werb) (books: Margret Rey & H.A. Rey)

Stars: Will Ferrell *(Ted; the man in the yellow hat)*, Frank *(George)*, Drew Barrymore *(Miss Maggie Dunlop)* ← the WEDDING SINGER ← WAYNE'S WORLD 2 ← FIRESTARTER / → MUSIC AND LYRICS, David Cross *(Junior Bloomsbury)*, Eugene Levy *(Clovis)* ← a MIGHTY WIND ← CLUB PARADISE ← HEAVY METAL / → OVER THE HEDGE, Joan Plowright *(Miss Plushbottom; opera diva)* ← DANCE WITH ME ← BRIMSTONE & TREACLE, Dick Van Dyke *(Mr. Bloomsberry)* ← DICK TRACY ← BYE BYE BIRDIE, Clint Howard *(balloon boy)* ← THAT THING YOU DO! ← GET CRAZY ← ROCK'N'ROLL HIGH SCHOOL ← COTTON CANDY

Storyline: Screen adaptation of the Stateside simian, who inadvertently arrives in the USA after taking up with Bloomsberry museum guide Ted and stowing away on his boat back from Africa. Having returned without a star curio to prevent his son profiting from the sale of the museum, he finds a mischievous star curio in George instead. *BG*

Movie rating: *6

Visual: dvd

Off the record: (see below)

JACK JOHNSON & Friends : Sing-A-Longs and Lullabies for the Film..

Feb 06. (cd) *Brushfire-Mercury; <87969> (9850967)* [1] [15]
– Upside down / Broken / People watching / Wrong turn / Talk of the town / Jungle gym / We're going to be friends / The sharing song / The 3 R's / Lullaby / With my own two hands / Questions / Supposed to be.

S/track review: Written for the curious adventures of an animated American monkey, although you'd never guess as much from first impressions; 'CURIOUS GEORGE' bears all the hallmarks of a regular JACK JOHNSON set, with positivist lyrics recounted in the drama-teacherly tones of a guy who – had he been born a generation earlier – could've made a sterling career at Jackanory. It's impossible not to warm to the man, even if you usually have a congenital aversion to easy-going surf-dudes. While primarily aimed at kids, the humanist principles of JOHNSON's art are readily applied all the way through from the proverbial cradle to the grave. And with a non-preachy emphasis on the environment (jazz-funk standard 'Three Is The Magic Number' is transformed into a 'Three R's green cross code with batucada-esque cowbell), he may just inspire a few mini eco-warriors along the way. The contributions of BEN HARPER make sure that the clear-eyed, almost religious parable-esque essence of a song like 'With My Own Two Hands', works as a kind of post-modern update on that old Assembly Hall chestnut, 'Kum Ba Ya', with the added advantage of an English language refrain. Here and throughout, the itchy amiability of JOHNSON's phrasing is a shamelessly easy complement to the strictly organic percussion and burnished keys, rendering song after song as mellow as a glass of Rioja. It mightn't be so easy to pick out one over another but "Friends" like G. LOVE and MATT COSTA add tone, timbre and moral support, the former lathering some foot stomping Special Sauce into 'Jungle Gym', the latter helping midwife the tender, finger-picked hush of 'Lullaby'. Just occasionally, the album sounds like 'Sesame Street' on a Deep South tour but then that's no bad thing, and certainly not enough to rouse you from the feel-good reverie you'll very likely be lost in. Figure in a wonderful cover of the White Stripes' 'We're Going To Be Friends', and you have an album that bridges the generation gap (several generation gaps) with unforced ease. *BG*

Album rating: *7

– spinoff hits, etc. –

JACK JOHNSON: Upside Down / Talk Of The Town (AOL version) / Lullaby (feat. Matt Costa) / ('A'-video)
May 06. (cd-s) *(9853873)* [38] [30]

☐ the CYRKLE segment
(⇒ the MINX)

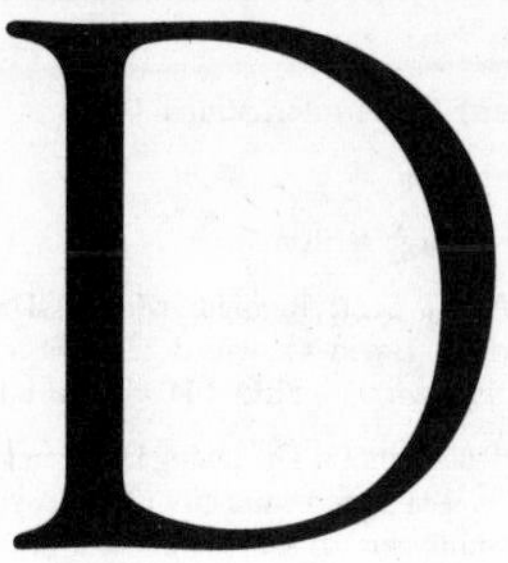

□ Evan DANDO
(⇒ the LEMONHEADS)

DANNY THE DOG

aka UNLEASHED

2005 (Fra/US 102m) Canal+ / Europa Corp. / Qian Yian (R)

Film genre: martial arts adventure

Top guns: dir: Louis Leterrier / s-w: Luc Besson

Stars: Jet Li *(Danny)*, Morgan Freeman *(Sam)* ← BLUES DIVAS ← LAST OF THE MISSISSIPPI JUKES ← JOHNNY HANDSOME, Bob Hoskins *(Bart)* ← SPICEWORLD ← the WALL / → BEYOND THE SEA, Kerry Condon *(Victoria)*, Christian Gazio *(paramedic)*, Michael Jenn *(Wyeth)*, Andy Beckwith *(Righty)*

Storyline: Danny is the titular prize fighter, big on violence but low in emotional maturity. His world consists of little more than illegal fighting and looking out for his mentor Bart, who regards him not so much like a dog as a human cash cow. When Bart falls into a coma after a car accident, Danny is forced to negotiate the outside world on his own, a task made easier with the help of benevolent piano tuner Sam. *BG*

Movie rating: *7

Visual: dvd

Off the record: MASSIVE ATTACK were formed in Bristol, England in 1987 by 3-D (Robert Del Naja), Mushroom (Andrew Vowles) and Daddy G (Grant Marshall). Having founded their own label, 'Wild Bunch' – named after the loose Bristol collective of DJ's, producers and musicians of which MASSIVE ATTACK were an integral part – five years earlier, they were subsequently snapped up by Virgin subsidiary, 'Circa' in 1990 and with only their second single, 'Unfinished Sympathy' – released under the revised moniker of Massive (to distance themselves from any affiliation with the UN Gulf War policy) – crashed into the Top 20. Featuring the velvet tones of Shara Nelson and luxuriant string arrangements to die for, this hypnotically beautiful track is oft cited as one of the most perfect singles ever crafted. While not boasting anything quite as tantalising, the classic debut album, 'Blue Lines', hit the the Top 20 in spring '91, a darkly sensual, spliff-heavy cocktail of sampla-delic dub, hip-hop, funk and soul that can quite possibly lay claim to be the Big Daddy of that much-maligned genre, trip-hop. Alongside the aforementioned Nelson, the record featured guest vocalists, Tricky (soon to carve out his own career in paranoid beats) and dub reggae veteran, Horace Andy. Nelson subsequently departed for a solo career and all was quiet from the Massive' camp until the autumn of '94, when they re-surfaced with the Nellee Hooper (Soul II Soul)-produced 'Protection' album. An even darker, slinkier creature, it featured an array of guest vocalists, most effectively employing Tracey Thorn on the aching 'Better Things' and the title track; Tricky, meanwhile, sounded almost catatonic on the spellbinding voodoo bass-psyche of 'Karmacoma' while the exotic tones of Nicolette graced a couple of tracks. More cohesive soundwise, the record was characterised by a haunting dub-reggae feel and while it was perhaps pushing it a bit to revamp a Doors track ('Light My Fire'), the claustrophobic brilliance of 'Spying Glass' (featuring Horace Andy in peerless form) more than made up for it. London dub producer, the Mad Professor, later gave it a bowel quaking, full-on dub reworking early in '95, the results surfacing as the mind scrambling 'No Protection'. In the summer of '97, the trio returned with their darkest, scariest track to date, 'Risingson', a solitary taster for the following year's long-awaited UK chart-topper, 'Mezzanine'. Yet again cleaning up across the critical board, MASSIVE ATTACK had created a work many regarded as the pinnacle of their career, an unflinchingly bleak, downbeat and introspective record mired in paranoia, despair and apocalytic pre-millennium tension. Nevertheless, 3-D, Mushroom and Daddy-G explored more musical possibilities than most bands of their ilk put together, even hooking up with Liz Fraser (of Cocteau Twins) on the track, 'Teardrops', subsequently a Top 10 hit. 1999 started a little painfully for the trio when Manfred Mann threatened a lawsuit against them for the use of his song 'Tribute' on their track 'Black Mark'; an out of court settlement was soon agreed on. However, that was the least of their problems, Mushroom opting to bail out in July that year. With Daddy G also departing on domestic duty, it was left to 3D to complete '100th Window' (2003), the band's fourth album and the only one not to develop significantly from its predecessor. That said, its brooding, stifling atmospherics were almost as compelling as 'Mezzanine', with Sinead O'Connor taking up the role that Shara, Tracey & Liz filled with such grace in the past. Unsurprisingly, the Irish singer brought a different dimension to that role, illuminating the album's darker corners with her burning vision, and nowhere more so than 'What Your Soul Sings'. Horace Andy also reported for duty once again, airing his timeless, genderless vocal chords on 'Name Taken' and 'Everywhen'. The baying industrio-grunge and abstract sonics of 'DANNY THE DOG' (2004) finally represented Massive's first soundtrack venture, a genre which they'd been gravitating towards – at least aesthetically – for years. *BG & MCS*

—

MASSIVE ATTACK

Oct 04. (cd) *E.M.I.; (<874393-2>)* **70** Nov04 ☐

– Opening title / Atta boy / P is for piano / Simple rules / Polaroid girl / Sam / One thought at a time / Confused images / Red light means go / Collar stays on / You've never had a dream / Right way to hold a spoon / Everybody's got a family / Two rocks and a cup of water / Sweet is good / Montage / Everything about you is new / The dog obeys / Danny the dog / I am home / The academy.

S/track review: MASSIVE ATTACK have always made music for films even if the source images have usually been confined to their own – or their listeners' – imaginations. Given the cinematic bent of their sound, it's perhaps difficult to believe that it took them fifteen years to get round to a full length soundtrack project (although they've laterally contributed specially commissioned pieces to the likes of 'Blade II' and 'Welcome To Sarajevo'). Unlike some artists, then, ROBERT "3D" DEL NAJA, GRANT "DADDY G" MARSHALL and ANDREW "MUSHROOM" VOWLES presumably didn't need to project their talents into the aesthetic mindset of a professional film composer. Instead they pretty much stuck to the musical policy of their latter-day albums, veering between gurning post-industrial territory and the glacially graceful sonic architecture they'd painstakingly chiselled out over the last decade or so. While the likes of 'Atta Boy', 'Simple Rules' and 'The Dog Obeys' come snarling out of the speakers with teeth bared, leashed to grungy, sub-New Order basslines, the aggro-distortion works better on 'One Thought At A Time', manacled to a hobbled, broken-backed beat, portentous timpani and an indulgent, naggingly folky melody. The likes of 'Polaroid Girl' sticks closest to the somnolent MASSIVE template but the dark, gentle grace of old really insinuates itself through orchestrated pieces like 'Sam' and the haunting, funereal title track, curiously hidden away near the end of the disc. Ditto 'Montage', the blinking, torn-hearted chords of which suggested that MASSIVE share more common ground with Radiohead than they might care to admit. Not quite on a par with the immaculate conception of their regular studio releases then, but pretty much what you might expect from a MASSIVE soundtrack. Given the limited time they had to create it (reportedly just over two months), it was also promising enough to suggest that they could easily make a full time career from film should they ever so desire. *BG*

Album rating: *5.5

Miles DAVIS

Born: 25th May 1926, Alton, Illinois, USA. As restlessly creative and supernaturally talented a figure as popular music – never mind jazz – has yet witnessed, trumpeter MILES DAVIS rung the changes in his chosen milieu with an unparalleled flair and a foresight bordering on the clairvoyant. As early as 1949 he was manipulating and changing the course of bebop, retaining its harmonic complexity while substituting a more laid-back lyricism for its frenetic tempo. The hugely influential session in question was belatedly released more than seven years later as 'Birth Of The Cool' (1958), by which point its casual languor had already influenced a generation of players. DAVIS' first soundtrack, for Louis Malle's pseudo-noir, 'Ascenseur Pour l'Echafaud' (1958), was released later in the year and displayed all the haunting grace of his more meditative work even if, by this point, he'd progressed to playing hard bop. More groundbreaking albums followed: noteably 'Kind Of Blue' (1959), 'Sketches Of Spain' (1960), redrawing the paramaters of jazz and re-imagining its possibilities. By the late 60s, DAVIS, together with sidemen like HERBIE HANCOCK and Ron Carter, had begun re-mapping jazz all over again, this time more radically and controversially than before. Using electric instruments, and welding his dazzling command of complex harmony onto rock and funk rhythms, the trumpeter alienated many of his more conservative fans but attracted new ones willing to ride with the all-out experimentation. Coming just after such evolutionary releases as 'In A Silent Way' (1969) and 'Bitches Brew' (1969), MILES' score for the boxing biopic, 'JACK JOHNSON' (1971) wasn't just another soundtrack, rather a crucial component of both his electric years and his career as a whole. With guitarist John McLaughlin matching DAVIS' fire note by greasy note, the album is widely regarded as the first comprehensive splicing of jazz and rock. While a 1972 car accident and its debilitating aftermath saw MILES withdraw completely from both performance and the recording studio during the latter half of the 70s, a change of record label and link-up with producer/multi-intrumentalist Marcus Miller saw him back on form by the mid-80s. Miller was closely involved in both comeback album, 'Tutu' (1986) and MILES' third soundtrack, 'SIESTA' (1987), the score to an obscure thriller set in Spain, and one which partly reprised the regal grace of 'Sketches . . . '. Like his final studio album, 'Doo-Bop' (1992), DAVIS' final soundtrack, 'DINGO' (1991), was posthumously released following his death on 28th September 1991. A collaboration with composer Michel LeGrand, 'DINGO' was the score to an Australian movie centering on a young trumpeter inspired by an older legend. That legend was, of course, DAVIS himself, the ailing star making both his acting debut and providing a fittingly poetic and metaphorical epitaph to a dazzling career. *BG*

- **filmography** (composer) {acting} –

Ascenseur Pour L'Echafaud *(1958 OST; see future edition)* / **Jack Johnson** *(1971 OST =>)* / Street Smart *(1987 w/ Robert Irving III)* / **Siesta** *(1987 OST w/ MARCUS MILLER =>)* / Scrooged *(1988 {p} OST by V/A + DANNY ELFMAN see; future editions =>)* / Symbiopsychotaxiplasm: Take One *(1991 w/ John Pearson)* / **Dingo** *(1992 {*} OST =>)* / posthumous:- **Red, White & Blues** *(2003 {p} on OST by V/A =>)*

DAWN OF THE DEAD

original title 'ZOMBI'

1978 sequel (US 126m) Target International (R)

Film genre: monster horror

Top guns: s-w + dir: George A. Romero

Stars: Ken Foree *(Peter)*, Scott Reiniger *(Roger)*, David Emge *(Stephen)*, Gaylen Ross *(Francine)*, David Crawford *(Dr. Foster)*, David Early *(Mr. Berman)*, Tom Savini *(Blades)* → FROM DUSK TILL DAWN

Storyline: The sequel to 'Night Of The Living Dead' from a decade previously, the flesh-eating zombies are rife in the city of Pennsylvania. Four survivors of the zombie-fied suburban apocalypse (two TV station employees and two SWAT team members) steal a helicopter and take refuge just outside Pittsburgh in a mega-mall, but after bikers spoil their little hideaway everything starts to go awry.

Movie rating: *7.5

Visual: video + dvd

Off the record: (see below)

—

the GOBLINS (additional composer: Dario Argento)

1978. (lp) *Cinevox; (MDF 33/121)* [–] Italy [–]
– L'Alba dei morti viventi / Zombi / Safari / Torte in faccia – Ai Margini della follia / Zaratozom / La caccia / Torassegmp / Oblio / Risveglio. *<(US/UK-iss.Jan89 on 'Varese Sarabande'+=; VC 81006)* – TENEBRE *(UK re-iss. Feb90 on 'Silva Screen' lp/c; CIA/+K7 5035)* – English titles: Dawn of the dead / Zombie / Safari / Pie in face – Edge of madness / Shriek / The hunt / Target shooting / Oblivion / Awakening. *(lp re-iss. Jul00 on 'Dagored'; RED 1171)*

S/track review: Dario Argento's offer to host George Romero in Rome as he wrote his sequel to 'Night Of The Living Dead' had many repercussions; the Italian director would ultimately help arrange the budget for 'DAWN OF THE DEAD' (taking a producer credit in the process), re-edit the film for Europe (re-titling it 'ZOMBI', inspiring the further re-titling of an unrelated Lucio Fulci movie as 'Zombi 2') and most importantly, bring in GOBLIN to produce the quintessential zombie soundtrack. Essentially the full GOBLIN score is for Argento's edit, as Romero elected to use only three of GOBLIN's cuts for his version, filling out the rest of the score with stock cues from the Music DeWolfe Library. The two edits differ according to the tastes of the two directors; when Argento elected to excise the more overtly comedic aspects of Romero's picture, the corresponding musical cues went out the window. Similarly, Romero found the GOBLIN score too overbearing in its entirety. Both versions are now commercially available, and both are classics in their own right. GOBLIN's score is one of the most eclectic in their oeuvre, opening with the understated majesty of 'L'Alba Dei Morti Viventi' ('Dawn Of The Dead'), evoking the slow, steady menace of the zombie hoards as its heartbeat rhythm and spiralling synth melodies gradually build the portentous, claustrophobic atmosphere. The staccato rhythms and rumbling drums of 'Zombi' are similarly tense, adding bongo and tribal percussion to hypnotising effect, while the title of 'Ai Margini Della Follia' ('Edge Of Madness') is apt but the tune is more soundscape than song. 'Zaratozom' finds GOBLIN on more familiar ground; a pounding rocker with Moroder-esque synths and double-tracked power rock lead guitar. 'La Caccia' ('The Chase') has a bizarre air of regality, 'Tirrassegno' ('Target Shooting') is a respectable stab at country music, and 'Oblivio' ('Oblivion') takes plaintive piano chords a la Harry Nilsson's version of 'Without You', and adds melancholy saxophone. Eclecticism aside, some of the GOBLIN music is surprisingly uncharacteristic for the Italian band, e.g. the weird tribalism of 'Safari', or the comedy barroom piano of 'Torte In Faccia' ('Pie In The Face'), and of course many listeners will not recognise GOBLIN's music as it doesn't feature in Romero's more widely seen cut. Listeners may likewise be surprised to find music they assumed to be GOBLIN is actually stock music, particularly S. Park's instantly recognisable 'Figment', so well associated with Romero's film that its use in the opening seconds of Edgar Wright's 'Shaun Of The Dead' instantly evokes the atmosphere of the original film. As great as GOBLIN's score is, the more 'Hollywood' horror tracks, like 'Cosmogony Part 1' and 'Sinistre' are just as evocative, with their own schlock-y appeal, while "comedy" tracks like polka oddity 'The Gonk', 'The Pretty Things' and ''Cause I'm A Man' are now inextricably linked with the movie, giving them a cult appeal of their own and making both collections essential items for any soundtrack aficionado. *SW*

Album rating: *7

DEAD MAN

1996 (US 134m b&w) Miramax Films (R)

Film genre: psychological western/road movie

Top guns: s-w + dir: Jim Jarmusch ← NIGHT ON EARTH ← MYSTERY TRAIN ← DOWN BY LAW / → YEAR OF THE HORSE → GHOST DOG: THE WAY OF THE SAMURAI → COFFEE AND CIGARETTES

Stars: Johnny Depp *(William Blake)* ← CRY-BABY / → FEAR AND LOATHING IN LAS VEGAS → the FUTURE IS UNWRITTEN, Gary Farmer *(nobody)* → GHOST DOG: THE WAY OF THE SAMURAI, Lance Henriksen *(Cole Wilson)* ← JOHNNY HANDSOME ← NEAR DARK / → TARZAN, Gabriel Byrne *(Charles Ludlow "Charlie" Dickinson)* ← the COURIER ← SIESTA ← GOTHIC / → the END OF VIOLENCE → STIGMATA, Mili Avital *(Thel Russell)*, Michael Wincott *(Conway Twill)* ← the CROW ← the DOORS / → STRANGE DAYS, Eugene Byrd *(Johnny "The Kid" Pickett)* → WENT TO CONEY ISLAND ON A MISSION FROM GOD . . . BE BACK BY FIVE → WHITEBOYS → 8 MILE, Robert Mitchum *(John Dickinson)*, **Iggy POP** *(Salvatore "Sally" Jenko)*, Crispin Glover *(train fireman)* ← EVEN COWGIRLS GET THE BLUES ← the DOORS ← WILD AT HEART, Alfred Molina *(trading post missionary)* → BOOGIE NIGHTS → MAGNOLIA → COFFEE AND CIGARETTES, Billy Bob Thornton *(Big George Drakoulious)* → PRIMARY COLORS → SOUTH OF HEAVEN, WEST OF HELL → → FRIDAY NIGHT LIGHTS, Jared Harris *(Benmont Tench)* ← NATURAL BORN KILLERS / → I SHOT ANDY WARHOL → TWO OF US, John Hurt *(John Scholfield)* ← EVEN COWGIRLS GET THE BLUES ← 1984 ← PIED PIPER / → the PROPOSITION, **Gibby Haynes** *(man with gun in alley)* → the DEVIL AND DANIEL JOHNSTON → YOU'RE GONNA MISS ME, Steve Buscemi *(barman)* ← AIRHEADS ← PULP FICTION ← RESERVOIR DOGS ← MYSTERY TRAIN ← the WAY IT IS / → the WEDDING SINGER → COFFEE AND CIGARETTES → ROMANCE & CIGARETTES

Storyline: Jim Jarmusch's monochrome, post-modern Western follows William Blake as he heads West with a promise of a job as an accountant. Upon arrival, he's told that the post is no longer available, and goes to drown his sorrows in the local watering hole where he becomes involved with an erstwhile prostitute and ends up on the run with a bounty on his head. A mysterious Native American subsequently takes him in, convinced he's the Blake of visionary legend rather than a humble number cruncher. *BG*

Movie rating: 8

Visual: video + dvd

Off the record: Gibby Haynes is leader of the Butthole Surfers, who had albums such as 'Locust Abortion Technician', 'Independent Worm Saloon' and 'Electriclarryland'. *MCS*

—

NEIL YOUNG

Feb 96. (cd) *Reprise; <(9362 46171-2)>* ☐ ☐
– Guitar solo, No.1 / The round stones beneath the earth / Guitar solo, No.2 / Why does thou hide thyself, clouds / Organ solo / Do you know how to use this weapon? / Guitar solo, No.3 / Nobody's story / Guitar solo, No.4 / Stupid white men / Guitar solo, No.5 / Time for you to leave, William Blake / Guitar solo, No.6.

S/track review: NEIL YOUNG begins this abstract experiment as he intends to go on, scraping and sawing at his strings amid desolate, distorted flurries of electric guitar. Save for the way he holds those melancholy notes, and despite the fact that the dialogue's Indian mysticism is a context tailor-made for the Canadian, this album is often barely recognisable as NEIL YOUNG. Probably a good thing, as he resists any temptation for sentimentality, creating instead a bleak, impressionistic canvas for Jarmusch's dark allegory. Save for some snatches of ghostly pump organ, it's also a determinedly minimalistic work, letting the spaces between the music do the talking rather than the music itself. Not an average YOUNG album, then, nor even an easy listen, but a fascinating oddity nonetheless. *BG*

Album rating: *4.5

DEAD MAN WALKING

1995 (US 122m) Polygram / Havoc / Working Title Films (R)

Film genre: religious/prison drama

Top guns: s-w + dir: Tim Robbins (au: Sister Helen Prejean)

Stars: Sean Penn *(Matthew Poncelet)* ← FAST TIMES AT RIDGEMONT HIGH / → I AM SAM, Susan Sarandon *(Sister Helen Prejean)* ← the ROCKY HORROR PICTURE SHOW ← JOE / → the BANGER SISTERS → ALFIE re-make → ROMANCE & CIGARETTES, Robert Prosky *(Hilton Barber)* ← THIEF, R. Lee Ermey *(Clyde Percy)*, Raymond J. Barry *(Earl Delacroix)* → WALK HARD: THE DEWEY COX STORY, Celia Weston *(Mary Beth Percy)*, Lois Smith *(Helen's mother)*, Roberta Maxwell *(Lucille Poncelet)* ← POPEYE, Margo Martindale *(Sister Colleen)* → WALK HARD: THE DEWEY COX STORY, Scott Wilson *(Chaplain Farley)* ← SOUL SURVIVOR ← GERONIMO: AN AMERICAN LEGEND ← ELVIS AND THE COLONEL: THE UNTOLD STORY ← YOUNG GUNS II ← JOHNNY HANDSOME ← BLUE CITY / → SOUTH OF HEAVEN, WEST OF HELL → DON'T LET GO → MONSTER, Barton Heyman *(Capt. Beliveau)* ← the BASKETBALL DIARIES ← ROADSIDE PROPHETS ← LIVING PROOF: THE HANK WILLIAMS JR. STORY, Jack Black *(Craig Poncelet)* → HIGH FIDELITY → SCHOOL OF ROCK → the PICK OF DESTINY → WALK HARD: THE DEWEY COX STORY, Steve Boles *(Sgt. Neal Trapp)* ← TRICK OR TREAT, Nesbitt Blaisdell *(warden Hartman)* → the MOTHMAN PROPHECIES, Eva Amurri *(Helen; 9 years old)* → the BANGER SISTERS

Storyline: Searingly powerful, Oscar-winning drama based on the autobiography of Sister Helen Prejean. Working among the Southern black poor, she naively stumbles into the role of befriending Matthew Poncelot, an unapologetic racist/would-be white supremacist convicted of the rape and murder of a (white) teenage couple. Awaiting execution on death row, the steely-eyed, bouffant-coiffed Poncelot is initially cocky and defiant, his appeal to Prejean centered on getting himself a reprieve. As the Sister feels her way through the anger (much of it directed her way) and grief of the victims' parents, and as it becomes clear there won't be any reprieve, she attempts to catalyse Poncelot's own truth and redemption in the face of his death. *BG*

Movie rating: *9

Visual: video + dvd

Off the record: The late **NUSRAT FATEH ALI KHAN** (b.13 Oct'48, Lyallpur, Punjab, Pakistan) remains the most revered singer in the Qawwali tradition, a Sufi rooted praise song designed to facilitate spiritual awareness in the listener. For KHAN, crucially, the listener was key; while his collaborations with western musicians and remixers brought flak from purists, his aim was to reach as wide an audience as possible. Despite a premature death at the age of only 49, he pretty much succeeded, drawing in non-Asian fans via collaborations with the likes of MICHAEL BROOK and MASSIVE ATTACK. A recording artist in Pakistan since the mid-70s, his entrée into the cultural sphere of western-aimed world music came via an appearance on the PETER GABRIEL-composed soundtrack for Martin Scorsese's 'The LAST TEMPTATION OF CHRIST' (1988). GABRIEL's 'Real World' label was also home to KHAN's first UK-released album, 'Mustt Must' (1990), from whence the title track was remixed by MASSIVE ATTACK and subsequently used in a Coca Cola ad. KHAN was also one of the first artists to sign to WOMAD Music, the publishing wing of GABRIEL's operation and a leading promoter for the use of global music in film. In 1994, the girthsome singer composed his first and only Bollywood soundtrack, to Shekhar Kapur's 'Bandit Queen', although he subsequently made an appearance in Rahul Rawail's '. . .Aur Pyaar Ho Gaya' (1997). Hollywood wise, his beguiling collaborations with Pearl Jam singer EDDIE VEDDER were the undisputed highlights of the soundtrack to Tim Robbins masterpiece, 'DEAD MAN WALKING' (1995). Even after his death from heart failure on 16th August 1997, KHAN was still in demand in the film world, with his voice used posthumously in the likes of Gurinder Chadha's 'Bend It Like Beckham' (2002). Charged with leading NUSRAT's ensemble after his death, nephew Rahat has also built on his uncle's celluloid inroads, contributing vocals to the James Horner-scored, Kapur-directed war epic, 'Four Feathers' (2002). *BG*

—

Various Artists: Music From And Inspired By . . .

Jan 96. (cd/c) *Columbia; <67522> (483534-2/-4)* 61
– Dead man walkin' (BRUCE SPRINGSTEEN) / In your mind (JOHNNY CASH) / Woman on the tier (I'll see you through) (SUZANNE VEGA) / Promises (LYLE LOVETT) / Face of love (NUSRAT FATEH ALI KHAN & EDDIE VEDDER) / The fall of Troy (TOM WAITS) / Quality of mercy (MICHELLE SHOCKED) / Dead man walking (a dream like this) (MARY CHAPIN CARPENTER) / Walk away (TOM WAITS) / Ellis unit one (STEVE EARLE) / Walkin blind (PATTI SMITH) / The long road (EDDIE VEDDER with NUSRAT FATEH ALI KHAN).

S/track review: Most of this is "Inspired By" rather than "From", but – for once – inspired is probably the right word. Assembling a cast of eccentrics and icons by personal request, Tim Robbins created an album in the image of both his own singer-songwriterly tastes and the clear-eyed, unshirking spirit of the movie. Given that the art of both BRUCE SPRINGSTEEN and JOHNNY CASH is so steeped in the vagaries of man already, you might be forgiven for thinking that their appearance on a project like this might seem just a little too contrived. You'd be wrong; Bruce gargles brass tacks like he's back on the 'Nebraska' sessions, assuming the take-it-or-leave-it outlaw mantle he wears so well and putting it to use on a title track which gets a potentially non-partisan audience thinking about his words rather than critics merely raving over them. And rather than the sombre interpretations JOHNNY CASH specialised in during his 'American' years, he tempers the deadly serious subtext with buckets of black humour and revivalist brio on 'In Your Mind'. Though they've been less picked over, STEVE EARLE's knocks have been almost as hard, and his 'Ellis Unit One' is, for this writer's money, the most piercing four minutes on the whole album, sung from the perspective of the (reluctant) executioner rather than the criminal, and named after Texas' own Death Row. TOM WAITS growls and stomps through his graveside jive, MICHELLE SHOCKED testifies on some fine religious funk and PATTI SMITH exhales the kind of ghoulish death row blues Nick Cave might've contributed, Cave being the most glaring omission from what is nevertheless a hugely impressive line-up, especially considering the all-original material. As Robbins implies in his notes, this volume isn't so much about music as narrative; it's NUSRAT FATEH ALI KHAN who channels the trouble of those narratives into pure, transfigurative sound, and while there are a handful of tasters here (EDDIE VEDDER is mesmerising on 'The Long Road'), his contributions are better served on the full-length score (see below). The 1998 'Legacy' addition adds the controlled sturm und drang of EDDIE VEDDER's 'Dead Man' (originally named 'Dead Man Walking' but usurped by SPRINGSTEEN's title), and a bonus DVD disc of the all-star benefit concert held in aid of Sister Helen Prejean and her humanitarian organisation, MVFR (Murder Victims' Families For Reconciliation). Aside from KHAN's climactic ululations, highlights include VEDDER covering Cat Stevens, the truly wired, staccato deliveries of ANI DiFRANCO, STEVE EARLE and LYLE LOVETT duetting over the unmistakable cadence of a Townes Van Zandt classic. *BG*

Album rating: *7

—

DAVID ROBBINS, EDDIE VEDDER, NUSRAT FATEH ALI KHAN, RY COODER & V.M. BHATT: Dead Man Walking – The Score

Mar 96. (cd/c) *Columbia; <67637> (484107-2/-4)* Apr96
– Face of love (NUSRAT FATEH ALI KHAN & EDDIE VEDDER) / Helen visits Angola prison (NUSRAT FATEH ALI KHAN & AMINA ANNABI) / Dudouk melody (a cool wind is blowing) / This is the day the Lord has made (REV. DONALD R. SMITH & THE GOLDEN GOSPEL CHOIR OF ST. FRANCIS) / Possum (NUSRAT FATEH ALI KHAN) / Shadow (NUSRAT FATEH ALI KHAN) / Helen faints – Helen's nightmare (DAVID ROBBINS & NUSRAT FATEH ALI KHAN) / Dudouk melody (I will not be sad in this world) / Sacred love (DAVID DUSING SINGERS) / The execution (DAVID ROBBINS & NUSRAT FATEH ALI KHAN) / The long road (EDDIE VEDDER & NUSRAT FATEH ALI KHAN) / Isa Lei (RY COODER & V.M. BHATT).

S/track review: The choice to soundtrack the final, ambivalent days of a death row inmate with the Sufi devotional music of qawwali was an interesting one. Ambitious also, in that it had never before been used so extensively in western film, even if its greatest ambassador, the late NUSRAT FATEH ALI KHAN, was no stranger to soundtracks, having previously contributed to the rich, multi-ethnic voicing of Peter Gabriel's 'Passion: Music For The LAST TEMPTATION OF CHRIST'. It's stating the obvious to say that this score was as groundbreaking as the movie, and that KHAN's passing so soon after it was recorded robbed the cinema world of what might have been a long and illustrious screen career, yet the loss is perhaps even greater in that no directors have since built upon KHAN's/DAVID ROBBINS' lead in developing qawwali's highly emotive, connective potential. 'DEAD MAN WALKING' isn't unadulterated qawwali, more a meeting between KHAN's genius for adapting the form for different cultural contexts (he'd already cheesed off purists with the infamous Massive Attack remix) and Robbins' conception of a "universal", multi-denominational sound. There's no question he achieves that ecumenical sound, and that the lunar tide of KHAN's voice is a powerful complement to EDDIE VEDDER (if you've had your appetite whetted by the various artists soundtrack, you'll be glad to know 'The Face Of Love' is treated to the full ten and fifteen minute versions bookending the main score; sheer bliss), French-Tunisian singer AMINA ANNABI and the Dusing Singers, yet they sound just as commanding apart. The Dusing Singers' solo recitation of Russian chorale, 'Sacred Love', is spine-shivering stuff, bringing home the reality of Poncelot's fate with an awesome spiritual charge, while KHAN's near a cappella, Michael Brook-produced vocal on 'Shadow' – backed only by harmonium – seals in its embrace both desolation and illumination. Some of the most affecting cues are likewise simple Armenian folk melodies performed by Robbins on solo dudouk. It might seem too easy to pick out the unbridled gospel of R. SMITH AND THE GOLDEN VOICES as a wrong turn, but whichever way you look at it – or listen to it – the happy clappy fervour sounds gauche under the circumstances. Still, that's a minor flaw in what otherwise ranks as an often brilliant search for the primordial impulse in all music, a work of solace, reconciliation and boundless possibility seen out by a beautiful piece from an album which first opened up so many of those possibilties: RY COODER & V.M. Bhatt's 'Meeting By The River' (1993). *BG*

Album rating: *7.5

DEAD SOLID PERFECT

1988 (US 97m TV) Home Box Office (HBO)

Film genre: sports drama

Top guns: dir: Bobby Roth ← BAJA OKLAHOMA ← HEARTBREAKERS / → the MAN INSIDE → BRAVE NEW GIRL / s-w: Dan Jenkins (+ au) ← BAJA OKLAHOMA

Stars: Randy Quaid *(Kenny Lee)* ← the LONG RIDERS ← BOUND FOR GLORY / → ELVIS, Kathryn Harrold *(Beverly T. Lee)*, Jack Warden *(Hubert "Bad Hair" Wimberly)*, Corinne Bohrer *(Jamie Rimmer)*, Brett Cullen *(Donny Smithern)*, DeLane Matthews *(Katie Beth Smithern)*, Larry Riley *(Spec)*, John M. Jackson *(Grover Scomer)* ← BAJA OKLAHOMA ← SID & NANCY ← LOCAL HERO / → GINGER ALE AFTERNOON, Linda Dona *(blonde)* ← BAJA OKLAHOMA / → SUMMER DREAMS: THE STORY OF THE BEACH BOYS

Storyline: Golfer Kenny Lee becomes a pro and discovers the temptations of the celebrity circuit. In the old days his main problem was avoiding the rough and bunkers, but now his troubles only seem to begin at the 19th hole when he runs into groupies and swingers after his money and his body. And poor Kenny just can't say no.
JZ

Movie rating: *6

Visual: video

Off the record: (see below)

—

TANGERINE DREAM

Mar 91. (cd) *Silva Screen; <(FILMCD 079)>* ☐ ☐
– Theme from "Dead Solid Perfect" / In the pond / Beverly leaves / Of cads and caddies / Tournament montage / A whore in one / Sand trap / In the rough / Nine iron / U.S. Open / "My name is Bad Hair" / In the hospital room / Welcome to Bushwood – Golfus interruptus / Deja vu (I've heard this before!) / Birdie / Divot / Kenny and Donny montage / Off to see Beverly / Phone to Beverly / "Nice shots" / Sinking putts / Kenny's winning shot.

S/track review: One of a handful of scores TANGERINE DREAM (at this point EDGAR FROESE, PAUL HASLINGER and RALPH WADEPHUL) produced for director Bobby Roth, this release consists of 22 short (only the new-agey theme tune breaks the three minute mark) and rudimentarily titled cues, and as such resembles a normal orchestral score album more than a collection of fully realised tunes. This is a mark of TANGERINE DREAM's latter day role as Hollywood scorers, and it's hard to imagine anyone but TD (or Randy Quaid) completists finding much of value here; with some tracks as short as 30 seconds, and even the longer tracks usually collections of snippets, it's difficult to get a sense of anything before it is over. The casual listener would also be hard pressed to match TD's shimmering synth score with a HBO golfing comedy starring the elder Quaid, but it is certainly representative of a strain of film soundtracks TD produced in the 80s and early 90s, the avatar of which is 'RISKY BUSINESS'. The titles of the tracks clash violently with the tone of the music, e.g. 'A Whore In One' is notably less bawdy than one might expect, although it does pick up when the slap bass arrives. 'U.S. Open' concedes a little fanfare, presumably to indicate the prestige of the event, before lapsing into tense and suspenseful ambience, while 'Kenny's Winning Shot' is predictably, blandly, euphoric. Although the tracks are mixed together in an attempt to create a cohesive whole, the tone of the tracks swings between mournful and upbeat, and any sense of cohesive drama is evidently left to the screen, rather than the speakers. This album is a good representation of TD's latter day output, very much of its time and ultimately of little value beyond its original use.
SW

Album rating: *3.5

DEADLY CARE

1987 (US 96m; TV) Universal Television

Film genre: medical melodrama

Top guns: dir: David Anspaugh

Stars: Cheryl Ladd *(Annie Halleran)*, Jennifer Salt *(Carol)*, Peggy McCay *(Mrs. Halloran)*, Belinda Balaski *(Terry)*, Jason Miller *(Dr. Miles Keefer)*, Beth Grant *(Madge)*, Joe Dorsey *(Mr. Halloran)*

Storyline: An intensive care nurse finds the pressures of work and home too much and begins taking drugs from her hospital. Her dependence grows worse after her sister dies and things come to a head when she almost causes a patient's death during an operation. With her job in the balance she realises she needs help, but she may be too far gone down the road to addiction for her friends and family to save her.
JZ

Movie rating: *5

Visual: none

Off the record: (see below)

—

TANGERINE DREAM

Dec 92. (cd) *Silva Screen; <SSD 1013> (FILMCD 121)* ☐ ☐
– "DEADLY CARE" Main theme / Paddles – Stolen pills / A strong drink – A bad morning / Wasted and sick / Hope for future / The hospital / In bed / Annie & father / More pills / In the Head nurse's office – At the father's grave / Clean and sober.

S/track review: One of the last TANGERINE DREAM projects to involve long-time member CHRISTOPHER FRANKE, 'DEADLY CARE', was made in the same year as their better known 'NEAR DARK' score. TD's music aims to match the character arc of Cheryl Ladd's character, as various addictions of her troubled nurse lead to alienation, depression and unemployment. The first two are perhaps necessary risks for any long term TANGERINE DREAM users, so the fit is apt. Having said that, 'DEADLY CARE' certainly falls on the right side of TD's descent into ambient impotence, and the music successfully invokes both the sterility of the hospital setting and the blankness of a drug induced fug. There is some drama created by the contrast between the spaced out sections ('Wasted And Sick', 'More Pills' etc.) and the urgent rhythms of the more tense scenes ('Paddles' / 'Stolen Pills' and 'In Bed'), but not enough to really hold the attention. As with most TD scores, there is a serious issue with datedness, and 'DEADLY CARE', with its reliance on bland synth sounds, rarely if ever transcends it's 80s TV movie setting. However, unlike some of the latter day TD soundtracks, 'DEADLY CARE' presents the full length tracks produced by TD, rather than re-edited cues culled from the originals, making it a slightly less obscure experience. Coupled with a insidiously subtle main theme, which is reprised twice (in 'Hope For The Future' and 'Clean And Sober') you have a lukewarm score which isn't as essential as TD's most famous, but certainly not as hard work as others.
SW

Album rating: *3.5

DEATH WISH

1974 (US 93m) Paramount Pictures (R)

Film genre: urban crime thriller

Top guns: dir: Michael Winner ← PLAY IT COOL / → DEATH WISH II → the WICKED LADY → SCREAM FOR HELP / s-w: Wendell Mayes (nov: Brian Garfield → DEATH WISH II →)

Stars: Charles Bronson *(Paul Kersey)* ← KID GALAHAD / → DEATH WISH II, Hope Lange *(Joanna Kersey)* ← WILD IN THE COUNTRY, Vincent Gardenia *(Frank Ochoa)* → DEATH WISH II → LITTLE SHOP OF HORRORS, Steven Keats *(Jack Toby)*, Stuart Margolin *(Aimes Jainchill)*, William Redfield *(Sam Kreutzer)*, Jeff Goldblum *(freak #1)* → NASHVILLE → THANK GOD IT'S FRIDAY → EARTH GIRLS ARE EASY → BARENAKED IN AMERICA, Hank Garrett *(Andrew McCabe)* → the JAZZ SINGER, Christopher Guest *(patrolman Jackson Reilly)* → the LONG RIDERS → THIS IS SPINAL TAP → LITTLE SHOP OF HORRORS → the PRINCESS BRIDE → a MIGHTY WIND, Helen Martin *(Alma Lee Brown)* ← COTTON COMES TO HARLEM / → a HERO AIN'T NOTHIN' BUT A SANDWICH → REPO MAN → HOUSE PARTY 2, Eric Laneuville *(mugger)* ← BLACK BELT JONES / → FEAR OF A BLACK HAT, Lawrence Hilton-Jacobs *(mugger)* ← CLAUDINE / → YOUNGBLOOD → the JACKSONS: AN AMERICAN DREAM → SOUTHLANDER

Storyline: This contentious, Michael Winner-directed thriller follows the increasingly violent adventures of self-styled vigilante and erstwhile liberal, Paul Kersey, as he takes random revenge for the killing of his wife and rape of his daughter. *BG*

Movie rating: *6.5

Visual: video + dvd

Off the record: (see below)

—

HERBIE HANCOCK

Dec 74. (lp) *Columbia; <PC 33199> C.B.S.; (80546)* □ □
– Death wish (main title) / Joanna's theme / Do a thing / Paint her mouth / Rich country / Suite revenge: (a) Striking back – (b) Riverside Park – (c) The alley – (d) Last stop – (e) 8th Avenue Station / Ochoa knose / Party people / Fill your hand. *(re-iss. Sep97 on 'Fopp'; FOPP 80456) <(cd-iss. Oct98 on 'Sony Jazz'; 491981-2)> <lp re-iss. Oct02; same>*

S/track review: While Michael Winner's notorious Charles Bronson vehicle can hardly be filed under pioneering black cinema, HERBIE HANCOCK's soundtrack has all the ingredients of a minor Blaxploitation classic. Like Miles Davis, HANCOCK was in the process of upsetting the jazz purists in the early to mid-70s with his excursions into funk and electronic experimentation; good news, of course, for his soundtrack work. And while this record isn't as immediate as either his studio albums from the same period or standard Blaxploitation fare, its moody charms – like Kersey's appetite for violence – reveal themselves in due course. Structured around a purring, four note bass part and embellished with HANCOCK's space-age piano stylings and typically ostentatious stings, the main title theme is a loping, kerb-crawling highlight. The gorgeous 'Joanna's Theme' builds from a mellow, elegiac ballad in the vein of Quincy Jones' 'Somethin's Cookin' into a slow-burning wah-wah funk piece, driven on by some great acoustic piano and string arrangements. 'Rich Country' is another luxurious, if incongruous cue, a lushly orchestrated, almost John Barry-esque affair. Granted, much of this score also comprises dark, minimalistic incidental music which doesn't function quite so well outside of the film, although score fans certainly won't be disappointed with the likes of 'Revenge Suite', a near ten minute epic climaxing in a soundclash of exploratory electronics and stray cowbells. *BG*

Album rating: *6

DEATH WISH II

1982 (US 93m) Cannon Films (R)

Film genre: crime thriller

Top guns: dir: Michael Winner ← DEATH WISH ← PLAY IT COOL / → the WICKED LADY → SCREAM FOR HELP / s-w: David Engelbach (au: Brian Garfield ← DEATH WISH)

Stars: Charles Bronson *(Paul Kersey)* ← DEATH WISH ← KID GALAHAD, Jill Ireland *(Geri Nichols)*, Vincent Gardenia *(Det. Frank Ochoa)* ← DEATH WISH / → LITTLE SHOP OF HORRORS, J.D. Cannon *(New York D.A.)* ← COTTON COMES TO HARLEM, Anthony Franciosa *(Herman Baldwin, L.A. police commissioner)* ← ACROSS 110th STREET, Ben Frank *(Inspector Lt. Mankiewicz)*, Robin Sherwood *(Carol Kersey)*, Laurence Fishburne III *(Cutter)* ← FAST BREAK ← CORNBREAD, EARL AND ME / → SCHOOL DAZE → WHAT'S LOVE GOT TO DO WITH IT → EVENT HORIZON → the SOUL OF A MAN, Charles Cyphers *(Donald Kay)* ← ELVIS: THE MOVIE ← TRUCK TURNER ← COOL BREEZE / → HONKYTONK MAN, Jim Begg *(tourist)* ← CATALINA CAPER ← IT'S A BIKINI WORLD ← the COOL ONES

Storyline: The trail of bodies switches from New York to L.A. as Paul Kersey and his family yet again attract punks and hoodlums like bees to a honeypot. This time it's his daughter Carol who's the unlucky one and her gruesomely inevitable demise sends Kersey back to his old ways, much to the annoyance of the police and streetcleaners who have to mop up all the blood and gore. *JZ*

Movie rating: *4.5

Visual: video + dvd

Off the record: **JIMMY PAGE** (see below)

—

JIMMY PAGE

Mar 82. (lp) *Swan Song; <SS 8511> (SSK 59415)* 50 Feb82 40
– Who's to blame / The chase / City sirens / Jam sandwich / Carole's theme / The release / Hotel rats and photostats / A shadow in the city / Jill's theme / Prelude / Big band, sax and violence / Hypnotizing ways (oh mamma). *<cd-iss. Dec99 on 'WEA'; 2745>*

S/track review: 1982 marked the return of rock music's best-loved guitarists, JIMMY PAGE. It'd been a year and a half since the death of his long-time Led Zeppelin colleague John Bonham died, which, in turn, led to the break-up of the world's greatest band. Zeppelin's final set, 'In Through The Out Door' (1979), possibly pointed the way PAGE, Plant and Co were heading, and with this OST the song certainly did not remain the same. With a basic rhythm backing of ex-Pilot bassist DAVE PATON and on/off Fairports drummer DAVE MATTACKS, 'DEATH WISH II', gets off to a rocking flyer via 'Who's To Blame', featuring a vocal by veteran 60s blues singer CHRIS FARLOWE; other vocal embarrassing contributions come via 'City Siren' and 'Hypnotizing Ways (Oh Mamma)'. PAGE's guitar licks feature prominently on the aforementioned, while he also gets a little funky on dirges such as 'The Chase' and 'Jam Sandwich'. You begin to seriously shout for Robert Plant. Most of the other tracks are down to the cold, eerie (and sometimes romantic!) orchestral score pieces such as 'Carole's Theme' plus the annoyingly piercing 'The Release', 'Hotel Rats And Photostats' and 'A Shadow In The City'. Only for ZEPPELIN/PAGE completists intent on getting rid of hard-earned cash – it'll cost you over £100 for the now rare CD. *MCS*

Album rating: *4.5

□ DECODER RING segment
(⇒ SOMERSAULT)

□ DEEP RED alt.
(⇒ PROFONDO ROSSO)

DELIVERANCE

1972 (US 109m) Warner Bros. Pictures (18)

Film genre: buddy film/drama

Top guns: dir: John Boorman ← CATCH US IF YOU CAN / s-w: James Dickey (+ nov)

Stars: Jon Voight *(Ed Gentry)* ← MIDNIGHT COWBOY, Burt Reynolds *(Lewis Medlock)* → the BEST LITTLE WHOREHOUSE IN TEXAS → BOOGIE NIGHTS → BROKEN BRIDGES, Ned Beatty *(Bobby Trippe)* → NASHVILLE → PURPLE PEOPLE EATER → HE GOT GAME, Ronny Cox *(Drew Ballinger)* → BOUND FOR GLORY, Bill McKinney *(mountain man)* → CLEOPATRA JONES, James Dickey *(Aintry Sheriff Bullard)*, Herbert Coward *(toothless man)*, Macon McCalman *(deputy queen)* → TIMERIDER: THE ADVENTURE OF LYLE SWANN

Storyline: John Boorman's disturbing take on the eternal nature versus culture debate, focusing on the hellish trials of four friends – led by headstrong He-man Lewis – who attempt to canoe a pristine stretch of Georgia's isolated Chattoga river before it's ruined by the construction of a dam. One of the group indulges in an impromptu jam session with a mute, worryingly inbred looking villager although it's the infamous male rape scene which really gives the locals a bad name. The incident occurs when the group are split up and two of them are cornered by gun-toting hillbillies. Things go from bad to worse as the increasingly difficult terrain tests the guys' already seriously shattered mettle. *BG*

Movie rating: *10

Visual: video + dvd

Off the record: 'Dueling Banjos' was actually written as 'Feuding Banjos' by Arthur "Guitar Boogie" Smith in 1955.

——

ERIC WEISSBERG & STEVE MANDELL (with MARSHALL BRICKMAN)

Jan 73. (lp) *Warners; <WB 2683> (K 46214)* [1] [ ]
– Dueling banjos / Little Maggie / Shuckin' the corn / Pony express / Old Joe Clark / Eight more miles to Louisville / Farewell blues / Earl's breakdown / End of a dream / Buffalo gals / Reuben's train / Riding the waves / Fire on the mountain / Eighth of January / Bugle call rag / Hard ain't it hard / Mountain dew / Rawhide. *(cd-iss. 1988; 246214) <(cd re-iss. May01 by MANDELL & WEISSBERG; 9362 48088-2)> <(cd re-iss. 2005; 2683-2)>*

S/track review: The aforementioned jam session remains one of cinema's most famous moments and the spiralling runs of ERIC WEISSBERG & STEVE MANDELL both opened the soundtrack and lent it its title, 'Dueling Banjos', a UK Top 20 hit in 1973. Together with MARSHALL BRICKMAN, WEISSBERG had originally cut the bulk of the album's tracks a decade earlier (on 'Elektra' set, 'New Dimensions') although their lightning-fast bluegrass had lost neither its relevance nor its country soul in the intervening years. Of the other tunes (most of them recognisably traditional and around 2 minutes long), 'Shuckin' The Corn', 'Pony Express' and 'Buffalo Gals' are exceptional. Virtuosity and energy come via the chugging of 'Reuben's Train' (at 3 minutes). Ditto the hoedown of 'Fire On The Mountain', while the echo of 'The Battle Of New Orleans' is rampant throughout the track, 'Eighth Of January'. Woody Guthrie's 'Hard Ain't It Hard' gets the speedy hillbilly treatment, while the banjo is king on closing cues, 'Mountain Dew' and 'Rawhide'. *BG & MCS*

Album rating: *7

– spinoff hits, etc. –

ERIC WEISSBERG: Dueling Banjos / End Of A Dream
Jan 73. (7") *<7659> (K 12223)* [2] Mar73 [17]
—— credited in the US both as ERIC WEISSBERG and 'DELIVERANCE' SOUNDTRACK, the latter also in UK (feat. ERIC WEISSBERG & STEVE MANDELL)

ERIC WEISSBERG: Dueling Banjos / Reuben's train
Mar 86. (7") *Old Gold; (OG 9574)* [-] [ ]

□ the DELLS segment
(⇒ NO WAY BACK)

DELUSION

1991 (US 100m) I.R.S. Releasing Corporation (R)

Film genre: crime thriller

Top guns: s-w: Carl Colpaert (+ dir), Kurt Voss ← BORDER RADIO / → SUGAR TOWN → DOWN AND OUT WITH THE DOLLS

Stars: Jim Metzler *(George O'Brien)*, Jennifer Rubin *(Patti)* ← the DOORS ← PERMANENT RECORD, Kyle Secor *(Chevy)*, Jerry Orbach *(Larry)*, Richard Jordan *(conference room executive)* ← DUNE / → SHOUT, Craig Sexton *(conference room executive)*, Tommy Redmond Hicks *(cop)* ← the FIVE HEARTBEATS / → WARMING BY THE DEVIL'S FIRE, Tracey Walter *(hotel desk clerk)* ← YOUNG GUNS II ← BATMAN ← REPO MAN ← HONKYTONK MAN ← TIMERIDER: THE ADVENTURE OF LYLE SWANN / → MAN ON THE MOON → HOW HIGH → MASKED AND ANONYMOUS

Storyline: Computer whizzkid Jim Metzler thinks he has it made as he zooms off to a new life in Nevada after pilfering half a million dollars from his company. His mood fades pretty sharpish, though, as a couple of deceptively innocent looking hitchhikers divest him of his ill-gotten gains and leave him to stew in the desert. *BG*

Movie rating: *5.5

Visual: video

Off the record: (see below)

——

BARRY ADAMSON

Aug 91. (cd/c/lp) *Elektra; <61127-2/-4> Ionic; (CD/C+/IONIC 004)* [ ] [ ]
– Delusion / Crossin' the line / Il solitario / Patti's theme / A settlin' kinda scam / Fish face / Go Johnny / The life we leave behind / An amendment / La cucaracha / Diamonds / George's downfall / Got to bet to win / The track with no name / Patti's theme (Two stage variation) / Death valley junction / These boots are made for walking.

S/track review: He covered John Barry's 'Goldfinger' back in his Magazine days; his first solo single was a version of Elmer Bernstein's 'The Man With The Golden Arm'; he contributed to the score of Derek Jarman's 'The Last Of England' (1987), and his debut album ranks as one of the most evocative soundtrack-to-an-imaginary film efforts ever recorded. Surprising, then, that it took BARRY ADAMSON so long to get his teeth into a real live, full length commission, where he could really get to "the place where the stomach churns.. underneath pictures", as he explained to web mag, A.V. Club', in 1998. Even taking into account a sensibility coloured by Manchester's infamously cheerless skies, it's fair to say that ADAMSON redefined the word brooding. Sure enough, much of 'DELUSION' is comprised of various shades of Morricone-inspired keyboard gloom, pensive Spanish guitar and paranoid, post-industrial soundwaves. As 'Moss Side Story' (1989) proved, though, it's an aesthetic that doesn't preclude humour, and ADAMSON isn't so reverent in his film buffery that he can't have some fun with his source material. He has 'La Cucaracha' jumping hoops in a circus of plod-hopping brass, and 'Fish Face' is surely as febrile a Latin-jazz workout as any Mancunian could hope to compose. He's also well versed in the kind of dynamic required to carry off the dovetailing quasi-opera of a cue like 'Il Soltario', while being au fait with sample culture, he almost gets away with an excess of dialogue and fragmentary sequencing that might grate in lesser hands. Buy this soundtrack, though, for the ANITA LANE-sung, proto-trip-hop jive that is 'These Boots Are Made For Walking', as stoned, petulant and generally reeking of nihilism as Nancy's was sassy. *BG*

Album rating: *6.5

DEMONLOVER

2002 (Fra 117m) Citizen / Cofimage / Elizabeth Films (18)

Film genre: erotic psychological thriller/mystery

Top guns: s-w (+ dir): Olivier Assayas → CLEAN (→ NOISE)

Stars: Connie Nielsen *(Diane De Monx)*, Charles Berling *(Herve Le Millinec)*, Chloe Sevigny *(Elise Lipsky)* ← KIDS / → DEATH OF A DYNASTY → the BROWN BUNNY, Gina Gershon *(Elaine Si Gibril)* ← the INSIDER ← TOUCH ← PRETTY IN PINK / → PREY FOR ROCK & ROLL, Dominique Reymond *(Karen)*, Jean-Baptiste Malartre *(Henri-Pierre Wolf)*, Edwin Gerard *(Edward Gomez)*

Storyline: Plots and intrigue abound in the world of corporate business as French firm VolfGroup try to buy out Japanese company TokyoAnime, whose animation films threaten to wipe out their market rivals. At the same time US firm Demonlover take an interest in VolfGroup and "double agent" Diane and rival Elaine do battle for their respective companies. When it transpires that Demonlover seems to own an illegal hard-core website, blackmail and murder are on the cards. *JZ*

Movie rating: *6

Visual: video + dvd

Off the record: (see below)

—

SONIC YOUTH // & Various Artists)

Nov 02. (cd) *S.N.D.; (72435 8 0180 28)* [–] French [–]
– Move away / Control freak / Safe in Hell / Electric noisefield / Slambient desire / Melodikim / Teknikal illprovisation / Superdead // Lovely head (GOLDFRAPP) / Dirge (DEATH IN VEGAS) / Hedgehoppers (DUB SQUAD) *[film version]* / Back to the primitive (SOULFLY).

S/track review: Their third crack at scoring (after 'MADE IN USA' and 'SUBURBI@'), SONIC YOUTH describe 'DEMONLOVER' as "the film score that you dream about doing" and by all accounts they were in their element recording it. Having previously selected 'Tunic' from their 'Goo' album for his movie 'Irma Vep', director Assayas was eager to collaborate more closely with THURSTON MOORE and Co., this time on a project inspired in part by Japanese Hentai pornography. While 'DEMONLOVER' was still in the script stages, SONIC YOUTH were invited to begin writing music, which was then played on set during filming. Assayas would in turn send the dailies to the band, and music inspired by this footage was returned to the set. Once filming was completed, the music was reprocessed and edited into the final cut along with music by other artists, including tracks by Neu!, Darkthrone, Ministry and A Silver Mt. Zion that are not included on the soundtrack release. Of SONIC YOUTH's original score, 'Move Away', a rhythmic slow builder with KIM GORDON vocals, is by far the most accessible track, though it still comes on like Can in a k-hole. In 'Control Freak', tinkling cymbals and throbbing waves of noise lapse into melancholy strummed guitar chords and distant feedback. Elsewhere, 'Safe In Hell' could be excerpted from an early Verve b-side, which could be a good thing, while 'Teknikal Illprovisation' sounds like Eraserhead in a rainforest, which probably isn't. GOLDFRAPP's 'Lovely Head', and 'Dirge' by DEATH IN VEGAS, both diverging significantly from SONIC YOUTH's abstractions, are intrinsically cinematic and create their own atmosphere without spoiling the general tone. The lofty poise of SONIC YOUTH is compromised less successfully by generic electronica from DUB SQUAD while the inclusion of SOULFLY's macho 'Back To The Primitive' knocks the collection severely off-balance. Ultimately, while not as wilfully obscure as some of SONIC YOUTH's releases, 'DEMONLOVER' is less satisfying as a solitary listening experience than many of their countless studio works, although this perhaps should be expected from a score so intrinsically linked to its source material. *SW*

Album rating: *5

□ Willy DeVILLE segment
(⇒ HOMEBOY)

□ the DEVIL'S SON-IN-LAW alt.
(⇒ PETEY WHEATSTRAW)

Neil DIAMOND

Born: 24 Jan'41, Brooklyn, New York, USA. The author of the MONKEES' signature, 'I'm A Believer' as well as a plethora of nicotine-stained karaoke favourites, NEIL DIAMOND began life as a Brill Building songwriter before racking up a string of mid-60s hits in his own right. An endearing combination of pop smarts and rootsier influences shaped classics like 'Kentucky Woman', 'Sweet Caroline' and 'Crackin' Rosie', although his first soundtrack, to Hal Bartlett's avian fantasy, 'JONATHAN LIVINGSTON SEAGULL' (1973), employed a more introspective approach in keeping with the post-hippy era and his own move towards a more overt singer-songwriter style. The album's multi-million selling success was repeated and even bettered with DIAMOND's soundtrack to the 'The JAZZ SINGER' (1980), an update of the 1927 Al Jolson original (starring Neil), and a record which spawned three US Top 10 hits. Strangely, considering the huge sales of these albums, DIAMOND has yet to score another film, although he did make an unexpected cameo appearance in critically slated slacker comedy, 'Saving Silverman' (2001), whose main characters were part of a NEIL DIAMOND tribute band. The ageing troubadour also garnered some belated street cred when American alt-rockers Urge Overkill covered his 1967 hit, 'Girl, You'll Be A Woman Soon', for the soundtrack to Quentin Tarantino's 'Pulp Fiction' (1995). *BG*

- **filmography** (composer) {acting} –

Jonathan Livingston Seagull *(1973 OST =>)* / **the Last Waltz** *(1978 {p} on OST by the BAND =>)* / **the Jazz Singer** *(1980 {*} + OST =>)* / Saving Silverman *(2001 {c})*

Manu DIBANGO

Born: 10 Feb'34, Douala, Cameroon. A titan of African-rooted jazz/funk and the one-time, self-confessed "Quincy Jones of African Paris", MANU DIBANGO stands alongside the likes of Fela Kuti as a commissar and cross-pollinator of African music. Wielding his trademark saxophone in the French capital as early as the mid-50s, DIBANGO spent the next decade shuttling between Paris, Cameroon, Belgium and the Congo, playing on the first African recordings in Europe and experimenting with various strands of world music before the term was even invented. His big break came in 1972 with 'Soul Makossa', a barnstorming Afro-Funk classic inspired by a rhythm native to Cameroon and written as a theme for that year's African Cup football extravaganza. The song was a global dancefloor hit, facilitating a move to New York and a period touring with Latino supergroup the FANIA ALL STARS. Around the same time he made his first move into film scoring with the soundtrack for African mercenary drama, 'COUNTDOWN AT KUSINI' (1976). Subsequently basing himself in West Africa where he led Ivory Coast's State Television Orchestra, DIBANGO scored acclaimed Senegalese drama, 'Ceddo' (1977). Back in France, he continued to work on the occasional score including 'Les Keufs' (1987), the controversial 'Comment Faire l'Amour Avec Un Noir Sans Se Fatiguer' aka 'How To Make Love To A Negro Without Getting Tired' (1989) and, with fellow Parisian-based Africans, Toure Kunda, 'Lumière Noire' (1994). While only the 1989 score made it to soundtrack, his collaborative recordings continued to draw acclaim, not least 'CubAfrica' (1998), an outstanding link-up with Cuba's Cuarteto Patria. Into the new millennium, DIBANGO scored a further couple of French movies, 'Nha Fala' (2002), and 'Le Silence De La Foretê' (2003). *BG*

- **filmography** (composer) {actor} –

Countdown At Kusini *(1975 OST =>)* / Ceddo *(1977)* / le Prix De La Liberte *(1978)* / Forty Deuce *(1982)* / les Keufs *(1987 w/ Francis Agbo, Raoul Agbo & Stephan Sirkis)* / How To Make Love To A Negro Without Getting Tired *(1989 OST; see future edition)* / Children Of Africa *(1993 TV {p} w/ ROY AYERS & HUGH MASEKELA)* / Lumiere Noire *(1994 w/ Avanos, Aziza & TOURE KUNDA)* / Black Dju *(1996 {c})* / Nha Fala *(2002)* / Kounandi *(2003)* / le Silence De La Foreta *(2003)*

DINGO

1991 (Aus/Fra 109m) AFFC / Dedre Films / Cine Cliq (PG)

Film genre: Jazz & Blues Musical drama

Top guns: dir: Rolf de Heer / s-w: Mark Rosenberg

Stars: Colin Friels *(John "Dingo" Anderson)*, **Miles DAVIS** *(Billy Cross)*, Bernadette Lafont *(Angie Cross)*, Helen Buday *(Jane Anderson)*, Joe Petruzzi *(Peter)*, Brigitte Catillon *(Beatrice Boulain)*, Bernard Fresson *(Jacques Boulain)*

Storyline: After a formative, runway run-in with jazz legend, Billy Cross, John 'Dingo' Anderson grows up dreaming of Paris in the wilds of Australia. When he isn't trapping dingos, he's playing trumpet with a local band but it isn't enough. Years of one-way correspondence make him even more despondent but, on the eve of his 33rd birthday, his wife pulls strings that he couldn't, setting up the trip of Anderson's lifetime. *BG*

Movie rating: *6

Visual: video

Off the record: Miles DAVIS (see own entry)

MILES DAVIS (& Michel LeGrand)

Feb 92. (cd) *Warners; <(7599 26438-2)>* ☐ ☐
– Kimberley trumpet / The arrival / Concert on the runway / The departure / Dingo howl / Letter as hero / Trumpet cleaning / The dream / Paris walking I / Paris walking II / Kimberley trumpet in Paris / The music room / Club entrance / The jam session / Going home / Surprise!

S/track review: Billing 'DINGO' as a MILES DAVIS album is perhaps a little disingenuous given that he only appears on half of it. The use of soundalike CHUCK FINDLEY on the other half means that viewers/listeners not au fait with either jazz or MILES DAVIS likely couldn't tell the difference. Still, it's the penultimate recording of the trumpeter's career (released just after his death on 28th September 1991) and the little attention it generates is usually in relation to DAVIS revisiting his past, or else the fact that it soundtracked his first – and last – major acting role. That the ailing legend looked to the 50s for inspiration is less surprising if you dig out 'Legrand Jazz' (1958), a buried treasure featuring DAVIS and a cast of contemporaries (John Coltrane, Ben Webster, Bill Evans and Donald Byrd to name but a few) performing what some regard as Michel LeGrand's career best arrangements. Thirty odd years later and in a completely different context, this reunion of DAVIS and LeGrand nevertheless sounds pretty much how you might expect, a combination of straightahead blowing and pensive abstraction. The French composer lays off the strings (although he does play keyboards), and 'The Arrival' – performed by DAVIS – establishes 'DINGO's main theme as a gaunt, haunted avowal of merciless heat and outback isolation. MILES revisits it in both 'The Dream' and 'Going Home', and it's the kind of deceptively diffident motif that spins around your brain for hours and days later. 'Concert On The Runway' is DAVIS in bustling, pre-'Kind Of Blue' hard bop mode, the first time he'd attempted any kind of regular jazz since the dawn of his electric phase. But FINDLEY – with whom DAVIS duels on 80s jazz-funk workout, 'The Jam Session' – also deserves a mention; he proves no slacker at bop-derived material himself on the sprightly 'Paris Walking I'. And if you've never heard MILES' laconic drawl, here's your chance; the dialogue makes him sound decades older than he was, but that only adds to the atmosphere. Not the first place to investigate MILES' soundtrack career but worthier of investigation than many critics admit. *BG*

Album rating: *6

☐ DIRTY THREE segment
(⇒ PRAISE)

DISCO GODFATHER

1979 (US 93m) Transvue Pictures Corp. (R)

Film genre: martial arts/crime caper/spoof

Top guns: s-w: J. Robert Wagoner (+ dir), Cliff Roquemore ← PETEY WHEATSTRAW

Stars: Rudy Ray Moore *(Tucker Williams)* ← PETEY WHEATSTRAW ← the MONKEY HUSTLE ← DOLEMITE / → JACKIE'S BACK! → BIG MONEY HUTLA, Carol Speed *(Noel)* ← DYNAMITE BROTHERS ← SAVAGE! ← the MACK ← BUMMER!, Jimmy Lynch *(Sweetmeat)* ← PETEY WHEATSTRAW ← DOLEMITE, Jerry Jones *(Dr. Fred Mathias)* ← DOLEMITE, Lady Reed *(Mrs. Edwards)* ← PETEY WHEATSTRAW ← DOLEMITE, James H. Hawthorne *(Stinger Ray)*, Leroy Daniels *(disco MC)* ← PETEY WHEATSTRAW, Julius J. Carry III *(Bucky)*, Dino Washington *(basketball player)* ← DOLEMITE, **Doc Watson** *(district councilman)* ← BANJOMAN, Keith David *(club patron)* → ROAD HOUSE → REALITY BITES, Jimmy Davis *(Prayer band)* ← JE T'AIME MOI NON PLUS

Storyline: Ex-cop Tucker Williams is now the resident DJ at the Blueberry Hill disco. When his nephew Bucky is introduced to the somewhat dubious delights of "angel dust" and comes back stoned out of his skull, Tucker decides to hit the streets once more to track down the pushers. Can he expose the bad guys and save New York from a drugs disaster or will he be visiting the angels himself? *JZ*

Movie rating: *3.5

Visual: video + dvd

Off the record: Doc Watson is the father of country artist, Merle Watson.

JUICE PEOPLE UNLIMITED

Sep 79. (lp) *Apple Juice; <AJ 152>* ☐ ☐-
– Disco Godfather / Shermanizing / One way ticket to hell / I never wanted to say goodbye / Spaced out.

S/track review: JUICE PEOPLE UNLIMITED were actually made up of top session players (ERNIE FIELDS JR., DAVID SHIELDS, PAUL JACKSON JR. and JAMES GADSON), disco superseding funk on this very rare groove chiller. The voice of RUDY RAY MOORE is also on show on 'DISCO GODFATHER', a vinyl junkie's stairway to mirrorball heaven. While the pieces seem to last forever, from the bubbly 'Shermanizing' to closer 'Spaced Out', this LP (due for a CD re-issue surely?) gets the listener into the groove. Although the film probably helped to kill off disco music (along with 'CAN'T STOP THE MUSIC', 'XANADU', 'The APPLE' and 'THANK GOD IT'S FRIDAY'), it has since achieved cult status. *MCS*

Album rating: *6

DISCO 9000

1977 (US 94m) Choice Inc. (PG)

Film genre: Dance-music drama

Top guns: dir: D'Urville Martin ← DOLEMITE / s-w: Roland S. Jefferson

Stars: John Poole *(Fass Black)*, Jeanie Bell *(Karen)* ← THREE THE HARD WAY ← TROUBLE MAN ← MELINDA, Cal Wilson *(Earl Ross)* ← FIVE ON THE BLACK HAND SIDE ← the FINAL COMEDOWN, Nicholas Lewis *(Bellamy)*, Harold Nicholas *(midget)* → the FIVE HEARTBEATS, Sidney Bagby *(Manny)*, Beverly Ann *(Denise)*, **Johnnie Taylor** *(Gene Edwards)* ← WATTSTAX, D'Urville Martin *(Stuffman)* ← DOLEMITE ← SHEBA, BABY ← FIVE ON THE BLACK HAND SIDE ← the SOUL OF NIGGER CHARLEY ← BLACK CAESAR ← BOOK OF NUMBERS ← HELL UP IN HARLEM ← the FINAL COMEDOWN ← WATERMELON MAN ← a TIME TO SING, Paula Sills *(Fass's attorney)* → NO WAY BACK

Storyline: Shady record producer Bellamy is convinced the only way to break into the L.A. music scene is to have his work played at Disco 9000, the top local nightspot (literally – it's in a penthouse). When owner Fass Black refuses to play ball, Bellamy resorts to more extreme measures to get his way, namely muggings, car trashings and theft. However, after a woman is killed, Black reckons enough is enough and plots his revenge. *JZ*

Movie rating: *4.5

Visual: none

Off the record: **JOHNNIE TAYLOR** (see below)

—

JOHNNIE TAYLOR

1977. (lp) *Columbia; <PS 35004>* ☐ ☐
– I don't know what I'd do without you / Toot your flute / Just a happy song / God is standing by / Disco 9000 / I love you woman / Right now. *<cd-iss. Sep01 on 'Westside'+=;* – JOHNNIE TAYLOR: Rated Extraordinare (tracks)

S/track review: A soul veteran (he had replaced Sam Cooke in the Soul Stirrers in 1957), JOHNNIE TAYLOR racked up a string of fine hits as the Stax label's top seller in the late 60s and early 70s before 'Disco Lady' became the first-ever platinum single in 1976 – and all but derailed him artistically. In fact the bass-driven, brass-trimmed number-one was more rooted in funky soul than the disco formula his record label subsequently encouraged him to pursue, and this soundtrack from the same period has been critically – and a little harshly – tainted by the lacklustre fare that followed. The funk-lite of the title track made #24 on the R&B charts, even if its "down at the disco" chorus limits its long-term appeal. Driven by the Muscle Shoals Horns, though, 'Just A Happy Song' is fine swinging Southern R&B. Elsewhere, the playing and production are faultless, there's a minimum of hissing hi-hats and popping-octave bass, and even the more ordinary material is listenable for TAYLOR's muscular, pliant and sassy baritone. Throwing off the curse of disco in the 80s, the Arkansas native would rediscover his classic strengths with a 16-year sequence of acclaimed Southern soul/blues albums prior to his premature death in 2000. Note that: JOHNNIE TAYLOR's 'Disco 9000' CD (released 2006) was a compilation not a re-issue. *ND*

Album rating: *5

☐ Willie DIXON segment
(⇒ GINGER ALE AFTERNOON)

DR. T & THE WOMEN

2000 (US/Ger 122m) Sandcastle / New Films / 20th Century Fox (R)

Film genre: romantic comedy drama

Top guns: dir: Robert Altman ← POPEYE ← NASHVILLE / s-w: Anne Rapp

Stars: Richard Gere *(Dr. T)* → the MOTHMAN PROPHECIES → I'M NOT THERE, Helen Hunt *(Bree)*, Farrah Fawcett *(Kate)*, Laura Dern *(Peggy)* ← WILD AT HEART ← LADIES AND GENTLEMEN, THE FABULOUS STAINS / → I AM SAM, Shelley Long *(Carolyn)*, Tara Reid *(Connie)* ← GIRL / → JOSIE AND THE PUSSYCATS, Kate Hudson *(Dee Dee)* ← ALMOST FAMOUS, Liv Tyler *(Marilyn)* ← THAT THING YOU DO! ← EMPIRE RECORDS ← HEAVY, Robert Hays *(Harlan)*, Matt Malloy *(Bill)* ← SOUTH OF HEAVEN, WEST OF HELL, Andy Richter *(Eli)* → POOTIE TANG, Lee Grant *(Dr. Harper)* ← the LANDLORD

Storyline: Dallas gynaecologist Sullivan Travis is surrounded by women: his neurotic wife, his moneyed clients, his soon-to-be-married lesbian daughter and his busybody of a sister-in-law, so just as well he ostensibly regards them as a higher species. His unruffled demeanour begins to flap as his spouse gets committed, the marriage looms and his golf course sojourns become more temptingly adulterous. *BG*

Movie rating: *5

Visual: video + dvd

Off the record: **LYLE LOVETT** (see own entry)

—

LYLE LOVETT

Sep 00. (cd) *Curb-M.C.A.; <088 112 381-2>* ☐ ☐
– Dr. T's theme / Opening credits / Mall women / The fountain / The bree shuffle / Golf cart love / The bridal shower / You've been so good up to now / She's already made up her mind / Lady of the lake / Dr. T's theme (reprise) / The screen door / The wedding / Go away with me / The crash / Ain't it somethin'.

S/track review: One of LYLE LOVETT's more desultory offerings defined in the differential between a 'Windham Hill'-esque main theme and hootenanny closer, the soundtrack initially suggests neo-classical pathos but soon beds in for an extended dose of bluesy shuffle, well oiled honky-tonk and western swing, not overly concerning itself with leitmotif development. Given the frantic, fractious nature of Altman's style, that's hardly surprising, but it all passes by innocuously enough. If vocals 'You've Been So Good Up To Now' and 'She's Already Made Up Her Mind' sound familiar, that's because they're both from LOVETT's 'Joshua Judges Ruth' album. Structurally, these songs don't acclimatise particularly well to the score, sounding like a lazy inversion of the usual ploy of tarting up compilations with ill-fitting incidental excerpts. More interesting are attempts at close-textured film music like 'The Screen Door' and 'The Crash', where a minimalist, dissonant dynamic rooted by bassist VIKTOR KAUSS and pianist MATT ROLLINGS really gets a chance to project beyond the Texas state boundary. *BG*

Album rating: *5.5

Thomas DOLBY

Born: Thomas Morgan Robertson, 14 Oct'58, Cairo, Egypt. The son of a British archeologist (hence his exotic birthplace), Thomas's penchant for electronic musical gadgetry developed while he was studying meteorology at college. Nicknamed "Dolby" by classmates for his technological wizardry, the boffin-like synth maestro began his professional musical life as a live sound mixer for the likes of the Fall before becoming a part-time member of Bruce Woolley & The Camera Club in 1979; DOLBY subsequently backed up punk starlet, Lene Lovich, penning her 1981 hit single, 'New Toy'. Early '81 also saw the release of DOLBY's own debut single, 'Urges', on tiny indie label, 'Armageddon'. It wasn't a hit, but DOLBY had created enough of a buzz for 'Parlophone' to snap him up later that year and furnish him with a minor UK hit in 'Europa And The Pirate Twins'. He was also canny enough to negotiate his own label, 'Venus In Peril' under 'Parlophone's sponsorship, launching it with a couple of flop singles, 'Airwaves' and 'Radio Silence', in the first half of '82. Ironically, DOLBY had more success that year with the million-selling 'Magic's Wand', an early hip-hop/electro classic he'd penned and produced for US rapper, Whodini. Despite his decidedly arty bent, DOLBY also twiddled knobs for such airbrushed rockers as Foreigner and Def Leppard. His own debut album, 'The Golden Age Of Wireless' (1982), sold moderately prior to the release of 'She Blinded Me With Science', an infectiously quirky ditty with an equally quirky video to match featuring idiosyncratic TV boffin, Magnus Pyke. While not even scraping the UK Top 40, the Americans (presumably much enamoured with its Great British "eccentricity") put it in the Top 5 via heavy MTV rotation and pushed the debut album (craftily re-titled after the hit single) into the Top 20. By contrast, his sophomore effort, 'The Flat Earth' (1984), made the UK Top 20 while barely making a mark in the States. This was largely due to the success of the kinetically funky 'Hyperactive' single, a Top 20 hit which nevertheless was unrepresentative of the more meditative soundscapes that characterised the album. Although DOLBY scored a further minor hit that year with a cover of Dan Hicks & The Charlatans' 'I Scare Myself', his chart success was patchy over the second half of the 80s. Instead, he concentrated on film scores (albeit for such ill-advised works as 'Fever Pitch' alongside Quincy Jones, 'HOWARD THE DUCK' and Ken Russell's 'GOTHIC'), collaborative work (with the critically acclaimed Ryuichi Sakamoto on 7", 'Field Work') and production duties for such stylistically diverse artists as George Clinton, Prefab Sprout and Joni Mitchell. Newly relocated to L.A. and married to Dynasty soap actress, Kathleen Beller, DOLBY set up a brief tenure with 'E.M.I.' for the 'Aliens Ate My Buick' (1988) album, released under the moniker Thomas Dolby & The Toy People. It met with a muted response and it'd be another four years – during which time he continued with film and production work (he featured in ROGER WATERS' 'The WALL: LIVE IN BERLIN') – before he re-emerged with the 'Astronauts And Heretics' (1992) album. Released on his new 'Giant' label ('Virgin' in the UK), the album was promoted with the almost MOR 'Close, But No Cigar', a UK Top 30 hit that introduced the most conventional pop/rock of his career. Despite the presence of such rock vets as JERRY GARCIA and Eddie Van Halen, the record flopped in DOLBY's adopted home country although it did spawn a further minor UK hit in 'I Love You Goodbye'. Re-released as a primer for "greatest hits" set, 'Retrospectacle' (1994), 'Hyperactive' was a UK hit all over again in early '94 although most of DOLBY's time was subsequently taken up with his computer software company, Headspace. *BG & MCS*

- **filmography** (composer) {acting} –

Fever Pitch *(1985 score w/ QUINCY JONES)* / **Howard The Duck** *(1986 {b} + OST w/ JOHN BARRY =>)* / **Gothic** *(1986 OST =>)* / **Rockula** *(1990 {*})* / **the Wall: Live In Berlin** *(1990 TV {p} OST by ROGER WATERS =>)* / the Gate To The Mind's Eye *(1994 OST => future edition)*

DOLEMITE

1975 (US 88m) Dimension Pictures (R)

Film genre: crime caper/comedy

Top guns: dir: D'Urville Martin → DISCO 9000 / s-w: Jerry Jones (story: Rudy Ray Moore)

Stars: Rudy Ray Moore *(Dolemite)* → the MONKEY HUSTLE → PETEY WHEATSTRAW → DISCO GODFATHER → JACKIE'S BACK! → BIG MONEY HUTLA, Lady Reed *(Queen Bee)* → PETEY WHEATSTRAW → DISCO GODFATHER, D'Urville Martin *(Willie Green)* ← SHEBA, BABY ← FIVE ON THE BLACK HAND SIDE ← the SOUL OF NIGGER CHARLEY → BLACK CAESAR ← BOOK OF NUMBERS ← HELL UP IN HARLEM ← the FINAL COMEDOWN ← WATERMELON MAN ← a TIME TO SING / → DISCO 9000, Jerry Jones *(Blakeley)* → DISCO GODFATHER, Dino Washington *(henchman)* → DISCO GODFATHER, William Bryant *(Mitchell)*, West Gale *(Reverend Gibbs)*, Jimmy Lynch *(Jimmy)* → PETEY WHEATSTRAW → DISCO GODFATHER, **James Ingram** *(keyboard player w/ Revelation Funk)*, Vince Barbi ← BLACK BELT JONES

Storyline: Comedic kingpin Dolemite is the baaadest ass in L.A.'s 4th Ward; his motto: "Dolemite is my name and fu**ing up muthafu**as is my game!". He might be languishing in jail but it's not long before Queen Bee, his portly right hand madame, has persuaded the governor to strike a deal. Told that his own nephew, Little Jimmy, has been fatally shot, he's asked to clean up the 'hood and take out his nemesis Willie Green while he's at it. Battling the wiles of corrupt cops, a sleazy mayor and a whore-mongering, black power-proseletysing preacher, Dolemite and his kung-fu fighting "bitches" reclaim the nightclub he lost in prison, prompting a final showdown with Green and his cronies. Along the way he gets plenty of opportunities to drop his favourite insults ("you no-business, born-insecure, jock-jawed muthafu**a!") and he also makes time to entertain the boys with a couple of his scatalogical rhymes, one, bizarrely enough, about the sinking of the Titanic, the other his infamous jungle fable, 'Signifyin' Monkey'. Hip hop is born. *BG*

Movie rating: *6

Visual: video + dvd

Off the record: (see below)

—

RUDY RAY MOORE & THE SOUL REBELLION ORCHESTRA (composer: Arthur Wright / & Various Artists)

Jul 75. (lp) *Generation International; <GEN 2501>* [ ] [–]
– Dolemite (BEN TAYLOR) / The queen / Do you still care (BEN TAYLOR) / The rumble / Mayor's get-away / Power of your love (MARY LOVE) / Willie Green / When we start making love (MARY LOVE) / The hitman / Ghetto expressions / Time is on our side (REVELATION FUNK) / Creeper / The jive jungle / Flatland. *<cd-iss. Jun06 on 'Relapse'+=; RR 6694>* – Dolemite (BEN TAYLOR w/ MOORE narration) – film version / Flatland – film version / Human tornado (from 'Human Tornado') / Miss Wonderful (from 'Human Tornado') / Dolemite radio spot (version 1) / Dolemite radio spot (version 2) / Human tornado radio spot.

S/track review: "The flyest man of all time" is how Ice-T describes RUDY RAY MOORE, the semi-legendary black comedian/singer/filmmaker whose x-rated material inspired countless hip hop samples. Self-financed from record sales, 'DOLEMITE' was his movie and soundtrack debut, the so-called Citizen Kane of blaxploitation, based around a character MOORE had introduced on his 1970 album, 'Eat Out More Often'. A born-bad mutha in the vein of Lightnin' Rod's 'Sport', Dolemite's maladjusted history is recounted in straight funk form by the mysterious BEN TAYLOR (NOT the son of James and Carly), and it's worth hearing if only for the plummy, tongue-stuffed-in-cheek backing vocals. MOORE himself doesn't have much of a singing voice, but then, it's probably what he does with it that counts, or rather what he says, peerless couplets like "I'm gonna tell my children's children what life is all about, and I'm hopin', yes hopin', they'll have enough soul to figure it out". Fans of the Last Poets will dig his swinging, exhortatory spoken-word track, 'Flatlands' (and, if you've got the recently re-issued CD, the bonus film version of the title theme); truth be told, the soundtrack could've done with more of them. As far as uncut blaxploitation funk goes, the pickings are slimmer than you'd imagine, and a name like the SOUL REBELLION ORCHESTRA (christened by RUDY himself) takes a lot of living up to. The band – composed entirely of anonymous sessioneers – are at their best accompanying MOORE; the instrumentals are tight if slightly one dimensional, often standing on the verge of getting it on with cheesy porno-funk. But there's some memorable stuff here: the clavinet-vamping 'Mayor's Get-Away', the syncopated squelch of 'The Hitman', the geeky-sweet soul of 'Willie Green'; at one point they even cheekily fall back on a snatch of 'Give It Up Or Turn It Loose'. REVELATION FUNK contribute the Stevie Wonder-esque 'Time Is On Our Side', but are probably more famous (infamous?) for spawning James Ingram. One lady who's got enough soul to figure it out for all of us is MARY LOVE, the relatively obscure Northern Soul dame turned gospel singer who'd previously recorded for 'Modern' and 'Roulette'. She doesn't stretch herself like she does on 'PETEY WHEATSTRAW', and while the recording budget for 'DOLEMITE' was equally miniscule, the sound isn't quite as satisfyingly ragged. The CD also comes with a rather lavish set of sleevenotes and the analogue-squiggling theme from mindwarping follow-up, 'Human Tornado' (previously only available as a disgustingly rare, $100 dollar single) but as the original masters were apparently untraceable, you can probably imagine what it sounds like. *BG*

Album rating: *6.5 (re-cd *7)

DONOVAN

Born: Donovan Philips Leitch, 10 May'46, Maryhill, Glasgow, Scotland (aged ten, his family moved to Hatfield, England). Finding an old acoustic guitar lying in someone's rubbish, the 14-year-old runaway unwittingly began his road to pop stardom. In 1964, while playing small gigs in Southend, DONOVAN was spotted by Geoff Stephens and Peter Eden, who immediately became his managers. Later that year, after performing on the 'Ready Steady Go!' pop show over three consecutive weeks, the denim-clad beatnik signed to 'Pye' records. His debut single, 'Catch The Wind' (issued around the same time as Dylan's 'The Times They Are A-Changin''), saw him break into the Top 5, later reaching Top 30 in America where he was enjoying the fruits of a burgeoning career. His follow-up, 'Colours', repeated the chart formula in the summer of '65, as did the debut album, 'What's Bin Did And What's Bin Hid'. Later in the year, the 'Universal Soldier' EP saw DONOVAN begin to develop his uncompromising anti-war stance, a theme which he touched on with his second album, 'Fairytale'. Initially heralded as Britain's answer to BOB DYLAN, he began to build on his folk/pop roots, progressing into flower-power with the classic, 'Sunshine Superman', in 1966. The album of the same name (issued only in the States) took DONOVAN to a creative high point and included the much revered, 'Season Of The Witch'. At the beginning of '67, yet another single 'Mellow Yellow' was riding high in the American hit parade, while 'Epistle To Dippy' soon followed suit. During this highly prolific period, which saw DONOVAN inspired by the transcendental meditation of guru Maharishi Mahesh Yogi, he released two sublime pieces of acid-pop in 'There Is A Mountain' and 'Jennifer Juniper'. The momentum continued with 'Hurdy Gurdy Man', another classic sojourn into psychedelia which hit Top 5 on both sides of the Atlantic. In 1969, DONOVAN contributed songs to and cameoed in the film 'If It's Tuesday, This Must Be Belgium' (he previously scored three tracks for 'Poor Cow' in 1967), while the man also collaborated with the JEFF BECK Group on 'Goo Goo Barabajagal' – this was his final 45 to make a major chart appearance. An album, 'Open Road' (1970), named after his new band, surprised many by cracking both the US & UK charts. In 1971, he recorded a double album of children's songs 'H.M.S. Donovan', which led to a critical backlash from the music press; his affiliation with the young ones continued when he starred in and wrote the music score for the movie, 'The PIED PIPER' (1972). His credibility was slightly restored with his co-writing credit for ALICE COOPER's 'Billion Dollar Babies' track. After a 3-year exile in Ireland for tax reasons, he set up home in California with his American wife Linda Lawrence and daughters Astrella Celeste and Oriole Nebula; he'd previously fathered two other children, Donovan Leitch Jnr. – star of the film 'GAS FOOD LODGING' – and actress-to-be, Ione Skye. DONOVAN enjoyed something of a renaissance in the early 90s when Happy Mondays' mainman Shaun Ryder sang his praises, leading to a comeback album, 'Donovan Rising'. He was still going strong in '96, releasing a well-received Rick Rubin-produced album, 'Sutras', for the R.C.A.-affiliated 'American' label. Nigh on a decade later, a near 60-year-old DONOVAN returned with 'Beat Cafe' (2004). *MCS & BG*

- **filmography** (composer) {acting} –

Chappaqua *(1966 {c} on OST by RAVI SHANKAR =>)* / **Don't Look Back** *(1967 {c+p} =>)* / Poor Cow *(1967 songs on score)* / **Festival** *(1967 {p} =>)* / If It's Tuesday, This Must Be Belgium *(1969 {p} songs on OST)* / **Cucumber Castle** *(1970 {c} OST by the BEE GEES =>)* / **the Pied Piper** *(1972 {*} OST =>)* / Brother Sun, Sister Moon *(1972 songs on OST)* / Aliens From Spaceship Earth *(1977 {*} + score)* / **Sgt. Pepper's Lonely Hearts Club Band** *(1978 {c} OST by V/A =>)* / the Secret Policeman's Other Ball *(1982 {c} OST by V/A =>)* / the Secret Policeman's Private Parts *(1984 {c})* / Walking After Midnight *(1988 {c})* / 84C MoPic *(1989 songs)* / L.I.E. *(2001 w/ Pierre Foldes & Georg Friedrich Handel)*

DON'T PLAY US CHEAP

1973 (US 90m) Yeah Inc.

Film genre: fantasy Musical comedy

Top guns: s-w + dir: **Melvin VAN PEEBLES**

Stars: Esther Rolle *(Miss Maybell)* → CLEOPATRA JONES, Avon Long *(David)*, Rhetta Hughes *(Earnestine)*, Mabel King *(house guest)* → the WIZ, Theresa Merritt *(house guest)* → the WIZ

Storyline: Inspired by the same incident which provided the material for Peebles' novel 'La Fête · Harlem', and centering on two infernal "imps" whose graduation to full demonic status depends on their breaking up a swinging party in Harlem. Matters are complicated when one of the satanic trainees is tempted by an all too human girl. *BG*

Movie rating: *2.5

Visual: video

Off the record: (see below)

MELVIN VAN PEEBLES

1973. (d-lp) *Stax; <STS 2-3006>* [ ] [-]
– You cut up the clothes in the closet of my dreams / Break that party & opening / Saturday night / The bowsers thing / The book of life / Quittin time / Ain't love grand / I'm a bad character / Know your business / Feast on me / Ain't love grand / Break that party / Someday it seems that it ain't just don't even pay to get out of bed / Quartet / The phoney game / It makes no difference / Bad character bossa nova / Quartet / The Washingtons thing / If you see a Devil, smash him. *<(d-cd re-mast.Apr02; SCD24 3006)>*

S/track review: Actually the soundtrack to a Broadway production rather than a film (although it belatedly appeared on video), this qualifies because it would've been the soundtrack to a film had director/composer MELVIN VAN PEEBLES been blessed with a distributor. It's also a funky good listen. It mightn't bear comparison with the epochal ' . . .SWEETBACK . . .' but as PEEBLES comments in the CD reissue's excellent sleevenotes: "It was a nice, warm, PG play. The other thing {Sweetback} was something else". As a stage production, most of the numbers are performed by actors although the spontaneity and soulfulness of the material checks any tendency to thespian stolidity. Among the assorted bluesy singalongs, call and response hollers, and bumptious interludes there were also some powerful stand-alone-tracks and at least one stone classic. Ex-Ikette JOSHIE JO ARMSTEAD's stunning 'You Cut Up The Clothes In The Closet Of My Dreams' remains as gutsy and sublime a gospel-inflected roots soul ballad as has ever appeared on any soundtrack, period. As such, it's worth the price of admission alone although former Pilgrim Traveler GEORGE McCURN's epic 'Quittin' Time' is as gritty an extra incentive as you could wish for. The thundering piano on both tracks is provided by an uncredited backing band which pads out the soundtrack with some lovely jazz-based instrumentals including the gorgeous 'Ain't Love Grand' (also performed as a haunting falsetto vocal by '..Sweetback..' actress Rhetta Hughes) and the cookin','Watermelon Man'-esque soul jazz of 'The Washingtons Thing'. Ironically, the only track which harked back to the subversive anarchy of PEEBLES' most famous work was wry closer, '(If You See A Devil') Smash Him'. You won't get any better advice than that. *BG*

Album rating: *6.5

– spinoff releases, etc. –

MELVIN VAN PEEBLES: The Melvin Van Peebles Collection

Oct 99. (d-cd) *Stax; <88040>* ☐ [–]
– (DON'T PLAY US CHEAP / SWEET SWEETBACK'S BAADASSSSS SONG)

☐ Nat DOVE & THE DEVILS segment (⇒ PETEY WHEATSTRAW)

DOWN AND OUT IN BEVERLY HILLS

1986 (US 103m) Buena Vista / Touchstone Films (R)

Film genre: domestic comedy

Top guns: s-w: Paul Mazursky (+ dir), Leon Capetanos (story/play: Rene Fauchois)

Stars: Nick Nolte *(Jerry Baskin)* → AFFLICTION → CLEAN → OVER THE HEDGE, **Bette MIDLER** *(Barbara Whiteman)*, Richard Dreyfuss *(Dave Whiteman)* ← AMERICAN GRAFFITI ← HELLO DOWN THERE, **LITTLE RICHARD** *(Orvis Goodnight)*, Tracy Nelson *(Jenny Whiteman)*, Elizabeth Pena *(Carmen)* ← TIMES SQUARE / → LA BAMBA → STRANGELAND → THINGS BEHIND THE SUN, Evan Richards *(Max Whiteman)*, Paul Mazursky *(Sidney Waxman)* ← a STAR IS BORN ← BLACKBOARD JUNGLE / → HEY HEY WE'RE THE MONKEES → TOUCH → WHY DO FOOLS FALL IN LOVE, Michael Greene *(Big Ed)* ← TO LIVE AND DIE IN L.A. ← NAKED ANGELS / → LAST MAN STANDING, Andre Philippe *(party guest)* ← BLACK BELT JONES

Storyline: When businessman Dave Whiteman sees hapless hobo Jerry drowning in his luxury swimming pool, he magnanimously decides to save him – big mistake. Jerry soon becomes an honorary member of Whiteman's dysfunctional family, but at first he gets on best with the mutt. He discovers that money doesn't buy happiness and Dave's very unhappy wife, shopaholic Barbara, starts an affair with him as does the housemaid. When Dave learns what's been going on when he's been at the office, he plans his revenge. *JZ*

Movie rating: *5.5

Visual: video + dvd

Off the record: (see below)

—

Various Artists // ANDY SUMMERS

Mar 86. (lp/c/cd) *M.C.A.; <MCA/+C/D 6160> (MCF/+C 3320)* [68] May86 ☐
– Great gosh a'mighty! (it's a matter of time) (LITTLE RICHARD) / California girls (DAVID LEE ROTH) / El tecalitleco (the MARIACHI VARGAS DE TECALITLAN) / I love L.A. (RANDY NEWMAN) / Tutti frutti (LITTLE RICHARD) // Down And Out In Beverly Hills theme / Search for Kerouac / Nouvelle cuisine / Wave hands like clouds / The mission blues / Jerry's suicide attempt. *<US cd-iss. Jun88; MCAD 31062>*

S/track review: A soundtrack of two halves you could say, side one featuring various artists such as LITTLE RICHARD, and side two the score by ex-Police guitarist ANDY SUMMERS. The aforementioned Richard Penniman provides two of the numbers, but there's really not much difference in style between movie hit, 'Great Gosh A'Mighty! (It's A Matter Of Time)' (written with Billy Preston) and its 50s original cloned counterpart, 'Tutti Frutti'. Typically for a film about Beverly Hills, there's two celebratory and jingoistic cuts, the Beach Boys' 'California Girls' by former Van Halen frontman DAVID LEE ROTH and 'I Love L.A.' (from 1983) by the effervescent RANDY NEWMAN. The curveball thrown in came by way of (Sergio) VARGAS' 'El Tecalitleco', a merengue star in Latin America, no less. ANDY SUMMERS – with some writing help alongside T. Humecke on two cues – gives the listener six instrumentals, the 5-minute cinematic 'Theme' and five other short'n'sweet ditties lasting in total 10 minutes (check out 'The Mission Blues'). Whether Andy was listening to Bernard Herrmann, John Barry or even Ryuichi Sakamoto is anyone's guess, but this was a marked transition for the one-time pop guitarist. *MCS*

Album rating: *5

– spinoff hits, etc. –

LITTLE RICHARD: Great Gosh A'mighty! (It's A Matter Of Time)

Feb 86. (7") *<52780> (MCA 1049)* [42] May86 [62]
(12"+=) *(MCAT 1049)* – ANDY SUMMERS: Down And Out In Beverly Hills theme.

TALKING HEADS: Once In A Lifetime – live

Apr 86. (7") *Sire; <29163>* [91] [–]

DOWN BY LAW

1986 (US/W.Ger 107m b&w) Black Snake / Island Pictures (R)

Film genre: buddy/road movie/comedy

Top guns: s-w + dir: Jim Jarmusch → MYSTERY TRAIN → NIGHT ON EARTH → DEAD MAN → YEAR OF THE HORSE → GHOST DOG: THE WAY OF THE SAMURAI → COFFEE AND CIGARETTES

Stars: **Tom WAITS** *(Zack)*, **John LURIE** *(Jack)*, Roberto Benigni *(Roberto)* → NIGHT ON EARTH → COFFEE AND CIGARETTES, Nicoletta Braschi *(Nicoletta)* → MYSTERY TRAIN, Ellen Barkin *(Laurette)* ← EDDIE AND THE CRUISERS ← TENDER MERCIES ← UP IN SMOKE / → SIESTA → JOHNNY HANDSOME → FEAR AND LOATHING IN LAS VEGAS, Billie Neal *(Bobbie)* → GIRL 6, Rockets Redglare *(Gig)* → CANDY MOUNTAIN → MYSTERY TRAIN → WHAT ABOUT ME, Vernel Bagneris *(Preston)* → RAY

Storyline: Zack, Jack and Roberto are three unlikely cellmates in sultry summertime New Orleans. Zack and Jack are both innocent of their crimes but are too lazy to protest, and Roberto is seemingly a somewhat confused Italian tourist. The pair take great delight at Roberto's hopeless attempts to speak English, but could he be the hero when the trio bust out of prison and head for the bayous, where there just happens to be an Italian girl who gives them food and shelter? *JZ*

Movie rating: *8

Visual: video + dvd

Off the record: Three songs not included on LURIE's soundtrack album are:- 'Jockey Full Of Bourbon' & 'Tango Till They're Sore' (both by TOM WAITS) and 'It's Raining' (by IRMA THOMAS). *MCS*

JOHN LURIE

Dec 86. (m-lp/m-cd) *Capitol; <90968> Made To Measure; (MTM 14/+CD)* ☐ May87 ☐
– What do you know about music, you're not a lawyer / Strangers in the day / Promenade du Maquereau / The invasion of Poland / Please come to my house / Are you warm enough? / Swamp part I / Swamp part II / Are you warm enough again? / The king of Thailand, the queen of stairs / A hundred miles from Harry / Nicoletta can't cook / Fork in the road. *<cd re-iss. Nov92 on 'Intuition'; INTU 3006> (cd re-iss. Apr96; same)* – VARIETY soundtrack *<cd re-iss. Nov99 on 'Strange & Beautiful'+=; SB 0011>* – JOHN LURIE: Variety

S/track review: JOHN LURIE's "fake jazz" (his words) complements this uneasy mini-score, 'DOWN BY LAW', an altogether deconstructive, avant-garde array of 13 vignettes over nearly 20 minutes. Featuring the man himself, he garners the likes of fellow ex-Lounge Lizard, ARTO LINDSAY and Tom Waits' sidekick, MARC RIBOT, but it's all a bit daunting musically speaking. A long way removed from his previous, chamber-music-styled OST, 'Stranger Than Paradise' (1984), 'DOWN BY LAW' sets out its avant-jazz stall with a degree of humour and irony. Tracks such as 'What Do You Know About Music, You're Not A Lawyer', 'Please Come To My House' and 'Fork In The Road' are indeed the highlights of LURIE's return to form. Whether it's everybody's taste is a matter of conjecture. *MCS*

Album rating: *6

DOWNHILL CITY

1999 (Ger/Fin 106m) Zweites Deutsches Fernsehen (S)

Film genre: romantic psychological drama

Top guns: s-w + dir: Hannu Salonen

Stars: Franka Potente *(Peggy)* → STORYTELLING, Teemu Aromaa *(Artsi)*, Andreas Brucker *(Hans)*, Michaela Rosen *(Doris)*, Sebastian Rudolph *(Sascha)*, Azel Werner *(Fabian)*, Janne Hyytiainen *(Sala)*

Storyline: Six people find their lives interwoven when they meet at a residential Berlin hotel – Downhill City. Artsi is a Finnish guitarist who is trying to relaunch his career; Fabien makes a living selling pizzas but dreams of becoming a writer; Sascha is an ex-con just out of prison; Hans and Peggy are a couple who drift further apart as time goes on; and Doris, who grows closer to Hans after the break-up of her last relationship. *JZ*

Movie rating: *5.5

Visual: dvd

Off the record: 22 PISTEPIRKKO were formed in Northern Finland (Utajarvi, to be exact) out of the ashes of punk outfit, Matti Mata & SS (c.1980). Naming themselves after a type of beetle, PK Keranen, his brother Asko Keranen and Espe Haverinen won Helsinki's Championship Of Rock in '82, quickly spreading their unique vision via a 6-track EP in 1983; a full set, 'Piano, Rumpu & Kukka' was released a year later. Moving to Helsinki, they teamed up with producer/guitarist, Riku Mattila, this partnership worked on three English-speaking sets, 'The Kings Of Hong Kong', their blues/country outing 'Bare Bone Nest' and their dark and moody major label debut, 'Big Lupu' (1991) – could any band have A-Ha-styled vocals fused with the rock of the Smashing Pumpkins or the Velvet Underground? During the first half of the 90s, 22-P concentrated on new electronic technology and buying some expensive gear. A lengthy break occurred, until 1994 & 1996's trip-hop/dub attempts, however 'Rumble City, La La Land' & 'Zipcode', failed to achieve their goals. After 1998's doodad-orientated 'Eleven' set and the 'DOWNHILL CITY' soundtrack, 22-P continuing their trend of selected ambience, drones and general experimental electronica, issuing what could've been considered their first 'summer', or, shudder 'pop' record. Simmering with day-glo warmth and a tentative ear for melodies, 'Rally Of Love' (2001) still maintained the group's instantly recognisible mix of beats, loops and samples et al, but this time with a melodic spin. Pretty much like Board Of Canada's trippy wavering psychedelic electro sound, but without being too sinister. *MCS*

22 PISTEPIRKKO

Jun 00. (cd) *Clearspot; (efa 05418-2)* ☐ ☐
– Fabian's theme / Downhill city / Fujisan / Say wrong / Let the Romeo weep / Snowy Dave – 99 / Doris drives away / Sascha's theme / Where's the home, Joey? / Coffee girl 2 / Truth / Fujisan – beatbox jam / Roundabout 2 / Tokyo – Aleksei Borisov remix.

S/track review: A Finnish-made film, so why not a veteran Finnish band (22 PISTEPIRKKO) to do the soundtrack?; Hanoi Rocks and er . . . Lasse Viron – was he not an Olympic gold medalist!? – were getting a bit too old for the job. Messrs PK KERANEN, ASKO KERANEN & ESPE HAVERINEN (of 22-P) were probably unlikely candidates for the score, having failed to garner much support outside Scandinavia (and the indie world) during their 20-year music tenure. 'DOWNHILL CITY' proved to be a little sketchy for the upwardly mobile 21st Century Schizoid Man (a reference to King Crimson), although their knowledge of how cinema scores work was tested on the opening orchestra-sampled piece, 'Fabian's Theme'. The follow-on title track was worth the admission price alone, its accentuated VU-reverbs emotional and ear-bashing in effective equal doses. 22-P's bluesy electro roots took hold with the uptempo, 150 rpm 'Let The Romeo Weep', a song that showcased the understated high-velocity vox of frontman PK – like Neil Tennant/Pet Shop Boys on speed; ANDY McCOY from the aforementioned Hanoi Rocks gets in on the act playing flamenco guitar. Calming things down somewhat, the PISTE' boys get all melancholy for 'Snowy Dave – 99' and the beatbox-driven 'Doris Drives Away'. The trio get all Ry Cooder-esque (in his Beefheart days no doubt!) on the eerie guitar-plucking, 'Sascha's Theme', while they find a lounge-lizard-in-the-living-room for 'Where's The Home, Joey?'. As effective and potentially classic as the aforementioned 'Downhill City' track, is 'Coffee Girl #2', its tinny-guitar-strumming a reprisal of earlier instrumental, 'Say Wrong'; track 11 'Truth' is also indie-cool. Like so many good (or great) albums, it takes several plays to get "into" the music, 'DC' seems to be of that ilk, although diversions such as the lengthy, beatbox jam version of 'Fujisan' get mixed in the mix so to speak. Ditto the techno-pop, Aleksei Borisov mix 'Tokyo'. Penultimate dirge, 'Roundabout 2', is fuzz-guitar personified and proves when 22-P rock they are in the groove, rather than the reverse. *MCS*

Album rating: *6.5

DRAWING RESTRAINT 9

2005 (US/Japan 135m) IFC Films / Wise Policy

Film genre: experimental/avant-garde fantasy/drama

Top guns: dir: Matthew Barney

Stars: Matthew Barney *(occidental guest)*, **BJORK** *(occidental guest)*, Sosui

Oshima *(captain)*, Tomoyuki Ogawa *(host)*, **Mayumi Miyata** *(sho player)*, Shiro Nomura

Storyline: A couple (finally!) board a whaling vessel, the Nisshin Maru, where they encounter a crew of labourers sculpting "the field", a mold filled with petroleum jelly. However, after the couple marry in a traditional Japanese-styled ceremony, a storm helps to break open the sculpture which in turn engulfs the newlyweds; with surprising results. *MCS*

Movie rating: *6

Visual: dvd

Off the record: San Franciscan-born filmmaker, Matthew "Cremaster" Barney, is the real-life partner of **BJORK**, and although they have a young daughter (born 2002), both have – unlike the film itself! – still to tie the knot. *MCS*

—

BJORK

Jul 05. (cd) *One Little Indian; (TPLP 459CD)* Aug05
– Gratitude / Pearl / Ambergris march / Bath / Hunter vessel / Shimenawa / Vessel Shimenawa / Storm / Holographic entrypoint / Cetacea / Antarctic return.

S/track review: BJORK's film work is not exactly extensive, in fact, it had been five long years since the Palme d'Or-winning musical, 'DANCER IN THE DARK' (aka 'Selmasongs' CD) took her from a trip-hopping pixie to become the brightest star (actress/singer/dancer) to emerge east of Hollywood. However, her return to celluloid via 'DRAWING RESTRAINT 9' with her arty filmmaker partner, Matthew Barney, wasn't the kind of comeback most fans or industry people were expecting. To describe the album as minimalist would be short-sighted, as at times there is a lot going on – all of the weird variety I might add. From organic opener, 'Gratitude' (featuring lo-fi "Bonnie Prince Billy" himself, WILL OLDHAM, and a children's choir!), it was clear the album was on a trip of its own, and most of it without the vox of BJORK. Track 2, 'Pearl', was all primal gasping over Japanese free-reed mouth organ – or something of that ilk – while 'Ambergris March' was defiantly upbeat and cinematic to the point of irritation. We finally hear BJORK on 'Bath', a whispering, multi-layered lullaby for the institutionalized; she can't get much "higher" than this. Many would say the opposite applies. By tracks 5 and 7, the brassic 'Hunter Vessel' and 'Vessel Shimenawa' respectively, I began to think that BJORK was taking too many studio tea-breaks or was she conducting, John Williams-like, overseeing her work if not exactly participating full-time as of old. And that's just the point. Why put the BJORK stamp on it, when she could have so easily – like so many film music collaborators before her! (too numerous to mention) – added say, MATTHEW BARNEY and sho mouth-organ man MAYUMI MIYATA. The latter sidekick is arguably too overbearing, but weirdly effective on sad laments, the abstract 'Shimenawa' and closing piece, 'Antarctic Return'. The album plays with every emotion under the sun, all highs and lows to combat the film's stark connections between life, death, sacrifice and transformation. Example the following two tracks. The first of these, the mind-blowing 'Storm' (easily the best thing on the set) BJORK projectiles her vocal chords as a "vessel" and at long last finally contributes something of worth. The second, the near 10-minute 'Holographic Entrypoint', is in contrast, theatrical, using traditional Noh singers and basic 10-rpm (rattles per minute, rather than revs), wood-block percussionists. Noh, or rather nohargh! came to mind, as did the Residents' 'Eskimo' album from '79. To end the sho – sho to speak! – BJORK got in another voca-a-a-l number, 'Cetacea', while the aforementioned 'Antarctic Return', left us all at sea. *MCS*

Album rating: *6

DUNE

1984 (US 137m) Universal Pictures (PG-13)

Film genre: sci-fi/space fantasy

Top guns: s-w: David Lynch (+ dir) → WILD AT HEART, Eric Bergren, Christopher de Vore, Rudolph Wurlitzer (story: Frank Herbert)

Stars: Francesca Annis *(Lady Jessica)* ← MACBETH / → UNDER THE CHERRY MOON, Leonardo Cimino *(the Baron's doctor)* ← COME BACK, CHARLESTON BLUE ← COTTON COMES TO HARLEM, Brad Dourif *(Piter De Vries)* → JUNGLE FEVER, Jose Ferrer *(Padishah Emperor Shaddam IV)*, Linda Hunt *(Shadout Mapes)* ← POPEYE, Freddie Jones *(Thufir Hawat)* ← NEVER TOO YOUNG TO ROCK ← SON OF DRACULA / → WILD AT HEART, Richard Jordan *(Duncan Idaho)* → DELUSION → SHOUT, Kyle MacLachlan *(Paul Usul Muad'Dib Atreides)* → the DOORS, Virginia Madsen *(Princess Irulan)* ← ELECTRIC DREAMS / → BRAVE NEW GIRL, Kenneth McMillan *(Baron Vladimir Harkonnen)* ← CARNY, Patrick Stewart *(Gurney Halleck)*, **STING** *(Feyd-Rautha)*, Paul Smith *(the Beast Rabban)* ← POPEYE ← the GOSPEL ROAD, Dean Stockwell *(Dr. Wellington Yueh)* ← PARIS, TEXAS ← HUMAN HIGHWAY ← PSYCH-OUT / → TO LIVE & DIE IN L.A. → TUCKER: THE MAN AND HIS DREAM → MADONNA: INNOCENCE LOST, Alicia Roanne Witt *(Alia)* → FOUR ROOMS, Sean Young *(Chani)* ← BLADE RUNNER / → EVEN COWGIRLS GET THE BLUES, Max Von Sydow *(Dr. Kynes)* ← FLASH GORDON / → UNTIL THE END OF THE WORLD → NONHOSONNO, Jack Nance *(Capt. Iakin Nefud)* ← FOOLS / → WILD AT HEART → the HOT SPOT

Storyline: Young Paul Atreides travels to planet Arrakis with his family to oversee production of the Spice drug, vital for interspace travel. After his father is murdered by the rival Harkonnen dynasty he is forced to flee into the inhospitable desert along with his mother Jessica. There he encounters the Fremen, who show him the secret of the giant worms which traverse the planet, and how to control them. Finally Paul and the Fremen seek revenge against the Harkonnens in a life or death struggle for control of the Spice. *JZ*

Movie rating: *6

Visual: video + dvd

Off the record: The men behind the soundtrack, **TOTO**, had been around the L.A. scene since 1978. Noted ex-session men, brothers Jeff and Steve Porcaro, Bobby Kimball, Steve Lukather, David Paich and David Hungate, took their name partly from the dog in 'The Wizard Of Oz' and partly from Kimball's real surname (Toteaux). After signing a worldwide deal for 'CBS-Epic', their debut single, 'Hold The Line' (from their eponymous 1978 debut album) became a massive seller, their blend/bland of airbrushed melody and supersession soft-rock going down a storm in America's heartlands. TOTO enjoyed moderate success with follow-ups, 'Hydra' (1979) and 'Turn Back' (1981), however things picked up dramatically with the monster selling, 'Toto IV' (1982). Highlights included, 'Rosanna' (a song written about Lukather's actress girlfriend, Rosanna Arquette), an AOR classic that lodged at No.2 in the US Billboard charts for 5 weeks; another 45, 'Africa', became another million seller and furnished them with their first No.1. In early 1984, Hungate was replaced by another Porcaro brother, Mike, while lead singer Kimball – during the recording of 'DUNE' – departed and was subsequently substituted by Dennis "Fergie" Fredericksen. *MCS*

—

TOTO

Dec 84. (lp/c/cd) *Polydor; <(823770-1/-4/-2)>*
– Prologue / Main title – /*3/*4/*5/- Robot fight / Leto's theme / The box / The floating fat man (the Baron) – /*10/- Trip to Arrakis – /*12/*13/- First attack / Prophecy theme (BRIAN ENO, DANIEL LANOIS & ROGER ENO) *[not on PEG cd]* – /*14/*15/*16/*17/- Dune (desert theme) *[track 28 on PEG]* / Paul meets Chani – /*19/*20/*21/- Prelude (take my hand) / Paul takes the water of life – /*24/- Big battle / Paul kills Feyd / Final dream – /*29/- Take my hand. *<cd re-iss. Jul94 on 'Universal'; E 823770-2)> <cd re-iss. ext.Oct97 on 'PEG Recordings'+= *; 015>* – 3. Guild report / 4. House Atreides / 5. Paul Atreides / 10. Departure / 12. Sandworm attack / 13. The betrayal – Shields down / 14. The Duke's death / 15. Sandworm chase / 16. The Freman / 17. Secrets of the Freman / 19. Destiny / 20. Riding the sandworm / 21. Reunion with Gurney / 24. The sleeper has awakened! / 29. Dune main title – demo version.

S/track review: Was 'Star Wars' (and sci-fi) composer John Williams apparently engaged elsewhere at the time? Who knows. David Lynch's subsequent choice on the seminal 'Blue Velvet' (1986) movie, Angelo Badalamenti, might well've been the inspired one here. With pomp-rockers Queen scoring – some would say an own-goal with – sci-fi feature, 'FLASH GORDON' (in 1980), soft-rock outfit TOTO were the surprise commission. What swung it was probably the fact that TOTO musician, DAVID PAICH, had a father (Marty Paich) in the film-composing business, a connection that led them both to collaborate on 'DUNE'. Other TOTO musicians were also present and correct on the 'DUNE' music mission, STEVE LUKATHER, brothers JEFF PORCARO, STEVE PORCARO and MIKE PORCARO attempting to still fit into this elaborate, fully-orchestrated work (by the Vienna Symphony Orchestra). 'Prologue' is basically that, dialogue to completely bamboozle you about "spice" and the film's plot; the 'Main Title' theme is segued in for balance. The quirky 'Robot Fight' is another short-n-sweet ditty, while 'Leto's Theme', 'The Box' (and others) continue the romantic-ish, orchestral reprisals. 'The Floating Fat Man (The Baron)' is as near to the sound of Rick Wakeman as you could get away with, but all too often the decent uptempo pieces were cut short. The Vienna Volksoper Choir get to gloriously shine on 'First Attack', but it's the two follow-on tracks that produce the "rock" element. BRIAN ENO (alongside musical associates brother ROGER ENO and DANIEL LANOIS) engage the ethereal, ambient element on 'Prophecy Theme', while TOTO – the band that is – finally get their musical two-pennorth in via 'Dune (Desert Theme)', although a little reminiscent of a medley of classical numbers. It was no surprise when this album failed commercially (compared to TOTO's previous pop works), having been released a month after their 'Isolation' set. A revamped, extended CD with extra tracks was issued in 1997, the makers annoyingly disregarding ENO's 'Prophecy Theme' piece. *MCS*

Album rating: *5.5

□ the DUST BROTHERS segment
(⇒ FIGHT CLUB)

DYNAMITE BROTHERS

1974 (US 90m) Independent International Pictures (R)

Film genre: martial arts/buddy film

Top guns: dir: Al Adamson / s-w: John D'Amato (story: Marvin Lagunoff, Jim Rein)

Stars: Alan Tang *(Larry Chin)*, Timothy Brown *(Stud Brown)* → NASHVILLE, James Hong *(Wei Chin)* → BOUND FOR GLORY → BLADE RUNNER → the KAREN CARPENTER STORY → WAYNE'S WORLD 2 → EXPERIENCE, Aldo Ray *(Burke)* ← RIOT ON SUNSET STRIP / → SHOCK 'EM DEAD, Carol Speed *(Sarah)* ← SAVAGE! ← the MACK ← BUMMER! / → DISCO GODFATHER, Don Oliver *(smiling man)*, Al Richardson *(Razor)*, Clare Nono *(Betty Fon)* → TRICK OR TREAT, Biff Yeager *(moustached thug)* → REPO MAN → SID & NANCY → STRAIGHT TO HELL → WALKER → ROADSIDE PROPHETS

Storyline: No sooner has Larry Chin hopped off a boat from Hong Kong than he finds himself handcuffed to the floral shirted Stud Brown. The unlikely Afro-Asia pairing ditch their captors and karate kick their way to Los Angeles, where Chin attempts to track down his long lost brother and Brown begins a relationship with a mute black hooker. Their garrulous host the Smiling Man is determined to prevent the local hoods – headed by a handlebar moustachioed, Blaxploitation dead ringer for Rikki Fulton's Supercop – from flooding the ghetto with dope, a ploy masterminded by Chin's mysterious older sibling. *BG*

Movie rating: *2

Visual: video

Off the record: **CHARLES EARLAND** (see below)

—

CHARLES EARLAND

May 74. (lp) *Prestige; <P 10082>* □ [-]
– Betty's theme / Never ending melody / Grasshopper / Shanty blues / Weedhopper / Razor J. / Snake / Kungfusion / Incense of essence. *<(UK + re cd-iss. Nov98 on 'Beat Goes Public'; CDBGPM 120)> <cd re-iss. Mar01 as 'At The Movies' on 'Prestige'+=; 24255-2>* – the Blackbyrds: CORNBREAD, EARL AND ME

S/track review: For colourful proof that the best Blaxploitation soundtracks accompanied the dodgiest films, look no further than CHARLES EARLAND's intrepid-score for 'The DYNAMITE BROTHERS', a garish – if endlessly chuckle-worthy – B-movie mish-mash of Bruce Lee and 'Black Caesar'. The Mighty Burner was at the top of his game in the late 60s/early 70s and, having already translated contemporary pop into sizzling soul-jazz, the Hammond heavyweight began embracing the kind of electronic technology which revolutionised the work of Miles Davis and Herbie Hancock at the turn of that decade. With synth wizard PATRICK GLEESON – who'd previously worked with Hancock – on hand (and jazz-funk surrealist Eddie Harris on remixing duties) EARLAND gets to grips with an ARP, sending out the kind of freaky Twilight Zone frequencies which just don't figure in other Blaxploitation soundtracks. 'Betty's Theme', a pimp-rolling electric piano groove perforated with surreptitious synth whistles, is one of the great 70s themes; it could've endured endless cop show re-runs without growing stale. Free of the main theme, EARLAND really stretches out. 'Never Ending Melody' is a fascinating, hall-of-mirrors collision of thundering tympani, woozy, elongated brass (courtesy of EDDIE HENDERSON, another Hancock alum and a psychiatrist to boot), electric guitar and the man's smoking organ runs. 'Weedhopper' twitches and lurches against a 'Rhubarb & Custard'-style bassline, desperate not to get buried alive under a blizzard of psych-guitar, libidinous trombone emissions and general electro weirdness – this is exactly the kind of stuff which would have sounded perfect in the screen adaptation of William Burroughs' 'Naked Lunch'. The epic 'Snake', wherein EARLAND dons a soprano sax, is another extended blast of trippy avant-funk. The sleeve credits dedicate it to GLEESON "for his unique contribution to its sound", and what a sound; a spacey, neo-free jazz decompression chamber echoing to mewling synth squiggles and grungy wah-wah bass. 'Kungfusion' – as its title suggests – is more typical Johnny Harris-influenced karate-soul jazz while 'Shanty Blues' is simply EARLAND burning as only he can. But it's all good, if criminally under-heard. A shame, as it's also currently one of the easiest Blaxploitation soundtracks to track down. Pure Dynamite. *BG*

Album rating: *8

☐ Charles EARLAND segment
(⇒ the DYNAMITE BROTHERS)

EAT THE RICH

1987 (UK 89m) Iron Fist Films (15)

Film genre: gangster/crime satire/comedy

Top guns: s-w: Peter Richardson (+ dir), Pete Richens

Stars: Lannah/Alan Pellay *(Alex)*, Nosher Powell *(Nosher)*, **LEMMY Kilmister** *(Spider)*, Ronald Allen *(Cmdr. Fortune)*, Robbie Coltrane *(Jeremy)* ← ABSOLUTE BEGINNERS ← GHOST DANCE ← SUBWAY RIDERS ← FLASH GORDON / → TUTTI FRUTTI, Sandra Dorne *(Sandra)*, Ron Tarr *(Ron)*, Jimmy Fagg *(Jimmy)*, Fiona Richmond *(Fiona)*, Rik Mayall *(Micky)* ← SHOCK TREATMENT / → BRING ME THE HEAD OF MAVIS DAVIS, Adrian Edmondson *(Charles)*, **Paul McCartney** *(banquet guest)* <= the BEATLES =>, Kathy Burke *(Kathy)* ← SID & NANCY / → STRAIGHT TO HELL → WALKER → KEVIN & PERRY GO LARGE, Dawn French *(Debbie Draws)*, Jennifer Saunders *(Lady Caroline)* → SPICEWORLD, Peter Richardson *(Henry)*, Pete Richens *(cafe owner)*, Miranda Richardson *(DHSS blonde)*, **Shane MacGowan** *(terrorist)* <= the POGUES =>, **Terence Wood** *(terrorist)*, Koo Stark *(Hazel)*, Nigel Planer *(DHSS manager)*, **Hugh Cornwall** *(Edgeley)*, **Sandie Shaw** *(Edgeley's girlfriend)* ← ABSOLUTE BEGINNERS, **Miles A. Copeland III** *(Derek)* ← BRING ON THE NIGHT, Simon Brint *(Dickie)*, Cathryn Harrison *(Joanna)* ← PIED PIPER, Rowland Rivron *(Star reporter)*, Neil Dickson *(Gerry)* → IT COULDN'T HAPPEN HERE, **Bill Wyman** *(toilet victim)* <= ROLLING STONES =>, **Steve Walsh** *(record executive)*

Storyline: A KGB general is determined to bring down that hated English Home Secretary, Nosher Powell, probably because of his dreadful suits. He finds an unlikely weapon in the form of Alex, a downtrodden waiter at an upper-class restaurant named Bastards. Fed-up Alex tries to start a revolution and begins his conquest of Britain by taking over the restaurant, which is swiftly re-named Eat The Rich. Will Karpov checkmate his opponent or will Alex realize he's just a pawn in the game? *JZ*

Movie rating: *5

Visual: video + dvd

Off the record: **Steve Walsh** was a member of Kansas.

—

MOTORHEAD (& Various) (score: SIMON BRINT *)

Nov 87. (lp/c/cd) *Filmtrax; (MOMENT/+C/CD 108)* ☐ ☐
– Eat the rich / Terrorists (*) / Built for speed / Nosher in the bar (DANNY ECCLESTON) / Nothing up my sleeve / Arriba salsa (*) / Doctor Rock / On the road – live / Pistol in my pocket (LANNAH) / Car approach (*) / Orgasmatron / Bess (WURZEL) / End titles theme (DANNY ECCLESTON).

S/track review: The mighty MOTORHEAD feature "heavily" on this OST to "Comic-Strip" Brit-flick, 'EAT THE RICH'. Comprising, at this stage, frontman/bassist LEMMY Kilmister, guitarist WURZEL (aka Michael Burston), guitarist PHILIP ANTHONY CAMPBELL and drummer PHIL "PHILTHY ANIMAL" TAYLOR (who'd just superseded Pete Gill after the 'Orgasmatron' set), MOTORHEAD were afforded several songs (including one Gary Moore-like effort, 'Bess', by WURZEL) to er . . . complement the movie. With four studio tracks ('Built For Speed', 'Nothing Up My Sleeve', 'Doctor Rock' & 'Orgasmatron') lifted from the previous year's Bill Laswell-produced 'Orgasmatron' set, the 'EAT THE RICH' OST was hardly innovative on the exclusivity front. MOTORHEAD's title track opened the set with all the guster and hard-rock traits one's been accustomed to over the previous decade or so; however, as a single it flopped. The aforementioned group songs (the beefed-up, speed-metal of 'Built For Speed', 'Nothing Up My Sleeve' & 'Doctor Rock', alongside the warts'n'all, doom-laden beast of 'Orgasmatron') were interspersed with unnecessary novelty noodles from the film's nerdy composer, SIMON BRINT, one-half of comedy duo, Raw Sex (alongside Rowland Rivron, the French & Saunders players). A live MOTORHEAD track, 'On The Road', kicks off side two, while disappointment lies ahead courtesy of a discopop, tongue-in-cheek Bananarama-esque song ('Pistol In My Pocket') by one of the movie's then-rising stars, LANNAH; better listened to on the "tranny" you could say. A second theme effort by additional scoresmith, DANNY ECCLESTON, literally finishes off the 'EAT THE RICH' platter. *MCS*

Album rating: *5.5

– spinoff releases, etc. –

MOTORHEAD: Eat The Rich / (non OST songs)

Nov 87. (7"/12") *G.W.R.; (GWR 6)* ☐ ☐

EBAN AND CHARLEY

2000 (US 86m) Monqui Films (R)

Film genre: psychological drama

Top guns: s-w + dir: James Bolton

Stars: Brent Fellows *(Eban)*, Giovanni Andrade *(Charley)*, Ellie Nicholson *(Sunshine)*, Drew Zeller *(Kevin)*, Pam Munter *(Eban's mother)*, Ron Upton *(Eban's father)*, Nolan V. Chard *(Charley's father)*

Storyline: Soccer coach Eban, a gay man in his late twenties, returns suddenly to his home town of Washington to live with his parents after an unspoken affair with one of his younger team-mates lands him in hot water. There, he meets Charley, a bored skatepunk teenager with an abusive father. The two strike up a relationship, as both characters' parents become increasingly wary of their intentions towards one another. *AS*

Movie rating: *5.5

Visual: dvd

Off the record: **Stephin MERRITT** (see own entry)

—

STEPHIN MERRITT

Jan 02. (cd) *Merge; <MRG 505> Sketchbook; (SKETCH 002)* ☐ Feb02 ☐
– Mother / Cricket problem / Some summer day / O Tannenbaum / Poppyland / Drowned sailors / Maria Maria Maria / Titles / This little ukulele / Tea party / Tiny flying player pianos / Mother remembered / Victorian robotics / Water torture / Greensleeves / Stage rain.

S/track review: The OST to James Bolton's complex and often misguided gay indie drama was composed by twee maverick troubadour STEPHIN MERRITT, and seems to fit in the film's downbeat, downtempo feel with hushed songs and sparse arrangements sometimes lasting no longer than two minutes. MERRITT takes the vocal reins on no less than six songs, but they're not his usual clap-along melodies, or even bittersweet tales of love and squalor. Instead, MERRITT seems to be awash in a "Leonard Cohen afterworld" with whispered lyrics of quiet controlling this low-key affair. The instrumentals are rather ambient and experimental, belonging to a world more akin with Robert Fripp and Jim O'Rourke than anything MERRITT has done before. Still, his indie electronic footprints are all over this and it is a formidable and healthy addition to any soundtrack collection. *AS*

Album rating: *6.5

the EDUCATION OF SONNY CARSON

1974 (US 104m) Paramount Pictures (R)

Film genre: urban crime drama/biopic

Top guns: dir: Michael Campus ← the MACK / s-w: Fred Hudson (au: Sonny Carson)

Stars: Rony Clanton *(Sonny Carson)* → RAPPIN' → JUICE, Don Gordon *(Pigliani)* ← the MACK, Joyce Walker *(Virginia)* ← WILLIE DYNAMITE ← SHAFT'S BIG SCORE!, Paul Benjamin *(Pops)* ← ACROSS 110th STREET ← MIDNIGHT COWBOY / → FRIDAY FOSTER → LEADBELLY → the FIVE HEARTBEATS, Thomas Hicks *(young Sonny)*, Mary Alice *(Moms)* → SPARKLE → BEAT STREET, **Linda Hopkins** *(Lil Boy's mother)* ← ROCKIN' THE BLUES / → HONKYTONK MAN, David Kernan *(judge)* ← FAREWELL PERFORMANCE

Storyline: Hugely influential biopic of late criminal turned activist/ black nationalist (Abubadika) Sonny Carson, mapping his descent from intellectually precocious high school student to petty criminal and fully paid up gang member who resorts to stealing flowers for his best friend's funeral. As New York smarts from economic freefall and vicious turf wars, Carson's personal point of illumination comes after he finds his own girlfriend hooked on heroin after a horrific stint in the slammer. *BG*

Movie rating: *5.5

Visual: video + dvd

Off the record: Linda Hopkins (b.14 Dec'24, New Orleans, Louisiana, USA) was a revered on-Broadway singer whose wide range of styles included gospel, blues and jazz. Having entered the charts in the early 60s, collaborating on two 45s alongside Jackie Wilson ('I Found Love' & 'Shake A Hand'), she continued to win awards for her musical stage work. At 77 years of age, she worked on the "Wild Women Blues" stage show which peaked in L.A. at a summer night at the Moca, 20th June, 2002. *MCS*

——

COLERIDGE TAYLOR PERKINSON (w/ LEON WARE)

1974. (lp) *Paramount; <PAS 1045>* ☐ [-]
– Where do I go from here? (Sonny Carson's theme) / The robbery and the chase / Exercise run / Girl, girl, girl (Sonny and Virginia) / Daydreams / The rumble / Funeral parlor / Please be there / Flashbulbs / Father and son / The junkies / A new direction / End title (Sonny's theme).

S/track review: The coming together of late Afro-American composer COLERIDGE-TAYLOR PERKINSON (whose non-classical credits included Rahsaan Roland Kirk, Donald Byrd and Barbara McNair's 'The Touch Of Time', B-side to one of 'Motown's rarest singles) and veteran writer/producer/solo artist LEON WARE is another of those pairings which, save for the birth pains of black cinema, would likely never have happened. Soul fans should thank their satin sheets it did; the pair were to link up again two years later on what arguably stands as the most underrated entry in Marvin Gaye's catalogue, 'I Want You' (1976), as well as WARE's de facto, equally pioneering and overlooked solo debut, 'Musical Massage' (1976). Fresh from jumpstarting his singing career on Quincy Jones' 'Body Heat', the dulcet balladeer handles no less than five tracks here, compared to only two for Lou Rawls with the similar composer-crooner framework used on 'The Soul Of Nigger Charley', Paramount's blaxbuster from the previous year. PERKINSON, for his part, specialised in scoring the more socially realistic strand of blaxploitation, films which were to influence contemporary directors like Spike Lee, as well as conscious hip hop artists like Lauryn Hill. Not for him, then, swaggering ostentation and hotwired chase funk. Despite the movie's unapologetic vérité style, his arrangements err on the side of Hollywood refinement (the gentle piano/vibes/woodwind melodies of 'Daydreams' or even 'Flashbulbs' might have been plucked from one of Pino Donaggio's lighter scores), especially when WARE's singing over them, and especially on the archetypal 70s weepie of a title theme: a domino-chain of string summits layered over a series of tasteful piano changes, with WARE's tenor the voice of plaintive humanism personified. On a purely dramatic level, the grievous horn/ woodwind charts, awkward jazz chords and bubbling percussion of 'Exercise Run' exemplify PERKINSON's sober, expressive touch, and it's only really on gangfight cue, 'The Rumble', that the man falls back on syncopated squelch. In fact it's a fairly imaginative piece of orchestral funk by 1974 standards, locked into contrapuntal melody and unusually bookended by restive, rhythmic woodwind. The heightened sensuality of the 'Motown/Marvin' connection, meanwhile, really begins to throb on side two, as WARE wallows in the strung out, red light sax soloing of 'Please Be There' and 'The Junkies'. An album's worth in a similar vein might've made it a classic, but alongside Gaye's own 'TROUBLE MAN', '. . .SONNY CARSON' remains one of the most satisfyingly mellow blax soundtracks out there. *BG*

Album rating: *6.5

ELECTRA GLIDE IN BLUE

1973 (US 114m) United Artists Pictures (18)

Film genre: cop/detective drama

Top guns: dir: **James William Guercio** / s-w: Robert Boris (+ story), Rupert Hitzig

Stars: Robert Blake *(John Wintergreen)*, Billy Green Bush *(Zipper Davis)* ← the SAVAGE SEVEN / → MACKINTOSH & T.J., Mitchell Ryan *(Det. Harve Poole)*, Jeannine Riley *(Jolene)*, Elisha Cook *(Crazy Willie)*, Royal Dano *(coroner)*, **Hawk Wolinski** *(VW bus driver)*, **Peter Cetera** *(Bob Zemko)*, **Terry Kath** *(killer)*, **Lee Loughnane** *(pig man)*, **Walter Parazaider** + other **Chicago** members, Nick Nolte *(hippy kid)*

Storyline: "Big John" Wintergreen isn't your average cop, a pint-sized Jack Nicholson with less of a wise ass and more of a heart, keen on introducing himself to his lawbreakers and given to diminutive chat-up lines. Tired of pounding the – beautifully shot – desert beat with his boorish redneck partner, he longs for the white Stetson, cigar-smoking status of detective work, a dream which draws closer to reality after he stumbles onto the scene of an apparent suicide. Taken under the wing of blustering senior Harve Poole, however, Wintergreen can neither quite talk the talk, or walk the walk, his lily-livered investigations in a hippy commune ("I want some information!"; "I got some information – you're standing in pig shit . . .") inspiring Poole to a show of customary police brutality. In the end it's all too much for Big John, who sees Poole for the phony he is, solving the case by old fashioned sympathy and intuition. And what does he get for his trouble? A finale cleverly inverting Easy Rider. *BG*

Movie rating: *6.5

Visual: video + dvd

Off the record: James William Guercio (see below)

——

Various Artists (composer: JAMES WILLIAM GUERCIO *)

Oct 73. (lp) *United Artists; <UA-LA 062H> (UAS 29486)* ☐ ☐
– Morning (*) / Prelude (*) / Meadow mountain top (MARK SPOELSTRA) / Overture (*) / Most of all (the MARCELS) / Jolene's dance (*) / Free from the Devil (MADURA) / The chase (*) / Song of sad bottles (MARK SPOELSTRA) / Monument valley (*) / Tell me (*). *<re-iss. Jan04 on 'Divine Recordings'; 355>*

S/track review: Not content with producing Blood, Sweat & Tears and Chicago, one-time session man and songwriter, JAMES WILLIAM GUERCIO, had the temerity to go and make one of the most enduring – and one of the most dryly amusing – cinematic oddities of the early 70s, an iconic, auteur-esque piece falling somewhere between 'Five Easy Pieces', 'Vanishing Point' and 'Chips'. Where else can you get to see a bearded Peter Cetera giving it some serious chase-funk welly before getting hauled in by the fuzz? From this vantage point, Cetera's limp 80s balladry seems a long way off. Complemented by a massive in-session orchestra, including sadly missed Moog man, PAUL BEAVER (ex-Beaver & Krause), guitarist LARRY CARLTON, drummer ROSS SALOMONE, bassist TERRY KATH and trombonist JAMES PANKOW (the latter two of Chicago), 'ELECTRA GLIDE . . .' encompasses more than a hint of jingoist leanings, albeit with a touch of irony and sarcasm (example the "God bless America" lyrics on 'Tell Me'). From opening cues, 'Morning' and 'Prelude', to the aforementioned side two finale, 'Tell Me' (think Ray Charles or Joe Cocker), the album will surprise the uninitiated among you. Side two also gets a little funky by way of blaxploitation-esque 'The Chase', although it's a tad too close to TV cop show scores for comfort. In stark contrast, two tracks ('Meadow Mountain Top' & 'Song Of Sad Bottles') by underrated, California-raised folksinger/guitarist, MARK SPOELSTRA, eased the tone somewhat – it was sad to hear of his passing (pancreatic cancer) on the 24th of February, 2007 (aged 66). On a lighter note, there are two further various artists on show: the soulful, doo-wop, but out of place the MARCELS, with the Alan Freed-Harvey Fuqua number, 'Most Of All', and 'Free From The Devil' by MADURA (aka guitarist ALAN DE CARLO, organist HAWK and drummer SALOMONE) – as close to Grand Funk Railroad as you'll ever hear. *BG & MCS*

Album rating: *6

☐ the ELECTRIC FLAG, AN AMERICAN BAND segment
(⇒ the TRIP)

the ELECTRIC HORSEMAN

1979 (US 120m) Columbia Pictures (PG)

Film genre: romantic modern western drama/comedy

Top guns: dir: Sydney Pollack / s-w: Robert Garland (+ story), Paul Gaer (+ story), Alvin Sargent (au: Shelly Burton)

Stars: Robert Redford *(Sonny Steele)*, Jane Fonda *(Hallie Martin)* ← STEELYARD BLUES, Valerie Perrine *(Charlotta)*, **Willie NELSON** *(Wendell Hickson)*, John Saxon *(Hunt Sears)*, Allan Arbus *(Danny Miles)*, Nicolas Coster *(Fitzgerald)*, Wilford Brimley *(farmer)* → TENDER MERCIES, Will Hare *(Gus Atwater)*, Basil Hoffman *(Toland)* → LAMBADA

Storyline: After downshifting from the rodeo ring to the soundbite world of advertising, jaded, faded, alcoholic cowboy Sonny Steele hits a new low, reduced to parody in Las Vegas atop an injured, drugged-up racehorse. Disgusted, he rides the horse down the main drag and into the desert, ultimately falling in love with the journalist covering his tracks. *BG*

Movie rating: *5

Visual: video + dvd

Off the record: **Willie NELSON** (see own entry)

——

WILLIE NELSON // DAVE GRUSIN

Dec 79. (lp/c) *Columbia; <JS/+T 36327> C.B.S.; (70177)* 52 Apr80 ☐
– Midnight rider / My heroes have always been cowboys / Mama don't let your babies grow up to be cowboys / So you think you're a cowboy / Hands on the wheel // Electro phantasma / Rising star / The electric horseman / Interlude – Tumbleweed morning / Disco magic / Freedom epilogue. *<(cd-iss. Jan89; CK 36327)>*

S/track review: A word of warning: this isn't exactly a country soundtrack, more a production of two halves. If you've an aversion to disco, proceed with caution, otherwise saddle up and gird your loins for a record which could only have come out of the late 70s and the newly superstar-spangled circumstances in which NELSON found himself. With his Outlaw records and standards landmark, 'Stardust' (1978), having raised his status to the point where his presence was requested at the White House, the genre-busting country icon was in the convenient position of being able to proposition Sydney Pollack about a role in his suitably offbeat, free spirit vs The Man cowboy film. So it was then, that NELSON ended up drawing encouraging notices for a typically freewheeling big screen debut alongside Robert Redford, backed by his own songs and DAVE GRUSIN's music. 'ELECTRIC HORSEMAN' is the first of several soundtracks NELSON put his name to over the ensuing decade, and – in a career which has seen a fair quota of eccentric albums – it's by far his most unlikely. Where 'Stardust' found him tripping the light fantastic without an orchestral crutch, here he's draped in extraneous arrangements. Neither 'Hands On The Wheel' nor 'My Heroes Have Always Been Cowboys' are short on strings, or the kind of baroque embellishments they could've done without, yet still NELSON transforms them. 'So You Think You're A Cowboy' gets off lighter, with a dusting of electric piano, and the ageless 'Mama Don't Let Your Babies Grow Up To Be Cowboys' comes rough'n'ready from his 1978 Outlaw collaboration, 'Waylon And Willie'. But if the album's worth hearing for anything, it's the rambunctious, harmonica-strafed cover of the Allman Brothers' 'Midnight Rider', which opens the whole thing. When the country finally does give way to 'Electro-Phantasma' half-way through, you can almost hear the orchestra exhaling with relief, going for broke on the kind of supper club disco that GRUSIN excelled at. He does disco for real on 'Disco Magic', clichéd but competent, with shades of Dan Hartman. The title theme itself is a classic piece of 70s score-funk which many DJs probably aren't even aware of, a riptide of break beats, wah-wah and siren string surges, with a wide-screen Western patina and electro-pulsing undercurrent. There might just be an argument for filing this one alongside 'Willie Nelson With Danny Davis And The Nashville Brass' (1980), but the fact is it still sounds better than most of the marketing comps passing as country soundtracks these days. Rhinestone cowboys rejoice. *BG*

Album rating: *6.5

– spinoff hits, etc. –

WILLIE NELSON: My Heroes Have Always Been Cowboys / **DAVE GRUSIN**: Rising star (love theme)

Jan 80. (7") *<11186> (CBS 8316)* 44 Mar80 ☐

☐ ELEPHANTS MEMORY segment
(⇒ MIDNIGHT COWBOY)

☐ Al ELIAS & Andy BADELE segment
(⇒ GORDON'S WAR)

□ Cass ELLIOT segment
(⇒ BEAUTIFUL THING)

□ Steve ELLIS segment
(⇒ LOOT)

□ Warren ELLIS segment
(⇒ the ASSASSINATION OF JESSE JAMES . . .)

Keith EMERSON

Born: 1 Nov'44, Lancashire, England. As one third of legendary prog supergroup Emerson Lake & Palmer, KEITH EMERSON became a byword for the kind of musical excess that incited punk musicians to kick out the moogs along with the jams. EMERSON himself held a particular fascination for the SEX PISTOLS, who allegedly once burned a lifesize effigy of him at one of their shows (although he has since met and befriended John Lydon). A precocious talent, EMERSON began playing professionally in his late teens as pianist in various R&B bands, before he first found real success playing Hammond organ in PP Arnold's backing band, the Nice. EMERSON's group split from Arnold and enjoyed success in their own right, recording several albums blending rock, jazz and classical influences, and establishing for the keyboardist a reputation as showman extraordinaire. An early trick was to stick a knife (gifted to EMERSON by Nice roadie LEMMY) into the keys of his Hammond, holding notes in order to play with more complexity, but also to facilitate the hijinks he would become famous for (he would later fix a board to his amplifier rig in order to throw his knives at it). It was hearing Walter Carlos's seminal 'Switched On Bach' album that proved the defining moment in his career, and EMERSON, purchasing one of the first modular Moog synthesizers with which the album was made, soon became the leading exponent of this new sound. From the very beginning EMERSON had made a habit of re-interpreting works by other composers in his own grandstanding style, often to stunning effect. The addition of the Moog to his arsenal catapulted EMERSON's appropriations into interstellar overdrive, and he never looked back. Throughout the course of his career, he would draw from a diverse list of "influences", ranging from Bach, Bartok and Bernstein's (Leonard and Elmer) to Beethoven, Berlioz and Bob (DYLAN), although he wasn't always diligent in crediting his sources. Following the break-up of the Nice, EMERSON joined with King Crimson's Greg Lake and Carl Palmer of Atomic Rooster to form ELP (the mooted involvement of JIMI HENDRIX was never realised due to his death). ELP were immediately a huge success, with the single 'Lucky Man' (groundbreaking synth solo and all) performing particularly well, and a number of definitively prog albums followed, including 'Tarkus', 'Trilogy', and what many consider to be their masterwork, 'Brain Salad Surgery'. By 1974, ELP and EMERSON in particular had long since left behind any notions of self-restraint. Their triple disc live album, 'Welcome Back My Friends To The Show That Never Ends', reflected the overindulgence that by this point was perhaps their defining attribute. EMERSON had taken to performing some songs strapped to a piano that was spun suspended from the ceiling of the venue, while others necessitated the unwieldy Moog synth being dragged round stadiums (one of thirteen EMERSON required). The release of 'Works Volume I' was followed by a grand rock folly to rank amongst the best of them, a tour accompanied by a full symphony orchestra who would eventually be abandoned at the roadside in the face of financial catastrophe. Following the close of the tour and the release of 'Works Volume II', ELP awoke to a world revolutionised by punk, which by its very nature demanded EMERSON's head on a pole. ELP's riposte was 1978's 'Love Beach', a contractual obligation that satisfied few and enraged many. EMERSON was crying all the way to the bank at this point, but he could also console himself with the knowledge that his 13-year reign as "Overall Best Keyboardist" in the annual reader's poll of Keyboard Magazine (on whose advisory board he holds a seat of honour) was by now well underway. Always at his best as an interpreter and arranger, it is perhaps no surprise that EMERSON began to find work as a composer of film scores. He had been approached to score Norman Jewison's 'The Dogs Of War' in 1976 but this project was eventually realised without him and EMERSON's first actual foray into scoring came with Dario Argento's 'INFERNO' in 1980, which remains an intriguing work. For the next five years EMERSON produced a variety of soundtracks, including Sly Stallone flop 'NIGHTHAWKS' and anime 'Harmagedon: Genma Taisen', rarely with the same success as his first attempt, often provoking derision and without fail controversy over his hiring. After 1984's underwhelming 'MURDEROCK' and an appearance as a talking head in Argento documentary 'World Of Horror', his scoring career went on hold for a while and solo albums 'Honky', 'Christmas Album' and 'Changing States' (aka 'Cream of Emerson Soup') were interspersed by sporadic attempts to recapture the glory of his 70s heyday. These included a new version of ELP with Palmer replaced by Cozy Powell, and alternative supergroup, 3, with Palmer, but not Lake. EMERSON returned briefly to his scoring career in 1989 with 'La CHIESA', which saw his work nestle alongside that of GOBLIN in an Argento penned horror. Five years later, he contributed original music for the short lived 'Iron Man' animated series, and in the interim period, the classic line-up of ELP reformed. The announcement of his retirement in 1994 following potentially calamitous nerve-grafting surgery was premature, and two albums of new material were enough to keep ELP on the road for much of the late 90s. Early in the new millennium, he contributed the score to a short film, 'The White Room', while ELP ground to a halt once again. EMERSON then reformed the Nice for a British tour, before forming the Keith Emerson Band and publishing his autobiography, 'Pictures Of An Exhibitionist'. A 2006 ELP tour was thwarted by management issues, while his most recent soundtrack work was for 'Gojira: Fainaru Uozo', intended as a 50th anniversary celebration of the Godzilla franchise. Fan reaction to EMERSON's score was typically less than charitable, but his reign as "Overall Best Keyboardist" remains unchallenged and he continues to tour. *SW*

- **filmography** (composer) –

Pictures At An Exhibition *(1972 {* ELP} OST by EMERSON, LAKE & PALMER =>)* / **Inferno** *(1978 OST =>)* / **Nighthawks** *(1981 OST =>)* / **Best Revenge** *(1982 OST =>)* / **Murderock** *(1984 OST =>)* / World Of Horror *(1985 {c} score w/ various others)* / **la Chiesa** *(1989 OST => w/ GOBLIN)* / **Message To Love: The Isle Of Wight Festival** *(1997 {p ELP} OST by V/A =>)* / Gojira: Fainaru uozu *(2004 score as KISU EMASON w/ others)*

– compilations, etc. –

KEITH EMERSON: At The Movies

Oct 05. (3xcd-box) *Castle; (756147)* □ [-]
– (nearly everything from INFERNO to La CHIESA)

the EMPEROR'S NEW GROOVE

2000 (US 79m) Walt Disney Pictures (G)

Film genre: animated children's/family fantasy

Top guns: dir: Mark Dindal / s-w: David Reynolds (story: Chris Williams, Mark Dindal / au: Roger Allers ← ANIMALYMPICS, Matthew Jacobs)

Voices: David Spade *(Emperor Kuzco / narrator)* ← REALITY BITES,

John Goodman *(Pacha)* ← COYOTE UGLY ← O BROTHER, WHERE ART THOU? ← BLUES BROTHERS 2000 ← TRUE STORIES ← SWEET DREAMS / → STORYTELLING → MASKED AND ANONYMOUS → OVERNIGHT → BEYOND THE SEA, **Eartha Kitt** *(Yzma)* ← FRIDAY FOSTER, Patrick Warburton *(Kronk)*, Wendie Malick *(Chica)*, Kellyann Kelso *(Chaca)*, Eli Russell Linnetz *(Tipo)*, Wendie Malick *(Chicha; Pacha's wife)* ← MADONNA: INNOCENCE LOST, **Tom Jones** *(theme song guy)* → RED, WHITE & BLUES

Storyline: Evil sorceress Yzma plans revenge on young Emperor Kuzco after she is dismissed from court for being too old and ugly. Her assistant Kronk inadvertently turns Kuzco into a talking llama and sends him out into the jungle to fend for himself. There Kuzco meets a farmer called Pacha who agrees to help him find another sorceror to reverse the spell, but things hot up when they find out that Yzma and Kronk are close on their trail and determined to put an end to Kuzco once and for all. *JZ*

Movie rating: *5

Visual: dvd

Off the record: Tom Jones (from the Welsh valleys) crawled his way up from working in the mines to the glittering showhalls of Las Vegas; his hits ranged from 'It's Not Unusual' & 'Delilah' in the sixties to 'Sex Bomb' at the turn of the noughties. *MCS*

STING & DAVID HARTLEY ** (score by JOHN DEBNEY *)

Nov 00. (cd) *Disney; <8 60689> (012278-2DNY)* ☐ Feb01 ☐
– Perfect world (TOM JONES & DAVID HARTLEY) / My funny friend and me (**) / Snuff out the light (Yzma's song) (EARTHA KITT & DAVID HARTLEY) / Walk the llama llama (GARY LEVOX, JAY DeMARCUS & JOE DON ROONEY) / Perfect world – reprise (TOM JONES & DAVID HARTLEY) / Run llama run (*) / One day she'll love me (STING & SHAWN COLVIN) / A new hope (*) / Beware the groove (*) / The jungle rescue (*) / Pacha's homecoming – The blue plate special (*) / The great battle – Friends forever (*).

S/track review: The big guns are wheeled out for this John Debney soundtrack and the results are suitably impressive. The CD is split into two sections, tracks 1-7 featuring STING, TOM JONES and David Hartley, whereas tracks 8-12 are purely instrumental. It is hard to choose which is the better half. TOM JONES kicks things off with 'Perfect World', a lively, snappy Latin American tune, and EARTHA KITT continues the upbeat theme with 'Snuff Out the Light'. In between the catchy Latin American pieces STING adds a softer touch with 'My Little Friend and Me' and performs a lovely duet with SHAWN COLVIN entitled 'One Day She'll Love Me'. Good as all these are, they are matched by John Debney's orchestral score in the last five tracks. He makes full use of the orchestra in a combination of Latin American and 'The Jungle Book' themes for each track. He creates suspense and the excitement of the chase by resorting to soft woodwind and light strings in a pizzicato style. And each track can be listened to as a piece of music in its own right and not just as an addendum to the film. An excellent CD with something for everyone. *JZ*

Album rating: *6.5

the END OF VIOLENCE

1997 (US/Fra/Ger 122m) Metro-Goldwyn-Mayer (R)

Film genre: urban drama

Top guns: dir: Wim Wenders ← PARIS, TEXAS / → TEATRO → BUENA VISTA SOCIAL CLUB → the MILLION DOLLAR HOTEL → the SOUL OF A MAN (+ story) / s-w: Nicholas Klein → the MILLION DOLLAR HOTEL (+ story)

Stars: Bill Pullman *(Mike Max)* ← SINGLES, Andie MacDowell *(Page Stockard)* → the MUSE, Gabriel Byrne *(Ray Bering)* ← DEAD MAN ← the COURIER ← SIESTA ← GOTHIC / → STIGMATA, Traci Lind *(Cat)*, Loren Dean *('Doc' Dean Brock)*, Daniel Benzali *(Brice Phelps)*, Frederic Forrest *(Ranger MacDermot)* ← TUCKER: THE MAN AND HIS DREAM ← ONE FROM THE HEART ← the ROSE / → SWEETWATER: A TRUE ROCK STORY, Udo Kier *(Zoltan Kovacs)* ← EVEN COWGIRLS GET THE BLUES ← SUSPIRIA / → NINA HAGEN = PUNK + GLORY → DANCER IN THE DARK → PIGS WILL FLY → 30 DAYS UNTIL I'M FAMOUS, Sam Fuller *(Louis Bering)*, Henry Silva *(Juan Emilio)* ← DICK TRACY ← MAN AND BOY / → GHOST DOG: THE WAY OF THE SAMURAI, K. Todd Freeman *(Six)*, Pruitt Taylor Vince *(Frank Cray)* ← HEAVY ← NATURAL BORN KILLERS ← WILD AT HEART ← SHY PEOPLE / → MONSTER, John Diehl *(Lowell Lewis)* ← WALKER, O-Lan Jones *(barmaid)* ← TOUCH ← NATURAL BORN KILLERS, Peter Horton *(Brian)* ← SINGLES, Rosalind Chao *(Claire)*, Nicole Parker *(Ade)* → BOOGIE NIGHTS → BROWN SUGAR, **Me'Shell NdegeOcello** *(Malike)* → STANDING IN THE SHADOWS OF MOTOWN, **Sam Phillips** *(singer)*

Storyline: Mike Max is a hotshot Hollywood producer jolted into a reconsideration of his career choice and lifestyle after he becomes the victim of a violent kidnapping uncomfortably close to the tone of his movies. *BG*

Movie rating: *5

Visual: video + dvd

Off the record: Soul singer **Me'Shell NdegeOcello** (b. Michelle Johnson, 29 Aug'68, Berlin, Germany) had her biggest success when she partnered John Cougar Mellencamp on his 1994 Top 3 hit, 'Wild Night', a Van Morrison cover; her album at the time was 'Plantation Lullabies'. **Sam Phillips** was actually Leslie Phillips (b. 1962, Glendale, California) and nothing to do with the legendary Elvis producer; her album released at the time was 'Martinis & Bikinis' (1994). *MCS*

RY COODER

Sep 97. (cd) *Outpost; <(OPD 30007)>* ☐ ☐
– Define violence / I'm leaving you / Seeds of violence / Observatory / I'm losing you / You shoot him! / Four weeks later / Mathilda / Six by numbers / Kinko's / Vamos Empezar / A night in L.A. / Pourquoi? / E-mail / Don't even know she got one (echoplex mix) / What a city! / Paige / The end of violence (end title).

S/track review: Composed and recorded at the peak of his pre-Buena Vista experimentalism, 'The END OF VIOLENCE' is perhaps RY COODER's most cinematic score, rich, dark and strange, full of the torpid subtlety which pervaded so much contemporary production in the mid-late 90s, yet still sounding surprisingly fresh ten years on. Much more so than the definitive bottleneck meditations of COODER's previous Wenders score, 'PARIS, TEXAS', it's a composite work, a sound cross-pollinated by artists as diverse and distinct as avant-gardist JAMES BLOOD ULMER, DJ/producer HOWIE B and veteran tenor saxophonist GIL BERNAL, as well as COODER regulars JIM KELTNER, JON HASSELL and FLACO JIMENEZ. Percussion protégé JOACHIM is almost as elemental in designing the sonics as papa, whose guitar sits out of the score for sustained periods. COODER Jr even gets co-writing credits on two of the record's most hypnotic pieces, 'Observatory' and 'Vamos Empezar', the latter as languid and liquid-cool a latin-jazz serenade as has graced any soundtrack since the genre's golden era, seduced by BERNAL's exquisite tone, phrasing and timing. The spirit of both Gil and Bill Evans, in fact, ghosts through the score's porous acoustics and hovers in the poise between the chords, lingering over the solo by 'Blue Note' pianist JACKY TERRASSON (on 'Pourquoi?') and the rare, very welcome piano arrangements of COODER himself. While he's ultimately responsible for the production and finished product, the studio manipulations of HOWIE B (credited with "mixing") and producer SUNNY D LEVINE ("programming and sampling") are very much at the heart of the score's multi-layered drift, surging to the fore on abstract centrepiece, 'You Shoot Him!', itself whooshing in on a quivering force-field à la Jack Nitzsche's 'PERFORMANCE', tarrying with a muttering, reed-scrawled mid-section and ultimately breaking down into a HASSELL-drilled braille of notes and pulses. The trumpet sculptor works more conventionally-vaporous magic on cues like 'What A City!' and the aforementioned 'Observatory', and – in only a few sparse phrases – brings COODER's end title, the cycle of themes which it ties up, and the whole score to a lucent, ingenuously metaphysical close. Wenders likens COODER's guitar to a camera, with which he "uncovers the music that the faces and the landscapes and the things on the screen are making deep down in themselves". COODER's achievement with 'The END OF VIOLENCE' is not only in having focused as clearly on uncovering that music of California's people and landscape as he did on '...TEXAS', but zooming in on it with such a complex, multi-layered lens. *BG*

Album rating: *7.5

Various Artists (score: RY COODER *)

Sep 97. (cd) *Outpost; <(OPD 30008)>*
– Define violence (*) / Shouldn't you know (dialogue – Traci Lind) / Every time I try (SPAIN) / Untitled heavy beat parts 1 & 2 (DJ SHADOW) / I'm not your baby (U2 & SINEAD O'CONNOR) / Strange world (dialogue – Bill Pullman) / Little drop of poison (TOM WAITS) / Disrobe (MEDESKI, MARTIN & WOOD) / Injured bird (MICHAEL STIPE & VIC CHESNUTT) / Bailare (el merecumbe) (RAUL MALO) / Me estas matando (LOS LOBOS) / Mr. Wobble (LATIN PLAYBOYS) / Theme for a trucker (WHISKEYTOWN) / Unintentional prayers (dialogue – Andie MacDowell) / You may feel me crying (ROY ORBISON) / Bad news (EELS) / Don't even know she got one (HOWIE B.) / In a heartbeat (dialogue – Bill Pullman).

S/track review: Stylistically much more diverse than the Various Artists soundtrack which accompanied 1992's 'TRESPASS', and obviously more in keeping with Wim Wenders' filmic vision, this does an impressive job of consolidating RY COODER's score. Setting the tone is his own 'Define Violence', further developed – after a droopy-eyed, country-ish interlude courtesy of SPAIN – by DJ SHADOW. As ever, SHADOW gets right under the skin of the film's bleak subtext; 'Untitled Heavy Beat' doesn't quite conjure the despair of 'Dark Days', but it's as insidious and ingratiating as his best work, building from a percussive scrapyard mêlée to a Led Zep-strength monster. The much touted U2 & SINEAD O'CONNOR effort, 'I'm Not Your Baby', initially comes across as flimsy in comparison, although its grungy, trip-hop approved minimalism builds its own quiet head of steam over the course. The mighty TOM WAITS proceeds to steal the show with 'Little Drop Of Poison', a head-scratching instalment of his finest gallows jazz, all lugubrious, quivering piano chords, furtive, creeping horns and bug-eyed, 60-a-day vocal rasping. Breakbeat jazz revivalists MEDESKI, MARTIN & WOOD lighten the mood at just the right moment, while (another fine if incongruous alt-country effort – courtesy of MICHAEL STIPE and VIC CHESNUTT – aside) RAUL MALO and LOS LOBOS embellish it with laissez-faire Latin exuberance. The grunge-blues-tech LATIN PLAYBOYS effort could've come from COODER, and the record's final third is by and large fairly low key. The big news is ROY ORBISON exhumed from the grave with 'You May Feel Me Crying'; as the title suggests, it's a typically ORBISON-esque tearjerker, rescued from oblivion and dressed up with some refined arrangements courtesy of BRIAN ENO. *BG*

Album rating: *6

the ENDLESS SUMMER

1966 (US 95m) Bruce Brown Films

Film genre: sports documentary

Top guns: s-w + dir: Bruce Brown

Stars: Mike Hynson *(principal surfer)* → RAINBOW BRIDGE, Robert August *(principal surfer)*, Lord "Tally Ho" Blears *(himself)*, Bruce Brown *(narrator)*, Terence Bullen *(South African guide)*

Storyline: Michael and Robert are two surfers who decide to live the ultimate dream – follow the summer sun around the globe and surf the best rollers of about four continents. Among the exotic locations they visit are Tahiti, Hawaii, Australia and Bognor Regis (only kidding) as they search for the "perfect wave" which they eventually find off the South African coast. Nice work if you can get it. *JZ*

Movie rating: *6

Visual: video + dvd

Off the record: The SANDALS (see own entry)

---

the SANDALS (composer: Bernie Henighen)

Jan 67. (lp) *World Pacific; <ST 1832>*
– Theme from The Endless Summer / Scrambler / 6-pac / Driftin' / Good Greeves / Decoy / Out front / Wild as the sea / Trailing / Jet black / Lonely road / TR-6. *<cd-iss. 1994 on 'Tri-Surf' diff. order +=; 1>* – The Endless Summer composite.

S/track review: Before the Beach Boys coined the phrase on a hits compilation LP in '74, 'The ENDLESS SUMMER' was the hot property of surf outfit, the SANDALS. Comprising JOHN BLAKELEY, WALTER GEORIS, GASTON GEORIS, JOHN GIBSON and DANNY BRAWNER, the SANDALS were on the crest of a proverbial wave during the sunny climes of the mid-60s. Mixing a sandy, beach-hut cocktail of the Ventures, the Shadows and dodgy western film tunes, the LP opens with the easy-listening theme. With the sound of revved-up motorbikes in the background, 'Scrambler' tears up the dirt track like some leather rebel rouser on a night out on the town (ditto 'TR-6'), while '6-Pac' shines out of the Shadows – so to speak; track 4, 'Driftin'', was actually scribed by a certain Hank Marvin – cut No.10, 'Jet Black,' stemming from breakaway Shad, Jet Harris. It was no surprise that 'The ENDLESS SUMMER' OST nearly generated enough beach-cred to hit the Top 100, its formulaic and derivative approach working its magic around many a teenage delinquent. Classics such as 'Out Front' and 'Wild As The Sea' (the latter the name of the re-issued CD double soundtrack comp.) just might be precursors to the likes of the Cramps, at least instrumentally. Now go find 'The LAST OF THE SKI BUMS'. *MCS*

Album rating: *6.5

– spinoff releases, etc. –

the SANDALS: Wild As The Sea: Complete Sandals 1964-1969

Feb 03. (cd) *Raven; <(RVCD 151)>* Mar03

ENGLAR ALHEIMSINS

UK title 'ANGELS OF THE UNIVERSE'

2000 (Ice/Ger/Scan 100m) Icelandic Film Corp. / Peter Rommel (15)

Film genre: psychological comedy drama

Top guns: dir: Fridrik Thor Fridriksson → NICELAND / s-w: Einar Mar Gudmundsson (+ nov)

Stars: Ingvar E. Sigurdsson *(Pall)*, Baltasar Kormakur *(Oli Beatle)* → 101 REYKJAVIK, Bjorn Jorundur Fridbjornsson *(Viktor)*, Hilmir Snaer Gudnason *(Petur)* → 101 REYKJAVIK, Margret Helga Johannsdottir *(Pall's mother)*, Theodor Juliusson *(Pall's father)*, Johann G. Johannsson *(policeman)*, Halldora Geirhardsdottir *(Dagny)*, Petur Einarsson *(Brynjolfur)* → 101 REYKJAVIK → NOI ALBINOI

Storyline: Based on a true (and at times comical) story of the writer's brother, Pall is an artistic but sensitive young man going through the pains of mental illness and schizophrenia after a break-up with girlfriend, Dagny. He quickly descends into bizarre and frightening behavoir, warranting his parents to commit him to an asylum, where he meets Oli, the man who wrote everything by the Beatles – or so he thinks! *MCS*

Movie rating: *7

Visual: dvd

Off the record: Hilmar Orn Hilmarsson (b.23 Apr'58) was once a collaborator with Genesis P-Orridge and his Psychic TV outfit (see future editions), while **SIGUR ROS** have their own entry. *MCS*

HILMAR ORN HILMARSSON / SIGUR ROS

Jan 01. (cd) *Krunk; (CDKRU 001)* [ ] [–]
– Aoflug – Draumur / Minning / Svarti hundurin og Skoska leikritio / Niourlaeging / Yfirim / Litbrigol / Stigio niour til: heljar / Snoo / Fero / Onnur minning / Bakslag / Mok / Schiller I Kina / Mattleysi / Kveoja / Bium bium bambalo (SIGUR ROS) / Danarfregnir og jardafarir (SIGUR ROS). *(UK-iss.Sep01 as 'ANGELS OF THE UNIVERSE' on 'Fat Cat'; FATOSTCD 01)* – Approach – Dream / Memory / The black dog and the Scottish play / Degradation / Over the bend / Colours / Journey to the underworld / Shave / On the road / Another memory / Relapse / Coma / Schiller in China / Helpless / Te morituri . . . / Bium bium bambalo (SIGUR ROS) / Death announcements and funerals (SIGUR ROS).

S/track review: Reykjavik-born rock musician turned neo-classical composer, Hilmar Orn Hilmarsson, was responsible for a barrel-load of scores before he was commissioned to do 'ENGLAR . . .' at the turn of the century; 'Born natturunnar' (aka 'Children Of Nature') in 1991 being his most revered to date. Apart from two closing tracks by his fellow countrymen, SIGUR ROS, HILMAR composed the bulk of the material, aided and augmented by a string section of sorts: Syzmon Kuran (violin), Kristjan Eldjarn (guitar) and Tomas M. Tomasson (bass) plus percussionists Birgir and Sigtryggur Baldursson. Atmospheric, haunting and ethereal have all been lavished praises – on many a modern-day composer in the past, but none more so than with the beautiful music that accompanied HILMAR's dozen or so pieces on 'ENGLAR ALHEIMSINS'. Not until track 5, the longer 'Yfirim' ('Over The Bend'), was the listener treated to an upbeat surge of Durutti Column-like rhythms, its pulsating backbeat of energy over crescendoed strings and eerie booms, riveting to the max. 'Litbrigol' ('Colours') displayed a Michael Nyman-type charm from his days in the Peter Greenaway stables, while 'Stigio Niour Til: Heljar' ('Journey To The Underworld'), might well have graced a Philip Glass score. This is not to say that Hilmar copied these iconic 20th-Century film composers, more so inhaling their vacuum-ous air that filled a plethora of symphonies and concert halls. If there were a complaint, it would be that the pieces were too short, non-concurrent and repetitive, although by the time HILMAR finished with 'Kveoja' ('Te Morituri . . .'), classical thoughts were put to one side for the dawning of SIGUR ROS. Tracks 16 & 17 ('Bium Bium Bambalo' & 'Danarfregnir Og Jardafarir' respectively) were darker interpretations from their recent 'Ny Batteri' EP, the former a lyrical arrangement of a much-loved Irish and Icelandic lullaby, while the latter was their prog-rock recital of the Icelandic radio service to chronicle their daily 'Death Announcements And Funerals'. This is where SIGUR ROS came of age. *MCS*

Album rating: *7.5

Brian ENO

Born: Brian Peter George St. John Le Baptiste De La Salle Eno, 15 May'48, Woodbridge, East Anglia, England. The bizarre electro-boffin beavering away in a cape and feather boa at the back of those old Roxy Music videos, and the man who pretty much singlehandedly invented the concept of ambient music, BRIAN ENO has also been a fairly prolific – if predictably enigmatic – film composer. After the short stint in Bryan Ferry's art-glam outfit, his preoccupation with sound and its constituent parts led the self-confessed "non-musician" into a series of aural experiments which, with the concept of using the studio itself as a compositional tool, not only revolutionised songwriting, but also intuitively married sound and melody to create the first bonafide "ambient" albums. All of which would have seismic implication for popular music in general and qualify ENO as a natural candidate for film scoring. His first brace of commissions, included Derek Jarman's homoerotic Roman drama, 'Sebastiane' (1976) and (with Michael Nyman) Peter Greenaway's 'Vertical Features Remake' (1978). Sandwiched somewhere inbetween these two landscape scores was his contribution to Derek Jarman's other new wave masterpiece, 'JUBILEE' (1977), although the majority of the OST was snatched by Adam & The Ants, Chelsea and other punks of the era. This coincided with some of his most enduring 70s studio work and, the fact that they were never issued in their own right set a frustrating precedent for almost all of his cinematic endeavour. Ironically, the widely available 'Music For Films' (1978) wasn't actually a soundtrack at all, rather a series of pieces for imaginary films, much the like the pseudonymous Passengers project he'd later work on with U2. If anything, ENO's film work became even more obscure in the 80s with scores for European arts documentaries, 'Egon Schiele – Exzess Under Bestrafung' (1981) and 'Hans: Het Leven Voor De Dood' (1983) as well as American docu, 'SL-1' (1983), on which he shared the credits with POPUL VUH, and German drama, 'Frevel' (1983). Slightly more high profile was his work with Toto on 'DUNE' (1984), although his part of the score was never released, nor was his work on Danish thriller 'Isolde' (1989). In fact, the only ENO score ever issued – with the exception of his work with BONO on 'The MILLION DOLLAR HOTEL' (2000) – was for Derek Jarman's posthumous biopic, 'GLITTERBUG' (1994). This despite accomplished work on the likes of Peter Greenaway's erotic drama, 'The Pillow Book' (1996) and Danish thriller, 'Fear X' (2003). If any interested parties are reading this, may we be so bold as to suggest at least a compilation of the man's filmic achievements? Pretty please? *BG*

- **filmography** (composer) –

Land Of The Minotaur *(1976)* / Sebastiane *(1976)* / **Jubilee** *(1977 OST w/ V/A =>)* / Alternative 3 *(1977 TV)* / Vertical Features Remake *(1978 w/ MICHAEL NYMAN)* / Egon Schiele – Exzess *(1981 OST w/ Anton Von Webern)* / SL-1 *(1983 w/ POPOL VUH)* / Hans: Het Leven Voor De Dood *(1983)* / Frevel *(1983)* / the Creation Of The Universe *(1984)* / Heat And Sunlight *(1987)* / Isolde *(1989)* / For All Mankind *(1990)* / Tong Tana – En Rasa Till Borneos Inre *(1991)* / **Glitterbug** *(1994 OST 'Spinner' w/ JAH WOBBLE =>)* / the Pillow Book *(1996)* / **the Million Dollar Hotel** *(2000 OST/score w/ BONO/U2, DANIEL LANOIS & the MDH BAND =>)* / Fear X *(2003)* / the Jacket *(2005)*

– compilations, etc. –

BRIAN ENO: Music For Films

Sep 78. (lp) *Polydor; (2310 623) E.G.; <EGS 105>* [55] [ ]
– Aragon / From the same hill / Inland sea / Two rapid formations / Slow water / Sparrowfall (1) / Sparrowfall (2) / Sparrowfall (3) / Alternative 3 / Quartz / Events in dense fog / 'There is nobody' / Patrolling wire borders / A measured room / Task force / M386 / Strange light / Final sunset. *(re-iss. Jan87 on 'E.G.' lp/c/cd; EGED/EGEDC/EEGCD 5)*

BRIAN ENO: Music For Films 2

Jan 87. (lp/c) *EG-Editions; (EGED/+C 35)* [ ] [–]
– The dove / Roman twilight / Matta / Dawn, marshland / Climate study / The secret place / An ending (ascent) / Always returning 1 / Signals / Under stars / Drift / Study / Approaching Taidu / Always returning 2.

ENTENDS-TU LES CHIENS ABOYER?

aka NO OYES LADRAR LOS PERROS?

1975 (Fra/Mex 85m) Films du Prosme

Film genre: rural drama

Top guns: s-w: Francois Reichenbach (+ dir), Carlos Fuentes, Jacqueline Lefevre (story: Juan Rulfo)

Stars: Ahui Camacho, Aurora Clavel, Ana De Sade, Gaston Melo, Salvador Sanchez, Salvador Gomez, Patrick Penn

Storyline: A poor Mexican peasant is forced to carry his sick boy on his back as he moves from village to village in search of a doctor to treat him. To keep the child entertained he recounts tales of the landscape, people and places they pass through, while of course keeping alert listening for those barking dogs. *JZ*

Movie rating: *4.5

Visual: none

Off the record: (see below)

—

VANGELIS PAPATHANASSIOU

Sep 75. (lp) *B.A.S.F.; (2129 852-3Y)* [–] French [–]
– Entends-tu les chiens aboyer? – part 1 / Entends-tu les chiens aboyer? – part 2. *(cd-iss. Jul85 by VANGELIS as 'Ignacio' on 'Phonogram'; 813304-2)* – Ignacio (IV parts). *(cd-iss. Apr93 on 'C.A.M.'; CSE 005)*

S/track review: Re-titled 'Ignacio' when issued on CD, this was actually one of VANGELIS' earlier soundtrack commissions. Split into two lengthy parts (totalling nearly 40 minutes), 'ENTENDS-TU LES CHIENS ABOYER?' is the synthesizer man's most space-aged release; possibly a precursor to his 'BLADE RUNNER' recorded several years later. At a time when composer VANGELIS was breaking through commercially all over Europe (his 1975 LP, 'Heaven And Hell' was just about to chart in the UK), the risky 'ENTENDS-TU . . .' disappointed his heyday Aphrodite's Child acolytes. With sporadic Gregorian chorales over neo-classical noodles, side one suffers from lack of direction: just as you think the piece is settling down it takes off on a Prog-like tangent. In stark contrast, side two kicks off rather groovily, but just like its flipside, it too (after about 4 minutes!) becomes monotonous and tinny. If this is your bag, go straight to "Film Soundtracks of Colombo" – or better still, rearrange the words: dry watching paint. *MCS*

Album rating: *3

☐ David ESSEX segment
(⇒ SILVER DREAM RACER)

EURYTHMICS

Formed: London, England . . . 1976 by Aberdonian Annie Lennox and Sunderland-born Dave Stewart. One of the defining acts of the 80s, and certainly one of the decade's better bands, EURYTHMICS grew out of late 70s power pop trio the Tourists (who also featured Stewart's erstwhile writing partner Pete Coombes). The unlikely duo's futuristic sound was at least partly down to Stewart's mastery of cutting edge studio techniques, while Lennox's vocals combined impressive depth and power with a chilly sensuality. It made for an alluring combination, all the more so in an era when over production and watered down songwriting was the norm. The melodic pulse and underlying menace of hits like 'Sweet Dreams (Are Made Of This)' and 'Here Comes The Rain Again' attracted the attention of film director Michael Radford, who invited the group to score his updated adaptation of George Orwell's '1984'. If EURYTHMICS' innovative electro-pop seemed tailor-made for Orwell's vision of dystopia, Stewart and Lennox were left dissatisfied with the amount of music actually heard in the movie's final cut. While both the film and the soundtrack stiffed in America, a spin-off single, 'Sexcrime (Nineteen Eighty-Four)', made the UK Top 5. If Lennox was to continue her relationship with the big screen in an acting capacity – making her debut in Hugh Hudson's period drama, 'Revolution' (1985) and appearing in Derek Jarman's 'Edward II' (1991) – Stewart was to specialise in film scoring following the EURYTHMICS' late 80s demise. His first commission was the soundtrack to obscure Dutch crime drama, 'Lily Was Here' (1989), the dreamy title theme of which – a collaboration with Dutch saxophonist Candy Dulfer – was a fair sized UK hit (Top 10) in early 1990. It was to be the first – and the most successful – in a string of film score credits, earned in tandem with his own short-lived Spiritual Cowboys outfit and subsequent solo work. In 1991, David was commissioned to write the music for Scottish TV mini-series, 'Jute City', his work complementing the harsh realties of life north of the border. While his soundtrack for little known Australian drama, 'No Worries' (1993) – a collaboration with Patrick Seymour – was only released down under, his orchestral score for Ted Demme's acerbic comedy, 'The Ref' (1994), was given a full American/British release. Even more high profile was Paul Verhoeven's controversial and critically lambasted stripper drama, 'Showgirls' (1995), for which Stewart composed the score on the alternative rock-slanted soundtrack. A bit part in teen computer drama, 'Hackers' (1995) marked his big screen acting debut, while Stewart once again hooked up with Ted Demme for the score (unreleased) to his romantic comedy, 'Beautiful Girls'. In Robert Altman's typically quirky Deep South comedy, 'Cookie's Fortune' (1999), the former EURYTHMICS man had finally scored a film of major note. It was an achievement he attempted to build upon in 2000 when he made his directorial debut with 'Honest', a London underworld crime comedy starring Brit girl band All Saints as gender-bending thieves. Although the movie was a given a warm critical reception at the Cannes Film Festival, its poor British box office performance didn't exactly boost the group's career. Undaunted, our Dave was back in 2004 with the score for Charles Shyer's 'ALFIE' remake, a collaboration with MICK JAGGER. Despite Stewart's prolific output, it was actually his erstwhile partner Annie Lennox, who was to gain official recognition for her film work, netting an Oscar for her theme to 'The Lord Of The Rings: Return Of The King' (2003). Prior to this, her only soundtrack credits were a contribution to 'Bram Stoker's Dracula' (1992) and a score for investigative documentary, 'Brother Minister: The Assassination Of Malcolm X' (1994). *BG*

— please note that there are only a few of the numerous DAVID A. STEWART soundtrack releases (see future edition)

- filmography (DAVE / ANNIE composer) {acting ANNIE} –

1984 *(1984 OST by EURYTHMICS =>)* / Revolution *(1985 {* ANNIE})* / the Room *(1987 TV {* ANNIE})* / Rooftops *(1989 w/ MICHAEL KAMEN; see future editions)* / the Long Way Home *(1989 docu {* ANNIE})* / Lily Was Here *(1990 OST by STEWART see; future editions)* / Edward II *(1991 {p ANNIE} on OST; see future editions)* / Jute City *(1991 OST by STEWART; see* *future editions)* / No Worries *(1993 OST by STEWART w/ Patrick Seymour; see future editions)* / the Ref *(1994 OST by STEWART see; future editions)* / Brother Minister: The Assassination Of Malcolm X *(1994 score by LENNOX & RICHIE HAVENS)* / Showgirls *(1995 OST by V/A & STEWART; see future editions)* / Apollo 13 *(1995 ANNIE on OST by V/A & James Horner; see future editions)* / Hackers *(1995 {b DAVID} OST by SIMON BOSWELL & V/A; see future editions)* / Beautiful Girls *(1996 score by STEWART / OST by V/A; see future editions)* / Crimetime *(1996 OST by STEWART; see future editions)* / Cookie's Fortune *(1999 OST by STEWART see; future editions)* / Honest *(2000 score by {d}{b} STEWART + ALL SAINTS =>)* / the Lord Of The Rings: The Return Of The King *(2003 LENNOX theme on OST by HOWARD SHORE; see future editions)* / **Alfie** *(2004 OST by MICK JAGGER & STEWART w/ V/A =>)*

EVEN COWGIRLS GET THE BLUES

1994 (US 101m) Fine Line Features (R)

Film genre: anarchic road movie/comedy

Top guns: s-w + dir: **Gus Van Sant** → GOOD WILL HUNTING → LAST DAYS (au: Tom Robbins)

Stars: Uma Thurman *(Sissy Hankshaw)* → PULP FICTION → CHELSEA WALLS → BE COOL, Rain Phoenix *(Bonanza Jellybean)*, John Hurt *(the Countess)* ← 1984 ← PIED PIPER / → DEAD MAN → the PROPOSITION, Noriyuki 'Pat' Morita *(the Chink)*, Keanu Reeves *(Julian Gitche)* ← BILL & TED'S BOGUS JOURNEY ← BILL & TED'S EXCELLENT ADVENTURE ← PERMANENT RECORD / → THUMBSUCKER, Lorraine Bracco *(Delores Del Ruby)* ← SING / → the BASKETBALL DIARIES → DEATH OF A DYNASTY, Angie Dickinson *(Miss Adrian)* ← CALYPSO JOE / → DUETS, Ed Begley Jr. *(Rupert)* ← STREETS OF FIRE ← THIS IS SPINAL TAP ← GET CRAZY ← ELVIS: THE MOVIE ← RECORD CITY / → a MIGHTY WIND, Carol Kane *(Carla)* ← the PRINCESS BRIDE, Sean Young *(Marie Barth)* ← DUNE ← BLADE RUNNER, Crispin Glover *(Howard Barth)* ← the DOORS ← WILD AT HEART / → DEAD MAN, Lin Shaye *(Rubber Rose Maid)* ← ROADSIDE PROPHETS ← PUMP UP THE VOLUME ← the LONG RIDERS / → LAST MAN STANDING → DETROIT ROCK CITY, Roseanne Arnold *(Madame Zoe)*, Buck Henry *(Dr. Dreyfuss)* ← the OWL AND THE PUSSYCAT ← CANDY ← the GRADUATE, Grace Zabriskie *(Mrs. Hankshaw)* ← WILD AT HEART, Udo Kier *(commercial director)* ← SUSPIRIA / → the END OF VIOLENCE → NINA HAGEN = PUNK + GLORY → DANCER IN THE DARK → PIGS WILL FLY → 30 DAYS UNTIL I'M FAMOUS, William Burroughs *(himself)* ← HOME OF THE BRAVE ← CHAPPAQUA, Heather Graham *(cowgirl Heather)* ← SHOUT / → BOOGIE NIGHTS → COMMITTED, Edward James Olmos *(musician at barbeque)* ← BLADE RUNNER / → SELENA → the ROAD TO EL DORADO, Scott Patrick Green *(pilgrim man)* → LAST DAYS, Lily Tomlin, Steve Buscemi, Faye Dunaway

Storyline: Gus Van Sant's adaptation of Tom Robbins' cult 70s novel has the unlikely heroine Sissy Henkshaw putting her unnaturally large thumbs to good use as the greatest hitchhiker on earth. She finally finds true love in in the form of Bonanza Jellybean, the ringleader of an errant band of cowgirls in deepest Oregon. *BG*

Movie rating: *4

Visual: video + dvd

Off the record: (see below)

---

k.d. LANG (co-composer: BEN MINK)

Nov 93. (cd/c) *Sire; <(9362 45433-2/-4)>* [82] [36]
– Just keep me moving / Much finer place / Or was I / Hush sweet lover / Myth / Apogee / Virtual vortex / Lifted by love / Overture / Kundalini yoga waltz / In perfect dreams / Curious soul astray / Ride of Bonanza Jellybean / Don't be a lemming polka / Sweet little Cherokee / Cowgirl pride.

S/track review: Coming just a year after her breakthrough album, 'Ingenue' (1992), k.d. LANG's soundtrack to this Gus Van Sant oddity bears, in its best moments, all the hallmarks of that record's smouldering classicism. Not least in the gorgeous 'Hush Sweet Lover' and 'Curious Soul Astray', yet having been recorded in the early 90s, there's a tendency to club-friendly fashion which hasn't weathered the years quite as well: exchange LANG's breathy croon for Shaun Ryder's Manc slur and 'Just Keep Me Moving' could easily take pride of place on a Happy Mondays album. Both LANG and longtime co-writer BEN MINK also obviously took the relative freedom of a film score to try out their more experimental whims; the likes of 'Kundalini Yoga Waltz' sounds exactly as you might expect . . . They also couldn't resist a bit of Morricone-esque, high noon moodiness, and why not; 'Ride Of Bonanza Jellybean' actually plays as one of the record's most haunting tracks. Fans of her more overtly country material should head straight for 'Sweet Little Cherokee', or else take the floor for hayloft hootenanny, 'Cowgirl Pride'. *BG*

Album rating: *5.5

– spinoff hits, etc. –

k.d. LANG: Just Keep Me Moving / In Perfect Dreams

Dec 93. (7"/c-s) *(W 0227/+C)* [ ] [59]
(12"/cd-s) *(W 0227 T/CD)* – ('A') / ('A'-wild planet mixes) / ('A'-moving mixes).

EVENT HORIZON

1997 (US 95m) Paramount Pictures (R)

Film genre: sci-fi horror

Top guns: dir: Paul Anderson / s-w: Philip Eisner

Stars: Laurence Fishburne *(Capt. Miller)* ← WHAT'S LOVE GOT TO DO WITH IT ← SCHOOL DAZE ← DEATH WISH II ← FAST BREAK ← CORNBREAD, EARL AND ME / → the SOUL OF A MAN, Sam Neill *(Dr. William Weir)*, Kathleen Quinlan *(Peters; med tech)* ← the DOORS, Joely Richardson *(Lt. Starck)*, Richard T. Jones *(Cooper)* ← WHAT'S LOVE GOT TO DO WITH IT, Jack Noseworthy *(Justin)* ← S.F.W. / → ELVIS, Sean Pertwee *(Smith)*, Jason Isaacs *(D.J.)*

Storyline: After a seven year absence the deep-space exploration ship Event Horizon suddenly appears in Neptune's orbit, broadcasting a distress signal. Scientist William Weir and a crew of seven go to investigate, but on arrival find that things on board ship are not as they should be. As fear and unease grip the crew, Weir must discover the nature of the evil presence on board before it is too late. *JZ*

Movie rating: *5

Visual: video + dvd

Off the record: (see below)

MICHAEL KAMEN & ORBITAL

Oct 97. (cd/c/lp) *London; <(828939-2/-4/-1)>* [ ] Sep97 [ ]
– The forward decks: a) Lewis and Clark, b) Neptune, c) Claire, d) First containment, e) Core, f) Metal, g) Second containment, h) Airlock / The main access corridor: a) Singularity, b) Ducts, c) Turbulence, d) Medical, e) Gravity drive / Engineering: a) Tomb, b) Blood, c) Countdown, d) Outer door, e) Bio scan / The Event Horizon: a) Weir, b) Event Horizon.

S/track review: The combination of film composer, Michael Kamen, and techno whizzkids, ORBITAL (aka: brothers PHIL & PAUL HARTNOLL) is a mixture of loud, deep orchestral music interspersed with futuristic synthesizer themes. It is designed to create the impression of fear and foreboding in an alien setting away from the safety of Earth. Unfortunately there is little variation in the music from beginning to end which rather affects the orchestra's attempts at creating suspense, mainly through long build-ups and then loud, staccato bursts after a sudden silence. This works for the first few times, but not when it is continually repeated throughout the score. The synthesized material does at least vary and partly succeeds in creating a sense of fear and strangeness. Titles such as 'Gravity Drive', 'Singularity' and 'Bio-Scan' are suitably futuristic but all-too similar in the music they contain. *JZ*

Album rating: *5

EVERYBREATH

1993 (US 90m) Columbia TriStar (R)

Film genre: psychological thriller

Top guns: s-w: (+ dir) Steve Bing, Andrew Fleming (+ story), Judd Nelson

Stars: Judd Nelson *(Jimmy)* ← BLUE CITY / → AIRHEADS → MR. ROCK'N'ROLL: THE ALAN FREED STORY, Joanna Pacula *(Lauren)*, Patrick Bauchau *(Richard)* ← PHENOMENA / → the BEATNICKS → RAY, Willie Garson *(Bob)*, Rebeca Arthur *(Mimi)*, Cynthia Brimhall *(Kris)*, John Pyper-Ferguson *(Hal)* → HARD CORE LOGO, Camille Cooper *(Sarah)*

Storyline: Actor Jimmy is rather confused after being hired by rich Richard to seduce his own wife Lauren. In the cold light of day, after much pain and humiliation, Jimmy realizes that the kinky couple were just using him, but he can't stop himself from meeting up with them again and finding some new stooges. But the fun and games get more serious when Lauren and Jimmy become allies against an ever-more demanding Richard. *JZ*

Movie rating: *5

Visual: video

Off the record: NILS LOFGREN was born on the 21st June '51, Chicago, Illinois, USA. Raised in Maryland, Washington DC by Italian/Swedish parents, the guitarist (who played with a thumb-pick rather than a flat pick) formed Paul Dowell & The Dolphin in 1969; two flop singles later, he folded the outfit and formed the harder-edged Grin. While building up their live reputation, LOFGREN sessioned for Neil YOUNG & Crazy Horse on 'After The Goldrush', the aforementioned group also employing him the following year as a part-time writer and session man on their brilliant eponymous debut. Meanwhile, Grin signed to 'Spindizzy' records (distributed by 'Columbia') and issued their self-titled debut LP in late summer '71. The record only managed to scrape into the US Top 200, as did their follow-ups, '1 + 1' and 'All Out' (the latter added Nils' younger brother Tom). In 1973, the group signed to 'A&M', although they subsequently split when Nils joined YOUNG & Crazy Horse for the sublime 'Tonight's The Night' (1975) set. Released the same year as 'Tonight . . .', LOFGREN's debut album found him finally hitting his groove with an irrepressible verve and a rock solid set of songs. Although the record failed to chart, LOFGREN enjoyed some belated chart success with the Al Kooper-produced 'Cry Tough' (1976). A more guitar-orientated affair, it made the UK Top 10 and the US Top 40, briefly elevating Nils to the level of recognition enjoyed by most of his peers. It wasn't to last though, the disappointing 'I Came To Dance' (1977) failing to maintain the momentum, while the much improved 'Nils' (1979) sold even less despite the lyrical suss of guest, Lou REED. A new deal with 'Backstreet-M.C.A.' failed to turn things around and early 80s sets, 'Night Fades Away' (1981) and 'Wonderland' (1983) made little impact. While 1983 had seen Nils again working with YOUNG (on the 'Trans' tour), LOFGREN initiated his marathon stint with Bruce SPRINGSTEEN's E-Street Band the following year. Independently released in the UK, 'Flip' (1985) was LOFGREN's final studio release of the decade, a frenetic set of high octane rockers which went down well with fans but again failed to cross over or break any new ground. The early 90s saw the singer/guitarist return with a new band (including ex-BAND man, Levon Helm) and a couple of albums in the space of two years, an uncharacteristically prolific burst of creativity no doubt fuelled by his long years as a sideman. 1993 saw LOFGREN's first foray into soundtrack work for the movie 'EVERYBREATH', while a further studio album, 'Damaged Goods', and the obligatory unplugged set, 'Acoustic Live', appeared in '95 and '97 respectively. The Mr. Nice of the rock establishment, LOFGREN remains one of the most respected, highly praised and in-demand guitarists around; the fact that his solo career never really took off only serves to fuel his cult status. *BG & MCS*

NILS LOFGREN

1993. (cd) *Stampede; <1006-2> Permanent; (PERMCD 28/1)* ☐ Oct94 ☐
– No return / Tender love / Take me home / No tomorrow / Dreams come true / Rainy nights / Alone / Tryin' not to fall / Good day for goodbyes / Lions wake / Out of the grave / A. lefty / Tough trails / Fallen into his hands. *(with free cd-ep+=; PERMCD 28/2)* – (non-OST tracks).

S/track review: It seems that playing guitar for some of rock's most revered legends (Neil Young, Bruce Springsteen and er . . . Ringo Starr) has taught NILS LOFGREN a few things about how to make a great album. 'EVERYBREATH' is peppered with howlin' blues licks, ear-shattering harmonica parts, smooth-as-silk ballads, and to-die-for guitar solos that all add up to a fine body of work. From the opening bars of the down'n'dirty 'No Return', through the delicate 'Tender Love' and jazz lounge-tinged 'Rainy Nights', to the final, gospel-accompanied, screeching notes of 'Fallen Into His Hands', 'EVERYBREATH' is an eclectic mix of styles that really complement each other. There is certainly a blues flavour throughout but LOFGREN shows off his versatility and scope without overdoing it, sounding too flamboyant, or committing the guitarist's cardinal sin of overindulgent soloing. Without setting the world alight, 'EVERYBREATH' has enough sumptuous guitar pieces and eloquently crafted songs to make it a worthwhile experience. *CM*

Album rating: *6

☐ EXPLOSIONS IN THE SKY segment
(⇒ FRIDAY NIGHT LIGHTS)

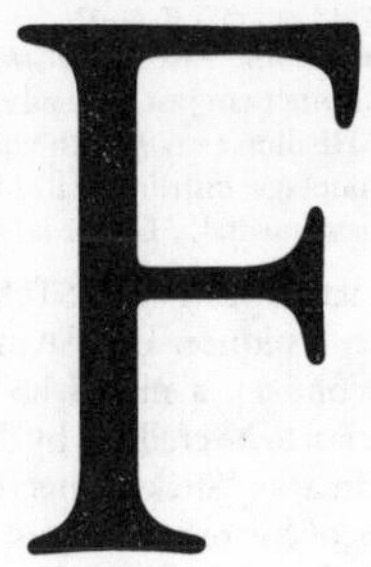

the FAMILY WAY

1966 (UK 115m) British Lion Film Corporation (AA)

Film genre: romantic comedy

Top guns: dir: Roy Boulting / s-w: Bill Naughton (+ nov: 'Honeymoon Deferred')

Stars: Hayley Mills *(Jenny Fitton)*, Hywel Bennett *(Arthur Fitton)* → LOOT → PERCY, John Mills *(Ezra Fitton)* → WHEN THE WIND BLOWS → WHO'S THAT GIRL, Marjorie Rhodes *(Lucy Fitton)* ← I'VE GOTTA HORSE → MRS. BROWN, YOU'VE GOT A LOVELY DAUGHTER, Avril Angers *(Liz Piper)* ← BE MY GUEST / → TWO A PENNY, John Comer *(Leslie Piper)*, Wilfred Pickles *(Uncle Fred)*, Barry Foster *(Joe Thompson)*, Liz Fraser *(Molly Thompson)* ← EVERY DAY'S A HOLIDAY / → UP THE JUNCTION / → the GREAT ROCK'N'ROLL SWINDLE, Andrew Bradford *(Eddie)* → FLASH GORDON → SID & NANCY, **Murray Head** *(Geoffrey Fitton)* → MADAME CLAUDE, Diana Coupland *(Mrs. Rose)*, Harry Locke *(Mr. Stubbs)* ← WHAT A CRAZY WORLD, Fanny Carby *(Mrs. Stone)* ← WHAT A CRAZY WORLD ← SOME PEOPLE

Storyline: Bookish and intense in the way only a 60s Brit film character can be, Arthur Fitton ties the knot with his virginal sweetheart Jenny but – after the marital bed literally collapses at the last moment – he suffers from a bad case of sexual stage fright. He also clashes constantly with his blue collar cliché of a father, under whose roof their lack of cash forces the couple to remain. When the days turn into weeks, and Jenny cracks and confesses all to her mother, it's only a matter of time before the local blue rinse brigade are gossiping about poor Arthur's shortcomings. *BG*

Movie rating: *7

Visual: video

Off the record: Singer-songwriter **Murray Head** is the older brother of actor Anthony Head, Prime Minister in TV's 'Little Britain'. *MCS*

PAUL McCARTNEY

Jun 67. (lp) *Decca; (LK/SKL 4847) London; <MS 82007>* Aug67
– Variations Nos.1-9 / Hymn to the child. *<cd-iss. 1995 on 'Polygram'+=; 528922> (cd-iss. May03 on 'XXI'+=; XXICD 21468) –* (extra variations, etc).

S/track review: Like many a talented rock star, PAUL McCARTNEY can't actually read or write musical notation; when he accepted the Boulting Brothers' commission for 'The FAMILY WAY', it was the first time he'd ventured beyond the security of his writing partnership with John Lennon (something which Lennon was apparently none too happy about), and he turned to Beatles producer GEORGE MARTIN for help. The soundtrack they came up with still stands as McCARTNEY's best, even if the decision to release it the same month as Sgt. Pepper's ensured it sank as quickly as Hywel Bennett's libido. Take away the heavy use of Colliery-dusted brass band and the familiar MARTIN strings, and there aren't many parallels with that album, with any Beatles material in fact. Much of this short (well under half an hour) but sweet soundtrack plays like a conventional orchestral film score, more likely to appeal to score buffs than Beatles fans. There's only one central melodic motif, 'Love In The Open Air', but it's elegiac in McCARTNEY's best tradition and robust enough to bear repeated variations. These include some gorgeous solo guitar and woodwind pieces and a swinging, Bacharach-like flight into mariachi waltz. Familiar electric guitar, bass, organ and drum arrangements kick the whole thing into gear on cues 7 and 9 (the score's so of-a-piece there aren't even any titles), with a rawer, Dick Dale-meets-the-Animals style vibe which Sir Paul hasn't hinted at since. What he did reprise was the symphonic ambition, going on to work with Carl Davis on 'Liverpool Oratario' (1991), which in turn inspired French Canadian quartet La Flûte Enchantée. Their interpretations of 'The FAMILY WAY' are included on the soundtrack's most recent CD re-issue – by Québécois label 'XXI' – alongside a whole suite of guitar orientated variations by another French Canadian composer/arranger, Carl Aubut, and his Claudel String Quartet. *BG*

Album rating: *6

– spinoff releases, etc. –

GEORGE MARTIN ORCHESTRA: Love In The Open Air / Theme From 'The Family Way'
1967. (7") *United Artists; (UP 1165)* –

FAR NORTH

1988 (US 90m) Alive Films (PG-13)

Film genre: rural domestic drama

Top guns: s-w (+ dir): **Sam Shepard** ← PARIS, TEXAS ← RENALDO AND CLARA ← ZABRISKIE POINT

Stars: Jessica Lange *(Kate)* ← SWEET DREAMS / → MASKED AND ANONYMOUS, Charles Durning *(Bertram)* ← the BEST LITTLE WHOREHOUSE IN TEXAS ← I WALK THE LINE / → DICK TRACY → O BROTHER, WHERE ART THOU?, Tess Harper *(Rita)* ← FLASHPOINT ← TENDER MERCIES / → BROKEN BRIDGES, Donald Moffat *(Uncle Dane)* ← ALAMO BAY, Ann Wedgeworth *(Amy)* ← SWEET DREAMS ← ELVIS AND THE BEAUTY QUEEN, Patricia Arquette *(Jilly)* → STIGMATA

Storyline: New Yorker Kate returns home to the Minnesota ranch when she learns that her poor daddy Bertram has landed in hospital thanks to Mel. Mel happens to be daddy's old horse, who deliberately tossed Bertram from the saddle for being grumpy and dictatorial. Now he orders Kate to shoot the unfortunate beast, but in the meantime she has to deal with the rest of her family, who seem to display every type of anti-social tendency between them. Can she pluck up courage to shoot the stallion or will she bite the bullet instead? *JZ*

Movie rating: *3.5

Visual: video

Off the record: The **RED CLAY RAMBLERS** (see below)

the RED CLAY RAMBLERS

Sep 89. (lp/c/c) *Sugar Hill; <(SH/+C/CD 8502)>*
– Far north / Blue Duluth / Amy's theme (kitchen) / Gourd, part 1 / Gourd, part 2 / Amy's theme (field) / Roll on buddy – montage / Gangar / Big ships / Katie's ride / Train through the big woods / Night harps / Run sister run / Camptown races – Amy's theme / Amy's theme (over the hill). *<(re-iss. Jan97 cd/c; SHCD/SHMC 8502)>*

S/track review: Formed in Chapel Hill, North Carolina in the early 70s, the RED CLAY RAMBLERS (here, comprising CLAY

BUCKNER on fiddles & harmonica, CHRIS FRANK on piano, guitar & accordion, JACK HERRICK multi-tasking, BLAND SIMPSON on piano and TOMMY THOMPSON on banjo) have earned a devoted following with an exuberant brew of old-time Appalachian folk, rock, jazz and show tunes, though this particular album's moody miscellany might not be the recipe to win new fans. The band's relationship with Sam Shepard has been one constant in its history of adventurous theatre and film projects; they first worked with the playwright off-Broadway on 'A Lie Of The Mind' with Harvey Keitel in 1985, and contributed the soundtrack to his subsequent 1993 film, 'Silent Tongue'. The score for 'FAR NORTH', though, is one of those soundtracks that probably shouldn't be set adrift without pictures; rootsy snatches of jigging fiddle, barrelhouse piano, plaintive accordion, slide guitar and muted trumpet are stylised with washes of echo, darkly overshadowed by portentous bass drones and death-knell drums. 'Gourd, pt.2' provides a refreshing interlude of banjo and guitar-hero histrionics, and a rattling, harp-led 'Train Through The Big Woods' briefly raises the temperature before succumbing to the theatrical atmospherics. About the only stable point, though, is the pervasive wistful waltz, 'Amy's Theme'. *ND*

Album rating: *4

☐ Jay FARRAR segment
(⇒ the SLAUGHTER RULE)

FAST BREAK

1979 (US 107m) Columbia Pictures (PG)

Film genre: sports comedy/drama

Top guns: dir: Jack Smight / s-w: Sandor Stern (story: Marc Kaplan)

Stars: Gabriel Kaplan *(David Greene)*, Harold Sylvester *(D.C.)* ← a HERO AIN'T NOTHIN' BUT A SANDWICH, Michael Warren *(Tommy "Preacher" White)* ← CLEOPATRA JONES, Bernard King *(Hustler)*, Reb Brown *(Bull)*, Mavis Washington *(Swish)*, Bert Remsen *(Bo Winnegar)* ← NASHVILLE ← the STRAWBERRY STATEMENT / → DICK TRACY, Randee Heller *(Jan)*, John Chappell *(Alton Gutkas)* ← KISS MEETS THE PHANTOM OF THE PARK / → HARD COUNTRY, K Callan *(Ms. Tidwell)* ← JOE, Laurence Fishburne III *(street kid)* ← CORNBREAD, EARL AND ME / → DEATH WISH II → SCHOOL DAZE → WHAT'S LOVE GOT TO DO WITH IT → EVENT HORIZON → the SOUL OF A MAN

Storyline: "The Best Guy On The Team Is A Girl!" Yep, you guessed it, when decent New York type David Greene is offered a coaching position at a Nevada college, he gathers up a motley selection of Big Apple waifs and strays as the core of his basketball team, one of whom happens to be a female in disguise. *BG*

Movie rating: *5

Visual: video

Off the record: **SYREETA** (b. 3 Aug'46, Pittsburgh, Pennsylvania, USA) didn't shine until she relocated to Detroit, home to 'Motown' records, whom she signed for as Rita Wright in the late 60s. With the help of STEVIE WONDER (her subsequent hubby), SYREETA proved to be a budding songwriter, supplying the man (and others) with several hits, including 'If You Really Love Me', 'Signed, Sealed, Delivered (I'm Yours)' & 'Superwoman'. Her eponymous debut album was released in 1972, while her collaborative sophomore set with her ex-husband, 'Stevie Wonder Presents Syreeta' (1974), spawned a UK Top 20 hit, 'Your Kiss Is Sweet'. Albums number three and four respectively ('One To One' 1977 and 'Rich Love, Poor Love' 1977) bombed commercially, but everything was back on course a few years later when she struck up a collaborative partnership with BILLY PRESTON. She retired from music in the mid-80s, only hitting the headlines once more when she died of cancer on the 6th of July, 2004. *MCS*

BILLY PRESTON & SYREETA

(score: David Shire & James Di Pasquale)

1979. (lp) *Motown; <M7-915 R1> (STML 12107)* [ ] [ ]
– Go for it (theme from "Fast Break") / Welcome to Cadwallader (instrumental) / More than just a friend / With you I'm born again (instrumental) / He didn't say / With you I'm born again / Books and basketball (montage; instrumental) / Half time (instrumental) / The big game (instrumental) / Go for it (disco).

S/track review: The late BILLY PRESTON's achievements are sometimes overlooked: a pioneer on clavinet and moog (and an influence on Stevie Wonder); a man who put the soul into the Beatles (the only musician to be credited by the band); a contributor to Rolling Stones landmarks 'Sticky Fingers' and 'Exile On Main Street'; and the author of his own string of influential space-funk No.1's. Having written the biggest hit of Joe Cocker's career ('You Are So Beautiful') in 1975, PRESTON was to ironically struggle to repeat his early 70s success over the latter half of the decade. Teamed with 'Motown' receptionist-turned-songwriter SYREETA, he finally reinvented himself as adult contemporary soul crooner on the transatlantic Top 5, 'With You I'm Born Again'. The partnership echoed the blueprint of Donny Hathaway and Roberta Flack, and the man who penned the claret-sighing melody was ace composer David Shire, he of the legendary 'Taking Of Pelham One Two Three' score, and fairly fresh from scooping a 'SATURDAY NIGHT FEVER' Grammy. And with percussionists like Funk Brothers EDDIE "BONGO" BROWN and JACK ASHFORD, and Brazilian supersessionist PAULINHO DA COSTA (another ' . . .NIGHT FEVER' veteran), as well as veteran jazzers RAY BROWN and VICTOR FELDMAN, and Funk Brother guitarist ROBERT WHITE on board, 'FAST BREAK' is a fairly respectable soundtrack for 1979, at least more respectable than the previous year's Beatles tribute/ fiasco, 'SGT. PEPPER'S LONELY HEARTS CLUB BAND', in which PRESTON appeared. FELDMAN and DA COSTA showboat with the rolling syncopation of 'Half Time' (which – at least for the first minute – sounds like a funk 45 from ten years previous), and BILLY and SYREETA 'Go For It' on the main theme, singing themselves dizzy on the "Disco" neo-remix: a great space-whooshing intro, Shire-arranged laser strings and as many breakdowns as you can bounce a basketball through. PRESTON's legendary organ-grinding only really gets a look in on the retro-jazzy 'Welcome To Cadwallader', SYREETA makes her own bid for disco-divadom on 'He Didn't Stay' and Shire supplies a couple of decent, late decade dance-funk instrumentals in 'Books And Basketball' and 'The Big Game', the latter speeding up into grandstanding 70s theme music. *BG*

Album rating: *6

– spinoff releases, etc. –

BILLY PRESTON & SYREETA: Go For It / With You I'm Born Again

Apr 79. (7") *(TMG 1139)* [ ] [ ]
(12"+=) *(TMG12 1139)* – (instrumental).

BILLY PRESTON & SYREETA: With You I'm Born Again / Go For It

Aug 79. (7") *<1460>* [ ] [–]

BILLY PRESTON & SYREETA: With You I'm Born Again

Aug 79. (7") *(TMG 1159)* [–] [2]

BILLY PRESTON & SYREETA: With You I'm Born Again

Nov 79. (7") *<1477>* [4] [–]

☐ José FELICIANO segment
(⇒ AARON LOVES ANGELA)

la FEMME DE MON POTE

aka My Best Friend's Girl

1983 (Fra 99m) Renn Productions / Sara-Films (18)

Film genre: romantic/seXual comedy

Top guns: s-w: Bertrand Blier (+ dir), Gerard Brach ← WONDERWALL / → SHY PEOPLE

Stars: Coluche *(Micky)*, Isabelle Huppert *(Viviane)*, Thierry Lhermitte *(Pascal)*, Daniel Colas *(the flirt)*, Francois Perrot *(the doctor)* ← MADAME CLAUDE, Farid Chopel *(the hoodlum)*

Storyline: The snow begins melting on the Alpine slopes as Viviane and Pascale have a steamy affair in their holiday chalet. But next morning Pascale is back at work and leaves Viviane in the company of his best friend Micky. Soon Micky's emotions get the better of him as Viviane seduces him (another day, another dope), but he's quickly guilt-ridden at what he's done to chum Pascale. How will the friends resolve their situation – share and share alike? *JZ*

Movie rating: *5.5

Visual: none

Off the record: **J.J. CALE** (b. Jean-Jacques Cale, 5 Dec'38, Oklahoma, USA. After a childhood spent immersing himself in the blues and rockabilly, CALE's first foray into the music business was as a country player in Nashville. When this came to little, CALE followed the bright lights and Tulsa musical compadres Russell Bridges (aka Leon Russell), Carl Radle (later of Derek & The Dominoes) and Jimmy Karstein to L.A. where he worked as an engineer for 'Liberty' records. Around this time he was also performing solo in L.A. clubs, releasing a one-off single for the label, 'Outside Looking In', around summer '66. CALE's most sought after artefact from this period, however, is his pseudo-psychedelic project, 'A Trip Down Sunset Strip', recorded under the moniker of the Leathercoated Minds. One track left over from this session was eventually revamped and released as 'After Midnight', a slow burning piano blues groove which was pivotal in getting CALE's career off the ground. Subsequently covered by ERIC CLAPTON in 1970 (who'd heard the track through Delaney & Bonnie), the single's success spurred on CALE to write full-time, who was now eking out a living back in Tulsa after another ill-fated period in Nashville. The result was 'Naturally' (1971), a backporch blend of country, blues, rockabilly and R&B which would serve the singer well over more than 30 years as a recording artist. Released on Leon Russell's 'Shelter' records, the set included a re-recorded 'After Midnight' as well as such CALE staples as 'Call Me The Breeze' (later covered by Lynyrd Skynyrd), 'Magnolia' (later covered by Poco and Jose Feliciano) and the languorous 'Crazy Mama' (CALE's Top 30 hit). The record also introduced CALE's trademark vocal style, a tersely minimalist, often barely audible drawl which complemented the unadorned music perfectly; interestingly, CALE's insistence that his voice be mixed down was drawn from his conviction that this would draw the listener in. Maybe there was something in this, most of CALE's albums pulsing with a subtly hypnotic power that was hard to resist. A follow-up set, 'Really' (1972), was more upbeat, recorded in various studios including Muscle Shoals where CALE cut the moody, horn-embellished R&B of 'Lies'. 'Okie' (1974) was a more organic affair, with several of the tracks recorded at CALE's house. Recorded in Nashville, 'Troubadour' (1976), became his first album to chart in the UK (Top 60) while the brassy swing of 'Hey Baby' enjoyed a brief tenure in the US Hot 100. The set also included the brooding road fever of 'Travelin' Light' (arguably one of CALE's finest moments, positively frenetic against the bulk of his work!) and his most famous track, 'Cocaine', covered, of course, to much success by ERIC CLAPTON. Yet again, CALE could've taken the bit between his teeth and made a shot at the big time on the back of the single's success; instead, he chose to spend the proceeds on building a studio in his Nashville home. '5' (1979) became CALE's highest charting album to date, making the UK Top 40, though you could hardly call this reticent studiophile a pop star. Shunning most publicity at any opportunity, it's just as well that it often took an interpretation by another artist for CALE's songs to gain radio airplay. Nevertheless, in the early 80s, he signed a major label deal with 'Phonogram International', releasing 'Grasshopper' (1982) and '#8' (1983); though they both sold fairly well in Britain, CALE was apparently unhappy and asked to be released from his contract. He then retired from the music business for the bulk of the 80s, although one LP did surface, the OST to French film, 'La FEMME DE MON POTE'. *BG & MCS*

J.J. CALE

Jun 84. (lp/c) *Mercury; (814 401-1/-4)* [–] French [–]
– Bringing it back / City girls / Mona / Right down here / The woman that got away / Ride me high / Starbound / You keep me hangin' on / Super blue / Magnolia.

S/track review: This rare French-only set is basically a J.J. CALE collection – not necessarily a "best of" as such – from his first six studio LPs. With three cues, 'The Woman That Got Away', 'Ride Me High' and 'Super Blue' (but sadly, no 'Cocaine'), his celebrated 1976 LP 'Troubadour' takes centre stage. Characterized by his cool, laid-back guitar style and husky vox, J.J. virtually breathes down the neck of "slowhand" Clapton on this trio of lazy blues-rock numbers. Funnily enough, the OST opens and closes with two songs ('Bringing It Back' and 'Magnolia') from CALE's classy debut, 'Naturally', the latter ballad up there with the man's greatest. One can tell there was eleven long years between his debut and 1982's, 'Grasshopper', an album that got lost somewhere in the mainstream pop melee, example two of its sharper cuts, 'City Girls' and 'You Keep Me Hangin' On'. Bringing up the rear are the three remaining tracks, 'Mona' (from CALE's '5' set), 'Right Down Here' (from 'Really') and 'Starbound' (from 'Okie'), all of them best served up "After Midnight". *MCS*

Album rating: *5.5

FIGHT CLUB

1999 (US 139m) Twentieth Century-Fox (R)

Film genre: psychological thriller/drama

Top guns: dir: David Fincher / s-w: Jim Uhls (au: Chuck Palahniuk)

Stars: Edward Norton (narrator), Brad Pitt *(Tyler Durden)* ← JOHNNY SUEDE / → the ASSASSINATION OF JESSE JAMES . . ., Helena Bonham Carter *(Marla Singer)*, **MEAT LOAF Aday** *(Robert 'Bob' Paulson)*, Zach Grenier *(Richard Chesler)* ← WORKING GIRL / → SWORDFISH, Jared Leto *(Angel Face)* ← BLACK AND WHITE, Eion Bailey *(Ricky)* → ALMOST FAMOUS, Pat McNamara *(Commissioner Jacobs)* ← CRIMES OF PASSION ← AMERICAN HOT WAX, Michael Shamus Wiles *(bartender in Halo)* → MAGNOLIA → ROCK STAR, Joel Bissonnette *(food court maitre D')* → LOOKING FOR LEONARD

Storyline: An anonymous narrator sleepwalks his way through airport lounges and his life in general, a hollow eyed, white collar insomniac who's so emotionally crippled he attends support groups for the terminally ill. Then he meets the mysterious Tyler Durden, a sexy, swaggering, and apparently amoral dude with a mission. Durden is everything Norton isn't, and his mission is to put corporately de-humanised automatons like him back in touch with their inner man through bare knuckle brawling. He also holds the key to Hollywood's most visceral dramatic twist in years. *BG*

Movie rating: *9

Visual: video + dvd

Off the record: The name of L.A.-born **MIKE SIMPSON** mightn't've meant much to the average music fan or cinemagoer, yet as one half of ace deconstructionist production duo the **DUST BROTHERS** (alongside **JOHN KING**), he's helped shape some of the best records of the last fifteen years, as well as one of the best soundtracks. Not to be confused with the Chemical Brothers' early incarnation, the **DUST BROTHERS** made their name on the American hip-hop scene of the late 80s/early 90s. By the time they came to record their opaque, industrial-groove score to David Fincher's Chuck Palahniuk adaptation, 'FIGHT CLUB' (1999), the duo had already racked up such achingly hip credits as the Beastie Boys' 'Paul's Boutique' and Beck's 'Odelay!' (as well as the painfully unhip likes of Hanson and the Rolling

Stones). The success of the cult Brad Pitt vehicle led SIMPSON into further commissions, for Todd Philips' 'Road Trip' (2000) and Canadian comedian Tom Green's unfortunately titled directorial debut, 'Freddy Got Fingered' (2001). Equally unfortunately, SIMPSON's score was passed over on the respective soundtracks in favour of the usual alternative rock selections. The lone DUST BRO's only other film project, Dennis Duggan's critically slated 'Saving Silverman' (2001), failed to generate a soundtrack at all. *BG*

---

the DUST BROTHERS

Jul 99. (cd) *Restless; <(01877-73715-2)>* □ □
– "Who is Tyler Durden?" / Homework / "What is Fight Club?" / Single serving Jack / Corporate world / Psycho boy Jack / Hessel, Raymond K. / Medulla oblongata / Jack's smirking revenge / Stealing fat / Chemical burn / Marla / Commissioner castration / Space monkeys / Finding the bomb.

S/track review: Back in the 90s, the DUST BROTHERS were the production duo du jour, feted for their sampladelic innovations with both the Beastie Boys and Beck, and in demand by acts as diverse as Hanson and White Zombie. Necessarily as fragmented as Edward Norton's mind, their 'FIGHT CLUB' soundtrack lists only sixteen cues but could've figured twice or three times that number. Most of them change tack with synapse-convulsing randomness, allowing little room for complacency and even less for the development of any real themes. It's DJ Shadow without the grand design, the Chemical Brothers with strobe-induced epilepsy. But it's an impressively dystopian achievement in its own right and invigorating enough in small doses, especially when it comes with dialogue as subversive – and as viciously funny – as the single, 'This Is Your Life'. Brutally extending and reifying 'Trainspotting's Sunday afternoon ennui, it offers Buddhist-style enlightenment on the wrong end of a bloody fist, pitching between 'Requiem For A Dream'-style gothtronica, back porch twang and Thievery Corporation-patented sitar. The one constant is a reliance on the kind of long, low, reptilian bass lines which sound like Darth Vader breaking particularly foul wind. That, and a range of beats to suit every occasion, from industrial jackboot to African percussion. To these bare bones they graft fleeting snatches of everything from monastic chant, mariachi brass, turntablist scratching, tabla-funk, grinding guitar riffs and sampled harp shimmer to clanging church bells and inevitably, that bloody sitar. The brothers are arguably at their most effective when they loosen up a bit, concocting a great, low rolling groove on 'Stealing Fat', at least until it shape shifts under an avalanche of electro-grunge freak out. Those looking for Beck/Beasties style mischief will have to content themselves with the vocoder buzz and cartoon casio of 'Space Monkeys'. In the final analysis, this is neither conventional film soundtrack nor thematic score, more an experiment in sonic collage. It's dark, queasy and relentless, and comes recommended with a couple of provisos; first rule: don't listen to this without first watching 'Fight Club', second rule: don't listen to this without first watching 'Fight Club'. *BG*

Album rating: *7

the FINAL COMEDOWN

1972 (US 83m) New World Pictures (R)

Film genre: political drama

Top guns: s-w: Oscar Williams (+ dir) → FIVE ON THE BLACK HAND SIDE → BLACK BELT JONES → TRUCK TURNER)

Stars: Billy Dee Williams *(Johnny Johnson)* → LADY SINGS THE BLUES → NIGHTHAWKS → BATMAN → the JACKSONS: AN AMERICAN DREAM, D'Urville Martin *(Billy Joe Ashley)* ← WATERMELON MAN ← a TIME TO SING / → HELL UP IN HARLEM → BOOK OF NUMBERS → BLACK CAESAR → the SOUL OF NIGGER CHARLEY → FIVE ON THE BLACK HAND SIDE → SHEBA, BABY → DOLEMITE → DISCO 9000, Celia Kaye *(Rene Freeman)*, Raymond St. Jacques *(Imir)* ← COOL BREEZE ← COTTON COMES TO HARLEM ← UP TIGHT / → COME BACK, CHARLESTON BLUE → BOOK OF NUMBERS, R.G. Armstrong *(Mr. Freeman)* → PAT GARRETT & BILLY THE KID → MEAN JOHNNY BARROWS → WHERE THE BUFFALO ROAM → DICK TRACY, Maidie Norman *(Mrs. Johnson)*, Ed Cambridge *(Dr. Smalls)* ← COOL BREEZE / → MELINDA → TROUBLE MAN – FRIDAY FOSTER → BILL & TED'S BOGUS JOURNEY, Pamela Jones *(Luanna)* → CORNBREAD, EARL AND ME, Cal Wilson → FIVE ON THE BLACK HAND SIDE → DISCO 9000, Nate Esformes → BLACK BELT JONES

Storyline: Johnny Johnson is the archetypal angry young Afro-American, forced into the arms of violent, pro-black extremists after being unfairly discriminated against in the job market. *BG*

Movie rating: *5

Visual: video

Off the record: (see below)

GRANT GREEN (composer: WADE MARCUS)

Jan 72. (lp) *Blue Note; <BST 84415>* □ □
– Past, present and future / The final comedown / Father's lament / Fountain scene / Soul food – African shop / Slight fear and terror / Afro party / Luanna's theme / Battle scene / Traveling to get to Doc / One second after death. *<(cd-iss. Apr03; 581678-2)>*

S/track review: Given that GRANT GREEN had been moving in increasingly funk and R&B-orientated circles since his late 60s comeback, it's not so surprising that he became the only jazz artist to record a bonafide Blaxploitation soundtrack for 'Blue Note' (actually his penultimate album for the label). While jazz critics have disregarded much of his latter period work, GREEN – at least on the main theme – is in smoking form here, sending his trademark flurries of quicksilver guitar rolling and tumbling over a steaming, stopcock organ groove. Although all too short at just over three minutes, it's another one of the great Blaxploitation themes and was included on the more professional of the Blax comps which proliferated in the late 90s. Back then, if your interest had been sufficiently piqued to sniff out the original soundtrack, you'd have had a tough, expensive search. Finally available on CD, 'The FINAL COMEDOWN' reveals a session in which GREEN, if anything, doesn't get enough space to stretch out. Not exactly known for his compositional skills, he leaves the writing to WADE MARCUS, an arranger who'd served time at 'Motown' during its Detroit heyday and went on to work with the likes of Stanley Turrentine and the Blackbyrds. While his Sabu Martinez-influenced percussion arrangements are pretty hardcore at times, the sleevenotes's grand claim that this is "one of the heaviest soundtracks ever recorded" can only be taken with a seriously funky dose of salt. Truth be told, things only really get nasty on opener, 'Past, Present And Future' and epic closer, 'Battle Scene', a heavy-duty chase workout where wire-taut wah-wah riffing joins forces with thundering timpani and teeth-rattling bongos for maximum collateral damage; GREEN was nothing if not versatile. Yet it's a shame there aren't more creative experiments like 'Slight Fear And Terror', where his more familiar walkin' blues style melds with a bass-heavy Blax groove; this is exactly the kind of stuff which a GRANT GREEN soundtrack suggests but which is mercilessly cut short after barely a minute. Still, this remains a fascinating entry in his catalogue, and it holds up surprisingly well against the competition. *BG*

Album rating: *6.5

□ Neil FINN segment
(⇒ RAIN)

FIRESTARTER

1984 (US 115m) Universal Pictures (R)

Film genre: sci-fi/horror thriller

Top guns: dir: Mark L. Lester ← CLASS OF 1984 ← ROLLER BOOGIE / s-w: Stanley Mann (au: Stephen King)

Stars: Drew Barrymore *(Charlene/Charly McGee)* → WAYNE'S WORLD 2 → the WEDDING SINGER → CURIOUS GEORGE → MUSIC AND LYRICS, David Keith *(Andy McGee)* ← the ROSE / → HEARTBREAK HOTEL → RAISE YOUR VOICE, George C. Scott *(John Rainbird)*, Martin Sheen *(Captain Hollister)* → a STRANGER IN THE KINGDOM, Freddie Jones *(Doctor Joseph Wanless)*, Heather Locklear *(Vicky Tomlinson McGee)* → ROCK'N'ROLL MOM → WAYNE'S WORLD 2, Art Carney *(Irv Manders)*, Louise Fletcher *(Norman Manders)* → the KAREN CARPENTER STORY, Moses Gunn *(Doctor Pynchot)*, Antonio Fargas *(taxi driver)* ← CAR WASH ← CORNBREAD, EARL AND ME ← FOXY BROWN ← CLEOPATRA JONES ← ACROSS 110th STREET ← SHAFT / → SOUL SURVIVOR, Curtis Credel *(Bates)* ← HARD COUNTRY

Storyline: Charly McGee is the young daughter of Andy and Vicky, who were in a top-secret experiment many years ago. Now Charly finds herself with an amazing ability to instigate fires merely by thought process, a talent which she must use to good effect before she is captured by The Shop, an underground government agency hell-bent on tracking the girl down to exploit her for their own evil means. *JZ*

Movie rating: *5

Visual: video + dvd

Off the record: (see below)

—

TANGERINE DREAM

Jul 84. (lp) *Varese Sarabande; <VSD 5251> M.C.A.; (MCF 3233)*
– Crystal voice / The run / Testlab / Charly the kid / Escaping point / Rainbirds move / Burning force / Between realities / Shop territory / Flash final / Out of the heat. *(re-iss. Jan89; MCA/+C 6163) (cd-iss. Apr90; DMCL 1899)*

S/track review: Up to now, German electronic prog-meisters TANGERINE DREAM had delivered a handful of thrilling film scores, among them the previous year's 'WAVELENGTH' and 'RISKY BUSINESS'. 'FIRESTARTER' suffered a little by comparison. It seemed the 'Dream was turning into a bit of a pop-synth nightmare, ruined by simple, melodious soundscapes rather than the "side A & side B" diversions of doom and gloom of their tour de force, non-OST LPs such as 'Rubycon' & 'Ricochet' (both 1975). The synthetic 80s were like that, simplistic to the point of non-entity and therefore dull. Only fellow Germans, Kraftwerk, were experimenting, but they didn't get their proverbial boots dirty in the ever-evolving cinematic world. Only in the second half of 'FIRESTARTER' do we hear the real TANGERINE DREAM come into play, EDGAR FROESE, CHRISTOPHER FRANKE and JOHANNES SMOELLING comfortably getting into top gear during one eerie track, 'Between Realities'; the upbeat 'Burning Force' is also worthy of a mention. However, the razor-sharp, ear-piercing shards of synth on tracks such as 'The Run', 'Testlab' & 'Escaping Point', basically irritate and annoy the hell out of me. On reflection, I'm not a big fan of 'FIRESTARTER' – "twisted firestarter" (couldn't resist it!). *MCS*

Album rating: *5

FIRST LOVE, LAST RITES

1997 (US 101m) Forensic Films / Toast Films (R)

Film genre: romantic drama

Top guns: s-w: **Jesse Peretz** (+ dir), **David Ryan** (story: Ian McEwan)

Stars: Natasha Gregson Wagner *(Sissel)* ← S.F.W. / → HIGH FIDELITY, Giovanni Ribisi *(Joey)* ← SUBURBI@ ← THAT THING YOU DO! / → the VIRGIN SUICIDES → MASKED AND ANONYMOUS → LOST IN TRANSLATION → COLD MOUNTAIN, Robert John Burke *(Henry)*, Eli Marienthal *(Adrian)* → the COUNTRY BEARS, Jeanetta Arnette *(Sissel's mom)*, Donal Logue *(Red)* ← MEDUSA: DARE TO BE TRUTHFUL / → the MILLION DOLLAR HOTEL, Hugh Joseph Babin *(Bob)*

Storyline: Peretz transplants the setting of Ian McEwan's short story from dreary England to the steamy torpor of Louisiana, where Joey and Sissel embark on an extended romantic tryst in a bayou shack. The intense, inexorable dynamic of infatuation takes precedence over any real plot. *BG*

Movie rating: *5.5

Visual: video + dvd

Off the record: **Jesse Peretz** + **David Ryan** (see **LEMONHEADS**).

—

SHUDDER TO THINK (featuring Various Artists)

Aug 98. (cd/c) *Epic; <EK/ET 69029> (491610-2/-4)*
– I want someone badly (feat. JEFF BUCKLEY) / Erecting a movie star (feat. LIZ PHAIR) / Diamonds, sparks and all / When I was born, I was bored (feat. BILLY CORGAN) / Appalachian lullaby (feat. NINA PERSSON) / Airfield dream / Automatic soup (feat. ROBIN ZANDER) / Lonesome dove / Speed of love (feat. JOHN DOE) / Day ditty (feat. ANGELA McCLUSKY) / The wedding is over (feat. LENA KARLSSON) / Jelly on the table (feat. MATT JOHNSON) / Just really wanna see you (feat. MIMI PARKER & ALAN SPARHAWK) / I want someone badly / Final dream.

S/track review: Given rookie director Jesse Peretz's credentials as a former Lemonhead and respected figure in the world of music video, the soundtrack to his debut feature was never going to be another alt-rock-by-numbers cash-in. At first glance, his choice of veteran punks SHUDDER TO THINK might've been unlikely (at least for an ostensible love story) but – given the band's major label blossoming on albums such as 'Pony Express Record' (1994) and '50,000 B.C.' (1997) – not unwise. In fact, with guitarist NATHAN LARSON's subsequent move into full-time film-scoring, it proved pretty prescient. The resulting soundtrack has endured as not only one of the D.C. outfit's most accomplished and diverse releases, but as one of the final recordings of the late JEFF BUCKLEY, whose burning blue vocal fearlessly explores the parameters of desire laid out in LARSON's deep soul ballad, 'I Want Someone Badly'. It's a great curtain raiser, indicative of both LARSON's emerging strengths as a songwriter and the imaginative collaborations to come. If the least – and most incongruous – of these ('When I Was Born, I Was Bored') is a spiky art-punk showcase for BILLY CORGAN, most of them resonate with a refreshingly un-ironic rock'n'roll years nostalgia, itself the dewy-eyed cross-weave knitting such disparate pairings together and the context for their broadcast over a crackly transistor radio in the movie itself. Cardigans gal NINA PERSSON is captivating on 'Appalachian Lullaby', a yodelling space-cast beamed against a clip-clop, mule and trap rhythm. Cue a ventriloquial, Louis Armstrong-style trumpet interlude before LARSON and co-writer CRAIG WEDREN launch themselves feet first into the Move-esque harmonies of 'Automatic Soup', marshalled by Cheap Trick's ROBIN ZANDER. WEDREN himself mainlines the spirit of Neil Diamond and Bruce Springsteen on 'Lonesome Dove' while MATT JOHNSON brings a claustrophobic authenticity to blues reprise, 'Jelly On The Table'. All in, it's a surprisingly heady trip, both in its reach and canny sequencing, and it evokes an endless series of references and reminiscences. A shame it also had to be their epitaph, at least in terms of a song based album. Although they moved deeper into film with a full blown score for Lisa Cholodenko's 'HIGH ART' (1998), LARSON's departure effectively called a halt to the group later the same year. His subsequent work on Todd Solondz' 'VELVET

GOLDMINE' (1998) and Kimberly Pierce's 'Boys Don't Cry' (1999) initiated a bonafide film composing career, a vocation which the pop cultural homage of 'FIRST LOVE, LAST RITES' presages in style. *BG*

Album rating: *8

FITZCARRALDO

1982 (W.Ger 158m) Zweites Deutsches Fernsehen (12)

Film genre: jungle adventure/drama

Top guns: s-w + dir: Werner Herzog

Stars: Klaus Kinski *(Brian Sweeney Fitzgerald / Fitzcarraldo)*, Claudia Cardinale *(Molly)*, Jose Lewgoy *(Don Aquilino)*, Paul Hittscher *(Capt. Orinoco Paul)*, Miguel Angel Fuentes *(Cholo – the mechanic)*, Peter Berling *(opera manager)*, Huerequeque Enrique Bohorquez *(cook)*, **Milton Nascimento** *(black man at opera house)*

Storyline: White-suited, white-haired dreamer/madman Brian Sweeney Fitzgerald is a little more unhinged than your average Irish adventurer, intoxicated by an outrageous plan to host Enrico Caruso and Sarah Bernhardt in his own deepest Amazonia opera house. With the rubber boom in full swing, Fizcarraldo plans to finance his scheme by mining an untapped seam in uncharted territory. To this end he mans a rusting hulk of a steamboat with a classically motley crew, taking courage in the gramophone records he blasts at an impassive jungle. Transfixing the natives like a Celtic Colonel Kurtz, the giant gringo uses his siren arias to enlist them in the most ambitious of all his schemes: a plan to hoist the ship over a hill and thus avoid an impassable waterfall. He needs an engineering miracle; after some fatal accidents and various death threats he gets an engineering miracle, as undoctored as it's presented on screen. Look out for a cameo from Brazilian MPB legend Milton Nascimento. *BG*

Movie rating: *9

Visual: video + dvd

Off the record: Klaus Kinski was not the director's first choice for the lead role, that went to Jason Robards and then Mick Jagger, although all the footage was destroyed by Herzog (see film documentary, 'Burden Of Dreams', for the whole picture). *MCS*

—

POPOL VUH (*) (& Various Composers **)

Nov 82. (lp) *ZYX; (20.021) Polydor; <PDH-I-6363>* [–] Swiss [ ]
– Wehe khorazin (*) / Emani (Verdi **) / Engel der luft (*) / Ridi pagliaccio (Caruso/Leoncavallo **) / O paradiso (Caruso/Meyerbeer) / Kind mit geige (trad.**) / Im garten der gemeinschaft (*) / Blasmusik (trad.**) / Tod und verklaerung (excerpt) (R. Strauss **) / Musik aus Burundi (trad.**) / Il sogno (Manon/Verdi **) / Quartett (Rigoletto/Verdi **) / Oh Mimi, tu piu non torni (Caruso/Puccini **) / Als lebten die engel auf erden (*) / A te o Cara, amor talora (I Puritani/Bellini **). *(cd-iss. Sep96 & Dec02 on 'Spalax'; 14876)*

S/track review: The most ambitious and fraught of all Werner Herzog's filmic visions, this man vs nature vs culture odyssey supplied plenty of off-camera Herzog-Kinski spats for the 'My Best Fiend' documentary. The soundtrack was equally excessive, fortifying the usual POPOL VUH dronescapes with scratchy operatic arias from the earliest decades of the 20th century. It's a contrast which mimicks the movie's force of will in the face of unknowable nature: FLORIAN FRICKE's organic hosannas drip-feeding from the darkness of the rainforest; Enrico Caruso's grandiloquent tenor temporarily stemming the tide, the magnificent straining of "civilisation". While the movie contextualises the concept with Kinski and his trusty gramophone pied-piping the natives, the soundtrack offers no such visual aid, leaving a blank canvas on which to interpret it. On first spin it's inevitably disorientating, especially if you're not an opera, or even a classical connoisseur. But the surface shock soon dissolves, melting from audacious juxtaposition into an exercise in possibility. If the Caruso and Verdi excerpts sound beamed in from another age today, they must have sounded just as alien to the natives in 1900s Iquitos, and FRICKE plays with the permeability of time. His opener 'Wehe Khorazin' is nothing if not a throwback to the late 60s grind of the Velvet Underground, sanctified with the kind of empyrean chorale and inner mounting chant he seemingly plucked from the spheres at will. In giving way to a diamantine falsetto from Verdi's 'Ernani', he hears the sacred in all music, regardless of when or why it was recorded. And as he did in the soundtrack to 'AGUIRRE, WRATH OF GOD', he affords the same respect to locally sourced cues like 'Kind Mit Geige' and 'Blasmusik' as he does a piece of Burundi drumming, itself segueing as timelessly into Verdi's 'Il Sogno' as Puccini glides into 'Als Lebten Die Engel Auf Erden', 'FITZCARRALDO's version of the spiralling guitar elegy FRICKE used on all his Herzog soundtracks. If there's one complaint with this album, beautifully packaged as it is (the 'S.P.V.' reissues cunningly use the same lavish sleevenote in all five Herzog/POPOL VUH soundtracks), it offers no label copy or any details at all for potential opera converts to get their teeth into, and beware, you might just be one of them. *BG*

Album rating: *7.5

FIVE ON THE BLACK HAND SIDE

1973 (US 96m) United Artists (PG)

Film genre: family/urban comedy drama

Top guns: dir: Oscar Williams ← the FINAL COMEDOWN / s-w: Charlie L. Russell

Stars: Leonard Jackson *(John Henry Brooks)* → CAR WASH, Clarice Taylor *(Gladys Ann Brooks)* → the WIZ, D'Urville Martin *(Booker T. Washington 'Sharrief' Brooks)* ← the SOUL OF NIGGER CHARLEY ← BLACK CAESAR ← HELL UP IN HARLEM ← BOOK OF NUMBERS ← the FINAL COMEDOWN ← WATERMELON MAN ← a TIME TO SING / → SHEBA, BABY → DOLEMITE → DISCO 9000, Glynn Turman *(Gideon)* → TOGETHER BROTHERS → a HERO AIN'T NOTHIN' BUT A SANDWICH, Virginia Capers *(Ruby)* ← TROUBLE MAN ← LADY SINGS THE BLUES ← NORWOOD / → HOWARD THE DUCK → WHAT'S LOVE GOT TO DO WITH IT, Tchaka Almoravids *(Fun Lovin')*, Frankie Crocker *(Rolls Royce)* ← JIMI HENDRIX ← CLEOPATRA JONES / → THAT'S THE WAY OF THE WORLD → BREAKIN' 2: ELECTRIC BOOGALOO, Janet DuBois *(Stormy Monday)*, Cal Wilson *(Hasaan)* ← the FINAL COMEDOWN / → DISCO 9000, Dick Anthony Williams *(Preston)* ← SLAUGHTER'S BIG RIP-OFF ← the MACK ← UP TIGHT!, Sonny Jim Gaines *(Sweet Meat)* → the FIGHTING TEMPTATIONS

Storyline: John Henry Brooks is the headstrong head of a black middle class household, forced to reconsider his chauvinistic ways and engage in some very 70s discussion in the wake of a backlash from his put upon family. *BG*

Movie rating: *6

Visual: video

Off the record: **H.B. BARNUM** (b.15 Jul'36, Houston, Texas, USA) was a producer/writer/arranger/multi-instrumentalist who started out in doowop group the Dootones (from the same L.A. scene as Don Julian's Meadowlarks) and went on to work with everyone from Frank Sinatra and Etta James to the Supremes and the Jackson 5 (and also recorded for 'Imperial', 'R.C.A.' and 'Capitol' in his own right); he also scored the music for 'Hit Man' (1972) and 'Big Daddy' (1973). *MCS*

—

H.B. BARNUM

Jan 02. (cd) *Beyond; <578256-2>* [ ] [–]
– Five on the black hand side (KEISA BROWN) / Kung fu funk –

John Henry / Freedom / Tell me you love me / The keep comin' / Gideon & morn / Black star barber shop / Sweet Meat / Stormy and Gladys / Playin' numbers / Temperance woman / Roof top fight / Fun Lovin' rap / Mama on the roof – Gail reads demands / Fun Lovin' arrives / Reception line dance / They keep comin' / I'll give you love.

S/track review: An obscure piece of kitchen sink comedy in the mould of John Berry's 'CLAUDINE' (1975), this is one of the rare black films of its era which didn't employ the gaudy tropes of blaxploitation (tagline: "You've been Coffy-tized, Blacula-rized and super-flied – but now you're gonna be glorified, unified and filled-with-pride.."), nor the heavy-duty chase funk to accompany them. There's plenty of rhythmic squelch, but more of a 60s jazz and soul slant than 'COFFY', 'BLACULA' et al. No surprise then, that the Gladys Knight connection extended to title theme performer and sometime Knight backing singer KEISA BROWN, as well as soundtrack composer Hidle Brown "H.B." BARNUM. BARNUM helms the movie with a bass-heavy, conscious soul powerhouse of a main title that could've, should've been a huge hit. Only ever issued as a single in lieu of a full soundtrack, it was a great advertisement for the rest of BARNUM's score, itself finally seeing the light of day in 2001. He gives his own weathered vocals a brief turn on 'Freedom' and a longer, harmonised showcase on excellent closer, 'I'll Give You Love'. And you've got to hand it to a man with the temerity to splice some cheesy Shaolin-funk with a snare-driven, bugle-call groove titled after a lead character with the same name as a legendary black railroad pioneer. But BARNUM writes and performs with the easy confidence of a decades-long track record; organ bossa, floating, Sly Stone-esque brass lines or 'Canteloupe Island'-era soul jazz, he applies his accumulated knowledge of black popular music with style and tenderness, and he's never out of his depth. A minor classic. BG

Album rating: *7.5

– spinoff releases, etc. –

KEISA BROWN: Five On The Black Hand Side / (instrumental)

1973. (7") *United Artists; <US-XW 338-V>* ☐ ⊟

FIVE SUMMER STORIES

1972 (US 94m) MacGillivray Freeman Films

Film genre: sports documentary

Top guns: s-w: Greg MacGillivray (+ dir), Jim Freeman

Stars: Billy Hamilton, Eddie Aikau, Sam Hawk, Butch Van Artsdalen, Jock Sutherland, Jeff Hakman, Terry Fitzgerald, Oberg, BK, Lynne Boyero, Gerry Lopez

Storyline: If you like surfing, sixties and psychedelia this one's for you. Most of the Californian coastline is covered, as miles and miles of surf and surfers are shown. The "cutting edge" comes in the commentary which takes a swipe at the increasingly commercialised society of the day, but water sports enthusiasts won't be "board" with this one. JZ

Movie rating: *6

Visual: none

Off the record: HONK were formed in Laguna Beach, California in 1970 by Steve Wood (keyboards & vocals), Don Whaley (bass), Tris Imboden (drums) and Mike Caruselle. Almost immediately the latter guy moved on to pastures new and was replaced by Richard Stekol (lead guitar & vocals) and subsequent addition, Craig Buhler (saxophones). A sixth member, the gorgeous Beth Fitchet (vocals & rhythm guitar), was soon welcomed into the fold by main song contributors Wood and Stekol, and this was the line-up who recorded debut LP/soundtrack, 'FIVE SUMMER STORIES'. In 1973, Whaley bailed out prior to their eponymous set for '20th Century' records. Once again a sextet (through adding Will Brady), HONK confusingly recorded a second eponymous LP for 'Epic', although it was apparently shelved by the company. While Tris later joined Chicago, he and the band maintained a steady following in and around Hollywood, where, in 2005, they still perform on occasion. MCS

—

HONK

1972. (lp) *Image; (ILP 721)* ⊟ Austra ⊟

– Creation / Blue of your backdrop / Brad and David's theme / High in the middle / Hum drums / Bear's country / Made my statement (love you baby) / Don't let your goodbye stand / Lopez / Blue of your backdrop instrumental / Tunnel of love / Pipeline sequence. *(UK cd-iss. Jan91 on 'GNP Crescendo'; GNPD 8027) <US lp-iss.2000 on 'Granite'; GR 7720>*

S/track review: Surf's up for Southern California's canyon-rock sextet, HONK, who bring visual stimuli to the feature-length film, 'FIVE SUMMER STORIES'. Specially prepared to complement each sequence, the LP (and later CD) follows a harmonious pattern that suggests influences from the likes of the early Eagles and latter-day Byrds or Chicago. Bypassing the short atmospheric intro, 'Creation', the music segues into the shiny bright, 'Blue Of Your Backdrop' song; the reprised take of RICHARD STEKOL's composition is track 10. Delightful and laid-back to the point of being horizontal, the instrumental 'Brad And David's Theme' is akin to a smooth Santana or Beach Boys number. The first of the group compositions, 'High In The Middle', saw HONK slide their geetars and yeehahs into Nashville territory and country-rock. For short'n'sweet follow-on cut, 'Hum Drums', TRIS IMBODEN exercises his kit, pre-Cozy Powell-like, while the DON WHALEY-penned 'Bear's Country' is just what one would imagine it to be. HONK could never be accused of favouring one particular genre; in fact, they could just about perform in any style, the funky Doobie Brothers-esque ballad 'Made My Statement (Love You Baby)' the prime example. The Doobies or indeed the Eagles would certainly have been proud of 'Don't Let Your Goodbye Stand', a track worth the admission price alone. The instrumental 'Lopez' (a sort of cocktail-lounge spot) is basically down to writer STEVE WOOD on keyboards, while HONK finally surround him with angel-like vibes. The aforementioned 'Brad And David's Theme' gets another treatment on track 11, 'Tunnel Of Love', a number annoyingly reminiscent of something or other from that era – help me somebody. The second group composition, 'Pipeline Sequence' (although it's CRAIG BUHLER not BETH FITCHET with pencil in hand), veers on hard rock only to drift, Steve Winwood-like (not-STEVE WOOD-like), into a keyboard versus percussion melange. MCS

Album rating: *6.5

☐ Roberta FLACK segment (⇒ BUSTIN' LOOSE)

FLASH GORDON

1980 (UK/US 115m) Universal Pictures (PG)

Film genre: comic-strip/sci-fi fantasy

Top guns: dir: Mike Hodges / s-w: Lorenzo Semple Jr. / adpt. Michael Allin ← TRUCK TURNER (comic strip: Alex Raymond)

Stars: Sam Jones *(Flash Gordon)*, Melody Anderson *(Dale Arden)* ← ELVIS: THE MOVIE, Topol *(Dr. Hans Zarkov)*, Max von Sydow *(Emperor Ming)* → DUNE → NONHOSONNO, Ornella Muti *(Princess Aura)*, Timothy Dalton *(Prince Barin)*, Brian Blessed *(Prince Vultan)* → TARZAN, Peter Wyngarde *(Klytus)*, Richard O'Brien *(Fico)* ← JUBILEE ← the ROCKY HORROR PICTURE SHOW / → SHOCK TREATMENT → SPICEWORLD, Philip Stone *(Zogi, the High Priest)* ← O LUCKY MAN! / → GREEN ICE, Andrew

Bradford *(Hawkman)* ← the FAMILY WAY / → SID & NANCY, Robbie Coltrane *(airport assistant)* → SUBWAY RIDERS → GHOST DANCE → ABSOLUTE BEGINNERS → EAT THE RICH → TUTTI FRUTTI, Viva *(Cytherian girl)* ← FORBIDDEN ZONE / → PARIS, TEXAS → NICO ICON, Imogen Claire *(special movement)* ← LISZTOMANIA ← the ROCKY HORROR PICTURE SHOW ← TOMMY / → SHOCK TREATMENT → HAWKS, Eddie Stacey *(Hawkman)* ← TOMMY / → 1984, Jim Carter *(Azurian man)* → TOP SECRET! → LIPSTICK ON YOUR COLLAR → HEARTLANDS, Burnell Tucker *(co-pilot)* ← FINDERS KEEPERS ← DATELINE DIAMONDS / → SCREAM FOR HELP, Trevor Ward *(Ardentian man)* ← ROCK FOLLIES OF '77

Storyline: Square-jawed quarterback Flash Gordon and his travel agent love interest Dale Arden get unwittingly blasted into space by deranged scientist Dr. Zarkoff, ending up at the imperial palace of evil dictator Ming The Merciless. Flash is summarily executed before being brought back to life by Ming's daughter, the delectable Princess Aura. Being an Aryan, all-American dude Flash prefers his travel agent and somehow resists Aura's advances. After a homoerotic whiplash duel, he makes up with the dashing Prince Barin and sets out to prevent Ming destroying planet earth. What happens next? – you'll have to wait for next week's episode, or maybe not! *BG*

Movie rating: *6

Visual: video + dvd

Off the record: **QUEEN** (see below)

—

QUEEN (score: Howard Blake)

Dec 80. (lp/c) *E.M.I.; (EMC/TCEMC 795) Elektra; <518>* [10] [23]
– Flash's theme / In the space capsule (the love theme) / Ming's theme (in the court of Ming the Merciless) / The ring (hypnotic seduction of Dale) / Football fight / In the death cell (love theme reprise) / Execution of Flash / The kiss (Aura resurrects Flash) / Arboria (planet of the Tree Men) / Escape from the swamp / Flash to the rescue / Vultan's theme (attack of the Hawk Men) / Battle theme / The wedding march / The marriage of Dale and Ming (and Flash approaching) / Crash dive on Mingo City / Flash's theme reprise (victory celebrations) / The hero. *(re-iss. 1984 lp/c; ATAK/TCATAK 26) (cd-iss. Jun88; CDP 746214-2) <US cd-iss. Aug91 on 'Hollywood'+=; 61203-2>* – Flash's theme. *(re-iss. Apr94 on 'Parlophone' cd/c; CD/TC PCSD 137)*

S/track review: It had to happen; by 1980, QUEEN had discovered the camp potential of new technology. Having already spruced up their ailing pomp-rock on 'The Game' (1980), Mike Hodge's kinky comic-strip adaptation presented an opportunity to really get stuck in to their synthesizers. As an electro-fied take on the classic QUEEN sound, the 'Flash' single appeared all the more cosmic in the wake of earthy hits like 'Crazy Little Thing Called Love' and 'Another One Bites The Dust'. And in FREDDIE MERCURY, the American football hunk turned saviour of the universe had found an equally outsized, cartoon-esque narrator. MERCURY wasn't going to save the singles charts from oblivion (he was 25 years too early) but it sounded like it. The segmented incidental music which filled up the rest of the soundtrack worked like a wet dream in the movie; transferred complete with dialogue as a bonafide QUEEN album, the critical concensus was as merciless as Ming himself. The brevity of the cues, the lack of any real themes (outside of the title), or any development of themes, can make for a fleeting, frustrating listen, especially if you haven't seen the film. Every band member is credited with "synth" but it's MERCURY who's most successful in manipulating his new toy, cranking out the Jean-Michel Jarre meets Vangelis melee of 'Football Fight' ("Are your men on the right pills?", asks Max von Sydow in his best Etonian accent) and the camp as boy scouts 'Vultan's Theme (Attack Of The Hawk Men)', as well as crafting the brief electro-orchestral snippet, 'The Kiss'. BRIAN MAY comes up with a real song, 'The Hero', as a swashbuckling coda, and works a few decent variations on his main title. And while he incorporates that unmistakable, finely buffed guitar sound into the rocking 'Battle Theme', the less said about its Rick Wakeman-like transmogrification into 'The Wedding March' the better. *BG*

Album rating: *4.5

– spinoff hits, etc. –

QUEEN: Flash / Football Fight

Nov 80. (7") *(EMI 5126) <47092>* [10] Jan81 [42]

FLASHPOINT

1984 (US 94m) HBO / Tri-Star / Silver Screen Partners (R)

Film genre: cop/detective mystery drama

Top guns: dir: William Tannen / s-w: Dennis Shryack, Michael Butler (au: George LaFountaine)

Stars: Kris KRISTOFFERSON *(Bobby Logan)*, Treat Williams *(Ernie Wyatt)* ← HAIR / → WHERE THE RIVERS FLOW NORTH, Rip Torn *(Sheriff Wells)* ← SONGWRITER ← ONE-TRICK PONY ← PAYDAY ← YOU'RE A BIG BOY NOW / → WHERE THE RIVERS FLOW NORTH → the INSIDER, Kevin Conway *(Brook)* → HOMEBOY, Kurtwood Smith *(Carson)* ← STAYING ALIVE ← ROADIE, Miguell Ferrer *(Roget)* → DERAILROADED, Jean Smart *(Doris)* → JUST MY IMAGINATION, Tess Harper *(Ellen)* ← TENDER MERCIES / → FAR NORTH → BROKEN BRIDGES, Roberts Blossom *(Amarillo)* → CANDY MOUNTAIN

Storyline: Bob and Ernie are two Texas border patrol officers, whose jobs are threatened by new radar technology. On patrol one day, they find a buried jeep with $1 million, a rifle and a skeleton. While Ernie wants to investigate the incident, Bob wants to take the money and run for the border. As tension builds between the pair they agree on a compromise but their investigations soon attract the attention of the FBI, who are killing anyone who might expose their cover-up. *JZ*

Movie rating: *4

Visual: video + dvd

Off the record: (see below)

—

TANGERINE DREAM (& Various Artist)

Dec 84. (lp/pic-lp/c) *EMI America; <ST 17141> Heavy Metal; (HM1 HP/PD/MC 29)* [ ] Feb85 [ ]
– Going west / Afternoon in the desert / Plane ride / Mystery tracks / Lost in the dunes / Highway patrol / Love phantasy / Madcap story / Dirty cross-roads / Flashpoint (the GEMS). *(cd-iss. Apr87; HM1 XD 29) (re-iss. cd Sep95 on 'One Way'; OW 18507)*

S/track review: If you've been commissioned to do five or six film scores in a few years (as TANGERINE DREAM were in the mid-80s), how do you make them different and appealing, if all you have at your disposal is an arpeggio-driven synth and a few other bits and bobs? The once innovative EDGAR FROESE, CHRISTOPHER FRANKE & JOHANNES SCHMOELLING, showed ideas were fast running out, 'FLASHPOINT' giving the impression of music-by-numbers, although quirky track 'Afternoon In The Desert' seems to contradict this somewhat. Where 'RISKY BUSINESS' (1983) and more so, 'FIRESTARTER' (1984), took on a progressive life of their own, this set got lost in the pop-synth melee, much like that of 'HEARTBREAKERS', from around the same time. When you think things can't get worse, they do when a Bruce Springsteen-esque group, the GEMS, take on the closing title track. I'm going to go away and swear now. *MCS*

Album rating: *4.5

FOOLS

1970 (US 93m) Translor Films / Cinerama (PG)

Film genre: romantic drama

Top guns: dir: Tom Gries / s-w: Robert Rudelson

Stars: Jason Robards *(Mathew South)* → PAT GARRETT & BILLY THE KID → MAGNOLIA, Katharine Ross *(Anais Appleton)* ← the GRADUATE / → DON'T LET GO, Scott Hylands *(David Appleton)*, Roy C. Jenson *(man in park)* → BUSTIN' LOOSE → HONKYTONK MAN, Mark Bramhall *(man in park)*, Marc Hannibal *(dog owner)*, Robin Menken *(hippie)* → the STRAWBERRY STATEMENT → THANK GOD IT'S FRIDAY → THIS IS SPINAL TAP → BODY ROCK, **Mimi Farina** *(herself)* ← FESTIVAL / → CELEBRATION AT BIG SUR → SING SING THANKSGIVING, Jack Nance *(hippie)* → DUNE → WILD AT HEART → the HOT SPOT, Joanna Cassidy → BLADE RUNNER → CLUB PARADISE

Storyline: Ageing actor Mathew South finds unexpected romance when he meets the much younger Anais, who unfortunately happens to be married to top San Francisco lawyer David Appleton. He's far from the ideal husband and it doesn't take much wooing from Matthew to send Anais into his arms. However, their affair is beset by the complications of the day's society and the jealous pursuit of the enraged hubby. *JZ*

Movie rating: *4

Visual: none

Off the record: Mimi Farina (b. Margarita Mimi Baez, 30 Apr'45, Palo Alto, California) – sister of JOAN BAEZ – was famous for her folk duo partnership with musician/author Richard Farina, although this was curtailed tragically in April 1966 when he died in a motorbike accident. Mimi remarried a few years later and went on to issue solo sets and tour prisons; she died of cancer on the 18th of July 2001. *MCS*

KENNY ROGERS AND THE FIRST EDITION (*) // SHORTY ROGERS *(instrumentals)*

1970. (lp) *Reprise; <RS 6429>* [–] promo [–]
– A poem I wrote for your hair (main title) (*) / Someone who cares (love theme) (KENNY ROGERS) / If you love (MIMI FARINA and KATHARINE ROSS) / A poem I wrote for your hair (zoo montage) (*) // Anais and Mathew / Up yours / Old time movies / Take a walk / Cajun source / Someone who cares.

S/track review: "Their concepts amount to a virtual definition of the phrase 'easy listening'," gushes Leonard Feather's sleevenote on KENNY ROGERS AND THE FIRST EDITION – and he means that in a good way. Even in an age when 'easy listening' has survived disgrace and ridicule to attain a kitsch appeal, though, it's hard to put up with the formulaic blandness of the FIRST EDITION's harmonies, never mind the fey hippyness ('A Poem I Wrote For Your Hair' is the theme song). The middle-of-the-road maestros were successful enough at the turn of the 70s to find their names dominating the soundtrack credits, though musicologists will note the less-celebrated presence of MIMI FARINA, once one of the stars of the Dylan-centred Greenwich Village folk scene; sad to report then, that FARINA's one song, delivered in unison with the actress KATHARINE ROSS, slips unmissed into the sugary swamp. SHORTY ROGERS (who had gone from star of the West Coast jazz scene with the likes of Art Pepper and Hampton Hawes to composer on 'The Love Boat' and 'Starsky & Hutch') musters some oomph on a healthy portion of instrumental jazz, without ever overstepping the genre's limited demands. His namesake KENNY ROGERS – no relation – would go on to immortality with kitsch of a different flavour, defining country hokum via 'Lucille' and 'The Gambler'. *ND*

Album rating: *3

FOR GOOD

2003 (NZ 96m) Arkles Entertainment (R16)

Film genre: psychological drama

Top guns: s-w + dir: Stuart McKenzie

Stars: Michelle Langston *(Lisa)*, Timothy Balme *(Grant Wilson)*, Miranda Harcourt *(mother)*, Tim Gordon *(father)*, Adam Gardiner *(flatmate)*, Charlie Bleakley *(Abbott)*

Storyline: Young New Zealand journalist Lisa interviews child murderer Grant Wilson as he is released from jail after ten years. Lisa shares many things in common with the murdered teenager and yet finds herself strangely drawn to her killer, causing friction with her own parents and those of the dead girl. Should Wilson be allowed to get on with a new life or should he always be treated as a murderer? *JZ*

Movie rating: *6

Visual: dvd

Off the record: SHAYNE CARTER was a founder of indie outfit, Straitjacket Fits, a band he formed in Brockville, Auckland, New Zealand in 1986 alongside a rhythm section of David Wood and John Collie; Andrew Brough was added in '87. Both CARTER (also ex-Bored Games) and Collie had been part of the legendary DoubleHappys, who for some time had been the darlings of Auckland having issued some quintessential releases including 1985's 'Cut It Out' EP. Signed to 'Flying Nun' records, the Straitjacket Fits followed in the established Kiwi tradition of the Chills, the Clean, etc., albeit they preferred their music with a bit more punch than many bands on the NZ scene. Although they debuted in 1987 with the 'Life In One Chord' EP, it would be another two years before the release of their first album, 'Hail', licensed for UK release by 'Rough Trade'. Despite featuring many songs previously released on the EP, the album also boasted a version of Leonard Cohen's 'So Long Marianne', a surprising but effective cover sitting comfortably with the band's darkly atmospheric garage drone. Subsequently securing a deal with 'Arista' records, the band released their follow-up set, 'Melt' (1991), although like the bulk of their musical countrymen, they failed to attract a wider crossover audience. Back on 'Flying Nun', for third set, 'Blow', the band finally gave up the ghost after a final single, 'If I Were You', in late '93. SHAYNE CARTER had already teamed up with Peter Jeffries (ex-This Kind Of Punishment) on a collaborative single for 'Flying Nun'; CARTER became leader of funk-rock act, Dimmer (in 2001), while he also scored the music for the movie, 'FOR GOOD'. *MCS*

SHAYNE CARTER (& Various Artists)

Apr 04. (cd) *Capitol; (CREC 1017)* [–] NewZ [–]
– Tracey's theme / Smoke (DIMMER) / Lisa's dream / Bo Diddley / I didn't mean to kill you / In the forest / I need your love (GOLDEN HARVEST) / The day thou gavest, Lord, is ended (SAINT CLEMENT, LES COMMANDEMENTS DE DIEU) / The abduction / If I were you (STRAITJACKET FITS) / Abbot Lisa – The Jazzdrums / Tracey's room / Lisa's room / Under the light (DIMMER) / The letter / Carride / Forgive our foolish ways (REPTON) / Smoke outro remix (NICK ROUGHAN).

S/track review: SHAYNE CARTER's deep, down and dirty score to 'FOR GOOD' lies somewhere between eerie and sinister. Augmented by friend and musician, ex-Skeptics bassist NICK ROUGHAN, the former DoubleHappys & Straitjacket Fits singer/guitarist, CARTER, finds his niche in the world of film composing. 'Tracey's Theme' opens the album, a track that highlights Shayne's astute acoustic guitar-plucking, backed incidentally by orchestral loops; the theme continues on track 12, 'Tracey's Room', albeit with piano substituting guitar. Awarded a couple of fresh tracks ('Smoke' & 'Under The Light') by his current indie-rock outfit, DIMMER, and one golden oldie by STRAITJACKET FITS ('If I Were You'), CARTER brings a nice diversity to the proceedings without searching too far in the minefield of worthy New Zealand acts; the outro remix version of 'Smoke' by his old mucker NICK ROUGHAN is a fitting finale to the set. One gets bogged down at times by the sheer experimental tenacity of CARTER's bleak recordings; only the rare disco-pop-fuelled Kiwi classic from the 70s, 'I Need Your Love' by GOLDEN HARVEST, shifts the mood from monotone morbidity to blinding banality – good guitar though. Bypassing the brief children's hymns, 'The Day Thou Gavest, Lord, Is Ended' and 'Forgive Our Foolish Ways', CARTER goes on a wigged-out grunge assault for 'The Abduction'. The treats are few and far between towards the end of the album, only 'Carride' – a disturbing, industrial-styled collision of noise and reverberating beats – takes the uneasy listener to his/her desired destination. Warning: fasten your seatbelts and leave the kids at home, 'FOR GOOD' is a long road leading nowhere. *MCS*

Album rating: *5.5

FOUR ROOMS

1995 (US 102m) Miramax Films (R)

Film genre: segmented comedy/farce

Top guns: s-w + dir: 'The Missing Ingredient':- Allison Anders ← GAS FOOD LODGING ← BORDER RADIO / → GRACE OF MY HEART → SUGAR TOWN → THINGS BEHIND THE SUN / 'The Wrong Man':- Alexandre Rockwell / 'The Misbehavers':- Robert Rodriguez → FROM DUSK TILL DAWN / 'The Man From Hollywood':- Quentin Tarantino ← NATURAL BORN KILLERS ← PULP FICTION ← RESERVOIR DOGS / → FROM DUSK TILL DAWN → JACKIE BROWN → KILL BILL: VOL.1 → KILL BILL: VOL.2

Stars: Tim Roth *(Ted the bellhop)* ← PULP FICTION ← RESERVOIR DOGS ← RETURN TO WATERLOO / → the MILLION DOLLAR HOTEL / 'The Missing Ingredient':- Valeria Golino *(Athena)*, Sammi Davis *(Jezebel)*, **MADONNA** *(Elspeth)*, Lili Taylor *(Raven)* → I SHOT ANDY WARHOL → a SLIPPING-DOWN LIFE → HIGH FIDELITY, Ione Skye *(Eva)* ← GAS, FOOD LODGING ← WAYNE'S WORLD / → WENT TO CONEY ISLAND ON A MISSION FROM GOD . . . BE BACK BY FIVE → SOUTHLANDER, Amanda De Cadenet *(Diana)* → GRACE OF MY HEART, Alicia Witt *(Kiva)* ← DUNE, Jennifer Beals *(Angela)* ← FLASHDANCE, + 'The Wrong Man':- David Proval *(Sigfried)*, 'The Misbehavers':- Antonio Banderas *(man)* ← TRUTH OR DARE / → EVITA → TAKE THE LEAD, Lana McKissack *(Sarah)*, Tamlyn Tomita *(wife)* → TOUCH, Danny Verduzco *(Juancho)*, Salma Hayek *(TV dancing girl)* → FROM DUSK TILL DAWN → 54 → ACROSS THE UNIVERSE / 'The Man From Hollywood':- Paul Calderon *(Norman)* ← PULP FICTION, Quentin Tarantino *(Chester)* ← PULP FICTION ← RESERVOIR DOGS ← EDDIE PRESLEY / → FROM DUSK TILL DAWN → GIRL 6, Marisa Tomei *(Margaret)* ← PLAYING FOR KEEPS / → ALFIE re-make, Kathy Griffin *(Betty)* ← PULP FICTION ← MEDUSA: DARE TO BE TRUTHFUL / → DILL SCALLION, Marc Lawrence *(Sam the bellhop)* ← GOIN' COCONUTS ← a PIECE OF THE ACTION, Bruce Willis *(Leo)* ← PULP FICTION / → BEAVIS AND BUTT-HEAD DO AMERICA → LAST MAN STANDING → the STORY OF US → OVER THE HEDGE

Storyline: It's New Year's Eve and newbie Ted is not having a good first night as a bellhop. Summoned to his first room, he encounters a coven of witches who need Ted for a "special ingredient" for their potion. Next he has to deal with a husband-and-wife situation gone completely out of control, and then runs into a gangster who forces him to babysit his two children from hell. Finally he meets a pompous film director whose guests indulge in a new version of Russian Roulette. Will Ted survive to tell the tale, or will his first night be his last? *JZ*

Movie rating: *5

Visual: video + dvd

Off the record: **COMBUSTIBLE EDISON** formed in Providence, Rhode Island, USA, late '91 after they featured in a show, 'The Tiki Wonder Hour'; in fact a two-hour long cabaret where they were billed as a 14-piece, Combustible Edison Heliotropic Oriental Mambo And Foxtrot Orchestra. Former Christmas members – an indie band – Liz Cox (bongos & vox), who adopted the name of Miss Lily Banquet and Michael Cudahy (aka guitarist The Millionaire) trimmed the line-up to a 5-piece, duly completed by his brother, Nick Cudahy (double bass), Peter Dixon (hi-fi organ) and Aaron Oppenheimer (trap drums & vibraharp). Taking their cue from legendary Mexican lounge muso, Juan Garcia Esquivel, 'Edison served their music up with a jazzy swing and a cool alternative twist, eccentrically kitted out in 40s/50s movie-style tuxedos. One of 'Sub Pop's less predictable signings, COMBUSTIBLE EDISON laid down their new style on debut album, 'I, Swinger' (1994), their own compositions lounging easily with their cover of Julie London's 'Cry Me A River'. A couple of years went by before the release of their follow-up, 'Schizophonic!' (1996), during which time the easy-listening revival was at its peak. Squeezed inbetween these two sets was probably 'EDISON's best achievement, the soundtrack to 'FOUR ROOMS'. *MCS*

COMBUSTIBLE EDISON (& ESQUIVEL *)

Sep 95. (cd) *Elektra; <61861-2>* [ ] [–]
– Vertigogo (opening theme) / Junglero / Four Rooms swing / Bewitched / Tea and Eva in the elevator / Invocation / Breakfast at Denny's / Strange brew / Coven of witches / The earthly Diana / Eva seduces Ted / Hallway Ted / Headshake rhumba / Skippen, Pukin, Sigfried / Angela / Punch drunk / Male bonding / Mariachi / Antes de medianoche / Sentimental journey (*) / Kids watch T.V. / Champagne and needles / Bullseye / Harlem nocturne (*) / The millionaire's holiday / Ted-o-vater / Vertigogo (closing credits) / "D" in the hallway / Torchy.

S/track review: COMBUSTIBLE EDISON (see above) were undeniably the kookiest, kitschiest, er . . . "rock" outfit to spring out of their initial indie trappings. With 29 tracks/ditties on show here, it would be exhausting to give the most comprehensive review of the album ever – but I'll try. For starters, 'Vertigogo' (the movie's opening theme), gets you thinking: where have I heard it before? You will be astounded to hear it subsequently featured on a TV ad for a certain washing powder (OK, Surf!); Miss Lily Banquette delivering her giddy "do-ya-dat-n-doy . . ." scat to wondrous effect. Only one of several numbers that go over the 2-minute mark, it was followed by some weird and wonderful tunes that were one-part absurd to two-parts exotic. If you can think Martin Denny, the Residents, Tortoise and the schizoid jazz half of Zappa, you might be halfway up the stairs to the "lounge" for a cocktail (example the trippy, 'Breakfast At Denny's'); ditto, 'Eva Seduces Ted'. Indeed, one was slightly 'Bewitched' by the whole thing, even when I heard their faithful rendition of the TV theme. Ahh! Nostalgia! For some ditties, you can get out your trusty Hawaiian trunks and sip your tequila sunrise out in the back yard, while others, such as the Lisa Gerrard-like, 'Invocation', are ethereal as one can get. If the film producer's plan was to get the likes of workaholic movie composer Danny Elfman there was no need, COMBUSTIBLE EDISON fitted the bill perfectly. This was a 'FORBIDDEN ZONE' of an album, a reference to the embryonic film journey taken with the Mystic Knights Of The Oingo Boingo many moons ago. If guitarist Dick Dale was your cup of lemon tea, 'Kids Watch TV' was another to get you rolling (or dancing!) in the aisles. CE even gave a few turns to their mentor, ESQUIVEL (see above), who in turn coolly whistled his way through a big-band version of the timeless 'Sentimental Journey', while giving a Forbidden Planet-meets-West Side Story-meets-Batman performance on 'Harlem Nocturne'. On a sad note, ESQUIVEL died on the 3rd January, 2002, aged 83. *MCS*

Album rating: *7

FOXY BROWN

1974 (US 91m) American International Pictures (R)

Film genre: crime thriller

Top guns: s-w + dir: Jack Hill ← COFFY

Stars: Pam Grier *(Foxy Brown)* ← COFFY ← COOL BREEZE ← BLACK

MAMA, WHITE MAMA ← BEYOND THE VALLEY OF THE DOLLS / → FRIDAY FOSTER → SHEBA, BABY → BUCKTOWN → BILL & TED'S BOGUS JOURNEY → JACKIE BROWN → BONES, Antonio Fargas *(Link Brown)* ← CLEOPATRA JONES ← ACROSS 110th STREET ← SHAFT / → CORNBREAD, EARL AND ME → CAR WASH → FIRESTARTER → SOUL SURVIVOR, Peter Brown *(Steve Elias)* ← RIDE THE WILD SURF, Terry Carter *(Michael Anderson)* ← BROTHER ON THE RUN ← NERO SU BIANCO, Kathryn Loder *(Katherine Wall)*, Harry Holcombe *(Judge Fenton)* → BOUND FOR GLORY, Fred Lerner *(Bunyon)* ← the SOUL OF NIGGER CHARLEY, Sid Haig *(Hays)* ← COFFY ← BLACK MAMA, WHITE MAMA ← IT'S A BIKINI WORLD ← BEACH BALL / → the FORBIDDEN DANCE → JACKIE BROWN → HOUSE OF 1000 CORPSES → KILL BILL: VOL.2 → the DEVIL'S REJECTS, Juanita Brown *(Claudia)* ← WILLIE DYNAMITE, Bob Minor *(Oscar)* ← COFFY, Jack Bernardi *(Tedeseo)* ← WILLIE DYNAMITE ← IT'S A BIKINI WORLD ← the WILD ANGELS ← BEACH BALL, Esther Sutherland *(nurse Crockett)* ← BLACK BELT JONES ← HELL UP IN HARLEM / → TRUCK TURNER

Storyline: First lady of Blaxploitation, Pam Grier, is the iconic Foxy Brown in this visceral slice of sex, violence and more violence. After going undercover as a prostitute to find the culprits behind her boyfriend's murder, Foxy enlists the help of local vigilantes to wreak her revenge. *BG*

Movie rating: *6

Visual: video + dvd

Off the record: (see below)

WILLIE HUTCH

Apr 74. (lp) *Motown; <M6 811ST> (STML 11269)* ☐ ☐
– Chase / Theme of Foxy Brown / Hospital prelude of love theme / Gimme me some of that good old love / Out there / Foxy lady / You sure know how to love your man / Have you ever asked yourself why (all about money game) / Whatever you do (do it good). *<cd-iss. 1996; 530 648-2>*

S/track review: It's probably fair to say that the late WILLIE HUTCH (who passed away as recently as 19th September 2005) died without ever really getting his full critical due. A multi-talented 'Motown' insider whose credits included the Jackson 5 ballad, 'I'll Be There', HUTCH seemed more than capable of emerging from the backroom shadows when he kicked off a solo career in the late 60s. Despite writing, producing and arranging two of the finest soundtracks in the blaxploitation canon, however, he remained a fringe figure, destined only for cult status. The second of his soundtracks, 'FOXY BROWN', is testament to that unsung talent, furthering the man's brand of street-tough soul showcased on 'The MACK' (1973). HUTCH's gauzy tenor – here sugared by a trio of female backing singers – thrives on that same combination of grit and sympathy which served Marvin Gaye so well in the 70s. He's also a mean guitarist, although his choppy riffing figures pretty low in the mix ('Motown', incidentally, never bothered releasing a re-mastered CD), and it's his voice, rather than any instrumental backing which is the prime focus here. Probably just as well given that wah-wah funk opener 'Chase' steers too close to Isaac Hayes' 'SHAFT' theme for comfort. Not so HUTCH's own main theme, a rolling soul groove where the harmonies of Maxine Willard, Julia Tillman and Carol Williams really come into their own, raising a halo for the Bobby Womack-like, bittersweet candour of Willie's singing. While the opulently soulful 'Give Me Some Of That Good Old Love' is exactly the kind of smouldering lover's man showcase which Gaye embraced in the mid-70s, 'Out There' boasts the kind of eminently sample-able bass line and Larry Young spaciness which characterised Gaye's own soundtrack masterpiece, 'TROUBLE MAN', right down to HUTCH's coitus interruptus vocal. Great stuff. Nor is Mr HUTCH afraid to experiment with the kind of electronically generated rhythms which set the metronomic tone of 'Foxy Lady' and 'You Sure Know How To Love Your Man'. Eddie Harris employed the same kind of tactics with more humour but perhaps not quite as much soul. And, in summing up HUTCH's achievement it's Soul – with a capital 'S' – which shouts loudest. Not as immediate as other blax soundtracks maybe, but with repeated listening, one of the genre's fondest. *BG*

Album rating: *6.5

– spinoff releases, etc. –

WILLIE HUTCH: Theme Of Foxy Brown / Give Me Some Of That Good Old Love

Mar 74. (7") *<1292>* ☐ ☐

FRANKIE'S HOUSE

1992 (Aus 185m or 60m x 4 TV mini) AFFC / ABC

Film genre: war docudrama

Top guns: dir: Peter Fisk / s-w: Andy Armitage, Matt Ford (auto/nov: 'Page After Page' by Tim Page)

Stars: Iain Glen *(Tim Page)*, Kevin Dillon *(Sean Flynn)*, Steven Vidler *(Steve Cotler)* → BAD EGGS, Alan David Lee *(Martin Stuart-Fox)*, Stephen Dillane *(Anthony Strickland)*, Alexandra Fowler *(Kate Richards)*, Caroline Carr *(Danielle Charasse)*

Storyline: Photojournalist Tim Page embarks on a series of adventures in war-torn Vietnam with his photographer-partner Sean Flynn. Always to be found where the action is thickest, the pair survive numerous close calls and tell their stories in the local brothel, Frankie's House. But as the fighting grows more intense and brutal, it may only be a matter of time before their luck runs out. *JZ*

Movie rating: *7

Visual: video

Off the record: JED LEIBER (see below)

JEFF BECK & JED LEIBER

Nov 92. (cd/c/lp) *Epic; (472494-2/-4) <EK/ET 53194>* ☐ Jan93 ☐
– The jungle / Requiem for the Bao-Chi / Hi-heel sneakers / Thailand / Love and death / Cathouse / In the dark / Sniper patrol / Peace island / White mice / Tunnel rat / Vihn's funeral / Apocalypse / Innocent victim / Jungle reprise.

S/track review: At first glance, the unlikely pairing of guitar legend JEFF BECK with unknown keyboard-player JED LEIBER, seemed a little uninspiring. However, it was JB's first foray into the world of film music as well as it was Jed's; they would reunite for 'Blue Chips' in 1994, although only the Various Artists featured on the OST. Opening track 'The Jungle' was a good enough beginning, its Morricone-meets-Tangerine Dream beats ruffled ever so slightly when BECK slides in with that distinctive guitar echo. The similar but lamenting, 'Requiem For The Bao-Chi', precedes an ill-fitting, out-of-context fuzz-guitar rendition of Robert Higginbotham's 'Hi-Heel Sneakers'. Pure mental. The film's Vietnam/War theme gets back on course via 'Thailand' and 'Love & Death', the latter a rocking, rollercoaster ride of extreme proportions. The sexy, 'Cathouse' (FRANKIE'S HOUSE's other subject matter), plucks all the right G-strings and strips away the bare bones of its hard-thrusting rock'n'roll sound. The best track on the album by far. It was all a bit of a damp squib from then on, the subsequent music retreating awkwardly on a mission to nowhere, with directions going everywhere but the right one. JEFF did get back on track on a few Cooder-esque ditties, the exception being the brightly-coloured intro of 'Innocent Victim'. War films and their music are best sampled through 'Apocalypse Now', 'Platoon' and even 'The KILLING FIELDS'. *MCS*

Album rating: *4

□ the FREEDOM segment
(⇒ NERO SU BIANCO)

□ FRENCH LESSON alt.
(⇒ the FROG PRINCE)

□ the FRENCH WOMAN alt.
(⇒ MADAME CLAUDE)

FRIDAY FOSTER

1975 (US 89m) American International Pictures (R)

Film genre: comic-strip thriller

Top guns: dir: Arthur Marks (+ story) ← BUCKTOWN / → the MONKEY HUSTLE / s-w: Oliver H. Hampton ← a TIME TO SING ← RIOT ON SUNSET STRIP ← CALYPSO HEAT WAVE

Stars: Pam Grier *(Friday Foster)* ← BUCKTOWN ← FOXY BROWN ← COFFY ← COOL BREEZE ← BEYOND THE VALLEY OF THE DOLLS / → SHEBA, BABY → BILL & TED'S BOGUS JOURNEY → JACKIE BROWN → BONES, Yaphet Kotto *(Colt Hawkins)* ← TRUCK TURNER ← ACROSS 110th STREET ← MAN AND BOY / → the MONKEY HUSTLE → the PARK IS MINE, Godfrey Cambridge *(Ford Malotte)* ← COME BACK, CHARLESTON BLUE ← COTTON COMES TO HARLEM ← WATERMELON MAN, Thalmus Rasulala *(Blake Tarr)* ← WILLIE DYNAMITE ← BLACULA ← COOL BREEZE / → CORNBREAD, EARL AND ME → BUCKTOWN → ADIOS AMIGO → LAMBADA → NEW JACK CITY, **Eartha Kitt** *(Madame Rena)* → the EMPEROR'S NEW GROOVE, Jim Backus *(Enos Griffith)* ← HELLO DOWN THERE ← ADVANCE TO THE REAR, Scatman Crothers *(Rev. Noble Franklin)* ← TRUCK TURNER ← BLACK BELT JONES ← SLAUGHTER'S BIG RIP-OFF ← LADY SINGS THE BLUES, Tierre Turner *(Cleve)* → CORNBREAD, EARL AND ME → BUCKTOWN → the CROW, Paul Benjamin *(Sen. David Lee Hart)* ← the EDUCATION OF SONNY CARSON ← ACROSS 110th STREET ← MIDNIGHT COWBOY / → LEADBELLY → the FIVE HEARTBEATS, Ted Lange *(Fancy Dexter)* ← BLACK BELT JONES ← WATTSTAX / → RECORD CITY, Edmund Cambridge *(Lt. Jake Wayne)* ← TROUBLE MAN ← MELINDA ← the FINAL COMEDOWN ← COOL BREEZE / → BILL & TED'S BOGUS JOURNEY, Julius Harris *(Monk Riley)* ← BLACK CAESAR ← HELL UP IN HARLEM ← TROUBLE MAN ← SUPERFLY ← SHAFT'S BIG SCORE! / → LET'S DO IT AGAIN, Carl Weathers *(Yarbro)* ← BUCKTOWN, Rosalind Miles *(Cloris Boston)* ← SHAFT'S BIG SCORE!

Storyline: From paparazzi to vigilante, our titular heroine rumbles a racist plot on a photo-journalistic assignment. Sent to shoot wealthy black figurehead Blake Tarr, she captures an attempted assassination on camera and, with the help of her P.I. boyfriend, uncovers a viper's nest of white supremicists out to pick off black politicians. *BG*

Movie rating: *5.5

Visual: video + dvd

Off the record: Eartha Kitt (b. Eartha Mae Keith, 17 Jan'27, North, South Carolina, USA) was the illegitimate daughter of a white farmer and a black/Cherokee mother, the latter relinquishing parental responsibility when she sent her away to live on the streets of Harlem aged only nine. By the 50s, Eartha's unique purring vocal style won her many famous fans around the world including Orson Welles who dubbed her "the most exciting girl in the world". A hit on the continent, especially gay Paris, the original "material girl" fashioned her way up the ladder of success, stopping off along the way for the odd chart entry; 'Under The Bridges Of Paris' was her first (and only) Top 10'er in the UK in 1955; single 'Santa Baby' and 'C'est Si Bon' had already made her a household name in the States. Her sex-kitten appeal was best tasted as the acidic Catwoman in the Batman TV series of the mid-60s, although her time would be spent mainly on the cabaret circuit. She starred in many Hollywood films including 'The Mark Of The Hawk' (1957), 'St. Louis Blues' (1958), 'FRIDAY FOSTER' (1975), 'Dragonard' (1987), 'Erik The Viking' (1989), 'Ill-Gotten Gains' (1998) and her most recent 'And Then Came Love' (2007), while her only really serious attempt at pop came via her 1989 collaboration with Bronski Beat on the hit 'Cha Cha Heels'. *MCS*

—

LUCHI DE JESUS

Dec 01. (cd) *Beyond: <57825-2>* □ [-]
– Friday Foster – main title (WARD L. CHANDLER) / Friday – Getting set / The assassinations – The pigeon – Hit / Mackin – Fancy pants – Glad rags / Skin city / Don't drop the soap – Final solution / Hasty exit – Wheels – Cat and mouse – Spider and fly / Be gay / Position #69 / Black widow / Be Shaft – Jericho – Super man / WW III / Friday – end titles.

S/track review: More famous for his work with Dennis Coffey on 'Black Belt Jones' (1974), LUCHI DE JESUS composed a raft of other more obscure, largely unreleased blaxploitation soundtracks among which 'FRIDAY FOSTER' was the penultimate, never issued on vinyl but highly coveted by DJ's and breaks freaks. A veteran arranger, producer and conductor who counted the likes of Chet Baker and Sarah Vaughan among his credits, DE JESUS had previously been a 'Mercury' A&R staffer alongside Quincy Jones. Here he's as handy with a vocoder as Pam Grier is with a camera, regurgitating laryngeal excretions in the insalubrious, neo-psychedelic mould of Eddie Harris, and – on standout track, 'Skin City' – backing them up with some great big band funk charts. Like fellow-arranger turned black cinema don, JJ Johnson, DE JESUS' heart is in jazz and when he's not tinkering with his vocoder, he's lining up banks of horns, on occasion even a solitary trumpet (check out the 'Mackin/Fancy Pants/Glad Rags' medley, the blazing solo in 'Skin City' and the Miles Davis-esque ballad, 'Position #69'). There's plenty of hard funk for blaxploitation addicts; two of the hardest – and shortest – cues are 'Black Widow' and 'WW III', a kettle-thundering groove with a trumpet breakdown. The only straight vocal is the main title, a Fender Rhodes bomb penned by Bodie Chandler, former music director at 'Hanna-Barbera' no less, and the man behind 'Down And Out In New York City' (the opener on James Brown's 'BLACK CAESAR' soundtrack). Harris buffs, early 70s Miles Davis aficionados and fans of Charles Earland's film stuff will especially appreciate this, and it's still possible to pick it up ridiculously cheap – get it while it lasts. *BG*

Album rating: *7

FRIDAY NIGHT LIGHTS

2004 (US 117m) Universal Pictures (PG-13)

Film genre: sports drama

Top guns: s-w: (+ dir) Peter Berg, David Aaron Cohen (book: H.G. Bissinger)

Stars: Billy Bob Thornton *(coach Gary Gaines)* ← SOUTH OF HEAVEN, WEST OF HELL ← PRIMARY COLORS ← DEAD MAN, Lucas Black *(Mike Winchell)* ← KILLER DILLER ← COLD MOUNTAIN ← ALL THE PRETTY HORSES ← SLING BLADE, Derek Luke *(Boobie Miles)* ← PIECES OF APRIL, Jay Hernandez *(Brian Chavez)*, Garrett Hedlund *(Don Billingsley)*, **Tim McGraw** *(Charles Billingsley)*, Connie Britton *(Sharon Gaines)*, Lee Thompson Young *(Chris Corner)*

Storyline: True-life account of the trials and tributations (set in 1988) of an American football team (the Permian Panthers) from the small, oil-town of Odessa, Texas. Setbacks a-plenty befall the high school buddies and their uncompromising coach, Gary Gaines, setbacks that included the loss of their star tailback, Boobie Miles. Will they make it to the interstate finals? *MCS*

Movie rating: *7

Visual: dvd

Off the record: EXPLOSIONS IN THE SKY (i.e. Mark Smith, Munaf Rayani, Christopher Hrasky and Michael James) from Austin, Texas, formed at the turn of the millennium, another tour de force on the post-rock climes once tread by MOGWAI, etc. Since the release of a homemade demo, 'How Strange, Innocence', two long-players for 'Temporary Residence' have been issued: 'Those Who Tell The Truth Shall Die..' (2001) and 'The Earth Is Not A Cold Dead Place' (2003). Number One country crooner (and spawn of ex-professional baseball player, Tug McGraw), **Tim McGraw** (b. 1 May'67, Delhi, Louisiana) had already starred in another sporting feature, 'Black Cloud' (2004); he went on to co-star in 2006 family film, 'Flicka' and is married to fellow country singer, Faith Hill. Tim's multi-platinum albums included 'Not A Moment Too Soon' (1994), 'All I Want' (1995), 'Everywhere' (1997), 'A Place In The Sun' (1999), 'Set This Circus Down' (2001), 'Tim McGraw And The Dancehall Doctors' (2002) & 'Live Like You Were Dying' (2004). *MCS*

—

EXPLOSIONS IN THE SKY (& Various Artists)

Oct 04. (cd) *Hip-O; <00036630-2>* ☐ ☐
– From West Texas / Your hand in mine / Our last days as children / An ugly fact of life / Home / Sonho dourado (DANIEL LANOIS) / To West Texas / Your hand in mine (goodbye) / Inside it all feels the same / Dop you ever feel cursed (DAVID TORN) / Lonely train / Seagull (BAD COMPANY) / The sky above, the field below (w/ BRIAN REITZELL) / A slow dance.

S/track review: With three post-rock albums behind them (see OTR above), Texas' own answer to Mogwai or Godspeed, EXPLOSIONS IN THE SKY were chosen by producer BRIAN REITZELL (the similar 'The VIRGIN SUICIDES' & 'LOST IN TRANSLATION') to supply the soundtrack. Both sombre and quietly uplifting at times (check out openers, 'From West Texas', 'Your Hand In Mine', 'Our Last Days As Children', 'An Ugly Fact Of Life' & 'Ugly'), the wistful quartet easing themselves into the proceedings while instrumentally painting that luminous landscape. Canadian guitarist DANIEL LANOIS was the first of three non-EITS artists to show, his track 'Sonho Dourado' full of trademark guitar licks, while also very reminiscent of a traditional lullaby lost somewhere between Ireland and the Deep South. By tracks 7 & 8 – virtually 1 & 2 reprised – thoughts were beginning to subside into a neverending ENO loop, anti-climactic and never quite getting over for a touchdown – so to speak! The following piece, 'Inside It All Feels The Same', was definitely trying to tell us something, we were going nowhere fast; DAVID TORN's 'Do You Ever Feel Cursed' was reading from the same songsheet, although COODER and Morricone fans might well love its sparse guitar echoes. Less EXPLOSIONS IN THE SKY more Asleep At The Wheel (a long-forgotten 70s bluegrass outfit) for zzz-zzz-top-yourself number, 'Lonely Train'; note of caution: not to be played while driving. Yes, time for a classic. 'Seagull' by BAD COMPANY (originally from their eponymous 1974 LP) masterfully segued into the set by REITZELL, and possibly the best ballad Paul Rodgers and Co ever released. Getting back into the spirit of things, EXPLOSIONS . . . played out the remainder of the soundtrack with two dirges, 'The Sky Above, The Field Below' and 'A Slow Dance', the latter self-explanatory beyond the field of duty. *MCS*

Album rating: *6

FRIENDS

1971 (UK 101m) Paramount Pictures (X)

Film genre: romantic teen drama

Top guns: dir: Lewis Gilbert / s-w: Jack Russell, Vernon Harris

Stars: Sean Bury *(Paul Harrison)*, Anicee Alvina *(Michelle LaTour)*, Toby Robins *(Mrs. Gardner)*, Ronald Lewis *(Mr. Harrison)*, Saddy Rebbot *(Pierre)*, Pascale Roberts *(Annie)*, Joan Hickson *(lady in bookshop)* ← MRS. BROWN, YOU'VE GOT A LOVELY DAUGHTER

Storyline: Paul is a neglected English lad who runs away from his home in Paris. Michelle is a neglected French lass who runs away from the orphanage to Paris. The pair meet up at the zoo and, after deciding that all adults are nasty and they love each other, they finish looking at the animals and run away together to a lonely Camargue cottage. But their idyllic life could be coming to an abrupt stop when Michelle announces there's a baby on the way. *JZ*

Movie rating: *3.5

Visual: video

Off the record: (see below)

—

ELTON JOHN (arranged & conducted by Paul Buckmaster)

Apr 71. (lp) *Paramount; (SPFL 269) <PAS 6004>* ☐ Mar71 36
– Friends / Michelle's song / Seasons / Variation on Michelle's song (A day in the country) / Can I put you on / Honey roll / Variation on Friends / I meant to do my work today (A day in the country) / Four moods / Seasons reprise.

S/track review: It'd been a prolific time for ELTON JOHN in the months leading up to the release of 'FRIENDS' in the spring of '71: his first two LPs ('Elton John' & 'Tumbleweed Connection') had gone platinum and Top 5 in the States, while his single 'Your Song' went Top 10 in the US and UK. It was quite incredible ELTON had any time for er . . . "FRIENDS", but he did have two in the shape of lyricist BERNIE TAUPIN and music arranger, PAUL BUCKMASTER, and it was mostly down to the hard work of the latter that this got off the ground (TAUPIN implied so in the sleevenotes). Straight from the opening hit single title track and follow-on number, 'Michelle's Song', the album (which was recorded in September 1970) has a nice easy-does-it, soft-rock approach, although the slightly uptempo 'Can I Put You On' and 'Honey Roll' put paid to that. Orchestral composer, BUCKMASTER puts in his melancholic two-pennorth in the first two and a half minutes of 'Seasons', while he's in full control of a few other variations (with sad film dialogue) and the 11-minute 'Four Moods'. All'n'all, very settling and after several listens, quite uplifting. After many years only issued on vinyl, the team at 'Polygram' decided it was time for a re-release under the guise of a 'Rare Masters' double-CD complete with early Sir ELTON material. *MCS*

Album rating: *6

– spinoff hits, etc. –

ELTON JOHN: Friends / Honey Roll

Apr 71. (7") *D.J.M.; (DJS 244) Uni; <55277>* ☐ Mar71 34

ELTON JOHN: Rare Masters

Oct 92. (d-cd/d-c) *Rocket; (<514138-2/-4>)* ☐ ☐
– (9 early tracks) / "Friends" soundtrack // (other songs).

Fred FRITH

Born: 17 Feb'49, Heathfield, Sussex, England. A founder member of Canterbury Scene pioneers Henry Cow, and long a dynamic man-in-demand on the American avant-garde scene, FRED FRITH, rather surprisingly, only recently began lending his talents to the film world. Having worked with as diverse an array of artists – including BRIAN ENO, John Zorn, Bill Laswell and the RESIDENTS – as stylistic constructs, largely on improvisational guitar, FRITH released his debut soundtrack, 'The TOP OF HIS HEAD' (1989). The man finally became the subject of his own documentary, 'STEP ACROSS THE BORDER' (1990), a film by Nicolas Humbert and Werner Penzel, while further OST releases came via 'MIDDLE OF THE MOMENT' (1995). In 'RIVERS AND TIDES: WORKING WITH TIME' (2001), he followed up by composing music for someone else's documentary, a portrait of artist Andy Goldsworthy by filmmaker Thomas Riedelsheimer, in which his skeletal, elemental score presented an atmospheric framework for Goldsworthy's environmental sculpture. FRITH has since worked with independent director, Alan Snitow, on the score for the documentary 'Thirst' (2004) and alongside profoundly deaf Scots percussionist, Evelyn Glennie. *BG & MCS*

- **filmography** (composer) –

Wolfsgrub *(1986)* / **the Top Of His Head** *(1989 OST =>)* / **Step Across The Border** *(1990 OST =>)* / Thea Und Nat *(1992)* / Before Sunrise *(1995 OST by V/A; see future edition)* / **Middle Of The Moment** *(1995 OST rel. 2004 =>)* / the Tango Lesson *(1997 w/ Sally Potter; see future edition)* / **Rivers And Tides: Working With Time** *(2001 OST =>)* / Thirst *(2004)* / Touch The Sound *(2004 w/ Evelyn Glennie)* / Drei Gegen Troja *(2005 TV)* / Time That Rests *(2007)*

FRITZ THE CAT

1972 (US 78m) Cinemathon Industries (X)

Film genre: animated seXual satire

Top guns: dir: (+ s-w) Ralph Bakshi → HEAVY TRAFFIC → AMERICAN POP (comic book: Robert Crumb)

Voices: Skip Hinnant *(Fritz)*, Rosetta LeNoire, John McCurry ← the LANDLORD, Phil Seuling, Judy Engles

Storyline: Satirical adult animation was the order of the day in this infamous adaptation of a Robert Crumb creation. Against Crumb's wishes, his dopey cat plays an oversexed drug fiend of a student in 60s New York. Fritz's decadent ways eventually lead to a violent run-in with the police and the death of his friend, prompting an archetypal cross-country, on-the-run road trip. *BG*

Movie rating: *7

Visual: video + dvd

Off the record: (see below)

—

Various Artists (composers: ED BOGAS * / RAY SHANKLIN **)

Jun 72. (lp) *Fantasy; <F 9405> (FAN 9406)* Sep72
– Black talk (CHARLES EARLAND) / Duke's theme (**) / Fritz the cat (*) / Mamblues (CAL TJADER) / Bo Diddley (BO DIDDLEY) / Bertha's theme (**) / Winston (*) / House rock (*) / The synagogue (arr. *) / Yesterdays (BILLIE HOLIDAY) / Love light of mine (the WATSON SISTERS) / The riot (*) / You're the only girl (I ever really loved) (* & **). <*(cd-iss. Nov96 +=; FCD 24745)*> – HEAVY TRAFFIC s/t *(lp re-iss. Oct99 on 'Moving Image Entertainment'; MIE 003)*

S/track review: Bakshi's marauding feline wasn't black but he was hep enough to have his escapades soundtrack'd by some of the best jazz/funk talent of his day. 'Fantasy' solo artist/sessioneer and Grateful Dead/Muhammad Ali associate MERLE SAUNDERS was charged with scoring the movie, even if the final credits went to ED BOGAS and RAY SHANKLIN (a 'Fantasy' arranger who'd previously reactivated 50s jazz label, 'Galaxy'). SAUNDERS roped in the rhythm section of Bernard Purdie and Chuck Rainey, at the time playing with Aretha Franklin. Franklin guitarist Cornell Dupree was also recruited, as was Arthur Adams – a veteran bluesman who'd worked with the likes of CHUCK BERRY, Lightnin' Hopkins and JAMES BROWN, and who went on to score an early 80s UK club hit with 'You Got The Floor' – and vibes legend CAL TJADER. As well as contributing the frantic 'Mamblues', an uncredited TJADER sounds like he's playing on 'Duke's Theme', a lengthy jazz-blues jam sanctified by what can only be SAUNDERS' ocean-deep electric piano (again uncredited!). This is about as good as it gets, but the rest of the album is serviceable enough, running though the chicken scratch and expletives of the title theme, the 'St. James Infirmary'-lite of 'Bertha's Theme' and the flaming, Charles Earland-like chase funk of 'The Riot'. The title of EARLAND's 'Black Talk' (1969) is actually one of a clutch of source tracks which make up the running time, including BO DIDDLEY's self-titled single from the early 60s (its doppleganger-strength similarity with early period Rolling Stones has to be heard to be believed), BILLIE HOLIDAY's searing 'Yesterdays' and a WATSON SISTERS' version of the spiritual, 'This Little Light Of Mine', used to better effect by Melvin Van Peebles. Hardly essential blaxploitation, and hardly as subversive as it could've been, but worth a punt. *BG*

Album rating: *6

□ Edgar FROESE
(⇒ TANGERINE DREAM)

the FROG PRINCE

US title 'FRENCH LESSON'

1985 (UK/US 90m) Enigma / Goldcrest Films (15)

Film genre: romantic/seXual comedy

Top guns: s-w: Brian Gilbert (+ dir), Posy Simmonds

Stars: Jane Snowden *(Jenny)*, Alexandre Sterling *(Jean-Phillipe)*, Diana Blackburn *(Ros)*, Oystein Wiik *(Niels)*, Jacqueline Doyen *(Mme. Peroche)*, Raoul Delfosse *(Mons. Peroche)*, Jeanne Herviale *(Madame Duclos)*

Storyline: British student Jenny is staying with the Peroche family while she studies at the Sorbonne in Paris. Jenny decides it's time to find the perfect man, fall in love, etc, etc, but who to choose? There is of course dashing local lad Jean-Phillipe, or the nice Norwegian Niels. So Jenny devises a series of tests for her potential Romeos to see who scores top marks. But how long will parochial Mme Peroche put up with Jenny's jiggery-pokery? *JZ*

Movie rating: *6

Visual: video

Off the record: (see below)

—

ENYA (w/ other artists)

Oct 85. (lp/c) *Island; (ISTA/ICT 10)* –
– The train to Paris / The first day / Mack the knife (JAZZ CLUB) / Let it be me (JAZZ CLUB) / With Jean-Phillipe / Jenny / Reflections / The Frog Prince / Dreams / The kiss / Sweet Georgia Brown (JAZZ CLUB) / Georgia on my mind (JAZZ CLUB) / A kiss by the fountain / Jenny & Roz / Les Flon-flons du bal (EDITH PIAF) / Epilogue. *(cd-iss. Aug95 on 'Spectrum' Germany; 551099-2)*

S/track review: This early solo effort from ENYA, following her departure from Clannad, is a dated relic featuring horrible 80s synthesizers which render many of the tracks indistinguishable from dreaded elevator Muzak. This is much more straightforward and unambiguous than her later work and mainly features snappy little keyboard ditties such as 'The First Day'. There is even the strong presence of an intrusive screaming saxophone on the likes of 'The Train To Paris' and 'The Kiss'. Bizarrely this soundtrack sits somewhere between the strings and synths of a gliding backing track to a Barry White song and the theme-tunes to late-night American cop shows (think Cagney & Lacey). 'Reflections' finally brings a touch of class to proceedings with its intricate layers and prominent Philip Glass-esque clarinet, whilst 'A Kiss By The Fountain' starts off nice enough with rhythmical laid-back pianos before the obligatory sax bursts in and spoils it. Elsewhere, there are also some playful jazz instrumental takes on famous standards such as 'Mack The Knife' and 'Georgia On My Mind' performed by JAZZ CLUB, as well as the engaging pomp of EDITH PIAF's 'Les Flon-Flons Du

Bal' to negotiate before this dreadful mess is done. Overall this has the feeling of a failed experiment, evident none more so than on the insipid ballad of the title track and 'Dreams', which are so dull and simple they sound like particularly bad hymns. This in turn made 'The FROG PRINCE' totally discernible from the atmospheric ambience that ENYA would go on to build a successful career around. *LF*

Album rating: *4.5

□ John FRUSCIANTE segment
(⇒ the BROWN BUNNY)

FUREUR

2003 (Fra 106m) Canal + / ADR / Gaumont

Film genre: romantic drama

Top guns: s-w + dir: Karim Dridi

Stars: Samuel Le Bihan *(Raphael Ramirez)*, Yann Tregouet *(Manu Ramirez)*, Nann Yu *(Chinh)*, Bounsy Luang Phinith *(Tony)*, Thomas Larget *(Monsieur Tran)*, Samart Payakarun *(Noi)*, Christian Mazucchini *(Desire)* ← NENETTE ET BONI

Storyline: Ex-boxer Raphael Ramirez now uses his hands to repair cars in his garage, while training his younger brother to follow in his footsteps. When his old rival Tony Tran (nationality undecided) makes an appearance it looks as if Raphael will be forced to don the gloves again, the reason being the beautiful Chinh, Tony's fiancee and Raphael's dream girl. The pair begin a tug of love for the girl but, just like in the ring, there can only be one winner – the loser will have to take it on the Chinh. *JZ*

Movie rating: *5

Visual: none

Off the record: JAH WOBBLE (b. John Wardle, 1958, Stepney, London, England). Might well have been a Sex Pistol after he borrowed Sid Vicious' bass, but was subsequently invited by John Lydon (the artist formerly known as Johnny Rotten) to join the man's breakaway outfit, Public Image Ltd (aka PiL). WOBBLE's contributions to their late 70s seminal albums 'Public Image' and 'Metal Box 1' were a little understated at the time, but one lasting impression of the bassist's memorable TV appearances was undoubtably his gap-toothed, Cheshire-cat grin for 'Death Disco' on BBC-TV's Top Of The Pops. Jah's sudden departure in 1980 was said to be due to Lydon's annoyance at his use of PiL rhythm tracks on his awful punk/dub debut, 'The Legend Lives On'. Subsequently flying out to Germany, WOBBLE cut the 'Full Circle' set with Can members, Holger Czukay and Jaki Liebezeit, while in 1983, he was the main thrust behind another collaboration, 'Snake Charmer', with the aforementioned Czukay and The EDGE (of U2). In the mid-80s, WOBBLE was forced to endure the trials of a "real" job when he worked for the London Underground (mind the gap, if indeed a musical one!). Sporadic releases also paid the bills, although it wasn't until 1991's comeback set, 'Rising Above Bedlam' (which introduced vocalist, Natacha Atlas of Transglobal Underground) that WOBBLE became a fully interested in the music scene once again. The bassman and his ever-expanding Invaders Of The Heart even hit the Top 40 with the beautiful 'Visions Of You' single featuring vocals by Sinead O'Connor. With WOBBLE's spiritual leanings now looming large over proceedings, 1994's 'Take Me To God' album hit the Top 20 following a rapturous appearance at the Glastonbury Festival. His subsequent collaborative contribution to the late Derek Jarman's 'GLITTERBUG' film compilation (album as 'Spinner') with BRIAN ENO was also worthy of note. WOBBLE even found time to form his own imprint, '30 Hertz', which went on to deliver most of his ethnic fusion albums; one of them, 'Molam Dub' (2000), featured a few cuts represented on the 'FUREUR' soundtrack. *MCS*

—

JAH WOBBLE

Apr 03. (cd) *EastWest; (2564-60165-2)* [–] French [–]
– Club scene / Club scene dub / Calm within the storm / Calm within the storm 2 / Lam saravane / Fight scene / Lovers' theme / Lam tang way dub / The courtship / Lam siphandone.

S/track review: JAH WOBBLE describes 'FUREUR' (Fury) as "a useless film, just sex and violence, but the music's good", and it's fair to say that WOBBLE's Asian-inflected dub probably works just as well, if not better, independently of the film. The majority of the soundtrack was recorded in tandem with filming, a situation which led to tensions between WOBBLE and an indecisive director, but the legendary dub bassist regardless delivered a typically dense but rewarding audio experience. Recycling three tracks featuring Paris-based, Laotian singing group MOLAM LAO from their collaborative 'Molam Dub' album, WOBBLE here mixes ethnic instruments, heavy dub rhythms and infectious vocal melodies in a way that immediately dispels any doubts about cultural imperialism, exploitation or general awfulness. If anyone else was at the helm, you'd be forgiven for expecting 'Club Scene Dub' to be an unnecessary retread of the opening track, but WOBBLE produces a blissed out four minutes of heavily treated drums and reverb-drenched guitar strums to wonky and entrancing effect. 'Calm Within The Storm' lays Spanish guitar (and Turkish sipsi!) over a low, rumbling bass line and the occasional gong. There's more creeping bass menace in 'Fight Scene', while 'Lovers' Theme' and 'The Courtship' are atmospheric but dismissible. The three tracks from 'Molam Dub' ('Lam Saravane', 'Lam Tang Way Dub' and 'Lam Siphandone') make a more lasting impression but still fit seamlessly in with the new tracks. With WOBBLE using studio downtime to start working on his 'Fly' album, it's easy to see this album as a bridge between the two, making it a worthwhile pursuit for fans of WOBBLE, while the casual listener might be better served seeking out 'Molam Dub' instead. *SW*

Album rating: *5

Peter GABRIEL

Born: 13 Feb'50, Cobham, Surrey, England. The frontman for the first, theatrical incarnation of prog pioneers Genesis, a successful solo star in his own right and a major player in the world music scene, PETER GABRIEL began dallying with film in the early 80s. After contributing the track 'Walk Through The Fire', to Taylor Hackford's 'An Officer And A Gentleman' (1982), he scored his first full length feature, Alan Parker's 'BIRDY' (1985), by remixing existing material from his two previous solo albums. Its success paved the way for 'Passion' (1989), GABRIEL's highly acclaimed score for Martin Scorsese's 'The LAST TEMPTATION OF CHRIST'. A completely original work and one which made compelling use of his increasing immersion in the – often obscure – musics of foreign cultures, this soundtrack is widely recognised as a world music milestone and one which launched the international careers of contributing artists like Youssou N'Dour and Nusrat Fateh Ali Khan. In fact, GABRIEL's involvement in his 'Real World' label and studios, as well as humanitarian and environmental work, took up much of his time in the 90s, and it'd be more than a decade before he undertook another movie project. Most fans and critics were in agreement that 'Long Walk Home' – Music From 'RABBIT-PROOF FENCE' (2002) was worth the wait. A soundtrack to Philip Noyce's acclaimed study of racist government policy in Australia, it employed all GABRIEL's empathy and imagination in translating the film's striking Aboriginal landscapes and cultural nuances. *BG*

- **filmography** (composer) –

Birdy *(1984 OST =>)* / the Secret Policeman's Third Ball *(1987 {p} on OST by V/A =>)* / **the Last Temptation Of Christ** *(1989 OST as 'PASSION' =>)* / **Woodstock '94** *(1995 {p} on OST by V/A =>)* / **My Generation** *(2000 {p} =>)* / **Rabbit-Proof Fence** *(2002 OST =>)*

Serge GAINSBOURG

Born: Lucien Ginzburg, 2 Apr'28, Paris, France. Provocateur extraordinare and icon of Gallic decadence, SERGE GAINSBOURG remains one of the most controversial yet best loved figures in the history of French popular song. From his earliest days as a boho-jazz performer, his unconventional appearance and manner, and his louche, mordant lyrics, polarized the public and most of the critics. Even as a series of inspired late 50s/early 60s 10" albums generated such prize winning songs as 'Le Poinçonneur De Lilas', GAINSBOURG remained an outsider, interpreting the works of outsider antecedents like Charles Baudelaire while other performers made his own songs more palatable. Undaunted, he diversified into acting with Brigitte Bardot vehicle, 'Voulez-Vous Danser Avec Moi?' (1959), and took major parts in Italian period dramas, 'La Rivolta Degli Schiavi' (1961), 'La Furia Di Ercole' (1961) and 'Sansone' (1961). He also initiated a highly prolific move into film composition with soundtrack EP's from 'Les Loups Dans La Bergerie' (1959), Jacques Doniol-Valcroze's 'L'eau A La Bouche' (1959), 'Strip-Tease' (1963) and Michel Boisrond's 'Comment Trouvez-vous Ma Soeur?' (1963) as well as unreleased scores for domestic features such as 'Week-end En Mer' (1962), 'Les Plus Belles Escroqueries Du Monde' (1963), 'Le Jardinier D'Argenteuil' (1965), 'L'Espion' (1966), 'Carré De Dames Pour Un As' (1966) and 'L'Une Et L'Autre' (1966). By the mid-60s, GAINSBOURG – newly enamoured of American rock'n'roll, Afro rhythms, Brazilian bossa nova and the wonderfully subversive possibilities of anglo-slang – was supplying material for the likes of Petula Clark, Marianne Faithfull and, most famously, France Gall, for whom he penned the Eurovision winning 'Poupée De Cire, Poupée De Son'. He was also writing songs for his erstwhile acting colleague Brigitte Bardot, with whom he began a high profile affair and recorded a series of duets, including the unforgettable 'Bonnie And Clyde'. His film career was also ticking over nicely with a glut of starring roles, in films for which he often composed the score into the bargain, among them 'Ce Sacre Grand-Pere' (1968), the TV musical 'ANNA' (1967), starring Jean-luc Goddard protégé Anna Karina, 'Le Pacha' (1968) – containing his great 45 'Requiem Pour Un Con', 'MISTER FREEDOM' (1969) and 'Slogan' (1969). While 'ANNA' and 'Le Pacha' both generated major hits in the shape of 'Sous Le Soleil Exactament' (sung by Karina) and 'Requiem Pour Un Con' respectively, the most pivotal film project of his career – given that it introduced him to his his future wife and muse, Jane Birkin – was perhaps 'Slogan'. While he'd initially recorded the infamous 'Je T'Aime Moi Non Plus' with Bardot, the actress' wariness of ensuing scandal had seen it shelved until Birkin came along. Bardot had been right about the scandal (the song was banned in many countries, including Britain) although its international success raised GAINSBOURG's profile to unprecedented levels and, with his landmark, Birkin-inspired concept set, 'Histoire De Melody Nelson' (1971), the singer sealed his legendary status. The new decade also saw the pair getting jiggy in Pierre Koralnik's notorious 'CANNABIS' (1970), a movie redeemed only by the wigged out, acid-orchestral brilliance of GAINSBOURG's soundtrack (composed in collaboration with the arranger of 'Histoire . . .', Jean-Claude Vannier), inspired in equal parts by JIMI HENDRIX and Bela Bartok and recently released as a two-on-one with 'Ce Sacre . . .', itself a combination of more traditional string pieces and vaguely psychedelic, semi-acoustic rock. More acting roles (usually alongside Birkin)/unreleased scores followed over the first half of the 70s including 'Trop Jolies Pour Etre Honnètes' (1972) and 'Sex Shop' (1972). In 1976, GAINSBOURG – at the height of his French celebrity – finally helmed his own production, titled after his steamy single, 'JE T'AIME, MOI NON PLUS', and featuring Birkin opposite Andy Warhol alumnus, Joe Dallesandro, as well as a cameo from a youthful Gérard Depardieu. The film's typically risqué subject matter (the relationship between a gay truck driver and an androgynous young waitress) caused yet another furore while the accompanying soundtrack provided a spin-off French hit in 'La Ballade De Johnny Jane'. GAINSBOURG subsequently worked on soundtracks for soft porn films 'MADAME CLAUDE' (1977) and 'Goodbye Emmanuelle' (1977), and continued scoring French features such as Patrice Leconte's tourist satire, 'Les Bronzés' (1978), which spawned another big French hit, 'Sea, Sex And Sun', Catherine Breillat's 'Tapage Nocturne' (1979) and Claude Berri's 'JE VOUS AIME' (1980), in which he made one of his increasingly rare acting appearances – opposite Catherine Deneuve – and which also saw a full soundtrack release. Into the 80s, Serge refused to grow old gracefully, continuing his directorial career with critically slated African drama, 'Equateur' (1983) and, more controversially, 'Charlotte For Ever' (1986), featuring his daughter Charlotte and coming hot on the heels of the infamous 'Lemon Incest' single and accompanying video. Later the same year, he composed the soundtrack for Bertrand Blier's 'Tenue De Soiree', starring Gerard Depardieu and, in 1990, completed his final film, 'Stan The Flasher'. Having already suffered a previous heart attack and having just undergone a liver operation, the hard living lothario suffered a second, fatal heart attack on 2nd March 1991. GAINSBOURG was posthumously honoured with one of his few film awards, a French Oscar for the theme song to 'Elisa', starring his latest (and final) protégé Vanessa Paradis. *BG*

- **filmography** (composer) {acting} -

Voulez-vous Danser Avec Moi? *(1959 {a})* / l'Eau A La Bouche *(1959 {p} OST EP future edition =>)* / les Loups Dans La Bergerie *(1960 OST EP w/ Alain Goraguer; future edition =>)* / Sansone *(1961 {a})* / la Rivolta Degli Schiavi *(1961 {a})* / En Passant Par Paris *(1962 TV {c})* / la Lettre Dans Un Taxi *(1962 TV)* / la Furia Di Ercole *(1962 {*})* / l'Inconnue De Hong Kong *(1963 {a})* / Strip-Tease *(1963 {p} OST EP future edition =>)* / Teuf-Teuf *(1963 TV {a})* / Comment Trouvez-vous Ma Soeur? *(1964 OST EP future edition =>)* / les Plus Belles Escroqueries Du Monde *(1964)* / Vidocq *(1966 {a} OST EP future edition =>)* / les Coeurs Verts *(1966 OST EP w/ Henri Renaud; see future edition =>)* / Estouffade A La Caraibe *(1966 {*})* / Carre De Dames Pour Un As *(1966 {b})* / le Jardinier d'Argenteuil *(1966 {a} OST EP w/ Michel Colombier; future edition =>)* / Lautlose Waffen *(1966)* / Noel A Vanguard *(1966 TV {*})* / **Anna** *(1967 TV {*} OST w/ Anna Karina =>)* / Vivre Le Nuit *(1967 {*})* / Valmy *(1967 TV {*})* / Si J'etais Un Espion *(1967 OST EP w/ Michel Colombier; future edition =>)* / l'Inconnu De Shandigor *(1967 {a} w/ Alphonse Roy)* / l'Horizon *(1967 w/ Michel Colombier; future edition =>)* / Toutes Folles De Lui *(1967 {c} w/ Georges Garvarentz)* / l'Une Et l'Autre *(1967)* / Ce Sacre Grand-Pere *(1968 {*} OST EP + on 'Cannabis'; see future edition =>)* / Paris N'existe Pas *(1968 {*})* / Erotissimo *(1968 {b})* / le Pache *(1968 single-only)* / Manon 70 *(1968)* / Mister Freedom *(1969 {a}; see future edition)* / Slogan *(1969 {*})* / les Chemins De Katmandou *(1969 {*})* / la Horse *(1970)* / Piggies *(1970 TV)* / **Cannabis** *(1970 {*} OST =>)* / 19 Djevojaka I Mornar *(1971 {*})* / Romance Of A Horsethief *(1971 {a})* / Sex-shop *(1972)* / Trop Jolies Pour Etre Honnetes *(1972)* / la Morte Negli Occhi De Gatto *(1973 {b})* / Projection Privee *(1973 w/ Jean-Claude Vannier)* / Bons Baisers De Tarzan *(1974 TV {a})* / Serieux Comme Le Plasir *(1975 {b})* / **Je T'aime Moi Non Plus** *(1976 [s-w + dir] OST =>)* / **Madame Claude** *(1977 OST =>)* / Goodbye Emmanuelle *(1977 OST; see future edition)* / Aurais Du Faire Gaffe . . . Le Choc Est Terrible *(1977)* / Melancholy Baby *(1979)* / Tapage Nocturne *(1979)* / **Je Vous Aime** *(1980 OST =>)* / Equateur *(1983)* / Mode In France *(1984)* / Tenue De Soiree *(1986 OST; see future edition)* / Charlotte For Ever *(1986 no OST)* / Stan The Flasher *(1990 single as GAINSBOURG)* / Roland Petit A Marseille *(1997 {*f} TV)*

– compilations, etc. –

SERGE GAINSBOURG: Le Cinema de Serge Gainsbourg – Musique de Films 1959-1990

Jul 02. (3xcd-box) *Universal France; (586 818-2)* [–] French [–]
– L'eau a la bouche / Angoisse / Black march / Les loups dans la bergerie – final / Cha-cha du loup / Strip-tease (par JULIETTE GRECO) / Some small chance / Rendez-vous a la calavados / Wake me at five / Solitude / Crazy-horse swing / Comment trouvez-vous ma souer? / Erotico-tico / No love for daddy / Rocking horse / Chanson du forcat / Vidocq flash-back / Scene de bal 2 / Valse du jardinier / Sous le soleil exactement (par ANNA KARINA) / Caressante / Woom woom woom / Breakdown suite // Elisa / L'horizon / Elisa – instrumental) / Manon / New delire / L'herbe tendre (par MICHEL SIMON) / Ce sacre grand-pere (generique) / Champeetre et pop / L'herbe tendre / Requiem pour un con / Psychatenie / Cadavres en serie / Oh beautiful America – Mister Freedom march / No no, yes yes / Freedom rock – Mister Freedom / La chanson de Slogan (par JANE BIRKIN) / Evelyne / La horse / L'alouette / Cannabis / Avant de mourir / Cannabis – instrumental / Derniere blessure / Un petit garcon nomme Charlie Brown // Sex-shop / Generique / Sex-radio-suite / Moogy-woogy – Close combat / L'amour en prive (par FRANCOISE HARDY) / Ballade de Johnny-Jane / Zanzibar / First class ticket – Yesterday on fender / Chanson du Chevalier blanc (par GERARD LANVIN) / Goodbye Emmanuelle / Sea, sex and sun / Melancholy suite / Tapage nocturne (par BIJOU) / Dieu fumeur de havanes (par CATHERINE DENEUVE) / Le physique et le figure / Travelling / Entrave / Stan – Elodie / Valse de l'eau-revoir (par JULIETTE GRECO) / Strip-tease (par NICO) / La fille qui fait tchic-ti-tchic (par MICHELE MERCIER) / La noyee (par ANNA KARINA) / Hier ou demain (par ANNA KARINA) / Goodbye Emmanuelle (version).

Vincent GALLO

Born: 11 Apr'62, Buffalo, New York, USA. Painter, singer, composer, determinedly improvisational method actor and all round underground renaissance man, VINCENT GALLO remains best known for his self-directed indie movie, 'BUFFALO '66' (1998), although his career actually stretches way back to the early 70s and his first band, the Blue Mood. After another teenage prog-rock vehicle, Zephyr, it wasn't long before he discovered punk and began hanging out with all the right people, holding down full and part-time roles in No Wave bands such as the Good and the Plastics. A move to downtown New York saw his own, short-lived solo project, the Nonsexuals as well as Gray, the band he formed with late NY artist Jean Michel Basquiat (and whose colourful activites he memorably describes on his official website). A former beau of MADONNA and a colleague of Andy Warhol not to mention the subject of a celeb-studded 1996 biopic, Basquiat was also the star of 'Downtown 81', an achingly hip snapshot of post-punk Manhattan and GALLO's acting debut (as himself). Although shot in the very early 80s, the film remained unreleased until 2000 when it was screened at the Cannes Film Festival. While this was GALLO's first acting role, his directorial debut had actually come a year earlier with an obscure short film, 'If You Feel Froggy, Jump' (1980), starring his then band Bohack. The very Run DMC-esque – and actually rather hilarious – shots of GALLO aka Prince Vince as one half of early 80s rap duo Trouble Deuce probably serve to underline the cultural fluidity of early 80s New York as much as they do the man's wandering talents, and it was but a short leap from here to his miasmic score for another, thespian-themed NY underground film, 'The WAY IT IS' (1986). GALLO also starred in the film himself, as did a young Steve Buscemi. While the only remaining print of the man's sophomore directing job, 'The Gun Lover' (1986), was damaged it is still possible to view his lead role in the little seen 'Doc's Kingdom', directed by the late Rob Kramer, as well as the equally obscure Portuguese film, 'A Idade Maior' (1990), in which GALLO plays a son whose father is conscripted into Portugal's wars in Angola and Mozambique. Much more high profile was a cameo appearance in gangster classic, 'Goodfellas' (1990), while a part in Claire Denis' short film, 'Keep It For Yourself' (1991), initiated a long term partnership with the French director which subsequently saw him starring in 'U.S. Go Home' (1994), 'NENETTE ET BONI' (1996) and most controversially, her sex'n'cannibalism study, 'TROUBLE EVERY DAY' (2001). In the meantime, GALLO scored his biggest roles to date alongside Johnny Depp and Faye Dunaway in Emir Kusturica's fishy comedy, 'Arizona Dream' (1993), and alongside Jeremy Irons and Meryl Streep in Billie August's 1993 adaptation of the Isabel Allende novel, 'The House Of The Spirits'. While parts as diverse as a cameo in Cuban emigre effort, 'The Perez Family' (1995), as a preacher in Rebecca Miller's psychological drama, 'Angela' (1995) and as a bungling crimimal in 'Palookaville' (1996) kept him in work, his portrayal as the doomed black sheep of a gangster dynasty in Abel Ferrara's 'The Funeral' (1996) was much more in keeping with GALLO's lone wolf style and Sicilian background. It was enough to land him a starring role in Keifer Sutherland's directorial debut, 'Truth Or Consequences, N.M.' (1997), another violent gangster piece. Then came GALLO's directorial debut proper, the aforementioned 'BUFFALO '66' (1998), where his gloriously unlikeable ex-con kidnaps Christina Ricci and memorably attempts to convince her family he once worked for the CIA. He also composed the acclaimed soundtrack, a corrollary to his debut solo album for UK electronica label, 'Warp'. While more low key roles followed – in Finnish director Mika Kaurismäki's 'L.A. Without A Map' (1998), Roland Joffe's 'Goodbye Lover' (1999), exploitaton flick, 'Freeway II: Confessions Of A Trickbaby' (1999) and Spanish space drama, 'Stranded' (2002) – the abrasive anti-hero resumed the off kilter coupling he'd initiated in 'BUFFALO '66' with 'Hide And Seek' (2000), 'Get Well Soon' (2001) and his 'Buffalo..' follow-up, 'The BROWN BUNNY' (2003), an abstruse road movie with Chloë Sevigny as his unlucky girlfriend. Love him or loathe him, GALLO remains one of the most prolific musican-cum-actors in the business, and at a significant and ever controversial remove from the majority of rock/pop stars who inevitably turn their hand to the big screen. *BG*

- filmography (composer) {acting} [s-w + dir] –

the Way It Is *(1986 {*} OST by GALLO =>)* / Doc's Kingdom *(1989 {*})* / a Idade Maior *(1990 {*})* / Goodfellas *(1990 {b})* / Arizona Dream *(1993 {*})* / the House Of The Spirits *(1993 {a})* / U.S. Go Home *(1994 {*})* / Angela *(1995 {*})* / the Perez Family *(1995 {a})* / Palookaville *(1995 {*})* / the Funeral *(1996 {*})* / **Nenette Et Boni** *(1996 {*} OST by TINDERSTICKS =>)* / Truth Or Consequences, N.M. *(1997 {*})* / **Buffalo '66** *(1998 [s-w + dir] {*} OST by GALLO =>)* / L.A. Without A Map *(1998 {*})* / Goodbye Lover *(1999 {b})* / Hide And Seek *(1999 {*})* / Freeway 2: Confessions Of A Trickbaby *(1999 {*})* / Get Well Soon *(2001 {*} + score w/ Ric Markmann)* / **Trouble Every Day** *(2001 {*} OST by TINDERSTICKS =>)* / Stranded *(2002 {*})* / **the Brown Bunny** *(2003 [s-w + dir] {*} OST by JOHN FRUSCIANTE & V/A =>)* / Indesiderabili, Gli *(2003 {*})* / Moscow Zero *(2006 {*})* / Oliviero Rising *(2007 {*})*

– compilations, etc. –

VINCENT GALLO: Recordings Of Music For Film

Jun 02. (cd/d-lp) *Warp; <(WARP CD/LP 96)>* ☐ ☐
– Her smell theme / The girl of her dreams / A brown lung hollering / The Way It Is waltz / Glad to be unhappy / Brown storm poem / Good bye sadness, hello death / Brown daisies / And a colored sky colored grey / Fishing for some friends / Six laughs once happy / Sunny and cloudy / No more papa mama / Fatty and Skinny / Her smell theme (reprise) / Lonely boy / A falling down Billy Brown / Drowning in brown / A somewhere place / A wet cleaner / Sixteen seconds happy / With smiles & smiles & smiles / A cold and grey summer day / DOWNTOWN '81:- Brown 69 / Dum beet / Me and her / IF YOU FEEL FROGGY, JUMP:- Ass fucker / Ass fucker (reprise) / I think the sun is coming out now.

□ GALLON DRUNK segment
(⇒ BLACK MILK)

□ Mike GARSON segment
(⇒ STIGMATA)

GAS FOOD LODGING

1992 (US 101m) Cineville / IRS Media (R)

Film genre: domestic coming-of-age drama

Top guns: s-w + dir: Allison Anders ← BORDER RADIO / → FOUR ROOMS → GRACE OF MY HEART → SUGAR TOWN → THINGS BEHIND THE SUN (au: Richard Peck)

Stars: Brooke Adams *(Nora)*, Ione Skye *(Trudi)* ← WAYNE'S WORLD / → FOUR ROOMS → WENT TO CONEY ISLAND ON A MISSION FROM GOD . . . BE BACK BY FIVE → SOUTHLANDER, Fairuza Balk *(Shade)* → ALMOST FAMOUS, James Brolin *(John)*, Robert Knepper *(Dank)* ← YOUNG GUNS II, David Landsbury *(Hamlet Humphrey)* → a STRANGER IN THE KINGDOM, Chris Mulkey *(Raymond)*, Jacob Vargas *(Javier)* → SELENA, Donovan Leitch *(Darius)* ← the IN CROWD ← BREAKIN' 2: ELECTRIC BOOGALOO / → I SHOT ANDY WARHOL, Chris Mulkey *(Raymond)* ← HEARTBREAK HOTEL ← TIMERIDER: THE ADVENTURE OF LYLE SWANN ← the LONG RIDERS / → SUGAR TOWN → MYSTERIOUS SKIN, Julie Condra *(Tanya)* → TOUCH, **J Mascis** *(Cecil)* ← 1991: THE YEAR PUNK BROKE / → GRACE OF MY HEART → THINGS BEHIND THE SUN, **Jeffrey McDonald** *(long haired boy)* <= REDD KROSS =>

Storyline: Single mum Nora tries her best to bring up her two very different teenage daughters in dry, dusty New Mexico. Trudi whiles away the hours with various romantic entanglements in between rebelling against her mother, while Shade spends her time in the dark at the local cinema, where she becomes friendly with projectionist Javier. What will mum say when Trudi finds herself pregnant to a runaway geologist? She could be in for a real rocky time of it. *JZ*

Movie rating: *6.5

Visual: video + dvd

Off the record: (see below)

J MASCIS & BARRY ADAMSON (& Various Artists)

Oct 92. (cd) *Mute-Elektra; <61424> Ionic-Mute; (IONIC 9CD)* ☐ ☐
– J MASCIS:- Untitled / Untitled / Untitled / Untitled / Untitled / Untitled / Untitled / Untitled / Flying clouds – instrumental / Sideways – instrumental / BARRY ADAMSON:- Soliloquy / Odio amor, odio amor / Shade // Insight (ANTAGONIST) / Maria (the MITCH GREEN EXPERIENCE feat. CARLOS) / Laverdad des nuda (BARRY ADAMSON) / Thunder (RENEGADE SOUNDWAVE) / Lament (NICK CAVE & THE BAD SEEDS) / Women respond to bass (RENEGADE SOUNDWAVE) / Trudis confession (BARRY ADAMSON) / Magic (LOUISE TOLLSON) / Cloud chamber (EASY) / We call it rock (the VELVET MONKEYS) / Los votos segradas (BARRY ADAMSON) / Love (VICTORIA WILLIAMS) / Sun before the dawn – instrumental (CRIME & THE CITY SOLUTION) / Untitled (BOYD RICE) / Untitled – reprise (J MASCIS).

S/track review: One thing you can say about 'GAS FOOD LODGING' is with over 70 minutes of playing time and 28 titles on display (several untitled in fact), one certainly gets value for money. That wouldn't be the case if the tracks were mere fillers. No, what we have here is an array of class acts, including two(!) score composers from the indie/alt-rock world: Dinosaur Jr.'s J MASCIS and ex-Nick Cave/Bad Seeds cohort, BARRY ADAMSON. The aforementioned 'Untitled' tracks (1-8) by J MASCIS kick off the long-player in horizontal, Pink Floyd-ish fashion, with only a hint of the era's grunge fixation. The introspective instrumentals (including titled tracks 9-10, 'Flying Clouds' & 'Sideways') are solo-guitar-driven with piano and percussion accompaniment, some are even too short to get into full swing – but that's not a complaint. Spread out over the remainder of the set, short cues by BARRY ADAMSON complement the somewhat eclectic selections, the man's keys/synths producing a 'Phantom . . . Opera'-like orchestra effect. The inclusion of the obscure, grindcore-metal dirge, 'Insight' (by ANTAGONIST), is a little baffling; the lyrical/vocal mess is indeed "out-of-tune" with the rest of the set. In contrast, follow-on number, 'Maria' (by the MITCH GREEN EXPERIENCE featuring CARLOS), is funky cool, exotic and arguably a pointer to the likes of lounge-lizards, Fun Lovin' Criminals. Another ambiguous and mystifying offering is delivered by unknown LOUISE TOLLSON and her cloned version of Olivia Newton-John's hit, 'Magic'; it would be unfair to compare the song with the fragility of VICTORIA WILLIAMS' 'Love' (track 25). If one was to pick out the highlight, it would have to be 'Thunder' by London's industrial

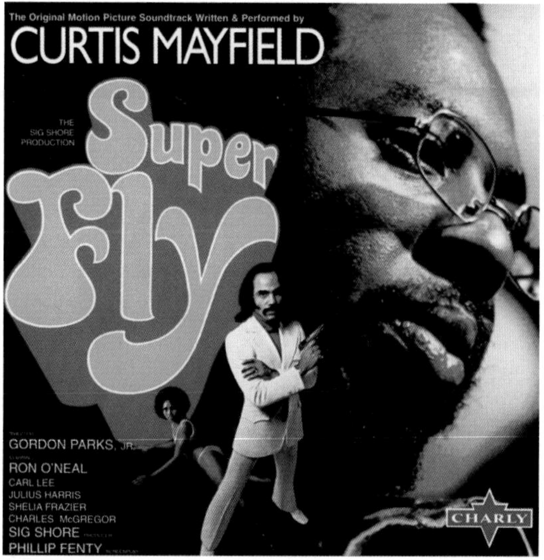

The quintessential blaxploitation movie, *Superfly* (1972) boasts an innovative, intelligent plot and impressive, moustachioed performance from Ron O'Neal as Youngblood Priest. Curtis Mayfield's soundtrack is almost universally regarded as the most accomplished and enduring of its era. On 'Freddie's Dead', 'Pusherman' and the title track he delivers devastating character analyses under a deceptively laid-back, soulful veneer.

Jimmy Page made his return to music in 1982 when he provided the soundtrack to Charles Bronson's second ultra-violent vigilante crime thriller. His guitar features prominently on 'Hypnotizing Ways (Oh Mamma)' and he gets a little funky on dirges 'The Chase' and 'Jam Sandwich'. Most of the other tracks on this rare album are made up of cold, eerie orchestral score pieces.

Isaac Hayes' 1971 Oscar-winning title ignited the whole blaxploitation genre and was a massive success for the legendary Stax record label. John Shaft – mean, lean and explosively charismatic – broke the mould in the genre and permanently altered Hollywood's portrayal of Afro-Americans. 'Theme From Shaft' throbbed with raw sexuality and omniscient cool, cocking up an even cooler one million sales and blueprinting wah-wah chic.

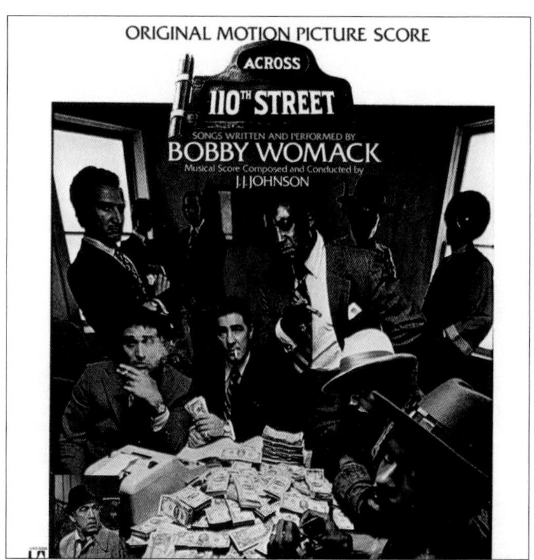

Bobby Womack's descent into his own drugs hell while working on Sly Stone's *There's A Riot Going On* (1972) makes this soundtrack's talk of junkies and pushers, living and dying, more than just idle ghetto speak. The title track ranks as one of the single most enduring pieces of blaxploitation music ever recorded and one of the best soul-funk singles ever released.

Tangerine Dream's soundtrack to Michael Mann's 1981 thriller merges pulsating electronic beats and piercing guitar work from start to finish. The 11-minute 'Diamond Diary' harked back to the Tangerine Dream of old that recorded mid-70s classics such as 'Phaedra', 'Rubycon' and 'Ricochet'.

Formed in Berlin in September 1967 by graphic designer Edgar Froese, Tangerine Dream have over 107 releases to their name, including studio albums, live recordings and soundtracks. Their pioneering use of synthesizers in their original 70s albums formed the basis for their international reputation, while their impact and influence on 80s cinema scores sealed it, bringing them to a much wider audience and providing a lucrative side business.

Nick Cave is one of the few talents of the post-punk generation who transcended the genre rather than stagnating. His sense of dark drama and poetic justice have served him well as a film composer, having contributed to *Ghosts . . . of the Civil Dead* (1988), for which he had written the screenplay, and latterly he has teamed up with fellow Bad Seed Warren Ellis to pen the scores to the anti-heroic western *The Proposition* (2007) and brooding *The Assassination of Jesse James by the Coward Robert Ford* (2007).

From smouldering Stax innovator to blaxploitation big gun, to unlikely *South Park* icon, Isaac Hayes has spun out his legendary career as stylishly as he's spun out countless cover versions. He combined atmosphere with hooks on his Grammy-winning soundtrack to *Shaft*, and more recently featured in the D.A. Pennebaker documentary *Only the Strong Survive* (2002).

Ry Cooder is one of American popular music's true renaissance men. A formidable talent for stringed instruments and an insatiably eclectic music taste have fuelled his outstanding soundtrack work, from Walter Hill's *The Long Riders* (1980) to *Primary Colors* (1998). Unfortunately, the OST to *Southern Comfort* (1981), one of his most famous works, is not available.

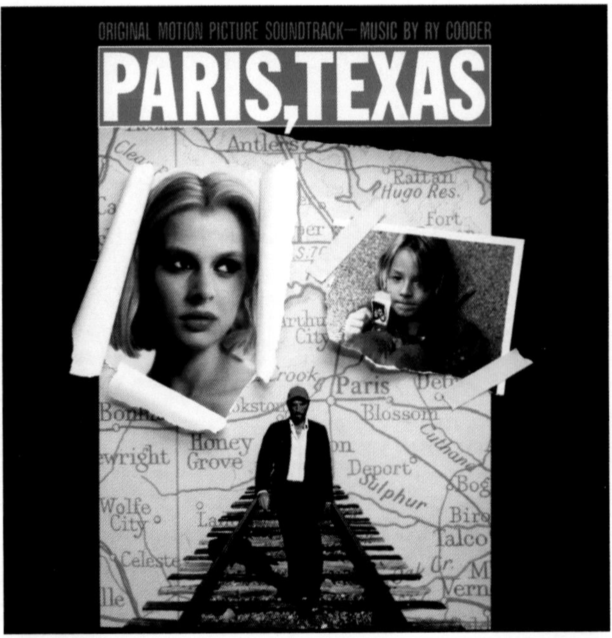

Wim Wenders' celebrated 1984 movie sees Harry Dean Stanton as Travis, the physically and emotionally lost lead character who stumbles out of the desert to confront his past. Ry Cooder's atmospheric score is the antithesis of 80s excess – a sparse, hallucinatory dialogue between him and his beloved slide guitar.

James Brown was one of the most influential artists in the evolution of popular music. He acted as a magnetic, hotwired conduit for the birth of Funk, reconnecting black and white music with its primal, polyrhythmic roots. His soundtrack to Larry Cohen's *Black Caesar* (1973) is one of the blaxploitation genre's most enduring and unfairly underrated documents.

Mark Knopfler is an atypically unassuming rock star who has sought rootsier terrain after the huge mid-80s success of Dire Straits. He is now an established film composer with a raft of successful soundtracks under his belt. He first moved into film with the *Local Hero* (1983) soundtrack, and distanced himself even further from his day job with conventional, orchestral scores such as *The Princess Bride* (1987), *Last Exit to Brooklyn* (1989) and more recently *Wag the Dog* (1997).

Curtis Mayfield's influence on the development of Soul, Funk, Hip-Hop and even Reggae is incalculable, and his back catalogue unimpeachable. His unadulterated falsetto, impeccable arrangements and elegant guitar playing found expression in the burgeoning blaxploitation genre, on soundtracks such as *Superfly* (1972), *Short Eyes* (1977) and *Piece of the Action* (1977).

Willie Hutch's songwriting talents figured in the vanguard of Motown's blaxploitation assault. He provided the classic soundtrack to Michael Campus' *The Mack* (1973), balancing the film's raw, uncut approach with Soul characterised by a lighter touch than the harder wah-wah funk of many blaxploitation scores. He followed up in similar style with the music for Jack Hill's iconic *Foxy Brown* (1974).

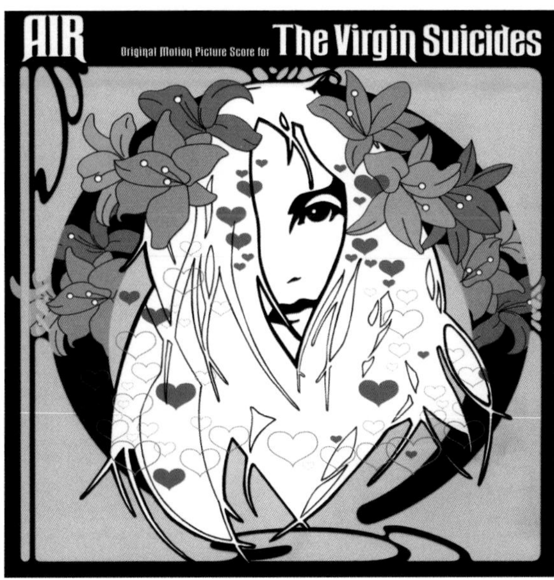

Gallic space-lounge duo Air provided the soundtrack to Sofia Coppola's 1999 directorial debut, a meta-comic tale of doomed youth. A group whose dolefully luxurious sound owes not a little to film scoring, they took their cues from the same primordial synth arsenal which made their *Moon Safari* (1998) set such an anachronistic triumph.

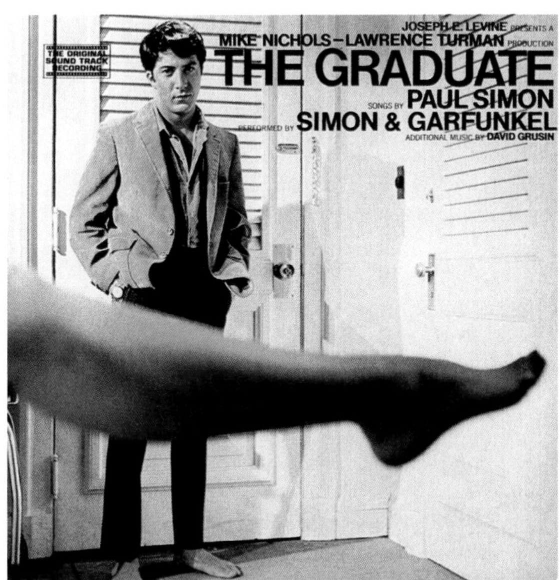

Mike Nichols' wry French New Wave-via-Hollywood take on intergenerational conflict and middle-class alienation featured one of the bestselling soundtracks of all time. Matchmaking previously released singles to onscreen action and marrying the bittersweet folk-pop of Simon & Garfunkel to Braddock's youthful ennui was a shrewd move that represented a seismic shift from traditional film scoring.

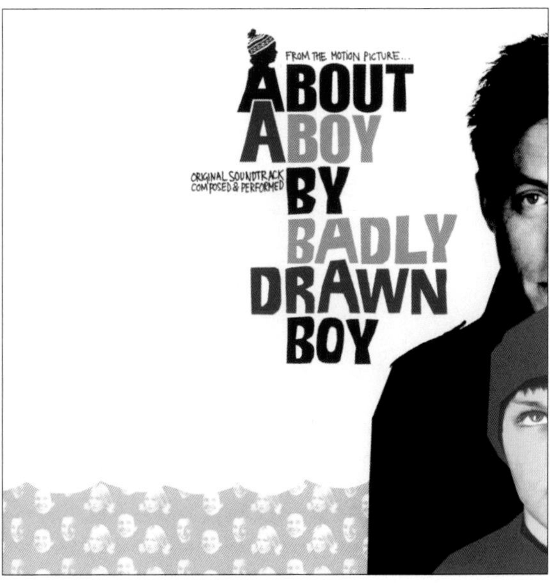

This 2002 adaptation of Nick Hornby's novel starred Hugh Grant as rich London playboy Will Freeman, pretending to be a single dad to pick up a girl. Badly Drawn Boy (aka Damon Gough) masterfully composed the full movie score as the unofficial follow-up to his acclaimed debut album. There is a roll-call of classic reference points and Funk and Jazz-influenced jams, which all point to Gough being a John Martyn for the Ikea generation.

Batman, Tim Burton's visionary 1989 re-imagining of the myth of the superhero, re-cast Bruce Wayne as a brooding anti-hero and saw Prince being given *carte blanche* to provide the movie's soundtrack, Danny Elfman's superb score withstanding. It's Prince's weakest album of the 80s, but given the bar-setting works which preceded it, its comic book funk spins an enjoyable web.

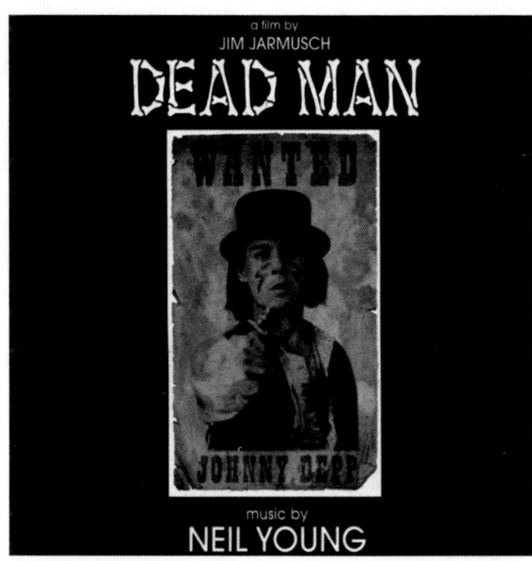

This monochrome, postmodern 1996 western directed by Jim Jarmusch follows Johnny Depp's William Blake, on the run with a bounty on his head. Neil Young begins this abstract experiment as he means to go on, scraping and sawing at his strings amid desolate, distorted flurries of electric guitar. Often barely recognisable as a Neil Young album, he creates a bleak, impressionistic canvas for Jarmusch's dark allegory.

Nick Cave wrote the screenplay to this 2005 Aussie western, directed by John Hillcoat, and he broke his decades-old film-scoring team to collaborate with Warren Ellis. A largely instrumental, dialogue-less score, Ellis' violin is the principal voice, chafing, droning and buzzing, and even Cave's vocals are terse and bleached. Certainly not a western score in the Morricone or Dylan vein, here the rhythm of life is not as powerful as the inevitability of betrayal and death.

On the cusp of global stadium-dom with their magnum opus, *The Dark Side Of The Moon*, Pink Floyd were unexpectedly roped in to provide another soundtrack for Barbet Schroeder, this time for *La Vallée* (1972). *Obscured By Clouds* is the final link in the band's occasionally messy transition from post-psychedelic pioneers to sleek prog-rock craftsmen. With the emphasis on songs rather than concepts and experiments, it is the most conventionally accessible album in the band's discography.

dub-meisters RENEGADE SOUNDWAVE, a record that marries the 'Pretty Vacant'-styled intro with a beatbox dub of Perry Como's 'It's Impossible'; it quite simply blows the stacks out. A close second also stems from Gary Asquith & Danny Briottet's RENEGADE SOUNDWAVE by way of Pil/Wobble-like, 'Women Respond To Bass', while NICK CAVE & THE BAD SEEDS shine out via 'Lament' (a track from 'The Good Son' album). The CAVE connection comes courtesy of some ex-Birthday Party members, CRIME & THE CITY SOLUTION, who contribute one melancholy, but exotic instrumental, 'Sun Before The Dawn'. If the Stooges or the 'Stones is one's bag, 'We Call It Rock' by Don Fleming's VELVET MONKEYS – from faux-soundtrack, 'Rake', with MASCIS in tow – might well see you through to the end. Meanwhile, 'Mute' records produce two more of their acts, the short-lived but well-named EASY via 'Cloud Chamber', and the imprint's ever-faithful industrialist, BOYD RICE, with a one-minute untitled cue; J MASCIS reprises his opening 'Untitled' (#1) to eclipse this infectious long-player. *MCS*

Album rating: *7.5

☐ Marvin GAYE segment (⇒ TROUBLE MAN)

☐ Ron GEESIN segment (⇒ the BODY)

☐ GEHEIMCODE: WILDGANSE alt. (⇒ CODENAME: WILDGEESE)

GERONIMO: AN AMERICAN LEGEND

1993 (US 115m) Columbia Pictures (PG-13)

Film genre: revisionist western biopic

Top guns: dir: Walter Hill ← TRESPASS ← JOHNNY HANDSOME ← CROSSROADS ← STREETS OF FIRE ← the LONG RIDERS / → LAST MAN STANDING / s-w: John Milius (+ story), Larry Gross ← STREETS OF FIRE

Stars: Wes Studi *(Geronimo)* ← the DOORS, Gene Hackman *(Brig. Gen. George Crook)*, Jason Patric *(Lt. Charles Gatewood)* ← RUSH, Robert Duvall *(Al Sieber)* ← TENDER MERCIES / → a SHOT AT GLORY, Matt Damon *(2nd Lt. Britton Davis)* → GOOD WILL HUNTING → ALL THE PRETTY HORSES → SPIRIT: STALLION OF THE CIMARRON, Rodney A. Grant *(Mangas)* ← the DOORS, Kevin Tighe *(Brig. Gen. Nelson Miles)* ← ROAD HOUSE, Steve Reevis *(Chato)* ← the DOORS, Stephen McHattie *(Schoonover)* ← BEST REVENGE, Scott Wilson *(Rodondo)* ← ELVIS AND THE COLONEL: THE UNTOLD STORY ← YOUNG GUNS II ← JOHNNY HANDSOME ← BLUE CITY / → SOUL SURVIVOR → DEAD MAN WALKING → SOUTH OF HEAVEN, WEST OF HELL → DON'T LET GO → MONSTER

Storyline: Charles Gatewood is the young cavalry officer ordered to track down and capture Geronimo, an escaped Chiricahua Apache leader who famously succeeds in outwitting a whole army with only a small band of fearless warriors. *BG*

Movie rating: *6

Visual: video + dvd

Off the record: (see below)

—

RY COODER

Apr 94. (cd/c) *Columbia; <CK/CT 57760> (475654-2/-4)* ☐ Jan94 ☐
– Geronimo: main title / Restoration / Goyakla is coming / Bound for Canaan (Sieber & Davis) (the 6th Cavalry) / Cibecue / The governor's ball: Get off the track – Danza – Battle cry of freedom / Wayfaring stranger / Judgement day / Bound for Canaan (Sieber & Davis) / Embudos / Sand fight / Army brass band: The young recruit – The girl I left behind me – Come come away / Yaqui village / I have seen my power / La vista / Davis / Train to Florida.

S/track review: Another fairly experimental score by RY COODER's standards and, being recorded the same year as his groundbreaking blues-via-the-Ganges link-up with V.M. Bhatt ('A Meeting By The River'), another pointer towards future world music explorations. Fittingly then, Tuvan throat singing maestros HUUN-HUUR-TU make one of their earliest appearances on record outside of their native land, intoning their strange, gutteral utterances over a fair chunk of the music – including the title theme – and adding to what would become a bulging CV of high profile global collaborations on both their own and COODER's part. 'Restoration' begins with some striking guitar/bouzouki arrangements, haunting chamber-folk of the highest order. Veteran COODER associate Van Dyke Parks takes centre stage on 'The Governor's Ball', a triptych of graceful, waltz-ish orchestrations – among which longtime COODER fans will also recognise a reprise of 'Rally Round The Flag' from 1980s 'The LONG RIDERS' – arranged with Parks' usual wit, panache and eccentricity, and a welcome respite from the dark atmospherics swirling around the rest of the score. Atmospherics which roam through Irish tin whistle, bouzouki, accordion and flute arrangements, as well as such obscure instrumentation as I-beam, cymbalum and tombak, in a score which can often seem slightly fractured. On the sleeve, director Walter Hill cites his desire to "valorise" two very different cultures through music; does COODER succeed? The answer is yes, probably, although divorced from the film, the juxtaposition of good-old-boy-marches/fanfares and disembodied dirges – and even a pretty, and glaringly out of place Spanish guitar solo – isn't often the easiest of listening. *BG*

Album rating: *7

Lisa GERRARD

Born: 12 Apr'61, Melbourne, Australia. As one half of Dead Can Dance alongside Brendan Perry, LISA GERRARD created some of the more esoteric 80s offerings from cult indie label, '4 a.d.'. Certainly esoteric enough to make her one of the most unlikely figures to move into Hollywood film scoring. With DCD she'd already scored 'El Niño De La Luna' (1989), the sophomore feature of noted Spanish director Augustín Villaronga and a film in which she also made her acting debut (appropriately enough, given DCD's über-Goth reputation, as a paranormal researcher). Although the group also contributed to the score of 'Baraka' (1992), Ron Fricke's psycho-global follow-up to 'Koyaanisqatsi' (1983), it was her creative partnership with Australian composer PIETER BOURKE (also of DCD fame) which set her on the road to Hollywood. In 1994, DEAD CAN DANCE released a concert film, 'TOWARD THE WITHIN', complete with interviews by GERRARD and Perry. While touring their 'Duality' (1998) album in the States, the pair were approached by director Michael Mann, who'd already licensed a couple of GERRARD's songs (from her mid-90s solo debut 'The Mirror Pool'), for the soundtrack to his Robert De Niro/Al Pacino head to head, 'Heat' (1995). The end result was a compelling combination of BOURKE's roiling, percussive ethnicisms and GERRARD's cerebral, ecstatic rumination, a soundtrack which illuminated Mann's Oscar-nominated expose, 'The INSIDER' (1999), in ways which even its authors mightn't have anticipated. Hans Zimmer was impressed enough to lure GERRARD into his high flying Media Ventures fold for work on Ridley Scott's Roman epic, 'Gladiator' (2000). Their collaborative efforts were enough to earn an Oscar nomination with GERRARD providing the haunting celestial yin to Zimmer's clamorous, Holst-inspired yang. Mann subsequently hired the GERRARD/BOURKE team for the score to his boxing biopic, 'Ali' (2001), and while only a fraction of their score made it on to the R&B weighted soundtrack, a second score-only disc filled out the missing pieces with some evocative ethno-ambience and dark kinetics alongside contributions from Malian superstar Salif Keita. While she continued to work with Zimmer on the likes of 'Black Hawk Down' (2001) and 'Tears Of The Sun' (2002), she finally struck out on her own with the hit Kiwi feature, 'WHALE RIDER' (2002), furnishing a soundtrack of typically ethereal, sub-aquatic sonic osmosis while keeping her trademark vocal ululations to a minimum. Fans of her gothic conjuring found more to savour in the most recent TV adaptation of Stephen King's 'Salem's Lot' (2004), a soundtrack which found her collaborating with Irish classical composer Patrick Cassidy (with whom she'd previously worked on the acclaimed '4 a.d.' album, 'Immortal Memory') on the title track aria and with composer Christopher Gordon on the main theme and much of the underscore. While GERRARD subsequently collaborated with another Media Ventures alumnus, Ilan Eshkeri, on the score to Guy Ritchie associate Matthew Vaughan's nu-gangster debut, 'Layer Cake' (2004), only a couple of cues made it to the 80s-centric soundtrack. This wasn't the case for short people-documentary 'A Thousand Roads' (2005), for which she was credited with the whole score alongside Jeff Rona, commissioned as they were by the Smithsonian Institute. 'Silver Tree' in 2006 was her most recent non-soundtrack release, albeit only available down under. *BG*

- **filmography** (composer) {acting} –

el Niño De La Luna *(1989 {*} w/ DEAD CAN DANCE)* / Baraka *(1993 w/ DEAD CAN DANCE on OST by Michael Stearns)* / **Toward The Within** *(1994 {p} OST by DEAD CAN DANCE =>)* / Nevada *(1997 w/ DEAD CAN DANCE)* / Nadro *(1998 w/ PIETER BOURKE)* / **the Insider** *(1999 OST w/ PIETER BOURKE =>)* / Gladiator *(2000 OST w/ Hans Zimmer; see future edition)* / Ali *(2001 OST w/ PIETER BOURKE + w/ V/A; see future edition)* / **Whale Rider** *(2002 OST =>)* / Salem's Lot *(2004 on OST by Christopher Gordon)* / Layer Cake *(2004 OST w/ Ilan Eshkeri & V/A =>)* / a Thousand Roads *(2005 OST w/ Jeff Rona; see future edition)*

GHOST DANCE

1983 (W.Ger/UK 96m w/b&w) Zweites Deutsches / Channel 4 (15)

Film genre: paranormal comedy/drama

Top guns: s-w + dir: Ken McMullen

Stars: Pascale Ogier *(Pascale)*, Leonie Mellinger *(Marianne)*, Robbie Coltrane *(George)* ← SUBWAY RIDERS ← FLASH GORDON / → ABSOLUTE BEGINNERS → EAT THE RICH → TUTTI FRUTTI, Dominique Pinon *(salesman/guide)*, Stuart Brisley *(action on water)*, Jacques Derrida *(himself)*, Ken McMullen *(voice of man)*

Storyline: Leonie and Pascale travel from London to Paris as they search for answers to matters of the mind. What is it that makes us who we are and what we think today? Deep in the psyche, what are the influences which shape our daily lives? People, places and ideas are discussed and philosopher Jacques Derrida gives his de-constructionist point of view in a film that is not for the cerebrally-challenged. *JZ*

Movie rating: *3

Visual: none

Off the record: **MICHAEL GILES**, etc. (see below)

—

MICHAEL GILES / JAMIE MUIR / DAVID CUNNINGHAM

Mar 96. (cd) *Piano; (PIANO 502)* ☐ ☐
– Ghost dance / Scratching the curve / Spillers village / Cascade / Screenwash / Mouthwork / Snake dance / The moving cymbal / Metalwork / Slow motion / Cargo / Pascale / Blue dance / Ghost Dance reprise / The trial.

S/track review: Recorded between 3rd & 6th of May, 1983, this was left on the proverbial shelf for a dozen years or so. The 'GHOST DANCE' OST featured two former King Crimson musicians MICHAEL GILES (on drums, assorted percussion, etc.) and JAMIE MUIR (assorted percussion, hand drums, etc.) plus a Flying Lizard, DAVID CUNNINGHAM (loops treatment, guitar & occasional percussion). GILES was an original member of Fripp's revolving-door outfit until late '69 (on one LP, 'In The Court Of The Crimson King'), while MUIR played on another Crimson classic, 'Larks' Tongues In Aspic' (1972); CUNNINGHAM, meanwhile, released a solo set before hitting the UK Top 5 in 1980 via an electro-monotone cover of 'Money' with the aforementioned Lizards. Experimental and improvised (much like the film itself), 'GHOST DANCE' commences with the title piece, an instrumental cue complete with thumb piano and kazoo. If listening to leaky pipes drip on garbage cans is one's cup of char, 'Scratching The Curve' will have one in musical heaven – but it's pure nausea. 'Spillers Village' is 7-plus minutes of eerie percussion, while 'Screenwash' is as close to "Frippertronics" as anything the bearded one managed to achieve in his late 70s/early 80s League Of Gentlemen period. Skipping through some extreme avant-garde machinations (the self-explanatory 'Metal Work' leads the way), there are little or no redeeming features in this 55-minute score, save for the 2-minute 'Pascale'. Closing number, 'The Trial', recalls a Chinese torture chamber; messrs. GILES, MUIR and CUNNINGHAM should undergo both experiences forthwith. *MCS*

Album rating: *1

GHOST DOG: THE WAY OF THE SAMURAI

1999 (Fra/Ger/US/Japan 116m) Bac Films / Filmcoopi / Canal+ (R)

Film genre: gangster/crime/martial arts drama

Top guns: s-w + dir: Jim Jarmusch ← YEAR OF THE HORSE ← DEAD MAN ← NIGHT ON EARTH ← MYSTERY TRAIN ← DOWN BY LAW / → COFFEE AND CIGARETTES

Stars: Forest Whitaker *(Ghost Dog)* ← JOHNNY HANDSOME ← GOOD MORNING, VIETNAM / → a LITTLE TRIP TO HEAVEN, John Tormey *(Louie)*, Cliff Gorman *(Sonny Valerio)*, Henry Silva *(Ray Vargo)* ← the END OF VIOLENCE ← DICK TRACY ← MAN AND BOY, Isaach de Bankole *(Raymond)* ← NIGHT ON EARTH / → COFFEE AND CIGARETTES, Tricia Vessey *(Louise Vargo)* → TROUBLE EVERY DAY, Frank Minucci *(Big Angie)*, Gene Ruffini *(old consigliere)*, Richard Portnow *(Handsome Frank)* ← FEAR AND LOATHING IN LAS VEGAS ← PRIVATE PARTS ← S.F.W. ← GOOD MORNING, VIETNAM ← ROADIE, Victor Argo *(Vinny)* ← the LAST TEMPTATION OF CHRIST ← the ROSE / → COYOTE UGLY, Gary Farmer *(nobody)* ← DEAD MAN, Damon Whitaker *(young Ghost Dog)*, Camille Winbush *(Pearline)*, Vinnie Vella *(Sammy the Snake)* → COFFEE AND CIGARETTES, Joe Rigano *(Joe Rags)* ← HEY, LET'S TWIST / → COFFEE AND CIGARETTES, Harry Shearer *(voice of Scratchy)* ← WAYNE'S WORLD 2 ← THIS IS SPINAL TAP ← ONE-TRICK PONY ← ANIMALYMPICS / → GIGANTIC (A TALE OF TWO JOHNS) → a MIGHTY WIND, Gano Grills *(gangsta in red)*, **the RZA** *(samurai in camouflage)* ← RHYME & REASON / → COFFEE AND CIGARETTES → BE COOL

Storyline: The hulking figure known only as Ghost Dog lives among his beloved carrier pigeons in a solitary rooftop retreat. When he's not reading or contemplating Bushido philosophy, he's out pulling off hits for his "retainer", a small time mobster named Louie. After unwittingly picking off his latest victim in the presence of Louie's boss's daughter, he's suddenly surplus to requirements, even if the comical hoods haven't reckoned with his medieval conception of communications technology. *BG*

Movie rating: *7

Visual: dvd

Off the record: RZA (see below)

RZA (w/ others incl. WU-TANG CLAN *)

Dec 99. (cd) *Victor; <VICP 60944>* [–] Japan [–]
– Ghost Dog theme (WITH DOGS & EFX) / Opening theme (raise your sword) instrumental / Flying birds / Samurai theme / Gangsters theme / Dead birds / Fast shadow – version 1 (*) / RZA #7 / Funky theme / RZA's theme / Samurai showdown (raise your sword) / Ghost Dog theme / Fast shadow – version 2 (*) / Untitled #8 *[not in film]* / Untitled #12 – free jazz *[not in film]* / Wu-world order – version 1 (*) *[not in film]. <re-iss. Nov01 on 'J.V.C.'; 81047>*

S/track review: It's just not fair: not only do the Japanese have all the best re-issues, they often get the hottest soundtracks as well. While the British and American markets had to make do with an inferior "inspired by" job, the land of expensive Tennent's lager released RZA's score in full. And what a score; if you're all blinged-out, or even if – like the inimitable Sonny Valerio – your appreciation of hip hop begins and ends with Public Enemy, this is sweet pigeon-feed for the soul. Pre-'KILL BILL' and hardly as unhinged as his allegedly angel-dust-inspired Bobby Digital debut, 'GHOST DOG: THE WAY OF THE SAMURAI' is instead a series of murky, Loch Ness-deep meditations and funky haikus. Throughout, RZA proves himself an endlessly adroit conjuror of mood, reconfiguring hip hop (and belatedly realising the promise of trip-hop) as a valid, hyperreal alternative to orchestral scoring, just as Johnny Mandel and Duke Ellington did with jazz back in the late 50s. And if there was a more haunting pre-millennial blues than the main theme, this reviewer has yet to hear it. Think DJ Shadow's 'Dark Days' meets Money Mark, a requiem for a century of broken dreams, rendered from ancient jazz, steel mill noise pollution and a woebegone keyboard loop. To these recurrent ingredients, the Shaolin-disposed scientist adds every secret weapon in his manuscript: Asiatic percussion, dungeon-esque strings, vintage blaxploitation (the mesmeric 'Funky Theme' reimagines Willie Hutch on mogodon), short-circuit electronica and beats as sharp and clean as a Samurai's blade (check the loop on 'RZA #7'). And it's not just Wu-Tang diehards who'll appreciate the distorted, freestyle aggro of 'Fast Shadow', as wild an epitaph for Ol' Dirty Bastard as we're likely to get. One of the soundtracks of the 90s and the beginning of a great film-scoring adventure. *BG*

Album rating: *8.5

Various Artists (score: RZA *) (dialogue: Forest Whitaker **)

Apr 00. (cd) *Epic; <EK 63794> (496146-2)* [84] [ ]
– Samurai code quote (**) / Strange eyes (SUNZ OF MAN) / 4 sho sho (NORTH STAR) / Zip code (BLACK NIGHTS) / Samurai code quote (**) / Cakes (KOOL G RAP & *) / Samurai code quote (**) / Don't test – Wu stallion (BANG GANG) / Walking through the darkness (TEKITHA) / The man (MASTA KILLAH & SUPERB) / Samurai code quote (**) / Walk the dogs (ROYAL FARM) / Stay with me (MELODIE & 12 O'CLOCK) / East New York stamp (JERU THE DAMAJA & AFU RA) / Samurai code quote (**) / Fast shadow (WU-TANG CLAN) / Samurai code quote (**) / Samurai showdown (*) / Samurai code quote (**).

S/track review: This domestic version of the soundtrack is basically an excuse for RZA to flex his production muscle on various Wu Tang affiliates, a kind of proxy Wu-Tang Killa Bees: 'The Swarm Volume 2'. An inspired-by job bolstered by dialogue and score pieces diluted with vocals for popular consumption, it's hardly, strictly speaking, a soundtrack at all, but with RZA's steadfast hand at the pump, "this is not just rock'n'roll". The only overt overlaps with the score CD are 'Samurai Showdown' and 'Fast Shadow', but with the help of SUNZ OF MAN, 12 O'CLOCK and BLUE RASPBERRY, the score's 'Funky Theme' becomes 'Strange Eyes', a weed-neurotic inversion of Rockwell's 80s paranoid anthem, 'Somebody's Watching Me'. The biggest non-Wu name is KOOL G RAP, who presides over one of two non-score standouts, 'Cakes'. Both this and 'Walking Through The Darkness' take their cues from vintage funk, the latter featuring longtime Clan crooner TEKITHA cooing over the looped intro to Bobby Womack classic, 'Across 110th Street' (with cute film dialogue for extra cheesiness). It's obvious but effective, and more of the same might've made a great album, maybe even a great imaginary soundtrack. As it is, this collection all but fails to sail into the movie's post-modern mystic. *BG*

Album rating: *5.5

GHOSTS … OF THE CIVIL DEAD

1988 (Aus 93m) Outlaw Values / Electric Pictures (18)

Film genre: crime/prison drama

Top guns: s-w: John Hillcoat (+ dir) → TO HAVE AND TO HOLD → the PROPOSITION, **Nick CAVE**, Evan English, Gene Conkie, **Hugo Race**

Stars: David Field *(Wenzil)* → TO HAVE AND TO HOLD → CHOPPER → ONE NIGHT THE MOON → SILENT PARTNER, Mike Bishop *(David Hale)*, Chris DeRose *(Jack Grezner)*, Kevin Mackey *(Glover)*, Dave Mason *(Lilly)*, **Nick CAVE** *(Maynard)*, Vincent Gil *(Ruben)*, Ian Mortimer *(Jack)*, **Mick HARVEY, Blixa Bargeld**

Storyline: Based on the revelations of former high security prison guard David Hale, Hillcoat's grim tale centres on a brutal, hi-tech correctional facility in the wastes of the Australian outback where the prison's highest authorities are implicated in an extended outbreak of violence. *BG*

Movie rating: *6.5

Off the record: Hugo Race was also of the Bad Seeds.

NICK CAVE, MICK HARVEY, BLIXA BARGELD

Mar 89. (cd/c/lp) *Ionic; (CD/C+/IONIC 3) Restless; <71433>* [ ] [ ]
– The news (voice: Michelle Babbit) / Introduction – A prison in the desert / David Hale – I've been a prison guard since I was 18 years old / Glover – I was 16 when they put me in prison / David Hale – You're danglin' us like a bunch of meat on a hook / Pop mix / Glover – We were united once / David Hale – The day of the murders / Lilly's theme ("a touch of warmth") / Maynard mix / David Hale – What I'm tellin' is the truth / Outro – The free world / Glover – One man released so they can imprison the rest of the world.

S/track review: Not for the faint hearted, the first full soundtrack from the compositional triumvirate of NICK CAVE, BLIXA BARGELD and MICK HARVEY is basically a string of violent, blood splattered spoken-word narratives and grisly revelations tenuously held together by bellows-like industrial reverb, bleak, high-pitched whistle and horror film strings. The running time may be only just over half an hour but if you're not in the mood, it can – forgive the pun – feel like a life sentence. The only light relief, in fact, is provided by 'Lily's Theme', a lilting, Astrud Gilberto-like bossa groove understatedly subtitled 'A Touch Of Warmth' and gloriously, crazily out of context. Elsewhere the chill is palpable and constant, seeping through the speakers. The predictably disembodied female vocals might have been of the happy psycho variety more usually heard prior to a gleeful, b-movie killing spree, but CAVE and Co's triumph was in creating the kind of unrelentingly portentous yet relatively subtle musical climate in which the graphic vignettes are able to take on the full, horrific weight of their implications. Haunting in all the wrong ways, inmate Kevin Mackey's quiet spoken attempts to analyze both his own condition and the authorities' wider agenda leave the deepest impression, lingering long after his parting shot – 'One Man Released So They Can Imprison The Rest Of The World' – fades into dissonance. *BG*

Album rating: *5.5

□ Michael GILES / Jamie MUIR / David CUNNINGHAM (⇒ GHOST DANCE)

GINGER ALE AFTERNOON

1989 (US 88m) NeoPictures / Skouras Pictures (R)

Film genre: romantic/domestic comedy

Top guns: dir: Rafal Zielinski / s-w: Gina Wendkos (+ play) → COYOTE UGLY

Stars: Dana Anderson *(Jesse Mickers)*, John M. Jackson *(Hank Mickers)* ← DEAD SOLID PERFECT ← LOCAL HERO / SID & NANCY ← LOCAL HERO, Yeardley Smith *(Bonnie)* ← MAXIMUM OVERDRIVE, Gene Butler *(radio DJ)*

Storyline: Nine months pregnant, "trailer-trash" Jesse finds out her layabout hubby, Hank, is been having it away with their young neighbour, Bonnie. When Jesse's labour begins, it's not the absent Hank who she turns to, but Bonnie, who's becomes her loyal friend. *MCS*

Movie rating: *3.5

Visual: video

Off the record: WILLIE DIXON (b. 1st July 1915, Vicksburg, Missouri, USA). The author of many of the most indelible urban blues songs – including the likes of 'Little Red Rooster', 'Back Door Man' and 'Spoonful' – and a pivotal figure in their dissemination as in-house overseer at 'Chess' records, WILLIE DIXON is a man whose towering influence on rock can be easily gauged by the number and pedigree of British bands for whom DIXON songs became a central part of their repertoire. Not least LED ZEPPELIN who were involved in two separate cases of alleged infringement, for both 'Bring It On Home' and 'Whole Lotta Love'. While his own recording career failed to match his achievements as a songwriter, DIXON's elder statesman of the blues stature saw him belatedly involved in cinema, recruited by the BAND alumnus ROBBIE ROBERTSON for his soundtrack to Oscar-winning Paul Newman sequel, 'The Color Of Money' (1986). This was followed by a soundtrack in his own right, 'GINGER ALE AFTERNOON', as well as a production credit for Bo Diddley's 'Who Do You Love' on the soundtrack to Richie Valens biopic, 'LA BAMBA'. Prior to his death on the 29th of January 1992, DIXON lost a leg to diabetes; he also made a handful of cameo screen appearances (usually as himself) in such minor fare as 'Night Of The Warrior' and 'Raw Justice'. *BG*

—

WILLIE DIXON

Oct 89. (lp/c/cd) *Varese Sarabande; <(VS/+C/CD 5234)>* □ □
– Miseries of memories / Wigglin' worm / I don't trust nobody / Earthquake and hurricane / The real thing / Move me, baby / Save my child (pt.1) / I just want to make love to you / Sittin' and cryin' the blues / Save my child (pt.2) / Shakin' the shake / That's my baby / Ginger ale blues / Save my child (pt.3) / Good understanding.

S/track review: As stated above, WILLIE DIXON, was a long-standing bluesman, highly regarded among his peers, although this haunting blues score – in more ways than one! – stretched even his most loyal following. Kicking off with 'Miseries Of Memories' probably didn't help matters, DIXON (accompanied by a soul-less harmonica) coming across like a languid version of 'Summertime'. Out of time by a good few decades or so, WILLIE's dance-craze song just didn't cut the ice – we'd had the twist, 'The SHAG' (or at least in the 1989 dance-craze movie), so why would we need to do the 'Wigglin' Worm', or did that come after the aforementioned dance. Whoever said DIXON could sing might just've been the most patronising bar steward ever. If you doubt one's critique sample 'I Don't Trust Nobody', a Dylan-esque type of chooglin', but without Zimmerman's unmistakable aura. Ditto 'That's My Baby'. Maybe I'm unfair to poke a little fun at a legendary bluesman, but at 74 he should've been thinking on the lines of retirement not experimenting with film soundtracks. Blues albums were comparable to British Rail trains, long-awaited and always too late to be taken seriously, BROWNIE McGHEE & SONNY TERRY's blaxploitation OST, 'BOOK OF NUMBERS' a prime example. DIXON's choice cuts came via 'The Real Thing', a real nu-blues number complete with his intricate lead guitar work. For me there's too much sad harmonica for one sitting, although DIXON's at his best when he narrates/recites (not sings!) part one of 'Save My Child'. Sporadically jazzy, the man reprises old chestnut 'I Just Want To Make Love To You' (for the film's love triangle theme), and takes much needed female accompaniment for closing track, 'Good Understanding'. 'GINGER ALE . . .' might not be to your taste, but at times it does have a bit of flavour. *MCS*

Album rating: *4

GIRL 6

1996 (US 107m) Fox Searchlight Pictures (R)

Film genre: psychological/seXual workplace comedy/drama

Top guns: dir: Spike Lee as below + → HE GOT GAME / s-w: Suzan-Lori Parks

Stars: Theresa Randle *(Judy; Girl 6)* ← CB4: THE MOVIE ← JUNGLE FEVER ← the FIVE HEARTBEATS, Isaiah Washington *(shoplifter)*, Spike Lee *(Jimmy)* ← CROOKLYN ← JUNGLE FEVER ← SCHOOL DAZE, Jenifer Lewis *(Lil; boss #1)* ← SHAKE, RATTLE & ROCK! tv ← WHAT'S LOVE GOT TO DO WITH IT ← BEACHES / → the PREACHER'S WIFE → the TEMPTATIONS → JACKIE'S BACK! → LITTLE RICHARD, Debi Mazar *(Girl #39)* ← EMPIRE RECORDS ← SINGLES ← JUNGLE FEVER ← the DOORS ← DOWNTOWN 81 / → the INSIDER → BE COOL, Peter Berg *(Bob; caller #1)* → DILL SCALLION, Joseph Lyle Taylor *(caller #3 / caller #16)* → HE GOT GAME, Michael Imperioli *(scary caller #30)* ← I SHOT ANDY WARHOL ← the BASKETBALL DIARIES ← JUNGLE FEVER / → LAST MAN STANDING → DISAPPEARING ACTS, Quentin Tarantino *(Q.T.; boss #1)* ← FROM DUSK TILL DAWN ← FOUR ROOMS ← PULP FICTION ← RESERVOIR DOGS ← EDDIE PRESLEY, **MADONNA** *(boss #3)*, John Turturro *(Murray the agent)* ← JUNGLE FEVER ← TO LIVE AND DIE IN L.A. / → GRACE OF MY HEART → HE GOT GAME → O BROTHER, WHERE ART THOU?, Thomas Byrd III *(caller #18)* → HE GOT GAME → RAY, **Coati Mundi** *(Martin; caller #8)* <= KID CREOLE & THE COCONUTS =>, Naomi Campbell *(Girl #75)* ← COOL AS ICE, Joie Susannah Lee *(switchboard operator)* ← CROOKLYN ← SCHOOL DAZE / → COFFEE AND CIGARETTES, Billie Neal *(Angela's mother)* ← DOWN BY LAW, John Cameron Mitchell *(Rob)* → HEDWIG AND THE ANGRY INCH, Leonard L. Thomas *(co-agent)* ← SCHOOL DAZE, Halle Berry *(herself)* ← CB4: THE MOVIE ← JUNGLE FEVER / → WHY DO FOOLS FALL IN LOVE → SWORDFISH, Mekhi Phifer *(himself)* → CARMEN: A HIP HOPERA → 8 MILE → HONEY, Gretchen Mol *(girl '12)* → FINDING GRACELAND, Novella Nelson *(Angela's aunt)* → MANNY & LO

Storyline: Theresa Randall is a would-be actress who at last gets an audition with director QT. Upset at the way she's treated, she walks out and gets a job as a phone-sex operator. At least here her boss is nice to her, but soon she becomes overly engrossed in her work and begins seeing Bob, one of her phone clients. Only Theresa's well-meaning neighbour Jimmy and her ex-fiancee seem to bring her back to the real world. *JZ*

Movie rating: *5.5

Visual: video + dvd

Off the record: Supermodel Naomi Campbell had a one-off solo hit (No.40) in UK 1994 with 'Love And Tears'.

—

PRINCE

Mar 96. (cd/c) *Paisley Park; <(9362 46239-2/-4)>* [75] [ ]
– She spoke to me / Pink cashmere / I count the days (the NEW POWER GENERATION) / Girls & boys / Streams of passion (the FAMILY) / Nasty girl (VANITY 6) / Erotic city / Hot thing / Adore / The cross / How come you don't call me anymore / Don't talk to strangers / Girl 6 (the NEW POWER GENERATION).

S/track review: The ever creative squiggle, The Artist Formerly Known As . . . PRINCE, has tinkered with as many musical hats as he has invented monikers throughout his career. 'GIRL 6', his fifth soundtrack after 'PURPLE RAIN' (1984), 'UNDER THE CHERRY MOON' (1986), 'BATMAN' (1989) and 'GRAFFITI BRIDGE' (1990), encompasses many of these styles. However, rather than creating a rich piece of work, 'GIRL 6' falls slightly flat with just a few flashes of brilliance. Recorded between the success of 'The Gold Experience' and his rather less well received 14th studio album 'Chaos and Disorder', this is a hash bash of tracks by PRINCE, the NEW POWER GENERATION and VANITY SIX. 'She Spoke To Me' is sweet as sugar jazz-influenced R&B recorded with the NEW POWER GENERATION and perfectly enjoyable it is; however, the problem is that it's just that. Similarly 'Pink Cashmere' is a slow and sultry contemporary ballad, which touches on what makes PRINCE reign (his glass-breaking high pitched vocals and funk sleaze) but it doesn't quite hit the mark. 'Count the Days', a harmonised gospel ballad featuring the NEW POWER GENERATION, suffers from the same tiresome US radio friendly AOR sound. However, PRINCE picks up the phallic mantle and redeems himself for 'Girls And Boys'. Sexy, funky and naughty with the sleaziest trumpets and a dash of French lyrics, lock up your daughter mama as PRINCE is cavorting at the microphone more heartily than a pole dancer. On 'Erotic City' too, he is on form with double entendres and racy metaphorical lyrics (creamy thighs?!) teamed with a drum machine beat and electronic slides and bleeps reminiscent of his 'Alphabet Street' era sound. Much like this is 'Hot Thing' with wild saxophone solos running in all directions and a thumping drum machine though his throne slips slightly on VANITY SIX's 'Nasty Girl', a middling danceable track, which is pure 80s throwback synth pop. If there's one thing you can't fault in PRINCE it's his eclecticism and willingness to experiment with a range of styles. Title track 'Girl 6' is a beautiful example of this. More modern and experimental, there are layers of scratching; light beat boxing and sampling lifted from the movie. 'The Cross' proves that songs do not have to be complex and that PRINCE can do ballads well. A single beat of a drum and elements of Egyptian guitar combine with emotional lyrics which build into a rocking crescendo. Despite his most valiant of efforts, this album failed to be his crowning glory. *SM*

Album rating: *6

GIRLS

1980 (Fra/Can/W.Ger 95m) Les Films Caneuram (X)

Film genre: coming-of-age seXual teen drama

Top guns: s-w: (+ dir) Just Jaeckin ← MADAME CLAUDE, Jean-Luc Voulfow

Stars: Anne Parillaud *(Catherine Flavin)*, Zoé Chauveau *(Annie)*, Charlotte Walior *(Suzanne)*, Isabelle Mejias *(Betty)*, Georg Burki *(Peter)*, Christophe Bourseiller *(Bernard)*, Philippe Klébert *(Jérôme)*

Storyline: Annie, Catherine and Suzanne at last say cheerio to High School and immediately go clubbing every night to celebrate. Boyfriends come and go like the tides, and the impressionable Betty, Suzanne's young sister, soon joins in the fun and gets a boyfriend of her own. Of course there's a price to be paid for all this tomfoolery and our questionable quartet soon begin to realize the relevance of "family planning". *JZ*

Movie rating: *4.5

Visual: none

Off the record: **ERIC STEWART** (b.20 Jan'45, Droylsden, Gt. Manchester, England) was a singer/guitarist with a couple of hit 60s pop acts (the Mindbenders and Hotlegs) long before his fruitful period with 70s art-rock supergroup, 10cc. A developing songwriter with the aforementioned British Invasion group Wayne Fontana & The Mindbenders, he left said band in 1968 to pursue other projects; he moonlighted with the embryonic Mandalaband. The following year, after co-investing in studios with Peter Tattersall and former Mindbenders songwriter, GRAHAM GOULDMAN, Eric formed the session trio, Hotlegs, alongside Kevin Godley and Lol Creme. However, their tenure was short-lived after they hit No.2 in 1970 with bubblegum/novelty record, 'Neanderthal Man'. In 1972, now trading as 10cc, the trio added the aforementioned GOULDMAN, signing to Jonathan King's newly formed 'UK' imprint in the process; STEWART also worked with Neil Sedaka around this time. The revamped quartet subsequently became a massive-selling outfit, making the Top 3 with the pastiche-like 'Donna' while the follow-up, 'Rubber Bullets', topped the charts. The group amassed an impressive series of hits during the 70s, including 'The Dean And I', 'Wall Street Shuffle' and 'Life Is A Minestrone', although they reached their pinnacle in 1975 (after signing to 'Mercury' records) by way of 'I'm Not In Love', a classy, sophisticated pop ballad lifted from their top selling album, 'The Original Soundtrack'. Further chart success came with 'Art For Art's Sake' and 'I'm Mandy, Fly Me', although Godley & Creme departed after the release of the accompanying 'How Dare You' (1976) set. Meanwhile, ERIC STEWART and GRAHAM GOULDMAN added Tony O'Malley, Rick Fenn and Stuart Tosh, scoring further hits with 'The Things We Do For Love', 'Good Morning Judge' and the woeful cod-reggae tune of 'Dreadlock Holiday' (their third UK No.1); needless to say, most of the spark had vanished by the time Eric released the soundtrack to the 1980 movie, 'GIRLS'. *MCS*

—

ERIC STEWART

Apr 80. (lp/c) *Polydor; (POLD/+C 5032)* [ ] [-]
– Girls opening music / Girls / Disco grindin' / Switch le bitch / Disco bumpin' / Aural exciter / Warm, warm, warm / Tonight / Snatch the gas / Your touch is soft / Trouble shared / Discollapse / Make the pieces fit.

S/track review: With his band 10cc all at sea and a near fatal car accident nearly killing him in January 1979, ERIC STEWART tried a new approach with the soundtrack to naughty French flick, 'GIRLS'. Released in the same month/year as fellow-10cc man Graham Gouldman's 'ANIMALYMPICS', 'GIRLS' didn't exactly inject any needed enthusiasm from critics or record buyers alike – but then again, the work of a pop-rock scoresmith was never an easy task. STEWART's smooth-talking vocals and AOR guitar-hooks are on display for the likes of the LP's best songs such as the flop singles, 'Girls' and 'Warm, Warm, Warm', but the remainder could well be described as B-sides – two of the LP's titles, 'Discollapse' & 'Switch Le Bitch', are indeed poignant to that fact. There's obvious references to the dancefloor via 'Disco Grindin'' and 'Disco Bumpin'', but with the movie's sexual theme, 'Aural Exciter' must take the proverbial limp biscuit. 10cc did have a subsequent revival of sorts in the mid 90s, but this solo work by STEWART is definitely not his best achievement – by a long way. *MCS*

Album rating: *3.5

– spinoff releases, etc. –

ERIC STEWART: Girls / Discollapse

Feb 80. (7") *(POSP 123)* [ ] [-]

ERIC STEWART: Warm, Warm, Warm / Switch Le Bitch

Aug 80. (7") *(POSP 155)* [ ] [-]

□ GIRLS AGAINST BOYS segment
(⇒ SERIES 7)

GLITTERBUG

1994 (UK 60m w/b&w) BBC / Dangerous To Know / Opal Films

Film genre: documentary biopic montage

Top guns: s-w + dir: Derek Jarman ← IN THE SHADOW OF THE SUN ← JUBILEE

Stars: Derek Jarman *(archive footage)*, etc.

Storyline: The film is a poignant epitaph to director/writer, Derek Jarman, who died of AIDS in 1994. It's basically a compilation of Jarman's home movies from between 1970 and 1986, without any real plot synopsis, and concentrates on his experiences in London before the onset of his illness. As well as charting his career we get an insider's view of the capital's party scene and holiday Super 8-mm footage from abroad shot in typical Jarman fashion – a flowing series of images representing all that he stood for. *JZ*

Movie rating: *5

Visual: video

Off the record: If you've been an ardent reader of the Great Rock Discography (especially 4, 5 and the Alternative editions) you'll have noticed my mistake when I billed this album 'Spanner'(!). I apologise for not looking closely enough at the title and more at the misleading "spanner/wrench" picture on the sleeve; and why not 'GLITTERBUG' anyway? *MCS*

BRIAN ENO & JAH WOBBLE: Spinner

Oct 95. (lp/c/cd) *All Saints; (AS/+C/CD 023) Gyroscope; <6614-2>* [71] [ ]
– Where we lived / Like organza / Steam / Garden recalled / Marine radio / Unusual balance / Space diary 1 / Spinner / Transmitter and trumpet / Left where it fell.

S/track review: This 'SPINNER' in the works – you could say – found the unlikely collaboration of solo ambient star (and ex-Roxy Music knob-twiddler), BRIAN ENO, turning over the master tapes to bass/dub soloist (and former John Lydon/PiL cohort), JAH WOBBLE. Not so much of a collaboration then, more of a patched-up companion piece to an unfinished project; and all'n'all both parties were extremely satisfied with the results. Not everyone was of that opinion, especially considering the high standards to which the listener had become accustomed in the work of ENO, and to a slightly lesser degree (at the time!), WOBBLE. There were of course the untouched ENO treatments such as opener 'Where We Lived', and others 'Garden Recalled' and 'Space Diary 1', not "Music For Films" per se, more "Music For unfinished Films", as most of ENO's complete cinematic scores ended up; Various Artists on each film have taken precedence over ENO's work on many occasions (i.e. 'JUBILEE' & 'Opera'). ENO and WOBBLE combine efforts on seven cuts, the best example of their distant interplay comes via 'Like Organza', a dubbed collision of bass and Eastern-inspired chimes. 'Steam' (with the added help of MARK FERDA on atmospheres/keyboards and JUSTIN ADAMS on guitar) might well have been inspired by electronic film composers, TANGERINE DREAM. Ditto 'Spinner' and 'Transmitter And Trumpet', both tracks augmented by the addition of Can's JAKI LIEBEZEIT on drums. With a few revisits to the proverbial turntable, the album begins to take shape (a little), the sparse, pitched-high bass on 'Marine Radio' nurtured with smooth effect, while 'Unusual Balance' is exactly what it says on the tin – a second half features vocals from SUSSAN DEYHIM. WOBBLE was finally in his element, an element of no holds barred experimentalism. 'Left Where It Fell' closed the ENO/WOBBLE workshop for the day (and quite possibly forever), its meandering jam-like rhythms of 7 minutes – 20 in total if you count the add-on eerie lounge piece – more akin to WOBBLE's fixation with everything dub and Eastern than of ENO's ambient muse. *MCS*

Album rating: *6

GOBLIN

Formed: Italy ... 1972. GOBLIN (aka Oliver, Cherry Five, IL REALE IMPERO BRITANNICO), and their supreme line-up of principal composer Claudio Simonetti (keyboards), Massimo Morante (guitars), Fabio Pignatelli (bass) and Agostino Marangolo (drums) are best known for their largely instrumental work with Dario Argento on his classic "giallo" slasher and horror films of the 1970s and 80s. Throughout the course of their diverse career, they would compose and perform numerous film and television soundtracks – although they would not always do both for particular projects – interspersing these with their own original albums. Originally influenced by seminal prog groups (Yes, Genesis, King Crimson, and Emerson, Lake & Palmer), they found little success in their first incarnation as Oliver (with Englishman Clive Haynes providing vocals, and drummer Carlo Bordini); a pilgrimage to England in 1974 at the behest of Yes producer Eddie Offord ended in disillusionment when they arrived in London to find Offord had just popped out for a lengthy tour of the USA. Returning to Italy the band found sanctuary with new label 'Cinevox', where they were perfunctorily renamed Cherry Five and put to work for the first time arranging and performing the work of film composers. Bordini refused to sign the new contract and was replaced by Walter Martino, while Haynes remained in the UK and was briefly replaced by Tony Tartarini. Cherry Five's unique sound began to garner them a reputation, and with an album of their own compositions pending, they were hired by Argento to replace jazz musician Giorgio Gaslini on the score for 'PROFONDO ROSSO' ('Deep Red') (1975). During the recording of the score, Martino left to join fusion band Libra but was soon replaced by Agostino Marangolo. In the same year as 'PROFONDO ...', the band recorded music written by Simonetti's father Enrico Simonetti, for Gamma (Salvatore Nocita, 1975). Renaming themselves GOBLIN – ostensibly to distinguish their work on the soundtrack from the release of Cherry Five's debut – was the first of many canonically problematic changes the band made. Although line-up changes, issues of legality and personal disputes would necessitate the use of various alter egos, retrospectives have collected many of these works under the GOBLIN banner, while there remain a few cases where the group's contribution to a score is suspected but not confirmed, notably Fabio Frizzio's soundtrack for Paura Nella Citta Dei Morti Viventi (City of the Living Dead) (Lucio Fulci, 1980). 'PROFONDO ROSSO's score was hugely successful in their home country (selling over 3 million copies to date), heralding a golden age for the band and for horror soundtracks. Pignatelli's distinctive funky bass and Simonetti's sinister arpeggiated synths were the defining elements, along with an experimental approach that belied their prog origins. The propulsive energy of their best scores ensured not only that their music was an essential and unignorable cinematic element, but that the music would transcend its origins and make them instantly recognisable favourites. As a group, GOBLIN's relationship with Argento would continue through 'SUSPIRIA' (1977), 'ZOMBI' (aka George Romero's 'DAWN OF THE DEAD' (1979) which Argento re-edited for Italy), 'La CHIESA' (with Keith EMERSON) (1989) directed by Michele Soavi but co-written with Argento, and 'NON HO SONNO' (2001). Simonetti worked individually on the scores for 'Phenomena' (aka 'Creepers') (Argento, 1985), Lamberto Bava's 'Demons' (1985) (another film co-written by Argento), and finally Argento's own 'Il Fantasma Dell'Opera' (1998) and

'Il Cartaio' (The Card Player) (2004). The first incarnation of GOBLIN produced two non-soundtrack albums, 'Roller' (1976) and 'Il Fantastico Viaggio Del "Bagarozzo" Mark' ('The Fantastic Voyage of Mark the Beetle', 1978) – both of which would later be pillaged for use in Argento's Italian cut of Romero's 'Martin' (aka 'Wampyr', 1977) and performed the score for 'PERCHE SI UCCIDON' (Mauro Macario, 1976), under the aforementioned pseudonym of IL REALE IMPERO BRITANNICO. This particular artifice was undertaken due to the controversial subject matter of the film. Lesser known soundtracks for 'La VIA DELLA DROGA' (aka 'The Heroin Busters') (1977) and 'Solamente Nero' ('The Bloodstained Shadow') (1978) followed, the latter of which is credited to Stelvio Cipriani, who completed the score GOBLIN had to abandon due to legal difficulties. They also recorded somewhat generic music written by Giorgio Farina for 1978 Italian TV programme 'Discocross'. Guitarist and sometime vocalist Massimo Morante quit after 'ZOMBI' in 1979 to pursue a frequently less than successful solo career, he was replaced by Carlo Pennisi, who was himself replaced by Marco Rinalduzzi in 1982. Before Simonetti followed Morante later in 1979, GOBLIN produced what is considered their least characteristic work, on Armenia Balducci's romance 'AMO NON AMO' (1979). The scores for 'SQUADRA ANTIGANGSTERS' (1979) (with singer Asha Puthli) and 1979 Italian television anthology series 'Sette Storie Per Non Dormire', while less renowned, were more likely successors to the work that made their name. Simonetti would find steady work composing and performing music for film, as did GOBLIN, now led by Fabio. Scores for 'PATRICK' (1979) and 'BUIO OMEGA' (1979) followed, while drummer Marangolo left after 'CONTAMINATION' (aka 'Alien Contamination') (1980). By this time Maurizio Guarini had replaced Simonetti, leaving Pignatelli the only original member. The addition of Derek Wilson (drums) and Mauro Lusini (sometime vocals), GOBLIN now entered their least rewarding phase, their own album 'Volo' (1982) meeting indifference – although the title track was used as the end theme for the 1982 Italian TV show 'Discoring' – while they produced scores for more and more obscure films, including one, 'Mo Deng Tian Shi' ('To Hell With The Devil', 1982) for a young John Woo. The nadir of the GOBLIN brand was reached with 'St Helens' (1981) for which the phrase "rarely heard" is a huge understatement, although the 'love theme' exists on collections as a warning to future generations. Luckily, the flame was still burning with founding members Morante and Simonetti, who reunited with Pignatelli to produce their last classic score, for Argento's 'TENEBRE', in 1982. In a neat reversal, the founding members of GOBLIN were unable to use the name as Pignatelli's aforementioned 'Volo' album was due at the same time as the score, although 'TENEBRE' has been retrospectively absorbed into the GOBLIN canon. While Pignatelli's GOBLIN continued into the 80s on scores for comedy 'Il Ras Del Quartiere' (1983) and thriller 'NOTTURNO' (1983), and the various former members would work together on scores, the glory days were clearly long gone. They found their work increasingly sidelined and even brutally edited down – Argento himself excised much of Simonetti's score for 'PHENOMENA' (1985) in favour of tracks by Iron Maiden and gothic rocker Andi Sex Gang. Although the original line-up has been recently restored, scoring Argento's soporific 'NO HO SONNO' (2002) the reunited GOBLIN have stated their belief that Argento's best work is behind him. This is either true, a reflection of his decreasing patronage, or both. GOBLIN however remain cautiously optimistic about future collaborations. Their most recent work has been a new studio album with Maurizio Guarini once again replacing Simonetti, entitled 'Back To The Goblin 2005', while they have seen a resurgence in appreciation – and appropriation – of their legendary music, with their theme for 'TENEBRE' sampled by French electronic duo Justice on their debut album. *SW*

- **filmography** (composers) –

Profondo Rosso *(1975 OST =>)* / **Perche Si Uccidono** *(1976 OST as IL REALE IMPERO BRITANNICO =>)* / **Suspiria** *(1977 OST =>)* / **la Via Della Droga** *(1977 OST =>)* / **Dawn Of The Dead – Zombi** *(1978 OST =>)* / Squadra Antimafia *(1978)* / **Patrick** *(1978 OST =>)* / **Squadra Antigangsters** *(1979 OST =>)* / **Amo Non Amo** *(1979 OST =>)* / **Buio Omega** *(1979 OST =>)* / L'Altro Inferno *(1980 no)* / **Contamination** *(1980 OST =>)* / the Comoedia *(1981 by SIMONETTI)* / St. Helens *(1981)* / I Nuova Barbari *(1982 OST by SIMONETTI =>)* / **Tenebre** *(1982 OST =>)* / **Notturno** *(1983 OST =>)* / Vai Alla Grande *(1983 by SIMONETTI)* / Conquest *(1983 OST by SIMONETTI =>)* / Dario Argento's World Of Horror *(1985 w/ SIMON BOSWELL, KEITH EMERSON, etc.)* / **Phenomena** *(1985 OST => + other w/ SIMONETTI, SIMON BOSWELL & V/A =>)* / Inferno In Diretta *(1985 by SIMONETTI)* / Demoni/Demons *(1985 OST by SIMONETTI & V/A =>)* / Morirai A Mezzanotte *(1986 OST by SIMONETTI =>)* / Vendetta Dal Futuro *(1986 by SIMONETTI)* / Camping Del Terrore *(1987 by SIMONETTI & Joel Goldsmith)* / Opera *(1987 OST by Various Classical => + OST by SIMONETTI w/ BRIAN ENO, ROGER ENO, DANIEL LANOIS & BILL WYMAN =>)* / Nightmare Beach *(1988 by SIMONETTI)* / Minaccia D'Amore *(1988 by SIMONETTI)* / Primal Rage *(1988 by SIMONETTI)* / College *(1989 TV by SIMONETTI)* / **la Chiesa** *(1989 OST w/ KEITH EMERSON =>)* / la Casa Del Sortilegio *(1989 TV by SIMONETTI as CLAUDE KING)* / la Casa Delle Anime Erranti *(1989 TV by SIMONETTI as CLAUDE KING)* / Vortice Mortale *(1993 by SIMONETTI)* / the Versace Murder *(1998 by SIMONETTI =>)* / **Nonhosonno** *(2001 OST =>)* / Apri Gli Occhi E . . . Sogna *(2002 by SIMONETTI)* / il Cartaio *(2004 OST by SIMONETTI =>)*

– compilations, etc. –

GOBLIN: Greatest Hits (film music)

1979. (lp/c) *Silva Screen; (ORL/ORK7 8305)* ☐ ☐ – Profondo Rosso / Witch / E Suono rock / Yell / Suspiria / Patrick *[not on cd]* / Zombi / Amo non amo / Disco China *[not on cd]* / Roller. *(cd-iss. 1987 +=;)* – Nocturne / Est / Connexion / Jennifer / St. Helene mountain / Life goes on / Helycopter.

GOBLIN: Goblin (their hits, rare tracks & outtakes collection 1975-1989)

Oct 95. (cd) *D.R.G.; <32904>* ☐ ☐ – Profondo Rosso (main title) / Death dies – M32 (original film version) / Profondo Rosso – M15 + M31 / Wampyr (finale) / Chi? (part 1 & 2) / Patrick – M32 bis + M1 + M34/34 bis/35 / Suspiria (main title) / La Via della droga – M1IV + M2 + M6 + 31 / L'Alba dei morti viventi / Buio omega – M6 + M25 + main title / St. Helen (love theme) / Contamination – M3 + M8 / Tenebre (main title) / Bass theme (from Notturno) / Phenomena – M12 + M15 (alt.) / La chiesa.

GOBLIN: Volume II 1975-1980

Feb 98. (cd) *D.R.G.; <32923>* ☐ ☐ – Profondo Rosso / Gianna (alt.take) / Deep shadows (film version – part 1) / Deep shadows (film version – part 2) / Death dies (film version – part 1) / Profondo Rosso (re-mix) / Black forest / Blind concert / Markos (alt.take) / The swan is a murderer (part 1) / The swan is a murderer (part 2) / Oliver / Il resvegno del serpente / Stunt cars / Connexion / Withy.

GOBLIN: Volume III 1978-1984

Jun 98. (cd) *D.R.G.; <32924>* ☐ ☐ – Buio omega (main title) / Strive after dark (suite) / Buio omega (alt.take suite) / Tenebre (remix) / Jennifer / Sleepwalking / Phenomena (alt.take) / E suono rock / La cascate di viridiana / La danza / Zombi (main title) / Zaratozom / L'Alba dei morti viventi / Amo non amo (main title) / Maniera / Yell.

GOBLIN: The Original Remixes Collection Vol1

May 99. (cd) *Family Affair; (FARCD 417)* ☐ ☐ – Profondo Rosso / Jennifer / Tenebre / Buio omega / Phenomena / Suspiria / Gamma / Flashing / Zombi / Death dies / Aquaman / Notte / Sleepwalking / Jennifer's friend.

GOBLIN: The Best Of Goblin, Vol.1

Sep 00. (d-cd) *Cinevox; (<CD-MDF 336>)* ☐ Dec02 ☐ – Profondo Rosso / Death dies / Mad puppet / Profondo Rosso (remix) / Suspiria / Sighs / Witch / Markos / Tenebre / Flashing / Waiting death / Tenebre (reprise) / Phenomena / Sleepwalking / The wind / Aquaman (live) / Snip snap (live) / Profondo Rosso (live) / Mark il Bagarozzo (live) / Notte (live) / Opera magnifica (live) / Le cascate di viridiana (live) / Un ragazzo d'Argento (live).

☐ the GODFATHER OF HARLEM alt. (⇒ BLACK CAESAR)

G'OLE!

1983 (UK 101m) Iveco / Lindbroke / Tyburn / Warner Bros. (PG)

Film genre: Sports documentary

Top guns: dir: Tom Clegg ← McVICAR / s-w: Stan Hey

Stars: Sean Connery *(narrator)*

Storyline: The official movie of the 1982 FIFA World Cup held in Spain. Football – or soccer to my Stateside compadres – is the main subject here, although emotions on and off the field are also the theme. Incidentally, Italy won the cup beating West Germany in the final. *MCS*

Movie rating: *7

Visual: video

Off the record: Rick WAKEMAN (see own entry)

RICK WAKEMAN

Apr 83. (lp/c) *Charisma; (CAS/+MC 1162)* ☐ ⊟
– International flag / The dove (opening ceremony) / Wayward spirit / Latin reel (theme from G'ole) / Red island / Spanish holiday / No possibla / Shadows / Black pearls / Frustration / Spanish montage / G'ole!

S/track review: Once the hero of many a Prog-rock aficionado (i.e. 'Journey To The Centre Of The Earth'), footie fan RICK WAKEMAN was probably the obvious choice to score such a project, having previously turned out 1976 Winter Olympics-themed 'WHITE ROCK' in '77. However, on 'G'OLE!', the results were something of a hit and miss, the overplay of staccato synths and percussion shied the album into touch. One of the only highlights came via the opening couple of minutes, 'International Flag', while the own-g'ole was flop single, 'Latin Reel (Theme From..)'. Thankfully, the CD version hasn't been released to date, so no injury time will be necessary. *MCS*

Album rating: *3.5

– spinoff releases, etc. –

RICK WAKEMAN: Latin Reel (Theme From G'ole!) / No Possibla
Apr 83. (7") *(CB 411)* ☐ ⊟

☐ GONG segment (⇒ CONTINENTAL CIRCUS)

GOOD WILL HUNTING

1997 (US 126m) Miramax Films (R)

Film genre: romantic coming-of-age/psychological drama

Top guns: dir: **Gus Van Sant** ← EVEN COWGIRLS GET THE BLUES / → LAST DAYS / s-w: Ben Affleck, Matt Damon (+ story)

Stars: Matt Damon *(Will Hunting)* ← GERONIMO: AN AMERICAN LEGEND / → ALL THE PRETTY HORSES → SPIRIT: STALLION OF THE CIMARRON, Robin Williams *(Sean McGuire)* ← GOOD MORNING, VIETNAM ← CLUB PARADISE, Ben Affleck *(Chuckie Sullivan)*, Minnie Driver *(Skylar)* → TARZAN → SOUTH PARK: BIGGER, LONGER & UNCUT, Stellan Skarsgard *(Gerald Lambeau)* → DANCER IN THE DARK, Casey Affleck *(Morgan O'Mally)* → COMMITTED, Cole Hauser *(Billy McBride)* → a SHOT AT GLORY, George Plimpton *(Henry Lipkin; psychologist)*, Harmony Korine *(Jerve)* ← KIDS / → LAST DAYS

Storyline: Will Hunting is a troubled young janitor at MIT University. As time goes by he finds himself increasingly at odds with the world and deeper in trouble with the police. However one day his life suddenly changes when he anonymously solves a complex maths equation set by Professor Lambeau for his students. Lambeau, astonished to find his test solved by a janitor, offers Hunting a chance to redeem himself if he'll take weekly maths lessons and speak to an unusual old pupil. *JZ*

Movie rating: *8

Visual: video + dvd

Off the record: ELLIOTT SMITH (see below)

Various Artists (songs: ELLIOTT SMITH * / score: DANNY ELFMAN **)

Nov 97. (cd) *Capitol; <(8 23338-2)>* 91 Mar98 ☐
– Between the bars – orchestral (*) / As the rain (JEB LOY NICHOLS) / Angeles (*) / No name #3 (*) / Fisherman's blues (the WATERBOYS) / Why do I lie? (LUSCIOUS JACKSON) / Will Hunting – main titles (**) / Between the bars (*) / Say yes (*) / Baker Street (GERRY RAFFERTY) / Somebody's baby (ANDRU DONALDS) / Boys better (the DANDY WARHOLS) / How can you mend a broken heart (AL GREEN) / Miss Misery (*) / Weepy donuts (**).

S/track review: You could cut this soundtrack into several slices, the biggest (at 40%) and best going to singer-songwriter ELLIOTT SMITH. Handpicked by fellow Portland-born filmmaker, Gus Van Sant (who incidentally, dabbled with lo-fi songwriting in the early 80s!), there were six SMITH numbers: an oldie from his 'Roman Candle' debut, 'No Name #3'; three from his most recent offering, 'Either/Or': 'Between The Bars', 'Angeles' and 'Say Yes' (four if one counts opener 'Between The Bars (orchestral)') plus a subsequent Best Song Oscar-nominee, 'Miss Misery'. If you liked your rock soft, and the music of Simon & Garfunkel (think 'The GRADUATE'), ELLIOTT was your man, his mellow, near-horizontal meanderings never gaining commercial approval until after his mysterious death on October 21st, 2003; his two albums since, the posthumous 'From A Basement On A Hill' (2004) and compilation 'New Moon' (2007) have both reached the US Top 30. On a different note entirely, prolific movie composer DANNY ELFMAN contributed a relatively small slice to the 'GOOD WILL . . .' pie, the forgettable 'Will Hunting (Main Titles)' and 'Weepy Donuts', the latter as close to Morricone's 'The Mission' OST as one could possibly get. The remainder were constructed of various artists from all over the place, Scotland providing two genuine folk-pop classics, 'Fisherman's Blues' by the WATERBOYS and 'Baker Street' by GERRY RAFFERTY. Portland's own newbies on the block, the DANDY WARHOLS delivered their post-grunge, 'Boys Better' in fine style, while New York lassies, LUSCIOUS JACKSON were caught out sounding like an indie Spice Girls for 'Why Do I Lie?'. Of the two covers, AL GREEN comes off best with the Bee Gees song, 'How Can You Mend A Broken Heart?', the other being the Robert Palmer-soundalike, ANDRU DONALDS on Jackson Browne's 'Somebody's Baby'; JEB LOY NICHOLS brought up the rear by contributing a bluegrass-meets-reggae(!) smoothie, 'As The Rain'. An eclectic song, but more so, an eclectic album. *MCS*

Album rating: *6.5

GOODBYE, COLUMBUS

1969 (US 105m) Warner Bros. (R)+(PG)

Film genre: romantic comedy drama

Top guns: dir: Larry Peerce ← the BIG T.N.T. SHOW / → HARD TO HOLD / s-w: Arnold Schulman → TUCKER: THE MAN AND HIS DREAM (au: Philip Roth)

Stars: Richard Benjamin *(Neil Klugman)*, Ali MacGraw *(Brenda Patimkin)*, Jack Klugman *(Ben Patimkin)*, Nan Martin *(Mrs. Ben Patimkin)*, Michael Meyers *(Ron Patimkin)*, Lori Shelle *(Julie Patimkin)*, Sylvie Strauss *(Aunt Gladys)*, Royce Wallace *(Carlotta)* → COOL BREEZE → WILLIE DYNAMITE → CROSSROADS, Michael Nouri *(Don Farber)* → FLASHDANCE, Monroe Arnold *(Uncle Leo)* → ALICE'S RESTAURANT

Storyline: Neil and Brenda are two young Jewish people who meet and fall in love. Brenda lives in style and elegance with her strict, well-to-do family while Neil has to work in the local library to make ends meet. They continue their affair in secret in case Brenda's parents stop her from seeing Neil, but eventually their differing lifestyles begin to prove too much for their already tenuous relationship. *JZ*

Movie rating: *8

Visual: video + dvd

Off the record: The **ASSOCIATION** formed in L.A. during the early part of '65. Combining the talents of Gary Alexander (guitar), Jim Yester (rhythm guitar), Ted Bluechel (drummer), Russ Giguere (percussion), Brian Cole (bass) and Terry Kirkman (flute), the psychedelic, sunshine pop band released their debut 45, 'Babe, I'm Gonna Leave You' on a small independent label. Soft-rock harmonies were much in evidence on their third 45, 'Along Comes Mary', a record which hit US Top 10 in the summer of '66; it was apparently laced with drug connotations (i.e. Mary = Marijuana?). A similarly-titled Top 5 album featured their first chart-topper, 'Cherish', while subsequent hits just kept rolling off the production line, including the ballad-esque 'Windy', a second US No.1. However, in the space of just over a year (and with the addition of multi-instrumentalist Larry Ramos, Jr. in 1967 to supplement the departure of guru-seeking Gary to India), the smart-suited ASSOCIATION had all but dried up. In early 1969, the 7-piece group (along came Gary again, this time as "Jules") took the misguided task of recording a soundtrack for the movie, 'GOODBYE, COLUMBUS'. Sadly, as the band's star faded into virtual obscurity, Brian Cole died of a heroin overdose on the 2nd of August 1972. *MCS*

---

the ASSOCIATION (score: CHARLES FOX *)

May 69. (lp) *Warner Bros; <(WS 1786)>* | 99 | Sep69 | ☐

– Goodbye, Columbus (vocal version) / How will I know you? (*) / Dartmouth? Dartmouth! (*) / Goodbye, Columbus (instrumental version) / Ron's reverie: a) Across the field, b) Carmen, Ohio (*) / It's gotta be real / A moment to share (*) / Love has a way (*) / A time for love (*) / So kind to me (Brenda's theme). *<cd-iss. Apr99 on 'WEA'; 10195> (UK cd re-iss. Feb06 on 'Collectors' Choice'; CCM-648)*

S/track review: The first question you'll ask yourself is: why were the ASSOCIATION given full sleeve credits on this one when they only contributed four tracks (under 11 minutes, worth!) to the album (CHARLES FOX gets five!). Maybe the people at 'Warner Bros' were trying to cash-in on the phenomenal success the group had on the run-up to this recording (see above); I suppose if it worked for SIMON & GARFUNKEL and Dave Grusin on the previous year's similarly wedding-themed 'The GRADUATE' (1968), why not with this one. Why, because as the sleevenotes suggest, 'GOODBYE, COLUMBUS' was handed to YESTER and Co to write in under a fortnight, record in under the same timescale and then worst of all, the company released it two months prior to the movie's premiere. Shambollocks. Anyway, of the four songs, if you count the JIM YESTER-penned, Pearl & Dean-like title track twice (vocal and wordless!), the ASSOCIATION produce their own blend of bland baroque pop. Of the other two cuts, LARRY RAMOS, JR. gets in a sort of pre-Jimmy Somerville ditty, 'It's Gotta Be Real', while TERRY KIRKMAN contributes finale crooner, 'So Kind To Me (Brenda's Theme)'. All ASSOCIATION tracks are effective in their own inimitable way (with possible musical links to the Fifth Dimension, the Grass Roots and the Turtles), but now we'll have to talk about where the rest fit in. Forgetting the jingo-istic, stars'n'stripes-waving 'Ron's Reverie', with cold dialogue that finally gets in the name of the film, we get back to the aforementioned CHARLES FOX. With a light orchestra and session players (which don't include the ASSOCIATION), the composer gets in some groove-a-delic numbers ('Dartmouth? Dartmouth!' included), and if its sounds funky enough for 'Barbarella', that's because he did that movie's score the year previously. The romanticism of 'A Moment To Share' is lovely and oh-so-60s, while 'A Time For Love' is awaiting the Mamas & The Papas to chime in. FOX would later become synonymous with a plethora of TV work including 'Love American Style', while he also co-wrote 'Killing Me Softly' for Roberta Flack. Now, is that everything? *MCS*

Album rating: *4.5

– spinoff hits, etc. –

the ASSOCIATION: Goodbye, Columbus

Mar 69. (7") *<(WB 7267)>* | 80 | Sep69 | ☐

GORDON'S WAR

1973 (US 90m) Palomar Pictures / 20th Century Fox (R)

Film genre: urban drama

Top guns: dir: Ossie Davis ← BLACK GIRL ← COTTON COMES TO HARLEM / → COUNTDOWN AT KUSINI / s-w: Howard Friedlander, Ed Spielman

Stars: Paul Winfield *(Gordon)* ← TROUBLE MAN ← SOUNDER / → a HERO AIN'T NOTHIN' BUT A SANDWICH → MIKE'S MURDER → BLUE CITY, Carl Lee *(Bee)* ← SUPERFLY ← the LANDLORD, David Downing *(Otis)*, Nathan C. Heard *(Big Pink)*, Tony King *(Roy Green)* ← SHAFT / → HELL UP IN HARLEM → BUCKTOWN → SPARKLE, Gilbert Lewis *(Spanish Harry)* ← ACROSS 110th STREET ← COTTON COMES TO HARLEM, Carl Gordon *(Luther the pimp)*, **Grace Jones** *(Mary)* → STRAIGHT TO HELL → SIESTA, Adam Wade *(hustler)* ← ACROSS 110th STREET ← COME BACK, CHARLESTON BLUE ← SHAFT / → CLAUDINE → PHANTOM OF THE PARADISE

Storyline: Together with his Black Panther-alluding posse of Vietnam vet vigilantes, ex-GI Gordon sets out to rid Harlem of drugs after arriving home to neighbourhood chaos and his wife dead from a heroin overdose. Bringing down his wrath with great vengeance and furious anger, he and his former platoon buddies battle Spanish Harry and Co with the kind of arsenal that an average 'Nam regiment could only dream about. *BG*

Movie rating: *4

Visual: video

Off the record: Jamaican-born, **Grace Jones**, was a model in the early 70s before moving into acting for blaxploitation movie, 'GORDON'S WAR' (1973). As a singer, she debuted with the album, 'Portfolio' (1976) and subsequently had a handful of hits: 'Private Life', 'Pull Up To The Bumper', etc. Her film work up to 'Siesta' included starring roles in 'Conan The Destroyer' (alongside Arnie), 'A View To A Kill' (with #2 Bond, Roger Moore) and who could forget her TV chat-show bout with presenter Russell Harty. *MCS*

AL ELIAS & ANDY BADELE (& Various Artists)

1973. (lp) *Buddah; <BDA 5137ST>* | ☐ | ☐

– Child of tomorrow (BARBARA MASON) / Just plain Luther / He'll be there / Roberta's theme / Harlem dreams / Come and dream some paradise (NEW BIRTH) / Tell that man to go to hell /

Child of tomorrow / Super shine number 9 (SISTER GOOSE AND THE DUCKLINGS) / Hot wheels (the chase) / Child of tomorrow (BARBARA MASON).

S/track review: Long lauded as one of the all-time great blaxploitation albums but never honoured with a reissue, 'GORDON'S WAR' should've been as big as 'SHAFT' or 'SUPERFLY', and usually commands its price accordingly. The film was blessed with one of the era's better politically slanted scripts, and the soundtrack's more of a team effort than most, co-written by Angelo Badalamenti no less, under a nom de plume (ANDY BADELE) years before he rose to prominence under David Lynch. BADDER THAN EVIL, an anonymous but demonically funky studio aggregate, perform the music, while a cast of famous and less famous soul artists sing themselves hoarse. The only vaguely household name is NEW BIRTH, the 70s boy-girl funk ensemble masterminded by producer Harvey Fugua, himself a one-time member of doo-wop pioneers the Moonglows and brother-in-law of Berry Gordy. The group had previously recorded a vocal version of the theme to Sidney Poitier's directorial debut, 'Buck And The Preacher', originally composed and performed by jazz legend Benny Carter (alongside Sonny Terry and Brownie McGhee). The NEW BIRTH version didn't make it into the film, or even score them a hit, but they finally got in on the blaxploitation game with the Fugua-arranged 'Come On And Dream Some Paradise', keeping it in the family with raw, career-definitive vocals from Leslie Wilson and sister-in-law, Ann Bogan. The last track on the group's final album before they moved to 'Buddah' themselves, the single – like 'Buck and The Preacher' before it – should've been a hit. For beat nuts and breaks fans, though, it's all about 'Hot Wheels (The Chase)', two minutes and fifty-nine seconds of tarmac-flaying rhythm. It stands as perhaps the definitive chase-funk theme, propelled by Stevie Wonder-style clavinet and boy-racer braggadocio. BARBARA MASON's orchestrated, pop-soul love theme gets her coupon on the sleeve but it's the boot-licking 'Super Shine #9' by SISTER GOOSE AND THE DUCKLINGS (give those gals a gold medallion for that name!) which you'll want to spin until your needle turns green, a cooing girlie-funk throwback in the spirit of the Vibrettes' 'Humpty Dump', lithe and populist enough even for World Cup Match Of The Day'.. Side Two boasts the sample-fest, 'Tell That Man To Go To Hell', living up to its title with a contortionist percussion break and some blazing sax improv. Which means Side One must pale in comparison, right? Hardly, well not if you're in the market for some excellent small band funk with mischievous hints of Eddie Harris, the languid purr of Isaac Hayes, and the cohesion of an instrumental suite. If you don't fancy lashing out on the original vinyl, you can pick up a re-press for around a tenner. *BG*

Album rating: *8.5

GOTHIC

1986 (UK 87m) Virgin Visions / Vestron Pictures (18)

Film genre: period-costume horror drama

Top guns: dir: Ken Russell ← CRIMES OF PASSION ← LISZTOMANIA ← TOMMY / s-w: Stephen Volk → OCTANE

Stars: Gabriel Byrne *(Lord Byron)* → SIESTA → the COURIER → DEAD MAN → the END OF VIOLENCE → STIGMATA, Julian Sands *(Percy Bysshe Shelley)* ← the KILLING FIELDS / → SIESTA → the MILLION DOLLAR HOTEL, Natasha Richardson *(Mary Shelley)* → CHELSEA WALLS, Myriam Cyr *(Claire Clairmont)* → I SHOT ANDY WARHOL, Timothy Spall *(Dr. John Polidori)* ← QUADROPHENIA / → STILL CRAZY → ROCK STAR, Alec Mango *(Murray)*, Andreas Wisniewski *(Fletcher)*, Dexter Fletcher *(Rushton)*

Storyline: On a stormy night in 1816, a group of poets and writers gather at Lord Byron's Swiss villa and are promised a night of terror by their host. Each guest, heavily under the influence of hallucinogenic drugs, tells a horror story to the rest as they explore the darkened rooms and corridors of Byron's home. But fear quickly turns to madness and depravity and the fine line between genius and insanity is stretched to the limit as the guests' inner demons take control. *JZ*

Movie rating: *5.5

Visual: video

Off the record: (see below)

THOMAS DOLBY

Feb 87. (cd/c/lp) *Virgin; (CD/TC+V 2417) <90607-1>* ☐ ☐
– Fantasmagoria / Byronic love / Shelleymania / Mary's theme / Party games / Gipsygirl / The crucifix / The fundamental source / Sin and buggery / Impalement / Skullpulse – Leech juice / Restless sleep 1, 2 + 3 / It's his! / A trickle of blood / Coitus per stigmata / Once we vowed eternal love / Riddled with guilt / Metamorphosis / The hangman / The beast in the crypt / The final séance / Funeral by the lake / No ghosts in daylight / The Devil is an Englishman. *(re-iss. 1988 lp/c; OVED/+C 229)*

S/track review: The "Hyperactive" THOMAS DOLBY was at the peak of his career in 1984 after his sophomore album, 'The Flat Earth', peaked at No.17 in the UK charts. 1985/86 had DOLBY working on two film-score projects, the disastrous 'HOWARD THE DUCK' (1986) – with John Barry – plus 'GOTHIC'. The latter was to be a long corridor away from his previous electro-pop antics, which ensured he would be pigeonholed alongside contemporaries Howard Jones and Nik Kershaw. For many film buffs, the nerdy DOLBY was an insane choice of composer, but classically at least, he pulled it off with dramatic, nay cinematic aplomb. At times eerily haunting, DOLBY only gets close to his pop past during 'Gipsygirl', where he definitely "scares himself", well . . . just a little bit. The annoying thing about the album, is the shortness of the 22 tracks, mostly orchestral/symphonic and indelibly "gothic", with an array of ye olde type instruments, i.e. harpsichord. This is indeed the dark side of the moon-head for DOLBY, shaking out the phantoms of his pop past with one foul swoop. Old masters Fritz Lang or Bernard Herrmann would be proud of the new DOLBY, the rock world was less enthusiastic; Gregorian chants from monks of various orders were not yet in vogue. 'The Devil Is An Englishman . . .' (a single, but extended!) is a prime example of taking hymnal praises too far. Track 19 (or somewhere thereabouts!), 'To The Grave', intros with film dialogue: "Is there no escape from this madhouse?" – the answer is plain to hear. *MCS*

Album rating: *4.5

– spinoff releases, etc. –

THOMAS DOLBY: The Devil Is An Englishman (extended) / Fantasmagoria
Feb 87. (12") *(VS 937-12)* ☐ [–]

☐ Graham GOULDMAN segment
(⇒ ANIMALYMPICS)

the GRADUATE

1967 (US 105m) Embassy Pictures Corporation (re-PG)

Film genre: romantic coming-of-age comedy/drama

Top guns: dir: Mike Nichols → WORKING GIRL → PRIMARY COLORS / s-w: Calder Willingham → LITTLE BIG MAN, Buck Henry → CANDY → the OWL AND THE PUSSYCAT (au: Charles Webb)

Stars: Dustin Hoffman *(Benjamin Braddock)* → MIDNIGHT COWBOY →

LITTLE BIG MAN → WHO IS HARRY KELLERMAN AND WHY IS HE SAYING THOSE TERRIBLE THINGS ABOUT ME? → the POINT! → DICK TRACY → WAG THE DOG, Anne Bancroft *(Mrs. Robinson)*, Katharine Ross *(Elaine Robinson)* → FOOLS → DON'T LET GO, William Daniels *(Mr. Braddock)*, Murray Hamilton *(Mr. Robinson)*, Elizabeth Wilson *(Mrs. Braddock)*, Walter Brooke *(Mr. McGuire)* → the LANDLORD, Alice Ghostley *(Mrs. Singleman)* → RECORD CITY → GREASE, Buck Henry *(hotel desk clerk)* → CANDY → the OWL AND THE PUSSYCAT → EVEN COWGIRLS GET THE BLUES

Storyline: Mike Nichols' wry, French New Wave via Hollywood take on inter-generational conflict and middle class alienation, following the hapless Benjamin Braddock as he gets lured into an affair with an older woman. His seedy trysts with the elder Mrs. Robinson soon make way for a genuine love affair with her daughter (Elaine), which, predictably, Robinson senior successfully calls a halt to. As Elaine girds her loins for an arranged marriage to someone else, Ben finally takes his destiny into his own hands. *BG*

Movie rating: *9

Visual: video + dvd

Off the record: (see below)

SIMON & GARFUNKEL (score: DAVE GRUSIN *)

Mar 68. (lp) *Columbia; <3180> C.B.S.; (70042)* [1] Oct68 [3]

– The sound of silence / The singleman party foxtrot (*) / Mrs. Robinson / Sunporch cha-cha-cha (*) / Scarborough fair – Canticle (interlude) / On the strip (*) / April come she will / The folks (*) / Scarborough fair – Canticle / A great effect (*) / The big bright green pleasure machine / Whew (*) / Mrs. Robinson / The sound of silence. *(re-iss. Feb84 lp/c; CBS/40 32359) (cd-iss. Dec85; CD 70042) (cd re-iss. Apr89 & Feb94; CD 32359) (lp re-iss. Nov98 on 'Simply Vinyl'; SVLP 39)*

S/track review: One of the best selling soundtracks of all time, boasting an iconic sleeve and some of the era's most iconic songwriting, this was also the prototype for matchmaking previously-released singles to onscreen action, a seismic shift from traditional film scoring. The concept was subsequently developed by 1969's 'Easy Rider', and eventually taken to its extreme with the anonymous, identikit compilations that pass for soundtracks in the 21st Century. Back then, marrying the bittersweet folk-pop of SIMON & GARFUNKEL to Braddock's youthful ennui was a shrewd move in itself. The duo hardly needed a boost to their commercial fortunes but 'The GRADUATE' massively widened their audience, ironically bridging exactly the kind of generation gap Nichols' film was making a comment on. As an opening shot, the churning, epochal 'Sound Of Silence' would invest any soundtrack with poetic portent, but it's 'Mrs. Robinson' which defined the movie, and by association, the soundtrack. One of the most buoyant tunes in the PAUL SIMON songbook, its freshman scat and breathless chorus are actually best sampled on the 'Bookends' album or the original single. Here the song is brutally truncated, split between miserly one minute alternate versions at either end of the score. 'April Come She Will' sounds as gorgeous as ever even if some of S&G's other contributions aren't so definitive; the 'Feelin' Groovy'-vintage 'Big Bright Green Pleasure Machine' remains as self-consciously hip-talking as the overrated 'Scarborough Fair – Canticle' is precious (although its stripped down acoustic/strings "Interlude" is a minor revelation). DAVE GRUSIN shamelessly goes for some olde-harpsichord textures himself on 'Whew', while the rest of his score lunges between ballroom formality, big band swing and low-slung blues. He gets it just about right with the baritone parping 'On The Strip', although describing it as a cross between Burt Bacharach and the Electric Flag is probably giving it more due than it deserves. Music to have affairs with your girlfriend's mum by. *BG*

Album rating: *6.5

– spinoff hits, etc. –

SIMON & GARFUNKEL: Scarborough Fair – Canticle / April Come She Will

Feb 68. (7") *<44465> (3317)* [11] Mar68 [ ]

SIMON & GARFUNKEL: Mrs. Robinson / Old Friends – Bookends

Apr 68. (7") *<44511> (3443)* [1] Jul68 [4]

– other bits & pieces, etc. –

SERGIO MENDES & BRASIL '66: Scarborough Fair

Nov 68. (7") *A&M; <986> (AMS 739)* [16] [ ]

the LEMONHEADS: Mrs. Robinson

Nov 92. (7"/c-s/10"/cd-s) *Atlantic; (A 7401/+C/TE/CD)* [–] [19]

□ Nick GRAVENITES, Mike BLOOMFIELD, Paul BUTTERFIELD & Maria MULDAUR (⇒ STEELYARD BLUES)

□ Grant GREEN segment (⇒ the FINAL COMEDOWN)

GREEN ICE

1981 (UK 116m) ITC Films International / Universal Pictures (PG)

Film genre: romantic/crime thriller

Top guns: dir: Ernest Day / s-w: Edward Anhalt, Ray Hassett, Anthony Simmons, Robert de Laurentiis (au: Gerald Browne)

Stars: Ryan O'Neal *(Joseph Wiley)* → MALIBU'S MOST WANTED, Anne Archer *(Holbrook)*, Omar Sharif *(Meno Argenti)* → TOP SECRET!, Philip Stone *(Jochim Kellerman)* ← FLASH GORDON ← O LUCKY MAN!, Domingo Ambriz *(Miguel)* → YOUNG GUNS II, John Larroquette *(Claude)*

Storyline: Electronics ace Joe Wiley takes a vacation after his divorce and heads for the escapist resort of Las Hadas. There he meets Lilian Holbrook, a wealthy socialite who spends her time searching for her missing sister, who in fact was murdered by Colombian soldiers. She is also friendly with villainous Meno Argenti, who is deep in the emerald smuggling game. Wiley must use his electronics expertise to mastermind a heist in Colombia and turn the tables on Argenti who will no doubt be green with envy. *JZ*

Movie rating: *4.5

Visual: video

Off the record: **BILL WYMAN** (see below)

BILL WYMAN

May 81. (lp/c) *Polydor; (POLS/+C 1031)* [ ] [–]

– Si si / Beach chase / Holbrooks house (Green Ice theme) / Floating (Cloudhopper theme) / Emerald guitars / Emerald vault / The water bottle / Noche de amor / Colombia (Green Ice opening titles) / Tenderness / Showdown / Cloudhoppers / Churchyard (Green Ice theme) / The mines / Sol y sombra / Miami arrival / Emerald waltz / Si si – reprise.

S/track review: More than a decade before finally quitting the Rolling Stones, BILL WYMAN was a busy man. 1980 found him producing and mixing a Buddy Guy/Junior Wells live album and doing promotional interviews for the Stones' 'Emotional Rescue', as well as knocking out his first film score in his French home studio. The result is neither as bad as might be feared, nor as good as it could be; working with long-time collaborator TERRY TAYLOR (who is still with him in WYMAN's ensemble the Rhythm Kings), he delivers a professional if derivative slate of synthesizer-based instrumentals, cannily polished by judicious shots of trumpet and Spanish guitar, as well as the accomplished orchestral arrangements of the veteran Ken Thorne (who'd scored the Beatles movie 'HELP!'). The album opens and closes with the perky faux-Caribbean jig that would later transmogrify into the bassist's Top 20 hit, 'Je Suis Un Rock Star', but its biggest disappointment comes with its proper songs; the wonderful MARIA MULDAUR's zestfully playful voice is still best known for 1974's 'Midnight At The Oasis', but here it struggles painfully to make anything of two WYMAN numbers ('Floating (Cloudhopper Theme)' & 'Tenderness') that – to put it kindly – are not going to be turning up in any classic repertoire. *ND*

Album rating: *5

– spinoff releases, etc. –

BILL WYMAN: Green Ice Theme / Cloudhoppers

Jun 81. (7") *(POSP 291)* □ [–]

GRIZZLY MAN

2005 (US/Can 103m) Discovery Docs / Lions Gate Films (R)

Film genre: nature documentary bio-pic

Top guns: s-w + dir: Werner Herzog ← COBRA VERDE ← NOSFERATU, THE VAMPYRE ← HERZ AUS GLAS ← AGUIRRE, WRATH OF GOD

Stars: archival: Timothy Treadwell + Amie Huguenard / Werner Herzog *(narrator)*, Franc G. Fallico *(medical examiner)*, Warren Queeney, Sam Egli, Willy Fulton, Marc Gaede, Marnie Gaede, Jewel Palovak, Carol Dexter, Val Dexter, Kathleen Parker, Larry Van Daele, David Letterman ← MAN ON THE MOON ← MEETING PEOPLE IS EASY ← PRIVATE PARTS ← BEAVIS AND BUTT-HEAD DO AMERICA

Storyline: This haunting Sundance prizewinner documents the final years of eccentric enthusiast Timothy Treadwell, an anti-heroic, sympathetic eccentric firmly in the Herzog tradition. A well intentioned, visibly troubled character, Treadwell sought refuge from humanity among the grizzly bears of Alaska, wild camping in the heart of their habitat every summer for more than a decade. The natives aren't shy in voicing their opinions about him, but his fearless footage – which forms a large part of the film – makes for compelling viewing, as do the revealing, often self-perpetuating, occasionally disturbing commentaries and raving monologues of Treadwell himself (hear 'That's My Story' on the soundtrack, if you can't see the film). *BG*

Movie rating: *8.5

Visual: dvd (Maple Pictures)

Off the record: (see below)

——

RICHARD THOMPSON

Sep 05. (cd) *Cooking Vinyl; <(COOKCD 360)>* □ Oct05 □
– Tim & the bears / Main title / Foxes / Ghosts in the maze / Glencoe / Parents / Bear swim / Twilight cowboy / The kibosh / Treadwell no more / Teddy bear / Small racket / Streamwalk / That's my story / Bear fight / Big racket / Corona for Mr. Chocolate / Main title revisited / Coyotes (DON EDWARDS).

S/track review: More than a decade and a half after his last, less than happy soundtrack experience (Taylor Hackford's forgotten comedy, 'SWEET TALKER'), RICHARD THOMPSON was lured back to the big screen with a more promising proposition, an opportunity to work with cinema survivor/ace documentarian Werner Herzog. Likely not dwelling too much on the daunting standards already set by German Prog-sters Popol Vuh, THOMPSON enlisted ubiquitous avant-gardists HENRY KAISER and JIM O'ROURKE, and spent two days improvising over footage in Berkeley's legendary Fantasy Studios. The reputation of KAISER and O'ROURKE might have predicted a departure out of left field in the mould of late 80s ensemble French / Frith / Kaiser / Thompson, but 'GRIZZLY MAN' is composed and performed largely within a modal folk-blues idiom, faithfully evoking the endless horizons of an Alaskan summer. Opener 'Tim & The Bears' and the main title intimate a more abstract 'LOCAL HERO', ironic given that Treadwell was anything but. It's an initial impression compounded by the inclusion of 'Glencoe', a very Scottish lament last heard as part of a medley on THOMPSON's 1981 album, 'Strict Tempo!'. As one of only two previously recorded compositions – the other being 'Coyotes', a yodelling eco-lament from veteran cowboy poet DON EDWARDS – it can hardly help but stand out (alongside the self-explanatory 'Twilight Cowboy'), and it's only when DANIELLE DeGRUTTOLA's cello makes its lugubrious entrance on 'Parents', that the gravity of Herzog's film begins to make itself felt. She soundtracks the movie's queasy finale with frenzied, atonal abrasions, and THOMPSON, KAISER and O'ROURKE generate their own existential symphony on 'Big Racket'. Such is the singularity of Herzog's project it would've generated the same impact even without the music, but THOMPSON and Co can boast an achievement that both fulfills the task at hand and stands up well against some of the man's lesser solo works. *BG*

Album rating: *6.5

□ Dave GROHL segment
(⇒ TOUCH)

□ James William GUERCIO segment
(⇒ ELECTRA GLIDE IN BLUE)

the GURU

1969 (UK/India 112m) Twentieth Century-Fox

Film genre: romantic comedy drama

Top guns: s-w: (+ dir) James Ivory (+ story), R. Prawer Jhabvala (+ story)

Stars: Michael York *(Tom Pickle)* ← SMASHING TIME / → 54, Rita Tushingham *(Jenny)* ← SMASHING TIME / → SWING, Utpal Dutt *(Ustad Zafar Khan)*, Madhur Jaffrey *(Begum Sahiba)*, Barry Foster *(Chris)*, Aparna Sen *(Ghazala)*, Zohra Segal *(Mastani)*, Saeed Jaffrey *(Murad)*

Storyline: Pop star Tom gets all in a Pickle when he goes on a sabbatical to India to learn the sitar from expert player Zafar Khan. There he meets fellow student Jenny who doesn't have Tom's talent but at least shows some respect to the sitar swami. Zafar takes the pair to meet the Supreme Guru and it remains to be seen whether the English couple will curry favour with him or regret their Passage To India. *JZ*

Movie rating: *4.5

Visual: video + dvd

Off the record: **USTAD VILAYAT KHAN** (see below)

——

USTAD VILAYAT KHAN

Feb 69. (lp) *R.C.A.; (SF 8025) <LSO 1158>* □ □
– Title music: Tom's arrival – The guru's house – Carriage chase / Jenny's theme (1) / The haunted palace: Arrival – The courtesan's ghost – Revels / Murder / Tom's boat song / Jenny's theme (2) / The pupil and his master: Rag bilawal / Arrival in Benaras / The begum's lament / Train journey / Jenny's theme (3) / Tom's boat song (reprise) / Concert in the haunted palace: Rag malkauns / Concert in the haunted palace: Rag yamani.

S/track review: First there was Ravi Shankar ('CHAPPAQUA' & 'CHARLY'), the "real" Guru of Indian music and culture, then there was India's 2nd greatest sitarist and composer USTAD VILAYAT KHAN, one-time collaborator with Satyajit Ray on the classical score for 'The Music Room'); incidentally Usted means maestro. Recorded in Bombay and conducted by V. Balsara, VILAYAT was augmented by his country's finest session players at the time: USTAD IMRAT KHAN (his younger brother) on sitar and surbahar, SHAKOOR KHAN (one for the older generation here!) on sarangi, PANDIT SHANTA PRASAD on tabla, singers FAYAZ AHMED KHAN and ZINDA HASAN KHAN plus a host of musicians playing Western instruments. It must also be noted that although actor Utpal Dutt does not actually play the sitar in the movie, he in fact "fingered" each action to meticulous levels. The 3-piece suite of 'Title Music' opens proceedings. 'Tom's Arrival' is bright enough to shine into any dark corridor of 'The Guru's House', while third segment 'Carriage Chase' is particularly interesting with the addition of funky percussion. The recurring 'Jenny's Theme' is interspersed in 3 excerpts throughout the set, while the 4-part 'The Haunted Palace': 'Arrival' in particular, brings to mind the psychedelic folk of the Incredible String Band, who were indeed dabbling with Eastern culture during the latter half of the 60s. 'The Courtesan's Ghost' drags eerily along, reminiscent of a dozy sacred cow wandering into someone else's backyard – the Jenny (played by Rita Tushingham) metaphors are strictly unintentional as one has not witnessed the movie for over three decades. The film's unique balance of cultures is best served by actor Michael York and his quintessentially English cue, 'Tom's Boat Song', a dirge both monotone and derivative of the times – think Syd Barrett on 'The Piper At The Gates Of Dawn'. 'The Pupil And His Master: Rag Bilawal' is indeed a lesson in sitar personified, while side two subsequently carries on with disguised "title music"; although "incidental" all have a tingling energy and variety that one hardly notices. 'Concert In The Haunted Palace' brings the curtain down in two parts, the shorter 'Rag Malkauns' (echoing chants et al) and the much longer (13-minute) 'Rag Yamani', the latter technically excellent and weirdly redolent of the end of a psychedelic night out. This has to be one of the most underrated soundtrack recordings of all time, but if there is one fault it's that it drives you to narcolepsy. All'n'all, by several listens you'll be humming "GURU" dirges for weeks, nae months to come. *MCS*

Album rating: *6.5

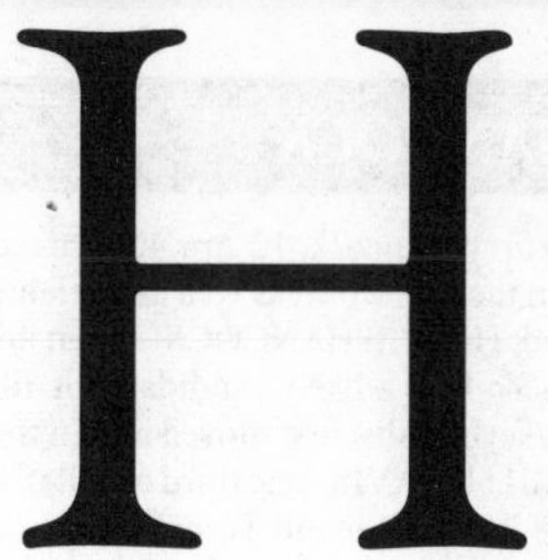

☐ Luke HAINES segment
(⇒ CHRISTIE MALRY'S OWN DOUBLE-ENTRY)

HAMMERS OVER THE ANVIL

1993 (Aus 95m) Harvey-Wright Enterprises / SAFC

Film genre: rural coming-of-age drama

Top guns: s-w: Ann Turner (+ dir), Peter Hepworth (story: Alan Marshall)

Stars: Charlotte Rampling *(Grace McAlister)*, Russell Crowe *(East Driscoll)* ← PROOF / → the INSIDER, Alexander Outhred *(Alan Marshall)*, Frankie J. Holden *('Bushman' Marshall)* ← PROOF, Jake D. Frost *(Joe Carmichael)*, Frank Gallacher *(Mr. Thomas, the preacher)* ← PROOF / → AMY → ONE PERFECT DAY, Alethea McGrath *(Mrs. Bilson)*, Amanda Douge *(Nellie Bolster)*, John Lee *(Charles McAlister)*, Syd Brisbane *(Duke; the dance caller)* → SILENT PARTNER → ONE PERFECT DAY

Storyline: Alan Marshall is a young lad living in the Outback at the turn of the last century. Crippled by polio from an early age, he has to wear leg braces which stops him from achieving his dream of riding a horse and makes him feel a bit of a loner. He befriends local horse breaker East Driscoll and soon finds himself a slightly unwilling go-between for Driscoll and his secret lover Grace McAllister. *JZ*

Movie rating: *6

Visual: video + dvd

Off the record: Frankie J. Holden (born Peter Brian) was in the band, Ol' 55.

NOT DROWNING, WAVING: Hammers

1994. (cd) *Rogues' Gallery; (RG 002)* [–] Austra [–]
– Hammer / Thoughts of Charlotte / Mist / The chase / Mrs. B's gate / Remember / Waltz / Mist / Cup of tea / Hammers / Young'uns / Walk with dad / Nellie's farewell / Stay / Preacher.

S/track review: The second of NOT DROWNING, WAVING's venture into film soundtracks (the first was 'PROOF' in '91). 'Hammers', as it was retitled, was also the band's final studio outing before founding member DAVID BRIDIE took cellist HELEN MOUNTFIELD and formed My Friend The Chocolate Cake. Together with guitarist JOHN PHILLIPS (no, not that one), the classically-trained BRIDIE, along with Rowan McKinnon (bass), James Southall & Russell Blakley (drums), they deliver 15 tracks of incidental music, what one would expect from an unexciting period-costume drama from the outback. Solemn ambient strings with more than a hint of lilting folk music (example 'Mist', 'Hammer' & 'Preacher') produce a type of worldly rock music only NDW could get away with. Incidentally, Russell Crowe (of 30 Odd Foot Of Grunts), briefly sings in the movie. *MCS*

Album rating: *5

□ John HAMMOND segment
(⇒ LITTLE BIG MAN)

Herbie HANCOCK

Born: Herbert Jeffrey Hancock, 12 Apr'40, Chicago, Illinois, USA. A living legend in the jazz world as well as a relentless explorer and musical vagabond, HERBIE HANCOCK's open ended approach to his art always made him a likely candidate for film scoring. It's a genre the pianist/keyboardist first moved into in the mid-60s during his tenure with MILES DAVIS. One third of Miles' crack 60s rhythm section alongside Ron Carter and Tony Williams, HANCOCK was the hottest pianist in America when he recorded his brilliant score for 'BLOW-UP' (1966), Michelangelo Antonioni's cult Swinging London-set thriller. By the early 70s, HANCOCK and DAVIS had gone their separate ways, although both were experimenting with the rhythmic possibilities of funk, rock and electronics. HANCOCK, in particular, embraced the polyrhythmic potential of funk, creating his own brand of electro-groove on the seminal 'Headhunters' (1974). It was into this cutting edge environment which his scores for the movies 'The SPOOK WHO SAT BY THE DOOR' (1973) and 'DEATH WISH' (1974) were born, soundtracks which pretty much qualified as prime Blaxploitation fare, even if the cult thrillers they soundtracked ('DEATH WISH' at least) couldn't be classified in strictly the same way. Although he went through a creatively fallow period in the late 70s/very early 80s, again the pianist convincingly reinvented himself by embracing the new musical ideas and technology of hip hop/electro. During this period, HANCOCK also scored his first film in almost a decade, the wartime drama, 'A Soldier's Story' (1984). While there was never a soundtrack release, a French single did appear featuring Patti LaBelle, who also acted in the movie. Yet of all HERBIE's soundtracks, the most familiar and best loved is undoubtedly ''Round Midnight' (1986), Bertrand Tavernier's all-star tribute to the life of Dexter Gordon, and a record unique among HANCOCK's scores in that it finds him in acoustic jazz mode. A comparatively fertile period in terms of his soundtrack work, the late 80s also found him composing the music for violent cop/gangster movies, 'Colors' (1988), 'Action Jackson' (1988) and 'Harlem Nights' (1989), while his songs have appeared on soundtracks to 'Jo Jo Dancer, Your Life Is Calling You' (1985), 'Livin' Large' (1991) 'Zoolander' (2001), 'Twins' (1989), 'Pallbearer' (1996) and 'Donnie Brasco' (1997) amongst others. More recently, HANCOCK contributed to Cliff Martinez' minimalist synth score for Hollywood narco-thriller, 'Traffic' (2000). *BG*

- **filmography** (composer) –

Blow-Up *(1966 OST =>)* / **the Spook Who Sat By The Door** *(1973 OST =>)* / **Death Wish** *(1974 OST =>)* / a Soldier's Story *(1984)* / Jo Jo Dancer, Your Life Is Calling *(1986)* / the George McKenna Story *(1986 TV)* / 'Round Midnight *(1986 OST see; future edition =>)* / Action Jackson *(1988 OST w/ V/A; see future edition)* / Colors *(1988 OST w/ V/A see; future editions =>)* / Harlem Nights *(1989)* / Livin' Large *(1991)* / Blue Note: A Story Of Modern Jazz *(1997 {p} OST by V/A; see future edition)*

HANNAH MED H

US title 'A DIFFERENT WAY'

2003 (Swe 98m) Canal + / Crone Film Prod. / Trianglefilm (R)

Film genre: romantic drama

Top guns: dir: Christina Olofson / s-w: Per Nilsson (+ au), + Annika Thor

Stars: Tove Edfeldt *(Hannah Andersen)*, Joel Kinnaman *(Andreas)*, Adnan Zorlak *(Edin)*, Bibjana Mustafaj *(Milena)*, Thomas Mork *(Jens Nosslin)*, Anna Larsson *(Anna)*, Neda Kocic *(Cattis)*, Anneli Martini *(Hannah's mother)*, Niels Andersen *(Hannah's father)*

Storyline: Teenage vegan Hannah Andersen flies the nest and begins her new life in the big bad world. Things begin innocently enough as she leaves her dreadful poetry in various shops and takes the huff with cars and pollution. However, when she meets schoolteacher Jens she starts getting strange phone calls and thinks that she's being followed. Things get even worse when it turns out that Jens is not who he says he is and actually likes her poetry. *JZ*

Movie rating: *4

Visual: dvd

Off the record: Still most famous in the UK for Jose Gonzales' cover of their 'Heartbeats' (as heard in Sony's "bouncing balls" ad), Swedish brother and sister act Olof Dreijer and Karin Dreijer Andersson (aka the KNIFE), have nevertheless achieved success mostly on their own terms. Notoriously unwilling to engage with the mainstream media, the KNIFE didn't perform live until the release of their third album and only allowed the 'Heartbeats' cover to be used by Sony in order to fund their own 'Rabid' records label, on which they have released all their own albums. They formed the KNIFE after Andersson's previous outfit Honey Is Cool failed to parlay critical appreciation into commercial success, although they have since remained wary of music industry machinations. The KNIFE'S eclectic, wonky electropop remains a required taste, although sales have proved much healthier, especially since their international breakthrough, 2006's 'Silent Shout', capitalised on the success of Gonzales' cover. *SW*

——

the KNIFE

Nov 03. (cd) *Rabid; (RABID 17)* [–] Sweden [–]
– Real life television / Hannah's conscious / Handy-man / High school poem / New Year's eve / Three boys / This is now / The bridge / Copenhagen / Wanting to kill / Jen's sneaking / Vegetarian restaurant / At the cafe / A different way / Poetry by night / Listen now.

S/track review: This 2003 score was the third full work by Sweden's the KNIFE, released on the band's own 'Rabid' imprint. International fans may recognise several tracks that were recycled as bonus tracks on the 2006 re-releases of their first two albums, 2001's eponymous debut and 2003's 'Deep Cuts'. However, 10 of the 16 tracks are exclusive to this release and they all are of comparable quality to those two albums. Diverse and eclectic, sometimes bemusingly so, the tunes here range from Depeche Mode for fluoro kids ('Real Life Television') to berserk eurodisco ('Handy Man' and 'New Years Eve'), taking in nondescript ambience ('Copenhagen') and Twin Peaks aping 50s guitar ('At The Cafe') along the way. The overwhelming feeling here is that most of these styles have been utilised better elsewhere, and the KNIFE only barely avoid invoking Wogan-at-Eurovison-style derision by dint of sheer variety. High NRG closer 'Listen Now' is a good litmus test for casual listeners, some of whom may be moved to tear off their own ears, while others will relish its gay abandon. For fans of the KNIFE, 'HANNAH MED H' is certainly worth tracking down – it's essentially a whole album of "new" material – although it's unlikely to convert any unbelievers. *SW*

Album rating: *6

HAROLD AND MAUDE

1971 (US 91m) Paramount Pictures (GP)

Film genre: romantic comedy

Top guns: dir: Hal Ashby ← the LANDLORD / → BOUND FOR GLORY → LET'S SPEND THE NIGHT TOGETHER / s-w: Colin Higgins → the BEST LITTLE WHOREHOUSE IN TEXAS

Stars: Bud Cort *(Harold Parker Chasen)* ← GAS-S-S-S ← BREWSTER McCLOUD ← the STRAWBERRY STATEMENT / → ELECTRIC DREAMS → SOUTH OF HEAVEN, WEST OF HELL → the MILLION DOLLAR HOTEL → COYOTE UGLY → the LIFE AQUATIC WITH STEVE ZISSOU, Ruth Gordon *(Maude)* → VOYAGE OF THE ROCK ALIENS, Vivian Pickles *(Mrs. Chasen)*, Cyril Cusack *(Glaucus; the sculptor)* ← 1984, Ellen Geer *(Sunshine Dore; third date)*, Charles Tyner *(Brig. Gen. / Uncle Victor Ball)*, Eric Christmas *(priest)* → PORKY'S REVENGE, Tom Skerritt as M.Borman *(motorcycle officer)* → UP IN SMOKE → SINGLES, Susan Madigan *(girlfriend)*, **Cat Stevens** *(man in front of Maude at funeral)*

Storyline: 20-year-old Harold has been born with a silver spoon, trouble is his snobby family have turned him into a morbid, self-destructive brat, obsessed with suicides and death. All this changes when he attends another funeral and meets a bohemian 79-year-old, Maude. Their world becomes entwined in a weird romance which leads to a marriage proposal on her 80th birthday – can it last? *MCS*

Movie rating: *9

Visual: video + dvd

Off the record: CAT STEVENS was born Stephen Demetre Georgiou, 21 Jul'48, Soho, London, England – son of a Greek restaurant owner and Swedish mother. While studying at Hammersmith college in 1965 and performing under the moniker Steve Adams, he met ex-Springfields singer Mike Hurst. The man produced CAT's first single 'I Love My Dog', which led to him being signed by Tony Hall to new Decca subsidiary label 'Deram'. The record reached the UK Top 30 but was surpassed the next year when follow-up, 'Matthew And Son' hit No.2. CAT's songs were soon being covered by many, including P.P. Arnold ('The First Cut Is The Deepest') and the Tremeloes ('Here Comes My Baby'). After a barren chart spell and recuperation from TB two years previously, STEVENS signed a new deal with 'Island' records in 1970 ('A&M' in America). He scored a comeback Top 10 hit with 'Lady D'Arbanville', which lent on the production skills of ex-Yardbird Keith Relf. The man stayed on for his follow-up to parent album, 'Mona Bone Jakon', the classic 1970 album 'Tea For The Tillerman'. CAT went on to become one of the biggest stars of the 70s, although his output never matched the scale of his previous work and 'Teaser And The Firecat' (1971), another collection of pleasant satisfying singer-songwriter musings. 'Catch Bull At Four' (1972) and 'Foreigner' (1973) sounded a trite overwrought and cluttered, a failing that marked the remainder of his output for 'Island' until his musical retirement in 1979 when he converted to the Muslim faith and changed his name to Yusaf Islam; he also married Fouzia Ali that September. He and his large family reside in London teaching his faith to a local primary school. Towards the end of the 80s, he controversally sided with the Ayatollah Khomeini who wanted the head of Satanic Verses writer Salman Rushdie. *MCS*

—

CAT STEVENS

1972. (lp) *A&M; <GP 216>* [-] Japan [-]
– Morning has broken / Wild world / I think I see the light / I wish, I wish / Trouble / Father and son / Miles from nowhere / Lilywhite / Where do the children play? / On the road to find out / Lady d'Arbanville / Tea for the tillerman.

CAT STEVENS

Dec 07. (lp) *Vinyl Films; <VFR 2007-3>* [ ] [-]
– Don't be shy / On the road to find out / I wish, I wish / Miles from nowhere / Tea for the tillerman / I think I see the light / Where do the children play? / If you want to sing out, sing out / If you want to sing out, sing out (banjo version) / Trouble / Don't be shy (alternate version) / If you want to sing out, sing out (instrumental). *<w/ free 7">* – Don't Be Shy (demo) / If You Want To Sing Out, Sing Out (alternate version)

S/track review: CAT STEVENS was on the crest of a wave during the making of 'H&M', albums 'Tea For The Tillerman' & 'Teaser And The Firecat' had both cracked the US Top 10. This made it highly unlikely that this OST would see light of day as it did contain a handful of cues from the aforementioned 'Tea For . . .': 'Where Do The Children Play?', 'Miles From Nowhere', 'On The Road To Find Out' & the title track, plus three from 1970s 'Mona Bone Jakon': 'I Think I See The Light', 'I Wish, I Wish' & 'Trouble'. Two new CAT songs surfaced on the film, 'Don't Be Shy' and 'If You Want To Sing Out, Sing Out', the latter subsequently becoming somewhat of a classic; the tracks became available on a CAT STEVENS collection 'Footsteps In The Dark' (1984). For many years, fans of the film had to be content with a Japanese-only (bootleg?) LP, which was in all intents and purposes just a basic compilation that left out the two fresh numbers and included songs not even in the film ('Morning Has Broken', 'Wild World', 'Father And Son', 'Lady D'Arbanville' & 'Lilywhite'). Since the film's critically lambasted release in 1971, it's become something of a cult classic, and so too has the unavailable soundtrack. Thanks to big fan and filmmaker, Cameron Crowe, the LP finally saw light towards the end of 2007, complete with a 36-page booklet and a free red-vinyl 7". While the movie shows its morbid fascination for death, 'HAROLD AND MAUDE' the soundtrack, is quite uplifting, especially in three takes of the joyous 'If You Want To Sing Out . . .'. *MCS*

Album rating: Japanese comp. *7 / new OST *9

☐ George HARRISON
(⇒ the BEATLES)

Mick HARVEY

Born: 29 Sep'58, Rochester, Melbourne, Australia. Right hand man of the indomitable NICK CAVE all the way through high school to the Bad Seeds, multi-instrumentalist, songwriter and arranger MICK HARVEY has also carved out a parallel, if fairly low key, career as a film composer. While his status as a Bad Seed found him performing along with CAVE and Co in Wim Wenders' 'Wings Of Desire' (1987), he also scored his first solo screen commissions the same year, for German documentary, 'Identity-Kid' (1987) and TV drama, 'Totes Geld'. This was followed by a collaboration with CAVE and BLIXA BARGELD on the haunting industrial score to the John Hillcoat-directed, CAVE-penned prison drama, 'GHOSTS . . . OF THE CIVIL DEAD' (1989). It was an impressive beginning and one which HARVEY consolidated with scores to Lucian Segura's 'Alta Marea' (1991) and – in collaboration with ALEX HACKE – German road movie 'Vaterland' (1992). The gorgeous orchestrations heard on Hillcoat's 'TO HAVE AND TO HOLD' (1996) still rank as one of HARVEY's most impressive achievements, making striking use of native singers in sympathy with the movie's Papua New Guinea setting and again written in collaboration with CAVE and BARGELD. While no soundtrack was issued from Segura's 'Go For Gold!' (1997), the new millennium saw HARVEY's talents officially recognised in his native Australia with an AFI nomination for his score to criminal biopic, 'CHOPPER' (2000), the soundtrack of which sandwiched the man's compositions between tracks from his old band the Birthday Party as well as Aussie veterans such as Rose Tattoo and Cold Chisel. Having finally found success back home, HARVEY went on to score race relations drama, 'AUSTRALIAN RULES' (2002). In 2005, MICK became a one-man band as he resurrected his solo career via comeback set, 'One Man's Treasure', a country album featuring covers as well as his own compositions. *BG*

- **filmography** (composer) {acting} –

Wings Of Desire *(1987 {p})* / **Identity-Kid** *(1988 TV score)* / **Ghosts . . . Of The Civil Dead** *(1989 {b} OST w/ NICK CAVE & BLIXA BARGELD =>)* / the Phantom Horsemen *(1990 score)* / **the Road To God Knows Where** *(1990 {p} w/ NICK CAVE & the BAD SEEDS)* / Alta Marea *(1991 OST =>)* / Vaterland *(1992 OST compilation incl. w/ 'Alta Marea' & ALEX HACKE =>)* / **To Have**

& To Hold *(1996 OST w/ NICK CAVE & BLIXA BARGELD =>)* / Go For Gold! *(1997 score)* / **Chopper** *(2000 OST w/ V/A =>)* / Planet Alex *(2001 {b})* / **Australian Rules** *(2002 OST =>)* / Frank Hurley: The Man Who Made History *(2004 TV score)* / Suburban Mayhem *(2006 score)* / Deliver Us From Evil *(2006 score w/ Joseph Arthur)*

– compilations, etc. –

MICK HARVEY: Alta Marea & Vaterland *(compilation)*

Mar 93. (cd) *Ionic-Mute; (<IONIC 6CD>)* □ Jul96 □
– ALTA MAREA: Overture / Avanti / Polaroid / Tereseuta / Tango della Alta Marea / La ultima spiaggia / Partenza / IDENTITY-KID: Vibes theme / Guitar theme / Waynesville / VATERLAND: Opening sequence / Flying / Abschieds theme / Dream sequence / Mountain (pt.1) / Mountain (pt.2) / End titles / TOTES GELD: Verfolgt / Westhafen / Mannfred / THE REAL POWER OF TELEVISION: Askenazi gitar A. / Magyar dallam / Hirado theme / Askenazi gitar B.

MICK HARVEY: Motion Picture Music '94-'05

Nov 06. (cd) *Fine Line – Mute; (LIONIC 19CD) <9345>* □ Feb07 □
– Two guitars / At Neville's gate / Cicaders / Homecoming / By the river / Face to face / Reuniting / Finale / Main theme / Three guitars / Noises – Fire / Piano theme / Setting sail / Antarctica / Things going wrong / The man who made pictures / In the wars / Papua – New Guinea / Things going wrong again / Back in Australia / Chimes / End titles / The stabbing / In the bar / The Polish market / In the bar again / The farewell song.

□ Donny HATHAWAY segment
(⇒ COME BACK, CHARLESTON BLUE)

HAWKS

1988 (UK/US 105m) Rank Films (15)

Film genre: road movie & buddy film

Top guns: dir: Robert Ellis Miller / s-w: Roy Clarke

Stars: Timothy Dalton *(Bancroft)*, Anthony Edwards *(Deckermensky, "Decker")* → MIRACLE MILE, Janet McTeer *(Hazel)* → VELVET GOLDMINE, Camille Coduri *(Maureen)*, Jill Bennett *(Vivian Bancroft)*, Robert Lang *(Walter Bancroft)* ← CATCH US IF YOU CAN, Geoffrey Palmer *(SAAB salesman)* ← O LUCKY MAN!, Connie Booth *(nurse Jarvis)*, Julie T. Wallace *(ward sister)*, Sheila Hancock *(Regina)*, Imogen Claire *(Paradise madame)* ← SHOCK TREATMENT ← FLASH GORDON ← LISZTOMANIA ← the ROCKY HORROR PICTURE SHOW ← TOMMY

Storyline: Bancroft and Decker are two terminally ill cancer patients who decide to have one last fling before their time is up. The aggressive Bancroft, complete with red clown's nose and stocking cap, goads the more reluctant Decker into escaping from hospital and heading to an Amsterdam whorehouse (where else?). On their travels they pick up Hazel and Maureen who are unaware of their illness, but together the foursome reveal their secrets to one another as time ticks inexorably onwards. *JZ*

Movie rating: *6

Visual: video

Off the record: Timothy Dalton squeezed this film into his schedule between two Bond films, 'The Living Daylights' and 'Licence To Kill'. *MCS*

BARRY GIBB (score: John Cameron)

Sep 88. (lp/c) *Polydor; (POLD/+C 5234)* □ -
– Moonlight madness / My eternal love / System of love / Where tomorrow is / In search of love / Cover you / The savage is loose / Not in love at all / Words of a fool / Distant strangers / Change / Letting go. *(cd-iss. 1998 Dutch +=; 837264-2)* – Celebration de la vie (alternate version 1) / Childhood days (Japanese extended mix) / Seagull's cry / Celebration de la vie (alternate version 2) / Celebration de la vie (alternate version 3) / Eternal love (closing theme) / Words of a fool – Marley Purt Drive (Bee Gees '91 soundcheck) / Siren chase.

S/track review: Prosaic, mundane, banal, pedestrian, and downright boring. Just some of the words that spring to mind when listening to the OST to 'HAWKS', which is written, produced and performed by BARRY GIBB. Any success he had as one third of the Bee Gees, a group built on perfect vocal harmonies and infectious pop tunes, just disappears into the mire of cheesy, faux-atmosphere, late-80s, overused-synth nonsense that is this soundtrack. It's disappointing when you think of the Bee Gees' contribution to the likes of 'SATURDAY NIGHT FEVER' and the way it captured a moment in time. Here though, 'System Of Love' sounds like BARRY GIBB is trying to disco dance Aerosmith into an early grave, while 'Words Of A Fool' is what you get if you drunkenly marry Elton John with Mike & The Mechanics in a Las Vegas chapel presided over by a one-eyed Phil Collins impersonator. Ghastly. Less said about the rest, the better. There's no emotion, no energy, no atmosphere, no adrenaline-pumping rollercoaster rides, no intensity, no suspense, no mystery, no verifiable traces of intelligent life or any semblance of helpful film narrative. The land of obscurity is a good place for this soundtrack, the bin is even better. Truly awful. *CM*

Album rating: *1

– spinoff releases, etc. –

BARRY GIBB: Childhood Days / Moonlight Madness

Aug 88. (7") *(PO 15)* □ -
(12"+=) *(PZ 15)* – Cover You.

Isaac HAYES

Born: 20 Aug'38, Covington, Tennessee, USA. From smouldering 'Stax' innovator to blaxploitation big gun to unlikely 'South Park' icon, ISAAC HAYES has spun out his legendary career as stylishly as he's spun out countless cover versions. As a prolific in-house songwriter and session musician at Memphis' soul powerhouse, 'Stax', he was well placed to make the transition from backroom boy to pioneering artist. In contrast to the usual singles plus filler of the average 60s soul album, HAYES specialised in audaciously extended, lavishly orchestrated covers, often featuring breathy monologues on the trials of romance. Visually, he cut just as as striking a figure, cultivating an aloof, sultan of soul-esque mystique through sheer physical presence and a wardrobe stuffed with extravagant dashikis. Yet it was his commitment to atmosphere over hooks which suggested an inevitable move into film composing: after an initial co-credit (with Wes Montgomery) on Norman Mailer's 'Maidstone' (1970), HAYES combined both atmosphere and hooks on his Grammy winning soundtrack to Gordon Parks' 'SHAFT' (1971). While the iconic theme tune deftly incorporated his imposing vocal style and love of orchestration into a killer wah-wah funk groove, scaling the US chart (UK Top 5) and bagging an Oscar, the bulk of the soundtrack was given over to characteristically lengthier pieces. As the first African American to be bestowed with an Academy Award, HAYES was suddenly hot stuff in the film world and the success opened a door into acting. His screen debut came with a major part in Italian blaxploitation-marketed effort, 'Uomini Duri' – aka 'THREE TOUGH GUYS' (1974), for which he also composed the score. More impressive was his starring role in Jonathan Kaplan's 'TRUCK TURNER' (1974), for which he created another classic blaxploitation soundtrack. While the shades-obsessed auteur could've conceivably gone on making great soundtracks indefinitely, the mid-70s implosion of the genre steered HAYES into the disco market and million dollar debts. Save for a part in obscure Canadian comedy, 'It Seemed Like A Good Idea At The Time' (1975), it was also the end of the man's acting career, at least until a memorable role in John Carpenter's 'Escape From New York' (1981). Cameos in 80s TV staples such as 'The A-Team' and 'Miami Vice' presaged a more prolonged acting career in low budget crime dramas and spy thrillers such as 'Mace' (1987), 'Nightstick' (1987), 'Counterforce' (1987), 'Dead Aim' (1988), 'Prime Target' (1991), 'Deadly Exposure' (1993) and 'Illtown' (1996). More high profile was his unlikely return to the ghetto-crusing days of yore, albeit with tongue planted firmly in cheek in Keenen Ivory Wayans' blaxploitation send-up, 'I'm Gonna Git You Sucka!' (1988). More satrically-themed fare followed in the shape of Mel Brooks' 'Robin Hood: Men In Tights' (1993) and rap satire, 'CB4: THE MOVIE' (1993), the latter especially timely given the avalanche of HAYES-sampling hip hop/trip-hop tracks. The renewed interest spurred the man to resume his long abandoned recording career and while his pair of mid-90s albums met with critical approval, there was no wholesale return to the charts just yet. At least not until his unlikely adoption as much loved character, Jerome "Chef" McElroy, on subversive TV animation, 'South Park'. As the show's top school dinner meister and in-house lothario, the singing Chef revisited HAYES' late 60s/early 70s golden era, with the man himself doing the voiceovers and handling the vocals. As well as appearing in the series' feature length movie, 'SOUTH PARK: BIGGER, LONGER & UNCUT' (1999), he featured on the spin-off album, 'Chef Aid', belatedly re-entering the UK singles chart and scoring an unlikely British No.1 with his inimitable contribution, 'Chocolate Salty Balls'. While his 90s acting CV included heavierweight material such as Mario Van Peebles' revisionist western, 'Posse' (1993) and Tim Reid's deep south race relations drama, 'Once Upon A Time ... When We Were Coloured' (1996), the 'South Park' exposure subsequently led to bigger budget roles including John Landis' 'BLUES BROTHERS 2000' (1998) and inevitably, the millennial remake of 'Shaft' (2000). It also engendered the even more belated return of his film composing skills, with HAYES concocting a revised 'Shaft' theme tune (a minor UK hit) and sharing the composing credits on similarly nostalgic Afro-American drama, 'Ninth Street' (1999), in which he also played a supporting role. As well as overseeing the arrangements on Alicia Keys' sassy debut album, 'Songs In A Minor', he subsequently landed parts in John Frankenheimer's 'Reindeer Games' (2000) and featured prominently in the D.A. Pennebaker rockumentary, 'ONLY THE STRONG SURVIVE' (2002). *BG*

- **filmography** (composer) {acting} –

Maidstone *(1970 score w/ WES MONTGOMERY)* / **Shaft** *(1971 OST =>)* / **Wattstax** *(1972 {p} on OST =>)* / **Save The Children** *(1973 {p} =>)* / **the Black Moses Of Soul** *(1974 {*p} =>)* / **Three Tough Guys** *(1974 {*} OST =>)* / **Truck Turner** *(1974 {*} OST =>)* / It Seemed Like A Good Idea At The Time *(1975 {*})* / Escape From New York *(1981 {*})* / Jailbait: Betrayed By Innocence *(1986 TV {*})* / Nightstick *(1987 {b})* / Counterforce *(1987 {a})* / Mace *(1987 {*})* / I'm Gonna Git You Sucka! *(1988 {*})* / Dead Aim *(1988 {b})* / Feuer, Eis & Dynamit *(1990 {b})* / Prime Target *(1991 {*})* / Guilty As Charged *(1992 {*})* / Final Judgement *(1992 {a})* / **CB4: The Movie** *(1993 {b} =>)* / Deadly Exposure *(1993 {*})* / Acting On Impulse *(1993 TV {a})* / Posse *(1993 {a})* / Robin Hood: Men In Tights *(1993 {a})* / Oblivion *(1994 {a})* / It Could Happen To You *(1994 {*})* / **Soul Survivor** *(1995 TV {*} =>)* / Illtown *(1996 {a})* / Flipper *(1996 {a})* / Once Upon A Time ... When We Were Colored *(1996 {b})* / Backlash: Oblivion 2 *(1996 {a})* / Six Ways To Sunday *(1997 {*})* / Uncle Sam *(1997 {*})* / **Blues Brothers 2000** *(1998 {p} =>)* / Ninth Street *(1999 {*} score w/ Wayne Hawkins)* / **South Park: Bigger, Longer & Uncut** *(1999 {v})* / Reindeer Games *(2000 {a})* / Shaft re-make *(2000 hit on OST by V/A =>)* / Dr. Doolittle 2 *(2001 {a})* / Book Of Days *(2003 {*})* / Dream Warrior *(2004 {a})* / **Hustle & Flow** *(2004 {a})* / Return To Sleepaway Camp *(2004 {a})*

HE GOT GAME

1998 (US 134m) 40 Acres & A Mule / Touchstone Pictures (R)

Film genre: urban/sports drama

Top guns: s-w (+ dir): Spike Lee ← GIRL 6 ← CROOKLYN ← JUNGLE FEVER ← SCHOOL DAZE

Stars: Denzel Washington *(Jake Shuttlesworth)* ← the PREACHER'S WIFE ← MO BETTER BLUES, Ray Allen *(Jesus Shuttlesworth)*, Milla Jovovich *(Dakota Burns)* → the MILLION DOLLAR HOTEL, Rosario Dawson *(Lala Bonilla)* ← KIDS / → JOSIE AND THE PUSSYCATS → CHELSEA WALLS → RENT, Hill Harper *(Coleman 'Booger' Sykes)*, Zelda Harris *(Mary Shuttlesworth)* ← CROOKLYN, Ned Beatty *(Warden Wyatt)* ← PURPLE PEOPLE EATER ← NASHVILLE ← DELIVERANCE, Joseph Lyle Taylor *(Crudup)* ← GIRL 6, Jim Brown *(Spivey)* ← THREE THE HARD WAY ← SLAUGHTER'S BIG RIP-OFF, Bill Nunn *(Uncle Bubba)* ← SCHOOL DAZE / → IDLEWILD, Thomas Jefferson Byrd *(Sweetness)* ← GIRL 6 / → RAY, John Turturro *(coach Billy Sunday)* ← GRACE OF MY HEART ← GIRL 6 ← JUNGLE FEVER ← TO LIVE AND DIE IN L.A. / → O BROTHER, WHERE ART THOU?, **Lonette McKee** *(Martha Shuttlesworth)* ← JUNGLE FEVER ← SPARKLE / → HONEY, Jennifer Esposito *(Ms. Janus)*, Leonard Roberts *(D'Andre Mackey)*, Roger Guenveur Smith *(Big Time Willie)* ← SCHOOL DAZE, **Coati Mundi** *(motel clerk)* <= KID CREOLE & THE COCONUTS =>, Saul Stein *(prison guard Books)* ← PINK AS THE DAY SHE WAS BORN, Felicia Finley *(Molly)* → TEMPTATION

Storyline: Serving a lengthy term for the accidental killing of his wife, Jack Shuttleworth is offered a reprieve if he can convince his basketball playing son, Jesus, to play for the prison governor's old college team. As a high-school prodigy, however, Jesus has more tempting offers to consider. *BG*

Movie rating: *6.5

Visual: dvd

Off the record: PUBLIC ENEMY formed in New York early 80s by Chuck D, a student at Adelphi University in Long Island. MC'ing for a local DJ crew, Spectrum City, Chuck met the outfit's mainman, Hank Shocklee (who would subsequently become PUBLIC ENEMY's co-producer), the pair subsequently teaming up for Bill Stephney's rap show on WBAU. Producing rough mixes and co-hosting the show, Chuck developed his hard hitting lyrical style while Shocklee undertook his earliest experiments in creating funky noise collages. The inimitable Flavor Flav (b. William Drayton) was an avid listener, eventually joining the show as a co-host; the stage was set for the formation of PUBLIC ENEMY. Mulling over the offer of a record deal from 'Def Jam' via Rick Rubin, Chuck eventually formulated the concept of the group alongside co-conspirators Shocklee and Stephney. With a brief to combine the caustic hip hop of RUN-D.M.C. and the radical attitude of the CLASH, they appointed DJ Terminator X (b. Norman Rodgers), Professor Griff (b. Richard Griffin) as 'Minister Of Information' and a militaristic back-up troupe named the S1W's (Security Of The First World). They also set up a formidable production team, the aptly monikered Bomb Squad, consisting of Chuck, Eric 'Vietnam' Sadler, Hank and his brother Keith. Taking their name from an early demo track (included in reworked form on the debut album), 'Public Enemy No.1', the group unleashed their debut album, 'Yo! Bum Rush The Show' (1987). The intent was clear from the start; the sleeve depicted the crew standing menacingly over a turntable in a darkened basement, their faces semi-submerged in shadows while the PE logo featured a sniper surrounded by a mock rifle sight. The music inside was equally uncompromising, by 1987 standards anyway. Chuck D was clearly a man who meant business, not another mealy-mouthed hip hop boaster. 'It Takes A Nation Of Millions To Hold Us Back' (1988) was PE's tour de force, hip hop's tour de force, even. The album went Top 10 in the UK, propelling PUBLIC ENEMY into the media spotlight. The group were already the subject of much controversy and following anti-semitic remarks made by Griff in a newspaper interview, the media circus went into overdrive. Although Griff and PUBLIC ENEMY soon parted ways, these events informed much of the group's new material. Chuck D's initial response was the inflammatory 'Fight The Power', the rapper railing against what he perceived to be a white, European conspiracy to wipe out the black race. The song was given added resonance after appearing in Spike Lee's 'Do The Right Thing' over scenes of race rioting'. Much of 'Fear Of A Black Planet' (1990) portrayed PE as victims, hounded by a predominantly white media and while there were accusations of racism,

Chuck had previously clearly stated that the group's agenda was not anti-white. With Sister Souljah now on board, 'Apocalypse '91 . . . The Enemy Strikes Black' was as militant as ever, at least lyrically. More commercial and with a cleaner production than PE's previous releases, the album reached the US Top 5. In the three years prior to the next album, Flav (who had been arrested on a domestic charge) again found himself on the wrong side of the law in late '93, following an incident with his neighbour. After a spell in rehab for drug addiction, Flav was back in action for 'Muse Sick-N-Hour Mess Age' (1994), and although the record was a relative success, PUBLIC ENEMY felt they had taken the concept to its limit, calling it a day the following year. Chuck D had always been peerless both as an entertainer and an educator, but it was the latter route that he subsequently chose for his post-PUBLIC ENEMY activities, lecturing on the college circuit as well as writing a book and hosting a news show on America's CNN. While this one-man think-tank is not on the ball 100% of time, he remains a fiercely articulate voice for the disenfranchised among the black community. PUBLIC ENEMY's legacy meanwhile, transcends all boundaries of race and culture, no hip hop artists have yet come close. *BG*

—

PUBLIC ENEMY

Apr 98. (cd/c/d-lp) *Def Jam; <(558130-2/-4/-1)>* [26] [50]
– Resurrection / He got game / Unstoppable / Shake your booty / Is your god a dog / House of the rising sun / Revelation 33 1/3 revolutions / Game face / Politics of the Sneaker Pimps / What you need is Jesus / Super agent / Go cat go / Sudden death (interlude).

S/track review: Following his contributions to filmmaking spoof, 'Burn Hollywood Burn' (1997), CHUCK D reactivated PUBLIC ENEMY (alongside FLAVOR FLAV, ERIC SADLER, HANK SHOCKLEE & GARY G-WIZ) for a full-length soundtrack which also doubled as a PE album. Despite the sleeve proviso "Public Enemy music ain't never been pretty, nor does it cater fully to popular tastes", the appearance of STEPHEN STILLS, the predictability of many of the samples and the paring back of the noise factor suggested otherwise. Still, if late 90s hip hop could have done with anything it was a bit of prettiness, and 'HE GOT GAME' earned PE the biggest UK hit of their career, reprising the vibe of prime De La Soul via Buffalo Springfield's 'For What It's Worth', the gospel voices of the Shabach Community Choir and a creaky STILLS vocal. 'Shake Your Booty' is higher in the cheese stakes, a FLAVOR FLAV nonsense rhyme which leans heavily on the Philly disco chestnut, 'Do It Anyway You Wanna'. It's great fun, but hardly sonic terrorism. 'House Of The Rising Son' cleverly modulates the intro to the Who's 'Won't Get Fooled Again' but when they resurrect Monty Norman's James Bond theme on 'Game Face', it suddenly seems like a lifetime since they tore up James Brown and copped Slayer riffs. Only the Danny Saber-produced 'Go Cat Go' harks back to past glories but the minimalist aesthetic – consolidated with the appearance of the Wu-Tang Clan's MASTA KILLA – frames CHUCK D's fury more effectively when it doesn't rely on such obvious source material: 'Revelation 33 1/3 Revolutions' vents its spleen over a quietly menacing baritone sax loop and teasing glimpses of what sounds like the JB's 'Blow Your Head'; 'Politics Of The Sneaker Pimps' takes on the trainer barons with a sinewy jazz guitar figure. But for all the gothic string credibility of a cut like 'Unstoppable' (featuring the mighty KRS-ONE), it's the colourful Lightnin' Rod/Gil Scott-Heron-esque phrasing of closer 'Sudden Death', which really shows how great hip hop can be when it looks to its own roots rather than lazy samples. *BG*

Album rating: *6.5

– spinoff hits, etc. –

PUBLIC ENEMY: He Got Game / (mix)

May 98. (c-s) *(568985-4)* [ ] [16]
(12"+=/cd-s+=) *(568985-1/-2)* – Resurrection (mixes).

HEARTBREAKERS

1984 (US 98m) Jethro Films / Orion (R)

Film genre: seXual/romantic drama

Top guns: s-w + dir: Bobby Roth → BAJA OKLAHOMA → DEAD SOLID PERFECT → the MAN INSIDE → BRAVE NEW GIRL

Stars: Peter Coyote *(Arthur Blue)* ← TIMERIDER: THE ADVENTURE OF LYLE SWANN / → BAJA OKLAHOMA → the MAN INSIDE → a LITTLE TRIP TO HEAVEN → COMMUNE, Nick Mancuso *(Eli Kahn)* → BLAME IT ON THE NIGHT → PAROLES ET MUSIQUE → NIGHT MAGIC → BRAVE NEW GIRL → IN THE MIX, Carole Laure *(Liliane)* ← FANTASTICA / → NIGHT MAGIC, Max Gail *(Charles King)*, James Laurenson *(Tony Ray)* ← the WALL ← the MONSTER CLUB / → the MAN INSIDE, Carol Wayne *(Candy Keen)*, Jerry Hardin *(Warren Williams)* ← HONKYTONK MAN, Carmen Argenziano *(Ron Bolt)* → BAJA OKLAHOMA

Storyline: Eli and Blue are two friends who both have women problems. Eli works for his father's clothes business but his good career prospects can't find him any woman worth more than a one night stand. Blue is a budding artist seemingly too immature for a committed relationship. Things soon become strained between the two friends when they both fall for the same woman, who forces them to grow up and see women in a different light. *JZ*

Movie rating: *6

Visual: video

Off the record: (see below)

—

TANGERINE DREAM

1985. (lp) *Virgin; (207 212-620)* [–] W.Ger [–]
– Heartbreakers / Footbridge to Heaven / Twilight painter / Gemini / Rain in New York City / Pastime / The loser / Breathing the night away / Desire / Thorny affair / Daybreak. *(UK cd-iss. Jun95 on 'Silva Screen'; FILMCD 163) <US cd-iss. Jun95 on 'Silva Screen'; 1039>*

S/track review: It'd been a busy period in the mid-80s for former electro-progsters TANGERINE DREAM (i.e. EDGAR FROESE, CHRISTOPHER FRANKE & JOHANNES SCHMOELLING), having released a number of non-OST sets and film scores such as 'WAVELENGTH', 'RISKY BUSINESS', 'FLASHPOINT' and 'FIRESTARTER'. This was slightly different to these aforementioned efforts, indeed this was a sort of "love album" (check out 'Footbridge To Heaven'), albeit in an S&M/fantasy way. Fuse Vangelis with Howard Jones and you'll be somewhere close to where 'HEARTBREAKERS' was intended to go. There are some nice pieces here ('Rain In New York City' a prime example), but it's just not Tangerine Dream, the Tangerine Dream we all loved so much in the mid-70s 'Rubycon' days. When they get all funky, even Level 42-esque with 'Pastime', it becomes downright unbearable. I'm not a fan of most of the 80s at the best of times, the main reason being the cheesy, AOR-rock direction most groups took. Did they all have to sound like (Jefferson) Starship in their 'Mannequin' fad. Maybe it's for another world, or even to be left hanging on the telephone. *MCS*

Album rating: *4

HEARTLANDS

2002 (UK/US 90m) Miramax Films (PG-13)

Film genre: road movie

Top guns: dir: Damien O'Donnell / s-w: Paul Fraser (story: **Richard Jobson** / au: Andrew Keyte)

Stars: Michael Sheen *(Colin)*, Mark Addy *(Ron)*, Jim Carter *(Geoff)* ←

LIPSTICK ON YOUR COLLAR ← TOP SECRET! ← FLASH GORDON, Celia Imrie *(Sonja)*, Ruth Jones *(Mandy)*, Phillipa Peak *(Sarah)*, Jane Robbins *(Sandra)*, Paul Shane *(Zippy)* ← LA PASSIONE, Mark Strong *(Ian)*, Jade Rhodes *(Ebony)*, Paul Popplewell *(Gulliver's kingdom soldier)* ← 24 HOUR PARTY PEOPLE

Storyline: Dozy darts player Colin finally realizes he's been throwing blanks when his wife Sandra runs off with team captain Geoff (and the rest of the squad) to Blackpool. Mounting his trusty old moped, Colin speeds after his beloved and along the way meets a variety of characters who all have plenty of advice for him. Despite a crushed moped, Colin finally arrives in Blackpool to confront the runaway couple, but can he finally hit the bull's-eye and win Sandra back? *JZ*

Movie rating: *5.5

Visual: dvd

Off the record: Richard Jobson was ex-Skids singer turned poet, author and screenwriter.

—

JOHN McCUSKER (*) / KATE RUSBY (**)

May 03. (cd) *Pure; (PRCD 11)* ☐ ☐
– Colin's farewell (*) / Sweet bride (**) / Weeping crisps (*) / The fairest of all yarrow (**) / I wonder what is keeping my true love (**/*) / Leafy moped (*) / William and Davy – instrumental (**) / Drowned lovers (**/*) / The wild goose (**/*) / Beer garden (*) / I saw that Sandra (*) / Let the cold wind blow (**) / Yodelling song (TIM O'BRIEN) / The brownies (*) / Over you now (**) / Round the next corner (* & TIM O'BRIEN) / The sleepless sailor (**).

S/track review: Twinning some of the best previously-recorded songs by Barnsley's "folk babe" KATE RUSBY with new material by her professional and domestic partner, Glasgow's JOHN McCUSKER (of the Battlefield Band), this is a wee gem that sparkles quite independently of the movie that shaped it. The pair were already the golden couple of folk, individually and collectively trailing a bagload of acclaim and awards, and 'HEARTLANDS' makes it easy to see why: in a pop culture a-shiver with agitated striving, this is music that won't be bullied into stridency or hurry or over-excitement. RUSBY's voice dances like an agile, pretty child, mixing easy simplicity with a husky edge that brings knowing and depth, and it shines in measured, crafty arrangements that value space and silence. The instrumentation is acoustic and focused, with fiddle and flute weaving around accordion and guitar on material that is either traditional ('I Wonder What Is Keeping My True Love', 'Drowned Lovers') or follows tradition with respect as well as imagination. With a couple of diversions to keep listeners on their toes ('Yodelling Song' brings whimsy and 'Round The Next Corner' bustles brassily) the album is both vibrant and soothing, and a beguiling demonstration that less is more. *ND*

Album rating: *7.5

HEAVY

1995 (US 104m) Cine 360 Inc. (R)

Film genre: romantic psychological drama

Top guns: s-w + dir: James Mangold → WALK THE LINE

Stars: Pruitt Taylor Vince *(Victor Modino)* ← NATURAL BORN KILLERS ← WILD AT HEART ← SHY PEOPLE / → the END OF VIOLENCE → MONSTER, Liv Tyler *(Callie)* → EMPIRE RECORDS → THAT THING YOU DO! → DR. T & THE WOMEN, Shelley Winters *(Dolly Modino)* ← PURPLE PEOPLE EATER ← ELVIS: THE MOVIE ← CLEOPATRA JONES ← WILD IN THE STREETS, **Deborah Harry** *(Delores)* <= BLONDIE =>, Joe Grifasi *(Leo)*, **Evan Dando** *(Jeff)* <= the LEMONHEADS =>, David Patrick Kelly *(grey man in hospital)* ← CROOKLYN ← the CROW ← WILD AT HEART ← the ADVENTURES OF FORD FAIRLANE / → LAST MAN STANDING, Marian Quinn *(Darlene)* → I SHOT ANDY WARHOL

Storyline: Set in a New York bar/diner owned by his mother, Victor is a shy, rotund, 30-something pizza-maker who subsequently salivates at the very sight of new waitress, the young and vivacious Callie. Resident waitress, Delores, takes the opposite approach to the newcomer and out of resentment makes an unwelcome pass at the more assertive Victor. Unfortunately for the big man, Callie has a boyfriend, a possessive car mechanic called Jeff. *MCS*

Movie rating: *7

Visual: video + dvd

Off the record: Evan Dando's past film history (aka a bit part in 1994's 'Reality Bites') was about as brief as his US chart appearances with the LEMONHEADS; they peaked at No.67 with 'Into Your Arms'. His godlike genius only apparently sinking in with British fans who were only too ready to buy the likes of 'Mrs. Robinson' (their version of that classic Simon & Garfunkel/'The Graduate' song and 'It's A Shame About Ray'. In this film he co-starred alongside rock chicks, **DEBORAH HARRY** and Liv Tyler, the latter the daughter of wide-mouthed, Aerosmith frontman Steven Tyler. *MCS*

—

Various Artists (score: THURSTON MOORE *)

Jul 96. (cd/c) *T.V.T.; <8000-2/-4> Cinerama; (0022642CIN)* ☐ Dec96 ☐
– Victor and Callie (*) / Hot coals (EVAN DANDO) / Pile up (the PLIMSOULS) / Boxcars (ROSIE FLORES) / Undertow (*) / Frying pan (EVAN DANDO) / Carry me (the VIDALIAS) / Howard is a drag (the RAKE'S PROGRESS) / My heart belongs to only one (BEN VAUGHN) / California thing (FREEDY JOHNSTON) / Kissing on the bridge (*) / Lost (the PLIMSOULS) / '74-'75 (the CONNELLS) / To dream of Sarah (ELENI MANDELL) / How much I've lied (EVAN DANDO) / Spinning goodbye (*) / Culinary institute (*).

S/track review: Could confuse the odd, neanderthal hard-rock fan, although there's nothing "HEAVY" about this easy-going collection. The conventional one-track-each, various artists soundtrack, 'HEAVY', is a mixture of score instrumentals featuring THURSTON MOORE (from SONIC YOUTH) and multi-contributions from the likes of EVAN DANDO (three) and re-formed power-pop outfit, the PLIMSOULS (er . . . two). THURSTON MOORE's donations – all five of them, including opener 'Victor And Callie' – were atmospheric, guitar-plucked instrumentals, bleak and laid-back to the point of being horizontal, while the ex-Lemonhead got to do his alt-country thing. DANDO strummed his way through a trio of covers, namely 'Hot Coals' (from the pen of Jeff Rymes), 'Frying Pan' (ditto: Victoria Williams) and 'How Much I've Lied' (written by his idol, Gram Parsons), all sounding a million miles away from his former indie-rock roots, and lying just about where Elvis Costello was with 'Almost Blue' in '81. One of America's unsung heroes, the PLIMSOULS (featuring leader, PETER CASE), had almost timed their mid-90s comeback to tie-in with the OST, tracks 'Pile Up' and 'Lost' kicking back the years and going for a sort of Beatles-meets-Stray Cats feel. Several other acts were on show, the pick of them being 'Boxcars' by ROSIE FLORES, a "Minnie The Moocher"-esque country number featuring a dreamy Hawaiian guitar. Featuring singer-songwriter, Charles Walston, the VIDALIAS (named so after Georgia's famous onions) were another new country-rock outfit, their Chris Isaak-esque 'Carry Me' also reminiscent of the Flying Burrito Brothers – the Gram Parsons connections just keep on a-comin'. Many will know the name of hard-working BEN VAUGHN as the man behind the theme tune to TV's award-winning 'Third Rock From The Sun', but here with 'My Heart Belongs To Only One' we have standard retro-fied Buddy Holly. Another solo artist around for a long time was FREEDY JOHNSTON, his number 'California Thing' probably celebrating his recent upgrade to 'Elektra' records. By far the most recognisable tune on the soundtrack was ''74-'75' by soft-rock aficionados the CONNELLS, originally a song from their 'Ring' set in 1993 and now a UK Top 20 hit. File under "where are they now". *MCS*

Album rating: *6.5

HEAVY TRAFFIC

1973 (US 76m) American International Pictures (X)

Film genre: animated seXual comedy drama

Top guns: dir: (+ s-w) Ralph Bakshi ← FRITZ THE CAT / → AMERICAN POP

Voices: Joseph Kaufmann *(Michael)*, Beverly Hope Atkinson *(Carole)*, Frank DeKova *(Angelo "Angie" Corleone)* → AMERICAN POP, Terri Haven *(Ida)*, Kim Hamilton

Storyline: 'FRITZ THE CAT' director Ralph Bakshi followed up with this hard-bitten animation (initially planned as an adaptation of Hubert Selby Jr.'s graphic novel, 'Last Exit To Brooklyn') centering on the adventures of Michael, an Italo-Jew who leaves his family mightily displeased after he marries a black woman. *BG*

Movie rating: *4

Visual: video + dvd

Off the record: (see below)

—

ED BOGAS & RAY SHANKLIN (& Various Artists)

Nov 73. (lp) *Fantasy; <F 9436>* [ ] [-]
– Scarborough fair (SERGIO MENDES & BRAZIL '66) / Scarborough street fair / Twist and shout (the ISLEY BROTHERS) / Angie's theme / Take five (DAVE BRUBECK QUARTET) / Carol's theme / Heavy traffic / What you sow / Maybellene (CHUCK BERRY) / Michael's Scarborough fair / Ballroom beauties / Ballroom dancers / Cartoon time / Ten-cent philosophy. *<cd-iss. Nov96 +=; FCD 24745>* – FRITZ THE CAT s/t *(lp re-iss. Feb00 on 'Moving Image Entertainment'; MIE 004)*

S/track review: A combination of original standards such as 'Take Five' (by DAVE BRUBECK QUARTET), 'Twist and Shout' (by the ISLEY BROTHERS), 'Maybellene' (by CHUCK BERRY) and Simon & Garfunkel's 'Scarborough Fair' (SERGIO MENDES & BRAZIL '66) are interspersed by jazzy-soul originals scored by 'Fantasy's in-house duo of ED BOGAS and RAY SHANKLIN; MERL SAUNDERS is on organ, keyboards & clavinet. The Godfather-esque, 'Angie's Theme' is basic run-of-the-mill score work, although most other tracks are rather in the groove and funky (example the title track plus 'What You Sow') or orchestral ('Ballroom Beauties' and 'Ballroom Dancers'). Closing track, 'Ten-Cent Philosophy', gets into the swing of things, quite literally, but it's just a cartoon after all, you shouldn't take it too seriously. *BG & MCS*

Album rating: *5.5

HELL UP IN HARLEM

1973 (US 94m) American International Pictures (R)

Film genre: gangster/crime thriller

Top guns: s-w + dir: Larry Cohen → BLACK CAESAR

Stars: Fred Williamson *(Tommy Gibbs)* → BLACK CAESAR → the SOUL OF NIGGER CHARLEY → THREE TOUGH GUYS → THREE THE HARD WAY → BUCKTOWN → MEAN JOHNNY BARROWS → ADIOS AMIGO → NO WAY BACK → MR. MEAN → FROM DUSK TILL DAWN → RIDE → CARMEN: A HIP HOPERA, D'Urville Martin *(Reverend Rufus)* ← the FINAL COMEDOWN ← WATERMELON MAN ← a TIME TO SING / → BOOK OF NUMBERS → BLACK CAESAR → the SOUL OF NIGGER CHARLEY → FIVE ON THE BLACK HAND SIDE → SHEBA, BABY → DOLEMITE → DISCO 9000, Tony King *(Zack)* ← GORDON'S WAR ← SHAFT / → BUCKTOWN → SPARKLE, Margaret Avery *(Sister Jennifer)* ← COOL BREEZE / → the JACKSONS: AN AMERICAN DREAM, Julius Harris *(Papa Gibbs)* ← TROUBLE MAN ← SUPERFLY ← SHAFT'S BIG SCORE / → BLACK CAESAR → FRIDAY FOSTER → LET'S DO IT AGAIN, Gloria Hendry *(Helen Bradley)* ← SLAUGHTER'S BIG RIP-OFF ← BLACK CAESAR ← ACROSS 110th STREET ← the LANDLORD / → BLACK BELT JONES, Gerald Gordon *(Mr. DiAngelo)*, James Dixon *(Irish)* → BLACK CAESAR, Esther Sutherland *(the cook)* → BLACK BELT JONES → FOXY BROWN → TRUCK TURNER

Storyline: Picking up the pieces where 'BLACK CAESAR' left off, Tommy Gibbs – with the help of his dad Papa Gibbs – pulls through after a botched assassination attempt contracted by corrupt District Attorney, DiAngelo. Tommy duly hires Papa as right hand man in his retooled racket, but doesn't count on the jealousy of chief hoodlum, Zach. Pissed off at being superseded, he goes on to slay both Tommy's ex-wife and, after Tommy has swapped Harlem for the good life in California with his new woman, Papa himself. Enraged, Tommy jets back to the Big Apple to take care of unfinished business. *BG*

Movie rating: *5

Visual: video

Off the record: **EDWIN STARR** was born Charles Hatcher, 21 Jan'42, Nashville, Tennessee, USA. Raised in Cleveland, Ohio, where he joined local group the Futuretones in 1957, his new act recorded a single for 'Tress' records, although subsequent releases were curtailed when he was drafted into the army. Posted to Germany, Edwin launched a revised solo singing career in local clubs, at a time when the Beatles were topping the charts. Returning to the States, he joined the Bill Doggett Combo (between 1963 and '65), before signing a solo deal for Detroit label 'Ric-Tic'. His debut 45, 'Agent Double-O Soul', clearly defined his R&B/soul roots and nearly broke him into US Top 20. After a couple more hits in the UK, where he had built up new following in the clubs, Edwin secured a contract with Berry Gordy's 'Tamla Motown' label. In 1969, the soul man had a US Top 10/UK Top 40 hit via '25 Miles', while the following year, he was No.1 in the States, via chanting, Norman Whitfield-penned peace anthem 'War' (a record which was later covered by BRUCE SPRINGSTEEN). Never quite emulating this triumph (although the OST to 'HELL UP IN HARLEM' came close critically), STARR did have another hit, 'Contact', a track to fire up the burgeoning 70s disco scene. Little was heard of Edwin throughout the next two decades – although he signed to briefly 'Virgin' records and sessioned for Stock, Aitken & Waterman – and sadly he passed away on the 2nd of April, 2003 – in Nottingham, England of all places. *MCS*

—

EDWIN STARR (composers: Freddie Perren & Fonce Mizell)

Jun 74. (lp) *Motown; <M 802V1> (STML 11260)* [ ] [ ]
– Ain't it hell up in Harlem / Easin' in / Big papa / Love never dies (Helen's love theme) / Don't it feel good to be free / Runnin' / Jennifer's love theme / Airport chase / Mama should be here too / Like we used to do / Ain't it hell up in Harlem (instrumental). *(<cd-iss. Mar01 & Aug01; 013739-2>)*

S/track review: Coinciding with 'Motown's move to Hollywood (a move mirrored by the film's plot), and after James Brown's score was rejected (mystifyingly, given the strength of its subsequent incaration as 'The Payback'), 'HELL UP IN HARLEM' inaugurated the brand-name partnership of FREDDIE PERREN and FONCE MIZELL. Writers, producers, arrangers and all-round backroom dudes of distinction, PERREN and MIZELL got their start as members of in-house hit-making aggregate the Corporation, fundamental to the early 70s success of the Jackson 5. Here, they split the composing credits and leave the singing to grizzly-voiced 'Motown' bruiser, EDWIN STARR. What was he good for? Absolutely everything that the label represented actually, top-flight soul delivered with conviction, wrapped in the kind of urbane arrangements PERREN and MIZELL made it their job to specialise in. Both the title theme and 'Easin' In' effectively bridged the gap between old and new 'Motown', taking up where Norman Whitfield/Barrett Strong left off. With 'Easin' In', especially, they hit the spot, conceiving it as a slinky distant cousin to STARR's monster No.1, 'War', arranging a halting yet cocksure bassline as pure rhythmic foreplay. They also vicariously live out the kind of

James Brown fantasy that had been too primal for the label in the past; 'Big Papa' is hardly a brand-new bag, but razor-choppy rhythm guitar and glam-gospel backing vocals make it perhaps the funkiest gutbucket growl in STARR's oeuvre. Add in the strongest of the album's two love themes and you have one of the most durable soundtrack A-sides of 1974. Side two slacks off a little, but PERREN and MIZELL stick their heads together for the bluesy extemporising of 'Runnin' and the cooing clavinet-funk of 'Airport Chase', while STARR charms despite himself on the Sly Stone-esque 'Like You Used To Do'. Although in the vanguard of blaxploitation scores, 'HELL UP IN HARLEM' surprisingly failed to bounce the singer back on to bigger and better things. PERREN and MIZELL, for their part, were just getting started. *BG*

Album rating: *8

– spinoff releases, etc. –

EDWIN STARR: Hell Up In Harlem / Don't It Feel Good To Be Free

Jun 74. (7") ☐ ⊟

EDWIN STARR: Big Papa / Like We Used To Do

Aug 74. (7") ☐ ⊟

a HERO AIN'T NOTHIN' BUT A SANDWICH

1978 (US 107m) New World Pictures (PG)

Film genre: urban drama

Top guns: dir: Ralph Nelson ← CHARLY / s-w: Alice Childress (+ au)

Stars: Cicely Tyson *(Sweets)* ← SOUNDER / → BUSTIN' LOOSE → IDLEWILD, Paul Winfield *(Butler)* ← GORDON'S WAR ← TROUBLE MAN ← SOUNDER / → MIKE'S MURDER → BLUE CITY, Larry B. Scott *(Benjie)* → FEAR OF A BLACK HAT, Helen Martin *(Mrs. Bell)* ← DEATH WISH ← COTTON COMES TO HARLEM / → REPO MAN → HOUSE PARTY 2, Glynn Turman *(Nigeria)* ← TOGETHER BROTHERS ← FIVE ON THE BLACK HAND SIDE, David Groh *(Cohen)*, Kevin Hooks *(Tiger)*, Kenneth Green *(Jimmy Lee)*, Arthur French *(security guard)* ← CAR WASH, Harold Sylvester *(doctor)* → FAST BREAK, Bill Cobbs *(bartender)* → ROADSIDE PROPHETS → the BODYGUARD → ROADSIDE PROPHETS → THAT THING YOU DO! → a MIGHTY WIND

Storyline: 70s Harlem, New York: Benjie is a black 13-year-old heroin addict, in denial about the extent of his problem and damning in his appraisal of the hypocrisy of friends and family. While his step- father Butler Craig tries his best to show his affections, enthusing about new opportunities for Afro-Americans, Benjie is jealous of his hold over his mother and scornful of his lowly position as a maintenance man; Butler himself admits he has no easy answers, is suspicious of social workers and psychobabble, and just wants a quiet life with a glass of whisky and a John Coltrane album. Number one target for Benjie's ire is teacher Nigeria Greene, the man responsible – along with put-upon jewish colleague Bernard Cohen (whom Greene regards as a gratuitous symbol of white authority) – for informing his family of his drug problem and, for Benjie, a man whose black nationalist rhetoric is so much sanctimonious hot air. *BG*

Movie rating: *4.5

Visual: none

Off the record: HUBERT LAWS is a much respected flautist/saxophonist who's worked with the likes of Mongo Santamaria, JJ JOHNSON, Miles Davis, Freddie Hubbard, Sergio Mendes and Gil Scott-Heron (notably on Scott-Heron's 1971 landmark, 'Pieces Of A Man') as well as icons like PAUL McCARTNEY and Leonard Bernstein, HUBERT LAWS started off in soundtracks in the late 70s, working with QUINCY JONES on 'The WIZ' (1978) and scoring this Alice Childress adaptation under his own steam. *BG*

—

HUBERT LAWS (score: Tom McIntosh)

Feb 78. (lp) *Columbia; <PS 35046>* ☐ ⊟
– School's out / I'm your fool – Butler's theme / Tiger's pad / Trackin' / Rehabilitation / Drop and pop / Somebody right now / Something to feel good / I can't leave you, Sweets / I'm your fool – Butler's theme reprise.

S/track review: Given the gritty subject matter and LAWS' jazz-funk pedigree, 'A HERO..' routinely gets bracketed under blaxploitation. There's no question the main theme, 'School's Out (Benji's Theme)' is funky enough, a loose-limbed, locktight aggregation of chukka-chukka rhythm guitar, ascending brass and LAWS' hide-and-seek filigree. Fans of his Scott-Heron stuff will lap it up, but the rest of the album is less about funk and more about jazz in its more tasteful guises. Not that he doesn't carry it off with aplomb, especially on the 'C.T.I.'-esque 'I'm Your Fool (Butler's Theme)'. Ex-pat Brit, VICTOR FELDMAN, mans the vibes on both 'Tiger's Pad' and the feisty 'Drop And Pop', while tenor saxophonist PLAS JOHNSON (himself an MOR session legend famous for performing on the original 'Pink Panther' theme and assorted other Hollywood scores, most Beach Boys albums and the Diana Ross soundtrack, 'LADY SINGS THE BLUES') takes the lead on 'Trackin''. No stranger to the classical world, LAWS also performs a lovely trio piece, 'Rehabilitation', blowing a melody from the Pino Donaggio school of pathos. Side B is much mellower if not quite as strong despite some luscious tenor phrasing and a reprise of 'Butler's Theme'. Overall, a fine soundtrack; re-issue please? *BG*

Album rating: *6

HERZ AUS GLAS

French title 'COEUR DE VERRE'

1976 (W.Ger 93m) New Yorker Films (18)

Film genre: experimental period-costume drama

Top guns: s-w + dir: Werner Herzog ← AGUIRRE, WRATH OF GOD / → NOSFERATU, THE VAMPYRE → COBRA VERDE → GRIZZLY MAN (au: Herbert Achternbush)

Stars: Josef Bierbichler *(Hias)*, Clemens Scheitz *(Adalbert)* → NOSFERATU, THE VAMPYRE, Stefan Guttler *(Huttenbesitzer)*, Sonja Skiba *(Ludmilla)*

Storyline: A small, 19th century Bavarian village slides into disorientation and madness after losing the secret of manufacturing the local ruby glass. Attempts to recreate the miracle formula are as doomed to failure as attempts to negotiate the plot in terms of a conventional narrative. Herzog famously hypnotised the entire cast, and the dilatory pace and intensity of performance are calculated for haunting, set-piece imagery rather than furnishing a storyline as such. *BG*

Movie rating: *6

Visual: video + dvd

Off the record: (see below)

—

POPOL VUH

Jan 77. (lp) *Brain; (0060.079)* ⊟ W.Ger ⊟
– Engel der Gegenwart / Blatter aus dem Buch der Kuhnheit / Das Lied von den hohen Bergen / Huter der Schwelle / Der Ruf / Singet, denn der Gesang vertreibt die Wölfe / Gemeinschaft. *(French-iss.1977 as 'COEUR DE VERRE' on 'Egg'; 900/536) (cd-iss. 1992 as 'COEUR DE VERRE' on 'Spalax'; SPA 14214) (cd-iss. 2005 on 'S.P.V.' +=; SPV 085-70182CD)* – Auf dem Weg – On the way (alternative guitar version) / Hand in hand in hand (Agape guitar version).

S/track review: Just as Herzog's movie is one of his most oblique and impenetrable, POPOL VUH's soundtrack isn't typical of their film work in general. The first Herzog/FLORIAN FRICKE collaboration to wholly feature the talents of ex-Amon Düül II man

DANNY FICHELSCHER (plus MATHIAS VON TIPPELSKIRCH), it's much more of a guitar/sitar-based album than 'AGUIRRE . . .' (1973) or even 'NOSFERATU' (1978). It's also arguably more one-dimensional than either of those records, and yet while it misses FLORIAN FRICKE's early, singular conception of electronica as a channel for communion with the unseen, under his beneficent direction a guitar is easily as esoteric as a moog. Most of the pieces are long, mantra-like slow-burners, rooted in Indian classical tradition and aflame with that Germanic combination of serenity, awe and misgiving which colours most of FRICKE's best work. In common with his other soundtracks, he also avails himself of Western folk and popular forms as resolution, as on the euphoric climax to opener 'Engel Der Gegenwart' and the latter part of 'Blatter Aus Dem Buch Der Künheit'. 'Hüter Der Schwelle', by contrast – and ironically given the proto-spiritual context – oppresses and entrances with the opiate potency of VU's 'Venus In Furs'. But it's the soundtrack tagline and penultimate track, 'Singet, Denn Der Gesang Vertreibt Die Wölfe' ('Sing, For Song Drives Away The Wolves'), which is perhaps most emblematic of FRICKE's intentions, elevating Herzog's weird science with cascades of pure liquid mercury. *BG*

Album rating: *6.5

– spinoff releases, etc. –

POPOL VUH: Sing, For Song Drives Away The Wolves *(revamped)*

May 93. (cd) *Milan; (13914-2) <35655-2>* □ Oct93 □
– Song of the high mountains / Pages from the book of daring / Dance of the Chassidim / Keepers of the threshold / Sing, for song drives away the wolves / Little warrior / Sweet repose / You shouldn't awake your beloved before it pleases her (Einsjager).

□ Boo HEWERDINE & Neil MacCOLL segment (⇒ TWENTYFOURSEVEN)

□ Monk HIGGINS segment (⇒ SHEBA, BABY)

HIGH ART

1998 (US 101m) October Films (R)

Film genre: romantic drama

Top guns: s-w + dir: Lisa Cholodenko → LAUREL CANYON

Stars: Ally Sheedy *(Lucy Berliner)* ← BLUE CITY / → SUGAR TOWN, Radha Mitchell *(Syd)*, Patricia Clarkson *(Greta)* → PIECES OF APRIL, Gabriel Mann *(James)* ← I SHOT ANDY WARHOL / → THINGS BEHIND THE SUN → JOSIE AND THE PUSSYCATS, Tammy Grimes *(Vera)* ← CAN'T STOP THE MUSIC, Bill Sage *(Arnie)* ← I SHOT ANDY WARHOL / → GLITTER → MYSTERIOUS SKIN, David Thornton *(Harry)*, Anh Duong *(Dominique)* ← I SHOT ANDY WARHOL ← the MAMBO KINGS, Rudolph Martin *(Dieter)* → SWORDFISH

Storyline: Syd's a svelte, ambitious young woman who's been made assistant editor on a New York photography magazine, hence the symbiotic strategies which ensue when she finds out her upstairs neighbour is semi-legendary yet reclusive photographer Lucy Berliner. Ushered into her coterie of narcotically inclined friends, the ostensibly heterosexual career girl persuades Berliner to shoot some material for her magazine as the pair slide into a relationship complicated – among other things – by the fact that Syd lives with her boyfriend. *BG*

Movie rating: *7

Visual: video + dvd

Off the record: (see below)

—

SHUDDER TO THINK

Jun 98. (cd) *Velvel; <(63467 79735-2)>* □ May99 □
– Opening / Dominoes / Cocoa butter / Mom's Mercedes / Photographic ecstasy / The gavial (RESERVOIR) / Noetony / ph balanced (for a lady) / Battle soaked (amnesian mix) / That's fat (JEEPJAZZ PROJECT) / She gives tone / Last lines / She might be waking up / Fools / End frame.

S/track review: As different from SHUDDER TO THINK's regular studio albums as it is from their 'FIRST LOVE, LAST RITES' soundtrack, 'HIGH ART' is a state-of-the-art, late 90s score which, despite sounding a little dated ten years on, won't let you off with a single listen. Less about scouring CRAIG WEDREN and NATHAN LARSON's record collection than extracting impressions contemporary enough to fit the era, the album exhales a tasteful frosting of ambient synth, treated instrumentation and vaporous trip-hop beats. At its most obvious – the swooning 'Fools'; the panting, Prince/George Michael-lite 80s throwback, 'Battle Soaked' (a remix, admittedly) – the music strays into frothy cappuccino land, but otherwise massages a delectably drowsy passage through your day; great for doing the ironing to. WEDREN especially, has a good handle on Fred Frith-style dilated air, surfing frequencies high enough to hypnotise but not quite strain your eardrums, emitting a sonic fog which hovers, lingers and resettles on cues like 'She Gives Tone'. WEDREN's also shrewd in manipulating the future-dub of 'Dominoes', but it's LARSON who dreams up those exalted, space-country melodies, shivering the skin on 'Cocoa Butter', 'Ph Balanced (For A Lady)' and 'Last Lines', and painting his rockabye retro sheen all over 'Photographic Essay'. He even dusts down his Paddy McAloon-esque vocals on the lovely 'She Won't Be Waking Up'. The glassy flow is – needlessly – interrupted only by WEDREN's aforementioned remix and a contribution from JEEPJAZZ PROJECT (the alias of Shane 'The Doctor' Faber, a writer/arranger who produced Digible Planets' Grammy-winning debut), looping the kind of treated harmonica in vogue years earlier. 'HIGH ART' never quite probes the sensory depths as thoroughly as say, Cliff Martinez's 'Solaris', but as an ambient score it floats well above the level of functional mood music. *BG*

Album rating: *6.5

the HIRED HAND

1971 (US 90m) Pando Company Inc. / Universal Pictures (R)

Top guns: dir: Peter Fonda / s-w: Alan Sharp

Stars: Peter Fonda *(Harry Collings)* ← EASY RIDER ← the TRIP ← the WILD ANGELS / → GRACE OF MY HEART → SOUTH OF HEAVEN, WEST OF HELL, Warren Oates *(Arch Harris)* → the BORDER, Verna Bloom *(Hannah Collings)* → ANIMAL HOUSE → HONKYTONK MAN → the LAST TEMPTATION OF CHRIST, Robert Pratt *(Dan Griffen)*, Severn Darden *(McVey)* ← VANISHING POINT ← MODEL SHOP, Ann Doran *(Mrs. Sorenson)* ← LIVE A LITTLE, LOVE A LITTLE, Ted Markland *(Luke)* → LAST MAN STANDING

Storyline: The lost genre of the hippy Western; we ain't never gonna see it's like again, son, and definitely not as Peter Fonda conceived it. This has been called the Wicker Man of Westerns and while that's probably a rope bridge too far, the two films share an ineffable sense of what's beyond. As the first, pizzicato-psyche strains of the composer's dulcimer echo into a high plains dawn, Fonda creates an unforgettable tableau of sun-dazzled rebirth and renewal. The subject is his character Harry Collings' young charge, Dan, who subsequently dies at the hand of a n'er do well named McVey. After dispensing some rough justice Collings and his sidekick Arch journey back to the farm where his wife has spent years trying to forget him. Ultimately, the ostensible simplicity of the plot, its themes of loyalty and gender, are subsumed into the dusty ambiente, with some mesmeric montage shot by the man who made Robert Altman's 'McCabe & Mrs Miller' such a murky pleasure. *BG*

Movie rating: *7.5

Visual: video + dvd

Off the record: A 60s sessioneer turned film scorer, **BRUCE LANGHORNE** initially made his way into the music business as a charismatic bit player on the Greenwich Village folk scene. In addition to studio session work for the likes of Tom Rush, John Sebastian and BOB DYLAN associates Richard & Mimi Farina, LANGHORNE famously played with DYLAN himself, contributing to 'The Freewheelin' Bob Dylan' (1963), 'Bringing It All Back Home' (1965) and the man's classic soundtrack, 'PAT GARRETT & BILLY THE KID' (1973). His own move into soundtrack composition presaged the latter work, a lost, recently recovered psych-country gem written to accompany Peter Fonda's directorial debut, 'The HIRED HAND' (1971). Scores to Fonda follow-up, 'Idaho Transfer' (1973), Bob 'Five Easy Pieces' Rafelson's 'Stay Hungry' (1976) – with BYRON BERLINE – and Jonathan Demme's 'Fighting Mad' (1976) followed in quick succession although only his work on Fonda vehicle, 'OUTLAW BLUES' (1977), made it to soundtrack, albeit with the aid of classical guy, Charles Bernstein. Following a score for Demme's breakthrough feature, 'Melvin And Howard' (1980), also unreleased, he moved into TV work and subsequently composed the music for two further movies, 'The Upstairs Neighbor' (1994) and 'The Argument' (1999). *BG*

—

BRUCE LANGHORNE

Nov 04. (cd) *Petite; <PTYT 002>* ☐ ☐
– Opening / Dead girl / Leaving del Norte / Riding thru the rain / Three teeth / Spring / Windmill / No further need / Arch leaves / Harry & Hannah / Ending. *<re-iss. Oct05 on 'Blast First Petite'; 30050>*

S/track review: 'The HIRED HAND' is one of those ravishing oddities that make the arcane world of soundtracks so addictive. It's an extended hymn to the silence and the Gods of the Old West and the Appalachians, scored by a veteran black accompanist/ session man who cut such a dash on the Greenwich Village folk scene that Bob Dylan was moved to pen 'Mr. Tambourine Man' in his honour. That it's been issued at all is – to soundtrack geeks and Dylan-ites alike – a miracle of Abraham-esque stature; even taking into account the vanished masters and sonic reconstruction ("the sound is not of the pristine, digital quality that we have come to expect from modern recordings", praise the Lord!), its inexhaustible depths argue a case that all composers should approach their task as amateurs, and follow BRUCE LANGHORNE's garage ethic to the letter. The music was recorded – by his girlfriend – on a Revox two-track and at least some of the magic comes from the vintage instruments, of which only a 1920 Martin guitar, fiddle and medieval-looking dulcimer survive. The Echoplex has long gone, but it lives on here in music of uncommon profundity, a sound that dissolves into the very DNA of the desert. There's no real indication of how LANGHORNE came up with this stuff, just 24 minutes of gloaming beatitude and unsolid air. Melodies are plucked out largely on the ancient strings, mantra-like in their humility, oscillating inside canyon-deep acoustics; Peter Fonda's unlikely pied piper brandishes his wooden recorder like a shamanic device, sending primordial whorls into a holy twilight. In fact, those premonitory bass notes would echo into LANGHORNE's work on that other luminous early 70s score, 'PAT GARRETT & BILLY THE KID'. The two soundtracks are different sides of the same saddle, even if 'The HIRED HAND' occupies a truly hallowed place in the greater Americana scheme of things, a hallucinatory refraction of Fonda's film and a mystic cowboy symphony in its own right. *BG*

Album rating: *8.5

HOMEBOY

1988 (US 118) Twentieth Century-Fox (R)

Film genre: sports drama

Top guns: dir: Michael Seresin / s-w: Mickey Rourke

Stars: Mickey Rourke *(Johnny Walker)* → JOHNNY HANDSOME → BUFFALO 66 → MASKED AND ANONYMOUS, Christopher Walken *(Wesley Pendergrass)* → WAYNE'S WORLD 2 → PULP FICTION → LAST MAN STANDING → TOUCH → the COUNTRY BEARS → ROMANCE & CIGARETTES → HAIRSPRAY re-make, Debra Feuer *(Ruby)* ← TO LIVE AND DIE IN L.A., Thomas Quinn *(Lou)*, Kevin Conway *(Grazziano)* ← FLASHPOINT, Anthony Alda *(Ray)*, Jon Polito *(Moe Fingers)* → the CROW → the SINGING DETECTIVE, Bill Slayton *(Bill)*, David Taylor *(Cannonball)*, Joseph Ragno *(Cotten's trainer)*, **Willy DeVille** *(Moe's bodyguard)* → BORN TO LOSE: THE LAST ROCK AND ROLL MOVIE, Matthew Lewis *(Cotten)*, **Ruben Blades** *(doctor)* → ALL THE PRETTY HORSES, Stephen Baldwin *(Luna Park drunk)* → LAST EXIT TO BROOKLYN

Storyline: Johnny Walker is an alcoholic down-and-out ex-boxer who is asked to go into the ring one last time to help debt-ridden Ruby keep her arcade. Meantime, gangster, Wesley Pendergrass, tries to enlist Johnny into taking part in an armed robbery which could make or break him. Knowing that just one blow to the head could potentially kill him, Johnny has a desperate choice to make. *JZ*

Movie rating: *5

Visual: video

Off the record: Willy DeVille (b. William Boray, 27 Aug'53, New York City, New York, USA). A singer-songwriter in the new wave/punk mould, Willy formed Mink DeVille in San Francisco, California around 1974 (he'd lived in London for the past few years), but relocated his new outfit to his native New York where they became favourites on the underground scene. Snapped up by 'Capitol' on the strength of a few tracks on the celebrated V/A collection, 'Live At CBGB'S', Mink DeVille broke through into the mainstream with their 1977 debut 45, 'Spanish Strollk'. A surprise UK chart hit in light of its characteristic Hispanic singing, crossed between Lou Reed and the more soulful R&B American singers, the track was one of the few highlights from their patchy eponymous debut set. Produced by Jack Nitzsche, the album failed to generate anticipated interest, although it was notable for the inclusion of Patti & The Emblems cover, 'Mixed Up, Shook Up Girl'. Follow-up set, 'Return To Magenta' (1978), fared little better, resulting in Willy relocated his musical endevours to Paris for the recording of third album, 'Le Chat Bleu' (1980). With each subsequent release, Mink (or just basically Willy solo) became an increasingly mainstream/AOR operation, culminating in a collaborative effort with MARK KNOPFLER, 'Storybook Love', from the soundtrack to 'The PRINCESS BRIDE' (1987). *MCS*

—

ERIC CLAPTON (w/ MICHAEL KAMEN & Various Artists)

Dec 88. (cd/c/lp) *Virgin; <791241-2> (CD/TC+/V 2574)* ☐ ☐
– Travelling east / Johnny / Call me if you need me (MAGIC SAM) / Bridge / Pretty baby (J.B. HUTTO & THE NEW HAWKS) / Dixie / Ruby's loft / I want to love you baby (PEGGY SCOTT & JO JO BENSON) / Bike ride / Ruby / Living in the real world (BRAKES) / Final flight / Dixie / Homeboy. *(cd+=)* – Country bikin' / Party / Training / Chase.

S/track review: Bluesman, ERIC CLAPTON, was no stranger to film scores by the time of this release, having contributed a couple of collaborative works, 'Edge Of Darkness' (1985) and 'Lethal Weapon' (1987). The music of the first few tracks of 'HOMEBOY' is a slow, lazy tempo very much in the blues mode, giving the impression of the hero's happy-go-lucky lifestyle in the film. The mood changes with a couple of rock numbers later on as the pace of the film quickens, and there is much more rhythm and beat from drums than before. Track 15 is an atmospheric mix of keyboard and drums which signifies the big fight and contains little in the way of melody, but for that reason it stands out more than any other track on the CD. The music ends with CLAPTON's solo version of 'Dixie' on electric guitar, a parody of Jimi Hendrix's 'Star Spangled Banner' and a brilliant end credits last track which makes the whole work a great listen for all blues and CLAPTON fans. *JZ*

Album rating: *6.5

□ HONK segment
(⇒ FIVE SUMMER STORIES)

HOOT

2006 (US 91m) New Line Cinema (PG)

Film genre: family comedy

Top guns: dir: (+ s-w) Will Shriner (nov: Carl Hiaasen)

Stars: Luke Wilson *(Officer David Delinko)* ← MASKED AND ANONYMOUS ← COMMITTED, Logan Lerman *(Roy Eberhardt)*, Brie Larson *(Beatrice Leap)*, Tim Blake Nelson *(Curly Branitt)* ← O BROTHER, WHERE ART THOU? ← THIS IS MY LIFE, Cody Linley *(Mullet Fingers)*, Neil Flynn *(Mr. Eberhardt)* ← MAGNOLIA, Kiersten Warren *(Mrs. Eberhardt)* ← DUETS, Jessica Cauffiel *(Kimberly)*, Robert Wagner *(Mayor Grandy)* ← DILL SCALLION, **Jimmy BUFFETT** *(Mr. Ryan)*

Storyline: Teenager Roy Eberhardt moves from Montana to Florida where he makes two unlikely friends in ace soccer player Beatrice and barefooted Mullet Fingers. They let Roy into their big secret – a colony of owls which they try to hide from property developer Chuck Muckle, who wants to take over the site for a new Pancake House. Aided by dimwitted cop Delinko, the kids must find a way to save the owls and prove the Pancake House is a big flop. *JZ*

Movie rating: *5

Visual: dvd

Off the record: Brie Larson (b. Brianne Sidonie Desaulniers, 1 Oct'89, Sacramento, California, USA) was a child actress turned pop singer – now where have we heard that before! (Hilary Duff, Lindsay Lohan) – who released an album, 'Finally Out Of P.E.' in 2005. Neil Flynn is the janitor from the cult TV sit-com, 'Scrubs'. *MCS*

Various Artists (incl. new songs by JIMMY BUFFETT (*) (score: PHIL MARSHALL, MICHAEL UTLEY & MAC McANALLY **)

Apr 06. (cd) *Mailboat; <MBD 2116>* □ [–]
– Wondering where the lions are (*) / Back of the bus (G. LOVE) / Barefootin' (* & ALAN JACKSON) / Florida (MOFRO) / Werewolves of London (*) / Let your spirit fly (RY CUMING) / Floridays (*) / Coming around (BRIE LARSON) / Funky Kingston (TOOTS & THE MAYTALS) / Good guys win (*) / Lovely day (MAROON 5 feat. BILL WITHERS & KORI WITHERS) / Happy ending (**).

S/track review: Featuring new recordings by amiable longtime Key West resident, JIMMY BUFFETT and various others, the 'HOOT' OST has an easy-going, laid-back-in-the-shade feel about it. Four of the five BUFFETT songs all stem from the pens of other artists: 'Wondering Where The Lions Are' (Bruce Cockburn), 'Werewolves Of London' (Warren Zevon), the freewheeling 'Good Guys Win' (by his band; Mac McAnally & Roger Guth) and 'Barefootin'' (Robert Parker); the one song written by himself is the cod-reggae 'Floridays'. About to tip his hat to the grand old age of sixty, Jimmy, unsurprisingly, sings mostly in a carefree, country/AOR fashion, befitting a man of his stature; the aforementioned ALAN JACKSON line-dancing duet of 'Barefootin'' the exception. Fellow Florida residents, MOFRO, get the Gomez/blue-eyed soul bug courtesy of a song about their beloved Sunshine State, while a new track by the cool RY CUMING ('Let Your Spirit Fly') is equally organic. Having discarded Special Sauce a few years back, G LOVE (aka Garrett Dutton) pops into the funk-rap mould by way of 'Back Of The Bus', knocks the socks off BRIE LARSON's Natalie Imbruglia-like 'Coming Around'. One of the highlights of 'HOOT' stems from the slick, neo-soul of MAROON 5 and their 'Lovely Day' rendition with the song's smooth soul-writer, BILL WITHERS (and his daughter KORI). With reggae a passion of BUFFETT and many of the Key West population, TOOTS & THE MAYTALS get down, courtesy of their early 70s nugget, 'Funky Kingston'; the steel drums, mouth-organ and guitar get into the fray via closing score instrumental, 'Happy Ending'. *MCS*

Album rating: *5.5

□ the HORSE FLIES segment
(⇒ WHERE THE RIVERS FLOW NORTH)

the HOT SPOT

1990 (US 120m) Orion Pictures (R)

Film genre: romantic crime thriller/drama

Top guns: dir: Dennis Hopper / s-w: Nona Tyson (au: Charles Williams)

Stars: Don Johnson *(Harry Madox)* ← ELVIS AND THE BEAUTY QUEEN ← ZACHARIAH, Virginia Madsen *(Dolly Harshaw)*, Jennifer Connelly *(Gloria Harper)* ← LABYRINTH ← PHENOMENA, Charles Martin Smith *(Lon Gulick)*, William Sadler *(Frank Sutton)*, Jerry Hardin *(George Harshaw)*, Barry Corbin *(sheriff)*, Jack Nance *(Julian Ward)* ← WILD AT HEART ← DUNE ← FOOLS

Storyline: Harry Madox is the kind of itinerant man's man who makes the ladies of smalltown Texas sweaty under their collars. While hatching a bank robbery, his hard-bitten patter lands him a job at a used car dealership, where he juggles relations with his boss' calculating, oversexed wife, Dolly, and the nubile secretary, Gloria. Although he eventually frees Gloria from the sinister clutches and intimate secrets of Frank Sutton, he's not quite as successful in freeing himself from a looming life sentence with Dolly. *BG*

Movie rating: *6.5

Visual: video + dvd

Off the record: Don Johnson kicked off his career in the early 70s via off-Broadway productions. After the success of the 'Miami Vice' series in the mid-80s, he increased his profile and returned to singing with a US Top 5 hit, 'Heartbeat'. *MCS*

Various Artists (composer: Jack Nitzsche)

Sep 90. (lp/c/cd) *Island; <PSCD 1085> Antilles; (AN/+C/CD 8755)* □ Oct90 □
– Coming to town (JOHN LEE HOOKER & MILES DAVIS) / Empty bank (TAJ MAHAL & MILES DAVIS) / Harry's philosophy (JOHN LEE HOOKER) / Dolly's arrival (TAJ MAHAL) / Harry and Dolly (JOHN LEE HOOKER, MILES DAVIS & TAJ MAHAL) / Sawmill (JOHN LEE HOOKER & MILES DAVIS) / Bank robbery (JOHN LEE HOOKER & MILES DAVIS) / Moanin' (JOHN LEE HOOKER) / Gloria's story (MILES DAVIS & BRADFORD ELLIS) / Harry sets up Sutton (JOHN LEE HOOKER & MILES DAVIS) / Murder (JOHN LEE HOOKER & MILES DAVIS) / Blackmail (JOHN LEE HOOKER & MILES DAVIS) / End credits (JOHN LEE HOOKER, MILES DAVIS & TAJ MAHAL).

S/track review: Exactly twenty years after 'JACK JOHNSON', and only a year before he was to bow out for good, MILES DAVIS made a career-capping return to both the big screen and the blues. This time around, John McLaughlin made way for JOHN LEE HOOKER, a Mississippi progenitor rather than a prodigious Yorkshireman. Completing an ersatz supergroup were TAJ MAHAL, slide guitarist ROY ROGERS, and a rhythm section of session godfather TIM DRUMMOND and legendary New Orleans drummer EARL PALMER. Hopper also surpassed himself by securing the services of veteran producer-turned-film composer Jack Nitzsche, who'd previously worked with ROGERS on 'One Flew Over The Cuckoo's Nest'. It's Jack Nitzsche's work on 'Blue Collar' (1978), though, which provides a more useful reference for the all-star jamming of 'The HOT SPOT'. There's no Beefheart-ed menace but there is HOOKER's lowdown moanin', a near constant, almost wordless commentary from the rambling larynx of a reluctant septuagenarian. Much sampled, it contributes enormously to the soundtrack's noir-ish, early hours torment, at times dissipating back into the blues' West African horizon or entering into indeterminate dialogue with DAVIS' horn. MILES, for his part, is economy personified, pacing spare, vaporous notes around HOOKER's wiry timing and gurgling trills, or MAHAL's National Steel. Only on 'Bank Robbery' – reprised on 'End Credits' – does he approach the ferocity of his sparring with McLaughlin, slicing bluesy lines over HOOKER's elastic boogie and cumulatively wresting the throb of electric blues back from the clutches of inept rock bands. It's blues as it was meant to be heard at the tail end of the 20th century, dark, seamless and hypnotic; great soundtrack music in other words, equally effective in the background or in your face. But it's also the sound of two of American popular music's greatest stylistic innovators confirming their continuing mutual relevance, a proposition so natural and innate that you'll find yourself wondering why they hadn't teamed up years before. *BG*

Album rating: *8

HOUSE OF 1000 CORPSES

2003 (US 88m) UMS / Lions Gate Films (R)

Film genre: occult/slasher horror

Top guns: s-w + dir: **Rob Zombie**

Stars: Sid Haig *(Captain J.T. Spaulding)* ← JACKIE BROWN ← the FORBIDDEN DANCE ← FOXY BROWN ← COFFY ← BLACK MAMA, WHITE MAMA ← IT'S A BIKINI WORLD ← BEACH BALL / → KILL BILL: VOL.2 → the DEVIL'S REJECTS, Bill Moseley *(Otis B. Driftwood)* → the DEVIL'S REJECTS, Sheri Moon *(Vera-Ellen / Baby Jane Bunny)* → the DEVIL'S REJECTS, Karen Black *(Gloria Teasdale / Mother Firefly)* ← NASHVILLE ← EASY RIDER ← YOU'RE A BIG BOY NOW, Dennis Fimple *(Hugo Z. Hackenbush; alias Grampa)* ← MACKINTOSH & T.J., Robert Mukes *(Rufus T. Firefly, aka R.J.)*, Irwin Keyes *(Emanuel Ravelli; alias Fiorello)*, Matthew McGrory *(Tiny; alias Baby Boy)* → the DEVIL'S REJECTS, Chris Hardwick *(Jerry Goldsmith)*, Erin Daniels *(Denise Willis)*, Jennifer Jostyn *(Mary Knowles)*, Rainn Wilson *(Bill Hudley)* ← ALMOST FAMOUS, Tom Towles *(Lt. George Wydall)*

Storyline: Two teenage couples drive round America to compile a roadside version of Fortean Times. They become intrigued when they learn about the legend of mysterious Dr Satan and set off to find the very tree he was hung from. However, a breakdown forces them to spend the night in a desolate old house with the creepy Firefly family, and as the night goes on the terrified teens look like becoming the main course for the crazy cannibals. *JZ*

Movie rating: *5

Visual: dvd

Off the record: (see below)

—

Various (score: ROB ZOMBIE & SCOTT HUMPHREY)

Mar 03. (cd) *Geffen; <(0694936342)>* [53] [ ]
– Howdy folks / House of 1000 corpses (ROB ZOMBIE) / Saddle up the mule / Everybody scream (ROB ZOMBIE) / Stuck in the mud / Holy Miss Moley / Who's gonna mow your grass? (BUCK OWENS) / Run, rabbit, run (ROB ZOMBIE) / Into the pit / Something for you men / I wanna be loved by you (HELEN KANE) / Pussy liquor (ROB ZOMBIE) / Scarecrow attack / My baby boy / Now I wanna sniff some glue (RAMONES) / Investigation and the smokehouse / The bigger the cushion / I remember you (SLIM WHITMAN) / Drive out the rabbit / Mary's escape / Little piggy (ROB ZOMBIE) / Ain't the only thing tasty / Dr. Satan / Brick house 2003 (ROB ZOMBIE feat. LIONEL RICHIE & TRINA) / To the house.

S/track review: As brutally stylized and emotionally one-dimensional as his cinematic debut, ROB ZOMBIE's score is perfectly suited to the movie it accompanies. For 'HOUSE OF 1000 CORPSES', ZOMBIE provided four exclusive full-band tracks, one older song (the title track, recycled from his earlier work 'The Sinister Urge') and one LIONEL RICHIE collaboration, as well as a handful of instrumental cues. The swampy industrial blues of ZOMBIE's full-band tracks evoke comparisons ranging favourably from Screamin' Jay Hawkins and Marilyn Manson (cf. 'Portrait Of An American Family') on one hand and unfavourably to Alabama 3 and Lordi (the Finnish Eurovision winners!) on the other. The best ('Run, Rabbit, Run' and 'Little Piggy') excuse the Lionel Richie cover, which isn't as clever as it thinks it is. Although subverting old pop songs is now a no-brainer for horror flicks, ZOMBIE has carefully chosen the few included here. 'Who's Gonna Mow Your Grass?' by BUCK OWENS becomes a tongue-in-cheek illustration of the weird family dynamic of his murderous characters, while the 1920s version of 'I Wanna Be Loved By You' is somehow completely at home here, something about its playful delirium chiming perfectly with ZOMBIE's hyper unreality. The inclusion of film dialogue (there are eight tracks of it here) is always risky, but when it's properly integrated (the 'NATURAL BORN KILLERS' score is a good example) it can gel a set of disparate songs into a cohesive listening experience. The excerpts on 'HOUSE OF . . .' put the non-ZOMBIE tracks into context and make the set flow together nicely on the first listen, although the repeat listener would inevitably find themselves skipping straight to the music, if they weren't annoyingly integrated. The score excerpts produced by ZOMBIE with long-time collaborator/producer SCOTT HUMPHREY are nicely handled pastiches of horror cliches, scraping strings and creepy noises. ROB ZOMBIE's take on the horror soundtrack is a well-crafted package, illustrating his affection for the genre, though being more a homage than a ground-breaker it doesn't add anything particularly new, simply turbo-charges what already worked. *SW*

Album rating: *5.5

HOWARD THE DUCK

1986 (US 111m) Universal Pictures (PG)

Film genre: comic-strip/sci-fi comedy

Top guns: s-w: Willard Huyck (+ dir) & Gloria Katz ← AMERICAN GRAFFITI (comic-strip: Steve Gerber)

Stars: Lea Thompson *(Beverly Switzler)*, Jeffrey Jones *(Dr. Walter Jenning)* → RAVENOUS → HOW HIGH, Paul Guilfoyle *(Lt. Welker)* → MANNY & LO, Tim Robbins *(Phil Blumbertt)* → TAPEHEADS → JUNGLE FEVER → HIGH FIDELITY → the PICK OF DESTINY, Chip Zien *(voice; Howard T. Duck)*, Ed Gale *(Howard T. Duck)* → BILL & TED'S BOGUS JOURNEY → O BROTHER, WHERE ART THOU?, Timothy M. Rose *(Howard T. Duck)*, Steve Sleap *(Howard T. Duck)*, Jordan Prentice *(Howard T. Duck)*, Mary Wells *(Howard T. Duck)*, Peter Baird *(Howard T. Duck)*, Lisa Sturz *(Howard T. Duck)*, Virginia Capers *(Cora Mae; secretary)* ← FIVE ON THE BLACK HAND SIDE ← TROUBLE MAN ← LADY SINGS THE BLUES ← NORWOOD / → WHAT'S LOVE GOT TO DO WITH IT, **Thomas Dolby** *(bartender in rock club)*, **the Cherry Bombs**:- Liz Sagal *(Ronette)* ← FLASHDANCE ← GREASE 2, Dominique Davalas *(Cal)*, Holly Robinson *(K.C.)* → the JACKSONS: AN AMERICAN DREAM, **Richard Edson**

(Ritchie) → WALKER → GOOD MORNING, VIETNAM → TOUGHER THAN LEATHER → WHAT ABOUT ME → STRANGE DAYS → the MILLION DOLLAR HOTEL → SOUTHLANDER, David Paymer *(Larry; scientist)* → ROCK'N'ROLL MOM, Miguel Sandoval *(cab driver)* ← REPO MAN / → SID & NANCY → STRAIGHT TO HELL → WALKER → JUNGLE FEVER, Nancy Fish *(bag lady)* ← BIRDY ← MORE AMERICAN GRAFFITI ← STEELYARD BLUES / → CANDY MOUNTAIN, John Fleck *(Pimples)* ← HARD ROCK ZOMBIES / → TAPEHEADS → CRAZY

Storyline: When a laboratory experiment goes wrong, the Dark Overlord of the Universe is transported to Earth with disastrous consequences. Luckily, unlikely superhero Howard the Duck also arrives and a series of amazing escapades follow as the superhero tries to stop the Dark Lord from destroying the Earth and conquering the universe. Howard, not necessarily a duck, just a turkey. *JZ*

Movie rating: *3

Visual: video + dvd

Off the record: Richard Edson was the original drummer for SONIC YOUTH.

___

THOMAS DOLBY // JOHN BARRY

Aug 86. (lp/c/cd) *M.C.A.; <MCA 6173> (MCF/+C/CD 3342)* [ ] Nov86 [ ]
– (THOMAS DOLBY):- Hunger city (DOLBY'S CUBE feat. CHERRY BOMB) / Howard the Duck (DOLBY'S CUBE feat. CHERRY BOMB) / Don't turn away / It don't come cheap (DOLBY'S CUBE feat. CHERRY BOMB) / I'm on my way // JOHN BARRY:- Lullaby of Duckland / Journey to Earth / You're the duckiest / Ultralight flight / Beddy-bye for Howard / Dark overlord.

S/track review: This cult 1986 OST combines the synthesizer skills of THOMAS DOLBY in the first five tracks with the instrumental ingenuity of John Barry in the last six. The first four tracks are sung by LEA THOMPSON and include the 'Howard The Duck' anthem and the moodier 'Don't Turn Away'. The style of music changes in 'I'm On My Way', a blues type number and changes again with the introduction of Barry's work. The track titles suggest the tone of the music – 'Lullaby Of Duckland' and 'Beddy-Bye For Howard' are slow tempo with romantic piano music, whereas 'Journey To Earth' and 'Dark Overlord' are much more upbeat, superhero-type pieces. Barry uses the orchestra with maximum effect – strings for suspense and tension, drums and brass for action and adventure all done in a slightly corny style parodying the John Williams 'Superman' theme. *JZ*

Album rating: *4.5

– spinoff releases, etc. –

THOMAS DOLBY: Howard The Duck / Don't Turn Away

Nov 86. (7"/12") *(MCA/+T 1092)* [–] [ ]

Willie HUTCH

Born: Willie Hutchinson, 6 Dec'46, Los Angeles, California, USA. A songwriter whose talents figured in the vanguard of 'Motown's blaxploitation assault, WILLIE HUTCH began his career writing for West Coast pop outfit Fifth Dimension. After polishing off the Jackson 5's 1970 No.1, 'I'll Be There', HUTCH was subsequently commandeered by 'Motown' kingpin Berry Gordy for further writing and production duties. While he'd actually begun a solo career a decade earlier, HUTCH finally established himself as a performing artist in his own right with a classic soundtrack to Michael Campus' 'The MACK' (1973), balancing the film's raw, uncut approach with empathetically orchestrated soul characterised by a lighter touch than the generally harder, wah-wah funk of many blaxploiation scores. While he followed up in similar style with the music for Jack Hill's iconic 'FOXY BROWN' (1974), HUTCH's profile dipped with the end of the blaxploitaiton era. He nevertheless continued to record in a solo capacity and, in tandem with writing and production work for other artists, belatedly returned to composing with contributions to Berry Gordy's blaxploitation/kung fu homage, 'The LAST DRAGON' (1985), and a score for obscure femme drama, 'Perfume' (1991). *BG*

- filmography (composer) –

the Mack *(1973 OST =>)* / **Foxy Brown** *(1974 OST =>)* / **the Last Dragon** *(1985 on OST by V/A =>)* / Perfume *(1991)*

□ I LOVE YOU, I LOVE YOU NOT alt.
(⇒ AMO NON AMO)

I WALK THE LINE

1970 (US 95m) Columbia Pictures (GP)

Film genre: cop/detective drama

Top guns: dir: John Frankenheimer / s-w: Alvin Sargent (au: Madison Jones)

Stars: Gregory Peck *(Sheriff Henry Tawes)*, Tuesday Weld *(Alma McCain)* ← WILD IN THE COUNTRY ← ROCK, ROCK, ROCK! / → THIEF → HEARTBREAK HOTEL → CHELSEA WALLS, Estelle Parsons *(Ellen Haney Tawes)* ← WATERMELON MAN / → DICK TRACY, Ralph Meeker *(Carl McCain)*, Lonny Chapman *(Bascomb)*, Charles Durning *(Deputy Wylie Hunnicutt)* → the BEST LITTLE WHOREHOUSE IN TEXAS → FAR NORTH → DICK TRACY → O BROTHER, WHERE ART THOU?, Jeff Dalton *(Clay McCain)*, Freddie McCloud *(Buddy McCain)*, Jane Rose *(Elsie)*

Storyline: Henry Tawes is a sheriff in deepest Tennessee, an upstanding citizen whose middle-aged hormones get the better of him as he turns a blind eye to the activities of local moonshiner Carl McCain so he can have his way with the man's daughter. Things take a violent turn for the worse when McCain kills one of his underlings and flees the state with his daughter in tow. *BG*

Movie rating: *6

Visual: video

Off the record: (see below)

JOHNNY CASH

Dec 70. (lp) *Columbia; <30397> C.B.S.; (70083)* □ Jun71 □
– Flesh and blood / I walk the line / Hungry / This town / This side of the law / Flesh and blood (instrumental) / 'Cause I love you / The world's gonna fall on you / Face of despair / Standing on the promises – Amazing grace. *<(cd-iss. Sep99 on 'Bear Family'+=; BCD 16130)>* – Little Fauss And Big Halsy soundtrack *(+ extra versions)*.

S/track review: Now the posthumous subject of his own Hollywood blockbuster, JOHNNY CASH maintained a sporadic relationship with film in his lifetime. Cut at the height of the man's prison revival, 'I WALK THE LINE' was the first – and the most downbeat – of two early 70s soundtracks, recorded in Nashville within weeks of each other. His 'Sun' breakthrough was once again the centrepiece but it's a solemn meditation without the whoop and spark of his jailhouse-rock. Only the defiant 'This Side Of The Law' and 'This Town' inhabit outlaw duds; 'The World's Gonna Fall On You' offers a clear-headed warning but for the most part, CASH – on the cusp of 40 – sounds like a man alternately wearied and consoled by his years, narrating aspects of his own life as much as the events of the film. 'Flesh And Blood' could be an open love letter to his new bride, June Carter, even as 'Hungry' distils the suffocation of routine and 'Face Of Despair' addresses ageing: "look at your September country" he admonishes in the reluctant voice of a juke-joint seer; he couldn't have known that some of his best creative days were still decades ahead of him. Accompaniment is minimal, as unobtrusive as his voice is biblical, and while the congregational singalongs are fine in the context of a CASH album, the orchestrations are less welcome, even if this is, after all, a soundtrack (and an all but forgotten and underrated one). *BG*

Album rating: *6.5

– spinoff hits, etc. –

JOHNNY CASH: Flesh And Blood / This Side Of The Law
Dec 70. (7") *<45269> (CBS 5364)* 54 Jan71 □

□ the IMPRESSIONS segment
(⇒ THREE THE HARD WAY)

IN THE NURSERY

Formed: Sheffield, England . . . 1982 by two sets of twins, Nigel and Klive Humberstone alongside Ant and Dolores Bennett. Specialising in military marching drum effects mixed with Cocteau Twins/Dead Can Dance-esque vocals and guitars mellowed down by romantic cello (bow on bass), this lot issued a string of low-key releases beginning with 1983's mini-set, 'When Cherished Dreams Come True'. Unfortunately, the group ran into a few problems with their follow-up 7", 'Witness To A Scream', the artwork printed wrongly and John Peel uncharacteristically fading the record out due to its poor quality. 'New European Records' (home of Death In June) took them on for a one-off 12", 'Sonority', this, and subsequent releases taking on a more orchestrated feel. During the second half of the 80s, IN THE NURSERY brushed aside charges of Fascist sympathies and concentrated on a prolific release schedule for the 'Sweatbox' imprint. By the time of 1990s 'Third Mind' ('Wax Trax' US) album, 'L'Espirit', ITN had fused their industrial sound with Ennio Morricone-type atmospherics, while 1992's 'Duality', saw them sampling the voice of actor, Richard Burton. Inevitably, the Humberstone brothers succumbed to world of film music, 'An AMBUSH OF GHOSTS' (1993), being their first of many scores to also hit the record shops. Side by side with a prolific domestic album return (from 1994's 'Anatomy Of A Poet' to 2007's 'Era'), they've combined re-hashed vintage/silent film OST's such as 'The Cabinet Of Dr. Caligari', 'Man With A Movie Camera', 'Hindle Wakes' & 'A Page Of Madness', to great effect. *MCS*

- filmography (composers) –

an Ambush Of Ghosts *(1993 OST =>)* / the Cabinet Of Dr. Caligari *(1996 OST of 1919 film; see future edition =>)* / Man With A Movie Camera *(1998 OST of 1929 film; see future edition =>)* / Hindle Wakes *(2000 OST of 1927 film; see future edition =>)* / a Page Of Madness *(2004 OST of 1926 film; see future edition =>)*

IN THE SHADOW OF THE SUN

1980 (UK 51m video) ICA Television

Film genre: experimental music movie

Top guns: dir: Derek Jarman ← JUBILEE / → GLITTERBUG

Stars: Christopher Hobbs, Andrew Logan, Karl Bowen, Graham Dowie, Lucy Su, Gerald Incandela, Luciana Martinez, Kevin Whitney

Storyline: A visual arts extravaganza highlighting the collective multi-layered, Super-8 work of filmmaker, Derek Jarman. Some of the non-linear material dates back to 1972-74, although the music was added much later. *MCS*

Movie rating: *5

Visual: video

Off the record: **THROBBING GRISTLE** (see below)

—

THROBBING GRISTLE

Feb 84. (lp) *Illuminated; (JAMS 35)* ☐ ☐
– In the shadow of the sun. *(<cd-iss. Oct93 on 'Grey Area-Mute'; TGCD 9>)*

S/track review: Probably the weirdest soundtrack ever to rise from the depths of alternative rock. In 1980, during a time when Londoners THROBBING GRISTLE and their nearest post-rock, industrial cousins, Cabaret Voltaire, were taking avant-garde music to new extremes. TG (GENESIS P-ORRIDGE, the delectable COSEY FANNI TUTTI, CHRIS CARTER and PETER 'SLEAZY' CHRISTOPHERSON) were responsible for some groundbreaking work during the early 80s, 'Second Annual Report' (1977) and the misleading '20 Jazz Funk Greats' (1979), among their best. 'IN THE SHADOW OF THE SUN' was nowhere near these classics. Basically one ambient track lasting a daunting 56 minutes (on the CD at least!), ringleader P-ORRIDGE took a backseat on the vocals front, bar some periodical screaming and shouting during loud crashing, blips and blops. This was hard work with no breather to shift the CD onwards, a near hour – like most of their early, controversial and pioneering stage sets – of woofs and tweeters. If their could be a comparison, maybe Eno or Pink Floyd might be close, although some pieces might well've been inspired by the Clangers of Tangerine Dream. Had to drop that one in – Tangerine Gristle, anyone? *MCS*

Album rating: *3.5

an INCONVENIENT TRUTH

2006 (US 95m) Paramount Classics (PG)

Film genre: environmental/political documentary

Top guns: dir: Davis Guggenheim

Stars: Al Gore *(himself)*, Billy West *(voice)*

Storyline: America's former Vice-President Al Gore raises his deeply shared concerns about global warming and the effects it might have on the human race. His campaign towards not only George Bush and the people of the United States, but to everyone everywhere is gripping and indeed, thought-provoking. But is it too late? *MCS*

Movie rating: *8

Visual: dvd

Off the record: On a subsequent date, 7th July, 2007, Al Gore was a leading figure in the global warming-associated "Live Earth" concert (featuring Genesis, Duran Duran, Metallica, Paolo Nutini, etc.) beamed to millions of people throughout the world. *MCS*

—

MICHAEL BROOK

Sep 06. (cd) *Canadian Rational; <CRBHE 005> Colosseum; (CST 8112-2)* ☐ ☐
– Main title [river view] / Science / Prof. Revelle / How could I spend my time? / Katrina / Election / Farm pt.1 / Farm pt.2 / Airport / Flood / Beijing / Tobacco / 1000 slide shows / Earth alone / Best unsaid (*) / Boom (*) / Carte noir (*). *<bonus tracks (*)>*

S/track review: With two previous OST releases under his belt, 'ALBINO ALLIGATOR' (1996) and 'AFFLICTION' (1998), "infinite" guitarist, MICHAEL BROOK, finally delivers his third full-length film score, 'An INCONVENIENT TRUTH'. Unlike the documentary movie, it's not all doom and gloom, BROOK's fusionist soundscapes set out as peaceful, atmospheric workouts. If there's any comparisons – on track 2, 'Science', for instance – there are echoes of fellow Canadian, Daniel Lanois, Passengers (the U2 offshoot) and Brian Eno, but most of the time, BROOK is out there in a "real" world of his own. With several of the cues taking a similar shape, there's not much to write home about here, 'How Could I Spend My Time?', 'Election', '1000 Slide Shows' and 'Earth Alone', being the exceptions to the rule. All instrumental of course, the majority of the tracks (and that includes a few extra tagged on at the end) average out at between 2 and 3 minutes. If one tends to nap after a quick bite to eat, the narcoleptic i-pod users among you are advised to steer clear of driving or using industrial equipment while listening to 'An INCONVENIENT TRUTH' – you have been warned. *MCS*

Album rating: *5.5

INFERNO

1980 (Ita 107m) produzioni intersound / 20th Century Fox (R)

Film genre: horror fantasy/mystery

Top guns: s-w: (+ dir) Dario Argento ← SUSPIRIA ← PROFONDO ROSSO / → TENEBRE → la CHIESA → NONHOSONNO

Stars: Eleonora Giorgi *(Sara)*, Gabriele Lavia *(Carlo)* ← PROFONDO ROSSO / → NONHOSONNO, Veronica Lazar *(the nurse)*, Leopoldo Mastelloni *(John; the butler)*, Irene Miracle *(Rose Elliot)*, Daria Nicolodi *(Countess Elise Stallone van Adler)* ← SHOCK ← PROFONDO ROSSO / → TENEBRE → PHENOMENA, Alida Valli *(Carol)*, Sacha Pitoeff *(Kazanian)*, Leigh McCloskey *(Mark Elliot)*

Storyline: Rose Elliot gets that tingly, hair-raising feeling when she buys a book which claims her apartment is the resting place of one of the sinister "Three Mothers". Rose does some snooping along with her friend Sara, but when they get close to knowing the Mothers' identity they are brutally murdered. Rose's brother Mark arrives from Rome and must solve the mystery before he too becomes a victim. Meanwhile, the enigmatic Professor Arnold is keeping mum about the Mothers' secrets. *JZ*

Movie rating: *6.5

Visual: video (1983) + dvd (2007)

Off the record: (see below)

—

KEITH EMERSON

Dec 80. (lp) *Atlantic; (K 50753) Cinevox; <CIA 33138>* ☐ ☐
– Inferno (main titles theme) / Rose's descent into the cellar / Taxi ride (Rome) / The library / Sarah in the library vaults / Bookbinder's delight / Rose leaves the apartment / Rose gets it / Elisa's story / A cat attic attack / Kazanian's tarantella / Mark's discovery / Mater tenebrarum / Inferno (finale) / Cigarettes, ices, etc. *(re-iss. Mar90 on 'Cinevox'; CIA 5022) (cd-iss. Feb98 on 'Cinevox'+=; CD-MDF 306)* – Inferno (outtakes suite).

S/track review: For the second part in his proposed "Three Mothers" trilogy (following 'SUSPIRIA' and preceding 'La Terza Madre'), director Dario Argento elected to overlook his house band Goblin in favour of a more "delicate" score from synth impresario KEITH EMERSON. The results are a mixed bag, with much of the score failing to rise above generic horror movie staples, with quiet, creeping piano melodies broken up by crashing sustained chords and string stabs to emphasise "drama". However rote, the score is nonetheless highly effective in establishing a thoroughly creepy mood and, even though some observers have noted its use in the film itself, sometimes undermines rather than underscores the shocks. EMERSON generally acquits himself quite well. The score picks up considerably when EMERSON lets rip and plays to his established strengths, i.e. ripping off classical sources in his own inimitable style. When at Argento's request, he reworks part of Verdi's 'Nabucco' (namely 'Va, Pensiero, Sull'ali Dorate') in 5/4 time for 'Taxi Ride (Rome)' the score rises above unfavourable comparisons to become notable in its own right. Here rattling pianos are overlayed with moog noodlings and intermittent bass and drums replicating the titular drive to startling and energetic effect. Elsewhere, choral voices introduced tentatively in the brilliantly titled 'Rose Gets It' pay off considerably in 'Mater Tenebrarum', a psycho burst of church organ and hysteric Latin that is so definitively Argento that it's hard to imagine even GOBLIN bettering it. Concluding with the suitably frenzied 'Inferno Finale' and synth tour de force 'Cigarettes, Ices, Etc.', EMERSON delivers a respectable – though thankfully not always too "delicate" – score that perhaps will appeal more to horror fans than to his own. *SW*

Album rating: *5

– spinoff releases, etc. –

KEITH EMERSON: The Taxi Ride / Mater Tenebrarum

Sep 80. (7") *(K 11612)* ☐ ☐ -

the INSIDER

1999 (US 157m) Touchstone Pictures (R)

Film genre: political/historical drama/thriller

Top guns: s-w: (+ dir) Michael Mann ← THIEF, Eric Roth (au: Marie Brenner)

Stars: Al Pacino *(Lowell Bergman)* ← DICK TRACY, Russell Crowe *(Jeffrey Wigand)* ← HAMMERS OVER THE ANVIL ← PROOF, Christopher Plummer *(Mike Wallace)* ← ROCK-A-DOODLE, Diane Venora *(Liane Wigand)* → LOOKING FOR AN ECHO, Philip Baker Hall *(Don Hewitt)* ← THREE O'CLOCK HIGH / → BOOGIE NIGHTS → MAGNOLIA, Lindsay Crouse *(Sharon Tiller)* ← PLACES IN THE HEART, Debi Mazar *(Debbie De Luca)* ← GIRL 6 ← EMPIRE RECORDS ← SINGLES ← JUNGLE FEVER ← the DOORS ← DOWNTOWN 81 / → BE COOL, Stephen Tobolowsky *(Eric Kluster)* ← ROADSIDE PROPHETS ← GREAT BALLS OF FIRE! / → the COUNTRY BEARS, Colm Feore *(Richard Scruggs)*, Bruce McGill *(Ron Motley)* ← CLUB PARADISE ← ANIMAL HOUSE, Gina Gershon *(Helen Caperelli)* ← TOUCH ← PRETTY IN PINK / → DEMONLOVER → PREY FOR ROCK & ROLL, Michael Gambon *(Thomas Sandefur)*, Rip Torn *(John Scanlon)* ← WHERE THE RIVERS FLOW NORTH ← SONGWRITER ← FLASHPOINT ← ONE-TRICK PONY ← PAYDAY ← YOU'RE A BIG BOY NOW, Lynne Thigpen *(Mrs. Williams)* ← STREETS OF FIRE ← GODSPELL, Clifford Curtis *(Sheikh Fadlallah)* → WHALE RIDER, Michael Moore *(himself)*

Storyline: Jeffrey Wigand is a research scientist for tobacco firm Brown and Williamson. After a major fall out with his employers, Wigand is approached by '60 Minutes' producer Lowell Bergman to spill the beans on the tobacco barons. Wigand agrees and does the interview, but at the last minute CBS pulls the plug on the show under pressure from their parent company. Wigand is left stranded as he tries to smoke out the truth. *JZ*

Movie rating: *8

Visual: dvd

Off the record: Russell Crowe (see 'PROOF')

—

LISA GERRARD & PIETER BOURKE
(additional score: GRAEME REVELL * & Various Artists)

Oct 99. (cd) *Sony; <63918> Columbia; (496458-2)* ☐ Mar00 ☐
– Tempest / Dawn of the truth / Sacrifice / The subordinate / Exile / The silencer / Broken / Faith / I'm alone on this (*) / LB in Montana (*) / Palladino montage (*) / Iguazu (GUSTAVO SANTAOLALLA) / Liquid moon / Rites – edit (JAN GARBAREK) / Safe from harm (Perfecto mix) (MASSIVE ATTACK) / Meltdown.

S/track review: It was inevitable as the sun rising that former Dead Can Dance mistress, LISA GERRARD, would step into the world of film music scores. Alongside one-time Dead Can Dance cohort, PIETER BOURKE, the Australian pair had previously contributed the score to 1998's 'Nadro'; however, 'The INSIDER' was their first feature to be awarded a release. Not content with having messrs GERRARD and BOURKE aboard, director and chief executive producer, Michael Mann, also saw the need for additional Antipodean composer, GRAEME REVELL (and others such as Argentina's GUSTAVO SANTAOLALLA, Norway's JAN GARBAREK and England's MASSIVE ATTACK), to be given extra tracks. But it was GERRARD and BOURKE that contributed the majority of the cues, ten in all. From the opening 'Tempest', a voice-versus-percussion track that could well've fitted on to the score of 'Gladiator' (Lisa's next neo-classical enterprise with Hans Zimmer), to Portishead-esque finale 'Meltdown', all tracks were eerily evocative and atmospherically cinematic. Pick of the bunch and worth the admission price alone is undoubtedly, 'Sacrifice' (another like 'Tempest' from Lisa & Pieter's 'Duality' set), a beautiful 7-plus minutes of sheer new age entropy, delivered in a way only gothic GERRARD can sing. Of the latter aforementioned offerings, the three consecutive REVELL excerpts ('I'm Alone On This', 'LB In Montana' & 'Palladino Montage') were short and a little incidental, but like all his soundtrack work, positively orchestral. SANTAOLALLA's 'Iguazu', meanwhile, was literally "plucked" from a lilting acoustic guitar, although the smoothness came via GARBAREK's saxy 'Rites'; Bristol tribe, MASSIVE ATTACK, secured their spot by way of an 8-minute Perfecto mix of their classic trip-hop number, 'Safe From Harm'. Good stuff all round. *MCS*

Album rating: *6

INTO THE WILD

2007 (US 141m) River Road Entertainment / Paramount Vantage (R)

Film genre: adventure docudrama

Top guns: s-w + dir: Sean Penn (au: Jon Krakauer)

Stars: Emile Hirsch *(Christopher J. McCandless)*, Marcia Gay Harden *(Billie McCandless)*, William Hurt *(Walt McCandless)*, Jena Malone *(Carine McCandless)* ← COLD MOUNTAIN, Catherine Keener *(Jan Burres)* ← WALKING AND TALKING ← JOHNNY SUEDE, Vince Vaughn *(Wayne Westerberg)* ← BE COOL ← THUMBSUCKER ← SOUTH OF HEAVEN, WEST OF HELL, Kristen Stewart *(Tracy)*, Hal Holbrook *(Ron Franz)* ← JONATHAN LIVINGSTON SEAGULL ← WILD IN THE STREETS

Storyline: College graduate Christopher J. McCandless gives his life savings to charity, looks out his survival handbook, and drives as far away from civilization as he can – the wilderness of Alaska. He keeps a diary of his mental and physical experiences as he settles down to live in an old bus. Soon, however, "Alexander Supertramp" finds the practical needs of food and shelter much more demanding than he imagined as he begins to grow hungrier, thinner and colder. *JZ*

Movie rating: *8.5

Visual: dvd

Off the record: **Eddie VEDDER** (see below & own biog)

—

EDDIE VEDDER

Sep 07. (cd) *J Records; <(88697 15944-2)>* [11] [ ]
– Setting forth / No ceiling / Far behind / Rise / Long nights / Tuolumne / Hard sun / Society / The wolf / End of the road / Guaranteed. *(hidden track +=)* – Guaranteed (humming vocal).

S/track review: While MICHAEL BROOK (see own entry) was credited with the score to 'INTO THE WILD', Pearl Jam's grungemeister EDDIE VEDDER was afforded this full OST, his debut solo album in fact. It'd been a dozen years since the PJ frontman last dabbled with film composing, although for 'DEAD MAN WALKING' (1995), the singer was only a bit player alongside the likes of David Robbins (director/actor Tim's brother), Nusrat Fateh Ali Khan, Ry Cooder & Springsteen; its star Sean Penn was now director here. By reading some tepid and somewhat unfair reviews for 'INTO THE WILD', one had some trepidations about what Eddie had let himself in for – one needn't have worried. From opening cue 'Setting Forth' (although only a minute and a half long!) to finale track, 'Guaranteed', all seemed well with the rootsy bard of alt-rock. Into the great wide open mind – one could say! – of ill-fated, Alaskan-bound Christopher J. McCandless, VEDDER puts his stamp and grizzly-voxed scent all over the project, performing lyrical on just about everything on display. The tracks that don't bear Eddie's hallmark are 'Hard Sun' (a classy cover of an Indio number written by Gordon Peterson, with backing vox by Sleater-Kinney's CORIN TUCKER) and the Springsteen-esque 'Society' (penned and co-performed by JERRY HANNAN). There's VEDDER on banjo for the short'n'sweet 'No Ceiling' and grunge unplugged-like for 'Far Behind' (another gem), while 'Rise' is both spiritual and uplifting. One's hairs at the back of one's neck begin to stand firm for the emotion-fuelled, 'Long Nights', by far the best song on the set and well up there alongside anything that even Pearl Jam have achieved. 'Tuolumne' is VEDDER's 'Bron-Y-Aur' moment (refer to Zeppelin if you must), while 'The Wolf' chant cries out like some disorientated banshee in the wilderness. VEDDER's versatility knows no boundaries here, 'End Of The Road' is both atmospheric and cinematic, while the aforementioned 'Guaranteed' gets into the spirit and soul of the peace-seeking McCandless. The only little let-down on 'INTO THE WILD' was that the album was only around half an hour in length – a mere trifle if one is honest. *MCS*

Album rating: *7

the INVISIBLE CIRCUS

2001 (US 92m) Fine Line Features (R)

Film genre: coming-of-age road movie/drama

Top guns: s-w + dir: Adam Brooks (nov: Jennifer Egan)

Stars: Jordana Brewster *(Phoebe)*, Cameron Diaz *(Faith)* ← FEAR AND LOATHING IN LAS VEGAS ← SHE'S THE ONE, Christopher Eccleston *(Wolf)* → 24 HOUR PARTY PEOPLE → REVENGERS TRAGEDY, Blythe Danner *(Gail)*, Camilla Belle *(Phoebe; age 10-12)*, Patrick Bergin *(Gene)* ← the COURIER, Moritz Bleibtreu *(Eric)*

Storyline: When 18-year-old Phoebe learns of her sister's apparent suicide in Portugal, she travels to Europe to find out the truth. In Paris she meets Faith's old boyfriend Wolf, who seems to know a lot more than he's letting on. Phoebe discovers that Faith ended up in Berlin as a Red Army anarchist before plunging to her death. As she follows in her sister's footsteps by having an affair with Wolf, it becomes clear that she too will meet her destiny on a Portuguese precipice. *JZ*

Movie rating: *5.5

Visual: video + dvd

Off the record: If one recalls a certain hit song in the mid-80s by the Dream Academy ('Life In A Northern Town') then one might also recall its charismatic guitar-strumming lead singer **Nick LAIRD-CLOWES** (b. 5 Feb'57, London, England). A runaway at the age of thirteen, he worked as an assistant sound engineer for the likes of PINK FLOYD, LED ZEPPELIN and the WHO; Nick subsequently bought the guitar once owned by his teen idol, the late, great Nick Drake; he also befriended JOHN LENNON. With his new band, Alphalfa, LAIRD-CLOWES inked a deal with 'E.M.I.' records, releasing a one-off set in the process. Relocating to New York, Nick subsequently dabbled with punk/new wave music for a while, eventually forming another outfit on his UK return, the Act, who released one LP, 'Too Late At 20' (for 'Hannibal' records). In 1983, LAIRD-CLOWES formed the Dream Academy (alongside multi-instrumentalist Kate St. John and keyboard-player Gilbert Gabriel) and inked a deal with 'Warner Bros.' records. With PINK FLOYD's David Gilmour at the controls, the trio's eponymous debut album (featuring the aforementioned transatlantic hit; an elegy for Nick Drake) was characterised by graceful arrangements and their self-professed love of adventurous pop; some reviewers took issue with what they regarded as polished pastiche. Much was also made of the group's flamboyant retro clothing which hardly helped them defend themselves against throwback accusations. The Dream Academy remained studiously unperturbed, working with Fleetwood Mac maestro Lindsey Buckingham on a follow-up set, 'Remembrance Days' (1987). Another collection of artfully refined pop, the record nevertheless failed to spawn a hit single never mind a success on the scale of their debut. Following 1991's swansong, 'A Different Kind Of Weather' (which included the musical reincarnation of Hare Krishna devotee, Poly Styrene, former X-Ray Spex singer!), the group folded with LAIRD-CLOWES increasingly dependent on hard drugs. Fighting back with the help of time spent at a Himalayan monastery, Nick was back again in the late 90s courtesy of Trashmonk. Signed to 'Creation' records, the group released one AOR-indie set, 'Mona Lisa Overdrive' (1999); Creation boss and big LAIRD-CLOWES fan, Alan McGee, took the same album – with a few bonus tracks – to his new 'Poptones' imprint for release in 2001. *MCS*

NICK LAIRD-CLOWES (& Various Artists)

Jan 01. (cd) *Chapter III; <CHA 1010-2>* [ ] [–]
– Espichel / Amsterdam / Beach / All change (TRASHMONK) / A long goodbye (WOODROW WILSON JACKSON III and PETRA HADEN) / Gun / Weather shy (YO LA TENGO) / Postcard / Fight / Trip / Betrayed / Gone / Evening / Afternoon / What about Africa (the UPSETTERS) / Stay away from Heaven (YO LA TENGO) / Chapel / On the way home (TRASHMONK).

S/track review: 'The INVISIBLE CIRCUS' was NICK LAIRD-CLOWES' maiden attempt at a film score; however, he needed a little help from his friends – so to speak (i.e. electric violinist BEN COLEMAN from No-Man, tabla/vocalist PANDIT DINESH, keyboard-player KENNY DICKENSON, double bass man CHUCHO MERCHAN, electronic percussionist REECE GILMORE and an orchestra conducted by Matt Dunkley). Three integrated, but run-of-the-mill tracks, 'Espichel', 'Amsterdam' and 'Beach', open the set, but it's not until his TRASHMONK gem, 'All Change' (taken from the album, 'Mona Lisa Overdrive'), that things kick off. Reminiscent of Public Image Ltd's ("eastern promise"-esque) 'Flower Of Romance', the track oozes class, but one can't help waiting for a certain John Lydon to chime in to LAIRD-CLOWES' vocals. Follow-on track, 'A Long Goodbye', by the mysterious WOODROW WILSON JACKSON III (featuring former that dog singer, PETRA HADEN) is basically a chant. One of indie-rock's finest, YO LA TENGO, are awarded two upbeat cues, 'Weather Shy' and 'Stay Away From Heaven', while the joker in the pack is undoubtably the UPSETTERS' excellent reggae dub tune, 'What About Africa'. LAIRD-CLOWES carries the derivative instrumental score on his proverbial back, all a little too worldly for his own good (although 'Trip' is nice). Thankfully, the OST closes with a second contribution from Nick's TRASHMONK, an edited-down version of the poignantly-titled 'On The Way Home'. *MCS*

Album rating: *6

IRREVERSIBLE

2002 (Fra 99m) 120 Films / Canal+ / Cinemas de la Zone (16)

Film genre: domestic crime drama

Top guns: s-w + dir: Gaspar Noe

Stars: Monica Bellucci *(Alex)*, Vincent Cassel *(Marcus)*, Philippe Nahon *(Philippe)*, Albert Dupontel *(Pierre)*, Jo Prestia *(le Tenia)*, Stephane Drouot *(Stephane)*, Jean-Louis Costes *(Fistman)*, Mourad Khima *(Mourad)*

Storyline: One long dark night of the flashback, Irreversible starts out grim and gets grimmer. With camera work so disorientating it shifts your centre of gravity, the film opens with a desperate trawl through a hardcore gay club and a savagely realistic, head-pulping attack with a fire extinguisher. Constantly folding back in upon itself, the reverse sequence plot reveals the motivation for the attack, an equally brutal rape of the protagonist's girlfriend. Caution advised. *BG*

Movie rating: *6.5

Visual: dvd

Off the record: THOMAS BANGALTER (see below)

THOMAS BANGALTER

Feb 03. (cd) *Roule; (ROULE 001CD) Virgin; <90705>* ☐ ☐
– Irreversible / Tempus edax rerum / Rectum / Night beats / Stress / Paris by night / Outrage / Outrun / Spinal scratch / Extra dry / Desaccords / Ventura – Into the tunnel / The end. *<re-cd+=; 826011>* – Mahler: Excerpt from Symphony No.9 in D Major (CZECH PHILHARMONIC ORCHESTRA) / Mon manege a moi (ETIENNE DAHO) / Beethoven: Excerpt from Symphony No.7 on A Major Op.92 (CZECH PHILHARMONIC ORCHESTRA).

S/track review: AIR having made their move into soundtracks in 1999, it was only a matter of time before contemporaries DAFT PUNK – or at least one half of them, THOMAS BANGALTER – followed. But if Sofia Coppola's 'The VIRGIN SUICIDES' had AIR's retrofied name written all over it, a commission for Gaspar Noé's shock-flick can't have been accepted lightly, especially by such a connoisseur of vocodered hedonism, the son of a man who turned Eurodisco into ageless, lowbrow art with the likes of 'Cuba' and 'D.I.S.C.O.'. Fans of BANGALTER's Stardust-spangled solo output will likewise find themselves adrift and disorientated in the sheer darkness of this music, in the suffocating drone of the main title, computer-glitch chattering of 'Stress' and the desolate requiem of 'Paris By Night'. Neither the moodiest Moroder reference nor classic synth-horror scoring device, however, can predict the truly nauseous pitch and wretch of a track like 'Rectum' – 'One More Time' this isn't. But it is powerful, no question, and mercilessly executed. Unlike say, 'FIGHT CLUB', the cues are also segued into a smoothly chartered journey by the DJ, albeit one which you likely won't want to undertake too often, and which suffers from some turbulence: when a more familiar BANGALTER emerges mid-way through, firing up the bpms, indulging in a bit of wheels-of-steel jiggery-pokery and slipping in some 12" vinyl from his back catalogue, the transition – exemplified by a chipper jazz guitar loop – isn't entirely convincing. Nor is the sudden downshift into Gallic pop with onetime Saint Etienne collaborator ETIENNE DAHO's 'Non Manege A Moi', or the Beethoven finale. A soundtrack of two halves, then, but proof that BANGALTER's disco evangelism has a darker, more accomplished side than he'd probably dared to imagine. *BG*

Album rating: *6.5

JACK JOHNSON

1971 (US 90m b&w) Big Fights Inc. (GP)

Film genre: sports documentary biopic

Top guns: dir: William Cayton / s-w: Alan Bodian

Stars: Brock Peters *(voice; Jack Johnson)* → BLACK GIRL → SLAUGHTER'S BIG RIP-OFF, Jack London *(himself)*, Pancho Villa *(himself)*, Victor McLaglen *(himself)*, James J. Jeffries *(himself)*, Jess Willard *(himself)*, + other boxers

Storyline: The fast life and wild times of black boxing legend Jack Johnson is the subject of this penetrating, Brock Peters narrated documentary, examining his rise to fame, struggles against race hatred and eventual exile in France. *BG*

Movie rating: *7

Visual: none

Off the record: (see below)

MILES DAVIS: A Tribute To Jack Johnson

Apr 71. (lp) *Columbia; <30455> C.B.S.; (70089)* ☐ May71 ☐
– Right off / Yesternow. *(re-imported Jan76; same) (cd-iss. Sep93; 471003-2)*

S/track review: Released the same year as the epochal 'Bitches Brew', this was the sound of worlds in collision, of rules being rewritten, reinvented. Just as Johnson had taken on whitey at his own game and given him a bloody nose, MILES DAVIS fearlessly squared up to the possibilities of jazz taking on rock music at its most primal. The results were electric, if not exactly pretty. As Rough Guide critic Ben Smith put it, "Jack Johnson managed to capture all of the sex and swagger of the boxing ring (plus some of the mess)". Yet even the mess – especially the mess – was compulsive listening as DAVIS – who wasn't averse to a few rounds in the ring himself – slugged it out with guitarist John McLaughlin to create what is often regarded as the definitive fusion of jazz and rock. The groove – in keeping with MILES' overarching late 60s/ early 70s vision and here flawlessly supplied by Billy Cobham and Michael Henderson – was all, but whereas on 'Bitches Brew' it had been dark and brooding, here it was louche, bluesy and swinging, getting off on McLaughlin's long, loping riffs. Like a prizefighter deep in the zone, DAVIS makes an unforgettable entrance a couple of minutes into the side-long 'Right Off', cranking out a searing high-register solo – one of the most astonishing of his long career – ablaze with that tribal, almost mystical energy which had made '..Brew' so intoxicating. He proceeds to knot it around the groove so tightly and mercilessly that McLaughlin's scuzzy lines are impelled to jab and snap for leg space. HERBIE HANCOCK's blunt, chalky Hammond stabs begin ratcheting up the tension on the quarter of an hour mark, while the groove finally breaks down five minutes later, with McLaughlin's hypnotic, spidery runs pointing towards an end game. 'Yesternow' is the hazy aftermath, all blurred vision and open wounds. While its endlessly repeated bass riff and rueful horn morphs into another muted, dissonant blues-funk workout and a haunting coda by way of an excerpt from 'In A Silent Way' (1969), the genesis and exact make-up of this second piece is even more complex than first appears, with two different line-ups and various overdubs, including sections from 'Right Off'. 'The Complete Sessions' (2003) box set opened up the picture further, comprehensively detailing the evolution of the two compositions which made the final cut of the soundtrack as well as a wealth of other material – previously unreleased and alternate takes included – which eventually turned up on subsequent landmarks like 'Live-Evil' (1971). As a primer for DAVIS' latter period career, it remains unsurpassed. Suffice to say, however, that the original album – regardless of its constituent parts – still sounds like nothing else. *BG*

Album rating: *9.5

– spinoff releases, etc. –

MILES DAVIS: Right Off / (part 2)

May 71. (7") *<45350>* ☐ [–]

MILES DAVIS: The Complete Jack Johnson Sessions

Sep 03. (5xcd-box) *Sony Jazz; <(CSK 86395)>* ☐ ☐
– Willie Nelson (6 takes) / Johnny Bratton (3 takes) / Archie Moore // Go ahead John (parts one / two A/B/C / one remake) / Duran (2 takes) / Sugar Ray // Right off (4 takes) / Yesternow (2 takes) / Honky tonk (2 takes) // Ali (2 takes) / Konda / Nem um talvez (2 takes) / Little high people (2 takes) / Nem um talvez (2 takes) / Selim / Little church (2 takes) // The mask (parts one & two) / Right off / Yesternow.

Joe JACKSON

Born: 11 Aug'54, Burton-On-Trent, Staffordshire, England. Steppin' out as a sardonic contemporary of ELVIS COSTELLO and Graham Parker before shrugging off the mainstream altogether, JOE JACKSON has been his own man for the best part of three decades, with admirers as artistically leagues apart as Tori Amos and Anthrax. His defiant eclecticism was always going to find a sympathetic redoubt in film, even if it's a field in which he hasn't been particularly well served. 'MIKE'S MURDER' (1984) is a case in point, a great soundtrack for what was by all accounts a fine film in its original print, and – despite enforced alterations – still is. Too much to stomach for preview audiences, the movie was toned down at the requests of its corporate overseers, finally seeing the light of day minus much of JACKSON's music as well as its original, 'Irreversible'-style chronology. John Barry had been drafted in for the music, although – with his original score hitting the shops months before the revisions were implemented – JACKSON at least had the consolation of a soundtrack release. Nor, despite a puckish retro-jazz score, was enough of his music used in the final cut of Francis Ford Coppola's 'TUCKER: THE MAN AND HIS DREAM' (1988), the second and final JACKSON soundtrack to see a commercial release. Parallel to an extended immersion in contemporary classical music, he nevertheless plugged away at film scoring for another decade or so, composing unreleased music for pre-'Friends' buddy film, 'Queen Of Logic' (1991), love triangular comedy, 'Three Of Hearts' (1993) and interactive thriller, 'I'm Your Man' (1998). Following on from his link-up with 'Star Trek' legend William Shatner (on a cover of Pulp's 'Common People' . . .), JACKSON made his feature debut with a piano playing cameo in the sophomore film of another British TV staple, Bill Paxton, a period golf drama going under the rather hopeful title, 'The Greatest Game Ever Played' (2005). *BG*

- filmography (composer) {actor} –

Mike's Murder *(1984 OST w/ John Barry =>)* / Private Eye *(1987 TV score)* / **Tucker: The Man And His Dream** *(1988 OST =>)* / Queens Logic *(1991 OST by V/A; see future edition)* / I'm Your Man *(1992 score)* / Three Of Hearts *(1993)* / the Greatest Game Ever Played *(2005 {c/p})*

JE T'AIME MOI NON PLUS

1976 (Fra 88m) President Films / Renn Productions / AMLF (X)

Film genre: erotic/seXual comedy drama

Top guns: s-w + dir: **Serge GAINSBOURG**

Stars: Jane Birkin *(Johnny)* ← CANNABIS ← SEX POWER ← MAY MORNING ← WONDERWALL ← BLOW-UP, Joe Dallesandro *(Krasky)* → ROCK & ROLL HEART ← CRY-BABY, Hugues Quester *(Padovan)*, Rene Kolldehoff *(Boris)*, Michel Blanc *(un ouvrier)* → BRIGADE MONDAINE, Gerard Depardieu *(man on horse)* → JE VOUS AIME, Jimmy 'Lover Man' Davis *(Moise)* → DISCO GODFATHER

Storyline: An androgynous, waif-thin waitress with a boy's name (Johnny) endures a mundane existence living and working in a dreary truck stop. Some unlikely colour comes into her life in the shape of beefcake garbage man, Krassky. Ignoring the warnings of her boss that he's actually gay, she proceeds to indulge their mutual attraction by less than conventional means, something that Krassky's lover isn't too happy about. *BG*

Movie rating: *5.5

Visual: video

Off the record: Joe Dallesandro is featured on the sleeve of the Smiths' eponymous debut set (taken from Andy Warhol's Flesh). *MCS*

SERGE GAINSBOURG: Je T'aime Moi Non Plus – "Ballade De Johnny-Jane"

1976. (lp) *Philips; (9101 030)* [–] French [–]
– Ballade de Johnny-Jane / Le camion Jaune / Banjo au bord du styx / Rock'n'roll autour de Johnny / L'abominable strip-tease / Joe Banjo / Je t'aime moi non plus / Je t'aime moi non plus au lac vert / Je t'aime moi non plus au motel / Ballade de Johnny-Jane (finale). *<cd-iss. Jun95 in Japan on 'Philips'; PHCA 1039>*

S/track review: One of SERGE GAINSBOURG's most controversial projects in a lifetime of controversy, 'Je T'Aime Moi Non Plus' took its title from the man's steamy 1969 megahit. It was also SERGE's directorial debut, in which his artistic schedule extended from the script to the music, perhaps the reason why the soundtrack relied so heavily on previous material. Time Out called it a "riotously bleak and brutalised love story", likely a compliment in the mighty GAINSBOURG's book. Love story or not, there are a full three versions of that iconic anthem here, all minus the nuisance-caller breathing: the even softer-focus-than-the-original 'Je T'Aime Moi Non Plus Au Lac Vert' is the most evocative, the kind of luscious pop that was Saint Etienne's pan et beurre back in the 90s. But the soundtrack's big (domestic) hit was 'Ballade De Johnny-Jane', a rolling, saloon-salon piano melody with a banjo coda i.e. exactly what you wouldn't expect to hear in a piece of caustic arthouse subversion, even from GAINSBOURG. It's difficult to imagine what Appalachian purists would make of a title like 'Banjo Au Bord Du Styx', but prepare to be amazed as Serge makes his grand Gallic bluegrass statement. Another priceless title – 'L'Abominable Strip-

Tease' – conceals some average 12-bar blues-rock. Like a hurried, sweaty tryst, there's a lot of repetitive movement here, and it's over all too soon. Good while it lasts though. *BG*

Album rating: *7

– spinoff releases, etc. –

SERGE GAINSBOURG: Ballade De Johnny-Jane / Joe Banjo
1976. (7") *(6042 131)* [–] French [–]

JE VOUS AIME

aka 'I Love You All'

1980 (Fra 100m) Renn Productions / AMLF

Film genre: romantic/psychological drama

Top guns: s-w: (+ dir) Claude Berri, Michel Grisolia

Stars: Catherine Deneuve *(Alice)* → PAROLES ET MUSIQUE → POLA X → DANCER IN THE DARK, Jean-Louis Trintignant *(Julien Tellier)*, Gerard Depardieu *(Patrick)* ← JE T'AIME MOI NON PLUS, **Alain Souchon** *(Claude)*, **Serge GAINSBOURG** *(Simon)*, Christian Marquand *(Victor)* ← CANDY, Isabelle Lacamp *(Dorothee)*, Thomas Langmann *(Thomas)*

Storyline: With yet another good man gone, handsome career mademoiselle and single mother Alice broods on her promiscuous, romantically interrupted life and loves, affording a window into her back pages through a non-chronological series of flashbacks. *BG*

Movie rating: *6

Visual: video

Off the record: **Alain Souchon** (b.27 May'44, Casablanca, Morocco) was a lyricist and French singer who worked on records with Laurent Voulzy. *MCS*

—

SERGE GAINSBOURG

Dec 80. (lp) *Philips; (6313 123)* [–] French [–]
– La fautive / Je vous salue Marie / La p'tite agathe / Dieu fumeur de havanes / La fautive (pianos) / Dieu fumeur de havanes / Papa Nono / Je pense queue / La fautive (orchestral).

S/track review: Ah, SERGE GAINSBOURG; the only man who could write an eye-wateringly poignant piece of orchestral pop and call it 'Sex-Shop'. That was 1972. By the end of the decade, he'd flirted with new wave, composed some incredible porno-funk/disco and managed to offend Algerian War veterans with an irreverent reggae remake of 'La Marseillaise'. He was at it again on 'JE VOUS AIME', reimagining 'Ave Maria' as francophone dub, even if his duet with a hesitant Catherine Deneuve is – the 'God Smokes Havanas' title, SERGE prefers Gitanes lyric aside – shockingly respectable balladry, one of his most conventional themes in years and one of the few SERGE songs you could actually take home to your mum. The organ instrumental isn't bad either. Depardieu isn't so pliant; he does hysterical, Gauloise-ravaged punk rock with a little help from BIJOU, the band who recorded GAINSBOURG's classic, proto-New Order theme for Catherine Breillat's 'Tapage Nocturne' (1979); hear it and weep. And, on opener 'La Fautive' and 'Je Pense Queue', SERGE does bubblegum soul, sounding not very guilty at all over a 'Stax'-style brass section and doo-wah-wah backing, recapitulating with familiar cracked-saloon piano. In other words, the kind of glorious ahistorical mess his soundtracks occasionally threatened to be, relying a little too much on repetition (filling out a whole two sides of soundtrack vinyl with original material wasn't one of his strong points) to be truly essential, but – like most of his albums – still thoroughly deserving of your euros. *BG*

Album rating: *6

Waylon JENNINGS

Born: 15 Jun'37, Littlefield, Texas, USA. Much like the class of early 70s Motown, country legend WAYLON JENNINGS fought for the right to gain full creative control over his records after a decade of studio compromise. In so doing, he unwittingly formed a bonafide musical movement dubbed outlaw country and encompassing free spirited brethren like WILLIE NELSON and KRIS KRISTOFFERSON. Five years or so earlier, the one time bass player for Buddy Holly had made his acting debut in 'NASHVILLE REBEL' (1966) a country musical which, despite content pretty faithful to the standards of its day, boasted a title which uncannily predicted the future career of its main protagonist. By the time of 'Moonrunners' (1975), a proto-Dukes Of Hazard, moonshine-themed comedy which JENNINGS both narrated and scored, he had become one of country's biggest stars and his involvement in the film mirrored his later work on the 'Dukes Of Hazard' TV series, for which he wrote the classic theme. His mid-70s status as chief outlaw also found JENNINGS composing the soundtrack for Roy Rogers' comeback movie, 'MACKINTOSH & T.J.' (1975), although it'd be another two decades before he'd be invloved in another feature film, a cameo appearance – alongside a clutch of younger country stars – in the big screen version of TV western series, 'Maverick' (1994). Like his contemporary (and onetime flatmate), JOHNNY CASH, JENNINGS finally succumbed to diabetes-related illness, passing away on the 13th of February, 2002. *BG*

- **filmography** (composer) {acting} –

Nashville Rebel *(1966 {*} OST =>)* / **Road To Nashville** *(1967 {*} =>)* / Travelin' Light *(1971 {p})* / Moonrunners *(1975 {a} score)* / **Mackintosh & T.J.** *(1975 OST =>)* / the Oklahoma City Dolls *(1981 TV {*})* / Stagecoach *(1986 TV {*})* / Maverick *(1994 {a})* / Tom Sawyer *(2000 {a})*

JOE

1970 (US 107m) Cannon Films (R)

Film genre: psychological urban drama

Top guns: dir: John G. Avildsen / s-w: Norman Wexler → SATURDAY NIGHT FEVER → STAYING ALIVE

Stars: Peter Boyle *(Joe Curran)* → STEELYARD BLUES → WHERE THE BUFFALO ROAM → WALKER → the IN CROWD, Dennis Patrick *(Bill Compton)*, Susan Sarandon *(Melissa Compton)* → the ROCKY HORROR PICTURE SHOW → DEAD MAN WALKING → the BANGER SISTERS → ALFIE re-make → ROMANCE & CIGARETTES, Patrick McDermott *(Frank Russo)*, Audrey Caire *(Joan Compton)*, K Callan *(Mary Lou Curran)* → FAST BREAK, Marlene Warfield *(Bellevue nurse)* → ACROSS 110th STREET

Storyline: High flying executive Bill Compton comes back to down to earth with a homicidal bump when a confrontation with the drug pushing boyfriend of his daughter goes too far. Blood on his hands, bewildered at his own brutality, he wanders into a random bar and falls into conversation with Joe, a blue-collar bigot to whom he unintentionally reveals all. As they scour New York searching for Bill's daughter, their vigilante odd-coupling ends in massacre at a hippie party. *BG*

Movie rating: *7.5

Visual: video + dvd

Off the record: A classically-trained pianist, composer, multi-instrumentalist, producer, arranger and songwriter (co-author of the famous Neil Diamond/Hollies hit, 'He Ain't Heavy, He's My Brother', itself inspired by the 1938 Spencer Tracy picture, 'Boys Town') **BOBBY SCOTT** (b.29 Jan'37, Mt. Pleasant, New York, USA) initially made his way in the music business as a jazz pianist for the likes of LOUIS PRIMA and Gene Krupa. He subsequently enjoyed a solo recording career and a one-off mid-50s hit (US) with 'Chain Gang' before penning the theme for the Shelagh Delaney play, 'A Taste Of Honey' (subsequently recorded by the Beatles on their UK debut album). His songwriting finally made it to the big screen in the late 60s/early 70s, featuring in both period melodrama, 'Slaves' (1969) and hippy backlash drama, 'JOE' (1970) – credited to JERRY BUTLER & EXUMA, as well as fact-based kids' film, 'Who Says I Can't Ride A Rainbow' (1971). As a contemporary of Quincy Jones at Mercury records, SCOTT played on many of JONES' albums, including his soundtrack to the multi-Oscar-nominated Alice Walker adaptation, 'The Color Purple' (1986). *BG*

—

JERRY BUTLER & EXUMA (composer: BOBBY SCOTT)

Dec 70. (lp) *Mercury; <SRM-1 605> (6338 029)* ☐ Jun71 ☐
– Where are you goin'? / The expiration of Frank / You can fly / Hey Joe / Compton's hangout / You don't know what's goin' on / It's a crock / When in Rome / Send the hippies to Hell / Where are you goin'?

S/track review: Though he played on Quincy Jones' classic score for 'The Pawnbroker' (1965) this was jazz pianist turned composer BOBBY SCOTT's highest profile soundtrack under his own name, and his most diverse. Having previously worked with the likes of Gene Krupa, Chet Baker and Roland Kirk, SCOTT found himself writing for soul legend JERRY BUTLER, former leader of the Impressions alongside CURTIS MAYFIELD. His old partner in harmony would at least partly define the sound of blaxploitation, but it was BUTLER, ironically, who got into the soundtrack game first, contributing a trio of vocal performances on the back of his pioneering Gamble & Huff productions. He may have been nicknamed "The Iceman", but on the meandering 'Where Are You Goin'' – released as a French single – his voice quakes with the lustre of tropical hardwood. He sounds even better backed by female harmonies and a Southern piano on 'You Can Fly'; much of the track's ten minutes-plus – and most of the vinyl – is taken up with tinder-crisp funk breaks and extended guitar jamming, rich pickings for DJs and samplers, performed by uncredited musicians. At least DEAN MICHAELS gets a credit for his performance on 'Hey Joe', not a cover of the Jimi Hendrix classic but a redneck country novelty brutally punctuated by expletive-bashing bleeps. More deserving of his credit is greatly underrated Bahamian singer EXUMA aka Tony McKay, signed by 'Mercury' in the hope of creating their own Dr John but destined for cult appreciation only. The self-penned 'You Don't Know What's Goin' On' – lifted from his 1970 debut album – is a great example of his voodoo-folk-reggae, not quite as chilling as 'Dambala' (brilliantly covered – along with McKay's 'Obeah Woman' – by Nina Simone on her 'R.C.A.' finale, 'It Is Finished') but arguably the most compelling three minutes on this soundtrack. The rest of the album is left to SCOTT's incidental music. His cues range from the loungey 'It's A Crock' to the grungy sitar piece, 'When In Rome'. 'Send The Hippies To Hell' is his showcase, a great title and a fine montage, packing in lightning-strike big-band jazz calibrated by burbling leatherback percussion in the mould of his mentor Quincy Jones, as well as hints of atonal tenor, solo snare rolls and tension aplenty. *BG*

Album rating: *5

Elton JOHN

Born: Reginald Kenneth Dwight, 25 Mar'47, Middlesex, England. A onetime Liberace of 70s super-songwriting who subsequently adapted himself to the slickness of adult contemporary, ELTON JOHN has covered more stylistic bases than most in his long career, and with more professional polish. While the chameleon-like piano thumper's early to mid 70s purple period turned up songs as ingratiatingly tenacious as 'Rocket Man', 'Candle In The Wind', 'Goodbye Yellow Brick Road', 'Philadelphia Freedom' and 'Don't Let The Sun Go Down On Me', the fact that he composed the score for obscure British teen fantasy, 'FRIENDS' (1971), remains less well known. More high profile was Elton's increasingly outrageous stage garb, as witnessed via his cameo appearance – as the outlandishly attired Pinball Wizard – in Ken Russell's film version of 'TOMMY' (1975). Unusually for such a major league star, however, his involvement in the world of film, either as composer or actor, was pretty much non-existent until the hugely successful Walt Disney animation, 'The LION KING' (1994). JOHN composed the film's score in tandem with lyricist Tim Rice, an achievement which earned them an Oscar for Best Original Song ('Can You Feel The Love Tonight'), and which they would expand upon for Julie Taymor's subsequent Broadway production. As well as making an appearance in the Spice Girls vehicle, 'SPICEWORLD' (1998), Elton went on to compose the score for Albert Brooks' Hollywood satire, 'The MUSE' (1999). Sir Elton (the man had received his CBE some years back) once again teamed up with Rice for the score to Dreamworks' Spanish conquistador animation, 'The ROAD TO EL DORADO' (2000). *BG*

- **filmography** (composer) {acting} –

Friends *(1971 OST w/ PAUL BUCKMASTER =>)* / **Born To Boogie** *(1972 {p} =>)* / **Tommy** *(1975 {*} on OST by the WHO =>)* / **All This And World War II** *(1976 {p} docu OST by V/A =>)* / **the Lion King** *(1994 OST w/ HANS ZIMMER & Tim Rice =>)* / **Spice World** *(1997 {c} =>)* / Women Talking Dirty *(1999 OST w/ V/A see; future editions =>)* / **the Muse** *(1999 OST =>)* / **the Road To El Dorado** *(2000 OST =>)* / **the Country Bears** *(2002 {v} OST by V/A =>)*

JOHNNY HANDSOME

1989 (US 94m) Columbia TriStar (R)

Film genre: crime drama

Top guns: dir: Walter Hill ← CROSSROADS ← STREETS OF FIRE ← the LONG RIDERS / → TRESPASS → GERONIMO: AN AMERICAN LEGEND → LAST MAN STANDING / s-w: Ken Friedman (au: 'The Three Worlds Of Johnny Handsome' by John Godey)

Stars: Mickey Rourke *(John Sedley)* ← HOMEBOY / → BUFFALO 66 → MASKED AND ANONYMOUS, Ellen Barkin *(Sunny Boyd)* ← SIESTA ← DOWN BY LAW ← EDDIE AND THE CRUISERS ← TENDER MERCIES ← UP IN SMOKE / → FEAR AND LOATHING IN LAS VEGAS, Elizabeth McGovern *(Donna McCarty)*, Morgan Freeman *(Lt. A.Z. Drones)* → LAST OF THE MISSISSIPPI JUKES → BLUES DIVAS → DANNY THE DOG, Forest Whitaker *(Dr. Steven Fisher)* ← GOOD MORNING, VIETNAM / → GHOST DOG: THE WAY OF THE SAMURAI → a LITTLE TRIP TO HEAVEN, Scott Wilson *(Mikey Chaimette)* ← BLUE CITY / → YOUNG GUNS II → ELVIS AND THE COLONEL: THE UNTOLD STORY → GERONIMO: AN AMERICAN LEGEND → SOUL SURVIVOR → DEAD MAN WALKING → SOUTH OF HEAVEN, WEST OF HELL → DON'T LET GO → MONSTER, Lance Henriksen *(Rafe Garrett)* ← NEAR DARK / → DEAD MAN → TARZAN, Jeffrey Meek *(Earl)*

Storyline: John Sedley is two-bit criminal nicknamed Johnny Handsome due to his deformed features. A plastic surgery op drastically improves his appearance as he's paroled from jail and ostensibly divorced from his dodgy past. *BG*

Movie rating: *5.5

Visual: video + dvd

Off the record: (see below)

—

RY COODER

Oct 89. (cd)(lp/c) *Warners; <(9 25886-2)>(WX 307/+C)* ☐ ☐
– Main theme / I can't walk this time – The prestige / Angola / Clip joint rhumba / Sad story / Fountain walk / Cajun metal / First week at work / Greasy oysters / Smells like money / Sunny's tune / I like your eyes / Adios Donna / Cruising with Rafe / How's my face / End theme. *<(cd re-iss. Feb95; same)>*

S/track review: Coming after 'CROSSROADS', this largely minimalist, impressionistic score was something of a relief, boasting a stark and unassuming main theme with sparse guitar and piano arrangements. Again, the spectre of 'PARIS, TEXAS' stalks this album, filling it with burning, vibrating echo and endless unstated suggestions and possibilities, not least in the likes of 'Cruising With Rafe' and the haunting 'Sunny's Tune', a twilight meditation drawn out by world- weary sax and resigned to its own, uncertain fate. Not for the first time on a COODER album, VAN DYKE PARKS works his magic with the arrangements, combining funky horn charts with tantalising snippets of 'Big Chief'-style New Orleans piano (courtesy of HAROLD BATTISTE) and syncopated drum rolls on 'Prestige', itself segued from the hollow piano ruminations of 'I Can't Walk This Time' and one of the album's more upbeat moments alongside the spry 'Clip Joint Rhumba'. *BG*

Album rating: *6.5

J.J. JOHNSON

Born: 22 Jan'24, Indianapolis, Indiana, USA. A fondly remembered and highly influential trombone legend in the jazz world and a major player during the blaxploitation era, J.J. JOHNSON's career can be pretty much divided into distinct segments. A mid-40s mainstay of Benny Carter's big band, JOHNSON went on to play with many of the bop era's key pioneers including Charlie Parker, MILES DAVIS and Sonny Rollins. By the early 70s, however, he was pouring all his energies into film scoring, initially collaborating with Quincy Jones on the soundtrack to Bill Cosby's debut feature, 'MAN AND BOY' (1971). Although there was no soundtrack release for his first solo score, 'Top Of The Heap' (1972), he excelled himself with his work on quasi-blaxploitation classic, 'ACROSS 110th STREET' (1972). While BOBBY WOMACK admittedly stole the show with the peerless theme, JOHNSON's dynamic instrumental funk was as deliciously uncut as any of the era. He almost replicated the feat with his driving orchestrations on 'CLEOPATRA JONES' (1973) and – with a post-Vandellas Martha Reeves handling vocals – his sterling work on Gilbert Moses' unsentimental pimp portrait, 'WILLIE DYNAMITE' (1974). With blaxploitation having run its course by the mid-70s, JOHNSON scored a further made-for-TV crime drama, 'Street Killing' (1976), before successfully resuming his jazz career. Tragically, he later committed suicide on 4th February 2001 after a battle with prostate cancer. *BG*

- **filmography** (composer) –

Man And Boy *(1971 OST =>)* / Top Of The Heap *(1972)* / **Across 110th Street** *(1972 OST w/ BOBBY WOMACK =>)* / **Cleopatra Jones** *(1973 OST =>)* / **Willie Dynamite** *(1974 OST =>)* / Street Killing *(1976 TV)*

JONATHAN LIVINGSTON SEAGULL

1973 (US 114m) Paramount Pictures (G)

Film genre: nature/family/children's adventure drama

Top guns: s-w + dir: Hall Bartlett (au: Richard D. Bach)

Voices: James Franciscus *(Jonathan)*, Juliet Mills *(Maureen)*, Richard Crenna *(father)*, Dorothy McGuire *(mother)*, David Ladd *(Fletcher)*, Philip Ahn *(Chang)* ← PARADISE, HAWAIIAN STYLE, Kelly Harmon *(Kimmy)*, Hal Holbrook *(the elder)* ← WILD IN THE STREETS / → INTO THE WILD

Storyline: Jonathan is a seagull who dreams of flying faster and higher than any other bird in the flock. One day he sets off into the clouds and flies around the world, eventually arriving at a bird's paradise where he meets his soul-mate Maureen. When Jonathan returns home to his flock, he finds he is no longer the same bird he was when he left. *JZ*

Movie rating: *4

Visual: video + dvd

Off the record: (see below)

—

NEIL DIAMOND

Oct 73. (lp/c) *Columbia; <KS 32550> C.B.S.; (CBS/40 69047)* [2] Jan74 [35]
– Prologue / Be / Flight of the gull / Dear father / Sky bird / Lonely looking sky / The Odyssey: Be – Lonely looking sky – Dear father / Anthem / Be / Skybird / Dear father / Be. *(cd-iss. 1986; CD 69047) <(re-iss. Dec90 on 'Columbia' cd/c/lp; 467607-2/-4/-1)>*

S/track review: From 1966 onwards, songwriter-turned-film composer, NEIL DIAMOND, was frequently hitting the top of the pop charts with songs such as 'Cracklin' Rosie' and 'Song Sung Blue'. 'JONATHAN . . .' was his escape from the limelight, although it still brought him a great deal of success and renewed credibility – in the movie world at least – having reached No.2 in the US. Arranged and conducted by prolific film composer in his own right, Lee Holdridge, with a plethora of classical backing musicians, JLS hit the right notes from day one; producer and musical director Tom Catalano and sound engineer Armin Steiner must also take credit. Opening with 'Prologue', Neil takes a back seat, letting the atmospheric orchestra set the lush, romantic tone. 'Be' – the first of four pieces of that name, and the longest by far – opens DIAMOND's singing account, his deep, spiritual voice and lyrics gracing every note. The theme and flow of the film continues with the instrumental, 'Flight Of The Gull', while 'Dear Father' (a prayer of sorts) shows the man in hymnal, minimalist lyricism mode. It must be said, NEIL takes on the role of Hall Bartlett's Jonathan Seagull character with some gusto. 'Sky Bird' (the instrumental piece) is a bright segue piece before the voice gets into full gear once again via the beautiful 'Lonely Looking Sky'. This piece and two others, the aforementioned 'Be' and 'Dear Father', get the reprised orchestral treatment by way of 'The Odyssey medley', 9 minutes-plus of Lee Holdridge at work. 'Anthem' is a surprise vocal/choral number, a piece to enchant the local church minister with its "Holy, Holy" approach and the weakest by far. 'Skybird' (the song) sees DIAMOND in "Una Paloma Blanca" mood, a melodious sing-a-long that cuts away all too soon. 'Dear Father' gets another instrumental run out, while the previously mentioned 'Be' (the Top 40 hit version/edit) ends what is a remarkable piece of music. Now "I'm A Believer". *MCS*

Album rating: *7

– spinoff releases, etc. –

NEIL DIAMOND: Be / Flight Of The Gull

Nov 73. (7") *<45942> (CBS 1843)* ☐ ☐

NEIL DIAMOND: Skybird / Lonely Looking Sky

Feb 74. (7") *<45998> (CBS 2191)* [75] Apr74 ☐

JOYRIDE

1977 (US 92m) American International Pictures (R)

Film genre: crime drama / road movie

Top guns: s-w: Joseph Ruben (+ dir), Peter Rainer

Stars: Desi Arnaz Jr. *(Scott)*, Robert Carradine *(John)* → the LONG RIDERS → WAVELENGTH → the LIZZIE McGUIRE MOVIE, Anne Lockhart *(Cindy Young)*, Melanie Griffith *(Susie)* ← ONE ON ONE / → WORKING GIRL, Cliff Lenz *(Henderson)*, Tom Ligon *(Sanders)*, Paul Fleming *(Big Ed)*

Storyline: Three young Californians get fed up with all the good weather and head north to Alaska to find work and adventure. They swiftly manage to lose their money and their jobs, but our intrepid trio form a plan – hold up the payroll office, capture a hostage and demand lots of money so they can get back home again. Needless to say it all goes badly wrong. Their Alaskan plan was surely half-baked. *JZ*

Movie rating: *4.5

Visual: video

Off the record: (see below)

—

ELECTRIC LIGHT ORCHESTRA (*) (& BARRY MANN ** & JIMMIE HASKELL ***)

Jun 77. (lp) *United Artists; <UA LA784-H>* ☐ ☐
– The best that I know how (**) / Tightrope (*) / Dancin' in Alaska (***) / Can't get it out of my head (*) / Boy blue (*) / Eatin' dog food (***) / The best that I know how – instrumental (***) / So fine (*) / The getaway (***) / Telephone line (*) / Rockaria! (*) / Train stuff (***) / The best that I know how – reprise (**).

S/track review: Jeff Lynne's ELECTRIC LIGHT ORCHESTRA headline this musical score to the film, 'JOYRIDE', although two other popular songwriters/composers (of the 60s), BARRY MANN and JIMMIE HASKELL, bring variety to this rare LP. ELO contribute six ready-made songs from a couple of magical mid-70s albums: from 1974's 'Eldorado' set, 'Can't Get It Out Of My Head' (a classic US Top 10 hit) & 'Boy Blue', and from 1976's 'A New World Record', four tracks, 'Tightrope', 'So Fine', 'Telephone Line' (another Top 10 smash) & 'Rockaria!'. If one was an ELO fan at the time (or indeed nowadays), these non-exclusive tracks would and should already be in their collection. Meanwhile, Brooklyn-born, Brill-Building songsmith BARRY MANN (with co-writer wife Cynthia Weil on board) delivers one solo number for openers, 'The Best That I Know How' (a song not too dissimilar to Jerry Ragovoy & Bert Berns' 'Piece Of My Heart'); two further renditions prolong the agony, the instrumental by the aforementioned HASKELL and the reprise. Not even getting an equal share of the billing on the LP's front cover, JIMMIE HASKELL – a man with more than a handful of rock film credits to his name, 'SURF PARTY' (1964), 'WILD ON THE BEACH' (1966) and 'ZACHARIAH' (1971) – gets all sentimental with four further cues, 'Dancin' In Alaska', 'Eatin' Dog Food', 'The Getaway' and 'Train Stuff'. Thank ELO for saving the day – again, and move to 'XANADU' for further adventures. *MCS*

Album rating: *4.5

☐ JUICE PEOPLE UNLIMITED segment (⇒ DISCO GODFATHER)

☐ Don JULIAN segment (⇒ SAVAGE!)

JUNGLE FEVER

1991 (US 131m) 40 Acres & A Mule / Universal Pictures (R)

Film genre: romantic urban drama

Top guns: s-w + dir: Spike Lee as below + → HE GOT GAME

Stars: Wesley Snipes *(Flipper Purify)* → DISAPPEARING ACTS, Annabella Sciorra *(Angie Tucci)*, Spike Lee *(Cyrus)* ← SCHOOL DAZE / → CROOKLYN → GIRL 6, Anthony Quinn *(Lou Carbone)* ← ACROSS 110th STREET, Ossie Davis *(the Good Reverend Doctor Purify)* ← SCHOOL DAZE ← COUNTDOWN AT KUSINI ← LET'S DO IT AGAIN / → BUBBA HO-TEP, Ruby Dee *(Lucinda Purify)* ← COUNTDOWN AT KUSINI ← WATTSTAX ← BLACK GIRL ← UP TIGHT!, John Turturro *(Paulie Carbone)* ← TO LIVE AND DIE IN L.A. / → GIRL 6 → GRACE OF MY HEART → HE GOT GAME → O BROTHER, WHERE ART THOU?, Samuel L. Jackson *(Gator Purify)* ← SCHOOL DAZE ← MAGIC STICKS / → JOHNNY SUEDE → JUICE → PULP FICTION → JACKIE BROWN → KILL BILL: VOL.1 → KILL BILL: VOL.2 → BLACK SNAKE MOAN, **Lonette McKee** *(Drew)* ← SPARKLE / → HE GOT GAME → HONEY, Frank Vincent *(Mike Tucci)* → SHE'S THE ONE, Tim Robbins *(Jerry)* ← TAPEHEADS ← HOWARD THE DUCK / → HIGH FIDELITY → the PICK OF DESTINY, Tyra Ferrell *(Orin Goode)* ← TAPEHEADS ← SCHOOL DAZE, Halle Berry *(Vivian)* → CB4: THE MOVIE → GIRL 6 → WHY DO FOOLS FALL IN LOVE → SWORDFISH, Michael Imperioli *(James Tucci)* → the BASKETBALL DIARIES → I SHOT ANDY WARHOL → GIRL 6 → LAST MAN STANDING → DISAPPEARING ACTS, Nicholas Turturro *(Vinny)*, Brad Dourif *(Leslie)* ← DUNE, **Queen Latifah** *(Lashawn)* → HOUSE PARTY 2 → JUICE → WHO'S THE MAN? → the COUNTRY BEARS → BROWN SUGAR → HAIRSPRAY re-make, Phyllis Yvonne Stickney *(Nilda)* → WHAT'S LOVE GOT TO DO WITH IT, Theresa Randle *(Inez)* ← the FIVE HEARTBEATS / → CB4: THE MOVIE → GIRL 6, Miguel Sandoval *(officer Ponte)* ← WALKER ← STRAIGHT TO HELL ← SID & NANCY ← HOWARD THE DUCK ← REPO MAN, Michael Badalucco *(Frankie Botz)* → O BROTHER, WHERE ART THOU?, Debi Mazar *(Denise)* ← the DOORS ← DOWNTOWN 81 / → SINGLES → GIRL 6 → EMPIRE RECORDS → the INSIDER → BE COOL, Charles Q. Murphy *(Livin' Large)* → CB4: THE MOVIE → MURDER WAS THE CASE → PAPER SOLDIERS → DEATH OF A DYNASTY → ROLL BOUNCE, Doug E. Doug *(friend of livin' large)*

Storyline: Although his name might lead you to believe he's a celebrity dolphin, Flipper Purify is actually a high flying Afro-American architect who impulsively gets it on with his Italian-American secretary. Both are otherwise romantically committed and must face the consequences, as well as the racial/prejudicial baggage of both themselves and their immediate families (and in Purify's case, narcotic baggage of his crackhead brother). *BG*

Movie rating: *7.5

Visual: video + dvd

Off the record: Doug E. Doug is a standup comedian.

—

STEVIE WONDER (score: Terence Blanchard)

May 91. (cd/c/lp) *Motown; <6291> (ZD/ZK/ZL 71750)* 24 56
– Fun day / Queen in the black / These three words / Each other's throat / If she breaks your heart / Gotta have you / Make sure you're sure / Jungle fever / I go sailing / Chemical love / Lighting up the candles.

S/track review: In the decade following his last great album, 'Hotter Than July' (1980), STEVIE WONDER generated a soundtrack-to-studio-album ratio of 50:50. There wasn't much to choose between the movie music and the regular stuff but at least 'JUNGLE FEVER' held the anticipation of two Afro-American icons in a filmic pow-wow. The results were nothing to chant about, but – simplified premise or no – the all-conquering STEVIE of the 70s briefly surfaced on the malaria-infectious title track, springing synth motif of 'Queen In The Black' and upfront 'Gotta Have You'. He also made a meaningful advance on his long tradition of soulsifying/quirkifying technology with 'Chemical Love', and even framed his still incredible voice with the burr of an upright bass and lap of a string section on 'Make Sure You're Sure'. The normally scrupulously polite soul-Bodhisattava even blurts out a neo-expletive ("pissed", as in angry); he really must've had a temperature. There are balmy hints of the deep balladry of old on 'Sailing', but both the showcase slowie, 'These Three Words', and the KIMBERLY BREWER-sung 'If She Breaks Your Heart', are ultimately just a little too bland to justifiably take their place in the WONDER pantheon. If anything, this soundtrack is overrated, talked up by critics desperate for another great, rather than merely good, STEVIE album. *BG*

Album rating: *5.5

– spinoff hits, etc. –

STEVIE WONDER: Gotta Have You

Jun 91. (7"/12") *<2081>* [92] [–]

STEVIE WONDER: Fun Day / (instrumental)

Sep 91. (7"/c-s) *(ZB/ZK 44957)* [–] [63]
(12"+=/cd-s+=) *(ZT/ZD 44958)* – ('A'remix) / ('A'-club mix).

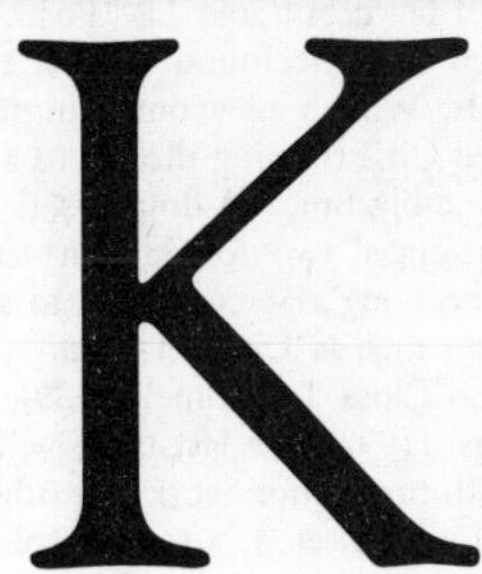

KAMIKAZE 1989

1982 (W.Ger 106m) Oase / Regina Ziegler / Trio Films (18)

Film genre: Crime fantasy/thriller

Top guns: s-w: Wolf Gremm (+ dir), Robert Katz (book: 'Murder On The 31st Floor' by Maj Sjowall + story: Per Wahloo)

Stars: Rainer Werner Fassbinder *(polizeileutnant Jansen)*, Gunther Kaufmann *(Anton)*, Boy Gobert *(Blue Panther; konzernchef)*, Arnold Marquis *(police chief)*, Richy Mueller *(neffe/nephew)*, Nicole Heesters *(Barbara)*, Brigitte Mira *(personal director)*, Petra Jokisch *(Elena)* ← ASPHALTNACHT, Franco Nero

Storyline: Set in Berlin 1989, a futuristic super cop attempts to solve a hoax bomb threat then a murder at the "Combine" (TV control unit) on the hidden 31st floor of a 30-storey building. *MCS*

Movie rating: *5

Visual: video

Off the record: Renowned German director, Rainer Werner Fassbinder, was also an actor; he committed suicide (o.d. 10th June 1982) shortly after the making of this movie. *MCS*

EDGAR FROESE

Oct 82. (lp) *Virgin; (V 2255)* [ ] [–]
– Videophonic / Vitamin 'C' / Krismopompas / Police disco / Intuition / Police therapy center / Blue panther / Snake bath / Unexpected death / Flying kamikaze / Tower block / The 31st floor. *(re-iss. Aug88; OVED 125) (cd-iss. Aug88; CDV 2255) <cd-iss. 1992 on 'Caroline'; CAROL 1626-2>*

S/track review: With two scores under his belt ('SORCERER' and 'THIEF') with electronic Prog-rock pioneers, TANGERINE DREAM, part-time solo artist EDGAR FROESE delivered his first OST. A brilliant and effective guitarist with a string of albums to his name (the most recent being 1979's 'Stuntman', FROESE chose a divergent musical route to that of TD. Augmented by long-time supporter KLAUS KRUGER on drums, EDGAR played – or dabbled with – every other digital instrument on the set, a set that included some dynamic but short formulaic tracks. *MCS*

Album rating: *5.5

Paul KELLY

Born: Paul Maurice Kelly, 13 Jan'55, Adelaide, Australia. Since his introduction to a musical career in 1974 via a public performance in Hobart (with trad-folklore number, 'Streets Of Forbes'), KELLY has led a plethora of bands from his inaugural incarnation as

Paul Kelly & The Dots (two LPs, 'Talk' 1981 & 'Manila' 1982). Flitting in the meantime from short-lived base, Melbourne, to Sydney, he recorded his debut solo LP, 'Post', in 1985, but this remained unreleased until he found a bona fide contract with 'Mushroom' records. With a new outfit in tow, the un-aptly-monikered Coloured Girls (tipping the hat to a certain Lou Reed song), KELLY hit the big time via double-set, 'Gossip' (1986), a record that also produced two Aussie chart entries, 'Darling It Hurts' & 'Before Too Long'. He continued to shine in his native Australia with albums such as 'Under The Sun' (1987 w/ the CGs), 'So Much Water, So Close To Home' (1989), 'Comedy' (1991) and 'Hidden Things' (1992), the last three with his third outfit, the Messengers. With production work and other activities in the pipeline (a book of poetry, etc.), a second solo album, 'Wanted Man' (1994), saw him find his lyrical folk roots once again. It was still a mystery as to how KELLY had never established himself in Britain and America (like so many other Australian acts, NICK CAVE, etc.), but that didn't deter him from trying. Subsequent albums flowed from KELLY's pen, while journeyman excursions into other music genres (i.e. techno and bluegrass, with Professor Ratbaggy & Uncle Bill, respectively) provided him with more directions than you could throw a boomerang at. Yet another outlet for PK's undoubted abilities was in the field of film music (having composed the music for 'Everynight ... Everynight' in 1994), the multi-talented singer-songwriter scoring for a string of Aussie flicks including 'SILENT PARTNER' (alongside GERRY HALE), 'LANTANA' and 'ONE NIGHT THE MOON' (all released in 2001). Described as Australia's equivalent to Bruce Springsteen, his eclectic post-millennium career continued with '. . .Nothing But A Dream' (2001), the double 'Ways & Means' (2004), the bluegrass 'Foggy Highway' (2005) with the Stormwater Boys and 'Stolen Apples' (2007).
MCS

- **filmography** (composer) {acting} –

Everynight . . . Everynight *(1994 promo-OST; future edition)* / **Silent Partner** *(2001 OST w/ GERRY HALE =>)* / **Lantana** *(2001 OST =>)* / **One Night The Moon** *(2001 {*} OST w/ KEV CARMODY & Mairead Hannan =>)* / Fireflies *(2004 TV on OST w/ V/A)* / Jindabyne *(2006 score)*

KIDS

1995 (US 91m) Sining Excalibur Films / Miramax Films (R)

Film genre: coming-of-age urban drama

Top guns: dir: Larry Clark → WASSUP ROCKERS (+ story w/ Jim Lewis) / s-w: Harmony Korine

Stars: Leo Fitzpatrick *(Telly)* → STORYTELLING, Justin Pierce *(Casper)* → LOOKING FOR LEONARD, Rosario Dawson *(Ruby)* → HE GOT GAME → JOSIE AND THE PUSSYCATS → CHELSEA WALLS → RENT, Chloe Sevigny *(Jenny)* → DEMONLOVER → DEATH OF A DYNASTY → the BROWN BUNNY, Sarah Henderson *(girl #1)*, Sajan Bhagat *(Paul)*, Billy Valdes *(Stanly)*, Harmony Korine *(club kid)* → GOOD WILL HUNTING → LAST DAYS

Storyline: A controversial day in the life of a group of New York teenagers, among whom Telly likes to think of himself as a womaniser, even if he doesn't realise he's infected his latest conquest, Jenny, with HIV. Once she realises her condition, she sets out to warn her wayward lover before he metes out a similar fate to another unsuspecting girl.
BG

Movie rating: *7

Visual: video + dvd

Off the record: The **FOLK IMPLOSION** (see below)

Various Artists / the FOLK IMPLOSION (*)

Jul 95. (cd/c) *London; <(828640-2/-4)>* [ ] Apr96 [ ]
– Casper (DANIEL JOHNSTON) / Daddy never understood (DELUXX FOLK IMPLOSION) * / Nothing gonna stop (*) / Jenny's theme (*) / Simean groove (*) / Casper, the friendly ghost (DANIEL JOHNSTON) / Natural one (*) / Spoiled (SEBADOH) * / Crash (*) / Wet stuff (*) / Mad fright night (LO DOWN) / Raise the bells (*) / Good morning captain (SLINT).

S/track review: "Caspar lives in a world without promise, sitting at home in his pyjamas, just wishing it would all go away somehow". DANIEL JOHNSTON had been imparting his tattered wisdom for years before 'KIDS', but his opening gambit still reads like a mid-90s slacker manifesto. Performed with catastrophic glee, 'Caspar' comes on like the Velvet Underground mangling Dylan's Chimes Of Freedom; the phantom, squeezebox epistle of 'Caspar The Friendly Ghost' is its imaginary friend. JOHNSTON may be the godfather of lo-fi, but the guilelessness of his art hasn't always been echoed by his disciples. Sometime scientists of the shambolic-like, side-project the FOLK IMPLOSION (featuring LOU BARLOW and JOHN DAVIS), became a main event after hitting a rich, dark seam of form on this soundtrack, but whose stealth in shifting between primeval splurge, orchestrated dissonance, and Can-esque death-march gives lie to the lo-fi cliches. 'Natural One' was the hit single, a half-sung hypno-groove putting a minor chord, Left Banke-sampling spin on Beck's thrift store economy. They bettered that with the Satie-sampling 'Wet Stuff' (a track that recalls nothing so much as forgotten blues mystics Masters Of Reality), the coma-inducing mesmerism of 'Nothing Gonna Stop', and the 'American Werewolf In London'-goes-trip-hop creepiness of 'Simean Groove'. That they failed to delve deeper into this electro-swamp fever remains one of the more disappointing legacies of an album which 'The Rough Guide To Rock' hails as "dazzling". Haunting is maybe a better adjective, but there's no denying that it's possibly the best original "indie" soundtrack of the 90s, crowned by the epic SLINT monologue, 'Good Morning Captain'.
BG

Album rating: *8

– spinoff hits, etc. –

the FOLK IMPLOSION: Natural One / (non-OST song)

Nov 95. (cd-s) *<850430-2>* [29] [–]

the FOLK IMPLOSION: Natural One / (Unkle mixes)

May 96. (12") *(LONX 382)* [–] [45]
(cd-s+=) *(LONCD 382)* – (Unkle No Skratch mix).

the KILLING FIELDS

1984 (UK 142m) Warner Bros. Pictures (R)

Film genre: political drama

Top guns: dir: Roland Joffe / s-w: Bruce Robinson (au: Sydney Schanberg)

Stars: Sam Waterson *(Sydney Schanberg)* ← RANCHO DELUXE ← MAHONEY'S LAST STAND, Dr. Haing S. Ngor *(Dith Pran)*, John Malkovich *(Alan 'Al' Rockoff, photographer)* ← PLACES IN THE HEART, Julian Sands *(Jon Swain)* → GOTHIC → SIESTA → the MILLION DOLLAR HOTEL, Craig T. Nelson *(Major Reeves, military attache)* ← WHERE THE BUFFALO ROAM, Spalding Gray *(U.S. consul)* → TRUE STORIES → BEACHES → STRAIGHT TALK → HOW HIGH, Athol Fugard *(Dr. Sundesval)*, Bill Paterson *(Dr. MacEntire)* → SPICEWORLD, Jay Barney *(Sydney Schanberg's father)* ← MISTER ROCK AND ROLL, Nell Campbell *(Beth)* ← the WALL ← SHOCK TREATMENT ← JUBILEE ← ROCK FOLLIES OF '77 ← LISZTOMANIA ← the ROCKY HORROR PICTURE SHOW

Storyline: Based on the real life events which conspired to keep Cambodian Dith Pran – an erstwhile source and translator for journalist Sidney Schanberg – at the mercy of Pol Pot's murderous Khmer Roughe. After being awarded the Pulitzer Prize for his reporting of the Vietnam War, Schanberg vows to free Pran against overwhelming odds.
BG

Movie rating: *8.5

Visual: video + dvd

Off the record: **MIKE OLDFIELD** (b.15 May'53, Reading, Berkshire, England) started playing guitar at the age of seven, and by 1968 he was part of folk-orientated outfit Sallyangie with sister Sally Oldfield. The duo signed to 'Transatlantic' records, who almost immediately issued their debut LP, 'Children Of The Sun', but after a flop single, 'Two Ships' (in September '69), they dissolved their partnership to concentrate on other projects. Following a spell in the short-lived Barefoot, Mike became the bassist for Kevin Ayers' band, the Whole World, appearing on two albums, 'Shooting At The Moon' (1971) and 'Whatevershebringswesing' (1972). It would be around this period, OLDFIELD started work on his own solo project, a project that would gain financial support from Richard Branson's newly formed 'Virgin' label. The album 'Tubular Bells' finally saw the light of day in May '73, immediately garnering critical acclaim from the music press. A near 50-minute concept piece, overdubbed many times by the multi-instrumentalist himself, the LP finally shot into the UK Top 3 a year later. Aided by a surprise US Top 10 single (an album excerpt) used in the horror movie, 'The Exorcist', 'Tubular Bells' repeated the feat Stateside. In September '74, his follow-up 'Hergest Ridge' was completed, and went straight to No.1. Critically lambasted by some commentators as "Son of Tubular Bells", it only managed to hit No.87 in America, OLDFIELD coming in for further flak as an orchestral Tubular Bells (conducted by David Bedford) was panned by the rock press. The period between 1975 and 1978 saw him branch into African and folk-type origins on the albums, 'Ommadawn' and 'Incantations', although at the same time he embarrassed his "rock" following by releasing mainly festive hit 45's. Nevertheless, his contribution to the 70s, in terms of both classical and rock fields, was arguably only matched by PINK FLOYD. The early 80s brought OLDFIELD a succession of more mainstream pop/rock albums, culminating with 1983's Top 10 'Crises' album, which spawned his biggest ever hit single, 'Moonlight Shadow' (it featured the celestial vocal chords of Maggie Reilly, a member of his band and new co-writing team). Surprisingly, his next single, 'Shadow On The Wall', bombed, although it did succeed in raising the profile of ex-Family frontman, Roger Chapman. OLDFIELD continued to achieve reasonable chart success throughout the remainder of the decade, even scoring the soundtrack to classic David Puttnam-produced movie, 'The KILLING FIELDS' (1984); his previous scores had been the rather low-key 'The Space Movie' (1980) and porn flick, 'Hot Dreams' (1983). *MCS*

MIKE OLDFIELD

Dec 84. (cd/c/lp) *Virgin; (CD/TC+/V 2328) Atlantic; <86009>* [97] [ ]
– Pran's theme / Requiem for a city / Evacuation / Pran's theme 2 / Capture / Execution / Bad news / Pran's departure / Worksite / The year zero / Blood sucking / The year zero 2 / Pran's escape – The killing fields / The trek / Boy's burial – Pran sees the Red Cross / Good news / Etude. *(re-iss. Jun88 lp/c; OVED/+C 183) <US cd-iss. 1990; 90591-2> (UK cd-iss. Jul00 on 'Virgin-VIP'; MIKECD 12)*

S/track review: Although MIKE OLDFIELD was reportedly unhappy with the compromises involved in scoring his one and only soundtrack, the end result suggested that film was an avenue which lent itself well to OLDFIELD's feel for composition. Scored largely on the Fairlight CMI synth/sampler – a state-of-the-art instrument in its day – this is dark and unwieldy stuff, sketching the film's murderous, inhumane themes. While the most accessible cues are those which feature the full orchestra, as on 'Pran's Departure' and 'Pran Sees The Red Cross' OLDFIELD skilfully employs ethnic melodies and instrumentation – much as he did in the late 70s – on the likes of 'Good News' and 'Etude' (inspired by a Spanish classical guitar piece), overlaying them with that trademark, clean-toned guitar. Of the more unsettling material, the creator of 'Tubular Bells' (after all used as the theme to a horror film) gathers claustrophobic choir arrangements, clanking percussion, 'Midnight Express'-style electro menace ('Evacuation') and ghostly, disembodied frequencies ('The Year Zero') for a score which you won't necessarily want to listen to every day but which will linger in your consciousness like a vaguely disturbing, fleetingly remembered dream. *BG*

Album rating: *5.5

– spinoff releases, etc. –

MIKE OLDFIELD: Etude / Evacuation

Nov 84. (7"/ext.12") *(VS 731/+12)* [ ] [-]

□ KING BLACK ACID segment
(⇒ the MOTHMAN PROPHECIES)

□ the KINKS
(⇒ Ray DAVIES)

□ Eartha KITT segment
(⇒ FRIDAY FOSTER)

□ the KNIFE segment
(⇒ HANNAH MED H)

Gladys KNIGHT

Born: 28 May'44, Atlanta, Georgia, USA. Earning initial exposure for her considerable vocal prowess via an American TV talent show 'Original Amateur Hour', at the tender age of 7, KNIGHT joined up with her siblings and cousins to form the first line-up of the Pips; named so after another of her cousins James "Pip" Woods. The group hit paydirt with 'Every Beat Of My Heart', a Bobby Robinson-produced nugget on 'Vee-Jay' records in 1962, the same year they renamed themselves, GLADYS KNIGHT & The Pips. The singing ensemble had a second hit with 'Letter Full Of Tears' and KNIGHT retired from touring to bring up her son Jimmy III and daughter Kenya. In 1966, she was forced back on the road to support her family, while the group signed to 'Motown'. It was there they produced hits such as 'I Heard It Through The Grapevine', 'If I Were Your Woman' and Grammy-winner 'Neither One Of Us (Wants To Be The First To Say Goodbye)'. It was only after leaving 'Motown' in 1972 for 'Buddah' records that KNIGHT and her loyal band scored their only US No.1 with 'Midnight Train To Georgia'. After she and the group laid down their Curtis Mayfield-penned soundtrack to 'CLAUDINE' (1974) – which featured Top 5 smash 'On And On' – her big acting break in the movies came via her starring role in 'PIPE DREAMS' (1976); it would net KNIGHT two Golden Globe nominations for Best Lead Actress and Best Song. Her thespian career was mostly small screen endeavours however, with roles in 'J.A.G.', 'New York Undercover' and 'The Jamie Foxx Show'. She even squeezed in an appearance playing herself on 'Baywatch'. She continued to record, solo and with the Pips, her most notable post-'Buddah' album being the 1980s Ashford & Simpson-penned 'About Love'. Towards the end of the 80s, Gladys also provided James Bond with a theme song for 'Licence To Kill'. KNIGHT currently directs the Grammy-award winning Choir Saints Unified Voices who perform at churches of Jesus Christ and the Latter-day Saints (Mormons) across America. *MR*

- **filmography** {acting} (composer) –

Save The Children *(1973 {p} =>)* / **Claudine** *(1974 OST to GLADYS KNIGHT & THE PIPS =>)* / **Pipe Dreams** *(1976 {*} OST =>)* / Desperado *(1987 {a})* / Licence To Kill *(1989 theme/hit on OST; see future edition)* / Twenty Bucks *(1993 {a})* / Hollywood Homicide *(2003 {a})* / Unbeatable Harold *(2006 {a})*

KNOCKED UP

2006 (US 130m) Apatow Pictures / Universal Pictures (R)

Film genre: romantic/SeXual comedy

Top guns: s-w + dir: Judd Apatow → WALK HARD: THE DEWEY COX STORY

Stars: Seth Rogen *(Ben Stone)*, Katherine Heigl *(Alison Scott)*, Paul Rudd *(Pete)* → WALK HARD: THE DEWEY COX STORY, Leslie Mann *(Debbie)* ← LAST MAN STANDING ← SHE'S THE ONE, Jason Segal *(Jason)* ← SLC PUNK, Jay Baruchel *(Jay)* ← ALMOST FAMOUS, Jonah Hill *(Jonah)*, Martin Starr *(Martin)* → WALK HARD: THE DEWEY COX STORY, Joanna Kerns *(Alison's mother)*, Harold Ramis *(Ben's dad)* ← AIRHEADS ← HEAVY METAL / → WALK HARD: THE DEWEY COX STORY, Kristen Wiig *(Jill)* → WALK HARD: THE DEWEY COX STORY, **Loudon Wainwright III** *(Dr. Howard)*

Storyline: Ben Stone is one of life's professional losers. Terminally unemployed, he spends his time smoking pot and watching internet movies. Then one night a beautiful woman, Karen, walks up to him in a bar and they have a one night stand. Ben then goes back to his old ways but suddenly he has to deal with the real world when two months later Karen appears on his doorstep and announces he's going to be a dad. Help! *JZ*

Movie rating: *8

Visual: dvd

Off the record: LOUDON WAINWRIGHT III (b. 5 Sep'46, Chapel Hill, North Carolina, USA) was the son of a journalist and served his musical apprenticeship on the US college and folk-club circuit following in the footsteps of BOB DYLAN and JOAN BAEZ. The budding singer/songwriter (hailed as the new DYLAN and later as the Woody Allen of folk, the Charlie Chaplin of rock and the male Melanie!) hitched to San Francisco in 1967 and signed to 'Atlantic' records two years later. After moving to 'Columbia' records in 1973, he scored a US Top 20 hit with the novelty song, 'Dead Skunk' (which allegedly took 15 minutes to write), lifted from the helpfully titled 'Album III'. His subsequent efforts, 'Attempted Moustache' and 'Unrequited', failed to consolidate his position and after an unsuccessful move to 'Arista' records, WAINWRIGHT relocated to London. He spent five years on 'Demon/Rounder', sometimes augmented by RICHARD THOMPSON on albums such as 'Fame And Wealth', 'I'm Alright' and 'More Love Songs'. Although still critically lauded, these albums were met with diminishing commercial returns; while WAINWRIGHT was admittedly not the greatest of singers, his inimitable comic satire usually compensated. Continuing to release fine material into the 90s, WAINWRIGHT released the 1995 set, 'Grown Man', featuring the hilarious 'IWIWAL (I Wish I Was A Lesbian)' which almost equalled his 'Dead Skunk' (this one took him eight! minutes to write) for deadpan humour. 1999's 'Social Studies' was pretty much what the title suggested although the tone was inimitably sardonic rather than academic, many of these topical sketches written especially for America's National Public Radio. A different beast altogether, 'Last Man On Earth' (2001) was an intensely personal and emotionally fraught affair written after the death of his mother. 'So Damn Happy' (2003) was back to irreverent business for Loudon, with his first live set in a decade. Featuring material culled largely from the 80s and 90s, and recorded at separate venues in California, the album was a highly enjoyable jaunt through the man's back pages with help from the likes of RICHARD THOMPSON and Van Dyke Parks. Apart from Loudon you can also hear other songs in the movie: 'Chelsea Dagger' (the FRATELLIS), 'We Are Nowhere And It's Now' (BRIGHT EYES), 'Smile' (LILY ALLEN), 'All Night' (DAMIAN MARLEY feat. STEPHEN MARLEY) and 'Shimmy Shimmy Ya' (the WU-TANG CLAN). *BG*

—

LOUDON WAINWRIGHT III: Strange Weirdos: Music From..

May 07. (cd) *Concord; <(CCD 30301)>* ☐ ☐
– Grey in L.A. / You can't fail me now / Daughter / Ypsilanti / So much to do / Valley morning / X or Y / Final frontier / Feel so good / Lullaby / Naomi / Doin' the math / Strange weirdos / Passion play.

S/track review: He's a funny man, is LOUDON WAINWRIGHT III. Anyone who caught the documentary on BBC4 a while back will be confident they know what to expect from this eternally ironic, singer-songwriterly patriarch. 'Grey In L.A.' is the track which sowed the seed of his quasi-soundtrack, an ode to leaden skies that's more than worthy of the Sunshine State's own in-house bard of sardonica, Randy Newman. Yet longtime LOUDON watchers should know to expect the unexpected. While Newman has been knocking out scores for donkeys years, this is WAINWRIGHT's first pop at a full soundtrack, a result of director Judd Apatow's having been "hooked" by a sighting, many moons ago on the David Letterman show, of "this scraggly guy with a beard", "who played a dark, funny song in which he threatened to commit suicide in order to make an ex-girlfriend feel guilty". The scrag and the beard have long gone but the black humour remains, reinstated for this album after having been largely divested from its music for use in the actual movie. In what has to count as a fairly unconventional film-scoring process, WAINWRIGHT – along with mercurial singer-songwriter/producer JOE HENRY – wrote songs inspired by the film which music supervisor Jonathan Karp would then strip of lyrics and synch their constituent parts with suitable dramatic moments. Here, though, we have the pooled genius of WAINWRIGHT and HENRY in its unexpurgated entirety, and the novelty of a quasi-score album with a full lyric sheet, one which simultaneously functions as de facto regular WAINWRIGHT album. Getting stuck into the mindset of scripted characters, plot and subtext gifts this most rambling of men a rare focus, eliciting such uncharacteristically searing, sober avowals of human trust and frailty as 'You Can't Fail Me Now', a song which Apatow credits with making the hair on his arms stand on end. As it turns out, the HENRY-partnered WAINWRIGHT is responsible for some of the most honest, unglamorous love songs of recent times. In strictly grammatical terminology, the title track might be regarded as a redundant modifier, but there's nothing redundant about its premise of two round pegs brave enough to make themselves fit into a square hole through mutual revelation. 'The Final Frontier', the track which makes most dramatic use of the Section Quartet, is also a moving meditation on bravery, the tenacity to brave the harsh reality (bounded by RICHARD THOMPSON's cauterising guitar) that is long term commitment, a reality which is inexorably worth braving, and one which, in the final analysis of 'Passion Play', transcends the ridiculousness of the life WAINWRIGHT has so often sent up: "We're gonna hang up the costumes, take off the make up, shut the dressing room door, Then it's me and you 1 disguised as 2 and twice as good as before". Long time fans can breathe easy, though, he's still sending life up on the likes of 'Feel So Good' ("I feel so bad it must be right, Have myself a nightmare every night, All of my friends are glad, Cause I feel so bad"). And WAINWRIGHT's unromantic eye reassuringly exorcises every last phantom of mystery and worry from pregnancy with the bumptious 'X Or Y', dusted clean by the matured, pump organ-piped Americana of his backing band (which also includes Van Dyke Parks on several tracks), itself coming into its own on spare, lucent productions like the oxymoronic, John Lennon-esque 'Lullaby', the gauzy smog of 'Valley Morning' and luscious HENRY instrumental, 'Naomi'. As well as being WAINWRIGHT's best album in years, 'Strange Weirdos' is as good an advert as any for the transformative power of soundtrack; maybe more artists should try the Loudon method. *BG*

Album rating: *7.5

Mark KNOPFLER

Born: 12 Aug'49, Glasgow, Scotland. An atypically unassuming rock star who's sought rootsier terrain after the huge mid-80s success of his band Dire Straits, MARK KNOPFLER is now an established film composer with a raft of successful soundtracks under his belt. Formed in London in the late 70s, Dire Straits were initially swept along by the momentum of the new wave movement, even if their brand of bluesy, Dylan-esque rock hardly qualified as punk rock. KNOPFLER first moved into film with the soundtrack for 'LOCAL HERO' (1983), just as his band were about to capture the mid-80s zeitgeist with their 'Brothers in Arms' album. If that record embodied such pivotal music industry shifts as the emergence of MTV and the CD market, 'LOCAL HERO' was pitched at the opposite end of the cultural spectrum; diffident and beguiling mood music for a movie championing the local over the corporate (so local, in fact, the main theme was adopted by Newcastle United football fans). Scores for both 'Comfort And Joy' and 'CAL' followed in 1984, movies set in Scotland and Northern Ireland respectively, and the latter, especially, distinguishing itself by its Celtic folk influences. While these soundtracks were recorded with key Dire Straits personnel, they were a world away from that band's ostentatious stadium fare, or at least its rockier elements. KNOPFLER distanced himself even further with more conventional, orchestral scores for 'The PRINCESS BRIDE' (1987) and 'LAST EXIT TO BROOKLYN' (1989), initiating a long term writing partnership with Guy Fletcher. Renewed activity in the Dire Straits camp, work with Chet Atkins and his own roots conglomeration the Notting Hillbillies, as well as a debut solo album proper (1996's 'Golden Heart') delayed further soundtrack work until the late 90s. Scores for American political satire 'WAG THE DOG' (1997) and British mid-life crisis drama 'METROLAND' (1997) confirmed that KNOPFLER's evocative guitar signature and understated approach were well suited to cinema, and in 2000/1, he took his fondness for native folk music a step further with the soundtrack to Scottish football drama, 'a SHOT AT GLORY'. Not one to blow his own trumpet, the quietly spoken northerner has indicated in at least one interview that he's not convinced of his own ability when it comes to soundtracks, an opinion that his impressive CV renders fairly groundless. *BG*

- **filmography** (composer) –

Local Hero *(1983 OST =>)* / Comfort And Joy *(1984 OST =>)* / **Cal** *(1984 OST =>)* / **the Princess Bride** *(1987 OST =>)* / **Last Exit To Brooklyn** *(1989 OST =>)* / **Wag The Dog** *(1997 OST =>)* / **Metroland** *(1997 OST w/ OST =>)* / **a Shot At Glory** *(2001 OST =>)*

– compilations, etc. –

MARK KNOPFLER: Screenplaying

Nov 93. (cd/c/lp) *Vertigo; (518327-2/-4/-1) / Warners; <45457-2/-4>* ☐ ☐
– Irish boy / Irish love / Father and son / Potato picking / The long road / A love idea / Victims / Finale – Last Exit To Brooklyn / Once upon a time . . . Storybook love / Morning ride / The friends' song / Guide my sword / A happy ending / Wild theme / Boomtown / The mist covered mountains / Smooching / Going home: theme from Local Hero. *(d-cd-iss. Oct00 on 'Universal'+=; E 546601-2)* – (Notting Hillbillies set).

☐ Al KOOPER segment
(⇒ the LANDLORD)

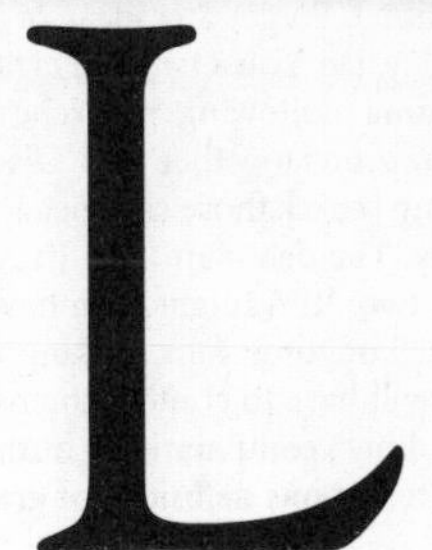

LA PASSIONE

1996 (UK 109m) Warner Bros. Pictures (15)

Film genre: domestic/sports melodrama

Top guns: dir: John B. Hobbs / s-w: **Chris Rea**

Stars: Thomas Orange *(young Jo)*, Sean Gallagher *(Jo)*, Jan Ravens *(Mama)*, Paul Shane *(Papa)*, Carmen Silvera *(Grandmother)*, Keith Barron *(Roy)*, Belinda Stewart-Wilson *(Dina)*, Anna Pernicci *(Fran)*, **Shirley Bassey** *(herself)*, Freddie Davis *(Uncle Valentino)*

Storyline: After making his fortune with a vanilla-scented aftershave inspired by a secret family recipe, a working class English boy fulfills his dreams of becoming a racing driver in Italy. *BG*

Movie rating: *6.5

Visual: video

Off the record: CHRIS REA was born 4th March '51, Middlesborough, England. An unassuming singer/songwriter/guitarist who's enjoyed a long and successful albums-based career, CHRIS REA belatedly joined the big league with his No.1 'Road To Hell' album in 1989. By then he'd already notched up two film composing credits, for Paul Lynch's black Canadian comedy, 'Cross Country' (1983) and West German drama, 'Auf Immer Und Ewig' (1986). Like MARK KNOPFLER, a fellow northerner whom he's often been compared with and who has also carved a separate career in film scoring, REA's mature, bluesy writing lent itself well to the demands of the big screen. He even made a cameo appearance in one of the most compelling films of the 90s, Neil Jordan's 'The Crying Game' (1992). The same year, REA scored the music for easygoing road movie 'Soft Top, Hard Shoulder'. A preoccupation with motion, travel and the open road has in fact been a recurring theme in his work, culminating in 'LA PASSIONE'. While REA wrote both the semi-autobiographical screenplay and the score, neither the film nor the soundtrack met with great critical or commercial success. Nor did 'Parting Shots' (1998), the Michael Winner comedy thriller in which REA played a dying photographer out for revenge. More recently, the singer underwent a battle with cancer, eventually re-emerging with his most acclaimed studio album in years, 'Dancing Down The Stony Road' (2002). *BG*

CHRIS REA

Nov 96. (cd/c) *East West; (0630-16695-2/-4)* 43 –
– La passione (film theme) / Dov'e il signore? / Shirley do you own a Ferrari? (w/ SHIRLEY BASSEY) / Girl in a sports car / When the grey skies turn to blue / Horses / Olive oil / Only to fly / You must follow / 'Disco' La Passione (vocals: SHIRLEY BASSEY) / Dov'e il signore? part two / Le Mans.

S/track review: Composed by CHRIS REA and performed largely by the Gavin Wright Film Orchestra, this lavishly arranged, theatrically minded score stands at a stark remove from the singer/guitarist's standard studio fare. Being recorded in 1996, it also comes with a mandatory SHIRLEY BASSEY duet (although admittedly she also appears in the film). Forget any ideas of Propellerheads-style chic, however; 'Shirley Do You Own A Ferrari?' is unashamedly sentimental melodrama wallowing in orchestral schmaltz. That said, the pair also step out together on "Disco' La Passione', an enjoyably campy romp (check those castanets!) in the best tradition of the Pet Shop Boys. The debonair 'Girl In A Sports Car' cruises halfway between the two; REA might even have had a hit with this back in the late 70s. Longtime fans looking for something a bit leaner and moodier will have to content themselves with 'Only To Fly' or 'You Must Follow', comparatively humble pickings next to the record's more ostentatious delusions of grandeur. *BG*

Album rating: *3.5

– spinoff hits, etc. –

CHRIS REA feat. SHIRLEY BASSEY: 'Disco' La Passione / (Adams & Gielen mix)

Nov 96. (c-s) *(EW 072C)* [41] [–]
(12"/cd-s) *(EW 072 T/CD)* – CHRIS REA: Horses.

CHRIS REA: Girl In A Sports Car / Dino

May 97. (c-s) *(EW 103C)* [ ] [–]
(cd-s+=) *(EW 103CD)* – Olive Oil.

LABYRINTH

1986 (UK/US 101m) TriStar Pictures (PG)

Film genre: family/children's fantasy

Top guns: s-w: Jim Henson (+ dir), Terry Jones, Edward C. Hume, John Varley, Lewis John Carlino (story: Dennis Lee)

Stars: David BOWIE *(Jareth)*, Jennifer Connelly *(Sarah)* ← PHENOMENA / → the HOT SPOT, Toby Froud *(Toby)*, Shelley Thompson *(stepmother)*, Christopher Malcolm *(father)* ← SHOCK TREATMENT, Natalie Finland *(fairy)*, Shari Weiser *(Hoggle)*, Rob Mills *(Ludo)*, David Barclay *(Didymus)*, Karen Prell *(the worm / junk lady)*, Brian Henson *(voice; Hoggle / Goblin)*, Michael Hordern *(the wiseman)* ← PIED PIPER

Storyline: George Lucas and Jim Henson team up to produce and direct this coming-of-age fantasy adventure. The tale features Sarah, who must try to rescue her little brother who has been abducted by goblins. Soon she encounters Jareth, who guides her ever-deeper into his magical kingdom where she must survive hidden traps and dangerous monsters until at last she stands before the enchanted castle at the heart of the Labyrinth. *JZ*

Movie rating: *6.5

Visual: video + dvd

Off the record: (see below)

—

DAVID BOWIE / TREVOR JONES (*)

Jun 86. (lp/c) *EMI America; (AML/TCAML 3104) <17206>* [38] Jul86 [68]
– Opening titles including Underground / Into the labyrinth (*) / Magic dance / Sarah (*) / Chilly down / Hallucination (*) / As the world falls down / The goblin battle (*) / Within you / Thirteen o'clock (*) / Home at last (*) / Underground (reprise). *(cd-iss. Sep86 & Feb90; CDP7 46312-2) (<cd re-iss. May04 on 'Fame'; CDFA 3322>)*

S/track review: The twelve tracks which make up this interesting and unusual work alternate between DAVID BOWIE songs and TREVOR JONES' synthesized orchestral pieces. JONES uses the instrumental pieces to emphasize the fairy-tale side of the film in tracks such as 'Into The Labyrinth' and 'Thirteen O'Clock'. Each track has a slightly different tone, darker in 'Hallucination' but warm and comforting in 'Home at Last', ensuring the music is not repetitive. DAVID BOWIE's six songs (co-produced by Arif Mardin), while continuing the fantasy theme, concentrate more on the developing relationship between his character Jareth and heroine Sarah, culminating in a haunting piece entitled 'Within You'. Other songs such as 'Magic Dance' and the final track 'Underground' threaten to become full-blown musical choruses at times but this suits the general air of quirkiness of JONES' soundtrack. BOWIE's distinctive voice blends well with this pop/fantasy mixture and makes this CD well worth a listen. *JZ*

Album rating: *6

– spinoff hits, etc. –

DAVID BOWIE: Underground / (instrumental)

Jun 86. (7"/7"sha-pic-d) *(EA/+P 216) <8323>* [21] [ ]

□ Nick LAIRD-CLOWES segment
(⇒ the INVISIBLE CIRCUS)

the LANDLORD

1970 (US 111m) United Artists Pictures (PG)

Film genre: romantic comedy/drama

Top guns: dir: Hal Ashby → HAROLD AND MAUDE → BOUND FOR GLORY → LET'S SPEND THE NIGHT TOGETHER / s-w: Bill Gunn (au: Kristin Hunter)

Stars: Beau Bridges *(Elgar Enders)* → SILVER DREAM RACER → ELVIS AND THE COLONEL: THE UNTOLD STORY, Lee Grant *(Joyce Enders)* → DR. T & THE WOMEN, **Pearl Bailey** *(Marge)*, Diana Sands *(Francine 'Fanny' Copee)* → WILLIE DYNAMITE, Marki Bey *(Lainie)*, Lou Gossett *(Copee)*, Douglas Grant *(Walter Gee Copee)*, Susan Anspach *(Susan Enders)*, Walter Brooke *(William Enders Sr.)* ← the GRADUATE, Melvin Stewart *(Prof. Duboise)*, Robert Klein *(Peter Coots)* → the OWL AND THE PUSSYCAT → the LAST UNICORN / → PRIMARY COLORS, Stanley Greene *(Heywood the butler)* → COTTON COMES TO HARLEM → the WIZ, Gloria Henry *(Gloria)* → ACROSS 110th STREET → BLACK CAESAR → SLAUGHTER'S BIG RIP-OFF → HELL UP IN HARLEM → BLACK BELT JONES, John McCurry *(Big John)* → FRITZ THE CAT, Oliver Clark *(Mr. Farcus)* → a STAR IS BORN, Louise Stubbs *(Louise)* → BLACK GIRL, Hector Elizondo *(Hector)* → BEACHES → HOW HIGH, Carl Lee *(Carl)* → SUPERFLY → GORDON'S WAR, Marlene Clark *(Marlene)*

Storyline: Rich socialite Elgar Enders decides to fly the nest and make a new home for himself. He takes the easy option of buying a whole tenement block, and as for the people already living there, well, he plans to evict them all. But when Elgar actually sets foot in the place and meets his evictees, he finds himself intrigued by their lives in contrast with the banal existence of his own parents. Throw in a little romance, and Elgar may compose himself to live and let live after all. *JZ*

Movie rating: *6.5

Visual: none

Off the record: Al KOOPER (see below)

—

Various Artists (music by AL KOOPER)

Aug 70. (lp) *United Artists; <UAS 5209> (UAS 29120)* [ ] Mar71 [ ]
– Brand new day (vocal by * & The MARTHA STEWART SINGERS) / The landlord (the LANDLORDS) / Car commercial / Walter G's boogaloo / Croquet game / Let me love you (vocal by LORRAINE ELLISON) / Rent party (tenor solo by JOE FARRELL) / Love theme (vocal by * & The MARTHA STEWART SINGERS) / Soul hoedown (the LANDLORDS) / Elgar's fantasy / Doin' me dirty (vocal by LORRAINE ELLISON) / Lainie's theme / Brand new day (vocal by The STAPLE SINGERS) / The axe / God bless the children (vocal by The STAPLE SINGERS).

S/track review: There can be few people with ears who haven't heard AL KOOPER's organ work on Dylan's 'Like A Rolling Stone'

(cooked up in the studio after more than one listen to Alan Price on 'House Of The Rising Sun') but the Brooklyn musician's contributions to many of the 20th Century's outstanding records remains under-celebrated. His first (and only) soundtrack finds him in top form, stretching out with exemplary taste and invention to shape an album that – if it wasn't for the tiresome (and puzzling) inclusion of a couple of tracks of abstract atmospherics – would walk into any self-respecting pop-soul record collection. The standouts are two gospel tracks, Jimmy Holiday's 'God Bless The Children' and KOOPER's own 'Brand New Day', both delivered with typically infectious passion by the STAPLE SINGERS. KOOPER surrounds himself with the cream of New York's session musicians, too: CHUCK RAINEY, ERIC GALE, AL ROGERS and FRANK OWENS, as well as the under-exposed husky soul voice of LORRAINE ELLISON, and produces them with the clarity to make the ordinary shine. But there is enough inspiration here (guitars that range from kora-like delicacy to twin electric leads, knockout horn charts and a constant sense of crafty dynamics) to rise far above the ordinary. *ND*

Album rating: *8

– spinoff releases, etc. –

AL KOOPER: Brand New Day / Love Theme From 'The Landlord'
Aug 70. (7") *<45179> (CBS 5146)* ☐ Mar71 ☐

k.d. LANG

Born: Kathryn Dawn Lang, 2 Nov'61, Consort, Alberta, Canada. One of the most interesting and consistently inventive female figures to emerge under the aegis of country in the last few decades, k.d. LANG has always sung to the tune of her spiritual mentor, Patsy Cline, rather than the Nashville establishment. A lesbian icon and an outspoken vegetarian, she nurtured her campy, unique vision of country from the alternative environs of Seymour Stein's 'Sire' rather than music row, netting the first of several Grammy awards in the late 80s. While her acting debut as a gay woman of Inuit descent in Percy Adlon's 'Salmonberries' (1991) prefigured her official "coming out" in 1992, LANG continued to challenge conventional ideas of gender and sexuality through her art, writing and performing the soundtrack to Gus Van Sant's 'EVEN COWGIRLS GET THE BLUES' in 1993 and scoring the music for 'Celluloid Closet', a 1995 film documenting Hollywood's presentation of homosexuality. In 1997 she took on the role of a gay film director in an American TV adaptation of the Mario Puzo novel, 'The Last Don', and subsequently starred alongside Ewan McGregor in the British/Candian thriller, 'Eye of the Beholder' (1999). Her songs, meanwhile, have appeared on soundtracks to films as diverse as 'SHAG: THE MOVIE' (1988), 'Coneheads' (1993), 'In Search Of Angels' (1994), 'Midnight In The Garden Of Good And Evil' (1997), 'Tomorrow Never Dies' (1997), 'Sweet November' (2001) and 'Home On The Range' (2004). *BG*

- **filmography** {acting} (composer) –

Black & White Night *(1988 {p} on OST by ROY ORBISON =>)* / Getting Married In Buffalo Jump *(1989 TV w/ Eric N. Robertson)* / Salmonberries *(1993 {*})* / **Even Cowgirls Get The Blues** *(1994 OST by LANG =>)* / Teresa's Tattoo *(1994 {a})* / the Celluloid Closet *(1995 w/ Carter Burwell)* / the Last Don *(1997 TV mini {a})* / Eye Of The Beholder *(1999 {*})*

☐ Bruce LANGHORNE segment
(⇒ the HIRED HAND)

Daniel LANOIS

Born: 19 Sep'51, Hull, Quebec, Canada. The producer of choice for U2 and assorted other veteran stars, DANIEL LANOIS is still best known for his work in shaping other artists' sound than for his own intermittent solo and film scoring work. A professional partnership with BRIAN ENO intially led LANOIS to work on such landmark albums as U2's 'The Unforgettable Fire' (1984) and 'The Joshua Tree' (1987), developing the organic, rarefied sound for which he remains so sought after. His trademark atmospherics also made him a prime candidate for cinematic projects, a fact obviously not lost on PETER GABRIEL who'd been sufficiently impressed with '. . .Fire' to hire LANOIS for his soundtrack to Alan Parker's 'BIRDY' (1984). The Canadian made his film scoring debut the same year, sharing the credits on low-budget domestic feature, 'The Surrogate' (1984). While the big name production credits (ROBBIE ROBERTSON, BOB DYLAN, etc.) continued to roll in, LANOIS kept his screen career ticking away with a National Geographic documentary, 'For All Mankind' (1989), composed of footage from assorted Nasa space missions, and another Canadian feature, 'Camilla' (1994). His mastery of spare, occasionally spiky, roots-rooted ambience was also showcased on Billy Bob Thornton's directorial debut, 'SLING BLADE' (1996), the first time his film work had made it to a bonafide soundtrack release. In 1998, LANOIS augmented friends WILLIE NELSON and EMMYLOU HARRIS on the former's Wim Wenders-directed short, 'TEATRO', which was also released on CD. LANOIS subsequently had a major hand in the BONO/U2-dominated soundtrack to Wenders' 'The MILLION DOLLAR HOTEL' (2000), writing (including the gorgeous 'Falling At Your Feet'), producing and even playing a bit of pedal steel. The new millennium also found him resuming his partnership with Thornton, contributing additional music to MARTY STUART's score for 'ALL THE PRETTY HORSES' (2000). *BG*

- **filmography** (composer) –

the Surrogate *(1984 w/ Pierre Marchand)* / For All Mankind *(1989)* / Camilla *(1994)* / **Sling Blade** *(1996 OST w/ V/A =>)* / **the Million Dollar Hotel** *(2000 OST w/ BONO, BRIAN ENO & MDH BAND =>)* / No Maps For These Territories *(2000 w/ BONO & The EDGE)*

LANTANA

2001 (Aus/Ger 121m) AFFC / Alamode Films (R)

Film genre: psychological mystery/drama

Top guns: dir: Ray Lawrence / s-w: Andrew Bovell

Stars: Anthony LaPaglia *(Det. Leon Zat)*, Geoffrey Rush *(John Knox)* ← STARSTRUCK / → the BANGER SISTERS, Barbara Hershey *(Dr. Valerie Somers)* ← BEACHES ← the LAST TEMPTATION OF CHRIST ← SHY PEOPLE, Kerry Armstrong *(Sonja Zat)* ← AMY / → ONE PERFECT DAY, Rachael Blake *(Jane O'May)*, Vince Colosimo *(Nik D'Amato)* ← CHOPPER, Peter Phelps *(Patrick Phelan)*, Daniella Farinacci *(Paula Daniels)*, Leah Purcell *(Claudia Weis)* → SOMERSAULT → the PROPOSITION

Storyline: The thick, twisty lantana plant has nothing on the plot of this one. After a woman's body is found in the undergrowth, detective Leon Zat is assigned to the case, but Zat is really a rat – he's cheating on his wife and seems close to a breakdown. His wife goes to see psychiatrist Valerie, who in turn suspects her own man of infidelity. Zat's mistress, Jane, lives next door to a couple called Nik and Paula, but when Valerie spots Nik acting suspiciously and then goes missing, the guilty party seems more obvious. But of course there's a twist in the tale. *JZ*

Movie rating: *8

Visual: dvd

Off the record: (see below)

PAUL KELLY (& Various Artists UK-only)

Sep 01. (cd) *E.M.I.; (535873-2)* [–] Austra [–]
– Lantana part 1 / Lantana part 2 / For Eleanor / What's happening to us / Through the window / Numb / Shortcut / Let's tangle. *(UK-iss.Aug02 on 'Cooking Vinyl'+=; COOKCD 238)* – Te busco (CELIA CRUZ) / Respeta mi tambo (LOS NARANJOS) / Que sabes tu de amor (JUANCYTO MARTINEZ) / Opening (BAMBOLEO) / Permiso que ilego van van (LOS VAN VAN).

S/track review: PAUL KELLY's brooding music might be just the thing to add weight to a tale of domestic angst, but you wouldn't want to hear it while you're chopping the onions. The soundtrack includes two lengthy slices of the extended jam session that threw up the bulk of the score, and it's sinister, uncomfortable stuff, featuring KELLY's spinoff outfit PROFESSOR RATBAGGY. Jazzy piano meanders over pulsing, unhurried bass figures, distorted guitars shriek and howl, and synths bluster and swirl like a nasty gale. KELLY remains one of those Antipodeans whose heroic status at home has not travelled, but this recording stands out as an expertly-crafted exercise in tension and menace, building around a simple theme that's insidiously infectious. The singer-songwriter's career has covered a wide range of other styles, too, from bluegrass to dub – but he is entirely absent from this schizophrenic soundtrack's other half. Sitting strangely next to the dark side are five absolutely top-notch salsa numbers, blaring out sunnily from veterans like LOS NARANJOS, LOS VAN VAN and the Queen of Salsa herself, CELIA CRUZ. The new generation of Cuban salsa artists are persuasively represented, too, with exhilarating tracks from JUANCYTO MARTINEZ and BAMBOLEO. But the whole thing adds up to an odd enough combination to explain the complete omission of these songs on versions of the CD. *ND*

Album rating: *6 / re-UK *7

□ Nathan LARSON
(⇒ SHUDDER TO THINK)

LAST EXIT TO BROOKLYN

1989 (Ger/US 100m) Neue Constantin Film / Cinecom Pictures (16/R)

Film genre: urban buddy drama

Top guns: dir: Uli Edel / s-w: Desmond Nakano ← BODY ROCK (au: Hubert Selby, Jr.)

Stars: Stephen Lang *(Harry Black)*, Jennifer Jason Leigh *(Tralala)* ← FAST TIMES AT RIDGEMONT HIGH / → RUSH → GEORGIA, Burt Young *(Big Joe)* ← ACROSS 110th STREET / → CROCODILE SHOES, Peter Dobson *(Vinnie)* ← SING, Jerry Orbach *(Boyce)*, Stephen Baldwin *(Sal)* ← HOMEBOY, Alexis Arquette *(Georgette)* → the WEDDING SINGER → CLUBLAND, Christopher Murney *(Paulie)* ← MAXIMUM OVERDRIVE ← the LAST DRAGON, Sam Rockwell *(Al)* → the ASSASSINATION OF JESSE JAMES . . ., Ricki Lake *(Donna)* ← WORKING GIRL ← HAIRSPRAY / → CRY-BABY → JACKIE'S BACK! → HAIRSPRAY re-make, Camille Saviola *(Ella)*, Mark Boone Junior *(Willie)* ← the WAY IT IS / → the BEATNICKS, Zette *(Regina)*

Storyline: A run-down Brooklyn neighbourhood is thrown into turmoil when the local factory workers go on strike and men's passions are aroused – in every sense. Bisexual Harry Black finds the temptations of power too much as he squanders the strike fund on transvestite Regina. Worker Big Joe batters his future son-in-law when he gets his daughter pregnant, and prostitute Tralala has little to sing about as she lurches from one desperate man to another. *JZ*

Movie rating: *7

Visual: video + dvd

Off the record: (see below)

—

MARK KNOPFLER

Nov 89. (lp/c/cd) *Vertigo; (838725-1/-4/-2) Warners; <25986>* [ ] [ ]
– Last exit to Brooklyn / Victims / Think fast / A love idea / Tralala / Riot / The reckoning / As low as it gets / Finale: Last exit to Brooklyn.

S/track review: While MARK KNOPFLER composed and produced the soundtrack to this Hubert Selby Jr. adaptation, it was collaborator and Dire Straits keyboardist GUY FLETCHER who performed the bulk of it. No surprise then, that this is the most atypical of all the man's soundtracks. It's also one of his most graceful, full of stately, finely chiselled orchestrations which stand up well next to the work of most Hollywood big shots. If the music is weighted with a melancholic gravitas in keeping with the film's grim storyline, it's a gravitas which never comes across as less than dignified despite the tawdriness of the subject matter. Comparisons with John Barry are difficult to avoid, especially on the main theme, itself almost as glacially haunting as some of Barry's own masterpieces. There's a sense that KNOPFLER was getting something out of his system here: he didn't return to soundtrack composition for the best part of a decade and, when he did, with 1997's 'WAG THE DOG', it was back to his more familiar, guitar-orientated approach. An interesting artifact then, albeit one more likely to appeal to serious film score fans. *BG*

Album rating: *5.5

the LAST GREAT WILDERNESS

2002 (UK/Den 95m) Sigma Films / Feature Film Company (18)

Film genre: buddy film/comedy

Top guns: dir: David Mackenzie → YOUNG ADAM → HALLAM FOE / s-w: Alastair Mackenzie, Michael Tait

Stars: Alastair Mackenzie *(Charlie)*, Jonny Phillips *(Vicente)*, Ewan Stewart *(Magnus)* ← WHITE CITY / → YOUNG ADAM, David Hayman *(Ruaridh)* ← ORDINARY DECENT CRIMINAL ← WALKER ← SID & NANCY, Victoria Smurfit *(Claire)* → ABOUT A BOY, Louise Irwin *(Morag)*, John Comerford *(Paul)* → YOUNG ADAM, Jane Stenson *(Flora)*, Sheila Donald *(Ellie)*, Ford Kiernan *(Eric)*, Martin Bell *(William)*, **the Pastels** *(house band; see below)*, **Jarvis Cocker** *(cameo)*

Storyline: Shades of The Wicker Man as outsider Charlie and his gaunt "Spanish" cousin find themselves the unannounced guests of a closed, unconventional community in deepest Scotland. Having ostensibly travelled north with the aim of torching his wife's lover's cottage, the often blackly comic chain of events at Moor Lodge conspire to change his mind and doubtless his perspective on life as the film lurches towards its gruesome climax. *BG*

Movie rating: *8

Visual: dvd

Off the record: The **PASTELS** formed in Glasgow, Scotland, 1982 by Stephen McRobbie, who chose to change his surname to Pastel. After a few indie outings, the band eventually settled for Alan McGee's 'Creation' records in late 1983 with a relatively stable line-up of Robbie, guitarist Brian Superstar (né Taylor), bassist Martin Hayward and drummer Bernice Simpson (the latter replacing Chris Gordon). An indie band in the truly classic sense of the term, the PASTELS' early mid-80s recordings such as 'Something Going On', 'Million Tears' and 'I'm Alright With You' were endearingly amateurish jingle-jangle/Velvet Underground-esque swathes of melodic noise, the latter the band's final single for 'Creation' before they moved to the small 'Glass' label. Around this time, the PASTELS, along with fellow Scottish (then) "shamblers" Primal Scream and a host of others, were forever immortalised via the dubious honour of having a track included on the NME's semi-legendary C86 compilation. Perhaps inspired by this modest scrape with indie stardom (though the band remain defiantly unambitious), the PASTELS soon adopted a more coherent, harmonious sound as evidenced on their trio of 'Glass' singles and the debut album

'Up For A Bit With . . .' (1987), which included a few choice moments from their earlier days. The group label-hopped yet again for the follow-up, signing with 'Chapter 22' for 1989's 'Sitting Pretty', arguably the band's most accomplished, if not exactly consistent work. With guest appearances by ubiquitous Glasgow scenesters like Eugene Kelly (once of the seminal Vaselines) and Teenage Fanclub's Norman Blake, the album featured some of the sweetest, juiciest moments in the PASTELS' chequered career. The album also saw David Keegan contributing guitar, the ex-Shop Assistants muso being a partner in Stephen's influential '53rd & 3rd' label (which signed Scots acts the Soup Dragons and BMX Bandits, amongst others). At the turn of the decade, the PASTELS line-up was stabilised to a core of Stephen, girlfriend Aggi Wright and Katrina Mitchell, with Keegan making occasional contributions. Signed to 'Paperhouse' records, the first release from the new-look PASTELS was a fine cover of American maverick Daniel Johnston's seminal 'Speeding Motorcycle', the group subsequently teaming up with another respected US underground figure, Jad Fair (HALF JAPANESE), on a collaborative eponymously-monikered album. Working with Galaxie 500 guru, Dean Wareham (on the 1994 EP, 'Olympic World Of Pastelism'), further illustrated the band's cultish kudos while 'Mobile Safari' (1995) was a wryly self-deprecating look at an indie band's lot. 'Illumination' (1997) and the long-awaited soundtrack follow-up, 'The LAST GREAT WILDERNESS' (2002), saw the kings/queens of anorak rock bow out on a high note. Highly influential, if never really groundbreaking, the PASTELS remain the Grandaddies (and mammies!) of the Glasgow indie music scene. *BG & MCS*

—

the PASTELS

Aug 03. (cd) *Geographic*; (<GEOG 018CD>) ☐ ☐
– Wilderness theme / Winter driving / Vincente's theme / Flora's theme / Charlie's theme / Everybody is a star / Flora again / Dark Vincente / Wilderness end theme / I picked a flower (feat. JARVIS COCKER).

S/track review: Released almost simultaneously with the soundtrack for 'YOUNG ADAM' (2003), 'The LAST GREAT WILDERNESS' invites inevitable comparison with David Byrne's dark masterpiece, not least because both films were directed by David Mackenzie, and both feature performances by Glasgwegian indie perennials. In his erudite sleevenote, chief PASTEL, STEPHEN McROBBIE talks about attempting to reflect a "neo-gothic Scottishness". He could easily have been talking about Byrne and friends' brooding orchestrations; and even if his own band's approximation of "homespun lushness" is in the gentler tradition of their C-86 heritage, there's a nebulous, spiritual continuity between the two scores. It's a kinship explicit in the pensive 'Vincente's Theme' and the miasmic electronics and repeating guitar figure of its bleaker variant, 'Dark Vincente'; a Northern soul born of genetic melancholy, suggesting an inherent native talent for conveying Scotland's psychological landscape as conceived in film. And despite McROBBIE's concern that the soundtrack not obstruct the movie's narrative, his music has luminous character enough to function as a great album in its own right. It mightn't be in the same league as Paul Giovanni's 'Wicker Man' (which McROBBIE cites in his notes, and which 'Flora's Theme' tantalisingly hints at), but its folky, jazz-tinged arrangements are sufficiently "neo-gothic" to intimate a Caledonian Tindersticks, while at the same time loose enough to accommodate the band's uber-twee tradition. Sly & The Family Stone's 'Everybody Is A Star' is ostensibly about as far removed in tone from Highland dislocation as it's possible to get, but McROBBIE and Co (with KATRINA MITCHELL coyly handling lead vocal, plus EUGENE KELLY, TOM CROSSLEY, ALLISON MITCHELL, BILL WELLS and LIZ DEW) re-imagine it as wasted pastoral, tucking it snugly into the middle of their score. What doesn't really fit (although it works just dandy in the movie's opening sequence) is 'I Picked A Flower', "a dirty pop song" commissioned by Mackenzie and co-written with Pulp's JARVIS COCKER. Performed live in the film by a Cocker-less PASTELS in drag (unmissable in itself), it's one of the Pulp legend's lower-key collaborations, and he handles it with typically low-key, deadpan humour, combining cautionary smut with a casual Bob Dylan reference. The PASTELS' first great soundtrack. *BG*

Album rating: *7.5

LAST MAN STANDING

1996 (US 101m) New Line Cinema (R)

Film genre: gangster/crime drama

Top guns: s-w: Walter Hill (+ dir) ← GERONIMO: AN AMERICAN LEGEN ← TRESPASS ← JOHNNY HANDSOME ← BLUE CITY ← STREETS OF FIRE ← the LONG RIDERS (story: Ryuzo Kikushima, Akira Kurosawa)

Stars: Bruce Willis *(John Smith)* ← FOUR ROOMS ← PULP FICTION / → BEAVIS AND BUTT-HEAD DO AMERICA → the STORY OF US → OVER THE HEDGE, Christopher Walken *(Hickery)* ← PULP FICTION ← WAYNE'S WORLD 2 ← HOMEBOY / → TOUCH → the COUNTRY BEARS → ROMANCE & CIGARETTES → HAIRSPRAY re-make, Bruce Dern *(Sheriff Ed Galt)* ← PSYCH-OUT ← the TRIP ← the WILD ANGELS / → ALL THE PRETTY HORSES → MASKED AND ANONYMOUS, William Sanderson *(Joe Monday)* ← BLADE RUNNER ← COAL MINER'S DAUGHTER, David Patrick Kelly *(Doyle)* ← HEAVY ← CROOKLYN ← the CROW ← WILD AT HEART ← the ADVENTURES OF FORD FAIRLANE, Karina Lombard *(Felina)* ← the DOORS, Ned Eisenberg *(Fredo Strozzi)*, Alexandra Powers *(Lucy Kolinski)*, Michael Imperioli *(Giorgio Carmonte)* ← GIRL 6 ← I SHOT ANDY WARHOL ← the BASKETBALL DIARIES ← JUNGLE FEVER / → DISAPPEARING ACTS, Leslie Mann *(Wanda)* ← SHE'S THE ONE / → KNOCKED UP, Lin Shaye *(the madame)* ← EVEN COWGIRLS GET THE BLUES ← ROADSIDE PROPHETS ← PUMP UP THE VOLUME ← the LONG RIDERS / → DETROIT ROCK CITY, Michael Greene *(Demayo)* ← DOWN AND OUT IN BEVERLY HILLS ← TO LIVE AND DIE IN L.A. ← NAKED ANGELS, Ted Markland *(Deputy Bob)* ← the HIRED HAND

Storyline: Walter Hill's adaptation of Akira Kurosawa's 'Yojimbo' – itself the inspiration for Sergio Leone's 'A Fistful of Dollars' – has two rival bootlegging gangs vying for control of the illegal alcohol trade in smalltown Texas. Unlike Clint Eastwood, John Smith actually has a name although his moral stock is just as low, playing the feuding gangs off against each other for his own monetary gain. *BG*

Movie rating: *5.5

Visual: video

Off the record: (see below)

—

RY COODER

Oct 96. (cd) *Verve*; *<(533415-2)>* ☐ Sep96 ☐
– Last man standing / Wanda / Jericho blues / Mexican highjack / Just between you and me / Hickery's back / Giorgio leaves town / Felina / We're quits – This is Hickery / Church – Ranger Tom Pickett / Five mile road / Jericho two-step / Smoke bath – Girl upstairs? / Felina drives / Gotta get her back / Lucy's ear / Bathtub / Where's the girl? / Find him / Icebox – Drive to Slim's – Slim's on fire / Hideout / This town is finished / Sunrise / I don't want to die in Texas / Somewhere in the desert (end title) / Sanctuary.

S/track review: Although Elmer Bernstein was originally commissioned for this one, his score was rejected and RY COODER was brought in at the last minute. While some critics cried foul, unwilling or unable to appreciate COODER's innovative approach, the end result was one of the man's most compelling soundtracks to date, cannily combining the darkness and dissonance of a work like 'TRESPASS' and the minimalism of 'PARIS, TEXAS' with his trademark roots and blues grit and consistent ability to conjure up forbidding Western environments. The Dixie-esque 'Jericho Blues' delights in the twang and stomp of COODER's best early 70s work, ditto its close cousin 'Jericho Two-Step'. The weightless, ozone-bleached reverb of the aforementioned 'PARIS, TEXAS' is at least partly reprised in the likes of 'Mexican Highjack', 'Church' and the gorgeous 'Sanctuary', while if you haven't actually seen the film, growling, apocalyptic cues such as 'Five Mile Road' and 'Smoke Bath', will have you furrowing your brow and wondering exactly what kind of action they were written to accompany. 'Felina' is the token concession to world influences, an extended meditation on bamboo flute, zarb and soenap flute, while 'Find Him' is far and away the most challenging piece here, an excerpt of screaming, shrieking, sax-bothering dissonance guaranteed to make the neighbours think you're carving up your cat for dinner. Sure, hearing a grainy blues number and a piece of experimental noise back to back and out of the movie's context is undoubtedly disconcerting, especially when they're combined into the same cue as in 'Hickey's Back'. Yet it's also strangely liberating, something which can't be said about many, if any soundtracks of recent times. Unlike many soundtracks it's also great value for money (if you can find a reasonably priced second-hand copy, that is), with a whopping 26 cues and 60 mins plus of music. *BG*

Album rating: *6.5

LAST OF THE SKI BUMS

1969 (US 86m) Universal Marion Corporation (G)

Film genre: sports documentary

Top guns: dir: Dick Barrymore

Stars: Dick Barrymore *(narrator)*, Ron Funk *(himself)*, Mike Zuettel *(himself)*, Ed Ricks *(himself)*

Storyline: On the road (or the ski slopes of Europe, to be exact!) with three of the world's finest downhill racers as they take on international competitors on the piste. Mine's a pint. *MCS*

Movie rating: *2.5

Visual: none

Off the record: (see below)

—

the SANDALS

1969. (lp) *World Pacific; <WPS 21884>* [ ] [–]
– Winter spell / Ski bum / Children of the sun / Agunus night / Yellow dove / Soul something / Coming down slow / Summer's gone / Return from the casino / Flowers to dance on / Water and stone / Porsche.

S/track review: The second and final surf-rock soundtrack instalment from the genre's original beach-bums, the SANDALS (e.g. WALTER GEORIS, GASTON GEORIS, JOHN BLAKELEY, JOHN GIBSON and DANNY BRAWNER). From the previous 'ENDLESS SUMMER' climes of bikinis and beach parties to 'The LAST OF THE SKI BUMS' and the icy pistes on snowy peaks, the group's studio destinations were conflicting to say the least. In only two years or so, the SANDALS had moved away from their Shadows-y guitar sound, opening track 'Winter Spell' the film's love theme of sorts, being the example. Swapping surf for psychedelia, the 4-plus minute 'Children Of The Sun', the shorter 'Agunus Night' and 'Yellow Dove' (think a non-vocal Love), are in marked contrast to anything the SANDALS set out to do way back in '64. There were spoilers on board though, the lightweight and Booker T.-esque 'Soul Something', as much use as a fart in a spacesuit – unwanted and indeed, unnecessary. With a mind-blowing hand-percussion intro, 'Return From The Casino', sets out a new stall for the quintet: heavy-blues in a style akin to Jethro Tull or Blue Cheer. It was clear by track 10, 'Flowers To Dance On', the group were having difficulties staying in one direction; in fact, the continental-styled 'Water And Stone' might well've been better suited to the likes of José Feliciano. From rock to exotic-lounge via the finale track, 'Porsche', the SANDALS were virtually "21st-century schizoid men" in the making – albeit, in a time capsule all on their own. *MCS*

Album rating: *5.5

– spinoff releases, etc. –

the SANDALS: Wild As The Sea: Complete Sandals 1964-1969
Feb 03. (cd) *Raven; <(RVCD 151)>* [ ] Mar03 [ ]

the LAST REBEL

1971 (US 90m) Spangler Pictures Ltd. (GP)

Film genre: western civil war drama

Top guns: dir: Denys McCoy / s-w: Lorenzo Sabatini (story: Lorenzo as Warren Kiefer)

Stars: Joe Namath *("Captain" Burnside Hollis)* ← NORWOOD, Jack Elam *(Matt)* → PAT GARRETT & BILLY THE KID, Woody Strode *(Duncan)*, Ty Hardin *(the sheriff)*, Victoria George *(Pearl)*, Renato Romano *(Deputy Virgil)*, Marina Coffa *(Camelia)*

Storyline: Two soldiers start a war of their own in Missouri as the real Civil War comes to an end. Hollis and Matt save a black man, Duncan, from a lynching, but trouble starts for the three when they find the best way to make money is to hustle at pool. When Hollis proves to be of Cincinnati Kid standard, Matt gets jealous of his big winnings and demands a share. Hollis and Duncan stick together but find themselves behind the 8-ball when Matt and his pals turn nasty. American football legend "Joe Namath is The Last Rebel" was the tagline. *JZ*

Movie rating: *3

Visual: none

Off the record: **ASHTON, GARDNER & DYKE** (see below)

—

JON LORD & TONY ASHTON (performed by ASHTON, GARDNER & DYKE)

1971. (lp) *Capitol; <SW 827>* [ ] [–]
– The last rebel / Surrender / Up the hill / Hanging / Stage coach ride / You, me and a friend of mine (instrumental) / Mood xylophone *[cd-only]* / Oh Matilda / The pool game / Hollis' getaway / Mother and daughter / The meal / String quartet *[cd-only]* / Ku Klux Klan *[cd-only]* / The pit & the knife fight / You, me and a friend of mine / Death whore / Graves to the graveyard / I'm dying for you. *<(cd-iss. Dec02 on 'Purple'+=; PUR 309)>* – You, me and a friend of mine (alt.) / Larry's theme *[not used in film]* / Pool game *[not used in film]* / The Last Rebel (alt unedited take) / Hollis' getaway (outtake) / Pianola shot / I'm dying for you (outtakes) / Hanging (outtake) / The meal (studio chat) / Up the hill (outtakes).

S/track review: Something of a curiosity this one, combining as it does the writing (and keyboard) talents of Deep Purple's JON LORD and ex-Remo Four singer, TONY ASHTON; the latter had been part of George Harrison's backing band on his 'WONDERWALL' soundtrack in '68. Alongside fellow English musicians, KIM GARDNER (bass; ex-Birds, ex-Creation) and ROY DYKE (drums; ex-Remo Four), a bluesy-rock trio was subsequently formed as ASHTON, GARDNER & DYKE, although only a Top 3 "one-hit-wonder" (Top 40 in America) made any commercial impact. That same year, 1971, also saw the US-only soundtrack release of 'The LAST REBEL', the trio's third set, albeit delivered in limited quantities. Performed with the addition of the Royal Liverpool Symphony Orchestra, ASHTON . . . (+ LORD), recorded the sessions in the autumn of 1970. The opening title track comes across as a funked-up Morricone-meets-Barry-styled dirge, a hybrid indeed of all things western. The unedited 'Surrender' track fuses a Dixie tune with keys that could scrape paint off any wagon, while 'Up The Hill' boasts AG&D's trademark barroom boogie. 'Hanging' strips away the cowboy connection in one fell swoop and, just where the novelty bass-versus-scat number 'Stage Coach Ride' goes, is anyone's guess – maybe jazz-loving Howard Moon of cult TV sitcom, 'The Mighty Boosh', would love it . . . then again. Collectors of rare soundtrack work should note that the original LP is worth a good $100 of your hard earned, while the 29-track CD re-issue (on 'Purple' records) can be obtained for a great deal less. While there's lots of junk on both sets, there's some good nostalgic pieces such as 'Oh Matilda' (referencing the Kennedy shooting!), a song which is another barroom breeze that sounds as if Alan Price just walked into the studio. Ditto 'You, Me And A Friend Of Mine (vocal)' – just add a measure of Joe Cocker. 'Hollis' Getaway' takes jazz-rock (and indeed classical music) to new extremes; the former genre was the ill-advised choice of AG&D when they subsequently released album number four, 'What A Bloody Long Day It's Been', to the bargain bins in '72. Fusing classical "Bolero-styled" symphonics with jazz on 'The Pit & The Knife Fight', plus the hard-rock fuzz on 'Graves To The Graveyard', is indeed a bridge too far. *MCS*

Album rating: *4 / re-CD *4.5

the LAST TEMPTATION OF CHRIST

1988 (US/Can 164m) Universal Pictures (R)

Film genre: religious/biblical drama

Top guns: dir: Martin Scorsese ← the LAST WALTZ / → FEEL LIKE GOING HOME → NO DIRECTION HOME / s-w: Paul Schrader ← LIGHT OF DAY / → TOUCH → AFFLICTION (au: Nikos Kazantzakis)

Stars: Willem Dafoe *(Jesus Christ)* ← TO LIVE AND DIE IN L.A. ← STREETS OF FIRE / → CRY-BABY → WILD AT HEART → AFFLICTION → OVERNIGHT → the LIFE AQUATIC WITH STEVE ZISSOU, Harvey Keitel *(Judas Iscariot)* ← the BORDER ← THAT'S THE WAY OF THE WORLD / → RESERVOIR DOGS → PULP FICTION → FROM DUSK TILL DAWN → FINDING GRACELAND → BE COOL, Barbara Hershey *(Mary Magdalene)* ← SHY PEOPLE / → BEACHES → LANTANA, Harry Dean Stanton *(Saul/Paul)* ← PRETTY IN PINK ← PARIS, TEXAS ← REPO MAN ← ONE FROM THE HEART ← the ROSE ← RENALDO AND CLARA ← RANCHO DELUXE ← PAT GARRETT & BILLY THE KID / → WILD AT HEART → FEAR AND LOATHING IN LAS VEGAS, **David BOWIE** *(Pontius Pilate)*, Verna Bloom *(Mary, mother of Jesus)* ← HONKYTONK MAN ← ANIMAL HOUSE ← the HIRED HAND, Andre Gregory *(John the Baptist)*, **John LURIE** *(James)*, Tomas Arana *(Lazarus / voice in the crowd)* → the BODYGUARD, Barry Miller *(Jerobeam)* ← FAME ← SATURDAY NIGHT FEVER, Gary Basaraba *(Andrew)* ← WHO'S THAT GIRL ← SWEET DREAMS ← ALAMO BAY, Victor Argo *(Peter)* ← the ROSE / → GHOST DOG: THE WAY OF THE SAMURAI → COYOTE UGLY, Alan Rosenberg *(Thomas)* → MIRACLE MILE → the TEMPTATIONS, Leo Burmester *(Nathaniel)* → FLY BY NIGHT / → SHAKE, RATTLE & ROLL: AN AMERICAN LOVE STORY, Peggy Gormley *(Martha; sister of Lazarus)* → FINDING GRACELAND

Storyline: The film looks at the nature of Jesus, debating whether he is a man, the Son of God, or both. Jesus is "tempted" by Satan during his 40 days in the wilderness and as he suffers on the cross. He is tormented by the guilt of working for the Romans, and as he hallucinates while himself on the cross, the life he might have chosen is shown to him, the greatest temptation of all. *JZ*

Movie rating: *7.5

Visual: video + dvd

Off the record: (see below)

—

PETER GABRIEL: Passion

Jun 89. (d-lp/cd) *Geffen; <24206> Real World; (RWLP/RWCD 1)* [60] [29]
– The feeling begins / Gethsemane / Of these, hope / Lazarus raised / Of these, hope – reprise / In doubt / A different drum / Zaar / Troubled / Open / Before night falls / With this love / Sandstorm / Stigmata / Passion / With this love – choir / Wall of breath / The promise of shadows / Disturbed / It is accomplished / Bread and wine. *(<cd re-mast.Jul02; RWCDR 1>)*

S/track review: PETER GABRIEL had come a long way since his early days as frontman provocateur with prog-rock kings, Genesis, and this was not his first venture into movie soundtracks, that went to the Alan Parker-directed 'BIRDY' (1984). Five years on, Martin Scorsese's controversial feature, 'The LAST TEMPTATION OF CHRIST', stirred up a hornet's nest of disapproval, religious zealots and bible-punchers foaming at the proverbial mouth towards any un-PC (that's Politically Catholic) remarks against the divine being – being in fact human. GABRIEL's 'Passion' stirred up something else. Retitled due to legal restraints, the album (recorded February '88 to March '99) was the first to be issued for his newly formed 'Real World' imprint. It'd been three long years since 'Sledgehammer' (and its award-winning video) hit the pop charts, 'Passion' completed a transitional period for the man, who had now firmly begun his righteous path into World Music. The multi-faceted PETER GABRIEL (synths, piano, percussion, bass & kitchen sink!) winds and weaves a tapestry of exotic sound, and talented musicians from places as far away as Turkey, Egypt, Pakistan and North Africa augment his cause to bring a graceful fusion and spirit to his musics; noted session people such as JON HASSELL, BILL COBHAM, NATHAN EAST and DAVID RHODES were also on board. Opener, 'The Feeling Begins', is a powerful dirge of borrowed Armenian melodies (as was the equally effective 'Before Night Falls'), its barrage of picturesque, Middle Eastern sounds setting the tone for the whole album. Dramatic, with experiemental twists and turns, 'Of These, Hope', reprised the thematic starter a few times, while some other pieces (mainly of the 3-minute variety) were reminiscent of Eno's ' . . .Bush Of Ghosts' period with David Byrne. 'A Different Drum' was in a league of its own, rhythmically uplifting, emotional in a joyous, near-tearful way courtesy of GABRIEL and YOUSSOU N'DOUR's dual vocals – not just the best track here, but one of the greatest soundtrack pieces of all time. The following 'Zaar' (a traditional Egyptian rhythm to fend off evil), shifts down a few gears, until some piercing guitars and string bring it back to life. Of the two collaborative tracks, 'Open' (with Indian icon, RAVI SHANKAR) and 'Stigmata' (with soloist NAHMOUD TABRIZI ZADEH), only the latter breaks any rhythmical mould. Indeed, some of the pieces can be quite solemn, sedate and even horizontal, taking several listens to filter through to mind and being, while a few tracks can be a little overbearing, like the 7-minute title track itself. The serene 'With This Love (choir)' seemed prised from Morricone's 'The Mission' (1986), while the brooding landscape of 'Disturbed', could well have fitted nicely on Bowie's 'Low' set, albeit with GABRIEL and Co's added percussion. All'n'all, exciting, relaxing, and worthy of further examination before you release this mortal coil. *MCS*

Album rating: *7

the LAST UNICORN

aka 'Das LETZTE EINHORN'

1982 (US/UK/W.Ger/Japan 84m) Jensen Farley Pictures (G)

Film genre: animated family/children's fantasy

Top guns: dir: Jules Bass, Arthur Rankin Jr. / s-w: Peter S. Beagle (+ au)

Voices: Alan Arkin *(Schmendrick)* ← CALYPSO HEAT WAVE, Jeff Bridges *(Prince Lir)* ← RANCHO DELUXE / → TUCKER: THE MAN AND HIS MUSIC → MASKED AND ANONYMOUS, Mia Farrow *(Unicorn / Amalthea)* ← the COMPLEAT BEATLES / → PRIVATE PARTS, Tammy Grimes *(Molly Grue)*, Robert Klein *(the Butterfly)* ← the OWL AND THE PUSSYCAT ← the LANDLORD / → PRIMARY COLORS, Angela Lansbury *(Mommy Fortuna)* ← BLUE HAWAII, Christopher Lee *(King Haggard)* ← the WICKER MAN ← the MAGIC CHRISTIAN, Keenan Wynn *(Captain Cully)* ← NASHVILLE ← BIKINI BEACH, Rene Auberjonois *(the Skull)* ← WHERE THE BUFFALO ROAM / → WALKER

Storyline: A unicorn and her trusty magician/wizard friend attempt to fend off the evil King Haggard, who wants to rid their fantasy kingdom of well, er.. unicorns – a type of white horse with a spiralled horn. *MCS*

Movie rating: *6

Visual: dvd

Off the record: In the early to late 70s, **AMERICA** – oft unfairly regarded as the poor man's Crosby, Stills & Nash – were responsible for several platinum-selling LPs, including 'America', (1972), 'Homecoming' (1972), 'Hat Trick' (1973), 'Holiday' (1974), 'Hearts' (1975), 'Hideaway' (1976) & 'Harbot' (1977), many of these featuring hits such as the chart-topping, 'A Horse With No Name' and 'Sister Golden Hair'. Around this production era, the trio consisted of Dan Peek, Gerry Beckley and Englishman Dewey Bunnell; the former two had been US Air Force based (in London) before they signed a record deal with 'Warner Bros.', AMERICA had a resurgence of sorts in 1982, when 'You Can Do Magic' reached the US Top 10, however this was without mainstay, Dan Peek. *MCS*

—

AMERICA: Das Letzte Einhorn (composer: JIMMY WEBB)

Nov 82. (lp) *Virgin; (206684)* [–] W.Ger [–]
– The last unicorn / Man's road / In the sea / Now that I'm a woman / That's all that I've got to say / The last unicorn – part 2 / The forest awakens: The unicorn – The forest – The hunters / Red soup / The red bull attacks / The cat / The tree / Haggard's unicorns / Bull-unicorn-woman / Unicorns in the sea / Unicorn and Lear. *(UK cd-iss. 1988 as 'THE LAST UNICORN' on 'Virgin'; 610388-2)*

S/track review: Rather a Unicorn with a name (Amalthea) than a sort of "Horse With No Name", soft-rockers AMERICA performed the score penned by "Wichita Lineman" songsmith, JIMMY WEBB. In fact, the latter even conducted the London Symphony Orchestra, augmented melodically by Messrs DEWEY BUNNELL, GERRY BECKLEY and the returning DAN PEEK (all on guitars). WEBB kept it AOR for the most part, restraining himself from appealing to the movie's main audience, the kids. 'The LAST UNICORN's best bits came via 'The Cat', 'Man's Road', 'Red Bull Attacks', 'In The Sea' and the MIA FARROW/JEFF BRIDGES tearful duet, 'That's All I've Got To Say', all effective and harmonious while relying on AMERICA's acoustic guitars and other assorted string and wind instruments; the solo MIA song 'Now That I'm A Woman' (I don't actually think it's her voice!) is another to represent the perspective of this fantasy tale. *MCS*

Album rating: *6.5

– spinoff releases, etc. –

AMERICA: The Last Unicorn / (instrumental)

1982. (7") *(105785-100)* [–] W.Ger [–]

□ Hubert LAWS segment
(⇒ a HERO AIN'T NOTHIN' BUT A SANDWICH)

□ LEADBELLY
(⇒ Rock Movies/Musicals..)

LEGEND

1985 (US/UK 89m) Universal Pictures (PG)

Film genre: Romantic fantasy adventure

Top guns: dir: Ridley Scott / s-w: William Hjortsberg

Stars: Tom Cruise *(Jack)* ← RISKY BUSINESS / → MAGNOLIA, Mia Sara *(Princess Lili)*, Tim Curry *(The Lord of Darkness)* ← TIMES SQUARE ← ROCK FOLLIES OF '77 ← the ROCKY HORROR PICTURE SHOW / → the WALL: LIVE IN BERLIN → JACKIE'S BACK!, David Bennett *(Honeythorn Gump)*, Alice Playten *(Blix)* ← HEAVY METAL, Billy Barty *(Screwball)* ← HARUM SCARUM ← ROUSTABOUT / → UHF, Cork Hubbert *(Brown Tom)* ← WHERE THE BUFFALO ROAM, Robert Picardo *(Meg Mucklebones)* ← GET CRAZY

Storyline: Young Jack embarks on a magical journey with his beautiful fairy princess (Lili) to see the only surviving unicorns. However, the Lord Of Darkness has other plans, as he tries to steal the girl and rid their world of the last unicorn, and thus all light. *MCS*

Movie rating: *6

Visual: video + dvd

Off the record: Jerry Goldsmith's original orchestral score was dropped to make way for a more contemporary TANGERINE DREAM.

—

TANGERINE DREAM

May 86. (lp/c) *M.C.A.; <(MCA/+C 6165)>* [96] Jan89 [ ]
– Is your love strong enough (BRYAN FERRY) / Opening / Cottage / Unicorn theme / Goblins / Fairies / Loved by the sun (vocal: JON ANDERSON) / Blue room / The dance / Darkness / The kitchen – Unicorn theme. *(re-iss. Jan90 on 'Silva Screen' lp/c/cd; FILM/+C/CD 045)*

S/track review: As previously mentioned, German electronic lords TANGERINE DREAM ('SORCERER', 'THIEF', 'FIRESTARTER', etc., behind them) won the battle to score the movie. Having said that, it's BRYAN FERRY and a recent UK hit single, 'Is Your Love Strong Enough', that cracks open the album. From then on in (bar the song 'Loved By The Sun' with his "highness!" JON ANDERSON of Yes on vocals), the 'DREAM flesh out the rest of a rather claustrophobic set. A series of New Age themes and melodies, uncharacteristic of FROESE and Co, led us into tales of Unicorns, Goblins, Fairies and er, a kitchen. Spooky synths, atmospheric arps and eerie electronics give the album a classical backdrop that pre-dates the work of Howard Shore for example. JOHANNES SCHMOELLING departed shortly after recording, as TD (EDGAR FROESE & CHRISTOPHER FRANKE) progressed even further into soundtrack work. *MCS*

Album rating: *6.5

– spinoff releases, etc. –

BRYAN FERRY: Is Your Love Strong Enough / (non-OST FERRY track)

Mar 86. (7"/12") *(FERRY/+X 4)* [–] [22]

the LEMONHEADS

Formed: Boston, Massachusetts, USA . . . 1983 as the Whelps by EVAN DANDO, JESSE PERETZ and Ben Deily. As metaphorical rags to near riches rock'n'roll stories go, the cautionary tale of the LEMONHEADS is a fairly compelling one. It begins ordinarily enough with just another melodic hardcore band releasing a series of albums for a Boston indie label. Neither was the inevitable power struggle (between DANDO and Deily) exactly unprecedented, yet it did mean that the unfeasibly chiselled features of DANDO were to become the most ubiquitous of the early to mid 90s. With the success of Nirvana opening the alternative floodgates, the LEMONHEADS looked a safe bet to become the next million selling guitar band, especially as DANDO's new position as chief songwriter and his fondness for prime country-rock had led to a mellowing of their sound. Signed to a major label ('Atlantic') and with DAVID RYAN having replaced Deily (and indie sex symbol Juliana Hatfield also temporarily on board), the band went down particularly well in the UK where their 1992 cover of Simon & Garfunkel's theme to 'The GRADUATE', 'Mrs. Robinson', became a Top 20 hit. Its success jumpstarted sales of breakthrough album, 'It's A Shame About Ray' (1992) and, with DANDO's flowing locks and all-American grin bearing down from seemingly every front cover in town, things looked rosy. Yet somehow the celebrity cachet didn't translate into anticipated sales, particularly in the US where the band barely charted. By the time he made a bit part appearance in one of the era's key Generation X movies, 'REALITY BITES' (1994), DANDO's drug abuse had spiralled out of control. His infamous solo appearance at the 1995 Glastonbury Festival was captured for posterity on UK documentary, 'GLASTONBURY: THE MOVIE' (1995), while the same year saw DANDO perform his one and only starring screen role – as Liv Tyler's slacker boyfriend – in slow moving James Mangold oddity, 'HEAVY' (1995). While the LEMONHEADS had been lurching towards their messy demise, original member JESSE PERETZ had been quietly forging a career in music video, counting his old band as clients alongside the likes of the Foo Fighters. He made his directorial feature debut in 1997 with 'FIRST LOVE, LAST RITES', an atmospheric adaptation of an Ian McEwan short story written in collaboration with fellow ex-Lemonhead, DAVID RYAN, who himself had joined another Boston indie band, Fuzzy. PERETZ followed up with 'The Chateau' (2001), a largely improvised comedy transplanting two Americn brothers to the South of France. *BG*

- **filmography** {acting} [dir + s-w] –

Reality Bites *(1994 {b EVAN} OST by V/A =>)* / **Heavy** *(1995 {* EVAN} OST by THURSTON MOORE & V/A =>)* / **Glastonbury: The Movie** *(1995 {p LEMONHEADS} =>)* / **First Love, Last Rites** *(1997 [s-w + dir: JESSE] [s-w + story: DAVID] OST by SHUDDER TO THINK =>)* / the Chateau *(2002 [story + dir: JESSE] score by NATHAN LARSON)*

LET'S DO IT AGAIN

1975 (US 112m) Warner Bros. Pictures (PG)

Film genre: urban comedy

Top guns: dir: Sidney Poitier → a PIECE OF THE ACTION → FAST FORWARD / s-w: Richard Wesley → FAST FORWARD (story: Timothy March → a PIECE OF THE ACTION → FAST FORWARD)

Stars: Sidney Poitier *(Clyde Williams)* ← TO SIR, WITH LOVE ← BLACKBOARD JUNGLE / → a PIECE OF THE ACTION, Bill Cosby *(Billy Foster)* ← MAN AND BOY / → a PIECE OF THE ACTION, Calvin Lockhart *(Biggie Smalls)* ← MELINDA ← COTTON COMES TO HARLEM / → WILD AT HEART, John Amos *(Kansas City Mack)* ← SWEET SWEETBACK'S BAADASSSSS SONG ← VANISHING POINT / → DISAPPEARING ACTS, Jimmie Walker *(Bootney Farnsworth)* ← SING SING THANKSGIVING / → MONSTER MASH: THE MOVIE, Denise Nicholas *(Beth Foster)* ← the SOUL OF NIGGER CHARLEY ← BLACULA / → a PIECE OF THE ACTION, Ossie Davis *(Elder Johnson)* → COUNTDOWN AT KUSINI → SCHOOL DAZE → JUNGLE FEVER → BUBBA HO-TEP, Mel Stewart *(Ellison)* ← STEELYARD BLUES, Julius Harris *(Bubbletop Woodson)* ← FRIDAY FOSTER ← BLACK CAESAR ← HELL UP IN HARLEM ← TROUBLE MAN ← SUPERFLY ← SHAFT'S BIG SCORE!, Lee Chamberlin *(Dee Dee Williams)* → BEAT STREET, Val Avery *(Lt. Bottomley)* ← BLACK CAESAR ← KING CREOLE, Jayne Kennedy *(girl at factory)* ← LADY SINGS THE BLUES / → BIG TIME, George Foreman *(factory worker!)*

Storyline: Following the harebrained schemes of Clyde Williams and Billy Foster (reactivating the celebrated Sidney Poitier/Bill Cosby partnership), this sequel to 'Uptown Saturday Night' centres around the hapless pair's attempts to turn a feeble boxer into a brawny heavyweight via hypnosis, thereby earning some cash for their local community association. Biggie Smalls is the local mobster persuaded into a risky bet, the very same who inspired the late Notorious B.I.G.'s alter ego. *BG*

Movie rating: *5

Visual: video + dvd

Off the record: (see below)

—

the STAPLE SINGERS (composer: CURTIS MAYFIELD)

Oct 75. (lp) *Curtom; <CU 5005>* [20] [–]
– Let's do it again / Funky love / A whole lot of love / New Orleans / I want to thank you / Big Mac / After sex / Chase. *<cd-iss. May02 on 'Spy'; SPY 45003-2> (UK cd-iss. Sep05 on 'Snapper'; SNAP 245CD)*

S/track review: Depicting Bill Cosby clutching a fat wad of greenbacks, Sidney Poitier twirling a pistol around his little finger and Jimmie Walker sitting not too pretty in the middle, the sleeve of 'LET'S DO IT AGAIN' is blaxploitation caricature with a mischievous glint in its eye. Ironically, it's pretty much unrepresentative of the music within, a showcase for the slickly combined might of two Chicago institutions: CURTIS MAYFIELD and the STAPLE SINGERS. But if there's more immaculately conceived Windy City soul than gospel grit, that doesn't stop MAVIS STAPLES from getting her freak-on in unprecedented style. MAYFIELD's self-confessed inspiration for this score was carnal rather than comedic, and it shows. Not even during their purple period at 'Stax' had the STAPLES clan put their vocal signature to such earthy material. Even the orchestrated soul of the title track leaves little to the imagination, a Marvin Gaye-patented invocation of sex as spiritual medicine, with MAVIS at her sultriest and MAYFIELD at his lushest. Released as a single, it mounted both the R&B and the pop charts, revitalising the STAPLES' stagnating career and maintained MAYFIELD's impressive soundtrack record. 'Funky Love' is even racier, although MAVIS' come-hither utterances are sanctified rather than seedy, while the explicitly titled 'After Sex' is actually a mellow confluence of ethereal harp, strings and wordless harmonies. The closest the record comes to real porno-funk is 'Big Mac', trippy disco with a side-order of dodgy panting. The baroque chase-funk of, erm, 'Chase' is a further, final reminder that this is a soundtrack rather than a straight album, yet at its best – on the righteous gospel-soul of 'I Want To Thank You' – 'LET'S DO IT AGAIN' is as uplifting as the STAPLES' more famous studio outings, and less one-dimensional. *BG*

Album rating: *7

– spinoff hits, etc. –

the STAPLE SINGERS: Let's Do It Again / After Sex
Oct 75. (7") *<0109>* [1] [–]

the STAPLE SINGERS: Let's Do It Again / New Orleans
Nov 75. (7") *(K 16657)* [–] [ ]

the STAPLE SINGERS: New Orleans / A Whole Lot Of Love
Feb 76. (7") *<0113>* [70] [–]

☐ LIALEH
(⇒ Rock Musicals/Movies)

☐ LIBRA segment
(⇒ SHOCK)

the LIFE AQUATIC WITH STEVE ZISSOU

2004 (US 118m) Touchstone Pictures / American Empirical Pictures

Film genre: sea adventure comedy

Top guns: s-w: Wes Anderson (+ dir), Noah Baumbach

Stars: Bill Murray *(Steve Zissou)* ← COFFEE AND CIGARETTES ← LOST IN TRANSLATION ← LITTLE SHOP OF HORRORS ← CADDYSHACK ← WHERE THE BUFFALO ROAM ← the RUTLES, Owen Wilson *(Ned Plimpton)*, Cate Blanchett *(Jane Winslett-Richardson)* ← COFFEE AND CIGARETTES / → I'M NOT THERE, Anjelica Huston *(Eleanor Zissou)*, Willem Dafoe *(Klaus Daimler)* ← OVERNIGHT ← AFFLICTION ← WILD AT HEART ← CRY-BABY ← the LAST TEMPTATION OF CHRIST ← TO LIVE AND DIE IN L.A. ← STREETS OF FIRE, Jeff Goldblum *(Alistair Hennessey)*, Michael Gambon *(Oseary Drakoulias)*, Noah Taylor *(Vladimir Wolodarsky)*, Bud Cort *(Bill Ubell)* ← COYOTE UGLY ← the MILLION DOLLAR HOTEL ← SOUTH OF HEAVEN, WEST OF HELL ← ELECTRIC DREAMS ← HAROLD AND MAUDE ← GAS-S-S-S ← BREWSTER McCLOUD ← the STRAWBERRY STATEMENT, **Seu Jorge** *(Pele dos Santos)*

Storyline: Steve Zissou is an eccentric, embattled oceanographer, outflanked by his swank rivals and ageing like a corked wine. The glory days may be behind him but his team of trusty assistants – lovingly kitted out in matching red beanies and tracksuits – stick by him on an expedition to revenge one of his crew mauled by a shark. Zissou's erratic leadership come under serious stress as he attempts to locate his fishy enemy in the animated depths while accommodating the entanglements of both a female journalist and a new crewman claiming to be his son. *BG*

Movie rating: *7.5

Visual: dvd

Off the record: **Seu Jorge** (see below)

—

Various Artists (score: MARK MOTHERSBAUGH *)

Dec 04. (cd) *Hollywood; <2061 62494-2> (5046 72751-2)* ☐ Feb05 ☐
– Shark attack theme (SVEN LIBAEK) / Loquasto International Film Festival (*) / Life on Mars? (DAVID BOWIE) / Starman (SEU JORGE) / Let me tell you about my boat (*) / Rebel rebel (SEU JORGE) / Zissou Society Blue Star Cadets – Ned's theme take 1 (*) / Gut feeling (DEVO) / Open sea theme (SVEN LIBAEK) / Rock'n'roll suicide (SEU JORGE) / Here's to you (JOAN BAEZ) / We call them pirates out here (*) / Search and destroy (IGGY AND THE STOOGES) / La nina de puerta oscura (PACO DE LUCIA) / Life on Mars? (SEU JORGE) / Ping Island – Lightning strike rescue op (*) / Five years (SEU JORGE) / 30 Century man (SCOTT WALKER) / The way I feel inside (the ZOMBIES) / Queen bitch (DAVID BOWIE).

S/track review: After his turn in 'City Of God', Favela survivor SEU JORGE became a media-style icon with an unlikely Hollywood sideline. As an unassuming bit-player in Bill Murray's motley crew of oceanic stooges, his sporadic outbursts of saudade-soaked David Bowie were an inspired touch in a movie content, by and large, to amble along on its charm. The songs were so popular that the original soundtrack was forgotten and superseded by an album's worth of SEU, topped up by additional Bowie covers not heard in the film. Even better, they had at least some rock critics taking umbrage: "polite acoustic samba treatments are no match for the ballsy rock originals", concluded a Mojo reviewer. Which is surely to miss the point; JORGE wasn't trying to match Bowie, he was initiating the man's sacred cows into the mysteries and subtleties of Brazilian music. The songs are still recognisably Bowie, but they're not rock, and to dismiss them as polite is to misunderstand the mission. To even be able to shoehorn English into Brazilian-Portuguese takes no little skill, skill that JORGE renders illusory, if not without typically playful artistic license. The freak-power sci-fi and hot tramp throb of the originals is transmuted into light and languor, illuminating what Bowie left unsaid. To material originally sneered in stylized cockney, the Rio native brings a timbre as rich and sage as mahogany, peeling back what even the Thin White Duke himself hailed as a "new level of beauty". And unlike harsher tongues, you don't need to grasp the wordplay or even understand a single word to indulge in the phonetic pleasure. This is the – too often misinformed – key to Brazilian music: you don't need to speak Portuguese to appreciate it. Despite creating some of the most sublime music on the planet, whole pantheons of Brazilian artists failed to find the mass Anglophone audience they deserved. The success of 'The LIFE AQUATIC . . .' proves that not only is it possible but it's actually happening, and that SEU JORGE might finally conquer where Jorge Ben, Gilberto Gil and even Tom Jobim were confined to relative cult status. *BG*

Album rating: *8

LIFESPAN

1974 (US/UK/Belg/Neth 85m) Whitepal Productions (18)

Film genre: sci-fi/fantasy thriller

Top guns: s-w: (+ dir) Alexander Whitelaw, Judith Rascoe, Alva Ruben

Stars: Hiram Keller *(Dr. Ben Land)* → COUNTRYMAN, Tina Aumont *(Anna)*, Klaus Kinski *(Nicholas Ulrich)* ← AGUIRRE, WRATH OF GOD / → MADAME CLAUDE → NOSFERATU, THE VAMPIRE → CODENAME: WILDGEESE → COBRA VERDE, Fons Rademakers *(Prof. van Arp)*, Eric Schneider *(Dr. Linden)*, Adrian Brine *(Dr. Winston)*

Storyline: A scientist (Dr. Land) living in Amsterdam may have the meaning to eternal life after he explores what happened to his fellow doctor who has just hung himself. When Land hooks up with old flame, Anna, his inner demons – including a sinister industrialist, Ulrich – experiment with the serum in old folks home. *MCS*

Movie rating: *5

Visual: video + dvd

Off the record: (see below)

—

TERRY RILEY: Les Yeux Fermés & Lifespan

Apr 07. (cd) *Elision Fields; <EF 101>* ☐ [–]
– (Les YEUX FERMES tracks) // G song / M – Music, I – Inside, C – Curved, E – Entrances / Slow melody in Bhairavi / In the summer / The oldtimer / Delay.

S/track review: TERRY RILEY's second outing as a film composer (his first being 'Les YEUX FERMÉS'), 'LIFESPAN' finally gets its belated release in 2007, doubled-up by US imprint 'Elision Fields' with the aforementioned 1972 set. One thinks the score to 'LIFESPAN' might well've been released back in '74, although minimalist composer, RILEY, more than likely owns the only copy or rare acetate – who knows? Structured more conventionally from its soundtrack predecessor, the set opens with the 3-minute 'G Song', a chord-scaling, church-organ-like dirge (complete with added sax) that Rick Wakeman would've been proud of. The percussion-intro'd follow-on piece, 'M I C E', is straight out of the John Cale canon, one even expects to hear Nico's VU/monotone vox droning out at any time (RILEY previously worked with Cale on a collaborative LP, 'Church Of Anthrax', in 1971). Ditto for 'Slow Melody In Bhairavi' – but without the percussive persuasion. Lengthier track, 'In The Summer' (clocking in at 6:40), chants meditatively and Pink Floyd-ianly over RILEY's unrelenting and grinding organ, while the uncharacteristically comic piece of the set, 'The Oldtimer', is both nauseating and novelty. 12:39 minutes long and track six finale, 'Delay', brings to mind Tangerine Dream, Cale (again!) and Italian Prog-rock soundtrack generals, Goblin, er . . . before their time! *MCS*

Album rating: *5.5

☐ LISZTOMANIA
(⇒ Rock Movies/Musicals..)

LITTLE BIG MAN

1970 (US 135m) National General Pictures (PG)

Film genre: revisionist western

Top guns: dir: Arthur Penn ← ALICE'S RESTAURANT / s-w: Calder Willingham (au: Thomas Berger)

Stars: Dustin Hoffman *(Jack Crabb)* ← MIDNIGHT COWBOY ← the GRADUATE / → WHO IS HARRY KELLERMAN AND WHY IS HE SAYING THOSE TERRIBLE THINGS ABOUT ME? → the POINT! → DICK TRACY → WAG THE DOG, Faye Dunaway *(Mrs. Louise Pendrake)* → the WICKED LADY → ALBINO ALLIGATOR, Martin Balsam *(Mr. Merriweather)*, Chief Dan George *(Old Lodge Skins)*, Richard Mulligan *(Gen. George A. Custer)*, Jeff Corey *(Wild Bill Hickok)*, Amy Eccles *(Sunshine)*, Kelly Jean Peters *(Olga Crabb)*, Ruben Moreno *(Shadow That Comes In The Night)* → COFFY, Bert Conway *(bartender)* ← ROCK, ROCK, ROCK! / → RANCHO DELUXE, Jack Mullaney *(card player)* ← SPINOUT ← TICKLE ME, M. Emmet Walsh *(shotgun guard)* ← ALICE'S RESTAURANT ← MIDNIGHT COWBOY / → BOUND FOR GLORY → BLADE RUNNER → CATCH ME IF YOU CAN → ALBINO ALLIGATOR

Storyline: 121 year old Jack Crabb, last survivor of Little Big Horn, recounts his life story to a historian. Kidnapped and adopted by the Cheyenne as an infant, Crabb was renamed Little Big Man and brought up in Indian fashion. Escaping back to "civilization", he marries and meets Buffalo Bill among others. By chance he ends up near Little Big Horn just as the notorious General Custer makes his last stand, but whose side will he join? *JZ*

Movie rating: *8

Visual: video + dvd

Off the record: **JOHN HAMMOND** (see below)

—

Dustin Hoffman (underscore: JOHN HAMMOND)

Jan 71. (lp) *Columbia; <S 30545>* ☐ ☐
– Jack Crabb and how he got to be named Little Big Man by the Human Beings. / The Indian education of Jack Crabb and the War against the whites. / The religious education of Jack Crabb at the hands of Rev. ans Mrs. Pendrake. The profane education of Jack Crabb at the hands of Mrs. Pendrake and Mr. Kane. / The loss of Olga, his Sweish bride, to the Indians and the subsequent search for her which leads him back among the Human Beings. / Jack Crabb rejoins the whites and participates in a War against the Indians. Jack Crabb gets discouraged. / Old Lodge Skins explains the difference between white men and Human Beings. Custer attacks and kills the ponies; Old Lodge Skins becomes invisible. / Jack Crabb goes crazy and joins Custer as a mule skinner and reverse barometer. Medicine Tail Coulee and Little Bighorn. / Old LOdge Skins prepares to die. But it rains and they go back to the teepee.

S/track review: This can only be described as a curio. An album of dialogue, mainly stemming from Dustin Hoffman (as Jack Crabb), a now established actor with starring roles in mainstream movies such as 'MIDNIGHT COWBOY' (1969) and 'The GRADUATE' (1968). Having seen the lengthy epic a long time ago, the soundtrack LP helped one to reminisce over certain scenes, especially the sexy reverend's wife Mrs Pendrake at er . . . bathtime; the witty Chief Dan George in deadpan sarcasm is also worthy of a mention. You might find yourself asking why the soundtrack's included here. Well, white bluesman JOHN HAMMOND did the underscore, and I mean underscore, bushwacked behind all the character dialogue and really unrepresented. HAMMOND (b. John Paul Hammond, 13 November '42, New York) was responsible for several folk/blues LPs on 'Vanguard' in the 60s before he signed a deal with Columbia records. I suppose his music at the time was going through a renaissance much like the movie's western revisionist themes. No proper songs then, just orchestral Dixie dirges, some guitar-pluckin' and er . . . did I mention the dialogue? *MCS*

Album rating: *1 music (*4 dialogue)

LITTLE FAUSS AND BIG HALSY

1970 (US 99m) Paramount Pictures (R)

Film genre: romanticised biker/sports drama

Top guns: dir: Sidney J. Furie ← WONDERFUL LIFE ← the YOUNG ONES / → LADY SINGS THE BLUES / s-w: Charles Eastman

Stars: Michael J. Pollard *(Little Fauss)* ← the WILD ANGELS / → DICK TRACY, Robert Redford *(Halsy Knox)*, Lauren Hutton *(Rita Nebraska)* → 54, Noah Beery Jr. *(Seally Fauss)*, Lucille Benson *(Mom Fauss)*, Ray Ballard *(the photographer)*, Linda Gaye Scott *(Moneth)* ← PSYCH-OUT, Ben Archibek *(Rick Nifty)*, Erin O'Reilly *(Sylvene McFall)*

Storyline: A tale of two speedway racers, one a geekish homeboy, the other a bare chested bit of rough with a taste for the drink and an eye for the ladies. The pair form and unlikely friendship but Little Fauss' luck goes from bad to worse as he breaks his leg in a crash and has to look on as Halsy takes over his license and even the girl Fauss figures he has a chance with. Karma begins to catch up with Halsy, however, as his woman gets pregnant and his diminutive buddy recovers from his injuries. *BG*

Movie rating: *6

Visual: none

Off the record: (see below)

—

JOHNNY CASH, CARL PERKINS, the TENNESSEE THREE

Nov 70. (lp) *Columbia; <S 30385> C.B.S.; (70087)* ☐ Sep71 ☐
– Rollin' free (JOHNNY CASH) / Ballad of Little Fauss and Big Halsy (CARL PERKINS) / Ballad of Little Fauss and Big Halsy (instrumental) (CARL PERKINS) / 7:06 union (instrumental) (CARL PERKINS) / Little man (JOHNNY CASH) / Little man (instrumental) (JOHNNY CASH) / Wanted man (BOB DYLAN) / Rollin' free (instrumental) (JOHNNY CASH) / True love is greater than friendship (CARL PERKINS) / Movin' (CARL PERKINS) / Little man (instrumental) (JOHNNY CASH) / True love is greater than friendship (instrumental) (CARL PERKINS) / Movin' (instrumental) (CARL PERKINS). *<(cd-iss. Sep99 on 'Bear Family'+=; BCD 16130)>* – JOHNNY CASH: I Walk The Line – soundtrack / (+ extra versions).

S/track review: With CARL PERKINS sharing both the cover and the songwriting credits, 'LITTLE FAUSS AND BIG HALSY' is the yang to 'I WALK THE LINE's yin. The rhythms are rambling, the lyrics unapologetic, projecting their time-honoured love-em-and-leave-em tropes onto Robert Redford and his speccy sidekick. JOHNNY CASH's basso profundo has a ball with the cavernous vowels of 'Rollin' Free', holding court in that high-horse drawl usually reserved for his juicier narratives. It's a voice which invests the odd-couple banality of PERKINS' title theme with the drama of a Greek myth, rumbling out its familiar melody like an irascible, backwoods Zeus. And just as he'd recorded the definitive 'Sunday Morning Coming Down' a few months earlier, CASH set Bob Dylan's 'Wanted Man' – the track which opened the live 'JOHNNY CASH AT SAN QUENTIN' (1969) – in stone as a proto-Outlaw anthem, a man-in-black mascot as enduring as 'A Boy Named Sue' or 'Ring Of Fire'. PERKINS supplied the instrumental '706 Union', a tribute to Sun Studios (and another CASH live staple), the stone country ballad, 'True Love Is Greater Than Friendship' (his only vocal), and generally continued to flourish under the aegis of his all-conquering partner. *BG*

Album rating: *7

– spinoff releases, etc. –

JOHNNY CASH: The Ballad Of Little Fauss And Big Halsy
May 72. (7"ep) *(EP 9155)* [–] [ ]

a LITTLE TRIP TO HEAVEN

2005 (Ice/US 86m) Palomar Pictures / Katapult Films (R)

Film genre: crime thriller/drama

Top guns: s-w: (+ dir) Baltasar Kormakur ← 101 REYKJAVIK, Edward Martin Weinman

Stars: Forest Whitaker *(Abe Holt)* ← GHOST DOG: THE WAY OF THE SAMURAI ← JOHNNY HANDSOME ← GOOD MORNING, VIETNAM, Julia Stiles *(Isold)* ← SAVE THE LAST DANCE, Jeremy Renner *(Fred)* → the ASSASSINATION OF JESSE JAMES . . ., Philip Jackson *(William)* ← GIVE MY REGARDS TO BROAD STREET, Peter Coyote *(Frank)* ← the MAN INSIDE ← BAJA OKLAHOMA ← HEARTBREAKERS ← TIMERIDER: THE ADVENTURE OF LYLE SWANN / → COMMUNE, Anne Reid *(Martha)*, Alfred Harmsworth *(Thor)*

Storyline: 'Quality Life' insurance investigator Abe Holt is all too aware of the fraudulent activity going on in his company. After overhearing his boss explain to a widow why she won't be paid out, he is reassigned to investigate the death of an ex-con in a car crash. His investigation leads him to a desolate village where he meets with Isold, the victim's sister – who just happens to be the $1 million beneficiary. As Holt finds out more about the truth of the accident, his suspicions about Isold and her husband Fred lead him to a fateful decision. *JZ*

Movie rating: *6

Visual: dvd

Off the record: (see below)

MUGISON: Little Trip

Jun 06. (cd) *Ipecac; (IPC 071)* [–] Icelan [–]
– Petur Gretarsson / Go blind / Little trip to Heaven / Watchdog / Mugicone / Piano for tombstones / Clip 10 / Alone in a hotel / Rush / Petur por Ben / Watchcat / My Nobel prize / Alone in the office / Mugicone part 2 / Stiff / Sammi & Kjartan.

S/track review: MUGISON's second excursion (or indeed "Little Trip") into the world of film scores, his first being 'NICELAND' a few years earlier. The multi-talented MUGISON (sometimes known as Mugimonkey) is probably just bubbling under Bjork and Sigur Ros as Iceland's best musical export. A short 30-second track, named after his drummer/percussionist 'Petur Gretarsson' opens the album, a unique feat repeated when he billed his guitarist on a longer trip, 'Petur Por Ben'; 'LITTLE TRIP' also shuts down proceedings with 'Sammi & Kjartan', named after respective trombonist Samuel Jon Samuelsson and trumpeter Kjartan Hakonarson. Quality jazz-styled instrumentals. Easily the best and his accessible "rock" song on the set, 'Go Blind', however, suffers in comparison with the likes of Kravitz or Plant, the English-phrasing RUNA ESTRADOTTIR is high-pitched to the max, but not exactly iconic; an extended bonus track (17) reprises the song and gets in a flamenco-styled guitar to boot. Going way back to the "title" track 3, MUGISON gives his dreamy, Hawaiian-guitar rendition of Tom Waits' 'Little Trip To Heaven'; "One From The Heart" indeed. The remainder of the cuts are solemn and sombre, typical examples being 'Alone In A Hotel' & 'Alone In The Office'; squeezed somewhere in between is the dustbowl, desert-like 'Rush'. 'Watchdog' and its companion piece, 'Watchcat', are pastel-funk instrumentals, while the Morricone-inspired (I think not!), 'Mugicone' takes the listener on its own "little trip to Heaven". Ditto – but with a heavier feel – for 'Mugicone Part 2'. Two further compositions must take pride of place here, the drum'n'bass'n'clink of 'Clip 10' and the choppy 'My Nobel Prize', the latter (with piano by Evitan) pushes out the barriers between Cage-like minimalist minimalism and neo-classical rock. An unusual one for Mike Patton (ex-Faith No More) and his 'Ipecac' imprint. *MCS*

Album rating: *6.5

LOCAL HERO

1983 (UK 112m) Enigma / Goldcrest / Warner Bros. Pictures (PG)

Film genre: rural comedy/drama

Top guns: s-w + dir: Bill Forsyth

Stars: Peter Riegert *(MacIntyre)* ← ANIMAL HOUSE, Burt Lancaster *(Felix Happer)*, Denis Lawson *(Gordon Urquhart)* ← ROCK FOLLIES OF '77, Fulton Mackay *(Ben)*, Peter Capaldi *(Danny Oldsen)* → NICELAND, Jenny Seagrove *(Marina)*, Norman Chancer *(Moritz)*, Alex Norton *(Watt)*, Rikki Fulton *(Geddes)*, John Jackson *(Cal)* → SID & NANCY → BAJA OKLAHOMA → DEAD SOLID PERFECT → GINGER ALE AFTERNOON

Storyline: Oil billionaire Felix Happer decides his next drilling project will be off Scotland's east coast. Standing in the way is the village of Ferness, so Happer sends negotiators Mac and Danny to offer the locals megabucks if they'll sell up. The prospect of riches is none too displeasing for the poor villagers, who quickly agree – all save one old man who lives in a shack on the beach. Ben Knox has decided he's not budging, so Happer himself must visit to pour oil on troubled waters. *JZ*

Movie rating: *8.5

Visual: video + dvd

Off the record: Denis Lawson is the uncle of Ewan McGregor.

MARK KNOPFLER

Apr 83. (lp/c) *Vertigo; (VERL/+C 4) Warners; <1/-4-23827>* [14] [ ]
– The rocks and the water / Wild theme / Freeway flyer / Boomtown / The way it always starts / The rocks and the thunder / The ceilidh and the northern lights / The mist covered mountains / The ceilidh: Louis' favourite Billy's tune / Whistle theme / Smooching / The rocks and the thunder / Going home (theme from 'Local Hero'). *(cd-iss. Jul84; 811 038-2) <US cd-iss. 1988; 2-23827>*

S/track review: Originally released in 1983, just before Dire Straits went global with 'Brothers In Arms' (1985), 'LOCAL HERO' was effectively MARK KNOPFLER's solo debut as well as his debut soundtrack. And while it's light years removed in both style and ambience from 'Brothers..' it does occasionally call to mind the band's 1982 album, 'Love Over Gold', a record characterised by the addition of Alan Clark's keyboards. While CLARK is also present here – along with 'Straits bassist JOHN ILLSLEY – his hammond, synth and piano playing serves as a context rather than a focal point, ghosting through fragments of Scottish folk tunes as surf breaks on a highland beach. KNOPFLER's guitar-picking is as evocative as ever, even more so for its restraint and reserve, and strikingly so on 'Wild Theme', where the bluff northerner begins his longtime love affair with Celtic roots themes. It's beguiling stuff, and if MICHAEL BRECKER's tasteful sax occasionally threatens to steer the whole thing into jazz-lite territory, a recurring sense of elemental warmth and strapping, luminscent melody keeps it all satisfyingly grounded. A soundtrack classic. *BG*

Album rating: *8.5

– spinoff releases, etc. –

MARK KNOPFLER: Going Home (Theme From 'Local Hero') / Smooching
Feb 83. (7"/12") *(DSTR 4/+12) <29725>* 56

MARK KNOPFLER: Wild Theme / Going Home (Theme From 'Local Hero')
Jul 83. (7") *(DSTR 5)* –

MARK KNOPFLER: Going Home (Theme Music Of The Crusader Challenge) / Wild Theme
Oct 86. (7") *(DSTR 14)* –
(12"+=) *(DSTR 14-12)* – Smooching.
(cd-s+=) *(DSCD 14)* – Comfort (from 'Comfort And Joy').

MARK KNOPFLER: Themes From Local Hero: Going Home / Wild Theme
Oct 93. (7"/c-s) *(VER/+MC 81)* –
(cd-s+=) *(VERCD 81)* – Comfort (from 'Comfort And Joy').

□ Nils LOFGREN segment (⇒ EVERYBREATH)

□ Frank LONDON segment (⇒ the SHVITZ)

the LONG RIDERS

1980 (US 100m) United Artists (R)

Film genre: historical/western outlaw drama

Top guns: dir: Walter Hill → STREETS OF FIRE → CROSSROADS → JOHNNY HANDSOME → TRESPASS → GERONIMO: AN AMERICAN LEGEND → LAST MAN STANDING / s-w: Bill Bryden, Steven Phillip Smith, James Keach, Stacy Keach

Stars: David Carradine *(Cole Younger)* ← BOUND FOR GLORY / → ROADSIDE PROPHETS → AMERICAN REEL → KILL BILL: VOL.1 → KILL BILL: VOL.2, Keith Carradine *(Jim Younger)* ← NASHVILLE, Robert Carradine *(Bob Younger)* ← JOYRIDE / → WAVELENGTH → the LIZZIE McGUIRE MOVIE, James Keach *(Jesse James)* ← FM / → WALK THE LINE, Stacy Keach *(Frank James)*, Dennis Quaid *(Ed Miller)* → GREAT BALLS OF FIRE!, Randy Quaid *(Clell Miller)* ← BOUND FOR GLORY / → DEAD SOLID PERFECT → ELVIS, Kevin Brophy *(John Younger)*, Harry Carey Jr. *(George Arthur)* → CROSSROADS, Christopher Guest *(Charlie Ford)* ← DEATH WISH / → THIS IS SPINAL TAP → LITTLE SHOP OF HORRORS → the PRINCESS BRIDE → a MIGHTY WIND, Pamela Reed *(Belle Starr)* → WHY DO FOOLS FALL IN LOVE, Lin Shaye *(Kate)* → PUMP UP THE VOLUME → ROADSIDE PROPHETS → EVEN COWGIRLS GET THE BLUES → LAST MAN STANDING → DETROIT ROCK CITY, James Remar *(Sam Starr)* ← the WARRIORS, Chris Mulkey *(Vernon Biggs)* → TIMERIDER: THE ADVENTURE OF LYLE SWANN → HEARTBREAK HOTEL → GAS, FOOD LODGING → SUGAR TOWN → MYSTERIOUS SKIN, **Ry COODER** *(guitarist)*

Storyline: Walter Hill's labour of love recreates the romantic misdeeds of the notorious James-Younger outlaw gang in the Old West of the 1870s, centering on the trials of the James brothers as they narrowly survive a botched bank robbery and go on the run. *BG*

Movie rating: *7

Visual: video + dvd

Off the record: (see below)

RY COODER

Jun 80. (lp/c) *Reprise; <HS 3448> (K/K4 56826)*
– The long riders / I'm a good old rebel / Seneca square dance / Archie's funeral (hold to God's unchanging hand) / I always knew that you were the one / Rally 'round the flag / Wildwood boys / Better things to think about / Jesse James / Cole Younger polka / Escape from Northfield / Leaving Missouri / Jesse James. *<(cd-iss. Jan96 on 'WEA'; 7599 23448-2)>*

S/track review: It's difficult to avoid the impression that in the early 80s, RY COODER was putting more heart and soul into his film composition than he was his regular studio albums. As it turned out, 'The LONG RIDERS' played as his best record since the celebrated 'Chicken Skin Music' four years earlier. Then again, with a classic outlaw re-make as a canvas, this was always going to be one to savour. As old-timey as COODER gets, some of this stuff feels like an audio transcription of some sepia-tinted photograph, particularly Civil War-era traditional adaptations like 'I'm A Good Old Rebel' and 'Seneca Square Dance' (at a push, you could almost imagine hearing the latter at a Scottish wedding). 'Rally Round The Flag' has the rambling, rootsy feel of COODER's early 70s material (not least because he'd already adapted the song for his 1972 set, 'Boomer's Story'), complete with the ragbag of unusual arrangements (sax, timbales, dulcimer, etc.) so beloved of American popular music's foremost curator. The score isn't without a sense of irony or humour, another COODER trademark, and 'Wildwood Boys', in particular has some great, gnarled outlaw lyrics which Waylon Jennings would have traded his beard for back in his heyday. Fans content to regard this as a proxy COODER studio set are spared any excess of film dialogue, and the brilliant version of trad outlaw ballad 'Jesse James', is far more consistently listenable than the dialogue excerpt of the same name. Beginning as an instrumental narrative spun out on banjo, mandolin, dulcimer and fiddle, a shrill tin whistle and boxy Irish percussion duly leads it into the kind of all-encompassing Americana jam only someone of COODER's musical mindset could conceive, a kind of Dixieland denouement brimful with parping trombone and jubilant cornet. All in, a classy RY COODER set, and one which conveyed both the end of a pivotal period in American history and the beginning of a new one in COODER's own career. *BG*

Album rating: *6.5

LOOKING FOR LEONARD

2001 (Can 87m) Boneyard Films / Frustrated Film Inc.

Film genre: crime caper/comedy drama

Top guns: s-w + dir: Matt Bissonnette, Steven Clark

Stars: Kim Huffman *(Jo)* ← LIPSTICK ON YOUR COLLAR, Joel Bissonnette *(Luka)* ← FIGHT CLUB, Benjamin Ratner *(Ted)*, Justin Pierce *(Chevy)* ← KIDS, Molly Parker *(Monica)* ← HARD CORE LOGO / → WHO LOVES THE SUN, Darcy Belsher *(Johnny)*, **Leonard COHEN** *(archive footage)*

Storyline: Eagle-eyed computer programmer Luka spots shoplifter Jo helping herself in a Montreal store. Confronting her, the two find they have a close affinity but their first kiss is interrupted by Jo's brother Johnny. In the ensuing fight Jo accidentally kills her brother and Luka does a runner, knowing he'll be suspected. Will Jo pursue Luka and continue her affair or will she go back to reading her beloved 'Beautiful Losers' and leave her Czech mate to face the music? *JZ*

Movie rating: *6

Visual: dvd

Off the record: **Leonard COHEN** (see own entry)

PORTASTATIC

May 01. (cd) *Merge; <MRG 490CD>* –
– Looking For Leonard theme / Stumbling music / Luka's theme / "Do you speak English?" / Stealing romance / Johnny's dead / Jo's plan / Luka's theme – shaker mix / Sweethearts organ mix / Funeral music / Only good people wonder if they're bad / The chase / A dead end / Sweethearts of the world.

S/track review: No doubt many indie-rock fans worldwide will know Superchunk's MAC McCAUGHAN is the man behind Tropicalia-inspired PORTASTATIC (example their post-millennium Brazilian artists' covers EP, 'De Mel, De Melão' for more). The 'Looking For Leonard Theme' kickstarts the album in colourful dirge-like aplomb and hints on nothing of what's to come. All instrumental, 'LOOKING FOR LEONARD', is both moody and cinematic, like a good film score should be in fact. Nostalgic and tipping a hat to South American exotic lounge giants such as Gilberto Gil, Os Mutantes and Caetano Veloso, McCAUGHAN (and guest violinist MARGARET WHITE) sets about putting his North Carolina slant on each take. Track 3, 'Luka's Theme' (repeated Shaker mix-like for track 8), is arguably the best thing here, its dreamy lo-fi, near-horizontal guitar-pickings throbbing amidst some backdrop organ. Trailed by some witty dialogue via "Do You Speak English?", the album oozes class on a grand scale; even the morbid but quirky 'Johnny's Dead' shines a little light. Ditto 'Funeral Music', which eventually draws the listener in after a minute or so, courtesy of some fuzz guitar by the Mac himself. The haunting 'Only Good People Wonder If They're Bad' (love the title) and 'A Dead End' sandwich McCAUGHAN's pièce de résistance, 'The Chase', a track in which the wistful guitarist also bangs the drums and percussion. The finale, 'Sweethearts Of The World', rounds off a remarkable score, taking us somewhere between a heaven and a helluva-nice-place. *MCS*

Album rating: *7

LOOT

aka LOOT – GIVE ME MONEY, HONEY

1970 (UK 101m) British Lion Film Corporation (15)

Film genre: crime caper/comedy

Top guns: dir: Silvio Narizzano / s-w: Ray Galton, Alan Simpson (play: Joe Orton)

Stars: Richard Attenborough *(Truscott)* ← the MAGIC CHRISTIAN, Lee Remick *(Fay)*, Hywel Bennett *(Dennis)* ← the FAMILY WAY / → PERCY, Milo O'Shea *(McLeavy)*, Roy Holder *(Hal)*, Dick Emery *(Bateman)* ← YELLOW SUBMARINE ← JUST FOR FUN, Jean Marlow *(the late Mrs. McLeavy)*

Storyline: Dennis and Hal are two lads with an eye for the main chance, which they get after they rob a bank: "We knock off anything – bodies, banks and birds!". Suspected by the police, they have to find a hiding place for the loot until the heat is off. They choose a coffin meant for Hal's recently deceased mum, and then hide said coffin in his dad's hotel. Meanwhile, the slightly insane Inspector Truscott investigates this grave crime and money-grabbing nurse Fay is also on the scene. Who will end up with the buried treasure? *JZ*

Movie rating: *5.5

Visual: video + dvd

Off the record: **STEVE ELLIS** (see below)

STEVE ELLIS (*) (music: KEITH MANSFIELD & Richard Willing Denton)

Dec 70. (lp) *C.B.S.; (70073)* □ [-]
– More, more, more (*) / Loot's the root (*) / Hey, hey, hey (*) / Where it's at (*) / Stealth in the night / Oh Fay! / We nearly were lovers / Police barricade / Mothers waltz (* & chorus) / The undertaker song (*) / Eyeball serenade / Loot's the root (*) / And more, more, more (*). *(<cd-iss. Jul01 on 'R.P.M.'; RPM 228>)*

S/track review: Two relatively big names of the late 60s crop up on the 'LOOT' soundtrack, STEVE ELLIS (former Love Affair singer turned solo artist) and songwriter/composer/pianist KEITH MANSFIELD (Love Affair producer); both were responsible for the group's five Top 20 teen-pop hits: 'Everlasting Love' (a No.1), 'Rainbow Valley', 'A Day Without Love', 'One Road' and 'Bringing On Back The Good Times'. 'LOOT' was a different kettle of fish – so to speak. Together with regular band, HOOKFOOT (who included CALEB QUAYE in the ranks), plus CLEM CATTINI, BIG JIM SULLIVAN and HERBIE FLOWERS in session, ELLIS and MANSFIELD worked on the score in the latter's house and also a studio in Hertfordshire. The LP opens its account with the brassy, laid-back, 'More, More, More' (think Georgie Fame or Alan Price fronting Blood, Sweat & Tears), one of many tracks that featured backing singers MADELINE BELL, DORIS TROY and SUE & SUNNY. Follow-on song, 'Loot's The Root', was – unbeknown to Steve! – lifted as a single; however, its overwhelming orchestra and horns somewhat overshadow the power of the singer's voice. 'Hey, Hey, Hey' and 'Where It's At' – poor lyrically, by anyone's standards – virtually mark time before ELLIS takes a rest to let MANSFIELD's funky orchestra get into full swing via 'Stealth In The Night'; set the remote to skip the embarrassingly quaint 'Oh Fay!', 'We Nearly Were Lovers' and movie dialogue skits, 'Police Barricade' & 'Eyeball Serenade'. The voice of STEVE ELLIS (and Chorus) returns to the scene of crime via 'Mothers Waltz', a mock cock-er-nee number that tries unsuccessfully to flaunt the swaggering satirical side of the film. 'The Undertaker Song' – with its hip and funky Hammond drowning out everything else – is down to MANSFIELD again, and not as it attributes on the LP sleeve, to ELLIS. And just why one needed to hear two more bookend versions of 'Loot's . . .' and 'More . . .' is anyone's guess – maybe it was to fill out the 31-minute playing time? ELLIS would subsequently form his own sur-named outfit, while he also fronted rock supergroup, Widowmaker, alongside ex-Mott The Hoople man, Ariel Bender. *MCS*

Album rating: *4

– spinoff releases, etc. –

STEVE ELLIS: Loot's The Root / More, More, More

Nov 70. (7") *(CBS 4992)* □ [-]

LOST IN TRANSLATION

2003 (US/Japan 102m) Focus Features / Momentum (R)

Film genre: psychological comedy/drama

Top guns: s-w + dir: Sofia Coppola ← the VIRGIN SUICIDES

Stars: Bill Murray *(Bob Harris)* ← LITTLE SHOP OF HORRORS ← CADDYSHACK ← WHERE THE BUFFALO ROAM ← the RUTLES / → COFFEE AND CIGARETTES → the LIFE AQUATIC WITH STEVE ZISSOU, Scarlett Johansson *(Charlotte)* ← MANNY & LO, Giovanni Ribisi *(John)* ← MASKED AND ANONYMOUS ← the VIRGIN SUICIDES ← FIRST LOVE, LAST RITES ← SUBURBI@ ← THAT THING YOU DO! / → COLD MOUNTAIN, Anna Faris *(Kelly)*, Fumihiro Hayashi *(Charlie)*, Akiko Takeshita *(Ms. Kawasaki)*, Catherine Lambert *(jazz singer)*, Yutaka Tadokoro *(commercial director)* ← TOKYO POP

Storyline: Bob and Charlotte find themselves thrown together in the cultural melting pot of Tokyo. Bob is a washed-up actor earning one last pay day doing a whiskey commercial; Charlotte is a young philosophy graduate tagging along with her photographer husband who's been sent out East. What will happen when an unlikely friendship forms and the pair find they've more in common than they first thought? *JZ*

Movie rating: *8

Visual: dvd

Off the record: (see below)

Various Artists (score: KEVIN SHIELDS * / BRIAN REITZELL & ROGER J. MANNING JR. **)

Sep 03. (cd) *Emperor Norton; <(ENR 7068-2)>* ☐ Feb04 ☐
– Intro – Tokyo / City girl (*) / Fantino (SEBASTIEN TELLIER) / Tommib (SQUAREPUSHER) / Girls (DEATH IN VEGAS) / Goodbye (*) / Too young (PHOENIX) / Kaze wo atsumete (HAPPY END) / On the subway (**) / Ikebana (*) / Sometimes (MY BLOODY VALENTINE) * / Alone in Kyoto (AIR) / Shibuya (**) / Are you awake? (*) / Just like honey (the JESUS & MARY CHAIN). *(hidden track +=)* – More than this (BILL MURRAY).

S/track review: Whatever happened to "likely lad" KEVIN SHIELDS, once pioneer of the late 80s shoegazing phase via his My Bloody Valentine (and part-timer w/ Experimental Audio Research)? Here's your answer, SHIELDS' filmatic debut and comeback of sorts, 'LOST IN TRANSLATION'. However, only 4 solo outings and a MY BLOODY VALENTINE nugget ('Sometimes' from 1991's 'Loveless' set) feature on the OST. 'City Girl' has that dreamy, picturesque appeal, dirgy guitar and dreamy vox, not too far removed from his MBV days. 'Goodbye' takes a leaf from the Brian Eno book of cinematic rock, while the short and sweet 'Ikebana' instrumental is just that. Ditto SHIELDS' foray into electronic knob-twiddling via 'Are You Awake?'. Two other score contributions ('On The Subway' & 'Shibuya') actually stem from the collaborative partnership of drummer/album's producer BRIAN REITZELL & ROGER J. MANNING JR (not the Jellyfish musician), although only the latter, with its haunting backdrop, is more than incidental. Of the various others, most all are recommended. 'Fantino' (a track from 2001) by multi-instrumentalist Frenchman SEBASTIEN TELLIER, fits like a glove into the concept of the movie, it's nearly King Crimson without the Frippertronic guitar effects. The funereal-paced 'Tommib' from SQUAREPUSHER (aka Tom Jenkinson), exudes some spiritual need, but it's all over too quickly. DEATH IN VEGAS ('Girls') is another sedate soundscape and not too far removed from the MBV/SHIELDS of old; the voice incidentally is by Susan Dillane. The English-singing Gallic outfit, PHOENIX and 'Too Young', give the impression – and a good one at that – of the great Todd Rundgren. Of course, AIR, are the greatest export from that country, the pair (straight from 'The VIRGIN SUICIDES' OST) get all Japanese with humming instrumental, 'Alone In Kyoto' – never have they sounded more 10cc. Japan does get its two-pennorth in via, 'Kaze Wo Atsumete' by HAPPY END, an early 70s duo (Takashi Matsumoto & Haroumi Hosono) influenced by James Taylor or even Gilbert O'Sullivan; Hosono would later form YMO (Yellow Magic Orchestra). The JESUS & MARY CHAIN closed the show with their timeless classic 'Just Like Honey', although if you persist a bit longer on the CD you'll hear bonus track 'More Than This' (the Roxy/Ferry track) karaoked by the film's leading man BILL MURRAY. *MCS*

Album rating: *7

☐ LOVE UNLIMITED ORCHESTRA segment
(⇒ TOGETHER BROTHERS)

Lyle LOVETT

Born: 1 Nov'57, Klein, Texas, USA. LYLE LOVETT was famous for two things really, his country-roots music and being the enviable hubby of Julia Roberts, although this was only for two years between 1993 and '95; his lanky looks and tall haircut would be no match for the beautiful actress – at least in the OTT tabloids. A revered singer-songwriter and guitarist, he quickly established himself after the release of his eponymous debut album for 'Curb' records in '86. His growth in stature among the elite of his genre has helped him sell a heap of records; several of them have sold by the million including 'Pontiac' (1988), 'Lyle Lovett & His Large Band' (1989), 'Joshua Judges Ruth' (1992), 'I Love Everybody' (1994), 'The Road To Ensenada' (1996), 'Step Inside This House' (1998) and 'Live In Texas' (1999). An actor in his own right, he's starred in movies such as 'Short Cuts' (1993), 'Bastard Out Of Carolina' (1996), 'The Opposite Of Sex' (1998), 'The New Guy' (2002) and '3 Days Of Rain' (2003), while his only full score/OST came courtesy of 'DR. T & THE WOMEN' (2000) – the Robert Altman connection continuing. *MCS*

- **filmography** {acting} (composer) –

Bill: On His Own *(1983 {p})* / the Player *(1992 {a})* / Short Cuts *(1993 {*})* / Prêt-à-Porter *(1994 {a})* / Bastard Out Of Carolina *(1996 {*})* / Breast Men *(1997 {a})* / **Fear And Loathing In Las Vegas** *(1998 {a} OST by V/A =>)* / the Opposite Of Sex *(1998 {*})* / Cookie's Fortune *(1999 {a})* / **Dr. T. & The Women** *(2000 OST =>)* / the New Guy *(2002 {*})* / 3 Days Of Rain *(2003 {*})* / **Be Here To Love Me: A Film About Townes Van Zandt** *(2004 {c} OST by VAN ZANDT =>)*, **Walk Hard: The Dewey Cox Story** *(2007 {c} =>)*

the LOVIN' SPOONFUL (w/ JOHN SEBASTIAN)

Formed: Greenwich Village, New York, USA . . . 1965 by JOHN SEBASTIAN and Zal Yanovsky. A light, frothy starter before the Summer Of Love's heavy psychedelic main course, the LOVIN' SPOONFUL were the court jesters of homegrown folk-pop, reeling off prepossessing hit after hit (the most famous being 'Daydream' and 'Summer In The City') through 1966 and into early '67. They were also the band of choice for Woody Allen's directorial debut, 'WHAT'S UP, TIGER LILY?' (1966), combining their trademark finger pickin' with uncharacteristically experimental elements on the soundtrack and also appearing in the film itself. Prior to Yanovsky's departure amid allegations that he'd informed on his drugs supplier, the band also recorded the soundtrack to Francis Ford Coppola's directorial debut, 'YOU'RE A BIG BOY NOW' (1967). The record was a more mature and enduring work than its predecessor, while its ingratiating theme tune was subsequently issued as the B-side to the band's penultimate, bittersweet hit, 'Six O'Clock'. While they belatedly regrouped for a one-off appearance in Paul Simon's 'ONE-TRICK PONY' (1980), the band remain one of the few 60s outfits not to have been tempted by the commercial carrot of reformation. Post 'Spoonful, the ever upbeat SEBASTIAN boosted his nascent solo career with an impromptu, crowd pleasing appearance at Woodstock, making it onto the accompanying soundtrack and Oscar winning documentary. He also featured prominently on the belatedly released 'CELEBRATION AT BIG SUR' (1971), a document of the 1969 Big Sur festival featuring an impressive cast of folk-rockers including JONI MITCHELL, NEIL YOUNG, JOAN BAEZ and CROSBY, STILLS & NASH, the very group SEBASTIAN had declined to join a few years earlier. If a one-off role in teen comedy, 'The Pom Pom Girls' (1976), didn't exactly constitute an acting career, the singer-songwriter made a return to screen composition with the appropriately titled 'Welcome Back', the hugely popular (US No.1) theme to mid-70s American show, 'Welcome Back Kotter'. Following further scores for early 80s TV movies, SEBASTIAN was credited on Canadian animation feature, 'The Care Bears Movie' (1985), and also contributed to follow-up, 'Care Bears: Adventure' (1987). *BG*

- **filmography** (composers) {acting} –

What's Up, Tiger Lily? *(1966 OST =>)* / **You're A Big Boy Now** *(1967 OST =>)* / **Woodstock** *(1970 {p JOHN} OST by V/A =>)* / **Celebration At Big Sur**

(1971 {p JOHN} =>) / the Pom Pom Girls *(1976 score by SEBASTIAN)* / **One-Trick Pony** *(1980 {c} OST by PAUL SIMON =>)* / the Act *(1982 TV score by SEBASTIAN)* / the Jerk, Too *(1984 TV score by SEBASTIAN)* / the Care Bears Movie *(1985 score by SEBASTIAN / OST by V/A)*

LUCIFER RISING

1972 (US/UK/W.Ger 29m short) Puck Films / BFF

Film genre: experimental/surrealist movie

Top guns: dir: Kenneth Anger

Stars: Kenneth Anger *(Lucifer)*, Donald Cammel *(Osiris)*, **Marianne Faithfull** *(Lilith)* ← STONES IN THE PARK ← DON'T LOOK BACK ← ANNA / → the WALL: LIVE IN BERLIN → ROCK AND ROLL CIRCUS, Myriam Gibril *(performer)*, **Bobby Beausoleil** *(footage)*

Storyline: Kenneth Anger's ritualised portrayal of Lucifer as the "LightGod", and his rising as the dawn of a new age, charted through heavily psychotropic, imagistic juxtaposition and Ancient Egyptian mythology. Primordial ooze and exploding magma herald the emergence of Isis and Osiris, nature and death, establishing the duality at the heart of Anger's mindset. Ritualistic, and richly symbolic in the mould of Sun Ra (flying saucers – over the Colossi of Memnon – present and correct), the blizzard of editing flashes between Luxor, Karnak, Gizeh and Stonehenge, in – apparently serendipitous – harmony with Beausoleil's kozmick blues. The video/dvd includes another Kenneth Anger short, 'Invocation Of My Demon Brother' (1969), a 12-minute episode featuring the Rolling Stones; Mick Jagger's brother Chris was set to play Lucifer, however arguments between CJ and Anger resulted in the latter taking over the devilish role. *BG & MCS*

Movie rating: *6

Visual: video + dvd (see above)

Off the record: **BOBBY BEAUSOLEIL** (see below)

BOBBY BEAUSOLEIL & the FREEDOM ORCHESTRA

Sep 04. (d-cd) *Arcanum Ent.; (AECD 0001)* [-] [ ]
– (parts I-VI) // LUCIFER RISING sessions:- Punjab's barber (excerpt by the ORKUSTRA) / Flash Gordon (excerpt by the ORKUSTRA) / Lucifer Rising recording session – 1967 (MAGICK POWERHOUSE OF OZ) / Lucifer Rising sessions – 1977-1978.

S/track review: An album with more baggage than an Airbus A380, BOBBY BEAUSOLEIL's masterpiece might never have surfaced at all; previous to the 2005 re-issue, it existed largely as a soundtrack holy grail, available only as a bootleg gleaned from a tiny vinyl pressing. Defying the kind of odds that would make Lucifer himself blanch ("obstacles that defy description", as he puts it in his notes), BEAUSOLEIL crafted a work of singular mystique, an ageless psychedelic mantra unsullied by commercial or contemporary considerations. Never mind 'Live At San Quentin', 'LUCIFER RISING' was actually written and recorded – on instruments built from scratch, by hand – while serving a life sentence at Tracy State Prison. Although BEAUSOLEIL had merely "hovered on the periphery of the [Charles] Manson circle" (according to Michael Moynihan's exhaustive sleevenotes), the sentence he received for another crime – "circumstantially unrelated" to the infamous Tate-LaBianca murders – reflected the infamy of such an association. The full story is recounted in the notes, which also document BEAUSOLEIL's initial meeting with Anger, their spiritual connection and subsequent collaboration. It's the kind of dark, saturnine genesis that inevitably colours every otherwordly note of this six-part headtrip. Think Popol Vuh if Klaus Kinski and Werner Herzog had actually acted out their mutual threats, or Pink Floyd if the late Syd Barrett had stayed on board. While Jimmy Page actually recorded 28 minutes of music for Anger's film (commissioned after Anger had decamped to London, and later rejected by the director), it's difficult to imagine it was as charged and enigmatic as this. Over crepuscular wells of electric keyboards and Fender-Rhodes, BEAUSOLEIL plucks out premonitory figures on his homecrafted, double-necked guitar/bass; a mariachi-esque trumpet sounds long and desolate, sublime and far from home in the prog maelstrom; the ironically named FREEDOM ORCHESTRA traverse parallel musical universes within universes, cross-filtering pockets of airless beauty, baroque debris and Hawkwind-esque turbulence. The metaphor of a trip is as cliched as prog-rock itself, but this soundtrack invokes as infinite a scenario as SUN RA's astral excursions, suggesting that BEAUSOLEIL's imagination expanded inversely to his material restriction. The man's earlier San Francisco experiments with his ORKUSTRA (alongside David LaFlamme, later of major label psych band It's A Beautiful Day) and MAGICK POWERHOUSE OF OZ emsembles (as well as FREEDOM ORCHESTRA rehearsals) are featured on the bonus disc, an evolution as fascinating as it is superbly packaged. *BG*

Album rating: *8.5

John LURIE

Born: 14 Dec'52, Worcester, Massachusetts, USA. Pretty much the definition of a cult composer/actor, JOHN LURIE graduated from New York's no wave scene to form an enduring partnership with Jim Jarmusch and even went on to be lavished with a Grammy nomination although he's always been more hipster anti-hero than Hollywood, appearing in some of the most influential independent films of the 80s. The seeds of the man's soundtrack work were sown in the late 70s when he formed neo-jazz (LURIE himself describes it as "fake jazz") outfit the Lounge Lizards, a band who improvised with diverse musical genres rather than within conventional jazz structures, and numbered Brazilian savant Arto Lindsay among its members. Ironically, the band was actually formed after LURIE figured he could raise money for a film he was working on by recording the music for it first. Besides acting and composing credits in DIY no-wave film 'The OFFENDERS' (1980) and an appearance as a homicidal saxophonist in Amos Poe's 'SUBWAY RIDERS' (1981), LURIE co-composed the soundtrack to Kathryn Bigelow's directorial debut, 'The Loveless'. Yet it was his work on the debut of Jim Jarmusch, 'Permanent Vacation' (1982), which would prove the more prescient of the two, initiating a strangely beautiful partnership and securing his screen future. While a kerb-crawling jazz score for Bette Gordon's 'Variety' followed in 1983, a part in Wim Wenders' 'PARIS, TEXAS' (1983), and, more notably, a starring role in Jarmusch's seminal 'Stranger Than Paradise' (1984), witnessed the birth of an unlikely neo-Beat icon. His rarefied string quartet score also announced the arrival of a serious compositional talent, a fact doubtless noted by 'Island' in their mid-80s signing of LURIE's latest Lounge Lizards incarnation. Punctuated by appearances in avant-garde docu 'Two Moon July' (1985) and, more bizarrely, MADONNA vehicle, 'Desperately Seeking Susan' (1985), LURIE followed up with another memorable character performance in Jarmusch's 'DOWN BY LAW', scoring the movie with an octet featuring both Lindsay and his Lounge Lizards replacement Marc Ribot. Co-star Roberto Benigni was to subsequently cast LURIE in his self-directed Satanic comedy, 'Il Piccolo Diavolo' (1988), a movie scored by John's brother Evan (another Lounge Lizards mainstay). The soundtrack to another Jarmusch masterpiece, 'MYSTERY TRAIN' (1989) came sandwiched between a more pious role as the Apostle James in Martin Scorsese's 'The LAST TEMPTATION OF CHRIST' (1988) and a bit part in David Lynch classic, 'WILD AT HEART' (1990). Unpredictable as ever, LURIE kicked off the 90s with his own TV series, 'Fishing With John', inviting uber-cool pals like Jarmusch, TOM WAITS, and Dennis Hopper on unlikely and reliably surreal global fishing trips, and enlisting some of them for the ethnically inclined soundtrack. While he shared the composing credits on obscure sci-fi flick, 'Genius' (1993) and scored Slovakian black comedy, 'Na Krasnom Modrom Dunaji' (1995), his next soundtrack to be blessed with a CD release was also the one which saw him nominated for an Oscar. Interspersed with songs from acts as diverse as Morphine and BOOKER T & THE MG's, his brief lounge-hound score for showbiz comedy 'Get Shorty' (1995) was the funky glue holding together one of the best soundtracks of that year. Save for minor parts in Wayne Wang's wryly observed Brooklyn snapshot, 'Smoke' (1995) and Abel Ferrara's 'New Rose Hotel' (1998), LURIE invested most of his creative energies in soundtrack work over the latter half of the 90s, composing the score for Wang's 'Smoke' follow-up, 'Blue In The Face' (1995), the debut feature from Alicia Silverstone's production company, 'Excess Baggage' (1997) and Lisa Krueger's coming-of-age drama, 'MANNY & LO' (1996). The latter was subsequently issued as a two-on-one CD with 'African Swim', an unreleased score which LURIE had retitled. Featuring the likes of Medeski, Martin & Wood and various Lounge Lizards alumni, this fiercely eclectic package is widely regarded as representing a career highlight although the man himself cites his band's belated studio set, 'Queen Of All Ears' (1998). While his score for that year's black comedy, 'Clay Pigeons' (1998) didn't make it onto the alt-country soundtrack, LURIE was indeed the mysterious creative force behind the the Legendary Marvin Pontiac, an Afro-Jewish alias pedalling the globetrotting mutant blues of 'Greatest Hits'. Pontiac's legendary "1952" track, 'I'm A Doggy', can in fact be heard in embryonic form on the belatedly released soundtrack to 'DOWNTOWN 81' (2000), an NY underground extravaganza starring a teenaged Jean-Michel Basquiat. On a more serious note, LURIE scored Steve Buscemi's gritty directorial follow-up, 'Animal Factory' (2000), although the soundtrack remains unreleased, as does the music for Paul Auster's 'Lulu On The Bridge' (1998), in which he shared composing credits with Graeme Revell. *BG*

- **filmography** {acting} (composer) –

the Offenders *(1980 {a} OST w/ V/A =>)* / **Subway Riders** *(1981 {*} OST w/ V/A =>)* / Permanent Vacation *(1982 {a} w/ Jim Jarmusch)* / the Loveless *(1982 w/ ROBERT GORDON)* / Variety *(1983 OST; see future edition)* / **Paris, Texas** *(1983 {a} OST by RY COODER =>)* / Stranger Than Paradise *(1984 {*} OST; see future edition)* / Desperately Seeking Susan *(1985 {a} OST by THOMAS NEWMAN)* / Two Moon July *(1985 docu {p})* / **Down By Law** *(1986 {*} OST =>)* / Il Piccolo Diavolo *(1988 {*})* / Police Story: Monster Manor *(1988)* / **the Last Temptation Of Christ** *(1988 {a} OST by PETER GABRIEL =>)* / **Mystery Train** *(1989 OST =>)* / **Wild At Heart** *(1990 {a})* / John Lurie And The Lounge Lizards Live In Berlin *(1992 {*p})* / Genius *(1993 w/ others)* / Na Krasnom Modrom Dunaji *(1995 w/ LOUNGE LIZARDS)* / Smoke *(1995 by Rachel Portman & Dmitry Shostakovich)* / Blue In The Face *(1995 OST w/ V/A =>)* / Get Shorty *(1995 OST w/ V/A =>)* / **Manny & Lo** *(1996 OST =>)* / Excess Baggage *(1997 OST =>)* / New Rose Hotel *(1998 {a} no OST by SCHOOLY D)* / Clay Pigeons *(1998 OST by V/A)* / Lulu On The Bridge *(1998 w/ GRAEME REVELL)* / Animal Factory *(2000)* / **Downtown 81** *(2000 on OST w/ V/A =>)* / Sleepwalk *(2001 {*})* / Face Addict *(2005)*

MACBETH

aka the TRAGEDY OF MACBETH

1971 (UK/US 140m) Columbia Pictures (AA/R)

Film genre: historical period-costume drama

Top guns: s-w: (+ dir) Roman Polanski, Kenneth Tynan (play: William Shakespeare)

Stars: Jon Finch *(Macbeth)* → BREAKING GLASS, Francesca Annis *(Lady Macbeth)* → DUNE → UNDER THE CHERRY MOON, Martin Shaw *(Banquo)*, Nicholas Selby *(Duncan)*, John Stride *(Ross)*, Stephan Chase *(Malcolm)*, Paul Shelley *(Donalbain)*, Terence Bayler *(Macduff)* → the RUTLES, Vic Abbott *(Cawdor)*, Keith Chegwin *(Fleance)*

Storyline: Polanski's Macbeth is a singularly tormented creation, deliberating over the pros and cons of evil under a claustrophobically grim colour scheme of rain-lashed browns, blacks and greys. Egged on by his wife, he unleashes the familiar spiral of violence and insomnia by murdering King Duncan and his friend Banquo. The Kingdom of Fife gets more mentions than at any time in screen history. *BG*

Movie rating: *7.5

Visual: video + dvd

Off the record: Keith Chegwin – he of subsequent Saturday morning kids' TV fame – makes his screen debut and the witches go naked. Hope this didn't influence the poor boy. *BG & MCS*

the THIRD EAR BAND: Music From Macbeth

Mar 72. (lp) *Harvest; (SHSP 4019)* ☐ ☐
– Overture / The beach / Lady Macbeth / Inverness: Macbeth's return – The preparation – Fanfare – Duncan's arrival / The banquet / Dagger & death / At the well – The prince's escape – Coronation – Come sealing tonight / Court dance / Fleance / Grooms' dance / Bear baiting / Ambush – Banquo's ghost / Going to bed – Blind man's bluff – Requiescant / Sere and yellow leaf / The cauldron / Prophesies / Wicca way. *(re-iss. Jan89 & Apr97 on 'Beat Goes On'; BGOLP 61) (cd-iss. Jul90; BGOCD 61) (cd re-iss. 1999 on 'Blueprint'; BP 312)*

S/track review: A decade before Michael Nyman's Renaissance with attitude, GLENN SWEENEY and his THIRD EAR BAND pretty much had the monopoly on medieval chamber improv. As oppressive as Nyman's approach was liberating, theirs was an aesthetic which chimed eerily with Polanski's infernal Shakespearean vision, a congruity all the more potent for the director's economy in applying it. More accessible and less frenetic than the baying, sawing string textures of the German TV soundtrack,

'ABÉLARD & HÉLOÏSE' (1970), the Anthony Asquith Award-nominated 'MACBETH' plugged in their sound with the addition of Elton John/Bowie arranger PAUL BUCKMASTER, electric guitar and some vintage VCS3 synth. Instead of the extended acoustic ragas TEB were famous – or rather obscure – for, this soundtrack democratically apportioned their compositions into an unheard-of sixteen tracks, several of them realising the potential for electrified discord; at its most atonal and uncompromising, some of the material ('Dagger And Death', 'Wicca Way', 'Ambush / Banquo's Ghost') could've slotted into the recent Morricone comp, 'Crime And Dissonance' (2005). But for the most part, any electric components are secondary to alternately droning/leaping curlicues from oboe and recorder, and the synth only really comes into its own when it traces the regal timbre of the woodwinds halfway through the 'Inverness' suite. It's surprisingly easy to imagine 'Inverness' or 'Court Dance' in a BBC costume drama, and for all the record's gothic menace, the fact that none other than an uncredited choirboy (played by Keith Chegwin in the film) sings the very 'Wicker Man'-esque 'Fleance' makes it difficult to be spooked for too long. *BG*

Album rating: *6

the MACK

1973 (US 110m) Cinerama Releasing Corporation (R)

Film genre: crime drama

Top guns: dir: Michael Campus → the EDUCATION OF SONNY CARSON / s-w: Robert J. Poole

Stars: Max Julien *(Goldie)* ← UP TIGHT! ← the SAVAGE SEVEN ← PSYCH-OUT, Richard Pryor *(Slim)* ← WATTSTAX ← LADY SINGS THE BLUES ← YOU'VE GOT TO WALK IT LIKE YOU TALK IT . . . ← WILD IN THE STREETS / → ADIOS AMIGO → CAR WASH → the WIZ → BUSTIN' LOOSE, Roger E. Mosley *(Olinga)* → LEADBELLY → BIG TIME, Don Gordon *(Hank)* → the EDUCATION OF SONNY CARSON, Carol Speed *(Lulu)* ← BUMMER! / → SAVAGE! → the DYNAMITE BROTHERS → DISCO GODFATHER, Dick Richard *(Pretty Tony)* ← UP TIGHT! / → SLAUGHTER'S BIG RIP-OFF → FIVE ON THE BLACK HAND SIDE, William Watson *(Jed)*, George Murdock *(Fatman)* → WILLIE DYNAMITE, Juanita Moore *(mother)* ← UP TIGHT! ← the GIRL CAN'T HELP IT, Paul Harris *(blind man)* ← ACROSS 110th STREET / → TRUCK TURNER, Christopher Brooks *(Jesus Christ)* → SPACE IS THE PLACE, Stu Gilliam *(announcer)* → BROTHERS

Storyline: Goldie – aka The Mack – is the Bay Area pimp fighting off the cops, drug pushers and his own peers in this lowlife parable which sacrificed flash for high intensity grit. *BG*

Movie rating: *5.5

Visual: video + dvd

Off the record: (see below)

—

WILLIE HUTCH

Apr 73. (lp) *Motown; <M 766L> (STMA 8003)* [ ] Aug73 [ ]
– Vampin' / Theme of The Mack / I choose you / Mack's stroll / The getaway (chase scene) / Slick / Mack man (got to get over) / Mother's theme (mama) / Now that it's all over / Brother's gonna work it out. *<cd-iss. 1996; 314 5303389-2>*

S/track review: The late WILLIE HUTCH might've graduated from 'Motown's back room rather than its famed production line but, in common with Stevie Wonder and Marvin Gaye, his 70s material was written, arranged, produced and performed by the man himself. Like Earth, Wind & Fire, Roy Ayers and Curtis Mayfield, HUTCH, by rights, should've seen his cinematic work leading to greater things. It wasn't to be. His legacy now lies in the two hugely influential soundtracks he recorded at the height of the black cinema jamboree: 'The MACK' and 'FOXY BROWN' (1974). It's mystifiying why 'The MACK's lead single, 'Brother's Gonna Work It Out', failed to break the Billboard Top 50; rolling syncopation, Alice Coltrane-style harp flourishes, swelling pre-disco strings and an unyieldingly positive message raise it to the era's creative, conscious soul heights. Shades of Gaye's 'What's Goin' On' illuminate HUTCH's phrasing, while the album version's mellifluous intro combines flute and guitar under a dialogue-excerpted debate on the unholy trinity of pimps, pushers and prostitutes. Everyone from Dr. Dre and Biggie Smalls to Moby and, most famously, the Chemical Brothers, have drawn on the song's luminous power to create something new, making it one of the era's most sampled tracks. Curiously for such a de facto theme, it was actually pushed to the end of the running order at the expense of 'Vampin', a derivative curtain-raiser. 'Theme Of The Mack' itself tempts with a gorgeously torpid horn arrangement before thundering into an old-skool soul groove, revealing HUTCH's vocals at their most rustically 'Stax'-like. The man's guitar playing is just as tenacious, corralling the hi-octane, hi-hat funk of 'The Getaway (Chase Scene)', and conceiving 'Mack Man (Got To Get Over)' as knotty, blaxploitation blues. And while James Brown paid tribute to his dear departed mom more emotively on 'BLACK CAESAR', with 'Mother's Theme (Mama)', HUTCH furthered the notion that behind every superbad blaxploitation mutha, was erm . . . a real mutha. HUTCH never did quite work it out in the fame stakes but 'The MACK' – one of blaxploitation's mellower soundtracks to one of its most uncompromising movies – was the nearest he came. And just for the record, it sounds nothing like Mark Morrison. *BG*

Album rating: *6.5

– spinoff hits, etc. –

WILLIE HUTCH: Brother's Gonna Work It Out / I Choose You
May 73. (7") *<1222> (TMG 862)* [67] Aug73 [ ]

WILLIE HUTCH: Slick / Mother's Theme (Mama)
Jul 73. (7") *<1252>* [65] [–]

MACKINTOSH & T.J.

1975 (US 96m) Penland Productions (PG)

Film genre: modern western

Top guns: dir: Marvin J. Chomsky / s-w: Paul Savage (+ story w/ Marshall Riggan & Dick Dragonette)

Stars: Roy Rogers *(Mackintosh)* ← the MAN, HIS WORLD, HIS MUSIC, Clay O'Brien *(T.J.)*, Billy Green Bush *(Luke)* ← ELECTRA GLIDE IN BLUE ← the SAVAGE SEVEN, Andrew Robinson *(Coley Phipps)*, Joan Hackett *(Maggie)*, Dennis Fimple *(Schuster)* → HOUSE OF 1000 CORPSES, James Hampton *(Cotton)* → PUMP UP THE VOLUME, Luke Askew *(Cal)* ← PAT GARRETT & BILLY THE KID ← EASY RIDER / → SOUTH OF HEAVEN, WEST OF HELL

Storyline: Worldly-wise ranch hand Mackintosh takes troubled youngster TJ under his wing at a farmstead out West. The kid needs a lot of TLC, and Mackintosh, with his stories of times gone by, eventually wins the trust and friendship of the boy. But the old man shows he's not just a storyteller when he takes on some hot-blooded hustlers in a good old-fashioned punch-up after he's "triggered" into action. *JZ*

Movie rating: *5

Visual: none

Off the record: Roy Rogers was the original singing cowboy on such early pioneering ditties such as 'Listen To The Rhythm Of The Range' (from the film, 'Under Western Stars' in 1938) and 'Buttons And Bows' (from Bob Hope's 'Son Of Paleface' 1952), etc., etc. *MCS*

—

WAYLON JENNINGS (& WILLIE NELSON ** / The WAYLORS *)

Mar 76. (lp) *RCA Victor; <APL1 1520>* ☐ ☐
– All around cowboy / Back in the saddle again (*) / Ride me down easy / Gardenia waltz (instrumental – feat. JOHNNY GIMBLE with *) / Bob Wills is still the king / Shopping (instrumental *) / (Stay all night) Stay a little longer (**) / Crazy arms (instrumental – * feat. RALPH MOONEY) / All around cowboy *[movie track]*.

S/track review: WAYLON JENNINGS and WILLIE NELSON's 'Wanted! The Outlaws' was just becoming the first-ever country music album to go platinum, setting the seal on their triumphant rebellion against the music industry establishment, and this enticing-looking oddity was never going to compete for attention. Frankly, there isn't too much to warrant it, either; it may be fair to suggest the hard-working composer's energies were focused elsewhere. The nine tracks here include WILLIE NELSON's cover of Bob Wills' 'Stay A Little Longer', which NELSON had recorded three years before, and which would become an indispensable and much-loved staple of his live show in stripped-down and speeded-up form. WAYLON's songs 'All Around Cowboy' (which appears twice), 'Ride Me Down Easy' and 'Bob Wills Is Still The King' fairly represent the singer's tough-guy sentimentality and guileless gusto, but they had all appeared on the previous year's 'Dreaming My Dreams' album. What's left is a clutch of expert and appealing instrumentals turned out by JENNINGS' road band the WAYLORS. Which may not really be enough. *ND*

Album rating: *4

MADAME CLAUDE

US aka the FRENCH WOMAN

1977 (Fra 105m) Orphee Arts / Columbia-Warner (X)

Film genre: seXual comedy drama

Top guns: dir: Just Jaeckin → GIRLS / s-w: Andre G. Brunelin (au: Jacques Quoirez)

Stars: Francoise Fabian *(Madame Claude)*, Dayle Haddon *(Elizabeth)* → PAROLES ET MUSIQUE, **Murray Head** *(David Evans)* ← the FAMILY WAY, Maurice Ronet *(Pierre)*, Klaus Kinski *(Alexander Zakis)* ← LIFESPAN ← AGUIRRE, WRATH OF GOD / → NOSFERATU, THE VAMPYRE → CODENAME: WILD GEESE → COBRA VERDE, Andre Falcon *(Paul)*, Robert Webber *(Howard)*, Francoise Perrot *(Lefevre)* → la FEMME DE MON POTE, Vibeke Knudsen *(Anne-Marie)*

Storyline: Madame Claude is ostenisbly the proprietress of a modelling agency whose covert trade in supplying high class whores to high ranking officials who really should know better is under threat from incriminating evidence. *BG*

Movie rating: *4

Visual: none

Off the record: Murray Head was more famous for his hit musical single, 'One Night In Bangkok' (from 'Chess').

SERGE GAINSBOURG

1977. (lp) *Philips; (9101 144)* ☐ French ☐
– Diapositivisme / Discophoteque / Mi corasong / Ketchup in the night / Fish-eye blues / Teleobjectivisme / Putain que ma joie demeure / Burnt island / Yesterday, yes a day (vocal: JANE BIRKIN) / Dusty lane / First class ticket / Long focal rock / Arabysance / Passage a tobacco / Yesterday on fender. *<cd-iss. Dec99 on 'Phantom' Japan; B00003 WGE4>*

S/track review: Released in the sonic limbo between his most abstruse concept set, 'L'Homme A Tete De Chou' (1976) and his Franco-reggae masterpiece, 'Aux Armes Et Caetera' (1978), 'MADAME CLAUDE' has always been the most fetishised of all SERGE GAINSBOURG soundtracks. Prior to its (Japanese) reissue in spring 2007, the original Japanese CD was going for silly money, with the original vinyl presenting ample opportunity for financial ruin. Few albums actually live up to the expectations the "crackhouse of record collecting" – as one waggish internet soul put it – imposes on them. This is one of them. It's a good Serge soundtrack, but it's not quite a great one. Unlike a somewhat recooked 'JE T'AIME MOI NON PLUS' (1976), though, the softcore disco-funk tropes are at least freshly written, generating some Concorde mileage from the faintly surreal convergence of Serge, Murray Head and Klaus Kinski (who, observed Time Out acidly, "looks like he'd give anything to be on a raft up the Amazon"). Titles like 'Ketchup In The Night' and 'Discophoteque' scream parody but the music is written and performed pretty much straight, the latter brazenly quoting from Philly disco nugget, 'Do It Any Way You Wanna'. It's fine, Deodato-esque stuff, full of creamy electric piano and bulbous bass, flying close to reggae on 'Dusty Lane' (Serge got even closer on 'Zanzibar', from the same year's 'Aurais Dû Faire Gaffe, Le Choc Est Terrible'; find it on the brilliant box set, 'Musique De Films') and perfected amid the percussive modulation and lead yelps of 'First Class Ticket'. But, well, it just isn't Serge the arch-provocateur, or even Serge the maverick. He does an equally straight take on Astor Piazzolla, again saving his humour for the title ('Corasong' . . .). You want some dive-bar blues-funk, what about 'Fish-Eye Blues'? Some acoustic guitar and steel drums? You've got – the rather fine actually – 'Burnt Island' (peerless title, especially if you happen to live in Fife). Just when you think he's going to leaf the 70s style-handbook dry, he pulls out the baroque organ weirdness of 'Putain Que Ma Joie Demeure' (don't ask about this title . . .) and medina-funk of Arabysance, punctuating swirling, coolly authentic Middle Eastern arrangements with aggravated clavinet. Then there's the JANE BIRKIN ballad, 'Yesterday Was A Day', one of the loveliest, most bittersweet and fragile in her Serge-penned oeuvre; that it's penned for a soft-porn film is just another GAINSBOURG-ian irony, sweeter than ever on the instrumental close-out, 'Yesterday On A Fender'. DJs get all hot and bothered about 'MADAME CLAUDE', and as a late-decade funk album it purrs like red leather. For the essential essence of GAINSBOURG the composer though, it's maybe not the best place to lose your cherry. *BG*

Album rating: *7.5

MADE IN USA

1987 (US 82m) Hemdale / TriStar Pictures / DeLaurentis (R)

Film genre: crime drama / road movie

Top guns: dir: Ken Friedman / s-w: Zbigniew Kempinski (+ story w/ Nick Wechsler)

Stars: Adrian Pasdar *(Dar)* → NEAR DARK → SHUT UP & SING, Chris Penn *(Tuck)* ← FOOTLOOSE / → RESERVOIR DOGS → MASKED AND ANONYMOUS, Judith Baldwin *(Dorie)* → BEACHES, Lori Singer *(Annie)* ← FOOTLOOSE, Marji Martin *(Ma Frazier)*, Tiny Wells *(Pa Frazier)* → DUDES, Jacqueline Murphy *(Cora)*, **Dean Paul Martin** *(Cowboy)*

Storyline: Tuck and Dar are two disillusioned buddies from Pennsylvania who decide to hit the highway after a coal mining disaster splits up their old town. They have no scruples about breaking the law to get what they want, and along with hot hitchhiker Annie they blaze a trail across the mid-west in a string of stolen cars on their way to the sunshine and sand of California's beaches. *JZ*

Movie rating: *4.5

Visual: video

Off the record: Tragically, **Dean Paul Martin** (member of 60s singing trio, Dino, Desi & Billy, and son of iconic Rat Pack crooner, Dean Martin) was killed on 21st March, 1987, when his plane crashed on San Gorgonio Mountain, California. *MCS*

—

SONIC YOUTH

Mar 95. (cd) *Warners-Rhino; <(8122 71591-2)>* ☐ ☐
– Mackin' for Doober / Full chrome logic / Secret girl / Cork mountain incident / Moustache riders / Tuck n Dar / Moon in the bathroom / Thought bubbles / Rim thrusters / Lincoln's gout / Coughing up tweed / Pre-poured wood / Hairpiece lullaby 1 & 2 / Pocketful of Sen-Sen / Smoke blisters 1 & 2 / The velvet plug / Giggles / Tulip fire 2 / The dynamics of bulbing / Smoke blisters 3 & 4 / O.J.'s glove or what? / Webb of mud 1, 2 & 3 / Bachelors in fur!

S/track review: In 1985/6, SONIC YOUTH were on a high, creative plain, when they enthusiastically agreed to write the score for 'MADE IN USA'; young Hollywood director Ken Friedman, had already tried out 'Secret Girl' (from SY's 'Evol' set) and discarded tracks by Southern-fried boogie band, the Outlaws. In a studio ('Spinhead') in the San Fernando Valley, SONIC YOUTH Messrs KIM GORDON, THURSTON MOORE, LEE RANALDO and STEVE SHELLEY constructed their (mono) experimental soundscapes around the film's rushes. Not all of their music (recorded October 1986) was used for the 1987 movie (much to THURSTON's dismay) and it took nigh on a decade for the OST to hit the shops. SONIC YOUTH had become America's underground darlings of the experimental jet-set, 'MADE IN USA' was not part of their masterplan and was put on the backburner until demand was high. First thing you notice when you handle the CD/Cass is the pseudo shop price sticker retailing at $0.00 – if only. It could be said 'MADE IN USA' is for the SY completist, but on closer inspection it's not too bad if you're into the avant garde and weird. Made up of short-ish, 1-2 minute instrumental soundbites, the band career through the odd tune. The exception to the rule being an excellent version of the aforementioned 'Secret Girl', Kim at her sexiest, if sounding a tad Patti Smith. Most of the tracks seem throwaway and quite annoyingly repetitive, take for instance 'Tuck N Dar', a proper song that reprises the previous two instrumentals. If there is any comparison, the desert sound of Ry Cooder on his 'Southern Comfort' mission, is not so far removed. Of the less cinematic pieces, 'Rim Thrusters' (mouth harp by Terry Pearson), is the most excitingly upbeat on show, hinting that they had not lost touch with rock'n'roll. Overall, there are of course 23 tracks here and however short, 'MADE IN USA' makes for a compelling collectors' piece rather than anything inspirational. If you want that and you're frustrated by the bleakness of the set, go find their 1988 classic, 'Daydream Nation'. *MCS*

Album rating: *4.5

the MAGIC CHRISTIAN

1969 (UK 95m) Commonwealth United Pictures (A)

Film genre: screwball satire/comedy

Top guns: s-w: Joseph McGrath (+ dir), Terry Southern ← EASY RIDER ← CANDY, plus Peter Sellers, John Cleese, Graham Chapman

Stars: Peter Sellers *(Sir Guy Grand)*, **Ringo Starr** *(Youngman Grand)* <= the BEATLES =>, Richard Attenborough *(Oxford coach)* → LOOT, Laurence Harvey *(Hamlet)*, Caroline Blakiston *(Esther)*, Christopher Lee *(ship's vampire)* → the WICKER MAN → the LAST UNICORN, Raquel Welch *(Priestess of the Whip)* ← a SWINGIN' SUMMER ← ROUSTABOUT, Spike Milligan *(traffic warden)* → CUCUMBER CASTLE, Wilfred Hyde-White *(Capt. Reginald K. Klaus)* → XANADU, Fred Emney *(Fitzgibbon)* ← BUNNY LAKE IS MISSING ← I'VE GOTTA HORSE, Dennis Price *(Winthrop)* ← PLAY IT COOL / → SON OF DRACULA, Leonard Frey *(Laurence Faggot)* → WHERE THE BUFFALO ROAM, Hattie Jacques *(Ginger Horton)*, Jeremy Lloyd *(Lord Hampton)* ← SMASHING TIME ← JUST FOR FUN, John Le Mesurier *(Sir John)* ← CUCKOO PATROL ← FINDERS KEEPERS, John Cleese *(director in Sotheby's)*, Frank Thornton *(police inspector)* ← GONKS GO BEAT ← IT'S TRAD, DAD! / → SIDE BY SIDE, Clive Dunn *(Sommelier)*, Patrick Cargill *(auctioneer)* ← HELP!, Graham Stark *(waiter at Chez Eduoard restaurant)* ← FINDERS KEEPERS, **Keith Moon** *(nun)* <= the WHO =>, Kenneth Connor ← CUCKOO PATROL ← GONKS GO BEAT, Roman Polanski *(drinker)*, Victor Maddern *(hot dog vendor)* ← CUCKOO PATROL ← BUNNY LAKE IS MISSING, Rita Webb *(woman in park)* ← MRS. BROWN, YOU'VE GOT A LOVELY DAUGHTER ← TO SIR, WITH LOVE / → PERCY → CONFESSIONS OF A POP PERFORMER, *(cameos)*:- Harry Carpenter, Michael Aspel, Alan Whicker, Yul Bruyner, Graham Chapman

Storyline: Sir Guy Grand, the richest man in the world, adopts Youngman to be his heir and takes him on a tour of Britain with a difference. Grand uses his immense wealth to show the greed and corruption of the establishment in a series of set-ups, including a massive cesspool full of tenners and a train with revolving Chinamen. The finale is a voyage on The Magic Christian, limited to only the extremely rich: whether they sail happily into the sunset is anyone's guess. *JZ*

Movie rating: *5

Visual: video + dvd

Off the record: Both Peter Sellers and Clive Dunn had hit singles, the latter subsequently topping the UK charts in December 1970 with the nauseating 'Grandad', a real 'Dad's Army' tune if ever there was one. *MCS*

—

Various Artists (composer: KEN THORNE *)

Apr 70. (lp) *Pye; (NSPL 28133) Commonwealth United; <CU 6004>* ☐ ☐
– Introduction (*) / Come and get it (BADFINGER) / Hamlet scene (*) / Hunting scene (*) / Carry on to tomorrow (BADFINGER) / Lilli Marlene (*) / Flip your wig or A Day In The Life (*) / Magic Christian waltz (*) / Come and get it (*) / Rock of ages (BADFINGER) / Newsreel march music (*) / Mad about the boy (PETER SELLERS) / Something in the air (THUNDERCLAP NEWMAN).

S/track review: Not much to 'The MAGIC CHRISTIAN' original sound track, in the way of minutes at least (under thirty). We have loads of movie dialogue (see above characters), a KEN THORNE score and more importantly, four pop songs. Three stem from Beatles signings BADFINGER (the McCartney-penned 'Come And Get It', 'Carry On To Tomorrow' & 'Rock Of Ages') and one from Pete Townshend-produced THUNDERCLAP NEWMAN (the classy chart-topper, 'Something In The Air'). The move into sophisticated and orchestral pop had been a heady solution for some post-psych/bubblegum bands, but BADFINGER and Speedy Keen's THUNDERCLAP pulled it off with ease. As for PETER SELLERS' camp rendition of Noel Coward's 'Mad About The Boy', well only time will tell if it matches Eartha Kitt's. Sarcasm aside, the THORNE orchestral compositions, mainly accompanied by marching bands and the aforementioned movie dialogue, was quite run-of-the-mill conventional. The confusing thing for some will be why the track known as 'Flip Your Wig' on the sleeve becomes 'A Day In The Life' on vinyl. What's more confusing, is the 'Apple' records cash-in of sorts by BADFINGER and Co (the Co being some ex-Beatles), when they issued their 'Magic Christian Music' LP (complete with their film contributions) a few months earlier than the official soundtrack. *MCS*

Album rating: *4.5

– spinoff hits, etc. –

THUNDERCLAP NEWMAN: Something In The Air / (non-OSTrack)
May 69. (7") *Track; (604 031) <2656>* 1 Aug69 37

BADFINGER: Come And Get It / Rock Of Ages

Dec 69. (7") *Apple; (APPLE 20) <1815>* 4 Jan70 7

BADFINGER: Magic Christian Music

Jan 70. (lp/c) *Apple; (SAPCOR/TCSAPCOR 12) <3364>* Mar70 55
– (3 tracks from the movie; the rest from period as the Iveys). *(<cd-iss. Oct91; CDP 798698-2>)*

☐ MAGNET segment
(⇒ the WICKER MAN)

MAGNOLIA

1999 (US 188m) New Line Cinema (R)

Film genre: psychological urban drama

Top guns: s-w + dir: Paul Thomas Anderson ← BOOGIE NIGHTS

Stars: Jason Robards *(Earl Partridge)* ← PAT GARRETT & BILLY THE KID ← FOOLS, Julianne Moore *(Linda Partridge)* ← BOOGIE NIGHTS, Tom Cruise *(Frank "T.J." Mackey)* ← LEGEND ← RISKY BUSINESS, Philip Seymour Hoffman *(Phil Parma)* ← BOOGIE NIGHTS / → ALMOST FAMOUS → COLD MOUNTAIN, John C. Reilly *(officer Jim Kurring)* ← BOOGIE NIGHTS ← GEORGIA / → the PICK OF DESTINY → WALK HARD: THE DEWEY COX STORY, Melora Walters *(Claudia Wilson Gator)*, Jeremy Blackman *(Stanley Spector)*, Philip Baker Hall *(Jimmy Gator)* ← the INSIDER ← BOOGIE NIGHTS ← THREE O'CLOCK HIGH, William H. Macy *(Donnie Smith)* ← BOOGIE NIGHTS ← WAG THE DOG ← COLIN FITZ LIVES! ← the LAST DRAGON, Michael Bowen *(Rick Spector)* ← JACKIE BROWN, Melinda Dillon *(Rose Gator)* ← SONGWRITER ← BOUND FOR GLORY, Alfred Molina *(Solomon Solomon)*, ← BOOGIE NIGHTS ← DEAD MAN / → COFFEE AND CIGARETTES, Emmanuel L. Johnson *(Dixon)*, Henry Gibson *(Thurston Howell)* ← a STRANGER IN THE KINGDOM ← the BLUES BROTHERS ← NASHVILLE, Michael Shamus Wiles *(Captain Muffy)* ← FIGHT CLUB / → ROCK STAR, Michael Murphy *(Alan Kligman, Esq.)* ← PRIVATE PARTS ← NASHVILLE ← DOUBLE TROUBLE, Miriam Margoyles *(Faye Barringer)* ← ELECTRIC DREAMS ← the APPLE, Bob Downey Sr. *(WDKK show director)* ← TO LIVE AND DIE IN L.A. ← YOU'VE GOT TO WALK IT LIKE YOU TALK IT . . ., Thomas Jane *(young Jimmy Gator)* ← BOOGIE NIGHTS, Ricky Jay *(Burt Ramsey / narrator)* ← BOOGIE NIGHTS / → LAST DAYS, Orlando Jones *(Worm)*, Danny Wells *(Dick Jennings)* ← the WOMAN IN RED ← GOIN' COCONUTS, Luis Guzman *(Luis)* ← BOOGIE NIGHTS ← SHORT EYES, Melora Walters *(Claudia Wilson Gator)* ← BOOGIE NIGHTS / → COLD MOUNTAIN, Patton Oswalt *(Delmer Darion)* → MAN ON THE MOON → CAKE BOY, Brad Hunt *(Craig Hansen)* ← CLUBLAND, Neil Flynn *(Stanley Berry)* → HOOT, Matt Gerald *(officer #2)* → IN THE MIX

Storyline: A highly ambitious three-hour plus sprawl through Los Angeles during the course of one day, taking in a vast array of characters including a chauvinistic sex therapist Frank/T.J., a dying man and his nurse, an estranged wife, a cop who's lost more than his gun and Donnie, a jilted former child gameshow prodigy. All lives interconnect (a la 'Pulp Fiction') during the course of the film, accumulating in a freak and bizarre weather phenomenon. *AS*

Movie rating: *9

Visual: video + dvd

Off the record: AIMEE MANN was born 8th September 1960, Richmond, Virginia, USA. After moving to Boston to attend the Berklee School of Music, one of Aimee's rather unlikely initial musical forays was working with Al Jourgensen's Ministry. This group, the Young Snakes (one 1982 EP exists), were around prior to her forming pop/rock outfit, 'Til Tuesday. While many of the songs on the debut set, 'Voices Carry' (1985), sprang from MANN's break-up with former lover, Michael Hausman (their drummer), the group's critically acclaimed third set, 'Everything's Different Now' (1989), was largely inspired by MANN's relationship with co-writer, Jules Shear. In spite of, or perhaps because of this "Rumours"-style emotional entanglement, the album was a compelling stepping stone to MANN's solo career and saw her developing into an accomplished and affecting songwriter. Yet the record sold poorly and the band dissolved amid record company hassles, MANN spending the next few years attempting to disentangle herself before embarking upon a solo career. She eventually emerged in autumn '93 with a new deal (on 'Imago') and album, 'Whatever', her eclectic, Beatles/Pretenders-like pop/rock drawing praise from such legendary songwriters as ELVIS COSTELLO, a personal friend and sometime collaborator. The record also provided her with her first major UK success, nudging into the Top 40, although just when it seemed as if MANN was finally beginning to establish herself as an artist in her own right, 'Imago' went bust. The ensuing hassles almost persuaded MANN to give it all up, 'Geffen' finally releasing a follow-up, 'I'm With Stupid', in 1995. She subsequently found herself without a recording contract once again, although some of her new material (including the Academy Award-winning 'Save Me' track) did surface on her 'MAGNOLIA' movie soundtrack in 1999. *BG & MCS*

AIMEE MANN (& Various Artists) (score: JON BRION *)

Jan 00. (cd) *Reprise; <9362 47583-2> (9362 47638-2)* 58 Mar00
– One / Momentum / Build that wall / Deathly / Driving sideways / You do / Nothing is good enough / Wise up / Save me / Goodbye stranger (SUPERTRAMP) / Logical song (SUPERTRAMP) / Dreams (GABRIELLE) / Magnolia (*).

S/track review: Praise was heaped upon MANN for her contribution to this film, where nine songs, some old, most new and accompanied by cover versions, won the LA-based singer-songwriter a plentiful amount of new fans. It's comforting then to know MANN is definitely the real deal. For example, the opening song on this sort-of mini-LP is a beautiful cover of Nilsson's 'One', displaying plenty of prowess on her part to make the song sound like her own. Two other covers are included on the set, both SUPERTRAMP songs 'Goodbye Stranger' and 'The Logical Song', although it's MANN's own compositions that really impress. Look out too for Jon Brion's orchestral score, also released on 'Reprise' records. *AS*

Album rating: *8

Taj MAHAL

Born: Henry St. Clair Fredericks, 17 May'40, New York City, New York, USA. A much respected elder statesman of the blues who – like his early partner RY COODER – has consistently striven to express the genre as part of a richer fabric of African-rooted forms, TAJ MAHAL can boast a pretty impeccable critical record and loyal fanbase if no real track record of crossover success. His earliest appearance on screen was an exuberant contribution to the Rolling Stones' 'ROCK AND ROLL CIRCUS' (1968), in which he dodged British musicians' union restrictions to perform. Although released in 1972, Martin Ritt's Oscar-nominated African-American drama, 'SOUNDER' was about as far from blaxploitation as it was possible to get, which no doubt suited its discerning soundtrack composer, MAHAL (with added contributions from Lightnin' Hopkins), just fine. His vibrant, traditionalist score was an impressive start to an occasional film composing career which saw him going on to score a 1976 follow-up, 'Sounder, Part Two' as well as gritty prison drama, 'BROTHERS' (1977), again more cerebral than the average blaxpoitation effort even if it did star 'SUPERFLY' antihero Ron O'Neal. While MAHAL himself had actually taken major acting parts in both instalments of 'SOUNDER', it would be 1991 before his next big screen appearance, a cameo in Keanu Reeves blockbuster, 'BILL & TED'S BOGUS JOURNEY' (1991). In tandem with a general early 90s resurgence, the bluesmeister also resurrected his long dormant talent for film scoring, providing the music for Anthony Drazan's award winning interracial drama, 'Zebrahead' (1992), as well as Langston Hughes' Broadway show, 'Mule Bone'. Through the 90s and into the noughties, MAHAL continued to act and compose, appearing in Tim Reid's 'Once Upon

A Time . . . When We Were Coloured' (1996), Maggie Greenwald's 'Songcatcher' (2000), as a DJ in road movie, 'Outside Ozona' (1998), which he also co-scored (as he did the same year with co-V/A OST, 'SCRAPPLE'), as a singer in Callie Khouri's chick flick, 'Divine Secrets Of The Ya-Ya Sisterhood' (2002) and, more recently, in blues comedy, 'KILLER DILLER' (2004). *BG*

- **filmography** (composer) {acting} –

Rock And Roll Circus *(1968 {p} on OST by the ROLLING STONES =>)* / **Sounder** *(1972 {*} OST =>)* / Sounder, Part Two *(1976 {*})* / **Brothers** *(1977 OST =>)* / Scott Joplin *(1977 TV {a})* / the Man Who Broke 1000 Chains *(1987 TV {a})* / **Bill & Ted's Bogus Journey** *(1991 {b} OST by V/A =>)* / Zebrahead *(1992 OST by V/A; see future edition)* / Once Upon A Time . . . When We Were Colored *(1996 {a})* / Blue Note: A Story Of Modern Jazz *(1997 TV {p} OST by V/A; see future edition)* / Outside Ozona *(1998 w/ Johnny Lee Schell)* / **Scrapple** *(1998 OST w/ V/A =>)* / Songcatcher *(2000 {a} OST by V/A =>)* / **Blues Odyssey** *(2002 {c} OST by V/A =>)* / Divine Secrets Of The Ya-Ya Sisterhood *(2002 {p})* / **Killer Diller** *(2004 {a})*

MAHONEY'S LAST STAND

aka MAHONEY'S ESTATE

1972 (Can 109m) International Film Distributors

Film genre: romantic road movie

Top guns: dir: Alexis Kanner (+ s-w), Harvey Hart, Terence Heffernan (+ s-w)

Stars: Alexis Kanner *(Leroy Mahoney)*, Maud Adams *(Miriam)*, Sam Waterston *(Felix)* → RANCHO DELUXE → the KILLING FIELDS

Storyline: Even the folks behind the CD soundtrack release haven't seen this film, nor, according to the sleevenotes, have they met anyone who has. Unsurprisingly we haven't seen it either although the storyline apparently revolves around city dweller Mahoney's journey back to the land and the romantic entanglement which ensues. *BG*

Movie rating: *3

Visual: none

Off the record: **RON WOOD & RONNIE LANE** (see below)

—

RON WOOD & RONNIE LANE

Sep 76. (lp/c) *Atlantic; <SD 36129> (K/K4 50308)* ☐ ☐
– Car radio / Tonight's number / From the late to the early / Chicken wired / I'll fly away / Title one / Just for a moment / Mona the blues / Hay tumble / Wooly's thing / Rooster funeral / Just for a moment. *(re-iss. Dec88 on 'Thunderbolt' lp/cd; THBL/CDTB 067) (pic-lp May89; THBL 067P) (lp re-iss. Feb99 on 'Get Back'; GET 517) (cd-iss. Feb01 on 'Burning Airlines'+=; PILOT 20)* – (5 extra tracks). *(cd re-iss. Apr01 on 'Soundport'; SP 1708)*

S/track review: Recorded in 1972 (and unreleased for four years due to legal reasons) amid the growing conflict of interest between the Faces (RON WOOD's outfit) and the stratospheric solo career of Rod Stewart, 'MAHONEY'S LAST STAND' is best approached as a rootsy primer for RONNIE LANE's solo career, and perhaps a glimpse into what the Faces would have sounded like had it been Stewart who'd departed rather than LANE. As Faces organist IAN McLAGAN (who appears on four tracks) admitted to Mojo, "Rod and Kenny {Jones, the band's drummer} would start rattling their car keys about 10 o'clock because they couldn't wait to get out of the studio and go clubbing, while the two Ronnies and I were happier getting high and playing music all night". He might've been referring to the recording of the Faces' magnum opus, 'A Nod's As Good As A Wink' (1971), but that image of LANE, WOOD and McLAGAN as the band's beating heart is hard to shake, and it's one which looms large over this soundtrack. In lieu of the usual inebriated braggadocio, the two Ronnies live out their grainiest Americana fantasies with a little help from famous pals. Inevitably, some of the tracks – the ballsy 'Car Radio' (featuring PETE TOWNSHEND), especially – sound like instrumental surplus from the aforementioned 'A Nod's As Good . . .', although the BOBBY KEYS/JIM PRICE-supplied brass arrangements on 'Tonight's Number' and especially the funky – bordering on the Afro-funky – 'Title One' make for an interesting twist on the Faces formula. And while there mightn't be a 'Debris' or a 'Richmond', LANE's wounded lyricism seeps from 'Just For A Moment' and the gorgeous 'From The Late To The Early', drawn out by WOOD's slide and rudimentary harmonica. The late guitarist also picks some mean banjo on his own favourite, 'Chicken Wired', the best homage to funky poultry since the Meters' 'Chicken Strut', and a track he subsequently re-recorded for his Slim Chance debut, 'Anymore For Anymore' (1974). Family man RIC GRECH takes the drum stool for the early Rolling Stones-esque 'Mona The Blues', and straps on his fiddle for 'Hay Tumble' and 'Rooster Funeral'. Fife-born 'Stones pianist IAN STEWART contributes some glorious honky-tonk plonking to 'Woody's Thing' and even producer Glyn Johns makes himself heard, stepping up for the a cappella chorus of 'I'll Fly Away'. The 'Burning Airlines' CD re-issue adds five out-takes (sourced on a reel titled 'Mahoney's Estate' according to the sleevenotes), three of which would later turn up as highlights of the Faces' underrated 'Ooh La La' (1973): 'My Fault' (with ROD STEWART scatting and chortling away in the absence of a full lyric sheet), an instrumental prototype of 'Just Another Honky' entitled 'Safety Pin Queen', and an early version of 'Flags And Banners' with the working title 'C&W Number'. A fascinating artefact. *BG*

Album rating: *6.5

☐ the MAMAS & THE PAPAS segment
(⇒ BEAUTIFUL THING)

MAN AND BOY

1971 (US 98m) Jemmin Productions / Levitt-Pickman Films (G)

Film genre: revisionist western drama

Top guns: dir: E.W. Swackhamer / s-w: Harry Essex, Oscar Saul (au: Rejean Ducharme)

Stars: Bill Cosby *(Caleb Revers)* → LET'S DO IT AGAIN → a PIECE OF THE ACTION, George Spell *(Billy Revers)*, Leif Erickson *(Sheriff Mossman)* ← ROUSTABOUT, Gloria Foster *(Ivy Revers)*, Douglas Turner-Ward *(Lee Christmas)*, John Anderson *(Stretch)* ← COTTON COMES TO HARLEM, Henry Silva *(Caine)* → DICK TRACY → the END OF VIOLENCE → GHOST DOG: THE WAY OF THE SAMURAI, Dub Taylor *(Atkins)* ← HOT ROD GANG / → FALLING FROM GRACE, Yaphet Kotto *(Nate Hodges)* → ACROSS 110th STREET → TRUCK TURNER → FRIDAY FOSTER → MONKEY HUSTLE → the PARK IS MINE, Shelley Morrison *(Rosita)*, Richard Bull *(Thornhill)*

Storyline: Black Civil War veteran Caleb Revers settles down on a small farm out West with his wife and son. They nurse a horse back to health, but are not best pleased when it's promptly stolen from its stable. Father and son go off in search of the animal, but soon they find themselves in a gunfight with the horse thieves as they hoof it south to the Mexican border. *JZ*

Movie rating: *4.5

Visual: video

Off the record: **J.J. JOHNSON** (see own entry)

—

J.J. JOHNSON (musical supervisor: QUINCY JONES)

Dec 71. (lp) *Sussex; <SXBS 7011>* ☐ ☐
– Theme from "Man And Boy" – Better days (BILL WITHERS) /

Slo-mo / Emancipation procrastination (monologue: Douglas Turner-Ward) / Pull, Jubal, pull / Man And Boy / Theme from "Man And Boy" – Better days / Country soul / Rosita / Trekkin' / Hard times, mister (Lee Christmas theme) / Man And Boy – end title.

S/track review: Legendary trombonist from big band/bebop times, J.J. JOHNSON (under the musical supervision of another giant, QUINCY JONES), made his inaugural film score debut with this Blaxploitation oddity, 'MAN AND BOY'. With a running-time of only around half-an-hour (the usual during this era), the LP has its moments courtesy of the funky 'Pull, Jubal, Pull' and the BILL "Ain't No Sunshine" WITHERS theme tune, 'Better Days' – a tune remarkably similar in parts to King Crimson's prog-classic, 'Moonchild' (substitute Moog for moody mouth-organ and orchestra!). Apart from two other main title instrumental themes and a 3-minute monologue by support actor, Douglas Turner-Ward, JOHNSON gets into the groove via highlights, 'Slo-mo', the self-descriptive 'Country Soul' (featuring great "geetar" and magical "moothy") and the John Barry-esque 'Rosita'. Incidentally, jazz crossover saxophonist, Grover Washington Jr., delivered his own rendition of the title track on his 1971 'Inner City Blues' set. *MCS*

Album rating: *5

the MAN INSIDE

French title 'L'AFFAIRE WALLRAFF'

1990 (Ger/Neth/US 93m) New Line Cinema (PG)

Film genre: psychological drama

Top guns: s-w + dir: Bobby Roth ← DEAD SOLID PERFECT ← BAJA OKLAHOMA ← HEARTBREAKERS / → BRAVE NEW GIRL (au: Gunter Wallraff)

Stars: Jurgen Prochnow *(Gunter Wallraff)*, Peter Coyote *(Henry Tobel)* ← BAJA OKLAHOMA ← HEARTBREAKERS ← TIMERIDER: THE ADVENTURE OF LYLE SWANN / → a LITTLE TRIP TO HEAVEN → COMMUNE, Nathalie Baye *(Christine)*, Dieter Laser *(Leonard Schroeder)*, Monique Van de Ven *(Tina Wallraff)*, James Laurenson *(Mueller)* ← HEARTBREAKERS ← the WALL ← the MONSTER CLUB

Storyline: Journalist Gunter Wallraff goes undercover as – a journalist! He's out to expose a rival tabloid's deliberate manipulation of the news for their own agenda. Soon Gunter realizes that the paper also has links with the intelligence agencies and is privy to state secrets, which raises the stakes considerably both for his story and his safety. *JZ*

Movie rating: *5

Visual: video

Off the record: (see below)

—

TANGERINE DREAM

1991. (cd) *E.M.I.; (795617-2)* [–] French [–]
– Wallraff's theme / Tendency of love / Addicted to the truth / World of the "standard" / Purposes of brevity / Tobel's death by the river / Taboo society / The drive to Hanover / Correlation of lies / Investigation / News and morality.

S/track review: Collectable, if only for its obscurity, this European thriller score is a pleasant, if dated, entry in the voluminous TANGERINE DREAM catalogue. Whereas the group's earlier soundtracks recalled the minimalism of Steve Reich with their reliance on sequenced melodies and riffs, here the duo of EDGAR FROESE and PAUL HASLINGER use their computers to ape a live band. As a result, the electronic rock of cues such as 'Wallraff's Theme' is a little too stiff to be truly suspenseful. 'Tendency For Love' is stronger, highlighting TANGERINE DREAM's knack for simple but affecting romantic themes built around soft synth pads and digital piano. This theme is given an edgier treatment on 'Addicted To The Truth', as zither-like keyboards negotiate choppy rhythms, sequenced bass and washes of distorted guitar. The theme is reprised again on the closing 'News And Morality', slowed down to a wistful piano lament. The New Age feel of some of the tracks, with their airy synth pads, clipped pan pipe effects and "ethnic" percussion, only reinforces the dated feel of this score. *SS*

Album rating: 4

MAN ON THE MOON

1999 (US 118m) Universal Pictures (R)

Film genre: showbiz biopic comedy drama

Top guns: dir: Milos Forman ← HAIR / s-w: Scott Alexander, Larry Karaszewski

Stars: Jim Carrey *(Andy Kaufman + Tony Clifton)* ← EARTH GIRLS ARE EASY, Danny DeVito *(George Shapiro)* ← the VIRGIN SUICIDES ← CAR WASH / → BE COOL, **Courtney LOVE** *(Lynne Margulies)*, Paul Giamatti *(Bob Zmuda)* ← PRIVATE PARTS ← SINGLES / → DUETS → STORYTELLING, Vincent Schiavelli *(Maynard Smith)*, Peter Bonerz *(Ed Weinberger)*, Jerry Lawler *(himself)*, Gerry Becker *(Stanley Kaufman)*, Leslie Lyles *(Janice Kaufman)*, George Shapiro *(Mr. Besserman)*, Bob Zmuda *(Jack Burns)*, Tracey Walter *(National Enquirer editor)* ← DELUSION ← YOUNG GUNS II ← BATMAN ← REPO MAN ← HONKYTONK MAN ← TIMERIDER: THE ADVENTURE OF LYLE SWANN / → HOW HIGH → MASKED AND ANONYMOUS, David Koechner *(National Enquirer reporter)* ← DILL SCALLION ← WAG THE DOG, Miles Chapin *(SNL assistant)* ← GET CRAZY ← HAIR, Judd Hirsch, Jeff Conaway, Christopher Lloyd, Marilu Henner, Lorne Michaels, Carol Kane *(themselves)*, David Letterman *(himself)* ← MEETING PEOPLE IS EASY ← PRIVATE PARTS ← BEAVIS AND BUTT-HEAD DO AMERICA / → GRIZZLY MAN, Patton Oswalt *(blue collar guy)* ← MAGNOLIA / → CAKE BOY, Brent Briscoe *(heavyset technician)* ← SLING BLADE / → CRAZY, Mews Small *(TM administrator)* ← AMERICAN POP ← THANK GOD IT'S FRIDAY, **Hal Blaine** *(Harrah's band)* ← GIRLS! GIRLS! GIRLS! / → the DR. JEKYLL & MR. HYDE ROCK 'N ROLL MUSICAL → BEAUTIFUL DREAMER: BRIAN WILSON AND THE STORY OF 'SMiLE', Brian Peck *(Friday's announcer)* ← the RETURN OF THE LIVING DEAD, Johnny Legend *(wild-haired guru)* ← YOUNG, HOT 'N' NASTY TEENAGE CRUISERS

Storyline: Biopic of American comedian Andy Kaufman, following his uncomfortable passage from controversial stand-up routines in small clubs to national fame and Saturday Night Live appearances before an untimely death from lung cancer. *BG*

Movie rating: *7

Visual: dvd

Off the record: **R.E.M.** (see own entry)

—

Various Artists incl. R.E.M. (*) (w/ dialogue **)

Nov 99. (cd/c) *Warners; <(9362 47483-2/-4)>* [ ] [ ]
– Mighty Mouse theme (here I come to save the day) (SANDPIPERS) / The great beyond (*) / Kiss you all over (EXILE) / Angela (theme from Taxi) (BOB JAMES) / Tony thrown out (**) / Man on the Moon (*) / This friendly world (*, ANDY & TONY) / Miracle (**) / Lynne & Andy (**) / Rose-Marie (ANDY KAUFMAN) / Andy gets fired (**) / I will survive (TONY CLIFTON) / Milk and cookies (**) / Man on the Moon (orchestral) / One more song for you (ANDY KAUFMAN).

S/track review: Scored by R.E.M. and also featuring two of the band's conventional songs, this can be classed as pretty much a bonafide R.E.M. soundtrack even if there's at least one other noteable contribution courtesy of producer/A&R man/all round jazz guru BOB JAMES, the man behind the original 'Taxi' theme, 'Angela' – included here in all its short (1 minute) but gossamer-sweet glory – and perhaps an influence on the score itself; it's actually difficult to believe STIPE and Co are behind as jazzy a cue as 'Tony Thrown Out'. The rest of the incidental music is fairly straightforward piano and orchestra material, pretty much what you might expect and evidence – particularly the elegiac 'Miracle' – that the band could probably more than handle a conventional film score in their own right. As for R.E.M's actual songs, the track which lent the film its name was probably one of the best on their landmark 1992 opus, 'Automatic For The People', and 'The Great Beyond' was the most impressive thing they'd come up with in years, more endearing than anything on their mid-late 90s albums. 'This Friendly World', for all its grating Jim Carrey vocal whoops, actually has a decent melody and a rootsy, 'Don't Go Back To Rockville'-style vibe. The ANDY/TONY KAUFMAN tracks can be either fast-forwarded or taken at face value: stand-up routines removed from their context. They're funny on first hearing (if not as funny – or as offensive – as the jokes themselves) but tedious if you plan on listening to the album more than once. A spare, orchestral version of 'Man On The Moon' rounds the whole thing off nicely, although it's hard to shake off the impression that this record is half substance/half filler. *BG*

Album rating: *5

– spinoff hits, etc. –

R.E.M.: The Great Beyond / Man On The Moon (live)

Dec 99. (c-s/cd-s) *(W 516 C/CD)* 57 Jan00 3

□ MANFRED MANN segment
(⇒ UP THE JUNCTION)

□ Aimee MANN segment
(⇒ MAGNOLIA)

MANNY & LO

1996 (US 88m) Pope Productions / Sony Pictures (R)

Film genre: domestic road movie

Top guns: s-w + dir: Lisa Krueger → COMMITTED

Stars: Scarlett Johansson *(Amanda)* → LOST IN TRANSLATION, Aleksa Palladino *(Laurel)* → STORYTELLING, **Mary Kay Place** *(Elaine)* ← JUST MY IMAGINATION ← MORE AMERICAN GRAFFITI ← BOUND FOR GLORY / → COMMITTED → KILLER DILLER, Glenn Fitzgerald *(Joey)*, Angie Phillips *(Connie)* → DUETS, Novella Nelson *(Georgine)* ← GIRL 6, Paul Guilfoyle *(Mr. Humphreys)* ← HOWARD THE DUCK

Storyline: Abandoned sisters Manny and Lo have had enough of foster homes and run away together, getting by through begging and stealing. All this changes when Lo finds herself pregnant and it becomes necessary to find somewhere to stay. They find an old cabin, and as the girls know nothing about childbirth they decide to kidnap shop assistant Elaine to act as midwife. Yet despite being kept in chains, Elaine seems happy to have at last found a role for herself tied to the youngsters. *JZ*

Movie rating: *7

Visual: video

Off the record: Tulsa-born **Mary Kay Place** released two country LPs in 1976 and 1977 respectively, 'Tonite! At The Capri Lounge Loretta Haggers' & 'Aimin' To Please', while she subsequently sang backing vocals on John Stewart's 1979 set, 'Bombs Away Dream Baby'. *MCS*

—

JOHN LURIE: African Swim // Manny & Lo

Feb 99. (cd) *Strange & Beautiful; <(SBM 0017)>* ☐ Mar99 ☐
– (AFRICAN SWIM tracks) // Manny & Lo (main titles) / Tiffany's bedroom / Driving into country / Manny with lunchbox / She's not a nurse / Manny leaves Lo / Monster trucks / Lo crawls through window / Wild Bill / Dream Elaine driving / Kidnapping Elaine / Hypnotize the lizard / Manny & Lo (end titles).

S/track review: Bypassing the music to JOHN LURIE's 'African Swim', a film that no longer exists (as it explains on the inner sleeve), the back-to-back CD tracks of 'MANNY & LO' find the guitarist/composer at his most effective and playful. Along with such session men luminaries as MARC RIBOT (guitar), BILL WARE (marimba), CHRIS WOOD (bass), BILLY MARTIN (percussion & drums), JOHN MEDESKI (Casio keyboards) and MATT ZIMBELMANN (guitar), LURIE discharges an eclectic and atmospheric soundtrack that encompasses a cocktail of musical genres from avant-jazz to punk-rock. The thirteen, mostly short'n'sweet tracks on 'MANNY & LO', open with the 2-minute (main title) theme and close with the lengthier, 6-minute equivalent (end title) track, a world-music-styled guitar-vs-marimba cue with backing chants by some of the players. Finished before they really get started, several of the instrumental dirges (including 'Tiffany's Bedroom', 'Monster Trucks', 'Lo Crawls Through Window', 'Dream Elaine Driving' & 'Hypnotize The Lizard') last under a minute each, making it difficult for the listener to register any emotion; also lasting under the minute mark is the JOHN LURIE-growled, Ramones-like 'She's Not A Nurse' – a welcome contrast. Down to just RIBOT, WOOD & MARTIN, the rockin' & rollin' of 'Kidnapping Elaine' captures the pure essence of 'MANNY & LO', lasting as it does 2:34 minutes. *MCS*

Album rating: *7.5 / MANNY & LO (*6)

□ MASSIVE ATTACK segment
(⇒ DANNY THE DOG)

□ MAVRO GALA alt.
(⇒ BLACK MILK)

MAXIMUM OVERDRIVE

1986 (US 97m) De Laurentiis Entertainment Group (R)

Film genre: sci-fi/horror disaster movie

Top guns: s-w + dir: Stephen King (+ story)

Stars: Emilio Estevez *(Bill Robinson)* ← REPO MAN / → YOUNG GUNS II → JUDGMENT NIGHT, Pat Hingle *(Hendershot)* ← ELVIS: THE MOVIE ← NORWOOD / → BATMAN, Laura Harrington *(Brett)*, Yeardley Smith *(Connie)* → GINGER ALE AFTERNOON, John Short *(Curtis)*, Ellen McElduff *(Wanda/June)*, J.C. Quinn *(Duncan)* ← TIMES SQUARE, Christopher Murney *(Camp Loman)* ← the LAST DRAGON / → LAST EXIT TO BROOKLYN, Leon Rippy *(Brad)* → YOUNG GUNS II, Giancarlo Esposito *(videoplayer)* → SCHOOL DAZE → NIGHT ON EARTH → KLA$H → FEEL THE NOISE, Frankie Faison *(Handy)* → MAXIMUM OVERDRIVE, Stephen King *(man at cashpoint)*

Storyline: Man's worst nightmares come true as cosmic forces animate the machine population of Wilmington, North Carolina. Lawnmowers get uppity, a drawbridge draws when it feels like it and trucks with no-one at the wheel terrorise law abiding citizens cowering in a diner. *BG*

Movie rating: *3.5

Visual: video + dvd

Off the record: AC/DC (see below)

—

AC/DC: Who Made Who

May 86. (lp/c) *Atlantic; <81650> (WX 57/+C)* [33] [11]
– Who made who / You shook me all night long / D.T. / Sink the pink / Ride on / Hells bells / Shake your foundations / Chase the ace / For those about to rock (we salute you). *(cd-iss. 1988; 781 650-2) (cd re-iss. Sep98 on 'E.M.I.'; 746299-2) (cd re-iss. Apr03 on 'Columbia'; 510769-2)*

S/track review: Once upon a time, AC/DC issued the kind of raging delinquent manifestos which comically recast hell as the best party in town and the Devil as one of the boys. By the mid-80s, their albums had become the equivalent of a quick fag round the back of the bike shed. Perhaps to remind us of just how sharp their horns had once been, horror writer Stephen King enlisted them for the soundtrack to his directorial debut. Rather than commissioning an album's worth of new music, he wisely compiled a proxy greatest hits set with a handful of new tracks as a sweetener. For those still in short trousers themselves in 1980, or not even born, the likes of 'Hells Bells' and the truly seismic 'You Shook Me All Night Long' are history lessons in the lost art of cod-demonic boogie rock. In these strange days of extreme metal and Norwegian church-burning, a band like AC/DC (ANGUS YOUNG, MALCOLM YOUNG, BRIAN JOHNSON, CLIFF WILLIAMS & SIMON WRIGHT) are a throwback to a more innocent time when most fans were savvy enough to take lyrics with a pinch of salt and a few slugs of tequila. A time when 'Highway To Hell' (1979) made it seem like punk had never happened. There's nothing from that album here, although the Bon Scott era is represented instead by the 1976 vintage blues, 'Ride On'. The soundtrack-only numbers comprise a couple of decent instrumentals and the title track, a typical 80s rock anthem tailored for the stadium circuit. If the title itself suggests a worrying move into religious philosophy, rest assured that it actually refers to the film's tongue-in-cheek, man vs machine storyline rather than humanity's origins. In lieu of a comprehensive AC/DC anthology (even after more than thirty years' worth of albums), this is still the next best thing. If you want more of the real pre-BRIAN JOHNSON thing, try out live performance documentary film, 'LET THERE BE ROCK', featuring the late, great Bon Scott. *BG*

Album rating: *7

– spinoff hits, etc. –

AC/DC: Who Made Who

May 86. (7"/7"sha-pic-d) *<89425> (A 9425/+P)* [16] [ ]
(12"+=/12"w-poster) *(A 9425T/+W)* – ('A'-Collectors mix).

MAY MORNING

aka 'ALBA PAGANA'

1970 (Ita 95m) Mondial Televisione Film

Film genre: psychological drama

Top guns: s-w: Ugo Liberatore (+ dir), George Crowther, Fulvia Gicca

Stars: Alessio Orano *(Valerio Montelli)*, Jane Birkin *(Flora)* ← SEX POWER ← WONDERWALL ← BLOW-UP / → CANNABIS → JE T'AIME MOI NON PLUS, John Steiner *(Roderick Rodney Stanton)* → SHOCK, Micaela Pignatelli *(Amanda)*, Ian Sinclair *(Professor Finlake)*, Rossella Falk *(Mrs. Finley)*

Storyline: Poor Italian student Valerio's attempts to fit in at Oxford just keep going from bad to worse. If only he could drink two pints in half a minute like the others! If only he didn't get caught with the tutor's beautiful daughter! If only his biggest enemy wasn't the daughter's real boyfriend! The final disaster occurs after an orgy of illicit passion when Valerio goes on a boat ride he'll never forget. *JZ*

Movie rating: *5

Visual: dvd (rare)

Off the record: Soundtrack debutantes, the **TREMELOES** had been on the go since 1958, when schoolboy Brian Poole (on vocals & guitar) roped in a few other likeminded lads from Barking, Essex, including rhythm guitarist Alan Blakley, drummer Dave Munden and guitarist Rick Westwood. Having turned pro towards the end of 1961, Brian Poole & The Tremeloes were almost immediately signed up by producer Mike Smith and 'Decca' records, who had the difficulty of choosing between them and a certain Liverpool band. Between the summers of '63 and '65, the quartet notched up a string of UK hits including, 'Twist And Shout', chart-topper 'Do You Love Me', 'Candy Man' & 'Someone, Someone', they even featured in the film. 'JUST FOR FUN' (1963). When Poole chose to take an ill-fated solo career in 1966, the TREMELOES regrouped and decided to carry on, bassist/vocalist Len "Chip" Hawkes (father of CHESNEY HAWKES, incidentally) being an inspired choice of replacement. In 1967, after their comeback single, 'Here Comes My Baby' (penned by Cat Stevens) hit the Top 5, the TREMELOES were back at the top of the charts with 'Silence Is Golden'. For the next two years, they continued to crack the Top 10 via, 'Even The Bad Times Are Good', 'Suddenly You Love Me', 'My Little Lady' and '(Call Me) Number One', all in their eyes, completely saccharine and manufactured. Dissatisfied with their bubblegum pastimes, the TREMELOES looked to further their "rock" credentials, and this was found in low-profile, Italian film, 'Alba Pagana' (i.e. 'MAY MORNING'). *MCS*

—

the TREMELOES (Italian score: Armando Trovajoli)

Nov 00. (cd) *Castle; (<CMRCD 025>)* [ ] [ ]
– May morning / All pull together / Till the sun goes down / Turn on with thee / I can't even breathe down here / May morning (reprise 1) / Anything / Think of what you said / Beer duel / Hard time / I'll take you home / Bunch of rapes / May morning (reprise 2) / I you know.

S/track review: Unissued for three decades, 'MAY MORNING' (recorded in February 1970 and scheduled for that August) was rescued from the vaults by the people at 'Castle' records. Complete with a Mellotron bought from Jeff Lynne (then of Idle Race) – it had been owned by the Beatles during their 'Sgt. Pepper' era – LEN HAWKES, ALAN BLAKLEY, RICK WESTWOOD and DAVE MUNDEN augmenting a new, textured sound to their once bubblegum roots. From the opening lines of the title track, the TREMELOES were indeed a different kettle of fish, although many of the songs are derivative of say, Badfinger, the Moody Blues or even the Small Faces (also example, 'Till The Sun Goes Down'). The swinging sixties had been left behind, or had they? The TREMELOES go 'round the "musical mulberry bush" like Traffic and the Spencer Davis Group did with their compositions from a certain 1968 movie. 'All Pull Together' is a sing-a-long of Beatles-vs-Strawbs variety, and although catchy in most respects, gets somewhat annoying with that Punch & Judy-vox interplay. That effective Mellotron is more evident on a handful of instrumentals, including 'Turn On With Thee', while the one-minute 'I Can't Even Breathe Down Here' (complete with mouth-organ) pre-dates Pink Floyd's 'Seamus' but with the howling dog himself. If you heard 'Anything' for the first time (5 and a bit minutes!), you'd be forgiven if you thought the Moody Blues, although when the harmonies subside into a psychedelic, guitar-vs-Mellotron wig-out in the middle, the mind is indeed . . . blown. 'Think Of What You Said' throws away the "heavy" shackles and returns to the TREMELOES croon-ballad of old. Only for Brian Poole fans here. That 'MORE'/ Pink Floyd-inspiration comes into the equation for 'Hard Time', a post-psychedelic dirge of hair-shaking proportions, just be careful with that wah-wah, Westwood. The Bo Diddley-esque 'I'll Take You Home' and 'Bunch Of Rapes', are effective enough, sort of marking time before a bright and sunny reprise of 'May Morning' floats (or flutes!) out of the speakers. Finale, 'I You Know' (think Beatles again!), completes, for what to many post-psych music fans, is a wee hidden treasure – the TREMELOES' best kept secret! *MCS*

Album rating: *7.5

Curtis MAYFIELD

Born: 3 Jun'42, Chicago, Illinois, USA. Like contemporaries JAMES BROWN and George Clinton, CURTIS MAYFIELD presided over the evolution of post-1950s African American popular music with a visionary talent and an intuitive sense of the music's relationship to cultural, social and political identity. His influence on the development of soul, funk, hip hop and even reggae is incalculable, his back catalogue pretty much unimpeachable. As leader of Chicago soul pioneers the IMPRESSIONS, MAYFIELD proved not only that it was possible for black artists to successfully write and perform their own material, but that it was possible to do it with a sense of dignity and community. As the optimism of the 60s gave way to the harsh realities of the 70s, MAYFIELD again anticipated the mood of the times with the searing funk realism of his debut solo single, '(Don't Worry) If There's A Hell Below We're All Going To Go', telling it like it was but retaining his vision of collective salvation. His unadulterated falsetto, impeccable arrangements and elegant guitar playing inevitably found expression in the burgeoning blaxploitation genre, a platform tailor made for MAYFIELD's conscious soul. His definitive soundtrack to Gordon Parks Jr's 'SUPERFLY' (1972) raised the bar in the wake of landmarks by both MELVIN VAN PEEBLES and ISAAC HAYES, vividly employing his gift for social commentary while sweetening the lyrical realism with a devastating finesse. It was a towering achievement, and one which, in the realm of cinema at least, MAYFIELD subsequently struggled to match. While follow-up, 'SUPERFLY T.N.T.' (1973) furnished him with a cameo role and a co-composing credit (alongside OSIBISA), MAYFIELD only really got stuck into film scoring in the mid-70s, creating musical backdrops for family orientated Afro-American fare like John Berry's 'CLAUDINE' (1974), Sidney Poitier's 'LET'S DO IT AGAIN' (1975) and the soul musical 'SPARKLE' (1976). These three soundtracks were credited to gospel/soul alumini GLADYS KNIGHT & The Pips, the STAPLE SINGERS and ARETHA FRANKLIN respectively. With his superior soundtrack to brutal prison drama, 'SHORT EYES' (1977), however, the man further underlined his talent for expressing the realities of human existence other artists preferred to pass over. Still, after scoring a further Poitier effort, 'a PIECE OF THE ACTION' (1977) – album by MAVIS STAPLES – and making an unlikely appearance in Robert Stigwood's Beatles fiasco, 'SGT. PEPPER'S LONELY HEARTS CLUB BAND' (1978), MAYFIELD chose to concentrate on his regular recording career, only returning to movie work with the inevitable blaxploitation update, 'The Return Of Superfly' (1990). Tragically, he was left paralysed the same year after being struck by a lighting rig at an open air concert, and, while continuing to work while confined to a wheelchair, finally succumbed to cancer on Boxing Day, 1999. *BG*

- **filmography** (composer) –

Superfly *(1972 OST =>)* / **Save The Children** *(1973 {p} =>)* / **Superfly T.N.T.** *(1973 {p} OST by OSIBISA =>)* / **Claudine** *(1974 OST by GLADYS KNIGHT & THE PIPS =>)* / **Let's Do It Again** *(1975 OST by the STAPLE SINGERS =>)* / **Sparkle** *(1976 OST by ARETHA FRANKLIN =>)* / **Short Eyes** *(1977 OST =>)* / **a Piece Of The Action** *(1977 OST by MAVIS STAPLES =>)* / **Sgt. Pepper's Lonely Hearts Club Band** *(1978 {p} =>)* / the Return Of Superfly *(1990 OST w/ V/A; future edition)*

☐ John McENTIRE segment (⇒ REACH THE ROCK)

☐ Brownie McGHEE segment (⇒ BOOK OF NUMBERS)

McVICAR

1980 (UK 99m) Brent Walker PLC (X)

Film genre: crime bio-pic/drama

Top guns: s-w + dir: Tom Clegg → G'OLE! (+ autobiog: John McVicar)

Stars: Roger Daltrey *(John McVicar)* <= the WHO =>, **Adam Faith** *(Walter Probyn)* ← STARDUST, Cheryl Campbell *(Sheila McVicar)* ← CHARIOTS OF FIRE, Steven Berkoff *(Ronnie Harrison)* → ABSOLUTE BEGINNERS → UNDER THE CHERRY MOON, Billy Murray *(Joey Davis)* ← ROCK FOLLIES ← PERFORMANCE ← UP THE JUNCTION ← WHAT A CRAZY WORLD, Ian Hendry *(Hitchens)*, Brian Hall *(Terry Stokes)*, Jeremy Blake *(Ronnie Johnson)*, Peter Jonfield *(Bobby Harris)* → the WALL, Tony Haygarth *(Rabies)* ← PERCY, Leonard Gregory *(Jimmy Collins)*, Georgina Hale *(Kate)*, Michael Feast *(Cody)* → VELVET GOLDMINE, James Marcus *(Sewell)*, David Beames *(policeman)* ← RADIO ON

Storyline: Having busted out of a maximum security prison with sidekick Walter Probyn, notorious train robber John McVicar comes to appreciate his common-law wife and their young son, so much so that he risks recapture with a final, retrial funding bank heist. *BG*

Movie rating: *6

Visual: video + dvd

Off the record: Adam Faith (b. Terence Nelhams, 23 Jun'40, Acton, London, England) was the British equivalent to the late Buddy Holly. Adam's hits kicked off towards the end of the 50s with UK chart-topper, 'What Do You Want', while follow-up, 'Poor Me', trod the same path. He performed two tracks and starred in the 1960 movie, 'Beat Girl' (music by John Barry), while he went on to have a string of Top 30 hits during the first half of the 60s. Adam will always be remembered for his lead role in early 70s TV series, 'Budgie', plus he also starred in rock movie, 'STARDUST' (1974). Adam died of a heart attack on the 8th of March, 2003. *MCS*

ROGER DALTREY

Jul 80. (lp/c) *Polydor; (POLD/+C 5034) <PD.1/.4 6284>* [39] Aug80 [22]
– Bitter and twisted / Just a dream away / Escape (part 1) / White City lights / Free me / My time is gonna come / Waiting for a friend / Escape (part 2) / Without your love / McVicar. *(cd-iss. Apr95; 527341-2)*

S/track review: Coming on the back of nostalgia WHO projects like 'QUADROPHENIA' (1979) and 'The KIDS ARE ALRIGHT' (1979), ROGER DALTREY's pet prison-flick was a more adventurous proposition, the most ambitious solo venture of his career in fact. While solo in name, in reality every WHO member – even new drummer KENNY JONES and tour keyboardist JOHN 'RABBIT' BUNDRICK – pitched in on one track or another. Unlike most of his 70s solo material, it also sounded like the WHO, albeit a WHO on the verge of redundancy. Fascinated by McVicar's life story, DALTREY had bought the rights to the man's book, co-produced the movie, took the lead role and performed most of the soundtrack. He'd also drafted in former Argent guitarist/freelance songslinger RUSS BALLARD, 'War Of The Worlds' mastermind JEFF WAYNE, and onetime Andrew Loog Oldham songwriting protégé BILLY NICHOLS, as well as the likes of HERBIE FLOWERS and DAVE MATTACKS. Fresh from dusting off Rainbow's rock-out classic, 'Since You've Been Gone', BALLARD struggled to match that standard here, coming up with the sub-Ruts bass-rocker, 'My Time Is Gonna Come', and 'Free Me', a horn-charted chugger which edged into the UK Top 40. DALTREY at least gives it the kind of iron-lunged intensity which his role demanded, but his passion is better directed on the bluesier NICHOLS-penned numbers: 'Waiting For A Friend' (ironically the only single which failed to chart), and the ballsy, valedictory title tune. The steely-eyed adonis actually sits out the best bit, a two-part WAYNE-written odyssey called 'Escape', one culled from the same turn-of-the-decade dystopia-electro ghetto as Barry De Vorzon's work on 'The Warriors' (1979). As a proxy final fling, though, DALTREY and Co would perhaps have done better to bow out with 'McVICAR' than 'Face Dances' (1981). *BG*

Album rating: *5.5

– spinoff releases, etc. –

ROGER DALTREY: Free Me / McVicar

Jul 80. (7") *(2001 980) <2105>* [39] Jun80 [53]

ROGER DALTREY: Without Your Love / Escape (part 2)

Sep 80. (7") *<2121>* [–] [20]

ROGER DALTREY: Without Your Love / (non-LP track) / Free Me

Oct 80. (7"m) *(POSP 181)* [55] [–]

ROGER DALTREY: Waiting For A Friend / Bitter And Twisted

Jan 81. (7") *<2153>* [–] [ ]

MEAN JOHNNY BARROWS

1976 (US 89m) Ramana Productions Inc. / Atlas Films (R)

Film genre: crime drama

Top guns: dir: Fred Williamson → ADIOS AMIGO → NO WAY BACK → MR. MEAN / s-w: Jolivett Cato, Charles Walker

Stars: Fred Williamson *(Johnny Barrows)* above + ← BUCKTOWN ← THREE THE HARD WAY ← THREE TOUGH GUYS ← HELL UP IN HARLEM ← the SOUL OF NIGGER CHARLEY ← BLACK CAESAR / → FROM DUSK TILL DAWN → RIDE → CARMEN: A HIP HOPERA, Roddy McDowall *(Tony Da Vinci)* ← ANGEL, ANGEL, DOWN WE GO ← HELLO DOWN THERE ← the COOL ONES / → CLASS OF 1984, Stuart Whitman *(Mario Racconi)* ← HOUND-DOG MAN / → the MONSTER CLUB, Jenny Sherman *(Nancy)*, Luther Adler *(Don Racconi)*, Mike Henry *(Carlo Da Vinci)*, Tony Caruso *(Don Da Vinci)*, R.G. Armstrong *(Richard)* ← PAT GARRETT & BILLY THE KID ← the FINAL COMEDOWN / → WHERE THE BUFFALO ROAM → DICK TRACY, Elliott Gould *(Professor Theodore Rasputin Waterhouse)*

Storyline: Johnny Barrows finds himself on the streets without a job after getting a dishonourable discharge from the army. He finds work in a mafia-run restaurant where gang boss Tony Da Vinci takes an interest in him, as he could be just the man to help him in his latest gang war. Cash-strapped Johnny agrees, but things go wrong when he gets a pizza the action he didn't expect. *JZ*

Movie rating: *3.5

Visual: video (no audio OST – but see below)

Off the record: This is more the fact the soundtrack music was lifted from a certain GORDON STAPLES LP of 1970, we at Strong HQ this was the first ever sampledelic OST; STAPLES would subsequently score 'GORDON'S WAR' a few years later. *MCS*

– associated releases, etc. –

GORDON STAPLES & THE MOTOWN STRINGS: Strung Out

1970. (lp) *Motown <MS 722>* [ ] [–]
– Strung out / Toonie / Sounds of the zodiac / The look of love / Get down / If your love were mine / It's got to be alrighty / From a heart that's true to only you / Someday we'll be together / The April fools.

GORDON STAPLES & THE MOTOWN STRINGS: Strung Out / Sounds Of The Zodiac

1970. (7") *<M 1180>* [ ] [–]

□ MELANIE segment
(⇒ ALL THE RIGHT NOISES)

MELINDA

1972 (US 109m) Metro-Goldwyn-Mayer (R)

Film genre: crime/martial arts drama

Top guns: dir: Hugh A. Robertson / s-w: Lonne Elder III → SOUNDER (au: Raymond Cistheri)

Stars: Calvin Lockhart *(Frankie J. Parker)* ← COTTON COMES TO HARLEM / → LET'S DO IT AGAIN → WILD AT HEART, Rosalind Cash *(Terry Davis)* → CORNBREAD, EARL AND ME → the MONKEY HUSTLE, Vonetta McGee *(Melinda)* → BLACULA → SHAFT IN AFRICA → BROTHERS → REPO MAN, Paul Stevens *(Mitch)*, Ross Hagen *(Gregg Van)* ← SPEEDWAY, Renny Roker *(Dennis Smith)* ← SKIDOO / → BROTHERS, Rockne Tarkington *(Tank)*, Judyann Elder *(Gloria)*, Lonne Elder III *(Lieutenant Daniels)*, Edmund Cambridge *(detective)* ← the FINAL COMEDOWN ← COOL BREEZE / → TROUBLE MAN → FRIDAY FOSTER → BILL & TED'S BOGUS JOURNEY, Jim Kelly *(Charles Atkins)* → BLACK BELT JONES → THREE THE HARD WAY, Jeannie Bell *(Jean)* → TROUBLE MAN → THREE THE HARD WAY → DISCO 9000, Earl Maynard *(member of karate group)* → BLACK BELT JONES → TRUCK TURNER

Storyline: Silver-tongued, kung-fu fighting DJ, Frankie J Parker, finds his titular girlfriend slain in his own apartment after a whirlwind romance, apparently targeted for her inside knowledge of a gangland hit. In the frame for her murder, he enlists the generous help of Terry, one of his past conquests, and sets out to nail the real killers. *BG*

Movie rating: *5.5

Visual: none

Off the record: JERRY PETERS (see below)

JERRY BUTLER / JERRY PETERS

1972. (lp) *Pride-MGM; <PRD 0006ST>* [ ] [–]
– Speak truth to the people (Frankie's theme) / Melinda – title theme / Part III / Tank's theme / Love is / Melinda – Latino / I can't let you go / The blues (dope pusher's theme) / Music for Tank's boat / Melinda – reprise.

S/track review: Although he entered film before Impressions' partner Curtis Mayfield, JERRY BUTLER's association with blaxploitation was relatively brief, reaching its zenith on this 1972 soundtrack, the same year his post-Gamble/Huff songwriting workshop generated the soul classic, 'Ain't Understanding Mellow'. Having already proved himself with contributions to John G. Avildsen thriller, 'JOE' (1970), BUTLER – in tandem with fellow producer/writer/arranger JERRY PETERS (a man whose credits number Marvin Gaye, Al Green, Herbie Hancock, Earth, Wind & Fire and Gladys Knight amongst others) – was given free rein to write and produce a whole album. It's a memorable pairing, and the two Jerrys aren't fazed by the directorial pedigree, Hugh A. Robertson being the Oscar-nominated editor of both 'MIDNIGHT COWBOY' and 'SHAFT'. Left to their own devices, they map out symphonic soul arrangements as silky, sophisticated and ultimately aspirational as Mayfield's, with an uncredited troupe of female backing singers lending gossamer-hosanna'd class to both the crème-café title theme and BUTLER's declamatory, sitar-tuned opening, 'Speak Truth To The People (Frankie's Theme)'. The ratio of vocals to instrumentals is surprisingly high for a blaxploitation record, yet some of 'MELINDA's best material is incidental, and the almost wholly vocal-free side two is uniformly compelling; BUTLER and PETERS configure a jazzier, less conspicuously Latino vision of War's 'Low Rider' ('I Can't Let You Go'), drowned in Fender Rhodes so deep you can't hear the bottom. Their pièce de résistance, though, is the cinematic, soul-psychedelic amplification of 'Frankie's Theme', prioritising and magnifying the sitar part (one which made an unlikely resurfacing in 80s pop), braking and accelerating the brass/string arrangements and fading the whole thing out in a haze of sustain and wailing souls. A fine blues motif ('Dope Pusher's Theme') and an epic slab of cauterised, clavinet-clucking chitlin' funk ('Part III') fill out a project more consistent and less indulgent than most of BUTLER's early-70s solo albums. Given the man's contributions to the soul canon – and his latter-day efforts in black music custodianship – ain't it a shame (travesty?) that neither 'JOE' nor 'MELINDA' have had a whiff of CD action. *BG*

Album rating: *7

MELODY

1971 (UK 103m) Hemdale Group / British Lion Film Corporation (A)

Film genre: children's romantic drama

Top guns: dir: Waris Hussein / s-w: Alan Parker → EVITA

Stars: Mark Lester *(Daniel)*, Tracy Hyde *(Melody)*, Jack Wild *(Ornshaw)* → PIED PIPER, Sheila Steafel *(Mrs. Latimer)* ← PERCY / → NEVER TOO YOUNG TO ROCK, Roy Kinnear *(Mr. Perkins)* ← HELP! / → PIED PIPER, Peter Walton *(Fensham)*, **John Gorman** *(Boys' Brigade captain)* → the MUSIC MACHINE, James Cossins *(headmaster)* ← PRIVILEGE, Kate Williams *(Mrs. Perkins)* → QUADROPHENIA, Neil Hallett *(man in hospital on TV)* ← GROUPIE GIRL

Storyline: Daniel and Melody are desperately in love and make heartfelt plans to get married; the only problem is that they're both ten years old. Unsurprisingly, their parents and even their friends aren't too impressed with all this although the happy couple remain undaunted. *BG*

Movie rating: *7

Visual: none

Off the record: John Gorman was one of the Scaffold, a trio of novelty-pop singers from Liverpool who had hits with 'Thank U Very Much' & 'Lily The Pink' in the flower-power-era 60s. *MCS*

—

the BEE GEES (score: Richard Hewson)

Jun 71. (lp) *Polydor; (2383 043) Atco; <SD33 363>* ☐ ☐
– In the morning / In the morning (reprise) / Melody fair / Melody fair (reprise) / Spicks and specks / Romance theme in F / Give your best / To love somebody / Working on it night and day / First of May / First of May (reprise) / Seaside banjo / Teachers chase / Teach your children (CROSBY, STILLS, NASH & YOUNG). *<cd-iss. 2002 in Japan'; POCP 2007>*

S/track review: The film's relative obscurity ensures that many people are unaware the BEE GEES actually had a soundtrack life before 'SATURDAY NIGHT FEVER', but here it is in all its 'Odessa'-period glory. While the likes of 'Melody Fair', 'First Of May' and 'To Love Somebody' were nothing fans hadn't heard before, the real draw of this soundtrack is still the one-off recording of the gorgeous 'In The Morning', BARRY GIBB's crowning glory and a song which had already been the subject of a stunning cover by Nina Simone. The remainder of the album includes pleasant orchestrations courtesy of Richard Hewson, a school choir version of 'Spicks And Specks' and the cheesily selected 'Teach Your Children' by CROSBY, STILLS, NASH & YOUNG. *BG*

Album rating: *6.5

☐ MERCURY REV segment
(⇒ BYE BYE BLACKBIRD)

Stephin MERRITT

Born: 1966, Canada. Singer-songwriter, producer and movie soundtrack composer, MERRITT is essentially the Magnetic Fields. Beginning recording in his teens, MERRITT didn't issue anything until his mid-twenties when, with help from fellow bandmates/ contributors Susan Amway, Claudia Gonson and Sam Davol, he recorded the electro-lo-fi indie pop album 'Magnetic Fields', which was to set the ball rolling for further releases such as 'New Despair' (1997) and the acclaimed '69 Love Songs' (1999). This prolific artist also formed an indie supergroup named the 6ths, with MERRITT taking a backseat this time rather than being at the forefront of all the action. More recently, as well as issuing music under the moniker of the Future Bible Heroes, MERRITT completed the Magnetic Fields' follow-up, simply entitled 'I' (2004). His first excursion into movie soundtrack making, saw him provide the score for 2000s difficult psychological gay drama 'EBAN AND CHARLEY' and 2003's Oscar-nominated urban comedy 'PIECES OF APRIL' (2003). No doubt there'll be more to come. *AS*

- **filmography** (composer) –

Eban And Charley *(2000 OST =>)* / **Pieces Of April** *(2003 OST =>)* / Tarnation *(2003 score w/ John Califra & Max Avery Lichtenstein)*

la METAMORPHOSE DES CLOPORTES

1965 (Fra/Ita 102m b&w) Les Films du Siecle (R)

Film genre: crime caper/thriller

Top guns: dir: Pierre Granier-Deferre / s-w: Michel Audiard, Albert Simonin (au: Alphonse Boudard)

Stars: Lino Ventura *(Alphonse Marechal)*, **Charles Aznavour** *(Edmond)* → CANDY, Irina Demick *(Catherine Verdier)*, Maurice Biraud *(Arthur)*, Georges Geret *(Rouquemonte)*, Pierre Brasseur *(Tonton)*, Francoise Rosay *(Gertrude)*

Storyline: Against his better judgement and only because he needs the cash, worldly criminal Alphonse Marechal is drawn into an art heist by a motley crew of petty associates. His worst fears are realised when the job is botched and he ends up going down for five years. Upon his release, he begins wreaking inevitable revenge on the "cloportes" – or creeps, in French slang – who let him down. *BG*

Movie rating: *6

Visual: none

Off the record: **JIMMY SMITH** (see below)

—

JIMMY SMITH

Oct 65. (lp) *Verve; (511 102)* [–] French [–]
– Blues pour Alphonse / Generique / Ballade pour un cloporte / Melodie pour Catherine / Theme pour Alphonse / Angoisse – Race track blues / Melodie pour Catherine (version 2) / Love theme / Requiem pour un cloporte / Generique (version 2). *(cd-iss. Nov02 & Mar05 on 'Universal'+=; 017186-2)* – JIMMY SMITH interprete . . .:- Melodie en Sous Sol (Any Number Can Win) / Les Felins (theme from Joy House) / Mission Impossible / Goldfinger / L'homme au Bras d'Or (The Man With The Golden Arm).

S/track review: The late Hammond legend JIMMY SMITH reinvented a fair few film themes in his time, but he only cut one original soundtrack. That it was for a French B-movie parody was par for the course (he later wrote a song for Gallic screen icon Alain Delon, entitled 'Delon's Blues'). A man with an organ fetish, director Pierre Granier-Deferre sensed that he could squeeze Twentieth Century Fox for the best player in Christendom. After broaching the subject at dinner with cigar-chewing Fox czar Darryl Zanuck, Granier-Deferre clocked Zanuck haranguing his secretary with the words he was so desperate to hear: "Hire Jimmy Smith for me!" Together with longtime guitarist QUENTIN WARREN and drummer BILLY HART, SMITH flew to Paris and improvised the soundtrack in a single night, working from the movement of the film rather than the dialogue. The music laid down in those wee small hours comprises SMITH's most obscure material, only reissued by 'Universal France' in 2002. It's also of historic interest in that – presumably down to logistical and financial considerations rather than purely creative ones – it goes against the grain of what he was doing at the time domestically. Having moved from 'Blue Note' to 'Verve' in 1963, the godfather of soul jazz was increasingly operating in a big band format behind arrangers like Lalo Schifrin and Oliver Nelson. Stripped down to a starker trio format, SMITH is necessarily more guarded and impressionistic here than on those small-combo classics of yore, but his playing is just as fiercely articulate. Interviewed in the sleevenotes, Granier-Deferre admits to the confounding of his expectations: "I was expecting a sharp sound from his electric organ, like Audiard's dialogues. The outcome was that he gave me speed, and tenderness, but not sharpness". He can't have been too disappointed; SMITH and his sidemen are dynamic enough to trace the nuances of pace and emotion on more dramatically weighted cues like 'Générique' and 'Thème Pour Alphonse', even if they can't understand the dialogue, and, even if they're not sharp, his heaving vamps are all the more explosive when he dives into them unexpectedly. And while SMITH flexes that famous right hand to great effect on opener 'Blues Pour Alphonse', fans of his bluesier, free-flowing jams material may find themselves frustrated by the record's preponderance of martial snare, walking-on-eggshells tension and erratic tempos. It's nevertheless fascinating to hear him nudging towards the avant-garde at times; not least in 'Requiem Pour Un Cloporte', where he wrenches some truly evil-sounding splurges from his Hammond. The inclusion – as bonus cuts – of the man's rollicking interpretations of themes to the likes of 'Mélodie En Sous Sol', 'Mission Impossible' and 'Les Félins' serve to highlight the stylistic disparity between the low-key compositions here and the film-related work he was cutting for 'Verve', and prove that he could handle both with the finesse that subsequently saw him nicknamed "The Cat". *BG*

Album rating: *6.5

METROLAND

1997 (UK/Fra/Spa 105m) BBC / Canal+ / Pandora Cinema (18)

Film genre: domestic/romantic comedy/drama (18)

Top guns: dir: Philip Saville / s-w: Adrian Hodges (au: Julian Barnes)

Stars: Christian Bale *(Chris)* → VELVET GOLDMINE → LAUREL CANYON → I'M NOT THERE, Lee Ross *(Toni)*, Emily Watson *(Marion)* → the PROPOSITION, Elsa Zylberstein *(Annick)*, Rufus *(Henri)*, Jonathan Aris *(Dave)*, Amanda Ryan *(Joanna)*, Ifan Meredith *(Mickey)*, John Wood *(retired commuter)*

Storyline: Bored daydreamer Chris sees the railway lines of life reach a junction when his old buddy Toni reappears after ten long years. While Chris has married and settled down, Toni has played the field around the world, reminding Chris of the good old days of revolutionary 1960s Paris. However, his wife Marion is not about to let him fly off into the sunset, and Chris must decide whether to stay in his safe, boring existence or jump off the rails once more. *JZ*

Movie rating: *6.5

Visual: video + dvd

Off the record: (see below)

—

MARK KNOPFLER (*) (& Various Artists)

May 98. (cd/c) *Mercury; (536912-2/-4) Warners; <47006>* ☐ Mar99 ☐
– Metroland theme (instrumental *) / Annick (*) / Tous les garcons et les filles (FRANCOISE HARDY) / Brats (*) / Blues Clair (DJANGO REINHARDT) / Down day (*) / A walk in Paris (*) / She's gone (*) / Minor swing (DJANGO REINHARDT AND THE QUINTETTE) / Du hot club de France (MINOR SWING) / Peaches (the STRANGLERS) / Sultans of swing (DIRE STRAITS) * / So you win again (HOT CHOCOLATE) / Alison (ELVIS COSTELLO) / Metroland (*).

S/track review: Fifteen years on from the triumphant faux-Celtic anthem of Local Hero, and it's surprising how little has changed. Dire Straits' unfocused wanderings were finally abandoned in 1995 (nearly a decade after their heyday) with MARK KNOPFLER vowing to concentrate on solo work and soundtracks. And this 1998 fable of thirty-something romantic crisis gives a fair demonstration of the Scots-born guitarist's continuing strengths and weaknesses. It would be harsh to demand cohesion from the music of a story that flits between the late 60s and late seventies, London and Paris, and the 14 tracks broadly divide into three categories. There is impeccably-chosen period pop (including ELVIS COSTELLO's poignant 'Alison', the STRANGLERS and the lovely FRANCOIS HARDY). Most pleasingly, the soundtrack stretches the timeframe to include DJANGO REINHARDT and STEPHANE GRAPPELLI, and KNOPFLER's own uncontestably-terrific DIRE STRAITS classic 'Sultans of Swing'. It also indulges the composer's flair for pastiche (remember 'Walk of Life'?), and he has fun with a perky bit of easy-listening jazz and a 'Wipeout'-style dance tune complete with manic cackling at the start of every chorus. Then there are a couple of new tracks (and a couple of fragments) featuring the full-blown and instantly recognisable KNOPFLER Thing, whose keyboard washes, lush-toned guitar and folky cadences are atmospheric and effective, if familiar. The main theme works a good deal better with soprano sax than with the singer's smoky, approximate vocal, but there's nothing here to change MARK KNOPFLER's enduring status as the thinking listener's Hank Marvin. *ND*

Album rating: *5.5

MIDDLE OF THE MOMENT

1995 (Swiss/Ger 80m b&w) Look Now! / Zorro Film

Film genre: people & places documentary

Top guns: dir: (+ s-w) Nicolas Humbert ← STEP ACROSS THE BORDER, Werner Penzel ← STEP ACROSS THE BORDER

Stars: Robert Lax *(performer)*, Sandra M'Bow *(performer)*, Aghail Ag Rhissa *(performer)*, Mutu Walat Rhabidine *(performer)*, Cirque O *(performers)*

Storyline: Clips from a two-year circumnavigation of the Northern Sahara form the basis of this "cinepoem". Its directors travelled the sands along with a French circus and an American poet/thinker, Robert Lax. Together they visited the settlements of the nomadic Tuareg and brought a small oasis of Western society to them. *JZ*

Movie rating: *7

Visual: video + dvd (2003)

Off the record: (see below)

—

FRED FRITH

1996. (cd) *RecRec; <ReR 14717>* [ ] [–]
– Le jour se leve / Moving / Digging for water / Portrait – Tam-Tam in Timia / Le cirque / Robert Lax is / Gnawa express Tanger / Bell song / Portrait II / Ghost stories / Portes ouvertes / Le cirque-oh! – Ghost dance – Portrait III / Le jour s'arrache / Middle of the moment (title theme). *<re-iss. Jun04 on 'Fred'; FRO 05>*

S/track review: Former Henry Cow stalwart, FRED FRITH, didn't just compose and arrange his avant-rock style of music, he virtually redesigned it to accompany any of his diverse projects. 'MIDDLE OF THE MOMENT' has many of the FRITH traits: stirring fretwork and ethnic ambience (North Africa comes under the spotlight here). The multi-talented/multi-instrumentalist FRITH is joined by TIM HODGKINSON on wind, MIKAELA DIETL and FABRIZIO APPELIUS on acerbic accordion, and, of course, the voices of the film's own poets ROBERT LAX and SANDRA M'BOW. Sampling the gorgeous throaty chords of a young native girl on 'Digging For Water', FRITH transgresses his musical routes straight from the start, while other field recordings of the roaming Tuareg people (IDAMIN WALAT AKHMUDAN, TSHANAK AG ABALBAL and the women from the Kel Iforas tribe) come into their own later on. CIRQUE O (JOSEFINA LEHMANN on violin, JOHANN LE GUILLERM on accordion & voice, ATTILA ZOMBORI on drums, percussion & guimbarde and BERTRAND DUVA on Tibetan rattles) also have a say in this hour-long soundtrack courtesy of 'Le Cirque', 'Le Cirque-oh! . . .'. If you want to hear Captain Beefheart-like African rhythms, best try out the 'Gnawa Express Tanger' & 'Portes Ouvertes', while the title theme finale showcases the accordion. Weird, but wonderful. *MCS*

Album rating: *7

MIDNIGHT COWBOY

1969 (US 113m w/b&w) United Artists (X)

Film genre: urban drama

Top guns: dir: John Schlesinger / s-w: Waldo Salt (au: James Leo Herlihy)

Stars: Jon Voight *(Joe Buck)* → DELIVERANCE, Dustin Hoffman *(Enrico "Ratso" Rizzo)* ← the GRADUATE / → LITTLE BIG MAN → the POINT! → WHO IS HARRY KELLERMAN AND WHY IS HE SAYING THOSE TERRIBLE THINGS ABOUT ME? → DICK TRACY → WAG THE DOG, Brenda Vaccaro *(Shirley)*, Sylvia Miles *(Cass)*, Barnard Hughes *(Towny)*, John McGiver *(O'Daniel)*, Ruth White *(Sally Buck)* ← CHARLY, Bob Balaban *(New York student)* → the STRAWBERRY STATEMENT, Paul Benjamin *(New York bartender)* → ACROSS 110th STREET → the EDUCATION OF SONNY CARSON → FRIDAY FOSTER → LEADBELLY → the FIVE HEARTBEATS, M. Emmet Walsh *(bus passenger)* → ALICE'S RESTAURANT → LITTLE BIG MAN → BOUND FOR GLORY → BLADE RUNNER → CATCH ME IF YOU CAN → ALBINO ALLIGATOR

Storyline: Would-be gigolo Joe Buck gets less than he bargained for after heading to New York to launch his career. On the skids, he winds up sharing a grim apartment with tubercular conman, Rico 'Ratso' Rizzo. An unlikely friendship blossoms, with Joe even taking a male client to help Rizzo realise his dreams. *BG*

Movie rating: *10

Visual: video + dvd

Off the record: Acid-rockers, **ELEPHANTS MEMORY**, were formed in New York City (East Village) in 1967, and for a time their original vocalist was CARLY SIMON. In 1969, with fresh female singer, Michal Shapiro, the ensemble of Zappa-influenced musicians (Shapiro, Stan Bronstein, Richard Sussman, Rick Frank, Richard Ayers, John Ward, Myron Yules, etc.) pieced together an eponymous debut LP in 1969. A sophomore album, 'Take It To The Streets' (1970) and a lucrative connection with JOHN LENNON on his 'Sometime In New York City' ensured their name was in lights for a short time; further LPs for 'Apple' ('Elephant's Memory') and 'R.C.A.' ('Angels Forever') had taken it a bit too far for many critics. *MCS*

——

Various Artists (score: JOHN BARRY *)

Jul 69. (lp) *United Artists; <5198> (UAS 29043)* [19] Dec69 [ ]
– Everybody's talkin' (NILSSON) / Joe Buck rides again (*) / A famous myth (the GROOP) / Fun city (*) / He quit me (LESLIE MILLER) / Jungle gym at the zoo (ELEPHANTS MEMORY) / Midnight cowboy (*) / Old man willow (ELEPHANTS MEMORY) / Florida fantasy (*) / Tears and joys (the GROOP) / Science fiction (*) / Everybody's talkin' (NILSSON). *(re-iss. Oct80 on 'Liberty'; LBR 1036) (cd-iss. Sep88 on 'E.M.I.'; CDP 748409-2) <cd-iss. 1989 on 'EMI America'; 48409> (cd re-iss. Jun96 on 'Premier'; PRMCD 6) (lp re-iss. Dec99 on 'Simply Vinyl'; SVLP 150)*

S/track review: One of the 60s best soundtracks, with an indelible combination of JOHN BARRY score and obscure rock, pop and psychedelia. BARRY's harmonica/acoustic guitar-fronted orchestrations – best heard on the galloping 'Joe Buck Rides Again' and the dreamy, drifting title theme – honour the film's seedy urban setting with the spirit of the Old West, while the inspired whimsy that is 'Florida Fantasy' ranks among the composer's most compelling oddities. It was NILSSON's (Fred Neil-penned) escapist eulogy, 'Everybody's Talkin', which became the movie's much covered calling card, however, included here in both its single version and as an abridged, harmonica-heavy coda. Elsewhere, the GROOP's weightless 'A Famous Myth' and the 7-minute+ jazz-rock psych-out of 'Old Man Willow' by ELEPHANTS MEMORY keep things interesting. Incidentally, the latter band were given full credit on a misleading re-issue on Neil Bogart's 'Buddah' records, which actually combined most of the band's 1969 debut set for the label with some songs (and re-vamped versions of 'Everybody's Talkin'' & 'Midnight Cowboy') from the movie. *BG & MCS*

Album rating: *7.5

– spinoff hits, etc. –

NILSSON: Everybody's Talkin'

Aug 69. (7") *RCA Victor; <0161> R.C.A.; (1876)* [6] Sep69 [23]

JOHN BARRY: Midnight Cowboy / Fun City

Aug 69. (7") *C.B.S.; (CBS 4448)* [ ] [ ]

FERRANTE & TEICHER: Midnight Cowboy

Oct 69. (7") *<50554> (UP 35050)* [10] [ ]

ELEPHANTS MEMORY: songs from Midnight Cowboy

Nov 69. (lp) *Buddah; <BDS 5038>* [ ] [–]
– Everybody's talkin' / Old man Willow / Midnight cowboy / Jungle gym at the zoo / Crossroads of the stepping stones / Don't put me on trial no more / Super heep / R.I.P. / Yogurt song / Band of love / Takin' a walk. *<cd-iss. Jun06 on 'Lemon'+=; 86>* – Hot dog man / Brief encounter.

MIDNIGHT COWBOY SOUNDTRACK: Midnight Cowboy / Fun City

Oct 80. (7") *(UP 634)* [–] [47]

– other bits & pieces, etc. –

the BEAUTIFUL SOUTH: Everybody's Talkin'

May 94. (7"/c-s/cd-s) *Go! Discs; (GOD/+MC/CD 113)* [–] [12]

MIKE'S MURDER

1984 (US 97m) Warner Bros. Pictures (R)

Film genre: crime drama

Top guns: s-w + dir: James Bridges ← URBAN COWBOY

Stars: Debra Winger *(Betty Parrish)* ← URBAN COWBOY ← THANK GOD IT'S FRIDAY, Mark Keyloun *(Mike)*, Darrell Larson *(Pete)*, Brooke Alderson *(Patty)* ← URBAN COWBOY, Paul Winfield *(Phillip)* ← a HERO AIN'T NOTHIN' BUT A SANDWICH ← GORDON'S WAR ← TROUBLE MAN ← SOUNDER / → BLUE CITY, Daniel Shor *(Richard)* → BILL &

TED'S EXCELLENT ADVENTURE → ELVIS AND THE COLONEL: THE UNTOLD STORY, Mark Brandon *(Ben)* → SWEETWATER: A TRUE ROCK STORY

Storyline: Betty Parrish is a bank-teller whose conventional life is turned upside down when her bisexual, drug dealing (and pro-tennis playing!) boyfriend is taken out by hit-men working for an L.A. big cheese. *BG*

Movie rating: *5.5

Visual: video

Off the record: Songs shelved:- 'Without You' (CHAZ JANKEL), 'Out Of The Business' (the TUBES), 'It's A Beautiful World' (DEVO), 'Get Down On It' (KOOL & THE GANG), 'Rebels Rule' (the STRAY CATS), 'Big Bird' (the B-52's) and 'L.A.C.A.' (ADAM'S/SHERMAN'S ALIAS). *MCS*

JOE JACKSON

Sep 83. (lp/c) *A&M; <SP/CS 4931> (AMLH/CAM 64931)* [64] [ ]
– Cosmopolitan / 1-2-3- go (this town's a fairground) / Laundromat Monday / Memphis / Moonlight / Zemeo / Breakdown / Moonlight theme.

S/track review: This probably wasn't a gratifying experience for JACKSON: when the much-revised movie eventually hit the streets long after the soundtrack, the bulk of the New Wave star's debut score had been replaced by the music of (the frankly more experienced) John Barry. And it's tempting to suggest that only diehard JOE JACKSON fans will prefer the angular contribution recorded here. The singer for whom JACKSON writes his vaulting, undeniably melodic cadences rarely sounds like he should be the composer himself; JACKSON's voice is most assured when he is sneering, and the in-your-face, shouty songs – suffused with parping keyboards and the spasmic bass of his hit 'Steppin' Out' (which was recorded the same year) – might work on a pop album, but surely jar in the cinema. Straying from the formula, 'Moonlight's gentle balladry serves to remind that JACKSON is no crooner. The second side of the album, by contrast, delivers three disciplined, atmospheric instrumentals much better suited to the job. Nothing groundbreaking, but 'Zemeo's understated jazzy development and authoritative execution is a deal more diverting than any of the braying songs. *ND*

Album rating: *5.5

– spinoff releases, etc. –

JOE JACKSON: Cosmopolitan / Breakdown
Aug 83. (7") *(AM 134)* [–] [ ]

JOE JACKSON: Memphis / Breakdown
Nov 83. (7") *<2601>* [85] [–]

MILANO CALIBRO 9

1972 (Ita 100m) Alpherat S.p.a. (18)

Film genre: crime/gangster thriller

Top guns: dir + s-w: Fernando Di Leo (+ story) (au: Giorgio Scerbanenco)

Stars: Gastone Moschin *(Ugo Piazza)*, Barbara Bouchet *(Nelly Bordon)*, Mario Adorf *(Rocco Musco)*, Frank Wolff *(police commissioner)*, Ivo Garrani *(Don Vincenzo)*, Luigi Pistilli *(Mercuri)*, Philippe Leroy *(Chino)*, Lionel Stander *(Americano)*, Mario Novelli *(Pasquale Tallarico)*

Storyline: Ugo Piazza is released from prison to find himself in the middle of some unwanted attention from his psychotic former gangster boss Rocco and the police, who are in the mind the ex-con has $300,000 of American drug baron money. *MCS*

Movie rating: *7.5

Visual: video + dvd

Off the record: OSANNA (see below)

OSANNA & LUIS E. BACALOV

1972. (lp) *Cosmo; (PILPS 9001)* [–] USA [–]
– Preludio / Tema / Variazione I (To Plinius) / Variazione II (My mind flies) / Variazione III (Shuum ...) / Variazione IV (Tredicesimo cortile) / Variazione V (Dianalogo) / Variazione VI (Spunti dallo spartito n. 14723/EY2 del Prof. Imolo Meninge) / Variazione VII (Posizione raggiunta) / Canzona (There will be time). *(cd-iss. Jun04 on Japanese 'Disk Union'; 7060)*

S/track review: Five years before Prog-rock counterparts Goblin scored their first of many scores, Italians OSANNA (who'd previously issued 'L'Uomo' in 1971 from their home base in Naples) were pioneers of the continental OST. Commissioned alongside prolific Argentina-born scoresmith, LUIS ENRIQUEZ BACALOV (who co-wrote 3 of the cues), OSANNA cut the set at the Fonorama Studios in Rome. Messrs DANILO RUSTICI, ELIO D'ANNA (on sax), LELLO BRANDI, LINO VAIRETTI and subsequent Goblin musician MASSIMO GUARINO, brought Prog-rock to the sunny Med via this splendid set of mostly short instrumental pieces. Opener 'Preludio' and follow-on track 'Tema', combine the orchestral work of BACALOV with subtle string and ARP 2600/ piano tones by OSANNA – very "space-age" neo-classical. If there are any comparisons, Brit-Prog-rock counterparts King Crimson, Van Der Graaf Generator, Pink Floyd, Jethro Tull and Colosseum would be the strongest. Vocals are in short supply, English being their chosen language on the likes of closing number, 'Canzona (There Will Be Time)', while the rest of the instrumental tracks are made up of 'Variazione' (I-VII). In 2004, the record was finally delivered in a glorious CD package, complete with a 12-page booklet. OSANNA went on to release three more studio sets, 'Palepoli' (1973), 'Landscape Of Life' (1974 US-only) and 'Suddance' (1978); in July 2006, they performed alongside Carl Palmer in a concert at Afragola. *MCS*

Album rating: *7

the MILLION DOLLAR HOTEL

2000 (Ger/US 122m) Icon / Road Movies / Kintop Pictures (R)

Film genre: cop/detective mystery

Top guns: dir: Wim Wenders ← BUENA VISTA SOCIAL CLUB ← TEATRO ← the END OF VIOLENCE ← PARIS, TEXAS / → the SOUL OF A MAN / s-w: Nicholas Klein ← the END OF VIOLENCE (+ story w/ Bono)

Stars: Milla Jovovich *(Eloise)* ← HE GOT GAME, Jeremy Davies *(Tom Tom)* ← RAVENOUS, Mel Gibson *(Detective Skinner)* → the SINGING DETECTIVE, Jimmy Smits *(Geronimo)*, Peter Stormare *(Dixie)* → DANCER IN THE DARK, Amanda Plummer *(Vivien)* ← PULP FICTION, Gloria Stuart *(Jessica)*, Tom Bower *(Hector)* ← a SLIPPING-DOWN LIFE, Donal Logue *(Charley Best)* ← FIRST LOVE, LAST RITES ← MEDUSA: DARE TO BE TRUTHFUL, Bud Cort *(Shorty)* ← SOUTH OF HEAVEN, WEST OF HELL ← ELECTRIC DREAMS ← HAROLD AND MAUDE ← GAS-S-S-S! ← BREWSTER McCLOUD ← the STRAWBERRY STATEMENT / → COYOTE UGLY → the LIFE AQUATIC WITH STEVE ZISSOU, Julian Sands *(Terence Scopey)* ← SIESTA ← GOTHIC ← the KILLING FIELDS, Harris Yulin *(Stanley Goldkiss)* → CHELSEA WALLS / ← CANDY MOUNTAIN ← GOOD TO GO, Tim Roth *(Izzy Goldkiss)* ← FOUR ROOMS ← PULP FICTION ← RESERVOIR DOGS ← RETURN TO WATERLOO, **Richard Edson** *(Joe)* ← STRANGE DAYS ← WHAT ABOUT ME ← TOUGHER THAN LEATHER ← GOOD MORNING, VIETNAM ← WALKER ← HOWARD THE DUCK / → SOUTHLANDER, Charlayne Woodard *(Jean Swift)* ← HAIR, Conrad Roberts *(Stix)* ← MAN ON THE MOON, **Bono** *(man in hotel lobby)* <= U2 =>, **Tito Larriva** *(Jesu)* ← FROM DUSK TILL DAWN ← ROAD HOUSE ← TRUE STORIES, **Jon Hassell** *(Hollow)*

Storyline: The usual Wenders-sponsored parade of beautiful losers people this L.A.-set tale, ostensibly a murder mystery focusing on FBI man Skinner's investigations into the suicide of a slumming artist, Izzy Goldkiss, who jumped to his death from the roof of the flophouse hotel which forms the movie's backdrop. *BG*

Movie rating: *5.5

Visual: video + dvd

Off the record: **Jon Hassell** (see below)

Various (composers: BRIAN ENO, DANIEL LANOIS & JON HASSELL)

Mar 00. (cd) *Interscope; <542395> Island; (CID 8094)* ☐ 13
– The ground beneath her feet (U2 with DANIEL LANOIS) / Never let me go (BONO & the MDH BAND) / Stateless (U2) / Satellite of love (MILLA JOVOVICH & the MDH BAND) / Falling at your feet (BONO & DANIEL LANOIS) / Tom Tom's dream (MDH BAND) / The first time (U2) / Bathtub (MDH BAND) / The first time – reprise (DANIEL LANOIS & the MDH BAND) / Tom Tom's room (BRAD MEHLDAU with BILL FRISELL) / Funny face (MDH BAND) / Dancin' shoes (BONO & the MDH BAND) / Amsterdam blue (cortege) (JON HASSELL, GREGG ARREGUIN, JAMIE MUHOBERAT & PETER FREEMAN) / Satellite of love – reprise (MDH BAND featuring DANIEL LANOIS, BILL FRISELL & GREG COHEN) / Satellite of love – Danny Saber remix (MILLA JOVOVICH with JON HASSELL & DANNY SABER) / Anarchy in the USA (TITO LARRIVA & the MDH BAND).

S/track review: Rather than his usual selection of specially commissioned cuts, director Wim Wenders assembled a supergroup of his favourite musicians and named them after his film. Consisting of BONO, DANIEL LANOIS, JON HASSELL, BRIAN ENO, jazz guitarist BILL FRISELL and lesser known names Greg Cohen, Brian Blade and Adam Dorn, the MDH band – in various permutations – achieved a level of continuity and cohesiveness perhaps absent from Wenders' soundtracks in the past. Unlike most supergroups, this egg-head aggregate also sounded pretty much the sum of its parts, although with BONO and U2 exerting the biggest influence, much of the album bore the rarefied fingerprint of the long-standing U2/ENO/LANOIS axis, from 'The Unforgettable Fire' onwards – 'The Ground Beneath Her Feet' (lyrics courtesy of Salman Rushdie) and especially the mantra-like 'Falling At Your Feet' are the kind of luminous meditations BONO and Co once specialised in but which have been conspicuous by their absence from their increasingly pedestrian studio albums. The instrumental interludes were given over to the jazzier impulses of FRISELL and HASSELL; in contrast to his more dissonant work with Ry Cooder, HASSELL's dreamy, diaphanous trumpet illuminated an imaginative cover of Lou Reed's 'Satellite Of Love' (with actress/supermodel Milla Jovovich showcasing her best Macy Gray impression) and lent his own 'Tom Tom's Dream' an authentic period charm. Even Jovovich's "beaver" dialogue excerpt was blessed with a chimerical ambience, an atmosphere gleefully shattered by a Spanish-language cover of the Sex Pistols' 'Anarchy In The UK' (with UK substituted by USA, duh!). Programme this out and you've got a soundtrack which remains the best proxy U2 album of the millennium so far. *BG*

Album rating: *7.5

the MINX

1969 (US 84m) Cambist Films

Film genre: cop/detective mystery or sexploitation flick

Top guns: s-w: Raymond Jacobs (+ dir), Herbert Jaffey

Stars: Jan Sterling *(Louise Baxter)*, Michael Beirne *(John Lawson)*, Robert Rodan *(Henry Baxter)*, William Gleason *(Detective Burke)*, Ned Cary *(Benjamin Thayer)*, Shirley Parker *(Terry)*, Adrienne Jalbert *(Nicole)*

Storyline: The Minx – plural, not singular – are a trio of good time girls with a difference, hired by corporate big wigs for their skill in sniffing out the competition's secrets. Contracted by John Lawson, their mission is to foil a takeover bid masterminded by his swaggering brother-in-law Henry Baxter, installed at the head of the family firm through marriage. *BG*

Movie rating: *4

Visual: none

Off the record: The **CYRKLE** (see below)

the CYRKLE

1970. (lp) *Amsterdam; <AMS 12007>* ☐ –
– Squeeze play / The Minx (vocal) / Murray the why / The rigging / The party / Nicole / It's a lovely game, Louise / The Minx (instrumental) / Something special / On the road / Walter's riff / The chase. *<(cd-iss. Mar03 on 'Sundazed'+=; SC 11106)>* – Terry's theme / Something special (alt. instr.) / Kites / Squeeze play (film version) / Murray the why (film version) / Nicole (film version) / Baxter's dangerous game / Terry's escape.

S/track review: Had 'The MINX' been released in the 70s, one can bet your dirty mac it would've dealt in prime porno-funk. Recorded during the summer of love, it's instead a typically 60s pornocopia of beat-group harmony, psych-jangle and sitar-groove. Whether it's worth the three-figure sum it fetches on the collector's market is another matter. Like British band Tomorrow, its unlikely creators the CYRKLE (i.e. TOM DAWES and DON DANNEMANN), are often remembered more for their soundtrack efforts than their regular releases (including a brace of US Top 10 hits) or their Beatles connection. With impressive adaptability but not much inspiration, they cover just about every base in American popular music, from doo-wop ('The Party') to bossa nova ('The Minx') to ironic Lee Hazelwood/Duane Eddy-style twang ('Walter's Riff'). Sixties buffs will appreciate the close harmonies of lead track 'Squeeze Play' (the film's original title), but soundtrack hounds and DJs have forked out the big bucks for the Indo-drone of 'Nicole' and a great bongos/kettle/snare face-off called, wait for it.. 'The Chase'. The best thing here by some margin, though, is the gentle pop-folkie, 'It's A Lovely Game Louise', an elegy for the film's fading lead, Jan Sterling. Among no less than 8 bonus tracks is an instrumental version of 'Kites' (a UK Top 10 hit for Simon Dupree And The Big Sound later the same year), the wild mono recording of 'Nicole' featured in the movie, a couple of previously unissued score freakouts and a superkitsch trailer ("even a minx can get turned on.. but good") with some dodgy sound effects. *BG*

Album rating: *5 (re-cd *6)

MIRACLE MILE

1989 (US 87m) Hemdale Pictures (R)

Film genre: sci-fi/disaster thriller

Top guns: s-w + dir: Steven de Jarnatt

Stars: Anthony Edwards *(Harry Washello)* ← HAWKS, Mare Winningham *(Julie Peters)* ← SHY PEOPLE ← ONE-TRICK PONY / → GEORGIA, John Agar *(Ivan Peters)*, Lou Hancock *(Lucy Peters)*, Mykel T. Williamson *(Wilson)*, Kelly Minter *(Charlotta)*, Kurt Fuller *(Gerstead)*, Alan Rosenberg *(Mike)* ← the LAST TEMPTATION OF CHRIST / → the TEMPTATIONS

Storyline: Shy musician Harry Washello must be the unluckiest man on the planet. Just when he meets his perfect woman and they fall in love, he misses his date with her and, as he searches here, there and everywhere for the elusive

Julie, he picks up a ringing payphone and learns a nuclear war has just started. Can Harry find his beloved in time to lead her to safety, or have his romantic plans been blown to atoms? *JZ*

Movie rating: *6.5

Visual: dvd

Off the record: (see below)

—

TANGERINE DREAM

Jul 89. (lp/cd) *Private; <2047-1/-2> Arista; (209/259 887)* ☐ ☐
– Teetering scales / One for the books / After the call / On the spur of the moment / All of a dither / Final statement / In Julie's eyes / Running out of time / If it's all over / People in the news / Museum walk. *(re-iss. cd Feb96; 260.016)*

S/track review: Between 1986 to 1991, EDGAR FROESE and TANGERINE DREAM newbie PAUL HASLINGER, kept up a prolific film-score workload in their desire to take over the world of electronic rock – or so it seemed. 'MIRACLE MILE' – unusually at the time for TD – was released to coincide with the movie and fused newfound pop-electro styles that embraced late 80s scores, 'DEADLY CARE' and 'Destination Berlin', while finding their retro-rock keys of old to boost their lagging fanbase. Opening sequence, 'Teetering Scales', bounced and writhed in 'DREAM fashion, while the repetitive 'One For The Books' was a little lighter on the ears. The eerie 'In Julie's Eyes' takes cues from the master of 'Halloween' horror John Carpenter, its spine-tingling effects take the duo into new boundaries. Frenetic percussion-bashing was the order of the day for 'After The Call', balanced perilously close to the synthetic, pseudo orchestra love ballad of 'On The Spur Of The Moment' – like the Art Of Noise meeting 10cc. 'All Of A Dither' presses the electro-funk button, but not in a Herbie Hancock kind of way, more like Level 42. Yes, this album is indeed of the schizoid variety, a pot-pourri of anything-goes electro, although highlights were the Vangelis-esque passages such as the oriental-tinged, 'Final Statement'. The lilting, soft-brushed 'If It's All Over' begged that very question, but there were a couple of uptempo dirges to go. Not a great TANGERINE DREAM album by any manner of means, but a good one nevertheless. *MCS*

Album rating: *5

MR. MEAN

1977 (Ita/US 98m) Lone Star Pictures International (R)

Film genre: crime drama

Top guns: dir: Fred Williamson ← NO WAY BACK ← ADIOS AMIGO ← MEAN JOHNNY BARROWS / s-w: Jeff Williamson

Stars: Fred Williamson *(Mr. Mean)* as above + ← BUCKTOWN ← THREE THE HARD WAY ← THREE TOUGH GUYS ← the SOUL OF NIGGER CHARLEY ← BLACK CAESAR ← HELL UP IN HARLEM / → FROM DUSK TILL DAWN → RIDE → CARMEN: A HIP HOPERA, Lou Castel, Pat Brocato, Angela Doria, Rita Silva, Raimund Harmstorf, David Mills, Antonio Maimone, Crippy Yocardo → WHITE "POP" JESUS, **the Ohio Players**

Storyline: The title hard man is a former mafia man on the straight and narrow who's unexpectedly handed a job to take out his former boss. *BG*

Movie rating: *2.5

Visual: video

Off the record: The **OHIO PLAYERS** stemmed from Dayton, Ohio, USA . . . 1959. This unit achieved a healthy reputation in soul/R&B circles as the backing band of the Falcons, an outfit fronted by one Wilson Pickett who together scored a US hit in 1962 with 'I Found Love'. With the core of Leroy 'Sugarfoot' Bonner, Clarence Satchell and Marshall Jones, with the addition of musicians from another local band, the Ohio Untouchables mutated into the OHIO PLAYERS. The talented troupe got their break as the house band for 'Compass' records, which eventually led to a deal with 'Capitol' records, and in 1969, they released their major label debut, 'Observations In Time'. The record made little commercial impression and the group moved on to 'Westbound' records, home to psychedelic funkster, George Clinton. Boasting a line-up of Bonner, Billy Beck, Satchell, Jones, Jimmy 'Diamond' Williams, Marvin 'Merv' Pierce and Ralph 'Pee Wee' Middlebrooks, the group hit the US Top 20 in early '73 with 'Funky Worm', scoring a minor chart placing with the attendant album, 'Pleasure'. The second instalment in their pain, pleasure, ecstasy trilogy ('Pain' had appeared in 1972), the OHIO PLAYERS concentrated squarely on the grinding groinal potential of the sinewy black groove which had come to be known as "funk". Later that summer, with the movement in full swing, the group scored a further Top 40 hit with 'Ecstasy'. Famed in funk circles for their notoriously pervy album sleeves as much as their music, the group didn't really infiltrate the conservatism of mainstream white music programming until the release of the anthemic 'Fire' in 1975. Now signed to 'Mercury' records, the 'Players hit No.1 with this classic slice of horny, Sly Stone-esque dancefloor delirium, the track's searing guitar work-out no doubt endearing them to rock fans. The accompanying album also topped the American charts and for a brief mid-70s period, the OHIO PLAYERS were almost as famous as JAMES BROWN; the irresistibly ebullient 'Love Rollercoaster' provided the group with a second No.1 later that year, following the minor chart success of the self-explanatory 'Sweet Sticky Thing' single. The album 'Honey' (1975) was equally sweet, certainly in commercial terms, narrowly missing the American top spot. The following year's 'Who'd She Coo' single and 'Contradiction' album both made the Top 20, while the 1977 compilation, 'Gold', neatly rounded up their most erotically essential, hip-grinding moments. As disco reared its orchestrated head in the late 70s, there wasn't a great demand for free-flowing funk and subsequent albums met with disappointing sales figures and chart positions. Through a constantly changing cast of labels and personnel, the group ploughed on through the 80s with minimal success. Even a brilliant 1997 cover of 'Love Rollercoaster' by the RED HOT CHILI PEPPERS wasn't enough to spark a full-scale revival although they remain one of the most respected outfits of funk's golden era. *BG*

—

the OHIO PLAYERS

Dec 77. (lp) *Mercury; <SRM 3707>* 68 –
– Mr. Mean / Fight me, chase me / The controller's mind / The big score / Magic trick / Good luck charm / Speak easy. *<cd-iss. 1994; 848350-2>*

S/track review: With their talent for dense, shifting arrangements and unusual time signatures, the OHIO PLAYERS (at this stage, CLARENCE SATCHELL, LEROY BONNER, BILLY BECK, MARVIN PIERCE, RALPH MIDDLEBROOK, MARSHALL JONES & JIMMY WILLIAMS) could easily have dropped a blaxploitation bomb. 'MR. MEAN' isn't it. Too late and a little too lackadaisical, it missed the boat by more than a few nautical miles. It is a diversion though, relegating the guitars and the sleaze, bringing on the keyboard-freaky jazz impulse. Two years on from the 'Honey' scandal (when a model's honey-dripping cover shot generated the kind of lurid gossip and conspiracy theory usually reserved for Led Zeppelin), the 'PLAYERS were still parading nude black women, albeit with a little more reserve. Inside 'MR. MEAN's gatefold sleeve, the wet permed lady looks suitably orgiastic in horse-riding get-up astride a film camera (of course . . .). If it's all very 70s soft-porn, the music isn't standard porno-funk, rather bass-heavy experimental grooves and endless ARP twiddling/Parliament-esque stringing. What makes the title track so damn catchy, though, is a high register guitar loop, as funky as the trademark frontline attack but far cleverer. Adding most weight to the band as prospective cinematic talents is 'Fight Me, Chase Me', an excellent action cue with a Latinate brass melody, aberrant gearbox tempos and even some stray cuíca grunts. The ARP-tickety, Dick Hyman-swooshing proto-electro of 'The Controller's Mind', meanwhile, is about as far removed from the band's trademark sound – and about as near to Herbie Hancock's 'The SPOOK WHO SAT BY THE DOOR' –

as they dared venture; more of this would've been dandy. It's only when they try just a little too hard to follow the tropes of black film music – 'The Big Score' – that it doesn't quite come off. Like Marvin Gaye's 'TROUBLE MAN', 'MR. MEAN' can be viewed as the jazz album they finally had the freedom to make; recommended for Clinton cadets and those of an abstract funk persuasion. Fans of the 'Love Rollercoaster' era – who're only really afforded the bumpin' 'Speak Easy' – won't find quite as many reasons to be funkful. *BG*

Album rating: *5

MODEL SHOP

1969 (US 90m) Columbia Pictures (M)

Film genre: romantic drama

Top guns: s-w + dir: Jacques Demy → PIED PIPER

Stars: Anouk Aimee *(Lola)*, Gary Lockwood *(George Matthews)* ← IT HAPPENED AT THE WORLD'S FAIR ← WILD IN THE COUNTRY, Alexandra Hay *(Gloria)* ← SKIDOO, Carol Cole *(Barbara)*, Tom Fielding *(Gerry)*, Severn Darden *(portly man)* → VANISHING POINT → the HIRED HAND, Neil Elliot *(Fred)*, **Jay Ferguson** *(Jay)*, Duke Hobbie *(David)* ← WINTER A-GO-GO, Fred Willard *(gas station attendant)* → THIS IS SPINAL TAP → HOW HIGH → a MIGHTY WIND → KILLER DILLER

Storyline: A day in the life of a disillusioned guy (George), who quits his mundane job and subsequently faces the wrath of his wife, the repossession of his car and the worry of an army call-up. He looks in other directions for some meaning to his life and ends up bedding French model, Lola. *MCS*

Movie rating: *6

Visual: video

Off the record: **SPIRIT** were formed in Los Angeles, 1964 as the Red Roosters, which, after an initial break became Spirits Rebellion. By 1967, SPIRIT (Randy California, his middle-aged, shaven-headed stepfather, Ed Cassidy, former Roosters Mark Andes, John Locke and **Jay Ferguson**), had signed to Lou Adler's 'Ode' records, releasing their eponymous debut soon after: a mellow melange of jazz and tripped-out blue rock that marked the band out from the bulk of the L.A. folk-rock pack of the late 60s. The quintet also looked different, noteably 40-something Cassidy resembling some ageing hippy Kojak. With the exuberant 'I Got A Line On You' single (from the follow-up album, 'The Family That Plays Together'), the band scored an unexpected Top 30 hit in '69, although the bulk of the record explored the grey area where jazz, rock and psychedelia met. Third LP, 'Clear' (also 1969), displayed a harder-edged sound although SPIRIT didn't really come into their own until they were paired with NEIL YOUNG producer David Briggs for the recording of post-psych, post 'MODEL SHOP' masterwork, 'Twelve Dreams Of Dr. Sardonicus' (1970). After fifth set, 'Feedback' (1972), SPIRIT gradually faded into obscurity but for the odd, very odd, surprise comeback. *MCS*

SPIRIT

Feb 05. (cd) *Sundazed; <(SC 6197)>* ☐ ☐
– The moving van / Mellow fellow / Now or anywhere / Fog / Green gorilla / Model shop I / Model shop II (clear) / The rehearsal theme / Song for Lola / Eventide / Coral / Aren't you glad.

S/track review: SPIRIT were only a year or so in the making when they were duly commissioned to score the music for 'MODEL SHOP'; and music it basically was, with only a hint of the standard song structure fans had witnessed on their late 60s, US Top 40 LPs, 'Spirit' & 'The Family That Plays Together'. Previously, SPIRIT had kept the psychedelic dream alive, although this did incorporate jazz-rock influences such as Soft Machine and Colosseum that were much more in evidence on the recordings for this soundtrack. However, due to the people at Lou Adler's 'Ode' HQ, the master tapes were shelved, making way for a rush-released third LP proper, 'Clear' (1969). It would be a long, long journey (36 years) until its bonafide release by 'Sundazed' (through 'Sony') in 2005. But was it worth it? Probably, yes, if you're a record collector completist, but no, if you're going to think this represented SPIRIT at the turn of the 70s. As previously hinted, there were only two proper songs on the 41-minute set, 'Now Or Anywhere' and 'Aren't You Glad'. The former sophomore outtake was a bluesy, stoner-rock dirge, while the latter number (different to the mix on 'The Family . . .' set) ended the CD on a high note with its screeching guitar solos and er, mono feedback. The rest of the album is cool, horizontal jazz-rock, with influences ranging from Pink Floyd, Frank Zappa, Miles Davis and the previously mentioned Soft Machine: Robert Wyatt would've been proud. Predominant highlights included the opener, 'The Moving Van', follow-on instrumental 'Mellow Fellow', the funky 'Green Gorilla' (with a chorus I might add) and the bass-laden 'Song For Lola', the latter something that just might've inspired the music for Bowie vehicle, 'The Man Who Fell To Earth'. Of the 'MODEL SHOP' title track in two parts and other passages, they basically filled out the album in a moody, incidental kind of way. JAY FERGUSON would subsequently form Jo Jo Gunne and have a solo career, before becoming a film composer in his own right. *MCS*

Album rating: *6

☐ MOGWAI segment
(⇒ ZIDANE: A 21st CENTURY PORTRAIT)

the MONKEY HUSTLE

1976 (US 89m) American International Pictures

Film genre: urban comedy drama

Top guns: dir: Arthur Marks ← FRIDAY FOSTER ← BUCKTOWN / s-w: Charles Johnson ← SLAUGHTER'S BIG RIP-OFF

Stars: Yaphet Kotto *(Big Daddy Foxx)* ← FRIDAY FOSTER ← TRUCK TURNER ← ACROSS 110th STREET ← MAN AND BOY / → the PARK IS MINE, Kirk Calloway *(Baby D)* ← the SOUL OF NIGGER CHARLEY, Thomas Carter *(Player)* → ALMOST SUMMER, Donn C. Harper *(Tiny)*, Lynn Caridine *(Jan-Jan)*, Lynn Harris *(Sweet Potato)*, Rudy Ray Moore *(Glitterin' Goldie)* ← DOLEMITE / → PETEY WHEATSTRAW → DISCO GODFATHER → JACKIE'S BACK! → BIG MONEY HUTLA, Patricia McCaskill *(Shirl)*, Rosalind Cash *(Mama)* ← CORNBREAD, EARL AND ME ← MELINDA

Storyline: A kind of garish, blaxploitation precursor to the Twyford Down fracas, with ghetto protestors battling the authorities over the proposed building of a freeway, kitted out in the latest street threads rather than army surplus and led by superlatively monikered local hustler Daddy Foxx. *BG*

Movie rating: *3

Visual: video on Orion 1996 / dvd on MGM/UA 2004

Off the record: **JACK CONRAD** (see below)

JACK CONRAD

Dec 01. (cd) *Beyond; <578251>* ☐ ☐
– Monkey hustle / Broken drum / Killer express freeway / Celebration / Sweet mama / Goldie and the long green / "D" to school / Foxxister transistor / Roller rink / Roller rink (pt.2) / Monkey hustle (M.T.) / Rubbish truck / Leon ambushed / Switch // (HARRY BETTS: Black Mama, White Mama *(tracks)*

S/track review: As one half of an excellent value two-on-one from the depths of the 'M.G.M.' vaults, released as part of the 'Soul Cinema' series, 'The MONKEY HUSTLE' is a generic but more than capable neo-blaxploitation effort from dramatic jack-of-all-trades JACK CONRAD. His titles – 'Killer Express Freeway', Broken

Drum', and our personal favourite, 'Foxxister Transistor' – might be overripe but the arrangements are pretty conventional mid-to-late-decade small group/dance funk. As usual with these kind of reissues, the sleevenotes offer endless paragraphs of plot but only the briefest info on the composer and zilch on the musicians (moan, moan, etc.); is this not a soundtrack? Or is it a DVD in disguise? We are, though, graced with the infomatic tidbit that CONRAD actually croons over his own music on the title. It's not the most memorable theme (the Hot Chocolate-like reprise just edges it) but at least he can sing, giving it a bit of sub-Larry Blackmon/Cameo yowl. '. . .Freeway' pulls over the rhythm to allow the horns more melodic width but the soundtrack only really kicks into gear once CONRAD wires in a mucky fuzz guitar to 'Celebration'; "you've got to have soul" testifies an ensemble chant, not like Bobby Byrd, you understand, but rocking all the same. Then it's hustle and flow all the way as CONRAD juggles with 'CAR WASH'-out-take-esque disco, circular scuzz-funk and the skeleton-clown jab of a clavinet. Why he didn't use the troll bass/jive horn melody of 'Block Party' for a main theme is anyone's guess, as is the question of why '. . .Transistor' sounds so familiar: it'll have you belting out 'Ain't No Mountain High Enough' before you realise you've got the wrong album. Chuck in a little pseudo-Amen Corner and it's almost Stars On 45. *BG*

Album rating: *6

MONSTER

2003 (US 109m) Newmarket Films / Media 8 Entertainment (R)

Film genre: romantic crime drama/biopic

Top guns: s-w + dir: Patty Jenkins

Stars: Charlize Theron *(Aileen Wuornos)*, Christina Ricci *(Selby Wall)* ← FEAR AND LOATHING IN LAS VEGAS ← BUFFALO 66 / → the FEARLESS FREAKS → BLACK SNAKE MOAN, Bruce Dern *(Thomas)*, Scott Wilson *(Horton Rohrbach)* ← DON'T LET GO ← SOUTH OF HEAVEN, WEST OF HELL ← DEAD MAN WALKING ← SOUL SURVIVOR ← GERONIMO: AN AMERICAN LEGEND ← ELVIS AND THE COLONEL: THE UNTOLD STORY ← YOUNG GUNS II ← JOHNNY HANDSOME ← BLUE CITY, Annie Corley *(Donna)*, Pruitt Taylor Vince *(Gene)* ← the END OF VIOLENCE ← HEAVY ← NATURAL BORN KILLERS ← WILD AT HEART ← SHY PEOPLE, Lee Tergesen *(Vincent Corey)*, Marco St. John *(Evan)*, Marc Macauley *(Will)*

Storyline: Monster tells the true-life story of Aileen Wuornos, a prostitute who murders her client after he brutally rapes her. With her girlfriend, Selby Wall, she tries to make ends meet but money is tight and steady work is hard to come by. Finally she embarks on a spree of robbery and murder, although it is only a matter of time before the net begins to close in on her and her grisly fate is assured. *JZ*

Movie rating: *8

Visual: dvd

Off the record: BT (see own entry)

—

BT

Jul 04. (cd w/dvd) *D.T.S.; <(6982960 1112-26)>* ☐ Feb04 ☐
– Childhood montage / Girls kiss / The bus stop / Turning tricks / First kill / Job hunt / Bad cop / "Call me daddy" killing / I don't like it rough / Ferris wheel / Ditch the car / Madman speech / Cop killing / News on TV / Courtroom. *(bonus w/ movie dvd)*

S/track review: This purely instrumental CD is hard to accurately classify and at times makes hard listening, but it is an excellent work well deserving repeat playing. BT/BRIAN TRANSEAU's ambient style contains different rhythms and melodies in each track and a variety of instruments are used, ranging from acoustic guitar to hurdy-gurdy, each with its own relationship to the characters and emotions in the film. Guitar and piano represent the two main characters in tracks such as 'Ferris Wheel' and 'Bus Stop' while the hurdy gurdy emphasises the darker emotions ('First Kill'). TRANSEAU puts most effort however into the synthesizer rhythms which show the emotions prevalent in the film – fear hate and revenge. Each track has some variation of these rhythms making the CD an excellent example of TRANSEAU's cutting-edge style. All in all, 'MONSTER', was indeed a splendid piece of work, incorporating dissonant orchestration and haunting, Beck-esque acoustica on a soundtrack light years removed from his dancefloor material of yore. *JZ*

Album rating: *6

☐ Rudy Ray MOORE segment
(⇒ DOLEMITE)

MORE

1969 (Fra 117m) Les Films du Losange (12)

Film genre: romantic crime drama

Top guns: s-w (+ dir): Barbet Schroeder → la VALLEE, Paul Gegauff → la VALLEE

Stars: Klaus Grunberg *(Stefan Bruckner)*, Mimsy Farmer *(Estelle Miller)* ← RIOT ON SUNSET STRIP / → CODENAME: WILDGEESE, Heinz Engelmann *(Dr. Ernesto Wolf)*, Michel Chanderli *(Charlie)*, Louise Wink *(Cathy)*, Henry Wolf *(Henry)*

Storyline: European counter-cultural shenanigans from Barbet Schroeder as young German Stefan heads for the fleshpots of 60s Paris where he meets fellow hipster Estelle. The couple subsequently strike out for Ibiza (at the time an idyllic hippy enclave rather than a tacky club ghetto) where drugs come between them; Estelle is revealed as a heroin addict while Stefan subsequently begins to lose his marbles on LSD. *BG*

Movie rating: *6

Visual: video

Off the record: (see below)

—

PINK FLOYD

Jul 69. (lp/c) *Columbia; (SCX/TCSCX 6346) Tower; <ST 5169>* 9 ☐
– Cirrus minor / The Nile song / Crying song / Up the Khyber / Green is the colour / Cymbaline / Party sequence / Main theme / Ibiza bar / More blues / Quicksilver / A Spanish piece / Dramatic theme. *(cd-iss. Apr87; CDP 746386-2) (re-iss. Sep95 on 'E.M.I.' cd/c; CD/TC EMD 1084)*

S/track review: One of the least written about and most underrated entries in the PINK FLOYD catalogue, this is another album routinely and lazily handed a paltry rating in most guides and – doubtless due to its soundtrack tag – too often passed over even by PF diehards. If nothing else it warrants closer listening for its transitional significance, coming as it did at a crucial juncture in the band's development. Newly Syd Barrett-less (1968's 'A Saucerful Of Secrets' had a few Syd contributions) and looking for a musical direction, Messrs WATERS, GILMOUR, WRIGHT and MASON made tentative inroads into more cohesive song structures without sacrificing the enigmatic allure of the Barrett years. The fact that 'MORE' was recorded contemporaneously with the studio portion of 'Ummagumma' (1969) makes comparisons inevitable, particularly with that album's 'Grantchester Meadows'. In its echoes and impressions of things to come, however, the album arguably bears more enduring comparison with their contributions to 'ZABRISKIE POINT' (1970). With ROGER WATERS beginning to assert his songwriting credentials there's that same sense of ruminating pastoralism, running through 'ZABRISKIE . . .' and extending to 'Wish You Were Here' (1975) and beyond. Here it manifests in deceptively bucolic fragments like 'Cirrus Minor' and the gorgeous 'Green Is The Colour', and the darker but no less evocative 'Cymbaline', a staple of their pre-'Dark Side Of The Moon' live sets. In 'Nile Song', the record also features one of PINK FLOYD's heaviest freak-outs, a proto-grunge monster which knocks the stuffing out of the record before a mood's even been set. In part, it's this schizophrenic tension – so different from their peerlessly sequenced classics of the mid-70s – which makes 'MORE' so frustrating and so compelling at the same time. But if it's largely a showcase for WATERS' emerging writing skills, it's also a rare platform for the idiosyncratic talents of his sidemen: MASON/WRIGHT and GILMOUR get their solo turns on 'Up The Khyber' (a decent jazz-rock excursion) and 'A Spanish Piece' (a fun flamenco romp complete with some Fawlty Towers-style Spanish muttering) respectively, while the instrumental 'Main Theme' is 'Floyd at their most elemental, a kinetic whirlpool of eddying electronics and spidery keyboards. Like Popol Vuh and Tangerine Dream, PF were a band born to make soundtracks and it's perhaps a pity they didn't create more stuff in this vein; in that sense the rockier 'Obscured By Clouds' (1972) – aka 'La VALLEE' – remains a missed opportunity. Some of the tracks are superfluous for sure, as are the remastered CD sleevenotes, basically a pointlessly extended plot synopsis for Schroeder's convoluted movie. If you're a PINK FLOYD fan, go back and give this a second chance. If you're a beginner, ignore the usual advice to start elsewhere; in some ways 'MORE's across-the-board eclecticism is actually more accessible than the often oppressive albums the band are better known for. *BG*

Album rating: *6

the MOTHMAN PROPHECIES

2002 (US 118m) Sony Pictures (PG-13)

Film genre: psychological sci-fi/fantasy thriller

Top guns: dir: Mark Pellington / s-w: Richard Hatem (nov: John A. Keel)

Stars: Richard Gere *(John Klein)* ← DR. T & THE WOMEN / → I'M NOT THERE, Laura Linney *(Connie Mills)* → the HOTTEST STATE, Will Patton *(Gordon Smallwood)*, David Eigenberg *(Ed Fleischman)*, Debra Messing *(Mary Klein)* → OPEN SEASON, Lucinda Jenney *(Denise Smallwood)* ← SUGAR TOWN ← GRACE OF MY HEART, Ann McDonough *(Lucy Griffin)*, Alan Bates *(Alexander Leek)* ← the WICKED LADY ← the ROSE, Bill Laing *(Indrid Cold)*, Nesbitt Blaisdell *(Chief Josh Jarrett)* ← DEAD MAN WALKING

Storyline: Routinely compared to an extended edition of 'The X-Files' (and based on the real life events which allegedly inspired the series), this genuinely unnerving chiller leads in with Washington Post journo John Klein and the bizarre fate of his wife. Two years after her death in a car crash, Klein uncovers disturbing parallels between her fevered bedside drawings and reported sightings of a moth-like apparition in Point Pleasant, West Virginia. In a 'Picnic At Hanging Rock' style time warp, Klein finds himself stranded near the town in the small hours. He doesn't have a clue where he is but local Gordon Smallwood is expecting him; Klein has apparently appeared at his door several times that week already. Disembodied phone calls, unexplained deaths and more supernatural sightings suggest that it'll take more than mothballs to solve the town's problems. *BG*

Movie rating: *7.5

Visual: dvd

Off the record: KING BLACK ACID were formed by former Hitting Birth leader, Daniel Riddle, initially as a one-man project. Forsaking his sonic industrial basslines for the guitar, and recruiting a number of friends and followers (Melinda DiCillo on keyboards, Nathan Jorg on bass, Roger Campos on guitar and Scott Adamo on drums), they have so far released three neo-psychedelic/space rock albums for 'Cavity Search' records: 'Womb Star Session' (1995), 'Royal Subjects' (1997) and 'Loves A Long Song' (2000). *MCS*

—

Various Artists (KING BLACK ACID * / TOMANDANDY **)

Jan 02. (d-cd) *Lakeshore; <LAK 33694-2> Colosseum; (CST 8087-2)* ☐ Mar02 ☐
– Half light [single] (LOW w/ **) / Wake up #37 (*) / Haunted (*) / One and only (*) / Collage (GLENN BRANCA) / Great spaces (*) / Rolling under (*) / Half life (*) / Soul systems burn (*) / Half light (LOW w/ **) // (**):- Movement 1: Composed of 12 members – Retrace – A new home – M.R.I. – Welcome to Point Pleasant / Movement 2: Point Pleasant – Seeing strange things – It's a voice and it's saying do not be afraid – He's wrong – Denver 9 / Movement 3: I had a dream like that – Not from human vocal chords – Zone of fear – Ring ring – Leek – Leek wouldn't see me / Movement 4: All at once, I understand, everything – Do you know that woman – The tape reveals – We are not allowed to know / Movement 5: It's how I ended up here – Airport – I have to go / Movement 6: We have dinner at 6, and we open presents at 8 – 12 o'clock call / Movement 7: The bridge / Movement 8: Mirror drone – John's theme – Cellos.

S/track review: Portland psych-sters KING BLACK ACID supply the moth's share of the tracks on disc one of this supernaturally good value double set, even if the overall effect is more soporific than scary (and definitely not "surreal" as the label hopefully claims). The name may suggest a grizzled aggregate of Hawkwind-vintage space-bandits, but DANIEL RIDDLE and Co specialise in lysergic-lite. At its most tasteful, on the likes of 'Wake Up #37', it's the personification of the acceptable face of latter-day "alternative" music, a memorably bland sonic broth of treated instrumentation and pallid vocals. RIDDLE only convinces when he either indulges his Pink Floyd fetish more fully (on the organic 'Rolling Under'), or, with the gorgeous 'Great Spaces', beams his electron melodies from some dark, distant star peopled by flickering holograms of Brian Eno and the Flying Pickets(!). And if that sounds frightening, it's nothing compared to the "interstitial sound design" by TOMANDANDY (TOM HADJU and ANDY MILBURN), techno boffins of Darth Vader-like severity whose credits include the likes of Roger Avary's 'Killing Zoë' (1994) and Oliver Stone's 'NATURAL BORN KILLERS' (1994). In addition to these thoroughly unpleasant snippets, they fill up disc two with an hour's worth of movie score, initially pledging solidarity with disc one's trip-tronica before plunging into electro-orchestral darkness. For the most part, the effect is studiedly, claustrophobically abstract: dark sonic shapes lunge out of the ether and take vicious swipes at your eardrum; a hollow piano note sounds a death-knell; dissonant transmissions, splintered samples, flinty guitar shards and infernal glitches promise disaster – as cue titles like 'Not From Human Vocal Chords' suggest, it's not something to spin while sipping your bedtime Horlicks. The strings occasionally swell into something less spectral but their mournful constancy is only really fleshed out in the final movement. TOMANDANDY are also credited on disc one opener, 'Half Light', presumably contributing the spook-whispering over LOW's keening guitar groove, while avant-garde veteran GLENN BRANCA shakes KING BLACK ACID out of their listlessness with the rivet-popping 'Collage'. *BG*

Album rating: *6.5

☐ MOTORHEAD segment
(⇒ EAT THE RICH + LEMMY)

MUGISON

Born: Orn Elius Gudmundsson, early 80s, Isafjordur, Iceland; nicknamed on holiday in Malaysia due to his karaoke-performing father, Muggi. MUGISON kicked off his solitary musical career with the unceremonious indie offering, the mini-CD, 'Lonely Mountain' (2003). What brought the connection between his trip-hop antics on that set, and the commission for 'NICELAND' (released on London's small 'Accidental' records – licensed from '12 Tonar'), is anyone's guess – Iceland was a possibility. A third set (his second for 'Accidental'), 'Mugimania! Is This Monkey Music?' (2005), tracked the same territory as its cinematic predecessor, although this time around there was no film. His second score, 'a LITTLE TRIP TO HEAVEN' (2005) – starring Forest Whitaker – found Muggi utilizing and wrestling with even more techno skills; without an OST, 'Myrin', was released the following year. With Icelandic groups going down a storm in the UK and US (SIGUR ROS, BJORK, Mum, etc.), it was no surprise that MUGISON would be included on performance documentary, 'Gargandi Snilld' – aka 'SCREAMING MASTERPIECE' (2005). *MCS*

- **filmography** (composer) {performer} –

Niceland *(2004 =>)* / **a Little Trip To Heaven** *(2005 =>)* / **Screaming Masterpiece** *(2005 {p} =>)* / Myrin *(2006)*

MURDEROCK – UCCIDE A PASSO DI DANZA

1984 (Ita 90m) Scena Films (R)

Film genre: crime mystery

Top guns: dir: Lucio Fulci / s-w: Gianfranco Clerici, Vincenzo Mannino, Roberto Gianviti

Stars: Olga Karlatos *(Candice Norman)*, Ray Lovelock *(George Webb)*, Claudio Cassinelli *(Dick Gibson)*, Cosimo Cinieri *(Lieutenant Borges)*, Giuseppe Mannajuolo *(Professor Davis)*, Belinda Busato *(Gloria Weston)*, Maria Vittoria Tolazzi *(Jill)*, Geretta Marie Fields *(Margie)*

Storyline: The Arts for Living Center rapidly becomes the Art of Dying Center as a succession of the world's top ballet dancers are chloroformed and stabbed through the heart with a needle. The police seem powerless to stop the murderer and so instructor Candice orders her few remaining students to ignore the fact they're being murdered and concentrate on their routines. What will happen when Candice starts getting nightmares about the killer and realizes she could be the next dying swan? *JZ*

Movie rating: *5

Visual: video as 'MURDER ROCK'

Off the record: (see below)

—

KEITH EMERSON

May 86. (lp/cd) *Chord; (CHORD/+CD 004)*
– Murderock / Tonight is your night / Streets to blame / Not so innocent / Prelude to Candice / Don't go in the shower / Coffee time / Candice / New York dash / Tonight is not your night / The spillone. *(cd-iss. Oct01 Italy on 'Cinevox'+=; CD MDF 345)* – Murderock (part 1) / Murderock (part 2) / Murderock (part 3) / Murderock (part 4).

S/track review: Also known as 'The Demon Is Loose' or, more aptly, 'Slashdance', 'MURDEROCK' is shamelessly blatant in its cynical blending of 'FLASHDANCE' and giallo slasher flick stylings. KEITH EMERSON's score reflects this in spades, although there is plenty for him to be ashamed of – even director Lucio Fulci was less than impressed with EMERSON's involvement, which was insisted upon by Fulci's producer. The producer perhaps expected EMERSON to bridge the generic gap, with his experience on Dario Argento's 'INFERNO' and his rock star pedigree, but the juxtaposition of the anaemic, aspirational rock of the first four tracks and the weak keyboard instrumentals of the rest of the score is less an inspired pairing and more an awkward arranged marriage. It's tempting to enjoy 'MURDEROCK' on an ironic level, so deadpan is the chest-thumping extravagance of tracks like 'Tonight Is Your Night', with its typically 80s male/female duet exclaiming "it's so good to be alive". That EMERSON has titled a later, instrumental track 'Tonight Is Not Your Night' is not clever enough to make up for the lack of imagination throughout. The closing quartet of 'Murderock – Parts 1-4' taken by themselves are interesting enough, representing cues used for the more horrifying scenes, but you get the sense that EMERSON created a score that is all too effective in replicating the bland power rock score of the mainstream films 'MURDEROCK' cribs from. The listener seems to be expected to buy it as a satirical approach, but in fact it's nothing more than a failed marketing ploy. *SW*

Album rating: *3

the MUSE

1999 (US 97m) October Films (PG-13)

Film genre: showbiz satire/comedy

Top guns: s-w: Albert Brooks (+ dir), Monica Johnson

Stars: Albert Brooks *(Steven Phillips)*, Sharon Stone *(Sarah Little)*, Andie MacDowell *(Laura Phillips)* ← the END OF VIOLENCE, Jeff Bridges *(Jack Warrick)*, Mark Feuerstein *(Josh Martin)*, Steven J. Wright *(Stan Spielberg)*, Bradley Whitford *(Hal)*, Stacey Travis *(Phyllis)* ← EARTH GIRLS ARE EASY, Cybill Shepherd *(herself)*, Jennifer Tilly *(herself)*, Lorenzo Lamas *(himself)* ← BODY ROCK ← GREASE, Rob Reiner *(himself)*, James Cameron *(himself)*, Martin Scorsese *(himself)*, Wolfgang Puck *(himself)*

Storyline: Writer Steven Phillips is desperate for inspiration after being told he's no longer the main man in Hollywood, bad news for his extravagant lifestyle. Meanwhile, his best friend Jack's career is catapulting to new heights, and he says it's all down to his muse, a real life woman called Sarah who visits him and just seems to 'make things happen'. Steven hires her on the spot but the price is high – after all, a daughter of Zeus expects a high standard of living. It's anyone's guess which will run out first – Jack's money or his wife. *JZ*

Movie rating: *5.5

Visual: dvd

Off the record: (see below)

—

ELTON JOHN

Aug 99. (cd) *Polygram; <546517-2>*
– Driving home / Driving to Universal / Driving to Jack's / Walk of shame / Better have a gift / The wrong gift / The aquarium / Are we laughing / Take a walk with me / What should I do / Back to the aquarium / Steven redecorates / To the guesthouse / The cookie factory / Multiple personality / Sarah escapes / Back to Paramount / Meet Christine / The muse / The muse – Jermaine Dupri remix.

S/track review: There isn't much to say about ELTON JOHN's score to 'The MUSE'. Most of the album consists of score items that barely pass the minute mark, not a usual trait for the once mighty Rocket Man. For what it's worth, these soundbites are light-hearted, bouncy affairs alternating between sweet piano pieces and orchestral manoeuvres that at least show off Sir Elton's versatility and ear for melody, even if some of the excerpts do sound like the fanfare at a royal wedding. Only two "proper" songs inhabit (or inhibit) the album. The first is the title-track performed by

ELTON JOHN, a record which is a kind of insipid, piano-led warble that has one of those annoying light snare drumbeats that characterised so much poor late-90s R&B ballads. The second is a remix by JERMAINE DUPRI that sounds almost exactly like the original, with the possible exception of a few additions of the aforementioned drumbeats. However, overall, 'The MUSE' has its delightful moments of grandeur, although hampered by a dreadful theme song. *CM*

Album rating: *4.5

MYSTERIOUS SKIN

2005 (US 99m) TLA Releasing / 1 More Film (NC-17)

Film genre: coming-of-age psychological drama

Top guns: s-w + dir: Gregg Araki ← SPLENDOR (au: Scott Heim)

Stars: Joseph Gordon-Levitt *(Neil McCormick)*, Brady Corbet *(Brian Lackey)*, Elisabeth Shue *(Mrs. McCormick)*, Michelle Trachtenberg *(Wendy Peterson)*, Jeff Licon *(Eric Preston)*, Chris Mulkey *(Mr. Lackey)* ← SUGAR TOWN ← GAS FOOD LODGING ← HEARTBREAK HOTEL ← TIMERIDER: THE ADVENTURE OF LYLE SWANN ← the LONG RIDERS, Bill Sage *(coach Heider)* ← GLITTER ← HIGH ART ← I SHOT ANDY WARHOL

Storyline: It's the summer of 1981 in Hutchinson, Kansas, and two 8-year-old boys encounter life-changing experiences during a little league baseball match; Brian, with – what he believes to have been – aliens while he was in an amnesiacal sleep and more shockingly, Neil with the paedophile coach. Ten years on, both get in touch with each other and set out to get rid of their nightmarish demons. *MCS*

Movie rating: *8

Visual: dvd

Off the record: ROBIN GUTHRIE (see below). **HAROLD BUDD** was born in L.A., 24th May 1936. Inspired by the buzz of telephone wires in his Mojave Desert town of Victorville, Southern Californian graduate with a degree in Musical Composition, BUDD was driven to write his first minimalistic works, 'The Candy-Apple Revision' and 'Unspecified D-Flat Major Chord & Lirio', around the late 60s. While teaching at the local Institute of Arts, he made an advance tape, 'Madrigals Of The Rose Angels', in 1971. Having signed to BRIAN ENO's 'Obscure' label in 1976, he finally delivered his solo debut, 'The Pavilion Of Dreams', albeit two years later. Yes, BUDD was a little slow in getting off the ground, and even slower on record with his pioneering take on post-rock, lo-fi dabblings. His subsequent landmark work with ENO resulted in a series of ambient-styled LPs, although he was best remembered for his collaborative set, 'The Moon And The Melodies' alongside Simon Raymonde, ROBIN GUTHRIE and Elizabeth Fraser (i.e. Cocteau Twins). In the 90s, now in his fifties, BUDD released some of his finest solo outings, 1993's 'Music For 3 Pianos' being his best received. While further collaborations with Xtc's Andy Partridge ('Through The Hill') kept his profile high, it would be his major-label signing to 'Atlantic' for 'The Room' (2000), that the 60-something composer would gain respect. Now semi-retired, but still issuing the odd album, BUDD and his elliptical piano are still in demand. The collaborative 'MYSTERIOUS SKIN' OST will probably be his last outing. *MCS*

—

ROBIN GUTHRIE / HAROLD BUDD

May 05. (cd) *Commotion; <CR 008> Rykodisc; (RCD 16058)* ☐ Jul05 ☐
– Neil's theme / The memories returning / Snowfall / Neil's farewell / Childhood lost / Halloween / A silhouette approaches / Goodbye to Wendy / Brian's nightmare – The unknown, part one / Twilight / The unknown, part two / The discovery / Loitering / The writing on the wall / One true love.

S/track review: The last time ambient-meisters ROBIN GUTHRIE and HAROLD BUDD collaborated – on a full-scale album at least – was two decades ago, towards the end of '86, when the HAROLD BUDD/Cocteau Twins collective gave us the delightful, though uninspiring 'The Moon And The Melodies' set; GUTHRIE had subsequently produced BUDD's 1988 solo album, 'The White Arcades' in Edinburgh, Scotland. With the Cocteaus and long-time partner/vocalist Elizabeth Fraser now a faint memory for the Grangemouth-born guitarist, the sonic soloist alongside American minimalist BUDD on keyboards, ignited their introduction to film scores via 'MYSTERIOUS SKIN'. In that distinctive reverberating style that graced so many a classic Cocteau Twins album, GUTHRIE shone out like the sun for dreamy opener 'Neil's Theme', although there were thoughts if only Liz would enter the fray; it seemed I'd been guilty of over-familiarising myself with their universally-acclaimed work. Track 2, 4 & 5, 'The Memories Returning', 'Neil's Farewell' and 'Childhood Lost', were clearly down to the soft, pastel tones of BUDD, like most of his lo-fi contributions, aesthetically pleasing. 'Snowfall', 'Halloween', 'Goodbye To Wendy' and most of Robin's treatments could well have fitted into any Cocteau Twins long-player, albeit with that incoherent warble of Fraser. Yes, I'm probably trying too much to find fault in such a haunting display of atmospheric soundscapes, but this is Sunday music for Saturday night people contemplating never going out from their safe bedsitter apartments. Track 10 and certainly their most melodic, 'Twilight', rises from the ashes without letting loose into a Mogwai-esque crescendo. And that's probably the problem – I need my sonic fix. 'MYSTERIOUS SKIN' – without opening credits piece by Sigur Ros – is at times musak while waiting in the lift on your way to Heaven, or is my imagination waiting for that ultimate trip. It would indeed be a pleasure to hop into that proverbial up escalator, especially i-pod-in-ear to CD highlight, 'Loitering' – truly delicious, and that Hawaiian arpeggio on follow-on track, 'The Writing On The Wall' – wow! *MCS*

Album rating: *7.5

NAKED ANGELS

1969 (US 88m) Favorite Films / International CAN (R)

Film genre: crime thriller + biker movie

Top guns: s-w: (+ dir) Bruce D. Clark, Marc Siegler

Stars: Michael Greene *(Mother)* → TO LIVE AND DIE IN L.A. → DOWN AND OUT IN BEVERLY HILLS → LAST MAN STANDING, Jennifer Gan *(Marlene)*, Richard Rust *(Fingers)*, Art Jenoff, Felicia Guy, Corey Fischer → BREWSTER McCLOUD, Howard Lester *(Skids)*, Tedd King, Leonard Coates, Penelope Spheeris → WAYNE'S WORLD

Storyline: Set in L.A., Mother is the leader of a tough biker gang. He falls foul of rival gang the Hotdoggers and ends up in prison after taking a beating from them. Out for revenge, he enlists the Angels and sets off into the desert to find his enemies and get even. Soon his manic, obsessive behaviour takes its toll on the rest of his gang and his girlfriend Marlene is ready to leave. *JZ*

Movie rating: *2.5

Visual: video / dvd in 2006

Off the record: **JEFF SIMMONS & RANDY STEIRLING** (see below). Interestingly enough, first-time actor Penelope Spheeris went on to direct cult rockumentary series, 'The DECLINE OF WESTERN CIVILIZATION', amongst others. *MCS*

—

JEFF SIMMONS (& RANDY STEIRLING)

Oct 69. (lp) *Straight; <STS 1056>* [ ] [–]
– Naked Angels theme / Ride into Vegas / Vegas boogie / Vegas pickup / Cop out / First desert ride / Rank / Boinin' (third ride) / Scots breath / Rat grind / Bar dream / Camper scene / Toccata for truck / End theme. *(UK cd-iss. Jan07 on 'Fallout'; FOCD 2035)*

S/track review: 'NAKED ANGELS' is the LP that Seattle native, JEFF SIMMONS, did before he partied and performed with Zappa & The Mothers. Little will also be known of his time spent as founder/leader of cult act, Puddin' & Pipe, or his association with the band, Ethiopia or Easy Chair; the latter won the local "Battle Of The Bands" in the summer of '68. And this is where SIMMONS met Frank Z. Jeff and his band secured a support slot to FZ himself, while also being part of a 'Straight/Bizarre' records Xmas bash alongside the Mothers Of Invention, Alice Cooper, the GTO's and Wild Man Fischer. While Zappa worked on Jeff's debut solo long-player, 'Lucille Has Messed My Mind Up', he also set the man up with session guitarist, RANDY STEIRLING, a guy who had worked with the Kingston Trio, Sly Stone and Neil Diamond. In 1969, prior to the release of SIMMONS' aforementioned cult classic, came another infectious masterpiece, 'NAKED ANGELS'. With its opening title track salvo – not so much Freak-out, more of a Wig-out – the instrumental acid-dirge has been regarded as the second-best biker theme ever. You can take one guess on the best: it was "born" around the same "wild" time. 'Ride Into Vegas' is basically what it says on the tin, a funky, psychedelic run-through of mellotron meeting lead guitar. 'Vegas Boogie' takes it one swing further, while 'Vegas Pickup' keeps on truckin', so to speak. 'Cop Out' is nothing but, and like most of the album, takes its cue from possibly Booker T & The MGs or even Iron Butterfly. The LP gets even funkier on track 8, 'Boinin (Third Ride)', a pounding acid-tinged piece of embryonic metal that would probably make future Swiss prog-sters Brainticket metamorphose before your very eyes. 'Scots Breath' is close to my heart, its bagpipe-sounding instruments taking on a sort of Area Code 615 meets the JSD Band. Down at the MCStrong bunker, we love the well-thought-out titles, 'Rat Grind' & 'Bar Dream' are basically what they say on the tin; 'Camper Scene' is definitely camper than any seen around at this time. 'Tocatta For Truck' gets all pseudo classical and it calls out for lyrics, although if Raspberries singer turned "All By himself" solo artist, Eric Carmen had got a hold of it, who knows. Vocal track, 'End Theme', bows out and "sets the controls for the heart of the sun" – well, sort of – but unlike Pink Floyd, SIMMONS' cinematic mission was all too brief. He would subsequently perform on some Zappa/Mothers early 70s albums, 'Chunga's Revenge', 'Waka/Jawaka' and the live 'Roxy & Elsewhere'. *MCS*

Album rating: *6

the NAKED APE

1973 (US 85m) Universal Pictures

Film genre: satirical docudrama

Top guns: s-w + dir: Donald Driver (au: Desmond Morris)

Stars: Johnny Crawford *(Lee)*, Victoria Principal *(Cathy)*, Dennis Olivieri *(Arnie)* → PHANTOM OF THE PARADISE → FORBIDDEN ZONE, Brett Parker, Diana Darrin, Norman Grabowski ← OUT OF SIGHT ← GIRL HAPPY ← ROUSTABOUT, Robert Ito, Marvin Miller, John Hillerman, Helen Horowitz

Storyline: The entire history of mankind in about an hour and a half, charting how we evolved out of the trees (some of us more successfully than others) and developed into who we are today. The message is very much one of human values and emotions triumphing over the artificial institutions of governments and authority, and there's a lot of monkey business in it too. *JZ*

Movie rating: *3.5

Visual: none

Off the record: (see below)

—

JIMMY WEBB (score)

Aug 73. (lp) *Playboy; <PS 125>* [ ] [–]
– 9 A.M., October 23, 4004 B.C. / D-minor toccata (J.S. Bach, P.D.) / Naked Ape theme (fingerpainting): Ape inventory / Carnivorock / Arnie's letter (my wife ran off with a jukebox) / Cathy's theme – Pair-bonding / Saturday suit (vocal by JIMMY WEBB) / Fingerpainting (vocal by JIMMY WEBB) / You brought a new kind of love to me (vocal by DONALD DRIVER) / Jesus loves me (vocal by CLYDIE KING) / Survival rag (vocal by DONALD DRIVER) / Gymnasts' ballet (fingerpainting) / Arnie's appeasement signals (Samurai sequence) / The elephant hunt / Naked Ape theme (fingerpainting): How like an angel.

S/track review: The 1970s were plain difficult for JIMMY WEBB, but there can have been few lower points than 'The NAKED APE'. More than five years after the phenomenal string of hits that secured his reputation as a great American songwriter ('By The Time I Get To Phoenix', 'Wichita Lineman', 'MacArthur Park', and all), the Oklahoman was increasingly frustrated by an audience indifferent to his performing talents. Having scored the 1971 western 'Doc', and soon to oversee a new Supremes LP, he snapped up this Hugh Hefner project like a man hell-bent on finding out whether Playboy turns out music any more successfully than JIMMY WEBB sells top-shelf magazines. The bilk of the soundtrack features the instrumental genre pastiches that underscore the movie's tiresome ironic lectures, while debutant director Donald Driver (who also wrote the screenplay, and was clearly intent on showcasing all his limitations at once) contributes hapless vocals on two unfunny ragtime songs. WEBB's own performances sound like they were recorded at the bottom of the pool in the Playboy mansion without managing to obscure the singer's shortcomings. That fine vocalist and former Raelette CLYDIE KING, by contrast, enhances one track that remains somehow untouched by the rubbish around it, the straight gospel 'Jesus Loves Me'. Another of WEBB's songs, 'Saturday Suit', would subsequently brush itself down and appear looking quite respectable on an Art Garfunkel album, while its writer probably still gives thanks that this movie's greatest virtue has been its forgettability. *ND*

Album rating: *2

the NAMESAKE

2006 (India/US 122m) Mirabai / Fox Searchlight Pictures (PG-13)

Film genre: family/domestic drama

Top guns: dir: Mira Nair / s-w: Sooni Taraporevala (nov: Jhumpa Lahiri)

Stars: Kal Penn *(Gogol Ganguli)*, Tabu *(Ashima Ganguli)*, Irfan Khan *(Ashoke Ganguli)*, Jacinda Barrett *(Maxine Ratliff)*, Zuleikha Robinson *(Moushumi Mazumdar)*, Gretchen Egolf *(Astrid)*, Ruma Guha Thakurta *(Ashoke's mother)*, Linus Roache *(Mr. Lawson)*, Brooke Smith *(Sally)* ← SERIES 7

Storyline: After their arranged marriage in Calcutta, Ashoke and Ashima head to New York to make their fortune. Soon a baby boy is on the way, and the happy couple name him Nikhil, though their pet name for him is Gogol. Fifteen years on, and scruffy, rebellious Gogol starts to reject his Indian ancestry in favour of the cool American lifestyle he's used to. How will he cope with new girlfriend Moushumi, who like himself is a child of two cultures? *JZ*

Movie rating: *8

Visual: dvd

Off the record: Linus Roache is the son of Coronation Street stalwart/soap actor, Bill Roache (aka Ken Barlow). **NITIN SAWHNEY** (see below). *MCS*

NITIN SAWHNEY (*) (& Various Artists)

Mar 07. (cd) *Rounder; <(11661 9072-2)>* ☐ ☐
– Shoes to America (*) / The Namesake opening titles (*) / First day in New York (*) / Jhiri jhiri choyetali (GEETA DUTT) / Flight IC408 (STATE OF BENGAL) / Airport grief (*) / Mo's affair (*) / Farewell ashoke (*) / Ashima becomes a widow (*) / Aftermath (*) / Ye mera divanapan hai (SUSHEELA RAMAN) / Baul song (LAKHAN DAS) / Taj Mahal (*) / The chosen one (the ELEMENTS & MYKILL MIERS) / Max arrives (*) / Boatman's song (KARTIK DAS) / Postales (FEDERICO AUBELE) / Amra reformed Hindus (PARTHA CHATTERJEE) / The Namesake reprise (*) / The same song (SUSHEELA RAMAN) / Falling (* feat. MATT HALES from AQUALUNG).

S/track review: While firmly in the socially/culturally aware tradition of the many TV and documentary commissions NITIN SAWHNEY has taken on in the past decade, 'The NAMESAKE' was, surprisingly perhaps, his first full soundtrack release. As godfather – along with Talvin Singh – of an Asian Underground scene peopled by the likes of Niraj Chag, Badmarsh & Shri and STATE OF BENGAL (featured here with the funky 'Flight IC408'), SAWHNEY has been composing cinematic music for much of his career, whether as accompaniment to screen images or not. His frequent orchestral collaborations (including his recent, newly imagined score for Franz Osten's silent Bombay melodrama, 'A Throw Of Dice'), dance projects and stage commissions have surely also served him well as a grounding to scoring such a high profile film, one conceived by such a fiercely independent yet Hollywood-savvy director like Mira Nair (and which she turned down Harry Potter for!). What's most surprising is the texture of SAWHNEY's score, or at least the opening portion of it, composed largely for acoustic guitar and flute (played by the hugely talented K. SRINIVASAN), borne – according to Nair's notes – out of his "casual strummings", "an ancient-modern tapestry that beautifully cradled the span of thirty years in the Ganguli family". It's a sound which seduces you from the first chords, full of grace and sunlight, unburdened by the electro-symphonic intensity and scale of some of his past projects. What makes its flighty melody even more tantalising is that there's so little of it, breezing through short one or two minute cues like snatched glimpses of some secluded, briefly glimpsed courtyard. The sequence of cues programmed mid-section are more reflective, pensive and orchestral (and the climactic ones embroidered with vocals, wordless and ecstatic from MITALI BHAWMIK; pallid and Chris Martin-ish from Aqualung's MATT HALES) but – contemporary production on closer 'Falling' aside – only on 'Mo's Affair' does he ramp up the arrangements to include drums to go with the Indian percussion and droning electric guitar to complement the violin and viola, creating a disorientating, quasi-psychedelic mood-upsetter in line with Nair's drama. Like all great directors, Nair instinctively knows how to put together her own soundtrack, magnifying the power of SAWHNEY's classical guitar-orientated motifs by insulating them with diverse but sympathetic source tracks, tracing the same journey from Calcutta to the Big Apple. Classic Bollywood inevitably gets a look-in – with an original in the shape of GEETA DUTT's delightful 'Jhiri Jhiri Choyetali', and a contemporary makeover with world music diva SUSHEELA RAMAN's 'Ye Mera Divanapan Hai' – as does the folk music of Bengal's wandering minstrel, UNESCO-flagged Baul culture. She gives space to hip young Argentinian singer-songwriter FEDERICO AUBELE, whose excellent if inevitably Gotan-ish 'Postales' swims well with the mood, but it's arguably venerable Anthropology professor PARTHA CHATTERJEE who steals the show with the brilliant 'Amra Reformed Hindus', his wry, bilingual erudition suggesting a sub-continental Jake Thackray. The opportunity of hand-picking her own scorer and her own music isn't something which Nair takes for granted and her parting shot – "This is the privilege of cinema: to bring together the sounds, voices, instruments of that which you love and make it one with image" – is perhaps one which lesser directors would do well to heed. About her only choice worth taking issue with is hip-hop cut, 'The Chosen One', sounding clichéd and forced in a context otherwise finely wrought and superbly sequenced. *BG*

Album rating: *8

the NATIVE AMERICANS

1994 (US 6x 44m epi.TV-mini) Total Marketing Services

Film genre: people documentary

Top guns: dir(s): Phil Lucas, John Borden, George Burdeau

Stars: Joy Harvo *(narrator)*, John Mohawk *(himself)*

Storyline: The Red Indians or the native Americans, these episodic chronicles take a look at several tribes and their territorial boundaries. *MCS*

Movie rating: *8

Visual: 6 episodic videos

Off the record: (see below)

—

ROBBIE ROBERTSON & THE RED ROAD ENSEMBLE: Music For..

Oct 94. (cd/c) *Capitol; <28295> (CD/TC EST 2238)* ☐ ☐
– Coyote dance / Mahk tchi (heartbeat drum song) / Ghost dance / The vanishing breed / It's a good day to die / Golden feather / Akua Tuta / Words of fire, deeds of blood / Cherokee morning song / Skinwalker / Ancestor song / Twisted hair.

S/track review: As a polished, muso variation on the kind of Enigma/Deep Forest-esque world fusion that was everywhere in the early to mid-90s, ROBBIE ROBERTSON's soundtrack inevitably sounds more dated than some of his other solo works, but it can at least claim the legitimacy of input from fellow contemporary Native American/Native American-descended artists, people like PURA FE (blues-singing descendent of the Tascarora tribe and founder of native a cappella group ULALI, also featured here), DOUGLAS SPOTTED EAGLE and the more instantly recognisable RITA COOLIDGE. ROBERTSON's deep-set strata of quasi-ambient programming, percussion and ethnic voicing are very 'Real World'-ly – the album's actually released on 'Capitol' but it wouldn't be at all surprising to see the familiar spectrum logo of Peter Gabriel's world music bastion – yet at the same time strangely passionless, as if the earnestness of intention has suffocated the end result. Much of the history here is pretty tragic but too often the poignancy of the Native American story doesn't really have room to breathe amid the overly sophisticated, overly studio-assisted music and lyrics which often border on the trite. Prominent bass and a smoke-signal keyboard melody lend the likes of 'Ghost Dance' and 'The Vanishing Breed' a certain grace but the soundtrack only really communicates the latent power of its subject on closer, 'Twisted Hair', where ROBERTSON pares the arrangements down to just a Lakota opera singer (BONNIE JO HUNT), his own wonderfully gruff voice and an unlikely spectral chorus of sampled crickets. A missed opportunity. *BG*

Album rating: *5.5

NEAR DARK

1987 (US 95m) DeLaurentiis Entertainment (R)

Film genre: gothic horror: western/vampire

Top guns: s-w + dir: Kathryn Bigelow

Stars: Adrian Pasdar *(Caleb Colton)* ← MADE IN USA / → SHUT UP & SING, Jenny Wright *(Mae)*, Lance Henriksen *(Jesse)* → JOHNNY HANDSOME → DEAD MAN → TARZAN, Bill Paxton *(Severin)* ← STREETS OF FIRE / → TRESPASS → DERAILROADED, Jenette Goldstein *(Diamondback)*, Tim Thomerson *(Loy Colton)* ← RHINESTONE ← HONKYTONK MAN ← CARNY ← RECORD CITY ← CAR WASH / → EDDIE PRESLEY → BAD CHANNELS, Joshua John Miller *(Homer)*, Marcie Leeds *(Sarah Colton)*

Storyline: Caleb Colton finally gets his chance to escape from his boring, smalltown lifestyle when he meets seductive drifter Mae. She introduces him to her "family" who turn out to be a gang of Hells Angel type vampires, wreaking havoc wherever they go. Caleb allows Mae to turn him into a vampire but he is not readily accepted by the others, and in a series of adventures he must prove himself loyal to his new "family" yet somehow save his real family back home from certain death. *JZ*

Movie rating: *8

Visual: video

Off the record: (see below)

—

TANGERINE DREAM

Nov 87. (lp/c/cd) *Silva Screen; <(FILM/+C/CD 026)>* ☐ Feb88 ☐
– Caleb's blues / Pick up at high noon / Rain in the third house / Bus station / Good times / She's my sister (resurrection 1) / Mae comes back / Father and son (resurrection 2) / Severin dies / Fight at dawn / Mae's transformation. *<(cd-iss. Jun90; VSD 47309)>*

S/track review: TANGERINE DREAM (EDGAR FROESE, CHRIS FRANKE and PAUL HASLINGER) got some rave reviews for this one, although some critics were still not convinced of their combination of "real" albums among their plethora of mid-80s film scores. If their standards were high it was due to their groundbreaking, mid-70s classics such as 'Phaedra', 'Rubycon' & 'Ricochet', while film work 'SORCERER' (1977) and 'THIEF' (1981) was equally up there with their best. Taking their previous album, 'Underwater Sunlight' (1986) and 'THREE O'CLOCK HIGH' (1987) as sort of benchmarks, this probably does sit in there, but I'm afraid for once you'll have to decide for yourself. 'Caleb's Blues' kicks off the set, an electro-pop instrumental that reminded me of something from JOHN PAUL JONES' 'SCREAM FOR HELP' (1985), simplistic and very unemotional; ditto 'Good Times'. FRANKE was to take his symphonic electronica on to new boundaries after he subsequently left the 'DREAM. There are a handful of appropriately eerie dirges here, including 'Pick Up A High Noon' and 'Mae Comes Back', but these are better sidelined with the movie. I'm not a fan, and anything was better than the cheesy theme song, 'Naughty Naughty' by JOHN PARR, shelved for the OST. *MCS*

Album rating: *6

NED KELLY

1970 (UK 103m) United Artists Pictures (AA)

Film genre: western/outlaw biopic

Top guns: s-w: (+ dir) Tony Richardson → the BORDER, Ian Jones

Stars: **Mick Jagger** *(Ned Kelly)* <= the ROLLING STONES =>, Allen Bickford *(Dan Kelly)*, Mark McManus *(Joe Byrne)*, Geoff Gilmour *(Steve Hart)*, Clarissa Kaye *(Ned's mother)*, Ken Goodlet *(Supt. Nicholson)*, Frank Thring *(Judge Barry)*, Bruce Barry *(George King)* → ABBA: THE MOVIE → PATRICK, Robert Bruning *(Sgt. Steele)*, Tony Bazell *(Mr. Scott)*, Diane Craig *(Maggie Kelly)*, Bill Hunter *(officer)* → RIKKI AND PETE → BAD EGGS

Storyline: Irish immigrant Ned Kelly finds it hard to make ends meet in the tough Australian Outback of the 19th century. When he is jailed for a crime he didn't commit it's the final straw, and he and his brothers become horse thieves when he's finally released. After a failed police ambush, Kelly's mother is arrested in the hope of drawing the gang out of hiding but a shoot-out in a saloon ends in tragedy for the family. "A Down Under Western". *JZ*

Movie rating: 4.5

Visual: video + dvd

Off the record: **Marianne Faithfull** was hospitalized after a drug overdose and her part was taken by Diane Craig. Mick Jagger wrote the song 'Brown Sugar' while on location. Mark McManus, step-brother of the Sweet's Brian Connolly, found fame in Scottish crime series, Taggart – he and his brother died in the mid 90s. *MCS*

—

SHEL SILVERSTEIN (& vocals: WAYLON JENNINGS *)

Jun 70. (lp) *United Artists; (UAS 29108) <UAS 5213>*
– Ned Kelly (*) / The wild colonial boy (vocal: MICK JAGGER) / Son of a scoundrel (*) / Shadow of the gallows (*) / Lonigan's widow (*) / Stoney cold ground (vocal: KRIS KRISTOFFERSON) / The Kelly's keep comin' (vocal: KRIS KRISTOFFERSON) / Ranchin' in the evening (*) / Blame it on the Kellys (*) / Pleasures of a Sunday afternoon (*) / Hey Ned (vocal: TOM GHENT). *(<cd-iss. Jan98 on 'Rhino'+=; RCD 10708>)* – (with dialogue). *(re-iss. Apr02 on 'Simply Vinyl'; SVLP 362)*

S/track review: A poet, much-loved children's author and the man who came up with 'A Boy Named Sue', 'Sylvia's Mother' and 'The Ballad Of Lucy Jordan', SHEL SILVERSTEIN was dogged by the tag of novelty writer – and this rollicking curio was never going to change that. Weighing in with rock-solid WAYLON JENNINGS – all ding-dong bass and growling story-song – it lurches through JAGGER's limping-elf impersonation of an acapella Irish folkie and caps that with KRISTOFFERSON's over-the-top japery on 'Son Of A Scoundrel' ("Was your grandma a whore/Was your grandpa a thief?") before JENNINGS returns just in time to prevent the ensemble being carted off to rehab. In fact, it's JENNINGS's album, rooted in a series of musically routine country-ish songs which let him describe and comment on the story with a deadpan narrative authority that would later become famous over seven series of 'The Dukes Of Hazzard'. Throw in a couple of interpolations by the equally-grizzled KRISTOFFERSON, some cheerfully eccentric folk and ethnic excursions and a burst of wayward whistling, and the whole thing must have represented a peak of career quirkiness for everyone involved – except SILVERSTEIN. The writer would plough on doggedly towards respectability, and he must have thought he'd got there twenty years later when one of his songs for 'Postcards From The Edge' was nominated for an Oscar. Stephen Sondheim won. *ND*

Album rating: *5.5

NENETTE ET BONI

1996 (Fra 103m) Canal+ / La Sept Cinema

Film genre: psychological coming-of-age drama

Top guns: s-w: Claire Denis (+ dir) → TROUBLE EVERY DAY, Jean-Pol Fargeau → POLA X → TROUBLE EVERY DAY

Stars: Alice Houri *(Nenette)* → TROUBLE EVERY DAY, Gregoire Colin *(Boni)*, Jacques Nolot *(Monsieur Luminaire)*, **Vincent GALLO** *(Vincenzo Brown; the baker)*, Malek Sultan *(Malek; le prof de boze)*, Valeria Bruni-Tedeschi *(the baker's wife)*, Gerard Meylan *(L'oncle)*, Alex Descas *(gynaecologist)* → TROUBLE EVERY DAY → COFFEE AND CIGARETTES, Christian Mazzuchini *(le receleur)* → FUREUR

Storyline: Nenette is a pregnant 14-year old girl on the run from her boarding school. Boni is her older brother, whom she turns to for support. Together they attempt to negotiate their own truce with their respective lives and that of Nenette's unborn child. *BG*

Movie rating: *6.5

Visual: video

Off the record: **Vincent GALLO** (see own entry)

TINDERSTICKS

Oct 96. (cd/lp) *This Way Up; (524300-2/-1) Bar None; <99>*
– Ma souer / La passerelle / Les gateaux / Camions / Nenette est la / Petites chiennes / Nosferatu / Petites gouttes d'eau / Les Cannes a peche / La mort de Felix / Nenette s'en va / Les bebes / Les fleurs / Rumba.

S/track review: While TINDERSTICKS (i.e. STUART STAPLES, DICKON HINCHLIFFE, DAVE BOULTER, MARK COLWILL, AL McCAULEY & NEIL FRAZER) were no stranger to instrumental pieces, the release of a full-length album largely bereft of STAPLES' stately croon was perhaps a bit of a gamble. Or at least an experiment, and one which turned out surprisingly well given the centrality of his vocal in the overall scheme of things. For the most part this is beguiling mood music, with only the most tantalising hint of STAPLES' lugubrious rumble. A sonorous Horace Silver-like bass part, brushed percussive shuffle and expectant, three-note piano motif recur like some half-remembered, vaguely ominous dream, skilfully knitting the whole thing together, serving as a palette for extra instrumental layers (like the droning pump organ on closer 'Rumba') and making way for eerie, loping diversions like 'Petites Chiennes'. The album's solitary vocal track, 'Petites Gouttes D'eau' (or 'Tiny Tears'; alas, STAPLES doesn't sing in French) is reassuringly lovelorn and luxuriantly arranged; it could easily sit alongside the cream of the band's albums. With or without its screen accompaniment, this is a record to be savoured, a kind of cocktail jazz-noir minus the kitsch affectation and with all the haunting grace of TINDERSTICKS' finest moments. *BG*

Album rating: *6.5

NERO SU BIANCO

aka BLACK ON WHITE

1969 (Ita 90m*) Lion Films (X)

Film genre: experimental/avant-garde drama

Top guns: s-w: Tinto Brass (+ dir), Gian Carlo Fusco, Franco Longo

Stars: Anita Sanders *(Barbara)*, Terry Carter *(the American)* → BROTHER ON THE RUN → FOXY BROWN, Nino Segurini *(Paolo)*, Di Grazia Umberto, **the Freedom:- Bobby Harrison, Ray Royer, Mike Lease, Steve Shirley** (themselves), Tinto Brass *(gynaecologist)*

Storyline: When Barbara is dropped off in Hyde Park she can't hide away from the attractions of trendy London Town. Avoiding a rock band perched in a tree, she takes the tube to the shops, which is when a black mystery man begins to follow her. Barbara begins to enjoy the thrill of the chase and leads her admirer on, but what will be the outcome as the pair are drawn closer together? *JZ*

Movie rating: *7

Visual: none

Off the record: **the FREEDOM** (see below)

---

the FREEDOM

Apr 69. (lp) *Atlantic; (ATL 08028)* [–] Italy [–]
– To be free / The better side / Attraction-Black on white – With you / The butt of deception / The truth is plain to see / Childhood reflections / Seeing is believing / You won't miss / Born again / Decidedly man / Relation / We say no / The game is over. *(UK-iss.Apr95 on 'Tenth Planet'; TP 011) (<cd-iss. May01 on 'Angel Air'+=; SJPCD 028>)* – The better side (working mix – single vocal) / The butt of deception (working mix) / Born again (dry version). *(cd re-iss. Nov02 on 'Moving Image Entertainment' += cd/lp; MIE 012 CD/LP)*

S/track review: A long lost curio of psychedelic rock, this 1968/9 score languished in the vaults for thirty years before it was quietly re-released. The band themselves were unaware of the score's original Italian release, which had become a sought-after rarity in the intervening years. Formed by sacked ex-members of Procol Harum, the FREEDOM (BOBBY HARRISON and RAY ROYER, plus MIKE LEASE & STEVE SHIRLEY) were hired to provide the score for director Tinto Brass before they had written any other songs or even played a gig (the first of the few gigs they played in their short existence would be for 'NERO SU BIANCO' producer Dino De Laurentiis's new year party). The set of songs they produced are an unexpected triumph that easily stand comparison to their previous, more famous band. The FREEDOM appear in the movie itself, performing their songs as a kind of commentary, in place of dialogue which is as scant as the clothing (even the band appear apparently nude at one point). Lyrically, the songs reflect the subject matter of the film, that is to say the cultural and sexual emancipation of a middle-class white housewife as she embarks on a voyage of self discovery, facilitated by means of sex with a black man (hence the title). Musically 'NERO SU BIANCO' is prime 60s psychedelia, swirling electric organ, chiming/wailing guitars and a tight, groovy as anything rhythm section, undiluted by avoiding thirty years of over-familiarity and re-appropriation. Two songs in and it becomes clear the score's obscurity is completely unjustified – after the epic 'Attraction – Black On White/With You' you realise it's a crime. 'Decidedly Man' helpfully retells the history of female sin from Adam's Eve to Cleopatra and beyond with attractively fuzzy guitars and wailing backing vocals. Closer 'The Game Is Over' features phased drums and vocals that could be mistaken for early Bowie, rounding up a set that for all its rarity has the reassuring familiarity of a lost relative. Often a so-called "lost classic" will fail to live up to its promise, but this record rarely disappoints (usually the fault of the slightly patronising lyrics) and often pleasantly surprises. The movie itself has, perhaps justifiably, all but vanished, ignored even by fans of Brass's later period of kitsch erotica (see 'Cosí Fan Tutte' and 'Frivolous Lola') – but fans of Procol Harum and English psychedelia in general will find plenty here to occupy their warped minds. *SW*

Album rating: *6

□ Michael NESMITH
(⇒ the MONKEES)

NETHERWORLD

1991 (US 87m; str8-to-vid) Full Moon Entertainment (R)

Film genre: supernatural horror

Top guns: dir: David Schmoeller (+ story) / s-w: Charles Band (+ story)

Stars: Michael C. Bendetti *(Corey Thornton)*, Denise Gentile *(Delores)*, Holly Floria *(Diane Palmer)*, Robert Burr *(Beauregard Yates)*, Robert Sampson *(Noah Thornton)*, Holly Butler *(Marilyn Monroe)*, Alex Datcher *(Mary Magdalene)*, David Schmoeller *(Billy C.)*, Anjanette Comer *(Mrs. Palmer)*, **David Bryan, Edgar Winter**

Storyline: Corey Thornton inherits a large estate after the death of his mysterious father. When reading through his papers, Corey is shocked to find his father was heavily into black magic and his last wish was to be brought back from the dead. When Corey discovers the brothel next door is really a witches' coven and stone hands appear out of the walls murdering people, he wonders whether his father's dream could become reality. *JZ*

Movie rating: *3.5

Visual: video + dvd

Off the record: DAVID BRYAN & EDGAR WINTER (see below).

—

DAVID BRYAN (featuring EDGAR WINTER)

1992. (cd) *Moonstone; <12940-2>* □ [-]
– Stranger to love / Tonk's place / Birds of a feather / Black magic river / Open door policy / My father's sins / The ceremony / Into the netherworld / If I didn't love you / Inherit the dead / Mirror image / What's your pleasure? / 100 reasons / Netherworld waltz.

S/track review: Many might have heard the name DAVID BRYAN bandied about in pop circles, but most will struggle to connect it with New Jersey rock giants, Bon Jovi. While singer JON BON JOVI had already committed himself to score the music for 'YOUNG GUNS II' (aka 'Blaze Of Glory') (1990), pianist BRYAN (born David Rashbaum), too, subsequently got on the proverbial soundtrack bandwagon. Augmented composer-wise by LARRY FAST (who'd already scored 'Jupiter Menace' in '84), there was also a sleeve credit to EDGAR WINTER, No.1 in the charts with 'Frankenstein', two decades past. EDGAR's soulful, ballad-rock vocals open the show on 'Stranger To Love', a track very much in the mould of Jovi – think 'Wanted Dead Or Alive', while others took on a Keith Emerson or Rick Wakeman approach. Like the movie itself, the music is haunting, ethereal and weird, each piece completely different to the last, fusing jazz and classical with BRYAN's piano-led dabblings. Track 3 for instance, 'Birds Of A Feather' is of particular interest with its diversions into neo-classical. WINTER shows us his roots (mainly white locks like his albino brother, Johnny), with easy-blues number, 'Open Door Policy', a brothel creep-er, indeed. Augmented by TONK'S HOUSE BAND, a band that included BRYAN, WINTER and TROY TURNER (guitar), HAROLD SCOTT (bass), STANLEY WATSON (drums) and NANCY BUCHAN (violin), the album threw up a few rock'n'roll concoctions, many reminiscent of past songs, 'If I Didn't Love You' (by EDGAR again) close enough to be 'Addicted To Love'. Anyway, not a bad set, but not a great one either. *MCS*

Album rating: *5

□ the NEW CHRISTY MINSTRELS segment
(⇒ ADVANCE TO THE REAR)

NICELAND

2004 (Ice/Den/Ger/UK 87m) Nimbus / TV2 / Tradewind / Zik Zak

Film genre: buddy comedy-drama/fantasy

Top guns: dir: Fridrik Thor Fridriksson ← ENGLAR ALHEIMSINS / s-w: Huldar Breidfjord

Stars: Martin Compston *(Jed)*, Gary Lewis *(Max)*, Kerry Fox *(Chloe)*, Peter Capaldi *(John)* ← LOCAL HERO, Shauna MacDonald *(Sandra)*, Timmy Lang *(Alex)*, Gudrun Maria Bjarnadottir *(Chloe)* ← 101 REYKJAVIK, Gudrun Gisladottir *(Ruth)*

Storyline: Youngsters, Jed and Chloe have mundane jobs working in a factory, their only goal in life seems to be seeking out Max, a man in-the-know they spot on telly – but does he have all the answers? *MCS*

Movie rating: *7

Visual: dvd

Off the record: Scottish actors are rife here (Compston, Lewis, Capaldi & MacDonald), heading a cast of interwoven Icelandic thespians. *MCS*

—

MUGISON

Sep 04. (cd) *Accidental; (AC 13CD)* □ [-]
– 2 birds / Move on / Love theme / I'm on fire / Later . . . with Jools Holland (out-take) / To the bank / I'd ask (acoustic version) / I'd ask theme / Sill – Song for hippies / Yfirheit (KIPPI KANINUS) / Mugigospel / Patrick Swayzee / Move on man (out-take) / I'd ask Jolly / Poke a pal (take 2) / Sun king / Blessud sorgin / Graturnar / Scrap yard / I'd ask (finale) / 47 sec symphony / Graturnar + voice.

S/track review: MUGISON's first cinematic offering (his second, 'a LITTLE TRIP TO HEAVEN' (2005) – aka 'Little Trip' – arrived a year or so later), saw the man from Iceland record the 22-song set in his hometown church. Soulful and heartwarming – on a laptop, lo-fi scale at least – 'NICELAND' opened its musical account with '2 Birds', a melancholy first take complete with female accompaniment and er . . . Muggi coughs. We go funky, pizzicato double bass and instrumental for track two, 'Move On', before we slide back to the campfire folk of 'Love Theme' – even Ry Cooder would be proud. 'I'm On Fire', 'To The Bank' and 'I'd Ask' (the latter thematic throughout), continued his bedsitter blues oft reminiscent of Will Oldham, Vincent Gallo and Scotsman Alasdair Roberts. MUGISON seems to take some degree of morbid mischief and funny fascination with mixing all this up with weird, Beatles/Gong-esque electronica noodlings, musical territory that at times seemed to complement, rather than hinder his lo-fi musings; the tracks 'Patrick Swayze' and 'Move Out Man, out-take', perhaps took it too far. 'Poke A Pal, take 2' (what happened to take 1, pal?) was far too short, although it did get the melodica man at the mic again. The most cinematic and Morricone-ish of all the record's numbers was undoubtably the wrist-cutting 'Sun King', while nearly everything else on the set just kept looking for the proverbial dust-bowl graveyard – somewhere far away, probably too far away for some people. As they say, it was an LP with two sides, I'd play side one . . . a lot. *MCS*

Album rating: *7

NIGHT ON EARTH

1991 (US 129m) Fine Line Features (R)

Film genre: urban comedy

Top guns: s-w + dir: Jim Jarmusch ← MYSTERY TRAIN ← DOWN BY LAW / → DEAD MAN → YEAR OF THE HORSE → GHOST DOG: THE WAY OF THE SAMURAI → COFFEE AND CIGARETTES

Stars: Gena Rowlands *(Victoria Snelling)* ← LIGHT OF DAY, Winona Ryder *(Corky)* ← GREAT BALLS OF FIRE! / → REALITY BITES, Giancarlo Esposito *(YoYo)* ← SCHOOL DAZE ← MAXIMUM OVERDRIVE / → KLA$H → FEEL THE NOISE, Rosie Perez *(Angela)* → MY GENERATION → the ROAD TO EL DORADO, Armin Mueller-Stahl *(Helmut Grokenberger)* → RED HOT, Roberto Benigni *(Gino)* ← DOWN BY LAW / → COFFEE AND CIGARETTES, Lisanne Falk *(rock manager)*, Beatrice Dalle *(blind woman)* → TROUBLE EVERY DAY → CLEAN, Isaach de Bankole *(Paris driver)* → GHOST DOG: THE WAY OF THE SAMURAI → COFFEE AND CIGARETTES, Alan Randolph Scott *(rock musician #1)*, Matti Pellonpaa * *(Mika)* + Kari Vaananen * *(man #1)* + **Sakari Kuosmanen** *(man #2)* ← LENINGRAD COWBOYS GO AMERICA / * → LENINGRAD COWBOYS MEET MOSES, **Anthony Portillo** *(rock musician #2)*

Storyline: Fed up with always getting the cab driver who knows everything? Here, five night-time taxi drivers in five different cities each pick up a motley collection of passengers as they go about their business. Sometimes it's the cabbies who tell their tales, sometimes the fares. In L.A., New York, Paris, Rome and Helsinki the languages may be different but the themes are always the same:- human interaction and what life is all about. That's a tenner please. *JZ*

Movie rating: *7

Visual: video + dvd

Off the record: **Sakari Kuosmanen** was a Finnish singer.

TOM WAITS

May 92. (cd/c) *Island; <(510929-2/-4)>*
– Back in the good old world / Los Angeles mood (chromium descensions) / Los Angeles theme (another private dick) / New York theme (hey, you can have that heart attack outside, buddy) / New York mood (a new haircut and a busted lip) / Baby, I'm not a baby anymore (Beatrice theme) / Good old world (waltz) / Carnival (Brunello del Montalcino) / On the old side of the world (vocal) / Good old world (gypsy instrumental) / Paris mood (un de fromage) / Dragging a dead priest / Helsinki mood / Carnival Bob's confession / Good old world (waltz vocal) / On the other side of the world (instrumental).

S/track review: It's surprising perhaps that the tremulous atmospheric of TOM WAITS have only been used to score two feature films, this and Francis Ford Coppola's 'ONE FROM THE HEART' (1982). Teaming up with Jim Jarmusch for this peculiar little quirk of a movie, WAITS took a couple of main codas: 'Good Old World', 'Theme' and 'Mood', and riffed a subtly different take for each of the quintet of vignettes. The results however, are disappointing by WAITS' standards. While 'Good Old World' is a by-the-book WAITS standard of junkyard thunks and backyard growls, it lacks an edge to make it as transcendent as so much of his back catalogue. It takes flashes of Joe Gore's razor-wire guitar to lift it past torpid. It does little more than setting a mood, but like the movie itself, it just doesn't go anywhere, each theme trundles along like a cab without a driver. You get the feeling this is less to do with WAITS but more to do with the slight nature of Jim Jarmusch's film. Considering what both men are capable of this is pretty ordinary. Can you imagine if WAITS soundtracked 'Broken Flowers' or 'DEAD MAN'? Now that would have been something. *MR*

Album rating: *4.5

NIGHTHAWKS

1981 (US 105m) Universal Pictures

Film genre: cop/detective/crime thriller (18)

Top guns: dir: Bruce Malmuth / s-w: David Shaber ← the WARRIORS (+ story w/: Paul Sylbert)

Stars: Sylvester Stallone *(Det. Sgt. Deke DaSilva)* → RHINESTONE, Billy Dee Williams *(Det. Sgt. Matthew Fox)* ← LADY SINGS THE BLUES ← the FINAL COMEDOWN / → BATMAN → the JACKSONS: AN AMERICAN DREAM, Rutger Hauer *(Reinhardt Heymar Wulfgar)*, Lindsay Wagner *(Irene)*, Nigel Davenport *(Peter Hartman)*, Persis Khambatta *(Shakka Holland)*, **Jellybean Benitez** *(DJ at Xenon)*, Luke Reilly *(conductor)* → PRIVATE PARTS → DANCER IN THE DARK

Storyline: New York cops, Deke DeSilva and Matthew Fox, are assigned to track down cold-blooded terrorist, Wulfgar, whose recent bombing campaign included blowing up a large department store in London. New York is his next target. *MCS*

Visual: video + dvd

Movie rating: *6

Off the record: Puerto Rican **"Jellybean" Benitez** (aka John) was the man behind MADONNA's breakthrough career, arranging hits such as 'Holiday' and 'Borderline'. *MCS*

KEITH EMERSON

Apr 81. (lp) *Backstreet; <BSR 5196> M.C.A.; (MCF 3107)*
– Nighthawks (main title) / Mean stalkin' / The bust / Nighthawking / The chase / I'm a man / The chopper / Tramway / I'm comin' in / Face to face / The flight of the hawk. *(re-iss. Jan89; MCA 1521) <US cd-iss. 2002 on 'Emersongs'; A 12802-2>*

S/track review: KEITH EMERSON's second stab at movie scores, his first being 'INFERNO' in 1978. The man himself was once renowned as the greatest keyboard player as part of 60s Classical-rock act, the Nice and 70s Prog-rock supergroup, Emerson, Lake & Palmer. This soundtrack release was a long way from the heady days of 'Tarkus', 'Trilogy' and 'Brain Salad Surgery'. Here, Keith was assisted by drummer NEIL SYMONETTE, bassist

KENDALL STUBBS, trumpeter GREG BOWEN, percussionist FRANK SCULLY, wind player JEROME RICHARDSON and a full orchestra. Action and suspense being the nature of the film, EMERSON's music succeeded in transporting us back there in the chilly streets of Manhattan. But for a few hiccups such as 'Nighthawking', featuring banal lyrics sung by PAULETTE WILLIAMS, the set was certainly his most accessible work since 'Fanfare For The Common Man'; even a playful cover of the Spencer Davis Group's 'I'm A Man' worked at this level. *MCS*

Album rating: *6.5

– spinoff releases, etc. –

KEITH EMERSON: I'm A Man / Nighthawks (main title)

Apr 81. (7") *(MCA 697)* [–] [ ]

(Harry) NILSSON

Born: Harry Nelson, 15 Jun'41, Brooklyn, New York, USA. Singular in his singing-songwriting talents, and with a penchant for elaborate orchestration, HARRY NILSSON composed at least one great soundtrack in his prematurely short lifetime, not to mention a handful of classic songs. One of these, his definitive version of Fred Neil's 'Everybody's Talkin', was elemental in the soundtrack success of John Schlesinger's 'MIDNIGHT COWBOY' (1969), although by this point he'd already recorded a whimsical score of his own, for Otto Preminger's dismal hippie yarn, 'SKIDOO' (1968), in which he also made a cameo appearance. Much, much better was NILSSON's soundtrack to TV animation, 'The POINT!' (1971), a hugely charming blend of dislocated melody and occasionally amusing, stoner-inspired dialogue. He subsequently landed a starring role (his one and only) in Freddie Francis' vampire spoof, 'SON OF DRACULA' (1974) as the punningly monikered Count Down, and while he also composed the score, he'd later comment that he only took the part in order to star opposite buddy RINGO STARR. The man's fourth and final score came with Robert Altman's 'POPEYE' (1980), where he combined with Van Dyke Parks to create a memorable clutch of amusing vignettes. Tragically, NILSSON died of a heart attack on 15th January 1994. *BG*

- **filmography** (composer) {acting} –

Skidoo *(1968 {a} OST =>)* / **the Point!** *(1971 TV OST =>)* / **Son Of Dracula** *(1974 {*} OST =>)* / **Popeye** *(1980 OST =>)* / the Telephone *(1987 [s-w])* / posthumous: **Who Is Harry Nilsson (And Why Is Everybody Talkin' About Him?)** *(2006 {*p} =>)*

1984

aka NINETEEN EIGHTY-FOUR

1984 (UK 110m) Umbrella-Rosenblum / Virgin (15)

Film genre: psychological/sci-fi/political satire/drama

Top guns: s-w: (+ dir) Michael Radford, Jonathan Gems (au: George Orwell)

Stars: John Hurt *(Winston Smith)* ← PIED PIPER / → EVEN COWGIRLS GET THE BLUES → DEAD MAN → the PROPOSITION, Richard Burton *(O'Brien)* ← CANDY, Suzanna Hamilton *(Julia)* ← BRIMSTONE & TREACLE, Cyril Cusack *(Charrington)* ← HAROLD AND MAUDE, Gregor Fisher *(Parsons)*, James Walker *(Syme)*, Andrew Wilde *(Tillotson)* → WHITE CITY, Janet Key *(instructress)* ← PERCY, Garry Cooper *(guard)* ← QUADROPHENIA / → BEAUTIFUL THING, Christine Hargreaves *(soup lady)* ← the WALL, Eddie Stacey *(executioner)* ← FLASH GORDON ← TOMMY

Storyline: In the totalitarian London of 1984, Winston Smith works in the records department of the Ministry of Truth, which rewrites history to suit the Party. When he discovers the Party has been lying to the people he begins to ask questions – putting him in danger with the Thought Police. When fellow worker Julia then begins taking an interest in Winston, he fears the worst, thinking her either a spy or another subversive. Either way, the dreaded Room 101 looms ever closer. *JZ*

Movie rating: *7.5

Visual: video + dvd

Off the record: (see below)

EURYTHMICS: 1984 – For The Love Of Big Brother

Nov 84. (lp/c) *Virgin; (V/TCV 1984) R.C.A.; <5349>* [23] [93]
– I did it just the same / Sexcrime (nineteen eighty-four) / For the love of Big Brother / Winston's diary / Greetings from a dead man / Julia / Doubleplusgood / Ministry of love / Room 101. *(re-iss. Jan88 lp/c; OVED/+C 207) (cd-iss. Apr89; CDV 1984) (cd re-iss. Dec95 on 'Virgin'VIP'; CDVIP 135) (cd re-iss. 2001 on 'Disky'; VI 646712)*

S/track review: 1984 was indeed a definitive year for EURYTHMICS (and indeed the group's songwriter, DAVID A. STEWART) as the group embarked on their first foray in the fickle film world. The duo of the aforementioned STEWART and his singing Scots-born wife, ANNIE LENNOX, had taken the pop industry by storm during the last few years when 'Sweet Dreams (Are Made Of This)' raced to the top of the US charts (No.2 in the UK), while four others ('Love Is A Stranger', 'Who's That Girl?', 'Here Comes The Rain Again' & 'Right By Your Side') also breached both Top 30s. Sadly, for the '1984' feature film (subtitled on the EURYTHMICS soundtrack, 'For The Love Of Big Brother'), there was a bit of a dispute between the filmmaker, Michael Radford, and 'Virgin' Films, who insisted on using the EURYTHMICS electro-pop score rather than Dominic Muldowney's orchestral one. The combination of both commissions are actually used in the movie, although different variations appear on a later Channel 4 version, the video and the subsequent DVD. Incidentally, the solo Dominic Muldowney OST was finally issued on CD in 1999. EURYTHMICS found it somewhat easier for a release date, although by all accounts the subsequent reviews and sales were pretty poor in comparison to their previous two sets, 'Sweet Dreams (Are Made Of This)' (1983) and 'Touch' (1983); 'In The Garden' (1981) was the group's debut LP. Far removed from the ethos of George Orwell's book it seems, EURYTHMICS become slaves to the rhythm from the onset, opener 'I Did It Just The Same': finds Annie scatting to a tribal dance rhythm. When one thinks of today's rather OTT, PC climate, follow-on track and hit single, 'Sexcrime (Nineteen Eighty-Four)', was hardly the topic to be chanting and dancing at the local disco; however, that's just what they did back in the yuppie, un-caring mid-80s. But it's still the album's saving grace (apart from the romantic, Jon Anderson-like hit ballad, 'Julia'), which doesn't say much for the rest of the album. Flitting between songs such as 'For The Love Of Big Brother' and unthreatening instrumentals, 'Winston's Diary' and 'Greetings From A Dead Man' (6 minutes of "poppapapa . . ."), the LP comes across as quite schizoid, but then again, the movie was about Orwell's dystopian novel. Beatbox at the ready, the re . . .re . . .petitive 'Doubleplusgood' is another to be short on lyrics, although Annie does get to shout instructions and numbers through that torturous voxbox. 'Ministry Of Love', meanwhile, is best left to STEWART as he described it as "Kraftwerk meeting African tribal meeting Booker T & The MGs". Finale cue, the chanting 'Room 101' (the place where one can throw all the worst things away!) sums it all up, making the '1984' OST a contender for the bargain bins, at least. For EURYTHMICS die-hards only; Orwell fans, meanwhile, are waiting for him turning in his proverbial grave. While EURYTHMICS continued to chart throughout the 80s (until the Annie/Dave partnership broke up),

STEWART carried on as a prolific film composer in his own right – but that's for another edition. *MCS*

Album rating: *4.5

– spinoff hits, etc. –

EURYTHMICS: Sexcrime (nineteen eighty-four) / I Did It Just The Same

Oct 84. (7") *(VS 728) <13956>* [4] [81]
(12"/12"pic-d) *(VS 728-12)* – ('A'-extended).

EURYTHMICS: Julia / Ministry Of Love

Jan 85. (7"/7"pic-d) *(VS 734)* [44] [–]
(12"+=) *(VS 734-12)* – ('A'-extended).

□ NO OYES LADRAR LOS PERROS? alt.
(⇒ ENTENDS-TU LES CHIENS ABOYER?)

NO WAY BACK

1976 (US 103m) Atlas Films (R)

Film genre: cop/detective drama

Top guns: s-w (+ dir): Fred Williamson ← ADIOS AMIGO ← MEAN JOHNNY BARROWS / → MR. MEAN

Stars: Fred Williamson *(Jess Crowder)* ← MEAN JOHNNY BARROWS ← BUCKTOWN ← THREE THE HARD WAY ← THREE TOUGH GUYS ← BLACK CAESAR ← HELL UP IN HARLEM / → MR. MEAN → FROM DUSK TILL DAWN → RIDE → CARMEN: A HIP HOPERA, Charles Woolf *(Pickens)* ← LADY SINGS THE BLUES, Tracy Reed *(Candy)* ← TRAIN RIDE TO HOLLYWOOD ← TROUBLE MAN / → CAR WASH → a PIECE OF THE ACTION, Virginia Gregg *(Mrs. Mildred Pickens)*, Stack Pierce *(Bernie)* ← CORNBREAD, EARL AND ME ← TROUBLE MAN ← COOL BREEZE, Argy Allen *(Pickens' brother)*, Paul Sills *(Crowder's secretary)* ← DISCO 9000, Don Cornelius ← CLEOPATRA JONES / → ROADIE → TAPEHEADS → JACKIE'S BACK!

Storyline: Black ex-cop Jesse Crowder is an L.A. private dick with few scruples when it comes to taking on a case, and he doesn't hesitate when a woman requests his services in tracking down her errant husband, despite the fact he's apparently bolted for Latin America with a young girl and a serious wad of pilfered cash. *BG*

Movie rating: *3

Visual: none

Off the record: The DELLS (see below)

—

the DELLS *[w/ non-s/t *]*

May 76. (lp) *Mercury; <SRM-1 1084>* [ ] [–]
– West Virginia symphony [*] / When does the lovin' start [*] / I'll make you my girl [*] / Life is the time [*] / Ain't no black and white in music [*] / No way back / Too late for love / You're the greatest [*] / Adventure / I'll try again [*] / Slow motion [*].

S/track review: The DELLS aren't the first group you think of when it comes to blaxploitation but the 50s doo-wop legends were still hungry enough – and sartorially sharp enough (no beards and jumpsuits for these cats, only nicknames like "Ice-Berg" and "Luca") – to cook up some serious funk. This isn't a full soundtrack; only three of the songs were recorded for the film (two if you consider that 'NO WAY BACK' runs over two parts), but they're all worth hearing, as is the rest of the album. The title track's about as heavy as anything the vocal quintet ever recorded, a multi-tempo grinder with a choppy, JBs-funky front and a sub-Mothership bottom, dominated by MARVIN "The Magnum" JUNIOR's Black & Decker rasp. 'Adventure' is its semi-instrumental reprise, driving, get-down disco-funk with mandatory clavinet, and likewise the most danceable few minutes in the group's catalogue; think Billy Preston covering Ray Barretto's 'Right On'. As a love theme, 'Too Late For Love', is fairly standard mid-70s DELLS, trademark harmonies supplying the kleenex to JUNIOR's wracked deliberations. Ivy Jo Hunter – mainstay of the early 'Motown' sound and co-writer of Martha & The Vandellas' 'Dancing In The Street' – supplies some fine Allen Toussaint-esque Southern funk in 'West Virginia Symphony', 'Ain't No Black And White In Music' and the brass-marshalled 'When Does The Lovin' Start', but it's the breathless, moon-eyed melodies and singing horn charts of producer and longtime associate Bobby Miller (hitmaker during the group's 60s stint at 'Chess') which brings out the collective street-corner crooner in these old pros. *BG*

Album rating: *6.5

NOI ALBINOI

alt. 'NOI THE ALBINO'

2003 (Ice/Den/UK/Ger 82m + 93m) Zik Zak Kvikmyndir / M&M (15)

Film genre: coming-of-age melodrama

Top guns: s-w + dir: **Dagur Kari**

Stars: Tomas Lemarquis *(Noi)*, Prostur Leo Gunnarsson *(Kiddi Beikon)* ← 101 REYKJAVIK, Elin Hansdottir *(Iris)*, Anna Fridriksdottir *(Lina)*, Hjalti Rognvaldsson *(Oskar)*, Petur Einarsson *(Prestur)* ← 101 REYKJAVIK ← ENGLAR ALHEIMSINS, Kjartan Bjargmundsson *(Gylfi)*, Gudmundur Olafsson *(Alfred Kennari)*

Storyline: Noi is a troubled but bright teenager living with his alcoholic father in a snowy and remote part of Iceland. To cope with boredom, the 17-year old punk/village idiot (delete as appropriate) rebels against authority, but then he meets petrol station worker, Iris, and plans his escape from the surrounding icy prison. *MCS*

Movie rating: *7

Visual: dvd (Artificial Eye) <Palm Pictures>

Off the record: SLOWBLOW is the project of independent film-maker/musician, **Dagur Kari Petursson** (b.12 Dec'73, France; raised Iceland) and his friend Orri Jonsson; already two albums in the can, including their excellent "eponymous" set. With the help of his short 40-minute film, 'Lost Weekend', Dagur graduated from the National Film School of Denmark in 1999; it went on to win nearly a dozen awards at various international festivals. After sweeping up rave reviews and awards for his feature-length debut, 'NOI . . .', Dagur subsequently wrote, directed and scored 'Voksne Mennesker' – 'Dark Horse' (2005) plus 'The Good Heart' (2007). *MCS*

—

SLOWBLOW (composer: DAGUR KARI)

Feb 04. (cd) *Kitchen Motors; (6)* [–] Icelan [–]
– Beginning / Hillbilly / Hole / Another beginning / Rainbow / Morgun / Piece of cake / Why Hawaii? / Maproom / Love on a couch / Dinner / Another hole / Date / Komdu litla barnid / Grave / Love on the phone / Groove / Sjoppa / Elegy / Aim for a smile.

S/track review: Wistful indie duo, SLOWBLOW (see above for other details), look for a warmer Hawaiian-style approach to balance the coldness of the bleak, Icelandic glaciers and fjords that surround the film's locations. It never happens. Two key words here are atmospheric and ethereal, and with twenty short-ish tracks, 'NOI ALBINOI', finds one kicking off one's snowboots for a snooze by the fireside. Peaceful to the point of horizontal (like Mogwai without the crescendos), SLOWBLOW choose to shift through an array of folky/bluegrass instruments such as box accordion, banjo, etc on opening short-takes, 'Beginning', 'Hillbilly', etc. With the majority of the cues never extending the two-minute mark, the lo-fi 'NOI . . .' never quite breaks the ice – so to speak. Think Robert Wyatt without the vox for 'Dinner', think watching paint dry for

'Another Hole' and think silent movie lullabies for 'Komdu Litla Barnid'. Like the latter and also penned by Sigridur Nielsdottir, 'Morgun' is akin to a post-millennium 'Three Blind Mice', while the variation continues via an avant-lounge workout, 'Piece Of Cake'. It's not that the album's bad, in fact in parts it's actually quite good, the uptempo and guitar-grungy 'Groove' being one highlight. Borrowed from Dmitri Shostakovich's lilting classical concerto for string-quartet, the 12-plus minute 'Elegy' is fine if you're stuck somewhere in Siberia – on a modern-day soundtrack it's akin to a game of Russian Roulette. Thankfully, messrs. DAGUR KARI and ORRI JONSSON get one final chance to redeem themselves by way of vocal cue, 'Aim For A Smile', although Iceland's top export Sigur Ros can rest easy. *MCS*

Album rating: *5.5

NON HO SONNO

2001 (Ita 117m) Opera Film Produzione / Medusa Produzione (18)

Film genre: psychological crime thriller/mystery/horror

Top guns: s-w: Dario Argento (+ dir) ← la CHIESA ← TENEBRE ← INFERNO ← SUSPIRIA ← PROFONDO ROSSO, Franco Ferrini ← la CHIESA, Carlo Lucarelli

Stars: Max von Sydow *(Ulisse Moretti)* ← DUNE ← FLASH GORDON, Stefano Dionisi *(Giacomo)*, Chiara Caselli *(Gloria)*, Rossella Falk *(Laura de Fabritiis)*, Roberto Zibetti *(Lorenzo)*, Paolo Maria Scalondro *(Chief Comm. Manni)*, Gabriele Lavia *(Dr. Betti)* ← INFERNO ← PROFONDO ROSSO

Storyline: Set in Turin, a prostitute at work discovers through finding and stealing a gruesome scrapbook, that her client has been a serial killer over the last two decades. She flees the scene and phones a friend to pick her up at the railway station. However, both are brutally murdered by the john, not before she whispers something about a dwarf to the ticket collector. Police detective, Ulisse Moretti, comes out of retirement to try and track down his old adversary before he commits more horrendous crimes. *MCS*

Movie rating: *6

Visual: dvd

Off the record: You might recall Von Sydow was also a star in another horror classic, 'The Exorcist', in 1973. *MCS*

GOBLIN

Dec 02. (cd) *Cinevox; (<CD-MDF 342>)* [–] Italy [–]
– Non ho sonno / Killer on the train / Endless love / Arpeggio – end title / Ulisse / Death farm / Movie soundtracks – The death farm animals: The pig – The cat – The swan – The rabbit / Inquiries / Associated dead / Final white week / Non ho sonno – main title.

S/track review: The much-anticipated GOBLIN return (and more so their reunion with filmmaker, Dario Argento) finally surfaced with this post-millennium gem, 'NON HO SONNO'. Keyboard-virtuoso, CLAUDIO SIMONETTI (now a film composer in his own right), guitarist MASSIMO MORANTE, bassist FABIO PIGNATELLI and drummer AGOSTINO MARANGOLO, all put their collective heads together for one last proverbial "stab" in the dark. Was it actually around a quarter of a century ago since 'PROFONDO ROSSO' (1975) and 'SUSPIRIA' (1977) reared their ugly head-less corpses. Italiano gallo was back in full gothic swing, however the prog-rock of old was replaced by Metallica-styled guitar dirges fused with classical piano tinkering and melodious choirs. This album rocked, right from the opening title track on to the creepy synth-biased, 'Killer On The Train', both atmospheric with that certain twist of the blade only GOBLIN could stick in. 'Endless Love' balanced up proceedings quite nicely, its female soprano (Vesna Duganova) producing a romantic opera-like touch to accompany that down'n'dirty, backstreet guitar that James Hetfield branded. In some respects some of the set, especially track four, 'Arpeggio (End Title)', is reminiscent of Keith Emerson's 80s scores, the comparison not too far off the mark, as both Emerson and GOBLIN had previously worked on another of Argento's movies, 'La CHIESA'. Once again, GOBLIN took their foot off the accelerator for the smoochy 'Ulisse', guitars and beautiful piano-tinkering feeling the pressure of a sexy saxophone (not in fact Kenny G, but AGOSTINO's brother ANTONIO). The multi-layered 'Death Farm' themes – electric guitar fighting percussion, bass and keys – ran through most of the remainder of the work, the follow-on 'Death Farm Animals' (tracks 7-10) variations were virtually 'NON HO SONNO' reprised in all but title. Although still effective, the recurring haunting variations cropped up on tracks 11-14, thus letting the album slide a little from the Richter scale it had climbed with ease. GOBLIN: we will not see their likes again! *MCS*

Album rating: *6.5

NOSFERATU, THE VAMPYRE

aka NOSFERATU, PHANTOM DER NACHT

1978 (W.Ger/Fra 107m) Centfox / Zweites Deutsches Fernsehen (16)

Film genre: gothic/occult horror drama

Top guns: s-w + dir: Werner Herzog ← HERZ AUS GLAS ← AGUIRRE, WRATH OF GOD / → COBRA VERDE → GRIZZLY MAN (au: Bram Stoker)

Stars: Klaus Kinski *(Count Dracula)* ← MADAME CLAUDE ← LIFESPAN ← AGUIRRE, WRATH OF GOD / → CODENAME: WILDGEESE → COBRA VERDE, Isabelle Adjani *(Lucy Harker)*, Bruno Ganz *(Jonathan Harker)*, Roland Topor *(Renfield)*, Walter Ladengast *(Dr. Van Helsing)*, Clemens Scheitz *(clerk)* ← HERZ AUS GLAS

Storyline: One of the most visually arresting and poignant portrayals of the blood lusting Count Dracula as he leaves the creepy seclusion of his Carpathian fortress and travels by sea to Western Europe, bringing plague and suspicious teeth marks in his wake. *BG*

Movie rating: *7.5

Visual: video + dvd

Off the record: (see below)

POPOL VUH: Brüder Des Schattens – Söhne Des Lichts

Nov 78. (lp) *Brain; (0060.167)* [–] W.Ger [–]
– Brüder des Schattens / Höre, der du wagst / Das Schloss des Irrtums / Die Umkehr. *(UK cd-iss. Feb97 on 'Spalax'; 14208)*

POPOL VUH: Nosferatu – On The Way To A Little Way

Nov 78. (lp) *PDU Pld.; (A 7005)* [–] W.Ger [–]
– Mantra 1 / Morning sun / Venus principle / Mantra 2 (choir) / Die Nacht der Himmel / Der Ruf der Rohrflöte / To a little way / Through pains to Heaven / On the way / Zwiesprache der Rohrflöte. *(UK cd-iss. Feb97 & Dec02 on 'Spalax'; 14212) (cd re-iss. May04 on 'S.P.V.'+=; SPV 085-70192CD)* – (both soundtracks).

S/track review: As with 'AGUIRRE...', POPOL VUH's music was as integral to Werner Herzog's F.W. Murnau remake as Klaus Kinski's pregnant silences, illuminating the director's often cryptic imagery. More sonically disembodied yet earthier than 'AGUIRRE...', FLORIAN FRICKE's third Herzog collaboration found him exploring instrumentally organic territory with wonderfully unsettling results. The soundtrack was actually released in various – and typically confusing and incomplete – incarnations before the 2002 'Spalax' reissue clarified matters, bringing together the disparate parts into one glossy, good value package. Those who've seen the film will be instantly transported back to the glowering skies of Eastern Europe by the likes of 'Die Umkehr' and opener 'Brüder Des Schattens', with an ominous funereal drone and regal orchestration heralding something very unpleasant indeed. While the track's hopeful coda anticipates the chiming, folkish pastoral of 'Morning Sun', its dark side is echoed in 'On The Way', which first appeared on the soundtrack's earliest 1978 version. While electronics continue to form the raw materials of recurring, theramin-haunted nightmares like 'Die Nacht Der Himmel', the man's interest in ethnic instrumentation had deepened further by the late 70s, expressed in extended sitar meditations and mantras such as 'Höre, Der Du Wagst'. *BG*

Album rating: *5

– spinoff releases, etc. –

POPOL VUH: Nosferatu – Music From The Werner Herzog Film
1985. (lp) *Nexus; (K22P 471)* [–] W.Ger [–]

NOT DROWNING, WAVING

Formed: Melbourne, Australia ... 1983/4 by DAVID BRIDIE (vocals & keyboards) and JOHN PHILLIPS (guitar). For a decade, the ensemble of rock-meets-ambient musicians (adding Rowan McKinnon on bass, Russell Bradley & James Southall on drums and Tim Cole as soundman) set out their prolific recording schedule including two group soundtracks, 'PROOF' (1991) and 'HAMMERS OVER THE ANVIL' (1992). Non-OST albums from the mid-80s 'Another Pond', 'The Little Desert' & 'Cold & The Crackle' showed promise, while highlights of their career stemmed from 'Claim' (1989), 'Tabaran' (1990) and 1994's farewell set 'Circus'. With the addition of cellist Helen Mountfield in '91, the band might well've established themselves as Australia's biggest export, but she and Bridie took off to form My Friend The Chocolate Cake. *MCS*

- filmography (composers) –

Hungry Heart *(1989 score by PHILLIPS)* / **Proof** *(1991 OST =>)* / Greenkeeping *(1992 score by PHILLIPS & BRIDIE)* / **Hammers Over The Anvil** *(1994 OST =>)* / God's Girls *(1995 score by PHILLIPS)* / What I Have Written *(1996 OST by BRIDIE & PHILLIPS with HELEN MOUNTFORT; see future edition)* / Mabo: Life Of An Island Man *(1997 score by PHILLIPS & BRIDIE)* / the Myth Of Fingerprints *(1997 OST by BRIDIE & PHILLIPS & V/A; see future edition)* / In A Savage Land *(1999 OST by BRIDIE; see future edition)* / Waiting At The Royal *(2000 TV score by BRIDIE)* / Tempted *(2001 OST by BRIDIE; see future edition)* / the Man Who Sued God *(2001 score by BRIDIE)* / the Men Who Would Conquer China *(2004 score by BRIDIE w/ Paul Anthony Smith)*

NOTTURNO

1983 (Ita 104m) La Sept Cinema / Zweites Deutsches (R)

Film genre: spy/crime drama

Top guns: s-w: Giorgio Bontempi (+ dir), Lucia Bruni

Stars: Tony Musante *(Jurek Rudinski)*, Claudio Cassinelli *(the contractor)*, Omero Antonutti *(Schwabe)*, Fiorenza Marchegiani *(Mary Ann Standish)*, Maurizio Merli *(Peter Wayne)*, West Buchanan *(Hackett)*, Susanna Martinkova *(Magdalena Rudinski)*

Storyline: Things look black for Jurek Rudinski as his ability to see in the dark lands him in trouble. When British secret servicemen kidnap his daughter, they force him into an assassination attempt of a top KGB man. Quite naturally our ace sniper is none too pleased with this turn of events but there seems nowhere to turn as he's hounded by agents on both sides. Will he do the deed and free his daughter or has he set his sights on another target? *JZ*

Movie rating: *5

Visual: video

Off the record: (see below)

GOBLIN

Apr 99. (cd) *Cinevox; (CD-MDF 320)* [ ] [–]
– Nocturne / Bass theme / Landing strip / Helycopter / Est / Landing strip (reprise) / Helycopter (reprise) / Nocturne (8-14).

S/track review: Fans of GOBLIN's tense horror soundtracks may find themselves a little disappointed by 'NOTTURNO'. Recorded by a later incarnation of the band, it has some of the eerie hallmarks of their best known work, but too often it veers towards easy-listening. Based around a driving guitar riff, opening salvo 'Nocturne', is the sound of a progressive rock band getting funky, with smears of synth and popping bass underlining a strident piano figure. Included as bonus tracks, a series of takes on 'Nocturne' demonstrate how the theme developed from ambient electronica to a more energetic rock number. For its opening few minutes, 'Bass Theme' has a late '70s jazz-funk feel, with supple bass runs and thin, high register synths. This makes way for a passage of lopsided piano and twinkling keyboard arpeggios, echoing their 'SUSPIRIA' soundtrack, albeit without the creeping dread. 'Landing Strip' is the sort of vaguely sinister lounge music that might play in lobby of a Soviet era Eastern European hotel, as cod-sophisticated saxophone wafts over vibraphone and piano chords. This mood continues with 'Helycopter', where what at first sounds like a standard romantic piano theme is slyly subverted by angular dischords. A sample of whirring helicopter blades and ominous synth usher in a melancholy saxophone solo, restoring the easy feel. By far the most interesting piece here is 'Landing Strip (reprise)', which bears little relation to the original track. As glassy synth pads shimmer and build in intensity, bowed cymbals squeak and whine, echoing and reverberating like wind whistling through a hall of mirrors. An atmospheric electro-acoustic dronescape – at least until the piano and saxophone return to reprise the theme – it offers a much more compelling side to GOBLIN (aka FABIO PIGNATELLI, ANTONIO MARANGOLO, AGOSTINO MARANGOLO & MAURIZIO GUARINI) than the bulk of this largely incidental soundtrack. *SS*

Album rating: *4.5

☐ Mary Margaret O'HARA segment (⇒ APARTMENT HUNTING)

O LUCKY MAN!

1973 (UK 186m) Columbia Pictures / Warner Brothers (18)

Film genre: political satire/comedy

Top guns: dir: Lindsay Anderson / s-w: David Sherwin

Stars: Malcolm McDowell *(Mick Travis / plantation thief)* → the COMPLEAT BEATLES → GET CRAZY → the DAVID CASSIDY STORY, Ralph Richardson *(Sir James Burgess / Monty)* → GIVE MY REGARDS TO BROAD STREET, Rachel Roberts *(Gloria Rowe / Madame Paillard / Mrs. Richards)*, Arthur Lowe *(Charlie Johnson / Mr. Duff / Dr. Munda)*, Helen Mirren *(Patricia)* → CAL, Graham Crowden *(Stewart / Prof. Millar / meths drinker)* ← PERCY, Peter Jeffrey *(factory chairman / prison governor)* → LIPSTICK ON YOUR COLLAR, Dandy Nichols *(tea lady / neighbour)* ← HELP!, Mona Washbourne *(neighbour / Sister Hallett / usher)* ← MRS. BROWN, YOU'VE GOT A LOVELY DAUGHTER ← TWO A PENNY ← FERRY 'CROSS THE MERSEY, Philip Stone *(Jenkins / Salvation Army major / interrogator)* → FLASH GORDON → GREEN ICE, Warren Clarke *(MoC / Warner / male nurse)* → TOP SECRET!, Mary MacLeod *(Mrs. Ball / salvationist / vicar's wife)* ← PIED PIPER / → BRIMSTONE & TREACLE, Bill Owen *(Supt. Barlow / Insp. Carding)*, Geoffrey Palmer *(doctor / Basil Keyes)* → HAWKS, Brian Glover *(foreman / power station guard)*, James Bolam *(Attenborough / doctor)*, **Alan Price** *(himself)* ← GET YOURSELF A COLLEGE GIRL, Patricia Lawrence *(clinic receptionist / Miss Hunter)* ← FERRY 'CROSS THE MERSEY, Hugh Thomas *(coffee salesman)* → BREAKING GLASS, Michael Medwin *(army captain / Duke of Belminster / power station technician)* ← I'VE GOTTA HORSE ← IT'S ALL HAPPENING ← the DUKE WORE JEANS, David Daker *(man at stag party / policeman / Munda's manservant)* → STARDUST, Jeremy Bullock *(young man)* ← SUMMER HOLIDAY ← PLAY IT COOL, Michael Elphick → STARDUST → QUADROPHENIA → BUDDY'S SONG, Lindsay Anderson *(film director)* → CHARIOTS OF FIRE

Storyline: Ambitious Mick Travis finally makes his mark on the world by landing a decent suit-and-tie job as a coffee salesman. Bright eyed and bushy tailed, Travis doesn't yet know what kind of world it is out there, and in the course of his travels across the country and up the social ladder he is seduced, tortured, used as a human guinea pig and finally jailed after working for a shady politician. O Lucky Man? *JZ*

Movie rating: *8

Visual: video + dvd

Off the record: **ALAN PRICE** (see below)

—

ALAN PRICE

Jul 73. (lp) *Warners; (K 46227) <BS 2710>* ☐ ☐
– O lucky man! / Poor people / Sell sell / Pastoral / Arrival / Look over your shoulder / Justice / My home town / Changes / O lucky man! *(<cd-iss. Oct96; 9362 46137-2>)*

S/track review: Lindsay Anderson took a unique approach for the second part of his Mick Travis trilogy, commissioning ALAN PRICE (of the Animals fame) to write songs in tandem with the development of the script itself, effectively using PRICE and his solo band as a greek chorus. PRICE appears in the film itself, punctuating the action with live performances before joining the narrative, playing himself. Essentially a modern retelling of Voltaire's 'Candide', Anderson's film is many things, but at heart it is a sprawling critique of capitalism, and PRICE's score is an excellent piece of detournment; performing a set of songs that wouldn't necessarily sound out of place on later Beatles albums, it would be easy enough on first listen to miss the tang of medicine in PRICE's spoonfuls of sugar. The nonchalant groove of PRICE's meat and potato rock belies the underlying satire and perfectly complements the tone of the film, which uses the innocence, optimism and naivety of main character Mick Travis to explore its somewhat darker themes. The mock triteness of some of the lyrics is an ironic counterpoint to some of the more vicious or blackly comic plot developments, as PRICE takes the role of conscience, questionable mentor or sage observer. The wry knowingness of the title track gives way to the deadpan delivery of lyrics such as "Poor people are poor people/They don't understand" before going on to presciently essay the capitalist "winner takes us all" mentality that was then in the ascendant with "Someone's got to win in the human race/If it isn't you it has to be me" ('Poor People'). PRICE delivers lines like "Sell, sell, sell/Everything you stand for" ('Sell Sell') set to a vampish boogie, with such lack of care that you almost forget that this is a bad thing. Similarly, on 'Justice' when he croons "Only wealth will buy you justice" the overriding effect is not of an indictment, but more a statement of natural fact, the insidious evolution of capitalist society once more ironically naturalised by PRICE's winning charm. 'Changes' puts new lyrics to the hymn, 'What A Friend We Have In Jesus' and then transforms it into a music hall boogie (in the film, the audience are invited with title cards in a selection of languages to sing along). A more spirited reprise of the title track closes the set, and the film itself, leaving the listener to draw their own conclusions – a risky gamble that didn't seem to pay off for either Anderson or PRICE, who failed to gain an Oscar nomination for this set, to star Malcolm McDowell's chagrin. Overall, an excellent soundtrack that sadly shares the fate of the film itself, rarely aired, often misunderstood and highly underrated. *SW*

Album rating: *6

– spinoff releases, etc. –

ALAN PRICE: Poor People / Arrival

Jul 73. (7") *(K 16293)* ☐ ☐

OCTANE

aka PULSE

2003 (UK/Lux 90m) Four Horsemen / Random Harvest (15)

Film genre: occult horror teen movie

Top guns: dir: Marcus Adams / s-w: Stephen Volk ← GOTHIC

Stars: Madeleine Stowe *(Senga Wilson)*, Norman Reedus *(recovery man)* ← OVERNIGHT ← the BEATNICKS ← REACH THE ROCK, **Bijou Phillips** *(backpacker)* ← ALMOST FAMOUS ← BLACK AND WHITE ← SUGAR TOWN, Mischa Barton *(Natasha 'Nat' Wilson)*, Jonathan Rhys-Meyers *(Marek)* ← VELVET GOLDMINE / → ELVIS, Leo Gregory *(joyrider)* → STONED

Storyline: Harassed mum Senga is determined to keep her daughter Nat out of trouble. Nat is equally determined to find some – which she does when she runs away with a group of hippies on their way to a music festival. However, the hippies turn out to be a vampire cult who cause car accidents and drink the blood of their victims. Never mind, Senga is hot on her wayward daughter's heels and sounds just the type to raise the stakes for the vampires. *JZ*

Movie rating: *4

Visual: dvd

Off the record: Bijou Phillips (b. 1 Apr'80, Greenwich, Conneticut) is the model turned singing daughter of Mamas & The Papas co-leader, JOHN PHILLIPS. She released only one Jerry Harrison-produced album for 'Almo Sounds', 'I'd Rather Eat Glass' (1999). *MCS*

—

ORBITAL

Oct 03. (cd/lp) *E.M.I.; (593784-2/-1)* ☐ ☐
– Octane / Through the night / Strangeness in the night / Preacher / Moments of crisis / Frantic / Breaking and entering / Chasing the tanker / Total paranoia / Confrontation / Initiation / Meet the father / Blood is thicker / The road ahead.

S/track review: ORBITAL (PHIL and PAUL HARTNOLL) were one of those acts whose music was frequently dubbed "cinematic". So it was inevitable that they'd turn their hand to an actual movie soundtrack. Following their theme for 'The Saint' in 1997 and an OST collaboration with Michael Kamen, 'EVENT HORIZON', 'OCTANE' is the electronica duo's first lone score. The subdued mood pieces of the OST retain that "cinematic" quality, but next to the rhythmic and textural invention of a HARTNOLL brothers' classic like 'The Box', with its 'Third Man'-like zither and spy movie guitar strings, they are distinctly underwhelming. Using a relatively limited palette of digital synthesizer sounds, some of which sound like presets, ORBITAL create a series of slow, ambient cues, based around slowly drifting synth pads. Certain themes recur – a pitch bent melodic figure, a Tangerine Dream-like arpeggio – but none are particularly memorable. Industrial hiss and static is used to add unease, while airy vocal sounds add a ghostly presence. The score is largely beat free – it's only on the later tracks that they introduce some percolating electronic rhythms. Easily the most interesting track here, 'Initiation' is a ghostly inversion of techno, with a dissolute vocal sample in place of a euphoric refrain, the percussion washed out, brittle. These more engaging pieces aside, 'OCTANE' is little more than background music: effective in the context of the film, easy to tune out on its own. *SS*

Album rating: *4.5

ODE

1999 (US 48m short b&w) Glass Eye Pix

Film genre: romantic drama

Top guns: s-w + dir: Kelly Reichardt (nov: Herman Raucher)

Stars: Kevin Poole *(Billy Joe McAllister)*, Heather Gottlieb *(Bobbie Lee Hartley)*, Jon Wurster

Storyline: Bobbie Lee and Billy Joe are two young lovers who are forced to keep their liaison a secret because of the religious beliefs of the society they come from. They have a special meeting place at Choctaw Ridge where they can be together privately, but of course the more times they meet the more chance there is of discovery and the inevitably tragic consequences. *JZ*

Movie rating: *5

Visual: none

Off the record: (see below)

—

WILL OLDHAM: Ode Music

Jan 00. (lp/cd) *Drag City; <(DC 183/+CD)>* ☐ ☐
– Ode #1 / Ode #2 / Ode #3 / Ode #4 / Ode #1a / Ode #1b / Ode #2a / Ode #5 / Ode #3a / Ode #4a. *<(re-iss. Apr04; same)>*

S/track review: An 'ODE' one this (sorry, couldn't resist it!). The multi-faceted WILL OLDHAM (actor, solo artist and er . . . beard) literally takes us through 10 'Ode' numbers – all instrumental, or "silent" music, as it states on the back cover. Will's acoustic guitar is king here, although the atmospheric background soundscapes of organ and muted pianos come over as a worthy contender to Oldham's Bonnie Prince Billy's title. Lo-fi and melancholic to the extreme, one can pick out the best reasonably easily; the 7+minute 'Ode #1' (which has two subsequent variations) sweeps through majestically, while the 4-minute 'Ode #2' (+ 2 mins. for 'Ode #2a') fuses elements of bluegrass and the Orient. With really only 5 different cues, this could be filed under the EP category, but adding up to a total of 33:45 minutes, one should probably give it LP status. *MCS*

Album rating: *5

☐ the OHIO PLAYERS segment
(⇒ MR. MEAN)

☐ Mike OLDFIELD segment
(⇒ the KILLING FIELDS)

Will OLDHAM

Born: 24 Dec'70, Louisville, Kentucky, USA. WILL OLDHAM, aka Palace, aka Bonnie Prince Billy, is one of the few "rock" artists to have begun his career in acting rather than the other way round, starring in John Sayles' critically acclaimed mining drama, 'Matewan', back in 1987. Following a further couple of appearances including a part in western, '1,000 Pieces Of Gold' (1991), OLDHAM swapped the big screen for the fringes of the alternative music scene. If the cultivation of an austere, roots miserabilist pedigree endeared him to indie and alt-country fans and critics, his wilfully obscure lyrics suggested a truly singular talent, one with almost as many aliases as narrative voices. While his film scoring career got off to a low key start with independent feature, 'The Broken Giant' (1996), he made a return to the screen – albeit in a peforming capacity – with 'Radiation' (1998) and a brief return to acting with a cameo in Harmony Korine's 'Julien Donkey-Boy' (1999). Early 2000 saw the release of 'ODE Music', OLDHAM's acoustic score to a Kelly Reichardt-directed short film. If it wasn't the most compelling of soundtrack debuts, he at least broadened his reach with the music for 'Slitch' (2003), another short film/ DVD directed by buddy Dianne Bellino. Composed in collaboration with the ubiquitous David Pajo and released under the moniker Continental Op (a pairing which made its debut with a one-off track on a 1997 compilation), the record featured some of OLDHAM's heaviest (as in noisy) material to date, appropriate for the man's casting as a gormless surfer dude. Even more obscure was 'Tripping With Caveh Vol.1' (2004), a DVD document of OLDHAM ingesting mushrooms with independent filmmaker Caveh Zahedi. Likewise 'Seafarers' (2004), an instrumental soundtrack EP written to accompany a maritime-themed documentary by Jason Misset. A soundtrack to the next Tom Cruise movie looks unlikely . . . *BG*

- filmography (composer) {acting} –

Matewan *(1987 {*} OST by MASON DARING; see future edition)* / Everybody's Baby: The Rescue Of Jessica McClure *(1989 TV {a})* / Thousand Pieces Of Gold *(1991 {a} OST by Gary Remal Malkin)* / the Broken Giant

(1998 score) / Radiation *(1998 {b})* / Julien Donkey-Boy *(1999 {b})* / **Ode** *(2000 OST =>)* / an Injury To One *(2002 score)* / Slitch *(2003 short {*} OST as CONTINENTAL OP; see future edition =>)* / Seafarers *(2004 OST-ep; see future edition)* / Junebug *(2005 {a})* / the Guatamalan Handshake *(2006 {*})* / Old Joy *(2006 {*})*

ONE ON ONE

1977 (US 98m) Warner Bros. Pictures (PG)

Film genre: sports drama

Top guns: dir: Lamont Johnson / s-w: Robby Benson, Jerry Segal

Stars: Robby Benson *(Henry Steele)*, Annette O'Toole *(Janet Hays)* → GIGANTIC (A TALE OF TWO JOHNS), G.D. Spradlin *(coach Moreland Smith)* ← ZABRISKIE POINT, Gail Strickland *(B.J. Rudolph)* ← BOUND FOR GLORY, Melanie Griffith *(the hitchhiker)* → JOYRIDE → WORKING GIRL, James G. Richardson *(Malcolm)* ← SUPERFLY T.N.T. ← SUPERFLY, Hector Morales *(Gonzales)*, James Houghton *(Jeff)* → I WANNA HOLD YOUR HAND → MORE AMERICAN GRAFFITI → PURPLE PEOPLE EATER

Storyline: Henry Steele may be the best basketball player in his home town, but he gets a rude awakening when he wins a scholarship in the big city. The basketball here is rough and tough and the object is to win at all costs. Poor Henry is soon way out of his depth and hard-nose coach Smith tries to get him thrown off campus. Luckily new girlfriend Janet is on hand to see Henry through. *JZ*

Movie rating: *5.5

Visual: video

Off the record: Melanie Griffith is the daughter of 'Marnie'/'The Birds' actress, Tippi Hedren, who was married to advertising executive, Peter Griffith. **SEALS & CROFT** (see below) *MCS*

SEALS & CROFT
(composer: Charles Fox, lyrics: Paul Williams)

Sep 77. (lp) *Warners; <3076> <K 56402)* ☐ Nov77 ☐
– The love theme from "One On One" (My fair share) / This day belongs to me / Janet's theme / John Wayne / Picnic / Flyin' / Reflections / Love conquers all / It'll be all right / Hustle / Time out / The party / The basketball game / This day belongs to me (reprise).

S/track review: SEALS & CROFT (aka JIM SEALS & DASH CROFT) were the main staple for AOR Americans who liked their soft-rock, er . . . soft. The duo had cut their teeth way back in the late 50s as members of instrumental combo the Champs, who were famous for the massive hit, 'Tequila'; this was pre Jim and Dash. After a time as the Dawnbreakers in the mid-60s, S&C formed their own breakaway outfit in 1969. Based in L.A., SEALS & CROFT amassed several top hits (including 'Summer Breeze' – also a hit for the Isley Brothers), although it was between 1972 and '73 that the duo gained their credibility as songwriters when LPs 'Summer Breeze' and 'Diamond Girl' were in the Top 10. For 'ONE ON ONE', SEALS & CROFT "sing the songs from the Originial Motion Picture Sound Track" (as it says on the package) and certainly this had all the feel of a late 60s, post-hippie score. Simon & Garfunkel had achieved many plaudits for their work with jazz muso Dave Grusin on 'The GRADUATE' (1968), while the similarly themed 'GOODBYE, COLUMBUS' (1969) – a collaboration between the Association and composer Charles Fox – fell a little short. So why did SEALS & CROFT choose the latter for another pop-vs.-orchestra collaboration? Was it the fact that talented lyricist Paul Williams (responsible for 'PHANTOM OF THE PARADISE') was also a player. Only a dull-oid will tell you. Mellow, sugary, summery, are all words that could describe the set, and words were all they had – as they say. From schmaltzy opener 'The Love Theme From One On One (My Fair Share)' (a minor US hit) to 'Love Conquers All' to 'This Day Belongs To Me', the listener is subjected to a barrage of romanticised Americana, once the property of Loggins & Messina, Firefall and dare one say it, Neil Sedaka. If you're looking for Charlie Fox to pull you from the cinders, the best the man could get was the track 'Basketball Game', scored possibly with 'Shaft' on his mind. When 'ONE ON ONE' only reached a meagre No.118 in the Billboard charts, it was inevitable that SEALS & CROFT were on their way out and after only two further unremarkable sets, they split in 1980. Rock and pop music had indeed moved on leaps and bounds. *MCS*

Album rating: *3.5

– spinoff hits, etc. –

SEALS & CROFT: My Fair Share
Oct 77. (7") *<8405>* 28 –

101 REYKJAVIK

2000 (Ice/Fra/Den/Nor 87m) 101 Limited / Icelandic Film Fund (18)

Film genre: seXual/romantic comedy

Top guns: s-w + dir: Baltasar Kormakur → a LITTLE TRIP TO HEAVEN (au: Hallgrimur Helgason)

Stars: Hilmir Snaer Gudnason *(Hlynur)* ← ENGLAR ALHEIMSINS, Hanna Maria Karlsdottir *(Berglind)*, Victoria Abril *(Lola Milagros)*, Baltasar Kormakur *(Thostur)* ← ENGLAR ALHEIMSINS, Thrudur Vilhjalmsdottir *(Hofi)*, Olafur Darri Olafsson *(Marri)*, Eyvindur Erlendsson *(Hafsteinn)*, Gudrun Maria Bjarnadottir *(Ingey)* → NICELAND, Prostur Leo Gunnarsson *(Brusi)* → NOI ALBINOI, Petur Einarsson *(Pabbi Magga)* ← ENGLAR ALHEIMSINS / → NOI ALBINOI

Storyline: Taking the 101 from the post-code to Reykjavik's oldest and most culturally elite district, we find a sad and drunken 28-year-old slacker who surfs for porn sites while living with his mother. In a sharp twist of fate, Hlynur is introduced, falls for and then has sex with his mother's lesbian Spanish dance teacher, who has come to stay over the Xmas holidays. Lola becomes pregnant, which obviously upsets the family tree somewhat in the fact that he, his mother and her new live-in girlfriend will bring up his baby; which would also be his brother(!). To makes matters worse, Hlynur's long-term squeeze, Hofi, is also up the proverbial duff. Suicide could be the only way out. *MCS*

Movie rating: *6.5

Visual: dvd

Off the record: **EINAR ORN BENEDIKTSSON** was once an integral part of Iceland's greatest exports, the Sugarcubes (featuring fellow singer and composer, BJORK). Much like in the '101 . . .' film itself, his life was prone to a little controversy, having married another, er . . . Sugarcube – and one-time member of embryonic Sugarcubes bands, Purrkur Pillnikk and K.U.K.L. – male! bassist Bragi Olafesson; Fleetwood Mac and Abba, it was not! *MCS*

DAMON ALBARN & EINAR ORN BENEDIKTSSON
(& Various Artists)

May 01. (cd) *E.M.I.; (<532989-2>)* ☐ Sep01 ☐
– 101 Reykjavik theme / 101 Reykjavik theme (remixed by EMILIANA TORRINI) / Bath (ATLANTA) / Frost (JOURNEY CLUB) / Bar beaten / Bar beaten (101 Terror City) (remixed by CURVER) / Flamenco Lola / Shooting gallery / Suitcase / Suitcase (101 hangovers) (remixed by HOH) / Bar hip hop / Teapot / Teapot mix (EGILL S) / Fireworks organ / New year #1 / New year #1 (remixed by BANG GANG) / New year #2 / Glacier memory / Morning beer / University / Dream scene / Stereo blasting (Lola) / Out of church / Man's world / Bar fight / Bar fight (remixed by MINUS & FINN B) / Big party / Glacier / Dub Lola / Reykjavik2K (by GUS GUS).

S/track review: The unique and unusual collaboration between a one-time crowned prince of Brit-Pop and Blur, DAMON ALBARN and the aforementioned "darling" of the Sugarcubes – in more ways than one! – EINAR ORN BENEDIKTSSON; the former had already collaborated on two other scores, 'RAVENOUS' (1999 with Michael Nyman) and 'ORDINARY DECENT CRIMINAL' (2000 with Various Artists). Together with a feast of Icelandic trip-hop mixers and buddies (including GUS GUS, MINUS and BANG GANG), the pair composed a series of sub-urban-ite big beats and techno trip-outs culminating in 30 tracks/dirges; a recurrent theme ('Lola') came via a boyhood songwriter hero of DAMONs, the "Godfather of Brit-Pop", Ray Davies, who had had a massive hit with the song in 1970. The pulsating 'Bar Beaten (101 Terror City)' – remixed by CURVER – could take pride in anybody's open-topped, convertible/motorised CD player ready to browbeat the neighbourhood into manic submission. The mouth organ-sampled (and repetitively-themed), 'Shooting Galley', 'Suitcase', 'Fireworks Organ', 'University', 'Dream Scene', 'Man's World' & 'Glacier' tracks, felt like a melancholy tribute to a long lost and nearly forgotten master of the harmonica, Larry Adler; ironically he died of cancer in August 2001, a few months after the score's release. Three excerpts of 'New Year', Kid Loco'd their way around the skull, the third BANG GANG version, the bounciest and more appealing to the ear. The Prodigy-like, punk-fuelled 'Bar Fight' and the remixed version by MINUS (reminiscent of Run-DMC's 'It's Tricky' and hopefully with kind permission, etc.) were album stick outs, alongside the Pop Group/Pigbag-sounding 'Big Party' – me thinks ALBARN at least, had a penchant for way-out 80s dance-rock. GUS GUS got in on the act courtesy of album finale, 'Reykjavik2k', a uplifting but moody Barry White-meets-Fad Gadget kind of groovebuster. Now you'll be asking – who the alice is Fad Gadget? *MCS*

Album rating: *7

OPEN SEASON

2006 (US 86m) Sony Pictures (PG)

Film genre: children's/family animation comedy

Top guns: dir: Roger Allers ← the LION KING, Jill Culton (+ story), Anthony Stacchi (+ story) / s-w: Steve Bencich ← BROTHER BEAR, Ron J. Friedman ← BROTHER BEAR, Nat Mauldin ← the PREACHER'S WIFE

Voices: Martin Lawrence *(Boog)* ← HOUSE PARTY II ← HOUSE PARTY, Ashton Kutcher *(Elliot)*, Gary Sinise *(Shaw)* ← ALBINO ALLIGATOR → RANSOM, Debra Messing *(Beth)* ← the MOTHMAN PROPHECIES, **Billy Connolly** *(McSquizzy)* ← OVERNIGHT ← STILL CRAZY ← the CONCERTS FOR THE PEOPLE OF KAMPUCHEA, Georgia Engel *(Bobbie)*, Jon Favreau *(Reilly)*, Jane Krakowski *(Giselle)* ← ALFIE re-make ← DANCE WITH ME,

Storyline: Boog is a domesticated grizzly bear content with the easy life – living from his days as a cub – in a comfy garage owned by park ranger Beth. However, when he frees and befriends a fast-talking, one-horned mule deer from a schizoid hunter, his world becomes somewhat more frantic as he takes to the woods just before Open Season. *MCS*

Movie rating: *5.5

Visual: dvd (score: Ramin Djawadi)

Off the record: PAUL WESTERBERG (see below)

PAUL WESTERBERG (* songs) (& Various Artists)

Sep 06. (cd) *Lost Highway; <B 000757902>* ☐ [–]
– Meet me in the meadow (*) / Love you in the fall (*) / I belong (*) / I wanna lose control (DEATHRAY) / Any better than this (*) / Wild wild life (TALKING HEADS) / Right to arm bears / Good day / All about me / Wild as I wanna be (DEATHRAY) * / Whisper me luck (*) / I belong (PETE YORN) *. *<diff.order 10"m-lp += (*); B 000757901>* – Wild as I wanna be (Replacements version) / I belong (piano/vocal version).

S/track review: Former Replacements frontman PAUL WESTERBERG takes full credit for the score (alongside a handful by Various Artists) on this easy-going semi-sequel to his '14 Songs' set. While he virtually dismissed the valid point of writing tracks for – what basically is – a family flick , WESTERBERG attempts to compose some easy-on-the-ear roots-pop dirges. 'Meet Me In The Meadow' kicks off the album in fine fettle, while 'Love You In The Fall' and 'I Belong' churn along nicely; the latter track (alternatively sung by PETE YORN) closes the set. The anthemic, Tom Petty-like 'Better Than This' carries the WESTERBERG torch but funnily enough is stopped in its tracks by TALKING HEADS' 'Wild Wild Life', while the sing-a-long 'Right To Arm Bears' shows Paul's lost none of his old rocking qualities. DEATHRAY are afforded two cues here, 'I Wanna Lose Control' and the PW-penned 'Wild As I Wanna Be', although they don't stand out as far as 'Any Better Than This' does. Ex-Del Fuegos mainman, Dan Zanes (who, incidentally, writes folk-tinged music for kids) might well've been a better choice of composer, but without the movie stills the music for 'OPEN SEASON' is worthy enough. *MCS*

Album rating: *6.5

ORBITAL

Formed: Sevenoaks, Kent, England ... late 80s by brothers Phil and Paul Hartnoll. United by a shared love of electro and punk, they were inspired by the outdoor party scene of '89 and named themselves after the infamous circular motorway which ravers used in delirious pursuit of their next E'd-up shindig. A home-produced 4-track demo, 'Chime', brought the band almost instant fame and remains one of their best-loved songs. Originally released on the small 'Oh-Zone' label, the track was given a full release in March 1990 on 'London' offshoot 'Ffrr', its subtly euphoric charms elevating 'Chime' into the Top 20 and the brothers onto a memorable 'Top Of The Pops' appearance where they sported defiant 'No Poll Tax' t-shirts. Although dance culture has since become increasingly politicized as a result of heavy-handed legislation, it was unusual at the time for a techno act to be so passionately anti-establishment, an ethos the Hartnoll brothers had carried over from their punk days and which would become a recurring theme throughout their career. Meanwhile, ORBITAL followed their debut with a trio of largely instrumental, synth-driven singles, the highlight being the pounding white noise of the Butthole Surfers-sampling 'Satan'. The track reached No.31 upon its release in August '91 although a subsequent live version stormed into the Top 5. Their untitled debut album, released in September of the same year, showcased cerebral electronic soundscapes which nevertheless retained a melancholy, organic warmth while their live shows moved feet and minds en masse. Alongside events like the Shamen's Synergy, which attempted to mix the spectacle of rock'n'roll with the communal energy of house, ORBITAL were pivotal in pioneering dance music in the live environment. Rather than reproducing the songs live on stage, they improvised, restructuring tracks which had been pre-set into sequencers. This spontaneity was enhanced by an innovative light show utilising state of the art technology, a heady combination that saw ORBITAL headline the Glastonbury festival two years running during the mid-90s. They were no less effective in the studio and their second untitled album was a finely tuned extension of the debut, encompassing such exotica as a sample from an Australian pedestrian crossing (!). With their third long player, 1994's cynically titled 'Snivilization', the music took on an uneasy paranoia, seething with a bitter undercurrent that railed against the state of humanity in general, as well as issues closer to home such as the much-hated Criminal Justice Bill. The record also introduced elements of drum'n'bass, a dalliance that continued with their 'In Sides' album. Preceded by the near-half-hour strangeness of 'The Box' single, the record marked the pinnacle of ORBITAL's sonic explorations, a luminous trip to the final frontiers of electronica. In spite of their experimentalism, a loyal following ensures that the duo are never short of chart success, the 'In Sides' album reaching No.5, while 1997 saw ORBITAL go Top 3 in the singles chart twice (first with the aforementioned live version of 'Satan' and then with their celebrated film version of 'The Saint'); 'EVENT HORIZON' (1997) was their first soundtrack release, a collaboration with film composer Michael Kamen. After a slight delay, ORBITAL were back in circulation with a fifth set, 'The Middle Of Nowhere' (1999), a happier affair that was premiered by hit single, 'Style'. Not content with sticking to their staple, ORBITAL tried to cross the boundaries on their 2001 album 'The Altogether', a strange mix of the group's previous six albums tempered by the arrival of guest vocalists et al. The 'OCTANE' (2003) soundtrack was also slightly below par, suitably atmospheric in its Tangerine Dream-esque meandering but lacking the dark menace and rhythmic celebration of their best work. It wasn't so much of a shock when the group announced their own demise in summer 2004, signing off with the backwards glance of 'Blue Album' (2004). *BG*

- **filmography** (composers) –

the Saint *(1997 hit theme)* / **Event Horizon** *(1997 OST w/ MICHAEL KAMEN =>)* / xXx *(2002 – on OST by V/A; see future editions =>)* / **Octane** *(2003 OST =>)*

ORDINARY DECENT CRIMINAL

2000 (Ire/UK/Ger 90m) Miramax Films (R)

Film genre: crime/gangster drama

Top guns: dir: Thaddeus O'Sullivan / s-w: Gerard Stembridge

Stars: Kevin Spacey *(Michael Lynch)* ← WORKING GIRL / → BEYOND THE SEA, Linda Fiorentino *(Christine Lynch)* ← SHOUT, Peter Mullan *(Stevie)* ← TRAINSPOTTING / → YOUNG ADAM, Stephen Dillane *(Det. Sgt. Noel Quigley)*, Helen Baxendale *(Lisa)*, David Hayman *(Tony Brady)* ← WALKER ← SID & NANCY / → the LAST GREAT WILDERNESS, Patrick Malahide *(Commissioner Daly)*, Gerard McSorley *(Harrison)*, David Kelly *(Fr. Grogan)*, Paul Ronan *(Billy Lynch)*, Colin Farrel *(Alec)*

Storyline: Michael Lynch is a devil-may-care, latter day Robin Hood who rules the roost in Dublin. With the help of his gang this criminal mastermind robs the rich and greedy and gives to the poor and needy. Everybody (including his two wives) loves him except of course for the police, who seemingly can do nothing to stop him. Then things suddenly go wrong and it looks like the game is up – unless Lynch can think up yet another masterplan to save himself from the clutches of the law. *JZ*

Movie rating: *4

Visual: dvd

Off the record: Kevin Spacey went on to star (and indeed sing) in the Bobby Darin biopic, 'BEYOND THE SEA' (2004).

—

Various Artists (score: DAMON ALBARN *)

Mar 00. (cd) *Atlantic; (<7567 83316-2>)* [ ] May00 [ ]
– One day at a time (* & ROBERT '3D' DEL NAJA) / Kevin on a motorbike (*) / Superfinger (LOWFINGER) / Mother of pearl (BRYAN FERRY) / I want you (SHACK) / Gopher mambo (YMA SUMAC) / Chase after gallery (*) / Eurodisco (BIS) / Bank job (*) / Dying isn't easy (*).

S/track review: Split half and half between Blur's DAMON ALBARN and a handful of Various Artists, 'ORDINARY DECENT CRIMINAL' is a fair cop – so to speak. After his unique collaboration with Michael Nyman on the previous year's 'RAVENOUS', the one-time prince of Brit-pop, ALBARN delivered his first solo outing since his stint on the excellent 'TRAINSPOTTING' soundtrack. Here on 'ODC', ALBARN opens with two and closes with two tracks, with one brassy short cut, 'Chase After Gallery', coming somewhere in between. 'One Day At A Time' (. . ."Sweet Jesus") is his trip-hop opening salva augmented by Massive Attack's 3D, a Beta Band-like dirge partly inspired from the Lena Martell gospel chart-topper from the mid-70s, while it also features star of the movie, Kevin Spacey, on Irish-accented dialogue and mirror-crooning. 'Kevin On A Motorbike' starts a bit like Roni Size, although the techno-blues of Moby possibly win out at the end of the day. Track No.9, 'Bank Job', is his most cinematic piece from the film, while he takes a hybrid of Blur gospel-ish ballads, 'Tender' & 'The Universal', to new heights with OST encore, 'Dying Isn't Easy'. Worth waiting for. Squeezed between the ALBARN tracks are the aforementioned V/A fillers, a good if not great selection probably picked by DAMON himself. LOWFINGER get freaky with the beat on the Black Grape-styled, 'Superfinger', weirdo dub-pop that just might've been too late to be picked up by the Brit-pop crowd. We go all suave and debonair for Mr BRYAN FERRY, who updates and sophisticates his old Roxy Music nugget, 'Mother Of Pearl'. Liverpool's SHACK bring Merseybeat up to date (they've been doing it virtually unnoticed for years!) courtesy of Rickenbacker delight, 'I Want You', while Scots indie technoid trio, BIS, fall flat on their proverbial dancefloor arses with 'Eurodisco'. There's always one surprise package, and here it goes to YMA SUMAC's Latino-gem, 'Gopher Mambo', altogether from another time (1954, to be exact!) and a song that might've been put to better use on Oingo Boingo's/(Danny Elfman's) fun-tastic 'FORBIDDEN ZONE' soundtrack. *MCS*

Album rating: *6

□ OSANNA segment
(⇒ MILANO CALIBRO 9)

□ OSIBISA segment
(⇒ SUPERFLY T.N.T.)

OSKAR UND LENI

1999 (Ger 89m b&w) Indigo Films

Film genre: buddy comedy

Top guns: s-w + dir: Petra Katharina Wagner

Stars: Christian Redl *(Oskar)*, Anna Thalbach *(Leni)*, Elisabeth Trissenaar *(Ella Grothe)*, Reiner Heise *(Heinz)*, Nadja Engel *(Tanja)*, Guenther Junghans *(Fritz Grothe)*, Wookie Mayer *(Maria; Leni's sister)*, Joachim Pail Assbock *(Romeo)*, Thomas Gerber *(Julia)*

Storyline: Oskar is a champion swimmer but does most of his ducking and diving running from the police. This is because he also happens to be an expert jewel thief wanted throughout Europe (it's not just Olympic rings that attract him). All this comes to a halt when Oskar is finally arrested and sent to jail, but will he come out reformed? When he makes eye contact with the beautiful call-girl Leni it seems like love at first sight – but can she track down Oskar before he disappears into the deep end? *JZ*

Movie rating: *5

Visual: none

Off the record: **SIMON JEFFES** was born on the 19th of February, 1949, in Sussex, England, although he was raised from an early age in Canada. Classically-trained, but with a love of folk-rock music, JEFFES saw a gap in the market to combine both genres, as his **PENGUIN CAFE ORCHESTRA** took shape. Picking out some pieces recorded between 1974-1976, the London-based group delivered their debut LP, 'Music From The Penguin Cafe' (1976), for Brian Eno's 'Obscure' imprint; they subsequently supported Kraftwerk at the Roundhouse in 1977. Four years later (during which time Simon spent working with Malcolm McLaren and Sid Vicious), the eponymous 'Penguin Cafe Orchestra' (1981) was finally released, its highlights including 'Air A Danser' and 'Telephone And Rubber Band', the latter probably known for its use on numerous TV commercials. Lead track on 1984's 'Broadcasting From Home', 'Music For A Found Harmonium', was another to garner the ensemble lots of praise, while the track was re-released in 1987 to coincide with 4th album, 'Signs Of Life' (1987); the latter album's Top 50 chart position was an indicator of PCO's increasing popularity as JEFFES also scored the music for the Australian movie, 'Malcolm' (1986). That benchmark of highbrow cultural quality, 'The South Bank Show', deemed to feature the group the following year, while a show at London's premier classical venue, the Royal Festival Hall, was recorded for posterity as 'When In Rome . . .' (1988). JEFFES and Co even worked with the Royal Ballet on a collaborative project, although a fifth PENGUIN CAFE ORCHESTRA studio effort, 'Union Cafe', didn't surface until 1993. While the 90s PENGUIN CAFE ORCHESTRA may be a more tastefully airbrushed proposition, JEFFES' stamp of offbeat originality makes damn near anything he turned his hand to worth more than a cursory listen. *MCS & BG*

---

the PENGUIN CAFE ORCHESTRA
(composer: SIMON JEFFES)

Oct 99. (cd) *Peregrina Music; <PM 50161>* ☐ ☐
– Life boat / Anotherone from the Porlock / Southern juke box music / Nothing really blue / Silver star of Bologna / Steady state / Oscar tango / Thorn tree wind / Red shorts / Air à danser.

S/track review: SIMON JEFFES, leader of the PENGUIN CAFE ORCHESTRA since its formation in 1972, had just passed away on December 11th, 1997 (brain tumour), and what better way to pay tribute to the man than afford his arty, avant-pop ensemble a full OST. Described as wistful and exuberant with a minimalist appeal, PCO deliver an album full of several past glories, revamped of course to appease both filmmaker and fan. So a compilation in many respects, 'OSKAR UND LENI', comprises of tracks via previous sets, mainly from 'Penguin Cafe Orchestra' ('Air A Danser' & 'Steady State'), 'Signs Of Life' ('Southern Juke Box Music' & 'Oscar Tango') plus 'Union Cafe' ('Life Boat', 'Nothing Really Blue', 'Anotherone From The Porlock', 'Thorn Tree Wind', 'Silver Star Of Bologna' & 'Red Shorts'). JEFFES' neo-classical airs and graces have always lent a little to the visual environs of film, but whether the music of 'OSKAR . . .' works to complement it, or the other way round, is strictly down to conjecture. Arguably, the best tracks are the melancholic but uplifting 'Southern Juke Box Music', 'Life Boat' (oh, that clarinet), 'Oscar Tango' and, of course, the movie's closing number 'Air A Danser'. *MCS*

Album rating: *7

OVER THE HEDGE

2006 (US 83m) DreamWorks / Paramount Pictures (PG)

Film genre: family/children's comedy animation

Top guns: dir: Tim Johnson, Karey Kirkpatrick (+ s-w w/ Len Blum ← PRIVATE PARTS ← HEAVY METAL, Lorne Cameron ← BROTHER BEAR, David Hoselton ← BROTHER BEAR

Voices: Bruce Willis *(RJ)* ← the STORY OF US ← BEAVIS AND BUTT-HEAD DO AMERICA ← LAST MAN STANDING ← FOUR ROOMS ← PULP FICTION, Garry Shandling *(Verne)*, Steve Carell *(Hammy)*, Wanda Sykes *(Stella)* ← POOTIE TANG, William Shatner *(Ozzie)*, Nick Nolte *(Vincent)* ← CLEAN ← AFFLICTION ← DOWN AND OUT IN BEVERLY HILLS, Thomas Haden Church *(Dwayne)*, Allison Janney *(Gladys)* ← PRIMARY COLORS ← PRIVATE PARTS ← WALKING AND TALKING / → HAIRSPRAY re-make, Eugene Levy *(Lou)* ← CURIOUS GEORGE ← a MIGHTY WIND ← CLUB PARADISE ← HEAVY METAL, Catherine O'Hara *(Penny)* ← a MIGHTY WIND ← DICK TRACY ← ROCK & RULE, **Avril Lavigne** *(Heather)*, Omid Djalili *(Tiger)*

Storyline: A group of animals and critters (including RJ the raccoon con artist) awake after their hibernation to find a new suburban community living Over The Hedge and their patch of the forest obliterated. It looks likely they'll have to venture across to find some food and a little adventure or two. *MCS*

Movie rating: *7

Visual: dvd

Off the record: Canadian-born **Avril Lavigne** has released two platinum albums to date, 'Let Go' (2004) and 'Under My Skin' (2006). She subsequently featured in two further films, 'Fast Food Nation' (2006) and 'The Flock' (2007). *MCS*

BEN FOLDS (* songs) / RUPERT GREGSON-WILLIAMS (** music)

May 06. (cd) *Sony Classical; <82876 83369-2>* ☐ ☐
– Family of me (*) / RJ enters the cave (**) / The family awakes (**) / Heist (*) / Lost in the supermarket (*) / Lets call it Steve (**) / Hammy time (**) / Still (*) / Play? (**) / Rockin' the suburbs – Over The Hedge version (* feat. WILLIAM SHATNER) / The inside heist (**) / RJ rescues his family (**) / Still – reprise (*).

S/track review: BEN FOLDS whittles from five down to one (alongside classical film composer, RUPERT GREGSON-WILLIAMS) for this kiddies computer animation OST. The six BF cues on parade show his blend of melodic pop to the max. From sentimental opener 'Family Of Me' to a version of the Clash's 'Lost In The Supermarket', singer/pianist BEN FOLDS (a man with several hit albums behind him from 1997's 'Whatever And Ever Amen' to 2005's 'Songs For Silverman') takes to film music like a duck to water. While songs 'Heist' and two takes of 'Still' are splendid, a golden oldie from 2001, 'Rockin' The Suburbs', gets the re-vamp treatment, the addition of Star Trek icon WILLIAM SHATNER an inspired move. Meanwhile, GREGSON-WILLIAMS balances proceedings with a playful score, the best cues come courtesy of 'Lets Call It Steve', 'Play?', 'Hammy Time' and 'The Family Awakens'. *MCS*

Album rating: *6.5

the OWL AND THE PUSSYCAT

1970 (US 96m) Columbia Pictures (R)

Film genre: romantic comedy

Top guns: dir: Herbert Ross → FOOTLOOSE / s-w: Buck Henry ← CANDY ← the GRADUATE (play: Bill Manhoff)

Stars: **Barbra Streisand** *(Doris)* → a STAR IS BORN, George Segal *(Felix)* → the LINDA McCARTNEY STORY, Robert Klein *(Barney)* ← the LANDLORD / → the LAST UNICORN → PRIMARY COLORS, Allen Garfield *(dress shop proprietor)* ← YOU'VE GOT TO WALK IT LIKE YOU TALK IT . . . → NASHVILLE → ONE-TRICK PONY → ONE FROM THE HEART → GET CRAZY → DICK TRACY, Roz Kelly *(Eleanor)* → YOU'VE GOT TO WALK IT LIKE YOU TALK IT . . . → NEW YEAR'S EVIL → AMERICAN POP, Jacques Sandulescu *(Rapzinsky)*, Jack Manning *(Mr. Weyderhaus)*, Grace Carney *(Mrs. Weyderhaus)*, Barbara Anson *(Ann Weyderhaus)*, Marilyn Chambers *(Barney's girl)*, Buck Henry *(man looking into Doubleday's bookshop)* ← CANDY ← the GRADUATE / → EVEN COWGIRLS GET THE BLUES

Storyline: Lightning paced Broadway adaptation pitting hard nosed prostitute Doris against speccy book clerk/aspiring writer Felix. After a hard day at the bookshop, Felix spies money changing hands and promptly informs the landlord. Out on her proverbial, leotard-clad ass, Doris forces her way into Felix's apartment and loosens a torrent of verbal abuse, accusing him of being, variously, homosexual, perverted, sneaky, creepy and just about every other adjective her limited vocabulary can come up with. While the learned Felix fights back with big words Doris doesn't care to understand, the sheer, gratuitous force of her personality drives him to the edge of a nervous breakdown before he finally succumbs to the charms of her "sexual disneyland". *BG*

Movie rating: *7

Visual: video + dvd

Off the record: **BLOOD, SWEAT & TEARS** (see below)

—

BLOOD, SWEAT & TEARS
(composer: RICHARD HALLIGAN; w/ dialogue)

Jan 71. (lp/c) *Columbia; <AS/BT 30401> C.B.S.; (70081)* ☐ Mar71 ☐
– The confrontation / The warmup / The seduction / The morning after / The Reunion.

S/track review: As funny and daring as this odd couple movie was for 1970, the soundtrack's extended dialogue – much of it consisting of heated argument and shouting! – makes for tedious listening. The instrumental interludes of jazz-rockers BLOOD, SWEAT & TEARS are far too thinly spread and locating them on vinyl is like sticking a quartz needle in a proverbial haystack. All that said, a top-of-their-game, 1970-vintage BS&T – on the back of classic hits 'You've Made Me So Very Happy' and 'Spinning Wheel' – almost make it worth persevering, and at least the main theme's unhurried brass motif – heard on the opening grooves of 'The Confrontation' (and repeated at both the tail end of 'The Seduction' and the beginning of 'The Reunion') – doesn't require any effort. Nor, admittedly, does the only non-instrumental piece, a minute or so of passable supperclub soul hustled almost out of sight on the end of the final cue on side two. Worthier of needle cruising is the welcome blast of Average White Band-strength jazz-funk – played over Barbra Streisand's night club/stripper scene – near the end of 'The Morning After', filled out with some lacerating electric guitar (and punctuated by one of the funnier dialogue skits, 'Cycle Sluts'). While most of the instances when the music – often just bubbling frustratingly out of earshot – breaks to the surface are so brief as to hardly warrant mention, if you can handle endless Streisand vs Segal bitching, there's a snippet of trio improv in there somewhere, accelerating to full horn arrangements, as well as a longer, funkier segment right at the end of 'The Warmup', with composer/arranger RICHARD HALLIGAN – the sole surviving member from the Al Kooper-era brass section – raking his trombone over BOBBY COLOMBY's stuttering break beats. Difficult easy listening. *BG*

Album rating: *4.5

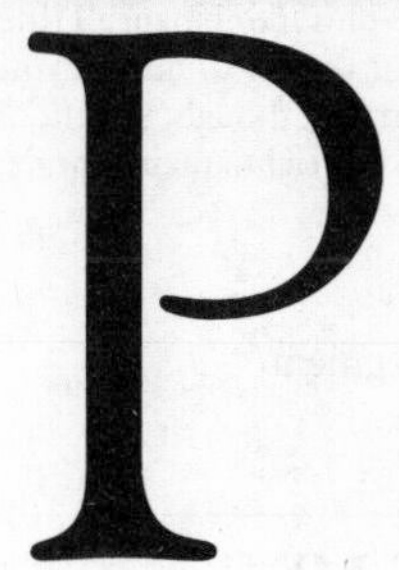

☐ Jimmy PAGE
(⇒ LED ZEPPELIN; Rockumentaries & Performance)

PARIS, TEXAS

1984 (US/W.Ger/Fra 147m) Tobis / Argos Films (R)

Film genre: road movie; drama

Top guns: s-w (+ dir): Wim Wenders → the END OF VIOLENCE → TEATRO → BUENA VISTA SOCIAL CLUB → the MILLION DOLLAR HOTEL → the SOUL OF A MAN, **Sam Shepard** ← RENALDO AND CLARA ← ZABRISKIE POINT / → FAR NORTH, L.M. Kit Carson

Stars: Harry Dean Stanton *(Travis)* ← REPO MAN ← ONE FROM THE HEART ← the ROSE ← RENALDO AND CLARA ← RANCHO DELUXE ← PAT GARRETT & BILLY THE KID / → PRETTY IN PINK → the LAST TEMPTATION OF CHRIST → WILD AT HEART → FEAR AND LOATHING IN LAS VEGAS, Nastassja Kinski *(Jane)* ← ONE FROM THE HEART, Dean Stockwell *(Walt)* ← HUMAN HIGHWAY ← PSYCH-OUT / → DUNE → TO LIVE AND DIE IN L.A. → TUCKER: THE MAN AND HIS DREAM → MADONNA: INNOCENCE LOST, Aurore Clement *(Anne Henderson)* → TROUBLE EVERY DAY, Hunter Carson *(Hunter)*, Bernhard Wicki *(Dr. Ulmer)*, **John LURIE** *(Slater)*, Viva Auder *(woman on TV)* ← FLASH GORDON ← FORBIDDEN ZONE / → NICO ICON

Storyline: Wim Wender's celebrated road movie trails the physically and emotionally lost lead character Travis as he staggers into a roadside outlet in deepest Texas. His brother Walt is informed of his whereabouts and drives out to collect him and bring him back to see his young son, Hunter. *BG*

Movie rating: *8.5

Visual: video + dvd

Off the record: (see below)

—

RY COODER

Feb 85. (lp) *Warners; <(9 25270-1)>* ☐ Dec84 ☐
– Paris, Texas / Brothers / Nothing out there / A cancion Mixteca / No safety zone / Houston in two seconds / She's leaving the bank / On the couch / I knew these people / Dark was the night. *<(cd-iss. May01; 9362 48088-2)>*

S/track review: Recorded 1983 but betraying nothing of that decade's misguided studio embellishments, RY COODER's atmospheric score is in fact, the antithesis of 80s excess – a sparse, hallucinatory dialogue between COODER and his beloved slide guitar. Scratching and gnawing at the strings, waiting tentatively as the vibrations dissolve into the dry desert air, COODER achieves an almost new-age-like ambience without the pseudo-spiritual baggage or the dippy experimentation. The traditional 'Cancion Mixteca' embellishes COODER's skeletal meditations with some structure, as well as a weight of Hispanic melancholy, vocals (in convincing Spanish) courtesy of Harry Dean Stanton. Stanton's compelling, 8-minute-plus monologue, 'I Knew These People', will have you searching out the DVD/video if you haven't already seen the film. The soundtrack, though, functions as an autonomous achievement in its own right, taking pride of place among its author's best work. *BG*

Album rating: *8.5

□ John PARISH segment
(⇒ ROSIE)

the PARK IS MINE

1986 (US/Can 102m TV) Astral Films / HBO

Film genre: military/urban drama

Top guns: dir: Steven Hilliard Stern / s-w: Lyle Gorch (au: Stephen Peters)

Stars: Tommy Lee Jones *(Mitch)* ← COAL MINER'S DAUGHTER / → NATURAL BORN KILLERS, Helen Shaver *(Valery)*, Yaphet Kotto *(Eubanks)* ← the MONKEY HUSTLE ← FRIDAY FOSTER ← TRUCK TURNER ← ACROSS 110th STREET ← MAN AND BOY, Lawrence Dane *(Commissioner Keller)*, Peter Dvorsky *(Dix)*, Eric Peterson *(Mike)*, Gale Garnett *(Rachel)*, Denis Simpson *(Richie)*

Storyline: Vietnam veteran Mitch decides the only way to draw attention to the plight of mentally and physically disabled ex-soldiers is to take over Central Park for 72 hours on Vets Weekend. With an array of weaponry suitable for an entire tank division, Mitch proceeds to hold off the entire NYPD but not intrepid reporter Valery Weaver, who sneaks in over a low wall. In desperation the Mayor sends in foreign mercenaries to flush Mitch out as he wins public opinion over to his side. *JZ*

Movie rating: *6

Visual: none

Off the record: (see below)

—

TANGERINE DREAM

Oct 91. (cd) *Silva Screen; (FILMCD 080) Silva America; <SSD 1004>* ☐ Mar92 ☐
– The park is mine – main title / Fatal fall – Funeral / The letter (parts 1 & 2) / Taking the park (parts 1 & 2) / Swatting S.W.A.T. / Love theme / Helicopter attack / Morning / We're running out of time / The claymore mine – Stalking / The final confrontation – The park is yours / Finale – End credits.

S/track review: The mid-80s were a prolific era for Berlin electro-prog trio, TANGERINE DREAM, a plethora of film commissions coming at them thick and fast (possibly too fast!), and not all of them finding an appropriate release date. 'The PARK IS MINE' was one such soundtrack excursion, recorded in '85 (with EDGAR FROESE, CHRISTOPHER FRANKE & JOHANNES SCHMOELLING) it finally touched basecamp at the tail end of '91, although allegedly without the group's go ahead. It shows, as the quality of the master tapes make way for 2-track stereo tapes used in the movie sequences. By the time of its eventual release by 'Silva Screen', both FRANKE and SCHMOELLING had left to take on their own solo/film careers, leaving FROESE at the helm. 'The PARK IS MINE' is thus old-style TANGERINE DREAM, bouncy, uptempo and er . . . un-cinematic, although some cuts here are just that – cuts (example the '. . .Main Title'). When the pace slows somewhat to, 'Fatal Fall – Funeral', the 'DREAM take on another guise, but this too, fades before the glory. 'The Letter' take a 'THIEF'-like musical stance, even the military-ish 'Taking The Park' and 'Swatting S.W.A.T.', prove unstoppable, true to the 'DREAM's once high standards. Eerie atmospherics, grinding guitars, pounding percussion are all on show, but there's something missing. Is it emotion? *MCS*

Album rating: *4.5

□ Gordon PARKS segment
(⇒ SHAFT'S BIG SCORE!)

□ the PASTELS segment
(⇒ the LAST GREAT WILDERNESS)

PAT GARRETT & BILLY THE KID

1973 (US 106m) Metro-Goldwyn-Mayer (R)

Film genre: revisionist/outlaw western

Top guns: dir: Sam Peckinpah / s-w: Rudy Wurlitzer → WALKER → CANDY MOUNTAIN

Stars: James Coburn *(Sheriff Pat Garrett)* ← CANDY / → WHITE ROCK → YOUNG GUNS II → AFFLICTION → SHAKE, RATTLE & ROLL: AN AMERICAN LOVE STORY, **Kris KRISTOFFERSON** *(William H. "Billy the Kid" Bonney)*, **Bob DYLAN** *(Alias)*, Richard Jaeckel *(Sheriff Kip McKinney)* ← FLAMING STAR, Katy Jurado *(Mrs. Baker)* ← STAY AWAY, JOE, Jason Robards *(Gov. Lew Wallace)* ← FOOLS / → MAGNOLIA, Chill Wills *(Lemuel)*, Slim Pickens *(Sheriff Colin Baker)* ← SKIDOO / → RANCHO DELUXE → HONEYSUCKLE ROSE, R.G. Armstrong *(Deputy Sheriff Bob Ollinger)* ← the FINAL COMEDOWN / → MEAN JOHNNY BARROWS → WHERE THE BUFFALO ROAM → DICK TRACY, John Beck *(John W. Poe)*, Richard Bright *(Holly)* → RANCHO DELUXE → HAIR → the IDOLMAKER → WHO'S THE MAN?, Harry Dean Stanton *(Luke)* → RANCHO DELUXE → RENALDO AND CLARA → the ROSE → ONE FROM THE HEART → REPO MAN → PARIS, TEXAS → PRETTY IN PINK → the LAST TEMPTATION OF CHRIST → WILD AT HEART → FEAR AND LOATHING IN LAS VEGAS, Jack Elam *(Alamosa Bill/Kermit)* ← the LAST REBEL, Paul Fix *(Pete Maxwell)*, **Rita Coolidge** *(Maria)* ← MAD DOGS & ENGLISHMEN ← VANISHING POINT / → a STAR IS BORN, Charlie Martin Smith *(Charlie Bowdre)* → AMERICAN GRAFFITI → COTTON CANDY → the BUDDY HOLLY STORY → MORE AMERICAN GRAFFITI → TRICK OR TREAT, Elisha Cook *(Cody)* ← BLACULA / → CARNY, Luke Askew *(Eno)* ← EASY RIDER / → MACKINTOSH & T.J. → SOUTH OF HEAVEN, WEST OF HELL, **Donnie Fritts** *(Beaver)* → a STAR IS BORN → SONGWRITER → the LIFE AND HARD TIMES OF GUY TERRIFICO, Aurora Clavel *(Ida Garrett)*, Rutanya Alda *(Ruthie Lee)* → RAPPIN', Matt Clark *(deputy sheriff J.W. Bell)* → OUTLAW BLUES → HONKYTONK MAN → SOUTH OF HEAVEN, WEST OF HELL

Storyline: Sam Peckinpah's masterful recreation of the Western legend and the legendary director's final shot at the genre. Billy the Kid is the charismatic outlaw who ignores the advice of his erstwhile partner-in-crime-turned-lawman, Pat Garrett, to hotfoot it to Mexico. Although caught and jailed, Billy's daring escape finds Garrett charged with tracking his old pal down for a final showdown. *BG*

Movie rating: *6.5

Visual: video + dvd

Off the record: Rita Coolidge & Donnie Fritts are catered for in other films (see lists above)

—

BOB DYLAN

Jul 73. (lp/c) *Columbia; <32460> C.B.S.; (CBS/40 69042)* 16 Sep73 29
– Main title theme (Billy) / Cantina theme (workin' for the law) / Billy 1 / Bunkhouse theme / River theme / Turkey chase / Knockin' on Heaven's door / Final theme / Billy 4 / Billy 7. *(re-iss. Mar82 lp/c; CBS/40 32098) <(cd-iss. Feb91 & Nov02 on 'Columbia'; CD 32098)>*

S/track review: Consistently given an inexplicably average rating in rock guides, this soundtrack isn't just another entry in BOB

DYLAN's catalogue worthy of purchase purely for 'Knockin' On Heaven's Door'; it's arguably one of the most evocative Western scores yet released and a key entry in DYLAN's brilliant creative spurt of the mid-70s. Backed by the likes of the Byrds' ROGER McGUINN, veteran fiddler BYRON BERLINE and even 'Stax' hero BOOKER T. JONES, DYLAN crafted a work of gentle regret and quiet power, largely instrumental but all the more effective for it. Moreover, the Mexican and Hispanic themes and melodies predict those of 1975's dazzling 'Desire', DYLAN's finest hour. It's no coincidence that ' . . .Heaven's Door', still one of the grizzled troubadour's most fully realised, best known and most covered (if always butchered) songs, is located here, and its air of resigned, lullaby-like fatalism blows through the rest of the score like sad-eyed tumbleweed. Not least in the reprise of 'Final Theme' where the melody is followed through and developed on flute and harmonium, a desert reverie every bit as fervent as Peckinpah's tortured devotion to his subject matter. On 'Billy 4', DYLAN sounds like he's been sleeping his his shoes for weeks, walking in the outlaw's very footsteps and condemned to the same fate. This is the sound of the man in his element, unbounded by affectation and the whims of musical, political or cultural fashion, and opened wide to an unforgiving American landscape, real or imagined. *BG*

Album rating: *7

– spinoff hits, etc. –

BOB DYLAN: Knockin' On Heaven's Door / Turkey Chase

Aug 73. (7") *<45913> (CBS 1762)* [12] Sep73 [14]

– other bits & pieces, etc. –

ERIC CLAPTON: Knockin' On Heaven's Door

Aug 75. (7") *R.S.O.; <513> (2090 166)* [ ] [38]

GUNS 'N ROSES: Knockin' On Heaven's Door / (studio version)

May 92. (7"/c-s/12"/cd-s) *Geffen; (GFS/+C/T/TD 21)* [–] [2]

DUNBLANE: Knockin' On Heaven's Door

Dec 96. (c-s/cd-s) *B.M.G.; (74321 44218-2)* [–] [1]

PATRICK

1978 (Aus 110m) Filmways Australasian / AIFC (18)

Film genre: sci-fi/horror thriller

Top guns: dir: Richard Franklin / s-w: Everett de Roche

Stars: Susan Penhaligon *(Kathy Jacquard)*, Robert Helpmann *(Dr. Roget)*, Rod Mullinar *(Ed Jacquard)*, Bruce Barry *(Dr. Brian Wright)* ← ABBA: THE MOVIE ← NED KELLY, Julia Blake *(Cassidy)*, Helen Hemingway *(Sister Williams)*, Robert Thompson *(Patrick)*

Storyline: Patrick murders his mother and her lover by electrocution. Three years later, he is in a coma, apparently traumatised by what he has witnessed. The authorities are not aware that it was Patrick who committed the crime. A newly arrived nurse looking after him comes to believe he is telepathic, as strange occurrences surround her. It seems Patrick is in danger. *DG*

Movie rating: *5

Visual: video + dvd

Off the record: (see below)

—

GOBLIN

1979. (lp) *Cinevox; (MDF 33/133)* [–] Italy [–]
– Patrick / Transmute / Bagliori di luce / Visioni / Snip snap / Metamorfosi / Follie / Vibrazioni / Metamorfosi II parte. *(cd-iss. Apr01 on 'Cinevox'+=; CD-MDF 330)* – Transmute / Visioni / Metamorfosi / Patrick / Transmute / Bagliori di luce / Patrick / Patrick / Patrick / Patrick (finale).

S/track review: This rarely sounds like what you might call a conventional horror film soundtrack. At times you'd imagine GOBLIN had scored a jaunty picture, rather than one chiefly concerned with death and the paranormal. The title track has strong, chiming guitars over an insistent keyboard line, but is spoiled by very odd effects which sound like nothing so much as air escaping a balloon at a very high pitch. Peculiar. 'Transmute' is essentially a variation on 'Patrick', but with the keyboard more pronounced, backed by an equally prominent bass line. It leads into 'Bagliori di luce', a slow synthesizer dominated track with more of the atmosphere you might expect. 'Visioni' has an almost pastoral feel, while 'Snip Snap' is basically funk. 'Metamorphosis' conjures memories of Rush's 'Xanadu', the guitar, synth and drums all sounding very familiar to anyone who's listened to 'A Farewell To Kings'. On 'Follie' an intricate guitar line leads to a choppy sequence backed by sustained synth chords before returning to the initial refrain. 'Vibrazioni' is a much slower tune, and more reflective in mood. There are further variations on these main tracks, which do little more than tweak the originals, though the reprise of 'Transmute' is more insistent than its initial outing. In all, some may think Brian May's symphonic score (not the Queen guitarist) for the original Australian release was more appropriate. *DG*

Album rating: *5.5

PELE

1977 (Fra/Mex 85m) Televisa

Film genre: sports documentary/biopic

Top guns: s-w: Francois Reichenbach (+ dir), Jacqueline Lefevre

Stars: Pele *(himself)* + a plethora of World Cup footballers

Storyline: One of many documentaries on the Brazilian legend, surveying his genius through archive match footage, and framing his celebrity with multifarious extra-curricular activities. *BG*

Movie rating: *6

Visual: video

Off the record: **SERGIO MENDES** (see below)

—

SERGIO MENDES (& Various Artists)

Mar 78. (lp) *Atlantic; <K 50410>* [ ] [–]
– O carocao do rei (The king's heart) / Meu mundo E uma bola (My world is a ball) (PELE) / Memorias (Memories) / Nascimento / Voltando a bauru (Back to bauru) (GERRY) / Cidade grande (Big city) / Cidade grande (Big city) (GRACINHA LEPORACE & PELE) / Alma Latina (Latin soul) / A tristeza do adeus (Sadness of goodbye) / Na bahia (In bahia) / Amore e agressao (Love and agression) / Meu mundo E uma bola (GRACINHA LEPORACE & PELE).

S/track review: What do you get if you cross God's greatest footballer, the coolest baritonist of all time and Brazilica godfather SERGIO MENDES? An album which could only have happened in the supersoul, football-mental 70s. How was it that a man whose ball control was cosmic enough to halt a Nigerian civil war, could just as effortlessly turn his hand to songwriting? In fact, PELE had a stockpile of songs, hundreds of them, a couple of which he'd recorded with Elis Regina on a 1969 EP, others which he reportedly supplied incognito to various Brazilian singers. With a bonafide solo album ('Ginga') finally released in 2006, now seems like as good a time as any to revisit a concept most of us in Blighty – where the words novelty hit and football squad have been interchangeable for decades – find difficult to take on board: a player talented enough to contribute to the soundtrack of his own documentary. Truth be told, his compositions almost outflank those of MENDES, the self-evident main theme, 'Meu Mundo É Uma Bola' ('My World Is A Ball') easing its way into your confidence on the kind of socially cohesive harmonies pivotal to so much Brazilian music; the Casio-cheesy variation – ironically subtitled 'Alma Latina (Latin Soul)' – is for lounge fantatics only. 'Cidade Grande', by contrast, is an introspective solo guitar piece, with flawless accompaniment from OSCAR CASTRO NEVES. SERGIO MENDES – also producer and arranger – takes over in the second half (no extra time, alas), supplying the luscious bossa, 'A Tristeza Do Adeus' ('The Sadness Of Goodbye'); with GERRY MULLIGAN offering up his most exquisitely toned blowing of the whole programme; even the mighty PELE can't compete. Atmospheric interlude, 'Na Bahia', is refreshingly underproduced, while a more familiar MENDES appears on 'Love And Aggression', a heavily percussive instrumental pitching MULLIGAN upfront amidst a melee of cross-rhythms. The beautiful game rarely sounded so sweet. *BG*

Album rating: *7

☐ the PENGUIN CAFE ORCHESTRA / Simon JEFFES segment (⇒ OSKAR UND LENI)

PERCHE SI UCCIDONO

US title 'PERCY IS KILLED'

1976 (Ita 92m) Mondial Televisione Film

Film genre: crime drama

Top guns: s-w + dir: Mauro Macario

Stars: Leonora Fani, Micky Pignatelli, Lia Dezman, Maurice Ronet, Beba Loncar, Marco Reims, Lucky Ross, Antonio Pierfederici, Antonio Rossi, Enrico Longodoria, Margherita Fumero → SQUADRA ANTIGANGSTERS

Storyline: Andrea plunges into a terrible existentialist crisis and, as with many young people, decides to resolve the problem by taking drugs. His girlfriend, who is less experienced than him, takes a dose that is too strong for her and dies. Luca, who is older and more together than Andrea, tries to help him but to no avail; Andrea cannot bear the pain and ends up committing suicide. *CD info*

Movie rating: *4

Visual: none

Off the record: **IL REALE . . .** (see below)

—

IL REALE IMPERO BRITANNICO // (shared score: Willy Brezza)

Mar 76. (lp) *Cinevox; (MDF 33/96)* [–] Italy [–]
– Epopea / Ammoniaca / Kalu' / Edda / Epopea (reprise) // My damned shit / Dodici e un quarto / Block / R.I.B. / Apotheke / Distrazioni. *(cd-iss. 1999; CD-MDF 321)*

S/track review: This little-known soundtrack is notable for a number of reasons. The 1976 Italian film (literally 'Why Do They Kill Themselves?') was a controversial if ultimately moralistic consideration of teen drug addiction, Satan worship and suicide. The score itself is a spirited, kitschy, mostly instrumental collection, including a song called 'My Damned Shit' which you would assume loses something in translation, except it's sung in (broken) English. Most intriguingly of all, 'IL REALE IMPERO BRITANNICO' ('The Real British Empire'), credited with performing the music, is in fact a pseudonym for the more well known GOBLIN, who co-wrote five of the eleven tracks here. However, it wouldn't be necessary to know that in order to enjoy this score, while fans of classic GOBLIN scores may be startled at the stylistic divergences here from the likes of 'PROFONDO ROSSO' and 'SUSPIRIA' which chronologically bookend this release. 'PERCHE SI UCCIDONO' features some of their least characteristic work, while retaining the quality that some of their more unlikely later scores sadly lack, and covers a broad range of styles from the light and melodic 'Ammoniaca' to the jazzy synth freak-out of 'Distrazioni'. If nothing else, this collection highlights GOBLIN's versatile range as session musicians, which at this point in their career may well have turned out to be their lot. However, the excellent musicianship on display across the board here does not obscure the fact that the GOBLIN co-written (with Fabio Frizzi) tracks stand out a mile, the opening 'Epopea', with its cop-show lead synth, towering over the cod funk of 'Apotheke'. The aforementioned 'My Damned Shit' is a bizarre sidestep, with it's Julio-Iglesias-at-drunken-karaoke vocals (good night and good luck to Tony Tartarini, erstwhile singer with GOBLIN in previous incarnation Cherry Five). That said, it would be easy to mistake some of the quintet of Willy Brezza-penned tunes that close the set for GOBLIN originals, particularly 'Block' and 'R.I.B.' which likely owe their quality to GOBLIN's unusual arrangement. The real gem here, though is 'Edda' with wordless vocals from what could be Minnie Riperton but is actually EDDA DELL'ORSO, the legendary vocalist on Ennio Morricone's most famous scores. The GOBLIN here are CLAUDIO SIMONETTI, FABIO PIGNATELLI and MASSIMO MORANTE. *SW*

Album rating: *5

PERCY

1971 (UK 103m) Anglo-EMI Films (X)

Film genre: seXual comedy

Top guns: dir: Ralph Thomas / s-w: Hugh Leonard, Terence Feely (au: Raymond Hitchcock)

Stars: Hywel Bennett *(Edwin Anthony)* ← LOOT ← the FAMILY WAY, Elke Sommer *(Helga)*, Britt Ekland *(Dorothy Chiltern-Barlow)* → the WICKER MAN → the MONSTER CLUB, Denholm Elliott *(Emmanuel Whitbread)* ← HERE WE GO ROUND THE MULBERRY BUSH / → BRIMSTONE & TREACLE → the WICKED LADY, Cyd Hayman *(Moira Warrington)*, Julia Foster *(Marilyn)*, Adrienne Posta *(Maggie Hyde)* ← UP THE JUNCTION ← HERE WE GO ROUND THE MULBERRY BUSH, Sue Lloyd *(Bernice)*, Patrick Mower *(James Vaile)*, Tracey Crisp *(Miss Elder)* ← TOOMORROW, Janet Key *(Hazel Anthony)* → 1984, Sheila Steafel *(Mrs. Gold)* → MELODY → NEVER TOO YOUNG TO ROCK, Arthur English *(pub comic)*, T.P. McKenna *(Meet The People compere)* ← FERRY 'CROSS THE MERSEY / → SILVER DREAM RACER, Graham Crowden *(Alfred Spaulton)* → O LUCKY MAN!, Rita Webb *(Mrs. Hedges)* ← the MAGIC CHRISTIAN ← MRS. BROWN, YOU'VE GOT A LOVELY DAUGHTER ← TO SIR, WITH LOVE / → CONFESSIONS OF A POP PERFORMER, Anthony Haygarth *(Purdey)* → McVICAR, George Best *(himself)*

Storyline: The Percy of the title is not actually a person at all but part of a person, or rather, a person's private parts. That person is Edwin Anthony and he has the dubious honour of undergoing the first ever penis transplant, duly dubbing his new friend Percy. Like the adopted child who becomes obsessed with finding their real parents, Edwin develops an unhealthy interest in Percy's previous owner. *BG*

Movie rating: *4.5

Visual: video + dvd

Off the record: (see below)

—

the KINKS

Mar 71. (lp) *Pye International; (NSPL 18365)* [ ] [–]
– God's children / Lola / The way love used to be / Completely / Running round town / Moments / Animals in the zoo / Just friends / Whip lady / Dreams / Helga / Willesden Green / God's children – end. *(re-iss. Oct87 on 'P.R.T.' lp/c/cd; PYL/PYM/PYC 6011) (cd re-iss. Oct89 on 'Castle'; CLACD 164) (cd re-mast.May98 on 'Essential'; ESMCD 510) (cd re-iss. Sep01 on 'Castle'; 321)*

S/track review: If there's a general critical concensus at all on the KINKS, it's that they went awry in "the sordid 70s". RAY DAVIES wasn't too keen on the 80s either ("hateful") but then a film – and hence a soundtrack – like 'PERCY' just couldn't have happened in the 80s. The early 70s actually turned up some of the man's greatest stand-alone songs, and three (four if you count the lounge-rock version of 'Lola') of them languish on this album. Not since 'Waterloo Sunset' had DAVIES nursed the inconsolable nostalgia in his soul as candidly as he did on 'Moments' and 'The Way Love Used To Be', pitching those quavering, crone-coy vocals into the embrace of acoustic guitar and orchestral tragedy. Strange kinds of love songs like these deserved a better context than a half-cocked tale of penis envy but, well, that's showbusiness for you. As a title theme, the sublime 'God's Children' is even less in tune with the film, preaching humanist wisdom and ramshackle harmony. It should've followed 'Lola' into the Top 10 (at a push, 'Dreams' could've done the same), but – given 'PERCY's contract-filling status and 'Pye's relative disinterest – it didn't even chart (although Mojo at least opened a soundtrack covermount with it a few years back). The instrumental 'Lola' retread featured here might be regarded as more filler than killer, but it makes the grade with some scything lead guitar work, cheesy organ and a brass coda fanfare, the kind of thing which might have made it onto DJ Spinna's 'Funk Rock' (2001) compilation. 'Running Around Town' sounds like a recidivist R&B take on the same song, while 'Animals In The Zoo' is a funkier, more cynical reprise of the universalist themes on 'God's Children'. DAVIES even predicts the Rockingbirds with the wry 'Willesden Green'. It's a familiar story – great music, appalling film, forgotten soundtrack – but one which shouldn't obscure one of the KINKS' most unsung achievements. BG

Album rating: *6.5

– spinoff releases, etc. –

the KINKS: God's Children / Moments

Apr 71. (7") *(7N 8001)* [ ] [–]
(7"m+=) *(7NX 8001)* – The Way Love Used To Be / Dreams.

the KINKS: God's Children / The Way Love Used To Be

Apr 71. (7") *Reprise; <1017>* [–] [ ]

☐ Jesse PERETZ
(⇒ the LEMONHEADS)

☐ Carl PERKINS segment
(⇒ LITTLE FAUSS AND BIG HALSY)

☐ Coleridge Taylor PERKINSON segment
(⇒ the EDUCATION OF SONNY CARSON)

PERMANENT RECORD

1988 (US 91m) Paramount pictures (PG-13)

Film genre: "generation x" coming-of-age/teen drama

Top guns: dir: Marisa Silver / s-w: Jarre Fees, Alice Liddle, Larry Ketron

Stars: Keanu Reeves *(Chris Townsend)* → BILL & TED'S EXCELLENT ADVENTURE → BILL & TED'S BOGUS JOURNEY → EVEN COWGIRLS GET THE BLUES → THUMBSUCKER, Alan Boyce *(David Sinclair)* → an AMBUSH OF GHOSTS, Michelle Meyrink *(M.G.)*, Jennifer Rubin *(Lauren)* → the DOORS → DELUSION, Pamela Gidley *(Kim)* ← DUDES / → S.F.W. → CAKE BOY, Barry Corbin *(Jim Sinclair)* ← HONKYTONK MAN ← the BEST LITTLE WHOREHOUSE IN TEXAS ← URBAN COWBOY, Kathy Baker *(Martha Sinclair)* → SHAKE, RATTLE & ROLL: AN AMERICAN LOVE STORY → COLD MOUNTAIN, Richard Bradford *(Principal, Leo Verdell)*, **Lou REED** *(himself)*, **Mark Springer** *(sailors audition)*

Storyline: The suicide of his popular and promising best friend hits high school student Chris Townsend very hard. While he is traumatised, he also finds it hard to cope with the realities of life, much in the same way as his dead friend. MCS

Movie rating: *6

Visual: video

Off the record: **Mark Springer** (the Pop Group) subsequently composed the score for 1991 gangster flick, 'London Kills Me'. MCS

JOE STRUMMER // Various Artists

May 88. (lp/c/cd) *Epic; <SE/+T 40879> (461161-1/-4/-2)* [ ] Jul88 [ ]
– Trash city / Baby the trans / Nefertiti rock / Nothin' 'bout nothin' / Theme from Permanent Record // 'Cause I said so (the GODFATHERS / Waiting on love (the BODEANS) / Wishing on another lucky star (J.D. SOUTHER) / All day and all of the night (the STRANGLERS) / Something happened (LOU REED).

S/track review: A record – permanent you could say – shared between ex-CLASH man, JOE STRUMMER, and a colourful array of various stars, from relative old-timer LOU REED to rock'n'roll cowpunks, the BODEANS. The album also featured a recent UK hit cover of the Kinks' 'All Day And All Of The Night', while major label newcomers (on 'Epic') the GODFATHERS' shined with spinoff flop 'Cause I Said So'. The aforementioned STRUMMER scored the first half, a mixture of loud and noisy rock that didn't quite have the bite of old; 'Trash City' failed to crack the charts. MCS

Album rating: *5

– spinoff releases, etc. –

JOE STRUMMER: Trash City / Theme From Permanent Record

Jun 88. (7"/7"s) *(TRASH/+P 1)* [–] [ ]
(12"+=/pic-cd-s+=) *(TRASH T/C 1)* – Nefertiti rock.

the GODFATHERS: 'Cause I Said So / (non-OST songs)

Jul 88. (7"/7"pic-d/12")(cd-s) *(GFT/+P/T 2)(CDGFT 2)* [–] [ ]

PETEY WHEATSTRAW

aka the DEVIL'S SON-IN-LAW

1977 (US 95m) Generation International Pictures (R)

Film genre: anarchic horror/fantasy comedy

Top guns: s-w + dir: Cliff Roguemore → DISCO GODFATHER

Stars: Rudy Ray Moore *(Petey Wheatstraw)* ← the MONKEY HUSTLE ← DOLEMITE / → DISCO GODFATHER → JACKIE'S BACK! → BIG MONEY HUTLA, Jimmy Lynch *(Jimmy)* ← DOLEMITE / → DISCO GODFATHER, Leroy Daniels *(Leroy)* → DISCO GODFATHER, Steve Wildman *(Steve)*, Ernest Mayhand *(Skillet)*, Ebony Wright *(Nell; Devil's daughter)*, Sy Richardson *(Petey's father)* → REPO MAN → SID & NANCY → STRAIGHT TO HELL → WALKER → TAPEHEADS → MYSTERY TRAIN, Lady Bee ← DOLEMITE / → DISCO GODFATHER, **Joe Williams** *(performer)* ← SING SING THANKSGIVING ← JAMBOREE

Storyline: Issuing forth fully formed from a watermelon (a real Watermelon Man you could say) during a tropical storm, Petey Wheatstraw is a born comedian, with a shit-kicking routine that fatally piques the envy of baaaad rivals Leroy and Skillet. All is not lost, though, as Satan offers him a devil's bargain: he'll bring Petey back to life – with added supernatural powers – if Petey marries his plug-ugly daughter. BG

Movie rating: *3.5

Visual: video

Off the record: Joe Williams (b. Joseph Goreed, 12 Dec'18, Cordele, Georgia, USA) was a big band jazz & blues singer who began his career with Lionel Hampton and progressed to the Count Basie Orchestra in the 50s. Joe died of natural causes in Las Vegas on 29th March, 1999.

—

NAT DOVE & THE DEVILS

Nov 77. (lp) *Magic Disc; <MD 112>* ☐ ⊟
– Petey Wheatstraw (vocal) / Ghetto St. USA (vocal) / Zombie march (instr.) / Loving you (instr.) / Walking theme (instr.) / Ghetto St. USA (instr.) / Joy (vocal) / Steve's den (instr.) / Loving you (instr.) / Petey Wheatstraw (instr.) / Junkie chase (instr.).

S/track review: RUDY RAY MOORE kept the cine-funk, the piss-poor karate and the ghetto jokes coming as late as 1977, with a little help from NAT DOVE & THE DEVILS. The sleeve suggests Hammer Horror-goes-to-Compton but the music – recorded at HB Barnum's Hollywood studio – is deep, heavy-duty soul with a backstreet charge, as rough and ready as MOORE's humour and all but unhampered by modern technology. The title theme – sung by MARY LOVE (imagine Joshie Jo Armstead with a migraine) – rips the lungs out of 'Disco Inferno', galloping along at the kind of lick that'd outpace a horseman of the apocalypse. DOVE himself sings like he's casting out demons, but LOVE's more than a match for him on the syncopated sparring of 'Ghetto St. U.S.A.'. She turns in defiant, bravura performances on the ballads, 'Loving You' and 'Joy', haunted by the tiered harmonies of mysterious backing trio, LE GRAND TROIS. Breaks fans usually pick up the soundtrack for 'Zombie March', a solid funk instrumental with flesh-eating bass and very un-undead-sounding horn charts. More of all this would've been great but DOVE seems to have run out of ideas halfway through. He fills up the empty vinyl with "instrumental versions", but – contrary bugger – sings on them anyway. Still, 'PETEY WHEATSTRAW' is about as old skool as it gets for the late 70s, and the least it deserves is a CD reissue. *BG*

Album rating: *6

☐ Tom PETTY segment
(⇒ SHE'S THE ONE)

PHENOMENA

US title 'CREEPERS'

1985 (Ita 110m) DACFilm Rome / New Line Cinema (R)

Film genre: crime/horror fantasy/thriller

Top guns: s-w: Dario Argento (+ dir), Franco Ferrini

Stars: Jennifer Connelly *(Jennifer Corvino)* → LABYRINTH → the HOT SPOT, Daria Nicolodi *(Frau Bruckner)* ← TENEBRE ← INFERNO ← SHOCK ← PROFONDO ROSSO, Donald Pleasence *(Prof. John McGregor)* ← the MONSTER CLUB ← SGT. PEPPER'S LONELY HEARTS CLUB BAND ← PIED PIPER, Dalila Di Lazzaro *(headmistress)*, Patrick Bauchau *(Insp. Rudolf Geiger)* → EVERYBREATH → the BEATNICKS → RAY, Fiore Argento *(Vera Brandt)*, Federica Mastroianni *(Sophie)*, Fiorenza Tessari *(Gisela Sulzer)*

Storyline: Teenager Jennifer finds her unusual talents called into play when she is enrolled at a Swiss boarding school. The Swiss police are baffled by a series of brutal murders and enlist the help of entomologist John McGregor, who uses insects to find clues. Jennifer is somehow able to communicate with bugs and beasties and helps the prof (and his pet chimp) track down the murderer. But as said murderer grows more desperate it's Jennifer who looks like being the next victim (unless she buzzes off). *JZ*

Movie rating: *6.5

Visual: video + dvd

Off the record: (see below)

—

Various Artists: Creepers (score: GOBLIN * / CLAUDIO SIMONETTI ** / SIMON BOSWELL ***)

Feb 86. (lp) *Heavy Metal; (HMILP 47) Enigma; <SJ 73205>* ☐ ☐
– Phenomena (**) / Flash of the blade (IRON MAIDEN) / Jennifer (*) / The quick and the dead (ANDI SEX GANG) / The wind (*) / Two tribes (FRANKIE GOES TO HOLLYWOOD) / Valley (BILL WYMAN & TERRY TAYLOR) / Sleepwalking (*) / Locomotive (MOTORHEAD) / You don't know me (ANDI SEX GANG) *[UK-only]* / Transmute (*) *[US-only]* / Jennifer's friends (*) / The maggots (***) / The naked and the dead (ANDI SEX GANG). *(cd-iss. Dec92 on 'Soundtrack Listeners Communications' Japan; SLCS 7149)*

—

GOBLIN

Feb 93. (cd) *Cinevox; (CD-MDF 303)* ☐ ⊟
– Phenomena / Jennifer / The wind / Sleepwalking / Jennifer's friends / Phenomena (film version 1) / Phenomena (film version 2) / Phenomena (piano solo – film version 3) / Sleepwalking (alt.) / The wind (film versions suite 1) / The wind ("Insects" film versions suite 2) / Jennifer's friends (alt.) / Jennifer (end titles). *(re-iss. Sep97 +=; CD-MDF 303)* – The monster child / Phenomena (video) / Phenomena (alt.)

S/track review: GOBLIN composer and synth player CLAUDIO SIMONETTI wrote and performed the title theme for 'PHENOMENA', a mix of operatic vocals, rumbling drums, SIMONETTI's trademark arpeggios, wailing electric guitar and a break disturbingly evocative of the 'Murder She Wrote' theme. Like the best GOBLIN themes, it is a unique and inventive tune, schlock-y and brazen but never boring. However, Director Dario Argento, dissatisfied with the rest of the original score produced by GOBLIN (i.e. SIMONETTI, FABIO PINATELLI, MASSIMO MORANTE, AGOSTINO MARANGOLO and MAURIZIO GUARINI) elected to throw metal and rock songs into the mix – including tracks by MOTORHEAD and IRON MAIDEN – as well as original music from BILL WYMAN and SIMON BOSWELL. BOSWELL, debuting as a film composer, was brought into score a sequence where Jennifer Connelly's character falls into a pit of decomposing bodies. For 'The Maggots' he called upon ANDI SEX GANG from the Sex Gang Children to provide tortured vocals, and the goth rocker then provided three more solo tracks for the soundtrack. While these and BILL WYMAN's contribution (a haunting guitar soundscape far removed from the Rolling Stones) compare unfavourably with most Argento/GOBLIN scores, the truth is that, SIMONETTI's excellent title theme aside, the Italian band's work here is not their best. The pan pipes and generic electric guitars on 'Jennifer' lack character, and 'Sleepwalking' is a directionless exercise in power rock drums and programmed synths. 'The Wind', however, showcases the reassuringly spooky operatic vocals of the title theme but these are then reprised less successfully in 'Jennifer's Friend' a close cousin of 'Sleepwalking' and similarly, unforgivably, boring. While the later GOBLIN release collects all the instrumental music produced for 'PHENOMENA' (summing up to 10 additional variants), the original release of the soundtrack included the five extant tracks that the rest of the GOBLIN tracks were based upon, along with most of the song soundtrack. This makes it the preferable purchase for fans of the film, or GOBLIN virgins. The GOBLIN track 'Transmute' which is included in some versions of the release is actually from their score for 'PATRICK' (1979). *SW*

Album rating: *5.5 (V/A *5)

John PHILLIPS

Born: 30 Aug'35, Parris Island, South Carolina, USA. The father figure of 60s pop sensations the MAMAS AND THE PAPAS, and the self-styled "Wolf King of L.A.", the hugely talented JOHN PHILLIPS was the songwriting genius behind such flower power anthems as 'California Dreamin', 'Monday, Monday' and 'Dedicated To The One I Love'. When the MAMAS AND THE PAPAS finally buckled under the weight of personal animosity and torrid intrigue, PHILLIPS retreated to his home studio to record a one-off solo album and notch up a co-composing credit (with Lionel Newman) on Mike Sarne's infamous Gore Vidal adaptation, 'Myra Breckinridge' (1970), as well as a songwriting credit on Robert Altman's 'BREWSTER McLOUD' (1970). While the failure of his solo debut sent PHILLIPS into a spiral of drug and alcohol abuse, he went on to work on the score to Edie Sedgwick documentary, 'Edie In Ciao! Manhattan' (1972), alongside the likes of Kim Fowley and Skip Battin, and subsequently scored Nicolas Roeg's DAVID BOWIE vehicle, 'The Man Who Fell To Earth' (1976). He was faced with a second flop, however, when his broadway musical, 'Man On The Moon', shut up shop after only a couple of performances. While PHILLIPS cleaned himself up in the 80s and went on to tour and record, his health finally failed him on March 18, 2001, when he died of a heart attack. His songwriting legacy was given a bit of a unlikely dusting down in 1996 via a teenaged CASS ELLIOT obsessive in Hettie McDonald's gay love story, 'BEAUTIFUL THING'. *BG*

- **filmography** (composer) –

Monterey Pop *(1968 {p w/ MAMAS & THE PAPAS} OST by V/A =>)* / Myra Breckinridge *(1970 OST w/ V/A & Lionel Newman; see future edition)* / **Brewster McCloud** *(1970 on OST by V/A / score: GENE PAGE =>)* / Edie In Ciao! Manhattan *(1972 w/ Skip Battin, Kim Fowley, RICHIE HAVENS & Kim Milford)* / the Man Who Fell To Earth *(1976)* / **Beautiful Thing** *(1997 OST by MAMAS & THE PAPAS =>)*

☐ John PHILLIPS
(⇒ NOT DROWNING, WAVING)

☐ PIANO MAGIC segment
(⇒ SON DE MAR)

a PIECE OF THE ACTION

1977 (US 140m) First Artists / Verdon Productions/ Warner Bros. (PG)

Film genre: Crime caper/comedy

Top guns: dir: Sidney Poitier ← LET'S DO IT AGAIN / → FAST FORWARD / s-w: Charles Blackwell (story: Timothy Marsh ← LET'S DO IT AGAIN / → FAST FORWARD)

Stars: Bill Cosby *(Dave Anderson)* ← LET'S DO IT AGAIN ← MAN AND BOY, Sidney Poitier *(Manny Durrell)* ← LET'S DO IT AGAIN ← TO SIR, WITH LOVE ← BLACKBOARD JUNGLE, James Earl Jones *(Joshua Burke)* ← CLAUDINE / → the LION KING → PRIMARY COLORS, Denise Nicholas *(Lila French)* ← LET'S DO IT AGAIN ← the SOUL OF NIGGER CHARLEY ← BLACULA, Hope Clarke *(Sarah Thomas)* ← BOOK OF NUMBERS / → BEAT STREET, Tracy Reed *(Nikki McLean)* ← CAR WASH ← NO WAY BACK ← TRAIN RIDE TO HOLLYWOOD ← TROUBLE MAN, Titos Vandis *(Bruno)*, Frances Foster *(Bea Quitman)*, Marc Lawrence *(Louie)* → GOIN' COCONUTS → FOUR ROOMS, Tamu Blackwell *(Cheryl)* ← CLAUDINE, Bryan O'Dell *(Roscoe)* → YOUNGBLOOD, Charles Walker *(parking lot attendant)* → GOIN' COCONUTS → ALMOST FAMOUS

Storyline: Wiseass crooks Dave Anderson and Manny Durrell swap con tricks for community service after being caught in the act by a retired cop. Coming to an informal arrangement rather than face official justice, they agree to impart some of their street wisdom to a bunch of no-hoper kids but don't bargain on the karmic consequences of one of their recent scams. *BG*

Movie rating: *4.5

Visual: video + dvd

Off the record: (see below)

—

MAVIS STAPLES (composer: CURTIS MAYFIELD)

Dec 77. (lp) *Curtom; <CU 5019>* ☐ [-]
– Chocolate city / Of whom shall I be afraid / Orientation / A piece of the action / Good lovin' daddy / 'Til blossoms bloom / Koochie, koochie, koochie / Getting deeper (instrumental). *(UK cd-iss. Mar06 on 'Snapper'; SNAP 263CD)*

S/track review: Released the same year as 'SHORT EYES' but coming from a different place entirely, this is more a companion piece to CURTIS MAYFIELD's earlier STAPLES collaboration, 'LET'S DO IT AGAIN'. Never mind that MAVIS was approaching the big four-0, her voice is smoking and her hormones raging on a record that's pretty much everything MAYFIELD's work with Aretha Franklin wasn't: raw, skanky, "dee-lish-us" . . . Allegedly brought in as a replacement for Roberta Flack and kept on a tight leash, she responded with one of the bravura performances of her career; 'Koochie, Koochie, Koochie' is the writhing apogee, drunk on double entendre and deep, dubby funk, but the nastiest couplets are on 'Good Lovin' Daddy'. And the steel drums are a nice touch; Fifty Cent would resurrect their lewd potential on his own 'P.I.M.P.' 'Getting Deeper' is MAYFIELD's attempt at a 'CAR WASH'-style set piece, a bustling, hi-hat-snuffling instrumental with ascendant, set-quasers-to-stun keyboards (Yello approximated a kind of 80s parallel with 'The Race'). CURTIS even makes an appointment with Dr Funkenstein on 'Chocolate City'; it's not a Parliament cover but – as Lightnin' Rod would put it – it's got its P-Funk shit down pat, or at least the chanted lyrics and Bernie Worrell bleeps. Lest he leave his right-hand arranger Rich Tufo with no syrupy strings to really get his charts into, MAYFIELD doesn't completely abandon the churchy pedigree: 'Of Whom Shall I Be Afraid' addresses the big man upstairs with righteous, secular-spiritual STAPLES fervour. Figure in the resolve-melting title track – pure-spun MAYFIELD silk – and you have another, near-flawless song cycle, one which lends credence to the claim that the Chicago soul don understood the dynamics of black cinema on a deeper level than many – if not all – of his peers. This album likewise should've launched MAVIS STAPLES as an A-list solo artist; a later attempt at a secular career was mired in mid-80s production, but this is a tantalising glimpse of what might have been. *BG*

Album rating: *7

PIECES OF APRIL

2003 (US 80m) Metro-Goldwyn-Mayer (PG-13)

Film genre: domestic/urban drama

Top guns: s-w (+ dir): Peter Hedges ← ABOUT A BOY

Stars: Katie Holmes *(April Burns)* ← the SINGING DETECTIVE, Patricia Clarkson *(Joy Burns)* ← HIGH ART, Derek Luke *(Bobby)* → FRIDAY NIGHT LIGHTS, Alison Pill *(Beth Burns)*, John Gallagher Jr. *(Timmy Burns)*, Oliver Platt *(Jim Burns)* ← WORKING GIRL, Alice Drummond *(Grandma Dottie)*, Sean Hayes *(Wayne)*, **Sisqo** *(Latrell)*, Lillias White *(Evette)*

Storyline: Shot on digital video, this tells the story of April, a kind-hearted bohemian twenty-something who lives in New York with her boyfriend Bobby and her terminally ill mother. It's the day of thanksgiving and April's family are visiting from Pennsylvania, but her oven is broken. Enlisting the help of two African American neighbours, she sets to cooking the meal as her judgemental family arrives to cause emotional havoc. *AS*

Movie rating: *7.5

Visual: dvd

Off the record: **Sisqo** (b. Mark Andrews, 9 Nov'78, Baltimore, Maryland, USA) was the silver-haired founder of the urban/R&B outfit, Dru Hill. After a reasonably fruitful time with the group (hits included 'Tell Me' from the 1996 feature, 'Eddie'), Sisqo went solo and had two million-seller, 'Incomplete' & 'Thong Song' both from his debut album, 'Unleash The Dragon' (1999). *MCS*

—

STEPHIN MERRITT (+ MAGNETIC FIELDS * & 6THS **)

Nov 03. (cd) *Nonesuch; <(7559 79860-2)>* ☐ Dec03 ☐
– All I want to know (*) / As you turn to go (**) / Dreams anymore (*) / Epitaph for my heart (*) / Heather Heather (*) / I think I need a new heart (*) / One April day / Stray with me (*) / The luckiest guy on the Lower East Side (*) / You you you you you (**).

S/track review: STEPHIN MERRITT returns for his second outing into movie soundtrack composing, keeping firmly in with the indie crowd. Unlike his previous effort, 'EBAN & CHARLEY', MERRITT donates songs from his previous band's releases, plus a few original compositions thrown in for good measure, the best of which being the song 'One Day In April', written, as you might imagine, exclusively for the film's soundtrack. Elsewhere his side-project group the 6THS' 'As You Turn To Go' makes a welcome appearance as do three of his songs from the much acclaimed MAGNETIC FIELDS album '69 Love Songs'. But it's the new stuff that will have fans and admirers purchasing this album; songs such as 'The Luckiest Guy On The Lower East Side' and 'Stray With Me' exaggerate MERRITT's great sense of dead-pan timing, and, although a little brief (at just over 25 minutes long), the new material on this notable soundtrack is just as good as MERRITT's previous output. *AS*

Album rating: *6.5

PIED PIPER

1972 (W.Ger/UK 90m) Sagittarius Productions / Goodtimes Enter.. (PG)

Film genre: mythical fantasy drama

Top guns: s-w: Jacques Demy (+ dir) MODEL SHOP, Andrew Birkin → FLAME, Mark Peploe (story: Brothers Grimm)

Stars: Jack Wild *(Gavin)* ← MELODY, **DONOVAN** *(the piper)*, Michael Hordern *(Melius; alchemist)* → LABYRINTH, John Hurt *(Franz)* → 1984 → EVEN COWGIRLS GET THE BLUES → DEAD MAN → the PROPOSITION, Cathryn Harrison *(Lisa)* → EAT THE RICH, Donald Pleasence *(the baron)* → SGT. PEPPER'S LONELY HEARTS CLUB BAND → the MONSTER CLUB → PHENOMENA, Roger Hammond *(Karl)*, Roy Kinnear *(burgermeister)* ← MELODY ← HELP!, Peter Vaughan *(bishop)*, Diana Dors *(burgermeister's wife)*, Mary MacLeod *(maidservant)* → O LUCKY MAN! → BRIMSTONE & TREACLE, Peter Eyre *(priest)* ← CATCH US IF YOU CAN, Gertan Klauber *(town crier)* ← DATELINE DIAMONDS / → BACKBEAT

Storyline: A Brothers Grimm fairy tale from the 19th Century – with a Robert Browning poem thrown in for good measure – about a mysterious, 14th Century Pied Piper of Hamelin who rids a town of all its rats, but when monies due are not forthcoming, he also rids the town of all its children. A dark tale, indeed. *MCS*

Movie rating: *6

Visual: video

Off the record: **DONOVAN** objected to his songs being released on a proposed soundtrack; three songs ('Sailing Homeward', 'The Pied Piper' and 'What A Waste Of Time', can be found on the LP, 'Donovan Volume 3'. In the can for 30 years or so, Donovan was finally persuaded by leading re-issue label, 'Rhino', to release the 'Pied Piper' album; can't review because it wasn't the official film soundtrack. *MCS*

– associated release, etc. –

DONOVAN: The Pied Piper

Mar 02. (cd) *Rhino; <78290>* [–] ☐
– I love my shirt / Happiness runs / Sun magic / People call me Pied Piper / Little boy in corduroy / Colours / Jackie Beanstalk / A funny man / Mandolin man and his secret / Nature friends / Wynken, Blynken and Nod / Little teddy bear / Voyage to the moon.

PIGS WILL FLY

2002 (Ger 102m) Workshop Leppin Moore Hoerner / ZDF (16)

Film genre: domestic abuse drama

Top guns: s-w: (+ dir) Eoin Moore, Nadya Derado

Stars: Andreas Schmidt *(Laxe)*, Thomas Morris *(Walter)*, Laura Tonke *(Inga)*, Kirsten Block *(Manuela)*, Alexis Lezin *(Stacey)*, Udo Kier *(Uncle Max)* ← DANCER IN THE DARK ← NINA HAGEN = PUNK + GLORY ← the END OF VIOLENCE ← EVEN COWGIRLS GET THE BLUES ← SUSPIRIA / → 30 DAYS UNTIL I'M FAMOUS, Hans-Peter Hallwachs *(father)*

Storyline: Laxe is a Berlin policeman struggling with the demons of a violent childhood, while he also is an abusive husband who beats his wife. Can he control his erratic behavoir or has the past left an indelible stain and scarred his mind for life. *MCS*

Movie rating: *7.5

Visual: dvd

Off the record: **CHRIS WHITLEY** was born in Houston on the 31st August, 1960, his career only really getting underway when he turned thirty (see review). Influenced in equal parts by Delta-Blues legend, Robert Johnson, John Coltrane and Chet Baker, WHITLEY finally got his break from Canadian singer-songwriter/producer, DANIEL LANOIS, who set up his solo debut for 'Columbia' records in 1991. Characterised by his long hair and skinny frame, WHITLEY was regarded – in the business at least (IGGY POP, TOM PETTY, SPRINGSTEEN, etc.) – as one of the best guitarists around. It's just a pity everyone else didn't quite see it that way. His best work included the aforementioned debut, 'Living With The Law' and 1998's 'Dirt Floor', while he was probably in his element when he was invited to appear in a performance documentary, 'HELLHOUND ON MY TRAIL – THE AFTERLIFE OF ROBERT JOHNSON'. He had just dusted off his umpteenth album, 'Soft Dangerous Shores' (2005), when he was diagnosed with lung cancer. Towards the fall of that year, he immediately cancelled all tour commitments and retired to his home in Houston. Sadly, the end was all too quick when he passed away on the 20th of November, 2005. Maybe now people will start buying his worthy back catalogue. *MCS*

—

WARNER POLAND and KAI-UWE KOHLSCHMIDT
featuring CHRIS WHITLEY

Feb 03. (cd) *Ulftone; (063)* [–] German [–]
– Crystaline / Laxe 01 / Dislocation blues / Please please / Breaking your fall / Gum / Frisco 01 / Fine day / Tijuana / Laxe 02 / Velocity (instrumental) / Velocity girl / Under the bridge / Frisco 03 / Summer's gone / Laxe 06 / Laxe on the run / Crystaline reprise / Fleamarket / Pinata baseball bat / Laxe 05 / Bridge song / Laxe 03 / Fine day *[film version]* / Frisco 02 / Crystalline *[film version]* / Keine titelinformation / Keine titelinformation *[data track]*.

S/track review: If Bruce Springsteen was ever going to get around to scoring a complete soundtrack, rather than the odd indulgence here and there, this is probably how he'd want it to sound. Another connection and inspiration was undoubtably Daniel Lanois, who produced his homecoming debut album, 'Living With The Law', way back in 1991; there were LPs issued earlier, but only in Belgium. However, this OST is down to – or rather featuring –

cool Texan-born blues-rocker, CHRIS WHITLEY, an unknown in some quarters although he already had several albums behind him including his previous effort, 'Rocket House', in 2001. As for German composers, WARNER POLAND and KAI-UWE KOHLSCHMIDT, little is known – maybe someone out there will inform me in time. Anyway, this is basically a CHRIS WHITLEY album, as his name is clearly the one emblazoned on the cover. 'PIGS WILL FLY' kicks off with 'Crystalline', a deep, soulful and self-reflective song that was characterised by his use of slide guitar. Interspersed with short instrumental 'Twin Peaks'-like dirges, the album flows with a rhythm that even Ry Cooder would be proud of. 'Dislocation Blues' and especially 'Breaking Your Fall', were worth the admission price alone, the latter would've graced any of his previous sets. Ditto the Lenny Kravitz-esque, 'Fine Day', while 'Velocity Girl' reverberates with a horizontal ease. Now that's what I call music – roots-styled, at least. The speakers blast out for glam-rock number, 'Summer's Gone', showing WHITLEY had more strings to his proverbial bow than one might have thought. 27 or so tracks span this album (around a dozen proper songs), so the listener is guaranteed his/her money's worth and there are definitely a few treasures lurking within. It's a pity the second half of the long-player didn't match up to the first, as there's just too many short pieces and reprise versions about. *MCS*

Album rating: *7

PINK FLOYD

Formed: London, England ... 1965 as the Abdabs by ROGER WATERS, Nick Mason and Richard Wright, in tandem with Clive Metcalfe, Juliet Gale and Keith Noble. The mercurial Syd Barrett subsequently replaced the latter three and the new look band took its moniker as a canny amalgamation of a relatively obscure bluesmen, Pink Anderson and Floyd Council. Yet far from being the average Brit blues boom combo, the PINK FLOYD – in spirit at least – went on to join the likes of SUN RA in travelling the spaceways of popular music. Unlike the legendary jazz seer, they somehow managed to translate their experimentation into some of the best selling albums of all time, not least 'The Dark Side Of The Moon' (1973), before transforming into one of the most bloated stadium rock dinosaurs of all time. While Barrett had brought an element of inspired whimsy to the band's seminal debut album, 'The Piper At The Gates Of Dawn' (1967), his infamous decline into serious mental illness changed their creative direction. Fifth member David Gilmour was brought in to bolster Barrett's loss while ROGER WATERS eventually took over Syd's role as principal songwriter. His was a world view far removed from Barrett's, however, and even in the early days, WATERS' writing replaced wide eyed surrealism with a sober compositional gravitas. The revamped 'Floyd expanded and strung out the band's original psychedelic vision into a much more fluid and sonically complex beast, with WATERS beginning to assert his songwriting dominance on the group's first feature-length soundtrack commission, to Barbet Schroeder's mediterranean road movie, 'MORE' (1969); short-film 'The COMMITTEE', was their celluloid debut. 'MORE' favoured an unexpectedly laidback and conventionally structured approach, employing all the rarefied atmospherics of their regular studio work but laying off the self indulgence. While the band had previously made their cinematic debut in Swinging London document, 'TONITE LET'S ALL MAKE LOVE IN LONDON' (1967), the Schroeder score was an impressive move into the wider film world and one which earned them a further brace of early 70s commissions. While WATERS himself collaborated with RON GEESIN on the score to anatomy documentary, 'The BODY' (1970), PINK FLOYD provided a considerable chunk of the score (alongside the likes of the Grateful Dead and John Fahey) for Michelangelo Antonioni's ambitious counterculture epic, 'ZABRISKIE POINT' (1970). This was followed by another Schroeder soundtrack, to hippy jungle drama, 'La VALLEE' (1972). With its closer emphasis on songwriting, the record – released under the title 'Obscured By Clouds' – was a final link from the freeform experimentation of the early years to the conceptual focus of the aforementioned 'The Dark Side Of The Moon' and beyond. And while they subsequently became one of the biggest rock bands in the world, they nevertheless continued to score the odd, obscure movie such as Swedish drama, 'Skaerselden' (1974) and British R.D. Laing-inspired drama, 'Knots' (1975). WATERS, however, hadn't played his trump card quite yet. With his creative grip over the band tightening, the man's dystopian vision and well publicised hatred of his own audience was finally given free reign on 'The WALL' (1979), a wildly ambitious and commercially successful concept set which was subsequently made into a partly animated, Alan Parker-directed film in 1982. Perversely, it even spawned a transatlantic No.1 single ('Another Brick In The Wall'), the first and only of the band's career. Yet it also marked the end of an era as WATERS finally departed amid lawsuits and recrimination, eventually resulting in a successful but – to date at least – creatively disappointing PINK FLOYD Mk III. In 1987, WATERS and Various Artists contributed to the animation movie, 'WHEN THE WIND BLOWS', and three years later the one-time PF mainman featured on Ennio Morricone's 'The Legend Of 1900'. *BG*

- **filmography** (composers) {performers} –

Tonite Let's All Make Love In London *(1967 {p} on OST by V/A =>)* / **the Committee** *(1968 score =>)* / **More** *(1969 OST =>)* / **Amougies** *(1970 {p} =>)* / **the Body** *(1970 OST by ROGER WATERS & RON GEESIN =>)* / **Zabriskie Point** *(1970 OST w/ V/A =>)* / **la Vallee** *(1972 OST 'Obscured By Clouds' =>)* / **Live At Pompeii** *(1974 {p})* / Skaerselden *(1974)* / Knots *(1975)* / **the Wall** *(1982 {c} video/dvd =>)* / **When The Wind Blows** *(1987 OST by WATERS & V/A =>)* / **the Wall: Live In Berlin** *(1990 [s-w + dir: WATERS] {*p WATERS} OST by ROGER WATERS & V/A =>)* / the Legend Of 1900 *(1998 WATERS on OST by Ennio Morricone)*

PIPE DREAMS

1976 (US 89m) AVCO Embassy Pictures (PG)

Film genre: rural drama

Top guns: s-w: Stephen Verona (+ dir), Jerry Ballew

Stars: Gladys KNIGHT *(Maria Wilson)*, Barry Hankerson *(Rob Wilson)*, Bruce French *(the Duke)*, Sherry Bain *(Loretta)*, Sylvia Hayes *(Sally)*, Carole Ita White *(Rosey Rottencrutch)*, Altovise Davis *(Lydia)* → CAN'T STOP THE MUSIC, Frank McRae *(Moose)* ← SHAFT IN AFRICA ← COOL BREEZE, Redmond Gleeson *(Hollow Legs)* → YOUNG GUNS II, Arnold Johnson *(Johnny Monday)* ← SHAFT / → AMERICAN HOT WAX → the FIVE HEARTBEATS, Sally Kirkland *(Two Street Betty)* ← HEY, LET'S TWIST / → a STAR IS BORN → HUMAN HIGHWAY → THANK YOU, GOOD NIGHT, Bobbi Shaw *(Slimey Sue)* ← the GHOST IN THE INVISIBLE BIKINI ← HOW TO STUFF A WILD BIKINI ← SKI PARTY ← BEACH BLANKET BINGO ← PAJAMA PARTY

Storyline: Maria Wilson swaps Atlanta for Alaska in an attempt to win back the affections of her husband Rob, an oil worker with an eye for the ladies. Most of the ladies in town are the kind you have to pay for, and while Maria resists the attentions of the local oil baron to get her on the game, one of his charges is driven to suicide. *BG*

Movie rating: *4

Visual: video

Off the record: Soul diva **Gladys KNIGHT** was at the time married to co-actor, Barry Hankerson (divorced 1979); he in turn was the uncle of late soul/ R&B singer, Aaliyah. *MCS*

—

GLADYS KNIGHT & THE PIPS (composers: Various)

Nov 76. (lp) *Buddah; <5676> (BDLP 5017)* [94] Dec76 [ ]
– So sad the song / Alaskan pipeline / Pot of jazz / I'll miss you / Nobody but you / Pipe dreams / Find a way / Follow my dreams / So sad the song (instrumental). *<cd-iss. Feb99 on 'Kama Sutra; 5676>*

S/track review: Two years after the success of 'CLAUDINE' (1974), GLADYS KNIGHT got hip to the mid-70s oil boom, making her screen debut as a big-city girl stranded in the frozen north with her real life husband. She didn't exactly strike black gold but, with Hollywood score legend Dominic Frontiere and Michael Masser on the arrangements/production, the soundtrack's well was deep enough to trade on the (transatlantic, summer '76) success of 'Midnight Train To Georgia'. The Southern heat of KNIGHT's alto defrosts 'Alaskan Pipeline' inside a few bars, extracting the kind of ensemble, earth-shovelling soul which Aretha Franklin's 'SPARKLE' (1976) lacked. Even the Goffin/Weil/Mann-calibre hits 'So Sad The Song' and 'Nobody But You' are better-than-average 70s soul, smooth enough to follow ' . . .Georgia' into the charts but – with 'Nobody . . .' at least – gutsy enough to deliver a gospel charge. Frontiere – a jazz accordionist in another life – comes up with a reasonable piano-led scat number, 'Pot Of Jazz' but the album sags in the middle: over-orchestrated James Cleveland (as in Reverend) ballads and a forgettable title theme (one of the least memorable themes to any 70s-vintage black film soundtrack and a disappointment from the man – Tony Camillo – who'd penned the Grammy winning ' . . .Georgia') divining KNIGHT's future career as an MOR artiste. *BG*

Album rating: *5.5

– spinoff hits, etc. –

GLADYS KNIGHT & THE PIPS: So Sad The Song / (instrumental)

Sep 76. (7") *<544> (BDS 448)* [47] Oct76 [20]

GLADYS KNIGHT & THE PIPS: Nobody But You / Pipe Dreams

Nov 76. (7") *(BDS 451)* [ ] Jan77 [34]

PLACES IN THE HEART

1984 (US 113m) Tri-Star Pictures (PG)

Film genre: rural period-costume melodrama

Top guns: s-w + dir: Robert Benton

Stars: Sally Field *(Edna Spalding)*, Lindsay Crouse *(Margaret Lomax)* → the INSIDER, Ed Harris *(Wayne Lomax)* → ALAMO BAY → SWEET DREAMS → WALKER → MASKED AND ANONYMOUS, Amy Madigan *(Viola Kelsey)* ← STREETS OF FIRE / → ALAMO BAY → CROCODILE SHOES, John Malkovich *(Mr. Will)* → the KILLING FIELDS, Danny Glover *(Moze)* → DREAMGIRLS, Yankton Hatten *(Frank)*, Lane Smith *(Albert Denby)* ← HONEYSUCKLE ROSE / → WHY DO FOOLS FALL IN LOVE, Terry O'Quinn *(Buddy Kelsey)*

Storyline: Edna Spalding finds her life turned upside down when her husband the sheriff is killed by a gunman. She's left in charge of a farm and her two young children with hardly a penny to her name. With the Depression at its height, she takes in a blind war veteran and a black journeyman to help pay the bills, but it all depends on the cotton crop surviving tornados, plummeting stock markets and even the KKK. Lucky white heather? *JZ*

Movie rating: *8

Visual: video + dvd

Off the record: DOC WATSON (see below)

—

DOC WATSON, MERLE WATSON & THE TEXAS PLAYBOYS (md: Howard Shore)

Apr 85. (lp) *Milan; (A 269)* [–] French [–]
– Cotton-Eyed Joe / Cotton-eyed Joe (reprise) / Ida red / Faded love / Lovesick blues / Cotton-eyed Joe / Sweetheart schottische / La golondrina / Right or wrong / First fiddle tune / Mexicali rose / Blessed assurance / Ida red (instrumental reprise) / Faded love (instrumental) / Mexicali rose (instrumental reprise) / Arkansas traveler / Right or wrong (reprise) / First fiddle tune (reprise) / In the sweet bye and bye / In the garden. *<(re-iss. Jan89 on 'Varese Sarabande'; STV 81229)>*

S/track review: Long before 'O BROTHER, WHERE ART THOU?' syringed a healthy dose of old-time music into the ears of the mainstream audience, this creditable little movie made a fair job of smuggling in the dungarees and bluegrass. Led by DOC WATSON, the endearing Appalachian guitarist who'd been unearthed in the 60s folk boom, it delivers a low-key, far from rumbustious and generally lovely trawl through standards like 'Cotton-Eyed Joe', 'Faded Love' and 'Mexicali Rose' as well as a waltz-heavy string of dance tunes. Arrangement and production are by Howard Shore (who would go on to score the 'Lord Of The Rings' trilogy), and the set-up is exemplary, down to the period-recording equipment and support from the TEXAS PLAYBOYS – featuring several of the veterans who'd backed the King of Western Swing, Bob Wills. The musicians rarely break sweat (a sizzling 'Arkansas Traveler' is one of the exceptions, and that lasts less than a minute), and WATSON's laid-back baritone is frankly a little genteel for Hank Williams' 'Lovesick Blues'. But when did sweat become a virtue? This is a plaintive, understated gem which bears witness that first-rate roots music could still hold its own in the days when John Malkovich and Ed Harris had hair. *ND*

Album rating: *7

the POINT!

1971 (US 74m TV) Murakami-Wolf Productions

Film genre: children's fantasy animation

Top guns: dir: Fred Wolf (+ anim.) / s-w: Norm Lenzer (au: **Harry Nilsson**)

Voices: Ringo STARR *(narrator)* <= the BEATLES =>, Dustin Hoffman *(narrator)* ← WHO IS HARRY KELLERMAN AND WHY IS HE SAYING THOSE TERRIBLE THINGS ABOUT ME? ← LITTLE BIG MAN ← MIDNIGHT COWBOY ← the GRADUATE / → DICK TRACY → WAG THE DOG, Paul Frees *(Oblio's father, etc.)* ← WILD IN THE STREETS, Mike Lookinland *(Oblio)*, Lennie Weinrib *(Count)* ← GOOD TIMES

Storyline: Nilsson's timeless children's fantasy, centering on the animated adventures of Oblio and his mate Arrow. Oblio is the unfortunate owner of a round head, not so clever in the land of Point where everyone else has a pointed bonce. Nilsson examines themes of prejudice and tribal mentality as Oblio is cast out (along with Arrow) and embarks on a voyage of self discovery through the "pointless forest". *BG*

Movie rating: *6

Visual: video + dvd

Off the record: Harry NILSSON (see below)

—

NILSSON

Feb 71. (lp) *R.C.A.; <LSP 4417> (SF 8166)* [25] Jan72 [46]
– Everything's got 'em / The town (narration) / Me and my arrow / The game (narration) / Poli high / The trial and banishment (narration) / Think about your troubles / The pointed man (narration) / Life line / The birds (narration) / P.O.V. waltz / The clearing in the woods (narration) / Are you sleeping? / Oblio's return (narration). *(re-iss. Jan78 on 'M.C.A.'; MCF 2826) (re-iss. Aug91 on*

'Edsel' lp+=/cd+=; ED/+CD 340) – Down to the valley / Buy my album. *(cd-iss. Aug00 on 'Camden'+=; 74321 75743-2)* – SKIDOO

S/track review: 'The POINT!' is unlike anything else HARRY NILSSON put his name to. Maybe just a little bit Beatles-y, but then his relationship with Lennon & McCartney was always one of mutual admiration, and 'Yellow Submarine' doesn't come close. Much of the record is narration, but that's a bonus – the man's a born storyteller, and his engrossing delivery, timing, rhythm and humour could've made him a 'Jackanory' icon. Ostensibly 60s in tone and message yet unmistakably of their decade, the music and lyrics are the karmic opposite of his other 1970 album, 'Nilsson Sings Newman' (and as soulful as 'SKIDOO' was disposable); the sweetness, warmth and nostalgic ache of songs like 'Everything's Got 'Em' and 'Me And My Arrow', glow dilated and drowsy through the darker moods of his later work. Imagine Brian Eno scuba diving with Mr Bean, and you'll come halfway to imagining the sub-aquatic 70s black hole from which the likes of 'Life Line' bubbles up. It's strange, gorgeous stuff, and you don't have to be a kid to enjoy it. Admittedly, he makes a record-breaking bid for the number of puns on the word "point", but there's method and message in NILSSON's madness, and likewise you don't have to be a kid to appreciate them. As an antidote to the chilliness of modern music and recording techniques, 'The POINT!' is indespensible, and ripe for rediscovery. So there you have it – as the man himself would say ". . .thank you and goodnight!". *BG*

Album rating: *7.5

– spinoff releases, etc. –

NILSSON: Down In The Valley / Buy My Album

Nov 70. (7") *<74-0362> (RCA 1987)* [ ] [ ]

NILSSON: Me And My Arrow / Are You Sleeping?

Mar 71. (7") *<74-0443>* [34] [–]

POLA X

1999 (Fra/Ger 134m) Canal+ / France 2 Cinema (18)

Film genre: psychological/romantic drama

Top guns: s-w (+ dir): Leos Carax, Jean-Pol Fargeau ← NENETTE ET BONI / → TROUBLE EVERY DAY (au: Herman Melville)

Stars: Guillaume Depardieu *(Pierre)*, Yekaterina Golubeva *(Isabelle)*, Catherine Deneuve *(Marie)* ← PAROLES ET MUSIQUE ← JE VOUS AIME / → DANCER IN THE DARK, Delphine Chuillot *(Lucie)*, Petruta Catana *(Razerka)*, Laurent Lucas *(Thibault)*, Patachou *(Margherite)*, Mihaella Silaghi *(the child)*

Storyline: The sleepy banks of the Seine are rudely awoken when scandal erupts in a quiet Normandy village. Pierre and Lucie are two young lovers destined to be married and live happily ever after, but all this changes when a haunting young woman, Isabelle, meets Pierre and tells him she's his half-sister. He immediately dumps lovelorn Lucie and heads off to Paris with Isabelle, where their relationship becomes much deeper. When Lucie also arrives the phrase "ménage à trois" becomes suitably fitting. *JZ*

Movie rating: *5.5

Visual: dvd

Off the record: **SCOTT WALKER** (see '30 CENTURY MAN')

SCOTT WALKER (& Various Artists)

Jun 00. (cd) *Barclay; (547608-2)* [–] French [–]
– The time is out of joint / Light / Meadow / The darkest forest / Extra blues (SMOG) / Never again / Iza kana zanbi (FAIRUZ) / Trang mo ben suo / Zai na yao yuan de di fang / The church of the apostles / Bombupper / River of blood / Blink (SONIC YOUTH) / Running / Closing / Isabel.

S/track review: From 60s pop pin-up to high priest of 21st Century avant-garde, very few artists have made the kind of musical metamorphosis that SCOTT WALKER has over the past 40 years. John Lennon never went anywhere near as far towards leftfield while David Sylvian never began from quite so far away. The soundtrack to French film 'POLA X' is similar to WALKER's previous album, 'Tilt', only here the stark experimentations are interspersed with beautiful orchestral maneuverings that reflect the versatility of the artist's imagination. His rousing baritone voice is used sparingly, making a brief appearance on 'The Time Is Out Of Joint', while the listener can only imagine what instruments or other implements are being used to create the sonic anarchy of 'Never Again' or 'The Church Of The Apostles'. WALKER contributes the majority of the work on 'POLA X' but he is helped out by a few other artists. SMOG sing a lament over plucked strings on 'Extra Blues' while SONIC YOUTH chip in with the stripped down, psychedelic folk of 'Blink'. Arguably the most interesting inclusion is 'Iza Kana Zanbi' by legendary Lebanese songstress FAIRUZ that adds a Middle-Eastern tangent to the progressive wanderings that make up the bulk of the soundtrack. 'POLA X' is a difficult soundtrack and takes several listens before it slips under the listener's skin but it's worth the effort for the contrast in styles and the sheer ingenuity of one of the few true geniuses that is still willing to try something that little bit different. *CM*

Album rating: *6.5

□ the POLYPHONIC SPREE segment
(⇒ THUMBSUCKER)

POPOL VUH

Formed: Munich, Germany ... 1969 by Florian Fricke. A classically-trained musician with a serious mystical bent, Fricke appropriated the name of a sacred Mayan text for his uncompromisingly experimental and deeply meditative 70s recordings, among which his film scores for director Werner Herzog figured prominently. Fricke's global wanderings and in-depth study of diverse ethnic cultures, religions and music served as the starting point for his experiments in sound, initially showcased on such pioneering classics as 'In Den Garten Pharads' (1972) and created with the help of a revolving cast of sidemen (including various personnel from fellow Germans Amon Duul). Having originally met Herzog back in his student days, Fricke subsequently linked up with the visionary director for his 1973 masterpiece, 'AGUIRRE, WRATH OF GOD'. Pivotal to the famous opening sequence (during the filming of which Herzog – as he later commented – "came to know his destiny") of Spanish conquistadors descending from the mist-shrouded heights of Machu Picchu were Fricke's mellotron-generated atmospherics, as resonantly mythical as El Dorado itself and a luminous canvas for the ensuing messianic delirium of Klaus Kinski's Don Lope De Aguirre. While the original soundtrack was belatedly released in 1976, the main theme, 'Aguirre 1', subsequently turned up on various re-issues and compilations amid the byzantine complexities of the POPOL VUH catalogue. While Fricke subsequently scored Herzog documentary, 'Die Grobe Ekstase Des Bildschnitzers Steiner' (1975) and made his acting debut with an appearance in the director's Grand Jury Prize winning 'The Enigma Of Kaspar Hauser' (1975), the pair's next major collaboration was the cult classic, 'HERZ AUS GLAS' (1976), in which Herzog infamously hypnotised the cast to achieve his desired – and admittedly compelling – result. The POPOL VUH soundtrack – released, at various times, under its English,

German and French titles – amplified the movie's mesmeric tone, employing a more rock-centric approach in line with the prior addition of another Amon Duul alumnus, Danny Fichelscher. Yet it was POPOL VUH's contributions to 'NOSFERATU, THE VAMPYRE' (1979) which many regard as their crowning cinematic achievement. To Herzog's sinister, stylized update of F.W. Murnau's silent classic, Fricke and Co provided music as timelessly evocative and ethereal as their work on 'AGUIRRE . . .' yet infinitely darker, with an ominous choral drone echoing against the bleak Carpathian landscapes and setting the scene for Kinski's unforgettably hollow eyed entrance. Again, there were complications with the soundtrack release although German label 'S.P.V.' finally issued the complete package on CD in 2004. And while a Wagner piece had been incorporated into 'NOSFERATU', in its use of classical opera the soundtrack to Herzog's second Amazonian odyssey, 'FITZCARRALDO' (1982), was something of a departure to say the least, alternating original Enrico Caruso excerpts with heavy ethnic percussion. Although POPOL VUH were, by this point, entering the final stage of their career, their legacy provided the music for what also turned out to be the final Herzog/Kinski collaboration and indeed the final film of Kinski's career. An imaginative adaptation of Bruce Chatwin's 1980 novel, 'The Viceroy Of Ouidah', 'COBRA VERDE' (1987) featured a haggard but still intense Kinski in the role of a Brazilian outlaw turned slaver, with a soundtrack which borrowed from POPOL VUH's final album, 'Spirit Of Peace' (1985). In addition to his work with Herzog, Fricke also scored German movie, 'Wintermaerchen' (1971) and – along with BRIAN ENO – the American documentary, 'SL-1' (1983), while POPOL VUH's music was subsequently used in a number of films after the group's mid-80s demise. *BG*

- filmography (composers) –

Lebenszeichen *(1968 {p FLORIAN})* / Auch Zwerge Haben Klein Angefangen *(1970 score FRICKE)* / Wintermaerchen *(1971)* / **Aguirre, Wrath Of God** *(1972 OST =>)* / the Enigma Of Kaspar Hauser *(1974 {p FLORIAN})* / die Grosse Ekstase Des Bildschnitzers Steiner *(1975)* / **Herz Aus Glas** *(1976 OST =>)* / **Nosferatu, The Vampyre** *(1978 OST =>)* / **Fitzcarraldo** *(1982 OST =>)* / SL-1 *(1983)* / **Cobra Verde** *(1987 OST =>)* / Al Gatun *(1990)* / il Gioco Delle Ombre *(1991)*

– compilations, etc. –

POPOL VUH: The Best Soundtracks From Werner Herzog Films

1991. (cd) *Bell; (BLR 84-710)* [–] German [–]
– Engel der luft / Wehe khorazin / Im garten der gemeinschaft / . . .Als lebten die engel auf erden / Lacrime di rei / Hore, der du wagst / Bruder des schattens – Sohne des lichts / Die umkehr.

POPOL VUH: Movie Music

1994. (cd) *Spalax; (14874)* [–] French [–]
– Das lied von den hohen bergen / Der ruf / Singet, denn der gesang vertreibt die wölfe / Bruder des schattens – Sohne des lichts / Lacrime di re / Im garten der gemeinschaft / Als lebten die engel auf erden / Eine andere welt / Wehe khorazin / Der tod des banditen / For you and me / Junge madchen ho, ziavi / Affenstunde / Letzte tage, letzte nachte.

POPOL VUH: Aguirre / Herz Aug Glas / Nosferatu

Oct 96. (3xcd-box) *Spalax; (14703)* [ ] [–]

PORKY'S REVENGE

1985 sequel-2 (Can/US 93m) Astral Bellevue / 20th Century Fox (R)

Film genre: seXual teen comedy

Top guns: dir: James Komack / s-w: Ziggy Steinberg

Stars: Dan Monahan *(Pee Wee Morris)*, Wyatt Knight *(Tommy Turner)*, Tony Ganios *(Meat Tuperello)*, Mark Herrier *(Billy)*, Kaki Hunter *(Wendy)* ← ROADIE, Scott Colomby *(Brian Schwartz)* ← CADDYSHACK, Nancy Parsons *(Ms. Beulah Balbricker)* ← WHERE THE BUFFALO ROAM, Chuck Mitchell *(Porky Wallace)*, Eric Christmas *(Mr. Carter)* ← HAROLD AND MAUDE

Storyline: It's third time unlucky for the Angel Beach jocks as one of their number unwittingly picks up the nice-legs-shame-about-the-face daughter of their old enemy, nightclub don Porky Wallace. Matters are complicated by the fact that their basketball coach is in hock to the guy, and under pressure to jeopardise the upcoming championship. *BG*

Movie rating: *3.5

Visual: video + dvd (Maple Pictures)

Off the record: DAVE EDMUNDS (see below)

Various Artists (incl. DAVE EDMUNDS *)

Mar 85. (lp/c) *Columbia; <+/JST 39983> C.B.S.; (CBS/40 70265)* [ ] Jul85 [ ]
– High school nights (*) / Do you want to dance (*) / Sleepwalk (JEFF BECK) / I don't want to do it (GEORGE HARRISON) / Stagger Lee (FABULOUS THUNDERBIRDS) / Blue suede shoes (CARL PERKINS) / Peter Gunn theme (CLARENCE CLEMONS) / Queen of the hop (*) / Love me tender (WILLIE NELSON) / Philadelphia baby (CRAWLING KING SNAKES) / Porky's revenge (*). *<cd-iss. 1985 on 'Mobile Fidelity'; MFCD 797> <cd re-iss. Apr04 on 'Legacy/ Columbia'+=; CK 90875> (UK cd-iss. May04 on 'Columbia'+=; 516491-2)* – Honey don't (CARL PERKINS) / Don't call me tonight (*).

S/track review: Those of a certain age will remember the original 'Porky's' films as a kind of Betamax rite-of-passage, stealthily consumed with a pilfered can of Kestrel. Readers of a slightly older vintage will recall DAVE EDMUNDS as an unlikely rock'n'roll savant, hailing – along with his poppier brethren Shakin' Stevens – from deepest Wales. Along with right-hand man, Nick Lowe, EDMUNDS was a major behind-the-scenes figure in the mid-late 70s pub-rock boom and a rockabilly rebel in his own right. The 80s were less kind to him although he did record this unlikely last gasp of a soundtrack to a last-gasp film, rounding up an even unlikelier posse of rock aristocrats and subjecting his homeboy rock'n'roll to a hammering 'Top Gun'-meets-'Axel F' treatment, at least on the title track. It's not quite as bad as it sounds, but it can't compete with 'High School Nights', a supremely guilty, more than pleasurable amalgam of Kenny Loggins, ELO and the Cars. EDMUNDS – backed by an erstwhile Allman Brother and a Santana renegade – also hams it up on 'Queen Of The Hop' and the shamelessly swooning 'Do You Wanna Dance'. In fact, it takes original daddy CARL PERKINS to remind EDMUNDS how it's done on a rare recording of 'Blue Suede Shoes', supported by the STRAY CATS; you couldn't date this to the 80s, thank God. JEFF BECK makes one of his sporadic soundtrack appearances with an enjoyable twang through 'Sleep Walk', the old Santo and Johnny hit from the late 50s, GEORGE HARRISON is pleasant if slight on the rare Bob Dylan song, 'I Don't Want To Do It', and WILLIE NELSON is in easy-listening mode on Elvis' 'Love Me Tender'; so much for the big hitters; most of them are shown up by the FABULOUS THUNDERBIRDS, veteran Texan rabble-rousers who crash through the New Orleans perennial, 'Stagger Lee'. The E Street Band's CLARENCE CLEMONS puts in a respectable sax spin on the 'Peter Gunn Theme', but, incredibly, it's actually ROBERT PLANT who really makes his Eddie Cochran fantasies come to life; his voice positively smoulders on 'Philadelphia Baby', making you wonder why he spent so many years warbling like a viking on helium. *BG*

Album rating: *6.5

– spinoff hits, etc. –

DAVE EDMUNDS: High School Nights / Porky's Revenge

Apr 85. (7") *<04762> (A 6277)* [91] Jul85 [ ]

DAVE EDMUNDS: Do You Want To Dance / Don't Call Me Tonight

Jul 85. (7") *<04923>* [ ] [–]

PORTASTATIC

Formed: Initially a 'Merge' records side-project of Superchunk's Mac McCaughan, PORTASTATIC were a slow-burning instrumental act who'd composed and released four albums since their classy 1994 debut, 'I Hope Your Heart Is Not Brittle'. Subsequent albums such as 'Slow Note From A Sinking Ship' (1995), 'The Nature Of Sap' (1997), were not as well received; Chapel Hill faves Superchunk (who'd given us the Steve Albini-produced 'No Pocky For Kitty' in '91 and 'Here's To Shutting Up' in '01) were also coming to end when PORTASTATIC drifted into movie soundtrack work via 'LOOKING FOR LEONARD' (2001). It helped somewhat that filmmaker, Matt Bissonnette and Steven Clark were huge fans of both Mac's indie outfits. Between their next Bissonnette film project, 'WHO LOVES THE SUN' (2006), PORTASTATIC were responsible for a handful of other sets, namely 'Summer Of The Shark' (2003), 'Autumn Was A Lark' (2003), 'Bright Ideas' (2005) & 'Be Still Please' (2006), the latter actually came out after the film. *MCS*

- filmography (composer)

Looking For Leonard *(2001 OST =>)* / **Who Loves The Sun** *(2006 OST =>)*

PRAISE

1999 (Aus 97m) Strand Releasing (18)

Film genre: romantic/seXual drama

Top guns: dir: John Curran / s-w: Andrew McGahan (+ au)

Stars: Peter Fenton *(Gordon Buchanan)*, Sacha Horler *(Cynthia Lamond)*, Marta Dusseldorp *(Rachel)*, Joel Edgerton *(Leo)*, Ray Bull *(Vass)*, Yvette Duncan *(Molly)* → GARAGE DAYS, **Gregory Perkins** *(Raymond)*, Leone Carmen *(Cathy)*, Skye Wansey *(Helen)* → CHOPPER

Storyline: The tainted love between Cynthia (a woman with eczema) and live-in lover Gordon (an unemployed asthmatic with an addiction to nicotine). When the latter's old flame reappears on the scene, his mind has to choose between body and soul. *MCS*

Movie rating: *6.5

Visual: dvd

Off the record: Peter Fenton was the Sydney-born singer, songwriter and guitarist with featured OST act, CROW, who incidentally split in 1998; **Gregory Perkins** is actually known as Tex Perkins, a solo artist once the singer of 80s/90s outfits, Beasts Of Bourbon and the Cruel Sea (the latter providing the unreleased soundtrack to 1994's 'Spider & Rose'). The **DIRTY THREE** were formed in Melbourne, Australia in 1992 by WARREN ELLIS, Mick Turner and Jim White. The instrumental trio played bars and clubs mainly as a side project and eventually their impressive tightknit musical gymnastics won them favour among the Australian press. A demo tape eventually worked its way across the globe to a small Boston indie, 'Poon Village', who subsequently issued the mini-set as 'Sad And Dangerous' late in '94. This helped them secure support slots to Pavement on their North American tour, which, in turn, spurred promoters to book them for that year's 'Lollapalooza' festival. NICK CAVE had been a celebrity fan for over a year now and he proved it by accompanying the DIRTY THREE on piano while they performed a live "soundtrack" to Carl Dreyer's silent movie, 'The Passion Of Joan Of Arc', at London's National Film Theatre. The punk crooner also collaborated with the trio on an 'X-Files' TV soundtrack album entitled 'Song In The Key Of X', while ELLIS and CAVE later co-wrote a song for the latter's soap-ish (so pure) pop buddy, Kylie Minogue. On the vinyl front, the DIRTY THREE were establishing themselves with each release. Signing to 'Big Cat' records ('Touch & Go' in the US), they issued two sets, 'The Dirty Three' (1995) and 'Horse Stories' (1996). Squeezed in between these well-received gems was a collaboration with WILL OLDHAM on his Palace release 'Arise Therefore'. A couple of years passed until the issue of their Steve Albini-produced 1998 set, 'Ocean Songs' (on ROBIN GUTHRIE's new imprint, 'Bella Union'), was heralded as their finest hour yet. The year 2000 clocked up another long-player, 'Whatever You Love, You Are', an at-times restrained work of art that experimented with melodious chamber rock jettisoning the violin to the forefront. Turner subsequently founded his own label, 'King Crab', while ELLIS went on to join Nick CAVE & The Bad Seeds (he also co-scored 'The PROPOSITION'). Around the same time (2005), White provided music for the alt-country documentary, 'SEARCHING FOR THE WRONG-EYED JESUS'. *MCS*

—

Various Artists (score: DIRTY THREE * / CROW **)

Apr 00. (cd) *Festival; (D 32054)* [–] Austra [–]
– I remember a time when once you used to love me (*) / Smoke! smoke! smoke! (that cigarette) (TEX WILLIAMS & HIS WESTERN CARAVAN) / Lights are yellow and the nights are slow (*) / The river looks lonely tonight (JOHN ELLIS) / You're so beautiful to know (**) / Somewhere else, some place good (*) / Flamenco festival (JUAN CESARE) / Toaster (*) / Once across a story bridge (**) / What did I do (JOHN ELLIS) / Summers lost heart (*) / Mano o mano (* & CARLOS GARDEL) / Devil in the hole (*) / The junk crammed up behind my eyes (**) / Xmas song (*) / King of the cowboys (JOHN ELLIS) / A strange holiday (*) / Mia Fora Thimame (ARIETA).

S/track review: Featuring predominantly Australian acts, 'PRAISE' alternates eight tracks from DIRTY THREE with music by CROW, JOHN ELLIS and others. Like Sonic Youth gone country, DIRTY THREE's instrumental music, shepherded by WARREN ELLIS' mercurial violin, sashays drunkenly from dignified waltz to deranged avant-garde noise. Of their eight featured tracks, three are recycled from previous albums ('I Remember A Time When Once You Used To Love Me', 'Toaster' and 'Devil In The Hole' from 'Horse Stories', 'Ocean Songs' and 'Sad & Dangerous' respectively), while five less frenzied new songs (including the beautiful, piano-led 'Lights Are Yellow And The Nights Are Slow') were written for the soundtrack. The tracks by CROW (featuring PETER FENTON) are diverting but nondescript instrumentals that, with the exception of 'The Junk Crammed Up Behind My Eyes', perhaps suffer by comparison to the superior DIRTY THREE material. WARREN ELLIS' father, bluegrass singer-songwriter JOHN ELLIS' has three songs featured here, coming across like recordings abandoned at the side of a dusty road somewhere, and charming enough. Of the other artists featured, TEX WILLIAMS' dryly comic 'Smoke! Smoke! Smoke! (That Cigarette)' is a great diversion, JUAN CESARE's 'Flamenco Festival' has an honest title and 'Mano O Mano' ('Hand In Hand') by CARLOS GARDEL, the Latin American "King Of Tango", is passionately sung, but non-Spanish speakers will be left guessing about what. The final track, 'Mia Fora Thimame's haunting lament by Greek singer ARIETA, also conceals DIRTY THREE's music hall take on 'I Remember A Time . . .' at the end. *SW*

Album rating: *5.5

PRAY FOR RAIN

Formed: San Francisco, California, USA . . . mid-80s by Dan Wool, a former punk guitarist from St. Louis, Missouri. Alongside Jim Woody on drums and Gary Brown on bass, PRAY FOR RAIN were discovered in a local club by 'REPO MAN' filmmaker Alex Cox. About to film biopic 'SID & NANCY' (1986), the director invited the trio to send in an instrumental score, which he duly used alongside various artists' songs by the POGUES, etc. This eclectic combination was also utilized for Cox's pseudo-spaghetti western follow-up, 'STRAIGHT TO HELL' (1987), their laid-back dustbowl delivery deliberately effective (and more so on the later re-issued double CD version!). Further scores arrived via 'Trust Me' (1989), the underscore for 'Zandalee' (1991) and 'No Secrets' (1991), the latter producing one of their best cues (although unknown) tacked onto the end credits. Their next project, 'ROADSIDE PROPHETS' (1992), saw Dan work alongside his surreal filmmaker sister, Abbe Wool; star roles went to musicians JOHN DOE (ex-X) and Adam Horovitz (of BEASTIE BOYS). 'Death And The Compass' (1992) reunited PRAY FOR RAIN with Cox, while the iconic man of independent celluloid also gave the trio work on 'The Winner' (1996), 'Three Businessmen' (1998) and 'Searchers 2.0' (2007). Underrated by everyone under the sun, PRAY FOR RAIN (who continued to work on a plethora of TV films) combine essential mood music for moody movies – a sort of modern-day Morricone. As a footnote, there is another Pray For Rain (or PFR due to legal reasons), a Christian pop-rock outfit who've been releasing "proper", non-soundtrack albums since 1992. *MCS*

- **filmography** (composers) –

Sid & Nancy *(1986 OST w/ POGUES & V/A =>)* / **Straight To Hell** *(1987 OST w/ POGUES & V/A =>)* / Trust Me *(1989)* / Zandalee *(1991)* / No Secrets *(1991)* / the Linguini Incident *(1992 on OST by THOMAS NEWMAN; see future editions =>)* / **Roadside Prophets** *(1992 OST w/ V/A =>)* / Death And The Compass *(1995 OST; see future editions =>)* / Love, Cheat & Steal *(1993 TV)* / Floundering *(1994 OST w/ V/A; see future editions =>)* / 18 Minutes In Albuquerque *(1994 TV)* / Car 54, Where Are You? *(1994)* / White Mile *(1994 TV) / My Dubious Sex Drive (1995)* / a Boy Called Hate *(1995)* / She Fought Alone *(1995 TV)* / Her Last Chance *(1996 TV)* / Sweet Dreams *(1996 TV)* / Pretty Poison *(1996 TV)* / the Winner *(1996 shelved w/ ZANDER SCHLOSS)* / the Three Lives Of Karen *(1997 TV)* / Any Mother's Son *(1997 TV)* / Perfect Body *(1997 TV)* / Standoff *(1998)* / Since You've Been Gone *(1998 TV)* / Nightmare In Big Sky Country *(1998)* / the Almost Perfect Bank Robbery *(1998 TV)* / Three Businessmen *(1998)* / Kurosawa: The Last Emperor *(1999)* / Late Last Night *(1999 TV)* / a Hard Look *(2000 TV)* / the Wednesday Woman *(2000 TV)* / Never Trust A Serial Killer *(2002)* / Mike Hama, Private Detective: Mike Hama Must Die! (2002 TV) / Journeyman *(2005 score as DAN WOOL)* / Searchers 2.0 *(2007 as DAN WOOL)*

the PREACHER'S WIFE

1996 re-make (US 124m) Touchstone Pictures (PG)

Film genre: romantic fantasy/drama/comedy

Top guns: dir: Penny Marshall / s-w: Nat Mauldin → OPEN SEASON, Allan Scott (au: Robert Nathan)

Stars: Denzel Washington *(Dudley 'Dud')* → HE GOT GAME, **Whitney Houston** *(Julia 'Jules' Biggs)* ← the BODYGUARD, Courtney B. Vance *(Reverend Henry Biggs)*, Gregory Hines *(Joe Hamilton)*, Justin Pierre Edmund *(Jeremiah 'Jer' Biggs / narrator)*, Jenifer Lewis *(Margueritte Coleman)* ← GIRL 6 ← SHAKE, RATTLE & ROCK! tv ← WHAT'S LOVE GOT TO DO WITH IT ← BEACHES / → the TEMPTATIONS → JACKIE'S BACK! → LITTLE RICHARD, Loretta Devine *(Beverly)* → I AM SAM → DREAMGIRLS, Taral Hicks *(teen)*, **Lionel Richie** *(Britsloe)* ← THANK GOD IT'S FRIDAY, Charlotte d'Amboise *(Debbie Paige)* ← the IN CROWD, **Shyheim Franklin** *(teen)*, **George Coleman** *(sax player)*, Melvyn Warren *(pianist)*

Storyline: The Rev. Henry Biggs is finding it hard to get into the Christmas spirit. The local youth centre has been swallowed up by slick property developer Joe Hamilton, and his own church may be next. For once, though, the big man upstairs heeds his plea and sends down an angel to help, or rather make a play for the attentions of his wife and therefore make the good reverend realise, in time honoured and wholesome style, that he has everything he needs right under his nose. *BG*

Movie rating: *5

Visual: video + dvd

Off the record: Shyheim Franklin (b.14 Nov'77, Brooklyn, NY) was discovered by the Wu-Tang Clan (their youngest affiliate) and released a handful of rap/hip-hop sets, kicking off with 'The Rugged Child' & the 1996 follow-up, 'The Lost Generation'. *MCS*

WHITNEY HOUSTON (composers: Various) (score: Hans Zimmer)

Dec 96. (cd/c) *Arista; <18951> (74321 44125-2/-4)* [1] [35]
– I believe in you and me / Step by step / Joy / Hold on, help is on the way / I go to the rock / I love the Lord / Somebody bigger than you and I / You were loved / My heart is calling / Who would imagine a king / He's all over me / The Lord is my shepherd (CISSY HOUSTON) / Joy to the world.

S/track review: Vocal gymnastics might have become the norm for a generation drip-fed on Pop Idolatry, but WHITNEY HOUSTON had the x-factor when many of the wannabes were still in nappies. The potential in those pipes was (and still is) prodigious but this soundtrack – like 'The BODYGUARD' before it – fails to fully realise it. For a gal trained in front of the pews, a gospel-centric project like 'The PREACHER'S WIFE' was surely a chance to reconnect with that inner mounting flame. Many of these songs, though, barely raise a flicker; penned by an unlikely cross section of pros, big guns and a solitary man of the cloth, they make a lot of noise but fail to preach beyond the converted, even if they are effective enough in the film itself. And as a showcase ballad, 'I Believe In You' is but a faint echo of 'I Will Always Love You', just as this soundtrack in general lacks the secular sex appeal of its predecessor. The Georgia Mass Choir bring out some of her best efforts but it takes the company of SHIRLEY CAESAR to really spur Whitney into a religious lather, giving it some frantic call-and-response muscle on 'He's All Over Me' (in a metaphorical sense, mind). Mom CISSY also puts in a gutsy shift with the Hezekiah Walker Choir on a bluesy 'The Lord Is My Shepherd', but this is one sermon where the spirit seems to have flown. *BG*

Album rating: *4.5

– spinoff hits, etc. –

WHITNEY HOUSTON: I Believe In You And Me / Step By Step

Dec 96. (c-s/cd-s) *<13293> (74321 46860-4/-2)* [4] Mar97 [16]

WHITNEY HOUSTON: Step By Step / (mixes)

Mar 97. (c-s/cd-s) *<13312> (74321 44933-4/-2)* [15] Dec96 [13]

WHITNEY HOUSTON: My Heart Is Calling

Jun 97. (c-s/cd-s) *<13362>* [77] [–]

Billy PRESTON

Born: 9 Sep'46, Houston, Texas, USA. An ace organist who accompanied some of the biggest names in rock history, BILLY PRESTON also achieved a brief period of solo fame in the early to mid 70s. Starting as he meant to go on, PRESTON took up the organ at the age of three (!) and played alongside gospel legend Mahalia Jackson before he'd even reached his teens. Billy even made it to the big screen, netting a cameo role as a pubescent W.C. Handy in a biopic of the famous composer entitled 'St. Louis Blues'. LITTLE RICHARD was the next star to take PRESTON under his wing, utilising his prodigious talents on a European tour. This in turn led to a deal with Sam Cooke's 'S.A.R.' label although the singer's untimely death saw him moving on to 'Vee-Jay' where he cut 'The Most Exciting Organ Ever' (1965). PRESTON's seemingly endless network of music biz connections (including RAY CHARLES) extended right to the top of the tree where the BEATLES (whom he'd first met in 1962 on the LITTLE RICHARD tour) were poised to sign him up to their recently inaugurated 'Apple' label in 1969. The organist recorded two albums for the ill-fated company, 'That's The Way God Planned It' (1969) and 'Encouraging Words' (1970), both produced by GEORGE HARRISON. PRESTON also appeared on the BEATLES' 'LET IT BE' album/film and was even co-billed (the only artist to ever enjoy such an honour) for his electric piano grooves on the band's No.1 single, 'Get Back'. Even after 'Apple's demise, the BEATLES connection continued as PRESTON contributed to HARRISON's classic double set, 'All Things Must Pass' (1970) and played at the guitarist's 1971 'CONCERT FOR BANGLADESH' in New York's Madison Square Garden. After inking a deal with 'A&M', Billy began recording a new album, 'I Wrote A Simple Song' (1971). By feeding a clavinet through a wah-wah pedal, he came up with the novel interstellar-funk of 'Outa-Space', a Grammy Award-winning, million- selling instrumental hit that missed the US No.1 spot by a whisker in the summer of '72. Follow-up set, 'Music Is My Life' (1972), finally provided the Afro-headed star with a No.1 single in the shape of 'Will It Go Round In Circles'. The most successful year of his career, 1973 also saw him scoring another huge, cosmic-themed hit with the Top 5 'Space Race'. Alongside his solo chart success, he continued to back up some of the biggest names in the business including Sly & The Family Stone, Carole King and the ROLLING STONES, PRESTON contributing to Jagger and Co's classic early 70s albums and going on to tour with them in the mid-70s. BP notched up his second No.1 in 1974, 'Nothing From Nothing', a track once again co-penned with songwriting partner Billy Fisher. The track's B-side, 'You Are So Beautiful', was a gospel-tinged ballad which subsequently furnished JOE COCKER with his biggest solo hit. Although the hits dried up in the latter half of the decade, PRESTON scored a one-off Top 5 in 1979 via 'With You I'm Born Again', a sophisticated duet with Motown stalwart Syreeta from their film score collaboration, 'FAST BREAK'. He went on to record a whole album of songs with STEVIE WONDER's ex, imaginatively titled 'Billy And Syreeta' (1981). 1982's 'Pressin' On' marked the end of his 'Motown' period, after which PRESTON disappeared from the spotlight. A touring stint with RINGO STARR in 1989 was followed by a brief period of recording for the UK-based 'Motorcity' label. Less promisingly, the early 90s saw the singer sentenced on drugs and assault charges. Billy eventually re-emerged with 'Minister Of Love', a return to the gospel roots of his childhood, while the movie world beckoned courtesy of his cameo in 'BLUES BROTHERS 2000' (1998). *MCS*

- **filmography** {acting} (composer), etc.-

St. Louis Blues *(1958 {b})* / **the Concert For Bangladesh** *(1972 {p} on OST by GEORGE HARRISON & V/A =>)* / Slaughter *(1972 single/theme on score)* / Twilight's Last Gleaming *(1977 theme on OST)* / **Sgt. Pepper's Lonely Hearts Club Band** *(1978 {*p} on OST by V/A =>)* / **Fast Break** *(1979 OST w/ SYREETA =>)* / Angel City *(1980 TV on OST)* / **Blame It On The Night** *(1984 {p})* / Wired *(1989 {p})* / **Blues Brothers 2000** *(1998 {p} on OST =>)* / Ticker *(2001 {p})* / **Concert For George** *(2003 {p} on OST by V/A =>)*

□ Alan PRICE segment
(⇒ O LUCKY MAN!)

PRIMARY COLORS

1998 (US/Fra/UK/Ger 143m) MCA/Universal Pictures (R)

Film genre: political satire/comedy

Top guns: dir: Mike Nichols ← WORKING GIRL ← the GRADUATE / s-w: Elaine May (au: Joe Klein)

Stars: John Travolta *(Gov. Jack Stanton)* ← PULP FICTION ← SHOUT ← STAYING ALIVE → URBAN COWBOY ← GREASE ← SATURDAY NIGHT FEVER / → SWORDFISH → BE COOL → HAIRSPRAY re-make, Emma Thompson *(Susan Stanton)* ← TUTTI FRUTTI, Billy Bob Thornton *(Richard Jemmons)* ← DEAD MAN / → SOUTH OF HEAVEN, WEST OF HELL → FRIDAY NIGHT LIGHTS, Adrian Lester *(Henry Burton)*, Kathy Bates *(Libby Holden)* ← DICK TRACY, Maura Tierney *(Daisy Green)* ← FLY BY NIGHT, Larry Hagman *(Gov. Fred Picker)* ← STARDUST, Paul Guilfoyle *(Howard Ferguson)*, Diane Ladd *(Mamma Stanton)* ← WILD AT HEART ← the WILD ANGELS, Caroline Aaron *(Lucille Kaufman)* ← THIS IS MY LIFE ← WORKING GIRL / → BEYOND THE SEA, Mykelti Williamson *(Dewayne Smith)* ← STREETS OF FIRE, Rob Reiner *(Izzy Rosenblatt)* ← THIS IS SPINAL TAP / → the STORY OF US, Allison Janney *(Miss Walsh)* ← PRIVATE PARTS ← WALKING AND TALKING / → OVER THE HEDGE → HAIRSPRAY re-make, Tommy Hollis *(William McCullison "Fat Willie")*, Robert Klein *(Norman Asher)* ← the LAST UNICORN ← the OWL AND THE PUSSYCAT ← the LANDLORD, Bianca Lawson *(Loretta)* → BONES → SAVE THE LAST DANCE, Geraldo Rivera *(himself)* ← HATED / → the U.S. VS. JOHN LENNON, Brian Markinson *(Randy Culligan)* → TAKE ME HOME: THE JOHN DENVER STORY, James Earl Jones (CNN voiceover) ← the LION KING ← a PIECE OF THE ACTION ← CLAUDINE

Storyline: Jack Stanton is a likeable, silver fox Southern governor with more than a few skeletons in his closet, a belly full of doughnuts and at least a passing resemblance to Bill Clinton. Desperate to work for someone who means it, or at least be fooled into thinking they mean it, idealistic campaign strategist Henry Burton finds himself in over his head when he hesitantly joins up for Stanton's presidential bid. After surviving one saucy revelation, the campaign faces a potentially fatal obstacle when Stanton's misadventures with a teenage girl are put to a paternity test. He's offered a reprieve when steel-balled lesbian Libby Holden digs the dirt on rival Fred Picker. Having been confined to the "booby hatch" after breaking down during George McGovern's campaign back in the 70s, however, she's unwilling to resort to underhand tactics. *BG*

Movie rating: *7

Visual: video + dvd

Off the record: (see below)

RY COODER (score w/ JOACHIM COODER)

Nov 98. (cd) *M.C.A.; <(MCD 11775)>* □ Apr98 □

– Camptown races / Not the best people / There will be a happy meeting in glory / Our position / Silbando mambo (PEREZ PRADO) / I like this porch / Wide sky (w/ JON HASSELL) / See that moon / Very close friend of mine / Long trip / Tennessee waltz / Don't break our hearts / Camptown races / You are my sunshine.

S/track review: God bless the good ol' US of A and God bless musicians who can interpret its contradictions as generously as RY COODER and Van Dyke Parks. Crusty old Americana is grist to both their mills, and it's not often they fail to make it fun for a contemporary audience, whether it's the martial minstrelsy of Stephen Foster, the triumphal folk-spiritual 'There Will Be A Happy Meeting In Glory' or a jazzy, tantalisingly Tex-Mex-tinged 'Tennessee Waltz'. Save your flag-waving, though, for an instrumental sashay through the old Jimmy Davis standard, 'You Are My Sunshine', so effective as soundtrack joie de vivre that the Coen brothers reprised it two years later on 'O BROTHER, WHERE ART THOU?'; here, COODER's arrangement is as balmy as country music gets, carried away on those lost-horizon guitar lines. The man's coterie of collaborators includes a veteran, JON HASSELL, and a more recent recruit in son JOACHIM; both assist in sculpting a more conventional work than COODER's ethnic-influenced scores of the pre-Buena Vista period. The subcontinental promise of RONU MAJUNDAR's flute in HASSELL's 'Wide open Sky', as well as the random inclusion of a scorching PEREZ PRADO mambo means it doesn't abandon the world thread completely, but there's just as much emphasis on the emotive subtleties of COODER's solo orchestral pieces, most obviously the poignant 'Don't Break Our Hearts'. Interestingly, JOACHIM's own cues – he's credited on at least four – seem to reference his dad's mid-80s masterpiece, 'PARIS, TEXAS', and why not; if you're going to follow in your old man's footsteps, you might as well start at the top, with a sound that instantly evokes the family name. Ultimately, as RY's last soundtrack to date, 'PRIMARY COLORS' brings it all back home, full circle from the civil war folk of 'The LONG RIDERS' almost two decades earlier. *BG*

Album rating: *6.5

the PRINCESS BRIDE

1987 (US 98m) Twentieth Century-Fox (PG)

Film genre: romantic children's/family fantasy comedy

Top guns: dir: Rob Reiner ← THIS IS SPINAL TAP / → the STORY OF US / s-w: William Goldman (+ au)

Stars: Cary Elwes *(Westley)*, Robin Wright *(Buttercup, the Princess Bride)* → the SINGING DETECTIVE → BREAKING AND ENTERING, Mandy Patinkin *(Inigo Montoya)* → DICK TRACY, Chris Sarandon *(Prince Humperdinck)*, Christopher Guest *(Count Tyrone Rugen)* ← LITTLE SHOP OF HORRORS → THIS IS SPINAL TAP ← the LONG RIDERS ← DEATH WISH / → a MIGHTY WIND, Peter Falk *(the grandfather)*, Wallace Shawn *(Vizzini)*, Fred Savage *(the grandson)*, Carol Kane *(Valerie)* → EVEN COWGIRLS GET THE BLUES, Andre the Giant *(Fezzik)*, Billy Crystal *(Miracle Max, the wizard)* ← ANIMALYMPICS, Peter Cook *(the Impressive Clergyman)* → GREAT BALLS OF FIRE!, Mel Smith *(the Albino)* ← BABYLON

Storyline: 'Scaling the Cliffs of Insanity and Battling Rodents of Unusual Size' – no, not the latest Japanese TV game show, but what two young lovers must overcome to be together. Beautiful Buttercup believes her beloved Westley to be dead, so she's about to marry the horrible Prince Humperdinck. However, Westley's very much alive and, with a little help from his friends the giant and the miracle man, he's determined to pluck Buttercup from the Prince and get his reward of a yucky smooch. *JZ*

Movie rating: *8

Visual: video + dvd

Off the record: (see below)

MARK KNOPFLER

Nov 87. (lp/c)(cd) *Warners; <25610> Vertigo (VERH/+C 53)(832864)* ☐ ☐
– Once upon a time . . . Storybook love / I will never love again / Florin dance / Morning ride / The friends' song (w/ GUY FLETCHER) / The cliffs of insanity / The swordfight / Guide my sword / The fireswamp and the rodents of unusual size / Revenge / A happy ending / Storybook love (w/ WILLY DeVILLE).

S/track review: Faced with scoring a movie as radically different from the Celtic provinciality of both 'CAL' and 'LOCAL HERO' as it was possible to get, KNOPFLER secured the services of new Dire Straits man GUY FLETCHER, and set about creating what was pretty much a conventional orchestral score. For someone who'd never tackled anything remotely like this before, the end result has to be considered a fairly impressive achievement. Endlessly inventive and convincing in conjuring a sense of fairytale wonder, the eddying arrangements faithfully chart the film's unfolding narrative and shiting moods without ever doubling back on themselves. KNOPFLER also proves that he can incorporate his quicksilver guitar playing into just about any musical format and while it isn't heard much, when it is, as on opener 'Once Upon A Time . . . Storybook Love', it dazzles. Not as warm as his previous soundtracks and perhaps not as enduring as a stand-alone album, but a rewarding listen nonetheless. *BG*

Album rating: *6

– spinoff releases, etc. –

MARK KNOPFLER & WILLY DeVILLE: Storybook Love (The Theme From 'The Princess Bride') / **MARK KNOPFLER & GUY FLETCHER:** The Friends' Song

Mar 88. (7"/c-s) *(VER/+MC 37)* ⊟ ☐
(cd-s+=) *(VERCD 37)* – Once upon a time . . . Storybook love.

PROFONDO ROSSO

UK title 'DEEP RED' / US video title 'the HATCHET MURDERS'

1975 (Ita 126m) Rizzoli / Seda Spettacoli films (18)

Film genre: Psychological mystery/horror-slasher

Top guns: s-w (+ dir): Dario Argento → SUSPIRIA → INFERNO → TENEBRE → la CHIESA → NONHOSONNO, Bernardino Zapponi

Stars: David Hemmings *(Marcus Day)* ← BLOW-UP ← BE MY GUEST ← LIVE IT UP ← SOME PEOPLE ← PLAY IT COOL / → la VIA DELLA DROGA, Daria Nicolodi *(Gianna Brezzi)* → SHOCK → INFERNO → TENEBRE → PHENOMENA, Gabriele Lavia *(Carlo)* → INFERNO → NONHOSONNO, Macha Meril *(Helga Ulmann)*, Eros Pagni *(Supt. Calcabrini)*, Giuliana Calandra *(Amanda Righetti)*, Glauco Mauri *(Prof. Giordani)*, Piero Mazzinghi *(Bardi)*

Storyline: Master of suspense and pioneer of Giallo/horror flicks, Dario Argento takes us to Rome, Italy, where concert pianist Marcus witnesses the brutal murder of a psychic. Does this have any bearing on the opening scene in which another murder is perspectively observed by a small child? Who knows? While police examine the case (and another killing of a paranormal investigator has taken place), Marcus and gorgeous reporter Gianni, become obsessed in tracing the killer before he targets them. *MCS*

Movie rating: *7.5

Visual: video + dvd

Off the record: Leading actor of the 60s/70s, David Hemmings, also combined a brief solo career when he issued a somewhat rare LP ('Happens') for 'M.G.M.' in 1967. *MCS*

GOBLIN

Apr 75. (lp) *Cinevox; (MDF 33.085)* ⊟ Italy ⊟
– Profondo rosso / Death dies / Mad puppet / Wild session / Deep shadows / School at night / Gianna. *(UK-iss.Jan89 on 'Silva Screen' lp/c; CIA/+K7 5005) (lp re-iss. Jun00 on 'Cinevox'; LPMDF 200)*

S/track review: Italian Prog-rockers GOBLIN (who'd also issued a one-off eponymous set as Cherry Five) were enticed by director Dario Argento to contribute alongside composer/conductor GIORGIO GASLINI for his groundbreaking 'PROFONDO ROSSO'. The Original Soundtrack became GOBLIN's official debut release and even topped the Italian charts, where they built up a large following; Britain and America took little notice – PFM were already making inroads. 'Profondo Rosso' (courtesy of opening title track) zoomed into focus with an ear-piercing keyboard and pulsating bass leading to a gothic-style organ that might well have inspired by Yes or even Barclay James Harvest. Track 2, 'Death Dies', was another highlight, it's music dynamically surging between jazz-blaxploitation sounds (think Isaac Hayes meets Herbie Hancock); it was later sampled by Beck. 'Deep Shadows', is somewhere between King Crimson and ELP, fast and furious to the extreme and well worth the admission price alone. The closing piano-led and romantic 'Gianni' suffers from Prog-rock over-indulgence. Overall, a great start to any group's musical campaign. *MCS*

Album rating: *6.5 / re-CD extended *7

– spinoff releases, etc. –

GOBLIN (& GIORGIO GASLINI *)

May 98. (cd) *Cinevox; (CD-MDF 301)* ☐ ☐
– Mad puppet's laughs (opening intro) / Profondo rosso / School at night (lullaby – music box version) (*) / Death dies / School at night (*) / School at night (lullaby – child version) (*) / Mad puppet / School at night (*) / School at night (lullaby – child version) (*) / Death dies (film version – part 1) / Profondo rosso / Gianna (alt.take) (*) / Profondo rosso / School at night (lullaby – celesta version) (*) / Death dies (film version – part 2) / Profondo rosso / Wild session (*) / Profondo rosso / Deep shadows (film version – part 1) (*) / Deep shadows (film version – part 2) (*) / Deep shadows (film version – part 3) (*) / Death dies (film version – part 3) / Gianna (album version) (*) / School at night (lullaby – echo version) (*) / Deep shadows (album version) (*) / School at night (album version) (*) / Profondo rosso (remix) / Profondo rosso (original sound effect).

PROOF

1991 (Aus 86m) House & Moorhouse Films / AFC / Film Victoria

Film genre: psychological comedy drama

Top guns: s-w + dir: Jocelyn Moorhouse

Stars: Hugo Weaving *(Martin)*, Genevieve Picot *(Celia)*, Russell Crowe *(Andy)* → HAMMERS OVER THE ANVIL → the INSIDER, Heather Mitchell *(Martin's mother)*, Jeffrey Walker *(young Martin)*, Frank Gallacher *(vet)* ← HAMMERS OVER THE ANVIL / → AMY → ONE PERFECT DAY, Frankie J. Holden *(Brian, the policeman)*, Daniel Pollock *(Gary, the punk)*, Saskia Post *(waitress)* ← DOGS IN SPACE, Cliff Ellen *(cemetery caretaker)*

Storyline: Martin is a blind man who trusts no-one, not even his mother. He wants to prove that the world he can see inside his head is the same as the real world outside, and so he takes photographs and describes them. When he befriends kitchen worker Andy, Martin at last feels that he has met someone he can trust – to the annoyance of his jealous housekeeper Celia, who begins a campaign of cruelty against him. *JZ*

Movie rating: *7

Visual: video + dvd

Off the record: Russell Crowe and his own rock outfit, 30 Odd Foot Of Grunts, wrote a song 'The Night That Davey Hit The Train' for co-actor Daniel Pollock who sadly committed suicide in 1992. *MCS*

NOT DROWNING, WAVING

Jan 92. (cd) *Alhambra; (A 8927)* ☐ ☐
– Walking music / Sexy music / Sad tune / Happy / Vet scene / Sad time / Flashback / Panic / Sexy band track / Walk / Sad. *(originally 1991 on 'Rogues' Gallery'; RG 001)* – (slightly diff. listings)

S/track review: Australia's award-winning NOT DROWNING, WAVING (unfairly unknown beyond Antipodean shores!) were a group responsible for two soundtrack releases during the early 90s, 'PROOF' and 'HAMMERS OVER THE ANVIL' (1992); incidentally, both films starred hard-man actor, Russell Crowe. NDW had been creating their own blend of cinematic rock since 1984 and, with four albums under their belt, including 1986's groundbreaking 'Claim', their filmatic course was obvious. Consisting of seven members, lyricist DAVID BRIDIE (keyboards), JOHN PHILLIPS (guitars & sampling), HELEN MOUNTFORT (cello), RUSSEL BRADLY (drums/percussion), ROWAN McKINNON (bass & acoustic guitar), JAMES SOUTHALL (percussion) and TIM COLE (sound production), NOT DROWNING, WAVING recorded 'PROOF' at the Pig Pen and Hothouse studios. Mostly instrumental (bar 'Sexy Music'), the listener is taken through an onslaught of eclectic dirges, emphasis being on post-80s rock. If there's any comparison, one could go back a decade to the double-percussion assault of fellow Aussie ensemble, Hunters & Collectors. The aforementioned 'Sexy Music (with vocals)' – and dialogue – could well've been from the pens of Icehouse or Crowded House, although lyrically, on this song's evidence at least, NDW come up trumps. Atmospheric, Bruce Hornsby-styled piano and folky, acoustic guitars litter the soundtrack, 'Sad Tune' being the prime example. 'Happy' and 'Vet Scene' take us up a notch or two on tempo, streaming U2-esque guitars battle with said keys, although the listener probably wins out. With blindness and deceit the movie's subject matter, 'Flashback' and 'Panic' – complete with dialogue on the former – gives us everything Martin goes through. Tracks 9-11 reprise 'Sexy . . .', 'Walk . . .' and 'Sad . . .', the instruments this time intertwined with HELEN MOUNTFORT's moody cello. Get 'PROOF' and listen – several times. *MCS*

Album rating: *6.5

the PROPOSITION

2005 (Austra/UK 104m) Columbia TriStar (MA)

Film genre: psychological western/outlaw drama

Top guns: dir: John Hillcoat ← TO HAVE AND TO HOLD ← GHOSTS . . .OF THE CIVIL DEAD / s-w: **Nick CAVE**

Stars: Guy Pearce *(Charlie Burns)* ← RAVENOUS ← a SLIPPING-DOWN LIFE, Ray Winstone *(Captain Stanley)* ← COLD MOUNTAIN ← SEXY BEAST ← LADIES AND GENTLEMEN, THE FABULOUS STAINS ← QUADROPHENIA / → BREAKING AND ENTERING, Emily Watson *(Martha Stanley)* ← METROLAND, David Wenham *(Eden Fletcher)* ← MOULIN ROUGE, John Hurt *(Jellon Lamb)* ← DEAD MAN ← EVEN COWGIRLS GET THE BLUES ← 1984, Danny Huston *(Arthur Burns)*, Leah Purcell *(Queenie)* ← SOMERSAULT ← LANTANA, David Gulpilil *(Jacko)* ← RABBIT-PROOF FENCE, Noah Taylor *(Brian O'Leary)* ← ALMOST FAMOUS ← DOGS IN SPACE, Tom Budge *(Samuel Stoat)* ← AUSTRALIAN RULES, Ralph Cotterill *(Dr. Bantrey)* ← SONS OF STEEL ← RIKKY AND PETE, Garry Waddell *(Officer Davenport)* ← CHOPPER ← SWEET TALKER ← 20th CENTURY OZ

Storyline: Captain Stanley has the unenviable job of bringing law and order to the particularly lawless Australian Outback of the 1880s. The biggest troublemakers are the Burns brothers, a notorious gang whose very mention sends the kangaroos scuttling for cover. Arthur is by far and away the worst of them, so when Stanley captures his naive younger brother Mikey and the older Charlie, he makes his Proposition:- Charlie must kill Arthur and Mikey won't hang – fair dinkum? *JZ*

Movie rating: *9

Visual: dvd

Off the record: **Nick CAVE** (see below + biog)

NICK CAVE & WARREN ELLIS

Mar 06. (cd) *Mute; (CDSTUMM 255)* <9305> ☐ ☐
– Happy land / The proposition pt.1 / Road to Banyon / Down to the valley / Moan thing / The rider pt.1 / Martha's dream / Gun thing / Queenie's suite / The rider pt.2 / The proposition pt.2 / Sad violin thing / The rider pt.3 / The proposition pt.3 / The rider song / Clean hands, dirty hands.

S/track review: 'The PROPOSITION' marked a significant departure for NICK CAVE, his first film score to break up the decades-old triumvirate of Blixa Bargeld, Mick Harvey and his big dark self. Gone then, are the weeping symphonies that filled 'TO HAVE AND TO HOLD' (1996). The congenital melancholy remains, but it's a sadness as harsh and glacial as a night in Death Valley. The partnership with director John Hillcoat (who'd been sitting on the idea of an Aussie western since 1979) likewise remains, but Dirty Three leader WARREN ELLIS is his musical collaborator this time around, extending their sometime live/studio partnership. In a largely instrumental, dialogue-less score, ELLIS' violin is the principal voice, chafing and sawing, droning and buzzing like an angry hornet; breaching the stony ground between the dour solemnity of English folk balladry and the ecstatic misgiving of Iranian spike fiddle master Kayhan Kalhor. In anticipation of what's not to come, the soundtrack leads in with 'Happy Land' of all things, that traditional spiritual beloved of dog-eared school violin primers. But the land ELLIS and CAVE inhabit sounds far from happy, a place where the rhythm of life isn't such a powerful thing, at least not as powerful as the inevitability of death and betrayal. What little rhythm there is takes the form of reptilian scrabbling and skin-crawling death rattles. Even CAVE's vocals are terse, bleached. On 'The Rider', an archetypal CAVE parable in three parts, he confides the lyrics in a pestilential whisper carried on some ill wind from the psych-scape of Lorca's 'Blood Wedding'. Only on 'The Rider Song' does the mood break: warm, weary piano chords flood like tears. For many artists, this would've brought closure, resolution. Not CAVE; he finishes on a typically uneasy note with another traditional adaptation: 'Clean Hands, Dirty Hands', queasily ruminating over the kinds of religious imagery he often ruminates over. Not the kind of album you're likely to dig out too often and not a Western score as Bernstein, Morricone, Dylan or anyone else conceived it, but one to savour if you find latter-day Bad Seeds' efforts too generous of spirit. *BG*

Album rating: *7

PSYCHO BEACH PARTY

2000 (Aus/US 95m) Strand Releasing (M)

Film genre: horror/teen mystery/comedy

Top guns: dir: Robert Lee King / s-w: Charles Busch (+ play)

Stars: Lauren Ambrose *(Florence 'Chicklet' Forrest)*, Thomas Gibson *(Kanaka)*, Nicholas Brendan *(Starcat)*, Kimberley Davies *(Bettina/Diane)*, Matt Keeslar *(Lars/Larry)* ← SPLENDOR, Charles Busch *(Capt. Monica Stark)*, Beth Broderick *(Mrs. Ruth Forrest)*, Amy Adams *(Marvel Ann)* → the SLAUGHTER RULE, Kathleen Robertson *(Rhonda)* ← SPLENDOR → I AM SAM, Buddy Quaid *(Junior)* ← CLUBLAND, Channon Roe *(Wedge Riley)* ← GIRL, Richard Fancy *(Dr. Wentworth / Dr. Edwards)* ← COME ON, GET HAPPY: THE PARTRIDGE FAMILY STORY ← TOUCH

Storyline: Florence Forrest doesn't quite fit in with the regular crowd at Malibu High, so instead she renames herself Chicklet and becomes the first female surfer on Malibu Beach. However, sun, sea and schizophrenia have the effect of turning cute Chicklet into foul-mouthed Anne and outspoken Tylene. Not only that, a series of brutal murders takes place on the beach at the same time and regulars Kanaka, Bettina and Lars are all suspects too. Where's Frankie when you need him? *JZ*

Movie rating: *5.5

Off the record: BEN VAUGHN (see below)

Various Artists (score: BEN VAUGHN *)

Sep 00. (cd) *Nettwerk; <(62428 40013-2)>* ☐ ☐
– Main title (*) / Tailspin (LOS STRAITJACKETS) / Marvel Ann on the prowl (*) / Wrestle (*) / Night crawler (the HALIBUTS) / Chicklet meets surfers (*) / Neenie's famous weenies (*) / Cha-wow-wow (HILLBILLY SOUL SURFERS) / Chicklet learns to surf (*) / Bombasteroid (FOUR PIECE SUIT) / Chicklet wipes out (*) / Mournful surfers (*) / Romantic beach scene (*) / Kanaka's shack (*) / Overboard (the FATHOMS) / Tempest (LOS STRAITJACKETS) / Mermaid love (MAN OR ASTRO-MAN?) / P-S-Y-C-H-O (Psycho) end title (*).

S/track review: Who better to invite to the 'PSYCHO BEACH PARTY' than Philadelphia-born, retro-surf-rocker BEN VAUGHN. This former punk had been touring the toilet circuit since the early 80s as the drummer with the Sickkidz. However, when pub-rock-roots outfit, the Morells, covered his 'The Man Who Has Everything' on their 1982 set, 'Shake And Push', things looked decidedly better. Subsequently finding a niche in the burgeoning retro-rockabilly market, his outfit the BEN VAUGHN Combo released a debut LP, 'The Many Moods Of . . .' (1985), for UK imprint 'Making Waves'. Garnering rave reviews from all and sundry, the album was sub-licensed to 'Restless' records, while one of the tracks, 'I'm Sorry (But So Is Brenda Lee)', was immediately borrowed by Marshall Crenshaw for his 'Downtown' set. Sadly, the Combo disbanded in '87 after only one further effort, 'Beautiful Thing'. As a solo artist, guitarist BEN VAUGHN delivered several worthy albums over the next decade, namely 'Blows Your Mind' (1988), 'Dressed In Black' (1990), 'Mood Swings' (1992), the backtracking 'Mono U.S.A' (1994), 'Kings Of Saturday Night' with Kim Fowley (1995) and 'Rambler '65' (1997); his early 90s scores for obscure documentaries, 'Favorite Mopar' (about muscle cars!) and 'Wild Girls Go Go Rama' – plus his recent award-winning instrumental theme(s) for hit sit-com, 'Third Rock From The Sun' – finally found their way on to 1995's self-explanatory 'Instrumental Stylings'. VAUGHN subsequently ventured across the ocean to Scotland, where he signed a deal with 'Shoeshine' records, releasing the first of two albums, 'A Date With . . .' in 1999. A tasty CV then, and one that paved the "waves" – so to speak – for his debut soundtrack proper, 'PSYCHO BEACH PARTY'. Taking a leaf from teen horror B-movies of the late 50s/early 60s (with a reference to the "BEACH PARTY" series), VAUGHN tipped his hat to the sounds of Johnny & The Hurricanes, Duane Eddy and Link Wray via album highlights, 'Main Title', 'Marvel Ann On The Prowl', 'Neenies Famous Weenies' and the Surfin' Bird-like, 'P-S-Y-C-H-O (Psycho)', although many cues only lasted a minute or two. The eleven VAUGHN numbers were interspersed with seven similarly-themed, retro-surf-rock acts, none more energetic than the Dick Dale-esque LOS STRAITJACKETS', with the 4-minute 'Tailspin'; the masked quartet are afforded a second instrumental by way of track 16, 'Tempest'. Meanwhile, the HILLBILLY SOUL SURFERS trio (led by Sherman LeRoi) and the cut, 'Cha-Wow-Wow', is as near to the Shadows playing lounge rock as one could imagine it. Ditto, the matching FOUR PIECE SUIT. In a rare vocal performance, the excellent MAN OR ASTRO-MAN? bring surf into the new millennium, courtesy of Felt-like song, 'Mermaid Love' – great guitar frets. Minnows, the HALIBUTS (on 'Night Crawler') and the FATHOMS (who go 'Overboard'), were indeed plucked from the bottom of the proverbial sea. *MCS*

Album rating: *5.5

☐ PUBLIC ENEMY segment
(⇒ HE GOT GAME)

☐ PULSE alt.
(⇒ OCTANE)

☐ Bernard "Pretty" PURDIE segment
(⇒ LIALEH)

☐ PURE COUNTRY: George Strait
(⇒ Rock Musicals & Pop Fiction)

□ QUEEN segment
(⇒ FLASH GORDON)

QUIET DAYS IN CLICHY

aka STILLE DAGE I CLICHY

1970 (Den 101m b&w) Valio-Filmi (18)

Film genre: erotic drama

Top guns: s-w + dir: Jens Jorgen Thorsen (nov: Henry Miller)

Stars: Paul Valjean *(Joey)*, Wayne Rodda *(Carl)*, Ulla Lemvigh-Muller *(Nys)*, Avi Sagild *(Mara)*, Susanne Krage *(Christine)*, Petronella *(Adrienne)*, Ben Webster *(himself; saxophonist)*

Storyline: It's lock-up-your-daughters time for the residents of Clichy, Paris, as literary ex-pat lothario Joey (aka Henry Miller) and his French partner in lust, Carl, turn their dingy flat into a veritable knocking shop. No real plot as such (save for an irate father coming to rescue his runaway teenage daughter) but plenty of virulent sexism, drunken debauchery, hot jazz and revelatory shots of 60s Paris. *BG*

Movie rating: *7

Visual: video

Off the record: Ben Webster was a big band entertainer born in Kansas City 1909 but died in Amsterdam in 1973.

—

COUNTRY JOE McDONALD (*) (& Various Artists)

Dec 70. (lp) *Vanguard; <VSD 79303> Sonet; (SNTF 622)* □ Jul71 □
– Quiet days in Clichy I (*) / Nys' love (*) / Hungry Miller and the hungry world (*) / Clichy (ANDY SUNDSTROM) / Behind the golden sun (YOUNG FLOWERS) / Luxembourg stomp (PAPA BUE'S VIKING JAZZ BAND) / Quiet days in Clichy II (*) / Blue miller (BEN WEBSTER) / Les Champs Elysses (ANDY SUNDSTROM) / Menilmontant (YOUNG FLOWERS) / Party beat (YOUNG FLOWERS) / Mara (*). *<(cd-iss. Apr98; VMD 79303)>*

S/track review: Often remembered more for his 'WOODSTOCK' shenanigans, leftist rhetoric and black humour than his – significant – contributions to music, COUNTRY JOE McDONALD was a canny choice for Thorsen's soundtrack; he certainly wasn't shy about expressing himself. A wandering rake's anthem, his title theme turns the air a bawdy, unhurried shade of blue, recounting Carl and Joey's unquiet exploits with deadpan incongruity. 'Nys' Love', by contrast, wouldn't have been out of place on 'The WICKER MAN' soundtrack, an erotic, equinoctial lament worked into a fertility-rites frenzy, and arguably the single most haunting recording McDONALD ever put his name to. Tenor saxophonist BEN WEBSTER is the other star presence; having decamped to Copenhagen in the mid-60s, the former Duke Ellington sideman was likewise a natural choice. He only gets one track, but it's a goodie, a smoky, tender tribute to his wayward countryman entitled 'Blue Miller'. ANDY SUNDSTROM's accordion pieces set the whole thing in at least some kind of traditional Parisian context and even the Cream/Hendrix-esque tracks from Danish band YOUNG FLOWERS bear repeated listening. Like that other 1970 milestone, 'PERFORMANCE', 'QUIET DAYS IN CLICHY' subsumes its disparate parts into a holistic-hedonistic world-within-a-world, one of substance, humour and longing rather than cheap titillation. The film's infamy (variously banned and condemned through the decades) still tends to overshadow the music, but while the movie plays as a surreal relic of a vanished mindset, the soundtrack still sounds as fresh today as it must've done in its libertine heyday. *BG*

Album rating: *7.5

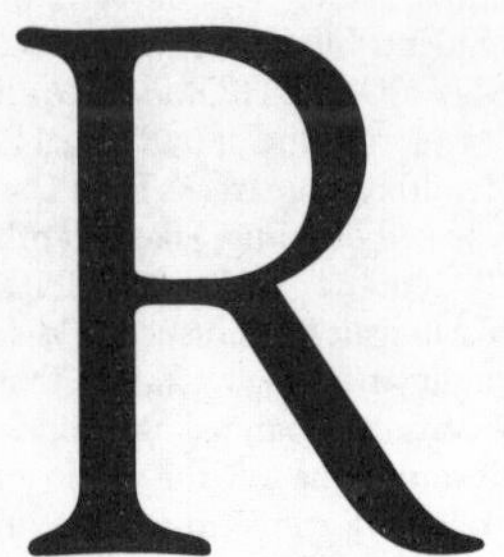

RABBIT-PROOF FENCE

2002 (Aus/UK 94m) Buena Vista / AFFC / HanWay Films (PG)

Film genre: rural period drama

Top guns: dir: Phillip Noyce / s-w: Christine Olsen (au: Doris Pilkington Garimara)

Stars: Everlyn Sampi *(Molly Craig)*, Tianni Sansbury *(Daisy)*, Laura Monaghan *(Gracie)*, David Gulpilil *(Moodoo, tracker)* → the PROPOSITION, Kenneth Branagh *(A.O. Neville; aka Mr. Devil)*, Deborah Mailman *(Mavis; Evans' servant)*, Jason Clarke *(Constable Riggs)*, Ningali Lawford *(Maud; Molly's mother)*, Garry McDonald *(Mr. Neal at Moore River)* ← MOULIN ROUGE ← the PIRATE MOVIE

Storyline: A haunting recreation of one girl's odyssey across the wastes of the Australian desert in defiance of the colonial authorities. Forcibly removed from her outback home along with her sister and cousin, 14-year old Molly Pilkington is transported 1200 miles to an orphanage for half-caste girls. Rather than acquiescing in insitutional attempts to mould her for God fearing servitude, she grabs her young relatives and makes a bid for freedom. *BG*

Movie rating: *8

Visual: dvd

Off the record: (see below)

—

PETER GABRIEL: Long Walk Home – music from the film . . .

Jun 02. (cd) *Real World; (PGCD 10) E.M.I.; <887131>* ☐ Apr02 ☐
– Jigalong / Stealing the children / Unlocking the door / The tracker / Running to the rain / On the map / A sense of home / Go away Mr. Evans / Moodoo's secret / Gracie's recapture / Crossing the salt pan / The return (pts.1-3) / Ngankarrparni (sky blue) / The rabbit-proof fence / Cloudless.

S/track review: Back in the summer of '89, PETER GABRIEL launched his 'Real World' label with a soundtrack (for Martin Scorsese's 'The LAST TEMPTATION OF CHRIST'). Since then, that familiar rainbow logo has become the nearest thing to a kitemark for world music. With this commission for Philip Noyce's award-winning drama being only his third film soundtrack in two decades, GABRIEL is clearly as discerning about his movie projects as he is about recording albums ("Deadlines are things that we pass through on the way to finishing", he once quipped) and selecting the artists he takes under his wing. In the collaborative, fusion-based spirit of 'Real World', many of those artists turn up here, even the late NUSRAT FATEH ALI KHAN. And 'Long Walk Home' is unmistakably in that fusion-based tradition, at least in comparison to GABRIEL's most recent solo album 'Up' (2002). Although some of the material here actually germinated from 'Up's work in progress, and despite the fact that both albums lead in with unusually aggressive, neo-industrial beats, this is necessarily a much more concentratedly impressionistic affair, haunted by its interminable horizons. As with 'BIRDY' (1985), GABRIEL meticulously assembles his eerie soundscapes from the bottom up, layering and counter-layering keyboards, sampled birdsong and Jocelyn Pook-arranged strings in an approximation of the quivering desert air and its bone-baked inhabitants. He wisely resists didgeridoo cliché, and instead it's the DHOL FOUNDATION who lend this music much of its rhythmic colour. The dry, booming clack of their cane sticks on goat hide somehow conjures the Australian outback as graphically as it does the Punjab, electrifying the climactic 'Running To The Rain'. 'RABBIT-PROOF FENCE' actresses Ningali and Myarn Lawford contribute authentic ethnic voicing to the more esoteric incidental material, including the title track, itself sandwiched between the choral harmony of 'Ngankarrapini (Sky Blue-reprise)' and the closing 'Cloudless'. Cannily saving his main melodic motifs until the final movement, GABRIEL and the BLIND BOYS OF ALABAMA raise the roof of the sky. Spellbinding. *BG*

Album rating: *7.5

RAIN

2001 (NZ 92m) Rose Road / New Zealand Film Commission (R)

Film genre: coming-of-age/domestic drama

Top guns: s-w + dir: Christine Jeffs (au: Kirsty Gunn)

Stars: Alicia Fulford-Wierzbicki *(Janey)*, Sarah Peirse *(Kate)*, Marton Csokas *(Cady)* → GARAGE DAYS, Alistair Browning *(Ed)*, Aaron Murphy *(Jim)*, David Taylor *(Sam)*, Chris Sherwood *(Ron)*, Claire Dougan *(Joy)*, Alison Routledge *(Heather)*

Storyline: Teenager Janey is on vacation with her parents and young brother in their beach house on the New Zealand coast. While dad Ed sits out the back on the booze, mum Kate starts chasing the local men and Janey is left on her own to look after young Jim. When photographer Cady shows up in his boat, Kate and Janey both take an interest in him and soon their jealous rivalry threatens to tear the family apart. *JZ*

Movie rating: *6.5

Visual: dvd

Off the record: **NEIL FINN** (see below)

—

NEIL FINN (& Various Artists)

Oct 01. (cd) *E.M.I.; (536964-2)* – NewZ –
– You don't know / Summer intro (EDMUND McWILLIAMS) / Summer of love (w/ EDMUND McWILLIAMS) / Mum in bed / Orange and blue / Red room / Cry wolf (LISA GERMANO) / The affair / Black Sally (HUMAN INSTINCT) / Boat dawn / Boat joyride / Kids floating / Batman / Shower / Phantom love (LISA GERMANO) / Drive home (w/ EDMUND McWILLIAMS) / Lucid dream (LIAM FINN).

S/track review: NEIL FINN had a little time on his hands after abandoning his long-time association with antipodean favourites, Crowded House (with brother Tim), in the late 90s (he'd also been an intergral part of New Zealand's finest, Split Enz, for whom he wrote 'I Got You'). Now a solo artist in his own right, Neil released his debut solo set, 'Try Whistling This' (1998), which was subsequently followed by 'One Nil' (2000) and the 'RAIN' soundtrack. Shared with various others, etc., the OST kicked off in fine fashion via 'You Don't Know', a record that was not too far removed from his Crowded House days. The first of a few score tracks featuring EDMUND McWILLIAMS, 'Summer Intro' and 'Summer Of Love', were bright and breezy affairs and did just what they said on the proverbial tin; their 'Drive Home' theme was equally effective. FINN took to film scores like a duck in water, the Beatles-esque 'Orange And Blue', delivering both sad vox and movie dialogue in equal measures – a modern-day '#9' but with melody. 'Red Room' twangs and twists into a solemn but uplifting gear shift, while 'The Affair' finds a Blue Nile kind of melancholy. In complete contrast, one of New Zealand's underrated bands, HUMAN INSTINCT get all Deep Purple/Black Sabbath with their late 60s rendition of Dennis Wilson's 'Black Sally'; the Beach Boys were not impressed. Indiana-born alt-songstress, LISA GERMANO, gets in two numbers, the violinist from the '4 a.d.' stable very avant-pop via longer piece 'Phantom Love'. Of the five FINN tracks on the second half of the set, the all-to-brief vocal 'Boat Joyride' is the most accessible, while 'Kids Floating' suggests why the man likes the aforementioned greasers HUMAN INSTINCT. His son, LIAM FINN (co-leader of NZ alt-pop band, Betchadupa), gets a shine in front of his dad courtesy of closing hum-a-long, Beatles-esque 'Lucid Dream'. Their musical family album was ever increasing. *MCS*

Album rating: *7

RANCHO DELUXE

1975 (US 93m) United Artists Pictures (R)

Film genre: comedy western

Top guns: dir: Frank Perry / s-w: Thomas McGuane

Stars: Jeff Bridges *(Jack McKee)* → the LAST UNICORN → TUCKER: THE MAN AND HIS DREAM → MASKED AND ANONYMOUS, Sam Waterston *(Cecil Colson)* ← MAHONEY'S LAST STAND / → the KILLING FIELDS, Elizabeth Ashley *(Cora Brown)*, Clifton James *(John Brown)*, Slim Pickens *(Henry Beige)* ← PAT GARRETT & BILLY THE KID ← SKIDOO / → HONEYSUCKLE ROSE, Charlene Dallas *(Laura Beige)*, Harry Dean Stanton *(Curt)* ← PAT GARRETT & BILLY THE KID / → RENALDO AND CLARA → the ROSE → ONE FROM THE HEART → REPO MAN → PARIS, TEXAS → PRETTY IN PINK → the LAST TEMPTATION OF CHRIST → WILD AT HEART → FEAR AND LOATHING IN LAS VEGAS, Richard Bright *(Burt)* ← PAT GARRETT & BILLY THE KID / → HAIR → the IDOLMAKER → WHO'S THE MAN?, Patti D'Arbanville *(Betty Fargo)*, Joe Spinell *(Mr. Colson)* → SORCERER → FORBIDDEN ZONE, Bert Conway *(Wilbur Fargo)* ← ROCK, ROCK, ROCK!

Storyline: Baulking at the thought of ever becoming upstanding citizenry, odd-couple cowboy slackers Cecil Colson and Jack McKee live a lackadaisical, parasitical life on the fat of Montana cattle. Determined not to give up his stock lightly, well-heeled rancher John Brown sets a couple of equally inadequate cowboys on their trail. When that fails, he hires a wily, witty ex-rustler-turned-private-dick to smoke them out. *BG*

Movie rating: *6

Visual: video + dvd

Off the record: (see below)

—

JIMMY BUFFETT

Mar 75. (lp) *United Artists; <LA 466-G>* ☐ ☐
– Rancho Deluxe – main title / (X-mas bonus; dialogue) / Ridin' in style / Left me with a nail to drive / (Rustler's that's us; dialogue) / Cattle truckin' / Countin' the cows ev'ry day / The wrangler / Rancho Deluxe – end title / Livingston Saturday night / (Dork; dialogue) / Some gothic ranch action / Wonder why you ever go home / (Hood ornament; dialogue) / Fifteen gears / Can't remember when I slept last / Rancho Deluxe. *<(cd-iss. Jan98 on 'Rykodisc'; RCD 10709)> <(cd re-iss. May04 on 'Varese Sarabande'; VSD 6573)>*

S/track review: A career throwback even at the time of recording, JIMMY BUFFETT's one and only full-length soundtrack offered up a bit of country rough at a time when he was cultivating Coral Reefer cool. Out went the steel drums and in came a chance to prove Nashville wrong. As 70s Western soundtracks go, 'RANCHO DELUXE' isn't quite 'The HIRED HAND' or 'PAT GARRETT & BILLY THE KID', but it's a solid attempt sitting just on the bearded side of Outlaw, "bouncing 'round the mountains" like BUFFETT had never been away. The man's congenital affection for the South spices his country with blues, swing and jazz (the contrarily titled "some gothic ranch action" is the one cue where he can't resist some film-score lounge-loafing), and with a barstool yarner like BUFFETT, it's not just the way he tells them, it's the wordplay he tells them with. He just about gets away with rhyming "Las Vegas glitter" and "kitty litter" on the mock-mawkish "Countin' The Cows Ev'ry Day', nutshells backwoods domestic strife as "another mobile home broken up" and comes up with the wry metaphor of driving a last nail into another romantic coffin instead of his car. Spruced up and minus its more controversial lyrics, 'Livingston Saturday Night' would even become a minor hit single on the back of the 'FM' soundtrack. But it's probably the rollicking instrumental, 'Fifteen Gears', and the Gram Parsons-esque honky tonk of 'Can't Remember When I Slept Last', which best sum up Jeff Bridges and his sidekick, and the freewheeling spirit of the film and soundtrack in general. It's a spirit and a music which you can't help thinking would take pride of place in the battered car stereo of The Dude, still Bridges' most memorable character (from 'The Big Lebowski'), and one which 'RANCHO DELUXE' haphazardly anticipates. Now look out 'HOOT', his part-OST released in 2006. *BG*

Album rating: *6.5

RANSOM

1996 (US 120m) Buena Vista / Touchstone Pictures (R)

Film genre: crime thriller

Top guns: dir: Ron Howard / s-w: Alexander Ignon, Richard Price (story: Cyril Hume, Richard Maibaum)

Stars: Mel Gibson *(Tom Mullen)*, Rene Russo *(Kate Mullen)*, Brawley Nolte *(Sean Mullen)*, Gary Sinise *(Det. Jimmy Shaker)* ← ALBINO ALLIGATOR / → OPEN SEASON, Delroy Lindo *(agent Lonnie Hawkins)* ← CROOKLYN ← MORE AMERICAN GRAFFITI, Lili Taylor *(Maris Conner)*, Liev Schreiber *(Clark Barnes)* ← WALKING AND TALKING, Donnie Wahlberg *(Cubby Barnes)*, Dan Hedaya *(Jackie Brown)*

Storyline: Multi-millionaire Tom Mullen's life is turned upside down when his young son Sean is kidnapped. The FBI are called in and advise Mullen to pay the $2 million ransom, but when the pay-off goes wrong Mullen, fearing for his son's life, goes on television to offer $2 million bounty for the kidnappers dead or alive. As the tension mounts, Mullen realises the kidnappers have a much closer link to his past than he could possibly have imagined. *JZ*

Movie rating: *7

Visual: video + dvd

Off the record: (see below)

—

James Horner // BILLY CORGAN

Nov 96. (cd/c) *Hollywood; <1 62086-2/-4>* ☐ ☐
– The kidnapping / Delivering the ransom / The quarry / A two million dollar bounty / Parallel stories / A fatal mistake / A dark reunion / The payoff – End credits // Rats / Worms / Spiders / Lizards / Worms part 2 / Squirrels with tails.

S/track review: James Horner has put together a dark, tense atmospheric piece which describes the drama and emotions involved in a kidnapping. From the beginning Horner uses the deep tones of brass, long, slow chords on violin and low, off-beat notes on piano to capture the mood – waiting, anxiety, fear. All of these themes are best demonstrated in 'Parallel Stories', the shortest track on the CD. As the kidnapping progresses, Horner's music slowly changes – his last two tracks, 'A Dark Reunion' and 'The Payoff' are more uptempo, hinting all will be well at the end. He introduces a flute solo midway through 'The Payoff' making the whole track much lighter in mood and finishes off with a flourishing fanfare as opposed to the darker pieces earlier. The last six tracks are performed by BILLY CORGAN (of Smashing Pumpkins) and MATT WALKER (ex-Filter). Titles such as 'Rats', 'Lizards' and 'Worms' emphasise the dark, nightmarish side of the world and the music, a sort of grunge/hip-hop mixture, does not make easy listening. This is a CD suitable for this film but not as a piece in itself. *JZ*

Album rating: *5

RAVENOUS

1999 (Czech/UK/US 100m) 20th Century Fox (R)

Film genre: western horror comedy/thriller

Top guns: dir: Antonia Bird *(took over from Milcho Manchevski & Raja Gosnell)* / s-w: Ted Griffin

Stars: Guy Pearce *(Capt. John Boyd)* ← a SLIPPING-DOWN LIFE / → the PROPOSITION, Robert Carlyle *(F.W. Colqhoun/ Col. Ives)* ← TRAINSPOTTING, Jeremy Davis *(Pvt. Toffler)* → the MILLION DOLLAR HOTEL, Jeffrey Jones *(Pvt. Hart)* ← HOWARD THE DUCK / → HOW HIGH, John Spencer *(Gen. Slauson)* ← ALBINO ALLIGATOR, Neal McDonough *(Pvt. Reich)*, Stephen Spinella *(Knox)*, David Arquette *(Pvt. Cleaves)* ← AIRHEADS

Storyline: Disgraced soldier John Boyd is sent to a remote army outpost in the Sierra Nevadas as punishment for his cowardice in the 1847 Mexican-American war. There his monotonous lifestyle is changed forever when Colquhoun, a bedraggled Scotsman, staggers into camp with tales of cannibalism amongst his group of settlers. Boyd and his motley soldier-companions learn about the legend of the Wendigo and as nerves become frayed it seems that Colquhoun may not be as innocent of cannibalism as he first claimed. *JZ*

Movie rating: *5.5

Visual: dvd

Off the record: Michael Nyman (see future edition)

—

DAMON ALBARN & MICHAEL NYMAN

Mar 99. (cd) *Virgin; <47126> E.M.I.; (522370-2)* ☐ Sep99 ☐
– Hail Columbia / Boyd's journey / Welcome to Fort Spencer (FOSTER'S SOCIAL ORCHESTRA) / Noises off (FOSTER'S SOCIAL ORCHESTRA) / Stranger at the window / Colquhoun's story / Weendigo myth (QUILTMAN) / Trek to the cave / He was licking me / The cave (MICHAEL NYMAN ORCHESTRA) / Run (MICHAEL NYMAN ORCHESTRA) / Let's go kill that bastard / The pit / Ives returns / Cannibal fantasy / Game of two shoulders / Checkmate / Martha and the horses / Ives torments Boyd and kills Knox / Manifest destiny / Saveoursoulissa / End titles.

S/track review: Blur's DAMON ALBARN and eclectic film composer Michael Nyman set the scene in the first two tracks by using only 19th Century instruments and uncomplicated tunes which would have been around at that time. FOSTER'S SOCIAL ORCHESTRA perform 'Welcome to Fort Spencer' and 'Noises Off' in an old-fashioned, slightly out-of-key style which gives the CD an authentic, contemporary feel. Squeeze box, fiddle and banjo are all prominent in these opening tracks. However the mood changes in 'Colquhoun's Story' which sees the combination of old instruments and new orchestra in a '3 Themes In 1' song. The modern contrasts with the old creating a macabre effect in keeping with the gruesome storyline. This can also be seen in 'Checkmate' later on in the CD. The rest of the OST is modern, the titles following the plot of the film. Track 13, 'The Pit', is a particularly compelling instrumental piece which shows Nyman at his best, and the inclusion of oddities such as 'Wendigo Myth', an Indian chant, ensures that the listener never quite knows what is coming next. *JZ*

Album rating: *6.5

☐ Chris REA segment
(⇒ LA PASSIONE)

REACH THE ROCK

1998 (US 100m) Gramercy Pictures (R)

Film genre: coming-of-age/teen movie

Top guns: dir: William Ryan / s-w: John Hughes ← PRETTY IN PINK

Stars: William Sadler *(Quinn)* ← TRESPASS ← RUSH ← BILL & TED'S BOGUS JOURNEY, Alessandro Nivola *(Robin)* → LAUREL CANYON, Bruce Norris *(Ernie)*, Karen Sillas *(Donna)*, Brooke Langton *(Lise)*, Richard Hamilton *(Ed)*, Norman Reedus *(Danny)* → OVERNIGHT → OCTANE

Storyline: Danny and Robin are two best friends drinking by the side of a river. Robin bets Danny he can't swim across and reach the rock on the other side. Danny accepts the bet but drowns halfway across, and Robin, blamed by all for his death, leaves town. Four years later, Robin suddenly returns and vandalises the shops in the main street. He is locked up for the night by Sergeant Quinn (Danny's uncle) and uses his phone call to contact his old girlfriend Lise. As the night draws on, Quinn, Robin and Lise talk about the past and what the future holds for them all. *JZ*

Movie rating: *5

Visual: dvd

Off the record: JOHN McENTIRE (see below)

—

JOHN McENTIRE (& Various Artists)

Mar 99. (cd) *Hefty; <(HEFT 14CD)>* ☐ ☐
– In a thimble (TORTOISE) / Criminal record / Overview / Stolen car / Drift (BUNDY K. BROWN) / Quinn goes to town / Window lights (the SEA AND CAKE) / Reverse migraine (POLVO) / Lise arrives / The kiss / Main title / Dreams of being king (DIANOGAH). *(lp-iss.Nov99; HEFT 014LP)*

S/track review: In his lengthy music career (from the early 90s onwards), JOHN McENTIRE was certainly prolific, having been an integral part of indie-jazz favourites Tortoise, the Sea And Cake, plus numerous production and collaborative works. In fact it was the excellent TORTOISE that kicked off McENTIRE's debut into scores. 'In The Thimble' was initially like their namesake, slow-paced, until the mood swung into math-rock bass'n'drums (n'guitar) rhythms. Cool start. Whether McENTIRE listened to film-music specialists Tangerine Dream for inspiration on track 2, 'Criminal Record', is anyone's guess, although his 'Overview' flows and twangs like every good Tortoise instrumental should. 'Stolen Car' ambiently drones away nicely and then ends abruptly after only a two-minute exercise, too short to go any distance. Annoying. McENTIRE's "shell-mate", BUNDY K BROWN's sole/soul contribution, 'Drift', gets all down'n'dirty with its drum'n'bass bending the ear into proverbial submission. The aforementioned the SEA AND CAKE (featuring leader Sam Prekop on vox) get into gear via 'Window Lights', a delightful indie-type number reminiscent of, say, Durutti Column – at a push! On the other hand, POLVO's 'Reverse Migraine' – complete with scale-y piano dirge – might've just utilised the latter word, while Chicago's DIANOGAH's 'Dreams Of Being King' was Tortoise in all but name – that's not a criticism. McENTIRE's remaining solo pieces ('Quinn Goes To Town', 'Lise Arrives', 'The Kiss' & 'Main Title') – all a little short – completed a horizontal album, nice for Sunday mornings or when you want some quiet, "own" time. *MCS*

Album rating: *6

☐ the RED CLAY RAMBLERS segment
(⇒ FAR NORTH)

☐ Martha REEVES segment
(⇒ WILLIE DYNAMITE)

☐ the RESIDENTS segment
(⇒ the CENSUS TAKER)

REVENGERS TRAGEDY

2002 (UK 109m) Northcroft Films / Exterminating Angel Films (R)

Film genre: period-costume comedy drama

Top guns: dir: Alex Cox ← WALKER ← STRAIGHT TO HELL ← SID & NANCY ← REPO MAN / s-w: Frank Cottrell Boyce ← 24 HOUR PARTY PEOPLE (play: Thomas Middleton)

Stars: Christopher Eccleston *(Vindici)* ← 24 HOUR PARTY PEOPLE ← the INVISIBLE CIRCUS, Eddie Izzard *(Lussurioso)* ← VELVET GOLDMINE / → ROMANCE & CIGARETTES → ACROSS THE UNIVERSE, Derek Jacobi *(the Duke)* → BYE BYE BLACKBIRD, Andrew Schofield *(Carlo)* ← SID & NANCY, Justin Salinger *(Ambitioso)* ← VELVET GOLDMINE, Marc Warren *(Supervacuo)*, Sophie Dahl *(Imogen)*, Diana Quick *(the Duchess)*, Margi Clarke *(Hannah)* ← 24 HOUR PARTY PEOPLE ← SOUL SURVIVOR, Anthony Booth *(Lord Antonio)* ← CONFESSIONS OF A POP PERFORMER, Paul Reynolds *(Junior)*, Stephen Graham *(2nd officer)* → THIS IS ENGLAND, Alex Cox *(Duke's driver)* ← IN HIS LIFE: THE JOHN LENNON STORY + (as above)

Storyline: Liverpool, 2011. Anti-hero Vindici has returned after 10 years to exact his revenge on The Duke, leader of the city's ruling family. The Duke poisoned Vindici's true love Gloriana when she refused his advances, and now he only has her skull to talk to in his hideaway. Meanwhile, there is trouble at court after the mysterious death of Lord Antonio's wife, while one of The Duke's sons is showing over-motherly affections to the Duchess. The scene is set for Vindici's terrible revenge. *JZ*

Movie rating: *6.5

Visual: dvd

Off the record: **CHUMBAWAMBA** were formed in Armly in Leeds ... 1980 by local vegan squatters, Dunstan Bruce (vocals), Alice Nutter (vocals, percussion), Lou Watts (vocals, keyboards), Mavis Dillon (trumpet), Harry Hamer (drums), Boff Whalley (vocals, guitar) and Danbert Nobacon (vocals, keyboards). In 1982, as Skin Disease, they featured on a single, 'Back On The Streets'. As CHUMBAWAMBA a year later, they toured with Crass, while also releasing three cassettes independently. In 1985/86, 'Wamba caused a little controversy by issuing records arguing the merits of the Band/Live Aid charity causes – needless to say, these were banned from radio airplay. 1987's 'Never Mind The Ballots: Here's The Rest Of Your Life', meanwhile, berated all parties in the forthcoming general election although obviously the Tories came in for the most disdain – as exampled on 'Mr Heseltine Meets His Public'. The same year, CHUMBAWAMBA railed against tabloid hypocrisy when they released 'Let It Be' under the moniker of Scab Aid. Perhaps as a reaction to yet another Conservative victory, the band released an album of traditional folk protest songs, 'English Rebel Songs 1381-1914' (1988), their Maddy Prior-meets-Crass sound rising with ease to the challenge. Discovering the subversive possibilities in the emerging rave culture, the band turned in the dancefloor-friendly 'Slap!' in summer 1990, although it took a pair-up with agit-hip hoppers Credit To The Nation for CHUMBAWAMBA to finally get their message across to a wider audience. Now signed to 'One Little Indian' records, the track in question, 'Enough Is Enough', gave the band a minor UK chart hit. Its call to challenge the rise of right-wing activism was echoed in a similarly successful follow-up, 'Timebomb'. The attendant album, 'Anarchy', reached the British Top 30, unimaginable ten years earlier. The once crustie band (but now without Mavis – replaced by Jude Abbot) signed to conglomorate, 'E.M.I.' in the mid-90s, obviously deciding to subvert the pop world from within (a likely story!). Not only did they come pretty damn close with the annoyingly infectious 'Tubthumping' (a No.2 UK hit!), but they broke the normally impenetrable American market. The accompanying album, 'Tubthumper' (1997) hit the US Top 5 (having earlier made the UK Top 20), proving that patience is a virtue, even for those committed to radical social change. Love them or loathe them (and there's never usually any waverers!), CHUMBAWAMBA are now something of an institution, their newfound pop/MTV-friendly sound ushering in a new era of chart topping protest, er, possibly . . . The faux anarchs were back in 2000 with a US album 'Wysiwyg' (aka What You See Is What You Get), a rambling, disjointed effort which saw no-one in particular pay attention. The band's one-time musical engineer, Neil Ferguson, became their official bass player on OST album, 'REVENGERS TRAGEDY' (without Boff). *SW*

—

CHUMBAWAMBA

Jan 03. (cd) *Mutt; (MUTTCD 003)* ☐ [-]
– Liverpool: drive with care / He did assault my brother! / That eternal eye / The very core of lust / Villian! strumpet! slapper! / Blurred / Lullaby demons / A slavish duke is baser than his slaves / Sweet angel of revenge / Ambition / Don't try this at home (Revengers version).

S/track review: Alex Cox's films invariably fail to live up to their conceptual promise, and even though there is always a certain charm to his failures, choosing CHUMBAWAMBA to score this film was one of his more perverse moves. Less than the sum of its parts, even the threat inherent in the idea of a CHUMBAWAMBA score isn't satisfyingly fulfilled. Rather than terrible, this is just relentlessly mediocre cod techno, better suited to a particularly downbeat early episode of Byker Grove than a futuristic take on a Jacobean play. In that sense, at least, CHUMBAWAMBA's score is appropriate in that the feeble attempts at melding electric guitars with derivative – and, more importantly, mundane – synths echo Cox's efforts to modernise the play. The inclusion of snippets of dialogue over the music further enhances the sense of amateurism and mock gravitas prevalent here, although they are preferable to the few appearances of ALICE NUTTER's impressively sub-Dido vocals. Ultimately, this is a collection that is unlikely to interest even CHUMBAWAMBA fans.

Album rating: *4

RIDE THE WILD SURF

1964 (US 101m) Columbia Pictures (PG)

Film genre: romantic/teen comedy drama

Top guns: dir: Don Taylor / s-w: Art Napoleon, Jo Napoleon

Stars: **FABIAN** *(Jody Wallis)*, Shelley Fabares *(Brie Matthews)* ← SUMMER LOVE ← ROCK, PRETTY BABY / → GIRL HAPPY → HOLD ON! → SPINOUT → CLAMBAKE → a TIME TO SING, Tab Hunter *(Steamer Lane)* → GREASE 2, Peter Brown *(Chase Colton)* → FOXY BROWN, Barbara Eden *(Augie Poole)* ← SWINGIN' ALONG, Susan Hart *(Lily Kilua)* → PAJAMA PARTY → the GHOST IN THE INVISIBLE BIKINI, John Anthony Hayes *(Frank Decker)* → WINTER A-GO-GO, James Mitchum *(Eskimo)*, Roger Davis *(Charlie)* → NASHVILLE GIRL, John Anthony Hayes *(Frank Decker)*

Storyline: Jodie, Steamer and Chase go for a complete change of scenery and move from the beaches of California to the beaches of Hawaii, just in time for the 'Last Ride' championship. Within a few seconds our guys have found some girls and fallen in love, so it's on with more practising on the big rollers. On the day of the competition one of their main rivals will be Eskimo – surely he doesn't stand a snowball's chance against the boys. *JZ*

Movie rating: *4.5

Visual: video

Off the record: JAN & DEAN (see 'DEADMAN'S CURVE')

JAN & DEAN (score: Stu Phillips)

Oct 64. (lp) *Liberty; <LST 7368> (LBY 1229)* **66** Apr65
– Ride the wild surf / Tell 'em I'm surfin' / Waimea Bay / She's my summer girl / The restless surfer / Skateboarding part 1 / Sidewalk surfin' / Surfin' wild / Down at Malibu beach / A surfer's dream / Walk on the wet side / The submarine races. *<(cd-iss. Nov04 on 'Beat Goes On'+=; BGOCD 636)>* – Folk 'n Roll (album by JAN & DEAN).

S/track review: JAN & DEAN's appeal was in their limitations. The grinning duo's successes didn't just sound like their friends the Beach Boys – they depended on the Beach Boys' gifts (though there was some reciprocity; DEAN TORRANCE can be heard on the falsetto lead of 'Barbara Ann'). Brian Wilson's subsequent journey from surf to sanitarium would generate some of the most influential ideas in pop, while JAN & DEAN remain frozen in an early-60s summer, their minor pop gems forever emblematic of a more innocent age. Gems are scarce, though, on this soundtrack. After some hit-and-miss singles overseen by a young Herb Alpert, JAN BERRY and DEAN TORRANCE had taken the refrain "two girls for every boy" to the top of the charts on the Wilson-penned 'Surf City', and nobody could accuse them of being slow to cash in. 'RIDE THE WILD SURF' was the fourth JAN & DEAN album to be released in 1964, and it followed the pattern of the others with a by-numbers mix of four WILSON originals and a deal of competent but makeweight musical fare like the saccharine 'A Surfer's Dream' and the would-be comic 'The Submarine Races'. The passing of surf music would leave the pair floundering (cue Dylan covers and a hopeful anthem for the next bandwagon, 'Folk City'), while BERRY's near-death experience in a car crash and subsequent rehabilitation made a ghoulishly compelling story. The imperfectly patched-up but admirably resolute pair continued to pop up on the nostalgia circuit until BERRY's death in 2004. *ND*

Album rating: *4.5

– spinoff hits, etc. –

JAN & DEAN: Ride The Wild Surf

Sep 64. (7") *<(LIB 55724)>* **16** Nov64

Terry RILEY

Born: 24 Jun'35, Colfax, California, USA. Graduating from Berkeley Music College, he played ragtime piano in a San Francisco saloon. In the late 50s, Terry stayed for a time in Europe while touring Scandinavia with various theatre projects. He worked with early minimalist, La Monte Young, before he set out on his own, recording the 'In C' album in 1964 (released 1968). This used many musicians and vocalists who performed tunes in staggered sequence over a repetitive array of chords, definitely a precursor to artists such as MIKE OLDFIELD, LAURIE ANDERSON, etc. In 1966, 'Reed Streams' came out on a small label, leading him to sign for 'Columbia' records. Early in the 70s, his work on 'A Rainbow In Curved Air' and 'Church Of Anthrax' (the latter with John Cale) highlighted his style of hypnotic electronics, while film scores included 'Les YEUX FERMES' (1972; released in France as 'Happy Ending') and 'LIFESPAN' (1974; left unissued until 2007). RILEY branched out in the 80s, working with Indian vocalist, Pandit Pranath, and the Kronos Quartet. An avant-garde "Godfather of minimalist muzak", he has, over the years, inspired a generation of figureheads such as JOHN CALE, LOU REED, DAVID BOWIE, BRIAN ENO, Philip Glass, as well as being a catalyst for "New Age" music. Homage was paid to RILEY via the WHO's classic track, 'Baba O'Riley'. *MCS & BG*

- filmography (composer) –

les Yeux Fermés *(1972 OST =>)* / la Chute D'un Corps *(1973 score)* / **Lifespan** *(1974 OST =>)* / No Man's Land *(1985 score)* / Pictures From A Revolution *(1991 score w/ William Eldridge)*

RISKY BUSINESS

1983 (US 99m) Geffen Pictures / Warner Bros. Pictures (R)

Film genre: teen crime comedy

Top guns: s-w + dir: Paul Brickman

Stars: Tom Cruise *(Joel Goodson)* → LEGEND → MAGNOLIA, Rebecca De Mornay *(Lana)* ← ONE FROM THE HEART / → RAISE YOUR VOICE, Joe Pantoliano *(Guido)* ← the IDOLMAKER / → EDDIE AND THE CRUISERS → SCENES FROM THE GOLDMINE → LA BAMBA → ROCK'N'ROLL MOM → the IN CROWD → BLACK AND WHITE, Richard Masur *(Rutherford)* ← TIMERIDER: THE ADVENTURE OF LYLE SWANN, Bronson Pinchot *(Barry)*, Curtis Armstrong *(Miles)* → MY DINNER WITH JIMI → RAY, Nicholas Pryor *(Joel's father)*, Janet Carroll *(Joel's mother)*

Storyline: When teenager Joel gets the run of the house, he thinks his dreams have come true. Money, cars and girls appear in various combinations and needless to say things soon get hopelessly out of control. Joel then decides to drive his dad's Porsche to Lake Michigan – and forgets to stop when he gets to the water! *JZ*

Movie rating: *6

Visual: video + dvd

Off the record: (see below)

TANGERINE DREAM (*) (& Various Artists)

Dec 83. (lp/c) *E.M.I.; <098620> Virgin; (V/TCV 2302)*
– Old time rock and roll (BOB SEGER) / The dream is always the same (*) / No future (get off the babysitter) (*) / Guido the killer pimp (*) / Lana (*) / Mannish boy (I'm a man) (MUDDY WATERS) / The pump (JEFF BECK) / D.M.S.R. (PRINCE) / After the fall (JOURNEY) / In the air tonight (PHIL COLLINS) / Love on a real train – Risky Business theme (*). *(cd-iss. May87; CDV 2302) (re-iss. Apr90 lp/c; OVED/+C 2302)*

S/track review: This soundtrack is very much a game of two halves, as excerpts from TANGERINE DREAM's electronic score sit next to salacious blues, funk and some truly horrid 80s rock. TD had long been renowned for their innovative use of sequencers, but with the advent of digital technology the group were able to programme complex melodies in addition to simple riffs and arpeggios, giving their music more structure. As a result, some of their pieces here recall the minimalism of Steve Reich and Phillip Glass, with shimmering melodic sequences that subtly shift in tone and texture. 'The Dream Is Always The Same', and 'Love On A Real Train' are quite beautiful pieces of ambient electronica, warm peals of electric piano and synthesised soprano swells slotting amongst the busy but delicate synthesiser lines. Less memorable are the electronic rock tracks 'No Future', 'Guido The Killer Pimp' and 'Lana', which, with their processed guitar licks and fantasy synth pads, sound a little dated. In their favour, the acid washes of white noise and industrial metal and metal effects successfully create a sinister and edgy atmosphere. The other half of the album consists of pop songs from the movie. BOB SEGER's 'Old Time Rock And Roll' is an enjoyably cheesy slice of bar band rock, while MUDDY WATERS' immortal 'Mannish Boy' needs little introduction. The live version included here is particularly rowdy, the crowd whooping in appreciation of the blues legend's sexual grandstanding. An early PRINCE b-side, 'D.M.S.R.' is a lean and sexy party track from the beginning of the Purple One's imperial phase. 'The Pump' sees JEFF BECK's flash and fire tempered by naff '80s production, while the JOURNEY power ballad 'After The Fall' is the sort of monstrosity best left in the '80s. Interestingly, if it weren't for the dreary vocals and bombastic drum fills, PHIL COLLINS' 'In The Air Tonight' would sit well alongside the TANGERINE DREAM tracks as mood music. The drum machine pulse, gloomy synth pads and sheet metal guitar of its opening bars are moodily atmospheric. Most of these tracks are available elsewhere, making this soundtrack primarily of interest to TD completists. *SS*

Album rating: *5.5

RIVERS AND TIDES – WORKING WITH TIME

2001 (Fin/Ger 90m) Piffl Medien GmbH (TV-G)

Film genre: art documentary

Top guns: dir: Thomas Riedelsheimer

Stars: Andy Goldsworthy (himself)

Storyline: A mesmerising, almost Zen-like document of Andy Goldsworthy's solitary eco-art, poetically shot by director Thomas Riedelsheimer. Both Goldsworthy and his organic creations make fascinating subjects; he's a man literally consumed with the cyclical power of nature, the relentless, cathartic processes of death and rebirth, sculpting from the land as a means of connecting and communing with it, as well as the people who've inhabited it – if he doesn't work he "doesn't know himself". Whether making endless attempts at a stone cairn before the tide comes in, feverishly entombing himself in a driftwood whorl or reinterpreting a dry stone wall, he's guided by the "liquid movement" he divines in all animate and inanimate things, endlessly recreating that same, snaking motif. So monk-ish in hue appears his vocation, in fact, and so in touch with seasonal and lunar rhythms that even his speech lilts hypnotically, it initially comes as something of a shock when the film cuts to Goldsworthy's boisterous family life (in a Scottish borders village), and a rare glimpse of humour. Nevertheless, it's clear that Goldsworthy's path is a spiritual one more than it is an artistic one, just as his honest, measured – and yes, earnest – explanation of that path – combined with Riedelsheimer's gorgeous landscapes, often shot like an open air ballet – is more like a meditation session than a film. *BG*

Movie rating: *8

Visual: dvd

Off the record: (see below)

—

FRED FRITH

Jul 03. (cd) *Winter & Winter; <91009-2>* [ ] [–]
– Part I / Part II / Part III / Part IV / Part V / Part VI / Part VII / Part VIII.

S/track review: Soundtrack becomes FRED FRITH. Chipping away at the compositional and improvisational limits of the guitar since the late 60s, counting the likes of John Zorn and Bill Laswell amongst his peers, the onetime Henry Cow founder has consistently concerned himself with the possibilities of sound over and above mere music. 'RIVERS AND TIDES' expands his remit to the world outside the studio, to the empty quarters where the land meets the sea. Even without music, Andy Goldsworthy's art makes for absorbing cinema; together with FRITH's atonal echoes, sound-songs and splintered notes, it's a veritable feast for the senses. FRITH's minimalist compositions likewise work apart from the images as a surprisingly compelling suite, one that given close attention yields up its rewards as surely and as patiently as a rainy Scottish spring or an icebound Nova Scotia. The trickle of water and the hum of vibrating air are FRITH's raw materials as much as they are Goldsworthy's, the canvas on which he maps the deceptive anarchy of the natural world. Quasi-Oriental barbs of violin, a cyclic, Bill Evans-esque piano chord, scattered percussive kindling; even the martial nightmarescape which ushers in 'Part III' is soothed with the balm of moving water, as the mysterious forces coursing through FRITH's soundscapes converge on 'Part VI', tracing sublime soprano sax lines in a desolate foreshore, contrapuntal melodies blown across the spray as a rangy berimbau notes the passing of time: as an evocation of Goldsworthy's "world beyond what words can define", it's nigh on clairvoyant. Those metaphysical impulses converge again on 'Part VIII', borne in on an unexpected flourish of Romany strings and pilgrim snares, before the whole is washed away, reclaimed. A mystical work under any definition of the term. *BG*

Album rating: *8

the ROAD TO EL DORADO

2000 (US 89m) DreamWorks (PG)

Film genre: family/children's animation comedy

Top guns: dir: Don Paul, Bibo Bergeron / s-w: Ted Elliott, Terry Rossio, Philip Lazebnik (story: Edmund Fong)

Voices: Kevin Kline *(Tulio)*, Kenneth Branagh *(Miguel)*, Rosie Perez *(Chel)* ← NIGHT ON EARTH / → MY GENERATION, Armand Assante *(Tzekel-Kan)* → LOOKING FOR AN ECHO, Edward James Olmos *(chief)* ← SELENA ← EVEN COWGIRLS GET THE BLUES ← BLADE RUNNER, Jim Cummings *(Cortes + others)*, Frank Welker *(Altivo + others)*, **Elton JOHN** *(narrator)*

Storyline: Con men Tulio and Miguel win a treasure map showing the location of the fabled city of El Dorado. Stowing away on Cortes' ship to the Americas, they are soon discovered and set adrift on a rowing boat along with their horse. Eventually they strike land and are relieved to find the local people take them for gods, except unfortunately for the evil priest who does his best to make them next in line for human sacrifice. *JZ*

Movie rating: *6

Visual: dvd

Off the record: (see below)

—

ELTON JOHN (lyrics: Tim Rice) (score: Hans Zimmer)

Mar 00. (cd) *DreamWorks; <(450 219-2)>* [63] Jun00 [ ]
– El Dorado / Someday out of the blue (theme from El Dorado) / Without question / Friends never say goodbye / The trail we blaze / 16th Century man / The panic in me / It's tough to be a god (duet with RANDY NEWMAN) / Trust me / My heart dances / Queen of cities / Cheldorado / The brig / Wonders of the new world.

S/track review: After achieving huge success with 'The LION KING' score, Sir ELTON JOHN put his name to another animated film in the shape of 'The ROAD TO EL DORADO', linking up once again with songwriter Tim Rice. Unlike the aforementioned 'LION KING', ' . . . EL DORADO' doesn't feel much like a soundtrack made to fit the film, instead it sounds like a collection of songs that have been manipulated a bit to fit the context. While 'The LION KING' evokes the sights, sounds and smells of the African plains through a well-crafted score, its successor fails to do anything similar for the jungles of South America. There is a hint of Latin flavour on one or two of the tracks, namely the title track and 'It's Tough To Be A God' (a duet with RANDY NEWMAN), but overall the album feels more akin to frontiers of the Wild West, with country guitars and ragtime piano underpinning many of the songs. If 'EL DORADO' is taken as an album instead of a soundtrack, then there are some outstanding ELTON JOHN songs that would compete with anything he has done since the early 90s. The title track has a rousing, sing-a-long chorus while '16th Century Man' and 'The Trail We Blaze' are thundering juggernauts; 'Queen of Cities' is a powerful, orchestra-backed ballad. However, songs such as 'Friends Never Say Goodbye' and 'Trust Me' fall off the tightrope and onto the safety net of sentimentalism that always accompany the soundtrack to animated films. ELTON JOHN fans will love some of the tracks, but the soundtrack, like the film itself, is sure to be swallowed up by obscurity while 'The LION KING' shines, both as a film and a vehicle for the artist's talents. *CM*

Album rating: *5.5

– spinoff hits, etc. –

ELTON JOHN: Someday Out Of The Blue / Cheldorado

Apr 00. (cd-s) *<459039>* 49 –

- ☐ Robbie ROBERTSON (the BAND)
- ☐ Smokey ROBINSON segment (⇒ BIG TIME)
- ☐ ROSE ROYCE segment (⇒ CAR WASH)

ROSIE

aka ROSIE: THE DEVIL IN MY HEAD

1998 (Belg 97m) Rime Time

Film genre: coming-of-age/teen drama

Top guns: s-w: Patrice Toye (+ dir), Lieve Hellinckx

Stars: Aranka Coppens *(Rosie)*, Sara de Roo *(Irene)*, Frank Vercruyssen *(Michel)*, Dirk Roofthooft *(Bernard Vermarcke)*, Joost Wijnant *(Jimi)*

Storyline: New inmate Rosie tells her life story to the warders of the juvenile detention centre. At first she lived with her "much older sister" Irene who just possibly could be her mum, and her gambling-mad brother Michel. However, when Irene turned her attention towards newcomer Bernard, Rosie was left out in the cold and decided to chat up the first good-looking young guy she found, in this case Jimi, whom she met on a bus. But what happened from that day till now when Rosie finds herself in the detention centre? *JZ*

Movie rating: *7.5

Visual: video + dvd

Off the record: **JOHN PARISH** (see below)

—

JOHN PARISH

Jan 99. (cd) *Swarf Finger; (<SF 034CD>)* ☐ Jun00 ☐
– Disturbance / Rosie Rosita / Pretty baby / Rosie takes Elvis / Secret / Irene talks about her prince / Burn rubber barons / Rosie reads Irenes palm / Pipeline disturbance / Accident / Rosita light a fire / More than a brother – Rosie dancing alone / I did it for you mama – end titles.

S/track review: Born in Yeovil, England, Bristol-based guitarist JOHN PARISH was an inspired choice to score this Flemish indie movie for his solo debut album. Through his embryonic Automatic Dlamini musings in the late 80s (that featured PJ Harvey) and/or his backing work with alt-rock singer PJ Harvey on their low-key, 50/50 collaboration 'Dance Hall At Louse Point' (1996), the filmmakers must've thought this connection to be enough for 'ROSIE'. 13 tracks over 35 minutes seems a little poor by today's standards, but I suppose soundtracks have their own unwritten rules. Shimmering, vibrato guitar – not too removed from Ry Cooder duelling with Fripp/King Crimson – could best describe a number of instrumentals here, track 2 'Rosie Rosita' included. Follow-on song, 'Pretty Baby', saw the cool, lo-fi vox of one ALISON GOLDFRAPP (with lyrics provided by Mauro Pawlowski), surely the best substitute one could hope for if newbie actress PJ was not available. The brooding, desert-bowl bleakness was everywhere here, that Ry Cooder-esque slide psycho-drilling the brain into submission a la, 'Rosie Takes Elvis'. Music and soft-spoken film dialogue excerpts fitted hand in glove on a few brow-beaten tracks such as 'Secret', 'Rosie Reads Irenes Palm' & 'Rosita Light A Fire', while highlights are undoubtedly the Neil Young-esque 'Burn Rubber Barons'. Never an easy listen by any manner of means, 'ROSIE' is like time spent on an industrial barren wasteland while getting ready for a storm – but the storm never comes. The closest the listener ever gets to crescendo or climax is "end title", 'I Did It For You Mama' (featuring violin solo by CLARE MacTAGGART) – Mogwai were apparently taking notes. JOHN PARISH has since released two albums for 'Thrill Jockey': 'How Animals Move' (2002) and 'Once Upon A Little Time' (2005). *MCS*

Album rating: *6

RUSH

1991 (US 120m) Metro-Goldwyn-Mayer (R)

Film genre: cop/detective drama

Top guns: dir: Lili Fini Zanuck / s-w: Peter Dexler (au: Kim Wozencraft)

Stars: Jason Patric *(Jim Raynor)* → GERONIMO: AN AMERICAN LEGEND, Jennifer Jason Leigh *(Kristen Cates)* ← LAST EXIT TO BROOKLYN ← FAST TIMES AT RIDGEMONT HIGH / → GEORGIA, Sam Elliott *(Larry Dodd)* ← ROAD HOUSE, Max Perlich *(Walker)* → SHAKE, RATTLE & ROCK! tv → GEORGIA, **Gregg Allman** *(Will Gaines)* → LIGHTNING IN A BOTTLE, Tony Frank *(Nettle)* ← YOUNG GUNS II ← SWEET DREAMS ← ALAMO BAY, William Sadler *(Monroe)* ← BILL & TED'S BOGUS JOURNEY / → TRESPASS → REACH THE ROCK, Dennis Burkley *(motorcycle guy)* ← the DOORS ← LAMBADA ← WHO'S THAT GIRL ← BUMMER! / → TOUCH

Storyline: Kristen Cates is a young, attractive and very green police recruit who gets more than she bargained for when she agrees to go undercover to nail a Texas drug kingpin. Both she and her mentor/lover Jim Raynor are drawn inexorably into addiction as they strive for authenticity among their underworld contacts. *BG*

Movie rating: *6.5

Visual: video + dvd

Off the record: **Gregg Allman** was formerly part of sibling outfit the Allman Brothers Band (albums included 'Eat A Peach'); he also briefly married CHER in 1977. *MCS*

—

ERIC CLAPTON

Jan 92. (cd) *Reprise; (<7599 26794-2>)* ☐ 24
– New recruit / Tracks and lines / Realization / Kristen and Jim / Preludin fugue / Cold turkey / Will Gaines / Help me up / Don't know which way to go (with BUDDY GUY) / Tears in Heaven. *(cd re-iss. Oct94; same)*

S/track review: Given that 'RUSH' was ERIC CLAPTON's first project following the accidental death of his son in 1991, this is a score which inevitably reflects some of the pain and loss CLAPTON must have been wrestling with at the time. While 'Tears In Heaven' all too poignantly makes explicit the man's grief, there's a muted intensity to much of this music which takes on an added weight in the knowledge of CLAPTON's personal tragedy. His dark, searing blues licks seem to exist in and of themselves, with only the most subtle of accompaniment and certainly no orchestration. CHUCK LEAVELL's piano contributes emotional colouring to the likes of 'Kristen And Jim', leaving that same sense of loss and regret hanging in the air – CLAPTON and his band only really break loose on 'Preludin Fugue' and 'Cold Turkey', and even then only for a few minutes. That said, the claustrophobic synth and percussion textures of 'Will Gaines' makes for an intriguing end-of-the-score section of the soundtrack. In contrast, the cathartic 'Help Me Up' comes as something of a relief, while 'Don't Know Which Way To Go', is an extended electric blues with vocals by BUDDY GUY. *BG*

Album rating: *6

– spinoff hits, etc. –

ERIC CLAPTON: Tears In Heaven / Tracks And Lines / (non-film tracks)

Jan 92. (7"/c-s/12"/cd-s) *<19038> (W 0081/+C/T/CD)* 2 5

□ David RYAN
(⇒ the LEMONHEADS)

RZA

Born: Robert Diggs, 5 Jul'66, Staten Island, New York, USA. The ubiquitous producer of the Wu-Tang Clan and, like sparring partners Method Man, Genius/GZA and the late Ol' Dirty Bastard, a man fond of an alias or two, RZA can justly claim to have revolutionised hip hop with his wayward troupe's pioneering debut album, 'Enter The Wu Tang: 36 Chambers' (1993). His raw, brooding collages also predicted his future career as an unlikely but successful film composer while his business acumen (including the establishment of pioneering solo deals for the individual Clan members) was the subject of a New York Times article. As well as fulfilling the role of writing/production mentor to the sprawling catalogue of Wu-Tang's extended family, the man also known as Bobby Digital released a fair few solo albums in his own right before moving into cinema. Given his martial arts obsession (the man actually performed at the ancient Shaolin temple in China!), it was perhaps inevitable that RZA was the composer of choice for indie director Jim Jarmusch's ghetto oddity, 'GHOST DOG: THE WAY OF THE SAMURAI' (1999). While the resulting soundtrack showcased the man's penchant for R&B and vintage soul alongside plenty of heavy duty Wu-Tang productions, his more abstract, BAFTA nominated contributions to Quentin Tarantino's 'KILL BILL: VOL.1' (2003) invested the reliably diverse soundtrack with an undercurrent of familiar menace. He made his big screen debut – alongside various other Wu-Tang alumni – the same year with appearances in comedy franchise, 'Scary Movie 3' and – chewing the fat with Bill Murray – in Jarmusch's b&w collage, 'COFFEE AND CIGARETTES', before resuming his scoring career with a credit on Afro-American aviation lark, 'Soul Plane' (2004), which starred his homie Method Man. Working alongside veteran producer George Drakoulias as well as co-composer Ramin Djawadi, RZA went on to compose the music for Wesley Snipes sequel, 'Blade: Trinity' (2004) and – in collaboration with Robert Rodriguez – the second instalment of 'KILL BILL: VOL.2' as well as another black comedy sequel, 'Barbershop 2: Back In Business' (2004), credited to the Wu-Tang Clan and scored in tandem with composer Richard Gibbs. A director in his own right, RZA also has a number of short film credits to his name as well as a full length kung fu effort, 'Z Chronicles' (2005). *MCS*

- **filmography** (composer) {performer} –

Ghost Dog: The Way Of The Samurai *(1999 OST =>)* / Luke's Freakfest: The Movie *(2001 {p w/ WU-TANG CLAN)* / **Coffee And Cigarettes** *(2003 {c} OST by V/A =>)* / **Kill Bill: Vol.1** *(2003 OST w/ V/A =>)* / Scary Movie 3 *(2003 {c})* / Barbershop 2: Back In Business *(2004 OST w/ WU-TANG CLAN see; future editions)* / **Kill Bill: Vol.2** *(2004 score w/ Robert Rodriguez + OST by V/A =>)* / Soul Plane *(2004 no OST w/ Chris Lennertz)* / Blade: Trinity *(2004 OST w/ V/A & Ramin Djawadi =>)*

the SANDALS

Formed: San Clemente, California, USA . . . 1962 out of the Twangs by Belgian-born siblings, Walter Georis (rhythm guitar) and Gaston Georis (keyboards). With their Shadows-meets-surf style apparent to all, the brothers and the other three musicians, John Blakley (lead guitar), John Gibson (bass) and Danny Brawner (drums), the Sandells – as they were briefly billed – inked a deal with 'World Pacific' records. In 1964, they debuted with the single, 'Out Front', and although it was a flop it found a fan in filmmaker, Bruce Brown. He commissioned the group to compose and perform the music for his documentary surf movie, 'The ENDLESS SUMMER' (1966). The West Coast sound had shifted by the time of its release; no longer were the flower children ready for the smooth, easy-listening of the Ventures, the SANDALS and their ilk. If they'd only managed to hear the rocking vibes displayed on the soundtrack, maybe minds would've been changed rather than being psychedelically altered. The group decided to call it a day in 1968, although they did leave behind the legacy of another film soundtrack, 'LAST OF THE SKI BUMS' (1969). While the Georis brothers found work in a new imprint, 'Tri-Surf', only Blakeley was to progress to better things as a member of Stoneground. *MCS*

- filmography {composers} –

the Endless Summer *(1966 OST =>)* / **Last Of The Ski Bums** *(1969 OST =>)*

SAVAGE!

aka BLACK VALOR

1973 (US/Mex 81m) New World Pictures (R)

Film genre: post-military adventure/drama

Top guns: dir: Cirio H. Santiago / s-w: Ed Medard

Stars: James Iglehart *(Savage)* ← BEYOND THE VALLEY OF THE DOLLS, Lada Edmund Jr. *(Vicki)*, Carol Speed *(Amanda)* ← the MACK ← BUMMER! / → the DYNAMITE BROTHERS → DISCO GODFATHER, Sally Jordan *(Sylvia)*, Aura Aurea *(China)*, Eddie Gutierrez *(Flores)*

Storyline: Universally pilloried action flick with ex-baseball star James Iglehart as Savage, a swashbuckling, womanising black activist who comes over to the cause of South American revolutionaries after initially being kidnapped by them. *BG*

Movie rating: *3.5

Visual: video

Off the record: **DON JULIAN** (see below)

—

DON JULIAN

Jun 73. (lp) *Money; <MS 1109>* ☐ –
– Title theme: Savage (with ARTHUR G. WRIGHT) / Lay it on your head / Where I'm coming from / It's a sad song / My favorite beer joint / Janitizio / Just kiss me. *<(UK+re-iss. Apr97 on 'Southbound' cd/lp; CD+/SEWM 114)>*

S/track review: "On The Streets Or On The Sheets, He's A Savage!" As blaxploitation taglines go, they don't come much kitschier. The "super soul soundtrack" found doo wop pioneer DON JULIAN in equally wild form, cooking up one of the genre's highest-octane title themes, a ten-minute, conga-frenzied epic with more time changes than a budget airlines flight. Don Cook's trombone provides the dramatic menace, Jimmy Vinson's flawless flute the nimble impressionist detail. Vinson is in equally smoking form on the slower, greasier numbers like 'Lay It On Your Head' and 'Where I'm Coming From', embellishing eerie, earthy basslines reminiscent of Cymande and complex structures echoing the prog-funk of Mandrill. Co-writer (and co-owner of the California-based 'Money' label which originally issued the album) Arthur Wright's 'It's A Sad Song' supplied a Spanish guitar interlude while 'Janitzio' (sampled by Warren G on his 1994 landmark, 'Regulate') boasts an earnest if curiously engaging, bi-lingual intro preaching chicano-on-black musical and racial harmony, and a latino-funk groove so louche and languid you can almost smell the tropical air and taste the rum. Run to the end of its groove all too soon, 'SAVAGE!' is testament to one of blaxploitation's most underrated players. In fact, JULIAN also recorded the music for – and starred in – one of the genre's most obscure films, 'Shorty The Pimp' (one of the last prints of which, according to blax website www.blaxploitation.com, is said to be in the possession of Quentin Tarantino), with a full soundtrack belatedly issued on 'Southbound' in 1998, the same year the man sadly passed away. *BG*

Album rating: *7

☐ Bobby SCOTT segment
(⇒ JOE)

SCRAPPLE

1998 (US 92m) Sweetwater Productions (R)

Film genre: gross-out comedy drama

Top guns: s-w: (+ dir) Christopher Hanson, Geoffrey Hanson, George Plamondon (story: Sean McNamara)

Stars: Geoffrey Hanson *(Al Dean)*, Ryan Massey *(Beth Muller; Tom's girlfriend)*, Buck Simmonds *(Tom Sullivan; aka Easy)*, Bunzy Bunworth *(Errol McNamara / pig catcher)*, L. Kent Brown *(Kurt Hinney)*, Grady Lee *(Phil Bandell)*, George Plamondon *(Ct Sloan)*, Luc Leestemaker *(Klauss)*, Christopher Hanson *(Rito)*

Storyline: The dreams and comedic schemes of a frazzled band of late 70s ski bums in the Colorado ski/hippie resort of Ajax. Small time drug dealer Al waits expectantly on a consignment of "Nepalese Temple Balls", the proceeds from which he hopes to fund a house for he and his paraplegic Vietnam Vet brother. The sacrificial "dharma piglet", however, has other ideas, scoffing the blow and getting Al in over his depth. *BG*

Movie rating: *6.5

Visual: video

Off the record: The film was nominated for the Grand Jury Prize at the corresponding Sundance Film Festival.

—

Various Artists incl. TAJ MAHAL *
(w/ the PHANTOM BLUES BAND **)

Dec 99. (cd) *Sweet H2O; <852>* ☐ ☐ –
– Sailin' shoes (SAM BUSH) / Farther on down the road (*) / One step ahead of the blues (J.J. CALE) / Over the hill (JOHN MARTYN) / Genesis (JORMA KAUKONEN) / Really love the rain (TOOTS HIBBERT) / Sunshine on my soul (**) / Dove (CYMANDE) / Moonburn (**) / Ajax piano rag (*) / Never let your fire go out (the RADIATORS) / Al's 5 speed (*) / The take out (WIDESPREAD PANIC) / Mud season (* & JOHNNY LEE SCHELL) / Dream your life, live your dreams (*) / Shanty (JONATHAN EDWARDS).

S/track review: Never mind the kind of nappy-wrapped nu-"punk" routinely used to soundtrack snowboarders' death-defying feats on late-night TV; as 'SCRAPPLE' summons just about enough energy to make clear, ski bums of a certain vintage would rather nod out to Little Feat covers. Scriptwriter/producer Geoffrey Hason's playlist of reggae-spiked doobie-folk is maybe a little bit too MOR for its own good but you can see what he's getting at. In some respects his taste is faultless – how often do you see either JORMA KAUKONEN, JOHN MARTYN or the mighty CYMANDE on soundtrack compilations? For those lucky, lucky people yet to discover MARTYN, 'Over The Hill' is only the beginning of a sublime adventure. CYMANDE's 'Dove' is a ten-minute hymn to the jungle gods, a masterpiece of progressive (fear not, in this case "prog" really is more than a four-letter word) enthno-rock that even Santana couldn't match. A mandolin version of 'Sailin' Shoes' takes a bit of getting used to, and it would've been great to see Lowell George here himself (licensing/budget considerations doubtless scuppered it), but veteran Newgrass Revivalist SAM BUSH isn't a bad choice as opener. The '82 vintage JJ CALE track ('One Step Ahead Of The Blues') is likewise a fair choice but, without wanting to nitpick (OK, wanting to nitpick), wouldn't one of his desert-madrigal meditations from the early 70s have fitted better? TOOTS HIBBERT likewise. Hanson's idea of who's carrying that 70s torch (what he terms a "slow-groovin' roots sound) might be questionable – Aussie rockers the RADIATORS? – but the contribution by "jam band", WIDESPREAD PANIC, is surprisingly evocative, all morning-dew guitar and the kind of plunging fiddle arrangements Scarlet Riviera worked on Bob Dylan's 'Desire'. It's roots legend TAJ MAHAL, though, who's the raison d'être behind the whole thing. Hanson had apparently asked him years before if he'd write a film score and, top bloke that he is, he kept his word. Backed by the PHANTOM BLUES BAND (featuring the likes of trumpeted country blues revivalist, ALVIN YOUNGBLOOD HEART), MAHAL lays down a clutch of specially composed score tracks ranging through impressively authentic roots reggae spiced with dobro ('Sunshine On My Soul' and 'Mud Season'), funk ('Moonburn') and – courtesy of pianist JON CLEARY – plenty of New Orleans moonshine. Add in MAHAL solo piece, 'Dream Your Life, Live Your Dreams', and you have a ski-stoner's wet snow dream of a compilation, taking MAHAL and co's roots-tropical vibes to altitudes they were probably never designed for. *BG*

Album rating: *7.5

SCREAM FOR HELP

1984 (US 88m) Miracle Films (18)

Film genre: psychological thriller

Top guns: dir: Michael Winner ← the WICKED LADY ← DEATH WISH II ← PLAY IT COOL / s-w: Tom Holland ← CLASS OF 1984

Stars: Rachael Kelly *(Christie Cromwell)*, Marie Masters *(Karen Cromwell Fox)*, David Brooks *(Paul Fox)* → the DOORS, Lolita Lorre *(Brenda Bohle)*, Corey Parker *(Josh Dealey)*, Tony Sibbald *(Bob Dealey)*, Rocco Sisto *(Lacey Bohle)*, Sandra Clark *(Janey)*, Antonio Cantafora as Michael Corby *(man at hotel)*, Burnell Tucker ← FLASH GORDON ← FINDERS KEEPERS ← DATELINE DIAMONDS

Storyline: 17-year-old Christie is convinced that her stepfather is trying to kill her wealthy mother. She dons the detective hat (and gets on her pushbike) to prove to her disbelieving mother and her sex-daft sister that he is also having an affair, while planning the deadly act of murder. Watch it at thanksgiving or Xmas and give this "turkey" a roasting. *MCS*

Movie rating: *1

Visual: video

Off the record: JOHN PAUL JONES (b. John Baldwin, 3 Jan'46, Sidcup, Kent, England. Raised by his music-performing/showbiz parents, John learned to play piano at an early age, subsequently taking up the bass to play with a band at boarding school. After a year stint with Jet Harris & Tony Meehan in 1963, he sessioned for the likes of LULU and the ROLLING STONES, however, his own solo single, 'Baja' (released April '64), failed to impress the buying public. It was while he was in the studio with DONOVAN in 1968, that he overheard guitarist JIMMY PAGE was looking for a bass player to join the New Yardbirds, who in turn became LED ZEPPELIN. The rest is indeed history . . . After the untimely death of their drummer, John Bonham in September 1980, all the remaining Led Zepp members went their own way, although John's long-standing friendship with JP and his association with filmmaker Michael Winner on the soundtrack to 'DEATH WISH II' (1982), saw the pair work together on 'SCREAM FOR HELP'. JPJ went on to become a top producer, working with the likes of the Mission, the Butthole Surfers and PETER GABRIEL, while putting out the odd sporadic solo set and a collaborative experiemental CD with Diamanda Galas. *MCS*

—

JOHN PAUL JONES

Mar 85. (lp/c) *Atlantic; <(7 80190-1/-4)>* ☐ ☐
– Spaghetti Junction / Bad child / Silver train / Crackback / Chilli sauce / Take it or leave it / Christie / When you fall in love / Here I am. *<cd-iss. Aug00 on 'WEA'; 2746>*

S/track review: There is no question when you see the sleeve (co-billed featuring JIMMY PAGE, JON ANDERSON, JOHN PAUL JONES), that its composer/performer JOHN PAUL JONES is definitely the former LED ZEPPELIN bassist turned multi-instrumentalist. Inside, it's a different matter. Two decent enough tracks come via the JONES/PAGE reunion: classy opener 'Spaghetti Junction' (sounding a little like Booker T & the MGs) and hard-rocker, 'Crackback', worthy of attention. The singing efforts of JPJ (sounding very KC & The Sunshine Band) were trial and error; the emphasis on the latter, while the unrecognisable Yes man JON ANDERSON finally broke his own falsetto vox, delivering 'Silver Train' and the goddamn awful 'Christie'. Of the other guest singers, only MADELINE BELL turns up trumps, while folk guitarist JOHN RENBOURN turns up for what essentially is a grisly Tangerine Dream-into-the-80s effort. 'SCREAM FOR HELP' – I'm still doing so! – is for LED ZEPPELIN completists only, and with the Japanese-only CD rising to $300 in places, this will also burn a hole in your pocket. *MCS*

Album rating: *4

☐ SEALS & CROFT segment
(⇒ ONE ON ONE)

the SECRET LIFE OF PLANTS

1979 (US 96m) Paramount Pictures (18)

Film genre: nature documentary

Top guns: dir: Walon Green / s-w: Michael Braun (au: Christopher Bird, Peter Tompkins)

Stars: Ashley Alexander as John Ashley Hamilton, + the plants!

Storyline: Lush documentary based on the famous book of the same name, positing that, yes, plants have feelings too, and that those feelings are finely tuned to both humans and animals, and their positive or negative intentions. *BG*

Movie rating: *5

Visual: none

Off the record: Walon Green was also screenwriter for feature films, 'SORCERER' and 'The BORDER'. *MCS*

—

STEVIE WONDER: Journey Through The Secret Life Of Plants

Nov 79. (d-lp/d-c) *Tamla Motown; <371> (TMSP/+TC-TMSP 6009)* [4] [8]
– Earth's creation / The first garden / Voyage to India / Same old story / Venus' flytrap and the bug / Ai no, sono / Seasons / Power flower / Send one your love (instrumental) / Race babbling / / Send one your love (vocal) / Outside my window / Black orchid / Ecclesiates / Kesse ye lolo de ye / Come back as a flower / A seed's a star – Tree (medley) / The secret life of plants / Tree / Finale. *<(d-cd-iss. 1986 & Sep95; 530106-2)>*

S/track review: Soundtracks composed by rock/pop stars are usually regarded, at best, as inessential diversions from the main event, at worst as pointless vanity projects. STEVIE WONDER not only made his a double, but (being about the only major soul artist not to have composed a blaxploitation score) filled it with experimental instrumentals inspired by a new-age book on the finer emotions of plants. It's the Stevie album everyone has heard of but few have actually sat though end to end, a flower-power anachronism even at the time of its release in 1979. Yet while the critics gave it a royal roasting, WONDER's strange creation refused to wilt, entwining its feathery roots with pop cultural lore and gradually assuming an outsider mystique fertilised by the intervening years. For all its bad press, the shockingly underrated ' . . .PLANTS' isn't quite as woolly or far removed from its predecessor, 'Songs In The Key Of Life' (1976), as received wisdom would have it. There's a definite continuum with regards to stylistic motifs like the minor-key, synthesised symphony of 'Ecclesiastes', and many of the vocal tracks could have nestled somewhere on 'Songs..'. 'Send One Your Love', 'Power Flower' and the title track – esoteric lyrics and Pink Floyd references aside – are ballads in his best 70s tradition, up there with 'Blame It On The Sun' and 'All In Love Is Fair'. 'Outside My Window' is a tree-hugging 'Isn't She Lovely', overlaid with a bizarre synth whistle rather than a gurgling baby, while the keening 'A Seed's A Star', is almost dancefloor strength (and surely qualifies as the only song ever to give vocodered voice to a tree and sample a cuckoo). He's way ahead of his time with the proto-electro of 'Race Babbling', and even anticipates the 70s old guard's 80s move into world music; successfully with kora piece, 'Kesse Ye Lolo De Ye', less so with the sub-continental noodling of 'Voyage To India' and the oriental pizzicato of 'Ai No, Sono'. Trippy counterparts to 'Sir Duke', the great 'Venus' Flytrap And The Bug' is another heavily modulated, 'A Bug's Life'-style spin on jazz heritage, while 'Seasons' is a loungey, gravity-free burlesque. WONDER's horti-musical journey will make more sense – at least in terms of the lyrics, which relate the plant-sensory ideas to STEVIE's time-honoured themes of peace, love and understanding – if you've read the book or at least seen the film. Some of it may be closer to Vangelis than R&B but, at a time when the reductionist tendencies of punk held sway, this remains a work of gloriously ridiculous ambition, and – taking WONDER's early 70s declaration of creative independence to its natural conclusion – about as far out from the original blueprint of motor city soul as any 'Motown' artist ever ventured. *BG*

Album rating: *7

– spinoff hits, etc. –

STEVIE WONDER: Send One Your Love / (instrumental)

Nov 79. (7") *<54303> (TMG 1146)* [4] [52]

STEVIE WONDER: Black Orchid

Jan 80. (7") *(TMG 1173)* [–] [63]

STEVIE WONDER: Outside My Window

Feb 80. (7") *<54308> (TMG 1179)* [52] Mar80 [52]

SERIES 7

full title 'SERIES 7: THE CONTENDERS'

2001 (US 86m) Blow Up Pictures / Killer Films / Open City Films (R)

Film genre: "reality TV" comedy thriller

Top guns: s-w: (+ dir) Daniel Minahan ← I SHOT ANDY WARHOL

Stars: Brooke Smith *(Dawn Lagarto)* → the NAMESAKE, Michael Kaycheck *(Tony Reilly)*, Glenn Fitzgerald *(Jeff Norman)*, Marylouise Burke *(Connie Trabucco)*, Richard Venture *(Franklin James)*, Merritt Wever *(Lindsay Berns)*, Nada Despotovich *(Michelle Reilly)* ← SMITHEREENS, Donna Hanover *(Sheila Berns)*, Jennifer Van Dyck *(Laura)*, Danton Stone *(Bob Berns)*

Storyline: The ultimate in reality TV is here as five new contenders battle series 6 winner Dawn in a game show where only the winner will escape death. Each contestant is given a gun but anything goes as the object of the game is to assassinate your rivals. For the winner fame and fortune, for the losers a TV death in front of billions. This time, Dawn is heavily pregnant and ex-boyfriend Jeff is one of her rival competitors. *JZ*

Movie rating: *6.5

Visual: dvd

Off the record: **GIRLS AGAINST BOYS** were formed in Washington DC, USA . . . 1988 out of Lunchmeat, then Soul Side (2/3 albums for 'Dischord' records) by Scott McCloud, Alexis Fleisig and Johnny Temple. Eli Janney, who'd been the latter act's soundman, joined as the band evolved into GIRLS AGAINST BOYS (future FUGAZI drummer Brendan Canty was also briefly involved, as was Amy Pickering). Their brand of hardcore industrial rock was first sampled on the 'Adult Swim' debut, 'Nineties Vs. Eighties' (1990), although it would be their second instalment a few years later, 'Tropic Of Scorpio', that tested the critical waters. Scott subsequently moved to New York to try out film school; the others subsequently followed suit as they signed a deal with 'Touch & Go'. Three albums garnering considerable European success were delivered during the mid 90s, 'Venus Luxure No.1 Baby' (1993), 'Cruise Yourself' (1994) and 'House Of GVSB' (1996), before their bass-heavy gutter sound was wanted by 'Geffen' records. In 1998, the 'Boys were on the threshold of mini-stardom with their sixth set, 'Freak*On*ICA', an album full of sexual sleaze and, of course, noise; their part-soundtrack to 'SERIES 7' (2001) was released at an awkward stage in their career. After their major label kerfuffel (which resulted in the band being dropped), GIRLS AGAINST BOYS delivered one of their finest albums to date (on the 'Jade Tree' imprint) in the form of 'You Can't Fight What You Can't See' (2002), a chugging thrash of a set for banging your head off the walls and shouting until your lungs capsized. *MCS*

—

GIRLS AGAINST BOYS (& Various Artists)

Apr 01. (cd) *Koch; <(KOCCD 8298)>* [ ] Jun01 [ ]
– It begins / One dose of truth / Let's get it on / Unlucky number / Creeping feeling / "I knew her . . ." / Whole world watching / Phone in / Tweaker / Love will tear us apart (JOY DIVISION) / Ray of hope / Sweetness of mine (JULIE STEPHANEK and ELI JANNEY) / The set-up / Turn it around / Death pact (ROBBIE KONDOR) / Wedding serenade (MENKING) / Dramatic re-creation / Nine lives / The contenders.

S/track review: When listening to 'SERIES 7', one cliched metaphor keeps springing to mind. An oasis in the desert. That is because in amongst the bland, horizon-less expanse of post-grunge noise, two songs offer welcome relief and quench the thirst of any weary listener. The first is the sheer Zeitgeist brilliance of JOY DIVISION's 'Love Will Tear Us Apart', while the second is the delicate ballad 'Sweetness Of Mine' by JULIE STEPHANEK and ELI JANNEY. The majority of the soundtrack is provided by GIRLS AGAINST BOYS, which to describe as uninspiring would be an understatement. The tracks are mostly score pieces made up of misplaced distortion and generic drum beats complete with sound clips that will either make you yawn or weep. They may fit the atmosphere of the film's scenes they represent, but as an independent listening experience it would be less painful to rub your ears with sandpaper. *CM*

Album rating: *4

SEX POWER

1970 (Fra/Gre 81m) Midem Productions (X)

Film genre: erotic/seXual comedy drama

Top guns: s-w + dir: Henry Chapier

Stars: Alain Noury *(boy)*, Juliette Villard *(girl in desert)*, Elga Anderson *(German girl)*, Jane Birkin *(mistress Jane)* ← WONDERWALL ← BLOW-UP / → MAY MORNING → CANNABIS → JE T'AIME MOI NON PLUS, Bernadette Lafont *(Cleopatra)* → DINGO

Storyline: A soft porn B-movie concerning the erotic and emotional journey of one young man as he drifts through an American landscape, both literal and imaginary. *SW*

Movie rating: *4

Visual: none (lost!)

Off the record: Aphrodite's Child (see below)

—

VANGELIS PAPATHANASSIOU

1970. (lp) *Philips; (6392 013)* [–] French [–]
– Introduction / Movement one / Movement two / Movement three / Movement four / Movement five / Movement six / Movement seven / Movement eight / Movement nine / Movement ten. *(cd-iss. 2000s on 'Platinum'+=; VPSP 803933)* – Poem Symphonique . . .

S/track review: For all intents and purposes, 'SEX POWER' is the 1970 debut solo album of VANGELIS PAPATHANASSIOU, still making waves, with singer Demis Roussos, in their band Aphrodite's Child. The film itself has been lost since its initial release (the director's other three films, two with unreleased scores by VANGELIS, share the same fate). The soundtrack is almost equally obscure, and for a long time it was almost impossible to find, the ultra rare vinyl something of a holy grail for VANGELIS fans, although bootlegged CDs now circulate. 'SEX POWER' originally consisted of two sides of vinyl, entitled '1ère partie' and '2ère partie', divided into eleven individual untitled tracks. (Two of these were released on a 7" single, usefully attributing track names; the A-side 'Djemilla' is track two of the first side of the album while B-side 'Third Love' is track five). The music itself is diverse and experimental, with the more obscure angles illuminated by light melodic pieces, giving the impression of a dream landscape perhaps better understood with reference to the long lost movie. Essentially one long sound collage, 'SEX POWER' mixes swirling piano melodies and matching vocal motifs with passages of industrial noise (particularly tracks eight and ten), interspersing them with sound effects (speeding motorcycles over plaintive guitar on track three) and choral interludes. Throughout, VANGELIS employs an intimidating range of styles and instrumentation (particularly percussion), and the experimental tone is perhaps that of a composer still searching for a distinctive voice. The piano and chimes of 'Djemilla' subtly prefigure his famous score for 'CHARIOTS OF FIRE', but only if 'CHARIOTS OF FIRE' was re-staged as a Bollywood orgy, otherwise 'SEX POWER' is merely a curio for fans only. *SW*

Album rating: *3.5

– spinoff releases, etc. –

VANGELIS PAPATHANASSIOU: Djemilla / Third Love
1970. (7") *Philips* [–] French [–]

SEXY BEAST

2000 (UK/Spa/US 88m) FilmFour / Record Picture Company (18)

Film genre: gangster/crime thriller

Top guns: dir: Jonathan Glazer / s-w: Louis Mellis, David Scinto

Stars: Ray Winstone *(Gary 'Gal' Dove)* ← LADIES AND GENTLEMEN, THE FABULOUS STAINS ← QUADROPHENIA / → COLD MOUNTAIN → the PROPOSITION → BREAKING AND ENTERING, Ben Kingsley *(Don Logan)*, Ian McShane *(Teddy Bass)* ← SOUL SURVIVOR, Amanda Redman *(DeeDee)*, Cavan Kendall *(Aitch)*, Julianne White (Jackie), James Fox *(Harry)*, Alvaro Monje *(Enrique)*

Storyline: Retired Cockney villain Gal was content living the high life with his missus in the Costa De Sol, until, that is, he receives a message from his old mucker, Don Logan. A psychopath in every sense of the word, Don insists in no uncertain terms that Gal is the only man for the job, a major robbery back in London. "Sometimes it's hard to say no". *MCS*

Movie rating: *7.5

Visual: dvd

Off the record: UNKLE / SOUTH (see below)

—

Various incl. UNKLE with SOUTH (*) (& ROQUE BANOS **)

Mar 01. (cd) *Edel; (0125782ERE) Beyond; <578198>* [ ] Jun01 [ ]
– Peaches (the STRANGLERS) / Lujon (HENRY MANCINI) / Cocaine and camcorders – original (*) / Logans run (*) / Psychosis (*) / Paranoid (*) / Suicide (*) / Daddy rollin' stone (DEAN MARTIN) // Gal & DeeDee (**) / Teddy the beast (**) / Party at the restaurant (**) / Sway (DEAN MARTIN).

S/track review: Released when UNKLE were still a fairly hip hyperlink between the dancefloor and the indie scene, 'SEXY BEAST' paired mainman James Lavelle with Mo' Wax-signed electro-organic trio SOUTH. Together they plough through much of the album's score, segued into one long, churning, half-hour segment. As befits his status as a guru of heavy-duty avant hip-hop, Lavelle can't resist more than a few dialogue samples loaded with the psycho-comic menace of Ben Kingsley. The man's barking, Francis Begbie-like logic fits the UNKLE dynamic like a straightjacket, manhandled by foot-thick, 'Phat Planet'-style basslines (Jonathan Glazer being the man behind the famous surfs-up Guinness ads) and filtered through 'Cocaine And Camcorders' and the wryly titled 'Logan's Run'. Kingsley's unhinged bald eagle also gets a monologue on 'Suicide', and while liberal borrowings on this scale might have sounded lazy, Logan's such a compellingly detestable character that they take a while to grow old. Spanish composer ROQUE BANOS is responsible for a couple of orchestral, classical guitar-dominated cues, sensibly laying off the dialogue save for a solitary choice quote from Logan and some less-than-effective pillow talk from Ray Winstone. He also supplies the big-band swing of 'Party At The Restaurant', an appetiser for DEAN MARTIN's ageless 'Sway', itself a predictable but effective closer. Shrewdly selected tracks from the STRANGLERS and HENRY MANCINI shore up the nothing-normal-under-the-sun mood. Beastly. *BG*

Album rating: *7.5

□ SHADES OF JOY segment (⇒ el TOPO)

SHAFT

1971 (US 100m) Metro-Goldwyn-Mayer (R)

Film genre: cop/detective thriller

Top guns: dir: Gordon Parks → SHAFT'S BIG SCORE! → LEADBELLY / s-w: Ernest Tidyman → SHAFT'S BIG SCORE!, John D.F. Black → TROUBLE MAN

Stars: Richard Roundtree *(John Shaft)* → SHAFT'S BIG SCORE! → SHAFT IN AFRICA, Moses Gunn *(Bumpy Jonas)* → SHAFT'S BIG SCORE! → CORNBREAD, EARL AND ME → AARON LOVES ANGELA, Charles Cioffi *(Lt. Victor Androzzi)*, Gwenn Mitchell *(Ellie Moore)* → BROTHER ON THE RUN, Christopher St. John *(Ben Buford)*, Camille Yarbrough *(Dina Greene)*, Lawrence Pressman *(Sgt. Tom Hannon)*, Ed Bernard *(Poerco)* → ACROSS 110th STREET → TOGETHER BROTHERS, Antonio Fargas *(Henry J. Jackson)* → ACROSS 110th STREET → CLEOPATRA JONES → FOXY BROWN → CORNBREAD, EARL AND ME → CAR WASH → FIRESTARTER → SOUL SURVIVOR, Tony King *(Davies)* → GORDON'S WAR → BUCKTOWN → HELL UP IN HARLEM → SPARKLE, **Adam Wade** *(brother #1)* → COME BACK, CHARLESTON BLUE → ACROSS 110th STREET → GORDON'S WAR → CLAUDINE → PHANTOM OF THE PARADISE, Ed Barth *(Tony)* → FAME, Arnold Johnson *(Cul)* → PIPE DREAMS → AMERICAN HOT WAX → the FIVE HEARTBEATS, Alan Weeks *(Gus)* → BLACK BELT JONES → TRUCK TURNER, Drew Bundini Brown *(Willy)* → SHAFT'S BIG SCORE! → AARON LOVES ANGELA

Storyline: Private detective John Shaft makes his screen debut and breaks the mould in this Blaxploitation blueprint, permanently altering Hollywood's portrayal of Afro-Americans. Mean, lean and explosively charismatic, Shaft is hired by Harlem big cheese Bumpy Jonas to rescue his kidnapped teenaged daughter. Jonas eventually reveals that it's the mob who are holding her and, amid the escalating threat of an all-out black versus white gangster feud, succeeds in getting Shaft to face down her kidnappers. *BG*

Movie rating: *8

Visual: video + dvd

Off the record: **Adam Wade** (b. Patrick Henry Wade, 17 Mar'35, Pittsburgh, Pennsylvania, USA) had another vocation in life as a lab assistant to Dr Jonas Salk, before he embarked on a singing career. In the early 60s, Wade had several smooth-and-silky hits for 'CoEd' records, including 'Ruby' (the film theme to 'Ruby Gentry'), 'Gloria's Theme' (from the feature, 'Butterfield 8'), 'Take Good Care Of Her', 'The Writing On The Wall' and 'As If I Didn't Know', the last three Top 10'ers. His subsequent work was an actor in the "blaxploitation" movies of the 70s, although he'll be best remembered as the first black TV talkshow host in 'Musical Chairs'. *MCS*

—

ISAAC HAYES

Aug 71. (d-lp) *Enterprise; <ENS 2-5002> Stax; (2659 007)* [1] Dec71 [17]
– Theme from "Shaft" / Bumpy's lament / Walk from Regio's / Ellie's love theme / Shaft's cab ride / Cafe Regio's / Early Sunday morning / Be yourself / A friend's place / Soulsville / No name bar / Bumpy's blues / Shaft strikes again / Do your thing / The end theme. *(re-iss. Oct89 on 'Stax'; SX2 021) <(cd-iss. Apr00; CDSXE 021)> (d-lp iss.Jun00 on 'Moving Image Entertainment'; MIE 002DLP)*

S/track review: With Melvin Van Peebles having lit the touch-paper, ISAAC HAYES' Oscar-winning title ignited the whole blaxploitation genre. 'Theme From Shaft' throbbed with raw sexuality and omniscient cool, clocking up an even cooler one million sales and blueprinting wah-wah funk chic. If the lyrics haven't aged so well, at least they're retrospectively amusing; a diverting missive from another world, when blowing your own macho trumpet was an art rather than a diatribe. The real paradox of this album lies in its relative lack of bite – HAYES might've fired off the ultimate blax theme but – in stark comparison with Van Peebles' anarchic cri de coeur – he meanders through much of the rest of the album without ever really breaking sweat. There's no jaw-clenching chase theme, no real soul-searching noir-jazz odyssey, but then this was charting new cine-soundtrack territory; much of the best was arguably yet to come, not least from Curtis Mayfield. In large part, he doles out the kind of smooth, orchestrated mood music with which he'd made his name at 'Stax', minus the songwriting muscle, monologues and revolutionary arrangements. Taken at face value, the likes of 'Ellie's Love Theme' and the loungey 'Café Reggio' are enjoyable enough while 'No Name Bar' flaunts a tougher, jazzier groove and the bluesy 'Soulsville' injects some much-needed grit, both lyrical and musical. The self-styled Black Moses only really comes close to the calibre of a 'Walk On By' or an 'Ike's Rap' when he allows both himself and the BAR-KAYS the space to stretch out on the epic 'Do Your Thing' (a full twenty, Funkadelic-influenced minutes' worth, although the re-mastered CD cuts it down to under five). Coming hot on the platform heels of their instrumental jam-fest, 'Gotta Groove' (1970), this was the sound of HAYES' sometime backing band at its gnarled, trippy zenith. *BG*

Album rating: *7

– spinoff hits, etc. –

ISAAC HAYES: Theme From "Shaft" / Cafe Regio's
Oct 71. (7") *<ENA 9038> (2025 069)* [1] Nov71 [4]

SHAFT IN AFRICA

1973 (US 112m) Metro-Goldwyn-Mayer (R)

Film genre: cop/detective/crime thriller

Top guns: dir: John Guillermin / s-w: Stirling Silliphant ← CHARLY

Stars: Richard Roundtree *(John Shaft)* ← SHAFT'S BIG SCORE! ← SHAFT, Frank Finlay *(slave dealer)* ← the BODY, Vonetta McGee *(Aleme)* ← BLACULA ← MELINDA / → BROTHERS → REPO MAN, Neda Arneric *(Jazar)*, Debebe Eshetu *(Wassa)*, Jacques Herlin *(Perreau)*, **James E. Myers** *(Det. Williams)* ← MRS. BROWN, YOU'VE GOT A LOVELY DAUGHTER, Spiros Focas *(Sassari)*, Frank McRae *(Oziot)* ← COOL BREEZE / → PIPE DREAMS, Thomas Baptiste *(Kopo)* → COUNTDOWN AT KUSINI → the MUSIC MACHINE

Storyline: Our man Shaft travels to deepest Ethiopia for the final instalment in the trilogy. Recruited to root out a gang of evil slave traders headed by Vincent Amafi, Shaft becomes embroiled in labyrinthine double crossing and intrigue, not to mention a hail of bullets from would-be assassins. *BG*

Movie rating: *6.5

Visual: video + dvd

Off the record: **James E. Myers** made his mark as Jimmy DeKnight when he co-wrote 'Rock Around The Clock' for Bill Haley & The Comets. *MCS*

—

JOHNNY PATE

Jul 73. (lp) *A.B.C.; <ABCX 793> Probe; (SPB 1077)* [ ] [ ]
– You can't even walk in the park / Are you man enough? – main title (FOUR TOPS) / Aleme finds Shaft / Shaft in Africa (Addis) / Headman / El jardia / Are you man enough? (FOUR TOPS) / Jazar's theme / Truck stop / Aleme's theme / El jardia (reprise) / Are you man enough? – end title (FOUR TOPS). *(re-iss. 1974 on 'A.B.C.'; ABCL 5035) (re-iss. Jun97 on 'Groove'; SHAFTLP 1) <cd-iss. 2004 'THE BEST OF SHAFT' on 'Hip-O'.*

S/track review: After the hastily assembled, home-grown soundtrack to 'SHAFT'S BIG SCORE' (1972), an outside contractor was once again brought in for Gordon Parks' rip-roaring finale. Was JOHNNY PATE man enough? The answer is a resounding Yo!; fresh from working on Blaxploitation's silky pièce de résistance, 'SUPERFLY' (1972), and armed with a CV stretching back to arranging engagements with the Impressions and an A&R stint at 'Verve', PATE masterfully rose to the challenge of taking the Funk back to Africa, concocting main theme arrangements heavy, heavy on the percussion, rooted with a killer drum loop, and broken down with conga and cowbell. As a cursory listen to the magnificent 'Ethiopiques' series (on French label, 'Buda Musique') will reveal, it sounds nothing like the funk actually coming out of Ethiopia at the time, but when it's this good, who cares. PATE gets even more tribal on 'Headman' and 'El Jardia', Cymande-style tropical mantras inlaid with shadowy woodwind and snake-charming brass, while his jazz credentials reveal themselves on mellow meditations 'Aleme's Theme' and 'Jazar's Theme'. But it's when the sub-Saharan motifs and PATE's big-band, Fender-powered funk tendencies clash head on – in the likes of irrepressible opener 'You Can't Even Walk In The Park' and 'Truck Stop' – that this soundtrack reaches malarial-strength fever pitch. And it's the FOUR TOPS who pump up the package to classic status with their gritty, last-gasp hit (played over the film's opening credits), just edging this record over the Isaac Hayes original. It's undoubtedly in the top flight of Blaxploitation albums, pretty much unique in its Afro-Funk references and not difficult to detect its continuing influence on the exalted likes of New York Afro-Beat curators the Daktaris amongst others. While it never was re-issued on CD, 'Hip-O' released the lion's share of the tracks on 'The Best Of Shaft', a package which – randomly, enough – also includes an obscure cover of the original 'SHAFT' theme by drum avatar (and 'LIALEH' composer), Bernard Purdie. *BG*

Album rating: *7.5

– spinoff hits, etc. –

the FOUR TOPS: Are You Man Enough?

Jun 73. (7") *<4354> (PRO 596)* [15] Jul73 [ ]

– other bits & pieces, etc. –

Various: The Best Of Shaft

Mar 99. (cd) *Hip-O; <(HIPD 4015-2)>* [ ] [ ]
– You can't even walk in the park (opening theme) / Theme from "Shaft" / Are you man enough? / Cafe Regio's / Ellie's love theme / Shaft in Africa (Addis) / Aleme finds Shaft / Headman / El jardia / Soulsville / Aleme's theme / Truck stop / Jazar's theme / Do your thing (long version) / Theme from "Shaft" (BERNARD BURDIE) / Are you man enough? (end credits version).

SHAFT'S BIG SCORE!

1972 (US 105m) Metro-Goldwyn-Mayer (R)

Film genre: cop/detective thriller

Top guns: dir: Gordon Parks ← SHAFT / → LEADBELLY / s-w: Ernest Tidyman ← SHAFT

Stars: Richard Roundtree *(John Shaft)* ← SHAFT / → SHAFT IN AFRICA, Moses Gunn *(Bumpy Jonas)* ← SHAFT / → CORNBREAD, EARL AND ME → AARON LOVES ANGELA, Joseph Mascolo *(Gus Mascola)* → the SPOOK WHO SAT BY THE DOOR, Drew Bundini Brown *(Willy)* ← SHAFT / → AARON LOVES ANGELA, Kathy Imrie *(Rita)*, Julius Harris *(Capt. Bollin)* → SUPERFLY → TROUBLE MAN → HELL UP IN HARLEM → BLACK CAESAR → FRIDAY FOSTER → LET'S DO IT AGAIN, Rosalind Miles *(Arna Ashby)* → FRIDAY FOSTER, Joe Santos *(Pascal)*, Wally Taylor *(Kelly)* ← COOL BREEZE ← COTTON COMES TO HARLEM / → CROSSROADS, Melvin Green Jr. *(Junior Gillis)*, Don Blakely *(Johnson)* → the SPOOK WHO SAT BY THE DOOR → SHORT EYES → PULP FICTION, Joyce Walker *(cigarette girl)* → WILLIE DYNAMITE → the EDUCATION OF SONNY CARSON, Evelyn Davis *(old lady)*

Storyline: Sequel to the blockbusting 'Shaft' with the supercool private detective attempting to investigate feuding Harlem gangsters after the police give him carte blanche to pinpoint the killers of local notable Carl Ashby. *BG*

Movie rating: *7.5

Visual: video + dvd

Off the record: (see below)

—

GORDON PARKS

Aug 72. (lp) *M.G.M.; <1SE 36ST> (2315 115)* [100] Oct72 [ ]
– Blowin' your mind (vocal: O.C. SMITH) / The other side / Smart money / First meeting / Asby-Kelly man / Don't misunderstand (vocal: O.C. SMITH) / Move on in (vocal: O.C. SMITH) / Symphony for Shafted Souls (the big chase): Take off – Dance of the cars – Water ballet (part I) – Water ballet (part II) – Call and response – The last amen.

S/track review: Despite the title claims to the contrary, this soundtrack was only going to obey the law of diminishing returns after Isaac Hayes scooped the Best Song Oscar for the theme to the first of the 'SHAFT' movies. Hayes may have headed off to become his own kind of Blaxploitation hero but director GORDON PARKS JR wasn't afraid to ramp up the amps for this Bond-like sequel. Employing the vocal stylings of O.C. SMITH and the trumpet talents of FREDDIE HUBBARD for his theme, 'Blowin' Your Mind' wasn't such a bad starting point. It may not have the tongue-in-cheek lyricism of Hayes' theme, but the song packs a punch in very much the same way; PARKS understands, like so many sequels, less is never, ever more and piles on the instruments to a furious climax. Indeed, there's little subtlety to PARKS' work but he was accompanying some pretty gaudy filmic set pieces, which doesn't stop this being an effective, emotive ride. This is no better illustrated than in the epic, 'Symphony For Shafted Souls', a mammoth instrumental suite that incorporates half a dozen pieces into a 13-minute trip. Nailing rapid fire beats into a web of wah-wah guitar and batteries of brutal minor brass stabs, it oozes grooves that have hip hop DJs everywhere foaming at their samplers. PARKS freely admits that the music for 'SHAFT'S BIG SCORE' was conceived, written and recorded in a little over two weeks. There are several clues that allude to this hurried process: the short running times, the formulaic structures and the almost identical employment of Hayes' original instrumentation – the rattle of the tambourine at exactly the same point in 'Blowin' Your Mind' as in 'Theme From Shaft' is almost endearing in its cheek. *MR*

Album rating: *6.5

Ravi SHANKAR

Born: Pandit Ravi Shankar, 7 Apr'20, Benares, India. Indian Classical maestro, so-called "Godfather Of World Music', and father to both Norah Jones and Anoushka Shankar (and uncle to legendary sitarist Ananda 'Dancing Drums' Shankar), RAVI SHANKAR is one of the most influential foreign musicians ever to make a mark on Western music, reserving his most ambitious and innovative fusions for the world of cinema. Mentored by Indian Classical pioneer Allaudin Khan, he began working in film and dance (a career which he forsook for the sitar) scoring in the mid-40s, composing the music for K.A. Abbas' politically charged debut, 'Dharti Ke Lal' (1946), as well as the Abbas-scripted 'Neecha Nagar' (1946). SHANKAR's most noted early work – perhaps the most highly regarded of his career – came on Satyajit Ray's seminal 'Pathar Panchali' (1955), a score recently making number four in an Observer Music Monthly 50 greatest soundtracks poll, with NITIN SAWHNEY revealing its significant influence on his own recent soundtrack for Mira Nair's 'The NAMESAKE' (2007). SHANKAR went on to net a best film-music award at the Berlin International Film Festival for his work on Tapan Sinha's 'Kabuliwala' (1956), and score the equally acclaimed 'Aparajito' (1957), following on from '. . .Panchali' as the second part of Ray's 'Apu Trilogy', itself completed with another SHANKAR-scored masterpiece, 'Apur Sansar' (1959). French-Canadian live action animated short, 'A Chairy Tale' (1957), was SHANKAR's first foreign commission, followed by James Ivory short, 'The Sword And The Flute' (1959). While continuing to work in Indian film, the early to mid 60s saw the sitarist expanding his horizons way beyond the Bombay music biz, regularly performing in the West and influencing a raft of first jazz and then rock musicians, most famously John Coltrane, Don Ellis and GEORGE HARRISON. 1996 brought a commission for Jonathan Miller's 'Alice In Wonderland' adaptation and, in his experimental, occasionally wild work on Conrad Rooks' autobiographical feature, 'CHAPPAQUA' (1966) – in which he also made a cameo – his first commercial soundtrack release. This was followed with an influential appearance at the 1967 'MONTEREY POP' festival, documented with the release of the D.A. Pennebaker-directed film the following year. 1968 also saw him scoring his first Hollywood feature in Ralph Nelson's Oscar-winning 'CHARLY', a sedate soundtrack compared to his heavily psychedelic work on 'VIOLA' – an obscure British film to which the soundtrack belatedly emerged in 1973 as 'Transmigration Macabre' – and his collaborations with HARRISON on 'WONDERWALL' (1969). In 1971, the same year he performed his groundbreaking 'Concerto For Sitar' with an Andre Previn-conducted London Symphony Orchestra, and featured as the subject of documentary, 'Raga', he teamed up with HARRISON in organising star-studded charity event, 'CONCERT FOR BANGLADESH', the 1972 soundtrack of which earned him a Grammy. Over the ensuing decade, SHANKAR returned to politicised Indian subject matter with Sampooran Singh Gulzar's 'Meera' (1979), Richard Attenborough's multi-Oscar winning biopic, 'Ghandi' (1982) and Mrinal Sen's desert fable, 'Genesis' (1986). While his soundtrack career subsequently tailed off, the sitar guru was the deserved subject of a 'South Bank Show' profile in 2001, and, following the death of his lifelong friend GEORGE HARRISON the same year, SHANKAR paid musical tribute in 2002 at the Royal Albert Hall memorial event, 'CONCERT FOR GEORGE', released on film in 2003. *BG*

- **filmography** (composer) {performer, etc.} –

Dharti Ke Lal *(1946)* / Neecha Nagar *(1946)* / Pather Panchali *(1955)* / Kabuliwala *(1956)* / en Djungelsaga *(1957)* / a Chairy Tale *(1957)* / Aparajito *(1958)* / Parash Pathar *(1958)* / the Sword And The Flute *(1959 w/ Ali Akbar Khan, Chatur Lal, T. Visvanathan & D.R. Parvatikar)* / Apur Sansar *(1959)* / Anuradha *(1960)* / Dheuer Pare Dheu *(1962)* / Go-Daan *(1963)* / the Psychedelics *(1966)* / **Chappaqua** *(1966 {a} OST =>)* / Alice In Wonderland *(1966 TV)* / **Viola** *(1967 OST in 1973 as 'Transmigration Macabre' =>)* / **Charly** *(1968 OST =>)* / **Monterey Pop** *(1968 {p} on OST by V/A =>)* / **Wonderwall** *(1969 on OST w/ GEORGE HARRISON =>)* / Sex And The Animals *(1969)* / Unterwegs Nach Kathmandu *(1971 TV {a} + score)* / Raga *(1971 {c})* / **the Concert For Bangladesh** *(1972 {p} on OST by GEORGE HARRISON & V/A =>)* / Meera *(1979 as PANDIT RAVISHANKAR)* / Gandhi *(1982 OST w/ George Fenton; see future edition)* / Genesis *(1986 OST; see future edition)* / Woodstock Diary *(1994 TV)* / Ravi Shankar: Between Two Worlds *(2001 {c} + score)* / the Song Of The Little Road *(2003 {c})* / **Concert For George** *(2003 {p} on OST by V/A =>)*

□ Ray SHANKLIN segment
(⇒ FRITZ THE CAT)

□ Elliott SHARP segment
(⇒ COMMUNE)

SHEBA, BABY

1975 (US 90m) American International Pictures (PG)

Film genre: cop/detective thriller

Top guns: s-w + dir: William Girdler (+ story w/ David Sheldon)

Stars: Pam Grier *(Sheba Shayne)* ← FRIDAY FOSTER ← FOXY BROWN ← COFFY ← COOL BREEZE ← BLACK MAMA, WHITE MAMA ← BEYOND THE VALLEY OF THE DOLLS / → BUCKTOWN → BILL & TED'S BOGUS JOURNEY → JACKIE BROWN → BONES, Austin Stoker *(Brick)*, D'Urville Martin *(pilot)* ← FIVE ON THE BLACK HAND SIDE ← the SOUL OF NIGGER CHARLEY ← BLACK CAESAR ← BOOK OF NUMBERS ← HELL UP IN HARLEM ← the FINAL COMEDOWN ← WATERMELON MAN ← a TIME TO SING / → DOLEMITE → DISCO 9000, Rudy Challenger *(Andy)* ← COOL BREEZE, Charles Kissinger *(Phil)*, Dick Merrifield *(Shark)*, Christopher Joy *(Walker)* ← CLEOPATRA JONES / → BIG TIME, Charles Broaddus *(Hammerhead)*

Storyline: The excellently monikered Sheba Shayne (trying saying that after a few babyshams) is a Chicago private eye who returns to her Southern home of Louisville, Kentucky, where local hoodlums are leaning on her father's loan business, and where she narrowly escapes death by car bomb. Out to teach whitey a lesson, Shayne ultimately locks horns with the gangster's main man, Pilot, donning a groovy little wetsuit number for some good, clean waterborne chase fun. *BG*

Movie rating: *4

Visual: video

Off the record: **MONK HIGGINS** (b. Milton Bland, 17 Oct'36, Menifee, Arkansas, USA) was the nearly-man of R&B having bubbled under the charts with sax instrumentals 'Who-Dun-It?' (in 1967) and 'Gotta Be Funky' (in 1972). A prolific hit songwriter for the likes of Bobby Bland, the Chi-Lites, etc., HIGGINS introduced his singing cousin Barbara Acklin to the pop world. In 1983, the man teamed up with blues guitarist Keb Mo to form Higgins' Whodunnit Band; sadly Monk died in L.A. on 3rd of July, 1986. *MCS*

—

MONK HIGGINS & ALEX BROWN

1975. (lp) *Buddah; <BDS 5634>* □ [–]
– B.B.D. / Three hoods / Sheba baby (feat. BARBARA MASON) / Get down Sheba / I'm in love with you (feat. BARBARA MASON) / Railroad / "Who the hell is that" / Heavyshot / A good man is gone (feat. BARBARA MASON) / Number one man / Sheba / The shark / Breast stroke / Speedboat / Good bye / She did it (feat. BARBARA MASON).

S/track review: This late-period Pam Grier vehicle came with a soundtrack by veteran writer/producer/arranger/multi-sampled saxophonist MONK HIGGINS. 'Buddah' kept it at least partly in-house with BARBARA MASON, the 60s soulsation who'd pitched up at the company after her old label, 'National General', had gone bust. She'd already made her blaxploitation debut on the 'GORDON'S WAR' soundtrack, and she frames Grier perfectly on a sultry, Randy Crawford-esque main theme that aligns itself with the first days of disco. To her credit, MASON actually took a late 70s career sabbatical rather than kowtow to the genre's more humiliating demands, and she sounds more at ease with the heavy soul of 'A Good Man Is Gone'. HIGGINS himself thrives on bass-trawling, disco-funk monsters like "Who In The Hell Is That?", experimenting with Bernie Worrell-style modulation on the freak-funky 'Speedboat' and another street-tough MASON vocal, 'She Did It'. The peachy 'Number One Man' chews the fat with Jimmy Cliff, Sly Stone and George Clinton at a New Orleans speakeasy, served by a sweet trombone solo by GEORGE BOHANAN, better known for his work with Diana Krall associates John Clayton and Jeff Hamilton. Ultimately, 'SHEBA, BABY' answers to the same eclectic jazz impulse as an Isaac Hayes soundtrack, especially on Side Two where the large cast of session players settle into a series of swinging, self-contained instrumentals. *BG*

Album rating: *7

SHE'S THE ONE

1996 (US 96m) Twentieth Century-Fox (R)

Film genre: romantic/urban comedy

Top guns: s-w + dir: Edward Burns

Stars: Jennifer Aniston *(Renee Fitzpatrick)* → ROCK STAR, Maxine Bahns *(Hope Fitzpatrick)*, Edward Burns *(Mickey Fitzpatrick)*, Cameron Diaz *(Heather Davis)* → FEAR AND LOATHING IN LAS VEGAS → the INVISIBLE CIRCUS, Mike McGlone *(Francis Fitzpatrick)*, John Mahoney *(Mr. Fitzpatrick)* ← REALITY BITES, Leslie Mann *(Connie)* → LAST MAN STANDING → KNOCKED UP, Malachy McCourt *(Tom)*, Amanda Peet *(Molly)*, Frank Vincent *(Ron; Renee's father)* ← JUNGLE FEVER, Beatrice Winde *(older woman)* → SPARKLE

Storyline: Mickey and Francis are the "Fighting Fitzpatricks", a pair of Irish-American brothers whose lifestyles are completely different. Mickey is a happy-go-lucky cab driver who enjoys the ultimate whirlwind romance with passenger Hope, while stockbroker Francis appears to be happily married to Renee and settled down. However, when it turns out that Francis is having an affair with Mickey's ex, Heather, complications begin and family loyalties are strained. *JZ*

Movie rating: *6

Visual: video + dvd

Off the record: TOM PETTY & THE HEARTBREAKERS formed in the mid-70s, almost immediately making an impact with songs such as 'American Girl', 'Anything That's Rock'n'Roll' and 'Breakdown', all taken from their eponymous 1977 LP. Platinum-selling albums such as 'You're Gonna Get It!' (1978), 'Damn The Torpedos' (1979), 'Hard Promises' (1981), 'Long After Dark' (1982) and 'Southern Accents' (1985), all proved worthy alongside competitors such as SPRINGSTEEN, DYLAN, YOUNG, etc. Sidelining a solo career (albums, 'Full Moon Fever' – 1989 & 'Wildflowers' – 1994) alongside time spent with the Traveling Wilburys, PETTY was never out of the limelight. Having never forgotten his band roots, he re-grouped the Heartbreakers for 'Into The Great Wide Open' (1991) and this soundtrack, the band were now Benmont Tench (keyboards), Mike Campbell (guitar), Howie Epstein (bass) and newcomer Steve Ferrone (drums). TOM PETTY was indeed the last Traveling Wilbury to compose the score for a movie. The other four older Wilburys had debuted much earlier: – Roy Orbison 'The FASTEST GUITAR ALIVE' (1968), George Harrison 'WONDERWALL' (1968), Bob Dylan 'PAT GARRETT & BILLY THE KID' (1973) and Jeff Lynne/ELO with half of 'JOYRIDE' (1977), before subsequently tackling other movie projects. One supposes it was about time PETTY (with the re-formed HEARTBREAKERS, of course) tried their hand at film composition, the blond from Gainesville, Florida having earlier appeared in movies such as concert-film 'FM' (1978), 'Made In Heaven' (1987) and about to star in 'The Postman' (1997). Incidentally, actor/novelist Michael McGlone released a critically acclaimed folk album, 'Hero', in 1999. *MCS*

TOM PETTY & THE HEARTBREAKERS

Aug 96. (cd/c) *Warners; <(9362 46285-2/-4)>* [15] [37]
– Walls (circus) / Grew up fast / Zero from outer space / Climb that hill / Change the locks / Angel dream (No.4) / Hope you never / Asshole / Supernatural radio / California / Hope on board / Walls (No.3) / Angel dream (No.2) / Hung up and overdue / Airport.

S/track review: 'SHE'S THE ONE', commendable as it was, saw a relaxed PETTY get back to the bare bones, Americana roots he once tracked. All the aforementioned Traveling Wilbury connections are here in PETTY's heart rather than in his soul. 'Walls (Circus)' is Dylan personified, although you can hear the background vox of Lindsey Buckingham alongside the ghosts of Roger McGuinn's Rickenbacker and Robert Palmer's 'Some Guys Have All The Luck'. Slow-burner – like life itself I suppose – 'Grew Up Fast' gets rid of the melancholic ruminations to become an out-and-out rock ballad. 'Zero From Outer Space' takes PETTY on to another level – he swears! – while the song – great as it is – is like a pastiche of many Rolling Stones songs with '19th Nervous Breakdown' and 'It's Only Rock'n'Roll' the ones that come to mind. PETTY once again takes the Dylan mantle but this time he metamorphoses into 'Cinnamon Girl'-period Neil Young using the brilliant HEARTBREAKERS as some sort of Crazy Horse backing. Ditto track 5, for the Lucinda Williams-penned 'Change The Locks', PETTY has a fun time with a post-'Weld'-ish grunge. Again, brilliant! The aforementioned alt-country girl from Lake Charles, Louisiana, lets PETTY and Co loose with a further song 'Asshole' (which subtlely rhymes "carrots" with "embarrassed"), a sort of post-'Strawberry Fields . . .' and a precursor to perhaps the weirdest of alt-rock's staples, the Handsome Family. No, really. Back to track 6, 'Angel Dream (No.4)', sees PETTY get all spiritual, in a way of Springsteen, Dylan or even Johnny Cash. Romantic love(lorn) songs come via, 'Hope You Never' and 'Supernatural Radio', are also effective, while the brighter, uptempo 'California' shines like its lyrics: "California's been good to me, Hope it doesn't fall into the sea"; oh! and there's a Dylan-like mouth-harp to get you all nostalgic. 'Hope On Board' is a short'n'bitter-sweet score instrumental that was the most cinematic of the set, and this preceded two further reprises of 'Walls (No.3)' and 'Angel Dream (No.2)'. You can 'Imagine' John Lennon for track No.14 (not No.9!), 'Hung Up And Overdue', while PETTY sadly ends the show with lounge-jazz ditty, 'Airport'. All'n'all, the album for me is as PETTY once sang, "Anything that's rock'n'roll's fine". *MCS*

Album rating: *6.5

– spinoff releases, etc. –

TOM PETTY & THE HEARTBREAKERS: Walls (circus) / Walls (No.3)

Sep 96. (c-s,cd-s) *<17593>* [–] [69]

TOM PETTY & THE HEARTBREAKERS: Walls (circus) / Hung Up And Overdue

Mar 97. (c-s) *(W 0371C)* [ ] [–]
(cd-s+=) *(W 0371CD)* – Walls (No.3).

SHOCK

alt. title 'SCHOCK'

1977 (Ita 90m) Tiranus (18)

Film genre: occult horror/thriller

Top guns: dir: Mario Bava / s-w: (+ story) Francesco Barbieri, Lamberto Bava, Dardano Sacchetti, Paolo Brigenti

Stars: Daria Nicolodi *(Dora Baldini)* ← PROFONDO ROSSO / → INFERNO → TENEBRE → PHENOMENA, John Steiner *(Bruno Baldini)* ← MAY MORNING, David Colin Jr. *(Marco)*, Ivan Rassimov *(Carlos)*

Storyline: After a long session with the psychiatrists, Dora and her new husband Bruno move back into her old house with her son Marco. But the house seems to contain someone else – the vengeful ghost of Dora's first husband Carlo. Soon the bangings and rattlings begin and young Marco starts behaving very oddly – as if he were Carlo come back to life. But how much of all this is real and how much is down to delusional Dora? *JZ*

Movie rating: *5

Visual: dvd

Off the record: LIBRA (see below)

—

LIBRA: Schock

Oct 77. (lp) *Cinevox; (MDF 113)* [–] Italy [–]
– The shock / L'Altalena rossa / (a) Transfert I, (b) Hypnos, (c) Transfert II / La baia / (a) La cantina, (b) The shock (ripresa), (c) Tema Di Marco I, (d) Tema Di Marco II / L'Incubo / Transfert III / Il fantasma suona il piano / (a) Transfert IV, (b) Tema Di Marco II (ripresa). *(cd-iss. 2001 += alt. movie versions; MDF 350)* – Il fantasma suona il piano (piano solo) / The shock / Tema Di Marco / Transfert IV.

S/track review: When you first hear this 'SHOCK'-horror OST by LIBRA, comparisons to Italian soundtrack/Prog-meisters Goblin crop up. The fact that drummer WALTER MARTINO was a Goblin original, and ex-Flea guitarist CARLO PENNISI and keyboard-player MAURIZIO GUARINI were subsequent members of said outfit, just might've had a hand in their similar sound. Formed in Rome, 1974, LIBRA released a debut LP ('Musica E Parole') for 'Ricordi', although at this stage none of the Goblin acolytes were present. Mainly a jazz-rock quintet with hints of PFM and funk, they surprisingly signed a deal with 'Motown' records in the States, who revised and re-released the set as 'Libra'. A second US-only LP ('Winter Days Nightmare' 1976) introduced MARTINO, although its failure to find a commercial niche resulted in the band returning to Italy. With a line-up of the aforementioned MARTINO, PENNISI and GUARINI, alongside originals SANDRO CENTOFANTI (keyboards) and DINO CAPPA (bass), LIBRA were commissioned to compose the score for 'SHOCK' (originally misspelt, 'Schock'). That unmistakable Goblin soundtrack sound was apparent from opening title, 'The Shock' (incidentally written by MARTINO), its frightening funk and kinky keyboards almost wicked to the extreme. In stark contrast, 'L'Altalena Rossa' (the first of several penned by MARTINO and CENTOFANTI) was a soft-pastel acoustic cue – ditto CENTOFANTI's contribution, 'La Baia'. The percussive noise experimentation on 'Transfert I – Hypnos – Transfert II', may have been a tad OTT, but the outlay was similar in shape to Italian Prog counterparts, PFM. Most of the pieces on board 'SHOCK' are indeed quite brief (the original LP itself only adds up to around half an hour), while a handful of cues are clumped together in segue-like fashion, making the record uneasy listening at times. Uncompromising and eerie – just like a good horror suspense flick should be – the excerpts 'Tema Di Marco I & II' are arguably the best pieces on show. The brooding 'L'Incubo' comes a close second, although it recalls the 'Atem' days of Tangerine Dream or even Krzysztof Komeda (composer of 'Rosemary's Baby'). The short-lived LIBRA (or . . . I LIBRA, in some circles) were much too complex a group for their own good. When simplicity was needed, oblique guitar vs bass vs keys vs drums seem to collide or get in the way of each other. One can only guess if the music matches the film visuals as one has not viewed the movie more than once. The CD version does add some alt. takes but the set as a whole leaves a somewhat bad and blood-soaked taste in one's mouth. *MCS*

Album rating: *4

SHORT EYES

1977 (US 104m) Film League (R)

Film genre: prison drama

Top guns: dir: Robert M. Young → ONE-TRICK PONY / s-w: Miguel Pinero (+ au)

Stars: Bruce Davison *(Clark Davis)* ← the STRAWBERRY STATEMENT / → DEADMAN'S CURVE → CRIMES OF PASSION → an AMBUSH OF GHOSTS → GRACE OF MY HEART, Jose Perez *(Juan)*, Nathan George *(Ice)*, Don Blakely *(El Raheem)* ← the SPOOK WHO SAT BY THE DOOR ← SHAFT'S BIG SCORE! / → PULP FICTION, Tony Di Benedetto *(Tony)*, **Shawn Elliott** *(Paco)* → BEAT STREET, Tito Goya *(Cupcakes)*, Miguel Pinero *(Go-Go)*, **Curtis MAYFIELD** *(Pappy)*, Luiz Guzman → BOOGIE NIGHTS → MAGNOLIA, Mark Margolis *(Mr. Morrison)* → WHERE THE RIVERS FLOW NORTH → I SHOT ANDY WARHOL, **Freddy Fender** *(himself)*, Yusef Bulos *(inmate)* → WHERE THE RIVERS FLOW NORTH

Storyline: Clark Davis is a child molester on the receiving end of his fellow inmates' wrath in this graphically brutal prison drama with a supporting cast of genuine hardcore cons. *BG*

Movie rating: *6.5

Visual: video + dvd

Off the record: Puerto Rican actor **Shawn Elliott** showed up on a handful of Broadway-style releases from 1962; he was the voice of Madeleine in the film, 'JACQUES BREL IS ALIVE AND WELL AND LIVING IN LONDON' (1975). **Freddy Fender** (b. Baldemar Garza Huerta, 4 Jun'37, San Benito, Texas, USA) was 37 years of age when he finally crossed-over into mainstream pop via chart-topper, 'Before The Next Teardrop Falls'. Country music had a new ambassador in 1975/6 when he followed the No.1 with further Top 50 hits, 'Wasted Days And Wasted Nights', 'Secret Love', 'Since I Met You Baby' & 'You'll Lose A Good Thing'. With an acting career ('The Milangro Beanfield War' in 1988) and a time spent with the Texas Tornados behind him, Fender retired out of the spotlight. With ill-health through lung cancer dogging him at the turn of the new millennium, Fender passed away on the 14th October, 2006. *MCS*

—

CURTIS MAYFIELD

Nov 77. (lp) *Curtom; <CU 5017> Warners; (K 56430)* [ ] Feb78 [ ]
– Do do wap is strong in here / Back against the wall / Need someone to love / A heavy dude / Short eyes / Freak, freak, free, free, free (*) / Break it down / Another fool in love / Father confessor. *(cd-iss. Jun96 on 'Charly'+= *; CPCD 8183)*

S/track review: After delivering the Blaxploitation bomb with 'SUPERFLY' (1972), CURTIS MAYFIELD became a regular dabbler in the world of film soundtracks. None of his subsequent projects achieved anything near the same success although all held their own against his regular studio sets, especially 'SHORT EYES', still one of his most obscure but also one of his heaviest and funkiest. Coming as it did in 1977, it marked something of a last hurrah for what, after all, had been an incredible two decades at soul's sharp end. 'Do Do Wap Is Strong In Here' (a US Top 30 R&B hit) remains one of the most striking openings to any MAYFIELD album and, in the grand tradition of both the man's caustic 70s commentary and the much older tradition of the prison ballad, it's about as close to the bone as anything he's written. On verse after devastating verse, that inimitable falsetto radiates a terrible beauty, telling it like Pappy sees it ("Ain't no heaven, ain't no heaven, this devil level") against a malevolent funk grind, delivering his revelations like an avenging angel. On 'Back Against The Wall', his tone isn't so much apocalyptic as despondent, lamenting the grim plight of a lifer, spiralling downwards into a slough of frenzied guitar soloing. 'Short Eyes / Freak, Freak, Free, Free, Free', meanwhile, warns of the protagonist's predatory threat and unflinchingly portrays his equally grim fate before morphing into a percussive instrumental coda. It's heavy stuff, and save for lighter moments like 'Another Fool In Love' or the falsetto slap-funk-n-tickle of 'A Heavy Dude' (prefiguring Prince, with MAYFIELD literally stretching his voice to breaking point), it pretty much stays that way till the end, signing off with the neo-Celtic folk influences and tortured guitar of 'Father Confessor'. *BG*

Album rating: *6.5

– spinoff releases, etc. –

CURTIS MAYFIELD: Do Do Wap Is Strong In Here / Need Someone To Love

Nov 77. (7") *<0131>* ☐ ⊟

a SHOT AT GLORY

2001 (US/UK 115m) Paramount / United International Pictures (15)

Film genre: sports drama

Top guns: dir: Michael Corrente / s-w: Denis O'Neill

Stars: Robert Duvall *(Gordon McLeod)* ← GERONIMO: AN AMERICAN LEGEND ← TENDER MERCIES, Michael Keaton *(Peter Cameron)* ← JACKIE BROWN ← BATMAN, Ally McCoist *(Jackie McQuillan)*, Brian Cox *(Martin Smith)*, Kirsty Mitchell *(Kate McQuillan)* ← the ACID HOUSE, Cole Hauser *(Kelsey O'Brian)* ← GOOD WILL HUNTING, Morag Hood *(Irene)*, Scott G. Anderson *(Alex)*, Libby Langdon *(Annie)*

Storyline: Second Division football club Kilnockie are told that it's make or break time by American owner Peter Cameron. Against the wishes of hard-bitten manager Gordon McLeod, ex-first division star Jackie McQuillan is signed to help the team win the cup. The fact that McQuillan's harum-scarum lifestyle ruined his career and his marriage to McLeod's daughter explains the manager's attitude, but as Kilnockie battle to a place in the final against Glasgow Rangers it's up to McQuillan to show what he can do to make amends. *JZ*

Movie rating: *6

Visual: dvd

Off the record: Ally McCoist (or "Coisty" to his fans) was an ex-Glasgow Rangers soccer star now working on TV's 'A Question Of Sport' and 'The Premiership'. In 1990, he sang with the Scotland World Cup Squad on mini-hit, 'Say It With Pride'. Other footballers in the film included Owen Coyle, Ally Maxwell, Claudio Reyna, Didier Agathe, John McVeigh, Andy Smith, Peter Heatherston plus Glasgow Celtic and Swedish idol, Henrik Larsson. *MCS*

—

MARK KNOPFLER

Oct 01. (cd) *Mercury; (548127-2) Warners; <48324>* ☐ Apr02 ☐
– Sons of Scotland / Hard cases / He's the man / Training / The new laird / Say too much / Four in a row / All that I have in the world / Sons of Scotland – quiet theme / It's over / Wild mountain thyme.

S/track review: MARK KNOPFLER's soundtracks can pretty much be divided into two camps: those which take conventional orchestral scoring as their reference point- 'LAST EXIT TO BROOKLYN', 'The PRINCESS BRIDE' – and those, the majority, which follow the man's penchant for bluesy acoustics and keenly felt Celtic folk. 'A SHOT AT GLORY' falls squarely into the latter category and is in fact, possibly his most accomplished attempt at combining the various roots styles he's pursued since leaving Dire Straits. That steely, signature guitar sound is never far away of course, and fans of his rockier days have at least one track, 'He's The Man', with which they can reminisce. Given the film's Scottish setting, it's no surprise that most of the other arrangements feature bhodran, whistle, bagpipes, accordion and fiddle, employed fairly traditionally for the most part, although KNOPFLER falls in with Scotland's thriving nu-folk scene by welding a strapping tempo and some peaty acid squelch onto 'Four In A Row'. The score works best, however, when he marries the gentler side of his guitar playing with subtle indigenous instrumentation, as on 'All That I Have In The World', and when he falls back into that deliciously reflective mode which made 'LOCAL HERO' so memorable and which so effortlessly carries the main theme here. *BG*

Album rating: *6

SHUDDER TO THINK

Formed: Washington, DC, USA . . . late 1986 by Stuart Hill, Chris Matthews, Mike Russell and CRAIG WEDREN. Hardly a typical 'Dischord' act, SHUDDER TO THINK began their career with a privately circulated demo, 'Curse, Spells, Voodoo, Mooses', in '89. The lads signed to FUGAZI/Ian MacKaye's operation and released 'Ten-Spot' as their debut album proper at the turn of the decade. Eschewing a straightforward hardcore sound for a more complex, awkwardly melodic approach, the quartet attracted a cult following with albums such as 'Funeral At The Movies' (1991) and 'Get Your Goat' (1992). Personnel ructions resulted in Matthews and Russell departing, being replaced by NATHAN LARSON and Adam Wade respectively, although things took a turn for the better as 'Epic' saw potential in the band's diverse musical talents. While 'Pony Express Record' (1994) might've made few concessions to their new major label status, the long-awaited '50,000 B.C.' was a far more immediate affair, putting an alternative twist on everything from rootsy rock to harmony-flowing power-pop/rock. A year on, SHUDDER TO THINK made a radical move into soundtrack work, no doubt alienating part of their loyal fanbase with the retro-pastiche of 'FIRST LOVE, LAST RITES' (1997) and the atmospheric score to 'HIGH ART' (1998). With LARSON bailing out for further soundtrack commissions and WEDREN opting for a solo/soundtrack career, SHUDDER TO THINK folded. Nathan relocated to Malmo, Sweden with girlfriend Nina Persson of the Cardigans (they duetted on a version of White Stripes' 'Dead Leaves And Dirty Ground' in the film 'God Willing'). *MCS*

- **filmography** (composers) –

First Love, Last Rites *(1997 OST =>)* / **High Art** *(1998 OST =>)* / Boys Don't Cry *(1999 OST by LARSON w/ V/A; see future editions)* / Tigerland *(2000 by LARSON)* / Wet Hot American Summer *(2001 by WEDREN w/ Theodore Shapiro)* / Prozac Nation *(2001 by LARSON)* / **Storytelling** *(2002 by LARSON; OST by BELLE & SEBASTIAN =>)* / the Chateau *(2002 by LARSON)* / Roger Dodger *(2002 by WEDREN)* / Dirty Pretty Things *(2002 OST by LARSON; see future editions)* / **Laurel Canyon** *(2003 score by WEDREN / OST by V/A =>)* / Lilja 4-ever *(2003 by LARSON)* / the Deal *(2003 by LARSON)* / **School Of Rock** *(2003 score by WEDREN / OST by V/A =>)* / the Woodsman *(2004 by LARSON)* / the Ranch *(2004 by LARSON)* / P.S. *(2004 OST by WEDREN w/ V/A see; future editions =>)* / a Love Song For Bobby Long *(2004 OST by LARSON w/ V/A; see future editions =>)* / Boxers And Ballerinas *(2004 by WEDREN)* / Palindromes *(2005 by LARSON)* / the Motel *(2005 by LARSON)* / the Baxter *(2005 OST by WEDREN, Theodore Shapiro & V/A see; future editions)* / Little Fish *(2005 by LARSON)* / God Willing *(2006 by LARSON)* / Beautiful Ohio *(2006 by WEDREN)* / Reno 911!: Miami *(2007 by WEDREN)* / Very Young Girls *(2007 by LARSON)*

– compilations, etc. –

NATHAN LARSON: Filmmusik

Sep 04. (cd) *Koch; <KOC-CD 5757>* ☐ ⊟
– Prozac ("Prozac Nation") / Boys ("Boys Don't Cry") / Operator ("Phone Booth") / Tigerland ("Tigerland") / You can take what's left of me ("Prozac Nation") / Night basketball ("Lilja 4-ever") / Fiction ("Storytelling") / A softer night ("Boys Don't Cry") / I want someone badly (bonus track) / The fawn ("Prozac Nation") / Small town jail ("Boys Don't Cry") / Mommy, are angels dead? ("Lilja 4-ever") / She might be waking up ("High Art") / Le pont de la tristesse ("The Chateau") / Mom's Mercedes ("High Art") / Balcony ("Prozac Nation") / Dirty pretty things ("Dirty Pretty Things") / Departure lounge ("Dirty Pretty Things") / Last lines ("High Art") / Walter ("The Woodsman") / Something like love ("Prozac Nation") / Rape and a burning polaroid ("Boys Don't Cry").

the SHVITZ

1993 (US 46m b&w) Five Points Media

Film genre: people documentary

Top guns: dir: Jonathan Berman → COMMUNE

Stars: Frank London & the Klezmatics *(performers)*, **Elliott Sharp** *(performer)*, **Marc Ribot** *(performer)*, **Jim Leff** *(performer)*, **Sebastian Steinberg** *(performer)*, **David Licht** *(performer)*, **Lorin Sklamberg** *(performer)*, **Alicia Svigals** *(performer)*, **Robert Musso** *(performer)*, **Greg Wall** *(performer)*, **Matt Darriau** *(performer)*, **Christopher Cauley** *(performer)*

Storyline: A look at a Jewish community in New York brought together in the unlikely meeting place of a traditional steam bath (shvitz). Artists and artisans sit in the sweltering heat and discuss their life and work, and what it means to be a Jew trying to balance old faiths and traditions with modern city life. *JZ*

Movie rating: *8

Visual: video + dvd

Off the record: Trumpeter **FRANK LONDON** had worked with the cream of the avant-garde crop (John Zorn, Gal Costa, DAVID BYRNE, They Might Be Giants, etc.) since the mid-80s, before he released 'The SHVITZ' and several subsequent albums in the 90s. *MCS*

—

FRANK LONDON: music from the movie The Shvitz

Apr 95. (cd) *Knitting Factory; <KNFCD 144>* ☐ [–]
– Bucket cue / Freaky guitar freylekhs / (How to) Sweat – part 1 / Emma Goldman's wedding: a) Desire, b) Dance to it / Now to the shvitz / V'erastikh li (Divine betrothal) (poem by Celia Dropken) / Take one / Full moon, ancient waters / Psycho-klezmer (from the repertoire of Naftulie Brandwein) / Kolomeyke / Coney Island heyday / V'erastikh li (Divine betrothal) – instrumental / Der neier freylekhs / Vus vet zayn (what will it be like when the Moshiach comes?) / Have another / It's hot in here! / (How to) Sweat – parts 1 & 2 – dance mix.

S/track review: Klezmer is a centuries old music form that originated in the Jewish tradition and is characterised by its expressive melodies intended to mirror the human voice. The soundtrack to 'The SHVITZ' is entirely based on this kind of music and led by FRANK LONDON, a trumpeter, bandleader and composer who has worked with several big name artists including John Cale, LL Cool J and Ben Folds Five, as well as beat poet Allen Ginsberg. LONDON is one of the world's foremost purveyors of this intriguing style of music with his New York-based band the KLEZMATICS. Obviously, the music has a very Middle Eastern feel and has many characteristics associated with religious music from that part of the world. Most of the music here is upbeat and LONDON has experimented by mixing various types of more mainstream music with the traditional klezmer sound. On '(How To) Sweat' he introduces turntables and drum loops to the sound with what can only be described as a rap over the top of it and 'V'erastikh Li (Divine Betrothal)' sounds like the Specials trying their hand at jazz, while 'Coney Island Heyday' mixes klezmer with big band swing jazz. Indeed, jazz seems to mingle effortlessly with klezmer on several of the tracks here to create some compelling sounds and emotions. As music to accompany a film, klezmer works extremely well due to its vibrancy and versatility, which is showcased here from the sinister forebodings of 'Psycho-Klezmer' and disorientating 'Take One' to the intimate 'Full Moon, Ancient Waters' and celebratory dance of 'Emma Goldman's Wedding'. Mysterious, intriguing and beautifully melodic, 'The SHVITZ' is one of those albums that comes along every once in a blue moon and reveals a fascinating music form that you have never heard before, inspiring you to explore it and reminding you that, when it comes to music, there are no boundaries. *CM*

Album rating: *8.5

SHY PEOPLE

1987 (US 120m) Cannon Group / Golan-Globus Productions (13)

Film genre: domestic melodrama

Top guns: s-w: Andrei Konchalovsky (+ dir), Gerard Brach ← la FEMME DE MON POTE ← WONDERWALL, Marjorie David

Stars: Jill Clayburgh *(Diana Sullivan)*, Barbara Hershey *(Ruth Sullivan)* → the LAST TEMPTATION OF CHRIST → BEACHES → LANTANA, Martha Plimpton *(Grace Sullivan)* → I SHOT ANDY WARHOL → COLIN FITZ LIVES!, Merritt Butrick *(Mike Sullivan)*, John Philbin *(Tommy Sullivan)* ← the RETURN OF THE LIVING DEAD / → GIRL, Don Swayze *(Mark Sullivan)*, Pruitt Taylor Vince *(Paul Sullivan)* → WILD AT HEART → NATURAL BORN KILLERS → HEAVY → the END OF VIOLENCE → MONSTER, Mare Winningham *(Candy)* ← ONE-TRICK PONY / → MIRACLE MILE → GEORGIA

Storyline: The perils of family environs are all too obvious here as middle-class journalist and mother, Diana, whisks her teenage junkie daughter and herself to start a new life – with a long-lost uncle and his "Deliverance-type" kin – in the bayous of Louisiana. *MCS*

Movie rating: *5.5

Visual: video

Off the record: (see below)

—

TANGERINE DREAM (additional score: Michael Bishop)

Nov 87. (lp/c/cd) *Varese; <VCD 47357> Silva Screen; (FILM/+C/ CD 027)* ☐ Jul88 ☐
– Shy people (vocals: JACQUIE VIRGIL) / Joe's place / The harbor (vocals: DIAMOND ROSS) / Nightfall / Dancing on a white moon (vocals: JACQUIE VIRGIL) / Civilized illusions / Swamp voices / Transparent days / Shy people (reprise).

S/track review: German electro-meisters, TANGERINE DREAM (i.e. EDGAR FROESE, CHRISTOPHER FRANKE and PAUL HASLINGER) were responsible for a plethora of cinematic soundtrack excursions around the same time, 'NEAR DARK', 'DEADLY CARE', 'DEAD SOLID PERFECT', etc. Here they tackle yet another lightweight American movie drama. Experimental to the point of bringing in some orchestration, FROESE and Co also add a few uncharacteristic vocal tracks, courtesy of JACQUIE VIRGIL (on the opening title track and the classy African-embossed 'Dancing On A White Moon') and DIAMOND ROSS on the throwaway, 'The Harbor'; their non-soundtrack album 'Tyger' was their only similar undertaking. At times beautifully crafted, encompassing both sweetness and power, the album's best moments are undoubtedly, 'Civilized Illusions' and 'Transparent Days'. *MCS*

Album rating: *6

SIESTA

1987 (UK/US 97m) Palace / Lorimar (18)

Film genre: psychological mystery/thriller

Top guns: dir: Mary Lambert → CLUBLAND / s-w: Patricia Louisianna Knop (au: Patrice Chaplin)

Stars: Ellen Barkin *(Claire)* ← DOWN BY LAW ← EDDIE AND THE CRUISERS ← TENDER MERCIES ← UP IN SMOKE / → JOHNNY HANDSOME → FEAR AND LOATHING IN LAS VEGAS, Gabriel Byrne *(Augustine)* ← GOTHIC / → the COURIER → DEAD MAN → the END OF

VIOLENCE → STIGMATA, Julian Sands *(Kit)* ← GOTHIC ← the KILLING FIELDS / → the MILLION DOLLAR HOTEL, Isabella Rossellini *(Marie)* → WILD AT HEART, Martin Sheen *(Del)*, Jodie Foster *(Nancy)* ← CARNY, **Grace Jones** *(Conchita)* ← STRAIGHT TO HELL ← GORDON'S WAR, Gary Cady *(Roger)*, Graham Fletcher-Cook *(Gary)* ← STRAIGHT TO HELL ← SID & NANCY ← ABSOLUTE BEGINNERS, Alexei Sayle *(cabbie)* → SWING

Storyline: Bloodied, bruised and memory-less at the end of a runway, American skydiver Claire wakes to an Iberian nightmare. She's definitely come to Spain for a rendevous with her former lover, but she's less sure about where the blood has come from. Dazed and confused, she wrestles with flashbacks and the prospect that the sangre on her hands is metaphorical as well as literal. *BG*

Movie rating: *5

Visual: video + dvd

Off the record: (see below)

—

MILES DAVIS & MARCUS MILLER

Feb 88. (lp/c/cd) *Warners; <(9 25655-1/-4/-2)>* ☐ ☐
– Lost in Madrid (pt.1): / Siesta – Kitt's kiss / Lost in Madrid (pt.2): Theme for Augustine – Wind – Seduction – Kiss / Submission / Lost in Madrid (pt.3): Conchita – Lament / Lost in Madrid (pt.4): Rat dance – The call / Claire – Lost in Madrid (pt.5): Afterglow / Los Feliz.

S/track review: If its title doesn't give it away first, the duende-rapt trumpet calls of 'Lost In Madrid Part 1' herald a mid-80s take on 'Sketches Of Spain'. The Gil Evans-orchestrated landmark was even used as a de facto soundtrack during filming, and its echo blows through MARCUS MILLER's score with the torrid lick of a Sirocco wind. Given the album's canonical status, it must've taken serious pelotas to apply the kind of synth programming which elevated 'Tutu' (1986), but DAVIS' sideman/producer/multi-instrumentalist saw it through with grace and aplomb even if, as the sleevenotes claim, a "punishing production schedule and movie budget did not properly allow MILLER to realise his musical vision". There's no point denying that the likes of 'Afterglow' and 'Lost In Madrid Part III' sound more like Ennio Morricone (and 'Conchita' like Peter Gabriel-meets-Vangelis) than MILES DAVIS, but MILLER's devotion to 'Sketches . . .' is obvious in the 'Solea'-esque rattling snares and classical-guitar flourishes of the title theme and the familiar arpeggios and symphonic counterpoint which open 'Lost In Madrid Part IV'. He can't hope to match the acoustic majesty of the past, and he doesn't try, but he's more than just a composer; 'SIESTA's lyricism owes almost as much to MILLER's playing as it does to DAVIS. The lazy hum of his baritone parts on 'Lost In Madrid Part II', 'Theme For Augustine' (the only track with a MILES credit) and elsewhere predict John Surman's mesmerising work on Emanuele Crialese's Mediterranean tone poem, 'Respiro' (2002). The man's management company apparently had a bit of a spat with 'Warners' over the cover credits but it's Gil Evans to whom 'SIESTA' is dedicated and, in the final instance perhaps, to whom it owes its mystery. *BG*

Album rating: *6.5

SIGUR ROS

Formed: Reykjavik, Iceland . . . by Jon Thor Birgisson, Georg Holm, Kjartan Sveinsson & Orri Pall Dyrason, although not all of the aforesaid members were present and correct at the time of their early 1994 inception. Four years and a couple of albums behind them, they finally garnered the recognition they strived for when 'Leit Af Lifi' (a song from 'Von Brigoi') topped the Icelandic charts for eight weeks. After a finalised line-up, the ethereal SIGUR ROS quickly returned to the studio in '99 and came up with 'Agaetis Byrjun' (1999), an album showcased in a spectacular radio broadcast at the Icelandic Opera House; around the same time, they struck a deal with London-based 'Fat Cat', who issued the much-celebrated 'Svefn-G-Englar' EP the same year. Crescendos of earth-quaking guitars (that didn't really sound like guitars at all), soft piano and Jon Thor's uniquely high-pitched falsetto vocals would appeal to Godspeed fans, while Prog-rocksters like Yes could even be cited as an influence. After selling loads of albums in their native Iceland, including their soundtrack collaboration here with composer Hilmar Orn Hilmarsson, they contributed two of their best works to the 'Vanilla Sky' (2001) movie. SIGUR ROS subsequently engrossed themselves in the mimbars of northern Iceland and recorded the wistful '()' in 2002. Yes, that's right – '()'. Just as the Beatles' eponymous album was christened the "White Album" by fans, SIGUR ROS' effort became known as the "Untitled Album", as no information was provided in the album sleeve and all tracks were, well, untitled. If it all sounded a bit pretentious, that's because it was, with Birgisson bordering on a line between childishness and pure musical poetry. 'Takk' (2004) went even further critically and commercially ('E.M.I.' in the UK and 'Geffen' in the US just might've been responsible), highlights on the transatlantic Top 30 entry undoubtably being 'Seaglopur' and hit single, 'Hoppipolla'. A few more scores were accredited to the men from Iceland, 'Villiljos' (2001), 'Hlemmur' (2002) and 'Immortel' (2004), while Various Artists performance sets, 'POPP I REYKJAVIK' (1998) and 'Gargandi Snilld' – or 'SCREAMING MASTERPIECE' (2005) to everyone outside the Scandics – spanned the pop-life of their existence. With SIGUR ROS on a creative high, they delivered a film about their homecoming, 'HEIMA' (2007). *MCS & AS*

- **filmography** (composers) {performers} –

Popp i Reykjavik *(1998 {p} on OST by V/A =>)* / **Englar Ahheimsins** *(2000 on OST w/ Hilmar Orn Hilmarsson =>)* / Villiljos *(2001 score w/ Valgeir Sigurdsson)* / Hlemmur *(2002 score)* / Immortel *(2004 score w/ Goran Vejvoda)* / **Screaming Masterpiece** *(2005 {p} on OST by V/A =>)* / **Heima** *(2007 {*p} =>)*

SILENT PARTNER

2001 (Aus 84m) Palace Films / AFC

Film genre: crime caper/comedy/drama

Top guns: dir: Alkinos Tsilimidos / s-w: Daniel Keene

Stars: David Field *(Bill)* ← ONE NIGHT THE MOON ← CHOPPER ← TO HAVE AND TO HOLD ← GHOSTS . . . OF THE CIVIL DEAD, Syd Brisbane *(John)* ← HAMMERS OVER THE ANVIL / → ONE PERFECT DAY

Storyline: Dog-fanciers John and Bill spend their nights and their wages getting drunk and losing at the local flapper track. When they get a chance to actually own a greyhound themselves they believe their bad luck has finally turned for the better. But their dog, Silent Partner, fluffs its first race and John and Bill take desperate measures, doping the mutt to the eyeballs for its next appearance. Their hare-brained scheme looks sure to go off the rails. *JZ*

Movie rating: *5

Visual: dvd

Off the record: (see below)

—

PAUL KELLY and GERRY HALE

Sep 01. (cd) *E.M.I.; (535569-2)* [–] Austra [–]
– Be careful what you pray for / Silver's theme / Is it a he or a she? / You can't take it with you (instrumental) / Silent partner / Teach me

tonight / Now's not the time for a hot sea bath / Silver's on the line / Ain't got the constitution / Better prospects / The gatekeeper / Forest funeral – Silver turns to lead / Little boy don't lose your balls / Silent partner (reprise) / Royal road / Ain't got the constitution (reprise) / Would you be my friend?

S/track review: Combining the musical talents of Australians PAUL KELLY and the relatively unknown bluegrass banjo strummer, GERRY HALE, 'SILENT PARTNER' was always going to be a bit of a gamble. Singer KELLY was revered in the land Down Under, while multi-instrumentalist HALE was a sidekick for the former's offshoot outfit, UNCLE BILL (featured here with augmented line-up PETER SOMERVILLE, STUART SPEED and ADAM GARE). There are several KELLY-only penned cues, the best of which must go to the Dylan-esque opener, 'Be Careful What You Pray For', the John Denver-esque 'Teach Me Tonight' (taken from KELLY's Uncle Bill set, 'Smoke') and the Brinsley Schwarz-like 'Little Boy Don't Lose Your Balls'. The instrumentals 'Silver's Theme' and 'Silver's On The Line' are very reminiscent of the work of Earl Scruggs, Eric Weissman or Barefoot Jerry, while 'Is It A He Or A She?' combines elements of Ry Cooder or Daniel Lanois. By far the most effective instrumental on board 'SILENT PARTNER' arguably stems from 'Ain't Got The Constitution', a recording that defines Outback bluegrass to a tee. While a handful of subsequent tracks on the set reprised the originals, the highlight of the latter half came by way of foggy-mountain-ish, 'Royal Road'. Expect to lose a substantial amount if you bet on this being released in Ol' Blighty. *MCS*

Album rating: *6

SILVER DREAM RACER

1980 (UK 101m) Rank Films (PG)

Film genre: romantic sports drama

Top guns: s-w + dir: David Wickes (story: Michael Billington)

Stars: David Essex *(Nick Freeman)* ← STARDUST ← THAT'LL BE THE DAY ← SMASHING TIME, Beau Bridges *(Bruce McBride)* ← the LANDLORD / → ELVIS AND THE COLONEL: THE UNTOLD STORY, Cristina Raines *(Julie Prince)* ← NASHVILLE, Clarke Peters *(Cider Jones)* ← the MUSIC MACHINE, Harry H. Corbett *(Wiggins)* ← WHAT A CRAZY WORLD ← SOME PEOPLE, Diane Keen *(Tina Freeman)* ← HERE WE GO ROUND THE MULBERRY BUSH, Lee Montague *(Jack Freeman)*, Sheila White *(Carol)* ← CONFESSIONS OF A POP PERFORMER ← MRS. BROWN, YOU'VE GOT A LOVELY DAUGHTER ← HERE WE GO ROUND THE MULBERRY BUSH ← the GHOST GOES GEAR, T.P. McKenna *(bank manager)* ← PERCY

Storyline: Nick Freeman is the lucky lad who gets to race his late brother's revolutionary new motor bike around the Silverstone circuit. The cheeky chappie's main rival is swaggering Yank Bruce McBride, whose head is several sizes too big for his helmet. Nick takes him down a peg or two by chatting up his girl Julie, but as race day looms, which of the two will triumph? A smashing ending is guaranteed. *JZ*

Movie rating: *3.5

Visual: video

Off the record: DAVID ESSEX (see below)

DAVID ESSEX & Various Artists
(* instrumentals arr. John Cameron)

Jun 80. (lp/c) *Mercury; (910963-1/-4)* [ ] [–]
– The dunes (*) / Silver dream machine (*) / Looking for something / The bike – part 1 (*) / Where is love (the REAL THING) / When I'm dancing (CLARKE PETERS) / Suzuki warlord (*) / Sea of love (VICTY SILVA) / The bike (*) / I think I'll always love you (VICTY SILVA) / The race (*) / Silver dream machine. *(re-iss. Jun82 lp/c; ERB/+C 7)*

S/track review: Seven years on from the innovative and still-beguiling single 'Rock On', gypsy David's undoubtable talents had settled into a more comfortably middle-of-the-road musical niche much as his acting had fallen away from the big screen challenges of 'THAT'LL BE THE DAY' and 'STARDUST'. ESSEX is probably just too genial a fellow to rattle around on the radical fringe for long, and there are plenty of pals like HERBIE FLOWERS and BARRY DE SOUZA – who can both be heard on 'Rock On' – helping him out on this unimpressive score. The likeably preposterous seven-minute disco-melodrama of 'Where Is Love?' is performed by the REAL THING (who'd been backing singers to ESSEX years before) and there are a couple of songs from session singer VICTY SILVA (who had been a musical stalwart of the West End when ESSEX was serving his stage apprenticeship). Untouched by punk, mainstream soundtrack music was still feeding on the fag-end of disco, so there's plenty of popping bass, hissing hi-hats and plastic keyboards, notably on the theme song (which, untrammelled by its similarity to Blondie's 'Dreaming', hustled its way to 4 in the UK singles chart). Apart from an extremely relaxed vocal performance on the laid-back 'When I'm Dancing' by CLARKE PETERS, who acts in the movie (and would go on to write the revue 'Five Guys Named Moe'), all that remains is some formulaic incidental music. *ND*

Album rating: *3.5

– spinoff hits, etc. –

DAVID ESSEX: Silver Dream Machine / (instrumental)
Apr 80. (7") *(BIKE 1)* [4] [–]

Shel SILVERSTEIN

Born: 25 Sep'30, Chicago, Illinois, USA. A satirical renaissance man with his finger in any number of creative pies, the late SHEL SILVERSTEIN intially made his name as a hot shot cartoonist for 'Playboy' magazine during its 60s heyday. He also trained his razor-sharp eye on the music scene, trying his hand at a variety of musical styles and honing his inimitable, irreverent songwriting style. Although it became synonymous with its performer, JOHNNY CASH, 'A Boy Named Sue' was actually SILVERSTEIN's creation and his most successful song along with 'Sylvia's Mother' and 'The Cover Of The Rolling Stone', tongue-in-cheek ditties which made 70s stars of Dr. Hook. While the man's own albums were never as big as the stars he wrote for, SILVERSTEIN achieved at least some musical success in his own right and even moved into film scoring with Tony Richardson's MICK JAGGER vehicle, 'NED KELLY' (1970) and Broadway turned Hollywood director Ulu Grosbard's 'WHO IS HARRY KELLERMAN AND WHY IS HE SAYING THOSE TERRIBLE THINGS ABOUT ME?' (1971). He went on to contribute his songwriting talents to Loretta Lynn biopic, 'COAL MINER'S DAUGHTER' (1980), Richard Marquand's failed finale, 'HEARTS OF FIRE' (1987) and Mike Nichols' 'Postcards From The Edge' (1990), for which his contribution, 'I'm Checking Out' (performed in the film by C&W act, Blue Rodeo), was nominated for an Oscar. A poet and children's author as well as a songwriter, SILVERSTEIN also collaborated with David Mamet for the screenplay to Mamet's 1988 crime comedy, 'Things Change'. One of popular culture's most adaptable talents passed away from a heart attack on 10th of May 1999. *BG*

- **filmography** (composer) {acting & s-w} –

Ned Kelly *(1970 OST w/ V/A =>)* / **Who Is Harry Kellerman And Why Is He Saying Those Terrible Things About Me?** *(1971 {a} OST w/ V/A =>)* / **Payday** *(1973 score w/others =>)* / Things Change *(1988 {s-w})*

Carly SIMON

Born: 25 Jun'45, New York City, New York, USA. The offspring of New York publisher Richard Simon (of Simon & Schuster), CARLY SIMON initially performed with her older sister before maturing into a bonafide singer-songwriter for the navel gazing eary 70s. While the gossip columns debated whether 'You're So Vain' was written about MICK JAGGER or Warren Beatty, Carly established herself as one of the most glamourous members of the era's piano plonking jet set, marrying singer-songwriter James Taylor into the bargain. Having enjoyed her greatest commercial success in the early to mid 70s, SIMON's initial involvement with the big screen not only revived a flagging career but created one of the most memorable and languidly sassy Bond themes in the series: 'Nobody Does It Better', as featured in Lewis Gilbert's 'The Spy Who Loved Me', made both the UK and US Top 10 in summer '77. A second hit from the world of movies came via 'Why', a double-header with Chic from 'Soup For One' (1982). As an active anti-nuclear campaigner, SIMON was subsequently featured in the documentary 'In Our Hands' (1984) alongside Taylor (whom she'd divorced by this point) and a raft of Hollywood stars, although it'd be almost a decade later before she'd score her first film, the Meryl Streep-Jack Nicholson head to head, 'Heartburn' (1986). While no soundtrack release was forthcoming, SIMON notched up another transatlantic hit (Top 20) with the airy title theme, 'Coming Around Again'. While the epic 'Let The River Run' – from her score to Nichols' 'WORKING GIRL' (1988) – narrowly failed to make it three in a row, an Oscar for Best Orginal Song was doubtless compensation enough. The turn of the decade found her teaming up with Nichols once again for 'Postcards From The Edge' (1990), sharing the composing credits with Howard Shore. After scoring Nora Ephron's directorial debut, 'THIS IS MY LIFE' (1992), SIMON diversified into opera with her own 'Romulus Hunt' (1993), authored a series of children's books and worked on the music to 'PRIMARY COLORS' (1998) with RY COODER. Of late, Carly has delivered songs for two soundtracks to Disney animations, 'Piglet's Big Movie' (2003) and 'Pooh's Heffalump Movie' (2005). *BG*

- **filmography** (composer) –

Taking Off *(1971 {p})* / the Spy Who Loved Me *(1977 hit theme by CARLY on OST by Marvin Hamlisch)* / Soup For One *(1982 hit theme by CARLY on OST by V/A & CHIC; see future editions)* / In Our Hands *(1984 {c})* / Perfect *(1985 {c})* / Heartburn *(1986 hit theme by CARLY)* / **Working Girl** *(1988 OST by CARLY w/ V/A =>)* / Postcards From The Edge *(1990)* / **This Is My Life** *(1992 OST =>)* / Piglet's Big Movie *(2003 OST w/ Carl Johnson see; future editions =>)* / Pooh's Heffalump Movie *(2005 on OST w/ Joel McNeely; see future editions)*

SIMON & GARFUNKEL

Formed: New York City, New York, USA . . . 1957 as Tom & Jerry by PAUL SIMON (b.13 Oct'41, Newark, New Jersey) and ART GARFUNKEL (b. 5 Nov'41, Queens, New York). Everyone and their granny's favourite pop-folk duo, SIMON & GARFUNKEL combined their considerable talents for a hugely successful run of singles and albums over the latter half of the 60s. The pair initially made headway in the film world via Mike Nichols' sex comedy, 'The GRADUATE' (1967), sharing soundtrack credits with Dave Grusin and scoring a UK Top 10 spin-off hit with the irrepressible theme tune, 'Mrs. Robinson'. While their greatest success, the record breaking 'Bridge Over Troubled Water' (1970), also marked the end of their partnership, a solo GARFUNKEL chose to build on his work with Nichols, landing a starring role in both the director's adaptation of 'Catch 22' (1970) and – opposite Jack Nicholson – his 1971 'Graduate' follow-up, 'Carnal Knowledge'. Despite encouraging critical notices, ART subsequently concentrated on his fairly successful 70s recording career, culminating in a massive UK No.1 with 'Bright Eyes', the haunting, sentimental theme to animal animation, 'Watership Down' (1979). SIMON, for his part, took time out from his own buoyant solo career to score Hal Ashby's high grossing sex satire, 'Shampoo', and take a major part in Woody Allen's acclaimed 'Annie Hall' (1977). He subsequently attempted to bring his songwriting and acting talents together in his own feature, 'ONE-TRICK PONY' (1980), writing the script into the bargain. If he didn't quite possess the dramatic gravitas necessary to carry off his gritty tale of a has-been musician lost in the brave new wave world, it was at least a decent attempt, with a soundtrack which served as a surrogate solo album for SIMON-starved fans. While his only other screen appearance of note came with a bit part in Ivan Reitman's political satire, 'Dave' (1993), GARFUNKEL, who'd made only intermittent forays into acting with Nicolas Roeg's 'Bad Timing' (1980) and Blaine Novak's 'GOOD TO GO' (1986), unexpectedly resumed his acting career with a bit part in the controversial Jennifer Chambers Lynch effort, 'Boxing Helena' (1993). Four years later, SIMON unveiled the most ambitious – and most commercially disastrous – project of his career: 'The Capeman' was a Broadway musical taking as its controversial subject matter the story of Puerto Rican killer turned writer, Salvador Agron, drawing protests from relatives of the man's victims and receiving a pasting from critics. To add insult to injury, the accompanying salsa and doo-wop influenced score, 'Songs From The Capeman' (1997), also performed poorly. *BG*

- **filmography** (composers) {acting} –

the Graduate *(1967 OST by SIMON & GARFUNKEL w/ DAVE GRUSIN =>)* / **Monterey Pop** *(1968 {p} OST by V/A =>)* / Catch-22 *(1970 {* ART})* / Carnal Knowledge *(1971 {* ART})* / Shampoo *(1975 score by PAUL)* / Annie Hall *(1977 {* PAUL})* / **the Rutles** *(1978 TV {* PAUL} OST by the RUTLES =>)* / Watership Down *(1979 hit theme by ART on OST by Angela Morley)* / Bad Timing *(1980 {* ART})* / **One-Trick Pony** *(1980 {* PAUL} [s-w: PAUL] OST by SIMON; =>)* / **Good To Go** *(1986 {* ART} OST by V/A =>)* / Mother Goose Rock'n'Rhyme *(1990 {p PAUL & ART})* / Dave *(1993 {a PAUL})* / Boxing Helena *(1993 {a ART})* / **54** *(1998 {b ART} OST by V/A =>)* / **Longshot** *(2000 {b ART} OST by V/A =>)*

□ Mike SIMPSON segment
(⇒ FIGHT CLUB)

SKIDOO

1968 (US 97m w/b&w) Paramount Pictures (M)

Film genre: gangster/crime caper

Top guns: dir: Otto Preminger ← BUNNY LAKE IS MISSING / s-w: Doran William Cannon

Stars: Jackie Gleason *(Tony Banks)*, Carol Channing *(Flo Banks)*, **Frankie AVALON** *(Angie)*, Michael Constantine *(Leech)*, Groucho Marx *("God")*, Fred Clark *(tower guard)* ← WHAT'S UP, TIGER LILY?, Frank Gorshin *(the man)* ← WHERE THE BOYS ARE / → RECORD CITY, John Phillip Law *(Stash)*, Peter Lawford *(the senator)*, Mickey Rooney *(Blue Chips Packard)* ← HOW TO STUFF A WILD BIKINI, Burgess Meredith *(the warden)* ← STAY AWAY, JOE, Cesar Romero *(Hechy)*, Phil Arnold *(mayor's husband)* ← GOOD TIMES ← HOLD ON! ← YOUR CHEATIN' HEART ← GO, JOHNNY, GO!, George Raft *(Capt. Garbaldo)*, Alexandra Hay *(Darlene Banks)* → the MODEL SHOP, Groucho Marx *(God)*, Slim Pickens *(switchboard operator)* → PAT GARRETT & BILLY THE KID → RANCHO DELUXE → HONEYSUCKLE ROSE, Robert Donner *(switchboard operator)* ← CATALINA CAPER / → VANISHING POINT, Luna *(God's mistress)* ← TONIGHT LET'S ALL MAKE LOVE IN LONDON / → ROCK AND ROLL CIRCUS, Richard Kiel *(Beany)* ← ROUSTABOUT ← EEGAH, Arnold

Stang *(Harry)* → HELLO DOWN THERE, Renny Roker *(prison guard)* → MELINDA → BROTHERS, **Harry NILSSON** *(tower guard)*

Storyline: Affably addled anti-establishment fare following the ridiculous adventures of Tony, a gangster who voluntarily gets himself admitted to prison at his bosses' behest. Rather than following their orders to nail a fellow con, he's serendipitously spiked with LSD and – together with jailed hippy, the Professor – turns on the rest of the inmates to the drug's dubious delights. *BG*

Movie rating: *5

Visual: video

Off the record: Peter Lawford, Cesar Romero, etc. had all featured in the original version of 'Ocean's Eleven' (1960).

NILSSON

Nov 68. (lp) *R.C.A.; <LSO 1152> (SF 8010)* ☐ Apr69 ☐
– The cast and crew / I will take you there / Skidoo – Commercials / Goodnight Mr. Banks – Let's get the hardware – Murder in the car wash / Angie's suite / The tree / Garbage can ballet / Tony's trip / Escape: Impossible – Green Bay Packers march / Man wasn't meant to fly / Escape: possible / Skidoo – Goodnight Mr. Banks (CAROL CHANNING). *(cd-iss. Sep00 on 'Camden-RCA'+=; 74321 75743-2)* – Nilsson:- The POINT! (tracks) / I will take you there (alt. mix) / Girlfriend / Down to the valley / Buy my album.

S/track review: HARRY NILSSON's penchant for whimsy isn't to all tastes and 'SKIDOO' takes the goof factor to unbearable levels, particularly on the opening 'The Cast And Crew' where the mercurial songwriter famously sings the movie's credits. This sounds like a bad idea on paper and be assured, it's even more tedious in reality. Even the trifling fantasia of 'Garbage Can Ballet' is more listenable. Elsewhere, NILSSON redeems himself to a certain extent with 'I Will Take You There' while George Tipton's orchestral arrangements – enhanced by obligatory sitar and tabla – pass by inconsequentially and CAROL CHANNING mercifully closes proceedings in squawking, sub-Eartha Kitt style. *BG*

Album rating: *4.5

the SLAUGHTER RULE

2002 (US 112m) Cowboy Pictures (R)

Film genre: coming-of-age/sports drama

Top guns: s-w + dir: Alex Smith, Andrew J. Smith

Stars: Ryan Gosling *(Roy Chutney)*, David Morse *(Gideon 'Gid' Ferguson)* ← DANCER IN THE DARK, Clea DuVall *(Skyla Sisco)* ← COMMITTED ← a SLIPPING-DOWN LIFE ← GIRL, David Cale *(Floyd; aka Studebaker)*, Eddie Spears *(Tracey Two Dogs)*, Kelly Lynch *(Evangeline Chutney)* ← ROAD HOUSE, Amy Adams *(Doreen)* ← PSYCHO BEACH PARTY, Ken White *(Russ Colfax)*, Noah Watts *(Waylon Walks Along)*, Geraldine Keams *(Gretchen Two-Dogs)*, **Wylie & The Wild West** *(Trails End House band)*

Storyline: The unfortunately named Roy Chutney comes of age in deepest Montana, where his life revolves around playing American football and coming to terms with the unexpected suicide of his absentee father. He subsequently takes up with Gideon "Gid" Ferguson's alternative six-man team after being dropped by his school, although his new coach's motives aren't as clean cut as they seem. *BG*

Movie rating: *6

Visual: dvd

Off the record: **JAY FARRAR** (see below)

JAY FARRAR (*) (& Various Artists)

Mar 03. (cd) *Bloodshot; <(BS 087)>* ☐ Jun03 ☐
– Open ground (*) / Gather (*) / Rank stranger (VIC CHESNUTT) / Frost heaves (*) / When I stop dreaming (FREAKWATER) / Odessa yodel (WYLIE & THE WILD WEST) / Highwood (*) / Gathering flowers for the master's banquet (BLOOD ORANGES) / Augusta (*) / To be young (is to be sad, is to be high) (RYAN ADAMS) / Buffalo jump (*) / West of Samoa (SPEEDY WEST & JIMMY BRYANT) / Freight (*) / Dark early (*) / Porchlight (NEKO CASE) / Tonight I think I'm gonna go downtown (JIMMIE DALE GILMORE & THE FLATLANDERS) / Cold chimes (*) / Gumption (*) / Killing the blues (MALCOLM GROUP HOLCOMBE) / Hangman (*) / Blue eyes (UNCLE TUPELO) / Open ground – reprise (*) / Will there be any stars in my crown? (PERNICE BROTHERS).

S/track review: When a clash of egos finally foreclosed the mighty Uncle Tupelo back in the mid 90s, the subsequent solo projects of Jeff Tweedy and JAY FARRAR presented case-studies in the divergent personalities which had defined alt-country: Tweedy as rambunctious rocker, FARRAR as austere troubadour. While Tweedy went on to run the gamut of American pop cultural reference and beyond with Wilco, embracing liberation as experimentation, FARRAR merely steadied his hand at the plough, braced himself against the chill wind of lonesomeness and kept the country faith. Viewed from another angle, both men could be said to have followed roughly similar solo career arcs, belatedly branching out from the crusty tropes of roots rock. They even made their soundtrack debuts the same year (with Tweedy supplying the music for Ethan Hawke's 'CHELSEA WALLS'). Yet it was arguably FARRAR's arcane baritone, wounded way beyond its years, that wove 'Tupelo into the seam of Great American Musical lore, and it's that voice which continues to define him both in relation to his erstwhile partner and in relation to whatever project he turns his hand to. And even if 'The SLAUGHTER RULE' features only one FARRAR vocal, 'Gather', it's the grainy locus for pretty much everything else on this soundtrack and one of the starkest and most affecting contexts for his art since the sublime 'March 16-20, 1992' (1993). Peppered throughout the soundtrack like rustic zen koans, the rest of FARRAR's contributions refreshingly distil a folky acoustic signature rather than labouring over songs. The ghost of Nick Drake and the spectre of John Fahey hover over his high, ringing finger-picking, raked by quavering echo, arching feedback, film dialogue and various shades of twang. Directors Alex and Andrew Smith pad out FARRAR's work with an imaginative collection of contemporary alt-country and assorted oddities from the vaults. Among the latter, SPEEDY WEST and JIMMY BRYANT's 'West Of Samoa' is the most gratiftyingly surreal, an intoxicating, Lord Of The Flies-goes-lounge lullaby, reconciling lap steel twang and the equatorial spook-jazz of Luis Carlos Vinhas. Alt-country forefathers the FLATLANDERS (aka JIMMIE DALE GILMORE, BUTCH HANCOCK and JOE ELY, a trio of "drumless psychedelic cowboys" in the words of legendary critic Robert Christgau) are also most haunted on 'Tonight I Think I'm Gonna Go Downtown', approximating Twilight Zone theremin with a musical saw. It's a great link back into FARRAR's own 'Cold Chimes', where the queasy frequencies are vaguely predictive of Richard G. Mitchell's work on 'GRAND THEFT PARSONS' (2003). The young bucks can't quite match that vintage, although RYAN ADAMS engagingly exiles himself just off Main Street with the R&B shuffle of 'To Be Young (Is To Be Sad, Is To Be High)', and NEKO CASE dusts down her best plaintive, prairie-wind falsetto for 'Porchlight'. MALCOLM HOLCOMBE lies prostrate somewhere in the middle, dragging his phlegmy wisdom across the gaping chasm of the years on 'Killing The Blues'. All told, it's an attractively offbeat entry point for alt-country novices, a must for FARRAR fans and compelling evidence that the man's at his best writing to a focused concept. *BG*

Album rating: *7.5

SLAUGHTER'S BIG RIP-OFF

1973 (US 93m) American International Pictures (R)

Film genre: gangster/crime thriller

Top guns: dir: Gordon Douglas ← FOLLOW THAT DREAM / s-w: Charles Johnson → the MONKEY HUSTLE

Stars: Jim Brown *(Slaughter)* → THREE THE HARD WAY → HE GOT GAME, Ed McMahon *(Duncan)*, Brock Peters *(Reynolds)* ← JACK JOHNSON ← BLACK GIRL, Don Stroud *(Kirk)* → the BUDDY HOLLY STORY, Gloria Hendry *(Marcia)* ← BLACK CAESAR ← ACROSS 110th STREET ← the LANDLORD / → HELL UP IN HARLEM → BLACK BELT JONES, Art Metrano *(Mario Burtoli)*, Russ McGinn *(Harvey)* → FOOTLOOSE, Scatman Crothers *(Cleveland)* ← LADY SINGS THE BLUES / → BLACK BELT JONES → TRUCK TURNER → FRIDAY FOSTER, Jackie Giroux *(Mrs. Duncan)* → TO LIVE AND DIE IN L.A., Judy Brown *(Norja)* → WILLIE DYNAMITE → THANK GOD IT'S FRIDAY, Richard Williams *(Joe Creole)* ← UP TIGHT! / → FIVE ON THE BLACK HAND SIDE → the MACK, **Pamela Miller** *(Burtoli's girl)* ← 200 MOTELS / → MAYOR OF THE SUNSET STRIP → FALLEN ANGEL → METAL: A HEADBANGER'S JOURNEY, J. Jay Saunders *(fry cook)* → CORNBREAD, EARL AND ME → THIEF → HOUSE PARTY

Storyline: Another chapter in the saga of the man known as Slaughter, as he attempts to outgun a posse of mobsters bent on his destruction. *BG*

Movie rating: *3.5

Visual: video + dvd

Off the record: **Pamela Miller** was in fact, Pamela Des Barres, ex-member of all-girl group(ies), the GTO's. *MCS*

JAMES BROWN (w/ co-composer: FRED WESLEY)

Jul 73. (lp) *Polydor; <PD 6015> (2391 084)* [92] Aug73 [ ]
– Slaughter theme / Tryin' to get over / Transmografpication / Happy for the poor / Brother rap / Big strong / Really, really, really / Sexy, sexy, sexy / To my brother / How long can I keep it up / People get up and drive your funky soul / King Slaughter / Straight ahead. <*(cd-iss. Aug96 & Sep98; 314 517136-2)*>

S/track review: The hardest-working man in showbusiness was apparently grafting harder than ever in 1973, chasing the 'Get On The Good Foot' album with two successive soundtracks and seeing another rejected. 'SLAUGHTER'S BIG . . .' doesn't quite measure up against BROWN's blaxploitation debut, 'BLACK CAESAR', but it definitely has its superbad moments. FRED WESLEY is once again credited as co-composer and – with BROWN at his most exhortatory, and WESLEY deep in his loping, slippery element – the scorching 'People Get Up And Drive Your Funky Soul' is the sound of two funk colossi splitting the atom. Swinging, roiling and relentless, it stands black and proud among the Godfather's crowning achievements. Even at its usually prohibitive price tag, 'SLAUGHTER'S . . .' is worth hunting out for this alone. Part of the reason the rest of the album pales in comparison is its regurgitation of older material, a policy which just doesn't cut it on a blaxploitation soundtrack. 'Happy For The Poor' is basically a speeded-up re-run of the – admittedly great – 1971 J.B.'s single, 'Gimme Some More', with added funky organ. 'Sexy, Sexy, Sexy' welds the backing track of BROWN's 1967 single, 'Money Won't Change You', to new lyrics and vocals while 'Brother Rapp' is pretty much a straight reprise of 1970s 'Brother Rapp (Part 1)' minus Alphonso Kellum's loose-limbed guitar and the original's dubbed applause. Elsewhere, WESLEY has himself a fine showcase on the jazzy 'Transmorgrapfication', while 'Slaughter Theme' is firmly in the tradition of BROWN's ministerial heavy heavy funk without ever really distinguishing itself. When the pair do make a conscious attempt to write orchestrated incidental material, as on 'Tryin' To Get Over' and 'To My Brother', the results are compelling if pretty incongruous next to the 60s-rooted re-records. Which is part of 'SLAUGHTER'S . . .' problem: airy epilogue 'Straight Ahead' is closest in spirit to the blithe instrumentals which glued '. . .CAESAR' together and which are absent from what is ultimately a fairly disjointed affair. As 'The Payback' (1974) would prove, JAMES BROWN wasn't the soundtrack slacker he's sometimes painted as. He mightn't have got the formula quite right here but over the course, his blaxploitation efforts pretty much equalled those of his peers; if not in innovation, then in sheer soul power. *BG*

Album rating: *6.5

– spinoff hits, etc. –

JAMES BROWN: Sexy, Sexy, Sexy / Slaughter Theme

Aug 73. (7") <*14194*> [50] [–]

SLING BLADE

1996 (US 135m) The Shooting Gallery / Miramax

Film genre: psychological melodrama

Top guns: s-w + dir: Billy Bob Thornton

Stars: Billy Bob Thornton *(Karl Childers)*, **Dwight YOAKAM** *(Doyle Hargraves)*, J.T. Walsh *(Charles Bushman)*, John Ritter *(Vaughan Cunningham)*, Lucas Black *(Frank Wheatley)* → ALL THE PRETTY HORSES → COLD MOUNTAIN → KILLER DILLER → FRIDAY NIGHT LIGHTS, Natalie Canerday *(Linda Wheatley)*, James Hampton *(Dr. Jerry Woolridge)*, Robert Duvall *(Karl's father)*, **Vic Chesnutt** *(Terence)*, **Col. Bruce Hampton** *(Morris)* → OUTSIDE OUT, Jim Jarmusch *(Frostee Cream boy)* ← LENINGRAD COWBOYS GO AMERICA ← CANDY MOUNTAIN ← STRAIGHT TO HELL / → YEAR OF THE HORSE → I PUT A SPELL ON ME → the FUTURE IS UNWRITTEN, Mickey Jones *(Monty Johnson)* ← LIVING PROOF: THE HANK WILLIAMS JR. STORY ← the BEST LITTLE WHOREHOUSE IN TEXAS

Storyline: Partially retarded Karl is released from mental hospital after murdering his mother and her lover when he was 12. Now apparently cured, he goes back to his home town where he befriends Frank and his mother Linda, who see him as a slow but kind, compassionate man. However things go wrong when Karl meets Linda's abusive boyfriend Doyle, who takes a strong dislike to him. As Karl grows closer to Frank, it's only a matter of time before things come to a head between himself and Doyle. *JZ*

Movie rating: *8

Visual: video + dvd

Off the record: **Vic Chesnutt** (b.12 Nov'65, Zebulon, Georgia, USA) was confined to a wheelchair since 1983 after a car crash left him paraplegic. He developed a distinctive singing/songwriting style so popular among fellow musicians that 'Columbia' released a tribute album, 'Sweet Relief – Gravity Of The Situation: The Songs Of Vic Chesnutt' (1996). Among the contributors were such luminaries as MADONNA, Smashing Pumpkins and R.E.M.; the latter connection had already proved pivotal in the direction of the man's career, with Michael Stipe having produced his first two albums, 'Little' (1989) and 'West Of Rome' (1991). Critics centred on the bitterness and vivid despair of the lyrics, Chesnutt trawling the depths of his psyche for 1994's 'Drunk'. *BG & MCS*

Various Artists (score: DANIEL LANOIS *)

Nov 96. (cd) *Island; <524 388-2>* [ ] [–]
– Asylum (*) / Jimmy was (*) / Bettina (*) / Soul dressing (BOOKER T. & THE M.G.'S) / Lonely one (TIM GIBBONS) / Blue waltz (*) / Secret place (*) / Darlin' (BAMBI LEE SAVAGE) / Shenandoah (* feat. EMMYLOU HARRIS) / Orange Kay (*) / Smothered in hugs (LOCAL H) / Phone call (RUSSELL WILSON and MARK HOWARD) / Omni (*) / The maker (*).

S/track review: Not DANIEL LANOIS' first soundtrack commission (check out the films, 'The Surrogate', 1984 and

'Camilla', 1994), but definitely his first to obtain a release. There's no doubt, the veteran guitarist from Quebec had all the right credentials and wore his Brian Eno (an old buddy and collaborator) influence firmly on his sleeve; opener 'Asylum' the prime example. More so for track 7, 'Secret Place', because the former Roxy Music guru operates an accomanying DX7 synth, track 13 'Omni' is of similar ilk but does not feature Eno. OK, the film is slow-paced, therefore, so is LANOIS' basic accompaniment, while feeling of desolation and isolation would be a good way to sum up the man's contributions. Augmented by the rhythm section of DARYL JOHNSON and BRIAN BLADE (like a handful of cuts), 'Jimmy Was' goes for a melodic, uptempo pace, although the beat is only a slow-train-coming away from tedium. On the other hand, 'Blue Waltz' finds a meeting place between Ry Cooder and David Gilmour, surely the best reverberating sound to ease out of the movie's backwoods setting. In complete contrast are the rocking intensity of 'Orange Kay' with the traditional, Appalachian collaboration 'Shenandoah' (accompanied by country great, EMMYLOU HARRIS) – hummin' hallelujah. Of the diverse various artists on show – and there aren't too many! – cool 60s cut, 'Soul Dressing', squeezed out by instrumental mods BOOKER T & THE MG'S, won hands down. Others such as growler TIM GIBBONS (on 'Lonely One'), the Weezer-esque LOCAL H (with 'Smothered In Hugs') and the sultry BAMBI LEE SAVAGE (with LANOIS-augmented 'Darlin''), were pot-pourri gone haywire. While producers and fellow Canadians, RUSSELL WILSON and MARK HOWARD got their two-pennorth in via the short 'Phone Call', an old LANOIS chestnut from 1989, 'The Maker' closed proceedings – it even had vocals. *MCS*

Album rating: *6

☐ SLOWBLOW segment
(⇒ NOI ALBINOI)

☐ Jimmy SMITH segment
(⇒ la METAMORPHOSE DES CLOPORTES)

☐ SMOKE segment
(⇒ the CANDY TANGERINE MAN)

SOMERSAULT

2004 (Austra 106m) Showtime / Red Carpet / Fortissimofilms (MA)

Film genre: romantic/coming-of-age/psychological drama

Top guns: s-w + dir: Cate Shortland

Stars: Abbie Cornish *(Heidi)* ← ONE PERFECT DAY, Sam Worthington *(Joe)* ← THUNDERSTRUCK, Lynette Curran *(Irene)*, Hollie Andrew *(Bianca)*, Erik Thomson *(Richard)*, Leah Purcell *(Diane)* ← LANTANA / → the PROPOSITION, Nathaniel Dean *(Stuart)*, Olivia Pigeot *(Nicole; Heidi's mother)*, Blake Pittman *(Karl)*

Storyline: Heidi is a gorgeous but mixed up 16-year-old, who incenses her mother when she tries to bed her tattooed live-in boyfriend. Obviously looking for love in all the wrong places, the blonde Heidi leaves her home and chooses another town (the resort of Jindabyne) to throw herself about. There, she finally gets it together with hard-drinking, rich farmer boy, Joe, but there's always something amiss with the lass (and her newfound colleagues) – is it just growing pains? *MCS*

Movie rating: *7.5

Visual: dvd

Off the record: **DECODER RING** hail from Sydney, and were instantly heralded as one of Australia's most promising acts after the release of two sets, 'Spooky Action At A Distance' (2002) and 'Decoder Ring' (2003) – both issued on 'Hello Cleveland / EMI'. Hard to categorize with their blend of ambient, electronica and cinema rock, it was befitting the quintet (Tom Schutzinger, Pete Kelly, Matt Fitzgerald, Kenny Davis Jnr and Ben Ely) would take the opportunity to get into film; they had contributed a track to the 'GARAGE DAYS' (2002) soundtrack. It was no surprise when they signed a deal with 'Bella Union', for the 'SOMERSAULT' commission – the label was owned by ROBIN GUTHRIE (ex-Cocteau Twins). Follow-up, 'Fractions' (2005), saw the band go totally independent again, described as "a sprawling rollercoaster of an album that spans dark electro, euphoric pop, intimate ballads and dancefloor anthems". *MCS*

—

DECODER RING

Mar 05. (cd) *Bella Union; (bellacd 93) Red Carpet; <20021>* ☐ Aug04 ☐
– Heidi's theme / Somersault / Snowflake / Rough sex / Carillion / Music box / More than scarlet / The Siesta Inn / You're hot / Higher higher / Alpine way / Naked snow / Electrocution (hydro mix) / Heidi's theme (reprise) / Somersault (score).

S/track review: The last successful ethereal indie band to come out of Antipodean shores was arguably Dead Can Dance (who incidentally featured cinematic vocalist/composer-to-be, Lisa Gerrard). Now take a bow to newbies, DECODER RING, a 5-piece that exudes contrasting levels of haunting and uplifting dirges and melodies; example if you will the lullaby-esque opener, 'Heidi's Theme', musak that even Mogwai and Explosions In The Sky would find hard to hi-crescendo-fi. The superseding title track (coolly sung by LENKA KRIPAC and actually the finale to the movie) was reminiscent of Vitamin C's sunny pop or Iceland's electronica-noodling Mum. 'Snowflake' carried on in a picturesque mission like the awakening of spring, while 'Rough Sex', transplanted the listener into deeper post-rock thoughts. LENKA (also the co-writer) was back on the mic for 'Music Box', a kind of pastel-shaped, Elizabeth Fraser-esque tune (see above for Robin Guthrie connection). Whoever said that the DECODER RING was genre-defying was certainly on the button, the three tracks that followed exemplified the statement: the bass beatbox and lullaby keys of 'More Than Scarlet' (reminiscent of Piano Magic/Glen Johnson), the Parisienne sidewalk of 'The Siesta Inn' and the schizoid introspective of mirrored dialogue, 'You're Hot', stunningly segued together for the soundtrack recording, although not for the film. Track Ten, 'Higher Higher', moves into Kid Loco and cinematic Blaxpolitation territory, funky to the max with also that eerie hint of cool that beats around your head and not necessarily the dancefloor. For the 'Ring's next trick, they conjured up the snowy, acoustic slow-burner, 'Alpine Way'; evidence of sorts that Australia did have a colder climate at times. To end a truly wonderful piece of work, DR produced three further beauties, the Eno-esque 'Electrocution (Hydro mix)', the reprised 'Heidi's Theme' and the score version of 'Somersault' title track, albeit with LENKA still contributing vocals. The only criticism levied at the CD was that it was a little short at just under 31 minutes, however, to balance this out, I heard the album before seeing the film and it can stand on its own with repetitive listenings, unlike many "Rock" scores of their ilk. *MCS*

Album rating: *8

SON DE MAR

trans: Sound Of The Sea

2001 (Spain 95m) Lolafilms (13)

Film genre: psychological/romantic drama

Top guns: dir: J.J. Bigas Luna / s-w: Rafael Azcona (au: Manuel Vicent)

Stars: Jordi Molla *(Ulises)*, Leonor Watling *(Martina)*, Eduard Fernandez

(Sierra), Sergio Caballero *(Xavier)*, Neus Agullo *(Roseta)*, Pep Cortes *(Basilo)*, Juan Munoz *(director instituto)*

Storyline: Lunas' lyrical tale of a literature teacher named Ulises, who arrives in an out of season coastal town with nothing more than school on his mind. Once there, his senses luxuriate in both the mystery of the sea and the local women, as he falls in love with one of his own students, Martina. Choosing Ulises at the expense of a wealthy admirer, she bears him a child, only to see him disappear as suddenly as he'd arrived. *BG*

Movie rating: *5.5

Visual: dvd

Off the record: **PIANO MAGIC** were formed in London, England . . . summer 1996 by mainstays Glen Johnson and Dick Rance. The oddly-titled PIANO MAGIC started as a casual activity with various members (Raechel Leigh and Dominic Chennell among them) coming and going whenever they wished. Johnson subsequently spent six months remixing tracks previously recorded and also took to developing new material featured on the band's demo recording which was sent to 'Che' records. That November, the band released their debut single, 'Wrong French', issued on 'Che'-associated imprint, 'i'. Their minimalist electronica lay somewhere between Kraftwerk and the Young Marble Giants; mototonik Krautrock with sweet'n'sour indie pop romance. A debut album, 'Popular Mechanics', was delivered in autumn 1997, its childlike approach to instrumentation and interpretation led to one John Peel becoming an admirer. With further personnel changes, PM released a four track 12" EP, 'The Fun Of The Century', in the winter months of '97. An album was not released for another eighteen months however, although fans were compensated by several classy singles/EP's including a split EP with Low and Transient Waves. The band now consisted of the ever present Johnson, alongside Charles Wyatt, Chris Overden and Paul Tronbohm. Finally released, 'A Trick Of The Sea' (1998) consisted of only two lengthy ambient tracks, both of which featured Lucy Gulland (the girlfriend of Ovenden). Not surprisingly, Johnson gave the band a little rest while he subsequently took PIANO MAGIC for a solo sojourn via 'Music For Annahbird' and 'Music For Rolex'. 'Low Birth Weight' was next off the production line, Johnson again utilising children's toys for instruments, while he assembled together Caroline Potter, Raechel Leigh (again) and Simon Rivers. 'Artists Rifles' (2000) was a concept record of sorts, the trials of war being the theme, while the 'SON DE MAR' soundtrack would be their next release. *AS & MCS*

—

PIANO MAGIC

Aug 01. (cd) *4 a.d.; (<MAD 2105CD>)* ☐ ☐
– (parts 1-6).

S/track review: PIANO MAGIC – "purveyors of fine radiophonic sounds since 1996" according to their website; "out of time, unfashionable and kinda weird looking", also according to their website – is the ongoing experiment of one GLEN JOHNSON, whose This Mortal Coil-inspired aesthetic has manifested itself in as many sonic guises and on as many cosmopolitan labels as he's seen international personnel come and go. More popular in Spain than he's ever been in the UK, in 2001 JOHNSON – by this point working with Seville native Miguel Marin and Frenchman Jerome Tchernayan – was contacted by Catalan director Bigas Luna to score his hallucinatory tale of love by the sea. The soundtrack runs for a meagre 37 minutes but – despite some judicious use of ticking clocks – appears even more fleeting than it is, dissolving time into lapping surf and tolling bells. There's no tracklisting, no info at all in fact, only credits from the film and an evocative still for the cover. If you haven't seen the movie, that still is all you have to go on in mentally constructing the kind of images which PM's liquid sound might accompany. What begins as an ambient funeral by a watery graveside, washes into a solemn but auspicious wake, lent dignity by James Topham's viola and hope by precipitative, pizzicato harp. The lunar moods ebb and pull with the unhurried rationale of fate, eroding sub-strata of loss and regret, and silting by degrees into a whumping rhythmic pulse; JOHNSON's tone poems are mystical (and yes, joyfully out of time, unfashionable and kinda weird-sounding), but magic's probably the wrong word. *BG*

Album rating: *7.5

SON OF DRACULA

1974 (UK 90m) Cinemation (PG)

Film genre: vampire/horror comedy

Top guns: dir: Freddie Francis / s-w: Jay Fairbank

Stars: **Harry NILSSON** *(Count Down)*, Dennis Price *(Van Helsing)* ← the MAGIC CHRISTIAN ← PLAY IT COOL, **Ringo Starr** *(Merlin the magician)* <= the BEATLES =>, Freddie Jones *(Dr. Frankenstein)* → NEVER TOO YOUNG TO ROCK → DUNE → WILD AT HEART, Suzanna Leigh *(Amber)* ← PARADISE, HAWAIIAN STYLE, **John Bonham** *(musician)*<= LED ZEPPELIN =>, **Peter Frampton** *(musician)* → SGT. PEPPER'S LONELY HEARTS CLUB BAND → ALMOST FAMOUS, **Keith Moon** *(musician)* <= the WHO =>, **Bobby Keyes** *(musician)* ← COCKSUCKER BLUES, **Jim Price** *(musician)* ← COCKSUCKER BLUES, **Klaus Voorman** *(musician)* ← the CONCERT FOR BANGLADESH / → POPEYE → WHITE STAR → CONCERT FOR GEORGE, **Ricki Farr** *(musician)*, Beth Morris *(Wendy)* ← THAT'LL BE THE DAY, Jenny Runacre *(woman in black)* → JUBILEE

Storyline: The ascension of Count Down – son of the late, great Count Dracula – to the Netherworld throne is complicated by the predictions of his mentor and astrological guide, Merlin the Magician. As written in the stars, the Count is smitten with Amber, a human temptress for the love of whom he undegoes treatment to make him human. With Baron Frankenstein also eager to be crowned king, Netherworld relations become strained. *BG*

Movie rating: *4

Visual: video

Off the record: Session man **Klaus Voorman, Bobby Keyes, Jim Price & Ricki Farr** found their way on to the movie, which included other stars of the day, **Peter Frampton, John Bonham, Ringo Starr, Keith Moon** and of course Harry NILSSON. *MCS*

—

NILSSON

May 74. (lp) *Rapple; (<APL-1 0220>)* ☐ Apr74 ☐
– It is he who will be King / Daybreak / At my front door / Count Down meets Merlin and Amber / Moonbeam / Perhaps this is all a dream / Remember (Christmas) / Intro: Without you / The Count's vulnerability / Down / Frankenstein, Merlin and the operation / Jump into the fire / The abdication of Count Down / The end (moonbeam).

S/track review: Released between his early 70s glory years and his lost Lennon weekend, this project effectively put a lid on HARRY NILSSON's season in the sun. There's a certain kitschy pleasure in the excess dialogue and – for those that haven't seen it (which, given that it closed the day it opened, has to be most of us) – an intimation of just how heroically wooden the film actually was; Ringo, especially, is volubly awful. The excerpts also give an immediate sense that the pair weren't exactly bending over backwards to write original music, to write any music. Instead, the odd couple raid Harry's recent chart albums – 'Nilsson Schmilsson' (1972) and 'Son Of Schmilsson' (1972) – and leave the incidental stuff to PAUL BUCKMASTER, he of the Third Ear Band, 'Space Oddity' and Elton John fame. Isolated from the dialogue, BUCKMASTER's fitful percussion, droning french horn and prepared piano arrangements would've made this soundtrack a more attractive proposition; as it is, they're partly buried under those groaning lines. One of the best opportunities to hear his score is 'The Abdication of Count Down', a brief 'Death Wish'-like finale. As for the NILSSON nuggets, the credits – GEORGE HARRISON, KLAUS VOORMAN, BOBBY KEYS, PETER FRAMPTON, CHRIS SPEDDING, NICKY HOPKINS, JIMMY WEBB, JIM KELTNER, HERBIE FLOWERS among them – read like a 70s supersession; 'Remember', 'Without

You' and 'The Moonbeam Song' are as subtly powerful as they were first time round but the very un-gothic, quasi-Caribbean music hall of 'Daybreak', was about the only incentive to buy this in 1974. Even that track has since been anthologised so, save for a great, 'Son Of Schmilsson'-inspired sleeve (STARR looking like he's just fluffed a casting for 'The Lord Of The Rings') and the BUCKMASTER cues, 'SON OF DRACULA' is pretty much collectors' bait. We await the CD version, hopefully with added versions, etc. *BG*

Album rating: *5.5

– spinoff hits, etc. –

NILSSON: Daybreak / Down

Apr 74. (7") *(APBO 0238) <APBO 0246>* ☐ 39

SORCERER

UK title 'WAGES OF FEAR'

1977 (US 121m) Paramount-Universal (PG)

Film genre: psychological jungle adventure

Top guns: dir: William Friedkin ← GOOD TIMES / → TO LIVE AND DIE IN L.A. / s-w: Walon Green → the BORDER (nov: Georges Arnaud / Henri-Georges Clouzot)

Stars: Roy Scheider *(Jackie Scanlon / "Juan Dominguez")*, Bruno Cremer *(Victor Manzon / "Serrano")*, Francisco Rabal *(Nilo)*, Ramon Bieri *(Corlette)*, Peter Capell *(Lartigue)*, Amidou *(Kassem / "Martinez")*, Joe Spinell *(Spider)* ← RANCHO DELUXE / → FORBIDDEN ZONE, Tom Signorelli *(bystander)* ← the TRIP / → THIEF → DICK TRACY

Storyline: Virtually a remake of the 1953 French movie, 'Le Salaire De La Peur' (Wages Of Fear), director William Friedkin moved on from classic horror flick, 'The Exorcist'. Four broke(n) exiles from various countries end up in Nicaragua and take on a well-paid but dangerous task of transporting nitroglycerin over jungle terrain. The misleading re-title did not help its critical or box-office appeal. *MCS*

Movie rating: *4

Visual: video + dvd

Off the record: Friedkin initially wanted Steve McQueen to play Scanlon, but things went awry when McQueen wanted then wife Ali MacGraw to be his co-star. *MCS*

—

TANGERINE DREAM

Jun 77. (lp/c) *M.C.A.; <2277> (MCF/+C 2806)* ☐ Jul77 25
– Main title / Search / The call / Creation / Vengeance / The journey / Grind / Rain forest / Abyss / The mountain road / Impressions of Sorcerer / Betrayal (Sorcerer theme). *(re-iss. Feb82 lp/c; MCL/+C 1646) (cd-iss. Aug92; MCLD 19159) <cd-iss. 1992; 10842>*

S/track review: Germany's TANGERINE DREAM were at their commercial peak when commissioned to do their first soundtrack release in 1976. Having previously charted in the UK with the groundbreaking 'Phaedra', 'Rubycon', 'Ricochet' and 'Stratosfear', the trio also reached the Top 30 with this effort. Not since the days of Louis & Bebe Barron's pioneering all-electronic score for the 1956 sci-fi classic, 'Forbidden Planet' (some 20 years earlier!), had we heard such synthetic rhythms. Unlike their more recent dabblings, composers EDGAR FROESE, PETER BAUMANN and CHRISTOPHER FRANKE broke with the tradition of lengthy, mostly one-sided pieces, and settled for a conventional and contemporary lay-out of 12 tracks. These eerie chunks of pulsating electronica – highlights being 'Search', 'The Journey', 'Grind', 'Rain Forest' and 'Betrayal' – encapsulated the uncompromising and bleak terrain of the South American environs – jazz excerpts from CHARLIE PARKER and KEITH JARRETT were not given light on the LP. PETER BAUMANN would be off on his own solo journey a year later, while the 'DREAM continued to issue a plethora of albums, including numerous soundtrack work. *MCS*

Album rating: *6.5

– spinoff releases, etc. –

TANGERINE DREAM: Betrayal / Grind

Aug 77. (7") *<40740>* ☐ –

the SOUL OF NIGGER CHARLEY

1973 sequel (US 110m) Paramount Pictures (R)

Film genre: western drama

Top guns: dir: Larry G. Spangler (+ story) / s-w: Harold Stone

Stars: Fred Williamson *(Charley)* ← BLACK CAESAR ← HELL UP IN HARLEM / → THREE TOUGH GUYS → BUCKTOWN → MEAN JOHNNY BARROWS → ADIOS AMIGO → THREE THE HARD WAY → MR. MEAN → FROM DUSK TILL DAWN → RIDE → CARMEN: A HIP HOPERA, D'Urville Martin *(Toby)* ← BLACK CAESAR ← BOOK OF NUMBERS ← HELL UP IN HARLEM ← the FINAL COMEDOWN ← WATERMELON MAN ← a TIME TO SING / → FIVE ON THE BLACK HAND SIDE → SHEBA, BABY → DOLEMITE → DISCO 9000, Denise Nicholas *(Elena)* ← BLACULA / → LET'S DO IT AGAIN → a PIECE OF THE ACTION, Pedro Armendariz Jr. *(Sandoval)*, Kirk Calloway *(Marcellus)* → the MONKEY HUSTLE, Fred Lerner *(Woods)* → FOXY BROWN, Richard Farnsworth *(Walker)* → RHINESTONE

Storyline: The continuing adventures of escaped slave turned cowboy Charley, now in the midst of the American Civil War: as a Yankee colonel keeps the Southern old guard in the lifestyle they're accustomed to by capturing AWOL Afro-Americans for their Mexican bolthole, Charley and his friend Toby do their damndest to put a soul-powered spanner in the works. *BG*

Movie rating: *5

Visual: none

Off the record: **DON COSTA** (see below)

—

DON COSTA (ORCHESTRA)

1973. (lp) *M.G.M.; <1SE 46ST>* ☐ –
– Main title – Charley / Main theme to Water Tower / A lonely summer (love theme) / Can you dig it? (working music) / Sometime day (vocal: LOU RAWLS) / The lonely summer / Train's comin' / Lord, it's a long time comin' / Fiesta (solo guitar: DANNY ZEFF) / Sandoval / Morning comes around (vocal: LOU RAWLS).

S/track review: DON COSTA, the so-called "Puccini of Pop", and a man better known for his work with Frank Sinatra and Paul Anka, was probably the most unlikely of all unlikely blaxploitation composers. He'd previously worked with B-movie don Mike Curb, but his involvement in an early 70s Fred Williamson film is still one of the era's odder commissions. There's no question that COSTA can cut the funk-mustard, though; on this evidence he might have enjoyed a handsome Hollywood run ('The SOUL OF NIGGER CHARLEY' was one of Paramount's highest grossing box office hits of 1973; the title ensured its rarity value). As it stands, this is his sole soundtrack release, recorded a decade before his heart – like the stress-ravaged tickers of too many composers before him – finally gave in. A past master of condensed melody, and having already worked on both Westerns (Arnold Laven's 'Rough Night In Jericho', Doris Day vehicle, 'The Ballad Of Josie') and a hard-bitten actioner (Don Siegel's 'Madigan'), COSTA has no problem steering his orchestra into ebullient sympho-funk territory. On 'Main Title –

Charley', his string section strikes a high-stepping balance between New York street and Western trail, arrangements deftly working in sitar and electric piano with melodic hints of Quincy Jones' 'Something's Cookin'. 'Main Theme To Water Tower' and the excellent 'Can You Dig It? (Working Music)' are more five o'clock shadow, the former prefacing its bridge with a spiny guitar solo, the latter bringing off an audacious chicken scratch-harpsichord hybrid. The too often underrated LOU RAWLS, meanwhile, calls it as coolly as Bill Withers on 'Sometime Day', an oxymoron that slides off RAWLS' tongue like super-saturated black coffee, against tight, small-band backing which breaks the orchestral programme nicely. While always intense, COSTA's pop savvy mean his cues are rarely overplayed, stitching together hush-holler gospel-invocation 'Lord, It's A Long Time Comin' (with uncredited female lead), a low-end-pot-boiler which Jones would've been only too proud to put his name to, a Mariachi-goes-Don Ellis cue titled 'Sandoval' and a solo guitar piece performed by veteran Flamenco authority DANNY ZEFF. Soul fans will get less mileage out of the love theme(s), but overall this is COSTA's high-water mark and – notwithstanding the PC-oops title – another 'M.G.M.' soundtrack that should've seen a CD reissue years ago. *BG*

Album rating: *7

SOUNDER

1972 (US 105m) Twentieth Century-Fox (G)

Film genre: coming-of-age/family drama

Top guns: dir: Martin Ritt / s-w: Lonne Elder III ← MELINDA / → BUSTIN' LOOSE (nov: William H. Armstrong)

Stars: Cicely Tyson *(Rebecca Morgan)* → a HERO AIN'T NOTHIN' BUT A SANDWICH → BUSTIN' LOOSE → IDLEWILD, Paul Winfield *(Nathan Lee Morgan)* → TROUBLE MAN → GORDON'S WAR → a HERO AIN'T NOTHIN' BUT A SANDWICH → MIKE'S MURDER → BLUE CITY, Kevin Hooks *(David Lee Morgan)* → AARON LOVES ANGELA, Carmen Mathews *(Mrs. Boatwright)*, **Taj MAHAL** *(Ike)*, James Best *(Sheriff Young)*, Janet MacLachlan *(Camille Johnson)* ← UP TIGHT!

Storyline: Deep South, depression-era drama as a tight-knit but poverty-stricken family are torn apart when patriarch Nathan is imprisoned for stealing a loaf of bread. Elder son David inadvertently kickstarts his overdue education when he tracks down the prison camp where his father is being held. *BG*

Movie rating: *8

Visual: video + dvd

Off the record: Taj MAHAL (see below)

—

TAJ MAHAL

1972. (lp) *Columbia; <S 31944> C.B.S.; (70123)* ☐ 1974 ☐
– Needed time / Sounder chase a coon / Needed time (hummin' and pickin') / Morning work – N' meat's on the stove / I'm running and I'm hapy / Speedball / Goin' to the country – Critters in the woods / Motherless children (hummin') / Jailhouse blues / Just workin' / Harriet's dance song / Two spirits reunited / David runs again / Curiosity blues / Someday be a change / Horseshoes / Cheraw / David's dream / Needed time (guitar) / Needed time (banjo and hand-clapping).

S/track review: On this, TAJ MAHAL's first – and all but forgotten – soundtrack, his instruments are credited like sidemen: National Steel Bodied Guitar, Harmonica, Banjo, Six-Holed Fife; a one-man band that chuckles at the very notion of an orchestral score. He may be as diligent, pioneering and exploratory an ethno-musicologist as longtime friend/collaborator Ry Cooder but 'SOUNDER' necessarily finds MAHAL presenting a series of brief, self-composed cues which abide solidly within the movie's Southern milieu, rotating its expression according to the accompaniment and lay of the land. Plenty of country blues and virtuoso banjo picking then, but also a couple of lovely solo Fife pieces, naturalistic and lighter than air, and inspired – as TAJ explains it in his sleeve notes – by the "union of the two spirits of vibration, that of sound (the ear) and of light (the eye)". His holistic, hippy-ish attitude to his art doesn't stop him shouting at the Devil, Robert Johnson-style, but it's on gregarious, drawling commentaries that his spirit really inhabits the music. Like Cooder, he's never had the strongest of voices, and while he can easily handle an a cappella like 'Someday Be A Change', he's just as effective with whistling or wordless lament, as on a soughing 'Motherless Children', the album's only non-original. The great LIGHTNIN' HOPKINS performs the main theme – a humble, gospel-supplication called 'Needed Time' – although it sounds like TAJ supplying the funky, syncopated handclaps on the instrumental closer. *BG*

Album rating: *6.5

SOUTH OF HEAVEN, WEST OF HELL

2000 (US 132m) Goldmount Pictures / Trimark Pictures (R)

Film genre: revisionist/outlaw western drama

Top guns: s-w: **Dwight YOAKAM** (+ dir), Stan Bertheaud (au: Otto Felix, Dennis Hackin)

Stars: Dwight YOAKAM *(Valentine Casey)*, Vince Vaughn *(Taylor Henry)* → THUMBSUCKER → BE COOL → INTO THE WILD, Billy Bob Thornton *(Brigadier Smalls)* ← PRIMARY COLORS ← DEAD MAN / → FRIDAY NIGHT LIGHTS, Bridget Fonda *(Adalyne Dunfries)* ← FINDING GRACELAND ← JACKIE BROWN ← TOUCH ← GRACE OF MY HEART ← SINGLES ← SHAG: THE MOVIE, Peter Fonda *(Shoshonee Bill)* ← GRACE OF MY HEART ← the HIRED HAND ← EASY RIDER ← the TRIP ← the WILD ANGELS, Paul Reubens *(Arvid Henry)* ← MOONWALKER ← BACK TO THE BEACH ← the BLUES BROTHERS / → OVERNIGHT → MAYOR OF THE SUNSET STRIP, Bud Cort *(agent Otis)* ← ELECTRIC DREAMS ← HAROLD AND MAUDE ← GAS-S-S-S ← BREWSTER McCLOUD ← the STRAWBERRY STATEMENT / → the MILLION DOLLAR HOTEL → COYOTE UGLY → the LIFE AQUATIC WITH STEVE ZISSOU, Bo Hopkins *(Uncle Angus)* ← MORE AMERICAN GRAFFITI ← AMERICAN GRAFFITI / → DON'T LET GO, Luke Askew *(Leland)* ← MACKINTOSH & T.J. ← PAT GARRETT & BILLY THE KID ← EASY RIDER, Joe Unger *(Nogales Sanchez)* ← the BODYGUARD ← ROAD HOUSE, Matt Clark *(Burl Dunfries)* ← HONKYTONK MAN ← OUTLAW BLUES ← PAT GARRETT & BILLY THE KID, Matt Malloy *(Harvey)* → DR. T & THE WOMEN, Michael Jeter *(Uncle Jude)* ← FEAR AND LOATHING IN LAS VEGAS ← HAIR, Scott Wilson *(Clete Monroe)* ← DEAD MAN WALKING ← SOUL SURVIVOR ← GERONIMO: AN AMERICAN LEGEND ← ELVIS AND THE COLONEL: THE UNTOLD STORY ← YOUNG GUNS II ← JOHNNY HANDSOME ← BLUE CITY / → DON'T LET GO → MONSTER, Noble Willingham *(Sheriff Harris)* ← GOOD MORNING, VIETNAM ← LA BAMBA ← LIVING PROOF: THE HANK WILLIAMS JR. STORY

Storyline: Critically savaged but surely destined at least for cult obscurity, the Twin Peaks-esque travails of Valentine Casey are played out in the border territory of Arizona when it was still lawless enough to be an admistrative headache. Unfortunate enough to have been brought under the wing of the ruthless Henry clan as a child, Casey has his erstwhile relatives come back to haunt him on Christmas eve; as sheriff of Los Tragos, he's forced to stand back as the firepower of clan chief Leland wins out during a bloody bank robbery. Although certified dead in the Cuban war, he – or his ghost – is subsequently witnessed engaged in cryptic banter with a fellow phantom accompanying an actress come to collect her deaf child. When the Caseys show up to spoil the party yet again, Valentine – together with his cross-dressing, sharp-shooting sidekick – vows to finish them off once and for all. *BG*

Movie rating: *5.5

Visual: dvd

Off the record: (see below)

—

DWIGHT YOAKAM

Oct 01. (cd) *Warners; <9362 48012-2>* [ ] [–]
– Words / Old friend / Who at the door is standing (with BEKKA BRAMLETT) / Good afternoon / Tears for two / Ma'am / The darkest hour / When you was shot / The first thing smokin' / How long was it / What's left of me / All anybody can do / Somewhere / A lotta good people / The last surrender / Show 'em your badge / No future in sight / Existence / It is well with my soul / Words – instrumental.

S/track review: There aren't many artists – never mind country artists – who've not only made the transition to acting but have ventured as far as the director's chair. Yet the critical consensus was that DWIGHT YOAKAM had overreached himself, what with writing the script, directing and scoring the movie, and putting together this partly "inspired by" soundtrack. The most obvious recent comparison would be Nick Cave's pet western. In as far as it's fair to compare two very different projects, Cave showed it could be done, and done convincingly. Granted, he didn't direct but his score dovetailed gracefully with his script. What you get here are snatches of score, ill-judged dialogue and underachieving big-name collaborations on a soundtrack which doesn't quite reflect the movie. Nothing unusual in itself but as YOAKAM proves with his elegant opening theme, he's more than capable of condensing high plains emotion in both a quasi-classical and a jazz idiom, and a further couple of equally strong themes would've rounded things out nicely. The creaking, atonal underscore glimpsed on some of the dialogue offcuts might've likewise been better served by being programmed in its entirety (released as a separate disc?), not sandwiched between slight country-pop like 'Tears For Two' and a flabby take on the old spiritual, 'Who At The Door Is Standing' (with BEKKA BRAMLETT). Gospel-wise, a sombre, Mexican brass and organ arrangement of 'The Darkest Hour' is more composed, as is the penultimate 'It Is Well With My Soul'. While Billy Gibbons' co-credit passes by fairly innocuously, Mick Jagger's contribution makes more of an impression in a tragi-cosmic, Gram Parsons kinda way. But YOAKAM approaches a more filmic tone when he's referencing roots legends off his own back, generating the Roy Orbison-esque grandeur of 'Somewhere', the Cooder-like fanfare of 'The Last Surrender' and the Allmans-vintage 'No Future In Sight'. *BG*

Album rating: *5.5

□ SPIRIT segment
(⇒ MODEL SHOP)

SPIRIT: STALLION OF THE CIMARRON

2002 (US 82m) DreamWorks (G)

Film genre: children's animated fantasy

Top guns: dir: Kelly Asbury, Lorna Cook / s-w: John Fusco ← YOUNG GUNS II ← CROSSROADS, Henry Mayo (+ story: Tom Sito)

Voices: Matt Damon *(Spirit)* ← ALL THE PRETTY HORSES ← GOOD WILL HUNTING ← GERONIMO: AN AMERICAN LEGEND, James Cromwell *(the Colonel)* ← the RUNNIN' KIND, Daniel Studi *(Little Creek)*, Matthew Levin *(Joe)*, Jeff LeBeau *(Murphy, railroad foreman)*, Chopper Bernet *(Sgt. Adams)*, John Rubano *(soldier)* ← LIGHT OF DAY, Charles Napier *(Roy)* ← the BLUES BROTHERS ← BEYOND THE VALLEY OF THE DOLLS, Michael Horse *(Little Creek's friend)*

Storyline: 'Dreamworks' animation higlighting the plight of Spirit, an Old West horse kicking against cruel white overlords. Run-ins with both the US cavalry and railroad slavery can't flatten his mane as he searches out his true love, a mare called Rain. As the Times put it, only "pony club fanatics" need apply. *BG*

Movie rating: *5.5

Visual: dvd

Off the record: A neo-Springsteen rocker turned Hollywood golden boy, **BRYAN ADAMS** (b. 5 Nov'59, Vancouver, Canada) has cornered the market for saccharine film themes with unprecedented success. Granted, there were early indications of ADAMS' future career when the track 'Heaven' (from his actually rather decent 'Reckless' album and a subsequent US No.1), was used in the abysmal teacher-student drama, 'A Night In Heaven' (1983). The man also made an early acting appearance in the Clint Eastwood's 1989 comedy, 'Pink Cadillac', although it was his trifling contribution to the high grossing Kevin Costner vehicle, 'Robin Hood: Prince Of Thieves' (1991) which had the movie execs in rapture. The song in question, '(Everything I Do) I Do It For You', sold millions around the world, earned ADAMS a Best Song Grammy and was nominated for an Oscar. The Canadian was duly recruited to come up with another blockbusting song for 1993's all-star update of 'The Three Muskateers'. The result was 'All For Love' (with STING & Rod Stewart), establishing his heavy handed balladry niche and making the appearance of the truly awful 'Have You Ever Really Loved A Woman' an inevitability. The latter was the showcase song for Francis Ford Coppola's 'Don Juan DeMarco' (1995) and the recipient of yet more award nominations. While 'I Finally Found Someone', penned for the 1996 Barbra Streisand vanity flick, 'The Mirror Has Two Faces', wasn't quite so successful, it was only a matter of time before ADAMS scored a whole soundtrack, collaborating with Hans Zimmer on the music for this innocuous animation. *BG*

—

BRYAN ADAMS: songs (music: Hans Zimmer)

May 02. (cd) *Universal; <493304-2> (493362-2)* [40] Jul02 [8]
– Here I am – end title / I will always return / You can't take me / Get off my back / Brothers under the sun / Don't let go (SARAH McLACHLAN) / This is where I belong / Here I am / Sound the bugle – instrumental / Run free – instrumental / Homeland main title – instrumental / Rain – instrumental / The long road back – instrumental / Nothing I've ever known / I will always return – finale.

S/track review: So smooth was BRYAN ADAMS' transition from journeyman rocker to Hollywood balladeer that it's difficult to see the join. Significantly, he's only released three original studio albums in the last fifteen years; much of his chart action has been generated by celluloid love songs priceless in their vacuity – if ADAMS could bottle his formula, he'd be an even richer man than he must be already. His link-up with 'Media Ventures' golden boy Hans Zimmer was as inevitable as George Bush's second term, with just as predictable a platform: ADAMS takes bloodless title theme ('Here I Am') into the charts for weeks on end, rasps through an album's worth of corporate schlock, and ZIMMER tags a few score excerpts onto the end. "Don't judge a thing till you know what's inside it" is one of his lyrical pearls of wisdom (from the dire 'You Can't Take Me'). Well, the sleeve doesn't bode well, and a thorough rummage around inside leaves judgement unavoidable: that this is the kind of professionally scripted, multi-tasking muzak that should've gone out of fashion in the 80s. It's hard to believe that one of ADAMS' army of co-writers, Robert 'Mutt' Lange, is the same man who helmed Ac/Dc's 'Highway To Hell' (1979). To be fair, 'Brothers Under The Sun' is at least cinematic and 'Get Off My Back' hints at the ADAMS of old, although even then its hook lumbers like a hobbled donkey. SARAH McLACHLAN makes a Shakespears Sister-like cameo on 'Don't Let Go', and Zimmer rolls out his usual electro-symphonic fusion. His orchestrations hawk more emotion – especially on the haunting, Vangelis-esque echo of 'The Long Road Back' – but it's nothing we haven't heard before. "Horribly close to Bambi" opined the Guardian's film review, and it's difficult not to regard the music as Bambi-like in turn. In two words, horseshit sandwich. *BG*

Album rating: *4

– spinoff hits, etc. –

BRYAN ADAMS: Here I Am – end title

Jul 02. (c-s) *(497743-4)* [-] [5]
(cd-s+=) *(497743-2)* – (soundtrack version).
(cd-s) *(497744-2)* – ('A') / (instrumental) / You can't take me (alt. version) / (video).

the SPOOK WHO SAT BY THE DOOR

1973 (US 102m) United Artists (PG)

Film genre: spy/political drama

Top guns: dir: Ivan Dixon ← TROUBLE MAN / s-w: Melvin Clay, Sam Greenlee (+ nov)

Stars: Lawrence Cook *(Dan Freeman)* ← TROUBLE MAN ← COTTON COMES TO HARLEM, J.A. Preston *(Dawson)*, Don Blakely *(Stud Davis)* ← SHAFT'S BIG SCORE! / → SHORT EYES → PULP FICTION, Paula Kelly *(Dahomey Queen)* ← TROUBLE MAN ← COOL BREEZE / → THREE TOUGH GUYS, Martin Golar *(Perkins)*, Anthony Ray *(Shorty)*, Joseph Mascolo *(Senator Hennington)* ← SHAFT'S BIG SCORE!, Elaine Aiken *(Mrs. Hennington)* → CADDYSHACK, Johnny Williams *(waiter)* → LOOKING FOR AN ECHO

Storyline: One of the most controversial, uncompromising and discursive black – if not quite blaxploitation – films of the early 70s (pulled from screens after a limited release), this Sam Greenlee-adapted cult classic takes up the story of Dan Freeman, an unassuming Korean vet who decides to take advantage of an apparent CIA equal opportunities policy. As the only black candidate to make it through the recruitment process, Freeman looks set for great things yet soon discovers that he's nothing but a cheap token to appease progressive sentiment, itself exploited by opportunistic politicians. Disillusioned not only with the CIA but with the dynamics of white power and the system in general, he gets angry and swaps government intelligence for ghetto activism, radicalizing and training – using acutely observed CIA methods – a Chicago gang he's been assigned as part of his new social services job. *BG*

Movie rating: *7

Visual: video

Off the record: (see below)

—

HERBIE HANCOCK

1973. (lp) *United Artists; <UAR 7370>* [ ] [-]
– Revolution / The spook who sat by the door (reprise) / Revenge / At the lounge / Training day / The stick up / Main theme / Underground / The spook who sat by the door / The big rip off / Recruiting / The pick up / It begins / (dialogue).

S/track review: Simmering in the same modal soup as 'Death Wish', but funkier, more inventive and generally drop-dead cooler, this is the one that should've been issued in the first place, a prelude to his 1974 masterpiece, 'Headhunters' and a premonition of his electro future shocks. Audio quality isn't the greatest but the suspect fidelity at least brings an authenticity to the deep-space bass, burbling keyboards and double-jointed drum fills, and much of the sample-hungry dialogue is conveniently crammed into one cue. It starts out as compellingly as any blaxploitation album, a countdown to hypno-funk with a payoff so hip – "Hang on brothers and sisters, liberation is near" – you can almost ignore the cliche. HANCOCK's canvases are anything but, probing nebulous depths between jazz and funk with the same restlessness that had driven him since he first plugged in with Miles Davis in the mid-late 60s. 'The SPOOK WHO SAT BY THE DOOR' itself quietly asserts as much improvisational scope as any blaxploitation title, landing quickfire wah-wah jabs, looping electric piano embouchoure around the limb-popping time signatures of drummer BILLY HART. It's that unrelenting, reptilian bass, though – all the way through 'Training Day', the psych-fi effects of 'The Stick Up' and 'The Big Rip Off' – which dominates this soundtrack, the throb of an inner-city revolt by no means outside the realm of possibilty in 1973; at times you can glimpse the innovations of Grandmaster Flash and the distant dawn of minimalist techno, revolution confined to the dancefloor. HANCOCK also echoes his own contemporaries further afield, within his own timeline; 'Recruiting' bends and loosens the bass till it's on Jamaican time while 'At The Lounge' echoes the murky Fender Rhodes experiments of Mulatu Astaque, brooding away at his dark-star jazz thousands of miles away on another continent. At just over half an hour, you don't get much for your money, but this is as ahead of its time as any of HANCOCK's solo records, and worth buying a turntable just to hear. *BG*

Album rating: *7.5

SQUADRA ANTIGANGSTERS

aka the GANG THAT SOLD AMERICA

1979 (Ita 90m*) Cinemaster (18)

Film genre: crime/gangster thriller

Top guns: s-w: Bruno Corbucci (+ dir), Mario Amendola

—

Stars: Tomas Milian *(Nico Giraldi)*, Enzo Cannavale *(Salvatore Esposito)*, **Asha Puthli** *(Fiona Strike)*, Gianni Musi *(Gitto Cardone)*, Margherita Fumero *(Maria Sole)* ← PERCHE SI UCCIDONO, Leo Gavero *(Don Vito)*

Storyline: Another in a series of 'Squadra Anti..' movies centered around foul-mouthed hippie cop, Nico Giraldi, and his horrible crime-busting compadres. *MCS*

Movie rating: *3.5

Visual: none

Off the record: Disco diva **Asha Puthli** hailed from New York via India and was more famous for her worldly jazz singing. She also appeared in the 1972 film, 'Savages', as Asha, the forest girl. *MCS*

—

GOBLIN (& Various Artists)

1979. (cd) *Cinevox; (MDF 33/131)* [-] Italy [-]
– The whip (ASHA PUTHLI) / The sound of money (ASHA PUTHLI) / Banoon / Stunt cars / Welcome to the boogie (vocals: CHARLIE CANNON) / Trumpet's flight / Sicilian samba / Disco China. *(cd-iss. Apr99 +=; CD-MDF 324)* – Squadra Antigangsters (movie take 1) / Squadra Antigangsters (movie take 2) / Trumpet's flight (alt.take).

S/track review: Up until now, Italian rock group GOBLIN (i.e. CLAUDIO SIMONETTI, FABIO PIGNATELLI, AGOSTINO MARANGOLO and CARLO PENNISI) were purveyors of everything Euro Prog-rock. Soundtrack albums for Giallo/suspense films such as 'PROFONDO ROSSO' (1975) and 'SUSPIRIA' (1977), had earned them a reputation as one of Italy's best exports since ELP-clones, PFM. However, GOBLIN took a step backwards for this jazzed-up, disco-orientated piece of pop-pourri. Here, everything hard and heavy is booted out for sterile, contemporary savoir faire. Right from openers, 'The Whip' and 'The Sound Of Money' (which feature Indian disco diva, ASHA PUTHLI), GOBLIN give the listener very little from their complex canon of old. Track 3, 'Banoon', takes cod-reggae into a new Police-like groove, but . . . er . . . without the Sting, while jazz-rock meets country 'Stunt Cars', gave us that good ole boy feel, better suited for The Dukes Of Hazzard TV series. Yet another vocal track, 'Welcome To The Boogie', featured unknown songsmith, CHARLIE CANNON, and just about did what it said on the tin. The only saving grace was the uptempo guitar/synth interplay on the classy jazz number, 'Trumpet's Flight'. Too little, too late. *MCS*

Album rating: *3 / cd+ *3.5

□ Edwin STARR segment
(⇒ HELL UP IN HARLEM)

STEALTH

2005 (US 121m) Phoenix Pictures / Columbia Pictures (PG-13)

Film genre: sci-fi thriller

Top guns: dir: Rob Cohen / s-w: W.D. Richter

Stars: Josh Lucas *(Lt. Ben Gannon)*, Jessica Biel *(Lt. Kara Wade)*, Jamie Foxx *(Lt. Henry Purcell)* ← RAY / → DREAMGIRLS, **Sam Shepard** *(Capt. George Cummings)* ← SWORDFISH ← ALL THE PRETTY HORSES ← RENALDO AND CLARA / → the ASSASSINATION OF JESSE JAMES . . ., Richard Roxburgh *(Dr. Keith Orbit)* ← MOULIN ROUGE! ← DOING TIME FOR PATSY CLINE, Joe Morton *(Capt. Dick Marshfield)* ← BLUES BROTHERS 2000 ← CROSSROADS, Ian Bliss *(Lt. Aaron Shaftsbury)*

Storyline: Three Navy pilots are none best pleased when they're told they're to have a fourth team member, Edi. It turns out that Edi is a hi-tech computer which controls an Unmanned Combat Aerial Vehicle (a robot plane to you and me). All goes well on the first mission but when the UCAV is struck by lightning it develops a mind of its own and promptly decides to begin World War III. It's up to the three human pilots to save the day and prove technology ain't everything. *JZ*

Movie rating: *4.5

Visual: dvd

Off the record: **Sam Shepard** was once a member of 'EASY RIDER' outfit, the Holy Modal Rounders. *MCS*

—

BT (additional scores: Trevor Morris * & Michael Dimattia **)

Aug 05. (cd) *Varese Sarabande; <302 066 676-2> (VSD 6676)* □ □
– Stealth main title / War machine (*) / Edi's arrival / The pilots' theme (*) / The joy of flight (*) / Edi's new data (**) / The vertical drop / Hellava 1st mission (*) / Lightning strike (*) / Thailand / Love theme / I'll tell you back at the boat / Quantum computer / Edi is the whole idea (**) / Flight to Tajikistan (**) / Tin man will prosecute / Attack at Tajikistan (*) / Henry's death / The aftermath / Kara's ejection / Camel hump (**) / Korean waterhole / Saving Edi (**) / Edi feels sorry (**) / Cummings' suicide (**) / DMZ (*) / Death of Col Yune (*) / Edi's sacrifice (*).

S/track review: 'STEALTH' was one of the biggest movie disasters of all time, losing almost a hundred million dollars upon its release. To suggest there is anything more than an incidental link between that fact and BT (BRIAN TRANSEAU)'s electro-symphonic OST would be irresponsible hyperbole, but the score is certainly appropriate to the overblown movie. A triumph of technology over substance, BT's music here puts all his pioneering production techniques to pedestrian rather than thrilling effect. TRANSEAU uses all the tricks in his arsenal: portentous/mock heroic orchestration (including judicious use of samples from Hans Zimmer's Media Ventures Library) and rote drums and bass, with elements of trance and small elements of glitch (the world-renowned BT stutter), too subtle to cause any real excitement to the untrained ear. The integration of orchestral and electronic music is, to be fair, well handled but speaks more of TRANSEAU's technical ability than any worthwhile innovation. There is bombast where necessary – punctuation to effect mounting tension (example 'Stealth Main Title' & 'Henry's Death') – and some interesting vocal layers ('Thailand' & 'Tin Man Will Prosecute'). Nowhere near as jarring as most scores that mix orchestral sounds with electronic elements, 'STEALTH' nonetheless fails to excise the elements of traditional action movie scores that are loud/brash or soft/cloying without any real thrill. The 'Love Theme' comes across in part like a musak version of Radiohead's 'Airbag', and the die is cast with the melodramatic new age vocals on the concluding 'EDI's Sacrifice' (EDI is the stealth plane, it stands for Extreme Deep Invader). The sense of self-satisfaction is evident, no mean feat in an instrumental medium, and the overriding feeling is that BT judges success in this field as merely achieving the swing of an action score, without the kick. Adequate, but more interesting – if technical expertise interests you – than astonishing. *SW*

Album rating: *4

– spinoff releases, etc. –

Various Artists

Jul 05. (cd) *Sony; <EK 94475> Epic-Sony; (520420-2)* □ □
– Make a move (INCUBUS) / Admiration (INCUBUS) / Neither of us can see (INCUBUS) / (She can) Do that (DAVID BOWIE AND BT) / Bullet-proof skin (INSTITUTE) / (L.S.F.) Lost souls forever (KASABIAN) / Bug eyes (DREDG) / Over my head (cable car) (the FRAY) / One day (TRADING YESTERDAY) *[bonus track]* / Different (ACCEPTANCE) *[bonus track]* / Nights in white satin (GLENN HUGHES featuring CHAD SMITH and JOHN FRUSCIANTE) / Aqueous transmission (INCUBUS).

□ STEELY DAN segment
(⇒ YOU'VE GOT TO WALK IT . . .)

STEELYARD BLUES

1973 (US 92m) Warner Bros. Pictures (PG)

Film genre: crime caper/comedy

Top guns: dir: Alan Myerson / s-w: Stevan Larner, David S. Ward

Stars: Jane Fonda *(Iris Caine)* → the ELECTRIC HORSEMAN, Donald Sutherland *(Jesse Veldini)* → ANIMAL HOUSE → RED HOT → COLD MOUNTAIN, Peter Boyle *(Eagle Thornberry)* ← JOE / → WHERE THE BUFFALO ROAM → WALKER → the IN CROWD, Garry Goodrow *(Duval Jax)* → AMERICAN HOT WAX → HARD TO HOLD → DIRTY DANCING, Howard Hesseman *(Frank Veldini)* → THIS IS SPINAL TAP, John Savage *(kid)* → HAIR, Dan Barrows *(Rocky)*, Morgan Upton *(police Capt. Bill)* → SPACE IS THE PLACE → BUCKTOWN → TUCKER: THE MAN AND HIS DREAM → the SPIRIT OF 76, Nancy Fish *(pool hall waitress)* → MORE AMERICAN GRAFFITI → BIRDY → HOWARD THE DUCK → CANDY MOUNTAIN, Mel Stewart *(black man in jail)* → LET'S DO IT AGAIN, Larry Hankin *(Bill the garbage truck driver)* ← the PHYNX / → AMERICAN HOT WAX

Storyline: When lifelong lounger Veldini gets out of prison yet again, he finally decides it's time to quit the rat race for ever (especially his pesky brother Frank, a lawyer). Recruiting a group of like-minded misfits, Veldini creates his version of Noah's Ark by restoring an old navy seaplane. But before they can fly off into the sunset Veldini must return to his old ways to smuggle a vital part out of the local navy base. *JZ*

Movie rating: *5

Visual: video

Off the record: (see below for score stars)

—

NICK GRAVENITES and MIKE BLOOMFIELD featuring PAUL BUTTERFIELD and MARIA MULDAUR

Feb 73. (lp) *Warner Bros.; <BS 2662>*
– Swing with it / Brand new family / Woman's love / Make the headlines / Georgia blues / My bag (the oysters) / Common ground / Being different / I've been searching / Do I care / Lonesome star blues / Here I come (there she goes) / If you cared / Theme from Steelyard Blues (Drive again). *<cd-iss. Oct03 on 'Pidm' Japan; 59670-2>*

S/track review: Why pick one major artist to write and play your music when you can have four? The majority of 'STEELYARD BLUES' was penned and performed by NICK GRAVENITES (vocal & guitar, plus production duties) and MIKE BLOOMFIELD (vocal & guitar), also featuring PAUL BUTTERFIELD (vocal & harmonica) and MARIA MULDAUR (vocal, guitar & claps!); others on session included MERLE SAUNDERS (organ & piano), JOHN KAHN (bass), CHRISTOPHER PARKER (drums) and guest vocalist ANNIE SAMPSON. If you love your blues and jazz you'll know most of these names. Chicago-born NICK GRAVENITES was usually the backseat driver in most of his previous work, having written songs for the likes of friend, Butterfield ('Born In Chicago'), Janis Joplin ('Buried Alive In The Blues'), etc.; his C.V. also stretched to performing with Muddy Waters, Howlin' Wolf, Charlie Musselwhite and MIKE BLOOMFIELD. With the latter ex-Paul Butterfield Blues Band member Buddy Miles, Barry Goldberg and Harvey Brooks, GRAVENITES formed the Electric Flag and recorded two psychedelic-blues albums ('A Long Time Comin'' & 'An American Music Band') in 1968. When this outfit split, Nick released a solo LP, 'My Labors' (1969) and even resurrected the band post-'STEELYARD . . .' for a 1974 set, 'The Band Kept Playing'. By this time, ex-Even Dozen/Jim Kwesin Jug Band singer MARIA MULDAUR was high in the chart with her best known number, 'Midnight At The Oasis'. 'STEELYARD BLUES' was another kettle of fish, starring Donald Sutherland (as the maniacal Jesse Veldini), all and sundry just had to get it right. With the blues still in vogue in some circles, the pairing of GRAVENITES and BLOOMFIELD was blistering, from the opening harmonica salvo and beats of 'Swing With It'. Follow-on track, 'Brand New Family', gets into the country-rock mode – well, everybody else was doing it, and just to emphasise their newly-found C&W leanings, GRAVENITES duets with MARIA MULDAUR on 'Woman's Love' (she had just split from her musician hubby, Geoff Muldaur). Getting back to the blues, Maria co-wrote 'Georgia Blues', while she also contributed the solo, 'Lonesome Star Blues' and with SAUNDERS, 'Do I Care'. You'd be mistaken to think Maria was the singer on the bluesy 'Common Ground' and 'If You Cared', that credit goes to the aforementioned (and very similar) ANNIE SAMPSON of Stoneground. Apart from the tongue-in-cheek, doo-wop ditty, 'My Bag (The Oysters)', the Canned Heat-cloned 'Being Different' and the Bo Diddley-esque 'I've Been Searching', most tracks are competent but conventional. Closing theme song ('Drive Again') is the most memorable from the film itself, where I think the aeroplane finally takes off. Shel Silverstein and indeed Dr. Hook & His Medicine Show would've been proud. *MCS*

Album rating: *6

- Chris STEIN
  (⇒ BLONDIE)

- Cat STEVENS segment
  (⇒ HAROLD AND MAUDE)

- Eric STEWART segment
  (⇒ GIRLS)

STIGMATA

1999 (US 103m) Metro-Goldwyn-Mayer (R)

Film genre: psychological/occult horror fantasy

Top guns: dir: Rupert Wainwright / s-w: Rick Ramage, Tom Lazarus ← SIDE BY SIDE: THE TRUE STORY OF A MAGICAL FAMILY (+ story)

Stars: Patricia Arquette *(Frankie Paige)* ← FAR NORTH, Gabriel Byrne *(Father Andrew Liernan)* ← the END OF VIOLENCE ← DEAD MAN ← the COURIER ← SIESTA ← GOTHIC, Jonathan Pryce *(Cardinal Daniel Houseman)* ← EVITA ← BREAKING GLASS / → BROTHERS OF THE HEAD, Nia Long *(Donna Chadway)* → ALFIE re-make, Thomas Kopache *(Father Durning)*, Rade Serbedzija *(Marion Petrocelli)*, Enrico Colantoni *(Father Dario)*, Ann Cusack *(Dr. Weston)*, Dick Latessa *(Father Gianni Delmonico)* → ALFIE re-make, Portia De Rossi *(Jennifer Kelliho)* ← GIRL

Storyline: Frankie Paige is a hair stylist whose routine life is transformed after being given rosary beads by her mother. She begins speaking a foreign language/tongue, comes under attack from mysterious forces, and develops stigmata wounds on her hands, feet and side. Father Kieran is the sceptical Vatican priest sent to investigate this possible miracle but he must act quickly if he is to save Frankie from the unbalancing forces of good and evil. *JZ*

Movie rating: *6

Visual: video + dvd

Off the record: A classically-trained pianist, **MIKE GARSON** (b. Jul'45, Brooklyn, New York) has accompanied some of the top names in jazz and recorded numerous jazz albums under his own steam. He was also a key member of David BOWIE's early to mid 70s touring band, memorably tinkling the ivories on 'Aladdin Sane' (1973). His film scoring career got off to a fairly low key start with 80s comedy, 'Life On The Edge' (1988), although he belatedly made it to soundtrack via, 'STIGMATA' (1999). *MCS*

Various Artists // BILLY CORGAN & MIKE GARSON

Aug 99. (cd) *Virgin; <7243 8 47753-2> (CDVUS 161)* Sep99
– Mary Mary (CHUMBAWAMBA) / Gramarye (REMY ZERO) / All is full of love (BJORK) / The pretty things are going to Hell (DAVID BOWIE) / Release (AFRO CELT SOUND SYSTEM feat. SINEAD O'CONNOR) / Inertia creeps (MASSIVE ATTACK) / Identify (NATALIE IMBRUGLIA) // Identify / Pop pop – Await – Reflect (pretty) / Reflect (clouds) – Truth / Of square waves – Random though / Reflection – Possession / Reflect (gray) – Of sine waves / Distrbnce (after sckhausen) – Reflect (pause) – Orah / Sustain – Identify (affectation) / All answers revealed – Reflect (devotion) / Purge – 10,000,000 voices – Reflect (purity) – Identify (peace) / Reflect (time) – Tree whispers.

S/track review: Collaborating with the Smashing Pumpkins' BILLY CORGAN, GARSON created an unsettling, claustrophobic series of cues located in the industrialised beatz landscape of the late 90s. The first half of the OST comprises modern, religion-oriented songs beginning with CHUMBAWAMBA's 'Mary Mary' and BOWIE's 'The Pretty Things Are Going To Hell'. Best of all is BJORK's 'All Is Full Of Love' and the unusual Afro-Celtic number 'Release' sung by SINEAD O'CONNOR. These modern, loosely religious songs help to emphasise the awkwardness of stigmata occurring in today's society. The second half of the CD is purely instrumental and mixes orchestra with synthesizer. This music is much moodier and deeper than the rock songs in the first half, as can be seen in track titles such as 'Of Square Waves / Random Thought' and 'Reflect'. Synthesizer noises and voices are used to create the impression that we are inside the mind of the heroine and understanding her moods and emotions as she suffers. Definitely a superior CD with loads of variation for everyone to enjoy. *JZ*

Album rating: *6

□ STILLE DAGE I CLICHY alt.
(⇒ QUIET DAYS IN CLICHY)

STING

Born: Gordon Matthew Sumner, 2 Oct'51, Wallsend, nr. Newcastle, England. A jazzer who somehow ended up in one of the New Wave's most successful bands, the Police, STING – unlike any rock/pop stars – had actually attended RADA, London's famous Royal Academy of Dramatic Art, prior to his big break. He'd even acted in TV commercials, although his first major screen part was as top mod bod, Ace Face, in the 1979 film version of 'Quadrophenia'. This was followed by a part in early Wim Wenders production, 'RADIO ON' (1980), to whose unreleased soundtrack he also contributed. Yet it was his work on Dennis Potter's malevolently brilliant black comedy, 'BRIMSTONE & TREACLE' (1982) which remain among the man's most memorable early cinematic endeavours. While the 1976 original (starring Michael Kitchen) was banned by the BBC, not making it to the screen until over a decade later, Richard Loncraine's 1982 remake starred STING in a convincingly demonic lead role. Although still a member of the Police at this point, his soundtrack contributions effectively represented his first bonafide solo efforts, even spawning a UK Top 20 single in the wonderfully warped 'Spread A Little Happiness'. Following a part in David Lynch's big budget sci-fi effort, 'DUNE' (1984), the man was the star of his own, Michael Apted-directed rockumentary, 'BRING ON THE NIGHT' (1986), following the touring adventures of the band he'd put together to record 'The Dream Of The Blue Turtles' album. In tandem with his new superstar solo status, STING continued to develop his acting career, taking a part in Meryl Streep vehicle, 'Plenty' (1985) and starring roles in Franc Roddam's slated Frankenstein update, 'The Bride' (1985) and Italian thriller, 'Julia And Julia' (1987). In between humanitarian efforts on behalf of Brazilian Indians, he returned to his native Newcastle for a starring role in Mike Figgis' directorial debut, 'Stormy Monday' (1988), and appeared in Terry Gilliam's fantastical follow-up, 'The Adventures Of Baron Munchausen' (1989). With his Grammy-winning recording career again reaching new heights in the early 90s, it'd be 1995 before the former Police chief starred in another feature film, namely black comedy, 'The Grotesque'; the release of the docu-film OST 'The Living Sea' went almost unnoticed. A part in Guy Ritchie's celebrated 'Lock, Stock And Two Smoking Barrels' (1998) found STING in gangster territory once again, albeit in London's East End rather than Newcastle, while the new millennium found him returning briefly to film scoring, sharing co-billing for nature documentary, 'Dolphins' (2000) and Disney animation, 'The EMPEROR'S NEW GROOVE'. *BG*

- **filmography** {acting} (composer) –

Quadrophenia *(1979 {*} =>)* / **Radio On** *(1980 {a})* / **Brimstone & Treacle** *(1982 {*} OST w/ V/A =>)* / **Dune** *(1984 {a} OST by TOTO =>)* / Plenty *(1985 {*})* / the Bride *(1985 {*})* / **Bring On The Night** *(1986 {*p} OST =>)* / Julia And Julia *(1987 {*})* / Stormy Monday *(1988 {*})* / the Adventures Of Baron Munchausen *(1989 {*})* / Resident Alien: Quentin Crisp In America *(1990 {*})* / Demolition Man *(1993 hit by STING)* / the Three Muskateers *(1993 hit by BRYAN ADAMS, ROD STEWART & STING; see future editions)* / the Grotesque *(1995 {*} =>)* / the Living Sea *(1995 OST; see future edition)* / Lock, Stock And Two Smoking Barrels *(1998 {a})* / Dolphins *(2000 OST w/ Steve Wood; see future edition)* / **the Emperor's New Groove** *(2000 OST w/ David Hartley & John Debney =>)*

– compilations, etc. –

STING: At The Movies

Mar 02. (cd) *A&M; (4 1535-2)* □ [-]
– De do do do, de da da da (the POLICE) *["the Last American Virgin"]* / I burn for you *["Brimstone & Treacle"]* / Need your love so bad *["Party Party"]* / Englishman in New York *["Stars And Bars"]* / Someone to watch over me *["Someone To Watch Over Me"]* / Demolition man (the POLICE) *["Demolition Man"]* / Shape of my heart *["the Professional"]* / All for love (w/ BRYAN ADAMS & ROD STEWART) *["the Three Muskateers"]* / The secret marriage *["Four Weddings And A Funeral"]* / The cowboy song *["Terminal Velocity"]* / It's probably me (w/ ERIC CLAPTON & MICHAEL KAMEN) *["Lethal Weapon 3"]* / Angel eyes *["Leaving Las Vegas"]* / Moonlight *["Sabrina"]* / My one and only love *["Leaving Las Vegas"]* / Fragile *["The Living Sea"]* / Murder by numbers *["Copycat"]* / Valparaiso *["White Squall"]*.

the STORY OF US

1999 (US 94m) Warner Bros. / Castle Rock (R)

Film genre: domestic/romantic comedy drama

Top guns: dir: Rob Reiner ← the PRINCESS BRIDE ← THIS IS SPINAL TAP / s-w: Jessie Nelson → I AM SAM, Alan Zweibel

Stars: Bruce Willis *(Ben Jordan)* ← BEAVIS AND BUTT-HEAD DO AMERICA ← LAST MAN STANDING ← FOUR ROOMS ← PULP FICTION / → OVER THE HEDGE, Michelle Pfeiffer *(Katie Jordan)* ← GREASE 2 / → I AM SAM → HAIRSPRAY re-make, Tim Matheson *(Marty)* ← ALMOST SUMMER ← ANIMAL HOUSE, Rob Reiner *(Stan)* ← PRIMARY COLORS ← THIS IS SPINAL TAP, Rita Wilson *(Rachel)* ← THAT THING YOU DO! / → RAISE YOUR VOICE, Paul Reiser *(Dave; Ben's literary agent)*, Julie Hagerty *(Liza)* ← JACKIE'S BACK! / → STORYTELLING, Colleen Rennison *(Erin Jordan; aged 10)*, Jake Sandvig *(Josh Jordan; aged 12)*, Jayne Meadows *(Dot)*, Tom Poston *(Harry)*, Betty White *(Lillian Jordan)*, Red Buttons *(Arnie)* ← YOUR CHEATIN' HEART, Art Evans *(George)* ← CB4: THE MOVIE ← TRESPASS ← SCHOOL DAZE ← YOUNGBLOOD ← BIG TIME ← LEADBELLY ← CLAUDINE

Storyline: After fifteen years of contented marriage, Ben and Katie realize that the excitement of first love has gone from their relationship. They decide on a trial separation to see how this will affect their feelings towards each other and whether they will get together again or ultimately drift apart forever. *JZ*

Movie rating: *5.5

Visual: dvd

Off the record: (see below)

ERIC CLAPTON with Marc Shaiman (& Various Performers)

Nov 99. (cd) *Reprise; <(9362 47603-2)>* □ Apr00 □
– Main title – (I) Get lost (ERIC CLAPTON) / A spoon is just a spoon / The girl in the pith helmet / Fighting / Empty nest / Keepin' out of mischief now (RUBY BRAFF & HIS NEW ENGLAND SONGHOUNDS) / Touching feet under the covers / Everything I love is in this bed / Dry cleaning – (I) Get lost (ERIC CLAPTON) / The shiek of Araby (TEDDY WILSON) / Family bed / Bust baby montage / Wonderful tonight – live edit (ERIC CLAPTON) / Silent drive to camp / Camp montage / Don't sit under the apple tree (the ANDREWS SISTERS) / Epiphany at the bistro / I hate the Kirbys / Love in Venice / Ben takes the apartment / Writing montage / Pictures on a wall / Classical gas (MASON WILLIAMS) / Let's go to chow fun.

S/track review: Guitar hero, ERIC CLAPTON, was no stranger to the art of film composition, having already given us the 'Lethal Weapon' series and 'Edge Of Darkness'. His collaborator here, Marc Shaiman, was essentially a session man (Yes, etc.) until he took on orchestral film work full-time (i.e. 'When Harry Met Sally', 'Misery' and 'Sister Act'). Although the music fits into the romantic/domestic mood of the movie, the E.C. we get here is the Slowhand "Tears In Heaven"-type (the latter a song from his 1991 score, 'RUSH'). That's not to say it's in any way bad, just a little sedate and easy-listening, alright for a sleep-in Sunday morning. Pointed out in the sleevenotes, director Rob Reiner was amazed at the artistry and professionalism of CLAPTON, and how he and Shaiman did everything over one long 10-hour day in the studio. '(I) Get Lost' opens CLAPTON's musical account in fine fettle, his amazing acoustic guitar-plucking and lovelorn wordplay both divine and elegant. Might well have made a hit single like the aforementioned 'Tears In Heaven'. Although Eric co-wrote the subsequent score instrumentals, his only other lyrical outings come via a second go at '(I) Get Lost' and a live edit of his classic, 'Wonderful Tonight' (not really in the film!). The rest of the score features soft and bluesy acoustic pieces, short'n'sweet and some augmented with a backing singer and a light orchestra. Of course, there are big let-downs courtesy of four vintage, non-Rock oldies: the big band sound of RUBY BRAFF & HIS NEW ENGLAND SONGHOUNDS and TEDDY WILSON, plus the squeaky-clean ANDREWS SISTERS with 'Don't Sit Under The Apple Tree' and on a slight upraised note, the perennial 'Classical Gas' by one-hit-wonder, MASON WILLIAMS. *MCS*

Album rating: *5

STORYTELLING

2001 (US 87m) Killer Films / New Line Cinema (R)

Film genre: buddy/ensemble black comedy drama

Top guns: s-w + dir: Todd Solondz

Stars: "Fiction":- Selma Blair *(Vi)* ← GIRL, Leo Fitzpatrick *(Marcus)* ← KIDS, Robert Wisdom *(Mr. Scott)* ← THAT THING YOU DO! / → MASKED AND ANONYMOUS → KILLER DILLER → RAY, Maria Thayer *(Amy)*, Angela Goethals *(Elli)* ← HEARTBREAK HOTEL, Tina Holmes *(Sue)* ← EDGE OF SEVENTEEN, Aleska Palladino *(Catherine)* ← MANNY & LO, "Non-Fiction":- Paul Giamatti *(Toby Oxman)* ← DUETS ← MAN ON THE MOON ← PRIVATE PARTS ← SINGLES, Mike Schank *(Mike the cameraman)* → BRITNEY, BABY, ONE MORE TIME, Xander Berkeley *(Mr. DeMarco)* ← TAPEHEADS ← WALKER ← STRAIGHT TO HELL ← SID & NANCY, Mark Webber *(Scooby Livingston)* ← WHITEBOYS / → CHELSEA WALLS → the HOTTEST STATE, John Goodman *(Marty Livingston)* ← the EMPEROR'S NEW GROOVE ← COYOTE UGLY ← O BROTHER, WHERE ART THOU? ← BLUES BROTHERS 2000 ← TRUE STORIES ← SWEET DREAMS / → MASKED AND ANONYMOUS → OVERNIGHT → BEYOND THE SEA, Julie Hagerty *(Fern Livingston)* ← the STORY OF US ← JACKIE'S BACK!, Noah Fleiss *(Brady Livingston)*, Franka Potente *(Toby's editor)* ← DOWNHILL CITY, Conan O'Brien *(himself)* ← BARENAKED IN AMERICA / → GIGANTIC (A TALE OF TWO JOHNS)

Storyline: A double bill split into "Fiction" and "Non-Fiction", the first following the misadventures of a college girl whose relationship with a cerebal palsy-afflicted classmate comes unstuck after his short story is ridiculed in class. She suffers a similar critical fate at the hands of her Afro-American, Pulitzer prize winning tutor and his lacky after writing about a sleazy encounter with him. The second film follows Toby Oxman, a geekish, thirty something would-be filmmaker as he shoots a documentary on teenage underachiever Scooby and the rest of his largely detestable family unit. His only ambitions being a vague idea of chat show fame, he makes for fairly pitiful subject matter, yet despite the reservations of Oxman's editor, the audience lap up the finished product. *BG*

Movie rating: *7

Visual: dvd

Off the record: BELLE AND SEBASTIAN were formed in Glasgow, Scotland ... early '96 by ex-choirboy/boxer!, Stuart Murdoch (the main songwriter) and Isobel Campbell, who met and recruited additional members Stuart David, Richard Colburn, Stevie Jackson and Chris Geddes in a local cafe. They borrowed the group name from a popular French 70s children's TV series about a young boy and his Pyrenees mountain dog. Two months into their career, the expanded outfit released a very limited (1000 copies) college financed album, 'Tigermilk', which gained sufficient airplay on national radio to ensure encroaching cult status. By the end of the year (and now with 7th member, Sarah Martin) they had unleashed their second set, 'If You're Feeling Sinister', which went on to sell in excess of 15,000 copies and gained much respect from end of the year critic polls. Since then, BELLE AND SEBASTIAN have hit the singles chart three times with a series of highly desirable EP's, 'Dogs On Wheels', 'Lazy Line Painter Jane' (with former Thrum larynx-basher Monica Queen in excellent form) and culminating with their critically acclaimed Top 40 entry, '3.. 6.. 9 Seconds Of Light'. The fact that they've scaled such giddy heights of indie stardom with only a minimum of promotion and a handful of gigs speaks volumes for the quality of their vintage twee C-86-esque sound. By late summer '98, expectations for a new album had reached fever pitch, critics unanimously hailing 'The Boy With The Arab Strap' as one of the year's finest (sadly, too late for the esteemed Mercury Prize) and helped ease it into the Top 20. After a two-year recording gap, B&S confidently returned with their fourth studio outing, the sublime, if not translucent 'Fold Your Hands Child, You Walk Like A Peasant'. On the eve of the release for this album they started doing press interviews – something that was frowned upon during their earlier years. The band also covered uncharted territory by issuing the album 'STORYTELLING' (2002), the "unofficial" soundtrack to the Todd Solondz film of the same name. A bleak look into American suburbia, the movie was a follow-up to the highly controversial (and highly uncomfortable) work 'Happiness'. It eventually got edited so much by the producers that Solondz vowed never to make another movie again. Unfortunately, with this tale, so went the B&S score, which didn't make the final cuts. *BG & MCS*

—

BELLE AND SEBASTIAN

Jun 02. (cd/lp) *Matador; <OLE 512> Jeepster; (JPR CD/LP 014)* ☐ 26
– Fiction / Freak / Dialogue: Conan, early Letterman / Fuck this shit / Night walk / Dialogue: Jersey's where it's at / Black and white unite / Consuelo / Dialogue: Toby / Storytelling / Dialogue: Class rank / I don't want to play football / Consuelo leaving / Wandering alone / Dialogue: Mandingo cliche / Scooby driver / Fiction (reprise) / Big John Shaft.

S/track review: Like so many before them, BELLE AND SEBASTIAN discovered that scoring a film wasn't all tea and scones. After going in "Armed with high hopes, dreams of great artistic endeavour and a copy of the 'PAT GARRETT & BILLY THE KID' soundtrack", recounts STEVIE JACKSON's notes, they found themselves "behaving like veteran hacks composing seventies style sitcom jingles on demand". Ah, the modesty of the indie bourgeoisie ... he winds up admitting it's "a cracking record" of course; if Scotland's best band ever (official these days), and a unit as steeped in cinematic style as B&S, couldn't come up with a decent soundtrack, who could? 'STORYTELLING' isn't on a par with Dylan's Mexicali blues, but it's (almost) everything you'd be entitled to expect. When JACKSON does dust down his harmonica on 'Fuck This Shit' (a more gratuitously incongruous title you couldn't hope for), it's more Bacharachian Sundance Kid than Billy The Kid but that's just fine. What he jokingly interprets as hackmanship is his band indulging – more than perhaps anywhere else in their catalogue – themselves and their record collections, avoiding parody through that sheer Glaswegian purity of intent; 'EASY RIDER'-era Byrds, Morricone at his most evocatively baroque, traces of Willis Jackson, Milton Nascimento and Michael Nyman even ... The only truly shameless moment is 'Wandering Alone', where JACKSON croons through a knowing Roy Orbison/Chris Isaak take-off. But you can't hold it against them; MURDOCH's lyrics carve out a leeway far beyond other songwriters, the kind of sorry insight that in a different place and time might've come from a haggard chansonnier. 'STORYTELLING' subtly admonishes Solondz himself, the winsomely barbed adieu of ISOBEL CAMPBELL, while 'Big John Shaft' tenderly examines the real-time plight of the film's lead against a warm, fuzzy funk riff, itself later fleshed out into the wonderful 'For The Price Of A Cup

Of Tea' (on 'The Life Pursuit'). A typically ingenuous piano melody conveys the main theme and its variations, immaculate chamber pop which puts the Hollywood score barons to shame. The record came in for a fair bit of flak from rock critics who don't quite understand soundtracks and who don't want their pet bands sullied by them. As B&S would go on to prove with their work on David Byrne's 'YOUNG ADAM', cinema flows silent in their veins, as it does in the blood of Glasgow brethren the Pastels and Mogwai. Only six minutes of 'STORYTELLING' was actually used in the film (Nathan Larson, formerly of Shudder To Think was composer of choice) but they rightly released it anyway, as it was conceived, cherry-picked dialogue and all. *BG*

Album rating: *7.5

STRAIGHT TALK

1992 (US 91m) Buena Vista (PG)

Film genre: romantic comedy

Top guns: dir: Barnet Kellman / s-w: Craig Bolotin (+ story), Patricia Resnick

Stars: **Dolly PARTON** *(Dr. Shirlee Kenyon)*, James Woods *(Jack Russell)* → the VIRGIN SUICIDES → BE COOL, Griffin Dunne *(Alan Riegert)* ← WHO'S THAT GIRL, Michael Madsen *(Steve Labell)* ← RESERVOIR DOGS ← the DOORS, Jerry Orbach *(Milo Jacoby)* ← DIRTY DANCING, Deirdre O'Connell *(Lily)* ← FALLING FROM GRACE, John Sayles *(Guy Girardi)*, Teri Hatcher *(Janice)*, Spalding Gray *(Dr. Erdman)* ← BEACHES ← TRUE STORIES ← the KILLING FIELDS / → HOW HIGH, Philip Bosco *(Gene Perlman)* ← WORKING GIRL, Irma P. Hall *(Ethel)* ← BOOK OF NUMBERS / → a SLIPPING-DOWN LIFE → DON'T LET GO, Charles Fleischer *(Tony)* ← DICK TRACY, Jane Lynch *(Gladys)* → a MIGHTY WIND, Jay Thomas *(Zim Zimmerman)*

Storyline: Shirlee Kenyon heads north to the Windy City to escape her windy boyfriend, and sets about finding work. When she turns up at the local radio station she is mistaken for the new talk show psychiatrist and plonked in front of a mic. Surprise surprise, Shirl is a 'natural' and the listeners love her, so she's hired under false pretences. However, reporter Jack Russell is not so sure – he begins to sniff out her past and discovers the truth. Will he reveal her secret or will a budding romance save Shirl from the doghouse? *JZ*

Movie rating: *5

Visual: video + dvd

Off the record: (see below)

—

DOLLY PARTON

Apr 92. (cd/c) *Hollywood; <61303-2/-4>* ☐ ☐
– Blue grace / The light of a clear blue morning / Dirty job / Blue me / Straight talk / Fish out of water / Burning / Livin' a lie / Thought I couldn't dance / Burning to burned / The light of a clear blue sky (reprise).

S/track review: For '9 To 5', DOLLY PARTON took country down to the discotheque, with irresistible results. Unfortunately, 'STRAIGHT TALK' smothers PARTON's songs in L.A. studio gloss. PARTON revisits one of her earliest songs, 'Light Of A Clear Blue Morning', and swaps its coat of many colours for a power suit and heels. Despite the best efforts of the pony-tailed session musicians, the uplifting Appalachian beauty of the chorus shines through. The rest of the album is much less successful. 'Dirty Job' sees PARTON try her hand at a rock number. She doesn't do too badly – rather than belt the song out in big-haired power-ballad style, she sings in a grainy lower register, throwing in some expertly controlled Tennessee twitters on the chorus. Sadly, the producer ruins it with tacky synthesised pan pipes, gated reverb drums and a sub-Clarence Clemens sax solo. 'Blue Me' has potential as a melancholy country swing ballad, but the cocktail jazz arrangement, complete with suspiciously fake double bass, brings it unpleasantly close to Ally McBeal territory. Similarly, there's a decent mandolin laced country number fighting to escape in 'Livin' A Lie'. The title track comes straight from the Billy Ocean book of yuppie soul music, with its plastic horns and mechanical rhythm, while 'Burning', a duet with BILL OWENS, underlines the redemptive qualities of PARTON's voice. But even she can't save 'Thought I Couldn't Dance' or the egregious 'Fish Out Of Water', where she raps – yes raps – over oleaginous guitar licks and naff synth hits. OWENS' 'Burning To Burned', benefits from a sparser treatment of just acoustic guitar and subdued orchestra. It's not a particularly memorable song, but PARTON's tender phrasing renders it more affecting that it should be. For all PARTON's charisma, 'STRAIGHT TALK' is ultimately sunk by the bombast and bad taste of her collaborators. *SS*

Album rating: *4

a STRANGER IN THE KINGDOM

1998 (US 112m) Kingdom Come Pictures (R)

Film genre: courtroom drama

Top guns: s-w: (+ dir) Jay Craven ← WHERE THE RIVERS FLOW NORTH, Don Bredes ← WHERE THE RIVERS FLOW NORTH (nov: Howard Frank Mosher ← WHERE THE RIVERS FLOW NORTH)

Stars: Ernie Hudson *(Rev. Walter Andrews)* ← The BASKETBALL DIARIES ← AIRHEADS ← the CROW ← ROAD HOUSE ← the JAZZ SINGER ← LEADBELLY, David Lansbury *(Charlie Kinneson)* ← GAS FOOD LODGING, Martin Sheen *(Sigurd Moulton)* ← FIRESTARTER, Jean Louisa Kelly *(Athena Allen)*, Bill Raymond *(Resolved Kinneson)* ← WHERE THE RIVERS FLOW NORTH, Sean Nelson *(Nathan Andrews)*, Henry Gibson *(Zack Burrows)* ← the BLUES BROTHERS ← NASHVILLE / → MAGNOLIA, Carrie Snodgress *(Ruth Kinneson)*, Tantoo Cardinal *(Heaven Fontaine)* ← WHERE THE RIVERS FLOW NORTH ← CANDY MOUNTAIN

Storyline: Set in the 50s, this post-WWII fact-based drama centres around a former army chaplain Walter Andrews, who's sent to become a minister of a rural town in Vermont. Commissioned over the phone, they soon realise they've hired a black man. When he befriends a young girl who is subsequently murdered, he's the first to come under suspicion. Let's now have order in the courtroom. *MCS*

Movie rating: *5.5

Visual: video + dvd

Off the record: In the 70s, Carrie Snodgress was the girlfriend of NEIL YOUNG (she's mother to his son, Zeke); she subsequently dated Young's producer, Jack Nitzsche. *MCS*

—

the HORSE FLIES

Dec 97. (cd) *Kingdom County; <own>* ☐ ☐
– The kingdom / Martian car / Bank robbery / Walt and Nat arrive / Claire arrives / Claire goes to Resolved's / Barbecue / Cockfight / Walt punches Harlan & Resolved in his cabin / Claire runs away / Claire fights with Resolved / Claire's premonition at the parsonage / The fair / Nat and Jim play ball in the graveyard / Attic / After church / Strip show / Kiss / Walt & Nat to Boston & Claire looks for Charlie / Claire's death & the funeral / Walt's arrest / Charlie at Harlan's garage / Doctor's testimony / Charlie and Athena walk / Nat walks in graveyard / Nat and Frenchy fight / Frenchy at Charlie's office / Frenchy testifies / Elijah's testimony and breakdown / Charlie proposes / Burying Pliny / Goodbyes / Gospel close – Hold on / End credit music – The fair.

S/track review: It's only lately in 2006 that the HORSE FLIES re-united, their split nearly a decade earlier caused by the cancer death of bassist JOHN HAYWARD. Having left behind an earlier score to 'WHERE THE RIVERS FLOW NORTH' (1994), the HORSE FLIES (husband and wife team JEFF CLAUS and JUDY HYMAN, banjoman RICH STEARNS, etc.) had established themselves as a band who could fit right in with the fickle world of film soundtracks. Their approach this time around was of the minimalist variety, fusing bluegrass folk and gothic roots music; however, unlike their last OST effort, the short dints and dirges spoiled the ebb and flow of their brooding sounds. Opening with 'The Kingdom' (one of only a trio of tracks over the 3-minute mark), the cue takes the listener on a conflicting, retro-fied mission of hope and despair. The warmth of HYMAN's characteristic electric violin-playing is centrepiece to most cuts, as is the guitar-plucking of hubby CLAUS, highlighted excellently on several of the 34 pieces. The HORSE FLIES bring tradition and invention to nearly every one of their atmospheric soundscapes, a marked difference to when the Red Clay Ramblers failed to generate much glow when they represented their trad-folk on the rural 'FAR NORTH' movie a decade previously. With lilting accordions, the odd banjo and soft percussion in the background, tracks like 'Burying Pliny' and 'The Fair' are testimony to the eclecticism of the band. If there's one gripe, it's that the pieces can be a little repetitive, but that's film music for you. *MCS*

Album rating: *6

□ Marty STUART segment
(⇒ ALL THE PRETTY HORSES)

SUPERFLY

1972 (US 93m) Warner Bros. Pictures (R)

Film genre: crime drama

Top guns: dir: Gordon Parks Jr. → THREE THE HARD WAY → AARON LOVES ANGELA / s-w: Phillip Fenty → SUPERFLY T.N.T.

Stars: Ron O'Neal *(Youngblood Priest)* → SUPERFLY T.N.T. → BROTHERS → YOUNGBLOOD, Carl Lee *(Eddie)* ← the LANDLORD / → GORDON'S WAR, Sheila Frazier *(Georgia)* → SUPERFLY T.N.T. → THREE THE HARD WAY, Julius Harris *(Scatter)* ← SHAFT'S BIG SCORE / → TROUBLE MAN → HELL UP IN HARLEM → BLACK CAESAR → FRIDAY FOSTER → LET'S DO IT AGAIN, Charles MacGregor *(Fat Freddie)* → ACROSS 110th STREET → THREE THE HARD WAY → THAT'S THE WAY OF THE WORLD → AARON LOVES ANGELA, Polly Niles *(Cynthia)*, Jim Richardson *(junkie)* → SUPER FLY T.N.T. → ONE ON ONE, **Curtis MAYFIELD** *(performer)*

Storyline: The quintessential Blaxploitation movie, boasting an innovative, intelligent plot: in an attempt to free himself from the clutches of the cocaine trade, impressively moustachioed drug dealer Youngblood Priest plans one last score primed to make him a million. Things get complicated, however, when one of his underlings cracks under police interrogation. *BG*

Movie rating: *6

Visual: video + dvd

Off the record: (see below)

—

CURTIS MAYFIELD

Aug 72. (lp) *Curtom; <CRS 8014ST> Buddah; (2318 065)* [1] Nov72 [26]
– Little child runnin' wild / Pusherman / Freddie's dead / Junkie chase / Give me your love (love song) / Eddie you should know better / No thing on me (cocaine song) / Think / Superfly / Superfly theme: Freddie's dead / Superfly (mix). *(re-iss. Nov74; BDLH 4018) (re-iss. Aug79 on 'R.S.O.'; RSS 5) (re-iss. Jun88 on 'Curtom' cd/c/lp; CD/ ZC+/CUR 2002) (cd re-iss. Jun94 on 'Charly'; CPCD 8039) (d-cd iss.Jun98 on 'Charly'+=; CDNEW 1302)* – (bonus tracks, etc.) *(cd re-iss. Mar01 on 'Snapper'; SNAP 005CD) <(d-cd iss.May02 on 'Snapper'+=; SNAD 507CD)> (d-cd-iss. Feb03 on 'Black Box'; BB 257) <lp re-iss. Jun03; same as>*

S/track review: Almost universally regarded as the most accomplished and enduring soundtrack of its era, 'SUPERFLY' is one of the few records of its kind to have retrospectively generated such serious kudos outside of the Blaxploitation ghetto. Unlike most artists' soundtrack excursions, it also stands as the most critically – and most commercially successful – album in CURTIS MAYFIELD's long and distinguished post-Impressions career. Rather than illuminating Gordon Parks Jr's plot, MAYFIELD's aim was to subvert what he interpreted as "a cocaine commercial". Fine-tuning the breakthrough he'd made with early 70s epics like the chilling '(Don't Worry) If There's A Hell Below We're All Going To Go', he downsized his piercing vision of human malaise from the societal to the individual. The likes of 'Freddie's Dead', 'Pusherman' and the title track deliver devastating character analyses under a deceptively laid-back, elegantly soulful veneer, in contrast to the preening, self-regarding throb of 'Theme From Shaft', Blaxploitation's opening gambit from a year previous. MAYFIELD's triumph, in even starker contrast to the sensory overload of Blaxploitation and 70s funk in general, is in his lightness of touch. At their most effective, Johnny Pate's arrangements – dictated by MAYFIELD himself – are a model of funky, creative economy; on the opening 'Little Child Runnin Wild', the orchestration is applied sparingly and mercilessly, with the precision of a surgeon's knife; on 'Pusherman', MAYFIELD's guitar is discursive and insidious but never gratuitous – there's a space in this music which sometimes speaks louder than the words, as incisive as they are. And his lyrics – transmitted in a vocal timbre characterised by emotional weight more than quality of tone – still dig deepest when he reprises the positive consciousness of his 60s and early 70s classics, as on the buoyant 'No Thing On Me (Cocaine Song)'. As unflinching socio-political treatise and definitive statement of artistic intent, 'SUPERFLY' is up there with Marvin Gaye's 'What's Going On' (1971) and Stevie Wonder's 'Innervisions' (1973), and there ain't too many soundtracks you can say that about. *BG*

Album rating: *9

– spinoff hits, etc. –

CURTIS MAYFIELD: Freddie's Dead (Theme From "Superfly")
Aug 72. (7") *<1975> (2011 141)* [4] Sep72 [ ]

CURTIS MAYFIELD: Superfly
Nov 72. (7") *<1978>* [–] [8]

CURTIS MAYFIELD: Superfly / Give Me Your Love (Love Song)
Feb 73. (7") *(2011 156)* [ ] [–]

SUPERFLY T.N.T.

1973 sequel (US 87m) Paramount Pictures (R)

Film genre: crime thriller

Top guns: dir: Ron O'Neal / s-w: Phillip Fenty ← SUPERFLY, Alex Haley

Stars: Ron O'Neal *(Priest)* ← SUPERFLY / → BROTHERS → YOUNGBLOOD, Roscoe Lee Browne *(Dr. Lamine Sonko)* ← UP TIGHT! / → EDDIE PRESLEY, Silvio Noto *(George; restaurant proprieter)*, Luigi Orso *(crew chief)*, Polly Niles *(Cynthia)*, Jacques Sernas *(Matty Smith)*, William Berger *(Lefevre)*, Robert Guillaume *(Jordan Gaines)* → the LION KING, Sheila Frazier *(Georgia)* ← SUPERFLY / → THREE THE HARD WAY, **Curtis MAYFIELD** *(himself)*, Jim Richardson *(junkie)* ← SUPERFLY / → ONE ON ONE

Storyline: Youngblood Priest is now a moustachioed ex-drug pusher languishing in a straight life in Rome. Fortunately, help from his existential crisis is at hand when a gun-running African revolutionary ropes him into overthrowing a dictator. *BG*

Movie rating: *2.5

Visual: video

Off the record: OSIBISA were formed in London, England . . . 1969 by Ghanaians Teddy Osei (on sax), his brother Mac Tontoh (bass) and friend Sol Amarfio (drums), alongside Caribbeans Wendell Richardson (a guitarist from Antigua), Robert Bailey (keyboardist from Trinidad) and Sparticus R (aka bassist Roy Bedeau from Grenada). Their unique blend of African rock and Santana-like rhythms, identified them from the rest of the early 70s funk and world music pack. Signed to 'M.C.A.' ('Decca' in the States), their first two critically-acclaimed sets ('Osibisa' 1971 & 'Woyaya' 1972) climbed the charts on both sides of the Atlantic, although third set, 'Heads' (1972), only reached #125. Next up for OSIBISA, the soundtrack to Blaxploitation feature 'SUPERFLY T.N.T.' (1973) was somewhat of surprise calling (CURTIS MAYFIELD must've declined the invitation?). With reggae and disco all the rage, the band subsequently succumbed to easy-listening type Afro-pop via two UK hits, 'Sunshine Day' & 'Dance The Body Music'. The critics never forgave them, although the group are still going strong today. *MCS*

OSIBISA

Jul 73. (lp) *Buddah; <BDS 5136ST> (2318 087)* ☐ Aug73 ☐
– T.N.T. / Superfly man / Prophets / The vicarage / Oye mama / Brotherhood / Come closer (if you're a man) / Kelele / La lla I la la. *<(cd-iss. Aug96 on 'Red Steel'; RMCCD 0196)>*

S/track review: The Afro-prog sounds of OSIBISA weren't the most obvious choice for the further adventures of Youngblood Priest but then – outside of Curtis Mayfield himself – who was? The group's ambitious arrangements, multiple breakdowns and time changes mean that unlike the pure-bred Sub-Saharan funk of say, Manu Dibango, they never really muster much momentum on a serious groove, even if their percussive agility is often dazzling. With members hailing from as far afield as Ghana, Guyana, Cameroon and Trinidad, OSIBISA operated more as a Trade Winds jazz-rock experiment, and 'SUPERFLY T.N.T.' often sounds like a more Afrocentric Santana, or – at its most indulgent – a black Jethro Tull (see the turgid 'Prophets'). Even with its wandering organ solos, the – admittedly overlengthy – title jam is proof that OSIBISA could adapt their style for film, parlaying dramatic, Pan-African brass over febrile rhythms. And while his band often pick up promising funk licks and just as often drop them in the next bar, at his fiercest, on the driving 'Oye Mama' and the compulsive 'Brotherhood', leader MAC TONTOH marshals his urbane warriors with the forbidding tone of a tribal chief. 'Superfly Man' (also a single) is a lot of fun for what it is, a breezy piece of Caribbean groove-folk, even if in this context it sounds like a parody, something like John Shaft goes to the cricket. There's also at least one excellent all-out African percussion track ('Kelele') which sounds like a field recording, and a haunting Afro-Islamic praise song, 'La Ila I La La'. OSIBISA's only soundtrack is usually written off as a mismatch but – if you can get past the cover shot of Ron O'Neal's hairy chest – it's definitely worth a punt. *BG*

Album rating: *6

– spinoff releases, etc. –

OSIBISA: Superfly Man / Prophets
Aug 73. (7") *(2011 179)* ☐ ☐

SUSPIRIA

1977 (Ita 97m) Seda Spettacoli (18)

Film genre: gothic/occult horror

Top guns: s-w: Dario Argento (+ dir) ← PROFONDO ROSSO / → INFERNO → TENEBRE → la CHIESA → NONHOSONNO, Daria Nicolodi

Stars: Jessica Harper *(Suzy Bannion)* ← PHANTOM OF THE PARADISE / → SHOCK TREATMENT, Alida Valli *(ballet mistress)*, Joan Bennett *(Madame Blanc)*, Stefania Casini *(Sara)*, Flavio Bucci *(Daniel)*, Miguel Bose *(Mark)*, Barbara Magnolfi *(Olga)*, Susanna Javicoli *(Sonia)*, Eva Axen *(Patty 'Pat' Hingle)*, Udo Kier *(Dr. Frank Mandel)* → EVEN COWGIRLS GET THE BLUES → the END OF VIOLENCE → NINA HAGEN = PUNK + GLORY → DANCER IN THE DARK → PIGS WILL FLY → 30 DAYS UNTIL I'M FAMOUS

Storyline: Another from the mind of Italian director, Dario Argento. Suzy, an American ballet dancer, arrives in Freiberg, Germany, to begin a course at the local Tans Academy. However, her attention is drawn by grizzly murders taking place and the evil that surrounds her. Psycho meets The Exorcist. *MCS*

Movie rating: *8.5

Visual: video + dvd

Off the record: **GOBLIN** (see Filmography)

GOBLIN (composer: Dario Argento)

Mar 77. (lp) *Cinevox; (MDF 33/108)* ☐ Italy ☐
– Suspiria / Witch / Opening to the sighs / Sighs / Markos / Black forest / Blind concert / Death valzer. *(UK-iss.Jan89 on 'Silva Screen' lp/c/cd; CIA/CIAK7/CDCIA 5005) (cd-iss. Sep97 +=; CD-MDF 305)* – Suspiria (celesta and bells) / Suspiria (narration) / Suspiria (intro) / Markos (alternate). *(cd-iss. Feb01 on 'Dagored'+=; RED 1271LP) <US cd-iss. Sep01 on 'Anchor Bay'; DV 11610>*

S/track review: A second venture into soundtrack work for Italian Prog-rocksters, GOBLIN (i.e. CLAUDIO SIMONETTI, FABIO PIGNATELLI, MASSIMO MORANTE & AGOSTINO MARANGOLO), their first being another Dario Argento horror flick, 'PROFONDO ROSSO' (1975). If there was ever a score to equally match the cinematic stills, then 'SUSPIRIA' was it. Creepy and unnerving from start to finish (and obviously inspired by 'The Exorcist'), GOBLIN create a jazzy Prog-rock vibe that was well ahead of its time. "Wicked" tracks were undoubtedly, 'Suspiria', 'Witch', 'Black Forest', 'Sighs' and the chime-friendly but funky, 'Markos'. The CD version adds a few title track takes culled from the movie, plus an alternate mix of 'Markos'; GOBLIN were never better. *MCS*

Album rating: *8.5

SVIDD NEGER

trans: 'Burnt Negro'

2003 (Nor 87m) Barentsfilm / Borealis / Oro Films (15)

Film genre: romantic comedy horror/drama

Top guns: dir: Erik Smith Meyer / s-w: Stein Elvestad

Stars: Kjersti Lid Gullvag *(Anna)*, Thor-Inge Gullvag *(Karl)*, Eirik Junge Eliassen *(Peder)*, Bjorn Granath *(Presten)*, Guri Johnson *(Ellen Margrethe)*, Isaka Sawadogo *(Faren)*, Kingsford Siayor *(Ante)*, Frank Jorstad *(Normann Haetta bongo utsi saus)*

Storyline: Controversial to the point of prosecution by the European Court of Human Rights in the Hague, the film and its immoral title (uncensored in Norway) were uneasy right from day one. The plot centers around Anna and her racist father, a man living in the outskirts of Norway as well as his mind, after he murdered his unfaithful ex-wife (who now haunts him) and her newly-born mulato child (whom he threw into the ocean). Anna, meanwhile, searches for love, and through a meeting with a hard-drinking woman, Ellen, and her son Peder, she thinks she's found the one. However, Ellen had adopted a black son, Kjell (who was coincidentally saved from the sea). Is there a connection? *MCS*

Movie rating: *6

Visual: dvd

Off the record: **ULVER** (meaning "wolves") were formed in Oslo, Norway in 1993 (vocalist Kristoffer "Garm" Rygg was a member of black metal outfit, Arcturus). ULVER were indeed black metal, although as their first three albums depicted, the trio (Garm, Jorn H. Scaeren and Tore Ylwizaker) incorporated Viking folk tales and an archaic Danish language set to ambient-styled guitar passages and unearthly vocals. The aforementioned "Black Metal Trilogie" consisted of 'Bergtatt – Et Eeventyr i 5 Capitler' (1994), 'Kvedssanger' – aka 'Twilight Songs' (1995) and 'Nattens Madrigal – Aate Hymne Til Ulven I Manden' (1996), were neo-classical in concept, while having that eerie feeling that one gets from too many Nordic nightcaps. Next on the ULVER agenda was the works of William Blake ('The Marriage Of Heaven And Hell'), although ULVER's version was completed in 1998 and somewhat different to their previous meanderings, while featuring the "talents" of Samoth and Insahn (from Emperor), Fenriz (from Darkthrone) and some unknown female on vocals. 'Metamorphosis' and 'Perdition City' followed in 1999 and 2000 respectively, while ULVER's first venture into soundtrack work came via 'Lyckantropen', a short Norwegian Grammy-nomination from 2002 (see future edition); 'SVIDD NEGER' followed suit. *MCS*

—

ULVER (score: Trond Nedberg)

Mar 04. (cd) *Jester; (TRICK 030)* ☐ Sep03 ☐
– Preface / Ante andante / Comedown / Surface / Somnam / Wild cat / Rock massif pt.1 / Rock massif pt.2 / Poltermagda / Mummy / Burn the bitch / Sick solilocky / Waltz of King Karl / Sadface / Fuck fast / Wheel of conclusion.

S/track review: Opening like a Godspeed You Black Emperor! intro over some disjointed orchestra and percussion section, 'Preface', shakes off the ambient black metal right from the start. Clint Mansell and Daniel Lanois (two fellow film score acolytes), might well have inspired the lush feel of tracks 2 & 3, 'Ante Andante' & 'Comedown', while 'Surface' was truly cinematic with its jazzy electro-beats and lilting saxophones – both melancholy and uplifting at the same time. Although ethereal and thematic from the outset, the album reaches some sort of meaning and climax during the screaming parts of track 6, 'Wild Cat' and the segued 'Rock Massif pt.1 & 2', the latter like John Barry in the studio with Godspeed! – now there's a thought. The only criticism I could level at the album is that each cut is just too damn short, and this is definitely the case with further pieces such as film descriptive 'Poltermagda', 'Mummy', 'Burn The Bitch' and 'Sick Solilocky': noise levels will have to be adjusted. ULVER take their newfound movie sensibilities a little too far for the quirky, downbeat, 'Waltz For King Karl' or the techno-fied 'Sadface'. But how could you fault their eclectic imagination and enterprise on any of the flowing instrumentals – including the appropriately-titled 'Wheel Of Conclusion' epic – from the near 33-minute set. ULVER certainly came of age with this classy work, possibly a bit too reminiscent of Clint Mansell's pieste de resistance from 2000, 'Requiem For A Dream': sadly only featured in a further "Symphonic Scores" edition. *MCS*

Album rating: *7.5

SWEET SWEETBACK'S BAADASSSSS SONG

1971 (US 97m) Cinemathon Industries (X)

Film genre: psychological/urban drama

Top guns: s-w + dir: **Melvin Van PEEBLES** ← WATERMELON MAN / → DON'T PLAY US CHEAP

Stars: Melvin VAN PEEBLES *(Sweetback)*, Rhetta Hughes *(old girlfriend)*, Simon Chuckster *(Beetle)*, Johnny Amos *(biker)* ← VANISHING POINT / → LET'S DO IT AGAIN → DISAPPEARING ACTS, Hubert Scales *(Mu-Mu)*, John Dullaghan *(Commissioner)*, Mario Peebles *(young Sweetback)* → RAPPIN'

Storyline: Catalyst for the whole Blaxploitation genre with Melvin Van Peebles producing, directing and starring as Sweetback, a sexually rampant and seriously pissed off black man on the run from the cops. His racist pursuers duly bear the brunt of his rage in a filmic explosion of suppressed anger which galvanised black audiences of the day. *BG*

Movie rating: *6.5

Visual: video + dvd

Off the record: (see below)

—

MELVIN VAN PEEBLES
(performed by EARTH, WIND & FIRE)

Jun 71. (lp) *Stax; <STS 3001>* ☐ ☐
– Sweetback losing his cherry / Sweetback getting it uptight and preaching it so hard the bourgeois reggin angel in Heaven turn around / Come on feet / Sweetback's theme / Hoppin' John / Mojo woman / Sanra Z / Reggin hanging on in there as best they can / Won't bleed me / The man tries running his usual game but Sweetback's Jones is so strong he wastes the hounds (yeah yeah and besides that will be coming back takin' names and collecting dues). *<(UK+re-iss. Apr97 on 'Ace-Stax' cd+=/lp+=; CDSXE/RXD 103)>* – (extra dialogue).

S/track review: Like its author's solo albums, this is more sonic cut-up than soundtrack, a blaxploitation blueprint which – in reality – bears little or no resemblance to any of the big-name scores which it supposedly inspired. Nor does it bear much resemblance to the jazz fusion with which EARTH, WIND & FIRE followed it up. But it does kick off as it means to go on: as controversially, gratuitously and calamitously as the film, pitching and reeling wildly between wailing siren, white noise and bordello funk. VAN PEEBLES' use of the old spiritual Wade In The Water, over the movie's most disturbing scenes, was infamously cited by Black Panther leader Huey P Newton in the critical fallout that accompanied the film's release, itself analysed in the extensive sleevenotes to the British Film Institute DVD. Ultimately, though, it's the explosive energy, desperation and anger invested in creating the polar opposite of the so-called 'Poitier persona' – as outlined by Post-Soul Black Cinema author William R Grant – that drives the soundtrack, with the titular anti-hero's hysterical, strangulated commentary disorientating the mix ever further, cat-called by sardonic female choirs: "They burned our mama, they beat our papa, they tricked our sisters, they chained our brothers"; "YEAH BUT THEY WON'T BLEED ME!". VAN PEEBLES wields the phrase like a mantra, driving himself on into the darkness ("blacker than a landlord's soul") in the relentless 'Come On Feet', from his 'A&M' album, 'Ain't Supposed To Die A Natural Death' (1970). The nearest thing to conventional cinematic funk is EW&F's 'Sweetback's Theme', a coyly sleazy, pimp-rolling organ groove which struts for a full seven minutes, resurfacing at anarchic angles. A couple of straight-up R&B numbers, 'Hoppin' John' and the sassy voodoo-funk of 'Mojo Woman' (dropped as a vinyl 45 in the film) punctuate the collage, as well as a mellow jazz instrumental, 'Sanra Z', but it's in its demented, radio-dial confusion that the music works its insurrectionary spell, sonically reproducing the convulsive cinematography: "With its handheld zooms, split screens, freeze frames and superimpositions, Sweetback was psychedelic soul on ice; not so much an escape from the grimy streets of Watts as an intensification", wrote critic Kodwo Eshun, heightened by "discordant tone clusters and brass fanfares". Yet while the movie is widely recognised as a watershed in black cinema ("the most important black American film of its age" argued Time Out), the soundtrack still hasn't had its full critical due, either in terms of its long-term influence on black music (hip-hopper Madlib liberally sampled VAN PEEBLES on his Quasimoto outings, and is currently working on a collaborative project), its conciliation of soul and the avant-garde and its anticipation of hip-hop's cut-and-paste culture to come. *BG*

Album rating: *9

SWEET TALKER

1991 (Aus 91m) Australian Film Commission / New Vision Pictures

Film genre: romantic comedy

Top guns: dir: Michael Jenkins / s-w: Tony Morphett (+ story w/ Bryan Brown)

Stars: Bryan Brown *(Harry Reynolds)* ← GIVE MY REGARDS TO BROAD STREET, Karen Allen *(Julie Maguire)* ← ANIMAL HOUSE, Justin Rosniak *(David Macguire)*, Chris Haywood *(Gerald Bostock)* ← DOGS IN SPACE, Bill Kerr *('Uncle' Cec)* ← the PIRATE MOVIE, Bruce Spence *(Norman Foster)* ← RIKKY AND PETE ← 20th CENTURY OZ / → QUEEN OF THE DAMNED, Bruce Myles *(Mayor Jim Scraper)*, Garry Waddell *(Bluey)* ← 20th CENTURY OZ / → CHOPPER → the PROPOSITION

Storyline: Fresh out of jail, sweet talking conman Harry Reynolds' latest scam is extracting cash for some bogus underwater archaeology off the Australian coastal town of Beachport. What he doesn't bargain for is falling under the spell of local widow and hotelier, Julie, for whose young son he unwittingly assumes the role of a father figure. *BG*

Movie rating: *5

Visual: video + dvd

Off the record: (see below)

RICHARD THOMPSON

May 92. (cd/c/lp) *Capitol; (CD/TC/+EST 2170) <C2/C4 94490>* ☐ ☐
– Put your trust in me / Persuasion / Roll up / The Dune ship / Conviction / Boomtown / Harry's theme / Sweet talker / To hang a dream on / Beachport / False or true.

S/track review: Less widely heard than his work on Werner Herzog's subsequent 'GRIZZLY MAN', RICHARD THOMPSON's debut soundtrack is at once a more song-based score but also – with the regular and keyboard-generated orchestrations of the title theme and 'The Dune Ship' – a more conventional one. What it lacks in the cohesion of a song cycle, it makes up for in sheer diversity, and at least two tracks stand confidently among the most accomplished of his solo career: Big Country-meets-Mike Oldfield opener, 'Put Your Trust In Me' is dyed-in-the-beard THOMPSON, stout-hearted, generous to a fault, erecting a granite-hewn bridge and chorus around that trademark trebly guitar, swapping the guitar for a mandolin on the Celto-bluegrass reprise, 'Harry's Theme'; 'Persuasion' makes sublime use of that same guitar sound, straying into 'LOCAL HERO' territory but never losing its sense of self on what has to rank as one of THOMPSON's most instantly evocative instrumentals, a track which Tim Finn was so taken with he dreamt up lyrics to it. With the likes of SIMON NICOL, DAVE MATTACKS and JOHN KIRKPATRICK on board, there's also a fair amount of traditional-minded material, while the part-symphonic 'Conviction' finds the man playing acoustic guitar and hammered dulcimer as FRAN BYRNE keeps the tempo on bhodran. Compounding the sense of listening to a compilation or a regular THOMPSON solo set rather than a score, the rest of the soundtrack crams in a tongue-in-cheek, 'Nashville'-style country rave-up sung by Chris Spedding associate JOHN ANDREW PARKS, an 80s rock hangover, 'To Hang A Dream On' (crudely mispelled in the CD booklet) and a jazzy instrumental. Still, until its best bits are anthologised, 'SWEET TALKER' repays the effort of hunting it down. *BG*

Album rating: *6

SWORDFISH

2001 (US 99m) Warner Brothers (R)

Film genre: crime caper/thriller

Top guns: dir: Dominic Sena / s-w: Skip Woods

Stars: John Travolta *(Gabriel Shear)* ← PRIMARY COLORS ← PULP FICTION ← SHOUT ← STAYING ALIVE ← URBAN COWBOY ← GREASE ← SATURDAY NIGHT FEVER / → BE COOL → HAIRSPRAY re-make, Hugh Jackman *(Stanley Jobson)*, Halle Berry *(Ginger)* ← WHY DO FOOLS FALL IN LOVE ← GIRL 6 ← CB4: THE MOVIE ← JUNGLE FEVER, Don Cheadle *(Agent Roberts)* ← THINGS BEHIND THE SUN ← BOOGIE NIGHTS ← ROADSIDE PROPHETS, Vinnie Jones *(Marco)*, **Sam Shepard** *(Senator Reisman)* ← ALL THE PRETTY HORSES ← RENALDO AND CLARA / → STEALTH → the ASSASSINATION OF JESSE JAMES . . ., Drea de Matteo *(Melissa)* → PREY FOR ROCK & ROLL, Rudolph Martin *(Axl Torvalds)* ← HIGH ART, Zach Grenier *(assistant director, Joy)* ← FIGHT CLUB ← WORKING GIRL, Camryn Grimes *(Holly)*, Angelo Pagan *(Torres)*, Timothy Omundson *(agent Thomas)* → CRAZY

Storyline: Intelligence agent Gabriel Shear knows there's billions of dollars worth of government funds locked away in a secret bank account codenamed Swordfish. The codes are encrypted to the hilt so expert hacker Stanley Jobson is enlisted to help with the e-burgling. Stanley's just out of jail and can't get to see his daughter Holly, but the chance of squillions of dollars could solve all that. However, the government feds are beginning to smell a cyber-rat, and agent Roberts is soon closing in fast on the conspirators. *JZ*

Movie rating: *5

Visual: dvd

Off the record: (see below)

PAUL OAKENFOLD: Swordfish <The Album> (w/ CHRISTOPHER YOUNG *)

Jun 01. (cd) *ffrr-Warners; <(4344 31169-2)>* ☐ Jul01 ☐
– Swordfish (intro) / The word – PMT remix (DOPE SMUGGLAZ) / Unafraid – Paul Oakenfold remix (JAN JOHNSTON) / Dark machine (w/ *) / New born – Paul Oakenfold mix (MUSE) / Chase (w/ *) / Harry Houdini / Kneel before your god (LEMON JELLY) / Lapdance – Paul Oakenfold Swordfish mix (N*E*R*D feat. LEE HARVEY & VITA) / Speed / Planet rock – Swordfish mix (vs. AFRIKA BAMBAATAA & SONIC SOUL FORCE) / Stanley's theme / Password / On your mind – Omaha mix (PATIENT SAINTS) / Get out of my life now (w/ AMOEBASSASSIN).

S/track review: PAUL OAKENFOLD's unassailable position as one of the UK's, nay the world's, original superstar DJs means he will forever have a place in many a young raver's heart. But the transition out from behind the decks has rarely been an easy one for even the biggest DJs. Many end up behind the scenes, providing futuristic soundtracks for blockbuster movies. This album is a mix of OAKENFOLD originals, a couple of esoteric originals from the likes of LEMON JELLY for the parts OAKENFOLD can't refresh himself, and a clutch of remixes. Many of these highly stylised reworkings are, to be frank, disastrous. MUSE get the epic trance makeover on 'New Born' to little effect, while the less heavy-handed remixes just manage to put the fire out in the originals. He manages to stunt the sleaze and rage of N.E.R.D.'s rabid 'Lapdance' and robs AFRIKA BAMBAATAA's legendary 'Planet Rock' of its brutal robot funk. Only his overhaul of DOPE SMUGGLAZ' 'The Word' really does both parties credit. Similarly, when it comes to creating his own sub-Leftfield, sub-Fatboy Slim, sub-Chemical Brothers big beats,

OAKENFOLD is found to be sadly lacking. If anything, this album should be a glaring indicator that OAKENFOLD should clearly stick to what he's best at: high-calibre, high-gloss trance. *MR*

Album rating: *3.5

□ SYREETA segment
(⇒ FAST BREAK)

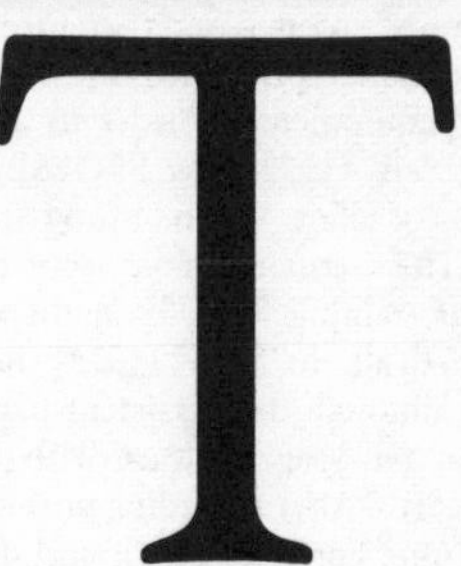

TANGERINE DREAM

Formed: Berlin, Germany . . . September 1967 by graphic designer EDGAR FROESE, TANGERINE DREAM have over 107 releases to their name, including studio albums, live recordings and of course, soundtracks. Their pioneering use of synthesizers in their original 70s albums formed the basis for their international reputation, while their impact and influence on 1980s cinema scores sealed it, bringing them to a much wider audience and providing a lucrative side business. Russian-born FROESE is the only constant member of a band that have seen several line-up changes and collaborations, while critical appreciation over the years has seen more highs and lows than a sine wave. For some, they are the grandfathers of modern electronic music. Others maintain that TANGERINE DREAM have been studiously avoiding a chorus for over 40 years. This, however, is an achievement in itself; anybody scorning whistle-able tunes for this long is clearly doing it on purpose. They were effectively synth colonisers; they effectively defined synth music for the modern age; variously euphoric, ponderous, ground breaking, pretentious, faceless and/or interminably long, for better or worse there are indelible traces of TANGERINE DREAM in all modern synth music. FROESE, a alumni of the Berlin Academy of Arts, harboured ambitions to bring visual art to music, and struggled at first to find a viable medium. Originally a guitarist, His composition for the inauguration of Salvador Dali's Christ statue in 1967 was "misunderstood", even as his personal friendship with Dali seemed to confer some artistic gravitas upon the young musician. Later that year FROESE began to assemble musicians to perform with him as TANGERINE DREAM, and just as quickly dissembled them and began again, eventually settling upon Klaus Schulze (drums) and Conrad Schnitzler (experimental electronics) to record 'Electronic Meditation' (1970) in a private studio. FROESE was surprised when the session brought his group a recording contract, especially since the members had almost immediately parted ways, Schulze for marriage, Schnitzler for want of proper musicianship. The guitarist quickly recruited drummer Christopher Franke, a tender 17 years of age, and organist Steve Schroyder. Their largely improvisational live performances set the tone for the recordings to come, second album 'Alpha Centauri' (1971) featuring a 22 minute long title track. Schroyder was shortly replaced by Peter Baumann, and the "classic" TD line-up was established. TD then began what would be a creatively and financially lucrative pursuit in scoring a German television version of 'Vampira' (1971), and then a programme entitled 'Geradeus Bis Zum Morgan' (1972), both of which remain unreleased on record and rarely, if ever, seen in their original form. No sooner was this line-up in place however, than FROESE strove to destabilise it, demanding his startled cohorts to abandon their instruments in favour of untested and therefore artistically exciting electronics. This proclamation belied the financial necessity of selling their "staid" equipment in order to afford a synthesiser. Their third album 'Zeit' (1972) saw FROESE, Franke and guest Peter Florian Fricke (of fellow German prog-sters, POPOL VUH) all on synthesiser. The German public were curiously unmoved by their innovations, raining food upon them in one early live excursion. Their fourth album 'Atem' (1973) was similarly received in their homeland, although the persistent patronage of DJ John Peel led them to a ten-year contract with Richard Branson's fledgling 'Virgin' records. After recording music for German movie 'Ein Fur Allemal' ('One For All', 1973), and dissatisfied with the German media and music industry's lack of appreciation for their progressive rock music, FROESE relocated to London, sensing correctly that international success lay ahead. He then spent the advance for their first 'Virgin' album, 'Phaedra' (1974) on a Moog synthesiser, once owned by a rich but technologically regressive MICK JAGGER. The 'Virgin' deal, and the critical appreciation for 'Phaedra' – which was dominated by synthesisers – encouraged TD to plow further into this new territory. They branched into theatrical scoring, providing musical accompaniment for 'Oedipus Tyrannus' in June of 1974, while Baumann departed briefly to be replaced by Michael Hoenig, before returning for 1975's 'Rubycon'. TD continued to split critics, internationally now, confounding some with their seemingly aimless and pretentious soundscapes, while others lauded their innovation, as their Laserium Light Show broke new ground in the live arena. Alt rock-critic godhead Lester Bangs in particular found it beneficial to the experience to ingest two bottles of cough syrup prior to the event. Their next studio effort, 'Stratosfear' (1976) – released soon after the live 'Ricochet' – saw them bring a more rhythmic structure to their experimentalism, which in turn brought them to the attention of 'Exorcist' director William Friedkin, who gave them their first major film scoring commission. Their score for 'SORCERER' (1977) was a success, and paved the way for more Hollywood work. TD's relative lack of vocals and a tangible rhythm section, allied with an emphasis on mood and atmosphere, were immediately a good match for scoring film and television; ironically, the same aspects that some critics found troubling were a positive boon in this arena. Add to this the rise of the synthesiser in the late 70s and 80s, and TD, with their dogged reliance on synthetic noise, were perfectly placed to dominate the market. Their ubiquity in soundtracks all through the 80s means that much of their music of this period can sound hopelessly dated, although it's presence on several cult movie soundtracks gives it a certain cache beyond the merely retro. Over the next ten years, TD would compliment their studio output with a huge amount of scoring work, although without Baumann who left due to "artistic differences" at the end of 1977, the vacancy filled by drummer Klaus Krieger. TD followed 'SORCERER' with many smaller scale projects in Germany, including 'Das Verbotene Spiel' (1979), a sci-fi TV movie, a short movie 'Game Over' (1978), 'Kneuss' (1978) and a documentary called 'Take It To The Limit' in 1980. English multi-instrumentalist Steve Joliffe joined for their studio album 'Cyclone' (1978), but departed after the more mainstream album was deemed a failure (the attempt at vocals, rare for TD, had not helped), and he clashed with FROESE over future plans. 'Force Majeure' (1979) was a critical success, although Krieger would no longer be a full-time member. Johannes Schmoelling, a trained pianist, joined then forming what would the next stable line-up, beginning with 'Tangram' (1980), critically mauled but commercially a hit. Their productivity continued unabated with studio albums 'Exit' (1981) and 'White Eagle' (1982). The soundtrack for 'Dead Kids' (1981) preceded the first work in an occasional but long lasting association with German TV detective series 'Tatort' which would see them provide music for future episodes. It was with the score for Michael Mann's 'THIEF' (1981) that TD's scoring career really took off, followed closely by 'Future War 198X' (1982), 'The Soldier' (1982), the FROESE solo 'KAMIKAZE 1989' (1982), 'WAVELENGTH' (1983) and another Michael Mann film 'The Keep' (1983). Symbolically enough, the expiration of their contract to 'Virgin' saw a definitive change in emphasis away from live performances, and towards fully embracing their burgeoning Hollywood career, continuing in earnest with 'RISKY BUSINESS' (1983), 'Spasms' (1983), 'Forbidden' (1984) and 'FIRESTARTER' (1984). Two more, for 'FLASHPOINT' (1984) and 'HEARTBREAKERS' (1985), came before there was a real reckoning, and the producers of 'LEGEND' (1985) decided that Jerry Goldsmith's traditional style score was too old fashioned, opting instead for FROESE's cutting edge synthesisers. This, in retrospect was the peak of TD's Hollywood career, although some consider the theme from quintessentially 80s tv show 'Streethawk' (1985) as an alternative highlight. Incredibly, during this period TD found time to produce studio albums 'Hyperborea' (1983) and 'Le Parc' (1985) (from which the 'Streethawk' theme was extracted) as well as two lesser known scores for 'The PARK IS MINE' (1985) and 'Vision Quest' (1985). The strain of such rampant creativity led to the departure of Schmoelling, replaced by Paul Haslinger in 1985. More scores, for 'City Of Shadows' (1986) and 'ZONING' (1986) preceded studio album 'Underwater Sunlight' (1986), which saw a new wave of critical appreciation for its more melodic content. Soundtracks for 'THREE O'CLOCK HIGH' (1987) and vampire horror flick 'NEAR DARK' (1987) maintained their winning streak, the latter remaining a cult favourite to this day. 1987 also saw TD scoring two TV movies, 'Tonight's The Night' and 'DEADLY CARE', while the score for 'SHY PEOPLE' (1987) saw the group work with female vocalists, a trend that continued with William Blake-inspired studio album 'Tyger' (1988). The score for video 'Canyon Dreams' (1988) was the last before Franke departed, another casualty of the superhuman workload. Following the addition of Ralph Wadephul, TD provided music for TV movie 'DEAD SOLID PERFECT' (1988), then studio album 'Optical Race' (1988) was the first of four albums that TD released on old member Baumann's label 'Private Music'; after Wadephul's speedy departure, they released the score for 'MIRACLE MILE' (1989), and studio albums 'Lily On The Beach' (1989) and 'Melrose' (1990). With yet more scores, for 'CATCH ME IF YOU CAN' (1989) and 'Destination Berlin' (1989), TD's work defined the law of diminishing returns. FROESE's son Jerome joined as a full time member in 1990 for the aforementioned 'Melrose', after which Haslinger left to pursue a solo film composing career. From this point, the FROESE's were the only full time members of TD, but they would continue to collaborate with other musicians on each project, including saxophonist Linda Spa and guitarist Zlatko Perica. TD's scores began to function at an increasingly mundane level; the ubiquity of their sound in the 1980s, and their gradual drift towards nondescript ambient noise left their music as little more than background noise. Music for Japanese TV show 'Mandala' (1990) is so obscure that TD may not have heard it, while the score for 'The MAN INSIDE' (1991) is indistinguishable from that of a bland workout video. The 1990s saw a merciful decrease in TD scores, which reflected both a steady decline in quality and relevance, and they began to concentrate on studio albums, 'Rockoon' (1992), 'Turn Of The Tides' (1994), 'Tyranny Of Beauty' (1995), 'Goblin's Club' (1996) and 'Ambient Monkeys' (1998), while the influence of the younger FROESE gave them a veneer of modernity. Nevertheless, they found meagre employment scoring for television, 'The Switch' (1993), 'Memphis PD: War On The Streets' (1996), and 'Luminous Visions' (1998) and documentary/art movies, 'Oasis' (1997), 'Transiberia' (1998), 'The Great Wall Of China' (1999). Documentary soundtracks for 'What A Blast: Architecture In Motion' (1999) and 'Mota Atma' (2003) have been well received by hardcore fans, if largely ignored by everybody else, while EDGAR FROESE has satisfied his tireless muse by "translating" Dante's 'Inferno' into a series of predictably grandiose concerts and albums. By now, TD's reputation as the godfathers of "new age" music means they have been increasingly marginalised by the mainstream press – although their early 70s work is still well regarded – and, as always, work continues apace. *SW*

- filmography (composers) –

Great Wall Of China *(1970 OST rel.2000; see future edition)* / **Sorcerer** *(1977 OST =>)* / Kneuss *(1978)* / **Thief** *(1981 OST =>)* / Dead Kids *(1981)* / Spasms *(1982)* / Identificazione Di Una Donna *(1982 w/ JOHN FOXX)* / Von Richtern und Anderen Sympathisanten *(1982 w/ KLAUS SCHULZE)* / the Soldier *(1982)* / **Kamikaze 1989** *(1982 OST by EDGAR FROESE =>)* / **Wavelength** *(1983 OST =>)* / **Risky Business** *(1983 OST w/ V/A =>)* / the Keep *(1983 OST rel.1997 see; future edition)* / **Firestarter** *(1984 OST =>)* / **Flashpoint** *(1984 OST =>)* / Street Hawk *(1984 TV series)* / **Heartbreakers** *(1984 =>)* / **Legend** *(1985 OST =>)* / Vision Quest *(1985 OST by V/A; see future edition)* / **the Park Is Mine** *(1985 TV OST =>)* / **Zoning** *(1987 OST =>)* / Red Nights *(1987)* / **Three O'Clock High** *(1987 OST =>)* / **Near Dark** *(1987 OST =>)* / **Shy People** *(1987 OST =>)* / Canyon Dreams *(1987 OST; see future edition)* / **Deadly Care** *(1987 TV OST =>)* / **Dead Solid Perfect** *(1988 TV OST =>)* / **Catch Me If You Can** *(1989 OST =>)* / **Miracle Mile** *(1989 OST =>)* / Destination Berlin *(1989 OST; see future edition)* / **the Man Inside** *(1990 OST =>)* / Highway To Hell *(1991)* / Oasis *(1997 OST; see future edition)* / What A Blast: Architecture In Motion *(1998 OST; see future edition)*

TARZAN

1999 (US 88m) Walt Disney Pictures (G)

Film genre: animated children's/family adventure

Top guns: dir: Kevin Lima, Chris Buck / s-w: Tab Murphy, Bob Tzudiker, Noni White, David Reynolds, Jeffrey Stepakoff (nov: 'Tarzan And The Apes' by Edgar Rice Burroughs)

Voices: Tony Goldwyn *(Tarzan)*, Minnie Driver *(Jane)* ← GOOD WILL HUNTING / → SOUTH PARK: BIGGER, LONGER & UNCUT, Glenn Close *(Kala)*, Lance Henriksen *(Kerchak; the gorilla king)* ← DEAD MAN ← JOHNNY HANDSOME ← NEAR DARK, Wayne Knight *(Tantor)*, Alex D. Linz *(young Tarzan)*, Rosie O'Donnell *(Terk)* ← JACKIE'S BACK!, Brian Blessed *(Clayton)* ← FLASH GORDON, Nigel Hawthorne *(Professor Porter)*

Storyline: Left to fend for himself in the African jungle after the death of his parents, the infant Tarzan is adopted by two gorillas, Kerchak and Kala. As he grows older he learns the ways of the jungle amongst his gorilla tribe, but his way of life is changed forever when he encounters Jane, who is studying wildlife along with her father and a hunter called Clayton. Tarzan must make the difficult choice between his desire to live with his gorilla family in the jungle or go to live with humans. *JZ*

Movie rating: *6

Visual: video + dvd

Off the record: (see below)

—

PHIL COLLINS (songs) & Mark Mancina (score)

May 99. (cd/c) *Disney; <8 60645> (010247-2/-4 DNY)* [5] Oct99 [ ]
– Two worlds / You'll be in my heart (w/ GLENN CLOSE) / Son of man / Trashin' the camp (ROSIE O'DONNELL) / Strangers like me / Two worlds (reprise) / Trashin' the camp (w/ 'N SYNC) / You'll be in my heart / Two worlds / A wonderous place / Moves like an ape, looks like a man / The gorillas / One family / Two worlds (finale).

S/track review: The OST to 'TARZAN' is atypical Disney production – repetition of several tracks with minor variations in an attempt to appeal to a different audience each time. However this Mark Mancina soundtrack is a pleasing mixture of pop and African style music, with upbeat, catchy numbers like PHIL COLLINS' 'Strangers As Me' and ROSIE O'DONNELL's 'Trashin' The Camp'. The instrumental score conveys the sense of being in touch with nature in 'A Wonderous Place' and living in harmony with the animals in 'The Gorillas'. The usual Disney themes of care, love and friendship are represented by tracks such as 'You'll Be In My Heart' and 'Son Of Man'. PHIL COLLINS' voice blends well with this type of music and, apart from the aforementioned track repetition, makes this CD a good listen especially with the soft, lilting instrumental pieces near the end. *JZ*

Album rating: *5.5

– spinoff hits, etc. –

PHIL COLLINS: You'll Be In My Heart / (version w/ GLENN CLOSE) / ROSIE O'DONNELL: Trashin' The Camp

Jun 99. (c-s/cd-s) *<860025> (010073 9/5 DNY)* [21] Nov99 [17]

□ Johnnie TAYLOR segment
(⇒ DISCO 9000)

TENEBRE

1982 (Ita 101m) Bedford Entertainment / Sigma Films (R)

Film genre: psychological slasher/horror thriller

Top guns: s-w: (+ dir) Dario Argento ← INFERNO ← SUSPIRIA ← PROFONDO ROSSO / → la CHIESA → NONHOSONNO

Stars: Anthony Franciosa *(Peter Neal)*, Christian Borromeo *(Gianni)*, John Saxon *(Bullmer)*, Mirella D'Angelo *(Tilde)*, Veronica Lario *(Jane McKerrow)*, Ania Pieroni *(Elsa Manni)*, John Steiner *(Christiano Berti)*, Eva Robins *(girl on beach)*, Daria Nicolodi *(Anne)* ← INFERNO ← SHOCK ← PROFONDO ROSSO / → PHENOMENA, Carola Stagnaro *(Detective Altieri)*, Marino Mase *(John)* ← CONTAMINATION

Storyline: The streets of Rome run red with blood as a maniacal killer goes on the rampage. The killer is obsessed with novelist Peter Neal (and red shoes, by the by) and it's Neal's arrival in the ancient city which has sparked off the killing spree. After various people connected to Neal have been stabbed, axed and garotted (some all at once) he is urged to leave town by the local police, but the kinky killer has one last deed to perform. *JZ*

Movie rating: *6.5

Visual: video + dvd

Off the record: (see below)

—

SIMONETTI, PIGNATELLI & MORANTE (aka GOBLIN)

Jul 83. (lp) *That's Entertainment; (TER 1064)* [ ] [–]
– Tenebre / Gemini / Slow circus / Lesbo / Flashing / Tenebre (reprise) / Waiting death / Jane mirror theme. *(cd-iss. 2000 on 'King' Japan +=; 2864)* – (other film versions & bonus tracks). *(lp re-iss. Jun01 on 'Dagored'; RED 1311)*

S/track review: Raising the bar they had themselves set with 'PROFUNDO ROSSO' and 'SUSPIRIA', 'TENEBRE' saw a reunited GOBLIN infect their distinctive style with elements of disco and insurgent electronic music for their third full collaboration with Dario Argento. Mixing their funk inflected, prog-rock style with electronic drums gave GOBLIN perhaps their most distinctive title track, a bombastic vocoder disco throb with unashamed power rock tendencies that decades later still sounds unlike anything you've ever heard. Argento was never renowned for his subtlety, and fittingly GOBLIN's real strength here doesn't lie in providing subtle background cues, but music that explodes into your ears with all the grace of a ripped jugular. That said, GOBLIN's work here proves that they can shamelessly toy with the emotions of the listener/viewer when they want to. The title track embodies the schlock appeal of Giallo movies, while the score as a whole deftly covers the entire gamut of classic horror soundtrack tricks, from warped music box melodies on 'Slow Circus', to doomy church organ on the title track and its various derivatives, and on to atmospheric washes and funky creeping bass on 'Gemini'. GOBLIN had the distinct advantage of doing all of these things before they were co-opted and bastardised for countless inferior films and scores, and the music here stands the test of time, both defining its epoch and transcending it. The closest they come to any kind of cheese is on the 'Don't Fear The Reaper' evoking 'Lesbo' which succeeds almost entirely on retrospective kitsch value, without ever crossing the razor sharp barrier into the irredeemably naff. As if in apology for this dalliance with the average, GOBLIN present 'Flashing' which morphs from atmospheric synth into a prime slice of classic electro – in the same year that Afrika Bambaataa was hatching 'Planet Rock' – before introducing what sounds suspiciously like trance synth. The reprise of the title track deconstructs the original, slowing down and drawing it out, bringing shimmering acoustic guitar and choppy electric guitar to the forefront. In addition to queering an already bizarre tune, this version is just as entrancing in its own right as the original, revealing that they really are singing "shoobie-do-wah" into their vocoders, after all. 'Waiting Death' is another re-imagining of the infinitely plunderable title track while 'Jane Mirror Theme' consists of flanged guitars and the now familiar arpeggiated organ riff. After this, there are several alternative versions of the preceding tracks, a slightly unnecessary track of sound effects which sounds more than a little like Tom Waits snoring and finally disco remixes of the title track and 'Flashing'. Although it is hard to imagine Argento's film without it, GOBLIN's music defies the limitations of the cinematic context: fans of John Carpenter's self-penned soundtracks and anyone who professes a scholarly approach to electronic music can't afford to ignore this soundtrack. *SW*

Album rating: *6.5

– spinoff releases, etc. –

GOBLIN: Tenebrae / Flashing

Jul 83. (12") *(STER 005EP)* ☐ ☐-

Sonny TERRY & Brownie McGHEE

Born: Saunders Terrell (24 Oct'11, Greensboro, North Carolina) and Walter Brown McGhee (30 Nov'15, Knoxville, Tennessee) respectively. One of the most fondly remembered duos in the history of American roots music, the late SONNY TERRY & BROWNIE McGHEE underwent familiar individual hardships before their partnership became the toast of the 60s folk revival. Accidentally blinded in both eyes by his mid teens, TERRY scratched a living as a street corner bluesman with a wildly expressive (and highly influential) harmonica habit. Described by legendary musicologist Alan Lomax as "that greatest of harp blowers", his subsequent link up with guitarist Blind Boy Fuller not only drew interest from record labels but catalysed his future partnership with BROWNIE McGHEE, a polio victim who himself overcame a major handicap to become one of the leading blues guitarists of his generation. Having initially met in 1939, the pair subsequently based themselves in New York where they recorded both together and independently for various labels. While TERRY made his acting debut in a post-war Broadway production, the man's harmonica was also much in demand by the likes of Woody Guthrie and Pete Seeger. As the 50s turned into the 60s, the duo increasingly catered to the enthusiastic demands of the folk crowd, releasing a series of acoustic folk and folk-blues albums and playing the requisite festivals. While McGHEE had also ventured onto the Broadway stage in the mid-50s, the pair's writing talents belatedly made it to the big-screen via Sidney Poitier's directorial debut, 'Buck And The Preacher' (1972) and thespian-turned-director Raymond St. Jacques' Deep South crime drama, 'BOOK OF NUMBERS' (1973). For his 1977 classic, 'Stroszek', iconic German director Werner Herzog substituted his usual soundtrack providers, POPOL VUH, for the rootsier tones of TERRY and Chet Atkins in what was to be the harmonica master's sole attempt at film scoring. While they'd acrimoniously put to bed their professional partnership in the mid-70s, TERRY and McGHEE made their belated screen acting debut with blues singing cameos in Steve Martin comedy, 'The Jerk' (1979). Into his seventh decade as a performer, TERRY subsequently passed away on 12th March, 1986 after a final appearance in multi-Oscar-nominated Alice Walker adapatation, 'The Color Purple' (1985). Although McGHEE's final screen appearance came a matter of months later in Alan Parker's demonic odyssey, 'Angel Heart' (1987), he was to survive his old sparring partner by a full decade, dying from cancer on 16th February 1996. *BG*

- filmography (composers) {acting} –

Festival *(1967 {p SONNY & BROWNIE} =>)* / Buck And The Preacher *(1972 both on s/t)* / Blues Under The Skin *(1973 {p SONNY})* / **Book Of Numbers** *(1973 OST by TERRY & McGHEE =>)* / Stroszek *(1977 no OST by TERRY & CHET ATKINS)* / the Jerk *(1979 {a+p SONNY & BROWNIE})* / **Hard Travelin'** *(1984 {c SONNY & BROWNIE} =>)* / the Color Purple *(1985 {p SAUNDERS SONNY TERRY} OST by QUINCY JONES see; future editions =>)* / Angel Heart *(1987 {a BROWNIE})*

THIEF

UK title 'VIOLENT STREETS'

1981 (US 122m) United Artists (15)

Film genre: post-noir crime caper/thriller

Top guns: s-w + dir: Michael Mann → the INSIDER (au: 'The Home Invaders' by Frank Hohimer)

Stars: James Caan *(Frank)* → DICK TRACY, Tuesday Weld *(Jessie)* ← I WALK THE LINE ← WILD IN THE COUNTRY ← ROCK, ROCK, ROCK! / → HEARTBREAK HOTEL → CHELSEA WALLS, **Willie NELSON** *(Okla)*, James Belushi *(Barry)* → LITTLE SHOP OF HORRORS → WAG THE DOG, Robert Prosky *(Leo)* → DEAD MAN WALKING, Tom Signorelli *(Attaglia)* ← SORCERER ← the TRIP / → DICK TRACY, Dennis Farina *(Carl)*, J.J. Saunders *(doctor)* ← CORNBREAD, EARL AND ME ← SLAUGHTER'S BIG RIP-OFF / → HOUSE PARTY, William L. Petersen *(Katz & Jammer barman)* → TO LIVE AND DIE IN L.A. → YOUNG GUNS II, Bruce A. Young *(mechanic #2)* → TRESPASS

Storyline: Frank's a slick but ageing, car salesman and professional diamond thief, worried in the knowledge he's still not pulled that final heist, a job that would secure a more settled life. Is crime boss, Leo, the man to give him that opportinity and is his new girlfriend really behind him? *MCS*

Movie rating: *7.5

Visual: video + dvd

Off the record: (see below)

—

TANGERINE DREAM

Apr 81. (lp/c) *Elektra; <5E/5C 521> Virgin; (V/TCV 2198)* ☐ 43
– Beach theme / Dr. Destructo / Diamond diary / Burning bar / Beach

scene *[UK-only]* / Scrap yard / Trap feeling / Igneous / Confrontation *[US-only]. (re-iss. Aug88 lp/c; OVED/+C 72) (cd-iss. Jun88; CDV 2198) (<cd re-iss. Aug95; TAND 12>)*

S/track review: It was four years since the release of TANGERINE DREAM's official debut soundtrack project, 'SORCERER' (1977). This time around, FROESE, FRANKE and SCHMOELLING, merge pulsating electronic beats and piercing guitar work from start to finish. Opener, 'Beach Theme', creates an easy, horizontal mood, before 'Dr. Destructo' bounces eerily between both ear sockets – excellent start. The third track and longest piece by far (at nearly 11 minutes!), 'Diamond Diary', harked back to the TANGERINE DREAM of old that gave us mid-70s classics such as 'Phaedra', 'Rubycon' and 'Ricochet'. The rest of the album – apart from the magical 'Igneous' that closed the set – floated mechanically somewhere between mediocrity and the fog that depicted Frank's violent streets. Note that PETER BAUMANN was incorrectly credited on the definitive CD edition, instead of JOHANNES SCHMOELLING. *MCS*

Album rating: *6.5

the THIRD EAR BAND

Formed: Canterbury, England in 1968 . . . originally as Giant Sun Trolley and Hydrogen Jukebox. Pigeonholed in the prog-meets-experimental box, the band went through several personnel changes before settling with jazz-lover Glenn Sweeney (drums, percussion, tabla), Richard Coff (violin, viola), Paul Minns (oboe, recorder) and Mel Davis (cello). Signing to 'Harvest' records (home to PINK FLOYD), the quartet kicked off their campaign in 1969 with the wholly instrumental, acoustic set, 'Alchemy'; Radio One disc jockey, John Peel, can be heard on Jew's harp. Described in some quarters as improvised chamber music, the free-of-electric crescendo-stoner outfit took their inspiration from Indian raga and psychedelia; the Soft Machine were doing similar things around the same era. THIRD EAR BAND's next LP (with Ursula Smith replacing Davis), the self-titled 'Third Ear Band' (aka 'Elements'), fared better, even reaching the lower rungs of the UK Top 50. It would be at this point that the same line-up were offered their first soundtrack work, albeit for German TV feature, 'ABÉLARD & HÉLOÏSE' (1970); this would remain unreleased until 1999. With the group ever-evolving (now Glenn Sweeney, his brother Colin Sweeney, Paul Minns, Paul Buckmaster, Simon House and Denim Bridges), they completed the score to Roman Polanski's 'MACBETH' feature in 1972, although Sweeney and Co disbanded not long after its recording. Returning to the fray late in the 80s, the THIRD EAR BAND (Sweeney, Minns, Allen Samuel and Mick Carter) went on to deliver a handful of albums for the Italian market. *MCS*

- **filmography** (composers) –

Abélard & Héloïse *(1970 OST =>)* / **Macbeth** *(1971 OST =>)*

THIS IS MY LIFE

1992 (US 105m) Twentieth Century Fox (PG-13)

Film genre: coming-of-age/showbiz comedy

Top guns: s-w: Nora Ephron (+ dir), Delia Ephron (au: Meg Wolitzer)

Stars: Julie Kavner *(Dottie Ingels)*, Samantha Mathis *(Erica Ingels)* ← PUMP UP THE VOLUME / → the THING CALLED LOVE, Gaby Hoffmann *(Opal Ingels)* → BLACK AND WHITE, Carrie Fisher *(Claudia Curtis)* ← the BLUES BROTHERS, Dan Aykroyd *(Arnold Moss)* ← the BLUES BROTHERS ← the RUTLES / → BLUES BROTHERS 2000, Bob Nelson *(Ed)*, Marita Geraghty *(Mia Jablon)*, Welker White *(Lynn)*, Caroline Aaron *(Martha Ingels)* ← WORKING GIRL / → PRIMARY COLORS → BEYOND THE SEA, Kathy Ann Najimy *(Angela)*, Tim Blake Nelson *(Dennis)* → O BROTHER, WHERE ART THOU? → HOOT, **Annie Golden** *(Marianne)* ← HAIR / → TEMPTATION

Storyline: The question of fame versus family rears its head for stand-up comedienne Dottie Ingels. When she and her young daughters move to New York her agent Claudia soon has her schedule mapped out, and most of it is on tour. Daughters Erica and Opal find themselves watching mum more on TV than in real life, and when they see her telling a chat show host all about her personal life the girls decide enough is enough! *JZ*

Movie rating: *5.5

Visual: video

Off the record: **Annie Golden** (b.19 Oct'51, Brooklyn, NY) was formerly of the Shirts, a pop new wave act who bubbled under the charts with the single, 'Tell Me Your Plans'. *MCS*

CARLY SIMON

Apr 92. (cd/c) *Qwest; <(7599 26901-2/-4)>* May92
– Love of my life / Back the way (Dottie's point of view) / Moving day / Easy on the eyes / Walking and kissing / The show must go on / Love of my life (Toots) / Back the way (girls' point of view) / Little troupers / The night before Christmas / This is my life suite: a) Pleasure and pain, b) Coming home, c) Uncle Peter / Love of my life (drive to the city).

S/track review: Singer-songwriter CARLY SIMON had an astounding track record with hit themes from the movies ('Nobody Does It Better' from the 1977 Bond movie, 'The Spy Who Loved Me', to 'Let The River Run' from 1988's 'WORKING GIRL'), but 'THIS IS MY LIFE' was her first complete solo OST album. With a Carly set, one knows what to expect: romantic love ballads, smooth, relaxing AOR tunes and a handful of the finest session people around (on this occasion, guitarist JIMMY RYAN, on synths & piano TEESE GOHL, drummer ANDY NEWMARK and bassist WILL LEE, plus the odd contribution from RUSS KUNKEL, RANDY BRECKER and TOOTS THIELEMANS). Opening number, 'Love Of My Life', namechecks Woody Allen, although it's basically a mother-to-daughter love song; it's reprised a further few times via TOOTS' harmonica version and the finale instrumental. Another track to display both sides of the movie's light-hearted domestic unrest is 'Back The Way', suffixed respectively as it was by the scatty '(Dottie's Point Of View)' and '(Girls' Point Of View)'. The first of several shortish instrumental cues comes via 'Moving Day', while others of that ilk such as 'Walking And Kissing', 'Little Troupers' and the longer 'This Is My Life Suite' basically fill time. It was no surprise that nothing was picked for release as a single, other songs such as 'Easy On The Eyes' (penned with Andy Goldberg), 'The Show Must Go On' and the festive 'The Night Before Christmas' too amiable and sentimental for even the hardened contemporary pop fan to take. *MCS*

Album rating: *3.5

Richard THOMPSON

Born: 3 Apr'49, London, England. A founder member of Fairport Convention, from 1967 until his departure early in 1971, THOMPSON was an important catalyst in the translation of English folk music into a rock format. He contributed many of Fairport's finest songs including 'Meet On The Ledge' and 'Sloth'. After session work for former Fairport friends, Sandy Denny and Iain Matthews, the bearded guitarist finally issued his 1972 debut

'Island' records album, 'Henry The Human Fly'. Just prior to this, he had worked with other ex-Fairport members Ashley Hutchings and Dave Mattacks who, as the Bunch, released the budget covers set, 'Rock On'. The following year, Richard teamed up both artistically and romantically with Glasgow-born Linda Peters, the couple becoming Richard & Linda Thompson after their marriage in 1974. Their first of seven albums together, 'I Want To See The Brights Lights Tonight', was acclaimed by many, and by rights, should have provided them with a hit single by way of the evocative title track. During the recording of their next album, 'Hokey Pokey' (1975), they converted to Sufism, even initiating their own Sufi community. Over the course of the next seven years, the "royal couple of British folk" created a string of finely crafted, harmony-laden albums, the pick of which was arguably 1982's 'Shoot Out The Lights'. The album featured the enduring 'Wall Of Death', appropriately enough the closing track on their final album together, their marriage already having floundered. Picking up the pieces, Richard went solo again the following year, recording 'Hand Of Kindness' for 'Hannibal' Records, a set which included the excellent 'Two Left Feet'. After finally achieving more widespread recognition, he moved to 'Capitol' records in the second half of the 80s and made significant inroads with the 1988 set, 'Amnesia'. THOMPSON gained a belated UK Top 40 solo success with his 1991 album, 'Rumour And Sigh', a wonderfully eclectic set running the gamut of THOMPSON's influences; on the back of this came his score to the film 'SWEET TALKER' (1991). 1994 saw the release of 'Mirror Blue', another critically acclaimed set including highlights such as 'Mingus Eyes' and 'The Way That It Shows'. His 1996 release, 'You? Me? Us?', introduced his son, Teddy, to the proceedings and offered up further classic tracks in the shape of 'Cold Kisses' and 'Woods Of Darney'. His home city of London was the lyrical core of THOMPSON's next work, 'Mock Tudor' (1999). After finally being dropped by 'Capitol', THOMPSON took the opportunity of going back to basics on 'The Old Kit Bag' (2003), casting an even more economical hand over the writing, recording and production than on its predecessor. 2005 was a relatively busy year for the guitarist with both a soundtrack to Werner Herzog's award-winning documentary, 'GRIZZLY MAN', and an all-acoustic solo album, 'Front Parlour Ballads', released within months of each other. The latter was THOMPSON's first set of wholly acoustic material since the traditional 'Strict Tempo', roundly praised as among the finest of his long solo career. In his time, THOMPSON (now a practising Muslim) has influenced many guitarists including Americans, Frank Black (of Pixies) and Bob Mould (of Husker Du and Sugar) and has come to be regarded as one of England's finest songwriting guitarists. *BG & MCS*

- **filmography** (composer) –

Sweet Talker *(1991 OST =>)* / **Grizzly Man** *(2005 OST =>)*

THREAT

2006 (US 90m) HIQI Media (R)

Film genre: urban drama

Top guns: s-w: (+ dir) Matt Pizzolo, Katie Nisa

Stars: Carlos Puga *(Jim)*, Keith Middleton *(Fred)*, Rebekka Takamizu *(Mekky)*, Kamouflage *(Desmond)*, Katie Nisa *(Kat)*, David R. Fisher *(Marco)*, Neil Rubenstein *(Ruby)*, Tony Dreannan *(Tony)*, **Rachel Rosen** *(punk rock girl)*, **Justin Brannan** *(straightedge kid)*

Storyline: Punk rocker Jim and hip hop revolutionary Fred live in New York's tough East Side. Jim has formed a gang called One Less Drunk who begin a campaign against drink drivers. When one of the gang has a run-in with a close friend of Fred, racial tension boils over and soon there is war on the streets between whites and blacks. Jim and Fred try their best to calm things down but the chaotic violence is rapidly spreading out of control. *JZ*

Movie rating: *6

Visual: dvd

Off the record: Justin Brannan & Rachel Rosen were both of the NYC metalcore outfit, Most Precious Blood; they've released three albums for 'Trustkill': 'Nothing In Vain' (2001), 'Our Lady Of Annihilation' (2003) and 'Merciless' (2005). **ATARI TEENAGE RIOT** were formed in West Berlin, Germany in 1992 by anti-Nazi cyberpunks **ALEC EMPIRE** (b. Alexander Wilke), Syrian-born punk goddess Hanin Elias and Swiss-born MC Carl Crack. With his 'Digital Hardcore' label as the main weapon of attack, EMPIRE waged war on what he saw as an increasingly corporate, decadently comatose German dance scene. His self proclaimed "lo-fi techno" owes more to the headfuck onslaught of radical hardcore punk (like X-Ray Spex or Crass) than any regular notion of "dance" music and ATARI TEENAGE RIOT's staunch anti-Nazi, anti-ecstasy stance has made EMPIRE a spokesman of sorts for the disillusioned Berlin underground scene. After a trio of fearsome albums, 'Delete Yourself' (1995), 'The Future Of War' (1997) and the well-received 'Burn, Berlin, Burn!' (1997), they secured support slots with big guns Rage Against The Machine and Wu-Tang Clan. In 1998, with a number of solo releases behind him, EMPIRE worked on ATR's comeback complete with a second female, the German/Japanese, face-painted, Nic Endo. A release schedule second to none was forthcoming by ATARI, EMPIRE, etc., notably the 'Rage' EP (a collaboration with RAtM's Tom Morello). Sadly, on the 6th of September, 2001, news filtered through that Carl Crack died in his Berlin flat. It was known for some time that the band were taking time out so that CARL could recover from drugs and alcohol abuse. EMPIRE's most recent album is 'Futurist' (2005), a lean towards punk-rock rather than hardcore electro. *MCS*

Various Artists incl. ALEC EMPIRE * / ATARI TEENAGE RIOT **

Jan 06. (cd) *Halo8; <02>* ☐ –

– Night of violence (*) / Start the riot (**) / Into the death (**) / Rage (** with TOM MORELLO & D-STROY) / Sick to death (**) / Get up while you can (**) / Gotta get out (*) / Common enemy (PANIC DHH) / Wanna peel (EC8OR) / Number seven with a bullet (BLEEDING THROUGH) / The great red shift (MOST PRECIOUS BLOOD) / One hell of a prize fighter (EIGHTEEN VISIONS) / Overcome (TERROR) / Drone (EYES LIKE KNIVES) / mPathik (QUEQUE) / hevN (QUEQUE) / I am the threat (KING DAVID) / Kids are united (**).

S/track review: 'THREAT' is the project that sees ALEC EMPIRE's youthful assertion that 'Riot Beats Create Riots' treated with the seriousness that he at least always believed it should be. EMPIRE's now defunct 'Digital Hardcore' label provide half the tracks here, and the other half are courtesy of NY hardcore label 'Trustkill' records (though the score on screen contains a lot more of EMPIRE and various other 'Digital Hardcore' acts). The industrial brutality of EMPIRE's more recent solo work is underwritten by the anime-and metal-sampling breakbeat frenzy of ten year old ATARI TEENAGE RIOT songs. Some people will struggle to get past ATR's straight faced imperatives to "Start the riot . . . now!", and in this context some of ATR's black humour and brutal exuberance is eclipsed by the overly sombre timbre of the rest of the collection. The juxtaposition of the DHR tracks with the more traditional and largely faceless metal and hardcore acts only highlights the conservatism of the latter while putting the former in an unflattering context (refer to ATR's 'Delete Yourself' album or EMPIRE's 'Miss Black America' instead). The effect of tracks by BLEEDING THROUGH and EIGHTEEN VISIONS is ironically soporific, so unremitting is their tuneless, uninspired dirge. The characterless drum and bass of King's Mob in-house beatmaker QUEQUE does nothing to lift the collection up from there; even his sampling of David Lynch's 'Lady In The Radiator Song' (from 'Eraserhead') is unremarkable, which is surely a botched opportunity. Much more interesting is 'I Am The Threat' by KING DAVID, written by punk singer and star of THREAT, David R Fisher, from his straight-edge character's perspective. This track is itself a riposte to rapper and fellow star of 'THREAT' Kamouflage's 'Am I A Threat', curiously not included here. ATARI TEENAGE RIOT's Sham 69 sampling 'Kids Are United' concludes this set with just the kind of infectious, gonzo energy and crackpot inventiveness (largely thanks to ATR's sadly deceased vocalist Carl Crack) that is conspicuously absent from the rest of the score. The title of the companion collection 'Music That Inspired THREAT' is somewhat misleading, as it consists of hardcore and metal tracks remixed especially for the collection by the likes of BILL YOUNGMAN, Dälek's OKTOPUS and EMPIRE himself. More consciously "underground" in sensibility than the similarly constructed soundtracks for 'Judgement Night' and 'Spawn', this album is prey to the same criticisms as the original soundtrack. The collaborations are rarely more than the sum of their parts, with many of the artists too close in sensibility if not in method for the remixes to be worthwhile. Somehow it's the remixes of seminal bands MINOR THREAT, AGNOSTIC FRONT and YOUTH OF TODAY that are the most underwhelming, while the lesser known acts are better served. Notable mentions go to OKTOPUS, whose reworking of Zak de la Rocha's old band INSIDE OUT re-stages their 'No Spiritual Surrender' in a dopey haze (re-titled 'Ghost In The Machine') and YOUNGMAN who re-edits JUDGE's 'Bringin' It Down' into a taut, glitchy throb. Overall, 'THREAT's strengths and its downfall are in its refusal to capitulate, and its lack of irony; subtlety and diversity are frowned upon, and this can make it an unforgiving, and, for the uninitiated, an easily dismissed experience. *SW*

Album(s) rating: *5 (+ inspired *4)

– spinoff release –

Various Artists: Music That Inspired The Movie..

Jan 06. (cd) *Halo 8; <01>* ☐ ⊟
– Pandemic (MOST PRECIOUS BLOOD vs. ALEC EMPIRE) / World at war (AGNOSTIC FRONT vs. SCHIZOID) / Ghost in the machine (INSIDE OUT vs. OKTOPUS) / World ablaze – Threat mix (KILLSWITCH ENGAGE vs. EDGEY) / Overkill (TERROR vs. ENDUSER) / Champagne enemaz (EIGHTEEN VISIONS vs. OTTO VON SCHIRACH) / Zolobovine (GORILLA BISCUITS vs. DEFRAGMENTATION) / Cannibal kitten (the ICARUS LINE vs. the END) / Slapped with an X (VOD vs. the TYRANT) / Bring it (JUDGE vs. BILL YOUNGMAN) / Stalwart carapace (YOUTH OF TODAY vs. EDGEY) / Deathbed (BLEEDING THROUGH vs. HECATE) / I know that you're lying (TODAY IS THE DAY vs. DARPH/NADER) / Star buried in my yard (GLASSJAW vs. ENDUSER) / Don't step (MINOR THREAT vs. HOLOCAUST).

THREE O'CLOCK HIGH

1987 (US 98m) Universal Pictures (13)

Film genre: teen/coming-of-age comedy/farce

Top guns: dir: Phil Joanou → RATTLE AND HUM / s-w: Richard Christian Matheson, Thomas Szollosi

Stars: Casey Siemaszko *(Jerry Mitchell)*, Anne Ryan *(Franny Perrins)*, Richard Tyson *(Buddy Revell)*, Stacey Glick *(Brei Mitchell)*, Jonathan Wise *(Vincent Costello)*, Jeffrey Tambor *(Mr. Rice)* → MALIBU'S MOST WANTED, Philip Baker Hall *(detective Mulvahill)* → BOOGIE NIGHTS → the INSIDER → MAGNOLIA, John P. Ryan *(Mr. O'Rourke)*, Liza Morrow *(Karen Clarke)*, Alice Nunn *(nurse Palmer)* ← WHO'S THAT GIRL? ← TRICK OR TREAT

Storyline: Another high school-theme'd feature from the 80s. Student nerd, Jerry Mitchell, has been delegated to interview class thug, Buddy Revell, on his violent past. However, his worse scenario arises when he is challenged by the bully to a fight outside after school. His inept trials and tribulations at averting the situation on the run up to three o'clock and the ever-pending time limit, make for a day to remember. *MCS*

Movie rating: *6.5

Visual: video + dvd

Off the record: (see below)

—

TANGERINE DREAM (+ score SYLVESTER LEVAY * etc)

Nov 87. (lp) *Varese Sarabande; <VS 47357>* ☐ ⊟
– It's Jerry's day today / 46-32-15 / No detention / Any school bully will do / Go to the head of the class / Sit (*) / The fight (*) / Jerry's decisions (*) / The fight is on (*) / Paper (*) / Big bright brass knuckles / Buying paper like it's going out of style / Dangerous trend / Who's chasing who? / Bonding by candlelight / You'll never believe it / Starting the day off right / Weak at the knees / Kill him (the football dummy) / Not so quiet in the library – Get lost in a crowd / Something to remember me by (JIM WALKER) / Arrival (RICK MORATTA & DAVID TICKLE). *<(UK+cd-iss. Oct90 also on 'Varese Sarabande'; VCD same>)*

S/track review: A near unique combination of Prog/electro champions TANGERINE DREAM, orchestral composer SYLVESTER LEVAY, and various others, made for a slightly schizoid soundtrack. TD's short compositions were mostly recorded in '86 and featured FROESE alongside FRANKE (and in a lesser respect, HASLINGER) on some dense, aggressive guitar atmospherics and beats; their longest piece being 'Go To The Head Of The Class' at just over 3 minutes. Squeezed and languishing somewhere in the middle of the group's multi-layered effects, were five symphonic stabs by LEVAY. Possibly a bad decision to include these tracks (and two closing pieces by a few unknowns) to what could have been a good TANGERINE DREAM set. *MCS*

Album rating: *4.5

THREE THE HARD WAY

1974 (US 89m) Allied Artists Pictures Corporation (R)

Film genre: crime thriller

Top guns: dir: Gordon Parks Jr. ← SUPERFLY / → AARON LOVES ANGELA / s-w: Eric Bercovici, Jerrold L. Ludwig

Stars: Jim Brown *(Jimmy Lait)* ← SLAUGHTER'S BIG RIP-OFF → HE GOT GAME, Fred Williamson *(Jagger Daniels)* ← THREE TOUGH GUYS ← the SOUL OF NIGGER CHARLEY ← BLACK CAESAR ← HELL UP IN HARLEM / → BUCKTOWN → MEAN JOHNNY BARROWS → ADIOS AMIGO → NO WAY BACK → MR. MEAN → FROM DUSK TILL DAWN → RIDE → CARMEN: A HIP HOPERA, Jim Kelly *(Mister Keyes)* ← BLACK BELT JONES ← MELINDA, Sheila Frazier *(Wendy Kane)* ← SUPERFLY T.N.T. ← SUPERFLY, Jay Robinson *(Monroe Feather)* → TRAIN RIDE TO HOLLYWOOD, Charles McGregor *(Charley)* ← ACROSS 110th STREET ← SUPERFLY / → THAT'S THE WAY OF THE WORLD → AARON LOVES ANGELA, Alex Rocco *(Lt. Di Nisco)* → VOICES → SCENES FROM THE GOLDMINE → THAT THING YOU DO!, Irene Tsu *(Pua)* ← PARADISE, HAWAIIAN STYLE, **the Impressions** (themselves), Jeannie Bell *(Polly)* ← TROUBLE MAN ← MELINDA / → DISCO 9000, Victor Brandt *(guard)* → I WANNA HOLD YOUR HAND → NEON MANIACS

Storyline: A sinister racist organisation plans some serious ethnic cleansing right in the heart of big town America. The tough guy African-American trio of the title set out to foil the fascists, whose fiendish plan to poison black folks through the water supply only increases the movie's hokum factor. *BG*

Movie rating: *5.5

Visual: none

Off the record: the IMPRESSIONS (see below)

—

the IMPRESSIONS

Jul 74. (lp) *Curtom; <CRS 8602ST>* ☐ ☐
– Having a ball / Make a resolution / Mister Keyes / On the move / Something's mighty, mighty wrong / That's what love will do / Three the hard way (chase theme) / Wendy. *(UK-iss.Nov01 on 'Get Back'; GET 8007)*

S/track review: With Curtis Mayfield busy smoothing Blaxploitation's rough edges, the IMPRESSIONS got their own piece of the black action pie with this unintentionally comedic Gordon Parks thriller. The presence of both Parks and Mayfield arranger RICH TUFO (on writing and production duties), as well as the ever-looming shadow of Mayfield himself, suggests exactly what this is going to sound like before you even get past the sleeve credits, but, well, first impressions (pun intended) don't always count, and TUFO has more than a few surprises up his sleeve. The band were actually on an upswing in 1974, with new singers RALPH JOHNSON and REGGIE TORIAN (alongside FRED CASH and SAM GOODEN) replacing Leroy Hutson, and scoring themselves a Top 20 hit with 'Finally Got Myself Together'. Had it been released as a single instead of the title theme, the crusading 'That's What Love Will Do' might have made the chart on its tail; while TUFO generally doesn't frame the band's pitch-and-pull vocals with the same razor-slick cool he did Mayfield's falsetto, his strings spit sparks here, riding call-and-response harmonies and frantic scat. Lead track – and de facto supporting theme – 'Make A Resolution' takes a similar tack without quite as much passion, while the ambitious two-part title theme 'Three The Hard Way (Chase & Theme)' manipulates the group's multiple vocal possibilities, layering in some buttery sax over the regulation hi-hat before taking it right down to almost reggae tempo (a blaxploitation avenue almost completely – and as TUFO proves, mistakenly – bypassed by other writers), sounding some quasi-dub echo in anticipation of a soul-deep harmony-roots refrain and Ernest Ranglin-esque guitar. Memorably sampled by Pete Rock, meanwhile, 'On The Move' is from the same bass/woodwind seed-bed as 'Freddie's Dead', slower and quirkier with trombone and a hammy jazz vocal/scat arrangement. 'Mister Keyes' tries Temptations-with-clavinet and the Lee Dorsey-esque bump-funk of 'Something's Mighty, Mighty Wrong' (flip-side of the single release) isn't bad either. Unlike say, his work on Aretha Franklin's 'SPARKLE', you can't accuse TUFO of playing it safe, and despite its low profile, 'THREE THE HARD WAY' repays more than one spin. If you can't turn up an original, note that sound quality on the Italian-manufactured re-press isn't the best. *BG*

Album rating: *6

– spinoff releases, etc. –

the IMPRESSIONS: Something's Mighty, Mighty Wrong / Three The Hard Way

Jun 74. (7") ☐ ☐

THREE TOUGH GUYS

1974 (Ita/US/Fra 92m) Paramount Pictures (PG)

Film genre: crime thriller

Top guns: dir: Duccio Tessari / s-w: Niccola Badalucco, Luciano Vincenzoni

Stars: Lino Ventura *(Father Charlie)*, **Isaac HAYES** *(Lee Stevens)*, Fred Williamson *(Joe Snake)* ← the SOUL OF NIGGER CHARLEY ← BLACK CAESAR ← HELL UP IN HARLEM / → THREE THE HARD WAY → BUCKTOWN → MEAN JOHNNY BARROWS → ADIOS AMIGO → NO WAY BACK → MR. MEAN → FROM DUSK TILL DAWN → RIDE → CARMEN: A HIP HOPERA, Paula Kelly *(Fay Collins)* ← the SPOOK WHO SAT BY THE DOOR ← TROUBLE MAN ← COOL BREEZE, Luciano Salce *(bishop)*, William Berger *(Capt. Ryan)*, Thurman Scott *(Tony Red)* ← ACROSS 110th STREET

Storyline: An Italian movie ('Uomini duri . . . altrimenti vi ammuchiamo') attempting to get on the Blaxploitation bandwagon and somehow roping Isaac Hayes into the action. Hayes plays Lee Stevens, who teams up with Father Charlie, an ex-con turned trainee priest, to find out who framed the good Father's friend. *BG*

Movie rating: *5.5

Visual: video

Off the record: (see below)

ISAAC HAYES: Tough Guys

Jun 74. (lp) *Enterprise; <ENS 7504> Stax; (STXH 5001)* ☐ ☐
– (title theme) / Randolph & Dearborn / The red rooster / Joe Bell / Hung up on my baby / Kidnapped / Run Fay run / Buns-o-plenty / (the end message). *<(d-cd-iss. Sep99 on 'Stax'+=; CDSXE2 095)>* – ISAAC HAYES: Truck Turner. *<(cd re-mast.Apr02; SCD24 7504)>*

S/track review: The most obscure of all ISAAC HAYES' soundtracks, 'THREE TOUGH GUYS' is also his most concise, clocking in at an incredible (at least for a master of overstatement like HAYES) half hour plus. Theoretically, that should mean it's also his most listenable and it probably is, but while it boasts a rocking main theme – combining the hi-hat foreplay of 'SHAFT' with the frazzled tropes of psychedelic soul and some exquisitely dated vocal phrasing – as well as a clutch of great instrumentals, it lacks a bonafide killer cut to raise it to classic status. The balmy, George Benson-esque jazz guitar lounging of 'Hung Up On My Baby' was indulged more extensively – if not quite as intoxicatingly – on HAYES' other summer '74 soundtrack, 'TRUCK TURNER'. The fact that it was also chosen as the B-side for the single release of that film's main theme underlines the interchangeability of the material on both albums. While the riff-heavy funk-rock and punchy horn charts of 'Joe Bell' recall 'SHAFT'-vintage Bar Kays, the percussive rattle and dissonant, wire-taut hum of 'Run Fay Run' was knotty and atmospheric enough to warrant inclusion on Quentin Tarantino's 'KILL BILL VOL.1' (2003). Well worth digging out on original vinyl, ' . . .TOUGH GUYS' was also re-packaged as a great-value 'Stax' two-fer with the aforementioned 'TRUCK TURNER'. *BG*

Album rating: *6.5

THUMBSUCKER

2005 (US 95m) Sony Pictures (R)

Film genre: coming-of-age/domestic comedy/drama

Top guns: s-w + dir: Mike Mills (au: Walter Kim)

Stars: Lou Taylor Pucci *(Justin Cobb)*, Tilda Swinton *(Audrey Cobb)* ← YOUNG ADAM, Vincent D'Onofrio *(Mike Cobb)* ← OVERNIGHT ← CHELSEA WALLS ← STRANGE DAYS, Vince Vaughn *(Mr. Geary)* ← SOUTH OF HEAVEN, WEST OF HELL / → BE COOL → INTO THE WILD, Keanu Reeves *(Perry Lyman)* ← EVEN COWGIRLS GET THE BLUES ← BILL & TED'S BOGUS JOURNEY ← BILL & TED'S EXCELLENT ADVENTURE ← PERMANENT RECORD, Benjamin Bratt *(Matt Schraam)*, Kelli Garner *(Rebecca)*

Storyline: High school student Justin finds the best way to forget his many problems is to suck his thumb. This does not escape the attention of the people round about him and inevitably turns him into a nerdy loner. Having a seriously weird family at home doesn't help things and even the school psychologist is at his wits' end. Then, one fateful day, Justin suddenly stops the thumb thing and becomes an overnight debating genius, but no-one can put their finger on why. *JZ*

Movie rating: *7

Visual: dvd

Off the record: The **POLYPHONIC SPREE** were formed in Dallas, Texas, USA ... 2000 by frontman/lyricist TIM DELAUGHTER in a bizarre postscript to the ill-fated Tripping Daisy outfit after the o.d. death of his bandmate Wes Berggren. With its twenty or so members (including former Tripping Daisy's Mark Pirro and Bryan Wakeland) plus DELAUGHTER's loose open-door policy, the Dallas congregation were established when they issued a cassette-only mini-LP, 'The Begining Stages Of . . .' (2000), before playing countless live shows in and around Texas. The independent label 'Good' issued the set, and, with their white sinuous robes, uplifting dreamy psychedelic gospel and quasi-religious overtones ("Jesus is love", and all that), the collective were soon becoming uber cult. It wasn't long before the British music press got their grubby little hands on the band – after all, they were still filthy with the overt favouritism and lazy handling of certain garage rock groups, it was refreshing to see around 23 robe-wearing happy Texans don the cover of a publication. The group added new material to their already existing mini-album and re-issued it as their debut LP, 'The Beginning Stages Of . . .' (2002). The music it contained – all in sections – was that of strange, breezy psychedelic pop in the vein of Mercury Rev or the Flaming Lips, but with the general communal ethos applied by the likes of Lambchop (who'd also boasted quite a line-up). After the clever pop/rock of Tripping Daisy, DELAUGHTER obviously had strong intentions of creating joyful Americana; a sometimes ecstatic blend of gospel, pop and lo-fi with warm instrumentation and DELAUGHTER's cracked vocals floating over the whole thing, the POLYPHONIC SPREE were a ray of sunshine that blasted into the often bleak world of American alt-rock. Slightly less shiny-happy-people and more you've-got-a-friend, 'Together We're Heavy' (2004) saw the robed revival continue while making at least some concession to life's darker side. *BG & MCS*

—

TIM DELAUGHTER / the POLYPHONIC SPREE
(. . .songs: ELLIOTT SMITH (*))

Sep 05. (cd) *Hollywood; <2061 62542-2> (342742-2)* ☐ Oct05 ☐
– The crash / Scream & shout / Slow halls / What would you let go / Empty rooms / Wonderful for you / The Rebecca fantasy / Thirteen (*) / Pink trash dream / The green lights / Debate montage (compliments of Tripping Daisy) / Trouble (*) / Skinny dip / Sourness makes it right / Some of the parts / Matt Schraam / Let's get lost (*) / Justin's hypnosis / The call of the wild / Wait and see / Move away and shine / Acceptance / Move away and shine (In A Dream version).

S/track review: Influenced by early 70s cult flick 'Harold And Maude' (score by Cat Stevens), 'THUMBSUCKER' filmmaker Mike Mills first thought of 90s singer-songwriter ELLIOTT SMITH when he imagined the movie's characters. When the pair met in 2003, it was agreed that ELLIOTT (who'd supplied several songs to 1997's 'GOOD WILL HUNTING') would record a handful of covers including John Lennon's 'Isolation' and Leonard Cohen's 'Sisters Of Mercy'. Sadly, a few months into recording his 'From A Basement . . .' set (and some 'THUMBSUCKER' tracks), ELLIOTT died that October (21st). For a while, Mills struggled with picking music, until that is, he witnessed a POLYPHONIC SPREE show. Glory be, the film and soundtrack found a new inner light. The combination of both POLYPHONIC SPREE cuts and ELLIOTT's recordings were, in the words of the director, "inspirational". TIM DELAUGHTER's congregation were the uplifting and spiritual factor right from opening track, 'The Crash', an exalting piece of hookline "la la la la la . . ." that catches one indubitably waving hands in mid air. 'Scream & Shout' is again Sunday school singing, but that's in no way a slight on the POLYPHONIC dress-sense or church-like chanting, it's simply because no one else (in the indie world at least) would be brave enough to attempt it. With tracks under a minute too short to get going – and there are several – one has to concentrate on fuller tracks such as the folkie 'What Would Let You Go', a number that could have had a stamp of approval from 'HAIR' or 'GODSPELL' aficionados. If you're also old enough to think of the Incredible String Band and Peter, Paul & Mary, you might just have the fusion right. If you were missing ELLIOTT at this stage, DELAUGHTER/'SPREE give a fine impression via 'Wonderful For You', the singer-songwriter finally gets rolling on a strummy rendition of Big Star's 'Thirteen' (can anyone remember Teenage Fanclub's version?). Only two other SMITH songs appear, Yusuf Islam's (or is that Cat Stevens') 'Trouble' and his own classic composition, 'Let's Get Lost'. Some will miss ELLIOTT in the same way they'll miss the now iconic Jeff Buckley. Back at the ranch, the POLYPHONIC SPREE get all 'Virgin Suicides' on us for track 10, 'The Green Lights', while the 'Debate Montage' celebrates the rebirth, of sorts of DELAUGHTER's old outfit, Tripping Daisy, albeit with that "la la la la la . . ." effect. With a piano-led intro similar to that of say.. Lennon's, but with a Flaming Lips feel (they've had that comparison levelled at them many times!), 'Sourness Makes It Right', and just about gets it right; 'Some Of The Parts' is reminiscent of something I can't put my finger on for now. Recorded in the First Unitarian Church, Philadelphia (of all places), 'The Call Of The Wild', is just pure spiritual punk rock gone haywire. 'Move Away And Shine' (in 2 versions) ends the show and is interspersed by the longest instrumental pop record in soundtrack history, the near 30-minute long, 'Acceptance', a lullaby for adults and without a doubt a cure for insomnia – take my word for it. *MCS*

Album rating: *7

TIMERIDER: THE ADVENTURE OF LYLE SWANN

1982 (US 94m) Zoomo Productions / Jensen Farley Pictures (PG)

Film genre: sci-fi western comedy

Top guns: s-w: (+ dir) William Dear, **Michael Nesmith**

Stars: Fred Ward *(Lyle Swann)* ← CARNY / → MASKED AND ANONYMOUS, Belinda Bauer *(Claire Cygne)* → FLASHDANCE → UHF, Peter Coyote *(Porter Reese)* → HEARTBREAKERS → BAJA OKLAHOMA → the MAN INSIDE → a LITTLE TRIP TO HEAVEN → COMMUNE, Richard Masur *(Claude Dorsett)* → RISKY BUSINESS, Tracey Walter *(Carl Dorsett)* → HONKYTONK MAN → REPO MAN → BATMAN → YOUNG GUNS II → DELUSION → MAN ON THE MOON → HOW HIGH → MASKED AND ANONYMOUS, Ed Lauter *(Padre Quinn)*, L.Q. Jones *(Ben Potter)* ← STAY AWAY, JOE, Chris Mulkey *(Daniels)* ← the LONG RIDERS / → HEARTBREAK HOTEL → GAS, FOOD LODGING → SUGAR TOWN → MYSTERIOUS SKIN, Macon McCalman *(Dr. Sam)* ← DELIVERANCE, William Dear *(3rd technician)*

Storyline: Moto-cross racer Lyle Swann unwittingly rides through a time-warp experiment and is transported back to the Wild West of the 1870s. It's not long before his bike attracts the attention of desperado Peter Coyote and his gang, who know the value of a quick getaway. Chased into Mexico, Lyle is mistaken for the Devil by the peasants, but it's the local priest and the voluptuous Clair who have to get him home. *JZ*

Movie rating: *4.5

Visual: video + dvd

Off the record: **MICHAEL NESMITH** (→ the MONKEES)

—

MICHAEL NESMITH

Aug 00. (cd) *Rio; <7528-2>* ☐ ☐
– The Baja 1000 / Lost in the weeds / Somewhere around 1875 / Scared to death / Silks and sixguns / Dead man's duds / Two Swanns at the pond / I want that machine / Escape to San Marcos / Claire's cabin / No jurisdiction / Murder at Swallow's camp / Claire's rescue / Up the hill to nowhere / Out of ammo / Reprise.

S/track review: Intermittently famous as one of the MONKEES, the heir to a corrective-fluid fortune (his mother invented Liquid Paper) and the inventor of MTV, MIKE NESMITH deserves much greater recognition for his achievements at the creative end of country music. While a string of songs like 'Different Drum' and 'Some Of Shelly's Blues' have become much-covered country standards, NESMITH's tangential, fresh take on the genre earns him a place alongside innovators like Gram Parsons and Roger McGuinn. Sadly, though, the soundtrack to his under-exposed time-travelling film (released on CD seventeen years after the film) is the one album the great man's fans can probably do without. This is the polymath as producer and co-screenwriter, and the composer comes off a poor second over fifteen instrumental tracks that cave in to the B-movie requirements of the day. There are hooks aplenty, and interesting ideas, but very little that can stand up to a wave of cheesy synth keyboards, permed-hair drumming and guitar hero callisthenics. The writing craft and the production are pretty well faultless – track titles like 'I Want That Machine' and 'Out Of Ammo' convey the functionality of the music, and you can certainly hear the energies and tensions of the unseen story – but you'd have to be a dedicated fan of mainstream 80s rock to appreciate this music without the formulaic celluloid it's clearly made for. *ND*

Album rating: *4

TINDERSTICKS

Formed: Nottingham, England ... 1988 as Asphalt Ribbons by Stuart Staples, Dave Boulter and Dickon Hinchcliffe, alongside Neil Fraser, Mark Colwill and Al McCauley. Long the connoisseur's choice as the most majestically miserable and preternaturally talented band in Britain, TINDERSTICKS make few concessions to joie de vivre and even less to fashion. After the almost universal critical praise lavished on their debut album, the band proceeded to plot an unswerving course through popular music's darker, more melancholy corners, places inhabited by intense individualists like NICK CAVE, JOHNNY CASH, SCOTT WALKER, TOM WAITS and Lee Hazlewood. If a 1993 cover of John Barry's 'We Have All The Time In The World' made plain their love of film music, it only confirmed what most fans already knew. Given their love of tasteful orchestration and celluloid meditation, it was probably only a matter of time before Staples and Co recorded a soundtrack of their own. That soundtrack was to be French director Clair Denis' 'NENETTE ET BONI' (1996), a low-key coming-of-age drama set in Marseilles. Denis' meditative directorial pace and TINDERSTICKS' brooding instrumentals proved such sympathetic bedfellows that the director commissioned them again for her considerably more controversial tale of everyday sex and cannibalism, 'TROUBLE EVERY DAY' (2001). *BG*

- filmography (composers) –

Nenette Et Boni *(1996 OST =>)* / **Trouble Every Day** *(2001 OST =>)*

TO HAVE AND TO HOLD

1996 (Aus 98m) AFC / Calypso Films / Palace Films (18)

Film genre: psychological romantic thriller/drama

Top guns: dir: John Hillcoat ← GHOSTS ...OF THE CIVIL DEAD / → the PROPOSITION / s-w: Gene Conkie

Stars: Tcheky Karyo *(Jack)*, Rachel Griffiths *(Kate Henely)* → AMY → STEP UP, Steve Jacobs *(Sal)*, Anni Finsterer *(Rose)* → BIGGER THAN TINA → QUEEN OF THE DAMNED, David Field *(Stevie)* ← GHOSTS ... OF THE CIVIL DEAD / → CHOPPER → ONE NIGHT THE MOON → SILENT PARTNER

Storyline: Against the lush backdrop of rural Papua New Guinea, the rough 'n' ready, recently widowed Jack begins a new romance with big city novelist Kate Henely. Once ensconced back in the jungle, however, the behaviour of her increasingly obsessive lover gives her reason to fear for her life. *BG*

Movie rating: *4.5

Visual: video + dvd

Off the record: (see below)

BLIXA BARGELD – NICK CAVE – MICK HARVEY

Feb 97. (cd) *Elektra; <69031> Ionic-Mute; (IONIC 15CD)* [ ] Aug98 [ ]
– To have and to hold / The jungle of love / Candlelit bedroom / Luther / A house in the jungle / Delerium / The river at night / Mourning song (RAUN RAUN THEATRE) / Romantic theme / Snow vision / Rose / The clouds / Noah's funeral / The fight / Kate leaves / We're coming – The riot / Murder / The red dress / I threw it all away (SCOTT WALKER) / To have and to hold – end titles. *(bonus track +=)* – Gangster bone (KEETY GENERAL).

S/track review: Having previously scored John Hillcoat's infamous 'GHOSTS ...OF THE CIVIL DEAD', NICK CAVE and Bad Seeds BLIXA BARGELD and MICK HARVEY were an obvious choice to soundtrack the man's torrid study of tropical fear and loathing. In stark contrast to 'GHOSTS ...', this was a fully-fledged orchestral score, as accomplished and nuanced as any Hollywood product and more deeply felt. It was also as mournful and meditative as anything in the CAVE canon, a precedent perhaps, for the man's quasi-religious masterpiece, 'The Boatman's Call' (1997). The main theme and the majority of the cues mourn disconsolately, adrift on HARVEY-arranged seas of aching, baying cellos and weeping violins, with only the child-like clamour of a native choir to connect them with the possibility of redemption and rebirth. Even some of the purely indigenous excerpts hang heavy with loss, especially the traditional 'Mourning Song' – performed by RAUN RAUN THEATRE – wherein the wracked sobbing sounds all too genuine. CAVE and Co were nevertheless far too canny a writing aggregate to rely on a wholly one-dimensional atmosphere, assuaging the sadness with the symbolic hope of church bells in 'Snow Vision' and the quicksilver cascade of a harp in 'The Clouds'. As well as incorporating avant-garde and found sound fragments into the orchestrations, they also tempered the cumulatively oppressive mood by alternating the classical pieces with percolating, sub-aquatic experiments like 'Luther' and 'Noah's Funeral'. While the segueing of SCOTT WALKER's typically lugubrious cover of Bob Dylan's 'I Threw It All Away' into the closing theme is a final classy touch, the programming of hidden ragga track, 'Gangster Bone' ends it all on a ridiculously incongruous note. *BG*

Album rating: *6.5

TO LIVE AND DIE IN L.A.

1985 (US 116m) MGM-UA / New Century Productions (R)

Film genre: cop/detective/crime thriller

Top guns: s-w: William Friedkin (+ dir) ← SORCERER ← GOOD TIMES, Gerald Petievich (+ au)

Stars: William Petersen *(Richard Chance)* ← THIEF / → YOUNG GUNS II, Willem Dafoe *(Eric 'Rick' Masters)* ← STREETS OF FIRE / → the LAST TEMPTATION OF CHRIST → CRY-BABY → WILD AT HEART → AFFLICTION → OVERNIGHT → the LIFE AQUATIC WITH STEVE ZISSOU, John Pankow *(John Vukovich)*, Debra Feuer *(Bianca Torres)* → HOMEBOY, John Turturro *(Carl Cody)* → JUNGLE FEVER → GIRL 6 →

GRACE OF MY HEART → HE GOT GAME → O BROTHER, WHERE ART THOU?, Darlanne Fluegel *(Ruth Lanier)*, Dean Stockwell *(Bob Grimes)* ← DUNE ← PARIS, TEXAS ← HUMAN HIGHWAY ← PSYCH-OUT / → TUCKER: THE MAN AND HIS DREAM → MADONNA: INNOCENCE LOST, Steve James *(Jeff Rice)* ← TIMES SQUARE, Jackie Giroux *(Claudia Leith)* ← SLAUGHTER'S BIG RIP-OFF, Robert Downey Sr. *(Thomas Bateman)* ← YOU'VE GOT TO WALK IT LIKE YOU TALK IT . . . / → BOOGIE NIGHTS → MAGNOLIA, Jane Leaves *(Serena)*, Michael Greene *(Jim Hart)* ← NAKED ANGELS / → DOWN AND OUT IN BEVERLY HILLS → LAST MAN STANDING

Storyline: Secret Service agent Richard Chance goes undercover in a counterfeiting ring to avenge the killing of his partner. William Friedkin scripted this flashy, violent crime thriller from a novel by ex-secret service agent Gerald Petievich. *DG*

Movie rating: *7

Visual: video + dvd

Off the record: WANG CHUNG (see below)

—

WANG CHUNG

Oct 85. (lp/c/cd) *Geffen; <24081> (GEF/40/CD 70271)* [85] Jan86 [ ]
– To live and die in L.A. / Lullaby / Wake up, stop dreaming / Wait / City of the angels / The red stare / Black-blue-white / Every big city. *(re-iss. Apr91 cd/c; GEF D/C 24081) (re-iss. Apr92 cd/c; GFL D/C 19055)*

S/track review: WANG CHUNG are best remembered for their hit single 'Dance Hall Days'. Previously known as Huang Chung, which apparently means "yellow bell" in Chinese, they changed their name after signing to Geffen records. It's been suggested that the company were worried people wouldn't be able to pronounce their original name. This is their only foray into soundtrack composition and it could be argued that shows in the structure of their efforts. There is a fifty-fifty split between songs and instrumental pieces, with a high tempo kept on all but 'The Red Stare', which builds from sparse piano to a brief guitar-led crescendo. Otherwise, we are firmly in 80s synth territory, backed by chugging drum tracks complemented with a guitar sound oddly reminiscent of that from 'Tinseltown In The Rain' by the Blue Nile. It can be argued that it is important for a soundtrack to capture a sense of time and place. WANG CHUNG (JACK HUES, NICK FELDMAN and DARRIN COSTIN) certainly achieve this: there are even "pan-pipes" to be heard on 'Wake Up, Stop Dreaming'. Listening to this (and watching the film) again after a good few years hurtles me back to my mid-teens. And that's not a bad thing. The main problem lies with JACK HUES' singing: there is something incongruous about William Petersen and John Pankow navigating the mean streets of L.A. while someone sings bad lyrics in a vaguely cockney accent over the hot and dusty images. It may have been wiser to stick to instrumentals, and leave the visuals alone. *DG*

Album rating: *5.5

– spinoff releases, etc. –

WANG CHUNG: To Live And Die In L.A. / Black-Blue-White

Oct 85. (7"/12") *<28891> (A/TA 6756)* [41] Jan86 [ ]

TO SIR, WITH LOVE

1967 (UK 105m) Columbia Pictures (A)

Film genre: urban coming-of-age/teen drama

Top guns: s-w + dir: James Clavell (au: E.R. Braithwaite)

Stars: Sidney Poitier *(Mark Thackeray)* ← BLACKBOARD JUNGLE / → LET'S DO IT AGAIN → a PIECE OF THE ACTION, Judy Geeson *(Pamela Dare)*, Christian Roberts *(Denham)*, **LULU** *(Barbara Pegg)*, Suzy Kendall *(Gillian Blanchard)*, Faith Brook *(Mrs. Evans)*, Patricia Routledge *(Clinty)*, Adrienne Posta *(Moira Jackson)*, Rita Webb *(Mrs. Joseph)* → MRS. BROWN, YOU'VE GOT A LOVELY DAUGHTER → the MAGIC CHRISTIAN → PERCY → CONFESSIONS OF A POP PERFORMER, Christopher Chittell *(Potter)*, Geoffrey Bayldon *(Weston)* ← TWO A PENNY / → BORN TO BOOGIE → the MONSTER CLUB, Avis Bunnage *(Rosie)*, **Michael Des Barres** *(Williams)* → MAYOR OF THE SUNSET STRIP, **the Mindbenders:- Ric Rothwell, Eric Stewart** *, **Bob Lang** *(performers)* → GIVE MY REGARDS TO BROAD STREET *

Storyline: Black engineer Mark Thackeray finds himself in a teaching post at a tough East End school after failing to get an engineering job. Needless to say he ends up teaching the Classroom From Hell, full of poor, angry, rebellious kids out to cause as many problems as they can for Teacher. Thackeray attempts to teach them respect and to behave like adults, while dealing with the class bully and an over-enthusiastic female student, who wants to give Sir more than an apple. *JZ*

Movie rating: *6.5

Visual: video + dvd

Off the record: LULU (see below + own biog)

—

Various Artists (instrumental score: RON GRAINER *)

Nov 67. (lp; stereo/mono) *Fontana; (S+/TL 5446) <SRF6/MGF2 7569>* [ ] Sep67 [16]
– To sir, with love (vocal by LULU) / School break dancing "Stealing my love from me" (vocal by LULU) / Thackeray meets faculty, then alone (*) / Music from lunch break "Off and running" (vocal by the MINDBENDERS) / Thackeray loses temper, gets an idea (*) / Museum outings montage "To sir, with love" (vocal by LULU) / A classical lesson (*) / Perhaps I could tidy your desk (*) / Potter's loss of temper in gym (*) / Thackeray reads letter about job (*) / Thackeray and Denham box in gym (*) / The funeral (*) / End of term dance "It's getting harder all the time" (vocal by the MINDBENDERS) / To sir, with love (vocal by LULU). *(cd-iss. May99 on 'Retroactive'; RECD 9004) <US cd-iss. 1999 on 'Sindrome'; 8935>*

S/track review: Although the score is really down to just one man, English orchestral composer RON GRAINER, there were a handful of pop tunes on display in this hip culture/youth movie. A teenager herself (at seventeen), Glasgow-born mop-top, LULU, provides the US chart-topping title track (3 times no less!) and a second Marcus London & Don Black song, 'Stealing My Love From Me'. While the latter failed to generate anything but a 60s upbeat, the former number has since become one of the Scots lassie's most revered singles to date. Once up there with the rest, Mancunians the MINDBENDERS (featuring future 10cc singer/guitarist, ERIC STEWART) contribute two quirky little dirges, 'Off And Running' and 'It's Getting Harder All The Time'. GRAINER, meanwhile, fits in the odd orchestral piece; the longest and best, 'A Classical Lesson', is virtually the theme represented playfully with harpsichord, percussion, etc. To be continued . . . *MCS*

Album rating: *5

– spinoff hits, etc. –

LULU: To Sir, With Love = (b-side of 'Let's Pretend')

Jun 67. (7") *Columbia; (DB 8221)* [11] [–]

LULU: To Sir, With Love

Aug 67. (7") *Epic; <10187>* [–] [1]

LULU: To Sir, With Love

Oct 67. (lp) *Epic; <26339>* [–] [24]
– (her film songs, etc.)

☐ TOGETHER? alt.
(⇒ AMO NON AMO)

TOGETHER BROTHERS

1974 (US 94m) 20th Century Fox (PG)

Film genre: crime thriller

Top guns: dir: William A. Graham / s-w: Jack DeWitt, Joe Greene

Stars: Ahmad Nurradin *(J.J.)*, Anthony Wilson *(Tommy)*, Nelson Sims *(A.P.)*, Kenneth Bell *(Mau Mau)*, Kim Dorsey *(Gri Gri)*, Owen Pace *(Monk)*, Ed Bernard *(Mr. Kool)*, Lincoln Kilpatrick *(Billy Most)* ← COOL BREEZE, Mwako Cumbaka *(Strokes McGee)* ← COFFY, Glynn Turman *(Dr. Johnson)* ← FIVE ON THE BLACK HAND SIDE / → a HERO AIN'T NOTHIN' BUT A SANDWICH

Storyline: Against a backdrop of Galveston, Texas, rather than the usual New York or L.A., a group of ghetto kids come together to track down the killer of a black policeman who's been a father figure to them. Although the group leader's five-year-old brother witnessed the killing, the trauma has left him mute, and the crime has to be solved by more traditional methods. *BG*

Movie rating: *4

Visual: none

Off the record: (see below)

—

the LOVE UNLIMITED ORCHESTRA
(composer: BARRY WHITE)

Jun 74. (lp) *20th Century; <ST 101> Pye Inter..; (NSPL 28203)* [96] [ ]
– Somebody's gonna off the man (vocal) / So nice to hear / Alive and well / Find the man bros. / You gotta case / Killer's lullaby / Theme from Together Brothers / Getaway / People of tomorrow are the children of today / Somebody's gonna off the man / The rip / Stick up / Dreamin' / Killer's back / Do drop in / Killer don't do it / Here comes the man / Dream on / Honey please, can't ya see / Can't seem to find him / People of tomorrow are the children of today (vocal). *<cd-iss. 1999 on 'Mercury'; 546217-2>*

S/track review: It's an irresistible cocktail: BARRY WHITE's carnal incantations, GENE PAGE's supercharged string arrangements and the momentum of the blaxploitaiton gravy train. 'TOGETHER BROTHERS' isn't the funkiest album in the canon, but it squares sophistication and grit in the argot of Isaac Hayes and Curtis Mayfield, and briefly – on the brilliant main theme – outflanks both. A staple of blaxploitation compilations, the theme's elegant, almost baroque melody line, thundering bass, feverish percussion and general highwire dynamics brand it all but unique among the competition, with one of the coolest codas to any 70s theme. WHITE doesn't sing on it; he doesn't need the exertion. Instead, the rotund lothario saves his love for 'Honey, Please Can't Ya See', and handles the heady lead-in, 'Somebody's Gonna Off The Man', coming on like a terminally disillusioned soapbox speaker with the weight of PAGE's shrill ostinato and pathos-drenched melody on his shoulders. Minus WHITE's profundo authority, PAGE convincingly rearranges the formula over a series of short cues rather than songs, alternately picking out brass, gyrating rhythm guitar and piano, chucking in gull-like screeds of lead, or occasionally playing it as pure incidental/experimental mood music (and employing at least some of the exotica he used on 'BLACULA'). Again, he's not shy of taking a page out of Hayes' book (check 'Dream On' or the guitar outro on 'You Gotta Case'), adapting a Morricone device (see 'Killer's Lullaby' / 'Killer Don't Do It') or slipping in a quaint orchestral piece a la 'BREWSTER McLOUD', but for the most part he concentrates on arrangements which were to prove highly influential among disco producers, as well as latter-day hip hop architects. *BG*

Album rating: *7

the TOP OF HIS HEAD

1989 (Can 110m) Films Transit Int. / Rhombus Media

Film genre: romantic comedy drama

Top guns: dir: (+ s-w) Peter Mettler

Stars: Stephen Ouimette *(Gus Victor)*, Christie MacFadyen *(Lucy Ripley)*, David Fox *(Uncle Hugo)*, Gary Reineke *(Berge; pursuer)*, Julian Richings *(Robert; henchman)* → HARD CORE LOGO → DETROIT ROCK CITY, Joey Hardin *(Joey; henchman)*, David Main *(Mr. Victor)*, Julie Wildman *(Mrs. Victor)*, Diana Barrington *(Yolanda)*, Alexander Malden *(Justin Miller)*, John Paul Young *(the car salesman)*

Storyline: Satellite dish salesman Gus finds his signals are confused when he meets beautiful conservationist Lucy. She shows him the flaws of his materialistic lifestyle and he begins to question the society he is so used to. Unfortunately this draws some unwelcome attention to himself just as Lucy vanishes and he notices he's being followed by the police. *JZ*

Movie rating: *6

Visual: video

Off the record: The John Paul Young here is Canadian, not the Australian singer famous for 'Love Is In The Air' in '78.

—

FRED FRITH

Apr 96. (lp/cd) *Crammed Discs – Made To Measure; (MTM 21)* [ ] Belgian [–]
– Title theme / Driving to the train (*) / Wheels within / Hold on hold / Lucy leaves a note / Gus escapes / Gravity's a rule / Channel change / Orbit / Fall to call / Underwater dream / This old Earth (JANE SIBERRY) / Donuts / The long drive / Lucy (*) / The premonition / Questions and answers / The performance / The way you look tonight – Title theme (conclusion). *(cd+= *)*

S/track review: Formerly of avant-rock band, Henry Cow, solo artist and multi-instrumentalist, FRED FRITH, comes up with his debut soundtrack, 'The TOP OF HIS HEAD'. Recorded between August and September, 1988, with augmentation from ANNE BOURNE (cello, accordion) and JEAN DEROME (sax), plus guests JANE SIBERRY (on vocals, guitar & accordion) and KEN MYHR (slide guitar) on 'This Old Earth', the album conjures up an unexpected treat. Fusing synths with, at times, industrial "rubber-band" guitar drones (from FRITH), 'The TOP OF HIS HEAD' showcases 2-3 minute soundbites rather than any prolonged songtracks. The eerie 'Driving To The Train' (like 'Lucy', not afforded a place on the LP version), 'Orbit' and 'Questions And Answers' all screech their way through some sort of imaginary pain barrier, but that's what experimental rock through the eyes of FF was all about – no pain, no gain. While there's also the voice of actress CHRISTIE MacFADYEN on parade, there's an unusual cover version: Dorothy Fields & Jerome Kern's 'The Way You Look Tonight' segued with the title theme finale. For something better from FRITH, try subsequent releases 'STEP ACROSS THE BORDER' (1990), 'MIDDLE OF THE MOMENT' (1995) and 'RIVERS AND TIDES' (2003). *MCS*

Album rating: *4.5

el TOPO

aka The Mole

1970 (Mex 124m, US 95m) Douglas Films (R)

Film genre: avant-garde hybrid western

Top guns: s-w + dir: Alejandro Jodorowsky

Stars: Alejandro Jodorowsky *(El Topo)*, Brontis Jodorowsky *(son of El Topo,* *as a boy)*, Alfonso Arau *(bandit #1)* → WALKER → COMMITTED, Jose Luis Fernandez *(bandit #2)*, Alf Junco *(bandit #3)*, Gerardo Cepeda *(bandit #4)*, Rene Barrera *(bandit #5)*, Rene Alis *(bandit #6)*, Federico Gonzales *(bandit #7)*, David Silva *(the colonel)*, Robert John *(Son of El Topo, as a man)*

Storyline: Dismissing Hollywood as "a child's industry", Alejandro Jodorowsky busied himself with material more in line with his conception of art as therapeutic "medicine". This cult surrealist western (critically midwifed by John Lennon, who hailed it as a masterpiece) takes the spirit of Leone and douses it in post-hippy religious visions, designed to enlighten exponentially in line with the viewer's "greatness". Dressed like a gunfighting biker, the hombre-guru with no name endures and ultimately fails an allegorical series of trials, ends up riddled with bullets and ultimately reborn amidst a community of cripples and outcasts. BG

Movie rating: *8

Visual: video + dvd

Off the record: **SHADES OF JOY** (see below)

—

SHADES OF JOY: Music Of El Topo

Dec 70. (lp) *Douglas; <Douglas 6>*
– The desert is a circle / Man of seven years / Flute in a quarry / Together / El Topo's dream / Slowest & saddest waltz / Freakout #1. *<(US + Italian re-iss. Aug04 on 'Dagored'; DAG 155CD)>*

S/track review: First up, the cover art: pure 70s and scary enough to double as a halloween mask. Actually, it looks like an Eagles' sleeve shot on bad acid (those eyes, woahhh). The music never quite matches that bearded glower – or the movie's reputation – but it's a fascinating smelting pot of psych-folk, funk and free jazz. In lieu of anyone taking much notice of the actual 'Apple'-issued music to Jodorowsky's film, the SHADES OF JOY record has become a kind of de facto soundtrack in its own right, one which – according to Mexican arranger/flautist/saxophonist MARTIN FIERRO – "takes up where Alejandro left off". Performed by a sizeable band including sometime Grateful Dead/obscure funk session man HOWARD WALES, it starts out as arcane pastoral, saddles up to some serious organ-burning and tails off with a Mariachi salute, all inside the first track. The recording venue was CBS studios, San Francisco rather than downtown Lagos but – as early as 1970 – those "bad cats" FIERRO talks up in his sleevenotes were also seemingly bad enough to dig African funk: with its heraldic brass arrangements, the excellent 'Flute In A Quarry' wouldn't be out of place on a latter-day Afro-Beat compilation. And since the soundtrack has only ever been available on LP, it's convenient that it sticks to the traditional A-side/B-side split; much of the 'Music Of El Topo' actually consists of weird, folk-idiomatic – occasionally bordering on the medieval – elegies, solemnly observed on flute, trumpet and piano, but Jodorowsky's surrealism really begins to sweat through the schizoid time-signatures on side 2, where the FIERRO-authored 'Freakout #1' (the only track not composed by Jodorowsky, apparently) whirls free-associative reeds, rabid yelps and WALES' staccato keys over a full half-side of vinyl without losing the place. Viva la 70s!! BG

Album rating: *7.5

– spinoff release –

ALEJANDRO JODOROWSKY

1970. (lp) *Apple; <3388>*
– Entierro de primer juguete / Bajo tierra / La catndral de los puercos / Los mewdigos sagrados / La nuerte es un nacimiento / Curios Mexicano / El agua viva / Vals fantasma / El alma nace en la sangre / Topo triste / Los dioses de Azucar / Las flores nacen en el barro / El infierno de Los Angeles prostitutos / Marcha de los ojos en el triangulos / Le miel de dolor / 300 conejos / Conocimiento a traves de la diluvio.

TOUCH

1997 (US 96m) Metro-Goldwyn-Mayer (R)

Film genre: romantic/religious satire/comedy

Top guns: s-w (+ dir): Paul Schrader ← the LAST TEMPTATION OF CHRIST ← LIGHT OF DAY / → AFFLICTION (au: Elmore Leonard → JACKIE BROWN → BE COOL)

Stars: Bridget Fonda *(Lynn Faulkner)* ← GRACE OF MY HEART ← SINGLES ← SHAG: THE MOVIE / → JACKIE BROWN → FINDING GRACELAND → SOUTH OF HEAVEN, WEST OF HELL, Christopher Walken *(Bill Hill)* ← LAST MAN STANDING ← PULP FICTION ← WAYNE'S WORLD 2 ← HOMEBOY / → the COUNTRY BEARS → ROMANCE & CIGARETTES → HAIRSPRAY re-make, Skeet Ulrich *(Juvenal; aka Charlie Lawson)* ← ALBINO ALLIGATOR, Tom Arnold *(August Murray)* → JACKIE'S BACK!, Gina Gershon *(Debra Lusanne)* ← PRETTY IN PINK / → the INSIDER → DEMONLOVER → PREY FOR ROCK & ROLL, Paul Mazursky *(Artie)* ← HEY HEY WE'RE THE MONKEES ← DOWN AND OUT IN BEVERLY HILLS ← a STAR IS BORN ← BLACKBOARD JUNGLE / → WHY DO FOOLS FALL IN LOVE, Lolita Davidovich *(Antoinette Baker)*, Janeane Garofalo *(Kathy Worthington)* ← REALITY BITES / → GIGANTIC (A TALE OF TWO JOHNS), **John DOE** *(Elwin Worrel)*, **LL Cool J** *(himself)* ← KRUSH GROOVE, Breckin Meyer *(Greg Czarnicki)* → 54, Richard Schiff *(Jerry)* ← GRACE OF MY HEART ← the BODYGUARD ← YOUNG GUNS II / → I AM SAM → RAY, Dennis Burkley *(hillbilly)* ← RUSH ← the DOORS ← LAMBADA ← WHO'S THAT GIRL ← BUMMER!, Julie Condra *(Shelly)* ← GAS, FOOD LODGING, Tamlyn Tomita *(prosecutor)* ← FOUR ROOMS, O-Lan Jones *(Bib Overalls)* ← NATURAL BORN KILLERS / → the END OF VIOLENCE, Anthony Zerbe *(Father Donahue)* ← BAJA OKLAHOMA ← KISS MEETS THE PHANTOM OF THE PARK, Richard Fancy *(judge)* → COME ON, GET HAPPY: THE PARTRIDGE FAMILY STORY → PSYCHO BEACH PARTY

Storyline: Promoter Bill Hill's eyes light up with dollar signs when he meets Juvenal, a rehab worker who also happens to be a miracle healer. However, Bill's sneaky plans involving producer Lynn Faulkner are put on hold with the appearance of the Rev. August Murray, who wants to free Juvenal from various corrupting influences and use him to promote his own hardline views. JZ

Movie rating: *5

Visual: video + dvd

Off the record: **DAVE GROHL** (see below)

—

DAVE GROHL

Mar 97. (cd) *Roswell; <(8 55632-2)>* Jun98
– Bill Hill theme / August Murray theme / How do you do / Richie Baker's miracle / Making popcorn / Outrage / Saints in love / Spinning newspapers / Remission my ass / Scene 6 / This loving thing (Lynn's song) / Final miracle / Touch.

S/track review: One question begs to be asked. How does DAVE GROHL (ex-Nirvana) find the time to do absolutely everything? Apart from being lead singer of the gigantic Foo Fighters, drumming for Queens Of The Stone Age on their 'Songs For The Deaf' album and creating his Probot side-project with Lemmy et al, and helping out on several other artists' albums, he also does soundtracks. Released in 1997, 'TOUCH' was GROHL's first attempt at scoring a film on his own, he had previously played drums for the early Beatles biopic, 'BACKBEAT' (1994), and went on to donate songs to the comedy 'Me, Myself & Irene', and shows a completely different side to the hard rocker we all know and love. Most of the tracks are instrumental with a few proper songs slotted in at appropriate intervals. 'Bill Hill Theme' and 'Spinning Newspapers' are instrumentals rooted in heavy rock with thumping drums and distorted guitar riffs. However, it is on tracks such as 'Making Popcorn' and 'Scene 6' that GROHL's ability and willingness to transcend genres really shines through. The former is a country-tinged ballad while the latter features a jarring, reggae style guitar over a jazz drum beat. He also shows that he can create edgy, atmospheric pieces on 'Outrage', 'Final Miracle' and 'August Murray Theme'. Proper song, 'How Do You Do' would sit well on any of the early Foo Fighters albums, while 'Touch', performed with LOUISE POST and LATE, is a touching love song. LATE also appear with JOHN DOE on another ballad, 'This Loving Thing (Lyn's Song)' and again with LOUISE POST on the instrumental 'Saints In Love'. 'TOUCH' is very much a film score as DAVE GROHL has produced all of the songs to fit the film rather than using it as a vehicle to promote his own material. The film, as a result, is better off because of this but none of the songs really shine if taken out of this context. Based on this evidence, GROHL could probably build a successful career scoring films, if only he could find the time. *CM*

Album rating: *6.5

□ the TOUCHABLES: Ken Thorne (⇒ Rock Musicals & Pop Fiction)

□ TRAFFIC segment (⇒ HERE WE GO 'ROUND THE MULBERRY BUSH)

□ the TREMELOES segment (⇒ MAY MORNING)

TRESPASS

1992 (US 103m) Universal Pictures (R)

Film genre: crime thriller

Top guns: dir: Walter Hill ← JOHNNY HANDSOME ← CROSSROADS ← STREETS OF FIRE ← the LONG RIDERS / → GERONIMO: AN AMERICAN LEGEND → LAST MAN STANDING / s-w: Bob Gale + Robert Zemeckis ← I WANNA HOLD YOUR HAND

Stars: Bill Paxton *(Vince)* ← NEAR DARK ← STREETS OF FIRE / → DERAILROADED, **ICE-T** *(King James)*, William Sadler *(Don)* ← RUSH ← BILL & TED'S BOGUS JOURNEY / → REACH THE ROCK, **ICE CUBE** *(Savon)*, Art Evans *(Bradlee)* ← SCHOOL DAZE ← YOUNGBLOOD ← BIG TIME ← LEADBELLY ← CLAUDINE / → CB4: THE MOVIE → the STORY OF US, De'voreaux White *(Lucky)* ← the BLUES BROTHERS, Bruce A. Young *(Raymond)* ← THIEF, Glenn Plummer *(Luther)* ← WHO'S THAT GIRL / → STRANGE DAYS, Stoney Jackson *(Wickey)* ← KNIGHTS OF THE CITY ← SWEET DREAMS ← STREETS OF FIRE ← ROLLER BOOGIE / → CB4: THE MOVIE, Tiny Lister *(Cletus)* ← BLUE CITY / → JACKIE BROWN, Tico Wells *(Davis)* ← the FIVE HEARTBEATS, James Pickens Jr. *(police officer Reese)*, Hal Landon Jr. *(Eugene De Long)* ← BILL & TED'S EXCELLENT ADVENTURE

Storyline: A couple of all-American firemen unexpectedly stumble upon a vicious gangland killing while attempting to locate some hidden gold in a disused warehouse. When they realise the execution has been witnessed first hand, the Afro-American hoods turn their attention to the firemen's merciless pursuit. *BG*

Movie rating: *5.5

Visual: video + dvd

Off the record: **ICE-T & ICE CUBE** (see own entries)

—

Various Artists (score: RY COODER *)

Dec 92. (cd/c) *Warners; <(7599 26978-2/-4)>* [82] Feb93 [ ]
– Trespass (ICE-T & ICE CUBE) / Gotta do what I gotta do (PUBLIC ENEMY) / Depths of Hell (ICE-T feat. DADDY NITRO) / I check my bank (SIR MIX-A-LOT) / I'm a playa (bitch) (PENTHOUSE PLATERS CLIQUE) / On the wall (BLACK SHEEP) / Don't be a 304 (AMG) / Gotta get over (taking loot) (GANG STARR) / You know what I'm about (LORD FINESSE) / I'm gonna smoke him (DONALD D.) / Quick way out (W.C. & THE MAAD CIRCLE) / King of the street (* & JIM KELTNER).

S/track review: RY COODER's 'King Of The Street' (with JIM KELTNER) features on the simultaneously released, gangsta rap showcase of a soundtrack alongside cuts from PUBLIC ENEMY, ICE CUBE and ICE-T, the latter two of whom also acted in the film itself and who give it big licks on the deranged duet of a title track. Even in the twilight of their first incarnation, PUBLIC ENEMY lay waste to the competition, grinding their funky organ with the great, Grant Green-sampling 'Gotta Do What I Gotta Do', while ICE-T checks in with a typically brutal survival tale. Yet the big guns don't necessarily have all the best ammunition here: PENTHOUSE PLAYERS CLIQUE contribute the great, if unashamedly misogynistic, wah-wah funk-hop of 'I'm A Playa (Bitch)' while BLACK SHEEP get in early on the jazz-rap crossover with 'On The Wall', making clever use of Jack Bruce's 'Statues'. LORD FINESSE raps against a funereal, DJ Shadow-esque backdrop which actually intensifies the darkness of the lyrics rather than leavening them, and DONALD D coasts over the kind of vintage old skool breakbeats and fat bass long ironed out of modern hip hop. As a various-artists soundtrack this works better than most, largely because it's a single genre effort, but also because it trains its blood-spattered sights on more than just the usual suspects; it's also a surprisingly good companion piece to COODER's score. *BG*

Album rating: *6.5

—

RY COODER

Jan 93. (cd/c) *Warners; <25399> WEA; (9362 45220-2/-4)* [ ] Dec92 [ ]
– Video drive-by / Trespass (main title) / East St. Louis toodle-o / Orgill Bros. / Goose and lucky / You think it's on now / Solid gold / Heroin / Totally boxed in / Give 'em cops / Lucy in the trunk / We're rich / King of the street / Party lights. *(re-iss. Feb95; same)*

S/track review: The most experimental RY COODER score to date, 'TRESPASS' is skeletal, unsettling and uncompromising, tracing the film's grim urban setting with only a core trio of COODER, longtime drummer JIM KELTNER and pioneering trumpeter JON HASSELL. COODER's playing on the relatively benign 'East St. Louis' recalls the serrated echo of U2's The Edge; you half expect to hear BONO's caterwaul break the spell at any second. Yet there really is nothing to hang onto here save isolated impressions and snatches of melody, pockets of reverb and instalments of clanking, sawing, wreckers-yard rhythm, with HASSELL's trumpet fissures sounding for all the world like a disembodied soul's dispatches from limbo; on the obliquely funky 'You Think It's On Now' his feral horn calls seem to trace a lineage back to 'Planet of the Apes' via 'Bitches Brew'. Save for the grungy title theme, 'Lucy In The Trunk' is probably the most solid of the instrumentals, futuristic, metronomic industrial blues expanded upon in the penultimate, dialogue-sampling 'King Of The Street'. After all this, Jr. Brown's droll country closer, 'Party Lights', sounds like it's been beamed in from some other, more sympathetic planet. *BG*

Album rating: *6

the TRIP

1967 (US 85m) American International Pictures (R)

Film genre: surreal psychological drama

Top guns: dir: Roger Corman ← the WILD ANGELS ← ROCK ALL NIGHT ← CARNIVAL ROCK / → GAS-S-S-S / s-w: Jack Nicholson → HEAD

Stars: Peter Fonda *(Paul Groves)* ← the WILD ANGELS / → EASY RIDER

→ the HIRED HAND → GRACE OF MY HEART → SOUTH OF HEAVEN, WEST OF HELL, Susan Strasberg *(Sally Groves)* → PSYCH-OUT → the RUNNIN' KIND, Bruce Dern *(John, guru)* ← the WILD ANGELS / → PSYCH-OUT → LAST MAN STANDING → ALL THE PRETTY HORSES → MASKED AND ANONYMOUS, Dennis Hopper *(Max)* → HEAD → EASY RIDER → HUMAN HIGHWAY → WHITE STAR → RUNNING OUT OF LUCK → STRAIGHT TO HELL, Salli Sachse *(Glenn)* ← THUNDER ALLEY ← the GHOST IN THE INVISIBLE BIKINI ← HOW TO STUFF A WILD BIKINI ← SKI PARTY ← BEACH BLANKET BINGO ← PAJAMA PARTY ← BIKINI BEACH ← MUSCLE BEACH PARTY / → WILD IN THE STREETS, Barboura Morris *(Flo)* ← the WILD ANGELS ← ROCK ALL NIGHT, Michael Blodgett *(lover)* → CATALINA CAPER → BEYOND THE VALLEY OF THE DOLLS → DISCO FEVER, Luana Anders *(waitress)* → EASY RIDER, Dick Miller *(Cash)* ← the WILD ANGELS ← WILD, WILD WINTER ← BEACH BALL ← SKI PARTY ← the GIRLS ON THE BEACH ← ROCK ALL NIGHT ← CARNIVAL ROCK / → TRUCK TURNER → I WANNA HOLD YOUR HAND → ROCK'N'ROLL HIGH SCHOOL → GET CRAZY → SHAKE, RATTLE & ROCK! tv, Luree Holmes *(Luree)* ← THUNDER ALLEY ← the GHOST IN THE INVISIBLE BIKINI ← HOW TO STUFF A WILD BIKINI ← SKI PARTY ← BEACH BLANKET BINGO ← PAJAMA PARTY ← BIKINI BEACH ← MUSCLE BEACH PARTY ← BEACH PARTY, Tom Signorelli *(Al)* → SORCERER → THIEF → DICK TRACY, Michael Nader ← HOW TO STUFF A WILD BIKINI ← SKI PARTY ← BEACH BLANKET BINGO ← PAJAMA PARTY ← BIKINI BEACH ← MUSCLE BEACH PARTY ← BEACH PARTY, Beach Dickerson ← G.I. BLUES ← LOVING YOU ← ROCK ALL NIGHT / → the SAVAGE SEVEN

Storyline: Roger Corman's drugsploitation feature plots a day (and night) trip in the life of advertising exec Paul Groves. After taking his medicine under the bearded eye of local acid guru John, he prances along Pacific shores, gets chased through the woods a la Lord Of The Rings, makes groovy love in a retina-scarring onslaught of psychedelic colour and freaks out a random woman in a local launderette. Dean Stockwell would give a far more visceral approximation of the horrors of LSD in the following year's 'PSYCH-OUT'. *BG*

Movie rating: *6

Visual: video + dvd

Off the record: The **ELECTRIC FLAG** (see below)

—

the ELECTRIC FLAG, AN AMERICAN MUSIC BAND

Jun 67. (lp; mono/stereo) *Tower; <T/ST 5908> C.B.S.; (63462)* ☐ Mar69 ☐
– Peter's trip / Joint passing / Psyche soap / M-23 / Synethesia / A little head / Hobbit / Inner pocket / Fewghh / Green and gold / The other Ed Norton / Flash, bam, pow / Home room / Peter gets off / Practice music / Fine jung thing / Senior citizen / Gettin' hard. *(UK-iss.Mar87 on 'Edsel'; ED 211) <cd-iss. 2003 on 'Fabulous'; FAB 142.2>*

S/track review: Fresh from the Paul Butterfield Blues Band and eager to engineer a situation more accommodating to his retiring nature, precocious guitarist MIKE BLOOMFIELD gathered together a supergroup of like-minded souls (including fellow 'Highway 61 Revisited' alum HARVEY BROOKS, BUTTERFIELD graduate NICK GRAVENITES, synth pioneer PAUL BEAVER, and charismatic drummer BUDDY MILES) and, under the banner of the ELECTRIC FLAG, AN AMERICAN MUSIC BAND, set about patenting his ambitious montage of blues, soul, jazz and psychedelia. That it was conceived in the shape of a soundtrack – one which Playboy magazine subsequently named score of the year – to Jack Nicholson's pre-'EASY RIDER' cause célèbre only underlined its zeitgeist credentials. Released the same month the band made their live entrance at the Monterey International Pop Festival, the soundtrack also served as something of a sounding board for their 1968 studio debut. And while some of it was actually dubbed over footage of the International Submarine Band (the fledgling country-rock vehicle of Gram Parsons), BLOOMFIELD's vision of American Music often comes across as more schizophrenic than cosmic, swerving crazily between fuzz-heavy garage rock, electronic freakout, trad jazz and neo-prog symphony. Main theme 'Peter's Trip' represents that vision at its grandest, all harpsichord flourish and brass fanfare, while PAUL BEAVER (of Beaver & Krause fame, and a man who also sessioned on Krysztof Komeda's soundtrack to the Oscar-winning horror, 'Rosemary's Baby') weighs in with some wild synth improv on 'Flash, Bam, Pow', itself subsequently used in 'EASY RIDER'. But it's difficult to avoid the impression that BLOOMFIELD, at heart, is something of a purist, and his grand plan really comes off when they bin the lysergic excess and simply let the constituent parts fuse naturally (on the propulsive Booker T-like jam, 'Fine Jung Thing') or else melt into each other, as on the gorgeous 'Green And Gold', one of the few tracks where his much vaunted use of a full horn section (a lead BUTTERFIELD was to follow) really comes into its own. Note that the garishly packaged 'Curb' US reissue shamelessly omits almost half the original soundtrack, including stinging highlights like 'Gettin' Hard'. *BG*

Album rating: *7

– spinoff releases, etc. –

the ELECTRIC FLAG: Peter's Trip / Green And Gold
Jul 67. (7") *<929>* ☐ [–]

TROUBLE EVERY DAY

2001 (Fra 102m) Canal+ / Rezo Films (16)

Film genre: seXual horror/thriller

Top guns: s-w: Claire Denis (+ dir) ← NENETTE ET BONI, Jean-Pol Fargeau ← POLA X ← NENETTE ET BONI

Stars: Vincent GALLO *(Shane Brown)*, Tricia Vessey *(June Brown)* ← GHOST DOG: THE WAY OF THE SAMURAI, Beatrice Dalle *(Core)* ← NIGHT ON EARTH / → CLEAN, Alex Descas *(Leo Semeneau)* ← NENETTE ET BONI / → COFFEE AND CIGARETTES, Florence Loiret-Caille *(Christelle)*, Nicolas Duvauchelle *(Erwan)*, Jose Garcia *(Choart)*, Raphael Neal *(Ludo)*, Helene Lapiower *(Malecot)*, Marilu Marini *(Friessen)*, Aurore Clement *(Jeanne)* ← PARIS, TEXAS, Alice Houri *(young girl on train)* ← NENETTE ET BONI

Storyline: Shane and June Brown aren't your average newlyweds, despite their choice of Paris as honeymoon destination. A choice which begins to take on sinister undertones as Shane searches for the scientist whose experiments have left him with some pretty gruesome appetites. *BG*

Movie rating: *5.5

Visual: dvd

Off the record: (see below)

—

TINDERSTICKS

Oct 01. (cd/lp) *Beggars Banquet; (BBQ CD/LP 225) <80225>* ☐ ☐
– Opening titles / Dream / Houses / Maid theme 1 / Room 321 / Computer / Notre Dame / Killing theme / Taxi to Core / Core on stairs – Love theme (Shane and June) / Maid theme (end) / Closing titles / Killing theme (alternate version) / Trouble every day.

S/track review: Both in subject matter and musical strategy, this is a far darker, more lugubrious (now there's an adjective that's never been used in the same breath as TINDERSTICKS before . . .) proposition than 'NENETTE ET BONI' (1996), the band's previous – and really rather groovy – soundtrack project. 'TROUBLE EVERY DAY' continued their relationship with French art-house director, Claire Denis, who was actually pretty fortunate in that STUART STAPLES, DICKON HINCHCLIFFE et al are one of only a slim cadre of artists who could even begin to attempt to elucidate the murky, oppressive emotional depths in her controversial tale of urban cannibalism. They do so by means of a heavily orchestrated – and almost wholly instrumental – score, book-ended by two vocal cues and punctuated by tentative, jazzy interludes. Not jazzy in the martini-chinking sense of 'NENETTE . . .' but in the portentous, Duende-rich sense of 'Sketches Of Spain'. It's not exactly a comfortable listen and the fact that even something as nominally doleful as a tolling bell gives intermittent relief in 'Notre Dame', imparts a flavour of the record's unrelenting despondency. STAPLES' funeral parlour croon is that despondency incarnate, embalming the soundtrack from both ends. Swathes of elegant, HINCHCLIFFE-arranged strings, spryly plucked violin and dolorous piano accompany STAPLES on the opening titles while HINCHCLIFFE joins him for a rare duet at the end. It's those recurring string motifs which carry much of the dramatic impetus, rising and swaying but always inevitably buckling under their own weight. Carpeted with creeping bongos and in counterpoint with ominous, oscillating cello, they achieve a catharsis of sorts on 'Killing Theme', yet so minimalist and filled with silence and shadows are some of these compositions that you may well find yourself checking your fuse box for a power cut. This is the sound of TINDERSTICKS in their element; they don't need actual songs to luxuriate in despair, and the lack of them shouldn't negate their achievement in what promises to be a rewarding cinematic career. *BG*

Album rating: *6.5

TROUBLE MAN

1972 (US 99m) 20th Century Fox (R)

Film genre: cop/detective adventure

Top guns: dir: Ivan Dixon / s-w: John D.F. Black ← SHAFT / → the SPOOK WHO SAT BY THE DOOR

Stars: Robert Hooks *(Mr. T)* → AARON LOVES ANGELA, Paul Winfield *(Chalky Price)* ← SOUNDER / → GORDON'S WAR → a HERO AIN'T NOTHIN' BUT A SANDWICH → MIKE'S MURDER → BLUE CITY, Bill Smithers *(Captain Joe Marx)*, Felton Perry *(Bobby Golden)*, Stack Pierce *(Collie)* ← COOL BREEZE / → CORNBREAD, EARL AND ME → NO WAY BACK, Paula Kelly *(Cleo)* ← COOL BREEZE / → the SPOOK WHO SAT BY THE DOOR → THREE TOUGH GUYS, Akili Jones *(Billy Chi)*, Larry Cook *(Buddy)* ← COTTON COMES TO HARLEM / → the SPOOK WHO SAT BY THE DOOR, Ralph Waite *(Pete Cockrell)* → the BODYGUARD, Tracy Reed *(policewoman)* → TRAIN RIDE TO HOLLYWOOD → NO WAY BACK → CAR WASH → a PIECE OF THE ACTION, Julius Harris *(Big)* ← SUPERFLY ← SHAFT'S BIG SCORE / → HELL UP IN HARLEM → BLACK CAESAR → FRIDAY FOSTER → LET'S DO IT AGAIN, Virginia Capers *(Macy)* ← LADY SINGS THE BLUES ← NORWOOD / → FIVE ON THE BLACK HAND SIDE → HOWARD THE DUCK → WHAT'S LOVE GOT TO DO WITH IT, Harrison Page *(bogus cop)* ← BEYOND THE VALLEY OF THE DOLLS, **Bill Henderson** *(Jimmy; pool room owner)*← COOL BREEZE ← CORNBREAD, EARL AND ME / → GET CRAZY, Edmund Cambridge *(Sam)* ← MELINDA ← the FINAL COMEDOWN ← COOL BREEZE / → FRIDAY FOSTER → BILL & TED'S BOGUS JOURNEY, Jean Bell *(Leona)* ← MELINDA / → THREE THE HARD WAY → DISCO 9000

Storyline: A super-suave private detective becomes embroiled in a turf war between opposing gangs after taking on a difficult case. *BG*

Movie rating: *4

Visual: video + dvd

Off the record: MARVIN GAYE was born Marvin Pentz Gay Jr., 2 Apr'39, Washington, D.C., USA, son of an apostolic minister. After being discharged from the army in '57, Marvin joined doo-wop outfit the Marquees, releasing two singles ('Hey Little School Girl', produced by Bo Diddley, & 'Baby You're The Only One') for the 'Okeh' label. The following year, Harvey Fuqua invited Marvin's group to become his new Moonglows, and after moving to 'Chess' land, Chicago, they recorded the 'Almost Grown' and 'Mama Loocie' singles. In 1960, Fuqua, who accompanied Marvin to motor city Detroit with the intention of becoming a solo artist, helped arrange for him to play session drums on 45s by the Miracles. In 1961, after more session work for 'Motown' artists such as the Marvelettes, Marvin signed as a solo artist to 'Tamla Motown' as well as marrying boss Berry Gordy's younger sister, Anna. Suffixing his surname with the letter E, MARVIN GAYE initially had his heart set on becoming a jazz balladeer, although an album, 'The Soulful Moods Of . . .' (1961), flopped and he was eventually cajoled into recording R&B/soul. The result was the rawer 'Stubborn Kind Of Fellow' single, an immediate success which provided young Marv with his first R&B Top 10 hit in 1962. 'Hitch Hike', 'Pride And Joy' and 'Can I Get A Witness' followed in quick succession, all charting in the Top 50 and establishing GAYE as one of Motown's foremost talents. Like most artists on the label, GAYE was assigned material by various writers (mainly the in-house team of Holland-Dozier-Holland), although even in those early days, many of his songs were self-penned, including the classic 'Wherever I Lay My Hat (That's My Home)' (later made famous again by English singer, Paul Young). In 1964, although still mainly a credible solo artist, Berry Gordy teamed him up with Mary Wells, and later Kim Weston, with whom he recorded the Top 20 soul-pop brilliance of 'It Takes Two' as well as recording a whole album of duets under a similar title. The mid-60s also saw him developing the super smooth vocal prowess that would become his trademark on such hits as 'How Sweet It Is (To Be Loved By You)' and 'One More Heartache'. The Weston alliance was dissolved in mid-'67 when GAYE found Philadelphia-born singer, Tammi Terrell, their charmed partnership yielding a three-year run of hits on both sides of the Atlantic and producing some of the most sublime duets in the history of soul ('Ain't No Mountain High Enough', 'You're All I Need To Get By', 'Ain't Nothing Like The Real Thing' etc.). Tragically, to the obvious dismay of Marvin, Tammi died of a brain tumour in March 1970, aged only 24. The previous year, Marvin had scored his biggest hit to date when 'I Heard It Through The Grapevine' hit No.1 in America and Britain, a brooding, experimental epic that became Motown's biggest selling record in the label's history. But Terrell's death hit Marvin hard and his subsequent work was to take on a considerably more introspective bent. Although Marvin didn't write it, the melancholy 'Abraham, Martin And John' single (released in spring 1970) was an indicator of the direction in which GAYE was heading. Taking his cue from STEVIE WONDER, Marvin decided to take complete control of his career, from the writing to the recording, making his first major artistic statement with 'What's Going On' (1971). A radical departure, the album (along with WONDER's early 70s material) changed the way soul music was made and challenged people's perceptions of the genre. Like a black 'Astral Weeks' (in feeling if not lyrically), the album was a lush, orchestral stream of consciousness collage, GAYE gazing into the ether and pleading for some kind of redemption for mankind. Addressing such pertinent issues as war, environmental disaster and God, 'Motown' were extremely reluctant to release the album, only relenting when GAYE threatened to leave the label. The singer was vindicated when the record became his biggest seller to date, as well as being recognised as one of the greatest albums in recording history. GAYE solved the problem of following up such a milestone by recording the soundtrack to 'TROUBLE MAN'. With a checkered career behind him throughout the rest of the 70s and early 80s, Marvin began sinking deeper into drug dependence and depression. Retreating to his parents' home in L.A., his depression and mood swings brought him into continual conflict with his father and after one particularly violent argument on the 1st of April 1984, Marvin, Snr. shot his son dead. It was a tragic end to the life of one of the most pivotal figures soul music has produced. *BG & MCS*

—

MARVIN GAYE

Dec 72. (lp) *Tamla Motown; <T322L> (STML 11225)* **14** Feb73 ☐
– Main theme from "Trouble Man" / "T" plays it cool / Poor Abbey Walsh / The break in (police shoot Big) / Cleo's apartment / Trouble man / Theme from "Trouble Man" / "T" stands for trouble / Main theme from "Trouble Man" / Life is a gamble / Deep-in-it / Don't mess with Mister "T" / There goes Mister "T". *(re-iss. Jul82 lp/c; STMS/CSTMS 5065) (re-iss. 1986 lp/c; WL/WK 72215) (cd-iss. Sep91; WD 72215) <(cd re-iss. Apr93; 530 097-2)>*

S/track review: Not the most famous blaxploitation soundtrack but definitely the coolest, the most cohesive, and possibly the most enduring of them all. The concept and composition was MARVIN GAYE's alone, but it helped that in JJ JOHNSON and GENE PAGE, he had two of the biggest blax arrangers on board for the ride. And what a ride; a queasy small-hours kerb crawl through the man's endlessly tormented soul. The story goes that GAYE wanted to be a black crooner, not a soul singer, and it's not so difficult to discern those ambitions in the brand of smooth, underbellied 70s soul he made his name with. But nowhere are those ambitions starker than they are here: taking the miasmic funk of 'Inner City Blues' as its starting point, the trippy, molasses-thick score oozes jazz ambition and uneasy class. The deceptively laid-back, shag-pile seduction of the arrangements croon in lieu of GAYE; his pained falsetto moans serve largely as instrumental texture, and when he does sing – on 'Trouble Man' itself – the effect is like being spiked with the finest cognac. Junkie paranoia, twisted sensuality, moral degradation; he conjures it all in glorious, jazz-inflected monochrome. The finger-snapping squelch of '"T" Plays It Cool' is as funky as it gets, but so liquid is the music's flow that, unusally for a blax soundtrack, singling out one piece over another is pointless. That this is also the only blaxploitation soundtrack to include a thank you to Jesus (as in Christ) probably says more about GAYE – and his troubled art – than any amount of critical evaluation. And regardless of critical opinion (in general, 'TROUBLE MAN' remains one of the most indefensibly underrated soundtracks ever released), MARVIN himself regarded it as his best. Make up your own mind. *BG*

Album rating: *8.5

– spinoff hits, etc. –

MARVIN GAYE: Trouble Man / Don't Mess With Mister "T"

Dec 72. (7") *<54228> (TMG 846)* 7 Mar73 □

TRUCK TURNER

1974 (US 91m) American International Pictures (R)

Film genre: crime thriller

Top guns: dir: Jonathan Kaplan / s-w: Michael Allin → FLASH GORDON, Leigh Chapman ← a SWINGIN' SUMMER, Oscar Williams ← BLACK BELT JONES ← the FINAL COMEDOWN (story: Jerry Wilkes)

Stars: Isaac HAYES *(Truck Turner)*, Yaphet Kotto *(Harvard Blue)* ← ACROSS 110th STREET ← MAN AND BOY / → FRIDAY FOSTER → the MONKEY HUSTLE → the PARK IS MINE, Nichelle Nichols *(Dorinda)*, Alan Weeks *(Jerry)* ← BLACK BELT JONES ← SHAFT, Paul Harris *(Richard Leroy Johnson aka Gator)* ← the MACK ← ACROSS 110th STREET, Sam Laws *(Nate)* ← COOL BREEZE / → GET CRAZY, Scatman Crothers *(Duke)* ← BLACK BELT JONES ← SLAUGHTER'S BIG RIP-OFF ← LADY SINGS THE BLUES / → FRIDAY FOSTER, Dick Miller *(Fogarty)* ← the TRIP ← the WILD ANGELS ← WILD, WILD WINTER ← BEACH BALL ← SKI PARTY ← the GIRLS ON THE BEACH ← ROCK ALL NIGHT ← CARNIVAL ROCK / → I WANNA HOLD YOUR HAND → ROCK'N'ROLL HIGH SCHOOL → GET CRAZY → SHAKE, RATTLE & ROCK! tv, Esther Sutherland *(Black Momma)* ← FOXY BROWN ← BLACK BELT JONES ← HELL UP IN HARLEM, Mel Novak *(doctor)* ← BLACK BELT JONES, Eddie Smith *(druggist)* ← BLACK BELT JONES, Clarence Barnes *(Toro)* ← BLACK BELT JONES, Earl Maynard *(Panama)* ← BLACK BELT JONES ← MELINDA, Jac Emil *(Reno)* ← BLACK BELT JONES ← WILLIE DYNAMITE, Earl Jolly Brown *(overweight bar person)* ← BLACK BELT JONES, Charles Cyphers *(drunk)* ← COOL BREEZE / → ELVIS: THE MOVIE → DEATH WISH II → HONKYTONK MAN

Storyline: Isaac Hayes plays Mack "Truck" Turner, a hard-nosed bounty hunter with a soft heart who heads off a vivid cast of pimps, gangsters and hit-men intent on taking him out once and for all. *BG*

Movie rating: *5.5

Visual: video + dvd

Off the record: Paris-born director Jonathan Kaplan is the son of film composer Sol Kaplan.

—

ISAAC HAYES

Jul 74. (d-lp) *Enterprise; <ENS-2 7507> Stax; (STXD 4001/2)* □ Aug74 □
– Main theme (Truck Turner) / House of beauty / Blue's crib / Driving in the sun / Breakthrough / Now we're one / The Duke / Dorinda's party / Pursuit of the pimpmobile / We need each other girl / A house full of girls / Hospital shootout / You're in my arms again / Give it to me / Drinking / The insurance company / End theme. *<(d-cd-iss. w/ 'THREE TOUGH GUYS')> <(cd re-mast.Apr02; SCD24 7505)>*

S/track review: With 'TRUCK TURNER', ISAAC HAYES once again wallowed in his mandatory four sides of vinyl, although the results, as with abbreviated predecessor, 'THREE TOUGH GUYS', actually outpaced 'SHAFT', the record so often touted as his celluloid masterpiece. Over a whopping seventeen tracks, and with typically studied abandon, Black Moses lives out more of his aural fantasies. While the bulk of them are mellow instrumentals, at least three of them are road-tested juggernauts: the boiling wah-wah, freeway-cruising strings and kitschy call-and-response of the title theme, the funk-rock grind of 'Breakthrough' and the brilliant proto-disco marathon, 'Pursuit Of The Pimpmobile'. One of HAYES' most enduring funk symphonies, 'Pursuit . . .' is as humorously well oiled as it is alliterative, as inventive and finely calibrated a balance of the orchestral and the rhythmic as the bald one ever engineered. And, despite a near ten-minute duration, it never runs out of gas. There's even a seven-minute psychedelic soul/jazz mindbender titled 'The Insurance Company'. It's all as sexy and larger than life as ever; even ISAAC's dreams "would blow the average man's mind", if you believe his boasts on 'A House Full Of Girls'. Yet while 'You're In My Arms Again' smoulders with downbeat eloquence, the man's rarely at his most compelling in Barry White mode, at least not within the relatively restricted confines of a soundtrack. And while jazzy, soft-top sketches like 'Blues Crib', 'Dorinda's Party' and the gorgeous 'We Need Each Other Girl', are effortlessly redolent of cloudless skies and the open road, HAYES can't shake that tendency to labour his point just a bit too coolly for sustained listening comfort. Still, another great Blaxploitation soundtrack, albeit one which could have been edited down to a single disc. *BG*

Album rating: *7

– spinoff releases, etc. –

ISAAC HAYES: Title Theme 'Truck Turner' / Hung Up On My Baby

Aug 74. (7") *<ENA 9104> (STXS 2004)* □ □

TUCKER: THE MAN AND HIS DREAM

1988 (US 110m) Paramount Pictures (PG)

Film genre: political biopic/drama

Top guns: dir: Francis Ford Coppola ← ONE FROM THE HEART ← YOU'RE A BIG BOY NOW / s-w: Arnold Schulman ← GOODBYE, COLUMBUS, David Seidler → COME ON, GET HAPPY: THE PARTRIDGE FAMILY STORY

Stars: Jeff Bridges *(Preston Tucker)* ← the LAST UNICORN ← RANCHO DELUXE / → MASKED AND ANONYMOUS, Joan Allen *(Vera Tucker)*, Martin Landau *(Abe Karatz)*, Frederic Forrest *(Eddie Dean)* ← ONE FROM THE HEART ← the ROSE / → the END OF VIOLENCE → SWEETWATER: A TRUE ROCK STORY, Dean Stockwell *(Howard Hughes)* ← TO LIVE AND DIE IN L.A. ← DUNE ← PARIS, TEXAS ← HUMAN HIGHWAY ← PSYCH-OUT / → MADONNA: INNOCENCE LOST, Mako *(Jimmy Sakuyama)*, Lloyd Bridges *(Senator Homer Ferguson)*, Nina Siemaszko *(Marilyn Lee Tucker)* → AIRHEADS, Christian Slater *(young Tucker)* ← LIVING PROOF: THE HANK WILLIAMS JR. STORY / → YOUNG GUNS II

→ PUMP UP THE VOLUME → MASKED AND ANONYMOUS, Marshall Bell *(Frank; press agent)* ← BIRDY / → DICK TRACY → AIRHEADS → a SLIPPING-DOWN LIFE, Jay O. Sanders *(Kirby; Tucker's attorney)* ← LIVING PROOF: THE HANK WILLIAMS JR. STORY, Morgan Upton *(Ingram)* ← MORE AMERICAN GRAFFITI ← BUCKTOWN ← SPACE IS THE PLACE ← STEELYARD BLUES / → the SPIRIT OF 76, **Patti Austin** *(Millie; Tucker's cook)* ← ONE-TRICK PONY ← the WIZ ← IT'S YOUR THING / → JACKIE'S BACK!

Storyline: All-American entrepreneur Preston Tucker is the man and making the ultimate car is his dream. The big automobile corporations have other ideas, defending their domination of the market with underhand tactics and a show trial engineered by corrupt politicians. *BG*

Movie rating: *7

Visual: video + dvd

Off the record: (see below)

JOE JACKSON

Nov 88. (lp/c/cd) *A&M; <(AMA/AMC/CDA 3917)>* ☐ ☐
– Captain of industry (overture) / Car of tomorrow . . . today! / No chance blues / (He's a) Shape in a drape / Factory / Vera / It pays to advertise / Tiger rag / Showtime in Chicago / Lone bank loan blues / Speedway / Marilee / Hangin' in Howard Hughes' hangar / The toast of the town / Abe's blues / The trial / Freedom swing – Tucker jingle / Rhythm delivery.

S/track review: As a man whose records have consistently fallen between the cracks in the pigeonhole wall, JOE JACKSON couldn't hope for a more amenable genre than soundtrack. In creating the music for Francis Ford Coppola's lavish portrait of a maverick, he got to immerse himself in period jazz while exploring as many stylistic sidetracks, compositional whims and counterwhims as dramatic device would allow. He'd already affirmed his fondness for the era with 1981's 'Jumpin Jive', here echoed on 'Rhythm Delivery', the rakish '(He's A) Shape In A Drape' (a Top 30 hit in the Netherlands, prime JACKSON country), and, with the artistic license of cinema, shaved into the aggro-slapstick of 'Tiger Rag'. It's the kind of prescribed freedom which sees pizzicato wit tempering the gravity of previous orchestral dalliances on Elfman-esque opening theme, 'Captain Of Industry'. Elsewhere it's a case of fine balance. 'Car Of Tomorrow – Today!' justifies its exclamation mark with trio elegance, R&B trio and big-band brashness, segueing in and out of an ornamented symphonic motif he'd develop – with typical JACKSON adaptability – into both a love theme and a creepy piece of underscore going by the wry title, 'Hangin' In Howard Hughes' Hangar'. He also managed to find space for it amidst the harmony-muted moans and satin soul of 'The Trial', an almost Quincy Jones-like montage drawing up the soundtrack's more reflective narrative strands. The bloodshot Ellington-ian shuffle of 'No Chance Blues' also mooches around on a second wind, but JACKSON's dynamic quirks are dovetailed most effectively with the film on the emblematic, mechanistic motifs of 'Factory' and especially 'Speedway', all woodblock counterpoint and bomb-ticking timpani breakdowns. It's a shame JOE JACKSON's profile was so low at the time of this commission; he could easily have gone on to rival the likes of Mark Isham. *BG*

Album rating: *7

– spinoff releases, etc. –

JOE JACKSON: (He's A) Shape In A Drape / Speedway

Aug 88. (7") *<1228> (AM 481)* ☐ ☐
(12"+=) *(AMY 481)* – Sometime in Chicago.

☐ Jeff TWEEDY
(⇒ WILCO)

TWENTYFOURSEVEN

1997 (UK 105 b&w) BBC / October Films / Scala Films (R)

Film genre: urban sports drama

Top guns: s-w: (+ dir) Shane Meadows → THIS IS ENGLAND, Paul Fraser

Stars: Bob Hoskins *(Alan Darcy)*, Danny Nussbaum *(Tim)*, James Hooton *("Wolfman" Knighty)*, Darren Campbell *(Daz)*, Justin Brady *(Gadget)*, Jimmy Hynd *(Meggy)*, Bruce Jones *(Tim's dad)*, Frank Harper *(Ronnie Marsh)* → KEVIN & PERRY GO LARGE → THIS IS ENGLAND

Storyline: Former boxer Alan Darcy sees the nobility of the boxing ring as the only way out for the unemployed, no-hoper youths in the grim Northern environs of suburban Nottingham. Employing his bluff, not inconsiderable charm he manages to get enough of them interested to form a team although inevitably dyed-in-the-wool attitudes threaten to scupper his efforts on the eve of the big match. *BG*

Movie rating: *6.5

Visual: video

Off the record: BOO HEWERDINE & NEIL MacCOLL had taken a year out (1997) from their normal Bible activities to produce a trio of film scores, the soccer-themed 'Fever Pitch', 'TWENTYFOURSEVEN' and 'Our Boy', the latter for television. HEWERDINE was of course former leader of Norwich-based indie-folk act, the Bible (albums, 'Walking The Ghost Back Home', 'Eureka' etc.) and a prolific solo star (albums, 'Evidence' – with Texan, Darden Smith – 'Baptism Hotel' and 'Ignorance'). MacCOLL (brother of singer Kirsty and son of iconic folk singer Ewan), also performed and co-wrote with Scots folkie, Eddi Reader, on her 'Mirmama' set of '92. *MCS*

Various (score: BOO HEWERDINE & NEIL MacCOLL *)

Mar 98. (cd/c) *Independiente; (ISOM 6 CD/MC)* ☐ ☐
– Tim & Darcy No.3 (*) / Wild night (VAN MORRISON) / Courtroom No.2 (*) / Monkey dead (SUN HOUSE) / Look at the fool (TIM BUCKLEY) / I wish I never saw the sunshine (BETH ORTON) / The Blue Danube waltz (VIENNA PHILHARMONIC ORCHESTRA) / North Country boy (CHARLATANS) / Blues No.3 (*) / Damaged (PRIMAL SCREAM) / Ramble on love (STRAUSS HOFMANNSTHAL GRAINGER) / Long time man (TIM ROSE) / Introitu (LES NOUVELLES POLYPHONIES CORSES) / Fruit tree (NICK DRAKE) / Funeral (*) / Broken stones (PAUL WELLER).

S/track review: Shane Meadows writes his sleevenotes like he directs his films, raw and unexpurgated. He readily admits that music was a way to allay first-day nerves on the shooting of his debut feature (" . . .it saved my fucking bacon") and naturally, his thumbnail sketches talk about how his choice of songs relate to particular scenes rather than why he loves the artists per se, but there's no arguing with his taste. Underrated Bible-man-turned-professional-song-slinger BOO HEWERDINE and sidekick NEIL MacCOLL supply the blues-folky, blink-and-you'll-miss-them score pieces. No musicians are credited but given that HEWERDINE worked with Danny Thompson on solo set, 'Baptism Hospital' (1996), chances are the fleshy acoustic bass parts are the work of the legend himself. Thompson provides a link to Meadows' choice of NICK DRAKE's 'Fruit Tree', and to the soundtrack's 70s singing-songwriting flavour in general: bluesy, late period TIM BUCKLEY and Woodstock-era VAN MORRISON both get a look in, while PAUL WELLER's moving Fender Rhodes elegy, 'Broken Stones' and PRIMAL SCREAM's 'Damaged' might as well be from the 70s. TIM ROSE's rasping murder ballad, 'Long Time Man', reverberates through misspent decades like a parable-following it up with the purifying chorale of LES NOUVELLES POLYPHONIES CORSES, is a masterstroke. Meadows' only misstep is 'The Blue Danube Waltz', too inextricably linked with Stanley Kubrick and deep-space mindwarping to count, but otherwise this is an evocative, highly personal lesson in various artistry. *BG*

Album rating: *7

- ULVER segment (⇒ SVIDD NEGER)
- UNDERWORLD segment (⇒ BREAKING AND ENTERING)
- UNKLE segment (⇒ SEXY BEAST)
- UNLEASHED alt. (⇒ DANNY THE DOG)

UP THE JUNCTION

1968 (UK 119m) Paramount Pictures (15)

Film genre: kitchen-sink drama

Top guns: dir: Peter Collinson / s-w: Roger Smith (book: Nell Dunn)

Stars: Suzy Kendall *(Polly)* ← UP JUMPED THE SWAGMAN, Dennis Waterman *(Peter)*, Adrienne Posta *(Rube)* ← HERE WE GO ROUND THE MULBERRY BUSH / → PERCY, Maureen Lipman *(Sylvie)*, Michael Gothard *(Terry)* → la VALLEE, Liz Fraser *(Mrs. McCarthy)* ← the FAMILY WAY ← EVERY DAY'S A HOLIDAY / → the GREAT ROCK'N'ROLL SWINDLE, Hylda Baker *(Winny)*, Alfie Bass *(Charlie)* ← HELP!, Susan George *(Joyce)*, Linda Cole *(Pauline)*, Jessie Robins *(Lil)* ← MAGICAL MYSTERY TOUR ← WHAT A CRAZY WORLD, Aubrey Morris *(Creely)* → the WICKER MAN, Stephen Whittaker *(Alf)* → CHASTITY, Billy Murray *(Ray)* ← WHAT A CRAZY WORLD / → PERFORMANCE → ROCK FOLLIES → McVICAR, **the Delcardos** *(pop group)*

Storyline: Originally a made-for-TV Wednesday Play in 1965, the story is actually based on a Brit novel by Nell Dunn. A well-heeled Chelsea chick Polly decides life is more real lived on the wrong side of the tracks, or at least the Thames. Moving to Battersea, she takes up with working class van driver Peter, gets a job in a factory and lends moral support to colleague Rube. Halliwell puts it more memorably: "An irritating heroine moves hygienically among motorbikes". *BG*

Movie rating: *5.5

Visual: video

Off the record: MANFRED MANN formed in London, England . . . late '62, initially as the Mann-Hugg Blues Band; they almost immediately named themselves MANFRED MANN after the band's bearded and bespectacled South African-born keyboard player. Manfred Mann and drummer Mike Hugg subsequently recruited Dave Richmond (bass), Mike Vickers (guitar, flute & sax) and Paul Jones (vocals), playing local gigs which secured them a deal with 'H.M.V.' records. Early in 1964, after two flop singles ('Why Should We Not' & 'Cock-A-Hoop'), MANFRED MANN – with Tom McGuinness superseding Richmond – had their first chart success, hitting the Top 5 with their harmonica-fuelled R&B classic, '5-4-3-2-1'. They continued to storm the charts throughout the 60s, reaching pole position three times with 'Doo Wah Diddy Diddy', 'Pretty Flamingo' and 'The Mighty Quinn' (1968). The line-up at this er junction was Mann, Hugg, McGuinness (guitar since '65), Klaus Voorman (who'd replaced Vickers via Jack Bruce in '66) and Mike D'Abo (who'd come in for solo-bound Jones late in '66). *MCS*

MANFRED MANN

Feb 68. (lp) *Fontana; (S+/TL 5460) Mercury; <SR 61159>* ☐ ☐
– Up the junction (vocal) / Sing songs of love / Walking around / Up the junction (instrumental) / Love theme (instrumental) / Up the junction (vocal & instrumental) / Just for me / Love theme (instrumental) / Sheila's dance / Belgravia / Wailing horn / I need your love / Up the junction (vocal). *(re-iss. 1970; 6852 005) (cd-iss. Nov99 on 'R.P.M.'+=; RPM 189)* – Sleepy hollow.

S/track review: You could sometimes be forgiven for wondering if MANFRED MANN ever existed at all. Neither their catchy line in stomp-pop singles nor highly regarded personnel (Jack Bruce, KLAUS VOORMAN) have earned them much retrospective coverage. In the mid-60s at least, they were high profile enough to make it onto a Burt Bacharach soundtrack (1965's 'What's New Pussycat?') and attract the attentions of future 'Italian Job' director, Peter Collinson. Despite Collinson's reservations, chief MANN and drummer MIKE HUGG transcended the 'Ready Steady Go!' appeal with 'UP THE JUNCTION'. It was their first post-'Sgt. Pepper's..' album and it shows: the title theme's kitchen-sink psyche is one part Lennon/McCartney, two parts Brian Wilson, infatuated with elongated vowels and harmonic premonition. Just as charming in moulding the Beatles' tropes are 'Just For Me' and 'Walking Round'. Minus the florid pretension, the latter could well have been another No.1, and you've got to hand it to MANN and HUGG for putting their film credentials where their harpsichord was (the soundtrack generated not a single hit). On the gorgeous 'Love Theme', the dapper gait of Bacharach himself silhouettes the orchestrations and brass arrangements, and their proficiency in hard swinging soul-jazz ('I Need Your Love' could be Les McCann) is another revelation, gilded by freaky VOORMAN reed parts on 'Sheila's Dance' and the eerie 'Wailing Horn'. The styles shift, reverse and converge with a cotton-wool-in-ether consistency, summed up in the Rip Van Winkle blues of 'Sleepy Hollow' (an addition to the CD). "The brittleness of pop music often gets lost on a film (but) the tunes of junction are the young kids of London.", comments Collinson in the sleevenotes. "The tunes will exist long after the picture has been forgotten". They exist, sure, but you don't hear much about them these days. *BG*

Album rating: *6.5 / re-CD *7

UP TIGHT!

1968 (US 104m) Paramount Pictures (M)

Film genre: urban drama

Top guns: s-w: Jules Dassin (+ dir), Ruby Dee, Julian Mayfield

Stars: Raymond St. Jacques *(B.G.)* → COTTON COMES TO HARLEM → COOL BREEZE → the FINAL COMEDOWN → COME BACK, CHARLESTON BLUE → BOOK OF NUMBERS, Ruby Dee *(Laurie)* → BLACK GIRL WATTSTAX → COUNTDOWN AT KUSINI → JUNGLE FEVER, Julian Mayfield *(Tank Williams)*, Frank Silvera *(Kyle)*, Roscoe Lee Browne *(Clarence)* → SUPERFLY T.N.T. → EDDIE PRESLEY, Juanita Moore *(Mama)* ← the GIRL CAN'T HELP IT / → the MACK, Max Julien *(Johnny)* ← the SAVAGE SEVEN ← PSYCH-OUT / → the MACK, Dick Anthony Williams *(Corbin)* → the MACK → SLAUGHTER'S BIG RIP-OFF → FIVE ON THE BLACK HAND SIDE, Janet MacLachlan *(Jeannie)* → SOUNDER, Ji-Tu Cumbuka *(Rick)* → BLACULA → BOUND FOR GLORY, **Ketty Lester** *(Alma)* → BLACULA → HOUSE PARTY 3, Leon Bibb *(Mr.*

Oakley), Robert DoQui *(street speaker)* → COFFY → NASHVILLE → FAST FORWARD → GOOD TO GO, Lonny Stevens → the PHYNX

Storyline: John Ford's 'The Informer' is transplanted to black urban America in the immediate wake of Martin Luther King's assassination, with militants rounding on a street sweeping vagrant who's dobbed them in to the cops. *BG*

Movie rating: *5.5

Visual: none

Off the record: **BOOKER T. & THE MG'S** (see below)

—

BOOKER T. AND THE MG'S

Feb 69. (lp; stereo/mono) *Stax; <STS 2006> (S+/XATS 1005)* [98] May69 [ ]
– Johnny, I love you / Cleveland now / Children, don't get weary / Tank's lament / Blues in the gutter / We've got Johnny Wells / Down at Ralph's joint / Deadwood Dick / Run Tank run / Time is tight. *(UK cd-iss. Jan90; CDXSE 024) <US cd-iss. 1992; SCD 8562-2>*

S/track review: BOOKER T and his 'Stax'-driving Memphis Group were on a roll in the late 60s, having just scored their biggest American hit since 'Green Onions' with a baroque organ treatment of Dominic Frontiere's 'Hang 'Em High' theme. It was to be a cinematic tour de force of their own making which would supply them with a follow-up. Rolling in on STEVE CROPPER's itchy guitar and BOOKER T. JONES' banks of climactic keys, 'Time Is Tight' remains, if only in terms of sheer feel-good simplicity, one of the era's greatest dancefloor instrumentals. It forms the centrepiece of the M.G.'s only soundtrack, one which arrived too early to be grouped under blaxploitation but which packs a gritty, soulful punch all the same. And while the famous quartet had split the writing credits in the past, here JONES – save for 'Time Is Tight itself – took full responsibility for the composing, as well as the production and arrangements. He even sings on jazzy lead track, 'Johnny, I Love You' (and hums the languid melody to 'Blues In The Gutter'), revealing a bluesy, versatile voice which begs the question of why it wasn't committed to vinyl more often. The late JUDY CLAY – an unsung sessioneer who scored a hit with William Bell and recorded a series of Northern Soul gems under her own steam – turns in one of the album's best performances on the ominous spiritual, 'Children, Don't Get Weary', her raw-as-uncured-leather vocal calling down JONES' funereal, 'House Of The Rising Son'-esque organ lines. The M.G.'s flex their sonic economy on dynamic interstices like 'We've Got Johnny Wells' and the conga-driven 'Cleveland Now', while the carnival-like groove of 'Deadwood Dick' underscores their versatility even if it doesn't gel with their Southern pedigree. *BG*

Album rating: *6.5

– spinoff hits, etc. –

BOOKER T. & THE MG'S: Time Is Tight / Johnny, I Love You

Mar 69. (7") *<STAX 0028>* [6] [–]

BOOKER T. & THE MG'S: Time Is Tight / (diff. B-side)

Apr 69. (7") *(STAX 119)* [–] [4]

☐ Midge URE segment
(⇒ WENT TO CONEY ISLAND . . .)

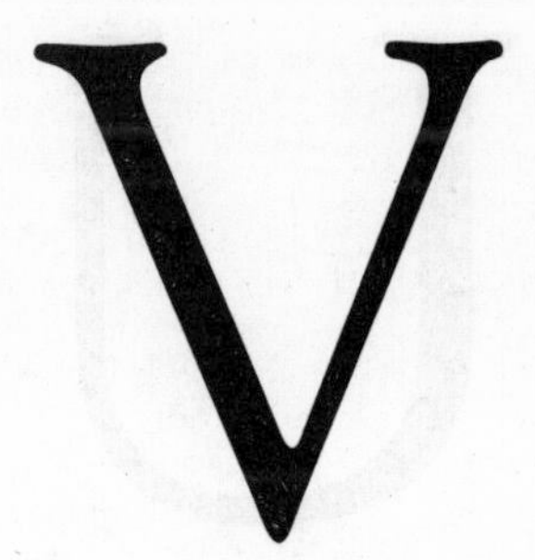

la VALLEE

aka 'The Valley'

1972 (Fra 106m) Les Films du Losange (12)

Film genre: seXual/psychological drama

Top guns: s-w: Barbet Schroeder (+ dir) ← MORE, Paul Gegauff ← MORE

Stars: Bulle Ogier *(Viviane)* ← les IDOLES / → CANDY MOUNTAIN, Michael Gothard *(Olivier)* ← UP THE JUNCTION, Jean-Pierre Kalfon *(Gaetan)* ← les IDOLES, Valerie Lagrange *(Hermine)* ← les IDOLES, Jerome Beauvarlet *(Yann)*, Monique Giraudy *(Monique)*

Storyline: Viviane is an adventurous kinda gal, married to a diplomat, but won't head off into the depths of the New Guinean jungle on a whim. Although ostensibly in search of bird feathers, she ends up falling in with a hippy commune. The Westerners get more than they bargain for, however, when the locals arrive on the scene. *BG*

Movie rating: *6

Visual: video + dvd

Off the record: (see below)

—

PINK FLOYD: Obscured By Clouds

Jun 72. (lp/c) *Harvest; (SHVL/TCSHVL 4020) <11078>* [6] [46]
– Obscured by clouds / When you're in / Burning bridges / The gold it's in the . . . / Wots . . . uh the deal / Mudmen / Childhood's end / Free four / Stay / Absolute curtains. *(cd-iss. Apr87; CDP 746385-2) (re-iss. Sep95 on 'E.M.I.' cd/c; CD/TC EMD 1083)*

S/track review: On the cusp of global stadium-dom with their magnum opus, 'The Dark Side Of The Moon', PINK FLOYD were unexpectedly roped in for another Barbet Schroeder soundtrack. If the finished (in under a week apparently) product hasn't been quite as historically ignored as 'MORE' (1969), their first effort for the director, it remains criminally conspicuous by its absence from most serious evaluations of the band's achievements. More lucid and generally more cohesive – if less interesting or alluring – than either 'MORE' or 'ZABRISKIE POINT' (1970), this is pretty much the final link in the band's occasionally messy transition from post-psychedelic pioneers to sleek prog-rock craftsmen. With its emphasis on songs as opposed to concepts or experiments, this is also – somewhat ironically – by far and away the most conventionally accessible (and most overtly "Rock") album in the band's discography. More so here than on any of their other late 60s/early 70s albums, there are glaring blueprints for the polished artistry which would make them internationally famous (hardly surprising when you consider that this was recorded smack dab in the middle of the protracted 'Dark Side . . .' sessions): 'Mudmen', with its spiralling sheets of GILMOUR-patented sound, predicts countless moments of 'FLOYD-ian majesty, while the same man's 'Childhood's End' would find a claustrophobic echo in 'Dark Side . . .'s 'Time'. The stoned incongruity of a title like 'Wot's . . . Uh The Deal', actually disguises a ballad of aching poignancy, perhaps the most affecting of its kind in the PINK FLOYD songbook. Crucially, WATERS' "chill winds" are offset by the nostalgia and resignation of RICK WRIGHT's jazzy piano chords, and, with both WRIGHT and GILMOUR's signature writ large all over a PINK FLOYD album for the first time in their career, it's this warmth which lends the record its immediacy. In fact, WATERS' only solo credit is 'Free Four', a galumphing death's head in jester's clothing and an unlikely single release. While the lyrics of 'Obscured By Clouds' at least suggest a linear sense of the movie's Heart Of Darkness-esque quest, closer 'Absolutely Curtains' is the only track to make its Papua New Guinean setting explicit, with disembodied keyboards and drum rolls ushering in a troupe of indigenous voices (a tactic also used by Nick Cave and Co on their largely orchestral – and rather fine – score to PNG-set drama, 'TO HAVE AND TO HOLD'). The 'Floyd would never sound quite so natural – or native – again. *BG*

Album rating: *6.5

– spinoff releases, etc. –

PINK FLOYD: Free Four / Stay

Jul 72. (7") *<3391>* [-] [ ]

Melvin VAN PEEBLES

Born: 21 Aug'32, Chicago, Illinois, USA. As an Afro American auteur whose cinematic innovations mutated into blaxploitation, MELVIN VAN PEEBLES remains justly famous. Save for his soundtrack to 'SWEET SWEETBACK'S BAADASSSSS SONG' (1971), his pioneering contributions to music remain less well known. Having relocated to Europe at the tail end of the 50s as Hollywood inroads eluded him, VAN PEEBLES' indulged creative talents which encompassed acting, editing, painting, film production and a series of novels. A grant from the French Cinema Center subsequently enabled the budding director to shoot an adaptation of one of his novels, 'La Permission', and release it as 'The Story Of A Three-Day Pass' (1967), writing the script and also composing the music. With the movie entered in the 1967 San Francisco Film Festival, VAN PEEBLES returned to America wielding an impressive CV. As well as a deal with 'Columbia' Pictures, he inked a recording contract with 'A&M', home to his first two albums: 'Br'er Soul' (1968), and follow-up, 'Ain't Supposed To Die A Natural Death' (1970). Disillusioned at what he saw as an apolitical black music scene out of step with oral, African-rooted tradition, he paired gonzoid proto-rap with frazzled funk and free jazz, inspiring the likes of the Last Poets and Gil Scott-Heron. While his soundtrack to racial satire, 'WATERMELON MAN' (the end result of his 'Columbia' deal), followed in 1970, it was his work on the aforementioned 'SWEETBACK . . .' (with a helping hand from a fledgling EARTH, WIND & FIRE) which confirmed him as a true cinematic and musical visionary. Against his raw, seminal tale of a sexually omnipotent black man defying the Man (mandatory viewing for Black Panther members!), he created a raging, disorientating maelstrom of a score, cutting up testifiying gospel, delirious, desperate dialogue, dapper jazz-funk and wicked soul with subversive, William Burroughs-esque glee. Yet while the cinematic revolution remained untelevised as Hollywood went on to have its sleazy way with blaxploitation (a term VAN PEEBLES himself recoils at), the multi-talented director turned his hand to theatre. While the lyrics of 'Ain't Supposed To Die . . .' formed the basis of the man's first – critically lauded – Broadway production, another stage project (and another adapataton from one of his 60s novels, 'The Party In Harlem)', 'DON'T PLAY US CHEAP' (1973), was also adapted for the big screen although its failure to find a distributor condemned it to relative obscurity. If the soundtrack wasn't quite as revelatory as its predecessor, it was another solid effort nonetheless, a more conventional combination of jazz, gospel, ensemble R&B celebration and the stunning, stratospheric soul of erstwhile Ikette Joshie Jo Armstead's 'You Cut Up The Clothes'. Although VAN PEEBLES continued to work on various music, theatre and literary projects, major screen productions remained elusive. His troubled relationship with Hollywood was again underlined when he chose to bail out of Richard Pryor vehicle, 'Greased Lightning' (1977), for which he'd penned the script. In between writing and acting for stage and television, the maverick thespian made his most unlikely career move to date, becoming a trader on the US Stock Exchange and even writing a book on the subject. In 1989 he returned to directing with the critically slated 'Identity Crisis', starring his son Mario, and, as well as parts in the likes of 'True Identity' (1991), 'Last Action Hero' (1993), 'Terminal Velocity' (1994) and 'Fist Of The North Star', he also acted in his son's directorial debut, the Afro American revisionist western, 'Posse' (1993). The father and son team again failed to convince the critics with 'Panther' (1995), Mario's adaptation of his father's historical novel. More successful was 'Le Conte Du Ventre Plein' (2000), VAN PEEBLES' award-winning return to the French screen which he wrote (adpated from another novel), directed and scored in his time-honoured renaissance man style. *BG*

- **filmography** [s-w + dir] (composer) {acting} –

the Story Of A 3-Day Pass *(1968 [s-w + dir] score)* / Slogan *(1969 [s-w])* / **the Watermelon Man** *(1970 [dir] OST =>)* / **Sweet Sweetback's Baadasssss Song** *(1971 [s-w + dir] {*} OST =>)* / **Don't Play Us Cheap** *(1973 [s-w + dir] OST =>)* / Just An Old Sweet Song *(1976 TV [s-w] score)* / Greased Lightning *(1977 [s-w])* / the Sophisticated Gents *(1981 TV [s-w] {a} score)* / America *(1986 {b})* / Taking Care Of Terrific *(1987 TV {*})* / O.C. And Stiggs *(1987 {a})* / Jaws: The Revenge *(1987 {a})* / Identity Crisis *(1990 [dir] {b})* / True Identity *(1991 {b})* / Boomerang *(1992 {b})* / Posse *(1993 {a} OST by V/A =>)* / Last Action Hero *(1993 {c} OST by V/A =>)* / Terminal Velocity *(1994 {a})* / Fist Of The North Star *(1995 {a})* / Erotic Tales: Vroom Vroom Vroooom *(1995 TV segment)* / Panther *(1995 {b} OST by V/A =>)* / Gang In Blue *(1996 [dir] {a})* / Calm At Sunset *(1996 TV {b})* / the Shining *(1997 TV mini {a})* / Riot *(1997 TV segment 'Homecoming Day' {a})* / Classified X *(1998 TV [s-w] {n})* / Love Kills *(1998 {a})* / Time Of Her Life *(1999 {a})* / Smut *(1999 {b})* / le Conte Du Ventre Plein *(2000 score)* / Antilles Sur Seine *(2000 {b})* / the Hebrew Hammer *(2003 {a})* / Blackout *(2007 {*})*

VANGELIS

Born: Evangelos Papathanassiou, 29 Mar'43, Volos, Greece. While VANGELIS broke big in the early 80s when his cultured electronics found a natural home on movie soundtracks, his film composing career had actually begun a decade earlier. After successfully following the evolution of popular music through the beat and progressive eras in his native Greece (noteably with Aphrodite's Child), he recorded the soundtrack to French adolescent awakening fantasy, 'SEX POWER' (1970), now the rarest and most sought after item in his catalogue. More French-directed fare was to follow, including scores for Francois Reichenbach's Mexican/French drama, 'No Oyes Ladrar Los Perros?'/'ENTENDS-TU LES CHIENS ABOYER?' (1975) and Frederic Rossif's 1976 nature documentary, 'la Fete Sauvage' (he'd previously worked with Rossif on his early 70s TV wildlife series, 'Apocalypse Des Animaux'). Through the latter half of the 70s, VANGELIS began developing the lofty synth signature which would become his trademark, recording increasingly impressive studio albums for 'R.C.A.' and 'Polydor'. While 1980 again found him composing for obscure foreign language films (none of which bore soundtrack releases), VANGELIS' big screen ambition finally reached creative and commercial fruition with his Oscar-winning score to 'CHARIOTS OF FIRE' (1981). Still one of the most recognisable themes in movie soundtrack history, this grandiose, slow motion epic made the Greek composer a household name and initated a sporadic relationship with big budget composition. While a tense, exploratory score (unreleased until the mid-90s) for Ridley Scott's cult sci-fi thriller, 'BLADE RUNNER', brought him more credibility and another Oscar nomination, VANGELIS spent most of the 80s scoring foreign documentaries and films with few official releases (the exception being the Japanese docu-drama, 'ANTARCTICA' in 1983). A new deal with 'Atlantic' and another link-up with Scott, '1492: Conquest Of Paradise' (1992), was the catalyst for his most successful score in years, pairing Columbus' visually arresting biopic with typically regal synth pieces and earning him the third Oscar nomination of his career. True to form, other scores around the same time were obscure foreign material such as Roman Polanski's bleak psycho-sexual drama, 'Bitter Moon' (featuring a very young and squirmingly awkward Hugh Grant) and a 1992 Latin American adaptation of Albert Camus' 'La Peste', before re-emerging with a big budget, historical epic a decade or so later. His score for Oliver Stone's 'Alexander' (2004) was generally better received than the film itself, revealing a more organic element to his sound and cementing his position as one of the most accomplished composers of his generation. *BG*

Note: the classical work of VANGELIS from the 90s (and a few nature films) are not included.

- filmography (composer) –

Sex Power *(1970 OST =>)* / Salut, Jerusalem *(1972)* / Amore *(1973)* / L'Apocalypse Des Animaux *(1973 TV OST see; future editions)* / **Entends-Tu Les Chiens Aboyer?** *(1975 OST =>)* / Crime And Passion *(1975)* / la Fete Sauvage *(1976 OST; see future edition)* / Mater Amatisima *(1980)* / Prkosna Delta *(1980)* / **Chariots Of Fire** *(1981 OST =>)* / Missing *(1982 OST see; future editions)* / **Blade Runner** *(1982 OST =>)* / Pablo Picasso *(1982)* / **Antarctica** *(1983 OST =>)* / the Bounty *(1984)* / Wonders Of Life *(1984 w/ Jean-Michel Jarre)* / Sauvage et Beau *(1984)* / Nosferatu a Venezia *(1988 w/ Luigi Ceccarelli)* / Francesco *(1989)* / the Third Solution *(1989)* / Bitter Moon *(1992)* / la Peste *(1992)* / 1492: Conquest Of Paradise *(1992 OST see; future editions)* / Kavafis *(1996)* / Alexander *(2004 OST see; future editions)*

– compilations, etc. –

VANGELIS: Themes

Jul 89. (lp/c)(cd) *Polydor; (LP/MC VGTV 1)(<839518-2>)* ☐ ☐
– End titles (from 'Blade Runner') / Main theme from 'Missing' / L'enfant / Hymn / Chung kuo / The tao of love / Theme from Antarctica / Love theme from Blade Runner / Opening titles from 'The Bounty' / Memories of green / La petite fille de la mer / Five circles / Chariots of fire.

□ Ben VAUGHN segment
(⇒ PSYCHO BEACH PARTY)

la VIA DELLA DROGA

1977 (Ita 90m*) Cinemaster S.r.l. (15)

Film genre: cop/detective thriller

Top guns: dir: Enzo G. Castellari / s-w: Massimo De Rita, Galliano Juso

Stars: Fabio Testi *(Fabio)*, David Hemmings *(Mike Hamilton)* ← PROFONDO ROSSO ← BLOW-UP ← BE MY GUEST ← LIVE IT UP ← SOME PEOPLE ← PLAY IT COOL, Sherry Buchanan *(Vera)*, John Loffredo *(Gianni, the boss)*, Wolfgango Soldati *(Girro)*

Storyline: Fabio is an undercover policeman who has wormed his way deep into an international drugs cartel in order to get close to the big men at the top. Along with Interpol agent Mike, he becomes involved in a vicious battle for control of the drugs scene in Rome which threatens to escalate into all-out war. Fabio and Mike realise that there's only one way to restore law and order – by meeting violence with violence. *JZ*

Movie rating: *6

Visual: video on Eurovidio / US dvd title 'HEROIN BUSTERS'

Off the record: (see below)

—

GOBLIN

Apr 99. (cd) *Cinevox; (CD-MDF 319)* ☐ ☐
– (main titles seq. 1-12 / finale).

S/track review: GOBLIN (i.e. CLAUDIO SIMONETTI, FABIO PIGNATELLI, MASSIMO MORANTE & AGOSTINO MARANGOLO) were fast becoming prolific score-meisters, already having renowned soundtrack LPs such as 'PROFONDO ROSSO' (1975) and 'SUSPIRIA' (1977) behind them. However, the score for 'La VIA DELLA DROGA' found itself for many years on the cutting-room floor, until that is, 'Cinevox' records, released the CD in 1999. Still without track names, the 13 untitled and mostly unrelated cues, gave GOBLIN fans that missing piece of their proverbial jigsaw. Track 1 saw the Italian quartet opt for the hard rock, Jimi Hendrix 'All Along The Watchtower'-inspired route, with even a hint of early Wishbone Ash thrown in – unintentionally of course. For the funk'n-bass-n' guitar interplay of tracks 3 and 10, GOBLIN take the jazz-rock trip, once the bastion of Weather Report, Billy Cobham and the Mahavishnu Orchestra, to namedrop a few. Santana-esque rhythms took over for the Latino-esque, title 4, while the follow-on cut shifting blissfully between the scales and some experiental prog. To say GOBLIN were now well ahead of their time rather than purveyors of Yes-meets-ELP prog, would be an understatement, the proof came thick and fast on the similar tracks 6, 7 & 12. It's the lead guitar riff that gets you thinking: where have I heard that before? In a "Loose Fit" sort of way, it predates the Happy Mondays by a good decade or so, although the gothic synths soon win the day. While titles 8 & 9 slide off the bat like some Cannon-styled TV cop drama, you've got to hold your breath slightly when you hear a few closing titles. The conga is king for #11 and perhaps a precursor to the alternative jazz-punks at the turn of the 80s. You'd be in no doubt with the finale, an upbeat number that could fit well in next to the likes of A Certain Ratio, 23 Skidoo or Pigbag; a reprise of the aforementioned opener spoils that theory slightly. *MCS*

Album rating: *6.5

VIOLA

1967 (UK ??m) unknown

Film genre: experimental/psychological drama

Top guns: dir: unknown

Stars: unknown (anybody?)

Storyline: The transmigration of the title presumably refers to the soul of the protagonist's dead wife who, the soundtrack sleevenotes reliably inform us, "has returned to life in the form of a cat that pursues him". *BG*

Movie rating: * unknown

Visual: none

Off the record: Look out for two further **RAVI SHANKAR** soundtracks, 'CHARLY' & 'CHAPPAQUA'.

—

RAVI SHANKAR: Transmigration Macabre

1973. (lp) *Spark; <SPA 06>* [–] [ ]
– Madness / Fantasy / Anxiety / Torment / Submission / Death / Transmigration / Retribution / Reflection. *(UK cd-iss. Jun97 on 'See For Miles'; SEECD 596) (UK cd re-iss. May06 on 'El – Cherry Red'; ACMEM 070CD)*

S/track review: The most obscure and psychedelic of all RAVI SHANKAR's scores, most recently exhumed by the rather fine 'él' label. There's no faulting their connoisseur's choice in reissues, but the sleevenotes might have offered more than one paragraph on the film over and above a brief plot synopsis. Still, a vengeful cat's better than nothing in getting a feel for what SHANKAR was trying to do here: with cues like 'Madness', 'Torment' and 'Death', you know it isn't going to be dinner party material. Ravi's conception of madness consists of disturbingly close mic'd percussion (think unnerving clanking on the back stairs after a 'Most Haunted' double bill), raked by nightmarish rushes of distortion approximating a cyber-elephant high on strychnine: the kind of flashback sonics which would've sent Tim Robbins round the bend in 'Jacob's Ladder' before he'd even been to Vietnam. For much of the score thereafter, SHANKAR holds up an almost constant level of threat with roiling, tolling bass drums behind bowels-of-Hades tabla and frantic, flying fingered sitar working itself into ever tighter neurotic knots, or conversely – with the simple ascending notes of 'Submission' – slowing down to a death knell. Powerful stuff, and all the more impressive for its thematic strength: even lighter cues like 'Fantasy' and the closing, more familiar-sounding soul-cycle of 'Transmigration', 'Retribution' and 'Reflection' maintain a phantasmagorical patina without sacrificing the narrative pulse. More than anything, 'Transmigration Macabre' is a fascinating window into the emotional reality of reinacarnation as imagined by someone steeped in Hindu tradition. *BG*

Album rating: *7.5

☐ VIOLENT STREETS alt.
(⇒ THIEF)

the VIRGIN SUICIDES

1999 (US 97m) Eternity Pictures / American Zoetrope (R)

Film genre: coming-of-age/teen drama/mystery

Top guns: s-w + dir: Sofia Coppola → LOST IN TRANSLATION (au: Jeffrey Eugenides)

Stars: James Woods *(Mr. Lisbon)* ← STRAIGHT TALK / → BE COOL, Kathleen Turner *(Mrs. Lisbon)* ← CRIMES OF PASSION, Kirsten Dunst *(Lux Lisbon)* ← WAG THE DOG / → GET OVER IT!, Josh Hartnett *(Trip Fontaine)*, Hanna Hall *(Cecilia Lisbon)*, Chelse Swain *(Bonnie Lisbon)*, A.J. Cook *(Mary Lisbon)*, Leslie Hayman *(Therese Lisbon)*, Scott Glenn *(Father Moody)* ← URBAN COWBOY ← MORE AMERICAN GRAFFITI ← NASHVILLE, Danny DeVito *(Dr. Horniker)* ← CAR WASH / → MAN ON THE MOON → BE COOL, Michael Pare *(adult Trip Fontaine)* ← EDDIE AND THE CRUISERS II: EDDIE LIVES! ← STREETS OF FIRE ← EDDIE AND THE CRUISERS, Jonathan Tucker *(Tim Weiner)* ← MR. MUSIC, Anthony DeSimone *(Chase Buell)*, **Robert Schwartzman** *(Paul Baldino)*, Hayden Christensen *(Joe Hill Conley)*, Melody Johnson *(Julie)* → ORIGINAL TEEN IDOL, Giovanni Ribisi *(narrator)* ← FIRST LOVE, LAST RITES ← SUBURBI@ ← THAT THING YOU DO! / → MASKED AND ANONYMOUS → LOST IN TRANSLATION → COLD MOUNTAIN

Storyline: A group of men try to fathom out the secrets of their old flames the Lisbon sisters. The girls seemed to have a happy, settled life at first, but all that changed when youngest sister Cecilia committed suicide. Their parents had taken them out of school and kept them housebound, much to the annoyance of sibling Lux who had just discovered that young men could be fun and interesting. What happened after Lux began sneaking away for clandestine meetings with the local lads is a mystery to all – until the dramatic finale. *JZ*

Movie rating: *7

Visual: video + dvd

Off the record: Score band, **AIR**, formed in Paris, France . . . 1995, Nicolas Godin and Jean-Benoît Dunckel cutting their proverbial teeth waking the neighbours up in a punk outfit called Orange. Preceded by a string of highly desirable 12" singles and a mini-set 'Premiers Symptomes', the Gallic duo's sublime 'Moon Safari' album ranks as one of 1998's most hypnotic, emotive and consistently listenable long players; the Moog was back. With the added kudos of being an essential purchase for any self-respecting fashion victim, the record's unearthly ELO-meets-Bacharach-meets-Carpenters hybrid had music journalists of all persuasions (with the possible exception of the metal press) reaching for the thesaurus. Those that portrayed AIR as mere faux-space-age lounge revivalists were surely missing the point, however; they might've doffed their cap to classic French pop but Messrs Godin and Dunckel were in the business of making music to last, serious business. No surprise, then, that the album made the UK Top 20, as did the attendant 'Kelly Watch The Stars' & 'Sexy Boy' singles. If there was a World Cup for music, AIR would definitely be in there with a shout, the French redrawing of contemporary musical battle lines continuing unabated. At the height of AIR's popularity, 'Virgin' squeezed out their 1997 mini-set for eager fans who surprisingly sent it into the UK Top 20. Sofia Coppola then came knocking. Incidentally, **Robert Schwartzman** (brother of Jason, drummer with Phantom Planet) has his own band, Rooney. *BG & MCS*

—

AIR

Feb 00. (cd/c/lp) *Astralwerks; <48848-2> Virgin; (CD/TC+/V 2910)* [ ] [14]
– Playground love (vocals: GORDON TRACKS) / Clouds up / Bathroom girl / Cemetary party / Dark messages / The word 'hurricane' / Dirty trip / Highschool lover / Afternoon sister / Ghost song / Empty house / Dead bodies / Suicide underground.

S/track review: A group whose dolefully luxurious sound owes not a little to classic film scoring, Gallic space-lounge duo AIR couldn't have been too surprised when directorial debutante Sofia Coppola hired them for her meta-comic tale of doomed youth. While the mid-noughties would see messieurs GODIN and DUNCKEL go on to work with French soundtrack don, Michel Colombier, here they more or less took their creative cues from the same primordial synth arsenal (or, as Rolling Stone memorably put it, "shag-carpet organ straight from the soundtracks of movies such as Un Homme et Une Femme") which made their 'Moon Safari' (1998) opus such an anachronistic triumph. Unshackled by the demands of a pop record, they use familiar ingredients to create something slightly more cerebral and impressionistic without ever really deviating from their bachelor pad-boffin blueprint. While opener 'Playground Love', was released as a single, only Gordon Tracks' vocal and Hugo Ferran's deliciously torpid sax actually distinguish it as such; with a bit of embellishment, the likes of 'Bathroom Girl' or even 'Clouds Up' could have performed the same function and, like much of this album, would've made great raw material for a 'Moon Safari Vol.2'. The muted modulations of 'Dark Messages' or whooshing sci-fi communiqués of 'Dirty Trip' represent les garçons at their most oblique, pretty much the kind of sonic debris you might expect from an AIR soundtrack. Yet no matter how frequently their knob-twiddling melancholy might hurl them into the orbit of classic Pink Floyd, they can't wring the warmth from their sound, so indelible and intoxicating is that analogue-acoustic patent. And, surprisingly, when they do step it up a gear the effect is truly stunning. In its almost cosmic continental aura (shades of Ennio Morricone's crime score classic, 'Svegliati E Uccidi') and disembodied dynamism, 'Dead Bodies' reprises that mysterious elixir of 60s/70s film music more evocatively than almost anything released since then; if that old "cathedral of sound" cliché is applicable anywhere, it's here. And if you've ever suspected AIR of Francophone archness, this irony-free tour de force will rob you of your assumptions faster than a Citroen C5 hurtling the wrong way down a one-way street. *BG*

Album rating: *7 / V/A *7.5

– spinoff hits, etc. –

AIR: Playground Love / Bathroom Girl

Feb 00. (c-s) *(VSC 1764)* [-] [25]
(cd-s+=) *(VSCDT 1764)* – ('A'-Vibraphone mix).
(12") *(VST 1764)* – ('A') / Nosferatu / Highschool prom.

Various Artists: (score: AIR *)

Mar 00. (cd/lp) *Emperor Norton; <(EMN 7029/+LP)>* [ ] [ ]
– Magic man (HEART) / Hello it's me (TODD RUNDGREN) / Everything you've done wrong (SLOAN) / Ce matin la (*) / The air that I breathe (the HOLLIES) / How can you mend a broken heart (AL GREEN) / Alone again (naturally) (GILBERT O'SULLIVAN) / I'm not in love (10CC) / A dream goes on forever (TODD RUNDGREN) / Crazy on you (HEART) / Playground love (vibraphone version) (*) / Come sail away (STYX).

WAG THE DOG

1997 (US 97m) Baltimore Pictures / New Line Cinema (R)

Film genre: political/media satire/comedy

Top guns: dir: Barry Levinson ← GOOD MORNING, VIETNAM / s-w: Hilary Henkin ← ROAD HOUSE, David Mamet (au: Larry Beinhart 'American Hero')

Stars: Dustin Hoffman *(Stanley Motss)* ← DICK TRACY ← WHO IS HARRY KELLERMAN AND WHY IS HE SAYING THOSE TERRIBLE THINGS ABOUT ME? ← the POINT! ← LITTLE BIG MAN ← MIDNIGHT COWBOY ← the GRADUATE, Robert De Niro *(Conrad Brean)* → JACKIE BROWN, Anne Heche *(Winifred Ames)* ← WALKING AND TALKING ← an AMBUSH OF GHOSTS, Woody Harrelson *(Sgt. William Schumann)* ← NATURAL BORN KILLERS, Denis Leary *(Fad King)* ← JUDGMENT NIGHT ← WHO'S THE MAN, **Willie NELSON** *(Johnny Green)*, Andrea Martin *(Liz Butsky)* ← CLUB PARADISE / → HEDWIG AND THE ANGRY INCH, Kirsten Dunst *(Tracy Lime)* → the VIRGIN SUICIDES, William H. Macy *(CIA agent Charles Young)* ← BOOGIE NIGHTS ← COLIN FITZ LIVES! ← the LAST DRAGON / → MAGNOLIA, Suzie Plakson *(Grace)*, John Michael Higgins *(John Levy)* → a MIGHTY WIND → KILLER DILLER, **Pops Staples** *(himself)* <= the STAPLE SINGERS =>, Jim Belushi *(himself)* ← LITTLE SHOP OF HORRORS ← THIEF, Harland Williams *(pet wrangler)* → BIG MONEY HUTLA, David Koechner *(director)* → DILL SCALLION → MAN ON THE MOON, **Merle Haggard** *(himself)* ← FROM NASHVILLE WITH MUSIC ← HILLBILLYS IN A HAUNTED HOUSE / → the LIFE AND HARD TIMES OF GUY TERRIFICO, Jason Cottle *(A.D.)* ← FALL AND SPRING / → the WEDDING SINGER, Jay Leno *(himself)* ← AMERICAN HOT WAX

Storyline: Oracular, often surreally hilarious satire as Mr President weasels out of a scandalous tryst with a teenaged "Firefly Girl", via the help of fast-talking, even faster-thinking political fixit man, Conrad Brean. Attempting to buy him time as he dallies in China on the premise of being ill, Brean concocts an imaginary set-to with Albania over a supposed terrorist threat. To ensure his smoke screen reaches prime time America, he enlists the services of excitable Hollywood producer Stanley Motss, overseeing some ludicrous studio footage of an Albanian peasant girl fleeing American bombs. As Johnny Green, meanwhile, Willie Nelson – hired to write a chest-beating anthem ("Albania's hard to rhyme") – looks conspicuously out of place among his Machiavellian chums. It all goes swimmingly until the war's declared prematurely over and the Brean/Motss axis have to come up with something new: a classic American war hero stuck behind enemy lines, whose priceless, Edgar Winter-penned theme tune, 'Good Ol' Shoe' brings a patriotic tear to decent American folks' eyes. What they don't know, of course, is that their trumped up hero is actually a psychopath jailed for raping a nun. While the plot thickens to pitch, Motss' neurotic craving for recognition eventually threatens his life. *BG*

Movie rating: *7

Visual: video + dvd

Off the record: Merle Haggard (b. 6 Apr'37, Oklahoma, USA) was a unique country singer in the fact that "the Okie from Muskogee" has actually lived the life of a C&W song:- he's been in prison (San Quentin when JOHNNY CASH performed there c.1968) and went through four D.I.V.O.R.C.E.'s; his current wife has stayed on course since September 1993. *MCS*

—

MARK KNOPFLER

Jan 98. (m-cd/m-c) *Mercury; (<536864-2/-4>)* □ □
– Wag the dog / Working on it / In the heartland / An American hero / Just instinct / Stretching out / Drooling national / We're going to war.

S/track review: A tiddler this, compared to some of the bonus-previously-unreleased-found-under-my-granny's-coalshed extras that clog up too many soundtracks. Over a succinct 24 minutes, MARK KNOPFLER noodles away evocatively in that unassuming northern way of his, covering the usual folk/blues/country bases but never outstaying his welcome. He even gets his middle-aged geezer freak on with the hammondeering title track, mumbling suggestively over a list of dance-craze double entendres from way back. The rest of the album is more tasteful, purely instrumental and, with such a stickler for perfection at the helm, instrumentally pure. Standout track 'In The Heartland' best sums it up, steeped in both the intimate grandeur of 'LOCAL HERO' and the cupid flourish of Dire Straits' 'Romeo and Juliet'. The whistling organ and 'Straits-esque bends of 'Stretching Out' isn't far behind, and as always, it's all about heart for this sultan of strings, a bloke-ish candour that colours every astutely plucked note; whether it's the right sound to accompany politically satirical comedy is a moot point. KNOPFLER offers comment on the movie's darker implications with the sombre, spaghetti-esque 'An American Hero' and 'We're Going To War', tempering the trademark warmth with martial underpinnings but tempering them both in turn by sticking in a bluegrass jam and calling it 'Drooling National'. Oh, and there's also a gloriously grumpy sleeve-shot of Robert De Niro as you've never seen him before, drinking tea and wearing a trilby. *BG*

Album rating: *6.5

□ WAGES OF FEAR alt.
(⇒ SORCERER)

Tom WAITS

Born: 7 Dec'49, Pomona, California, USA. Though, incredibly, he's claimed in the past that his own work is too mainstream, the one man experiment in sound that is TOM WAITS will fit comfortably into even the most stringent definition of the term musical maverick. WAITS spent most of the 70s reeling off post-Beat, neon-frazzled commentaries on the seedier side of American lowlife, tragi-comic portraits set to his own brand of spiked cocktail jazz. In fact, his inimitable piano playing actually earned him his first break in the movies, tinkling the ivories in both Sylvester Stallone's 'Paradise Alley' (1978) and forgotten horror flick, 'Wolfen' (1981). It was Francis Ford Coppola's 'ONE FROM THE HEART' (1982), however, which really kickstarted his long relationship with film. WAITS' efforts on his own 1977 album, 'Foreign Affairs', was reportedly Coppola's inspiration and he commissioned him for the soundtrack. While the film was an expensive failure and the anticipated musical chemistry between WAITS and Crystal Gayle never really materialised, the album was nevertheless another impressive entry on his CV and the subject of an Academy Award nomination. In tandem with a serious leftfield turn in WAITS' recording career, the Coppola association continued through the early to mid-80s with minor roles in 'The Outsiders' (1983), 'Rumble Fish' (1983) and 'The Cotton Club' (1984). His first major screen part came via Jim Jarmusch and his cult classic, 'DOWN BY LAW' (1986), where he played a surly, rootless DJ framed for a crime he didn't commit, contributing his own 'Jockey Full Of Bourbon' (from 1985's 'Raindogs' album) to the soundtrack. Another convincing role opposite Jack Nicholson in Depression era drama, 'Ironweed' (1987), announced his entry into mainstream cinema, and if none of these parts strayed too far from WAITS' rank outsider aesthetic, the piano man finally played himself in his own conceptual TV concert film, 'BIG TIME' (1988). While his 1987 album, 'Frank's Wild Years', was actually a soundtrack for a stage production co-written by WAITS and his wife, playwright Kathleen Brennan, the man's next outside scoring job was the music for Jim Jarmusch's droll taxi driving oddity, 'NIGHT ON EARTH' (1992). If memorable turns in enjoyable failures such as 'Cold Feet' (1989) and 'At Play In The Fields Of The Lord' (1991) didn't exactly raise his profile, the early 90s found him with typically subversive roles in two of his biggest Hollywood movies to date, 'The Fisher King' (1991) and as an insect-eating lunatic in Coppola's huge horror re-invention, 'Bram Stoker's Dracula'. A part in Robert Altman's acclaimed 'Short Cuts' – as the wonderfully named Earl Piggot – followed in 1993, while musically, WAITS also contributed the brilliant 'Little Drop Of Poison' to Wim Wenders' 1997 effort, 'The END OF VIOLENCE'. More recently, he appeared in superhero send-up 'Mystery Men' and took much of the plaudits for his Palme D'Or-winning chinwag with IGGY POP in Jarmusch's 'COFFEE AND CIGARETTES' (2003). At the time of writing, WAITS was rumoured to be cast as a wandering soothsayer in the film 'Domino', an apt metaphor for his vagabond-like movie career and talent for blackly surreal pearls of wisdom. He mightn't be the most famous "rock star" (those are serious inverted commas) in the movies but few actors can muster the gruff intensity of TOM WAITS at his bizarre best. *BG*

- **filmography** {acting} (composer) –

Paradise Alley *(1978 {a} 2 tracks on OST by Bill Conti)* / Wolfen *(1981 {a})* / **One From The Heart** *(1982 {*} OST w/ CRYSTAL GAYLE =>)* / the Outsiders *(1983 {a})* / Prenom: Carmen *(1983 score)* / Rumble Fish *(1983 {a} OST by STEWART COPELAND =>)* / the Cotton Club *(1984 {a})* / Streetwise *(1985 score)* / Coffee And Cigarettes *(1986 short {*})* / **Down By Law** *(1986 {*} OST by JOHN LURIE =>)* / **Candy Mountain** *(1987 {*} score)* / Ironweed *(1987 {a})* / Wohin? *(1988 score)* / **Big Time** *(1988 {*p} [s-w] OST =>)* / Cold Feet *(1989 {*})* / Bearskin: An Urban Fairytale *(1989 {*})* / the Two Jakes *(1990 {a} OST by VAN DYKE PARKS =>)* / Queens Logic *(1991 {a})* / the Fisher King *(1991 {a})* / At Play In The Fields Of The Lord *(1991 {*})* / Until The End Of The World *(1991 {p} see future edition)* / **Night On Earth** *(1992 OST =>)* / Bram Stoker's Dracula *(1992 {a})* / Short Cuts *(1993 {*} OST by ANNIE ROSS, etc. =>)* / Mystery Men *(1999 {a})* / Big Bad Love *(2001 OST w/ TOM WAITS + by V/A =>)* / Long Gone *(2003 on score)* / **Coffee And Cigarettes** *(2003 {c*})* / Domino *(2005 {b})* / Wristcutters: A Love Story *(2007 {*})*

Rick WAKEMAN

Born: 18 May'49, Perivale, Middlesex, England. Pioneering the concept of stacking keyboards on top of each other for live performances, playing mellotron on DAVID BOWIE's 'Space Oddity' and appearing on Channel 4's 'Countdown' up to twenty times a year are but a few of RICK WAKEMAN's many proud achievements. After establishing himself as a session player par excellence (playing as many as eighteen sessions a week with the likes of Black Sabbath, Cat Stevens and Cilla Black, among many others), producing the theme tune for TV's 'Ask Aspel' and achieving minor success with the Strawbs, WAKEMAN found real fame with Yes in 1971. After leaving Yes for the first time in 1973 (subsequently re-joining and re-leaving many times), the ever prolific WAKEMAN focused on a solo career which, after the false start of 1971's 'Piano Vibrations' (essentially a glorified piece of session work), started in earnest with 'The Six Wives Of Henry VIII', and to date encompasses over 80 studio, live and soundtrack releases. Concept albums based around Jules Verne's 'Journey To The Centre Of The Earth' and 'King Arthur' (later performed on ice at Wembley) followed before WAKEMAN made his first proper foray into the world of movies, with 1975's 'LISZTOMANIA' (though WAKEMAN had contributed, with members of the Strawbs, to the soundtrack of 1972 movie 'Zee & Co', 'LISZTOMANIA' was his first full score). Ken Russell's movie, released in the same year as his 'TOMMY' and also starring Roger Daltrey of the WHO in the lead role, featured WAKEMAN reinterpreting the works of Liszt and Wagner in the fledgling tradition of symphonic rock, while he portrayed the character of Thor onscreen. WAKEMAN later denounced the album following the unwelcome interference of his record label and the film's production company (in a presumably unrelated incident he was forced, while in full Thor body makeup, to rebuff the amorous attentions of several men in a pub toilet). His score for the theatrical release of 'WHITE ROCK', a documentary about the 1976 Winter Olympics, was well received, while in 1979 a selection from his 'King Arthur And The Knights Of The Round Table' album was used to soundtrack the BBC's Election Night coverage for the first time, starting a tradition only since interrupted once, in 2001. After a brief sojourn with Yes from 1977-78, WAKEMAN returned to dramatic scoring in style with 1981's 'The BURNING', a slasher movie that launched the careers of the Weinstein brothers, and still represents for many the creative pinnacle of WAKEMAN's scoring career. The keyboard wizard followed this with sci-fi B-movie 'She', before returning to sport for 'G'OLÉ!', the official film of the 1982 World Cup (WAKEMAN also scored the next World Cup movie 'Hero', in 1986). 1984 brought another project for Ken Russell, and the opportunity for WAKEMAN to briefly stretch his acting muscles once more in 'CRIMES OF PASSION' (he also delivered the mediocre soundtrack, based on Dvorak's 9th Symphony) and, always happy to be working, WAKEMAN also that year supplied the theme for TV's 'Database'. In 1987, WAKEMAN continued to display the versatility of his music, which adorned both a TV adaptation of Thomas Hardy's short story 'The Day After The Fair' and some of anthology horror film 'Creepshow 2'. 'Phantom Power' (1990), an ill-advised challenge to Lloyd Webber's rock opera throne, was written for a re-release of the 1925 silent film 'Phantom Of The Opera', after which WAKEMAN took a break from scoring to set up his own record label 'Ambient' on which he would release many, many records of limited, or "niche", appeal. Soundtracks for the Harry Palmer films 'Bullet To Beijing' and 'Midnight In St Petersburg', low rent additions to a classic series shot back to back in 1995, were unlikely to gain WAKEMAN any new fans, while he launched a new label 'Hope', specialising in Christian music. Returning once more to record with Yes in 1996, WAKEMAN left before touring commenced again, only to rejoin in 2002. His recent scoring of the straight-to-dvd docu-drama 'Aleister Crowley – The Wickedest Man In The World: In Search Of The Great Beast 666', led to him issuing a statement defending his involvement as a Christian, and making it clear he did not support Crowley's views. Most recently, two films from screenwriter Douglas Ford, 'Out Of Reach' and 'The HAB Theory', feature WAKEMAN scores, and with Yes mooted to tour once more, the synth legend shows no sign of slowing down. *SW*

- **filmography** (composer) {acting} –

Lisztomania *(1975 OST =>)* / **White Rock** *(1977 OST =>)* / **the Burning** *(1981 OST =>)* / **G'Olé!** *(1983 OST =>)* / **Crimes Of Passion** *(1984 {b} OST =>)* / Creepshow 2 *(1987 w/ LES REED)* / Day After The Fair *(1987 TV)* / the Phantom Of The Opera *(1925! re-score as 'Phantom Power' 1991; see future edition)*

WALKER

1987 (US/Nicaragua 94m) Universal Pictures (R)

Film genre: historical biopic/docudrama/satire

Top guns: dir: Alex Cox ← STRAIGHT TO HELL ← SID & NANCY ← REPO MAN / → REVENGERS TRAGEDY / s-w: Rudy Wurlitzer ← PAT GARRETT & BILLY THE KID / → CANDY MOUNTAIN

Stars: Ed Harris *(William Walker)* ← SWEET DREAMS ← ALAMO BAY ← PLACES IN THE HEART / → MASKED AND ANONYMOUS, Marlee Matlin *(Ellen Martin)*, Peter Boyle *(Commodore Cornelius Vanderbilt)* ← WHERE THE BUFFALO ROAM ← STEELYARD BLUES ← JOE / → the IN CROWD, Richard Masur *(Ephraim Squier)*, Blanca Guerra *(Yrena)*, Rene Auberjonois *(Major Siegfried Hennington)* ← the LAST UNICORN ← WHERE THE BUFFALO ROAM, Keith Szarabajka *(Timothy Crocker)*, Sy Richardson *(Capt. Hornsby)* ← STRAIGHT TO HELL ← SID & NANCY ← REPO MAN ← PETEY WHEATSTRAW / → TAPEHEADS → MYSTERY TRAIN, Xander Berkeley *(Byron Cole)* ← STRAIGHT TO HELL ← SID & NANCY / → TAPEHEADS → STORYTELLING, John Diehl *(Stebbins)* → the END OF VIOLENCE, **Joe STRUMMER** *(Faucett)*, Gerrit Graham *(Norvell Walker)* ← PHANTOM OF THE PARADISE / → SHAKE, RATTLE & ROCK! tv, **Edward Tenpole Tudor** *(Doubleday)* ← STRAIGHT TO HELL ← SID & NANCY ← ABSOLUTE BEGINNERS ← the GREAT ROCK'N'ROLL SWINDLE, Norbert Weisser *(Prange)*, **Zander Schloss** *(Huey)* <= the CIRCLE JERKS =>, **Spider Stacy** *(Davenport)* <= the POGUES =>, Kathy Burke *(Annie Mae)* ← STRAIGHT TO HELL ← EAT THE RICH ← SID & NANCY / → KEVIN & PERRY GO LARGE, David Hayman *(Father Rossiter)* ← SID & NANCY / → ORDINARY DECENT CRIMINAL → the LAST GREAT WILDERNESS, **Richard Edson** *(Turley)* ← HOWARD THE DUCK / → GOOD MORNING, VIETNAM → TOUGHER THAN LEATHER → WHAT ABOUT ME → STRANGE DAYS → the MILLION DOLLAR HOTEL → SOUTHLANDER, Milton Selzer *(judge)* ← SID & NANCY ← LADY SINGS THE BLUES / → TAPEHEADS, **Dick Rude** *(Washburn)* ← STRAIGHT TO HELL ← SID & NANCY ← REPO MAN / → ROADSIDE PROPHETS → LET'S ROCK AGAIN!, Miguel Sandoval *(Parker French)* ← STRAIGHT TO HELL ← SID & NANCY ← HOWARD THE DUCK ← REPO MAN / → JUNGLE FEVER, Biff Yeager *(Max; carpetbagger)* ← STRAIGHT TO HELL ← SID & NANCY ← REPO MAN ← DYNAMITE BROTHERS / → ROADSIDE PROPHETS, Alfonso Arau *(Raousset)* ← el TOPO / → COMMITTED

Storyline: Satirical portrait of 19th Century manifest destiny maniac William Walker, whose self-righteousness increasingly turns to madness as he assists a liberal victory in the Nicaraguan civil war. After assuming the presidency, it's not long before he's legalizing slavery, decreeing that English become the official language and commandeering the passenger ships of his patron Cornelius Venderbilt. It all ends in flames, though, as he regales his bedraggled subjects with a final prophecy: "No matter how much you fight, or what you think, we'll be back." *BG*

Movie rating: *5.5

Visual: video + dvd

Off the record: Edward Tenpole Tudor nearly replaced Johnny Rotten in the SEX PISTOLS when the latter singer became John Lydon and formed Public Image Ltd (witness 'The GREAT ROCK'N'ROLL SWINDLE'). One person he did replace was 'ROCKY HORROR PICTURE SHOW's writer/star, Richard O'Brien, in TV gameshow 'The Crystal Maze' c.1994/5. In 1981, Eddie's post-punk-pop group, Tenpole Tudor, had a UK Top 50 album, 'Eddie, Old Bob, Dick & Garry' (named after their four members), featuring three hits, 'Swords Of A Thousand Men', 'Wunderbar' & 'Throwing My Baby Out With The Bathwater'. *MCS*

JOE STRUMMER

Feb 88. (cd/c/lp) *Virgin; <90686-2/-4/-1> (CD/TC+/V 2497)* ☐ ☐
– Filibustero / Omotepe / Sandstorm / Machete / Viperland / Nica libre / Latin romance / The unknown immortal / Musket

waltz / The brooding side of madness / Tennessee rain / Smash everything / Tropic of no return / Tropic of Pico. *<cd-iss. Jul05 on 'Astralwerks'+=; 7763-2>* – Brooding side of madness – new extended Outer Limits mix / Straight shooter / Filibustero – Freestyle mix.

S/track review: The 'Astralwerks' re-issue trumpets JOE STRUMMER's solo soundtrack as "Spaghetti Western inspired". Truth be told, the late CLASH frontman's full-blown foray into scoring was largely a blend of Cuban, Mexican and Nuyorican styles, relentlessly tasteful and often verging on Latin jazz: both lead track 'Filibustero' and the feline 'Nica Libre' could've featured in Fernando Trueba documentary, 'CALLE 54' (2000); 'Machete' sounds like an Antonio Forcione instrumental; and 'Latin Romance' borders on elevator territory. In contrast to the chaotic satire of the film itself, only occasionally did he hint at the howling anarchy of 'STRAIGHT TO HELL' (1986), but even then – on the likes of 'Sandstorm' or maybe 'Straight Shooter', one of three bonus cuts on the reissue – the effect is more spaghetti slimline range than a plate of mama's full-fat bolognese. That's not to say this isn't a skilfully crafted score, inspired in places, but for those that care about such things, it sounds nothing like JOE STRUMMER as most of us know and love him; even the Latinate tracks on 'Sandinista!' (1980) are only tendentially related to most of the material here. In fact, save for the blinking, recurring portent that is 'The Brooding Side Of Madness' (the most effective cue in the film), the cumulative slickness of the arrangements and 80s production is such that it's something of a relief when he starts singing on standout track, 'The Unknown Immortal', and downsizes to the folkier, Celtic-influenced likes of 'Tennessee Rain' and 'Smash Everything', or, on 'Tropic Of Pico' – a Solentiname naif painting in sound – to simple Spanish guitar. This is when his empathy with Nicaragua and its centuries of imperialist woe really gets under your skin, just as Bob Dylan did with border country in his peerless 'PAT GARRETT & BILLY THE KID' (1973), a record which Mr. STRUMMER was reportedly enamoured of himself. *BG*

Album rating: *6 / re-CD *6.5

WALKING AND TALKING

1996 (US/UK/Ger 86m) Miramax Films (R)

Film genre: romantic urban comedy/drama

Top guns: s-w + dir: Nicole Holofcener

Stars: Catherine Keener *(Amelia)* ← JOHNNY SUEDE / → INTO THE WILD, Anne Heche *(Laura)* ← an AMBUSH OF GHOSTS / → WAG THE DOG, Todd Field *(Frank)*, Liev Schreiber *(Andrew)* → RANSOM, Kevin Corrigan *(Bill)* ← BANDWAGON / → BUFFALO '66 → DETROIT ROCK CITY → CHELSEA WALLS, Randall Batinkoff *(Peter)*, Vincent Pastore *(Laura's Devil-seeing patient)* ← the BASKETBALL DIARIES ← WHO'S THE MAN? ← BLACK ROSES / → JOE'S APARTMENT, Allison Janney *(gum puller)* → PRIVATE PARTS → PRIMARY COLORS → OVER THE HEDGE → HAIRSPRAY re-makew

Storyline: Amelia's down in the dumps because her friend Laura seems to have found Mister Perfect while she's desperate for a date. She even goes out with Bill, the geek from the video store, whose idea of a good time is going to a monster club convention. Just to rub things in, her cat expires from cancer and even Bill gives up on her, but things begin to change when she learns that Laura's Mister P is not as wonderful as he first seemed. *JZ*

Movie rating: *7

Visual: video + dvd

Off the record: **BILLY BRAGG** was born Steven William Bragg on the 20th December '57 in Barking, Essex, England. Inspired by the CLASH, he formed Peterborough-based R&B/punk band, Riff Raff, in 1977. After releasing a string of indie 7" singles, (including the wonderfully titled 'I Wanna Be A Cosmonaut'), the band split in 1981, BRAGG incredibly going off to join the army. Thankfully, a career in the military wasn't to be though, and he bought himself out after only 90 days. Complete with amplifier and guitar, he busked around Britain, finally furnished with some studio time in 1983 courtesy of 'Charisma' indie subsidiary, 'Utility'. The result was 'Life's A Riot With Spy Vs Spy', and with the help and distribution of new label 'Go! Discs', the record finally hit the UK Top 30 in early '84. BRAGG's stark musical backdrop (for the most part, a roughly strummed electric guitar) and even starker vocals, belied a keen sense of melody and passionate, deeply humane lyrics. 'The Milkman Of Human Kindness' was a love song of the most compassionate variety which illustrated that Billy approached politics from a humanist perspective rather than a soapbox. After seeing firsthand how Thatcher had decimated mining communities, BRAGG's songs became more overtly political. 'Brewing Up With Billy Bragg' (1984) opened with the fierce 'It Says Here', but again the most affecting moments were to be found on heartfelt love songs like the wistful 'St. Swithin's Day'. It would be another two years before he released a new album, in the interim taking time to make his Top Of The Pops debut and play a lead role in the political 'Red Wedge' campaign. A well intentioned but ultimately hopeless initiative to persuade people to vote Labour, BRAGG toured alongside the Style Council, the Communards and Morrissey. As the Conservatives romped home to another sickening victory, BRAGG licked his wounds and bounced back with a third album, 'Talking With The Taxman About Poetry' (1986). His most successful and accomplished release to date, the record spawned the classic single, 'Levi Stubbs' Tears' as well as the Johnny Marr collaboration, 'Greetings To The New Brunette'. Recording a cover of 'She's Leaving Home' with Cara Tivey, BRAGG found himself at No.1 when the song was released as the B-side to Wet Wet Wet's cover of 'With A Little Help From My Friends', the not inconsiderable proceeds going to the Childline charity. BRAGG's next album, 'Worker's Playtime' (1988), saw a move away from the sparse accompaniment of old, while lyrically the record focused more on matters of the heart than the ballot box. 'The Internationale' (1990), meanwhile, was BRAGG's most political work to date, while 'Don't Try This At Home' (1991), enlisted a cast of musicians to flesh out the sound, a tactic that elicited mixed results. A 5-year hiatus (in which time he became a dad), Billy returned to the Top 20 with 'William Bloke' (1996), his first for 'Cooking Vinyl' records. *BG & MCS*

Various Artists (new score: BILLY BRAGG *)

Sep 96. (cd) *TVT Soundtrax; <TVT 8050-2>* ☐ [–]
– She's got a new spell / Not given lightly (FRENTE) / Anticipated anger scene (*) / Going home (GREENHOUSE 27) / Fourteenth of February (*) / 2AM (CATHERINE) / Argue in the kitchen scene (*) / The diving bell (JOE HENRY) / Must I paint you a picture (BILLY BRAGG) / Requiem (PAL SHAZAR) / Alone for the moment (the SEA AND CAKE) / Notice mole scene (*) / Wings of desire (JERRY BURNS) / Small wonder (SHRIMP BOAT) / You wake up my neighbourhood (BILLY BRAGG) / Driving home scene (*).

S/track review: Picture BILLY BRAGG and chances are it's one of a fist in the air, soapbox-standing, Socialist, protesting troubadour with an ear for a tune and an intense hatred of anything that hints remotely at blue blood. What is often overlooked is BRAGG's ability to write charming, melodic pieces that capture the essence of a particular feeling or moment. Think 'A Lover Sings' or (that Kirsty MacColl song) 'A New England'. 'WALKING AND TALKING' sees BRAGG at his best in this respect, with classics such as 'She's Got A New Spell', 'You Wake Up My Neighbourhood' and 'Must I Paint You A Picture', side by side with score cue, 'Fourteenth Of February'. However, outside of these tracks, the soundtrack lacks much in the way of vibrancy or class. FRENTE's 'Not Given Lightly' is a wistful tune, reminiscent of a Sixpence None The Richer B-side, while the 'The Diving Bell' by JOE HENRY is a folk-tinged ballad that could easily be a Bob Dylan throwaway. PAL SHAZAR's feisty 'Requiem' may be the only other highlight on an album that is good without being great, hardly exciting the Bard of Barking's more devout parishioners. *CM*

Album rating: *5.5

☐ WANG CHUNG segment
(⇒ TO LIVE AND DIE IN L.A.)

☐ WAR segment
(⇒ YOUNGBLOOD)

WATERMELON MAN

1970 (US 100m) Columbia Pictures (R)

Film genre: urban comedy

Top guns: dir: **Melvin VAN PEEBLES** / s-w: Herman Raucher

Stars: Godfrey Cambridge *(Jeff Gerber)* → COTTON COMES TO HARLEM → COME BACK, CHARLESTON BLUE → FRIDAY FOSTER, Estelle Parsons *(Althea Gerber)* → I WALK THE LINE → DICK TRACY, Howard Caine *(Mr. Townsend)*, Mantan Moreland *(cashier)*, D'Urville Martin *(bus driver)* ← a TIME TO SING / → the FINAL COMEDOWN → HELL UP IN HARLEM → BOOK OF NUMBERS → BLACK CAESAR → the SOUL OF NIGGER CHARLEY → FIVE ON THE BLACK HAND SIDE → SHEBA, BABY → DOLEMITE → DISCO 9000, Kay Kimberley *(Erica)*, Kay E. Kuter *(Dr. Wainwright)* → GRAND THEFT PARSONS, Charles Lampkin *(Dr. Catlin)*, ← CORNBREAD, EARL AND ME, **Paul H. Williams** *(employment office clerk)* → PHANTOM OF THE PARADISE → the DOORS, **Melvin VAN PEEBLES** *(sign painter)*

Storyline: Melvin Van Peebles turned the tables on racism and kickstarted his career in this tale of a white bigot who wakes up one morning to find that his skin has turned black. *BG*

Movie rating: *6

Visual: video + dvd

Off the record: (see below)

MELVIN VAN PEEBLES

1970. (lp) *Beverly Hills; <BHS 26>* ☐ ☐
– Love, that's America / Great guy / Eviction scene / Soul'd on you / Where are the children / Erica's theme / Fugue 1 / Fugue 2 / Fugue 3.

S/track review: Great title! But the credit for that should probably go to Herbie Hancock, whose much-covered 1962 classic is entirely absent here. MELVIN VAN PEEBLES, by contrast, makes music in which his vigour is the outstanding feature, like this soundtrack's 'Soul'd On You', which finds him delivering a would-be comically over-wrought vocal on a hapless musical steal of 'Heard It Through The Grapevine'. Long before the Blaxploitation boom that would kick off with his own 'SWEET SWEETBACK'S BAADASSSSS SONG', VAN PEEBLES had established that he was a movie director who would write his own music – and sing on it too, by golly. And while it's hard to deny a man his creative expression, it's also possible VAN PEEBLES – an interesting character who was writing French plays in 1960s Paris – might have prospered better with more frugal marshalling of his talents. Mercifully his vocal on the opening so-loose-it's-saggy blues workout 'Love, That's America' is actually shouted, and the satirical polemic that results turns out to be the one memorable thing on the album. Elsewhere, apart from an embarrassing lullaby sung by ESTELLE PARSONS, it's generic instrumental stuff with added quirks that, like everything else, are hard to make out through the hapless production. Guess who was the producer. *ND*

Album rating: *4

☐ Roger WATERS
(⇒ PINK FLOYD)

WAVELENGTH

1983 (US 87m) New World Pictures (PG)

Film genre: Sci-fi/space movie

Top guns: s-w + dir: Mike Gray

Stars: Robert Carradine *(Bobby Sinclair)* ← the LONG RIDERS ← JOYRIDE → the LIZZIE McGUIRE MOVIE, **Cherie Currie** *(Iris Longacre)* <= the RUNAWAYS =>, Keenan Wynn *(Dan)*, James Hess *(Col. James MacGruder)*, Cal Bowman *(Gen. Milton Ward)*, Bobby Di Cicco *(Marvin Horn)* ← I WANNA HOLD YOUR HAND

Storyline: Fading rock musician, Bobby Sinclaire, and his lover Iris *(played by "real" rock musician, Cherie Currie!)*, discover small benign extraterrestrials held captive by an unscrupulous American government – where have I heard that one before? When it is time for some experiments, it is also time for the couple, E.T.-like to send them home. *MCS*

Movie rating: *5.5

Visual: video

Off the record: (see above)

TANGERINE DREAM

1983. (lp/c) *Silva Screen; <STV/CTV 81207>* ☐ ☐
– Alien voices / Wavelength (main title) / Desert drive / Mojave (end title) / Healing / Breakout / Alien goodbyes / Spaceship / Church theme / Sunset drive / Airshaft / Alley walk / Cyro lab / Running through the hills / Campfire theme / Mojave (end title reprise). *(UK cd-iss. Jan89 also on 'Varese Sarabande'; VCD 47223)*

S/track review: TANGERINE DREAM'S third official soundtrack effort (the first two being 'SORCERER' in 1977 and 'THIEF' in 1981), marked a switch into minimalistic soundscapes, which the trio (EDGAR FROESE, CHRISTOPHER FRANKE & JOHANNES SCHMOELLING) had been experimenting with during the previous decade. Melody and accessibility were key words for what had been a little trial of sorts for the Euro-tronic synth-meisters. Guitarist FROESE, who had recently delivered his own "solo" soundtrack, 'KAMIKAZE 1989', was still creating that ambient, New Age feel to 'Dream's compositions; example the main title theme and the glorious, 'Alien Goodbyes'. *MCS*

Album rating: *5.5

the WAY IT IS

1986 (US 80m b&w) Spring

Film genre: crime mystery

Top guns: s-w + dir: Eric Mitchell

Stars: Kai Eric *(Orpheus)*, Boris Major *(Eurydice)*, **Vincent GALLO** *(Victor)*, Mark Boone Jr. *(Hank)* → LAST EXIT TO BROOKLYN → the BEATNICKS, Steve Buscemi *(Willy)* → MYSTERY TRAIN → RESERVOIR DOGS → PULP FICTION → AIRHEADS → the WEDDING SINGER → COFFEE AND CIGARETTES → ROMANCE & CIGARETTES → the FUTURE IS UNWRITTEN, Jessica Stutchbury *(Vera)*

Storyline: As Vincent Gallo himself put it "Eric would ask a bunch of Lower East Side actors to portray a bunch of Lower East Side actors mimicking Jean Cocteau's Orpheus". Matters are complicated when the lead actress dies in mysterious circumstances, leaving the rest of the cast under suspicion. *BG*

Movie rating: *3

Visual: none

Off the record: (see below)

VINCENT GALLO

1992. (ltd-lp) *Rojo; <RJ 1001>* ☐ ☐
– Her smell theme / One day in May / The girl of her dreams / A brown lung hollering / The brown blues / The Way It Is waltz / Glad to be unhappy / Brown storm poem / Goodbye sadness hello death / Brown Italy / Drowning in brown / And a colored sky colored grey / Fishing for some friends / The dark and slow brown / Six laughs once happy / Sunny and cloudy / No more papa mama / Fatty and Skinny / Somewhere brown downtown / Brown orpheus / Her smell theme (reprise).

S/track review: Originally released six years after the film in a vinyl-only pressing of 1000 copies, VINCENT GALLO's debut soundtrack was belatedly issued on CD in 2002 as a significant chunk of 'Warp's 'Music For Film' anthology (and hot on the heels of his acclaimed solo debut, 'When'). In the anthology's brutally candid sleevenotes, GALLO describes how, way back in the early 80s, the debut album of his band Bohack came out "sounding like it was recorded in some primitive claustrophobic netherworld". Organic might be a better adjective than primitive, but 'The WAY IT IS' sounds summoned from similarly murky depths, so contingent is it upon echo and unvoiced misgiving. And, despite being recorded a decade and a half earlier, this record pretty much provided the blueprint for the soundtrack to GALLO's directorial debut, 'BUFFALO 66' (1998), an artistic arc which – with the inclusion of even earlier, previously unreleased excerpts from 'DOWNTOWN 81' – is easier to chart within the wider context of the anthology. Armed with his trusty Ampex 350 two-track, the amateur auteur recorded himself, for the most part, picking out oblique guitar and bass parts, leaving their vibrations hanging in the air like a judge passing sentence. He answers the strangely bovine-like pleas of 'A Brown Lung Hollering' with a series of cold, metallic clanks, and rings up the sum total of his minor-chord disaffection with the trill of a cash register-like bell on 'Six Laughs Once Happy'. Yet as adept as he is at dank, basement minimalism, he tempers it with hints of chamber jazz, Bohemian lyricism – most obviously in the dolefully elegant clarinet melody to 'Her Smell Theme' – and out-of-orbit ambience. Some of his mellotron experiments even suggest a Lower East Side Popol Vuh, especially 'Good Bye Sadness, Hello Death', the title of which – along with such joyfully monikered fragments as 'Glad To Be Unhappy' and 'Fishing For Some Friends' – tells its own story. Like Tindersticks, GALLO specialises in alchemising misery, even if he rarely completes the process. *BG*

Album rating: *6

Jimmy WEBB

Born: 15 Aug'46, Elk City, Oklahoma, USA. A master of the songwriting art, JIMMY WEBB penned some of the 60s biggest, most ornate hits before emerging from the anonymity of label credits to forge a low-key performing career in his own right. As adept at epic balladry as soaring, Bacharach-esque pop, WEBB was famously a millionaire by the time he was 21, furnishing hugely successful material for GLEN CAMPBELL, Fifth Dimension and Richard Harris amongst others. Yet despite the highly lucrative and Grammy-winning nature of his trade, WEBB longed for the recognition and kudos of the stars he was writing for. In tandem with the beginnings of his own solo career among the burgeoning, L.A. based singer-songwriter set, he began composing for films, a natural enough move given the often highly elaborate, atmospheric sweep of his pen. While WEBB had previously worked on the theme music for romantic comedy, 'How Sweet It Is!' (1968), his first full commission was an unreleased score for Frank Perry's analytical western, 'Doc' (1971). The man's budding celluloid career wasn't boosted any with his involvement in a critically lambasted adaptation of Desmond Morris' best-selling potted-anthropolgy classic, 'The NAKED APE' (1973), despite a brave effort to complement the film's skewed humour. It'd be 1979 before he worked in film again, scoring Robert Markowitz's romantic drama, 'VOICES'. Three years later, he collaborated with AMERICA on the soundtrack to much loved kids animation, 'The LAST UNICORN' (1982). With the meandering folk-rockers (better known for their early 70s hit, 'A Horse With No Name') having previously contributed to the songwriter's unreleased 1976 album, 'Jim, The World's Greatest Lover', WEBB returned the favour by composing and arranging the film's haunting score. His music for Vietnam POW drama, 'The Hanoi Hilton' (1987) remains unreleased, as does his score to low budget road movie, 'The Clean And The Narrow' (2000), with WEBB tending to concentrate on intermittent, critically acclaimed solo recordings and theatre work over the last couple of decades. *BG*

- **filmography** (composer) –

Doc *(1971)* / **the Naked Ape** *(1973 OST =>)* / **Voices** *(1979 OST w/ V/A =>)* / **the Last Unicorn** *(1982 OST by AMERICA =>)* / the Hanoi Hilton *(1987)* / the Clean And Narrow *(2000)*

☐ Craig WEDREN
(⇒ SHUDDER TO THINK)

☐ Eric WEISSBERG, Marshall BRICKMAN & . . .
(⇒ DELIVERANCE)

WENT TO CONEY ISLAND ON A MISSION FROM GOD . . . BE BACK BY FIVE

1998 (US 94m) Evenmore Entertainment / Phaedra Cinema (R)

Film genre: psychological/buddy comedy/drama

Top guns: s-w: (+ dir) Richard Schenkman, Jon Cryer

Stars: Jon Cryer *(Daniel)* ← DUDES ← PRETTY IN PINK, Rick Stear *(Stan)*, Rafael Baez *(Richie)*, Ione Skye *(Gabby)* ← FOUR ROOMS ← GAS, FOOD LODGING ← WAYNE'S WORLD / → SOUTHLANDER, Frank Whaley *(Skee-ball Weasel)* ← PULP FICTION ← the DOORS / SHAKE, RATTLE & ROLL: AN AMERICAN LOVE STORY → CHELSEA WALLS → the HOTTEST STATE, Peter Gerety *(Maurice)*, Akili Prince *(Julie)*, Aesha Waks *(Cindy Goldclang)*, Jesse Lenat *(Jojo)* → TO HELL AND BACK, Eugene Byrd *(teenage friend)* ← WHITEBOYS ← DEAD MAN / → 8 MILE, Wilson Jermaine Heredia *(Darcy)* → RENT

Storyline: The mission, which Daniel and Stan decide to accept, is to find their long-lost friend Richie, last seen wandering around babbling incoherently at Coney Island amusement park (luckily closed). On a freezy winter's day they meet a succession of oddball characters and remember the early days with their elusive chum. Will they find their buddy after their roller-coaster ride through life's ups and downs? *JZ*

Movie rating: *6.5

Visual: dvd

Off the record: MIDGE URE was born James Ure, 10 Oct'53, Cambuslang, nr. Glasgow, Scotland. Although he's fallen out of the limelight in recent years, MIDGE URE was one of the 80s most visible Scottish pop/rock stars as the suave lead singer of synth-poppers Ultravox. Almost a decade before the band reached their commercial peak, URE was making his first mark in the music business as the lead singer of teenybop heart-throbs, Slik. Originally formed as Salvation, the group topped the UK chart with 'Forever And Ever' in 1974. Dissatisfied with their bubblegum pop sound, URE subsequently turned down an offer to join an early incarnation of the SEX PISTOLS before eventually teaming up with erstwhile Pistol, Glen Matlock, to form the Rich Kids; during this period he was also part of the Zones and PVC2. The aforementioned project lasted one album, 'Ghosts Of Princes In Towers' (1978), before Midge went on to front a revamped version of Ultravox in spring '79. Originally led by John Foxx and trading in Roxy Music-style art-rock, Ultravox benefited from the injection of new creative blood and became part of the burgeoning synth-led New Romantic movement. All glacial European glamour and grandiose pretension, 1981's 'Vienna' single made the band a household name and URE a pop star. With his talent for taking po-faced but melodic art-pop to the masses, he also had a hand in the success of Visage, the Steve Strange-fronted act which scored with the classic 'Fade To Grey' around the same time. Ever the musical magpie, Midge had even found time to replace Gary Moore as a touring guitarist with Thin Lizzy at the turn of the decade. Hardly surprising then, that he initiated his own solo career in 1982 with the single, 'I Can't Even Touch You'. Although it flopped, a follow-up cover of Tom Rush's 'No Regrets' made the Top 10, while a link-up with Japan's Mick Karn via 'After A Fashion' scraped into the Top 40 a year later. Fans would have to hold their breath for a full album as URE subsequently teamed up with Bob Geldof to co-write and co-ordinate the Band Aid famine relief project in late '84. The resulting track, 'Do They Know It's Christmas', wiped the floor with the Xmas No.1 competition, selling millions in the process and spurring Geldof on to initiate Live Aid the following summer. Mid '85 also marked URE's first solo No.1, 'If I Was', a markedly pop-hued departure from his Ultravox work. With the band temporarily put on ice, the singer had also recorded a debut solo album, 'The Gift' (1985), whence sprang an additional two minor hits, 'That Certain Smile' and 'Call Of The Wild'. Following the dissolution of Ultravox in 1987, URE concentrated on a full-time solo career and released sophomore set, 'Answers To Nothing' (1988). While it made the Top 40, the album failed to spawn a major hit and for the first time in his lengthy career, Midge's Midas touch looked to be deserting him. 'Cold Cold Heart' furnished the commercially ailing star with his first Top 20 hit in over 5 years as 'Arista' attempted to relaunch his career in 1991. Although the accompanying album, 'Pure', scraped the Top 40, it'd be a further half-decade before URE again re-emerged. Predictably, 'Breathe' (1996) failed to resuscitate the man's domestic fortunes although after being used in a European ad campaign, the title track scaled both the German and Italian charts in 1999! The new millennium, meanwhile, found Midge completing the soundtrack to acclaimed drama, 'WENT TO CONEY ISLAND . . .', as well as releasing a fifth solo album, 'Move Me'. *BG & MCS*

—

MIDGE URE

Oct 00. (cd) *Evenmore; <none>* ☐ ☐
– The Gabby variations / High noon on 103rd Street / Surgery / Stan's disco / Stealing candy / Arriving at Coney / Midday suite / Bumper cars – Locket stealing / Pawnshop – Jerry Mahoney / Finding Richie again / Allegra / Richie calls his mom / Wedding / Lost point (GIRLFRIEND) / Return to Skeeball.

S/track review: MIDGE URE was of course a man more famous for other activities. In his backseat involvement with Band Aid, Live Aid, 80s-era Ultravox and his solo UK chart-topper, 'If I Was', he finally delivered his one and only soundtrack to 1998's 'WENT TO CONEY ISLAND . . .'. Far removed from the rock-pop-synth of the aforementioned Ultravox, this OST is composed, produced and performed (not sung!) by URE himself; this was bar one track, 'Lost Point', by new-ish melancholia duo, GIRLFRIEND (aka Robin Cryer & actor Phil Hyland). From opening cue, 'The Gabby Variations', to closing number, 'Return To Skeeball', Midge gets engrossed in some dirty electronica, while short-ish pieces in between such as the self-explanatory 'High Noon' (very Morricone!) & 'Stan's Disco', show his versatility. Follow-on cue, 'Stealing Candy', switches disco into techno-rave, as does the longer Tortoise-like dirge, 'Midday Suite'. Turning the volume and tempo down somewhat, the medley of 'Bumper Cars / Locket Stealing' keeps the pace flowing if not sedate. Ditto the Tangerine Dream-like 'Pawnshop / Jerry Mahoney', the longest track on the CD at nearly 5 minutes. Not included on the CD is a garbageband rendition of Adam & The Ant's 'Ant Music'. Not the greatest of rock soundtracks, but then again it's not the worst, showing URE had an unexpected knowledge of things cinematic. *MCS*

Album rating: *4.5

☐ Howard WERTH & AUDIENCE segment (⇒ BRONCO BULLFROG)

☐ Paul WESTERBERG segment (⇒ OPEN SEASON)

WHALE MUSIC

1994 (Can/US 107m) Alliance Atlantis Communications

Film genre: psychological drama

Top guns: dir: Laurence Horricks (+ s-w), Richard J. Lewis (au: Paul Quarrington)

Stars: Maury Chaykin *(Desmond Howl)*, Cyndy Preston *(Claire Lowe)* → MADONNA: INNOCENCE LOST, Paul Gross *(Daniel Howl)*, Ken Welsh *(Kenneth Sexston)*, Jennifer Dale *(Fay Ginzburg-Howl)*, Blu Mankuma *(Mookie Saunders)*, Alan Jordan *(Sal Goneau)*, **Jim Byrnes** *(Dewey Moore)*

Storyline: Retired rock star Desmond Howl lives the life of a hermit on the Canadian coast. Nowadays his only dream is to create whale music in his recording studio in the hope of attracting the giant creatures to the shoreline. However the only thing he manages to attract is young runaway Claire, who tries to integrate him back into society and win his heart. *JZ*

Movie rating: *6.5

Visual: video

Off the record: **RHEOSTATICS** had been on the go since 1980 when they were actually billed as Rheostatics And The Trans Canada Soul Patrol. Formed in Etobicoke, Ontario, Canada, the line-up finally settled down to the quartet of strumming vocalists Dave Bidini and Martin Tielli, plus bassist/vocalist Tim Vesely and drummer Dave Clark. A long-awaited debut LP, mischievously titled 'Greatest Hits' was finally in the shops in 1987, a favourite among the alternative college brigade due to the fact it enveloped a jangly cult hit, 'The Ballad Of Wendel Clark Parts I & II'. A four-year hiatus was eventually broken when the quartet released their "fishy" sophomore set, 'Melville' (1991), a complex affair that harboured a cover of Gordon Lightfoot's 'The Wreck Of Edmund Fitzgerald'. It also led to a contract with 'Capitol' records. Naming their third album, 'Whale Music' (1992), after the Rock novel by Paul Quarrington, it was no surprise then, that when the book was turned into a movie shortly afterwards, RHEOSTATICS were commissioned to do the score. The confusion sets in when there were actually two 'WHALE MUSIC' albums on release, several instrumental tracks from the score landing on 1994's lyrical piece 'Introducing Happiness', released prior to the soundtrack itself. When Clark left for other waters, and the band found they were dropped by 'Sire', the remaining trio recruited multi-instrumentalist, Don Kerr. Although never quite chalking up significant sales worldwide, RHEOSTATICS are Canada's nearly-lads, the ones that got away, but ever so Tragically Hip. *MCS*

—

the RHEOSTATICS (score: George Blondheim)

Nov 94. (cd) *Sire; <245836-2>* ☐ Canada ☐
– Song of congregation / Find me Mookie Saunders / Torque torque / Desmond's reflections / Dez's lament – Claire / Ocean courtship / Song of flight / Fried brain / Song of danger / Song of courtship / Goodbye, Claire / Song of sadness / Euqrot euqrot / End title / Deconstruct me, Claire.

S/track review: With a tale about a Brian Wilson-type eccentric music guru in hiding, it's hardly surprising RHEOSTATICS sound like the Beach Boys, albeit with a prog-rock tint (think Yes circa 'Roundabout'). There was plenty evidence to support this unusual fusion, example the multi-layered 'Torque Torque' (subliminally reversed later in the set), from which you can just about hear

Jon Anderson and Co shining through. Alongside the odd synth'd "whale noises", symphonic pop gets its fair share, three versions of the Canadian hit single 'Claire' are masterfully produced out of the hat when things get a little melancholy in places; 10cc would be proud of you lads. If there was ever an album so appropriately titled it has to be 'WHALE MUSIC', the strong elements exuding from the very mammal's being and always in the forefront. Ok, composer, George Blondheim, does get in several orchestral pieces, the best being 'Desmond's Reflections' and 'Ocean Courtship', but they seem to fit in to the RHEOSTATICS moods. The trouble with the album, is that it goes in too many directions, with rock shanties overlapping most of the latter half of the album includes 'Song Of Courtship' and 'Song Of Sadness' – think Hank Marvin playing folk music. A fine album, not a great one, and a word to the wise: watch you don't buy the 1992 'Capitol' records 'Whale Music', although the OST is a bit pricey. *MCS*

Album rating: *6

– spinoff hits, etc. –

the RHEOSTATICS: Claire

1994. (cd-s) [–] Canada [–]

WHALE RIDER

2002 (NZ 101m) New Zealand Film Commission (PG-13)

Film genre: teen/domestic drama

Top guns: s-w + dir: Niki Caro (au: Witi Ihimaera)

Stars: Keisha Castle-Hughes *(Pai)*, Rawiri Paratene *(Koro)*, Vicky Haughton *(Nanny Flowers)*, Grant Roa *(Uncle Rawiri)*, Cliff Curtis *(Porourangi)* ← the INSIDER, Mana Taumaunu *(Hemi)*, Rawinia Clarke *(Miro)*, Roi Taimana *(Rewi)*, Rachel House *(Shilo)*, Tammy Davis *(Dog)*

Storyline: The Whangara people of eastern New Zealand believe that they are descended from Paikea, who hitched a lift from a friendly whale when his canoe capsized. Since then the chief has always been the first-born male of the ruling family, but when mum and baby boy die in childbirth, daughter Pai should by rights take over. However, grandfather Koro is determined to maintain tradition and insists that a boy becomes chief. It's up to Pai to give grandad a bit of a fight. *JZ*

Movie rating: *7.5

Visual: dvd

Off the record: (see below)

LISA GERRARD: Whalerider

Jul 03. (cd) *4 a.d.; (CAD 2304CD) <72304>* [ ] Jun03 [ ]
– Paikea legend / Journey away / Rejection / Biking home / Ancestors / Suitcase / Pai calls the whales / Reiputa / Disappointed / They came to die / Pai theme / Paikea's whale / Empty water / Waka in the sky / Go forward.

S/track review: As stated on the back cover itself, 'WHALE RIDER' (or 'Whalerider') is composed and arranged by Melbourne-born LISA GERRARD, her first solo OST after her outings with Pieter Bourke (see 'The INSIDER') and the disbandment of Dead Can Dance. Her ethereal vox had been utilized to great effect on Hans Zimmer's score to Ridley Scott's sword-and-sandal epic, 'Gladiator' (2000), to pick out one highlight from her move into film music. 'WHALE RIDER' starts as it means to go on with 'Paikea Legend', a track full of what you might expect: eerie whale-like noises (the dialogue is by the movie's rising star, Keisha Castle-Hughes). Taking virtually the same theme, 'Journey Away' adds local Maori percussion to the forefront. What one does miss is GERRARD's distinctive vocal cords, but these shortish stints garner only a sort of new age water music. Track 4, 'Biking Home' (with actor Rawiri Paratene speaking at the end), is pleasantly bright and uplifting and yes, Lisa's cherished voice finally gets in on the act. Ditto 'Ancestors' and 'Suitcase'. With further intro dialogue from Keisha, 'Pai Calls The Whales' finally sees GERRARD competing with orchestra, while follow-on track, 'Reiputa', just carries on the theme. If there's one shallow gripe, it's that most of the good pieces are stopped in their tracks before they get into full flow. The aptly-titled 'Disappointed' & 'They Came To Die' are indeed darker and funereal, but rather than taking the music forward, they drown in their own proverbial tears. PHIL POMEROY's piano on 'Pai Theme' has another touch of classical about it, rather than any rock ethos; the brief 'Empty Water' is also too short. KERIANA THOMSON & THE WANANGA BOYS call to arms on 'Paikea's Whale', and it's thanks to the people of Ngati Kondhi, Whangara, performing the Haka on two tracks ('Waka In The Sky' & finale 'Go Forward'), that gave the set a little oomph and spirit. But one can hear this sound (minus orchestra of course) during an All Blacks rugby team warm-up. On its own without the aid of the film, 'WHALE RIDER' fails to come to the surface for long periods of time. Is that its intention. *MCS*

Album rating: *5.5

WHAT'S UP, TIGER LILY?

1966 (US/Japan 80m) American International Pictures (PG)

Film genre: spy spoof/comedy

Top guns: s-w: Senkichi Taniguchi (+ dir), Woody Allen (+ dir), Kazuo Yamada

Stars: Tatsuya Mihashi *(Phil Moskowitz)*, Mie Hama *(Terri Yaki)*, Akiko Wakabayashi *(Suki Yaki)*, Tadeo Nakamaru *(Shepherd Wong)*, Susumu Kurobe *(Wing Fat)*, Woody Allen *(narrator/host/voices)*, **the LOVIN' SPOONFUL:- John Sebastian, Zal Yanovsky, Joe Butler, Steve Boone** *(performers)*

Storyline: For his debut feature Woody Allen resourcefully grafted a whole new script onto an existing Japanese spy movie, tracing the proto-Austin Powers antics of agent Phil Moskowitz as he attempts to prevent a top secret salad recipe falling into the wrong hands. *BG*

Movie rating: *6

Visual: video + dvd

Off the record: The **LOVIN' SPOONFUL** (see own entry)

---

the LOVIN' SPOONFUL

Sep 66. (lp) *Kama Sutra; <KLP/+S 8053>* [ ] [–]
– (introduction to Flick) / POW / Gray prison blues / POW revisited / Unconscious minuet / Fishin' blues / Respoken / A cool million / Speakin' of spoken / Lookin' to spy / Phil's love theme / (end title).

S/track review: Coming hot on the heels of the LOVIN' SPOONFUL's monster No.1, 'Summer In The City', this soundtrack materialised at the height of the band's fame, recorded in a stop-gap between tours. As such it has the lightweight but durable stamp of the JOHN SEBASTIAN school of songwriting, with the same jug-band jam feel which made even their flimsiest early efforts a pleasure. The opening Woody Allen dialogue is funny once or twice but best skipped over for 'Pow!', a fast-talking, harmonica-wailing blast of a main title, developed in a Greek/ Middle Eastern-tinged instrumental version. The other highlight is 'Fishin' Blues', a traditional folk tune covered by John Martyn (on his 1968 album, 'The Tumbler') amongst others, here performed in typically excitable style but deliciously revisited as a loping, bass-and-mandolin epilogue. 'Respoken' is the sole track in the wistful, woolly-head pop vein of the hit singles while the evocative 'Lookin' To Spy' achieves at least some success in translating the 'SPOONFUL's airy acoustics into film score noir. The incongruously titled 'Phil's Love Theme', meanwhile, betrays unlikely echoes of the kind of apocalyptic folk which Uncle Tupelo would carry off so well in the early 90s. Worth picking up in its own right, this album was most recently packaged with 'YOU'RE A BIG BOY NOW' as a good value two-fer. *BG*

Album rating: *5

WHEN THE WIND BLOWS

1986 (UK/Belg 80m) Film Four / Penguin Books / TVC London (PG)

Film genre: post-nuclear animation drama

Top guns: dir: Jimmy T. Murakami / s-w: Raymond Briggs (+ au)

Voices: Peggy Ashcroft *(Hilda Bloggs)*, John Mills *(Jim Bloggs)* ← the FAMILY WAY / → WHO'S THAT GIRL, Robin Houston *(announcer)*, James Russell, **David Dundas, Matt Irving**

Storyline: A very British animation, and ultimately a crushingly poignant one as Jim Bloggs – ever the optimist and the kind of good citizen who follows government directives to the letter, and has a bit of trouble with his abbreviations – and his wife Hilda – a matronly pensioner who grumbles about communists and beatniks when she's not reminiscing about WWII – literally waste away in the pathetic ruins of their home after a nuclear strike. *BG*

Movie rating: *5.5

Visual: video + dvd

Off the record: David Dundas (b. 2 Jun'45, Oxford, England) was actually the son of a marquess. DD had a one-off Top 3 hit in 1976 with TV-ad promoted single, 'Jeans On' (the follow-up, 'Another Funny Honeymoon', scraped into the Top 30), while he subsequently co-scored the music to the cult black-comedy flick, 'Withnail & I' (1987). **Matt Irving** played in the bands for Paul Young and Manfred Mann's Earth Band. *MCS*

Various Artists // ROGER WATERS & THE BLEEDING HEART BAND

Oct 86. (cd/c/lp) *Virgin; (CD/TC+/V 2406)* [ ] [-]
– When the wind blows (DAVID BOWIE) / Facts and figures (HUGH CORNWALL) / Brazilian (GENESIS) / What have they done (SQUEEZE) / The shuffle (PAUL HARDCASTLE) // The Russian missile / Towers of faith / Hilda's dream / The American bomber / The Anderson shelter / The British submarine / The attack / The fallout / Hilda's hair / Folded flags. *(re-iss. 1989 lp/c; OVED/+C 259)*

S/track review: Released the same year he finally left 'FLOYD, this quasi-solo project paved the way for ROGER WATERS' 'Radio K.A.O.S.' (1987). His session-anonymous BLEEDING HEART BAND turn out latter-period 'Floyd tropes aplenty – keening female backing vocals, tasteful sax mewling, Gilmour-ian guitar canvases; but the titular wind seems to have blown any real hooks right out the studio window. The World Trade Center-referencing 'Towers Of Faith' starts out relatively promisingly before spinning into snail-paced oblivion. Even the soulful tones of PAUL CARRACK can't bring much character to the pleasant but ultimately forgettable 'Folded Flags', with WATERS clumsily adapting 'Hey Joe' for the global stage. While his lyrics righteously pick their way through a minefield of religion and geopolitics, the harrowing dialogue excerpts reminisce on WWII as a subtext for the horrors of the nuclear age. In fact, the incidental pieces – which work perfectly in the film – are actually more engaging: the all-too-brief acoustic picking of 'Hilda's Dream', the nightmarish conflagration of screaming dissonance, Band Aid-style bells and red brick nostalgia that is 'The Attack'. Elsewhere, DAVID BOWIE supplies a functional theme tune while bloodless contributions from HUGH CORNWELL and PAUL HARDCASTLE prove that, in the 80s, the soulless chill of the Cold War wasn't confined to politics. GENESIS at least generate some period cheese with their Harold Faltermeyer-esque synth oddysey, 'The Brazilian'. Not so much the sound of a nuclear war as an under-reported border skirmish. *BG*

Album rating: *5

– spinoff hits, etc. –

DAVID BOWIE: When The Wind Blows / (instrumental)

Nov 86. (7"/7"sha-pic-d) *(VS/+S 906)* [44] [-]
(ext.dance-12"+=) *(VS 906-12)* – (dub).

WHERE THE BUFFALO ROAM

1980 (US 98m) Universal Pictures (R)

Film genre: buddy biopic/satire

Top guns: dir: Art Linson ← AMERICAN HOT WAX story / s-w: John Kaye ← AMERICAN HOT WAX (stories: Hunter S. Thompson → FEAR AND LOATHING IN LAS VEGAS)

Stars: Bill Murray *(Dr. Hunter S. Thompson)* ← the RUTLES / → CADDYSHACK → LITTLE SHOP OF HORRORS → LOST IN TRANSLATION → COFFEE AND CIGARETTES → the LIFE AQUATIC WITH STEVE ZISSOU, Peter Boyle *(Carl Lazlo, Esq.)* ← STEELYARD BLUES ← JOE / → WALKER → the IN CROWD, Bruno Kirby, Jr. *(Marty Lewis)* ← ALMOST SUMMER / → THIS IS SPINAL TAP → BIRDY → GOOD MORNING, VIETNAM → the BASKETBALL DIARIES → a SLIPPING-DOWN LIFE, Rene Auberjonois *(Harris)* → the LAST UNICORN → WALKER, R.G. Armstrong *(Judge Simpson)* → MEAN JOHNNY BARROWS ← PAT GARRETT & BILLY THE KID ← the FINAL COMEDOWN / → DICK TRACY, Danny Goldman *(porter)* ← the STRAWBERRY STATEMENT, Leonard Frey *(desk clerk)* ← the MAGIC CHRISTIAN, Rafael Campos *(Rojas)*, **DeWayne Jessie** *(superfan)* ← ANIMAL HOUSE ← THANK GOD IT'S FRIDAY ← CAR WASH ← SPARKLE, Leonard Gaines *(Blackie)*, Mark Metcalf *(Dooley)* ← ANIMAL HOUSE, Sonny Davis *(Stephanian)* → ROADIE → BAD CHANNELS, Nancy Parsons *(head nurse)* → PORKY'S REVENGE, Sunny Johnson *(Lil; nurse)* → ANIMAL HOUSE → FLASHDANCE, Craig T. Nelson *(cop on stand)* → the KILLING FIELDS, Cork Hubbert *(bell captain)* → LEGEND, Richard M. Dixon *(candidate)* ← GOOD TO SEE YOU AGAIN, ALICE COOPER

Storyline: Aviator shades forever shielding his eyes from common decency, a cigarette holder jammed into the corner of his mouth and sporting a wardbrobe's worth of tasteless shirts, Hunter S. Thompson forges gonzo journalism as an apparent byproduct of chaos as a life choice. He records it all on his trusty dictaphone in a voice which conjures an institutionalised Bugs Bunny, lurching from one frazzled misassignment to the next, joyfully divesting both his interviewees and fellow writers of their egos while trying his best to avoid the manic attentions of errant attorney Lazlo. The subsequent 'FEAR AND LOATHING IN LAS VEGAS' was another attempt to put Thompson's surreal humour on display. *BG*

Movie rating: *7

Visual: video + dvd

Off the record: DeWayne Jessie was performer Otis Day in the anarchic comedy feature, 'ANIMAL HOUSE'. *MCS*

Various Artists (score: NEIL YOUNG *)

Mar 80. (lp) *Backstreet; <5126>* [ ] [-]
– Buffalo stomp (*) / Ode to wild Bill, No.1 (*) / All along the watchtower (JIMI HENDRIX) / Lucy in the sky with diamonds (BILL

MURRAY) / Ode to wild Bill, No.2 (*) / Papa was a rolling stone (the TEMPTATIONS) / Home, home on the range (*) / Straight answers (dialogue; BILL MURRAY) / Highway 61 revisited (BOB DYLAN) / I can't help myself (sugar pie, honey bunch) (the FOUR TOPS) / Ode to wild Bill, No.3 (*) / Keep on chooglin' (CREEDENCE CLEARWATER REVIVAL) / Ode to wild Bill, No.4 (*) / Buffalo stomp refrain (*).

S/track review: Some of NEIL YOUNG's more obscure film work, for one of Bill Murray's most underrated performances. Coming as it did after the ferociousness of 'RUST NEVER SLEEPS' (1979), as YOUNG basked in multiple Rolling Stone awards, 'WHERE THE BUFFALO ROAM' was always going to signal another lurch towards the ditch. His orchestrations – performed by the Wild Bill Band Of Strings – aren't quite as self-consciously bombastic as his earlier 'Harvest' album, but even taking into account the humour and the cinematic sang-froid, they're indicative of that famous restlessness beginning to assert itself. YOUNG's basic premise for the solo pieces is to take a stars'n'stripes icon – in this case the old cowboy folk song, 'Home On The Range' – and mete out the same caustic treatment Jimi Hendrix unleashed on 'The Star Spangled Banner', splicing them with Van Dyke Parks-styled orchestral passages. He dubs it 'Ode To Wild Bill' and rations it over four versions, none more than a few bars long but all worth hearing for more than just novelty value. YOUNG also performs the first verse of 'Home On The Range' a capella, a surprisingly tender interlude with echoes of 'Helpless'. Save for the CREEDENCE wild card, 'Keep On Chooglin', the rest of the album gets nil points for imagination, although Murray's gleeful trashing of some overrated Beatles is worth sitting through at least once. *BG*

Album rating: *5.5

WHERE THE RIVERS FLOW NORTH

1994 (US 104m) Caledonia Pictures (PG-13)

Film genre: rural drama

Top guns: s-w: (+ dir) Jay Craven → a STRANGER IN THE KINGDOM / Don Bredes → a STRANGER IN THE KINGDOM (au: Howard Frank Mosher → a STRANGER IN THE KINGDOM)

Stars: Rip Torn *(Noel Lord)* ← FLASHPOINT ← SONGWRITER ← ONE-TRICK PONY ← PAYDAY ← YOU'RE A BIG BOY NOW / → the INSIDER, Tantoo Cardinal *(Bangor)* ← CANDY MOUNTAIN, Bill Raymond *(Wayne Quinn)* → a STRANGER IN THE KINGDOM, Mark Margolis *(New York Money)* ← SHORT EYES / → I SHOT ANDY WARHOL, Michael J. Fox *(Clayton Farnsworth)* ← LIGHT OF DAY ← CLASS OF 1984, George Woodard *(Mitchell)*, Yusef Bulos *(Armand)* ← SHORT EYES, John Griesemer *(Henry Coville)* → a STRANGER IN THE KINGDOM, Treat Williams *(Champ's manager)* ← FLASHPOINT ← HAIR

Storyline: It's 1927, and Noel Lord, a Vermont logger from the fictional region of Kingdom County, stands in the way of a power company intent on the building of a dam – at any cost. Pressurised with money and other bribes, Noel asks the advice of his Indian friend, Bangor, but even that doesn't budge the stubborn man. *MCS*

Movie rating: *5

Visual: video + dvd

Off the record: The **HORSE FLIES** (see below)

—

the HORSE FLIES

Aug 94. (cd/c) *Alcazar; <119>* [ ] [–]
– People go under (opening credits) / People go under in pieces / The woods / The town / Carnival lips (Kingdom common fair) / Charleston (Kingdom common) / People go under in pieces 2 (Noel closes dam game) / Cutting the trees / Warmth of your love (Bangor leaves) / The boat / The distempered bear waltz / The storm trucks / The bug loop / Log death / I flew far from water (burial) / Warmth of your love (end credits).

S/track review: Fusing innovation with a sense of tradition, genre-bending quintet, the HORSE FLIES, deliver their inaugural soundtrack to a film about the cold backwoods of Vermont. Looking remarkably like the main characters in the movie, the gothic-bluegrass outfit had released a handful of albums (including 'Human Fly' in '87 and 'Gravity Dance' in '92) before this commission, all wholly unique and creating quite a buzz in the folk music world. 'WHERE THE RIVERS FLOW NORTH' befits a band in cinematic transition, the fiddle-playing of JUDY HYMAN a feature on highlights such as 'The Storm Trucks' and 'Woods'. Her finger-pickin', banjo-strumming husband JEFF CLAUS also gets in on the act courtesy of the atmospheric, 'Charleston', while he also garners the others – banjo wizard RICHIE STEARNS, bassist JOHN HAYWARD and accordionist/keyboard-player PETER DODGE; but without percussionist Taki Masuko – to delight the listener with 'Warmth Of Your Love'. While instrumentation was at the forefront of this and every good HORSE FLIES set (CLAUS was the vocalist), there are sparse movements of sound accompanied by electronics (crickets and loons) that seems to lend a spiritual hand to the brooding, old-timey themes. An excellent album if one demands peace, love and a cabin in the forest. On a sad note, HAYWARD died of cancer in '97; the band subsequently splitting for other projects. *MCS*

Album rating: *7

WHITE ROCK

1977 (UK 76m) Shueisha / Worldmark Productions (PG)

Film genre: sports documentary

Top guns: s-w + dir: Tony Maylam

Stars: James Coburn *(narrator)* ← PAT GARRETT & BILLY THE KID ← CANDY / → YOUNG GUNS II → AFFLICTION → SHAKE, RATTLE & ROLL: AN AMERICAN LOVE STORY

Storyline: Director Tony Maylam takes the viewer to the 1976 Winter Olympics at Innsbruck, Austria, where the tuned-up athletes are ready to compete on snow and ice to search for that elusive gold medal. *MCS*

Movie rating: *5.5

Visual: video

Off the record: **RICK WAKEMAN** (see own entry)

—

RICK WAKEMAN

Jan 77. (lp/c) *A&M; (AMLH/CAM 64614) <SP 4614>* [14] Feb77 [ ]
– White rock / Searching for gold / The loser / The shoot / Lax'x / After the ball / Montezuma's revenge / Ice run. *(cd-iss. 1988; CDA 4614)*

S/track review: Former/current Yes keyboard wizard RICK WAKEMAN (he of pompous Prog classics, 'The Six Wives Of Henry VIII' and 'Journey To The Centre Of The Earth') took this commission as his 5th official project/album. The showman was no stranger to a bit of white rock, in fact, the long-haired extrovert had ill-advisedly taken his 1975 work, 'Myths & Legends Of King Arthur . . .', not on the road, but onto ice; appropriate venue – Wembley Pool. 'WHITE ROCK' was not his first score, that came via Ken Russell's (classical) rock bio-pic, 'LISZTOMANIA' (also 1975), which he shared credits with WHO frontman, ROGER

DALTREY. With all this experience behind him, and a recent UK Top 10 album, 'No Earthly Connection', pianist WAKEMAN (along with trusty drummer, TONY FERNANDEZ, and a little choir!) got back to basics for this mood-setting UK Top 20 OST. Highlights were undoubtedly the rock-fuelled title track, and others such as 'Lax'x', 'After The Ball' and the Romany-esque, 'Montezuma's Revenge'. A few decades later – with WAKEMAN no longer holding the rights to the soundtrack for some unearthly reason – he re-scored the entire set and released it as 'White Rock II' (1999). A unique development, indeed. *MCS*

Album rating: *6.5 / re-score *5.5

– spinoff releases, etc. –

RICK WAKEMAN: After The Ball / White Rock

Jun 77. (7") <1937> [–] [ ]

RICK WAKEMAN: White Rock II *(re-score)*

Jun 99. (cd) *Music Fusion; (MFCD 004) Musea; <4396>* [ ] 2001 [ ]
– Oriental iceman / Ice pie / Dancing on snowflakes / Nine ice groove / In the frame / Harlem slalom / Frost in space.

☐ Chris WHITLEY segment
(⇒ PIGS WILL FLY)

☐ WHO IS HARRY KELLERMAN AND WHY IS HE SAYING THOSE TERRIBLE THINGS ABOUT ME?
(⇒ Rock Musicals & Pop Fiction)

WHO LOVES THE SUN

2006 (Can 94m) Inferno Pictures Inc. / Christal Films

Film genre: domestic drama

Top guns: s-w + dir: Matt Bissonnette ← LOOKING FOR LEONARD

Stars: Lukas Haas *(Will Morrison)* ← LAST DAYS, Molly Parker *(Maggie Claire)* ← LOOKING FOR LEONARD ← HARD CORE LOGO, Adam Scott *(Daniel Bloom)* ← GIRL, R.H. Thomson *(Arthur Bloom)*, Wendy Crewson *(Mary Bloom)*

Storyline: Writer Daniel thinks he's seen a ghost when his inseparable childhood pal Will shows up after a mere five years' absence. Everything then comes out in the washing when Daniel admits to having had an affair with Will's wife Maggie, which caused Will to go off in the huff when he found out. As the ex-buddies square up for fisticuffs who should appear on the scene but the femme fatale herself, and she's none too pleased with Will's disappearing act either. *JZ*

Movie rating: *5.5

Visual: dvd

Off the record: (see below)

—

PORTASTATIC

Jun 06. (cd) *Merge; <MRG 277>* [ ] [–]
– Will's return / The sunset rock / Maggie at the dock / Fighting music / Seems like a long time ago / The search for Daniel / Nice one / Lively chase / Snake music / Nice strums / Do you want to know? / Maggie and Mary / Stretch waltz / Tremolo chase / A bit pastoral / Just like a real book / Is that Mars? / Will's return complete / Fishing music / Once nice piano / Last kiss music / Older summers.

S/track review: It'd been exactly five years since PORTASTATIC's last soundtrack attempt, 'LOOKING FOR LEONARD', although their previous album was the stunning 'Bright Ideas' in 2005. With mainman and multi-instrumentalist, MAC McCAUGHAN, shutting up the Superchunk shop for good to concentrate on his PORTASTATIC project, 'WHO LOVES THE SUN' (the title taken from a Velvet Underground song) bodes well for indie lo-fi in general. Gone is the Tropicalia/bossa nova beats that fenced-in their previous score, and in its place, luscious pastoral chamber pop complemented by a backing band of sorts (LAURA THOMAS on violin, CARRIE SHULL on oboe & English horn, TIM SMITH on flute, CHRIS EUBANK on cello & bass, LEE WATERS on drums, etc.). All of the instrumental pieces (twenty-two in total) are under three minutes, including several that don't make the minute mark. One can immediately hear (or think) Penguin Cafe Orchestra, Belle And Sebastian, or indeed any followers of the orchestral backing delights of the late, great, Nick Drake. Not everything on parade is melancholic: 'Fighting Music' for one, 'Lively Chase' is another, two tracks that stoke up the fire with a charming upbeat and flowing melody. The beauty of the film doesn't escape McCAUGHAN and Co at any stage, the repetitious and thematic 'Do You Want To Know?' and 'Stretch Waltz', cousins or even next-door neighbours in a musical sense. Although nothing strikes out as a wondrous individual track, the album/score as a whole – well produced and arranged – is an intimate introspection of modern-day domesticity. *MCS*

Album rating: *6

the WICKED LADY

1983 re-make (UK 98m) Columbia Pictures / United Artists (18)

Film genre: period-costume adventure/drama

Top guns: s-w: Michael Winner (+ dir) ← DEATH WISH II ← PLAY IT COOL / → SCREAM FOR HELP, Leslie Arliss (au: Magdalen King-Hall)

Stars: Faye Dunaway *(Lady Barbara Skelton)* ← LITTLE BIG MAN / → ALBINO ALLIGATOR, Alan Bates *(Jerry Jackson)* ← the ROSE / → the MOTHMAN PROPHECIES, John Gielgud *(Hogarth)* ← CHARIOTS OF FIRE, Denholm Elliott *(Sir Ralph Skelton)* ← BRIMSTONE & TREACLE ← PERCY ← HERE WE GO ROUND THE MULBERRY BUSH, Prunella Scales *(Lady Kinsclere)*, Oliver Tobias *(Kit Locksby)*, Glynis Barber *(Caroline)*, Joan Hickson *(Aunt Agatha)*, Derek Francis *(Lord Kingsclere)* ← FAREWELL PERFORMANCE, David Gant *(clergyman in church)* → SEEING DOUBLE

Storyline: Lady Barbara Skelton is the wicked woman in question, who steals bridegroom Sir Ralph away from her own sister Caroline. Soon bored with being a wealthy housewife, she takes up with dashing Captain Jackson, a notorious highwayman, and joins him on his nefarious exploits on Merrie England's rutted roads. But how long can she go undetected as her reputation grows and the hangman's noose draws ever tighter round her slender neck? *JZ*

Movie rating: *3.5

Visual: video

Off the record: TONY BANKS (b. Anthony George Banks, 27 Mar'50, East Heathly, Sussex, England) is better known for being stalwart keyboard-wizard with prog-rockers, Genesis. For three decades from their early incarnation in the mid-60s as the Garden Wall, the classically-trained BANKS and Co (i.e. PETER GABRIEL, Michael Rutherford, and later members PHIL COLLINS and Steve Hackett, etc.), hit the right chord with university students and mellotron fanatics alike on magical LPs from 'Trespass' & 'Nursery Cryme' (1970/71) to 'Invisible Touch' & 'We Can't Dance' (1986/91), with of course, the peerless 'Foxtrot' (1972), 'Selling England By The Pound' (1973), 'The Lamb Lies Down On Broadway' (1974) & 'Trick Of The Tail' (1976) squeezed in between. After co-writing his first movie score to 1978's 'The Shout' (alongside bassist Rutherford), Tony branched out as solo artist, releasing his inaugural LP, 'A Curious Feeling' (1979), which nearly reached the UK Top 20. BANKS delivered a second solo effort, 'The Fugitive' (with his vocals!), in 1983, while he also composed the music for 'The WICKED LADY' and subsequent Hollywood sequel, '2010: The Year We Made Contact'. The latter score didn't find favour with the film's producers, but was recycled for excerpts to 1985's 'Starship'; Tony produced another score to 'Quicksilver' (1986), and although it featured Marillion singer Fish, it was only available via a compilation. In 1989, and as always the force behind Genesis (incidentally, the trio issued a live one-off comeback set in 2007), Tony "popped-out" courtesy of a mainstream rock album under the title and billing, 'Bankstatement'. *MCS*

—

TONY BANKS (orchestra: Christopher Palmer)

Jun 83. (lp) *Atlantic; (A 0073) <80073-1>* ☐ ☐
– The Wicked Lady / Spring / The chase / Caroline / Jerry Jackson / Repentance / Kit / Barbara / Prelude to The Wicked Lady / Portrait of Jerry Jackson / Caroline's theme / Scherzo / Pastorale / The Wicked Lady / Kit's theme / Finale.

S/track review: As in most tales and legends (or yarns in this case), there were always two sides to every story, so for the context of 'The WICKED LADY' LP soundtrack (side one: TONY BANKS solo on 8-track, side two: arrangements & orchestrations by Christopher Palmer & London's National Philharmonic conducted by Stanley Black), there was no exception to the rule. While Tony's "other side" was of the symphonic film score variety and unappealing to any sane Genesis disciple (Led Zeppelin's JIMMY PAGE and JOHN PAUL JONES had also been tried-and-tested by filmmaker, Michael Winner, on 'DEATH WISH II' and 'SCREAM FOR HELP' respectively), side one had all the traits of BANKS' elaborate keyboard style – albeit "un-progged" if not unplugged. The distinctive opening title track comes off best, the rest are simple and reticent by comparison, while the theme is revisited on numerous occasions (example 'Repentance' & 'Barbara'). BANKS was certainly playing it a little risqué and close to one's self-indulgent chest on this occasion, but while Genesis were still a revelation in the commercial stakes, did he really care? *MCS*

Album rating: *3.5

– spinoff releases, etc. –

TONY BANKS: The Wicked Lady / (part 2)

May 83. (7") *(A 9825)* ☐ ☐

the WICKER MAN

1973 (UK 86m) British Lion Film Corporation (X)

Film genre: occult horror mystery/thriller

Top guns: dir: Robin Hardy / s-w: Anthony Shaffer

Stars: Edward Woodward *(Sgt. Neil Howie)*, Christopher Lee *(Lord Summerisle)* ← the MAGIC CHRISTIAN / → the LAST UNICORN, Britt Ekland *(Willow)* ← PERCY / → the MONSTER CLUB, Ingrid Pitt *(librarian)*, Lindsay Kemp *(Alder MacGregor)* → JUBILEE → VELVET GOLDMINE, Diane Cilento *(Miss Rose)*, Roy Boyd *(Broome)*, Russell Waters *(harbour master)*, Aubrey Morris *(gardener/gravedigger)* ← UP THE JUNCTION, Walter Carr *(school master)*, **Magnet:- Paul Giovanni** *(vocals, acoustic guitar)*, **Andrew Tompkins** *(acoustic guitar)*, **Peter Brewis** *(harmonica, recorder)*, **Bernard Murray** *(hand drum)*, **Ian Cutler** *(violin)*, **Michael Cole** *(concertina)* / Barbara Ann Brown *(woman with baby)* → TUTTI FRUTTI → the ACID HOUSE → the YOUNG PERSON'S GUIDE TO BECOMING A ROCK STAR

Storyline: The mysterious disappearance of a young girl in a remote Scottish island sparks off an investigation headed by Police Sergeant Howie. The righteous officer of the law subsequently uncovers all manner of debauchery in the pastoral, cultish community – led by the eccentric Lord Summerisle – including wanton sexuality/naturism, pagan blasphemy and ultimately, witchcraft and human sacrifice. *MCS*

Movie rating: *9.5

Visual: video + dvd

Off the record: MAGNET (see below)

—

PAUL GIOVANNI (composer) – (performed by MAGNET)

Jun 98. (red-lp/cd) *Trunk; (BARKED 4/+CD)* ☐ ☐
– The Wicker Man (main title) / Corn riggs / Landlord's daughter / Festival photos / Loving couples / Willow's song / Maypole song / Beetle / Ruined church sequence / Corn riggs & fireleap / Fireleap (reprise) / Graveyard sequence – Tinker of Rye / Tinker of Rye (part 2) / Festival / Masks / Hobby horse & tarring / Search 1 – baa, baa, black sheep / Search 2 / Hand of glory / Procession / Chop chop / Horn at cave – Cave chase / The anoiting / Hum / Approach / Summer is a coming in / The Wicker Man (end title).

S/track review: With all things pagan and "twindie" (to borrow Paul Morley's wry labelling of the nu/avant/psych/wyrd/electronic-folk scene) occupying an ever greater cultural/religious space in 21st-century Britain, the momentum which finally saw the movie retrieved from cult obscurity to Region 2 DVD, and which has inspired at least two major music festivals, inevitably ended up in a dodgy Hollywood remake with a conventional Angelo Badalamenti score. The original soundtrack – which itself had no small part in driving the film's cult – is a different beast entirely. Despite a raft of covers, references and live performances (including a festival show in Brussels featuring original Pentanglers Danny Thompson and Jacqui McShee), and regardless of the fact the film and its music unwittingly captured a deep, dark seam of the British/Western imagination, the soundtrack isn't quite the proto-twindie manifesto it's often claimed to be; it's far too singular, surreal and unashamedly licentious for that, praise the Lord Summerisle. And let's thank the Old Gods that we have it at all; in an ironic extension of the controversy surrounding the film, the recent history of the soundtrack(s) is almost as tortuous. Righteously hailing it as "the unholy grail" and "the last great unreleased soundtrack of a generation", the enterprising Jonny Trunk (of estimable screen kitsch/nostalgia/exotica repository, 'Trunk Records') had the foresight to tap into latent Wicker Man fever by releasing it on instantly collectable vinyl (as well as CD) in 1998, having mastered the album from the mono "music and effects tapes" languishing in Pinewood Studios. Sound quality therefore isn't the best, and, as the tapes were from the shorter original cut of the film, there's no 'Gently Johnny' at all, but – with everything from raucous/crazed/libidinous laughter, stray comments ("that's disgusting!") and licking flames worked into the narrative flow – you get a more visceral, holistic listening experience closer to an actual viewing. It's now deleted alas, so unless you want to hunt for second-hand copies on ebay you'll have to go with the lavish 'Silva Screen' version released in 2002. Fascinatingly and painstakingly annotated by Associate Musical Director GARY CARPENTER, it offers eight stereo, studio masters intended for the original (and ultimately shelved) soundtrack back in the 70s. In one of cult film's most quoted and enduring myths (about the only myth the movie doesn't have is an 'Exorcist'/'Omen'-style curse), the tapes had been feared lost to progress, dumped in a landfill smoothed over with a motorway. Yet here are those ethereal, ale-swilling anthems of – not quite – yore, digitally transferred through the endeavour of wandering composer/prolific ethno-musicologist David Fanshawe. In his notes, CARPENTER dispells the confusion over the name of the band credited in the different prints: half the musicians hired were members of CARPENTER's folk-rock band, Hocket, although for the film they originally adopted the nom de plume, Lodestone. When it transpired there was already a band of that name, CARPENTER and co came up with the MAGNET moniker, credited on subsequent prints. More surprisingly, according to CARPENTER, late songwriter/composer/lead vocalist PAUL GIOVANNI "couldn't read a note of music" (thus CARPENTER's handling of the arrangements and orchestration), translating his requirements more directly. Given the mavericks who've worked a similar strategy on soundtracks in the past, perhaps it isn't so surprising that he came up with something as stunning as 'Gently Johnny', a carnal pastoral with empyrean, multi-layered backing vocals and a guitar part similar to Country Joe's work on another early 70s classic, 'QUIET DAYS IN CLICHY'; for CARPENTER, the "resultant harmonies which, as no one actually seemed to be singing them, are a continuing source of wonder". As a Wicker icon, the track vies with 'Willow's Song' and the Rabbie Burns-adapted 'Corn Rigs', the latter a lustier tribute to rustic love scripted with Nordic lyre, recorder and ostinato violin, the former a truly sublime four-plus minutes of adult fairytale, earthed and aroused by a throbbing tom-tom, checked by that same ostinato and ultimately elevated to a higher plane on Lesley Mackie's tantalising curlicues (voiced in the film by either Rachel Verney – also the voice of 'Lullaby' – or veteran jazz singer Annie Ross, according to which account you read). These three tracks form the core of the soundtrack's legend but what to make of 'The Landlord's Daughter'? Described as "quite a rude song.. utterly filthy, in fact" by director Robin Hardy in a recent Guardian article, it is indeed rather bold but also, by turns, absurd, hilarious and utterly compelling. GIOVANNI's vocals – sung in a winsome-cum-strapping tone and unplaceable accent – aren't often given their full due in creating the soundtrack's allure, but on '..Daughter' it's difficult to locate him at all: to the cod-sea shanty/oompa wheeze of a concertina, the priceless Wicker Man Chorus take turns singing Britt Ekland's charms in archival accents emphasized to the point of surreality. If you've never supped Tartan Special in a woolly turtleneck, you'll want to soon. Trilling fertility ditty, 'Maypole', derives from a parallel seam of eccentricity; "a twisted, ridiculous tune with loads of weird melodies" is how Mike Lindsay of electro-folkies Tunng described it in the same Guardian article, the man behind one of at least two unlikely cover versions (the other a John Cale-produced effort by the Medaeval Babes). Even a kilted Christopher Lee – duetting with an entertainingly Scottish-consonant-straining Diane Cilento (worth it for the rolled 'r' in "work" alone) – gets a shot at singing with 'The Tinker Of Rye', his quarry-deep basso profundo bumped up to a full three verses. Martial brass arrangements fill out the rest of the – restored mono – tracks, along with an ensemble adaptation of the pre-mediaeval 'Sumer Is A-Cumen In', tailing off with Edward Woodward's chilling dialogue excerpt: "Oh God! Oh Jesus Christ!". The 'Silva Screen' version then presents its own montage of mono incidental music, leading in with the hugely evocative opening title, adapted from the Glencoe Massacre-inspired Burns tune, 'The Highland Widows' Lament', and beautifully sung by Mackie. While CARPENTER regards the rock guitar (and presumably the organ as well) arrangements of 'Cave Chase' (here subsumed into 'Searching For Rowan') as "a mistake", they give a heady flavour of the film's era and arguably fit like a March hare with the rest of the decontextualised traditional stuff. Ulitimately, 'The WICKER MAN' is the kind of magical musical arcana that could only have happened in the unique creative environment of the 70s, and probably only happened in Britain. The next time you hear your favourite rock/pop legend harping on about how the place was a musical desert before punk came along, dig up this soundtrack and kick out the Summerisle jams, or at least get yer antlers out. "The soundtrack world's 'Dark Side Of The Moon'." *BG*

Album rating: *10

– spinoff releases, etc. –

PAUL GIOVANNI (music and songs) – (performed by MAGNET)

Sep 02. (cd) *Silva Screen; (FILMCD 330) <1141>*
– Corn rigs (*) / The landlord's daughter (*) / Gently Johnny (*) / Maypole (*) / Fire leap (*) / The tinker of Rye (*) / Willow's song (*) / Procession (*) / Chop chop (*) / Lullaby (*) / Festival – Mirie it is – Sumer is a-cumen in / Opening music – Loving couples – The ruined church (*) / The masks – The hobby horse / Searching for Rowan / Appointment with the Wicker Man / Sunset.

WILLIE DYNAMITE

1974 (US 102m) Universal Pictures (R)

Film genre: crime drama

Top guns: dir: Gilbert Moses / s-w: Ron Cutler, Joe Keyes Jr.

Stars: Roscoe Orman *(Willie Dynamite)*, Diana Sands *(Cora)* ← the LANDLORD, Thalmus Rasulala *(Robert Daniels)* ← BLACULA ← COOL BREEZE / → FRIDAY FOSTER → CORNBREAD, EARL AND ME → BUCKTOWN → ADIOS AMIGO → LAMBADA, Joyce Walker *(Pashen)* ← SHAFT'S BIG SCORE! / → the EDUCATION OF SONNY CARSON, Roger Robinson *(Bell)*, Juanita Brown *(Sola)* → FOXY BROWN, George Murdock *(Celli)* ← the MACK, Norma Donaldson *(Honey)* ← ACROSS 110th STREET / → STAYING ALIVE → HOUSE PARTY → the FIVE HEARTBEATS, Marcia McBroom *(Pearl)* ← JESUS CHRIST SUPERSTAR ← COME BACK, CHARLESTON BLUE ← BEYOND THE VALLEY OF THE DOLLS, Judith Brown *(Gorgia)* ← SLAUGHTER'S BIG RIP-OFF / → THANK GOD IT'S FRIDAY, Richard Lawson *(Sugar)* → STREETS OF FIRE, Ken Lynch *(Judge No.1)* ← ACROSS 110th STREET, Royce Wallace *(Willie's mother)* ← COOL BREEZE ← GOODBYE, COLUMBUS / → CROSSROADS, Albert Hall *(Pointer)* ← COTTON COMES TO HARLEM / → LEADBELLY, Jack Bernardi *(Willie's lawyer)* ← IT'S A BIKINI WORLD ← the WILD ANGELS ← BEACH BALL / → FOXY BROWN, Leslie McRae *(competing prostitute)* ← COFFY ← BUMMER!, Jac Emil *(pimp)* → BLACK BELT JONES → TRUCK TURNER

Storyline: The polar opposite of the swashbuckling blaxploitation hero, Willie Dynamite is a pimp who struggles to maintain his street cred, Cora is an ex-prostitute turned social worker who busies herself with his redemption. *BG*

Movie rating: *5.5

Visual: none

Off the record: MARTHA REEVES (b.18 Jul'41, Eufaula, Alabama, USA) was better known for her time on 'Motown' records with the Vandellas. Formed in Detroit, Michigan, 1960 as the Del-Phis, she got together with high school pals Rosalynd Ashford and Annette Sterling Beard. Although the trio cut a one-off side for 'Chess' subsidiary 'Check-Mate' while still at school, their big break came after REEVES landed herself a job as A&R secretary at the aforementioned 'Motown' imprint. When singer Mary Wells failed to show up for a MARVIN GAYE session, the trio were called in at short notice to back GAYE on two tracks, 'Stubborn Kind Of Fellow' and 'Hitch Hike'. They also recorded a track of their own, 'I'll Have To Let Him Go', releasing it in September '62 under the moniker, Martha & The Vandellas (named after Detroit's Van Dyke street and REEVES' heroine, Della Reese). The single stiffed but a follow-up, 'Come And Get These Memories', made the US Top 30. Cue the entrance of 'Motown' songsmiths par excellence, Holland-Dozier-Holland who proceeded to cook up the searing 'Heat Wave' as the group's first Top 5 hit in late '63. One of the definitive singles in the 'Motown' pantheon and a key record in developing the label as a brand name, the song worked up a delirious aural sweat with a killer combination of thundering brass, hollering handclaps and fervent call and response vocals. The winning formula was repeated in early '64 with the Top 10 'Quicksand', after which Beard was replaced by ex-Velvelette, Betty Kelly. Successive singles, 'Live Wire' and the less frenetic 'In My Lonely Room' hovered on the edges of the Top 40 yet the group hit paydirt after taking on a song rejected by labelmate Kim Weston. Penned by GAYE, Ivy Jo Hunter and REEVES' erstwhile boss, Mickey Stevenson, 'Dancing In The Street' was subsequently moulded in the Vandellas style and shimmied its way to No.2 that autumn. Possibly the premier dancefloor anthem of 60s soul, the track was dusted down two decades later by rock stalwarts DAVID BOWIE and MICK JAGGER who performed the song at Live Aid and duly sent it to the top of the UK chart. The headlong rush of 'Nowhere To Run' found them back in the Top 10 in 1965 and over the ensuing three years they sporadically hit the Top 10 with 'I'm Ready For Love' and 'Jimmy Mack'. Early 68's 'Honey Chile' was the first track released under the expanded moniker, Martha Reeves & The Vandellas, apeing the fashion in which the Supremes had becmome DIANA ROSS & the Supremes a year earlier. While REEVES may have won this token concession, hers was a constant battle with label boss, Berry Gordy over what she saw as preferential treatment for the Supremes and especially ROSS. Whatever, 'Honey Chile' was the last Holland-Dozier-Holland track prior to their departure from 'Motown' and the Vandellas' commercial fortunes became progressively bleaker as they made do with lesser material. The group's last major success came in early '71 with the near Top 10 hit, 'Forget Me Not' before they finally called it a day late the following year. By the time of the split, REEVES was the only original remaining member. Profoundly affected by her experiences at 'Motown', she was struggling with drug dependence and emotional problems, having already suffered her first breakdown in 1969 (ironically, re-issues of both 'Dancing In The Street' and 'Nowhere To Run' hit the Top 5 in the UK around the same time). REEVES left the label after a final 1973 single, 'No One There', signing to 'M.C.A.' as a solo artist and cutting a couple of critically praised but unsuccessful albums. *BG*

—

J.J. JOHNSON (w/ MARTHA REEVES & THE SWEET THINGS *)

1974. (lp) *M.C.A.; <MCA 393>* [ ] [–]
– Willie D (*) / Willie Chase / King Midas (*) / Willie escapes / Passion's dilemma / Keep on movin' on (by *) / Make it right / Parade strut / Gospel family / Willie D (by *). *<cd-iss. 2004 on 'Hip-O';*

S/track review: One of blaxploitation's more thoughtfully scripted efforts also came with one of its better if lesser-known soundtracks, pairing jazz veteran J.J. JOHNSON with soul superstar MARTHA REEVES. Musically single after the 1973 break-up of the Vandellas and performing with backing aggregate the SWEET THINGS, REEVES brought the full quota of her hard-bitten experience and gentle yet sultry authority to bear on JOHNSON's itchy, febrile arrangements, animating lyricist Gilbert Moses III's portrait of a likeable pimp to the extent that we're sympathising with the rascally 'Willie D' before the first track's even halfway through. Drawing on an even more venerable pedigree, JOHNSON had made an unlikely but hugely impressive leap into film composition with the likes of 'ACROSS 110TH STREET' (1972) and 'CLEOPATRA JONES' (1973), and he more than kept up that momentum on this, his final blax effort. The man's dynamic, percussively complex instrumentals boast breaks to rival the Incredible Bongo Band without ever relinquishing the sophistication of his jazz background or falling back on cliché. A slyly imaginative arranger, he rarely relied solely on the stock-in-trade armoury of vibes, flutes, Rhodes, guitar, etc., but threw in instrumental curveballs like jews harp or, on 'Passion's Dilemma', a snuffling, snorting baritone sax. 'Parade Strut' pits wah-wah funk against martial brass and snares, harking back to the Deep South as readily as 'Gospel Family', while the title track cannily combines the bittersweet slickness of Motown with the bongo fury of primetime funk. Inevitably, though, it's REEVES who takes the final plaudits, turning in some of her strongest post-Vandellas performances on the ballads 'King Midas' and 'Keep On Movin' On'. 100% dynamite (or near enough!). *BG*

Album rating: *7.5

□ Bobby WOMACK segment
(⇒ ACROSS 110th STREET)

the WOMAN IN RED

1984 (US 87m) Orion Pictures (PG-13)

Film genre: romantic comedy

Top guns: s-w: Gene Wilder (+ dir), Jean-Loup Dabadie ← ANNA, Yves Robert (+ play)

Stars: Gene Wilder *(Teddy Pierce)*, Charles Grodin *(Buddy)*, Joseph Bologna *(Joey)*, Judith Ivey *(Didi Pierce)*, Michael Huddleston *(Mikey)* → BAD CHANNELS, Kelly LeBrock *(Charlotte)*, Gilda Radner *(Ms. Milner)* ← ANIMALYMPICS ← the RUTLES, Kyle T. Heffner *(Richard)* ← FLASHDANCE, Michael Zorek *(Shelly)*, Danny Wells *(maitre d')* ← GOIN' COCONUTS / → MAGNOLIA, Thom Matthews *(Erik)* → the RETURN OF THE LIVING DEAD

Storyline: Theodore Pierce's life is turned on its head when he espies the voluptuous Charlotte having a "breath of fresh air" over a grate. All thoughts of the wife are also blown away as the infatuated Theodore desperately tries to get a date with Miss Red Dress. He enlists the help of his workmates to think up Machiavellian plots (they fail miserably) and gets his comeuppance when he mistakenly dates the dreadful Ms Milner. Will Theodore ever get his girl or will the Itch run another seven years? *JZ*

Movie rating: *3

Visual: video + dvd

Off the record: (see below)

—

STEVIE WONDER (score: John Morris)

Sep 84. (lp/c) *Motown; <6108> (ZL/ZK 72285)* [4] [2]
– The woman in red / It's you (w/ DIONNE WARWICK) / It's more than you (instrumental) / I just called to say I love you / Love light in flight / Moments aren't moments (DIONNE WARWICK) / Weakness (w/ DIONNE WARWICK) / Don't drive drunk. *(cd-iss. Oct87; ZD 72285)*

S/track review: That a soundtrack generated the biggest single in STEVIE WONDER's chart history is ironic, more so if you consider it arrived during one of the most fallow periods in his career. Routinely written off as MOR sap, 'I Just Called To Say I Love You' is arguably ripe for revision – those weird keyboard melodies alone render it a period oddity. Still, off-kilter romance is one thing, sexual chemistry another; 'The Woman In Red' is no 'Boogie On Reggae Woman', and perhaps STEVIE – and definitely Gene Wilder – was getting too long in the tooth for this kind of thing. A beaming back-cover shot has him surrounded by state-of-the-art keyboards, but all the assorted 80s studio effrontery in the world can't mask weak songwriting – the flimsiness of the material wafts through this soundtrack like cheap perfume, gagging the DIONNE WARWICK collaborations especially. With STEVIE's transcendental energies largely taken up with the recording of 'In Square Circle' (1985), longtime fans were left with slim pickings: only the wriggling electro melodies of 'Love Light In Flight' and the bizarre 'Don't Drive Drunk' – the most unlikely public service broadcast in the history of soul and all the more unlikely in that it resembles an outtake from '. . .SECRET LIFE OF PLANTS' (1979) – hint that he was once a pioneer in his field. *BG*

Album rating: *5.5

– spinoff hits, etc. –

STEVIE WONDER: I Just Called To Say I Love You / (instrumental)

Aug 84. (7"/12") *<1745> (TMG/+T 1349)* [1] [1]

STEVIE WONDER: Love Light In Flight / It's More Than You

Nov 84. (7"/12") *<1769> (TMG/+T 1364)* [17] [44]

STEVIE WONDER: Don't Drive Drunk / (instrumental)

Dec 84. (7"/12") *(TMG/+T 1372)* [–] [62]

Stevie WONDER

Born: Steveland Judkins Morris, 13 May'50, Saginaw, Michigan, USA. A blind child prodigy who developed into a Motown soul seer, STEVIE WONDER – along with contemporaries such as MARVIN GAYE, ISAAC HAYES and Sly Stone – was at least partly responsible for the elevation of black American music from being primarily a dance format to rivalling the conceptualism and complexity of white rock. It's difficult to overestimate the man's contribution to popular music, and although his unrelentingly positive approach probably precluded him from recording a Blaxploitaiton soundtrack, his entry into film scoring was from an entirely different – and, in WONDER'S case, entirely appropriate – angle. While he appeared in teen surf movies, 'MUSCLE BEACH PARTY' (1964) and 'BIKINI BEACH' (1964) during his first flush of 'Motown' fame and also made an unlikely appearance in infamous ROLLING STONES rockumentary, 'COCKSUCKER BLUES' (1972), it wasn't until after his astonishing quintet of 70s classics – 'Music Of My Mind' (1972), 'Talking Book' (1972), 'Innervisions' (1973), 'Fulfillingness' First Finale' (1974) and 'Songs In The Key Of Life' (1976) – that he recorded his debut soundtrack. Ironically, perhaps, this extended creative spurt was finally brought to an end as he embarked on the three year recording of 'Journey Through The SECRET LIFE OF PLANTS' (1979). Ostensibly the soundtrack to Walon Green's esoteric and visually dazzling documentary on the finer emotions of plants, it was also a follow-up to the career high of 'Songs In The Key Of Life', and as such was regarded as a self-indulgent disappointment. In retrospect, it's probably best bracketed with other endearingly excessive late 70s doubles like MARVIN GAYE's 'Here My Dear', cult favourites with unique qualities passed over at the time. It'd be 1984 before STEVIE attempted another score, recording the occasionally brilliant music for Gene Wilder's mid-life crisis comedy, 'The WOMAN IN RED', duetting with Dionne Warwick on a number of tracks and scoring a transatlantic No.1 with the ballad, 'I Just Called To Say I Love You'. The latter would be the penultimate No.1 of his career (to date) and by the release of the soundtrack to Spike Lee's 'JUNGLE FEVER' (1991), WONDER was no longer the kind of major league chart star he'd been for the preceeding two decades. While the record showed flashes of his past genius, it wasn't quite the return to form which his fans had been waiting on. And if his song contributions to the soundtrack for kids animation, 'The Adventures Of Pinocchio' (1996) weren't quite as high profile as they once might have been, WONDER remains a genuine living legend whose concert appearances remain all the more valuable given the passing away of his own role model, RAY CHARLES. *BG*

- filmography (composer) –

Muscle Beach Party *(1964 {c})* / **Bikini Beach** *(1964 {c})* / **Cocksucker Blues** *(1972 {*} =>)* / **the Secret Life Of Plants** *(1979 OST =>)* / **the Woman In Red** *(1984 OST =>)* / the Last Radio Station *(1986)* / **Jungle Fever** *(1991 OST =>)* / the Adventures Of Pinocchio *(1996 songs on OST by Rachael Portman w/ BRIAN MAY =>)*

WONDERWALL

1969 (UK 82m) Compton-Cameo Films (AA)

Film genre: romantic/seXual drama

Top guns: dir: Joe Massot → the SONG REMAINS THE SAME → DANCE CRAZE / s-w: G. Cabrera Infante → VANISHING POINT (au: Gerard Brach → la FEMME DE MON POTE → SHY PEOPLE)

Stars: Jack MacGowran *(Prof. Oscar Collins)*, Jane Birkin *(Penny Lane)* ← BLOW-UP / → SEX POWER → MAY MORNING → CANNABIS → JE T'AIME MOI NON PLUS, Richard Wattis *(Perkins)* ← BUNNY LAKE IS MISSING ← UP JUMPED A SWAGMAN ← PLAY IT COOL / → TAKE ME HIGH, Iain Quarrier *(young man)*, Irene Handl *(Mrs. Peurofoy)* ← SMASHING TIME ← JUST FOR FUN / → the GREAT ROCK'N'ROLL SWINDLE → ABSOLUTE BEGINNERS, Sean Lynch *(Riley)*, Beatrix Lehmann *(mother)*, Bee Duffell *(Mrs. Charmer)*, Anita Pallenberg *(girl at party)* → CANDY → PERFORMANCE → le BERCEAU DE CRISTAL

Storyline: Psychedelic voyeurism is on the menu as butterfly collector and professor, Oscar Collins, enjoys copious views of his gorgeous neighbour Penny through a crack in the wall. The film remained unreleased until much later. *BG*

Movie rating: *5.5

Visual: video + dvd

Off the record: (see below)

—

GEORGE HARRISON: Wonderwall Music

Nov 68. (lp; stereo/mono) *Apple; (S+/APCOR 1) Zapple; <ST 3350>* □ Jan69 49
– Microbes / Red lady too / Tabla and Pavajak / In the park / Drilling a hole / Guru Vandana / Greasy legs / Ski-ing / Gat Kirwani / Dream scene / Party Seacombe / Love scene / Crying / Cowboy music / Fantasy sequins / On the bed / Glass box / Wonderwall to be here / Singing om. *(cd-iss. Jun92; CDSAPCOR 1) <US cd-iss. Jun92 on 'Capitol'; C2 98706>*

S/track review: Famous as the first "official" solo album by a Beatles member as well as the first album to appear on the band's newly formed 'Apple/Zapple' label, this dense, pioneering experiment continues to divide fans and critics. Wholly instrumental save for religious chanting, the GEORGE HARRISON album comprises just under twenty cues, with recordings split between Bombay and London. That geographical dichotomy extends to the music with an East-meets-West splicing of Indian instrumentation, conventional rock guitar, tape loops and general studio trickery punctuated with moments of Beatles-style whimsy and ranging from the cheroot-chewing 'Cowboy Museum' to the hypnotic, waggishly titled 'Wonderwall To Be Here'. As a soundtrack, it has weathered the years better than the film; as a virgin foray into world music fusion it was literally decades ahead of its time. *BG*

Album rating: *5

WORKING GIRL

1988 (US 115m) 20th Century Fox (R)

Film genre: romantic workplace comedy

Top guns: dir: Mike Nichols ← the GRADUATE / → PRIMARY COLORS / s-w: Kevin Wade

Stars: Melanie Griffith *(Tess McGill)* ← JOYRIDE ← ONE ON ONE, Harrison Ford *(Jack Trainer)* ← BLADE RUNNER ← MORE AMERICAN GRAFFITI ← AMERICAN GRAFFITI ← ZABRISKIE POINT, Sigourney Weaver *(Katherine Parker)*, Alec Baldwin *(Mick Dugan)* → GREAT BALLS OF FIRE!, Joan Cusack *(Cyn)* → HIGH FIDELITY → SCHOOL OF ROCK, Philip Bosco *(Oren Trask)* → STRAIGHT TALK, Nora Dunn *(Ginny)* → SHAKE, RATTLE & ROCK! tv, Oliver Platt *(Lutz)* → PIECES OF APRIL, James Lally *(Turkel)* ← MAGIC STICKS, Olympia Dukakis *(personnel director)* ← the IDOLMAKER, Kevin Spacey *(Bob Speck)* → ORDINARY DECENT CRIMINAL → BEYOND THE SEA, Ricki Lake *(bridesmaid)* → HAIRSPRAY → LAST EXIT TO BROOKLYN → CRY-BABY → JACKIE'S BACK! → HAIRSPRAY re-make, Zach Grenier *(Jim)* → FIGHT CLUB → SWORDFISH, Amy Aquino *(Alice Baxter)* → the SINGING DETECTIVE, Caroline Aaron *(petty marsh secretary)* → THIS IS MY LIFE → PRIMARY COLORS → BEYOND THE SEA, Suzanne Shepherd *(Trask receptionist)*

Storyline: Tess McGill is an ambitious Wall Street secretary whom fortune rescues from a scheming boss injured in a skiing accident. Finally given her shot at the big time, it's an often hilarious case of poor girl made good as she works her way up the ladder with the help and affection of high roller Jack Trainer. *BG*

Movie rating: *7.5

Visual: video + dvd

Off the record: (see below)

—

CARLY SIMON (*) (& Various Artists)

Feb 89. (lp/c/cd) *Arista; (2/4 09767) <8593>* 45 Mar89 □

– Let the river run (*) / In love – instrumental (*) / The man that got away (BOB MOUNSEY, GEORGE YOUNG, CHIP JACKSON & GRADY TATE) / The scar – instrumental (*) / Let the river run (ST. THOMAS CHOIR OF MEN AND BOYS) / Lady in red (CHRIS DE BURGH) / Carlotta's heart (*) / Looking through Katherine's house (*) / Poor butterfly – instrumental (SONNY ROLLINS) / I'm so excited (POINTER SISTERS).

S/track review: Following her unreleased score and hit theme ('Coming Around Again') for 'Heartburn' (1986), 'WORKING GIRL' was the nearest thing to a CARLY SIMON soundtrack. Its main theme wasn't a hit, but it finally won her an Oscar (the peerless 'Nobody Does It Better' was nominated but beaten by Barbra Streisand), and it's not difficult to see why Hollywood fawned over its torchy melody. A decade and a half later, the choral breast-beating and pseudo-religious imagery sound way out of time, like much of this album. It's a patchy, incoherent listen, leaping crazily from the St. Thomas Choir Of Men And Boys to CHRIS DE BURGH's slip-on shuffle, 'Lady In Red', and from SONNY ROLLINS balladry to the tinny, hyperactive R&B of the POINTER SISTERS. The rest of SIMON's score is largely competent, big-budget movie music, tasteful to the point of distraction. Her piano-playing dominates the elegiac 'In Love', and she at least varies the mood with some muzak and wordless vocalising on 'Carlotta's Heart', and 'Looking Through Katherine's House', but this one's for 80s diehards only. *BG*

Album rating: *5

– spinoff releases, etc. –

CARLY SIMON: Let The River Run

Feb 89. (7") *<9793>* 49 –

CARLY SIMON: Let The River Run / Carlotta's Heart

Mar 89. (7"/12"/cd-s) *(112/612/662 124)* – □

□ Gary WRIGHT segment (⇒ BENJAMIN)

□ Robert WYATT segment (⇒ the ANIMALS FILM)

□ Bill WYMAN (⇒ the ROLLING STONES)

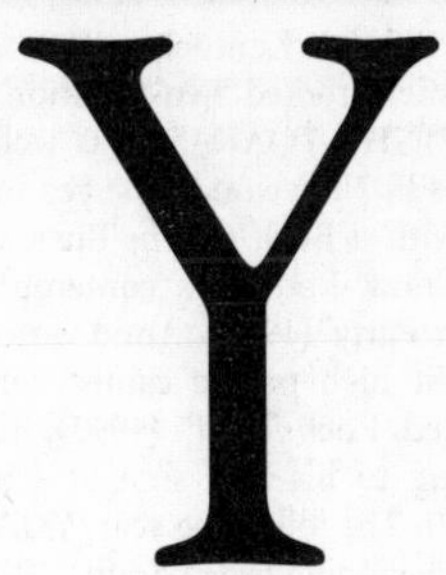

les YEUX FERMÉS

trans: the Eyes Closed

1972 (Fra 118m) Delfilm

Film genre: psychological drama

Top guns: s-w: (+ dir) Joël Santoni, Claude Breuer, Jeanne Bronner

Stars: Gérard Desarthe *(Yvan)*, Lorraine Rainer *(Xénie)*, Jean Carmet *(Raoul)* → NIGHT MAGIC, Marcel Dalio *(le vieux monsieur)*, Lucien Raimbourg *(Pépère)*, Dominique Labourier *(Caroline)*

Storyline: With nothing better to do, out-of-work actor Yvan masquerades as a blind person, although it's not long before his risky deception turns into a living nightmare as he has to keep up the illusion. Sadly, his world becomes a complete fantasy as he hallucinates himself into oblivion. *MCS*

Movie rating: *4

Visual: none

Off the record: (see below)

TERRY RILEY: Happy Ending

Jul 72. (lp) *Warners; <K 46125>* – French –

– Journey from the death of a friend / Happy ending. *<cd-iss. Apr07 on 'Elision Fields'+=; EF 101>* – TERRY RILEY: Lifespan

S/track review: Godfather of Minimalism and Improvisation, TERRY RILEY, is the man behind this independent film score. Responsible for minimalism in its "purest" form via the celebrated 'Rainbow In Curved Air' album, the composer takes the listener on two long trips (or indeed movements) in the shape of the 18 minute 25 second side, 'Journey From The Death Of A Friend' and the 18:26 flipside, 'Happy Ending'; the latter was the original title of the French-only release. The aforementioned 'Journey From . . .' track finds its way through a repetitive cacophony of sombre electric organ that reverberates, Tangerine Dream-like, into the brain of the (un-easy) listener. Fusing classical, free-jazz and prog-rock elements, and gradually stretching out the harmonic feel to the musak, RILEY finally achieves his subdued goal. With the track around 14:40 into its complex workout, the music spills out like lava from a volcano, every key and tape loop altogether crescendo-like in their new wayward structure. With "eyes closed" once again (as best sampled), track/side two, 'Happy Ending', reinforces RILEY's barrage of sound by way of added sax appeal; thankfully it lets up for sporadic interludes. Some might appreciate the effort and creativity that RILEY puts into his work, but as they say in some Byrne-ing circles . . . "this ain't no party". *MCS*

Album rating: *6

Dwight YOAKAM

Born: 23 Oct'56, Pikeville, Kentucky, USA. Having established himself as a Bakersfield-rooted neo-traditionalist in L.A. rather than Nashville, DWIGHT YOAKAM was well placed to employ his transferable skills in Hollywood. The year after he first topped the country chart with a Buck Owens duet, he made his acting debut in director Frank Roddam's contemporary cowboys and Indians drama, 'War Party' (1989). Amid various countrymentary appearances, his first high profile cameo came in John Dahl's cult desert-noir, 'Red Rock West' (1993), the Dennis Hopper connection extending to his first shot at scoring, on Hopper's own 'Chasers' (1994). The following year, YOAKAM took his first starring role in award winning rodeo drama, 'Painted Hero' (1995), its plot of flight and murky family background foreshadowing his own writing debut to come. In the meantime he put in his most powerful supporting role as a misanthropic drunk in Billy Bob Thornton's acclaimed directorial debut, 'SLING BLADE' (1996), following it up with starring roles in obscure thriller, 'The Little Death' (1996), Richard Linklater's underrated heist film, 'The Newton Boys' (1998) and acclaimed Doctor Death-style serial killer feature, 'The Minus Man' (1999). Finally, at the turn of the millennium, YOAKAM masterminded his own movie, the equally underrated 'SOUTH OF HEAVEN, WEST OF HELL' (2000). A deadpan neo-metaphysical western fable scripted, directed and scored by YOAKAM himself, it also cast the country renaissance man in its leading role as an enigmatic sheriff. While the soundtrack release squandered its potential, the haunting theme ranks among YOAKAM's most accomplished compositions. He even moved into co-production with Thornton comedy, 'Waking Up In Reno' (2001), returning to lead parts in David Fincher's high-tension thriller, 'Panic Room' (2002) and – assuming his favourite roles of mysterious outsider/sheriff – in, respectively, '3-Way' (2004) and Tommy Lee Jones' border drama, 'The Three Burials Of Melquiades Estrada' (2005). While his country hits might have dried up (he now co-ordinates his music activities from his own label), YOAKAM still enjoys a relatively high screen profile, starring in hi-octane actioner, 'Crank' (2006) and as another hugely unlikeable villain opposite Salma Hayek and Penelope Cruz in femme comedy Western, 'Bandidas' (2006). *BG*

- **filmography** (composer) {acting} [s-w + dir] –

War Party *(1989 {b})* / Red Rock West *(1992 {a})* / Roswell *(1994 TV {a})* / Chasers *(1994 score w/ Pete Anderson)* / the Little Death *(1995 {a})* / Painted Hero *(1995 {*})* / Don't Look Back *(1996 TV {*})* / **Sling Blade** *(1996 {*} OST by DANIEL LANOIS =>)* / Painted Hero *(1997 {*})* / the Newton Boys *(1998 {a} OST by V/A; see future editions)* / When Trumpets Fade *(1998 TV {a})* / the Minus Man *(1999 {*})* / **South Of Heaven, West Of Hell** *(2000 {*} [s-w + dir] OST =>)* / Panic Room *(2002 {*} OST by HOWARD SHORE see; future editions =>)* / Hollywood Homicide *(2003 {a})* / 3-Way *(2004 {*})* / the Three Burials Of Melquiades Estrada *(2005 {*})* / Wedding Crashers *(2005 {a})* / Bandidas *(2006 {*})* / Crank *(2006 {*})*

Neil YOUNG

Born: 12 Nov'45, Toronto, Ontario, Canada. The troubadour's troubadour, NEIL YOUNG remains surpassed only by perhaps BOB DYLAN or VAN MORRISON as the most important and influential singer-songwriter in modern history. Like those two, his sometimes contrary and taciturn nature always made any real diversion into acting unlikely, although he has composed a handful of soundtracks and made the occasional directorial effort and screen appearance. The first of these, 'JOURNEY THROUGH THE PAST' (1972) was hardly the most auspicious of celluloid starts; the weakest of his early 70s albums, it accompanied a failed experimental film of the same name. More promising was his score for a failed 1980 biopic of the late Hunter S. Thompson, 'WHERE THE BUFFALO ROAM' (1980), and while his collaboration with Tom Lavin on the score to Dennis Hopper's 'Out Of The Blue' (1981), remains unreleased, YOUNG himself made his low-key and predictably off-kilter directorial debut with 'HUMAN HIGHWAY' (1982). Credited under his favourite alias, Bernard Shakey, YOUNG also acted in the film and co-composed the score (again unreleased) with help from songs by DEVO. He also took bit parts in Alan Rudolph's romantic fantasy, 'Made In Heaven' (1987) – embellishing Mark Isham's score with a handful of tracks – and Steven Kovacs' hippy era drama, ''68' (1988). Two years later, he teamed upwith Rudolph once more for his final feature appearance – actually one of his biggest parts – in the director's easygoing private eye flick, 'Love At Large' (1990). YOUNG's subsequent critical and commercial rebirth saw him concentrating on his recording career in the 90s although he did find time to create the most compelling – if oblique – film score of his career, for Johnny Depp vehicle, 'DEAD MAN' (1995). As unpredictable as ever, YOUNG confounded critics and fans once again with the release of 'GREENDALE' (2003), a rambling, Shakey-directed musical and soundtrack offering a bleary and often heavy handed snapshot of small town life. *BG*

- **filmography** (composer) –

Celebration At Big Sur *(1971 {p by CSN&Y} =>)* / **Journey Through The Past** *(1972 [dir] {*p} OST =>)* / **the Last Waltz** *(1978 {p} OST by the BAND =>)* / **Rust Never Sleeps** *(1979 {*p} OST 'Live Rust' =>)* / **Where The Buffalo Roam** *(1980 OST w/ V/A =>)* / Out Of The Blue *(1981 w/ Tom Lavin)* / **Human Highway** *(1982 [dir] {*} w/ DEVO)* / Made In Heaven *(1987 {b} BUFFALO SPRINGFIELD songs on OST by Mark Isham & V/A; see future edition)* / '68 *(1988 {b})* / Love At Large *(1990 {a} OST by Mark Isham; see future edition)* / **Dead Man** *(1995 OST =>)* / **Year Of The Horse** *(1997 {*p} associated OST =>)* / **My Generation** *(2000 {p w/ CSN&Y} =>)* / **Greendale** *(2003 [s-w + dir] {b} OST =>)* / **Heart Of Gold** *(2006 {*p} =>)*

YOUNG ADAM

2003 (UK/Fra 98m) Scottish Screen / HanWay Films / Sveno (18)

Film genre: seXual crime thriller

Top guns: s-w + dir: David Mackenzie ← the LAST GREAT WILDERNESS / → HALLAM FOE(au: Alexander Trocchi)

Stars: Ewan McGregor *(Joe Taylor)* ← MOULIN ROUGE ← VELVET GOLDMINE ← TRAINSPOTTING ← LIPSTICK ON YOUR COLLAR, Tilda Swinton *(Ella Gault)* → THUMBSUCKER, Peter Mullan *(Les Gault)* ← ORDINARY DECENT CRIMINAL ← TRAINSPOTTING, Emily Mortimer *(Cathie Dimly)*, Jack McElhone *(Jim Gault)*, Therese Bradley *(Gwen)*, Ewan Stewart *(Daniel Gordon)* ← the LAST GREAT WILDERNESS ← WHITE CITY, Stuart McQuarrie *(Bill)* ← TRAINSPOTTING, John Comerford *(jury foreman)* ← the LAST GREAT WILDERNESS

Storyline: David McKenzie's adaptation of Alexander Trocchi's novel, centering on the sexual pecadillos and rootless, claustrophobic existence of barge worker Joe, who subsequently embarks on an ill-advised affair with his workmate's wife. *BG*

Movie rating: *6.5

Visual: dvd

Off the record: (see below)

DAVID BYRNE: Lead Us Not Into Temptation

Sep 03. (cd/lp) *Thrill Jockey; (<THRILL 133/+LP>)* ☐ ☐
– Body in a river / Mnemonic discordance / Seaside smokes /

Canal life / Locks & barges / Haitian fight song (HUNG DRAWN QUARTET) / Sex on the docks / Inexorable / Warm sheets / Dirty hair / Bastard / The lodger / Ineluctable / Speechless / The Great Western Road.

S/track review: Perhaps it's because he was feeling the pull of his Scottish roots (this was recorded at Glasgow's CaVa studios), or because the spicy yang of his more Latin-tinged work was beginning to smother his artistic yin, but this is at once the darkest and most compelling music DAVID BYRNE has composed since leaving Talking Heads. It might also have something to do with the fact that various members of some of Scotland's finest bands – BELLE & SEBASTIAN, MOGWAI, the DELGADOS were backing him up. As a soundtrack to a Trocchi adaptation, this couldn't be more on the nail, but it also evokes an infinity of alternate scenarios, so raw and condensed is its sense of melancholy. 'Sex On The Docks' literally wrings the pathos from its melody, carrying its wounded piano thread onto the next cue. The nearest comparison would have to be Tindersticks' soundtrack excursions, if only for the preponderance of world-weary strings and tendency to neo-jazz shuffle. It's a lazy approximation, however, for the singularity of BYRNE's achievement. The lanky musical polymath even sings, or at least contributes a woozy, barely comprehensible vocal on the appropriately titled 'Speechless', and also handles lead vocals on the closing 'Great Western Road', presumably named after Glasgow's famous thoroughfare. And before you begin marvelling at how the cream of Scotland's indie crop managed such a blistering cover of Charles Mingus' 'Haitian Fight Song' – tight and swinging beyond the call of duty – a close reading of the sleeve credits reveal that an entirely different set of musicians played on this, the score's sole upbeat moment. All told, probably the best soundtrack release of 2003, or even this decade. *BG*

Album rating: *8.5

YOUNG GUNS II

1990 sequel (US 105m) Twentieth Century Fox (PG-13)

Film genre: outlaw western

Top guns: dir: Geoff Murphy / s-w: John Fusco ← CROSSROADS / → SPIRIT: STALLION OF THE CIMARRON

Stars: Emilio Estevez *(William H. Bonney/"Billy The Kid")* ← MAXIMUM OVERDRIVE ← REPO MAN / → JUDGMENT NIGHT, Kiefer Sutherland *(Josiah Gordon "Doc" Scurlock)*, Lou Diamond Phillips *(Jose Chavez y Chavez)* ← LA BAMBA, Christian Slater *(Arkansas Dave Rudabaugh)* ← TUCKER: THE MAN AND HIS DREAM ← LIVING PROOF: THE HANK WILLIAMS JR. STORY / → PUMP UP THE VOLUME → MASKED AND ANONYMOUS, William Petersen *(Pat Garrett)* ← TO LIVE AND DIE IN L.A. ← THIEF, Alan Ruck *(Hendry French)*, James Coburn *(John Chisum)* ← WHITE ROCK ← PAT GARRETT & BILLY THE KID ← CANDY / → AFFLICTION → SHAKE, RATTLE & ROLL: AN AMERICAN LOVE STORY, Robert Knepper *(Deputy Carlyle)* → GAS, FOOD LODGING, Viggo Mortensen *(John W. Poe)* → ALBINO ALLIGATOR, Scott Wilson *(Governor Lew Wallace)* ← JOHNNY HANDSOME ← BLUE CITY / → ELVIS AND THE COLONEL: THE UNTOLD STORY → GERONIMO: AN AMERICAN LEGEND → SOUL SURVIVOR → DEAD MAN WALKING → SOUTH OF HEAVEN, WEST OF HELL → DON'T LET GO → MONSTER, Leon Rippy *(Bob Ollinger)* ← MAXIMUM OVERDRIVE, Tracey Walter *(Beever Smith)* ← BATMAN ← REPO MAN ← HONKYTONK MAN ← TIMERIDER: THE ADVENTURE OF LYLE SWANN / → DELUSION → MAN ON THE MOON → HOW HIGH → MASKED AND ANONYMOUS, Jenny Wright *(Jane Greathouse)* ← the WALL, Tony Frank *(judge Bristol)* ← SWEET DREAMS ← ALAMO BAY / → RUSH, Balthazar Getty *(Tom O'Folliard)* → RED HOT, Richard Schiff *(Rat Bag)* → the BODYGUARD → GRACE OF MY HEART → TOUCH → I AM SAM → RAY, Jack Kehoe *(Ashmun Upson)* ← DICK TRACY ← CAR WASH, Redmond Gleeson *(Murphy man)* ← PIPE DREAMS, Domingo Ambriz *(valquero #1)* ← GREEN ICE, **Jon Bon Jovi** *(pit inmate)*

Storyline: With only three of the original five "Young Guns" remaining, namely Billy The Kid, Doc Scurlock and Jose Chavez y Chavez, the trio take on new recruits (Arkansas Dave Rudabaugh, Tom O'Folliard and Hendry French), but their sojourn to New Mexico is curtailed by government agents including Pat Garrett. The question is though, was Billy The Kid killed by Garrett way back in 1881 or has he become the movie's narrator, Brushy Bill Roberts? *MCS*

Movie rating: *5.5

Visual: video + dvd

Off the record: JON BON JOVI (b. John Bongiovi, 2 Mar'62, Sayreville, New Jersey, USA). After a career as the wet-permed heart-throb fronting the hard rock band of his own name, JON BON JOVI spent much of the 90s carving out a semi-successful niche in Hollywood. From humble beginnings in a New jersey studio, Bon Jovi (the band) went on to forge one of the most distinctive sounds of the 80s metal boom. Their melodic, anthemic and highly accessible songwriting became increasingly rootsy as the decade wore on, a trend exemplified in JON BON JOVI's contribution to 'YOUNG GUNS II'. His acting career got really underway playing the object of an older woman's affections in 'Moonlight And Valentino' (1995), before going on to secure a fairly similar role as a Casanova actor in John Duigan's failed romantic comedy, 'The Leading Man' (1996). Despite the latter's poor box office performance, BON JOVI was back as a womanising bartender in Friends-style comedy, 'Little City' (1997), and as a small town mechanic in Ed Burns' working-class drama, 'No Looking Back' (1998). Appearances in 'Homegrown' (1998), the all-star war drama, 'U-571' (2000) and especially 'Row Your Boat' (1998); 'Vampires: Los Muertos' (2002), confirmed a move towards grittier, less romantic parts. The lure of rock'n'roll was to prove too strong, however, and with the successful reformation of Bon Jovi in 2000, JON's acting took a back seat in favour of his original vocation. *BG*

—

JON BON JOVI: Blaze Of Glory / Young Guns II
*(score: ALAN SILVESTRI *)*

Aug 90. (cd/c/lp) *Vertigo; <(846 473-2/-4/-1)>* [3] [2]
– Billy get your guns / Miracle / Blaze of glory / Blood money / Santa Fe / Justice in the barrel / Never say die / You really got me now / Bang a drum / Dyin' ain't much of a livin' / Guano city. *(re-iss. Apr95 cd/c; same)*

S/track review: At the beginning of his band's ten year hiatus during the 1990s, JON BON JOVI tried his hand at the soundtrack for western sequel, 'YOUNG GUNS II'. Musically, it does not stray far from the power ballad/epic rock templates that Bon Jovi followed so faithfully at the peak of their big haired power, save for a dash of C&W sounds. Think bad pirate copies of 'Wanted (Dead Or Alive)'. The title track, 'Blaze Of Glory', reached number 1 in the US, as well as landing the singer a Grammy nomination, and deservedly so because, taken individually, this anthemic battle-cry is BON JOVI at his lung bursting, pompous best. Unfortunately, most of the other material on offer sounds like 'Blaze Of Glory's poor cousins and collectively suffocate the stand out track. The album is packed full of Western clichés, with an overkill of slide guitar and references to sleeping under the stars, good versus evil, God, death, whiskey, and of course, guns, lots and lots of guns. Indeed, if tumbleweed had a sound it would be on there. A few friends have been dragged along to try and lend some credibility to the proceedings. JEFF BECK lays down guitar solos on most of the tracks, which are good but you don't get the feeling he has had to try very hard. The same could be said for ELTON JOHN, who appears on two tracks, 'Billy Get Your Gun' and 'Dyin' Ain't Much Of A Living', playing piano on both and lending vocals to the latter. LITTLE RICHARD makes a cameo appearance on 'You Really Got Me Now', the only other song on the album worthy of mention, with vocals and a ragtime piano shot straight out of a bourbon soaked saloon. BON JOVI has always had aspirations to be Bruce Springsteen in his songwriting but, while he may have come close a few times in the past, he doesn't have the subtlety or poetic qualities of The Boss. This is clearly evident on 'YOUNG GUNS II' where songs about the harshness of the world and the good people down on their luck sound patronizing and hackneyed. On the other hand, the film itself doesn't take itself too seriously and maybe that's the best way to approach the soundtrack. *CM*

Album rating: *4.5

– spinoff hits, etc. –

JON BON JOVI: Blaze Of Glory / JON BON JOVI & LITTLE RICHARD: You Really Got Me Now

Jul 90. (7") *<875896> (JBJ 1)* [1] [13]
(12"+=/cd-s+=) *(JBJ T/CD 1)* – Blood money.

JON BON JOVI: Miracle / Blood Money

Oct 90. (c-s) *<878392>* [12] [–]

JON BON JOVI: Miracle / Bang A Drum

Nov 90. (7"/c-s) *(JBJ/+C 2)* [–] [29]
(12"+=/cd-s+=) *(JBJ T/CD 2)* – Dyin' ain't much of a livin' / (interview).

YOUNGBLOOD

1978 (US 90m) American International Pictures (R)

Film genre: urban drama

Top guns: dir: Noel Nosseck / s-w: Paul Carter Harrison

Stars: Lawrence Hilton-Jacobs *(Rommel)* ← CLAUDINE ← DEATH WISH / → the JACKSONS: AN AMERICAN DREAM → SOUTHLANDER, Bryan O'Dell *(Youngblood)* ← a PIECE OF THE ACTION, Ren Woods *(Sybil)* ← CAR WASH ← SPARKLE / → HAIR → XANADU, Tony Allen *(hustler)*, Vince Cannon *(Corelli)*, Art Evans *(junkie)* ← BIG TIME ← LEADBELLY ← CLAUDINE / → SCHOOL DAZE → TRESPASS → CB4: THE MOVIE → the STORY OF US, Ann Weldon *(Mrs. Gordon)*, T.K. Carter *(Bubba Cosell)*, Ron O'Neal *(gym teacher)* ← BROTHERS ← SUPERFLY T.N.T. ← SUPERFLY

Storyline: A Vietnam vet returns to Watts, picks up his old crime traits and educates a youngster on the ways of crime. Trouble is just around the corner when a gang member o.d.'s. *BG*

Movie rating: *4.5
Visual: none

Off the record: **WAR** were formed in 1969 out of Compton/South Bay, L.A. outfit the Creators. An eclectic R&B combo with a strong Latino influence, the group released a few singles in the mid-60s but failed to make much of an impact outside of their native California. They did, however, pre-figure their soul/blues/rock partnership with white R&B merchant ERIC BURDON by hooking up with Love sax player Tjay Contrelli for a series of local club dates (actual recordings of this bizarre partnership are rumoured to exist although they've never been commercially released). In 1968, the Creators metamorphasised into the Nightshift, the group subsequently backing up American football figurehead, Deacon Jones, who was attempting to re-invent himself as a club crooner. WAR were saved from such a fate by producer/songwriter Jerry Goldstein, who introduced the band to ex-ANIMALS singer ERIC BURDON, fresh from England and looking to get hip to the West Coast scene. Renaming themselves WAR, the group (who at this stage comprised Lonnie Jordan, Howard Scott, Charles Miller, Harold Brown, Lee Oskar, B.B. Dickerson and Papa Lee Allen) recorded two albums with BURDON, 'Eric Burdon Declares War' (1970) and 'Black Man's Burdon' (1970). Though the strangely infectious rhythms of Top 3 hit, 'Spill The Wine', boded well, the debut sounded stodgy and directionless despite its US Top 20 success. The group nevertheless toured America and Europe to critical acclaim and mass adulation, while the follow-up album showed more promise. The union was to be short-lived however, and following the death of close friend JIMI HENDRIX in September 1970, BURDON bailed out of the tour. WAR battled on alone, fulfilling their live commitments and beginning work on their own album. Although the group were still officially working as BURDON's backing band, Goldstein (now their manager) secured them a separate deal with 'United Artists'. The eponymous 'War' was released in spring '71, a promising collection of soul, funk, gospel and jazz, underpinned with the group's trademark latino rhythms. One of WAR's secret weapons was the Danish-born Oskar, his harmonica playing at its bittersweet best on the beautiful 'Back Home', a sun-kissed, hymn-like ballad which stands among the cream of WAR's mellower work. Their more experimental tendencies emerged on 'War Drums' and 'Fidel's Fantasy', the latter a bizarre spoken monologue berating Cuban leader Fidel Castro, its mocking message driven on a hypnotic groundswell of insistent piano and latin percussion. There were apparently fears for Allen's (writer and narrator) safety after the record's release; WAR were certainly big enough to attract unwanted attention, especially after the considerable success of 'All Day Music' (1971). For many fans the consummate WAR set, it was certainly their most consistent, boasting the seminal spookiness of 'Slippin' Into Darkness', a shadowy blues/funk epic which had the atmosphere of an old-time confessional, alongside the defiant funk clarion call of 'Get Down' and the groovy 'Nappy Head'. Upon its release as a single, 'Slippin' . . .' eventually hit the Top 20, becoming WAR's first gold release as well as boosting sales of the album and cementing the group's position as one of the foremost funk/soul attractions in America. It came as little surprise then, when WAR scaled the US charts with their third set, 'The World Is A Ghetto' (1973), the record spawning two Top 10 singles in the compelling mock-Western fantasy of 'Cisco Kid' and the title track. 'Deliver The Word' (1973) and 'Why Can't We Be Friends' (1975) both went Top 10, continuing WAR's singles chart success with a gold disc for the latter's title track (a heartfelt plea for an end to racial segregation which was even beamed into space for US and Russian astronauts' listening pleasure!). The brilliant 'Low Rider' meanwhile, became one of only two WAR singles to break the UK Top 20. Things started to go awry in the latter half of the decade, beginning with a move to 'Blue Note' records. Though 'Platinum Jazz' (1977) was the label's only platinum release, musically it fell way short of expectations with its noodling, instrumental hotch-potch of old and previously unreleased tracks. 'Galaxy' (1978) wasn't much of an improvement, the group found all at sea attempting to come to grips with the all-pervasive disco revolution. *BG*

—

WAR

Jul 78. (lp/c) *United Artists; <LA 904-H> M.C.A.; (MCF/+C 2804)* [69] Dec79 [ ]
– Youngblood (livin' in the streets) / Sing a happy song / Keep on doin' / The Kingsmen sign / Walking to war / This funky music makes you feel good / Junk yard / Superdude / Youngblood & Sybil / Flying machine (the chase) / Searching for Youngblood & Rommel / Youngblood (livin' in the streets) – reprise. *<cd-iss. 1996 on 'Avenue'; R2 72289>*

S/track review: Coming as late as it did, it's debatable whether 'YOUNGBLOOD' counts as blaxploitation at all. It certainly never gets mentioned in commentaries on black film and looks to have even been conveniently written out of most retrospectives of WAR themselves. All of which is a funky shame; this album arguably deserves mention in the same breath as the soundtrack efforts of Willie Hutch, Roy Ayers, JJ Johnson, Don Julian et al. By 1978, there were few old-guard funk bands kicking grooves as hard or as organic as the title theme, 'Youngblood (Livin' In The Streets)'. A ten-minute-plus monster and a distant cousin of 'War Is Coming! War Is A Coming!', it thunders on a relentless piano riff, descends into an extended deep synth coda, and echoes to close-harmonies as ominous as only WAR could marshal. 'Flying Machine' (a tune which has occasionally featured on blax comps), is the album's other tour de force, a brilliant, near eight-minute masterclass in Latin jazz. Rarely were WAR (i.e. LEE OSKAR, LONNIE JORDAN, HOWARD SCOTT, HAROLD BROWN, MORRIS DICKERSON, CHARLES MILLER & THOMAS ALLEN) so fluid; LONNIE JORDAN's piano lines dip and snake from spry, seductive repetition to blistering improv, ranks of syncopated percussion duck and weave, a flute traces helium arabesques and a synth swells to climax, applied with the kind of economy that might've saved funk from a slow death. Bookended between these epics, the likes of 'Sing A Happy Song' and the Fatback-like 'Keep On Doin' are more in the mould of their era, lifted clear of the competition by the urbane rhythms. The accent's likewise on rhythm with lithe, dialogue-fronting cues such as 'The Kingsmen Sign', 'Junk Yard' and, wait for it. 'Superdude', while 'Walking To War' shudders to a stethoscope pulse and dissonant sound effects. The only real mis-step is the verging-on-parody P-Funk of 'This Funky Music Makes You Feel Good'. The last great blaxploitation album? – you decide. *BG*

Album rating: *7.5

YOU'RE A BIG BOY NOW

1966/7 (US 96m) Seven Arts Pictures (15)

Film genre: coming-of-age/urban comedy

Top guns: s-w + dir: Francis Ford Coppola → ONE FROM THE HEART → TUCKER: THE MAN AND HIS DREAM (au: David Benedictus)

Stars: Peter Kastner *(Bernard Chanticleer)*, Elizabeth Hartman *(Barbara Darling)*, Geraldine Page *(Margery Chanticleer)*, Julie Harris *(Miss Nora Thing)*, Rip Torn *(I.H. Chanticleer)* → PAYDAY → ONE-TRICK PONY → SONGWRITER → FLASHPOINT → WHERE THE RIVERS FLOW NORTH → the INSIDER, Karen Black *(Amy)* → EASY RIDER → NASHVILLE → GYPSY 83 → HOUSE OF 1000 CORPSES, Tony Bill *(Raef)*, Michael Dunn *(Richard Mudd)*, Dolph Sweet *(patrolman Francis Graf)*

Storyline: Francis Ford Coppola's tentative directorial debut follows the fortunes of Bernard Chanticleer as he ups sticks to New York where – with the help of new friend Tony – he gets his first taste of wine, women and song. The inevitable pain of his first real romantic attachment makes way for a more stable relationship as he finally sloughs his adolescent skin. *BG*

Movie rating: *6

Visual: video

Off the record: Francis Ford Coppola produced this movie for his UCLA film school thesis at a cost of over $750,000.

---

the LOVIN' SPOONFUL

Apr 67. (lp; mono/stereo) *Kama Sutra; <KLP/+S 8058> (KLP 402)* [ ] May67 [ ]
– You're a big boy now / Lonely (Amy's theme) / Wash her away / Kite chase / Try and be happy / Peep show percussion / Girl, beautiful girl / Darling be home soon / Dixieland big boy / Letter to Barbara / Barbara's theme / Miss Thing's thang / March / The finale. *<(cd-iss. Sep99 on 'Camden'+=; 74321 69952-2)>* – WHAT'S UP TIGER LILY

S/track review: The LOVIN' SPOONFUL's second and final soundtrack came a full year after 'WHAT'S UP . . .', released as the original chemistry faded with ZAL YANOVSKY's ignominious exit. It's nevertheless an accurate barometer of where the YANOVSKY-less band were at and where JOHN SEBASTIAN the songwriter and future solo artist was headed. The roots jam sessions had become heavier, bluesier and less frequent while the song-based material had become more self-consciously sophisticated, exemplified in the autumnal, Bacharach-esque 'Lonely (Amy's Theme)'. SEBASTIAN's evolution as a writer is equally apparent on the gorgeous, uncharacteristically introspective hit single, 'Darling Be Home Soon' (reprised in unlikely, parping circus-parade style on 'March'), its keening strings anticipating the orchestration so glaring by its absence on the earlier score. Despite diversions into whimsical lounge and vintage jazz, this is more cohesive as an album and, more importantly for rookie director Martin Scorsese, it translated the agony and the ecstasy of his main character's growing pains with the sad-eyed, heavy-lidded sympathy – or the "pastel states of mind" as one critic put it – which would increasingly become SEBASTIAN's trademark. *BG*

Album rating: *6

– spinoff hits, etc. –

the LOVIN' SPOONFUL: Darling Be Home Soon

Feb 67. (7") *<220> (KAS 207)* [15] [44]

YOU'VE GOT TO WALK IT LIKE YOU TALK IT OR YOU'LL LOSE THAT BEAT

1971 (US 85m) JER Pictures (15)

Film genre: avant-garde comedy/satire

Top guns: s-w + dir: Peter Locke

Stars: Zalman King *(Carter Fields)*, Allen Garfield *(Herby Moss)* ← the OWL AND THE PUSSYCAT / → NASHVILLE → ONE-TRICK PONY → ONE FROM THE HEART → GET CRAZY → DICK TRACY, Suzette Green *(Susan)*, Richard Pryor *(wino)* ← the PHYNX ← WILD IN THE STREETS / → LADY SINGS THE BLUES → WATTSTAX → the MACK → ADIOS AMIGO → CAR WASH → the WIZ → BUSTIN' LOOSE, Robert Downey Sr. *(head of ad agency)* → TO LIVE AND DIE IN L.A. → BOOGIE NIGHTS → MAGNOLIA, Liz Torres *(singer in men's room)*, Roz Kelly *(girl in park)* ← the OWL AND THE PUSSYCAT / → NEW YEAR'S EVIL → AMERICAN POP, Peter Locke *(thief/purse snatcher)*

Storyline: Why exactly is it that countless rock, pop and jazz artists have turned out so much decent – often great – music to utterly forgotten films? You'll be hard pressed to find anyone who's ever seen this movie; even the soundtrack sleevenotes barely mention it. It allegedly centres (not a little 'FRITZ THE CAT'-like, if the sleeve is anything to go by) on the misadventures of a hippy bruised and abandoned by life's iniquities. Oh, and Wes Craven did the editing.. *BG*

Movie rating: *4

Visual: none

Off the record: STEELY DAN (see below)

WALTER BECKER & DONALD FAGEN: You Gotta Walk It Like You Talk It

Oct 71. (lp) *Visa; <IMP 7005>* [ ] [–]
– You gotta walk it like you talk it / Flotsam and jetsam / War and peace / Roll back the meaning / You gotta walk it like you talk it – reprise / Dog eat dog / Red giant – Green dwarf / If it rains. *(UK-iss.Mar78 on 'Spark'; SRLP 124) (cd-iss. Sep92 on 'See For Miles'; SEECD 357) (cd re-iss. Aug06 on 'El'; 79)* – (tracks in different order).

S/track review: There aren't many rock acts who started out in soundtracks, or more accurately, who blueprinted their sound in film. But then STEELY DAN were never your average rock act. Their common denominator was jazz and pop, their world-view far too weary and their original calling professional song-slinging. They picked up this obscure Richard Pryor gig during their short-lived membership of Jay & The Americans, with stalwart Long Islander KENNY VANCE on vocals and production. It didn't set the world alight but it did save them from nostalgia-circuit oblivion, pairing WALTER BECKER and DONALD FAGEN with rhythm guitarist DENNY DIAZ, and patenting the stylistic quirks of what would become STEELY DAN. The most striking thing about it is how much the boyish wonders sound like an L.A. act before they'd even moved there. A Laurel Canyon ballad from the concrete canyons of New York, the VANCE-sung 'If It Rains' could easily have slipped incognito amidst the FM harmonies of 'Can't Buy A Thrill' (1972). The near Crosby, Stills & Nash-mellow 'Roll Back The Meaning' and the tumbling jazz-piano chords of 'Dog Eat Dog' likewise, expounding FAGAN's casually erudite cynicism as an opening gambit. In fact, anyone with a soft spot for easy rolling, early-period 'DAN can welcome this record as a debut before the debut; most bands would have to consider themselves fortunate to be blessed with the talent incubating here. That the loose roots-pop occasionally gives way to quasi-quadrophonic indulgence like 'War & Peace' (it is a soundtrack after all) is about the only note of caution to be sounded in what has to rank as an essential addition to the already Mount Rushmore-strength STEELY DAN legacy. And how – at least in the 'El' (aka 'Cherry Red' subsidiary) reissue – can a man resist sleevenote tidbits like BECKER & FAGAN being in a band called Leather Canary with Chevy Chase . . . *BG*

Album rating: *6.5

Z

ZIDANE: A 21st CENTURY PORTRAIT

2006 (Fra/Ice 90m) Universal Pictures

Film genre: Sports documentary

Top guns: dir: Douglas Gordon, Philippe Parreno

Stars: Zinedane Zidane *(himself)*, Ronaldo, etc.

Storyline: Celebrating the legendary French footballer, Zidane, one of the most talented and gifted players the world has ever seen. The viewer will also see through ZZ's life (on and off-the-field) perspective plus the Spanish LIga match – 23 April, 2005 – between his club, Real Madrid and Villareal. Only two other footballers have so far managed to be the subject of moviemakers, Pele and (George) Best. 'Zidane' was initially shown at the Cannes Film Festival then the Toronto Film Festival. *MCS*

Movie rating: *6

Visual: dvd

Off the record: **MOGWAI** – i.e. Stuart Braithwaite (guitar & vocals), Dominic Aithison (bass & guitar), Martin Bulloch (drums), John Cummings (guitar) and now Barry Burns (multi) – were named after the wee furry creatures in the film, 'Gremlins'. The band have been on the go since 1995, initially setting their sonic pace with a string of independent singles and EPs. 1997's 'Mogwai Young Team' (for Glasgow's 'Chemikal Underground' imprint), pushed away all the traditional barriers that a post-guitar-rock band should have. Dynamic, but at the same time melodic (think Slint, My Bloody Valentine or Pixies), MOGWAI delivered crescendo after meteoric-rock crescendo on further studio albums such as 'Come On Die Young' (1999), 'Rock Action' (2001), 'Happy Songs For Happy People' (2003) and 'Mr. Beast' (2006). *MCS*

MOGWAI

Oct 06. (cd) *Play It Again Sam; (PIASX 067)* ☐ ☐
– Black spider / Terrific speech 2 / Wake up and go berserk / Terrific speech / 7:25 / Half time / I do have weapons / Time and a half / It would have happened anyway / Black spider 2. *(..+ bonus track)*

S/track review: With a second album in a year (complementing their non-OST set, 'Mr. Beast'), it seemed Glasgow indie-rock act MOGWAI were getting a little prolific in their old age. 'ZIDANE' opened the album's account with a couple of so-lo-fi numbers, 'Black Spider' (an outtake from 'Rock Action') and 'Terrific Speech 2', while 'Wake Up And Go Berserk' created a lightly-tinted sonic screech that mellowed-out with finger-plucking guitars and lilting keyboards. Reprising 'Terrific Speech' for track 4, MOGWAI matched past glittering glories like 'Summer' and 'Cody'. Lasting just over five minutes(!), chilled-out track '7:25' (an outtake from

'Come On Die Young'), led into the appropriately titled 'Half Time', a slow-shifting, stirring and sensitive work – much like the man Zidane, himself. A further two instrumental pieces, 'I Do Have Weapons' and 'It Would Have Happened Anyway', created impassioned, contemplative music for a lethargic generation – and why not. Closing number, 'Black Spider 2' (a term probably used to describe his footwork), did not end as it suggested after four minutes – it you wait a while you'll get around 25 minutes of added sonic experimentations. Try to stop listening to Tangerine Dream, lads! *MCS*

Movie rating: *6

☐ ZOMBI alt.
(⇒ DAWN OF THE DEAD)

☐ the ZOMBIES segment
(⇒ BUNNY LAKE IS MISSING)

ZONING

1986 (W.Ger 89m) Scala-Z Films / Cine International

Film genre: sci-fi/crime thriller

Top guns: s-w: (+ dir) Ulrich Krenkler, Angelika Hacker

Stars: Norbert Lamla *(Due)*, Hubertus Gertzen *(Ozzy)*, **Dieter Meier**, Veronika Wolff, Eleonore Weisgerber

Storyline: Fired from their jobs as construction workers, Ozzy and Due hide out in the basement of their skyscraper workplace, where they loot anything that's valuable. When the pair infiltrate the company's computer, their little 4-day jaunt gets a little more serious. *MCS*

Movie rating: *3

Visual: video + dvd

Off the record: Dieter Meier is of Swiss duo, Yello.

—

TANGERINE DREAM

1996. (cd) *Repertoire; (REP 4595-WY)* [–] W.Ger [–]
– The conspiracy / Skyscraper / Headhunter / Downtown Chicago / Fading and turning / Affluent society / Stairway affair / Good choice, bad timing / Bachelor of crime / Unfit for consumption / Days of grief and glory / Eyewitness news / Missing link.

S/track review: Mystery surrounds the production of this score, recorded in 1994, released in 1996, for what appears to have been a movie filmed in 1986 (when the line-up was EDGAR FROESE, Christopher Franke and Paul Haslinger). The released soundtrack reportedly only vaguely resembles the actual movie score, and it seems likely that EDGAR FROESE revisited his original music a decade later (possibly for a video release), re-recording, remixing and adding new music with his son JEROME FROESE, as he went (the father/son team pulled a similar trick in 2002, revising TD's 'Optical Race', 'Lily On The Beach' and 'Melrose' albums). The intrigue is purely scholarly though, because the music itself does not justify more than passing interest, and the presumably modernising influence of FROESE junior – most clearly felt on opener 'The Conspiracy' and closer 'Missing Link' – amounts to an embarrassing dalliance with rubbish, dated electro. An EDGAR FROESE solo album in all but name (the track 'Eyewitness News' was retitled 'Descent Like A Hawk' for a compilation of FROESE's solo works), 'ZONING' contains music that at one time would have been associated with terrestrial TV night-screens, and programmed drums better suited to 80s computer racing games. As ever with TD, characterless washes of synth pervade (see most tracks, particularly 'Affluent Society' and 'Stairway Affair'), while occasional classical guitars ('Headhunter', 'Fading And Turning') and saxophone ('Headhunter' again) intervene only to enhance the sensation of listening to tarted-up muzak. The only real mystery worth considering is why FROESE and son bothered to revisit it. *SW*

Album rating: *2

C

F

G

H

I

J

K

T